Who's Who in America®

Who's Who in America®

2000

Millennium Edition

Since 1899

54th Edition

Volume 3
Indexes

MARQUIS
Who'sWho® 121 Chanlon Road
New Providence, NJ 07974 U.S.A.

Who'sWho in America®

Marquis Who's Who®

Managing Director Thomas M. Bachmann

Editorial Director Fred Marks   **Managing Editor** Robert Docherty

Editorial

Senior Editor	Maurice Brooks
Assistant Editors	Danielle M.L. Barry
	Donald Bunton
	Josh Samber
	Mary San Giovanni
	Elissa Strell
	Paul M. Zema

Editorial Services

Managers	Karen Chassie
	Debra Krom
Creative Project Manager	Michael Noerr
Assistant Creative Project Managers	William R. Miller
Production Supervisor	Jeanne Danzig

Editorial Support

Manager	Debby Nowicki
Coordinator	J. Hector Gonzalez
Clerk	Sola Osofisan

Mail Processing

Supervisor	Kara A. Seitz
Staff	Betty Gray
	Jill S. Terbell

Database Operations

Director, Production & Training	Mark Van Orman
Assistant Managing Editor	Matthew O'Connell
Assistant Manager	Patrick Gibbons

Research

Senior Managing Research Editor	Lisa Weissbard
Freelance Coordinator	Debra Ayn
Associate Research Editors	Susan Eggleton
	Oscar Maldonado
Assistant Research Editor	Stephen J. Sherman

Published by Marquis Who's Who, a member of the Lexis-Nexis Group.

President and Chief Executive Officer Lou Andreozzi

Vice President and Publisher Randy H. Mysel

Vice President, Database Production Dean Hollister

Marquis Who's Who
121 Chanlon Road
New Providence, New Jersey 07974
1-908-464-6800
www.marquiswhoswho.com

WHO'S WHO IN AMERICA is a registered trademark of Reed Publishing (Nederland) B.V., used under license.
Library of Congress Catalog Card Number 49-48186
International Standard Book Number   0-8379-0199-5 (set, Classic Edition)
                                            0-8379-0202-9 (volume 3, Classic Edition)
                                            0-8379-0203-7 (set, Deluxe Edition)
                                            0-8379-0206-1 (volume 3, Deluxe Edition)
Internationl Standard Serial Number   0083-9817

Manufactured in the United States of America

Table of Contents

Introduction

The *Who's Who in America* Geographic and Professional Indexes provide access to biographical information in the 54th Edition through two avenues in alphabetical form—geography and profession. Each Biographee entry contains name and occupational description. A dagger symbol (†) indicates a new name first appearing in the 54th Edition.

The Geographic Index lists names in the United States under state and city designations, as well as Biographees in American territories. Canadian listings include provinces and cities. Names in Mexico and other countries appear by city. Biographees whose addresses are not published in their sketches are found under Address Unpublished.

The Professional Index includes thirty-eight categories ranging alphabetically from Agriculture to Social Science. Within each area, the names appear under geographic subheadings. Names without published addresses appear at the end of each professional area listing under Address Unpublished. If the occupation does not fall within one of the specified areas, the name is listed under Unclassified.

Some Biographees have professions encompassing more than one area; each of these appears under the field best suited to the Biographee's occupation. Thus, while most bankers are listed under Finance: Banking Services, investment bankers are found in Finance: Investment Services. A Biographee with two or more diverse occupations is found under the area that best fits his or her professional profile.

The Retiree Index lists the names of those individuals whose biographical sketches last appeared in the 51st, 52nd, or 53rd Edition of *Who's Who in America.*

The Necrology lists Biographees of the 53rd Edition whose deaths were reported to Marquis prior to the close of the compilation of this edition of *Who's Who in America.*

Alphabetical Practices

Names are arranged alphabetically according to the surnames, and under identical surnames according to the first given name. If both surname and first given name are identical, names are arranged alphabetically according to the second given name.

Surnames beginning with De, Des, Du, however capitalized or spaced, are recorded with the prefix preceding the surname and arranged alphabetically under the letter D.

Surnames beginning with Mac and Mc are arranged alphabetically under M.

Surnames beginning with Saint or St. appear after names that begin Sains, and are arranged according to the second part of the name, e.g. St. Clair before Saint Dennis.

Surnames beginning with Van, Von, or von are arranged alphabetically under the letter V.

Compound surnames are arranged according to the first member of the compound.

Many hyphenated Arabic names begin Al-, El-, or al-. These names are alphabetized according to each Biographee's designation of last name. Thus Al-Bahar, Neta may be listed either under Al- or under Bahar, depending on the preference of the listee.

Also, Arabic names have a variety of possible spellings when transposed to English. Spelling of these names is always based on the practice of the Biographee. Some Biographees use a Western form of word order, while others prefer the Arabic word sequence.

Similarly, Asian names may have no comma between family and given names, but some Biographees have chosen to add the comma. In each case, punctuation follows the preference of the Biographee.

Parentheses used in connection with a name indicate which part of the full name is usually deleted in common usage. Hence Chambers, E(lizabeth) Anne indicates that the usual form of the given name is E. Anne. In such a case, the parentheses are ignored in alphabetizing and the name would be arranged as Chambers, Elizabeth Anne. However, if the name is recorded Chambers, (Elizabeth) Anne, signifying that the entire name Elizabeth is not commonly used, the alphabetizing would be arranged as though the name were Chambers, Anne. If an entire middle or last name is enclosed in parentheses, that portion of the name is used in the alphabetical arrangement. Hence Chambers, Elizabeth (Anne) would be arranged as Chambers, Elizabeth Anne.

Where more than one spelling, word order, or name of an individual is frequently encountered, the sketch has been entered under the form preferred by the Biographee, with cross-references under alternate forms.

Geographic Index

†New name in *Who's Who in America*, 54th Edition

UNITED STATES

ALABAMA

Albertville
Johnson, Clark Everette, Jr. *judge*
†Patterson, Jeffery Allen *realtor*
†Rice, Fuhrman D. (Runt) *retired paper executive*
Sheets, Dorothy Jane *retired school librarian and educator*

Alexander City
Gade, Marvin Francis *retired paper company executive*
Powers, Runas, Jr. *rheumatologist*
Shuler, Ellie Givan, Jr. *retired military officer, military museum administrator*

Andalusia
Albritton, William Harold, IV *lawyer*
Fuller, William Sidney *lawyer*
Patterson, Edwin *minister*
†Rich, Lonnie Keven *art educator, artist*
Taylor, James Marion, II *automotive wholesale executive*
Windham, Susan Kay Harper *early childhood educator*

Anniston
Ayers, Harry Brandt *editor, publisher, columnist*
Harwell, Edwin Whitley *judge*
Klinefelter, James Louis *lawyer*
Landholm, Dawn Renae *land use planner*
Smith, Judith Day *early childhood educator*
Woodrow, Randall Mark *lawyer*

Arab
Hall, Atlee Burpee *researcher*
Hammond, Ralph Charles *real estate executive*

Ashland
Ingram, Kenneth Frank *retired state supreme court justice*

Athens
Hawley, Harold Patrick *educational consultant*
†Ruf, Donnie Lee *delivery service driver*
Williams, Timothy Dale *reference librarian*
Wilson, Lucy Lynn Willmarth *postal service administrator*

Auburn
Alderman, Charles Wayne *university dean*
Aldridge, Melvin Dayne *electrical engineering educator*
Amacher, Richard Earl *literature educator*
Andelson, Robert Vernon *social philosopher, educator*
Bailey, Wilford Sherrill *retired parasitology educator, science administrator, university president*
Ball, Donald Maury *agronomist, consultant*
Barker, Kenneth Neil *pharmacy administration educator*
Clark, Janet Eileen *political scientist, educator*
Cochran, John Euell, Jr. *aerospace engineer, educator, lawyer*
†Ellis, Cliff *college basketball coach*
Galbraith, Ruth Legg *retired university dean, home economist*
Gilbert, Armida Jennings *American literature educator*
Govil, Narendra Kumar *mathematics educator*
Harvey, James Mathews, Jr. *instructional media producer, columnist*
Havens, Carolyn Clarice *librarian*
Housel, David *athletic director*
Irwin, John David *electrical engineering educator*
Jaeger, Richard Charles *electrical engineer, educator, science center director*
Klesius, Phillip Harry *microbiologist, researcher*
Kribel, Robert Edward *academic administrator, consultant physicist*
Lechner, Norbert Manfred *architect, educator*
Lewis, Walter David *historian*
Lishak, Lisa Anne *secondary education educator*
Littleton, Taylor Dowe *humanities educator*
Marsh, David *university swimming coach*
McEldowney, Rene *health care educator, consultant*
Miller, Wilbur Randolph *university educator and administrator*
Millman, Richard George *architect, educator*
Muse, William Van *academic administrator*
Owens, John Murry *dean*
Parsons, Daniel Lankester *pharmaceutics educator*
†Penaskovic, Richard John *religious studies educator*
Philpott, Harry Melvin *former university president*
Reeve, Thomas Gilmour *physical education educator*
Samford, Thomas Drake, III *lawyer*
Shore, Eric *coach*
Straiton, T(homas) Harmon, Jr. *librarian*
Tolbert, Clinton Jame *machinist, army officer*
†Tullier, Michael Joseph *nonprofit blood center administrator*
Turnquist, Paul Kenneth *agricultural engineer, educator*
Voitle, Robert Allen *college dean, physiologist*
Walsh, William Kershaw *textile engineering educator*
Zallen, Harold *corporate executive, scientist, former university official*

Bay Minette
†Cabaniss, Charlotte Jones *library services director*
Granade, Fred King *lawyer*

Bessemer
Bains, Lee Edmundson *state official*
Stephens, Betsy Bain *retired elementary school educator*

Birmingham
Acker, William Marsh, Jr. *federal judge*
Adams, Alfred Bernard, Jr. *environmental engineer*
Agee, Claudia *clerk, receptionist, tax consultant*
Akers, Ottie Clay *lawyer, publisher*
Alford, Margie Searcy *lawyer*
Allen, Christopher C. *publishing executive*
Allen, Lee Norcross *historian, educator*
Allen, Maryon Pittman *former senator, journalist, lecturer, interior and clothing designer*
Allman, Richard Mark *physician, gerontologist*
Appleton, Joseph Hayne *civil engineer, educator*
†Armstrong, Robert R., Jr. *federal judge*
Arrington, Richard, Jr. *mayor*
Avent, Charles Kirk *medical educator*
Baker, David Remember *lawyer*
Barker, Thomas Watson, Jr. *energy company executive*
Barrett, Ellen Colby *magazine editor*
Barrow, Richard Edward *architect*
Benditt, Theodore Matthew *humanities educator*
Bennett, James Patrick *healthcare executive*
Bennett, Joe Claude *pharmaceutical executive*
†Bennett, Thomas B. *federal judge*
Berg, Thomas Charles *law educator*
Berte, Neal Richard *college president*
Blackburn, Sharon Lovelace *federal judge*
Blan, Ollie Lionel, Jr. *lawyer*
Boardman, Mark Seymour *lawyer*
Boomershine, Donald Eugene *bureau executive, development official*
Booth, Rachel Zonelle *nursing educator*
Booth, Wendy Christina *nursing educator*
Bowron, Richard Anderson *retired utilities executive*
Bradley, John M(iller), Jr. *forestry executive*
Branham, Grady Eugene *principal*
Braswell, Walter E. *prosecutor*
Bridgers, William Frank *physician, educator*
†Bridges, James Edward, Jr. *dean*
Brough, James A. *airport terminal executive*
†Brouwer, Bert *art educator*
Brown, Ephraim Taylor, Jr. *lawyer*
Bruno, Ronald G. *food service executive*
Bueschen, Anton Joslyn *physician, educator*
Bugg, Charles Edward *biochemistry educator, scientist*
Bulow, Jack Faye *library director*
Bunt, Randolph Cedric *mechanical engineer*
Burden, Cedric Jerome *English educator*
Caldwell, Tom O. *pediatric physician*
Callahan, Alston *physician, author*
Campbell, Charles Alton *manufacturing corporate executive*
Campbell, Elizabeth Todd *judge*
Carlton, Eric L. *lawyer*
Carlton, Michael *magazine editor*
Carmichael, Mary Alice *artist, genealogist*
Carruthers, Thomas Neely, Jr. *lawyer*
Carter, Frances Tunnell (Fran Carter) *fraternal organization administrator*
Carter, John Thomas *retired educational administrator, writer*
Casebeer, Linda Louise *medical educator*
Casey, Ronald Bruce *journalist*
Caulfield, James Benjamin *pathologist, educator*
Chin, Kai Chi *financial analyst*
Chrencik, Frank *chemical company executive*
Clarke, Juanita M. Waiters *education educator*
†Clayton, Orville Woolford *surgeon*
Clemmons, Nancy Washington *library administrator*
Clemon, U. W. *federal judge*
†Cohen, Benjamin *federal judge*
Coleman, Brittin Turner *lawyer*
Comer, Donald, III *investment company executive*
Cooper, Jerome A. *lawyer*
Cooper, John Allen Dicks *medical educator*
Cooper, Karen René *health facility administration nurse*
Cooper, Max Dale *physician, medical educator, researcher*
Cooper, N. Lee *lawyer*
Copeland, Hunter Armstrong *real estate executive*
Corts, Thomas Edward *university president*
Crenshaw, James Faulkner *physician*
Crichton, Douglas Bentley *editor, writer*
Cullen, William Zachary *lawyer*
Culp, Charles Allen *financial executive*
Currie, Larry Lamar *insurance company executive*
Curtis, John J. *medical educator*
Daniel, Kenneth Rule *former iron and steel manufacturing company executive*
Davenport, Horace Willard *physiologist*
Davis, Julian Mason, Jr. *lawyer*
DeGaris, Annesley Hodges *lawyer, educator*
Denson, William Frank, III *lawyer*
Devane, Denis James *health care company executive*
Diethelm, Arnold Gillespie *surgeon*
Dodd, Donald Bradford *museum administrator, historian*
Dougherty, Dana Dean Lesley *television producer, educator*
Dowdey, Benjamin Charles *physician*
Drummond, Garry N. *mining company executive*
Dubovsky, Eva Vitkova *nuclear medicine physician, educator*
Edmonds, William Fleming *retired engineering and construction company executive*
Edwards, Margaret McRae *college administrator, lawyer*
Elgavish, Ada *molecular, cellular biologist*
Elgavish, Gabriel Andreas *physical biochemistry educator*
Elmets, Craig Allan *dermatologist*
Espey, Linda Ann Glidewell *accountant*
Fallon, Harold Joseph *physician, pharmacology and biochemistry educator*
Farley, Joseph McConnell *lawyer*
Fayne, Gwendolyn Davis *air force officer, English educator*
Finley, Sara Crews *medical geneticist, educator*
†Fix, R. Jobe *plastic and reconstructive and hand surgeon*
Fleming, Frank *sculptor*
Floyd, John Alex, Jr. *editor, marketing executive, horticulturist*
†Foley, David E. *bishop*
Foster, Arthur Key, Jr. *lawyer*
Francavilla, Donna T. *news reporter*
Fraser, Robert Gordon *diagnostic radiologist*
Friedel, Robert Oliver *physician*
Friedlander, Michael J. *neuroscientist, animal physiologist, medical educator*
Friend, Edward Malcolm, III *lawyer, educator*
Fullmer, Harold Milton *dentist, educator*
Gale, Fournier Joseph, III *lawyer*
Garner, Robert Edward Lee *lawyer*
George, Frank Wade *small business owner, antiquarian book dealer*
Gilchrist, William Aaron *architect*
Gilmore, Catherine Rye *arts administrator*
Givhan, Robert Marcus *lawyer*
†Glosecki, Stephen Orin *English educator, folklorist*
Goldberg, Edward Jay *general contractor*
Goldenberg, Robert L. *obstetrician*
Goldman, Jay *industrial engineer, educator, former dean*
Goldstein, Debra Holly *judge*
Goodner, Jacob B., Jr. (Jay Goodner) *marketing professional*
Goodrich, Thomas Michael *lawyer, engineering and construction executive*
Grant, Walter Matthews *lawyer, corporate executive*
Greenwood, P. Nicholas *lawyer*
Griffin, Eleanor *magazine editor*
Gross, Iris Lee *association executive*
Guin, Junius Foy, Jr. *federal judge*
Hall, Robert Alan *financial company executive*
Hames, Carl Martin *educational administrator, art dealer, consultant*
Hamilton, Virginia Van der Veer *historian, educator*
Hammond, C(larke) Randolph *healthcare executive*
Hanson, Victor Henry, II *newspaper publisher*
Harbert, Bill Lebold *construction corporation executive*
Hardman, Daniel Clarke *accountant*
Harris, Aaron *management consultant*
Harris, Elmer Beseler *electric utility executive*
Hawk, Beverly Gale *political scientist, educator*
Haworth, Michael Elliott, Jr. *investor, former aerospace company executive*
Hecker, William Fulham, Jr. *architect*
Hendley, Dan Lunsford *retired university official*
Hickson, Marcus Lafayette, III *communication educator, consultant*
Hidy, George Martel *chemical engineer, executive*
†Hill, David Geoffrey *college administrator*
Hill, Samuel Richardson, Jr. *retired medical educator*
Hill, Stan Wayne *video producer*
Hinton, James Forrest, Jr. *lawyer*
Hirschowitz, Basil Isaac *physician*
Holmes, Suzanne McRae *nursing supervisor*
Holton, J(erry) Thomas *concrete company executive*
Horsley, Richard David *banker*
Howell, William Ashley, III *lawyer*
Hull, William Edward *theology educator*
Hutchins, William Bruce, III *utility company executive*
Ingram, Margi *real estate broker*
Irons, George Vernon, Sr. *history educator*
Irons, William Lee *lawyer*
Johnson, Creighton Ernest *insurance company executive, retired*
Johnson, Joseph H., Jr. *lawyer*
Jones, D. Paul, Jr. *banker, lawyer*
†Jones, G. Douglas *prosecutor*
Jones, Moniaree Parker *occupational health nurse*
†Joseph, David B. *pediatric urologist*
Kapanka, Heidi *emergency physician*
Keller, Armor *artist, arts advocate*
Kelly, David Reid *pathologist*
Kennedy, Joe David, Jr. (Joey Kennedy) *editor*
King, Charles Mark *dentist, educator*
Kirkley, D. Christine *non-profit organization administrator*
Kirklin, John Webster *surgeon*
Koopman, William James *medical educator, internist, immunologist*
Kracke, Robert Russell *lawyer*
Kuehn, Ronald L., Jr. *natural resources company executive*
†Kuzniecky, Ruben Itamar *neurologist, educator*
Lacy, Alexander Shelton *lawyer*
Lide, Neoma Jewell Lawhon (Mrs. Martin James Lide, Jr.) *poet*
Lloyd, Lewis Keith, Jr. *surgery and urology educator*
Lochridge, Stanley Keith *cardiovascular and thoracic surgeon*
Loftin, Sister Mary Frances *religious organization administrator*
Logan, J. Patrick *lawyer*
Long, Thad Gladden *lawyer*
Luckie, Robert Ervin, Jr. *advertising executive*
Lynch, Kevin *publishing executive*
Lynne, Seybourn Harris *federal judge*
Makarov, Yuri Viktorovich *electrical engineering educator, researcher*
Manson-Hing, Lincoln Roy *dental educator*
Marchase, Richard Banfield *cell biologist, educator*
Marks, Charles Caldwell *retired investment banker, retired industrial distribution company executive*
Massey, Richard Walter, Jr. *investment counselor*
Max, Rodney Andrew *lawyer, mediator*
Mc Callum, Charles Alexander *university official*
McCarl, Henry Newton *economics and geology educator*
McLain, David Andrew *internist, rheumatologist*
McMahon, John J., Jr. *metal processing company executive*
Mc Millan, George Duncan Hastie, Jr. *lawyer, former state official*
McWhorter, Hobart Amory, Jr. *lawyer*
Meezan, Elias *pharmacologist, educator*
Miller, Dennis Edward *health medical executive*
Mills, William Hayes *lawyer*
Mitchell, Tamara O. *judge*
Molen, John Klauminzer *lawyer*
Montgomery, John Atterbury *research chemist, consultant*
Moran, William Madison *fundraising executive*
Morgan, Hugh Jackson, Jr. *bank executive*
†Morin, Bode Joseph *curator, historian, industrial archeologist*
Morrisey, Michael A. *health economics educator*
Morrison, Gregg Scott *minister, college administrator*
Morton, Marilyn Miller *genealogy and history educator, lecturer, researcher, travel executive, director*
Murrell, Susan DeBrecht *librarian*
Nash, Warren Leslie *banker*
Neal, Phil Hudson, Jr. *manufacturing company executive*
Nelson, Edwin L. *federal judge*
Nepomuceno, Cecil Santos *physician*
Nettles, Bert Sheffield *lawyer*
Newton, Alexander Worthy *lawyer*
Newton, Don Allen *chamber of commerce executive*
Nielsen, Leonard Maurice *physician assistant*
Norris, Robert Wheeler *lawyer, military officer*
Northen, Charles Swift, III *banker*
Nunn, Grady Harrison *political science educator emeritus*
Nunnelley, Carol Fishburne *editor newspaper*
Oakes, Walter Jerry *pediatric neurosurgeon*
O'Brien, Dellanna West *religious organization administrator*
Oglesby, Sabert, Jr. *retired research institute administrator*
Omura, George Adolf *medical oncologist*
†O'Neil, Peter V. *provost*
Oparil, Suzanne *cardiologist, educator, researcher*
Pacifico, Albert Dominick *cardiovascular surgeon*
Page, John Gardner *research administrator, scientist*
Palmer, Robert Leslie *lawyer*
Parker, Israel Frank *national association consultant*
Parker, John Malcolm *management and financial consultant*
Pearson, Richard L. *lawyer*
Pedersen, Paul Bodholdt *psychologist, educator*
Peeples, William Dewey, Jr. *mathematics educator*
Perry, Helen *home care nurse, educator*
Pfister, Roswell Robert *ophthalmologist*
Pittman, Constance Shen *physician, educator*
Pittman, James Allen, Jr. *physician, educator*
Pizitz, Richard Alan *retail and real estate group executive*
Pohost, Gerald Michael *cardiologist, medical educator*
Pointer, Sam Clyde, Jr. *federal judge*
Powell, Curtis Everett *music educator, college official*
Powell, William Arnold, Jr. *retired banker*
Powers, Edward Latell *accountant*
Price, Rosalie Pettus *artist*
Privett, Caryl Penney *lawyer*
Propst, Robert Bruce *federal judge*
†Putnam, Terry Michael *magistrate judge*
Quintana, Jose Booth *health care executive*
Raabe, William Alan *tax author and educator*
Ramey, Craig T. *psychology educator*
Redden, Lawrence Drew *lawyer*
Refinetti, Roberto *psychologist*
Reynolds, W(ynetka) Ann *academic administrator, educator*
Richards, J. Scott *rehabilitation medicine professional*
Richey, V. L. *steel company executive*
Robin, Theodore Tydings, Jr. *lawyer, engineer, consultant*
Robinson, Edward Lee *retired physics educator, consultant*
Roby, Jasper *bishop*
Rogers, Ernest Mabry *lawyer*
Rotch, James E. *lawyer*
Roth, William Stanley *hospital foundation executive*
Rountree, Asa *lawyer*
Rouse, John Wilson, Jr. *technology consultant*
Rubright, James Alfred *oil and gas company executive, lawyer*
Rushton, William James, III *insurance company executive*
Russell, Richard Olney, Jr. *cardiologist, educator*
Rynearson, W. John *foundation administrator*
Savage, Laura Lou *ministry consultant*
Scarritt, Thomas Varnon *newspaper editor*
Schafer, James Arthur *physiologist*
Schloder, John E. *museum director*
Schroeder, Harry William, Jr. *physician, scientist*
Scott, Owen Myers, Jr. *nuclear engineer*
Seitz, Karl Raymond *editor*
Selfe, Edward Milton *lawyer*
Sellers, Fred Wilson *accountant*
Sheppard, Scott *magazine publisher*
Shores, Janie Ledlow *retired state supreme court justice*
Skalka, Harold Walter *ophthalmologist, educator*
Sklenar, Herbert Anthony *industrial products manufacturing company executive*
Smith, Edward Samuel *federal judge*
Smith, John Joseph *lawyer*
Smith, Steve Allen *nursing administrator*
Smitherman, David Conrad *medical marketing professional*
Spahn, James Francis *marketing professional*
Spence, Paul Herbert *librarian*
Stabler, Lewis Vastine, Jr. *lawyer*
Stallworth, Anne Nall *writer, writing educator*
Stephens, Deborah Lynn *health facility executive*

Stephens, James T. *publishing executive*
Stephens, Jerry Wayne *librarian, library director*
Stevenson, Edward Ward *retired physician, surgeon, otolaryngologist*
Stewart, Joseph Grier *lawyer*
Stone, Edmund Crispen, III *banker*
Styslinger, Lee Joseph, Jr. *manufacturing company executive*
Sydnor, Edgar Starke *lawyer*
Szygenda, Stephen A. *electrical and computer engineering educator, researcher*
Taub, Edward *psychology researcher*
Threadcraft, Hal Law, III *pastor, counselor*
Tieszen, Ralph Leland, Sr. *internist*
Timberlake, Marshall *lawyer*
Todd, Judith F. *lawyer*
Todsen, Dana Rognar *health care executive*
Tucker, Thomas James *investment manager*
Vinson, Laurence Duncan, Jr. *lawyer*
Wallace, Carl Jerry *zoo director*
Warnock, David Gene *nephrologist*
Weatherly, Robert Stone, Jr. *banker*
Weeks, Arthur Andrew *lawyer, law educator*
Weinsier, Roland Louis *nutrition educator and director*
†Westerfield, Richard *music director*
Wood, Clinton Wayne *middle school educator*
Wrinkle, John Newton *lawyer*
Young, Thomas Richard *sales professional*
Zahl, Paul Francis Matthew *dean*
Zeiger, Herbert Evan, Jr. *neurosurgeon*

Bremen
Weathersby, Cecil Jerry *accounting and finance manager*

Brewton
†Reynolds, Harold Mark *language educator*

Camden
Lewis, Robert Henry *lay worker*

Camp Hill
Hennies, Clyde Albert (Lou) *military officer, state official, military academy administrator*

Centre
Clark, Kathleen Vernon *special education educator*

Chapman
Miller, James Rumrill, III *finance educator*

Clanton
Davenport, Betty *special education educator*

Clayton
Jackson, Lynn Robertson *lawyer*

Collinsville
Beasley, Mary Catherine *home economics educator, administrator, researcher*

Cordova
Anthony, Yancey Lamar *minister*

Crossville
Blessing, Maxine Lindsey *secondary education educator*

Cullman
Freeman, Chester Willie *small business owner*
Munger, James Guy *protective services executive*
Poston, Beverly Paschal *lawyer*

Cusseta
Striblin, Lori Ann *critical care nurse, Medicare coordinator, nursing educator*

Dadeville
Adair, Charles Robert, Jr. *lawyer*
Barnes, Ben Blair *company executive, electrical engineer*
Oliver, John Percy, II *lawyer*

Daphne
Baugh, Charles Milton *biochemistry educator, college dean*
Bennett, Anne Marie *nursing administrator*
†Henson, Pamela Taylor *secondary education educator, biology*
Hilley, Joseph Henry *lawyer*

Dauphin Island
Levenson, Maria Nijole *retired medical technologist*
Porter, John Finley, Jr. *physicst, conservationist, retired educator*

Decatur
Bennett, Rebecca Eaton *artist*
Blackburn, John Gilmer *lawyer*
Caddell, John A. *lawyer*
Michelini, Sylvia Hamilton *auditor*
Ragland, Wylheme Harold *minister, health facility administrator*
Simmons, Robert Burns *history and political science educator*
Talley, Richard Woodrow *accountant*
Taylor, Paul *retired engineer*

Demopolis
Dinning, Woodford Wyndham, Jr. *lawyer*
Lloyd, Hugh Adams *lawyer*

Dothan
Ameter, Brenda K. *English educator*
Cross, Steven Jasper *finance educator*
Garner, Alto Luther *retired education educator*
Jackson, Alisa Simmons *geriatrics nurse, administrator*
Mocker, Hans Walter *physicist*
Singletary, William Barry *manufacturing company executive*
Wright, Burton *sociologist*

Dozier
Grantham, Charles Edward *broadcast engineer*

Elberta
Brennan, Lawrence Edward *electronics engineer*

Elmore
Williams, Glenda Carlene *writer*

Enterprise
Parker, Ellis D. *retired career officer, aviation executive*
Patterson, Albert Love III *career military officer*
Rikard, Yvonne H. *elementary educator*

Epes
Zippert, John *association administrator, editor, publisher*

Evergreen
†Castleberry, Carolyn P. *mental health therapist and counselor*

Fairfield
Hamrick, Leon Columbus *surgeon, medical director*
Lloyd, Barbara Ann *nurse, educator*

Fairhope
Brumback Patterson, Cathy Jean *psychologist*
Ottensmeyer, David Joseph *retired neurosurgeon, retired healthcare executive*
†Propp, Sheila Margaret *newspaper editor*
†Suddeth, Betty Fisher *librarian*

Florence
Burford, Alexander Mitchell, Jr. *retired physician*
Davis, Ernestine Bady *nurse educator, administrator*
Eich, Wilbur Foster, III *pediatrician*
Foote, Avon Edward *webmaster, communications educator*
Gartman, Max Dillon *language educator*
Johnson, Johnny Ray *mathematics educator*
Kyzar, Patricia Parks *maternity nurse*
Potts, Robert Leslie *academic administrator*
Richardson, Ruth Delene *business educator*
Tease, James Edward *judge*
Zarate, Ann Gairing *academic administrator, lawyer*

Foley
Breed, Eileen Judith *small business owner*
Russell, Ralph Timothy *insurance company executive, mayor*
St. John, Henry Sewell, Jr. *utility company executive*
Wood, Linda Sherrill *secondary education educator*

Fort Mc Clellan
Baker, Robert Vernon, Jr. *retired military officer, military trainer*
†Ryder, Donald J. *military career officer*
†Wooten, Ralph G. *career officer*

Fort Payne
Harris, Melba Iris *secondary school educator, state agency administrator*

Fort Rucker
Caldwell, John Alvis, Jr. *experimental psychologist*
Glushko, Gail Marie *physician, military officer*
†Jones, Anthony Ray *military career officer*

Gadsden
Arnold, Don Carl *pastor, religious organization executive*
Lefelhocz, Irene Hanzak *nurse, business owner*
Sledge, James Scott *judge*
Young, Fredda Florine *steel manufacturing manager*

Gallant
Lively, Brenda Mae R. *women's health nurse*

Gordo
McKnight, William Baldwin *physics educator*

Greensboro
Massey, James Earl *clergyman, educator*

Guin
†Lolley, Steven V. *banker*

Gulf Shores
Wallace, John Loys *aviation services executive*

Guntersville
Hefner, W. G. (Bill Hefner) *former congressman*
Patterson, Harold Dean *retired superintendent of schools*
Sparkman, Brandon Buster *educator, writer, consultant*

Hartselle
Slate, Joe Hutson *psychologist, educator*
Smith, Pamela Rodgers *elementary education educator*

Harvest
Norman, Ralph Louis *physicist, consultant*

Hayden
Graves, Marie Maxine *public relations executive, OSHA consultant*

Homewood
Hart, Virginia Wade *elementary education educator*

Hoover
†Anyanwu, Victor O. *criminologist, political scientist*
Cole, Charles DuBose, II *law educator*
Crater, Timothy Andrews *physician*
Hemmings, Robert Leslie *chemical engineer*
Wyers, Mary Shuttlesworth *secondary school educator, coach*

Hueytown
Allison, Robert Arthur *race car owner, retired professional stock car driver*

Huntsville
Accardi, James Roy *prosecutor*
Allan, Barry David *research chemist, government official*
Bendickson, Marcus J. *company executive*
Black, Daniel Hugh *retired secondary school educator*
Boykin, Betty Ruth Carroll *mortgage loan officer, bank executive*
Bramon, Christopher John *aerospace engineer*
Bridwell, G. Porter *retired aerospace engineer*
Burns, Pat Ackerman Gonia *information systems specialist, software engineer*
Campbell, Jonathan Wesley *astrophysicist, aerospace engineer*
Chassay, Roger Paul, Jr. *engineering executive, project manager*
Childs, Rand Hampton *data processing executive*
Componation, Paul Joseph *industrial and systems engineer, educator*
Cornatzer, William Eugene *retired biochemistry educator*
Costes, Nicholas Constantine *aerospace technologist, university educator, retired government official*
Daly, Cecily A. *author, educator*
Decher, Rudolf *physicist*
De Shields, Carla Veonecia *county official*
Dimmock, John Oliver *university research center director*
Emerson, William Kary *engineering company executive*
Franz, Frank Andrew *university president, physics educator*
Freas, George Wilson, II *computer consultant*
Gillani, Noor Velshi *atmospheric scientist, researcher, educator*
Graves, Benjamin Barnes *business administration educator*
Gray, Ronald W. *business executive*
†Greene, Paul W. *federal judge*
†Hall, Elizabeth Murchie *retired special education educator, consultant*
Heidish, Louise Oridge-Schwallie *transportation specialist, marketing professional*
Hession, Alice Irene *principal*
Hoppe, Lea Ann *elementary education educator*
Huber, Donald Simon *physician*
Huckaby, Gary Carlton *lawyer*
Hunter, Herbert Erwin *aerospace engineer*
†Jedlovic, Gary J. *meteorologist, remote sensing scientist*
Johnson, Charles Leslie *aerospace physicist, consultant*
Kestle, Wendell Russell *cost and economic analyst, consultant*
Kim, Young Kil *aerospace engineer*
King, Olin B. *electronics systems company executive*
Krueger, Kathleen Susan *special education administrator*
Kuehn, Robert John, Jr. *air force officer*
Leslie, Lottie Lyle *retired secondary education educator*
Loux, Jean McCluskey *housewife, registered nurse*
Loux, Peter Charles *anesthesiologist*
Lundquist, Charles Arthur *university official*
McAuley, Van Alfon *aerospace mathematician*
McClendon, Dennis Edward *retired air force officer*
Mc Donough, George Francis, Jr. *retired aerospace engineer, consultant*
McIntyre-Ivy, Joan Carol *data processing executive*
Miller, Carol Lynn *librarian*
Miller, Walter Edward *physical scientist, researcher*
Mohan, Tungesh Nath *television and film producer, film educator*
Moore, Fletcher Brooks *engineering company executive*
Morgan, Beverly Hammersley *middle school educator, artist*
Morgan, Ethel Branman *accountant, retired electronics engineer*
Morgan, Timothy Wayne, Sr. *district attorney*
Motz, Kenneth Lee *former farm organization official*
Noble, Ronald Mark *sports medicine facility administrator*
Nuessle, William Raymond *surgeon*
Olstead, Christopher Eric *aerospace executive, talent manager*
Parnell, Thomas Alfred *physicist*
Potter, Ernest Luther *lawyer*
Quick, Jerry Ray *academic administrator*
Reece, Wanda G. *space station training engineer, writer*
Richter, William, Jr. *technical management consulting executive*
Robb, David Metheny, Jr. *art historian*
Roberts, Frances Cabaniss *history educator*
Robinson, Isaiah, Jr. *minister*
Schonberg, William Peter *aerospace, mechanical, civil engineering educator*
Schroer, Bernard Jon *industrial engineering educator*
Shafer, Roberta W. Crow (Robbie Shafer) *human resources executive, career marketing consultant, venture capital consultant*
Smith, Robert Earl *space scientist*
Spor, Mary W. *English educator*
Stephens, (Holman) Harold *lawyer*
Stuhlinger, Ernst *physicist*
Theisen, Russell Eugene *electrical engineer*
Vaughan, Otha H., Jr. *retired aerospace engineer, research scientist*
Vaughan, William Walton *atmospheric scientist*
Vinz, Frank Louis *electrical engineer*
Watson, Raymond Coke, Jr. *engineering executive, academic administrator*
Watts, William Park *naval officer*
White, John Charles *historian*
Williamson, Donald Ray *retired career Army officer*
†Wolfe, Jackie Lee, Jr. *protective services professional*
Wright, John Collins *retired chemistry educator*
Wu, Ying Chu Lin Susan *engineering company executive, engineer*
Yang, Hong-Qing *mechanical engineer*

Hurtsboro
Bouilliant-Linet, Francis Jacques *global management consultant*

Irondale
Karr, Beverly Ann *counselor*

Jacksonville
Austin, Dan *retired dean*
Boswell, Rupert Dean, Jr. *retired academic administrator, math educator*
Browder, John Glen *former congressman, educator*
Dunaway, Carolyn Bennett *retired sociology educator*
Fairleigh, James Parkinson *music educator*
Fairleigh, Marlane Paxson *retired business consultant, educator*
Hale, Judy Ann *education educator*
Horton, Gloria Ann *English educator*
Hubbard, William James *library director*
McGee, Harold Johnston *academic administrator*
Merrill, Martha *instructional media educator*

Jasper
Bevill, Tom *retired congressman, lawyer*

Lillian
Moyer, Kenneth Evan *psychologist, educator*

Livingston
DeMay, Patricia Ann *elementary educator, education educator*
Green, Asa Norman *university president*

Loachapoka
Schafer, Elizabeth Diane *historian, writer*
Schafer, Robert Louis *agricultural engineer, researcher*

Madison
Adams, Gary Lee *systems engineer*
Barbour, Blair Allen *electro-optical engineer, researcher*
Dannenberg, Konrad K. *aeronautical engineer*
Evensen, Alf John *engineer, researcher, sales executive*
Hawk, Clark Williams *mechanical and aerospace engineering educator*
Reddy, Thikkavarapu Ramachandra *electrical engineer*

Maxwell AFB
†Ellis, Edward R. (Buster) *career officer*
Kane, Robert Barry *career officer*
Kinnan, Timothy Alan *air force officer*
Kline, John Alvin *academic administrator*
†Rosa, John William *career officer*
Wendzel, Robert Leroy *political science educator*

Mc Calla
Gentry, Vicki Paulette *museum director*

Meridianville
Oberhausen, Joyce Ann Wynn *aircraft company executive, artist*

Midfield
Bush, Dennis *radio personality*

Mobile
Adams, Jeffrey Paul *insurance agent, insurance company executive*
Armbrecht, William Henry, III *retired lawyer*
Atkinson, William James, Jr. *retired cardiologist*
Ballard, Michael Eugene *lawyer*
Bell, John *state agency executive*
†Bodie, Belin Frederick *dermatologist*
Booker, Larry Frank *accountant*
Bostwick, Robert O. *municipal staff member*
Brandon, Jeffrey Campbell *physician, interventional radiologist, educator*
Braswell, Louis Erskine *lawyer*
Brogdon, Byron Gilliam *physician, radiology educator*
Butler, Charles Randolph, Jr. *federal judge*
Byrd, Mary Jane *education educator*
Callahan, Sonny (H.L. Callahan) *congressman*
Cashdollar, Dick *protective services official*
†Cassady, William E. *federal judge*
Clark, Jack *retired hospital company executive, accountant*
†Clark, Veronica Ann Wilds (Ronni Patriquin Clark) *journalist*
Clausell, Deborah Deloris *artist, songwriter*
Cochran, Samuel M. *protective services official*
Coker, Donald William *economic, management, banking, evaluation & healthcare consultant*
Conrad, Marcel Edward *hematologist, educator*
Copeland, Lewis *principal*
Cox, Emmett Ripley *federal judge*
Cummings, James M. *urology educator*
Dansak, Daniel Albert *medical educator, consultant*
DeBakey, Ernest George *physician, surgeon*
†Delaney, Caldwell *museum director*
Delaney, Thomas Caldwell, Jr. *city official*
Durizch, Mary Lou *radiology educator*
Edwards, Jack *former congressman, lawyer*
Eichold, Samuel *medical educator, medical museum curator*
Floyd, Cinthia Ann *secondary school educator, coach*
Foster, J. Don *lawyer*
Goff, William M., Jr. *art director, graphic designer*
Guarino, Anthony Michael *pharmacologist, educator, consultant, counselor*
Hamid, Michael *electrical engineering educator, consultant*
Hamner, Eugenie Lambert *English educator*
Hand, William Brevard *federal judge*
Harris, Benjamin Harte, Jr. *lawyer*
Hearin, William Jefferson *newspaper publishing company executive*
Helmsing, Frederick George *lawyer*
Holland, Lyman Faith, Jr. *lawyer*
Holmes, Broox Garrett *lawyer*
Howard, Alex T., Jr. *federal judge*
Jones, Daniel Hare *librarian, consultant*
Kahn, Gordon Barry *retired federal bankruptcy judge*
Kimbrough, William Adams, Jr. *lawyer*
Lindsey, Bebe Gustin *fundraiser*
Lipscomb, Oscar Hugh *archbishop*
Lyons, George Sage *lawyer, oil industry executive, former state legislator*
†Mahoney, Margaret A. *federal judge*
McCall, Daniel Thompson, Jr. *retired judge*
McCann, Clarence David, Jr. *special events coordinator, museum curator and director, artist*
McCleery, Winston Theodore *computer consulting company executive*
McElhaney, Lynne Meyer *chemistry and biology educator*
†Miller, John C. H., Jr. *lawyer*
†Milling, Bert William, Jr. *magistrate judge*
Moore, Robert J. *United States marshal*
Murchison, David Roderick *lawyer*
Parmley, Loren Francis, Jr. *medical educator*
Parsley, Brantley Hamilton *librarian*
Peplowski, Celia Ceslawa *librarian*
Perkins, Marie McConnell *real estate executive*
Perry, Nelson Allen *radiation safety engineer, radiological consultant*
Pittman, Virgil *federal judge*
Richelson, Paul William *curator*
†Rodgers, Patricia Mansfield *librarian*
Rodning, Charles Bernard *surgeon*
Roedder, William Chapman, Jr. *lawyer*
†Sauer, David Kennedy *English educator*

Marcey, Jean LaVerne *educational association administrator*
Matsui, Dorothy Nobuko *elementary education educator*
Mattison, Elisa Sheri *organizational psychologist*
†McKay, Thomas W. *petroleum engineer*
Meddleton, Daniel Joseph *health facility administrator*
Molinari, Carol V. *writer, investment company executive, educator*
Munson, Vivian Ruth *lawyer*
Nielsen, Jennifer Lee *molecular ecologist, researcher*
O'Regan, Deborah *association executive, lawyer*
Overly, Frederick Dean *civilian military employee, entrepreneur*
Owens, Robert Patrick *lawyer*
Patrick, Leslie Dayle *hydrologist*
Pearson, Larry Lester *journalism educator, internet presence provider*
Perkins, Joseph John, Jr. *lawyer*
Porcaro, Michael Francis *advertising agency executive*
Pressley, James Ray *electrical engineer*
Price, Margaret Ruth *financial services company executive*
Rasmuson, Elmer Edwin *banker, former mayor*
Rieger, Steven Arthur *state legislator, business consultant*
Risley, Todd Robert *psychologist, educator*
Roberts, John Derham *lawyer*
Rollins, Alden Milton *documents librarian*
Rose, David Allan *investment manager*
Rosenfeld, Harry Leonard *rabbi*
†Ross, Herbert A. *federal judge*
Ross, Wayne Anthony *lawyer*
Rylander, Robert Allan *financial service executive*
Schnell, Roger Thomas *business owner, state official, retired career officer*
Sedwick, John W. *judge*
Selby, Jerome M. *mayor*
Shadrach, (Martha) Jean Hawkins *artist*
Shultz, Delray Franklin (Lucky Shultz) *management consultant*
Singleton, James Keith *federal judge*
Spencer, Ted *museum director*
Strohmeyer, John *writer, former editor*
Sullivan, George Murray *transportation consultant, former mayor*
Teague, Bruce Williams *chiropractor*
Teal, Gilbert Earle, II *lawyer, coast guard officer*
Thomas, Lowell, Jr. *author, lecturer, former lieutenant governor, former state senator*
Thrasher-Livingston, Kara Scott *program director*
Trevithick, Ronald James *underwriter*
†Udland, Duane S. *protective services official*
Udland, Dwane *protective services official*
von der Heydt, James Arnold *federal judge, lawyer*
Wagstaff, Robert Hall *lawyer*
Watts, Michael Arthur *materials engineer*
Wedel, Millie Redmond *secondary school educator*
Weinig, Richard Arthur *lawyer*
Wohlforth, Eric Evans *lawyer*
Wolf, Aron S. *medical director, psychiatrist*
Wolf, Patricia B. *museum director*

Arctic Village
Tritt, Lincoln C. *writer, educator, musician*

Barrow
Parkin, Sharon Kaye *bookkeeper*

Bethel
McMahon, Craig Roger *lawyer*
Selby, Naomi Ardean *women's health nurse, medical/surgical nurse*

Chiniak
Griffin, Elaine B. *educator*

Eagle River
Brooks, Stuart Dale *building consultant*
Cotten, Samuel Richard *former state legislator, fisherman*

Eielson AFB
†Crawford, Tommy F. *career officer*

Elmendorf AFB
Luckett, Byron Edward, Jr. *chaplain, career officer*

Fairbanks
Alexander, Vera *dean, marine science educator*
Beistline, Earl Hoover *mining consultant*
Berry, Kathryn Allen *editor in chief science publication*
Blake, Robert Philip *human services administrator, music therapist*
Brody, Bonnie *clinical social worker*
Burch, Barbara Jean *special education educator, administrator*
Davis, Charles Lee *fire marshal*
Doran, Timothy Patrick *educational administrator*
Duffy, Lawrence Kevin *biochemist, educator*
Falk, Marvin William *historian, bibliographer*
Fathauer, Theodore Frederick *meteorologist*
†Fenton, Thomas E., Jr. *federal judge*
Fischer, Robert Edward *meteorologist*
Hopkins, David Moody *geologist*
Jonaitis, Aldona Claire *museum administrator, art historian*
†Kaniecki, Michael Joseph *bishop*
Kessel, Brina *ornithologist, educator*
Kleinfeld, Andrew Jay *federal judge*
Krauss, Michael Edward *linguist*
Kunz, Michael Lenney *archaeologist*
Lind, Marshall L. *academic administrator*
Lingle, Craig Stanley *glaciologist, educator*
McNutt, Stephen Russell *volcanologist, geophysical scientist*
Mitchell, Susan E. *editor, desktop publisher*
Reichardt, Paul Bernard *provost, chemistry educator*
Roederer, Juan Gualterio *physics educator*
†Ruff, Doyle C. *airport manager*
Thompson, Daniel Emerson *vending machine service company executive*
Tilsworth, Timothy *retired environmental/civil engineering educator*
Weller, Gunter Ernst *geophysics educator*
White, Robert Gordon *research director, biology educator*
Wilkniss, Peter E. *foundation administrator, researcher*
Wood, William Ransom *retired university president, city official, corporate executive*

Fort Richardson
†Cash, Dean W. *military career officer*

Gakona
†Ainsworth, Cynthea Lee *folklorist*

Girdwood
†Trauter, John James *real estate executive*

Glennallen
Smelcer, John E. *publishing company executive*

Haines
Kaufman, David Graham *construction company executive*

Homer
Beach, Geo *journalist, poet*
Scruggs, Mary Ann *women's health nurse*

Indian
Wright, Gordon Brooks *musician, conductor, educator*

Juneau
Botelho, Bruce Manuel *state attorney general, mayor*
†Burke, Marianne King *state agency administrator, financial executive*
Bushre, Peter Alvin *investment company executive*
Cary, Suzanne *elementary education educator*
Cole, Charles Edward *lawyer, former state attorney general*
†Collins, Patricia A. *lawyer, judge*
†Condon, Wilson Leslie *commissioner*
Crane, Karen R. *director Alaska State Library*
†Dauenhauer, Richard Leonard *writer*
DeRoux, Daniel Grady *artist*
†Holloway, Shirley J. *state agency administrator*
Johnson, Mark Steven *public health administrator*
Kato, Bruce *curator*
†King, Robert Wilson *gubernatorial staff member*
†Kirkpatrick, Willis F. *state banking and securities administrator*
Knowles, Tony *governor*
Kohring, Victor H. *state legislator, construction executive*
Lauber, Mignon Diane *food processing company executive*
†Martin, Robert, Jr. *state agency administrator*
Meacham, Charles P. *president, capital consulting*
†Miller, David C. *airport manager*
Nave, Thomas George *lawyer*
†Perdue, Karen *state agency administrator*
Robinson, David B. *psychiatrist*
Romesburg, Kerry D. *state education administrator*
Ruotsala, James Alfred *historian, writer*
Schorr, Alan Edward *librarian, publisher*
Smith, Charles Anthony *businessman*
Twomley, Bruce Clarke *commissioner, lawyer*
Ulmer, Frances Ann *state official*
†Warfel, Michael W. *clergy member*
Wilbur, Robert L. *biologist, science editor*

Ketchikan
†Chenhall, Donald R. *airport manager*
†Dunning, David Michael *history educator*
Laurance, Leonard Clark *marketing researcher, educator and consultant*
McDermott, David (John) *artist, writer, photographer*

Kodiak
Croyle, Douglas Eugene *career officer*
Jamin, Matthew Daniel *lawyer, magistrate judge*
Ott, Andrew Eduard *lawyer*

Ninilchik
Oskolkoff, Grassim *Native American Indian tribal chief*

Nome
Dunaway, Samantha Jo *secondary school educator*
McCoy, Douglas Michael *social services administrator, clergyman*
Sloan, Patrice S. *artist*

Nondalton
Gay, Sarah Elizabeth *lawyer*

North Pole
Chamberland, Anna Margaret Pickett *communitcations professional, small business owner*
Fleming, Carolyn Elizabeth *religious organization administrator, interior designer*
James, Jeannette Adeline *state legislator, accountant*
†Prax, Glenn Michael *financial consultant*

Sitka
Carlson, Susan Spevack *medical director, family physician*
Ross, Dona Ruth *education program director, retired*

Soldotna
Franzmann, Albert Wilhelm *wildlife veterinarian, consultant*

Sterling
Frusetta, James Walter *historian*
Steckel, Barbara Jean *retired city financial officer*

Talkeetna
Stubblefield, Bobette Lynn *business administrator*

Tuntutuliak
Daniel, Barbara Ann *elementary and secondary education educator*

Valdez
Todd, Kathleen Gail *physician*

Wasilla
Moore, Toni Floss *elementary education educator*

Wrangell
Kraft, Richard Joe *sales executive*

ARIZONA

Apache Junction
Bracken, Harry McFarland *philosophy educator*
Cameron, Janice Carol *executive assistant*
Coe, Anne Elizabeth *artist*
Ransom, Evelyn Naill *language educator, linguist*
Winslow, Lillian Ruth *nurse*

Arizona City
Donovan, Willard Patrick *retired elementary education educator*
Ross, Lanson Clifford, Jr. *religion educator, author*

Avondale
Huffman, Thomas Patrick *secondary education educator*
Rosztoczy, Ferenc Erno *business executive*
SantaVicca, Edmund Frank *information scientist*
Thompson, Bonnie Ransa *secondary educator, chemistry educator*

Benson
Collmer, Russell Cravener *data processing executive, educator*

Bisbee
Eppele, David Louis *columnist, author*
Gustavson, Carrie *museum director*
Johnson, Heidi Smith *science educator*
Milton, John P. *ecologist, educator, author, photographer*
Stiles, Knute *artist*

Bowie
Burke, Ruth *writer*

Buckeye
Burton, Edward Lewis *retired industrial procedures and training consultant, educator*

Bullhead City
†Bettendorf, Jerry *airport administrator*
†Hicks, Norm *airport operations executive*

Carefree
Alexander, Judd Harris *retired paper company executive*
Birkelbach, Albert Ottmar *retired oil company executive*
Byrom, Fletcher Lauman *chemical manufacturing company executive*
Galda, Dwight William *financial company executive*
Giolito, Caesar Augustus *public relations executive, consultant*
Hook, William Franklin *retired radiologist*
Hutchison, Stanley Philip *lawyer, retired*
Wise, Paul Schuyler *insurance company executive*

Casa Grande
Houle, Joseph Adrien *orthopedic surgeon*
Hutchison, Pat *nurse, administrator*
McGillicuddy, Joan Marie *psychotherapist, consultant*
Rutherford, Linda Marie *corporate recruiter*

Cave Creek
†Kastelic, Robert L. *education educator*
LeNeau, Thomas Ervin *retired gas company executive*
O'Reilly, Thomas Eugene *human resources consultant*
†Valentine, Margo *secondary education educator*

Chandler
Barnard, Annette Williamson *elementary school principal*
†Barrett, Craig R. *computer company executive*
Bies, Roger David *cardiologist*
Brunello-McCay, Rosanne *sales executive*
†Eckstat, Arthur Gene *consultant*
Farley, James Newton *manufacturing executive, engineer*
Fordemwalt, James Newton *microelectronics engineering educator, consultant*
Goyer, Robert Stanton *communication educator*
Graham, Anita Louise *correctional and community health nurse*
Markey, James Kevin *lawyer*
Matus, Nancy Louise *artist*
Miller, Robert Carl *retired library director*
Myers, Gregory Edwin *aerospace engineer*
Robrock, James Lawrence *plastic surgeon*
Rowe, Ernest Ras *education educator, academic administrator*
Rudibaugh, Melinda Campbell *mathematics educator*
Shousha, Annette Gentry *retired critical care nurse*
Stewart, Nancy Sue Spurlock *educator*
Sue, Lawrence Gene *statistician*

Coolidge
Shih, Marie *metaphysical healer*

Cortaro
Fossland, Joeann Jones *professional speaker, personal coach*

Cottonwood
Izzo, Mary Alice *real estate broker*
Peck, Donald Harvey *chiropractor*

Davis Monthan A F B
†Corley, John D. W. *military officer*
Miller, Charles Wallace *historian, environmental geologist*

Dewey
Burch, Mary Lou *organization consultant, housing advocate*

Douglas
Dusard, Jay *photographer*

Dragoon
Woosley, Anne I. *cultural organization administrator*

Duncan
Ouzts, Eugene Thomas *minister, secondary education educator*

Eagar
McCain, Buck *artist*
Saunders, James Harwood *accountant*

Flagstaff
Aurand, Charles Henry, Jr. *music educator*
Bertoldo, Joseph Ramon *lawyer*
Block, M. Juliann McCarthy *school psychologist*
Bolin, Richard Luddington *industrial development consultant*
†Castillo, Diana May *religious organization administrator*
Cline, Platt Herrick *author*
Colbert, Edwin Harris *paleontologist, museum curator*
†Connell, Charles W. *provost*
Cowser, Danny Lee *lawyer, mental health specialist*
Drickamer, Lee Charles *zoology educator*
Eide, Joel S. *museum director*
Evans, Ronald Allen *lodging chain executive*
Fox, Michael J. *museum director*
Giovale, Virginia Gore *medical products ecexutive, civic leader*
Gliege, John Gerhardt *lawyer*
Hammond, Howard David *retired botanist and editor*
Helford, Paul Quinn *communications educator, academic administrator*
Hooper, Henry Olcott *academic administrator, physicist*
Lockwood, Chris A. *business educator, consultant*
Lovett, Clara Maria *university administrator, historian*
Maxwell, Mary Susanna *psychology educator*
McDonald, Craydon Dean *psychologist*
Millis, Robert Lowell *astronomer*
Mullens, William Reese *retired insurance company executive*
Phillips, Arthur Morton, III *botanist, consultant*
Price, Peter Wilfrid *ecology educator, researcher*
Ratzlaff, Vernon Paul *elementary education educator, consultant*
Reyhner, Jon Allan *education educator*
Sanders, Meg *women's basketball coach*
Shoemaker, Carolyn Spellmann *planetary astronomer*
Siegmund, Mark Alan *editor, publisher, business consultant, design scientist*
Smith, Zachary Alden *political science and public administration educator*
Somerville, Mason Harold *mechanical engineering educator, university dean*
Stoops, Daniel J. *lawyer*
†Tanaka, Kenneth Lloyd *planetary geologist*
Venedam, Richard Joseph *chemist, educator*
†Verkamp, Stephen L. *federal judge*
†Walka, Joseph J. *economics educator*
†Weston, Laurie Beth *psychiatrist*
Wetzel, Wendy Sue *women's health nurse practitioner, holistic health nurse*

Fort Huachuca
Adams, Frank *education specialist*
Clark, Brian Thomas *mathematical statistician, operations research analyst*
Kelly, Maureen Ann *management accountant*
Tyler, Cecilia K. *army officer*

Fountain Hills
Gifford, Ray Wallace, Jr. *physician, educator*
Herzberger, Eugene E. *retired neurosurgeon*
Humes, Charles Warren *counselor, educator*
Tyl, Noel Jan *baritone, astrologer, writer*
York, Tina *painter*

Fredonia
Pickett-Trudell, Catherine *family therapist*

Ganado
Chamberlin, Ed *curator*

Gilbert
Bourne, Elfreda O. *community health nurse*
Conger-White, Christine Kathleen *utilization management coordinator*
Duran, Michael Carl *bank executive*
Earnhardt, Hal J., III *automotive executive*
Handy, Robert Maxwell *patent lawyer*
Kenney, Thomas Frederick *broadcasting executive*
Larson, Dorothy Ann *business educator*

Glendale
Altersitz, Janet Kinahan *principal*
Baum, Phyllis Gardner *travel management consultant*
Bellah, C. Richard *lawyer*
Bret, Donna Lee *elementary education educator*
Cassidy, Barry Allen *physician assistant, clinical medical ethicist*
Collins, Richard Francis *microbiologist, educator*
Edwards, Vicki Ann *elementary school assistant principal*
Galletti, Marie Ann *English language and linguistics educator*
Harris, Warren Lynn *development engineer*
Ingham, Edward A. *career officer*
Joseph, Gregory Nelson *media critic, writer*
Landrum, Larry James *computer engineer*
Lopez, Steven Richard *small business owner, consultant*
Louk, Donna Pat *elementary education educator, music educator*
Ricks, David Artel *business educator, editor*
Shimek, John Anton *legal investigation business owner, educator*
Sims, Glenn *sociologist, educator*
Throp, George Lawrence *secondary education educator, mathematics educator*
Trejos, Franklin Anthony *physician assistant*
Tuman, Walter Vladimir *Russian language educator, researcher*
Zinn, Dennis Bradley *magician, actor, corporate skills trainer*

Goodyear
Asadi, Robert Samir *high school principal*
Bailey, Thomas Everett *engineering company executive*

Grand Canyon
Arnberger, Robert *federal administrator*
Bryant, Leland Marshal *business and nonprofit executive*

Green Valley
Barich, Dewey Frederick *emeritus educational administrator*
Bates, Charles Carpenter *oceanographer*
Blickwede, Donald Johnson *retired steel company executive*
Brewington, Arthur William *retired English language educator*
Brissman, Bernard Gustave *insurance company executive*
Crystall, Joseph N. *communications company executive*
Dingle, Albert Nelson *meteorology educator*
Dmytryshyn, Basil *historian, educator*
Egger, Roscoe Lynn, Jr. *consultant, former IRS commissioner*
Friedman, Edward David *lawyer, arbitrator*
Gilliam, Mary *travel executive*
Johnson, Onalee H. *retired nursing educator*
Miner, Earl Howard *retired trust banker*
Nasvik-Dennison, Anna *artist*
Page, John Henry, Jr. *artist, educator*
Pike, George Harold, Jr. *religious organization executive, clergyman*
Ramette, Richard Wales *chemistry educator*
Smith, Raymond Lloyd *former university president, consultant*
White, Herbert Spencer *research library educator, university dean*

Hereford
Hirth, John Price *metallurgical engineering educator*
Schenk, Quentin Frederick *retired social work educator, mayor, psychologist*

Holbrook
†O'Hop, Suzanne Elizabeth *educator*
Palmer, Arthur Arvin *dean, rancher*
†Passer, Gary Louis *college president*

Kingman
McAfee, Susan Jacqueline *county official*
†Wickstrom, Clifton Duane *county executive, educator*

Lake Havasu City
Barbieri, Arthur Robert *insurance agent, former chemical company official*
Shervheim, Lloyd Oliver *insurance company executive, lawyer*

Lake Montezuma
Burkee, Irvin *artist*

Luke AFB
†Barry, John L. *military officer*

Many Farms
Hamilton, Jimmy Ray *secondary education educator*

Mesa
Anderson, Herschel Vincent *librarian*
Boyd, Leona Potter *retired social worker*
Brown, Wayne J. *mayor*
Carter, Sally Packlett *elementary education educator*
†Christiansen, Larry K. *college president*
Colbert, George Clifford *college official*
†Darling, Sandra Kay *educational consultant, school administrator*
DeRosa, Francis Dominic *chemical company executive*
Evans, Don A. *healthcare company executive*
Fiorino, John Wayne *podiatrist*
†Fleisher, Mark *health care executive*
Frisk, Jack Eugene *recreational vehicle manufacturing company executive*
Garwood, John Delvert *former college administrator*
Hagen, Nicholas Stewart *medical educator, consultant*
Hiatt, Holly Marlane *history educator*
Johnson, Doug *advertising and public relations executive*
Kaida, Tamarra *art and photography educator*
Klosowski-Gorombei, Deborah Ann *nursing administrator, flight nurse*
Lengeman, William Irving, III *writer*
Luth, William Clair *retired research manager*
Mason, Marshall W. *theater director, educator*
McCollum, Alvin August *real estate company executive*
Mead, Linda McCullough *secondary education educator, adult educator*
Mead, Tray C. *museum director*
Murphy, Edward Francis *sales executive*
Philbrick, Douglas Robert *principal, librarian, educator, mental health professional*
Ramirez, Janice L. *assistant school superintendent*
Rummel, Robert Wiland *aeronautical engineer, author*
Sanders, Aaron Perry *radiation biophysics educator*
Shelley, James LaMar *lawyer*
Simpson, John Berchman, Jr. *clergy member, chaplain, retired law enforcement officer, retired newspaper editor*
Squire, Bruce M. *lawyer*
Stott, Brian *software company executive*
Tennison, William Ray, Jr. *financial planner, stockbroker, resort owner*
Tindle, Charles Dwight Wood *broadcasting company executive*
Wong, Willie *former mayor, automotive executive*

Miami
†Ladendorff, Linda Hardin-Reed *early childhood education educator*

Morenci
Subia, Eva M. *medical/surgical and community health nurse*

Nogales
Castro, Raul Hector *lawyer, former ambassador, former governor*

Oracle
Brusca, Richard Charles *zoologist, researcher, educator*
Rush, Andrew Wilson *artist*

Oro Valley
Loeh, Corinne Rachow *artist*
Oro, Debra Ann *dentist*
Tinker, Robert Eugene *minister, educational consultant*

Page
Hart, Marian Griffith *retired reading educator*
Leus McFarlen, Patricia Cheryl *water chemist*

Paradise Valley
Cussler, Clive Eric *author*
Day, Richard Putnam *marketing, strategic planning and employee benefits consultant, arbitrator*
Denning, Michael Marion *entrepreneur, computer company executive*
De Shazor, Ashley Dunn *business consultant*
Doede, John Henry *investment company executive*
Duff, James George *retired financial services executive*
Grimm, James R. (Ronald Grimm) *multi-industry executive*
Heller, Jules *artist, writer, educator*
Kilgore, L(eRoy) Wilson *minister*
Levetown, Robert Alexander *lawyer*
McKinley, Joseph Warner *health science facility executive*
†Meland, N. Bradley *plastic surgeon*
Polson, Donald Allan *surgeon*
Ratkowski, Donald J. *mechanical engineer, consultant*
Russell, Paul Edgar *electrical engineering educator*
Targovnik, Selma E. Kaplan *physician*
Turner, William Cochrane *international management consultant*
Unruh, James Arlen *former business machines company executive*

Payson
Lasys, Joan *medical nurse, writer, educator, publisher*

Peoria
Keesling, Karen Ruth *lawyer*
Lichtenberg, Larry Ray *chemist, consultant, researcher*
Morrison, Manley Glenn *real estate investor, former army officer*
Moshier, Mary Baluk *patent lawyer*
Saunders, James *management and training consultant*
Schindler, William Stanley *retired public relations executive, consultant*
Willard, Garcia Lou *artist*

Phoenix
Ainge, Danny Ray *professional basketball coach*
Allen, John Rybolt L. *chemist, biochemist*
Allen, Robert Eugene Barton *lawyer*
†Allen, Verna L. *state commissioner*
Alsentzer, William James, Jr. *lawyer*
Amavisca, Edward Dean *electrical engineer*
Amoako, James Kwaku *transportation services executive, financial analyst*
Anderson, Milada Filko *manufacturing company executive*
Arbetman, Jeffrey Farrell *lawyer*
Armstrong, Nelson William, Jr. *gaming company executive*
Aschaffenburg, Walter Eugene *composer, music educator*
Aybar, Charles Anton *aviation executive*
Bachus, Benson Floyd *mechanical engineer, consultant*
Bain, C. Randall *lawyer*
Baker, William Dunlap *lawyer*
Bakker, Thomas Gordon *lawyer*
Banerjee, Ajoy Kumar *engineer, constructor, consultant*
Barela, Bertha Cicci *elementary education educator, artist*
Barnes, Stephen Paul *financial planner*
†Baugh, James A. *mathematics educator, retired army officer*
†Baum, Redfield T., Sr. *federal judge*
Bayless, Betsey *state official*
Begam, Robert George *lawyer*
Bell, Jay Stuart *baseball player*
Bellus, Ronald Joseph *marketing and communications executive*
Benach, Sharon Ann *physician assistant*
Benes, Andrew Charles *professional baseball player*
†Berman, Tressa Lynn *anthropologist, writer*
Bidwill, William V. *professional football executive*
Bishop, C. Diane *state agency administrator, educator*
†Bivens, Donald Wayne *lawyer, judge*
†Blum, David Elias *neurlogist*
Bluth, Don *animator, director, screenwriter*
Bodney, David Jeremy *lawyer*
Bolin, Vernon Spencer *microbiologist, consultant*
Bolin, Vladimir Dustin *chemist*
Boozer, James L. *federal agency administrator*
Borel, James David *anesthesiologist*
Bostwick, Todd William *city archaeologist*
Bouma, John Jacob *lawyer*
Bradley, Gilbert Francis *retired banker*
Broomfield, Robert Cameron *federal judge*
Brown, James Carrington, III (Bing Brown) *public relations and communications executive*
Brunacini, Alan Vincent *fire chief*
†Buffmire, Donald K. *internist*
Burchard, John Kenneth *chemical engineer*
Burchfield, Don R. *counselor, youth services administrator*
Burg, Jerome Stuart *financial planning consultant*
Burgoyne, David Sidney *psychiatrist*
Burke, Timothy John *lawyer*
Buscha, Ralph Victor *security firm executive*
Butler, Byron Clinton *obstetrician, gynecologist*
Cain, Robert Joseph *elementary school educator*
Camous, Louise Michelle *secondary education educator, sister*
Canby, William Cameron, Jr. *federal judge*
Carpenter, Carol Settle *communications executive*
Carroll, Earl Hamblin *federal judge*
Carter, Ronald Martin, Sr. *pharmaceutical company executive*
Case, David Leon *lawyer*
Chan, Michael Chiu-Hon *chiropractor*
Charlton, John Kipp *pediatrician*
Chisholm, Tom Shepherd *environmental engineer*
Christensen, Bradford William *state official*
Clements, John Robert *real estate professional*
Cohen, Jon Stephan *lawyer*
Colangelo, Bryan *professional sports team executive*
Colangelo, Jerry John *professional basketball team executive*
Colburn, Donald D. *lawyer*
Cole, George Thomas *lawyer*
Condo, James Robert *lawyer*
Conrad, John Regis *lawyer, engineering executive*
Conway, David Antony *management executive, marketing professional*
Cook, Mary Margaret *steamfitter*
Cooledge, Richard Calvin *lawyer*
Coppersmith, Sam *lawyer*
Copple, William Perry *federal judge*
Cristiano, Marilyn Jean *speech communication educator*
Crockett, Clyll Webb *lawyer*
Culnon, Sharon Darlene *reading specialist, special education educator*
Curcio, Christopher Frank *city official*
Curley, Sarah Sharer *federal bankruptcy judge*
Currie, Constance Mershon *investment services professional*
Daniel, James Richard *accountant, computer company financial executive*
Daniels, Barbara Ann *non-profit organization executive*
Darby, Wesley Andrew *minister, educator*
Daughton, Donald *lawyer*
Davies, David George *lawyer*
DeBartolo, Jack, Jr. *architect*
Deeny, Robert Joseph *lawyer*
DeMichele, Mark Anthony *stage director, educator, actor*
De Michele, O. Mark *utility company executive*
Derdenger, Patrick *lawyer*
Derouin, James G. *lawyer*
Desser, Kenneth Barry *cardiologist, educator*
De Valeria, David Alan *architect, sculptor*
DeWall-Owens, Karen Marie *marketing consultant*
Dewane, John Richard *retired manufacturing company executive, consultan*
DiCiccio, Sal *city official*
Dignac, Geny (Eugenia M. Bermudez) *sculptor*
Dillenberg, Jack *public health officer*
Donnelly, Charles Robert *retired college president*
Dorland, Byrl Brown *retired civic worker*
Doto, Irene Louise *statistician*
Drain, Albert Sterling *business management consultant*
Drakulich, Martha *arts educator*
DuMoulin, Diana Cristaudo *marketing professional*
Dunipace, Ian Douglas *lawyer*
Durrant, Dan Martin *lawyer*
Duyck, Kathleen Marie *poet, musician, retired social worker*
Eaton, Berrien Clark *retired lawyer, author*
Edens, Gary Denton *broadcasting executive*
Ehmann, Anthony Valentine *lawyer*
Ehst, Eric Richard *aerospace engineer*
Elien, Mona Marie *air transportation professional*
Ellison, Cyril Lee *literary agent, retired publisher*
Elmore, James Walter *architect, retired university dean*
Esahak, George Michael *lawyer*
Everett, James Joseph *lawyer*
Everroad, John David *lawyer*
Faul, Gary Lyle *electrical engineering supervisor*
Feinstein, Allen Lewis *lawyer*
Feldman, Stanley George *state supreme court justice*
Fenzl, Terry Earle *lawyer*
Fine, Charles Leon *lawyer*
Fishburne, John Ingram, Jr. *obstetrician-gynecologist, educator*
Fitzgerald, Joan *principal*
Fitzgerald-Verbonitz, Dianne Elizabeth *nursing educator*
Fitzsimmons, (Lowell) Cotton *professional basketball executive, broadcaster, former coach*
Flickinger, Don Jacob *patent agent*
Frank, John Paul *lawyer, author*
Franke, William Augustus *corporate executive*
Freyermuth, Clifford L. *structural engineering consultant*
Fugiel, Frank Paul *insurance company executive*
Fulk, Roscoe Neal *retired accountant*
Fullmer, Steven Mark *systems engineer*
Gaffney, Donald Lee *lawyer*
Gaines, Francis Pendleton, III *lawyer*
†Garagiola, Joe, Jr. *baseball team executive*
†Garcia-Buñuel, Luis *neurologist*
Genrich, Mark L. *newspaper editorial writer, columnist*
Gerber, Rudolph Joseph *judge, educator*
Gibbs, William Harold *finance company executive*
Giedt, Bruce Alan *paper company executive*
Gilbert, Donald Roy *lawyer*
†Gillom, Jennifer *professional basketball player*
Gladner, Marc Stefan *lawyer*
Godwin, Mary Jo *editor, librarian consultant*
Goldberg, Morris *internist*
Goldenthal, Nathan David *physician*
Goldman, Charles *electromechanical engineer*
Goldstein, Stuart Wolf *lawyer*
Gossell, Terry Rae *advertising agency executive, small business owner*
Grafe, Warren Blair *cable television executive*
Griller, Gordon Moore *court administrator*
Grinell, Sheila *museum director*
†Gronseth, Daniel Edward *park ranger*
Gunty, Christopher James *newspaper editor*
Gwozdz, Kim Elizabeth *interior designer*
Halpern, Barry David *lawyer*
Hamilton, Darden Cole *flight test engineer*
Hamilton, Ronald Ray *minister*
Hanley, Fred William *librarian, educator*
Hardin, Terrence Armstrong *radio broadcasting manager*
Hardy, Charles Leach *federal judge*
Harnett, Lila *retired publisher*
Harrison, Mark Isaac *lawyer*
Harte, John Joseph Meakins *bishop*
Hassett, Brian Thomas *administrator local chapter of United Way*
Hawkins, Jasper Stillwell, Jr. *architect*
Hayden, William Robert *lawyer*
Hays, E. Earl *youth organization administrator*
Healy, Barbara Anne *insurance company executive, financial planner*
Hemond, Roland A. *professional baseball team executive*
Henely, Geraldine Josephine *medical/surgical nurse*
Herranen, Kathy *artist, graphic designer*
Hicks, Bethany Gribben *judge, lawyer, commissioner*
Hicks, William Albert, III *lawyer*
Hienton, James Robert *lawyer*
Hoecker, Thomas Ralph *lawyer*
†Holdsworth, John H. *marketing professional*
Holloway, Edgar Austin *retired diversified business executive*
†Houseworth, Richard Court *state agency administrator*
Hoxie, Joel P. *lawyer*
Hudson, Laura Lyn Whitaker *scientific researcher*
Huffman, Edgar Joseph *oil company executive*
Hughes, Robert Edward *elementary education educator*
Hull, Jane Dee *governor, former state legislator*
Huntwork, James Roden *lawyer*
Hutchinson, Ann *development director*
Jacobson, Albert Dale *pediatrician, accountant*
Jacobson, (Julian) Edward *lawyer*
James, Charles E., Jr. *lawyer*
Jansen, Donald William *lawyer, legislative administrator*
Jirauch, Charles W. *lawyer*
Johnson, Kevin Maurice *professional basketball player*
Johnson, Mary *museum director*
Johnson, Pam *newspaper editor*
Johnson, Randall David (Randy Johnson) *professional baseball player*
Johnston, Logan Truax, III *lawyer*
Jorgensen, Gordon David *engineering company executive*
Jungbluth, Connie Carlson *accountant, tax professional*
Kail, Konrad *physician*
Kaiser, Robert Blair *journalist*
Kaliszek, Andrew Wojciech *mechanical engineer*
Kandell, Howard Noel *pediatrician*
Kaufman, Roger Wayne *state judge*
†Keegan, Lisa Graham *state education agency adminstrator*
Kelley, Patricia Austin *publishing executive*
Kidd, Jason *professional basketball player*
Kimball, Bruce Arnold *soil scientist*
King, Felton *bishop*
King, Jack A. *lawyer*
Klahr, Gary Peter *lawyer*
Klausner, Jack Daniel *lawyer*
Knoller, Guy David *lawyer*
Koester, Berthold Karl *lawyer, law educator, retired honorary German consul*
Kolbe, John William *newspaper columnist*
Komando, Kimberly Ann *computer company executive, radio and television host*
Kopp, David Eugene *manufacturing company executive*
Kreutzberg, David W. *lawyer*
Krueger, John Charles *financial planner, investment advisor*
Kuivinen, Ned Allan *pathologist*
Kupel, Douglas Edward *historian*
Kurn, Neal *lawyer*
Kurtz, Joan Helene *pediatrician*
†Kuzma, George Martin *bishop*
Land, George A. *philosopher, writer, educator, consultant*
Lang, Patricia Ann *school nurse*
Laufer, Nathan *cardiologist*
Lawrence, William Doran *physician*
Leach, John F. *newspaper editor, journalism educator*
Le Clair, Douglas Marvin *lawyer, educator, judge*
Lee, Richard H(arlo) *lawyer*
Leeland, Steven Brian *electronics engineer*
Lemon, Leslie Gene *retired diversified services company executive*
Leonard, Elizabeth Lipman *psychologist*
Leonard, Jeffrey S. *lawyer*
Lewis, Orme, Jr. *investment company executive, land use advisor*
Lidman, Roger Wayne *museum director*
Linderman, William Earl *elementary school educator, writer*
Lingner, Doug *city official*
Linxwiler, Louis Major, Jr. *retired finance company executive*
Lowry, Edward Francis, Jr. *lawyer*
Lubin, Stanley *lawyer*
Lyon, William James *sociology educator*
Lyons, Lionel Dale *city equal opportunity director*
Madden, Paul Robert *lawyer*
Maimon, Elaine Plaskow *English educator, university provost*
Manning, Daniel Ricardo *professional basketball player*
Manning-Weber, Claudia Joy *medical radiography administrator, consultant*
Marks, Merton Eleazer *lawyer*
Martone, Frederick J. *state supreme court justice*
Martori, Joseph Peter *lawyer*
†Mathis, Virginia *federal judge*
McClelland, Norman P. *food products executive*
McClennen, Crane *judge*
Mc Clennen, Louis *lawyer, educator*
McCoy-Shay, Donna Carol *telecommunication manager*
McDougall, Roderick Gregory *lawyer*
McGuire, Gerard Joseph *engineering executive*
McKeighen, Ronald Eugene *physicist*
McKelvey, Tanya Hope *biologist, physical anthropologist*
McNamee, Stephen M. *federal judge*
McRae, Hamilton Eugene, III *lawyer*
Meister, Frederick William *state official, lawyer*
Melinosky, Karen Elizabeth *special education educator*
Melner, Sinclair Lewis *insurance company executive, retired*
Meridith, Denise Patricia *government official*
Merlin Kearfott, DuVal *health consultant*
Merritt, Nancy-Jo *lawyer*
Mertes, Sharon Colleen *women's health nurse*
Meschkow, Jordan Mark *patent lawyer*
Meyers, Howard Craig *lawyer*
Meyerson, Bruce Elliot *lawyer*
†Michael, Hermann *music director*
†Miller, Cheryl DeAnn *professional basketball coach, broadcaster*
Miller, Eleanor Louise *lawyer*
Miller, Louis Rice *lawyer*
Miller, Michael Jon *survey engineer, local government manager*
Miller, William *broadcast executive*
Minor, Willie *college department chair*
Mitchell, Wayne Lee *health care administrator*
†Montague, Gray *performing company executive*
Montague, Sidney James *real estate developer*
†Mooreman, Robert G. *federal judge*
Morrison, Richard Neely *deacon*
Mousel, Craig Lawrence *lawyer*
Moya, Patrick Robert *lawyer*
Moyer, Alan Dean *retired newspaper editor*
Mullen, Daniel Robert *finance executive*
Murphy, John W. *foundation executive*
†Murrell, Adrian Bryan *professional football player*
Myers, Cindy L. *museum director*
Myers, Robert David *judge*
Napolitano, Janet Ann *state attorney general*

Nelson, John councilman, engineering executive
Newman, Lois Mae marketing executive
†Nielsen, George B.
Nielson, Theo Gilbert law enforcement official, university official
Nijinsky, Tamara actress, puppeteer, author, librarian, educator
Nishioka, Teruo (Ted Nishioka) electrical engineer
North, Patrick broadcasting executive
North, Warren James government official
†Noyes, Francie state official
O'Brien, Thomas Joseph bishop
Olsen, Alfred Jon lawyer
Olson, Robert Howard lawyer
Oppedahl, John Fredrick publisher
O'Steen, Van lawyer
Palmer, Alice Eugenia retired physician, educator
Papp, Harry science association administrator
Pasholk, Paul Douglas retail executive, government official
Perry, Lee Rowan retired lawyer
Pettis, Bridget basketball player
Pettle, Cecile city director
Piatt, Malcolm Keith, Jr. medical center administrator
Platt, Warren E. lawyer
Plattner, Richard Serber lawyer
†Plummer, Jason Steven (Jake) professional football player
Pogson, Stephen Walter lawyer
Price, Charles Steven lawyer
Prieto, Vicente chiropractor
Quayle, James Danforth (Dan) former vice president United States, entrepreneur
Quayle, Marilyn Tucker lawyer, wife of former vice president of United States
Rathwell, Peter John lawyer
Rau, David Edward real estate company executive
Reed, Wallace Allison physician
Refo, Patricia Lee lawyer
Reyes, Anna Maria broadcast executive
Rimsza, Skip mayor
Rister, Gene Arnold humanities educator
Roe, William Thomas behaviorial engineer, educator, researcher
†Roenick, Jeremy professional hockey player
Romley, Richard M. lawyer
Rosen, Sidney Marvin lawyer
Rosenblatt, Paul Gerhardt judge
Rowley, Beverley Davies medical sociologist
Rudolph, Gilbert Lawrence lawyer
Saffo, Mary Beth biologist
St. Clair, Thomas McBryar mining and manufacturing company executive
Savage, Stephen Michael lawyer
Scarbrough, Ernest Earl stockbroker, financial planner
Schabow, John William accountant
Schatt, Paul newspaper editor
Schaumburg, Donald Roland art educator, ceramic artist
Schiffner, Charles Robert architect
†Schilling, John Michael education director
Schroeder, Mary Murphy federal judge
Seamons, Quinton Frank lawyer
Sebold, Duane David food manufacturing executive
Seiler, Steven Lawrence health facility administrator
Sherk, Kenneth John lawyer
Showalter, Buck (William Nathaniel Showalter, III) major league baseball team manager
Sibbio, Michael Gregory promoter, concept developer, audio technical consultant
Siebert, Dave councilman
Silver, Roslyn O. judge, federal
Silverman, Alan Henry lawyer
†Silverman, Barry G. federal judge
Simpson, Charles Robert marketing professional
Singer, Jeffrey Alan surgeon
†Sitver, Morton federal judge
Sliger, Herbert Jacquemin, Jr. lawyer
Smith, Stuart Robert foundation executive
Smith-Hart, Ann Aurelia instructional services administrator
Smock, Timothy Robert lawyer
Snare, Carl Lawrence, Jr. business executive
Snell, Richard holding company executive
Solheim, Karsten golf equipment company executive
Solomon, John Davis aviation executive
Sourbrine, Richard Don, II architect
Stahl, Louis A. lawyer
Steckler, Phyllis Betty publishing company executive
Stern, Richard David investment company executive
Stern, Stanley psychiatrist
Steward, Lester Howard psychiatrist, academic administrator, educator
Storey, Lee A. lawyer
Storey, Norman C. lawyer
Strand, Roger Gordon federal judge
Subach, James Alan information systems company executive, consultant
Sullivan, Martin Edward museum director
Sullivan, Mary Kathleen nurse
Swann, Eric Jerrod professional football player
Teets, John William retired diversified company executive
Thompson, Joel Erik lawyer
Thompson, Terence William lawyer
Timms, Michele professional basketball player
Tkachuk, Keith professional hockey player
Tobin, Vincent Michael professional football coach, former sports team executive
Udall, Calvin Hunt lawyer
Ulrich, Paul Graham lawyer, author, publisher, editor
Upson, Donald V. financial executive, retired
Uthoff, Michael dancer, choreographer, artistic director
Van Arsdale, Dick professional basketball team executive
Van Horssen, Charles Arden manufacturing executive
Van Kilsdonk, Cecelia Ann retired nursing administrator, volunteer
Veit, William Arthur financial planner
Vu, Eric Tin neurobiologist, researcher
Walker, Richard K. lawyer
Wall, Donald Arthur lawyer
Weber, Fredric G. broadcast executive
Weil, Louis Arthur, III newspaper publishing executive
Welliver, Charles Harold hospital administrator
Wendel, O. Theodore, Jr. university associate provost
West, Tony state official
Wheeler, Steven M. lawyer
Whisler, James Steven lawyer, mining and manufacturing executive
White, Edward Allen electronics company executive
†Whitlow, Donna Mae daycare and primary school administrator
Whitlow, William La Fond minister, theology school planter
Williams, A. Cody councilman
Williams, Aeneas Demetrius professional football player
Williams, Arleen Rolling pediatrics nurse
Williams, Joyce Marilyn artist, business owner
Williams, Matt (Matthew Derrick Williams) professional baseball player
Williams, Quinn Patrick lawyer
Wilson, Stephen Rip public policy consultant
Winslow, Paul David architect
Winthrop, Lawrence Fredrick lawyer
Witherspoon, James Donald biology educator
†Wold, Kimberly G. legislative staff member
Wolf, G. Van Velsor, Jr. lawyer
Wolf, Irna Lynn psychologist
Wood, Barbara Butler secondary language arts and television production educator
Woods, Bobby Joe transportation executive
Woods, Donald Peter real estate executive, marketing professional
Woods, Grant lawyer, former state attorney general
Woolf, Michael E. lawyer
Wright, Richard Oscar, III pathologist, educator
†Wu, Jianguo ecologist, educator
Yarnell, Michael Allan lawyer
Yearley, Douglas Cain mining and manufacturing company executive
Zerella, Joseph T. pediatric surgeon

Pima
Shafer, James Albert health care administrator

Pine
Gurney, Evalyn Hartung retired secondary school educator

Portal
Zweifel, Richard George curator

Prescott
Anderson, Arthur George laboratory director, former computer company executive, consultant
Anderson, Parker Lynn editorial columnist, playwright
†Anderson, Walter Lee environmental educator, artist, photographer
Beaumont, Roderick Fraser education consultant
Bieniawski, Zdzislaw Tadeusz Richard engineering educator emeritus, writer, consultant
Brown, James Isaac rhetoric educator
Chesson, Eugene, Jr. civil engineering educator, consultant
Goodman, Gwendolyn Ann nursing educator
Goodman, Mark N. lawyer
Gose, Richard Vernie lawyer
Hasbrook, A. Howard aviation safety engineer, consultant
Kahne, Stephen James systems engineer, educator, academic administrator, engineering executive
Kleindienst, Richard Gordon lawyer
Martinez, Anthony Joseph real estate appraiser
Mc Cormack, Fred Allen state social services administrator
Moore, Elizabeth Jane banker
Morrison, Gladys Mae pilot training firm executive
Moses, Elbert Raymond, Jr. speech and dramatic arts educator
Osborn, DeVerle Ross insurance company executive
Palmer, Robert Arthur private investigator
Parkhurst, Charles Lloyd electronics company executive
Rheinish, Robert Kent university administrator
Rindone, Joseph Patrick clinical pharmacist, educator
Stasack, Edward Armen artist
White, Brittan Romeo manufacturing company executive
Willoughby, James Russell artist, author

Prescott Valley
Cole, Susie Cleora retired government employee relations official
Peoples, Esther Lorraine elementary education educator
Wynn, Robert Raymond retired engineer, consultant

Rio Verde
Jordan, Richard Charles engineering executive
Ramsey, David Selmer retired hospital executive

Roll
Jorajuria, Elsie Jean elementary education educator

Sacaton
Stephenson, Larry Kirk stategic planner, management, geography educator

Safford
Riddlesworth, Judith Himes elementary and secondary education educator

San Manuel
Hawk, Dawn Davah secondary education educator
Hawk, Floyd Russell secondary school educator
Lemley, Diane Claire Beers principal

Scottsdale
Adams, Robert Granville marketing professional
Allison, Stephen Galender broadcast executive
Angle, Margaret Susan lawyer
Baker, Jeffrey Charles telecommunications executive
Ball, Donald Edmon architect
Berry, Charles Richard lawyer
Biglin, Karen Eileen library director
Blanchet, Jeanne Ellene Maxant artist, educator, performer
Blinder, Martin S. business consultant, art dealer
Boat, Ronald Allen business executive
Bonner, Thomas Neville history and higher education educator
Bragg, David Gordon physician, radiology educator
Braun, Stephen Hughes psychologist
Brown, Shirley Margaret Kern (Peggy Brown) interior designer
Budge, Hamer Harold mutual fund company executive
Buel, Jeffrey A. pharmaceutical executive
Buri, Charles Edward lawyer
Burke, Richard Kitchens lawyer, educator
Burr, Edward Benjamin life insurance company executive, financial executive
Carpenter, Betty O. writer
Chase, James Keller retired artist, museum director, educator
Clement, Richard William plastic and reconstructive surgeon
Comfort, Clifton C. management consultant, fraud examiner
Cormie, Donald Mercer investment company executive
Cunningham, Gilbert Earl business owner
Dalton, Howard Edward retired accounting executive
Dobronski, Mark William judge, justice of the peace
Doglione, Arthur George data processing executive
Donaldson, Scott English language educator, writer
Doyle, Michael Joseph mining executive
Draeger, Kenneth W. high technology company executive
Eckelman, Richard Joel engineering specialist
Eide, Imogene Garnett nursing consultant
Esquer, Deborah Anne elementary education educator
Evans, Tommy Nicholas physician, educator
Everingham, Harry Towner editor, publisher
Fennelly, Jane Corey lawyer
Ferree, John Newton, Jr. fundraising specialist, consultant
Fink, Joel Charles dermatologist, retired
Fisher, John Richard engineering consultant, former naval officer
Fosgate Heggli, Julie Denise producer
Fratt, Dorothy artist
Freedman, Stanley Marvin manufacturing company executive
Friedman, Shelly Arnold cosmetic surgeon
Friesen, Oris Dewayne software engineer, historian
Frischknecht, Lee Conrad retired broadcasting executive
Gans, Eugene Howard cosmetic and pharmaceutical company executive
Garfield, Ernest bank consultant
Garling, Carol Elizabeth real estate executive and developer
Gilson, Arnold Leslie retired engineering executive
Gookin, Thomas Allen Jaudon civil engineer
Gray, Walter Franklin retired banker
Grenell, James Henry retired manufacturing company executive
Grier, James Edward hotel company executive, lawyer
†Grimm, Phillip Henry electronic security company executive
†Grogan, James J. real estate company executive
Gwinn, Mary Dolores business developer, philosopher, writer, speaker
Hansen, Donald W. insurance and financial services executive
Harrison, Harold Henry physician, scientist, educator
Henry, Lois Hollender psychologist
Hill, Louis Allen, Jr. former university dean, consultant
Hill, Robert Martin police detective, forensic document examiner, consultant, lecturer
Hockmuth, Joseph Frank physicist, psychotherapist
Holliger, Fred Lee oil company executive
Hooker, Jo interior designer
Howard, William Gates, Jr. electronics company executive
Inman, William Peter lawyer
Itkin, Robert Jeffrey lawyer
Jacobson, Frank Joel cultural organization administrator
Jann, Donn Gerard minister
Johnson, Micah William television newscaster, director
Kane-Villela, Grace McNelly maternal, women's health and pediatrics nurse
Kiehn, Mogens Hans aviation engineer, consultant
Kizziar, Janet Wright psychologist, author, lecturer
Kjellberg, Betty J. association administrator
Kleppe, Shirley R. Klein artist
Klien, Wolfgang Josef architect
Krupp, Clarence William lawyer, personnel and hospital administrator
Kübler-Ross, Elisabeth physician
Lang, Margo Terzian artist
Lee, Dennis Turner civil engineer, construction executive
†Leighton, William D. plastic and reconstructive surgeon
Lillestol, Jane Brush career development company executive
Lillo, Joseph Leonard osteopath, family practice physician
Lloyd, Eugene Walter retired construction company executive
†Lloyd, Sally-Heath Fahnestock artist
Luke, David Kevin investment company executive
Malsack, James Thomas retired manufacturing company executive
Mayer, Robert Anthony retired college president
Mc Knight, William Warren, Jr. publisher
McPherson, Donald J. metallurgist
Meyers, Marlene O. hospital administrator
Mousseux, Renate language educator
Mueller, Gerald Damon Adent publisher, editor
Muller, H(enry) Nicholas, III foundation executive
Mybeck, Richard Raymond lawyer
Myers, Clay retired investment management company executive
Nadler, Henry Louis pediatrician, geneticist, medical educator
Newman, Marc Alan electrical engineer
†Novicki, Donald Edward urologic surgeon
O'Berry, Carl Gerald former air force officer, electrical engineer
O'Donnell, William Thomas management consultant
Olwin, John Hurst retired surgeon
Orford, Robert Raymond consulting physician
Perry, David Niles public relations executive
Peshkin, Samuel David lawyer
Peterson, John Willard composer, music publisher
Pitcher, Helen Ione advertising director
Ragland, Samuel Connelly industrial engineer, management consultant
Ralston, Joanne Smoot public relations counseling firm executive
Reins, Ralph Erich automotive components supply company executive
Reznick, Richard Howard pediatrician
Roberts, Jean Reed lawyer
Roberts, Peter Christopher Tudor engineering executive
Roe, Richard C. industry consultant, former home furnishings manufacturing executive
Rosenthal, Charles Louis artist, educator
Rudd, Eldon retired congressman, political consultant
Rutes, Walter Alan architect
Sanderson, David R. physician
Scherzer, Joseph Martin dermatologist
Scholder, Fritz artist
Sears, Alan Edward lawyer
Simmons, Julie Lutz artist
Sirven, Joseph Ignatius neurologist
Smith, Leonard Bingley musician
Soleri, Paolo architect, urban planner
Starr, Phillip Henry psychiatrist, educator
Swanson, Robert Killen management consultant
Swartz, Melvin Jay lawyer, author
Swetnam, Monte Newton petroleum exploration executive
Titus, Jon Alan lawyer
†Trojanowski, Deborah A. plastic surgeon
Troxell, Mary Theresa (Terry Troxell) geriatrics services professional
Tyner, Neal Edward retired insurance company executive
Vairo, Robert John insurance company executive
Van Dusen, Peter artist
Walsh, Edward Joseph toiletries and food company executive
Warnas, Joseph John municipal official
Weil, John David teleservices executive
Wolf, Anne K. sales and marketing executive
Wong, Astria Wor cosmetic business consultant
Wright, C. T. Enus former academic administrator

Sedona
Becker, Wesley Clemence psychology educator emeritus
Bolton, Robert Floyd construction executive
Catterton, Marianne Rose occupational therapist
Chicorel, Marietta Eva publisher
Eggert, Robert John, Sr. economist
Goldberg, Melvyn retired educator
Gregory, James retired actor
Griffin, (Alva) Jean entertainer
Hawkins, David Ramon psychiatrist, writer, researcher
Iverson, Wayne Dahl landscape architect, consultant
Prather, Richard Scott author
Reno, Joseph Harry retired orthopedic surgeon
Rhines, Marie Louise composer, violinist
Shors, Clayton Marion cardiologist
Stoufer, Ruth Hendrix community volunteer
Thorne, Kate Ruland writer, publisher, editor
Ware, Peggy Jenkins photographer, writer, artist, dancer
Wolfe, Al marketing and advertising consultant

Sierra Vista
Cowger, Phyllis nurse
Ford, Frederick Jay clergyman
Lutes, Todd Oakley political science educator
Michelich, Joanna Kurdeka academic administrator
Morrow, Bruce William educational administrator, business executive, consultant, author
Plum, Richard Eugene retired flight engineer
Ricco, Raymond Joseph, Jr. computer systems engineer
Sizemore, Nicky Lee computer scientist
Smith, Donna Nadine army noncommissioned officer

Snowflake
Freyermuth, Gundolf S. writer

Sonoita
Cook, William Howard architect

Springerville
Geisler, Sherry Lynn magistrate

Sun City
Farwell, Albert Edmond retired government official, consultant
Jackson, Randy computer networking executive
Lapsley, James Norvell, Jr. minister, pastoral theology educator
Lutin, David Louis real estate development and finance consultant
Oppenheimer, Max, Jr. foreign language educator, consultant
Pallin, Samuel Lear ophthalmologist, educator
Park, Francis Wood, III retired minister
Randall, Claire church executive
Roberts, Anna Ruth financial consultant
Thompson, Betty Jane small business owner
Treece, James Lyle lawyer
Vander Molen, Jack Jacobus engineering executive, consultant
Van Horssen, Arden Darrell retired manufacturing executive

Sun City West
Berkenkamp, Fred Julius management consultant
Bowkett, Gerald Edson editorial consultant, writer
Calderwood, William Arthur physician
Cohen, Abraham J. (Al Cohen) educational administrator
Coté, Ralph Warren, Jr. mining engineer, nuclear engineer
Forbes, Kenneth Albert Faucher urological surgeon
Forti, Lenore Steimle business consultant
Madson, John Andrew architect
†Manville, Greta C. writer
Mc Cune, John Francis, III retired architect
Mc Donald, Barbara Ann psychotherapist
O'Brien, Gerald James utilities executive
Person, Robert John financial management consultant
Pipitone, Phyllis L. psychologist, educator, author
Schrag, Adele Frisbie business education educator
Stevens, George Richard business consultant, public policy commentator
Suttles, Virginia Grant advertising executive
Wasmuth, Carl Erwin physician, lawyer
Williams, William Harrison retired librarian
Woodruff, Neil Parker agricultural engineer

Sun Lakes
Houser, Harold Byron epidemiologist
Richardson, Robert Carleton engineering consultant
Smith, Eleanor Jane university chancellor, retired, consultant
Thompson, Loring Moore retired college administrator, writer

Surprise
Black, Robert Frederick former oil company executive
Clark, Lloyd historian, educator
Eriksen, Otto Louis retired manufacturing company executive
Shipley, Linda Diane Stuff gerontology and medical/surgical nurse
Veigel, Jon Michael science administrator

Taylor
Kerr, Barbara Prosser solar device designer

Teec Nos Pos
Smith, Mark Edward music educator

Tempe
Adelson, Roger Dean history educator, editor, historian
Alisky, Marvin Howard political science educator
Allen, Charles Raymond television station executive
Anand, Suresh Chandra physician
Arters, Linda Bromley public relations consultant, writer, lecturer
Balanis, Constantine Apostle electrical engineering educator
Bauer, Ernst Georg physicist, educator
Berman, Neil Sheldon chemical engineering educator
Bjork, Robert Eric language professional educator
Blankenship, Robert Eugene chemistry educator
Brack, O. M., Jr. English language educator
Bristol, Stanley David mathematics educator
†Bucklin, Leonard Herbert lawyer
Buseck, Peter Robert geochemistry educator
†Chambers, Anthony Hook Literature educator
Clevenger, Jeffrey Griswold mining company executive
†Codell, Julie Francia university administrator
Coor, Lattie Finch university president
Cortright, Barbara Jean writer
Cowley, John Maxwell physics educator
Doebler, Bettie Anne language educator, researcher, writer
Douglas, Michael publishing executive
Downs, Floyd L. mathematics educator
Evans, Lawrence Jack, Jr. lawyer
Farber, Bernard sociologist, educator
Ferry, David Keane electrical engineering educator
Forsyth, Ben Ralph academic administrator, medical educator
Ger, Shaw-Shyong accountant
Glick, Milton Don chemist, university administrator
Golshani, Forouzan computer science and engineering educator
Gordon, Leonard sociology educator
Goronkin, Herbert physicist
†Gruzinska, Aleksandra language educator
Guinouard, Donald Edgar psychologist
Guinouard, Philip Andre restaurant executive
Guzzetti, Barbara Jean education educator
Hackett, Edward John sociology educator and researcher
Harris, Mark English educator, author
Hempfling, Gregory Jay mechanical engineer
Herald, Cherry Lou research educator, research director
†Hestenes, David physics educator
Hickson, Robin Julian mining company executive
Hoke, Judy Ann physical education educator
Hoppensteadt, Frank Charles educator, mathematician, university administrator
Ihrig, Edwin Charles, Jr. mathematics educator
Iverson, Peter James historian, educator
Johanson, Donald Carl physical anthropologist
Juvet, Richard Spalding, Jr. chemistry educator
Karady, George Gyorgy electrical engineering educator, consultant
Kaufman, Herbert Mark finance educator
Kaufman, Irving retired engineering educator
Kenyon, David Lloyd architect, architectural firm executive
Kinney, Raleigh Earl artist
Lange, Lynette Patricia nurse
Lein, Randy coach
Lombardi, Eugene Patsy orchestra conductor, violinist, educator, recording artist
Lounsbury, John Frederick geographer, educator
Lunsford, Jack William community colleges official
MacKinnon, Stephen R. Asian studies administrator, educator
Mahajan, Subhash electronic materials educator
Mason, Terence K. critical care nurse
Matheson, Alan Adams law educator
Mathews, Wilma Kendrick public relations executive
Matthews, Gertrude Ann Urch retired librarian, writer
Maynard, Michael librarian
McKeever, Jeffrey D. computer company executive
McKelvy, Michael John materials chemist, research scientist
Mc Sheffrey, Gerald Rainey architect, educator, city planner
Mense, Allan Tate research and development engineering executive
Metcalf, Virgil Alonzo economics educator
Miller, Warren Edward political scientist
Missimer, Denise Louise mental health nurse
Montero, Darrel Martin social worker, educator
Moore, Carleton Bryant geochemistry educator
Moore, Rob professional football player
Nagrin, Daniel dancer, educator, choreographer, lecturer, writer
Nigam, Bishan Perkash physics educator
Oakes, Thomas Chapas financal analyst
O'Neil, Michael Joseph opinion survey executive, marketing consultant
Overman, Glenn Delbert college dean emeritus
Owens, Michael L. radio station executive
Pany, Kurt Joseph accounting educator, consultant
Patten, Duncan Theunissen ecologist educator
Pettit, George Robert chemistry educator, cancer researcher
Péwé, Troy Lewis geologist, educator
Pijawka, David environmental educator, researcher
Poe, Jerry B. financial educator
Presley-Holloway, Marsha Ann planetary scientist
Quadt, Raymond Adolph metallurgist, cement company executive
Raby, William Louis author
Rankin, William Parkman educator, former publishing company executive
Rice, Ross R(ichard) political science educator
Richards, Gale Lee communication educator
Robertson, Samuel Harry, III transportation safety research engineer, educator
Roy, Asim business educator
Ruiz, Vicki Lynn history educator
Sabine, Gordon Arthur educator, writer
Sackton, Frank Joseph public affairs educator
Saunders, Karen Estelle secondary school educator
Schneller, Eugene Stuart health adminstration and policy educator
Schroder, Dieter Karl electrical engineering educator
Scott, Judith Myers elementary education educator
Severe, Salvatore Francis school psychologist
Shaw, Milton Clayton mechanical engineering educator
Shimpock, Kathy Elizabeth lawyer, writer
Si, Jennie engineering educator
Simmons, Howard Lee education educator
Simon, Sheldon Weiss political science educator
Smith, Carol Estes city councilman
Smith, David John physicist, educator
Smith, Harvey Alvin mathematics educator, consultant
Snyder, Bruce Fletcher coach
Snyder, Lester M. sports association executive
Spritzer, Ralph Simon lawyer, educator
Starrfield, Sumner Grosby astrophysics educator, researcher
Stephenson, Frank Alex engineer, consultant
Sullivan-Boyle, Kathleen Marie association executive
Tambs, Lewis Arthur diplomat, historian, educator
†Taylor, Nora Annesley humanities educator, art historian
Thorne, Charlie Turner women's collegiate basketball coach
Turk, Rudy Henry artist, retired museum director
Uttal, William R(eichenstein) psychology and engineering educator, research scientist
Vandenberg, Edwin James chemist, educator
Wallen, Carl J. education educator
†Warner, Michael Dennis educator
Wehinger, Peter Augustus astronomer, educator
Weigend, Guido Gustav geographer, educator
Weiler, Dorothy Esser librarian
†Wentz, Richard Eugene religious studies educator
Wesbury, Stuart Arnold, Jr. health administration and policy educator
White, Kevin M. athletic director
Williams, James Eugene management consultant
Wills, J. Robert academic administrator, drama educator, writer
Yau, Stephen Sik-sang computer science and engineering educator, computer scientist, researcher

Thatcher
Heaton, Debbie Ann mental health services worker

Tonalea
Francisco, Irving landmark administrator

Tonopah
Brittingham, James Calvin nuclear engineer

Tubac
Fey, John Theodore retired insurance company executive
Miller, Frederick Robeson banker

Tucson
Abrams, Herbert Kerman physician, educator
Acker, Loren Calvin medical instrument company executive
Acker, Robert Flint microbiologist
Alberts, David Samuel physician, pharmacologist, educator
Alpert, Joseph Stephen physician, educator
Andersen, Luba electrologist, electropigmentologist
Anderson, Rachael Keller library administrator
Angel, James Roger Prior astronomer
Armstrong, R(obert) Dean entertainer
Arnell, Walter James William mechanical engineering educator, consultant
Austin, John Norman classics educator
Baldwin, Ira Lawrence retired bacteriologist, educator
Ballou, Kenneth Walter retired transportation executive, university dean
†Bannard, Ann sculptor
Barrett, Bruce Richard physics educator
Bartlett, David Carson state legislator
Barton, Stanley Faulkner management consultant
†Bautzmann, Nancy Annette artist
Beach, Lee Roy psychologist, educator, academic administrator
Bell, Alan lawyer, environmental health activist
Ben-Asher, M. David physician
Bennett, Pamela Yvonne diabetes resource nurse, pediatrics nurse
Bergamo, Ron marketing executive
Best, Gary Thorman commercial real estate broker
Betteridge, Frances Carpenter retired lawyer, mediator
Bilby, Richard Mansfield federal judge
Billings, Richard Bruce economics educator, consultant
Birkby, Walter Hudson forensic anthropologist, consultant
Block, Michael Kent economics and law educator, public policy association executive, former government official, consultant
Blue, James Guthrie retired veterinarian
Bodinson, Holt conservationist
Bonvincini, Joan M. university women's basketball coach
Boyse, Edward Arthur research physician
Brainerd, Charles J(on) experimental psychologist, applied mathematician, educator
Brasswel, Kerry tax accountant, horsewoman
Breckenridge, Klindt Duncan architect
Brewer, Barbara Bagdasarian nursing administrator
†Briggs, Laura humanities
Broadfoot, Albert Lyle physicist
Brooks, Donald Lee civil engineering and scientific consulting firm executive
Brosin, Henry Walter psychiatrist, educator
Brown, Don museum director
Browning, William Docker federal judge
Brunton, Daniel William mechanical engineer
Bryan, Gordon Redman, Jr. retired naval officer
†Bryan, Judith Hager travel consultant, educator
Bryning, Susan Mary critical care nurse, adult nurse practitioner
Burg, Walter A. airport terminal executive
Burrows, Benjamin retired physician, educator
Butcher, Russell Devereux author, photographer
Cain, Shannon Margaret fundraising executive
†Canfield, John Douglas English educator, writer, consultant
Capp, Michael Paul physician, educator
Case, Richard W. sports association executive
Casper, Wayne Arthur state government official, educator
Cate, Rodney Michael academic administrator
†Chalmers, David J. philosophy educator
Chidester, Otis Holden retired secondary education educator
†Childs, Richard Francis scientist, educator, retired
Citron, David Sanford physician
Clarke, James Weston political science educator, writer
Coates, Wayne Evan agricultural engineer
Code, Arthur Dodd astrophysics educator
Coffman, Roy Walter, III publishing company executive
Cogut, Theodore Louis environmental specialist, meteorologist
Conant, Howard Somers artist, educator
Cook, Paul Christopher engineering psychologist
Cortner, Hanna Joan science administrator, research scientist, educator
Cox, Robert Gene management consultant
Cox, Stephen F. retired publishing company executive
Crawford, David L. astronomer
Crawford, Michael city council
Cuello, Joel L. biosystems engineer, educator
Cutrone, Lawrence Gary school system administrator, consultant, writer
Dahood, Roger English literature educator
Dalen, James Eugene physician, educator
D'Antonio, James Joseph lawyer
Davies, Roger geoscience educator
Davis, James Luther retired utilities executive, lawyer
Davis, Richard Calhoun dentist
Davis, Stanley Nelson hydrologist, educator
Deluca, Dominick medical educator, researcher
Dessler, Alexander Jack space physics and astronomy educator, scientist
De Young, David Spencer astrophysicist, educator
Dickinson, Robert Earl atmospheric scientist, educator
Dinnerstein, Leonard historian, educator
Dinsmore, Philip Wade architect
Dobbs, Dan Byron lawyer, educator
Dodd, Charles Gardner physical chemist
Dolph, Wilbert Emery lawyer
Done, Robert Stacy consultant
Dufner, Max retired German language educator
Dyer-Raffler, Joy Ann special education diagnostician, educator
Eckdahl, Donald Edward manufacturing company executive
Eckhardt, August Gottlieb law educator
Eribes, Richard dean
Evans, Arthur Haines, Jr. educational consultant, researcher
Ewy, Gordon Allen cardiologist, researcher, educator
Fang, Li-Zhi physicist, educator
Fasel, Hermann F. aerospace and mechanical engineering educator
Feliciano, José entertainer
†Fiora, Nancy federal judge
Fontana, Bernard Lee retired anthropologist, writer, consultant
Foran, Kevin Richard television station executive
Fortman, Marvin law educator, consultant
Fritts, Harold Clark dendrochronology educator, researcher
Froman, Sandra Sue lawyer
Furlow, Mary Beverley English language educator
Gantz, David Alfred lawyer, university official
Garner, Girolama Thomasina retired educational administrator, educator
Garza, Elizeo director solid waste management, Tucson
Geistfeld, Ronald Elwood retired dental educator
Gerhart, Dorothy Evelyn insurance executive, real estate professional
Giesser, Barbara Susan neurologist, educator
Giorgi, Peter Bonnard educator
Glaser, Steven Jay lawyer
Gourley, Ronald Robert architect, educator
Graham, Anna Regina pathologist, educator
Grayeski, Mary Lynn chemist, foundation administrator
Green, Richard Frederick astronomer
Green, Robert Scott biotechnology company executive
Griffen, Agnes Marthe library administrator
Grimes, James Cahill retired publishing executive, advertising executive
Grubb, L(ewis) Craig investment company executive, consultant
Gruhl, James energy scientist
Guice, John Thompson retired career officer
Hale, William Bryan, Jr. newspaper editor
Hamilton, Ruth Hellmann design company owner
Hanson, George music director, conductor
Harinck, John Gordon sales executive, hydraulics engineer
Harrington, Roger Fuller electrical engineering educator, consultant
Harris, David Thomas immunology educator
Harrison, Edward Robert physicist, educator
Hartmann, William Kenneth astronomy scientist
Hawke, Robert Francis dentist
Hay, Richard Le Roy geology educator
Haynes, Caleb Vance, Jr. geology and archaeology educator
Hays, James Fred geologist, educator
Heins, Marilyn college dean, pediatrics educator, author
Heller, Frederick retired mining company executive
Herrnstadt, Richard Lawrence American literature educator
Hershberger, Robert Glen architect, educator
Hildebrand, John G(rant) neurobiologist, educator
Hill, Henry Allen physicist, educator
Hiskey, J. Brent metallurgical engineer, educator
Hoffmann, William Frederick astronomer
Hogle, Jerrold Edwin English language educator
Horan, Mary Ann Theresa nurse
Howard, Robert Franklin observatory administrator, astronomer
Hoyt, Charlee Van Cleve management executive
Hruby, Victor Joseph chemistry educator
Hubbard, William Bogel planetary sciences educator
Huggins, Delma Bustamante community nurse, family nurse practitioner
Hull, Herbert Mitchell plant physiologist, researcher
Hunt, Bobby Ray electrical engineering educator, consultant
Hunten, Donald Mount planetary scientist, educator
Hurt, Charlie Deuel, III dean, educator
Hutchinson, Charles Smith, Jr. book publisher
Hyams, Harold lawyer
Ibarra, Jose city council
†Inman, Billie Jo (Andrew) writer, retired English educator
Irvin, Mark Christopher real estate consultant, broker and developer
Jackel, Lawrence publishing company executive
Jackson, Kenneth Arthur physicist, researcher
Jacome, Felipe Carlos anthropologist
Jamison, Harrison Clyde former oil company executive, petroleum exploration consultant
Jeffay, Henry biochemistry educator
Jefferies, John Trevor astronomer, astrophysicist, observatory administrator
Jeter, Wayburn Stewart retired microbiology educator, microbiologist
Johnson, Christopher Gardner technology educator
Johnson, John Gray retired university chancellor
Johnson, Robert Bruce company director
Jones, Frank Wyman management consultant, mechanical engineer
Jones, John Stanley director special projects, Tucson
Kaltenbach, C(arl) Colin dean, educator
Kany, Judy C(asperson) health policy analyst, former state senator
Karkoschka, Erich planetary science researcher, writer
Karson, Catherine June computer programmer, consultant
Katakkar, Suresh Balaji hematologist, oncologist
Kaucher, James William lawyer
Kearney, Joseph Laurence retired athletic conference administrator
Kerr, Frederick Hohmann health care company executive
Kerwin, William James electrical engineering educator, consultant
Kessler, John Otto physicist, educator
†Kiefer, Frederick P. English educator
Kiersch, George Alfred geological consultant, retired educator
Kimble, William Earl lawyer
King, Marcia management consultant
Kingsolver, Barbara Ellen writer
Kinney, Robert Bruce mechanical engineering educator
Kmet, Rebecca Eugenia Patterson pharmacist
Kotin, Paul pathologist
Krider, E. Philip atmospheric scientist, educator
†Kruse, Diane Viewing college library director
Labelle, James William retired pediatrician
Labiner, David M. neurologist
Lacagnina, Michael Anthony judge
Lamb, Willis Eugene, Jr. physicist, educator
Langendoen, Donald Terence linguistics educator
Langum, W. Sue civic worker
Larson, L. Jean educational administrator
Law, John Harold biochemistry educator
Leal, Steve city council
Leavitt, Jerome Edward childhood educator
Lehrling, Terry James real estate broker
Lesher, Robert Overton lawyer
Levenson, Alan Ira psychiatrist, physician, educator
Lewis, Wilbur H. educational management consultant
Likins, Peter William university administrator
Lombard, Richard Spencer lawyer
Lomicka, William Henry investor
Longan, George Baker, III real estate executive
†Lowe, Jonathan F. writer
Lunine, Jonathan Irving planetary scientist, educator
Lyman, Darlice Murphy critical care nurse
Macleod, Hugh Angus McIntosh optical science educator, physicist, consultant
Madden, James A. gifted and talented educator
Magnotto, Rebecca Adiutori community and mental health nurse
Maker, Carol June gifted and talented educator
Malmgren, René Louise educational theater administrator
Marcialis, Robert Louis planetary astronomer
Marcus, Frank Isadore physician, educator
Marcus, Janet city council
†Marlar, James M. federal judge
Marquez, Alfredo C. federal judge
Martin, June Johnson Caldwell journalist
Martin, Paul Edward retired insurance company executive
Mason, Judith Ann freelance writer
Masters, William Howell physician, educator
McAllister, Patricia L. nurse
McCabe, Monica Jane oncological nurse
McCanless, Lauri Lynn neonatal and pediatrics nurse
McConnell, Robert Eastwood architect, educator
McCormick, Floyd Guy, Jr. agricultural educator, college administrator
Mc Donald, John Richard lawyer
McEwen, Alfred Sherman planetary geologist
Meehan, Michael Joseph lawyer
Meeker, Robert Eldon retired manufacturing company executive
Mercker, Mary Alice aviation school administrator
Metcalfe, Darrel Seymour agronomist, educator
Meyerson, Ronald L. director of operations, Tucson
Miller, George mayor
Milward, Hendree Brinton, Jr. management and public administration educator
Mishler, William, II political science educator
Mitchell, Robert Campbell nuclear consultant
Moreno, Manuel D. bishop
Morrow, James Franklin lawyer
Mullikin, Vernon Eugene aerospace executive
Nadler, George L. orthodontist
Nanz, Robert A. biochemist
Nation, James Edward retired speech pathologist
Negley, Floyd Rollin genealogist, retired army officer and civilian military employee
Nelson, Edward Humphrey architect
Neuman, Shlomo P. hydrology educator
Nugent, Charles Arter physician
Ogilvie, T(homas) Francis engineer, educator
†Ollason, Lawrence federal judge
Olson, Lute university athletic coach
†Oro, Robert John dentist, consultant, writer
Osterberg, Charles Lamar marine radioecologist, oceanographer
Pace, Thomas M. lawyer
Paez, Antonio Contreras director transportation Tucson
Parmenter, Robert Haley physics educator
Partridge, William Russell retired federal executive
Peeler, Stuart Thorne petroleum industry executive and independent oil operator
†Penner, Jonathan David English educator, writer
Pepper, Ian L. environmental microbiologist, research scientist, educator
Peters, Charles William research and development company manager
Polan, David Jay lawyer

Powell, Richard C. *physicist, educator, researcher*
Powers, Stephen *educational researcher, consultant*
Prince, John Luther, III *engineering educator*
Puente, Tito Anthony *orchestra leader, composer, arranger*
Rabuck, Donna Fontanarose *English writing educator*
Reid, Charles Phillip Patrick *academic administrator, researcher, educator*
Reinmuth, Oscar MacNaughton *physician, educator*
Renard, Kenneth George *civil engineer*
Rhoads, Preston Mark *pharmacist, consultant*
Rich, Bobby *broadcast personality, radio programmer*
Riggs, Frank Lewis *foundation executive*
Roemer, Elizabeth *astronomer, educator*
Rogers, John Alvin *retired technical educator, writer, publisher*
Roll, John McCarthy *judge*
Roos, Nestor Robert *consultant*
Root, Nile *photographer, educator*
Rose, Hugh *management consultant*
Ross, Mark L. *mortgage broker*
Ross, Robert *health agency administrator*
Rountree, Janet Caryl *astrophysicist*
Rubendall, Richard Arthur *civil engineer*
Russ, Joanna *author*
Rutter, George B., Jr. *career officer*
Salmon, Sydney Elias *medical educator, director*
Sampliner, Linda Hodes *psychologist, consultant*
Sander, Eugene George *vice provost, dean*
Sankovich, Joseph Bernard *cemetery management consultant*
Sarlat, Gladys *public relations consultant*
Schaefer, John Paul *chemist, corporate executive*
Schaffer, Richard E(nos) *artist, registrar*
Schannep, John Dwight *brokerage firm executive*
Schorr, S. L. *lawyer*
Schulman, Elizabeth Weiner *financial consultant*
Scott, Shirley *city council*
Scotti, James Vernon *astronomer*
Seaman, Arlene Anna *musician, educator*
Seay, Suzanne *financial planner, educator*
Sells, Kevin Dwayne *marine engineer*
Semm, Kurt Karl *obstetrics and gynecology researcher*
Sewell, Charles Robertson *geologist, exploration company executive, investor*
Shannon, Robert Rennie *optical sciences center administrator, educator*
Shropshire, Donald Gray *hospital executive*
Sibley, William Austin *neurologist, educator*
Sickel, Joan Sottilare *foundation administrator*
Smith, David Mitchell *fire and explosion consultant*
Smith, David Wayne *psychologist, educator*
Smith, Gordon Eugene *pilot*
Smith, Josef Riley *internist*
Smith, Vernon Lomax *economist, researcher*
Sohnen-Moe, Cherie Marilyn *business consultant*
Solomon, Vita Petrosky *artist*
Soren, David *archaeology educator, cinema author*
Sprague, Ann Louise *space scientist*
Stearns, Elliott Edmund, Jr. *retired surgeon*
Stein, Mary Katherine *writer, editor, photographer, communications executive*
Stini, William Arthur *anthropologist, educator*
Stoffle, Carla Joy *university library dean*
Strausfeld, Nicholas James *neurobiology and evolutionary biology researcher, educator*
Strittmatter, Peter Albert *astronomer, educator*
Strong, John William *lawyer, educator*
Sundt, Harry Wilson *construction company executive*
Swalin, Richard Arthur *scientist, company executive*
Tang, Esther Don *development consultant, retired social worker*
Taveggia, Thomas Charles *management consultant*
†Terlizzi, Raymond T. *federal judge*
Thompson, Raymond Harris *retired anthropologist, educator*
Tifft, William Grant *astronomer*
Tindall, Robert Emmett *lawyer, educator*
Tirrell, John Albert *organization executive, consultant*
Toland, Florence Winifred *printing company executive, retired business educator*
Tomoeda, Cheryl Kuniko *academic researcher*
Tretschok, Dale Deege *lawyer*
Underwood, Jane Hainline Hammons *anthropologist, educator*
Vanatta, Chester B. *retired business executive, educator*
Vicker, Ray *writer*
Vidal, Delia *medical/surgical and oncological nurse*
Villa, Jacqueline Irene *newspaper editor*
Volgy, Thomas John *political science educator, organization official*
Wahlke, John Charles *political science educator*
Walker, Franklin Curtis *national park administrator*
Wallach, Leslie Rothaus *architect*
Warren, Bacil Benjamin *writer, publisher*
Waterman, David Moore *lawyer*
Weaver, Albert Bruce *university administrator*
Weber, Charles Walter *nutrition educator*
Weber, Samuel *editor, retired*
Weil, Andrew Thomas *physician, educator*
Weinstein, Ronald S. *physician, pathologist, educator*
Weller, Cheryl K. *Internet service provider executive, educator*
Wheeler, Jeanette Norris *entomologist*
White, Jane See *journalist*
Whiting, Allen Suess *political science educator, writer, consultant*
Wickham, John Adams, Jr. *retired army officer*
Williams, John Charles, II *data processing executive*
Willoughby, Stephen Schuyler *mathematics educator*
Wilson, Teresa Ann *maternal/newborn nurse*
Winarski, Daniel James *mechanical engineer, educator*
Winfree, Arthur Taylor *biologist, educator*
Witte, Marlys Hearst *internist, educator*
Witten, Mark Lee *lung injury research scientist, educator*
Wolfe, William Jerome *librarian, English language educator*
Wolff, Sidney Carne *astronomer, observatory administrator*
Woolfenden, James Manning *nuclear medicine physician, educator*
Yassin, Robert Alan *museum administrator, curator*
Yocum, Harrison Gerald *horticulturist, botanist, educator, researcher*
Young, Donald Allen *writer, consultant*
†Zapata, Frank *federal judge*
Zube, Ervin Herbert *landscape architect, geographer, educator*
†Zwolinski, Malcolm John *natural resources educator*

Vail
Hunnicutt, Robert William *engineer*
Reichlin, Seymour *physician, educator*
Saul, Kenneth Louis *retired utility company executive*

Waddell
Turner, Warren Austin *state legislator*

West Sedona
Lane, Margaret Anna Smith *property manager developer*

Wickenburg
Baker, Carolyn *musician*

Window Rock
Hathaway, Loline *zoo and botanic park curator*

Winslow
Kaliher, Michael Dennis *librarian, historian*
Wolfe, Janice Kay *oncological nurse*

Youngtown
Gross, Al *electrical engineer, consultant*

Yuma
Desmond, Leif *writer*
Hilgert, Arnie *management and marketing educator*
Hossler, David Joseph *lawyer, law educator*
Hudson, John Irvin *retired career officer*
†Irwin, Jay R. *federal judge*
Jack, Dixie Lynn *software consultant, social worker*
Martin, James Franklin *physician, lawyer*
†Nelson, Rodney *writer, editor*
Norton, Dunbar Sutton *economic developer*
Rivera, Jaime Arturo *secondary education educator, principal*
Stuart, Gerard William, Jr. *investment company executive, city official*
Talbot, Devon Vvictor *precious metals dealer, writer*

ARKANSAS

Alma
†Dyer, V. Jeffrey *principal*

Arkadelphia
Bass, Carol Ann (Mitzi Bass) *English language educator*
Butler, Dartha Jean *middle school educator*
Dunn, Charles DeWitt *academic administrator*
Elrod, Ben Moody *academic administrator*
†Fendley-Herbert, Debi Lynn *artist, art educator*
Grant, Daniel Ross *retired university president*
Halaby, Raouf Jamil *English and art educator, consultant*
Mueller, Gene Albert *dean, social sciences educator*
Sandford, Juanita Dadisman *sociologist, educator, writer*
Thomas, Herman L. *school system administrator*
Webster, Robert Lee *accounting educator, researcher*

Batesville
Carius, Robert Wilhelm *mathematics and science educator, retired naval officer*
Harkey, John Norman *judge*
Logan, Michael J. *veterinary medical officer*

Bella Vista
Cooper, John Alfred, Jr. *community development company executive*
Fite, Gilbert Courtland *historian, educator, retired*
Johnson, A(lyn) William *chemistry educator, writer, researcher, consultant*
Medin, Myron James, Jr. *city manager*
Musacchia, X(avier) J(oseph) *physiology and biophysics educator*
Pogue, William Reid *former astronaut, foundation executive, business and aerospace consultant*
Rose, Donald L. *physician, educator*
Sutherland, Gail Russell *retired industrial equipment manufacturing company executive*

Bentonville
Glass, David D. *department store company executive, professional baseball team executive*
Glover, Deborah Joyce *school psychologist, consultant*
Higham, Paul H. *marketing professional*
Ingram, Dale *consumer products company executive*
Rhoads, Robert K. *lawyer, retail executive*
Walton, S. Robson *discount department store chain executive*
†White, Nick *retail executive*

Berryville
Brown, Frances Louise (Grandma Fran Brown) *artist, art gallery owner*

Blytheville
†Davidson, Michael W. *psychologist*
Fendler, Oscar *lawyer*
Slowik, Richard Andrew *air force officer*

Brookland
†Angleman-Noble, Sharon Ann *journalist*

Camden
Bradshaw, Otabel *retired primary school educator*
Owen, Larry Gene *academic administrator, educator, electronic and computer integrated manufacturing consultant*

Cedarville
Whitaker, Ruth Reed *retired newspaper editor*

Cherokee Village
Hollingsworth, John Alexander *retired science and mathematics educator, writer, consultant*

Clarksville
Mooney, Robbi Gail *operations officer*
Pennington, Donald Harris *musician, retired physician*

Conway
Daugherty, Billy Joe *banker*
Die, Ann Marie Hayes *college president, psychology educator*
Hatcher, Joe Branch *executive search consulting company executive*
Hays, Steele *retired state supreme court judge*
Horton, Finis Gene *financial services company executive*
Horton, Joseph Julian, Jr. *academic dean, educator*
Johnson, James Douglas (Jim Johnson) *lawyer*
†Knipscheer, Carol S. *English language educator*
Maakestad, Erik Paul *artist, educator*
Mc New, Bennie Banks *economics and finance educator*
Moore, Herff Leo, Jr. *management educator*
Morgan, Charles Donald, Jr. *manufacturing executive*
Petersen, Laddian Walter *flight operations director*
Plotkin, Helen Ann *writer, editor*
Polk, William Allen *city planner, architect*
Reddin, George *religious organization administrator*
†Ruehle, Jon *sculptor*
Thompson, Winfred Lee *university president, lawyer*
Titlow, Larry Wayne *physical education and kinesiology educator*

Crofton
Parsley, Robert Charles *minister*

Crossett
Hubbell, Billy James *lawyer*
†Smith, Connie Simpson *secondary school educator*

Dermott
Bynum, Judith Lane *special education educator*

Des Arc
Branham, Elizabeth Mullen *educational administrator*

El Dorado
Barnes, Harry F. *federal judge*
Lee, Vernon Roy *minister*
†Shepherd, Bobby E. *federal judge*
Vaughan, Odie Frank *oil company executive*
Watkins, Jerry West *retired oil company executive, lawyer*

Enola
Brown, Lois Heffington *health facility administrator*

Eureka Springs
Dragonwagon, Crescent (Ellen Zolotow) *writer*

Fayetteville
Ahlers, Glen-Peter, Sr. *law library director, educator, consultant*
Andrews, John Frank *civil and environmental engineering educator*
Bassett, Woodson William, Jr. *lawyer*
Bennett, Sonja Quinn *administrative assistant*
Blair, Gary *women's collegiate basketball coach*
Brady, Robert *communications educator*
Brown, Connell Jean *retired animal science educator*
Brown, Craig Jay *ophthalmologist*
Burggraf, Frank Bernard, Jr. *landscape architect, retired educator*
Cook, Doris Marie *accountant, educator*
Copeland, John Dewayne *law educator*
Davis, Wylie Herman *lawyer, educator*
Dockery, Robert Gerald *minister*
Dulan, Harold Andrew *former insurance company executive, educator*
Evans, William Lee *biologist*
Ferritor, Daniel E. *educator*
Gaddy, James Leoma *chemical engineer, educator*
Gatewood, Willard Badgett, Jr. *historian*
Grammer, Frank Clifton *oral surgeon, researcher*
Green, Thomas James *archaeologist*
Hay, Robert Dean *retired management educator*
Hendren, Jimm Larry *federal judge*
Jackson, Robert Lee *real estate agent*
Jones, Euine Fay *architect, educator*
Kellogg, David Wayne *agriculture educator, researcher*
Lacy, Claud H. Sandberg *astronomer*
Levine, Daniel Blank *classical studies educator*
Lieber, Michael *physics educator*
Madison, Bernard L. *mathematics educator*
Malone, David Roy *state senator, university administrator*
Marquardt, Stephen Alan *ironworks company executive*
Masterson, Michael Rue *journalist, educator, editor*
McDonnell, John *coach*
Mc Gimsey, Charles Robert, III *anthropologist*
Morris, Justin Roy *food scientist, consultant, enologist, research director*
Musick, Gerald Joe *entomology educator*
Naseem, Hameed Ahmad *educator*
Orr, Betsy *business education educator*
Pearson, Charles Thomas, Jr. *lawyer*
†Restrepo, Luis Fernando *Latin-American literature educator*
†Richardson, Nolan *university athletic coach*
Riggs, Robert Dale *plant pathology/nematology educator, researcher*
Rosenberg, Leon Joseph *marketing educator*
Scharlau, Charles Edward, III *natural gas company executive*
Schoppmeyer, Martin William *education educator*
Scifres, Charles Joel *agricultural educator*
Shafer, Carol Larsen *retired book reviewer*
Simpson, Ethel Chachere *archivist*
Thornton, Mitchell Aaron *engineering educator, consultant*
Van Patten, James Jeffers *education educator*
VanWinkle, John Ragan *lawyer*
Waters, H. Franklin *federal judge*
Webb, Lynne McGovern *communication educator, consultant*
White, John Austin, Jr. *engineering educator, chancellor*
Wilkins, Charles L. *chemistry educator*
Williams, Doyle Z. *university dean, educator*
Williams, Miller *poet, translator*
Wilson, Charles Banks *artist*

Forrest City
Creasey, Katherine Yvonne *family nurse practitioner*
Stipe, John Ryburn *bank executive*

Fort Huachuca
†Sutten, Charles G., Jr. *career military officer*

Fort Smith
†Banks, David R. *health products executive*
Banks, David Russell *health care executive*
Coleman, Michael Dortch *nephrologist*
Craig, David Clarke *financial advisor, instructor*
Decker, Josephine I. *health clinic official*
Dotson, Donald L. *lawyer*
Drolshagen, Leo Francis, III *radiologist, physician*
Flanders, Donald Hargis *manufacturing company executive*
Gooden, Benny L. *school system administrator*
Harper, S. Birnie *business brokerage company owner*
Hembree, Hugh Lawson, III *diversified holding company executive*
Holmes, Paul Kinloch, III *prosecutor*
Howell, James Tennyson *allergist, immunologist, pediatrician*
Husarik, Stephen *music educator*
Miles, Travis Anthony *state senator*
Montgomery, M. Darlene *secondary education educator, English educator*
Paxton, Jackie Lee *education educator, writer, consultant*
Pollan, Carolyn Joan *state legislator, job research administrator*
Qualls, Robert L. *manufacturing executive, banker, former state official, educator*
Snider, James Rhodes *radiologist*
Stites, Beverly R. *judge*
Taylor, James Lynn (Jimmie Taylor) *real estate executive*
Young, Robert A., III *freight systems executive*

Gillett
Wood, Edward Ephraim, Jr. *park administrator*

Glenwood
Klopfenstein, Philip Arthur *high school educator*

Greenbrier
†Burgin, Karen Jean *special education educator*
Reed, James David *minister, social worker*

Greenwood
Walters, Bill *state senator, lawyer*

Hampton
Copley, Stephen Jean *minister*

Harrison
Pinson, Jerry D. *lawyer*

Hartford
Roller Hall, Gayle Aline *gifted and talented education educator*

Heber Springs
Rawlings, Paul C. *retired government official*

Helena
Roscopf, Charles Buford *lawyer*

Hindsville
Peirce, Carole *secondary school educator*

Holiday Island
Epley, Lewis Everett, Jr. *lawyer*

Hot Springs
Brinson, Harold Thomas *retired university president emeritus*

Hot Springs National Park
Baer, Kenneth Peter *farmer cooperative executive*
†Clontz, Jerry Michael *sales administrator*
Craft, Kay Stark *real estate broker*
Farley, Roy C. *rehabilitation researcher, educator*
Farris, Jefferson Davis *university administrator*
Hutchison, Donna McAnulty *humanities educator*
Lauber, Joseph Lincoln *publisher's representative*
McDaniel, Ola Jo Peterson *social worker, educator*
Schroeder, Donald Perry *retired food products company executive*
Stuber, Irene Zelinsky *writer, researcher*
Tanenbaum, Bernard Jerome, Jr. *corporate executive*
Wallace, William Hall *economic and financial consultant*
Wennerstrom, Arthur John *aeronautical engineer*

Huntsville
Carr, Gerald Paul *former astronaut, business executive, former marine officer*
Musick, Pat *artist, sculptor, art educator*

Jefferson
Casciano, Daniel Anthony *biologist*
Hart, Ronald Wilson *radiobiologist, toxicologist, government research executive*
Schwetz, Bernard Anthony *toxicologist*

Jonesboro
Calaway, Dennis Louis *insurance company executive, real estate broker, financial executive*
Christiano, Melissa *artist, educator*
Elkins, Francis Clark *history educator, university official*
†Guffey, Marsha Kidd *grant writer, consultant*
Humway, Ronald Jimmie *state agency administrator*
Jones, Kenneth Bruce *surgeon*
King, Dorothy Jackson *psychologist, marriage-family counselor, therapist*
†Kumar, Bangaroswamy Vijaya *neurologist*
†Lavers, Norman *adult education educator*
Nelsen, Evelyn Rigsbee Seaton *retired educator*
Peters, Mary Helen *real estate agent*
Smith, Eugene Wilson *retired university president and educator*
Tims, Robert Austin *data processing official, pilot*

Leachville
Adams, Eddie *company executive*

Little Rock
†Alexander, Don *state official*
Anderson, Joel E., Jr. *university administrator*
Anderson, Philip Sidney *lawyer*
Arnold, Morris Sheppard *judge*
Arnold, Richard Sheppard *federal judge*

Ziegler, Raymond Stewart *retired architect*

Anaheim
Bavasi, William Joseph *professional sports team executive*
Bennett, Genevieve *artist*
Bowman, Jeffrey R. *protective services official*
Carvajal, Jorge Armando *endocrinologist, internist*
Collins, Terry *professional baseball manager*
Daly, Tom *mayor*
DiSarcina, Gary Thomas *baseball player*
Edmonds, James Patrick (Jim Edmonds) *baseball player*
Fenton, Donald Mason *retired oil company executive*
Fielder, Cecil Grant *professional baseball player*
Finley, Chuck (Charles Edward Finley) *baseball player*
Franklin, Cheryl Jean *engineer, author*
Gaston, Randall Wallace *police chief*
Guajardo, Elisa *counselor, educator*
Hill, David *city human resources director*
Jackson, David Robert *school system administrator*
Jung, Charlene *city treasurer*
Kallay, Michael Frank, II *medical devices company official*
Kariya, Paul *professional hockey player*
Keller, Kent Eugene *advertising and public relations executive*
Kimme, Ernest Godfrey *communications engineer*
Lano, Charles Jack *retired financial executive*
Loeblich, Helen Nina Tappan *paleontologist, educator*
McDowell, Jack Burns *professional baseball player*
Miller, Jean Ruth *retired librarian*
Nelipovich, Sandra Grassi *artist*
Nguyen, Tai Anh *minister*
Noorda, Raymond J. *computer software company executive*
Rubenstein, David H. *media manufacturing executive*
Salmon, Timothy James *professional baseball player*
Selanne, Teemu *hockey player*
Settgast, Leland G. *religion educator, minister*
Sohl, Lee *municipal official*
Stark, Milton Dale *sports association executive*
Tavares, Tony *professional hockey and baseball leagues executive*
Valdez, James Gerald *automotive aftermarket executive*
Vaughn, Maurice Samuel (Mo Vaughn) *professional baseball player*
Watson, Oliver Lee, III *aerospace engineering manager*

Angwin
Maxwell, Donald Malcolm *college president, minister*
Ness, Bryan Douglas *biologist, educator*

Antioch
Adams, Liliana Osses *music performer, harpist*
Bedell, Jay Dee *educator, writer*
Cakebread, Steven Robert *minister, chef*
Chu, Valentin Yuan-ling *author*
Richards, Gerald Thomas *lawyer, consultant, educator*

Apple Valley
Beller, Gerald Stephen *professional magician, former insurance company executive*
Fisher, Weston Joseph *economist*
Ledford, Gary Alan *real estate developer*
Mays, George Walter, Jr. *educational technology educator, consultant, tutor*
Nolan, Ruth Marie *technical writer*
Tishner, Keri Lynn *secondary education educator*

Aptos
Bohn, Ralph Carl *educational consultant, retired educator*
Dobey, James Kenneth *banker*
Heron, David Winston *librarian*
Howe, Susan Leone *artist, printmaker, design consultant*
Mechlin, George Francis *electrical manufacturing company executive*
Penny, Steve *media producer, speaker*
Schy, Gay *artist, investor*
Swenson, Kathleen Susan *music and art educator*
†Winters, Paul Andrew *editor*
†Wolff, Jean Walton *writer, artist*

Arcadia
Anderson, Holly Geis *women's health facility administrator, commentator, educator*
Baillie, Charles Douglas *banker*
Baltz, Patricia Ann (Pann Baltz) *elementary education educator*
†Boeskin, Bryan Edward *public administrator*
Broderick, Donald Leland *electronics engineer*
Danziger, Louis *graphic designer, educator*
Dodds, Dale Irvin *chemicals executive*
Forward, Dorothy Elizabeth *legal assistant*
Freedman, Gregg *real estate appraisal company executive*
Gallup, Janet Louise *human resources development executive*
Gamboa, George Charles *oral surgeon, educator*
Gelber, Louise C(arp) *lawyer*
Kalm, Arne *investment banker*
Kenvin, Roger Lee *writer, retired English educator*
Massier, Paul Ferdinand *mechanical engineer*
Mc Cormack, Francis Xavier *lawyer, former oil company executive*
Razor, Beatrice Ramirez (Betty Razor) *enterostomal therapy nurse, educator, consultant*
Sleeter, John William Higgs *physician, health service administrator*
Sloane, Beverly LeBov *writer, consultant*
Yen, Wen-Hsiung *language and music professional educator*
Zimmerman, Amy J. *producer, director*

Arcata
Anderson, William Thomas *art educator, artist*
Barratt, Raymond William *biologist, educator*
Bowker, Lee Harrington *academic administrator*
Emenhiser, JeDon Allen *political science educator, academic administrator*
Hise, Mark Allen *dentist*
Janssen-Pellatz, Eunice Charlene *healthcare facility administrator*
McCrone, Alistair William *university president*
Swanson, Carolyn Rae *news reporter, counselor*
Zielinski, Melissa L. *museum director*

Aromas
Nutzle, Futzie (Bruce John Kleinsmith) *artist, author, cartoonist*

Arroyo Grande
†Battles, Lara *counselor, psychotherapist*
†del Campo, Robert A. *federal judge, lawyer*
Nay, Joan McNeilly *retired English educator, university administrator*
Oseguera, Palma Marie *retired marine corps officer, reservist*

Artesia
†Choo, Michael Owen *executive, consultant*

Atascadero
Cotter, Cornelius Philip *political scientist, educator*
Lamore, Bette *rehabilitation counselor, motivational speaker*
Ogier, Walter Thomas *retired physics educator*

Atherton
Amdahl, Gene Myron *computer company executive*
Bales, Royal Eugene *philosophy educator*
Baran, Paul *computer executive*
Barker, Robert Jeffery *financial executive*
Chetkovich, Michael N. *accountant*
Ferris, Robert Albert *lawyer, venture capitalist*
Goodman, Sam Richard *electronics company executive*
King, Jane Cudlip Coblentz *volunteer educator*
Lane, Joan Fletcher *educational administrator*
Lowry, Larry Lorn *management consulting company executive*
†Oakes, David Duane *medical educator*
Rosen, Charles Abraham *electrical engineer, consultant*
Starr, Chauncey *research institute executive*

Atwater
DeVoe, Kenneth Nickolas *food service executive*

Auburn
Hanowell, Ernest Goddin *physician*
Hess, Patrick Henry *chemist*
Jeske, Howard Leigh *retired life insurance company executive, lawyer*
Leonard, Angeline Jane *psychotherapist*
Sun, Haiyin *optical engineer, educator*
Warren, Marshall Thomas *protective service official*

Avenal
Barr, Maurice Alan *elementary education educator*

Avila Beach
Kamm, Herbert *journalist*
McLaren, Archie Campbell, Jr. *marketing executive*

Azusa
Felix, Richard E. *academic administrator*
Forbes, Judie *program manager*
†Palm, Daniel Carl *political science educator*
Sambasivam, Samuel E. *computer science and mathematics educator*
Shoemaker, Melvin Hugh *religious educator*
Smith, Beverly *nursing educator*
Works, Madden Travis, Jr. (Pat Works) *operations executive, author, skydiving instructor, skydiving publications executive*

Bakersfield
Akers, Tom, Jr. *cotton broker, consultant*
Amerine, Wendy L. *community health and gerontology nurse*
Anderson, Cliffton *science educator*
Arciniega, Tomas Abel *university president*
Bacon, Leonard Anthony *accounting educator*
Barmann, Bernard Charles, Sr. *lawyer*
Boyd, William Harland *historian*
Brummer, Steven E. *police chief*
Clark, Thomas Sullivan *lawyer*
Dorer, Fred Harold *chemistry educator*
Enriquez, Carola Rupert *museum director*
†Etcheverry, Louis P. *federal judge*
Farr, G(ardner) Neil *lawyer*
Grabski, Daniel Alexis *psychiatrist*
Hamann, Janet Marian *educational psychology educator*
Hart, Donald Milton *automotive and ranching executive, former mayor*
Hefner, John *principal*
Hodash, Bob (Robert A. Hodash) *principal*
Ice, Marie *education educator*
†Johnson, Deborah Valerie Germaine *parish administrator*
Kegley, Jacquelyn Ann *philosophy educator*
Kind, Kenneth Wayne *lawyer, real estate broker*
†Krishnamurthy, Sriram *planner*
Litherland, Donna Joyce *counselor*
Lundquist, Gene Alan *cotton company executive*
Martin, George Francis *lawyer*
McAlister, Michael H. *architect*
McMillan, Leonard David *family life specialist, consultant, lecturer*
Murillo, Velda Jean *social worker, counselor*
Osterkamp, Dalene May *psychology educator, artist*
Owens, Buck (Alvis Edgar, Jr.) *singer, musician, songwriter, broadcast executive*
Peterson, Pamela Carmelle *English language educator*
Powell, Patricia Ann *secondary school educator*
Price, Robert Otis *mayor*
Reep, Edward Arnold *artist*
Schmidt, Joanne (Josephine Anne Schmidt) *language educator*
Singer, George Milton *clinical psychologist*
Thomas, Tom Eldon *corrections educator*
Tornstrom, Robert Ernest *lawyer, oil company executive*
Watkins, Judith Ann *nurse administrator*
Weygand, Leroy Charles *service executive*
Wong, Wayne D. *nutritionist*
Young, John Byron *retired lawyer*
Zeviar-Geese, Gabriole *stock market investor*

Balboa Island
Petersen, Richard Craig *dentist*

Baldwin Park
Barry(Branks), Diane Dolores *podiatrist*

Banning
Finley, Margaret Mavis *retired elementary school educator*
Holmes, John Richard *physicist, educator*
Swick, Sean Bowman *software developer*

Barstow
Jones, Nathaniel *bishop*
†Mahlum, Kirtland L. *federal judge*

Bayside
Bank, Ron *principal*
Cocks, George Gosson *retired chemical microscopy educator*

Beale AFB
†Simpson, Charles N. *military officer*

Beaumont
†Mayer, Harvey Ethan *educator*

Bell Canyon
Labbett, John Edgar *senior financial executive*

Bellflower
Cook, Karla Joan *elementary education educator*
Martin, Melissa Carol *radiological physicist*

Belmont
Carlson, Gary R. *publishing executive*
†Keller, Eric Trent *real estate manager*
Morris, Bruce Dorian *technical writer, literary historian, educator*
Orszag, Peter Richard *economist*

Belvedere
Benet, Carol Ann *journalist, career counselor, teacher*

Belvedere Tiburon
Behrman, Richard Elliot *pediatrician, neonatologist, university dean*
Buell, Edward Rick, II *lawyer*
Caselli, Virgil P. *real estate executive*
Cook, Robert Donald *financial service executive*
Cooke, James Barry *civil engineer, consultant*
Denton, Charles Mandaville *corporate consultant*
Hudnut, David Beecher *retired leasing company executive, lawyer*
Kramer, Lawrence Stephen *journalist*

Benicia
Cummings, Barton *musician*
Garrop, Barbara Ann *elementary education educator*
Lipsky, Ian David *mechanical engineering executive*
Nelson, Elmer Kingsholm, Jr. *educator, writer, mediator, consultant*
Shannonhouse, Sandra Lynne Riddell *sculptor*
Szabo, Peter John *investment company executive, financial planner, mining engineer, lawyer*
von Studnitz, Gilbert Alfred *state official*

Bereley
Chamberlain, Owen *nuclear physicist*

Berkeley
Abel, Carlos Alberto *immunologist*
Adelman, Irma Glicman *economics educator*
Alhadeff, David Albert *economics educator*
Alpen, Edward Lewis *biophysicist, educator*
Alter, Robert B. *comparative literature educator and critic*
Alvarez, Walter *geology educator*
Ames, Bruce N(athan) *biochemist, molecular biologist*
Anderson, John Richard *entomologist, educator*
Anderson, William Scovil *classics educator*
Arveson, William Barnes *mathematics educator*
Auerbach, Alan Jeffrey *economist*
Baas, Jacquelynn *art historian, museum administrator*
Bacon, Elizabeth Morrow *librarian, writer, editor, educator*
Bagdikian, Ben Haig *journalist, emeritus university educator*
Baldwin, Bruce Gregg *botany educator, researcher*
Barker, Horace Albert *biochemist, microbiologist*
Barnett, R(alph) Michael *theoretical physicist, educational agency administrator*
Barrett, Reginald Haughton *biology educator, wildlife management educator*
Bartlett, Neil *chemist, educator*
Bartlett, Paul A. *organic chemist*
Barton, Babette B. *lawyer, educator*
Bea, Robert G. *civil engineering educator*
Bell, Alexis T. *chemical engineer*
Bellah, Robert Neelly *sociologist, educator*
Bender, Richard *university dean, architect, educator*
Benedict, Burton *retired museum director, anthropology educator*
Berdahl, Robert Max *academic administrator, historian, educator*
Berger, Stanley Allan *mechanical engineering educator*
Bergman, George Mark *mathematician, educator*
Bergman, Robert George *chemist, educator*
Berkner, Klaus Hans *laboratory administrator, physicist*
Berlekamp, Elwyn Ralph *mathematic educator, electronics company executive,*
Bern, Howard Alan *science educator, research biologist*
Berry, William Benjamin Newell *geologist, educator, former museum administrator*
Bickel, Peter John *statistician, educator*
Birdsall, Charles Kennedy *electrical engineer*
Birman, Alexander *physicist, researcher*
†Black, Richard W. *director, financial aid*
Blackwell, David H. *statistics educator*
Blake, Laura *architect*
Bloom, Robert *language professional educator*
Bogy, David B(eauregard) *mechanical engineering educator*
Bolt, Bruce Alan *seismologist, educator*
Bond, Thomas Moore, Jr. *labor mediation and arbitration executive*
Bowker, Albert Hosmer *retired university chancellor*
Bragg, Robert Henry *physicist, educator*
Brandes, Stanley Howard *anthropology educator, writer*
Braun, Benjamin *basketball coach*
Brayton, Robert K. *computer science educator*
Breslauer, George William *political science educator*
Brewer, Leo *physical chemist, educator*
Brixey, Shawn Alan *digital media artist, media educator, director*
Brocchini, Ronald Gene *architect*
Brodersen, Robert W. *engineering educator*
Bronstein, Arthur J. *linguistics educator*
Browne, G.M. Walter Shawn Browne *journalist, chess player*
Buckland, Michael Keeble *librarian, educator*
Bucklin, Louis Pierre *business educator, consultant*
Budinger, Thomas Francis *radiologist, educator*
Buffler, Patricia Ann *epidemiology educator, retired dean*
Bukowinski, Mark Stefan Tadeusz *geophysics educator*
Burch, Claire Rita *writer*
Burger, Edmund Ganes *architect*
Burnside, Mary Beth *biology educator, researcher*
Buxbaum, Richard M. *law educator, lawyer*
Cairns, Elton James *chemical engineering educator*
Callenbach, Ernest *writer, editor*
Calloway, Doris Howes *nutrition educator*
Canfield, Judy Ohlbaum *psychologist*
Cantor, Rusty Sumner *artist*
Cardwell, Kenneth Harvey *architect, educator*
Carmichael, Ian Stuart Edward *geologist, educator*
Carpenter, Kenneth John *nutrition educator*
Casida, John Edward *entomology educator*
†Cedars, Michael G. *plastic surgeon*
Cerny, Joseph, III *chemistry educator, scientific laboratory administrator, university dean and official*
Chamberlin, Michael John *biochemistry educator*
Chandler, David *scientist, educator*
Chang-Hasnain, Constance Jui-Hua *educator*
Cheit, Earl Frank *economist, educator*
Chemsak, John Andrew *entomologist*
Chern, Shiing-Shen *mathematics educator*
†Chetin, Helen Campbell *writer*
Chew, Geoffrey Foucar *physicist*
Chodorow, Nancy Julia *sociology educator*
Choper, Jesse Herbert *law educator, university dean*
Chopra, Anil Kumar *civil engineering educator*
Chorin, Alexandre Joel *mathematician, educator*
Cieslak, William *academic administrator*
Clark, John Desmond *anthropology educator*
Clarke, John *physics educator*
Cline, Thomas Warren *molecular biologist, educator*
Cohen, Marvin Lou *physics educator*
Cohn, Theodore Elliot *optometry educator, vision scientist*
Colson, Elizabeth Florence *anthropologist*
Cooper, William Secord *information science educator*
Costa, Gustavo *Italian language educator*
Cozzarelli, Nicholas Robert *molecular biologist, educator*
Crews, Frederick Campbell *humanities educator, writer*
Cross, Kathryn Patricia *education educator*
Curtis, Garniss Hearfield *geology educator*
Cutter, David Lee *pharmaceutical company executive*
Dahlsten, Donald Lee *entomology educator, university dean*
Danton, Joseph Periam *librarian, educator*
Davidson, Donald Herbert *philosophy educator*
Davis, Marc *astrophysics educator*
Day, Lucille Lang *health facility administrator, educator, author*
De Goff, Victoria Joan *lawyer*
Dekel, Eddie *economics educator*
Denn, Morton Mace *chemical engineering educator*
Diamond, Marian Cleeves *anatomy educator*
Diamond, Richard Martin *nuclear chemist*
Diamond, Sara Rose *writer, sociologist, lecturer*
Dornfeld, David Alan *engineering educator*
Dresher, Paul Joseph *composer, music educator, performer*
Duesberg, Peter Heinz Hermann *molecular biology educator*
Duhl, Leonard *psychiatrist, educator*
†Dunbar, Ian Fraser *veterinarian, animal behaviorist*
Dundes, Alan *writer, folklorist, educator*
Eisenberg, Melvin A. *law educator*
†Ellis, Ella Thorp *writer, retired educator*
Ely, Robert Pollock, Jr. *physics educator, researcher*
Enoch, Jay Martin *vision scientist, educator*
Falkner, Frank Tardrew *physician, educator*
Feeley, Malcolm M. *law educator, political scientist*
Feller, David E. *law educator, arbitrator*
Finnie, Iain *mechanical engineer, educator*
Fleming, Graham Richard *chemistry educator*
Foster, George McClelland, Jr. *anthropologist*
Fowler, Thomas Kenneth *physicist*
Fraenkel-Conrat, Heinz Ludwig *cell biology educator*
Fréchet, Jean Marie Joseph *chemistry educator*
Freedman, David Amiel *statistics educator, consultant*
Freedman, Mervin Burton *psychologist, educator*
Freedman, Sarah Warshauer *education educator*
Frenkel, Edward Vladimir *mathematician, educator*
Friedman, Mendel *hospital administration executive*
Frisch, Joseph *mechanical engineer, educator, consultant*
Fuerstenau, Douglas Winston *mineral engineering educator*
Fulton, Katherine Nelson *journalist, consultant*
†Gable, Cate M. *communications company executive*
Gaillard, Mary Katharine *physics educator*
Gall, Donald Arthur *minister*
Garrison, William Louis *civil engineering educator*
Genn, Nancy *artist*
Getz, Wayne Marcus *biomathematician, researcher, educator*
Gilbert, Neil Robin *social work educator, author, consultant*
Gilbert, Richard Joseph *economics educator*
Glaser, Donald Arthur *physicist*
Glenny, Lyman Albert *retired education educator*
Goldhaber, Gerson *physicist, educator*
Goldsmith, Werner *mechanical engineering educator*
Goodman, Corey Scott *neurobiology educator, researcher*
Gordley, James Russell *law educator*
Graburn, Nelson Hayes Henry *anthropologist, educator*
Gray, Paul Russell *electrical engineering educator*
Grimes, Ruth Elaine *city planner*
Grossman, Elmer Roy *pediatrician*
Grossman, Lawrence Morton *nuclear engineering educator*
Guest, Barbara *author, poet*
Hack, Elizabeth *artist*
Hafey, Joseph Michael *health association executive*
†Haggstrom, Jane *mental health nursing educator, administrator*
Hahn, Erwin Louis *physicist, educator*
Halbach, Edward Christian, Jr. *legal educator*
Haley, George Patrick *lawyer*

Franklin, Carl *director*
Fraser, Brendan *actor*
Frears, Stephen *film director*
Freeman, Morgan *actor*
†Friedkin, William *film director*
Friendly, Ed *television producer*
Gabler, Lee *talent agency executive*
†Gabriel, Jeanette Hanisee *curator, art historian*
Gambrell, Thomas Ross *investor, retired physician, surgeon*
†Garber, Victor *stage and film actor*
Garr, Teri (Ann) *actress*
Gelbart, Larry *writer, producer*
George, Lynda Day *actress*
Gerber, William Norman *motion picture executive*
Gibson, Brian *film director*
Gillard, Stuart Thomas *film and television director, writer*
Gish, Annabeth *actress*
†Glazer, Guilford *real estate developer*
Glenn, (Theodore) Scott *actor*
Gless, Sharon *actress*
Glover, Danny *actor*
Glover, John *actor*
Goldblum, Jeff *actor*
Goldman, Larry *public relations executive*
Goldman, William *writer*
Goldsmith, Bram *banker*
Goodman, John *actor*
Goodman, Mark Paul *physician*
Grant, Hugh *actor*
Grant, Michael Ernest *educational administrator, institutional management educator*
Graves, Peter *actor*
Grazer, Brian *film company executive*
Grey, Brad *producer, agent*
Griffith, Andy (Andrew Samuel Griffith) *actor*
Grushow, Sandy *broadcast executive*
Guest, Christopher *actor, director, screenwriter*
Hackford, Taylor *film director, producer*
Hagman, Larry *actor*
Haile, Lawrence Barclay *lawyer*
Hallstrom, Lasse *director*
Hamlin, Harry Robinson *actor*
Hanks, Tom *actor*
†Hansen, Tom *lawyer*
Hanson, Curtis *director, writer*
†Harlin, Renny (Renny Lauri Mauritz Harjola) *film director*
Harris, Fran *sportscaster, former basketball player*
Harvey, Simon *actor, writer*
Haskell, Peter Abraham *actor*
Hawke, Ethan *actor*
Hawn, Goldie *actress*
Headly, Glenne Aimée *actress*
†Heaton, Patricia *actress*
Hefner, Hugh Marston *editor-in-chief*
Heller, Paul Michael *film company executive, producer*
Henderson, Florence (Florence Henderson Bernstein) *actress, singer*
Henry, Buck *actor, writer*
†Hergott, Alan *laywer*
Heston, Charlton (John Charlton Carter) *actor*
†Hewitt, Jennifer Love *actress, singer*
Hill, David *broadcast executive*
Hill, Michael J. *film editor*
Hill, Walter *film director, writer, producer*
Hilton, Barron *hotel executive*
Himelstein, Susan *psychologist*
Hogan, Steven L. *lawyer*
†Holland, Agnieszka *film director, screenwriter*
Hopkins, Sir Anthony (Philip) *actor*
†Hopper, Dennis *actor, writer, photographer, film director*
Horwin, Leonard *lawyer*
Howard, Ron *director, actor*
Hoy, William *film editor*
Hughes, John W. *film producer, screenwriter, film director*
Hulce, Tom *actor*
†Hunane, Kevin *talent agent*
Hunt, Linda *actress*
Hurd, Gale Anne *film producer*
†Hurt, William *actor*
Huston, Anjelica *actress*
Hutton, Timothy *actor*
Idle, Eric *actor, screenwriter, producer, songwriter*
Ingels, Marty *theatrical agent, television and motion picture production executive*
Israel, Richard Stanley *investment banker*
†Jacobson, Craig *lawyer*
Jaffe, F. Filmore *lawyer, retired judge*
Jagger, Mick (Michael Philip Jagger) *singer, musician*
Joffe, Roland *film director*
Jones, Terry *film director, author*
Jordan, Glenn *director*
Kahn, Madeline Gail *actress*
Kane, Carol *actress*
Karpman, Harold Lew *cardiologist, educator, author*
†Kasdan, Lawrence Edward *film director, screenwriter*
Kaufman, Philip *film director*
Keaton, Diane *actress*
Keitel, Harvey *actor*
Keith, David Lemuel *actor*
Kellman, Barnet Kramer *film, stage and television director*
Kemper, Victor J. *cinematographer*
Khaiat, Laurent E. *producer, films*
Kilmer, Val *actor*
Kingsley, Ben *actor*
†Kingston, Alex(andra) *actress*
Kinski, Nastassja (Nastassja Nakszynski) *actress*
Klein, Arnold William *dermatologist*
†Konchalovsky, Andrei *film director*
†Korn, Henry *museum administrator*
Kozak, Harley Jane *actress*
Kravitz, Ellen King *musicologist, educator*
Kravitz, Hilard L(eonard) *physician*
†Kravitz, Lenny *singer, guitarist*
Kuhn, Michael *motion picture company executive*
Lahti, Christine *actress*
†Landis, John David *film director, writer*
Lane, Nathan (Joseph Lane) *actor*
Lange, Jessica *actress*
Langella, Frank *actor*
LaPaglia, Anthony *actor*
Lavin, Linda *actress*
Leary, Denis *comedian*
†Leder, Mimi *television director*
†Lee, Ang *filmmaker*
Lee, Jason Scott *actor*
†Lehmann, Michael Stephen *film director*
Leigh, Jennifer Jason (Jennifer Leigh Morrow) *actress*
Lemmon, Jack (John Uhler Lemmon, III) *actor*
Lesser, Gershon Melvin *physician, lawyer, medical and legal media commentator*
Levant, Brian *film director*
Levingston, John Colville Bowring *telecommunications executive*
Levy, Peter *cinematographer*
†Levy, Richard Brian *lawyer*
Lewis, Juliette *actress*
Limato, Edward Frank *talent agent*
Lindo, Delroy *actor*
Linkletter, Arthur Gordon *radio and television broadcaster*
†Linney, Laura *actress*
Liotta, Ray *actor*
Litman, Brian David *communications executive*
Lloyd, Emily (Emily Lloyd Pack) *actress*
Loggia, Robert *actor*
Lond, Harley Weldon *editor, publisher*
Long, Shelley *actress*
Lopez, Jennifer *actress, dancer, singer*
Lott, Ronnie (Ronald Mandel Lott) *retired professional football player, T.V. broadcaster*
Louis-Dreyfus, Julia *actress*
†Lourd, Bryan *talent agent*
Lovett, Richard *talent agency executive*
Lowell, Carey *actress*
Lowry, Dick M. *director*
Lumet, Sidney *film director*
Lynch, David K. *film director, writer*
Lyne, Adrian *film director*
Lynn, Jonathan Adam *film director, writer, actor*
Mac Dowell, Andie (Rose Anderson Mac Dowell) *actress*
MacLachlan, Kyle *actor*
MacMillan, Kenneth *cinematographer*
Madsen, Michael *actor*
Malkovich, John *actor*
†Manheim, Camryn *television and film actress*
†Mann, Michael K. *producer, director, writer*
Manulis, Martin *film producer*
Manus, Willard *writer, journalist, critic*
Margulies, Julianna *actress*
†Martin, Kellie (Noelle) *actress*
Martin, Steve *comedian, actor*
Masterson, Mary Stuart *actress*
Mastrantonio, Mary Elizabeth *actress*
Masur, Richard *actor*
Matheson, Tim *actor*
Mathis, Samantha *actress*
Matlin, Marlee *actress*
Matovich, Mitchel Joseph, Jr. *motion picture producer, executive*
Matzdorff, James Arthur *investment banker, financier*
Mazursky, Paul *screenwriter, theatrical director and producer*
McAlpine, Andrew *production designer*
†McDaniel, James *actor*
McDermott, Dylan *actor*
McGagh, William Gilbert *financial consultant*
†Mc Tiernan, John *film director*
Mechanic, William M. *television and motion picture industry executive*
Menkes, John Hans *pediatric neurologist*
Metcalf, Laurie *actress*
Milius, John Frederick *film writer, director*
Miner, Steve *film director*
†Minghella, Anthony *film director*
Moelleken, Brent Roderick Wilfred *surgeon*
Moffat, Donald *actor*
†Mohajer, Dineh *cosmetics company executive*
†Monosson, Ira Howard *physician*
Montalban, Ricardo *actor*
Moore, Demi (Demi Guynes) *actress*
Moore, Dudley Stuart John *actor, musician*
Moore, Julianne *actress*
Moore, Mary Tyler *actress*
Moore, Michael *film director*
Moriarty, Cathy *actress*
Morissette, Alanis *musician*
†Moser, Franklin George *neuroradiologist, researcher*
Mulroney, Dermot *actor*
Murphy, Eddie *comedian, actor*
Murray, Bill *actor, writer*
Najimy, Kathy *actress*
Nava, Gregory *film director*
Neeson, Liam *actor*
Neill, Sam *actor*
Nelson, Judd *actor*
Nicholas, Frederick M. *lawyer*
Nicita, Rick *agent*
Nimoy, Leonard *actor, director*
Norris, Chuck (Carlos Ray) *actor*
Novak, Kim (Marilyn Novak) *actress*
Novak, Maximillian Erwin *English language educator*
†Noyce, Phillip *film director*
†Nyman, Michael S. *company executive*
Oakley, Bill *television producer*
O'Connor, Carroll *actor, writer, producer*
†O'Connor, David *talent agent*
O'Donnell, Chris *actor*
O'Keefe, John Francis *fundraiser*
Olin, Lena Maria Jonna *actress*
Ormond, Julia *actress*
Ovitz, Michael S. *communications executive*
Pacino, Al (Alfredo James Pacino) *actor*
Palminteri, Chazz *actor*
Paltrow, Gwyneth *actress*
Pantoliano, Joe *actor*
Parker, Alan William *film director, writer*
Parker, Mary-Louise *actress*
Parker, Sarah Jessica *actress*
Patinkin, Mandy *actor*
Patric, Jason *actor*
Pavlik, John Michael *performing arts association executive*
Paymer, David *actor*
Penderecki, Krzysztof *composer, conductor*
Perkins, Elizabeth Ann *actress*
Perlman, Rhea *actress*
Perry, Luke (Coy Luther Perry, III) *actor*
Petersen, Wolfgang *film director*
Pfeiffer, Michelle *actress*
Pinchot, Bronson *actor*
Pinkett, Jada *actress*
Pitt, Brad *actor*
Platt, Oliver *actor*
Plummer, (Arthur) Christopher (Orme) *actor*
†Polanski, Roman *film director, writer, actor*
Pollak, Kevin *actor*
†Portman, Natalie *actress*
Presley, Priscilla *actress*
Priestley, Jason *actor*
†Priselac, Thomas M. *health facility administrator*
Proft, Pat *screenwriter, film producer*
Ptak, John *talent agent*
Pullman, Bill *actor*
Quinn, Aidan *actor*
Rabe, David William *playwright*
†Raimi, Samuel M. *film director*
Ramer, Bruce M. *lawyer*
Rapke, Jack *agent*
Reese, Della (Deloreese Patricia Early) *singer, actress*
Reeve, Christopher *actor*
Reeves, Keanu *actor*
Reiner, Annie *writer, psychotherapist*
Reiner, Carl *director, actor, writer*
Reiner, Rob *director, writer, actor*
†Reuben, Gloria *actress*
Rhames, Ving (Irving) *actor*
Ricci, Christina *actress*
Richardson, Patricia *actress*
Rickman, Alan *actor*
Riess, Gordon Sanderson *management consultant*
Rifkin, Arnold *film company executive*
Riley, Jack *actor, writer*
†Rivers, Joan *entertainer*
Robbins, Tim(othy Francis) *director, actor*
Roberts, Julia Fiona *actress*
Roberts, Tony (David Anthony Roberts) *actor*
Rodman, Francis Robert *psychoanalyst, writer*
Roeg, Nicolas Jack *film director*
Roget, Cristiane *producer, publisher, film distribution executive*
Ronstadt, Linda Marie *singer*
†Root, Stephen Don *actor*
Rosenberg, Philip *production designer*
Rosenzweig, Richard Stuart *publishing company executive*
Rosky, Burton Seymour *lawyer*
Roth, Eric *screenwriter*
†Rothman, Thomas Edgar *production executive*
Rowan, Keith Patterson *communications executive, consultant*
Ruehl, Mercedes *actress*
†Rush, Geoffrey *actor*
Rush, Herman E. *television executive*
Russell, Irwin Emanuel *lawyer*
†Russell, Keri *actress*
Russell, Kurt Von Vogel *actor*
Russo, Rene *actress*
Ryan, Meg *actress*
Saget, Bob *actor, comedian*
St John, Martin *marketing consultant*
Sams, David Ronald *television and music producer*
Sanford, Isabel Gwendolyn *actress*
Sarandon, Susan Abigail *actress*
Scacchi, Greta *actress*
Schaefer, Susan G. *lawyer*
Schepisi, Fred *producer, director, screenwriter*
Schlesinger, John Richard *film, opera and theater director*
Schneider, Charles I. *newspaper executive*
Schneider, Rob *actor*
Schroeder, Barbet G. *director*
Schulian, John (Nielsen Schulian) *screenwriter, author*
Schulman, Tom *screenwriter*
Scott, Deborah L. *costume designer*
†Scott, Ridley *film director*
Seeger, Melinda Wayne *realtor*
Seidel, Joan Broude *stockbroker, investment advisor*
Seiff, Stephen S. *ophthalmologist*
Seymour, Jane *actress*
†Shadyac, Thomas *film director*
Shapell, Nathan *financial and real estate executive*
Sharif, Omar (Michael Shalhoub) *actor*
Shepard, Kathryn Irene *public relations executive*
Shepard, Sam (Samuel Shepard Rogers) *playwright, actor*
Shoemaker, Bill (William Lee Shoemaker) *retired jockey, horse trainer*
Short, Martin *actor, comedian*
Shue, Elisabeth *actress*
Silverman, Jonathan *actor*
†Simpson, Michael *talent agent*
†Singleton, John *director, screenwriter*
Sinise, Gary *actor, director*
Skerritt, Tom *actor*
Smith, Jaclyn *actress*
†Smith, Kevin *film director, writer*
Smith, Roy Forge *art director, production designer*
Smith, Will *actor, rapper*
Snipes, Wesley *actor*
Snyder, David L. *film production designer*
Sobelle, Richard E. *lawyer*
Sonnenfeld, Barry *director, cinematographer*
Sorvino, Mira *actress*
Sorvino, Paul *actor*
Spacek, Sissy (Mary Elizabeth Spacek) *actress*
Spader, James *actor*
Spheeris, Penelope *film director*
Spielberg, Steven *motion picture director, producer*
Spivak, Jacque R. *bank executive*
Stallone, Sylvester Enzio *actor, writer, director*
Stambler, Irwin *publishing executive*
Stamos, John *actor*
Steenburgen, Mary *actress*
Stefano, Joseph William *film and television producer, author*
Steinkamp, William *film editor*
Stewart, Patrick *actor*
Stiller, Ben *actor, director*
Stoltz, Eric *actor*
Stowe, Madeleine *actress*
Streep, Meryl (Mary Louise Streep) *actress*
Streisand, Barbra Joan *singer, actress, director*
Summers, Andy (Andrew James Somers) *popular musician*
Sutherland, Donald *actor*
Sutherland, Kiefer *actor*
Swayze, Patrick *actor, dancer*
Taggart, Sondra *financial planner, investment advisor*
Tamkin, Curtis Sloane *real estate development company executive*
Taylor, Lili *actress*
Thompson, Caroline Warner *film director, screenwriter*
Thompson, Emma *actress*
Thompson, Larry Angelo *producer, lawyer, personal manager*
Thorin, Donald E. *cinematographer*
Thornton, Billy Bob *actor, director*
Thurman, Uma Karuna *actress*
Tilly, Jennifer *actress*
Toffel, Alvin Eugene *corporate executive, business and governmental consultant*
Towne, Robert *screenwriter*
Travis, Nancy *actress*
Trueba, Fernando *film director and producer, screenwriter*
Tucci, Stanley *actor*
†Tucker, Chris *comedian, actor*
Turner, Kathleen *actress*
†Turteltaub, Jon *film director*
†Turturro, Nicholas *actor*
†Tyler, Liv *actress, model*
Underwood, Blair *actor*
†Underwood, Ronald Brian *director, producer*
Urich, Robert *actor*
Van Ark, Joan *actress*
Van Damme, Jean-Claude (Jean-Claude Van Varenberg) *actor*
Van de Kamp, Andrea Louise *academic administrator*
Van Dyke, Dick *actor, comedian*
Van Sant, Gus, Jr. *director, screenwriter*
Victor, Robert Eugene *real estate corporation executive, lawyer*
Wagner, Lindsay J. *actress*
Walker, William Tidd, Jr. *investment banker*
Ward, David Schad *screenwriter, film director*
Ward, Sela *actress*
Warren, Lesley Ann *actress*
Weaver, Sigourney (Susan Alexandra Weaver) *actress*
Weber, Jeffrey Randolph *record producer*
Weber, Steven *actor*
Weir, Peter Lindsay *film director*
†Weisz, Rachel *actress*
Weller, Peter *actor*
White, Betty *actress, comedienne*
Widaman, Gregory Alan *financial executive, accountant*
Wilder, Gene *actor, director, writer*
Williams, Robin *actor, comedian*
Willis, Walter Bruce *actor, singer*
Willson, James Douglas *aerospace executive*
Winger, Debra *actress*
Winkler, Henry Franklin *actor*
Winkler, Irwin *motion picture producer*
Winningham, Mare *actress*
Winters, Shelley (Shirley Schrift) *actress*
Winthrop, John *wines and spirits company executive*
Wise, Robert *film producer, director*
Wood, Elijah *actor*
Woods, James Howard *actor*
Wright, Robin *actress*
Wu, Yusen (John Woo) *film director*
Yaryan, Ruby Bell *psychologist*
Yomtov, Michelle Rene *journalist*
Yuan, Robin Tsu-Wang *plastic surgeon*
Zane, Billy *actor*
Zanuck, Richard Darryl *motion picture company executive*
Zarem, Abe Mordecai *management consulting executive*
Zerbe, Anthony *actor*
†Zeta-Jones, Catherine *actress*
†Zwick, Edward M. *director, producer, scriptwriter*

Big Bear Lake

†Carlsen, Russell Arhtur *city manager*
Hendler, Rosemary Nielsen *business owner, digital artist*
Miles, Vera *actress*

Bishop

Kelley, William *author, screenwriter*
Naso, Valerie Joan *automotive dealership executive, travel company operator*

Bloomington

Llanusa, Steven Michael *elementary education educator*

Blythe

Bryant, Gary Jones *minister*
Hansen, Randall Glenn *school psychologist, consultant*
Thomas, Marcella Elaine *elementary education educator*

Bodega

Hedrick, Wally Bill *artist*

Bodega Bay

Allard, Robert Wayne *geneticist, educator*
Clegg, James Standish *physiologist, biochemist, educator*
Cohen, Daniel Morris *museum administrator, marine biology researcher*
Hand, Cadet Hammond, Jr. *marine biologist, educator*
King, Leland W. *architect*

Bolinas

Harris, Paul *sculptor*
Lerner, Michael Albers *educator*
Okamura, Arthur Shinji *artist, educator, writer*
Remen, Rachel Naomi *pediatrician, psycho-oncologist*

Bonita

Barnard, Arlene *retired secondary education educator*
Curtis, Richard Earl *former naval officer, former company executive, business consultant*
Deane, Debbe *psychologist, journalist, editor, consultant*
Wood, Fergus James *geophysicist, consultant*

Boonville

Hanes, John Ward *sculptor, civil engineer consultant*

Boulder Creek

Billings, Judith Diane *elementary education educator*

Bradbury

Christensen, Donn Wayne *insurance executive*
Greenstein, Jesse Leonard *astronomer, educator*

Brawley

Jaquith, George Oakes *opthalmologist*

Brea

Greytak, Lee Joseph *financial services and real estate development company executive*
Herzing, Alfred Roy *computer executive*
Natsuyama, Harriet Hatsune *mathematician*
Pearson, April Virginia *lawyer*
Pierpoint, Karen Ann *marriage, family and child therapist*
Ramsey, Nancy Lockwood *nursing educator*
Schlose, William Timothy *health care executive*
Shen, Gene Giin-Yuan *organic chemist*

Spiegel, Ronald Stuart *insurance company executive*
Stegemeier, Richard Joseph *oil company executive*

Brentwood
Albers, Lucia Berta *land developer*

Brisbane
England, Cheryl *publisher, editorial director*
Orban, Kurt *foreign trade company executive*

Buena Park
Papin, Nancy Sue *educational computer coordinator*
Parker, Larry Lee *electronics company executive, consultant*
Turkus-Workman, Carol Ann *educator*
Underwood, Thomas Woodbrook *communications company executive*
Wiersema, Harold LeRoy *aerospace engineer*

Burbank
Ackerman, Mitchell *television executive*
Allen, Tim (Timothy Allen Dick) *actor, comedian*
Ancier, Garth Richard *television broadcast executive*
Arkoff, Samuel Z. *motion picture executive, producer*
†Bader, Diedrich *actor*
†Bello, Maria *actress*
Berman, Bruce *entertainment company executive, television producer*
†Black, Carole *broadcast executive*
Bowen, John Pearson *video tape editor*
Bower, Richard James *minister*
Bright, Kevin S. *producer*
Brillstein, Bernie J. *producer, talent manager*
Brogliatti, Barbara Spencer *television and motion picture executive*
†Carey, Drew *actor*
Chaffee, James Albert *protective services official*
Clements, Ronald Francis *animation director*
Cole, Paula *pop singer, songwriter*
Cook, Richard W. *motion picture company executive*
Cooke, John F. *entertainment company executive*
Cooke, Philip Howard *television director, producer*
†Cortese, Dan *actor*
†Costello, Elvis (Declan Patrick McManus) *musician, songwriter*
Costner, Kevin *actor*
Crane, David *producer*
Cunningham, Robert D. *lawyer*
Daly, Robert Anthony *former film executive*
Dargan, John Henry *strategic planner*
de Cordova, Frederick Timmins *television producer, director*
†DeLuise, David *actor*
DeMieri, Joseph L. *bank executive*
DiBonaventure, Lorenzo *film company executive*
Disney, Roy Edward *broadcasting company executive*
Donner, Richard *film director, producer*
†Dunning, Debbe *actress*
Eisner, Michael Dammann *entertainment company executive*
†Ferguson, Craig *actor*
Fogerty, John Cameron *musician, composer*
Garcia, Daniel P. *real estate manager*
Gibson, Mel *actor, director*
†Gilpin, Peri *actress*
Godwin, Annabelle Palkes *retired early childhood education educator*
Gold, Stanley P. *diversified investments executive*
Goldstein, Kenneth F. *entertainment executive, software executive*
†Green, Judson C. *marketing agency executive*
Guy, Buddy *blues guitarist*
Hartshorn, Terry O. *health facility administrator*
Hashe, Janis Helene *editor*
†Holder, Donald *lighting designer*
†Hooper, Tobe *film director*
Hope, Bob *actor, comedian*
Ingram, James *popular musician*
†Innes, Laura *actress*
Jonas, Tony *television executive*
Joseff, Joan Castle *manufacturing executive*
†Karn, Richard Wilson *actor*
Kauffman, Marta *producer*
Kellner, Jamie *broadcasting executive*
Kelly, Michael Joseph *academic administrator, consultant*
†Kinney, Kathy *actress*
†Kleiser, (John) Randal *motion picture director*
Lamas, Lorenzo *actor, race car driver*
Lang, K. D. (Katherine Dawn Lang) *country music singer, composer*
†Lehr, John *actor*
Leno, Jay (James Douglas Muir Leno) *television personality, comedian, writer*
Levinson, Barry L. *film director*
Lieberfarb, Warren N. *broadcast executive*
†Liss, Walter C. *television station executive*
Liss, Walter C., Jr. *television station executive*
Litvack, Sanford Martin *lawyer*
†Lloyd, Eric *actor*
Marinace, Kenneth Anthony *financial advisor*
Mather, Ann *international entertainment company executive*
McConaughey, Matthew *actor*
Mc Mahon, Ed *television personality*
Mestres, Ricardo A., III *motion picture company executive*
†Miller, Christa *actress*
Miller, Clifford Albert *merchant banker, business consultant*
†Milmore, Jennifer *actress*
†Mitchell, Daryl (Chill Mitchell) *actor*
†Mitchell, Joni (Roberta Joan Anderson) *singer, songwriter*
Naidorf, Louis Murray *architect*
Noddings, Sarah Ellen *lawyer*
Ohlmeyer, Donald Winfred, Jr. *film and television producer*
†Orbit, William *record producer*
Osterwald, Bibi (Margaret Virginia Osterwald) *actress*
Petersen, Gladys *accounting clerk, writer*
Raulinaitis, Pranas Algis *electronics executive*
†Rawlinson, Joseph *foundation executive*
Razouk, Rashad Elias *retired chemistry educator*
Renner, Andrew Ihor *surgeon*
Robertson, Richard Trafton *entertainment company executive*
Rosen, Eden Ruth *promoter, merchandiser, consultant, writer*
Roth, Joe *motion picture company executive*
Roth, Peter *broadcast executive*
Sanborn, David *alto saxophonist*
Schneider, Peter *film company executive*
†Schumacher, Joel *director, writer*
Schumacher, Thomas *film company executive*
Schwartz, Allen Marvin *production company executive*
Semel, Terry *former entertainment company executive*
Shriver, Maria Owings *news correspondent*
†Shuler Donner, Lauren *film producer*
Silver, Joel *film producer*
†Snyder, Liza *actress*
Steiger, Rod *actor*
†Stiles, Ryan *actor*
Sweeney, Anne M. *cable television company executive*
Tatum, Thomas Deskins *film and television producer, director*
Teague, Jane Lorene *lay worker*
Thomason, Harry *film and television producer*
Thompson, Lea *actress*
Thyret, Russ *recording industry executive*
Tritt, Travis *country music singer, songwriter*
Volk, Robert Harkins *aviation company executive*
Walters, Kenneth C. *retired educator*
Wise, Woodrow Wilson, Jr. *small business owner*
Wolper, David Lloyd *motion picture and television executive*
†Wonder, Stevie (Stevland Morris) *singer, musician, composer*
Wu, Shu-Lin Sharon *animation educator*
York, Michael (Michael York-Johnson) *actor*

Burlingame
Chen, Basilio *engineering executive*
Costa, John Anthony *loan assistant*
Cotchett, Joseph Winters *lawyer, author*
†Garnett, Katrina A. *information technology executive*
Gradinger, Gilbert Paul *plastic surgeon*
Heath, Richard Raymond *investment executive*
Hepler, Kenneth Russel *manufacturing executive*
Hotz, Henry Palmer *physicist*
Mahoney, Ann Dickinson *fundraiser*
Mendelson, Lee M. *film company executive, writer, producer, director*
Most, Nathan *mutual fund executive*
Nadell, Andrew Thomas *psychiatrist*
Ocheltree, Richard Lawrence *lawyer, retired forest products company executive*
Peel, Fred Welch, Jr. *law educator, writer*
Raffo, Susan Henney *elementary education educator*
Sadilek, Vladimir *architect*
Schwantes, Robert Sidney *international relations executive*
Stofflet, Mary Kirk *museum curator, writer*
Tanzi, Carol Anne *interior designer*
Voelker, Elizabeth Anne *artist*
Ward, William Reed *composer, educator*
Ziegler, R. W., Jr. *lawyer, consultant*

Byron
Alexander, Frank *publisher, editor*

Calabasas
Bernhard, Sandra *actress, comedienne, singer*
†Dunphy, Jerry Raymond *television news anchor, lyric writer*
Goldfield, Emily Dawson *finance company executive, artist*
Hosseiniyar, Mansour M. *software engineer, financial consultant*
Iacobellis, Sam Frank *retired aerospace company executive*
Landau, Martin *actor*
Laney, Michael L. *manufacturing executive*
Larese, Edward John *company executive*
Levy, Dena Christine *television producer, director*
Menteer, David Hilton *producer, production manager*
Phillips, Teddy Steve, Sr. *conductor, saxophone player, production company executive*
†Sperber, Burton S. *construction executive*

Caliente
Rankin, Helen Cross *cattle rancher, guest ranch executive*

Calistoga
Dillon, James McNulty *retired banker*
Moorhouse, Douglas C. *retired engineering executive*
Ogg, Robert Danforth *corporate executive*

Camarillo
Alexander, John Charles *editor, writer*
Cleary, Thomas Charles *technology company executive*
Cobb, Roy Lampkin, Jr. *retired computer sciences corporation executive*
Denmark, Bernhardt *manufacturing executive*
DePatie, David Hudson *motion picture company executive*
Doebler, Paul Dickerson *publishing management executive*
Evans, James Handel *university administrator, architect, educator*
Faulconer, Kay Anne *communications executive, dean*
Field, Jeffrey Frederic *designer*
Frayssinet, Daniel Fernand *software company executive*
Halperin, Kristine Briggs *insurance sales and marketing professional*
Kiser, Nagiko Sato *retired librarian*
Lam, Cheung-Wei *electrical engineer*
MacAlister, Robert Stuart *oil company executive*
MacDonald, Norval (Woodrow) *safety engineer*
Parker, Allan Leslie *marketing executive*
Parker, Theodore Clifford *electronics engineer*
Rieger, Elaine June *nursing administrator*
Street, Dana Morris *orthopedic surgeon*
Vannix, C(ecil) Robert *programmer, systems analyst*
Weiss, Carl *aerospace company executive*

Cambria
Blundell, William Edward *journalist, consultant*
DuFresne, Armand Frederick *management and engineering consultant*
Harden, Marvin *artist, educator*
Morse, Richard Jay *human resources and organizational development consultant, manufacturers' representative company executive*
Salaverria, Helena Clara *educator*

Cameron Park
Frazer, Lance William *writer*

Camp Pendleton
Admire, John H. *career officer*
Branson-Berry, Karen Marie *nurse*

Campbell
†Beyer, Casey K. *legislative staff member*
Nicholson, Joseph Bruce *real estate developer*
Ross, Hugh Courtney *electrical engineer*
Tseng, Alexander *medical oncologist*

Campo
Beierle, Herbert Leonard *dean*

Canoga Park
Destler, Dave M. *publisher, editor, journalist*
Kivenson, Gilbert *engineering consultant, patent agent*
Lederer, Marion Irvine *cultural administrator*
McAuley, Milton Kenneth *author, book publisher*
Peirson, George Ewell *film producer, writer, art director, educator*
Rosenfeld, Sarena Margaret *artist*
†Song, Yanming *artist*

Canyon Lake
Knight, Vick, Jr. *author, educator, counselor*
Schilling, Frederick Augustus, Jr. *geologist, consultant*

Capitola
Barna, Arpad Alex *electrical engineering consultant*
Sprenkel, Joanne Noce *employee health nurse*

Capo Beach
Ely-Chaitlin, Marc Eric *government official*
Hallowell, John H *minister*

Cardiff By The Sea
Karr, Marie Aline Christensen *executive*
Sargent, J(ean) McNeil *artist, art educator*
Sheldon, Deena Lynn *television camera operator*

Carlsbad
Anderson, Paul Irving *management executive*
Bartok, Michelle *cosmetic company executive*
Billingsley, William Scott *accountant, controller*
Brown, Jack *magazine editor*
Buckley, Greta Paula *auditor*
Crooke, Stanley Thomas *pharmaceutical company executive*
Diaz, David *illustrator*
Dziewanowska, Zofia Elizabeth *neuropsychiatrist, pharmaceutical executive, researcher, educator*
Gardner, David Chambers *education educator, psychologist, business executive, author*
Halberg, Charles John August, Jr. *mathematics educator*
Haney, Robert Locke *retired insurance company executive*
Hrenoff, Natalia Olympiada *nurse*
Kauderer, Bernard Marvin *retired naval officer*
Lange, Clifford E. *librarian*
Liddicoat, Richard Thomas, Jr. *professional society administrator*
McCracken, Steven Carl *lawyer*
†Missett, Judi Sheppard *dancer, jazzercise company executive*
Mitchell, Thomas Edward, Jr. *communications cabling executive*
Moore, Terry Wayne *high technology venture management consultant*
Peasland, Bruce Randall *financial executive*
Peckham, Donald *computer company executive*
Smith, Warren James *optical scientist, consultant, lecturer*
Tompane, Mary Beth *management consultant*
Weiss, Egon Arthur *retired library administrator*
Wilson, Donald Grey *management consultant*

Carmel
Allan, Robert Moffat, Jr. *corporate executive, educator*
Alsberg, Dietrich Anselm *electrical engineer*
Andreason, Sharon Lee *sculptor*
Aurner, Robert Ray, II *oil company, auto diagnostic, restaurant franchise and company development executive*
Bohannon-Kaplan, Margaret Anne *publisher, lawyer*
Bonfield, Andrew Joseph *tax practitioner*
Chung, Kyung Cho *Korean specialist, scholar, educator, author*
Elmstrom, George P. *optometrist, writer*
Evans, Charlotte Mortimer *communications consultant, writer*
Faul, George Johnson *former college president*
Faul, June Patricia *education specialist*
Felch, William Campbell *internist, editor*
Jordan, Edward George *business investor, former college president, former railroad executive*
Kenna, Michael *photographer*
Koeppel, Gary Merle *publisher, art gallery owner, writer*
Krugman, Stanley Lee *international management consultant*
Loper, D. Roger *retired oil company executive*
Merrill, William Dickey *architect*
Mollman, John Peter *book publisher, consultant electronic publishing*
Morain, Mary Stone Dewing *volunteer association executive*
Parker, Donald Henry *psychologist, author*
Reese, William Albert, III *psychologist, clinical neuropsychologist*
Robinson, John Minor *lawyer, retired business executive*
Shapiro, Stephen George *screenwriter, photographer*
Smith, Gordon Paul *management consulting company executive*
Steele, Charles Glen *retired accountant*
Vagnini, Livio Lee *chemist, forensic consultant*
Wolf, Dorothy Joan *poet*

Carmel Valley
Meckel, Peter Timothy *arts administrator, educator*
Wolfe, Maurice Raymond *retired museum director, educator*

Carmichael
Areen, Gordon E. *finance company executive*
Givant, Philip Joachim *mathematics educator, real estate investment executive*
Goodin, Evelyn Marie *writer*
Halpenny, Diana Doris *lawyer*
Jarrett, Ronald Douglas *lawyer, nurse*
McHugh, James Joseph *retired naval officer, retired associate dean*
Probasco, Calvin Henry Charles *clergyman, college administrator*
Rich, Albert Clark *solar energy manufacturing executive*
Sahs, Majorie Jane *art educator*
Wagner, Carruth John *physician*

Carpinteria
Fisher, John Crocker *physicist*
Hansen, Robert William *artist, educator*
Schmidhauser, John Richard *political science educator*
Wheeler, John Harvey *political scientist*

Carson
Chan, Peter Wing Kwong *pharmacist*
Hirsch, Gilah Yelin *artist, writer*
Hope, Ellen *clinical sciences educator*
Kowalski, Kazimierz *computer science educator, researcher*
Quijada, Angélica María *elementary education educator*
Zimmerer, Kathy Louise *university art gallery director*

Castro Valley
Bennett, Shoshana Stein *post partum counselor, consultant, lecturer*
Denning, Eileen Bonar *management consultant*
Erwin, Frances Suzanne *artist*
Knight, Andrew Kong *visual artist, educator*
Morrison, Glenn Leslie *minister*
Palmer, James Daniel *inspector*

Castroville
Guglielmo, Eugene Joseph *software engineer, consultant*

Cathedral City
Jackman, Robert Alan *retail executive*
Konwin, Thor Warner *financial executive*

Cayucos
Hedlund, James Lane *retired psychologist, educator*
Theurer, Byron W. *aerospace engineer, business owner*

Cedar Ridge
Bruno, Judyth Ann *chiropractor*

Century City
Feiman, Thomas E. *investment manager*
†Fili-Krushel, Patricia *broadcast executive*
Spirt, Mitchell Jeffrey *internist, gastroenterologist, medical consultant*
Wilson, Pete *former governor*

Cerritos
Ayloush, Cynthia Marie *financial executive*
Rice, Barbara Pollak *advertising and marketing executive*
Sarno, Maria Erlinda *lawyer, scientist*
Subramanya, Shiva *aerospace systems engineer*

Chatsworth
Hage, Stephen John *radiology administrator, consultant*
Lu, Guiyang *electrical engineer*
Miller, Robert Steven *secondary school educator*
Sherman, Robert *communications executive, producer*
Stephenson, Irene Hamlen *biorhythm analyst, consultant, editor, educator*
Weisbrod, Ken (Joseph Louis Weisbrod) *marketing professional*
Wells, Annie *photographer*

Chico
Allen, Charles William *mechanical engineering educator*
Burks, Rocky Alan *independent living center executive, consultant*
Dorman, N.B. *writer*
Ediger, Robert Ike *botanist, educator*
Esteban, Manuel Antonio *university administrator, educator*
Etz, (Helen) Jane *hospital utilization*
Houx, Mary Anne *investments executive*
King, Claudia Louan *film producer, lecturer*
Kistner, David Harold *biology educator*
Livingston, Myran Jay *author, film writer, director and producer*
McNall, Scott Grant *sociology educator*
Moore, Brooke Noel *philosophy educator*
Olsen, Robert Arthur *finance educator*
Robinson, Beulah Lobdell *retired educator*
Rodrigue, Christine M(ary) *geography educator, business consultant*
Van Auken, Stuart *marketing educator*
Vaught, Tony Steven *aquaculturist*
Ward, Chester Lawrence *physician, retired county health official, retired military officer*
†Williams, Mark Grayson *artist*

China Lake Nwc
Bennett, Jean Louise McPherson *physicist, research scientist*
Long, Andre Edwin *law educator, lawyer*

Chino
Determan, John David *lawyer*
†Forsyth, Barbara Jean *elementary reading specialist, writer, poet*
Goodman, Lindsey Alan *furniture manufacturing executive, architect*
Koestel, Mark Alfred *geologist, photographer*
Pfuntner, Allan Robert *entomologist*
Yochem, Barbara June (Runyan) *sales executive, lecturer*

Chino Hills
Hemenway, Stephen James *record producer, author*

Chiriaco Summit
Myers, William Elliott *financial consultant*

Chula Vista
Allen, David Russell *lawyer*
Allen, Henry Wesley *biomedical researcher*
Blankfort, Lowell Arnold *newspaper publisher*

Cohen, Elaine Helena *pediatrician, pediatric cardiologist*
Hanson, Eileen *principal*
†Kowit, Steve Mark *poet, educator*
Livziey, James Gerald *secondary school educator*
Maggi, Gayle J.B. *secondary school educator*
Manary, Richard Deane *manufacturing executive*
Quisenberry, Robert Max *architect, industrial designer*
Santee, Dale William *lawyer, air force officer*
Scozzari, Albert *portfolio manager*
Smith, Peggy O'Doniel *physicist, educator*
Tilden, Kevin Archer *communications executive*
Trujillo, Teófilo-Carlos *writer, publisher, history educator*
Vess, Ronald Wayne *librarian*
Vignapiano, Louis John *municipal official*
Wolk, Martin *physicist, electronics engineer*
Wyatt, Edith Elizabeth *elementary education educator*

Citrus Heights
Barth, Sharon Lynn *nurse*
Leisey, Donald Eugene *educational materials company executive, educator*
Stadley, Pat Anna May Gough (Mrs. James M. Stadley) *author*

City Of Industry
Churchill, James Allen *lawyer*
†Requeno, Nestor Danilo *strategic planner*
Scritsmier, Jerome Lorenzo *manufacturing company executive*

Claremont
Ackerman, Gerald Martin *art historian, consultant*
Alexander, John David, Jr. *college administrator*
Ansell, Edward Orin *lawyer*
Atlas, Jay David *philosopher, consultant, linguist*
Barnes, Richard Gordon *English literature educator, poet*
Bekavac, Nancy Yavor *academic administrator, lawyer*
Benjamin, Karl Stanley *art educator*
Bjork, Gordon Carl *economist, educator*
Blizzard, Alan *artist*
Borcherding, Thomas Earl *economist*
†Brint, Steven Gregory *sociologist, educator*
Burns, Richard Dean *history educator, publisher, author*
Casanova, Aldo John *sculptor*
†Chávez-Silverman, Suzanne *Latin American studies educator*
Coleman, Courtney Stafford *mathematician, educator*
Cooke, Kenneth Lloyd *mathematician, educator*
Davis, Nathaniel *humanities educator*
Doty, Horace Jay, Jr. *theater administrator, arts consultant*
Douglass, Enid Hart *educational program director*
†Dunye, Cheryl *artist, film maker*
Dym, Clive Lionel *engineering educator*
Faranda, John Paul *college administrator*
Fossum, Robert H(eyerdahl) *retired English literature educator*
Fucaloro, Anthony Frank *dean*
Gabriel, Earl A. *osteopathic physician*
Gann, Pamela Brooks *academic administrator*
Goodrich, Norma Lorre (Mrs. John H. Howard) *French and comparative literature educator*
Hartford, Margaret Elizabeth (Betty Hartford) *social work educator, gerontologist, writer*
Helliwell, Thomas McCaffree *physicist, educator*
Henriksen, Melvin *mathematician, educator*
Herschensohn, Bruce *film director, writer*
Jaffa, Harry Victor *political philosophy educator emeritus*
Johnson, Jerome Linné *cardiologist*
Kibler, Ray Franklin, III *minister*
Kroll, C(harles) Douglas *minister*
Kubota, Mitsuru *chemistry educator*
Kucheman, Clark Arthur *religion educator*
Leeb, Charles Samuel *clinical psychologist*
Liggett, Thomas Jackson *retired seminary president*
Likens, James Dean *economics educator*
Lofgren, Charles Augustin *legal and constitutional historian, history educator*
Macaulay, Ronald Kerr Steven *linguistics educator, former college dean*
Maguire, John David *academic administrator, educator, writer*
Martin, Jay Herbert *psychoanalysis and English educator*
McClelland, Harold Franklin *economics educator*
McKirahan, Richard Duncan, Jr. *classics and philosophy educator*
Mezey, Robert *poet, educator*
Molinder, John Irving *engineering educator, consultant*
Monson, James Edward *electrical engineer, educator*
Moss, Myra Ellen (Myra Moss Rolle) *philosophy educator*
Mullikin, Harry Copeland *mathematics educator*
Pedersen, Richard Foote *diplomat and academic administrator*
Phelps, Orme Wheelock *economics educator emeritus*
Pinney, Thomas Clive *retired English language educator*
Platt, Joseph Beaven *former college president*
Purves, William Kirkwood *biologist, educator*
Reiss, Roland Martin *artist, educator*
Riggs, Henry Earle *academic administrator, engineering management educator*
Rossum, Ralph Arthur *political science educator*
Roth, John King *philosopher, educator*
Sanders, James Alvin *minister, biblical studies educator*
Sontag, Frederick Earl *philosophy educator*
Stanley, Peter William *academic administrator*
Stark, Jack Lee *academic administrator*
Strauss, Jon Calvert *academic administrator*
Tanenbaum, Basil Samuel *engineering educator*
Taylor, Roy Lewis *botanist, educator*
Tengbom, Luverne Charles *religion educator*
Tilden, Wesley Roderick *author, retired computer programmer*
†Ulitin, Vladimir Gregor *retired Russian language and literature educator*
Valdez, Arnold *dentist, lawyer*
Warder, Michael Young *think tank executive*
Wents, Doris Roberta *psychologist*
Wettack, F. Sheldon *academic administrator*
Wheeler, Geraldine Hartshorn *historian*
Woodress, James Leslie, Jr. *English language educator*
†Wright, Jonathan Charles *biology educator, researcher*
Wykoff, Frank Champion *economics educator*

Young, Howard Thomas *foreign language educator*
Yurist, Svetlan Joseph *mechanical engineer*
Zornes, Milford *artist*

Clayton
Bower, Fay Louise *retired academic administrator, nursing educator*

Cloverdale
Neuharth, Daniel J., II *psychotherapist*

Clovis
Mort, Gary Steven *physical education educator*
Shields, Allan Edwin *writer, photographer, retired educator*
Smith, William Clarke *clergyman*
Terrell, Howard Bruce *psychiatrist*

Coalinga
Frame, Ted Ronald *lawyer*
Harris, John Charles *agriculturalist*

Colton
Brown, Jack H. *supermarket company executive*
Dybowski, Douglas Eugene *education educator, economist*
Slider, Margaret Elizabeth *elementary education educator*
Witman-Glenn, Laura Kathleen *writer, security guard, silent alarm monitor*

Colusa
Carter, Jane Foster *agriculture industry executive*

Compton
Drew, Sharon Lee *sociologist*
Golleher, George *food company executive*
Janeway, Barbara *public relations executive*
Shiloh, Allen *writer, postal employee*
Wang, Charles Ping *scientist*
Williams, Vivian Lewie *college counselor*

Concord
Albrecht, Donna G. *author*
Bellson, Louis Paul *drummer*
Cassidy, John Joseph *hydraulic and hydrologic engineer*
Crocker, Kenneth Franklin *data processing consultant*
Davis, Robert Leach *retired government official, consultant*
Hammond, Blaine Randol *priest*
Hearst, John Eugene *chemistry educator, researcher, consultant*
Jones, Gerald Edward *religion educator*
Koffler, Herbert *health plan administrator, educator*
Lee, Low Kee *electronics engineer, consultant*
MacDonald, Angus *writer, editor*
McConnell, Rob *jazz musician, composer*
Padget, John E. *management professional*
†Robert, Cavett McNeill, Jr. *neurosurgeon*
Thompson, Jeremiah Beiseker *international medical business executive*
Travers, Judith Lynnette *human resources executive*

Cool
Sheridan, George Groh *English and history educator*

Corona
Hagmann, Lillian Sue *violin instructor*
Steiner, Barbara Anne *secondary school educator*
Wetsch, Peggy A. *information systems specialist, publisher, educator, nurse*

Corona Del Mar
Bird-Porto, Patricia Anne *personnel director*
Brandt, Rexford Elson *artist*
Britten, Roy John *biophysicist*
Crump, Spencer *publisher, business executive*
Delap, Tony *artist*
Freeman, Richard Dean *new business start-up service company executive*
Helphand, Ben J. *actuary*
Hill, Melvin James *oil company executive*
Hinderaker, Ivan *political science educator*
Menke, Cathleen Vejsicky *management executive, educator*
Muller, David Webster *architectural designer*
†Quinlan, Francis E. *lawyer*
Richmond, Ronald LeRoy *aerospace engineer*
Terrell, A. John *university telecommunications director*
Wolf, Karl Everett *aerospace and communications corporation executive*
Yeo, Ron *architect*

Coronado
Allen, Charles Richard *retired financial executive*
Axelson, Joseph Allen *professional athletics executive, publisher*
Brunton, Paul Edward *retired diversified industry executive*
Butcher, Bobby Gene *retired military officer*
Crilly, Eugene Richard *engineering consultant*
Dalton, Matt *retired foundry executive*
Hostler, Charles Warren *international affairs consultant*
Hubbard, Donald *marine artist, writer*
Neblett, Carol *soprano*
Perrill, Frederick Eugene *information systems executive*
Raushenbush, Walter Brandeis *law educator*
Rizza, Joseph Padula *naval officer, former president maritime academy*
Sack, Edgar Albert *electronics company executive*
Stockdale, James Bond *writer, research scholar, retired naval officer*
Wagener, Hobart D. *retired architect*
Weiss-Cornwell, Amy *interior designer*
Worthington, George Rhodes *retired naval officer*

Corralitos
Short, Harold Ashby *imaging engineer*

Corte Madera
Kratka-Schneider, Dorothy Maryjohanna *psychotherapist*

Costa Mesa
Anderson, Jon David *lawyer*
†Austin, David John *curriculum developer, writer*
Bender, Edward Erik *geology educator, researcher*
Botello, Troy James *arts administrator, educator*

Brady, John Patrick, Jr. *electronics educator, consultant*
Buchtel, Michael Eugene *optical mechanical engineer*
Caldwell, Courtney Lynn *lawyer, real estate consultant*
Calise, William Joseph, Jr. *lawyer*
Carpenter, Frank Charles, Jr. *retired electronics engineer*
Currie, Robert Emil *lawyer*
Damsky, Robert Philip *communications executive*
Daniels, James Walter *lawyer*
Davis, Don H. *electronics executive*
DeMille-Camacho, Dianne Lynne *mathematics educator, administrator*
Dinkel, John George *magazine editor*
Dougherty, Betsey Olenick *architect*
Frieden, Clifford E. *lawyer*
Gardin, John George, II *psychologist*
Goldstein, Michael Gerald *lawyer*
Hamilton, James William *lawyer*
Hamilton, Phillip Douglas *lawyer*
Hay, Howard Clinton *lawyer*
Hugo, Nancy *county official, alcohol and drug addiction professional*
Jabbari, Ahmad *publishing executive*
Jansen, Allan W. *lawyer*
Jones, H(arold) Gilbert, Jr. *lawyer*
Klein, (Mary) Eleanor *retired clinical social worker*
Kolanoski, Thomas Edwin *financial company executive*
Lopata, Martin Barry *business executive*
Medina-Puerta, Antonio *scientist*
Muller, Jerome Kenneth *photographer, art director, editor*
Paine, David M. *public relations executive*
Panaccione, Bruce Roy *systems analyst, geographer*
Renne, Janice Lynn *interior designer*
Reveal, Ernest Ira, III *lawyer*
Rudolph, George Cooper *lawyer*
Schaaf, Douglas Allan *lawyer*
Tanner, R. Marshall *lawyer*
Tennyson, Peter Joseph *lawyer*
Thurston, Morris Ashcroft *lawyer*
Trivelpiece, Craig Evan *computer electronics executive*

Cotati
Hill, Ray Allen *educator*

Covina
Colley, Janet Scritsmier *investment consultant*
Cottrell, Janet Ann *controller*
Fillius, Milton Franklin, Jr. *food products company executive*
More, Blake *writer, poet*
Straw, Ellen Katrina *English educator, writer*
Takei, Toshihisa *otolaryngologist*

Coyote
Keeshen, Kathleen Kearney *public relations consultant*

Crescent City
Carter, Neville Louis *geophysicist, educator*
Hight, Harold Philip *retired security company executive*
Ruffer, Joyce Sellars *poet, artist*

Crestline
Douglas, Cindy Holloway *mortgage company executive*
Merrill, Steven William *research and development executive*

Crockett
†Adams, Carol Jean *educator*
Leporiere, Ralph Dennis *quality engineer*

Cromberg
Kolb, Ken Lloyd *writer*

Culver City
Abarbanell, Gayola Havens *financial planner*
Bancroft, Anne (Mrs. Mel Brooks) *actress*
Berland, James Fred *software company executive*
†Besson, Luc *film director*
Binder, Bettye B. *author, lecturer*
Boonshaft, Hope Judith *public relations executive*
Boorman, John *film director, producer, screenwriter*
Brooks, James L. *writer, director, producer*
Brooks, Mel *producer, director, writer, actor*
Buyse, Emile Jules *film company executive*
Calley, John *motion picture company executive, film producer*
Clodius, Albert Howard *history educator*
Copeland, Stewart *composer, musician*
Crowe, Cameron *screenwriter, film director*
Davidson, Valerie LaVergne *institute administrator*
Davis, George Osmond *communications executive*
†Devlin, Dean *producer, writer, actor*
Eckel, James Robert, Jr. *financial planner*
†Ewing, Elisabeth Anne Rooney *priest*
†Ewing, James E. *priest*
Feingold, Benjamin S. *broadcast executive*
Feltheimer, Jon *entertainment company executive*
Fisher, Lucy J. *motion picture company executive*
†Grant, Joan Julien *artist, poet*
Gregg, David Paul *information storage media specialist*
Guber, Peter *producer*
Hu, Lincoln *media technology executive, computer scientist*
†Jacobs, Sidney J. *rabbi, journalist*
Jaffe, Stanley Richard *film producer, director*
Johnson, Earvin (Magic Johnson) *professional sports team executive, former professional basketball coach*
†Kaplan, Andy *broadcast executive*
Kumar, Anil *nuclear engineer*
Leve, Alan Donald *electronic materials manufacturing company owner, executive*
†Litewka, Albert Bernard *communications and publishing company executive*
Littlefield, Warren *television executive*
Maltzman, Irving Myron *psychology educator*
Mark, Laurence Maurice *film producer*
†Marshall, Garry *film producer, director, writer*
Marshall, (C.) Penny *director, actress*
McNeill, Daniel Richard *writer*
Mehlman, Lon Douglas *information systems specialist*
Morgan, Paul Evan *architect*
Moss, Eric Owen *architect*
Netzel, Paul Arthur *fundraising management executive, consultant*

Pascal, Amy *film company executive*
Pavitt, William Hesser, Jr. *lawyer*
Pittard, William Blackburn (Billy Pittard) *television graphic designer*
Pollack, Sydney *film director*
Rose, Margarete Erika *pathologist*
†Sakai, Richard *motion picture and television executive, producer*
Sensiper, Samuel *consulting electrical engineer*
Stark, Ray *motion picture producer*
Stoughton, W. Vickery *healthcare executive*
Tang, Yin Sheng *physicist*
†Tannenbaum, Eric *broadcast executive*
Tisch, Steven E. *movie producer*
Trebek, Alex *television game show host*
Walsh, Thomas A. *production designer*
Wigan, Gareth *film company executive*
Williams, Kenneth Scott *entertainment company executive*
Wood, Paul Nigel *film and television engineer*

Cupertino
Adams, Jo-Ann Marie *lawyer*
Baab, Carlton *advertising executive*
Burg, John Parker *signal processing executive*
Cleary, William T. *marketing executive*
Compton, Dale Leonard *retired space agency executive, consultant*
Davis, Barbara Joyce Wiener *accountant, investment manager, financial consultant, educator*
Fenn, Raymond Wolcott, Jr. *retired metallurgical engineer*
Fletcher, Homer Lee *librarian*
Flynn, Ralph Melvin, Jr. *sales executive, marketing consultant*
Hill, Claudia Adams *tax consultant*
Holmes, Richard Albert *software engineer, consultant*
Horn, Christian Friedrich *venture capital company executive*
Kvamme, Mark D. *marketing professional*
Mattathil, George Paul *communications specialist, consultant*
Mishelevich, David Jacob *medical company executive, consultant*
Nelson, Richard Burton *physicist, engineer, former patent consultant*
Quirke, Lillian Mary *retired art educator*
Russi, John Joseph *priest, educational administrator*
Simon, Nancy Ruth *lawyer*
Suiter, Thomas *advertising executive*
Supan, Richard Matthew *finance company executive*
Tice, Bradley Scott *humanities educator*
Togasaki, Shinobu *computer scientist*

Cypress
Barman, Robert John *home electronics company executive*
Bloom, Julian *artist, editor*
Dorn, Marian Margaret *educator, sports management administrator*
Edmonds, Ivy Gordon *writer*
Friess, Donna Lewis *children's rights advocate, writer*
George, Patricia Byrne *artist*
Grant, Alan J. *business executive, educator*
Hall, Georgianna Lee *special education educator*
Magdosku, Christopher Lee *civil engineer*
Olschwang, Alan Paul *lawyer*
Osgood, Frank William *urban and economic planner, writer*
Sillman, George Douglas *computer programmer analyst*

Daggett
Bailey, Katherine Christine *artist, writer*

Daly City
†Baladi, Naoum Abboud *surgeon*
Boccia, Barbara *lawyer*
Civitello-Joy, Linda Joan *association executive*
Dee, Jon Facundo *financial services executive*
Hargrave, Sarah Quesenberry *consulting company executive*
Reuss von Plauen, Prince-Archbishop Heinrich XXVI *Metropolitan, nursing, legal consultant, psychologist, educator*
Shaw, Richard Eugene *cardiovascular researcher*

Dana Point
Bullock, Harvey Reade *screenwriter*
Furst, Raymond Bruce *engineer, consultant*
Kesselhaut, Arthur Melvyn *financial consultant*
Lang, George Frank *insurance executive, consultant, lawyer*
Mardian, Robert Charles, Jr. *restauranteur*
Montanus, Mary Rosamond *accountant*
Reed, David Andrew *foundation executive*

Danville
Amon, William Frederick, Jr. *biotechnology company executive*
Behring, Kenneth E. *professional sports team owner*
Gorman, Russell William *marketing executive, consultant*
Handa, Eugenie Quan *graphic designer*
Mattoon, Henry Amasa, Jr. *advertising and marketing consultant, writer*
Puffer, Sharon Kaye *residential loan officer*
Randolph, Kevin H. *marketing executive*
Sekera, Cynthia Dawn *secondary education educator*

Davis
Addicott, Fredrick Taylor *retired botany educator*
Akesson, Norman Berndt *agricultural engineer, emeritus educator*
Ardans, Alexander Andrew *veterinarian, laboratory director, educator*
Baldwin, Ransom Leland *animal science educator*
Barbour, Michael G(eorge) *botany educator, ecological consultant*
Bartosic, Florian *lawyer, arbitrator, educator*
Baskin, Ronald Joseph *cell biologist, physiologist, biophysicist educator, dean*
Beadle, Charles Wilson *retired mechanical engineering educator*
Beagle, Peter Soyer *writer*
Black, Arthur Leo *biochemistry educator*
Brandt, Harry *mechanical engineering educator*
Brown, Arthur Carl, Jr. *retired minister*
Bruch, Carol Sophie *lawyer, educator*
Bruening, George E. *virologist*
†Bunch, Richard Alan *writer, educator*
Cahill, Thomas Andrew *physicist, educator*
Cardiff, Robert Darrell *pathology educator*
Carter, Harold O. *agricultural economics educator*

Chancellor, William Joseph *agricultural engineering educator*
Cheney, James Addison *civil engineering educator*
Cliver, Dean Otis *microbiologist, educator*
Cohen, Lawrence Edward *sociology educator, criminologist*
Colvin, Harry Walter, Jr. *physiology educator*
Conn, Eric Edward *plant biochemist*
Cook, Roberta Lynn *agricultural economist, specialist*
Day, Howard Wilman *geology educator*
Dorf, Richard Carl *electrical engineering and management educator*
Dykstra, Daniel James *lawyer, educator*
Enders, Allen Coffin *anatomy educator*
Epstein, Emanuel *plant physiologist*
Ernst, Ralph Ambrose *poultry specialist*
Feeney, Floyd Fulton *legal educator*
Feeney, Robert Earl *research biochemist*
Fowler, William Mayo, Jr. *rehabilitation medicine physician*
†Francis, Mark Owen *landscape architecture educator*
Freedland, Richard Allan *retired biologist, educator*
Fridley, Robert Bruce *agricultural engineering educator*
Gardner, Murray Briggs *pathologist, educator*
Gates, Bruce Clark *chemical engineer, educator*
Ghausi, Mohammed Shuaib *electrical engineering educator, university dean*
Gifford, Ernest Milton *biologist, educator*
Ginosar, D. Elaine *elementary education educator*
Goldstone, Jack Andrew *sociologist*
Green, Bonnie Jean *early childhood administrator*
Green, Melvin Martin *geneticist*
Grey, Robert Dean *academic administrator, biology educator*
Grossman, George Stefan *library director, law eductor*
Groth, Alexander Jacob *political science educator*
Hakimi, S. Louis *electrical and computer engineering educator*
Harper, Lawrence Vernon *human development educator*
Hawke, Deborah Sue *academic counselor*
Hawkes, Glenn Rogers *psychology educator*
Hayden, John Olin *English literature educator, author*
Hays, Myrna Mantel *educational association administrator, fashion consultant*
†He, Pingnian *physiologist, researcher*
Hedrick, Jerry Leo *biochemistry and biophysics educator*
Henderson, Mark Gordy *lawyer*
Hess, Charles Edward *environmental horticulture educator*
Hoffman, Michael Jerome *humanities educator*
Hollinger, Mannfred Alan *pharmacologist, educator, toxicologist*
Horwitz, Barbara Ann *physiologist, educator, consultant*
Imwinkelried, Edward John *law educator*
Jett, Stephen Clinton *geography and textiles educator, researcher*
Johnson, Kevin Raymond *lawyer, educator*
Jones, Edward George *neuroscience professor, department chairman*
Juenger, Friedrich Klaus *lawyer, educator*
Jungerman, John Albert *physics educator*
Kado, Clarence Isao *molecular biologist*
Kaplan, Douglas Allen *county official*
Keizer, Joel Edward *theoretical scientist, educator*
Kester, Dale Emmert *pomologist, educator*
King, Janet Carlson *nutrition educator, researcher*
Kofranek, Anton Miles *floriculturist, educator*
Krener, Arthur J. *systems engineering educator*
Krone, Ray Beyers *civil and environmental engineering educator, consultant*
Laidlaw, Harry Hyde, Jr. *entomology educator*
Larock, Bruce Edward *civil engineering educator*
Lazarus, Gerald Sylvan *physician, university dean*
Learn, Elmer Warner *agricultural economics educator, retired*
Levy, Bernard C. *electrical engineer, educator*
Lewis, Jonathan *health care association administrator*
Lofland, Lyn Hebert *sociology educator*
Major, Clarence Lee *novelist, poet, educator*
Manoliu, Maria *linguist, educator*
Mason, William A(lvin) *psychologist, educator, researcher*
McHenry, Henry Malcolm *anthropologist, educator*
Meyer, Margaret Eleanor *microbiologist, educator*
Morgan, Charles Edward Phillip *bank executive*
Motley, Michael Tilden *communication educator*
Moyle, Peter Briggs *fisheries and biology educator*
Mukherjee, Amiya K *metallurgy and materials science educator*
Murphy, Terence Martin *biology educator*
Musolf, Lloyd Daryl *political science educator, institute administrator*
Nash, Charles Presley *chemistry educator*
Oakley, John Bilyeu *law educator, lawyer, judicial consultant*
Olsson, Ronald Arthur *computer science educator*
Orlob, Gerald Thorvald *civil engineer, engineering educator, reseacher*
Owings, Donald Henry *psychology educator*
Painter, Ruth Robbins *retired environmental biochemist*
Palmer, Philip Edward Stephen *radiologist*
Petersen, Roland *artist, printmaker*
Plopper, Charles George *anatomist, cell biologist*
Pritchard, William Roy *former university system administrator*
Qualset, Calvin O. *plant genetics and agronomy educator*
Rhode, Edward Albert *veterinary medicine educator, veterinary cardiologist*
Richman, David Paul *neurologist, researcher*
Rick, Charles Madeira, Jr. *geneticist, educator*
Rost, Thomas Lowell *plant biology educator*
†Rothchild, Donald Sylvester *political science educator*
Rothstein, Morton *historian, retired educator*
Schenker, Marc Benet *preventive medicine educator*
Schneeman, Barbara Olds *nutritionist*
Schoener, Thomas William *zoology educator, researcher*
Sharrow, Marilyn Jane *library administrator*
Shelton, Robert Neal *physics educator, researcher*
Sillman, Arnold Joel *physiologist, educator*
Skinner, G(eorge) William *anthropologist, educator*
Smiley, Robert Herschel *university dean*
Smith, Michael Peter *social science educator, researcher*
Spindler, George Dearborn *anthropologist, educator, author, editor*
Steffey, Eugene Paul *veterinary medicine educator*
Stern, Judith S. *nutritional researcher, educator*
Storm, Donald John *archaeologist, historian*
Stowell, Robert Eugene *pathologist, retired educator*
Stumpf, Paul Karl *biochemistry educator emeritus*
Sumner, Daniel Alan *economist, educator*
Swift, Richard G(ene) *composer, educator*
†Thurston, William Paul *mathematician*
Tinney, Thomas Milton, Sr. *genealogical research specialist*
Troy, Frederic Arthur, II *medical biochemistry educator*
Tsai, Chih-Ling *management educator*
Turnlund, Judith Rae *nutrition scientist*
Uyemoto, Jerry Kazumitsu *plant pathologist, educator*
Vanderhoef, Larry Neil *academic administrator*
Vermeij, Geerat Jacobus *marine biologist, educator*
Volman, David Herschel *chemistry educator*
Von Behren, Ruth Lechner *adult day health care specialist, retired*
Waddington, Raymond Bruce, Jr. *English language educator*
Wang, Shih-Ho *electrical engineer, educator*
Watt, Kenneth Edmund Ferguson *zoology educator*
Wegge, Leon Louis François *retired economics educator*
Williams, Hibbard Earl *medical educator, physician*
Williams, William Arnold *agronomy educator*
Williamson, Alan Bacher *English literature educator, poet, writer*
Willis, Frank Roy *history educator*
Wolk, Bruce Alan *law educator*
Woodruff, Truman O(wen) *physicist, emeritus educator*
Wooten, Frederick (Oliver) *applied science educator*
Wydick, Judith Brandli James *volunteer*
Wydick, Richard Crews *lawyer, educator*

Deer Park
Hodgkin, John E. *pulmonologist*

Del Mar
Boynton, Robert Merrill *retired psychology educator*
Comrie, Sandra Melton *human resource executive*
Cooper, Martin *electronics company executive*
Faludi, Susan C. *journalist, scholarly writer*
Farquhar, Marilyn Gist *cell biology and pathology educator*
Kaye, Peter Frederic *television editor*
Lesko, Ronald Michael *osteopathic physician*
Randall, Chandler Corydon *church rector*
Seitman, John Michael *lawyer, arbitrator, mediator*
Smith, Robert Hamil *author, fund raiser*
†Walshok, Mary Lindenstein *academic administrator, sociology educator*
Wilkinson, Eugene Parks *nuclear engineer*

Delano
Lucas, Stephanie Heune *elementary education educator*

Desert Hot Springs
Halasz, Stephen Joseph *retired electro-optical systems engineer*
Hall, Anthony R. *photographer*
†Price, Cynthia Rose *elementary educator, entrepreneur*

Diamond Bar
Domeño, Eugene Timothy *elementary education educator, principal*
Gong, Carolyn Lei Chu *real estate agent*
Mirisola, Lisa Heinemann *air quality engineer*

Diamond Springs
Tarbet, Urania Christy *artist, writer*

Dinuba
Leps, Thomas MacMaster *civil engineer, consultant*
McKittrick, Joseph Terrence *school administrator, educator*

Dixon
Molina Villacorta, Rafael Antonio *technology management investment company executive*

Downey
Baumann, Theodore Robert *aerospace engineer, consultant, army officer*
Brooks, Lillian Drilling Ashton *adult education educator*
Carrico, Deborah Jean *special education teacher*
Demarchi, Ernest Nicholas *aerospace engineering administrator*
†Diaz, Consuleo *medical executive*
Duzey, Robert Lindsey *lawyer*
Gogolin, Marilyn Tompkins *educational administrator, language pathologist*
Gong, Henry, Jr. *physician, researcher*
Grooms, Henry Randall *civil engineer*
Hackney, Jack Dean *physician*
Hart-Duling, Jean Macaulay *clinical social worker*
Huff, Ricky Wayne *sales executive*
Magnes, Harry Alan *physician*
Nash, Richard Eugene *aerospace engineer*
Nichols, Mark Edward *engineer*
Rose, Susan M. *rehabilitation nurse*
Ruecker, Martha Engels *retired special education educator*
Schoettger, Theodore Leo *city official*
White, Michael Lee *executive producer, writer*

Downieville
Forbes, Cynthia Ann *small business owner, marketing educator*

Duarte
Balon, Thomas William *exercise physiologist*
Comings, David Edward *physician, medical genetics scientist*
Driskill, James Lawrence *minister*
Kovach, John Stephen *oncologist, research center administrator*
Lundblad, Roger Lauren *research director*
Ohno, Susumu *research scientist*
Probst, John Elwin *chaplain, minister*
Smith, Steven Sidney *molecular biologist*
Sollenberger, Donna Kay Fitzpatrick *hospital and clinics executive*
Tse, Man-Chun Marina *special education educator*
Vaughn, James English, Jr. *neurobiologist*

Dublin
Cope, Kenneth Wayne *chain store executive*
Murdock, Steven Kent *business consultant, educator*
Whetten, John D. *food products executive*

Dunlap
Gair, Kevin Lindsey *learning director, educator*

Edwards
Brand, Vance Devoe *astronaut, government official*
Deets, Dwain Aaron *aerospace technology executive*
Garcia, Andrew B. *chemical engineer*
Hamlin, Edmund Martin, Jr. *engineering manager*

Edwards AFB
†Reynolds, Richard V. *career officer*

El Cajon
Brown, Marilynne Joyce *emergency nurse*
Harvey, Elaine Louise *artist, educator*
McClure, Donald Edwin *electrical construction executive, consultant*
Palafox, Mari Lee *private school educator*
Pollock, Richard Edwin *former county administrator*
Rose, Raymond Allen *computer scientist*
Silverberg, Lewis Henry *legal consultant*
Spiegel, Charles (Louis S.J. Spiegel) *psychology educator*
Summers, Stanley Eugene *mechanical engineer*
Thigpen, Mary Cecelia *city official, consultant*
Thomas, Esther Merlene *elementary education educator*

El Centro
Flock, Robert Ashby *retired entomologist*
Patterson, Melissa *elementary education educator*
†Schmitt, Joseph E. *federal judge*
Steensgaard, Anthony Harvey *federal agent*

El Cerrito
Addison, Alonzo Church *graphics visualization executive, educator, consultant*
Cooper, William Clark *physician*
Garbarino, Joseph William *labor arbitrator, economics and business educator*
Griffith, Ladd Ray *retired chemical research director*
Komatsu, S. Richard *architect*
Kuo, Ping-chia *historian, educator*
Schilling, Janet Naomi *nutritionist, consultant*
Siri, William E. *physicist*
Smith, Eldred Reid *library educator*

El Dorado Hills
Davies, William Ralph *service executive*
Schlachter, Gail Ann *publishing company executive*

El Macero
†Andrews, Neil Corbly *surgeon*
Raventos, Antolin *radiology educator*
Wheeler, Douglas Paul *conservationist, government official, lawyer*

El Monte
Deaver, Sharon Mae *special education educator*
Glass, Jean Ann *special education services professional*
Hwang, Tzu-Yang *minister*
Last, Marian Helen *social services administrator*
Wallach, Patricia *mayor*

El Segundo
Autolitano, Astrid *consumer products executive*
Banuk, Ronald Edward (Ron) *mechanical engineer*
Barad, Jill Elikann *family products company executive*
Bauer, Jerome Leo, Jr. *chemical engineer*
Beach, Roger C. *oil company executive*
Begert, Matthew *engineering company official*
Brown, Lorraine Ann *office manager*
†Codon, Dennis P. *lawyer*
Conrad, Paul Francis *editorial cartoonist*
Cordner, Tom *advertising executive*
Criss, William Sotelo *electronics company executive*
Gregg, Lucius Perry, Jr. *aerospace executive*
Halloran, James Vincent, III *technical writer*
†Hamel, Michael A. *military officer*
Honeycutt, Van B. *computer services company executive*
Katz, Lew *advertising executive*
Kostoulas, Ioannis Georgiou *physicist*
Lantz, Norman Foster *electrical engineer*
Mathur, Ashok *telecommunications engineer, educator, researcher*
Maxwell, Floyd Dawson *research engineer, consultant*
McDonald, Rosa Nell *federal research and budgets manager*
McKee, John Morrison *broadcast executive*
McQuillin, Richard Ross *management consultant*
Mirza, Zakir Hussain *aerospace company consultant*
Mo, Roger Shih-Yah *electronics engineering manager*
Pettersen, Thomas Morgan *accountant, finance executive*
Pugay, Jeffrey Ibanez *mechanical engineer*
Rock, Angela *volleyball player*
Tamrat, Befecadu *aeronautical engineer*
†Wilkinson, Sylvia Jean *writer, educator*
Williams, Theodore Earle *industrial distribution company executive*

El Sobrante
Gilbert, William Marshall *retired biologist, educator*
Withrow-Gallanter, Sherrie Anne *construction and audio company executive*

Elk Grove
Crapo, Sheila Anne *telecommunications company professional, artist*
Landon, JoJene Babbitt *special education educator*
McDavid, Douglas Warren *systems consultant*
McIntyre-Ragusa, Mary Maureen *social services consultant*
Sparks, Jack Norman *college dean*
Vang, Timothy Teng *church executive*
Weagraff, Patrick James *psychology educator, writer*

Elverta
Betts, Barbara Lang *lawyer, rancher, realtor*

Emeryville
Bresler, Boris *consulting engineer*
Chilvers, Robert Merritt *lawyer*
Fenwick, James H(enry) *editor*
Finney, Lee *negotiator, social worker*
Greene, Albert Lawrence *hospital administrator*
Hurst, Deborah *pediatric hematologist*
Lewis, Martha Nell *expressive arts therapist, massage therapist, instructor*
Masri, Merle Sid *biochemist, consultant*
McEachern, Alexander *electronics company executive*
Nady, John *electronics company executive*
Penhoet, Edward *biochemicals company executive*
Smith, Christopher Allen *technology company executive, marketing professional*
Taylor, William James (Zak Taylor) *lawyer*
Weaver, Velather Edwards *small business owner*
Zwoyer, Eugene Milton *consulting engineering executive*

Encinitas
Breslaw, Cathy Lee *artist, educator*
Burgin, George Hans *computer scientist, educator*
Chavez, Cesar T. *ophthalmologist, cosmetic surgeon*
Deuble, John L., Jr. *environmental science and engineering services consultant*
†Farrell, Warren Thomas *author*
Frank, Michael Victor *risk assessment engineer*
Galiley, C. Jerome *secondary education educator*
Goldberg, Edward Davidow *geochemist, educator*
McNeil, Dee Dee *singer, songwriter*
Morrow, Charles Tabor *aerospace consulting engineer*
Motoyama, Hiroshi *science association administrator*
Perine, Robert Heath *artist, writer*
Satur, Nancy Marlene *dermatologist*
Smith, Benjamin Eric *venture capitalist, executive*
Williams, Michael Edward *lawyer*

Encino
Aaronson, Robert Jay *aviation executive*
Acheson, Louis Kruzan, Jr. *aerospace engineer and systems analyst*
Bach, Cynthia *educational program director, writer*
Badham, Julia Aileen *artist*
Baker, William Morris *cultural organization administrator*
Bekey, Shirley White *psychotherapist*
Costea, Nicolas Vincent *physician, researcher*
Davenport, Alfred Larue, Jr. *manufacturing company executive*
Dor, Yoram *accountant, firm executive*
Franklin, Bonnie Gail *actress*
Friedman, George Jerry *aerospace company executive, engineer*
Fuld, Steven Alan *financial advisor, insurance specialist*
Gasich, Welko Elton *retired aerospace executive, management consultant*
Greenberg, Allan *advertising and marketing research consultant*
Gross, Sharon Ruth *forensic psychologist, researcher*
Hawthorne, Marion Frederick *chemistry educator*
Hoefflin, Richard Michael *lawyer, judicial administrator, contractor*
Holman, Harland Eugene *retired motion picture company executive*
House-Hendrick, Karen Sue *nursing consultant*
Hunt, Peter Huls *theatrical director, theatrical lighting designer*
Jones, John Harding *photographer*
Kent, Thomas Edward *lawyer*
Knuth, Eldon Luverne *engineering educator*
Lowy, Jay Stanton *music industry executive*
Luna, Barbara Carole *financial analyst, accountant, appraiser*
Medak, Peter *film director*
Nielsen, Leslie *actor*
O'Donnell, Scott Richard *aviation administrator*
Olmos, Edward James *actor*
Phelps, Michael Edward *biophysics educator*
Pryor, Richard *actor, writer*
Rawitch, Robert Joe *journalist, educator*
Roderick, Robert Lee *aerospace executive*
Rose, Doyle *broadcast executive*
Smith, Selma Moidel *lawyer, composer*
Sperber, David Sol *lawyer*
Stanton, Harry Dean *actor*
Thorpe, Gary Stephen *chemistry educator*
Vigdor, James Scott *distribution executive*
Vogel, Susan Carol *nursing administrator*
Webster, David Arthur *life insurance company executive*
Westmore, Michael George *make-up artist*
Woskow, Robert Marshall *management consultant*
Zsigmond, Vilmos *cinematographer, director*

Escalon
Barton, Gerald Lee *farming company executive*

Escondido
Allen, Donald Vail *investment executive, writer, concert pianist*
Bergsma, Derke Peter *minister, religious studies educator*
Briggs, Edward Samuel *naval officer*
Collins, George Timothy *computer software consultant*
Daniels, Richard Martin *public relations executive*
Devine, Walter Bernard *naval architect, marine engineer*
Everton, Marta Ve *retired ophthalmologist*
†Friedman, Alan Howard *education educator, writer*
Gentile, Robert Dale *optometrist, consultant*
Ghandhi, Sorab Khushro *electrical engineering educator*
Killmar, Lawrence E. *wild animal park site curator*
Kilmer, Maurice Douglas *marketing executive*
Moore, Marc Anthony *university administrator, writer, retired military officer*
Newman, Barry Ingalls *retired banker, lawyer*
Raher, Richard Ray *minister*
Rich, Elizabeth Marie *nursing educator*
Rockwell, Elizabeth Goode *dance company director, consultant, educator*
Sampson, Richard Arnim *security professional*
Sternberg, Harry *artist*
Tomomatsu, Hideo *chemist*

Etna
Auxentios, (Bishop Auxentios) *clergyman*

Eureka
Daniels, Madeline Marie *psychotherapist, author*
Kriger, Peter Wilson *healthcare administrator*
Lollich, Leslie Norlene *journalist, educator*
Marak, Louis Bernard, Jr. *artist, educator*
†Nord, Larry B. *federal judge*
Welling, Gene B. *dental association executive*

Fair Oaks
Chernev, Melvin *retired beverage company executive*
Davidson, (Marie) Diane *publisher*
Lemke, Herman Ernest Frederick, Jr. *retired elementary education educator, consultant*
Nolan, Mark Gregory *advertising executive*
Smiley, Robert William *industrial engineer*
†Staley, James Kelly *secondary school educator*
Yarrigle, Charlene Sandra Shuey *realtor, investment counselor*

Fairfax
Codoni, Frederick Peter *editor*
Toney, Anthony *artist*

Fairfield
Atiba, Joshua Olajide O. *internist, pharmacologist, oncologist, educator*
Honeychurch, Denis Arthur *lawyer*
Kirkorian, Donald George *college official, management consultant*
Moore, Marianna Gay *law librarian, consultant*
†Suga, Steven Hidenori *neurologist*

Fall River Mills
Caldwell, Walter Edward *editor, small business owner*

Fallbrook
Bryant, Don Estes *economist, scientist*
Cralley, Lester Vincent *retired industrial hygienist, editor*
David, Ward Stanton *bank officer, retired federal agency executive*
Evans, Anthony Howard *university president*
Freeman, Harry Lynwood *accountant*
Higbee, Donald William *electronics company executive*
Johnston, Betty *writer*
Ragland, Jack Whitney *artist*
Tess, Roy William Henry *chemist*

Felicity
Istel, Jacques Andre *mayor*

Felton
Kulzick, Kenneth Edmund *retired lawyer, writer*

Ferndale
†Silver, Emily Ann *artist, educator*

Fish Camp
Schneider, Arthur Paul *retired videotape and film editor, author*

Flintridge
Fry, Donald Owen *broadcasting company executive*
†Johnston, Oliver Martin, Jr. *animator*
Otte, Carel *geologist*
Pickering, William Hayward *physics educator, scientist*
Read, William McClain *retired oil company executive*
†Thomas, Franklin Rosborough *retired animator*

Folsom
Aldridge, Donald O'Neal *military officer*
Anderson, Jeffrey Lee *physician, anesthesiologist, consultant*
Campbell, Ann Marie *artist*
Emery, Nancy Beth *lawyer*
Ettlich, William F. *electrical engineer*
Ewing, Russell Charles, II *physician*

Fontana
De Tomaso, Ernest Pat *general building contractor, developer*

Forest Ranch
Morrison, Martha Kaye *photolithography engineer, executive*

Forestville
Kielsmeier, Catherine Jane *school system administrator*

Fort Bragg
Galli, Darrell Joseph *management consultant*
Lehan, Jonathan Michael *judge*

Fort Irwin
Burns, Julian H(all), Jr. *military officer*
Strunz, Kim Carol *military officer*
†Webster, William G., Jr. *army officer*

Fortuna
Fisher, Bruce David *elementary school educator*

Foster City
Ball, John Paul *publishing company executive*
Berman, Daniel K(atzel) *educational consultant, university official*
Brankamp, Robert George *biosystems specialist*
Carter, William Gerald *non-profit corporation executive*
Evans, Darrell J. *higher education educator*
Ham, Lee Edward *civil engineer*
Josephine, Helen Bowden *librarian*
Lonnquist, George Eric *lawyer*
Lutvak, Mark Allen *computer company executive*
†McHenry, Julie *communications executive*
†McManus, Dana C. *construction company executive*
Miller, Jon Philip *research and development organization executive*
Nugent, Denise Smith *holistic health care consultant*
Owens, Gwendolyn Rennetta *speech and language therapist*
Thomlinson, Ralph *demographer, educator*
Zaidi, Iqbal Mehdi *biochemist, scientist*

Fountain Valley
Berman, Steven Richard *software engineer*
Davis, Jeremy Matthew *chemist*
Einstein, Stephen Jan *rabbi*
Khalessi, Mohammad R. *structural engineer, researcher*
Lonegan, Thomas Lee *retired restaurant corporation executive*
Mauldin, Jean Humphries *aviation company executive*

†Purdy, Leslie *community college president*
Smith, Marie Edmonds *real estate agent, property manager*
Treadway-Dillmon, Linda Lee *athletic trainer, actress, stuntwoman*
Tu, John *engineering executive*

Frazier Park
Nelson, Harry *journalist, medical writer*

Fremont
Baker, Paul Thornell *anthropology educator*
Buswell, Debra Sue *small business owner, programmer, analyst*
Cummings, John Patrick *lawyer*
†Eastin, Delaine Andree *state agency administrator*
Engelbart, Doug *engineering executive*
Feinberg, Richard Alan *clinical psychologist*
Gill, Stephen Paschall *physicist, mathematician*
Jensen, Paul Edward Tyson *business educator, consultant*
Kuhlman, Gloria Jean *mental health and geriatric nurse, educator*
Lahri, Rajeeva *electronics executive*
Le, Thuy Trong *research scientist, educator*
Lee, Chan-Yun *physicist, process engineer, educator*
Li, Wenbin *physicist, engineer*
†Liang, Christine *import company executive*
Loarie, Thomas Merritt *healthcare executive*
Lydon, Daniel T. *city official*
Morrison, Gus (Angus Hugh Morrison) *mayor, engineer*
Perkins, Jan *municipal official*
Reeves, Carla Marianne *women's health, nurse midwife*
Steckler, Craig Theodore *law enforcement official*
Steinmetz, Seymour *pediatrician*
Torian, Henry *automotive executive*
Tribus, Myron *retired quality counselor, engineer, educator*
Wang, Stanley *electronics executive*
†Weinstein, Marta *packaging services company executive*
Wu, James Chen-Yuan *aerospace engineering educator*
Yee, Keith Philip *accountant*
Zajac, John *semiconductor equipment company executive*

Fresno
Antrim, Minnie Faye *residential care facility administrator*
†Beck, Dennis L. *magistrate judge*
†Best, Hollis G. *federal judge*
Blum, Gerald Henry *department store executive*
Bohl, Allen *coach*
Bond, Thomas Ross *television assistant director*
†Burnett, Lynn Barkley *health science educator*
Buzick, William Alonson, Jr. *investor, lawyer, educator*
Chandler, Bruce Frederick *internist*
Coleman, Donald Gene *education educator*
Coyle, Robert Everett *federal judge*
Crocker, Myron Donovan *federal judge*
Dackawich, S. John *sociology educator*
Dandoy, Maxima Antonio *education educator emeritus*
Darden, Edwin Speight, Sr. *architect*
Dauer, Donald Dean *investment executive*
Diestelkamp, Dawn Lea *county superior court manager*
Donaldson, George Burney *environmental consultant*
†Dorian, Brett J. *federal judge*
Emrick, Terry Lamar *financial business consultant*
Ewell, A. Ben, Jr. *lawyer, businessman*
Ezaki-Yamaguchi, Joyce Yayoi *renal dietitian*
Falcone, Alfonso Benjamin *physician and biochemist*
Ganulin, Judy *public relations professional*
Garrison-Finderup, Ivadelle Dalton *writer*
Genini, Ronald Walter *history educator, historian*
Gorman, Michael Joseph *library director, educator*
Gump, Barry Hemphill *chemistry and food science educator*
Haak, Harold Howard *university president*
Hart, Russ Allen *telecommunications educator*
†Harvey, Raymond Curtis *conductor*
Hill, Pat *coach*
Holmes, Albert William, Jr. *physician*
Howard, Katsuyo Kunugi *counselor, educator, consultant*
Howe, Ronald Evans *minister*
Huddleston, Forest Willis *retired mental healing counselor*
Huffman, David George *electrical engineer*
Huizenga, Edward Richard *mortgage banker*
†Ishii, Anthony W. *judge*
Jamison, Oliver Morton *retired lawyer*
Kallenberg, John Kenneth *librarian*
Kauffman, George Bernard *chemistry educator*
Keen, Derl Walter *child development educator*
Klassen, Peter James *academic administrator, history educator*
Kouymjian, Dickran *art historian, Orientalist, educator*
Kus, James Stedry *geography educator, archaeologist*
Lambe, James Patrick *lawyer*
Lawless, John Howard *minister*
Leigh, Hoyle *psychiatrist, educator, writer*
Levine, Philip *poet, retired educator*
Levy, Joseph William *department stores executive*
Mettee, Stephen Blake *publishing executive*
Michael, James Daniel *computer scientist*
Moyer, J. Keith *newspaper editor*
†Mullins, Cathy Layne *poet, bartender, manager*
Munyon, William Harry, Jr. *architect*
O'Berg, Robert Myron *minister*
O'Brien, John Conway *economist, educator, writer*
O'Connor, Kevin John *psychologist*
†Ortiz, John Michael *provost*
Palmer, Samuel Copeland, III *lawyer*
Patnaude, William E. *architect*
Patterson, James *mayor*
Patton, Jack Thomas *family practice physician*
Petrochilos, Elizabeth A. *writer, publisher*
Pings, Anthony Claude *architect*
Pinkerton, Richard LaDoyt *management educator*
Putman, Robert Dean *golf course architect*
Rank, Everett George *government official*
Redmond-Stewart, Audrey A. *small business owner*
†Rimel, Whitney *federal judge*
Ryan, Charlotte Muriel *family nurse practitioner*
Sherr, Morris Max *lawyer*
Shmavonian, Gerald S. *entertainment executive*
Smith, Richard Howard *banker*
Smith, V. Roy *neurosurgeon*
†Snyder, Sandra M. *federal magistrate judge*
Steinbock, John Thomas *bishop*

Tellier, Richard Davis *management educator*
Thompson, Leonard Russell *pediatrician*
Wanger, Oliver Winston *federal judge*
†Waters, Charles R. *executive editor*
Welty, John Donald *academic administrator*
Wilson, James Ross *communications educator, broadcasting executive*
Winchester, Ed *protective services official*
Xiong, Tousu Saydangnmvang *minister*

Fullerton
Aston, Edward Ernest, IV *dermatologist*
Ayala, John *librarian, dean*
Bakken, Gordon Morris *law educator*
Barchi, Barbara Ann *education and training services consultant*
Boyum, Keith Orel *political scientist, consultant*
Brattstrom, Bayard Holmes *biology educator*
Curran, Darryl Joseph *photographer, educator*
Curry, Denise *university women's basketball coach*
Donoghue, Mildred Ransdorf *education educator*
Duncan, Griff *opera company executive*
Everett, Pamela Irene *legal management company executive, educator*
Goldstein, Edward David *lawyer, former glass company executive*
Gordon, Milton Andrew *academic administrator*
Gunness, Robert Charles *chemical engineer*
Hershey, Gerald Lee *psychologist*
Hollander, Gerhard Ludwig *computer company executive*
Hopping, Richard Lee *college president emeritus*
Jones, Claris Eugene, Jr. *botanist, educator*
†Junn, Ellen N. *psychology educator*
Kaisch, Kenneth Burton *psychologist, priest*
Karson, Burton Lewis *musician*
Kim, Sang Koo *pastor, educator*
Lewandoski, Robert Henry *editor, publisher*
Macaray, Lawrence Richard *art educator*
†Martinez, Vera *academic administrator*
Miller, Arnold *electronics executive*
†Milo, Albert J. *librarian*
Moerbeek, Stanley Leonard *lawyer*
†Morton, Michael James *software engineer*
Nitta, Douglas *family practice physician*
O'Donnell, Edith J. *educational and information technology consultant, author, musician*
Oh, Tai Keun *business educator*
Parsons, Rodney Hunter *lawyer*
Peralta, Joseph Soriano *financial planner*
Pullen, Rick Darwin *dean*
Roberts, Mark Scott *lawyer*
Sa, Julie *council woman*
Shapiro, Mark Howard *physicist, educator, academic dean, consultant*
Smith, Ephraim Philip *academic administrator, former university dean, educator*
Snider, Jane Ann *elementary school educator*
Steward, Marsh, Jr. *obstetrician, gynecologist*
Sugarman, Michael *physician, rheumatologist*
†Traphagan, John Willis *anthropologist*
†Wan, Julia Chang *science educator*
Wiley, David Cole *producer*
Woodhull, Patricia Ann *artist*

Galt
†Nunes, Judy Omai *artist*

Garden Grove
Ballesteros, Juventino Ray, Jr. *minister*
Bell, Melodie Elizabeth *artist, massage therapist*
Clarke, S. Gordon *clergyman*
Dornan, Robert Kenneth *former congressman*
McKee, Kathryn Dian Grant *human resources consultant*
Radosevich, Sharon Kay *critical care nurse*
†Schuller, Robert Harold *clergyman, author*
Sherrard, Raymond Henry *retired government official*
Virgo, Muriel Agnes *swimming school owner*
Williams, J(ohn) Tilman *insurance executive, real estate broker, city official*

Garden Valley
Price, Lew Paxton *writer, engineer, scientist*

Gardena
Kanner, Edwin Benjamin *electrical manufacturing company executive*
Rubin, Lawrence Ira *podiatrist*

Georgetown
Lengyel, Cornel Adam (Cornel Adam) *author*

Gilroy
Borton, George Robert *retired airline captain*
Katemopoulos, Mildred Josephine *executive secretary*
McCarty, Robert Clarke *mathematician*
McGrogan, Michael Patrick *molecular and cell biologist*

Glen Ellen
Hurlbert, Roger William *information service industry executive*
Rockrise, George Thomas *architect*

Glendale
Bitterman, Melvin Lee *real estate developer*
Courtney, Howard Perry *clergyman*
Cross, Richard John *banker*
Curtis, Allan Craig *video and film production executive, consultant*
Darnell, Roger Kent *writer/producer*
de Grassi di Santa Cristina, Leonardo *art historian, educator*
Dohring, Doug *marketing executive*
Dohring, Laurie *marketing executive*
Empey, Donald Warne *educational administrator*
Garcia, Serafin Montealto *physician*
Hadley, Paul Ervin *international relations educator*
Herzer, Richard Kimball *franchising company executive*
Hess, Richard Lowell *broadcast executive*
Hoffman, Donald M. *lawyer*
†Holstad, Scott Cameron *writer, network specialist*
Horton, Kathryn Lynne *marketing executive*
Hughes, Margaret Jane *nurse*
Kay, Alan *computer scientist*
Kazanjian, Phillip Carl *lawyer, business executive*
Kessler-Hodgson, Lee Gwendolyn *actress, corporate executive*
Lathe, Robert Edward *management and financial consultant*
Levy, Ezra Cesar *aerospace scientist, real estate broker*

MacDonald, Kirk Stewart *lawyer*
Martin, John Hugh *lawyer, retired*
Martinetti, Ronald Anthony *lawyer*
Michelson, Lillian *motion picture researcher*
Misa, Kenneth Franklin *management consultant*
Moorhead, Carlos J. *former congressman*
Odier, Pierre Andre *educator, writer, photographer, artist*
Scott, A. Timothy *lawyer*
Simpson, Allyson Bilich *lawyer*
Sitomer, Sheila Marie *television producer, director*
†Smith, Robert A., II *leasing executive, foundation administrator*
Spatny, Mark Scott *production designer, production manager*
Sprosty, Joseph Patrick *weapons specialist, producer, writer, consultant*
Stanfill, Latayne Colvett *non-fiction writer*
Stemmer, Jay John *safety engineer, consultant*
Toscano, Oscar Ernesto *lawyer*
Tripoli, Masumi Hiroyasu *financial consultant and diplomat*
Vilnrotter, Victor Alpár *research engineer*
Whalen, Lucille *academic administrator*

Glendora
Acevedo, Elizabeth Morrison *special education educator*
Barrett, Thomas Joseph *sales executive, computer systems consultant*
Cahn, David Stephen *cement company executive*
Cerullo, Rudy Michael, II *psychology, theology educator, minister*
Day-Gowder, Patricia Joan *retired association executive, consultant*
Haile, Benjamin Carroll, Jr. *retired chemical and mechanical engineer*
Lasko, Allen Howard *pharmacist*
O'Hagan, William Gordon *state agency administrator*
Phillips, Jill Meta *novelist, critic, astrologer*
Richey, Everett Eldon *religion educator*
Schiele, Paul Ellsworth, Jr. *educational business owner, writer*
†Thomas, Andree K *assistant vice president*

Gold River
Andrew, John Henry *lawyer, retail corporation executive*
Gray, Myles McClure *retired insurance company executive*
Milani, Diva *marketing and communications executive*

Goleta
Koart, Nellie Hart *real estate investor and executive*
Thom, Richard David *aerospace executive*
Tulin, Marshall P(eter) *engineering educator*
Winslow, Norman Eldon *business executive*

Granada Hills
Aller, Wayne Kendall *psychology educator, researcher, computer education company executive, property manager*
Lehtihalme, Larry (Lauri) K. *financial planner*
McCraven, Carl Clarke *health service administrator*
Shoemaker, Harold Lloyd *infosystem specialist*

Granite Bay
Borum, William Donald *engineer*
Flora, Edward Benjamin *research and development company executive, mechanical engineer*
Hartmann, Frederick Howard *political science educator emeritus*
Holtz, Sara *lawyer, consultant*
Manzo, Salvatore Edward *retired business developer*

Grass Valley
Hawkins, Richard Michael *lawyer*
Hutcherson, Christopher Alfred *marketing, recruiting and educational fundraising executive*
McDonnell, MaryAnn Margaret *medical marketing executive*
Ozanich, Charles George *real estate broker*
Pasten, Laura Jean *veterinarian*
Robbins, Dale Alan *minister*

Greenbrae
Blatt, Morton Bernard *medical illustrator*
Elder, Rex Alfred *civil engineer*
Levy, S. William *dermatologist*
Parnell, Francis William, Jr. *physician*
†Ramirez, Archimedes *neurosurgeon*

Greenfield
Munoz, John Joseph *retired transportation company executive*

Gridley
Tanimoto, George *agricultural executive, farmer*

Grover Beach
Edwards, Patrick Michael *sales consultant*

Gualala
Gaustad, Edwin Scott *historian*
Ring, Alice Ruth Bishop *retired physician*

Guerneville
Grassa, Rosemarie Lucia *massage therapist*
Weese, Bruce Eric *pharmaceutical sales executive*

Hacienda Heights
Love, Daniel Joseph *consulting engineer*
Sim, John Kim-Chye *minister*

Half Moon Bay
Fennell, Diane Marie *marketing executive, process engineer*
Hinthorn, Micky Terzagian *volunteer, retired*
Lambert, Frederick William *lawyer, educator*
Robertson, Abel L., Jr. *pathologist*

Hanford
†Harris, Mildred Staeger *retired broadcast executive*
Zack, Teresa Ison *civil engineer*

Happy Camp
†Jefferson, Peggy Lee *English educator*

Harbor City
Ackerson, Bradley Kent *physician*

Kwan, Benjamin Ching Kee ophthalmologist
Lee, Grace Tze information services company executive

Hawthorne
Burns, Brent Emil electrical engineer
Gruenwald, James Howard association executive, consultant
Hunt, Brian L. program manager
Perry, James Gregory sales and marketing executive
Roberts, George Christopher manufacturing executive

Hayward
Dance, Maurice Eugene college administrator
Duncan, Doris Gottschalk information systems educator
Funston, Gary Stephen publishing and advertising executive
Gin, Hal Gabriel university administrator
Harris, Penelope Claire children's center administrator, consultant
Hunnicutt, Richard Pearce metallurgical engineer
Jordahl, Kathleen Patricia (Kate Jordahl) photographer, educator
Jun, Jong Sup public administration educator
Kahn, Arlene Judy Miller nurse, educator
Laycock, Mary Chappell gifted and talented education educator, consultant
McCune, Ellis E. retired university system chief administrator, higher education consultant
Minzner, Dean Frederick aviation company executive
Pearce-Percy, Henry Thomas physicist, electronics executive
Ramsdell, Kristin Romeis librarian, researcher
Rees, Norma S. academic administrator
Smith, John Kerwin lawyer

Healdsburg
Allman, Gregg musician
Canfield, Grant Wellington, Jr. management consultant
Eade, George James retired air force officer, research executive, defense consultant
Erdman, Paul Emil author
Glad, Joan Bourne clinical psychologist, educator
Kamm, Thomas Allen air transportation company executive
Myers, Robert Eugene writer, educator

Hemet
Berger, Lev Isaac physicist, educator
Bible, Frances Lillian mezzo-soprano, educator
Coad, Dennis Lawrence real estate broker
Lawrence, Paula Denise physical therapist
Minnie, Mary Virginia social worker, educator, retired
Rowe, Mary Sue accounting executive

Hercules
†Guevara, A.P. network consultant

Hermosa Beach
McDowell, Edward R. H. chemical engineer
†McQuiggan, David K. computer company executive
Wickwire, Patricia Joanne Nellor psychologist, educator

Hesperia
Butcher, Jack Robert (Jack Risin) manufacturing executive
Du Lac, Lois Arline writer

Highland
†Odell, Brenda W. principal
†Vanderveer, David Bryan artist

Highlands
Lee, Robert Erich information technology consultant

Hillsborough
Blume, John August consulting civil engineer
Hower, Donna Wilson elementary education educator
Keller, John Francis retired wine company executive, mayor
Kraft, Robert Arnold retired medical educator, physician
Schapiro, George A. electronics company executive
Westerfield, Putney management consulting executive
Willoughby, Rodney Erwin retired oil company executive
Zimmerman, Bryant Kable retired lawyer

Hollister
Grace, Bette Frances certified public accountant
Smith, George Larry analytical and environmental chemist
Spencer, Douglas Lloyd chemist, manufacturing executive
Turpin, Calvin Coolidge retired university administrator, educator

Hollywood
Adjenian, Robert publisher
†Berman, Richard Keith television producer, film producer
Blakeney, Karen Elizabeth social work administrator, consultant
Byrnes, James Bernard museum director emeritus
Caine, Michael actor
Crow, Sheryl singer/songwriter, musician
Curry, Daniel Francis Myles filmmaker
†Drudge, Matt journalist
Fischer, Dale Susan judge
Fisher, Joel Marshall political scientist, legal consultant, educator
Freilich, Jeff television producer, writer, director
†Huang, Wen-xiang artist, educator
Kurlander, Carl Litman screenwriter
Marshall, Conrad Joseph entrepreneur
Melchior, Ib Jorgen author, television and motion picture writer, director
Miles, Joanna actress, playwright
Parks, Robert Myers appliance manufacturing company executive
Roberts, Mel (Melvin Richard Kells) retired film editor
Salzman, David Elliot entertainment industry executive
Sarley, John G. broadcast executive, writer
Schmidt, Arthur film editor
Secada, Jon musician
Shurtleff, C. Michael writer

†Smith, Pamela Jaye writer, producer, consultant
Thomas, Tony producer
†Wald, Harlan Ira plastic surgeon, lawyer
Walling, Mary Jo Anne women's health nurse

Hopland
Jones, Milton Bennion agronomist, educator

Huntington Beach
Berry, Kim Lauren artist
Boysen, Lars financial consultant
Davidson-Shepard, Gay secondary education educator
De Massa, Jessie G. media specialist
Frye, Judith Eleen Minor editor
Hayden, Ron L. library director
†Hazelton, Astor Miller artist
Jackle, Karen Dee real estate executive
Kovach, Ronald footwear manufacturing executive
Lans, Carl Gustav architect, economist
Leveton, Ian Sinclair civil engineer
Licata, Paul James health products executive
†Lieberman, Phillip E. data company executive
MacCauley, Hugh Bournonville banker
†Nichter, Larry Steven medical educator, plastic surgeon
Olsen, Greg Scott chiropractor
Rook, Douglas Brian cable television executive, recruiter
Shishkoff, Muriel Mendelsohn educational writer
Stillman, Alfred William, Jr. design and support engineer
Strutzel, J(od) C(hristopher) escrow company executive
Thomas-Cote, Nancy Denece office products manufacturing company executive
Wing, Roger management consultant
Wolzinger, Renah medical products executive, music company executive
†Yglesias, Kenneth Dale college president

Huntington Park
Veis, Fred Alan special education educator

Idyllwild
Schneider, Paul writer

Imperial
O'Leary, Thomas Michael lawyer

Imperial Beach
Merkin, William Leslie lawyer

Indian Wells
Harris, Milton M. distributing company executive
Kelley, John Paul communications consultant
Reed, A(lfred) Byron retired apparel and textile manufacturing company
Trotter, F(rederick) Thomas retired academic administrator

Indio
Ellis, Lee publisher, editor
Houghton, Robert Charles secondary education educator
York, Douglas Arthur manufacturing and construction company executive

Industry
†Osuala, Chima Iheanyichukwu microbiologist

Inglewood
Alaniz, Miguel José Castañeda library director
Bryant, Kobe basketball player
Dixon, Tamecka professional basketball player
Dymally, Mervyn Malcolm retired congressman, international business executive
Epstein, Marsha Ann public health administrator, physician
Ferraro, Ray hockey player
†Harper, Derek professional basketball player
Harris, Del William professional basketball coach
Jackson, Philip Douglas professional basketball coach
Kupchak, Mitchell professional sports team executive
Leslie, Lisa professional basketball player
Lewis, Roy Roosevelt physicist
Mabika, Mwadi basketball player
McGee, Pamela basketball player
O'Neal, Shaquille Rashaun professional basketball player
Rice, Glen Anthony professional basketball player
Robinson, Larry Clark professional hockey coach
Rodman, Dennis Keith basketball player
Roski, Edward P. professional sports team executive
Sharman, William professional basketball team executive
Toler, Penny professional basketball player
Vario, Joyce graphic designer
†Woolridge, Orlando professional basketball coach

Inverness
Welpott, Jack Warren photographer, educator

Inyokern
Bass, Nancy Agnes airport executive
Stallknecht-Roberts, Clois Freda publisher, publicist

Ione
Sparrowk, Cora Catherine lay church leader

Irvine
Abu-Mostafa, Ayman Said computer consultant
Adams, Mark coach
Aigner, Dennis John economics educator, consultant
Alcone, Matt advertising executive
Alspach, Philip Halliday manufacturing company executive
Ayala, Francisco José geneticist, educator
Bander, Myron physics educator, university dean
Bartkus, Richard Anthony magazine publisher
Basler, Richard Alan medical consultant
Bastiaanse, Gerard C. lawyer
Beach, Christopher John American literary arts educator
Beckman, Arnold Orville analytical instrument manufacturing company executive
Bennett, Bruce Michael mathematician, educator, musician
Berryhill, Georgia Gene graphic designer, educator
Bershad, Neil Jeremy electrical engineering educator
Block, Sandra Linda special education educator
Bradshaw, Ralph Alden biochemistry educator

Bron, Walter Ernest physics educator
Brueske, Charlotte poet, composer
†Buenavista, Joseph Constante sales manager
Burton, Michael Ladd anthropology educator
Cahill, Richard Frederick lawyer
Chacon, Michael Ernest computer networking specialist
Christopher, Steven Lee religious studies educator
Chronley, James Andrew real estate executive
Clark, Bruce Robert geology consultant
Clark, Karen Heath lawyer
Clark, Michael Phillip English educator
†Click, James H. automotive executive
Cohen, Robert Stephen drama educator
†Colombatto, Martin J. technology company executive
Connolly, John Earle surgeon, educator
Crowley, Daniel Francis, Jr. transportation and logistics executive
Currivan, Bruce Joseph electronics engineer
Curtis, Jesse William, Jr. retired federal judge
Cushman, Robert Fairchild political science educator, author, editor
Danziger, James Norris political science educator
Demetrescu, Mihai Constantin research scientist, educator, computer company executive
†Doan, Patrick Toai Van writer, foundation administrator
Dossett, Lawrence Sherman professional services company official
Dzyaloshinskii, Igor Ekhielievich physicist
Fan, Hung Y. virology educator, consultant
Feldstein, Paul Joseph management educator
Felton, Jean Spencer physician
†Fernandez, Aurelio sales executive
Fisher, Lawrence N. lawyer
Fitch, Walter M(onroe) molecular biologist, educator, evolutionist
Fleischer, Everly Borah academic administrator
Fouste, Donna H. association executive
Freeman, Linton Clarke sociology educator
Fukui, Naoki theoretical linguist
Fybel, Richard D. lawyer
Garretson, Steven Michael PC support manager
Gauntlett, David Allan lawyer
Giannulli, Mossimo designer, apparel business executive
Greenberger, Ellen psychologist, educator
Gupta, Sudhir immunologist, educator
Guymon, Gary LeRoy civil engineering educator, consultant
†Haggerty, Charles A. electronics executive
Hardie, Robert C. newspaper publishing executive
†Hartmann, Dale Walter librarian
Herbert, Gavin Shearer health care products company executive
Hine, Robert Van Norden, Jr. historian, educator
Hoffman, Donald David cognitive and computer science educator
Hubbell, Floyd Allan physician, educator
Hufbauer, Karl George historian of science
Huff, C(larence) Ronald public policy and criminology educator
Jacobsen, Eric Kasner consulting engineer
Jeffers, Michael Bogue lawyer
†Johnson, Benjamin Arlen religious studies educator
Jones, Joie Pierce acoustician, educator, writer, scientist
Jordan, Michelle Henrietta public relations company executive
Key, Mary Ritchie (Mrs. Audley E. Patton) linguist, author, educator
Kinsman, Robert Preston biomedical plastics engineer
Kleeman, Nancy Gray Ervin special education educator
Kluger, Ruth German language educator, editor
Knight, Patricia Marie optics researcher
Korc, Murray endocrinologist
Kraemer, Kenneth Leo architect, urban planner, educator
Krieger, Murray English language educator, author
Laird, Wilbur David, Jr. bookseller, editor
Larson, Kirk David pomologist and extension specialist
Lave, Charles Arthur economics educator
Lawton, Michael James entomologist, pest management specialist
Lenhoff, Howard Maer biological sciences educator, academic administrator, activist
Lesonsky, Rieva editor
†Lightburn, Jeffrey Caldwell corporate communications executive
Lillyman, William John German language educator, academic administrator
†Lindenfelser, Timothy L. marketing professional
Lindquist, Raymond Irving clergyman
Luce, R(obert) Duncan psychology educator
Maddy, Penelope Jo philosopher
†Manian, Vahid manufacturing operations executive
Maradudin, Alexei A. physics educator
Margolis, Julius economist, educator
Mason, Roger Deen archaeologist
Mc Culloch, Samuel Clyde history educator
McLaughlin, Calvin Sturgis biochemistry educator
Miledi, Ricardo neurobiologist
Moghadam, Amir consultant, educational administrator
Muller, Edward Robert lawyer
Murata, Margaret Kimiko music historian, educator
Nalcioglu, Orhan physics educator, radiological sciences educator
†Nicholas, Henry Thompson, III engineering executive
Nomura, Masayasu biological chemistry educator
Orme, Melissa Emily mechanical engineering educator
Overman, Larry Eugene chemistry educator
Peltason, Jack Walter foundation executive, educator
Petrasich, John Moris lawyer
Phalen, Robert Franklynn environmental scientist
Power, Francis William newspaper publisher
Puzder, Andrew F. lawyer
Quilligan, Edward James obstetrician, gynecologist, educator
Rachlis, Arnold Israel rabbi, religion educator
†Ranjan, Priya economist
Rentzepis, Peter M. chemistry educator
Ristau, Kenneth Eugene, Jr. lawyer
Rollans, James O. service company executive
Ross, Amy Ann experimental pathologist
Rosse, James N. newspaper publishing executive
Rowland, Frank Sherwood chemistry educator
†Ruehle, William J. technology company executive
Ruttencutter, Brian Boyle manufacturing company executive
Rynn, Nathan physics educator, consultant
Salesky, William Jeffrey corporate executive

Samueli, Henry electrical engineering educator, entrepreneur
Schonfeld, William Rost political science educator, researcher
Schuetz, John Michael sales executive
Seller, Gregory Erol marketing executive, writer, consultant
Shusterman, Neal Douglas author, screenwriter
Silverman, Paul Hyman science administrator, former university official
Sirignano, William Alfonso aerospace and mechanical engineer, educator
Sklansky, Jack electrical and computer engineering educator, researcher
Sowder, Kathleen Adams marketing executive
Specter, Richard Bruce lawyer
Sperling, George cognitive scientist, educator
Stack, Geoffrey Lawrence real estate developer
Steward, Oswald neuroscience educator, researcher
Stricklin, Guy Michael construction company executive
Stubberud, Allen Roger electrical engineering educator
†Sunoo, Harold W. Asian studies educator
Sutton, Dana Ferrin classics educator
Thomas, Joseph Edward lawyer
Thornton, Robert Lee aircraft manufacturing company executive
Ting, Albert Chia bioengineering researcher
Tobis, Jerome Sanford physician
Toledano, James lawyer
Tully, John Peter land use planner
van-den-Noort, Stanley physician, educator
Van Mason, Raymond dancer, choreographer
Wallis, Richard Fisher physicist, educator
Webb, Louis automotive company executive
Weinstein, Gerald D. dermatology educator
Weissbard, Samuel Held lawyer
Weissenberger, Harry George lawyer
White, Douglas Richie anthropology educator
White, Stephen Halley biophysicist, educator
Wiener, Jon history educator
Wiley, Matthew Forrest real estate broker
Williams, James E. food products manufacturing company executive
Williams, S. Linn lawyer
Wintrode, Ralph Charles lawyer
Wolff, Geoffrey Ansell novelist, critic, educator
Yin, Hong Zhen neuropathologist, researcher
Zack, James G(ordon), Jr. construction claims executive, consultant

Jackson
Steele, John Roy real estate broker

Joshua Tree
Styles, Beverly entertainer

Keene
Rodriguez, Arturo Salvador labor union official

Kelsey
Rankin, Graham M. educator, consultant

Kelseyville
Sandmeyer, E. E. toxicologist, consultant

Kensington
Appelman, Evan Hugh retired chemist
Connick, Robert Elwell retired chemistry educator
Littlejohn, David writer
Loran, Erle artist
Oppenheim, Antoni Kazimierz mechanical engineer
Stent, Gunther Siegmund molecular biologist, educator

Kentfield
Blum, Joan Kurley fundraising executive
Bruyn, Henry Bicker physician
Halprin, Anna Schuman (Mrs. Lawrence Halprin) dancer

Kenwood
Podboy, John Watts clinical, forensic psychologist
Richardson, Mary Weld education administrator, development consultant

King City
Bolles, Donald Scott lawyer

Kingsburg
Olson, Maxine Louise artist, lecturer

La Canada
Baines, Kevin Hays planetary scientist, astronomer
Paniccia, Patricia Lynn journalist, writer, lawyer, educator
Tookey, Robert Clarence consulting actuary

La Canada Flintridge
Costello, Francis William lawyer
Price, Humphrey Wallace aerospace engineer
Racklin, Barbara Cohen fundraising consultant
Wallace, James Wendell lawyer

La Crescenta
Fisk, Irwin Wesley financial investigator
Klint, Ronald Vernon math educator, financial consultant
Peterson, John Edward minister
Phillips, Mary Linda actress
Sanders, David Clyde management and marketing consultant

La Habra
Ahn, Peter Pyung-choo dean
Chase, Cochrane advertising agency executive
Kent, Jeffrey Donald lawyer
Lundberg, Lois Ann political consultant, property manager executive
Oliver, Joyce Anne journalist, editorial consultant, columnist
Schoppa, Elroy accountant, financial planner
Woyski, Margaret Skillman retired geology educator

La Habra Heights
Agajanian, Gilda pianist

La Honda
Henderson, D. Austin computer scientist
Melvin, Jay Wayne computer programmer

La Jolla
Alksne, John F. *dean*
Alvariño De Leira, Angeles (Angeles Alvariño) *biologist, oceanographer*
†Ande, Jan Lee *educator, poet*
Andre, Michael Paul *physicist, educator*
Anthony, Harry Antoniades *city planner, architect, educator*
Antin, David *poet, critic*
†Armstrong, Elizabeth Neilson *curator*
Arnold, James Richard *chemist, educator*
Asmus, John Fredrich *physicist*
Attiyeh, Richard Eugene *economics educator*
Backus, George Edward *theoretical geophysicist*
Baesel, Stuart Oliver *architect*
Bardwick, Judith Marcia *management consultant*
Barrett-Connor, Elizabeth Louise *epidemiologist, educator*
Bastien, Jane Smisor *music educator*
Bavasi, Peter Joseph *angling service executive*
Beebe, Mary Livingstone *curator*
Benson, Andrew Alm *biochemistry educator*
Bergan, John Jerome *vascular surgeon*
Berger, Wolfgang H. *oceanographer, marine geologist*
Bernstein, Michael Alan *history educator, department chairman*
Beutler, Ernest *physician, research scientist*
Block, Melvin August *surgeon, educator*
Bloom, Floyd Elliott *physician, research scientist*
Boger, Dale L. *chemistry educator*
Brooks, Charles Lee, III *computational biophysicist, educator*
Brown, Stuart I. *ophthalmologist, educator*
Buckingham, Michael John *oceanography educator*
Burbidge, E. Margaret *astronomer, educator*
Burbidge, Geoffrey *astrophysicist, educator*
Cain, William Stanley *psychologist, educator*
Carmichael, David Burton *physician*
Case, Kenneth Myron *physics educator*
Castleman, Breaux Ballard *health management company executive*
Cavenee, Webster K. *director*
Chang, William Shen Chie *electrical engineering educator*
Cheverton, William Kearns *science corporation executive, consultant*
Chien, Shu *physiology and bioengineering educator*
Chrispeels, Maarten Jan *biology educator*
Churg, Jacob *pathologist*
Coburn, Marjorie Foster *psychologist, educator*
Coler, Myron A(braham) *chemical engineer, educator*
Conn, Robert William *engineering science educator*
Continetti, Robert E. *chemistry educator*
Copley, David C. *newspaper publishing company executive*
Copley, Helen Kinney *newspaper publisher*
Counts, Stanley Thomas *aerospace consultant, retired naval officer, retired electronics company executive*
Covington, Stephanie Stewart *psychotherapist, writer, educator*
Cox, Charles Shipley *oceanography researcher, educator*
†Craig, Jenny *weight management executive*
Cunningham, Bruce Arthur *biochemist*
Dalessio, Donald John *physician, neurologist, educator*
Davies, Hugh Marlais *museum director*
Davis, Russ Erik *oceanographer, educator*
Diamant, Joel Charles *internist*
Dixon, Frank James *medical scientist, educator*
Doolittle, Russell Francis *biochemist, educator*
Dorsey, Dolores Florence *corporate treasurer, business executive*
Drake, Hudson Billings *aerospace and electronics company executive*
Dreilinger, Charles Lewis (Chips Dreilinger) *dean*
Driscoll, Charles Frederick *physics educator*
†Dynes, Robert C. *academic administrator*
Edelman, Gerald Maurice *biochemist, neuroscientist, educator*
Edgington, Thomas S. *pathologist, educator, molecular biologist*
Edwards, Charles Cornell *physician, research administrator*
Erie, Steven Philip *political science educator*
Farson, Richard Evans *psychologist*
Fisher, Robert Lloyd *retired marine geologist and oceanographer*
Fishman, William Harold *cancer research foundation executive, biochemist*
Foley, L(ewis) Michael *real estate executive*
Freedman, David Noel *religion educator*
†Freedman, Michael Hartley *mathematician, educator*
Friedmann, Theodore *physician*
Frieman, Edward Allan *academic administrator, educator*
Fung, Yuan-Cheng Bertram *bioengineering educator, author*
Garland, Cedric Frank *epidemiologist, educator*
Geckler, Richard Delph *metal products company executive*
Geiduschek, E(rnest) Peter *biophysics and molecular biology educator*
Gilbert, James Freeman *geophysics educator*
Gill, Gordon N. *medical educator*
Gittes, Ruben Foster *urological surgeon*
Glass, Christopher Kevin *physician*
Goel, Ajay *molecular biophysicist, researcher*
Goguen, Joseph Amadee *computer science educator*
Guillemin, Roger C. L. *physiologist*
Halkin, Hubert *mathematics educator, research mathematician*
Hall, Harold Robert *retired computer engineer*
Hallin, Daniel Clark *communications educator*
Hamburger, Robert N. *pediatrics educator, consultant*
Han, Jiahuai *medical researcher*
Harkins, Edwin L. *music educator, performer*
Harris, Philip Robert *management and space psychologist*
Harris, T. George *magazine editor*
Havis, Allan Stuart *playwright, theatre educator*
Haxo, Francis Theodore *marine biologist*
Hazzard, Mary Elizabeth *nurse, educator*
Helinski, Donald Raymond *biologist, educator*
Helstrom, Carl Wilhelm *electrical engineering educator*
Hoston, Germaine Annette *political science educator*
†Howe, Fanny Quincy *poet*
Inverarity, Robert Bruce *artist*
Itano, Harvey Akio *biochemistry educator*
Jeub, Michael Leonard *financial executive*
Johnson, Allen Dress *cardiologist*
Judd, Lewis Lund *psychiatrist, educator*
Kadonaga, James Takuro *biochemist*
Katzman, Robert *medical educator, neurologist*
Keeney, Edmund Ludlow *physician*
Kent, Paula *public relations, marketing and management consultant, lecturer*
Kirchheimer, Arthur E(dward) *lawyer, business executive*
Kitada, Shinichi *biochemist*
Klinman, Norman Ralph *immunologist, medical educator*
Knauss, John Atkinson *former federal agency administrator, oceanographer, educator, former university dean*
Knowlton, Nancy *biologist*
Knox, Elizabeth Louise *community volunteer, travel consultant*
Knox, Robert Arthur *oceanographer, academic administrator*
Kolodner, Richard David *biochemist, educator*
Lal, Devendra *nuclear geophysics educator*
Lane, Sylvia *economist, educator*
Langacker, Ronald Wayne *linguistics educator*
Lauer, James Lothar *physicist, educator*
Lee, Jerry Carlton *university administrator*
Lerner, Richard Alan *chemistry educator, scientist*
Levenstein, Roslyn M. *advertising consultant, writer*
†Levinsky, Frieda Libby *language educator*
Levy, Ralph *engineering executive, consultant*
Lewin, Ralph Arnold *biologist*
Lobert, Jürgen Michael *research chemist*
Longuet-Higgins, Michael Selwyn *mathematician, physicist*
Low, Mary Louise (Molly Low) *documentary photographer*
MacDougall, John Douglas *earth science educator*
Malhotra, Vivek *medical educator*
Mandler, George *psychologist*
Mandler, Jean Matter *psychologist, educator*
Martin, James John, Jr. *retired consulting research firm executive, systems analyst*
Masys, Daniel Richard *medical school director*
Mathews, Kenneth Pine *physician, educator*
McCammon, James Andrew *chemistry educator*
McDonald, Marianne *classicist*
McIlwain, Carl Edwin *physicist*
Merrim, Louise Meyerowitz *artist, actress*
Miller, Stanley Lloyd *chemistry and biochemistry educator*
Miller, Stephen Herschel *surgery educator*
Milstein, Laurence Bennett *electrical engineering educator, researcher*
Mirsky, Phyllis Simon *librarian*
Mitry, Darryl Joseph *educator, writer, strategic advisor*
Miyoshi, Masao *English literature educator, writer*
Morse, Jack Hatton *management consultant*
Mullin, Michael Mahlon *Biology and oceanography educator*
Mullis, Kary Banks *biochemist*
Nakamura, Robert Motoharu *pathologist*
Nelson, Craig Alan *management consultant*
Newmark, Leonard Daniel *linguistics educator*
†Nicolaides, Becky Marianna *history educator*
Nicolaou, K. C. *chemistry educator*
Nierenberg, William Aaron *oceanography educator*
Nyhan, William Leo *pediatrician, educator*
Ogdon, Wilbur *composer, music educator*
Ohkawa, Tihiro *physicist*
Olafson, Frederick Arlan *philosophy educator*
Oldstone, Michael Beaureguard Alan *immunologist*
O'Neil, Thomas Michael *physicist, educator*
Onuchic, José Nelson *biophysics educator, electrical engineer*
Oreskes, Naomi *science historian*
Patton, Stuart *biochemist, educator*
Peebles, Carol Lynn *immunology researcher*
Penner, Stanford Solomon *engineering educator*
Peterson, Laurence E. *physics educator*
Pollard, Thomas Dean *cell biologist, educator*
Pratt, George Janes, Jr. *psychologist, author*
Purdy, Kevin M. *estate planner*
Rearden, Carole Ann *clinical pathologist, educator*
Rebek, Julius, Jr. *chemistry educator, consultant*
Reed, James Anthony *hotel industry executive, consultant*
Resnik, Robert *medical educator*
Reynolds, Roger Lee *composer*
Richard, Rae Linda *nurse practitioner, vascular access specialist*
Ride, Sally Kristen *physics educator, scientist, former astronaut*
Rights, Clyde Siewers *obstetrician and gynecologist*
Ripley, Stuart McKinnon *real estate consultant*
Rosen, Judah Ben *computer scientist*
Rosenblatt, Murray *mathematics educator*
Rosenbluth, Marshall Nicholas *physicist, educator*
Rosenfeld, Michael G. *medical educator*
Rudee, Mervyn Lea *engineering educator, researcher*
Rudolph, Walter Paul *engineering research company executive*
Ruoslahti, Erkki *medical research administrator*
Saier, Milton H., Jr. *biology educator*
Schiller, Herbert Irving *social scientist, author*
Schimmel, Paul Reinhard *biochemist, biophysicist, educator*
Schmid-Schoenbein, Geert Wilfried *biomedical engineer, educator*
Schudson, Michael Steven *communications educator*
Sclater, John George *geophysics educator*
Seegmiller, Jarvis Edwin *biochemist, educator*
Shakespeare, Frank *ambassador*
Sham, Lu Jeu *physics educator*
Sharpless, K. Barry *chemist, educator*
Shor, George G., Jr. *geophysicist, oceanographic administrator, engineer*
Shuler, Kurt Egon *chemist, educator*
Siegan, Bernard Herbert *lawyer, educator*
Silva, Ernest R. *visual arts educator, artist*
Silverstone, Leon Martin *cariologist, neuroscientist, educator, researcher*
Simnad, Massoud T. *engineering educator*
Somerville, Richard Chapin James *atmospheric scientist, educator*
Spiegelberg, Hans Leonhard *medical educator*
Spiess, Fred Noel *oceanographer, educator*
Spiro, Melford Elliot *anthropology educator*
Squire, Larry Ryan *neuroscientist, psychologist, educator*
Starr, Ross Marc *economist, educator*
Steinberg, Daniel *preventive medicine physician, educator*
Stevens, Paul Irving *manufacturing company executive*
Stone, Donald D. *investment and sales executive*
Stone, William Ross *research and development company executive, physicist*
Sung, Kuo-Li Paul *bioengineering educator*
Sung, Lanping Amy *biomedical engineer*
Tan, Eng Meng *immunologist, biomedical scientist*
Taylor, Susan Serota *biochemistry researcher*
Teirstein, Paul Shepherd *physician, health facility administrator*
Terras, Audrey Anne *mathematics educator*
Terry, Robert Davis *neuropathologist, educator*
Thal, Leon Joel *neuroscientist*
Tietz, Norbert Wolfgang *clinical chemistry educator, administrator*
Timmer, Charles Peter *agricultural and development economist*
Todd, Harry Williams *aircraft propulsion system company executive*
Tsien, Roger Yonchien *chemist, cell biologist*
Van Lint, Victor Anton Jacobus *physicist*
Verma, Inder M. *biochemist*
Waddy, Lawrence Heber *religious writer*
Walker, Richard Hugh *orthopaedic surgeon*
Wall, Frederick Theodore *retired chemistry educator*
Watson, Kenneth Marshall *physics educator*
Weigle, William Oliver *immunologist, educator*
Wertheim, Robert Halley *national security consultant*
Wesling, Donald Truman *English literature educator*
West, John Burnard *physiologist, physicuan, educator*
Whitaker, Eileen Monaghan (Eileen Monaghan) *artist*
White, Halbert Lynn, Jr. *economist, educator, consultant*
Wilkie, Donald Walter *biologist, aquarium museum director*
Wilkins, Floyd, Jr. *retired lawyer, consultant*
Williams, Forman Arthur *engineering science educator, combustion theorist*
Wolf, Jack Keil *electrical engineer, educator*
Wright, Andrew *English literature educator*
Wulbert, Daniel Eliot *mathematician, educator*
Wyle, Ewart Herbert *clergyman*
Yen, Samuel S(how)-C(hih) *obstetrics and gynecology educator, reproductive endocrinologist*
York, Herbert Frank *physics educator, government official*
Zyroff, Ellen Slotoroff *information scientist, classicist, educator*

La Mesa
Allen, David Charles *computer science educator*
Bailey, Brenda Marie *accountant*
Black, Eileen Mary *elementary school educator*
Bourke, Lyle James *electronics company executive, small business owner*
Freeland, Robert Frederick *retired librarian*
Hansen, Grant Lewis *retired aerospace and information systems executive*
Lasater, Marie *intensive care nurse*
Ligon, Patti-Lou E. *real estate investor, educator*
Reiff, Theodore Curtis *construction executive*
Schlador, Paul Raymond, Jr. *insurance agent*
Schmidt, James Craig *retired bank executive, bankruptcy examiner*
Tarson, Herbert Harvey *university administrator emeritus*
Wohl, Armand Jeffrey *cardiologist*

La Mirada
Feldman, Roger Lawrence *artist, educator*
Pike, Patricia Louise *psychology educator*

La Palma
Akubuilo, Francis Ekenechukwu *secondary school educator*

La Puente
Goldberg, David Bryan *biomedical researcher*
Hitchcock, Fritz *automotive company executive*
Ogden, Jean Lucille *sales executive*
Sheridan, Christopher Frederick *human resources executive*

La Quinta
Atkins, Honey Jean *retired business executive*
Barr, Roger Terry *sculptor*
†Calvin, James Willard *thoracic and vascular surgeon*
Hartley, Celia Love *nursing educator, nursing administrator*
Peden, Lynn Ellen *marketing executive*

La Verne
Chu, Esther Briney *retired history educator*
Coray, Jeffrey Warren *assistant principal, instructor*
Cozad, Lyman Howard *city manager*
Fleck, Raymond Anthony, Jr. *retired university administrator*
Hwang, Cordelia Jong *chemist*
McDonough-Treichler, Judith Dianne *medical educator, consultant*
Morgan, Stephen Charles *academic administrator*
Neher, Mary Timmons *nursing administrator, educator*
Neher, Robert Trostle *biology educator*
†Somvichian, Kamol *political science educator*

Lafayette
Alexander, Kenneth Lewis *editorial cartoonist*
Dethero, J. Hambright *banker*
Hemphill, Norma Jo *special event planning and tour company executive*
James, Muriel Marshall *author, psychotherapist*
Kahn, Robert Irving *management consultant*
Koetser, David *export company executive*
Krueger, Robert Edward *manufacturing executive, mechanical engineer*
Lewis, Sheldon Noah *technology consultant*
Monheit, Molly Jane *artist, writer*
Peters, Ray John *surveyor*
Reynolds, Harry Lincoln *physicist*
Shurtleff, Akiko Aoyagi *artist, consultant*
Stewart, Leslie Mueller *editor, writer*
†Thomas, Ramsay Berry *secondary educator*

Laguna Beach
Batdorf, Samuel B(urbridge) *physicist*
Bent, Alan Edward *political science educator, administrator*
Bezar, Gilbert Edward *retired aerospace company executive, volunteer*
Blacketer, James Richard *artist*
Bushman, Edwin Francis Arthur *engineer, plastics consultant, rancher*
Calderwood, James Lee *former English literature educator, writer*
Camp, Joseph Shelton, Jr. *film producer, director, writer*
DiGenova, Silvano Antonio *rare coin and fine art dealer*
Ghiselin, Brewster *author, English language educator emeritus*
Hanauer, Joe Franklin *real estate executive*
Larson, Harry Thomas *electronics engineer, executive, consultant*
Linhart, Eddie Gene *aerospace executive*
Mirone-Bartz, Dawn *secondary school and community college educator*
Pelton, Virginia Lue *small business owner*
Powers, Runa Skötte *artist*
Ryder, Virginia Pinkus *retired school system administrator*
Segard, Hubert J. *international marketing company executive, consultant*
Simons, Barry Thomas *lawyer*
Taylor, Theodore Langhans *author*

Laguna Hills
Banuelos, Betty Lou *rehabilitation nurse*
Bell, Sharon Kaye *small business owner*
Green, Leon, Jr. *mechanical engineer*
Hammond, R. Philip *chemical engineer*
Henderson, Marsha Roslyn Thaw *clinical social worker*
Hussey, William Bertrand *retired foreign service officer*
Iberall, Arthur Saul *physicist, publisher*
Ierardi, Stephen John *physician*
James, Sidney Lorraine *television executive*
Lederer, Jerome *aerospace safety consultant, engineer*
McClure, Hal H. *travel film producer*
Miller, Eldon Earl *corporate business publications consultant, retired manufacturing company executive*
Mirman, Irving R. *scientific adviser*
Noble, Marion Ellen *retired home economist*
†Ortiz, Alfred T. *financial executive*
Pelton, Harold Marcel *mortgage broker*
Reinglass, Michelle Annette *lawyer*
Rodriguez, Graciela Pilar *psychotherapist*
Rossiter, Bryant William *chemistry consultant*
Walker, Virginia L. *art educator*
Wheatley, Melvin Ernest, Jr. *retired bishop*
Widyolar, Sheila Gayle *dermatologist*

Laguna Niguel
Apt, Charles *artist*
Axon, Donald Carlton *architect*
Coleman, Roger Dixon *bacteriologist*
Greenberg, Lenore *public relations professional*
†King, Richard Maurice, Jr. *consultant*
Malott, John Raymond *writer, consultant*
Meyers, Theda Maria *textile company executive*
Nelson, Alfred John *retired pharmaceutical company executive*
Shifrin, Bruce Carl *electrical engineer*
Smith, Leslie Roper *hospital and healthcare administrator*
Sturdevant, Charles Oliver *physician, neuropsychiatrist*
York, James Orison *real estate executive*

Laguna Woods
Epley, Thelma Mae Childers *retired gifted and talented education educator*
Ross, Mathew *psychiatry educator*
Saudek, Martha Folsom *artist, educator*

Lagunitas
Holman, Arthur Stearns *artist*
Mann, Karen *consultant, educator*

Lake Arrowhead
Barnett, Michael *sports agent, business manager*
Beckman, James Wallace Bim *economist, marketing executive*
Fitzgerald, John Charles, Jr. *investment banker*
Hubbard, Jeffrey Charles *educational administrator*

Lake Forest
Hertweck, Galen Fredric *minister*
Larsen, Robert Ray *healthcare executive, surgeon*
Sheehy, Jerome Joseph *electrical engineer*
Wetenkamp, Herbert Delos, Jr. *publisher*

Lake Hughes
La Mont, Tawana Faye *camera operator, video director*

Lake Isabella
Fraser, Eleanor Ruth *radiologist, administrator*

Lake Sherwood
Steadman, Lydia Duff *elementary school educator, symphony violinist*

Lakeport
Jones, Brenda Gail *school district administrator*

Lakewood
Barton, Billie Jo *artist, educator*
Robbins, Daniel Charles *music educator*

Lancaster
Bohannon, Linda Sue *special education educator*
Cooper, James Ralph *engineering executive*
Hodges, Vernon Wray *mechanical engineer*
Roths, Beverly Owen *organization executive*
Swart, Bonnie Blount *artist*

Landers
Landers, Vernette Trosper *writer, educator, association executive*

Larkspur
Finkelstein, James Arthur *management consultant*
Greenberg, Myron Silver *lawyer*
Kirk, Gary Vincent *investment advisor*
Maier, Peter Klaus *business executive*
Napoles, Veronica Kleeman *graphic designer, consultant*
Ratner, David Louis *retired law educator*
Saxton, Lloyd *psychologist, author*
Selandia, Elizabeth *acupuncturist, Oriental medicine physician*

Lee Vining
McQuilkin, Geoffrey James *enviromental association administrator*

Lemon Grove
Mott, June Marjorie school system administrator

Lemoore
Krend, William John secondary education educator

Lewiston
McColm, George Lester international agricultural consultant, journalist

Linden
Smith, Donald Richard editor, publisher

Lindsay
Sanchez, Ruben Dario minister, family counselor, parochial school educator, writer

Livermore
Alcock, Charles Roger science educator
Alder, Berni Julian physicist
Bennett, Alan Jerome electronics executive, physicist
Bjorkholm, John Ernst physicist
Brieger, Stephen Gustave management consultant
Campbell, John Hyde laser materials researcher, consultant
Carley, James French chemical and plastics engineer
Cassens, Nicholas, Jr. ceramics engineer
Christensen, Richard Monson mechanical engineer, materials engineer
Cook, Robert Crossland research chemist
Edmondo, Douglas Brian marine engineer
Ellsaesser, Hugh Walter retired atmospheric scientist
Futch, Archer Hamner retired physicist
Hill, John Earl mechanical engineer
Hiskes, Dolores G. educator
Hooper, Edwin Bickford physicist
Johnson, Roy Ragnar electrical engineer
Kidder, Ray Edward physicist, consultant
King, Ray John electrical engineer
Kirkwood, Robert Keith applied physicist
Leith, Cecil Eldon, Jr. retired physicist
Love, Sandra Rae information specialist
Max, Claire Ellen physicist
Nuckolls, John Hopkins physicist, researcher
Roshong, Dee Ann Daniels dean, educator
Schalit, Michael research librarian
Schock, Robert Norman geophysicist
Seward, James Pickett internist, educator
Sheem, Sang Keun fiber optics engineering professional
Shotts, Wayne J. nuclear scientist, federal agency administrator
Tarter, Curtis Bruce physicist, science administrator
Williams, David Michael manufacturing executive
Wilson, James Ricker physicist, consultant
Wong, Joe physical chemist

Livingston
Fox, Robert August food company executive

Lodi
Bishop-Graham, Barbara secondary school educator, journalist
†Miller, Barry Lee strategic planner
Nusz, Phyllis Jane retired fundraising consultant, meeting planner
Schulz, Laura Janet writer, retired secretary

Loma Linda
Aloia, Roland Craig scientist, administrator, educator
Behrens, Berel Lyn physician, academic administrator
Bell, Denise Louise newspaper reporter, photographer, librarian
Betancourt, Hector Mainhard psychology scientist, educator
Brandstater, Murray Everett physiatrist
Bull, Brian Stanley pathology educator, medical consultant, business executive
Bullock, Weldon Kimball health facility administrator, pathologist, pathology educator
Chan, Philip J. medical educator
Coggin, Charlotte Joan cardiologist, educator
Feller, Ralph Paul dentist, educator
Green, Lora Murray immunologist, researcher, educator
Hinshaw, David B., Sr. retired hospital administrator
Hinshaw, David B., Jr. radiologist
Joyce, Vicki Marie special education educator
Kirk, Gerald Arthur nuclear radiologist
Klooster, Judson academic administrator, dentistry educator
†Krick, Edwin Harry, Sr. medical educator, preventive medicine physician
Llaurado, Josep G. nuclear medicine physician, scientist
Llerandi Phipps, Carmen Guillermina nutritionist and dietitian
Longo, Lawrence Daniel physiologist, obstetrician-gynecologist
Mace, John Weldon pediatrician
†Moorhead, J. David health facility administrator
Rendell-Baker, Leslie anesthesiologist, educator
Roberts, Walter Herbert Beatty anatomist
Slater, James Munro radiation oncologist
Slattery, Charles Wilbur biochemistry educator
Stilson, Walter Leslie radiologist, educator
Strother, Allen biochemical pharmacologist, researcher
Wilcox, Ronald Bruce biochemistry educator, researcher
Young, Lionel Wesley radiologist

Lomita
Balcom, Orville engineer

Lompoc
Cockrell-Fleming, Shelia Yvette public health nurse

Long Beach
Adler, Jeffrey D. political consultant, public affairs consultant, crisis management expert
Aldrich, David Lawrence public relations executive
Alkon, Ellen Skillen physician
Anatol, Karl W. E. provost
Anderson, Garry Michael diagnostic radiologist
Anderson, Gerald Verne retired aerospace company executive
Armstrong, Joanna education educator
Aston, Steven Wesley production manager
Bauer, Roger Duane chemistry educator, science consultant
Beebe, Sandra E. retired English language educator, artist, writer
Beljan, John Richard university administrator, medical educator
Berke, Irving obstetrician-gynecologist, military officer
Best, Gary Allen special education educator
Blazey, Michael Alan educator
Boccia Rosado, Ann Marie paralegal
Bond, Frances Curtis retired editor
Bontá, Diana M. city manager
Bos, John Arthur retired aircraft manufacturing executive
Boychuk, Dallas university head women's basketball coach
Brault, G(ayle) Lorain healthcare executive
Burroughs, Gary L. city official
Byles, Torrey Koppe communications technolgy specialist
Calhoun, John R. lawyer
Crane, Steven financial company executive
Crivaro, John Pete family practice physician
Cummings, Darold Bernard aircraft engineer
Dawson, Frances Emily poet, nurse
Dillon, Michael Earl engineering executive, mechanical engineer, educator
†Domingo-Forasté, Douglas classics educator
Donald, Eric Paul aeronautical engineer, inventor
Dublin, Stephen Louis secondary school educator, singer, musician
Duke, Phyllis Louise Kellogg Henry school administrator, management consultant
Elftman, Susan Nancy physician assistant, childbirth-lactation educator
Elliott, John Gregory aerospace design engineer
Ellis, Harriette Rothstein editor, writer
Feldman, Stephen academic administrator
Ferreri, Michael Victor optometrist
Fleming, Jane Williams retired educator, author
Friis, Robert Harold epidemiologist, health science educator
Gimmillaro, Brian university head women's volleyball coach
Glenn, Constance White art museum director, educator, consultant
Gunderson, Bernice Blower retired nurse, genealogy researcher
Hall, Phyllis Charlene therapist, counselor
Hancock, John Walker, III banker
Hext, Kathleen Florence internal audit college administrator
Higginson, John retired military officer
Hirshtal, Edith concert pianist, educator, chamber musician
Hobgood, E(arl) Wade college dean
Jager, Merle LeRoy aerospace engineer
Jeffery, James Nels protective services official
Johnson, Philip Leslie lawyer
Johnson, William Harry international management consultant
Keller, J(ames) Wesley credit union executive
Kelly, Chuck H. singer, writer, trombonist
†Kelly, Wayne Fred journalism educator
Kumar, Rajendra electrical engineering educator
Kurnick, Nathaniel Bertrand oncologist-hematologist, educator, researcher
Kwaan, Jack Hau Ming retired physician
Lathrop, Irvin Tunis retired academic dean, educator
Lauda, Donald Paul university dean
Lodwick, Michael Wayne lawyer
Loganbill, G. Bruce logopedic pathologist
Looney, Gerald Lee medical educator, administrator
Lowentrout, Peter Murray religious studies educator
Luman, Robert M. protective services official
Macer, George Armen, Jr. orthopedic hand surgeon
Maxson, Robert C. university president
McDonough, Patrick Dennis academic administrator
McGann, John Milton real estate executive
McGaughey, Charles Gilbert retired research biochemist
McGuire, James Charles aircraft company executive
Moran, Edgar M. physician, educator
Morrow, Sharon R. financial advisor
Moss, Elizabeth Lucille (Betty Moss) transportation company executive
Muchmore, Don Moncrief museum, foundation, educational, financial fund raising and public opinion consulting firm administrator, banker
Myers, John Wescott aviation executive
Nelson, Harold Bernhard museum director
Nguyen, Huong Tran English language professional, federal agency official
Nielsen, Pamela Jeanne artist, writer
†Nuiry, Octavio Emilio advertising executive
O'Neill, Beverly Lewis mayor, former college president
Palacios, Alana Sue computer programmer
Patino, Douglas Xavier foundation, government agency, and university administrator
Perkowitz, Simon architect
Pineda, Anselmo neurosurgery educator
Porter, Priscilla elementary education educator
Reed, Charles Bass chief academic administrator
Robinson, Michael R. aeronautical engineer
Rosenberg, Jill realtor, civic leader
Russell, Thomas Arthur lawyer
Ruszkiewicz, Carolyn Mae newspaper editor
Ruth, Steven J. architectural firm executive
Sato, Eunice Noda former mayor, consultant
Schick, Susan F. municipal official, developer
Schinnerer, Alan John entrepreneur
Schneider, Duane Bernard English literature educator, publisher
Scott, Bruce Laurence physicist, educator
Shoji, June Midori import and export trading executive
Skelly, John Joshua retired clergyman, fundraiser
Small, Richard David research scientist
†Snider, Clifton Mark English educator, writer, poet
Snow, James Harry metallurgist, educator, aircraft planning executive
Sosoka, John Richard consulting firm executive, engineer
Stemmer, Edward Alan surgeon, educator
Swatek, Frank Edward microbiology educator
Tabrisky, Phyllis Page physiatrist, educator
Taylor, Reese Hale, Jr. lawyer, former government administrator
Todd, Malcolm Clifford surgeon
Vander Lans, John Anthony city prosecutor
†Van Gorder, Chris medical executive
VavRosky, Mark James career officer, educator
Viola, Bill artist, writer
Walker, Linda Ann financial planner
†Waters, Jim Great Elk storyteller, artist
White, Katherine Elizabeth retired pediatrician
†Wilcox, David Cornell ballet company director
Williams, David Alexander pilot
Wise, George Edward lawyer
Yousef, Fathi Salaama communication studies educator, management consultant

Los Alamitos
Booth, John Nicholls minister, magician, writer, photographer
†Burke, Jan Helene author
Hanson, Larry Keith plastics company executive
Peters, Samuel Anthony lawyer

Los Altos
Abrams, Arthur Jay physician
Barker, William Alfred physics educator
Beer, Clara Louise Johnson retired electronics executive
Bell, Chester Gordon computer engineering company executive
Bell, Richard G. lawyer
Bergrun, Norman Riley aerospace executive
Carr, Jacquelyn B. psychologist, educator
Carsten, Jack Craig venture capitalist
Castellino, Ronald Augustus Dietrich radiologist
Cranston, Alan former senator
Farber, Geraldine Ossman civic worker
Garman, Jon Kent anesthesiologist
Gonzales, Richard Robert academic administrator
Hall, Charles Frederick space scientist, government administrator
Halverson, George Clarence business administration educator
Hammond, Donald Leroy computer company executive
Heymann, Stephen marketing management consultant
Jones, Robert Thomas aerospace scientist
Kazan, Benjamin research engineer
Keller, James Warren college administrator
Martin, Leonardo San Juan urologist, surgeon
Miller, Ronald Grant author, critic
Moll, John Lewis electronics engineer, retired
Nivison, David Shepherd Chinese and philosophy educator
Orman, Nanette Hector psychiatrist
Orr, Susan Packard business owner
Peterson, Victor Lowell aerospace engineer, management consultant
Sanchez, Marla Rena controller
Sharpe, Roland Leonard engineering company executive, earthquake and structural engineering consultant
Spiller, Gene Alan nutritionist, clinical human nutrition research consultant, research center administrator, writer, editor
Sun, Bill Kawo-Hwa energy consulting company executive
Thurber, Emily Forrest political consultant
Weir, Robert H. lawyer
Wilbur, Colburn Sloan foundation administrator, chief executive officer
Zebroski, Edwin Leopold consulting engineer

Los Altos Hills
Alexander, Katharine Violet lawyer
Cameron, Eleanor Cranston Fowle author
Esber, Edward Michael, Jr. software company executive
Fondahl, John Walker civil engineering educator
Johnson, Penelope Anne university dean
van Tamelen, Eugene Earle chemist, educator

Los Angeles
†Aaron, Benjamin law educator, arbitrator
Aaron, Paul film and television producer and director
Abdou, Mohamed A. mechanical, aerospace, and nuclear engineering educator
Abdul-Jabbar, Kareem (Lewis Ferdinand Alcindor) retired professional basketball player, sports commentator
Abernethy, Robert John real estate developer
Abraham, F(ahrid) Murray actor, educator
Abrams, Norman law educator, university administrator
Adamek, Charles Andrew lawyer
Adams, Thomas Merritt lawyer
Adamson, Arthur Wilson chemistry educator
Adell, Hirsch lawyer
Adelman, Andrew A. city manager
Adler, Erwin Ellery lawyer
Adler, Sara arbitrator, mediator
Afifi, Abdelmonem A. biostatistics educator, academic dean
†Ahart, Alan M. bankruptcy judge
Alarcon, Arthur Lawrence federal judge
Alexander, Jeffrey Charles sociology educator
Alkana, Ronald Lee neuropsychopharmacologist, psychobiologist
Alkon, Paul Kent English language educator
Allen, Michael John Bridgman English educator
Allen, William Richard retired economist
Aller, Lawrence Hugh astronomy educator, researcher
Allerton, Samuel Ellsworth biochemist
Allison, Laird Burl business educator
Allums, Henriene elementary education educator
Alpers, Edward Alter history educator
Álvarez, Rodolfo sociology educator, consultant
Alwan, Abeer electrical engineering educator
Amdur, Judith Devorah artist, cook
Amey, Rae television and video developer, producer
†Amiel, Jon film director
Amos, John actor, producer, director
Anawalt, Patricia Rieff anthropologist
Andersen, Ronald Max health services educator, researcher
Anderson, Austin Gilman economics research company consultant
Anderson, Daryl actor
Anderson, Kathryn D. surgeon
Anderson, Kenneth Jeffery family financial planner, accountant, lawyer
Anderson, Loni Kaye actress
†Anderson, Paul Thomas (Paul Thomas, IV) film director
Anderson, Richard Norman actor, film producer
Anderson, Robert Marshall retired bishop
Anderson, Roy A. aerospace company executive
Anderson, W. French biochemist, physician
Angeloff, Dann Valentino investment banking executive
Ansley, Julia Ette educator, poet, writer, consultant
Antin, Michael lawyer
Antonovich, Michael D. city manager
Apfel, Gary lawyer
Apple, Jacqueline B (Jacqueline B. Apple) artist, writer, educator
Appleby, Joyce Oldham historian
April, Rand Scott lawyer
Apt, Leonard physician
†Araki, Gregg film director, cinematographer
Arbib, Michael Anthony neuroscientist, educator, cybernetician
Arbit, Beryl Ellen legal assistant
Archerd, Army (Armand Archerd) columnist, television commentator
Archie, Carol Louise obstetrician and gynecologist, educator
†Arkin, Adam actor
Armistead, Thomas Boyd, III television and film producer
Armstrong, Lloyd, Jr. university official, physics educator
Armstrong, Orville judge
Arnold, Dennis B. lawyer
Arnold, Jeanne Eloise anthropologist, archaeologist, educator
Arnold, Skip performance artist
Arquette, Rosanna actress
Ash, Roy Lawrence business executive
Ashforth, Alden musician, educator
Ashley, Sharon Anita pediatric anesthesiologist
Askanas-Engel, Valerie neurologist, educator, researcher
Atluri, Satya N(adham) aerospace engineering educator
Avary, Roger Roberts film director, writer
Badie, Ronald Peter banker
Bahr, Ehrhard Germanic languages and literature educator
Bailey, Julia Nancy geneticist
Bain, Conrad Stafford actor
Baird, Lourdes G. federal judge
Bakeman, Carol Ann travel and administrative services manager, singer
Baker, Guy coach
Baker, Robert Frank molecular biologist, educator
†Ballard, Carroll film director, cinematographer
Ballard, Glen composer
Bangs, Cate (Cathryn Margaret Bangs) film production designer, interior designer
Bangs, John Wesley, III law enforcement administrator
Banks, Melissa Richardson fund raising professional
Barker, Robert William television personality
Barnes, Priscilla actress
Baron, Melvin Farrell pharmacy educator
Barrett, Cynthia Townsend neonatologist
Barrett, Jane Hayes lawyer
Barretta-Keyser, Jolie professional athletics coach, author, film and TV casting director
†Barron, Stephanie museum curator
Barry, Gene actor
Barrymore, Drew actress
Barth, Uta artist, educator
Bartoletti, Barbara Marie corporate secretary
Barton, Alan Joel lawyer
Barza, Harold A. lawyer
Basch, Darlene Chakin clinical social worker
Basil, Douglas Constantine author, educator
Bates, Marcia Jeanne information scientist educator
Baum, Michael Lin lawyer
Bauman, John Andrew law educator
Baumann, Richard Gordon lawyer
Bauml, Franz Heinrich German language educator
Bayless, Raymond Gordon writer, artist, parapsychologist
Baylor, Elgin Gay professional basketball team executive
Beal, Graham William John museum director
Beam, William Washington, III data coordinator
Beard, John Jackson, III journalist
Beard, Ronald Stratton lawyer
Beart, Robert W., Jr. surgeon, educator
Beatty, Ned actor
Beck, John Christian physician, educator
Becker, Donald Paul surgeon, neurosurgeon
†Becker, Harold film director, producer
Bekey, George Albert computer scientist, educator, engineer
Bell, Lee Phillip television personality, television producer
Belleville, Philip Frederick lawyer
Belnap, David F. journalist
Beltramo, Michael Norman management consultant
†Belzer, Richard comedian, TV show host, actor
†Bender, Charles William lawyer
Bender, Dean public relations executive
Bendix, Helen Irene lawyer
Bennett, Charles Franklin, Jr. biogeographer, educator
Bennett, Fred Gilbert lawyer
Bennis, Warren Gameliel business administration educator, author, consultant
Benson, Sidney William chemistry researcher
Benty, Cameron Todd magazine editor
Berenbaum, Michael Gary foundation adminstrator, theology educator
Bergman, Nancy Palm real estate investment company executive
Berman, Geoffrey Louis turnaround management company executive
Berman, Myles Lee lawyer
Berman, Saul Jay strategic consultant
Bernacchi, Richard Lloyd lawyer
Bernhard, Herbert Ashley lawyer
Bernson, Hal city councilman
Bernstein, Sol cardiologist, educator
Bernstein, William film company executive
Berry, Richard Douglas architectural educator, urban planner and designer
Berry, Stephen Joseph reporter
Berst, Charles Ashton English educator
Bessman, Samuel Paul pediatrician, biochemist
Best, Roger Norman inventor, real estate manager, consultant
Bezemer, Cal Gene composer
Bhaumik, Mani Lal physicist
Bialosky, Marshall Howard composer
Bice, Scott Haas lawyer, educator
Biederman, Donald Ellis lawyer
Bierstedt, Peter Richard lawyer, entertainment industry consultant
Biles, John Alexander pharmacology educator, chemistry educator
Billig, Franklin Anthony chemist
†Bird, Antonia film director
Bird, Peter geology educator
Birren, James Emmett university research center executive
Bishop, Sidney Willard lawyer
Black, Donna Ruth lawyer
Black, Lisa Hartman (Lisa Hartman Black) actress, singer
Blackman, Lee L. lawyer

Blahd, William Henry *physician*
Blakely, Edward James *economics educator*
Blencowe, Paul Sherwood *lawyer*
Blitz-Weisz, Sally *speech pathologist*
Bloch, Paul *public relations executive*
Block, Amanda Roth *artist*
†Block, Robert N. *federal judge*
Blodgett, Julian Robert *small business owner*
Bloomberg, Stu *broadcast executive*
Bluestone, David Allan *pediatrician*
Blumberg, Grace Ganz *law educator, lawyer*
Bobrow, Michael Lawrence *architect*
Bodey, Bela *immunomorphologist*
Bodkin, Henry Grattan, Jr. *lawyer*
Bodnar, Jackie Sue *molecular biologist, geneticist*
Boehm, Barry William *computer science educator*
Bogaard, William Joseph *lawyer*
Bogart, Paul *film director*
Bogen, Andrew E. *lawyer*
Bohle, Sue *public relations executive*
Boime, Albert Isaac *art history educator*
Bok, Dean *cell biologist, educator*
Bomes, Stephen D. *lawyer*
Bondareff, William *psychiatry educator*
Bonner, Robert Cleve *lawyer*
Borenstein, Daniel Bernard *physician, educator*
Borenstein, Mark A. *lawyer*
Borko, Harold *information scientist, psychologist, educator*
Borneman, John Paul Jay *pharmaceutical executive*
Borsch, Frederick Houk *bishop*
Borsting, Jack Raymond *business administration educator*
Bortman, David *lawyer*
Bosl, Phillip L. *lawyer*
Bosley, Tom *actor*
Boswell, James Douglas *medical research executive*
Bothwell, Dorr *artist*
Bottjer, David John *earth sciences educator*
Bowlin, Michael Ray *oil company executive*
Bowman, C. Michael *physician*
Boyarsky, Benjamin William *journalist*
Boyd, Malcolm *minister, religious author*
†Boyer, Paul D. *biochemist, educator*
Boyett, Joan Reynolds *arts administrator*
Boyle, Barbara Dorman *motion picture company executive*
†Boyle, Danny *film director*
Boynton, Donald Arthur *title insurance company executive*
Bradley, Lawrence D., Jr. *lawyer*
Bradshaw, Carl John *investor, lawyer, consultant*
Bradshaw, Murray Charles *musicologist*
Branca, John Gregory *lawyer, consultant*
Brandler, Jonathan M. *lawyer*
Braun, David A(dlai) *lawyer*
Braunstein, Glenn David *physician, educator*
Brecht, Albert Odell *library and information technology administrator*
Breidenbach, Francis Anthony *lawyer*
Breslow, Lester *physician, educator*
Bressan, Paul Louis *lawyer*
†Brest, Martin *film director*
Breuer, Melvin Allen *electrical engineering educator*
Breuer, Stephen Ernest *temple administrator*
Brickwood, Susan Callaghan *lawyer*
Bringardner, John Michael *lawyer, clergyman*
Brittenham, Skip *lawyer*
Broad, Eli *financial services executive*
Brolin, James (James Brunderlin) *actor*
Brotman, David Joel *architectural firm executive*
Broussard, Thomas Rollins *lawyer*
Brown, Elliott Rowe *physicist*
Brown, James Kevin *professional baseball player*
†Brown, Jason Robert *composer, arranger*
Brown, Kathleen *state treasurer, lawyer*
Brown, Sally Ann *research scientist*
Brownridge, J. Paul *city manager*
Brubaker, William Rogers *sociology educator*
†Bruce, William A. *airport executive*
Bruneau, Marie-Florine *French educator*
Buchman, Mark Edward *banker*
Bucy, Richard Snowden *aerospace engineering and mathematics educator, consultant*
Bufford, Samuel Lawrence *federal judge*
Burch, Robert Dale *lawyer*
Burgess, J. Wesley *neuropsychiatrist*
Burke, Robert Bertram *lawyer, political consultant, lobbyist*
Burman, Sheila Flexer Zola *special education educator*
Burns, Marvin Gerald *lawyer*
Burns, Robert Ignatius *historian, educator, clergyman*
Burrows, James *television and motion picture director, producer*
Burton, Tim *film director*
Butler, Brett *comedian, actress*
Butterworth, Robert Roman *psychologist, researcher, media therapist*
Byers, Nina *physics educator*
Byrd, Christine Waterman Swent *lawyer*
Byrd, Marc Robert *florist*
Byrne, Gabriel *actor*
Byrne, Gerard Anthony *publishing company executive, marketing consultant*
Byrne, Jerome Camillus *lawyer*
Byrne, William Matthew, Jr. *federal judge*
Caffey, H. David *music educator*
†Callaghan, Sheila *playwright, graphic designer*
Calman, Craig David *writer, actor, director*
Campbell, Kenneth Eugene, Jr. *vertebrate paleontologist*
†Campbell, Martin *film director, producer, writer*
Campion, Robert Thomas *manufacturing company executive*
Campo, Todd Russell *principal, law enforcement educator*
†Campos, Bruno *actor*
Camron, Roxanne *editor*
Caprioli, Joseph *ophthalmologist*
Capron, Alexander Morgan *lawyer, educator*
†Caram, Eve La Salle *English educator, writer*
Carey, Chase *broadcast executive*
Cariou, Len Joseph *actor, director*
Carlin, George Denis *comedian*
Carlip, Hillary *author, screenwriter*
Carlson, Robert Edwin *lawyer*
Carmen, Julie *actress*
Carnesale, Albert *university chancellor*
Caroompas, Carole Jean *artist, educator*
Carothers, A. J. *scriptwriter*
Carr, James Patrick *lawyer*
Carr, Willard Zeller, Jr. *lawyer*
Carrey, Neil *lawyer, educator*
Carter, Emily Ann *physical chemist, researcher, educator*
Carter, Janice Joene *telecommunications executive*
Cartwright, Brian Grant *lawyer*
†Cassavetes, Nick *film director, actor*
Castro, Leonard Edward *lawyer*
Cates, Gilbert *film, theater, television producer and director*
Cathcart, David Arthur *lawyer*
Cecchetti, Giovanni *poet, educator, literary critic*
Cerrell, Joseph R. *political scientist, consultant*
Chacko, George Kuttickal *systems science educator, consultant*
Chaffin, Cean *producer*
Champagne, Duane Willard *sociology educator*
Champlin, Charles Davenport *television host, book critic, writer*
Chan, David Ronald *tax specialist, lawyer*
Chan, Jackie *actor, director, writer*
Chandor, Stebbins Bryant *pathologist*
Chang, Henry Chung-Lien *library administrator*
Chapman, Orville Lamar *chemist, educator*
†Chapman, Rosalyn M. *federal judge*
Charles, Ray (Ray Charles Robinson) *musician, singer, composer*
Charwat, Andrew Franciszek *engineering educator*
Chassman, Leonard Fredric *labor union administrator*
Chavez, Victor Edwin *judge*
†Chazen, Stephen I. *oil company executive*
†Chedid, John G. *bishop*
Chen, Peter Wei-Teh *mental health services administrator*
Cheng, Hsien Kei *aeronautics educator*
Cheng, Tsen-Chung *electrical engineering educator*
Cherkin, Adina *interpreter, translator*
Chernesky, John Joseph, Jr. *retired naval officer, healthcare executive*
Cherry, James Donald *physician*
Chiate, Kenneth Reed *lawyer*
Chick, Laura *councilwoman*
Chin, Llewellyn Philip *lawyer*
Christol, Carl Q(uimby) *lawyer, political science educator*
Christopher, James Roy *executive director*
Christopher, Warren *lawyer, former government official*
†Chrzanowski, Joseph *language educator*
Chu, Morgan *lawyer*
Cicciarelli, James Carl *immunology educator*
Ciccone, Amy Navratil *art librarian*
Cisneros, Henry G. *former federal official, broadcast executive*
Clark, Burton Robert *sociologist, educator*
Clark, Rufus Bradbury *lawyer*
Clark, William Arthur V. *geographer, demographer*
Clarke, Peter *communications and health educator*
Cleary, William Joseph, Jr. *lawyer*
Clemente, Carmine Domenic *anatomist, educator*
Cochran, Johnnie L., Jr. *lawyer*
Cohan, John Robert *retired lawyer*
Cohen, Arthur M. *education educator*
Cohen, Cynthia Marylyn *lawyer*
Cohen, Ellis Avrum *producer, author, investigative journalist*
Cohen, Leonard (Norman Cohen) *poet, novelist, musician, songwriter*
Cohen, S(tephen) Marshall *philosophy educator*
Cohen, William Alan *marketing educator, author, consultant*
Cole, Natalie Maria *singer*
Coleman, Charles Clyde *physicist, educator*
Coleman, Paul Jerome, Jr. *physicist, educator*
Coleman, Rexford Lee *lawyer, educator*
Collias, Nicholas Elias *zoology educator, ornithologist*
Collier, Charles Arthur, Jr. *lawyer*
Collins, Audrey B. *judge*
Coln, William Alexander, III *pilot*
Comrie, Keith Brian *city administrative officer*
†Condon, William (Bill) *director, writer, producer*
Conley, Darlene Ann *actress*
Coombs, Robert Holman *behavioral scientist, medical educator, therapist, author*
Cooper, Edwin Lowell *anatomy educator*
Cooper, Leon Melvin *lawyer*
Cordova, Jeanne Robert *publisher, journalist, activist*
Corea, Chick (Armando Corea) *pianist, composer*
Corman, Julie Ann *producer, director*
Corman, Marvin Leonard *surgeon, educator*
Corman, Roger William *motion picture producer, director*
Cornwall, John Michael *physics educator, consultant, researcher*
Coroniti, Ferdinand Vincent *physics educator, consultant*
Cortinez, Veronica *literature educator*
†Coston, Suzanne *television producer*
Cote, Richard James *pathologist, researcher*
Craft, Cheryl Mae *neurobiologist, anatomist, researcher*
Cram, Donald James *chemistry educator*
Crippens, David Lee *broadcast executive*
Crockett, Donald Harold *composer, university educator*
Crombie, Douglass Darnill *aerospace communications system engineer*
Cromwell, James *actor*
Crosby, Peter Alan *management consultant*
Cuadra, Carlos Albert *information scientist, management executive*
Curry, Daniel Arthur *judge*
D'Accone, Frank Anthony *music educator*
†Dahl, John *film director*
Dalis, Peter T. *athletic director*
Dana, Lauren Elizabeth *lawyer*
Daniels, John Peter *lawyer*
Dann, Francis Joseph *dermatologist, educator*
Darby, G(eorge) Harrison *lawyer*
Darby, Michael Rucker *economist, educator*
Darden, Christopher A. *lawyer, actor, writer*
Darling, Juanita Marie *correspondent*
Dash, Stacey *actress*
Davidson, Ezra C., Jr. *physician, educator*
Davidson, Herbert Alan *Near Eastern languages and cultures educator*
Davidson, Robert C., Jr. *manufacturing executive*
Davies, Kelvin James Anthony *research scientist, educator, consultant, author*
Davis, Edmond Ray *lawyer*
Davis, Marvin *petroleum company executive, entrepreneur*
Davis, Paul Milton *communications administrator*
Dawson, Adam *private investigator, former newspaper editor*
Dawson, John Myrick *plasma physics educator*
DeBard, Roger *investment executive*
De Brier, Donald Paul *lawyer*
de Castro, Hugo Daniel *lawyer*
De Cherney, Alan Hersh *obstetrics and gynecology educator*
Dechter, Bradley Graham *music arranger, orchestrator*
†DeDominic, Patty (Lee DeDominic) *personnel executive*
Dekmejian, Richard Hrair *political science educator*
Del Olmo, Frank *newspaper editor*
Del Toro, Benicio *actor*
†DeLuca, Michael *film company executive*
DeLuce, Richard David *lawyer*
Delugach, Albert Lawrence *journalist*
DeMartini, Frank Thomas *film company executive, lawyer*
Demsetz, Harold *economist, educator*
Denham, Robert Edwin *lawyer, investment company executive*
Depp, Johnny *actor*
Detels, Roger *epidemiologist, physician, former university dean*
Deukmejian, George *lawyer, former governor*
Dewey, Donald Odell *university dean*
Dhir, Vijay K. *mechanical engineering educator*
Diamond, Jared Mason *biologist*
Diamond, Stanley Jay *lawyer*
Dickson, Robert Lee *lawyer*
Dignam, William Joseph *obstetrician, gynecologist, educator*
Di XX Miglia, Gabriella *artist, conservationist*
Doll, Lynne Marie *public relations agency executive*
†Domino, Fats (Antoine Domino) *pianist, singer, songwriter*
Donen, Stanley *film director*
Donovan, John Arthur *lawyer*
Donovan, Thomas B. *judge*
Dorman, Albert A. *consulting engineer executive, architect*
Dosamantes-Beaudry, Irma *psychology educator*
Douglas, Ileana *actress*
Dows, David Alan *chemistry educator*
Dr. Dre, (Andre Young) *rapper, record producer*
Drescher, Fran *actress*
Drew, Paul *entrepreneur*
Drewry, Elizabeth *newspaper publishing executive*
Dreyfuss, John Alan *health facility administrator*
Driscoll, John J. *city manager*
Drummond, Marshall Edward *business educator, university administrator*
Dryden, Mary Elizabeth *law librarian, writer, actress*
Dudziak, Mary Louise *law educator, lecturer*
Duffy, Patrick *broadcast executive*
Duffy, Patrick Sean *television production executive*
Dummett, Clifton Orrin *dentist, educator*
DuMont, James Kelton, Jr. *actor, producer*
Dunn, Arnold Samuel *biochemistry educator*
Dunn, Bruce Sidney *materials science educator*
Dworsky, Daniel Leonard *architect*
Dwyre, William Patrick *journalist, public speaker*
Dyck, Andrew Roy *philologist, educator*
†Dyer, Michael George *educator in computer science*
Eckardt, Richard William *lawyer*
Ecklund, Judith Louise *academic administrator*
Edgerton, Bradford Wheatly *plastic surgeon*
Edwards, Kathryn Inez *instructional media consultant*
Edwards, William H., Sr. *retired hotel corporation executive*
†Eick, Charles F. *federal judge*
Eisenberg, David Samuel *molecular biologist, educator*
†Elfman, Jenna *actress*
Ellickson, Bryan Carl *economics educator*
Elliott, John Ed *economics educator*
Elliott, Robert S(tratman) *electrical engineer, educator*
Ellsworth, Frank L. *non-profit executive*
Elrod, Lu *music educator, actress, author*
Emanuel, William Joseph *lawyer*
Emmeluth, Bruce Palmer *investment company executive, venture capitalist*
Engel, William King *neurologist, educator*
English, Stephen Raymond *lawyer*
Engoron, Edward David *food service consultant, television and radio broadcaster*
Enstrom, James Eugene *cancer epidemiologist*
Erickson, Richard Beau *insurance and financial company executive*
†Espey, John Jenkins *writer, English educator*
Estrin, Gerald *computer scientist, engineering educator, academic administrator*
Etra, Donald *lawyer*
Ettenger, Robert Bruce *physician, nephrologist*
Ewing, Edgar Louis *artist, educator*
Faal, Edi M. O. *lawyer*
Fahey, John Leslie *immunologist*
Fairbank, Robert Harold *lawyer*
Farmer, Robert Lindsay *lawyer*
Faroudja, Philippe Yves *television director*
†Farrell, Joseph *movie market analyst, producer, entertainment research company executive, writer, sculptor, designer*
Faulwell, Gerald Edward *insurance company executive*
Feig, Stephen Arthur *pediatrics educator, hematologist, oncologist*
Feigen, Brenda S. *literary manager, lawyer, motion picture producer*
Fein, Irving Ashley *television and motion picture executive*
Feldman, Frances Lomas *educator, consultant*
Fenning, Lisa Hill *federal judge*
Ferrell, Conchata Galen *actress, acting teacher and coach*
Ferry, Richard Michael *executive search firm executive*
Fickett, Edward Hale *architect, planner, arbitrator*
Field, Richard Clark *lawyer*
Field, Ted (Frederick Field) *film and record industry executive*
Fielding, Jonathan E. *pediatrician*
Fields, Bertram Harris *lawyer*
Figlin, Robert Alan *physician, hematologist, oncologist*
Finch, Caleb Ellicott *neurobiologist, educator*
Finegold, Sydney Martin *microbiology educator*
Firstenberg, Jean Picker *film institute executive*
Fischer, Alfred George *geology educator*
Fish, Barbara *psychiatrist, educator*
Fishburne, Laurence, III *actor*
Fisher, Barry Alan Joel *protective services official*
Fisher, Richard N. *lawyer*
Fishman, Arnie *marketing executive, consultant, film producer*
Fitzgerald, Tikhon (Lee R. H. Fitzgerald) *bishop*
Flanagan, Fionnula Manon *actress, writer, producer*
Flanigan, James J(oseph) *journalist*
†Fleder, Gary *film director, producer*
†Fleischmann, Ernest Martin *music administrator*
Fleming, Arthur Wallace *physician, surgeon*
Fleming, Macklin *judge, author*
†Flockhart, Calista *actress*
Flynn, Elizabeth Anne *advertising and public relations company executive*
Fogelman, Alan Marcus *internist*
Fohrman, Burton H. *lawyer*
†Foley, David *television and film actor*
Follick, Edwin Duane *law educator, chiropractic physician*
Follmer, John Scott *visual effects producer, supervisor*
†Fong, Matthew Kipling *state official*
Fontenote-Jameson, Belinda *museum director*
Foote, Christopher Spencer *chemist, educator*
Ford, Chris *professional basketball coach*
Ford, Donald Hainline *lawyer*
Forness, Steven Robert *educational psychologist*
Foster, Jodie (Alicia Christian Foster) *actress*
Foster, Mary Christine *motion picture and television executive*
Fowler, Vincent R. *dermatologist*
Fox, Saul Lourie *physician, researcher*
Frackman, Russell Jay *lawyer*
Fragner, Matthew Charles *lawyer*
Frame, John Fayette *sculptor*
Franceschi, Ernest Joseph, Jr. *lawyer*
Francis, Merrill Richard *lawyer*
Francis-Bruce, Richard *film editor*
Franz, Dennis *actor*
†Franz, Elizabeth *actress*
Fraser, Brad *playwright, theatrical director, screenwriter*
Frasier, S. Douglas *medical educator*
Fredman, Howard S *lawyer*
Freehling, Allen Isaac *rabbi*
Fried, Burton David *physicist, educator*
Friedlander, Sheldon Kay *chemical engineering educator*
Friedman, Alan E. *lawyer*
Friedman, Nathan Baruch *physician*
Friedman, Robert Lee *film company executive*
Friedman, Russell Peter *grief recovery educator, restaurant manager*
Frimmer, Paul Norman *lawyer*
Fromkin, Victoria Alexandra *linguist, phonetician, educator*
Fry, Michael Graham *historian, educator*
Fukushima, Teiichiro *obstetrician and gynecologist, educator*
Fulco, Armand John *biochemist*
Fuller, Larry *choreographer, director*
Furlong, Thomas Castle *newspaper editor*
Furlotti, Alexander Amato *real estate development company executive*
Furth, George *actor, playwright*
†Gabriel, Ronald Samuel *child neurologist*
Galanos, James *fashion designer*
Galanter, Ruth *city official*
Gale, Robert Peter *physician, scientist, researcher*
Gallo, Jon Joseph *lawyer*
Galton, Stephen Harold *lawyer*
Gambino, Jerome James *nuclear medicine educator*
Ganas, Perry Spiros *physicist*
Garcetti, Gilbert I. *prosecutor*
Garcia, Andy *actor*
Garland, G(arfield) Garrett *sales executive, golf professional*
Garofalo, Janeane *actress, comedienne*
†Garrett, Brad *actor, comedian*
Garrison, P. Gregory *diversified financial services company executive*
Garry, William James *magazine editor*
Garza, Oscar *newspaper editor*
Gauff, Lisa *broadcast journalist*
Gavin, Delane Michael *television writer, producer, director*
Gebb, Sheldon Alexander *lawyer*
Gebhart, Carl Grant *security broker*
Geller, Stephen Arthur *pathologist, educator*
Gentile, Joseph F. *lawyer, educator*
Georgesco, Victor *printing company executive*
Gest, Howard David *lawyer*
Getlin, Josh *reporter*
Getty, Estelle *actress*
Ghez, Andrea Mia *astronomy and physics educator*
Ghil, Michael *atmospheric scientist, geophysicist*
Giannotta, Steven Louis *neurosurgery educator*
Gibbs, Marla (Margaret Gibbs) *actress*
Giffin, Margaret Ethel (Peggy Giffin) *management consultant*
Gilbert, Robert Wolfe *lawyer*
Gillespie, Mike J. *university baseball coach*
Gillis, Nelson Scott *financial executive*
Gilman, John Joseph *research scientist*
Gilman, Nelson Jay *library director*
Gilmore, Mikal George *critic, journalist, author*
Girman, Tanya Lynn *dietitian*
Girvin, Shirley Eppinette *elementary education educator, journalist*
Glass, Herbert *music critic, lecturer, editor*
Glazer, Michael *lawyer*
Glick, Earl A. *lawyer*
Glitz, Dohn George *biochemistry educator*
Glushien, Morris P. *lawyer, arbitrator*
Gold, Arnold Henry *judge*
Goldberg, Harvey *financial executive*
Goldberg, Herb *psychologist, educator*
Goldberg, Jackie *councilwoman*
Goldman, Allan Bailey *lawyer*
Goldman, Benjamin Edward *lawyer*
Goldschmidt, Walter Rochs *anthropologist, educator*
Goldsmith, Jerry *composer*
Goldwyn, Ralph Norman *financial company executive*
Göllner, Marie Louise *musicologist, educator*
Golomb, Solomon Wolf *mathematician, electrical engineer, educator, university official*
Gómez, Ricardo Juan *philosophy educator*
Gonick, Harvey Craig *nephrologist, educator*
Good-Black, Edith Elissa (Pearl Williams) *writer*
Gooding, Cuba, Jr. *actor*
Goodman, David Bryan *musician, educator*
Goodman, Max A. *lawyer, educator*
Gordon, Basil *mathematics educator*
Gordon, David Eliot *lawyer*
Gordon, Malcolm Stephen *biology educator*
†Gordon, Mark, II *film producer*
Gordy, Berry *entrepreneur, record company executive, motion picture executive*
Gorman, Joseph Gregory, Jr. *lawyer*
Gorman, Lillian R. *human resources executive*
Gorney, Roderic *psychiatry educator*
Gorski, Roger Anthony *neuroendocrinologist, educator*
Gosfield, Margaret *educator, educational administrator, consultant, editor*

Gothold, Stuart Eugene *school system administrator, educator*
Gottfried, Ira Sidney *management consulting executive*
Gould, Charles Perry *lawyer*
Gould, David *lawyer*
Gould, Elliott *actor*
Grammer, Kelsey *actor*
Grausam, Jeffrey Leonard *lawyer*
†Gray, Bruce Gordon *sculptor*
†Gray, Ryan Christopher *writer, editor, graphic artist*
Green, Kenneth Norton *law educator*
†Green, Richard E. *real estate company executive*
Green, William Porter *lawyer*
Greenberg, Barry Michael *talent executive*
Greenberg, Ira Arthur *psychologist*
Greenberger, Martin *computer and information scientist, educator*
Greene, Alvin *service company executive, management consultant*
Grey, Joel *actor*
Griffey, Linda Boyd *lawyer*
Griffithe, Todd Allen *television associate director*
Griffiths, Barbara Lorraine *psychologist, writer*
†Griffiths, Rachel *actress*
Grimwade, Richard Llewellyn *lawyer*
Grinnell, Alan Dale *neurobiologist, educator, researcher*
Grobe, Charles Stephen *lawyer, accountant*
Grose, Elinor Ruth *retired elementary education educator*
Gross, Allen Jeffrey *lawyer*
†Gross, Matt G. *executive*
Grossman, Dorothea G. *consulting services administrator, poet*
Grosz, Philip J. *lawyer*
Groves, Martha *newspaper writer*
Grudzielanek, Mark James *professional baseball player*
Gudea, Darlene *publishing company executive*
Gurash, John Thomas *insurance company executive*
Gurfein, Peter J. *lawyer*
Guy, Jasmine *actress*
Guze, Phyllis Arlene *internist, educator, academic administrator*
Gyemant, Robert Ernest *lawyer*
Hackman, Gene (Eugene Alden) *actor*
Haglund, Thomas Roy *research biologist, consultant, educator*
Hahn, James Kenneth *lawyer*
Haines, Randa *film director*
Hale, Kaycee *research marketing professional*
†Haley, Roslyn Trezevant *educational program director*
Halkett, Alan Neilson *lawyer*
Hall, Clarence Albert, Jr. *geologist, educator*
Hamilton, Beverly Lannquist *investment management professional*
Hamilton, Patricia Rose *artist's agent*
Hammond, Teena Gay *editor*
†Hancock, Herbert Jeffrey (Herbie Hancock) *composer, pianist, publisher*
†Handley, William Ross *English educator*
Handy, Lyman Lee *petroleum engineer, chemist, educator*
Handzlik, Jan Lawrence *lawyer*
Hansell, Dean *lawyer*
Hanson, John J. *lawyer*
Harberger, Arnold Carl *economist, educator*
Harris, F. Chandler *retired university administrator*
Harris, Richard A. *film editor*
Harris, Theodore Edward *mathematician, educator*
Hart, John Lewis (Johnny Hart) *cartoonist*
Hartke, Stephen Paul *composer, educator*
Hartsough, Gayla Anne Kraetsch *management consultant*
Harvey, Jackson *film producer*
Harvey, James Gerald *educational counselor, consultant, researcher*
Hatter, Terry Julius, Jr. *federal judge*
Haughton, James Gray *medical facility administrator, municipal health department administrator, consultant, physician*
Hauk, A. Andrew *federal judge*
Havel, Richard W. *lawyer*
Hawley, Philip Metschan *retired retail executive, consultant*
Hayes, Byron Jackson, Jr. *retired lawyer*
Hayes, Robert Mayo *university dean, library and information science educator*
Hayutin, David Lionel *lawyer*
Haywood, L. Julian *physician, educator*
Hedlund, Paul James *lawyer*
Hein, Leonard William *accounting educator*
Heinke, Rex S. *lawyer*
Helgeland, Brian *film director, writer, producer*
Helgeson, Duane Marcellus *retired librarian*
Heller, Philip *lawyer*
Helper, Lee *public relations executive*
Helsper, James Thomas *surgical oncologist, researcher, educator*
Hemminger, Pamela Lynn *lawyer*
Hemmings, Peter William *orchestra and opera administrator*
Henderson, Jai *museum director*
Henriksen MacLean, Eva Hansine *former anesthesiology educator*
†Herek, Stephen *film director, producer*
Hernandez, Mike *city official*
Hershman, Jerome Marshall *endocrinologist*
Hess, Frederick Scott *artist*
Heyck, Theodore Daly *lawyer*
Heyler, Grover Ross *retired lawyer*
Hieronymus, Edward Whittlesey *lawyer*
Highberger, William Foster *lawyer*
Hight, B. Boyd *lawyer*
Highwater, Jamake *author, lecturer*
Hill, Bonnie Guiton *company executive*
Hiller, Arthur *motion picture director*
†Hillman, Stephen J. *federal judge*
†Hiltzik, Michael *journalist*
Hinerfeld, Robert Elliot *lawyer*
Hines, William Everett *publisher, producer, cinematographer, writer*
Hirsch, Barry L. *lawyer*
Hirsch, Judd *actor*
Hoang, Duc Van *theoretical pathologist, educator*
†Hoblit, Gregory *film director, television executive*
Hockney, David *artist*
Hodal, Melanie *public relations executive*
Hofert, Jack *consulting company executive, lawyer*
Hoffenberg, Marvin *political science educator, consultant*
Hoffman, Neil James *academic administrator*
Holden, Nate *city councilman*
Holden, William Willard *insurance executive*
Holdsworth, Ray W. *architectural firm executive*
Holland, Gary Norman *ophthalmologist, educator*
Holliday, Thomas Edgar *lawyer*
Holt, James Franklin *retired numerical analyst, scientific programmer analyst*
Holtzman, Robert Arthur *lawyer*
Hopkins, Henry Tyler *museum director, art educator*
†Hopkins, Stephen *film director, producer*
Horning, Robert Alan *securities broker*
Horovitz, Adam *recording artist*
Horowitz, Ben *medical center executive*
Horowitz, David Charles *consumer commentator, newspaper columnist*
Horwitz, David A. *physician, scientist, educator*
Hospers, John *philosophy educator*
Hotchkiss, Vivian Evelyn *employment agency executive*
Hotz, Robert Lee *science writer, editor*
Hough, Steven Hedges *lawyer*
Houk, Kendall Newcomb *chemistry educator*
House, John William *otologist*
Houston, Ivan James *insurance company executive*
Hovanessian, Shahen Alexander *electrical engineer, educator*
Hovannisian, Richard G. *Armenian and Near East history educator*
Howard, Nancy E. *lawyer*
Howe, Con Edward *city manager*
Howe, John Thomas *film director, educator*
Hsiao, Chie-Fang *neuroscientist*
†Hsu, Kylie *language educator*
Huang, Sung-cheng *electrical engineering educator*
Hubbard, John Randolph *university president emeritus, history educator, diplomat*
Hubbs, Donald Harvey *foundation executive*
Huben, Brian David *lawyer*
Hudson, Christopher John *publisher*
Hudson, Jeffrey Reid *lawyer*
Hufstedler, Seth Martin *lawyer*
Hufstedler, Shirley Mount (Mrs. Seth M. Hufstedler) *lawyer, former federal judge*
Hummel, Joseph William *hospital administrator*
Humphreys, Robert Lee *advertising agency executive*
Hundley, Norris Cecil, Jr. *history educator*
Hundley, Todd Randolph *professional baseball player*
Hunt, Peter Roger *film director, writer, editor*
Hupp, Harry L. *federal judge*
Hurt, William Holman *investment management company executive*
Hurwitz, Lawrence Neal *investment banking company executive*
Hutchins, Joan Morthland *manufacturing executive, farmer*
Hwang, John Dzen *municipal official*
†Hyams, Peter *film director, producer, cinematographer*
Hyman, Milton Bernard *lawyer*
Hymers, Robert Leslie, Jr. *pastor*
Iafrate, Gerald Carl *motion picture company executive, lawyer*
Iamele, Richard Thomas *law librarian*
Ideman, James M. *federal judge*
Ignarro, Louis J. *pharmacology educator*
Igo, George Jerome *physics educator*
Ilanit, Tamar *psychologist*
Incaudo, Joseph August *engineering company executive*
Inman, James Russell *claims consultant*
Intriligator, Michael David *economist, educator*
Iovine, Jimmy *recording industry executive*
Irani, Ray R. *oil and gas and chemical company executive*
Ireland, Kathy *actress*
Irving, Jack Howard *technical consultant*
Irwin, Philip Donnan *lawyer*
Israel, David *journalist, screenwriter, producer*
Itoh, Tatsuo *engineering educator*
Ivey, Judith *actress*
†Jackson, Janet Damita *singer, dancer*
Jackson, Kingsbury Temple *educational contract consultant*
†Jackson, Michael (Joseph) *singer*
†Jackson, Mick *film director, producer*
Jacobs, Randall Brian *lawyer*
Jacobs, Stephen Jay *musician, composer, writer*
Jacobsen, Laren *programmer, analyst*
Jacobson, Edwin James *medical educator*
Jacobson, Sidney *editor*
Jaffe, Sigmund *chemist, educator*
Jalali, Behnaz *psychiatrist, educator*
James, William J. *lawyer*
James, William Langford *aerospace engineer*
Jamison, Dean Tecumseh *economist*
Janofsky, Leonard S. *lawyer, association executive*
Janowski, Karyn Ann *artist*
Jarc, Frank Robert *printing company executive*
Jarmon, Lawrence *developmental communications educator*
Jarvik, Lissy F. *psychiatrist*
†Jarvik, Murray Elias *psychiatry, pharmacology educator*
Jelliffe, Roger Woodham *cardiologist, clinical pharmacologist*
†Jennings, Willbur *musician, popular*
†Jeunet, Jean-Pierre *film director*
†Johnson, Betsey Lee *fashion designer*
Johnson, Cage Saul *hematologist, educator*
Johnson, Charles Floyd *television executive, producer*
†Johnson, Davey (David Allen Johnson) *baseball team manager*
Johnson, E. Eric *insurance executive*
†Johnson, Earl, Jr. *judge, author*
Johnson, John Patrick *neurosurgeon, educator*
Johnson, Jonathan Edwin, II *lawyer*
Johnson, Keith Liddell *chemical company executive*
Johnson, Michael Marion *judge*
Johnston, Roy G. *consulting structural engineer*
Johnston, Ynez *artist*
Jones, Doug *travelog producer*
Jones, Janet Dulin *writer, film producer*
Jordan, Robert Leon *lawyer, educator*
Jorgensen, Paul Alfred *English language educator emeritus*
Judge, Mike *animator*
Kaback, Elaine *career counselor, consultant*
Kadison, Stuart *lawyer and educator*
Kadner, Carl George *biology educator emeritus*
Kahan, Sheldon Jeremiah (Christopher Reed) *musician, singer*
Kahane, Jeffrey *music director*
Kalaba, Robert Edwin *applied mathematician*
Kamil, Elaine Scheiner *physician, educator*
Kamine, Bernard Samuel *lawyer*
Kandal, Terry R. *sociology educator, consultant*
Kaplan, Isaac Raymond *chemistry educator, corporate executive*
Kaplan, Jonathan Stewart *film director, writer*
Kaplan, Nadia *writer*
Kaplan, Samuel *pediatric cardiologist*
Karatz, Bruce E. *business executive*
Karplus, Walter J. *engineering educator*
Karros, Eric Peter *baseball player*
Karst, Kenneth Leslie *legal educator*
Katleman, Harris L. *television executive*
Katz, Jerry Paul *corporate executive*
Katz, Roger *pediatrician, educator*
Katz, Ronald Lewis *physician, educator*
Kaula, William Mason *geophysicist, educator*
Kaye, Barry *investment company executive*
Kaye, Jhani *radio station manager, owner production company*
Keach, James P. *actor*
Kelleher, Robert Joseph *federal judge*
Keller, William D. *federal judge*
Kellerman, Sally Claire *actress*
Kelley, David E. *producer, writer*
Kelley, Harold Harding *psychology educator*
Kelly, Arthur Paul *physician*
Kelly, Henry Ansgar *English language educator*
Kelly, Maureen H. *actress*
Kemp, Anthony Maynard *English educator*
Kendig, Ellsworth Harold, Jr. *retired corporate lawyer*
Kennedy, George *actor*
Kennelly, Sister Karen Margaret *college president*
Kent, Susan *library director, consultant*
Kenyon, David V. *federal judge*
Kerman, Barry Martin *ophthalmologist, educator*
†Kerndt, Peter Reynolds *physician*
†Kersels, Martin *artist*
†Kershner, Irvin *film director*
Ketchum, Robert Glenn *photographer, print maker*
†Kiang, Ching-Hwa *chemical engineering educator*
Kidman, Nicole *actress*
Kiekhofer, William Henry *lawyer*
Kilburn, Kaye Hatch *medical educator*
Kindel, James Horace, Jr. *lawyer*
King, Duane Harold *museum administrator*
†King, George H. *judge*
King, Michael *syndicated programs distributing company executive*
Kirsner, Robert Shneider *Dutch and Afrikaans educator*
Kirwan, R. DeWitt *lawyer*
Kivelson, Margaret Galland *physicist*
Klauss, Kenneth Karl *composer, educator*
Kleeman, Charles Richard *medical educator, nephrologist, researcher*
Klein, Benjamin *economics educator, consultant*
Klein, Jeffrey S. *lawyer, media executive*
†Klein, Jim *company executive*
Klein, Joan Dempsey *judge*
Klein, Snira L(ubovsky) *Hebrew language and literature educator*
Kleinberg, Marvin H. *lawyer*
Kleiner, Arnold Joel *television station executive*
Kleingartner, Archie *founding dean, educator*
Kleinrock, Leonard *computer scientist*
Kline, Lee B. *architect*
Kline, Richard Stephen *public relations executive*
Klinger, Allen *engineering and applied science educator*
Klinger, Marilyn Sydney *lawyer*
Klowden, Michael Louis *lawyer*
Knapp, Cleon Talboys *business executive*
Knopoff, Leon *geophysics educator*
Knotts, Don *actor*
Kobe, Lan *medical physicist*
Koch, Richard *pediatrician, educator*
Koelzer, George Joseph *lawyer*
Koffler, Stephen Alexander *investment banker*
Koga, Rokutaro *physicist*
Kolve, V. A. *English literature educator*
Korn, Lester Bernard *business executive, diplomat*
†Kornwasser, Joseph K.
Korsch, Barbara M. *pediatrician*
Kory, Michael A. *graphics computer animator*
Kovacs, Laszlo *cinematographer*
Kraft, Scott Corey *correspondent*
Krag, Olga *interior designer*
Kramer, Barry Alan *psychiatrist*
Kreitenberg, Arthur *orthopedic surgeon, consultant*
Kresa, Kent *aerospace executive*
Kristof, Kathy M. *journalist*
Krueger, Robert William *management consultant*
Krupp, Edwin Charles *astronomer*
Kuechle, John Merrill *lawyer*
Kuehl, Hans Henry *electrical engineering educator*
Kunc, Joseph Anthony *physics and engineering educator, consultant*
Kupchick, Alan Charles *advertising executive*
Kupietzky, Moshe J. *lawyer*
Kupperman, Henry John *lawyer*
Kurtz, Swoosie *actress*
Kuwayama, George *retired curator*
Laaly, Heshmat Ollah *chemist, roofing materials executive, consultant*
Laba, Marvin *management consultant*
Labiner, Gerald Wilk *physician, medical educator*
La Force, James Clayburn, Jr. *economist, educator*
Laird, David *humanities educator emeritus*
†Lal, Vinay *history educator*
Landen, Sandra Joyce *psychologist, educator*
Landing, Benjamin Harrison *pathologist, educator*
Lansing, Sherry Lee *motion picture production executive*
Lappen, Chester I. *lawyer*
Larson, Karin Louise *financial analyst*
Lasorda, Thomas Charles (Tommy Lasorda) *professional baseball team manager*
Lasswell, Marcia Lee *psychologist, educator*
Latham, Joseph Al, Jr. *lawyer*
Latzer, Richard Neal *investment company executive*
Lauchengco, Jose Yujuico, Jr. *lawyer*
†Laudicina, Salvatore Anthony *film industry executive*
Laventhol, David Abram *newspaper editor*
Lavin, Laurence Michael *lawyer*
Lavin, Stephen Michael *basketball coach*
Lawton, Eric *lawyer, photographer, visual artist, writer*
Layton, Harry Christopher *artist, lecturer, consultant*
Lazarus, Mell *cartoonist*
Leach, Britt *actor*
Leal, George D. *engineering company executive*
Lear, Norman Milton *producer, writer, director*
Le Berthon, Adam *lawyer*
Lee, Burns Wells *public relations executive*
Lee, James Jui-Chang *public relations executive*
Lee, Shi-Chieh (Suchi Lee) *international tax specialist*
Lee, Stan (Stanley Martin Lieber) *cartoon publisher, writer*
†Leeka, Andrew B. *hospital executive*
Lehan, Richard D'Aubin *English language educator, writer*
†Lehmkuhl, Lynn *publishing executive*
Leibert, Richard William *special events producer*
Leibow, Ronald Louis *lawyer*
Leigh, Janet (Jeanette Helen Morrison) *actress*
Leighton, Robert *film editor*
Leijonhufvud, Axel Stig Bengt *economics educator*
Leiweke, Timothy *sports executive, marketing professional*
Lem, Richard Douglas *painter*
Lenard, Michael Barry *merchant banker, lawyer*
Leo, Malcolm *producer, director, writer*
Lesser, Joan L. *lawyer*
Lettich, Sheldon Bernard *director, screenwriter*
Letts, J. Spencer *federal judge*
Letwin, Leon *legal educator*
Leung, Frankie Fook-Lun *lawyer*
Levey, Gerald Saul *physician, educator*
Levine, C. Bruce *lawyer*
Levine, Jesse E. *publishing executive*
Levine, Michael *public relations executive, author*
Levine, Philip *classics educator*
Levine, Raphael David *chemistry educator*
Levine, Robert Arthur *economist, policy analyst*
Levine, Thomas Jeffrey Pello *lawyer*
†Levinsohn, Gary *producer*
Levy, Michael Lee *neurosurgeon*
Lew, Ronald S. W. *federal judge*
Lewin, Klaus J. *pathologist, educator*
Lewis, Charles Edwin *physician, educator*
†Lewis, Mary Ann *nursing educator*
Li, Gerald *architect, film producer and director*
Li, Lilia Huiying *journalist*
Liang, Jing *pharmacologist*
Liebeler, Wesley J. *law educator, lawyer*
Lieber, David Leo *university president*
Lim, David Jong-Jai *otolaryngology educator, researcher*
Lim, Larry Kay *university official*
Lin, Thomas Wen-shyoung *accounting educator, researcher, consultant*
Lin, Tung Hua *civil engineering educator*
Lindholm, Dwight Henry *lawyer*
Lindley, F(rancis) Haynes, Jr. *foundation president emeritus, lawyer*
Lindsey, William C. *engineering educator*
Link, George Hamilton *lawyer*
Linsk, Michael Stephen *real estate executive*
†Lionnet, Francoise *educator*
Lipsig, Ethan *lawyer*
†Little, Carole *women's apparel company executive*
Liu, Don *ophthalmologist, medical researcher*
†Lloyd, Jake *actor*
Loeb, Ronald Marvin *lawyer*
Loehwing, Rudi Charles, Jr. *publicist, radio broadcasting executive, journalist*
Löfstedt, Bengt Torkel Magnus *classics educator*
London, Andrew Barry *film editor*
Long, Gregory Alan *lawyer*
Longmire, William Polk, Jr. *physician, surgeon*
Lopez-Navarro, Eduardo Luis *family therapist*
Lowenthal, Abraham Frederic *international relations educator*
Lu, John Kuew-Hsiung *physiology educator, endocrinologist*
Lublinski, Michael *lawyer*
Lubman, Richard Levi *physician, educator, research scientist*
Lucente, Rosemary Dolores *educational administrator*
Lund, James Louis *lawyer*
†Lunden, Joan *television personality*
Lyman, John *psychology and engineering educator*
Lynch, Beverly Pfeifer *education and information studies educator*
Lynch, Martin Andrew *retail company executive*
Lynch, Patrick *lawyer*
Lynn, Katherine Lyn *quality engineer, chemist*
Mabee, John Richard *physician assistant, educator*
MacGraw, Ali *actress*
Mack, Brenda Lee *sociologist, public relations consulting company executive, media executive*
Mack, J. Curtis, II *civic organization administrator*
MacKenzie, John Douglas *engineering educator*
MacLaughlin, Francis Joseph *lawyer*
†MacLeod, William Bentley *economics and law educator*
†Madden-Lunsford, Kerry Elizabeth *writer*
†Madwin, Paul M. *retired sales executive*
Mager, Artur *retired aerospace company executive, consultant*
Magner, Rachel Harris *banker*
Maher, Bill *talk show host, comedian, producer*
Mahony, Cardinal Roger M. *archbishop*
†Maida, Carl Albert *anthropologist*
Main, Laurie (Laurence George Main) *actor*
Maker, Janet Anne *author, lecturer*
Maki, Kazumi *physicist, educator*
Malamuth, Neil Moshe *psychology and communication educator*
Malcolm, Dawn Grace *family physician*
Malden, Karl (Malden Sekulovich) *actor*
Malecki, Edward Stanley, Jr. *political science educator*
†Malick, Terrence (David Whitney, II) *film director*
†Malik, Terrence (David Whitney, II) *director, writer, producer*
Mall, William John, Jr. *aerospace executive, retired air force officer*
Malone, Nancy *actor, director, producer*
Maloney, Robert Keller *ophthalmologist, medical educator*
Maltin, Leonard *television commentator, writer*
†Mamer, John William *adult education educator*
Manatt, Charles Taylor *lawyer*
Mancino, Douglas Michael *lawyer*
Mandel, Joseph David *academic administrator, lawyer*
Manella, Nora M. *US district judge*
Mann, Delbert *film, theater, television director and producer*
Mann, Nancy Louise (Nancy Louise Robbins) *entrepreneur*
Mann, Wesley F. *newspaper editor*
Manolakas, Stanton Peter *watercolor artist*
Maquet, Jacques Jerome Pierre *anthropologist, writer*
Marc, David *American studies educator*
†March, Kathleen Patricia *bankruptcy judge*
Marciano, Maurice *apparel executive*
Marcus, Stephen Howard *lawyer*
Margol, Irving *personnel consultant*
†Margosis, Daniel I. *television writer, producer*
Margulies, Lee *newspaper editor*
Markham, Charles Henry *neurologist*
Markland, Francis Swaby, Jr. *biochemist, educator*
Marlin, Robert Matthew *secondary school educator*

Marmarelis, Vasilis Zissis engineering educator, author, consultant
Marmor, Judd psychiatrist, educator
Maronde, Robert Francis internist, clinical pharmacologist, educator
Marrow, Deborah foundation executive, art historian
Marshall, Arthur K. lawyer, judge, arbitrator, educator, writer
Marshall, Consuelo Bland federal judge
Marshall, Mary Jones civic worker
Martin, Albert Carey architect
Martin, J(ohn) Edward architectural engineer
†Martin, Shane Patrick education educator, consultant
Martinez, Miguel Acevedo urologist, consultant, lecturer
Masters, Lee broadcast executive
Masterson, William A. judge
Mathias, Alice Irene health plan company executive
Matthau, Walter actor
Mattingly, Gary city manager
May, Lawrence Edward lawyer
McAniff, Edward John lawyer
McCabe, Edward R. B. academic administrator, educator, physician
McCluggage, Kerry television executive
McClure, William Owen biologist
McDermott, John E. lawyer
McDermott, Thomas John, Jr. lawyer
McGraw, Deloss Holland illustrator, painter
Mc Guire, Dorothy Hackett actress
†McKellen, Ian actor
McKellop, Harry Alden biomechanical engineering educator
McKinzie, Carl Wayne lawyer
McKnight, Frederick L. lawyer
McLane, Frederick Berg lawyer
McLarnan, Donald Edward banker, corporation executive
†McMahon, James W. federal magistrate judge
Mc Pherson, Rolf Kennedy clergyman, church official
McQueen, Justus Ellis (L. Q. Jones) actor, director
McRae, Marion Eleanor critical care nurse
Medearis, Miller lawyer
Meduski, Jerzy Wincenty nutritionist, biochemist
Meecham, William Coryell engineering educator
Mellinkoff, David lawyer, educator
Mellinkoff, Sherman Mussoff medical educator
Mellor, Ronald John history educator
Meloan, Taylor Wells marketing educator
Mendel, Jerry Marc electrical engineering educator
Merlis, George television producer
Merrifield, Donald Paul university chancellor
Metheny, Pat jazz musician
Metzger, Robert Streicher lawyer
Meyer, Michael Edwin lawyer
Meyer, Russ film producer, director
Michael, William Burton psychologist, educator
Michaud, Michael Gregg publishing executive, writer
Michel, Donald Charles editor
Mihan, Richard retired dermatologist
Milchan, Arnon film producer
Miles, Jack (John Russiano) journalist, educator
Miles, Richard Robert art historian, writer
Milgrim, Darrow A. insurance broker, recreation consultant
Millard, Neal Steven lawyer
Miller, Gary Douglas aerospace company executive, former urban planning consultant
Miller, Milton Allen lawyer
†Miller, Percy record company executive
Milligan, Sister Mary theology educator, religious consultant
Milsome, Douglas cinematographer
Mintz, Marshall Gary lawyer
Mintz, Ronald Steven lawyer, photojournalist
Mirisch, Lawrence Alan motion picture agent
Mirren, Helen actress
Mishell, Daniel R., Jr. physician, educator
Mishkin, Marjorie Wong aviation and marketing consultant
Mitchell, Theodore R. academic administrator
Mock, Theodore Jaye accounting educator
Mockary, Peter Ernest clinical laboratory scientist, researcher, medical writer
Moe, Stanley Allen architect, consultant
Moffatt, Robert Henry accountant, publisher, writer, consultant
Mohr, John Luther biologist, environmental consultant
Molleur, Richard Raymond lawyer
Moloney, Stephen Michael lawyer
Mondesi, Raul baseball player
Montoya, Velma economist, policy consultant
Moonves, Leslie television company executive
Moore, Donald Walter academic administrator, school librarian
Moore, Ronald Bruce visual effects producer
Moore, Walter Dengel rapid transit system professional
†Moorhouse, Jocelyn Denise film director
Mooser, Stephen author
Moran, Thomas Harry university administrator
Moreno, Rita actress
Morgan, Dirck broadcast journalist
Morgenthaler, Alisa Marie lawyer
Morgner, Aurelius economist, educator
Mori, Allen Anthony university dean, consultant, researcher
Morris, Karen Ann critical care nurse, administrator
Morris, Sharon Hutson city manager
Morrison, Donald Graham business educator, consultant
Morrow, Winston Vaughan financial executive
Mortensen, Richard Edgar engineering educator
Morton, Joe actor
Mosich, Anelis Nick accountant, author, educator, consultant
Mosk, Richard Mitchell lawyer
Moskowitz, Joel Steven lawyer
Mossman, Thomas Mellish, Jr. television manager
Mottek, Frank broadcaster, journalist
Moxley, John Howard, III physician
Moy, Gwendolyn C.I. community health nurse, educator
Moy, Ronald Leonard dermatologist, surgeon
Moyer, Craig Alan lawyer
Mueller, Carl Richard theater arts educator, author
Muldaur, Diana Charlton actress
Mulligan, Richard M. actor, writer
†Mulligan, Robert Patrick film director, producer
Mulryan, Lenore Hoag author, art curator
Munitz, Barry foundation administrator
Muntz, Eric Phillip aerospace engineering and radiology educator, consultant
Murphy, Philip Edward broadcast executive
Murray, Alice Pearl data processing company executive
Murray, James Patrick newspaper columnist
Myers, Barton architect
Myers, Katherine Donna writer, publisher
Nadler, Gerald engineering educator, management consultant
Naef, Weston John museum curator
Nakanishi, Don Toshiaki Asian American studies educator, writer
Nathwani, Bharat Narottam pathologist, consultant
Neal, Howard broadcasting executive
Neal, Joseph C., Jr. church administrator
Neely, Sally Schultz lawyer
Neiter, Gerald Irving lawyer
Nelson, Bryce Eames journalist, educator
Nelson, Grant Steel lawyer, educator
Nelson, Howard Joseph geographer, educator
Nelson, James Augustus, II real estate executive, architect, banker
Nelson, Mark Bruce interior designer
Nettleton, Lois actress
Neufeld, Elizabeth Fondal biochemist, educator
Neufeld, Mace film company executive
Neufeld, Naomi Das pediatric endocrinologist
Neutra, Dion architect
Newhart, Bob entertainer
Newman, Anita Nadine surgeon
Newman, Craig Alan media executive, lawyer
Newman, David Wheeler lawyer
Newman, Michael Rodney lawyer
Newmar, Julie Chalane actress, dancer, real estate businesswoman
Nibley, Robert Ricks retired lawyer
Nicholas, William Richard lawyer
Nicholson, Jack actor, director, producer
Niemeth, Charles Frederick lawyer
Niese, William A. lawyer, newspaper publishing executive
Niles, John Gilbert lawyer
Nissenson, Allen Richard physician, educator
Nobe, Ken chemical engineering educator
Noble, Ernest Pascal physician, biochemist, educator
Noble, James Wilkes actor
Noble, Richard Lloyd lawyer
Nocas, Andrew James lawyer
Noce, Walter William, Jr. hospital administrator
Nochimson, David lawyer
Nodal, Adolfo V. city manager
Noguchi, Thomas Tsunetomi author, forensic pathologist
†Norman, Marc screenwriter, producer
Norris, William Albert former federal judge
†Norton, Edward actor
†Norwood, Brandy singer, actress
†Nunez, Victor film director, producer, writer
Ochoa, Armando bishop
O'Connell, Kevin lawyer
O'Connor, Kevin Thomas archdiocese development official
†O'Connor, Pat film director
O'Daniel, Damon Mark development assistant
O'Day, Anita Belle Colton entertainer, singer
O'Donnell, Pierce Henry lawyer
Ogle, Edward Proctor, Jr. investment counseling executive
Okeh, Samson Ewruje psychiatric nurse
Okrent, David engineering educator
Olah, George Andrew chemist, educator
Oldman, Gary actor
Olivas, Daniel A. lawyer
†Olivier, Kathy college basketball coach
Olmsted, Sallie Lockwood executive
†Olowokandi, Michael professional basketball player
Olsen, Frances Elisabeth law educator, theorist
Onak, Thomas Philip chemistry educator
O'Neal, Tatum actress
†O'Neil, W. Scott publishing executive
O'Neill, Russell Richard engineering educator
Orbach, Jerry actor, singer
Orchard, Henry John electrical engineer
Ordin, Andrea Sheridan lawyer
O'Reilly, Richard Brooks journalist
Orme, Antony Ronald geography educator
Orsatti, Alfred Kendall organization executive
O'Toole, James Joseph business educator
Owen, Michael Lee lawyer
Packard, Robert Charles lawyer
Paez, Richard A. judge
Palazzo, Robert P. lawyer, accountant
Papiano, Neil Leo lawyer
Parham, Linda Diane occupational therapist, researcher, educator
†Park, Chan Ho professional baseball player
Park, Sam-Koo transportation executive
Parker, John William pathology educator, investigator
Parker, Robert George radiation oncology educator, academic administrator
Parks, Debora Ann private school director
Parks, Michael Christopher journalist
Parmelee, Arthur Hawley, Jr. pediatric medical educator
Parsky, Gerald Lawrence lawyer
Pasich, Kirk Alan lawyer
Passaro, Edward, Jr. surgeon, educator
†Pastor, Jennifer sculptor
Patel, Chandra Kumar Naranbhai communications company executive, educator, researcher
Patron, Susan Hall librarian, writer
Paulson, Donald Robert chemistry educator
Paxton, Bill actor, writer, director
Pearce, Joan DeLap research company executive
Pearl, Judea computer scientist, educator
Peck, Austin H., Jr. lawyer
Pedersen, Norman A. lawyer
Pederson, Con animator
†Pedroarias, Ricardo Jose Spanish educator
Peña, Elizabeth actress
Penn, Christopher actor
Penn, Sean actor
†Perez, Denise Therese editor
Perlmutter, Donna music and dance critic
Perloff, Joseph Kayle cardiologist
Perrine, Richard Leroy environmental engineering educator
Perry, Ralph Barton, III lawyer
Perry, Robert Michael international engineering company executive
Perry, William Joseph food processing company executive
Petak, William John systems management educator
Peters, Aulana Louise lawyer, former government agency commissioner
Peters, Brock actor, singer, producer
Peters, Richard T. lawyer
Petersen, Robert E. publisher
†Pettibon, Raymond video artist
Pfaelzer, Mariana R. federal judge
Phelps, Barton Chase architect, educator
†Philips, Chuck journalist
Phillips, Geneva Ficker editor
Phillips, Keith Wendall minister
Phillips, Lou Diamond actor, director
†Phillips, Virginia A. federal judge
Phinney, Bernard O. research scientist, educator
Pierskalla, William Peter university dean, management-engineering educator
Pike, Malcolm Cecil preventive medicine educator
†Pinkus, Steve roofing contractor
Pircher, Leo Joseph lawyer
Plate, Thomas Gordon newspaper columnist, educator
Poindexter, William Mersereau lawyer
Pollack, Daniel concert pianist
Polley, Terry Lee lawyer
Pollock, John Phleger lawyer
Polon, Linda Beth elementary school educator, writer, illustrator
†Pondel, Roger S. public relations executive
Ponty, Jean-Luc violinist, composer, producer
†Poole, Robert William, Jr. foundation executive
Pope, Alexander H. non-profit administrator, former lawyer
Port, Sidney Charles mathematician, educator
Portenier, Walter James aerospace engineer
Porter, Verna Louise lawyer
Pottenger, Mark McClelland computer programmer
Powell, James Lawrence museum director
Power, John Bruce lawyer
Prejean, Kattie Calvin educational administrator
Preonas, George Elias lawyer
Presant, Sanford Calvin lawyer, educator, author, lecturer
Pressman, Jacob rabbi
Preston, Martha Sue pharmaceutical company executive
Pritsker, Keith Wayne lawyer
Pugsley, Robert Adrian law educator
†Pujol, Ernesto artist
Pulec, Jack Lee otolaryngologist
Quinn, Tom communications executive
Rabinovitz, Jason film and television consultant
Rabinovitz, Joel lawyer, educator
Rachelefsky, Gary Stuart medical educator
Radloff, William Hamilton editor, writer
Rae, Matthew Sanderson, Jr. lawyer
Rafeedie, Edward, Sr. federal judge
Raghavan, Derek oncologist, medical researcher and educator
Ramer, Lawrence Jerome corporation executive
Ramo, Simon engineering executive
Rankaitis, Susan artist
Raphael, Frederic Michael author
Rappeport, Ira J. lawyer
Rath, Howard Grant, Jr. lawyer
Rathbun, John Wilbert American studies educator
Rauch, Lawrence Lee aerospace and electrical engineer, educator
Raven, Bertram H(erbert) psychology educator
Ray, Gilbert T. lawyer
Rea, William J. judge
Reagan, Nancy Davis (Anne Francis Robbins) volunteer, wife of former President of United States
Reagan, Ronald Wilson former President of United States
Real, Manuel Lawrence federal judge
Reardon, John E. broadcast executive
Rector, Margaret Hayden writer
Reed, George Ford, Jr. investment executive
Reeves, Barbara Ann lawyer
Reich, Kenneth Irvin journalist
Reiss, Howard chemistry educator
Rense, Paige editor, publishing company executive
Renwick, Edward S. lawyer
†Resnick, Lynda art company executive
†Reuben, David Burt medical educator
Reynolds, Burt actor, director
†Reynolds, Gene television producer, director
†Reynolds, Kevin film director, writer
Reynoso, Cruz lawyer, educator
Rhys-Davies, John actor
Rice, Susan F. fundraising counsel executive
Rich, Alan music critic, editor, author
Rich, Andrea Louise museum executive
Richardson, Arthur Wilhelm lawyer
Richardson, Douglas Fielding lawyer
Richardson, John Vinson, Jr. library and information science educator
Riche, Wendy television producer
Richmond, Ray S(am) journalist
Rickles, Donald Jay comedian, actor
Rimoin, David Lawrence physician, geneticist
Ring, Michael Wilson lawyer
Rinsch, Charles Emil insurance company executive
Riordan, George Nickerson investment banker
Riordan, Richard J. mayor
Ritter, John(athan) (Southworth) actor
Ritvo, Edward Ross psychiatrist
†Robbins, Brian Quinn federal judge
Robert, Patrick playwright
†Roberts, Norman C. company executive
Roberts, Robert Winston social work educator, dean
Roberts, Sidney biological chemist
Robison, William Robert lawyer
†Robitaille, Luc professional hockey player
†Robles, Ernest federal judge
Rodnick, Eliot Herman psychologist, educator
Rodriguez, Edward John educational software developer
†Rodriguez, Ensor physician, scientist
Roeder, Richard Kenneth business owner, lawyer
Roemer, Milton Irwin physician, educator
Rogger, Hans Jack history educator
Romo, Cheryl Annette writer, editor
Roney, John Harvey lawyer, consultant
Rosenberg, Howard Anthony journalist
Rosenberger, Carol concert pianist
Rosenthal, Sol lawyer
Rosett, Arthur Irwin lawyer, educator
Ross, Herbert David film director
Ross, Marion actress
Rosser, James Milton academic administrator
Rosten, Irwin writer, producer, director
Rotello, Gabriel journalist
Roth, Tim actor
Rothenberg, Alan I. lawyer, professional sports association executive
Rothman, Claire Lynda entertainment executive
Rothman, Frank lawyer, motion picture company executive
Rouse, Richard Hunter historian, educator
Roussey, Robert Stanley accountant, educator
Rubin, Bruce Joel screenwriter, director, producer
Rubin, Stanley Creamer producer
Rubinstein, Moshe Fajwel engineering educator
Rudolph, Alan film director
Rudolph, Jeffrey N. museum director
Ruskin, Joseph Richard actor, director
†Russell, Barry federal judge
†Russell, Bill coach
Russell, James Brian broadcast executive, media consultant
Russell, Pamela Redford writer, film documentarian
Rust, Patricia Joan television production company executive, writer/producer
Rutter, Marshall Anthony lawyer
Ryan, Stephen Joseph, Jr. ophthalmology educator, university dean
Saar, Alison sculptor
Sackman, Dave marketing executive
Safonov, Michael George electrical engineering educator, consultant
Sager, Philip Travis academic physician, cardiac electrophysiologist
†Salem, Hadi thoracic surgeon
Saltzman, Barry actor
Saltzman, Joseph journalist, producer, educator
Salvaty, Benjamin Benedict lawyer
Samet, Jack I. lawyer
Sample, Steven Browning university executive
San Giacomo, Laura actress
Sargent, Joseph Daniel motion picture and television director
Sarnat, Bernard George plastic surgeon, educator, researcher
Sarnoff, Thomas Warren television executive
Sarris, Greg Native American educator
Sawyer, Charles Henry anatomist, educator
Saxe, Deborah Crandall lawyer
Sayles, John Thomas film director, writer, actor
Saylor, Mark Julian editor
Scates, Allen Edward coach
Schaefer, William David English language educator
Scheibel, Arnold Bernard psychiatrist, educator, research director
Schelbert, Heinrich Ruediger nuclear medicine physician
Schiff, Martin physician, surgeon
Schine, Wendy Wachtell foundation administrator
Schipper, Merle art historian and critic, exhibition curator
Schmidt, Karl A. lawyer
Schmitz, John Anthony systems analyst
Schnabel, Rockwell Anthony ambassador
Schnebelen, Pierre resort planner and developer, consultant
Schneider, Edward Lewis medicine educator, research administrator
Scholtz, Robert Arno electrical engineering educator
Schubert, Mark university swimming coach
Schulberg, Budd author
Schutz, John Adolph historian, educator, former university dean
Schwabe, Arthur David physician, educator
Schwartz, Leon foreign language educator
Schwartz, William Benjamin educator, physician
Schwarzenegger, Arnold Alois actor, author
Schwimmer, David actor
Scott, Kelly newspaper editor
Scott, Robert Lane chemist, educator
Scott, Tony film director
Scoular, Robert Frank lawyer
Scully, Vincent Edward sports broadcaster
See, Carolyn English language educator, novelist, book critic
Seeman, Melvin sociologist, educator
Segil, Larraine Diane materials company executive
Selleck, Tom actor
Sellin, Paul Roland retired English literature educator
†Setian, Nerses Mikail bishop, former apostolic exarchate
Settles, F. Stan, Jr. engineering educator, manufacturing executive
Seymour, Michael production designer
†Shakely, John Bower (Jack Shakely) foundation executive
†Shammas, Carole historian, educator
Shank, Russell librarian, educator
Shanks, Patricia L. lawyer
Shapazian, Robert Michael publishing executive
Shapiro, Marvin Seymour lawyer
Shapiro, Mel playwright, director, drama educator
Shapiro, Robert Leslie lawyer
Shapley, Lloyd Stowell mathematics and economics educator
Shatner, William actor
Shaw, David Lyle journalist, author
†Shea, Fran broadcast executive
Shea, Jack television and film director, producer, writer
Shearer, Derek Norcross international studies educator, diplomat, administrator
Sheehan, Lawrence James lawyer
Sheffield, Gary Antonian professional baseball player
Sheinbaum, Stanley K. economist
Sheppard, William Vernon engineering and construction executive
Sherfy, Bradley L. golf coach
Sherman, Eric director, writer, educator
Shi, Wenyuan microbiologist
Shideler, Ross Patrick foreign language and comparative literature educator, author, translator, poet
Shinozuka, Masanobu civil engineer, educator
Shire, David Lee composer
Shneidman, Edwin S. psychologist, educator, thanatologist, suicidologist
Shortz, Richard Alan lawyer
Shultz, John David lawyer
Shuster, Alvin journalist, newspaper editor
Siegel, David Aaron accountant
Siegel, Michael Elliot nuclear medicine physician, educator
Siegel, Sheldon C. physician
Sigband, Norman Bruce management communication educator
Silbergeld, Arthur F. lawyer
Silver, Ron actor, director
Silverman, Bruce Gary advertising executive
Silverman, Leonard M. university dean, electrical engineering educator
Silverman, Treva writer, producer, consultant
Silverstone, Alicia actress
Simkhovich, Boris Zalman biochemist, researcher
Simmons, Jean actress
Simpson, O. J. (Orenthal James Simpson) former professional football player, actor, sports commentator
Sinay, Hershel David publisher
Sinay, Joseph retail executive
Slaughter, John Brooks university administrator

Slavitt, Earl Benton *lawyer*
Sloane, Robert Malcolm *university administrator*
Smathers, James Burton *medical physicist, educator*
Smight, Alec Dow *film editor, consultant*
Smith, Ann Delorise *municipal official*
Smith, Emil L. *biochemist, consultant*
Smith, Jean Webb (Mrs. William French Smith) *civic worker*
Smith, Lane Jeffrey *automotive journalist, technical consultant*
Smith, William Ray *retired biophysicist, engineer*
Smits, Jimmy *actor*
Snyder, Arthur Kress *lawyer*
Snyder, Christina A. *lawyer*
†Sobieszek, Robert A. *photographer, educator*
†Sokoloff, Kenneth Lee *economics educator*
Solomon, George Freeman *psychiatrist, retired educator*
†Sommers, Stephen *film director*
Sonnberg, Mark *television executive*
Sonnenschein, Ralph Robert *physiologist*
†Spangler, Mary *college president*
Spelling, Aaron *film and television producer, writer, actor*
Sperling-Orseck, Irene *publishing company executive*
Spindler, Paul *corporate executive, consultant*
Spinotti, Dante *cinematographer*
Spitzer, Peter George *information systems executive, consultant*
Spofford, Robert Houston *advertising agency executive*
Squire, Molly Ann *organizational psychologist*
†Stacy, Hollis *professional golfer*
Stamm, Alan *lawyer*
Stancill, James McNeill *finance educator, consultant*
Stapleton, Jean (Jeanne Murray) *actress*
Steckel, Richard J. *radiologist, academic administrator*
Steel, Ronald Lewis *author, historian, educator*
Steele, Bruce Carl *editor*
Steele, Victoria Lee *librarian*
†Stein, Jay Joseph *urologist*
Steinberg, Warren Linnington *school principal*
Steinbrecher, Edwin Charles *writer, association director, film producer, astrologer*
Stellwagen, Robert Harwood *biochemistry educator*
Stephens, George Edward, Jr. *lawyer*
Stergion, Monica Lee *information technology management consultant*
Sterling, Donald T. *professional basketball team executive*
Stern, Leonard Bernard *television and motion picture production company executive*
Stern, Mitchell *broadcast executive*
Stern, Ruth Szold *business executive, artist*
Stern, Sandor *film writer, director*
Stern, Walter Eugene *neurosurgeon, educator*
Stevens, Eleanor Sandra *domestic services executive*
Stevens, George, Jr. *film and television producer, writer, director*
Stevenson, Robert Murrell *music educator*
Stewart, James M. *insurance and securities broker*
Stockwell, Robert Paul *linguist, educator*
Stone, George *artist, art educator*
Stone, Lawrence Maurice *lawyer, educator*
Stormes, John Max *instructional systems developer*
Storms, Lester C. (C Storms) *retired veterinarian*
Straatsma, Bradley Ralph *ophthalmologist, educator*
Strack, Stephen Naylor *psychologist*
Straw, Lawrence Joseph, Jr. *lawyer*
Strawn, Judy C. *public relations professional*
Streiker, Susan L. *law librarian*
Strock, Herbert Leonard *motion picture producer, director, editor, writer*
Stromberg, Ross Ernest *lawyer*
Strong, George Gordon, Jr. *litigation and management consultant*
Stuppi, Craig *lawyer*
Sudarsky, Jerry M. *industrialist*
Sullivan, Cornelius Wayne *marine biology educator, university research foundation,government agency administrator*
Sullivan, Peter Meredith *lawyer*
Sumner, James DuPre, Jr. *lawyer, educator*
Sutherland, Michael Cruise *librarian*
Svorinich, Rudy, Jr. *councilman*
Swartz, Roslyn Holt *real estate investment executive*
Swit, Loretta *actress*
Sylvester, Richard Russell *economist, management executive*
Szego, Clara Marian *cell biologist, educator*
Szwarc, Michael *polymer scientist*
Tabachnick, Norman Donald *psychiatrist, educator*
Takasugi, Robert Mitsuhiro *federal judge*
Tamkin, S. Jerome *business executive, consultant*
Tan, Zhiqun *biomedical scientist*
Tarantino, Quentin *film director, screenwriter*
Tardio, Thomas A. *public relations executive*
Tarr, Ralph William *lawyer, former federal government official*
Tarses, Jamie *television network executive*
Tatum, Jackie *parks and recreation manager, municipal official*
Taylor, Charles Ellett *biologist*
Taylor, Leigh Herbert *college dean*
Taylor, Minna *lawyer*
Teele, Cynthia Lombard *lawyer*
Tellem, Susan Mary *public relations executive*
Tennant, John Randall *management advisory company executive*
Tennenbaum, Michael Ernest *private investor*
Territo, Mary C. *health facility administrator, oncologist*
Terzian, Shohig Garine Sherry *mental health facility administrator*
Tevrizian, Dickran M., Jr. *federal judge*
Thoman, John Everett *architect, mediator*
Thomas, Betty *director, actress*
†Thompson, Andrea *actress*
Thompson, Earl Albert *economics educator*
Thompson, Richard Frederick *psychologist, neuroscientist, educator*
Thompson, Sada Carolyn *actress*
Thoren-Peden, Deborah Suzanne *lawyer*
Thorne, Richard Mansergh *physicist*
Thorpe, Douglas L. *lawyer*
Thrower, Norman Joseph William *geographer, educator*
Tinsley, Walton Eugene *retired lawyer*
Title, Gail Migdal *lawyer*
Titus, Edward Depue *psychiatrist, administrator*
Tobisman, Stuart Paul *lawyer*
Toledo, Robert *football coach*
Toman, Mary Ann *federal official*
Tomash, Erwin *retired computer equipment company executive*
Tompkins, Ronald K. *surgeon*
Torres-Gil, Fernando M. *federal official, academic administrator*
Totten, George Oakley, III *political science educator*
Touber, Joshua Samuel *technology consultant*
Toulmin, Stephen Edelston *humanities educator*
Tourtellotte, Wallace William *neurologist, educator*
Townsend, Barbara *actress*
Townsend, Robert *film director*
Treister, George Marvin *lawyer*
Trembly, Cristy *television executive*
Trimble, Phillip Richard *law educator*
Trimble, Stanley Wayne *hydrology and geography educator*
Triqueneaux, Laurent E. *photography agency owner*
Troy, Joseph Freed *lawyer*
†Troy, Nancy J. *art history educator*
Trumbull, Stephen Michael *entrepreneur*
Trygstad, Lawrence Benson *lawyer*
Tugend, Jennie Lew *film producer*
Tulloch-Reid, Elma Deen *nurse, consultant*
Tulsky, Fredric Neal *journalist*
Turchin, Carolyn *judge*
Turner, Craig *journalist*
Turner, Ralph Herbert *sociologist, educator*
Tuthill, Walter Warren *retail and financial executive*
Tuttle, Rick *city controller*
Tyler, Richard *fashion designer*
Tyson, Cicely *actress*
Udwadia, Firdaus Erach *engineering educator, consultant*
Ufimtsev, Pyotr Yakovlevich *physicist, electrical engineer, educator*
Ukropina, James R. *lawyer*
Ullman, Tracey *actress, singer*
Unterman, Thomas *newspaper publishing company executive, lawyer*
Urena-Alexiades, Jose Luis *electrical engineer*
Urioste, Frank J. *film editor*
Valentine, Dean *broadcast executive*
Valenzuela, Manuel Anthony, Jr. *lawyer*
van Dam, Heiman *psychoanalyst*
Van de Kamp, John Kalar *lawyer*
†Van Der Beek, James *actor*
Vanderet, Robert Charles *lawyer*
Van Der Meulen, Joseph Pierre *neurologist*
Vander Naald Egenes, Joan Elizabeth *business owner, educator*
†Vangelisti, Paul Louis *poet*
Van Horne, R. Richard *oil company executive*
Vargas, Diana L *television station executive*
Vaughn, William Weaver *lawyer*
Verdon, Gwen (Gwyneth Evelyn) *actress, dancer, choreographer*
Ver Steeg, Donna Lorraine Frank *nurse, sociologist, educator*
Villablanca, Jaime Rolando *medical neuroscientist, educator*
Villard, Dimitri Serrano *film producer, investment company executive*
Volpert, Richard Sidney *lawyer*
von Kalinowski, Julian Onesime *lawyer*
von Neumeyer Hull, LeAnne *public relations and communication executive, research consultant, writer*
Vredevoe, Donna Lou *research immunologist, microbiologist, educator*
Vuckovic, Gojko Milos *public administration scholar*
†Wachowski, Andy *film director*
†Wachowski, Larry *film director*
Wachs, Joel *city councilman*
Wade, Michael Robert Alexander *marketing specialist*
Wagner, Christian Nikolaus Johann *materials engineering educator*
Wagner, Darryl William *lawyer*
Wagner, William Gerard *university dean, physicist, consultant, information scientist, investment manager*
Wainess, Marcia Watson *legal management consultant*
Waite, Ralph *actor*
Waits, Thomas Alan *composer, actor, singer*
Walcher, Alan Ernest *lawyer*
Walker, Charles Montgomery *lawyer*
Walla, Catherine Anne *nursing administrator, educator*
Wallach, Howard Frederic *psychiatrist*
†Wallock, Terrence J. *corporate lawyer*
Walsh, John *museum director*
Walsh, John Harley *medical educator*
Walters, Rita *councilwoman*
Walton, Brian *labor union executive*
Ward, Leslie Allyson *journalist, editor*
†Wardlow, Bill *record industry consultant, entertainer*
Warner, James *broadcast executive*
Waterman, Michael Spencer *mathematics educator, biology educator*
Waters, Laughlin Edward *federal judge*
Waterston, Samuel Atkinson *actor*
Watkins, Sydney Lynn *pharmaceutical sales consultant*
†Watson, Emily *actress*
Watson, Sharon Gitin *psychologist, executive*
Wayte, (Paul) Alan *lawyer*
Wazzan, A(hmed) R(assem) Frank *engineering educator, dean*
Webber, Peggy *actress, producer, director, writer*
Weber, Charles L. *electrical engineering educator*
Weber, Eugen *historian, educator, author*
Webster, Jeffery Norman *science and technology policy analyst*
Wei, Jen Yu *physiologist, researcher, educator*
Weil, Robert Irving *arbitrator, mediator, retired judge*
Weiner, Leslie Philip *neurology educator, researcher*
Weinman, Glenn Alan *lawyer*
Weinstein, Irwin Marshall *internist, hematologist*
Weinstock, Harold *lawyer*
Weiser, Stanley *screenwriter*
Weiss, Martin Harvey *neurosurgeon, educator*
Weiss, Walter Stanley *lawyer*
Welborne, John Howard *railway company executive, lawyer*
Welch, Lloyd Richard *electrical engineering educator, communications consultant*
Welch, Raquel *actress*
Welles, Melinda Fassett *artist, educational psychologist*
Welsh, John *actor*
Wendlandt, Wendy Ann *political organizer*
Werner, Gloria S. *librarian*
Wessling, Robert Bruce *lawyer*
West, Robert Johnson *appraisal company executive*
Westheimer, David Kaplan *novelist*
Weston, John Frederick *business educator, consultant*
Wexler, Robert *university administrator*
Wheat, Francis Millspaugh *retired lawyer*
Whitaker, Forest *actor, director, producer*
White, Robert Joel *lawyer*
Whitmore, Bruce G. *lawyer*
Whitten, Charles Alexander, Jr. *physics educator*
Whybrow, Peter Charles *psychiatrist, educator, author*
Wigmore, John Grant *lawyer*
Wilbraham, Craig *broadcast executive*
Wilhoit, Julie *women's collegiate basketball coach*
Wilkinson, Alan Herbert *nephrologist, medical educator*
Willes, Mark Hinckley *media industry executive*
Williams, David Welford *federal judge*
Williams, Donald Clyde *lawyer*
Williams, John *coach*
Williams, Julie Ford *mutual fund officer*
Williams, Richard Thomas *lawyer*
Williams, Robert Martin *economist, consultant*
Williams, Ronald Dean *minister, religious organization executive*
Williams, Walter David *aerospace executive, consultant*
†Williams, William J. *educator, consultant, writer*
Williamson, Edwin Lee *wardrobe and costume consultant*
†Williamson, Kevin *writer, producer, director*
Willner, Alan Eli *electrical engineer, educator*
Wills, John Elliot, Jr. *history educator, writer*
Wilson, Charles Zachary, Jr. *newspaper publisher*
Wilson, Donald Kenneth, Jr. *lawyer, publisher*
Wilson, Gayle Ann *civic worker*
Wilson, Mable Jean *paralegal*
Wilson, Miriam Geisendorfer *retired physician, educator*
Wilson, Myron Robert, Jr. *retired psychiatrist*
Wilson, Stephen Victor *federal judge*
Windham, Timothy Ray *lawyer*
Wine, Mark Philip *lawyer*
Winkler, Howard Leslie *investment banker, business and financial consultant*
Winterowd, Walter Ross *English educator*
Winters, Barbara Jo *musician*
Winthrop, Kenneth Ray *insurance executive*
†Wistrich, Andrew J. *federal judge*
Withers, Hubert Rodney *radiotherapist, radiobiologist, educator*
†Witherspoon, (Laura Jean) Reese *actress*
Wittmann, Otto *art museum executive*
Wittrock, Merlin Carl *educational psychologist*
Wlaschin, Ken *cultural organization administrator, writer*
Woelffer, Emerson Seville *artist*
Wolf, Alfred *rabbi*
Wolfen, Werner F. *lawyer*
Wolinsky, Leo C. *newspaper editor*
Wong, James Bok *economist, engineer, technologist*
Woodland, Irwin Francis *lawyer*
Woodley, David Timothy *dermatology educator*
Woolf, Nancy Jean *neuroscientist, educator*
Wooten, Cecil Aaron *religious organization administrator*
Wortham, Thomas Richard *English language educator*
Wright, Bernard *artist*
Wright, Donald Franklin *retired newspaper executive*
†Wright, Joan Frances *surgeon*
Wright, Kenneth Brooks *lawyer*
Wu, Ching-Fong *gastroenterologist*
Wu, Li-Pei *banker*
Wu, Qingyun *Chinese language and literature educator*
Wudl, Fred *chemistry educator*
Wurtele, Morton Gaither *meteorologist, educator*
Wyatt, James Luther *drapery hardware company executive*
†Wylie, Pamela Jane *writer, producer, consultant, small business owner*
Yamamoto, Joe *psychiatrist, educator*
Yanai, Michio *meteorologist, educator*
Yang, Bingen *mechanical engineering educator*
Yang, Yang *science educator*
Yates, Peter *director, producer*
Yeh, William Wen-Gong *civil engineering educator*
Yen, Teh Fu *civil and environmental engineering educator*
York, Gary Alan *lawyer*
Yoshiki-Kovinick, Marian Tsugie *author*
Young, Caprice Yvonne *municipal official*
Young, Charles Edward *university chancellor emeritus*
Young, Sean *actress*
Youpa, Donald G. *broadcast executive*
Zawacki, Bruce Edwin *surgeon, ethicist*
Zeitlin, Maurice *sociology educator, author*
Zelikow, Howard Monroe *management and financial consultant*
Zelon, Laurie Dee *lawyer*
Zemeckis, Robert L. *film director*
Ziffren, Kenneth *lawyer*
Ziskin, Laura *film producer*
†Zurzulo, Vincent P. *federal judge*

Los Banos
Castellano, Valen Edward *biologist*
Peterson, Stanley Lee *artist*

Los Gatos
Cohen, James Robert *oncologist, hematologist*
Dahlberg, Thomas Robert *author, attorney, educator, software company executive*
Dunham, Anne *educational institute director*
Meyers, Ann Elizabeth *sports broadcaster*
Naughten, Robert Norman *pediatrician*
Naymark, Sherman *consulting nuclear engineer*
Pfeiffer, Gerald G. *human resources specialist*
Rissanen, Jorma Johannes *computer scientist*
Rogers, Franklin Robert *former language educator, writer*
Rosenheim, Donald Edwin *electrical engineer*
Seligmann, William Robert *lawyer, author*
Tinsley, Barbara Sher *historian, educator, writer*

Los Osos
Allison, Ralph Brewster *psychiatrist*
Polk, Benjamin Kauffman *retired architect, composer, educator*
Topp, Alphonso Axel, Jr. *environmental scientist, consultant*

Lucerne Valley
Johnson, Jane Oliver *artist*

Madera
Kellam, Becky *business educator, consultant*

Von Prince, Kilulu Magdalena *retired occupational therapist, sculptor*

Magalia
Sincoff, Steven Lawrence *chemistry educator*

Malibu
Aiken, Lewis Roscoe, Jr. *psychologist, educator*
Almond, Paul *film director, producer, writer*
Baskin, Otis Wayne *business educator*
Bedrosian, Edward *electrical engineer*
Bowman, Bruce *art educator, writer, artist*
Chester, Arthur Noble *physicist*
Clewett, Raymond Winfred *mechanical design engineer*
†Collings, Michael Robert *poet, educator*
Crawford, Natalie Wilson *applied mathematician*
Darraby, Jessica L. *lawyer, educator, writer*
Davenport, David *university president, lawyer*
Ensign, Richard Papworth *transportation executive*
Fulton, Norman Robert *credit manager*
Harris, Ed(ward Allen) *actor*
Hill, Lawrence Sidney *management educator*
Hooper, Catherine Evelyn *senior development engineer*
Jeffrey, Francis *software developer, forecaster*
Jenden, Donald James *pharmacologist, educator*
Kmiec, Douglas William *government official, law educator, columnist*
Krueger, Kenneth John *corporate executive, nutritionist, educator*
MacLeod, Robert Fredric *editor, publisher*
Margerum, J(ohn) David *chemist*
Monsma, Stephen Vos *political scientist, educator*
Moore, John George, Jr. *medical educator*
Morgenstern, Leon *surgeon*
Ortiz, Geoffrey *stock broker, retirement planning specialist*
Palacio, June Rose Payne *nutritional science educator*
Pepper, David M. *physicist, educator, author, inventor*
Phillips, Ronald Frank *academic administrator*
Ratliff, James Conway *hospitality consultant*
Smith, George Foster *retired aerospace company executive*
Stalzer, Mark Anthony *computer scientist*
Stockwell, Dean *actor*
Trakh, Mark *university head women's basketball coach*
Vereen, Ben *actor, singer, dancer*
Vickers, Deborah Janice *electrical engineer, researcher*

Mammoth Lakes
Buchanan, Lee Ann *public relations executive*
Shekhar, Stephen S. *obstetrician, gynecologist*

Manhattan Beach
Blanton, John Arthur *architect*
Bradburn, David Denison *engineer, retired air force officer*
Curran, Janet S. *advertising executive*
Deutsch, Barry Joseph *consulting and development company executive*
Devitt-Grasso, Pauline Virginia *civic volunteer, nurse*
Lee, Gloria Deane *artist, educator*
Lucas, Suzanne *statistician, entrepreneur*
Posner, Judith Lois *art dealer*
Ricardi, Leon Joseph *electrical engineer*
Schoenfeld, Lawrence Jon *real estate developer, asset lender*
Stern, Daniel Alan *business management consultant*
Trager, Russell Harlan *advertising consultant*

Manteca
Hirning, Fredric Carl *pharmacist*

Marina
Cornell, Annie Aiko *nurse, administrator, retired army officer*
Grenfell, Gloria Ross *freelance journalist*
Shane, William Whitney *astronomer*

Marina Del Rey
Allmon, Michael Bryan *financial consultant*
Banks, Ernest (Ernie Banks) *retired professional baseball player*
Collins, Russell Ambrose *advertising executive, creative director*
Dankanyin, Robert John *international business executive*
Engel, Geoffrey Byron *editor*
Evans, Thomas R. *magazine publisher*
Frank, Ann-Marie *sales administration executive*
†Glen, Paul Michael *management consultant, educator*
Gold, Carol Sapin *international management consultant, speaker*
Goldaper, Gabriele Gay *clothing executive, consultant*
Heisser-Metoyer, Patricia *psychologist, organizational consultant*
Holland, Robin Jean *personnel company executive*
Kiraly, Karch (Charles Kiraly) *professional volleyball player*
Lange, Gerald William *book artist, typographer*
Lott, Davis Newton *advertising agency executive, publisher*
Orr, Ronald Stewart *lawyer*
Rojany, Lisa Adrienne *publishing company executive*
†Sehdeva, Jagjit S. *surgeon*
Stebbins, Gregory Kellogg *foundation executive*
Steffes, Kent *volleyball player*
Stiess, Walter George *retired surgeon*
Strum, Stephen B. *oncologist*
Touch, Joseph Dean *computer scientist, educator*
Wineman, Paul Raymond, Jr. *contract negotiator*

Marshall
Evans, Robert James *architect*

Martinez
Bray, Absalom Francis, Jr. *lawyer*
DeWolfe, Martha Rose *singer, songwriter, publisher*
McKnight, Lenore Ravin *child psychiatrist*
Meyer, Jarold Alan *oil company research executive*
Tong, Siu Wing *computer programmer*
Uilkema, Gayle Burns *county official, mayor, councilwoman, business educator*
Williams, Charles Judson *lawyer*

Marysville
Babao, Donna Marie community health, psychiatric nurse, educator
Gray, Katherine marriage and family counselor and support therapist, writer, educator
Myers, Elmer psychiatric social worker

Mcclellan AFB
Herrlinger, Stephen Paul flight test engineer, air force officer, educator
†Wiedemer, Michael P. military officer

Mckinleyville
Berry, Glenn educator, artist
Thueson, David Orel pharmaceutical executive, researcher, educator, writer

Mendocino
Rappaport, Stuart Ramon lawyer
†Sharkey, Virginia Grace artist
Woelfel, Robert William broadcast executive, mayor

Menifee
Kandus, Richard Jay adult education educator

Menlo Park
Alsop, Stewart communications executive
†Altman, Drew E. foundation executive
Arthur, Greer Martin maritime container leasing firm executive
Bader, W(illiam) Reece lawyer
Baez, Joan Chandos folk singer
Bourne, Charles Percy information scientist, educator
Boyarski, Adam Michael physicist
Bremser, George, Jr. electronics company executive
Bukry, John David geologist
Bull, James Robert publishing executive
†Cardozo, Oscar F. engineering executive
Chin, Albert Kae research physician
Clair, Theodore Nat educational psychologist
Coats, William Sloan, III lawyer
Cook, Paul Maxwell technology company executive
Craig, Gordon Alexander historian, educator
Crandall, Nelson David, III lawyer
Crane, Hewitt David science advisor
Creswell, Donald Creston management consultant
Dorset, Phyllis Flanders technical writer, editor
Edson, William Alden electrical engineer
Ehrlich, Thomas educator
Evans, Bob Overton electronics executive
Fairbank, Jane Davenport editor, civic worker
Fenton, Noel John venture capitalist
Fischer, Michael Ludwig environmental executive
Friend, David Robert chemist
Fuhrman, Frederick Alexander physiology educator
Funkhouser, Lawrence William retired geologist
Glaser, Robert Joy retired physician, foundation executive
Goodman, Beatrice May real estate professional
Gunderson, Robert Vernon, Jr. lawyer
Hoagland, Laurance Redington, Jr. investment executive
Hoffman, Thomas Edward dermatologist
Holzer, Thomas Lequear geologist
Honey, Richard Churchill retired electrical engineer
†Johansen, Bob think-tank executive
Jorgensen, Paul J. research company executive
Kaufman, Christopher Lee lawyer
Kirk, Cassius Lamb, Jr. lawyer, investor
Kohne, Richard Edward retired engineering executive
Kovachy, Edward Miklos, Jr. psychiatrist
Kuwabara, James Shigeru research hydrologist
Lachenbruch, Arthur Herold geophysicist
Lane, Laurence William, Jr. retired ambassador, publisher
Levenson, Milton chemical engineer, consultant
Lindzey, Gardner psychologist, educator
Lockton, David Ballard business executive
Lucas, Donald Leo private investor
Luepke, Gretchen geologist
Madison, James Raymond lawyer
McCarthy, Roger Lee mechanical engineer
†McCown, George E. venture banking company executive
McDonald, Warren George accountant, former savings and loan executive
Millard, Richard Steven lawyer
Morrison, David Fred freight company executive
Neumann, Peter Gabriel computer scientist
Nichols, Alan newspaper publishing executive
Nichols, William Ford, Jr. foundation executive, business executive
O'Brien, Raymond Francis transportation executive
Pake, George Edward research executive, physicist
Pallotti, Marianne Marguerite foundation administrator
Paustenbach, Dennis James environmental toxicologist
Phipps, Allen Mayhew management consultant
Quigley, Philip J. telecommunications industry executive
†Root, Jonathan David company executive
Saffo, Paul communications executive
Salmon, Vincent acoustical consultant
Sauers, William Dale lawyer, playwright
Schleh, Edward Carl business analyst
Schmidt, Chauncey Everett banker
Schnebly, F(rancis) David aerospace and electronics company executive
Scott, Michael Dennis lawyer
Shah, Haresh Chandulal civil engineering educator
Shen, Nelson Mu-Ching fiber optics communications scientist
Shows, Winnie M. speaker, author, consultant
†Shulman, Lee S. foundation executive
Sparks, Robert Dean medical administrator, physician
Speidel, John Joseph physician, foundation officer
Steiger, Bettie Alexander information industry specialist
Taft, David Dakin chemical executive
Taylor, Robert P. lawyer
Tokheim, Robert Edward physicist
Vane, Sylvia Brakke anthropologist, publisher, cultural resource management company executive, writer
Vickers, Roger Spencer physicist, environmental mapping director
Walsh, William Desmond investor
Wegner, Judith Welch law educator, dean
Westcott, Brian John manufacturing executive
White, Cecil Ray librarian, consultant
Wolfson, Mark Alan investor, business educator
Wright, Rosalie Muller magazine and newspaper editor

Merced
Boese, Sandra Jean publishing executive
Olsen, David Magnor chemistry and astronomy educator

Middletown
Downing, James Christie lawyer

Midway City
McCawley, William Dale, II accountant, writer, ethnohistorian

Mill Valley
Baker, Malcolm marketing executive
Benezet, Louis Tomlinson retired psychology educator, former college president
Clark, Edgar Sanderford insurance broker, consultant
Crews, William Odell, Jr. seminary administrator
Davis, Linda Jacobs municipal official
DuBose, Francis Marquis clergyman
Gianturco, Paola management consulting company executive
Harner, Michael James anthropologist, educator, author
Harris, Jeffrey Saul physician executive, consultant
Jones, Pirkle photographer, educator
Leslie, Jacques Robert, Jr. journalist
McFarlane, William John management consultant
McNamara, Stephen newspaper executive
Nemir, Donald Philip lawyer
†Owings, Alison June writer, journalist
Padula, Fred David filmmaker
Premo, Paul Mark oil company executive
†Smith, Karen Randlev educator, writer
Stubblefield, Jerry Mason religious educator, minister
Taylor, Rose Perrin social worker
Wallerstein, Robert Solomon psychiatrist
Ware, David Joseph financial consultant
Winskill, Robert Wallace manufacturing executive

Millbrae
Honor, Nicholas Kelly disc jockey, accountant
Lande, James Avra lawyer, contracts manager
Mank, Edward Warren marketing professional
Palmer, Patricia Ann Texter English language educator
Rosenthal, Herbert Marshall lawyer

Milpitas
Berkley, Stephen Mark computer peripherals manufacturing company executive
†Brown, Michael A. computer hardware company executive
Corrigan, Wilfred J. data processing and computer company executive
Duque, Ricardo German analytical chemist
Fenner, Peter David communications executive
Granchelli, Ralph S. company executive
†Larson, Greg Edward city manager
Leonardi, Rosarius Roy special education educator
McDonald, Mark Douglas electrical engineer
Mian, Guo electrical engineer
Nishimura, Koichi electronics manufacturing company executive
Parruck, Bidyut electrical engineer
Roddick, David Bruce construction company executive
Sobeck, Gerald Robert quality assurance professional, professional baseball scout
Wang, Huai-Liang William mechanical engineer
Wheeler, William R. technical advisor
Wolters, Christian Heinrich systems engineer

Mineral
Hoofard, Jane Mahan Decker elementary education educator

Mission Hills
Baril, Nancy Ann gerontological nurse practitioner, consultant
Cramer, Frank Brown engineering executive, combustion engineer, systems consultant
Krieg, Dorothy Linden soprano, performing artist, educator
McFarland-Esposito, Carla Rae nursing executive
Weber, Francis Joseph archivist, museum director

Mission Viejo
Corey, Jo Ann senior management analyst
Dergarabedian, Paul energy and environmental company executive
Dillon, Francis Patrick human resources executive, management and sales consultant
Faley, Robert Lawrence retired instruments company executive
Gilbert, Heather Campbell manufacturing company executive
Harris, Ruby Lee realtor
Ljubicic Drozdowski, Miladin Peter consulting engineer
McGinnis, Joán Adell retired secondary school educator
Sabaroff, Rose Epstein retired education educator
Samuelson, Norma Graciela architectural illustrator, artist
Sanz, Kathleen Marie management consultant
Sessions, Don David lawyer
Subramanian, Sundaram electronics engineer
Teitelbaum, Harry English educator
Wilson, Eleanor McElroy county official

Modesto
Bairey, Marie principal
Berry, John Charles clinical psychologist, educational administrator
Bucknam, Mary Olivia Caswell artist
Cofer, Berdette Henry public management consulting company executive
Crawford, Charles McNeil winery science executive
Gallo, Ernest vintner
Goldberg, Robert Lewis preventive and occupational medicine physician
Gunter, William Dayle, Jr. physicist
Harrison-Scott, Sharlene Marie elementary education educator
Mayhew, William A. judge
†McManus, Michael S. federal judge
Moe, Andrew Irving veterinarian
Morrison, Robert Lee physical scientist
Naeve, Catherine Ann secondary education educator
Owens, Jack Byron lawyer
Piccinini, Robert M. grocery store chain executive
Sibitz, Michael William school superintendent
†Sill, Anna Laura retired language educator

Smith, Heather Lynn psychotherapist, recreational therapist
Tidball, Lee Falk elementary education educator
Whiteside, Carol Gordon foundation executive

Moffett Field
Baldwin, Betty Jo computer specialist
Cohen, Malcolm Martin psychologist, researcher
Dacles-Mariani, Jennifer Samson engineering educator
Erzberger, Heinz aeronautical engineer
Greenleaf, John Edward research physiologist
Haines, Richard Foster psychologist
Kerr, Andrew W. aerodynamics researcher
Lissauer, Jack Jonathan astronomy educator
McCroskey, William James aeronautical engineer
McDonald, Henry (Harry McDonald) research center administrator
Morrison, David science administrator
Ragent, Boris physicist
Salama, Farid astrophysicist, spectroscopist, research scientist
Statler, Irving Carl aerospace engineer
Strawa, Anthony Walter research scientist

Mojave
Shelby, Tim Otto secondary education educator

Monarch Beach
de Beixedon, S(usan) Yvette psychologist
Dougherty, Elmer Lloyd, Jr. retired chemical engineering educator, consultant

Monrovia
Adler, Fred Peter electronics company executive
Andary, Thomas Joseph biochemist
Edwards, Kenneth Neil chemist, consultant
Huffey, Vinton Earl clergyman
Jemelian, John Nazar management consultant
Kimnach, Myron William botanist, horticulturist, consultant
Mac Cready, Paul Beattie aeronautical engineer
Pray, Ralph Emerson metallurgical engineer

Montara
Wall, Glennie Murray historic preservation professional

Monte Rio
Pemberton, John de Jarnette, Jr. lawyer, educator

Montebello
Cabrera, Carmen secondary education educator
Kolbeck, Sister Ann Lawrence school principal
Meeker, Arlene Dorothy Hallin (Mrs. William Maurice Meeker) manufacturing company executive
Norkin, Mark Mitchell sales executive

Montecito
Burgee, John Henry architect
Levinson, Betty Zitman artist
Meghreblian, Robert Vartan manufacturing executive, physicist
Wheelon, Albert Dewell physicist

Monterey
Allen, Karen Jane actress
Barrett, Archie Don consultant , former federal official
Black, Robert Lincoln pediatrician
Boger, Dan Calvin statistical and economic consultant, educator
Bomberger, Russell Branson lawyer, writer
Butler, Jon Terry computer engineering educator, researcher
Caldwell, Joni psychology educator, small business owner
Collins, Curtis Allan oceanographer
Cutino, Bert Paul restaurant co-founder, chef
Di Girolamo, Rosina E. education educator
Fenton, Lewis Lowry lawyer
†Frampton, James Scott career officer
†Garrett, William L. federal judge
Gilpin, Henry Edmund, III photographer, educator
Gotshall, Cordia Ann publishing company executive, distributing executive
Haddad, Louis Nicholas paralegal
Karsh, Yousuf photographer
Keene, Clifford Henry medical administrator
Kennedy-Minott, Rodney international relations educator, former ambassador
Krasno, Richard Michael educational organization executive, educator
Marto, Paul James retired mechanical engineering educator, consultant, researcher
Matthews, David Fort military weapon system acquisition specialist
†Morgan, Edwin Philip academic administrator
Newberry, Conrad Floyde aerospace engineering educator
Oder, Broeck Newton school emergency management consultant
Peet, Phyllis Irene women's studies educator
Reneker, Maxine Hohman librarian
Ryan, Sylvester D. bishop
Schrady, David Alan operations research educator
Shropshire, Helen Mae retired historian
Shull, Harrison chemist, educator
Stern, Gerald Daniel lawyer
†Sunde, Douglas plastic surgeon
von Drachenfels, Suzanne Hamilton writer
Wright, Mary Rose state park superintendent

Monterey Park
Amezcua, Charlie Anthony social science counselor
Chan, Daniel Siu-Kwong psychologist
Chang, Jonathan Lee orthopedist, educator
Crawford, Philip Stanley bank executive
Gomez, Sylvia pediatric critical care nurse
Groce, Ewin Petty lawyer
Lin, Lawrence Shuh Liang accountant
Meysenburg, Mary Ann principal
Montag, David Moses telecommunications company executive
†Moreno, Ernest H. college president
Smith, Betty Denny county official, administrator, fashion executive
Stapleton, Jean journalism educator
Szeto, Paul (Cheuk-Ching) religious mission executive
Tseng, Felix Hing-Fai accountant
Waiter, Serge-Albert retired civil engineer
Wilson, Linda librarian

†Win, George Chin chiropractor

Montrose
Greenlaw, Roger Lee interior designer
Twitchell, Theodore Grant music educator and composer

Moorpark
Bahn, Gilbert Schuyler retired mechanical engineer, researcher
Brunner, Robert Francis composer, conductor
Bush, June Lee real estate executive
Hall, Elton Arthur philosophy educator
Kavli, Fred manufacturing executive
Young, Victoria E. occupational health and pediatrics nurse practitioner, lawyer

Moraga
Allen, Richard Garrett health care and education consultant
Coleman, Henry James, Jr. management educator, consultant
Frey, William Rayburn healthcare educator, consultant
Haag, Carol Ann Gunderson marketing professional, consultant
Ittner, Helen Louise entrepreneur
Lester, Jacob Franklin liberal arts educator
Lu, Matthias priest, educator
Sestanovich, Molly Brown writer

Moreno Valley
†Brown, Frederick Courtney writer
Gull, Paula Mae renal transplant coordinator, nephrology nurse, medical-surgical nurse
Iweka, Vanessa Ann nurse midwife, educator
†McClellan, Barry Dean city manager
Mullen, Terri Ann special education educator
Twedell, Lester Ralph, Jr. secondary school educator
Wilson, Robert Michael Alan writer

Morgan Hill
Dixon, Lani Gene critical care nurse
Foster, John Robert lawyer
Freimark, Robert (Bob Freimark) artist
Halopoff, William Evon industrial designer, consultant

Morongo Valley
Lindley, Judith Morland cat registry administrator

Morro Bay
Eggertsen, Paul Fred psychiatrist
O'Neill, Margaret E. psychological counselor
Wagner, Peter Ewing physics and electrical engineering educator

Moss Landing
Brewer, Peter George ocean geochemist
Clague, David A. geologist
Lange, Lester Henry mathematics educator

Mount Shasta
Heller, Joseph health professional
Mariner, William Martin chiropractor

Mountain View
Andreessen, Marc communications company executive
Barksdale, James Love communications company executive
†Beaudry, Guy G. company executive, lawyer
†Belluzzo, Richard E. computer company executive
Bills, Robert Howard political party executive
Boyd, Dean Weldon management consultant
Casey, Richard L. pharmaceutical executive
Castor, Jon Stuart electronics company executive
Ching, Andy Kwok-yee minister
Clark, Jim communications executive
Clark, Jonathan L. photographer, printer, publisher
Clinton, John Philip Martin communications executive
Craig, Joan Carmen secondary school educator, drama teacher
Crowley, Jerome Joseph, Jr. investment company executive
Cusumano, James Anthony pharmaceutical company executive
de Urioste, George Adolfo, IV software company executive
Di Muccio, Mary-Jo retired librarian
†Duggan, Kevin Charles city manager
Emmons, Victoria Ann hospital administrator, marketing consultant
Feld, Donald H. network consultant
Hamilton, Judith Hall computer company executive
Heffelfinger, David Mark optical engineer
Johnson, Conor Deane mechanical engineer
Karp, Nathan political activist
Klein, Harold Paul microbiologist
Kobza, Dennis Jerome architect
Koo, George Ping Shan business consultant
†Kriens, Scott G. information technology executive
Lee, Murlin E. solutions manager
Loew, Gilda Harris research biophysicist, biology research executive
Maas, Joan Louise training and development consultant
McCormac, Billy Murray physicist, research institution executive, former army officer
Mc Nealy, Scott computer company executive
Michalko, James Paul library association administrator
†Pearl, Samuel N. plastice surgery
Perkins, Nancy Jane industrial designer
Polese, Kim software company executive
Qureishi, A. Salam computer software and services company executive
Savage, Thomas Warren engineering director
†Seidman, Saul William neurology surgeon
Serra, Patricia Janet social services administrator
Smith, Lonnie Max diversified industries executive
Subramanian, Ravi electrical engineer
Warren, Richard Wayne obstetrician and gynecologist
†Watson, Ian telecommunications company executive, investor

Murphys
Moody, Frederick Jerome mechanical engineer, consultant thermal hydraulics

Murrieta
Froelich, Wolfgang Andreas neurologist

Spangler, Lorna Carrie pharmacy technician
Steiling, Daniel Paul retired railroad conductor, writer

Napa
Battisti, Paul Oreste county supervisor
Buchanan, Teri Bailey communications executive
Chiarella, Peter Ralph vintner
Chung, Dae Hyun retired geophysicist
†Dow, Philip Donovan poet, educator
Ervin, Margaret Howie elementary education educator, special education educator
Garnett, William photographer
Hennings, Dorothy Ann financial adviser
Ianziti, Adelbert John industrial designer
Jones, Wayne Ross agronomist
Kuntz, Charles Powers lawyer
Lee, Margaret Anne social worker, psychotherapist
Loar, Peggy Ann foundation administrator
Meredith, Joseph Charlton retired military officer, librarian, tree farmer
Moore, William Joseph retired educator
Norman, Sheri Hanna artist, educator, cartographer
Price, John James, Jr. retired orthopaedic surgeon, forensic reporter
Rada, Alexander university official
Renfrow, Patricia Anne secondary education educator
Sedlock, Joy psychiatric social worker
Smith, Robert Bruce former security consultant, retired career officer
Strock, David Randolph brokerage house executive
Wycoff, Charles Coleman writer, retired anesthesiologist
Zimmermann, John Paul plastic surgeon

National City
Morgan, Jacob Richard cardiologist
Potter, J(effrey) Stewart property manager

Nevada City
†Cassella, Dennis Gene county official

Newark
Ferber, Norman Alan retail executive

Newbury Park
Bleiberg, Leon William surgical podiatrist
Fredericks, Patricia Ann real estate executive
Kocen, Lorraine Ayral accountant
McCune, Sara Miller foundation executive, publisher

Newhall
Heekin, Valerie Anne telecommunications technician

Newman
Carlsen, Janet Haws retired insurance company owner, mayor

Newport Beach
Adams, William Gillette lawyer
Allen, Russell G. lawyer
Anyomi, Samuel Mawuena Kweku business educator
Armstrong, Robert Arnold petroleum company executive
Baskin, Scott David lawyer
Bennett, Bruce W. construction company executive, civil engineer
Bissell, George Arthur architect
Black, William Rea lawyer
Bren, Donald L. real estate company executive
Brown, Giles Tyler history educator, lecturer
Cano, Kristin Maria lawyer
†Cheng, Yuhua electrical engineer
Chihorek, John Paul electronics company executive
†Chong, John Kenneth plastic surgeon
Clark, Thomas P., Jr. lawyer
Cook, Marcy Lynn mathematics educator, consultant
Copenbarger, Lloyd Gaylord lawyer
Cosgrove, Cameron technology executive
Cox, (Charles) Christopher congressman
Crean, John C. retired housing and recreational vehicles manufacturing company executive
Dean, Paul John magazine editor
†de Garcia, Lucia marketing professional
Dovring, Karin Elsa Ingeborg author, poet, playwright, communication analyst
Fawcett, John Scott real estate developer
Frederick, Dolliver H. merchant banker
Garra, Raymond Hamilton, II marketing executive
Gellman, Gloria Gae Seeburger Schick marketing professional
Gerken, Walter Bland insurance company executive
Giannini, Valerio Louis investment banker
Greenfield, James M. fund raiser
Hancock, S. Lee lawyer
Harley, Halvor Larson banker, lawyer
Harris, Brent Richard investment company executive
Hinshaw, Ernest Theodore, Jr. private investor, former Olympics executive, former financial executive
Huffman, John Abram, Jr. minister
Indiek, Victor Henry finance corporation executive
Jacobs, Donald Paul architect
Johnson, Thomas Webber, Jr. lawyer
†Johnson, William S. financial planning company executive, educator
Jones, Roger Wayne electronics executive
Joyce, Stephen Francis human resource executive
Kallman, Burton Jay foods association director
Katayama, Arthur Shoji lawyer
Kenney, William John, Jr. real estate development executive
Kienitz, LaDonna Trapp city librarian, city official
Knobbe, Louis Joseph lawyer
Kraus, John Walter former aerospace engineering company executive
†Laidlaw, Victor D. construction executive
Lawson, Thomas Cheney fraud examiner
†Lee, Christopher Michael information technology specialist
Lipson, Melvin Alan technology and business management consultant
Logan, April Charise lawyer
Mallory, Frank Linus lawyer
Mandel, Maurice, II lawyer, educator
Marcoux, Carl Henry former insurance executive, writer, historian
Mayfield, Lori Jayne marketing professional
McClune, Michael Marlyn real estate executive
McCue, Dennis Michael management consultant
McEvers, Duff Steven lawyer
McGee, James Francis lawyer
McMahon, Brian publishing executive
Millar, Richard William, Jr. lawyer
Mink, Maxine Mock real estate executive
Morisseau, Nan Kruger television personality
†Nitta, Katharine plastic surgeon
Pepe, Stephen Phillip lawyer
Phillips, Layn R. lawyer
Poole, Thomas Richard endowment capital campaign director, fund raising counsel
Randolph, Steven insurance and estate planner
Richardson, Walter John architect
Robinson, Hurley surgeon
Rogers, Robert Reed manufacturing company executive
Rooklidge, William Charles lawyer
Schnapp, Roger Herbert lawyer
Shamoun, John Milam plastic surgeon
Sharbaugh, W(illiam) James plastics engineer, consultant
Shonk, Albert Davenport, Jr. advertising executive
Spisak, John Francis environmental company executive
Spitz, Barbara Salomon artist
Stephens, Michael Dean hospital administrator
Sutton, Thomas C. insurance company executive
Thorp, Edward Oakley investment management company executive
Toren, Mark state official, econometrician
Tow, Marc Raymond lawyer, real estate investor
Van Mols, Brian publishing executive
Wagner, John Leo lawyer, former magistrate judge
Weber, Mark Edward editor, historian
†Wendt, James Robert plastic surgeon
Wentworth, Diana von Welanetz author
Wentworth, Theodore Sumner lawyer
Whittemore, Paul Baxter psychologist
Wolf, Alan Steven lawyer
Wood, George H. investment executive
Wyatt, Brett Michael secondary school educator
Zalta, Edward otorhinolaryngologist, physician

Newport Coast
Pavony, William H. retail executive, consultant
Swan, Peer Alden scientific company executive, bank director

North Fork
Flanagan, James Henry, Jr. lawyer

North Highlands
Hope, Gerri Danette telecommunications management executive

North Hills
Boeckmann, H. F. automotive executive
Tomko, Regina Jacqueline nurse practitioner

North Hollywood
Baker, Rick make-up artist
Balmuth, Bernard Allen retired film editor
Boulanger, Donald Richard financial services executive
Chang, Wung researcher, lecturer, business advisor
Diller, Phyllis actress, author
Feola, Louis broadcast executive
Grasso, Mary Ann theater association executive
Horowitz, Zachary I. entertainment company executive
Jaeger, Sharon Ann chiropractor
Knoll, William Lee animation director
Koran, Dennis Howard publisher
Kuter, Kay E. writer, actor
Lindheim, Richard David television company executive
McMartin, John actor
Neill, Ve make-up artist
Null, Thomas Blanton recording producer
Patterson, James Franklyn physics educator
Powell, Stephanie visual effects director, supervisor
Powers, Melvin publishing executive
Reynolds, Debbie (Mary Frances Reynolds) actress
Schlosser, Anne Griffin librarian
Schultz, Phyllis May financial property manager
Smothers, Dick actor, singer
Smothers, Tom actor, singer
Walker, Mallory Elton tenor
Wannebo, Ode religious organization executive, opera-concert singer, educator
†Warzel, Peter international entertainment company consultant
Woyt, James Charles (Jim Woyt) actor

Northridge
Bassler, Robert Covey artist, educator
Bradshaw, Richard Rotherwood engineering executive
†Bregen, Louis music professional
Chen, Joseph Tao historian, educator
Curzon, Susan Carol university administrator
Dart, John Seward journalist, author
dePaolis, Potito Umberto food company executive
†Douglas, Crerar religious studies educator
Falk, Heinrich Richard theater and humanities educator
Flores, William Vincent Latin American studies educator
†Hall, Donald E. English educator
Harwick, Betty Corinne Burns sociology educator
Kiddoo, Robert James engineering service company executive
Logan, Lee Robert orthodontist
Matsumoto, Shigemi opera soprano, voice educator
Paulson, Nancy Lee health facility consultant
Ruley, Stanley Eugene cost analyst
†Shaw, Victor N. educator
Stout, Thomas Melville control systems engineer
Stratton, Gregory Alexander computer specialist, administrator, mayor
Syms, Helen Maksym educational administrator
Tanis, Norman Earl retired university dean, library expert
Torgow, Eugene N. electrical engineer
Watson, Julia women's studies and liberal studies educator
Weatherup, Wendy Gaines graphic designer, writer
†Yasuda, Roderick K. cardiothoracic surgeon

Norwalk
Armstrong, David Ligon psychiatrist

Novato
Danse, Ilene Homnick Raisfeld physician, educator, toxicologist
†Fraser, Margot consumer products company executive
Leaton, Marcella Kay insurance representative, business owner
Lewin, Werner Siegfried, Jr. lawyer
†Morrissey, Michael Patrick educational research consultant, educator
Patterson, W. Morgan college president
Pfeiffer, Phyllis Kramer publishing executive
Simon, Lee Will astronomer
†White, Linda Lee Locy secondary educator

Oak Park
Connolly, Thomas Edmund educator

Oakhurst
Bonham, Clifford Vernon retired social work educator
Cantwell, Christopher William artist
Carlin, Sidney Alan music publisher, arranger

Oakland
Alba, Benny artist
Alford, Joan Franz entrepreneur
Allen, Jeffrey Michael lawyer
Anderson, Brother Mel academic administrator
Anderson, Robert Thomas anthropologist, researcher, physician
Anthony, Elaine Margaret real estate executive, interior designer
Armstrong, Saundra Brown federal judge
Atkinson, Richard Chatham university president
Barlow, William Pusey, Jr. accountant
Beasley, Bruce Miller sculptor
Benham, Priscilla Carla religion educator, college president
Bjork, Robert David, Jr. lawyer
Bogues, Tyrone Curtis (Muggsy Bogues) professional basketball player
Bowman, Alison Frances writer
†Brazil, Wayne D. federal judge
†Brevetti, Francine Clelia journalist
Brewster, Andrea B. artist
†Brown, Edmund Gerald, Jr. (Jerry Brown) mayor, former governor
Brown, Stephen Lawrence environmental consultant
Brust, David physicist
Burdick, Claude Owen pathologist
Burnison, Boyd Edward lawyer
Burt, Christopher Clinton publisher
Carlesimo, P. J. (Peter J. Carlesimo) professional basketball coach
Caulfield, W. Harry health care industry executive, physician
Cherry, Lee Otis scientific institute administrator
Ching, Eric San Hing health care and insurance administrator
Christopher, L. Carol communication researcher, freelance writer
Cohan, Christopher professional sports team executive
Collen, Morris Frank physician
Collins, James Francis toxicologist
Conway, Nancy Ann editor
Crane, Robert Meredith health care executive
Crocker, Joy Laksmi concert pianist and organist, composer
Crowley, Thomas B., Jr. water transportation executive
Cummins, John Stephen bishop
Cushman, Karen Lipski writer
Dailey, Garrett Clark publisher, lawyer
DeFazio, Lynette Stevens dancer, choreographer, educator, chiropractor, author, actress, musician
De Ford, Douglas Atmetlla biochemical, biomechanical and industrial engineer
Deming, Willis Riley lawyer
De Vos, George Alphonse psychologist, anthropologist
Diaz, Sharon education administrator
Drexel, Baron Jerome lawyer
DuMont, Virginia Peterson educator, writer
Earle, Sylvia Alice research biologist, oceanographer
Eckbo, Garrett landscape architect, urban designer
Elgin, Gita psychologist
Elliott, Jack folk musician
Erlich, Reese William journalist
Farrell, Kenneth Royden economist
Firoozabady, Ebrahim plant scientist
Foley, Jack (John Wayne Harold Foley) poet, writer, editor
Frey, Viola sculptor, educator
Fries, Lita Linda school system administrator
Gaus, Clifton R. healthcare executive
Goldstine, Stephen Joseph college administrator
Gomes, Wayne Reginald academic administrator
Gonzalez, Arthur Padilla artist, educator
Gordon, David Jamieson tenor
Griego, Elizabeth Brownlee college dean
Griffin, Betty Jo elementary school educator
Haiman, Franklyn Saul author, communications educator
†Hamer, Forrest Michael psychologist
Hancock, Nannette Beatrice Finley mental health educator, consultant
Harper, Rob March artist, educator
Harpster, Robert Eugene engineering geologist
Haskell, Arthur Jacob retired steamship company executive
†Hawkins, Robert B. think tank executive
Helvey, Julius Louis, II finance company executive
Heydman, Abby Maria dean
Heywood, Robert Gilmour lawyer
Hoffman, George Alan consulting company executive
†Hofman, Ken professional sports team executive
Howard, Bradford Reuel travel company executive
Howe, Art (Arthur Henry Howe, Jr.) professional baseball manager
†Jellen, Edward D. federal judge
Jensen, D. Lowell federal judge, lawyer, government official
Johnson, Kenneth F. lawyer
Jukes, Thomas Hughes biological chemist, educator
Kelso, David William fine arts publishing executive, artist
Killebrew, Ellen Jane (Mrs. Edward S. Graves) cardiologist
King, Cary Judson, III chemical engineer, educator, university official
Kint, Arne Tonis industrial engineer, mechanical engineer
Koplin, Donald Leroy health products executive, consumer advocate
Lawrence, David M. health facility administrator
Lepowsky, William Leonard mathematics and statistics educator
Leslie, Robert Lorne lawyer
Levine, Marilyn Anne artist
Linford, Rulon Kesler physicist, engineer
Long, William Joseph software engineer
Lubliner, Irving mathematics educator, consultant
Lusby, Grace Irene infection control nurse practitioner
MacKay, Nancy librarian, oral historian
Macmeeken, John Peebles foundation executive, educator
Madabhushi, Govindachari Venkata retired civil engineer
Matsumoto, George architect
Mayers, Eugene David philosopher, educator
McCarthy, Steven Michael lawyer
†McCloskey, Mark educator
McKinney, Judson Thad broadcast executive
Melchert, James Frederick artist
Mendelson, Steven Earle lawyer
Mikalow, Alfred Alexander, II deep sea diver, marine surveyor, marine diving consultant
Miller, Barry research administrator, psychologist
Miller, Kirk Edward lawyer, health foundation executive
Miller, Thomas Robbins lawyer, publisher
Musgrove, George city official
Musihin, Konstantin K. electrical engineer
Narell, Irena freelance writer, history educator
Nathan, Laura E. sociology educator
Nebelkopf, Ethan psychologist
Newsome, Randall Jackson judge
Ng, Lawrence Ming-Loy pediatrician
Nicol, Robert Duncan architect
Oberti, Sylvia Marie Antoinette rehabilitation counselor and administrator, career advisor, textile consultant
O'Connor, Paul Daniel lawyer
O'Hara, Delia Iglauer family nurse practitioner
Parrott, Joel zoo director
Patten, Bebe Harrison minister, chancellor
Patton, Roger William lawyer, educator
Patton, Warren Andre public relations executive, journalist
Perlmutter, Martin Lee interactive media producer, recruiter, consultant, writer
†Phillips, Keith Anthony (Tony) professional baseball player
Pister, Karl Stark engineering educator
Potash, Jeremy Warner public relations executive
Potash, Stephen Jon public relations executive
Power, Dennis Michael museum director
Quinby, William Albert lawyer, mediator, arbitrator
Raines, Timothy professional baseball player
Randisi, Elaine Marie accountant, educator, writer
Randle, Ellen Eugenia Foster opera and classical singer, educator
Rath, Alan T. sculptor
Reynolds, Kathleen Diane Foy (KDF Reynolds) transportation executive
Rhein, Timothy J. transportation company executive
St. Jean, Garry professional basketball coach
Samuels, Joseph, Jr. police chief
Saunders, Ward Bishop, Jr. retired aluminum company executive
Schacht, Henry Mevis writer, consultant
Schomer, Howard retired clergyman, educator, social policy consultant
†Schott, Stephen C. professional sports team executive
Schrag, Peter editor, writer
†Serin, Judith Ann English educator
Sharpton, Thomas physician
†Sheridan, John Lucas artist, art consultant
Sidney, William Wright retired aerospace company executive
Silverberg, Robert author
Skaff, Andrew Joseph lawyer, public utilities, energy and transportation executive
Solomon, Norman author, columnist
Spitzer, Matthew L. retired retail store executive
†Starks, John Levell professional basketball player
Stewart, John Lincoln university administrator
Stromme, Gary L. law librarian
Sullivan, G. Craig household products executive
†Tchaikovsky, Leslie J. bankruptcy judge
Thompson Stanley, Trina lawyer
Tomlinson-Keasey, Carol Ann university administrator
Tran, Nguyet T. accountant
Tsztoo, David Fong civil engineer
Tyndall, David Gordon business educator
Vallerga, Bernard A. engineering administrator
Wade, Bill airport executive
Wallace, Elaine Wendy lawyer
Wallis, Eric G. lawyer
Warrick, Brooke marketing executive
Wendlinger, Robert Matthew communications and memory consultant
Whitsel, Richard Harry biologist, entomologist
Wilken, Claudia judge
Winslow, Thomas Scudder, III naval architect, marine consultant
Wong, Ivan Gynmun seismologist
Wood, James Michael lawyer
Wood, Larry (Mary Laird) journalist, author, university educator, public relations executive, environmental consultant
Zelmanowitz, Julius Martin mathematics educator, university administrator

Occidental
Rumsey, Victor Henry electrical engineering educator emeritus

Oceanside
†Aponte, Jose A. library director
Asato, Susan Pearce business executive, educator
Burney, Victoria Kalgaard corporate business executive, consultant, civic worker
Clark, Arthur Bryan engineer
Curtin, Thomas Lee ophthalmologist
Delienne, Jacquelyn E. e-commerce developer and publisher, management consultant, electronic comme
Garfin, Louis actuary
Garruto, John Anthony cosmetics executive
Haley, Thomas John retired pharmacologist
Hertweck, Alma Louise sociology and child development educator
Hertweck, E. Romayne psychology educator
Howard, Robert Staples newspaper publisher
Humphrey, Phyllis A. writer
Jones, Barbara Dean substance abuse counselor
L'Annunziata, Michael Frank chemist, consultant
Lyon, Richard mayor, retired naval officer
Peck, Paul Lachlan minister
Pena, Maria Geges academic services administrator
Roberts, James McGregor retired professional association executive

Rosier, David Lewis investment banker
Sarkisian, Pamela Outlaw artist
Stewart, Kenneth Malcolm retired anthropologist, researcher
Swoger, James Wesley magician
Taverna, Rodney Elward financial services company executive

Oildale
Gallagher, Joseph Francis marketing executive

Ojai
Paxton, Glenn Gilbert composer
Weill, Samuel, Jr. automobile company executive
Weyl, Nathaniel writer

Ontario
Ariss, David William, Sr. real estate developer, consultant
Bernard, Alexander airport police official
Carlson, Ralph William, Jr. food products company executive
Coney, Carole Anne accountant
Dastrup-Hamill, Faye Myers city official
†Drinkwater, Peter L. airport executive
†Evans, Daniel Joseph journalist
Hull, Jane Laurel Leek retired nurse, administrator
Johnson, Maurice Verner, Jr. agricultural research and development executive
Kahn, Mario Santamaria international marketing executive
Kennedy, Mark Alan middle and secondary school educator
†McAfee, I. Paul, III editor
Peters, Jacqueline Mary secondary education educator
Wagner, Rob Leicester newspaper editor, writer
Wright, Charles Lee information systems consultant

Orange
Achauer, Bruce Michael plastic surgeon
Andrews, Charles wholesale distribution executive
Anzel, Sanford Harold orthopedic surgeon
Armentrout, Steven Alexander oncologist
Barr, Ronald Jeffrey dermatologist, pathologist
Batchelor, James Kent lawyer
Becker, Juliette psychologist, marriage and family therapist
Berk, Jack Edward physician, educator
Brown, Tod David bishop
Buhler, Richard Gerhard minister
Crumley, Roger Lee surgeon, educator
DiSaia, Philip John gynecologist, obstetrician, radiology educator
Doti, James L. academic administrator
Eagan, Robert T. oncologist
Fisher, Mark Jay neurologist, neuroscientist, educator
Fisk, Edward Ray retired civil engineer, author, educator
Fletcher, James Allen video company executive
†Foltz, Eldon Lercy neurosurgeon, educator
Furnas, David William plastic surgeon
Gardin, Julius Markus cardiologist, educator
Godeke, Raymond Dwight insurance company executive, accountant
Hamilton, Harry Lemuel, Jr. academic administrator
Kathol, Anthony Louis finance executive
Kim, Moon Hyun physician, educator
Korb, Lawrence John metallurgist
Lindskoog, Kathryn Ann writer, educator
Lott, Ira Totz pediatric neurologist
Luck, Kenneth Leverett healthcare executive, author
MacArthur, Carol Jeanne pediatric otolaryngology educator
Maier, John Mark organizational leadership educator
Mc Farland, Norman Francis bishop
Miller, Jay Anthony minister
Monsees, James Eugene engineering executive, consultant
Morgan, Beverly Carver physician, educator
Mosier, Harry David, Jr. physician, educator
Roden, Donald R. medical products executive
Rowen, Marshall radiologist
†Sawdei, Milan A. lawyer
Smith, Jack Daryl accountant, stockbroker
Starr, Richard William retired banker
Talbott, George Robert physicist, mathematician, educator
Thompson, William Benbow, Jr. obstetrician, gynecologist, educator
Underwood, Vernon O., Jr. grocery stores executive
Vatcher, James Gordon retired physician
Vaziri, Nosratola Dabir internist, nephrologist, educator
Vice, Charles Loren electromechanical engineer
Wilson, Archie Fredric medical educator
Yeager, Myron Dean English language educator, business writing consultant
Yu, Jen medical educator
Zweifel, Donald Edwin editor, civic affairs volunteer, consultant

Orangevale
Webb, Andrew Howard minister

Orinda
Bach, Martin Wayne stockbroker, owner antique clock stores
Baker, Don Robert chemist, inventor
Berens, E. Ann writer, mental health and youth advocate
Dorn, Virginia Alice artist, art gallery director
Epperson, Stella Marie artist
Fisher, Robert Morton foundation administrator, university administrator
Gilbert, Jerome B. consulting environmental engineer
Glasser, Charles Edward university president
Heftmann, Erich biochemist
Rosenberg, Barr Marvin investment advisor, economist
Somerset, Harold Richard retired business executive
Spraings, Violet Evelyn psychologist
Welch, Thomas Andrew retired lawyer, arbitrator
Woolsey, David Arthur leasing company executive

Oroville
Shelton, Joel Edward clinical psychologist
Tamori, David Isamu secondary education educator

Oxnard
Dimitriadis, Andre C. health care executive
Gay, Marilyn Fanelli Martin television producer, talk show hostess
Hamm, George Ardeil retired secondary education educator, hypnotherapist, consultant
Harrower, Thomas Murray electro-mechanical design engineer
Hayashi, Alan T. mathematics educator
Herrera, Sandra Johnson school system administrator
Niesluchowski, Witold S. cardiovascular and thoracic surgeon
O'Connell, Hugh Mellen, Jr. retired architect
O'Hearn, Michael John lawyer
Oncken, Ellen Lorraine minister, speaker
Poole, Henry Joe, Jr. business executive
Snasdell, Susan Kathleen computer company executive
Sweet, Harvey theatrical, scenic and lighting designer
Takasugi, Nao state official, business developer
Woodworth, Stephen Davis investment banker
Zigman, Paul Edmond environmental consultant, executive

Pacific Grove
Adams, Margaret Bernice retired museum official
Bailey, Stephen Fairchild museum director and curator, ornithologist
Davis, Robert Edward retired communication educator
Eadie, Margaret L. educational and career consultant
Epel, David biologist, educator
Fleischman, Paul children's author
Wangberg, Elaine Gregory university administrator

Pacific Palisades
Abrams, Richard Lee physicist
Abzug, Malcolm flight mechanics engineer
Albert, Eddie (Edward Albert Heimberger) actor
†Anwyl-Davies, Marcus John judge, arbitrator
Cale, Charles Griffin lawyer, investor
Chesney, Lee Roy, Jr. artist
Claes, Daniel John physician
Csendes, Ernest chemist, corporate and financial executive
Dean, Ronald Glenn lawyer
Diehl, Richard Kurth retail business consultant
Dignam, Robert Joseph retired orthopaedic surgeon
Fabray, Nanette actress
Fisher, Frances actress
Flattery, Thomas Long lawyer, legal administrator
Garwood, Victor Paul retired speech communication educator
Georges, Robert Augustus emeritus professor, researcher, writer
Greene, Warren W. anesthesiologist
†Grimstad, Kirsten Julia educator
Hadges, Thomas Richard media consultant
Hagenbuch, Rodney Dale stock brokerage house executive
Herman, Elvin E. retired consulting electronic engineer
Holman, Bill composer
Hooley, James Robert oral and maxillofacial surgeon, educator, dean
Jennings, Marcella Grady rancher, investor
†Kirkgaard, Valerie Anne writer, producer, consultant
Klein, Joseph Mark retired mining company executive
Lagle, John Franklin lawyer
Longaker, Richard Pancoast political science educator emeritus
McGinn, James Thomas writer, producer
Middleton, James Arthur oil and gas company executive
Mulryan, Henry Trist mineral company executive, consultant
Nash, Gary Baring historian, educator
Pitkin, Roy Macbeth editor
Price, Frank motion picture and television company executive
Purcell, Patrick B. consultant
Rothenberg, Leslie Steven lawyer, ethicist
†Sasaki, John Eric art company executive
Schwartz, Murray Louis lawyer, educator, academic administrator
Sevilla, Stanley lawyer
Zivelonghi, Kurt Daniel computer graphics artist, art director, designer

Pacoima
†Buzzetti, George Howard small business owner, chemical miller

Palm Desert
Ayling, Henry Faithful writer, editor, consultant
Bowlin, Eve Sallee retired ob-gyn nurse practioner
Chambers, Milton Warren architect
Crider, Jeffrey John public relations executive
Godfrey, Alden Newell communications educator
Gullander, Werner Paul retired consultant, retired corporate executive
Hannon, Violet Marie surgical nurse
Hester, Gerald LeRoy retired school system administrator
Hoffmann, Joan Carol retired academic dean
Kaufman, Charlotte King artist, retired educational administrator
Kern, Paul Alfred advertising company executive, research consultant, realtor, financial analyst
Krallinger, Joseph Charles entrepreneur, business advisor, author
McKissock, Paul Kendrick plastic surgeon
Moroles, Jesus Bautista sculptor
Morrison, Robert Thomas aerospace engineering and marketing consultant
Osborne, Bartley Porter, Jr. aeronautical engineer
Ponder, Catherine clergywoman
Ryan, Allyn Cauagas author, educator
Sausman, Karen zoological park administrator
Sexson, Stephen Bruce educational writer, educator
Singer, Gerald Michael lawyer, educator, author, arbitrator and mediator
Spirtos, Nicholas George lawyer, financial company executive
Wiedle, Gary Eugene real estate management company executive

Palm Springs
Arnold, Stanley Norman manufacturing consultant
Boyajian, Timothy Edward public health officer, educator, consultant
Browning, Norma Lee (Mrs. Russell Joyner Ogg) journalist
FitzGerald, John Edward, III lawyer
Gill, Jo Anne Martha middle school educator
Hartman, Rosemary Jane special education educator
Hearst, Rosalie philanthropist, foundation executive
Jamison, Warren writer, lecturer, publisher
Jones, Milton Wakefield publisher
Jumonville, Felix Joseph, Jr. physical education educator, realtor
Kimberling, John Farrell retired lawyer
Lougheed, Arthur Lawrence investment advisor, tax and pension consultant
Loya, Ranaldo senior physician assistant
Lunde, Donald Theodore physician
Mann, Zane Boyd editor, publisher
Maree, Wendy painter, sculptor
Minahan, John English author
Owings, Thalia Kelley elementary school educator
Satcher, Clement Michael Art education educator
Seale, Robert McMillan office services company executive
Weil, Max Harry physician, medical educator, medical scientist

Palmdale
Anderson, R(obert) Gregg real estate company executive
Hummer-Sharpe, Elizabeth Anastasia genealogist, writer
Luther, Amanda Lisa producer
Moore, Everett LeRoy library administrator
Moule, William Nelson electrical engineer
Reichman, Dawn Leslie lawyer, educator, deputy sheriff
Smith, Maureen McBride laboratory administrator

Palo Alto
Allen, Louis Alexander management consultant
Allen, Vicky sales and marketing professional
Amylon, Michael David physician, educator
Andersen, Torben Brender optical researcher, astronomer, software engineer
Anderson, Charles Arthur former research institute administrator
Bagshaw, Malcolm A. radiation oncologist, educator
Balzhiser, Richard Earl research and development company executive
Bensch, Klaus George pathology educator
Beretta, Giordano Bruno computer scientist, researcher
Berg, Olena investment company executive, former federal official
Bohrnstedt, George William educational researcher
Bolitho, Louise Greer educational administrator, consultant
Botstein, David geneticist, educator
Bradley, Donald Edward lawyer
Breiner, Sheldon geophysics educator, business executive
Breyer, James William venture capitalist
Briggs, Winslow Russell plant biologist, educator
Brigham, Samuel Townsend Jack, III lawyer
†Briskin, Mae writer
Britton, M(elvin) C(reed), Jr. physician, rheumatologist
Brown, David Randolph electrical engineer
Brown, Robert McAfee minister, religion educator
Case, Robbie education educator, author
Chase, Robert Arthur surgeon, educator
Chen, Stephen Shi-hua pathologist, biochemist
Chow, Winston engineering research executive
Climan, Richard Elliot lawyer
Cohen, Karl Paley nuclear energy consultant
Colligan, John C. (Bud Colligan) multimedia company executive
Cooke, John P. cardiologist, medical educator, medical researcher
Cotsakos, Christos Michael internet financial services company executive
Cutler, Leonard Samuel physicist
Dafoe, Donald Cameron surgeon, educator
†Daniels, Keith Allen materials engineering manager
Date, Elaine Satomi physician
Datlowe, Dayton Wood space scientist, physicist
Davis, Glenn communications company executive
DeLustro, Frank Anthony biomedical company executive, research immunologist
Dement, William Charles sleep researcher, medical educator
Desai, Kavin Hirendra pediatrician
Diffie, Whitfield computer and communications engineer
Donaldson, Sarah Susan radiologist
Donnally, Robert Andrew lawyer, real estate broker
Early, James Michael electronics research consultant
Eggers, Alfred John, Jr. research corporation executive
Eisenstat, Benjamin artist
Eitner, Lorenz Edwin Alfred art historian, educator
Eleccion, Marcelino security executive, computer consultant, music consultant, editor, writer, lecturer, artist
Eng, Lawrence Fook biochemistry educator, neurochemist
Ernst, Wallace Gary geology educator
Eulau, Heinz political scientist, educator
Fann, James Ilin cardiothoracic surgeon
Farber, Eugene Mark psoriasis research institute administrator
Farquhar, John William physician, educator
Ferrell, Mark Stephen flight nurse
Flanagan, Robert Joseph economics educator
Flory, Curt Alan research physicist
Forbes, Alfred Dean religious studies researcher, biomedical consultant
Fox, Lorraine Susan marketing professional
Fried, Louis Lester information technology and management consultant
Fries, James Franklin internal medicine educator
Fujitani, Martin Tomio software quality engineer
Furbush, David Malcolm lawyer
Garland, Harry Thomas research administrator
Gliner, Erast Boris theoretical physicist
Goff, Harry Russell retired manufacturing company executive
Goldstein, Avram pharmacology educator
Goldstein, Mary Kane physician
Gouraud, Jackson S. energy company executive
Grubb, William Francis X. consumer software executive, marketing executive
Haisch, Bernhard Michael astronomer
Halperin, Robert Milton retired electrical machinery company executive
Hamilton, David Mike publishing company executive
†Hamilton, Joe executive
Harris, Edward D., Jr. physician
Haslam, Robert Thomas, III lawyer
Hays, Marguerite Thompson physician
Hecht, Lee software company executive
Hellyer, Constance Anne (Connie Anne Conway) writer, musician
Herrick, Tracy Grant fiduciary
Hewlett, William (Redington) manufacturing company executive, electrical engineer
Hodge, Philip Gibson, Jr. mechanical and aerospace engineering educator
Holman, Halsted Reid medical educator
Hubert, Helen Betty epidemiologist
Jamison, Rex Lindsay medical educator
Jamplis, Robert Warren surgeon, medical foundation executive
Johnson, Horace Richard electronics company executive
Johnson, Noble Marshall research scientist
Joy, Bill computer company executive
Kelley, Robert Suma systems engineer
Kelly, Charles Eugene, II gastroenterologist, researcher
Kelsey, Edith Jeanine psychotherapist, consultant
Kennedy, W(ilbert) Keith, Jr. electronics company executive
Kiser, Stephen artist, educator
Klotsche, John Chester lawyer
Kohler, Fred Christopher tax specialist
Kolarov, Krasimir Dobromirov computer scientist, researcher
Koomen, Cornelis Jan telecommunications, micro and consumer electronics executive
Kott, Joseph transportation executive, consultant, educator
Kung, Frank F. biotechnology and life sciences venture capital investor
Lamport, Leslie B. computer scientist
Lane, Alfred Thomas medical educator
Lane, William Kenneth physician
Lau, John Hon Shing manufacturing executive
Laurie, Ronald Sheldon lawyer
Lender, Adam electrical engineer
Lesser, Henry lawyer
Levinson, Kathy multimedia executive
†Levitin, Daniel Joseph cognitive science researcher, journalist
Linna, Timo Juhani immunologist, researcher, educator
Litt, Iris Figarsky pediatrics educator
Lo, Yee On composer
Loewenstein, Walter Bernard nuclear power technologist
London, A(lexander) L(ouis) retired mechanical engineering educator
Loveless, Edward Eugene education educator, musician
Maffly, Roy Herrick medical educator, retired
Mahmood, Aamer computer system architect
Mansour, Tag Eldin pharmacologist, educator
Mario, Ernest pharmaceutical company executive
Markkula, A. C., Jr. entrepreneur, computer company executive
Martin, Roger John computer scientist
Massey, Henry P., Jr. lawyer
McCluskey, Lois Thornhill photographer
McHugh, Stuart Lawrence research scientist
Mendelson, Alan Charles lawyer
Michie, Sara H. pathologist, educator
Miller, Michael Patiky lawyer
Moffitt, Donald Eugene transportation company executive
Mommsen, Katharina retired German language and literature educator
Moretti, August Joseph lawyer
Nau, Charles John lawyer
Neil, Gary Lawrence pharmaceutical company research executive, biochemical pharmacologist
Nopar, Alan Scott lawyer
Nordlund, Donald Craig corporate lawyer
Nycum, Susan Hubbell lawyer
Oki, Brian Masao software engineer
O'Rourke, C. Larry lawyer
Oshman, M. Kenneth computer company executive
Panofsky, Wolfgang Kurt Hermann physicist, educator
Parker, Thomas G. educator
Pasahow, Lynn H(arold) lawyer
Patterson, Robert Edward lawyer
Perlman, Steve multimedia broadcast executive
Phair, Joseph Baschon lawyer
Pierce, John Robinson electrical engineer, educator
Polan, Mary Lake obstetrics and gynecology educator
Pooley, James lawyer, author
Quate, Calvin Forrest engineering educator
Quraishi, Marghoob A. management consultant
Ragan, Charles Ransom lawyer
Rejman, Diane Louise manufacturing systems applications analyst
Rheingold, Howard multimedia executive
Rich, Lesley Mosher artist
Rinsky, Arthur C. lawyer
Roberts, Lawrence Gilman telecommunications company executive
Rosaldo, Renato Ignacio, Jr. cultural anthropology educator
Rulifson, Johns Frederick computer company executive, computer scientist
Salvatierra, Oscar, Jr. transplant surgeon, urologist, educator
Sanders, William John research scientist
Sawyer, Wilbur Henderson pharmacologist, educator
Saxena, Arjun Nath physicist
Schreiber, Everett Charles, Jr. chemist, educator
Schrier, Stanley Leonard physician, educator
Schurman, David Jay orthopedic surgeon, educator
Scitovsky, Anne Aickelin economist
Scoledes, Aristotle Georgius Michale retired science and technology educator, research consultant
Seethaler, William Charles international business executive, consultant
Shelton, Robert Charles electrical engineer
Shuer, Lawrence Mendel neurosurgery educator
Skeff, Kelley Michael health facility administrator
Small, Jonathan Andrew lawyer
Smith, Glenn A. lawyer
Smith, Pamela Iris consulting company executive
Spira-Solomon, Darlene Joy industrial chemist, researcher, department manager
Staprans, Armand electronics executive
Strober, Samuel immunologist, educator
Szczerba, Victor Bogdan electrical engineer, sales engineer
Taimuty, Samuel Isaac physicist
Taylor, John Joseph nuclear engineer
Theeuwes, Felix physical chemist
Thom, David Hinton family physician, medical educator
Tiffany, Joseph Raymond, II lawyer
Tsien, Richard Winyu biology educator
Tune, Bruce Malcolm pediatrics educator, renal toxicologist
Urquhart, John medical researcher, educator

Van Atta, David Murray *lawyer*
Van Derveer, Tara *university athletic coach*
Varney, Robert Nathan *retired physicist, researcher*
Walker, Ann Yvonne *lawyer*
Walker, Carolyn Peyton *English language educator*
Waller, Peter William *public affairs executive*
Watkins, Dean Allen *electronics executive, educator*
Weakland, Anna Wu *artist, art educator*
Weng, Wen-Kai *physician, medical researcher*
Wheeler, Raymond Louis *lawyer*
†Whitfield, Roy A. *pharmaceutical executive*
Winkleby, Marilyn A. *medical researcher*
Wohlmut, Thomas Arthur *communications executive*
Wolf, Christopher Robin *biotechnology executive*
Wong, Y(ing) Wood *real estate investment company executive, venture capital investment company executive*
Youngdahl, Paul Frederick *mechanical engineer*
Zarins, Christopher Kristaps *surgery educator, vascular surgeon*

Palomar Mountain
Day, Richard Somers *author, editorial consultant*

Palos Verdes Estates
Basnight, Arvin Odell *public administrator, aviation consultant*
Benson, Francis M. *production engineer, radio producer*
Fischer, Robert Blanchard *university administrator, researcher*
Friesz, Mary Lee *poet, self-employed*
Hara, Tadao *educational administrator*
Hughs, Mary Geraldine *accountant, social service specialist*
Joshi, Satish Devdas *organic chemist*
Lazzaro, Anthony Derek *university administrator*
Mackenbach, Frederick W. *welding products manufacturing company executive*
Manning, Christopher Ashley *finance educator, consultant*
Mennis, Edmund Addi *investment management consultant*
Paulikas, George Algis *retired physicist*
Smith, Stephen Randolph *aerospace executive*
Sun, Teresa Chi-Ching *foreign languages and literature educator*
Toftness, Cecil Gillman *lawyer, consultant*
Wisdom, William Russell *radiologist*

Palos Verdes Peninsula
Barab, Marvin *financial consultant*
Baxter, Betty Carpenter *educational administrator*
Christie, Hans Frederick *retired utility company subsidiaries executive, consultant*
Copeland, Phillips Jerome *former academic administrator, former air force officer*
Cubillos, Robert Hernan *church administrator, philosophy educator*
Denke, Paul Herman *aircraft engineer*
Frassinelli, Guido Joseph *retired aerospace engineer*
Gaines, Jerry Lee *secondary education educator*
Giles, Allen *pianist, composer, music educator*
Grant, Robert Ulysses *retired manufacturing company executive*
Haynes, Moses Alfred *physician*
King, Nancy *communications educator*
Leone, William Charles *retired manufacturing executive*
Lima, Luis Eduardo *tenor*
Lorenz, Cynthia *gerontology, cardiology nurse*
Lowi, Alvin, Jr. *mechanical engineer, consultant*
Mirels, Harold *aerospace engineer*
Pfund, Edward Theodore, Jr. *electronics company executive*
Rechtin, Eberhardt *retired aerospace executive, retired educator*
Seide, Paul *civil engineering educator*
Slayden, James Bragdon *retired department store executive*
Slusser, Robert Wyman *aerospace company executive*
Spinks, John Lee *retired engineering executive*
Thomas, Claudewell Sidney *psychiatry educator*
Thomas, Hayward *manufacturing company executive*
Wang, Tony Kar-Hung *automotive and aerospace company executive*
Weiss, Herbert Klemm *retired aeronautical engineer*
Wilson, Theodore Henry *retired electronics company executive, aerospace engineer*
Yeomans, Russell Allen *lawyer, translator*

Panorama City
Curtis, Rosanne Jeanne *medical facility administrator*
Henrickson, Mark *social worker, priest*
Loudon, Craig Michael *video specialist*

Paradise
Fulton, Len *publisher*
†Haws, Hale Louis *medical consultant*
Learned, Vincent Roy *electrical engineer , educator*
†Likley, Katherine *retail executive*
Livesay, Linda Lee Kell *geriatrics nurse, nursing administrator*
Wilder, James D. *geology and mining administrator*

Paramount
Cohn, Lawrence Steven *physician, educator*

Pasadena
Abelson, John Norman *biology educator*
Adams, Elaine *art agent, publicist, writer*
Ahrens, Thomas J. *geophysicist*
Albee, Arden Leroy *geologist, educator*
Albert, Sidney Paul *philosophy and drama educator*
Allen, Clarence Roderic *geologist, educator*
Ammirato, Vincent Anthony *lawyer*
Anderson, Don Lynn *geophysicist, educator*
Arnott, Robert Douglas *investment company executive*
Arrieta, Marcia *poet, editor, publishing executive, educator*
Ashley-Farrand, Margalo *lawyer, mediator, private judge*
Axelson, Charles Frederic *retired accounting educator*
Bakaly, Charles George, Jr. *lawyer, mediator*
Baldeschwieler, John Dickson *chemist, educator*
Baltimore, David *academic administrator, microbiologist, educator*
Barnard, William Marion *psychiatrist*
Barnes, Charles Andrew *physicist, educator*
Barrett, Robert Mitchell *electrical engineer*
Baum, Dwight Crouse *investment banking executive*
Bean, Maurice Darrow *retired diplomat*
Beauchamp, Jesse Lee (Jack Beauchamp) *chemistry educator*
Beaudet, Robert Arthur *chemistry educator*
Beer, Reinhard *atmospheric scientist*
Bejczy, Antal Károly *research scientist, research facility administrator*
Bercaw, John Edward *chemistry educator, consultant*
Berger, Jay Vari *executive recruiter*
Bergholz, Richard Cady *political writer*
†Bertani, Lillian Elizabeth T. *biologist, researcher, educator*
Blandford, Roger David *astronomy educator*
Boehm, Felix Hans *physicist, educator*
Boochever, Robert *federal judge*
Boulos, Paul Fares *civil and environmental engineer*
Breckinridge, James Bernard *optical science engineer, program manager*
Bridges, William Bruce *electrical engineer, researcher, educator*
Brooks, Edward Howard *college administrator*
Brown, David R. *academic administrator*
Buck, Anne Marie *library director, consultant*
Buck, Francis Scott *pathologist, educator*
Bunt Smith, Helen Marguerite *lawyer*
Butler, Octavia Estelle *free-lance writer*
Caillouette, James Clyde *physician*
Caine, Stephen Howard *data processing executive*
Caldwell, William Mackay, III *business executive*
Calleton, Theodore Edward *lawyer*
Cappello, Eve *international business consultant*
Carey, Keith Grant *editor, publishing executive*
Carroll, William Jerome *civil engineer*
Cass, Glen Rowan *environmental engineer*
Cepielik, Elizabeth Lindberg *educator*
Chahine, Moustafa Toufic *atmospheric scientist*
Chamberlain, Willard Thomas *retired metals company executive*
Chan, Daniel Chung-Yin *lawyer*
Chan, Sunney Ignatius *chemist*
Chandy, K. Mani *computer science educator*
†Cienfuegos, Mauricio *professional soccer player*
Cohen, Marshall Harris *astronomer, educator*
Crowley, John Crane *real estate developer*
Culick, Fred Ellsworth Clow *physics and engineering educator*
Dallas, Saterios (Sam) *aerospace engineer, researcher, consultant*
D'Angelo, Robert William *lawyer*
Davidson, Eric Harris *molecular and developmental biologist, educator*
Davidson, Norman Ralph *biochemistry educator*
Davis, Lance Edwin *economics educator*
Davis, Mark E. *chemical engineering educator*
Dayton, Sky *communications company executive*
†Del Prado, Sergio *professional soccer team executive*
Dervan, Peter Brendan *chemistry educator*
Diehl, Digby Robert *journalist*
Dougherty, Dennis A. *chemistry educator*
Duxbury, Thomas Carl *planetary scientist*
†Dyck, Peter *neurosurgeon*
Elachi, Charles *aerospace engineer*
Elliot, David Clephan *historian, educator*
Epstein, Bruce Howard *lawyer, real estate broker*
Epstein, Samuel *geologist, educator*
Everhart, Thomas Eugene *retired university president, engineering educator*
Falick, Abraham Johnson *printing company executive*
Farr, Donald Eugene *engineering scientist*
Fay, Peter Ward *history educator*
Ferber, Robert Rudolf *physics researcher, educator*
Fernandez, Ferdinand Francis *federal judge*
Finnell, Michael Hartman *corporate executive*
Franklin, Joel Nicholas *mathematician, educator*
Frautschi, Steven Clark *physicist, educator*
Freise, Earl Jerome *univeristy administrator, materials engineering educator*
Friedl, Randall Raymond *environmental scientist*
Fu, Lee-Lueng *oceanographer*
Fultz, Brent Thomas *materials scientist, educator, researcher*
Garrett, Duane David *hospitality executive*
Gavalas, George R. *chemical engineering educator*
†Gerber, Merrill Joan *writing educator*
Giem, Ross Nye, Jr. *surgeon*
Gill, Gene *artist*
Gillis, Christine Diest-Lorgion *financial planner, stockbroker*
Gilman, Richard Carleton *retired college president*
Girod, Erwin Ernest *internist*
Goodstein, David Louis *physics educator*
Goodwin, Alfred Theodore *federal judge*
Gould, Roy Walter *engineering educator*
Gray, Harry Barkus *chemistry educator*
Griesche, Robert Price *hospital purchasing executive*
Grubbs, Robert Howard *chemistry educator*
Gurnis, Michael Christopher *geological sciences educator*
Haight, James Theron *lawyer, corporate executive*
Hale, Charles Russell *lawyer*
Hall, Cynthia Holcomb *federal judge*
Hanson, Noel Rodger *management consultant*
Harmsen, Tyrus George *librarian*
Harvey, Joseph Paul, Jr. *orthopedist, educator*
Hatheway, Alson Earle *mechanical engineer*
Heer, Ewald *engineer*
Heindl, Clifford Joseph *physicist*
Helander, Terrill Webb *educational psychologist*
Hemann, Raymond Glenn *research company executive*
Hilbert, Robert S(aul) *optical engineer*
Hitlin, David George *physicist, educator*
Holbrook, Sally Davis *author*
Hopkins, Philip Joseph *journalist, editor*
Horner, Althea Jane *psychologist*
Housner, George William *retired civil engineering educator, consultant*
Howe, Graham Lloyd *photographer, curator*
Hunt, Gordon *lawyer*
Ingersoll, Andrew Perry *planetary science educator*
†Iturbide, Graciela *photographer*
Jacobs, Joseph John *engineering company executive*
Jastrow, Robert *physicist*
Jennings, Paul Christian *civil engineering educator, academic administrator*
Johnson, Barbara Jean *retired lawyer, judge*
Jones, Jennifer *actress*
Kaplan, Gary *executive recruiter*
Kevles, Daniel Jerome *history educator, writer*
Knauss, Wolfgang Gustav *engineering educator*
Knowles, James Kenyon *applied mechanics educator*
Koch, Albin Cooper *lawyer*
Koenig, Marie Harriet King *public relations director, fund raising executive*
Konishi, Masakazu *neurobiologist, educator*
Koonin, Steven Elliot *physicist, educator, academic administrator*
Kousser, J(oseph) Morgan *history educator*
Kozinski, Alex *federal judge*
Ledyard, John Odell *economics educator, consultant*
Leonard, Nelson Jordan *chemistry educator*
Levy, David Steven *college administrator*
Lewis, Edward B. *biology educator*
Lewis, Nathan Saul *chemistry educator*
Liebau, Frederic Jack, Jr. *investment manager*
Liepmann, Hans Wolfgang *physicist, educator*
Lingenfelter, Sherwood Galen *university provost, anthropology educator*
Linstedt, Walter Griffiths *lawyer, banker*
Lisoni, Gail Marie Landtbom *lawyer*
List, Ericson John *environmental engineering science educator, engineering consultant*
Little, Paul Edward *communications executive, city official*
Li Vigni, Shana Margaret Veronica Reichl *disc jockey*
Logan, Francis Dummer *lawyer*
Mandel, Oscar *literature educator, writer*
Marble, Frank E(arl) *engineering educator*
Marcus, Rudolph Arthur *chemist, educator*
Marlen, James S. *chemical-plastics-building materials manufacturing company executive*
Marrow, Marva Jan *photographer, writer, video and multimedia producer, web designer, publisher*
Marsden, Jerrold Eldon *mathematician, educator, engineer*
Martin, Craig Lee *engineering company executive*
Mathies, Allen Wray, Jr. *physician, hospital administrator*
Mc Carthy, Frank Martin *oral surgeon, surgical sciences educator*
Mc Duffie, Malcolm *oil company executive*
Mc Koy, Basil Vincent Charles *theoretical chemist, educator*
Mead, Carver Andress *computer science educator*
Meye, Robert Paul *retired seminary administrator, writer*
Meyerowitz, Elliot Martin *biologist, educator*
Miklusak, Thomas Alan *psychiatrist, psychoanalyst*
Miller, Charles Daly *self-adhesive materials company executive*
Mosher, Sally Ekenberg *lawyer, musician*
Mueth, Joseph Edward *lawyer*
Munger, Edwin Stanton *political geography educator*
Myers, R(alph) Chandler *lawyer*
Nackel, John George *health care director*
Neal, Philip Mark *diversified manufacturing executive*
Nelson, Dorothy Wright (Mrs. James F. Nelson) *federal judge*
Neugebauer, Gerry *retired astrophysicist, educator*
Neugebauer, Marcia *physicist, administrator*
North, Wheeler James *marine ecologist, educator*
O'Connor, William Charles *automobile agency finance executive*
Oemler, Augustus, Jr. *astronomer*
Olson, Diana Craft *image and etiquette consultant*
Opel, William *medical research administrator*
Otoshi, Tom Yasuo *electrical engineer, consultant*
Ott, George William, Jr. *management consulting executive*
Owen, Ray David *biology educator*
Parker, Robert Allan Ridley *government administrator, astronaut*
Pashgian, Margaret Helen *artist*
Patterson, Mark Jerome *computer software designer*
Pattie, Steven Norris *advertising executive, artist, author*
Patton, Richard Weston *retired mortgage company executive*
Perez, Reinaldo Joseph *electrical engineer*
Peter, Kenneth Shannon *elementary school educator*
Pianko, Theodore A. *lawyer*
Pings, Cornelius John *educational consultant, director*
Pitts, Ferris Newcomb *physician, psychiatry educator*
Plott, Charles Raymond *economics educator*
Politzer, Hugh David *physicist, educator*
Presecan, Nicholas Lee *environmental and civil engineer, consultant*
Raichlen, Fredric *civil engineering educator, consultant*
Revel, Jean-Paul *biology educator*
Roberts, John D. *chemist, educator*
†Rosenfeld, Harold Lee *plastic surgeon*
Roshko, Anatol *aeronautic engineer*
Roth, Irma Doris Brubaker *editor*
Rymer, Pamela Ann *federal judge*
Sabersky, Rolf Heinrich *mechanical engineer*
Saffman, Philip G. *mathematician*
Sakoguchi, Ben *artist, art educator*
Samson, Sten Otto *x-ray crystallographer, consultant, researcher*
Sandage, Allan Rex *astronomer*
Sano, Roy I. *bishop*
Sargent, Wallace Leslie William *astronomer, educator*
Savedra, Jeannine Evangeline *art educator, artist*
†Schaller, Anthony Josef *technology management executive*
Schieldge, John Philip *physicist, researcher*
Schlinger, Warren Gleason *retired chemical engineer*
†Schmid, Sigi *professional soccer coach*
Schmidt, Maarten *astronomy educator*
Schwarz, John Henry *theoretical physicist, educator*
Scudder, Thayer *anthropologist, educator*
Seinfeld, John Hersh *chemical engineering educator*
Sekanina, Zdenek *astronomer*
Shalack, Joan Helen *psychiatrist*
Sharp, Robert Phillip *geology educator, researcher*
Sharp, Sharon Lee *hospice nurse*
Shuster, Marguerite *minister, educator*
Siemon-Burgeson, Marilyn M. *education administrator*
Simon, Marvin Kenneth *electrical engineer, consultant*
Smith, Howard Russell *manufacturing company executive*
Smith, Michael Robert *electro-optical engineer, physicist*
Soloway, Jay Stephen *consulting firm executive*
Spector, Phil *record company executive*
Staehle, Robert L. *foundation executive*
Stevens, Roy W. *sales and marketing executive*
Stevenson, David John *planetary scientist, educator*
Stewart, Homer Joseph *engineering educator*
Stolper, Edward Manin *secondary education educator*
Stone, Edward Carroll *physicist, educator*
Strick, Ruth Cochran *career counselor*
Talt, Alan R. *lawyer*
Tanner, Dee Boshard *retired lawyer*
Tashima, Atsushi Wallace *federal judge*
Thomas, Joseph Fleshman *architect*
Thorne, Kip Stephen *physicist, educator*
Tirrell, David A. *research scientist, educator*
Todd, John *mathematician, educator*
†Tolaney, Murli *environmental engineering executive*
Tollenaere, Lawrence Robert *retired industrial products company executive*
Tombrello, Thomas Anthony, Jr. *physics educator, consultant*
Torres, Ralph Chon *minister*
Trussell, R(obert) Rhodes *environmental engineer*
Ulrich, Peter Henry *banker*
Van Karnes, Kathleen Walker *realtor*
van Schoonenberg, Robert G. *corporate lawyer*
Varshavsky, Alexander Jacob *molecular biologist*
Vaughn, John Vernon *banker, industrialist*
Vogt, Rochus Eugen *physicist, educator*
Walendowski, George Jerry *accounting and business educator*
Wardlaw, Kim A.M. *federal judge*
Wasserburg, Gerald Joseph *geology and geophysics educator*
Watkins, John Francis *management consultant*
Wayland, J(ames) Harold *biomedical scientist, educator*
Weisbin, Charles Richard *nuclear engineer*
Westphal, James Adolph *planetary science educator*
Whitham, Gerald Beresford *mathematics educator*
Wilcox, Roberta Moat *music educator*
Wood, Lincoln Jackson *aerospace engineer*
Wu, Theodore Yao-Tsu *engineer*
Wyatt, Joseph Lucian, Jr. *lawyer, author*
Yamarone, Charles Anthony, Jr. *aerospace engineer, consultant*
Yao, Xiaotian Steve *electrical engineer, optical scientist*
Yariv, Amnon *electrical engineering educator, scientist*
Yau, Kevin Kam-ching *astronomer*
Yeager, Caroline Hale *radiologist, consultant*
Yeh, Paul Pao *electrical and electronics engineer, educator*
Yeomans, Donald Keith *astronomer*
Yohalem, Harry Morton *lawyer*
Zammitt, Norman *artist*
Zewail, Ahmed Hassan *chemistry and physics educator, editor, consultant*
Zirin, Harold *astronomer, educator*

Paso Robles
Boxer, Jerome Harvey *computer and management consultant, vintner, accountant*
Brown, Benjamin Andrew *journalist*
Gruner, George Richard *retired secondary education educator*
Knecht, James Herbert *lawyer*
Rocha, Marilyn Eva *clinical psychologist*

Pebble Beach
Burkett, William Andrew *banker*
Carns, Michael Patrick Chamberlain *air force officer*
Ference, Helen Marie *nursing consultant*
Harvie, J. Jason *administrative aide, private secretary*
Ketcham, Henry King *cartoonist*
Kim, Han Pyong *dentist, researcher*
Klevan, Robert Bruce *music educator*
Mauz, Henry Herrward, Jr. *retired naval officer*
Maxeiner, Clarence William *lawyer, construction company executive*
Mortensen, Gordon Louis *artist, printmaker*
Rivette, Gerard Bertram *manufacturing company executive*

Penn Valley
Morgenthaler, John Herbert *chemical engineer*
Throner, Guy Charles, Jr. *engineering executive, scientist, engineer, inventor, consultant*

Penngrove
Chadwick, Cydney Marie *writer, art projects executive*

Penryn
Bryson, Vern Elrick *nuclear engineer*

Petaluma
Carr, Les *psychologist, educator*
Cuggino, Michael Joseph *financial executive*
Daniel, Gary Wayne *motivation and performance consultant*
Eck, Robert Edwin *physicist*
Frederickson, Arman Frederick *minerals company executive*
Fuller-McChesney, Mary Ellen *sculptor, writer, publisher*
†Ghane, Kamran *computer engineer*
†Hass, Robert L. *writer, educator*
Herlihy, James Edward *retail executive*
Hill, Debora Elizabeth *author, journalist, screenwriter*
James, Mary Spencer *nursing home health administrator*
†Knight, Arthur Winfield *English educator*
†Knight, Kit Marie *poet, writer, movie critic*
McChesney, Robert Pearson *artist*
McKibben, James Denis *marketing and sales executive*
Pronzini, Bill John (William Pronzini) *author*
Reichek, Jesse *artist*
Skalagard, Hans Martin *artist*
Skup, David Alan *insurance company executive*

Phelan
Erwin, Joan Lenore *artist, educator*

Pico Rivera
Brotman, Richard Dennis *counselor*
Donoghue, John Charles *software management consultant*
Harwick, Wayne Thomas *economist*

Piedmont
Cole, Peter William *financial executive*
Hoover, Robert Cleary *retired bank executive*
Hughes, James Paul *physician*
Hurley, Morris Elmer, Jr. *management consultant*
McCormick, Timothy Brian Beer *lawyer*
Putter, Irving *French language educator*
Solomon, Neal Edward *management consultant, executive recruiter, social theorist, author*
Willrich, Mason *energy industry executive*
Wood, Wayne Barry *photojournalist*

Pine Mountain
Edwards, Sarah Anne *radio, cable TV personality, clinical social worker*

Pinole
Gerbracht, Robert Thomas (Bob Gerbracht) *painter, educator*
Grogan, Stanley Joseph *educational and security consultant*
Harvey, Elinor B. *child psychiatrist*
Naughton, James Lee *internist*

Pismo Beach
Brisbin, Robert Edward *insurance agency executive*
Saveker, David Richard *naval and marine architectural engineering executive*

Placentia
Gobar, Alfred Julian *economic consultant, educator*
Linnan, Judith Ann *psychologist*
Nettleship, William Allan *sculptor*

Placerville
Beneš, Norman Stanley *meteorologist*
Burnett, Eric Stephen *environmental consultant*
Craib, Kenneth Bryden *resource development executive, physicist, economist*
McIntosh, Paul Eugene *county government official*
Nesbitt, Paul Edward *historian, author, educator*
Palmieri, Rodney August *state agency administrator, pharmacist*
Wickline, Marian Elizabeth *former corporate librarian*

Playa Del Rey
Berry, Jeffrey Alan *film director*
Blomquist, Carl Arthur *medical and trust company executive, insurance executive*
Clow, Lee *advertising agency executive*
Coots, Laurie *advertising executive*
Kuperman, Robert Ian *advertising agency executive*
†Reed, Timothy Max *secondary education educator*
Tai, Frank *aerospace engineering consultant*
Weir, Alexander, Jr. *utility consultant, inventor*

Pleasant Hill
Ashby, Denise Stewart *speech educator, communication consultant*
†Edelstein, Mark Gerson *college president*
Gardner, Nord Arling *management consultant administrator*
Hassid, Sami *architect, educator*
Hopkins, Robert Arthur *retired industrial engineer*
Lundgren, Susan Elaine *counselor, educator*
†McQueen, Geoffrey Pierce *lawyer*
Newkirk, Raymond Leslie *management consultant*
Richard, Robert Carter *psychologist*
Stevenson, James D(onald), Jr. *psychologist, counselor*
Toms, Kathleen Moore *nurse*

Pleasanton
Aladeen, Lary Joe *secondary school educator*
Burd, Steve *food service executive*
Choy, Clement Kin-Man *research scientist*
Davis, Ron Lee *clergyman, author*
Denavit, Jacques *retired physicist*
Eby, Frank Shilling *retired research scientist*
Fehlberg, Robert Erick *architect*
Goddard, John Wesley *cable television company executive*
Jarnagan, Harry William, Jr. *project control manager*
Majure, Allison Scott *product marketing professional*
Novak-Lyssand, Randi Ruth *engineer, computer scientist*
Petrone, Joseph Anthony *business consultant, writer*
†Plaisance, Melissa *retail executive*
Ruppert, Paul Richard *telecommunications executive*
Scott, G. Judson, Jr. *lawyer*
Shen, Mason Ming-Sun *medical center administrator*
Smith, Gary *marketing executive*
Staley, John Fredric *lawyer*
Weiss, Robert Stephen *medical manufacturing company financial executive*
Whisnand, Rex James *association executive*

Plymouth
Andreason, John Christian *lawyer*

Pollock Pines
Johnson, Stanford Leland *marketing educator*
Rickard, Margaret Lynn *library consultant, former library director*

Pomona
Ambrose, William Wright, Jr. *college dean, accounting educator, tax researcher*
Aurilia, Antonio *physicist, educator*
Bernau, Simon John *mathematics educator*
Bidlack, Wayne Ross *nutritional biochemist, toxicologist, food scienti*
Demery, Dorothy Jean *secondary school educator*
†Dishman, Rose Marie Rice *academic administrator, researcher*
Fine, Aubrey Howard *educator*
Garrity, Rodman Fox *psychologist, educator*
Kauser, Fazal Bakhsh *aerospace engineer, educator*
Keating, Eugene Kneeland *animal scientist, educator*
Lyon, Carolyn Bartel *civic worker*
McDonough, Julie Marie *mortgage company executive, consultant*
Palmer, Robert Alan *lawyer, educator*
Patten, Thomas Henry, Jr. *management, human resources educator*
Suzuki, Bob H. *university president*
Teague, Lavette Cox, Jr. *systems educator, consultant*
Vo, Huu Dinh *pediatrician, educator*

Port Hueneme
Haddad, Edmonde Alex *public affairs executive*
Hedvig, Michael Elliott *management consultant*

Porterville
†Golightly, Douglas Raymond *artist*
Hayes, Shirley Ann *special education educator*
Mullen, Rod *nonprofit organization executive*

Portola Valley
Cooper, John Joseph *lawyer*
Dixon, Andrew Derart *retired academic administrator*
Garsh, Thomas Burton *publisher*
Graham, William James *packaging company executive*
Kuo, Franklin F. *computer scientist, electrical engineer*
Millard, Stephens Fillmore *electronics company executive*
Moses, Franklin Maxwell *retired chemical marketing executive*
Oscarson, Kathleen Dale *writing assessment coordinator, educator*
Purl, O. Thomas *retired electronics company executive*
Ward, Robert Edward *retired political science educator and university administrator*

Poway
Berger, Newell James, Jr. *security professional*
Burnworth, Randy James *video company executive*
Dean, Richard Anthony *mechanical engineer, engineering executive*
Dollen, Charles Joseph *clergyman, writer*
Hadley, Theresa Iguico *medical/surgical and psychiatric nurse*
Rudolph, Charles Herman *computer software development executive*
Shippey, Lyn *reading center director*
Tello, Donna *tax strategist*
Vitti, Anthony Mark *secondary education educator*
Wirt, Sherwood Eliot *writer, minister*
†Yousefian, Shahram *chemist*

Prunedale
Garman, Dale S., Jr. *sculptor*

Quartz Hill
McKain, Mary Margaret *musician*
Nettelhorst, Robin Paul *academic administrator, writer*
Noble, Sunny A. *business owner*

Ramona
Bennett, James Chester *computer consultant, real estate developer*
Cooper, James Melvin *healthcare executive, consultant*
Hoffman, Wayne Melvin *retired airline official*
Jordan, David Francis, Jr. *retired judge*
Vaughn, Robert Lockard *aerospace and astronautics company executive*

Rancho Cordova
Alenius, John Todd *insurance executive*
Darlington, Ronald Lawrence *English language educator*
Hendrickson, Elizabeth Ann *retired secondary education educator*
Lynch, Robert Berger *lawyer*
†Martin, Rafael M., Sr. *construction company executive*
Meigel, David Walter *retired career officer, retired musician*

Rancho Cucamonga
Bucks, Charles Alan *airline industry consultant, former executive*
Horton, Michael L. *mortgage company executive, publishing executive*
Robertson, Carey Jane *musician, educator*
Shields, Andrea Lyn *psychologist, educator*
Southard, Burton M. *political and public affairs consultant*

Rancho Dominguez
Janura, Jan Arol *apparel manufacturing executive*

Rancho La Costa
Handel, William Keating *advertising and sales executive*

Rancho Mirage
Bennett, Grover Bryce *engineering consultant*
Deiter, Newton Elliott *clinical psychologist*
Doi, Lois *psychiatric social worker*
Ford, Betty Bloomer (Elizabeth Ford) *health facility executive, wife of former President of United States*
Ford, Gerald Rudolph, Jr. *former President of United States*
Foster, David Ramsey *soap company executive*
Goldie, Ray Robert *lawyer*
Greenbaum, James Richard *liquor distributing company executive, real estate developer*
Kiser, Roberta Katherine *medical records administrator, education educator*
Kramer, Gordon *mechanical engineer*
Lacey, Beatrice Cates *psychophysiologist*
Lacey, John Irving *psychologist, physiologist, educator*
Leydorf, Frederick Leroy *lawyer*
Olderman, Murray *columnist, cartoonist*
Reuben, Don Harold *lawyer*
Rotman, Morris Bernard *public relations consultant*
Stenhouse, Everett Ray *clergy administrator*
Vaughan, Joseph Robert *lawyer*

Rancho Murieta
Irelan, Robert Withers *retired metal products executive*
Ragsdale, Christina Ann *public relations executive, consultant*

Rancho Palos Verdes
Hillinger, Charles *journalist, writer*
Marlett, De Otis Loring *retired management consultant*
Raue, Jorg Emil *electrical engineer*
Rubenstein, Leonard Samuel *communications executive, ceramist, painter, sculptor, photographer*
Savage, Terry Richard *information systems executive*
Schach, Barbara Jean *elementary education educator*

Rancho Santa Fe
Affeldt, John Ellsworth *physician*
Baker, Charles Lynn *management consultant*
Best, Jacob Hilmer (Jerry), Jr. *hotel chain executive*
Creutz, Edward Chester *physicist, museum consultant*
Dieffenbach, AliceJean *artist*
Gruenwald, George Henry *new products development management consultant, writer*
Jordan, Charles Morrell *retired automotive designer*
Kessler, A. D. *business, financial, investment and real estate advisor, consultant, lecturer, author, broadcaster, producer*
LaBonté, C(larence) Joseph *financial and marketing executive*
Matthews, Leonard Sarver *advertising and marketing executive*
McNally, Connie Benson *editor, publisher, antiques dealer*
Peterson, Nad A. *lawyer, retired corporate executive*
Polster, Leonard H. *investment company executive*
Rible, Morton *financial services and manufacturing executive*
Rockoff, S. David *radiologist, physician, educator*
Ruiz, Ramon Eduardo *history educator*
Schirra, Walter Marty, Jr. *business consultant, former astronaut*
Simon, William Leonard *film and television writer and producer, author*
Sommer-Bodenburg, Angela *author, artist*
Step, Eugene Lee *retired pharmaceutical company executive*
†Woolley, Roger Swire *lawyer*

Rancho Santa Margarita
†Butte, Kenneth Michael *executive*
Curtis, John Joseph *lawyer*
Miller, Elliot Ivan *editor*
Montana, Joseph C., Jr. *former professional football player*
Munsell, Joni Anne *middle school educator*
†Pruett, Scott *race car driver*

Red Bluff
Kennedy, James William, Jr. (Sarge Kennedy) *special education administrator, consultant*

Redding
†Bay, Richard M. *federal judge*
†Campbell, Barth Lynn *theology educator*
Drake, Patricia Evelyn *psychologist*
Emmerson, Red *sawmill owner*
†Grant, James Martin *academic administrator*
Nicholas, David Robert *minister, college president*
Potter, James Vincent *educator*
Shadish, William Raymond *plastic surgeon, retired*
†Shea, John F. *construction executive, contractor*
Skrocki, Edmund Stanley, II *health fair promoter, executive*
Streiff, Arlyne Bastunas *business owner, educator*

Redlands
Adey, William Ross *physician*
Appleton, James Robert *university president, educator*
Bangasser, Ronald Paul *physician*
Barnes, A. Keith *management educator*
†Burgess, Charlotte Gaylord *dean*
Burgess, Larry Eugene *library director, history educator*
Coleman, Arlene Florence *nurse practitioner*
Griesemer, Allan David *retired museum director*
Hanson, Gerald Warner *retired county official*
Healy, Daniel Thomas *secondary education educator*
Jennings, Irmengard Katharina *academic administrator*
Langer, Richard Charles *minister*
†McAllister, Bruce Hugh *writer and educator*
Musmann, Klaus *librarian*
Richardson, A(rthur) Leslie *former medical group consultant*
Sexton, Kathryn Louise *nursing administrator*
Skomal, Edward Nelson *aerospace company executive, consultant*
Stuart, Robert Lee *English language educator*
Wang, Colleen Iona *medical association administrator, writer*

Redondo Beach
Ball, William Paul *physicist, engineer*
Battles, Roxy Edith *novelist, consultant, educator*
Brodsky, Robert Fox *aerospace engineer*
Buchta, Edmund *engineering executive*
Cardin, Suzette *nursing educator*
Cohen, Clarence Budd *aerospace engineer*
Davis, Lowell Livingston *cardiovascular surgeon*
Foster, John Stuart, Jr. *physicist, former defense industry executive*
Hawkins, Harold Stanley *pastor, police chaplain, school director*
Kagiwada, Reynold Shigeru *advanced technology manager*
Kronenberg, Jacalyn (Jacki Kronenberg) *nurse administrator*
Lake, Bruce Meno *applied physicist*
Lytal, Patricia Lou *art educator*
Marsee, Stuart (Earl) *educational consultant, retired*
Moretti, Constance Walton *author, genealogist*
Naples, Caesar Joseph *law/public policy educator, lawyer, consultant*
Reed, John E. *producer, consultant*
Sabin, Jack Charles *engineering and construction firm executive*
Sackheim, Robert Lewis *aerospace engineer, educator*
Shellhorn, Ruth Patricia *landscape architect*
Woike, Lynne Ann *computer scientist*

Redway
Branzei-Velasquez, Sylvia Carol *secondary education educator*

Redwood City
Ellis, Eldon Eugene *surgeon*
Ellison, Lawrence J. *computer software company executive*
Foley, Patrick *air courier company executive*
Gagarin, Dennis Paul *advertising agency executive*
Harrington, Walter Howard, Jr. *judge*
Herrin, Stephanie Ann *retired aerospace engineer*
Heuman, Donna Rena *lawyer*
Itnyre, Jacqueline Harriet *systems analyst*
Kovacevic, Brenda L. *sales administrator*
Morrison, Murdo Donald *architect*
Nacht, Sergio *biochemist*
Neville, Roy Gerald *scientist, chemical management and environmental consultant*
†O'Keefe, Donald Martin *county protective services officer*
Oppel, Andrew John *computer systems consultant*
Rohde, James Vincent *software systems company executive*
Rothhammer, Craig Robert *social worker, consultant*
Rowland, John Arthur *lawyer*
Shoemaker, Dorothy Hays *technical writer*
Silvestri, Philip Salvatore *lawyer*
Sollman, George Henry *telecommunications company executive*
Spangler, Nita Reifschneider *volunteer*
Stone, Herbert Allen *management consultant*
Tight, Dexter Corwin *lawyer*
Tooley, Terry L(ee) *software company executive*
Waller, Stephen *air transportation executive*
Wang, Chen Chi *electronics company, real estate, finance company, investment services, and international trade executive*
Wilhelm, Robert Oscar *lawyer, civil engineer, developer*

Redwood Shores
Howard, Karen Lynn *marketing executive*
Kertzman, Mitchell E. *software company executive*
Martin-O'Neill, Mary Evelyn *advertising, marketing, business writing, sales training consultant*

Reedley
Carey, Ernestine Gilbreth (Mrs. Charles E. Carey) *writer, lecturer*
Dick, Henry Henry *minister*

Rescue
Ackerly, Wendy Saunders *construction company executive*

Reseda
Alenikov, Vladimir *motion picture director and writer*
Anstad, Neil *director*
†Brooks, Robert Eugene *management consultant*
Chavez, Albert Blas *financial executive*
Hoover, Pearl Rollings *nurse*
Leahy, T. Liam *marketing and management consultant*
Moss, Debra Lee *special education educator*

Rialto
Bauza, Christine Diane *special education educator*
Straight, James Wesley *secondary education educator*
Walker, Jeanne Claire *retired English educator, writer*

Richmond
Barashkov, Nickolay Nickolayevich *polymer chemist, researcher*
Beall, Frank Carroll *science director and educator*
Dolberg, David Spencer *business executive, lawyer, scientist*
Doyle, William Thomas *retired newspaper editor*
Huckeby, Karen Marie *graphic arts executive*
Jobs, Steven Paul *computer corporation executive*
Kaune, James Edward *ship repair company executive, former naval officer*
Kirk-Duggan, Michael Allan *retired law and computer sciences educator*
†Lasseter, John P. *film director, computer animator*
Quenneville, Kathleen *lawyer*
Thomas, John Richard *chemist*
Wessel, Henry *photographer*

Ridgecrest
Lepie, Albert Helmut *chemist, researcher*
Matulef, Gizelle Terese *secondary education educator*
Pearson, John *mechanical engineer*
Roberts, Jerry Bill *publishing company executive*

Rio Linda
Lebrato, Mary Theresa *lawyer, psychologist*

Riverbank
Ingram, Robert M. *communications company executive*

Riverside
Aderton, Jane Reynolds *lawyer*
Adrian, Charles Raymond *political science educator*
†Alberts, Robert W. *federal judge*
Allen, William Merle *university administrator, museum director*
Anderson, Jolene Slover *small business owner, publishing executive, consultant*
Auth, Judith *library director*
Balow, Irving Henry *retired education educator*
Barnes, Martin McRae *entomologist*
Bartnicki-Garcia, Salomon *microbiologist, educator*
Beni, Gerardo *electrical and computer engineering educator, robotics scientist*
Bricker, Neal S. *physician, educator*
†Bulloch, Kathleen Louise *educational professional*
Burgess, Curt *psychologist, computer scientist, educator*
Carpenter, Susan Ann *financial planner*
Cavers-Huff, Dasiea Yvonne *philosopher*
Chang, Janice May *lawyer, administrator, notary public*
Childs, Donald Richard *pediatric endocrinologist*
Clegg, Michael Tran *genetics educator, researcher*
Darling, Scott Edward *lawyer*
Decker, Catherine Helen *English language educator*
Diamond, Richard *secondary education educator*
Elliott, Emory Bernard *English language educator, educational adminstrator*
Erwin, Donald Carroll *plant pathology educator*
Eyman, Richard Kenneth *psychologist, educator*
Fagundo, Ana Maria *creative writing and Spanish literature educator*
Finan, Ellen Cranston *secondary education educator, consultant*
Foreman, Thomas Elton *drama critic*
Geraty, Lawrence Thomas *academic administrator, archaeologist*
†Goldberg, Mitchel R. *federal judge*
Gordon, Jerry Arthur *retired family services organization administrator*
Graves, Patrick Lee *lawyer*
Green, Harry Western, II *geology-geophysics educator, university official*
Green, Jonathan William *museum administrator and educator, artist, author*
Griffin, Keith Broadwell *economics educator*
Hall, Anthony Elmitt *crop ecologist*
Harrison, Ethel Mae *financial executive*
Hendrick, Irving Guilford *dean, education educator*
Hodgen, Maurice Denzil *foundation executive*
Howe, Vernon Wesley *mathematics educator*
Jung, Timothy Tae Kun *otolaryngologist*
†Jury, Meredith A. *federal judge*
†Kauffman, Kristina Marie *political science educator*
Keen, Noel Thomas *plant pathology educator*

GEOGRAPHIC INDEX 5501 CALIFORNIA

Korzec, Patricia Ann museum administrator
†Kronenfeld, Judy Zahler humanities educator, writer
Kummer, Glenn F. manufactured housing executive
Lacy, Carolyn Jean elementary education educator, secondary education educator
Linaweaver, Walter Ellsworth, Jr. physician
Loveridge, Ronald Oliver mayor
Marlatt, Michael James lawyer
Mc Cormac, Weston Arthur retired educator, retired career officer
Mc Laughlin, Leighton Bates, II journalism educator, former newspaperman
McQuern, Marcia Alice newspaper publishing executive
Medel, Rebecca Rosalie artist
Moore, John Alexander biologist
Naugle, Charlotte June principal, educator
†Naugle, David N. federal judge
Nicol, Colleen municipal official
Norman, Anthony Westcott biochemistry educator
Opotowsky, Maurice Leon newspaper editor
Orbach, Raymond Lee physicist, educator
Page, Albert Lee soil science educator, researcher
Petrinovich, Lewis Franklin psychology educator
†Pianca, Marina educator, researcher, writer
Przytycki, Józef Henryk mathematician
Rabenstein, Dallas Leroy chemistry educator
Ratliff, Louis Jackson, Jr. mathematics educator
Robbins, Karen Diane editor
†Rodrigue, George P. editor
Rosenthal, Robert psychology educator
Ross, Delmer Gerrard historian, educator
Schwartz, Bernard Julian lawyer
Seyfert, Howard Bentley, Jr. podiatrist
Sheppard, Howard Reece accountant
Sherman, Irwin William biological sciences educator
Smith, Jeffry Alan health administrator, physician, consultant
Snyder, Henry Leonard history educator, bibliographer
Sokolsky, Robert Lawrence journalist, entertainment writer
Spencer, William Franklin, Sr. soil scientist, researcher
Talbot, Prue biology educator
Timlin, Robert J. judge
Turk, Austin Theodore sociology educator
Van Dalen, Gordon John physicist
Van Gundy, Seymour Dean nematologist, plant pathologist, educator
Warren, Katherine Virginia art gallery director
White, Clara Jo graphoanalyst
White, Robert Stephen physics educator
Whyld, Steve municipal official
Wild, Robert Lee physics educator
Williams, Pamela R. elementary school administrator
Yacoub, Ignatius I. university dean
Yamamoto, Stanly Tokio city attorney
Zappe, John Paul city editor, educator, newspaper executive
Zentmyer, George Aubrey plant pathology educator

Rocklin
Dwyer, Darrell James financial executive
Gans, Dennis Joseph information technology solutions specialist
Tovar, Nicholas Mario mechanical engineer

Rodeo
Emmanuel, Jorge Agustin chemical engineer, environmental consultant

Rohnert Park
Arminana, Ruben academic administrator, educator
Babula, William university dean
Byrne, Noel Thomas sociologist, educator
Criswell, Eleanor Camp psychologist
Haslam, Gerald William writer, educator
Lord, Harold Wilbur electrical engineer, electronics consultant
†Merril, Charles Hall social science educator
Phillips, Peter Martin sociologist, educator, media researcher
Robinson, Louise Evette marriage family child counselor
Schafer, John Francis retired plant pathologist
†Tortorici, Peter Christopher metallurgical engineer
Trowbridge, Dale Brian educator

Rolling Hills Estates
Allbee, Sandra Moll real estate broker
Bradford, Susan Anne political consultant, writer
Chuang, Harold Hwa-Ming banker
Clewis, Charlotte Wright Staub mathematics educator
Diaz-Zubieta, Agustin nuclear engineer, executive
Kline, Frank Menefee psychiatrist
Leake, Rosemary Dobson physician
Rumbaugh, Charles Earl arbitrator, mediator, educator, lawyer, speaker
Wong, Sun Yet engineering consultant

Rosamond
Trippensee, Gary Alan aerospace executive

Rosemead
Bryson, John E. utilities company executive
Bushey, Richard Kenneth utility executive
Danner, Bryant Craig lawyer
Gibson, Frances nurse
Rosenblum, Richard Mark utility executive

Roseville
†Cohen, Michael Wayne physician
Gray, Robert Donald retired mayor
Hennessey, David Patrick banker
Lungren, Daniel Edward former state attorney general
†Reichmann, Peter Iván mathematician
†Spampinato, Francis Cesidio, Jr. federal administrator
Witt, Denise Marcia writer, public relations specialist

Ross
Goulet, William Dawson marketing professional
Rosenbaum, Michael Francis securities dealer
Way, Walter Lee anesthetist, pharmacologist, educator

Rough And Ready
Nix, Barbara Lois real estate broker

Rowland Heights
Allen, Delmas James anatomist, educator, university administrator
†Shear, Walter L. retired English educator

Rutherford
Eisele, Milton Douglas viticulturist
Staglin, Garen Kent finance and computer service company executive

Sacramento
Achtel, Robert Andrew pediatric cardiologist
†Adelman, Rick professional basketball coach
Alarcon, Richard state senator, former councilman
Aldrich, Thomas Albert former brewing executive, consultant
Allan, William George painter, educator
†Allen, Sonny professional basketball coach
Alpert, Dede Whittleton (Dede Alpert) state legislator
Baccigaluppi, Roger John agricultural company executive
Baltake, Joe film critic
Bankowsky, Richard James English educator
Basconcillo, Lindy insurance and financial services company executive
Benfield, John Richard surgeon
Bennett, Lawrence Allen psychologist, criminal justice researcher
Betts, Bert A. former state treasurer, accountant
Bezzone, Albert Paul structural engineer
Blackman, David Michael lawyer
Blake, D. Steven lawyer
Block, Alvin Gilbert journal executive editor
Bobrow, Susan Lukin lawyer
Bolton-Holifield, Ruthie basketball player
Booze, Thomas Franklin toxicologist
Bottel, Helen Alfea columnist, writer
Boylan, Richard John psychologist, hypnotherapist, researcher, behavioral scientist, educator
Brookman, Anthony Raymond lawyer
Burgess, Linda basketball player
Burns, John Francis state official, educator
Burrell, Garland E., Jr. federal judge
Burton, Randall James lawyer
†Bustamante, Cruz M. state official
Byears, Latasha professional basketball player
Callahan, Ronald federal investigator, historian
Capps, Cindy M. computer systems analyst
Carleone, Joseph aerospace executive
Carr, Gerald Francis German educator
Carrel, Marc Louis lawyer, policy advisor
Cavigli, Henry James petroleum engineer
Cerezo, Abraham Johnson social worker
Chapman, Loring psychology, physiology educator, neuroscientist
Chapman, Michael William orthopedist, educator
Cole, Glen David minister
Collins, William Leroy telecommunications engineer
Contreras, Dee (Dorthea Contreras) municipal official, educator
Cosgrove, James artist, industrial designer
Costamagna, Gary fire chief City of Sacramento
Crabbe, John Crozier telecommunications consultant
Crimmins, Philip Patrick metallurgical engineer, lawyer
Dahl, Loren Silvester retired federal judge
Dahlin, Dennis John landscape architect, environmental consultant
Dalkey, Fredric Dynan artist
†Damrell, Frank C., Jr. judge
Davis, Gray governor
Dedrick, Kent Gentry retired physicist, researcher
Drachnik, Catherine Meldyn art therapist, artist, counselor
Drown, Eugene Ardent federal agency administrator
Dunaway, Margaret Ann (Maggie Dunaway) state agency consultant
Dunlap, John Daniel, III association administrator
Dunnett, Dennis George state official
Endicott, William F. journalist
Enomoto, Jerry Jiro protective services official
†Fansler, Brian Caldwell budget analyst
†Favre, Gregory publishing executive
Felderstein, Steven Howard lawyer
Filloy, Beverlee Ann Howe clinical social worker
Forsyth, Raymond Arthur civil engineer
Fox, Ned professional sports team owner
Franz, Jennifer Danton public opinion and marketing researcher
Frey, Charles Frederick surgeon, educator
Friedman, Morton Lee lawyer
Friery, Thomas P. city treasurer
Garcia, Edward J. federal judge
†Gawthrop, Daphne Wood performing company executive
Gerth, Donald Rogers university president
Glackin, William Charles arts critic, editor
Gottfredson, Don Martin criminal justice educator
Gray, Walter P., III archivist, consultant
Gray-Fuson, Joan Lorraine lawyer
Grossman, Marc Richard media consultant
Hackett, Louise personnel services company executive, consultant
Hackney, Robert Ward plant pathologist, nematologist, parasitologist, molecular geneticist, commercial arbitrator
Hallenbeck, Harry C. architect
Hammond, Lauren Rochelle senate consultant
Hardmon, Lady professional athlete
†Harris, Robert M. college president
Harris, Wilson psychiatrist, research scientist
Hayward, Fredric Mark social reformer
†Heaphy, Janis D. newspaper executive
Helmick, D.O. protective services official
Herman, Irving Leonard business administration educator
Hodgkins, Francis Irving (Butch Hodgkins) county official
†Hollows, Gregory G. federal judge
Holmes, Robert Eugene state legislative consultant, journalist
Houpt, James Edward lawyer
†Howes, Edward Herbert educator
Hunt, Dennis public relations executive
Ishmael, William Earl land use planner, civil engineer
James, Robert William lawyer, government executive
Janigian, Bruce Jasper lawyer, educator
Jones, Bill state official, rancher
Karlton, Lawrence K. federal judge
Keiner, Christian Mark lawyer
Kelley, Lisa Stone public guardian, conservator
Kellough, Richard Dean educator
Killian, Richard M. library director
†Klein, Christopher M. federal judge
Kline, Fred Walter retired communications company executive
Knight, William J. (Pete Knight) state senator, retired air force officer
Knudson, Thomas Jeffery journalist
Kolkey, Daniel Miles judge
Lake, Molly Anne state official
LaMont, Sanders Hickey journalist
Larsen, Kenneth Marshall art and human services advocate, consultant
Lasley, Mona Carol elementary education educator, consultant
Lathi, Bhagawandas Pannalal electrical engineering educator
Law, Nancy Enell school system administrator
Leslie, (Robert) Tim state legislator
Levi, David F. federal judge
Liberty, John Joseph librarian
Lionakis, George architect
Lippold, Roland Will surgeon
†Lockyer, Bill state attorney general
Lopes, Brenda M. state agency administrator
†Lucas, Donna communications executive
Lukenbill, Gregg real estate developer, sports promoter
Lundstrom, Marjie newspaper editor
Lynch, Peter John dermatologist
Mack, Edward Gibson retired business executive
Majesty, Melvin Sidney psychologist, consultant
Malloy, Michael Patrick law educator, author, consultant
McClatchy, James B. editor, newspaper publisher
McElroy, Leo Francis communications consultant, journalist
McKeag, Jane Dickson judge
McKim, Harriet Megchelsen education educator
McLennan, Geoffrey Thomas state agency real estate executive
Merwin, Edwin Preston health care consultant, educator
Meyer, Rachel Abijah foundation director, artist, theorist, poet
Moulds, John F. federal judge
Muehleisen, Gene Sylvester retired law enforcement officer, state official
Neville, Monica Mary state assembly program executive
Newland, Chester Albert public administration educator
Nice, Carter conductor, music director
†Nowinski, Peter A. federal judge
Nussenbaum, Siegfried Fred chemistry educator
Nye, Gene Warren retired art educator
O'Leary, Marion Hugh university dean, chemist
Oliva, Stephen Edward resource conservationist, lawyer
Peck, Ellie Enriquez retired state administrator
Peck, Raymond Charles, Sr. driver behavior research specialist and research administrator
Petrie, Geoff professional basketball team executive
Phillips, Dana Wayne lawyer
Piert, Edwyna Patrice child care worker
Post, August Alan economist, artist
†Potts, Erwin Rea newspaper executive
†Powers, William Edwards, Jr. hand surgeon
Pruitt, Gary B. newspaper executive
Putney, Mary Engler federal auditor
†Quackenbush, Chuck insurance commissioner
Quinn, Francis A. bishop
Ramirez, Graciela women's health nurse
Reed-Graham, Lois L. administrator, secondary education educator
Reiber, Gregory Duane forensic pathologist
†Reynolds, Jerry Owen sports team executive
Robbins, Stephen J. M. lawyer
Roberts, James E. civil engineer
Roberts, Paul Dale health services administrator
Root, Gerald Edward planning and operational support administrator
Rosenberg, Dan Yale retired plant pathologist
Ross, Terence William architect
Rounds, Barbara Lynn psychiatrist
†Rualo, Hector Ramos investment management executive
Russell, David E. judge
Russell, Newton Requa retired state senator
Sawiris, Milad Youssef statistician, educator
Schmidt, Gregory Palmer secretary California senator, historian
Schmitz, Dennis Mathew English language educator
Schwartz, Milton Lewis federal judge
†Seave, Paul L. prosecutor
Sequeira, Jim utilites administrator, municipal official
Serna, Joe, Jr. mayor
Shapero, Harris Joel pediatrician
Sharma, Arjun Dutta cardiologist
Shaw, Eleanor Jane newspaper editor
Shelley, Susanne Mary lawyer, mathematics educator
Simeroth, Dean Conrad chemical engineer
†Smith, Marie B. college president
Soble, Mark Richard lawyer
Soriano, Bernard C. engineering executive
Starr, Kevin librarian, educator
Steinhaus, Patricia university administrator
†Stenzel, Larry Gene writer
Stevens, Charles J. former prosecutor, lawyer
Stevenson, Thomas Ray plastic surgeon
Stoker, Mike Brian state agency executive
Stuart, David R. academic administrator
Styne, Dennis Michael physician
Swatt, Stephen Benton communications executive, consultant
Tashjian, Gregory Kimball Thaddeus political consultant, writer
Terhune, C.A. state official
Thomas, Jim professional basketball team executive
Tranum, Jean Lorraine freelance writer
Trounstine, Philip John state official
Tubbs, William Reid, Jr. public service administrator
Twiss, Robert Manning prosecutor
Van Camp, Brian Ralph judge
Venegas, Arturo, Jr. chief police
Venema, Jon Roger educator, pastor
Waks, Dennis Stanford lawyer
Waller, Larry Gene mortgage banking executive
Walsh, Denny Jay reporter
Walston, Roderick Eugene state government official
Walters, Daniel Raymond political columnist
Wasserman, Barry L(ee) architect
†Webber, Chris, III (Mayce Edward Christopher Webber) professional basketball player
Weigand, William Keith bishop
Welch, Robin A. maternal/women's health and medical/surgical nurse
Wender, Deborah Elizabeth policy consultant, social worker
West, Irma Marie retired occupational health physician
†Whetzel, Thomas Porter plastic surgeon
Wickland, J. Al, Jr. petroleum product executive, real estate executive
Wilks-Owens, Dixie Rae conference/meeting planner, workforce preparation specialist
Wishek, Michael Bradley lawyer
Wolfman, Earl Frank, Jr. surgeon, educator
Wroten, Walter Thomas lawyer
Zaidi, Emily Louise retired elementary school educator
Zeff, Ophelia Hope lawyer
Zeman, Valerie Denise home economics educator
Zil, J. S. psychiatrist, physiologist
Zimmerman, Katherine Louise hypnotherapist
†Zito, Michael Steven educational administrator

Saint Helena
Allegra, Antonia editor, writer
Herber, Steven Carlton physician
Spann, Katharine Doyle marketing and communications executive

Salinas
†Bans, Phil retired corporate security professional
Chester, Lynne foundation executive, artist
Feller, Robert counselor
Phillips, John P(aul) retired neurosurgeon
Puckett, Richard Edward artist, consultant, retired recreation executive
Spinks, Paul retired library director
Stevens, Wilbur Hunt accountant
Taylor, Steven Bruce agriculture company executive
Wong, Walter Foo county official

San Andreas
Arkin, Michael Barry lawyer, arbitrator, writer
Breed, Allen Forbes correctional administrator
Millsaps, Rita Rae elementary school educator

San Anselmo
Ellenberger, Diane Marie nurse, consultant
Mudge, Lewis Seymour theologian, educator, university dean
Murphy, Barry Ames lawyer
Torbet, Laura author, artist, photographer, graphic designer

San Bernardino
Barnes, Gerald R. bishop
Beeler, Bulah Ray medical/surgical nurse
Birge, Anne Constantin protective services official
†Brown-Stigger, Alberta Mae nurse
Burgess, Michael library science educator, publisher
Crowell, Samuel Marvin, Jr. education educator
Dean, Lee protective services executive
De Haas, David Dana emergency physician
Farmer, Wesley Steven police officer
French, Kirby Allan transportation engineer, computer programmer
Holtz, Tobenette aerospace engineer
Kuehn, Klaus Karl Albert ophthalmologist
†Larkin, Donald James, Jr. county government official
Maul, Terry Lee psychologist, educator
Mian, Lal Shah entomologist, educator
Norton, Ruth Ann education educator
Pendleton, Ronald Kenneth education educator
†Roop, Ophelia Georgiev library director
Ruml, Treadwell English language educator
Seitz, Victoria Ann apparel merchandising and marketing educator
Stout, Dennis Lee district attorney
Tacal, Jose Vega, Jr. public health official, veterinarian
Traynor, Gary Edward association administrator
Whitney, David prosecutor
Willis, Harold Wendt, Sr. real estate developer

San Bruno
Bradley, Charles William podiatrist, educator
Corbett, Gerard Francis electronics executive
Ebersole, Priscilla Pier mental health nurse, geriatrics nurse
Kell-Smith, Carla Sue federal agency administrator
Olson, Julie Ann systems consultant, educator

San Carlos
Eby, Michael John marketing research and technology consultant
Fleishman, Alan Michael marketing consultant
Gutow, Bernard Sidney packaging manufacturing company executive
Jones, Georgia Ann publisher
Komissarchik, Edward computer scientist
Mark, Lillian Gee educational administrator
Morrison, Ellen M. writer, researcher
Oliver, Nancy Lebkicher artist, retired elementary education educator
Schumacher, Henry Jerold museum administrator, former career officer, business executive
Sullivan, Shirley Ross (Shirley Ross Davis) art collector
Symons, Robert Spencer electronic engineer
†Torregian, Sotère poet

San Clemente
†Alter, Robert A. hotel executive
Anderson, Michael Robert marketing representative
Clark, Earnest Hubert, Jr. tool company executive
Cramer, Eugene Norman nuclear power engineer, computer educator
Fall, John Robert management and information technology consultant
†Hulce, Randy C. hotel executive
Petruzzi, Christopher Robert business educator, consultant
Singer, Kurt Deutsch news commentator, author, publisher
Stenzel, William A. consulting services executive
White, Stanley Archibald research electrical engineer

San Diego
Aaron, Cynthia G. judge
Abrams, Reid Allen surgeon, educator
Adams, Loretta marketing executive
Addis, Thomas Homer, III professional golfer
†Adler, Louise DeCarl bankruptcy judge
Akeson, Wayne Henry orthopedic surgeon, educator
Alpert, Michael Edward lawyer
Anderson, Karl Richard aerospace engineer, consultant
Anderson, Paul Maurice electrical engineering educator, researcher, consultant
Andreos, George Phillip lawyer

Angelo, Sandra McFall *television and video producer, writer*
Archibald, James David *biology educator, paleontologist*
Asaro, V. Frank *lawyer*
Ashton, Tamarah M. *special education educator*
Backer, Matthias, Jr. *obstetrician-gynecologist*
Bailey, David Nelson *pathologist, educator*
Baird, Mellon Campbell, Jr. *electronics industry executive*
Bakko, Orville Edwin *retired health care executive, consultant*
Bales, Robert Freed *social psychologist, educator*
†Barnhart, Douglas E. *construction company executive*
Barone, Angela Maria *artist, researcher*
†Battaglia, Anthony J. *federal judge*
Baxter, Robert Hampton, III *insurance executive*
Beathard, Bobby *professional football team executive*
Beattie, Geraldine Alice (Geri Beattie) *advocate*
Beauchamp, Miles Philip *newspaper editor-columnist, education consultant*
Beaumont, Mona *artist*
Bell, Gene *newspaper publishing executive*
Bennett, Ronald Thomas *photojournalist*
Bernstein, Sanford Irwin *biology educator*
Beyster, John Robert *engineering company executive*
Bieler, Charles Linford *development director, zoo executive director emeritus*
Binmoeller, Kenneth Frank *physician, surgeon*
†Birnbaum, Aaron S *marketing professional*
Blade, Melinda Kim *archaeologist, educator, researcher*
Blakemore, Claude Coulehan *banker*
Blum, John Alan *urologist, educator*
Bochy, Bruce *professional sports team manager, coach*
Borden, Diane Lynn *communications educator*
†Bowens, Thella *senior aviation director*
Bowie, Peter Wentworth *judge, educator*
Brandes, Raymond Stewart *history educator*
Branson, Harley Kenneth *finance executive*
Brewster, Rudi Milton *state judge*
Brim, Sue *community health nurse*
Brimble, Alan *business executive*
Brom, Robert H. *bishop*
Brooks, John White *lawyer*
†Brooks, Reuben B. *federal judge*
Brose, Cathy *principal*
Brown, Alan J. *electrical engineer*
Brown, Darrell *broadcast executive*
Bruggeman, Terrance John *financial corporate executive*
Bryan, John Rodney *management consultant*
Burge, David Russell *concert pianist, composer, piano educator*
Burke, Arthur Thomas *engineering consultant*
Burke, John *science technology company executive*
Bussard, Robert William *physicist*
Butler, Geoffrey Scott *systems engineer, educator, consultant*
Butler, William H. *military officer*
Buzunis, Constantine Dino *lawyer*
Callahan, LeeAnn Lucille *psychologist*
Campbell, Ian David *opera company director*
Cantor, Charles Robert *biochemistry educator*
Carleson, Robert Bazil *public policy consultant, corporation executive*
Carleton, Mary Ruth *foundation administrator, consultant*
Carney, John Michael *professional football player*
Castruita, Rudy *school system administrator*
Caughlin, Stephenie Jane *organic farmer*
Chamberlin, Eugene Keith *historian, educator*
Chambers, Henry George *orthopedic surgeon*
Charles, Carol Morgan *education educator*
Chatroo, Arthur Jay *lawyer*
Chavez, Gilbert Espinoza *bishop*
Chen, Carlson S. *mechanical engineer*
Chen, Kao *consulting electrical engineer*
Christiansen, David K. *hospital administrator*
Clague, Christopher K(arran) *economics educator*
Clauson, Gary Lewis *chemist*
Clement, Betty Waidlich *literacy educator, consultant*
Clifton, Mark Stephen *administrator*
Cobble, James Wikle *chemistry educator*
Cobianchi, Thomas Theodore *engineering and marketing executive, educator*
Colling, Kenneth Frank *hospital administrator*
Conly, John Franklin *engineering educator, researcher*
Conte, Julie Villa *nurse, administrator*
Coox, Alvin David *history educator*
Copeland, Robert Glenn *lawyer*
Cota, John Francis *utility executive*
†Coulter, Borden McKee *retired management consultant*
Cowen, Donald Eugene *retired physician*
Cox, Kim Carroll *lawyer, broadcaster*
Crick, Francis Harry Compton *science educator, researcher*
Crocker, Valerie Marian *mechanical engineer*
Crook, Sean Paul *aerospace systems program director*
Crumpler, Hugh Allan *author*
Daley, Arthur Stuart *retired humanities educator*
Damoose, George Lynn *lawyer*
Darmstandler, Harry Max *real estate executive, retired air force officer*
Da Rosa, Alison *travel editor*
Davis, James McCoy *real estate executive*
Davis, John Warren *program integrator*
Davis, William Albert *theme park director*
Delawie, Homer Torrence *architect*
DeMaria, Anthony Nicholas *cardiologist, educator*
Demeter, Steven *neurologist, publishing company executive*
Devine, Brian Kiernan *pet food and supplies company executive*
DiRuscio, Lawrence William *advertising executive*
Disney, Michael George *financial services executive*
Dolan, James Michael, Jr. *zoological society executive*
Donahoe, Jim *broadcast executive*
Donley, Dennis Lee *school librarian*
Donnelly, Edward James, Jr. *medical services company executive*
Downing, David Charles *minister*
Downs, Kathleen Anne *healthcare consultant*
Duddles, Charles Weller *food company executive*
Dunn, David Joseph *financial executive*
Dwyer, Lauraine Theresa *ambulatory care administrator, rehabilitation nurse*
Dyer, Charles Richard *law librarian, law educator*
Early, Ames S. *healthcare system executive*
Eckhart, Walter *molecular biologist, educator*
Edwards, Darrel *psychologist*

Edwards-Tate, Laurie Ellen *homecare services company executive, educator*
Eimers, Jeri Anne *therapist*
Emerick, Robert Earl *sociologist, educator*
Enright, William Benner *judge*
Evans, Ersel Arthur *consulting engineer executive*
Evans, John Joseph *management professional, writer, consultant*
Farmer, Janene Elizabeth *artist, educator*
Fauchier, Dan R(ay) *construction management consultant, mediator, arbitrator, educator*
Fay, Helyn *college counselor*
Feinberg, Lawrence Bernard *university dean, psychologist*
Fike, Edward Lake *newspaper editor*
Fisher, Frederick Hendrick *oceanographer emeritus*
Fleischmann, Paul *youth minister*
Flettner, Marianne *opera administrator*
Frasch, Brian Bernard *lawyer*
Frederick, Norman L., Jr. *electrical engineer*
Freedman, Jonathan Borwick *journalist, author, lecturer*
Freeman, Myrna Faye *county schools official*
Friedenberg, Richard Myron *radiology educator, physician*
Friedman, Paul Jay *radiologist, chest radiologist, educator*
Froman, Veronica Zasadni *career officer*
Garcia, Stephanie Brown *aerospace company pricing manager*
Garrison, Betty Bernhardt *retired mathematics educator*
Gastil, Russell Gordon *geologist, educator*
Geffe, Philip Reinhold *electrical engineer, consultant*
Gengor, Virginia Anderson *financial planning executive, educator*
Georgakakos, Konstantine Peter *research hydrologist*
Getis, Arthur *geography educator*
Gilliam, Earl B. *federal judge*
Glickenhaus, Mike *radio station executive*
Golding, Brage *former university president*
Golding, Susan *mayor*
Goltz, Robert William *physician, educator*
Gonzalez, Irma Elsa *federal judge*
Goodall, Jackson Wallace, Jr. *restaurant company executive*
Goode, John Martin *manufacturing company executive*
Gray, Gavin Campbell, II *computer information engineer, computer consultant*
Gray-Bussard, Dolly H. *energy company executive*
Green, Kevin Patrick *career officer*
Greene, John M. *physicist*
Greenspan, Ralph Jay *biologist*
Gross, Jeffrey *software engineer*
Grosser, T.J. *administrator, developer, fundraiser*
Guinn, Stanley Willis *lawyer*
Gulliver, Edward Quentin *marine consultant, writer*
Gwinn, Casey *city attorney San Diego, California*
Gwynn, Anthony Keith (Tony Gwynn) *professional baseball player*
Halasz, Nicholas Alexis *surgeon*
Hale, David Fredrick *health care company executive*
Hales, Alfred Washington *mathematics educator, consultant*
Hamburg, Marian Virginia *health science educator*
Harbaugh, James Joseph *professional football player*
†Hargrove, John James *bankruptcy judge*
Harwood, Ivan Richmond *pediatric pulmonologist*
Hayes, Alice Bourke *university official, biology educator*
Hayes, Claude Quinten Christopher *research scientist*
Hayes, Robert Emmet *retired insurance company executive*
Hays, Garry D. *academic administrator*
Heath, Berthann Jones *education administrator*
Henderson, John Drews *architect*
Henig, Suzanne *retired educator, writer, editor*
†Herzog, Lawrence Arthur *city planning educator*
Hills, Linda Launey *advisory systems engineer*
Hobbs, Marvin *engineering executive*
Hoffman, Robert James *retired electronics engineer*
Hoffman, Trevor William *professional baseball player*
Holl, Walter John *architect, interior designer*
Hooper, Robert Alexander *television producer, international educator*
Hourani, Laurel Lockwood *epidemiologist*
†Howard, Mildred *sculptor*
Howard, William Matthew *educator, lawyer, arbitrator, author*
Hoye, Walter Brisco *retired college administrator*
Huang, Chien Chang *electrical engineer*
Huang, Kun Lien *software engineer, scientist*
Huff, Marilyn L. *federal judge*
Hunt, Robert Gary *medical consultant, oral and maxillofacial surgeon*
Hutcheson, J(ames) Sterling *lawyer*
Intriere, Anthony Donald *physician*
Ivans, William Stanley *electronics company executive*
Jacoby, Irving *physician*
Jamieson, Stuart William *surgeon, educator*
Jeffers, Donald E. *retired insurance executive, consultant*
†Johnson, Grace Alexander *anthropologist, curator*
Johnson, LaMont *composer, musician, producer, consultant*
Johnson, Michael Edward *communication consultant, magician*
Johnson, Vicki R. *insurance company executive*
Jones, Clyde William *anesthesiologist*
Jones, Napoleon A., Jr. *judge*
Jones, Ronald H. *computer information systems executive*
Jong, Theresa Ann *human resource executive*
Kaback, Michael *medical educator*
Kaplan, George Willard *urologist*
Kaufman, Julian Mortimer *broadcasting company executive, consultant*
Keep, Judith N. *federal judge*
Keith, Norman Thomas *aerospace company administrator*
Kendrick, Ronald H. *banker*
Kiesler, Charles Adolphus *psychologist, academic administrator*
Klein, Herbert George *newspaper editor*
Klinedinst, John David *lawyer*
Koehler, John Edget *entrepreneur*
Koski, Donna Faith *poet*
Kraft, William Armstrong *retired priest*
Krejci, Robert Harry *non-profit organizations development consultant*
Kripke, Kenneth Norman *lawyer*
Kropotoff, George Alex *civil engineer*
Krulak, Victor Harold *newspaper executive*
Krull, Kathleen *juvenile fiction and nonfiction writer*
Kuc, Joseph A. *education educator, consultant*
Lakier, Nancy S. *health care consultant*

Lane, Gloria Julian *foundation administrator*
Langer, Eva Marie *audio video systems manager*
Lao, Lang Li *nuclear fusion research physicist*
Larson, Mark Devin *communications executive*
Lathrop, Mitchell Lee *lawyer*
LeBeau, Charles Paul *lawyer*
Le Blanc, Deborah Sims *public administration educator*
Lederer, Richard Henry *writer, educator, columnist*
Legrand, Shawn Pierre *computer systems programmer*
Lehrer, Merrill Clark *retail store executive*
Leopold, George Robert *radiologist*
Lesinski, John Anthony *pharmacist*
Levy, Jerome *dermatologist, retired naval officer*
Lewis, Alan James *pharmaceutical executive, pharmacologist*
Lewis, Gerald Jorgensen *judge*
Lewis, Shirley Jeane *psychology educator*
†Lindbergh, Anne Spencer Morrow (Mrs. Charles Augustus Lindbergh) *author*
Lindh, Patricia Sullivan *banker, former government official*
Ling, David Chang *international book dealer*
Linn, Edward Allen *writer*
Linton, Roy Nathan *graphic arts company executive*
Livingston, Stanley C. *architect*
Lomeli, Marta *elementary education educator*
Longenecker, Martha W. *museum director*
Loper, Warren Edward *computer scientist*
Lovelace, Susan Ellen *professional society administrator*
Lucchino, Lawrence *sports team executive, lawyer*
†Magadan, David Joseph *professional baseball player*
Magnus, Robert *military officer*
Maier, Paul Victor *pharmaceutical executive*
†Maier-Lorentz, Madeline Marie *nurse educator*
March, Marion D. *writer, astrologer, consultant*
Markowitz, Harry M. *finance and economics educator*
Marple, Stanley Lawrence, Jr. *electrical engineer, signal processing researcher*
†Marshall, Lawrence F. *neurologist, surgeon*
†Martén, Roger Evan *screenwriter*
†Martin, Bruce Daniel *engineering executive*
Martinez, John Stanley *entrepreneur*
Masotti, Louis Henry *management educator, consultant*
Mayer, James Hock *mediator, lawyer*
McCarthy, Kevin *broadcast executive*
McCarty, Judy *city councilwoman*
Mc Comic, Robert Barry *real estate development company executive, lawyer*
McEvoy, Pamela T. *clinical psychologist*
McGinnis, Robert E. *lawyer*
McGraw, Donald Jesse *biologist, historian of science, writer*
†McKeon, John Aloysius (Jack) (Jack McKeon) *professional baseball team executive*
McLeod, John Hugh, Jr. *mechanical and electrical engineer*
McManus, Paul Robert *audio recording engineer*
Means, Natrone Jermaine *professional football player*
Mendoza, Stanley Atran *pediatric nephrologist, educator*
Metcalf, Eric Quinn *professional football player*
Meyer, Paul I. *lawyer*
Meyers, James William *federal judge*
Miller, William Charles *lawyer*
Mir, Marilyn *retired educator*
Mittermiller, James Joseph *lawyer*
Mohan, Chandra *research biochemistry educator*
Moore, Edward, Jr. *career officer*
Moores, John *professional sports team executive*
Moossa, A. R. *surgery educator*
Morgan, Mark Quenten *astronomer, astrophysics educator*
Morgan, Neil *author, newspaper editor, lecturer, columnist*
Morris, Grant Harold *law educator*
Morris, Henry Madison, Jr. *education educator*
Morris, Sandra Joan *lawyer*
†Moskowitz, Barry T. *judge*
Mosteller, James Wilbur, III *data processing executive*
Munroe, Ronald L. *architect*
Murray, Colette Morgan *executive search executive*
Myers, Douglas George *zoological society administrator*
Myers, Randall Kirk (Randy Myers) *professional baseball player*
Myrland, Doug *broadcast executive*
Nagao, Norris Sadato *political science educator, consultant*
Nassif, Thomas Anthony *business executive, former ambassador*
Nenner, Victoria Corich *nurse, educator*
Neuman, Tom S. *emergency medical physician, educator*
Neumann, Linda Kay *marketing executive*
Nielsen, Leland C. *federal judge*
Noehren, Robert *organist, organ builder*
Nordt, Sean Patrick *clinical toxicologist*
†North, Robert L. *computer software executvie*
Noziska, Charles Brant *lawyer*
Nugent, Robert J., Jr. *fast food company executive*
Nyiri, Joseph Anton *sculptor, art educator*
O'Laughlin, Joanie *broadcast executive*
O'Leary, John Joseph *security firm executive*
†Olichney, John Michael *neurosciences educator*
Oliphant, Charles Romig *physician*
O'Malley, Edward *physician, consultant*
O'Malley, James Terence *lawyer*
Orgel, Leslie Eleazer *chemist*
Ortiz, Antonio Ignacio *public relations executive*
Osby, Robert Edward *protective services official*
Overton, Marcus Lee *performing arts administrator, actor, writer*
Owen, Charles Theodore *journalist, publisher*
Owsia, Nasrin Akbarnia *pediatrician*
Paderewski, Sir Clarence Joseph *architect*
†Panos, Reed Gregory *plastic surgeon*
†Papas, Leo S. *federal judge*
Parthemore, Jacqueline Gail *physician, educator*
Partida, Gilbert A. *executive*
Payne, Margaret Anne *lawyer*
Pecsok, Robert Louis *chemist, educator*
Petersen, Martin Eugene *museum curator*
Peterson, Paul Ames *lawyer*
Pfeffer, Rubin Harry *publishing executive*
†Philipp, Adam Lief Kakimoto *lawyer*
Pierson, Albert Chadwick *business management educator*
Pincus, Howard Jonah *geologist, engineer, educator*
Pincus, Robert Lawrence *art critic, cultural historian*
Piskor, Chrystal Lea *service company owner*

Pitt, William Alexander *cardiologist*
†Porter, Louisa S. *federal judge*
Powell, Robert Francis *manufacturing engineer*
Pray, Ralph Marble, III *lawyer*
Prescott, Lawrence Malcolm *medical and health science writer*
Preston, David Raymond *lawyer*
Prodor, Leah Marie *secondary education educator*
Pugh, Richard Crawford *lawyer*
Purcifull, Robert Otis *insurance company executive*
Pyatt, Kedar Davis, Jr. *research and development company executive*
Quinn, Edward J. *broadcasting company executive*
Radke, Jan Rodger *pulmonologist, physician executive*
Ranney, Helen Margaret *physician, educator*
Ray, Albert *family physician*
Ray, Gene Wells *industrial executive*
Rea, Amadeo Michael *ethnobiologist, ornithologist*
Reading, James Edward *transportation executive*
Reinhard, Christopher John *merchant banking, venture capital executive*
Reynolds, Hallie Bellah *elementary education educator*
Rhoades, John Skylstead, Sr. *federal judge*
Rice, Clare I. *electronics company executive*
Richards, Thomas R. *military officer*
Riedy, Mark Joseph *finance educator*
†Riley, Michael (Mike Riley) *professional football coach*
Risser, Arthur Crane, Jr. *zoo administrator*
Ristine, Jeffrey Alan *reporter*
Robins, Mitchell James *accountant, management consultant*
Robinson, David Howard *lawyer*
Rodgers, Janet A. *nursing educator, dean*
Rodin, Alvin Eli *retired pathologist, medical educator, author*
Roeder, Stephen Bernhard Walter *chemistry and physics educator*
Romano, Albert *retired educator, statistical consultant*
Roseman, Charles Sanford *lawyer*
Rosen, Peter *health facility administrator, emergency physician, educator*
Ross, Terry D. *lawyer*
Ross, Vonia Pearl *insurance agent, small business owner*
Rowe, Peter A. *newspaper columnist*
Sabatella, Elizabeth Maria *clinical therapist, educator, mental health facility administrator*
Sabin, Gary Byron *financial company executive, investment advisor*
St. Clair, Hal Kay *electrical engineer*
St. George, William Ross *lawyer, retired naval officer, consultant*
Saito, Frank Kiyoji *import-export firm executive*
Samuelson, Derrick William *lawyer*
Sanders, Jerry *protective services official*
Sanders, Reginald Laverne (Reggie Sanders) *professional baseball player*
Sannwald, William Walter *librarian*
Sauer, David Andrew *writer, computer consultant*
Savitripriya, Swami *Hindu religious leader, author*
†Savvas, Minas *English educator*
Sceper, Duane Harold *lawyer*
Schade, Charlene Joanne *adult and early childhood education educator*
Schaechter, Moselio *microbiology educator*
Schmidt, Joseph David *urologist*
Schmidt, Terry Lane *health care executive*
Schorr, Martin Mark *forensic examiner, psychologist, educator, screenwriter*
Schuck, Carl Joseph *lawyer*
Schwartz, Alfred *university dean*
Schwartz, Edward J. *federal judge*
Schwertly, Harvey Kenneth, Jr. *computer electronics educator*
Scorgie, Glen Given *religious studies educator*
Seagren, Stephen Linner *oncologist*
Seau, Junior (Tiana Seau, Jr.) *professional football player*
Seegall, Manfred Ismar Ludwig *retired physicist, educator*
Sell, Robert Emerson *electrical engineer*
Sesonske, Alexander *nuclear and chemical engineer*
Shackelford, Gordon Lee, Jr. *physics educator*
Shapiro, Philip Alan *lawyer*
Sheaffer, Richard Allen *electrical engineer*
Shearer, William Kennedy *lawyer, publisher*
Shelton, Dorothy Diehl Rees *lawyer*
Shneour, Elie Alexis *biochemist*
†Siegal, Barbara Leatrice *visual artist*
Skwara, Erich Wolfgang *novelist, poet, educator, literary critic*
Slate, John Butler *biomedical engineer*
Slater, Leonard *writer, editor*
Slomanson, William Reed *law educator, legal writer*
Smith, Raymond Edward *retired health care administrator*
Smith, Steven Ray *law educator*
Smith, Stuart Craig *television and corporate writer and producer*
Snaid, Leon Jeffrey *lawyer*
Snyder, David Richard *lawyer*
†Sohn, Steven S. *physician*
Sorby, J(oseph) Richard *artist, educator*
†Spanos, Alexander Gus *professional football team executive*
Spanos, Dean A. *business executive*
Springer, Wayne Richard *research biochemist, healthcare system official*
Stafford, Mike *broadcast executive*
Stallings, Valerie Aileen *councilwoman*
Steen, Paul Joseph *retired broadcasting executive*
Stein, Eleanor Benson (Ellie Stein) *playwright*
†Stein, Greg *legislative staff member*
Sterrett, James Kelley, II *lawyer*
Stevens, George L. *city councilman*
Stewart-Pérez, Renice Ann *writer*
Stiska, John Charles *lawyer*
Stone, Thomas Edward *defense consultant, retired rear admiral*
Stoorza Gill, Gail *corporate professional*
Storer, Norman William *sociology educator*
Sullivan, Michelle Cornejo *lawyer*
Sullivan, William Francis *lawyer*
Taylor, George Allen *advertising agency executive*
Taylor, Tony S. *research scientist*
Tedeschi, Ernest Francis, Jr. *retired naval officer, naval company executive*
Thomas, Charles Allen, Jr. *molecular biologist, educator*
Thompson, David Renwick *federal judge*
Thompson, Gordon, Jr. *federal judge*
Thornton, Wayne Allen *naval officer, engineer*
Tidwell, Geoffrey Morgan *medical company executive*

Tillinghast, Charles Carpenter, III *marketing company executive*
Tom, Lawrence *engineering executive*
†Toth, Simone Lee *reporter*
†Towers, Kevin *baseball team executive*
†Trageser, James Michael *editor*
Tricoles, Gus Peter *electromagnetic engineer, physicist, consultant*
Turrentine, Howard Boyd *federal judge*
Underwood, Anthony Paul *lawyer*
Vallbona, Marisa *public relations counselor*
Valliant, James Stevens *lawyer*
Vanderbilt, Kermit *English language educator*
†Varela, José Hector *public defender*
Vargas, Juan *city official*
Vaughn, Billy Eldridge *psychology educator, publisher*
Vause, Edwin Hamilton *research foundation administrator*
Viterbi, Andrew James *electrical engineering and computer science educator, business executive*
Wadlington, W. M. *software company executive*
Waitt, Ted W. *computer company executive*
Walker, Donald Ezzell *retired academic administrator*
Wallace, Helen Margaret *physician, educator*
Wallace, J. Clifford *federal judge*
Walton, Bill (William Theodore Walton, III) *sportscaster, former professional basketball player*
Ward, Charles Raymond *systems engineer*
Warden, Barbara *city councilwoman*
Ward-Steinman, David *composer, music educator, pianist*
Warner, John Hilliard, Jr. *technical services, military and commercial systems and software company executive*
Wasserman, Stephen Ira *physician, educator*
Wear, Byron *councilman*
Weber, Stephen Lewis *university president*
Weeks, John Robert *geographer, sociology educator*
Wehrli, John Erich *biotechnology executive*
Welch, Arnold DeMerritt *pharmacologist, biochemist*
Whitehead, Marvin Delbert *plant pathologist*
Whitmore, Sharp *lawyer*
Wiesler, James Ballard *retired banker*
Wight, Nancy Elizabeth *neonatologist, educator*
Willerding, Margaret Frances *mathematician*
Wilson, Richard Allan *landscape architect*
Winner, Karin *newspaper editor*
Witt, John William *lawyer*
Wood, Hadley Hesse *French language educator*
Woodford, Mary Imogene Steele *secondary school educator*
Wright, Jon Alan *physicist, researcher*
Yarber, Robert Earl *writer, retired educator*
Youngs, Jack Marvin *cost engineer*
Zakarin, Keith *lawyer*
Ziegaus, Alan James *public relations executive*

San Dimas
Cameron, Judith Lynne *secondary education educator, hypnotherapist*
Lindly, Douglas Dean *elementary school educator, administrator*
Peters, Joseph Donald *filmmaker*
Zhang, Guotai *process engineer, researcher, ethylene furnace specialist*

San Fernando
Aguilar, Julia Elizabeth *real estate associate, writer*
Bridges, Robert McSteen *mechanical engineer*
Chiu, Dorothy *pediatrician*
Douglass, Ramona Elizabeth *medical sales professional*
McCraven, Eva Stewart Mapes *health service administrator*

San Francisco
Achtenberg, Roberta *former federal official*
Adamson, Mary Anne *geographer, systems engineer*
Adler, Nancy Elinor *psychologist, educator*
†Ahern, Joseph A. *television station executive*
Albino, Judith Elaine Newsom *university president*
Aldinger, William F., III *banker*
Aldrich, Michael Ray *library curator, health educator*
Alexander, Mary Elsie *lawyer*
Alexander, Robert C. *lawyer*
Allen, Bruce John *writer, activist*
Allen, Jose R. *lawyer*
Allen, Paul Alfred *lawyer, educator*
Alsup, William *lawyer*
Amend, William John Conrad, Jr. *physician, educator*
Ammiano, Tom *county and municipal official*
Anders, George Charles *journalist, author*
Anderson, David E. *zoological park administrator*
Angell, James Browne *electrical engineering educator*
Anschutz, Philip F. *transportation executive, communications executive*
Anthony, Metropolitan, of Sourozh (Anthony Emmanuel Gergiannakis) *bishop*
Apatoff, Michael John *finance executive*
Arbuthnot, Robert Murray *lawyer*
Archer, Richard Joseph *lawyer*
Auerback, Sandra Jean *social worker*
August-deWilde, Katherine *banker*
Autio, Rudy *artist educator*
Axtell, Keith Elton *federal agency administrator*
Babcock, Jo *artist, educator*
Backus, John *computer scientist*
Bainton, Dorothy Ford *pathology educator, researcher*
Baker, Cameron *lawyer*
Baker, Dusty (Johnnie B. Baker, Jr.) *professional baseball team manager*
Baker, Kenneth *art critic, writer*
Balin, Marty (Martyn Jerel Buchwald) *musician*
Bancel, Marilyn *fund raising management consultant*
Bancroft, James Ramsey *lawyer, business executive*
†Barayon, Ramon Sender *writer*
Barbagelata, Robert Dominic *lawyer*
Barber, James P. *lawyer*
Barnum, Alexander Stone *journalist*
Barondes, Samuel Herbert *psychiatrist, educator*
Batchelor, Karen Lee *English language educator*
Bates, William, III *lawyer*
Batlin, Robert Alfred *editor*
Bauer, Michael *newspaper editor*
Baumhefner, Clarence Herman *banker*
Baxter, Marvin Ray *state supreme court justice*
Baxter, Ralph H., Jr. *lawyer*
Beall, Dennis Ray *artist, educator*
Bechtel, Riley Peart *engineering company executive*
Bechtel, Stephen Davison, Jr. *engineering company executive*
Beck, Edward William *lawyer*
Bedford, Daniel Ross *lawyer*
Bee, Robert Norman *banker*
Benet, Leslie Zachary *pharmacokineticist*
Bennett, William *oboist*
Bensinger, David August *dentist, university dean*
Benvenutti, Peter J. *lawyer*
Berggruen, John Henry *art gallery executive*
†Bernstein, Gerald William *management consultant, researcher*
Bertain, G(eorge) Joseph, Jr. *lawyer*
Bertram, Phyllis Ann *lawyer, communications executive*
Bishop, John Michael *biomedical research scientist, educator*
Bitterman, Mary Gayle Foley *broadcasting executive*
Blackburn, Elizabeth Helen *molecular biologist*
Blanc, Maureen *public relations executive*
Bliss, Marian Alice *information systems professional*
†Blood, Brian Ellis *artist*
†Boas, Nancy M. *curator*
†Boehlke, Christine *public relations executive*
†Boehlke, William Fredrick *public relations executive*
Boles, Roger *otolaryngologist*
Bonapart, Alan David *lawyer*
Bondoc, Rommel *lawyer*
Bonds, Barry Lamar *professional baseball player*
Bookin, Daniel Henry *lawyer*
Booth, Forrest *lawyer*
Borowsky, Philip *lawyer*
Boucher, Harold Irving *retired lawyer*
Bourne, Henry R. *biochemistry professor*
Boutin, Peter Rucker *lawyer*
Boyd, William Sprott *lawyer*
Boyer, Herbert Wayne *biochemist*
Boyle, Antonia Barnes *audio producer, writer*
Bracken, Thomas Robert James *real estate investment executive*
Brandin, Alf Elvin *retired mining and shipping company executive*
Breeden, David *clarinetist*
†Brennan, Joan Stevenson *federal judge*
Bridges, Robert Lysle *retired lawyer*
Bridgman, Richard Darrell *lawyer*
Briggs, Susan Shadinger *lawyer*
Briscoe, John *lawyer*
Broadway, Nancy Ruth *landscape design and construction company executive, consultant, model and actress*
Bromley, Dennis Karl *lawyer*
†Bronstein, Phil *executive editor*
Brooke, Pegan Struthers *artist, art educator*
Brooks, William George *aeronautical engineer*
Broome, Burton Edward *insurance company executive*
Brower, David Ross *conservationist*
†Brown, Amos Cleophilus *minister*
†Brown, Cabot *private equity investor*
Brown, Donald Wesley *lawyer*
Brown, Eric Joel *biomedical researcher*
Brown, Geoffrey Francis *public defender, lawyer*
Brown, Janice Rogers *state supreme court justice*
†Brown, Robert Elliott *lawyer*
Brown, Walter Creighton *biologist*
Brown, Willie Lewis, Jr. *mayor, former state legislator, lawyer*
Browning, James Robert *federal judge*
Bruen, James A. *lawyer*
Buckner, John Knowles *pension administrator*
Buidang, George (Hada Buidang) *educator, administrator, consultant, writer*
Bull, Henrik Helkand *architect*
Burden, James Ewers *lawyer*
Burgess, Leonard Randolph *business administration and economics educator, writer*
Burgess, Robert *software company executive*
Burlingame, Alma Lyman *chemist, educator*
Burns, Brian Patrick *lawyer, business executive*
Bushnell, Roderick Paul *lawyer*
Butenhoff, Susan *public relations executive*
Butz, Otto William *political science educator*
Caccamo, Aldo M. *oil industry executive*
Cain, Leo Francis *retired special education educator*
Callison, Russell James *lawyer*
Calvin, Dorothy Ver Strate *computer company executive*
Campbell, Scott Robert *lawyer, former food company executive*
Campisi, Dominic John *lawyer*
Canales, James Earl, Jr. *foundation administrator*
Caniparoli, Val William *choreographer, dancer*
Cape, Ronald Elliot *retired biotechnology company executive*
†Carlisle, Henry C. *author*
Carlson, John Earl *lawyer*
†Carlson, Thomas Edward *bankruptcy judge*
Carson, Jay Wilmer *pathologist, educator*
Carter, George Kent *oil company executive*
Carter, John Douglas *lawyer*
Cartmell, Nathaniel Madison, III *lawyer*
Castro, Joseph Ronald *physician, oncology researcher, educator*
Cavanagh, John Charles *advertising agency executive*
†Cepeda, Orlando *retired professional baseball player*
Chadwick, Whitney *writer, art historian, educator*
†Chan, Daisy S. W. *manufacturing engineer*
Chao, Cedric C. *lawyer*
Chapin, Dwight Allan *columnist, writer*
Chartrand, April Martin *designer*
Chase, Marilyn *journalist*
Cheatham, Robert William *lawyer*
Cheitlin, Melvin Donald *physician, educator*
Chen, Joan (Chen Chong) *actress*
Cheng, Kwong Man *structural engineer*
Cheng, Wan-Lee *mechanical engineer, industrial technology educator*
Cherny, Robert Wallace *history educator*
Chesney, Maxine M. *judge*
Chiaverini, John Edward *construction company executive*
Chin, Ming *state supreme court justice*
Chin, Sue Soone Marian (Suchin Chin) *conceptual artist, portraitist, photographer, community affairs activist*
Chong, Rachelle B. *lawyer, federal communications commissioner*
Clark, Richard Ward *trust company executive, consultant*
Clarke, Richard Alan *electric and gas utility company executive, lawyer*
†Clementi, Mark Anthony *clinical and sport psychologist, educator*
Clever, Linda Hawes *physician*
Clopton, Karen Valentia *lawyer, president civil services commission*
Close, Sandy *journalist*
Cluff, Lloyd Sterling *earthquake geologist*
Cobbs, Price Mashaw *social psychiatrist*
Coffin, Judy Sue *lawyer*
Cohn, Nathan *lawyer*
Coleman, Thomas Young *lawyer*
Collas, Juan Garduño, Jr. *lawyer*
†Collins, Dennis Arthur *foundation executive*
Colwell, Kent Leigh *venture capitalist*
Conti, Samuel *federal judge*
Cook, John C. *lawyer*
Coombe, George William, Jr. *lawyer, retired banker*
Corcoran, Maureen Elizabeth *lawyer*
Corkery, Paul Jerome *author, editor*
Corrigan, Robert Anthony *academic administrator*
Costa-Zalessow, Natalia *foreign language educator*
Cousineau, Philip Robert *writer, filmmaker*
Coye, Molly Joel *state agency administrator*
Crawford, Roy Edgington, III *lawyer*
Crosby, Kathryn Grandstaff (Grant Crosby) *actress*
Cruse, Allan Baird *mathematician, computer scientist, educator*
Cumming, George Anderson, Jr. *lawyer*
Curley, John Peter *sports editor*
Curtis, David Lambert *rheumatologist, educator*
Dachs, Alan Mark *investment company executive*
Dallman, Mary F. *physiology educator*
Danziger, Bruce Edward *structural engineer*
David, George *psychiatrist, economic theory lecturer*
Davies, Paul Lewis, Jr. *retired lawyer*
Davis, J. Steve *advertising agency executive*
Davis, James Wesley *university program administrator, artist, writer, composer*
Davis, Roger Lewis *lawyer*
Dawson, Chandler Robert *ophthalmologist, educator*
Debas, Haile T. *gastrointestinal surgeon, physiologist, educator*
de Hostos, Eugenio Luis *cell biologist*
Deicken, Raymond Friedrich *neuropsychiatrist, clinical neuroscientist*
Delacote, Goery *museum director*
Del Campo, Martin Bernardelli *architect*
†Dell, Robert Michael *lawyer*
Dellas, Robert Dennis *investment banker*
De Lutis, Donald Conse *investment manager, consultant*
Demarest, David Franklin, Jr. *banker, former government official*
DeMuro, Paul Robert *lawyer*
Derr, Kenneth T. *oil company executive*
DeSoto, Lewis Damien *art educator*
deWilde, David Michael *executive search consultant, financial services executive, lawyer*
Diamond, Philip Ernest *lawyer*
Dickey, Glenn Ernest, Jr. *sports columnist*
Dickinson, Eleanor Creekmore *artist, educator*
Dickinson, Wade *physicist, oil company executive, educator*
Diekmann, Gilmore Frederick, Jr. *lawyer*
Dill, Kenneth Austin *pharmaceutical chemistry educator*
†Dillon, Millicent Gerson *writer*
Doan, Mary Frances *advertising executive*
Dolby, Ray Milton *engineering company executive, electrical engineer*
Donnally, Patricia Broderick *newspaper editor*
Donnici, Peter Joseph *lawyer, law educator, consultant*
Donovan, Charles Stephen *lawyer*
Dorfman, Paul Michael *bank executive*
Draper, William Henry, III *business executive*
Dreibelbis, Ellen Roberts *artist*
Drexler, Fred *insurance executive*
Drozd, Leon Frank, Jr. *lawyer*
Dryden, Robert Eugene *lawyer*
Du Bain, Myron *foundation administrator*
Dugoni, Arthur A. *orthodontics educator, university dean*
Dullea, Charles W. *university chancellor emeritus, priest*
Dunn, Richard Joseph *retired investment counselor*
Dunne, Kevin Joseph *lawyer*
Dupont, Colyer Lee *television and film producer, video and film distributing company executive*
Dupree, Stanley M. *lawyer*
Duscha, Julius Carl *journalist*
Düzgünes, Nejat A. *biophysicist, microbiologist*
Eastham, Thomas *foundation administrator*
Eastwood, Susan *medical scientific editor*
Eaton, Jerry *television executive*
Eckersley, Norman Chadwick *bank executive*
Edgar, James Macmillan, Jr. *management consultant*
Edginton, John Arthur *lawyer*
Edwards, Robin Morse *lawyer*
Egan, Patricia Jane *former university development director, writer*
Elderkin, E(dwin) Judge *retired lawyer*
Enfield, D(onald) Michael *insurance executive*
Eng, Catherine *health care facility administrator, physician, medical educator*
Engelmann, Rudolph Herman *electronics consultant*
Engleman, Ephraim Philip *rheumatologist*
Entriken, Robert Kersey *retired management educator*
Epstein, Charles Joseph *physician, medical geneticist, pediatrics and biochemistry educator*
Epstein, John Howard *dermatologist*
Epstein, Leon Joseph *psychiatrist*
Ericson, Bruce Alan *lawyer*
†Ermatinger, John *apparel executive*
Eschmeyer, William Neil *marine scientist*
Estes, Carroll Lynn *sociologist, educator*
Etheridge, Melissa Lou *singer, songwriter*
Falk, Steven B. *newspaper publishing executive*
Faron, Fay Cheryl *private investigator, writer*
Fergus, Gary Scott *lawyer*
Ferlinghetti, Lawrence *poet*
Festinger, Richard *music educator, composer*
Field, John Louis *architect*
Finberg, James Michael *lawyer*
Finberg, Laurence *pediatrician, educator, dean*
Finck, Kevin William *lawyer*
Fine, Marjorie Lynn *lawyer*
Finefrock, James Alan *editor*
†Finley, Karen *actress*
Fisher, Donald G. *casual apparel chain stores executive*
Fishman, Robert Allen *neurologist, educator*
Fitzpatrick, William Peter *computer programmer, analyst, state legislator*
Fleishhacker, David *school administrator*
Flittie, Clifford Gilliland *retired petroleum company executive*
Fogel, Paul David *lawyer*
Folberg, Harold Jay *lawyer, mediator, educator, university dean*
Forsythe, Janet Winifred *lawyer*
Foster, David Scott *lawyer*
Foye, Laurance Vincent *physician, hospital administrator*
Frank, Anthony Melchior *federal official, former financial executive*
Fredericks, Dale Edward *lawyer*
Freeman, Marshall *publishing executive*
Freeman, Tom M. *lawyer*
Freud, Nicholas S. *lawyer*
Freund, Fredric S. *real estate broker, property manager*
Frick, Oscar Lionel *physician, educator*
Friedman, K. Bruce *lawyer*
Friedman, Meyer *physician*
Friese, Robert Charles *lawyer*
Fromm, Hanna *educational administrator*
Fu, Karen King-Wah *radiation oncologist*
Fuller, James William *financial director*
Fuller, William P. *president Asia Foundation*
Furst, Arthur *toxicologist, educator*
Furth, Frederick Paul *lawyer*
Gaither, James C. *lawyer*
Gale, Michael Jonathan *entrepreneur*
Ganong, William F(rancis) *physiologist, physician*
Garchik, Leah Lieberman *journalist*
Gardner, James Harkins *venture capitalist*
Garvey, Joanne Marie *lawyer*
Gaut, Norman Eugene *software firm executive*
Gelhaus, Robert Joseph *lawyer, publisher*
Gellin, Gerald Alan *dermatologist*
George, Donald Warner *online columnist and editor, freelance writer*
George, Ronald M. *state supreme court chief justice*
George, Vance *conductor*
German, William *newspaper editor*
Gerwick, Ben Clifford, Jr. *construction engineer, educator*
Gibbs, Patricia Hellman *physician*
Gillette, Frankie Jacobs *retired savings and loan executive, social worker, government administrator*
Ginn, Sam L. *telephone company executive*
Giovinco, Joseph *nonprofit administrator, writer*
Glassberg, Alan Burnett *physician*
Glazer, Jack Henry *lawyer*
Glynn, Robert D., Jr. *energy-based holding company*
Goldberg, Fred Sellmann *advertising executive*
†Goldman, Richard N. *foundation administrator*
†Goode, Barry Paul *lawyer*
Goode, Erica Tucker *internist*
Gooding, Charles Arthur *radiologist, physician, educator*
Gordon, Judith *communications consultant, writer*
Gowdy, Franklin Brockway *lawyer*
Grager, Steven Paul *life insurance and trust consultant*
Graham, Toni *writer*
Graysmith, Robert *political cartoonist, author*
Grayson, Ellison Capers, Jr. *human resources executive*
Greber, Robert Martin *financial investments executive*
†Green, Bartley Crocker *advertising executive*
Green, Robert Leonard *hospital management company executive*
Greene, John Clifford *dentist, former university dean*
Greenspan, Deborah *oral medicine educator*
Greenspan, Francis S. *physician*
Greenspan, John S. *dentistry educator, scientist, administrator*
Gresham, Zane Oliver *lawyer*
Greyson, Clifford Russell *internist*
Grodsky, Gerold Morton *biochemistry educator*
Grose, Andrew Peter *foundation executive*
Grossman, William *medical researcher, educator*
Grove, Douglas David *insurance company executive*
Grubb, David H. *construction company executive*
Gruber, George Michael *accountant, financial systems consultant*
Grumbach, Melvin Malcolm *physician, educator*
Guggenhime, Richard Johnson *lawyer*
Gund, George, III *financier, professional sports team executive*
Gunn, Thom(son) (William) *poet*
Gyani, Mohan *communications company executive*
Haas, Peter E., Sr. *company executive*
Haas, Robert Douglas *apparel manufacturing company executive*
Haerle, Paul Raymond *judge*
Hagenbuch, John Jacob *investment banker*
Hahner, Linda R. R. *artist, creative director*
Hall, Paul J. *lawyer*
Hall, Zach Winter *academic administrator*
Halliday, John Meech *investment company executive*
Halloran, Michael James *lawyer*
Hallstrom, Robert Chris *government actuary*
Hamburger, Ronald Owen *structural engineering executive*
Handler, Evelyn *science administrator*
Handlery, Paul Robert *hotel executive*
Hannawalt, Willis Dale *retired lawyer*
Hanschen, Peter Walter *lawyer*
Hara, George *software company executive*
†Hardiman, David Alexander *music educator*
Hardison, Donald Leigh *architect*
Harlan, Neil Eugene *retired healthcare company executive*
Harrington, Charlene Ann *sociology and health policy educator*
Hastings, Edward Walton *theater director*
Havel, Richard Joseph *physician, educator*
Haven, Thomas Edward *lawyer*
†Hawthorne, Mark R. *investigator, educator*
Hayes, Randall L. *environmental organizer, lecturer*
Hazen, Paul Mandeville *banker*
Heafey, Edwin Austin, Jr. *lawyer*
Heilbron, David M(ichael) *lawyer*
Hellman, F(rederick) Warren *investment advisor*
Henderson, Dan Fenno *lawyer, law educator*
Henderson, Nancy Grace *marketing and technical documentation executive*
Henderson, Thelton Eugene *federal judge*
Heng, Donald James, Jr. *lawyer*
†Henshaw, Guy Runals *management consultant*
Henson, Ray David *legal educator, consultant*
Herbert, Chesley C. *psychiatrist, educator*
Hering, William Marshall *medical organization executive*
Herlihy, Thomas Mortimer *lawyer*
Herringer, Frank Casper *diversified financial services company executive*
Hershman, Lynn Lester *artist*
Herskowitz, Ira *educator, molecular geneticist*
Heuring, Wayne Robert *newspaper journalist*
†Hewitt, Conrad W. *state superintendent of banks*
Heyman, Melvin Bernard *pediatric gastroenterologist*
Heyneman, Donald *parasitology and tropical medicine educator*
Hickman, Maxine Viola *social services administrator*
†Hiemstra, Marvin Roy *poet, humorist, literary consultant*

Higashida, Randall Takeo radiologist, neurosurgeon, medical educator
High, Thomas W. energy services executive
Hill, Greg newspaper bureau chief
Hills, Austin Edward vineyard executive
Hilton, Stanley Goumas lawyer, educator, writer
Hinman, Frank, Jr. urologist, educator
Hinman, Harvey DeForest lawyer
Hoadley, Walter Evans economist, financial executive, lay worker
Hobbs, C. Fredric artist, filmmaker, author
Hochschild, Adam writer, commentator, journalist
†Hoffman, Auren company executive
Hoffman, Julien Ivor Ellis pediatric cardiologist, educator
Hofmann, John Richard, Jr. lawyer
Holden, Frederick Douglass, Jr. lawyer
Holmes, Irvin R., Jr. marketing professional
Homer, Barry Wayne lawyer
Hoppe, Arthur Watterson columnist
†Hor, Johnson contractor
Horan, Joseph Patrick interior designer
Horne, Grant Nelson public relations consultant
Howard, Carl (Michael) lawyer
Howard, David E. artist
Howe, Drayton Ford, Jr. lawyer
Howitt, David Andrew human resources executive
Howley, Peter Anthony communications executive
Hsieh, Michael Thomas venture capitalist
Hsu, John Chao-Chun retired pediatrician
Hudner, Philip lawyer, rancher
Hudson, Mark Woodbridge lawyer
Hull, Cordell William business executive
Hunt, James L. lawyer
Hunter, William Dennis lawyer
Huntting, Cynthia Cox artist
Hurabiell, John Philip, Sr. lawyer
Hurley, Mark Joseph bishop
Iacono, James Michael research center administrator, nutrition educator
Illston, Susan Y. judge
Irwin, William Rankin lawyer
Jacobs, John Howard professional society administrator
Jacobs, Rodney L. bank executive
Jacobus, Arthur dance company administrator
Jaffe, Robert Benton obstetrician, gynecologist, reproductive endocrinologist
James, David Lee lawyer, international advisor, author
James, George Barker, II apparel industry executive
†James, Maria-Elena federal judge
Jan, Lily Yeh physiology, biochemist
†Jay, Cheryl Ann neurology educator
Jenkins, Bruce sportswriter
Jensen, Ronald H. medical educator
Jewett, George Frederick, Jr. forest products company executive
Jimenez, Josephine Santos portfolio manager
Johns, Richard Seth Ellis lawyer
Johns, Roy (Bud Johns) publisher, author
Johnson, Camille media executive
Johnson, Herman Leonall research nutritionist
Johnson, Martin Wayne lawyer
Johnson, Reverdy lawyer
Jones, J. Gilbert research consultant
Jones, Stanton William management consultant
Joseph, Allan Jay lawyer
†Julius, Daniel J. university administrator, educator
Jung, David Joseph law educator
Junker, Howard Henry periodical editor
Kahle, Brewster communications executive
Kahn, Linda McClure actuary, consultant
Kallgren, Edward Eugene lawyer
†Kamer, Larry public relations executive
Kan, Yuet Wai physician, investigator
Kane, Mary Kay law educator, college dean
Kaplan, Alvin Irving lawyer, adjudicator, investigator
Kasanin, Mark Owen lawyer
Katz, Hilliard Joel physician
Kaufman, Barbara municipal official
Kaufman, Jonathan Allan (Jon) public relations executive
†Kazalia, Marie Ann writer
Keeney, Ralph Lyons information systems specialist, educator
Kehlmann, Robert artist, critic
†Kelleher, Kevin Paul journalist
Keller, Edward Lowell electrical engineer, educator
Kelly, J. Michael lawyer
Kelly, Kevin editor
Kelly, Regis Baker biochemistry educator, biophysics educator
Kemp, Alson Remington, Jr. lawyer, legal educator
Kemp, Jeanne Frances office manager
Kendall, Robert Daniel priest, theology educator
Kennard, Joyce L. state supreme court justice
Kennedy, Raoul Dion lawyer
Kent, Jeffrey Franklin baseball player
Kern, John McDougall lawyer
Kerner, Michael Philip lawyer
Khosla, Ved Mitter oral and maxillofacial surgeon, educator
Kiefer, Renata Gertrud physician, epidemiologist, economist, international health management consultant
Kielarowski, Henry Edward marketing executive
†Kilgore, Eugene Sterling, Jr. surgeon
Kimport, David Lloyd lawyer
†Kimpton, Bill hotel executive
†Kind, Gabriel Matthew plastic surgeon
†King, Alonzo artistic director, choreographer
Klammer, Joseph Francis management consultant
Kleeman, Michael Jeffrey telecommunications and computer consultant
Klein, Jeffrey editor-in-chief
Klein, Marc S. newspaper editor and publisher
Kleinberg, David Lewis education administrator
Kline, Howard Jay cardiologist, educator
Klott, David Lee lawyer
Knapp, Charles Lincoln law educator
Knebel, Jack Gillen lawyer
Knutzen, Martha Lorraine lawyer
Koeppel, John A. lawyer
Koffel, Martin M. engineering company executive
Kolb, Felix Oscar physician
Komater, Christopher John artist
Kozloff, Lloyd M. university dean, educator, scientist
Kramer, Steven G. ophthalmologist
Kreitzberg, Fred Charles construction management company executive
Krevans, Julius Richard university administrator, physician
Kriken, John Lund architect
Krippner, Stanley Curtis psychologist
Kuhl, Paul Beach lawyer
Kuhns, Craig Shaffer business educator
Kurtz, Larry corporate communications executive
LaBelle, Thomas Jeffrey academic administrator
Ladar, Jerrold Morton lawyer
Lai, Him Mark writer
Lamberson, John Roger insurance company executive
Landahl, Herbert Daniel biophysicist, mathematical biologist, researcher, consultant
Landis, Richard Gordon retired food company executive
Lane, Fielding H. lawyer
†Langford, F. Steele federal judge
Langton, Daniel Joseph English, writing educator, poet
Lara, Adair columnist, writer
Larsen, Loren Joseph retired pediatric orthopedic surgeon
Larson, John William lawyer
Larson, Mark Allan financial executive
Lasky, Moses lawyer
†LaTour, Thomas W. hotel executive
Lau, Elizabeth Kwok-Wah writer
Lau, Fred H. protective services official
Leal, Susan city official
LeBlanc, Tina dancer
Lee, Ivy, Jr. public relations consultant
Lee, John Jin lawyer
Lee, Pamela Anne bank executive, accountant, business analyst
Lee, Philip Randolph medical educator
Legge, Charles Alexander federal judge
†LeGrady, George photographer, educator
Leung, Kason Kai Ching computer specialist
Levada, William Joseph archbishop
Levine, Norman Gene insurance company executive
Levit, Victor Bert lawyer, foreign representative, civic worker
Leviton, Alan Edward museum curator
Lewis, Andrea Elen editor
Libbin, Anne Edna lawyer
Lim, Robert Cheong, Jr. surgeon, educator
Lin, Tung Yen civil engineer, educator
Lindsay, George Edmund museum director
Lindstrom, Gregory P. lawyer
Lippitt, Elizabeth Charlotte writer
Littlefield, Edmund Wattis mining company executive
Livsey, Robert Callister lawyer
Lo, Bernard education educator
Lobdell, Frank artist
Lombardi, David Ennis, Jr. lawyer, lecturer, mediator
Lo Schiavo, John Joseph university executive
Lotito, Michael Joseph lawyer
Louie, David A. television journalist
Low, Randall internist, cardiologist
Lowndes, David Alan programmer analyst
Lucia, Marilyn Reed physician
Luckoff, Michael broadcast executive
Luft, Harold S. health economist
Luikart, John Ford investment banker
Lull, Robert John nuclear medicine physician, educator
Lustgarten, Celia Sophie freelance consultant, writer
†Lyon, David William research executive
MacGowan, Eugenia lawyer
Mack, Ronald Brand pediatric dentist, clinician, educator, writer, lecturer
MacNaughton, Angus Athole finance company executive
Madson, David John fundraising executive
Maffre, Muriel ballet dancer
Magowan, Peter Alden professional baseball team executive, grocery chain executive
Mahoney, Michael James investment executive
Maibach, Howard I. dermatologist
Mandra, York T. geology educator
Maneatis, George A. retired utility company executive
Mann, Bruce Alan lawyer
Manning, Jerome Alan lawyer
Manson, Malcolm Hood educational administrator
†Mao, Stephen Tsing executive
Marchant, David Judson lawyer
Marcus, Richard Leon lawyer, educator
Marcus, Robert aluminum company executive
Margulis, Alexander Rafailo physician, educator
Marino, Richard J. publishing executive
Marmysz, John Alexander philosophy educator, consultant
†Marshall, Carolyn D. journalist, author
Marshall, John Paul broadcast technologist
Marshall, Scott advertising agency executive
Marston, Michael urban economist, asset management executive
Martel, John Sheldon lawyer, author
Martin, Fred artist, college administrator
Martin, John L. airport executive
†Martin, William John, III psychotherapist, artist
Martinson, Ida Marie nursing educator, nurse, physiologist
Marvin, David Keith international relations educator
Mason, Cheryl White lawyer
Mason, Dean Towle cardiologist
Massaro, Mike advertising executive
Mathes, Stephen John plastic and reconstructive surgeon, educator
Mattern, Douglas James electronics reliability engineer
Mattes, Martin Anthony lawyer
Matthews, Gilbert Elliott investment banker
Maxim, David Nicholas artist
Mayer, Patricia Jayne financial officer, management accountant
Mayeri, Beverly artist, ceramic sculptor, educator
McAninch, Jack Weldon urological surgeon, educator
McClintock, Jessica fashion designer
†McClure, Thomas Allan physician
McCorkle, Horace Jackson physician, educator
McElhinny, Harold John lawyer
†McGegan, Nicholas music director
McGettigan, Charles Carroll, Jr. investment banker
McGrath, Patrick Joseph bishop
McGuckin, John Hugh, Jr. lawyer
McKelvey, Judith Grant lawyer, educator, university dean
Mc Laughlin, Jerome Michael lawyer, shipping company executive
McNally, Thomas Charles, III lawyer
McNamara, Thomas Neal lawyer
Meadows, John Frederick lawyer
Meister, Gerry Smith social studies educator
Mellor, Michael Lawton lawyer
Merrill, Harvie Martin manufacturing executive
Metz, Mary Seawell retired university dean, retired college president
Metzler, Roger James, Jr. lawyer
Meyer, Keith John marketing professional
Meyer, Thomas James editorial cartoonist
Mihan, Ralph George lawyer
Miller, John Nelson banker
Miller, William Napier Cripps lawyer
Mills, Thomas Cooke psychiatrist
Millstein, David J. lawyer
†Mimi, Haas volunteer
Minar, Paul G. design consultant
Minnick, Malcolm David lawyer
Minor, Halsey multimedia company executive
Minor, Halsey M. computer company executive
Minton, Torri journalist
Mitchell, Bruce Tyson lawyer
Monson, Arch, Jr. fire alarm manufacturing company executive
Montali, Dennis federal judge
Montney, Marvin Richard writer, poet, playwright
Moore, Scott Michael lawyer
Morgan, Christina venture capital firm executive
Morgan, Michael Brewster publishing company executive
Moris, Lamberto Giuliano architect
Morrissey, John Carroll, Sr. lawyer
Mosk, Stanley state supreme court justice
Moss, Douglas Mabbett military officer, airline pilot, test pilot
Muegge, Lyn advertising executive
Muench, Marcus Oliver hematologist
Mumford, Christopher Greene corporate financial executive
†Munroe, Tapan economist, educator, consultant
Muranaka, Hideo artist, educator
Murdoch, Colin cultural organization administrator
Murphy, Kathleen Anne Foley advertising agency executive
Musfelt, Duane Clark lawyer
Musser, Sandra G. retired lawyer
Mussman, William Edward, III lawyer
Mustacchi, Piero physician, educator
Myers, Howard Milton pharmacologist, educator
Nachman, Gerald Weil columnist, critic, author
Naegele, Carl Joseph university academic administrator, educator
Nee, D. Y. Bob think tank executive, engineering consultant
Needleman, Jacob philosophy educator, writer
Nelson, Jonathan computer communications company executive
Nelson, Matthew Sherwood computer communications company executive
Nen, Robert Allen (Robb Nen) professional baseball player
Newirth, Richard Scott cultural organization administrator
Nguyen, Ann Cac Khue pharmaceutical and medicinal chemist
Nichols, Richard Alan ecologist
Nicholson, William Joseph forest products company executive
Nicoll, Roger Andrew pharmacology and physiology educator
Ninkovich, Thomas owner research firm, consultant
Nix, Katherine Jean medical case manager
Noonan, John T., Jr. federal judge, legal educator
Norbeck, Jane S. nursing educator
Nord, Paul Elliott accountant
O'Connor, G(eorge) Richard ophthalmologist
O'Connor, Sheila Anne freelance writer
Odgers, Richard William lawyer
Offer, Stuart Jay lawyer
Olds, John Theodore banker
Olejko, Mitchell J. lawyer
Oliver, John Edward bank strategic management and training consultant
Olshen, Abraham Charles actuarial consultant
Olson, Walter Gilbert lawyer
O'Neill, Michael academic administrator
O'Rourke, Dennis advertising executive
Orrick, William Horsley, Jr. federal judge
Osterhaus, William Eric television executive
Otus, Simone public relations executive
Oxarart, Frank broadcast executive
Palmer, William Joseph accountant
Pantaleo, Jack writer, composer, social worker, harpist
Parker, Diana Lynne restaurant manager, special events director
Parker, Harry S., III art museum administrator
†Pastreich, Peter orchestra executive director
Patel, Marilyn Hall judge
Paterson, Richard Denis financial executive
Paul, Don writer, musician
Pazour, Don publishing executive
Penskar, Mark Howard lawyer
Perkins, Herbert Asa physician
Perlman, David science editor, journalist
Perlman, Susan Gail organization executive
Peters, Raymond Robert bank executive
Peterson, Rudolph A. banker
Peterson, Wayne Turner composer, pianist
Petrakis, Nicholas Louis physician, medical researcher, educator
Pfau, George Harold, Jr. stockbroker
Philipsborn, John Timothy lawyer, author
Phillips, Steve lawyer, past president board of education
Phillips, Theodore Locke radiation oncologist, educator
Phillips, Thomas Embert artist
Piccolo, Richard Andrew artist, educator
Piel, Carolyn Forman pediatrician, educator
Pimentel, Benjamin Impelido journalist
†Pipes, Sally C. think-tank executive
Pitts, Orion Clark theatre educator
Pollack, Jeffrey Lee restaurateur
Poole, Gordon Leicester lawyer
Pope, Carl professional society administrator
Popofsky, Melvin Laurence lawyer
Probert, Colin advertising executive
Pulido, Mark A. pharmaceutical and cosmetics company executive
Quick, William Thomas author, screenwriter
Raciti, Cherie artist
Raeber, John Arthur architect, construction consultant
Raedeke, Linda Dismore geologist
Ralston, Henry James, III neurobiologist, anatomist, educator
Ramey, Drucilla Stender legal association executive
Ramos, Charles Joseph (Joe Ramos) wealth management consultant
Rankin, Jimmie R. neuroscience nurse
Rascón, Armando artist
†Raskin, Neil Hugh neurology educator
Raven, Robert Dunbar lawyer
Ream, James Terrill architect, sculptor
Reding, John Anthony lawyer
Redo, David Lucien investment company executive
Reed, Robert Daniel publisher
Reese, John Robert lawyer
Rembe, Toni lawyer
Renfrew, Charles Byron lawyer
Renne, Louise Hornbeck lawyer
Rice, Denis Timlin lawyer
Rice, Dorothy Pechman (Mrs. John Donald Rice) medical economist
Rice, Jonathan C. retired educational television executive
Richards, Norman Blanchard lawyer
Riley, Benjamin Kneeland lawyer
Riney, Hal Patrick advertising executive
Rippel, Clarence W. academic administrator
Risse, Guenter Bernhard physician, historian, educator
†Roberts, Jerry newspaper editor
Robertson, Armand James, II judge
Robertson, J. Martin lawyer
Rock, Arthur venture capitalist
Roe, Benson Bertheau surgeon, educator
Roethe, James Norton lawyer
Rogoff, Alice Elizabeth writer, editor
Roloff, John Scott artist, art educator
Roman, Stan G. lawyer
Romeo, Roberta H. McNeill nurse educator
Rosales, Suzanne Marie hospital coordinator
Rosch, John Thomas lawyer
Rosen, Moishe religious organization founder
Rosen, Sanford Jay lawyer
Rosenbaum, Ernest Harold internist, oncologist, educator
Rosenberg, Claude Newman, Jr. investment adviser
Rosenberg, Richard Morris banker
Rosenheim, Daniel Edward journalist, television news director
Rosinski, Edwin Francis health sciences educator
Rosner, Robert Mendel securities analyst
Ross, David A. art museum director
Rossetto, Louis editor, publisher
Rossmann, Antonio lawyer, educator
Rouda, Robert E. dentist
Rubenstein, Steven Paul newspaper columnist
Rubin, Michael lawyer
Rudolph, Abraham Morris physician, educator
Runnicles, Donald conductor
Rusher, William Allen writer, commentator
Russoniello, Joseph Pascal lawyer
Rutschke, Annamarie administrative technician
Ryland, David Ronald lawyer
†Sabean, Brian R. professional baseball team executive
Sachs, Marilyn Stickle author, lecturer, editor
Salomon, Darrell Joseph lawyer
Salvadore, Tony broadcast executive
Sano, Emily Joy museum director
†Sarti, Edward R. lawyer, accountant
Sassone, Marco Massimo artist
Satin, Joseph language professional, university administrator
Saunders, Debra J. columnist
Savage, Michael John Kirkness oil company and arts management executive
Savage, Thomas Joseph executive development company executive, priest
Scarlett, Randall H. lawyer
Schaffer, Jeffrey L. lawyer
Schiller, Francis neurologist, medical historian
Schlegel, John Peter academic administrator
Schlesinger, Norma Honig art historian, writer
Schmid, Rudi (Rudolf Schmid) internist, educator, scientist
Schmidt, Robert Milton physician, scientist, educator, administrator
Scholten, Paul obstetrician, gynecologist, educator
Schrier, Eric publisher
Schrock, Theodore R. surgeon
†Schroffel, Bruce university executive
Schwartz, Louis Brown legal educator
Schwarz, Glenn Vernon editor
Schwarzer, William W federal judge
Seabolt, Richard L. lawyer
Seavey, William Arthur lawyer, vintner
Seebach, Lydia Marie physician
Seegal, John Franklin lawyer
Seelenfreund, Alan distribution company executive
Seneker, Carl James, II (Kim Seneker) lawyer
Sevier, Ernest Youle lawyer
Sevilla, Carlos A. bishop
Shackley, Douglas John fire alarm company executive
Shadwick, VirginiaAnn Greer librarian
Shapiro, Larry Jay pediatrician, scientist, educator
Sheinfeld, David composer
Shenk, George H. lawyer
Shepherd, John Michael lawyer
Sherry, Robert Joseph lawyer
Shinefield, Henry Robert pediatrician
Shor, Samuel Wendell Williston naval engineer
Shorenstein, Walter Herbert commercial real estate development company executive
Shreibman, Henry M. religious educator
Shulgasser, Barbara writer
Shushkewich, Kenneth Wayne structural engineer
Sias, John B. multi-media company executive, newspaper publisher, publishing executive
Siegel, Patricia Ann association management specialist
Silk, Thomas lawyer
Silverman, Mervyn F. health science association administrator, consultant
Silverstein, Richard advertising agency executive
Singer, Allen Morris lawyer
Small, Marshall Lee lawyer
Smegal, Thomas Frank, Jr. lawyer
Smelick, Robert Malcolm investment bank executive
Smith, David Elvin physician
Smith, Kerry Clark lawyer
Smith, Lloyd Hollingsworth physician
Smith, Robert Charles political science educator, researcher
Smuin, Michael choreographer, director, dancer
Sneed, Joseph Tyree, III federal judge
Snow, Tower Charles, Jr. lawyer
Soberon, Presentacion Zablan state bar administrator
Sokolow, Maurice physician, educator
†Solomon, Gina Michelle physician
Sparer, Malcolm Martin rabbi
Sparks, John Edward lawyer
Sparks, Thomas E., Jr. lawyer
Spencer, William H. ophthalmologist
Spiegel, Hart Hunter retired lawyer
Sproul, John Allan retired public utility executive
Stamper, Robert Lewis ophthalmologist, educator
Stanzler, Jordan lawyer
Staring, Graydon Shaw lawyer

Stauffer, Thomas Michael university president
Steer, Reginald David lawyer
Steinberg, Michael music critic, educator
Steinman, John Francis psychiatrist
Stephens, Elisa art college president, lawyer
Stephenson, Charles Gayley lawyer
Stinnett, Terrance Lloyd lawyer
Stotter, Lawrence Henry lawyer
Stowell, Christopher R. dancer
Stratton, Richard James lawyer
Strock, James Martin entrepreneur, writer
Stroup, Stanley Stephenson lawyer, educator
Strupp, Joseph Paul reporter
Sugarman, Myron George lawyer
Sullivan, James N. fuel company executive
Sullivan, Robert Edward lawyer
Susskind, Teresa Gabriel publisher
Sussman, Brian Jay meteorologist, weather broadcaster
Sutcliffe, Eric lawyer
Suter, Ben lawyer
Sutton, John Paul lawyer
Sweet, Cynthia Kay business administrator
Swing, William Edwin bishop
Talbot, Stephen H. television producer, writer
Tank, Man-Chung civil engineer
Tarnoff, Peter business consultant
Taylor, Belinda Carey magazine editor, writer
Taylor, John Lockhart city official
†Taylor, (Paul) Kent poet, medical researcher
Taylor, Sabrena Ann author, visual artist
†Taylor, Wendy editor
Terr, Abba Israel allergist, immunologist
Terr, Lenore Cagen psychiatrist, writer
Thacher, Carter Pomeroy diversified manufacturing company executive
Thistlethwaite, David Richard architect
Thomas, William Geraint museum administrator
Thompson, Charlotte Ellis pediatrician, educator, author
Thompson, Robert Charles lawyer
Thornton, D. Whitney, II lawyer
Tiano, Anthony Steven television producer, book publishing executive
Timmins, James Donald venture capitalist
Tingle, James O'Malley lawyer
Tobin, Gary Allan cultural and community organization educator
Tobin, James Michael lawyer
Tobin, Shannon R. media trade show producer
Tomasson, Helgi dancer, choreographer, dance company executive
Tonini, Leon Richard sales professional
Torme, Margaret Anne public relations executive, communications consultant
Torrey, Ella King academic administrator
Trautman, William Ellsworth lawyer
Traynor, John Michael lawyer
Trejo, JoAnn medical researcher
Trowbridge, Thomas, Jr. mortgage banking company executive
Truett, Harold Joseph, III (Tim Truett) lawyer
Turner, Marshall Chittenden, Jr. venture capitalist, consultant
Turner, Ross James investment corporation executive
Tyau, Gaylore Choy Yen business educator
Tyran, Garry Keith banker
Ullman, Myron Edward, III retail executive
Uri, George Wolfsohn accountant
Ury, Claude Max educational consultant, book reviewer
Valentine, William Edson architect
Vallee, Jacques Fabrice venture capitalist
Van Dyck, Wendy dancer
Van Dyke, Craig psychiatrist
Van Etten, Peter Walbridge hospital administrator
Van Hoesen, Beth Marie artist, printmaker
van Hoften, James Dougal Adrianus business executive, former astronaut
Veitch, Stephen William investment counselor
Venning, Robert Stanley lawyer
Vick, Edward Hoge, Jr. advertising executive
Villa, Carlos Pedro artist, activist, educator
Vogt, Evon Zartman, III (Terry Vogt) merchant banker
Volpe, Peter Anthony surgeon
Vreeland, Robert Wilder electronics engineer
Wade, Booker television executive
Walker, Ralph Clifford lawyer
Walker, Vaughn R. federal judge
Walker, Walter Herbert, III lawyer, writer
Wall, Brian Arthur sculptor
Wall, James Edward telecommunications, petroleum and pharmaceutical executive
Wallerstein, Ralph Oliver physician
Walsh, Francis Richard law educator, lawyer, arbitrator
Wang, Wayne film director
Wang, William Kai-Sheng law educator
Ward, Doris M. recorder/ assessor, San Francisco
Warmer, Richard Craig lawyer
Warner, Harold Clay, Jr. banker, investment management executive
Warner, Rollin Miles, Jr. economics educator, real estate broker
Watanabe, Larry Geo biomaterials scientist
Watkins, Rufus Nathaniel newspaper professional
Watts, Malcolm S(tuart) M(cNeal) physician, medical educator
Way, E(dward) Leong pharmacologist, toxicologist, educator
Weaver, Sara Lee sales executive
Weber, Arnold I. lawyer
Weihrich, Heinz management educator
Weiner, Peter H. lawyer
Welsh, Stacey Lau investment banker
Wentz, Jeffrey Lee information systems consultant
Werb, Zena cell biologist, educator
Werdegar, Kathryn Mickle state supreme court justice
Werner, William Arno architect
Wernick, Sandra Margot advertising and public relations executive
Wertheimer, Robert E. paper company executive
Wescott, William Burnham oral maxillofacial pathologist, educator
†West, Alice Clare artist
Whalen, Philip Glenn poet, novelist
Whelan, John William lawyer, law educator, consultant
Whitaker, Clem, Jr. advertising and public relations executive
Whitehead, David Barry lawyer
Wilbur, Brayton, Jr. distribution company executive
Wild, Nelson Hopkins lawyer
Wiley, Thomas Glen retired investment company executive
Willner, Jay R. consulting company executive
Willson, Prentiss, Jr. lawyer
Wilner, Paul Andrew journalist
Wilson, Allan Byron graphics company executive
Wilson, Charles B. neurosurgeon, educator
Wilson, Ian Robert food company executive
Wilson, Matthew Frederick newspaper editor
Wilson, Robert Llewellyn clinical psychologist, educator
†Winans, Allan Davis poet, private investigator
Winblad, Ann investment company executive
Wingate, C. Keith legal educator
Winn, Steven Jay critic
Wintroub, Bruce Urich dermatologist, educator, researcher
Wirthlin, Milton Robert, Jr. periodontist
Witter, Wendell Winship financial executive, retired
Wolaner, Robin Peggy internet and magazine publisher
Wolfe, Burton H. non-profit organization executive
Wolfe, Cameron Withgot, Jr. lawyer
Wolff, Sheldon radiobiologist, educator
Wood, Robert Warren lawyer
Woods, James Robert lawyer
Worthington, Bruce R. lawyer
Wrona, Peter Alexander structural engineer
Wyle, Frederick S. lawyer
Wyllie, Loring A., Jr. structural engineer
Wyse, Roger Earl physiologist
Yaki, Michael J. municipal official
Yamakawa, David Kiyoshi, Jr. lawyer
Yamamoto, Keith Robert molecular biologist, educator
Yamamoto, Michael Toru journalist
†Yao, John Sen physician
Yin, Dominic David police officer, educator, lawyer
Young, Bryant Llewellyn lawyer, business executive
Yuan, Shao Wen aerospace engineer, educator
Zellerbach, William Joseph retired paper company executive
Zhu, Bo-qing cardiovascular research specialist
Ziering, William Mark lawyer
Zimmerman, Bernard judge
Zippin, Calvin epidemiologist, educator
Zobel, Jan A. tax consultant

San Gabriel
Bilecki, Ronald Allan financial planner
Chen, John Calvin child and adolescent psychiatrist
Kettemborough, Clifford Russell computer scientist, consultant, manager
Terry, Roger pathologist, consultant
Wong, John Wing-Chung psychiatrist

San Jacinto
Jones, Marshall Edward, Jr. retired environmental educator

San Jose
Abenroth, Donna Jean community health nurse
Ackerman, Arlene Alice accountant, business consultant, artist, writer
Anderson, Edward Virgil lawyer
Arvizu, Charlene Sutter elementary education educator
Avakoff, Joseph Carnegie medical and legal consultant
†Bain, Linda L. academic administrator
Ball, James William check cashing company executive
Beizer, Lance Kurt lawyer
Beverett, Andrew Jackson marketing executive
Bohn, Robert Herbert lawyer
Brough, Bruce Alvin public relations and communications executive
Brown, Barbara Mahone communications educator, poet, consultant
Bunn, Charles Nixon strategic business planning consultant
Callan, Josi Irene museum director
Cao, Jie-Yuan electronics engineer, researcher
Caret, Robert Laurent university president
Carey, Peter Kevin reporter
Carruth, Patti Jo nursing director
Castagnetto, Perry Michael retail sales executive
Castellano, Joseph Anthony chemist, management consulting firm executive
Cedolini, Anthony John psychologist
†Ceppos, Jerome Merle newspaper editor
†Cerritos, Ronald professional soccer player
Chamberlin, Donald Dean computer engineer
Chambers, John T. computer company executive
Chandramouli, Ramamurti electrical engineer
Chastain, Robert Lee educational psychologist
Clark, William Frederick lawyer
Cohen, D. Ashley clinical neuropsychologist
Collett, Jennie principal
Contos, Paul Anthony engineer, investment consultant
†Coons, Larry R. public parks administrator
Craford, M. George physicist, research administrator
Cruz, B. Robert academic administrator
Cryer, Rodger Earl educational administrator
Cummins, Charles Fitch, Jr. lawyer
Cunnane, Patricia S. medical facility administrator
Dafforn, Geoffrey Alan biochemist
Dalis, Irene mezzo-soprano, opera company administrator, music educator
Damphousse, Vincent professional hockey player
Dando, Pat city official
Delucchi, George Paul accountant
Dennison, Ronald Walton engineer
Doan, Xuyen Van lawyer
Doctor, Kenneth Jay editor
Dougherty, John James computer software company executive, consultant
Duncan, Gloria Celestine elementary educator
Eigler, Donald Mark physicist
Elder, Robert Laurie newspaper editor
Ellner, Michael William art educator
Elsorady, Alexa Marie secondary education educator
Estabrook, Reed artist, educator
Eyerman, David John software engineer
Faggin, Federico electronics executive
Finnigan, Robert Emmet business owner
Fiscalini, Frank city councilman
Forster, Julian physicist, consultant
Gale, Arnold David pediatric neurologist, consultant
Gallar, John Joseph mechanical engineer, educator
Gallo, Joan Rosenberg city attorney
Geschke, Charles M. computer scientist, computer company executive
Gill, Hardayal Singh electrical engineer
Gillett, Paula humanities educator
Gilmore, Helen Carol computer specialist, executive
Goldstein, Robin lawyer
†Gonzales, Ron mayor, former county supervisor
Granneman, Vernon Henry lawyer
Greenstein, Martin Richard lawyer
Grin, Leonid conductor
†Grube, James R. federal judge
Gruber, John Balsbaugh physics educator, university administrator
Gunther, Barbara artist, educator
Hall, Robert Emmett, Jr. investment banker, realtor
Hannon, Timothy Patrick lawyer, educator
Haque, Mohammed Shahidul electrical engineer
†Harris, Jay Terrence newspaper editor
Hernández, Fernando Vargas lawyer
Hill, Anna Marie manufacturing executive
Hills, Alan R. artistic director
Hind, Harry William pharmaceutical company executive
Hoang, Loc Bao electrical engineer
Hodgson, Gregory Bernard software systems architect
Hodgson, Peter John music educator, composer
†Hoff, Marcian Edward, Jr. electronics engineer
Holyer, Erna Maria adult education educator, writer, artist
Huang, Francis Fu-Tse mechanical engineering educator
Hutcheson, Jerry Dee manufacturing company executive
†Infante, Edward A. federal judge
Ingle, Robert D. newspaper editor, newspaper executive
Ingram, William Austin federal judge
Israel, Paul Neal computer design engineer, author
Jackson, Patrick Joseph insurance executive
Jacobson, Albert Herman, Jr. industrial and systems engineer, educator
Jacobson, Raymond Earl electronics company entrepreneur and executive
Jordan, Bernice Bell elementary education educator
Joshi, Janardan Shantilal surgeon
Karin, Mardi Ross surgeon
Katzman, Irwin lawyer
Kennedy, George Wendell prosecutor
Kertz, Marsha Helene accountant, educator
Kiggins, Mildred L. telemarketing firm executive
Kirk, Donald Evan electrical engineering educator, dean
Kramer, Richard Jay gastroenterologist
Kraw, George Martin lawyer, essayist
Kwock, Royal architect
Leavy, Paul Matthew management consultant
Levy, Salomon mechanical engineer
Light, Jane Ellen librarian
Lopez, Angelo Cayas freelance illustrator
Love, Amy Dundon business executive, marketing and sales executive
Loventhal, Milton writer, playwright, lyricist
Martin, Bernard Lee former college dean
McDowell, Jennifer sociologist, composer, playwright, publisher
McEnery, Tom professional sports team executive
McManis, James lawyer
Mee, C(harles) Denis physicist
Mendenhall, Carrol Clay physician
Merriam, Janet Pamela special education educator
Migielicz, Geralyn photojournalist
Mitchell, David Walker lawyer
Moates, Betty Carolyn microbiologist, computer consultant
Monia, Joan management consultant
†Monica, Martin J. law enforcement officer, educator
Morawitz, Hans physicist
Morgan, Marilyn federal judge
Morgan, Robert Hall lawyer
Morgridge, John P. computer business executive
Morimoto, Carl Noboru computer system engineer, crystallographer
Morrison, William Fosdick business educator, retired electrical company executive
Mulvey, Gerald John telecommunication engineering administrator, meteorologist educator
†Nahat, Dennis F. artistic director, choreographer
Neptune, John Addison chemistry educator, consultant
Nguyen, Lam Duc business executive, consultant
†Nguyen, Lan Ba cultural center administrator, educator
Nguyen, Long Duc artist
Nguyen, Thinh Van physician
Nicholls, Bernard Irvine hockey player
Nielsen, Christian Bayard lawyer
Nimmagadda, Rao Rajagopala materials scientist, researcher
Nolan, Owen professional hockey player
Okerlund, Arlene Naylor university official
Okita, George Torao pharmacologist educator
†Orr, Dominic information technology company executive
Ostrom, Philip Gardner computer company executive
†Ourmazdi, Behzad physician, educator
Panelli, Edward Alexander retired state supreme court justice
Parkin, Stuart S. P. materials scientist
Patnoe, Shelley Elizabeth psychologist, writer
Pausa, Clements Edward electronics company executive
Payne, Gregory physical education educator
Pflughaupt, Jane Ramsey secondary school educator
Piazza, Duane Eugene biomedical researcher, college official
Pitts, William Clarence physicist
Press, Barry Harris Jay plastic surgeon, educator
†Quinn, Brian professional soccer coach
Richards, Lisle Frederick architect
Rosendin, Raymond Joseph electrical contracting company executive
Rostoker, Michael David micro-electronics company executive, lawyer
Rothblatt, Donald Noah urban and regional planner, educator
Rubinfien, Elisabeth Sepora journalist
Schmidt, Cyril James librarian
Schroeder, William John electronics executive
Scifres, Donald Ray semiconductor laser, fiber optics and electronics company executive
Scott, Edward William, Jr. computer software company executive
Shaw, Charles Alden engineering executive
†Shuster, Diana artistic director
Shuster, Dianna musical theatre company executive, choreographer
Sidener, Margaret Weil Leathers foundation administrator
Silver, Roberta Frances (Bobbi Silver) educator, writer
Simons, Roger Mayfield tax specialist
Smith, Charles Richard high technology marketing executive
Smith, Rodney electronics executive
Soos, Richard Anthony pastor
Stapleton, Beverly Cooper aerospace company executive
Stein, Arthur Oscar pediatrician
Steinberg, Charles Allan electronics manufacturing company executive
Stewart, Melinda Jane judge
†Takizawa, Gregory Hidaeki telecommunication industry executive
Tanaka, Richard Koichi, Jr. architect, planner
Taylor, Kendrick Jay microbiologist
†Toepfer, Karl Eric theatre arts educator
Tonseth, Ralph G. airport executive
Towery, James E. lawyer
Tran, Jack Nhuan Ngoc gas and oil reservoir engineer
†Trumbull, Patricia V. federal judge
Valentine, Ralph Schuyler chemical engineer, research director
†Van Selst, Mark G.A. psychology educator
Vernon, Mike professional hockey player
Vieira, Linda Marie administrative and technical coordinator, endoscopy technician
Ware, James W. federal judge
Warnock, John Edward computer company executive
Waterer, Bonnie Clausing high school educator
Weeker, Ellis emergency physician
†Weissbradt, Arthur S. federal judge
Westendorf, Elaine Susan social worker
Whitney, Natalie White primary school educator
Whyte, Ronald M. federal judge
Williams, Spencer Mortimer federal judge
Winslow, Frances Edwards city official
Winters, Harold Franklin physicist
Wise, Joseph Stephen secondary education educator, artist
Woolls, Esther Blanche library science educator
Wu, Dongping (Don Wu) optical and electrical engineer
Wughalter, Emily Hope physical education educator
†Wynalda, Eric professional soccer player
Yoshizumi, Donald Tetsuro dentist
Zaro, Brad A. research company executive, biologist
Zhang, Jianping electrical engineer

San Juan Bautista
Fort, Robert Bradley minister

San Juan Capistrano
Botway, Lloyd Frederick computer scientist, consultant
Brown, Robert G. lawyer
Brown, Stephanie Cecile librarian, writer
Burns, Toni Anthony artist
Fisher, Delbert Arthur physician, educator
Grayson, Robert Allen marketing executive, educator
Hough, J. Marie real estate company official
Kleiner, Richard Arthur writer, editor
Korb, Robert William former materials and processes engineer
Olson, Cal Oliver golf architect
Paul, Courtland Price landscape architect, planner
Peterson, Fred McCrae retired librarian
Robinson, Daniel Thomas brokerage company executive
White, Beverly Jane cytogeneticist

San Leandro
Chilcoat, Dale Allen artist, visual and performing arts educator
Ley, David Chanpannha secondary mathematics and ESL educator
Nehls, Robert Louis, Jr. school system administrator
Newacheck, David John lawyer
Pansky, Emil John entrepreneur
Stallings, Charles Henry physicist

San Lorenzo
†Clum, Gerard W. academic administrator
Glenn, Jerome T. secondary school principal
Lantz, Charles Alan chiropractor, researcher
Morrison, Martin (Earl) computer systems analyst
Schultz, Frederik Emil academic administrator

San Luis Obispo
Anderson, Warren Ronald electrical engineering educator
Bailey, Philip Sigmon, Jr. university official, chemistry educator
Baker, Warren J(oseph) university president
Blakeslee, Diane Pusey financial planner
Bunge, Russell Kenneth writer, poet, editor
Busselen, Steven Carroll journalist, editor
Campbell, Renoda Gisele human resources administrator
Carr, Roxanne Marie mortgage company executive
Culbertson, James Thomas psychologist
Dalton, Linda Catherine university administrator
†Davidson, Frances film and video producer
Deasy, Cornelius Michael architect
Dickerson, Colleen Bernice Patton artist, educator
Ericson, Jon Meyer academic administrator, rhetoric theory educator
Grismore, Roger physics educator, researcher
Hafemeister, David Walter physicist
Haile, Allen Cleveland educator and administrator
Hasslein, George Johann architectural educator
Hempenius, Gerald Edward real estate broker
Jamieson, James Bradshaw foundation administrator
Lang, Martin Traugott mathematics educator
Mette, Joe museum director
Ruggles, Joanne Beaule artist, educator
Sachs, Robert Michael author
Seeber, James J. sociology educator
Shlaudeman, Harry Walter retired ambassador
Sullivan, Thomas James retired manufacturing company executive
Vanderspek, Peter George management consultant, writer
Waller, Julia Reva financial aide counselor

San Luis Rey
Melbourne, Robert Ernest civil engineer
Williams, Elizabeth Yahn author, lecturer, lawyer

San Marcos
Andersen, Robert health products, business executive
Barnes, Howard G. communications executive, film and video producer
†Boggs, George Robert academic administrator
Branch, Robert Hardin radio and television educator, broadcast executive
Carroll, William publisher
Cater, Judy Jerstad librarian
Ciurczak, Alexis librarian

Coleman, Robert Trent *social worker, rehabilitation consultant*
Harmon, Harry William *architect, former university administrator*
Jeffredo, John Victor *aerospace engineer, manufacturing company executive, inventor*
Knight, Edward Howden *retired hospital administrator*
Lilly, Martin Stephen *university dean*
†O'Doherty, Fergal Columba *English educator, researcher*
Purdy, Alan Harris *biomedical engineer*
Rolle-Rissetto, Silvia Maria *foreign languages educator, writer, artist*
†Yuan, Yuan *English educator, translator*

San Marino
Babcock, Catherine Marly *public relations executive*
Baldwin, James William *lawyer*
Benzer, Seymour *neuroscience educator*
Cranston, Howard Stephen *lawyer, management consultant*
Darian, Craig Charles *executive film producer*
Footman, Gordon Elliott *educational administrator*
Galbraith, James Marshall *lawyer, business executive*
Grantham, Richard Robert *real estate company consultant*
Hull, Suzanne White *retired administrator, author*
Karlstrom, Paul Johnson *art historian*
Lashley, Virginia Stephenson Hughes *retired computer science educator*
Medearis, Roger Norman *artist*
Meyer, William Danielson *retired department store executive*
Mortimer, Wendell Reed, Jr. *judge*
Mothershead, J. Leland, III *dean*
Ridge, Martin *historian, educator*
Robertson, Mary Louise *archivist, historian*
Rolle, Andrew F. *historian, educator, author*
Skotheim, Robert Allen *museum administrator*
Steadman, John Marcellus, III *English educator*
Thorpe, James *humanities researcher*
Tomich, Lillian *lawyer*
Wark, Robert Rodger *art curator*
Zall, Paul Maxwell *retired English language educator, consultant*

San Mateo
Bell, Frank Ouray, Jr. *lawyer*
Bell, Leo S. *retired physician*
Bonnell, William Charles *secondary education educator*
†Brink, Robert Ross *plastic surgeon*
Castleberry, Arline Alrick *architect*
Chester, Sharon Rose *photographer, natural history educator, writer, illustrator*
Danker, Mervyn Kenneth *director of education*
Diehr, David Bruce *social service administrator*
Fellows, Ward Jay *philosophy educator, minister*
Gombocz, Erich Alfred *biochemist*
Graham, Howard Holmes *financial executive*
Grammater, Rudolf Dimitri *retired construction executive*
Grill, Lawrence J. *lawyer, accountant, corporate/banking executive*
Helfert, Erich Anton *management consultant, author, educator*
Huxley, Mary Atsuko *artist*
Johnson, Charles Bartlett *mutual fund executive*
Johnson, Rupert Harris, Jr. *finance company executive*
Kenney, William Fitzgerald *lawyer*
Kidera, George Jerome *physician*
Lamson, Kristin Anne *finance company executive*
Landry, Richard *publishing executive*
Leong, Carol Jean *electrologist*
Monaco, Daniel Joseph *lawyer*
Motoyama, Catherine Tomoko *communications educator*
Nazzaro, David Alfred *sales executive*
Patnode, Darwin Nicholas *academic administrator, professional parliamentarian*
Petit, Susan Yount *French and English educator*
Potts, David Malcolm *population specialist, administrator*
Richens, Muriel Whittaker *AIDS therapist, counselor and educator*
Rollo, F. David *hospital management company executive, health care educator*
Sorensen, Dorothy Allan *nursing administrator*
†Speirn, Sterling K. *foundation administrator*
Trabitz, Eugene Leonard *aerospace company executive*
Van Kirk, John Ellsworth *cardiologist*
von Doepp, Christian Ernest *psychiatrist*
Wong, Otto *epidemiologist*

San Pablo
Colfack, Andrea Heckelman *elementary education educator*
†Thompson, Sandra Leniese *publishing company executive, consultant*
Woodruff, Kay Herrin *pathologist, educator*

San Pedro
†Berg, Deborah Jean *construction management owner*
Crutchfield, William Richard *artist, educator*
Ellis, George Edwin, Jr. *chemical engineer*
Fritzsche, Kathleen (Dragonfire Fritzsche) *performing arts educator*
Gammell, Gloria Ruffner *professional association administrator*
Keller, Larry A. *city manager*
McCarty, Frederick Briggs *electrical engineer*
Simmons, William *physicist, retired aerospace research executive*
Strasen, Barbara Elaine *artist, educator*

San Rafael
Badgley, John Roy *architect*
Bartz, Carol *software company executive*
Bertelsen, Thomas Elwood, Jr. *investment banker*
Clark, Charles Sutter *interior designer*
Djordjevich, Michael *insurance company executive*
Dykstra, Edie M. *human resource director*
Eekman, Thomas Adam *Slavic languages educator*
Fink, Joseph Richard *college president*
Freitas, David Prince *lawyer*
Friesecke, Raymond Francis *health company executive*
Gould, R(ichard) Martin (Richard Martin Goldman) *marketing consultant, researcher*
Gryson, Joseph Anthony *orthodontist*
Hart, Mickey *rock musician*
Heller, H(einz) Robert *financial executive*
Henry, Marie Elaine *poet*
Keegan, Jane Ann *insurance executive, consultant*
Kennedy, James Waite *management consultant, author*
Latno, Arthur Clement, Jr. *telephone company executive*
Ligare, Kathleen Meredith *strategy and marketing executive*
Lucas, George W., Jr. *film director, producer, screenwriter*
Morehouse, Valerie Jeanne *librarian*
Murphy, George *special effects expert*
Nelson, James Carmer, Jr. *writer, advertising executive*
Roffman, Howard *motion picture company executive*
Roulac, Stephen E. *real estate consultant*
Sansweet, Stephen Jay *journalist, author, marketing executive*
Santana, Carlos *guitarist*
Saunders, Kathryn A. *retired data processing administrator*
Squires, Scott William *special effects expert, executive*
†Sybinsky, Estrella Besinga *political science educator*
Thomas, Mary Ann McCrary *counselor, school system administrator*
Thompson, John William *international management consultant*
Thompson, Peter Layard Hailey, Sr. *golf course architect*
Tosti, Donald Thomas *psychologist, consultant*
Trepp, Leo *rabbi*
Wright, Frederick Herman Greene, II *computer systems engineer*
Zaleski, Brian William *computer programmer, analyst*

San Ramon
Davis, John Albert *lawyer*
Dickerson, Cynthia Rowe *marketing firm executive, consultant*
Freed, Kenneth Alan *lawyer*
Garcia, Michael Joseph *telecommunications company executive*
Litman, Robert Barry *physician, author, television and radio commentator*
Moore, Justin Edward *data processing executive*
Rogula, James Leroy *consumer products company executive*
Rose, Joan L. *computer security specialist*
Schofield, James Roy *computer programmer*

San Simeon
Jennings, Mark Russell *biologist*

Santa Ana
Adams, John M. *library director*
Amoroso, Frank *retired communication system engineer, consultant*
Barr, James Norman *federal judge*
Bauer, Bruce F. *aerospace engineer*
Baugh, Coy Franklin *corporate executive*
Bentley, William Arthur *electro-optical consultant, engineer*
Boynton, William Lewis *electronic manufacturing company official*
†Cagle, Thomas M. *electronics engineer*
Capizzi, Michael Robert *prosecutor*
Chenhalls, Anne Marie *nurse, educator*
Cheverton, Richard E. *newspaper editor*
Danoff-Kraus, Pamela Sue *shopping center development executive*
Dean, William Evans *aerospace industry executive*
Dillard, John Martin *lawyer, pilot*
Dunn, Edward Thomas, Jr. *lawyer, educator*
†Eddy, Charles Christopher *educator*
†Edwards, Elgin C. *federal judge*
Fay-Schmidt, Patricia Ann *paralegal*
Ferguson, Warren John *federal judge*
Foster, Julian Francis Sherwood *political science educator*
Frost, Winston Lyle *lawyer, educator*
Glazier, Ron *zoological park administrator*
†Haldeman, Scott *neurology educator*
Harley, Robison Dooling, Jr. *lawyer, educator*
Holtz, Joseph Norman *marketing executive*
Hoops, Alan *health care company executive*
Jack, Minta Sue *hospital department head*
Kato, Terri Emi *elementary school and gifted and talented educator*
Katz, Tonnie *newspaper editor*
Kelly, James Patrick, Jr. *retired engineering and construction executive*
Lawrence, David Norman *broadcasting executive, consultant*
Myers, Marilyn Gladys *pediatric hematologist and oncologist*
Pincombe, Jodi Doris *health facility administrator*
Pratt, Lawrence Arthur *thoracic surgeon, foreign service officer*
Richard, Robert John *library director*
Riddle, Lynne *judge*
Ryan, John Edward *federal judge*
St. Clair, Carl *conductor, music director*
Schiff, Laurie *lawyer*
Schulte Shields, Mary Ann *finance executive*
Shahin, Thomas John *dry cleaning wholesale supply company executive*
Smith, Keith Larue *research company executive*
Storer, Maryruth *law librarian*
Stotler, Alicemarie Huber *judge*
Sudbeck, Robert Francis *music educator, philosophy educator*
Tanaka, Richard I. *computer products company executive*
Taylor, Gary L. *federal judge*
Treshie, R. David *newspaper publishing executive*
Verhaegen, Terri Lynn Foy *middle school educator*
Waaland, Irving Theodore *retired aerospace design executive*
†Walters, Paul *protective services official*
Wang, Jian-Ming *research scientist*
Watts, Judith-Ann White *academic administrator*
Williams, Cleveland *municipal or county official*
†Wilson, John James *federal judge*
Yuen, Andy Tak Sing *electronics executive*
Zaenglein, William George, Jr. *lawyer*
Zepeda, Susan Ghozeil *county official*

Santa Barbara
Ackerman, Marshall *publishing company executive*
†Adizes, Ichak *management consultant, author*
Ahlers, Guenter *physicist, educator*
Ah-Tye, Kirk Thomas *lawyer*
Aijian, Haig Schuyler *pathologist, educator*
Aldisert, Ruggero John *federal judge*
Allaway, William Harris *retired university official*
Anderson, Donald Meredith *bank executive*
Arnold, Michael Neal *real property appraiser, consultant*
Atwater, Tanya Maria *marine geophysicist, educator*
Badash, Lawrence *science history educator*
Barbakow, Jeffrey *health facility administrator*
Bartlett, James Lowell, III *investment company executive*
Ben-Dor, Giséle *conductor, musician*
Beutler, Larry Edward *psychology educator*
Bischel, Margaret DeMeritt *physician, managed care consultant*
Blasingame, Benjamin Paul *electronics company executive*
Bliss, Lee *English language educator*
Bock, Russell Samuel *author*
Boehm, Eric Hartzell *information management executive*
Boles, Deborah Ann *gerontology nurse*
Bongiorno, James William *electronics company executive*
Boyan, Norman J. *retired education educator*
Brant, Henry *composer*
Brantingham, Barney *journalist, writer*
Bridges, B. Ried *lawyer*
Brodhead, James E(aston) *actor, writer*
Brown, J'Amy Maroney *journalist, media relations consultant, investor*
Brownlee, Wilson Elliot, Jr. *history educator*
Bruice, Thomas C. *chemist, educator*
Campbell, Robert Charles *minister, theology educator*
Campbell, William Steen *publishing executive, writer, speaker*
Carlson, Arthur W. *lawyer*
Cathcart, Linda *art historian*
Cavat, Irma *artist, educator*
Chafe, Wallace LeSeur *linguist, educator*
Chmelka, Bradley Floyd *chemical engineering educator*
Christman, Arthur Castner, Jr. *scientific advisor*
Cirone, William Joseph *educational administrator*
Clinard, Marshall Barron *sociologist, educator*
Coldren, Larry Allen *engineering educator, consultant*
Collins, Robert Oakley *history educator*
Comanor, William S. *economist, educator*
Conley, Philip James, Jr. *retired air force officer*
Cooper, Saul *producer, public relations executive*
Crawford, Donald Wesley *philosophy educator, university official*
Crispin, James Hewes *engineering and construction company executive*
Crowell, John C(hambers) *geology educator, researcher*
Cunningham, Julia Woolfolk *author*
Dauer, Francis Watanabe *philosophy educator*
Davidson, Eugene Arthur *author*
Davidson, Roger H(arry) *political scientist, educator*
Delaney, Paul William *English language educator*
Del Chiaro, Mario Aldo *art historian, archeologist, etruscologist, educator*
Dennison, Richard Leon *entertainment company executive*
Doutt, Richard Leroy *entomologist, lawyer, educator*
Duffy, Andrew Enda *language educator*
Dunne, Thomas *geology educator*
Duntley, Linda Kathleen Day *network executive, artist, educator, author, educator, researcher*
Egan, Susan Chan *security analyst*
Egenolf, Robert F. *lawyer*
Eguchi, Yasu *artist*
Emmons, Robert John *corporate executive*
†Enders, Jody *French educator*
Enelow, Allen Jay *psychiatrist, educator*
Erasmus, Charles John *anthropologist, educator*
Erickson, Robert Allen *English literature educator*
Falstrom, Kenneth Edward *lawyer*
Fingarette, Herbert *philosopher, educator*
Fisher, Matthew P. A. *physicist*
Fisher, Steven Kay *neurobiology educator*
Fleming, Brice Noel *retired philosophy educator*
Focht, Michael Harrison *health care industry executive*
Ford, Peter C. *chemistry educator*
Fredrickson, Glenn Harold *chemical engineering and materials educator*
French, Mark *women's basketball coach university level*
Frizzell, William Kenneth *architect*
Gaines, Howard Clarke *retired lawyer*
Gibney, Frank Bray *publisher, editor, writer, foundation executive*
Gillquist, Peter Edward *church organization executive*
Gordon, Helen Heightsman *English language educator, writer, publisher*
Gossard, Arthur Charles *physicist*
Gunn, Giles Buckingham *English educator, religion educator*
Gutmann, Barbara Lang *nurse, educator*
Hanley, Kevin Lance *maintenance manager*
Hansen, Robert Gunnard *philatelist, entrepreneur*
Hedgepeth, John M(ills) *aerospace engineer, mathematician, engineering executive*
Heeger, Alan Jay *physicist*
Helgerson, Richard *English literature educator*
Herlinger, Daniel Robert *hospital administrator*
Howorth, David *producer, director*
Hsu, Immanuel Chung Yueh *history educator*
Hubbard, Arthur Thornton *chemistry educator, electro-surface chemist*
Iselin, Donald Grote *civil engineering and management consultant*
Israel, Barry John *lawyer*
Israelachvili, Jacob Nissim *chemical engineer*
Jochim, Michael Allan *archaeologist*
Johnsen, Eugene Carlyle *mathematician and educator*
Karpeles, David *museum director*
Keator, Carol Lynn *library director*
Kendler, Howard H(arvard) *psychologist, educator*
Kennedy, John Harvey *chemistry educator*
Klakeg, Clayton Harold *cardiologist*
Kohn, Roger Alan *surgeon*
Kohn, Walter *educator, physicist*
Kokotovic, Petar V. *electrical and computer engineer, educator*
Korenic, Lynnette Marie *librarian*
Kram, Mark Lenard *hydrogeologist, environmental geochemist*
Kramer, Edward John *materials science and engineering educator*
Kroemer, Herbert *electrical engineering educator*
Kruger, Kenneth Charles *architect*
Kryter, Karl David *research scientist*
Kuehn, David Laurance *music academy administrator*
Lambrecht, Frank Laurent *medical entomologist, parasitology researcher*
Lange, Hope *actress*
Langer, James Stephen *physicist, educator*
Lawrance, Charles Holway *civil and sanitary engineer*
Lennox Buchthal, Margaret Agnes *retired neurophysiologist*
Lim, Shirley Geok Lin *English language educator, author*
Looper, Kevin Charles *non-profit executive*
Luyendyk, Bruce Peter *geophysicist, educator, institution administrator*
Macdonald, Ken Craig *geophysicist*
Mac Intyre, Donald John *college president*
Marcus, Marvin *mathematician, educator*
Marcuse, Harold *history educator*
Martzen, Philip D. *physicist, software developer*
Mayer, Richard Edwin *psychology educator*
Mc Coy, Lois Clark *emergency services professional, retired county official, magazine editor*
McEwen, Willard Winfield, Jr. *lawyer, judge*
McGee, James Sears *historian*
Mehra, Rajnish *finance educator*
Meinel, Aden Baker *optics scientist*
Meriam, James Lathrop *mechanical engineering educator*
Metzinger, Timothy Edward *lawyer*
Minc, Henryk *mathematics educator*
†Mitchell, Shawne Maureen *author*
Mitra, Sanjit Kumar *electrical and computer engineering educator*
†Morgan, Alfred Vance *management consulting company executive*
†Mosely, Jack Meredith *thoracic surgeon*
Nelson, Sonja Bea *paralegal*
Newman, Morris *mathematician*
O'Dowd, Donald Davy *retired university president*
Peale, Stanton Jerrold *physics educator*
Philbrick, Ralph *botanist*
Pilgeram, Laurence Oscar *biochemist*
Potter, David Samuel *former automotive company executive*
Prager, Elliot David *surgeon, educator*
Prindle, William Roscoe *consultant, retired glass company executive*
Redick, Kevin James *cultural organization administrator*
Renehan, Robert Francis Xavier *Greek and Latin educator*
Riblet, Robin L. *judge*
Rockwell, Don Arthur *psychiatrist*
Rose, Mark Allen *humanities educator*
Russell, Charles Roberts *chemical engineer*
Russell, Jeffrey Burton *historian, educator*
Scalapino, Douglas James *physics educator*
Schneider, Edward Lee *botanic garden administrator*
Schultz, Arthur Warren *communications company executive*
Segal, Helene Rose *editor*
Shackman, Daniel Robert *psychiatrist*
Shames, Henry Joseph *lawyer*
Shreeve, Susanna Seelye *educational planning facilitator*
Silverander, Carol Weinstock *manufacturing executive*
Simons, Stephen *mathematics educator, researcher*
Simpson, Curtis Chapman, III *lawyer*
Sinsheimer, Robert Louis *retired university chancellor and educator*
Smith, Michael Townsend *author, editor, stage director*
Smith, Robert Nathaniel *broadcasting executive, lawyer*
Snyder, Allegra Fuller *dance educator*
Sprecher, David A. *university administrator, mathematician*
Stirling, Clark Tillman *lawyer*
Strahler, Arthur Newell *former geology educator, author*
Swalley, Robert Farrell *structural engineer, consultant*
Tapper, Joan Judith *magazine editor*
Tilton, David Lloyd *savings and loan association executive*
Tilton, George Robert *geochemistry educator*
Tirrell, Matthew *chemical engineering, materials science educator*
Tucker, Shirley Lois Cotter *botany educator, researcher*
Turner, Henry A. *retired political science educator, author*
VanderMey, Randall John *English language educator*
Veigele, William John *physicist*
Wade, Glen *electrical engineer, educator*
Wallin, Lawrence Bier *artist*
†Warner, John Jeffrey *mining executive*
Wayland, Newton Hart *conductor*
Wilkins, Burleigh Taylor *philosophy educator*
Wilson, Leslie *biochemist, cell biologist, biology educator*
Wooldridge, Dean Everett *engineering executive, scientist*
Yang, Henry T. *university chancellor, educator*
Zaleski, James Vincent *electronics executive*
Zimmerman, Everett Lee *English educator, academic administrator*

Santa Clara
Aguinsky, Richard Daniel *software and electronics engineer*
Alexander, George Jonathon *law educator, former dean*
Benhamou, Eric A. *computer company executive*
Carlsen, John Richard *engineer*
Carter, Dennis Lee *marketing professional*
Chan, Shu-Park *electrical engineering educator*
†Chastain, Brandi Denise *professional soccer player*
de la Roza, Gustavo Luis *pathologist*
DuMaine, R. Pierre *bishop*
Dunlap, F. Thomas, Jr. *lawyer, electronics company executive*
Elkus, Richard J., Jr. *electronics company executive*
Falgiano, Victor Joseph *electrical engineer, consultant*
Fernbach, Stephen Alton *pediatrician*
Field, Alexander James *economics educator*
Filo, David *computer communications executive*
Goldstein, Jack *health science executive, microbiologist*
Gozani, Tsahi *nuclear physicist*
Grove, Andrew S. *electronics company executive*
Gupta, Rajesh *industrial engineer, quality engineer*
Halla, Brian *electronics company executive*
Halmos, Paul Richard *mathematician, educator*
Hanks, Merton Edward *professional football player*

†Powell, Sandy *costume designer*
Reiner, Thomas Karl *manufacturing company executive*
Rich, Gareth Edward *financial planner*
Schlessinger, Laura *radio talk show host*
†Schroder, Rick *actor*
Sheen, Charlie (Carlos Irwin Estevez) *actor*
Shore, Howard Leslie *composer*
Silberman, Irwin Alan *retired public health physician*
†Sonders, Scott Aleksander *writer, educator*
Sting, (Gordon Matthew Sumner) *musician, songwriter, actor*
Strauss, John *public relations executive*
Tesh, John *television talk show host, musician*
Tsiros, John Andreas *accountant*
Weiss, Julie *costume designer*
Wilcox, Robert Kalleen *journalist*
Williams, John Towner *composer, conductor*
Winkler, Lee B. *business consultant*
Yasnyi, Allan David *communications company executive*
Zemplenyi, Tibor Karol *cardiologist*

Shingle Springs
Guay, Gordon Hay *postal service executive, marketing educator, consultant*

Sierra Madre
Converse, Elizabeth Sheets *artist, writer*
Dewey, Donald William *magazine publisher, editor, writer*
Lyle, John Tillman *architect, landscape architecture educator*
MacGillivray, MaryAnn Leverone *marketing professional*
Nation, Earl F. *retired urologist, educator*

Signal Hill
Jarman, Donald Ray *retired public relations professional, minister*
Vandament, William Eugene *retired academic administrator*

Silverado
Mamer, James Michael *secondary education educator*

Simi Valley
Ahsan, Omar Faruk *computer engineer, manager, consultant*
Bullock, Donald Wayne *elementary education educator, educational computing consultant*
Harris, Richard Anthony Sidney *trust company executive*
Hunt, Mark Alan *museum director*
Jackson, Thirston Henry, Jr. *retired adult education educator*
Kearns, Albert Osborn *minister*
Killion, Jack Charles *newspaper columnist*
McBride, Joyce Browning *accountant*
Rehart, Margaret Lee *controller*
Shawn, Eric *software and consumer products company executive*
Shirilla, Robert M. *bank executive*
Weiser, Paul David *manufacturing company executive*
Whitley, David Scott *archaeologist*

Solana Beach
Agnew, Harold Melvin *physicist*
Arledge, Charles Stone *former aerospace executive, entrepreneur*
Beard, Ann Southard *government official, travel company executive*
Beck-von-Peccoz, Stephen George Wolfgang *artist*
Brody, Arthur *industrial executive*
DeMarco-Dennis, Eleanor (Poppy DeMarco-Dennis) *elementary education educator, community activist*
Derbes, Daniel William *manufacturing executive*
Ernst, Roger Charles *former government official, natural resources consultant, association executive*
Friedman, Maurice Stanley *religious educator*
Gildred, Theodore Edmonds *ambassador*
Parker, John Brian *broadcast executive*
Watson, Jack Crozier *retired state supreme court justice*
Zwick, Shelly Crittendon *lawyer*

Solvang
Chandler, E(dwin) Russell *clergyman, author*
Morrow, Richard Towson *lawyer*

Somerset
Setzekorn, William David *retired architect, consultant, author*

Somis
Kehoe, Vincent Jeffré-Roux *photographer, author, cosmetic company executive*

Sonoma
Allen, Rex Whitaker *architect*
Anderson, Gunnar Donald *artist*
Beckmann, Jon Michael *publisher*
Bow, Stephen Tyler, Jr. *insurance and computer industry consultant*
Broderick, Harold Christian *interior designer*
†Canan, Janine Burford *psychiatrist, poet*
Hass, Robert Michael *editor*
Hobart, Billie *education educator, consultant*
Jayme, William North *writer*
Kizer, Carolyn Ashley *poet, educator*
Markey, William Alan *health care administrator*
Muchmore, Robert Boyer *engineering consultant executive*
Pollack, Phyllis Addison *ballerina*
Scott, John Walter *chemical engineer, research management executive*
Stadtman, Verne August *former foundation executive, editor*
Woodbridge, John Marshall *architect, urban planner*

Sonora
Efford, Michael Robert *police administrator, educator*
Erich, Louis Richard *physician*
Mathias, Betty Jane *communications and community affairs consultant, writer, editor, lecturer*
Patterson, Paul Edward *minister*
Sharboneau, Lorna Rosina *artist, educator, author, poet, illustrator*
Wheeler, Elton Samuel *financial executive*

Soquel
Murray, Barbara Olivia *writer, retired psychologist*

South Dos Palos
Hirohata, Derek Kazuyoshi *career officer*

South Gate
Mosby, Dorothea Susan *municipal official*

South Lake Tahoe
Darvas, Endre Peter *artist*
†Miller, Kerry Lee *city manager*
Nason, Rochelle *conservation organization administrator*
Prescott, Barbara Lodwich *educational administrator*
†Reece, Monte M. *federal judge*

South Pasadena
Askin, Walter Miller *artist, educator*
Girvigian, Raymond *architect*
Kopp, Eugene Howard *electrical engineer*
†Lima, Donald Roger *computer programmer*
Lowe, Richard Gerald, Jr. *computer programming manager*
†Maguire, Theresa Louise *library director*
Man, Lawrence Kong *architect*
Mantell, Suzanne Ruth *editor*
†Remy, Ray *state government official*
White, W. Robin *author*
White-Thomson, Ian Leonard *mining company executive*
Zimmerman, William Robert *entrepreneur, engineering based manufacturing company executive*

South San Francisco
Allen, Robert *wholesale distribution executive*
Blethen, Sandra Lee *pediatric endocrinologist*
Canova-Davis, Eleanor *biochemist, researcher*
Dixit, Vishva M. *pathology educator*
Grannuci, Leo *marketing professional*
Levinson, Arthur David *molecular biologist*
Lewis, Jason Alvert, Jr. *communications executive*
Rodriguez, Roman *physician, child psychiatrist, educator*
Shelton, Leslie Habecker *adult literacy program director*
Walsh, Gary L. *consumer products company executive*

Spring Valley
Blackwell, Garland W(ayne) *retired military officer*
Long, David Michael, Jr. *biomedical researcher, cardiothoracic surgeon*
Roberts, Carolyn June *medical school department manager*

Springville
Meredith, Marilyn *writer, writing educator*

Stanford
Abrams, Herbert LeRoy *radiologist, educator*
Allen, Matthew Arnold *physicist*
Almond, Gabriel Abraham *political science educator*
Amemiya, Takeshi *economist, statistician*
Andersen, Hans Christian *chemistry educator*
Anderson, Annelise Graebner *economist*
Anderson, Martin Carl *economist*
Anderson, Theodore Wilbur *statistics educator*
Andreopoulos, Spyros George *writer*
Arrow, Kenneth Joseph *economist, educator*
Atkin, J. Myron *science educator*
Aziz, Khalid *petroleum engineering educator*
Babcock, Barbara Allen *lawyer, educator*
Baker, Keith Michael *history educator*
Baker, Patricia Ann *publishing executive*
Baldwin, Robert Lesh *biochemist, educator*
Bandura, Albert *psychologist*
Baron, James Neal *organizational behavior and human resources educator, researcher*
Basch, Paul Frederick *international health educator, parasitologist*
Bauer, Eugene Andrew *dermatologist, educator*
Baylor, Denis Aristide *neurobiology educator*
†Beaty, Shannon Michelle *financial consultant*
Beaver, William Henry *accounting educator*
Berg, Paul *biochemist, educator*
Berger, Joseph *author, educator, counselor*
Bjorkman, Olle Erik *plant biologist, educator*
Blaschke, Terrence Francis *medicine and molecular pharmacology educator*
Blau, Helen Margaret *molecular pharmacology educator*
Blumenkranz, Mark Scott *surgeon, researcher, educator*
Bonner, William Andrew *chemistry educator*
Boskin, Michael Jay *economist, government official, university educator, consultant*
Boudart, Michel *chemical engineer, chemist, educator*
Bracewell, Ronald Newbold *electrical engineering educator*
Bradshaw, Peter *engineering educator*
Brauman, John I. *chemist, educator*
Breitrose, Henry S. *communications educator*
Brest, Paul A. *law educator*
Brinegar, Claude Stout *retired oil company executive*
†Brody, Richard Alan *political science educator, researcher*
Brown, Byron William, Jr. *biostatistician, educator*
Bryson, Arthur Earl, Jr. *retired aerospace engineering educator*
Bube, Richard Howard *materials scientist*
Bunzel, John Harvey *political science educator, researcher*
Campbell, Allan McCulloch *bacteriology educator*
Cannon, Robert Hamilton, Jr. *aerospace engineering educator*
Carlsmith, James Merrill *psychologist, educator*
Carlson, Robert Codner *industrial engineering educator*
Carlson, Robert Wells *physician, educator*
Carnochan, Walter Bliss *retired humanities educator*
Chaffee, Steven Henry *communication educator*
Cohen, Albert *musician, educator*
Cohen, Harvey Joel *pediatric hematology and oncology educator*
Cohen, Stanley Norman *geneticist, educator*
Cohen, William *law educator*
Coleman, Robert Griffin *geology educator*
Collman, James Paddock *chemistry educator*
Conquest, (George) Robert (Acworth) *writer, historian, poet, critic, journalist*
Cork, Linda Katherine *veterinary pathologist, educator*
Cover, Thomas M. *statistician, electrical engineer, educator*
Cox, Donald Clyde *electrical engineering educator*
Damon, William Van Buren *developmental psychologist, educator, writer*
Dantzig, George Bernard *applied mathematics educator*
Davis, Mark M. *microbiologist, educator*
Davis, Ronald Wayne *genetics researcher, biochemistry educator*
Deal, Bruce Elmer *physical chemist, educator*
Dekker, George Gilbert *literature educator, literary scholar, writer*
Derksen, Charlotte Ruth Meynink *librarian*
Djerassi, Carl *chemist, educator, writer*
Donohue, John Joseph *law educator*
Dunlop, John Barrett *foreign language educator, research institution scholar*
Dutton, Robert W. *electrical engineer*
Duus, Peter *history educator*
Efron, Bradley *mathematics educator*
Egbert, Peter R. *ophthalmologist, educator*
Ehrlich, Anne Howland *research biologist*
Ehrlich, Paul Ralph *biology educator*
Elliott, David Duncan, III *science research company executive*
Enthoven, Alain Charles *economist, educator*
Eshleman, Von Russel *electrical engineering educator*
Eustis, Robert Henry *mechanical engineer*
Falkow, Stanley *microbiologist, educator*
Fee, Willard Edward, Jr. *otolaryngologist*
Feigenbaum, Edward Albert *computer science educator*
Fetter, Alexander Lees *theoretical physicist, educator*
Francke, Uta *medical geneticist, genetics researcher, educator*
Frank, Joseph Nathaniel *comparative literature educator*
Franklin, Gene Farthing *engineering educator, consultant*
Franklin, Marc Adam *law educator*
Fredrickson, George Marsh *history educator*
Friedman, Gary David *epidemiologist*
Friedman, Lawrence M. *law educator*
Friedman, Milton *economist, educator emeritus, author*
Fuchs, Victor Robert *economics educator*
Fuller, Joseph Barry *company executive*
Gage, Nathaniel Lees *psychologist, educator*
Gardner, John William *writer, educator*
Gelpi, Albert Joseph *English educator, literary critic*
George, Alexander Lawrence *political scientist, educator*
Gere, James Monroe *civil engineering educator*
Gibbons, James Franklin *electrical engineering educator*
Gibson, Count Dillon, Jr. *physician, educator*
Girard, René Noel *author, educator*
Giraud, Raymond Dorner *retired language professional*
†Glasser, Theodore L. *journalism educator*
Glazer, Gary Mark *radiology educator*
Goldstein, Dora Benedict *pharmacologist, educator*
Goldstein, Paul *lawyer, educator*
Goodman, Joseph Wilfred *electrical engineering educator*
Gray, Robert M(olten) *electrical engineering educator*
Greenberg, Joseph H. *anthropologist, linguist*
Gross, Richard Edmund *education educator*
Guerard, Albert Joseph *retired modern literature educator, author*
Gunther, Gerald *lawyer, educator*
Hall, Robert Ernest *economics educator*
Hanawalt, Philip Courtland *biology educator, researcher*
Harbaugh, John Warvelle *applied earth sciences educator*
Harris, Donald J. *economics educator*
Harris, Stephen Ernest *electrical engineering and applied physics educator*
Harrison, Walter Ashley *physicist, educator*
Harrison, Wendy Jane Merrill *university official*
Henriksen, Thomas Hollinger *university official*
Hentz, Vincent R. *surgeon*
Herring, William Conyers *physicist, emeritus educator*
Herrmann, George *mechanical engineering educator*
Herzenberg, Leonard Arthur *medical educator*
Hesselink, Lambertus *electrical engineering and physics educator*
Hewett, Thomas Avery *petroleum engineer, educator*
Hickman, Bert George, Jr. *economist, educator*
Hilgard, Ernest Ropiequet *psychologist*
Hlatky, Mark Andrew *cardiologist, health services researcher*
Holloway, Charles Arthur *public and private management educator*
Holloway, David James *political science educator*
Howell, James Edwin *economist, educator*
Huntington, Hillard Griswold *economist*
Inkeles, Alex *sociology educator*
Jameson, Antony *aerospace engineering educator*
Jardetzky, Oleg *medical educator, scientist*
Johnson, John J. *historian, educator*
Johnston, Bruce Foster *economics educator*
Kailath, Thomas *electrical engineer, educator*
Kane, Thomas Reif *engineering educator*
Kays, William Morrow *university administrator, mechanical engineer*
Keller, Arthur Michael *computer science researcher*
Keller, Joseph Bishop *mathematician, educator*
Keller, Michael Alan *librarian, educator, musicologist*
Kendig, Joan Johnston *neurobiology educator*
Kennedy, David Michael *historian, educator*
Kennedy, Donald *environmental science educator, former academic administrator*
Kino, Gordon Stanley *electrical engineering educator*
Kirst, Michael Weile *education educator, researcher*
Klima, Roger Radim *physiatrist*
Knuth, Donald Ervin *computer sciences educator*
Kornberg, Arthur *biochemist*
Kornberg, Roger David *biochemist, structural biologist*
Kovach, Robert Louis *geophysics educator*
Krauskopf, Konrad Bates *geology educator*
Krueger, Anne O. *economics educator*
Kruger, Charles Herman, Jr. *mechanical engineering educator*
Krumboltz, John Dwight *psychologist, educator*
Kurz, Mordecai *economics educator*
Laitin, David Dennis *political science educator*
Lau, Lawrence Juen-Yee *economics educator, consultant*
†Laughlin, Robert B. *physics educator*
Lazear, Edward Paul *economics and industrial relations educator, researcher*
Leavitt, Harold Jack *management educator*
Lehman, (Israel) Robert *biochemistry educator, consultant*
Lepper, Mark Roger *psychology educator*
Levinthal, Elliott Charles *physicist, educator*
Levitt, Raymond Elliot *civil engineering educator*
Lewis, John Wilson *political science educator*
L'Heureux, John Clarke *English language educator*
Lieberman, Gerald J. *statistics educator*
Linvill, John Grimes *engineering educator*
Lipset, Seymour Martin *sociologist, political scientist, educator*
Little, William Arthur *physicist, educator*
Loftis, John (Clyde), Jr. *English language educator*
Lohnes, Walter F. W. *German language and literature educator*
Long, Sharon Rugel *molecular biologist, plant biology educator*
Lyman, Richard Wall *foundation and university executive, historian*
Lyons, Charles R. *drama educator and critic*
Maccoby, Eleanor Emmons *psychology educator*
Macovski, Albert *electrical engineering educator*
Madix, Robert James *chemical engineer, educator*
Maharidge, Dale Dimitro *journalist, educator*
Manley, John Frederick *political scientist, educator*
Mann, J. Keith *arbitrator, law educator, lawyer*
March, James Gardner *social scientist, educator*
Mark, James B. D. *surgeon*
Marmor, Michael Franklin *ophthalmologist, educator*
Martin, Roger Lloyd *educator, management consultant*
Matson, Pamela Anne *environmental science educator*
McCarthy, John *computer scientist, educator*
McCarty, Perry Lee *civil and environmental engineering educator*
McCluskey, Edward Joseph *engineering educator*
McConnell, Harden Marsden *biophysical chemistry researcher, chemistry educator*
McDevitt, Hugh O'Neill *immunology educator, physician*
McDonald, John Gregory *financial investment educator*
McDougall, Iain Ross *nuclear medicine educator*
Mc Lure, Charles E., Jr. *economist*
Mc Namara, Joseph Donald *researcher, retired police chief, novelist*
Meier, Gerald Marvin *economics educator*
Melmon, Kenneth Lloyd *physician, biologist, pharmacologist, consultant*
Merigan, Thomas Charles, Jr. *physician, medical researcher, educator*
Metzenberg, Robert L. *education educator*
Middlebrook, Diane Wood *English language educator*
Miller, Daniel James *systems engineer*
Miller, William Frederick *research company executive, educator, business consultant*
Moin, Parviz *mechanical engineering educator*
Montgomery, David Bruce *marketing educator*
†Montgomery, Mike *university basketball coach*
Mooney, Harold Alfred *plant ecologist*
Moravcsik, Julius Matthew *philosophy educator*
Moses, Lincoln E. *statistician, educator*
Moss, Richard B. *pediatrician*
Naimark, Norman M. *academic administrator*
Newman-Gordon, Pauline *French language and literature educator*
Noll, Roger Gordon *economist, educator*
North, Robert Carver *political science educator*
Oberhelman, Harry Alvin, Jr. *surgeon, educator*
Olshen, Richard A. *statistician, educator*
Ornstein, Donald Samuel *mathematician, educator*
Orr, Franklin Mattes, Jr. *petroleum engineering educator*
Ortolano, Leonard *civil engineering educator, water resources planner*
†Osheroff, Douglas Dean *physicist, researcher*
Palm, Charles Gilman *university official*
Parkinson, Bradford Wells *astronautical engineer, educator*
Paul, Benjamin David *anthropologist, educator*
Payne, Anita Hart *reproductive endocrinologist, researcher*
Pease, Roger Fabian Wedgwood *electrical engineering educator*
Perkins, David D(exter) *geneticist, educator*
Perl, Martin Lewis *physicist, engineer, educator*
Perloff, Marjorie Gabrielle *English and comparative literature educator*
Perry, John Richard *philosophy educator*
Pfeffer, Jeffrey *business educator*
Pope, Norris *publishing executive*
Porterfield, James Temple Starke *business administration educator*
Raffin, Thomas A. *physician*
Raisian, John *academic administrator, economist*
Rakove, Jack Norman *history educator*
Reitz, Bruce Arnold *cardiac surgeon, educator*
Reynolds, Clark Winton *economist, educator*
Reynolds, William Craig *mechanical engineer, educator*
Ricardo-Campbell, Rita *economist, educator*
Richter, Burton *physicist, educator*
Risser, James Vaulx, Jr. *journalist, educator*
Roberts, Donald Frank, Jr. *communications educator*
Roberts, Donald John *economics and business educator, consultant*
Roberts, Paul V. *civil and environmental engineering educator*
Robinson, Paul Arnold *historian, educator, author*
Rosenberg, Saul Allen *oncologist, educator*
Rosenthal, Myer Hyman *anesthesiologist*
Ross, John *physical chemist, educator*
Roster, Michael *lawyer*
†Rowen, Henry Stanislaus *economics educator*
Rubenstein, Edward *physician, educator*
Rudd, Peter *physician, medical educator*
Salisbury, David Francis *science and technology writer*
Saloner, Garth *management educator*
Schatzberg, Alan Frederic *psychiatrist, researcher*
Scheller, Richard H. *molecular and cellular physiology educator*
Schendel, Stephen Alfred *plastic surgery educator, craniofacial surgeon*
Schneider, Stephen Henry *climatologist, environmental policy analyst, researcher*
Schoen, Richard Melvin *mathematics educator, researcher*
Scott, Kenneth Eugene *lawyer, educator*
Scott, W(illiam) Richard *sociology educator*
Seligman, Thomas Knowles *museum administrator*
Shapiro, Lucille *molecular biology educator*
Shaw, Herbert John *physics educator emeritus*

Sheehan, James John historian, educator
Shepard, Roger Newland psychologist, educator
Shooter, Eric Manvers neurobiology educator, consultant
Shortliffe, Edward Hance internist, medical informatics educator
Shultz, George Pratt former government executive, economics educator
Siegman, Anthony Edward electrical engineer, educator
Silverman, Frederic Noah physician
Simons, Thomas W., Jr. history educator
Smelser, Neil Joseph sociologist
Sofaer, Abraham David lawyer, legal advisor, federal judge, law educator
Solomon, Ezra economist, educator
Somerville, Chris plant biologist, educator
Sorrentino, Gilbert English language educator, novelist, poet
Spence, Andrew Michael dean, finance educator
Spicer, William Edward, III physicist, educator, engineer
Spiegel, David psychiatrist
Spitz, Lewis William historian, educator
Spreiter, John Robert engineering researcher, educator, space physics scientist
Springer, George Stephen mechanical engineering educator
Spudich, James A. biology educator
Stamey, Thomas Alexander physician, urology educator
Stansky, Peter David Lyman historian
Steele, Charles Richard biomedical and mechanical engineering educator
Steele, Shelby writer, educator
Steidle, Edward humanities educator
Stone, William Edward unversity adminstrator
Street, Robert Lynnwood civil, mechanical and environmental engineer
Strena, Robert Victor university research laboratory manager
Strober, Myra Hoffenberg education educator, consultant
Stryer, Lubert biochemist, educator
Sulloway, Frank Jones psychologist, historian
Taube, Henry chemistry educator
Taylor, John Brian economist, educator
Taylor, Richard Edward physicist, educator
Teller, Edward physicist
Thompson, George Albert geophysics educator
Traugott, Elizabeth Closs linguistics educator and researcher
Triska, Jan Francis retired political science educator
Trost, Barry Martin chemist, educator
Tsai, Stephen Wei-Lun aeronautical educator
Ullman, Jeffrey David computer science educator
Van Dyke, Milton Denman aeronautical engineering educator
Van Horne, James Carter economist, educator
Veinott, Arthur Fales, Jr. universtiy research administrator
Vincenti, Walter Guido aeronautical engineer, emeritus educator
Vitousek, Peter M. botany educator, research ecologist
Wagoner, Robert Vernon astrophysicist, educator
Walt, Martin physicist, consulting educator
Wang, Suwen physicist, consultant
Waymouth, Robert chemistry educator
Weissman, Irving L. medical scientist
Wender, Paul Anthony chemistry educator
White, Robert Lee electrical engineer, educator
Whittemore, Alice biostatistician
†Wilson, John Long physician
Wojcicki, Stanley George physicist, educator
Wolff, Tobias (Jonathan Ansell Wolff) author
Yanofsky, Charles biology educator
Zajonc, Robert B(oleslaw) psychology educator
Zare, Richard Neil chemistry educator
Zimbardo, Philip George psychologist, educator, writer

Stockton

Addie, Harvey Woodward retired secondary education educator, music director
Biddle, Donald Ray aerospace company executive
Blewett, Robert Noall lawyer
Blodgett, Elsie Grace association executive
Chavez, Edward police chief
Curtis, Orlie Lindsey, Jr. lawyer
DeRicco, Lawrence Albert college president emeritus
Dolgow, Allan Bentley consulting company executive
Dornbush, Vicky Jean medical billing systems executive
Dunning, John university volleyball coach
Foster, Colleen library director
Gallagher, Tim parks and recreation director
Giottonini, James B. public works director Stockton, California
Goldstrand, Dennis Joseph business and estate planning executive
Hepper, Iona Lydia gallery owner
Jacobs, Marian advertising agency owner
Jantzen, J(ohn) Marc retired education educator
†Lawrence, James Russell information systems specialist
Limbaugh, Ronald Hadley history educator, history center director
Lovell, Emily Kalled journalist
Lutz, Reinhart English language educator, writer
Mathre, Lawrence Gerhard minister, federal agency administrator
McNeal, Dale William, Jr. biological sciences educator
Meissner, Katherine Gong city clerk
Pinkerton, Steven James city director housing and redevelopment
Ratto, Douglas C. protective services official
Samsell, L. Patrick municipal official
Samsell, Lewis Patrick municipal finance executive
Sorby, Donald Lloyd university dean
Taylor, Francis Michael auditor, municipal official
Tregle, Linda Marie dance educator
Vargo, Richard Joseph accounting educator, writer
Viscovich, Sir Andrew John educational management consultant
Whiteker, Roy Archie retired chemistry educator

Studio City

Bull, David fine art conservator
Carsey, Marcia Lee Peterson television producer
Chambers, Clytia Montllor public relations consultant
Devane, William actor
Duffield, Thomas Andrew art director, production designer
Frumkin, Simon political activist and columnist
Gautier, Dick actor, writer
Hasselhoff, David actor
Herrman, Marcia Kutz child development specialist
Jacobs, Ronald Nicholas television and motion picture producer/director
Kaye, Lori travel academy executive, consultant
Kenney, H(arry) Wesley, Jr. producer, director
Lamothe, Irene Elise television producer, distributor
Lasarow, William Julius retired federal judge
†Mandabach, Caryn television producer
Miller, Charles Maurice lawyer
Nelson, Anna Masterton writer, digital effects artist
Parish, James Robert author, cinema historian
Pressman, Michael film director
Richman, Peter Mark actor, painter, writer
Sertner, Robert Mark producer
Shavelson, Melville writer, theatrical producer and director
Spencer, James H. art director, production designer
Sylbert, Paul production designer, art director
Sylbert, Richard production designer, art director
Taylor, Jack G., Jr. art director
Thomas, Wynn P. art director, production designer
Tomkins, Alan art director, production designer
Werner, Tom television producer, professional baseball team executive
Whitney, Steven writer, producer
Wissner, Gary Charles motion picture art director, production designer

Summerland

Calamar, Gloria artist
Cannon, Louis Simeon journalist, author
Hall, Lee Boaz publishing company consultant, author
Mitchell, Maurice B. publishing executive, educator

Sun Valley

Casey, Paul Arnold writer, composer, photographer
Dergrigorian, Ronald water microbiologist
†Kamins, Philip E. diversified manufacturing company executive
Mayhue, Richard Lee dean, pastor, writer
Stitzinger, James Franklin religion educator, library director

Sunnyvale

Alich, John Arthur, Jr. manufacturing company executive
Armistead, Robert Ashby, Jr. scientific research company executive
Can, Sumer research electrical engineer
Crabill, Linda Jean municipal government official
DeMello, Austin Eastwood astrophysicist, concert artist, poet, writer
Devgan, Onkar Dave N. technologist, consultant
Evans, Barton, Jr. analytical instrument company executive
Fairweather, Edwin Arthur electronics company executive
Gordon, Marc Stewart pharmacist, scientist
Green, Marjorie automotive distribution, import and manufacturing company executive
Kempf, Martine voice control device manufacturing company executive
Kim, Wan Hee electrical engineering educator, business executive
Lewis, John Clark, Jr. manufacturing company executive
†Lin, Chong Ming engineer
Linn, Gary Dean golf course architect
†Lopatin, Sergey Dmitrievich microelectronic scientist, electrochemist
Ludgus, Nancy Lucke lawyer
Majumder, Sabir Ahmed physical and analytical chemist
McReynolds, Stephen Paul lawyer
Peline, Val P. engineering executive
Robbins, James Edward electrical engineer
Sanders, Walter Jeremiah, III electronics company executive
Simon, Ralph E. electronics executive
Thissell, James Dennis physicist
Woolsey, Roy Blakeney electronics company executive
Yin, Gerald Zheyao technology and business executive
Zahrt, William Dietrich, II lawyer

Sunset Beach

Bettis, John Gregory songwriter

Susanville

†Kellison, Craig M. federal judge

Sylmar

Corry, Dalila Boudjellal internist
Foster, Dudley Edwards, Jr. musician, educator
Froelich, Beverly Lorraine foundation director
Lisalda, Sylvia Ann primary education educator
Madni, Asad Mohamed engineering executive
Munro, Malcolm Gordon obstetrician, gynecologist, educator
Scheib, Gerald Paul fine art educator, jeweler, metalsmith
Shaw, Anthony physician, pediatric surgeon
Tully, Susan Balsley pediatrician, educator
Yguado, Alex Rocco economics educator
Ziment, Irwin medical educator

Tarzana

Brook, Winston Rollins retired audio-video design consultant
Easton, Sheena rock vocalist
Evans, Colleen Marie home health administrator
†Haberkorn, John G. small business owner
Handelsman, Yehuda endocrinologist, internal medicine physician
Hansen, Robert Clinton electrical engineering consultant
Macmillan, Robert Smith electronics engineer
Meyers, Robert Allen chemist, publisher
Rinsch, Maryann Elizabeth occupational therapist
Yablun, Ronn secondary education educator, small business owner

Tehachapi

Badgley, Theodore McBride psychiatrist, neurologist
†Dewar, Robert Earl artist
Mitchell, Betty Jo writer, publisher
Smith-Thompson, Patricia Ann public relations consultant, educator

Temecula

Buzbee, John Duffie, Jr. sales executive
Coram, David James marketing professional
Kinsler, Bruce Whitney air traffic controller, consultant, air traffic control engineer, air defense engineer, air traffic control automation specialist, branch manager
Locklin, William Ray financial planner
Minogue, Robert Brophy retired nuclear engineer
†Overman, John W.J. physician
Petersen, Vernon Leroy communications and engineering corporations executive
Randall, John Albert, III elementary and secondary education educator
Rosenstein, Robert Bryce lawyer, financial advisor

Temple City

Costa, George George (Adel George Costandy) physician
Matsuda, Stanley Kazuhiro secondary education educator
Perkins, Floyd Jerry retired theology educator
Provenzano, Maureen Lynn secondary school educator
Robbins, William Curtis, Jr. television and motion picture producer, director, writer, news reporter, cameraman
Weidaw, Kenneth Roe musician, educator, consultant

Templeton

Guenther, Robert Stanley, II investment and property executive
Shahan, Sherry Jean author, educator

Terra Bella

Gletne, Jeffrey Scott forester

The Sea Ranch

Hayflick, Leonard microbiologist, cell biologist, gerontologist, educator, writer

Thousand Oaks

Allen, David Harlow business educator, logistician, consultant
Binder, Gordon M. health and medical products executive
Buyalos, Richard Paul, Jr. physician
Cipriano, Patricia Ann secondary education educator, consultant
Cobb, Shirley Ann public relations specialist, journalist
Deisenroth, Clinton Wilbur electrical engineer
Dougherty, Gerard Michael lawyer
Emerson, Alton Calvin retired physical therapist
Forti, Corinne Ann corporate communications executive
Geiser, Thomas Christopher lawyer
Glieberman, Cary Hirsch film producer, director, writer
Gregory, Calvin insurance service executive
Herman, Joan Elizabeth healthcare company executive
Heyer, Carol Ann illustrator
Horton, Kenneth investor
Jessup, Warren T. retired lawyer
†Johnson, Shirley Amagna systems analyst
Klein, Jeffrey Howard oncologist, internist
Knight, Jeffrey Richard small business owner
Krumm, Charles Ferdinand electrical engineer
Lark, M. Ann management consultant, strategic planner, naturalist
Malmuth, Norman David scientist, program manager
Monis, Antonio, Jr. (Tony Monis) electric industry executive
Noonan, Daniel Christopher consultant
†Powe, Larry Kenneth clinical researcher
Relkin, Michele Weston artist
Rooney, Mickey (Joe Yule, Jr.) actor
Schaeffer, Leonard David healthcare executive
Sherman, Gerald nuclear physicist, financial estate adviser, financial company executive
Sladek, Lyle Virgil mathematician, educator
†Tierney, Nathan Llywellyn educator
Trover, Ellen Lloyd lawyer
Walker, Lorenzo Giles surgeon, educator

Tiburon

Bauch, Thomas Jay lawyer, educator, former apparel company executive
Cook, Lyle Edwards retired fund raising executive, consultant
Harary, Keith research scientist, writer, science journalist
Widman, Gary Lee lawyer, former government official

Toluca Lake

Morris, Janet Eloise webdesigner, poet
Mracky, Ronald Sydney marketing and promotion executive, travel consultant
Ragan, Ann Talmadge media and production consultant, actor
Runquist, Lisa A. lawyer
Rustam, Mardi Ahmed film and television producer, publisher

Torrance

Adelsman, (Harriette) Jean newspaper editor
Brasel, Jo Anne physician
Buckley, James W. librarian
†Burnham, Daniel Patrick manufacturing company executive
Cai, Khiem Van technologist, researcher, administrator
Culton, Paul Melvin retired counselor, educator, interpreter
Deason, Edward Joseph lawyer
Dickerson, Joe Bernard principal, educator
Emmanouilides, George Christos physician, educator
Enright, Stephanie Veselich investment company executive
Everts, Connor artist
Gilbert, Scott advertising executive
Grollman, Julius Harry, Jr. cardiovascular and interventional radiologist
Hammer, Terence Michael physician
Harmon Brown, Valarie Jean hospital laboratory director, information systems executive
Harness, William Edward tenor
†Hennig, Alfred W. lawyer
Hoagland, Albert Joseph, Jr. psychotherapist, hypnotherapist, minister
Hollander, Daniel gastroenterologist, medical educator
Houston, Samuel Robert statistics educator, consultant
†Howroyd, Janice Bryant personnel placement executive
Itabashi, Hideo Henry neuropathologist, neurologist
Johnson, Einar William lawyer
Kasari, Leonard Samuel quality control professional, concrete consultant
Kaufman, Sanford Paul lawyer
Krout, Boyd Merrill psychiatrist
Kucij, Timothy Michael engineer, musician, minister
Lee, James King technology corporation executive
Mann, Michael Martin electronics company executive
Matsunaga, Geoffrey Dean lawyer
Mazzolini, James William engineering administrator
McNamara, Brenda Norma secondary education educator
Medley, Nancy May nurse
Mehringer, Charles Mark medical educator
Mende, Howard Shigeharu mechanical engineer
Moore, Christopher Minor lawyer
Myhre, Byron Arnold pathologist, educator
Perrish, Albert steel company executive
Prell, Joel James medical group administrator
Rogers, Howard H. chemist
Savitz, Maxine Lazarus aerospace company executive
Signorovitch, Dennis J. communications executive
Sloan, Michael Dana information systems specialist
Sorstokke, Susan Eileen systems engineer
Stabile, Bruce Edward surgeon
Tabrisky, Joseph radiologist, educator
Talmo-Wang, Regina Marie social studies educator
Tanaka, Kouichi Robert physician, educator
Wylie, Richard Thornton aerospace engineer
†Yu, Kian-Ti Tiu pediatrician, educator
Zhao, Mingjun physicist, research scientist

Trabuco Canyon

Jessup, R. Judd health care executive

Tracy

Dittman, Deborah Ruth real estate broker
Green, Brian Gerald marketing executive
Hay, Dennis Lee lawyer
Nelson, Kenneth Arthur electrical engineer

Travis AFB

†Rasmussen, Craig P. career officer
†Rodgers, Lee P. career officer
†Roser, Steven A. career officer

Trinidad

Marshall, William Edward historical association executive

Truckee

Forsen, Harold Kay retired engineering executive
Johnston, Bernard Fox author, foundation executive
Todd, Linda Marie nutrition researcher, financial consultant, pilot

Tujunga

Mayer, George Roy educator

Tulare

Baradat, Raymond Alphonse recording industry executive
Vickrey, Herta Miller microbiologist

Turlock

Ahlem, Lloyd Harold psychologist
Amrhein, John Kilian retired dean
Hughes, Marvalene academic administrator
Parker, John Carlyle retired librarian and archivist, editor
Stensether, John Eldon minister
Twaddell, Karen Grace elementary education educator
Volk, Gregory Thomas secondary education educator
Wallström, Wesley Donald bank executive
Williams, Delwyn Charles telephone company executive

Tustin

Bartlett, Arthur Eugene franchise executive
Crouch, Paul Franklin minister, church official
†Del Campo, C. Alicia theater scholar
†De Veirman, Geert Adolf engineer
Greene, Wendy Segal special education educator
Hester, Norman Eric chemical company technical executive, chemist
Kraft, Henry R. lawyer
Madory, Richard Eugene lawyer
Pauley, Richard Heim real estate counselor
Prizio, Betty J. property manager, civic worker
Sinnette, John Townsend, Jr. research scientist, consultant
Zhu, Peter Chaoquan chemist

Twain Harte

Kinsinger, Robert Earl property company executive, educational consultant

Twentynine Palms

Clemente, Patrocinio Ablola psychology educator
Fultz, Philip Nathaniel management analyst

Ukiah

Eversole, Walter Robert funeral director
Lohrli, Anne retired English language educator, author
McAllister, (Ronald) Eric pharmaceutical executive, physician, software developer
McClintock, Richard Polson dermatologist
Toms, Michael Anthony broadcast journalist, editor, writer, producer

Union City

Cobos, José Manuel Spanish language educator
Lewis, Mark Earldon city manager
Lockhart, Patsy Marie secondary education educator
Nacario, Robert John educational administrator

Universal City

Baker, Richard Eugene corporate executive
†Bratt, Benjamin actor
Costello, Richard Neumann advertising agency executive
Devin, Richard film industry executive
Geffen, David recording company executive, producer

Gumpel, Glenn J. *association executive*
†Harmon, Angie *actress*
†Hill, Steven *actor*
Horak, Jan-Christopher *film studies educator, curator*
Katzenberg, Jeffrey *motion picture studio executive*
Kay, Kenneth Jeffrey *entertainment company executive*
†LaBelle, Patti *singer*
Lansbury, Angela Brigid *actress*
Lovett, Lyle *musician*
†Merkerson, S. Epatha *actress*
Meyer, Ron *agent*
Midler, Bette *singer, entertainer, actress*
Paul, Charles S. *motion picture and television company executive*
Reitman, Ivan *film director, producer*
†Simonds, Robert *producer*
Wasserman, Lew R. *film, recording and publishing company executive*

Upland
Boswell, Dan Alan *health maintenance organization executive, health care consultant*
Chaney, Robert Galen *religious organization executive*
Deppisch, Paul Vincent *data communications executive*
Goodman, John M. *construction executive*
Graw, LeRoy Harry *purchasing-contract management company executive*
Jones, Nancy Langdon *financial planning practitioner*
Lewis, Goldy Sarah *real estate developer, corporation executive*
Porrero, Henry, Jr. *construction company executive*

Upper Lake
Scobey, Jan (Jeannette Marie Scobey) *jazz musician, store owner, author*
Twitchell, Kent *mural artist*

Vacaville
Dailey, Dawn Elaine *public health service official*
Dedeaux, Paul J. *orthodontist*
Ford, John T., Jr. *art, film and video educator*
Russell, Rhonda Cheryl *piano educator*
Sawyer, Nelson Baldwin, Jr. *credit union executive*
†Yerkes, Jay Alan *financial planner*

Valencia
Simmons, Ann Lorraine *actor*
Volpe, Eileen Rae *special education educator*

Vallejo
Feil, Linda Mae *tax preparer*
Hudak, Paul Alexander *retired engineer*
Kleinrock, Robert Allen *physician*
McGowan, Thomas Randolph *retired religious organization executive*

Valley Ford
†Clowes, Garth Anthony *electronics executive, consultant*

Valley Glen
Ghent, Peer *management consultant*

Valley Springs
Vitrac, Jean-Jacques Charles *international business consultant*

Valley Village
Bench, Johnny Lee *retired professional baseball player*
Toussaint, Christopher Andre *video producer, director, writer*

Van Nuys
Allen, Stephen Valentine Patrick William *television comedian, author, pianist, songwriter*
Arabian, Armand *arbitrator, mediator, lawyer*
Boyd, Harry Dalton *lawyer, former insurance company executive*
Cochran, Anne Westfall *public relations executive*
Fisher, Earl Monty *utilities executive*
Fox, James Michael *orthopedic surgeon*
†Freeman, Margaret H. *English educator*
Freiberg, Robert Jerry *laser physicist, engineer, technology administrator, consultant*
Graham, Roger John *photography and journalism educator*
Josephs, Alice Ruth *retired executive secretary*
Kagan, Stephen Bruce (Sandy Kagan) *network marketing executive*
Lagasse, Bruce Kenneth *structural engineer*
Mohr, Anthony James *judge*
Sandel, Randye Noreen *artist*
Simon, David Harold *retired public relations executive*
Sludikoff, Stanley Robert *publisher, writer*
Stender, Charles Frederick *test pilot*
Westbrook, G. Jay *hospice nurse, grief counselor*
Zucker, Alfred John *English language educator, academic administrator*

Vandenberg AFB
†Perryman, Gerald F., Jr. *military officer*

Venice
Bengston, Billy Al *artist*
Bill, Tony *producer, director*
Davis, Kimberly Brooke *art gallery director*
Dixon, Neil Edward *elementary school educator, paleoanthropologist*
Eliot, Alexander *author, mythologist*
Eversley, Frederick John *sculptor, engineer*
Garabedian, Charles *artist*
Hartley, Corinne *painter, sculptor, educator*
†Mikesekk, Richard Hugh *real estate*
Padilla, Mario René *literature educator, writer, actor*
Seger, Linda Sue *script consultant, lecturer, writer*
Shelton, Peter T. *artist*

Ventura
Abul-Haj, Suleiman Kahil *pathologist*
Arant, Eugene Wesley *lawyer*
Arita, George Shiro *biology educator*
Bircher, Andrea Ursula *psychiatric-mental health nurse, educator, clinical nurse specialist*
Bray, Laurack Doyle *lawyer*
English, Woodrow Douglas *lawyer*
Gartner, Harold Henry, III *lawyer*
Gaynor, Joseph *chemical engineer, technical-management consultant*
Kent, Theodore Charles *psychologist*
Kirman, Charles Gary *photojournalist*
Lovell, Frederick Warren *pathologist, medical legal consultant*
Moran, Rita Jane *music, drama, restaurant critic, travel writer*
Naurath, David Allison *engineering psychologist, researcher*
Okuma, Albert Akira, Jr. *architect*
Renger, Marilyn Hanson *elementary education educator*
Robinson, William Franklin *retired legal consultant*
Ruebe, Bambi Lynn *interior, environmental designer*
Smith, Bill *city manager*
Villaveces, James Walter *allergist, immunologist*
Zuber, William Frederick *thoracic and vascular surgeon*

Victorville
Lagomarsini, George Caesar *engineering and mathematics educator, consultant*
Peterson, Leroy *retired secondary education educator*
Quadri, Fazle Rab *lawyer, government official*
Sedeño, Eugene Raymond *electronics engineer, consultant*

Villa Grande
Shirilau, Mark Steven *utilities executive*

Villa Park
Britton, Thomas Warren, Jr. *management consultant*
Buffington, Linda Brice *interior designer*
Hawe, David Lee *consultant*

Visalia
Crowe, John T. *lawyer*
Goulart, Janell Ann *elementary education educator*
Hart, Timothy Ray *lawyer, dean*
Heidbreder, Gail *architect, educator*
Keenan, Robert Joseph *trade association executive*
Madden, Wanda Lois *nurse*
Neeley, James K. *credit agency executive*
Riegel, Byron William *ophthalmologist*
Rodriguez, Carlos *fire chief*
Taylor, Helen Shields *civic worker*

Vista
Beversdorf, Anne Elizabeth *astrologer, Jyotishi, author, educator*
Cavanaugh, Kenneth Clinton *retired housing consultant*
Ferguson, Margaret Ann *tax consultant*
Fuhlrodt, Norman Theodore *retired insurance executive*
Helmuth, Philip Alan *tax consultant*
Hofmann, Frieder Karl *biotechnologist, consultant*
Klungness, Elizabeth Jane *publisher, writer, retired accountant*
Tiedeman, David Valentine *education educator*

Walnut
Caudron, John Armand *accident reconstructionist, forensic investigator*
Chaney, Gene Paul Russ *trade association administrator*
Craig, Karen Lynn *accountant, controller*
Dibell, Marta Lee *foreign language educator*
McKee, Catherine Lynch *law educator, lawyer*
Shannon, Cynthia Jean *biology educator*
Spencer, Constance Marilyn *secondary education educator*
Tan, Colleen Woo *communications educator*

Walnut Creek
Acosta, Julio Bernard *obstetrician, gynecologist*
Ausenbaum, Helen Evelyn *social worker, psychologist*
Barnett, David Hughes *software engineer, computer systems architect*
Boland, Margaret Camille *financial services administrator, consultant*
Borenstein, Daniel Asa *newspaper political editor*
Bristow, Lonnie Robert *physician*
Burgarino, Anthony Emanuel *environmental engineer, consultant*
Carver, Dorothy Lee Eskew (Mrs. John James Carver) *retired secondary education educator*
Cervantez, Gil Lawrence *venture capital company executive*
Coit, R. Ken *financial planner*
Conger, Harry Milton *mining company executive*
Crandall, Ira Carlton *consulting electrical engineer*
Curtin, Daniel Joseph, Jr. *lawyer*
Dasovich, E. Martin *accountant*
De Benedictis, Dario *arbitrator, mediator*
DeBoer, David James *transportation executive*
Duke, Ellen Kay *community activist, playground professional*
Epstein, Judith Ann *lawyer*
Fridley, Saundra Lynn *internal audit executive*
Fuller, Glenn Straith *minister*
Garlough, William Glenn *marketing executive*
Garrett, James Joseph *lawyer, partner*
Ginsburg, Gerald J. *lawyer, business executive*
Hallock, C. Wiles, Jr. *athletic official*
Hamlin, Kenneth Eldred, Jr. *retired pharmaceutical company executive*
Jones, Orlo Dow *lawyer, drug store executive*
Kang, Isamu Yong *nuclear medicine physician*
Keith, Bruce Edgar *political analyst, genealogist*
Kuhl, Ronald Webster *marketing executive*
Lagarias, John Samuel *engineering executive*
Lee, William Chien-Yeh *electrical engineer*
Long, Robert Merrill *retail drug company executive*
Mackay, Patricia McIntosh *counselor*
McCauley, Bruce Gordon *financial consultant*
McGrath, Don John *banker*
Medak, Walter Hans *lawyer*
Mitgang, Iris Feldman *lawyer, educator*
Moore, John D. *management consultant*
Nolan, David Charles *lawyer, mediator*
Pagter, Carl Richard *lawyer*
Palmer, Vincent Allan *construction consultant*
Rhody, Ronald Edward *banker, communications executive*
Satz, Louis K. *publishing executive*
Seaborg, David Michael *evolutionary biologist*
Shastid, Jon Barton *wine company executive*
Sheen, Portia Yunn-ling *retired physician*
Skaggs, Sanford Merle *lawyer*
Stapp, Olivia Brewer *opera singer*
Stover, W. Robert *temporary services executive*
Trousdale, Stephen Richard *newspaper editor*
Wilkins, Sheila Scanlon *management consultant*
Williams, Michael James *health care services consultant*
Wolf, Harry *retired dean and educator*
Wu, Tse Cheng *research chemist*
†Yake, Daniel Glen *civil engineer*

Washington
Gonzales, Daniel Richard *defense and technology analyst*

Watsonville
Alfaro, Felix Benjamin *physician*
Brown, Alan Charlton *retired aeronautical engineer*
Condon, Thomas Joseph *editor, writer*
†Eadie, Charles D. *city planner, consultant, writer*
†Hannula, Tarmo *photographer*
Hansen, Elizabeth Jean *appraiser, author*
Hernandez, Jo Farb *museum curator, consultant*
Pye, David Thomas *specialty retail company executive*
Solari, R. C. *retired heavy construction company executive*
†Watts, David H. *construction company executive*

Weed
Kyle, Chester Richard *mechanical engineer*

Weimar
Ing, Clarence Sinn Fook *preventive medicine physician, ophthalmic surgeon*
Kerschner, Lee R(onald) *academic administrator, political science educator*

West Covina
Adams, Sarah Virginia *family counselor*
Collins, Beverly Ann *obstetrical, gynecological nurse practitioner*
Franden, Blanche M. *nursing educator*
McHale, Edward Robertson *retired lawyer*
Musich, Robert Lorin *motivational speaker*
Pollak, Erich Walter *surgeon, educator*
Shiershke, Nancy Fay *artist, educator, property manager*
Torres, Esteban Edward *former congressman, business executive*
West, Edward Alan *graphics communications executive*

West Hills
Centorino, James Rocco *science educator, composer*
†Davidorf, Jonathan Michael *ophthalmologist*
Godsil, Richard William *minister*
Koerber, John Robert *computer programmer*
Struhl, Stanley Frederick *real estate developer*
Tennen, Ken *lawyer*

West Hollywood
Annakin, Kenneth Cooper *film director, writer*
Bloom, Claire *actress*
Blumofe, Robert Fulton *motion picture producer, association executive*
Cage, Nicolas (Nicolas Coppola) *actor*
†Chillida, Eduardo *sculptor*
†De Palma, Brian Russell *film director, writer*
Eastman, Donald *church officer*
Eger, Denise Leese *rabbi*
Einstein, Clifford Jay *advertising executive*
Etessami, Rambod *endodontist*
Feidelson, Marc *advertising executive*
Finstad, Suzanne Elaine *writer, producer, lawyer*
Gates, Lisa *private chef, caterer*
Grasshoff, Alex *writer, producer, director*
Harper, Robert *actor*
Henley, Don *singer, drummer, songwriter*
Hill, Jack *motion picture director, writer, educator*
Hoffenblum, Allan Ernest *political consultant*
Holt, Dennis F. *media buying company executive*
Jaglom, Henry David *actor, director, writer*
Kingsley, Patricia *public relations executive*
Krabbe, Jeroen Aart *actor*
Madonna, (Madonna Louise Veronica Ciccone) *singer, actress*
Males, William James *film producer, make-up artist*
McGaughey, Emmett Connell *advertising agency executive*
McLaughlin, Stephen *sound recording engineer*
Perry, Troy D. *clergyman, church administrator*
Shaye, Robert Kenneth *cinema company executive*
Sherman, Robert B(ernard) *composer, lyricist, screenwriter*
Thaw, Mort *writer*
Verhoeven, Paul *film director*
Wilson, Nancy Linda *church officer*

West Sacramento
Lloyd, Sharon *marketing professional*
McGagin, Nancy *public affairs executive*
Solomon, Russell *retail products executive*
†Teal, Joyce Raley *grocery chain executive*
Teel, James E. *supermarket and drug store retail executive*
Teel, Joyce *supermarket and drugstore retail executive*
Teel, Michael J. *supermarket chain executive*

Westlake Village
Caligiuri, Joseph Frank *retired engineering executive*
Cammalleri, Joseph Anthony *financial planner, retired air force officer*
Caren, Robert Poston *aerospace company executive*
Catrambone, Eugene Dominic *magazine editor*
Colburn, Keith W. *electronics executive*
Cucina, Vincent Robert *retired financial executive*
DeLorenzo, David A. *food products executive*
Detterman, Robert Linwood *financial planner*
Fredericks, Ward Arthur *venture capitalist, food industry consultant*
Munson, John Backus *computer systems consultant, retired computer engineering company executive*
Murdock, David H. *diversified company executive*
Smyth, Glen Miller *management consultant*
†Swink, Greg *computer software executive*
Troxell, Lucy Davis *consulting firm executive*
Valentine, Gene C. *securities dealer*
Vinson, William Theodore *lawyer, diversified corporation executive*
Weisman, Martin Jerome *manufacturing company executive*
†Woodard, Matthew Jay *martial arts instructor*

Westminster
Allen, Merrill James *marine biologist*
Armstrong, Gene Lee *systems engineering consultant, retired aerospace company executive*
Begg, Cynthia I. *health facility administrator*
Gylseth, Doris (Lillian) Hanson *retired librarian*
Luong, Khanh Vinh Quoc *nephrologist, researcher*
Milligan, Ronald Edgar *journalist*
†Reasonover, Robert Pretceille (Huy-manh Nguyen) *real estate broker, educator*
Rupel, Daniel Patrick *retailing executive*
†Salaymeh, Muhammad Tawfik *surgeon*
Smith, William Hugh, Sr. *retired audit manager, consultant*

Westport
Anderson, Terry Marlene *civil engineer*

Whitley Heights
Lawrence, Sanford Hull *physician, immunochemist*

Whittier
Arcadi, John Albert *urologist*
Ash, James Lee, Jr. *academic administrator*
Briney, Allan King *retired radiologist*
Caro, Evelyn Inga Rouse *writer*
Connick, Charles Milo *retired religion educator, clergyman*
De Lorca, Luis E. *educational administrator, educator, speaker*
Harvey, Patricia Jean *educator, administrator, retired*
Korf, Leonard Lee *theater arts educator*
Lillevang, Omar Johansen *civil engineer*
†Long, Peggy Jo *principal*
Lowe, Oariona *dentist*
Maxwell, Raymond Roger *accountant*
McKenna, Jeanette Ann *archaeologist*
Meardy, William Herman *association executive*
Prickett, David Clinton *physician*
Scheifly, John Edward *retired lawyer*
Shackelford, Anastasia Marie *secondary school educator*
Tunison, Elizabeth Lamb *education educator*
Welsh, William Daniel *family practitioner*
Zanetta, Joseph Michael *university administrator, lawyer*

Williams
Ratzlaff, Ruben Menno *religion educator, minister*

Willits
Akins, George Charles *accountant*
Handley, Margie Lee *business executive*

Wilton
Harrison, George Harry, III (Hank Harrison) *publishing executive, author*

Windsor
†Drake, Glendon Frank *writer*
Gomez, Edward Casimiro *physician, educator, vintner*
Smith, Maynard Dwight *minister*

Woodlake
Lippmann, Bruce Allan *rehabilitative services professional, educator*

Woodland
†Breeden, Michael Edward *defender*
Butler, Patricia Lacky *mental health nurse, educator, consultant*
Stormont, Clyde Junior *laboratory company executive*

Woodland Hills
Anaya, Richard Alfred, Jr. *accountant, investment banker*
Babayans, Emil *financial planner*
Baker, Joe Don *actor*
Barrett, Robert Matthew *lawyer, law educator*
Beasley, Larry *newspaper publishing executive*
Berry, Carol Ann *insurance executive*
Blanchard, William Henry *psychologist*
Bonassi, Jodi *artist, marketing consultant*
Brozowski, Laura Adrienne *mechanical engineer*
Burke, Tamara Lynn *marketing professional*
DeWitt, Barbara Jane *journalist*
Ennis, Thomas Michael *management consultant*
Evigan, Greg *actor, musician*
Firestone, Morton H. *business management executive*
Fitzpatrick, Dennis Michael *information systems executive*
Floyd, Brett Alden *mortgage banker*
Fox, Stuart Ira *physiologist*
†Funari, Robert Glenn *health care services executive*
Gill, Keith Hubert *lawyer*
Gonzalez, Michael Joe *multimedia producer*
†Gray, Laura *human resources specialist*
†Greenwald, Arthur M. *federal judge*
Halamandaris, Harry *aerospace executive*
Harmon, David *finance company executive*
Harris, Sigmund Paul *physicist*
Herdeg, Howard Brian *physician*
Hoch, Orion Lindel *corporate executive*
Horne, Lena *singer*
†Inocencio, E. Bing *college president*
Johnson-Champ, Debra Sue *lawyer, educator, writer, artist*
Kinkade, Kate *magazine editor, insurance executive*
Klugman, Jack *actor*
†Lax, Kathleen Thompson *bankruptcy judge*
Levy, Norman *motion picture company executive*
Lund, Robert W. *newspaper editor*
Meeks, Crawford Russell, Jr. *mechanical engineer*
Morishita, Akihiko *trading company executive*
Mund, Geraldine *judge*
Nierenberg, Norman *urban land economist, retired state official*
Parrott, Dennis Beecher *sales executive*
Pickard, Dean *philosophy and humanities educator*
Pregerson, Harry *federal judge*
†Preston, John Elwood *lawyer*
Randall, Craig *financial and business management consultant, accountant, computer specialist*
Richards, Benness Melvin *airline pilot*
Robertson, Alexander, IV *lawyer*
Shuster, Fred Todd *journalist, commentator*
Small, Michael *composer*
Stoll, Leonard Peter *aerospace business administrator, consultant*
Strote, Joel Richard *lawyer*
Taubitz, Fredricka *financial executive*
Taylor, Rowan Shaw *music educator, composer, conductor*
Weider, Joseph *wholesale distribution executive*

Wester, Keith Albert film and television recording engineer, television executive
Yackle, Albert Reustle aeronautical engineer
†Yates, Gary L. marriage and family therapist
Zeitlin, Herbert Zakary retired college president, real estate company excutive

Woodside
Ashley, Holt aerospace scientist, educator
Blum, Richard Hosmer Adams educator, writer
Frank, Victor Robert electrical engineer
Freitas, Antoinette Juni insurance company executive
Gates, Milo Sedgwick retired construction company executive
Isaacson, Robert Louis investment company executive
Lee, Hamilton H. education educator
Martin, Joseph, Jr. retired lawyer, former ambassador
†Miller, John Johnston pediatric rheumatologist
Spitzer, Walter Oswald epidemiologist, educator
Taylor, Robert William research director

Yorba Linda
Forth, Kevin Bernard beverage distributing industry consultant
Hutchins, James Leigh quality assurance professional
Kennedy, Robert P. civil engineer
Lunde, Dolores Benitez retired secondary education educator
Naulty, Susan Louise archivist
Porcello, Leonard Joseph engineering research and development executive
Vilardi, Agnes Francine real estate broker

Yosemite National Park
Forgang, David M. museum curator

Yountville
Damé-Shepp, Diane art management administrator
Helzer, James Dennis hospital executive
Jones, Thomas Robert social worker
Kay, Douglas Casey leasing consultant
†Paquet, Gary Michael Sebastian company executive

Yreka
Beary, Shirley Lorraine retired music educator
Fiock, Shari Lee event planner, entrepreneur, publishing executive
Smith, Vin sports editor, business owner, novelist

Yuba City
Dalpino, Ida Jane secondary education educator
Doscher, Richard John protective services official
Kemmerly, Jack Dale retired state official, aviation consultant
Lefever, Eric Bruce anesthesiologist
Perry, Phillip Edmund middle school educator
†Skiles, Margaret S. plastic surgeon

Yucaipa
Horn, Paul Ervin minister

Yucca Valley
†Martin, George Leonard federal judge

COLORADO

Alamosa
Layton, Terry Wayne college basketball coach
Rickey, June Evelyn Million retired educator

Arvada
Bert, Carol Lois educational assistant
Deere, Cyril Thomas retired computer company executive
Eaves, Sally Ann logistics director, research administrator
Halley, Diane Esther artist
Hammond-Blessing, DiAnn A. elementary education educator
Holden, George Fredric brewing company executive, policy specialist, author
Knight, William V. geologist
Laidig, Eldon Lindley financial planner
Loomis, Christopher Knapp metallurgical engineer
Martin, Robert Gregory chemist
Peck, Kenneth E. lawyer
Reynolds-Sakowski, Dana Renee science educator
Wambolt, Thomas Eugene financial consultant
Williams, Marsha Kay data processing executive
Young, Bonnie Darline primary school educator
Zetterman, Polly Davis retired secondary school educator

Aspen
Alstrom, Sven Erik architect
Berkó, Ferenc photographer
Caudill, Samuel Jefferson architect
Ewing, Wayne Hilley film producer, director, writer
Finster, Brent Edwin public safety communications administrator
Hansen, Steven Alan construction executive
Harth, Robert James music festival executive
Hayes, Mary Eshbaugh newspaper editor
McDade, James Russell management consultant
McGrath, J. Nicholas lawyer
Oden, Robert Rudolph surgeon
Peirce, Frederick Fairbanks lawyer
Pullen, Margaret I. genetic physicist
Shipp, Dan Shackelford lawyer
Soldner, Paul Edmund artist, ceramist, educator
†Young, Henry executive director
Zinman, David Joel conductor

Aurora
Barnes, Raymond Edward fire department official
Battaglia, Frederick Camillo physician
Bauman, Earl William accountant, government official
Bennion, Scott Desmond physician
Bobrick, Steven Aaron marketing executive
Brinkmeyer, Dotty Stewart maternal/child nurse
†Brown, Anne Sherwin speech pathologist
Dawes, Douglas Charles retired career officer
Dooley, J. Gordon food scientist
Fedak, Barbara Kingry technical center administrator
Gardner, Sandra Lee nurse, outreach consultant
†Gieskieng, Janice Carol assistant principal
Halford, Sharon Lee legal studies administrator, victimologist, educator
Harlan, Raymond Carter communication executive, computer application developer
Jarvis, Mary G. principal
Johnson, Geraldine Esch language specialist
Lochmiller, Kurtis L. real estate entrepreneur
Magalnick, Elliott Ben retail medical supply company executive
Miller, Sarah Pearl librarian
Moser, Jeffery Richard economic director, public affairs and public management executive, artist, writer, former state official
Munro, Michael Donald air transportation executive, retired military officer
Nicholas, Thomas Peter library administrator, community television consultant, producer
†Nichols, Clyde Richard clergyman, company executive
Nora, Audrey Hart physician
Osterberg, Jorj O. retired civil engineer
Reitan, Harold Theodore management consultant
Richardson, Charles H. lawyer
Savage, Eric Wayne multimedia developer
Schilling, Edwin Carlyle, III lawyer
Schwartz, Lawrence aeronautical engineer
Sheffield, Nancy city neighborhood services director
Sherlin, Jerry Michael retired hydro meteorological technician
†Slater, Dick Dale radiologist
Starr, Nancy Barber pediatric nurse practitioner
Tauer, Paul E. mayor, educator
Vessels, Kevin Daryl mental health clinician, inventor
Vincent, Verne Saint protective services official
Volpe, Richard Gerard insurance accounts executive, consultant
Welch, Richard LeRoy personal improvement company executive
Young, Donna L. city official
Young, Gordon elementary education educator
Zuschlag, Nancy Hansen environmental science/nature resources educator

Bailey
Van Dusen, Donna Bayne communication consultant, educator, researcher

Basalt
Weill, Hans physician, educator

Bayfield
Giller, Edward Bonfoy retired government official, retired air force officer

Boulder
Albritton, Daniel Lee atmospheric scientist
Alldredge, Leroy Romney retired geophysicist
Anderson, Ronald Delaine education educator
Armstrong, David Michael biology educator
Bailey, Dana Kavanagh radiophysicist, botanist
Baker, Daniel Neil physicist
Bangs, F(rank) Kendrick former business educator
Barchilon, Jacques foreign language educator, researcher, writer
Barnes, Frank Stephenson electrical engineer, educator
Bartlett, David Farnham physics educator
Baugh, L. Darrell financial executive
Baughn, William Hubert former business educator and academic administrator
Begelman, Mitchell Craig astrophysicist, educator
Beylkin, Gregory mathematician
Bierman, Sandra Lee artist
Bintliff, Barbara Ann law librarian, educator
Birkenkamp, Dean Frederick editor, publishing executive
Boggs, Marcus Livingstone, Jr. publisher, novelist, editor
Bolen, David B. ambassador, former corporation executive
Bolomey, Roger Henry sculptor
Borysenko, Joan psychologist, biologist
Bourne, Lyle Eugene, Jr. psychology educator
Bowers, John Waite communication educator
Brakhage, James Stanley filmmaker, educator
Breddan, Joe systems engineering consultant
Breed, Michael Dallam environmental, population, organismic biology educator
Brown, Jack D(elbert) chemist, researcher
Brues, Alice Mossie physical anthropologist, educator
Bryson, Gary Spath cable television and telephone company executive
Buechner, John C. academic administrator
Byerly, Radford, Jr. science policy official
Callen, Lon Edward county official
Calvert, Jack George atmospheric chemist, educator
Carlson, Devon McElvin architect, educator
Cathey, Wade Thomas electrical engineering educator
Cech, Thomas Robert chemistry and biochemistry educator
Chappell, Charles Franklin meteorologist, consultant
Chong, Albert Valentine artist, educator
Clark, Alan Fred physicist
Clark, Melvin Eugene chemical company executive
Clifford, Lawrence M. real estate company executive
Clifford, Steven Francis science research director
Colbert, Elbert Lynn dentist, recording artist
Conti, Peter Selby astronomy educator
Copeland, Poppy Carlson psychotherapist
Corbridge, James Noel, Jr. law educator
Cornell, Eric Allin physics educator
Corotis, Ross Barry civil engineering educator, academic administrator
Cowley, Gerald Dean architect
Cristol, Stanley Jerome chemistry educator
Crow, Edwin Louis mathematical statistician, consultant
Danilov, Victor Joseph museum management program director, consultant, writer, educator
De Fries, John Clarence behavioral genetics educator, institute administrator
Derr, Vernon Ellsworth retired government research administrator
Dilley, Barbara Jean college administrator, choreographer, educator
Dryer, Murray physicist
Dubin, Mark William educator, neuroscientist
Dubofsky, Jean Eberhart lawyer, retired state supreme court justice
Duckworth, Guy musician, pianist, educator
Dumas, Jeffrey Mack lawyer
DuVivier, Katharine Keyes lawyer, educator
Echohawk, John Ernest lawyer
Enarson, Harold L. university presidentemeritus
†Evans, Hugh Williams retired mining engineer, consultant
Fenster, Herbert Lawrence lawyer
Fiflis, Ted James lawyer, educator
Fink, Robert Russell music theorist, former university dean
Fisher, Joseph Stewart management consultant
Fleming, Rex James meteorologist
Flowers, William Harold, Jr. lawyer
Frey, Julia Bloch French language educator
Friedman, Pamela Ruth Lessing art consultant, financial consultant
Gaines, James Russell magazine editor, author
Garstang, Roy Henry astrophysicist, educator
Glover, Fred William artificial intelligence and optimization research director, educator
Goldstein, Michael Aaron finance educator
Gonzalez-del-Valle, Luis Tomas Spanish language educator
Gossard, Earl Everett physicist
Gray, William R. lawyer
Greenberg, Edward Seymour political science educator, writer
Greene, David Lee physical anthropologist, educator
Gupta, Kuldip Chand electrical and computer engineering educator, researcher
Hall, John Lewis physicist, researcher
Hammell, Grandin Gaunt real estate consultant
Hanley, Howard James Mason research scientist
Hanna, William Johnson electrical engineering educator
†Hatfield, Steven Michael data processing executive
Hauser, Ray Louis research engineer, entrepreneur
Hawkins, Brian L. academic administrator, educator
Hawkins, David philosophy and history of science, educator
Healy, Alice Fenvessy psychology educator, researcher
Healy, James Bruce cooking school administrator, writer
Heath, Josephine Ward foundation administrator
Hermann, Allen Max physics educator
Hildner, Ernest Gotthold, III solar physicist, science administrator
Hill, Boyd H., Jr. medieval history educator
Hill, David Allan electrical engineer
Hoffman, Charles Fenno, III architect
Hofmann, David John atmospheric science researcher, educator
Hogg, David Clarence physicist
Holzer, Thomas E. physicist
Horii, Naomi editor
†Hurd, Jerrie writer
Iris (Silverstein), Bonnie artist, writer, educator
Jerritts, Stephen G. management consultant
Jessor, Richard psychologist, educator
Johnson, Maryanna Morse business owner
Jonsen, Richard Wiliam educational administrator
Joselyn, Jo Ann space scientist
Joy, Edward Bennett electrical engineer, educator
Kapteyn, Henry Cornelius physics and engineering educator
Kelley, Bruce Dutton pharmacist
Kellogg, William Welch meteorologist
Kimmel, Mark writer, retired venture capital company executive
King, Edward Louis retired chemistry educator
Kintsch, Walter psychology educator, director
Kisslinger, Carl geophysicist, educator
†Knierim, Willis M. educator
Koch, Tad Harbison chemistry educator, researcher
Kompala, Dhinakar Sathyanathan chemical engineering educator, biochemical engineering researcher
†Krysl, Marilyn English educator
Kuchar, Theodore conductor, academic administrator, musician
Lally, Vincent Edward atmospheric scientist
Lattes, Raffaele physician, educator
LaVelle, Betty Sullivan Dougherty legal professional
LeMone, Margaret Anne atmospheric scientist
Lemp, John, Jr. telecommunications engineer
Leone, Stephen Robert chemical physicist, educator
†Lightfoot, William Carl performing arts association executive, symphony musician
Limerick, Patricia Nelson history educator
Lineberger, William Carl chemistry educator
Little, Charles Gordon geophysicist
Low, Boon Chye physicist
MacDonald, Alexander Edward meteorologist
Maier, Edward Karl foreign language educator
Main, Gloria Jean Lund history educator
Main, Jackson Turner history educator
Malde, Harold Edwin retired federal government geologist
Malone, Michael William electronics executive, software engineer
Mancino, John Gregory software company executive
Marshall, James Kenneth academic administrator
Martin, Phillip Dwight bank consulting company executive, mayor
Martinez, Jose Rafael writer, educator, poet
Matthews, Eugene Edward artist
†Mavrogianes, Mark educator
McCray, Richard Alan astrophysicist, educator
Mc Intosh, J(ohn) Richard biologist, educator
Meagher, James Francis atmospheric research executive
Mehalchin, John Joseph entrepreneur, finance executive
Meier, Mark Frederick research scientist, glaciologist, educator
Meier, Thomas Joseph museum director, author
Melicher, Ronald William finance educator
Menken, Jane Ava demographer, educator
Menn, Lise linguistics educator
Meyer, Andrea Peroutka small business owner
Middleton-Downing, Laura psychiatric social worker, artist, small business owner
Miller, Harold William nuclear geochemist
†Mitchell, David S. writer, editor, publisher, educator
Monarchi, David Edward management scientist, information scientist, educator
Moore, George Barnard poet, educator
Morris, John Theodore planning official
Moses, Raphael Jacob lawyer
Mycielski, Jan mathematician, educator
Neinas, Charles Merrill athletic association executive
Oromaner, Daniel Stuart marketing consultant
Ostrovsky, Lev Aronovich physicist, oceanographer, educator
Pankove, Jacques Isaac physicist
Peters, Max Stone chemical engineer, educator
Peterson, Courtland Harry law educator
Peterson, Roy Jerome physics educator
Porzak, Glenn E. lawyer
Prescott, David Marshall biology educator
Reitsema, Harold James aerospace engineer
Rienner, Lynne Carol publisher
Robinson, Peter paleontology educator, consultant
Roble, Raymond Gerald science administrator
Rodriguez, Juan Alfonso technology corporation executive
Roellig, Leonard Oscar physics educator
Rood, David S. linguistics educator
†Rosato, Antonette visual artist
Sani, Robert LeRoy chemical engineering educator
Sarson, John Christopher television producer, director, writer
Schaffer, Joel Lance dentist
Schlander, Mark D. financial consultant
Schneider, Nicholas McCord planetary scientist, educator, textbook author
Schnell, Russell Clifford atmospheric scientist, researcher
Secunda, David Abraham outdoor products sales executive
Sedei Rodden, Pamela Jean therapist
Seebass, Alfred Richard, III aerospace engineer, educator, university dean
Serafin, Robert Joseph science center administrator, electrical engineer
Shanahan, Eugene Miles flow measurement instrumentation company executive
Shumick, Diana Lynn computer executive
Sirotkin, Phillip Leonard educational administrator
Skaar, Daniel (Leif) engineering executive
Smith, Ernest Ketcham electrical engineer
Snow, Theodore Peck astrophysics educator
Sodal, Ingvar Edmund electrical engineer, scientist
Spangler, Timothy Chester meteorologist, program director
Staehelin, Lucas Andrew cell biology educator
Stanton, William John, Jr. marketing educator, author
Stepanek, Joseph Edward industrial development consultant
Strauch, Richard G. electrical engineering educator
Sutton, Philip D(ietrich) psychologist
Symons, James Martin theater and dance educator
Tary, John Joseph engineer, consultant
Tatarskii, Valerian Il'Ich physics researcher
Taylor, Allan Ross linguist, educator
Tharp, Richard athletic director
Thomas, Daniel Foley financial services company executive
Thomas, Gary Edward science educator, researcher
Timmerhaus, Klaus Dieter chemical engineering educator
Tolbert, Bert Mills biochemist, educator
Trenberth, Kevin Edward atmospheric scientist
Uberoi, Mahinder Singh aerospace engineering educator
Waldman, Anne Lesley poet, performer, editor, publisher, educational administrator
Warner, Richard psychiatrist
Washington, Warren Morton meteorologist
White, Gilbert F(owler) geographer, educator
Wieman, Carl E. physics educator
Williams, James Franklin, II university dean, librarian
†Wilmarth, Richard poet
Wilson, Kenneth Allen educator
Zavorotny, Valery Ustimovich physicist, researcher

Breckenridge
Katz, Jeri Beth lawyer
O'Reilly, Thomas Mark real estate executive
Sbragia, Gary W. communications company executive

Broomfield
Affleck, Julie Karleen accountant
Ekey, Carrie Rae elementary education educator
Little, Mark Douglas secondary school educator
Lybarger, John Steven human resources development consultant, trainer
Lybarger, Marjorie Kathryn nurse
Sissel, George Allen manufacturing executive
Steinhauser, John Stuart (Jack Steinhauser) oil company executive
Von Star, Brenda Lee primary care family nurse practitioner

Brush
Gabriel, Donald Eugene science educator

Buena Vista
Herb, Edmund Michael optometrist, educator

Calhan
Fuller, Janice Marie secondary school educator
Henderson, Freda LaVerne elementary education educator

Canon City
Baumann, Ernst Frederick college president
Cochran, Susan Mills librarian
Fair, Annie May geological computer specialist
Honaker, Charles Ray health facility administrator
McBride, John Alexander retired chemical engineer
Mohr, Gary Alan physician
Perrin, Cynthia Suzanne secondary education educator
Romano, Rebecca Kay counselor
Trogden, Kathy Ann nursing administrator
Williamson, Edward Henry chaplain, army officer

Carbondale
Cowgill, Ursula Moser biologist, educator, environmental consultant
Linden, Susan Pyles marketing executive

Castle Rock
Bell, Brian Mayes lawyer
Eppler, Jerome Cannon private financial advisor
Thornbury, John Rousseau radiologist, physician

Cherry Hills Village
Meyer, Milton Edward, Jr. lawyer, artist
Stapleton, Katharine Hall (Katie Stapleton) food broadcaster, author

Cheyenne Mountain Air Station
†Baptiste, Thomas L. career officer

Cheyenne Wells
Palmer, Rayetta J. technology coordinator, educator

Colorado Springs
Adams, Bernard Schroder retired college president
Adams, Deborah Rowland lawyer

Adnet, Jacques Jim Pierre astronautical and electrical engineer, consultant
Anderson, Paul Nathaniel oncologist, educator
Armstrong, Lance professional cyclist
Artl, Karen Ann business owner, author
Badger, Sandra Rae health and physical education educator
Ball, Jennifer Leigh writer, editor
Barbre, Erwin S. publishing company executive
Barrowman, Mike Olympic athlete, swimmer
Barton, Gregory Mark Olympic athlete, kayak racer
Beard, Amanda swimmer, Olympic athlete
Bennett, Brian Richard investment broker
†Bennett, Brooke Olympic athlete
Bergman, Yaacov performing company executive
Berkoff, David Olympic athlete, swimmer
Biondi, Matt Olympic athlete, swimmer
Bishop, Leo Kenneth clergyman, educator
Blackburn, Alexander Lambert author, English literature educator
Botsford, Beth swimmer, Olympic athlete
Bowen, Clotilde Marion Dent retired army officer, psychiatrist
Bowers, Zella Zane real estate broker
Bressan, Robert Ralph accountant
Bridges, Gerald Dean religious organization executive
Brooks, Glenn Ellis political science educator, educational administrator
Brooks, Timothy Joe career military officer
Bruce, Douglas E. real estate investor
Budington, William Stone retired librarian
Buell, Bruce Temple lawyer
Burgess, Greg Olympic athlete, swimming
Burnley, Kenneth Stephen school system administrator
Bybee, Rodger Wayne science education administrator
Byrd, Chris amateur boxer
Cameron, Paul Drummond research facility administrator
Campbell, Frederick Hollister retired lawyer, historian
Carlton, Steven Norman retired professional baseball player
Child, Joseph Alan minister
Christensen, C(harles) Lewis real estate developer
Cimino, Jay automotive company executive
Clifford, Walter Jess microbiologist, immunologist
Comes, Robert George research scientist
Corry, Charles Elmo geophysicist, consultant
Cousar, Ronny city official
Cramer, Owen Carver classics educator
Dassanowsky, Robert von writer, editor, educator, producer
Davis, Richard Shermer, Jr. aerospace company operations manager
Dello Joio, Norman olympic athlete, equestrian
Diebel, Nelson Olympic athlete, swimmer
Dinerstein, Marc J. career military officer
†Dolan, Tom Olympic athlete
Donovan, Anne coach
Driscoll, David Lee chiropractor
Ehrhorn, Richard William electronics company executive
Evans, Janet Olympic swimmer
Everson, Steven Lee lawyer, real estate executive
Eyman, Roger Allen minister
Fahey, Henry Martin information technology executive
Fisher, Robert Scott lawyer
Ford, James Carlton human resources executive
Forgan, David Waller retired career officer
Fortune, James Michael network analyst
Foth, Bob Olympic athlete, riflery
Fox, Douglas Allan retired religion educator
Fox, Gwen artist, educator
Freeman, J. P. Ladyhawk underwater exploration, security and transportation executive, educator, fashion model
Gagne, Margaret Lee accounting educator
Goehring, Kenneth artist
Granato, Catherine (Cammi Granato) hockey player
Guy, Mildred Dorothy retired secondary school educator
†Haislett, Nicole Olympic athlete
Hall, Nechie Tesitor advertising and public relations executive
Hallenbeck, Kenneth Luster numismatist
Hanifen, Richard Charles bishop
Hawley, Nanci Elizabeth social services administrator
Heffron, Michael Edward software engineer, computer scientist
Hinkle, Betty Ruth educational administator
Hoffman, John Raleigh physicist
Homan, Ralph William finance company executive
James, Wayne Edward electrical engineer
†Jones, Vernon Dale educator
Kendall, Phillip Alan lawyer
Killian, George Ernest educational association administrator
King, Peter Joseph, Jr. retired gas company executive
Kramer, Lorne C. protective services official
Kubida, William Joseph lawyer
†Kwan, Michelle figure skater
Leasure, Robert Ellis writer, photographer
LeMieux, Linda Dailey museum director
Lewey, Scot Michael gastroenterologist
Lewis, Steve Olympic athlete, track and field
Lipinski, Tara Kristen figure skater
Lokken, Steven Lee chiropractor, nutritionist
†Lorenz, Stephen R. career officer
Loux, Gordon Dale organization executive
Loux, Jonathan Dale business development consultant
MacDougall, Malcolm Edward lawyer
MacLeod, Richard Patrick foundation administrator
Makepeace, Mary Lou mayor
†Manning, George Weston psychiatrist
Markert, Clement Lawrence biology educator
Mehlis, David Lee publishing executive
Michels, Patricia A. insurance agent
Miller, Zoya Dickins (Mrs. Hilliard Eve Miller, Jr.) civic worker
Milton, Richard Henry retired diplomat, children's advocate
Mitchell, John Henderson management consultant, retired career officer
Mohrman, Kathryn academic administrator
Moltzan, Nicoline G. nurse, administrator
Moorhouse, Mary Frances rehabilitation nurse
Morales, Pablo Olympic athlete, swimmer
Morris, Jason Olympic athlete
Mullen, James H. city manager
Murray, Ty (King of the Cowboys) professional rodeo cowboy
Navarro, Manuel protective services official
Nolan, Barry Hance publishing company executive
Noyes, Richard Hall bookseller
†Oelstrom, Tad J. lieutenant general United States Air Force
Ogrean, David William sports executive
Olin, Kent Oliver banker
O'Shields, Richard Lee retired natural gas company executive
Palermo, Norman Anthony lawyer
Phibbs, Harry Albert interior designer, professional speaker, lecturer
Pickett, David Franklin, Jr. technology company executive
Plunkett, Michael C. psychotherapist
Purvis, Randall W. B. lawyer
Rhode, Kim Olympic athlete
Rhodes, Daisy Chun writer, researcher, oral historian
Rhodes, Eric Foster arbitrator, employee relations consultant, writer
Roach, Cynthia Whittig nursing educator
Robinson, Robert James retired manufacturing executive
Robinson, Ronald Alan manufacturing executive
Rochette, Edward Charles retired association executive
Rogers, Steven Ray physicist
Rothenberg, Harvey David educational administrator
Rouse, Jeff Olympic athlete, swimmer
Rouss, Ruth lawyer
Ruch, Marcella Joyce retired educator, biographer
Russel, Richard Allen telecommunications consultant, aerospace engineer, nuclear engineer, electrical engineer, retired naval officer
Sanders, Summer former olympic athlete, television correspondent
Sawyer, Thomas William air force officer
Sceats, D(onald) James, Jr. neurological surgeon
Schaeffer, Reiner Horst career officer, retired librarian, foreign language professional
Scherr, James E. sports association executive
Schultz, Richard Dale national athletic organizations executive
Schwartz, Donald chemistry educator
Shade, Linda Bunnell university chancellor
Shafer, Dallas Eugene psychology gerontology educator, minister
Silliman, Brian Allen numismatist, authenticator
Simmons, George Finlay mathematics educator
Sinclair, William Donald church official, fundraising consultant, political activist
†Smith, Steven Alan newspaper editor
†Speirs, Alfred C. plastic and reconstructive surgeon
Stavig, Mark Luther English language educator
†Stewart, Melvin Olympic athlete, swimmer
Stienmier, Saundra Kay Young aviation educator
Stoen, J. Thomas energy company executive, land developer, investor
Thomas, Debi (Debra J. Thomas) ice skater
Todd, Harold Wade association executive, retired air force officer
Trimble, Donna Denise clinical therapist
Tueting, Sarah hockey player
†Valdez, Troy business executive
Van Dyken, Amy swimmer, Olympic athlete
Vayhinger, John Monroe psychotherapist, minister
Watkins, Lois Irene English educator
Watts, Oliver Edward engineering consultancy company executive
Watz, Hallet N. emergency physician
West, Ralph Leland veterinarian
Whalin, W. Terry author, editor
Wheeler, Larry Richard accountant
Wheeler, Stephen Frederick municipal court administrator
White, Deborah Sue Youngblood lawyer
Wilcox, Rhoda Davis elementary education educator
Wilkins, Christopher Putnam conductor
†Wilson, Todd Andrew college administrator in public relations
Witte, Robert Alan electrical engineer
Yaffe, James author
Zapel, Arthur Lewis book publishing executive
Zelenek, David S. city official
Ziemer, Rodger Edmund electrical engineering educator, consultant

Columbine Valley
Wittbrodt, Edwin Stanley consultant, former bank executive, former air force officer

Commerce City
Hanson, Edward Alvin technical writer
Trujillo, Lorenzo A. lawyer, educator

Conifer
Kalla, Alec Karl writer, rancher

Cortez
Meredith, Richard Stephen psycotherapist, educator
Winterer-Schulz, Barbara Jean art designer, author

Craig
Violette, Glenn Phillip transportation engineer

Crestone
†Manno, Angela Linda artist

Cripple Creek
Swanson, Erik Christian museum director

Deer Trail
Malson, Verna Lee special education educator

Delta
Wendt, John Arthur Frederic, Jr. lawyer

Denver
Abo, Ronald Kent architect
Abram, Donald Eugene federal magistrate judge
Abramovitz, Michael John lawyer
Adelman, Jonathan Reuben political science educator, consultant
Adler, Charles Spencer psychiatrist
Aikawa, Jerry Kazuo physician, educator
†Aisenberg, Bennett S. lawyer
Alcott Tempest Temple, Leslie artist
Alfers, Stephen Douglas lawyer
Allen, Robert Edward, Jr. physician assistant
†Alvarado, Linda G. construction company executive
Anderson, John David architect
Antonoff, Steven Ross educational consultant, author
Archibold, John Ewing lawyer, consultant
Arp, Elizabeth Kench psychotherapist, social worker
Ashton, Rick James librarian
Atkins, Dale Morrell retired physician
Austin, H(arry) Gregory lawyer
Avrit, Richard Calvin defense consultant
Axley, Hartman underwriter
Babcock, Lewis Thornton federal judge
Baca, Kelly Mae marketing communications director
Bain, Donald Knight lawyer
Bain, James William lawyer
Balboa, Marcelo soccer player
Barber, Larry Eugene financial planner
Barger, Louise Baldwin religious organization administrator
Barker, Fred research geologist, scientific editor
Barkman, Debra Rae nephrology nurse
Barz, Richard L. microbiologist
Bates, James Robert newspaper editor
†Baumgartner, Bruce airport administrator
Bautista, Michael Phillip school system administrator
Bearden, Thomas Howard news program producer, correspondent
Beatty, Michael L. lawyer
Beckman, L. David university chancellor
Belitz, Paul Edward lawyer
Bell, Steven H. financial company executive
Benson, Robert Eugene lawyer
Benton, Auburn Edgar lawyer
Berger, William Merriam Bart investment management company executive
Berkey, Douglas Bryan dental educator, researcher, gerontologist, clinician
Berland, Karen Ina psychologist
Bichette, Alphonse Dante professional baseball player
†Biester, Doris J. hospital executive
Billig, Shelley Hirschl educational research and training consultant
Bishop, Tilman Malcolm state senator, retired college administrator
Blair, Andrew Lane, Jr. lawyer, educator
Blatter, Frank Edward travel agency executive
Blish, Eugene Sylvester trade association administrator
Blitz, Stephen M. lawyer
Blunk, Forrest Stewart lawyer
†Borchers, Richard M. federal judge
Bowden, Randall Glen academic adminstrator
Boyd, Dawn Andrea Williams airline employee, artist
Boylan, Michelle Marie Obie medical surgical nurse, hospital administrator
Bradley, Jeff(rey Mark) arts critic
Brantigan, Charles Otto surgeon
†Bravo, Paul professional soccer player
Brega, Charles Franklin lawyer
Briney, Walter George rheumatologist
Britton, Dennis A. newspaper editor, newspaper executive
†Brooke, James Bettner news correspondent
†Brooks, Sidney B. bankruptcy judge
Brown, Keith Lapham retired ambassador
Brown, Mark Ransom financial advisor
Browne, Spencer I. mortgage company executive
Brownlee, Judith Marilyn priestess, psychotherapist, psychic
Brownson, Jacques Calmon architect
†Brumbaugh, Roland John bankruptcy judge
Bryan, A(lonzo) J(ay) service club official
Bukowiecki, Sister Angeline Bernadette nun
Bunn, Paul A., Jr. oncologist, educator
Burdick, Robert W. newspaper editor
Burford, Anne McGill lawyer
Burke, Kenneth John lawyer
Burns, Alexandra Darrow (Sandra Burns) health program administrator
Burrell, Calvin Archie minister
Burshtan, John Willis television producer
Butler, David lawyer
Bye, James Edward lawyer
Byrne, Thomas J. lawyer
Cain, Douglas Mylchreest lawyer
Campagna, Timothy Nicholas institute executive
Campbell, David Neil physician, educator
Campbell, Leonard Martin lawyer
Cannon, Elizabeth Anne special education educator
Carlson, Robert Ernest freelance writer, architect, lecturer
Carr, James Francis lawyer
Carraher, John Bernard lawyer
Carrigan, Jim R. arbitrator, mediator, retired federal judge
Carver, Craig R. lawyer
Cashman, Michael Richard small business owner
Cassidy, Samuel H. lawyer, lieutenant governor, state legislator
Castilla, Vinivio Soria professional baseball player
Ceci, Jesse Arthur violinist
Chamberlain, Adrian Ramond transportation engineer
Chapman, Gerald Wester educator
Chappell, Willard Ray physics educator, environmental scientist
Chaput, Charles J. archbishop
Cheris, Elaine Gayle Ingram business owner
Cheroutes, Michael Louis lawyer
Christopher, Daniel Roy lawyer
Churchill, Mair Elisa Annabelle medical educator
†Clark, Lori DeVito environmental scientist
Clark, Patricia Ann federal judge
Clayton, Mack Louis surgeon, educator
Clinch, Nicholas Bayard, III business executive
Cobban, William Aubrey paleontologist
Cockrell, Richard Carter retired lawyer
Coffelt, Janice Litherland contracting officer
Cohen, Cheryl Denise municipal official
Cohn, Aaron I. anesthesiologist, educator
Colvis, John Paris aerospace engineer, mathematician, scientist
Commander, Eugene R. lawyer
Conger, John Janeway psychologist, educator
Conroy, Thomas Francis insurance company executive
Cook, Albert Thomas Thornton, Jr. financial advisor
†Cooke, Paul Lewis state fire marshall
Cooper, Larry S. carpet industry consultant
Cooper, Paul Douglas lawyer
Cope, Thomas Field lawyer
Cordova, Donald E. lawyer
Cotherman, Audrey Mathews management and policy consultant, administrator
Craine, Thomas Knowlton non-profit administrator
Crow, Nancy Rebecca lawyer
Cubbison, Christopher Allen editor
Cutter, Gary Raymond biostatistician
Dallas, Sandra correspondent, writer
Dance, Francis Esburn Xavier communication educator
Daniel, Wiley Y. lawyer
Danos, Robert McClure retired oil company executive
†D'Antoni, Mike professional basketball coach
Dauer, Edward Arnold law educator
†Davidson, Donetta state government official
Dean, James Benwell lawyer
Decker, Peter Randolph rancher, former state official
De Gette, Diana Louise lawyer, congresswoman
Deitrich, Richard Adam pharmacology educator
DeLaney, Herbert Wade, Jr. lawyer
Dempsey, Howard Stanley lawyer, mining executive, investment banker
DeMuth, Alan Cornelius lawyer
DePew, Marie Kathryn retired secondary school educator
DeVine, B. Mack management consultant
Devitt, John Lawrence consulting engineer
†Dicks, Patricia K. state senate employee
Doida, Stanley Y. dentist
Dominick, Peter Hoyt, Jr. architect
Donder, Pauline Veronica legal secretary
Dorr, Robert Charles lawyer
Dowdle, Patrick Dennis lawyer
Drake, Lucius Charles, Jr. school administrator, university consultant, educator
Drake, Sylvie (Jurras Drake) theater critic
Driggs, Margaret educator
Dubroff, Henry Allen newspaper editor
Ducker, Bruce novelist, lawyer
†Dunham, Joan Roberts administrative assistant
†Dunham, Stephen Sampson lawyer
Dunn, Randy Edwin lawyer
East, Donald Robert civil engineer
Eaton, Gareth Richard chemistry educator, university dean
Ebel, David M. federal judge
Edelman, Joel medical center executive
Edwards, Daniel Walden lawyer
†Ehnes, Jack state insurance commissioner
Ehret, Josephine Mary microbiologist, researcher
Eiberger, Carl Frederick trial lawyer
Eickhoff, Theodore Carl physician
Eklund, Carl Andrew lawyer
Ellis, Sylvia D. Hall development and library education consultant
Engdahl, Todd Philip newspaper editor
Espenlaub, Margo Linn women's studies educator, artist
Faatz, Jeanne Ryan educational association director
Fagin, David Kyle natural resource company executive
Falkenberg, William Stevens architect, contractor
†Fassler, Karen Kay human resources specialist
Faxon, Thomas Baker lawyer
Fay, Richard James mechanical engineer, executive, educator
Featherstone, Bruce Alan lawyer
Felter, Edwin Lester, Jr. judge
Fennessey, Paul Vincent pediatrics and pharmacology, educator, research administrator
Fielden, C. Franklin, III early childhood education consultant
Filley, Christopher Mark neurologist
Finegan, Cole lawyer
Flanders, George James mechanical engineer, engineering development manager
Forsberg, Peter professional hockey player
Fortune, Lowell lawyer
Foster, Norman Holland geologist
Fredmann, Martin ballet artistic director, educator, choreographer
Freiheit, Clayton Fredric zoo director
Frevert, Donald Kent hydraulic engineer
Frontera, Michael P. municipal official
Fryt, Monte Stanislaus petroleum company executive, speaker, advisor
Fugate, Ivan Dee banker, lawyer
Fujioka, Jo Ann Ota educational administrator, consultant
Fulginiti, Vincent university dean
Fulkerson, William Measey, Jr. college president
Fuller, Kenneth Roller architect
Gabow, Patricia Anne internist
Gallagher, Dennis Joseph municipal official, state senator, educator
Gallegos, Larry Duayne lawyer
Gampel, Elaine Susan investment management analyst and consultant
Garcia, June Marie library director
Gates, Charles Cassius rubber company executive
Gebhard, Bob professional baseball team executive
Geiser, Elizabeth Able publishing company executive
Gibbs, Ronald Steven obstetrician-gynecologist
Giesen, John William advertising executive
Giffin, Glenn Orlando, II music critic, writer, newspaper editor
Gloss, Lawrence Robert fundraising executive
Goldberg, Hillel rabbi, educator
Golitz, Loren Eugene dermatologist, pathologist, clinical administrator, educator
†Gonzales, Richard L. fire department chief
Gould, Marty Leon minister, writer, composer
Graham, Pamela Smith artist, distributing company executive
Grant, Patrick Alexander lawyer, association administrator
Grant, William West, III banker
Green, Larry Alton physician, educator
Greenberg, David Ethan communications consultant
Greenberg, Pamela Thayer public policy specialist
Greenspahn, Barbara university administrator, law educator, librarian
Grissom, Garth Clyde lawyer
Groff, JoAnn organization administrator
Grossman, Arnold Joseph writer, producer
†Groth, Mark Adam audio visual specialist, photographer
Grounds, Vernon Carl seminary administrator
Gustus, Stacey A. legal secretary
Hafenstein, Norma Lu educator, administrator
Hagen, Glenn W(illiam) lawyer
Hakeem, Muhammad Abdul artist, educator
Halgren, Lee A. academic administrator
Hall, Richard Murray, Jr. finance executive, consultant
Hamblin, Kenneth Lorenzo radio talk show host, columnist
†Hamilton, Barry Alan aerospace engineer, software engrineer
Hand, Dale L. pharmacist
Harken, Alden Hood surgeon, thoracic surgeon
Harris, Dale Ray lawyer
Harris, Howard Jeffrey marketing and printing company executive

Englewood
Aarestad, Norman O. *oncologist*
Aguirre, Vukoslav Eneas *environmental engineer*
Albrecht, Duane Taylor *veterinarian*
Anderson, Peggy Rees *accountant*
Bardsley, Kay *historian, archivist, dance professional*
Beake, John *professional football team executive*
Bingham, Paris Edward, Jr. *electrical engineer, computer consultant*
Bondi, Bert Roger *accountant, financial planner*
Bowlen, Patrick Dennis *holding company executive, lawyer, professional sports team executive*
†Brett, Stephen M. *lawyer, entertainment company executive*
Brierley, James Alan *research administrator*
Brown, Steven Harry *corporation health physicist, consultant*
Burg, Michael S. *lawyer*
Carter, Dale Lavelle *professional football player*
†Chavez, Lloyd G. *automotive executive*
Chesser, Al H. *union official*
Cooper, Sharon Marsha *marketing, advertising executive*
Cooper, Steven Jon *healthcare management consultant, educator*
Corboy, James McNally *investment banker*
Craw, Nicholas Wesson *motor sports association executive*
Dahl, Gardar Godfrey, Jr. *geologist, consultant*
†Davis, Terrell *football player*
Dawson, Eugene Ellsworth *university president emeritus*
Eccles, Matthew Alan *golf course and landscape architect*
Ellsworth, Joseph Cordon *real estate executive, lawyer*
Elway, John Albert *professional football player*
Erickson, William Hurt *retired state supreme court justice*
Figa, Phillip Sam *lawyer*
Greenagel, Debra *travel agency executive*
†Harbaugh, Teresa Gabriel *publisher, artist*
Harding, Wayne Edward, III *software company executive, accountant*
Hardy, Wayne Russell *insurance and investment broker*
Haupenthal, Laura Ann *clinical psychologist*
Hendrick, Hal Wilmans *human factors educator*
Hindery, Leo Joseph, Jr. *media company executive*
†Irwin, Mark *writer, educator*
Joffe, Barbara Lynne *computer applications systems manager, computer artist, project management professional*
Jones, Glenn Robert *cable systems executive*
Karr, David Dean *lawyer*
Katz, Michael Jeffery *lawyer*
Kelsall, David Charles *otologist*
Lake, Stanley James *security consulting company executive, motel chain executive, locksmith*
†Lessey, Samuel Kenric, Jr. *foundation administrator*
Lidstone, Herrick Kenley, Jr. *lawyer*
Mahoney, Gerald Francis *manufacturing company executive*
Malone, John C. *telecommunications executive*
†McCrary, Brian Fountain *physician*
McReynolds, Gregg Clyde *lawyer*
Murdock, Michelle Marie *marketing executive*
Neiser, Brent Allen *public affairs consultant*
Nelson, Barbara Louise *secondary education educator*
Nuce, Madonna Marie *career officer*
O'Brien, James B. *broadcast executive*
†Peck, Charles *hotel executive*
†Platt, John B. *hotel executive*
Reese, Monte Nelson *agricultural association executive*
Rodin, Mike *lawyer, corporate*
Rosser, Edwin Michael *mortgage company executive*
Runice, Robert E. *retired corporate executive*
Saliba, Jacob *manufacturing executive*
†Schmahl, John Howard *counseling*
Schwartz, Michael Lee *financial planner, consultant*
Shaddock, Paul Franklin, Sr. *human resources director*
Shanahan, Mike *professional football coach*
Shannon, Richard Stoll, III *financial executive*
†Sharpe, Shannon *professional football player*
Shields, Marlene Sue *elementary school educator*
Sims, Douglas D. *bank executive*
†Smith, Neil *professional football player*
Smyth, David Shannon *real estate investor, commercial and retail builder and developer*
Sprincz, Keith Steven *financial services company professional*
Steinhauser, John William *retired lawyer*
Syke, Cameron John *lawyer*
Thompson, Robert Frank, Jr. *career officer*
†Vallin, Travis L. *state government administator*
Van Loucks, Mark Louis *venture capitalist, business advisor*
Wagner, David James *lawyer*
Ward, Milton Hawkins *mining company executive*
Whiteaker, Ruth Catherine *retired secondary education educator, counselor*
Wiegand, Robert, II *lawyer*
Wynar, Bohdan Stephen *librarian, author, editor*
Zernial, Susan Carol *educator, consultant, acquisitions editor*

Erie
Alpers, John Hardesty, Jr. *financial planning executive, retired military officer*
Dilly, Marian Jeanette *humanities educator*

Estes Park
Arnold, Leonard J. *construction executive*
†Berkeley, Seamus Osborne *artist, consultant*
Blumrich, Josef Franz *aerospace engineer*
Bridges, Douglas M. *musician, small business owner*
Guest, Linda Sand *education educator*
Johnson, Carol Lynn *secondary school counselor*
Jones, A. Durand *park administrator*
Moore, Omar Khayyam *experimental sociologist*
Ojalvo, Morris *civil engineer, educator*
Stanton, Lea Kaye *elementary school educator, counselor*
Webb, Richard C. *engineering company executive*

Evergreen
Berger, Sue Anne *secondary education educator, chemist*
Dobbs, Gregory Allan *journalist*
†Grunska, Gerald P(aul) *former secondary educator, sports official*
Haun, John Daniel *petroleum geologist, educator*
Heyl, Allen Van, Jr. *geologist*
Jesser, Roger Franklyn *former brewing company engineering executive, consultant*
Lang, Brian Joseph *museum curator*
McEldowney, Roland Conant *gold mining company executive*
Newkirk, John Burt *metallurgical engineer, administrator*
Phillips, Adran Abner (Abe Phillips) *geologist, oil and gas exploration consultant*
Rodolff, Dale Ward *sales executive, consultant*
White, John David *composer, theorist, cellist*

Fallbrook
Spahn, Warren *retired baseball player*

Flagler
†Bredehoft, Thomas Evan *newspaper publisher*

Florissant
McCaslin, Kathleen Denise *child abuse educator*

Fort Carson
Boylan, Steven Arthur *career officer*
Chomko, Stephen Alexander *archaeologist*
†Riggs, John M. *army officer*

Fort Collins
Bamburg, James Robert *biochemistry educator*
Benjamin, Stephen Alfred *veterinary medicine educator, environmental pathologist, researcher*
Bennett, Jacqueline Beekman *school psychologist*
Bennett, Thomas LeRoy, Jr. *clinical neuropsychology educator*
Bernstein, Elliot Roy *chemistry educator*
Berwanger, Eugene Harley *history educator*
Brown, Ronald Laming *lawyer*
Burns, Denver P. *forestry research administrator*
Cermak, Jack Edward *engineer, educator*
Christiansen, Norman Juhl *retired newspaper publisher*
Collen, Tom *coach*
Cook, Dierdre Ruth Goorman *school administrator, secondary education educator*
Crabtree, Loren William *provost, academic administrator, history educator*
Curthoys, Norman P. *biochemistry educator, consultant*
Daniel, Janis Sue *women's health nurse*
Driscoll, Richard Stark *land use planner*
Edgeman, Rick Lee *statistics educator, consultant*
Eitzen, David Stanley *sociologist, educator*
Elkind, Mortimer Murray *biophysicist, educator*
Emslie, William Arthur *electrical engineer*
Ernest, Douglas Jerome *librarian*
Ewing, Jack Robert *accountant*
Fixman, Marshall *chemist, educator*
Fletcher, Charles Rickey *public affairs specialist*
Follett, Ronald Francis *soil scientist*
Fotsch, Dan Robert *elementary education educator*
Frink, Eugene Hudson, Jr. *business and real estate consultant*
Fromm, Jeffery Bernard *lawyer*
Gandy, Hoke Conway *judge, state official*
Gillette, Edward LeRoy *radiation oncology educator*
Gilmore, Timothy Jonathan *paralegal*
Grandin, Temple *livestock equipment designer, educator*
Grigg, Neil S. *civil engineering educator*
Gubler, Duane J. *research scientist, administrator*
Guest, Richard Eugene *psychologist*
Halvorson, Ardell David *soil scientist*
Harper, Judson Morse *university administrator, consultant, educator*
Heermann, Dale Frank *agricultural engineer*
Heird, James C. *agricultural studies educator*
Hinz, Shirley Sorensen *administrative secretary*
Hu, Edna Gertrude Fenske *pediatrics nurse*
Jaros, Dean *university official*
Johnson, Robert Britten *geology educator*
Kaufman, Harold Richard *mechanical engineer and physics educator*
Keim, Wayne Franklin *retired agronomy educator, plant geneticist*
Kinnison, Robert Wheelock *retired accountant*
Kleinschnitz, Barbara Joy *oil company executive, consultant*
Koessel, Donald Ray *retired banker*
Ladanyi, Branka Maria *chemist, educator*
Lameiro, Gerard Francis *corporate strategist*
Lumb, William Valjean *veterinarian*
Maga, Joseph Andrew *food science educator*
†Marecaux, Marie Laure *consultant*
Mc Clellan, William Monson *library administrator, retired*
Mesloh, Warren Henry *civil and environmental engineer*
Meyers, Albert Irving *chemistry educator*
Mielke, Paul William, Jr. *statistician*
Morgan, David Allen *electronic engineer*
Mortvedt, John Jacob *soil scientist*
Mosier, Arvin Ray *chemist, researcher*
Newlin, Douglas Randal *learning products engineer*
Ogg, James Elvis *microbiologist, educator*
Pape, Arnis Weston *minister*
Patton, Carl Elliott *physics educator*
Peterson, Gary Andrew *agronomics researcher*
Richardson, Everett Vern *hydraulic engineer, educator, administrator, consultant*
Roberts, Archibald Edward *retired career officer, author*
Rolston, Holmes, III *theologian, educator, philosopher*
Roos, Eric Eugene *plant physiologist*
Schendel, Winfried George *insurance company executive*
Schumm, Stanley Alfred *geologist, educator*
Seidel, George Elias, Jr. *animal scientist, educator*
†Simons, Stephen Richard *artist*
Smith, Dwight Raymond *ecology and wildlife educator, writer*
Smith, Gary Chester *meat scientist, researcher*
Smith, Nina Maria *mental health nurse, administrator, consultant*
Smith, Ralph Earl *virologist*
†Snyder, Carol Jeanne *agricultural economist*
Sons, Raymond William *journalist*
Stephens, Taylor Lane *insurance company executive*
Suinn, Richard Michael *psychologist*
Switzer, Ralph V., Jr. *accounting and taxation educator*
Thies, Margaret Diane *nurse*
Thomas, Jeanette Mae *public accountant*
Tremblay, William Andrew *English language educator*
Walsh, Richard George *agricultural economist*
Weimer, Dawn *sculptor*
Weiser, Timothy L. *athletic director*
Williamson, Samuel Chris *research ecologist*
Woolhiser, David Arthur *hydrologist*
Yates, Albert Carl *academic administrator, chemistry educator*

Fort Garland
Boyer, Lester Leroy, Jr. *architecture educator, consultant*
Leighninger, David Scott *cardiovascular surgeon*

Fort Morgan
Gibbs, Denis Laurel *radiologist*

Franktown
Smith, James Micheal *marketing executive*

Fraser
Hibbs, John David *software executive, engineer, business owner*

Georgetown
Hildebrandt-Willard, Claudia Joan *banker*
Stern, Mort(imer) P(hillip) *journalism and communications educator, academic administrator, consultant*

Glendale
Childs, John David *computer hardware and services company executive*

Glenwood Springs
Callier, Maria Cecile *writer, actress*
Reinisch, Nancy Rae *therapist, consultant*
Walker, Robert Harris *historian, author, editor*

Golden
Bergeron, Sheila Diane *retired science educator, educational consultant*
Bickart, Theodore Albert *university president*
Bradley, James Alexander *software engineer, researcher*
Carney, Deborah Leah Turner *lawyer*
Christensen, Robert Wayne *oral maxillofacial surgeon, minister*
Clausen, Bret Mark *industrial hygienist, safety professional*
Coakley, William Thomas *utilities executive*
Coors, William K. *brewery executive*
Dickinson, Carol Rittgers *arts administrator, writer, executive director*
†Dubois, Jean Hall *writer*
Eber, Kevin *science writer*
Eckley, Wilton Earl, Jr. *humanities educator*
Ervin, Patrick Franklin *nuclear engineer*
Fahey, Barbara Stewart Doe *public agency administrator*
Freeman, Val LeRoy *geologist*
Furtak, Thomas Elton *physicist, educator, author, consultant*
Gentry, Donald William *mine engineering executive*
Hager, John Patrick *metallurgy engineering educator*
Hopper, Sally *state legislator*
Hubbard, Harold Mead *retired research executive*
Hughes, Marcia Marie *lawyer, mediator, trainer*
Hutchinson, Richard William *geology educator, consultant*
Jackson, Richard Brooke *judge*
Kennedy, George Hunt *chemistry educator*
Kopel, David Benjamin *lawyer*
Krauss, George *metallurgist*
Kuehn, Carl Peter *information technology consultant, statistician*
Leonard, Mary Jo *occupational health nurse*
Lindsay, Nathan James *aerospace company executive, retired career officer*
Lyons, Cherie Ann *educational administrator, author*
Mathews, Anne Jones *consultant, library educator and administrator*
Mueller, William Martin *former academic administrator, metallurgical engineering educator*
Napier, Anne Hess *psychotherapist, mental health nurse*
O'Connor, Patricia Eryl *telecommunications consultant*
Olson, Marian Katherine *emergency management executive, consultant, publisher*
Petrick, Alfred, Jr. *mineral economics educator, consultant*
Quirke, Terence Thomas, Jr. *genealogist, retired geologist*
Sacks, Arthur Bruce *environmental and liberal arts educator*
Sloan, Earle Dendy, Jr. *chemical engineering educator*
Snead, Kathleen Marie *lawyer*
Sneed, Joseph Donald *philosophy educator, author*
†Stevenson, Cynthia Mary *school system administrator*
Stewart, Frank Maurice, Jr. *federal agency administrator*
Tegtmeier, Ronald Eugene *physician, surgeon*
Tilton, John Elvin *mineral economics educator*
Truly, Richard H. *academic administrator, former federal agency administrator, former astronaut*
Wei, Su-Huai *physicist*
Weimer, Robert Jay *geology educator, energy consultant, civic leader*
Wellisch, William Jeremiah *social psychology educator*
White, James Edward *geophysicist*
Wilson, James Robert *lawyer*
Woods, Sandra Kay *manufacturing executive*
Woolsey, Robert Eugene Donald *mineral economics, mathematics and business administration educator*
Yarar, Baki *metallurgical engineering educator*

Granby
Johnson, William Potter *newspaper publisher*

Grand Junction
Armstrong, Linda Jean (Gene) *writer, artist*
Bacon, Phillip *geographer, author, consultant*
Bergen, Virginia Louise *principal, language arts educator*
Butcher, Duane Clemens *economist, consultant*
Duray, John Robert *physicist*
Fay, Abbott Eastman *history educator*
Freeman, Neil *accounting and computer consulting firm executive*
Gustafson, Kirk *performing company executive*
McCarthy, Mary Frances *hospital foundation administrator*
Moberly, Linden Emery *educational administrator*
Nelson, Paul William *real estate broker*
Pantenburg, Michel *hospital administrator, health educator, holistic health coordinator*
†Robb, James M. *federal judge*
Rutz, Richard Frederick *physicist, researcher*
Rybak, James Patrick *engineering educator*
Skogen, Haven Sherman *investment company executive*

Greeley
Brown, Hank *former senator, university administrator*
Camp, Ronald Stephen *educational technologist, television producer, educator*
Conway, Rebecca Ann Koppes *lawyer*
Duff, William Leroy, Jr. *university dean emeritus, business educator*
†Embry, Marcus *English educator*
Engle, Cindy *medical transcriptionist*
Fadner, Willard Lee *physics educator, researcher*
Green, Vickie Lee *gifted and talented educator, music educator*
Griffin, Peggy *university administrator*
Hart, Milford E. *psychotherapist, counselor*
Houtchens, Barnard *lawyer*
Jones, Loretta Lucek *chemistry educator, writer*
Kerr, Robert James *mediator, educational consultant*
Linde, Lucille Mae (Jacobson) *motor-perceptual specialist*
Mader, Douglas Paul *quality engineering manager*
Mason, Carolyn Sue *career coordinator*
Miller, Diane Wilmarth *human resources director*
Morgensen, Jerry Lynn *construction company executive*
Ross, Rosann Mary *psychotherapist, educator*
Schrenk, Gary Dale *foundation executive*
Smith, Jack Lee *bank executive*
Smythe, Valerie Ann *special education educator*
†Thompson, Paul N. *college president*
Ursyn, Anna *computer graphics artist, educator*
†Walch, Robert Anton *physics educator*
Willis, Connie (Constance E. Willis) *author*
Worley, Lloyd Douglas *English language educator*

Green Mountain Falls
Faber, Michael Warren *lawyer*

Greenwood Village
Arenberg, Irving Kaufman Karchmer *ear surgeon, educator, entrepeneur*
Barnard, Rollin Dwight *retired financial executive*
Bowen, Peter Geoffrey *arbitrator, investment advisor, business management lecturer*
Davidson, John Robert (Jay) *banking executive*
Dymond, Lewis Wandell *lawyer, mediator, educator*
Peterson, Ralph R. *engineering executive*
Poe, Robert Alan *lawyer*
Ramsey, John Arthur *lawyer*
Walker, Eljana M. du Vall *civic worker*

Guffey
Ward, Larry Thomas *social program administrator*

Gunnison
Myers, Rex Charles *history educator, retired college dean*
Venturo, Frank Angelo *communications educator, college offical*

Highlands Ranch
Boraz, Robert Alan *dentist, surgery and pediatrics educator*
Breuer, Werner Alfred *retired plastics company executive*
Bublitz, Deborah Keirstead *pediatrician*
Jeffryes, Mark Allen *elementary school educator, administrator*
Massey, Leon R. (R.L. Massey) *professional association administrator*
Mierzwa, Joseph William *lawyer, legal communications consultant*

Idaho Springs
Block, Kerry Reagan *special education educator*
Kelley, Louanna Elaine *newspaper columnist, researcher*

Idalia
†Rossbach, Lucille K. *secondary education educator, reading specialist*

Idledale
Brown, Gerri Ann *physical therapist*

Indian Hills
Johnston, Laurance Scott *foundation director*

Kersey
Guttersen, Michael *ranching and investments professional*

Kremmling
Lewis, Charles D. *rancher, consultant*

La Junta
Strong, Mayda Nel *psychologist, educator*

La Veta
Zehring, Peggy Johnson *artist*

Lafayette
†Kelly, John Fitzgerald *software developer*
Middlebrooks, Eddie Joe *environmental engineer*
Short, Ray Everett *minister, sociology educator emeritus, author, lecturer*

Lakewood
Allen, Sam Raymond *organization development specialist*
Babel, Deborah Jean *social worker, paralegal*
Bettinghaus, Erwin Paul *cancer research center administrator*
Boyd, John Garth *manufacturing production and operations consultant*
Cambio, Irma Darlene *nursing consultant*
Danzberger, Alexander Harris *chemical engineer, consultant*
Downey, Arthur Harold, Jr. *lawyer, mediator*
Elkins, Lincoln Feltch *petroleum engineering consultant*
Forrest, Kenton Harvey *science educator, historian*
Foster, David Mark *retired bishop*

GEOGRAPHIC INDEX 5515 CONNECTICUT

Guyton, Samuel Percy *retired lawyer*
Hall, Larry D. *energy company executive, lawyer*
Heath, Gary Brian *manufacturing firm executive, engineer*
Hickman, Ruth Virginia *Bible educator*
Isely, Henry Philip *association executive, integrative engineer, writer, educator*
Johnstone, James George *engineering educator*
Joy, Carla Marie *history educator*
Karlin, Joel Marvin *allergist*
Keatinge, Cornelia Wyma *architectural preservationist consultant, lawyer*
Keller, Shirley Inez *accountant*
Knott, William Alan *library director, library management and building consultant*
†Kourlis, Thomas A. *state commissioner*
Mc Bride, Guy Thornton, Jr. *college president emeritus*
McElwee, Dennis John *lawyer, former pharmaceutical company executive*
Morton, Linda *mayor*
Orullian, B. LaRae *bank executive*
Parker, John Marchbank *consulting geologist*
Porter, Lael Frances *communication consultant, educator*
Priest, Terrance Lee *logistics professional*
Rhamy, Jennifer Frances *marketing professional*
Richards, Robert Charles *management consultant*
Rosa, Fredric David *construction company executive*
Thome, Dennis Wesley *lawyer*
Thomson, Marjorie Belle Anderson *sociology educator, consultant*
Vogt, Hugh Frederick *minister, college administrator*
West, Marjorie Edith *elementary education educator*
Wolfe, Brian Augustus *retired sales executive, small business owner*
Woodruff, Kathryn Elaine *English language educator*

Larkspur
Bierbaum, J. Armin *petroleum company executive, consultant*

Littleton
Anderson, Darrell Edward *psychologist, educator*
Bachman, David Christian *orthopedic surgeon*
Bass, Charles Morris *financial and systems consultant*
Benkert, Mary Russell *pediatrics nurse, researcher*
Bowe, Roger Lee *small business owner*
Bragg, Albert Forsey *retired airline captain*
Brychel, Rudolph Myron *engineer, consultant*
Bush, Stanley Giltner *secondary school educator*
†Butler, Dena Louise *mathematics educator*
Choquette, Philip Wheeler *geologist, educator*
Dolan, Patrick Thomas *English educator*
Doty, Della Corrine *organization administrator*
Eberhardt, Gretchen Ann *lawyer, hearing officer*
Feist, Edward Joseph *secondary education educator*
Fisher, Louis McLane, Jr. *management consultant*
Forstot, Stephan Lance *ophthalmologist*
Gertz, David Lee *homebuilding company executive*
Greenberg, Elinor Miller *college official, consultant*
Greenspan, Stephen Howard *retired psychology educator*
Hadley, Marlin LeRoy *direct sales financial consultant*
Haley, John David *petroleum consulting company executive*
Hammerschmidt, Marilyn Kay *health services administrator*
Harney, Patricia Rae *nuclear analyst*
Hayes, Roger Matthew *deputy sheriff*
Hopping, William Russell *hospitality industry consultant and appraiser*
Huffman, Donna Lou *interior designer*
Kazemi, Hossein *petroleum engineer*
Keely, George Clayton *lawyer*
Keogh, Heidi Helen Dake *advocate*
Kleinknecht, Kenneth Samuel *retired aerospace company executive, former federal space agency official*
Kullas, Albert John *management and systems engineering consultant*
Lening, Janice Allen *physical education educator*
†Lesh-Laurie, Georgia Elizabeth *university administrator, biology educator, researcher*
Miller, Betty Sue *counselor*
Milliken, John Gordon *research economist*
Newell, Michael Stephen *finance company executive, international finance, protective services consultant*
Norman, Marcia Macy *writer, realtor*
Panasci, Nancy Ervin *speech pathologist, cookbook writer, communications consultant*
Paull, Richard Allen *geologist, educator*
Plusk, Ronald Frank *manufacturing company executive*
Price, Gayl Baader *residential construction company administrator*
Riley, Mary Jane *computer scientist*
Rinkenberger, Richard Krug *physical scientist, geologist, consultant*
Ryan, Evonne Ianacone *capital management company executive*
Smith, Derrin Ray *information systems company executive*
Spelts, Richard John *lawyer*
Treybig, Edwina Hall *sales executive*
Truhlar, Doris Broaddus *lawyer*
Udevitz, Norman *publishing executive*
Ulrich, John Ross Gerald *aerospace engineer*
Vail, Charles Daniel *veterinarian, consultant*
VanderLinden, Camilla Denice Dunn *telecommunications industry manager*
Wallisch, Carolyn E. *principal*
Whalen, Cathryn Ann *reading specialist*
Whitehouse, Charles Barton *avionics educator*
Williams, Sally *landscape designer*

Loma
†Young, David Bennion *artist*

Lone Tree
Bauer, Randy Mark *management training firm executive*

Longmont
Davis, Donald Alan *author, news correspondent, lecturer*
Dierks, Richard Ernest *veterinarian, educational administrator*
Ford, Byron Milton *computer consultant*
Jones, Beverly Ann Miller *nursing administrator, retired patient services administrator*
Kaminsky, Glenn Francis *deputy chief of police retired, business owner, teacher*
†Keene, Samuel James, Jr. *reliability engineer researcher, educator*
King, Jane Louise *artist*
McEachern, Susan Mary *information technology specialist*
Muench, Lothar Wilhelm *electrical engineer, consultant*
Nevling, Harry Reed *health care human resources executive*
Ralston, Paula Jane *nurse*
Simpson, Velma Southall *insurance agent*
Thompson, Michael James *news editor*
Ulrich, John August *microbiology educator*
Walker, Kathleen Mae *health facility administrator*

Louisville
Brault, James William *physicist*
Day, Robert Edgar *retired artist, educator*
Ferguson, Gary L. *public relations executive*
Raymond, Dorothy Gill *lawyer*
Shively, Merrick Lee *pharmaceutical scientist, consultant*
Slater, Shelley *telecommunications company administrator*
Sontag, Peter Michael *travel management company executive*
†Spagnola, Robert G. *lawyer, business management educator*
Tetlow, William Lloyd *infotech consultant*
Willette, Donald Corliss *reverend*

Loveland
Balsiger, David Wayne *television-video director, researcher, producer, writer*
Carter, Laura Lee *academic librarian, psychotherapist*
Hughes, Edwin Strode *public relations executive*
Rodman, Alpine C. *arts and crafts company executive*
Rodman, Sue A. *wholesale Indian crafts company executive, artist, writer*
Taylor, Marian Alecia *manufacturing development engineer*
Weresh, Thelma Faye *sculptor, artist*

Lyons
Brown, Michael DeWayne *lawyer*
†Spring, Kathleen *writer*

Manitou Spgs
Slivka, Michael Andrew *lawyer*

Monument
Breckner, William John, Jr. *retired air force officer, corporate executive, consultant*
Karasa, Norman Lukas *home builder, developer, geologist*
Miele, Alfonse Ralph *former government official*

Morrison
Myers, Harry J., Jr. *retired publisher*
Routson, Clell Dennis *manufacturing company executive*
Solin, David Michael *state official*

Nederland
†Border, William Lawson *artist*

New Castle
†Spuhler, Jacilyn E. *librarian*

Niwot
Garvan, Stephen Bond *artist manager*
Rinehart, Frederick Roberts *publisher*

Northglenn
Peters, LeRoy Richard *materials management consulting company executive*

Olathe
Shriver, Allen Keith *electrical engineer, contractor, executive*

Pagosa Springs
Howard, Carole Margaret Munroe *retired public relations executive*

Palmer Lake
Harrington, Judith Regina *English language educator*

Parker
Greenberg, Morton Paul *lawyer, consultant, insurance broker, underwriter*
Jankura, Donald Eugene *hotel executive, educator*
Lembeck, James Peter *nutritionist, writer, consultant*
Nelson, Marvin Ray *retired life insurance company executive*

Peterson AFB
†Arnold, Brian A. *career officer*
†Drennan, Jerry M. *military officer*
†Hinson, Robert C. *career officer*
†Kelly, Rodney P. *military officer*
†Pettit, Donald *career officer*

Placerville
Monferrato, Angela Maria *entrepreneur, investor, writer, designer*
Reagan, Harry Edwin, III *lawyer*

Pueblo
Alt, Betty L. *sociology educator*
Altman, Leo Sidney *lawyer*
Avery, Julia May *speech pathologist, organizational volunteer*
Bates, Charles Emerson *library administrator*
Chandler, Kris *computer consultant, educator*
Cress, Cecile Colleen *retired librarian*
Farley, Thomas T. *lawyer*
Geisel, Henry Jules *lawyer*
Giffin, Walter Charles *retired industrial engineer, educator, consultant*
Hawkins, Robert Lee *health facility administrator*
Heizer, Ida Ann *retired real estate broker*
Henning, William Thomas *museum director*
Humes, James Calhoun *lawyer, communications consultant, author, professor*
Kelly, William Bret *insurance executive*
Lewallen, William Marvin, Jr. *ophthalmologist*
Lightell, Kenneth Ray *education educator*
Meek, Charles Ronald
Mou, Thomas William *physician, medical educator and consultant*
Noblit, Betty Jean *publishing technician*
O'Callaghan, Robert Patrick *lawyer*
Occhiato, Michael Anthony *city official*
Poole, Rita Ann *secondary education educator*
Rawlings, Robert Hoag *newspaper publisher*
Sisson, Ray L. *retired dean*
†Swanson, Bret Robert *elementary education educator*
Tafoya, Arthur N. *bishop*
Vega, Jose Guadalupe *psychologist, clinical director*
White, Rodney Curtis *paralegal, legal assistant*
†Wong, Leslie Eric *academic administrator*

Ridgway
Lathrop, Kaye Don *nuclear scientist, educator*
Weaver, Dennis *actor*

Rocky Ford
†Mendenhall, Harry Barton *lawyer*

Rollinsville
Burandt, Gary Edward *advertising agency executive*

Salida
Miller, Marian Lofton *artist, musician*

San Luis
Wardlaw, Diane *graphic designer*

Schriever AFB
†Looney, William R., III *career officer*

Silverthorne
Ponder, Herman *geologist*

Silverton
Denious, Sharon Marie *publisher*

Snowmass
Lovins, L. Hunter *public policy institute executive*

Snowmass Village
Bancroft, Paul, III *investment company executive*
Beeman, Malinda Mary *artist, program administrator*
Le Buhn, Robert *investment executive*
Mattis, Louis Price *pharmaceutical and consumer products company executive*

South Fork
Foster, Bruce Dudley *retired clergyman*

Sterling
Christian, Roland Carl (Bud Christian) *retired English language and speech communications educator*
Gustafson, Randall Lee *city manager*
Hunter, Frank A. *secondary education educator*
Jones, Daniel Lee *software development company executive*
Jones, Laurie Ganong *sales and marketing executive*
Widhalm, Michele Ann *reporter, writer*

Strasburg
†Nesland, Matt J. *journalist, photojournalist*

Swink
Rockwell, Virginia Considine *school counselor*

Telluride
Groeneveld, David Paul *plant ecologist, hydrologist*
Hadley, Paul Burrest, Jr. (Tabbit Hadley) *domestic engineer, photographer*
Kuehler, Jack Dwyer *engineering consultant*
Smith, Samuel David *artist, educator*

Thornton
Hendren, Debra Mae *critical care nurse*
†Roberts, Steven L. *human resources specialist*

Trinidad
Potter, William Bartlett *business executive*

Twin Lakes
†Zadeh, Firooz E. *author, real estate developer*

U S A F Academy
Coppock, Richard Miles *nonprofit association administrator*
†DeBerry, Fisher *college football coach*
Krise, Thomas Warren *military officer, English language educator*
Morris, Steven Lynn *career officer, aeronautical engineering educator*
Newmiller, William Ernest *English educator*

Vail
Bevan, William Arnold, Jr. *emergency physician*
Knight, Constance Bracken *writer, realtor, corporate executive*
†McFadden, Joseph Tedford *retired neurosurgeon, writer*
McGee, Michael Jay *fire marshal, educator*
Spaeh, Saundra Lee (Smith)
Vosbeck, Robert Randall *architect*

Westcliffe
Jones, Daniel Edwin, Jr. *bishop*
Merfeld, Gerald Lydon *artist*

Westminster
Dalesio, Wesley Charles *former aerospace educator*
Eaves, Stephen Douglas *educator, vocational administrator*
Liard, Jean-Francois *cardiovascular physiologist, researcher, educator*
Wade, Rodger Grant *financial systems analyst*
Wirkkala, John Lester *cable company executive*

Wheat Ridge
Barrett, Michael Henry *civil engineer*
Brown, Steven Brien *radiologist*
Gerlick, Helen J. *tax practitioner, accountant*
Hashimoto, Christine L. *physician*
LaMendola, Walter Franklin *human services, information technology consultant*
Leino, Deanna Rose *business educator*
Nichols, Vicki Anne *financial consultant, librarian*
Scherich, Erwin Thomas *civil engineer, consultant*
Wilcox, Mary Marks *Christian education consultant, educator*

Woodland Park
Cockrille, Stephen *art director, business owner*
Sallquist, Gary Ardin *minister, non-profit executive*
Stewart, Robert Lee *retired army officer, astronaut*

Yellow Springs
†Sholtis, Michelle Lea *potter, educator*

CONNECTICUT

Ansonia
Dvoretzky, Israel *dermatologist*
Kerpa, Gary J. *computer science consultant*
Rubin, Larry Jeffrey *occupational rehabilitation professional*
Yale, Jeffrey Franklin *podiatrist*

Ashford
McCaughtry, Charles H. *artist, painter*
Spencer, Editha Mary (Hayes) *artist*
Spencer, Harold Edwin *retired art educator, art historian, painter*

Avon
Boucher, Louis Jack *retired dentist, educator*
†Dodd, David K. *banker*
Hickey, Kevin Francis *healthcare executive*
Kling, Phradie (Phradie Kling Gold) *small business owner*
Mazur, Edward John, Jr. *insurance agent*
McIlveen, Walter *mechanical engineer*
Stowe, Joyce Lundy *life insurance company official, educator*
Weiss, Robert Michael *dentist*
Wiechmann, Eric Watt *lawyer*

Berlin
Carroll, Adorna Occhialini *real estate executive*

Bethany
Childs, Brevard Springs *religious educator*
†Weber, Katharine *writer*

Bethel
Ajay, Abe *artist*
DeLugo, Ernest Mario, Jr. *electrical engineer*
Kurfehs, Harold Charles *real estate executive*

Bloomfield
†Carstensen, Fred V. *economics educator*
Day, John G. *lawyer*
De Maria, Anthony John *electrical engineer*
Ervin, Billy Maxwell *aerospace executive*
Foster, Benjamin, Jr. *educational administrator*
Hammer, Alfred Emil *artist, educator*
Handel, Morton Emanuel *management consultation executive*
Hilsenrath, Baruch M. *principal*
Johnson, Linda Thelma *information specialist*
Kaman, Charles Huron *diversified technologies corporation executive*
Kissa, Karl Martin *electrical engineer*
†Klinger, Douglas Evan *money management executive*
Leonberger, Frederick John *electrical engineer, photonics manager*
Less, Anthony Albert *retired naval officer*
Mackey, William Arthur Godfrey *analytical testing company executive*
Mark, Henry Allen *lawyer*
Nye, Edwin Packard *mechanical engineering educator*
Reid, Hoch *lawyer*
Wetstone, Howard Jerome *physician, administrator*

Bolton
Banas, Conrad Martin *mechanical engineer, chief scientist*

Branford
Cohen, Myron Leslie *business executive, mechanical engineer*
De Gennaro, Richard *retired library director, library advisor*
Glick, Marion Shepherd *psychology, educator*
Hayes, Samuel Perkins *social scientist, educator*
LeVasseur, Lee Allan *fine artist*
McCurdy, Larry Wayne *automotive parts company executive*
Milgram, Judith Lee *art educator, administrator, artist*
Resnick, Idrian Navarre *foundation administrator*
Smith, Richard Emerson (Dick Smith) *make-up artist*
Vietzke, Wesley Maunder *internist, educator*
Wegener, Peter Paul *engineering educator, author*
Whitaker, Thomas Russell *English literature educator*

Bridgeport
Agee, Kevin Jerome *minister*
Allen, Richard Stanley (Dick Allen) *English language educator, author*
Brunale, Vito John *aerospace engineer*
†Bruner, Evans *management consultant*
Byrd, Charles Everett *clergyman*
Chih, Chung-Ying *physicist, consultant*
Ciszak, Lynn Marie *city planner*
Despres, Robert Leon *urban planner*
Dworkin, Irma-Theresa *school system administrator, researcher, educator*
Egan, Edward M. *bishop*
Eginton, Warren William *federal judge*
Ettre, Leslie Stephen *chemist*
†Fitzsimmons, Holly B. *federal judge, educator*
Freeman, Richard Francis *banker*
Gagnon, Robert James, Jr. *manufacturing engineer*
Henderson, Albert Kossack *publishing company executive, dairy executive, consultant*
Hendricks, Edward David *speaker, educator, consultant*
Hmurcik, Lawrence Vincent *electrical engineering educator*
Lymm, Peter Jay *hospital administrator*
Mahmud, Shireen Dianne *photographer*
†Menke, Richard Xavier *military officer*
†Mijensohn, Daniel E. *neurosurgeon*
Nevas, Alan Harris *federal judge*

Rubenstein, Richard Lowell *theologian, educator*
Schwartz, James Peter *real estate broker*
Semple, Cecil Snowdon *retired manufacturing company executive*
Sheridan, Eileen *librarian*
Shiff, Alan Howard William *federal judge*
Skowron, Tadeusz Adam *physician*
Sobh, Tarek Mahmoud *computer science educator, researcher*
Stokes, Charles Junius *economist, educator*
Trefry, Robert J. *healthcare administrator*
van der Kroef, Justus Maria *political science educator*
Walsh, Charles Hagen *columnist, writer*
Ward, Thomas Joseph *association executive, lecturer, researcher, writer*
Watson, David Scott *financial services executive*
Williams, Ronald Doherty *lawyer*

Bristol
Adamle, Mike *sports commentator*
Aldridge, David *sports announcer*
Barnes, Carlyle Fuller *manufacturing executive*
Barnes, Wallace *manufacturing executive*
Beil, Larry *sports announcer*
Berman, Chris *sports anchor*
Bernstein, Al *sports commentator*
Bernstein, Bonnie *reporter*
Corso, Lee *former football coach, football analyst*
Cyphers, Steve *reporter*
Eisen, Rich *reporter*
†Furniss, Keith Richard *educational administrator*
Gammons, Peter *columnist*
Hickingbotham, Nancy Bennett *nursing case manager*
Kernan, John William *auto racing reporter*
Kiper, Mel *sports commentator*
Kremer, Andrea *sports correspondent*
Malone, Mark *sports reporter*
Melrose, Barry James *sportscaster, former professional hockey team coach*
Miller, Jon *sports commentator*
Morgan, Joe Leonard *investment company executive, former professional baseball player*
Morganti, Al *reporter*
Nessler, Brad R. *sports commentator*
Pallotti, Robert Michael *minister*
Parsons, Benny *auto racing commentator*
Patrick, Bill *sports network host*
Patrick, Dan *sportscaster*
Patrick, Mike *sports commentator*
Pidto, Bill *sports network anchorman*
Punch, Jerry *sports reporter*
Raftery, Bill *basketball analyst*
Ravech, Karl *sports anchor, reporter*
Reynolds, Harold Craig *professional baseball player*
Roberts, Jimmy *sports correspondent*
Roberts, Robin *sportcaster*
Saunders, John *broadcast network host*
Schwarz, Mark *sports correspondent*
Scott, Stuart *sports anchor*
Steiner, Charles Harris *sports broadcaster, journalist*
Thorne, Gary *sports commentator*
Varsha, Bob *sports commentator*
Visser, Lesley *sports correspondent*

Broad Brook
Kement, Isabella Viniconis *retired construction company executive*

Brookfield
Cohen, Mark Steven *dentist*
Foncello, Martin John, Jr. *business and intelligence analyst, consultant*
Reynolds, Jean Edwards *publishing executive*
Schetky, Laurence McDonald *metallurgist, researcher*
Stern, Michael Lawrence *psychologist*

Brooklyn
Dune, Steve Charles *lawyer*

Burlington
Sonn, Gay *mathematics educator*

Canaan
Capecelatro, Mark John *lawyer*

Centerbrook
Simon, Mark *architect*

Central Village
Wilson, Aurele Paula *mental health nurse*

Cheshire
Bozzuto, Michael Adam *wholesale grocery company executive*
Burton, Robert William *retired office products executive*
†Cassagneres, Everett *engineer, consultant, pilot*
Eppler, Richard Andrew *chemical engineer, educator, consultant*
Maddaloni, Betty *elementary education educator*
Martin, Glen Matthew *architect, landscape*
McKee, Margaret Jean *federal agency executive*
Pettine, Linda Faye *physical therapist*
Rowland, Ralph Thomas *retired architect*
Saad, Edward Theodore *architect*

Chester
Cobb, Hubbard Hanford *magazine editor, writer*
Feldmann, Shirley Clark *psychology educator*
Frost-Knappman, (Linda) Elizabeth (Elizabeth Frost Knappman) *publishing company executive*
Harwood, Eleanor Cash *librarian*
Hays, David Arthur *theater producer, stage designer*

City Place
Nolan, John Blanchard *lawyer*

Clinton
Harris, Doris Ann *nurse*
Hershatter, Richard Lawrence *lawyer, author*

Cobalt
Stevens, Robert Edwin *bank executive, former insurance company executive*

Colebrook
Ash, Hiram Newton *graphic designer*
Fuller, Renee Nuni *psychologist, educational publisher*

Mc Neill, William Hardy *retired history educator, writer*

Collinsville
Ford, Dexter *retired insurance company executive*

Columbia
Malchiodi, Joanne Marie *elementary education educator, reading consultant*
Orr, Jim (James D. Orr) *columnist, writer, publicist*

Cornwall Bridge
Pfeiffer, Werner Bernhard *artist, educator*

Cos Cob
Barnard, Charles Nelson *editorial consultant, author*
Duncalf, Deryck *retired anesthesiologist*
Hauptman, Michael *broadcasting company executive*
Kane, Jay Brassler *banker*
Kane, Margaret Brassler *sculptor*
Snowdon, Jane Louise *industrial engineer*
Sorese, Denise Powers *reading consultant, educator*
Yudain, Carole Gewirtz *public relations consultant, writer, editor, historian, photojournalist, audio-visual producer, educator*
Zang, Joseph Albert, Jr. *chemical engineer, consultant*

Coventry
Foster, Lloyd Arthur *principal*

Cromwell
Darius, Franklin Alexander, Jr. (Chip Darius) *health administrator, educator, consultant*
Trowbridge, Phillip Edmund *surgeon, educator*

Danbury
Anderson, Alan Reinold *real estate executive, communications consultant*
Arbitelle, Ronald Alan *elementary school educator*
Baker, Leonard Morton *manufacturing company executive*
Baruch, Eduard *management consultant*
Burns, Jacqueline Mary *laboratory administrator*
Chaifetz, David Harvey *lawyer*
†DiBiccari, Grace *pastor*
Dornfeld, Sharon Wicks *lawyer*
Edelstein, David Simeon *historian, educator*
Edmunds, Robert Thomas *retired surgeon*
Fuller, Cassandra Miller *applications specialist*
Geoghan, Joseph Edward *lawyer, chemical company executive*
Gezurian, Dorothy Ellen *accounting executive*
Gogliettino, John Carmine *insurance broker*
Hawkes, Carol Ann *university dean*
Heller, Maryellen *special education educator*
Izzo, Lucille Anne *sales representative*
Jennings, Alfred Higson, Jr. *music educator, actor, singer*
Joyce, William H. *chemist*
Kurien, Santha T. *psychiatrist*
Leish, Kenneth William *publishing company executive*
Lichtenberger, H(orst) William *chemical company executive*
Malino, Jerome R. *rabbi*
McNabb, Frank William *consumer products company executive*
Murray, Stephen James *lawyer*
Pankulis, Pauline Johnson *nursing administrator, geriatrics nurse*
Pastor, Stephen Daniel *chemistry educator, researcher*
Perun, John Joseph, Jr. *information systems professional*
Proctor, Richard Jerome, Jr. *business educator, accountant, expert witness*
Rafferty, James Paul *telecommunications executive*
Roach, James R. *university president*
Saghir, Adel Jamil *artist, painter, sculptor*
Scalzo, Robert Edward *middle school mathematics educator*
Selfridge, John William *publishing executive*
Skolan-Logue, Amanda Nicole *lawyer, consultant*
Soviero, Joseph C. *chemical company executive*
Toland, John Willard *historian, writer*
Tolor, Alexander *psychologist, educator*
†Walker, Michael James *surgeon*
Williamson, Brian David *information systems executive, consultant*
Wright, Marie Anne *management information systems educator*
Zirn, Jonathan Russell *dermatologist, dermatopathologist*

Darien
Bays, John Theophanis *consulting engineering*
Beach, Stephen Holbrook *lawyer*
Britton, Robert Austin *manufacturing company executive*
Brooke, Avery Rogers *publisher, writer*
Brown, James Shelly *lawyer*
Chyung, Chi Han *management consultant*
Cowherd, Edwin Russell *management consultant*
Dale, Erwin Randolph *lawyer, author*
Dordelman, William Forsyth *food company executive*
Forman, J(oseph) Charles *chemical engineer, consultant, writer*
Glenn, Roland Douglas *chemical engineer*
Hailey, Arthur *author*
Hartong, Hendrik J., Jr. *transportation company executive*
Kobak, James Benedict *management consultant*
Koontz, Carl Lennis, II *investment counselor*
Kutz, Kenneth John *retired mining executive*
Look, Alice *writer, producer, journalist*
Mapel, William Marlen Raines *retired banking executive*
Marshall, Susan Lockwood *civic worker*
Moltz, James Edward *brokerage company executive*
Morse, Edmond Northrop *investment management executive*
Prince, Kenneth Stephen *lawyer*
Schell, James Munson *financial executive*
Smith, Elwin Earl *mining and oil company executive*
Sprole, Frank Arnott *retired pharmaceutical company executive, lawyer*
†Welsh, John Francis *retired advertising executive*
Woodring, Thomas Joseph *publisher*
Ziegler, William, III *diversified industry executive*

Deep River
Hieatt, Allen Kent *language professional, educator*
Hieatt, Constance Bartlett *English language educator*

Zack, Steven Jeffrey *master automotive instructor*

Derby
†Augusta, Judith Wood *librarian*

Devon
Spinelli, Viola June *healthcare management consultant*

Durham
Hicks, Norman William *physical science educator*
Russell, Thomas James *critical care supervisor*

East Berlin
†Pelton, Timothy Noble *management consultant*

East Glastonbury
Smith, David Clark *research scientist*

East Granby
Scanlon, Lawrence Eugene *English language educator*

East Haddam
Borton, John Carter, Jr. (Terry Borton) *theatrical producer*
Clarke, Cordelia Kay Knight Mazuy *managment executive, consultant*
Clarke, Logan, Jr. *management consultant*

East Hampton
†Jamsheed, Jacqueline Tahminey *financial manager*
Tucceri, Clive Knowles *science writer and educator, consultant*

East Hartford
Barredo, Rita M. *auditor*
Bonin, Paul Joseph *real estate and banking executive*
Cassidy, John Francis, Jr. *industrial technology executive*
Conwell, Theresa Gallo *financial services representative*
Day, William Hudson *mechanical engineer, turbomachinery company executive*
Dutka, Linda Semrow *psychiatric and addictions nurse*
Foyt, Arthur George *electronics research administrator*
Franklin, Robert Richard *retired federal agency administrator, farmer*
Henry, Paul Eugene, Jr. *minister*
LeJambre, Charles R. *aeronautical engineer*
Milo, George Thomas *administrator*
Murphy, Ann Burke *retired systems analyst*
Pfeifer, Howard Melford *mechanical engineer*
Pudlo, Frances Theresa *executive assistant*
Pudlo, Virginia Mary *medical surgical nurse*
Rhie, Chae Myung *mechanical engineer, aeronautical engineer, aerospace engineer*
Scholsky, Martin Joseph *priest*
Whiston, Richard Michael *lawyer*
Zacharias, Robert M. *mechanical engineer, aeronautical engineer, aerospace engineer*
Zampiello, Richard Sidney *metals and trading company executive*

East Haven
Conn, Harold O. *physician, educator*

Easton
Enos, Randall *cartoonist, illustrator*
Lorenz, Lee Sharp *cartoonist*
Maloney, John Joseph *writer*
Meyer, Alice Virginia *state official*
Nusim, Roberta *publisher*
Pendagast, Edward Leslie Jr. *physician*

Ellington
Setzer, Herbert John *chemical engineer*

Enfield
Berger, Robert Bertram *lawyer*
Dyer, Joseph Edward *company executive*
Folmsbee, Patricia Hurley *reading consultant*
Loomis, Janice Kaszczuk *artist*
Oliver, Bruce Lawrence *information systems specialist, educator*
Reuter, Joan Copson *program director*
Squires, William Allen *distribution company executive*

Essex
Burris, Harriet Louise *emergency physician*
Goff, Christopher Wallick *pediatrician*
Grover, William Herbert *architect*
Miller, Elliott Cairns *retired bank executive, lawyer*
Thompson, George Lee *consulting company executive*

Fairfield
Ambrosino, Ralph Thomas, Jr. *retired telecommunications executive*
Barone, Rose Marie Pace *writer, retired educator, entertainer*
Beers, Anne Cole *real estate broker*
Booth, George Keefer *finanical service executive*
Boskello, Dennis Jon *elementary education educator*
Boskello, Margo Lynn *elementary education educator*
Brett, Arthur Cushman, Jr. *banker*
Bryan, Barbara Day *retired librarian*
Bullard, Roger Perrin *artist*
Bunt, James Richard *electric company executive*
Burd, Robert Meyer *hematologist, oncologist, educator*
Caruso, Daniel F. *lawyer, judge, former state legislator*
Cernera, Anthony Joseph *academic administrator*
Cole, Richard John *marketing executive*
Cox, Richard Joseph *former broadcasting executive*
Daley, Pamela *lawyer*
Dean, George Alden *advertising executive*
DeCarlo, Deena M. *mortgage company executive*
Denniston, Brackett Badger, III *lawyer*
Detmar-Pines, Gina Louise *business strategy and policy educator*
Doris, Eugene Patrick *athletics director*
Dunham, Christopher Scott *librarian*
Eigel, Edwin George, Jr. *mathematics educator, retired university president*
Eigel, Marcia Duffy *editor*
Everett, Wendy Ann *toy designer*
Fash, Michael William *cinematographer, director*

Ford, Maureen Morrissey *civic worker*
Gad, Lance Stewart *investment advisor, lawyer, private investor*
Harkrader, Milton Keene, Jr. *corporate executive*
Hauck, Madeline (Agnes) *special and adult basic education educator*
Heineman, Benjamin Walter, Jr. *lawyer*
Hodgkinson, William James *marketing company executive*
Kaff, Albert Ernest *journalist, author*
Kelley, Aloysius Paul *university administrator, priest*
Koutas, Samuel Demetrios *human resources executive*
LaFollette, Ernest Carlton *lawyer*
Levine, Stanley Walter *chemical company executive*
Lumbard, Joseph Edward, Jr. *federal judge*
Luther, David Byron *energy company executive*
McCain, Arthur Williamson, Jr. *retired pension investment consultant*
Mead, Philomena *mental health nurse*
Michael, Mary Amelia Furtado *retired educator, freelance writer*
Miles, Leland Weber *university president*
†Morehouse, Sarah McCally *political science educator*
Murphy, Eugene F. *aerospace, communications and electronics executive*
Newton, Lisa Haenlein *philosophy educator*
†Paolini, Claire Jacqueline *dean, educator*
Regan, Thomas Joseph *Roman Catholic priest*
†Rinaldi, Nicholas M. *educator in English language*
Rosenman, Stephen David *obstetrician and gynecologist*
Shaffer, Dorothy Browne *retired mathematician, educator*
Simpson, W(ilburn) Dwain *physicist, corporate executive, computer systems, telecommunications, environmental, and advanced fueling systems consultant*
Spence, Barbara E. *publishing company executive*
Sutphen, Harold Amerman, Jr. *retired paper company executive*
Trager, Philip *photographer, lawyer*
Welch, John Francis, Jr. (Jack Welch) *electrical manufacturing company executive*
Wexler, Herbert Ira *retail company executive*

Falls Village
Collins, Robert G(eorge) *literature educator, writer*
Cronin, Robert Lawrence *sculptor, painter*
Gaschel-Clark, Rebecca Mona *special education educator*
Purcell, Dale *college president, consultant*
Purcell, Mary Louise Gerlinger *retired educator*
Toomey, Jeanne Elizabeth *animal activist*

Farmington
Anderson, Buist Murfee *lawyer*
Besdine, Richard William *medical educator, scientist*
Bigler, Harold Edwin, Jr. *investment company executive*
Bronner, Felix *physiologist, biophysicist, educator, painter*
Cooperstein, Sherwin Jerome *medical educator*
Deckers, Peter John *dean*
Donaldson, James Oswell, III *neurology educator*
Flynn, Daniel Francis *investment company executive*
Gossling, Harry Robert *orthopaedic surgeon, educator*
Grunnet, Margaret Louise *pathology educator*
Hermann, Robert Jay *manufacturing company engineering executive, consultant*
Hinz, Carl Frederick, Jr. *physician, educator*
Jestin, Heimwarth B. *retired university administrator*
Katz, Arnold Martin *medical educator*
Kedderis, Pamela Jean *academic administrator*
LaGanga, Donna Brandeis *sales and marketing executive*
†Lasser, Jay Andrew *psychiatrist*
Liebowitz, Neil Robert *psychiatrist*
Mandell, Joel *lawyer*
Massey, Robert Unruh *physician, university dean*
McCann, John Joseph *lawyer*
Miller, Crystal C. *intravenous therapy nurse*
†Minges, James Seth *consulting engineer, planner*
Moran, John Joseph *retired food and beverage company executive*
Murphy, Joanne M. *computer company executive*
†Ort, Eric D. *fundraising executive*
Osborn, Mary Jane Merten *biochemist*
Raisz, Lawrence Gideon *medical educator, consultant*
Rothfield, Lawrence I. *microbiology educator*
Rothfield, Naomi Fox *physician*
Schenkman, John Boris *pharmacologist, educator*
Smith, Cary Christopher *artist*
Spencer, Richard Paul *biochemist, educator, physician*
Testa, John Anthony *medical researcher, consultant*
Walker, James Elliot Cabot *physician*

Georgetown
Roberts, Priscilla Warren *artist*

Glastonbury
†Andrews, Bryant Aylesworth *software company executive*
Budd, Edward Hey *retired insurance company executive*
†Cavanaugh, Marianne *secondary educator*
Goodwin, Rodney Keith Grove *international bank and trade company executive*
†Guzzi, R. James, Jr. *health care fraud consultant*
Hamlin, Kathryn F. *geriatrics nurse, administrator*
Hatch, D. Patricia P. *principal*
Juda, Richard John *anesthesiologist*
Schneiderman, Joan Ellen *psychotherapist*
Schroth, Peter W(illiam) *lawyer, management and law educator*
Singer, Paul Richard *ophthalmologist*
Tomlinson, Richard Giles *author, consultant*

Goshen
†Morris, John M. *insurance agency administrator*

Greens Farms
Deford, Frank *sportswriter, television and radio commentator, author*
McManus, John Francis, III *advertising executive*
St. Marie, Satenig *writer*

Greenwich
Adrian, George Panaitisor *graphic designer*
Allen, Paul Howard *financial institutions investor*
Amen, Robert Anthony *investor and corporate relations consultant*

Zikmund, Barbara Brown minister, seminary president, church history educator

Higganum
de Brigard, Emilie anthropologist, consultant
Twachtman-Cullen, Diane communication disorders and autism specialist

Ivoryton
Bendig, William Charles editor, artist, publisher
Osborne, John Walter historian, educator, author

Kent
White, Roger Bradley priest

Lakeville
Estabrook, Robert Harley journalist
Jones, Ronald David lawyer

Lebanon
Ajemian, Cheryl Bloom audit consultant

Ledyard
Haase, William R., IV urban planner
White, Harold R. insurance and health care inforamtion company executive

Litchfield
Booth, John Thomas investment banker
Kenagy, Robert Coffman planning consulting company executive
Shrady, Alexander James S. accountant

Lyme
Bessie, Simon Michael publisher
Bloom, Barry Malcolm pharmaceutical consultant
Hoyt, Charles King architect, editor

Madison
Azarian, Martin Vartan publishing company executive
Cappetta, Anna Maria art educator
Carlson, Dale Bick writer
Clendenen, Corinna Pakenham art critic, writer, auctioneer
Clendenen, William Herbert, Jr. lawyer
Egbert, Emerson Charles retired publisher
Golembeski, Jerome John wire and cable company executive
Houghton, Alan Nourse association executive, educator, consultant
Ingis, Gail interior designer, educator, writer, photographer, artist
Keim, Robert Phillip retired advertising executive, consultant
Kronauer, Lisa Elliott art director
Langdon, Robert Colin dermatologist, educator
Passero, Virginia Ann retired nursing educator
Platt, Sherman Phelps, Jr. publishing consultant
Purcell, Bradford Moore publishing company executive
Snell, Richard Saxon anatomist

Manchester
Brazeal, Earl Henry, Jr. electrical engineer
Gaines, Robert Martin lawyer
Galasso, Francis Salvatore materials scientist
†Jacobson, Charles Edward, Jr. urologist
Stull, Daniel Richard retired research thermochemist, educator, consultant

Mansfield Center
Aldrich, Robert Adams agricultural engineer
Liberman, Alvin Meyer psychology educator
Merrill, Denise state legislator
Petrus, Robert Thomas internet distribution executive, real estate executive

Marion
Perkins, James Winslow international business consultant, builder, contractor

Meriden
Bertolli, Eugene Emil sculptor, goldsmith, designer, consultant
Giosa, Richard Peter pulmonary medicine physician
Horton, Paul Chester psychiatrist
†Johnson, James principal
Lowry, Houston Putnam lawyer
Molder, Sybil Ailene occupational health nurse
Mule, Donna Kemish human services coordinator
Muzyczka, Kathleen Ann family and consumer sciences educator
Pepe, Richard Kane nurse anesthetist
Reitz, H(oward) Wesley construction company executive
Smits, Helen Lida physician, administrator, educator

Middle Haddam
Beaulieu, Dennis E. videographer
Dart, John Robert horticulturist

Middlebury
Arnold, William Parsons, Jr. retired internist
Davis, Joanne Fatse lawyer

Middletown
Abelove, Henry historian, literary critic
Arnold, Herbert Anton German language educator
Balay, Robert Elmore editor, reference librarian
Bennet, Douglas Joseph, Jr. university president
Buel, Richard Van Wyck, Jr. history educator, writer, editor
Carrington, Virginia Gail (Vee Carrington) professional society administrator, librarian
Comfort, William Wistar mathematics educator
Crites, Stephen Decatur religion educator
Fry, Albert Joseph chemistry educator
Gerber, Murray A. molding manufacturing company executive
Gillmor, Charles Stewart history and science educator, researcher
Haake, Paul chemistry, biochemistry and history of science educator
Hager, Anthony Wood mathematics educator
Kerr, C(larence) William retired university administrator
†McCormick, Elizabeth Johnston college official
Meyer, Priscilla Ann Russian language and literature educator
Meyers, Arthur Solomon library director
Miller, Richard Alan economist, educator
Morris, Jonathan Ira biology educator
Narad, Joan Stern psychiatrist
Novick, Stewart Eugene physical chemist, educator
Osborne, Raymond Lester, Jr. radiologist
Pomper, Philip history educator
Quattro, Mark Henry lawyer, developer
Reed, Joseph Wayne American studies educator, artist
Reid, James Dolan mathematics educator, researcher
Scheibe, Karl Edward psychology educator
†Schwarcz, Vera history educator
Sease, John W(illiam) chemistry educator
Shapiro, Norman Richard Romance languages and literatures educator
Slotkin, Richard Sidney American studies educator, writer
Smith, Brian Condray manufacturing executive
Upgren, Arthur Reinhold, Jr. astronomer, educator
Valentine, George Edward dentist
Wensinger, Arthur Stevens language and literature educator, author
Winston, Krishna Ricarda foreign language professional

Milford
Antosz, Candace Elizabeth health promotion educator
Berchem, Robert Lee, Sr. lawyer
Calabrese, Anthony marine biologist
Cox, Robert Claude retird educator and school system administrator
Curt, Denise Morris artist, limner, photographer
Dodd, Alan Charles art educator
Fischer, David Seymour internist, consultant
Fontaine, Ronald Gerard librarian
Grogins, Jack Lawrence state judge
Haigh, Charles criminal justice educator
Hanlon, James Allison confectionery company executive
Khoury, Robert John international leadership management consultant
Muth, Eric Peter ophthalmic optician
Myers, David Richard youth organization financial executive
Olson, Harold Roy computer company executive
Taylor, Charles Henry psychoanalyst, educator
Wall, Robert Emmet educational administrator, novelist

Monroe
Kranyik, Elizabeth Ann secondary education educator
Magazian, Victor Edward private investigator
Roberge, Cecelia Ament nursing administrator, rehabilitation nurse
Turko, Alexander Anthony biology educator, hypnotherapist
Wheatley, Sharman B. art educator, artist

Moodus
Cumming, Robert Emil editor
Steinkamp, Dorothy DeMauro nursing educator

Mystic
Antipas, Constantine George lawyer, civil engineer
Carr, James Revell museum executive, curator
Chiang, Albert Chinfa polymer chemist
Connell, Hugh P. foundation executive
Johnston, Waldo Cory Melrose museum director
†McCabe, Edward Owen photoprocessing executive
Rogers, Brian Deane retired librarian
Smith, Norman Clark fund raising and non-profit management consultant
Thompson, Robert Allan aerospace engineer

Naugatuck
Flannery, Joseph Patrick manufacturing company executive
Mannweiler, Mary-Elizabeth painter
Stauffer, Elizabeth Clare elementary education educator, music choral director, consultant

New Britain
Baskerville, Charles Alexander geologist, educator
Bozek, Thomas state legislator
Brownstein, Julian M. advertising and public relations executive
Bruemmer, Lorraine Venskunas funeral director, real estate broker, nurse
Cline, John Carroll clinical psychologist
Cotten-Huston, Annie Laura psychologist, educator
Czajkowski, Eva Anna aerospace engineer, educator
Davidson, Phillip Thomas retail company executive
Deckert, Clinton Allen artist
Dimmick, Charles William geology educator
Emeagwali, Gloria Thomas humanities educator
Hampton, John James university dean, consulting company executive
Judd, Richard Louis academic administrator
Kot, Marta Violette artist, art educator
Margiotta, Mary-Lou Ann software engineer
Meskill, Thomas J. federal judge
Pearl, Helen Zalkan lawyer
Rohinsky, Marie-Claire modern languages educator
Rosa, Peter Manuel university administrator, researcher
Sarisley, Edward F. engineering technology educator, consultant
Sohn, Jeanne librarian
Tomaiuolo, Nicholas Gregory librarian, educator
Weddle, Stephen Shields manufacturing company executive

New Canaan
Antupit, Samuel Nathaniel art director
Bartlett, Dede Thompson company executive
†Batchelor, David Henry Lowe marketing consultant
Burns, Ivan Alfred grocery products and industrial company executive
Caesar, Henry A., II sculptor
Cohen, Richard Norman insurance executive
Crossman, William Whittard retired wire cable and communications executive
Dean, Robert Bruce architect
†Ervin, Wilma Jean painter, photographer
Gilbert, Steven Jeffrey venture capitalist, screenwriter, lawyer
Grace, Julianne Alice investor relations firm executive
Halverstadt, Robert Dale mechanical engineer, metals manufacturing company
Hodgson, Richard electronics company executive
Kennedy, John Raymond pulp and paper company executive
Kovatch, Jak Gene artist
Lione, Susan Garrett consultant
MacEwan, Nigel Savage merchant banker
Marcus, Edward economist, educator
McClure, Grover Benjamin management consultant
McIvor, Donald Kenneth retired petroleum company executive
Mc Mennamin, George Barry advertising agency executive
Means, David Hammond retired advertising executive
Mountcastle, Kenneth Franklin, Jr. retired stockbroker
Norman, Christina Reimarsdotter secondary education language educator
Noxon, Margaret Walters community volunteer
Oatway, Francis Carlyle corporate executive
Penny, Susan Caroline Voelker investment manager
Pike, William Edward business executive
Prescott, Peter Sherwin writer
Rendl-Marcus, Mildred artist, economist
Richards, Walter DuBois artist, illustrator
Richardson, Dana Roland video producer
Risom, Jens furniture designer, manufacturing executive
Rutledge, John William former watch company executive
Sachs, John Peter carbon company executive
Silbey, Paula J. public relations consultant, writer
Snyder, Nathan entrepreneur
Stack, J. William, Jr. management consultant
Sweeny, Kenneth S. graphic design consultant
Thacher, Barbara Auchincloss history educator
Thomsen, Donald Laurence, Jr. institute executive, mathematician
Vasta, Vincent Joseph, Jr. lawyer
Wallace, Kenneth Donald lawyer
Ward, Richard Vance, Jr. management executive
White, Richard Booth management consultant
Ylvisaker, James William insurance executive

New Fairfield
Daukshus, A. Joseph systems engineer
Meyers, Abbey S. foundation administrator

New Haven
Abdelsayed, Wafeek Hakim accounting educator
Ackerman, Bruce Arnold lawyer, educator
Adair, Robert Kemp physicist, educator
Adanti, Michael J. academic administrator
Aghajanian, George Kevork medical educator
Alexander, Bruce Donald real estate executive, educator
Alexandrov, Vladimir Eugene Russian literature educator
Altman, Sidney biology educator
Anderson, Carl Albert academic administrator, lawyer
Anderson, John Frederick science administrator, entomologist, researcher
Apfel, Robert Edmund mechanical engineering educator, applied physicist, research scientist
Apter, David Ernest political science and sociology educator
†Ariyan, Stephen surgeon
†Arons, Marvin Shield plastic and hand surgeon
Aronson, Peter Samuel medical scientist, physiology educator
Arterton, Janet Bond judge
Askenase, Philip William medicine and pathology educator
Aylor, Donald Earl biophysicist, research meteorologist, plant pathology educator and reseacher
Bailey, William Harrison artist, educator
Baker, Robert Stevens organist, educator
Barash, Paul George anesthesiologist, educator
Bartlett, Beatrice Sturgis modern China historian, educator
Beardsley, G(eorge) Peter pediatric oncologist, biochemical pharmacologist
Behrman, Harold Richard endocrinologist, physiologist, educator
Bell, Wendell sociologist, educator, futurist
Belt, David Levin lawyer
Benfer, David William hospital administrator
†Benjamin, Donna Miller university official, elementary education educator
Benjamin, Martin anthropologist
Bennett, Scott Boyce librarian
Bennett, William Ralph, Jr. physicist, educator
Berliner, Robert William physician, medical educator
Berner, Robert Arbuckle geochemist, educator
Berson, Jerome Abraham chemistry educator
Birnbaum, Irwin Morton lawyer
Blatt, Sidney Jules psychology educator, psychoanalyst
Bloom, Harold humanities educator
Blum, John Morton historian
Bly, Mark John dramaturg, playwriting educator
Bolognia, Jean Lynn academic dermatologist
Borroff, Marie English language educator
Boyer, James Lorenzen physician, educator
Bracken, Paul political science educator
Brainard, William Crittenden economist, educator, university official
Braverman, Irwin Merton dermatologist, educator
Bromley, David Allan physicist, engineer, educator
Brooks, Peter (Preston) French and comparative literature educator, writer
Brown, Thomas Huntington neuroscientist
Brownell, Kelly David psychologist, educator
Bruder, Charles Irwin psychologist, researcher
Brünger, Axel Thomas biophysicist, researcher, educator
Buck, Donald Tirrell finance educator
Buckley, Richard Bennett asset management company executive
Bunney, Benjamin Stephenson psychiatrist
Burns, Ellen Bree federal judge
Burrow, Gerard Noel physician, educator
Burt, Robert Amsterdam lawyer, educator
Buss, Leo William biologist, educator
Byck, Robert Samuel psychiatrist, educator
Cabranes, José Alberto federal judge
Cadman, Edwin Clarence health facility administrator, medical educator
Calabresi, Guido federal judge, law educator
Carr, Cynthia lawyer
Casten, Richard Francis physicist
Chandler, William Knox physiologist
Child, Irvin Long psychologist, educator
Chilton, William David architect
Chupka, William Andrew chemical physicist, educator
Clark, Elias law educator
Clarke, Fred W., III architect, architectural firm executive
Coe, Michael Douglas anthropologist, educator
Cofrancesco, Donald George health facility administrator
Cohen, Donald Jay pediatrics, psychiatry and psychology educator, administrator
Cohen, Lawrence Baruch neurobiologist, educator
Cohen, Lawrence Sorel physician, educator
Cohen, Morris Leo retired law librarian and educator
Coleman, Joseph Emory biophysics and biochemistry educator
Collins, William F., Jr. neurosurgery educator
Comer, James Pierpont psychiatrist, educator
Condon, Thomas Brian hospital executive
Conklin, Harold Colyer anthropologist, educator
Cooney, Leo Mathias, Jr. geriatrician, educator
Cooper, Dennis Lawrence oncologist, educator
Cooper, Jack Ross pharmacology educator, researcher
Craig, William Emerson lawyer
Crakes, Gary Michael economics educator
Crothers, Donald Morris biochemist, educator
Crowder, Robert George psychology educator
Cunningham, Walter Jack electrical engineering educator
†Dabrowski, Albert S. federal judge
Davey, Lycurgus Michael neurosurgeon
Days, Drew S., III lawyer, law educator
Dechant, Virgil C. fraternal organization administrator
De Lio, Anthony Peter lawyer
Demos, John Putnam history educator, writer, consultant
Diers, Donna Kaye nurse educator
Dittes, James Edward psychology of religion educator
Donaldson, Robert Macartney, Jr. physician
Doob, Leonard William psychology educator, academic administrator
Dorsey, Peter Collins federal judge
DuBois, Arthur Brooks physiologist, educator
Duke, Steven Barry law educator
Dupré, Louis retired philosopher, educator
Dworski, Sylvia modern languages educator
Dyson, William R. state legislator, educator
Edelson, Marshall psychiatry educator, psychoanalyst
Ellickson, Robert Chester law educator
Ember, Carol R. anthropology educator, author
English, Mark Edward Latin educator
Erikson, Kai sociologist, educator
Erlich, Victor Slavic languages educator
†Evenson, Robert Eugene economics educator
Feinstein, Alvan Richard physician, educator
†Feinstein, Rochelle artist, educator
Ferholt, J. Deborah Lott pediatrician
Fikrig, Erol rheumatologist, medical educator
Fischer, Michael John computer science educator
Fiss, Owen M. law educator
Fleck, Stephen psychiatrist
Freed, Daniel Josef law educator
Freedman, Gerald Stanley radiologist, healthcare administrator, educator
French, Richard Frederic retired music educator
Fried, Charles A. accountant, financial executive
Friedlaender, Gary Elliott orthopedist, educator
Gallup, Donald Clifford bibliographer, educator
Galston, Arthur William biology educator
Garen, Alan biophysics professor
Garner, Wendell Richard psychology educator
Garvey, Sheila Hickey theater educator
Genel, Myron pediatrician, educator
Geselowitz, Michael Norman anthropologist
Giebisch, Gerhard Hans physiology educator
Gilbert, Creighton Eddy art historian
Gildea, Brian Michael lawyer
Glaser, Gilbert Herbert neuroscientist, physician, educator
Glier, Ingeborg Johanna German language and literature educator
†Golan, Romy educator
Goldman-Rakic, Patricia Shoer neuroscience educator
Goldstein, Abraham Samuel lawyer, educator
Goodrich, Isaac neurosurgeon, educator
Gordon, John Charles forestry educator
Gordon, Robert Boyd geophysics educator
Górniak-Kocikowska, Krystyna Stefania philosopher, educator
Graedel, Thomas Eldon chemist, researcher
Gralla, Howard Irwin graphic designer
Grausman, Philip sculptor
Greene, Liliane French educator, editor
Greenfield, James Robert lawyer
Griffith, Ezra Edward Holman health facility administrator, educator
Gross, Ian academic pediatrician, neonatologist
Haddad, Gabriel G. physician, pediatrics educator
Hadley, Nancy Lynne community foundation executive
Hallo, William Wolfgang Assyriologist
Handschumacher, Robert Edmund biochemistry educator
Hansmann, Henry Baethke law educator
Harries, Karsten philosophy educator, researcher
Harrison, Henry Starin real estate educator, entrepreneur
Hartman, Geoffrey H. language professional, educator
Haskins, Caryl Parker scientist, author
†Haverland, Michael Robert architect
Hayden, Dolores author, architect, educator
Heninger, George Robert psychiatry educator, researcher
Herbert, Peter Noel physician, medical educator
Hersey, George Leonard art history educator, retired
Herzenberg, Arvid physicist, educator
Hickey, Leo J(oseph) museum curator, educator
Hines, Roberta Leigh medical educator
Hoffer, Paul B. nuclear medicine physician, educator
Hoffleit, Ellen Dorrit astronomer
Hoffman, Joseph Frederick physiology educator
Hoge, Michael Alan psychologist
Hohenberg, Pierre Claude research physicist
Holder, Angela Roddey lawyer, educator
Hollander, John humanities educator, poet
Holmes, Frederic Lawrence science historian
Holquist, James Michael Russian and comparative literature educator
Horstmann, Dorothy Millicent retired physician, educator
Horváth, Csaba chemical engineering educator, researcher
Howe, Roger Evans mathematician, educator
Hughes, Vernon Willard physics educator, researcher
Huwiler, Joan P. public relations executive, consultant
Hyman, Paula E(llen) history educator
Igarashi, Peter nephrologist, educator, researcher

St. George, Judith Alexander *author*

Old Saybrook
Dewdney, Anthony Edward *quality assurance professional, auditor*
Huftalen, Lisa Freeman *corporate executive, graphic designer*
Jensen, Oliver Ormerod *editor, writer*
Knobelsdorff, Kristina Louise Marie *English language educator*
Peszke, Michael Alfred *psychiatrist, educator*
Phillips, William E. *advertising agency executive*
Spencer, William Courtney *foundation executive, international business executive*

Orange
†Davis, David Brion *historian, educator*
Douskey, Theresa Kathryn *health facility administrator*
Fasanella, Rocko Michael *ophthalmologist*
Lobay, Ivan *mechanical engineering educator*
Miller, Henry Forster *architect*
Randall, Arthur Raymond *building contractor*

Plainville
Glassman, Gerald Seymour *metal finishing company executive*

Plantsville
Roy, Ralph Lord *clergyman*

Plymouth
Hall, William Smith, Jr. *land surveyor*

Portland
Chapman, Allen Floyd *management educator, college dean*
D'Oench, Russell Grace, Jr. *publishing consultant*

Preston
Gibson, Margaret Ferguson *poet, educator*

Prospect
Powell, Raymond William *financial planner, school administrator*
Thornley, Wendy Ann *educator, sculptor*

Redding
Isley, Alexander Max *graphic designer, lecturer*
Russell, Allan David *lawyer*

Ridgefield
Bernstein, William Robert *banker*
Brewster, Carroll Worcester *former academic administrator*
Bye, Arthur Edwin, Jr. *landscape architect*
Byrne, Daniel William *biomedical research consultant, biostatistician, computer specialist, educator*
Colen, Helen Sass *plastic surgeon*
Dimos, Helen *landscape designer*
Forbes, James Wendell *publishing consultant*
Fricke, Richard John *lawyer*
Grozinger, Karl Georg *chemist, researcher*
Knortz, Herbert Charles *retired conglomerate company executive*
Kromer, Ann Marie *artist*
Leonard, Sister Anne C. *superintendent, education director*
Levine, Paul Michael *paper industry executive, consultant*
Lodewick, Philip Hughes *equipment leasing company executive*
McConnell, John Edward *electrical engineer, company executive*
Mesznik, Joel R. *investment banker*
Nodland, Borge Heming *physicist*
†Pitman, Ann Bridgman *artist*
Sadow, Harvey S. *health care company executive*
Sen, Pabitra N. *physicist, researcher*
Sobol, Bruce J. *internist, educator, researcher*
Stoddard, William Bert, Jr. *economist*
†Swartout, Torin Sherwin Roberts *transportation executive, real estate broker*
Tomanic, Joseph P(aul) *retired research scientist*
Wallace, Ralph *superintendent*
Wyton, Alec *composer, organist*

Riverside
Battat, Emile A. *management executive*
Becker, Don Crandall *retired newspaper executive*
Coulson, Robert *retired association executive, arbitrator, author*
Geismar, Richard Lee *communications executive*
McSpadden, Peter Ford *retired advertising agency executive*
Olshan, Kenneth S. *business executive, advisor, writer*
Otto, Charles Edward *health care administrator*
Powers, Claudia McKenna *state legislator*

Rockville
†Ciparelli, Peter Francis *library director*

Rocky Hill
Chu, Hsien-Kun *chemist, researcher*
Chuang, Frank Shiunn-Jea *engineering executive, consultant*
Dubin, Joseph William *union representative*
Griesé, John William, III *astronomer, mental health advocate*
Hoffman, Penny Joan *adult nurse practitioner, administrator*
McCullough, Jefferson Walker *industrial engineering consultant*
Roy, Thomas David *accountant*
Tietjen, Scott Phillips *computer programmer, analyst*

Rogers
Boomer, Walter Eugene *marine officer*

Rowayton
Raikes, Charles FitzGerald *retired lawyer*

Roxbury
Gurney, Albert Ramsdell *playwright, novelist, educator*
Styron, Rose Burgunder *human rights activist, poet, journalist*

Salem
Diamond, Sigmund *editor, educator*

Salisbury
Block, Zenas *management consultant, educator*
Kilner, Ursula Blanche *genealogist, writer*
White, Norval Crawford *architect*

Sharon
Gordon, Nicholas *broadcasting executive*
Gottlieb, Richard Matthew *psychiatrist, consultant*
Kahn, Paul Frederick *executive search company executive*
†Nweeia, Martin Thomas *dentist, musician, composer, anthropologist*

Shelton
Asija, S(atya) Pal *lawyer*
†Coughlin, Karen A. *health care company executive*
Lewis, Peter David *artist, educator*
Pagliaro, Frank Carl, Jr. *collection agency executive, city official*
Wham, William Neil *publisher*

Sherman
Cohn, Jane Shapiro *public relations executive*
Valeriani, Richard Gerard *news broadcaster*

Simsbury
Adams, (Lewis) Dean *theater director*
Calvert, Lois Wilson *civic worker*
Long, Ann Marie *health facility administrator*
†Mogck, Derek Leonard
Roberts, Celia Ann *librarian*
Roman, Robin *anesthesiologist*

Somers
Blake, Stewart Prestley *retired ice cream company executive*
Hooper, Donald Robert *retired corporate chief executive*

South Kent
Samartini, James Rogers *retired appliance company executive*

South Windsor
Coullard, Chad *information systems specialist*
Famiglietti, Nancy Zima *computer executive*
Hobbs, David Ellis *mechanical engineer*

Southbury
Atwood, Edward Charles *economist, educator*
Leonard, John Harry *advertising executive*
Marchese, Ellen *consultant*
Morehead, Frederick Ferguson *retired physical chemist*
Rubin, Jacob Carl *mechanical research engineer*
Wescott, Roger Williams *anthropologist*
Wilson, Carolyn Elizabeth *nursing administrator*
Wilson, Geraldine O'Connor *psychologist*

Southington
Burkhardt, Dolores Ann *library consultant*
Kassey, Jacquelyn Marie Bonafonte *pediatrics nurse*

Southport
Damson, Barrie Morton *oil and gas exploration company executive*
Hill, David Lawrence *research corporation executive*
Moore, Roy Worsham, III *lawyer*
Schadt, James Phillip *investment company executive*
Sheppard, William Stevens *investment banker*
Taylor, James Blackstone *aviation company executive*
Walker, Charles Dodsley *conductor, organist*
Wheeler, Wilmot Fitch, Jr. *diversified manufacturing company executive*
Wilbur, E. Packer *investment company executive*

Stamford
Allaire, Paul Arthur *office equipment company executive*
Amarilios, John Alexander *lawyer, real estate consultant*
Anderson, Susan Stuebing *business equipment company executive*
Apfelbaum, Marc *lawyer*
Ast, Steven Todd *executive search firm executive*
Barker, James Rex *water transportation executive*
†Barr, Charles F. *lawyer, reinsurance company executive*
Barreca, Christopher Anthony *lawyer*
Baylis, Robert Montague *investment banker*
Beck, Angel C. *columnist, educator*
Beyman, Jonathan Eric *information officer*
Birenbaum, Jonathan *lawyer*
Block, Ruth *retired insurance company executive*
Bowen, Patrick Harvey *lawyer, consultant*
Brakeley, George Archibald, Jr. *fundraising consultant*
Breakstone, Robert Albert *consumer products, information technology and consulting executive*
Britt, Glenn Alan *media company executive*
Broadhurst, Austin, Jr. *executive recruiter*
†Brown, Stephen Bernard *corporate lawyer*
Brown, W. Michael *publishing company executive*
Burston, Richard Mervin *business executive*
Calarco, Vincent Anthony *specialty chemicals company executive*
Caldwell, Philip *retired automobile manufacturing company executive, retired financial services company executive*
Carten, Francis Noel *lawyer*
Casper, Stewart Michael *lawyer*
Cassetta, Sebastian Ernest *industry executive*
Chamberlain, Jill Frances *financial service executive*
Chickering, Howard Allen *insurance company executive, lawyer*
Chisolm, Barbara Wille *world affairs organization executive*
Christophe, Cleveland Aleridge *investment company executive*
Cochran, David MacDuffie *management consultant*
Coleman, Ernest Albert *plastics and materials consultant*
Collins, Joseph Jameson *communications executive*
Conover, Harvey *retired publisher*
Cook, Colin Burford *psychiatrist*
Courter, Jeanne Lynn *materials scientist*
Critelli, Michael J. *lawyer, manufacturing executive*
Daleo, Robert *communications executive*
Dederick, Ronald Osburn *lawyer*
Dell, Warren Frank, II *management consultant*
Della Rocco, Kenneth Anthony *lawyer*
Dennies, Sandra Lee *city official*
Di Maria, Valerie Theresa *public relations executive*
Dolian, Robert Paul *lawyer*
Donahue, Donald Jordan *mining company executive*
Duncan, Thomas Webb *magazine publishing executive*
Evans, Robert Sheldon *manufacturing executive*
Everhart, Judd *public relations executive*
Fein, Ronnie *writer, journalist*
Ferguson, Ronald Eugene *reinsurance company executive*
Fickenscher, Gerald H. *chemicals company executive*
Filter, E. Margie *business equipment manufacturing executive*
Frank, Laura Jean *computer scientist*
†Fredo, Bart *educator*
Frese, Alan D.R. *publishing executive*
Fuchs, Hanno *communications consultant, lawyer*
Gagnon, Monique Francine *pediatrician*
Gladstone, Herbert Jack *manufacturing company executive*
Godfrey, Robert R. *financial services executive*
Goodhue, Peter Ames *obstetrician and gynecologist, educator*
Gromults, Joseph Michael, Jr. *internist*
Gross, Ronald Martin *forest products executive*
Haber, Judith Ellen *nursing educator*
Harrington, Richard J. *newspaper publishing executive*
Harris, Wiley Lee *financial services executive*
Hawley, Frank Jordan, Jr. *venture capital executive*
Hedge, Arthur Joseph, Jr. *corporate executive*
†Herlands, E. Ward *poet, printmaker*
Hollander, Milton Bernard *corporate executive*
Hood, Edward Exum, Jr. *retired electrical manufacturing company executive*
Hudson, Harold Jordon, Jr. *retired insurance executive*
Jacobson, Ishier *retired utility executive*
James, John Whitaker, Sr. *financial services executive*
Jason, J. Julie *money manager, author, lawyer*
Karp, Steve *producing director*
Kellogg, Tommy Nason *reinsurance corporation executive*
Kerr, Ian *public relations executive*
Kingsley, John McCall, Jr. *manufacturing company executive*
Kinnear, James Wesley, III *retired petroleum company executive*
Kinsman, Robert Donald *art museum administrator, cartoonist*
Kisseberth, Paul Barto *retired publishing executive*
Klein, Neil Charles *physician*
Klenk, Rosemary Ellen *pediatrician*
Knag, Paul Everett *lawyer*
Koch, Robert *art educator*
Koproski, Alexander Robert *real estate executive*
Kweskin, Edward Michael *lawyer*
Lennard, Gerald *metal products executive*
Livolsi, Frank William, Jr. *lawyer*
Loh, Arthur Tsung Yuan *finance company executive*
Lowman, George Frederick *lawyer*
Lupia, David Thomas *corporate financial advisor, management consultant*
Lynch, John T. *management consultant*
Maarbjerg, Mary Penzold *office equipment company executive*
Malloy, Dannel Patrick *mayor*
Margolis, Emanuel *lawyer, educator*
Marlowe, Edward *research company executive*
Marsden, Charles Joseph *financial executive*
Martin, Patrick *business equipment company executive*
†McClave, Wilkes, III *business executive*
McGrath, Richard Paul *lawyer*
McGuire, Bartlett *sports association executive*
Mc Kinley, John Key *retired oil company executive*
McNamara, Francis Joseph, Jr. *foundation executive, lawyer*
McNear, Barbara Baxter *retired financial communications executive, consultant*
McWilliams, Thomas Henry *life reinsurance underwriter professional*
Megrue, Suzanne Jacobsen *primary education educator*
Merritt, William Alfred, Jr. *lawyer, telecommunications company executive*
Miklovic, Daniel Thomas *research director*
Miller, Wilbur Hobart *business diversification consultant*
Motroni, Hector John *manufacturing executive*
Munera, Gerard Emmanuel *manufacturing company executive*
Murphy, Robert Blair *management consulting company executive*
Nevans, Roy Norman *food products executive, producer*
Nichols, Ralph Arthur *lawyer*
Nierenberg, Roger *symphony conductor*
Nightingale, William Joslyn *management consultant*
Ogden, Dayton *executive search consultant*
Olson, Richard E. *publishing executive, paper company executive*
O'Malley, Thomas D. *diversified company executive*
Padilla, James Earl *lawyer*
Pansini, Michael Samuel *tax and financial consultant*
Parker, Jack Steele *retired manufacturing company executive*
Paul, Richard Stanley *lawyer*
†Peppers, Donald Alan *marketing consultant, writer*
Perle, Eugene Gabriel *lawyer*
†Peters, Clifford Simpson *secondary school educator*
Peterson, Carl Eric *metals company executive, banker*
Philipps, Edward William *banker, real estate appraiser*
Pollock, Duncan *advertising executive*
Popelyukhin, Aleksey *actuary, researcher*
†Raphael, Brett *artistic director, choreographer*
Rapp, James Allen *marketing executive*
Reade, Lewis Pollock *business executive, retired diplomat, engineer*
Rilla, Donald Robert *social services administrator*
Rose, Richard Loomis *lawyer*
Rowe, William John *newspaper publishing executive*
Rudman, Joan Eleanor *artist, educator*
Sadove, Stephen Irving *consumer products company executive*
Sahota, Gurcharn Singh *mechanical engineer*
Sarbin, Hershel Benjamin *management consultant, business publisher, lawyer*
Sarner, Richard Alan *lawyer*
Sayers, Richard James *newspaper editor*
Schechter, Audrey *medical, surgical nurse*
Schmitz, Robert Allen *publishing executive, investor*
Shapiro, Bruce *psychiatrist*
Sherman, Norman Mark *advertising agency executive*
Silver, Charles Morton *communications company executive*
Silver, R. Philip *metal products executive*
Sisley, G. William *lawyer*
Skidd, Thomas Patrick, Jr. *lawyer*
Spindler, John Frederick *lawyer*
Stapleton, James Francis *lawyer*
Steeneck, Regina Aultice *information systems specialist*
Stillings, Irene Ella Grace Cordiner *organization executive*
Strosahl, William Austin *artist, art director*
Sveda, Michael *management and research consultant*
Taylor, Stephen Hosmer *sports entertainment executive, photographer*
Teeters, Nancy Hays *economist*
Teitell, Conrad Laurence *lawyer, author*
Thoman, G. Richard *computer company executive*
Tierney, Patrick John *information services executive*
Tregurtha, Paul Richard *marine transportation and construction materials company executive*
Trivisonno, Nicholas Louis *communications company executive, accountant*
Tully, Daniel Patrick *financial services executive*
Veronis, Peter *publisher*
Vivian, Jay (R.L. Vivian, Jr.) *retirement funds manager*
Vos, Frank *advertising and marketing executive*
Wallfesh, Henry Maurice *business communications company executive, editor, writer*
Walsh, Thomas Joseph *neuro-ophthalmologist*
†Waxberg, Jonathan Abel *urologic surgeon, oncologist*
Weitzel, William Conrad, Jr. *lawyer*
Wheeler, Wesley Dreer *marine engineer, naval architect, consultant*
Wilensky, Julius M. *publishing company executive*
Wilhelm, Gayle Brian *lawyer*
Wunsch, Bonnie Rubenstein *fraternal organization executive*
Yardis, Pamela Hintz *computer consulting company executive*
Yonkman, Fredrick Albers *lawyer, management consultant*
Younskevicius, Adriana *law librarian*

Stonington
Mantz, Arlan W. *physics educator*
Pottie, David Laren *magazine publisher*
Rees, Charles H. G. *retired financial officer, investor, consultant*
Stoddard, Alexandra *designer, writer, lecturer*
Van Rees, Cornelius S. *lawyer*

Storrs
Nieforth, Karl Allen *university dean, educator*
Stevens, Nancy *coach*

Storrs Mansfield
Abramson, Arthur Seymour *linguistics educator, researcher*
Allen, John Logan *geographer*
Anderson, Gregory Joseph *botanical sciences educator*
Auriemma, Geno *university athletic coach*
Austin, Philip Edward *university president*
Azaroff, Leonid Vladimirovitch *physics educator*
Bartram, Ralph Herbert *physicist*
Birdman, Jerome Moseley *drama educator, consultant*
Bobbitt, James McCue *chemist*
Britner, Preston Arthur, IV *developmental psychologist, educator*
Buck, Ross Workman *communication sciences educator, psychology educator, writer*
Calhoun, Jim *college basketball coach*
Charters, Ann *biographer, editor, educator*
Chinn, Peggy Lois *nursing educator, editor*
Cohen, Marcia Alice *special education administrator*
Coons, Ronald Edward *historian, educator*
†Crow, Laura Jean *design educator, costume designer*
Cyr, Juliette Mary *molecular biology researcher*
Deb, Somnath *software company executive*
Devereux, Owen Francis *metallurgy educator*
DiBenedetto, Anthony Thomas *engineering educator*
Gilmour, Robert S. *political science educator*
Glasser, Joseph *manufacturing and marketing executive*
Gutteridge, Thomas G. *academic administrator, consultant and labor arbitrator*
Jensen, Helene Wickstrom *retired nutritionist, educator*
Jones, Clyde Adam *art educator, artist*
Kattamis, Theodore Zenon *metallurgy educator, material enginerring*
Katz, Leonard *psychology educator*
Kerr, Kirklyn M. *university administrator, veterinary pathologist, researcher*
Klemens, Paul Gustav *physicist, educator*
Koths, Jay Sanford *floriculture educator*
†Ladd, Everett Carll *political science educator, author*
Laufer, Hans *developmental biologist, educator*
Lee, Tsoung-Chao *education educator*
Long, Richard Paul *civil engineering educator, geotechnical engineering consultant*
Marcus, Harris Leon *materials science educator*
Marcus, Philip Irving *virology educator, researcher*
McEachern, William Archibald *economics educator*
Perez-Escamilla, Rafael *nutritionist*
Pitkin, Edward Thaddeus *aerospace engineer, consultant*
Reed, Howard Alexander *historian, educator*
Rimland, Lisa Phillip *writer, composer, lyricist, artist*
Romano, Antonio *microbiologist*
Rosen, William *English language educator*
Schuster, Todd Mervyn *biophysics educator, biotechnology company executive*
Shaffer, Jerome Arthur *philosophy educator*
Skauen, Donald Matthew *retired pharmaceutical educator*
Slater, James Alexander *entomologist, educator*
Smith, Robert Victor *university administrator*
Stevens, Norman Dennison *retired library director*
Stwalley, William Calvin *physics and chemistry educator*
Tucker, Edwin Wallace *law educator*
Zirakzadeh, Cyrus Ernesto *political science educator*

Stratford
Chase, J. Vincent *shopping center executive, justice of the peace*
Conti-O'Brien, Yvonne *elementary education educator*
Cowperthwaite, John Milton, Jr. *architect, construction consultant*
Douglas, Karin Nadja *engineer*

Feinberg, Dennis Lowell *dermatologist*
Hageman, Richard Philip, Jr. *educational administrator*
Hall, Shelley Stevenson *special education educator*
Kassapoglou, Christos *aeronautical engineer*
Kaufman, Jess *communication, financial and marketing consultant*
Rock, William Booth *producer, announcer*
Russell, Cynthia Pincus *social worker, educator*
Salzberg, Emmett Russell *new product developer*
†Sipprell, George Sidney *engineering professional*
Walker, Gladys Lorraine *author*
Weisz, Sandor Ferenc *business machines company executive, industrial designer, educator, consultant*

Suffield
†Alfano, Charles T., Jr. *lawyer*
Bianchi, Maria *critical care specialist, adult nurse practitioner, acute care nurse practitioner*
Charkiewicz, Mitchell Michael, Jr. *economics and finance educator*
D'Aleo, Penny Frew *special education educator, consultant*
Friedman, Dian Debra *elementary education educator*
Tobin, Joan Adele *writer, scholar*

Tariffville
Johnson, Loering M. *design engineer, historian, consultant*

Thomaston
Mühlanger, Erich *ski manufacturing company executive*

Thompson
Fisher, William Thomas *business administration educator*

Tolland
Simons, Barry *underwriter, insurance consultant*
Wilde, Daniel Underwood *computer engineering educator*
†Wyman, Nancy S. *state legislator*

Torrington
Adorno, Monica S. *taxpayer representative*
Drobena, Thomas John *minister, educator*
Kucharek, Wilma Samuella *minister*
Leard, David Carl *lawyer*
Lippincott, Walter Edward *law educator*
†McKenzie, Kathleen Julianna *artist*
Sexton, Diana Elizabeth *communications company executive*
Wall, Robert Anthony, Jr. *lawyer*

Trumbull
FitzGerald, James W. (Jay) *magazine publisher*
Garelick, Melvin Stewart *engineering educator, aerospace engineer*
Gladki, Hanna Zofia *civil engineer, hydraulic mixer specialist*
Lang, James Richard *education consultant*
London, Michael Jeffrey *public relations executive*
Nevins, Lyn (Carolyn A. Nevins) *educational supervisor, trainer, consultant*
Norcel, Jacqueline Joyce Casale *educational administrator*
Reeves, Edmund Hoffman, III *food products executive*
Renz, William Franklin *real estate investor*
Schmitt, William Howard *cosmetics company executive*
Seitz, Nicholas Joseph *magazine editor*
Smith, Gail Marie *special education educator, educational consultant*
Tarde, Gerard *magazine executive*
Watson, Donald Ralph *architect, artist, educator, author*
Weiner, Mary Lou *elementary education educator*

Uncasville
†Bunnel, Charles Franklin *personnel director, lobbyist*

Vernon Rockville
Brooks, Neil H. *physician*
Herbst, Marie Antoinette *former state senator*
Marmer, Ellen Lucille *pediatric cardiologist*
McKeever, Brian Edward *general contractor*
†Obroski, Paulo *public administration coordinator*
Polifroni, Elizabeth Carol *nurse, educator*
Roden, Jon-Paul *computer science educator*
Williams, Julius Penson *composer, conductor*
Wolff, Gregory Steven *insurance company executive*

Voluntown
Thevenet, Patricia Confrey *social studies educator*

Wallingford
Cohen, Gordon S. *health products executive*
Dunkle, Lisa Marie *clinical research executive*
Fleming, James Stuart, Jr. *pharmaceutial company manager*
Hay, Leroy E. *school system administrator*
Kaplan, Harold Paul *physician, health science facility administrator*
Lauttenbach, Carol *artist*
Molinoff, Perry Brown *biologist, science administrator*
Spero, Barry Melvin *medical center executive*

Warren
Abrams, Herbert E. *artist*

Washington
Darlow, George Anthony Gratton *investor*
Leab, Daniel Joseph *history educator*

Washington Depot
Mandler, Susan Ruth *dance company administrator*
Pendleton, Moses Robert Andrew *dancer, choreographer*
Tracy, Michael Cameron *choreographer, performer, educator*

Waterbury
†Adamski, Richard Franklyn *writer, mental health consultant, technical theatre assistant*
†Arias, Bridget Carser *elementary educator*
Bellemare, David John *architectural designer*
Brown, Lillian Hill *retired educator*
Colbenson, Mary Elizabeth Dreisbach *materials engineer*
Dudrick, Stanley John *surgeon, scientist, educator*
†Eisen, Steven Leslie *neurologist*
†Epstein, Carl Plakcy *public information officer*
Fielding, Howard William *newspaper editor, columnist*
Fischbein, Charles Alan *pediatrician*
Glass, Robert Davis *judge*
Goettel, Gerard Louis *federal judge*
Holub, Barbara Ann *rehabilitation nurse*
†Jorge, Juan B. *cultural organization administrator, writer*
†Kelly, Maura Anne *political reporter*
Leever, Harold *chemical company executive*
Luedke, Frederick Lee *manufacturing company executive*
MacLeod, Glen Gary *English language educator*
Marano, Richard Michael *lawyer*
Meyer, Judith Chandler Pugh *history educator*
†Ogrodnik, Lana Kathleen *real estate broker*
Oliver, Eugene Alex *speech and language pathologist*
Ostrov, Melvyn R. *physician*
Pape, William James, II *newspaper publisher*
Peterson, W(alter) Scott *ophthalmic surgeon*
Phillips, Walter Mills, III *psychologist, educator*
Plummer, John Mitchell *postal clerk*
†Richard, Peter Wayne *educator*
Rosa, Domenico *mathematics educator*
Sherwood, James Alan *physician, scientist, educator*
Smith, Ann Youngdahl *museum administrator*
Titus, Curtis Vest *lawyer*
Tomaszek, Thomas Richard *manufacturing executive*
Zasada, Mary Eileen *nursing project leader*

Waterford
Commire, Anne *playwright, writer, editor*
Hinerfeld, Lee Ann *veterinarian*
Hinkle, Muriel Ruth Nelson *naval warfare analysis company executive*
Johnson, Gary William *environmental scientist*
Patnode, Mark W. *artist, graphic designer*
Walsh, Peter Joseph *multimedia marketing professional*
White, George Cooke *theater director, foundation executive*

Watertown
Wuthrich, Paul *electrical engineer, researcher, consultant*

West Cornwall
Jones, Mark Richard *financial advisor*
Klaw, Barbara Van Doren *author, editor*
Klaw, Spencer *writer, editor, educator*
Prentice, Tim *sculptor, architect*

West Granby
Conland, Stephen *publishing company executive*

West Hartford
†Collins, Alma Jones *English educator, writer*
Conard, Frederick Underwood, Jr. *lawyer*
DeLibero, Mary Smellie *insurance company professional, pianist, soprano*
Doran, James Martin *retired food products company executive*
Dunn, Robert Elbert *education consultant, principal*
Echols, Ivor Tatum *retired educator, assistant dean*
Gingold, George Norman *insurance company executive, lawyer*
Glotzer, Mortimer M. *quality assurance consultant*
Gryc, Stephen Michael *composer, music educator*
†Ivey, Elizabeth S. *acoustician, physicist*
†Jamil, S. Selina *eduator*
Jones, Allison *basketball coach*
Leshem, Osnat Alice *institutional resource clinician*
Markham, Sister M(aria) Clare *chemistry educator, educational director*
Scott, Mary Elizabeth *management consultant*
Storm, Robert Warren *lawyer*
Swerdloff, Ileen Pollock *lawyer*
Welna, Cecilia *mathematics educator*
White, Joan Michelson *artist*
†Yueh, Chai-Lun *voice educator, opera singer*

West Hartland
Perkins, Bob(by) F(rank) *geologist, dean*

West Haven
Allen, Jerry L. *university dean, communication educator*
Borrell, Paul Nicholas *sales executive*
Bowerman, Richard Henry *utility company executive, lawyer*
Debeyssey, Mark Sammer *molecular and cellular biologist*
DeNardis, Lawrence J. *academic administrator*
Ellis, Lynn Webster *management educator, telecommunications consultant*
Ezekowitz, Michael David *physician*
Farquharson, Patrice Ellen *primary school educator*
Glen, Robert Allan *history educator*
Kern, Bernadette *rehabilitation services educator, consultant*
†L'Heureux, Amy Elizabeth *school psychologist*
Linemeyer, David Lee *molecular biologist*
Perlmutter, Lynn Susan *neuroscientist*
Simone, Angela Paolino *elementary education educator*
†Solano, Mona *elementary education educator*

West Redding
†Holder, Barbara June *educator in English and literature*

West Simsbury
Morest, Donald Kent *neuroscientist, educator*

Westbrook
Douglas, Hope M. *psychotherapist, forensic hypnotist*
Dundas, Philip Blair, Jr. *lawyer*

Weston
Alcosser, Lois Harmon *cultural organization administrator*
Bellin, Harvey Forrest *television producer, director*
Bleifeld, Stanley *sculptor*
Boesch, Diane Harriet *elementary education educator*
Cadmus, Paul *artist, etcher*
Cohen, Fred Howard *lawyer, investment company executive*
Daniel, James *curator, business executive, writer, former editor*
Diforio, Robert George *literary agent*
Fredrik, Burry *theatrical producer, director*
Kilty, Jerome Timothy *playwright, stage director, actor*
Kimmelman, Gregory M. *television producer and director*
Laikind, Donna *psychotherapist, consultant*
Levien, Roger Eli *strategy and innovation consultant*
Murray, Thomas Joseph *advertising executive*
Offenhartz, Edward *aerospace executive*
Oliver, Sandra *art dealer, painter*
Swenson, Eric Pierson *retired publishing company executive*
Thompson, N(orman) David *insurance company executive*
Zimmerman, Bernard *investment banker*

Westport
Aasen, Lawrence Obert *public relations executive*
Albani, Suzanne Beardsley *lawyer*
†Allen, Michael G. *management consultant*
Altman, Lawrence Gene *biologist*
Barton, James Miller *lawyer, international business consultant*
†Battenfeld, John Leonard *educator, journalist*
Blau, Barry *marketing executive, financial investor*
Brandt, Kathy A. *public relations and events management executive, secondary school educator*
Bronson, Carole *publishing executive*
Brooks, Andrée Aelion *journalist, educator, author*
Burns, John Joseph *pharmacology educator*
Chernow, Ann Levy *artist, art educator*
Clausman, Gilbert Joseph *medical librarian*
Cramer, Allan P. *lawyer*
Davis, Joel *publisher*
Daw, Harold John *lawyer*
Densen-Gerber, Judianne *psychiatrist, lawyer, educator*
†Fash, Victoria R. *Healthcare company executive*
Ferris, Roger Patrick *architect*
Fisher, Leonard Everett *artist, writer, educator*
Frankel, Paul Warren *insurance executive, physician*
Frey, Dale Franklin *financial investment company executive, manufacturing company executive*
Gallagher, Michael Robert *consumer products company executive*
Gold, Richard N. *management consultant*
Hagelstein, Robert Philip *publisher*
Hayden, Vern Clarence *financial planner*
Hotchner, Aaron Edward *author*
Jacobs, Jeffrey Lee *lawyer, education network company executive*
Kelly, Paul Knox *investment banker*
†Klein, Woody *writer, editor, educator*
Knopf, Alfred, Jr. *retired publisher*
Kosakow, James Matthew *lawyer*
Kurz, Mitchell Howard *marketing communications executive*
Lopker, Anita Mae *psychiatrist*
Martin, Ralph Guy *writer*
Mc Bride, Thomas Frederick *lawyer, former university dean, government official*
McCormack, Donald Paul *newspaper consultant*
McElroy, Abby Lucille Wolman *financial consultant*
McFarland, Richard M. *executive recruiting consultant*
McKane, David Bennett *business executive*
Meinke, Alan Kurt *surgeon*
Milton, Catherine Higgs *public service entrepreneur*
Murphy, Thomas John *publishing executive*
Nathan, Irwin *business systems company executive*
Nedom, H. Arthur *petroleum consultant*
Nolte, Richard Henry *political science researcher, consultant*
O'Keefe, John David *investment specialist*
O'Leary, James John *economist*
Rastegar, Farzad Ali *investment banker*
Razzano, Pasquale Angelo *lawyer*
Ready, Robert James *financial company executive*
Reilly, Anne Caulfield (Nancy Reilly) *painter*
Rodiger, W. Gregory, III *financial executive*
Rogan, Stephen Joseph *software implementation consultant*
Rose, Reginald *television writer, producer*
Ross, John Michael *editor, magazine publisher*
Sacks, Herbert Simeon *psychiatrist, educator, consultant*
Saxl, Richard Hildreth *lawyer*
Schriever, Fred Martin *management consultant, financial investor*
Sheiman, Ronald Lee *lawyer*
†Siff, Marlene Ida *artist, designer*
Solum, John Henry *flutist, educator, author*
Stashower, Michael David *retired manufacturing company executive*
Stewart, Martha Kostyra *editor-in-chief, lecturer, author*
†Strmecki, Marin J. *foundation executive*
Swiggart, Carolyn Clay *lawyer*
Walton, Alan George *venture capitalist*
Wayne, Kurt Christopher *architect*
Wayne, Neil Russell *investment management company executive*
Weissman, Robert Evan *information services company executive*

Wethersfield
†Armstrong, John J. *state agency administrator*
Edwards, Kenneth S. *principal*
Franco, Carole Ann *international consultant*
Jenks, Dennis *publishing executive*
Karwic, Richard A. *management consultant, educator*
†Mann, Edward H. *state official*
Osborne, Louise *publishing executive*

White Plains
Turner, Stephen Miller *lawyer, oil company executive*

Whitneyville
Miller, Walter Richard, Jr. *banker*

Willimantic
Carter, David George, Sr. *university administrator*
Enggas, Grace Falcetta *university administrator*
Mann, Prem Singh *economics educator*
Peagler, Owen F. *college administrator*
†Perch, Theodore Lesco *library director, artist*
Stoloff, David L. *education educator*

Willington
Rogers, Diana Florence *research scientist*

Wilton
Adams, Thomas Tilley *lawyer*
Bishop, William Wade *advertising executive*
Black, Rita Ann *communications executive*
Brown, James Thompson, Jr. *computer information scientist, logistics specialist*
Campbell, Robert Ayerst *accounting company executive*
Caravatt, Paul Joseph, Jr. *communications company executive*
Cassidy, George Thomas *international business development consultant*
Cook, Jay Michael *accounting company executive*
Copeland, James E., Jr. *financial service executive*
Eisen, Glenn Philip *management consultant, teacher*
Flesher, Margaret Covington *corporate communications consultant*
Forger, Robert Durkin *retired professional association administrator*
Greene, Howard Roger *educational consultant*
Grunewald, Donald *former college president, educator*
Healy, James Casey *lawyer*
Hersh, Ira Paul *tax and financial planning consultant*
†Hughes, Joan Mottola *education association representative*
Juran, Joseph Moses *engineer*
Kangas, Edward A. *accounting firm executive*
Kenton, James Alan *healthcare products executive*
Kovak, Ellen B. *public relations firm executive*
Kriss, Patricia Anne *health services executive*
Lamb, Frederic Davis *retired lawyer*
Martimucci, Richard Anthony *engineering company executive*
Maruyama, Karl Satoru *graphic designer*
†McCracken, Douglas M. *consultant company executive*
Mc Dannald, Clyde Elliott, Jr. *management consultation company executive*
Nickel, Albert George *advertising agency executive*
Oberstar, Helen Elizabeth *retired cosmetics company executive*
†Parrett, William G. *consultant company executive*
Paulson, Loretta Nancy *psychoanalyst*
Pethley, Lowell Sherman *management consultant*
Poundstone, Sally *library director*
Scheinman, Stanley Bruce *international financial executive, lawyer*
Sideroff, Barry *advertising executive*
Slater, Ralph Evan *lawyer*
Van Riper, Robert Austin *writer, retired public relations executive*
Weiland, Juliette Marie *public relations executive, freelance writer and photographer*

Winchester
Firimita, Florin Ion *artist, educator, curator*

Windsor
Ferraro, John Francis *business executive, financier*
Garde, Anand Madhav *materials scientist*
Goldman, Ethan Harris *retail executive*
Kamerschen, Robert Jerome *consumer products executive*
Koussa, Harold Alan *insurance account executive*
Mangold, John Frederic *manufacturing company executive, former naval officer*
Morelli, Carmen *lawyer*
Sears, Sandra Lee *computer consultant*

Windsor Locks
Heisler, Elwood Douglas *hotel executive*
Trubia, Michael Leo *retired army officer, business administrator*

Winsted
†Finch, Frank Herschel, Jr. *lawyer*

Wolcott
Gerace, Robert F. *secondary school principal*
Regan, Michael Frederick *school psychologist*

Woodbridge
Alvine, Robert *industrialist, entrepreneur, international business leader*
Bondy, Philip Kramer *physician, educator*
Ecklund, Constance Cryer *French language educator*
Kleiner, Diana Elizabeth Edelman *art history educator, administrator*
†Menchaca, Frank *editorial director*
Nolan, Victoria *theater director*
Ostfeld, Alexander Marion *advertising agency executive*
†Roche, Raymond Laird *artist*
Van Sinderen, Alfred White *former telephone company executive*

Woodbury
Fiederowicz, Walter Michael *lawyer*
Marsching, Ronald Lionel *lawyer, former precision instrument company executive*
Moeckel, Henry Theodore *architect*
Skinner, Brian John *geologist, educator*

Woodstock
Boote, Alfred Shepard *marketing researcher, educator*
Susla, Jeffrey Jonathan *English language educator*

Woodstock Valley
Allaby, Stanley Reynolds *clergyman*

DELAWARE

Bear
Cairns, Sara Albertson *physical education educator*
Davis, Richard Frank *state legislator*
Hersi, Dorothy Talbert *education educator*
Stewart, Shirley Anne *assistant principal*

Bethany Beach
Gale, Robert L. *educational association administrator, consultant*

Bridgeville
Burns, Vicki Lynn *writer, poet*

Camden Wyoming
Porterfield, Craig Allen *psychologist, consultant*

Claymont
Doto, Paul Jerome accountant
Lewis, George Withrow business executive
†Morra, Daniel Rocco physician

Dagsboro
Lally, Richard Francis aviation security consultant, former association executive, former government official

Delmar
Madden, Cynthia Ann pediatric and family nurse practitioner, educator
Tasker, John Baker veterinary medical educator, college dean

Dover
†Amato, Anthony J. director state aviation department
Angstadt, F. V. language arts and theatre arts educator
Bair, Myrna Lynn state senator
Bookhammer, Eugene Donald state government official
Braverman, Ray Howard secondary school educator
Britt, Maisha Dorrah protective services official
Carey, V. George farmer, state legislator
Carper, Thomas Richard governor
Cook, Nancy W. state legislator
Delauder, William B. academic administrator
Deuble, Lottie Edwards missionary, receptionist
DeVane, Jackie head coach women's basketball
Ellingsworth, Alan D. police superintendent
Ennis, Bruce Clifford lawyer
Flayhart, William Henry history educator
Freel, Edward J. state official
Gorum, Jacquelyne W. dean, social work educator
Hartnett, Maurice A., III judge
Henry, Margaret Rose state legislator
Hoff, Samuel Boyer political science educator
Jones, Jay Paul environmental engineer
Lorton, Lewis researcher, computer executive, dentist
Lowell, Howard Parsons government records administrator
Maroney, Jane P. state legislator
Minner, Ruth Ann state official
Olagunju, Amos Omotayo computer science educator, consultant
Ornauer, Richard Lewis retired educational association administrator
Pelzer, Linda Lee English language educator
Richman, Joseph Herbert public health services official
Smith, Charles Nathaniel academic administrator
Smyth, Joel Douglas newspaper executive
Stone, F. L. Peter lawyer
Streetman, Lee George sociology educator, criminology educator
†Sylvester, Gregg C. state official, physician
†Tarburton, John F. state agency administrator
†Taylor, Stan corrections department commissioner
Taylor, Suzonne Berry Stewart real estate broker
Twilley, Joshua Marion lawyer
Vaughn, James T. former state police officer, state senator
Wagner, Nancy Hughes secondary school educator, state legislator
Warner, Raymond Melvin county official
Wasfi, Sadiq Hassan chemistry educator
Wetherall, Robert Shaw librarian
Williams, Donna Lee H. state agency adminstrator
Wilson, Clealyn Bullock elementary education educator
Wilson, Samuel Mayhew surgeon
Wisneski, Sharon Marie critical care nurse, educator
†Woodruff, Sheri L. state official

Fenwick Island
Dickerson, Joseph Alfred retired sales executive

Frederica
Schulz, David A. author

Georgetown
Holland, Randy James state supreme court justice
Pippin, Kathryn Ann state agency administrator

Greenville
DeWees, Donald Charles securities company executive
Dombeck, Harold Arthur insurance company executive
Levitt, George retired chemist
Reynolds, Nancy Bradford duPont (Mrs. William Glasgow Reynolds) sculptor

Harrington
Quillen, George R. state legislator

Hockessin
Mills, George Alexander retired science administrator
Sawin, Nancy Churchman educator, artist, historian

Laurel
Kile, Kenda Jones educational consultant

Lewes
Adams, John Pletch orthopaedic surgeon
Boyer, John Strickland biochemist, biophysics
Fried, Jeffrey Michael health care administrator
Nehrling, Arno Herbert, Jr. retired chemical company executive
Smith, George H.P. retired elementary educator

Lincoln
Ashley, Linda Ann nurse

Milford
Ferrari, Mercedes V secondary education educator
Sherman, Jane Ehlinger nursing educator
Trott, Edward Ashley reproductive endocrinologist
Walls-Culotta, Sandra L. educational administrator
†Wilkerson, Pamela Helen nurse
Yindra, Meredith Kaye nursing administrator, realtor

Millsboro
Derrickson, Shirley Jean Baldwin elementary school educator
Townsend, P(reston) Coleman agricultural business executive

Millville
McCabe, Margaret Clark family practice nurse

Montchanin
Freytag, Richard Arthur banker
Hall, Robert Paul social services administrator
†Melloy, Joseph Patrick, Sr. consulting company executive
Olney, Robert C. diversified products manufacturing executive

New Castle
Almquist, Don illustrator, artist
†Amari, Jane editor
Bellenger, George Collier, Jr. physics educator
Brzoska, Denise Jeanne paralegal
Cansler, Leslie Ervin retired newspaper editor
Cope, Maurice Erwin art history educator
†Doberstein, Audrey K. college president
†Epstein, Jonathan Daniel journalist
Spence, Terry R. state legislator

Newark
Allen, Herbert Ellis environmental chemistry educator
Amick, Steven Hammond senator, lawyer
Baiul, Oksana figure skater
Bareford, William John chemical engineer
Barteau, Mark Alan chemical engineering and chemistry educator
Bergström, Anna foreign language educator
Bolton, Carile Orville Bogy auditor, accountant
Brown, Hilton visual arts educator, artist
Buchanan, Thomas Steven biomechanics educator
Bunkše, Edmunds Valdemārs geographer, educator, consultant
Burmeister, John Luther chemistry educator, consultant
Byrne, John Michael energy and environmental policy educator, researcher
Campbell, Linzy Leon molecular biology researcher, educator
Carter, Mae Riedy retired academic official, consultant
Cason, June Macnabb musician, educator, arts administrator
Cawley, Charles M. banker
Cheng, Alexander Hung-Darh engineering educator, consultant
Christy, Charles Wesley, III industrial engineering educator
†Cole, Peter linguistics educator
Collins, George Edwin computer scientist, mathematician, educator
Colton, David Lem mathematician, educator
Curtis, James C. cultural organization administrator/history educator
Daniels, William Burton physicist, educator
Day, Robert Androus English language educator, former library director, editor, publisher
DeCherney, George Stephen research scientist, research facility administrator
†Desi, Laurence physician
DiRenzo, Gordon James sociologist, psychologist, educator
Doberenz, Alexander R. nutrition educator, chemist
Esrey, Elizabeth Gove Goodier chemist, biologist
Evans, Dennis Hyde chemist, educator
Evenson, Paul Arthur physics educator
†Gates, Barbara T. English literature educator
Giacco, Alexander Fortunatus chemical industry executive
Godwin, Ralph Edward computer operator
Goodman, Susan English language educator
†Gore, Genevieve Walton company executive
Gore, Robert W. electronics executive
Graham, Frances Keesler (Mrs. David Tredway Graham) psychologist, educator
Grayson, Richard Andrew aerospace engineer
Gronka, M(artin) Steven educational association executive, film and television producer
†Grossman, Jonathan Hamilton English literature educator, researcher
Gulick, Walter Lawrence psychologist, former college president
Halio, Jay Leon language professional, educator
Homer, William Innes art history educator, art expert, author
Hunsperger, Elizabeth Jane art and design consultant, educator
Hutton, David Glenn environmental scientist, consultant, chemical engineer
Jenkins, McKay Bradley English language educator, journalist
Jordan, Robert Reed geologist, educator
Kasprzak, Lucian Alexander physicist, researcher, technical manager
Keene, William Blair state education official
Kleinman, R. E. mathematician, educator
Lathrop, Thomas Albert language educator
†Lemay, J.A. Leo American literature educator
Lemole, Gerald Michael surgeon
Lewis, Horacio Delano consultant, educator
Lomax, Kenneth Mitchell agricultural engineering educator
Lynch, Thomas Gregory educational program administrator
Mangone, Gerard J. international and maritime law educator
Martin, Tina basketball coach
Mather, John Russell climatologist, educator
McLain, William Tome principal
Mitchell, Peter Kenneth, Jr. educational consultant, association administrator
Molz, Robert Joseph manufacturing company executive
Murray, Richard Bennett physics educator
†Nahera, Kristina Luckanish educator
Neal, James Preston state senator, project engineer
Ness, Norman Frederick astrophysicist, educator, administrator
Nye, John Calvin agricultural engineer, educator
Palley, Marian Lief political science educator
Poplos, Charles Mitchell, III social science educator, educational technologist
Protokowicz, Nora Jane nursing administrator
Roselle, David Paul university president, mathematics educator
Rowe, Charles Alfred artist, designer, educator
Sandler, Stanley Irving chemical engineering educator
Satinoff, Evelyn educator
Schiavelli, Melvyn David academic administrator, chemistry educator, researcher
Sparks, Donald Lewis soil chemistry educator
Stark, Robert Martin mathematician, civil engineer, educator
Steiner, Roger Jacob linguistics educator, author, researcher
Stiner, Frederic Matthew, Jr. accounting educator, consultant, writer
Szeri, Andras Z. engineering educator
Thureen, Dean Richard molecular biologist
Tolles, Bryant Franklin, Jr. history and art history educator
Townsend, Brenda S. educational association administrator
Trofimenko, Swiatoslaw chemist, researcher, consultant
†Unger, Donald G. psychologist, educator
Venezky, Richard Lawrence English language educator
Walker, Jeanne Murray English educator
Wetlaufer, Donald Burton biochemist, educator
†Wilder, Margaret G. urban policy educator
Wolters, Raymond historian, educator
Woo, S. B. (Shien-Biau Woo) former lieutenant governor, physics educator
Wu, Jin oceanographer, educator, engineer
Yan, Xiao-Hai science center director, educator
Zank, Gary Paul phyicist

Newport
†Bayard, Richard H. political party official
Kirkland, Joseph J. research chemist

Odessa
Pulinka, Steven M. historic site director

Rehoboth Beach
Johnson, Kermit Douglas minister, retired military officer
McCartney, James Harold retired newspaper columnist, educator, journalist
Truitt, Suzanne real estate broker
Warden, Richard Dana government labor union official

Rockland
Harvey, Andre sculptor
Levinson, John Milton obstetrician, gynecologist
Rubin, Alan A. pharmaceutical and biotechnology consultant

Seaford
Petrea, Patricia Beth special education educator

Smyrna
Hutchison, James Arthur, Jr. architectural and engineering company executive

Wilmington
†Ahn, James Jongho legislative aide
Amsler, Karen Marie medical technologist, scientist
Arrington, Charles Hammond, Jr. retired chemical company executive
Athreya, Balu H. pediatrics educator
Aungst, Bruce Jeffrey pharmaceutical company scientist
Bader, John Merwin lawyer
†Baker, Pamela W. accountant
Balick, Helen Shaffer retired judge
Battaglia, Basil Richard political party official, company executive
Baumann, Julian Henry, Jr. lawyer
Benes, Solomon biomedical scientist, physician
Benson, Barbara Ellen state agency administrator
Blevins, Patricia M. state legislator
Bounds-Seemans, Pamella J. artist
Brady, M. Jane state attorney general
Brown Leatherberry, Thomas Henry gospel music company executive, clergy member
Bruni, Stephen Thomas art museum director
Busche, Robert Marion chemical engineer, consultant
Carey, John Patrick, III lawyer
Carpenter, Edmund Nelson, II retired lawyer
Caruso, Nicholas Dominic protective services official
Cason, Roger Lee retired chemical company executive, educator, consultant
Chipman, Bruce Lewis English language educator
Clark, Esther Frances law educator
Collins, Francis Winfield chemical company executive
Connelly, Donald Preston electric and gas utility company executive
Copper, William P. composer, computer consultant
Cornelison, Floyd Shovington, Jr. retired psychiatrist, former educator
Crittenden, Eugene Dwight, Jr. chemical company executive
Curran, Barbara Sanson lawyer
D'Angelo, Arthur E. advertising agency executive
Del Pesco, Susan Marie Carr state judge
†DeMatteis, Claire state director
Devine, Donn lawyer, genealogist, former city official
DiLiberto, Richard Anthony, Jr. lawyer
Du Pont, Pierre Samuel, IV lawyer, former governor of Delaware
Eichler, Thomas P. state agency administrator
Eleuterio, Marianne Kingsbury retired genetics educator
Elliott, Roxanne Snelling educational consultant to independent schools
Emanuel, Abraham Gabriel photo processing company executive, consultant
Emmert, Richard Eugene retired professional association executive
Farnan, Joseph James, Jr. federal judge
Fenton, Wendell lawyer
Frelick, Robert Westcott physician
Gebelein, Richard Stephen judge, former state attorney general
George, Orlando John, Jr. state representative, college administrator
Gewirtz, Leonard Benjamin rabbi
Gibson, Joseph Whitton, Jr. retired chemical company executive
Gilliam, James H., Jr. lawyer, private investor, consultant
Goldberg, Morton Edward pharmacologist
Goldstein, Jack Charles lawyer
Graves, Thomas Ashley, Jr. educational administrator
Green, James Samuel lawyer
Griffin, Jo Ann Thomas retired financial planner, tax specialist
Grossman, Jerome Kent lawyer, accountant
Gunzenhauser, Stephen Charles conductor
†Hall, Gene M. consumer protection agency administrator
Harley, Robison Dooling physician, educator
Harris, Robert Laird minister, theology educator emeritus
Herdeg, John Andrew lawyer
†Hockersmith, Charles Edwin information technology educator
†Holliday, Charles O., Jr. chemical company executive
Holtzman, Arnold Harold chemical company executive
Howard, Richard James mycology researcher
Hurley, William Joseph chemical company executive
Ianni, Francis Alphonse state official, former army officer
Igwe, Godwin Joseph chemical engineer
Ikeda, Satoshi thoracic and cardiovascular surgeon
Inselman, Laura Sue pediatrician
Jacobs, Jack Bernard judge
Jezl, Barbara Ann chemist, automation consultant
†Ji, Zhenghua computer engineer
Johns, Emerson Thomas chemical company executive
Kalil, James, Sr. investment executive
Kane, Edward Rynex retired chemical company executive, corporate director
Kaye, Neil Scott psychiatrist
Kennedy, William James pharmaceutical company executive
Kerr, Janet Spence physiologist, pharmacologist
Kimmel, Morton Richard lawyer
Kirk, Richard Dillon lawyer
Kirkpatrick, Andrew Booth, Jr. lawyer
Klayman, Barry Martin lawyer
Kneavel, Ann Callanan humanities educator, communications consultant
Kneavel, Thomas Charles, Jr. psychologist
Kohler, Frederick William, Jr. pharmacist
Kristol, Daniel Marvin lawyer
Krol, John A. retired diversified chemicals executive
Kutemeyer, Peter Martin industrial engineering executive
Kwolek, Stephanie Louise chemist
Lahvis, Sylvia Leistyna art historian, educator, curator
Laird, Walter Jones, Jr. investment professional
Latchum, James Levin federal judge
†Lazar, Kathleen Ellen clinical psychologist
Lerner, Alfred real estate and financial executive
Lewis, Mary Therese artist
Liew, Fah Pow mechanical engineer
Linderman, Jeanne Herron priest
Longobardi, Joseph J. federal judge
Macel, Stanley Charles, III lawyer
Magee, Thomas Hugh lawyer
Maggard, Woodrow Wilson, Jr. management consultant
Maley, Patricia Ann preservation planner
Malik, John Stephen lawyer
Marcali, Jean Gregory chemist, retired
Maxwell, Audrey L. healthcare administrator
McBride, David Clinton lawyer
McDonough, Kenneth Lee disease management company executive
McKelvie, Roderick R. federal judge
Meitner, Pamela lawyer, educator
Mekler, Arlen B. lawyer, chemist
Michel, Sandra Seaton writer
†Milbury-Steen, Sally (Sarah) Louise administrator not-for-profit association, advocate
Moore, Carl Gordon chemist, educator
Morgan, Craig Douglas orthopaedic surgeon
Morris, Ronald Anthony county official
†Mullaney, Timothy P. United States marshall
Murphy, Arthur Thomas systems engineer
Nelson, Dewey Allen neurologist, educator
Newell, Katherine Claiborne librarian
Nwankwo, Emeka Obioma chemical engineer, educator, entrepreneur
Olson, Leroy Calvin retired educational administration educator
Parshall, George William research chemist
Patton, James Leeland, Jr. lawyer
Pell, Sidney epidemiologist
Perdue, James food products executive
Perez, Eduardo Hector mechanical engineering consultant
Perse, Aria Leon international business advanced technologies executive
Peterson, Russell Wilbur former association executive, former state governor
Pollock, Paul Edward insurance executive
Porter, John Francis, III banker
Porter, Kenneth Wayne actuary
Reeder, Charles Benton economic consultant
Robertson, David Wayne pharmaceutical company executive
Robinson, Sue L(ewis) federal judge
†Rodgers, Stephen John lawyer, consultant
Rogoski, Patricia Diana financial executive
Rose, Selwyn H. chemical company executive
Roth, Jane Richards federal judge
Rothrock, Richard Edward sculptor, stone specialist
Rothschild, Steven James lawyer
Rudge, Howard J. corporate lawyer
St. Clair, Jesse Walton, Jr. retired savings and loan executive
Salinger, Frank Max lawyer
†Saltarelli, Michael A. priest
Salzstein, Richard Alan biomedical engineer, bioprocessing engineer
Schwartz, Marshall Zane pediatric surgeon
Schwartz, Murray Merle federal judge
Sganga, John B. furniture holding company executive
Shapiro, Irving Saul lawyer
Shevchuck, Harry retired image systems consultant
Shipley, Samuel Lynn advertising and public relations executive
†Simon, Elisabeth Page nonprofit organization administrator
Sleet, Gregory M. lawyer
Sly, John Eugene advertising and marketing consultant
Smith, Craig Bennett lawyer
Smith, S(tewart) Gregory ophthalmologist, inventor, product developer, consultant, author
Smook, Malcolm Andrew chemist, chemical company executive
Stapleton, Walter King federal judge
Stein, Robert Benjamin biomedical researcher, physician
†Tankersley, Julianne Grandell elementary and secondary education educator
†Thomes, Harry Scott real estate consultant
Thurman, Herman Robert, Jr. structural engineer
Tigani, Bruce William lawyer
Trainham, James A., III chemical engineer
Trostle, Mary Pat judge
Uffner, Michael S. retail automotive executive
Vajk, Hugo manufacturing executive
Vary, Eva Maros retired chemical company executive

Vattilana, Joseph William retired chief state safety inspector
Veasey, Eugene Norman chief justice
Wachstein, Joan Martha dental hygienist
Wallace, Jesse Wyatt pharmaceutical scientist
Walsh, Joseph Thomas state supreme court justice
†Walsh, Peter J. federal judge
Ward, Rodman, Jr. lawyer
†Wasserman, Edel scientist, executive
Wells, James Robert pharmaceutical company executive
Wesler, Ken theater company manager
Wheeler, M. Catherine organization executive
Wier, Richard Royal, Jr. lawyer, inventor
Willard, John Martin lawyer
Williams, Evelyn Lois chemicals executive, safety consultant
Williams, Richmond Dean library appraiser, consultant
Woods, Robert A. chemical company executive
Woolard, Edgar S., Jr. chemical company executive
Wright, Caleb Merrill federal judge
Wright, Vernon Hugh Carroll bank executive
Ziolkowska-Boehm, Aleksandra writer

Winterthur

Hummel, Charles Frederick museum official
Lanmon, Dwight Pierson museum director

DISTRICT OF COLUMBIA

Bolling AFB

†Dendinger, William J. career officer, chaplain
Hallion, Richard Paul aerospace historian, museum consultant
†Jones, Hiram L. (Doc) career officer, chaplain
†Mabry, Earl W. military officer
Randolph, Leonard McElRoy, Jr. career officer
†Wyrick, Michael K. military officer

Fort Mcnair

†Chilcoat, Richard Allen army officer, university president
†Clodfelter, Mark A. air force officer, educator
†Engel, Richard L. career officer
Swihart, James W., Jr. diplomat

Washington

Aaron, David L. diplomat
Aaron, Henry Jacob economics educator
Aaronson, David Ernest lawyer, educator
Abbott, Alden Francis lawyer, government official, educator
Abbott, Corinne fundraiser
†Abbott, Ernest B. emergency management administrator
Abel, Elie reporter, broadcaster, educator
Abeles, Charles Calvert retired lawyer
Abelson, Philip Hauge physicist
Abercrombie, Neil congressman
Abernathy, Charles Owen toxicologist
Ablard, Charles David lawyer
Able, Edward H. association executive
Abler, Ronald Francis geography educator
Abraham, Katharine Gail economics educator
Abraham, Spencer senator
Abrams, Elliott think-tank executive, writer, foreign affairs analyst
Abramson, Jill newspaper publishing executive
Abshire, David Manker diplomat, research executive
Acheson, David Campion lawyer, author, policy analyst
Acheson, Eleanor Dean federal government official
Ackerman, F. Kenneth, Jr. health facility administrator
Ackerman, Gary Leonard congressman
Ackerman, Kenneth David federal agency administrator
†Ackerman, Michael W. career officer
Ackerson, Nels J(ohn) lawyer
†Adam, Nancy Elizabeth library and information manager
Adams, A. John Bertrand public affairs consultant
Adams, Lee Stephen lawyer, banker
Adams, Lorraine reporter
†Adams, Patrick O. career officer
Adams, Robert Edward journalist
†Adams, Roger C. lawyer
Adamsons, Uldis government official
Aderholt, Robert B. congressman
Adler, Howard, Jr. lawyer
Adler, Howard Bruce lawyer
Adler, Robert Martin lawyer
Affens, Steven Charles television photojournalist
Affronti, Lewis Francis, Sr. microbiologist, educator
Agres, Theodore Joel editor
†Aguirre-Baca, Francisco publisher
Aguirre-Sacasa, Francisco Xavier international banker, diplomat
Aguirre-Sacasa, Rafael Eugenio marketing executive
Ahl, Alwynelle Self zoology, ecology and veterinary medical executive
Ahmann, Mathew Hall social action organization administrator, consultant
Ain, Sanford King lawyer
Aisenberg, Irwin Morton lawyer
Akaka, Daniel Kahikina senator
Akey, Steven John public relations executive
Akhter, Mohammad Nasir physician, government public health administrator
Alatis, James Efstathios university dean emeritus
Alberts, Bruce Michael federal agency administrator, foundation administrator, biochemist
Albertson, Terry L. lawyer
†Albicker, Robert federal official
Albrecht, Kathe Hicks art historian, visual resources manager
Albright, Joseph William army officer
Albright, Madeleine Korbel federal official, diplomat, political scientist
Alexander, Arthur Jacob economist
†Alexander, Brad L. legislative staff member
Alexander, Clifford Joseph lawyer
Alexander, Dawn Alicia public relations executive
Alexander, Donald Crichton lawyer
Alexander, Joseph Kunkle, Jr. physicist
†Alexander, Mary K. electronics company executive
Allan, Richmond Frederick lawyer
Allard, A. Wayne senator, veterinarian
Allard, Nicholas W. lawyer
Allbritton, Joe Lewis diversified holding company executive
Allen, Edward Lawrence, Jr. government relations executive, lobbyist
Allen, Frederick Warner federal agency executive
†Allen, Melissa J. federal agency administrator
Allen, Richard Vincent international business consultant, bank executive
Allen, Thomas H. congressman, lawyer
Allen, William Hayes lawyer
Allen, William Jere minister
Allen, William L. editor
Allnutt, Robert Frederick management consultant, corporate director
Alperovitz, Gar author, educator
†Altenburg, John D., Jr. career officer
†Altenhofen, Jane Ellen federal agency administrator, auditor
Alton, Bruce Taylor educational consultant
Altschul, Alfred Samuel airline executive
Alvarez, Aida federal agency administrator
Alvarez, Scott G. federal official
Alward, Ruth Rosendall nursing consultant
Ambach, Gordon Mac Kay educational association executive
Ambrose, Myles Joseph lawyer
Ames, Frank Anthony percussionist, film producer
Amling, Frederick economist, educator, investment manager
Amolsch, Arthur Lewis publishing executive
†Anarde, Russell J. career officer
Andersen, Robert Allen retired government official
Anderson, Beverly Jacques academic administrator
Anderson, David Turpeau government official, judge
Anderson, Dean William educational administrator
Anderson, Donald Morgan entomologist
†Anderson, Edward G., III army officer
†Anderson, Frank J., Jr. career officer
Anderson, Frederick Randolph, Jr. lawyer, law educator
Anderson, John Bayard lawyer, educator, former congressman
Anderson, Samuel David government affairs consultant
Andewelt, Roger B. federal judge
Andrew, Joseph Jerald lawyer, political party official
†Andrews, James E. career officer
Andrews, John Frank editor, author, educator
Andrews, Laureen E. foundation administrator
Andrews, Lewis Davis, Jr. trade association executive
Andrews, Mark Joseph lawyer
Andrews, Robert E. congressman
Anfinson, Thomas Elmer government financial administrator
Angier, Natalie Marie science journalist
Angula, Helmut Kangulohi Namibian government official
Ansary, Cyrus A. investment company executive, lawyer
Anschuetz, Norbert Lee retired diplomat, banker
Anthony, Sheila Foster government official
Anthony, Virginia Quinn Bausch medical association executive
†Antonelli, Angela Maria policy analyst
Apostolos-Cappadona, Diane Pan religion and art educator
Apperson, Bernard James lawyer
Apple, Martin Allen scientific federation executive, educator
Apple, Raymond Walter, Jr. journalist
Applebaum, Harvey Milton lawyer
Appleberry, James Bruce higher education association executive
Apud, Jose Antonio psychiatrist, psychopharmacologist, educator
Arana, Marie editor, writer
Arapian, Linda pediatrics nurse
Arbit, Terry Steven lawyer
Archer, Glenn LeRoy, Jr. federal circuit judge
Archer, William Reynolds, Jr. (Bill Reynolds) congressman
Archibald, George reporter
Arena, Kelli news correspondent
Arend, Anthony Clark international relations educator
Arent, Albert Ezra lawyer
Arkilic, Galip Mehmet mechanical engineer, educator
Arling, Bryan Jeremy internist
Arling, Donna Dickson social worker
Arlook, Ira Arthur non-profit association executive
Armacost, Michael Hayden research institution executive, ambassador
Armaly, Mansour F(arid) ophthalmologist, educator
†Armstrong, Alexandra financial advisor
Armstrong, David Andrew federal agency official, retired army officer
†Armstrong, Michael J. federal agency administrator
†Armstrong, Robert retired federal agency administrator
†Armstrong, Spence M. aerospace technology administrator
Arndt, Richard Tallmadge writer, consultant
Arnez, Nancy Levi educational leadership educator
Arnold, G. Dewey, Jr. accountant
Arnold, Gary Howard film critic
Arnold, William Edwin foundation administrator, consultant
Arnovitz, Benton Mayer editor
Arundel, John Howard financial consultant
Aschheim, Joseph economist, educator
Ashcroft, John David senator
Ashe, Lincoln Emil police officer
Ashton, Richard M. federal lawyer
Asker, James Robert magazine editor
Åslund, Anders economist
Atcheson, Richard editor
Atherton, Alfred Leroy, Jr. former foreign service officer
Atherton, Charles Henry federal commission administrator
Atlas, Liane Wiener writer
Atlas, Terry journalist
Attaway, David Henry retired federal research administrator, oceanographer
Attkisson, Sharyl T. newscaster, correspondent, writer
†Attridge, Patrick J. federal judge
Atwood, James R. lawyer
Atwood, John Brian federal agency administrator
Audrey-Taylor, Davida secondary education educator
Auerbach, Stuart Charles development loan fund administrator, journalist
Augustyn, Frederick John, Jr. librarian
Aukofer, Frank Alexander journalist
Auld, Albert Michael sculptor
Aultman, William Robert career officer
Auten, John Harold government official
Avery, Byllye Yvonne health association administrator
Avil, Richard D., Jr. lawyer
Axelrod, Jonathan Gans lawyer
Ayer, Donald Belton lawyer
†Ayres, David T. senatorial administrator
Ayres, Edward Hutchinson editor
Ayres, Mary Ellen government official
Ayres, Richard Edward lawyer
Azcuenaga, Mary Laurie government official
†Babb, Valerie M. English educator, writer
Babbitt, Bruce Edward federal official
Babby, Ellen Reisman education administrator
Babby, Lon S. lawyer
Babcock, Charles R. columnist
Baca, Edward Dionicio national guard officer
Bachman, David M. ophthalmologist
Bachman, Kenneth Leroy, Jr. lawyer
Bachman, Leonard physician, retired federal official
Bachrach, Eve Elizabeth lawyer
Bachula, Gary R. federal official
Bachus, Spencer T., III congressman, lawyer
†Backlin, Jim legislative staff member
Bacon, Elinor R. goverment agency administrator
†Bacon, Kenneth H. federal agency administrator, editor, journalist
Bader, John Burkhardt political scientist, educator
Bader, Rochelle Linda (Shelley Bader) educational administrator
Bader, William Banks historian, foundation executive, former corporate executive
Baer, Michael Alan political scientist, educator
†Baer, William J. lawyer
Bagge, Carl Elmer association executive, lawyer, consultant
Bahr, Morton trade union executive
†Bahret, Mary Ellen press secretary
Bailey, Betty L. federal agency administrator
Bailey, Charles Waldo, II journalist, author
Bailey, Nancy Joyce educator
Bainum, Peter Montgomery aerospace engineer, consultant
†Baird, Brian N. congressman
†Baker, D. James oceanographic and atmospheric administrator
Baker, Emily Lind editor, digital library specialist
Baker, James Robert federal agency administrator
†Baker, Jennifer L. strategic communications consultant
Baker, Richard Hugh congressman
Baldacci, John Elias congressman
Baldyga, Leonard J. retired diplomat, international consultant
Balfour, Ana Maria office manager
Ball, (Robert) Markham lawyer
Ballard, Frederic Lyman, Jr. lawyer
†Ballard, Joe N. career officer
Ballenger, Thomas Cass congressman
Ballentine, J. Gregory economist
Ballou, Jeffrey Pierre producer
Balutis, Alan federal agency administrator
Balz, Daniel John newspaper editor, journalist
Bandow, Douglas Leighton editor, columnist, policy consultant
Banta, James Elmer physician, epidemiologist, university dean
Banzhaf, John F., III legal association executive, lawyer
Baquet, Charles R., III federal agency administrator
Baran, Jan Witold lawyer, educator
Barber, Ben Bernard Andrew journalist
Barcia, James A. congressman
Bardin, David J. lawyer
†Barlow, Larry S. federal agency administrator
Barnes, Dennis Norman lawyer
Barnes, Donald Michael lawyer
Barnes, Frederic Wood, Jr. journalist
Barnes, James A. journalist
Barnes, Mark James lawyer
Barnes, Michael Darr lawyer, think tank executive
Barnes, Peter lawyer
Barnes, Shirley Elizabeth foreign service officer
Barnet, Richard Jackson author, educator
Barnett, Arthur Doak political scientist, educator
Barnett, Robert Bruce lawyer
†Baronas, Jean Marie computer systems engineer, educator
†Barr, Mari R. federal agency administrator
Barr, Michael Blanton lawyer
Barr, Robert Laurence, Jr. congressman, lawyer
Barr, William Pelham lawyer, former attorney general of United States
Barram, David J. federal agency administrator
Barrett, Lake H. energy industry executive
Barrett, Laurence Irwin public relations executive, writer
Barrett, Richard David university director, consultant, bank executive
Barrett, Thomas M. congressman
Barrett, William E. congressman
Barringer, Philip E. retired government official
Barr-Kumar, Raj architect
Barron, Jerome Aure law educator
Barrow, Robert Earl retired agricultural organization administrator
Barry, Donald J. government official
Barry, Donald James government official
Barry, John J. labor union leader
Barshefsky, Charlene diplomat
Bartlett, Charles Leffingwell foundation executive, former newspaperman
Bartlett, John Laurence lawyer
Bartlett, Michael John lawyer
Bartlett, Roscoe G. congressman
Bartnoff, Judith judge
Barto, Cheryl educational association administrator, researcher
Barton, William Russell government official
Baruch, Jordan Jay management consultant
Basch, Richard Vennard photographer, producer, writer, director
Bass, Charles F. congressman
Basseches, Robert Treinis lawyer
Bassin, Jules foreign service officer
Batdorf, Lynn Robert horticulturist
Bateman, Herbert Harvell congressman
Bateman, Paul William government official, business executive
Bates, John Cecil, Jr. lawyer
Batla, Raymond John, Jr. lawyer
Battle, Lucius Durham retired educational institution administrator, former diplomat
Baucus, Max S. senator
Baxter, Nevins Dennis bank consultant
Bayh, Evan senator, former governor
Bayly, John Henry, Jr. judge
Beach, Milo C. art museum director
Beach, Walter Eggert retired publishing organization executive
Beale, Betty (Mrs. George K. Graeber) columnist, writer
Beard, Lillian B. McLean physician, consultant
Beatty, Richard Scrivener lawyer
Becerra, Xavier congressman, lawyer
†Beck, Peter Michael economics researcher
Becker, Brandon lawyer
†Becker, Jerome David writer
Becker, Mary Louise political scientist
Beckham, Edgar Frederick educational consultant
Beckwith, Edward Jay lawyer
Beddow, Richard Harold judge
Bedini, Silvio A. historian, author
Bednash, Geraldine Polly association executive
†Beecher, Donna D. human resources administrator
Beecher, William Manuel government official
†Beers, Rand narcotics and law enforcement administrator
Beeson, Virginia Reed naval officer, nurse
Beghe, Renato federal judge
Beisner, John Herbert lawyer
Beizer, Robert A. lawyer
†Bekhechi, Mohammed Abdelwahab lawyer
Bell, Hubert Thomas government official
Bell, James Frederick retired lawyer
Bell, Robert G. federal agency official
Bell, Stephen Robert lawyer
Bellamy, Joe David English language educator, writer
Beller, Herbert N. lawyer
Beller, Melanie federal agency administrator
Bellinger, Edgar Thomson lawyer
Bello, Judith Hippler lawyer
Bellows, Michael Donald foreign service officer
Belman, A. Barry pediatric urologist
Belman, Murray Joel lawyer
Belson, James Anthony judge
Beltz, William Albert publisher
Bender, David Ray library association executive
Benedick, Richard Elliot diplomat
†Benedict, Carol Ann educator
Benedict, Lawrence Neal foreign service officer
Beneke, Patricia Jane federal agency administrator
Benica, Sherry Lynn pediatric critical care nurse
Benken, Eric W. career officer
Bennett, Alexander Elliot lawyer
Bennett, Betty T. English language educator, university dean, writer
Bennett, Carl Roosevelt secondary education teacher
†Bennett, Douglas Philip real estate executive, lawyer
Bennett, Robert F. senator
†Bennett-Maccubbin, Justen Michael journalist, producer
Bentley, James Daniel hospital association executive
Bentley, James Luther journalist
†Benton, Marjorie Craig federal agency administrator
Bentsen, Kenneth E., Jr. congressman
Bercovici, Martin William lawyer
Berendzen, Richard astronomer, educator, author
Beresford, Douglas Lincoln lawyer
Bereuter, Douglas Kent congressman
Berg, Stephen Warren government official
†Berger, Jonathan M. legislative staff member
Berger, Melvin Gerald lawyer
Berger, Paul S. lawyer
Berger, Robert Martin urologist
†Berger, Samuel R. federal official
Bergmann, Barbara Rose economics educator
†Bergren, Scott C. career officer
Bergsten, C. Fred economist
Berkley, Shelley congresswoman
Berl, Joseph M. lawyer
Berlack, Evan Raden lawyer
Berman, Ellen Sue energy and telecommunications executive, theatre producer
Berman, Howard Lawrence congressman
Berman, Marshall Fox lawyer
Bern, Paula Ruth columnist
Berner, Frederic George, Jr. lawyer
Berner, Keith foundation administrator executive
Bernhard, Berl lawyer
Bernstein, Aaron magazine editor
Bernstein, Edwin S. judge
Bernstein, Joan Z. government official
Bernstein, Lionel M. gastroenterologist, educator
Bernstein, Mitchell Harris lawyer
Bernthal, Frederick Michael association executive
Berrington, Craig Anthony lawyer
Berry, Marion congressman
Berry, Mary Frances federal agency administrator, history and law educator
Berry, Morrell John cultural organization administrator
Berryman, Richard Byron lawyer
Berube, Raymond P. federal agency administrator
Berz, David R. lawyer
Besen, Stanley Martin economist
Besozzi, Paul Charles lawyer
Best, Judah lawyer
Betancourt L., Antonio L. association executive
Bice, David F. career officer
Biddle, Catharina Baart artist
Biddle, Livingston Ludlow, Jr. former government official, author, consultant
Biddle, Timothy Maurice lawyer
Biden, Joseph Robinette, Jr. senator
Biechman, John Charles federal agency official
Bienenstock, Arthur Irwin physicist, educator, government official
Bierly, Eugene Wendell meteorologist, science administrator
Bierman, James Norman lawyer
Bigelow, Donald Nevius educational administrator, historian, consultant
Biggert, Judith Borg congresswoman, lawyer
†Biggs, Jeffrey Robert educator
Bilbray, Brian P. congressman
Bilirakis, Michael congressman, lawyer, business executive
Biller, Morris (Moe Biller) union executive
Billington, James Hadley historian, librarian
†Biltchik, David Ellis business consultant
Bingaman, Jeff senator
Binkley, Marilyn Rothman educational research administrator
Birdsall, Nancy professional association administrator
Birnbaum, Norman author, humanities educator
Birnbaum, S. Elizabeth lawyer
Birnkrant, Henry Joseph lawyer
Biro, Susan Lori lawyer
Bishop, James Dodson lawyer, mediator
Bishop, Sanford Dixon, Jr. congressman
Bishop, Wayne Staton lawyer
Bishop, William Peter research scientist
Biskupic, Joan reporter
Biter, Richard M. federal official
Bittman, William Omar lawyer
Black, Stephen Franklin lawyer

Blackwelder, Brent Francis environmentalist
Blagojevich, Rod R. congressman
Blair, James Pease photographer
Blair, Louis Helion foundation executive
Blair, Margaret Mendenhall research economist, consultant
Blair, Robert Allen business executive, lawyer
Blair, Thomas Delano inspector general Smithsonian Institution
Blair, Warren Emerson retired federal judge
Blair, William Draper, Jr. conservationist
Blair, William McCormick, Jr. lawyer
Blake, Jonathan Dewey lawyer
Blanchard, Bruce environmental engineer, government official
Blanchard, Charles Alan lawyer, former state senator
Blasier, Cole political scientist
Blazek-White, Doris lawyer
Bleakley, Peter Kimberley lawyer
Bleicher, Samuel Abram lawyer
Bliss, Donald Tiffany, Jr. lawyer
Blitzer, Charles educational administrator
Bloch, Richard Isaac labor arbitrator
Bloch, Stuart Marshall lawyer
Block, Herbert Lawrence (Herblock) editorial cartoonist
Blodgett, Todd Alan publisher, marketing executive
†Bloom, Bruce hotel executive
Bloomfield, Maxwell Herron, III history and law educator
Bloomfield, Sara museum director
Blum, Margaret D. federal agency administrator
Blumenauer, Earl congressman
Blumenfeld, Jeffrey lawyer, educator
Blumenthal, Ronnie lawyer
†Blumer, Dennis Hull lawyer
Blunt, Roy D. congressman
Bluth, B. J. (Elizabeth Jean Catherine Bluth) sociologist, aerospace technologist
†Blyth, Jonathan J. legislative staff member
Boaz, David Douglas foundation executive
Bodansky, Robert Lee lawyer
Bode, Barbara foundation executive, Internet consultant, entrepreneur
Bodner, John, Jr. lawyer
Boehlert, Sherwood Louis congressman
Boehm, Steven Bruce lawyer
Boehner, John A. congressman
†Boergers, David Paul energy executive
†Boesel, Charles Mather communications professional
Bogard, Lawrence Joseph lawyer
†Bogdanovich, Michele L. legislative staff member
Boggs, George Trenholm lawyer
Boggs, Thomas Hale, Jr. lawyer
Bohlke, Gary Lee lawyer, playwright
Boland, Christopher Thomas, II lawyer
†Bolden, Betty labor relations administrator
Bolden, Charles F., Jr. career officer
Bolling, Landrum Rymer retired academic administrator, writer, consultant
Bolton, John Robert lawyer, former government official
Bond, Christopher Samuel (Kit Bond) senator, lawyer
Bond, Julian civil rights leader
Bonde, Count Peder Carlsson investment company executive
†Bonham, (Andrew) Kent legislative staff member
Bonilla, Henry congressman, broadcast executive
Bonior, David Edward congressman
Bonner, Walter Joseph lawyer
Bono, Mary congresswoman
Bonosaro, Carol Alessandra professional association executive, former government official
Bonvillian, William Boone lawyer
Book, Edward R. consultant, retired association executive
Bookbinder, Hyman H(arry) public affairs counselor
Boone, Theodore Sebastian lawyer
Boorstin, Daniel Joseph historian, lecturer, educator, author, editor
Borelli, John religious organization professional
Borenstein, David Gilbert physician, author
Boright, John Phillips science administrator
Born, Brooksley Elizabeth lawyer
Borsari, George Robert, Jr. lawyer, broadcaster
Borski, Robert Anthony congressman
Borut, Donald J. professional society administrator
Borwick, Richard management consultant
Boskey, Bennett lawyer
Boss, Lenard Barrett lawyer
Boswell, Leonard L. congressman
†Bosworth, Stephen Warren ambassador
Boucher, Frederick C. congressman, lawyer
Boucher, Wayne Irving policy analyst
Boughton, James Murray economist
Bourne, Peter Geoffrey physician, educator, author
Bowen, Margareta Maria interpretation and translation educator
Bowie, Calvert S. architect
Bowman, Dorothy Louise artist
Boxer, Barbara senator
†Boyagian, Levon legislative administrator
Boyd, F. Allen, Jr. farmer, congressman
Boyd, Francis R. geophysicists
Boyd, Stephen Mather arbitrator, mediator, lawyer
Boyette, Van Roy lawyer, consultant
Boyle, John Edward Whiteford cultural organization administrator
Boyle, Patrick Kevin journalist
Bradford, William Allen, Jr. lawyer
Bradford, William Hollis, Jr. lawyer
Bradlee, Benjamin Crowninshield executive editor
Bradley, Amelia Jane lawyer
Bradley, Melvin LeRoy communications company executive
Brady, Kevin congressman
†Brady, Robert A. congressman
Bragg, Lynn Munroe federal agency administrator
Brahms, Thomas Walter engineering institute executive
Brame, Joseph Robert, III lawyer
Bramson, Leon social scientist, educator
†Bramucci, Raymond L. employment and training executive
Brandt, Carl David research virologist
Branegan, James Augustus, III journalist
Brannan, Beverly Wood curator of photography
Brant, Donna Marie journalist
Brazaitis, Thomas Joseph journalist
Breaux, John B. senator, former congressman
Breed, Joseph Illick financial economist
Bregman, Arthur Randolph lawyer, educator
†Breitman, Richard David historian, educator, writer
Brennan, Robin Lynn producer
Brenner, Daniel Leslie lawyer
Brenner, Janet Maybin Walker lawyer
Brenner, Robert David federal agency administrator
Bresee, James Collins federal agency scientist
Bresnahan, Thomas J. radio station executive
Bretzfelder, Deborah May museum exhibit designer, photographer
Breul, Jonathan Dutro government official
Brewster, Bill K. business executive, former congressman
Brewster, Robert Charles diplomat, consultant
Breyer, Stephen Gerald United States supreme court justice
Brick, Barrett Lee lawyer
Brickhouse, Eugene A. federal agency administrator
Briggs, Alan Leonard lawyer
†Briggs, Ethel D. federal agency administrator
Brightup, Craig Steven lobbyist
Brimmer, Andrew Felton economic and financial consultant
Brinkmann, Robert Joseph lawyer
Brintnall, Michael Arthur association executive, political scientist
Bristo, Marca healthcare executive
Britton, Katherine Lela Quainton lawyer
Britton, Leann G. federal official
Brobeck, Stephen James consumer advocate
Brock, Gerald Wayne telecommunications educator
Broder, David Salzer reporter
Brody, Kenneth David investment banker
†Bromwich, Michael Ray federal official
Bronstein, Alvin J. lawyer
Brooke, Edward William lawyer, former senator
Brooks, Daniel Townley lawyer
†Brooks, John W. military officer
Brosnan, Carol Raphael Sarah retired arts administrator, musician
Brotzman, Donald Glenn government official, lawyer
Broun, Elizabeth art historian, museum administrator
Broun, Richard Hadas government administrator
†Brown, Alvin housing and urban development administrator
Brown, Bradford Clement government relations public affairs executive
Brown, Charles Freeman, II lawyer
Brown, Corrine congresswoman
Brown, Dale Susan government administrator, educational program director, writer
Brown, David Nelson lawyer
Brown, Donald Arthur lawyer
Brown, Doreen Leah Hurwitz development company executive
Brown, Elizabeth Ann foreign service officer
Brown, George Leslie legislative affairs and business development consultant, former manufacturing company executive, former lieutenant governor
Brown, Harold former secretary of defense, corporate director
†Brown, Jeanette L. environmental protection administrator
Brown, John Carter art and education consultant, federal agency administrator
Brown, John Patrick newspaper executive, financial consultant
Brown, June Gibbs government official
Brown, Lester Russell research institute executive
Brown, Louis physicist, researcher
†Brown, Mark Malloch bank executive
Brown, Michael Arthur lawyer
Brown, Norman Allen consultant, educator
Brown, Pamela Wedd artist
Brown, Preston lawyer
†Brown, Richard E., III military officer
Brown, Sherrod congressman, former state official
†Brown, Stuart L. tax specialist
†Brown, Terrence J. federal agency administrator
Brownback, Sam senator
Browne, Richard Cullen lawyer
Browner, Carol federal agency administrator
Brownstein, Philip Nathan lawyer
Bruce, E(stel) Edward lawyer
Bruggink, Eric G. federal judge
Brunsvold, Brian Garrett lawyer, educator
Brush, Peter Norman retired federal agency administrator, lawyer
Bryan, Richard H. senator
Bryant, Arthur H. lawyer
Bryant, Edward congressman
Bryant, Thomas Edward physician, lawyer
Bryant, William B. federal judge
Bryson, William Curtis federal judge
Brzezinski, Zbigniew political science educator, author
Buc, Nancy Lillian lawyer
†Bucella, Donna A. federal official
Buchan, Douglas Charles petroleum company executive, government official
†Buchholz, Douglas David military officer
Bucholtz, Harold Ronald lawyer
Buck, Carolyn J. federal official
Buckelew, Robin Browne aerospace engineer
Buckley, James Lane federal judge
Buckley, Jeremiah Stephen lawyer
†Buckley, Jill legislative and public affairs administrator
Buckley, John Joseph, Jr. lawyer
Buechner, Jack W(illiam) lawyer, government affairs consultant
Buergenthal, Thomas lawyer, educator, international judge
Bulger, Roger James academic health center executive
Bumpers, Dale L. former senator, former governor
Burack, Michael Leonard lawyer
†Burbano, Fernando federal agency administrator
Burchfield, Bobby Roy lawyer
Burdette, Robert Bruce lawyer
Burge, Heidi basketball player
Burgess, David lawyer
Burgin, Walter Hotchkiss, Jr. educational administrator
Burka, Robert Alan lawyer
Burke, John priest
†Burki, Shahid Javed bank executive
Burnett, Arthur Louis, Sr. judge
†Burnette, Thomas N. career officer
Burnham, David Bright writer, educator
Burns, Conrad Ray senator
Burns, David Mitchell writer, musician, former diplomat
†Burns, R. Nicholas federal official
Burns, Stephen Gilbert lawyer
†Burns, William Stuart legislative administrator
Burr, Richard M. congressman
Burris, Boyd Lee psychiatrist, psychoanalyst, physician, educator
Burris, James Frederick federal research administrator, educator
Burson, Charles W. federal official, former state attorney general
Burt, Jeffrey Amsterdam lawyer
Burtless, Gary Thomas economist, consultant
Burton, Dan L. congressman
Burton, Douglas Gray magazine editor
Burton, William Joseph engineering executive
Burwell, David Gates transportation executive
Busby, David lawyer
Busby, Morris D. ambassador
Buscemi, Peter lawyer
Buss, Patricia Arnold plastic surgeon
†Buster, Kendall art educator
Butler, J. Bradway lawyer
Butler, Michael Francis lawyer
Butler, Steven Bailey journalist
Butterworth, Ritajean Hartung broadcast executive
Buyer, Steve Earle congressman, lawyer
Buzzell, Robert Dow management educator
Byers, Paul Heed television news producer, consultant
Byrd, Robert Carlyle senator
Byrne, Leslie Larkin former federal agency administrator, former congresswoman
Byron, Michael J. career officer
Byron, William James management educator, former university president
Cacciavillan, Agostino archbishop
Cafritz, Robert Conrad art historian, critic, consultant
Cagney, Michael Joseph foundation adminstrator
Calamaro, Raymond Stuart lawyer
Caldera, Louis Edward federal official
Caldwell, John L. international company executive
Caldwell, Willard E. psychologist, educator
Calhoun, John Alfred social services administrator
Calhoun, Noah Robert oral maxillofacial surgeon, educator
Calhoun-Senghor, Keith lawyer
Calingaert, Michael nonprofit organization executive
Callahan, Debra Jean environmental organization executive
Callahan, John J. federal official
Callaway, Clifford Wayne physician
†Callear, Mildred O. federal agency administrator
Callender, Clive Orville surgeon
Calvani, Terry lawyer, former government official
Calvert, Ken congressman
Cameron, Don R. educational association administrator
Cameron, Duncan Hume lawyer
Camp, Dave congressman
†Campbell, Arthur C. federal agency adminstrator
Campbell, Ben Nighthorse senator
Campbell, Bruce James
†Campbell, Douglas J. legislative staff member
Campbell, James Albert Barton association executive, retired marketing executive
Campbell, James Sargent lawyer
Campbell, Thomas J. congressman
†Campbell, William H. career officer
Campiglia, Michael Edward association executive
Canady, Charles Terrence congressman, lawyer
Canes, Michael Edwin trade association administrator, economist
Canfield, Edward Francis lawyer, business executive
†Cannon, Charles C., Jr. military career officer
Cannon, Christopher B. congressman
Canter, Howard Raphael nuclear engineer
Cantor, Herbert I. lawyer
†Cantú, Norma V. federal official
Caplin, Mortimer Maxwell lawyer, educator
Caponiti, James federal government official
Capps, Lois Ragnhild Grimsrud congresswoman, school nurse
†Capuano, Michael Everett congressman
Card, James Conrad coast guard officer
Cardin, Benjamin Louis congressman
Carey, E. Fenton federal agency associate administrator
Carey, Sarah Collins lawyer
†Carey, Wilhelmina Cole management consultant
Carhart, Homer W(alter) research scientist
Carioti, Bruno M. civil engineer
Carlin, John William archivist, former governor
Carliner, David lawyer
Carlisle, Margo Duer Black government official
Carlson, Bruce career officer
†Carlson, Melinda Suzanne librarian
Carlson, Richard Warner journalist, diplomat, federal agency administrator, broadcast executive
†Carlton, Bruce J. transportation company executive
Carlton, Paul Kendall, Jr. air force officer, physician
Carmody, Margaret Jean retired social worker
Carneal, George Upshur lawyer
Carney, Robert Thomas lawyer
Carome, Patrick Joseph lawyer
Carpenter, Sheila Jane lawyer
†Carpenter, Shirley M. (Sam) career officer
Carpenter, Ted Galen political scientist
Carr, Bob former congressman, lawyer
†Carr, Bobby G. legislative staff member
Carr, Carolyn Kinder deputy director National Portrait Gallery
Carr, David Michael editor, writer
Carr, Lawrence Edward, Jr. lawyer
Carr, Marie Pinak book distribution company executive
Carr, Timothy Bernard librarian
Carroll, J. Speed lawyer, financial executive
Carrow, Milton Michael lawyer, educator
Carson, Julia M. congresswoman
Carter, Barry Edward lawyer, educator, administrator
Carter, Jean Anne psychologist
Carter, William Joseph lawyer
Carter, Yvonne Johnson writer, editor, English educator
Carver, George Allen, Jr. lawyer
Casciano, John P. federal military program director
Case, Larry D. agricultural education specialist
Casey, Bernard J. lawyer
†Casey, George W. military career officer
Cashen, Henry Christopher, II lawyer, former government official
Casserly, Charley professional football team executive
Casserly, James Lund lawyer
Cassidy, Robert Charles, Jr. lawyer
Casstevens, Kay L. federal official
Castle, Michael N. congressman, former governor, lawyer
†Castro, Laura Ellen accountant
Catlett, D. Mark federal official
Catoe, Bette Lorrina physician, health educator
Cavanagh, John Henry political economist
Caws, Peter James philosopher, educator
Cazan, Matthew John political science educator
Cebe, Juanita academic administrator
†Celeste, Richard F. ambassador, former governor
Cenkner, William religion educator, academic administrator
†Cha, Victor D. government educator, consultant
Chabot, Elliot Charles lawyer
Chabot, Herbert L. judge
Chabot, Steven J. congressman
Chafee, John Hubbard senator
Chafetz, Marc Edward lawyer
†Chaitovitz, Samuel judge
Chalkley, Jacqueline Ann retail company executive
Chamberlin, John Charlton federal agency administrator
Chambers, Letitia Pearl Caroline public policy consulting firm executive
Chambliss, Saxby congressman
Chameides, Steven B. lawyer
Chan, Wai-Yee molecular geneticist
Chan, Wing-Chi cultural organization administrator, musicologist
Chandler, John Wesley educational consultant
Chanin, Michael Henry lawyer
Chanin, Robert Howard lawyer
Chapman, James L. (Jim Chapman) former congressman
Chapoton, John Edgar lawyer, government official
Charles, Leslie Bermann government official
Charles, Robert Bruce lawyer
Charlton, Gordon Randolph physicist
Chavez-Thompson, Linda labor union administrator
Checchi, Vincent Victor economist
Cheetham, Alan Herbert paleontologist
Chen, John Shaoming architecture educator
Cheney, Lynne V. humanities educator, writer
Cheney, Stephen A. career officer
Cheng, Tsung O. cardiologist, educator
Chenoweth, Helen P. congresswoman
Cherry, Robert Newton, Jr. army officer, health physicist
†Chesser, Judy Lee federal agency administrator, lawyer
Cheston, Sheila Carol lawyer
Chiang, George Djia-Chee engineer, educator
Chiapella, Anne Page epidemiologist
Chiazze, Leonard, Jr. biostatistician, epidemiologist, educator
Chiechi, Carolyn Phyllis federal judge
Chierichella, John W. lawyer
Chilcote, Samuel Day, Jr. trade association administrator
Childress, Kerri J. federal agency administrator
Childs, Timothy Winston writer
Chilman, Catherine Earles Street social welfare educator, author
Chin, Allen E., Sr. athletic administrator, educator
Chin, Cecilia Hui-Hsin librarian
Cho, Sung Yoon law librarian
Chopko, Mark E. lawyer
Chorba, Timothy A. former ambassador to Singapore
Chrétien, Raymond A. J. ambassador
Christaldi, Brian lawyer
Christensen, Donna Marie congresswoman
Christenson, Ronald L. military officer
Christian, Betty Jo lawyer
Christian, Ernest Silsbee, Jr. lawyer
Christian, Mary Jo Dinan educator, real estate professional
Chu, David S. C. economist
Chubb, Talbot Albert physicist
Chused, Richard Harris law educator
Cicconi, James William lawyer
†Cicotello, Thomas Matthew property manager
Cikovsky, Nicolai, Jr. curator, art history educator
†Cima, Gay Gibson English educator
Clagett, Brice McAdoo lawyer, writer
Claiborne, William journalist
†Clampitt, Susan federal agency administrator
†Clapp, Charles E., II senior judge
Clark, Dick former senator, ambassador, foreign affairs specialist
†Clark, Donald Scott federal official
†Clark, Jamie Rappaport fish and wildlife service administrator
Clark, John Franklin lawyer
Clark, LeRoy D. legal educator, lawyer
Clark, Robert William, III lawyer
Clay, Don Richard environmental consulting firm executive
Clay, William Lacy congressman
†Claypool, Robert T. military career officer
Clayton, Eva M. congresswoman, former county commissioner
Clearfield, Sidney religious organization executive
Cleary, Manon Catherine artist, educator
Clegg, Roger Burton lawyer
Cleland, Joseph Maxwell (Max Cleland) state official
Cleland, Max senator
†Clem, Ralph S. career officer
Clement, Bob congressman
Clemmer, Dan Orr librarian
Clevenger, Raymond C., III federal judge
Clift, Eleanor magazine correspondent
Cline, William Richard economist, educator
Clinton, Hillary Rodham First Lady of United States, lawyer
Clinton, William Jefferson President of the United States
Clodius, Robert LeRoy economist, educator
Close, David Palmer lawyer
†Close, George F., Jr. career officer
Clurman, Michael newspaper publishing executive
Clyburn, James E. congressman
Clymer, Adam newspaper editor
Coats, Daniel Ray former senator
Cobb, Calvin Hayes, Jr. lawyer
Cobb, Jane Overton legislative staff member
Cobble, Steven Bruce political consultant, strategist
Cobbs, Nicholas Hammer lawyer
Coburn, Tom A. congressman
Cocco, Marie Elizabeth journalist
Cochran, John Thomas professional association executive
Cocke, Erle, Jr. international business consultant
Coelho, Tony former congressman
Coerper, Milo George lawyer, priest
Coffey, Timothy physicist, think-tank executive
Coffield, Shirley Ann lawyer, educator
Coffin, Laurence Edmondston, Jr. landscape architect, urban planner
†Cohen, Bonnie R. government official
Cohen, David public affairs specialist, educator
Cohen, Edward Barth lawyer
Cohen, Jordan Jay medical association executive
Cohen, Louis Richard lawyer
Cohen, Marc Jacob researcher
Cohen, Mary Ann judge

Eisner, Howard *engineering educator, engineering executive*
Eisner, Neil Robert *lawyer*
Eisner, Peter Norman *journalist, author, news agency executive*
Eizenstat, Stuart E. *ambassador, lawyer*
†Elcano, Mary S. *lawyer, federal agency administrator*
Elder, Mary Louise *librarian*
Elfin, Mel *magazine editor*
Elgart, Mervyn L. *dermatologist, educator*
Elias, Thomas Sam *botanist, author*
El Khadem, Hassan Saad *chemistry educator, researcher*
Elkinton, Steven *government agency administrator*
Ellicott, John LeMoyne *lawyer*
†Elliott, Carol C. *career officer*
Elliott, Edwin Donald, Jr. *law educator, federal administrator, environmental lawyer*
Elliott, Emerson John *education consultant, policy analyst*
Elliott, Lee Ann *government official*
Elliott, Robert John *lawyer*
Elliott, Thomas Michael *executive, educator, consultant*
†Elliott, Warren G. *lawyer*
Ellis, Courtenay *lawyer*
Ellis, Steven George *public relations/corporate communication executive*
Ellis, Winford G. *career officer*
Elmer, Brian Christian *lawyer*
Elrod, Eugene Richard *lawyer*
Elsasser, Glen Robert *journalist*
Elsey, George McKee *foundation administrator*
Ely-Raphel, Nancy *diplomat*
Emerson, Jo Ann *congresswoman*
Emmett, Robert Addis, III *lawyer*
Emperado, Mercedes Lopez *librarian*
Engel, Eliot L. *congressman*
Engel, John *lawyer*
Engel, Ralph *manufacturers association executive*
Engle, Jane *research nurse*
English, Philip Sheridan *congressman*
Enzi, Michael Bradley *senator, accountant*
Epps, Charles Harry, Jr. *orthopaedic surgery educator*
Epps, Roselyn Elizabeth Payne *pediatrician, educator*
Epstein, Gary Marvin *lawyer*
Epstein, Kalman Noel *newspaper publishing company executive*
Epstein, Lionel Charles *lawyer*
Epstein, Sidney *editor*
Epstien, Jay Alan *lawyer*
Erdreich, Ben Leader *federal agency executive*
Erlanger, Steven Jay *journalist*
Ershler, William Baldwin *biogerontologist, educator*
Erumsele, Andrew Akhigbe *development policy analyst*
Eshoo, Anna Georges *congresswoman*
Esposito, Mark Alan *stock market executive*
Esslinger, John Thomas *lawyer*
Etheridge, Bob *congressman*
†Ettenson, Gordon Michael *air force officer*
Etters, Ronald Milton *lawyer, government official*
Etzel, Ruth Ann *pediatrician, epidemiologist*
Etzioni, Amitai *sociologist, educator*
Evans, Charles Hawes, Jr. *immunologist, health science administrator*
Evans, Lane *congressman*
Evans, Rowland, Jr. *columnist, commentator*
Evans, Thomas William *lawyer*
Evelyn, Douglas Everett *museum executive*
Everett, Ralph Bernard *lawyer*
Everett, Robinson Oscar *federal judge, law educator*
Everett, Terry *congressman*
†Everly, Rebecca D. *lawyer*
Ewing, Kevin Andrew *lawyer*
Ewing, Ky Pepper, Jr. *lawyer*
Ewing, Thomas William *congressman, lawyer*
Fadiman, Anne *writer, editor*
Faherty, Robert Louis *publishing executive*
Fahey, John M., Jr. *book publishing executive*
Fahrenkopf, Frank Joseph, Jr. *lawyer*
Fain, Cheryl Ann *translator, editor*
Fainberg, Anthony *physicist*
Fairbanks, David Nathaniel Fox *physician, surgeon, educator*
Fairbanks, Richard Monroe, III *lawyer, former ambassador at large*
Fairchild, Samuel Wilson *professional services company executive, former federal agency administrator*
Falci, Kenneth Joseph *food and nutrition scientist*
Faleomavaega, Eni Fa'auaa Hunkin *congressman*
†Faletti, Tom *legislative staff member*
Faley, R(ichard) Scott *lawyer*
Falk, David Benjamin *lawyer, professional athletic representative*
†Falk, Diane M. *research director, librarian, editor, writer*
Falk, James Harvey, Sr. *lawyer*
Falk, John Mansfield *shareholder*
Falkner, Juliette *federal agency administrator*
Falter, Vincent Eugene *retired army officer, consultant*
Farabow, Ford Franklin, Jr. *lawyer*
Farley, John Joseph, III *federal judge*
Farmer, Donald A(rthur), Jr. *lawyer*
Farmer, Greg *former federal agency administrator*
†Farr, George F. *federal official*
Farr, Judith Banzer *writer, literature educator*
Farr, Sam *congressman*
Farrell, Joseph Michael *steamship company executive*
Farrell, Michael W. *state supreme court justice*
†Farrell, Richard T. *human resources administrator*
Fasman, Zachary Dean *lawyer*
Fattah, Chaka *congressman, former state legislator*
Faucheux, Ronald Anthony *publisher, editor*
Fauntleroy, Carma Cecil *arts administration executive*
Faust, Marcus G. *lawyer*
Faux, Jeff (Geoffrey Peter Faux) *economist, writer*
Fay, William Michael *federal judge*
Fedders, John Michael *lawyer*
Feffer, Gerald Alan *lawyer*
Feierstein, Mark Barry *diplomat*
Feinberg, Kenneth Roy *lawyer, law educator*
Feingold, Russell Dana *United States senator, lawyer*
Feinstein, Dianne *senator*
†Feinstein, Frederick Lee *lawyer*
†Felbinger, Claire Louise *adult education educator, administrator*
Feld, Karen Irma *columnist, journalist, broadcaster, public speaker*
†Felder, Richard Bruce *pipeline safety administrator*
Feldhaus, Stephen Martin *lawyer*
Feldman, Bruce Allen *otolaryngologist*
Feldman, Clarice Rochelle *lawyer*
Feldman, Mark B. *lawyer*
Feldman, Roger David *lawyer*
Feldman, Sandra *labor union administration*
Fels, Nicholas Wolff *lawyer*
Fendrich, Roger Paul *lawyer*
Fenn, Peter Huntington *political consultant, media producer, educator*
Ferguson, Thomas *federal agency administrator*
Ferguson, Thomas Crooks *lawyer*
Fern, Alan Maxwell *art historian, museum director*
Ferrand, Louis George *lawyer*
Ferrara, Peter Joseph *federal official, lawyer, author, educator*
Ferrara, Ralph C. *lawyer*
Ferrara, Steven *educational researcher, test developer*
Ferren, John Maxwell *lawyer*
Ferris, George Mallette, Jr. *investment banker*
Ferris, William Reynolds *folklore educator*
Fertig-Dykes, Susan Beatrice *communications executive, human resourses professional*
Feshbach, Murray *demographer, educator*
Fetters, J. Michael *museum administrator*
Feuerstein, Donald Martin *lawyer*
Feulner, Edwin John, Jr. *research foundation executive*
Fialka, John Joseph *journalist*
Field, Andrea Bear *lawyer*
Fielding, Fred Fisher *lawyer*
Fields, Stuart Howard *labor relations specialist*
Fields, Suzanne Bregman *syndicated columnist*
Fields, Wendy Lynn *lawyer*
Fifer Canby, Susan Melinda *library administrator*
Filner, Bob *congressman*
Finelsen, Libbi June *lawyer*
Fineman, Howard David *political correspondent*
Finerty, Martin Joseph, Jr. *military officer, researcher, association management executive*
Fingerhut, Marilyn Ann *federal agency administrator*
Fink, Lois Marie *art historian*
Fink, Matthew Pollack *trade association executive, lawyer*
Finkel, Adam *government agency administrator*
Finkel, Eugene Jay *lawyer*
Finkelstein, James David *physician*
Finkle, Jeffrey Alan *professional association executive*
Finley, Julie Hamm *political party official*
Finley, Skip *media consultant, communications executive*
Fiorini, John E., III *lawyer*
Fischer, Stanley *economist, educator*
Fischetti, Michael Joseph *accounting educator*
Fishburne, Benjamin P., III *lawyer*
Fishel, Andrew S. *director, federal*
Fisher, Bart Steven *lawyer, educator, investment banker*
Fisher, Benjamin Chatburn *lawyer*
Fisher, Miles Mark, IV *education and religion educator, minister*
Fisher, Raymond Corley *lawyer*
Fisher, Robert Dale *stockbroker, retired naval officer*
Fisher, Stephen Todd *naval officer*
Fisher, Wesley Andrew *research administrator, Eurasian studies specialist*
Fisher, William P. *association executive*
Fitts, C. Austin *investment adviser*
FitzGerald, William Henry G. *diplomat, corporation executive*
Fitz-Hugh, Glassell Slaughter, Jr. *bank executive*
Fitzmyer, Joseph Augustine *theology educator, priest*
Fitzpatrick, James Franklin *lawyer*
Fitz-Pegado, Lauri J. *telecommunications executive*
Flack, Ronald David *diplomat, public service educator, banker*
Flagg, Ronald Simon *lawyer*
Flaherty, Sister Mary Jean *dean, nursing educator*
Flanagan, Francis Dennis *retired corporate executive*
Flannery, Ellen Joanne *lawyer*
Flannery, John Philip *lawyer*
Flattau, Edward *columnist*
Flattau, Pamela Ebert *research psychologist, consultant*
Fleischaker, Marc L. *lawyer*
Fleisher, Eric Wilfrid *retired foreign service officer*
Fleit, Martin *lawyer*
†Fletcher, (Robert) Ernie *congressman*
Flintoff, Corey Alan *radio newscaster, writer*
Flood, Mark Damien *finance educator*
Flowe, Carol Connor *lawyer*
Flynn, Cathal *federal agency amdinistrator*
Flynn, Nancy Marie *government executive*
Flyzik, James J. *federal official*
Foard, Douglas W. *educational association administrator*
Foer, Sara *public relations spokesperson, consultant*
Fogarty, John Patrick Cody *lawyer*
Fogel, J(oan) Cathy *lawyer*
Fogleman, Guy Carroll *physicist, mathematician, educator*
†Foglesong, Robert H. *lieutenant general United States Air Force*
Foglietta, Thomas Michael *diplomat, former congressman*
Fois, Andrew *lawyer, educator*
Foley, Mark Adam *congressman*
†Foley, Maurice B. *federal judge*
Foley, Robert Matthew *lawyer*
†Foley, Thomas Stephen *diplomat, former speaker House of Representatives*
Fontheim, Claude G.B. *lawyer, advisor*
Forbes, Michael P. *congressman*
Ford, Harold Eugene *congressman*
Ford, William R. *federal agency administrator*
Foreman, Carol Lee Tucker *consumer advocate*
Forester, John Gordon, Jr. *lawyer*
Forgey, Benjamin Franklin *architecture and art critic*
Forrest, Herbert Emerson *lawyer*
Forrest, Sidney *clarinetist, music educator*
Forrester, Patricia Tobacco *artist*
Foscarinis, Maria *lawyer*
Fosdick, Cora Prifold (Cora Prifold Beebe) *government official*
Fosler, R. Scott *academic administrator*
Fossella, Vito John *congressman*
Foster, C(harles) Allen *lawyer*
†Foster, Serrin Marie *non-profit organization executive*
†Foust, Robert Schmertz *legislative director*
Fowler, J. Edward *lawyer*
Fowler, James D., Jr. *marketing and human resources consulant*
Fowler, Raymond Dalton *professional association executive, psychologist*
Fowler, Tillie Kidd *congresswoman*
Fowler, William E., Jr. *government official*
Fox, Jon D. *congressman*
Fox, Lynn Smith *federal government official*
Fox, Sarah *lawyer*
Frahm, Veryl Harvey, Jr. *laboratory manager*
Francke, Gloria Niemeyer *pharmacist, editor, publisher*
Franco, Robert *economist*
Francois, Francis Bernard *association executive, lawyer*
Frank, Arthur J. *lawyer*
Frank, Barney *congressman*
Frank, Isaiah *economist, educator*
Frank, Richard Asher *lawyer, health products executive*
Frank, Theodore David *lawyer*
Frankle, Edward Alan *lawyer*
Franklin, Barbara Hackman *business executive, former government official*
†Franklin, Cabe Gerard *information systems specialist*
Franklin, Hardy R. *retired library director*
Franklin, Peter Charles *brigadier general*
†Franz, Marian C. *association administrator*
Franz, Wanda *association administrator*
†Franzel, Brent Steven *lawyer*
Franzen, Byron T. (John Franzen) *media specialist*
Frawley Bagley, Elizabeth *government advisor, ambassador*
Frederick, Robert Melvin *farm organization executive*
Freedman, Jay Weil *lawyer*
Freedman, Walter *lawyer*
Freeh, Louis Joseph *federal agency administrator*
Freeman, Chas. W., Jr. *government official, ambassador, author*
Freeman, Milton Victor *lawyer*
Freeman, Robert Turner, Jr. *insurance executive*
Freer, Robert Elliott, Jr. *lawyer*
Freije, Philip Charles *lawyer*
Frelinghuysen, Rodney P. *congressman*
†French, Richard Vaughn *federal agency administrator*
Freund, Deborah Miriam *transportation engineer*
Fricke, Heinz *conductor*
Friday, Elbert Walter, Jr. *federal agency administrator, meteorologist*
Fried, Bruce Merlin *health services director*
†Fried, Daniel *ambassador*
Fried, Edward R. *government official*
Friedan, Betty *author, feminist leader*
Friedlander, Bernice *federal program administrator*
Friedlander, James Stuart *lawyer*
Friedman, Alvin *lawyer*
Friedman, Arthur Daniel *electrical engineering and computer science educator, investment management company executive*
Friedman, Daniel Mortimer *federal judge*
Friedman, Frank Bennett *lawyer*
†Friedman, Gregory H. *energy administrator*
Friedman, Herbert *physicist*
Friedman, Miles *trade association executive, financial services company executive, university lecturer*
†Friedman, Paul Lawrence *lawyer*
Friend, William L. *oil industry executive*
Frist, William H. *senator, surgeon*
Fritts, Edward O. *broadcast executive*
Fritz, Thomas Vincent *association and business executive*
Fromm, Hans *gastroenterologist, educator, researcher*
Frost, Edmund Bowen *lawyer*
Frost, Jonas Martin, III *congressman*
†Frost, Molly Spitzer *Chinese culture educator*
Frost, S. David *retired naval officer*
Fry, Louis Edwin, Jr. *architect*
Fuhrman, Ralph Edward *civil and environmental engineer*
†Fuhrman, Russell L. *career officer*
Fujito, Wayne Takeshi *international business company executive*
Fulbright, Harriet Mayor *foundation administrator*
Fuller, Edwin Daniel *hotel executive*
Fuller, Kathryn Scott *environmental association executive, lawyer*
Fulton, Kenneth Ray *professional association administrator*
†Fulton, Scott C. *federal agency administrator*
†Funches, Jesse L. *financial administrator*
Funderburk, David Britton *consultant, former congressman and ambassador*
†Furchgott, David Max *cultural programs executive*
Furgol, Edward Mackie *museum curator, historian*
Furgurson, Ernest Baker, Jr. (Pat Furgurson) *writer*
Futey, Bohdan A. *federal judge*
Futrell, John William *legal association administrator, lawyer*
Fygi, Eric J. *federal government lawyer*
Gable, Edward Brennan, Jr. *lawyer*
Gaff, Jerry Gene *academic administrator*
Gaffney, Susan *federal official*
Gaguine, Benito *lawyer*
Gainer, Ronald Lee *lawyer*
Gainer, Terrance W. *police official*
Gajarsa, Arthur J. *judge*
Gale, Joseph H. *federal judge*
Gall, Mary Sheila *federal agency administrator*
Gallagher, George R. *judge*
Gallegly, Elton William *congressman*
Gallegos, Lou *federal agency administrator*
Gallo, Anthony Ernest *economist, agribusiness author*
Galloway, Joseph Lee, Jr. *writer, journalist*
Galloway, William Jefferson *former foreign service officer*
Galson, Steven Kenneth *preventive medicine specialist*
Gans, Curtis B. *think tank administrator*
Ganske, J. Greg *congressman, plastic surgeon*
†Gansler, Jacques Singleton *executive in acquisition and technology*
Gantt, Harvey B. *former mayor*
Garaufis, Nicholas G. *federal official*
Garavelli, John Stephen *biochemistry research scientist*
Gardiner, David *federal agency administrator*
Garland, Merrick Brian *federal judge*
Garrett, Theodore Louis *lawyer*
Garrish, Theodore John *lawyer*
Gart, Murray Joseph *journalist*
Garthoff, Raymond Leonard *diplomat, diplomatic historian*
†Gartzke, Dana G. *legislative administrator*
Garvey, Jane *federal aviation administrator*
Garvey, John Leo *lawyer, educator*
Gasch, Oliver *judge*
Gati, Toby T. *international advisor*
Gatons, Anna-Marie Kilmade *government official*
Gaviria Trujillo, Cesar *international organization administrator, former president of Colombia, economist*
Gearan, Mark D. *federal agency administrator*
†Gee, Robert W. *energy administrator*
†Geer, Dennis F. *insurance executive*
Geisel, Harold Walter *diplomat*
Gejdenson, Sam *congressman*
Gekas, George William *congressman*
Gelb, Joseph Donald *lawyer*
Gelbard, Alene H. *demographer, policy analyst*
Gelbard, Robert Sidney *ambassador*
Geller, Kenneth Steven *lawyer*
Gellhorn, Ernest Albert Eugene *lawyer*
Gelmann, Edward Paul *oncologist, educator*
†Genetti, Albert J., Jr. *army officer*
Genia, Vicky *psychologist*
Geniesse, Robert John *lawyer*
†Gensler, Gary *federal agency administrator*
Gentner, Paul LeFoe *architect, consultant*
†Gentry, Pamela
Genz, Michael Andrew *lawyer*
George, Joey Russell *lawyer*
George, W. Peyton *lawyer*
Georgine, Robert Anthony *union executive*
Gephardt, Richard Andrew *congressman*
Gerber, Joel *federal judge*
Gernert, Jeffrey Jared *psychologist*
Gershman, Carl Samuel *foundation administrator*
Gerson, Stuart Michael *lawyer*
Gertzman, Stephen F. *lawyer*
Gessaman, Donald Eugene *consultant, former government executive*
Gest, Kathryn Waters *public affairs professional*
†Gettinger, Stephen H. *journalist*
Geyer, Georgie Anne *syndicated columnist, educator, author, biographer, TV commentator*
Giacconi, Riccardo *astrophysicist, educator*
Giallorenzi, Thomas Gaetano *optical engineer*
†Gianni, Gaston L., Jr. *federal agency administrator*
Gibbons, James Arthur *congressman*
Gibbons, Martha Blechar *psychotherapist, educator, consultant*
Gibbons, Sam Melville (Sam Gibbons) *business executive, former congressman*
Gibbs, Lawrence B. *lawyer*
Gibson, Florence Anderson *talking book company executive, narrator*
Gibson, Paul Raymond *international trade and investment development executive*
Gibson, Reginald Walker *federal judge*
Gibson, Thomas Fenner, III *public affairs strategist, political cartoonist*
Gideon, Kenneth Wayne *lawyer*
Gierke, Herman Fredrick, III *federal judge*
†Giffin, Gordon D. *ambassador, lawyer*
Gifford, Prosser *library administrator*
Gigot, Paul Anthony *newspaper columnist*
Gilbert, Charles Richard Alsop *physician, medical educator*
Gilchrest, Wayne Thomas *congressman, former high school educator*
Gildenhorn, Joseph Bernard *lawyer, businessman, former diplomat*
Giles, Patricia Cecelia Parker *retired art educator, graphic designer*
Gilfoyle, Nathalie Floyd Preston *lawyer*
†Gill, Clair F. *military career officer*
†Gill, Shayne H. *legislative staff member*
Gilliam, Arleen Fain *labor union administrator, finance executive*
Gillingham, Robert Fenton *federal agency administrator, economist*
Gilliom, Judith Carr *government official*
Gillmor, Paul E. *congressman, lawyer*
Gilman, Benjamin Arthur *congressman*
Ginsberg, Marc C. *former diplomat, investment company executive*
Ginsburg, Charles David *lawyer*
Ginsburg, Douglas Howard *federal judge, educator*
Ginsburg, Gilbert J. *lawyer, law educator*
Ginsburg, Martin David *lawyer, educator*
Ginsburg, Mitchell Paul *international economist*
Ginsburg, Ruth Bader *United States supreme court justice*
†Gioconda, Thomas F. *career officer*
Glancz, Ronald Robert *lawyer*
Glaser, Howard B. *lawyer*
Glaser, Vera Romans *journalist*
Glasgow, Norman Milton *lawyer*
Glass, Andrew James *newspaper editor*
†Glass, Wayne *legislative staff member*
Glassman, James Kenneth *editor, writer, publishing executive*
Glauthier, T. J. *federal official*
Gleiman, Edward Jay *federal agency administrator*
†Glenn, Harry J. *legislative administrator*
Glick, Leslie Alan *lawyer*
Glickman, Daniel Robert *federal official*
†Glover, Jere Walton *lawyer*
Gnehm, Edward W., Jr. *ambassador*
Gobeli, Virginia C. *national program leader*
Gober, Hershel W. *government official*
Godsey, John Drew *minister, theology educator emeritus*
Godson, Roy Simon *political scientist, think tank executive*
Godwin, Kimberly Ann *federal agency administrator, lawyer*
Goelzer, Daniel Lee *lawyer*
†Goetz, Peter *safety board director*
Gold, Peter Frederick *lawyer*
Goldberg, Joseph Philip *government official*
Goldberg, Kirsten Boyd *science journalist*
Goldberg, Seth A. *lawyer*
Goldblatt, Steven Harris *law educator*
Golden, Cornelius Joseph, Jr. *lawyer*
Golden, Gregg Hannan Stewart *lawyer*
Golden, John Joseph, Jr. *information systems executive*
†Golden, Olivia A. *health and science agency administrator*
Goldfarb, Ronald Lawrence *lawyer*
Goldfield, Edwin David *statistician*
Goldhaber, Jacob Kopel *retired mathematician, educator*
Goldin, Daniel S. *federal agency administrator*
Goldman, Aaron *foundation executive, writer*
Goldschmid, Harvey Jerome *law educator*
Goldsmith, Willis Jay *lawyer*
Goldson, Alfred Lloyd *oncologist, educator*
Goldson, Amy Robertson *lawyer*
Goldstein, Allan Leonard *biochemist, educator*
Goldstein, Frank Robert *lawyer*
Goldstein, Laurence Alan *trade association executive*
Goldstein, Michael B. *lawyer*
Goldstein, Murray *health organization official*
Goler, Robert I. *museum curator*

Hug, James Edward *religious organization administrator*
Hughes, Kent Higgon *economist*
Hughes, Marija Matich *law librarian*
Hughes, Morris Nelson, Jr. *foreign service officer*
†Hughes, Patrick M. *career officer*
Hughes, Thomas Lowe *foundation executive*
Hugler, Edward C. *lawyer, federal and state government*
Hull, Marion Hayes *communications educator, researcher*
Hulshof, Kenny *congressman*
Hume, Brit (Alexander Britton Hume) *journalist*
Hume, Ellen Hunsberger *media analyst, journalist*
Hungate, Joseph Irvin, III *computer scientist*
Hunnicutt, Charles Alvin *lawyer*
Hunt, Albert R. *newspaper executive*
†Hunter, Milton *army officer*
Huntoon, Carolyn Leach *physiologist*
Huntress, Wesley Theodore, Jr. *scientist*
Huntsman, Lawrence Darrow *lawyer*
Hurley, John Arthur *government official*
Hussain, Syed Taseer *biomedical educator, researcher*
Huston, John Wilson *air force officer, historian*
Hutchinson, Asa *congressman*
Hutchinson, Tim *senator*
Hutt, Peter Barton *lawyer*
Hyde, Henry John *congressman*
Hyde, Howard Laurence *lawyer*
Hyman, Lester Samuel *lawyer*
Hynes, Terence Michael *lawyer*
Ibañez, Alvaro *patent design company executive, artist*
†Ibish, Yusuf Hussein *retired educator*
Igasaki, Paul M. *federal agency administrator*
†Ihrie, John Richard, III *art educator*
Ikenberry, Stanley Oliver *education educator, former university president*
Imam, M. Ashraf *materials scientist, educator*
Indyk, Martin S. *diplomat*
Ingold, Catherine White *academic administrator*
Ingram, Richard Thomas *educational association executive*
Inhofe, James M. *senator*
Innerst, Preston Eugene *newspaper editor, journalist*
Inouye, Daniel Ken *senator*
†Inslee, Jay R. *congressman, lawyer*
Insprucker, Nancy Rhoades *air force officer*
Ireland, Patricia *association executive*
Irish, Leon Eugene *lawyer, educator, non-profit executive*
Irizarry, Estelle Diane *foreign language educator, author, editor*
Irvine, Reed John *media critic, corporation executive*
†Irving, Clarence L., Jr. (Larry Irving) *federal official*
Irwin, Paul Garfield *former minister, humane society executive*
Isaacs, Amy Fay *political organization executive*
†Isakson, Johnny *congressman*
Isbell, David Bradford *lawyer, legal educator*
Isenbergh, Max *lawyer, musician, educator*
†Isom, Charles L. *legislative staff member*
Istook, Ernest James, Jr. (Jim Istook) *congressman, lawyer*
Ivers, Donald Louis *judge*
Ivey, William James *foundation executive, writer, producer*
Ivins, Steven David *editor*
†Izard, C. Douglass *tax specialist*
Jackson, Jesse, Jr. *congressman*
Jackson, Jimmy Joe *litigation consultant*
Jackson, John Howard *lawyer, educator*
†Jackson, Mary Ellen *librarian, consultant*
Jackson, Neal A. *lawyer*
Jackson, Patricia Pike *association executive*
Jackson, Shirley Ann *federal agency administrator, physicist*
Jackson, Thomas Penfield *federal judge*
Jackson Lee, Sheila *congresswoman*
Jacobs, David E. *federal agency administrator*
Jacobs, Julian I. *federal judge*
Jacobsen, Hugh Newell *architect*
†Jacobsen, Magdalena Gretchen *mediator, federal agency executive*
Jacobsen, Raymond Alfred, Jr. *lawyer*
Jacobson, Allen H. *economist*
Jacobson, David Edward *lawyer*
Jacobson, Michael Faraday *consumer advocate, writer*
Jacoby, Lowell Edwin *career officer*
Jagoda, Barry Lionel *media adviser, communications consultant*
Jamar, Steven Dwight *law educator*
James, Charles Clinton *science education educator, consultant*
James, Estelle *economics educator*
Jameson, Paula Ann *lawyer*
Jamme, Albert Joseph *archaeologist, educator*
Jani, Sushma Niranjan *pediatrics and child and adolescent psychiatrist*
Jarvis, Charlene Drew *council member*
Jaspersen, Frederick Zarr *economist*
Javits, Joshua Moses *lawyer*
Jefferson, William L. (Jeff Jefferson) *congressman*
Jeffords, James Merrill *senator*
Jeffress, Charles N. *government agency administrator*
Jehani, Ahmed *lawyer*
Jenkins, John Smith *academic dean, lawyer*
Jenkins, Robert Emerson *coach*
Jenkins, William L. (Bill Jenkins) *congressman*
Jensen, James E. *director congressional and government affairs*
Jenson, William G. *federal agency adminstrator*
Jepsen, Peter Lee *court reporter*
Jernigan, Robert Wayne *statistics educator*
Jessup, Philip Caryl, Jr. *lawyer, museum executive*
Jeweler, Robin *lawyer*
Joe, Thomas *think-tank*
John, Chris *congressman*
Johnson, Arlene Lytle *government agency official*
Johnson, David Raymond *lawyer*
Johnson, Eddie Bernice *congresswoman*
†Johnson, Eric *legislative administrator*
†Johnson, Jacqueline *Native American program administrator*
Johnson, James A. *financial organization executive*
†Johnson, Jay L. *career officer*
Johnson, Jay Withington *former congressman*
Johnson, Nancy Lee *congresswoman*
Johnson, Norma Holloway *federal judge*
Johnson, Oliver Thomas, Jr. *lawyer*
Johnson, Omotunde Evan George *economist*
Johnson, Philip McBride *lawyer*
Johnson, Richard Clark *lawyer*
Johnson, Richard Tenney *lawyer*
Johnson, Robert Henry *political science educator*
†Johnson, Robert L. *broadcast executive*
Johnson, Robert Louis *cable television company executive*
Johnson, Samuel (Sam Johnson) *congressman*
Johnson, Timothy Peter *senator*
†Johnson, Victor Charles *association executive*
Johnston, Gerald Samuel *physician, educator*
Johnston, John Bennett, Jr. *former senator*
Johnston, Kenneth John *astronomer, scientific director naval observatory*
Jones, Aidan Drexel *lawyer*
Jones, Boisfeuillet, Jr. *lawyer, newspaper executive*
Jones, George Fleming *foundation executive*
Jones, Howard St. Claire, Jr. *electronics engineering executive*
Jones, Philip Howard *broadcast journalist*
Jones, Stanley Boyd *health policy analyst, priest*
†Jones, Stephanie Tubbs *congresswoman, lawyer*
Jones, Walter Beaman, Jr. *congressman*
Jones, William Bowdoin *political scientist, retired diplomat, lawyer*
Jones-Wilson, Faustine Clarisse *education educator emeritus*
Jordan, Anne E. Dollerschell *journalist*
Jordan, Irving King *university president*
†Jordan, Larry R. *career officer*
Jordan, Mary Lucille *commissioner*
Jordan, Robert Elijah, III *lawyer*
†Jordan, Samantha *legislative staff member*
Jordan, Sandra *public relations professional*
Jordan, Vernon Eulion, Jr. *lawyer, former association official*
Joseph, Daniel Mordecai *lawyer*
Joseph, James Alfred *ambassador*
Josephson, Diana Hayward *government agency official*
Journey, Drexel Dahlke *lawyer*
Joyce, Anne Raine *editor, director of publications*
Joyner, Christopher Clayton *international relations educator*
Judd, Jacqueline Dee (Jackie Judd) *journalist, reporter*
Juliana, James Nicholas *ordnance company executive*
Kabel, Robert James *lawyer*
Kafka, Gerald Andrew *lawyer*
Kahlow, Barbara Fenvessy *statistician*
Kahn, Edwin Leonard *lawyer*
Kahn, Michael *stage director*
Kahn, Walter Kurt *engineering and applied science educator*
Kailian, Aram Harry *architect*
Kaiser, Philip Mayer *diplomat*
Kaiser, Robert Greeley *newspaper editor*
†Kak, Neeraj *public health specialist*
Kaludis, George *management consultant, book company executive, educator*
Kamber, Victor Samuel *political consultant*
Kamensky, John Michael *federal agency administrator*
Kammerer, Joseph T. *government official*
†Kane, Allen *postal service executive*
Kane, Annette Pieslak *religious organization executive*
Kanjorski, Paul Edmund *congressman, lawyer*
Kant, Gloria Jean *neuroscientist, researcher*
Kanter, Arnold Lee *international businesss consultant, policy analyst*
Kanuk, Leslie Lazar *management consultant, educator*
Kapetanakos, Christos Anastasios *science administrator, physics educator*
†Kaplan, Keith Jacob *physician*
Kapp, Robert Harris *lawyer*
Kappaz, Michael H. *engineering company executive*
Kaptur, Marcia Carolyn *congresswoman*
Karcher, Donald Steven *medical educator*
†Karl, Jonathan David *television journalist*
Karle, Isabella L. *chemist*
Karle, Jerome *physicist, researcher*
Karnas, Fred G., Jr. *government agency administrator*
Karpan, Kathleen Marie *former state official, lawyer, journalist*
Karpinski, Gene Brien *non-profit group administrator, think tank executive*
Kasich, John R. *congressman*
Kass, Benny Lee *lawyer*
†Kassiday, Joel David *legislative staff member*
Kasten, Robert W., Jr. *former senator*
Katson, Roberta Marina *economist*
Katz, John W. *lawyer, state official*
†Katz, Mitchell Jay *public affairs specialist*
Katz, Sherman E. *lawyer*
Katzen, Sally *lawyer, government official*
Katzmann, Robert Allen *law educator, non-profit association executive, political scientist*
Kauzlarich, Richard Dale *ambassador, foreign service officer*
Kavanaugh, Everett Edward, Jr. *trade association executive*
Kavulich, John Steven, II *international marketing executive*
Kazin, Michael *history educator, writer*
Keaney, Thomas Addis *strategic studies educator*
Kearney, Stephen Michael *corporate treasurer*
Kearns, Kevin Lawrence *political association executivc, lawyer*
Keating, Robert B. *ambassador*
Keeley, Robert Vossler *retired academic administrator, retired ambassador*
Keeney, John C. *lawyer*
Keeney, John Christopher, Jr. *lawyer*
†Keenum, Mark E. *legislative chief of staff*
Keeny, Spurgeon Milton, Jr. *association executive*
Keevey, Richard Francis *government official, educator*
†Keilty, Bryan T. *government agency administrator*
Keiner, R(obert) Bruce, Jr. *lawyer*
Kelley, Edward Watson, Jr. *federal agency administrator*
Kellison, James Bruce *lawyer*
†Kellogg, Joseph J., Jr. *military career officer*
Kelly, Marguerite Stehli *fashion executive, consultant*
†Kelly, Raymond W. *federal agency administrator*
Kelly, Sue W. *congresswoman*
Kelly, Timothy T. *television station executive*
Kelly, William Charles, Jr. *lawyer*
Kelso, Gwendolyn Lee *silver appraiser, consultant*
Keltz, Amy Lynn *political science organization administrator*
†Kemble, Penn *government official*
Kemp, Geoffrey Thomas Howard *international affairs specialist*
Kemp, John D. *professional society administrator*
Kempley, Rita A. *film critic, editor*
Kempner, Jonathan L. *professional society administrator*
Kempster, Norman Roy *journalist*
Kendall, David E. *lawyer*
Kendall, Gene R. *military officer, federal agency administrator*
Kendall, Peter Landis *television news executive*
Kendrick, John Whitefield *economist, educator, consultant*
Kennan, Stephanie Ann *advisor*
Kennard, Mary Elizabeth *lawyer*
Kennard, William Earl *federal agency administrator, lawyer*
Kennedy, Anthony McLeod *United States supreme court justice*
†Kennedy, Claudia J. *military officer*
†Kennedy, Craig *foundation administrator*
Kennedy, Edward Moore *senator*
Kennedy, Eugene Richard *microbiologist, university dean*
†Kennedy, Henry H. *judge*
Kennedy, Jerry Wayne *lawyer*
Kennedy, Patrick F. *federal official*
Kennedy, Patrick J. *congressman*
Kennedy, Robert Emmet, Jr. *history educator*
Kennelly, Barbara B. *former congresswoman, federal agency administrator*
†Kenney, Dennis Jay *criminal justice researcher, educator*
Kenney, Robert James, Jr. *lawyer*
Kent, M. Elizabeth *lawyer*
Kerber, Frank John *diplomat*
Kern, John Worth, III *judge*
Kerr, Stuart H. *lawyer, think tank executive*
†Kerr, T. Michael *federal official*
Kerrey, Bob (J. Robert Kerrey) *senator*
†Kerrick, Donald L. *career officer*
Kerry, John Forbes *senator*
†Kerwin, Cornelius Martin *dean, public affairs educator*
Kessler, Gladys *federal judge*
Kessler, Judd Lewis *lawyer*
Ketchum, James Roe *curator*
Keune, Russell Victor *architect, architectural association executive*
Keyes, Arthur Hawkins, Jr. *architect*
Khadduri, Majid *international studies educator*
Khozeimeh, Issa *electrical engineer*
Kibler, Virginia Mary *economist*
Kies, Kenneth J. *lawyer*
†Kievenaar, Henry A. *military career officer*
Kiko, Philip George *lawyer*
Kilborn, Peter Thurston *journalist*
Kilburn, Edwin Allen *lawyer*
Kildee, Dale Edward *congressman*
Kilgore, Edwin Carroll *retired government official, consultant*
Kilian, Michael David *journalist, columnist, writer*
†Killefer, Nancy *federal agency administrator*
Kilpatrick, Carolyn Cheeks *congresswoman*
†Kim, John Chan Kyu *electrical engineer*
†Kim, Sook Cha *artist*
†Kim, Sung Yup *diplomat*
†Kimball, Marc Kennedy *press secretary*
†Kimble, Melinda L. *environmental administrator*
Kimmitt, Joseph Stanley *political consultant*
Kimmitt, Robert Michael *lawyer, banker, diplomat*
Kind, Ron *congressman*
King, Gwendolyn S. *retired utility company executive, former federal official*
King, Larry (Larry Zeiger) *broadcaster, radio personality*
King, Llewellyn Willings *publisher, lecturer, journalist, commentator*
King, Nina Davis *journalist*
King, Patricia Ann *law educator*
King, Peter Thomas *congressman, lawyer*
King, Rufus *lawyer*
King, Warren R. *judge*
Kingston, Jack *congressman*
Kinsey, Mark A. *government official*
Kiplinger, Knight A. *journalist, publisher*
Kirk, Donald *journalist*
Kirkien-Rzeszotarski, Alicja Maria *academic administrator, researcher, educator*
Kirkpatrick, Jeane Duane Jordan *political scientist, government official*
Kirsch, Laurence Stephen *lawyer*
†Kiss, Tibor *military attache*
Kissel, Peter Charles *lawyer*
Kitfield, James Crawford *foreign policy correspondent, writer*
Kittrie, Nicholas N(orbert Nehemiah) *law educator, international consultant, author*
Kitzmiller, William Michael *government official*
Kizer, Kenneth Wayne *physician, educator, administrator*
†Klaits, Joseph A. *education program director, historian*
Klarfeld, Peter James *lawyer*
Klass, Philip Julian *technical journalist, electrical engineer*
Klawiter, Donald Casimir *lawyer*
Kleczka, Gerald D. *congressman*
Kleiman, Devra Gail *zoologist, zoological park research scientist*
†Klein, Bill *legislative staff member*
Klein, Michael Roger *lawyer, business executive*
Klein, Perry Ian *electronics engineer*
Klein, Philipp Hillel *electronic materials consultant*
Kline, Norman Douglas *federal judge*
Klink, Ron *congressman, reporter, newscaster*
Klosson, Michael *foreign service officer*
†Knapp, Andrew C. *political association administrator*
Knapp, Charles Boynton *economist, educator, institute president*
Knapp, George M. *lawyer*
Knapp, Patrick *women's basketball coach*
Knapp, Richard Maitland *association executive*
Knapp, Rosalind Ann *lawyer*
Knauer, Leon Thomas *lawyer*
Knebel, John Albert *lawyer, former government official*
Knezo, Genevieve Johanna *science and technology policy researcher*
Knight, Athelia Wilhelmenia *journalist*
Knight, Edward S. *lawyer, federal official*
Knippers, Diane LeMasters *association president*
†Knisely, Robert A. *federal agency administrator*
Knollenberg, Joseph (Joe Knollenberg) *congressman*
Knopman, Debra Sara *hydrologist, policy analyst*
Koch, George William *lawyer*
Koch, Kathleen Day *lawyer*
†Koehnke, Donna R. *federal agency administrator*
Koenig, Harold Martin *former United States Navy surgeon general*
Koering, Marilyn Jean *anatomy educator, researcher*
Kohl, Herbert *professional sports team executive, former senator*
Kolb, Charles Chester *humanities administrator*
Kolbe, James Thomas *congressman*
†Kollar-Kotelly, Colleen *district judge*
Koller, Shirley Leavitt *sculptor*
Kolman, Mark Herbert *lawyer*
Komer, Robert William *government official, consultant*
Konschnik, David Michael *lawyer*
Konselman, Douglas Derek *lawyer*
Konstantinov, Tzvetan Krumov *musician, concert pianist, educator*
Koppel, Ted *broadcast journalist*
Korn, David *educator, pathologist*
†Korner, Jules Gilmer, III *senior judge*
Kornheiser, Anthony I. *journalist*
Kornicker, Louis S. *museum curator*
Korologos, Tom Chris *government affairs consultant, former federal official*
Korth, Fritz-Alan *lawyer*
Koskinen, John Andrew *federal government executive*
Kossak, Shelley *think-tank executive*
Kotz, Samuel *statistician, educator, translator, editor*
Kouts, Herbert John Cecil *physicist*
Kovach, Eugene George *government official, consultant*
Kovacic, William Evan *law educator*
Kraemer, Jay Roy *lawyer*
Kraemer, Sylvia Katharine *government official, historian*
Kramek, Robert E. *United States Coast Guard officer*
Kramer, Andrew Michael *lawyer*
Kramer, Constance Ann *songwriter*
Kramer, Franklin David *lawyer*
Kramer, Jay Harlan *physiologist, researcher, educator*
Kramer, Kenneth Bentley *federal judge, former congressman*
Kramer, Robert *dean*
Kramer, William David *lawyer*
Krasnow, Erwin Gilbert *lawyer*
Kratovil, Jane Lindley *think tank associate, developer/fundraiser*
†Kraus, Margery *management consultant*
Krebs, Martha *physicist, federal science agency administrator*
Krebs, Rockne *artist*
Kreidler, Charles W(illiam) *linguist, educator*
Kreig, Andrew Thomas *trade association executive*
Kreinheder, Hazel Fuller *genealogist, historian*
Krepinevich, Andrew F. *organization administrator*
Kressley, Larry *foundation administrator*
Kriesberg, Simeon M. *lawyer*
†Kripowicz, Robert S. *energy administrator*
Kristol, Irving *social sciences educator, editor*
Kristol, William *editor, publisher*
Kroener, William Frederick, III *lawyer*
Krol, Joseph John, Jr. *career officer*
Krombein, Karl vonVorse *entomologist*
Kronstein, Werner J *lawyer*
†Krulak, Charles Chandler *marine officer*
Krulfeld, Ruth Marilyn *anthropologist, educator*
Krump, Gary Joseph *lawyer*
Ku, Charlotte *professional association administrator*
Kucinich, Dennis J. *congressman*
Kuder, Armin Ulrich *lawyer*
†Kudlacz, Michael S. *career officer*
Kuh, Charlotte Virginia *economist*
Kullberg, John Francis *foundation administrator*
Kundanis, George *congressional aide*
Kung, David Shean-Guang *plastic surgeon*
Kuperman, Frances Pergericht *lawyer*
Kurin, Richard *museum program director*
Kurtz, Howard *journalist, author*
†Kurtzer, Daniel *ambassador*
Kurtzke, John Francis, Sr. *neurologist, epidemiologist*
Kusnet, David *speechwriter, commentator*
Kutscher, Ronald Earl *retired federal government executive*
Kuykendall, Steven T. *congressman*
Kybal, Elba Gómez del Rey *economist, non-profit organization executive*
Kyhos, M. Gaither Galleher *private school educator*
Kyhos, Thomas Flynn *lawyer*
Kyl, Jon L. *senator*
Labandeira, Conrad Christopher *paleobiologist*
†Lachance, Janice Rachel *federal agency administrator, lawyer*
Laczko, Brian John *theater director*
Laden, Ben Ellis *economist*
Laden, Susan *publisher, consultant*
†Ladner, Benjamin *university president*
Laessig, Walter Bruce *publishing executive*
La Falce, John Joseph *congressman, lawyer*
†Lago, Marisa *federal agency administrator*
LaHaye, Beverly *cultural organization administrator*
LaHood, Ray *congressman*
Laird, Melvin Robert *former secretary of defense*
Lamb, Brian P. *broadcast executive*
Lambert, Jeremiah Daniel *lawyer*
Lambert, Steven Charles *lawyer*
Lamberth, Royce C. *federal judge*
Lambro, Donald Joseph *columnist*
Lamm, Carolyn Beth *lawyer*
†Lampe, George P. *retired military officer*
Lampl, Peggy Ann *social services administrator*
Lampson, Nick *congressman*
Landers, James Michael (Jim Landers) *news correspondent*
Landfield, Richard *lawyer*
Landrieu, Mary L. *senator*
Landsburg, Alexander Charles *naval architect, researcher*
Lane, Bruce Stuart *lawyer*
Lane, Herman Eugene *human resource manager*
Lane, John Dennis *lawyer*
Lane, Mark *lawyer, educator, author*
†Lane, Maury *communications director*
Lane, Neal Francis *federal administrator, physics researcher, former university provost*
Lange, William Michael *lawyer*
Langston, Edward R., Jr. *career officer*
†Lankler, Gregory M. *legislative administrator*
Lantos, Thomas Peter *congressman*
Lanza, Kenneth Anthony *foreign service officer*
LaPidus, Jules Benjamin *educational association administrator*
Laporte, Gerald Joseph Sylvestre *lawyer*
Lapp, Douglas Martin *director national science resource center*
Laqueur, Walter *history educator*
Lardner, George, Jr. *journalist, author*
Lardy, Nicholas Richard *economics educator*
Largent, Steve *congressman, former professional football player*
†LaRiche, Jeffrey T. *museum administrator*
†Larkin, Barbara Mills *federal agency administrator*
Laro, David *judge*

†La Rocque, Gene Robert retired naval officer, government official, author
Larroca, Raymond G. lawyer
Larsen, Richard Gary accounting firm executive
†Larson, Alan Philip federal official
Larson, Charles Fred trade association executive
Larson, George Charles magazine editor, writer
†Larson, John Barry congressman, insurance executive
La Sala, James labor union administrator
Lash, Jonathan non-profit environment/development executive
Lash, Myles Perry hospital administrator, consultant
Lash, Terry R. federal agency administrator
Lasko, Joel company executive
†Laster, Gail W. lawyer
Lastowka, James Anthony former federal agency executive, lawyer
Latham, Peter Samuel lawyer
Latham, Tom congressman
Latham, Weldon Hurd lawyer
†Lathen, Deborah A. federal agency administrator
Latimer, Allie B. retired lawyer
LaTourette, Steven C. congressman
†Lattimore, Patricia administration and management administrator
Laughlin, Felix B. lawyer
Laughlin, Gregory H. (Greg Laughlin) former congressman
Laughlin, James Harold, Jr. lawyer
Lautenberg, Frank R. senator
Lavelle, Joseph P. lawyer
Lavine, Henry Wolfe lawyer
Lawson, Jennifer broadcast executive
Lawson, Richard Laverne trade association executive, retired military officer
†Layden, John F. federal agency chairman
Lazarus, Arthur, Jr. lawyer
Lazarus, Kenneth Anthony lawyer
Lazio, Rick A. congressman, lawyer
Leach, James Albert Smith congressman
Leaf, Howard Westley retired air force officer, military official
†Leahy, Daniel F. federal agency administrator
Leahy, Patrick Joseph senator
Leary, Thomas Barrett lawyer
LeBlanc, James Leo business executive, consultant
Lebow, Irwin Leon communications engineering consultant
LeBrecht, Thelma Jane Mossman reporter
Ledley, Robert Steven biophysicist
Lee, Barbara congresswoman
Lee, Carol Frances lawyer
Lee, Charlyn Yvonne chemical engineer
Lee, Shew Kuhn retired optometrist
Leeds, Charles Alan publishing executive
Leffall, LaSalle D(oheny), Jr. surgeon
Le Goc, Michel Jean-Louis business educator
Lehman, Donald Richard physicist, educator
Lehmberg, Robert Henry research physicist
Lehner, George Alexander, Jr. lawyer
Lehrer, James Charles television journalist
Leibach, Dale W. public relations executive
Leibold, Arthur William, Jr. lawyer
Leigh, Monroe lawyer
Leiter, Richard Allen law educator, law librarian
†Lemmon, David press secretary
Lenczowski, John political science educator
Lenhart, James Thomas lawyer
Lennon, John Edward broadcast executive
Lent, Norman Frederick, Jr. former congressman
Lentini, Joseph Charles government agency management analyst
LeoGrande, William Mark political science educator, writer
Leon, Donald Francis university dean, medical educator
Leonard, H. Jeffrey finance executive
Leonard, Will Ernest, Jr. lawyer
Leshy, John D. lawyer, legal educator, government official
Lessard, Arnold Fred international business executive
Lessenco, Gilbert Barry lawyer
Lessin, Lawrence Stephen hematologist, oncologist, educator
Lessy, Roy Paul, Jr. lawyer
Leubsdorf, Carl Philipp newspaper executive
Levenson, Alan Bradley lawyer
Levey, Robert Frank newspaper columnist
Levin, Carl senator
Levin, Edward M. lawyer, government administrator
Levin, Peter J. hospital administrator, public health professor
Levin, Sander M. congressman
Levine, Henry David lawyer
Levinson, Daniel Ronald lawyer
Levinson, Nanette Segal international relations educator, administrator
Levinson, Peter Joseph lawyer
Levitt, Arthur, Jr. federal agency administrator, securities and publishing executive
Levitt, Mark Howard government official
Levy, David Corcos museum director
Levy, David Matthew lawyer
Levy, Mark Irving lawyer
Levy, Michael B. business educator
Lew, Jacob federal official
Lewis, Anne McCutcheon architect
Lewis, Charles Jeremy congressman
Lewis, Charles Joseph journalist
Lewis, David John lawyer
Lewis, Douglas art historian
Lewis, Eleanor Roberts lawyer
†Lewis, Fred P. career officer
Lewis, Henry Donald fundraising consultant
Lewis, John R. congressman
†Lewis, John Van Dusen federal agency administrator, anthropologist
Lewis, Lorraine general counsel
Lewis, Robert David Gilmore editor
Lewis, Robert John Cornelius Koons university library director, consultant
Lewis, Ron congressman
Lewis, William Henry, Jr. lawyer
Lewis, William Walker management consultant
†Lewis, Wilma Antoinette prosecutor, former federal agency administrator
†Libin, Alexander Viktorovich psychologist, researcher, writer
Lichtman, Allan Jay historian, educator, consultant
Liebenson, Herbert economist, trade association executive
Lieber, Robert James political science educator, writer
Lieberman, James federal agency administrator
Lieberman, Joseph I. senator
Liebman, Ronald Stanley lawyer
Liederman, David Samuel child welfare administrator
Lilienthal, Alfred M(orton) author, historian, editor
Lilly, William Eldridge government official
Lim, Joseph Edward lawyer
Limon, Lavinia social services administrator
Lin, William Wen-Rong economist
Lincoln, Blanche Lambert senator
Lindberg, Tod Marshall editor, writer
Linder, John E. congressman, dentist
Lindquist, Robert John accountant, financial investigator
Lindsey, Alfred Walter federal agency official, environmental engineer
Lindsey, Lawrence Benjamin economist
Lindsey, Seth Mark lawyer, federal agency administrator
†Linehan, Lou Ann state official
Ling, Geoffrey Shiu Fei neurologist, pharmacologist, educator
†Linn, Johannes bank executive
Linn, Richard lawyer
Linowitz, Sol Myron lawyer
†Linton, Gordon J. federal agency administrator
Lipinski, William Oliver congressman
Lipstein, Robert A. lawyer
Lipton, Eric reporter
†Lisaius, Kenneth Allen communications specialist
Lisboa-Farrow, Elizabeth Oliver public and government relations consultant
Lissakers, Karin Margareta federal agency administrator
Lister, Harry Joseph financial company executive, consultant
Litan, Robert Eli lawyer, economist
Litke, Arthur Ludwig business executive
Littell, Richard Gregory lawyer
Littig, Lawrence William psychologist, educator
Little, John William plastic surgeon, educator
†Liu, Xiaozhu Drew institute administrator, editor
Livingood, Wilson S. law enforcement official
Livingston, Donald Ray lawyer
Livingston, Robert Gerald university official, political scientist
Livingston, Robert Linlithgow, Jr. (Bob Livingston, Jr.) former congressman
LLubién, Joseph Herman psychotherapist, counselor
Loach, Robert Edward federal agency administrator
LoBiondo, Frank A. congressman
Lobron, Neil Richard federal civil servant
†Lockwood, Maggie L. press secretary
Lockyer, Charles Warren, Jr. corporate executive
Loeb, G. Hamilton lawyer
Loeffler, Robert Hugh lawyer
Loevinger, Lee lawyer, science writer
Lofgren, Zoe congresswoman
†Lofton, James H. legislative staff
†Logan, Ann D. financial company executive
Loker, Elizabeth St. John newspaper executive
Lombard, Judith Marie human resource policy specialist
Lombardo, Fredric Alan pharmacist, educator
†Long, Nancy writer, lawyer
†Longest, Henry L., II research and development administrator
Longin, Thomas Charles education association administrator
Loosbrock, Carol Marie information management professional
Lopatin, Alan G. lawyer
†Lori, William E. bishop
Lorsung, Thomas Nicholas news service editor
Lott, Trent senator
Lotze, Evie Daniel psychodramatist
Lourie, Alan David federal judge
Love, Margaret Colgate lawyer
Lovell, Malcolm Read, Jr. public policy institute executive, educator, former government official, former trade association executive
Low, Stephen foundation executive, educator, former diplomat
Lowe, Harry museum director
Lowe, Mary Frances federal government official
Lowe, Randall Brian lawyer
Lowenstein, James Gordon former diplomat, international consultant
Lowey, Nita M. congresswoman
Loy, Frank Ernest government official
Loy, James M. coast guard officer
Lubar, Jeffrey Stuart journalist, trade association executive
Lubic, Robert Bennett lawyer, arbitrator, law educator
Lubick, Donald Cyril lawyer
Lucas, C. Payne development organization executive
Lucas, Frank D. congressman
Lucas, George Ramsdell, Jr. philosophy educator
Lucas, James Walter federal government official
†Lucas, Ken congressman
Lucas, Steven Mitchell lawyer
Luce, Gregory M. lawyer
Luciano, Peter Joseph professional society administrator
Luck, Andrew Peter federal agency administrator
†Ludecke, Kristen M. press secretary
†Luedtke, Thomas associate administrator procurement for NASA
Luessenhop, Alfred John neurosurgeon, educator
Lugar, Richard Green senator
Luhrs, Caro Elise internal medicine physician, administrator, educator
Luikart, Fordyce Whitney management consultant
†Lundsager, Meg federal agency administrator
†Lupia, Eugene A. military officer
Lupo, Raphael V. lawyer
Lurding, Donald Scott business executive
Lustig, Nora Claudia researcher
Luther, William P. congressman
Luti, William Joseph career officer
Luttwak, Edward Nicolae academic, writer policy and business consultant
Luxenberg, Steven Marc newspaper editor
Lybecker, Martin Earl lawyer
Lydon, Thomas J. federal judge
†Lyles, Lester L. director
Lynch, Robert L. art association administrator
Lyness, Richard Mark journalist, editor
Lynker, John Paul newscaster
Lynn, Barry William religious organization executive
Lynn, D. Joanne physician, ethicist, health services researcher
†Lynn, James Thomas investment banker, insurance company executive, government executive, lawyer
Lynn, William James, III federal agency administrator
Lyons, Dennis Gerald lawyer
Lyons, James Robert federal official
MacBeth, Angus lawyer
MacDonald, Bruce Walter aerospace engineer, government official
Macdonald, David Robert lawyer, fund administrator
MacDonald, Gary Alan lawyer
MacDonald, John Thomas educational administrator
MacDonald, William Lloyd architectural historian
MacIntyre, John Alexander financial planner
Mack, Connie, III (Cornelius Mack) senator
Mack, Julia Cooper judge
Mack, Raymond Francis newspaper executive
MacKay, Kenneth Hood, Jr. (Buddy MacKay) federal official
MacLaury, Bruce King research institution executive
MacLeish, Roderick novelist, screenwriter, television producer
Macleod, John Amend lawyer
†MacLeod, Laurel A. lobbyist, researcher
†Maco, Paul S. securities and exchange administrator
Macomber, John D. industrialist
Madden, Jerome Anthony lawyer
Madden, Murdaugh Stuart lawyer
Maddock, Jerome Torrence information services specialist
Mader, David federal agency administrator
†Madison, Christopher King communications director
Maechling, Charles, Jr. lawyer, diplomat, educator, writer
†Magaw, John W. federal law enforcement official
Magee, Charles Thomas international consultant, retired diplomat
Magielnicki, Robert L. lawyer
Magrath, C. Peter educational association executive
Mahar, Ellen Patricia law librarian
†Maher, John Joseph, III military career officer
Maher, Patrick Joseph retired utility company executive
†Mahr, Thomas D. legislative staff member
Maillett, Louise Elizabeth government official
†Majak, Roger administration executive
Majev, Howard Rudolph lawyer
Makris, Andreas composer
Malcom, Shirley Mahaley science association executive
Malek, Frederic Vincent finance company executive
Malia, Gerald Aloysius lawyer
†Mallan, John Powers retired educator
Malone, Julia Louise news reporter, national correspondent
Maloney, Carolyn Bosher congresswoman
Malveaux, Floyd Joseph academic dean
Mamer, Louisan Elizabeth home economist, journalist
Manatos, Andrew Emanuel public relations executive
Mann, Charles Roy statistician
Mann, Donegan lawyer
Mann, John L. federal agency administrator
Mann, Marion physician, educator
Mann, Roger Ellis food service and real estate and business development executive
Mann, Thomas Edward political scientist
Mansfield, Edward Patrick, Jr. advertising executive
Manson, Joseph Lloyd, III lawyer
Manzullo, Donald A congressman, lawyer
Mao, Ho-kwang geophysicist, educator
Maraniss, David journalist
Marans, J. Eugene lawyer
Marburg-Goodman, Jeffrey Emil lawyer
Marcotte, Michael Steven municipal administrator
Marcum, Deanna Bowling library administrator
Marcuss, Rosemary Daly economist
Marcuss, Stanley Joseph lawyer
Marfiak, Thomas F. career officer
Marfiak, Thomas Fletcher naval officer
Margeton, Stephen George law librarian
Margolis, Daniel Herbert lawyer
Margolis, Lawrence Stanley federal judge
Marinaccio, Charles Lindbergh lawyer
Mariotte, Michael Lee environmental activist, environmental publication director
Mark, Hans Michael physicist, government official
Markey, Edward John congressman
Marks, Herbert Edward lawyer
Marks, Jonathan Bowles lawyer, mediator, arbitrator
Marks, Leonard Harold lawyer
Marks, Richard Daniel lawyer
Marquez, Awilda Rose federal official
Marquez, Joaquin Alfredo lawyer
Marr, Phebe Ann historian, educator
Marriott, John Willard, Jr. lodging and senior living executive
Marsh, Caryl Amsterdam museum exhibitions curator, psychologist, advisor
Marshall, Ann Louise pastoral counselor
Marshall, Brian Laurence trade association executive
Marshall, C. Travis manufacturing executive, government relations specialist
Marshall, William, III think tank executive
Martin, David Briton Hadden, Jr. lawyer
Martin, David Standish education educator
†Martin, Edith Waisbrot computer scientist, aerospace and electronics company executive
Martin, Guy lawyer
Martin, Jerry Lee organization executive, educator
Martin, John Joseph journalist
†Martin, Julie A. insurance executive
†Martin, Kate Abbott lawyer
Martin, Keith lawyer
Martin, Ralph Drury lawyer, columnist
Martin, Susan Katherine librarian
†Martinage, Ashley E. legislative staff member
Martinez, Eluid government official
Martinez, Herminia S. economist, banker
Martinez, Matthew Gilbert congressman
†Martinez, Ricardo federal agency administrator
Martuza, Robert L. neurosurgeon
Marumoto, William Hideo management consultant
Marvel, L. Paige judge, lawyer
Mascara, Frank congressman
Masi, Dale A. research company executive, social work educator
Mason, Brian Harold geologist, curator
Mason, Dwight Newell law administrator
†Masten, Charles C. federal agency administrator
Masters, Edward E. association executive, former foreign service officer
Mastromarco, Dan Ralph lawyer
Matheson, Michael J. federal official
Mathews, Jessica Tuchman policy researcher, columnist
Mathias, Charles McCurdy lawyer, former senator
Mathias, Edward Joseph merchant banker
Mathis, John Prentiss lawyer
Matsui, Robert Takeo congressman
Mattar, Philip institute director, editor
Mattingly, J. Virgil, Jr. federal lawyer
†Maude, Timothy J. career officer
†Maury, Samuel L. association executive
Maxa, Rudolph Joseph, Jr. journalist
Maxted, William C. dean
Maxwell, David E. academic executive, educator
Maxwell, David Ogden former government official and financial executive
May, Clifford Daniel director, newspaper editor, journalist
May, Felton Edwin bishop
May, Stephen writer, former government official
†May, Sterling Randolph health association executive
May, Timothy James lawyer
Mayer, Haldane Robert federal chief judge
Mayer, Martin career officer
Mayer, Neal Michael lawyer
†Mayer, Susan telecommunications company executive
Mayers, Daniel Kriegsman lawyer
Mayfield, Richard Heverin lawyer
Maynes, Charles William foundation administrator
Mayo, George Washington, Jr. lawyer
Mazo, Mark Elliott lawyer
Mazzaferri, Katherine Aquino lawyer, bar association executive
Mc Afee, William government official
McAllister, Jennifer Rae financial controller
McAllister, William Howard, III newspaper reporter, columnist
McAteer, J. Davitt federal agency administrator
McAvoy, John Joseph lawyer
McBee, Susanna Barnes journalist
McBride, Jonathan Evans executive search consultant
McBride, Martha Gene Shultz editor, actress
McBride, Michael Flynn lawyer
McCaffrey, Barry Richard federal official, retired army officer
McCain, John Sidney, III senator
†McCam, Shelia federal agency administrator
McCann, Michael F. industrial hygienist
McCarthy, Abigail Quigley writer, columnist, educator
McCarthy, David Jerome, Jr. law educator
†McCarthy, John F. healthcare administrator
McCarthy, Karen P. congresswoman, former state representative
McClain, William Thomas lawyer
McCollam, William, Jr. utility company executive
Mc Collum, Ira William, Jr. (Bill Mc Collum) congressman
McConnell, Addison Mitchell, Jr. (Mitch McConnell, Jr.) senator, lawyer
McCormally, Kevin Jay editor
†McCoy, Helen Thomas civilian military employee
McCoy, Jerry Jack lawyer
McCrabb, Donald Raymond lay minister
McCreight, Robert Edwin federal agency administrator, educator
McCrery, James (Jim McCrery) congressman
McDaniels, William E. lawyer
McDavid, Janet Louise lawyer
Mc Dermott, Albert Leo lawyer
McDermott, Edward Aloysious lawyer
McDermott, James A. congressman, psychiatrist
McDiarmid, Robert Campbell lawyer
Mc Donald, John Warlick diplomat, global strategist
†McDonald, Patricia Ann legislative administrator
McDowell, Charles R. columnist, news analyst, lecturer
†McDuffie, John M. military officer
McElveen, Joseph James, Jr. author, journalist, public broadcasting executive
McElveen, Junius Carlisle, Jr. lawyer
McEnroe, John Patrick, Jr. professional tennis player, commentator
McEntee, Gerald W. labor union official
McEwen, Gerald Noah, Jr. bio scientist executive
†McGarey, Patrick O. legislative staff member
Mc Giffert, David Eliot lawyer, former government official
†McGill, Michael S. legislative staff member
McGinley, Edward Stillman, II former naval officer, engineering executive
McGinnies, Elliott Morse psychologist, educator
McGinnis, James Michael physician
McGinty, Kathleen federal official
McGovern, James P. congressman
McGovern, Michael Barbot lawyer
McGrath, Kathryn Bradley lawyer
McGrath, Mary Helena plastic surgeon, educator
McGraw, Lavinia Morgan retired retail company executive
Mc Grory, Mary columnist
McGue, Christie federal official
McGuire, Patricia A. lawyer, academic administrator
McGuire, Roger Alan retired foreign service officer
McHugh, James Lenahan, Jr. lawyer
McHugh, John Michael congressman, former state senator
McIlwain, John Knox real estate investment administrator
McInnis, Scott Steve congressman, lawyer
McIntosh, David M. congressman
McIntyre, Bernice Kay lawyer, management consultant
McIntyre, Carl Henry, Jr. lawyer
McIntyre, Douglas Carmichael, II congressman
McIntyre, Mike congressman
Mc Kay, Emily Gantz civil rights professional
McKee, Alan R. foreign service officer
†McKelvie, Darina C. federal agency administrator
McKeon, Howard P. (Buck McKeon) congressman, former mayor
McKeown, Joe women's basketball coach
†McKinley, Craig R. air force officer
McKinney, Cynthia Ann congresswoman
McKinney, James DeVaine, Jr. lawyer
McLaughlin, John broadcast executive, television producer, political commentator, journalist
Mc Lean, George Francis philosophy of religion educator, clergyman
McLean, R. Bruce lawyer
McLellan, Joseph Duncan critic, journalist
McLucas, William Robert federal agency director
McMahon, Debra Brylawski management consultant
McMahon, Joseph Einar lawyer, consultant
McMahon, Neil Michael real estate executive
†McMahon, Timothy J. career officer
McMichael, Guy H., III federal official
McNamara, Robert Strange former banking executive, cabinet member
McNeil, Patricia Wentworth federal agency executive
McNicol, David Leon federal official
McNulty, Michael Robert congressman
McNulty, Robert Holmes non-profit executive
Mc Phee, Henry Roemer lawyer
Mc Pherson, Harry Cummings, Jr. lawyer

McQueen, James T. *federal agency administrator*
McReynolds, Mary Armilda *lawyer*
McShane, Franklin John, III *nurse anesthetist, army officer*
McSteen, Martha Abernathy *organization executive*
†McTaggart, Timothy Robert *state agency administrator, lawyer*
Mead, Gilbert D(unbar) *geophysicist, lawyer*
†Mead, Kenneth Minor *federal agency administrator*
Means, Marianne *political columnist*
Means, Thomas Cornell *lawyer*
Mears, Walter Robert *journalist*
Medalie, Richard James *lawyer*
Medalie, Susan Diane *lawyer, management consultant*
Mederos, Carolina Luisa *transportation policy consultant*
Medish, Mark *federal government official*
Meehan, Martin Thomas *congressman, lawyer*
Meek, Carrie P. *congresswoman*
Meekers, Dominique Armand *health and demographics researcher*
Meeks, Gregory Weldon *congressman*
Meggers, Betty J(ane) *anthropologist*
Mehle, Roger W. *federal agency administrator*
Meijer, Paul Herman Ernst *educator, physicist*
Melamed, Arthur Douglas *lawyer*
Melamed, Carol Drescher *lawyer*
Melendez, Sara E. *non-profit organization executive*
Melendy, David Russell *broadcast journalist*
Mellor, John Williams *economist, policy consultant firm executive*
†Mellow, Jane E. *legislative administrator*
Meloy, Sybil Piskur *lawyer*
Melton, Carol A(nne) *media executive*
Meltzer, Alan David *lawyer*
Menard, Edith *English language educator, artist, poet, actress*
Mencher, Bruce Stephan *judge*
Menczer, William B. *government agency executive*
Mendelsohn, Martin *lawyer*
Menendez, Adolfo *engineering company executive*
Menendez, Robert *congressman, lawyer*
†Menig, Janet *federal government executive*
Menkel-Meadow, Carrie Joan *law educator*
Menzer, Robert Everett *toxicologist, educator*
Meredith, Pamela Louise *lawyer*
Merow, James F. *federal judge*
Merry, Robert William *publishing executive*
Meserve, Richard Andrew *lawyer*
Messenger, Jon Carleton *government project manager*
Messner, Howard Myron *professional association executive*
Meszar, Frank *publishing executive, former army officer*
Metcalf, Jack *congressman, retired state senator*
Metz, Craig Huseman *legislative administrator*
Metz, Helen Chapin *Middle East analyst*
Metz, Ronald Irwin *retired priest, addictions counselor*
†Metz, Thomas Frederic *military career officer*
Meurlin, Keith W. *airport manager*
Meyer, Alden Merrill *environmental association executive*
Meyer, Armin Henry *retired diplomat, author, educator*
Meyer, Cord *columnist*
Meyer, Dennis Irwin *lawyer*
Meyer, Laurence Harvey *federal official*
Meyer, Lawrence Robert *journalist*
Meyerhoff, James Lester *medical researcher*
Meyers, Tedson Jay *lawyer*
Meyers, Wayne Marvin *microbiologist*
Meyerson, Adam *foundation executive*
Meyerson, Christopher Cortlandt *law scholar*
†Mezo, Ronald S. *retail executive, small business consultant*
Michaels, Gary David *lawyer*
Michaelson, Martin *lawyer*
Michaud, Michael Alan George *diplomat, writer*
Michel, James H. *ambassador, lawyer*
Michel, Paul Redmond *federal judge*
Michelman, Kate *advocate*
Middendorf, J. William, II *investment banker*
Mielke, James Edward *geochemist*
Miklaszewski, James Alan *television news correspondent*
Miles, David Michael *lawyer*
Miles, Richard *diplomat*
Millar, James Robert *economist, educator, university official*
Millender-McDonald, Juanita *congresswoman, former school system administrator*
Miller, Alan Stanley *ecology center administrator, law educator*
Miller, Andrew Pickens *lawyer*
Miller, Carl Frank *financial executive, vending controller*
Miller, Charles A. *lawyer*
Miller, Christine Odell Cook *judge*
Miller, Dan *congressman*
Miller, Evan *lawyer*
†Miller, Gary G. *congressman*
Miller, Gay Davis *lawyer*
Miller, George *congressman*
Miller, G(eorge) William *merchant banker, business executive*
Miller, H. Todd *lawyer*
Miller, Herbert John, Jr. *lawyer*
Miller, Iris Ann *landscape architect, urban designer, educator*
Miller, James Clifford, III *economist*
Miller, Jeanne-Marie Anderson (Mrs. Nathan J. Miller) *English language educator, academic administrator*
Miller, John Francis *association executive, social scientist*
Miller, John T., Jr. *lawyer, educator*
Miller, Judith A. *federal official*
Miller, Kerry Lee *lawyer*
Miller, Loye Wheat, Jr. *journalist, corporate communications specialist*
Miller, Marcia E. *federal government official*
Miller, Margaret Alison *education association administrator*
Miller, Mark Karl *journalist*
Miller, Marshall Lee *lawyer*
Miller, Mary Hotchkiss *lay worker*
Miller, Robert Allen *hotel executive*
Miller, Warren Lloyd *lawyer*
Miller, William Green *ambassador*
Millian, Kenneth Young *public policy consultant*
Millie, Harold Raymond *editor*
Millon, Henry Armand *fine arts educator, architectural historian*
Mills, Kevin Paul *lawyer*
Milstein, Elliott Steven *law educator, academic administrator*
Minarik, Joseph John *economist, researcher*
Minge, David *congressman, lawyer, law educator*
Mink, Patsy Takemoto *congresswoman*
Minkoff, Alice Sydney *interior designer, showroom owner*
Minnich, Nelson Hubert Joseph *historian, educator*
Mintz, Seymour Stanley *lawyer*
Mishkin, Barbara Friedman *lawyer*
Misner, Robert David *electronic warfare and magnetic recording consultant, electro-mechanical company executive*
Missar, Charles Donald *librarian*
Mitchell, Andrea *journalist*
Mitchell, Brian Keith *professional football player*
Mitchell, Roy Shaw *lawyer*
Mixter, Christian John *lawyer*
Mlay, Marian *retireed government official*
Moakley, John Joseph *congressman*
Moates, G. Paul *lawyer*
Modiano, Albert Louis *gas, oil industry executive*
Moe, Richard Palmer *lawyer*
Moe, Ronald Chesney *public administration researcher*
Moler, Elizabeth Anne *lawyer*
†Molitoris, Jolene M. *federal agency administrator*
Mollohan, Alan B. *congressman, lawyer*
Monagan, John Stephen *writer, lecturer, retired congressman and lawyer*
Money, Arthur Lewis *electronics executive*
Moniz, Ernest Jeffrey *government official, former physics educator*
Monkman, Betty Claire *curator*
Monroe, Robert Rawson *engineering construction executive*
Montgomery, George Cranwell *lawyer, former ambassador*
Mooney, Marilyn *lawyer*
Moore, Amy Norwood *lawyer*
Moore, Bob Stahly *communications executive*
†Moore, Dennis *congressman*
Moore, Elvi *performing company executive*
Moore, George S., Jr. *government, executive*
Moore, Jacquelyn Cornelia *labor union official, editor*
Moore, Jerry *retired religious organization administrator*
Moore, Marsha Lynn *elementary education educator*
Moore, Miles David *journalist*
Moore, Robert Madison *food industry executive, lawyer*
†Moore, William F. *military officer*
Moran, James Patrick, Jr. *congressman, stockbroker*
Moran, Jerry *congressman*
More, John Herron *lawyer, classicist*
Morehouse, David Frank *geologist*
Morella, Constance Albanese *congresswoman*
Moreno, G(ilberto) Mario *federal agency administrator*
Morgan, Linda Joan *federal agency administrator*
†Morgan, Ronald E. *federal air traffic director*
Moring, John Frederick *lawyer*
†Moritz-Ridenour, Amy *research center administrator*
Morningstar, Richard L. *diplomat*
Morris, Craig Allen *international marketing specialist*
Morris, Daniel Kearns *journalist*
†Morris, Joann Sebastion *federal agency adminstrator*
Morrison, Bruce Andrew *government executive, former congressman*
Morriss, Nicholas Anson *financial consultant*
†Morse, Jerome Samuel *government administrator, trade specialist*
Morse, M. Howard *lawyer*
Morse, Richard McGee *historian*
†Mosely, Teed M. *career officer*
Moser, Donald Bruce *magazine editor*
Moses, Alfred Henry *lawyer, former ambassador*
Moskowitz, Faye Stollman *educator*
†Mosley, Raymond A. *federal agency administrator*
Moss, Madison Scott *editor*
Moss, Thomas Henry *science association administrator*
Mossel, Patricia L. *opera executive*
Mosso, Lyle David *accountant*
Mostoff, Allan Samuel *lawyer, consultant*
Moulton, David Aubin *library director*
Moyer, Homer Edward, Jr. *lawyer*
Moynihan, Daniel Patrick *senator, educator*
Mrazek, David Allen *pediatric psychiatrist*
Mtewa, Mekki *foundation administrator*
†Muasher, Marwan J. *Jordanian diplomat*
Muckenfuss, Cantwell Faulkner, III *lawyer*
Mueller, Sharon Lee (Sherry Mueller) *educational organization executive*
Muhn, B.G. *artist, educator*
Muir, J. Dapray *lawyer*
Muir, Patricia Allen *professional association administrator*
Mujica, Barbara Louise *foreign language educator, author*
Muldrow, Tressie Wright *psychologist*
Mulhollan, Daniel Patrick *research director*
†Mulloy, Patrick Aloysius *lawyer*
Munasinghe, Mohan *development economist*
†Munoz, George *federal agency administrator*
Munsell, Elsie Louise *lawyer*
Munson, Richard Jay *congressional policy analyst*
Murett, Robert B. *career officer*
Murkowski, Frank Hughes *senator*
Murphy, Betty Southard (Mrs. Cornelius F. Murphy) *lawyer*
Murphy, Emalee Godsey *lawyer*
Murphy, Gerald *retired government official, consultant*
Murphy, John Condron, Jr. *lawyer*
Murphy, Kathryn Marguerite *archivist*
Murphy, Lezell Wanda *stock market analyst*
†Murphy, Patrick M. *legislative staff member*
Murphy, Sean Patrick *lawyer*
Murphy, Shaun Edward *bank executive*
Murphy, Terence Roche *lawyer*
Murr, James Coleman *retired federal government official*
Murray, Alan Stewart *publishing executive*
Murray, Christopher Charles, III *architect*
Murray, James Joseph, III *association executive*
Murray, John Einar *lawyer, retired army officer, federal official*
Murray, Patty *senator*
Murray, Robert Fulton, Jr. *physician*
Murry, Harold David, Jr. *lawyer*
Murtha, John Patrick *congressman*
†Musick, Anthony *financial executive*
Musil, Robert Kirkland *professional society administrator*
Mutter, Carol A. *career officer*
Myers, Elissa Matulis *publisher, association executive*
Myers, James R. *lawyer*
†Myers, Margaret E. *performance assessment director*
Myers, Marjorie Lora *elementary school principal*
Myrick, Sue *congresswoman, former mayor*
Nabholz, Joseph Vincent *biologist, ecologist*
Nace, Barry John *lawyer*
Nader, Ralph *consumer advocate, lawyer, author*
Nadler, Jerrold Lewis *congressman, lawyer*
Nagorski, Zygmunt *political scientist*
†Naher, Raymond *federal agency administrator*
Nahmad, Albert H. *United States federal commissioner, manufacturing executive*
Nakhleh, Emile A. *political science educator*
Namorato, Cono R. *lawyer*
Nangle, John Francis *federal judge*
Napier, John Light *lawyer*
†Napolitano, Grace F. *congresswoman*
Narasaki, Karen Keiko *civil rights organization executive, lawyer*
Natalie, Ronald Bruce *lawyer*
Navarro, Bruce Charles *lawyer*
†Navas, William Antonio, Jr. *retired military officer, civil engineer*
Naylor, Brian *news correspondent*
†Naylor, Mary A. *legislative staff member*
Neal, Charlie *sports broadcaster*
Neal, Darwina Lee *government official*
Neal, Richard Edmund *congressman, former mayor*
†Neal, Robert L., Jr. *director*
Neas, Lindsey Rutledge *legislative assistant*
Nebeker, Frank Quill *federal judge*
Neff, William L. *lawyer*
Neimark, Sheridan *lawyer*
Nelson, Alan Phillip *nuclear energy scientist*
Nelson, Alan Ray *internist, medical assocation executive*
Nelson, Candice Jean *political science educator*
Nelson, Gaylord Anton *former senator, association executive*
Nelson, George Driver *astronomy and education educator, former astronaut*
Nelson, Jacqueline Dunham *elementary education educator*
Nelson, John Howard (Jack Howard Nelson) *journalist*
Nelson, Lars-Erik *newspaperman*
Nelson, Robert Louis *lawyer*
Nemeroff, Michael Alan *lawyer*
Nemfakos, Charles Panagiotis *government official*
†Nesmith, Jeff *journalist*
Ness, Andrew David *lawyer*
Nethercutt, George Rector, Jr. *congressman, lawyer*
Nethery, John Jay *government official*
Neufeld, Michael John *curator, historian*
Neumann, Ronald Eldredge *diplomat*
Neviaser, Robert Jon *orthopaedic surgeon, educator*
Newman, Kurt Douglas *pediatric surgeon*
Newman, Monroe *retired economist, educator*
Newman, Pauline *federal judge*
†Newsom, Eric D. *federal official*
Newsome, Steven Cameron *museum director*
Newton, David George *diplomat*
Newton, Hugh C. *public relations executive*
Newton, Virginia *archivist, historian, librarian*
Ney, Robert W. *congressman*
Nicely, Olza M. (Tony) *insurance company executive*
Nichols, Henry Eliot *lawyer, savings and loan executive*
†Nichols, Rob *legislative staff member*
Nicholson, Jim *political organization administrator*
Nicholson, Richard Selindh *educational association administrator*
†Nickens, Paula *political organization administrator*
Nickles, Donald (Don Nickles) *senator*
†Nicogossian, Arnauld E.T. *federal agency administrator*
Nightingale, Elena Ottolenghi *geneticist, physician, administrator*
Nikkel, Ronald Wilbert *social services administrator*
Niskanen, William Arthur, Jr. *economist, think tank executive*
Noble, Lawrence Mark *federal government agency lawyer*
Nolan, David Brian *lawyer*
Nolan, John Edward *lawyer*
Noland, Marcus *economist, educator*
Norberg, Charles Robert *lawyer*
Norcross, David Frank Armstrong *lawyer*
Nordhaus, Robert Riggs *lawyer*
Nordlinger, Gerson, Jr. *investor*
Norland, Donald Richard *retired foreign service officer*
Norman, William Stanley *travel and tourism executive*
†Northington, Larry W. *career officer*
Northup, Anne Meagher *congresswoman*
Norton, Eleanor Holmes *congresswoman, lawyer, educator*
Norton, Floyd Ligon, IV *lawyer*
Norton, Gerald Patrick *lawyer*
Norton, James J. *union official*
Norwood, Charles W., Jr. *congressman*
†Novak, Jana *legislative staff member*
Novak, Michael (John) *religion educator, author, editor*
Novak, Robert David Sanders *newspaper columnist, television commentator*
†Novak, Vicki A. *human resources specialist*
Novitch, Mark *physician, educator, retired pharmaceutical executive*
Nowak, Judith Ann *psychiatrist*
Nuland, Anthony C. J. *lawyer*
Nussle, James Allen *congressman*
Nutter, Franklin Winston *lawyer*
Nutting, Wallace Hall *army officer*
Nwagbaraocha, Joel Onukwugha *academic administrator, educator*
Oakley, Diane *insurance executive, benefit consultant*
Oakley, Phyllis Elliott *diplomat*
Oakley, Robert Louis *law librarian, educator*
Oberdorfer, Louis F. *federal judge*
Oberstar, James L. *congressman*
Obey, David Ross *congressman*
†Obrecht, Margaret M. H. *cultural organization administrator*
†O'Brien, Edwin F. *bishop*
O'Brien, Richard Francis *advertising agency executive*
O'Brien, Timothy Andrew *writer, journalist, lawyer*
O'Bryon, James Fredrick *defense executive*
Ochmanek, David Alan *defense analyst*
Ochs, Charlie *broadcast executive*
O'Connor, Charles P. *lawyer*
O'Connor, Jennifer *lawyer*
O'Connor, John Dennis *academic administrator*
O'Connor, John Jay, III *lawyer*
O'Connor, Sandra Day *United States supreme court justice*
O'Connor, Thomas Edward *petroleum geologist, world bank officer*
O'Connor, Tom *corporate executive, management consultant*
O'Day, Paul Thomas *trade association executive*
O'Dell, Michael James *social sciences specialist*
†Odgers, Everett G. *career officer*
Odle, Robert Charles, Jr. *lawyer*
Odom, William Eldridge *army officer, educator*
O'Donnell, Terrence *lawyer*
O'Donovan, Leo Jeremiah *university president, theologian, priest*
Oehme, Wolfgang Walter *landscape architect*
Oertel, Goetz K. H. *physicist, professional association administrator*
Oertel, Yolanda Castillo *pathologist, educator, diagnostician*
Offutt, Susan Elizabeth *economist*
Oge, Margo Tsirigotis *environmentalist*
Ogg, Clayton Wallace *economist*
Ogilvie, Donald Gordon *bankers association executive*
Oh, John Kie-Chiang *political science educator, university official*
O'Hara, Clifford Bradley *commission administrator*
O'Hara, James Thomas *lawyer*
†Ohle, David H. *military career officer*
†Okin, Carol J. *federal agency administrator*
Olcott, John Whiting *aviation executive*
Olender, Jack Harvey *lawyer*
Oliver, LeAnn Michelle *government official*
Oliver, William Albert, Jr. *paleontologist*
Oliver-Simon, Gloria Craig *human resources advisor, consultant, lawyer*
Olmstead, Cecil Jay *lawyer*
Olson, Charles Eric *economist*
†Olson, Lyndon Lowell, Jr. *ambassador*
Olson, Theodore Bevry *lawyer*
Olson, Walter Justus, Jr. *management consultant*
Olver, John Walter *congressman*
O'Malley, Susan *professional basketball team executive*
Oman, Ralph *lawyer*
O'Neil, Joseph Francis *association executive*
O'Neil, John H., Jr. *lawyer*
†O'Neill, Richard P. *economist, director*
O'Neill, Richard Paul *federal agency administrator*
O'Neill, William Patrick *lawyer*
Onek, Joseph Nathan *lawyer*
Ongman, John Will *lawyer*
Ooms, Van Doorn *economist*
Opfer, George J. *federal agency executive*
Oppenheimer, Franz Martin *lawyer*
Oran, Elaine Surick *physicist, engineer*
O'Reilly, Kenneth William *military officer*
Orr, J. Scott *newspaper correspondent*
Orr, Paul Welles *government relations consultant*
Orski, C. Kenneth *consulting company executive, lawyer, publisher*
Ortiz, Solomon P. *congressman*
Ortner, Donald J. *biological anthropologist, educator*
Ose, Douglas *congressman*
Osgood, Barbara Travis *conservationist, sociologist*
Osnos, David Marvin *lawyer*
Osten, Janice Anne *education chief nurse*
Ostrov, Jerome *lawyer*
O'Sullivan, Judith Roberta *lawyer, author*
O'Sullivan, Lynda Troutman *lawyer*
O'Toole, Francis J. *lawyer*
Ottaway, David Blackburne *journalist*
Ottley, William Henry *professional association director, consultant*
Overbeck, Gene Edward *retired airline executive, lawyer*
Overman, Dean Lee *lawyer, investor, author*
Overman, Eric Mario *international trade and finance consultant*
Oweiss, Ibrahim Mohamed *economist, educator*
Owen, Henry *former ambassador, consultant*
Owen, Roberts Bishop *lawyer, arbitrator*
Owendoff, James M. *federal agency administrator*
Owens, Major Robert Odell *congressman*
Oxley, Michael Garver *congressman*
Oyler, Gregory Kenneth *lawyer*
Ozer, Martha Ross *school psychologist*
Paal, Douglas H. *educational association administrator*
Packard, Ronald C. *congressman*
Padden, Preston *broadcast executive*
Padgett, Nancy Weeks *law librarian, consultant, lawyer*
Padilla, David Joseph *lawyer, diplomat*
Page, Clarence E. *newspaper columnist*
Page, Harry Robert *business administration educator*
Page, Robert Wesley *engineering and construction company executive, federal official*
Page, Tim *music critic*
Paige, Hilliard Wegner *corporate director, consultant*
Painter, William Hall *law educator*
†Palast, Geri Deborah *federal agency administrator, Lawyer*
Pallone, Frank, Jr. *congressman*
Palmer, Robert E. *science administrator*
Palmer, R(obie Marcus Hooker) Mark *banker*
Palmer, Stacy Ella *periodical editor*
Palmer, Steven O. *federal official*
Palumbo, Benjamin Lewis *public affairs consulting company executive*
†Pamerleau, Susan L. *military officer*
Pancake, John *newspaper editor*
Panzer, Mary Caroline *museum curator*
Paper, Lewis J. *lawyer, educator*
Papkin, Robert David *lawyer*
Parde, Duane Arthur *association executive*
Pari, Brigitta Gulya *federal government official*
Park, Alice Mary Crandall *genealogist*
Park, Frances Mihei *author, food products executive*
Parr, Carolyn Miller *federal judge*
†Parris, Mark Robert *ambassador*
Parris, Robert *composer*
Pascrell, William J., Jr. *congressman*
Pashayev, Hafiz Mir Jalal *diplomat, physics educator*
†Pasini, Ralph *career officer*
†Pass, Jeffrey Ryan *researcher*
Passage, David *diplomat*
Pastor, Edward *congressman*
Patchan, Joseph Jerry *lawyer*
Pate, Michael Lynn *lawyer*
Patrick, Janet Cline *personnel company executive*
Patrick, Richard M. *professional hockey team executive*
Patron, June Eileen *former government official*

Roybal-Allard, Lucille *congresswoman*
Royce, Edward R. (Ed Royce) *congressman*
Roycroft, Howard Francis *lawyer*
Royle, David Brian Layton *television producer, journalist*
†Rubin, Eric S. *foreign service officer*
†Rubin, James P. *public affairs administrator*
Rubin, Kenneth Allen *lawyer*
Rubin, Robert E. *former secretary of treasury*
Rubin, Seymour Jeffrey *lawyer, judge, educator*
Rubinoff, Ira *biologist, research administrator, conservationist*
Rubinoff, Roberta Wolff *government administrator*
†Rucker, Kelly *legislative staff member*
Ruckman, Roger Norris *pediatric cardiologist*
Rudder, Catherine Estelle *political science association administrator*
Ruddy, Frank *lawyer, former ambassador*
†Rudesill, Dakota Sundance *legislative assistance*
Rudman, Warren Bruce *former senator, lawyer, think tank executive*
Ruehle, Charles Joseph *pathologist, military officer*
†Ruf, Frederick John *humanities educator*
Rugh, William Arthur *diplomat*
Ruiz, Vanessa *state judge*
Rule, Charles Frederick (Rick Rule) *lawyer*
†Rundquist, Paul Stanley *government policy analyst, educator*
Rupel, Dimitrij *diplomat*
Rusch, Jonathan Jay *lawyer*
Ruscio, Domenic *legislative consultant, public affairs specialist*
Rush, Bobby L. *congressman*
Rushnell, Squire Derrick *television executive*
Rushton, Emory Wayne *government official*
†Rushton, H. Gil *pediatrician, urologist, educator*
Russell, Mark *comedian*
Russell, Michael James *lawyer*
Russell, William Joseph *educational association administrator*
Russert, Timothy John *broadcast journalist, executive*
Russin, Jonathan *lawyer, consultant*
Rust, William David, Jr. *retired structural engineer*
Rutstein, David W. *lawyer, food products executive*
Ruttenberg, Charles Byron *lawyer*
Ruttinger, George David *lawyer*
Ruwe, Robert P. *federal judge*
Ryan, David Alan *computer specialist*
Ryan, Frederick Joseph, Jr. *lawyer, public official*
Ryan, John E. *federal agency administrator*
Ryan, Joseph *lawyer*
†Ryan, Judith Margaret *scripture scholar, educator*
†Ryan, Mary A. *diplomat*
Ryan, Norbert R., Jr. *career military officer*
†Ryan, Paul *congressman*
Ryerson, Paul Sommer *lawyer*
†Rymland, Richard Sylvan *real estate developer*
Ryn, Claes Gösta *political science educator, author, research institute administrator*
Ryun, Jim *congressman*
Sabo, Martin Olav *congressman*
Sabshin, Melvin *psychiatrist, educator, medical association administrator*
Sacher, Steven Jay *lawyer*
Sachs, Stephen Howard *lawyer*
Sackler, Arthur Brian *lawyer*
Sacksteder, Frederick Henry *former foreign service officer*
†Saffuri, Khaled Ahmad *cultural organization executive*
Safire, William *journalist, author*
Sagalkin, Sanford *lawyer*
Sagawa, Shirley Sachi *lawyer*
Salamon, Linda Bradley *English literature educator*
Salem, George Richard *lawyer*
Salhani, Claude *photojournalist*
Salisbury, Dallas L. *research institute executive*
Salmon, Matt *congressman*
Salmon, William Cooper *mechanical engineer, engineering academy executive*
Saltzburg, Stephen Allan *law educator, consultant*
Samet, Andrew *government official*
Samet, Kenneth Alan *hospital administrator*
Samuel, Howard David *union official*
Samuels Lasner, Mark *book and art collector*
Samuelson, Kenneth Lee *lawyer*
Sanchez, Jose Luis, Jr. *physician researcher, army officer*
Sanchez, Loretta *congresswoman*
Sanchez, Rafael Antonio *chemical engineer*
Sandefur, James Tandy *mathematics educator*
Sanders, Bernard (Bernie Sanders) *congressman*
†Sanders, David G. *federal agency administrator*
Sanderson, Fred Hugo *economist*
Sandler, Sumner Gerald *medical educator*
Sandlin, Max Allen, Jr. *congressman*
Sanford, Bruce William *lawyer*
Sanford, Marshall (Mark Sanford) *congressman*
Sankaran, Shubha Silver *musician, information management consultant*
Sansalone, William Robert *biochemistry educator, researcher*
Santorum, Rick *senator*
Santos, Leonard Ernest *lawyer*
†Saperstein, David Nathan *rabbi, lawyer, educator*
Saperstein, Marc Eli *religious history educator, rabbi*
Sarbanes, Paul Spyros *senator*
Sass, Neil Leslie *toxicologist*
Sasser, James Ralph (Jim Sasser) *ambassador, former senator*
Satcher, David *public health service officer, federal official*
†Satloff, Robert B. *think-tank executive*
Satterlee, Peter Hamilton *communications executive, military officer*
Sattler, Stephen Charles *writer, editor, communications consultant*
Sausser, Gail Dianne *lawyer*
Savage, Phillip Hezekiah *federal agency administrator*
Sawhill, Isabel Van Devanter *economist*
Sawyer, Forrest *newscaster*
Sawyer, Thomas C. *congressman*
Saxton, H. James *congressman*
Sayler, Robert Nelson *lawyer*
Sayre, Edward Vale *chemist*
Sayre, Robert Marion *ambassador*
Sazima, Henry John *oral and maxillofacial surgery educator*
Scalia, Antonin *United States supreme court justice*
Scanlon, Terrence Maurice *public policy foundation administrator*
Scarborough, Joe *congressman*
Scarbrough, Frank Edward *government official*
†Schaap, Aletta Johanna *artist*
Schad, Theodore MacNeeve *science research administrator, consultant*
Schaefer, Dan L. *former congressman*
Schaefer, James Lee *television news producer*
Schaffer, Robert (Bob Schaffer) *congressman*
Schaffner, Joan Elsa *law educator*
Schafrick, Frederick Craig *lawyer*
†Schakowsky, Janice *congresswoman*
Schall, Alvin Anthony *federal judge*
Schapiro, Mary *federal agency administrator, lawyer*
Schatz, Thomas Andrew *nonprofit organization executive, lawyer*
Schechter, Geraldine Poppa *hematologist*
Scheibel, Kenneth Maynard *journalist*
Schenker, Carl Richard, Jr. *lawyer*
Scheppach, Raymond Carl, Jr. *association executive, economist*
Scheraga, Joel Dov *economist*
Schick, Michael William *public affairs consultant*
Schieffer, Bob *broadcast journalist*
Schiff, Margaret Scott *newspaper publishing executive*
Schiff, Stefan Otto *zoologist, educator*
Schiffer, Lois Jane *lawyer*
Schifter, Richard *lawyer, government official*
†Schindler, Sol *foreign affairs analyst, writer*
Schlagel, Richard H. *philosophy educator*
Schlesinger, B. Frank *architect, educator*
Schlesinger, James Rodney *economist*
Schley, Wayne Arthur *political consultant*
Schlickeisen, Rodger Oscar *non-profit environmental organization executive*
†Schlitt, Lyn M. *lawyer*
Schloss, Howard Monroe *federal agency administrator*
Schmeltzer, David *lawyer*
Schmeltzer, Edward *lawyer*
Schmidt, Berlie Louis *agricultural research administrator*
†Schmidt, Derek Larkin *legislative aide*
Schmidt, Richard Marten, Jr. *lawyer*
Schmidt, William Arthur, Jr. *lawyer*
†Schmitt, John K. *army officer*
†Schmitten, Rolland Arthur *government official*
†Schneider, Cynthia Perrin *ambassador, art history educator*
Schneider, Mark Lewis *government official*
Schneider, Matthew Roger *lawyer*
Schneiter, George Robert *government executive*
Schoenberg, Mark George *government agency administrator*
Schor, Laurence *lawyer*
Schorr, Lisbeth Bamberger *child and family policy analyst, author, educator*
Schram, Martin Jay *journalist*
Schram, Susan Gale *agriculturist, consultant*
Schriever, Bernard Adolph *management consultant*
Schroeder, Patricia Scott (Mrs. James White Schroeder) *trade association administrator, former congresswoman*
Schubert, Richard Francis *consultant*
Schuerch, William *federal agency official*
Schultz, Todd R. *science administrator*
Schultze, Charles Louis *economist, educator*
Schumer, Charles Ellis *senator*
Schwaab, Richard Lewis *lawyer, educator*
Schwartz, Daniel C. *lawyer*
†Schwartz, Norton A. *military officer*
Schwartz, Victor Elliot *lawyer*
Schwartzman, Andrew Jay *lawyer*
Schwelb, Frank Ernest *court of appeals judge*
†Scott, Bruce K. *army officer*
Scott, Evelyn Fuller *customer service professional*
Scott, Gary Thomas *historian*
Scott, Raymond Peter William *chemistry research educator, writer*
Scott, Robert Cortez *congressman, lawyer*
Scott, Thomas Jefferson, Jr. *lawyer, electrical engineer*
Scott-Finan, Nancy Isabella *government administrator*
†Scowcroft, Brent *retired air force officer, government official*
Scriven, Wayne Marcus *lawyer*
Seagrave, Pia Seija *English language educator, editor, poet*
Searing, Marjory Ellen *government official, economist*
Sears, John Patrick *lawyer*
Sears, Mary Helen *lawyer*
Seats, Peggy Chisolm *marketing executive*
Seck, Mamadou Mansour *ambassador, career officer*
†Seed, Charles J. *accountant*
Segal, Donald E. *lawyer*
Segal, Phyllis Nichamoff *lawyer*
Seidel, Samuel Learned Richard Carton *governmental researcher*
Seidenberg, Ivan G. *telecommunications company executive*
Seidman, L(ewis) William *television commentator, publisher*
Seldman, Neil Norman *cultural organization administrator*
Selin, Ivan *entrepreneur*
†Selinger, Robin L.B. *physics educator*
Sellin, Theodore *foreign service officer, consultant*
Seneff, Michael Geren *critical care physician*
Senior, William Curtis *editor*
Sensenbrenner, Frank James, Jr. *congressman, lawyer*
Sentelle, David Bryan *federal judge*
Serafin, Barry D. *television news correspondent*
Serrano, Jose E. *congressman*
Sessions, Jefferson Beauregard, III *senator*
Sethness, Charles Olin *international financial official*
Severino, Roberto *foreign language educator, academic administration executive*
Sewell, John Williamson *research association executive*
†Sewer, Loán C. *legislative staff member*
Sha, Richard Chih-Tung *literature educator*
Shadegg, John B. *congressman*
Shafer, Raymond Philip *lawyer, business executive*
Shaffer, David James *lawyer*
†Shaffron, J. Janet *legislative administrator*
Shaheen, Michael Edmund, Jr. *lawyer, government official*
Shakow, David Joseph *lawyer, educator*
Shalala, Donna Edna *federal official, political scientist, educator, former university chancellor*
Shales, Thomas William *television and film critic, writer, journalist*
Shalowitz, Erwin Emmanuel *civil engineer*
Shanahan, Sheila Ann *pediatrician, educator*
Shands, Henry Lee *plant geneticist, administrator*
Shane, Jeffrey Neil *lawyer*
Shanks, Hershel *editor, writer*
Shanks, Judith Weil *editor*
Shannon, Donald Hawkins *retired newspaperman*
Shapero, Donald Campbell *physicist, government official*
Shapiro, George Howard *lawyer*
Shapiro, Michael Henry *government executive*
Shapiro, Nelson Hirsh *lawyer*
†Shapiro, Robert J. *economic affairs executive*
Shapiro, Walter Elliot *political columnist*
Sharpe, Rochelle Phyllis *journalist*
Sharples, Ruth Lissak *public relations specialist, video producer*
Shaw, Anesther O(live) *university administrative staff member*
Shaw, Bernard *television journalist*
Shaw, E. Clay, Jr. (Clay Shaw) *congressman*
Shaw, Gaylord *newspaper executive*
Shaw, Russell Burnham *author, journalist*
Shaw, William Frederick *statistician*
†Shaw, William J. *hotel facility executive*
Shays, Christopher *congressman*
†Shea, Donald William *military officer*
Shea, Patrick A. *lawyer*
Shear, Natalie Pickus *public relations executive*
Shearer, Alan *newspaper editor*
Shearer, Paul Scott *government relations professional*
Shearin, Morris Lee *minister*
Sheavly, Robert Bruce *social worker*
Sheehan, Michael Andrew *diplomat*
Sheehan, Michael Terrence *arts administrator, historian, consultant*
Sheehan, Neil *reporter, scholarly writer*
†Sheehy, Daniel Edward *arts administrator, musician*
Sheeler, Harva Lee *law librarian*
Shelby, Richard Craig *senator, former congressman*
Shelley, Herbert Carl *lawyer*
Shelly, Christine Deborah *foreign service officer*
†Shelton, Henry H. *federal agency administrator*
Shelton, L. Robert *federal official*
†Shelton-Colby, Sally *federal agency administrator*
Shenefield, John Hale *lawyer*
Shenon, Philip *journalist*
Shepherd, Alan J. *construction executive, management consultant*
Sherman, Bradley James *congressman*
Sherman, Charles Edwin *broadcasting executive, educator*
Sherman, Lawrence Jay *lawyer*
Sherman, Nancy *philosophy educator*
†Sherwood, Donald Lewis *congressman*
Sherzer, Harvey Gerald *lawyer*
Shestack, Alan *museum administrator*
†Shibley, Gail *public affairs director transportation department*
Shihata, Ibrahim Fahmy Ibrahim *bank executive, lawyer*
Shimkus, John Mondy *congressman*
Shine, Kenneth Irwin *cardiologist, educator*
Shinn, David Hamilton *diplomat*
Shinolt, Eileen Thelma *artist*
†Shinseki, Eric Ken *vice chief of staff United States Army*
Shlaes, John B. *consultant*
Shogan, Robert *news correspondent*
Shon, Frederick John *nuclear engineer*
Shosky, John Edwin *communications consultant, speechwriter*
†Shows, Ronnie *congressman*
Shrader, Carl Michael *photography and pre-press production executive*
Shribman, David Marks *editor*
Shrier, Adam Louis *investment firm executive, consultant*
Shrier, Diane Kesler *psychiatrist*
Shrinsky, Jason Lee *lawyer*
Shriver, Robert Sargent, Jr. *lawyer*
Shulman, Stephen Neal *lawyer*
Shumate, John Page *diplomat*
Shuster, Bud *congressman*
Sibolski, Elizabeth Hawley *academic administrator*
Sibolski, John Alfred, Jr. *educational association executive*
Siciliano, Rocco Carmine *institute executive*
†Sidak, Joseph Gregory *law educator*
Sidey, Hugh Swanson *correspondent*
Sidransky, Herschel *pathologist*
Siebert, Thomas L. *lawyer, former ambassador*
Siegel, Allen George *lawyer*
Siegel, Frederic Richard *geology educator*
Siegel, Lloyd Harvey *architect, real estate developer, consultant*
Siegel, Michael Eric *judicial center official*
Siegel, Richard David *lawyer, former government official*
Siegel, Robert Charles *broadcast journalist*
Sierck, Alexander Wentworth *lawyer*
Sieverts, Frank Arne *association executive*
†Signer, William Alan *consultant*
Silberg, Jay Eliot *lawyer*
Silver, Brian Quayle *broadcast journalist, musician, educator*
Silver, David *financial executive, lawyer*
Silver, Harry R. *lawyer*
Silver, Jonathan Moses *investment management executive*
†Silverman, Harold M. *pharmacologist, healthcare executive, educator*
Silverman, Marcia *public relations executive*
†Silvia, Stephen John *political science educator*
†Simes, Anastasia Ryurikov *artist*
Simes, Dimitri Konstantin *international affairs expert and educator*
Simmons, Anne L. *federal official*
Simmons, Edwin Howard *marine corps officer, historian*
Simon, Gary Leonard *internist, educator*
Simon, Jeanne Hurley *federal commissioner*
Simon, Kenneth Mark *lawyer*
Simons, Barbara M. *lawyer*
†Simons, Carol Lenore *magazine editor*
Simons, Lawrence Brook *lawyer*
Simpich, George Cary *investment banker*
Simpkins, Robert Allyn *business consultant*
Simpson, Charles Reagan *retired judge*
Simpson, Campbell H. *ambassador*
†Simpson, Jacqueline Angelia *law librarian*
Simpson, John M. *lawyer*
Simpson, Louis A. *insurance company executive*
†Simpson, Michael K. *congressman*
Sims, Robert Bell *professional society administrator, public affairs official, newspaper publisher*
Singer, Daniel Morris *lawyer*
Singer, Maxine Frank *biochemist, scientific research company executive*
Singerman, Phillip A. *federal agency administrator*
Singleton, Harry Michael *lawyer*
Sinkford, Jeanne Craig *dentist, retired dean, educator*
Sisco, Joseph John *management consultant, corporation director, educator, government official*
Sisisky, Norman *congressman, soft drink bottler*
†Sitilides, John *government relations executive, policy analyst*
Skaggs, David E. *association administrator, lawyer, educator*
Skeen, Joseph Richard *congressman*
Skelly, Thomas P. *federal agency executive*
Skelton, Isaac Newton, IV (Ike Skelton) *congressman*
Skinner, Robert Earle, Jr. *civil engineer, engineering executive*
†Sklarew, Myra *humanities educator, poet*
Skodon, Emil Mark *diplomat*
Skol, Michael *management consultant*
†Skolfield, Melissa T. *government official*
Skolnick, Judith A. Colton *artist*
Skolnik, Merrill I. *electrical engineer*
Slade, John Danton *lobbyist*
Slagle, Larry B. *human resources specialist*
†Slakey, Francis *association administrator, physics educator*
Slater, Rodney E. *federal official*
Slatkin, Leonard Edward *conductor, music director, pianist*
Slaughter, Louise McIntosh *congresswoman*
Slenker, Richard Dreyer, Jr. *broadcast executive*
†Slocombe, Walter Becker *government official, lawyer*
Sloyan, Patrick Joseph *journalist*
Sly, Ridge Michael *physician, educator*
Small, Lawrence M. *financial organization executive*
Smith, Adam *congressman*
†Smith, Amy Capen *economist*
Smith, Brian William *lawyer, former government official*
Smith, Bruce David *archaeologist*
Smith, Bruce R. *English language educator*
Smith, Christopher Henry *congressman*
Smith, D. Adam *congressman*
Smith, D(aisy) Mullett *publisher*
Smith, Daniel Clifford *lawyer*
Smith, Daniel Martin *nonprofit research organization administrator*
Smith, Dean *communications advisor, arbitrator*
Smith, Donald Eugene *executive*
Smith, Dwight Chichester, III *lawyer*
Smith, Elaine Diana *foreign service officer*
Smith, Frank *councilman*
†Smith, Gene *legislative staff member*
Smith, Gordon Harold *senator*
Smith, Jack Carl *foreign trade consultant*
Smith, James Michael *telecommunications executive, lawyer*
Smith, Lamar Seeligson *congressman*
Smith, Lee Elton *surgery educator, retired military officer*
Smith, Marshall Savidge *government official, academic dean, educator*
Smith, Mignon C. *publishing executive*
†Smith, Nancy M. *federal agency administrator*
Smith, Nick *congressman, farmer*
Smith, Philip Meek *science policy consultant, writer*
Smith, Raymond Charles, Jr. *naval officer*
Smith, Richard Hewlett, II *senior analyst*
Smith, Robert Clinton *senator*
Smith, Roy Philip *judge*
Smith, Stephen Grant *journalist*
Smith, Steven Grayson *military officer*
Smith, Stuart Seaborne *writer, government official, union official*
Smith, Wendy Haimes *federal agency administrator*
Smith, William Lee *federal administrator, educator*
†Smittcamp, Lisa M. *state official*
Smoot, Oliver Reed, Jr. *lawyer, trade association executive*
Smuckler, Ralph Herbert *university dean, political science educator*
†Smulkstys, Inga *operations and management executive*
Smyth, Paul Burton *lawyer*
Smythe-Haith, Mabel Murphy *consultant on African economic development, speaker, writer*
Snow, Robert Anthony *journalist*
Snowe, Olympia J. *senator*
†Snyder, Daniel *professional sports team executive, communications executive*
Snyder, James P. *audio and digital television technician, videographer engineer, editor*
Snyder, John Michael *lobbyist, public relations director*
Snyder, Vic *congressman, physician*
Sohn, Louis Bruno *lawyer, educator*
Solecki, Ray *government agency administrator*
Solinger, Janet W. *museum executive*
Solinger, Janet Weiland *cultural association director*
Soller, R. William *association executive, pharmacologist*
Solomon, Elinor Harris *economics educator*
Solomon, George M. *newspaper editor*
Solomon, Gerald Brooks Hunt *former congressman*
Solomon, Henry *university dean*
Solomon, Julie Robin *language educator*
Solomon, Richard Harvey *political scientist*
Solomon, Rodney Jeff *lawyer*
Solomon, Sean Carl *geophysicist, lab administrator*
Solomons, Mark Elliott *lawyer, art dealer, entrepreneur*
Sombrotto, Vincent R. *postal union executive*
Somerville, Walter Raleigh, Jr. *government official*
Sommer, Alphonse Adam, Jr. *lawyer*
Sommerfelt, Soren Christian *foreign affairs, international trade consultant, former Norwegian diplomat, lawyer*
Sonde, Theodore Irwin *lawyer*
†Sonderquist, Randy *public information officer*
†Sonneborn, Daniel Atesh *composer, ethnomusicologist, producer, author*
Sonnenfeldt, Helmut *former government official, educator, consultant, author*
Souder, Mark Edward *congressman*
Soule, Jeffrey Lyn *urban planner, consultant*
†Soule, Robert R. *program analysis administrator*
†Soutter, Catherine Patricia *nurse*
Spaeder, Roger Campbell *lawyer*
Spaeth, Steven Michael *lawyer*
Spagnolo, Samuel Vincent *internist, pulmonary specialist, educator*
†Spalter, Jonathan H. *government information officer*
†Sparks, Kenneth R. *association executive*
Spears, David D. *trading commission executive*
Specter, Arlen *senator*
Spector, Eleanor Ruth *government executive*
Spector, Phillip Louis *lawyer*
Spence, Floyd Davidson *congressman*
Spence, Sandra *professional administrator*
Sperling, Godfrey, Jr. *journalist*
Spilhaus, Athelstan Frederick, Jr. *oceanographer, association executive*

Watson, George Henry, Jr. journalist, broadcaster
Watson, Harlan L(eroy) federal official, physicist, economist
Watson, Jack H., Jr. lawyer
Watt, Melvin L. congressman, lawyer
Wattenmaker, Richard Joel archive director, art scholar
Watters, Thomas Robert geologist, museum administrator
Watts, J. C., Jr. congressman
Waxman, Henry Arnold congressman
Waxman, Seth Paul lawyer
Wayne, Stephen J. government educator, academic director, writer
Weadon, Donald Alford, Jr. lawyer
†Weaver, Paul A., Jr. career officer
Webb, Robert Kiefer history educator
Webber, Richard John lawyer
Webre, Septime ballet company artistic director, choreographer
Webster, Christopher White foreign service officer
Webster, Robert Kenly lawyer
Webster, Thomas Glenn psychiatrist
Webster, William Hedgcock lawyer
Wegener, Mark Douglas lawyer
†Weglarczyk, Bartosz journalist
Wehe, David Carl real estate developer
†Wehrle, Joseph H., Jr. military officer
Weidenfeld, Edward Lee lawyer
Weil, Stephen Edward museum official
Weinberger, Caspar Willard publishing executive, former secretary of defense
Weiner, Kenneth Brian lawyer
Weiner, Timothy Emlyn newspaper journalist
Weingold, Allan B. obstetrician, gynecologist, educator
Weinman, Howard Mark lawyer
Weinmann, Eric retired lawyer
Weinstein, Allen educator, historian, non-profit administrator
Weinstein, Diane Gilbert federal judge, lawyer
Weinstein, Harris lawyer
Weinstein, Kenneth N. federal government administrator
Weintraub, Sidney economist, educator
Weirich, Richard Denis government official
Weisberg, Stuart Elliot federal official, lawyer
Weisgall, Jonathan Michael lawyer
Weiss, Arnold Hans lawyer, consultant
Weiss, David Alan international trade consultant
Weiss, Gail Ellen legislative staff director
Weiss, Mark Anschel lawyer
Weiss, Paul philosopher, educator
Weiss, Paul Thomas management consultant, editor-in-chief, public manager
Weiss, Stephen J. lawyer
Weissman, Cheryl Ann editor
†Weissman, Stephen Richard political scientist, policy analyst, advocate
Weissman, William R. lawyer
Weiswasser, Stephen Anthony lawyer, broadcast executive
Welch, Charles David diplomat
†Welch, Laura Stewart physician, internist
Weldon, David Joseph, Jr. congressman, physician
Weldon, W(ayne) Curtis congressman
Wellen, Robert Howard lawyer
Weller, Gerald C. congressman
Welles, Judith public affairs executive
Wells, Linton, II government official
Wells, Samuel Fogle, Jr. research center administrator
Wells, Thomas B. federal judge
Wellstone, Paul senator
Wendt, E. Allan ambassador
Wenner, Charles Roderick lawyer
†Wenzel, Bob federal agency administrator
Werkman, Sidney Lee psychiatry educator
Werntz, Carl Weber physics educator
Wertheim, Mitzi Mallina technology company executive
Wertheimer, Fredric Michael public policy advocate
West, Gail Berry lawyer
West, Jake labor union administrator
West, Robert MacLellan science education consultant
West, Togo Dennis, Jr. federal official, former aerospace executive
†Weston, Craig P. military officer
Wetherill, George West geophysicist, planetary scientist
Wexler, Anne government relations and public affairs consultant
Wexler, Robert congressman
Weygand, Bob A. congressman
Weyrich, Paul Michael political organizations executive
Whalen, Laurence J. federal judge
Wheeler, Thomas Edgar communications technology executive
Wheelock, Arthur Kingsland, Jr. art historian
Whelan, Roger Michael lawyer, educator
Whitaker, A(lbert) Duncan lawyer
White, Byron R. former United States supreme court justice
†White, Daryl W. information officer
†White, Evelyn human resources administrator
White, George government official, physical scientist
White, George Malcolm architect
White, John federal agency administrator
White, John Arnold physics educator, research scientist
White, John Kenneth politics educator
White, Lee Calvin lawyer
White, Margit Triska financial advisor
White, Martha Vetter allergy and immunology physician, researcher
White, Robert M., II newspaper executive, editor, columnist
White, Robert Mayer meteorologist
White, Robert Roy retired chemical engineer
White, Roy Martin engineering manager
†White, Stanley legislative administrator
Whitehead, Alfred K. labor union administrator
Whitfield, Edward (Wayne Whitfield) congressman
Whiting, Richard Albert lawyer
Whitmore, Frank Clifford, Jr. geologist
Whittlesey, Judith Holloway public relations executive
Whitworth, Horace Algernon mechanical engineer
†Wholey, Dennis Matthew television talk show host
Wicker, Roger F. congressman
Wides, Burton V. lawyer
Wiener, Jerry M. psychiatrist
Wiese, John Paul federal judge
Wiessler, Judy Burton news editor
†Wiggins, Sandra Lynn human resources executive
Wilcher, Shirley J. lawyer
Wilderotter, James Arthur lawyer
Wilensky, Gail Roggin economist
Wiles, William Wharton retired federal government official
Wiley, Richard Emerson lawyer
†Wilf, Peter Daniel paleobiologist
Wilhelm, Peter G. aeronautical and astronautical engineer
Wilhide, Peggy C. public affairs administrator
Wilkins, Amy P. publishing executive
†Wilkinson, Quintin Stanley poet, speaker
Wilkinson, Ronald Sterne science administrator, environmentalist, historian
Will, George Frederick editor, political columnist, news commentator
Willard, Richard Kennon lawyer
Willauer, Whiting Russell consultant
†Williams, Anthony A. mayor
Williams, B. John, Jr. lawyer, former federal judge
Williams, Earl Patrick, Jr. editor, freelance writer
Williams, Eddie Nathan research institution executive
Williams, Frances Elizabeth secondary education educator
Williams, James R., III broadcast executive
Williams, John Edward lawyer
Williams, Julie Lloyd lawyer
Williams, Karen Hastie lawyer, think tank executive
Williams, Lawrence Floyd conservation organization official
†Williams, Leaford Clemetson writer, political scientist
Williams, Maurice Jacoutot development organization executive
Williams, Michael J. career officer
Williams, Ronald L. pharmaceutical association executive
Williams, Stephen Fain federal judge
Williams, Thomas Raymond lawyer
†Williams, Tony J. legislative staff member
Williams, Wesley Samuel, Jr. lawyer
Williams-Bridgers, Jacquelyn federal government official
Williamson, Darlene Swanson speech pathologist
Williamson, Michael Stanley photojournalist, writer
Williamson, Richard Hall federal association executive
Williamson, Rushton Marot, Jr. information technology project manager
Williamson, Thomas Samuel, Jr. lawyer
Willis, Arnold Jay urologic surgeon, educator
Willmore, Robert Louis lawyer
Wilner, Thomas Bernard lawyer
Wilson, Charles (Charlie Wilson) former congressman
Wilson, Ewen Maclellan economist
Wilson, Gary Dean lawyer
Wilson, Glen Parten professional society administrator
Wilson, Heather Ann congresswoman
Wilson, Joseph Charles, IV ambassador
†Wilson, Kevin M. legislative staff member
Wilson, Michael Moureau lawyer, physician
Wilson, Ronald Lawrence professional hockey coach
†Wilson, Ross political advisor
Wilson, William Stanley oceanographer
Wimberly, John William, Jr. minister
Wine, L. Mark lawyer
†Wingate, Heather legislative staff member
Winkler, Vera Cortada (Nina Winkler) government executive
Winner, Lara E. database manager
Winograd, Morley Alec government consultant, retired sales executive
†Winokur, Robert S. federal agency administrator
Winslow, Rosemary English language educator
Winston, Judith Ann lawyer
Winter, Douglas E. lawyer, writer
Winter, Harvey John government official
†Winter, Michael Alex federal agency administrator
Winter, Roger Paul government official
Winter, Thomas Swanson editor, newspaper executive
Winters, Sam federal agency administrator, lawyer
Wintrol, John Patrick lawyer
Wippel, John Francis philosophy educator
Wirth, Timothy Endicott foundation official, former senator
Wirtz, William Willard lawyer
Wise, Robert Ellsworth, Jr. (Bob Ellsworth) congressman
Wise, Sandra Casber lawyer
Wise, William Harvey, IV human service executive
Wiseman, Alan M(itchell) lawyer
Wiseman, Laurence Donald foundation executive
Wiss, Marcia A. lawyer
Witajewski, Robert M. diplomat
Witcover, Jules Joseph newspaper columnist, author
Withrow, Mary Ellen federal agency administrator
Withuhn, William Lawrence museum curator, railroad economics and management consultant
Witt, James Lee federal agency administrator, director
Wofford, Harris Llewellyn former senator, national service executive
Wogaman, John Philip minister, educator
Wolanin, Barbara Ann Boese art curator, art historian
Wolanin, Thomas Richard educator, researcher
Wolf, Frank R. congressman, lawyer
Wolf, Patrick John political science educator
Wolfe, Leslie R. think-tank executive
†Wolfensohn, James David international public officer
Wolff, Alan William lawyer
Wolff, Elroy Harris lawyer
Wolff, Paul Martin lawyer
Wolin, Neal Steven lawyer
Wollenberg, J. Roger lawyer
Won, Delmond J.H. commissioner
†Wood, Bernard Anthony anthropology educator
Wood, John Martin lawyer
Woodall, Samuel Roy, Jr. lawyer
Woodfin, Jane Dee lawyer, legislative director
Woodruff, Judy Carline broadcast journalist
Woodward, Robert Forbes retired government official, consultant
Woodward, Robert Upshur newspaper reporter, writer
Woodworth, Ramsey Lloyd lawyer
Woolley, John Edward trade association executive
Woolsey, Lynn congresswoman
Woosley, Raymond pharmacology and medical educator
Wooten, Michael Eric United States Marine officer
†Worden, Robert Leo government agency administrator, researcher
Work, Charles Robert lawyer
Work, Jane Magruder professional society administrator
Worsley, James Randolph, Jr. lawyer
Worth, Melvin H. surgeon, educator
Worthy, K(enneth) Martin lawyer
Worthy, Patricia Morris municipal official, lawyer
Wortley, George Cornelius government affairs consultant, investor
Woteki, Catherine Ellen nutritionist
Wouk, Herman writer
Wraase, Dennis Richard utilities company executive, accountant
Wray, Robert lawyer
†Wright, Bruce A. military officer
†Wright, Christopher J. federal agency administrator
Wright, Lawrence A. federal judge
†Wright, Lisa Lyons media specialist
Wright, Wiley Reed, Jr. lawyer, retired judge, mediator
Wrigley, William David protection services official
Wu, Carl Cherng-Miin ceramic engineer
Wu, David congressman
Wu, Frank H. law educator, journalist
Wubbena, Kurt Wilharm interior designer
Wulf, William Allan computer information scientist, educator, federal agency administrator
Wulff, Roger LaVern museum administrator
Wurtzel, Alan Leon retail company executive
Wyden, Ron senator
Wynn, Albert Russell congressman
Wyss, John Benedict lawyer
Wytkind, Edward federal agency administrator
Yablon, Jeffery Lee lawyer
†Yalowitz, Kenneth Spencer ambassador
Yambrusic, Edward Slavko lawyer, consultant
Yardley, Jonathan journalist, columnist
Yates, John Melvin ambassador
†Yeager, Brooks policy and international affairs administrator
Yellen, Janet Louise government official, economics educator
Yellen, John Edward archaeologist
Yerick, Martin R. lawyer
Yerkes, David Norton architect
Yochelson, Ellis L(eon) paleontologist
Yochelson, Kathryn Mersey art researcher
Yock, Robert John federal judge
Yoder, Hatten Schuyler, Jr. petrologist
Yoder, Mary Jane Warwick psychotherapist
Yoder, Ronnie A. judge
Yoskowitz, Irving Benjamin merchant banker
†Yost, Paul A., III legislative staff
Yost, Paul Alexander, Jr. foundation executive, retired coast guard officer
Young, C. W. (Bill Young) congressman
Young, Donald Alan physician
Young, Donald E. congressman
Young, Loretta Ann auditor
Young, Peter Robert librarian
Young, Thomas Wade journalist
Young, Vincent Arron publicist
Youtcheff, John Sheldon physicist
Yulish, Charles Barry public relations executive
Yurow, John Jesse lawyer
Yzaguirre, Raul Humberto civil rights leader
Zaffos, Gerald federal agency executive
†Zaidman, Steven associate official Federal Aviation Administration
Zausner, L. Andrew lawyer
Zax, Leonard A. lawyer
Zechman, Edwin Kerper, Jr. medical facility administrator
Zeidman, Philip Fisher lawyer
Zeifang, Donald Paul lawyer
Zelnick, Carl Robert writer, educator
†Zenker, Wendy financial executive
Zenowitz, Allan Ralph government official
†Zettler, Michael E. military officer
Zielinski, Paul Bernard grant program administrator, civil engineer
Zietz, Karyl Lynn Kopelman writer, opera critic, television correspondent, producer, documentary filmmaker
Ziglar, James W. federal official, lawyer, investment banker
Zimmerman, Carole Lee public relations professional
Zimmerman, Edwin Morton lawyer
Zipp, Joel Frederick lawyer
Zobel, Rya Weickert federal judge, legal administrator
Zok, James J. federal agency administrator
Zollar, Carolyn Catherine lawyer
Zuckman, Harvey Lyle law educator
†Zuern, Theodore Francis priest
Zukowska-Grojec, Zofia Maria cardiovascular physiologist, educator
Zulberti, Carlos Alberto planning executive
Zwach, David Michael foreign service officer
Zwadiuk, Oleh radio executive
Zweben, Murray lawyer, consultant

FLORIDA

Alachua
Gaines, Weaver Henderson lawyer
Marston, Robert Quarles university president
Neubauer, Hugo Duane, Jr. software engineer
Schneider, Richard T(heodore) optics research executive, engineer
†Tilton, John Ellsworth ceramic artist

Altamonte Springs
Heindl, Phares Matthews lawyer
Hoogland, Robert Frederics lawyer
Hull, John Doster retired insurance company executive
Huyett, Debra Kathleen elementary education educator
Poland, Phyllis Elaine secondary school educator, consultant
Seykora, Margaret S. psychotherapist
Siddiqui, Farooq Ahmad protein biochemist
†Woods, Abraham Lincoln, III urologist

Amelia Island
Jesser, Benn Wainwright chemical engineering and construction company executive

Anna Maria
Dielman, Ray Walter radiologic scientist, clinical herbalist
Kaiser, Albert Farr diversified corporation executive

Apalachicola
Cronkite, Mary Sue Riddle journalist, fiction writer
Galloway, Brenda Mabrey school system administrator

Apopka
Calhoun, Emily Mitchell elementary education educator
Leslie, John William public relations and advertising executive
Webb, Erma Lee nurse educator

Arcadia
Schmidt, Harold Eugene real estate company executive

Atlantic Beach
Buell, Victor Paul marketing educator, author, editor
Filips, Nicholas Joseph management consultant
Herge, Henry Curtis, Sr. education educator, dean emeritus
Walker, Richard Harold pathologist, educator

Atlantis
Gough, Carolyn Harley library director
Stone, Ross Gluck orthopaedic surgeon

Auburndale
Wean, Karla Denise middle school educator, secondary education educator

Aventura
Babson, Irving K. publishing company executive
Cerri, Robert Noel photographer
Cohen, Alex retired publisher
Fishman, Barry Stuart lawyer
Golden, Alfred business owner
Kliger, Milton Richard financial services executive
McRoberts, Jeffrey Alan nursing administrator

Babson Park
Hodapp, Shirley Jeaniene curriculum administrator
Morrison, Kenneth Douglas author, columnist

Bal Harbour
Ash, Dorothy Matthews civic worker
Horton, Jeanette municipal government official

Bartow
Andress, Lucretia Ann King health care executive

Bay Harbor Islands
†Kitner, Harold artist, educator
Patrick, Marty lawyer
Rosenbluth, Morton periodontist, educator

Bay Pines
Johnson, David Porter infectious diseases physician
Keskiner, Ali psychiatrist
Law, David Hillis physician
Stewart, Jonathan Taylor psychiatrist, educator
Weaver, Thomas Harold health facility administrator

Belle Glade
Alvarez, Jose Florencio food products executive, mechanical engineer
Waddill, Van Hulen entomology educator

Belleair
Imparato, Edward Thomas writer
Lasley, Charles Haden cardiovascular surgeon, health and fitness consultant

Belleview
Bellis, Arthur Albert financial executive, government official

Beverly Hills
†Denis, Heidi Anfinson library administrator
Larsen, Erik art history educator

Big Pine Key
Cooper, John Charles writer, educator

Boca Grande
Baldwin, William Howard lawyer, retired foundation executive
Brock, Mitchell lawyer
Dyche, David Bennett, Jr. retired management consultant
Hayes, Scott Birchard raw materials company executive
Heffernan, John William retired journalist

Boca Raton
Agler, Richard Dean rabbi
Alvarado, Ricardo Raphael retired corporate executive, lawyer
Arden, Eugene retired university provost
Bainton, Donald J. diversified manufacturing company executive
Barbarosh, Milton Harvey merchant banking executive
Barnes, Donald Winfree financial services executive
Bartunek, Kenneth Steven finance educator
Baumgarten, Diana Virginia gerontological nurse
Beber, Robert H. lawyer, financial services executive
Beck, Crafton music director
Beck, Louis S. hotel executive
Boggess, Jerry Reid protective services official
Borg, Dean Jeremy real estate developer
Brennan, Teresa Mary Isabel social theory educator, writer
Breslauer, Charles S. chemical company executive
Buckstein, Mark Aaron lawyer, educator
Camilleri, Michael lawyer, educator
Cannon, Herbert Seth investment banker
Caputi, Marie Antoinette university official
Carr-Allen, Elizabeth real estate and mortgage broker, metaphysician
Catanese, Anthony James academic administrator
†Chestnov, Richard Franklin private investor
Cohen, Melvyn Douglas securities company executive
Cohn, Jess Victor psychiatrist
Collins, Robert Arnold English language educator
Comisky, Ian Michael lawyer
Connor, Frances Partridge retired education educator
Connor, Leo Edward special education administrator
†Cope, Daniel package good industry executive

Demes, Dennis Thomas religious studies educator
Dolan, Dan communications executive
Dorfman, Allen Bernard international management consultant
Douglas, Andrew legal nurse
Doyle-Kimball, Mary freelance writer, editor
Dunhill, Robert W. advertising direct mail executive
†Engle, Stephen Douglas history educator
Erdman, Joseph lawyer
Fels, Robert Alan psychotherapist
Fengler, John Peter television producer, director, advertising executive
Ferris-Waks, Arlene Susan financial analyst
Fetter, Richard Elwood retired industrial company executive
Feuerlein, Willy John Arthur economist, educator
Frank, Stanley Donald publishing company executive
Frank, William Edward, Jr. executive recruitment company executive
†Franklin, Ronald neuropsychologist
Friend, Harold Charles neurologist
Gagliardi, Raymond Alfred physician
Gale, Marla social worker
Garelick, Martin retired transportation executive
Gold, Catherine Anne Dower music history educator
Golis, Paul Robert lawyer
†Goray, Gerald Allen investor, business executive, lawyer
Gralla, Eugene natural gas company executive
Greenfield-Moore, Wilma Louise social worker, educator
Guglielmino, Lucy Margaret Madsen education educator, researcher, consultant
Guillama-Alvarez, Noel Jesus healthcare company executive
Han, Chingping Jim industrial engineer, educator
Hersh, Sid real estate developer
†Hoppenstein, Abraham Solomon investment and merchant banker, consultant
Houraney, William George marketing and public relations executive
Ingwersen, Martin Lewis shipyard executive
Innes-Brown, Georgette Meyer real estate and insurance broker
Jaffe, Leonard Sigmund financial executive
Jessup, Jan Amis arts volunteer, writer
Jessup, Joe Lee business educator, management consultant
Johnson, James Robert ceramic engineer, educator
Johnson, Martin Allen publisher
Karmelin, Michael Allen financial executive
Kassner, Herbert Seymore lawyer
Kauffman, Alan Charles lawyer
Keil, Charles Emanuel corporation executive
Kelley, Eugene John business educator
†Keusch, Cristina Frexes plastic surgeon
Kewley, Sharon Lynn systems analyst, consultant
Keyes, Daniel author
Kirkbride, Patricia Capell educational administrator
Kitzes, William Fredric lawyer, safety analyst, consultant
Klein, Robert manufacturing company executive
Knudsen, Rudolph Edgar, Jr. insurance company executive
Konrad, Agnes Crossman retired real estate agent, retired educator
Kramer, Cecile E. retired medical librarian
Lagin, Neil landscape designer, consultant
Landry, Michael Gerard investment company executive
Langbort, Polly retired advertising executive
Latané, Bibb social psychologist
Leary, William James educational administrator
Lerner, Theodore Raphael dentist
Levenson, David Irwin endocrinologist
Levine, Irving Raskin news commentator, university dean, author, lecturer
Levine, Richard A. physician
Lin, Y. K. engineer, educator
Lynn, Eugene Matthew insurance company executive
MacFarland, Richard B. lawyer
Markin, Alex chemical company executive, mergers and acquisitions consultant
Marrese, Barbara Ann nurse, educator, program planner
McFarren, Naza artist
McLeod, John Wishart architect
McQueen, Scott Robert broadcasting company executive
Miller, Eugene university official, business executive
Miller, William library administrator
Monroe, William Lewis human resources executive
Morris, Jill Carole psychotherapist
O'Donnell, Joseph Michael electronics executive
Ortlip, Mary Krueger artist
Ortlip, Paul Daniel artist
Parker, Kim Anne English educator
Pelish, Susan Marion sculptor, painter
Pepper, Beverly artist, sculptor
Perez, Jorge Luis manufacturing executive
Perlick, Lillian counselor, therapist
Rabinowitz, Wilbur Melvin container company executive, consultant
Racine, Brian August intellectual property lawyer
Rebel, Amy Louise elementary education educator
Reid, George Kell biology educator, researcher, author
Reinstein, Joel lawyer
Resnick, Robert physicist, educator
Reynolds, George Anthony, Jr. engineering executive
Richardson, R(oss) Fred(erick) insurance executive
Rosner, M. Norton business systems and financial services company executive
Ross, Donald Edward university administrator
Ross, Fred Michael organic chemist
Rothberg, June Simmonds retired nursing educator, psychotherapist, psychoanalyst
Saffir, Leonard public relations executive
Samuels, William Mason physiology association executive
Sarna, Helen Horowitz retired librarian, educator
Schechterman, Lawrence business consultant
Schmoke, L(eroy) Joseph, III entrepreneur
Sena, John Michael insurance agent
Siegel, David Burton lawyer
Siegel, Ned Lawrence real estate developer
Sigel, Marshall Elliot financial consultant
Singer, Merle Elliot rabbi
Skurnick, Sam stockbroker, investment manager
Spencer, James Gray marketing professional
Stein, Irvin orthopedic surgeon, educator
Su, Tsung-Chow Joe engineering educator
Tennies, Robert Hunter headmaster
Van Alstine, Ruth Louise medical language specialist, writer
†Weiner, Howard Marc physician
Weissbach, Herbert biochemist
Wertheimer, Esther sculptor
Wichinsky, Glenn Ellis lawyer
Wiesenfeld, John Richard chemistry educator
Willis, John Alexander lawyer
Zaleznak, Bernard D. physician
Zuckerman, Sidney retired allergist, immunologist

Bokeelia
†Hausman, Gerald Andrews writer
Winterer, Victoria Thompson hospitality executive
Winterer, William G. hotel executive

Bonita Springs
Dacey, George Clement retired laboratory administrator, consultant
†DiSerafino, Reneé Marie elementary education educator
Finger, Iris Dale Abrams elementary school educator
Johnson, Franklyn Arthur academic administrator
Katzen, Raphael consulting chemical engineer
Olander, Ray Gunnar retired lawyer
Sargent, Charles Lee manufacturing company executive
Snedden, James Douglas retired health service management consultant
Trudnak, Stephen Joseph landscape architect

Boynton Beach
Allison, Dwight Leonard, Jr. investor
Armstrong, Jack Gilliland lawyer
Ashley, James MacGregor management consultant
Babler, Wayne E. retired telephone company executive, lawyer
Balis, Moses Earl biochemist, educator
Bartholomew, Arthur Peck, Jr. accountant
Berman, Ruth Sharon chiropractor
Birkenstock, Joyce Ann artist
Bloede, Merle Huie civic worker
Bryant, Donald Loyd insurance company executive
Caras, Joseph Sheldon life insurance company executive
Costa, Terry Ann educational administrator
Cotton, John Pierce principal
Farace, Virginia Kapes librarian
Fields, Theodore consulting medical radiation physicist
Force, Elizabeth Elma retired pharmaceutical executive, consultant
Ganz, Samuel human resource and management professional
Gill, Milton Randall minister
Glickman, Franklin Sheldon dermatologist, educator
Harwood, Bernice Baumel artist, community volunteer
Heckelmann, Charles Newman (Charles Lawton) author, publishing consultant
Jacobs, C. Bernard banker
Jensen, Reuben Rolland former automotive company executive
Klein, Bernard publishing company executive
Koteen, Jack management consultant, writer
Kronman, Joseph Henry orthodontist
Lentin, Dennis Henry communications executive
Miller, Emanuel retired lawyer, banker
Mittel, John J. economist, corporate executive
Pataky, Paul Eric ophthalmologist
Peltzie, Kenneth Gerald hospital administrator, educator
Polinsky, Janet Naboicheck state official, former state legislator
Rogers, John S. retired union official
†Rosenstein, David Alan plastic surgeon
Saxbe, William Bart lawyer, former government official
Srinath, Latha physician
Sterman, Gail K. Mendelson public relations specialist
Stubbins, Hugh A(sher), Jr. architect
Vesely, Alexander civil engineer

Bradenton
Aerts, Cindy Sue nurse
Baker, Walter Louis retired engineering company executive
Beall, Robert Matthews, II retail chain executive
Blankenship, Dwight David business owner
Corey, Kay Janis business owner, designer, nurse
Doyle, William Jay, II business consultant
Ellman, Norman Kenneth psychologist, psychoanalyst
Feeley, John Paul retired paper company executive
Friedrich, Robert Edmund retired electrical engineer, corporate consultant
Garrison, Richard Neil artist
Gurian, Mal telecommunications executive
Hall, Ralph C. retired architect, mechanical engineer
Keane, Gustave Robert architect, consultant
Lister, Thomas Mosie composer, lyricist, publishing company executive, minister
Lopacki, Edward Joseph, Jr. lawyer
Mandell, Marshall physician, allergist, consultant
†Marram, Ellen R. food products executive
Maynard, Donald Nelson horticulturist, educator
†McClish, Jerry F. artist
McFarland, Richard Macklin retired journalist
McGarry, Marcia community service coordinator
Myette, Jeré Curry nursing administrator
Nelson, Ralph Erwin investment company executive, coin dealer
Patterson, Homer Stephen electronics maintenance supervisor
Pedersen, Norman Arno, Jr. retired headmaster, literary club director
Phelan, John Densmore insurance executive, consultant
Prettyman, Jon Allison urban planner
Price, Edgar Hilleary, Jr. business consultant
Rehmann, Elizabeth Schultz health system executive
Robinson, Hugh R. retired marketing executive
Roehl, Nancy Leary marketing professional, educator
Scott, Gary LeRoy photographic manufacturing executive, photographer
Seim, Andrew investment company executive, venture capitalist
Sprenger, Thomas Robert retired orthopedic surgeon
Stewart, Priscilla Ann Mabie art historian, educator
Taylor, Carol rehabilitation nurse
Thompson, Barbara Storck state official
Tilbe, Linda MacLauchlan nursing administrator
Voorhees, Stephanie Robin Nee Faught retired art educator
White, Dale Andrew journalist
Woodson-Howard, Marlene Erdley former state legislator

Brandon
Curry, Clifton Conrad, Jr. lawyer
†Hall, Robert Dale mathematician, educator, physicist
Lafferty, Beverly Lou Brookover retired physician, consultant
Pomeroy, Wyman Burdette business owner, consultant
Straub, Susan Monica special education educator
Tittsworth, Clayton (Magness) lawyer

Brooksville
Anderson, Richard Edmund city manager, management consultant
Capps, David Edward, Jr. assistant dean
Harvey, Joseph Howard mathematics educator, musician
Linn, James Eldon, II insurance company executive
Melli, Richard George bishop
Miller, Kenneth Edward mechanical engineer, consultant
Schutte, Carla Daniels elementary education educator
Smith, Margaret Ann health care executive

Bushnell
Panzetta, John Cosmo clinical chaplain

Cantonment
Crook, Penny Loraine investment broker

Cape Canaveral
†Albright, Judith Anne writer
Bell, James Bacon business executive
Field, Thomas Harold software engineer

Cape Coral
Brevoort, Richard William public relations executive
Buthman, Nancy Smith nurse practitioner, critical care nurse
Dietrich, Jonathan Austin chemical process engineer
Lane, William C., Jr. principal
Longo, Paul Albert retired industrial engineer, consultant
Martin, Benjamin Gaufman ophthalmologist
Peters, Donald Cameron construction company executive
Smith, Bruce William safety engineer
Vilardi, Charles Ronald elementary education educator
West, John Merle retired physicist, nuclear consultant

Captiva
Ronald, Peter utility executive

Carrabelle
Campbell, Thomas Emory author, researcher

Carrollwood
O'Keefe, Fredrick Rea bishop, consultant, educator, writer

Cassadaga
Haydu, John N. psychic counselor

Casselberry
Lucas, Robert William human resources consultant, writer
Medin, A. Louis computer company executive
Pollack, Robert William psychiatrist
Sokol, I. Scott political and fundraising executive
Vincent, Thomas James retired manufacturing company executive

Cedar Key
Starnes, Earl Maxwell urban and regional planner, architect

Celebration
Renard, Meredith Anne marketing and advertising professional

Chattahoochee
Ivory, Peter B. C. B. medical administrator

Chuluota
Hatton, Thurman Timbrook, Jr. retired horticulturist, consultant

Citrus Springs
Tillery, Billy Carey writer, poet

Clearwater
Bairstow, Frances Kanevsky labor arbitrator, mediator, educator
Bertram, Frederic Amos architect
Birmingham, Richard Gregory lawyer
Bomstein, Alan Charles construction company executive
Brady, Sheila Ann manufacturing company executive
Bramante, Pietro Ottavio physiology educator, retired pathology specialist
†Brown, Richard Christopher epidemiologist
Campolettano, Thomas Alfred contract manager
Caronis, George John insurance executive
Cheek, Michael Carroll lawyer
Chisholm, William DeWayne retired contract manager
Clingerman, Edgar Allen, Sr. financial services executive
Conover, Dorothy Nancy Lever medical practice administrator, nurse
Cowles, Sandra Lynne metallurgical engineer
Davidson, Joan Gather psychologist
Devoe, Charles Louis, II sales and marketing consultant
Fine, A(rthur) Kenneth lawyer
Flagg, Helen Clawson writer
Fraser, John Wayne insurance executive, consultant, underwriter
Free, E. LeBron lawyer
Grala, Jane M. securities firm executive
Hallam, Arlita Warrick quality of life administrator
Hoel, Robert Fredrick, Jr. construction executive, civil engineer
Hoornstra, Edward H. retail company executive
Hopen, Anton John lawyer
Horowitz, Harry I. podiatrist
Houtz, Duane Talbott hospital administrator
Howes, James Guerdon airport director
†Johnson, Randall C. mortgage banker
Johnson, Timothy Augustin, Jr. lawyer
Keyes, Benjamin B. therapist
Kumar, Anita reporter
Lokys, Linda J. dermatologist
Loos, Randolph Meade financial planner
Mattice, Howard LeRoy education educator
Maxwell, Richard Anthony retail executive
McAllister, Charles John nephrologist, medical administrator
Moore, Matthew Stafford librarian
Peters, Robert Timothy circuit judge
Peterson, James Robert retired engineering psychologist
Pope, Fred Wallace, Jr. lawyer
Raymund, Steven A. computer company executive
Rinde, John Jacques internist
St. Clair, Jane Elizabeth management executive
Sandefer, G(eorge) Larry lawyer
Sassouni, Chris Garo financial consultant
Scarne, John game company executive
Smith, Marion Pafford avionics company executive, retired
Stettner, Jerald W. retail drugs stores executive
Stewart, Michael Ian orthodontist
Stilwell, Charlotte Finn vocational counselor
Sutton, Sharon Jean surgical nurse
Tanner, Craig Richard fire and explosion engineer
Teets, Charles Edward international business consultant, lawyer
Tragos, George Euripedes lawyer
Turley, Stewart retired retail company executive
VanMeer, Mary Ann publisher, writer, researcher
†Walker, William Russell artist
Whedon, George Donald medical administrator, researcher
Wyllie, Alfred Linn real estate broker, mortgage broker
Yoho, Robert Wayne company executive

Clermont
Cox, Margaret Stewart photographer

Cocoa
Drake, James Alfred higher education administrator
Gamble, Thomas Ellsworth academic administrator
†King, Maxwell Clark academic administrator
Luecke, Conrad John aerospace educator
Maddison, Ronald Charles physicist
McLendon, Dorothy school psychologist
Papa, Michael Joseph real estate broker

Cocoa Beach
Blum, June artist, curator
Choromokos, James, Jr. former government official, consultant
Herbstman, Loretta sculptor
Wirtschafter, Irene Nerove tax consultant

Coconut Creek
Godofsky, Stanley lawyer
Limmer, Ezekiel retired federal agency administrator, economist
Yormark, Alanna Katherine pediatrics nurse

Coconut Grove
Denaro, Gregory lawyer
Katz, Lawrence Sheldon lawyer
La Forge, Raymond Bernard, Jr. marketing and sales consultant
McAmis, Edwin Earl lawyer
Softness, John public relations executive
Sweeny, Donna Bozzella writer, editor
Taylor, J(ames) Bennett management consultant

Coleman
Crenshaw, Tena Lula librarian

Cooper City
Waganheim, Arthur Brian marketing executive

Coral Gables
Arcos, Cresencio S. ambassador
†Balaban, John poet, educator in English, translator
Bannard, Walter Darby artist, art critic
Bishopric, Susan Ehrlich public relations executive
Blumberg, Philip Flayderman real estate developer
†Bourgoignie, Marie Helene educator
Buell, Rodd Russell lawyer
Burini, Sonia Montes de Oca apparel manufacturing and public relations executive
Cano, Mario Stephen lawyer
Carney, Martin Joseph, Jr. university administrator
Criss, Cecil M. chemistry educator
†Currier, Susan Anne computer software company executive
Dunn, Charles Anthony family physician
Einspruch, Norman Gerald physicist, educator
Ely, John Hart lawyer, university dean
†Evarist, Milian, Jr. insurance company executive
Feiler, Michael Benjamin lawyer
Freedman, Anne Beller public speaking and marketing consultant
Groome, Kimberly VonGonten administrative assistant
†Hamilton, J. Leonard college basketball coach
Hertz, Arthur Herman business executive
Higginbottom, Samuel Logan retired aerospace company executive
Hoffman, Carl H(enry) lawyer
†Jones, Susan Tamny fundraising executive
Kline, Jacob biomedical engineering educator
Kniskern, Joseph Warren lawyer
Labati, Ferne women's basketball coach
Lampert, Wayne Morris corporate financier
Landon, Robert Kirkwood philanthropist, retired insurance company executive
Leblanc, Roger Maurice chemistry educator
Lewis, Elisah Blessing university official
Lomonosoff, James Marc marketing executive
†Lopez, Ruben engineer, educational administrator
Lott, Leslie Jean lawyer
Mitchell, David Benjamin lawyer, mediator, arbitrator
Moss, Ambler Holmes, Jr. academic administrator, educator, lawyer, former ambassador
Nacknouck, James D. management executive
Nunez-Portuondo, Ricardo investment company executive
Pastoriza, Julio lawyer
Perez, Josephine psychiatrist, educator
Quillian, Warren Wilson, II pediatrician, educator
Rodriguez, Nestor Joaquin insurance broker
Rosenn, Keith Samuel lawyer, educator
Roy, Joaquin humanities and international affairs educator

Sacasas, Rene *lawyer*
Saffir, Herbert Seymour *structural engineer, consultant*
Schaiberger, George Elmer *microbiologist educator*
Shipley, Vergil Alan *political science educator*
Stano, Carl Randolph (Randy Stano) *newspaper editor, art director, educator*
Steinberg, Alan Wolfe *investment company executive*
Stover, James Howard *real estate executive*
Suarez, George Michael *urologist*
Telepas, George Peter *lawyer*
Thornton, John William, Sr. *lawyer*
†Trowbridge, Mark Alan *educational consultant*
Warburton, Ralph Joseph *architect, engineer, planner, educator*
Weiner, Morton David *banker, insurance agent*
Wolf, Aizik Loft *neurosurgeon*
Yarger, Sam Jacob *dean, educator*
Young, Tzay Y. *electrical and computer engineering educator*

Coral Springs
Bachove, Jason Frost *musician*
Bosted, Dorothy Stack *public relations executive*
Burg, Ralph *art association executive*
Carrington, J(oseph) P(eter) (Jossif Peter Bartolotti) *nutritionist, psychoanalyst, research scientist, educator*
Colton, Susan Adams *educational administrator*
†Dajani, Badr Mustafa *neurologist*
Dzieduszko, Janusz Wladyslaw *electrical engineer*
Furman, Mark Evan *human performance scientist*
Heydet, Nathalie Durbin *gifted and talented education educator*
Levitz, John Blase *investment management consultant*
†Miller, Karl Frederick *insurance manager*
Murray, John Ralph *former college president*
Polin, Alan Jay *lawyer*
Richardson, Peter Mark James *town official*
Sanders, Marc Andrew *computer technical consultant*
Schultz, Joel Sidney *architect*
Sommerer, John *accountant*
Swiller, Randolph Jacob *internist*
Tharp, Karen Ann *insurance agent*
†Tomeo, Louis Anthony *county official*
Valasquez, Joseph Louis *industrial engineer*
†Yalamanchi, Bose *surgeon*

Crawfordville
Black, B. R. *retired educational administrator, consultant*

Crestview
Scott, George Gallmann *accountant*

Crystal River
Hoge, James Cleo *retired priest and school administrator*
Schlumberger, Robert Ernest *accountant*

Dade City
Currier, Douglas Gilfillan, II *urban planner*
Feld, Harvey Joel *pathologist*

Dania
Dodge, Richard Eugene *oceanographer, educator, marine life administrator*
†Satin, Claire Jeanne *sculptor, illustrator*
Weissman-Berman, Deborah *sandwich composites engineer, researcher*

Davie
†Gonzalez, Richard *quality performance professional*
Johnson, Jimmy *professional football coach*
Jones, Eddie J. *professional football team executive*
Marino, Daniel Constantine, Jr. *professional football player*
†McDuffie, Otis James (O.J.) *professional football player*
Morris, Joseph Raymond *business and economics educator*
Speiller-Morris, Joyce *English educator*
Wannstedt, David Raymond *professional football team coach*
Webb, Richmond Jewel *professional football player*

Daytona Beach
Adams, John Carter, Jr. *insurance executive*
Alcott, Amy Strum *professional golfer*
Alvarez, Marianne *artist, photographer, educator*
Amick, William Walker *golf course architect*
†Ammaccapane, Danielle *professional golfer*
Andrews Reeves, Donna *golfer*
Bodine, Brett *professional race car driver*
Braim, Paul Francis *history educator, writer*
Bronson, Oswald Perry *religious organization administrator, clergyman*
Burton, Brandie *professional golfer*
Cardwell, Harold Douglas, Sr. *rehabilitation specialist*
Carmona, José Antonio *Spanish language educator, English language educator*
Chesnut, Nondis Lorine *screenwriter, consultant, reading and language arts educator*
Craven, Ricky *professional race car driver*
Davidson, Herbert M. (Tippen), Jr. *newspaper owner*
†Davies, Laura *golfer*
†DeLuca, Annette *professional golfer*
Di Nicolo, Roberto *allergist*
Duma, Richard Joseph *microbiologist, physician, pathologist, researcher, educator*
Dunagan, Walter Benton *lawyer, educator*
†Dunn, Moira C. *golf professional*
Earnhardt, (Ralph) Dale *professional race car driver*
Ebbs, George Heberling, Jr. *university executive*
†Figg-Currier, Cindy *professional golfer*
Gewirtz, Jeffrey Brian *lawyer*
Goldberg, Paul Bernard *gastroenterologist, clinical researcher*
Gordon, Jeff *race car driver*
†Hartsell, Horace Ed *college president*
Hastings, Mary Lynn *real estate broker*
Inkster, Juli *professional golfer*
Jacobson, Ira David *aerospace engineer, educator, researcher*
†Kane, Lorie *professional golfer*
King, Betsy *professional golfer*
Klein, Emilee *professional golfer*
Lampe, Harriett Richmond *retired educator, artist*
Libby, Gary Russell *museum director*
Mallon, Meg *professional golfer*

Mc Collister, John Charles *writer, clergyman, educator, executive producer*
McGann, Michelle *professional golfer*
Millar, Gordon Halstead *mechanical engineer, agricultural machinery manufacturing executive*
Neitzke, Eric Karl *lawyer*
Neumann, Liselotte *professional golfer*
Obeng, Morrison Stephen *computer scientist, educator*
O'Reilly, Don *reporter, writer, photographer*
Patterson, Roger Lewis *psychologist*
Pepper, Dottie *professional golfer*
Perschmann, Lutz Ingo *property manager, real estate consultant*
†Robbins, Kelly *professional golfer*
†Rudd, Ricky *professional race car driver*
Salter, Leo Guilford *mental health services professional*
Schrader, Ken *professional race car driver*
Scott, John Brooks *research institute executive, retired*
Sheehan, Patty *professional golfer*
Simatos, Nicholas Jerry *aerospace company executive, consultant*
†Sloane, James Robert *chemical engineer*
Smith, Ann Marie *nurse educator*
Sorenstam, Annika *professional golfer*
Speed, Lake *professional race car driver*
Spencer, Jimmy *professional race car driver*
†Steinhauer, Sherri *professional golfer*
Stephenson, Jan Lynn *professional golfer*
†Tschetter, Kris *professional golfer*
†Votaw, Ty M. *golf association commissioner*
Wallace, Rusty *race car driver*
†Wanjohi, Elsie Wairimu *communications educator*
Webb, Karrie *professional golfer*
Whitworth, Kathrynne Ann *professional golfer*
Yarborough, William Caleb *former professional stock car race driver*

Debary
Schaeffer, Barbara Hamilton *retired rental leasing company executive, writer*
†Tauber, James G. *fire chief*

Deerfield Beach
Areskog, Donald Clinton *retired chiropractor*
Brown, Colin W(egand) *lawyer, diversified company executive*
Davis, Ronald P. *secondary school educator*
King, Don *boxing promoter*
Laser, Charles, Jr. *oil company executive*
Levitan, David M(aurice) *lawyer, educator*
†Moore, Terrence Raenale *city administrator*
Moran, James M. *automotive sales executive*
Moran, Patricia Genevieve *corporate executive*
Nolan, Lone Kirsten *financial advisor*
Rung, Richard Allen *lawyer, retired air force officer, retired educator*
Solomon, Barry Jason *healthcare administrator, consultant*
Tyson, Mike G. *professional boxer*

Deland
Becker, Herbert Lawrence *writer, accountant*
Brakeman, Louis Freeman *retired university administrator*
Caccamise, Alfred Edward *real estate executive*
Caccamise, Genevra Louise Ball (Mrs. Alfred E. Caccamise) *retired librarian*
Dascher, Paul Edward *university dean, accounting educator*
Duncan, Pope Alexander *college administrator*
Fant, Clyde Edward, Jr. *religion educator*
Gill, Donald George *education educator*
Horton, Thomas Roscoe *business advisor*
Hupalo, Meredith Topliff *artist, illustrator*
Langston, Paul T. *music educator, university dean, composer*
Lee, Howard Douglas *academic administrator*
Morland, Richard Boyd *retired educator*
†Pleus, Michael P.
Sanders, Edwin Perry Bartley *judge*
Sorensen, Jacki Faye *choreographer, aerobic dance company executive*
Tedros, Theodore Zaki *educator, real estate broker, appraiser*
†Wilkes, Glenn Newton *athletics educator, consultant*
Wilson, Susan *geriatrics nurse*

Delray Beach
Blankenheimer, Bernard *economics consultant*
Borkosky, Bruce Glenn *psychologist*
Burbank, Kershaw *writer*
Case, Manning Eugene, Jr. *food products executive*
Chavin, Walter *biological science educator and researcher*
Drimmer, Bernard E. *research physicist*
Dye, Thomas Roy *political science educator*
Erenstein, Alan *emergency room nurse, medical education consultant*
Fuente, David I. *office supply manufacturing executive*
Gaffey, Thomas Michael, Jr. *retired consumer products executive*
Gatewood, Robert Payne *financial planning executive*
Goldenberg, George *retired pharmaceutical company executive*
Haros, Joann *critical care nurse*
Hegstrom, William Jean *mathematics educator*
Himmelright, Robert John, Jr. *rubber company executive*
†Klein, Marilyn (Lynn) *interior designer, volunteer*
Larry, R. Heath *lawyer*
Lerner, Norman *photographer, educator*
Levinson, Harry *psychologist, educator*
Liguori, Joseph John, Jr. *fire fighter, paramedic consultant*
Love, Marsha Lynn *interior decorator*
†Lucà-Moretti, Maurizio *scientist, nutrition researcher*
Mayer, Marilyn Gooder *steel company executive*
Mills, Agnes Eunice Karlin *artist, printmaker, sculptor*
Mueller, Gerry *retired computer company executive*
Randall, Priscilla Richmond *travel executive*
Reef, Arthur *industry business consultant*
Rippeteau, Darrel Downing *architect*
Robinson, Brenda Kay *editor, public relations professional*
Robinson, Richard Francis *writer, author*
Rosenfeld, Steven Ira *ophthalmologist*
Ross, Beatrice Brook *artist*
Rowland, Robert Charles *writer, clinical psychotherapist, researcher*

Saffer, Alfred *retired chemical company executive*
Salsberg, Arthur Philip *publishing company executive*
†Scott, James Lawrence *retired human resources executive, consultant*
Seder, Arthur Raymond, Jr. *lawyer*
Shister, Joseph *arbitrator, educator*
Shute, Melodie Ann *community services administrator*
Smith, Charles Oliver *engineer*
Smith, John Joseph, Jr. *textile company executive, educator*
Sondak, Arthur *management consultant*
Stewart, Patricia Carry *foundation administrator*
Walker, Fred Elmer *broadcasting executive*
Zarwyn, Berthold *physical scientist*

Deltona
Bondinell, Stephanie *counselor, former educational administrator*
Morgan, Shirley Ann *information systems executive*
Neal, Dennis Melton *middle school administrator*
Tiblier, Fernand Joseph, Jr. *municipal engineering administrator*

Destin
Asher, Betty Turner *academic administrator*
De Revere, David Wilsen *professional society administrator*
Horne, Thomas Lee, III *entrepreneur*
Najarian, Betty Jo *music educator*

Dover
Pearson, Walter Donald *editor, columnist*

Dundee
Johnson, Gordon Selby *consulting electrical engineer*

Dunedin
Allison, Brooke Hastings *artist*
Espy, Charles Clifford *English language educator, author, consultant, lecturer, administrator*
Flemm, Eugene William *concert pianist, educator, conductor, chamber musician*
†Foley, Wendy H. *library director*
Gambone, Victor Emmanuel, Jr. *internist*
Metcalf, Robert John Elmer *industrial consultant*
Rosa, Raymond Ulric *retired banker*
Samson, Jerome *communications executive, software engineer*
Simmons, Patricia Ann *pharmacist, consultant*
Tweedy, Robert Hugh *retired equipment company executive*
Weber, Ellen Schmoyer *pediatric speech pathologist*
Zschau, Julius James *lawyer*

Dunnellon
Dixon, W(illiam) Robert *retired educational psychology educator*
Sawick, Karen Ann *real estate salesperson*

Eglin AFB
Franzen, Larry William *aerospace electronics engineer*
Head, William Christopher *military officer, health care administrator*
†Kostelnik, Michael C. *career officer*
†Richardson, Douglas J. *career officer*
Snyder, Donald Robert, III *electronic imaging engineer*
Stewart, J. Daniel *air force development and test center administrator*
Word, Jennifer Tracy Shannon *air force officer*

Ellenton
Edson, Herbert Robbins *retired foundation and hospital executive*
Murray, Constance Yvonne *gerontology and geropsychiatric nurse, administrator*

Englewood
Brainard, Paul Henry *musicologist, retired music educator*
Curtis, Caroline A. S. *community health and oncology nurse*
Dowdell, Michael Francis *critical care and anesthesia nurse practitioner*
Heintz, Mary Ethel *business owner*
Lahiff, Marilyn J. *nursing administrator*
Lantz, Joanne Baldwin *academic administrator emeritus*
Schultz, Arthur Joseph, Jr. *retired trade association executive*
Seeley, David William *minister*
Simis, Theodore Luckey *investment banker, information technology executive*
Sisson, Robert F. *photographer, writer, lecturer, educator*
Tracy, Lois Bartlett *painter*
Urka, Martin C. *soil scientist*

Estero
Brown, William Robert *association executive, consultant*
Brush, George W. *college president*

Eustis
Alfrey, Lydia Jean *musician educator*
Chorosinski, Eugene Conrad *writer, poet, author*
Pinkston, Isabel Hay *minister, writer, educator, therapist*

Fernandina Beach
Barlow, Anne Louise *pediatrician, medical research administrator*
Burns, Stephen Redding *golf course architect*
D'Agnese, John Joseph *sanitation, public health and pest management consultant*
DelPesco Thornton, Nancy Rose *artist, educator*
Eaton, Henry Taft *forest products executive, consultant*
Fishbaugh, Carole Sue *secondary school educator*
Kurtz, Myers Richard *hospital administrator*
Lilly, Wesley Cooper *marine engineer, ship surveyor*
Rogers, Robert Burnett *naval officer*

Fisher Island
Bandler, Richard *advertising executive*
Ventura, Richard Eugene *human resources executive*

Flagler Beach
Wadsworth, Frances Faulkner *retired educator*

Floral City
Wise, Lawrence George *human resources executive*

Fort Lauderdale
Abraham, Rebecca Jacob *finance educator*
Adams, Daniel Lee *lawyer*
Adams, Salvatore Charles *lawyer, speaker, financial consultant, radio and television commentator*
Alpert, Martin Jeffrey *chiropractic physician*
Ambrose, Judith Ann *designer*
Austin, Scott Raymond *lawyer*
Azrin, Nathan Harold *psychologist*
Barnard, George Smith *lawyer, former federal agency official*
Barnes, William Douglas *advertising executive*
Bartelstone, Rona Sue *gerontologist*
Bethel, Marilyn Joyce *librarian*
Bird, Linda W. *realtor*
Bishop, George Williams, III *supply company executive*
Bogenschutz, J. David *lawyer*
Brawer, Marc Harris *lawyer*
Bunnell, George Eli *lawyer*
Bustamante, Nestor *lawyer*
Calhoun, Peggy Joan *fundraising executive*
Cantwell, John Walsh *advertising executive*
Carney, Dennis Joseph *former steel company executive, consulting company executive*
Carter, James Thomas *contractor*
Carton, Cristina Silva-Bento *elementary educator*
Cash, Ralph Eugene *psychologist*
Cassidy, Terrence Patrick, Jr. *engineering consultant*
†Catinella, Frank Peter *cardiovascular and thoracic surgeon*
Caulkins, Charles S. *lawyer*
Ceasar, Mitchell *lawyer*
Ciccarelli, Dino *professional hockey player*
Clark, Mary Ellen *Olympic athlete*
Cobb, David Keith *business executive*
Collins, Ronald William *psychologist, educator*
Cooney, David Francis *lawyer*
Costello, John H., III *business and marketing executive*
Cox, Linda Susan *allergist, immunologist*
Cummings, Virginia (Jeanne) *retired real estate company executive*
Danzig, Sheila Ring *marketing and direct mail executive*
Danzig, William Harold *marketing executive*
Dean, Marilyn Ferwerda *nursing consultant, administrator*
Devol, George Charles, Jr. *manufacturing executive*
Donoho, Tim Mark *entrepreneur*
Dorn, Samuel O. *endodontist*
Dressler, Robert A. *lawyer*
Dutko, Michael Edward *lawyer*
†Dworin, Micki (Maxine) *automobile dealership executive*
Easton, Robert Morrell, Jr. *optometric physician*
†Edmund, Norman W. *educational researcher*
Eisner, Will *publishing company executive*
Enriquez, Cristino Catud *radiologist, internist, cardiologist*
Ephraim, Charles *lawyer*
Etling, Terry Douglas *state agency administrator*
Eynon, Steven Scott *minister*
†Faust, Charles *hotel executive*
Feld, Joseph *construction executive*
Feldman, Myrna Lee *elementary education educator*
Fine, Howard Alan *travel industry executive*
Fischler, Abraham Saul *education educator, retired university president*
Fishe, Gerald Raymond Aylmer *engineering executive*
Ford, Edward Charles (Whitey Ford) *retired baseball player*
Galvez-Jimenez, Nestor *neurologist*
Garver, James Amos *municipal official*
Gerbino, John *advertising executive*
Geronemus, Diann Fox *social work consultant*
Gianguzzi, Joseph Custode *sculptor*
Glantz, Wendy Newman *lawyer*
Golden, E(dward) Scott *lawyer*
Gonzalez, Jose Alejandro, Jr. *federal judge*
Goodstein, Richard George *sales executive*
Greenberger, Sheldon Lee *newspaper advertising executive*
Groshart, Caroline King *technical writer, editor*
Gude, Nancy Carlson *computer consultant*
Halpern, Steven Jay *editor, newspaper columnist, freelance writer*
Hanbury, George Lafayette, II *academic administrator*
Hargrove, John Russell *lawyer*
Hartz, Deborah Sophia *editor, critic*
Heath, Thomas Clark *lawyer*
Hershenson, Miriam Hannah *librarian*
Hess, George Franklin, II *lawyer*
Hester, Julia A. *lawyer*
Hirsch, Jeffrey Allan *lawyer*
Hoines, David Alan *lawyer*
Honahan, H(enry) Robert *motion picture theatre executive*
Horowitz, Kenneth A. *communications executive, entrepreneur*
Huizenga, Harry Wayne *entrepreneur, entertainment corporation executive, professional sports team executive*
Huysman, James David *healthcare executive, consultant*
†Hymann, Paul G., Jr. *federal judge*
James, Gordon, III *lawyer*
Jotcham, Thomas Denis *marketing communications consultant*
Judd, James *performing company executive*
Kaplan, Elissa *social worker, children's counselor, consultant*
Kemper Littman, Marlyn *information scientist, educator*
Kennedy, Beverly (Kleban) Burris *financial consultant, tv and radio talk show host*
†King, Nathaniel Bregman *aviation construction company executive*
†Klein, Stacy Lynn *educator*
Koch, Katherine Rose *communications executive*
Krathen, David Howard *lawyer*
Kreizinger, Loreen I. *lawyer, nurse*
Kropp, Stacy Anne *small business owner*
Kubler, Frank Lawrence *lawyer*
Kurzenberger, Dick *health services executive*
†LaMarr, Jack Paul *lawyer*
Lataif, Lawrence P. *lawyer*
LeRoy, Miss Joy *model, designer*
Lewis, Ovid C. *dean, law educator, lawyer*
Lilley, Mili Della *insurance company executive, entertainment management consultant*
Lister, Mark Wayne *clinical laboratory scientist*

Lobeck, William E. rental company executive
Lodwick, Gwilym Savage radiologist, educator
Loos, John Thompson business owner
Magrino, Peter Frank lawyer
Mannino, Robert medical educator
Mastronardi, Corinne Marie lawyer
Maucker, Earl Robert newspaper editor, newspaper executive
Maxwell, Sara Elizabeth psychologist, educator, speech pathologist, director
McAusland, Randolph M. N. arts administrator
McCan, James Lawton education educator
McGinnis, Patrick Bryan mental health counselor
McGreevy, Mary retired psychology educator
Meeks, William Herman, III lawyer
Miller, Jerome M. civic worker
Miller, Stephen Warren dean
Mintz, Joel Alan law educator
Moraitis, Karen Karl real estate broker
Morse, Edward J. automotive executive
Moss, Stephen B. lawyer
Nash, James Lee poet, security official
†Nero, Peter pianist, conductor, composer, arranger
Niehaus, Robert James investment banking executive
Nyce, John Daniel lawyer
Olen, Milton William, Jr. marketing executive
Oliet, Seymour endodontics educator, dean, dentist
Ornstein, Libbie Allene primary school educator
Page, Earl Michael management specialist
Pallans, Mark David city official, telecommuncations specialist
Pallowick, Nancy Ann special education educator
Palmer, Marcia Stibal food and wine retailer, interior designer, real estate investor
Pettijohn, Fred Phillips retired newspaper executive, consultant
Pohlman, Randolph A. business administration educator, dean
Price, Judith nursing educator
Ramos-Moll, Ervin career officer, federal agency administrator
Randi, James (Randall James Hamilton Zwinge) magician, writer, educator
†Ray, Raymond B. federal judge
Reisinger, Sandra Sue columnist
Rendon-Pellerano, Marta Ines dermatologist
Rentoumis, Ann Mastroianni psychotherapist
Richmond, Gail Levin law educator
Riggs, Donald Eugene librarian, university official
Roettger, Norman Charles, Jr. federal judge
Rose, Norman retired lawyer, retired accountant
Roselli, Richard Joseph lawyer
Rosen, Barry Howard museum director, history educator
†Salanga, Virgilio Dizon neurologist, educator
Satz, Michael lawyer
Schear, Betty Z. engineering executive, consultant
Schrader, Robert George lawyer
Schreiber, Alan Hickman lawyer
Schulte, Frederick James newpaper editor
†Seltzer, Barry S. federal judge
Sherman, Richard Allen lawyer
Shoemaker, William Edward financial executive
Snow, Lurana S. judge
Soeteber, Ellen journalist, newspaper editor
Sorensen, Allan Chresten service company executive
Spann, Ronald Thomas mediator
Spungin, Charlotte Isabelle retired secondary education educator, writer
Stadtmiller, Marguerita W. advertising executive
Stankee, Glen Allen lawyer
Stone, Edward Durell, Jr. landscape architect and planner
Sutton, Douglas Hoyt nurse
Tanner, Travis travel company executive
Thayer, Charles J. investment banker
Tripp, Norman Densmore lawyer
Turner, Hugh Joseph, Jr. lawyer
†Valliere, Flora Lee law firm official
Vladem, Paul Jay investment advisor, broker
Washington, Alice Hester human services professional
†Welton professional soccer player
Whitmore, Douglas Michael physician
Wich, Donald Anthony, Jr. lawyer
Wietor, Michael George real estate executive, commodity trading advisor, export purchasing agent
Williams, Roslyn Patrice marketing executive
Williamson, William Paul, Jr. journalist
Wojcik, Cass decorative supply company executive, former city official
†Wortmann, Ivo professional soccer coach
†Young Olson, Brenda elementary education educator
Zikakis, John P. consultant, educator, researcher, biochemist
†Zlatkin, Michael Brian physician
Zloch, William J. federal judge
Zumbano, Anthony Ralph risk, claims management executive

Fort Myers

Adams, Todd Porter financial and investment advisor
Allen, Richard Chester retired lawyer, educator
Antonic, James Paul international marketing consultant
Arnall, Robert Esric physician, medical administrator
Barbour, William Rinehart, Jr. retired book publisher
Brown, Earl Kent historian, clergyman
Canham, Pruella Cromartie Niver retired educator
†Chambers, Jim Arthur educator
Colasurd, Richard Michael lawyer
Colgate, Doris Eleanor retailer, sailing school owner and adminstrator
Dalton, Anne lawyer
Dean, Jean Beverly artist
†Demers, Nora Egan immunologist, biologist, educator
Diers, Hank H. drama educator, playwright, director
Disney, Ralph L(ynde) retired industrial engineering educator
Fisher, Michael Bruce lawyer
Frank, Elizabeth Ahls art educator, artist
Fromm, Winfield Eric retired corporate executive, engineering consultant and investor
†Fulker, Edmund management consultant
Gorelik, Alla piano educator
Griffin, Jerry J. chaplain
Gustafson, Jim broadcast executive
Hartman, Earl Kenneth writer
Heath, Glenn Edward planner
Hopple, Jeanne M. adult nurse practitioner
Horecker, Bernard Leonard retired biochemistry educator
Housel, Natalie Rae Norman physical therapist
Jacobi, Fredrick Thomas newspaper publisher
Johnson, Sally A. nurse, educator
Kelley, Michael James medical services executive, author
Kish, Elissa Anne educational administrator, consultant
Koehler, Robert Brien priest
Laboda, Gerald oral and maxillofacial surgeon
Mac Master, Harriett Schuyler retired elementary education educator
†Manning, John E. port authority chairman
Massa, Conrad Harry religious studies educator
Mc Grath, William Restore transportation planner, traffic engineer
Medvecky, Robert Stephen lawyer
Mergler, Harry Winston engineering educator
Milaski, John Joseph business transformation industry consultant
Miner, Thelma Smith retired American literature educator
Missimer, Thomas Michael geologist
Moeschl, Stanley Francis electrical engineer, management consultant
Morse, John Harleigh lawyer
Newland, Jane Lou nursing educator
†Pascotto, Robert Daniel cardiovascular/thoracic surgeon
Pearson, Paul Holding insurance company executive
Peterson, Rodney Delos mediator, forensic economist
Powell, Richard Pitts writer
Ranney, Mary Elizabeth business executive
Rose, Susan A. Schultz retired theological librarian
Schoonover, Jack Ronald judge
Schwartz, Carl Edward artist, printmaker
Scott, Kenneth Elsner mechanical engineering educator
Sechrist, Chalmers Franklin, Jr. electrical engineering educator
Shafer, Robert Tinsley, Jr. judge
Simmons, Vaughan Pippen medical consultant
†Sneddon, Robert J. educator elementary schools
Snelling, Lonie Eugene, Jr. minister
Steier, Michael Edward cardiac surgeon
†Swartz, George T. federal judge
Warner, Elizabeth Jane Scott exceptional education educator
†Wassersug, Stephen Robert environmental consultant
Wendeborn, Richard Donald retired manufacturing company executive
Whittaker, Douglas Kirkland school system administrator
Williams, Suzanne pediatric nurse practitioner
Workman, Susan Barnett mental health center administrator

Fort Myers Beach

Oerter, Al motivational speaker
Tatarian, Mary Linda retailer, real estate broker

Fort Pierce

Arnold, Donna F. business educator
Bynum, Henri Sue education and French educator
Calvert, David Victor soil science educator
Garment, Robert James clergyman
Gawel, Maureen Saltzer newspaper executive
Ginns, David Richard county official
Lucy, Donald Michael business and accounting educator, accountant
†Lynch, Frank J. federal judge
†Massey, Edwin R. college president
Norton, Robert Howard entertainer, musical arranger, author
Partenheimer, Robert Chapin emergency physician
Peterson, Barbara Owecke artist, nurse, realtor
Rice, Mary Esther biologist
Solon, Leonard R(aymond) physicist, educator, consultant
Steel, Philip S. architect, artist
Stock, Grace Emma civic volunteer
Thoma, Richard William chemical safety and waste management consultant
†Walker, Dennis artist

Fort Walton Beach

Bergschneider, John city engineer
†Buckroth, Mari Beth counselor
Cooke, Fred Charles real estate broker
Culver, Dan Louis federal agency administrator
Day, George Everette lawyer, retired military officer
Fallin, Barbara Moore human resources director
†Hill, Carol Jean library director
†Muehlberger, Gerald L. physician
Rogers, Steven Charles electronics technician
Sanders, Jimmy Devon public administration and health services educator
Stevenson, Mary Eva Blue retired elementary education educator
Villecco, Judy Diana substance abuse, mental health counselor, director

Gainesville

Abbaschian, Reza materials science and engineering educator
Abbott, Thomas Benjamin speech educator
Alexander, Stewart Murray (Buddy Alexander) golf coach
Anderson, Richard McLemore internist
Anderson, Timothy J. chemical engineering educator
Andrew, Edward Raymond physicist
App, James Leonard assistant dean
Baker, Bonnie Barbara mental health and school counselor, educator
Balabanian, Norman electrical engineering educator
Barber, Charles Edward newspaper executive, journalist
Bartlett, Rodney J. chemistry and physics educator
Bedell, George Chester retired publisher, educator, priest
†Belz, Richard A. federal judge
Bernard, H. Russell anthropology educator, scientific editor
Berns, Kenneth Ira physician
Besch, Emerson Louis physiology educator, past academic administrator
Boyes, Patrice Flinchbaugh lawyer, environmental executive
Brandi, Andy tennis coach
†Brodeur, Michael Stephen dean
Brown, Myra Suzanne librarian
Brown, William Samuel, Jr. communication sciences and disorders educator
Bryan, Robert Armistead university administrator, educator
Burridge, Michael John veterinarian, educator, research administrator
†Butler, Henry James academic administrator, consultant
Bzoch, Kenneth Rudolph speech and language educator, department chairman
Candelas, Teresa Bush special education educator
Capaldi, Elizabeth Ann Deutsch psychological sciences educator
Capehart, Barney Lee industrial and systems engineer
Carr, Glenna Dodson economics educator
Carr, Thomas Deaderick astronomer/physics educator, science administrator
Catasus, Jose Magin Perez school psychologist
Chait, Andrea Melinda special education educator
Challoner, David Reynolds university official, physician
Cheek, Jimmy Geary university administrator, agricultural education and communications educator
Cluff, Leighton Eggertsen physician
Coleman, Mary Stallings retired chief justice
Conner, Kathryn Gamble nurse
Conrad, Joseph Henry animal nutrition educator
Coordsen, Karen Gail medical/surgical nurse
Copeland, Edward Meadors, III surgery educator
Cousins, Robert John nutritional biochemist, educator
Creel, Austin Bowman religion educator
Cristescu, Nicolaie Dan engineering educator
Danforth, Glenn R. magazine publisher
Davis, George Kelso nutrition biochemist, educator
Davis, John Allen, Jr. (Jeff Davis) financial planner
Delfino, Joseph John environmental engineering sciences educator
Der-Houssikian, Haig linguistics educator
Dewsbury, Donald Allen historian of psychology, comparative psychologist
Dickinson, Joshua Clifton, Jr. museum director, educator
Dilcher, David Leonard paleobotany educator, research scholar
Dinculeanu, Nicolae mathematician
†Donovan, Billy university basketball boach
Drucker, Daniel Charles engineer, educator
Drury, Kenneth Clayton biological scientist
Duvenhage, Ian head tennis coach
Edwardson, John Richard retired agronomist
Emch, Gerard Gustav mathematics and physics educator
†Farber, Erich A. mechanical engineer
Fossum, Jerry George electrical engineering educator
Freeland, James M. Jackson lawyer, educator
†Gaintner, Richard J. health facility administrator
Gelband, Craig Harris physiologist, pharmacologist
Gets, Lispbeth Ella educational administrator
†Gilbert, Pamela Katherine literature educator
Gordon, Richard M. Erik retailing executive, educator
Grant, Elizabeth Jane Thurmond graphic design educator, consultant
Gravenstein, Joachim Stefan anesthesiologist, educator
Green, Eleanor Myers veterinarian, educator
Greer, Melvin medical educator
Gutekunst, Richard Ralph microbiology educator
Hall, David Walter botanist
Hanrahan, Robert Joseph chemist, educator
Hanson, Harold Palmer physicist, government official, editor, academic administrator
Haring, Ellen Stone (Mrs. E. S. Haring) philosophy educator
Heflin, Martin Ganier foreign service officer, international political economist
Henson, (Betty) Ann media specialist, educator
Himes, James Albert veterinary medicine educator emeritus
Hollien, Harry Francis speech and communications scientist, educator
Holloway, Paul Howard materials science educator
Hope, George Marion vision scientist
Hornberger, Robert Howard psychologist
Houchen, Constance Elaine nursing administrator
Hoy, Marjorie Ann entomology educator
Humphrey, Stephen college dean
Huszar, Arlene Celia lawyer, mediator
Iasemidis, Leonidas D. neuroscience educator
Isaacs, Gerald William retired agricultural engineering educator, consultant
Israel, Jerold Harvey law educator
Jackson, LaTrelle D. psychologist, educator
Jacobs, Alan Martin physicist, educator
Jaeger, Marc Julius physiology educator, researcher
Javid, Nikzad Sabet dentist, prosthodontist educator
†Johnston, Otto William German language and literature educator
Jones, David Alwyn geneticist, botany educator
Jones, Elizabeth Nordwall county government official
Jones, Richard Lamar entomology educator
Jones, Tom track and field coach
Kaimowitz, Gabe Hillel civil rights lawyer
Kaplan, John photojournalist, consultant, educator
Katritzky, Alan Roy chemistry educator, consultant
Keesling, James Edgar mathematics educator
Kerslake, Kenneth Alvin artist, printmaker, art educator
Klauder, John Rider physics educator
Kurrus, Thomas William lawyer
Kurzweg, Ulrich Hermann engineering science educator
Lampotang, Samsun medical educator
Law, Mark Edward electrical engineer, educator
Limacher, Marian Cecile cardiologist
Lindholm, Fredrik Arthur electrical engineering educator
Lombardi, John V. university administrator, historian
Lowenstein, Ralph Lynn university dean emeritus
Mahla, Michael E. anesthesiologist, educator
Malasanos, Lois Julanne Fosse nursing educator
Malvern, Lawrence Earl engineering educator, researcher
Maple, Marilyn Jean educational media coordinator
†Maria, Bernard L. pediatric neurologist
Maurer, Virginia Gallaher law educator
McClellan, Richard Augustus small business owner
McCluskey, Charles James, Jr. physician assistant
McFarlane, Neil Frazer health administrator
Mead, Frank Waldreth taxonomic entomologist
Meredith, Julia Alice nematologist, biologist, researcher
Meyer, Harvey Kessler, II retired academic administrator
Micha, David Allan chemistry and physics educator
Milanich, Jerald Thomas archaeologist, museum curator
Modell, Jerome Herbert anesthesiologist, educator
Morgan, Anne Barclay artist, author
†Murray, Kate Shakeshaft artist
Nair, Ramachandran P.K. agroforestry educator, researcher
Neiberger, Richard Eugene pediatrician, nephrologist, educator
Neims, Allen Howard univeristy dean, medical scientist
†Nell, Terril A. horticulturalist, educator
Neugroschel, Arnost electrical engineering educator
Niblack, Nancy Lee Parham insurance agent, financial consultant
†Nichols, Linda Rose educator, program administrator
Nicoletti, Paul Lee veterinarian, educator
Noffsinger, William Blake computer science educator, academic administrator
Nozzi, Dom urban planner
Oberlander, Herbert insect physiologist, educator
Odum, Howard T. emeritus environmental science educator
Ohanian, Mihran Jacob nuclear engineering educator, research dean
Ohrn, Nils Yngve chemistry and physics educator
Opdyke, Neil Donald geology educator
Oppenheim, Paul vocational educator
Owens, Robin Shane clergyman
Palovcik, Reinhard Anton research neurophysiologist
Paul, Maurice M. federal judge
Paul, Ouida Fay music educator
Pearce, Joseph Huske industrial engineer
Peebles, Peyton Zimmerman, Jr. electrical engineer, educator
Person, Willis Bagley chemistry educator
Pfaff, William Wallace medical educator
Phillips, Winfred Marshall dean, mechanical engineer, academic administrator
Polasek, Edward John electrical engineer, consultant
Pop, Emil research chemist
Popenoe, Hugh Llywelyn soils educator
Price, Donald Ray university official, agricultural engineer
Proctor, Samuel history educator
Purcifull, Dan Elwood plant virologist, educator
Quesenberry, Kenneth Hays agronomy educator
Randall, Malcom health care administrator
Reeves, Tracey Elizabeth director
Reynolds, Richard Clyde physician, educator
Rhoton, Albert Loren, Jr. neurological surgery educator
Robertson, James Cole consultant
Rosenbloom, Arlan Lee physician, educator
Ross, Julia Carol basektball coach
Rubin, Melvin Lynne ophthalmologist, educator
Sah, Chih-Tang electrical and computer engineering educator
Schelske, Claire L. limnologist, educator
Schiebler, Gerold Ludwig physician, educator
Schmeling, Gareth classics educator
Schmertmann, John Henry civil engineer, educator, consultant
Schmidt-Nielsen, Bodil Mimi (Mrs. Roger G. Chagnon) physiologist
Schneider, Richard Harold university dean, educator
Schwartz, Michael Averill pharmacy educator, consultant
Shaeff, Gary William anthropologist, computer consultant
Sheng, Yea-Yi Peter oceanographic engineer, educator, researcher
Sherif, S. A. mechanical engineering educator
Siegel, Robert James communications executive
Singer, Robert Norman motor behavior educator
Singley, John Edward, Jr. environmental scientist, consultant
Sisler, Harry Hall chemist, educator
Small, Natalie Settimelli pediatric mental health counselor
Small, Parker Adams, Jr. pediatrician, educator
Smith, Alexander Goudy physics and astronomy educator
Smith, David Thornton lawyer, educator
Smith, Jo Anne writer, retired educator
Smith, Wayne Hilry forest resources and conservation educator
†Spurrier, Steve university athletic coach, former professional football player
Stehli, Francis Greenough geologist, educator
Stein, Jay M. planning and design educator, consultant
Stephan, Alexander F. German language and literature educator
Stern, William Louis botanist, educator
Sullivan, Neil Samuel physicist, researcher, educator
Suzuki, Howard Kazuro retired anatomist, educator
Talbert, James Lewis pediatric surgeon, educator
Taylor, William Jape physician
Teitelbaum, Philip psychologist
Teixeira, Arthur Alves food engineer, educator, consultant
Thompson, Neal Philip food science and nutrition educator
Thornton, J. Ronald technology center director
Tillman, Michael Gerard lawyer
Trickey, Samuel Baldwin physics educator, researcher, university administrator
Tulenko, James Stanley nuclear engineer, educator
Tumlinson, James H., III agriculturist
Van Alstyne, W. Scott, Jr. lawyer, educator
Varnes, Jill Tutton university official, health educator
Verink, Ellis Daniel, Jr. metallurgical engineering educator, consultant
Viessman, Warren, Jr. academic dean, civil engineering educator, researcher
von Mering, Otto Oswald anthropology educator
Wagner, Eric Armin sociology educator
Walker, Robert Dixon, III surgeon, urologist, educator
Watson, Robert Joe hospital administrator, retired career officer
Westphal, Roger Allen electrical engineer
Wethington, John Abner, Jr. retired nuclear engineering educator
Weyrauch, Walter Otto law educator
White, Jill Carolyn lawyer
White, Susie Mae school psychologist
Widmer, Charles Glenn dentist, researcher
Wilcox, Charles Julian geneticist, educator
Williams, Hiram Draper artist, educator
Willocks, Robert Max retired librarian
Wing, Elizabeth Schwarz museum curator, educator
†Wyatt-Brown, Anne Marbury linguistics educator
Wyatt-Brown, Bertram historian, educator
York, E. Travis academic administrator, former university chancellor, consultant
York, Vermelle Cardwell real estate broker and developer
Yost, Richard Alan chemistry educator

Young, David Michael *biochemistry and molecular biology educator, physician*
Zerner, Michael Charles *chemistry and physics educator, consultant, researcher*

Goulds
Cooper, Kenneth Stanley *educational administrator*

Graceville
Collier, Evelyn Myrtle *elementary school educator*
Kinchen, Thomas Alexander *college president*
Murrell, Irvin Henry, Jr. *librarian, minister*

Green Cove Springs
Norton, Joan Jennings *English language educator*
†Slade, Tom *industrial paint manufacturing company executive, political party official*
Watson, Thomas Campbell *economic development consulting company executive*
Yelton, Eleanor O'Dell *retired reading specialist*

Greenacres
Diaz, Raul *psychologist*

Gulf Breeze
DeBardeleben, John Thomas, Jr. *retired insurance company executive*
French, Jere Stuart *landscape architect*
Jenkins, Robert Berryman *real estate developer*
Larson, Kurt Paul *fire chief*
MacKenzie, Malcolm Robert *personnel management consultant*
McDonald, Marianne M. *artist*
Milford, Stephen Alan *management consultant*
Strength, Janis Grace *management executive, educator*
†Twiss, Dorothy Gleason *English educator, poet*

Gulf Stream
Nalen, Craig Anthony *government official*
Stone, Franz Theodore *retired fabricated metal products manufacturing executive*

Gulfport
Athanson, Mary Catheryne *school system administrator*
Davis, Ann Caldwell *history educator*
Keistler, Betty Lou *accountant, tax consultant*
Kruse, James Joseph *merchant banker*
Marshall, Nathalie *artist, writer, educator*

Haines City
Clement, Robert William *retired air force officer*
Mc Dougall, Dugald Stewart *retired lawyer*
Ware, Clarkie May Flake *civic worker*

Hallandale
Contney, John Joseph *trade association administrator*
Geller, Bunny Zelda *poet, writer, publisher, sculptor, artist*
Haspel, Arthur Carl *podiatrist, surgeon*
Price, Ruthe Geier *actress, writer, educator*

Havana
Macmillan, Tyler Lash *state agency administrator*
Whitehead, Lucy Grace *health facility administrator*

Heathrow
Darbelnet, Robert Louis *automobile association executive*

Hernando
Cooper, Harry Edwin *historian*

Hialeah
Bolanos, Rolando D. *protective services officer*
Deloach, Daniel *city clerk*
Dominik, Jack Edward *lawyer*
Economides, Christopher George *pathologist*
Edelcup, Norman Scott *management and financial consultant*
Farach, Ruben *city administrator*
Gomez, Luis Carlos *manufacturing executive*
Grahm, Charles Morton *sales executive*
Hernandez, Roland *broadcast executive*
Horsley, Ernest *city administrator*
Koreman, Dorothy Goldstein *physician, dermatologist*
Legg, Morris Burke *secondary school educator*
†Martinez, Raul L. *mayor, publisher*
Phelps, Dorothy Frink *civic worker*
Proctor, Thomas F. Goldsmith *sales executive, publishing executive*
Shaw, Steven John *retired marketing educator, academic administrator*
Worth, James Gallagher *engineer, chemist*

Hialeah Gardens
Stewart, Burch Byron *laboratory director*
†Tarafa, Roberto M. *construction company executive*

Highland Beach
Frager, Albert S. *retired retail food company executive*
Karp, Richard M. *advertising and communication executive*
Schor, Stanley Sidney *mathematical sciences educator*
Settler, Eugene Brian *record company executive*
Stimson, Frederick Sparks *Hispanist, educator*
Summers, James Irvin *retired advertising executive*
†Tolf, Robert Walter *writer*
Zagoria, Sam D(avid) *arbitrator, author, educator*

Hilliard
Nelson, Tommy Leon *poet*

Hillsboro Beach
McGarry, Carmen Racine *historian, artist*

Hobe Sound
Casey, Edward Paul *manufacturing company executive*
Craig, David Jeoffrey *retired manufacturing company executive*
DeHority, Edward Havens, Jr. *retired accountant, lawyer*
Etherington, Edwin Deacon *lawyer, business executive, educator*
Havens, Oliver Hershman *lawyer, consultant*
Hotchkiss, Winchester Fitch *retired investment banker*
Markoe, Frank, Jr. *lawyer, business and hospital executive*
Matheson, William Lyon *lawyer*
McChristian, Joseph Alexander *international business executive*
Parker, H. Lawrence *investor, rancher, retired investment banker*
Simpson, Russell Gordon *lawyer, mayor, counselor to not-for-profit organizations*
Vanderbilt, Oliver Degray *financier*

Holiday
Swatos, William Henry, Jr. *sociologist, priest*

Hollywood
Anger, Paul *newspaper editor*
Angstrom, Wayne Raymond *communications executive*
Bivens, Constance Ann *retired elementary education educator*
†Carter, Richard Leland *neurosurgeon*
Cowan, Irving *real estate owner, developer*
Duffner, Lee R. *ophthalmologist*
Fell, Frederick Victor *publisher*
Fischler, Shirley Balter *retired lawyer*
Foreman, Edwin Francis *economist, real estate broker*
Giulianti, Mara Selena *mayor, civic worker*
Goldberg, Icchok Ignacy *retired special education educator*
Harringer, Olaf Carl *architect, museum consultant*
Korngold, Alvin Leonard *broadcasting company executive*
Ladin, Eugene *communications company executive*
Matasa, Claude George *researcher, science administrator, educator*
†Mostel, Claire Roberta *county official*
Nicolas, Carl-Richard *commodities trading company executive, translator*
Ohms, Cosmo *recording and production company executive*
†Perryman, Richard Allan *cardiac surgeon*
Roseman, Mark Alan *lawyer*
Sadowski, Carol Johnson *artist*
Shane, Doris Jean *respiratory therapist, administrator*
Shapiro, Samuel Bernard *management consultant*
Staller, Aileen J. *neurosurgical nurse clinician*
Tannen, Ricki Lewis *lawyer, depth psychologist/analyst, educator*
Tucker, Nina Angella *hospital administrator*
Valdes, Jacqueline Chehebar *neuropsychologist, consultant, researcher*
Weinberg, Marcy *psychologist*

Holmes Beach
Dunne, James Robert *academic administrator, management consultant, business educator*

Homestead
Bachmeyer, Steven Allan *secondary education educator*
Crouse, John Oliver, II *journalist, publisher*
Ring, Richard G. *national park service administrator*
Roberts, Larry Spurgeon *biological sciences educator, zoologist*
Willner, Eugene Burton *food and liquor company executive*

Homosassa
Acton, Norman *international organization executive*
Nagy, Albert N. *entrepreneur, consultant*

Homosassa Springs
Burch, Annetta Jane *writer*

Hudson
Stash, Janet *nursing consultant*

Hurlburt Field
†Holland, Charles R. *military officer*
Ingram, Shirley Jean *social worker*

Hutchinson Island
Wegman, Harold Hugh *management consultant*

Indialantic
Button, Kenneth John *physicist*
Lewis, Richard Stanley *author, former editor*
Pavlakos, Ellen Tsatiri *sculptor*

Indian Creek
Shula, Don Francis *former professional football coach, team executive*

Indian Harbor Beach
Clark, John F. *aerospace research and engineering educator*
Covault, Craig *editor*
Haggis, Lewanna Strom *educator, author, consultant*
Harrington, Peter Tyrus *emergency management company executive, public relations consultant, author, photographer*
Koenig, Harold Paul *management consultant, ecologist, evangelist, writer*
Osmundsen, Barbara Ann *sculptor*
Scanlon, Charles Francis *retired army officer, defense consultant, author*
Traylor, Angelika *stained glass artist*
Van Arsdall, Robert Armes *engineer, retired air force officer*
†Wagner, Susan Preston *nursing educator*

Indian Rocks Beach
†Kephart, Robert Dennis *publisher*
Rocheleau, James Romig *retired university president*

Inverness
Cook, George *songwriter*
Esquibel, Edward V. *psychiatrist, clinical medical program developer*
Mavros, George S. *clinical laboratory director*
Nichols, Sally Jo *geriatrics nurse*
Stone, Fred Lyndon *human resources administrator*

Islamorada
Boruszak, James Martin *insurance company executive*
Pritchard, Robert Jerome *resort owner, retired*
†Whyatt, Frances (Shylah Boyd) *poet, novelist*

Jacksonville
Aftoora, Patricia Joan *transportation executive*
Agnew, Samuel Gerard *orthopaedic traumatologist*
Akers, James Eric *medical practice marketing executive*
Allen, Ronald Wesley *financial executive*
Anderson, John Quentin *rail transportation executive*
Ansbacher, Lewis *lawyer*
Arbogast, Gordon Wade *systems engineer, executive, educator, consultant*
Baldwin, David Gregory *technical support representative*
Bartholomew, John Niles *church administrator*
Beattie, Donald A. *energy scientist, consultant*
†Beitz, William Charles *religious charity executive*
Belin, Jacob Chapman *paper company executive*
Bennett, Charles Edward *former congressman, educator*
Bennett, Michael Wayne *social services administrator, consultant*
Beytagh, Francis Xavier, Jr. *law educator*
Black, Susan Harrell *federal judge*
Blackburn, Robert McGrady *retired bishop*
Bodkin, Ruby Pate *corporate executive, real estate broker, educator*
Boyer, Tyrie Alvis *lawyer*
Boylan, Kevin Bernard *neurologist*
Bradford, Dana Gibson, II *lawyer*
Brady, James Joseph *economics educator*
†Brott, Thomas Gordon *neurologist*
Brown, Lloyd Harcourt, Jr. *newspaper editor*
†Brunell, Mark Allen *football player*
Bryan, Joseph Shepard, Jr. *lawyer*
†Cannon, Carl N. *publisher*
Capers, Dominic *professional football coach*
Carithers, Hugh Alfred *physician, retired*
Carver, Joan Sacknitz *university dean*
†Chambers, Jack A. *educator*
Cloud, Linda Beal *retired secondary school educator*
Cole, Linda Sue *grants planner, computer software professional*
Commander, Charles Edward *lawyer, real estate consultant*
Constantini, JoAnn M. *information management consultant*
†Corcoran, James Joseph, Jr. *health plan administrator, physician*
Coughlin, Tom *professional football coach*
Criser, Marshall M. *lawyer, retired university president*
Davis, A. Dano *grocery store chain executive*
Delaney, John Adrian *mayor*
Delaney, Kevin Francis *retired naval officer*
Dornan, Kevin William *lawyer*
Dorsher, Peter T. *physician*
Dundon, Margo Elaine *museum director*
Eden, F(lorence) Brown *artist*
Edwards, Marvin Raymond *investment counselor, economic consultant*
Ehrlich, Raymond *lawyer*
Ejimofor, Cornelius Ogu *political scientist, educator*
Farkas, Andrew *library director, educator, writer*
Farmer, Guy Otto, II *lawyer*
Fawbush, Andrew Jackson *lawyer*
Feinglass, Neil Gordon *anesthesiologist*
Francis, James Delbert *oil company executive*
Francis, Miles N., Jr. *muncipal official*
Frazier, Rosa Mae *medical/surgical and hemodialysis nurse*
Fulton-Quindoza, Debra Ann *nurse practitioner*
†Funk, Jerry A. *federal judge*
Getman, Willard Etheridge *lawyer, mediator*
Glover, Nathaniel, Jr. *sheriff*
Glover, Richard Bernard *foundation administrator*
Godfrey, John Munro *economic consultant*
†Goldman, Stephen Lewis *occupational physician*
Gooding, David Michael *lawyer, mediator*
Gorman, James Francis *systems analyst*
Groom, Dale *physician, educator*
Halverson, Steven Thomas *lawyer, construction executive*
Hamilton, Susan Owens *transportation company executive, lawyer*
Hartmann, Frederick William *newspaper editor*
Hartzell, Charles R. *research administrator, biochemist, cell biologist*
Haskell, Preston Hampton, III *construction company executive*
Hatch, Donald James (Jim Hatch) *business leadership and planning executive*
Hawkins, James Douglas, Jr. *structural engineer, architect*
†Hearle, Edward F.R. *retired management consultant*
Hecht, Frederick *physician, researcher, author, educator, consultant*
Held, Edwin Walter, Jr. *lawyer*
Helganz, Beverly Buzhardt *counselor*
Hill, James Clinkscales *federal judge*
Hipps, Alberta *city councilwoman*
Hodges, William Terrell *federal judge*
Holliday, Patricia Ruth McKenzie *evangelist*
Holzendorf, King, Jr. *city councilman*
Huddleston, John Franklin *obstetrics and gynecology educator*
Jackson, Julian Ellis *food company executive*
†Johnson, Crystal Maria *primary school educator*
Johnson, Douglas William *physician, radiologist, oncologist*
Johnson, Leland "Lee" Harry *social services administrator*
Jones, Harold C. *director agriculture*
Joos, Olga Martin-Ballestero de *language educator*
Joyce, Edward Rowen *retired chemical engineer, educator*
Keefe, Kenneth M., Jr. *lawyer*
Kelalis, Panayotis *pediatric urologist*
Kelso, Linda Yayoi *lawyer*
Kent, John Bradford *lawyer*
Kilbourne, Krystal Hewett *rail transportation executive*
Kinne, Frances Bartlett *chancellor emeritus*
Kitchens, Frederick Lynton, Jr. *insurance company executive*
Korn, Michael Jeffrey *lawyer*
Lake, Carnell Augustino *professional football player*
Lane, Edward Wood, Jr. *retired banker*
Leapley, Patricia Murray *dietitian*
Legler, Mitchell Wooten *lawyer*
Lestage, Daniel Barfield *retired naval officer, physician*
Lewis, Richard Harlow *urologist*
Liebtag, Benford Gustav, III (Ben Liebtag) *engineer, consultant*
Lindner, Carl Henry, Jr. *financial holding company executive*
Lipkovic, Peter *chief medical examiner*
Lluberas, Manuel F. *biologist*
Longino, Theresa Childers *nurse*
Loomis, Henry *former broadcasting company executive, former government official*
Loomis, Jacqueline Chalmers *photographer*
Lyon, Wilford Charles, Jr. *insurance executive*
†Magill, Sherry *foundation administrator*
Main, Edna (June) Dewey *education educator*
Mann, Timothy *corporate executive*
Marion, Gail Elaine *reference librarian*
Mason, William Cordell, III *hospital administrator*
Mass, M. F. *allergist, immunologist*
McBurney, Charles Walker, Jr. *lawyer*
McGehee, Frank Sutton *paper company executive*
McWilliams, John Lawrence, III *lawyer*
Melton, Howell Webster, Sr. *federal judge*
Milbrath, Robert Henry *retired petroleum executive*
Milton, Joseph Payne *lawyer*
Mishael, Rochelle Jaaziel *retired correctional officer*
Mizrahi, Edward Alan *allergist*
Monsky, John Bertrand *investment banking executive*
Moore, David Graham *sociologist, educator*
Moore, John Henry, II *federal judge*
Morehead, Charles Richard *insurance company executive*
Morgan, William Newton *architect, educator*
Morris, Max King *foundation executive, former naval officer*
Moseley, James Francis *lawyer*
Moses, Daniel *writer, singer*
Motsett, Charles Bourke *sales and marketing executive*
Mousa, Sam E. *municipal official*
Mueller, Edward Albert *retired transportation engineer executive*
Mullaney, Richard A. *lawyer*
Nimmons, Ralph Wilson, Jr. *federal judge*
Ohnsman, David Robert *insurance consultant*
Osborn, Marvin Griffing, Jr. *educational consultant*
Park, Christopher S. *chairman civil service board*
Parker, David Forster *real estate development consultant*
Paryani, Shyam Bhojraj *radiologist*
Pavlick, Pamela Kay *nurse, consultant*
Pearce, Jennifer Sue *real estate appraiser*
Phillips, Mary Kleyla *lawyer*
Pillans, Charles Palmer, III *lawyer*
Piotrowski, Sandra A. *elementary education educator*
Potter, William *city executive*
†Proctor, George L. *federal judge*
Rice, Charles Edward *bank executive*
Rice, James Philip *surgeon*
Rinaman, James Curtis, Jr. *lawyer*
Rinehart, Harry Elmer *retired sales executive*
Roberts, Lynwood *county official*
Rogers, Betty Gravitt *research company executive*
Rubens, Linda Marcia *home health services administrator*
Rue, Douglas Michael *technical application consultant*
Rumpel, Peter Loyd *architect, educator, artist*
Russell, David Emerson *mechanical engineer, consultant*
Sadler, Luther Fuller, Jr. *lawyer*
Saltzman, Irene Cameron *perfume manufacturing executive, art gallery owner*
Sandercox, Robert Allen *college official, clergyman*
Sanders, Marion Yvonne *geriatrics nurse*
Scales, Marjorie Lahr *pastoral counselor*
Schlageter, Robert William *museum administrator*
Schlesinger, Harvey Erwin *judge*
Schramm, Bernard Charles, Jr. *advertising agency executive*
Schultz, Frederick Henry *investor, former government official*
Sederbaum, William *marketing executive*
Short, Howard Elmo *church history educator*
Shoup, James Raymond *computer systems consultant*
Sibley, Richard Carl *real estate executive*
Siegel, Steven Douglas *oncologist*
†Siegmund, Susan *legislative staff member*
Simms, Jacqueline Kamp *secondary education educator*
Simpson, Charles Eugene *physician, military officer*
Slade, Thomas Bog, III *lawyer, investment banker*
Smith, Ivan Huron *architect*
†Snyder, Howard T. *federal judge*
Snyder, John Joseph *bishop*
Soud, Ginger *city councilwoman*
Stanley, Helen Camille *composer, musician*
†Steele, John E. *federal judge*
Stein, Jay *retail executive*
Stephenson, Samuel Edward, Jr. *retired physician*
Stone, Dennis J. *law educator, dean, lawyer*
Swartz, Stephen Arthur *banker, lawyer*
Tardona, Daniel Richard *ethologist, naturalist, writer, park ranger, educator*
†Taylor, Fred *professional football player*
Thorsteinsson, Gudni *physiatrist*
Tjoflat, Gerald Bard *federal judge*
Toker, Karen Harkavy *physician*
Tomlinson, William Holmes *management educator, retired army officer*
Townsend, Heather Marie *family nurse practitioner*
Turner, Robert Carlton *manufacturing company executive*
Vane, Terence G., Jr. *mortgage company executive, lawyer*
Vincent, Norman Fuller *broadcasting executive*
†Wallace, Steven R. *college president*
Wallis, Donald Wills *lawyer*
Wallizada, Wassy A. *physician*
Walters, John Sherwood *retired newspaperman*
Weaver, Wayne *professional sports team executive*
Welch, Philip Burland *electronics and office products company executive*
White, Edward Alfred *lawyer*
Wiles, Jon W(hitney) *education educator, consultant*
Williams, Lance Lamont *legislative assistant*
Wilson, C. Nick *health educator, consultant, researcher, lecturer*
Yamane, Stanley Joel *optometrist*
Zahra, Ellis E. *lawyer*

Jacksonville Beach
Forrest, Allen Wright *tax and financial services firm executive, accountant, financial planner*
Jones, Herman Otto, Jr. *corporate professional*
Pugh-Marzi, Sherrie *daycare center administrator*

Jasper
McCormick, John Hoyle *lawyer*

Jay
Brecke, Barry John *weed scientist, researcher, educator*

Weaver, Lynn Edward academic administrator, consultant, editor

Melbourne Beach
Costa, Manuel Antone recreational facility manager
Walker, Harriette Katherine religious administrator

Melrose
Burt, Alvin Victor, Jr. journalist
Harley, Ruth artist, educator

Merritt Island
Deardoff, R. Bruce automotive executive
Johnson, Clarence Traylor, Jr. circuit court judge
McClanahan, Leland academic administrator
Smith, David Edward business executive
Thomas, James Arthur retired government official, electrical engineer
Thompson, Hugh Lee academic administrator
Walter, George Anthony elementary education educator

Miami
Albright, John D. emergency room and telemetry nurse
Alexenberg, Mel artist, art educator
Allen, Charles Norman television, film and video producer
Alonso, Antonio Enrique lawyer
Alvarez, Raul Alberto internist
Amos, Betty Giles restaurant company executive, accountant
Anderson, Douglas Richard ophthalmologist, educator, scientist, researcher
Anscher, Bernard manufacturing executive, investor, management consultant
Arango, Jorge Sanin architect
Argibay, Jorge Luis information systems firm executive and founder
Arison, Micky cruise line company executive, sports team executive
Armstrong, James Louden, III lawyer
Astigarraga, Jose I(gnacio) lawyer
Atkins, C(arl) Clyde federal judge
Balás, Irene Barbara artist
Balmaseda, Liz columnist
Banas, Suzanne middle school educator
†Bandstra, Ted E. federal judge
Barkett, Rosemary federal judge
Barry, Dave columnist, author
Barthel, William Frederick, Jr. elctrical engineer, electronics company executive
Bastian, James Harold air transport company executive, lawyer
Batcheller, Joseph Ann entrepreneur
Batista, Alberto Entimio marketing professional
Baumberger, Charles Henry lawyer
Beck, Morris allergist
Beckham, Walter Hull, Jr. lawyer, educator
Beckley, Donald K. fundraiser
†Benitiz, Manny manufacturing company executive
Bennett, Olga Salowich civic worker, graphic arts researcher, consultant
Berger, Steven R. lawyer
†Berkman, Ronald M. dean, educator
Berley, David Richard lawyer
Berman, Bruce Judson lawyer
Bishopric, Karl investment banker, real estate executive, advertising executive
Bitter, John university dean emeritus, musician, businessman, diplomat
Black, Creed Carter newspaper executive
Blackburn, Roger Lloyd lawyer
Blanco, Josefa Joan-Juana (Jossie Blanco) social services administrator
Blanco, Luciano-Nilo physicist
Blumberg, Edward Robert lawyer
†Boles, John professional baseball coach, manager
Bolooki, Hooshang cardiac surgeon
Borkan, William Noah biomedical electronics company executive
Borstelmann, Stephen Matthew radiologist
Brady, Steven Michael lawyer
Brinkman, Paul Del(bert) foundation executive
Brito, Maria Cristina sculptor, educator
Bronis, Stephen J. lawyer
Brown, Stephen Thomas magistrate judge
Brownell, Edwin Rowland banker, civil engineer, land surveyor
Burnett, Henry lawyer
†Burnett, Keitha Denise social studies educator
Burns, M. Anthony transportation services company executive
Cagen, Edward Leslie surgeon, physician
Cai, Yong chemist
Camacho, Alfredo accountant
Camner, Howard author, poet
Capraro, Franz accountant
Carollo, Joe mayor
Carter, Harriet Vanessa public relations specialist, congressional aide
Casariego, Jorge Isaac psychiatrist, psychoanalyst, educator
Cassel, John Michael plastic surgeon
Cassileth, Peter Anthony internist
Catanzaro, Tony dancer
Cates, Nelia Barletta de diplomat of Dominican Republic
Chang-Mota, Roberto electrical engineer
Chaplin, Harvey wine and liquor wholesale executive
Chapman, Alvah Herman, Jr. newspaper executive
Chen, Chun-fan biology educator
Cherry, Andrew Lawrence, Jr. social work educator, researcher
Chirovsky, Nicholas Ludomir economics educator, historian, author
Chisholm, Martha Maria dietitian
Chisholm, Robert E. architect
†Chung, Bongkil Asian studies educator
Clark, Ira C. hospital association administrator, educator
Clarke, Jay Marion editor, author
Clarke, Mercer Kaye lawyer
Clarkson, John G. academic administrator, ophthalmologist
Cohen, Eugene Erwin university health institute administrator, accounting educator emeritus
Cohen, Jeffrey Michael lawyer
Cohen, Sanford Irwin physician, educator
Cole, Todd Godwin management consultant transportation
Collins, Susan Ford leadership consultant
Colsky, Andrew Evan lawyer, mediator, arbitrator
Colwin, Arthur Lentz biologist, educator
†Concha, Mauricio epidemiologist, educator, neurologist
Cosgrove, John Francis lawyer, state legislator
Cristol, A. Jay federal judge
Cruz, Javier F. architect
Cubas, Jose M(anuel) advertising agency executive
Cullom, William Otis trade association executive
Dady, Robert Edward lawyer
Dann, Oliver Townsend psychoanalyst, psychiatrist, educator
David, Christopher Mark lawyer
Davidson, Joy Elaine mezzo-soprano
Davis, Edward Bertrand federal judge
Davis, Richard Edmund facial plastic surgeon
Day, Kathleen Patricia financial planner
Deaktor, Darryl Barnett lawyer
Dean, Stanley Rochelle psychiatrist
†DeCristofaro, John George artist, designer
de la Guardia, Mario Francisco electrical engineer
de Leon, John Louis public defender
Dellapa, Gary J. airport terminal executive
†DeMueller, Lucia investment consultant
Denison, Floyd Gene insurance executive
DePasquale, Laura artist, art education administrator
Dessler, Gary S. business educator, author, consultant, administrator
D'Gabriel, Carlos Leonardo retired travel executive
Dickason, John Hamilton retired foundation executive
Dickey, Arden newspaper publishing executive
Dombrowski, David baseball team executive
Donelan, Mark Anthony physicist
Dorion, Robert Charles entrepreneur, investor
Dottin, Erskine S. education educator
Dribin, Michael A. lawyer
†Dube, Robert L. federal judge
Duncanson, Harry Richard accountant, financial executive
Dursum, Brian A. museum curator, art educator
Dye, H. Michael marketing executive
Dyer, John Martin lawyer, marketing educator
Eaglstein, William Howard dermatologist, educator
Eftekhari, Nasser physiatrist
Ehrlich, Morton international finance executive
Eisdorfer, Carl psychiatrist, health care executive
England, Arthur Jay, Jr. lawyer, former state justice
Engle, Mary Allen English physician
Engle, Ralph Landis, Jr. internist, educator
Ersek, Gregory Joseph Mark lawyer, business administrator
Escotet, Miguel-Angel psychologist, educator
Esteves, Vernon Xavier financial consultant, investment advisor
Etling, Russell Hull museum executive, production company executive
Evans, Peter Kenneth advertising executive
Fain, Richard David cruise line executive
Farcus, Joseph Jay architect, interior designer
Farmer, Hiram Leander physical education educator
Fay, Peter Thorp federal judge
Feito, Jose architect
Fern, Emma Elsie state agency administrator
Fernandez, Isabel Lidia human resources specialist
Ferrell, Milton Morgan, Jr. lawyer
Fichtner, Margaria journalist
Fishel, Peter Livingston accounting business executive
Fishman, Lewis Warren lawyer, educator
Fitzgerald, John Thomas, Jr. religious studies educator
Fitzgerald, Lynne Marie Leslie family therapist
Fletcher, John Greenwood II state judge
Flinn, David Lynnfield financial consultant
Fontes, J. Mario F., Jr. lawyer
Foote, Edward Thaddeus, II university president, lawyer
Fort-Brescia, Bernardo architect
Foster, Kathryn Warner newspaper editor
Fox, Gary Devenow lawyer
Freeman, Gill Sherryl judge
Freshwater, Michael Felix surgeon, educator
Fromkin, Ava Lynda management consultant, healthcare risk management services
Frost, Philip insurance company executive
Fuertes, Raul A. psychologist, educator
Furst, Alex Julian thoracic and cardiovascular surgeon
Gabor, Frank insurance company executive
Ganz, William Israel radiology educator, medical director, researcher
†Garber, Barry L. magistrate judge
Garrett, Richard G. lawyer
Gaylis, Norman Brian internist, rheumatologist, educator
Geis, Tarja Pelto educational coordinator, consultant, counselor, teacher, professor
Gelband, Henry pediatric cardiologist
George, Stephen Carl reinsurance executive, educator, consultant
Gibb, Robin vocalist, songwriter
Giller, Norman Myer banker, architect, author
Gindy, Benjamin Lee insurance company executive
Ginsberg, Myron David neurologist
Gittelson, George physician
Glaser, Luis biochemistry educator
Glenn, Frances Bonde dentist
Glogower, Michael Howard public housing senior functional specialist
Godofsky, Lawrence lawyer
†Gold, Alan Stephen judge, lawyer, educator
Goldberg, Bernard R. news correspondent
Goldstein, Burton Jack psychiatrist
Gomez, Ivan A. lawyer
Gong, Edmond Joseph lawyer
Gonzalez, Manuel John investment broker, international trade executive
Goodnick, Paul Joel psychiatrist
†Goodwin, Jarrad otolaryngologist, educator
Gragg, Karl Lawrence lawyer
Graham, Donald Lynn federal judge
Granata, Linda M. lawyer
†Gray, Christopher John history educator, human rights activist
Greenleaf, Walter Franklin lawyer
Greer, Alan Graham lawyer
Gross, Leslie Jay lawyer
Grossman, Robert Louis lawyer
Guerra, Charles Albert financial consultant and executive
Guerra, Roland regional property manager
Haar, Ana Maria Fernández advertising and public relations executive
Hall, Andrew Clifford lawyer
Hall, Miles Lewis, Jr. lawyer
Hallbauer, Rosalie Carlotta business educator
Halsey, Douglas Martin lawyer
Hampton, John Lewis retired newspaper editor
Hampton, Mark Garrison architect
Hanna, Ronald Everette art educator, consultant
Hardaway, Timothy Duane basketball player
Harper, Kenneth Charles clergyman
Harris, Douglas Clay newspaper executive
Hartz, Steven Edward Marshall lawyer
Hector, Louis Julius lawyer
Heggen, Arthur William insurance company executive
Heiens, Richard Allen education foundation executive
Henderson, William Eugene education educator
Hendrickson, Harvey Sigbert retired accounting educator
†Henry, John W. professional sports team executive
Heuer, Robert Maynard, II opera company executive
†Hewitt, Thomas F. hotel executive
Hickey, John Heyward lawyer
Hicks, Dorothy Jane obstetrician and gynecologist, educator
Highsmith, Shelby federal judge
Higley, Bruce Wadsworth orthodontist
Hills, Lee foundation administrator, newspaper executive, consultant
Himburg, Susan Phillips dietitian, educator
Hirsch, Milton Charles lawyer
Hodgetts, Richard Michael business management educator
Hoeveler, William M. federal judge
Hoffman, Larry J. lawyer
Houlihan, Gerald John lawyer
Howard, Elsie Sterling marketing executive
Howell, Ralph Rodney pediatrician, educator, geneticist
Hoy, William Ivan minister, religion educator
Huang, Dongzhou civil engineering educator, scientist, engineer
Huber, Michael Frederick journalist, educator
Hudson, Robert Franklin, Jr. lawyer
Humphries, Joan Ropes psychologist, educator
Ibarguen, Alberto newspaper executive
Imperato, Joseph John lawyer, composer
Iver, Robert Drew dentist
†Jaouhari-McCune, Cynthia nurse, childbirth educator
†Johnson, Linnea Ruth federal judge
Jones, William Kinzy materials engineering educator
Kanet, Roger Edward political science educator, university administrator
Karl, Robert Harry cardiologist
Karlan, Sandy Ellen judge
Kassewitz, Ruth Eileen Blower retired hospital executive
Kehoe, James W. federal judge
Kenin, David S. lawyer
Kim, James Jupyung surgeon, orthopedist, medical educator
King, James Lawrence federal judge
Kislak, Jean Hart art director
†Kitsos, Constantine Nicholas plastic surgeon
Klein, Peter William lawyer, corporate officer, investment company executive
Klock, Joseph Peter, Jr. lawyer
Knight, Kenneth Vincent leisure company executive, entrepreneur, venture capitalist
Koller, William Carl neurology educator
Kooima, Linda Kay neonatal and pediatrics nurse
Korchin, Judith Miriam lawyer
†Kotsay, Mark Steven baseball player
Kregg, Judith Lynne accountant
Krissel, Susan Hinkle university official
Kuczynski, Pedro-Pablo investor
Kuehne, Benedict P. lawyer
Kunce, Avon Estes vocational rehabilitation counselor
Kurzban, Ira Jay lawyer
Kwiat, David Mark educator, actor
Lampen, Richard Jay lawyer, investment banker
Landy, Burton Aaron lawyer
Lapidus, Morris retired architect, interior designer
Lasseter, Kenneth Carlyle pharmacologist
Lavin, David accountant, educator
Lawrence, David, Jr. journalist, early childhood development advocate
Lawson, Eve Kennedy ballet mistress
Layton, Robert Glenn radiologist
LeBow, Bennett S. communications executive
Le Duc, Albert Louis, Jr. management consultant
Lee, J. Patrick academic administrator
Leeds, Robert dentist
Lefton, Donald E. hotel executive
Lemberg, Louis cardiologist, educator
León, Eduardo A. diplomat, business executive
Levitt, Ronald Larry public relations consulting executive
†Lewis, Clifton principal
Lewis, John Milton cable television company executive
Lichacz, Sheila Enit diplomat, artist
Liebes, Raquel import/export company executive, educator
Lipcon, Charles Roy lawyer
Llanes, José Ramón corporate professional, educator
†Lokeshwar, Balakrishna Loknath cancer biologist, educator
Long, Maxine Master lawyer
Lopez-Munoz, Maria Rosa P. land development company executive
Louis, Paul Adolph lawyer
Love, Mildred Allison retired secondary school educator, historian, writer, volunteer
Maddern, David artist
Maher, Stephen Trivett lawyer, educator
Maidique, Modesto Alex academic administrator
Malinin, Theodore medical educator, researcher
Marcus, Joy John pharmacist, consultant, educator
Marcus, Stanley federal judge
†Mark, Robert A. federal judge
Marks, Shirley I. artist
Martinez, Luis Osvaldo radiologist, educator
Martinez, Walter Baldomero architect
Mau, James Anthony sociologist, academic administrator, educator
Maynard, Cecil Darwin, III auditor, accountant
McCabe, Robert Howard college president
McKeehan, Mildred Hope nurse
Mc Kenzie, John Maxwell physician
McLaughlin, Margaret Brown educator, writer
Mehta, Eileen Rose lawyer
Mendez, Jesus history educator, education administrator
Merrill, George Vanderneth lawyer, investment executive
Miller, Gene Edward newspaper reporter and editor
Miller, Pamela Gardiner performing arts company executive
Miller, Raymond Vincent, Jr. lawyer
Milne, Edward Lawrence biomedical engineer
Milstein, Richard Craig lawyer
Mintz, Daniel Harvey diabetologist, educator, academic administrator
Mittleberg, Eric Michael pharmaceutical administrator
†Montes-Bradley, Saul Mariano foundation administrator
Mooers, Christopher Northrup Kennard physical oceanographer, educator
Moore, Kevin Michael federal judge
Moorman, Rose Drunell county administrator, systems analyst
Moreno, Federico Antonio federal judge
Morgan, Dahlia museum director
Morgan, Marabel author
Morin, James Corcoran editorial cartoonist
Morphonios, Martha Monsalve pharmacist
Mourning, Alonzo professional basketball player
Mudd, John Philip lawyer
Muench, Karl Hugo clinical geneticist
Muir, Helen journalist, author
Munn, Janet Teresa lawyer
Myers, Kenneth M. lawyer
Nachwalter, Michael lawyer
Nagin, Stephen E. lawyer, educator
Nathanson, Andrew E(ric) film location coordinator
Natoli, Joe newspaper publishing executive
Nesbitt, Lenore Carrero federal judge
Nestor Castellano, Brenda Diana real estate executive
Neuman, Susan Catherine public relations and marketing consultant
Newlin, Kimrey Dayton international trade consultant, political consultant, personal computer analyst
Newman, Terrie Lynne advertising and marketing executive
Norton, Susan Marlene real estate agent
Nuernberg, William R(ichard) lawyer
Nunez-Lawton, Miguel G. international finance specialist
†Ojeda, Jose Antonio, Jr. county official
O'Laughlin, Sister Jeanne university administrator
Ortiz, Loida A. communications executive
Osinski, Martin Henry healthcare consultant
Ostlund, H. Gote atmospheric and marine scientist, educator
Page, Larry Keith neurosurgeon, educator
†Palermo, Peter R. federal judge
Papper, Emanuel Martin anesthesiologist
Parnes, Edmund Ira oral and maxillofacial surgeon
Parrish, Richard Kenneth, II medical educator
Patarca, Roberto immunologist, molecular biologist, physician
Paul, Robert lawyer
Pearlman, Michael Allen lawyer
Pena, Guillermo Enrique lawyer
Perry, E. Elizabeth social worker, real estate manager
Pfenniger, Richard Charles, Jr. lawyer
†Pfund, Randy (Randell Pfund) sports team executive, former professional basketball coach
Pham, Si Mai cadiothoracic surgeon, medical educator
Plater-Zyberk, Elizabeth Maria architectural educator
Podhurst, Aaron Samuel lawyer
Polen-Dorn, Linda Frances communications executive
Pomeranz, Felix accounting educator
Pope, John Edwin, III newspaper sports editor
Porter, Charles King advertising executive
Porter, Terry professional basketball player
Portland, Charles Denis publishing executive
Poston, Rebekah Jane lawyer
Potter, James Douglas pharmacology educator
Price, Barbara Gillette college administrator, artist
Prussin, Jeffrey A. management consultant
Pubillones, Jorge transit adminstration administrator
Quentel, Albert Drew lawyer
Quirantes, Albert M. lawyer
Raffel, Leroy B. real estate development company executive
Raines, Jeff biomedical scientist, medical research director
Ramirez de la Piscina, Julian diversified financial services company executive
Reed, Alfred composer, conductor
Richards, Bobbie Jo secondary education educator
Riecken, Ellnora Alma retired music educator
Riley, Patrick James professional basketball coach
Risi, Louis J., Jr. business executive
†Rivera, David M. government official
Rivero, Andres insurance executive
Roddenberry, Stephen Keith lawyer
Rodriguez, Ray broadcast executive
Rojas, Raul Eduardo executive, economist
Roman, Agustin A. clergyman
Rosenberg, Mark B. political science educator, university official
Rosenthal, Stanley Lawrence meteorologist
Rosinek, Jeffrey judge
Rotenberg, Don Harris chemist
Rothchild, Howard Leslie advertising executive
Rothman, David Bill lawyer
Routh, Donald K(ent) psychology educator
Rubens, Jeffrey David investment executive
Rubin, Bruce Stuart public relations executive
Rundle, Katherine Fernandez states attorney
Russell, Elbert Winslow neuropsychologist
Russell, James Webster, Jr. newspaper editor, columnist
Sacher, Barton Stuart lawyer
Sackner, Marvin Arthur physician
Saland, Deborah psychotherapist, educator
Salazar-Carrillo, Jorge economics educator
Salvaneschi, Luigi real estate and development executive, business educator
Samole, Myron Michael lawyer, management consultant
Sanchez, Javier Alberto industrial engineer
Sanchez, Robert Francis journalist
Sargent, Joanne Elaine lawyer
Sarnoff, Marc David lawyer
Satuloff, Barth accounting executive, dispute resolution professional
Saunders, Norman Thomas military officer
Savage, James Francis editor
Scerpella, Ernesto Guillermo physician researcher
Scheer, Mark Jeffrey lawyer
Scheinberg, Peritz neurologist
Schiff, Eugene Roger medical educator, hepatologist
Schofield, Calvin Onderdonk, Jr. bishop
Schor, Olga Seemann mental health counselor, real estate broker
Schuette, Charles A. lawyer
Schwartz, Gerald public relations and fundraising agency executive
†Scott, Thomas Emerson, Jr. prosecutor
†Serure, Alan plastic and reconstructive surgeon
Sharpstein, Richard Alan lawyer

†Shebert, Robert T. *neurologist, pathologist*
Sherman, Beatrice Ettinger *business executive*
Shevin, Robert Lewis *judge*
Shusterman, Nathan *life underwriter, financial consultant*
†Sigars-Malina, L. Janá *lawyer*
Silber, Norman Jules *lawyer*
Simmons, Sherwin Palmer *lawyer*
Skolnick, S. Harold *lawyer*
Smiley, Logan Henry *journalist, public concern consultant*
Smith, Stanley Bertram *clinical pathologist, allergist, immunologist, anatomic pathologist*
Sonenreich, Steven Douglas *hospital administrator*
†Sorrentino, Charlene H. *federal judge*
Spear, Laurinda Hope *architect*
Spencer, Richard Thomas, III *healthcare industry executive*
Spratt, Stephen Michael *county government official*
Stansell, Leland Edwin, Jr. *lawyer, educator*
Starr, Ivar Miles *lawyer*
Stein, Allan Mark *lawyer*
Steinback, Robert Lamont *newspaper columnist*
Steinberg, Marty *lawyer*
Stephan, Egon, Sr. *cinematographer, film equipment company executive*
Stern, Joanne Thrasher *elementary school educator*
Stiehm, Judith Hicks *university official, political science educator*
Stokes, Paul Mason *lawyer*
Stone, Ronald William *veterinarian*
Strickland, Thomas Joseph *artist*
Stuchins, Carol Mayberry *nursing executive*
Sugarbaker, Everett Van Dyke *surgical oncologist*
Sussex, James Neil *psychiatrist, educator*
Tamayo, Raquel *medical/surgical nurse*
Tang, Walter Zhonghong *environmental engineer*
Taylor, Adam David *real estate executive*
†Taylor, Dorothy Lee *sociology educator*
Tejada, Francisco *physician, educator*
Telesca, Francis Eugene *architect*
Temple, Jack Donald, Jr. *physician, medical educator*
Terilli, Samuel A., Jr. *newspaper publishing executive*
Thompson, Allen Joseph *construction executive, civil engineer*
Thornburg, Frederick Fletcher *diversified business executive, lawyer*
Thornton, Sandi Tokoa *elementary education educator*
Toro, Carlos Hans *insurance/financial products marketing executive*
Torres, Hugo R. *financial analyst, international credit analyst, telecommunications analyst*
Torres, Milton John *industrial engineering educator*
Touby, Kathleen Anita *lawyer*
Trippe, Kenneth Alvin Battershill *shipping industry executive*
Tschumy, Freda Coffing *artist, educator*
Ungaro-Benages, Ursula Mancusi *federal judge*
Urban, Alan Gene *painter, art executive*
†Valdes, Juan Carlos *marketing executive*
Valle, Laurence Francis *lawyer*
VanBrode, Derrick Brent, IV *trade association administrator*
Van Vliet, Carolyne Marina *physicist, educator*
Van Wyck, George Richard *insurance company executive*
Venet, Claude Henry *architect, acoustic engineer*
Vento, M. Thérèse *lawyer*
Villarreal, Juan De Dios *management consultant*
Walters, David McLean *lawyer*
Walton, Rodney Earl *lawyer*
Warren, Emily P. *retired secondary school educator*
Wax, William Edward *photojournalist*
Weinstein, Andrew H. *lawyer*
Weiser, Ralph Raphael *business executive*
Weiser, Sherwood Manuel *hotel and corporation executive, lawyer*
Wells, Daniel Ruth *physics educator*
†Wenski, Thomas Gerard *priest*
Wheeler, Harold Austin, Sr. *lawyer, former educational administrator*
Wheeler, Steve Dereal *neurologist*
Whisenand, James Dudley *lawyer*
Whitaker, Cynthia Ellen *managed healthcare nurse*
†Whitehead, John *poet*
Whittington, Robert Wallace *corporate professional, pianist*
Wickstrom, Karl Youngert *publishing company executive*
Winship, Blaine H. *lawyer*
Wolff, Grace Susan *pediatrician*
†Wright, Pamela Jean *administrator*
Wright, Robert Thomas, Jr. *lawyer*
Yaffa, Jack Ber *healthcare administrator, educator, surgeon*
Zanakis, Steve H. *management science/information systems educator*
Zand, Lloyd Craig *radiologist*
Zwerling, Leonard Joseph *physician, educator*

Miami Beach
Arkin, Stanley Herbert *retired construction executive, consultant*
Barroso, Eduardo Guillermo *surgeon, educator*
Blakley, John Clyde *telecommunications consultant*
Carmichael, Lynn Paul *family practice physician*
Crisci, Mathew G. *marketing executive, writer*
Danzis, Rose Marie *emeritus college president*
Gitlow, Abraham Leo *retired university dean*
Gordon, Jack David *senator, foundation executive*
Gottleib, Karla Lewis *writer, college official*
†Hair, Gilbert Martin *foundation administrator*
Hecht, Donn *songwriter, screenwriter, agent*
Katzenstein, Thea *retail executive, jewelry designer*
Krieger, Bruce Phillip *medical educator*
LaVorgna, Judith Phelps *educational administrator*
Lazović, Gavrilo *internist*
Lehrman, David *orthopedic surgeon*
Lehrman, Irving *rabbi*
†Makovsky, Randy D. *urologist*
Mandri, Daniel Francisco *psychiatrist*
Marcus, Arthur Jay *architect*
Maulion, Richard Peter *psychiatrist*
McManus, Michael Edward *artist, educator*
Nixon, Daniel David. *physician*
Paresky, David S. *travel company executive*
Perkel, Robert Simon *photojournalist, educator*
Ratzan, Kenneth Roy *physician*
Rube, Miriam Shoshana *principal, educator*
Sayfie, Eugene Joe *cardiologist, internist, educator*
†Sharlach, Jeffrey *public relations executive*
Tiller, J. Howell *physician*
Webb, Roy *television producer, writer*
Wernick, Nissim *rabbi*

Miami Lakes
Fletcher, Carlos Alfredo Torres *video and film production company executive*
Rodriguez, Manuel Alvarez *pathologist*
Sharett, Alan Richard *lawyer, environmental litigator, mediator and arbitrator, law educator*
Zwigard, Bruce Albert *brokerage house executive*

Miami Shores
Favalora, John Clement *bishop*
McCarthy, Edward Anthony *archbishop*
Sunshine, Edward Robert *theology educator*

Micanopy
Cripe, Wyland Snyder *veterinary medicine educator, consultant*

Micco
Cognata, Joseph Anthony *retired football commissioner*

Miccosukee Cpo
Humphrey, Louise Ireland *civic worker, equestrienne*

Milton
McKinney, George Harris, Jr. *training systems analyst*
Moorer, Lela Irene *elementary education educator*
Seaton, Carolle Carter *educator, writer*

Miramar
Gallinaro, Nicholas Francis *business executive*
Gauwitz, Donna Faye *nursing educator*
†Lee-Murphy, Karen Simone *education specialist*
Militello, Lawrence *nursing home adminstrator*

Monticello
Hooks, Mary Linda *adult education educator*

Montverde
Bloder, Lisa W. *critical care nurse, mental health nurse*
Harris, Martin Harvey *aerospace company executive*

Morriston
Adams, Kelly Lynn *emergency physician*

Mount Dora
Borg, Henry Franklin *retired manufacturing company executive*
Foote, Nathan Maxted *retired physical science educator*
Hart, Valerie Gail *writer*
Hensinger, Margaret Elizabeth *horticultural and agricultural advertising and marketing executive*
Moretto, Jane Ann *nurse, public health officer, consultant*
Myren, Richard Albert *criminal justice consultant*
Scharfenberg, Margaret Ellan *retired elementary educator*
Schnatterly, Michael Dean *priest*
Shyers, Larry Edward *mental health counselor, educator*
Trussell, Charles Tait *columnist*

Mulberry
Bowman, Hazel Lois *retired English language educator*
Mueller, Michael Lee *editor*
Oettinger, Kathleen Linda *artist, writer*

Naples
Abbott, John Sheldon *law school dean and chancellor emeritus*
Alpert, Hollis *writer*
Baldwin, Ralph Belknap *retired manufacturing company executive, astronomer*
Barkley, Marlene A. Nyhuis *nursing administrator*
Barnhill, Howard Eugene *insurance company executive*
Barter, Robert Henry *physician, retired educator*
Beam, Robert Thompson *retired lawyer*
Benedict, Manson *chemical engineer, educator*
Berman, Robert S. *marketing consultant*
Berry, Donald Lee *accountant*
Biondo, Michael Thomas *retired paper company executive*
Blakely, John T. *lawyer*
Bornmann, Carl Malcolm *lawyer*
†Breitenstein, David E. *newswriter*
Brooks, Joae Graham *psychiatrist*
Brown, Cindy Lynn *critical care nurse, emergency nurse, family nurse practitioner*
Bush, John William *federal transportation official*
Capelle-Frank, Jacqueline Aimee *writer*
Card, Orson Scott (Byron Walley) *writer*
Cardillo, John Pollara *lawyer*
†Carneiro, Ronaldo Dos Santos *surgeon*
Censits, Richard John *business consultant*
Chartrand, Robert Lee *information scientist*
Cimino, Richard Dennis *lawyer*
Clapp, Roger Howland *retired newspaper executive*
Clark, Kenneth Edwin *psychologist, former university dean*
Clarke, John Patrick *retired newspaper publisher*
Cobb, Brian Eric *broadcasting executive*
Conrad, Kelley Allen *industrial and organizational psychologist*
Corkran, Virginia B. *realtor*
Craighead, Rodkey *banker*
Crehan, Joseph Edward *lawyer*
Davis, Sidney Fant *lawyer, author*
de Saint Phalle, Thibaut *investment banker, educator, lawyer, financial consultant*
Eldridge, David Carlton *art appraiser*
Elliott, Edward *investment executive, financial planner*
Emerson, John Williams, II *lawyer*
Evans, Elizabeth Ann West *retired realtor*
Finley, Jack Dwight *investments and consultation executive*
Franco, Anthony M. *public relations executive*
Frazer, John Howard *tennis association executive, retired manufacturing company executive*
Gaskins, William Darrell *ophthalmologist*
Ghorayeb, Fay Elizabeth *nurse educator, secondary education educator*
Gillespie, Jacquelyn Randall *psychologist*
Gilman, John Richard, Jr. *management consultant*
Grove, William Johnson *physician, surgery educator*
Gushman, John Louis *former corporation executive, lawyer*
Hainsworth, Melody May *information professional, researcher*
Hampton, Philip McCune *banker*
Handy, Charles Brooks *accountant, educator*
Hedberg, Paul Clifford *broadcasting executive*
Hooper, John Allen *retired banker*
Humphreville, John David *lawyer*
Ivancevic, Walter Charles *former gas distribution company executive*
Jaffe, Marvin Eugene *pharmaceutical company executive, neurologist*
Johnson, Kennett Conrad *advertising agency executive*
Johnson, Walter L. *transportation company executive*
Johnson, Zane Quentin *retired petroleum company executive*
Jones, Richard Wallace *interior designer*
Kapnick, Harvey Edward, Jr. *retired corporate executive*
Kay, Herbert *retired natural resources company executive*
Kempers, Roger Dyke *obstetrics and gynecology educator*
Kennedy, Donald Davidson, Jr. *retired insurance company executive*
†Kibria, Eshan *neurologist, engineer*
Kleinrock, Virginia Barry *public relations executive*
Kley, John Arthur *banker*
Lange, George Willard, Jr. *lawyer, trust banker*
Larson, Wilfred Joseph *chemical company executive*
Leitner, Alfred *mathematical physicist, educator, educational film producer*
Leverenz, Humboldt Walter *retired chemical research engineer*
Lewis, Gordon Gilmer *golf course architect*
Lewis, Marianne H. *psychiatric nurse practitioner*
Lichtwardt, Harry E.
Loft, Bernard Irwin *education educator, consultant*
Marcy, Jeannine Koonce *retired educational administrator*
Marshall, Charles *communications company executive*
Martinuzzi, Leo Sergio, Jr. *banker*
McCaffrey, Judith Elizabeth *lawyer*
McCarthy, Joseph Harold *consultant, former retail food company executive*
McDonell, Horace George, Jr. *instrument company executive*
Mc Queen, Robert Charles *retired insurance executive*
Megee, Geraldine Hess *social worker*
Mehaffey, John Allen *marketing, newspaper management and advertising executive*
Moore, Mechlin Dongan *communications executive, marketing consultant*
Mutz, Oscar Ulysses *manufacturing and distribution executive*
†Nelson, John Charles *retired educator*
Norins, Leslie Carl *publisher*
Oliver, Robert Bruce *retired investment company executive*
Ordway, John Danton *retired pension administrator, lawyer, accountant*
Osias, Richard Allen *international financier, investor, real estate investment executive, corporate investor*
Pancero, Jack Blocher *restaurant executive*
Parish, John Cook *insurance executive*
Parker, Thomas Lee *business executive*
Petersen, David L. *lawyer*
†Poehlmann, Christopher Eric *artist, designer*
Putzell, Edwin Joseph, Jr. *lawyer, mayor*
Raia, Theodore John, Jr. *retired military career officer and radiologist*
Reed, John Franklin *instrument manufacturing company executive*
Roberts, William B. *lawyer, business executive*
Rowe, Herbert Joseph *retired trade association executive*
Rowe, Jack Field *retired electric utility executive*
Savage, Robert Heath *advertising executive*
Schauer, Wilbert Edward, Jr. *lawyer, manufacturing company executive*
Seaman, Christopher *perfoming arts company executive*
Sekowski, Cynthia Jean *corporate executive, contact lens specialist*
Sharpe, Robert Francis *equipment manufacturing company executive*
Shields, Bruce Maclean *management consultant*
Siddall, Patricia Ann *retired English language educator*
Sigman, Susan Bell *educator, writer*
Slaff, Allan Paul *naval officer, university administrator, educator*
Smith, Numa Lamar, Jr. *lawyer*
Snyder, Marion Gene *lawyer, former congressman*
Sowman, Harold Gene *ceramic engineer, researcher*
Stevens, William Kenneth *lawyer*
Stewart, Harris Bates, Jr. *oceanographer*
Strauss, Jerome Manfred *lawyer, banker*
Suziedelis, Vytautas A. *engineering corporation executive*
Taishoff, Lawrence Bruce *publishing company executive*
Tanner, Robert Hugh *engineer, consultant*
Tarbutton, Lloyd Tilghman *motel executive, franchise consultant*
Terenzio, Peter Bernard *hospital administrator*
Thomas, Gary Lynn *financial executive*
Thompson, Didi Castle (Mary Bennett) *writer, editor*
†Tymann, Jack T. *technology company executive*
Vanderslice, Thomas Aquinas *electronics executive*
von Arx, Dolph William *food products executive*
Walker, Patricia D. *critical care nurse*
Weeks, Richard Ralph *marketing educator*
Wemple Kinder, Suzanne Fonay *historian, educator*
Westman, Carl Edward *lawyer*
Wheeling, Robert Franklin *computer consultant*
White, Roy Bernard *theater executive*
White, Warren Wurtele *retired retailing executive*
Williams, Edson Poe *retired automotive company executive*
Williams, George Earnest *engineer, retired business executive*
Wodlinger, Mark Louis *broadcast executive*
Wyant, Corbin A. *newspaper publisher*

Navarre
Wesley, Stephen Burton *training professional*

New Port Richey
Carter, David Ray *lawyer*
Focht, Theodore Harold *lawyer, educator*
Hanahan, James Lake *insurance executive*
Hauber, Frederick August *ophthalmologist*
Hlad, Gregory Michael *psychometrist, assessment services coordinator*
Hu, Chen-Sien *surgeon*
Oosten, Roger Lester *medical manufacturing executive*
Sebring, Marjorie Marie Allison *former home furnishings company executive*

New Smyrna Beach
Claridge, Richard *structural engineer*
Grummer, Eugene Merrill *commodity futures market development executive*
Hauser, Sara Nooney *writer, educator*
Jesup, Cynthia Smith (Cindy Jesup) *elementary education educator*
Kolodinsky, Richard Hutton *lawyer*
Ledbetter, Benton L. *sculptor*
Leeper, Doris Marie *sculptor, painter*
Shaffer, Joye Coy *reading specialist*
Skove, Thomas Malcolm *retired manufacturing company financial executive*

Newberry
Smith, Michael Steven *data processing executive*

Niceville
Litke, Donald Paul *business executive, retired military officer*
Phillips, Richard Wendell, Jr. *air force officer*
Rasmussen, Robert Dee *real estate appraiser*
Zoghby, Guy Anthony *lawyer*

Nocatee
Turnbull, David John (Chief Piercing Eyes-Penn) *cultural association executive*

Nokomis
Albano, Anthony William *retired career officer, secondary school educator*
Beck, George William *retired industrial engineer*
Brisbin, Sterling G. *engineering executive, consultant*
Hawley, Phillip Eugene *investment banker*
Holec, Anita Kathryn Van Tassel *civic worker*
Lockledge, Jack E. *principal, retired*
Meyerhoff, Jack Fulton *financial executive*
Novak, Robert Louis *civil engineer, pavement management consultant*
Wendt, Lloyd *writer*

North Bay Village
Solomon, Norman Frank *finance company executive*

North Fort Myers
†Woodbridge, Norma Jean *registered nurse, writer*

North Lauderdale
Stunson, John *city manager*

North Miami
Averch, Harvey Allan *economist, educator, academic administrator*
Bonham-Yeaman, Doria *law educator*
†Klinger, Donald E. *educator*
Kopenhaver, Lillian Lodge *journalism educator*
Markson, Daniel Ben *real estate developer, consultant, syndicator*
Polley, Richard Donald *microbiologist, polymer chemist*
Roslow, Sydney *marketing educator*
Stills, Stephen *musician, vocalist, composer*
Sundel, Martin *social work educator, psychologist*
Vogel, Barry Robert *university official*

North Miami Beach
Ballman, Donna Marie *lawyer*
Capdevielle, Xavier O. *builder, constructor*
Ginsberg, Burton *lawyer*
Slewett, Robert David *lawyer*
Snihur, William Joseph, Jr. *lawyer*
Sorosky, Jeri Ruth *academic administrator*

North Palm Beach
†Connor, John Thomas *retired bank and corporate executive, lawyer*
†Coyle, Dennis Patrick *lawyer*
Crawford, Roberta *association administrator*
Edwards, William James *broadcasting executive*
Frevert, James Wilmot *financial planner, investment advisor*
Hayman, Richard Warren Joseph *conductor*
Hushing, William Collins *retired corporate executive*
Koffler, Warren William *lawyer*
Lavine, Alan *columnist, writer*
Lynch, William Walker *banker*
Portera, Alan August *elementary education educator*
Shaw, Stephen Ragsdale *trust investment executive*
Sooy, William Ray *electrical engineer, systems analyst*
Staub, W. Arthur *health care products executive*
Stein, Mark Rodger *allergist*
Woodard, Wallace William, III *quality advocate*

North Port
†Coleman-Triana, Karen L. *media specialist*
Galterio, Louis *healthcare information executive*

Oakland Park
Adams, Nancy Ann *school system administrator*
Kilpatrick, Clifton Wayne *book dealer*
Krauser, Janice *special education educator*

Ocala
Adel, Garry David *lawyer*
Altenburger, Karl Marion *allergist, immunologist*
Booth, Jane Schuele *real estate broker, executive*
DeLong, Mary Ann *educational administrator*
Forgue, Stanley Vincent *physics educator*
Fredericks, William John *chemistry educator*
Hunter, Oregon K., Jr. *physiatrist*
†Knief, Helen Janett *artist*
Kofink, Wayne Alan *minister*
Lamon, Kathy Lynn *nursing administrator*
Layton, William Gene *emergency medical service administrator*
Leek, Jay Wilbur *management consultant*
Lincoln, Larry William *automotive executive*
Pimpinella, Ronald Joseph *retired surgeon*
Robinson, Susan *conductor, musician*
Stickeler, Carl Ann Louise *professional parliamentarian*
Stock, Stephen Michael *broadcast journalist*
Thompson, Raymond Edward *lawyer*

Ocklawaha
Silagi, Barbara Weibler corporate administrator

Ocoee
Davis, Elena Denise accountant

Odessa
Cobb, Terri Reamer (Ceci Cobb) film and video producer

Okeechobee
Bishop, Sid Glenwood union official
Chilcutt, Dorthe Margaret art educator, artist
Selmi, William, Jr. lawyer

Oldsmar
Brunner, George Matthew management consultant, former business executive
Burrows, William Claude aerospace executive, retired air force officer
Craft Davis, Audrey Ellen writer, educator
MacLeod, Donald Martin corporate professional
Rogers, James Virgil, Jr. retired radiologist and educator
Thompson, Mack Eugene history educator

Ona
Rechcigl, Jack Edward soil and environmental sciences educator

Opa Locka
Conner, Laban Calvin retired librarian
Hopton, Janice elementary school principal
Light, Alfred Robert lawyer, political scientist, educator
Rushin, Jerry broadcast executive

Orange Park
Brown, Linda Lockett nutrition management executive, nutrition consultant
Enney, James Crowe former air force officer, business executive
Gadapee, Brett Ronald English language educator, coach
Glenn, Steven Claude financial executive
Goss, William Allan author, speaker
Holloman, Marilyn Leona Davis nurse nonprofit administrator
Hudson, William Mark insurance company executive, owner
Kennedy, James Frederick artist
Myers, Bertina Satterfield secondary education business educator, administrator
Ratzlaff, Judith L. secondary school educator
Reemelin, Angela Norville dietitian consultant
Rice, Ronald James hospital administrator
Rodgers, Billy Russell chemical engineer, research scientist
†Roman, Theresa Kay educational administrator
Stevens, David Michael retired naval officer
Walsh, Gregory Sheehan optical systems professional

Orlando
Allen, William Riley lawyer
Allison, Anne Marie retired librarian
†Andrew, Brian J. information technology company executive
Armacost, Robert Leo management educator, former coast guard officer
Arnett, Warren Grant interior designer
Ashington-Pickett, Michael Derek construction company executive, journalist
Baggott, Brenda Jane Lamb elementary educator
†Bailey, William Ray transportation planner
†Baker, David A. federal judge
Baker, Peter Mitchell laser scientist and executive, educator
Barlow, Nadine Gail planetary geoscientist
Barros, Nélio Baptista biological oceanographer
Bevc, Frank Peter electrical engineer
Bias, Kimberly Vance special education educator
Blackford, Robert Newton lawyer
Blue, Joseph Edward physicist
Blum, Richard Arthur writer, media educator
†Bond, William L. career officer
Boyar, Jay Mitchell film critic
Bridgett, Noel William convalescent center administrator
†Briskman, Arthur B. federal judge
Brookes, Carolyn Jessen early childhood education educator
Brownlee, Thomas Marshall lighting manufacturing company executive
Bundy, David John engineering executive
Bussey, John W., III lawyer
Butler, John Paul sales professional
Capouano, Albert D. lawyer
Cawthon, Frank H. retired construction company executive
Chotas, Elias Nicholas lawyer
Christiansen, Patrick T. lawyer
Cirello, John utility and engineering company executive
Clinton, Stephen Michael academic administrator
Colbourn, Trevor retired university president, historian
Comfort, Iris Tracy writer
Connolly, Joseph Francis, II educational executive, government consultant
Conti, Louis Thomas Moore lawyer
Conway, Anne Callaghan federal judge
Crane, Glenda Paulette private school educator
Crawford, Patricia Ann education educator
Davis, Duane Lee marketing educator
Davis, H. Alan retired airline captain, consultant
Davis, Marvin Arnold manufacturing company executive
Deo, Narsingh computer science educator
De Vos, Daniel G. sports team executive, marketing professional
Diefenbach, Dale Alan law librarian, retired
Dietz, Robert Lee lawyer
Downs, David Rutherford minister
Drehoff, Diane Wyble electrical engineer, marketing manager
Dunn, William Bruna, III journalist
DuRose, Richard Arthur lawyer
Eagan, William Leon lawyer
Ellis, James Jolly landscape resort official
Fawsett, Patricia Combs federal judge
†Ferrara, Katherine June executive television producer
Ford, Kisha basketball player
Gabriel, John sports team executive
†Gianini, Paul C., Jr. college university
†Glazebrook, James G. federal judge
Gokee, Donald LeRoy clergyman, author
Gold, I. Randall lawyer
Golinkin, Webster Fowler media executive
Grady, Thomas J. retired bishop
Grant, Joanne Cummings film company executive
Gray, Anthony Rollin capital management company executive
Gray, J. Charles lawyer, cattle rancher
Grecsek, Matthew Thomas software developer
Green, Joal Fekete Stafford library media specialist
Guest, Larry Samuel newspaper columnist
Hall, Lawrie Platt consumer products executive, public community corporate philanthropy executive
Handley, Leon Hunter lawyer
Hardaway, Anfernee Deon (Penny Hardaway) professional basketball player
Hardesty, Stephen Don secondary education educator
Hartley, Carl William, Jr. lawyer
Haxton, David computer graphics educator, computer animator, photographer
Healy, Jane Elizabeth newspaper editor
Hedrick, Steve Brian psychotherapist
Hendry, Robert Ryon lawyer
Henry, William Oscar Eugene lawyer
Higgins, Robert Frederick lawyer
†Hillenmeyer, John medical center executive
Hitt, John Charles academic administrator
Hollis, Judy Wilson curriculum resource educator
Hornick, Richard Bernard physician
Howe, John Wadsworth bishop
†Hubbard, Susan Mary writer, English educator
Ispass, Alan Benjamin utilities executive
†Janzen, Lee professional golfer
Jasica, Andrea Lynn investor, former mortgage banking executive
†Jenneman, Karen S. federal judge
Johnson, Kraig Nelson lawyer, mediator
Jontz, Jeffry Robert lawyer
Kelaher, James Peirce lawyer
Kindlund, Newton Carlton retail executive
†Koonce, Jefferson Michael psychologist, university official, consultant
Krouse, Helene June nursing educator
Kruczek, Mike coach
Laning, Richard Boyer naval officer, writer, retired
Layish, Daniel T. internist
Lee, Joe R. food service executive
Lefkowitz, Ivan Martin lawyer
Leonhardt, Frederick Wayne lawyer
Levreault, Kathryn Sue school system official, information specialist
Llewellyn, Ralph Alvin physics educator
†Lopez Cruz, Humberto J. foreign language educator
Losey, Ralph Colby lawyer
Lowndes, John Foy lawyer
Mallette, Phyllis Spencer Cooper medical/surgical nurse
Managhan, James L., Jr. entrepreneur, entertainer
Marsh, Malcolm Roy, Jr. electronics engineer
Martinez, Melquiades R. (Mel Martinez) lawyer
Maupin, Elizabeth Thatcher theater critic
Metz, Larry Edward lawyer
Mock, Frank Mackenzie lawyer
Moltzon, Richard Francis manufacturing executive
Moore, Yolanda basketball player
Morgan, Mary Ann lawyer
†Moriarty, Michael Eugene retired humanities educator
Morrisey, Marena Grant art museum administrator
Nadeau, Robert Bertrand, Jr. lawyer
Neff, A. Guy lawyer
Neiman, Norman aerospace business and marketing executive
O'Farrell, Mark Theodore religious organization administrator
O'Keefe, Maurice Timothy editor, photographer
Okun, Neil Jeffrey vitreoretinal surgeon
Palanca, Terilyn software industry analyst
Palmer, William D. lawyer
Pantuso, Vincent Joseph food service consultant
Pauley, Bruce Frederick history educator
Pearlman, Louis Jay aviation and promotion company executive
†Peck, Carolyn professional basketball coach
Polite, Edmonia Allen consultant
Ponder, James Alton clergyman, evangelist
Popp, Gregory Allan lawyer
Puerner, John newspaper publishing executive
Qadri, Yasmeen educational administrator, consultant
Quinn, Jane journalist
Quinn, Sondra science center executive
Raffa, Jean Benedict author, educator
†Ramos Fonseca, Luis A. neurological surgeon
Randall, Roger Paul religious organization consultant
Rattman, William John electronics and eletro-optic engineer
Reagan, Larry Gay college vice president
Reed, John Alton lawyer
Reese, Charles Edgar columnist
Reinhart, Richard Paul lawyer
Reis, Melanie Jacobs women's health nurse, educator
Renee, Lisabeth Mary art educator, artist, galley director
Rivera, Richard Edwin restaurant chain executive
†Rivers, Glenn Anton (Doc) professional basketball coach, former basketball player
Robertson, Lorna Dooling artist, real estate developer
Rolle, Christopher Davies lawyer
†Rosen, Harris hotel company executive
Rosenbach, Leopold engineer, consultant
Rush, Fletcher Grey, Jr. lawyer
Safcsak, Karen medical/surgical nurse
Salzman, Gary Scott lawyer
Scott, Kathy Lynn peri-operative nurse
Sharkey, Colleen Mary sports association administrator
Sharp, George Kendall federal judge
Sheaffer, William Jay lawyer
Shirek, John Richard retired savings and loan executive
Shub, Harvey Allen surgeon
Silfvast, William T. laser physics educator, consultant
Simmons, Cleatous J. lawyer
Sims, Roger W. lawyer
Skambis, Christopher Charles, Jr. lawyer
Sloan, Steve athletic director
†Softic, Tanja artist
Spears, Robert Edward instructional technologist
Spoonhour, James Michael lawyer
Stewart, Harry A. lawyer
Swedberg, Robert Mitchell opera company director
Taitt, Earl Paul psychiatrist, army officer
Ting, Robert Yen-ying physicist
†Trumble, Eric R. pediatric neurosurgeon
Urban, James Arthur lawyer
Vander Weide, Bob professional sports team executive
Vander Weide, Cheri DeVos sports team executive, marketing professional
†Velez, Diana historian, educator
Vining, F(rancis) Stuart architect, consultant
Wagner, Lynn Edward lawyer
Wall, Arthur Edward Patrick editor
Walsh, James Anthony (Tony Walsh) theater and film educator
Warren, Dean Stuart artist
Watson, Barry Lee real estate and mortgage broker, investor, contractor, builder, developer
Watson, Jimmy Lee academic administrator
Weiss, Christopher John lawyer
Whitehill, Clifford Lane lawyer
Whitehouse, Gary industrial engineer, educator, university provost
Whitworth, Hall Baker, Jr. cardiologist
Wilkins, (Jacques) Dominique professional basketball player
Williams, Pat professional basketball team executive
Wilson, William Berry lawyer
Witengier, Mary Joan MacGilvray retired special education educator, physical therapist
Witty, John Barber health care executive
Woodard, Clara Veronica nursing home official
Wunder, James George, III educator
Wutscher, Heinz Konrad horticulturist
Yates, Leighton Delevan, Jr. lawyer
Yesawich, Peter Charles advertising executive
Young, George Cressler federal judge

Ormond Beach
Boyle, Susan Jean Higle elementary school educator
Burt, Wallace Joseph, Jr. insurance company executive
Burton, Alan Harvey city official
Coke, C(hauncey) Eugene consulting company executive, scientist, educator, author
Connors, Michele Perrott wholesale beverage company executive
Cromartie, Robert Samuel, III thoracic surgeon
†Frank, Robert E. artist
Hodkinson, Sydney Phillip composer, educator
Kanfer, Julian Norman biochemist, educator
Lively, Carol A. professional society administrator
Logan, Sharon Brooks lawyer
Morris, Carol Bishop mathematics educator
Raimondo, Louis John psychiatrist
Shepard, Janie Ray (J. R. Shepard) software development executive
Stogner, William Louis pharmaceutical company sales executive
Thompson, Stephen Joseph construction executive
Truitt, Richard byron landscape architect
Wendelstedt, Harry Hunter, Jr. umpire

Osprey
Allen, George Howard publishing management consultant
Coates, Clarence Leroy, Jr. research engineer, educator
Gross, James Dehnert pathologist
Halladay, Laurie Ann public relations consultant, former franchise executive
Harrington, Nancy Regina O'Connor volunteer
Lin, Edward Daniel anesthesiologist, inventor
Maddocks, Robert Allen lawyer, manufacturing company executive
Metzger, Sidney communications engineering
Petrik, Gerd pharmaceutical executive
Robinson, Sally Winston artist

Oviedo
Brethauer, William Russell, Jr. claim investigator
Hyslop, Gary Lee librarian
MacKenzie, Charles Sherrard academic administrator
Tabiryan, Nelson V. optical engineer, research scientist
Whitworth, Hall Baker forest products company executive
Worthington, Daniel Glen lawyer, educator

Palatka
Baldwin, Allen Adail lawyer, writer

Palm Bay
Bigda, Rudolph A. business and financial consultant
Boley, Andrea Gail secondary school educator
Galitello-Wolfe, Jane Maryann artist, writer
Herro, John Joseph software specialist
Seifer, Ronald Leslie psychologist
Sheets, Fredrick Sidney career officer, retired, auditor
Simpson, Philip Lockwood English educator

Palm Beach
Adler, Frederick Richard lawyer, financier
Andrews, Holdt investment banker
Bagby, Joseph Rigsby financial investor
Bagby, Martha L. Green real estate holding company, novelist, publisher
Baum, Selma customer relations consultant
Bishop, Warner Bader finance company executive
Black, Leonard Julius retail store consultant
Blades, John Michael museum director
Callaway, Trowbridge banker
Chittick, Elizabeth Lancaster association executive, women's rights activist
Chopin, L. Frank lawyer
Cohen, Aaron Mitchell producer, publisher, writer
Cook, Edward Willingham diversified industry executive
Curry, Bernard Francis former banker, consultant
DiMartino, Christina writer
Donnell, John Randolph retired petroleum executive
Elson, Suzanne Goodman community activist
Feldman, Leonid Ariel rabbi
Fitilis, Theodore Nicholas portfolio manager
Floyd, Raymond Loran professional golfer
Ford, Thomas Patrick lawyer
Graubard, Seymour lawyer
Gundlach, Heinz Ludwig investment banker, lawyer
Habicht, Frank Henry retired industrial executive
Halmos, Peter entrepreneur
Hope, Margaret Lauten civic worker
Hopper, Arthur Frederick biological science educator
Isenberg, Abraham Charles shoe manufacturing company executive
Jackson, John Tillson retired corporate executive
Johnson, Theodore Mebane investment executive
Krois, Audrey artist
†Lappin, Bob music director, conductor
Lickle, William Cauffiel publisher
Mandel, Carola Panerai (Mrs. Leon Mandel) foundation trustee
Miller, Richard Jackson lawyer
Moloney, Thomas Walter consulting firm executive
Monath, Norman publishing company executive
Myers, Eugene Ekander art consultant
Oder, Frederic Carl Emil retired aerospace company executive, consultant
Pryor, Hubert editor, writer
Rauch, George Washington lawyer
Rinker, Ruby Stewart foundation administrator
Roberts, Margaret Harold editor, publisher
Roberts, Margot Markels business executive
Rukeyser, M.S., Jr. television consultant, writer
Rumbough, Stanley Maddox, Jr. industrialist
Shepherd, Charles Clinton real estate executive
Simon, Harold radiologist
Smith, Lloyd Hilton independent oil and gas producer
Snedeker, Sedgwick lawyer
Steere, Anne Bullivant retired student advisor
Tremain, Alan hotel executive
Wenzel, Joan Ellen artist
Winkler, Joseph Conrad former recreational products manufacturing executive
Wirtz, Willem Kindler garden and lighting designer, public relations consultant
Zeller, Ronald John lawyer

Palm Beach Gardens
†Andrade, William Thomas professional golfer
Awtrey, Jim L. sports association executive
Bonifazi, Stephen chemist
Bower, Ruth Lawther retired mathematics educator
Christian, Robert Henry architect
Colussy, Dan Alfred aviation executive
Couples, Frederick Steven professional golfer
Daly, John professional golfer
Druck, Kalman Breschel public relations counselor
Duval, David Robert golfer
Falk, Bernard Henry trade association executive
Furyk, James Michael professional golfer
Giordano, Andrew Anthony retired naval officer
Haas, Jay professional golfer
Hannon, John Robert investment company executive
Harnett, Joseph Durham oil company executive
Hayes, Neil John lawyer
Henninger, Brian professional golfer
Herrick, John Dennis financial consultant, former law firm executive, retired food products executive
Horton, Edward Carl retired military officer, public administrator
Howard, Melvin financial executive
Huston, John professional golfer
Jacobsen, Peter Erling professional golfer
Kahn, David Miller lawyer
Keppler, William Edmund multinational company executive
Klein, Gail Beth Marantz freelance writer, dog breeder
Langer, Bernhard professional golfer
†Leonard, Justin professional golfer
†Lickliter, Frank Ray, II professional golfer
†Love, Davis Milton, III professional golfer
†Maggert, Jeffrey Allan professional golfer
Mendelson, Richard Donald former communications company executive
Merritt, Jean consulting firm executive
†Mickelson, Phil professional golfer
Miller, John Laurence professional golfer
Montgomerie, Colin professional golfer
O'Connell, Anthony J. bishop
Olazabal, Jose Maria professional golfer
†O'Meara, Mark professional golfer
Orr, Joseph Alexander educational administrator
†Ozaki, Jumbo professional golfer
Parnevik, Jesper Bo golfer
Perry, James Kenneth professional golfer
Pumphrey, Gerald Robert lawyer
Robb, David Buzby, Jr. financial services company executive, lawyer
†Roberts, Loren Lloyd professional golfer
Rosenfeld, Carson retired leasing company executive
Shapiro, Steven David dermatologist
Stankowski, Paul Francis golfer
Strange, Curtis Northrop professional golfer
Van Sickle, John Davis logistics engineer, naval officer
†Verplank, Scott Rachal professional golfer
Wackenhut, Richard Russell security company executive
†Westwood, Lee professional golfer
Woods, Tiger (Eldrick Woods) professional golfer

Palm City
Ammarell, John Samuel retired college president, former security services executive
Derrickson, William Borden manufacturing executive
Hennessy, Dean McDonald lawyer, multinational corporation executive
Henry, David Howe, II retired diplomat
Huntington, Earl Lloyd lawyer, retired natural resources company executive
Mc Hale, John Joseph baseball club executive
Sloan, Richard artist
Spears, Doris Ann Hachmuth entrepreneur, writer, publisher, real estate and management consultant
Wirsig, Woodrow magazine editor, trade organization executive, business executive
Wishart, Ronald Sinclair retired chemical company executive

Palm Coast
Dickson, David Watson Daly retired college president
DiUlus, Frederick Alfonso-Edward business educator
Farrell, Joseph Christopher retired mining executive, services executive
Patz, Edward Frank retired lawyer

Palm Harbor
Banwart, George Junior food microbiology educator
Curreri, John Robert mechanical engineer, consultant
Dunbar, David Wesley bank executive
Fanning, Wanda Gail retired elementary school educator
Fernandez, Joseph Anthony educational administrator
Fischer, John Jules clergy member, theology educator, writer
Giavis, Theodore Demetrios commercial illustrator, artist
Grace, John Eugene business forms company executive
Hoppensteadt, Jon Kirk law librarian

Katzen-Guthrie, Joy *performance artist, engineering services executive*
McDonald, Peggy Ann Stimmel *retired automobile company official*
Metsch, Werner Walter *mechanical engineer, consultant*
Murphy, Lester F(uller) *lawyer*
†Paolilli, Almonte Louis *librarian*
†Ross, Jay Howard *plastic surgeon*
Ruskin, Les D. *chiropractor*
Slorah, Patricia Perkins *anthropologist*
Smith, W. James *health facility administrator*
Thomas, Patrick Robert Maxwell *oncology educator, academic administrator*

Palmetto
Compton, Charles Daniel *chemistry educator*
Patton, Ray Baker *financial consultant, real estate broker*
Rains, Gloria Cann *environmentalist company executive*

Panama City
Byrne, Robert William *lawyer*
D'Arcy, Gerald Paul *engineering executive, consultant*
†McWhorter, Susan Carol *English language educator*
Mulligan, Barbara Laird Welch *school system administrator*
Patterson, Christopher Nida *lawyer*
Schuler, Burton Silverman *podiatrist*
Shelton, Karl Mason *management consultant*
Smith, Erlinda Fay *occupational therapist*
Smith, Jani Marie *special education educator*
Smith, Larry Glenn *retired state judge*
Staab, Diane D. *lawyer*
Stark, S. Daniel, Jr. *convention and visitors bureau executive*
Wade, Larry Edward *evangelist, academic administrator*
Wallace, Arnold Lynn *English educator, writer*
Walters, George John *oral and maxillofacial surgeon*

Panama City Beach
Kapp, John Paul *lawyer, physician, educator*
Roberts, Paul Craig, III *economics educator, author, columnist*
Schafer, John Stephen *foundation administrator*
Shugart, Cecil Glenn *retired physics educator*

Parkland
Brancaleone, Salvatore Joseph *nutritionist, consultant*
Janice, Barbara *illustrator*

Patrick A F B
Gal, Richard John *industrial engineer*
Haggis, Arthur George, Jr. *retired military officer, educator, publisher*

Paxton
Kearns, John William (Bill Kearns) *electronics inventor and executive*

Pembroke Pines
Abbott, Linda Joy *stained glass artisan, educator*
Herzog, Richard F. *retired science educator*
Kater, Kathryn M. *critical care nurse*
Mason, Mitchell Gary *emergency nurse*
Motes, Joseph Mark *cruise and convention promotion company executive*
†Robinson, Howard Neil *plastic surgeon*

Penney Farms
Bronkema, Frederick Hollander *retired minister and church official*
Meyer, Marion M. *editorial consultant*

Pensacola
Abercrombie, Charlotte Manning *reading specialist, supervisor*
Andrews, Edson James, Jr. *radiologist*
Arnold, Barry Raynor *philosophy educator, minister, ethicist, counselor*
†Bare, Charles Lambert *education director*
Bowden, Jesse Earle *newspaper editor, author, cartoonist, journalism educator*
Bozeman, Frank Carmack *lawyer*
Bullock, Ellis Way, Jr. *architect*
Burke-Fanning, Madeleine *artist*
Carper, William Barclay *management educator*
Clare, George *safety engineer, systems safety consultant*
Coker, William Sidney *historian, educator*
Collier, Lacey Alexander *federal judge*
Commins, Ernest Altman (Ernie Commins) *certified financial planner*
Cooper, Elva June *artist, writer*
Cox, Amie C. *publisher*
Dauser, Kimberly Ann *physician assistant*
Davis, Ryan Wesley *military officer, navigator*
DeMaria, Michael Brant *psychologist*
Dillard, Robert Perkins *pediatrician, educator*
Foster, Virginia *retired botany educator*
Franklin, Godfrey *adult education educator*
Furlong, George Morgan, Jr. *health care foundation executive, retired naval officer*
Galloway, Sharon Lynne *special education educator*
Geeker, Nicholas Peter *lawyer, judge*
George, Katie *lawyer*
Hanline, Manning Harold *internist*
Hutto, Earl *retired congressman*
Johnson, Alfred Carl, Jr. *former navy officer*
Klepper, Robert Kenneth *writer, silent film historian, journalist*
Levin, David Harold *lawyer*
Long, H. Owen *retired economics educator, fiction writer*
Love, Robert William, Jr. *retired physician, government administrator*
†Lovoy, Joseph T. *investment advisor*
Maddock, Lawrence Hill *retired language educator*
Marsh, William Douglas *lawyer*
Marx, Morris Leon *academic administrator*
McCann, Mary Cheri *medical technologist, horse breeder and trainer*
McLeod, Stephen Glenn *education educator, language educator*
McQueen, Rebecca Hodges *health care executive, consultant*
Moulton, Wilbur Wright, Jr. *lawyer*
Novotny, Susan M. *judge*
Olsen, John Richard *education consultant*
Ramsey, William Edward *retired naval officer, space systems executive*
Rasmussen, Robert *museum director*
Ricard, John H. *bishop, educator*
Rubardt, Peter Craig *conductor, educator*
Sargent, James O'Connor *freelance writer*
Serangeli, Deborah S. *healthcare facility administrator*
Shimmin, Margaret Ann *women's health nurse*
Sisk, Rebecca Benefield *educator, business owner*
Soloway, Daniel Mark *lawyer*
Steinhoff, Raymond O(akley) *consulting geologist*
†Symonds, Ronald Delbert *retired military physician*
Taggart, Linda Diane *women's health nurse*
Vinson, C. Roger *federal judge*
Vuksta, Michael Joseph *surgeon*
Walker, Peggy Jean *social work agency administrator*
White, William Clinton *pathologist*
Woolf, Kenneth Howard *architect*

Pineland
Donlon, Josephine A. *diagnostic and evaluation counseling therapist, educator*
Donlon, William James *lawyer*

Pinellas Park
Di Salvatore, Chris Allen *mechanical engineer*
Hall, Charles Allen *aerospace and energy consultant*
Perry, Paul Alverson *utility executive*
Tower, Alton G., Jr. *pharmacist*
West, Wallace Marion *cultural organization administrator*

Placida
Grissom, Joseph Carol *retired leasing and investments business executive*
Wood, Yvonne McMurray *nursing educator*

Plant City
Buchman, Kenneth William *lawyer*
Hixon, Andrea Kaye *healthcare quality specialist*
Knoderer, David Letterfly *artist, educator*
Mathis-Sales, Helen *nurse*
McDaniel, James Roosevelt *municipal official*

Plantation
Appel, Antoinette Ruth *neuropsychologist*
Ballantyne, Maree Anne Canine *artist*
Buck, Thomas Randolph *retired lawyer, financial services executive*
Chou, Chung-Kwang *bio-engineer*
Ferris, Robert Edmund *lawyer*
†Fish, Michael *psychologist*
Garrett, Linda Silverstein *financial planner*
Gonshak, Isabelle Lee *nurse*
Lehman, Joan Alice *real estate executive*
†Maingot, Anthony Peter *sociology educator*
Newburge, Idelle Block *psychotherapist*
Ramos, Manuel Antonio, Jr. *pulmonologist*
†Schmidt, Andrew Lytle *pool and spa contracting company executive*
Sterling, Carol Barbara *social worker, psychotherapist*
Tingley, Floyd Warren *physician*

Pomona Park
Garcia, Mary Elizabeth *Spanish and English as second language educator*

Pompano Beach
Bliznakov, Emile George *biomedical research scientist*
Bookbinder, Robert Max *superintendent of schools*
Brands, Robert Franciscus *marketing executive*
Calevas, Harry Powell *management consultant*
Danziger, Terry Leblang *public relations and marketing consultant*
Donnelly, Michael Joseph *management consultant*
Elder, Robert Lee *professional golfer*
Forman, Harriet *nursing publication executive*
Fritsch, Billy Dale, Jr. *construction company executive*
Gilchrist, William Risque, Jr. *economist*
Grigsby-Stephens, Klaron *corporate executive*
Johnson, Dorothy Curfman *elementary education educator*
Kester, Stewart Randolph *banker*
Legler, Bob *publishing company executive*
MacLaren, Neil Moorley, Jr. *musician, music educator*
Miller, A. Edgar, Jr. *dermatologist*
Mulvey, John Thomas, Jr. *financial consultant*
Noland, Josh *recording company executive*
Pigott, Melissa Ann *social psychologist*
Rifenburgh, Richard Philip *investment company executive*
Roberts, Karen Barbara *art educator*
Roen, Sheldon R. *publisher, psychologist*
Saleeby, Cherie Lee *sculptor*
Schwartz, Joseph *retired container company executive*
Shang, Charles Yulin *medical physicist*
Shulmister, M(orris) Ross *lawyer*
†Slovin, Bruce *diversified holding company executive*
Szilassy, Sandor *retired lawyer, library director, educator*
Thaung *journalist*
Waldman, Alan I. (Alawana) *songwriter, composer, lyricist, computer programmer, emergency medicine provider*
Walsh, Thomas Francis, Jr. *producer, writer, director*
Wilson, Arthur Jess *psychologist, educator*

Ponte Vedra
Davis, Kim McAlister *real estate sales executive, real estate broker*
Moore, Philip Walsh *appraisal company executive*
Watson, John Lawrence, III *former trade association executive*
Wood, Quentin Eugene *oil company executive*

Ponte Vedra Beach
Azinger, Paul *professional golfer*
Brink, John William *financial corporation executive*
Cook, John *professional golfer*
de Selding, Edward Bertrand *retired banker*
Elkington, Steve *professional golfer*
Elston, William Steger *food products company executive*
Fiorentino, Thomas Martin *transportation executive, lawyer*
Forsman, Dan Bruce *professional golfer*
Frost, David *professional golfer*
Gold, Keith Dean *advertising and design executive*
Green, Norman Kenneth *retired oil industry executive, former naval officer*
Hamilton, William Berry, Jr. *shipping company executive*
Kuhn, Bowie K. *lawyer, former professional baseball commissioner, consultant*
Nadler, Sigmond Harold *physician, surgeon*
O'Brien, Raymond Vincent, Jr. *banker*
†Patterson, Oscar, III *university program administrator*
Pavin, Corey Allen *professional golfer*
Ramsey, William Dale, Jr. *marketing and technology consultant*
ReMine, William Hervey, Jr. *surgeon*
Rodriguez, Chi Chi (Juan Rodriguez) *professional golfer*
Roland, Melissa Montgomery *accountant*
†Sluman, Jeff *professional golfer*
Spence, Richard Dee *paper products company executive, former railroad executive*
Van Nelson, Nicholas Lloyd *business council executive*
Wadkins, Lanny *professional golfer*
Washington, MaliVai *professional tennis player*
Weinstein, George William *retired ophthalmology educator*
Wu, Hsiu Kwang *economist, educator*

Port Charlotte
Clark, Keith Collar *musician, educator*
Gendzwill, Joyce Annette *retired health officer*
Labousier, Susan Evelyn *choreographer, dancer*
Leslie, John *artist, designer, photographer, sculptor*
Mulligan, Louise Eleanore *retired English literature educator*
Munger, Elmer Lewis *civil engineer, educator*
Reynolds, Helen Elizabeth *management services consultant*
Sheahan, Joan A. *long term care nursing administrator*
Soben, Robert Sidney *systems scientist*
Spatz, Hugo David *film producer*
Von Holden, Martin Harvey *psychologist*
Wall, Edward Millard *environmental consulting executive*

Port Orange
Hiatt, Charles F., II *secondary education educator*
Horváth, Michael Joseph *curator*
Parish, Lynn Race *medical technologist*
Willhoit-Rudt, Marilyn Jean *medical resources company executive*

Port Richey
Mueller, Lois M. *psychologist*

Port Saint Joe
Burke, Sabrina Nelson *sales and marketing professional*

Port Saint Lucie
Augelli, John Pat *geography educator, author, consultant, rancher*
Hambel, Henry Peter *clinical hypnotherapist, forensic security consultant, educator*
Huang, Denis Kuo Ying *chemical engineer, consultant*
Jackson, George Mark *writer, photographer*
Olson, Edward Charles *entrepreneur, conservationist, writer, environmental consultant, banker, business consultant, foundation administrator*
Sommers, Robert Thomas *editor, publisher, author*
Wedzicha, Walter *foreign language educator*
Westman, Steven Ronald *rabbi*

Port Salerno
Martin, Dale *vocational rehabilitation executive*

Princeton
Cottrill, Mary Elsie *family nurse practitioner*

Punta Gorda
Beever, James William, III *biologist*
Beever, Lisa Britt-Dodd *transportation and environmental planner, researcher*
Bowman, Willard Nelson, Jr. *architect*
Bulzacchelli, John G. *financial executive*
Clinton, Mariann Hancock *educational association administrator*
Goodman, Donald C. *university administrator*
Graham, William Aubrey, Jr. *real estate broker*
Harrington, John Vincent *retired communications company executive, engineer, educator*
Haswell, Carleton Radley *banker*
Hill, Richard Earl *academic administrator*
Kavanaugh, Frank James *film producer, educator*
Knoble, William Avery *government finance officer, accountant*
Koll, Richard Leroy *retired chemical company executive*
O'Donnell, Mary Murphy *nurse epidemiologist, consultant*
Piacitelli, John Joseph *county official, educator, pediatrician*
†Rohrbach, David Franklin *chemistry educator*
Smith, Marilyn Patricia *city government official, management consultant and facilitator*
Truby, John Louis *computer, management and trucking consultant*
Wolff, Diane Patricia *author, journalist, producer*
Wood, Emma S. *nurse practitioner*

Quincy
Laughlin, William Eugene *electric power industry executive*

Ramrod Key
Clark, John Russell *marine biologist*

Reddick
Corwin, Joyce Elizabeth Stedman *construction company executive*

Ridge Manor
Cameron, Kristen Ellen Schmidt *nurse, construction company executive, educator, writer*

River Ranch
Swett, Albert Hersey *retired lawyer, business executive, consultant*

Riverview
Till, Beatriz Maria *international business consultant, translator*

Rockledge
Sutton, Betty Sheriff *elementary education educator*

Roseland
Canterbury-Counts, W. Douglas *psychologist*

Royal Palm Beach
Curphey, Geraldine Casterline *church musician, retired*
†Robinson, Dolores Olivia *educational consultant, grantwriter*

Safety Harbor
Banks, Allan Richard *artist, art historian, researcher*
Banks, Holly Hope *artist*
Fay, Carolyn M. *education marketing business owner*
Slevin, Patrick Jeremiah *paralegal*

Saint Augustine
Adams, William Roger *historian*
†Baker, Harold Wayne *retired news editor, anchor*
Bishop, Claire DeArment *small business owner, former librarian*
Dale, Chuck *landmark staff member*
Fevurly, Keith Robert *educational administrator*
Gillilland, Thomas *art gallery director*
Greenberg, Michael John *biologist, editor*
†Hall, Robert *art educator, artist*
Keys, Leslee Frances *historic preservation planner*
LeBeau, H. Alton, Jr. *confectionary company executive*
Marsolais, Harold Raymond *trade association administrator*
Matzke, Frank J. *architect, consultant*
McCarty, Doran Chester *religious organization administrator*
†Naughton, René Patricia *primary school educator*
Nolan, David Joseph *author, historian*
Nolan, Joseph Thomas *journalism educator, communications consultant*
Poland, Richard Clayton *law educator*
Proctor, William Lee *college president*
Robbins, Rima *journalist, public relations consultant*
Rountree, John Griffin Richardson *association and retail executive*
Sappington, Sharon Anne *retired school librarian*
Theil, Henri *economist, educator*
Tuseo, Norbert Joseph John *marketing executive, consultant*

Saint Cloud
Everett, Woodrow Wilson *electrical engineer, educator*
Kandrac, Jo Ann Marie *school administrator*
Shuman, Barbara *social studies educator*

Saint Leo
Hale, Charles Dennis *education educator*

Saint Pete Beach
Bauman, Tatjana *pathologist, consultant*
DeLorenzo, David Joseph *retired public relations executive*
Garnett, Stanley Iredale, II *lawyer, utility company executive*
Hurley, Frank Thomas, Jr. *realtor*

Saint Petersburg
Allshouse, Merle Frederick *educational organization administrator*
Armacost, Peter Hayden *academic administrator*
†Armstrong, Kenneth *corporate lawyer*
Arnold, Jay *retired engineering executive, educator*
Bailey, Robin Keith *physician assistant, perfusionist*
Baiman, Gail *real estate broker*
Barca, James Joseph *fire department administrative services executive*
Barnes, Andrew Earl *newspaper editor*
Barney, Linda Susan *manufacturing specialist*
Battaglia, Anthony Sylvester *lawyer*
Battaglia, Brian Peter *lawyer*
Belich, John Patrick, Sr. *journalist*
Benbow, Charles Clarence *retired writer, critic*
Bercu, Barry B. *pediatric endocrinologist*
Betzer, Susan Elizabeth Beers *family physician, geriatrician*
Blumenthal, Herman Bertram *accountant*
Boggs, Wade Anthony *professional baseball player*
Brown, Jacqueline Ley White *retired lawyer*
Bryant, Laura Militzer *artist*
Buchan, Russell Paul *publisher, gas company executive, entrepreneur*
Byrd, Isaac Burlin *fishery biologist, fisheries administrator*
Callahan, James K. *fire chief*
Canseco, Jose *professional baseball player*
Carrere, Charles Scott *lawyer*
Carroll, Charles Michael *music educator*
Clark, Carolyn Chambers *nurse, author, educator*
Cole, Sally Ann *critical care nurse*
Collins, Carl Russell, Jr. *corporate services*
Collins, Paul Steven *vascular surgeon*
Connelly, David O'Brien *museum administrator, journalist*
Corty, Andrew P. *publishing executive*
Cretekos, George Nick *district assistant*
Donovan, Denis Miller *psychiatrist, author, lecturer*
Edwards, Fred L., Jr. *writer, consultant*
Elson, Charles Myer *law educator*
Emerson, William Allen *retired investment company executive*
Erlinger, Melvin Herbert *pastor, educator*
Escarraz, Enrique, III *lawyer*
Fassett, John D. *retired utility executive, consultant*
Fischer, David J. *mayor*
Fishman, Mark Brian *computer scientist, educator*
Foley, Michael Francis *newspaper executive*
Franke, Thomas *investment company executive*
Freeman, Corinne *financial services, former mayor*
†French, Thomas *journalist*
Galbraith, John William *securities company executive*
Galucki, Frances Jane *nursing educator, medical/surgical nurse*
Godbold, Francis Stanley *investment banker, real estate executive*
Good, Robert Alan *physician, educator*
Griffin, Dennis Joseph *middle school principal*
†Griggs, Catherine M. *educator*
Grube, Karl Bertram *judge*

Haiman, Robert James *newspaper editor, journalism educator, media consultant*
†Hamilton, John McFarland *plastic surgeon, bank director*
Hansel, Paul George *physicist, consultant*
Harrell, Roy G., Jr. *lawyer*
Hines, Andrew Hampton, Jr. *utilities executive*
Hoche, Philip Anthony *life insurance company executive*
Hooker, Robert Wright *journalist*
Houser, Ruth G. *data communications manager*
Jacob, Bruce Robert *law educator*
James, Thomas A. *investment company executive*
Jenkins, Robert Norman *newswriter, editor*
Johnson, Edna Ruth *editor*
Jordan, William Reynier, Sr. *therapist, poet*
Julien, Jeffrey P. *investment company executive*
Kaiser, Greg Christopher *pediatric gastroenterologist*
Kent, Allen *library and information sciences educator*
Kiefner, John Robert, Jr. *lawyer, educator*
†Krause, James R. *urologist*
Kubiet, Leo Lawrence *newspaper advertising and marketing executive*
†Kuttler, Carl Martin, Jr. *academic administrator*
Lamar, William Fred *chaplain, educator*
Lanitis, Tony Andrew *market researcher*
Lauber, Christopher Joseph *sports event promoter*
Layton, William George *management consultant, human resources executive, export-import executive*
Liebert, Larry Steven *journalist*
Ling, Chung-Mei *retired pharmaceutical company executive*
Linhart, Joseph Wayland *retired cardiologist, educational administrator*
MacMillan, Duncan Jay *music educator, pianist*
Maier, Karl George *estate and financial planner*
Mann, Sam Henry, Jr. *lawyer*
Martin, Susan Taylor *newspaper editor*
Martindale, Robert Warren *retired military officer, biomedical administrator*
McGriff, Fred (Frederick Stanley McGriff) *baseball player*
Meisels, Gerhard George *academic administrator, chemist, educator*
Metz, Robert Edward *quality assurance executive*
Metzger, Kathleen Ann *computer systems specialist*
Meyer, Robert Allen *human resource management educator*
Mills, William Harold, Jr. *construction company executive*
Moneypenny, Edward William *petroleum exploration and production executive*
Moody, Lizabeth Ann *law educator*
Morgan, Avery A. *electrical engineer*
Morgan, Rebecca C. *lawyer, educator*
Mueller, O. Thomas *molecular geneticist, pediatrics educator*
Mussett, Richard Earl *city official*
Naimoli, Vincent Joseph *diversified operating and holding company executive*
Naughton, James Martin *journalist*
Nussbaum, Leo Lester *retired college president, consultant*
Oman, Robert Milton *writer, consultant, educator*
Pardoll, Peter Michael *gastroenterologist*
Patterson, Eugene Corbett *retired editor, publisher*
Peterson, Eric Lang *art appraiser, art consultant, gallery owner*
†Peterson, Sheryl Swan *academic administrator, psychologist*
Pittman, Robert Turner *retired newspaper editor*
Putnam, J. Stephen *financial executive*
Raissi, Joseph *financial planner*
Ransom, Brian Charles *artist, educator, musician, composer*
Reilly, Tracy Lynn *language professional/educator, English*
Remke, Richard Edwin *lumber company executive*
Roales, Judith *newspaper publisher*
Roney, Paul H(itch) *federal judge*
Root, Allen William *pediatrician, educator*
Rosenblum, Martin Jerome *ophthalmologist*
Ross, Howard Philip *lawyer*
†Rothschild, Larry *professional baseball executive*
Rummel, Harold Edwin *real estate development executive*
Schultz, G. Robert *lawyer*
Scott, Kathryn Fenderson *lawyer*
Scott, Lee Hansen *retired holding company executive*
Serrie, Hendrick *anthropology and international business educator*
Sheen, Robert Tilton *manufacturing company executive*
Shi, Feng Sheng *mathematician*
Silver, Lawrence Alan *marketing executive*
Smith, Betty Robinson *elementary education educator*
Smyth, Walter G. *real estate broker*
Southworth, William Dixon *retired education educator*
Squires, Patricia Eileen Coleman *freelance journalist, writer*
Stephens, Darrel W. *protective services official*
Tash, Paul Clifford *newspaper editor*
Turner, Robert H. *administrator*
VanButsel, Michael R. *real estate broker and developer*
Walker, Brigitte Maria *translator, linguistic consultant*
Walker, Lola H. *religious organization administrator*
Wasserman, Susan Valesky *accountant*
Wedding, Charles Randolph *architect*
Westall, Sandra Thornton *special education educator*
White, Charles Ronald *psychiatrist*
Williams, Larry Ross *surgeon*
Wright, Fred W., Jr. *writer*

San Mateo
Wood, Shelton Eugene *college educator, consultant, minister*

Sanford
Oostwouder, Peter Henry *family physician*
Smith, Vicki Lynn *lawyer*
Wright, Stephen Caldwell *English language educator*

Sanibel
Bailey, John Turner *public relations executive*
Ball, Armand Baer *former association executive, consultant*
Brodbeck, William Jan *marketing consultant, speaker*
Courtney, James Edmond *real estate developer*
Crown, David Allan *criminologist, educator*
Gibson, Roy L. *city planner*

Hasselman, Richard B. *retired transportation company executive*
Herriott, Donald Richard *optical physicist*
Keogh, Mary Cudahy *artist*
Kiernan, Edwin A., Jr. *lawyer, corporation executive*
Lautenbach, Terry Robert *information systems and communications executive*
Perkinson, Diana Agnes Zouzelka *interior design firm import company executive*
Rogstad, John Thomas *retired pharmaceuticals executive*
Sappenfield, Charles Madison *architect, educator*
Walton, Chelle Koster *travel writer*

Santa Rosa Beach
Gilmore, Beverly J *retired journalist, gallery owner*
Wright, John Peale *retired banker*

Sarasota
†Ainslie, Kimble Fletcher *scholar, research consultant, writer*
Altabe, Joan Augusta Berg *artist, writer, art and architecture critic*
†Arias, Oscar David *computer programmer*
Arreola, John Bradley *diversified financial service company executive, financial planner*
Atwell, Robert Herron *higher education executive*
Aull, Susan *physician*
Bailey, Robert Elliott *financial executive*
Balliett, John William *entrepreneur, real estate executive*
Bassis, Michael Steven *academic administrator*
Bausch, James John *foundation executive*
Beck, Robert Alfred *hotel administration educator*
Benedick, James Michael *psychotherapist*
Bennett, Lois *real estate broker*
Berkoff, Charles Edward *pharmaceutical executive*
Bernfield, Lynne *psychotherapist*
Bewley, David Charles *financial planner*
Biegel, Alice Marie *secondary school educator*
†Bjaland, Leif *artistic director, conductor*
Blanchard, Leonard Albert *management consultant, writer*
Blucher, Paul Arthur *lawyer*
Bonn, Theodore Hertz *computer scientist, consultant*
Burdick, Eugene Allan *retired judge, lawyer, surrogate judge*
Burkett, Helen *artist*
Bushey, Alan Scott *retired insurance holding company executive*
Byron, E. Lee *real estate broker*
Byron, H. Thomas, Jr. *veterinarian, educator*
Carr, Patricia Ann *community health nurse*
Cashin, Patricia Jeanne (Pat Cashin) *artist, educator*
Castle-Hasan, Elizabeth E. *religious organization administrator*
Christ-Janer, Arland Frederick *college president*
Christopher, William Garth *lawyer*
Close, Michael John *lawyer*
Conetta, Tami Foley *lawyer*
Cooper, William Ewing, Jr. *retired army officer*
Covert, Michael Henri *healthcare facility administrator*
Cummings, Erika Helga *business consultant*
Davis, Louis Poisson, Jr. *lawyer, consultant*
Dearden, Robert James *retired pharmacist*
Deutsch, Sid *bioengineer, educator*
Dillon, Rodney Lee *lawyer*
Dlesk, George *retired pulp and paper industry executive*
†Doenecke, Justus D. *history educator*
Drenz, Charles Francis *retired army officer*
Dryce, H. David *accountant, consultant*
Eachus, Joseph J(ackson) *computer scientist, consultant*
Ebitz, David MacKinnon *art historian, museum director*
Fawks, David Robert *psychiatric clinical nurse specialist*
Feder, Allan Appel *management executive, consultant*
Fendrick, Alan Burton *retired advertising executive*
Garland, Richard Roger *lawyer*
Gauch, Eugene William, Jr. *former air force officer*
Gilbert, Perry Webster *emeritus educator*
Giordano, David Alfred *internist, gastroenterologist*
Gittelson, Bernard *public relations consultant, author, lecturer*
Goldsmith, Stanley Alan *lawyer*
Gordon, Sanford Daniel *economics educator*
†Graham, Braun H. *plastic surgeon*
Graham, Douglas John *museum curator, banker, artist, poet*
†Graper, William Peter *cardiac surgeon*
Greenfield, Robert Kauffman *lawyer*
Gugino, Carl Frank *orthodontist, educator*
†Gurney, Frank Irving *transportation executive*
Gurvitz, Milton Solomon *psychologist*
Hackl, Alphons J. *publisher*
Harmon, (Loren) Foster *art consultant*
Harvey, Donald Phillips *retired naval officer*
Heiser, Rolland Valentine *former army officer, foundation executive*
Hennemeyer, Robert Thomas *diplomat*
Herb, F(rank) Steven *lawyer*
Highland, Marilyn M. *principal*
Hoffman, Heinz Joseph *aerospace scientist, management consultant*
Hoffman, Oscar Allen *retired forest products company executive*
Hrones, John Anthony *mechanical engineering educator*
Huff, Russell Joseph *public relations and publishing executive*
Hummel, Dana D. Mallett *librarian*
†Ihde, Aaron John *history of science educator emeritus*
†Jackson, Jody *journalist*
Jelks, Mary Larson *retired pediatrician*
Jones, Sally Daviess Pickrell *writer*
Jones, Tracey Kirk, Jr. *minister, educator*
Kelly, Debra Ann *adult education educator*
Kelly, John Love *public relations executive*
Kimbrough, Robert Averyt *lawyer*
Kozma, Karen Jean *nurse, educator*
Krate, Nat *artist*
Lambert, John Phillip *financial executive, consultant*
Landis, Edgar David *retired services business company executive*
Larsen, Lawrence Bernard, Jr. *priest, pastoral psychotherapist*
Lee, Ann McKeighan *secondary school educator*
Lengyel, Alfonz *art history, archeology and museology educator*
Lindsay, David Breed, Jr. *aircraft company executive, former editor and publisher*
Long, Robert Radcliffe *fluid mechanics educator*

Loomis, Wesley Horace, III *former publishing company executive*
Mackey, Leonard Bruce *lawyer, former diversified manufacturing corporation executive*
Magenheim, Mark Joseph *physician, epidemiologist, educator*
Mahadevan, Kumar *marine laboratory director, researcher*
Makau, John *artist*
Marino, Eugene Louis *publishing company executive*
Matthews, Lynn O. *publisher*
Mattran, Donald Albert *management consultant, educator*
Matz, Kenneth H., Jr. *retired newscaster*
McCollum, John Morris *tenor*
†McFarlin, Diane Hooten *newspaper editor*
Meyer, B. Fred *small business executive, home designer and builder, product designer*
Middleton, Norman Graham *social worker, psychotherapist*
Miles, Arthur J. *financial planner, consultant*
Minette, Dennis Jerome *financial computing consultant*
Miranda, Carlos Sa *food products company executive*
Mitchell, John Noyes, Jr. *retired electrical engineer*
Morris, Gordon James *financial company executive, consultant*
Mullane, John Francis *pharmaceutical company executive*
Myerson, Albert Leon *physical chemist*
North, Marjorie Mary *columnist*
O'Malley, Thomas Anthony *gastroenterologist, internist*
Pender, Michael Roger *engineering consultant*
Petrie, George Whitefield, III *retired mathematics educator*
Phillips, Elvin Willis *lawyer*
Pierce, Richard Harry *research director for laboratory*
Pollack, Joseph *diversified company executive*
Poppel, Harvey Lee *strategic management consultant, investment banker*
Prade, Jean Noël Cresta *entrepreneur*
Proffitt, Waldo, Jr. *newspaper editor*
Raimi, Burton Louis *lawyer*
Retzer, Mary Elizabeth Helm *retired librarian*
Roberts, Don E. *accountant*
Ross, Gerald Fred *engineering executive, researcher*
Roth, James Frank *manufacturing company executive, chemist*
Salomone, William Gerald *lawyer*
Scheitlin, Constance Joy *real estate broker*
Schmidt, James Harvey *plastic surgeon*
†Schumacher, James Matthew *neurosurgeon*
Schwartz, Norman L. *lawyer*
Seibert, Russell Jacob *botanist, research associate*
Shulman, Arthur *communications executive*
Simon, Joseph Patrick *food services executive*
Skelton, Howard Clifton *advertising and public relations executive*
Skelton, Winifred Karger *advertising agency executive, painter*
Slocum, Donald Hillman *product development executive*
Smith, Mark Hallard *architect*
Spencer, Lonabelle (Kappie Spencer) *political agency administrator, lobbyist*
†Steenfatt, Gertraude *community health nursing administrator*
Stickler, Daniel Lee *health care management consultant*
Sturtevant, Ruthann Patterson *anatomy educator*
Tamberrino, Frank Michael *professional association executive*
Taplin, Winn Lowell *historian, retired senior intelligence operations officer*
Tate, Manley Sidney *real estate broker*
Thompson, Annie Figueroa *academic director, educator*
Tucci, Steven Michael *health facility administrator, physician, recording industry executive*
Veinott, Cyril George *electrical engineer, consultant*
Venit, William Bennett *electrical products company executive, consultant*
Wadsworth, Dyer Seymour *lawyer*
Weeks, Albert Loren *author, educator, journalist*
Welch, John Dana *urologist, arts association executive*
Westcott, Joan Clark *poet*
Wetstone, Janet Meyerson *designer, journalist*
White, Jeffrey Lloyd *radiotherapy physicist*
White, Will Walter, III *public relations consultant, writer*
Williams, Julia Rebecca Keys *secondary school educator*
Wilson, Kenneth Jay *writer*
Wilson, Marsha L. *consultant*
Wilson, Ned Bruce *university academic administrator*
Winterhalter, Dolores August (Dee Winterhalter) *art educator*
Wise, Warren Roberts *retired lawyer*
Yonker, Richard Aaron *rheumatologist*
†Zentner, Arnold Stuart *psychiatrist*

Sebastian
Becker, Jim *gem historian, jeweler*
Gangemi, Gaetano Tommaso, Sr. *computer company executive*
Mauke, Leah Rachel *counselor*
Mauke, Otto Russell *retired college president*
Muller, Henry John *real estate developer*
Pieper, Patricia Rita *artist, photographer*
White, Thomas Patrick *county official, small business owner*

Sebring
McCollum, James Fountain *lawyer*
Sherrick, Daniel Noah *real estate broker*
Shinholser, Olin Wilson *judge*
Trombley, Michael Jerome *lawyer*

Seffner
†Allen, Claudette A. *educational administrator*

Seminole
Jarrard, Marilyn Mae *nursing consultant, nursing researcher*
Schwartzberg, Roger Kerry *osteopath, internist*
Wilson, Marc Burt *engineering educator*

Silver Springs
Sundstrom, Harold Walter *public relations executive*

South Bay
Oeffner, Barbara Dunning *biographer, educator, screenwriter*

Spring Hill
Aldrich, David Alan *accountant*
Burnim, Kalman Aaron *theatre educator emeritus*
Martin, Gary J. *retired business executive, mayor*
Weber, Mary Linda *preschool educator*

Starke
†Solze, Richard C. *real estate appraiser*

Steinhatchee
Grubbs, Elven Judson *retired newspaper publisher*

Stuart
Ankrom, Charles Franklin *golf course architect, consultant*
Belanger, Robert Eugene *lawyer*
Campazzi, Earl James *physician*
Conklin, George Melville *retired food company executive*
Delagi, Edward Francis *physician, retired educator*
Donohue, Edith M. *human resources specialist, educator*
Erlick, Everett Howard *broadcasting company executive*
Haserick, John Roger *retired dermatologist*
Hutchinson, Janet Lois *historical society administrator*
Jaffe, Jeff Hugh *retired food products executive*
Laska, Paul Robert *protective services official, writer, educator*
Leibson, Irving *retired industrial executive*
Lysen, Lucinda Katherine *nutrition support nurse, dietitian*
Maktouf, Samir *education company executive*
McKenna, Sidney F. *retired technical company executive*
Mulcahy, Albert Lee, III *civil engineer, environmental engineer*
O'Connor, Francis X. *financial executive*
Patterson, Robert Arthur *physician, health care consultant, retired health care company executive, retired air force officer*
Proctor, Gail Louise Borrowman *home health nurse, educator, women's health nurse*
Shane, Robert Samuel *chemical engineer, consultant*
Snider, Harlan Tanner *former manufacturing company executive*
White, Donald Francis *financial planner, insurance agent*

Summerland Key
Muth, John Fraser *economics educator*

Sun City Center
Calviello, Joseph Anthony *research electrophysicist, consultant*
Crow, Harold Eugene *physician, family medicine educator*
Fleischman, Sol Joseph, Sr. *retired television broadcasting executive*
Gummere, Walter Cooper *educator, consultant*
Hall, John Fry *psychologist, educator*
Jeffries, Robert Joseph *retired engineering educator, business executive*
McGrath, John Francis *utility executive*
Steele, Richard J. *management consultant*
Swatosh, Robert Beryl *retired army officer, nuclear physicist*

Sunny Isles Beach
Adrian, Manuella *research scientist, administrator*

Sunrise
Bure, Pavel *professional hockey player*
Cronin, Mary Haag *real estate referral agent*
Groover, Sandra Mae *business executive*
McLean, Kirk *professional hockey player*
Murray, Bryan Clarence *professional sports team executive*
Thompson, Yaakov *rabbi*
Torrey, William Arthur *professional hockey team executive*

Surfside
Hastings, Lawrence Vaeth *lawyer, physician, educator*

Tallahassee
Abele, Lawrence Gordon *biology educator, university administrator*
Adams, James Alfred *natural science educator*
Adams, Perry Ronald *former college administrator*
Allaire, Joseph Leo *French educator*
Anderson, John Roy *grouting engineer*
Anstead, Harry Lee *state supreme court justice*
Arce, Pedro Edgardo *chemical engineering educator*
Ashler, Philip Frederic *international trade and development advisor*
Aurell, John Karl *lawyer*
†Bailey, Suzanne K. *health care consultant*
Barker, Jeanne Wilson *principal, computer educational consultant*
Barnett, Martha Walters *lawyer*
Baum, Werner A. *former academic administrator, meteorologist*
Beck, Earl Ray *historian, educator*
Bell, John Tedford *civil engineer*
Bert, Clara Virginia *home economics educator, administrator*
†Blanton, Faye Wester *legislative staff member*
Bowden, Bobby *university athletic coach*
†Bower, Beverly Lynne *education educator*
Boyd, Joseph Arthur, Jr. *lawyer*
Braswell, Jackie Boyd *state agency administrator*
Brennan, Leonard Alfred *research scientist, administrator*
†Bridger, Carolyn Ann *pianist, music educator*
Burkman, Ernest, Jr. *education educator*
Burnette, Ada M. Puryear *educational administrator*
†Bush, John Ellis *governor*
Butterworth, Robert A. *state attorney general*
Bye, Raymond Erwin, Jr. *academic administrator*
Caspar, Donald Louis Dvorak *biophysics and structural biology educator*
Choppin, Gregory Robert *chemistry educator*
Clarkson, Julian Derieux *lawyer*
Coe, Thomas R. *police chief*
Coloney, Wayne Herndon *civil engineer*
Conti, Lisa Ann *epidemiologist, veterinarian*
Crawford, Bob *state commissioner*

Crider, Irene Perritt *education educator, small business owner, consultant*
Crow, Jack E. *physics administrator*
Curtin, Lawrence N. *lawyer*
Dadisman, Joseph Carrol *newspaper executive*
D'Alemberte, Talbot (Sandy D'Alemberte) *academic administrator, lawyer*
Dall, Sasha Raoul Xola *evolutionary ecologist, researcher*
Daniels, Irish C. *principal*
Dariotis, Terrence Theodore *lawyer*
Davis, Bertram Hylton *retired English educator*
Davis, Larry Michael *military officer, health-care manager, consultant*
Davis, William Howard *lawyer*
DeFoor, J. Allison, II *state agency officer, lawyer*
Deutsch, Alleen Dimitroff *university administrator*
Dillingham, Marjorie Carter *foreign language educator*
Doan, Petra Leisenring *urban planner, educator*
Dorn, Charles Meeker *art education educator*
Drayton, Carey M. *police administrator*
Ehlen, Martin Richard *state agency administrator, management analyst*
Ervin, Robert Marvin *lawyer*
Farmer, Claudette *collegiate basketball coach*
Foss, Donald John *university dean, research psychologist*
France, Belinda Takach *lawyer, business owner*
Friedmann, E(merich) Imre *biologist, educator*
Gabor, Jeffrey Alan *insurance and financial services executive*
Garretson, Peter P. *historian, educator*
Gilmer, Robert *mathematics educator*
Golden, Leon *classicist, educator*
†Grant, Sydney Robert *educator*
Griffith, Elwin Jabez *lawyer, university administrator*
Grimes, Stephen Henry *retired state supreme court justice*
Gunter, William Dawson, Jr. (Bill Gunter) *insurance company executive*
Gupta, Madhu Sudan *electrical engineering educator*
Halpern, Paul G. *history educator*
Hammer, Marion Price *association executive*
Harbin, Merline Johnson *social service agency administrator*
†Harding, James Raymond, II *special education educator*
Harding, Major Best *state supreme court chief justice*
Harper, George Mills *English language educator*
†Harris, Katherine *state official*
Harrison, Thomas James *electrical engineer, educator*
Harsanyi, Janice *soprano, educator*
Hatchett, Joseph Woodrow *federal judge*
Hayward, Patricia Carroll *university administrator*
Hedstrom, Susan Lynne *maternal women's health nurse*
Herbert, Adam William, Jr. *chancellor*
Herndon, Roy Clifford *physicist*
Herskovitz, S(am) Marc *lawyer*
Hicken, Russell Bradford *art dealer, appraiser*
Holcomb, Lyle Donald, Jr. *retired lawyer*
Holcomb, Terri Lynn *computer graphic consultant*
Holcombe, Randall Gregory *economics educator*
†Holtzclaw, Mark Alexander *social worker*
Howard, Louis Norberg *mathematics educator*
Hult, Gert Tomas Mikael *international business executive, educator*
Humphries, Frederick S. *university president*
Hunt, John Edwin *insurance company executive, consultant*
Hunt, Mary Alice *library science educator*
Ivlev, Boris Ivanovich *physicist*
Jenks, Frederick Lynn *English educator, university program administrator*
Johnson, Benjamin F., VI *real estate developer, consulting economist*
Kemper, Kirby Wayne *physics educator*
Kerns, David Vincent *lawyer*
Kessler, Mitzi Lyons *artist*
Kogan, Gerald *state supreme court justice*
Koontz, Christine Miller *research faculty*
Ladd, Kristi Lynn *special education educator*
Laird, Doris Anne Marley *humanities educator, musician*
Laird, William Everette, Jr. *economics educator, administrator*
Leavell, Michael Ray *computer programmer, analyst*
Leeper, Zane H. *company executive, consultant*
†Leon, Karen Renée *elementary education educator*
Lick, Dale Wesley *adult education educator*
Lipner, Harry *retired physiologist, educator*
Lisenby, Dorrece Edenfield *realtor*
Long, Michael Christian *forester*
Loper, David Eric *geophysics educator, mathematics educator*
Maguire, Charlotte Edwards *retired physician*
Mandelkern, Leo *biophysics and chemistry educator*
Mang, Douglas Arthur *lawyer*
Manley, Walter Wilson, II *lawyer*
Marshall, Alan George *chemistry and biochemistry educator*
Marshall, Marilyn Josephine *lawyer*
Mason, Robert McSpadden *technology management educator, consultant*
Mayo, John *dean*
McBride, Donna Jannean *publisher*
†McCarty, Ann Darice *scientist*
McConnell, Michael *opera company director*
McCord, Guyte Pierce, Jr. *retired judge*
McCrimmon, Barbara Smith *writer, librarian*
McNeely, Robert A. *lawyer*
Meredith, Michael *science educator, researcher*
Miller, Gregory R. *lawyer*
Miller, John Samuel, Jr. *lawyer*
Miller, Morris Henry *lawyer*
Milligan, Robert Frank *state agency administrator*
Mills, Belen Collantes *early childhood education educator*
†Moore, Dennis D. *English educator*
Morgan, Constance Louise *real estate executive*
Morgan, Lucy Ware *journalist*
Morgan, Robert Marion *educational research educator*
Mortham, Sandra Barringer *former state official*
Moulton, Grace Charbonnet *physics educator*
Mustian, Middleton Truett *hospital administrator*
Nam, Charles Benjamin *sociologist, demographer, educator*
Navon, Ionel Michael *mathematics educator*
†Nelson, Bill *state treasurer*
Noah, Belinda Gail *lawyer*
Onokpise, Oghenekome Ukrakpo *agronomist, educator, forest geneticist, agroforester*
Overton, Benjamin Frederick *state supreme court justice*
Owens, Joseph Francis, III *physics educator*
Owens, Steven Mark *health education educator*
Palladino-Craig, Allys *museum director*
Paredes, James Anthony *anthropologist, educator*
Patterson, Michael P. *prosecutor*
Penson, Edward Martin *management consulting company executive*
Pfeffer, Richard Lawrence *geophysics educator*
†Phelps, John B. *legislative official*
Pond-Koenig, donalee *artist*
Presmeg, Norma Christine *mathematics educator, researcher*
Ramsey, Sally Ann Seitz *retired state official*
Raymond, Leland Francis *editor, desktop publisher*
Rikvold, Per Arne *physics researcher and educator*
Riley, Kenneth Jerome *athletic director*
Robbins, Jane Borsch *library science educator, information science educator*
Roberts, Michael Joseph *journalist*
Robson, Donald *physics educator*
Ryll, Frank Maynard, Jr. *professional society administrator*
†Sapp, Lauren B. *librarian, educator*
Saunders, Ron *lawyer, former state legislator*
Schrieffer, John Robert *physics educator, science administrator*
Schroeder, Edwin Maher *law educator*
Scott, Brenda D. *writer*
Semrau, Sue *university head women's basketball coach*
Serow, William John *economics educator*
Shaw, Leander Jerry, Jr. *state supreme court justice*
†Sherill, William C. *federal judge*
Sittig, Dennis Wayne *poet, paper hanger*
Skagfield, Hilmar Sigurdsson *business executive*
Smith, Clayton Alexander *college administrator*
Spooner, Donna *public administrator*
Sprouse, James Dean *nurse anesthetist*
Stafford, William Henry, Jr. *federal judge*
Standley-Burt, Nancy Vilma *psychologist, educator*
Stino, Farid Kamal Ramzi *biostatistician, educator, researcher, consultant*
Stinson, Stanley Thomas *computer consultant*
Summers, Frank William *librarian*
Summers, Lorraine Dey Schaeffer *librarian*
Sundberg, Alan Carl *former state supreme court justice, lawyer*
Sushko, Yuri *physicist researcher*
Thagard, Norman E. *astronaut, physician, engineer, educator*
Thomas, James Bert, Jr. *government official*
Thompson, Gregory Lee *social sciences educator*
Thompson, Jean Tanner *retired librarian*
Tookes, James Nelson *real estate investment company executive*
Tourtet, Christiane Andrée *writer, artistic photographer, poetess*
Turnbull, Marjorie Reitz *foundation executive, state legislator*
Valencic, Cynthia *foundation administrator*
Varn, Herbert Fred *state agency administrator*
Venable, Lisa Anita *computer programmer*
Walborsky, Harry M. *chemistry educator, consultant*
Webster, Peter David *judge*
Wells, Charles Talley *state supreme court justice*
†Wetherell, Thomas Kent *college president*
Whitney, Glayde Dennis *psychologist, educator, geneticist*
Wilkins, (George) Barratt *librarian*
†Wilson, Damian Michael *management analyst*
Wu, Tien-Shuenn *engineer, researcher, consultant*
Zachert, Martha Jane *retired librarian*
Zaiser, Kent Ames *lawyer*
Zirps, Fotena Anatolia *psychologist, researcher*

Tamarac
Auletta, Joan Miglorisi *construction company executive, mortgage and insurance broker*
Brown, Ted Leon, Jr. *investment company executive*
†Krause, John L. *optometrist*

Tampa
Abell, Jan Meisterheim *architect*
Able, James Augustus, Jr. *writer*
Adams, Henry Lee, Jr. *federal judge*
Adkins, Edward Cleland *lawyer*
Afield, Walter Edward *psychiatrist, service executive*
Aitken, Thomas Dean *lawyer*
Alexander, William Olin *finance company executive*
†Alstott, Michael Joseph (Mike Alstott) *professional football player*
Anderson, Robert Henry *educator*
Anton, John Peter *philosopher, educator*
Arfsten, Betty-Jane *nurse*
Ashe, Reid *publishing executive*
Ault, Jeffrey Michael *investment banker*
Ayers, Charles Allen *insurance risk management executive*
Barkin, Marvin E. *lawyer*
Barksdale-Ladd, Mary Alice *education educator*
Barness, Lewis Abraham *physician*
†Barrett, Stephen Michael *editor*
Barton, Bernard Alan, Jr. *lawyer*
Battle, Jean Allen *writer, educator*
Baynes, Thomas Edward, Jr. *judge, lawyer, educator*
Becatti, Lance Norman *finance company executive*
Becker, Alison Lea *lawyer*
Bedford, Robert Forrest *anesthesiologist*
Behnke, Roy Herbert *physician, educator*
Benjamin, Robert Spiers *foreign correspondent, writer, publicist*
Biles, (Lee) Thomas *religious organization executive, clergyman*
Binford, Jesse Stone, Jr. *chemistry educator*
Bittle, Polly Ann *nephrology nurse, researcher*
Bokor, Bruce H. *lawyer*
Bondi, Joseph Charles, Jr. *education educator, consultant*
Boutros, Linda Nelene Wiley *medical/surgical nurse*
Bowen, Thomas Edwin *cardiothoracic surgeon, retired army officer*
Brackin, Phyllis Jean *recruiting professional*
Bradish, Warren Allen *internal auditor, operations analyst, management consultant*
Bradley, Charles Ernest *educational leadership consultant, music educator*
Branch, William Terrell *urologist, educator*
Brookins, Wayne *municipal official*
†Brooks, Stuart Merrill *medical educator*
Brown, Steven Thomas *communications company official*
Brown, Troy Anderson, Jr. *electrical distributing company executive*
Buchert, Ronald V. *retired military career officer*
Bucklew, Susan Cawthon *federal judge*
Bukantz, Samuel Charles *physician, educator*
Bunker-Soler, Antonio Luis *physician*
Butler, Paul Bascomb, Jr. *lawyer*
Callan, Joseph Patrick *social service administrator*
Callen, David H. *hotel executive*
Campbell, David Ned *retired electric utility executive, business consultant*
Campbell, Richard Bruce *lawyer*
Cannella, Deborah Fabbri *elementary school educator*
Carnahan, Robert Paul *civil engineer, educator, researcher, consultant*
Carter, James A. *finance executive*
Catoe, Paul *cultural organization administrator*
Cavanagh, Denis *physician, educator*
Christensen, Kenneth Jussi *computer science and engineering educator*
Christopher, Wilford Scott *public relations consultant*
Clark, Michael Earl *psychologist*
Cohen, Frank Burton *wholesale novelty company executive*
Corbitt, Doris Orene *real estate agent, dietitian*
†Corcoran, Clement Timothy, III *bankruptcy judge*
Costin, John Edward *graphic artist*
Dail, Joseph Garner, Jr. *judge*
Daks, Peter A. *telecommunications company executive*
Davis, Blondell Gilliam *business manager, evangelist, artist, author*
Davis, Helen Gordon *former state senator*
Davis, Richard Earl *lawyer*
†Dilfer, Trent *professional football player*
Doliner, Nathaniel Lee *lawyer*
Donelan, Peter Andrew *dermatologist*
Dungy, Tony *professional sports team executive*
†Dunne, Peter Benjamin *university administrator*
Edberg, Judith Florence *music educator*
Eddy, Colette Ann *aerial photography studio owner, photographer*
Eichberg, Rodolfo David *physician, educator*
Ellwanger, Thomas John *lawyer*
England, Lynne Lipton *lawyer, speech pathologist, audiologist*
Ferlita, Ross *municipal government official*
Ferlita, Theresa Ann *clinical social worker*
Flagg, Barry David *insurance, corporate benefits, estate planning consultant*
Flom, Edward Leonard *retired steel company executive*
Flynn, Michael Patrick *radiologist*
Franzen, Lavern Gerhard *bishop*
Freedman, Sandra Warshaw *former mayor*
Frias, Jaime Luis *pediatrician, educator*
Friedlander, Edward Jay *journalism educator*
Fritzsche, R. Wayne *corporate executive*
Gardner, J. Stephen *lawyer*
Genter, John Robert *grocery industry executive*
Germany, John Fredrick *lawyer*
Gifford, Donald Arthur *lawyer*
Gilbert, Leonard Harold *lawyer*
Gilbert-Barness, Enid F. *pathologist, pathology and pediatrics educator*
Givens, Paul Edward *industrial engineer, educator*
Givens, Paul Ronald *former university chancellor*
Glazer, Malcolm *professional sports team executive*
†Glenn, Paul M. *federal judge*
Glickman, Ronnie Carl *state official, lawyer*
Gonzalez, Alan Francis *lawyer*
Gossett, Forrest Scott *publishing executive*
†Graham, Laurel Diane *sociology educator*
Grammig, Robert James *lawyer*
Greco, Dick A. *mayor, hardware company executive*
Greenfield, George B. *radiologist*
Greenhalgh, Terry Lamont *marketing executive*
Grendys, Edward Charles *obstetrician-gynecologist, gynecologic oncologist*
Grimes, David Lynn *communications company executive*
Hadden, John Randolph *sales and marketing executive*
Hadden, John Winthrop *immunopharmacology educator*
Hanford, Agnes Rutledge *financial adviser*
Hanford, Grail Stevenson *writer*
Hanisee, Mark Steven *employee benefits professional*
Hankenson, E(dward) Craig, Jr. *performing arts executive*
Hankinson, Tim *soccer coach*
Harriman, Malcolm Bruce *investment advisor*
Hartmann, William Herman *pathologist, educator*
Heck, James Baker *university official*
†Heckman, Gary Walter *military career officer*
Hegarty, Thomas Joseph *academic administrator, history educator*
†Heide, Kathleen Margaret *criminology educator, psychotherapist*
Henard, Elizabeth Ann *controller*
Henning, Rudolf Ernst *electrical engineer, educator, consultant*
Hernandez, Gilberto Juan *accountant, auditor, management consultant*
Heuer, Martin *temporary services executive*
Hickman, Hugh V. *science educator, researcher*
Highsmith, Jasper Habersham *sales executive*
Hillman, James V. *pediatrician*
Hinsch, Gertrude Wilma *biology educator*
Holder, Anna Maria *holding company executive*
Holder, Ben R. *protective services official*
Holder, Harold Douglas, Sr. *investor, industrialist*
Holfelder, Lawrence Andrew *pediatrician, allergist*
Holmes, Dwight Ellis *architect*
Hoover, Betty-Bruce Howard *private school educator*
Howey, John Richard *architect*
Hubbell, David Smith *surgeon, educator*
Humphries, J. Bob *lawyer*
Hunter, Larry Lee *electrical engineer*
Ihde, Mary Katherine *mathematics educator*
Ingalls, Rick Lee *fundraising consulting executive*
Jablonski, Carol Jean *communication professional, educator*
Jacobs, Timothy Andrew *epidemiologist, international health consultant, medical missionary*
†Jenkins, Elizabeth A. *federal judge*
Jennewein, James Joseph *architect*
Johnson, Anthony O'Leary (Andy Johnson) *meteorologist, consultant*
Johnson, Ewell Calvin *research and engineering executive*
Johnson, James E. *airport executive*
Jones, John Arthur *lawyer*
Jreisat, Jamil Elias *public administration and political science educator, consultant*
Justice, Eunice McGhee *missionary, evangelist*
Kass, Emily *art museum administrator*
Kaufman, Ronald Paul *physician, school official*
Kaw, Autar Krishen *mechanical engineer, educator*
Kelly, Thomas Paine, Jr. *lawyer*
King, Jack Howell *transportation engineering executive*
Kovac, Michael G. *engineering educator*
Kovachevich, Elizabeth Anne *federal judge*
LaCasse, James Phillip *lawyer*
Lakdawala, Sharad R. *psychiatrist*
Lane, Robin *lawyer*
Leavengood, Victor Price *telephone company executive*
Levine, Jack Anton *lawyer*
†Liedke, Guy Arthur *public administrator*
Liller, Karen DeSafey *public health educator*
Lim, Daniel Van *microbiology educator*
Litschgi, A. Byrne *lawyer*
Locker, Raymond Duncan *editor*
Lockey, Richard Funk *allergist, educator*
Lowe, Peter Stephen *non-profit company executive*
Lozner, Eugene Leonard *internal medicine educator, consultant*
Luber, Amanda Kimmer *public relations executive, marketing professional*
Luddington, Betty Walles *library media specialist*
Lykes, Joseph T., III *investments manager*
Lyman, Gary Herbert *epidemiologist, cancer researcher, educator*
MacDonald, Thomas Cook, Jr. *lawyer, mediator*
Mahan, Charles Samuel *public health service officer*
Major, Jim *broadcasting executive*
Malone, John I. *pediatrics educator, biomedical researcher*
Mangiapane, Joseph Arthur *consulting company executive, applied mechanics consultant*
Manion, Beatrice (B.C. Manion) *journalist*
Martin, Gary Wayne *lawyer*
Matheny, Charles Woodburn, Jr. *retired army officer, retired civil engineer*
McAdams, John P. *lawyer*
Mc Alister, Linda Lopez *educator, philosopher*
McClurg, Douglas P. *lawyer*
McConnell, Joan Tronco *municipal government official*
McCook, Kathleen de la Peña *university educator*
†McCoun, Thomas B., III *federal judge*
McIntosh, Martha Ann *retired teacher, director of religious education*
McKay, Richard James *lawyer*
†McKinney, Patricia J. *automobile company executive*
McQuigg, John Dolph *lawyer*
†Meincke, John W. *career officer*
Mellish, Gordon Hartley *economist, educator*
Menendez, Manuel, Jr. *judge*
Merryday, Steven D. *federal judge*
Metcalf, Ralph *director sanitation department*
Michaels, John Patrick, Jr. *investment banker, media broker*
Miller, Bonnie Sewell *marketing professional, writer*
Miller, Charles Leslie *civil engineer, planner, consultant*
†Miller, Randy E. *journalism educator, writer*
Mitchell, Mozella Gordon *English language educator, minister*
Moreland, Don *protective services official*
Muroff, Lawrence Ross *nuclear medicine physician, educator*
Murtagh, Frederick Reed *neuroradiologist, educator*
Nagera, Humberto *psychiatrist, psychoanalyst, educator, author*
Nesmith, William Leonard *protective services official*
Neusner, Jacob *humanities and religious studies educator*
Nevsimal, Ervin L. *elementary education educator*
Nickerson, Hardy Otto *football player*
Nord, Walter Robert *business administration educator, researcher, consultant*
Noriega, Fernando, Jr. *municipal official*
Oehler, Richard Dale *lawyer*
Olson, John Karl *lawyer*
Olson, Robert Eugene *physician, biochemist, educator*
O'Neill, Albert Clarence, Jr. *lawyer*
Ortinau, David Joseph *marketing specialist, educator*
Pasetti, Louis Oscar *dentist*
Paskay, Alexander L. *federal judge, law educator*
Pekas, Bradley Scott *geological engineer, consultant*
Perret, Gerard Anthony, Jr. *orthodontist*
Pfeiffer, Eric Armin *psychiatrist, gerontologist*
Piper, John Richard *political science educator*
†Pizzo, Mark A. *federal judge*
Poe, William Frederick *insurance agency executive, former mayor*
Pollara, Bernard *immunologist, educator, pediatrician*
Posner, Gary Philip *physician, medical software company executive*
Powers, Pauline Smith *psychiatrist, educator, researcher*
Preto-Rodas, Richard A. *retired foreign language educator*
Price, Douglas Armstrong *chiropractor*
Purcell, Henry, III *real estate developer*
Reading, Anthony John *physician*
Reese-Brown, Brenda *primary education educator, mathematics specialist*
Roberson, Bruce H. *lawyer*
Roberts, Edwin Albert, Jr. *newspaper editor, journalist*
Robinson, John William, IV *lawyer*
Rogal, Philip James *physician*
Rosenkranz, Stanley William *lawyer*
Rowlands, David Thomas *pathology educator*
†Ruas, Ernesto Jose *plastic surgeon*
†Rubin, Steven J. *English studies educator, academic administrator*
Russell, Diane Elizabeth Henrikson *career counselor*
Ruth, Daniel John *journalist*
Sakiewicz, Nick *professional sports team executive*
Sanchez, Mary Anne *retired secondary school educator*
†Sanchez-Ramos, Juan R. *physician, medical educator*
†Sandstrom, James E. *military career officer*
Schine, Jerome Adrian *retired accountant*
Schmidt, Paul Joseph *physician, educator*
Schnitzlein, Harold Norman *anatomy educator*
Schonwetter, Ronald Scott *physician, educator*
†Schoomaker, Peter J. *military officer*
Schwenke, Roger Dean *lawyer*
Scott, Charles Francis *health facility administrator*
†Sergay, Stephen Michael *neurologist*
†Shawkey, Gary Alan *manufacturing executive, consultant*
Sheridan, Richard *neonatologist*
Shevy, Allen Earl, Jr. *publishing executive*
Shons, Alan Rance *plastic surgeon, educator*
Siegel, Richard Lawrence *allergist, immunologist, pediatrician*
Sigety, Charles Birge *investment company executive*
Silbiger, Martin L. *radiologist, medical educator, college dean*

Silver, Paul Robert *marketing executive, consultant*
Sinnott, John Thomas *internist, educator*
Smith, Mark A. *physician, educator*
Smith, W. Gordon *magazine editor*
Snyder, James Robert *professional sports executive*
Sparkman, Steven Leonard *lawyer*
Spellacy, William Nelson *obstetrician, gynecologist, educator*
Stallings, (Charles) Norman *lawyer*
Steiner, Geoffrey Blake *lawyer*
Stephens, Robert David *environmental engineering executive*
Stiles, Mary Ann *lawyer, author, lobbyist*
Streeter, Richard Barry *academic official*
Studer, William Allen *county official*
Tapp, Mamie Pearl *educational association administration*
Tatum, William Otis, IV *neurologist*
Taub, Theodore Calvin *lawyer*
Taylor, Austin Randall *sales executive*
Teblum, Gary Ira *lawyer*
Tewksbury, Russell Baird *Internet and new media consultant, educator*
Thelen, Gil *newspaper editor*
Theodoropoulos, Demetrios *medical geneticist, allergist*
Thomas, Wayne Lee *lawyer*
†Thompson, Sandra Jean *writer, editor*
Trunnell, Thomas Newton *dermatologist*
Tully, Darrow *newspaper publisher*
Tykot, Robert Howard *social sciences educator, archaeologist*
Vanden, Harry Edwin *political science educator*
Vanderburg, Paul Stacey *insurance executive, consultant*
Veasey, Byron Keith *information systems consultant*
Wade, Thomas Edward *electrical engineering educator, university research administrator*
Wagner, Frederick William (Bill Wagner) *lawyer*
Waller, Edward Martin, Jr. *lawyer*
Walling, Arthur Knight *orthopedist*
Watkins, Joan Marie *osteopath, occupational medicine physician*
Watson, Roberta Casper *lawyer*
Weiner, Irving Bernard *psychologist*
Wells, Karen Elaine *plastic surgeon, educator*
Whatley, Jacqueline Beltram *lawyer*
White, Nancy G. *journalism educator*
Williams, Thomas Arthur *biomedical computing consultant, psychiatrist*
Williams, Yvonne G. *corporate trainer*
Wilson, Charles R. *lawyer*
†Wilson, Thomas G. *federal judge*
Witwer, Bruce *newspaper editor*
Wyman, Richard Thomas *information services consultant*
Young, Gwynne A. *lawyer*
Zelinski, Joseph John *engineering educator, consultant*

Tarpon Springs
Byrne, Richard Hill *counselor, educator*
Crismond, Linda Fry *public relations executive*
Georgiou, Ruth Schwab *retired social worker*
Jackel, Simon Samuel *food products company executive*
Mueller, Willys Francis, Jr. *retired pathologist*
Padberg, Daniel Ivan *agricultural economics educator, researcher*
Parks, Karl Eaton, Jr. *publisher*
Wilson, Robert William *aerospace/defense systems company executive*

Tavernier
Lupino, James Samuel *lawyer*

Temple Terrace
DeHainaut, Raymond Kirk *international studies educator*
Kashdin, Gladys Shafran *painter, educator*
Rink, Wesley Winfred *banker*
Schmaltz, Lawrence Gerard *engineer, consultant*
†Scruggs, Charles Eugene *language linguistics educator*

Tequesta
Holmes, Melvin Almont *insurance company executive*
Peterson, James Robert *retired writing instrument manufacturing executive*
†Ragno, Nancy Nickell *educational writer*
Seaman, William Bernard *physician, radiology educator*
Swets, John Arthur *psychologist, researcher*
Turrell, Richard Horton, Sr. *retired banker*
Vollmer, James E. *high technology management executive*

Tierra Verde
Gaffney, Thomas Francis *investment company executive*
Schmitz, Dolores Jean *primary education educator*

Titusville
Bartley, Larry Durand *computer systems planner, mayor*
Bush, Patricia Eileen *education educator*
Furci, Joan Gelormino *early childhood education educator*
Hardister, Darrell Edward *insurance executive*
Hartung, Patricia McEntee *therapist*
Linscott, Jacqueline C. *education consultant, retired educator*
Shafer, Lorene Leggitt *real esate agent*

Treasure Island
Dunn, Craig Andrew *entertainer, conductor, composer, educator*
Foote, Frances Catherine *association executive, living trust consultant*
Williams, Bonnie Lee *city official*

Tyndall AFB
†Arnold, Larry K. *major general United States Air Force*
†Hunter, James D. (Jim) *brigadier general Canadian Air Force*
†Rubus, Gary M. *career officer*
†Stromquist, Kenneth J., Jr. *brigadier general United States Air Force*

Valrico
Benjamin, Sheila Pauletta *secondary education educator*
Dillard, Nancy Rose *naval officer*
Foster, Michael Paul *sales and marketing representative*
Parrado, Peter Joseph *real estate executive*

Venice
Appel, Wallace Henry *retired industrial designer*
Baga, Margaret Fitzpatrick *nurse, medical office manager*
Barritt, Evelyn Ruth Berryman *nurse, educator, university dean*
Berger, Bernard Ben *environmental and civil engineer, former educator and public health officer*
Bluhm, Barbara Jean *communications agency executive*
Buckley, John William *financial company executive*
Concordia, Charles *consulting engineer*
Corrigan, William Thomas *retired broadcast news executive*
Freibott, George August *physician, chemist, priest*
Hackett, Edward Vincent *investment research company executive*
Hays, Herschel Martin *electrical engineer*
Hrachovina, Frederick Vincent *osteopathic physician and surgeon*
Jamrich, John Xavier *retired university administrator*
Leidheiser, Henry, Jr. *retired chemistry educator, consultant*
†Liang, Daniel S. *surgeon*
McEntee, Robert Edward *management consultant*
Miller, Allan John *lawyer*
Myers, Virginia Lou *education educator*
†Nevins, John J. *bishop*
Ogan, Russell Griffith *business executive, retired air force officer*
O'Keefe, Robert James *retired banker*
†Pike, Nancy M. *librarian*
Przemieniecki, Janusz Stanislaw *engineering executive, former government senior executive and college dean*
†Ross, Robert Roy, Jr. *urologic surgeon*
Shaw, Bryce Robert *author*
Thomas, David Ansell *retired university dean*
Thomas, Terence Patrick *writer, researcher, electronics design engineer*
Torrey, Richard Frank *utility executive*
Williams, Justin *retired government official*
Xanthopoulos, Philip, Sr. *brokerage house executive*

Vero Beach
Ahrens, William Henry *architect*
Allik, Michael *diversified industry executive*
Anderson, Rudolph J., Jr. *lawyer*
Baker, Richard H. *retired geneticist, educator*
Binney, Jan Jarrell *publishing executive*
Burdette, Carol Janice *gerontology nursing administrator*
Burton, Arthur Henry, Jr. *insurance company executive*
Cartwright, Alton Stuart *electrical manufacturing company executive*
Christy, Nicholas Pierson *physician*
Clawson, John Addison *financier, investor*
Cochrane, William Henry *municipal administration executive*
Cooke, Robert Edmond *physician, educator, former college president*
Danforth, Arthur Edwards *finance executive*
†Duncan, Joseph Wayman *business economist*
Fetter, Robert Barclay *retired administrative sciences educator*
Fisher, Andrew *management consultant*
Furrer, John Rudolf *retired manufacturing business executive*
Gibson, James Elliott *architect*
Glassmeyer, Edward *investment banker*
Goff, Michael Harper *retired lawyer*
Grobman, Arnold Brams *retired biology educator and academic administrator*
Grobman, Hulda Gross (Mrs. Arnold B. Grobman) *retired health sciences educator*
Hubner, Robert Wilmore *retired business machines company executive, consultant*
Janicki, Robert Stephen *retired pharmaceutical company executive*
Koontz, Alfred Joseph, Jr. *financial and operating management executive, consultant*
Mackall, Laidler Bowie *lawyer*
MacTaggart, Barry *retired corporate executive*
McCauley, James Kelly, Jr. *chemical engineer*
McCrystal, Ann Marie *community health nurse, administrator*
McGee, Humphrey Glenn *architect*
McNamara, John J(oseph) *advertising executive, writer*
Menk, Carl William *executive search company executive*
Mosier, William Arthur *psychologist, medical educator, medical administrator*
Nichols, Carl Wheeler *retired advertising agency executive*
Parkyn, John William *editor, writer*
Reed, Sherman Kennedy *chemical consultant*
Riefler, Donald Brown *financial consultant*
Ritterhoff, C(harles) William *retired steel company executive*
Schmidt, Ted *talent agent, entertainment producer*
Schulman, Harold *obstetrician, gynecologist, perinatologist*
Schwarz, Berthold Eric *psychiatrist*
†Scott, Charlotte Patricia *artist*
Sheehan, Charles Vincent *investment banker*
Thomas, Milton John, Jr. *economist*
Thompson, William David *investment banking executive*
Torres, Terry Terol *mechanical engineer, general contractor*
Tullis, Chaillé Handy *interior designer, volunteer*
Whitney, J. Lee *home health care administrator, retired*
Wiegner, Edward Alex *multi-industry executive*
Wilcox, Harry Wilbur, Jr. *retired corporate executive*
Wilson, Robert James Montgomery *investment company executive*

Village Of Golf
Bates, Edward Brill *retired insurance company executive*
Boer, F. Peter *chemical company executive*

Wellington
Beshears, Charles Daniel *insurance executive, retired*
†Elmquist, John Gunnar *plastic surgeon, general surgeon*
Knudsen, Raymond Barnett *clergyman, association executive, author*
Kravetz, Cheryl DuPree *reporter*
McGee, Lynne Kalavsky *principal*
Reddy, Vardhan Jonnala *surgeon*

Wesley Chapel
Donovan, Brian Joseph *oil industry executive*
Holloway, Marvin Lawrence *retired automobile club executive, rancher, vintager*
Mendelsohn, Louis Benjamin *financial analyst*

West Melbourne
Fetner, Suzanne *small business owner*
Robsman, Mary Louise *education educator*

West Palm Beach
Aaron, M. Robert *electrical engineer*
Abdo, Deborah J. *school administrator*
Abernathy, Barbara Eubanks *counselor*
Ackerman, Paul Adam *pharmacist*
Alea, Jorge Antonio *physician*
Alimanestianu, Calin *retired hotel consultant*
Aron, Jerry E. *lawyer*
Atkinson, Regina Elizabeth *medical social worker*
Baker, Bernard Robert, II *lawyer*
Barnhart, Forrest Gregory *lawyer*
Beall, Kenneth Sutter, Jr. *lawyer*
Bohn, Barbara Ann *laboratory director*
Borchers, Karen Lily *museum administrator*
Brumback, Clarence Landen *physician*
Chopin, Susan Gardiner *lawyer*
Clark, Claudia Pia *preschool administrator*
†Clark, David William *lawyer, councilman*
Corts, Paul Richard *college president*
Cox-Gerlock, Barbara *academic administrator, consultant*
Craft, Jerome Walter *plastic surgeon, health facility administrator*
D'Angelo, Andrew William *retired civil engineer*
Davis, Paul B. *mechanical engineer, civil engineer, retired*
Davis, Shirley Harriet *social worker, editor*
DeMoss, Nancy *foundation administrator*
Dunston, Leigh Everett *lawyer*
Engh, Fredric Charles *educational association administrator*
Eppley, Roland Raymond, Jr. *retired financial services executive*
Eschbach, Jesse Ernest *federal judge*
Fairbanks, Richard Monroe *broadcasting company executive*
Flanagan, L. Martin *lawyer*
Freudenthal, Ralph Ira *toxicology consultant*
†Friedman, Steven H. *federal judge*
Gillette, Frank C., Jr. *mechanical engineer*
Glinski, Helen Elizabeth *operating room nurse*
Goetz, Cecelia Helen *lawyer, retired judge*
Grantham, Kirk Pinkerton *lawyer, insurance company executive*
Gronlund, Robert B. *art collector, fund raising consultant*
†Hale, Marie Stoner *artistic director*
Herring, Grover Cleveland *lawyer*
Hill, Thomas William, Jr. *lawyer, educator*
Holloway, Edward Olin *human services manager*
Holt, Richard Duane *lawyer*
Hurley, Daniel T. K. *federal judge*
Jenkins, Stanley Michael *stockbroker*
Johnston, Harry A., II *former congressman*
Kamen, Michael Andrew *lawyer*
Kapnick, S. Jason *oncologist*
Khouri, George George *ophthalmologist*
Koch, William I. *energy company executive*
Laura, Robert Anthony *coastal engineer, consultant*
Layman, David Michael *lawyer*
Livingstone, John Leslie *accountant, management consultant, business economist, educator*
McAfee, William James *lawyer*
McCluskey, Neil Gerard *gerontologist, educator, literary agent*
Mendelow, Gary N. *physician, emergency consultant*
Montgomery, Robert Morel, Jr. *lawyer*
Moore, George Crawford Jackson *lawyer*
Mrachek, Lorin Louis *lawyer*
Nelson, Richard Henry *manufacturing company executive*
Newmark, Emanuel *ophthalmologist*
Nolan, Richard Thomas *clergyman, educator*
O'Flarity, James P. *lawyer*
O'Hara, Thomas Patrick *managing editor*
Olsak, Ivan Karel *civil engineer*
Oppenheim, Justin Sable *business executive*
Orlovsky, Donald Albert *lawyer*
Orr-Cahall, Christina *art museum director, art historian*
Paine, James Carriger *federal judge*
Palen, Frank Simon *lawyer*
Passy, Charles *arts critic*
Player, Gary Jim *professional golfer, businessman, golf course designer*
Pottash, A. Carter *psychiatrist, hospital executive*
Rafaidus, David Martin *health and human services planner*
Robertson, Sara Stewart *portfolio manager*
Robinson, Raymond Edwin *musician, music educator, writer*
Ronan, William John *management consultant*
Royce, Raymond Watson *lawyer, rancher, citrus grower*
Ryskamp, Kenneth Lee *federal judge*
Saraf, Shevach *electronics executive*
Sears, Edward Milner, Jr. *newspaper editor*
Sklar, William Paul *lawyer, educator*
Smith, Betsy Keiser *telecommunications company executive*
Smith, David Shiverick *lawyer, former ambassador*
†Smith, Pamela Sandlian *library director*
Stauderman, Bruce Ford *advertising executive, writer*
Stern, Harold Peter *business executive*
Storch, Barbara Jean Cohen *librarian*
Sturrock, Thomas Tracy *botany educator, horticulturist*
†Susman, Edward S. *freelance writer*
Tanzer, Jed Samuel *lawyer, financial consultant*
Taylor Dye, Judy Angie *engineer, consultant*
Terwillegar, Jane Cusack *librarian, educator*
Thomashow, Steven Roy *military officer, intelligence officer*
Turner, Arthur Edward *college administrator*
Vecellio, Leo Arthur, Jr. *construction company executive*
Vitunac, Ann E. *judge*
Wagner, Arthur Ward, Jr. *lawyer*
Wisnicki, Jeffrey Leonard *plastic surgeon*
Witt, Gerhardt Meyer *hydrogeologist*
Wright, Donald Conway *editorial cartoonist*
Zisson, James Stern *investment management consultant*

Weston
Atlas, David *meteorologist, research scientist*
Austin, Grant William *real estate appraiser*
Boles, Eric Paul *staffing company executive*
Casey, George Edward, Jr. *construction executive*
Gordon, Lori Heyman *psychotherapist, author, educator*
Holtzman, Gary Yale *administrative and financial executive*
Randolph, Jennings, Jr. (Jay Randolph) *sportscaster*

Wildwood
†Terry, Ernest Lee *clergyman, international evangelist*

Wilton Manors
Daly, Susan Mary *lawyer*

Windermere
Hylton, Hannelore Menke *retired manufacturing executive*

Winter Garden
Clifford, Margaret Louise *psychologist*
Earls, Irene Anne *art history educator*

Winter Haven
Burns, Arthur Lee *architect*
†Bybee, Charles Forrest *writer, poet*
Chase, Lucius Peter *lawyer, retired corporate executive*
Clement, Elizabeth Stewart *artist*
Gage, Robert Clifford *minister*
Gobie, Henry Macaulay *philatelic researcher, retired postal executive*
Honer, Richard Joseph *surgeon*
Leedy, Gene Robert *architect*
Mc Anulty, Mary Catherine Cramer *retired principal, educator*
O'Connor, R. D. *retired health care executive*
Peck, Maryly VanLeer *college president, headmaster, chemical engineer*
Porter, Howard Leonard, III *health and education policy consultant*
Rossbacher, John Robert *retired insurance broker, musician, writer*
Small, Norman Morton *speech and humanities educator, theater producer*
Trickett, Jennifer Beatrice *medical and surgical nurse*
Turnquist, Donald Keith *orthodontist*
West, Mary Elizabeth *psychiatric management professional*

Winter Park
Arman Gelenbe, Deniz *concert pianist*
Benedict, Dorothy Jones *genealogist, researcher*
Bevc, Carol-Lynn Anne *financial officer*
Blair, Mardian John *hospital management executive*
Bornstein, Rita *academic administrator*
Brooten, Kenneth Edward, Jr. *lawyer*
Builder, J. Lindsay, Jr. *lawyer*
Bush-Counts, Christine Gay *dental hygienist*
Conrad, Judy L. *insurance company executive*
Coulter, Fredrik Vladimir *accountant, consultant*
DiBacco, Richard Paul *vocational case manager*
Douglas, Kathleen Mary Harrigan *psychotherapist, educator*
Fluno, John Arthur *entomologist, consultant*
Fowler, Mark Stapleton *lawyer, corporation counsel*
Granzig, William Walker *clinical sexologist, educator*
Hill, Elizabeth Starr *writer*
Johannes, Virgil Ivancich *electrical engineer*
Kerr, James Wilson *engineer*
Kost, Wayne L. *business executive*
Kraft, Kenneth Houston, Jr. *insurance agency executive*
Markland, Barbara Carolyn *administrative assistant*
Mason, Aimee Hunnicutt Romberger *retired philosophy and humanities educator*
McDowell, Annie R. *retired counselor*
McKean, Thomas Wayne *dentist, retired naval officer*
Mica, John L. *congressman*
Myers, Norman Lewis *fund development consultant*
Olsson, Nils William *former association executive*
Pineless, Hal Steven *neurologist*
Plane, Donald Ray *management science educator*
Rogers, Rutherford David *librarian*
Ruggiero, Laurence Joseph *museum director*
Seymour, Thaddeus *English educator*
Spake, Ned Bernarr *energy company executive*
Starr, Martin Kenneth *management educator*
Strawn, Frances Freeland *real estate executive*
Swan, Richard Gordon *retired mathematics educator*
Therrien, Francois Xavier, Jr. *business and tax consultant*
Velazquez, Anabel *medical services executive*
Wisler, Willard Eugene *retired health care management executive*

Winter Springs
San Miguel, Manuel *painter, historian, composer, poet*
San Miguel, Sandra Bonilla *social worker*
Stone, George Francis, III *army officer*

Yalaha
Brown, Paula Kinney *heating and air conditioning contractor*

Yulee
†Citino, Scott Bradley *wildlife veterinarian*

Zephyrhills
Martindale, Carla Joy *librarian*
†McGavern, Melanie Lynn *veterinarian*
Powell, David Thomas, Jr. *retired association administrator*

GEORGIA

Adel
Darby, Marianne Talley *elementary school educator*

Adrian
McCord, James Richard, III *chemical engineer, mathematician*

Albany
Barnes, David Benton *school psychologist*
Carter-Wommack, Barbara *retired educator*

Ezeamii, Hyacinth Chinedum public administration educator
†Goad, Danny Harlan industrial engineer
†Hodge, Richard L. federal judge
†Hollis, Lois B. history and political science educator
Keith, Carolyn Austin secondary school counselor
Marbury, Ritchey McGuire, III engineering executive, surveyor
McKissock, Gary Samuel career officer
McManus, James William chemist, researcher
Paschal, James Alphonso counselor, educator secondary school
Peach, Paul E. physician, medical facility administrator
Sands, W. Louis federal judge

Alpharetta
Adams, Rex M. telecommunications executive
Ashley, John Bryan software executive, management consultant
Balows, Albert microbiologist, educator
Bobo, Genelle Tant (Nell Bobo) office administrator
Brands, James Edwin finance executive
Butts, Carol Henderson personnel consultant
Clary, Ronald Gordon insurance agency executive
Desai, Hiren D. software engineer
Dovey, Laurie Lee magazine editor, writer, photographer
Edmondson, Damon Wayne financial analyst, consultant
Esher, Brian Richard environmental company executive
Eubanks, Omer Lafayette data communications consultant, systems engineer
Fowler, Vivian Delores insurance company executive
Friedman, Lee Gary network media solutions architect
Johnson, Roger Warren chemical engineer
Kurtz, Robert Arthur finance company executive
Mock, Melinda Smith orthopedic nurse specialist, consultant
Needle, Charles Richard photographer
Rettig, Terry veterinarian, wildlife consultant
Watts, William David corporate executive, business owner
Wise, Steven Lanier lawyer, clergyman
Wu, Wayne Wen-Yau artist
Zimmermann, John financial consultant

Americus
Bearden, Denise G(odwin) humanities educator, secondary education educator
Capitan, William Harry university president emeritus
Fuller, Millard Dean charitable organization executive, lawyer
Hooks, George Bardin state senator, insurance and real estate company executive
Isaacs, Harold history educator
McGrady, Clyde A. secondary school principal
Mecke, William Moyn public affairs consultant
Nichols, Harold James university dean
Stanford, Henry King college president
Worrell, Billy Frank health facility administrator

Andersonville
Boyles, Frederick Holdren historian

Aragon
Hardin, Sherrie Ann Asfoury commercial photographer

Athens
Adams, Michael Fred university president, political communications specialist
Agee, Warren Kendall journalism educator
Agosin, Moises Kankolsky zoology educator
Albersheim, Peter biology educator
Allinger, Norman Louis chemistry educator
Anderson, Wyatt Wheaton biology educator
Andrews, Grover Jene adult education educator, administrator
Arabnia, Hamid Reza computer scientist, educator
Avise, John Charles geneticist, educator
Baile, Clifton A. biologist, researcher
Bamber, Linda Smith accounting educator
Beaird, James Ralph law educator, dean
Black, Clanton Candler, Jr. biochemistry educator, researcher
Boudinot, Frank Douglas pharmaceutics educator
Clements, Robert Donald sculptor
Clute, Robert Eugene political and social science educator
Coley, Linda Marie secondary school educator
Corey, Stephen Dale magazine editor, poet, educator
Crowley, John Francis, III university dean
Crowther, Ann Rollins dean, political science educator
Darvill, Alan G. biochemist, botanist, educator
DerVartanian, Daniel Vartan biochemistry educator
DeZurko, Edward Robert retired art educator
Diaz, Manuel university tennis coach
Douglas, Dwight Oliver university administrator
†Dowling, John Clarkson educator
Dunn, Delmer Delano political science educator
Edison, Diane artist, educator, administrator
Ellington, Charles Ronald lawyer, educator
Eriksson, Karl-Erik Lennart biochemist, educator
Feldman, Edmund Burke art critic
Fincher, Cameron Lane education educator
Fink, Conrad Charles journalism educator, communications consultant
†Franklin, Rosemary F. English educator
Freer, Coburn English language educator
Garbin, Albeno Patrick sociology educator
Giles, Norman Henry educator, geneticist
Hellerstein, Nina Salant French literature and language educator
Herbert, James Arthur artist, filmmaker
Hester, Albert Lee retired journalism educator
Hildebrand, Don science foundation executive
Hillenbrand, Martin Joseph diplomat, educator
Hofer, Charles Warren strategic management, entrepreneurship educator, consultant
Holder, Howard Randolph, Sr. broadcasting company executive
Houser, Ronald Edward lawyer, mediator
Huszagh, Fredrick Wickett lawyer, educator, information management company executive
Hynds, Ernest journalism educator
Jackson, Thomas Harold, Jr. public relations administrator
Johnson, Michael Kenneth chemistry educator
†Jones, Betty Kay academic administrator
Kamerschen, David Roy economist, educator
Kaufman, Glen Frank art educator, artist
Kent, Robert B. artist, educator
Kretzschmar, William Addison, Jr. English language educator
Landau, David Paul physics educator
Landers, Andy head coach women's basketball
Langdale, George Wilfred soil scientist, researcher
†Larson, Edward John law educator, lawyer, historian
Law, S. Edward engineering educator, researcher
Lawson, Bonnie Hulsey retired psychotherapist
Levine, David Lawrence social work educator
Logan, Dayton Norris retired minister
Mamatey, Victor Samuel history educator
Marable, Robert Blane secondary education agriculture educator
Marks, Henry Lewis poultry scientist
McCutcheon, Steven Clifton environmental engineer, hydrologist
Miller, Herbert Elmer accountant
Miller, Lois Kathryn virology educator
Miller, Ronald Baxter English language educator, author
Moore, Rayburn Sabatzky American literature educator
Morrison, Darrel Gene landscape architecture educator
†Morrow, John H., Jr. history educator
Nelson, Stuart Owen agricultural engineer, researcher, educator
Nute, Donald E., Jr. philosophy educator
Olsen, Richard James artist, art educator
O'Toole, Laurence Joseph political science educator, researcher
Paul, William Dewitt, Jr. artist, educator, photographer, museum director
Pavlik, William Bruce psychologist, educator
Payne, William Jackson microbiologist, educator
Pelletier, S. William chemistry educator
Pettis, Victoria Elaine secondary school educator
Plummer, Gayther L(ynn) climatologist, ecologist, researcher
Posey, Loran Michael pharmacist, editor
Potter, William Gray, Jr. library director
Puckett, Elizabeth Ann law librarian, law educator
Reid, Leonard N. academic administrator
Rosen, Sidney psychologist
Russell, J. Thomas dean
†Sachs, Margarget V. law educator
Schaefer, Henry Frederick, III chemistry educator
Shaw, James Scott astronomy educator
Smagorinsky, Peter education educator
Speering, Robin educator, computer specialist
Spurgeon, Edward Dutcher law educator
Staub, August William drama educator, theatrical producer, director
Sumner, Malcom Edward agronomist, educator
Swayne, David Eugene avian pathologist, researcher
Teague, Frances Nicol English language educator
Tesser, Abraham social psychologist
Thomas, Howard Lamar chef, consultant, writer
Tollner, Ernest William agricultural engineering educator, agricultural radiology consultant
Tyler, David Earl veterinary medical educator
Wallace, Jeff tennis coach
West, Marsha elementary school educator
Yamaguchi, Yukio chemistry research scientist
Yegidis, Bonnie Lee social work educator, university dean
Yen, William Mao-Shung physicist
Younts, Sanford Eugene university administrator
Zinkhan, George Martin, III marketing educator

Atlanta
Aaberg, Thomas Marshall, Sr. academic administrator, ophthalmology educator
Aaron, Henry L. (Hank Aaron) professional baseball team executive
Abdel-Khalik, Said Ibrahim nuclear and mechanical engineering educator
Abrams, Bernard William construction manufacturing and property development executive
Abrams, Edward Marvin construction company executive
Abrams, Harold Eugene lawyer
Ackerman, F. Duane utility company executive
Aczel, Mollie Goodman educational administrator
†Adams, Corey Emile planner, analyst
Adams, David Porterfield, III business appraiser
Affonso, Dyanne D. dean, nursing educator
†Ahlquist, Jeffrey strategy consultant
Aldridge, John lawyer
Alexander, Cecil Abraham college official, architect, consultant
Alexander, Kent B. lawyer
Alexander, Miles Jordan lawyer
Alexander, Robert Wayne medical educator
Allen, Ivan, Jr. office products company owner
†Allen, Natalie cable news anchor
Ambrose, Samuel Sheridan, Jr. urologist
Ames, William Francis mathematician, educator
Anderson, Ray C. carpet company executive
†Anthony, Jacquelyn A. political scientist, educator
Arani, Ardy A. professional sports marketing executive, lawyer
Archard, Douglas Bruce foreign service officer
Armanios, Erian Abdelmessih aerospace engineer, educator
Ashby, Eugene Christopher chemistry educator
Atkinson, A. Kelley insurance company executive
Attridge, Richard Byron lawyer
Austin, Judy Essary scriptwriter
Averitt, Richard Garland, III financial services company executive
Axon, Michael education association field representative
Babcock, Peter Heartz professional sports executive
Bacon, Louis Albert retired consulting civil engineer
Bahl, Roy Winford economist, educator, consultant
Bailey, Joy Hafner counselor, educator
Bainbridge, Frederick Freeman, III architect
Bakay, Roy Arpad Earle neurosurgeon, educator
Baker, Anita Diane lawyer
Baker, Edward L., Jr. physician, science facility executive
Baker, Jerry Herbert executive search consultant
Baker, Thurbert E. state attorney general
Baldwin, Daniel Flanagan mechanical engineer, researcher, educator
Bales, Virginia Shankle health administration
Ballard, Wiley Perry III hematologist, oncologist
Bankoff, Joseph R. lawyer
Barker, William Daniel hospital administrator
Barkoff, Rupert Mitchell lawyer
Barksdale, Richard Dillon civil engineer, educator
Barnes, Harry G., Jr. human rights activist, conflict resolution specialist, retired ambassador
Barnett, Crawford Fannin, Jr. internist, educator, cardiologist, travel medicine specialist
Barron, Patrick Kenneth bank executive
Bassett, Peter Q. lawyer
Batson, Richard Neal lawyer
Baum, Stanley M. lawyer
Baylor, Don Edward professional baseball manager
†Beegle, Philip H., Jr. plastic and reconstructive surgeon
Bell, Griffin B. lawyer, former attorney general
Bell, Jack Atkins percussionist, educator
Bellamy, Walter Jones retired basketball player
Bellanca, Joseph Paul engineering construction executive
Benario, Herbert William classics educator
Benatar, Leo packaging company executive
Benham, Robert state supreme court justice
Bennett, Jay D. lawyer
Benston, George James accountant, economist
Berenato, Agnus McGlade women's basketball coach
Bergonzi, Al company executive
Bevington, E(dmund) Milton electrical machinery manufacturing company executive
Bevington, Paula Lawton facilities management consulting executive
Bibb, Daniel Roland antique painting restorer and conservator
Bickerton, Jane Elizabeth university research coordinator
Bihary, Joyce federal judge
Billington, Barry E. lawyer
Birch, Stanley Francis, Jr. federal judge
Bird, Francis Marion, Jr. lawyer
Bird, Wendell Raleigh lawyer
Birdsong, Alta Marie volunteer
Bisher, James Furman journalist, author
Black, Kenneth, Jr. retired insurance executive and educator, author
Blackburn, William Stanley lawyer
Blackstock, Jerry B. lawyer
Blackwell, Michael Sidney broker, financial services executive
†Blank, Arthur M. home and lumber retail chain executive
Blankenship, Samuel Max physicist
†Blaylock, Mookie (Daron Oshay Blaylock) professional basketball player
†Bledsoe, Susan McCallum operations manager, stockbroker
Bloodworth, A(lbert) W(illiam) Franklin lawyer
†Blount, Benroe Wayne physician
Blumenthal, Anna Catherine English educator
Boeke, Eugene H., Jr. construction executive
Boisseau, Richard Robert lawyer
Bolch, Carl Edward, Jr. corporation executive, lawyer
Boman, John Harris, Jr. retired lawyer
Bonds, John Wilfred, Jr. lawyer
Bondurant, Emmet Jopling, II lawyer
Boone, Bret Robert professional baseball player
Booth, Gordon Dean, Jr. lawyer
Bourne, Henry Clark, Jr. electrical engineering educator, former academic official
Bowden, Henry Lumpkin, Jr. lawyer
Bowers, Patricia Newsome communications executive
Boyd, Kenneth Wade publishing company executive, consultant
Boyle, Robert Daniel management consultant, program management and business process reengineering
Bradley, William Hampton lawyer
Brady, Kimberly Ann editorial director
Bragdon, Katherine McCoy urban planner, civilian military employee
Brandenburg, David Saul gastroenterologist, educator
Brandt, Gene Stuart fundraising consultant
Brannon, Lester Travis, Jr. lawyer
Braswell, Cruse C., Jr. public relations executive
Bratton, James Henry, Jr. lawyer
Brecher, Armin G. lawyer
Bridgewater, Herbert Jeremiah, Jr. radio host
Bright, David Forbes academic administrator, classics and comparative literature educator
†Brill, Gerrilyn G. federal judge
†Brizendine, Robert E. federal judge
Brooks, David William farmer cooperative executive
Brooks, James Joe, III accountant
Brooks, Jeffrey Martin marketing and sales executive
Broome, Claire Veronica epidemiologist, researcher
Brothers, June Esternaux Scott forest products company executive
Brown, John Robert lawyer, priest, philanthropist
Brown, Lorene B(yron) library educator, educational administrator
Brown, Sarah M. artist, gallery owner, educator, publisher
Brown-Olmstead, Amanda public relations executive
†Bruckner, William J. lawyer
Buck, Lee Albert retired insurance company executive, evangelist
Bump, Gerald Jack executive recruiter
Buoch, William Thomas corporate executive
Burge, William Lee retired business information executive
Burgess, Chester Francis, III journalist, television producer
Burke, William A. broadcast executive
Burns, Thomas Samuel history educator
Bush, John Kendall management consultant
Butte, Anthony Jeffrey healthcare executive
†Byington, William W., Jr. federal judge
Byrne, Granville Bland, III lawyer
Cabey, Alfred Arthur, Jr. business owner, publisher
Cadenhead, Alfred Paul lawyer
Calabria, Deb Flanagan playwright, director
Calise, Anthony John aerospace engineering educator
Callahan, Harry Morey photographer
Callner, Bruce Warren lawyer
Cameron, Rondo economic history educator
Camp, Jack Tarpley, Jr. federal judge
Campbell, Bill mayor
Campbell, Colin McLeod journalist
Campbell, Pollyann S. lawyer
Candler, John Slaughter, II retired lawyer
Capone, Antonio psychiatrist
Capron, John M. lawyer
Carey, Gerald John, Jr. research institute director, former air force officer
Cargill, Robert Mason lawyer
Carley, George H. state supreme court justice
Carlisle, Patricia Kinley mortgage company executive, paralegal
Carlos, Michael C. wine, spirits and linen service wholesale executive
Carlson, Robert Lee engineering educator
Carnes, Julie Elizabeth federal judge
Carson, Christopher Leonard lawyer
Carter, Jimmy (James Earl Carter, Jr.) former President of United States
Casarella, William Joseph physician
Cavallaro, Joseph John microbiologist
Cavin, Kristine Smith lawyer
†Chace, William M. university executive
Chace, William Murdough university administrator
Chambers, Anne Cox newspaper executive, former diplomat
Chambers, Robert William financial company executive
Champion, Charles Howell, Jr. retired army officer
Chandler, Robert Charles healthcare consultant
Chapman, Hugh McMaster banker
Chapman, Paul H. author
†Chapman, William S. state agency administrator
Chasen, Sylvan Herbert computer applications consultant, investment advisor
Cheatham, Richard Reed lawyer
†Chen, Joie cable news anchor
Chilivis, Nickolas Peter lawyer
Chilton, Horace Thomas pipeline company executive
Chisholm, Tommy lawyer, utility company executive
Choa, Walter Kong technical service professional
†Chopp, Rebecca S. provost
†Chumbley, Robert Edward artistic director
Clarke, Thomas Hal lawyer
Clements, James David retired psychiatry educator, physician
Clemons, Julie Payne telephone company manager
Clifton, David Samuel, Jr. research executive, economist
Clough, Gerald Wayne academic administrator
Cohen, Ezra Harry lawyer
Cohen, George Leon lawyer
Cohen, N. Jerold lawyer
Cohn, Bob public relations executive
Cole, Johnnetta Betsch university president emeritus, educator
†Cole, Robert S. hotel executive
Cole, Thomas Winston, Jr. chancellor, college president, chemist
Coleman, David Michael religious organization executive
Collier, Diana Gordon publishing executive
Collins, Steven M. lawyer
Compans, Richard W. microbiology educator
Comstock, Robert Donald, Jr. real estate executive
Cone, Frances McFadden data processing consultant
Connelly, Terrence John, Sr. television station executive
Connor, Charles William airline pilot
Cook, Christopher Dixon communications company executive
Cook, Philip Carter lawyer
Cooper, Clarence federal judge
Cooper, Frederick Eansor lawyer
Cooper, Gerald Rice clinical pathologist
Cooper, James Russell retired law educator
Cooper, Jerome Maurice architect
Cooper, Thomas Luther retired printing company executive
Copeland, John Alexander, III physicist
Copen, Melvyn Robert management educator, university administrator
Cornell, John Robert lawyer
Cornwell, William John lawyer
Corr, James Vanis furniture manufacturing executive, investor, lawyer, accountant
Correll, Alston Dayton, Jr. forest products company executive
†Cossack, Roger newscaster
†Cotton, Stacey W. federal judge
†Cousins, William Luke transportation administrator
Cox, Bobby (Robert Joe Cox) professional baseball manager
†Cox, Cathy state official
Cramer, Howard Ross geologist, environmental consultant
†Cravey, Pamela J. librarian
Cremins, Bobby college basketball coach
Crews, William Edwin lawyer
Croft, Terrence Lee lawyer
Crutchfield, Carolyn Ann physical therapy educator
Cupp, Robert Erhard golf course architect, land use planner
Curran, Christopher economics educator
Curran, James W. epidemiologist, educator, academic administrator
Curry, Toni Griffin counseling center executive, consultant
Curtis, Philip Kerry real estate developer
Curtiss, Jeffery Steven organizational development executive
Cutshaw, Kenneth Andrew lawyer
Dahlberg, Alfred William electric company executive
Dalton, John Joseph lawyer
D'Andrea, Frances Mary special education educator
Darden, Claibourne Henry, Jr. marketing research professional
Davis, Eleanor Kay museum administrator
Davis, Frank Tradewell, Jr. lawyer
Davis, Lawrence William radiation oncologist
Davis, Michael medical educator
Davis, Sterling Evan television executive
Dean, Andrew Griswold epidemiologist
†Deane, Richard H., Jr. federal judge
DeConcini, Barbara association executive, religious studies educator
†Decosta, Benjamin airport administrator
Delahanty, Edward Lawrence management consultant
Delaney-Lawrence, Ava Patrice secondary school educator
del Rosario, Remedios K. commissioner water department Atlanta
Denham, Vernon Robert, Jr. lawyer
Dennison, Daniel Bassel chemist
Denny, Richard Alden, Jr. lawyer
Deremer, Susan René artist
Despriet, John G. lawyer
Diedrich, Richard Joseph architect
Dietz, Arthur Townsend investment counseling company executive
Dobbins, Michael A. city planning and development commissioner
Dobes, William Lamar, Jr. dermatologist
Dobrzyn, Janet Elaine quality management professional
Dobson, Bridget McColl Hursley television executive and writer
†Domingo, Esther music educator
Donoghue, John Francis archbishop
†Dorsey, David Frederick dean, humanities educator
Dotson, Robert Charles news correspondent
Dougherty, John Ernest judge
Douglas, John Lewis lawyer

Douglas, (Charles) Lee executive vice president basketball team
Dowda, William F. internist
Doyle, Michael Anthony lawyer
Drake, Miriam Anna librarian, educator
Draper, Stephen Elliot lawyer, engineer
Drewry, Joe Samuel Jr. design engineer
Driver, Walter W., Jr. lawyer
Drummond, Jere A. telecommunications company executive
DuBose, Charles Wilson lawyer
Dudley, Perry, Jr. wireless communications administrator
†Duffey, Lee communications company executive
Duffey, William Simon, Jr. lawyer
Dunahoo, Charles religious publisher, religious organization administrator, consultant, human resource director
Dunlap, Donald Kelder rental company executive
Dunn, John Clinton writer, editor, organization executive
Duques, Ric information services executive
Durrett, James Frazer, Jr. lawyer
Dykes, John Henry, Jr. retired finance executive
Dysart, Benjamin Clay, III environmental consultant, conservationist, engineer
Eason, William Everette, Jr. lawyer
Easterly, David Eugene communications executive
Eckert, Charles Alan chemical engineering educator
Eckl, William Wray lawyer
Edelhauser, Henry F. physiologist, ophthalmic researcher, educator
Edmondson, James Larry federal judge
†Edson, Margaret playwright
Edwards, Louis Ward, Jr. diversified manufacturing company executive
Edwards, Stephen Allen lawyer
Egan, Michael Joseph retired lawyer, state legislator
Ehrlich, Jeffrey data processing company executive
†Eidecker, Martina Elisabeth foreign language educator
Eidson, James Anthony lawyer
Elliott, Lester Franklyn plastic surgeon
Ellis, Elmo Israel broadcast executive, consultant, columnist
†Ellis, U. Bertram, Jr. information technology company executive
Ellison, Earl Otto computer scientist
Elsas, Louis Jacob, II medical educator
El-Sayed, Mostafa Amr chemistry educator
Emerson, James Larry beverage company executive
Endicott, John Edgar international relations educator
England, John Melvin lawyer, clergyman
Epstein, David Gustav lawyer
†Estes, Joseph O'Bryant, II mortgage corporation executive
Etheridge, Jack Paul arbitrator, mediator, former judge
†Evans, Dorinda art history educator
Evans, Orinda D. federal judge
Farley, Charles P. public relations executive
Farmer, Mary Bauder small business owner, artist, painter
Farnham, Clayton Henson lawyer
Fash, William Leonard retired architecture educator, college dean
†Fehsenfeld, Martha Dow writer, editor
Feldman, Joel Martin magistrate judge
Fellows, Henry David, Jr. lawyer
Felton, Jule Wimberly, Jr. lawyer
Ferguson, Erik Tillman transportation consultant
Fernandez, Henry A. lawyer, consultant
Ferris, James Leonard academic administrator
Ferriss, Abbott Lamoyne sociology educator emeritus
Finkelstein, David Ritz physicist, educator, consultant
Finley, Sarah Maude Merritt social worker
Fiorentino, Carmine lawyer
Fitzgerald, John Edmund civil engineering educator
Fleming, Julian Denver, Jr. lawyer
Fleming, Sidney Howell psychiatrist, educator
Fletcher, Norman S. state supreme court justice
†Flynn, Marty J. investment company administrator
Foerster, David Wendel, Jr. counselor, consultant, human resources specialist
Forbes, Theodore McCoy, Jr. arbitrator, mediator, retired lawyer
†Ford-Roegner, Patricia A. health services professional
Foreman, Edward Rawson lawyer
Forrestal, Robert Patrick banker, lawyer
Forrester, J. Owen federal judge
†Fortin, Judy cable news anchor
Fortin, Raymond D. lawyer
Foster, Roger Sherman, Jr. surgeon, educator, health facility administrator
†Fox, Jack financial service executive
Fox, Lloyd Allan insurance company executive
Fox, Ronald Forrest physics educator
Fox-Genovese, Elizabeth Ann Teresa humanities educator
Franco, Ramon S. plastic surgeon
Frank, Erica preventive medicine physician
Franklin, Charles Scothern lawyer
Franks, Tommy Ray army officer
Fredo, Peter W. public relations executive
Freedman, Louis Martin dentist
Freeman, Richard Cameron federal judge
French, Michael Bruce beverage company executive
Frizzell, Rick Dale corporate creative director
Frost, Norman Cooper retired telephone company executive
Frye, Billy Eugene university administrator, biologist
Furnad, V. R. (Bob Furnad) television news executive
Galambos, John Thomas medical educator, internist
Galarraga, Andres Jose professional baseball player
Galloway, Thomas D. dean
Gambrell, David Henry lawyer
Ganaway, George Kenneth psychiatrist, psychoanalyst
Garner, Edwin Bruce government official
†Garner, J. Wayne state agency administrator
Garner, Thomas Emory, Jr. health insurance executive
Garrett, Franklin Miller historian
Garrow, David Jeffries historian, author
†Gates, Jeff writer
†Gayle, Helene D. federal agency administrator, pediatrician
Gayles, Joseph Nathan, Jr. administrator, fund raising consultant
Gaylor, James Leroy biomedical research director
Gearon, John Michael professional basketball team executive
Gelardi, Robert Charles trade association executive, consultant
Genberg, Ira lawyer
Gentry, David Raymond engineer
Gerst, Steven Richard healthcare director, physician
Gibson, Althea retired professional tennis player, golfer, state official
†Gibson, Michael artist
Giddens, Don Peyton engineering educator, researcher
Gilmer, Harry Wesley publishing executive, educator
Girth, Marjorie Louisa lawyer, educator
Gladden, Joseph Rhea, Jr. lawyer
Glaser, Arthur Henry lawyer
Glavine, Tom (Thomas Michael Glavine) professional baseball player
Glover, John Trapnell real estate executive
Goldman, John Abner rheumatologist, immunologist, educator
Goldstein, Burton Benjamin, Jr. communications executive
Goldstein, Elliott lawyer
Goldstein, Jacob Herman retired physical chemist
Gonzalez, Emilio Bustamante rheumatologist, educator
Gonzalez-Pita, J. Alberto lawyer
Goodman, Seymour Evan computer science and international studies educator, researcher, consultant
Goodwin, George Evans public relations executive
Gordon, Frank Jeffrey medical educator
Grady, Kevin E. lawyer
Graham, Matt Patrick minister, librarian
Green, Holcombe Tucker, Jr. investment executive
Greenblatt, Edward Lande lawyer
Greer, Bernard Lewis, Jr. lawyer
Gregory, Mel Hyatt, Jr. retired insurance company executive
Griffin, Clayton Houstoun retired power company engineer, lecturer
Grogan, Paula Cataldi newspaper editor
Gross, Stephen Randolph accountant
†Grubic, Adrianne journalist
Grumet, Priscilla Hecht fashion specialist, consultant, writer
Guberman, Sidney Thomas painter, writer
Guest, Rita Carson interior designer
Gunn, Robert Burns physiology educator
Haas, George Aaron lawyer
Haddad, Wassim Michael aerospace engineer, educator
Hale, Jack K. mathematics educator, research center administrator
†Hall, Rebekah A. journalist, editor
Hall, Wilbur Dallas, Jr. medical educator
Halwig, Nancy Diane banker
Hamm, (Charles) Stan(ley) telecommunications company executive
Hammill, Dick advertising and marketing executive
Hanna, Frank Joseph credit company executive
Hardegree, Gloria Jean Fore health services administrator
Harkey, Robert Shelton lawyer
Harmer, Don Stutler physics and nuclear engineering educator
Harness, William Walter lawyer
Harney, Thomas C. lawyer
†Harper, William Lloyd federal judge
Harris, Econ Nigel rheumatologist, internist
Harris, Henry Wood cable television executive
†Harris, Mark I. neurologist
Harrison, George Brooks research engineer, retired career officer
Harrison, John Raymond foundation executive, retired newspaper executive
Hartle, Robert Wyman retired foreign language and literature educator
Harvard, Beverly Joyce Bailey protective service official
Hassett, Robert William lawyer
Hasson, James Keith, Jr. lawyer, law educator
Hatcher, Charles Ross, Jr. cardiothoracic surgeon, medical center executive
Haverty, Rawson retail furniture company executive
Hawkins, Robert Garvin management educator, consultant
Hays, William Grady, Jr. corporate financial and bank consultant
Head, William Carl lawyer, author
Healy, Maureen marketing executive
Hearn-Youngblood, Peggy Elaine organist
Heimburger, Elizabeth Morgan psychiatrist
Henderson, Albert John federal judge
Henderson, Charles William health and medical publishing executive
Henry, Ronald James Whyte university official
Henry, William Ray business administration educator
Henson, Howard Kirk lawyer
Henson, Michele state legislator
Henwood, William Scott lawyer
Hiers, Mary A. museum director
Higgins, Richard J. educational administrator
Hill, Donald Dee management consultant, lecturer, writer
Hill, Paul Drennen lawyer, banker
Hiller, George Mew financial advisor, investment manager, lawyer
Hines, Preston Harris state supreme court justice
Hodges, Dewey Harper aerospace engineer, educator
Hodgson, Reginald Hutchins, Jr. corporate executive
Hoff, Gerhardt Michael lawyer, insurance company executive
Hoffman, Fred L. human resources professional
Hoffman, Michael William lawyer, accountant
Hogan, John Donald college dean, finance educator
Hogue, Carol Jane Rowland epidemiologist, educator
Holden, Laurence Preston artist
Hollis, Timothy Martin bank executive
Honaman, J. Craig health facility administrator
Hopkins, Donald Roswell public health physician
Hopkins, George Mathews Marks lawyer, business executive
Horowitz, Ira R. gynecologic oncologist
Hough, Leslie Seldon educational administrator
House, Donald Lee, Sr. software executive, private investor, management consultant
Howard, Harry Clay lawyer
Howard, Pierre state official
Howell, Hilton Hatchett, Jr. business executive
Hudspeth, Gregg William landscape architect
Hug, Carl Casimir, Jr. pharmacology and anesthesiology educator
†Hugee, Elton Bernard university official, retired military enlisted man
Hughes, James Mitchell epidemiologist
Hulbert, Daniel Joyce theater critic, entertainment writer
Hull, Frank Mays federal judge
Hunstein, Carol state supreme court justice
Hunt, Willis B., Jr. federal judge
Hunter, Douglas Lee media executive, former elevator company executive
Hunter, Forrest Walker lawyer
Hyde, Richard Lee investigator
Hyle, Charles Thomas marketing specialist
Iacobucci, Guillermo Arturo chemist
Ignatonis, Sandra Carole Autry special education educator
Ingram, Roland Harrison, Jr. physician, educator
Irvin, Thomas T. state commissioner of agriculture
Isaf, Fred Thomas lawyer
Israili, Zafar Hasan scientist, clinical pharmacologist, educator
Ivester, Melvin Douglas beverage company executive
Ivey, Michael Wayne mortgage broker
Izard, John lawyer
Jackson, Geraldine entrepreneur
Jackson, Richard Joseph epidemiologist, public health physician, educator
Janney, Donald Wayne lawyer
Jeffery, Geoffrey Marron medical parasitologist
Jenkins, Albert Felton, Jr. lawyer
Johns, Michael Marieb Edward otolaryngologist, academic administrator
Johnson, Carl Frederick marriage and family therapist
Johnson, Ellis Lane mathematician
Johnson, Richard Clayton engineer, physicist
Johnson, Ronald Carl chemistry educator
Johnson, Tom broadcasting executive
Johnson, W. Thomas, Jr. media executive
Johnson, Weyman Thompson, Jr. lawyer
Johnson, Wyatt Thomas, Jr. (Tom Johnson) cable news executive
Johnston, Summerfield K., Jr. food products executive
Jones, Frank Cater lawyer
Jones, Herbert Cornelius, III otolaryngologist
Jones, J. Kenley journalist
Jones, Joseph W. foundation administrator
†Jones, Larry Wayne "Chipper" baseball player
Jones, Mark Mitchell plastic surgeon
Jones, Walter Edward communications executive
Jurkiewicz, Maurice John surgeon, educator
†Kahn, A. David federal judge
Kahn, Bernd radiochemist, educator
Kalafut, George Wendell distribution company executive, retired naval officer
Kamm, Laurence Richard television producer, director
Kanov, Mark radio station executive
†Kaplan, Richard N. broadcast executive, cable
Karp, Herbert Rubin neurologist, educator
Kasten, Stanley Harvey sports association executive
Katz, Joel Abraham lawyer, music consultant
Keiller, James Bruce college dean, clergyman
Kelley, James Francis lawyer
Kelly, Carol White company executive
Kelly, James Michael lawyer
Kelly, James P. delivery service executive
Kelly, William Watkins educational association executive
Kennedy, James C. publishing and media executive
Kenney, Belinda Jill Forseman electronics executive
Kent, Philip communications executive
Keough, Donald Raymond investment company executive
Kerr, Nancy Helen psychology educator
Kieh, George Klay political science educator, consultant
Killorin, Edward Wylly lawyer, tree farmer
Killorin, Robert Ware lawyer
King, Coretta Scott (Mrs. Martin Luther King, Jr.) educational association administrator, lecturer, writer, concert singer
King, Frederick Alexander neuroscientist, educator
King, K(imberly) N(elson) computer science educator
King, Marian Emma health and physical education educator
King, Philip Jerome internet retailer, music business consultant
Kingsbury, Michael Bryant organist, retired elementary and secondary education educator
†Kintzel, Roger publisher
Kinzer, William Luther lawyer
Kitchens, Joyce Ellen lawyer, assistant county guardian
Kitchens, William H. lawyer
Klamon, Lawrence Paine lawyer
†Klehr, Harvey political science educator
Klein, Luella Voogd obstetrics-gynecology educator
†Kline, Lowry F. lawyer
Kloer, Philip Baldwin television critic
Kneisel, Edmund M. lawyer
Knight, Deidre Elise Mosteller literary agent
Knight, W. Donald, Jr. lawyer
Knowles, Marjorie Fine lawyer, educator, dean
Knox, Charles Courtenaye composer
Kokko, Juha Pekka physician, educator
Kolb, Derek Andrew information systems specialist
Komerath, Narayanan Menon aerospace engineer
Koplan, Jeffrey Powell physician
Kravitch, Phyllis A. federal judge
Ku, David Nelson medical educator
Kuntz, Marion Lucile Leathers classicist, historian, educator
Kuse, James Russell chemical company executive
L'Abate, Luciano psychologist
Lackland, Theodore Howard lawyer
La Farge, Timothy plant geneticist
Lamon, Harry Vincent, Jr. lawyer
Landau, Michael B. law educator, musician, author
Landess, Mike (Malcolm Lee Landess, III) television news anchorman
Landon, James Henry lawyer
Laney, James Thomas former ambassador, educator
Langdale, Noah Noel, Jr. research educator, former university president
Lanier, George H. lawyer
Laubscher, Robert James consumer products company executive
Lawson, A(bram) Venable retired librarian
Lee, John Everett physician
Lee, R(aymond) William, Jr. retired apparel company executive
Lehfeldt, Martin Christopher nonprofit association executive
Lehrer, Robert Nathaniel retired educator, executive, consultant
Leipold, Cynthia A. Ney critical care nurse, nursing administrator
Leonard, David Morse lawyer
Lester, Charles Turner, Jr. lawyer
Levy, Daniel economics educator
Levy, David lawyer
Lewcock, Ronald Bentley architect, educator
Lide, Janet Elizabeth graphic designer, artist
Liebmann, Seymour W. construction consultant
Lin, Ming-Chang physical chemistry educator, researcher
Linkous, William Joseph, Jr. lawyer
Lipman, Bernard internist, cardiologist
Lipshutz, Robert Jerome lawyer, former government official
Lnenicka, Wade Sheridan purchasing official, councilman
Lobb, William Atkinson financial services executive
Lockett, Jennifer Elisabeth middle school educator
Long, Leland Timothy geophysics educator, seismologist
Long, Maurice Wayne physicist, electrical engineer, radar consultant
Lotito, Nicholas Anthony lawyer
†Love, Gay manufacturing executive
Lower, Robert Cassel lawyer, educator
Lubin, Michael Frederick physician, educator
Lucero, Michael sculptor
Ludovice, Peter John chemical engineer
Luker, Ralph Edlin history educator
Lybarger, Jeffrey Allen epidemiology research administrator
†Macomson, Eric David pharmacist
Maddux, Greg(ory Alan) professional baseball player
Mafico, Temba Levi Jackson Old Testament and Semitic languages educator, clergy
Mahan, James S. communications company executive
Malhotra, Naresh Kumar management educator
Malone, James Hiram graphic artist, painter, writer
Malone, Perrillah Atkinson (Pat Malone) retired state official
†Malone, Richard Harlan consultant
Manley, Audrey Forbes college president, physician
Manley, Frank English language educator
Manley, Lance Filson data processing consultant
Maple, Terry L. county official
Marcus, Bernard retail executive
Marks, James S. public health service administrator
Marks, Marilyn company executive
Marshall, John Treutlen lawyer
Marshall, Thomas Oliver, Jr. lawyer
Martin, David Edward health sciences educator
Martin, James Francis state legislator, lawyer
Martin, Ron newspaper editor-in-chief
Martin, Virve Paul licensed professional counselor
Martinez, Tino Max financial services company executive
Marvin, Charles Arthur law educator
Mashburn, Guerry Leonard marketing professional
Mashburn, Sylvia Anita Smith communications executive, state official
Massey, Charles Knox, Jr. advertising agency executive
†Massey, James E. federal judge
Massey, Walter Eugene physicist, science foundation administrator
†Matlock, Kent company executive
Mauldin, Earle communications company executive
McCarty, Deborah Ownby city commissioner, lawyer
McChesney, Michael C. computer network security company executive
McCormick, Donald Bruce biochemist, educator
McDowell, David Lynn mechanical engineering educator
McDuffie, Frederic Clement physician
†McFall, John artistic director
McGowan, John Edward, Jr. clinical microbiology educator, epidemiologist, infectious diseases specialist
McHugh, Gene television executive
McLean, Ephraim Rankin information systems educator
McLean, James Albert artist, educator
McMahon, Donald Aylward investor, corporate director
McMaster, Belle Miller religious organization administrator
McMichael, Robert Henry protective services official
McNabb, Dianne Leigh investment banker, accountant
McNeill, Thomas Ray lawyer
McPherson, Judy Beth education educator
McQueen, Sandra Marilyn educator, consultant
McTier, Charles Harvey foundation administrator
McVey, Walter Lewis lawyer, educator
Meindl, James Donald electrical engineering educator, administrator
†Meltz, David Barry law educator
Mequirk, Terry broadcast executive
Merdek, Andrew Austin publishing/media executive, lawyer
Meyer, Ellen L. academic administrator
Middleton, Jarvis Darnell city commissioner
†Miles, Sid R. state agency administrator
Milhous, David Matthew television network editor
Millar, John Donald occupational and environmental health consultant, educator
Miller, Zell Bryan former governor
Millikan, James Rolens cleaning service executive, musician, composer
Minner, Thomas marketing executive
Minor, Winston L. city fire chief
Mitch, William Evans nephrologist
Mitchell, Stephen Milton manufacturing executive
Mobley, John Homer, II lawyer
Moderow, Joseph Robert lawyer, package distribution company executive
Moeling, Walter Goos, IV lawyer
Moon, Anne Trippe secondary school educator
Moore, Henry Rogers consulting engineer, retired railroad executive
Moore, Melinda public health physician
Moore, Philip Nicholas author
Moses, Edwin former track and field athlete
Moss, Dan, Jr. stockbroker
Moss, Sandra Hughes legal administrator
Moulthrop, Edward Allen architect, artist
Moye, Charles Allen, Jr. federal judge
Moynihan, James J. architectural firm executive
Mull, Gale W. lawyer
Muller, William Manning corporate lawyer
†Mullin, Leo Francis airline executive
†Murnane, George, III business executive
Murphy, James Jeffrey electronics executive
Murphy, Margaret Hackett federal judge
Murphy, Richard Patrick lawyer
Murphy, Thomas Bailey state legislator
Muth, Richard Ferris economics educator
Mutombo, DiKembe (Dikembe Mutombo Mpolondo Mukamba Jean Jacque Wamutombo) professional basketball player
Myrick, Bismarck diplomat
Nash, Charles D. investment banker

Neil, Robert F. broadcast executive
Nelson, Brian James broadcast journalist
Nelson, Linda Carol corporate chief executive
Nelson, Robert Earl, Jr. financial services company executive
Nemeroff, Charles Barnet neurobiology and psychiatry educator
Nemhauser, George L. industrial, systems engineer, operations research educator
Nerem, Robert Michael engineering educator, consultant
Newkirk, Isaac L. communications executive
Newton, Floyd Childs, III lawyer
Neylan, John Francis, III nephrologist, educator
Nichols, Joseph J., Sr. surgeon
Nie, Zenon Stanley manufacturing company executive
Nimmons, M(ajor) Stuart, III architect
Norris, Mary Penn elementary education educator
Nunn, Samuel (Sam Nunn) former senator
O'Brien, Mark Stephen pediatric neurosurgeon
O'Haren, Thomas Joseph financial services executive
O'Kelley, William Clark federal judge
Oliker, Vladimir mathematician, educator
†Oliver, Thomas hotel executive
Oplinger, Kathryn Ruth computer specialist
Oppenlander, Robert retired airline executive
Orenstein, Walter A. health facility administrator
Orr, John Mark senior planner Athens-Clarke County
Ortiz, Jay Richard Gentry lawyer
†Ortman, Mary Fallon public relations company official
Ottley, John K. publisher
Overstreet, Jim public relations executive
Owen, Robert Hubert lawyer, former real estate broker
Pace, Wayne H. communications executive
Pannell, Robert D. lawyer
†Papp, Daniel Stephen international affairs educator
Paquin, Jeffrey Dean lawyer
Paris, Demetrius Theodore electrical engineering educator
Parko, Edith Margaret special education educator
Parko, Joseph Edward, Jr. emeritus educator
Parsons, Leonard Jon marketing educator, consultant
Parsonson, Peter Sterling civil engineer, educator, consultant
Partain, Eugene Gartly lawyer
Patterson, William Robert lawyer
Pattillo, Manning Mason, Jr. academic administrator
Patton, Carl Vernon academic administrator, educator
Payne, Maxwell Carr, Jr. retired psychology educator
Payne, Nettleton Switzer, II neurosurgeon
Peacock, George Rowatt retired life insurance company executive
Peacock, Lamar Batts retired physician
Pence, Ira Wilson, Jr. material handling research executive, engineer
Petersen-Frey, Roland manufacturing executive
Petty, E. James community service director
†Philen, Rossanne McElroy medical epidemiologist
Philipp, Alicia community foundation executive
Phillips, Barry lawyer
Phillips, Debbie Jean managed care nurse
Phillips, John David media company executive
Phillips, William Russell, Sr. lawyer
Piassick, Joel Bernard lawyer
Pike, Larry Samuel lawyer
Pilcher, James Brownie lawyer
Pitts, Marcellus Theadore civil engineer, consultant
Pless, Laurance Davidson lawyer
Plummer, Michael Kenneth financial consultant
Podgor, Ellen Sue law educator
Poe, H. Sadler lawyer
Polk, James Ray journalist
Porter, Alan Leslie industrial and systems engineering educator
Pratt, Harry Davis retired entomologist
Pratt, Michael Francis physician and surgeon, otolaryngologist
Price, Edward Warren aerospace engineer, educator
Prince, David Cannon lawyer
Prince, Larry L. automotive parts and supplies company executive
Pryor, Shepherd Green, III lawyer
Pucci, Mark Leonard public relations professional
Puckett, Susan newspaper editor
Pulgram, William Leopold architect, space designer
Purcell, Ann Rushing state legislator, office manager medical business
Raby, Kenneth Alan lawyer, retired army officer
Raines, Tim D. real estate corporation executive
Ramsey, Ira Clayton retired pipeline company executive
Raper, Charles Albert retired management consultant
Ratliff, Hugh Donald industrial engineering educator
Reda, James Francis business consultant
Reed, Glen Alfred lawyer
Reed, James Whitfield physician, educator
Reedy, Edward K. research operations administrator
Regenstein, Lewis Graham conservationist, author, lecturer, speech writer
Reid, Antonio (L. A. Reid) musician, songwriter
Reid, Joseph William consultant
Reith, Carl Joseph apparel industry executive
Renford, Edward J. hospital administrator
Rex, Christopher Davis classical musician
Rhodes, Thomas Willard lawyer
Rich, Robert Regier immunology educator, physician
Richey, Thomas S. lawyer
Richtarik, Marilynn Josephine English language educator
Riddle, Marnita Marie medical nurse
Riggs, Gregory Lynn lawyer
Rink, Christopher Lee information technology consultant, photographer
†Riordan, Bridget Guernsey educational administrator
Robbins, James communications executive
Roberson, Timothy Randall public relations professional
†Roberts, Chuck cable news anchor
Roberts, Edward Graham librarian
Robertson, Kimberly Harden social welfare administrator
Robinson, Florence Claire Crim composer, conductor, educator
†Robinson, Hugh, Jr. federal judge
Robinson, Jeffery Herbert design and building company executive
Robison, Carolyn Love retired librarian
Robison, Richard Eugene architect
Rock, John Aubrey gynecologist and obstetrician, educator
Rodenbeck, Sven Erich environmental engineer, consultant
†Rodriguez, Rocio artist
Rogers, Brenda Gayle educational administrator, educator, consultant
Rogers, C. B. lawyer
Rojas, Carlos Spanish literature educator
Rollins, Howard Alonzo, Jr. psychology educator
Rosenberg, Mark L. health facility administrator
Rosenfeld, Arnold Solomon newspaper editor
Roth, Teresa Ann broadcast executive
†Rountree, Neva B. business executive
Rucker, Kenneth Lamar law enforcement officer, educator
Rusher, Derwood H., II lawyer
Ryan, J. Bruce health care management consulting executive
Salay, Cindy Rolston technical specialist, nurse
Salo, Ann Sexton Distler lawyer
Salomone, Jeffrey Paul surgeon, educator
†Sanders, Keith Alan neurologist
Sands, Jerome D. investment company executive
Sands, Robert O. lawyer
Sansone, Victor broadcast executive
Savell, Edward Lupo lawyer
†Savidge, Martin cable news anchor
Scarpucci, Penelope Alderman fundraising executive
Schadl, John Scott marketing consultant
Schafer, Ronald William electrical engineering educator
Schewe, Donald Bruce archivist, library director
Schimberg, Henry Aaron soft drink company executive
Schneeberger, Helen Haynes artist
Schroder, Jack Spalding, Jr. lawyer
Schuerholz, John Boland, Jr. professional baseball executive
Schulte, Jeffrey Lewis lawyer
Schulze, Horst H. hotel company executive
Schuppert, Roger Allen university official
Schwartz, Arthur Jay lawyer
Schwartz, William A(llen) broadcasting and cable executive
Schwartz, William B., Jr. ambassador
Schwarz, Patrick Joseph screenwriter
Scott, William Fred cultural organization administrator
Scovil, Roger Morris international business consultant
Sears, Leah J. state supreme court justice
Seffrin, John Reese health science association administrator, educator
Seretean, Martin B. (Bud Seretean) carpet manufacturing company executive
Sexson, William Robert pediatrician, educator
Shannon, David Thomas, Sr. reitred academic administrator
Sherman, Roger Talbot surgeon, educator
Sherry, Henry Ivan marketing consultant
Sherwood, Deborah Grace travel executive
Sheth, Jagdish Nanchand business administration educator
Shoob, Marvin H. federal judge
Sibley, Celestine (Mrs. John C. Strong) columnist, reporter
Sibley, Horace Holden lawyer
Sibley, James Malcolm retired lawyer
Simpson, Allan Boyd real estate company executive
†Sinclair, Robert P., Jr. accountant
Sink, John Davis leadership consultant, scientist
Sitter, John Edward English literature educator
Ski, Frank radio disc jockey
Skillrud, Harold Clayton minister, retired bishop
†Slater, Niall Ward classics educator
Smith, Alexander Wyly, Jr. lawyer
Smith, David Doyle international management consultant, consulting engineer
Smith, Eleanor Van Law paralegal
Smith, Glenn Stanley electrical engineering educator
Smith, James Louis, III lawyer
Smith, Jay publishing executive
Smith, Jeffrey Michael lawyer
Smith, Joseph Newton, III retired architect, educator
Smith, Lawrence A. lawyer
Smith, Michael Vincent surgeon
Smith, Robert Boulware, III vascular surgeon, educator
Smith, Sidney Oslin, Jr. lawyer
Smith, Steven Delano professional basketball player
Smoltz, John Andrew professional baseball player
Snarey, John Robert psychologist, researcher, educator
Snelling, George Arthur banker
Söderberg, Bo Sigfrid business executive
Somers, Fred Leonard, Jr. lawyer
Spalten, David Elliot lawyer
Spangler, Dennis Lee physician
Spiegel, John William banker
Spillett, Roxanne social services administrator
Spitznagel, John Keith microbiologist, immunologist
Spivey, Ted Ray English educator
Stacey, Weston Monroe, Jr. nuclear engineer, educator
Stallings, Ronald Denis lawyer
Stamps, Thomas Paty lawyer, consultant
Stancell, Arnold Francis chemical engineering educator, retired oil executive
Starr, Charles Christopher foundation executive, priest
Stegall, Marbury Taylor psychiatric, mental health nurse
Steinhaus, John Edward physician, medical educator
Stephenson, Mason Williams lawyer
Stewart, Jeffrey B. lawyer, commodity trading advisor
Stewart, Michael McFadden professional speaker
Stimpert, Michael Alan agricultural products company executive
Stokes, Mack (Marion) Boyd bishop
Stone, Matthew Peter lawyer
Stormont, Richard Mansfield hotel executive
Strauss, Robert David lawyer
Streeb, Gordon Lee diplomat, economist
Strekowski, Lucjan chemistry educator
Stubbs, Thomas Hubert company executive
Su, Kendall Ling-Chiao engineering educator
Sullivan, Terrance Charles lawyer
Summerlin, Glenn Wood advertising executive
Surber, Eugene Lynn architect
Sutton, Berrien Daniel beverage company executive
Swann, Jerre Bailey lawyer
Sweeney, Neal James lawyer
Swift, Frank Meador lawyer
Tanner, W(alter) Rhett lawyer
Tarver, Jackson Williams newspaper executive
Taylor, George Kimbrough, Jr. lawyer
†Taylor, Mark state official
Taylor, Mary Rose television anchor, journalist
Tedder, Daniel William chemical engineering educator
Teepen, Thomas Henry newspaper editor, journalist
Teja, Amyn Sadrudin chemical engineering educator, consultant
Tennant, Thomas Michael lawyer
Thacker, Stephen Brady medical association administrator, epidemiologist
Tharpe, Frazier Eugene journalist
Thaxton, Mary Lynwood librarian
Thomas, Barbara Ann record company executive
Thomas, James Edward, Jr. brokerage house executive
Thomas, Kenneth Eastman cardiothoracic surgeon
Thomas, Mable communications company executive, former state legislator, councilwoman
Thompson, Hugh P state supreme court justice
Thompson, Larry Dean lawyer
Thompson, Nils Roy, III investment company executive
Thompson, Wallace Reeves, III physical education educator
Thorp, Benjamin A., III paper manufacturing company executive
Thuesen, Gerald Jorgen industrial engineer, educator
Thumann, Albert association executive, engineer
Tidwell, George Ernest federal judge
Tillman, Mary Norman urban affairs consultant
Tissue, Mike medical educator, respiratory therapist
Togut, Torin Dana lawyer
Tomaszewski, Richard Paul market representation manager
Toner, Michael F. journalist
†Toomey, Kathleen E. state agency administrator
Tucker, Cynthia Anne journalist
Tullis, Bill broadcasting company executive, sound engineer, music producer
Tummala, Rao Ramamohana engineering educator
Turner, Michael Griswold advertising executive, writer
Turner, Ted (Robert Edward Turner) television executive
Tuschhoff, Christian liberal studies educator, paramedic
Uys, Jurgen Peter Brinker securities analyst
Vachon, Reginald Irenee mechanical engineer
Van Assendelft, Onno Willem hematologist
Vanegas, Jorge Alberto civil engineering educator
Varner, Chilton Davis lawyer
Verner, Linda Hogan manager cardiac surgery operating room
Verrill, F. Glenn advertising executive
Vigtel, Gudmund museum director emeritus
Volentine, Richard J., Jr. lawyer
Wakefield, Stephen Alan lawyer
Wald, Michael Leonard economist
Walden, Philip Michael recording company executive, publishing company executive
Walker, Betsy Ellen consulting and systems integration company executive
Walker, Jennie Louise research director
Walker, Robert broadcast executive
Walsh, W. Terence lawyer
Walter, John newspaper editor
Walton, Carole Lorraine clinical social worker
Walton, Jim sports news network executive
Ward, Horace Taliaferro federal judge
†Ward, Jackie M. computer company executive
Ward, Janet Lynn magazine editor, sports wire reporter
Wartell, Roger Martin biophysics educator
†Waters, Lou anchorman, correspondent
Waters, William Carter, III internist, educator
Watt, John Reid retired mechanical engineering educator
Watts, Anthony Lee bank executive
Weed, Roger Oren rehabilitation services professional, educator
Weiss, Jay M(ichael) psychologist, educator
Weisz, Peter R. lawyer
Wertheim, Steven Blake orthopedist
West, Benjamin B. advertising executive
Westerhoff, John Henry, III clergyman, theologian, educator
White, Ann Wells community activist
White, Gayle Colquitt religion writer, journalist
†White, Jacinta Victoria book distribution company owner
White, Ortrude B. architect
White, Perry Merrill, Jr. orthopedic surgeon
White, Ronald Leon financial management consultant
Whitley, Joe Dally lawyer
Whitmer, William Eward retired accountant
Whitt, Richard Ernest reporter
Wiesenfeld, Kurt Arn physicist, educator
Wilkens, Leonard Randolph, Jr. (Lenny Wilkens) professional basketball coach
Wilkes, George Gardner, Jr. landscape architect
Wilkins, J. Ernest, Jr. mathematician
Williams, David Howard lawyer
Williams, James Bryan banker
Williams, Neil, Jr. lawyer
Williams, Ralph Watson, Jr. retired securities company executive
Willis, Isaac dermatologist, educator
Wilson, Frank Lyndall surgeon
Wilson, James Hargrove, Jr. lawyer
Wilson, Norman Eugene adminstrator department Georgia penal institution
Winchester, Jesse Gregory commercial real estate company executive
Winer, Ward Otis mechanical engineer, educator
Withrow, William N., Jr. lawyer
Witty, Robert Wilkes insurance services company executive
Wolbrink, James Francis real estate investor
Wolensky, Michael K. lawyer
Womack, Mary Pauline lawyer
Wong, Ching-Ping chemist, materials scientist, engineer, educator
†Woodard, John Leonard neuropsychologist, researcher
Woodard, John Roger urologist
†Worley, David lawyer
Wright, Daniel wine specialist, consultant
Wright, Peter Meldrim lawyer
Wu, De Ting mathematics educator, researcher, writer
Wyvill, J. Craig research engineer, program director
Yancey, Asa Greenwood, Sr. physician
Yancey, Carolyn Dunbar educational policy maker
Yarnell, Jeffrey Alan retired regional credit executive
Yates, Ella Gaines library consultant
Yoculan, Suzanne gymnastics coach
Yoganathan, Ajit Prithiviraj biomedical engineer, educator
Young, Michael Anthony lawyer
Zink, Charles Talbott lawyer
Zinn, Ben T. engineer, educator, consultant
Zumpe, Doris ethologist, researcher, educator
Zunde, Pranas information science educator, researcher

Augusta

†Barfield, W. Leon federal judge
Barnard, Druie Douglas, Jr. former congressman, former bank executive
Barton, Raymond Oscar, III concrete company executive
Bloodworth, William Andrew, Jr. academic administrator
Bowen, Dudley Hollingsworth, Jr. federal judge
Bradberry, Edward opera company executive
Chandler, Arthur Bleakley pathologist, educator
Cooney, William J. lawyer
Cremer, Thomas Gerhard music educator
Cundey, Paul Edward, Jr. cardiologist
†Dalis, John S. federal judge
†Davies, Kimberly Ann sociology educator
Davison, Frederick Corbet foundation executive
Dolen, William Kennedy allergist, immunologist, pediatrician, educator
Feldman, Elaine Bossak medical nutritionist, educator
†Flythe, Starkey Sharp writer
Gadacz, Thomas Roman surgery educator
Gambrell, Richard Donald, Jr. endocrinologist, educator
Gillespie, Edward Malcolm hospital administrator
Given, Kenna Sidney surgeon, educator
Grigsby, R. Kevin social work and psychiatry educator
Guill, Margaret Frank pediatrics educator, medical researcher
Hakim, Fares Samih physician
†Hauenstein, Jill Pledger Hodges psychiatrist
Hilson, Diane Niedling nursing administrator
Hooks, Vendie Hudson, III surgeon
Ingham, Robert Francis marketing professional
Kirch, Darrell Gene dean
Lambert, Vickie Ann dean
Lee, Emma McCain counselor
Loomis, Earl Alfred, Jr. psychiatrist
Loring, David William neuropsychologist, researcher
Luxenberg, Malcolm Neuwahl ophthalmologist, educator
MacLeod, James L. minister, finance executive, gallery owner
Mahesh, Virendra Bhushan endocrinologist
Mansberger, Arlie Roland, Jr. surgeon
Martin, Willie Pauline elementary school educator, illustrator
Mayberry, Julius Eugene realty company owner, investor
Meyer, Carol Frances pediatrician, allergist
Miller, Jerry Allan, Jr. pediatrician
†Mode, Donald G. urologist, medical director
Moore, Nancy Fischer elementary school educator
Morgante, John-Paul management consultant
†Morris, William Shivers, III newspaper executive
Ownby, Dennis Randall pediatrician, allergist, educator, researcher
Pallas, Christopher William cardiologist
Parrish, Robert Alton retired pediatric surgeon, educator
Powell, James Kevin financial planner
Prisant, L(ouis) Michael cardiologist
Pryor, Carol Graham obstetrician, gynecologist
Rasmussen, Howard medical educator, medical institute executive
Rosen, James Mahlon artist, art historian, educator
Rowland, Arthur Ray librarian
Ryan, James Walter physician, medical researcher
Sansbury, Barbara Ann Pettigrew nursing administrator
Tedesco, Francis Joseph university administrator
Whittemore, Ronald Paul hospital administrator, retired army officer, nursing educator
Woodhurst, Robert Stanford, Jr. architect
Woods, Gerald Wayne lawyer
Wray, Betty Beasley allergist, immunologist, pediatrician

Austell

Halwig, J. Michael allergist

Avondale Estates

Carroll, Jane Hammond artist, author, poet
Fowler, Andrea teachers academy administrator

Bainbridge

Chambers, Heidi Kniskern English educator
Goodyear, Nancy L. biology educator
Hodges, Benjamin, Jr. management consultant
Kwilecki, Paul photographer
†Provence, Daniel Joseph realtor, farmer

Baldwin

Smith, John Andrew veterinarian

Barnesville

Hatcher, Wayne academic administrator
Kennedy, Harvey John, Jr. lawyer

Baxley

Reddy, Yenamala Ramachandra metal processing executive
Reddy, Yenemala Jaysimha mechanical engineer

Berkeley Lake

†Cooke, Marguerite K. nurse, mayor

Big Canoe

†Helms, Vernon Lamar telecommunications executive

Blackshear

Vaughan, Mittie Kathleen journalist

Bogart

Butts, David Phillip science educator

Bonaire

Griffin, Barbara Conley kindergarten and adult educator, antique store owner, retailer

Bowdon
Henson, Diana Jean *county official*

Bremen
McBrayer, Laura Jean H. *school media specialist*

Brooks
Buzzard, Sir Anthony Farquhar *religion educator*

Brunswick
Alaimo, Anthony A. *federal judge*
†Brinson, Cora Katherine *principal*
Brubaker, Robert Paul *food products executive*
Crowe, Hal Scott *chiropractor*
†Graham, James E. *federal judge*
Harper, Janet Sutherlin Lane *educational administrator, writer*
Hicks, Virginia Hobson *bookstore owner, educator*
Hopwood, Vicki Jeane *medical center official*
Iannicelli, Joseph *chemical company executive, consultant*
Lyons, Kathleen Marie *elementary school educator*
Mills, Margie Batley *home health care executive*
Mitchell, Dorothy Harvey *healthcare administrator*
Talbott, Mary Ann Britt *secondary education educator*
Thomas, Versie Lee *nursing educator*
†Willis, Faith M. *sociology educator, researcher*

Buford
Byrd, Larry Donald *behavioral pharmacologist*
Carswell, Virginia Colby *primary school educator, special education educator*
Garwood, Robert Ashley, Jr. *network communications analyst*
†Hesketh, Thomas R. *chemical engineer*
Rowe, Audrey *paralegal*

Cairo
Jordan, Randall Warren *optometrist*

Calhoun
Smith, Janice Self *family nurse practitioner*

Canton
Hasty, William Grady, Jr. *lawyer*
Sperin, Amelia Harrison *medical/surgical and pediatric nurse*

Carrollton
Aanstoos, Christopher Michael *psychology educator*
Arons, Myron Milford *psychology educator*
Barron, Purificacion Capulong *nursing administrator, educator*
Beard, Charles Edward *library director, consultant*
†Caress, Stanley Malcolm *political science educator*
Dunnavant, Tracy Lynn *planning administrator*
Goodson, Carol Faye *librarian*
Gustin, Ann Winifred *psychologist*
Harden, Gail Brooks *elementary school educator*
Ingle, Richard Maurice *research scientist*
Kielborn, Terrie Leigh *secondary education educator*
Noe, Kenneth William *historian, educator*
Richards, Roy, Jr. *wire and cable manufacturing company executive*
Sethna, Beheruz Nariman *university president, marketing, management educator*
Sullivan, Robert R. *marketing professional*

Cartersville
Barnett, Harold Thomas *school system superintendent*
Harris, Joe Frank *former governor*

Chamblee
Fried, Lawrence Philip *insurance company executive*
Lass, Teresa Lee *secondary school and special education educator*

Chatsworth
Beasley, Troy Daniel *secondary education educator*

Clarkesville
Dowden, Thomas Clark *telecommunication executive*

Clarkston
Love, Nancy Lorene *communication and political strategist, educator*
Wieck, Stewart Douglas *publisher, writer*

Clayton
English, Cheryl Ann *medical technologist*

Cleveland
Barrett, David Eugene *judge*
†Harris, Kevin J. *political science educator, consultant*

Cochran
Halaska, Thomas Edward *academic administrator, director, engineer*

College Park
Charania, Barkat *real estate consultant*
Fahy, Nancy Lee *food products marketing executive*
†Kirk, Thomas *chiropractor*
Mays, Jill Duncan *social services administrator, counselor*

Columbus
Amos, Daniel Paul *insurance executive*
Amos, Paul Shelby *insurance company executive*
Andrews, Gerald Bruce *retired textile executive*
Averill, Ellen Corbett *secondary education science educator, administrator*
Brinkley, Jack Thomas *lawyer, former congressman*
Brinkley, Jack Thomas, Jr. *lawyer*
Brown, Frank Douglas *academic administrator*
Butler, Charles Thomas *museum director, curator*
Carmack, Comer Aston, Jr. *steel company executive*
Chan, Philip *dermatologist, army officer*
Cloninger, Kriss, III *insurance company executive*
Collins, Wayne Winford *protective services official*
Diaz-Verson, Salvador, Jr. *investment advisor*
Duncan, Frances Murphy *retired special education educator*
Dunson, Diane Elaine *elementary education educator, computer specialist*
Edwards, Joan Annette *elementary art educator*
Elliott, James Robert *federal judge*
Ellis, Patrick R. *municipal official*
†Fluellen, Abraham P. *researcher*
Gore, James Arnold *biology educator, aquatic ecologist, hydrologist*
Harp, John Anderson *lawyer*
Heard, William T. *automotive executive*
Huff, Lula Eleanor *controller, accounting educator*
Jinright, Noah Franklin *vocational school educator*
Johnson, Herman James *correctional facility administrator*
Kerr, Allen Stewart *psychologist*
Kilgore, J. Donald *coroner*
Land, Martin J. *city official*
Laney, John Thomas, III *federal judge*
Lasseter, Earle Forrest *lawyer*
Leebern, Donald M. *distilled beverage executive*
†Loudermilk, Joey M. *insurance corporation executive, corporate lawyer*
Miller, Luther C. *protective services official*
Mize, Larry Hogan *professional golfer*
Montgomery, Anna Frances *elementary school educator*
Newton, Gwendolyn Stewart *elementary school educator*
Page, William Marion *lawyer*
Patrick, Carl Lloyd *theatre executive*
Polleys, Hardwick, Jr. *lawyer*
Segrest, Roger W. *auditor, municipal official*
Sims, Guy Willis *superintendent schools*
†Slaughter, William L. *federal judge*
Tate, Charles W. *information system specialist, municipal official*

Conley
Marcus, James Elbert *manufacturing company executive*

Conyers
Burman, Marsha Linkwald *lighting manufacturing executive, manpower development professional*
DeVane, Patricia Ann Doss *educational administrator*
Hungerford, Lugene Green *physicist*
Kelly, John Hubert *diplomat, business executive*
Kilkelly, Brian Holten *lighting company executive*
Mc Clung, Jim Hill *light manufacturing company executive*
Mc Intosh, James Eugene, Jr. *interior designer*
Pearce, Sara Margaret Culbreth *middle school educator*
Smith, William Lester *sales executive*
Spearman, Maxie Ann *financial analyst, administrator*
†Vaighn, Arthur Augustus *state agency administrator*

Covington
Wilson, Guy Harris, Jr. *minister*

Crawford
Bower, Douglas William *pastoral counselor, psychotherapist, clergyman*

Cumming
Enterline, Susan Carole *elementary educator, writer*
†Fuqua, Jane Boyd *principal*

Cuthbert
Treible, Kirk *college president*

Dahlonega
Friedman, Barry David *political scientist, educator*
Jones, William Benjamin, Jr. *electrical engineering educator*
Meyer, Sylvan Hugh *editor, magazine executive, author*

Dallas
Williams, Gary Randall *lawyer*

Dalton
Alexander, Burt Edward *management executive*
Bouckaert, Carl *manufacturing executive*
Bundros, Thomas Anthony *utilities executive*
Evans, Thomas Passmore *business and product licensing consultant*
Forsee, Joe Brown *library director*
Frerichs, Joy Roberta *elementary education educator*
Hutcheson, John Ambrose, Jr. *history educator*
†Laughter, Bennie M. *corporate lawyer*
Saul, Julian *retail executive*
Shaw, Robert E. *carpeting company executive*
Winter, Larry Eugene *accountant*

Danielsville
Bond, Joan *elementary school educator*

Dawsonville
Jorgensen, Alfred H. *computer software and data communications executive*

Decatur
Anderson, Jonpatrick Schuyler *financial consultant, therapist, archivist*
Apolinsky, Stephen Douglas *lawyer*
Bain, James Arthur *pharmacologist, educator*
Baker, Stephen Monroe *school system administrator*
Brown, W. Virgil *internal medicine educator*
Bullock, George Daniel *energy consultant*
Cirou, Joseph Philip *priest, organist, educator*
Dillingham, William Byron *literature educator, author*
Downs, Jon Franklin *drama educator, director*
Frank, Ronald Edward *marketing educator*
Garrett, Gloria Susan *social services professional*
Gay, Robert Derril *public agency director*
Gericke, Paul William *minister, educator*
Gregory, Sharon E. *neonatal clinical nurse specialist*
Hagood, Susan Stewart Hahn *clinical dietitian*
Hagood, Thomas Richard, Jr. *minister, publisher*
Hale, Cynthia Lynette *religious organization administrator*
Hamilton, Frank Strawn *jazz musician, folksinger, composer and arranger, educator*
Hawkins, Janice Edith *medical/surgical clinical nurse specialist*
Hill, Thomas Glenn, III *dermatologist*
Hinman, Alan Richard *public health administrator, epidemiologist*
Jones, Sherman J. *academic administrator, management educator, investment executive*
Keaton, Mollie M. *elementary school educator*
Knight, Walker Leigh *editor, publisher, clergyman*
Losh, Charles Lawrence *vocational education administrator*
Major, James Russell Richards *historian, educator*
Manners, George Emanuel *business educator, emeritus dean*
Middleton, James Boland *lawyer*
Myers, Clark Everett *retired business administration educator*
Myers, Orie Eugene, Jr. *university official*
Rausher, David Benjamin *internist, gastroenterologist*
Rodgers, Richard Malcolm *management accountant*
Ross, Valdor Wendell *operating room nurse*
Shaw, Jeanne Osborne *editor, poet*
Shulman, Arnold *judge, lawyer*
Solomon, Hilda Pearl *wholesale executive*
†Veach, Daniel Lee *editor*
Whitesides, Thomas Edward, Jr. *orthopaedic surgeon*
Williams, Rita Tucker *lawyer*
Young, James Harvey *historian, educator*

Demorest
Lytle, Timothy Fenner *philosophy educator*

Dillard
Wilkinson, Albert Mims, Jr. *lawyer*

Doraville
Wempner, Gerald Arthur *engineering educator*

Douglas
Sims, Rebecca Littleton *lawyer*

Douglasville
Henley, Lila Jo *school social worker, consultant, retired*
Landy, Lois Clouse *principal, counselor*
Paterson, Paul Charles *private investigator, security consultant*
Vance, Sandra Johnson *secondary school educator*

Dublin
Claxton, Harriett Maroy Jones *retired English language educator*
Doster, Daniel Harris *retired counselor, minister*
Folsom, Roger Lee *healthcare administrator*
Greene, Jule Blounte *lawyer*
Sumner, Lorene Knowles Hart *retired medical/surgical and rehabilitation nurse*

Duluth
Burns, Carroll Dean *insurance company executive*
Colwell, Gene Thomas *engineering educator*
Cooke, Steven John *chemical engineer, consultant, scientist*
†Garner, Karen Burnette *artist, administrative assistant*
Hibben, Celia Lynn *psychiatric mental health nurse practitioner*
Holutiak-Hallick, Stephen Peter, Jr. *retired career officer, businessman, educator*
Johnston, William David *biotechnology executive*
Neuman, Ted R. *principal*
Reed, Ralph Eugene, Jr. *association executive, writer*
Rogers, William Brookins *financial consultant, business appraiser*
Sloan, Donnie Robert, Jr. *lawyer*
Street, David Hargett *investment company executive*

Dunwoody
Callison, James W. *former lawyer, consultant, airline executive*
Clark, Faye Louise *drama and speech educator*
Hanna, Vail Deadwyler *critical care nurse*
La Motte, Louis Cossitt, Jr. *medical scientist, consultant*
†Whitt, Jeffrey E. *nuclear energy industry executive*

East Point
Cheves, Harry Langdon, Jr. *physician*
Fuller, Ora *nursing administrator, health care executive*
Gloster, Hugh Morris *retired college president, college association consultant*
McMullan, James Franklin *financial planner*

Eastman
Wiggins, James L. *lawyer*

Ellenwood
Walker, F. Darlene *writer, researcher*

Epworth
Walker, Sarah Harriet *English educator, administrator*

Fairburn
†Brooks, Janice Willena *educator*

Fayetteville
Brown, L(arry) Eddie *tax practitioner, real estate broker, financial planner*
Fleckenstein, James William *elementary school educator*
Harris, Glenda Stange *medical transcriptionist, writer*
Johnson, Donald Wayne *lawyer*
Phillips, Gary Lee *principal*
Turnipseed, Barnwell Rhett, III *journalist, public relations consultant*

Fitzgerald
Lewis, Charles Wesley *secondary education educator, English educator*

Flowery Branch
Monroe, Melrose *retired banker*

Folkston
Crumbley, Esther Helen Kendrick *realtor, retired secondary education educator*

Forest Park
†Fisher, George A., Jr. *career officer*

Fort Benning
Alles, Rodney Neal, Sr. *information management executive*
†Ernst, Carl F. *career officer*
†Martinez-Lopez, Lester *physician, commander*

Fort Gillem
†Fisher, George Alexander, Jr. *lieutenant general United States Army*

Fort Gordon
†Griffin, Robert F. *military career officer*
Zelazny, Robert Claire *army officer*

Fort Mcpherson
†Pickler, John M. *career officer*
†Schwartz, Thomas A. *military officer*
†Shadley, Robert D. *army officer*

Fort Stewart
†Riley, James Clifford *military career officer*

Fort Valley
Stumbo, Helen Luce *retail executive*
†Swartwout, Joseph Rodolph *obstetrics and gynecology educator, administrator*

Franklin
Lipham, William Patrick *principal, educator*

Fremont
Macaluso, Mary Margaret *nurse, educator*

Gainesville
Burd, John Stephen *academic administrator, music educator*
Ferguson, David Robert *energy research manager*
Gravitt, Nancy Canup *realtor*
Leet, Richard Hale *oil company executive*
†McDade, Dina Catherine *nursing educator*
Schuder, Raymond Francis *lawyer*
†Strother, John R., Jr. *federal judge*
Taylor, Mary Jane *art educator, artist*
Thompson, Jeffery Elders *health care administrator, minister*
Turner, John Sidney, Jr. *otolaryngologist, educator*

Garfield
Fountain, Edwin Byrd *minister, educator, librarian, poet*

Glynco
†Basham, W. Ralph *federal agency administrator*
Church, Barbara Ryan *organizational psychologist*
Mihal, Sandra Powell *distance learning specialist*

Grayson
Hollinger, Charlotte Elizabeth *medical technologist, tree farmer*
Mitchell, Laura Anne Gilbert *family nurse practitioner*
Nease, Judith Allgood *marriage and family therapist*

Griffin
Canup, Sherrie Margaret *foreign languages educator*
Doyle, Michael Patrick *food microbiologist, educator, administrator*
Duncan, Ronny Rush *agriculturist, turf researcher, consultant*
Georgiev, Goshko Atanasov *agrometeorologist, researcher*
Marshall, Allen Wright, III *communications executive, financial consultant*
Shuman, Larry Myers *soil chemist*

Grovetown
Baldwin, James Edwin *civil engineer, land development executive*
Bledsoe, Tommy Dalton *minister*
Muzik, Nancy Lynn *chemist*

Hamilton
Byrd, Gary Ellis *lawyer*
Chewning, Martha Frances MacMillan *lawyer*

Hapeville
Bugg, Owen Bruce *state agency administrator*
†Dhara, Venkata Ramana *physician, educator*

Hawkinsville
Mixon, Julia Jean Sanders *primary school educator*
Sheffield, Gloria Carol *elementary education educator*

Hinesville
Carter, Georgian L. *minister*
†Wise, Carl Stamps *accounting educator*

Hogansville
Spradlin, Charles Leonard *secondary school educator*

Hull
Melton, Charles Estel *retired physicist, educator*

Indian Springs
Lamb, Deryle Jean *preservationist*

Jasper
Dewey, Edward Allen *retired construction company executive*
Ledford, Shirley Louise *practical nurse*
Marger, Edwin *lawyer*
Sutter, Jean *sculptor*

Jekyll Island
Hicks, Leslie Elizabeth *museum curator*
McKinley, Douglas Webster (Webb McKinley) *consultant*
Murphy, F. Warren *museum director*

Jersey
Batchelor, Joseph Brooklyn, Jr. *electronics engineer, consultant*

Jonesboro
Dame, Laureen Eva *nursing administrator*
Dawson, Lewis Edward *minister, retired military officer*
King, Glynda Bowman *state legislator*
Smith, Robyn Doyal *elementary and middle school educator*
Ziegler, Robert Oliver *retired special education educator*

Anantha Narayanan, Venkataraman *physics educator*
†Andrews, Christine Marie *graphic designer*
Aquadro, Jeana Lauren *graphic designer, educator*
Belles, Martin Russel *manufacturing engineer*
Billet, Donald Franklin *civil engineer, consultant*
Boland, John Kevin *bishop*
Bowman, Catherine McKenzie *lawyer*
Brandner, Christine Marie *curator, artist*
Burnett, Robert Adair *university administrator, history educator*
Cadle, Farris William *land title abstractor*
Caldwell, John Walter *United States marshal*
Cartledge, Raymond Eugene *retired paper company executive*
†Clary, Warren Upton *neurosurgeon*
Coberly, Patricia Gail *elementary education educator, adult education educator*
Coffey, Thomas Francis, Jr. *writer*
Croom, John Henry, III *utility company executive*
Davis, Chris *aerospace company executive*
Dickerson, Lon Richard *library administrator*
DiClaudio, Janet Alberta *health information administrator*
Dixon, Harry D., Jr. (Donnie Dixon) *prosecutor*
Dodge, William Douglas *insurance company consultant*
Eaves, George Newton *lecturer, consultant, research administrator*
†Edeawo, Gale Paula *publishing company executive, writer*
Edenfield, Berry Avant *federal judge*
Foley, Marilyn Lorna *artist*
Forbes, Morton Gerald *lawyer*
Froelicher, Franz *chemist, geologist, environmental consultant*
Gabeler-Brooks, Jo *artist*
Giblin, Patrick David *retired banker*
Gillespie, Daniel Curtis, Sr. *retired non-profit company executive, consultant*
†Graham, Patrick Samuel *air transportation executive*
Granger, Harvey, Jr. *retired manufacturing company executive*
†Greco, Richard Jude *plastic and reconstructive surgeon*
Greenberg, Philip B. *symphony orchestra conductor and music director*
Harold, Fran Powell *historic site director*
Haywood, John William, Jr. *engineering consultant*
†Hemphill, John Michael *neurologist*
Hill, Dorothy Bennett *community activist*
Horan, Leo Gallaspy *physician, educator*
Howard, Constance Adair *bank officer*
Hsu, Ming-Yu *engineering educator*
Jenkins, Mark Guerry *cardiologist*
†Jones, William Randolph *history educator*
†Kalantari, Behrooz *political science educator*
Krahl, Enzo *retired surgeon*
†Lamar, W. Davis, Jr. *federal judge*
Leighton, Richard Frederick *retired dean*
Lessard, Raymond William *bishop*
Lindqvist, Gunnar Jan *management consultant, international trade consultant*
Moore, William Theodore, Jr. *judge*
Nawrocki, H(enry) Franz *propulsion technology scientist*
†Neely, C. Michael *graphic designer, illustrator*
Oelschig, Augusta Denk *retired artist, art educator*
Otter, John Martin, III *television advertising consultant, retired*
Painter, Paul Wain, Jr. *lawyer*
Peer, George Joseph *metals company executive*
Potts, Glenda Rue *music educator*
Ramage, James Everett, Jr. *respiratory and critical care physician, educator*
Rawson, William Robert *lawyer, retired manufacturing company executive*
Roth, Richard Harrison *petrochemical inspection company executive*
Rousakis, John Paul *former mayor*
Rowan, Richard G. *academic administrator*
†Samir, Sami A. *food service executive*
Schafer, Thomas Wilson *advertising agency executive*
Scott, Walter Coke *retired sugar company executive, lawyer*
Shang, Xuhong *art educator, artist*
Shealy, Catherine Clarke *elementary school educator*
Sheehy, Barry Maurice *management consultant*
Simonaitis, Richard Ambrose *chemist*
Spitz, Seymour James, Jr. *retired fragrance company executive*
†Spradley, Dorothy Radford *art educator, sculptor*
Sprague, William Wallace, Jr. *retired food company executive*
Standbridge, Peter Thomas *retired insurance company executive*
Stillwell, Walter Brooks, III *lawyer*
Strauser, Beverly Ann *education educator*
Thomas, Dwight Rembert *writer*
Thompson, Larry James *gifted educatin educator*
Trosten, Leonard Morse *lawyer*
Walter, Paul Hermann Lawrence *chemistry educator*
Webb, James Calvin *minister*
Windom, Herbert Lynn *oceanographer, environmental scientist*
Wirth, Fremont Philip, Jr. *neurosurgeon, educator*
Zoller, Michael *otolaryngologist, head and neck surgeon, educator*

Scottdale
Borochoff, Ida Sloan *real estate executive, artist*

Sea Island
Brown, Ann Catherine *investment company executive*
LaWare, John Patrick *retired banker, federal official*
Leisure, George Stanley, Jr. *lawyer*
Revoile, Charles Patrick *lawyer*

Shannon
Williams, Thresia Wayne Matthews *occupational health nurse*

Sharpsburg
Wooten, Tina Helen Wilhelm *medical/surgical and oncological nurse*

Smarr
Evans, Rosemary King (Mrs. Howell Dexter Evans) *librarian, educator*

Smyrna
Atkins, William Austin, Sr. (Bill Atkins) *former state legislator*
Head, John Francis, Jr. *distributing company executive*
Lubker, John William, II *manufacturing executive, civil engineer*
Mc Kenzie, Harold Cantrell, Jr. *retired manufacturing executive*
Murray, Barry Wayne *economics educator*
Passantino, Richard J. *architect*

Snellville
Brueckner, Lawrence Terence *orthopedic surgeon*
Elleby, Gail *management consultant*
Gerson, Martin Lyons *secondary school educator*

Social Circle
Penland, John Thomas *import and export and development companies executive*

South Jesup
Wilcox, Ronald Wayne *minister*

Statesboro
Bacon, Martha Brantley *small business owner*
Beasley, John Julius *child and family development educator*
Brown, John Howard *economics educator*
Cram, Rusty *basketball coach*
Davenport, Ann Adele Mayfield *home care agency administrator*
†Flynn, Richard McDonnell *English educator*
Green, Edward Thomas, Jr. *education educator*
Henry, Nicholas Llewellyn *college president, political science educator*
Mobley, Cleon Marion, Jr. (Chip Mobley) *physics educator, real estate executive*
Murkison, Eugene Cox *business educator*
Parrish, Benjamin Emmitt, II *insurance executive*
Parrish, John Wesley, Jr. *biology educator*
Ragans, Rosalind Dorothy *textbook author, retired art educator*
Rodell, Paul Arthur *history educator*
Stone, Ralph Kenny *lawyer*
Wilhoite, Laura J. *occupational health nurse*

Stockbridge
Davis, Raymond Gilbert *retired career officer, real estate developer*
Friedman, Robert Barry *physician*
Grimes, Richard Allen *economics educator*

Stone Mountain
Boothe, Edward Milton *aeronautical engineer, pilot*
Bowers, Michael Joseph *former state attorney general*
Dees, Julian Worth *retired academic/research administrator*
Denney, Laura Falin *insurance company executive*
†Moseley, Clifford Longstaff *industrial hygienist*
Nelson, Larry Keith *document investigation laboratory executive*
Speed, Billie Cheney (Mrs. Thomas S. Speed) *retired editor, journalist*

Sugar Hill
Draughon, Deborah *writer*
Jordan, Henry Hellmut, Jr. *management consultant*

Summerville
Connelly, Lewis Branch Sutton *lawyer*
Spivey, Suzan Brooks Nisbet *association administrator, medical technologist*
Wright, Kevin Douglas *veterinarian*

Suwanee
†Anderson, Jamal Sharif *professional football player*
†Chandler, Christopher Mark (Chris) *professional football player*
Colgan, George Phillips *real estate developer, real estate analyst*
†Dickerson, Eric Demetric *former professional football player*
Mathis, Terance *professional football player*
Puente, Jose Garza *safety engineer*
Reeves, Daniel Edward *professional football coach*
Shihady, Diane Divis *speech pathologist*
Smith, Taylor *professional football team executive*
Tuggle, Jessie Lloyd *professional football player*
†White, Gregory Dale *environmental consultant*

Swainsboro
Malone, Frankie Wheeler *primary school educator*

Sylvania
Martin, Charles Wade *pastor*

Thomaston
McPhail, Charles L., Jr. *school system support personnel*
Smith, Debra Joan *informatics nurse, critical care nurse*

Thomasville
Flowers, Langdon Strong *foods company executive*
Flowers, William Howard, Jr. *food company executive*
Mc Mullian, Amos Ryals *food company executive*
Stepanek, David Leslie *financial services company executive*
Watt, William Vance *surgeon*

Thomson
Smith, Robert L. *principal*
Wilson, Donna Owen *author, artist*

Tifton
Austin, Max Eugene *horticulture educator*
Dorminey, Henry Clayton, Jr. *allergist*
Johnson, Edith Scott *English educator, writing consultant*

Tiger
DuBois, Karen York *secondary school educator*

Toccoa
Austin, Robert Brendon *civil engineer*
Maypole, John Floyd *real estate holding company executive*
Scott, Louyse Hulsey *school social worker*
Thomas, Maurice W(illiam), Jr. *composer, lyricist*
van der Veur, Paul W. *humanities educator*

Toccoa Falls
Alford, Paul Legare *college and religious foundation administrator*
Diehl, Donna Rae *education educator*
Reese, David George *adult education educator*
Williams, Donald T. *English educator*

Tucker
Armstrong, Edwin Alan *lawyer*
Baker, Russ *executive search firm owner*
Broucek, William Samuel *printing plant executive*
†Brown, Betsy S. *hotel executive*
†Giavaras, Faith E. *minister*
†Guimbellot, Bobby E. *hotel executive*
McNair, Nimrod, Jr. *foundation executive, consultant*
Reed, Barbara Alford *pain management nurse, consultant*
Twining, Henrietta Stover *retired English language educator*
Valk, Henry Snowden *physicist, educator*

Tunnel Hill
Martin, Teresa Ann Hilbert *special education educator*
†McNelley, Judy Anne *small business owner*

Tyrone
Slocum, Sheila Jean *missionary*

Union City
†Arnold, Dorothy Harrison *assistant principal*

Valdosta
Bailey, Hugh Coleman *university president*
Bridges, James A. *vocational school educator*
Bright, Joseph Converse *lawyer*
†Capps, Susan Marie *elementary school educator*
Grissino-Mayer, Henri Dee *research scientist*
Halter, H(enry) James, Jr. (Diamond Jim Halter) *retail executive*
Marinelli, Linda Floyd *nurse educator*
Onwuegbuzie, Anthony John *mathematician, educator*
Robertson, Dale Wayne *minister*
Sherman, Henry Thomas *retired physician*
Vincent, Kay Louise *community health nursing director*
Waldrop, Mary Louise *nursing educator*

Vidalia
Fortner, Billie Jean *small business owner*
Joyner, Jo Ann *geriatrics nurse*

Warner Robins
Duntz, David W. *career officer*
Lavdas, Leonidas G. *meteorologist, religion educator*
Nugteren, Cornelius *air force officer*

Washington
Mansfield, Norman Connie *bookkeeper*

Watkinsville
Johnson, Norman James *physician, lawyer, medicolegical consultant*
Nichols, William Curtis *psychologist, family therapist, consultant*

West Point
Glover, Clifford Clarke *retired construction company executive*

Willacoochee
Gillis, Judy Wingate *elementary educator*

Winder
Hutchins, Cynthia Barnes *special education educator*
McLemore, Michael Kerr *lawyer, minister*

Winterville
Anderson, David Prewitt *retired university dean*
Shockley, W. Ray *travel trade association executive*

Woodstock
Aromin, Mercedes Fung *portfolio manager, investment advisor, consultant*
Austin, John David *retired financial executive*
Collins, David Browning *religious institution administrator*
Everiss, Dana Ford *middle school educator*
†Tull, Trent Ashley *director activities*

Young Harris
Putnam, Joanne White *college financial aid administrator, bookkeeper*

Zebulon
Watson, Forrest Albert, Jr. *lawyer, bank executive*

HAWAII

Aiea
Munechika, Ken Kenji *research center administrator*
Uyehara, Harry Yoshimi *library educator*
Walker, Welmon, Jr. (Rusty Walker) *publisher, consultant*

Camp H M Smith
†Blair, Dennis Cutler *career officer*
†Miller, Thomas G. *career officer*
Surface, Stephen Walter *water treatment chemist, environmental protection specialist*
Teare, Richard Wallace *ambassador*

Captain Cook
Link, Matthew Richard *video producer*

Eleele
Takanishi, Lillian K. *elementary school educator*

Ewa Beach
Kea, Jonathan Guy *instrumental music educator*
Lewis, Mary Jane *communication specialist, video producer, writer*
Neudorf, Howard Fred *family physician*

Fort Shafter
†Donald, James E. *military career officer*
Maruoka, Jo Ann Elizabeth *information systems manager*

Haiku
Riecke, Hans Heinrich *architect*

Haleiwa
Austen, Shelli Oetter *radio news anchor, consultant*

Hanalei
Helder, David Ernest *artist, educator*
Schaller, Matthew Fite *architect*

Hawaii National Park
Gray, Elizabeth Marie *biologist*
Nicholson, Marilyn Lee *arts administrator*
Swanson, Donald Alan *geologist*

Hickam AFB
†Dunn, Michael M. *military officer*
Miller, David Allen *air force officer, observatory administrator*
†Polk, Steven R. *military officer*
Sandstrom, Dirk William *air force officer, hospital administrator*

Hilo
Best, Mary Lani *university program coordinator*
Clark, Janet *retired health services executive*
Gersting, Judith Lee *computer science educator, researcher*
Griep, David Michael *astronomical scientist, researcher*
Ushijima, John Takeji *state senator, lawyer*

Honolulu
Abbott, Isabella Aiona *biology educator, retired*
Acoba, Simeon Rivera, Jr. *judge*
Akinaka, Asa Masayoshi *lawyer*
Alm, Steve *prosecutor*
Amor, Simeon, Jr. *photographer*
Arbeit, Wendy Sue *researcher, writer*
Asai-Sato, Carol Yuki *lawyer*
Ashford, Clinton Rutledge *judge*
Ashton, Geoffrey Cyril *geneticist, educator*
Astriab, Steven Michael *army officer*
Aung-Thwin, Michael Arthur *history educator*
Baker, Helen Doyle Peil *realtor*
Baker, Kent Alfred *broadcasting company executive*
†Ball, Robert Jerome *classics educator*
Belknap, Jodi Parry *graphic designer, writer, business owner*
Bender, Byron Wilbur *linguistics educator*
Betts, Barbara Stoke *artist, educator*
Betts, James William, Jr. *financial analyst, consultant*
Bitterman, Morton Edward *psychologist, educator*
†Blair, Robert C. *federal judge*
Bloede, Victor Carl *lawyer, academic executive*
Boas, Frank *lawyer*
Bogart, Louise Berry *education educator*
Boggs, Steven Eugene *lawyer*
Bopp, Thomas Theodore *university administrator, chemistry educator*
Bornhorst, Marilyn *Democrat party chariwoman*
Bossert, Philip Joseph *information systems executive*
Botsai, Elmer Eugene *architect, educator, former university dean*
Brady, Stephen R.P.K. *physician*
Brennan, Jerry Michael *economics educator, statistician, researcher, clinical and forensic psychologist*
Bronster, Margery S *state attorney general*
Cachola, Romy Munoz *state representative*
Cain, Raymond Frederick *landscape architect, planning company executive*
Callies, David Lee *lawyer, educator*
Camara, Jorge de Guzman *ophthalmologist, humanitarian, educator*
†Carey, W. David P. *hotel executive*
Carson, Hampton Lawrence *geneticist, educator*
Case, James Hebard *lawyer*
Cattell, Heather Birkett *psychologist*
Cayetano, Benjamin Jerome *governor, former state senator and representative*
Chambers, Kenneth Carter *astronomer*
Chang, Rodney Eiu Joon *artist, dentist*
Char, Vernon Fook Leong *lawyer*
Chesne, Edward Leonard *physician*
Cho, Lee-Jay *social scientist, demographer*
Chock, Clifford Yet-Chong *family practice physician*
Choy, Herbert Young Cho *federal judge*
Chuck, Walter G(oonsun) *lawyer*
Chun Oakland, Suzanne Nyuk Jun *state legislator*
Clarke, Robert F. *utilities company executive*
Couch, John Charles *diversified company executive*
Cowan, Stuart Marshall *lawyer*
Cox, Richard Horton *civil engineering executive*
Deaver, Phillip Lester *lawyer*
Devaney, Donald Everett *law enforcement official*
Devens, Paul *lawyer*
DeVilbiss, Jonathan Frederick *airline analyst*
DiLorenzo, Francis X. *bishop*
Dods, Walter Arthur, Jr. *bank executive*
Dougherty, Raleigh Gordon *manufacturer's representative*
Dreher, Nicholas C. *lawyer*
Dyen, Isidore *linguistic scientist, educator*
Ellis, George Richard *museum administrator*
Ezra, David Alan *federal judge*
Fasi, Frank Francis *state senator*
†Faucher, David F. *federal judge*
Feher, Steve Joseph Kent *design engineer, research developer*
Fischer, Joel *social work educator*
Fitz-Patrick, David *endocrinologist, educator*
Flanagan, John Michael *editor, publisher*
Flannelly, Kevin J. *psychologist, research analyst*
Flannelly, Laura T. *mental health nurse, nursing educator, researcher*
Flynn, Joan Mayhew *librarian*
Fong, Hiram Leong *former senator*
Fukushima, Barbara Naomi *financial consultant*
Fullmer, Daniel Warren *psychologist, educator, retired*
Furst, Dan (Daniel Christopher Furst, III) *producer, writer, actor*
Furuyama, Renee Harue *association executive*
Gallup, James Donald *physician*
Gary, James Frederick *business and energy advising company executive*
†Gatti, Jim *editor*
Gay, E(mil) Laurence *lawyer*
Gee, Chuck Yim *dean*
Gelber, Don Jeffrey *lawyer*
Gillin, Malvin James, Jr. *lawyer*

Gillmar, Jack Notley Scudder real estate company executive
Gillmor, Helen federal judge
Goldstein, Sir Norman dermatologist
Goo, Vince women's collegiate basketball coach
Gormley, Francis Xavier, Jr. social worker
†Goto Sabas, Jennifer state official
Greenberg, Marvin retired music educator
Greenfield, David W. zoology educator
Haig, David M. property and investment manager
Haight, Warren Gazzam investor
Hale, Nathan Robert architect
Halloran, Richard Colby writer, former research executive, former news correspondent
Hamada, Duane Takumi architect
Harris, Jeremy mayor
Hatfield, Elaine Catherine psychology educator
Hawke, Bernard Ray planetary scientist
†Hays, John Tennyson, III import, export company executive
Hays, Ronald Jackson career officer
†Heen, Walter Meheula retired judge, political party executive
Heller, Ronald Ian lawyer
Herbig, George Howard astronomer, educator
Hipp, Kenneth Byron lawyer
Hirono, Mazie Keiko state official
Ho, Reginald Chi Shing medical educator
Ho, Stuart Tse Kong investment company executive
Hoag, John Arthur retired bank executive
Hook, Ralph Clifford, Jr. business educator
Howes, William Craig English educator
Hu, Joseph Kai Ming insurance company executive
Hughes, Robert Harrison former agricultural products executive
Ihrig, Judson La Moure chemist
Inaba, Lawrence Akio educational director
Ishikawa-Fullmer, Janet Satomi psychologist, educator
Jellinek, Roger editor
Johnson, Lawrence M. banker
Jordan, Amos Azariah, Jr. foreign affairs educator, retired army officer
Joseph, Robert David astronomer, educator
Kadohiro, Jane Kay educator, nurse, diabetes consultant
Kahikina, Michael Puamamo social services administrator, state legislator
Kamemoto, Fred Isamu zoologist
Kamemoto, Garett Hiroshi reporter
Kane, Thomas Jay, III orthopaedic surgeon, educator
Katayama, Robert Nobuichi lawyer
Katz, Alan Roy public health educator
Kawachika, James Akio lawyer
Kay, Alan Cooke federal judge
Kay, Elizabeth Alison zoology educator
Keil, Klaus geology educator, consultant
Keir, Gerald Janes banker
Keith, Kent Marsteller academic administrator, corporate executive, government official, lawyer
Kelley, Richard Roy hotel executive
†Kellogg, Judith Lillian English educator
Keogh, Richard John firearms and explosives consultant
Khan, Mohammad Asad geophysicist, educator, former energy minister and senator of Pakistan
Kim, Joung-Im communication educator, consultant
King, Arthur R., Jr. education educator, researcher
†King, Lloyd federal judge
Kitagawa, Audrey Emiko lawyer, retired
†Kitamura, Michael state director
Klobe, Tom art gallery director
Knowlton, Edgar Colby, Jr. linguist, educator
Kohloss, Frederick Henry consulting engineer
Koide, Frank Takayuki electrical engineering educator
Kong, Laura S. L. geophysicist
Krauss, Bob newspaper columnist, author
Kroll, Sandra L. healthcare facility administrator
Kudo, Emiko Iwashita former state official
Kunishige, Lynn Leiko Kimura secondary education educator
Kupchak, Kenneth Roy lawyer
Kuroda, Yasumasa political science educator, researcher
†Kurren, Barry M. federal judge
Lamoureux, Charles Harrington botanist, arboretum administrator
Laney, Leroy Olan economist, banker, educator
Langhans, Edward Allen drama and theater educator
Lau, Charles Kwok-Chiu architect, architectural firm executive
Lau, Eugene Wing Iu lawyer
Lau, H. Lorrin physician, inventor
Lau, Jeffrey Daniel lawyer
Laughlin, Charles William agriculture educator, research administrator
Lee, Candie Ching Wah retail executive
Lee, Marcia Ellen insurance agent
Lee, Yeu-Tsu Margaret surgeon, educator
Levinson, Steven Henry state supreme court justice
Lilly, Michael Alexander lawyer, author
Lin, Shu electrical engineering educator
Lindsay, Karen Leslie insurance company executive
Linman, James William retired physician, educator
Loeffler, Richard Harlan retail and technology company executive
Loh, Edith Kwok-Yuen oncology nurse, health education specialist
Louie, David Mark lawyer
Luke, Lance Lawton real estate and construction consultant
Lum, Jean Loui Jin nurse educator
Mader, Charles Lavern chemist
Mandel, Morton molecular biologist
Mark, Shelley Muin economist, educator, government official
Marsella, Anthony Joseph psychologist, educator
Masters, Elaine educator, writer
Masuchika, Glenn Norio librarian, university official, book reviewer
Matayoshi, Coralie Chun lawyer, bar association executive
Matthews, Norman Sherwood, Jr. insurance company executive
†Mattoch, Ian L. lawyer
Mau, William Koon-Hee financier
†Mau-Shimizu, Patricia Ann lawyer
Meagher, Michael radiologist
Meech, Karen Jean astronomer
Metz, James Robert mathematics educator
Midkiff, Robert Richards financial and trust company executive, consultant
Miike, Lawrence Hiroshi public health officer
Miller, Clifford Joel lawyer
Miller, Richard Sherwin law educator
Miyamoto, Craig Toyoki public relations executive
Miyasaki, Shuichi lawyer
Mizokami, Iris Chieko mechanical engineer
Moccia, Mary Kathryn social worker
Moody, John Henry minister, hospital chaplain, clinical pastoral educator
Moody, Raymond Albert foreign language educator
Moon, Ronald T. Y. state supreme court justice
Moore, Ernest Carroll, III lawyer
Moore, Willis Henry Allphin history and geography educator
Moreno-Cabral, Carlos Eduardo cardiac surgeon
Moroney, Michael John lawyer
†Morrison, Charles think-tank executive
Morse, Richard social scientist
Mortimer, Kenneth P. academic administrator
Nakabayashi, Nicholas Takateru retired retail executive
Nakayama, Paula Aiko state supreme court justice
Nelson, Jeanne Francess secondary education educator
Nelson, Marita Lee anatomist
Ng, Wing Chiu accountant, computer software consultant, educator, activist
Niles, Geddes Leroy private investigator
Nishimura, Pete Hideo oral surgeon
Nordyke, Eleanor Cole population researcher, public health nurse
†Obata, Randy executive assistant to governor of Hawaii
Ogawa, Dennis Masaaki American studies educator
Ogburn, Hugh Bell chemical engineer, consultant
Oishi, Stephen Masato physician
Okada, Ronald Masaki insurance agent
Okimoto, Glenn Michiaki state official
Okinaga, Lawrence Shoji lawyer
Olsen, Harris Leland real estate and international business executive, educator, diplomat
O'Neill, Charles Kelly marketing executive, former advertising agency executive
Pacific, Joseph Nicholas, Jr. educator
Paige, Glenn Durland political scientist, educator
Palia, Aspy Phiroze marketing educator, researcher, consultant
Pang, Herbert George ophthalmologist
Parker, R. E., Jr. career officer
Pence, Martin federal judge
Perkins, Frank Overton university official, marine scientist
Pfeiffer, Robert John business executive
Pickens, Frances Jenkins jewelry/metal artist, art educator
Pien, Francis D. internist, microbiologist
Pilar, L. Prudencio R. financial services executive
†Popper, Jordan S. physician
Potts, Dennis Walker lawyer
Quinn, William Francis lawyer
Raleigh, Cecil Baring geophysicist
Rambo, A. Terry anthropologist, researcher
Rapson, Richard L. history educator
Rautenberg, Robert Frank consulting statistician
Reber, David James lawyer
Rehg, Kenneth Lee linguistics educator
Reinke, Stefan Michael lawyer
Rexner, Romulus publishing executive
Riggs, Fred Warren political science educator
Roberson, Kelley Cleve health care financial executive
Robinson, Robert Blacque foundation administrator
Roehr, Kathleen Marie nursing administrator
Rogers, Dwane Leslie retired management consultant
Roseberry, Edwin Southall state agency administrator
Rosendal, Hans Erik meteorologist
Sagawa, Yoneo horticulturist, educator
Saiki, Patricia (Mrs. Stanley Mitsuo Saiki) former federal agency administrator, former congresswoman
Sato, Glenn Kenji lawyer
Sato, Richard Michio consulting engineering company executive
Schatz, Irwin Jacob cardiologist
Scheerer, Ernest William dentist
Schoenke, Marilyn Leilani foundation administrator
Scott, David Irvin minister
Seely, Marilyn Ruth state agency administrator
Seidensticker, Edward George Japanese language and literature educator
Sekine, Deborah Keiko systems analyst, programmer
Sharma, Santosh Devraj obstetrician, gynecologist, educator
Shen, Edward Nin-Da cardiologist, educator
Shigetomi, Keith Shigeo lawyer
Shimabukuro, Elton Ichio sales professional
Shoji, Dave women's collegiate volleyball coach
Simonds, John Edward newspaper editor
Singer, Hersh marketing executive
Smales, Fred Benson corporate executive
Smith, Albert Charles biologist, educator
Smith, Barbara Barnard music educator
Smyser, Adam Albert newspaper editor
Solidum, James finance and insurance executive
Sorenson, Perry resort facility executive
Souza, Joan of Arc educational administrator
Sparks, Robert William retired publishing executive
Statler, Oliver Hadley writer
Steinhoff, Patricia Gayle sociology educator
Stephan, John Jason historian, educator
Stephenson, Herman Howard retired banker
Strickland, John Arthur Van minister
†Strode, Walter Sterling urologist
Sugiki, Shigemi ophthalmologist, educator
Suh, Dae-Sook political science educator
Sumida, Kevin P.H. lawyer
Sutton, Charles Richard architect, designer
Szumotalska Stamper, Ewa psychologist
Takumi, Roy Mitsuo state representative
Tamura, Neal Noboru dentist, consultant
Tatibouet, Andre Stephan condominium and resort management firm executive
Tehranian, Majid political economy and communications educator
Terminella, Luigi critical care physician, educator
Tharp, James Wilson lawyer
Thomas, Verneda Estella retired perfusionist
Timbers, Judith Ann academic administrator, writer
Tito, Maureen Louise educational administrator
Topping, Donald M. English language professional, educator
Turbin, Richard lawyer
Twigg-Smith, Thurston newspaper publisher
Uhl, Philip Edward marine artist
Usui, Leslie Raymond retired clothing executive
Varley, Herbert Paul Japanese language and cultural history educator
Varner, Helen communication educator
Vercauteren, Richard Frank career officer
Vidal, Alejandro Legaspi architect
Vogel, Carl-Wilhelm Ernst biomedical scientist, clinical pathologist
Vroom, Jennifer Galleher history educator
Wageman, Lynette Mena librarian
†Wakatsuki, Lynn Y. commissioner
Wallach, Stephen Joseph cardiologist
Wang, Jaw-Kai agricultural engineering educator
Weight, Michael Anthony lawyer, former judge
Weiner, Ferne psychologist
White, Emmet, Jr. retirement community administrator
White, Gary Richard electrical engineer, plant operator
Williams, Carl Harwell utilities executive
Williams, Mark Riley video producer, director
†Wilson, Charles Robert port captain, harbor master
Wilson, William James healthcare executive
Witeck, John Joseph labor union representative, educator
Wolff, Herbert Eric banker, former army officer
Wong, Alfred Mun Kong lawyer
Woo, Vernon Ying-Tsai lawyer, real estate developer, judge
Wright, Chatt Grandison academic administrator
Yamada, Stephen Kinichi lawyer, real estate developer
Yamamoto, Harry Yoshimi biochemist, educator
†Yamashita, Francis Isami magistrate judge
Yamato, Kei C. international business consultant
Yang, David Chie-Hwa business administration educator
Yap, Frank, Jr. lawyer
Yee, Alfred Alphonse structural engineer, consultant
Yeh, Raymond Wei-Hwa architect, educator
†Yim, Mario K.M. financial planner
Yoshihara, Elva nursing educator
Zaleski, Halina Maria animal scientist

Kaaawa
Baldridge, Melinda E. psychiatric nurse specialist

Kahului
Nishimoto, Marc Makoto research chemist
Richardson, Robert Allen lawyer, educator
Shaw, Virginia Ruth clinical psychologist

Kailua
Amos, Wally entrepreneur
Bone, Robert William writer, photojournalist
†Johnson, Ronald Charles psychology educator
Lundquist, Dana Richard healthcare executive
Tokumaru, Roberta principal
Young, Jacqueline Eurn Hai state legislator, consultant

Kailua Kona
Ashley, Darlene Joy psychologist
Clewett, Kenneth Vaughn college official
Diama, Benjamin retired educator, artist, composer, writer
Feaver, Douglas David retired university dean, classics educator
Luizzi, Ronald wholesale distribution executive
Martin, William Charles retired lawyer, law educator
Scarr, Sandra Wood psychology educator, researcher
Spitze, Glenys Smith retired educator
Wageman, Virginia Farley editor, writer
Zimmerman, William Irving lawyer
Zola, Michael S. lawyer

Kalaupapa
Alexander, Dean museum director

Kamuela
Mc Dermott, John Francis, Jr. psychiatrist, physician
Young, Ernest park administrator

Kaneohe
Donahoe, Peter Aloysius lawyer
Fisette, Scott Michael golf course designer
Fukumoto, Geal S. investment representative
Hanson, Richard Edwin civil engineer
Ikeda, Moss Marcus Masanobu retired state education official, lecturer, consultant
Lange-Otsuka, Patricia Ann nursing educator
McGlaughlin, Thomas Howard publisher, retired naval officer
Westerdahl, John Brian nutritionist, health educator

Kapaa
Chimoskey, John Edward physiologist, medical educator
Kahn, Martin Jerome art gallery owner
Outcalt, David Lewis academic administrator, mathematician, educator, consultant

Kapaau
Jankowski, Theodore Andrew artist
McFee, Richard electrical engineer, physicist

Keaau
Kawachika, Jean Keiko middle school educator

Kihei
Burns, Richard Gordon retired lawyer, writer, consultant
†McCullough-Dieter, Carol Mae database administrator
Wright, Thomas Parker computer science educator
†Yamada, Shige artist

Koloa
Cobb, Rowena Noelani Blake real estate broker

Kula
Rohlfing, Frederick William lawyer, travel executive, political consultant, retired judge

Lahaina
Conover, Robert Warren retired librarian
Sato, Tadashi artist

Laie
Allen, Merle Maeser, Jr. lawyer

Lanai City
Black, Anderson Duane writer, business consultant
Keenan-Abilay, Georgia Ann service representative

Lihue
†Cabanting, Judy Bayuca elementary educator
Lai, Waihang art educator
Lenthall, Judith Faith non-profit corporation administrator
Lovell, Carol museum director
Pironti, Lavonne De Laere developer, fundraiser
Shigemoto, April Fumie English educator secondary school
Stephens, Jack writer, photographer
Stevens, Robert David librarian, educator
Tanaka, Leila Chiyako lawyer

Makawao
Lester, John James Nathaniel, II (Sean Lester) engineer, environmental analyst, human rights activist

Mililani
Gardner, Sheryl Paige gynecologist
Kiley, Thomas rehabilitation counselor
Magee, Donald Edward retired national park service administrator
Neff, Pamela Marie medical/surgical nurse

Ocean View
Gilliam, Jackson Earle bishop

Pahoa
Lewis, Jack (Cecil Paul Lewis) publishing executive, editor
Satterwhite, Sharon mental health nurse

Paia
†Loomis, James Cook educator

Papaikou
Andrasick, James Stephen agribusiness company executive
Buyers, John William Amerman agribusiness and specialty foods company executive

Pearl City
Hodgson, Lynn Morrison marine biologist
Kanenaka, Rebecca Yae microbiologist
Lee, Kenneth secondary education educator
Matsuoka, Eric Takao mathematics educator
Rhinelander, Esther Richard secondary school educator
Roberts, Norman Frank English composition and linguistics educator
Sue, Alan Kwai Keong dentist
Tokuno, Kenneth Alan college dean, poet

Pearl Harbor
Clemins, Archie R. naval career officer
Mirick, Robert Allen military officer

Pukalani
Fredericksen, Walter Mailand behavioral and ocean sciences educator emeritus

Puunene
Kubota, Gaylord museum director
Tocho, Lee Frank mechanical engineer

Schofield Barracks
†Campbell, James L. military career officer
Chau, Hung engineer, educator

Tripler Army Medical Center
Adams, Nancy R. nurse, military officer
Uyehara, Catherine Fay Takako (Yamauchi) physiologist, educator, pharmacologist

Wahiawa
Kiyota, Heide Pauline clinical psychologist

Waialua
Singlehurst, Dona Geisenheyner horse farm owner

Waianae
Hiapo, Patricia Kamaka lay worker
Kakugawa, Terri Etsumi osteopath
Pinckney, Neal Theodore psychologist, educator

Waikoloa
Switaj, Carmen Marie administrative assistant

Wailuku
Baker, Rosalyn Hester economic development administrator
Isbell, Alan Gregory editor, writer, publisher
Kinaka, William Tatsuo lawyer
Savona, Michael Richard physician

Waimanalo
†Okimoto, Dean J. farmer, marketing consultant

Waipahu
Casey, James Leroy curriculum director

IDAHO

American Falls
Newlin, L. Max parks and recreation director

Bancroft
Larsen, Aileen principal
Pristupa, David William secondary education educator

Bellevue
Pearson, Robert Greenlees writing services company executive

Boise
†Alcorn, James M. state insurance administrator
Andrus, Cecil Dale academic administrator
Appleton, Steven R. electronics executive
Baird, Donald Robert secondary school educator
Barber, Phillip Mark lawyer
Beaumont, Pamela Jo marketing professional
Beebe, Stephen A. agricultural products company executive
Benavides, Mary Kathleen anesthesiologist, nutritional consultant
Benham, James H. state official
Black, Pete retired state legislator, educator
Bolles, Charles Avery librarian

†Boren, Robert Reed *communication educator*
Boyle, Larry Monroe *federal judge*
Brownfield, Shelby Harold *soil scientist*
Burton, Lawrence DeVere *agriculturist, educator*
Caufield, Marie Celine *religious organization administrator*
Cenarrusa, Pete T. *secretary of state*
Cleary, Edward William *retired diversified forest products company executive*
Craig, Kara Lynn *chief executive officer*
Doolittle, Michael Jim *lawyer*
Driscoll, Michael P. *bishop*
†Eastland, Larry L. *entertainment and theme park development executive*
Ellis-Vant, Karen McGee *elementary and special education educator, consultant*
Erickson, Robert Stanley *lawyer*
†Ewing, Jack *communications executive*
†Gee, Gavin M. *state government official*
†Gellert, Edward Bradford *advertising agency executive*
Geston, Mark Symington *lawyer*
Gray, Lonna Irene *indemnity fund executive*
Harad, George Jay *manufacturing company executive*
Hawkins, James Victor *state official*
Heitman, Gregory Erwin *state official*
Hendren, Merlyn Churchill *investment company executive*
Hoagland, Samuel Albert *lawyer, pharmacist*
Hoffman, William Kenneth *retired obstetrician, gynecologist*
Holleran, John W. *lawyer*
Huckstead, Charlotte Van Horn *retired home economist, artist*
Hunsucker, (Carl) Wayne *architectural firm executive, educator*
Ilett, Frank, Jr. *trucking company executive, educator*
Jones, Donna Marilyn *real estate broker, legislator*
Kemp, J. Robert *beef industry consultant, food company executive*
Kempthorne, Dirk Arthur *governor*
Khatain, Kenneth George *psychiatrist, former air force officer*
Lance, Alan George *state attorney general*
Lawrence, Ralph Alan *minister*
Lee, Roger Ruojia *semiconductor engineer*
Leonard, John William, Jr. *engineering executive*
Leroy, David Henry *lawyer, state and federal official*
Littman, Irving *forest products company executive*
Lodge, Edward James *federal judge*
Long, William D. *grocery store executive*
Maloof, Giles Wilson *academic administrator, educator, author*
McClary, James Daly *retired contractor*
McDevitt, Charles Francis *state supreme court justice*
Mc Quade, Henry Ford *state justice*
Meyer, Christopher Hawkins *lawyer*
Michael, Gary G. *retail supermarket and drug chain executive*
Minnich, Diane Kay *state bar executive*
Mock, Stanley Clyde *certified financial planner, investment advisor*
Myers, William Gerry, III *lawyer*
Nelson, Thomas G. *federal judge*
Nelson, Willard Gregory *veterinarian, mayor*
Noack, Harold Quincy, Jr. *lawyer*
Nuttall, Michael Lee *engineer, educator*
Olson, Richard Dean *researcher, pharmacology educator*
†Orien, Harold Andrew *customer service representative*
Otter, Clement Leroy *lieutenant governor*
Overgaard, Willard Michele *retired political scientist, jurisprudent*
†Pappas, Jim D. *chief bankruptcy judge*
†Park, William Anthony (Tony) *lawyer*
Peterson, Eileen M. *state agency director, administrator*
†Pimble, Toni *artistic director, choreographer, educator*
Pomeroy, Horace Burton, III *accountant, corporate executive*
Pon-Brown, Kay Migyoku *research and development project administrator*
Porter, Barbara Reidhaar *accounting executive*
Randall, Sherri Lee *accountant*
Richardson, Betty H. *prosecutor*
Risch, James E. *lawyer*
Ruch, Charles P. *academic administrator*
Saldin, Thomas R. *lawyer, consumer products company executive*
Shurtliff, Marvin Karl *lawyer*
†Spalding, James C. *state official*
†Starry, Pamela Faye *elementary educator*
†Stead, Jerre L. *telecommunications company executive*
Sullivan, James Kirk *retired forest products company executive*
Swanson, Kenneth J. *museum administrator*
†Takasugi, Patrick A. *state agency administrator*
Terteling, Carolyn Ann *city official*
Thornton, John S., IV *retired bishop*
Trott, Stephen Spangler *federal judge, musician*
True, Leland Beyer *civil engineer, consultant*
VanHole, William Remi *lawyer*
Wells, Merle William *historian, state archivist*
Wentz, Catherine Jane *elementary education educator*
†Williams, J. D. *state controller*
†Williams, Mikel H. *magistrate judge*
Wilson, Jack Fredrick *retired federal government official*
Winmill, B. Lynn *judge*
Yang, Baiyin *adult education educator*

Bonners Ferry
McClintock, William Thomas *health care administrator*

Burley
King, Janet Felland *family nurse practitioner*

Caldwell
Attebery, Louie Wayne *English language educator, folklorist*
Hendren, Robert Lee, Jr. *academic administrator*
Kerrick, David Ellsworth *lawyer*
Lonergan, Wallace Gunn *economics educator, management consultant*

Coeur D Alene
Adams, Elinor Ruth *retired laboratory technician*
Dahlgren, Dorothy *museum director*
Dunnigan, Mary Ann *former educational administrator*
Griffith, William Alexander *former mining company executive*
Medved, Sandra Louise *elementary education educator*
†Rosdahl, Nils *educator*
Sanderson, Holladay Worth *domestic violence advocate*
Strimas, John Howard *allergist, immunologist, pediatrician*
West, Robert Sumner *surgeon*

Donnelly
†Edwards, Lydia Justice *state official*

Driggs
Cantwell, William Patterson *lawyer*

Eagle
Kenyon, Kendra Sue *organizational consultant*
Tschacher, Darell Ray *mortgage banking executive*

Harrison
Carlson, George Arthur *artist*

Hayden
Morris, Mary Ann *bookkeeper*

Hayden Lake
Wogsland, James Willard *retired heavy machinery manufacturing executive*

Homedale
Patterson, Beverly Ann Gross *fund raising consultant, grant writer, federal grants administrator, social services administrator, poet*

Idaho Falls
Call, Joseph Rudd *accountant*
Daniher, John M. *retired engineer*
Harris, Darryl Wayne *publishing executive*
Harvego, Edwin Allan *mechanical engineer*
Jacobsen, Richard T *mechanical engineering educator*
Kirkland, Judy Joylene *computer specialist*
Leverett, Margaret Ann *women's health nurse practitioner*
LoPiccolo, John *conductor, music director*
Miller, Gregory Kent *structural engineer*
Paik, Seungho *mechanical engineer*
Parkinson, Howard Evans *insurance company executive*
Riddoch, Hilda Johnson *accountant*
Riemke, Richard Allan *mechanical engineer*
Thorsen, James Hugh *aviation director, airport manager, retired*
Thorsen, Nancy Dain *real estate broker*
Whittier, Monte Ray *lawyer*
Williams, Phyllis Cutforth *retired realtor*

Inkom
Ambrose, Tommy W. *chemical engineer, executive*

Jerome
Feiss, Hugh Bernard *priest, religious educator*
†Ricketts, Virginia Lee *historian, researcher*

Kellogg
Haller, Ann Cordwell *secondary school educator*

Ketchum
Ziebarth, Robert Charles *management consultant*

Kimberly
Maschek, Roger Alan *counselor*

Lewiston
Aherin, Darrel William *lawyer*
Peterson, Philip Everett *legal educator*
Scott, Linda Byrne *artist*
Smith, Phyllis Mae *healthcare consultant, educator*
Tait, John Reid *lawyer*

Menan
Webb, Marilyn McCoy *middle school educator*

Middleton
Brown, Ilene De Lois *special education educator*

Moscow
Anderson, Clifton Einar *writer, communications consultant*
Bitterwolf, Thomas Edwin *chemistry educator*
Bobisud, Larry Eugene *mathematics educator*
Butterfield, Samuel Hale *former government official and educator*
DeShazer, James Arthur *biological engineer, educator, administrator*
Force, Ronald Wayne *librarian*
Goetschel, Roy Hartzell, Jr. *mathematician, researcher*
Goszczynski, Stefan *chemistry educator*
Greever, William St. Clair *educator, historian*
Harris, Robert Dalton *history educator, researcher, writer*
Hatch, Charles R. *university dean*
Hendee, John Clare *university research educator*
Hoover, Robert Allan *university president*
Jackson, Melbourne Leslie *chemical engineering educator and administrator, consultant*
Jankowska, Maria Anna *librarian, educator*
Johnson, Brian Keith *electrical engineering educator*
Kennedy, Mary Virginia *diplomat*
Miller, Maynard Malcolm *geologist, educator, research institute director, explorer, state legislator*
Roberts, Lorin Watson *botanist, educator*
Scott, James Michael *research biologist*
Shreeve, Jean'ne Marie *chemist, educator*
Stumpf, Bernhard Josef *physicist*
Vincenti, Sheldon Arnold *law educator, lawyer*
Woodall, David Monroe *research engineer, dean*

Mountain Home
Graves, Karen Lee *high school counselor*
Hiddleston, Ronal Eugene *drilling and pump company executive*
Krueger, Candice Jae *assistant principal*

Mountain Home A F B
Borchert, Warren Frank *elementary education educator*
†Schmidt, Randall M. *military official*

Nampa
Botimer, Allen Ray *retired surgeon, retirement center owner*
Franklin, Leonard G. *engineer*
Heidt, Raymond Joseph *insurance company executive*
Hopkins, Martha Jane *education educator*
Kloosterhuis, Robert John *publishing association company executive*
Lodahl, Michael Eugene *religion educator*
Redfield, David Allen *chemistry educator*
Shaffer, Mary Louise *art educator*

New Plymouth
Matthews-Burwell, Vicki *elementary education educator*

Plummer
Matheson, Donna Jane *communications executive, editor*

Pocatello
Bott-Graham, Michelle Lynn *behavior therapist*
Bowen, Richard Lee *academic administrator, political science educator*
†DeTienne, Darcy A. *university administrator*
Eichman, Charles Melvin *career assessment educator, school counselor*
Hazen, Dean Scott *meteorologist*
Hillyard, Ira William *pharmacologist, educator*
Jackson, Allen Keith *museum administrator*
†Larsen, Stephen Allan *endowment administrator, financial planner*
McCune, Mary Joan Huxley *microbiology educator*
Pemberton, Cynthia Lee A. *physical education educator*
Sagness, Richard Lee *education educator, former academic dean*
Seeley, Rod Ralph *physiology educator*
Smith, Evelyn Elaine *language educator*
Spadafore, Gerald Joseph *psychology educator*
Stanek, Alan Edward *music educator, performer, music administrator*
Van Pelt, Tamise Jo *English educator*
†Wahl, Russell Edward *philosphy educator*

Post Falls
Brede, Andrew Douglas *research director, plant breeder*
Grassi, James Edward *Christian ministry executive director*
Mikles, Chris *secondary school educator*

Rexburg
Terry, Steven Spencer *mathematics educator, consultant*

Saint Anthony
Blower, John Gregory *special education educator*

Salmon
†Nisbet, Marian Frances *community and political activist*
Snook, Quinton *construction company executive*
Wiederrick, Robert *museum director*

Shelley
Thompson, Sandra Jane *secondary school educator*

Soda Springs
†Clark, Trent L. *federal affairs manager*

Stanley
Kimpton, David Raymond *natural resource consultant, writer*

Sun Valley
†Bieker, Fred William *plastic surgeon*
Briley, John Richard *writer*

Troy
Hepler, Merlin Judson, Jr. *real estate broker*

Twin Falls
Anderson, Marilyn Nelle *elementary education educator, librarian, counselor*
Fanselow, Julie Ruth *writer*
Halsell, George Kay *music educator*
Hohnhorst, John Charles *lawyer*
Jones, Douglas Raymond *farming executive, state legislator*
Shuss, John Logan *surgeon*
†Studebaker, William Vern *sports and literature educator, writer*
Tolman, Steven Kay *lawyer*
Woods, James C. *museum director*
Yost, Kelly Lou *pianist*

Wilder
Culton, Sarah Alexander *psychologist, writer*
Olsen, Helen May *author*

ILLINOIS

Abbott Park
Allen, Steven Paul *microbiologist*
Bush, Eugene Nyle *pharmacologist, research scientist*
Coughlan, Gary Patrick *pharmaceutical company executive*
Fath, Michael John *pharmaceutical/health care stategic planner*
Frazier, Douglas Byron *health care consultant*
Geist, Jill Marie *medical writer*
Jeng, Tzyy-Wen *biochemist*
Lussen, John Frederick *pharmaceutical laboratory executive*
†Robbins, Paul LaVerne *pharmaceutical executive*
Young, Jay Maitland *product manager health care products*

Addieville
Utke, Robert Ahrens *minister*

Addison
Baillie-David, Sonja Kirsteen *controller*
Brunken, Gerald Walter, Sr. *manufacturing company executive*
†Christopher, Doris *consumer products executive*
†Kelsay, Bruce D. *school psychologist*
†Leiber, Annete Perone *artist, art association administrator*
McDonald, David Eugene *package car driver*
Nedza, Sandra Louise *manufacturing executive*

Aledo
Prosser, Wesley Lewis *advertising and public relations executive*

Alton
Dickey, Keith Winfield *dentist, dental educator*
Fortado, Robert Joseph *librarian, educator*
Hoagland, Karl King, Jr. *lawyer*
Kisabeth, Tim Charles *obstetrician, gynecologist*
Schnabel, John Henry *retired music educator*
Struif, L. James *lawyer*
Talbert, Hugh Mathis *lawyer*

Alvin
Story, Judith K. *adult day care owner, administrator*

AMF Ohare
Kalcevic, Timothy Francis *airline pilot, educator*

Anna
Wolfe, Martha *elementary education educator*

Antioch
Dahl, Laurel Jean *human services administrator*
Zeman, Don *secondary education educator, coach*

Argenta
†Bowman, Cynthia D. *library director*

Argo
Castellano, Christine Marie *lawyer*

Argonne
Blander, Milton *chemist*
Carpenter, John Marland *engineer, physicist*
Chang, Yoon Il *nuclear engineer*
Derrick, Malcolm *physicist*
DiMelfi, Ronald J. *materials scientist*
Fields, Paul Robert *retired research nuclear chemist, consultant*
Green, David William *chemist, educator*
Haupt, H. James *mechanical design engineer*
Herzenberg, Caroline Stuart Littlejohn *physicist*
Katz, Joseph Jacob *chemist, educator*
Kumar, Romesh *chemical engineer*
Lawson, Robert Davis *theoretical nuclear physicist*
Masek, Mark Joseph *laboratory administrator*
Mattas, Richard Frank *nuclear energy industry executive*
Miller, Shelby Alexander *chemical engineer, educator*
Morss, Lester Robert *chemist*
Panchal, Chandrakant B. *chemical engineer, researcher*
Perlow, Gilbert J(erome) *physicist, editor*
Peshkin, Murray *physicist*
Sabau, Carmen Sybile *chemist*
Saricks, Christopher Lee *transportation analyst*
Schiffer, John Paul *physicist*
Schriesheim, Alan *research administrator*
†Sedlet, Jacob *chemist*
Steindler, Martin Joseph *chemist*
Stock, Leon Milo *chemist, educator*
Till, Charles Edgar *nuclear engineer*

Arlington Heights
Baumann, Daniel E. *newspaper executive*
Biestek, John Paul *lawyer*
Burdsall, Deborah Patterson *geriatrics nurse, educator*
Catrambone, Kathy *journalist*
†Chen, Wen *software engineer, researcher*
Church, Herbert Stephen, Jr. *retired construction company executive*
Crawford, Robert W., Jr. *furniture rental company executive*
DeDonato, Donald Michael *obstetrician/gynecologist*
Dickau, John C. *religious organization executive*
Di Prima, Stephanie Marie *educational administrator*
Gabrielsen, Carol Ann *employment consulting company executive*
Griffin, Jean Latz *writer, political strategist, small business owner*
Hudson, Ronald Morgan *aviation planner*
Hughes, John *chemical company executive*
Lampinen, John A. *newspaper editor*
Lewin, Seymour Zalman *chemistry educator, consultant*
Li, Norman N. *chemicals executive*
Lobo, Philip Anthony *radiation oncologist*
Nerlinger, John William *trade association administrator*
Paddock, Robert Young *retired publisher*
Payne, Thomas, II *market research company executive*
Placek-Zimmerman, Ellyn Clare *school system administrator, educator, consultant*
†Placik, Otto Joseph *plastic surgeon*
Pochyly, Donald Frederick *physician, hospital administrator*
Pollin, Pierre Louis *executive chef*
Ray, Douglas Kent *newspaper executive*
Ricker, Robert S. *religious organization administrator*
†Ruder, John Regan *physician*
Shetty, Mulki Radhakrishna *oncologist, consultant*
Shuman, Nicholas Roman *journalist, educator*
Smith, Norman Obed *physical chemist, educator*
Spohr, Frederick Stephen *sales professional*
Tongue, William Walter *economics and business consultant, educator emeritus*
Walter, Robert Irving *chemistry educator, chemist*

Ashland
Benz, Donald Ray *nuclear safety engineer, researcher*

Auburn
Burtle, Debra Ann *needlework and gift shop owner*
Burtle, Paul Walter *farmer*

Aurora
Alschuler, Sam *retired lawyer*

Belcher, La Jeune *automotive parts company executive*
Camic, David Edward *lawyer*
†Cano, Juventino *manufacturing company executive*
Cochran, William Michael *librarian*
Easley, Pauline Marie *retired elementary school educator*
Etheredge, Forest DeRoyce *former state senator, university administrator*
Halfvarson, Lucille Robertson *music educator*
Halloran, Kathleen L. *financial executive, accountant*
†Kheshgi-Genovese, Zareena *psychotherapist, educator*
Lee, Robert Hugh *management executive*
McCleary, Scott Fitzgerald *lawyer*
McKenzie, John W. *mathematician, educator*
Nelson, Kay Hoyle *communication educator*
Settles, William Frederick *secondary and university educator, administrator*
Sloan, Michael Lee *secondary education educator*
†Stallons, James C. *secondary education educator*
Stephens, Steve Arnold *real estate broker*
†Thompson, John Tyrus *secondary education educator, consultant*
Toler, Randall Douglas *computer consultant*
Zarle, Thomas Herbert *academic administrator*

Bannockburn
Slavin, Craig Steven *management and franchising consultant*

Barrington
Bash, Philip Edwin *publishing executive*
Cass, Robert Michael *lawyer, consultant*
Chung, Joseph Sang-hoon *economics educator*
Dykla, K.H.S. Edward George *retired social services administrator*
Fowler, Susan Michele *real estate broker, entrepreneur*
Francis, Philip Hamilton *management consultant*
Furst, Warren Arthur *retired holding company executive*
Groesch, John William, Jr. *marketing research consultant*
Hicks, Jim *secondary education educator*
Koten, John A. *retired communications executive*
Kroha, Bradford King *electronics manufacturing corporation executive*
Lee, William Marshall *lawyer*
Leon, Edward *investor*
Lessman, Robert Edward *lawyer*
Mathis, Jack David *advertising executive*
Murphy, Robert *search firm executive*
Nadolski, Stephanie Lucille *artist, designer*
Perry, I. Chet *petroleum company executive*
Porter, Stuart Williams *investment company executive*
Riendeau, Diane *secondary school educator*
Ross, Frank Howard, III *management consultant*
Schaefer, Mary Ann *health facility administrator, consultant*
Stephens, Norval Blair, Jr. *marketing consultant*
Stoutenburg, Jane Sue Williamson *nurse practitioner, fund raiser, actress*
Sturm, Sherri Charisse *marketing and developmental researcher, actuary*
Tobin, Dennis Michael *lawyer*
White, Jeffrey Paul *lawyer*
Wood, Andrée Robitaille *archaeologist, researcher*
Wyatt, James Frank, Jr. *lawyer*
Wynn, Thomas Joseph *judge, educator*

Bartlett
Robinson, Jack Fay *clergyman*
Robinson, Lois Hart *retired public relations executive*

Bartonville
Graves, Carol Kenney *construction company executive*

Batavia
Bardeen, William Allan *research physicist*
Bicknell, Brian Keith *dentist*
Chrisman, Bruce Lowell *physicist, administrator*
Jonckheere, Alan Mathew *physicist*
Lach, Joseph Theodore *physicist*
Peoples, John, Jr. *physicist, researcher*
†Quigg, Chris *physicist*
Schilling, Arlo Leonard *bank executive*
Thompson, Juul Harold *lawyer, educator*
Witherell, Michael S. *physicist*

Beardstown
Gross, Shirley Marie *artist, farm manager*

Bedford Park
Wenstrup, H. Daniel *chemical company executive*

Beecher
Barber, Robert Owen *village administrator*
Termuende, Edwin Arthur *retired chemistry educator*

Belleville
Bailey, Susan Carol *commercial banking executive*
Bauman, John Duane *lawyer*
Berkley, Gary Lee *newspaper publisher*
Boyle, Richard Edward *lawyer*
Brian, Patricia Ann *social services administrator*
Coghill, William Thomas, Jr. *lawyer*
Connors, Jimmy (James Scott Connors) *professional tennis player*
Ferguson, John Marshall *retired federal magistrate judge*
Fietsam, Robert Charles *accountant*
Franks, David Bryan *internist, emergency physician*
Gregory, Wilton D. *bishop*
Heiligenstein, Christian E. *lawyer*
Hess, Frederick J. *lawyer*
Holbrook, Thomas Aldredge *state legislator*
James, Ernest Wilbur *lawyer*
Kramer, Andrew Joseph *clergyman*
Looman, Gary John *minister*
Parham, James Robert *lawyer*
Taylor, Lynne M. *medical/surgical nurse*
Tinoco, Patricia Ann *elementary education educator*
Waller, Paul Pressley, Jr. *lawyer*
Wittenbrink, Boniface Leo *priest*

Bellwood
McCullough-Wiggins, Lydia Statoria *pharmacist, consultant*

Belvidere
Britt, Ronald Leroy *manufacturing company executive*
Luhman, William Simon *community development administrator*

Bensenville
Demouth, Robin Madison *lawyer, corporate executive*
Leach, Donald Paul *small business owner*
Lewis, Darrell L. *retail executive*
Matera, Richard Ernest *minister*
Naker, Mary Leslie *export transportation company executive*

Benton
Foreman, James Louis *retired judge*
†Frazier, Phillip M. *federal judge*
Gilbert, J. Phil *federal judge*
Glasco, Sue Alice *retired educator*

Berwyn
Gordon, Dolores Joan *retired emergency medical technician*
Lofquist, Lisa Willson *occupational therapist, business owner*
Misurec, Rudolf *physician, surgeon*

Bethalto
Gallinot, Ruth Maxine *educational consultant*
Wilson, Sandra Jean *principal*

Bethany
Syfert, Samuel Ray *retired librarian*

Bloomingdale
Konopinski, Virgil James *industrial hygienist*
Pelant, Barney Frank *international business consulting executive*
Richard, David Dean *publishing executive*
Wolfe, Carl Dean *electrical engineer*

Bloomington
Axley, Dixie L. *insurance company executive*
Bragg, Michael Ellis *lawyer, insurance company executive*
Brown, Jared *theater director, educator, writer*
Callis, Bruce *insurance company executive*
Carlson, David Noel *landscape architect, sculptor*
Casey-Beich, Micheal Louanna *artist*
Curry, Alan Chester *insurance company executive*
Daily, Jean A. *marketing executive, spokesperson*
Dickson, Robert Frank *nursing home executive*
Engelkes, Donald John *insurance company executive*
Friedman, Joan M. *accounting educator*
Godt, Earl Wayne, II *technology education educator*
Goebel, William Mathers *lawyer*
Harms, David Jacob *agricultural consultant*
Hinojosa, David *fraud examiner*
Hoyt, Don, Sr. *home builder, former association executive*
Johnson, Earle Bertrand *insurance executive*
Joslin, Roger Scott *insurance company executive*
Kelly, Timothy William *lawyer*
Key, Otta Bischof *retired educator*
Lauritson, Judy Marie *nursing consultant*
Lord, Timothy Charles *philosophy educator*
Merwin, Davis Underwood *newspaper executive*
Myers, Minor, Jr. *academic administrator, political science educator*
Olson, Rue Eileen *librarian*
Rodman, Raymond G. *insurance company executive*
Rust, Edward Barry, Jr. *insurance company executive, lawyer*
Shelley, Edward Herman, Jr. *retired insurance company executive*
Simpson, J. Christopher *academic administrator*
Sullivan, Laura Patricia *lawyer, insurance company executive*
Switzer, Jon Rex *architect*
Trefzger, Richard Charles *surgeon*
Vayo, David Joseph *composer, music educator*
Ward, Jon David *insurance company executive*
Watkins, Lloyd Irion *university president*
Webb, O. Glenn *farm supplies company executive*

Blue Island
Yager, Vincent Cook *banker*

Bolingbrook
Caddy, Edmund H.H., Jr. *architect*
Katsianis, John Nick *financial executive*
Malicay, Manuel Alaban *physician*
Price, Theodora Hadzisteliou *individual and family therapist*
Relwani, Nirmal Murlidhar (Nick Relwani) *mechanical engineer*
Willadsen, Michael Chris *marketing professional, sales executive*

Bone Gap
Putt, Jerry Wayne *municipal official*

Bourbonnais
Bahls, Gene Charles *agricultural products company executive*
Koehler, Frank James *city manager*
Peters, Betty A. *physical education educator*

Bradford
†Jason, Mary L. *librarian*

Bradley
Anderson, Janice Lee Ator *secondary education mathematics educator*
Marsh, Carla A. *document control group leader*

Bridgeport
Legg, Ronald Otis *oil company executive*
McMillen, Julie Lynn *educator*

Bridgeview
Parmer, Dan Gerald *veterinarian*

Broadview
Christopher, Alexander George *transportation company executive*
Cousins, William Thomas *industrial engineer, educator*

Brookfield
Dornhecker, Sandra Lee *human resources executive, consultant*
Hansen, Donald Marty *journalist, accountant*
Pick, Richard Samuel Burns *educator, composer*
Rabb, George Bernard *zoologist*
Stejskal, Joseph Frank, Jr. *carbohydrate chemist*

Buffalo Grove
Dimond, Robert Edward *publisher*
Johnson, Craig Theodore *portfolio manager*
Kole, Julius S. *lawyer*
Leonetti, Michael Edward *financial planner*
Serbus, Pearl Sarah Dieck *former freelance writer, former editor*
Shields, Patrick Thomas, Jr. *retired property manager*
Tracy, Allen Wayne *management consultant*
Wigodner, Byron I. *pharmaceutical executive*

Burbank
Juodvalkis, Egle *writer*

Burr Ridge
Bottom, Dale Coyle *management consultant*
Finnegan, James John, Jr. *editor, publisher*
Greulich, Robert Charles *insurance company marketing executive*
Rosenberg, Robert Brinkmann *technology organization executive*
Sund, Jeffrey Owen *publishing company executive*

Byron
Oneil, Susan Jean *media specialist*

Cahokia
Healy, Steven Michael *accountant, city official*
†Hoffman, Marc Olin *state official*
Trikha, Ajit *psychiatrist*
Wade, Susan Kaye *elementary education educator*

Calumet City
Jandes, Kenneth Michael *superintendent of schools*
Kovach, Joseph William *management consultant, psychologist, educator*
Palagi, Robert Gene *college administrator*
Self, Madison Allen *chemical company executive*
Strubbe, Thomas R. *insurance industry executive*

Carbondale
Ammon, Harry *history educator*
Bauner, Ruth Elizabeth *library administrator, reference librarian*
Benjamin-Kruge, Siona *artist, educator*
Buckley, John Joseph, Jr. *health care executive*
Burr, Brooks Milo *zoology educator*
†Chavasse, Philippe *foreign languages educator*
Clemons, John Robert *lawyer*
Cordoni, Barbara Keene *special education educator*
Dixon, Billy Gene *academic administrator*
Eynon, Thomas Grant *sociology educator*
Gilbert, Glenn Gordon *linguistics educator*
†Gilbert, Sharon L. *education educator*
Guernsey, Thomas Franklin *law educator*
Hahn, Lewis Edwin *philosopher, retired educator*
Hart, James Warren *university athletic director, restaurant owner, former professional football player*
Helstern, Linda Lizut *university administrator, poet*
Hofling, Charles Andrew *anthropologist, linguist, educator*
Jaehnig, Walter Bruno, Jr. *communications educator*
Johnson, Elmer Hubert *sociologist, researcher in criminology*
Jugenheimer, Donald Wayne *advertising and communications educator, university administrator*
Koch, David Victor *librarian, administrator*
Koch, Loretta Peterson *librarian, educator*
Lit, Alfred *experimental psychologist, vision science educator, engineering psychology consultant*
Little, Judy Ruth *English educator*
Livengood, Joanne Desler *healthcare administrator*
Mead, John Stanley *university administrator*
Molino, Michael Robert *English educator*
Riley, Peter Christopher *aeronautics company official*
Rubin, Harris B. *psychology educator*
Sanders, John Theodore *academic administrator*
Simon, Paul *former senator, educator, author*
Snyder, Carolyn Ann *university dean, librarian*
Somit, Albert *political educator*
Stetter, John *publishing executive*
Webb, Howard William, Jr. *retired humanities educator, university official*
Whitlock, John Joseph *museum director*
Williams, George Harvey *author*
Wotiz, John Henry *chemist, educator*

Carlinville
Bellm, Joan *civic worker*
Goudy, Josephine Gray *social services administrator*
Koplinski, Sarah E. Pruitt *college development director*
Pride, Miriam R. *college president*

Carlyle
Kottmeyer, Martin S. *farmer, writer*

Carol Stream
Choice, Priscilla Kathryn Means (Penny Choice) *gifted education educator, international consultant*
Darling, Lawrence Dean *engineering computing executive*
Gale, Neil Jan *internet consultant, computer consultant*
Gaukel, Erich John *magazine editor*
Kearns, Janet Catherine *corporate secretary*
LaPorte, Stephen Walter *police officer*
Myra, Harold Lawrence *publisher*
Schmerold, Wilfried Lothar *dermatologist*
Shorney, George Herbert *publishing executive*
Taylor, Kenneth Nathaniel *publishing executive, author*
Trafimow, Jordan Herman *orthopedist*

Carrollton
Strickland, Hugh Alfred *lawyer*

Carterville
Dews, Henry *environmental educator, minister, recycler*
Poshard, Glenn W. *former congressman*

Carthage
Erbes, John Robert *engineering executive*
Glidden, John Redmond *lawyer*
Moore, Richard Alan *optometrist*

Catlin
Phillips, Diana Dawn *nurse*

Centralia
Davidson, Karen Sue *computer software designer*

Champaign
Aiken, Michael Thomas *academic administrator*
Aniello, Anthony Joseph *information system executive*
Arnould, Richard Julius *economist, educator, consultant*
†Arwine, Alan Troy *political educator*
Bailey, Andrew Dewey, Jr. *accounting educator*
Baker, Jack Sherman *architect, designer, educator*
Batzli, George Oliver *ecology educator*
Bentley, Orville George *retired agricultural educator, dean emeritus*
Birmingham, Carolyn *recreation educator*
Brighton, Gerald David *accounting educator*
Buschbach, Thomas Charles *geologist, consultant*
Cammack, Trank Emerson *retired university dean*
Cartwright, Keros *hydrogeologist, researcher*
Christians, Clifford Glenn *communications educator*
Clark, Roger Gordon *educational administrator*
Cribbet, John Edward *law educator, former university chancellor*
Crum, Becky Sue *supervisor, educator*
Davis, James Henry *retired psychology educator*
Due, John Fitzgerald *economist, educator emeritus*
Dulany, Elizabeth Gjelsness *university press administrator*
Eriksen, Charles Walter *psychologist, educator*
Espeseth, Robert D. *park and recreation planning educator*
Flora, Kent Allen *small business owner*
Frampton, George Thomas, Sr. *legal educator*
Fredrickson, L(awrence) Thomas *composer*
Freedman, Philip *physician, educator*
Friedberg, Maurice *Russian literature educator*
†Ganguly, Ananda Roop *business management educator*
Garvey, John Charles *violist, conductor, retired music educator*
Gross, David Lee *geologist*
Guttenberg, Albert Ziskind *planning educator*
Hayasaki, Yoshi *coach*
Hays, Robert Glenn *journalism educator*
Hellmer, Lynne Beberman *education educator*
Herendeen, Robert Albert *environmental scientist*
Herzog, Beverly Leah *hydrogeologist*
Hopkins, Lewis Dean *planner, educator*
Humphreys, Lloyd Girton *research psychologist, educator*
Jackson, Billy Morrow *artist, retired art educator*
Johnson, Lawrence Eugene *lawyer*
Kanfer, Frederick H. *psychologist, educator*
Kindt, John Warren, Sr. *lawyer, educator, consultant*
Klausner, Robert David *facial, plastic and cosmetic surgeon*
Knox, Charles Milton *purchasing agent, consultant*
Koenker, Diane P. *history educator*
Korst, Helmut Hans *mechanical engineer, educator*
Kotoske, Roger Allen *artist, educator*
Krause, Harry Dieter *law educator*
†Kroner, Fred L. *journalist*
Lawrence, Gordon Ray *army noncommissioned officer*
Levin, Geoffrey Arthur *botanist*
Lyon, James Cyril *chemical society executive*
Maggs, Peter Blount *lawyer, educator*
Mamer, Stuart Mies *lawyer*
Mann, Lawrence Robert *university administrator*
Mc Cord, John Harrison *lawyer, educator*
McCulloh, Judith Marie *editor*
Meyer, August Christopher, Jr. *broadcasting company executive, lawyer*
Mies, John Charles *internet industry executive*
Miller, Gregory Allen *psychology educator*
Miller, Harold Arthur *lawyer*
Nesbitt, Juanita *occupational health nurse, medical and surgical nurse*
Nowak, John E. *law educator*
O'Neill, John Joseph *speech educator*
Orr, Daniel *educator, economist*
Perry, Kenneth Wilbur *accounting educator*
Peterson, Roger Lyman *insurance company executive*
Rawles, Edward Hugh *lawyer*
Richards, Daniel Wells *company executive*
Ridlen, Samuel Franklin *agriculture educator*
Riley, Robert Bartlett *landscape architect*
Rosenblatt, Karin Ann *cancer epidemiologist*
Rotunda, Ronald Daniel *law educator, consultant*
Sanderson, Glen Charles *science director*
Schoenfeld, Hanns-Martin Walter *accounting educator*
Schowalter, William Raymond *college dean, educator*
†Searsmith, Kelly Lin *English language educator, writer*
Selby, Barbara Kenaga *bank executive*
Simmons, Ralph Oliver *physics educator*
Slichter, Charles Pence *physicist, educator*
Smith, Ralph Alexander *cultural and educational policy educator*
Smith, Robert Lee *agriculturalist*
Smith, Stanley Edward, Jr. *obstetrician-gynecologist*
Spice, Dennis Dean *venture capitalist*
Spodek, Bernard *early childhood educator*
Sprenkle, Case Middleton *economics educator*
Stone, Victor J. *law educator*
Tracey, Terence John *psychology educator*
Triandis, Harry Charalambos *psychology educator*
Turner, Ron *coach*
Ward, James Gordon *education administration educator*
Wasserman, Stanley *statistician, educator*
Watts, Robert Allan *publisher, lawyer*
Wentworth, Richard Leigh *editor*
Whitaker, Stephen Taylor *geologist, oil exploration consultant*
Wills, Bart Francis *insurance company executive*
Wolfram, Stephen *physicist, computer company executive*

Charleston
Ankenbrand, Larry Joseph *physical education educator*
Boshart, Jeffrey Glenn *sculptor, educator*
Cooper, George Kile *business educator*
Dey, Suhrit K. *mathematician, researcher*

Havey, J. Michael *psychologist, educator*
†Hedges, Edith Rittenhouse *nutrition and home economics educator*
Jones, George Hilton *retired history educator, writer*
Jorns, David Lee *university president*
Kaufman, Susan Jane *journalist, educator*
†Kunkel, Robert Anthony *business educator*
Lee, Young Sook *philosopher, educator*
McCormick, Frank Grady *English educator*
Moler, Donald Lewis *educational psychology educator*
Rich, Steven Wayne *director alumni affairs*
Rives, Stanley Gene *university president emeritus*
Surles, Carol D. *academic administrator*
†Young, Bailey Kilbourne *history educator*

Chatham
Chew, Keith Elvin *healthcare services administrator*
Hoots, Charles Wayne *principal*

Chester
Welge, Donald Edward *food manufacturing executive*

Chicago
Abcarian, Herand *surgeon, educator*
Abelson, Herbert Traub *pediatrician, educator*
Abrams, Lee Norman *lawyer*
Abt, Ralph Edwin *lawyer*
Abt, Sylvia Hedy *dentist*
Acker, Ann *lawyer*
Acker, Frederick George *lawyer*
Acs, Joseph Steven *transportation engineering consultant*
Adair, Wendell Hinton, Jr. *lawyer*
Adelman, Stanley Joseph *lawyer*
Adelman, Steven Herbert *lawyer*
Adelson, Duffie Ann *music school administrator*
Adler, Mortimer Jerome *philosopher, author*
Agarwal, Gyan Chand *engineering educator*
Agema, Gerald Walton *broadcasting company executive*
Aggarwal, Suresh Kumar *mechanical and aerospace engineering educator*
†Agoos, Jeff *professional soccer player*
Ahern, Joseph A. *television station executive*
Aitay, Victor *concert violinist, music educator*
Akers, Michelle Anne *soccer player*
Akos, Francis *violinist*
Al-Chalabi, Margery Lee *economic development services company executive*
†al-Chalabi, Suhail Abdul-Jabbar *transportation executive*
Alesia, James H(enry) *judge*
Aliber, Robert Z. *economist, educator*
Allard, Jean *lawyer, urban planner*
Allen, Belle *management consulting firm executive, communications company executive*
Allen, Janice M. *interior designer, nurse, office manager, actress, model*
†Allen, Julie Michelle *secondary education educator*
Allen, Richard Blose *legal editor, lawyer*
Allen, Ronald Jay *law educator*
Allen, Thomas *alderman*
Allen, Thomas Draper *lawyer*
Almeida, Richard Joseph *finance company administrator*
Almen, Lowell Gordon *church official*
Alonzi, Loreto Peter *finance executive*
Alschuler, John Haas *architect*
Altman, Edith G. *sculptor*
Amato, Isabella Antonia *real estate executive*
Amberg, Thomas L. *public relations executive*
Amonte, Anthony Lewis *professional hockey player*
Amstadter, Laurence *retired architect*
Andersen, Burton Robert *physician, educator*
Andersen, Wayne R. *federal judge*
Anderson, David Albert *lawyer*
Anderson, Edgar Ratcliffe, Jr. *career officer, hospital administrator, physician*
Anderson, Hugh George *bishop*
Anderson, J. Trent *lawyer*
Anderson, John Thomas *lawyer*
Anderson, Jon Stephen *newswriter*
Anderson, Kimball Richard *lawyer*
Anderson, Laurel Alma *nursing educator*
Anderson, Lorraine *secondary education educator*
Anderson, Philip Vernon *retired pastor*
Anderson, William Cornelius, III *lawyer*
Andreoli, Kathleen Gainor *dean, nurse*
Andrews, Robert Lee *clergyman, architect*
Angst, Gerald L. *lawyer*
Annable, James Edward *economist*
Anthony, Michael Francis *lawyer*
Antonio, Douglas John *lawyer*
Anvaripour, M. A. *lawyer*
Appel, Nina Schick *law educator, dean*
Applebaum, Edward Leon *otolaryngologist, educator*
Arditti, Fred D. *economist, former educator*
Arekapudi, Vijayalakshmi *obstetrician-gynecologist*
Arena, Bruce *professional soccer coach*
Argeros, Anthony George *lawyer*
Armstrong, Edwin Richard *lawyer, publisher, editor*
Aronson, Howard Isaac *linguist, educator*
Aronson, Virginia L. *lawyer*
Arpino, Gerald Peter *performing company executive*
Artner, Alan Gustav *art critic, journalist*
Ash, J. Marshall *mathematician, educator*
†Ashman, Martin C. *federal judge*
Aspen, Marvin Edward *federal judge*
Astrachan, Boris Morton *psychiatry educator, consultant*
Athas, Gus James *lawyer*
Atristain-Carrion, Ramiro Javier *investment company executive*
Auerbach, Marshall Jay *lawyer*
Augustynski, Adam J. *lawyer*
Avery, Robert Dean *lawyer*
Axley, Frederick William *lawyer*
Ayman, Iraj *international education consultant*
Babcock, Lyndon Ross, Jr. *environmental engineer, educator*
Bacher, Robert Newell *church official*
Badel, Julie *lawyer*
Baer, John Richard Frederick *lawyer*
Baetz, W. Timothy *lawyer*
Baglivo, Mary L. *client services administrator*
Bailar, Barbara Ann *statistician, researcher*
Bailar, John Christian, III *public health educator, physician, statistician*
Bailey, Robert, Jr. *advertising executive*
Bailey, Robert Short *lawyer*
Baird, Douglas Gordon *law educator*
Baird, Ellen Taylor *art historian, educator*
Baker, Bruce Jay *lawyer*
Baker, James Edward Sproul *retired lawyer*
Baker, Pamela *lawyer*
Baker, Robert J. *medical academic dean, surgeon*
Bakwin, Edward Morris *banker*
Baldwin, Shaun McParland *lawyer*
Balk, Robert A. *medical educator*
Ball, Neal *management consultant, philanthropist*
Balsam, Theodore *physician*
Baltic, Scott Michael *magazine editor*
Balzekas, Stanley, Jr. *museum director*
Ban, Stephen Dennis *natural gas industry research institute executive*
Banerjee, Prashant *industrial engineering educator*
Baniak, Sheila Mary *accountant*
Banks, Deirdre Margaret *church organization administrator*
Banks, William J. P. *alderman*
Banoff, Sheldon Irwin *lawyer*
Baptist, Allwyn J. *health care consultant*
Barber, Edward Bruce *medical products executive*
Barbour, Claude Marie *minister*
Bard, John Franklin *consumer products executive*
Barker, Emmett Wilson, Jr. *trade association executive*
Barker, Walter Lee *thoracic surgeon*
Barker, William Thomas *lawyer*
†Barliant, Ronald *federal judge*
Barnard, Robert N. *lawyer*
Barnes, James Garland, Jr. *lawyer*
Barney, Carol Ross *architect*
Barr, Emily *television station executive*
Barr, John Robert *lawyer*
Barr, Sanford Lee *dentist*
Barrett, Roger Watson *lawyer*
Barriger, John Walker, IV *transportation executive*
Barron, Howard Robert *lawyer*
Barrow, Charles Herbert *investment banker*
Barry, Norman J., Jr. *lawyer*
†Barry, Richard A. *public relations executive*
Bartholomay, William C. *insurance brokerage company executive, professional baseball team executive*
Barton, John Joseph *obstetrician, gynecologist, educator, researcher*
Bartter, Brit Jeffrey *investment banker*
Baruch, Hurd *lawyer, arbitrator*
Basden, Cameron *ballet mistress, dancer*
Bashwiner, Steven Lacelle *lawyer*
Bassiouny, Hishan Salah *surgeon, educator*
Batlivala, Robert Bomi D. *oil company executive, economics educator*
Batlle, Daniel *nephrologist*
Bauer, William Joseph *federal judge*
Baugher, Peter V. *lawyer*
Baughman, Verna Lee *anesthesiologist*
Baum, Bernard Helmut *sociologist, educator*
†Baumgardt, Justi Michelle *soccer player*
Baumhart, Raymond Charles *Roman Catholic church administrator*
Baworowsky, John Michael *academic administrator*
Bayer, Gary Richard *advertising executive*
Beane, Marjorie Noterman *academic administrator*
Beattie, Ted Arthur *zoological gardens and aquarium administrator*
Beavers, William M. *alderman*
Beban, Gary Joseph *real estate corporation officer*
Beck, Irene Clare *educational consultant, writer*
Beck, Philip S. *lawyer*
Beck, Robert Lee *bookstore owner*
Beck, Robert N. *nuclear medicine educator*
Beck, Rodney Roy *baseball player*
Becker, Gary Stanley *economist, educator*
Becker, Michael Allen *physician, educator*
Becker, Robert Allen *data processing executive*
Becker, Theodore Michaelson *lawyer*
Beeby, Thomas H. *architect*
Beecher, William John *zoologist, museum director*
Beem, Jack Darrel *lawyer*
Bell, Clark Wayne *business editor, educator*
Bell, David Arthur *advertising agency executive*
Bell, Kevin J. *zoological park administrator*
Belluschi, Anthony C. *architect*
Benak, James Donald *lawyer*
Bender, Janet Pines *artist*
Bennett, Lerone, Jr. *magazine editor, author*
Bennett, Robert William *law educator*
Bensinger, Peter Benjamin *consulting firm executive*
Benson, Irene M. *nurse*
Benson, Sally Jean *development manager*
Benson, Sara Elizabeth *real estate broker, real estate appraiser*
Bent, Geoffrey Steven *artist, librarian*
Benzon, Honorio Tabal *anesthesiologist*
Berendi, Erlinda Bayaua *physician surgeon*
Berens, Mark Harry *lawyer*
Berenzweig, Jack Charles *lawyer*
†Berger, Jack Chandler *retired physician, surgeon, psychiatrist, educator*
Berger, Robert Michael *lawyer*
Bergonia, Raymond David *venture capitalist*
Berk, Harlan Joseph *numismatist, writer, antiquarian*
Berkoff, Mark Andrew *lawyer*
Berland, Abel Edward *lawyer, realtor*
Berman, Arthur Leonard *state senator*
Berman, Howard Allen *rabbi*
Bernardini, Charles *alderman*
Berner, Robert Lee, Jr. *lawyer*
Berning, Larry D. *lawyer*
Bernstein, H. Bruce *lawyer*
Berolzheimer, Karl *lawyer*
Bess, Ronald W. *advertising executive*
Betts, Henry Brognard *physician, health facility administrator, educator*
Betz, Hans Dieter *theology educator*
Betz, Ronald Philip *pharmacist*
Beugen, Joan Beth *communications company executive*
Bevington, David Martin *English literature educator*
Bidwell, Charles Edward *sociologist, educator*
Biebel, Paul Philip, Jr. *lawyer*
Biederman, Jerry H. *lawyer*
Bierig, Jack R. *lawyer, educator*
Biggles, Richard Robert *marketing executive*
Biggs, Robert Dale *Near Eastern studies educator*
Bilandic, Michael A. *state supreme court justice, former mayor*
Birnbaum, Barry William *special education educator*
Bishop, Oliver Richard *state official*
Bitner, John Howard *lawyer*
Bixby, Frank Lyman *lawyer*
Black, Robert Durward *television producer*
Blair, Edward McCormick *investment banker*
Blankenship, Edward G. *architect*
Blatt, Richard Lee *lawyer*
Blauser, Jeffrey Michael *professional baseball player*
Bloch, Ralph Jay *professional association executive*
Block, Neal Jay *lawyer*
Block, Philip Dee, III *investment counselor*
Bloom, Benjamin S. *education educator*
Blount, Michael Eugene *lawyer*
†Bluestone, Jeffrey Allen *immunology educator, researcher*
Blumberg, Avrom Aaron *physical chemistry educator*
Blume, Paul Chiappe *lawyer*
Blumenthal, Carlene Margaret *vocational-technical school educator*
Blust, Larry D. *lawyer*
Blutter, Joan Wernick *interior designer*
Boardman, Robert A. *lawyer*
Boardman, William Penniman *lawyer, banker*
Boatman, Elizabeth Artle *information systems specialist, municipal official*
Bobins, Norman R. *banker*
†Bobrick, Edward A. *federal judge*
Bocci, Raymond Perry *auditor*
Bockelman, John Richard *lawyer*
Bodenstein, Ira *federal government lawyer*
Bodine, Laurence *lawyer, editor, marketer*
Boehnen, Daniel A. *lawyer*
Boers, Terry John *sportswriter, radio and television personality*
Boggess, Thomas Phillip, III *graphic arts company executive*
Boggs, Joseph Dodridge *pediatric pathologist, educator*
Bohn, Charlotte Galitz *retired real estate executive*
Bolaños, Anita Marie *lawyer*
Bolger, David P. *bank executive*
Boncher, Mary *talent agent*
Bonham, Russell Aubrey *chemistry educator*
Bonow, Robert Ogden *medical educator*
Bookstein, Abraham *information science educator*
Booth, Thomas Collins *musician*
Booth, Wayne Clayson *English literature and rhetoric educator, author*
Borenstine, Alvin Jerome *search company executive*
Boris, James R. *investment company executive*
Bornholdt, Laura Anna *university administrator*
Boshes, Louis D. *physician, scientist, educator*
Bott, Harold Sheldon *accountant, management consultant*
Bourdon, Cathleen Jane *executive director*
†Bouson, J. Brooks *English educator*
Bowe, William John *lawyer*
Bowen, William Joseph *management consultant*
Bower, Glen Landis *lawyer*
Bowman, Barbara Taylor *institute president*
Bowman, James Edward *physician, educator*
Bowman, Leah *fashion designer, consultant, photographer, educator*
Bowman, Tina Marie Davis *pediatric nurse*
Boyce, David Edward *transportation and regional science educator*
Boyda, Debora *advertising executive*
Boyer, John William *history educator, dean*
Bracken, Kathleen Ann *nurse*
Bradburn, Norman M. *behavioral science educator*
Braddock, David Lawrence *health science educator*
†Bradley, Bob *professional soccer coach*
Brady, Catherine Rawson *software company executive*
Braidwood, Robert John *archaeologist, educator*
Brake, Cecil Clifford *retired diversified manufacturing executive*
Bramnik, Robert Paul *lawyer*
Brandt, William Arthur, Jr. *consulting executive*
Bransfield, James Joseph *surgeon*
Bratcher, Juanita *journalist*
†Bregoli-Russo, Mauda Rita *language educator*
†Brendler, Charles Burgess *urologist*
Brennan, James Joseph *lawyer, banking and financial services*
Bresnahan, James Francis *medical ethics educator*
Brewster, Gregory Bush *telecommunications educator*
Breyer, Norman Nathan *metallurgical engineering educator, consultant*
Brice, Roger Thomas *lawyer*
Bridewell, David Alexander *lawyer*
Bridgman, Thomas Francis *lawyer*
Brinkman, John Anthony *historian, educator*
Brizzolara, Charles Anthony *lawyer*
Brodsky, William J. *options exchange executive*
Brooker, Thomas Kimball *oil company executive*
Brooks, Gwendolyn *writer, poet*
†Broski, David C. *chancellor*
Brotman, Barbara Louise *columnist, writer*
Brouse, John Ammon, Jr. *fiber optics engineer*
Brown, Alan Crawford *lawyer*
Brown, Charles Eric *health facility administrator, biochemist*
†Brown, Delores *academic administrator*
Brown, Donald James, Jr. *lawyer*
Brown, Faith A. *communications executive*
Brown, Gregory K. *lawyer*
Brown, Richard Holbrook *library administrator, historian*
Brown, Steven Spencer *lawyer*
Browning, Don Spencer *religion educator*
Brubaker, Charles William *architect*
†Bruce, Debra M. *poet, English language educator*
Brueschke, Erich Edward *physician, researcher, educator*
Brumback, Charles Tiedtke *retired newpaper executive*
Brummel, Mark Joseph *magazine editor*
Bruner, Stephen C. *lawyer*
Brusky, Linda L. *middle school mathematics and science educator*
Bryan, John Henry *food and consumer products company executive*
Bryan, William Royal *finance educator*
Bua, Nicholas John *retired federal judge*
Buchanan, John *city official*
Buckle, Frederick Tarifero *international holding company executive, political and business intelligence analyst*
Buckley, Janice Marie *school administrator*
Buckley, Joseph Paul, III *polygraph specialist*
Bucklo, Elaine Edwards *United States district court judge*
Buehler, Evelyn Judy *poet*
Bueschel, David Alan *management consultant*
Bugielski, Robert Joseph *state legislator*
Bulger, Brian Wegg *lawyer*
Buniak, Raymond *educational professional*
Bunn, William Bernice, III *physician, lawyer, epidemiologist*
Burack, Elmer Howard *management educator*
Burditt, George Miller, Jr. *lawyer*
Burgdoerfer, Jerry *lawyer*
Burke, Edward M. *alderman*
Burke, Thomas Joseph, Jr. *lawyer*
Burkey, Lee Melville *lawyer*
Burnett, Walter, Jr. *city official*
Burns, James B. *prosecutor*
Burns, Terrence Michael *lawyer*
Burt, Robert Norcross *diversified manufacturing company executive*
Burt-Bradley, Della Ann *English educator, consultant*
Burton, Raymond Charles, Jr. *transportation company executive*
Busey, Roxane C. *lawyer*
Bush, Crystal Reed *lawyer*
Bushman, Mary Laura Jones *developer, fundraiser*
Buss, Daniel Frank *environmental scientist*
Bussman, Donald Herbert *lawyer*
Butler, Robert Allan *psychologist, educator*
Bynoe, Peter Charles Bernard *real estate developer, lawyer*
Cacioppo, John Terrance *psychology educator, researcher*
Cadieux, Dennis Barry *religious organization administrator, minister*
Cahill, Kathleen *broadcast executive*
†Calcagno, Anne *writer, educator*
Calenoff, Leonid *radiologist*
Callahan, Michael J. *chemicals and manufacturing company executive*
Callaway, Karen A(lice) *journalist*
Calvanico, Joseph James *financial company executive*
Campbell, Bruce Crichton *hospital administrator*
Campbell, Gavin Elliott *real estate investor and developer*
Camper, John Jacob *press secretary*
†Campos-Pons, Maria Magdalena *artist*
Cannon, Bennie Marvin *physical education educator*
Cappo, Joseph C. *publisher*
Carlin, Dennis J. *lawyer*
Carlson, LeRoy Theodore, Jr. *telecommunications industry executive*
Carlson, Richard Gregory *accountant*
Carlson, Stephen Curtis *lawyer*
Carlson, Walter Carl *lawyer*
Carlton, Dennis William *economics educator*
Caro, William Allan *physician*
Carpenter, Allan *author, editor, publisher*
Carpenter, David William *lawyer*
Carren, Jeffrey P. *lawyer*
Carroll, James J. *lawyer*
Carroll, William Kenneth *law educator, psychologist, theologian*
Cary, Arlene D. *retired hotel company sales executive*
Cascino, Anthony Elmo, Jr. *lawyer, insurance executive*
Case, Donni Marie *investment company executive*
Cass, Edward Roberts (Peter) *hotel and travel marketing professional*
Cassel, Douglass Watts, Jr. *lawyer, educator, journalist*
Castillo, Mario Enrique *artist, educator*
Castillo, Ruben *judge*
Castorino, Sue *communications executive*
Cha, Soyoung Stephen *mechanical engineer, educator*
Chakrabarty, Ananda Mohan *microbiologist*
Chaleff, Carl Thomas *brokerage house executive*
†Chambers, Donald Arthur *biochemistry and molecular medicine educator*
Chambers, Richard Leon *retired Turkish language and civilization educator*
Champagne, Ronald Oscar *academic administrator, mathematics educator*
Chandler, Kent, Jr. *lawyer*
Chandler, Michael D. *city official*
Chang, Sung-Jin James *management consultant*
Chang, Yi-Cheng *insurance agent*
Chapman, Alger Baldwin *finance executive, lawyer*
Charles, Allan G. *physician, educator*
Chatterton, Robert Treat, Jr. *reproductive endocrinology educator*
Cheely, Daniel Joseph *lawyer*
Chefitz, Joel Gerald *lawyer*
Chemers, Robert Marc *lawyer*
Chen, Wai-Kai *electrical engineering and computer science educator, consultant*
Cherney, James Alan *lawyer*
Cherry, Robert Steven, III *municipal agency administrator*
Chico, Gery J. *lawyer, school system administrator*
Chiles, Stephen Michael *lawyer*
Chinitz, David Evan *literature educator*
Cho, Wonhwa *biomedical researcher*
Chookaszian, Dennis Haig *financial executive*
†Chorengel, Bernd *international hotel corporation executive*
Christian, John M. *lawyer*
Christiansen, Richard Dean *newspaper editor*
Christianson, Stanley David *corporate executive*
Chudzinski, Mark Adam *lawyer*
Chung, Paul Myungha *mechanical engineer, educator*
Cipinko, Scott J. *lawyer, general counsel, secretary*
Cizza, John Anthony *insurance executive*
Clark, James Allen *lawyer, educator*
Clark, John Whitcomb *diagnostic radiologist*
†Clarke, Jay A. *art historian, curator*
Clarke, Philip Ream, Jr. *investment banker*
Clayton, Robert Norman *chemist, educator*
Clemens, Richard Glenn *lawyer*
Clevenger, Penelope *international business consultant*
Clinton, Edward Xavier *lawyer*
Cloonan, James Brian *investment executive*
Closen, Michael Lee *law educator*
Coar, David H. *federal judge*
Coase, Ronald Harry *economics educator*
Coe, Donald Kirk *university official*
Coe, Fredric L. *physician, educator, researcher*
Cohen, Christopher B. *lawyer*
Cohen, Edward Philip *microbiology and immunology educator, physician*
†Cohen, Ira *legislative staff member*
Cohen, Jerome *psychology educator, electrophysiologist*
Cohen, Melanie Rovner *lawyer*
Cohen, Melvin R. *physician, educator*
Cohen, Ted *philosophy educator*
Cohler, Bertram Joseph *social sciences educator, clinical psychologist*
Cohn, Bernard Samuel *anthropologist, historian, educator*
Cohodes, Eli Aaron *publisher*
†Cole, Dana T. *adult educator, researcher*
Cole, Stephen Salisbury *bank executive*
Coleman, Roy Everett *secondary education educator, computer programmer*
Collen, Sheldon Orrin *lawyer*
Collens, Lewis Morton *university president, legal educator*
Colley, Karen J. *medical educator, medical researcher*
Collins, Harvey Taliaferro *chemist*
Colom, Vilma *alderman*
Colten, Harvey Radin *pediatrician, educator*
Combs, Ronald T. *music educator*

Comiskey, Michael Peter lawyer
Conant, Howard Rosset steel company executive
Conidi, Daniel Joseph private investigation agency executive
Conklin, Thomas William lawyer
Conlon, Patrick C. family nurse practitioner
Conlon, Suzanne B. federal judge
Connelly, John Dooley social service organization executive
Connelly, Mary Jo lawyer
Connors, Dorsey television and radio commentator, newspaper columnist
Conrad, John R. corporate executive
Consey, Kevin Edward museum administrator
†Conte, Lou artistic director, choreographer
Conviser, Richard James law educator, lawyer, publications company executive
Conway, James Joseph physician
Conway, Michael Maurice lawyer
Cook, Richard Borreson architect
Cooper, Charles Gilbert toiletries and cosmetics company executive
Cooper, Ilene Linda magazine editor, author
Cooper, Stuart Leonard chemical engineering educator, researcher, consultant
Cooper, Wylola retired special education educator
Copeland, Edward Jerome lawyer
Coppersmith, Susan Nan physicist
Corbett, Frank Joseph advertising executive
Corcoran, James Martin, Jr. lawyer, writer, lecturer
Cornell, Rob hotel executive
Corwin, Sherman Phillip lawyer
Costa, Erminio pharmacologist, cell biology educator
Costello, John William lawyer
Costin, J(oseph) Laurence, Jr. information services executive
Cotter, Daniel A. diversified company executive
Coughlan, Kenneth Lewis lawyer
Coulson, William Roy lawyer
Covalt, Robert Byron chemicals executive
Covey, Frank Michael, Jr. lawyer, educator
Cox, Allan James management consultant and sports executive
Cox, Charles C. economist
†Cox, Daniel T. management consultant
Coy, Patricia Ann special education director, consultant
Coyle, Thomas marketing executive
Crane, Barbara Bachmann photographer, educator
Crane, Mark lawyer
Crane, Peter Robert botanist, geologist, paleontologist, educator
†Crane, R.H. poet, editor
Craven, George W. lawyer
Crawford, Dewey Byers lawyer
Crawford, Jean Andre clinical therapist
Crawford, William F. corporate executive, consultant
Creighton, Neal foundation administrator, retired army officer
Cremin, Susan Elizabeth lawyer
Crenshaw, Carol charitable organization administrator
Cressey, Bryan Charles lawyer
Crihfield, Philip J. lawyer
Crisham, Thomas Michael lawyer
†Cromwell, Amanda Caryl soccer player, coach
Cronin, James Watson physicist, educator
Cropsey, Joseph political science educator
Cross, Chester Joseph lawyer, accountant
Cross, Robert Clark journalist
Crossan, John Robert lawyer
Crown, James Schine investment executive
Crown, Lester manufacturing company executive
Csar, Michael F. lawyer
Cudahy, Richard D. federal judge
Cui, Ke-hui embryologist, obstetrician, gynecologist
Cullen, Charles Thomas historian, librarian
Culp, Kristine Ann dean, theology educator
†Cumings, Bruce history educator, writer
Cummings, Maxine Gibson elementary school educator
Cunningham, Robert James lawyer
Cunningham, Thomas Justin lawyer
Curran, Barbara Adell retired law foundation administrator, lawyer, writer
Currie, David Park lawyer, educator
Curwen, Randall William journalist, editor
Cusack, John Thomas lawyer
Custer, Charles Francis lawyer
Dabrowski, Edward John television technical director
Daffron, Sandra Ratcliff professional society administrator
Daley, Richard Michael mayor
Daley, Vincent Raymond, Jr. real estate executive, consultant
Daly, Patrick F. real estate executive, architect
Dam, Kenneth W. lawyer, law educator
Dancewicz, John Edward investment banker
Daniels, John Draper lawyer
Darby, Edwin Wheeler retired newspaper financial columnist
†Dardai, Shahid Moinuddin computer science educator
Darnall, Robert J. steel company executive
Darr, Milton Freeman, Jr. banker
Datta, Rathin chemical engineer
Davidson, Richard Laurence geneticist, educator
Davidson, Stanley J. lawyer
Davis, Concelor Dominquez mental health therapist, counselor
Davis, Danny K. congressman
Davis, DeForest P. architectural engineer
†Davis, Floyd Asher neurologist
Davis, Jack Wayne, Jr. internet publisher
Davis, Michael W. lawyer
Davis, Muller lawyer
Davis, Scott Jonathan lawyer
Davison, Richard physician, educator
Daze, Eric professional hockey player
DeBat, Donald Joseph media consultant, columnist
Debus, Allen George history educator
DeCarlo, William S. lawyer
Decker, Richard Knore lawyer
De Francesco, John Blaze, Jr. public relations company executive
Degroot, Leslie Jacob medical educator
†de Hoyos, Debora M. lawyer
Deitrick, William Edgar lawyer
De Leonardis, Nicholas John bank executive, financial lecturer, educator
Deli, Anne Tynion financial services executive
Deliford, Mylah Eagan mathematics educator
Delp, Wilbur Charles, Jr. lawyer
Dembowski, Peter Florian foreign language educator
DeMiles, Edward agent
DeMoss, Jon W. insurance company executive, lawyer
Dempsey, Mary A. library commissioner, lawyer
†Denlow, Morton federal judge
Dent, Thomas G. lawyer
Deorio, Anthony Joseph surgeon
Derlacki, Eugene L(ubin) otolaryngologist, physician
†deRoulet, Daniel N. college dean
Desjardins, Claude physiologist, dean, administrator
D'Esposito, Julian C., Jr. lawyer
Despres, Leon Mathis lawyer, former city official
Detuno, Joseph Edward lawyer
Deutsch, Thomas Alan ophthalmologist, educator
de Vos, Peter Jon ambassador
DeWolfe, John Chauncey, Jr. lawyer
DeWyn, Kenneth Lee development executive, arts administrator, actor
Diamond, Seymour physician
Diamond, Shari Seidman psychology educator, law researcher
Diaz-Arce, Raul soccer player
DiCicco, Tony soccer coach
Dickerson, Martha Ann health facility administrator
Diefenbach, Viron Leroy dental, public health educator, university dean
Dietler, Michael David archaeologist, educator
Digangi, Al marketing executive
Ditkowsky, Kenneth K. lawyer
Dix, Rollin C(umming) mechanical engineering educator, consultant
Dixon, Lorraine city official
Dixon, Stewart Strawn lawyer
Dobrick, Jo-Anne business executive, environmental consultant
Dobrov, Gregory W. adult education educator, researcher
Dockterman, Michael lawyer
Doetsch, Virginia Lamb former advertising executive, writer
Doherty, Brian Gerard alderman
Dolan, Thomas Christopher professional society administrator
Dold, Robert Bruce journalist
Dombkowski, Thomas Raymond public health administrator
Dompke, Norbert Frank retired photography studio executive
Doniger, Wendy history of religions educator
Donlevy, John Dearden lawyer
Donnell, Harold Eugene, Jr. professional society administrator
Donnelley, James Russell printing company executive
Donohoe, Jerome Francis lawyer
Donovan, Dianne Francys journalist
Doolittle, Sidney Newing retail executive
Dorman, Jeffrey Lawrence lawyer
†Douglas, Charles W. lawyer
Downing, Robert Allan lawyer
Doyle, John Robert lawyer
Draft, Howard Craig advertising executive
Drechney, Michaelene secondary education educator
Drexler, Richard Allan manufacturing company executive
Dropkin, Allen Hodes lawyer
Drymalski, Raymond Hibner lawyer, banker
†Ducar, Tracy soccer player
Dudash, Linda Christine insurance executive
Duell, Daniel Paul artistic director, choreographer, lecturer
Duff, Brian Barnett federal judge
Duhl, Michael Foster lawyer
Duncan, John Patrick Cavanaugh lawyer
Dunea, George nephrologist, educator
Dupont, Todd F. mathematics and computer science educator
Durchslag, Stephen P. lawyer
Dwyer, Dennis D. information technology executive
Dykstra, Paul Hopkins lawyer
Dyrud, Jarl Edvard psychiatrist
Dyson, Marv broadcast executive
Early, Bert Hylton lawyer, legal search consultant
Easterbrook, Frank Hoover federal judge
Eastham, Dennis Michael advertising executive
Eastman, Dean Eric science research executive
Eaton, John C. composer, educator
Ebert, Roger Joseph film critic
Echols, M(ary) Evelyn travel consultant
Eddy, David Latimer banker
Edelman, Alvin lawyer
Edelman, Daniel Joseph public relations executive
Edelsberg, Sally C. physical therapy educator and administrator
Edelstein, Teri J. art history educator, art federation administrator
Egan, Kevin James lawyer
Eggert, Russell Raymond lawyer
Eimer, Nathan Philip lawyer
Einoder, Camille Elizabeth secondary education educator
Eisenmann, Dale Richard dental educator
Ekdahl, Jon Nels lawyer, corporate secretary
Elbaz, Sohair Wastawy library director, consultant
Elden, Gary Michael lawyer
Ellison, Jeffrey Alan educator
Ellwood, Scott lawyer
†Elshtain, Jean Bethke social and political ethics educator
Elson, Alex lawyer, educator, arbitrator
Elwin, James William, Jr. dean, lawyer
†Emmanuel, Rahm federal official
Enenbach, Mark Henry community action agency executive, educator
Engel, Philip L. insurance company executive
English, Henry L. not-for-profit association executive
English, John Dwight lawyer
Eppen, Gary Dean business educator
Epstein, David M. publishing executive
Epstein, Raymond engineering and architectural executive
Epstein, Richard A. law educator
Epstein, Sidney architect and engineer
Epstein, Stephen Roger financial executive
Epstein, Wolfgang biochemist, educator
Erber, Thomas physics educator
Erdös, Ervin George pharmacology and biochemistry educator
Erens, Jay Allan lawyer
Erlebacher, Albert history educator
Ernest, J. Terry ocular physiologist, educator
Espat, N. Joseph surgeon
Espinosa, Gustavo Adolfo radiologist, educator
Esrick, Jerald Paul lawyer
Essex, Joseph Michael visual communication planner
Evans, Earl Alison, Jr. biochemist
Evans, Mariwyn periodical editor
Evans, Thelma Jean Mathis internist
Even, Francis Alphonse lawyer
Everhart, Bruce radio station executive
Fabisch, Gale Warren civil engineer
Fagan, Elizabeth Ann medical researcher, hepatologist
Fahn, Jay commercial bank executive, consultant, art dealer
Fahner, Tyrone C. lawyer, former state attorney general
Fahnestock, Jean Howe retired civil engineer
Fair, Hudson Randolph recording company executive
Fairchild, Thomas E. federal judge
Falkof, Melvin Milton food products executive
Falkowski, Patricia Ann investment consultant, financial analyst
†Falls, Robert Arthur artistic director
Fano, Ugo physicist, educator
Fanta, Paul Edward chemist, educator
Farber, Bernard John lawyer
Farina, Dennis actor
Farr, Marcia Elizabeth English and Linguistics educator
Farrakhan, Louis religious leader
†Fawcett, Joy Lynn soccer player
Fazio, Peter Victor, Jr. lawyer
Feder, Robert television and radio columnist
Feeley, Henry Joseph, Jr. (Hank Feeley) artist, former advertising agency executive
Fein, Roger Gary lawyer
Feiner, Arlene Marie librarian, researcher, consultant
Feingold, Daniel Leon anesthesiologist
Feinstein, Fred Ira lawyer
Feldman, Scott M. lawyer
Feldstein, Charles Robert fund raising consultant
Fellows, Jerry Kenneth lawyer
Felsenthal, Steven Altus lawyer
Felton, Cynthia educational administrator
Fennessy, John James radiologist, educator
Fensin, Daniel diversified financial service company executive
Fenton, Clifton Lucien investment banker
Ferencz, Robert Arnold lawyer
Ferguson, Bradford Lee lawyer
Ferguson, Donald John surgeon, educator
Ferguson, Leonard Price (Bear Ferguson) advertising executive, consultant
Ferguson, Margaret Geneva author, publisher, real estate broker
Ferrini, James Thomas lawyer
Fetridge, Clark Worthington publisher
Field, Karen Ann (Karen Ann Schaffner) real estate broker
Field, Marshall business executive
Field, Robert Edward lawyer
†Fiks, Arsen Phillip physician, researcher
Filpi, Robert Alan lawyer
Fina, Paul Joseph lawyer
Finke, Robert Forge lawyer
Finley, Harold Marshall investment banker
Fish, Stanley Eugene university dean, English educator
Fisher, Eugene marketing executive
Fisher, Herbert Hirsh lawyer
Fisher, Lawrence Edgar market research executive, anthropologist
Fisher, Lester Emil zoo administrator
Fitch, Frank Wesley pathologist educator, immunologist, educator, administrator
Fitch, Morgan Lewis, Jr. intellectual property lawyer
Fitzgerald, Robert Maurice financial executive
Fitzpatrick, Christine Morris legal administrator, former television executive
Fitzpatrick, Mark professional hockey player
Fizdale, Richard advertising agency executive
Flagg, Michael James communications and graphics company executive
Flaherty, Emalee Gottbrath pediatrician
Flanagan, Joseph Patrick advertising executive
Flanagan, Patrick Sean Liam priest
Flanagin, Neil lawyer
Flaum, Joel Martin federal judge
Fleischer, Cornell Hugh history educator
Fleming, Richard H. finance executive
Fligg, James Edward retired oil company executive
Flock, Jeffrey Charles news bureau chief
Floyd, Tim professional basketball coach, former collegiate basketball coach
Flynn, John J. museum curator
Fogel, Henry orchestra administrator
Fogel, Robert William economist, educator, historian
Foley, Joseph Lawrence sales executive
Forbes, John Edward financial consultant
Formeller, Daniel Richard lawyer
Fornek, Scott Patrick journalist
Fort, Jeffrey C. lawyer
Fortune, Michael Joseph religion educator
Foster, James Reuben investment company executive
Foster, Teree E. law educator, dean
†Fotopoulos, Danielle soccer player
Foudree, Bruce William lawyer
†Foudy, Julia Maurine soccer player
Fowler, George Selton, Jr. architect
Fox, Elaine Saphier lawyer
Fox, Paul T. lawyer
Franch, Richard Thomas lawyer
Francois, William Armand packaging company executive, lawyer
†Frangipane, Amy Christina media planner
Franke, Richard James retired investment banker
Frankel, Bernard advertising executive
Franklin, Cory Michael medical administrator, educator
Franklin, Richard Mark lawyer
Frankson-Kendrick, Sarah Jane publisher
Frano, Andrew Joseph lawyer, civil engineer
Fraumann, Willard George lawyer
Frazin, Rhona Sondra non-profit executive
Freed, Karl Frederick chemistry educator
Freed, Mayer Goodman law educator
Freedman, Walter G. corporate services executive
Freehling, Stanley Maxwell investment banker
Freeman, Charles E. state supreme court justice
Freeman, Lee Allen, Jr. lawyer
Freeman, Leslie Gordon anthropologist, educator
Freeman, Louis S. lawyer
†Freeman, Paul Douglas symphony conductor
Freeman, Susan Tax anthropologist, educator, culinary historian
Freidheim, Cyrus F., Jr. management consultant
Freidheim, Ladonna dance company director
Freitag, Frederick Gerald osteopathic physician
Fremon, David Kent writer, consultant
Fried, Josef chemist, educator
Friedlander, Patricia Ann marketing professional
Friedman, Lawrence Milton lawyer
Friedman, Roselyn L. lawyer
Friedrich, Paul anthropologist, linguist, poet
Friend, Robert Nathan financial counselor, economist, market technician
Frisch, Henry Jonathan physics educator
Frohman, Lawrence Asher endocrinology educator, scientist
Fromm, Erika (Mrs. Paul Fromm) clinical psychologist
Fross, Roger Raymond lawyer
†Frydman, Lucio chemist, researcher, educator
Fuchs, Elaine V. molecular biologist, educator
Fulgoni, Gian Marc market research company executive
Fullagar, William Watts lawyer
Fuller, Harry Laurance oil company executive
Fuller, Jack William writer, publishing executive
Fuller, Perry Lucian lawyer
Fullmer, Paul public relations counselor
Fultz, Dave meteorology educator
Funk, Carla Jean library association executive
Furcon, John Edward management and organizational consultant
Furlane, Mark Elliott lawyer
Furlong, Patrick David educator, researcher
Furth, Yvonne advertising executive
†Gabarra, Carin Leslie professional soccer player
Gabinski, Theri city official
†Gaetti, Gary baseball player
Gaines, Anne Farley artist, art educator
Gaines, William Chester journalist
Galante, Jorge Osvaldo orthopedic surgeon, educator
Gall, Betty Bluebaum office services company executive
Galowich, Ronald Howard real estate investment executive, venture capitalist
Gannon, Sister Ann Ida retired philosophy educator, former college administrator
Garber, Daniel Elliot philosophy educator
Garber, Samuel Baugh lawyer, retail company executive
Gardiner, Judith Kegan English language and women's studies educator
Gardner, Howard Alan travel marketing executive, travel writer and editor
Gardunio, Joseph landscaping company executive
Garner, Ted artist
Garr, Daniel Frank restaurateur
Garrigan, Richard Thomas finance educator, consultant, editor
Garth, Bryant Geoffrey law educator, foundation executive
Gearen, John Joseph lawyer
Gecht, Martin Louis physician, bank executive
Geha, Alexander Salim cardiothoracic surgeon, educator
Geiman, J. Robert lawyer
Gelman, Andrew Richard lawyer
Genetski, Robert James economist
Geoga, Douglas Gerard real estate development company executive, lawyer
George, Francis Cardinal archbishop
Geraldson, Raymond I. lawyer
Geraldson, Raymond I., Jr. lawyer
†Gerber, Lawrence lawyer
Gerber, Phillip advertising executive
Gerbie, Albert Bernard obstetrician, gynecologist, educator
Gerbie, S. Ralph real estate executive, property investor
Gerdes, Neil Wayne library director
Geren, Gerald S. lawyer
Gerlits, Francis Joseph lawyer
Gerske, Janet Fay lawyer
Gerstman, George Henry lawyer
Gerstner, Robert William structural engineering educator, consultant
Gertz, Elmer lawyer, author, educator
Gertz, Theodore Gerson lawyer
Gettleman, Robert William judge
Gewertz, Bruce Labe surgeon, educator
Giampietro, Wayne Bruce lawyer
Gibbons, William John lawyer
Gibson, McGuire archaeologist, educator
Giesen, Richard Allyn business executive
Gilbert, Debbie Rose entrepreneur
Gilbert, Howard N(orman) lawyer
Gilbert, Vincent Newton publisher
Giles, Percy Z. city official
Gilford, Steven Ross lawyer
†Gilfoyle, Timothy Joseph historian
Gilman, Sander Lawrence German language educator
Gilmour, Doug professional hockey player
Gilson, Jerome lawyer, writer
Gin, Jackson architect
Gindilis, Viktor Mironovitch geneticist, researcher
Gingiss, Benjamin Jack retired formal clothing stores executive
Ginsberg, Norman Arthur physician
Ginsburg, Norton Sydney geography educator
Giovacchini, Peter Louis psychoanalyst
Gislason, Eric Arni chemistry educator
†Gittins, Anthony J. anthropologist, theology educator
†Giustino, Maryanne public relations executive
Gladden, James Walter, Jr. lawyer
Gladden, Robert Wiley corporate executive
Glasser, James J. leasing company executive, retired
Gleeson, Paul Francis lawyer
Glenn, Cleta Mae lawyer
Glenner, Richard Allen dentist, dental historian
Glieberman, Herbert Allen lawyer
Goddu, Roger retail executive
Goepp, Robert August dental educator, oral pathologist
Golan, Stephen Leonard lawyer
Gold, Allan Harold architect, structural engineer, educator
Goldberg, Arnold Irving psychoanalyst, educator
Goldberg, Sherman I. banking company executive, lawyer
Goldblatt, Stanford Jay lawyer
Golden, Bruce Paul lawyer
Golden, Lily Oliver educator
Golden, William C. lawyer
Goldman, Louis Budwig lawyer
Goldman, Michael P. lawyer
Goldring, Norman Max advertising executive
Goldsborough, Robert Gerald publishing executive, author
Goldschmidt, Lynn Harvey lawyer
Goldsmith, Ethel Frank medical social worker
Goldsmith, John Anton linguist, educator
Goldsmith, Julian Royce geochemist, educator
Goldwasser, Eugene biochemist, educator
Golomb, Harvey Morris oncologist, educator
Golter, Christina Rita marketing specialist, consultant
Gomer, Robert chemistry educator
Good, Sheldon Fred realtor
Goodman, Gary Alan lawyer
Gordon, Ellen Rubin candy company executive

Gordon, Howard Lyon advertising and marketing executive
Gordon, James S. lawyer
Gordon, William A. lawyer
Gorman, John R. auxiliary bishop
Gorter, James Polk investment banker
Gossett, Philip musicologist
Gottlieb, Gidon Alain Guy law educator
Gottschall, Joan B. judge
Gould, John Philip economist, educator
Gould, Samuel Halpert pediatrics educator
Graber, Doris Appel political scientist, editor, author
Graber, Thomas M. orthodontist
Grace, Mark Eugene baseball player
Grady, John F. federal judge
Graham, David F. lawyer
Graham, Patricia Albjerg education educator, foundation executive
Gralen, Donald John lawyer
Granato, Jesse D. alderman
Grant, Burton Fred lawyer
Grant, Dennis newspaper publishing executive
Grant, Robert McQueen humanities educator
Grant, Robert Nathan lawyer
Graupe, Daniel electrical and computer engineering educator, systems and biomedical engineer
Graves, Robert Lawrence mathematician, educator
Gray, Dawn Plambeck work-family consultant
Gray, Hanna Holborn history educator
Gray, Milton Hefter lawyer
Gray, Richard art dealer, consultant, holding company executive
Grayck, Marcus Daniel lawyer
Grayhack, John Thomas urologist, educator
Greeley, Andrew Moran sociologist, author
Green, RuthAnn marketing and management consultant
Greenberg, Bernard entomologist, educator
Greenberg, Steve brokerage house executive
Greenberger, Ernest lawyer
Greene, Robert Bernard, Jr. (Bob Greene) broadcast television correspondent, columnist, author
Greenfield, Michael C. lawyer
Gregg, Lauren women's soccer coach
Griffin, Lawrence Joseph lawyer
Griffith, Donald Kendall lawyer
Griffiths, Robert Pennell banker
Gross, Hanns history educator
Gross, Theodore Lawrence university administrator, author
Grossi, Francis Xavier, Jr. lawyer, educator
Grossman, Lisa Robbin clinical psychologist, lawyer
Grossman, Robert Mayer lawyer
Grosso, James Alan information technology executive
Gruber, William Paul journalist
Grund, David Ira lawyer
Grunsfeld, Ernest Alton, III architect
Guastafeste, Roberta Harrison cellist
†Gunning, Tom art educator
Gupta, Krishna Chandra mechanical engineering educator
Guralnick, Sidney Aaron civil engineering educator
Guthman, Jack lawyer
Gutmann, David Leo psychology educator
Gutstein, Solomon lawyer
†Guzman, Ronald A. federal judge
Haas, Howard Green retired bedding manufacturing company executive
Hackl, Donald John architect
Haddix, Carol Ann Mighton journalist
Haderlein, Thomas M. lawyer
Haffner, Charles Christian, III retired printing company executive
Hahn, David Bennett hospital administrator, marketing professional
Hahn, Frederic Louis lawyer
Hales, Daniel B. lawyer
Haley, George Romance languages educator
Hall, Joan M. lawyer
Hallinan, Joseph Thomas journalist, correspondent
Halloran, Michael John lawyer
Halpern, Jack chemist, educator
Hamada, Robert S(eiji) economist, educator
Hamarstrom, Patricia Ann director, animation/multimedia specialist
Hambrick, Ernestine retired colon and rectal surgeon
Hamister, Donald Bruce retired electronics company executive
Hamm, Mariel Margaret soccer player
Hammesfahr, Robert Winter lawyer
Hanika, Stephen D. advertising executive
Hanlon, Cyril Rollins physician, educator
Hannah, Wayne Robertson, Jr. lawyer
Hannay, William Mouat, III lawyer
Hanrath, Linda Carol librarian, archivist
Hansen, Bernard J. alderman
Hansen, Carl R. management consultant
Hansen, Claire V. financial executive
Hanson, Floyd Bliss applied mathematician, computational scientist, mathematical biologist
Hanson, Martin Philip mechanical engineer, farmer
Hanson, Ronald William lawyer
Hardaway, Ernest, II oral and maxillofacial surgeon, public health official
Hardgrove, James Alan lawyer
†Hards, Richard Charles artist
Harrington, Carol A. lawyer
Harrington, James Timothy lawyer
Harris, Chauncy Dennison geographer, educator
Harris, Donald Ray lawyer
Harris, Gregory Scott management services executive
Harris, Irving Brooks cosmetics executive
Harris, Jules Eli medical educator, physician, clinical scientist, administrator
Harris, Neil history educator
†Harris, Rivkah liberal arts educator
Harris, Ronald William commodities trader
Harrold, Bernard lawyer
Hart, Pamela Heim banker
Hart, William Thomas federal judge
Hartnett, James Patrick engineering educator
Harvey, Elizabeth Schroer lawyer
Harvey, Paul news commentator, author, columnist
Harvey, Ronald Gilbert research chemist
Haselkorn, Robert virology educator
Hast, Malcolm Howard medical educator, biomedical scientist
Hatton, Stephen Barth chemical company executive, information executive
Haupt, Roger A. advertising executive
Hawkins, Loretta Ann secondary school educator, playwright
Hayden, Harrold Harrison information company executive
Haydock, Walter James banker
Hayes, David John Arthur, Jr. legal association executive
Hayes, Jacqueline Crement real estate broker and developer
Hayes, John T. lawyer, accountant
Hayes, Richard Donald architect
Hayes, Richard Johnson association executive, lawyer
Hayes, William Aloysius economics educator
Hayward, Thomas Zander, Jr. lawyer
Head, Louis Rollin surgeon
Head, Patrick James lawyer
Headrick, Daniel Richard history and social sciences educator
Heagy, Thomas Charles banker
†Healy, Sondra Anita consumer products company executive
Heatwole, Mark M. lawyer
Hebel, Doris A. astrologer
Heckman, James Joseph economist, econometrician, educator
Hefner, Christie Ann publishing and marketing executive
Hefner, Philip James theologian
Heidrick, Robert Lindsay management consultant
†Height, David Joseph consumer products executive, lawyer
Heindl, Warren Anton law educator, retired
Heinecken, Robert Friedli art educator, artist
Heineman, Ben Walter corporation executive
Heinz, John Peter lawyer, educator
Heinz, William Denby lawyer
Heisler, Quentin George, Jr. lawyer
Heller, Paul medical educator
Heller, Reinhold August art educator, consultant
Hellie, Richard Russian history educator, researcher
Hellman, Samuel radiologist, physician, educator
Helman, Robert Alan lawyer
Helmbold, Nancy Pearce classical languages educator
Helmholz, R(ichard) H(enry) law educator
Helms, Byron Eldon associate director of research, biology and physiology administrator
Heltne, Paul Gregory museum executive
Hendrix, Ronald Wayne physician, radiologist
Hengstler, Gary Ardell publisher, editor, lawyer
Henikoff, Leo M., Jr. academic administrator, medical educator
Henning, Joel Frank lawyer, author, publisher, consultant
Henriquez-Freeman, Hilda Josefina fashion design executive
Henry, Brian Thomas lawyer
Henry, Frederick Edward lawyer
Herbert, Victor James foundation administrator
Herbert, William Carlisle lawyer
Herbst, Arthur Lee obstetrician, gynecologist
Herman, Sidney N. lawyer
Herman, Stephen Charles lawyer
Hermann, Donald Harold James lawyer, educator
Herseth, Adolph Sylvester (Bud Herseth) classical musician
Herzog, Fred F. law educator
Hess, Sidney J., Jr. lawyer
Hester, Thomas Patrick lawyer, business executive
Heuer, Michael Alexander dean, endodontist educator
Hickcox, Leslie Kay health educator, consultant, counselor
Hickey, Jerome Edward investment company executive
Hickey, John Thomas, Jr. lawyer
Hickman, Frederic W. lawyer
Hicks, Cadmus Metcalf, Jr. financial analyst
Hidding, Gezinus Jacob information technology and strategy educator
Hier, Daniel Barnet neurologist
Higgins, Jack editorial cartoonist
Hildebrand, Roger Henry astrophysicist, physicist
Hill, Gary video artist
Hilliard, David Craig lawyer, educator
Hillman, Jordan Jay law educator
Himmelfarb, John David artist
Hinkelman, Ruth Amidon insurance company executive
Hinojosa, Raul physician, ear pathology researcher, educator
Hirsch, James Alan executive director
Hirsch, Martin Alan dentist
Hirsch, Syrola Ruth gerontology rehabilitation nurse
Hirshman, Harold Carl lawyer
Hoban, George Savre lawyer
Hochhalter, Gordon Ray advertising communications executive
Hodes, Scott lawyer
Hoey, Rita Marie public relations executive
Hofer, Roy Ellis lawyer
Hoff, John Scott lawyer
Hoffman, Richard Bruce lawyer
Hoffman, Valerie Jane lawyer
Hogarth, Robin Miles business educator, university official
Holabird, John Augur, Jr. retired architect
Holderman, James F., Jr. federal judge
Holland, Eugene, Jr. lumber company executive
Holli, Melvin George history educator
Hollins, Mitchell Leslie lawyer
Hollis, Donald Roger banking consultant
Holmes, Colgate Frederick hotel executive
Holzer, Edwin advertising executive
Homans, Peter psychology and religious studies educator
Honig, George Raymond pediatrician
Hoover, Paul poet
Horne, John R. farm equipment company executive
Horowitz, Fred Lee dentist, administrator, consultant
Horwich, Allan lawyer
Horwitz, Irwin Daniel otolaryngologist, educator
Hoseman, Daniel lawyer
Hoskins, Richard Jerold lawyer
Houk, James Charles physiologist, educator
Howard, Christy J. actuary
Howe, Jonathan Thomas lawyer
Howell, R(obert) Thomas, Jr. lawyer, former food company executive
Hubbard, Elizabeth Louise lawyer
Huckman, Michael Saul neuroradiologist, educator
Hudik, Martin Francis hospital administrator, educator, consultant
Hughes, John Russell physician, educator
Hummel, Gregory William lawyer
Hunt, Lawrence Halley, Jr. lawyer
Hunter, James Galbraith, Jr. lawyer
Hunter, J(ames) Paul English language educator, literary critic, historian
Huntley, Robert Stephen newspaper editor
Husar, John Paul newspaper columnist, television panelist, broadcaster
Husting, Peter Marden advertising consultant
Huston, DeVerille Anne lawyer
Huston, John Lewis chemistry educator
Huston, Steven Craig lawyer
Hutchison, Clyde Allen, Jr. chemistry educator
Huyck, Margaret Hellie psychology educator
Hyman, Michael Bruce lawyer
Ida, Shoichi artist
Ingham, Norman William Russian literature educator, genealogist
Ingram, Donald insurance company executive
Iqbal, Zafar Mohd cancer researcher, biochemist, pharmacologist, toxicologist, consultant, molecular biologist
Isaacs, Roger David public relations executive
Istock, Verne George banker
Jachna, Joseph David photographer, educator
Jackowiak, Patricia lawyer
Jackson, Gregory Wayne orthodontist
Jackson, Jesse Louis civic and political leader, clergyman
Jacobson, Harold LeLand lawyer
Jacobson, Marian Slutz lawyer
Jacobson, Richard Joseph lawyer
Jacover, Jerold Alan lawyer
Jager, Melvin Francis lawyer
Jahn, Helmut architect
Jahns, Jeffrey lawyer
Jain, Nemi Chand chemist, coating scientist, educator
Jakstas, Alfred John museum conservator, consultant
Jakubowski, Thad J. bishop
Jambor, Robert Vernon lawyer
†James, Thomas W. federal judge
Janecek, Lenore Elaine insurance specialist, consultant
Jaramillo, Carlos Alberto civil engineer
Jares, Terryl Lynn musician
Jean, Kenneth conductor
Jegen, Sister Carol Frances religion educator
Jensen, Harold Leroy physician
Jernstedt, Richard Don public relations executive
Jerome, Jerrold V. insurance company executive
Jersild, Thomas Nielsen lawyer
Jester, Jack D. lawyer
Jezuit, Leslie James manufacturing company executive
Jibben, Laura Ann state agency administrator
Jilhewar, Ashok gastroenterologist
Jock, Paul F., II lawyer
Joehl, Raymond Joseph surgeon, educator
†John, Nancy R. librarian, writer
Johnson, Barbara Elaine Spears education educator
Johnson, Caroline Janice insurance company executive
Johnson, Donald Harry, Jr. government official, educator
Johnson, Douglas Wells lawyer
Johnson, Gary Thomas lawyer
Johnson, Glenn Thompson judge
Johnson, Janet Helen Egyptology educator
Johnson, Lael Frederic lawyer
Johnson, Mary Ann computer training vocational school owner
Johnson, Maryl Rae cardiologist
Johnson, Richard Fred lawyer
Johnson, Shirley Elaine management consultant
Johnston, Sheryl L. communications executive
Jonas, Harry S. professional society administrator
Jonasson, Olga surgeon, educator
†Jones, Cobi professional soccer player
Jones, Dorothy F. judge
Jones, Linda communications educator
Jones, Richard Jeffery physician, educator
†Jones, R(oger) Kent civil engineer, educator
Jones, Trina Wood special education educator
Jordan, Michelle Denise lawyer
Joseph, Robert Thomas lawyer
Joslin, Rodney Dean lawyer
Judge, Bernard Martin editor, publisher
Junewicz, James J. lawyer
Kahrilas, Peter James medical educator, researcher
Kaiserlian, Penelope Jane publishing company executive
Kallick, David A. lawyer
Kamerick, Eileen Ann financial executive, lawyer
Kamin, Chester Thomas lawyer
Kamin, Kay Hodes financial planner, lawyer, entrepreneur, educator
Kaminsky, Richard Alan lawyer
Kamyszew, Christopher D. museum curator, executive educator, art consultant
Kanne, Michael Stephen federal judge
Kanter, Burton Wallace lawyer
Kaplan, Jared lawyer
Kaplan, Jonathan Harris healthcare business transformation and information technology specialist
Kaplan, Kalman Joel psychologist, educator
Kaplan, Morton A. political science and philosophy educator
Kaplan, Sidney Mountbatten lawyer
Karanikas, Alexander English language educator, author, actor
Karu, Gilda M(all) lawyer, government official
Kass, Leon Richard educator
Kastel, Howard L. lawyer, business executive
Kathrein, Michael Lee leasing company executive, real estate company executive
Katz, Adrian Izhack physician, educator
†Katz, Erwin I. federal judge
Katz, Stuart Charles lawyer, concert jazz musician
Kaufman, Edward Phillip psychotherapist
Kawitt, Alan lawyer
Kaye, Richard William utility company executive
Kazenas, Susan Jean consultant
Kearney, John Walter sculptor, painter
Kearney, Lynn Marilyn Haigh arts administrator, curator
Keating, Terry Michael commercial banker
Keenan, James George classics educator
†Keller, Deborah Kim soccer player
Kelly, Arthur Lloyd management and investment company executive
Kelly, Charles Arthur lawyer
†Kelly, Curtis Hartt publishing executive
Kelly, Gerald Wayne chemical coatings company executive
†Kelly, Janet Langford lawyer
Kelly, Jerry Bob social services administrator
Kelly, Michael Thomas educator
Kelly, Robert Francis real estate consultant
Kempf, Donald G., Jr. lawyer
Kennedy, Eugene Cullen psychology educator, writer
Kennedy, Lawrence Allan mechanical engineering educator
Kenney, Frank Deming lawyer
Kenny, Edmund Joyce lawyer
Kerbis, Gertrude Lempp architect
Keroff, William B. advertising agency executive
Kerros, Edward Paul stage director, playwright
Keryczynskyj, Leo Ihor lawyer, county official, educator
†Keys, Arlander federal judge
Kikoler, Stephen Philip lawyer
Kim, Mi Ja dean
Kim, Michael Charles lawyer
Kindzred, Diana communications company executive
King, Andre Richardson architectural graphic designer
King, Billie Jean Moffitt former professional tennis player
King, Clark Chapman, Jr. lawyer
King, Michael Howard lawyer
King, Sharon Louise lawyer
Kinnamon, Ron administrator
Kins, Juris lawyer
Kinzie, Raymond Wyant banker, lawyer
Kipper, Barbara Levy corporate executive
Kirby, William Joseph corporation executive
Kirkland, John Leonard lawyer
Kirkpatrick, Anne Saunders systems analyst
Kirsch, Jeffrey Scott securities executive
Kirschner, Barbara Starrels pediatric gastroenterologist
Kirsner, Joseph Barnett physician, educator
Kisor, Henry Du Bois newspaper editor, critic, columnist
Kissel, Richard John lawyer
Kite, Steven B. lawyer
Kitt, Walter psychiatrist
Kittle, Charles Frederick surgeon
Klapperich, Frank Lawrence, Jr. investment banker
Klaviter, Helen Lothrop magazine editor
Klebba, Raymond Allen property manager
†Kleckner, Robert A. accounting firm executive
Kleiman, Kelly (Ruth B.) non-profit organization consultant, lawyer
Klein, Melvyn Norman lawyer, investment executive
Klein, Robert Marshall lawyer
Klenk, James Andrew lawyer
Klenk, Timothy Carver lawyer
Kleppa, Ole J. chemistry educator
Klopack, Kenneth Barthon art educator, artist
Klues, Jack communications executive
Knapp, Donald Roy musician, educator
Knight, Christopher Nichols lawyer
Knight, James Atwood consulting executive
Knoblauch, Mark George librarian, consultant
Knowles, Thomas William business educator, consultant
Knox, James Edwin lawyer
Knox, James Marshall lawyer
Knox, Lance Lethbridge venture capital executive
Kobs, James Fred advertising agency executive
Koch, Carole Jackson human resources executive
Kocoras, Charles Petros federal judge
Koenig, Bonnie international non-profit organization consultant
Koester, Robert Gregg record company executive
Koga, Mary artist, photographer, social worker
Kohlstedt, James August lawyer
Kohn, Shalom L. lawyer
Kohn, William Irwin lawyer
Kohrman, Arthur Fisher pediatrics educator
Kolb, Gwin Jackson language professional, educator
Kolek, Robert Edward lawyer
Kolmin, Kenneth Guy lawyer
Kopec, John William research scientist
Koppe, William Paul deputy sheriff
Koppes, Steven Nelson science writer, editor
Kos, Heather Anne management consultant
Kosokoff, Jeffrey Eugene librarian
Kotulak, Ronald newspaper science writer
Kouvel, James Spyros physicist, educator
Kozak, John W. lawyer
Kramer, Anthony Ferdinand real estate company executive
Kramer, Ferdinand mortgage banker
Kramer, Weezie Crawford broadcast executive
Kramm, Deborah Lucille lawyer
Kraus, Herbert Myron public relations executive
Krause, Jerry (Jerome Richard Krause) professional basketball team executive
Kravitt, Jason Harris Paperno lawyer
†Kreis, Jason professional soccer player
Kriss, Robert J. lawyer
Krivkovich, Peter George advertising executive
Kroll, Barry Lewis lawyer
Krueger, Bonnie Lee editor, writer
Kubida, Judith Ann museum administrator
Kubistal, Patricia Bernice educational consultant
Kuchta, John Albert manufacturing executive
Kuczmarski, Susan Smith management consulting company executive
Kuczwara, Thomas Paul postal inspector, lawyer
Kudish, David J. financial executive
Kudo, Irma Setsuko not-for-profit executive director
Kuhn, Ryan Anthony information industry investment banker
†Kukoc, Toni professional basketball player
Kullberg, Duane Reuben accounting firm executive
Kunkle, William Joseph, Jr. lawyer
Kupcinet, Irv columnist
Kurty, John Thomas secondary school administrator
Kuta, Jeffrey Theodore lawyer
Kyle, Robert Campbell, II publishing executive
Lach, Alma Elizabeth food and cooking writer, consultant
Lach, Donald F. history educator, author
Lach, Michael C. educator
†La Franco, Frank Paul ophthalmologist, educator
Laidlaw, Andrew R. lawyer
Lampert, Steven A. lawyer
Landers, Ann (Mrs. Esther P. Lederer) columnist
Landes, William M. law educator
Landow-Esser, Janine Marise lawyer
Landsberg, Jill Warren lawyer, consultant to government agencies
Lane, Kenneth Edwin retired advertising agency executive
Lane, Ronald Alan lawyer
Laner, Richard Warren lawyer
Lannert, Robert Cornelius manufacturing company executive
Lapidus, Dennis real estate developer
†Lara-Valle, Julio medical educator, physician
Larsen, Paul Emanuel religious organization administrator
Larson, Allan Louis political scientist, educator, lay church worker
Larson, Mark Allen educator
Larson, Nancy Celeste computer systems manager
Larson, Paul William public relations executive
Laski, James J. city clerk
†Lassar, Scott R. lawyer
Lathon, Sheraine church administrator

Latimer, Kenneth Alan *lawyer*
Lauderdale, Katherine Sue *lawyer*
Laumann, Anne Elizabeth *dermatologist*
Laumann, Edward Otto *sociology educator*
Laurino, Margaret *alderman*
LaVelle, Arthur *anatomy educator*
Lawler, James Ronald *French language educator*
Lazar, Ludmila *concert pianist, pedagogue*
Lazar, Richard Beck *physician, medical administrator*
Lazarus, George Milton *newspaper columnist*
Leavitt, Victoria Seyferth *marketing professional*
LeBaron, Charles Frederick, Jr. *lawyer*
†Leckey, Andrew A. *financial columnist*
Lederman, Leon Max *physicist, educator*
Lee, Marva Jean *counselor, physical education educator, consultant*
Lee, Raphael Carl *plastic surgeon, biomedical engineer*
LeFevre, Perry Deyo *minister, theology educator*
Leff, Alan Richard *medical educator, researcher*
Leff, Deborah *non-profit executive*
Leff, Donna Rosene *journalism educator*
†Lefkow, Joan H. *federal judge*
Lefkow, Joan Humphrey *judge*
Lehman, George Morgan *food sales executive*
Leigh, Sherren *communications executive, editor, publisher*
Leighton, George Neves *retired federal judge*
Leinenweber, Harry D. *federal judge*
Leisten, Arthur Gaynor *lawyer*
Lennes, Gregory *manufacturing and financing company executive*
Lerner, Alexander Robert *association executive*
†Lerner, Wayne *health care executive*
Levar, Patrick *alderman*
Levenfeld, Milton Arthur *lawyer*
Leventhal, Bennett Lee *psychiatry and pediatrics educator, administrator*
Levi, John G. *lawyer*
Levin, Arnold Murray *social worker, psychotherapist*
Levin, Charles Edward *lawyer*
Levin, Jack S. *lawyer*
Levin, Michael David *lawyer*
Levine, Donald Nathan *sociologist, educator*
Levine, Laurence Harvey *lawyer*
Levi-Setti, Riccardo *physicist, director*
Levitan, Valerie F. *medical research facility executive*
Levy, Donald Harris *chemistry educator*
Lewert, Robert Murdoch *microbiologist, educator*
Lewis, Charles A. *investment company executive*
Lewis, Philip *educational and technical consultant*
Lewis, Phillip Harold *museum curator*
Lewis, Ramsey Emanuel, Jr. *pianist, composer*
Lewis, Sylvia Gail *journalist*
Lewy, Ralph I. *hotel executive*
Leyhane, Francis John, III *lawyer*
Liao, Shutsung *biochemist, oncologist*
Lichten, Nancy G. *chemical company executive*
Lichtenbert, Robert Henry *philosopher educator and writer*
†Lichtor, Terry *neurosurgeon, neuro-oncologist*
Lieb, Michael *English educator, humanities educator*
Liebenow, Franklin Eastburn, Jr. *English literature educator*
Liggio, Carl Donald *lawyer*
Lilly, Kristine Marie *soccer player*
Lim, Len Gui Remolona (Mark Lim) *critical care and emergency nurse*
Lin, Chin-Chu *physician, educator, researcher*
Lin, James Chih-I *biomedical and electrical engineer, educator*
Lind, Jon Robert *lawyer*
Lindberg, George W. *federal judge*
Lindberg, Richard Carl *editor, author, historian*
Linde, Ronald Keith *corporate executive, private investor*
Linden, Henry Robert *chemical engineering research executive*
Lindquist, Susan Lee *biology and microbiology educator*
Lindskog, Norbert F. *business and health administration educator, consultant*
Ling, Kathryn Wrolstad *health association administrator*
Linklater, William Joseph *lawyer*
Lipinski, Ann Marie *newspaper editor*
Lippe, Melvin Karl *lawyer*
Lippman, Jessica G. *clinical psychologist, educator*
Lipton, Lois Jean *lawyer*
Lipton, Richard M. *lawyer*
Lishka, Edward Joseph *insurance underwriter*
Littman, Margaret Rachel *writer, magazine*
Litweiler, John Berkey *writer, editor*
Litwin, Burton Howard *lawyer*
Liu, Ben-chieh *economist*
Lloyd, William F. *lawyer*
Lochbihler, Frederick Vincent *lawyer*
Lockwood, Gary Lee *lawyer*
Loesch, Katharine Taylor (Mrs. John George Loesch) *communication and theatre educator*
Logan, David Samuel *investment banker*
†Lohmiller, Jeffrey Joseph *veterinarian, educator*
Loney, Mary Rose *airport administrator*
Longman, Gary Lee *accountant*
Longworth, Richard Cole *journalist*
Look, Dona Jean *artist*
Looman, James R. *lawyer*
Loomis, Salora Dale *psychiatrist*
Looney, Claudia Arlene *academic administrator*
†López, Cecilia Luisa *educational association administrator*
Lorch, Kenneth F. *lawyer*
Lorenz, Hugo Albert *retired insurance executive, consultant*
Lorie, James Hirsch *business administration educator*
†Lotocky, Innocent Hilarius *bishop*
Loughnane, David J. *lawyer*
†Love, Richard H. *art historian, art gallery executive*
Lowery, Sharon A. *travel industry executive*
Lowrie, William G. *oil company executive*
Lowry, Donald Michael *retired lawyer*
Lowry, James Hamilton *management consultant*
Lubawski, James Lawrence *health care consultant*
Lubin, Donald G. *lawyer*
Lucas, Robert Emerson, Jr. *economist, educator*
†Lumpkin, John Robert *public health physician, state official*
Lundberg, George David, II *medical editor in chief, pathologist*
Lundergan, Barbara Keough *lawyer*
Luning, Thomas P. *lawyer*
Lurain, John Robert, III *gynecologic oncologist*
Luthringshausen, Wayne *brokerage house executive*
Lutter, Paul Allen *lawyer*
†Lutzer, Erwin Wesley *clergyman, author*
Lyerla, Bradford Peter *lawyer*
Lyman, Arthur Joseph *financial executive*
Lynch, Edward Francis *professional sports team executive*
Lynch, John Peter *lawyer*
Lynch, William Thomas, Jr. *advertising agency executive*
Lyne, Sheila *public health commissioner, sister*
Lynn, Laurence Edwin, Jr. *university administrator, educator*
Lynnes, R. Milton *advertising executive*
Lyon, Jeffrey *journalist, author*
†Lysakowski, Richard Stanley *secondary education educator, economic analyst*
Lythcott, Marcia A. *newspaper editor*
MacCarthy, Terence Francis *lawyer*
MacDougal, Gary Edward *corporate director, foundation trustee*
Mack, Alan Wayne *interior designer*
Macklin, Jeanette *secondary education educator*
MacLane, Saunders *mathematician, educator*
†MacMillan, Shannon Ann *soccer player*
†MacPhail, Andrew B. *professional sports team executive*
Macsai, John *architect*
Maczulski, Margaret Louise *marketing event professional, meeting manager*
Madansky, Albert *statistics educator*
Madden, Bartley Joseph *economist*
Madigan, John William *publishing executive*
Madsen, Dorothy Louise (Meg Madsen) *writer*
Magdovitz, Ethan H. *information architect*
Maggio, Michael John *artistic director*
Magnus, Kathy Jo *religious organization executive*
†Magoon, Patrick M. *healthcare executive*
Mahaffey, John Christopher *association executive*
Maher, David Willard *lawyer*
Mahowald, Anthony Peter *geneticist, developmental biologist, educator*
Makinen, Marvin William *biophysicist, educator*
Makkai, Adam *linguistics educator, poet*
Malik, Raymond Howard *economist, scientist, corporate executive, inventor, educator*
Malinowski, Arthur Anthony *lawyer, labor arbitrator*
Malkin, Cary Jay *lawyer*
Mallory, Robert Mark *controller, finance executive*
Mancoff, Neal Alan *lawyer*
Mandly, Charles Robert, Jr. *lawyer*
Manelli, Donald Dean *screenwriter, film producer*
Manning, Blanche M. *federal judge*
Manny, Carter Hugh, Jr. *architect, foundation administrator*
Mansfield, Karen Lee *lawyer*
†Manuel, Jerry *manager professional athletics*
Manzo, Edward David *patent lawyer*
Marco, Guy Anthony *librarian, educator*
Marcus, Joseph *child psychiatrist*
Margoliash, Emanuel *biochemist, educator*
Margolis, Rob *publisher*
Marick, Michael Miron *lawyer*
Marin, Vincent Arul *infosystems executive*
Marks, Jerome *lawyer*
†Markus, Vasyl *author, editor*
Marovich, George M. *federal judge*
Marovitz, James Lee *lawyer*
Marroquin-Merino, Victor Miguel *lawyer*
Marsh, Jeanne Cay *social welfare educator, researcher*
Marshall, Cody *bishop*
Marshall, Donald Glenn *English language and literature educator*
Marshall, John David *lawyer*
Martin, Arthur Mead *lawyer*
†Martin, Dennis Dale *religious studies educator*
Martin, Gary Joseph *medical educator*
Martin, Robert C. *marketing professional*
Martin, Wesley George *electrical engineer*
Martinez, Josemaria Espino *computer services administrator*
Marty, Martin Emil *religion educator, editor*
Marvel, Kenneth Robert *lawyer, corporate executive*
Marwedel, Warren John *lawyer*
Marx, David, Jr. *lawyer*
†Mason, Earl Leonard *food products executive*
Mason, Henry Lowell, III *lawyer*
Mason, Richard J. *lawyer*
†Mason, Sandra Renee *dean*
Massura, Eileen Kathleen *family therapist*
Matanky, James E. *real estate developer*
Matanky, Robert William *lawyer*
Matasar, Ann B. *former dean, business and political science educator*
Mateles, Richard Isaac *biotechnologist*
Mathieu-Harris, Michele Suzanne *association executive*
Matsuda, Takayoshi *surgeon, biomedical researcher*
Matthei, Edward Hodge *architect*
Mattos Neto, Sebastiao De Souza *lawyer*
Mattson, Stephen Joseph *lawyer*
May, J. Peter *mathematics educator*
Mayer, Frank D., Jr. *lawyer*
Mayer, Raymond Richard *business administration educator*
Maynard, George Fleming, III *consultant to philanthropy organizations*
McAuliffe, Richard L. *church official*
McCabe, Charles Kevin *lawyer, author*
McCaleb, Malcolm, Jr. *lawyer*
McCallister, Richard Anthony *business consulting company executive*
McCarron, John Francis *columnist*
Mc Carter, John Wilbur, Jr. *museum executive*
McCausland, Thomas James, Jr. *brokerage house executive*
McClain, Lee Bert *corporate lawyer, insurance executive*
McClure, James Julius, Jr. *lawyer, former city official*
McConahey, Stephen George *securities company executive*
McConnell, E. Hoy, II *advertising/public policy executive*
McConnell, James Guy *lawyer*
McCormack, Robert Cornelius *investment banker*
McCoy, John Bonnet *banker*
McCracken, Thomas James, Jr. *lawyer*
McCray, Curtis Lee *university president*
McCrohon, Craig *lawyer*
McCrone, Walter Cox *research institute executive*
McCue, Judith W. *lawyer*
McCullagh, Grant Gibson *architect*
McCulloh, Gerald William *theology educator*
McCullough, Richard Lawrence *advertising agency executive*
McCurry, Margaret Irene *architect, interior and furniture designer, educator*
McDaniel, Charles-Gene *journalism educator, writer*
McDermott, John H(enry) *lawyer*
McDermott, Robert B. *lawyer*
McDonald, Theresa Beatrice Pierce (Mrs. Ollie McDonald) *church official, minister*
McDonald, Thomas Alexander *lawyer*
McDonough, John Michael *lawyer*
McDougal, Alfred Leroy *publishing executive*
McDowell, Orlando *educator*
McGarr, Frank James *retired federal judge, dispute resolution consultant*
Mc Gimpsey, Ronald Alan *oil company executive*
McGinn, Bernard John *religious educator*
McGrail, Jeane Kathryn *artist, educator, poet, curator*
McKay, Neil *banker*
McKee, Keith Earl *manufacturing technology executive*
McKenzie, Robert Ernest *lawyer*
McKinley, Vicky Lynn *biology educator*
†McKinney, Peter *plastic surgeon*
McLaughlin, T. Mark *lawyer*
McLees, John Alan *lawyer*
†McManus, James Laughlin *writer, educator*
McMenamin, John Robert *lawyer*
McNally, Andrew, IV *publishing executive*
McNeely, Carol J. *dentist*
McNeill, G. David *psychologist, educator*
McNeill, Thomas B. *retired lawyer*
McVisk, William Kilburn *lawyer*
McWhirter, Bruce J. *lawyer*
McWilliams, Dennis Michael *lawyer*
Meade, Robin Michele *news anchor, reporter*
Mecklenburg, Gary Alan *hospital executive*
Mehlman, Mark Franklin *lawyer*
Melamed, Leo *investment company executive*
Melikian, Grigory Borisovich *science educator*
Mell, Richard F. *city official*
Melton, David Reuben *lawyer*
Meltzer, Bernard David *law educator*
Meltzer, Robert Craig *lawyer, educator*
Meltzer, Sharon Bittenson *English language and humanities educator*
Mendelsohn, Zehavah Whitney *data processing executive*
Menon, Siva Kumar *physical therapist*
Mercer, David Robinson *cultural organization administrator*
Merrill, Thomas Wendell *lawyer, law educator*
Merwin, Peter Matthew *teacher, writer*
Messner, Leonard Vincent *optometrist, educator*
Metz, Charles Edgar *radiology educator*
Meyer, Michael Jon *education educator, writer*
Meyer, Michael Louis *lawyer*
Meyer, Peter *physicist, educator*
Meyers, Lynn Betty *architect*
Michaels, Richard Edward *lawyer*
†Michaels, Robert A. *real estate development company executive*
Michalak, Edward Francis *lawyer*
Migala, Lucyna Jozefa *broadcast journalist, arts administrator, radio station executive*
Mikesell, Marvin Wray *geography educator*
Mikovich, Terry *home health facility administrator*
Mikva, Abner Joseph *lawyer, retired federal judge*
†Milbrett, Tiffeny Carleen *professional soccer player*
Miles, Roberta *jazz singer, artist*
Miletich, Ivo *library and information scientist, bibliographer, educator, linguist, literature research specialist*
Miller, Angela Perez *bilingual and special education educator*
Miller, Bernard J., III *advertising executive*
Miller, Bernard Joseph, Jr. *advertising executive*
Miller, Charles S. *clergy member, church administrator*
Miller, Edward Boone *lawyer*
Miller, Ellen *advertising executive*
Miller, Jay Alan *civil rights association executive*
Miller, John Leed *lawyer*
Miller, Merton Howard *finance educator*
Miller, Oscar *economics educator*
Miller, Patrick William *research administrator, educator*
Miller, Paul J. *lawyer*
Miller, Stephen Ralph *lawyer*
Millichap, Joseph Gordon *neurologist, educator*
Millner, Robert B. *lawyer*
Milnikel, Robert Saxon *lawyer*
Miner, Thomas Hawley *international entrepreneur*
Minichello, Dennis *lawyer*
Minkowycz, W. J. *mechanical engineering educator*
Minneste, Viktor, Jr. *retired electrical company executive*
Minnick, Malcolm L., Jr. *clergy member, church administrator*
Minogue, John P. *academic administrator, priest, educator*
Minow, Josephine Baskin *civic worker*
Minow, Newton Norman *lawyer, educator*
Mintzer, David *physics educator*
Mirkin, Bernard Leo *clinical pharmacologist, pediatrician*
Mironovich, Alex *publisher*
Mirza, David Brown *economist, educator*
Mirza, Leona Lousin *educator*
Mitchell, Dennis L. *artist, educator*
Mitchell, Lee Mark *communications executive, investment fund manager, lawyer*
Mittendorf, Robert *physician, epidemiologist*
Mlotek, Herman Victor *former religious education educator*
Moawad, Atef *obstetrician, gynecologist, educator*
Mobbs, Michael Hall *lawyer*
Modesto, Mark *advertising professional*
Moffatt, Joyce Anne *performing arts executive*
Montgomery, Charles Barry *lawyer*
Montgomery, Charles Howard *retired bank executive*
Montgomery, William Adam *lawyer*
Moor, Roy Edward *finance educator*
Moore, Joseph Arthur *alderman, lawyer*
†Moore, Nancy Gaye *dance historian*
Moore, Vernon John, Jr. *pediatrician, lawyer, medical consultant*
Mora, Carol Ann *early childhood educator, lecturer*
Moran, James Byron *federal judge*
Moran, John Thomas, Jr. *lawyer*
Morardini, Michael Robert *baseball player*
Morency, Paula J. *lawyer*
Moretti, Robert James *psychologist, educator*
Morewitz, Stephen John *behavioral scientist, consultant, educator*
Morgan, Wesley James *personnel executive*
Morrill, R. Layne *real estate broker, executive, professional association administrator*
Morris, Naomi Carolyn Minner *medical educator, administrator, researcher, consultant*
Morris, Norval *criminologist, educator*
Morris, Ralph William *chronopharmacologist*
Morrison, Portia Owen *lawyer*
Morrissey, George Michael *judge*
Morrow, Richard Martin *retired oil company executive*
Morsch, Thomas Harvey *lawyer*
Moss, Gerald S. *dean, medical educator*
Muchin, Allan B. *lawyer*
Mugnaini, Enrico *neuroscience educator*
Mullan, John Francis (Sean Mullan) *neurosurgeon, educator*
Mullen, Charles Frederick *health educator*
Mullen, J. Thomas *lawyer*
Muller, Kurt Alexander *lawyer*
Muller, Leon *writer*
Mulligan, Robert William *university official, clergyman*
Mullins, Obera *microbiologist*
Mulvihill, Terence Joseph *investment banking executive*
Mumford, Manly Whitman *lawyer*
Munoz, Mario Alejandro *civil engineer, retired consultant*
Munoz, Ricardo *alderman*
Murata, Tadao *engineering and computer science educator*
Murdock, Charles William *lawyer, educator*
Murphy, Ellis *association management executive*
Murphy, Hugh *city official*
Murphy, Michael Emmett *retired food company executive*
Murphy, Thomas W. *city official*
Murray, Daniel Richard *lawyer*
Murtaugh, Christopher David *lawyer*
Mustoe, Thomas Anthony *physician, plastic surgeon*
Muthuswamy, Petham Padayatchi *pulmonary medicine and critical care specialist*
Myers, Lonn William *lawyer*
†Myers, Mary A. *public relations executive, consultant*
Nachman, Norman Harry *lawyer*
Naclerio, Robert Michael *otolaryngologist, educator*
Nagel, Sidney Robert *physics educator*
Nahrwold, David Lange *surgeon, educator*
Najita, Tetsuo *history educator*
Nambu, Yoichiro *physics educator*
Napleton, Robert Joseph *lawyer*
Narahashi, Toshio *pharmacology educator*
Nash, Donald Gene *commodities specialist*
Natarus, Burton F. *government executive*
Nault, William Henry *publishing executive*
Neal, Steven George *journalist*
Nebenzahl, Paul *fundraising executive, museum executive*
Nechin, Herbert Benjamin *lawyer*
Needleman, Barbara *newspaper executive*
Neff, John Hallmark *art historian*
Nelson, Harry Donald *telecommunications executive*
Nelson, Richard David *lawyer*
Nelson, Thomas George *consulting actuary*
Neubauer, Charles Frederick *investigative reporter*
Neumeier, Matthew Michael *lawyer*
Newey, Paul Davis *lawyer*
Newlin, Charles Fremont *lawyer*
Newman, Wade Davis *trade association executive*
Nichol, Norman J. *manufacturing executive*
Nicholas, Ralph Wallace *anthropologist, educator*
Nickels, John L. *state supreme court justice*
Nims, John Frederick *writer, educator*
Nissen, William John *lawyer*
Nitikman, Franklin W. *lawyer*
Nora, Gerald Ernest *lawyer*
Nord, Henry J. *transportation executive*
Nord, Robert Eamor *lawyer*
Nordberg, John Albert *federal judge*
Nordland, Gerald *art museum administrator, historian, consultant*
Norgle, Charles Ronald, Sr. *federal judge*
Notebaert, Richard C. *telecommunications industry executive*
Notz, John Kranz, Jr. *arbitrator and mediator, retired lawyer*
Novak, Mark *lawyer*
Novak, Marlena *artist, educator, writer, curator*
Nowacki, James Nelson *lawyer*
Nussbaum, Bernard J. *lawyer*
Nussbaum, Martha Craven *philosophy and classics educator*
Nyhus, Lloyd Milton *surgeon, educator*
Oates, James G. *advertising executive*
O'Brien, Brien Michael *investment firm executive*
O'Brien, James Phillip *lawyer*
O'Brien, Patrick William *lawyer*
Ocasio, Billy *alderman*
O'Connell, Daniel Craig *psychology educator*
O'Connor, James John *retired utility company executive*
O'Connor, Patrick J. *city official*
O'Connor, William Michael *executive search company executive*
O'Dell, James E. *newspaper publishing executive*
Oehme, Reinhard *physicist, educator*
Oesterle, Eric Adam *lawyer*
O'Flaherty, Paul Benedict *lawyer*
Ogui, Koshin *Buddhist minister*
O'Hagan, James Joseph *lawyer*
Oka, Takeshi *physicist, chemist, astronomer, educator*
O'Leary, Daniel Vincent, Jr. *lawyer*
Olian, Robert Martin *lawyer*
Olins, Robert Abbot *communications research executive*
Oliver, Harry Maynard, Jr. *retired brokerage house executive*
Oliver, Roseann *lawyer*
Olivo, Frank *city official*
Olk, Frederick James *county official, paralegal*
O'Loughlin, Donna *editor periodical*
Olsen, Edward John *geologist, educator*
Olsen, Rex Norman *trade association executive*
Olson, Patricia Joanne *artist, educator*
Olson, Roy Arthur *government official*
O'Malley, John Daniel *law educator, banker*
O'Neill, Timothy P. *law educator*
Ong, Michael King *mathematician, educator, banker*
O'Reilly, Charles Terrance *university dean*
Orin, Stuart I. *lawyer*
Oryshkevich, Roman Sviatoslav *physician, physiatrist, dentist, educator*
Osborn, William A. *investment company executive*
Osborne, Karen Lee *educator*
O'Shaw, Robert (Bob) *city official*
Osiyoye, Adekunle *obstetrician, attorney medical and legal consultant, gynecologist, educator*
Oskouie, Ali Kiani *chemical and environmental engineer*
Osmond, Lynn *architecture executive*
Osowiec, Darlene Ann *clinical psychologist, educator, consultant*
†Overbeck, Carla Werden *soccer player, coach*
Overgaard, Mitchell Jersild *lawyer*

Overton, George Washington *lawyer*
Overton, Jane Vincent Harper *biology educator*
Owens, Charles A. *cardiovascular and interventional radiologist*
Oxtoby, David William *chemistry educator*
Pacchini, Mark *advertising executive*
Pachman, Daniel J. *physician, educator*
Padberg, Helen Swan *violinist*
Page, Ernest *medical educator*
Paitich, Olivia *executive assistant*
Pallasch, Abdon Maxim, III *journalist*
Pallasch, B. Michael *lawyer*
Pallmeyer, Rebecca Ruth *federal judge*
Palmer, John Bernard, III *lawyer*
Palmer, Martha H. *counseling educator*
Palmer, Patrick Edward *radio astronomer, educator*
Palmer, Robert Towne *lawyer*
Pandit, Bansi *nuclear engineer*
Panich, Danuta Bembenista *lawyer*
Pantuso, Michael Vincent *graphic design company executive*
Pappas, George Demetrios *anatomy and cell biology educator, scientist*
Pappas, Philip James *real estate company executive*
Paprocki, Thomas John *lawyer, priest*
Parcells, Frederick R. *product management*
Parcells, Margaret Ross *deputy auditor general*
Parisi, Joseph (Anthony) *magazine editor, writer-consultant, educator*
Park, Thomas Joseph *biology researcher, educator*
Parkhurst, Todd Sheldon *lawyer*
†Parks, Carolyn Lightford *public administrator*
Parks, Corrine Frances *insurance agency owner*
†Parlow, Cynthia Marie *soccer player*
Parrish, Overton Burgin, Jr. *pharmaceutical corporation executive*
Partridge, Mark Van Buren *lawyer, educator, writer*
Pascal, Roger *lawyer*
Patel, Homi Burjor *apparel company executive*
Patterson, Roy *physician, educator*
Pattishall, Beverly Wyckliffe *lawyer*
Paul, Arthur *artist, graphic designer, illustrator, art and design consultant*
Paul, Ronald Neale *management consultant*
Paulus, Michael John *bank executive, economist*
Pavalon, Eugene Irving *lawyer*
Peerman, Dean Gordon *magazine editor*
Pell, Wilbur Frank, Jr. *federal judge*
Pelton, Russell Meredith, Jr. *lawyer*
Peltzman, Sam *economics educator*
Peres, Judith May *journalist*
Perlberg, Jules Martin *lawyer*
†Perlberg, Mark *poet, educator*
Perlman, Carole Lachman *education professional*
Perlmutter, Norman *finance company executive*
Peruzzi, William Theodore *anesthesiologist, intensivist, educator*
Peters, Gordon Benes *musician*
Petersen, Donald Sondergaard *lawyer*
Petersen, William Otto *lawyer*
Peterson, Bradley Laurits *lawyer*
Peterson, Ronald Roger *lawyer*
Peterson, Terry *city official*
Petitan, Debra Ann Burke *educator, education counselor, design engineer, writer, author*
†Petrillo, Nancy *public relations executive*
†Petty, Linda C. *academic administrator, educator*
Phelan, Mary Helen *artist, educator*
Phelps, Richard William *journal editor, consultant*
Philipson, Morris *university press director*
Phillips, Frederick Falley *architect*
Phillips, Gene Daniel *English language educator*
†Phillips, Keith *Spanish language educator*
Pick, Ruth *research scientist, physician, educator*
Piderit, John J. *university educator*
Piecewicz, Walter Michael *lawyer*
Piekarski, Victor J. *lawyer*
Pierson, Don *sports columnist*
Pigozzi, Raymond Anthony *architect*
Pilarski, Jeffrey H. *graphic designer, consultant*
Pilchen, Ira A. *editor*
Pimentel, Julio Gumeresindo *lawyer, accountant*
Pincus, Theodore Henry *public relations executive*
Pinsky, Michael S. *lawyer*
Pinsky, Steven Michael *radiologist, educator*
Pitt, George *lawyer, investment banker*
Pitt, Judson Hamilton *publisher, author*
Pizer, Howard Charles *sports and entertainment executive*
Plank, Betsy Ann (Mrs. Sherman V. Rosenfield) *public relations counsel*
Platzman, George William *geophysicist, educator*
Plotkin, Manuel D. *management consultant, educator, former corporate executive and government official*
Plotnick, Harvey Barry *publishing executive*
Plotnik, Arthur *author, editorial consultant*
Plunkett, Paul Edmund *federal judge*
Poe, Gertie LaVerne *sales executive*
Pokorni, Orysia *musician*
Polaski, Anne Spencer *lawyer*
Polk, Lee Thomas *lawyer*
Pollak, Raymond *general and transplant surgeon*
Pollock, Alexander John *banker*
Pollock, Earl Edward *lawyer*
Pollock, George Howard *psychiatrist, psychoanalyst*
Pollock, Sheldon Ivan *language professional, educator*
Pond, Joel Patrick *veterinary technician*
Ponné, Nanci Teresa *entertainment promoter, writer*
Pope, Daniel James *lawyer*
Pope, Kerig Rodgers *magazine executive*
Pope, Michael Arthur *lawyer*
Pope, Richard M. *rheumatologist*
†Porento, Gerald John *lawyer*
Posner, Richard Allen *federal judge*
Poston, Carol Hoaglan *English educator, writer*
Poznanski, Andrew Karol *pediatric radiologist*
Preble, Robert Curtis, Jr. *insurance executive*
Preece, Lynn Sylvia *lawyer*
Preisler, Harvey D. *medical facility administrator, medical educator*
Prendergast, Carole Lisak *musician, educator*
Presser, Stephen Bruce *lawyer, educator*
Price, Henry Escoe *broadcast executive*
Price, Paul L. *lawyer*
Price, William S. *lawyer*
Primm, Earl Russell, III *publishing executive*
Prinz, Richard Allen *surgeon*
Prior, Gary L. *lawyer*
Pritzker, Robert Alan *manufacturing company executive*
Pritzker, Thomas Jay *lawyer, business executive*
Prochnow, Douglas Lee *lawyer*
Prochnow, Herbert Victor, Jr. *lawyer*
Proctor, Barbara Gardner *advertising agency executive*
Provus, Barbara Lee *executive search consultant*
Pruter, Robert Douglas *editor*
Pugh, Roderick Wellington *psychologist, educator*
†Pukelis, Larry S. *art educator*
Pump, Bernard John *finance company executive*
Pumper, Robert William *microbiologist*
Quaal, Ward Louis *broadcast executive*
Quade, Victoria Catherine *editor, writer, playwright, producer*
Quebe, Jerry Lee *architect*
Rabin, Joseph Harry *marketing research company executive*
Rachwalski, Frank Joseph, Jr. *financial executive*
Radler, Franklin David *publishing holding company executive*
Rajan, Fred E. N. *clergy member, church administrator*
Ramsey-Goldman, Rosalind *physician*
Ran, Shulamit *composer*
Rankin, James Winton *lawyer*
Ranney, George A., Jr. *lawyer*
Raphaelson, Joel *retired advertising agency executive*
Rasin, Rudolph Stephen *corporate executive*
Ratner, Carl Joseph *theater director*
Ratner, Gerald *lawyer*
Rauschenberg, Mary Edna *accountant*
†Razov, Ante *professional soccer player*
Reda, Robert Salvatore *lawyer*
Reddy, Janardan K. *medical educator*
Redmond, Richard Anthony *lawyer*
Ree, Donna *social services administrator, educator*
Reece, Beth Pauley *commodities broker*
Reed, John Shedd *former railway executive*
Reed, Keith Allen *lawyer*
Reed, Vastina Kathryn (Tina Reed) *child psychotherapist, educator*
Reedy, Jerry Edward *editor, writer*
†Regenstein, Joseph, Jr. *foundation executive*
Regensteiner, Else Friedsam (Mrs. Bertold Regensteiner) *textile designer, educator*
Rehage, Kenneth J. *educational association administrator*
Reich, Allan J. *lawyer*
Reicin, Ronald Ian *lawyer*
Reid, Daniel James *public relations executive*
Reiffel, Leonard *physicist, scientific consultant*
Reilly, Joan Rita *nurse practitioner, educator, school nurse*
Reilly, Robert Frederick *valuation consultant*
Reinke, John Henry *educational administrator, clergyman*
Reinsdorf, Jerry Michael *professional sports teams executive, real estate executive, lawyer, accountant*
Reiter, Michael A. *lawyer, educator*
Reitman, Jerry Irving *advertising agency executive*
Relias, John Alexis *lawyer*
Replogle, Robert L. *cardiovascular and thoracic surgeon*
Reschke, Michael W. *real estate executive*
Resnick, Donald Ira *lawyer*
Reum, James Michael *lawyer*
Reynolds, Frank Everett *religious studies educator*
Reynolds, Ruth Carmen *school administrator, secondary school educator*
Rhind, James Thomas *lawyer*
Rhodes, Charles Harker, Jr. *lawyer*
Rice, Charles Lane *surgical educator*
Rice, Judith C. *city commissioner*
Rice, Linda Johnson *publishing executive*
Rice, William Edward *newspaper columnist*
Rich, S. Judith *public relations executive*
Richards, Linda *pharmaceutical company executive*
Richardson, John Thomas *academic administrator, clergyman*
Richardson, Julieanna Lynn *cable television executive*
Richardson, William F. *lawyer*
Riches, Kenneth William *nuclear regulatory engineer*
Richman, Harold Alan *social welfare policy educator*
Richman, John Marshall *retired lawyer, business executive*
Richmond, James G. *lawyer*
Richmond, William Patrick *lawyer*
Rieger, Mitchell Sheridan *lawyer*
†Rieger, Pearl Beverly *psychoeducational diagnostician, consultant*
Rielly, John Edward *educational association administrator*
Riggleman, James David *professional baseball team manager*
Rikoski, Richard Anthony *engineering executive, electrical engineer*
Riley, Jack T., Jr. *lawyer*
Rissman, Burton Richard *lawyer*
Ritchie, Albert *lawyer*
Rizowy, Carlos Guillermo *lawyer, educator, political analyst*
Rizzi, Joseph Vito *banker*
Rizzo, Ronald Stephen *lawyer*
Robbins, Henry Zane *public relations and marketing executive*
Robbins, Kenneth Carl *biochemist*
Roberts, John Charles *law school educator*
Roberts, Theodore Harris *banker*
†Roberts, Tiffany Marie *soccer player*
†Robertson, Donna V. *architect, educator, dean*
Robin, Richard C. *lawyer*
Robins, Joel *company executive*
Robinson, June Kerswell *dermatologist, educator*
Robinson, Samira E. Watson *marketing executive, writer*
Robinson, Theodore Curtis, Jr. *lawyer*
Roche, James McMillan *lawyer*
Rodgers, James Foster *association executive, economist*
Roeper, Richard *columnist*
Rogers, Desiree Glapion *utilities executive*
Rohrman, Douglass Frederick *lawyer*
Roizen, Nancy J. *physician, educator*
Roizman, Bernard *virologist, educator*
Rollhaus, Philip Edward, Jr. *manufacturing company executive*
Rooney, Matthew A. *lawyer*
†Ropp, Daniel Nels *actuary*
Ropski, Gary Melchior *lawyer*
Rosemarin, Carey Stephen *lawyer*
†Rosemond, Thomas W., Jr. *federal judge*
Rosen, George *economist, educator*
Rosen, Sherwin *economist, educator*
Rosen, Steven Terry *oncologist, hematologist*
Rosenbaum, Jonathan Daniel *film critic*
Rosenbaum, Michael A. *investor relations consultant*
Rosenberg, Gary Aron *real estate development executive, lawyer*
Rosenberg, Sheli *broadcast executive*
Rosenbloom, Lewis Stanley *lawyer*
Rosenbloom, Steve *sportswriter*
Rosenblum, Victor Gregory *political science and law educator*
Rosenbluth, Marion Helen *educator, consultant, psychotherapist*
Rosenfield, Robert Lee *pediatric endocrinologist, educator*
Rosenheim, Edward Weil *English educator*
Rosenheim, Margaret Keeney *social welfare policy educator*
Rosenthal, Albert Jay *advertising agency executive*
Rosenthal, Ira Maurice *pediatrician, educator*
Rosner, Jonathan Lincoln *physicist, educator*
Rosner, Robert *astrophysicist*
Ross, Darius Alexander *merger and acquisition specialist*
Ross, Michael *publishing executive*
Ross, Michael Neil *publishing executive*
Rosso, Christine Hehmeyer *lawyer*
Roston, David Charles *lawyer*
†Roth, Robert A. *newspaper executive*
Roth, Sanford Irwin *pathologist, educator*
Rothman-Denes, Lucia Beatriz *biology educator*
Rothstein, Ruth M. *county health official*
Rotman, Carlotta Hayes Hill *physician*
Roupp, Albert Allen *architect*
Roustan, Yvon Dominique *lawyer, real estate broker*
Rovell, Michael Jay *lawyer*
Rovner, Ilana Kara Diamond *federal judge*
Rovner, Jack Alan *lawyer*
Rowder, William Louis *lawyer*
†Rowe, John W. *company executive*
Rowe, John William *utility executive*
Rowe, Randall Keith *real estate executive*
Rowley, Janet Davison *physician*
Roy, David Tod *Chinese literature educator*
Royster, Darryl *computer programmer and analyst*
Rozenblat, Anatoly Isaacovich *scientist, inventor*
Rozran, Jack Louis *courier service executive*
Rubenstein, Eric Davis *real estate executive*
Rubin, Robert J. *lawyer*
Rudnick, Ellen Ava *health care executive*
Rudnick, Paul David *lawyer*
Rudstein, David Stewart *law educator*
Rudy, Lester Howard *psychiatrist*
Rugai, Virginia A. (Ginger) *city official*
Rugo, Steven Alfred *architect*
Rumsfeld, Donald Henry *former government official, corporate executive*
Rundio, Louis Michael, Jr. *lawyer*
Runkle, Martin Davey *library director*
Rupert, Donald William *lawyer*
Rury, John Leslie *education educator*
Russell, Lillian *medical, surgical nurse*
Russell, Paul Frederick *lawyer*
Russo, Gilberto *engineering educator*
Rutkoff, Alan Stuart *lawyer*
Ruxin, Paul Theodore *lawyer*
Ryan, Leo Vincent *business educator*
Ryan, Patrick G. *insurance company executive*
Ryan, Thomas F. *lawyer*
Rychlak, Joseph Frank *psychology educator, theoretician*
Rymer, William Zev *research scientist, administrator*
Rynkiewicz, Stephen Michael *journalist*
Sabbagha, Rudy E. *obstetrician, gynecologist, educator*
Sabin, Neal *broadcast executive*
Sachs, Robert Green *physicist, educator, laboratory administrator*
Sacks, Terence Julius *writer, editor, consultant*
Sagarin, James Leon *rabbi, author, editor*
Sager, William Frederick *retired chemistry educator*
Saliga, Pauline Andrea *administrator*
Saller, Richard Paul *classics educator*
Sampson, Ronald Alvin *advertising executive*
†Samuels, Fern Jacqueline *artist, educator*
Sandberg, Ryne *former professional baseball player*
Sanders, David P. *lawyer*
Sanders, Jacquelyn Seevak *psychologist, educator*
Sanders, Richard Henry *lawyer*
Sandlow, Leslie Jordan *physician, educator*
Sandor, Richard Laurence *financial company executive*
†Sandroff, Howard *composer, sound artist*
Santangelo, Mario Vincent *dentist*
Santiago, Benito Rivera *professional baseball player*
Sarauskas, Paul Justas *lawyer*
Saul, Bradley Scott *communications, advertising and entertainment executive*
Saunders, George Lawton, Jr. *lawyer*
Saunders, Terry Rose *lawyer*
Savard, Denis Joseph *former professional hockey player, coach*
Sawyier, David R. *lawyer*
Scalish, Frank Anthony *labor union administrator*
Scanlan, Thomas Cleary *publishing executive, editor*
Schade, Stanley Greinert, Jr. *hematologist, educator*
Schaefer, Helene G(eraldine) *social services professional*
Schafer, Michael Frederick *orthopedic surgeon*
Schar, Stephen L. *lawyer*
Scheinkman, José Alexandre *economics educator*
Scherman, Timothy Harris *language educator*
Schieser, Hans Alois *education educator*
Schiller, Donald Charles *lawyer*
Schiller, Eric M. *lawyer*
Schillinger, Edwin Joseph *physics educator*
Schilsky, Richard Lewis *oncologist, researcher*
Schimberg, A(rmand) Bruce *retired lawyer*
Schimberg, Barbara Hodes *organizational development consultant*
Schindel, Donald Marvin *lawyer*
Schink, James Harvey *lawyer*
Schippers, David Philip *lawyer*
Schirn, Janet Sugerman *interior designer*
Schlickman, J. Andrew *lawyer*
Schlitter, Stanley Allen *lawyer*
Schlossman, John Isaac *architect*
Schmeltzer, John Charles *financial writer*
Schmetterer, Jack Baer *federal judge*
Schmitz, Edward Henry *distribution company executive*
Schneider, Dan W. *lawyer, consultant*
Schneider, Jorge *psychiatrist, dean*
Schneider, Robert E., II *lawyer*
Schneider, Robert Jerome *lawyer*
Schneider, Wesley Clair *marketing communications company executive*
Schommer, Carol Marie *principal*
Schoonhoven, Ray James *retired lawyer*
Schornack, John James *accountant*
Schoumacher, Bruce Herbert *lawyer*
Schreck, Robert A., Jr. *lawyer*
Schriver, John T., III *lawyer*
Schroeder, Charles Edgar *banker, investment management executive*
Schroeder, Douglas Fredrick *architect*
Schubert, Helen Celia *public relations executive*
Schubert, William Henry *curriculum studies educator*
Schueppert, George Louis *financial executive*
Schug, Kenneth Robert *chemistry educator*
Schuler, James Joseph *vascular surgeon*
Schulfer, Roche Edward *theater executive director*
Schulhofer, Stephen Joseph *law educator, consultant*
Schulman, Sidney *neurologist, educator*
Schulte, Bruce John *lawyer*
Schulte, David Michael *investment banker*
Schulte, Stephen Charles *lawyer*
†Schultz, John L. *writer, educator*
Schultz, Paul Neal *electronic publishing executive*
Schulz, Keith Donald *corporate lawyer*
Schumann, Adolph Alfred, Jr. *architect*
Schumer, William *surgeon, educator*
Schupp, Ronald Irving *clergyman, civil and human rights leader*
Schuster, Bertram *recruiter, management consultant, publisher*
Schwab, James Charles *urban planner*
Schwartz, Alan Gifford *sport company executive*
Schwartz, Charles Phineas, Jr. *financial and business consultant, lawyer*
Schwartz, Donald Lee *lawyer*
†Schwartz, John David *federal judge*
Schwartz, John Norman *health care executive*
Schwartzberg, Hugh Joel *lawyer, corporate executive, educator*
Schwartzberg, Joanne Gilbert *physician*
†Schwoy, Laurie Annette *soccer player*
Sciarra, John J. *physician, educator*
Scogland, William Lee *lawyer*
Scommegna, Antonio *physician, educator*
Scott, Karen Ann *dentist*
Scott, Stephen Brinsley *theater producer*
Scotti, Michael John, Jr. *medical association executive*
Scribner, Margaret Ellen *school evaluator, senior consultant*
Scrimshaw, Susan Crosby *dean*
Scurry, Briana Collette *soccer player*
Seaman, Irving, Jr. *public relations consultant*
Sedelmaier, John Josef *film director, cinematographer*
Seebert, Kathleen Anne *international sales and marketing executive*
Seeler, Ruth Andrea *pediatrician, educator*
Seifert, Timothy Michael *infosystems specialist*
Seitzinger, Sean Christopher *strategic consultant*
Selfridge, Calvin *lawyer*
Senior, Richard John Lane *textile rental service executive*
Serritella, James Anthony *lawyer*
Serritella, William David *lawyer*
Serwer, Alan Michael *lawyer*
Sfikas, Peter Michael *lawyer, educator*
Shadur, Milton I. *judge*
Shadur, Robert H. *lawyer*
Shafer, Eric Christopher *minister*
Shambaugh, George Elmer, III *internist*
Shank, William O. *lawyer*
Shannon, Iris Reed *nursing educator*
Shannon, Peter Michael, Jr. *lawyer*
Shapey, Ralph *composer, conductor, educator*
Shapiro, Harold David *lawyer, educator*
Shapiro, Stephen Michael *lawyer*
Shapo, Marshall Schambelan *lawyer, educator*
Shaughnessy, Edward Louis *Chinese language educator*
Shedlock, James *library director, consultant*
Shen, Virginia Shiang-lan *Spanish language educator*
Shepherd, Daniel Marston *executive recruiter*
Shepherd, Stewart Robert *lawyer*
Shere, Dennis *publishing executive*
Sherman, Joseph J. *newspaper publishing executive*
Shieh, Ching-Long *structural engineering executive*
Shields, Thomas Charles *lawyer*
Shields, Thomas William *surgeon, educator*
Shiller, Helen *alderman, adult education educator*
Shindler, Donald A. *lawyer*
Shirley, Virginia Lee *advertising executive*
Short, Marion Priscilla *neurology educator*
Shott, Susan *medical biostatistician, educator*
Sibener, Steven Jay *chemistry educator*
Siegel, Howard Jerome *lawyer*
Siegler, Mark *internist, educator*
Sigal, Michael Stephen *lawyer*
Sigler, Hollis *artist, educator, author*
Silberman, Alan Harvey *lawyer*
Sills, Thomas W. *physical science educator*
Silva, Cheryl Lynn *financial economist*
Silvia, John Edwin *economist*
Simon, Bernece Kern *social work educator*
Simon, John Bern *lawyer*
Simon, Mordecai *religious association administrator, clergyman*
Simon, Seymour *lawyer, former state supreme court justice*
Simovic, Laszlo *architect*
Simpson, John Alexander *physicist*
Singer, Emel *staffing industry executive*
Singh, Manmohan *orthopedic surgeon, educator*
Siska, Richard Stanly *marketing professional*
Siske, Roger Charles *lawyer*
Sive, Rebecca Anne *public affairs company executive*
Skala, Gary Dennis *electric and gas utilities executive management consultant*
Skilling, Raymond Inwood *lawyer*
Skilling, Thomas Ethelbert, III *meteorologist, meteorology educator*
Sklarsky, Charles B. *lawyer*
†Skoien, Gary *real estate company executive*
Skolnick, Sherman Herbert *media host/producer, researcher, court reformer*
Skrebneski, Victor *photographer*
Sladen, Bernard Jacob *psychologist*
Slansky, Jerry William *investment company executive*
Smith, Adrian Devaun *architect*
Smith, Craig Malcolm *architect, consultant*
Smith, David Waldo Edward *pathology and gerontology educator, physician*
Smith, Earl Charles *nephrologist, educator*
Smith, Gordon Howell *lawyer*
Smith, J. Clarke *telecommunications industry executive*
Smith, John Gelston *lawyer*
Smith, Mary Ann *alderman*
Smith, Michele *lawyer*
Smith, Raymond Thomas *anthropology educator*
Smith, Sam Pritzker *columnist, author*
Smith, Scott Clybourn *media company executive*
Smith, Stan Vladimir *economist, financial service company executive*
Smith, Tefft Weldon *lawyer*
Smithburg, William Dean *food manufacturing company executive, retired*
Smrcina, Catherine Marie *nursing administrator, researcher*
Sneed, Michael (Michele) *columnist*

Snider, Lawrence K. lawyer
Snodgrass, Klyne Ryland seminary educator
†Snow, Randy J. librarian, English educator
Snyder, Jean Maclean lawyer
So, Frank S. educational association administrator
†Sobrero, Kathryn Michele soccer player
Sochen, June history educator
Socol, Michael Lee obstetrician, gynecologist, educator
Socolofsky, Jon Edward banker
†Socolow, Daniel James foundation administrator
Solaro, Ross John physiologist, biophysicist
Solis, Daniel S. city official
†Solomon, Jack Avrum lawyer, automotive distributor, art dealer
Solovy, Jerold Sherwin lawyer
†Solwitz, Sharon writer, educator
Sonderby, Susan Pierson chief federal bankruptcy judge
Sopranos, Orpheus Javaras manufacturing company executive
Sorensen, Leif Boge physician, educator
Sorensen, W. Robert clergy member, church administrator
Sorgel, Sylvia financial services executive
Sosa, Samuel (Sammy Sosa) professional baseball player
Soto, Ramona training specialist
Spagnolo, Joseph A., Jr. state agency administrator
Spain, Richard Colby lawyer
†Spangehl, Stephen Douglas educator, accrediting agency administrtor
Sparberg, Marshall Stuart gastroenterologist, educator
Spargo, Benjamin H. educator, renal pathologist
Spearman, David Leroy elementary education educator, administrator
Spears, Jackson E., Jr. investment banker
Spector, David M. lawyer
Spellmire, George W. lawyer
Spindler, George S. lawyer, oil industry executive
Spiotto, James Ernest lawyer
†Spoerri, Robert C. real estate company executive
†Springer, Jerry television talk show host
Sproger, Charles Edmund lawyer
Squires, John Henry judge
Sresty, Guggilam Chalamaiah environmental engineer
Stack, John Wallace retired lawyer
Stack, Paul Francis lawyer
Stack, Stephen S. manufacturing company executive
Stanton, Benjamin R. investment company executive
†Staples, Thori Yvette soccer player
Stark, Henry technology educator
Starkman, Gary Lee lawyer
Stead, James Joseph, Jr. securities company executive
Stecich, John Patrick structural engineer
Steck, Theodore Lyle biochemistry and molecular biology educator, physician
Steele, Glenn Daniel, Jr. surgical oncologist
Stein, Robert Allen legal association executive, law educator
Steinberg, Morton M. lawyer
†Steinberg, Salme Elizabeth Harju university president, historian
Steiner, Donald Frederick biochemist, physician, educator
Steinfeld, Manfred furniture manufacturing executive
Steingraber, Frederick George management consultant
Stern, Carl William, Jr. management consultant
Stern, Richard Gustave author, educator
Sternberg, Paul retired ophthalmologist
Sternstein, Allan J. lawyer
Stetler, David J. lawyer
Steven, Donald Anstey educator, composer
Stevens, Mark banker
Stevens, Paul G., Jr. brokerage house executive
Stevenson, Adlai Ewing, III lawyer, former senator
Stewart, Patricia Ann banker
Stewart, S. Jay chemical company executive
Stifler, Venetia Chakos dancer, choreographer, dance educator
Stigler, Stephen Mack statistician, educator
Stillman, Nina Gidden lawyer
Stirling, James Paulman investment banker
Stocking, George Ward, Jr. anthropology educator
Stoll, John Robert lawyer, educator
Stone, Alan container company executive
Stone, Bernard Leonard vice mayor, alderman, lawyer
Stone, Geoffrey Richard law educator, lawyer
Stone, James Howard management consultant
Stone, Roger Warren container company executive
Stone, Steven Michael sports announcer, former baseball player
Storb, Ursula Beate molecular genetics and cell biology educator
Stotler, Edith Ann grain company executive
Stover, Leon (Eugene) anthropology educator, writer, critic
Stowell, Joseph, III academic administrator
Strauch, Gerald Otto surgeon
Strauss, Jeffrey Lewis healthcare executive
Streeto, Joseph Michael catering company official
Streff, William Albert, Jr. lawyer
†Streiffer, Jen soccer player
†Strick, Jeremy curator
Strobeck, Charles LeRoy real estate executive
Strong, Dorothy Swearengen educational administrator
Strubel, Ella Doyle advertising and public relations executive
Strubel, Richard Perry manufacturing company executive
Struggles, John Edward management consultant
Stumpf, David Allen pediatric neurologist
Suarez, Ray city official
Sulkin, Howard Allen college president
Sullivan, Bernard James accountant
Sullivan, Marcia Waite lawyer
Sullivan, Peggy (Anne) librarian
Sullivan, Thomas Patrick lawyer
Sumner, William Marvin anthropology and archaeology educator
Sussman, Arthur Melvin law educator
Sutter, William Paul lawyer
Svanborg, Alvar geriatrics educator, researcher
Swaney, Thomas Edward lawyer
Swanson, Don Richard university dean
Swanson, Patricia K. university official
Sweeney, James Raymond lawyer
Sweet, Charles Wheeler executive recruiter
Swerdlow, Martin Abraham physician, pathologist, educator
Swibel, Steven Warren lawyer
Swift, Edward Foster, III investment banker
Swonk, Diane Catherine economist
Szczepanski, Slawomir Zbigniew Steven lawyer
Tabin, Julius patent lawyer, physicist
Taccarino, John Robert psychology educator
Talbot, Pamela public relations executive
Tallchief, Maria ballerina
Tanner, Helen Hornbeck historian
Tao, Mariano biochemistry educator
Taraszkiewicz, Waldemar physician
Tardy, Medney Eugene, Jr. otolaryngologist, facial plastic surgeon
Tarun, Robert Walter lawyer
Taub, Richard Paul social sciences educator
†Taylor, Bernice academic administrator
Taylor, Roger Lee lawyer
Teichner, Lester management consulting executive
Tekmetarovic, Lisa economics educator
Telfer, Margaret Clare internist, hematologist, oncologist
Temple, Donald retired allergist and dermatologist
†Terkel, Studs (Louis Terkel) author, interviewer
Teruya, Jun hematologist, clinical pathologist
Tessing, Louise Scire graphic designer
Thaden, Edward Carl history educator
†Thall, Robert photographer, educator
Theobald, Edward Robert lawyer
Theobald, Thomas Charles banker
Thies, Richard Brian lawyer
Thomas, Bertha Sophia office manager, paralegal
Thomas, Cherryl T. city buildings commissioner
Thomas, Dale E. lawyer
Thomas, Frank Edward professional baseball player
Thomas, Frederick Bradley lawyer
Thomas, John Thieme management consultant
Thomas, Leona Marlene health information educator
Thomas, Richard Lee banker
Thomas, Stephen Paul lawyer
Thompson, George Everet graphic designer, educator
Thompson, James Robert, Jr. lawyer, former governor
Thompson, Kenneth Roy management educator
Thorne-Thomsen, Thomas lawyer
Thurston, Stephen John pastor
Tigerman, Stanley architect, educator
Tillman, Dorothy Wright alderman
Tipp, Karen Lynn Wagner school psychologist
Tobaccowala, Rishad marketing professional
Tobin, Calvin Jay architect
Tobin, Michael Alan architect, real estate developer
Tobin, Thomas F. lawyer
Tocklin, Adrian Martha insurance company executive, lawyer
Toll, Daniel Roger corporate executive, civic leader
Tomaino, Joseph Carmine former retail executive, former postal inspector
Tomita, Tadanori neurosurgeon
Toohey, James Kevin lawyer
Topinka, Judy Baar state official
Torgersen, Torwald Harold architect, designer
Torshen, Jerome Harold lawyer
Totlis, Gust John retired title insurance company executive
Towson, Thomas D. securities trader
Trapani, Catherine special education and educational psychologist
Trapp, James McCreery lawyer
Travis, Dempsey Jerome real estate executive, mortgage banker
Trenary, Michael chemistry educator
Trienens, Howard Joseph lawyer
Tripp, Marian Barlow Loofe retired public relations company executive
Trost, Eileen Bannon lawyer
Troutman, Arenda alderman
Truran, James Wellington, Jr. astrophysicist
Truskowski, John Budd lawyer
Tryban, Esther Elizabeth lawyer
Tsou, Tang political science educator, researcher
Tucker, Bowen Hayward lawyer
Tuckson, Reed V. academic administrator
Turkevich, Anthony Leonid chemist, educator
Turner, La Ferria Maria business consultant, financial consultant
Turner, Michael Stanley physics educator
Turner-Coleman, Shirley A. city official
Turow, Scott F. lawyer, author
Tyner, Howard A. publishing executive, newspaper editor, journalist
Tyree, James C. insurance company executive
Udeani, George Ogbonna pharmacist, educator
Ultmann, John Ernest physician, educator
Underwood, Robert Leigh venture capitalist
Ungaretti, Richard Anthony lawyer
†Unsworth, Richard Timothy writer
Upshaw, Harry Stephan psychology educator
Vagnieres, Robert Charles, Jr. architect
Valaskovic, David William architect, designer
Valerio, Joseph M. architectural firm executive, educator
Van Demark, Ruth Elaine lawyer
Van Den Hende, Fred J(oseph) human resources executive
VanderBeke, Patricia K. architect
Vander Wilt, Carl Eugene banker
Vanecko, Robert Michael surgeon, educator
Van Eron, Kevin Joseph organizational development consultant
Van Pelt, Robert Irving firefighter
Van Valen, Leigh biologist, educator
Varro, Barbara Joan editor
Varwig, David Lee investment banker
Velisaris, Chris Nicholas financial analyst
†Venturini, Tisha Lea professional soccer player
Verschoor, Curtis Carl business educator, consultant
Vertreace, Martha Modena English educator, poet
Veverka, Donald John lawyer
Vinci, John Nicholas architect, educator
Visotsky, Harold Meryle psychiatrist, educator
Vita, Steven Edward poet
Vitale, David J. banker
Vitale, Gerald Lee financial services executive
Vladem, Steven Allen author, motivational speaker
Vogelzang, Jeanne Marie professional association executive, attorney
Vondruska, Eloise Marie librarian
von Rhein, John Richard music critic, editor
Von Roenn, Kelvin Alexander neurosurgeon
Vrablik, Edward Robert import/export company executive
Vree, Roger Allen lawyer
Vroustouris, Alexander inspector general
Vukas, Ronald publishing executive
Vyn, Kathleen A. small business owner
Wackerle, Frederick William management consultant
Wadden, Richard Albert environmental engineer, educator, consultant, research director
Wade, Edwin Lee writer, lawyer
Wade, Nigel editor in chief
Wade, Suzanne management consultant
Wagner, Joseph M. church administrator
Wagner, Mark Anthony videotape editor
Wagner, Rose Mary librarian
Wahlen, Edwin Alfred lawyer
Waintroob, Andrea Ruth lawyer
Waite, Dennis Vernon investor relations consultant
Waite, Norman, Jr. lawyer
Walberg, Herbert John psychologist, educator, consultant
†Walker, Joan H. public relations executive
Walker, Ronald Edward psychologist, educator
Walker, Thomas Ray city transportation commissioner
Walker-Ricks, Gloria Deloise secondary education educator
Wall, James McKendree minister, editor
Wall, Michael Joseph academic administrator
Wall, Robert F. lawyer
Wallerstein, Mitchel Bruce foundation executive
Wallingford, Anne writer, editor, project developer
Walsh, Michael S. lawyer
Walter, Priscilla Anne lawyer
Walters, Lawrence Charles advertising executive
Waltz, Jon Richard lawyer, educator, author
Wander, Herbert Stanton lawyer
Wang, Albert James violinist, educator
Wanke, Ronald Lee lawyer
Ward, Michael W. lawyer
Wardropper, Ian Bruce museum curator, educator
Warfield, William Caesar singer, actor, educator
Wasan, Darsh Tilakchand university official, chemical engineer educator
Wasiolek, Edward literary critic, language and literature educator
Watson, MaryFrances Elizabeth management consultant, librarian
Watson, Robert R. lawyer
Waxler, Beverly Jean anesthesiologist, physician
Wayman, David Anthony state agency administrator
Weaver, Donna Rae company executive
Weaver, Timothy Allan lawyer
Webb, Dan K. lawyer
Weber, Daniel E. association executive
Weber, Donald B. advertising and marketing executive
Weber, Hanno architect
Webster, David Macpherson lawyer
Webster, James Randolph, Jr. physician
Webster, Ronald D. communications company executive
Weclew, Victor T. dentist
†Wedoff, Eugene R. federal judge
Weese, Benjamin Horace architect
Weigand, Russell Glen fundraising consulting firm executive
Weil, Roman Lee accounting educator
Weiman, Heidi early childhood education educator
Weinberg, David B. investor
Weinberg, Lila Shaffer writer, editor
Weinberg, Meyer humanities educator
Weinkopf, Friedrich J. lawyer
Weinsheimer, William Cyrus lawyer
Weintraub, Joseph Barton publishing executive
Weir, Bryce Keith Alexander neurosurgeon, neurology educator
Weis, Mervyn J. physician, gastroenterologist
Weisberg, Lois arts administrator, city official
Weiss, Robert Alan surgeon
Weissman, Michael Lewis lawyer
Weitzman, Robert Harold investment company executive
Weldon-Linne, C. Michael pathologist, microbiologist
Wellington, Robert Hall manufacturing company executive
Wells, Joel Freeman editor, author
Wells, Samuel Alonzo, Jr. surgeon, educator
Welsh, Kelly Raymond lawyer, telecommunications company executive
Werner, William Norman internist, hospital administrator
†Westcott, Robert Frederick consultant
Wetzel, Franklin Todd spinal surgeon, educator, researcher
Wexler, Richard Lewis lawyer
†Whalen, Sarah Eve soccer player
Whalen, Wayne W. lawyer
†Whidmayer, Christopher A. legislative staff member
White, Linda Diane lawyer
White, R. Quincy lawyer
Whitington, Peter Frank pediatrics educator, pediatric hepatologist
Wick, Lawrence Scott lawyer
Wiecek, Barbara Harriet advertising executive
Wied, George Ludwig physician
Wier, Patricia Ann publishing executive, consultant
Wiggins, Charles Henry, Jr. lawyer
Wikman, Thomas S. music director
Wilber, David James cardiologist
Wilcox, Mark Dean lawyer
Wildman, Max Edward lawyer
Wilhelm, David C. political organization administrator
Will, Jon Nicholson small business owner, financial consultant
Williams, Ann Claire federal judge
Williams, Edward Joseph banker
Williams, Elynor A. public affairs specialist
Williams, George Howard lawyer, association executive
Williams, Mark H. marketing communications executive
Williams, Richard Lucas, III electronics company executive, lawyer
Williams-Ashman, Howard Guy biochemist, educator
Williamson, Richard Salisbury lawyer
Willoughby, William Franklin, II physician, researcher
Willson, Mary F. ecology researcher, educator
Wilmouth, Robert K. commodities executive
Wilson, Anne Gawthrop artist, educator
Wilson, Clarence Sylvester, Jr. lawyer, educator
Wilson, Richard Harold government official
Wilson, Thomas W. market research company executive
Wine-Banks, Jill Susan lawyer
Winfrey, Oprah television talk show host, actress, producer
Wingfield-Hyrams, Carlene English educator
Winkelman, Lois Anaya womens health nurse
Winkler, Charles Howard lawyer, investment management company executive
Winnie, Alon Palm anesthesiologist, educator
†Winninghoff, Albert C. M. advertising company executive
Winston, Roland physicist, educator
Winton, Jeffrey Blake arbitrator
Wirszup, Izaak mathematician, educator
Wirtz, William Wadsworth real estate and sports executive
Wisenberg, Sandra Leah writer
Wishner, Maynard Ira finance company executive, lawyer
Witcoff, Sheldon William lawyer
Witrod, Sister Mary Rosalita nursing home administrator
Wittenberg, Jon Albert accountant
Witwer, Samuel Weiler, Jr. lawyer
Wiwchar, Michael bishop
Wolf, Charles Benno lawyer
Wolf, Linda advertising executive
Wolf-Chase, Grace Annamarie astronomer, astrophysicist
Wolfe, David Louis lawyer
Wolfe, Sheila A. journalist
Wolfson, Larry Marshall lawyer
Wolin, Jeffrey Alan artist
Wolpert, Edward Alan psychiatrist
Wood, James Nowell museum director and executive
Wood Prince, William Norman investments and real estate professional
Woods, Robert Archer investment counsel
Wooldridge, Patrice Marie marketing professional, martial arts and meditation educator
Wooten-Bryant, Helen Catherine principal
Workman, Robert Peter artist, cartoonist
Wright, Helen Kennedy professional association administrator, publisher, editor, librarian
Wright, Judith Margaret law librarian, educator
Wycliff, Noel Don journalist, newspaper editor
Wyszynski, Richard Chester musician, conductor, educator
Yacktman, Donald Arthur financial executive, investment counselor
Yale, Seymour Hershel dental radiologist, educator, university dean, gerontologist
Yamada, Takeshi artist, language and cultural consultant, educator
Yao, Tito Go pediatrician
Yapoujian, Nerses Nick manufacturing executive
Yates, Sidney Richard former congressman, lawyer
York, Donald Gilbert astronomy educator, researcher
Young, James Eugene management consultant
Young, Keith Lawrence lawyer
Young, Lauren Sue Jones education educator
Young, Ronald Faris commodity trader
Youngman, Owen Ralph newspaper executive
Yu, Anthony C. religion and literature educator
Zabel, Sheldon Alter lawyer, law educator
Zagel, James Block federal judge
Zajicek, Jeronym music educator
Zaremski, Miles Jay lawyer
Zaslow, Jeffrey Lloyd syndicated columnist
Zeid, Paula Klein metals broker
Zeid, Philip L. metal recycling executive
Zekman, Pamela Lois (Mrs. Fredric Soll) reporter
Zell, Samuel transportation leasing company executive
Zellner, Arnold economics and statistics educator
Zemm, Sandra Phyllis lawyer
Zenner, Sheldon Toby lawyer
Zimmerman, Martin E. financial executive
Zimmermann, Polly Gerber emergency nurse
Zimny, Robert Walter metal processing executive
Zisman, Lawrence S. internist
Zlatoff-Mirsky, Everett Igor violinist
Zolno, Mark S. lawyer
Zonis, Marvin political scientist, educator
Zonka, Constance Z. educational organization administrator
Zorn, Eric John newspaper columnist
Zucaro, Aldo Charles insurance company executive
Zukowsky, John Robert curator

Chicago Heights
Bohlen, Jeffrey Brian protective services official
Cifelli, John Louis lawyer
Dowden, Craig Phillips human resources executive
Galloway, Sister Mary Blaise mathematics educator

Cicero
Kociolko, John Stephen town official
†Kreuz, Jeanette C. accountant, school official
Levin, Michael David musician
Welborn, Sarah photographer, writer, poet

Clarendon Hills
Moritz, Donald Brooks mechanical engineer, consultant

Coal City
†Franciskovich, Jolene Ann library administrator
Major, Mary Jo dance school artistic director

Collinsville
Morris, Calvin Curtis architect
Pallozola, Christine non-profit historic site administrator

Columbia
Megahy, Diane Alaire physician

Country Club Hills
Scherer, George Robert secondary education educator

Crestwood
Cowie, Norman Edwin credit manager
Morissette, Carol Lynne healthcare consultant

Crete
Langer, Steven human resources management consultant and industrial psychologist
Scott, Whitney writer

Crystal Lake
Althoff, J(ames) L. construction company executive
Anderson, Lyle Arthur manufacturing company executive
Bishop, James Francis lawyer
Chamberlain, Charles James railroad labor union executive
Dabkowski, John electrical engineering executive
†Davidson, Shirley Jean elementary and secondary educator
Fleming, Marjorie Foster freelance writer, artist
Haemmelmann, Keith Alan minister
Halperin, Richard George information technology executive
Keller, William Francis publishing consultant

Knox, Susan Marie *paralegal*
Linklater, Isabelle Stanislawa Yarosh-Galazka (Lee Linklater) *foundation administrator*
Pearson, Nels Kenneth *retired manufacturing company executive*
Smyth, Joseph Vincent *manufacturing company executive*
Wood, Leslie Ann *retail administrator*

Danville
Arnold, Scott Gregory *computer information systems specialist*
Ball, James S. *orchestra conductor, educator, musician*
Blan, Kennith William, Jr. *lawyer*
Brumaghim, Paul *small business owner*
Colwell, Sue Ellen *English educator*
Craig, Hurshel Eugene *agronomist*
†Fines, Gerald D. *federal judge*
Kettling, Virginia *health facility administrator*
Konsis, Kenneth Frank *forester, educator*
Prabhudesai, Mukund M. *pathology educator, laboratory director, researcher, administrator*
†Steward, Irene A. *academic administrator*

Darien
†Beardon, Richard *beverage company executive*
Gardner, Howard Garry *pediatrician, educator*
Klassek, Christine Paulette *behavioral scientist*

De Kalb
Hanna, Nessim *marketing educator*

Decatur
Andreas, Glenn Allen, Jr. *agricultural company executive*
Bluhm, Myron Dean *sales professional*
Bradshaw, Billy Dean *retail executive*
Braun, William Joseph *life insurance underwriter*
†Buck, Christopher George *religion educator, writer*
Cain, Richard Duane *small business owner*
Decker, Charles Richard *investment executive*
Dunn, John Francis *lawyer, state representative*
Erlanson, Deborah McFarlin *state program administrator*
Forster, Lance Allen *technical researcher animal science*
Heisler, Harold Reinhart *management consultant*
Koucky, John Richard *metallurgical engineer, manufacturing executive*
Kraft, Burnell D. *agricultural products company executive*
Moorman, John A. *librarian*
Morgan, E. A. *church administrator*
Morrison, Barbara *nursing educator*
Perry, Anthony John *retired hospital executive*
Reising, Richard P. *lawyer*
Requarth, William Henry *surgeon*
Rockefeller, Margaretta Fitler Murphy (Happy Rockefeller) *widow of former vice president of United States*
Staley, Henry Mueller *manufacturing company executive*
Sweet, Arthur *orthopedist*
Vigneri, Joseph William *lawyer*
Womeldorff, Porter John *utilities executive*

Deerfield
Abbey, G(eorge) Marshall *lawyer, former health care company executive, general counsel*
Bagley, Thomas Steven *private equity investor*
Barker, Barbara *real estate professional*
Benjamin, Lawrence *food service executive*
Berman-Hammer, Susan *public relations executive*
Boyd, Joseph Don *financial services executive*
Chromizky, William Rudolph *accountant*
Cruikshank, John W., III *life insurance underwriter*
Cutchins, Clifford Armstrong, IV *lawyer*
Dawson, Suzanne Stockus *lawyer*
Dennison, Terry Alan *management consultant*
Gaither, John F. *lawyer*
Gash, Lauren Beth *lawyer, state legislator*
Graham, William B. *pharmaceutical company executive*
Guttman, Arnold R. *chemist, educator*
Howell, George Bedell *equity investing and managing executive*
†Jorndt, Louis Daniel *retail drug store chain executive*
Karp, Gary *marketing and public relations executive*
Kingdon, Henry Shannon *physician, biochemist, educator, executive*
†Kohn, David Lupo *legislative staff member*
Lifschultz, Phillip *financial and tax consultant, accountant, lawyer*
Loucks, Vernon R., Jr. *medical technologies executive*
Marsh, Miles L. *paper company executive*
Oettinger, Julian Alan *lawyer, pharmacy company executive*
Ringler, James M. *cookware company executive*
Russell, William Steven *finance executive*
Sanner, John Harper *retired pharmacologist*
Scheiber, Stephen Carl *psychiatrist*
Scott, Theodore R. *lawyer*
Serwy, Robert Anthony *accountant*
Staubitz, Arthur Frederick *lawyer, healthcare products company executive*
Stavropoulos, Rose Mary Grant *community activist, volunteer*
Vollen, Robert Jay *lawyer*
Wallace, Rick *marketing professional*
Wolf, Andrew *food manufacturing company executive*
Woodbridge, John Dunning *history and church history educator*
Zywicki, Robert Albert *electrical distribution company executive*

Dekalb
Baker, William *British literature educator*
†Banovetz, James M. *public administration educator, consultant*
Bickner, Bruce *food products executive*
Bukonda, Ngoyi K. Zacharie *health care management educator*
Coakley, Michael James *university administrator*
Crosser, Carmen Lynn *marriage and family therapist, clinical social worker, consultant*
Davidson, Kenneth Lawrence *lawyer, educator*
Dorn, Gordon Joseph *artist, art educator*
Healey, Robert William *school system administrator*
James, Marilyn Shaw *secondary education educator, social service worker*
Kimball, Clyde William *physicist, educator*
Kind, Joshua B. *history educator*
King, Kenneth Paul *secondary education educator*
Kuropas, Myron Bohdon *elementary education educator*
La Tourette, John Ernest *academic administrator*
Lippold, Neal William *criminal justice educator*
Lorence, William George *county engineer, consultant*
Marcano, Rosita Lopez *education educator*
Merritt, Helen Henry *retired art educator, ceramic sculptor, art historian*
†Merwin, Donald Miles *retired phone worker, politician*
Monat, William Robert *university official*
†Moody, Jesse Carroll *educational administrator*
Morrison, Harriet Barbara *retired education educator*
Niemi, John Arvo *adult education educator*
Quinney, Richard *sociology educator*
Rossing, Thomas D. *physics educator*
Skeels, Jack William *economics educator, consultant*
Sons, Linda Ruth *mathematics educator*
Stoia, Dennis Vasile *industrial management educator*
†Stryk, Lucien Henry *writer*
Studwell, William Emmett *librarian, writer*
Troyer, Alvah Forrest *seed corn company executive, plant breeder*
Tucker, Watson Billopp *lawyer*
Vance Siebrasse, Kathy Ann *newspaper publishing executive*
Williams, Hope Denise *administrator, business consultant*
Witmer, John Harper, Jr. *lawyer*
Zar, Jerrold H(oward) *biology educator, university dean, statistician*

Des Plaines
Appelson, Marilyn Irene *director of college development*
Arena, Blaise Joseph *research chemist*
†Baerenklau, Alan H. *hotel executive*
Banach, Art John *graphic artist*
Brodl, Raymond Frank *lawyer, former lumber company executive*
Carroll, Barry Joseph *manufacturing and real estate executive*
Clapper, Marie Anne *magazine publisher*
Coburn, James LeRoy *educational administrator*
Cucco, Ulisse P. *obstetrician, gynecologist*
Decker, William Alexander *editor*
Frank, James S. *automotive executive*
Grahn, Barbara Ascher *publisher*
†Henrikson, Arthur Allen *political cartoonist, educator*
Hlavacek, Roy George *publishing executive, magazine editor*
Holtz, Michael P. *hotel executive*
Jacobs, William Russell, II *lawyer*
Jakubek, Helen Majerczyk *retired secondary school educator*
Larrimore, Randall Walter *manufacturing company executive*
Lee, Bernard Shing-Shu *research company executive*
Meinert, John Raymond *clothing manufacturing and retailing executive, investment banker*
Mueller, Kurt M. *hotel executive*
Pannke, Peggy M. *long term care insurance agency executive*
Quellmalz, Frederick *foundation executive, editor*
Quintanilla, Antonio Paulet *physician, educator*
Rosenson, Irwin Dale *accountant*
Stokes, Robert Allan *science research facility executive, physicist*
Torchia, H. Andrew *hotel executive*
Winfield, Michael D. *engineering company executive*
Zamirowski, Thaddeus Andrew, Jr. *family physician*

Dixon
Polascik, Mary Ann *ophthalmologist*
Shaw, Thomas Douglas *newspaper executive*

Dolton
Whitehurst, Steven Laroy *telecommunications administrator*

Dorsey
Hinkle, Jo Ann *English language educator*

Downers Grove
Beres, Michael John *plant engineer*
†Canitz, Henry Charles *food company executive*
†Cantu, Carlos *holding company executive*
†Capek, Brenda Joyce *social worker*
Clement, Paul Platts, Jr. *performance technologist, educator*
Colbert, Marvin Jay *retired internist, educator*
Feeney, Don Joseph, Jr. *psychologist*
Gioioso, Joseph Vincent *psychologist*
Hasen-Sinz, Susan Katherine *state agency administrator, actress*
Holt, William Harold, Jr. *film producer, consultant*
Hsiao, Ming-Yuan *nuclear engineer, researcher*
Hubbard, Lincoln Beals *medical physicist, consultant*
Kellum, Carmen Kaye *apparel company executive*
Kirkegaard, R. Lawrence *architectural acoustician*
†Kunnemann, Nancy Bush *special education educator*
LaRocca, Patricia Darlene McAleer *middle school mathematics educator*
Martan, Joseph Rudolf *lawyer*
Melesio, Kathryn Mary *oncological nurse, educator*
Morefield, Michael Thomas *financial executive*
Pollard, C. William *environmental services administrator*
Pollard, Charles William *diversified services company executive*
Powers, Anthony Richard, Jr. *educational sales professional*
Punt, Leonard Cornelis *educational services company executive*
Ruffolo, Paul Gregory *police officer, educator*
Saricks, Joyce Goering *librarian*
Schwemm, John Butler *printing company executive, lawyer*
Shen, Sin-Yan *physicist, conductor, acoustics specialist, music director*

Du Quoin
Atkins, Aaron Ardene *lawyer*

Dundee
Ulakovich, Ronald Stephen *real estate developer*
Weck, Kristin Willa *bank executive*

Dunlap
Hanard, Patricia Ann *family nurse practitioner*
Leetz, John Richard *health care executive*
Reinsma, Harold Lawrence *design consultant, engineer*

Dupo
Gallamore, Betty Lou *nurse*

East Hazel Crest
Ruyle-Hullinger, Elizabeth Smith (Beth Ruyle) *association executive*

East Moline
Polios, Nancy Louise *secondary school educator*
Silliman, Richard George *retired lawyer, retired farm machinery company executive*
Taylor, Byron Keith *industrial engineer*

East Saint Louis
Beatty, William Louis *federal judge*
†Cohn, Gerald B. *federal judge*
†Finch, Janet Mitchell *academic administrator*
Martin, Betty J. *speech, language pathologist*
†Meyers, Kenneth J. *federal judge*
Proud, Clifford J. *judge*
Riley, Paul E. *judge*
Stiehl, William D. *federal judge*
Wright, Katie Harper *educational administrator, journalist*

Edelstein
†Hickey, Bernard J. *bank executive*

Edinburg
†Jones, Kenneth D. *secondary education educator, coach*

Edwardsville
Crowder, Barbara Lynn *judge*
Dietrich, Suzanne Claire *instructional designer, communications consultant*
†Drucker, Mark Lewis *public administration educator, consultant*
Gauen, Patrick Emil *newspaper correspondent*
†Hampton, Phillip Jewel *artist, educator*
Hulbert, Linda Ann *health sciences librarian*
Lazerson, Earl Edwin *academic administrator emeritus*
Malone, Robert Roy *artist, art educator*
May, Mary Louise *elementary education educator*
Nehring, Wendy Marie *pediatrics nurse*
Rikli, Donald Carl *lawyer*
Riley, Dawn C. *educational philosopher, researcher*
Swalley, Gary William *history educator*

Effingham
Heth, Diana Sue *therapist*
Pickett, Steven Harold *elementary education educator*

Elburn
Hansen, H. Jack *management consultant*
Willey, James Lee *dentist*

Elgin
Beyer, Karen Haynes *social worker*
Dodohara, Jean Noton *music educator*
Duffy, John Lewis *retired Latin, English and reading educator*
Eineke, Alvina Marie *public health nurse*
Freeman, Corwin Stuart, Jr. *investment adviser*
Hopkins, John Kendall *college administrator, architect*
Juergensmeyer, John Eli *lawyer*
Kelly, Matthew Edward *association executive, retired*
Kirkland, Alfred Younges, Sr. *federal judge*
Koepke, Donald Herbert *retired mechanical engineer and real estate professional*
Machowicz, Michele A. *secondary education educator, consultant*
Mason, Stephen Olin *nonprofit association administrator*
Matthaeus, Renate G. *high school principal*
Nelson, John Thilgen *retired hospital administrator, physician*
Nolen, Wilfred E. *church administrator*
O'Connor, Peggy Lee *communications manager*
Parks, Patrick *English language educator, humanities educator*
Roeser, Ronald O. *lawyer, consultant*
Rogers, Carleton Carson, Jr. *trade show and convention executive*
Schmalholz, Deborah Lynn *education educator*
Wilson, Robert Byron *manufacturing executive*
Zack, Daniel Gerard *library director*

Elk Grove Village
Bandel, David Brian *accountant*
Field, Larry *paper company executive*
Flaherty, John Joseph *quality assurance company executive*
Meyer, Raymond Joseph *former college basketball coach*
Nadig, Gerald George *manufacturing executive*
Sanders, Joe Maxwell, Jr. *pediatrician, association administrator*
Stein, David Timothy *minister*

Elmhurst
†Babyar, Margaret *school counselor*
Baker, Robert I. *business executive*
Begando, Joseph Sheridan *retired university chancellor, educator*
Berry, James Frederick *lawyer, biology educator*
Betinis, Emanuel James *physics and mathematics educator*
Blain, Charlotte Marie *physician, educator*
Burton, Darrell Irvin *engineering executive*
Choyke, Phyllis May Ford (Mrs. Arthur Davis Choyke, Jr.) *management executive, editor, poet*
Cureton, Bryant Lewis *college president, educator*
Dallas, Daniel George *social worker*
Daugherty, Richard Allen *musician, retired educator*
Duchossois, Richard Louis *manufacturing executive, racetrack executive*
Fornatto, Elio Joseph *otolaryngologist, educator*
Hildreth, R(oland) James *foundation executive, economist*
†Hookham, Eleanor King *painter*
King Hookham, Eleanor *artist*
Moffitt, Ray *social worker, consultant*
Noffs, David Sharrard *foundation administrator*
Pruter, Margaret Franson *editor*
Webster, Douglas Peter *emergency physician*
†Young, Wendy Unrath *musician*

Elmwood Park
Fiore, Mercia V. *author*

Eureka
Hearne, George Archer *academic administrator*
Vijitha-Kumara, Kanaka Hewage *computer science educator*
West, Nancy Lee *music educator, performance artist, entertainer*

Evanston
Abnee, A. Victor *trade association executive*
Achenbach, Jan Drewes *engineering educator, scientist*
Allred, Albert Louis *chemistry educator*
Bankoff, Seymour George *chemical engineer, educator*
Bareiss, Erwin Hans *computer scientist, mathematician, nuclear engineer, educator*
Bashook, Philip G. *medical association executive, educator*
Basolo, Fred *chemistry educator*
Bazant, Zdenek Pavel *structural engineering educator, scientist, consultant*
Beatty, William Kaye *medical bibliography educator*
Beck, Eva-Carol *musician*
Bellow, Alexandra *mathematician, educator*
Belytschko, Ted Bohdan *civil and mechanical engineering educator*
Bienen, Henry Samuel *political science educator, university executive*
Bishop, David Fulton *library administrator*
Bobco, William David, Jr. *consulting engineering company executive*
Borcover, Alfred Seymour *journalist*
Bordwell, Frederick George *chemistry educator*
Boye, Roger Carl *academic administrator, journalism educator, writer*
Braeutigam, Ronald Ray *economics educator*
Brazelton, William Thomas *chemical engineering educator*
Buchbinder-Green, Barbara Joyce *art and architectural historian*
Butt, John Baecher *chemical engineering educator*
Carr, Stephen Howard *materials engineer, educator*
Cassell, Frank Hyde *business educator*
Cates, Jo Ann *library administrator, writer*
Catlett, George Roudebush *accountant*
Cheng, Herbert Su-Yuen *mechanical engineering educator*
Christian, Richard Carlton *university dean, former advertising agency executive*
Cohen, Jerome Bernard *materials science educator*
Cole, Douglas *retired English literature educator*
Conger, William Frame *artist, educator*
Corey, Gordon Richard *financial advisor, former utilities executive*
Crawford, James Weldon *psychiatrist, educator, administrator*
Crawford, Susan *library director, educator, author*
Crook, Stephen Richard *sales and marketing management consultant*
†Cubbage, Alan Kennett *academic administrator*
Dallos, Peter John *neurobiologist, educator*
Daskin, Mark Stephen *civil engineering educator*
Davis, Stephen Howard *applied mathematics educator*
Devinatz, Allen *mathematician, mathematics educator*
Downing, Joan Forman *editor*
Duncan, Robert Bannerman *strategy and organizations educator*
Durst, Gary Michael *management trainer, speaker*
Eberley, Helen-Kay *opera singer, classical record company executive, poet*
Enroth-Cugell, Christina Alma Elisabeth *neurophysiologist, educator*
Felknor, Bruce Lester *editorial consultant, writer*
Fessler, Raymond R. *metallurgical engineering consultant*
Fine, Arthur I. *philosopher*
Fine, Morris Eugene *materials engineer, educator*
Fisher, Neal Floyd *religious organization administrator*
Fitzgerald, Mary Joan *music educator*
Fourer, Robert Harold *industrial engineering educator, consultant*
Frazer, Ricardo Amando *program director*
Freeman, Arthur J. *physics educator*
Frey, Donald Nelson *industrial engineer, educator, manufacturing company executive*
Friedman, Hans Adolf *architect*
Fryburger, Vernon Ray, Jr. *advertising and marketing educator*
Galvin, Kathleen Malone *communications educator*
Gasper, George, Jr. *mathematics educator*
Gibbons, William Reginald, Jr. *poet, novelist, translator, editor*
†Goldman, Lawrence H. *construction company executive*
Goldstick, Thomas Karl *biomedical engineering educator*
Goodyear, Julie Ann *marketing and fundraising specialist*
Gordon, Julie Peyton *foundation administrator*
Gordon, Robert James *economics educator*
Gormley, R(obert) James *retired lawyer*
Greenberg, Douglas Stuart *history educator*
Haberman, Shelby Joel *statistician, educator*
Haddad, Abraham Herzl *electrical engineering educator, researcher*
Hannan, Bradley *educational publishing consultant and executive*
Haring, Olga Munk *retired medical educator, physician*
Hemke, Frederick L. *music educator, university administrator*
Hennessy, Margaret Barrett *health care executive*
Herron, Orley R. *college president*
Howard, Kenneth Irwin *psychology educator*
Hughes, Edward F. X. *physician, educator*
Hurter, Arthur Patrick *economist, educator*
Ibers, James Arthur *chemist, educator*
Ingersoll, Robert Stephen *former diplomat, federal agency administrator*
Ionescu Tulcea, Cassius *research mathematician, educator*
Irons, William George *anthropology educator*
†Jacobs, Donald P. *dean, banking and finance educator*
Jacobs, Norman Joseph *publishing company executive*
Jennings, Francis P. *historian, writer*
Jerome, Joseph Walter *mathematics educator*
Johnson, David Kenneth *historian*
Johnson, David Lynn *materials scientist, educator*
Jones, Dorothy Vincent *diplomatic historian*

Jones, Robert Russell *magazine editor*
Kalai, Ehud *decision sciences educator, researcher in economics and decision sciences*
†Kapranov, Mikhail M. *mathematician, educator*
Karlins, M(artin) William *composer, educator*
Keer, Leon Morris *engineering educator*
Keith, Thomas Warren, Jr. *marketing executive*
Khandekar, Janardan Dinkar *oncologist, educator*
King, Robert Charles *biologist, educator*
Kliphardt, Raymond A. *engineering educator*
Klotz, Irving Myron *chemist, educator*
Krizek, Raymond John *civil engineering educator, consultant*
Krulee, Gilbert Koreb *computer scientist, educator*
Kuenster, John Joseph *magazine editor*
Kujala, Walfrid Eugene *musician, educator*
Kung, Harold Hing-Chuen *engineering educator*
Laff, Ned Scott *English educator, university administrator*
Lafont, Cristina *educator*
Lambert, Joseph Buckley *chemistry educator*
Langsley, Donald Gene *psychiatrist, medical board executive*
Langsley, Pauline Royal *psychiatrist*
Larson, Roy *journalist, publisher*
Lavengood, Lawrence Gene *management educator, historian*
Lee, Der-Tsai *electrical engineering and computer science educator, researcher, consultant*
†Lems, Kristin *English language educator, songwriter*
Letsinger, Robert Lewis *chemistry educator*
Lewis, Dan Albert *education educator*
Liu, Shu Qian *biomedical engineer, researcher, educator*
Liu, Wing Kam *mechanical and civil engineering educator*
Marhic, Michel Edmond *engineering educator, entrepreneur, consultant*
Markowitz, Judith Ann *owner small business*
Matkowsky, Bernard Judah *applied mathematician, educator*
McCleary, Elliott Harold *magazine editor*
McCoy, Marilyn *university official*
McDonough, Bridget Ann *music theatre company director*
Meshii, Masahiro *materials science educator*
Miller, Deborah Jean *computer training and document consultant*
Miller, Thomas Williams *former university dean*
Moore, Wallace David *minister, religious organization administrator*
Morrison, John Horton *lawyer*
Moskos, Charles C. *sociology educator*
Murphy, Gordon John *electrical engineer*
Musa, Samuel Albert *university executive*
Myerson, Roger Bruce *economist, game theorist, educator*
Nakoneczny, Michael Martin *artist*
Neuschel, Robert Percy *management consultant, educator*
Novales, Ronald Richards *zoologist, educator*
Oakes, Robert James *physics educator*
†Okal, Emile Andre *geophysicist, educator*
Olmstead, William Edward *mathematics educator*
Olson, Gregory Bruce *materials science and engineering educator, academic director*
Ottino, Julio Mario *chemical engineering educator, scientist*
Otwell, Ralph Maurice *retired newspaper editor*
Peck, Abraham *editor, writer, educator, magazine consultant*
Peponis, Harold Arthur *insurance agent, broker*
Pople, John Anthony *chemistry educator*
Porter, Robert Hugh *economics educator*
Prince, Thomas Richard *accountant, educator*
Protess, David Lewis *journalism educator*
Rasco, Kay Frances *antique dealer*
Raymond, Frank Joseph *association executive*
Reimer, Bennett *music educator, writer*
Reiter, Stanley *economist, educator*
Robinson, R. Clark *mathematician, educator*
Rolfe, Michael N. *management consulting firm executive*
Rubenstein, Albert Harold *industrial engineering and management sciences educator*
Saari, Donald Gene *mathematician*
Sachtler, Wolfgang Max Hugo *chemistry educator*
Salzman, Arthur George *architect*
Schank, Roger Carl *computer science and psychology educator*
Schwartz, Theodore B. *physician, educator*
Schwarzlose, Richard Allen *journalism educator*
Scott, Walter Dill *management educator*
Seeskin, Kenneth Robert *philosophy educator*
Seidman, David N(athaniel) *materials science and engineering educator*
Shah, Surendra Poonamchand *engineering educator, researcher*
Shanas, Ethel *sociology educator*
Sheridan, James Edward *history educator*
Shriver, Duward Felix *chemistry educator, researcher, consultant*
Silverman, Richard Bruce *chemist, biochemist, educator*
Sims, William Ronald *advertising executive*
Smith, Spencer Bailey *engineering and business educator*
Sobel, Alan *electrical engineer, physicist*
Spears, Kenneth George *chemistry educator*
Sprang, Milton LeRoy *obstetrician, gynecologist, educator*
Stern, Louis William *marketing educator, consultant*
Sundquist, Eric John *American studies educator*
Taam, Ronald Everett *physics and astronomy educator*
Taflove, Allen *electrical engineer, educator, researcher, consultant*
Takahashi, Joseph S. *neuroscientist*
Tanner, Martin Abba *statistics and human oncology educator*
Thrash, Patricia Ann *educational association administrator*
Tornabene, Russell C. *communications executive*
Traisman, Howard Sevin *pediatrician*
Ulmer, Melville Paul *physics and astronomy educator*
Vanderstappen, Harrie Albert *Far Eastern art educator*
Vanneman, Edgar, Jr. *retired lawyer*
Van Ness, James Edward *electrical engineering educator*
Vaynman, Semyon *materials scientist, educator*
Ver Steeg, Clarence Lester *historian, educator*
Vick, Nicholas A. *neurologist*
Villa-Komaroff, Lydia *molecular biologist, educator, university official*
Wagner, Durrett *former publisher, picture service executive*
Walker, Harold Blake *minister*
Wang, Jian-Sheng *materials scientist*
Weber, Arnold R. *academic administrator*
Weertman, Johannes *materials science educator*
Weertman, Julia Randall *materials science and engineering educator*
Wefler, Wilson Daniel *publisher, editor, management consultant*
Weil, Irwin *Slavic languages and literature educator*
Well, Irwin *language educator*
Wessels, Bruce W. *materials scientist, educator*
Whitaker, Charles F. *journalism educator*
White, Sylvia Frances *gerontology home care nurse, consultant*
White, Willmon Lee *magazine editor*
†Wilhelm, Frank Leo *publisher, writer*
Williams-Monegain, Louise Joel *retired science educator, ethnographer*
Wills, Garry *journalist, educator*
Wright, Donald Eugene *retired librarian*
Wright, John *classics educator*
Wu, Tai Te *biological sciences and engineering educator*
Xia, Zhihong *mathematics educator*
Yoder, Frederick Floyd *fraternity executive*
Yoder, John Clifford *producer, consultant*
Zarefsky, David Harris *academic administrator, communication studies educator*
Zelinsky, Daniel *mathematics educator*
Ziomek, Jonathan S. *journalist, educator*
Zolomij, Robert William *landscape architect, consultant*

Evanton
Olkowski, June *women's collegiate basketball coach*

Evergreen Park
†Daw, Maureen Bridgette *special education educator, administrator*
Zumerchik, John *urologist*

Fairfield
Arakkal, Antony Lona *engineering executive, researcher*
Smith, Terry G. *insurance sales professional*

Fairview Heights
Grace, (Walter) Charles *prosecutor*
Harrison, Moses W., II *state supreme court justice*

Flat Rock
Marx, Michael William *English educator*

Flossmoor
Ferreira, Daniel Alves *secondary education Spanish language educator*
Gevers, Marcia Bonita *lawyer, lecturer, mediator, consultant*
Lis, Edward Francis *pediatrician, consultant*
Pierce, Shelby Crawford *management and oil industry consultant*
Schillings, Denny Lynn *history educator*

Forest Park
Hatch, Edward William (Ted Hatch) *health care executive*
Orland, Frank J. *oral microbiologist, educator*

Forsyth
Dreyer, Alec Gilbert *independent power producer*

Fox Lake
Vida, Diane *high school administrator*

Fox River Grove
Abboud, Alfred Robert *banker, consultant, investor*
Kenzle, Linda Fry *writer, artist*

Frankfort
Hattendorf, Diane Lynn *principal*
Huff, John David *church administrator*

Franklin Park
Blanchard, Eric Alan *lawyer*
Currie, Leah Rae *special education educator*
Dean, Howard M., Jr. *food company executive*
Simpson, Michael *metals service center executive*
†Watson, Robert Edward *librarian, information specialist*

Freeport
Pascoe, E(dward) Rudy *insurance sales executive*
Phillips, Spencer Kleckner *retired surgeon*
Weaver, Michael Glenn *pharmacist*

Galena
Alexander, Barbara Leah Shapiro *clinical social worker*
Burkhart, John Ernest *minister, religion educator*
Crandall, John Lynn *insurance consultant, retired insurance company executive*
Hermann, Paul David *retired association executive*

Galesburg
†Bailey, Stephen *history educator*
Conway, Lowava Denise *data processing administrator*
Hane, Mikiso *history educator*
Haywood, Bruce *retired college president*
Kowalski, Richard Sheldon *hospital administrator*
Litvin, Martin Jay *author, lecturer*
McCrery, David Neil, III *lawyer*
Sandborg, Shirlee J. *health science facility professional*
Sunderland, Jacklyn Giles *former alumni affairs director*

Galva
†Heck, Melody Ann *library director*

Gardner
Coulter, Julienne Ellen *secondary education educator, consultant*

Gays
Finley, Gary Roger *financial company executive*

Geneseo
Allen, Leonard Brown *retired tax manager*
Brown, Mabel Welton *lawyer*

Geneva
Barney, Charles Richard *transportation company executive*
Goulet, Charles Ryan *retired insurance company executive*
Irwin, John Thomas *retired counselor*
Kallstrom, Charles Clark *dentist*
Lazzara, Dennis Joseph *orthodontist*
Mishina, Mizuho *artist*
Pershing, Robert George *telecommunications company executive*
Weigand, Jan Christine *elementary education educator, computer specialist*
Young, Jack Allison *financial executive*

Genoa
Brown, Katherine Jane *editor, retired, chamber of commerce executive*
Cromley, Jon Lowell *lawyer*
Naden, Vernon Dewitt *manufacturing executive*

Gibson City
Welch, Melanie Gay *administrative assistant*

Gillespie
†Alepra, Sherry Jo *elementary school educator*

Gilman
Ireland, Herbert Orin *engineering educator*

Glen Ellyn
Agruss, Neil Stuart *cardiologist*
Baloun, John Charles *wholesale grocery company executive, retired*
Barrett, Carolyn Hernly *paralegal*
Carson, Andrew Doyle *research psychologist*
Cvengros, Joseph Michael *manufacturing company executive*
Dieter, Raymond Andrew, Jr. *physician, surgeon*
Drafke, Michael Walter *business educator, consultant*
Frateschi, Lawrence Jan *economist, statistician, educator*
Georgalas, Robert Nicholas *English language educator*
Grundy, Roy Rawsthorne *marketing educator*
Hudson, Dennis Lee *lawyer, retired government official, arbitrator, educator*
Jens, Elizabeth Lee Shafer (Mrs. Arthur M. Jens, Jr.) *civic worker*
Kirkpatrick, Clayton *former newspaper executive*
Lischer, Ludwig Frederick *retired consultant, former utility company executive*
Logan, Henry Vincent *transportation executive*
Mooring, F. Paul *physics editor*
Murphy, Jerome Eugene *communications consultant*
†Nilsson, Ronald Allan *academic administrator*
Parkhurst, Edwin Wallace, Jr. *healthcare management consultant*
Patten, Ronald James *retired university dean*
†Rusnack, William *petroleum company executive*
Taylor, Robert Rowe *communications executive, consultant*
Ulrich, Werner *patent lawyer*

Glencoe
Baer, Joseph Winslow *retired lawyer, mediator, arbitrator*
†Blonsky, Eugene Richard *neurologist*
Cole, Kathleen Ann *advertising agency executive, retired social worker*
Glink, Ilyce Renée *writer, publishing executive*
Grossweiner, Leonard Irwin *physicist, educator*
Hickey, John Thomas *retired electronics company executive*
Joseph, Donald Louis *management consultant*
Milloy, Frank Joseph, Jr. *surgeon*
Morris, Robert Barrett *city manager*
Morrissey, Terri Jo *artist*
Nebenzahl, Kenneth *rare book and map dealer, author*
Niefeld, Jaye Sutter *advertising executive*
Silver, Ralph David *financial consultant and arbitrator*
Webb, James Okrum, Jr. *insurance company executive*

Glendale Heights
Pimental, Patricia Ann *neuropsychologist, consulting company executive, author*
Silver, Marc Laurence *marketing and advertising executive*
Spearing, Karen Marie *physical education educator, coach*

Glenview
Berkman, Michael G. *lawyer, chemical consultant*
Biedron, Theodore John *newspaper advertising executive*
Bradtke, Philip Joseph *architect*
Braun, Eunice Hockspeier *author, religious order executive, lecturer*
Corley, Jenny Lynd Wertheim *elementary education educator*
Coulson, Elizabeth Anne *physical therapy educator, state representative*
Faig, Kenneth Walter *actuary, publisher*
Farrell, W. James *manufacturing company executive*
Feldman, Burton Gordon *printing company executive*
Franklin, Lynne *business communications consultant, writer*
Gillis, Marvin Bob *investor, consultant*
Goldmann, Morton Aaron *cardiologist*
Hutter, Gary Michael *environmental engineer*
Kinigakis, Panagiotis *research scientist, engineer, author*
Levin, Donald Robert *business and finance executive, motion picture producer, professional sports team owner*
Livingston, Richard Alan *retired secondary education educator*
Logani, Kulbhushan Lal *civil and structural engineer*
Mabley, Jack *newspaper columnist, communications consultant*
Mack, Stephen W. *financial planner*
Marmet, Gottlieb John *lawyer*
Mukoyama, James Hidefumi, Jr. *securities executive*
†Nelson, Paul Alfred *philosopher, editor*
Nichols, John Doane *diversified manufacturing corporation executive*
Panarese, William C. *civil engineer*
Parker, James John *engineering and marketing manager*
Ptak, Frank S. *manufacturing executive*
Rorig, Kurt Joachim *chemist, research director*
Russell, Henry George *structural engineer*
Schulman, Alan Michael *small business owner*
Smith, Harold B. *manufacturing executive*
Taylor, D(arl) Coder *architect, engineer*
Traudt, Mary B. *elementary education educator*
Van Zelst, Theodore William *civil engineer, natural resource exploration company executive*
Winett, Samuel Joseph *manufacturing company executive*
Witting, Christian James, Jr. (Chris Witting) *broadcast executive*

Glenwood
Christopher, Claude *minister*

Godfrey
Ford, Terry Lynn *fire department executive*
King, Ordie Herbert, Jr. *oral pathologist*
McDaniels, John Louis *retired mathematics educator*
Miller, Donald Edward *banking executive*
†Woods, Karen Dies *educator*

Golf
Fellingham, Warren Luther, Jr. *retired banker*

Grand Chain
†Ulrich, Eugene J. *music educator, composer*

Grand Ridge
Goodchild, Rosina Ann *community health nurse*

Granite City
Eftimoff, Anita Kendall *educational consultant*
Humphrey, Owen Everett *retired education administrator*
Raczkiewicz, Paul Edward *hospital administrator*

Grayslake
Johnson, Margaret H *welding company executive*
Nicholas, Willadene Louise *artist*
Schmoll, George Frederick, III *research engineer*
Taylor, Sharen Rae (McCall) *special education educator*
†Thomas, Roberta M. *librarian*

Greenville
Flowers, Creole Duane *publishing executive*
Junod, Daniel August *podiatrist*

Griggsville
†Dunham, Charlotte Ann *English language educator*

Gurnee
Murgatroyd, Eric Neal *data processing executive*
Sommerlad, Robert Edward *environmental research engineer*
Southern, Robert Allen *lawyer*
†Theard, Clausel *language educator*
Theis, Peter Frank *engineering executive, inventor*
Weber, James Stuart *management educator*

Hampshire
Hirn, Doris Dreyer *health service administrator*

Hanover
Bleveans, John *lawyer*

Hanover Park
Michel, Lynn Francine *critical care nurse*
Schoeld, Constance Jerrine *financial planner*
Winterstein, James Fredrick *academic administrator*

Harrisburg
Endsley, Jane Ruth *nursing educator*
Rushing, Philip Dale *retired social worker*

Harvel
Zimmerman, Donald Dean *farmer, farm manager*

Harvey
Dunn, Eraina Burke *non-profit organization administrator, city official*
Heilicser, Bernard Jay *emergency physician*
Liem, Khian Kioe *medical entomologist*
†Saldana, John Wesley, Jr. *songwriter, publisher*

Havana
Holmes, Lois Rehder *composer, piano and voice educator*
Sinnock, Elizabeth Anne *bank officer*

Hazel Crest
Chapman, Delores *elementary education educator*
Potts, Clifford Albert *retired educator, church musician*

Hennepin
Bumgarner, James McNabb *judge*

Herrin
Tibrewala, Sushil *physician*

Highland
Franklin, Patricia Lynn *special education educator*

Highland Park
Bakalar, John Stephen *printing and publishing company executive*
Bluefarb, Samuel Mitchell *physician*
Burman, Diane Berger *organization development consultant*
Dubin, Arthur Detmers *architect*
Gordon, Paul *metallurgical educator*
Greenblatt, Miriam *author, editor, educator*
Harris, Thomas L. *public relations executive*
Herbert, Edward Franklin *public relations executive*
Hoffman, Sharon Lynn *adult education educator*
Johnson, Curtis Lee *publisher, editor, writer*
Karol, Nathaniel H. *lawyer, consultant*
Liebow, Phoebe Augusta Recht *nursing educator, school nurse*
Mehta, Zarin *music festival administrator*
Nathan, Robert Burton *life insurance agent*
Pattis, S. William *publisher*
Ruder, David Sturtevant *lawyer, educator, government official*

Rudo, Milton *retired manufacturing company executive, consultant*
Rutenberg-Rosenberg, Sharon Leslie *retired journalist*
Saltzberg, Eugene Ernest *physician, educator*
Scheuzger, Thomas Peter *audio engineer*
Slavick, Ann Lillian *art educator, arts*
Smith, Malcolm Norman *manufacturing company executive*
Uhlmann, Frederick Godfrey *commodity and securities broker*
Zywicki, Cindy Mary *nurse*

Highwood
Brown, Lawrence Haas *banker*

Hillsboro
Herrmann, Jane Marie *physical therapist*
McCafferty, Marlyn Jeanette *elementary education educator*
Mulch, Robert F., Jr. *physician*

Hillside
†Payton, Roger *logistics company executive*

Hines
Best, William Robert *physician, educator, university official*
Folk, Frank Anton *surgeon, educator*
Hagarty, Eileen Mary *pulmonary clinical nurse specialist*
Wetherald, Dawn Margaret *surgical nurse*
Zvetina, James Raymond *pulmonary physician*

Hinsdale
Akins, Marilyn Parker *interior designer*
Anderson, Harry Frederick, Jr. *architect*
Beatty, Robert Alfred (R. Alfred) *surgeon*
Bloom, Stephen Joel *distribution company executive*
Brandt, John Ashworth *fuel company executive*
Burrows, Donald Albert *college dean, artist, painter,*
Butler, Margaret Kampschaefer *retired computer scientist*
Carlini, James *management consultant*
Cohen, Burton David *franchising executive, lawyer*
Copley, Stephen Michael *materials science and technology engineer, consultant*
Dederick, Robert Gogan *economist*
Denton, Ray Douglas *insurance company executive*
Dussman, Judith Ann *publishing executive*
Finley, Robert Coe, III *interventional cardiologist, consultant, educator*
Gallagher, John Pirie *retired corporation executive*
Kaminsky, Manfred Stephan *physicist*
Kazan, Robert Peter *neurosurgeon*
Kinney, Kenneth Parrish *retired banker*
Lavine, Lorette Pauline *nursing educator, maternal/women's health nurse*
Lebedow, Aaron Louis *consulting company executive*
Lowenstine, Maurice Richard, Jr. *retired steel executive*
Nibeck, Susan Nelson *real estate sales agent*
Paloyan, Edward *physician, educator, researcher*
Pawley, Ray Lynn *zoological park and environmental consultant*
†Smith, Jared Russell William *research executive*
Stastny, John Anton *real estate executive*
Taylor, T(homas) Roger *educational consultant, educator*
Unikel, Eva Taylor *interior designer*
Whitney, William Elliot, Jr. *advertising agency executive*
Zaccone, Suzanne Maria *sales executive*

Hoffman Estates
Dennis, Steven P. *retail executive*
Fitzpatrick, Ellen *economist, consultant*
†Geller, Bruce *music publisher, composer*
Martinez, Arthur C. *retail company executive*
Nicholas, Arthur Soterios *manufacturing company executive*
Pagonis, William Gus *retired army general*
Ramunno, Thomas Paul *financial consultant*
Roach, William Russell *training and education executive*
Schulz, Michael John *fire and explosion analyst, consultant*
Weston, Roger Lance *banker*

Homer
Gilhaus, Barbara Jean *secondary education home economics educator*

Homewood
Bultema, Janice Kay *healthcare executive*
Dietch, Henry Xerxes *judge*
†Heron, Frances Dunlap *author, educator*
Lyttle, Christopher Sherman *medical sociologist*
MacMaster, Daniel Miller *retired museum official*
Parker, Eugene Newman *retired physicist, educator*
Pedersen, Walter *minister*
Reed, Michael A. *agricultural products supplier*

Hopedale
Birky, John Edward *banker, consultant, financial advisor*

Hoyleton
Schnake, Betty Berniece *nursing educator, retired*

Hudson
Mills, Frederick VanFleet *art educator, watercolorist*
Mills, Lois Jean *company executive, former legislative aide, former education educator*

Huntley
Plunkett, Melba Kathleen *manufacturing company executive*
Van Horn, John Henry *secondary school educator*

Ina
Weston, Kevin David *adult education educator*

Indianhead Park
Frisque, Alvin Joseph *retired chemical company executive*
Johnson, (Mary) Anita *physician, medical service administrator*
Lundin, Shirley Matcouff *early childhood and adult educator, consultant*
†Strojny, Ronald P. *lawyer*

Ingleside
Krentz, Eugene Leo *university president, educator, minister*

Inverness
Hetzel, William Gelal *executive search consultant*
Victor, Michael Gary *lawyer, physician*

Itasca
Boler, John *manufacturing executive*
Carter, Eleanor Elizabeth *business manager*
Ellis, Harold Donald *auto repair company executive*
Garratt, Reginald George *electronics executive*

Jacksonville
Findley, Paul *former congressman, author, educator*
Hansmeier, Barbara Jo *elementary education educator*
Johns, Beverley Anne Holden *special education administrator*
Kirchhoff, Michael Kent *economic development executive*
Loughary, Thomas Michael *dentist*
Marshall, James Paul *mathematics educator*
Moe-Fishback, Barbara Ann *counseling administrator*
Pfau, Richard Anthony *college president*
Scott, Fred Dacon *surgeon*
†Ware, Jon Dean *retail executive*
Welch, Rhea Jo *special education educator*
Woodworth, Harold G. *minister*

Jerseyville
Graham, Lester Lynn *radio journalist*

Joliet
Bartow, Barbara Jené *university program administrator*
Bartz, William Walter *musician*
Boyer, Andrew Ben *lawyer*
Caamano, Kathleen Ann Folz *gifted education professional*
Chalmers, Diana Jean *office administrator*
Chamberlain, Jeffrey Scott *history educator*
Cochran, Mary Ann *nurse educator*
Colonna, William Mark *accountant*
Copeland, Charlene Carole *lawyer*
Ellebracht, Harold Mark *marine engineer*
Holmgren, Myron Roger *social sciences educator*
Holzrichter, Fred William *foundation executive*
†Imesch, Joseph Leopold *bishop*
Johnston, James Robert *library director*
Kaffer, Roger Louis *bishop*
Layman, Dale Pierre *medical educator, author, researcher*
Lenard, George Dean *lawyer*
†Lewis, Gregory Austin *urologist*
O'Connell, James Joseph *port official*
Ring, Alvin Manuel *pathologist, educator*
Russow, Cheryl Ann *nurse*
Scott, Linda Ann *assistant principal, elementary education educator*
Starner, Barbara Kazmark *marketing, advertising and export sales executive*
†Wilson, Reed J. *legislative staff member*

Kampsville
Sutton, Cynthia Ann *executive director museum*

Kankakee
Bowling, John C. *academic administrator*
Call, Cary C. *transportation specialist*
Dalton, Ronnie Thomas *theology educator*
Dodson, Carl Edward *nuclear engineer, real estate agent, executive, minister, assistant superintendent*
Elliott, Kathy Bradshaw *judge*
Gurney, Pamela Kay *social services official*
Kanouse, Donald Lee *wastewater treatment executive*
Schroeder, David Harold *healthcare facility executive*
Wasser, Larry Paul *hematologist, oncologist*
Wintrode, Kelly Rose *elementary education educator*

Kenilworth
Bowen, Gilbert Willard *minister*
Clary, Rosalie Brandon Stanton *timber farm executive, civic worker*
Cook, Stanton R. *media company executive*
Corrigan, John Edward, Jr. *banker, lawyer*
Dixon, Carl Franklin *lawyer*
Edson, Wayne E. *retired dentist, consultant*
Guelich, Robert Vernon *retired management consultant*
McKittrick, William Wood *lawyer*
Weiner, Joel David *retired consumer packaged goods products executive*

Kildeer
Harrod, Scott *consulting manufacturing executive*

La Grange
Hubert, Jean-Luc *chemicals executive*
Jaffe-Notier, Peter Andrew *secondary education educator*
Kerr, Alexander Duncan, Jr. *lawyer*
Mehlenbacher, Dohn Harlow *civil engineer*
Mermigas, Diane Cynthia Stefanos *business journalist*
Mikolyzk, Thomas Andrew *librarian*
Morelli, Anthony Frank *pediatric dentist*
†Moskal, Stephen L., Jr. *librarian*

La Grange Park
Brown, Helen Sauer *fund raising executive*
Calhamer, Allan Brian *retired postal worker*
Carroll, Thomas John *retired advertising executive*

Lafox
Seils, William George *lawyer*

Lake Bluff
Anderson, Roger E. *bank executive*
Borling, John Lorin *military officer*
Burns, Kenneth Jones, Jr. *lawyer, consultant*
Fortuna, William Frank *architectural engineer, architect*
Marino, William Francis *telecommunications industry executive, consultant*
Preschlack, John Edward *management consultant*
Schreiber, George Richard *association executive, writer*
Sweetser, Marie-Odile Gauny *retired foreign language educator*

Van Clay, Mark *schools superintendant*

Lake Forest
Adelman, Pamela Bernice Kozoll *education educator*
Barnes, Sandra Henley *publishing company executive*
Beitler, Stephen Seth *private equity and venture capital executive*
Bell, Charles Eugene, Jr. *industrial engineer*
Bernthal, Harold George *healthcare company executive*
Bransfield, Joan *principal*
Brown, Cameron *insurance company consultant*
Brown, Sharon Gail *company executive, consultant*
Burnham, Duane Lee *retired pharmaceutical company executive*
Carter, Donald Patton *advertising executive*
Chieger, Kathryn Jean *recreation company executive*
Covington, George Morse *lawyer*
Crowley, Anna Avra *secondary education educator, historian*
Davidson, Richard Alan *data communications company executive*
Deters, James Raymond *retired manufacturing and services company executive*
Dur, Philip Alphonse *automotive executive, retired naval officer*
Eckert, Ralph John *insurance company executive*
Emerson, William Harry *lawyer, retired, oil company executive*
Fetridge, Bonnie-Jean Clark (Mrs. William Harrison Fetridge) *civic volunteer*
Frederick, Virginia Fiester *state legislator*
Fromm, Henry Gordon *retired manufacturing and marketing executive*
Hamilton, Peter Bannerman *business executive, lawyer*
Hammar, Lester Everett *health care manufacturing company executive*
Holzman, Esther Rose *perfume company executive*
Hotchkiss, Eugene, III *retired academic administrator*
Hough, Richard T. *chemical company executive*
Jaeger, Jeff Todd *professional football player*
Jones, Gordon Kempton *dentist*
Jones, Philip Newton *physician, medical educator*
Kenly, Granger Farwell *marketing consultant, college official*
Kenzenkovic, Kevin G. *management consultant*
Keyser, Richard Lee *distribution company executive*
Kozitka, Richard Eugene *retired consumer products company executive*
Lambert, John Boyd *chemical engineer, consultant*
Larsen, Peter N. *leisure products manufacturing executive*
Larson, Peter N. *company executive*
Levy, Nelson Louis *physician, scientist, corporate executive*
McCaskey, Edward W. *professional football team executive*
McCaskey, Michael B. *professional football team executive*
McClellan, Mart Gaynor *orthodontist*
Miller, Arthur Hawks, Jr. *librarian, consultant*
Mitchell, Richard Charles *human resources executive*
Mohr, Roger John *advertising agency executive*
Moylan, Stephen Craig *architect*
O'Mara, Thomas Patrick *manufacturing company executive*
Palmer, Ann Therese Darin *lawyer*
Pawl, Ronald Phillip *neurosurgery educator*
Peterson, Donald Matthew *insurance company executive*
Price, John Edward *religion educator*
Rand, Kathy Sue *public relations executive*
Raudabaugh, Joseph Luther *management consultant*
Reichert, Jack Frank *manufacturing company executive*
Reichert, Norman Vernon *financial services consultant*
Ross, Robert Evan *bank executive*
Salter, Edwin Carroll *retired physician*
Schulze, Franz, Jr. *art critic, educator*
Sikorovsky, Eugene Frank *retired lawyer*
Smith, Sidney Talbert *biomedical engineer*
Swanton, Virginia Lee *author, publisher, bookseller*
Taylor, Barbara Ann Olin *educational consultant*
Tyler, W(illiam) Ed *printing company executive*
Weston, Arthur Walter *chemist, scientific and business executive*
Wilbur, Richard Sloan *physician, executive*
†Yanella, Donald *educator*
†Zamer, William E. *biologist, educator*

Lake Villa
Anderson, Milton Andrew *chemical executive*
Sikora, Evelyn Marie *psychiatric and substance abuse nurse*

Lake Zurich
Dixon, John Fulton *village manager*
Krolopp, Rudolph William *retired industrial designer, consultant*
Schmitz, Shirley Gertrude *marketing and sales executive*
Schultz, Carl Herbert *real estate management and development company executive*
Teeters, Joseph Lee *mathematician, consultant*

Lansing
Ansary, Hassan Jaber *transportation executive*
Guzak, Debra Ann *special education educator*
Hill, Philip *retired lawyer*
Kaplan, Huette Myra *business educator, training consultant*
Olson, Jaynie L. *secondary school counselor*
Stuart, Robert *container manufacturing executive*

Lemont
Chen, Shoei-Sheng *mechanical engineer*
Dillon, Phillip Michael *construction company executive*
Galati, Michael Bernard *lay church worker*
Williams, Jack Marvin *research chemist*

Lewistown
Shank, Glenna Kaye *medical/surgical nurse, educator*

Libertyville
Baske, C. Alan *manufacturing company executive*
Beeler, Thomas Joseph *lawyer, general management consultant*
Bell, Robert Matthew *pharmaceutical company consultant*
†Belluomini, Ronald Joseph *secondary education educator, poet*

Bermingham, John Scott *associate dean*
Burrows, Brian William *research and development manufacturing executive*
Conklin, Mara Loraine *public relations executive*
Feit, Michael *controller*
Harding, James Warren *finance company executive*
Hattis, Albert Daniel *business executive, retired educator, journalist*
Kremkau, Paul *principal*
Munson, Norma Frances *biologist, ecologist, nutritionist, educator*
O'Leary, Timothy Francis *real estate developer*
Rallo, Douglas *lawyer*
Rancourt, John Herbert *pharmaceutical company executive*
Ranney, George Alfred *lawyer, former steel company executive*
Rucker, Dennis Morton Arthur *telecommunications executive*
True, Raymond Stephen *writer, editor, analyst, consultant*

Lincoln
Wilson, Robert Allen *religion educator*

Lincolnshire
Bayly, George V. *manufacturing executive*
Caballero, Mario Gustavo *investment company executive, gaming executive*
Dobrin, Sheldon L. *architect*
Galatz, Henry Francis *lawyer*
Giza, David Alan *lawyer*
Goldin, Sol *marketing consultant*
Hebda, Lawrence John *data processing executive, consultant*
Hughes, William Franklin, Jr. *ophthalmologist, emeritus educator*
Kramer, Alexander Gottlieb *financial director*
Martin, John Driscoll *school administrator*
Mathieson, Michael Raymond *controller*
Pappano, Robert Daniel *financial company executive*
Schauble, John Eugene *physical education educator*
†Sheble, Ronald Walter *financial manager*
Simes, Stephen Mark *pharmaceutical products executive*
Stern, Gerald Joseph *advertising executive*

Lincolnwood
Donovan, John Vincent *consulting company executive*
Grant, Paul Bernard *industrial relations educator, arbitrator*
Greenblatt, Deana Charlene *elementary education educator*
Krejcsi, Cynthia Ann *textbook editor*
†Lewis, Harriet Gerber *plumbing fixtures manufacturing company executive*
Pattis, Mark R. *publishing company executive*

Lindenhurst
Rose, William *retired business executive*

Lisle
Birck, Michael John *manufacturing company executive, electrical engineer*
Bradna, Joanne Justice *manufacturer's representative*
Fortier, Mardelle LaDonna *English educator*
Kirshbaum, Jon Alan *information systems consultant, retired educational administrator*
Koford, Stuart Keith *electronics executive*
Krehbiel, Frederick August, II *electronics company executive*
Kubo, Gary Michael *advertising executive*
Long, Charles Franklin *corporate communications executive*
McCaul, Joseph Patrick *chemical engineer*
Mehaffey, Scott Alan *landscape architect*
Myers, Daniel N. *lawyer, association executive*
Reum, W. Robert *manufacturing executive*
Sandrok, Richard William *lawyer*
Simpson, Jayne Lou *academic administrator*
Smith, Sydney David *data processing executive*
Staab, Thomas Eugene *chemist*
Tyson, Kirk W. M. *management consultant*
Vora, Manu Kishandas *chemical engineer, quality consultant*
Ware, George Henry *botanist*

Litchfield
Best, Karen Magdalene *legal secretary*
Deaton, Beverly Jean *nursing administrator, educator*
Talley, Hayward Leroy *communications executive*

Lockport
Bhatti, Neeloo *environmental scientist*
McIntyre, John Andrew *environmental and economic planner, geography educator*

Lombard
Ahlstrom, Ronald Gustin *artist*
Beideman, Ronald Paul *chiropractic physician, college dean*
Burdett, James Richard *golf products innovator*
Chopores, John Leslie *software specialist, educator*
Cihak, Erwin Frank *retired securities trader, real estate developer*
Goodman, Elliott I(rvin) *lawyer*
Holgers-Awana, Rita Marie *electrodiagnosis specialist*
Hudson, Samuel Campbell, Jr. *art educator, artist, sculptor*
Kasprow, Barbara Anne *biomedical scientist, writer*
Miczuga, Mark Norbert *metal products executive*
O'Shea, Patrick Joseph *lawyer, electrical engineer*
Sheehan, Dennis William, Sr. *lawyer, business executive*
Swanson, Bernet Steven *consulting engineer, former educator*
Velardo, Joseph Thomas *molecular biology and endocrinology educator*
Willis, Douglas Alan *lawyer*
Yeager, Phillip Charles *transportation company executive*

Long Grove
Ausman, Robert K. *surgeon, research executive*
Beach, Robert Mark *biologist*
Connor, James Richard *foundation administrator*
Conway, John K. *lawyer*
Dajani, Esam Zapher *pharmacologist*
Freeland, Marcia Stephan *nursing educator*
Liuzzi, Robert C. *chemical company executive*
Obert, Paul Richard *lawyer, manufacturing company executive*

Van Der Bosch, Susan Hartnett *real estate broker*

Louisville
Edwards, Ian Keith *retired obstetrician, gynecologist*

Macomb
†Adams, John Quincy *educator, consultant*
Anderson, Richard Vernon *ecology educator, researcher*
Bauerly, Ronald John *marketing educator*
†Colvin, Daniel L. *English educator*
Dexter, Donald Harvey *surgeon*
Goehner, Donna Marie *retired university dean*
Hallwas, John Edward *English language educator*
Hayes, Paul Robert *special education educator*
Hogan, Kenneth James *lawyer*
Hopper, Stephen Rodger *hospital administrator*
†Kyllonen Rose, Julie Frances *college program administrator*
Maguire, Dave *real estate owner, manager*
McLean, Deckle *journalism educator*
North, Teresa Lynn *agricultural educator*
Rao, Vaman *economics educator*
Walzer, Norman Charles *economics educator*
Witthuhn, Burton Orrin *university official*

Madison
Pope, Sarah Ann *elementary education educator*

Mahomet
Bosworth, Douglas LeRoy *international company executive, educator*
Kennedy, Cheryl Lynn *museum director*

Manteno
Balgeman, Richard Vernon *radiology administrator, alcoholism counselor*

Mapleton
†Dailey, Alice Beatrice *postmaster*
Hayes, Debra Troxell *family nurse practitioner*
Wendelin, Barbara Lynn *elementary school educator*

Marengo
Franks, Herbert Hoover *lawyer*

Marion
Crane, Hugh Wingate *railroad executive*
Howell, Catherine Jeanine *retired secondary education educator*
†Munas, Fil A. *psychiatric physician*
Powless, Kenneth Barnett *lawyer*
Wilkins, Sondra Ann *mental health nurse, educator*

Markham
Peacock, Marilyn Claire *primary education educator*

Marseilles
Van Horn, John Kenneth *health physicist, consultant*

Marshall
Cork, Donald Burl *electrical engineer*
Mitchell, George Trice *physician*

Maryville
Stark, Patricia Ann *psychologist, educator*

Mason City
Breedlove, Jimmie Dale, Jr. *elementary education educator*

Matteson
Goyak, Elizabeth Fairbairn *retired public relations executive*
Keenan, Robert Arthur *financial executive*
Pedziwater, Kaye Lynn *elementary education educator*

Mattoon
†Bays, Mona Rae *librarian*
Horsley, Jack Everett *lawyer, author*
†Keown, Michele L. *computer training specialist, business educator*
Maris, Charles Robert *surgeon, otolaryngologist*
Phipps, John Randolph *retired army officer*

Maywood
†Anderson, Douglas E. *neurosurgeon*
Baldwin, Allan Oliver *information scientist, higher education executive*
Bilek, Arthur John *criminologist*
Blumenthal, Harold Jay *microbiologist, educator*
Canning, John Rafton *urologist*
Celesia, Gastone Guglielmo *neurologist, neurophysiologist, researcher*
Cera, Lee Marie *veterinarian*
Ellington, Mildred L. *librarian*
Farley, Robert Hugh *police detective, child abuse consultant*
Freeark, Robert James *surgeon, educator*
Hanin, Israel *pharmacologist, educator*
Hart, Cecil William Joseph *otolaryngologist, head and neck surgeon*
Hindle, Paula Alice *nursing administrator*
Light, Terry Richard *orthopedic hand surgeon*
Newman, Barry Marc *pediatric surgeon*
Pickleman, Jack R. *surgeon*
Slogoff, Stephen *anesthesiologist, educator*
Tobin, Martin John *pulmonary and critical care physician*
†Woody, Lisa Ellen *occuational medicine physician*

Mc Gaw Park
†Feather, William L. *corporate lawyer*
Knight, Lester B. *healthcare company executive*
Wolfson, Marsha *internist, nephrologist*

Mc Leansboro
Brinkley, William John *secondary education educator*

Mchenry
Dodds, David William *superintendent*
Kenyon, Patricia Mae *poet*
Koehl, Camille Joan *accountant*
McKinley, James Frank, Jr. *manufacturing executive*
Sheft, Mark David *market analyst, consultant, product manager*
†Shelton, Kevin Patrick *secondary education educator*

Melrose Park
†Bernick, Carol Lavin *corporate executive*
Bernick, Howard Barry *manufacturing company executive*
Cernugel, William John *consumer products and special retail executive*
Douglas, Kenneth Jay *food products executive*
†Hillert, Richard Walter *composer, educator, author*
†Lavin, Bernice E. *cosmetics executive*
Quirk, Donna Hawkins *financial analyst*
Shturmakov, Alexander Joseph *automotive industry executive*
Umans, Alvin Robert *manufacturing company executive*
White, Linda Sue *cardiology technician*

Mendota
Stamberger, Edwin Henry *farmer, civic leader*

Millstadt
Fowler-Dixon, Deborah Lea *family physician*

Minooka
Nellett, Gaile H. *university level educator*

Mokena
Maiotti, Dennis Paul *manufacturing company executive*
Sangmeister, George Edward *lawyer, consultant, former congressman*

Moline
Arnell, Richard Anthony *radiologist*
Badur, Diana Isabel *English language educator*
Becherer, Hans Walter *agricultural equipment manufacturing executive*
Carls, Judith Marie *physical education educator, golf coach*
Cleaver, William Lehn *lawyer*
Cottrell, Frank Stewart *lawyer, manufacturing executive*
Harrington, Roy Edwards *agricultural engineer, author*
†Healy, Donald Eugene, Jr. *special education educator, consultant*
Johnson, Mary Lou *lay worker*
Larson, Richard James *computer network systems executive*
Luebbers, Rita Mary *religious education director*
Malicki, Gregg Hillard *agricultural equipment manufacturing executive*
Middleton, Marc Stephen *corporate insurance risk manager*
Morrison, Deborah Jean *lawyer*
Parise, Marc Robert *banker*
†Schwiebert, Deborah Johnson *marketing executive*
Skromme, Arnold Burton *educational writer, engineering consultant*
Smith, David William
†Washington, Helene Maria *eduator*

Monmouth
Kirk, Sherwood *librarian*

Mooseheart
Ross, Donald Hugh *fraternal organization executive*

Morrison
Gallagher, John Robert, Jr. *county official*

Morton
Corey, Judith Ann *educator*
Grisham, George Robert *mathematics educator*

Morton Grove
Blanchard, James Arthur *engineer, computer systems specialist, financial planner*
Farber, Isadore E. *psychologist, educator*
McKenna, Andrew James *paper distribution and printing company executive, baseball club executive*

Mount Carmel
Fornoff, Frank J(unior) *retired chemistry educator, consultant*
Wheatley, Joan Mercedese *telemetry care nurse*

Mount Carroll
Leemon, John Allen *lawyer*

Mount Olive
Rogers, Ke'an Seth *elementary school educator*

Mount Prospect
Avila, Arthur Julian *metallurgical engineer*
Cohn, Bradley M. *lawyer*
Garvin, Paul Joseph, Jr. *toxicologist*
Gerlitz, Curtis Neal *business executive*
O'Connor, Nan G. *social worker*
Pulsifer, Edgar Darling *leasing service and sales executive*
Rogers, Richard F. *construction company executive, architect, engineer*
†Sayers, Gale *computer company executive, retired professional football player*
Scott, Norman Laurence *engineering consultant*
Thulin, Adelaide Ann *design company executive, interior designer*

Mount Vernon
Harvey, Morris Lane *lawyer*
Stephen, Richard Joseph *oral and maxillofacial surgeon*
Withers, W. Russell, Jr. *broadcast executive*
Wittmeyer, Richard Arthur *management consulting company executive*

Mount Zion
Burns, B. Thomas *broadcasting executive*

Mundelein
Ackley, Robert O. *lawyer*
Kincaid, Cynthia June *school psychologist*
Meehan, Jean Marie Ross *occupational health and safety management consultant*
Mills, James Stephen *medical supply company executive*
Smith McKee, Maureen Jacquelene *marketing professional*
Terris, William *publishing executive*

Murphysboro
Gersbacher, Eva Elizabeth *special education administrator*
Hall, James Robert *secondary education educator*
McCann, Maurice Joseph *lawyer*
Merz, Kathy Maureen *elementary education educator*
Millar, Barbara Lee *technical writer, school administrator*

Naperville
Arzoumanidis, Gregory G. *chemist*
Balasi, Mark Geoffrey *architect*
†Bremer, Michael Stewart *management consultant*
Burton, Kay Fox *retired secondary education educator, guidance counselor*
Coplien, James O. *engineering researcher*
Cowlishaw, Mary Lou *state legislator*
Craigo, Gordon Earl *quality systems consultant*
Crawford, Raymond Maxwell, Jr. *nuclear engineer*
Desch, Theodore Edward *retired health insurance company executive, lawyer*
Fawell, Harris W. *lawyer former congressman*
Florence, Ernest Estell, Jr. *special education educator*
†Fritz, Lee D. *software company executive*
Fritz, Roger Jay *management consultant*
Frizelis, Karen Lynn *adult nurse practitioner*
Fuhrer, Larry *management consultant, finance company executive*
Garg, Vijay Kumar *telecommunications engineer*
Grimley, Jeffrey Michael *dentist*
†Hellmuth, John S. *healthcare executive*
†Huffman, Louise Tolle *elementary education educator*
Katai, Andrew Andras *chemical company executive*
Kimmel, Frank Edward *engineer*
Koeppe, Eugene Charles, Jr. *electrical engineer*
Krishnamachari, Sadagopa Iyengar *mechanical engineer, consultant*
L'Allier, James Joseph *educational multimedia company executive, instructional designer*
Landwehr, Arthur John *minister*
Larson, Mark Edward, Jr. *lawyer, educator, financial advisor*
Martin, Joan Ellen *secondary education educator*
Modery, Richard Gillman *marketing and sales executive*
†Moore, Brian Michael *newspaper copy editor, journalist*
Penisten, Gary Dean *entrepreneur*
Perez-Reyes, Edward *molecular physiologist*
Peters, Boyd Leon *agricultural engineer*
PoPolizio, Vincent *retired secondary education educator*
Raccah, Dominique Marcelle *publisher*
Ramirez, Martin Ruben *architect, engineer, educator, cognitive scientist, consultant*
Rosenmann, Daniel *physicist, educator*
Rosenthal, Edward Leonard *secondary school educator*
Schaack, Philip Anthony *retired beverage company executive*
†Schaeffer, Joan L. *theater company executive*
Schanstra, Carla Ross *technical writer*
Sellers, Gregory Jude *physicist*
Sellers, Lucia Sunhee *marketing professional*
Shaw, Michael Allan *lawyer, mail order company executive*
Sherren, Anne Terry *chemistry educator*
Spiotta, Raymond Herman *editor*
Tan, Li-Su Lin *accountant, insurance executive, investment consultant*
Vanagas, Rimantas Andrius (Ray Vanagas) *entrepreneur*
Wake, Richard W. *food products executive*
Wake, Thomas G. *food products executive*
Wake, William S. *wholesale distribution executive*
Wilde, Harold Richard *college president*
Worden, William Patrick *deacon*

Niles
Fillicaro, Barbara Jean *business owner, consultant*
Gillet, Pamela Kipping *special education educator*
†Herb, Marvin J. *food products executive*
Obermann, George *engineering executive*

Normal
Ball, Linda Ann *secondary education educator*
Bender, Paul E. *title insurance executive*
†Brosnahan, Leger Nicholas *English educator*
Cooley, William Emory, Jr. *radiologist*
†Elledge, Jim *poet, literature educator*
Fry, Terry L. *English educator*
Gottschalk, Keith Edward *journalist*
Hesse, Douglas Dean *English educator*
Jones, Graham Alfred *mathematics educator*
Matsler, Franklin Giles *retired education educator*
Parry, Sally Ellen *academic administrator, english educator*
Parton, Thomas Albert *speech-language pathologist*
Pritner, Calvin Lee *actor, educator*
Skibo, James M. *anthropologist, educator*
Spears, Larry Jonell *lawyer*
†Stith, Rodney W. *mathematics educator*
†Strand, David Arthur *psychologist*
†Veney, Cassandra *political science educator*
†Vogt, W. Paul *dean*

North Chicago
Albach, Richard Allen *microbiology educator*
†Barsano, Charles P. *medical educator, dean*
Beer, Alan Earl *physician, medical educator*
Booden, Theodore *dean*
†de Lasa, José M. *lawyer*
Ehrenpreis, Seymour *pharmacology educator*
Freese, Uwe Ernest *physician, educator*
Gall, Eric Papineau *physician, educator*
Hawkins, Richard Albert *medical educator, administrator*
Kim, Yoon Berm *immunologist, educator*
Kovacek, Duane Michael *secondary school educator*
Kringel, John G. *health products company executive*
Kyncl, John Jaroslav *pharmacologist*
Loga, Sanda *physicist, educator*
Nair, Velayudhan *pharmacologist, medical educator*
Rogers, Eugene Jack *medical educator*
Rudy, David Robert *physician, educator*
Schneider, Arthur Sanford *physician, educator*
Sierles, Frederick Stephen *psychiatrist, educator*
Taylor, Michael Alan *psychiatrist*
Wiesner, Dallas Charles *immunologist, researcher*

North Riverside
Mockus, Joseph Frank *electrical engineer*
Sedlak, S(hirley) A(gnes) *freelance writer*

Northbrook
†Abbott, Boyce *temporary help company executive*
Adler, Robert *electronics engineer*
Afterman, Allan B. *accountant, educator, researcher, consultant*
Bueche, Wendell Francis *agricultural products company executive*
Clarey, John Robert *executive search consultant*
Colton, Frank Benjamin *retired chemist*
†D'Arcy, Thomas P. *real estate company executive*
Day, Emerson *physician*
Dilling, Kirkpatrick Wallwick *lawyer*
Elleman, Barbara *editor*
Feibel, Frederick Arthur *finanical consultant*
Fischer, Aaron Jack *accountant*
Fowler, Robert Edward, Jr. *agricultural products company executive*
†Fowler, Robert F., Jr. *chemicals executive*
Glabe, Elmer Frederick *food scientist*
Gratalo, John, Jr. *mortgage banker, business owner*
Green, David *manufacturing company executive*
Harris, Neison *manufacturing company executive*
Hecker, Lawrence Harris *industrial hygienist*
Hestad, Marsha Anne *educational administrator*
Hicks, Judith Eileen *nursing administrator*
Hill, Thomas Clarke, IX *accountant, systems specialist, entrepreneur*
Hirsch, Lawrence Leonard *physician, retired educator*
Huebner, Emily Ann *home healthcare administrator, consultant*
Kahn, Sandra S. *psychotherapist*
Keehn, Silas *retired bank executive*
Klemens, Thomas Lloyd *editor*
Lapin, Harvey I. *lawyer*
Lenon, Richard Allen *chemical corporation executive*
Lever, Alvin *health science association administrator*
Levy, Arnold S(tuart) *real estate company executive*
Lewis, Evelyn *management consultant*
Lezak, Jeffrey Mayer *mortgage broker*
Liddy, Edward M. *insurance company executive*
Magad, Samuel *orchestra concertmaster, conductor*
Mandel, Karyl Lynn *accountant*
McGinn, Mary Jovita *lawyer, insurance company executive*
Michna, Andrea Stephanie *real estate consultant and developer*
Milligan, Robert Lee, Jr. *computer company executive*
Newman, Lawrence William *financial executive*
Noeth, Carolyn Frances *speech and language pathologist*
Pesmen, Sandra (Mrs. Harold William Pesmen) *editor*
Pollak, Jay Mitchell *lawyer*
Polsky, Michael Peter *mechanical engineer*
†Rijos, John P. *hospitality company executive*
Roehl, Kathleen Ann *financial executive*
Ross, Debra Benita *jewelry designer, marketing executive*
Rotchford, Patricia Kathleen *lawyer*
Saunders, Kenneth D. *insurance company executive, consultant, arbitrator*
Sayatovic, Wayne Peter *manufacturing company executive*
Scanlon, Edward F. *surgeon, educator*
Schmidt, Arthur Irwin *steel fabricating company executive*
Sernett, Richard Patrick *lawyer*
Shape, Steven Michael *insurance executive, lawyer*
Singer, Norman Sol *food products executive, inventor*
Slattery, James Joseph (Joe Slattery) *actor*
Snader, Jack Ross *publishing company executive*
Stearns, Neele Edward, Jr. *diversified holding company executive*
Stewart, Charles Leslie *lawyer*
Sudbrink, Jane Marie *sales and marketing executive*
Turner, Lee *travel company executive*
Wajer, Ronald Edward *management consultant*
Wallace, Harry Leland *lawyer*
Weinstein, Ira Phillip *advertising executive*
Young, R. James *marketing executive*
Young, Susan Jean *music specialist*

Northfield
Bruns, Nicolaus, Jr. *retired agricultural chemicals company executive, lawyer*
Carlin, Donald Walter *retired food products executive, consultant*
Giffin, Mary Elizabeth *psychiatrist, educator*
Glass, Henry Peter *industrial designer, interior architect, educator*
Hadley, Stanton Thomas *international manufacturing and marketing company executive, lawyer*
Heise, Marilyn Beardsley *public relations company executive*
Kleinman, Burton Howard *real estate investor*
Larson, Donald Harold *information systems executive*
Porter, Helen Viney (Mrs. Lewis M. Porter, Jr.) *lawyer*
Pratt, Murray Lester *information systems specialist*
Schneider-Criezis, Susan Marie *architect*
Seaman, Jerome Francis *actuary*
Shabica, Charles Wright *geologist, earth science educator*
Smart, Jackson Wyman, Jr. *business executive*
Smeds, Edward William *retired food company executive*
Stein, Paula Jean Anne Barton *hotel real estate consultant*
Stepan, Frank Quinn *chemical company executive*
Wise, William Jerrard *lawyer*

Northlake
Haack, Richard Wilson *retired police officer*

O'Fallon
Bjerkaas, Carlton Lee *technology services company executive*
Cecil, Dorcas Ann *property management executive*
Herrington, James Patrick *secondary education educator*
Jenner, William Alexander *meteorologist, educator*
Ottwein, Merrill William George *real estate company executive, veterinarian*

Oak Brook
Baker, Robert J(ohn) *hospital administrator*
Barnes, Karen Kay *lawyer*
Bennett, Margaret Airola *lawyer*
Cannon, Patrick Francis *public relations executive*
Christian, Joseph Ralph *physician*
Congalton, Susan Tichenor *lawyer*

Degerstrom, James Marvin *retired engineering executive*
DeLorey, John Alfred *printing company executive*
Dmowski, W. Paul *obstetrician, gynecologist*
Duerinck, Louis T. *retired railroad executive, attorney*
Getz, Herbert A. *lawyer*
Goodwin, Daniel L. *real estate company executive*
†Greenberg, Jack M. *food products executive*
Hand, Roger *physician, educator*
Higgens, William John, III (Trey Higgens) *sales executive*
Hodnik, David F. *retail company executive*
Holsinger, Wayne Townsend *retail executive, retired*
John, Richard C. *enterprise development organization executive*
Johnson, Grant Lester *lawyer, retired manufacturing company executive*
Kelly, Donald Philip *entrepreneur*
Kostrubala, Mark Anthony *writer*
Lane, James Frederick, IV *publishing executive*
Loughead, Jeffrey Lee *physician*
Michelsen, John Ernest *software and internet services company executive*
Miller, Robert Stevens, Jr. *finance professional*
Mlsna, Kathryn Kimura *lawyer*
Morello, Josephine A. *microbiology and pathology educator*
Muschler, Audrey Lorraine *insurance broker*
Nelson, Robert Eddinger *management and development consultant*
Noel, Tallulah Ann *healthcare industry executive*
Quinlan, Michael Robert *fast food franchise company executive*
Rathi, Manohar Lal *pediatrician, neonatologist*
Ring, Leonard M. *lawyer*
Risk, Richard Robert *health care executive*
Turner, Fred L. *fast food company executive*
Veitch, Stephen Boies *city manager*
Veno, Ronald James, Jr. *travel industry executive*
Warnock, William Reid *lawyer*
Wheeler, Paul James *real estate executive*
Wigginton, Adam *marketing professional*
Xu, Tao *mechanical engineer*
Young, Steven Scott *managing director*

Oak Forest
Hull, Charles William *special education educator*
Jashel, Larry Steven (L. Steven Rose) *entrepreneur, media consultant*
Kogut, Kenneth Joseph *consulting engineer*
Lee, David Chang *physician*

Oak Lawn
†Casey, James B. *librarian*
Gordon, Edward Earl *management consultant*
Kenny, Mary Alice *lawyer, law librarian*
†Leon, Jay *educator*
Wright, Steven Randall *minister*

Oak Park
Adelman, William John *university labor and industrial relations educator*
Andre, L. Aumund *management consultant*
Brackett, Edward Boone, III *orthopedic surgeon*
Burhoe, Brian Walter *automotive service executive*
Cary, William Sterling *retired church executive*
Clark, John Peter, III *engineering consultant*
Devereux, Timothy Edward *advertising agency executive*
Forst, Edmund Charles, Jr. *communications educator, consultant*
Gerson, Gary Stanford *rabbi*
†Goergen, Juana Iris *Latin American studies educator*
Goold, Florence Wilson *occupational therapist*
Hallstrand, Sarah Laymon *denomination executive*
Kahn, Peter R. *secondary school educator*
Kosanavich, Lisa A. *interior designer, industrial designer*
Lunney, Daniel Thomas *chaplain, bereavement coordinator*
Morkovin, Mark Vladimir *aerospace and mechanical engineer*
Reed, Charles Allen *retired anthropologist*
Schubert, Blake H. *lawyer, investor*
Spartz, Alice Anne Lenore *retired retail executive*
Varchmin, Thomas Edward *environmental health administrator*
Worley, Marvin George, Jr. *architect*

Oakbrook Terrace
Anderson, Stephen Francis *insurance company executive*
Becker, Robert Jerome *allergist, health care consultant*
Berry, Lynn Marina *healthcare administrator*
Buntrock, Dean Lewis *waste management company executive*
Cason, Marilynn Jean *technological institute official, lawyer*
Catalano, Gerald *accountant, oil company executive*
Ciccarone, Richard Anthony *financial executive*
Fenech, Joseph Charles *lawyer*
Keller, Dennis James *management educator*
LaForte, George Francis, Jr. *lawyer*
O'Brien, Walter Joseph, II *lawyer*
Shalek, James Arthur, Jr. *insurance agent, financial consultant*
Singhal, Vivek Kumar *management consultant*
Tibble, Douglas Clair *lawyer*

Oglesby
Zeller, Francis Joseph *dean*

Okawville
Pomeroy, Bruce Marcel *critical care nurse, educator*

Olympia Fields
Haley, David Alan *preferred provider organization executive*
Kasimos, John Nicholas *pathologist*
Menees, John Robert *mechanical engineer*
Sprinkel, Beryl Wayne *economist, consultant*
Villari, Jack C. *performing arts executive, arts entrepreneur*

Onarga
Wilken, Caroline Doane *critical care, emergency, recovery room, and medical/surgical nurse*

Oregon
Abbott, David Henry *manufacturing company executive*
Cain, Vernon *information services executive*
Cargerman, Alan William *lawyer*
Clement, John Edward Strausz *minister, religious organization administrator*

Orion
Magee, Elizabeth Sherrard *civic organization volunteer*
Nicholson, Tom Cotton *school district administrator*

Orland Park
Anderson, Arthur Rodney *secondary education educator*
Capstaff, Genevieve MacKeeby *humanities educator*
English, Floyd Leroy *telecommunications company executive*
Gittelman, Marc Jeffrey *manufacturing and financial executive*
Kahn, Jan Edward *manufacturing company executive*
Knop, Charles Milton *electrical engineer*
Price, Nancy Molander *educational administrator, school psychologist*
Rasmason, Frederick Charles, III *emergency nurse*
Schultz, Barbara Marie *insurance company executive*

Oswego
Van Etten, Edythe Augusta *retired occupational health nurse*
Weilert, Ronald Lee *data processing executive*

Ottawa
Breipohl, Walter Eugene *real estate broker*
Thornton, Edmund B. *philanthropist*

Palatine
Aleksandras, Deloris Niles *retired nursing educator*
Brod, Catherine Marie *foundation administrator*
Butler, John Musgrave *business financial consultant*
Castle, Grace Eleanor *legal investigator*
Cesario, Robert Charles *franchise executive, consultant*
†Chalupa, Vlastislav John *retired bank executive*
Compton, David Bruce *international management consultant*
Crawford, Annmarie *writer, model, actress, photographer*
Fitzgerald, Gerald Francis *retired banker*
†Fitzgerald, Peter Gosselin *senator, lawyer*
†Fleenor, Juliann Evans *English language educator, writer*
Fortunato, Nancy *artist*
Hellyer, Timothy Michael *protective services officer*
Keres, Karen Lynne *English language educator*
Medin, Lowell Ansgard *management executive*
Miletto, David Gregory *artist*
Nixon, Wayne Robert *engineering manager*
Pohl, Frederik *writer*
Rembusch, Joseph John *psychologist, management consulting company executive*
Spinner, Lee Louis *accountant*
Stephens, LaVerne C. *middle school educator*
Walker, Sally Y. *educational association administrator*

Palos Heights
Nederhood, Joel H. *church organization executive, minister, retired*
Swanson, Warren Lloyd *lawyer*

Palos Hills
Crawley, Vernon Obadiah *academic adminstrator*
Johnson, Audrey Ann *options trader, stockbroker*
Vasiliauskas, Edmund *chemistry educator*

Palos Park
Nelson, Lawrence Evan *business consultant*
Nicholls, Richard Allen *middle school social studies educator*

Pana
Waddington, Irma Joann *music teacher*

Paris
Sisson, Marilyn Sue *writer*

Park Forest
Billig, Etel Jewel *theater director, actress*
Cribbs, Maureen Ann *artist, educator*
Goodrich, John Bernard *lawyer, consultant*
Moore, D(eane) Stanley *educator*
Steinmetz, Jon David *mental health executive, psychologist*
Williams, Jack Raymond *civil engineer*

Park Ridge
Bailey, Marianne Therese *social service administrator*
Bales, Edward Wagner *consultant, former manufacturing executive*
Bitran, Jacob David *internist*
Boe, Gerard Patrick *health science association administrator, educator*
Bridges, Jack Edgar *electronics engineer*
Carr, Gilbert Randle *retired railroad executive*
Charewicz, David Michael *photographer*
Cochin, Rita R. *nurse*
Ewald, Robert Frederick *insurance association executive*
Fried, Walter *hematologist, educator*
Hegarty, Mary Frances *lawyer*
Herting, Robert Leslie *pharmaceutical executive*
Jennrich, Judith A. *critical care nurse, nursing educator*
Johnson, Kenneth Stuart *publisher, printer*
†Joyce, Teri *church organization administrator*
Kenney, John Patrick *dentist*
Kleckner, Dean Ralph *trade association executive*
LaRue, Paul Hubert *lawyer*
Lesiak, Lucille Ann *graphic designer*
Mangun, Clarke Wilson, Jr. *public health physician, consultant*
McIntosh, Don Leslie *electrical engineer*
Orlow, Daniel John *photographer, artist*
Rojek, Kenneth John *health facility administrator, hospital*
Sersen, Howard Harry *interior designer, cabinetry consultant*
Weber, Philip Joseph *retired manufacturing company executive*

Pecatonica
Merkel, Richard Eugene *retired pilot*

Pekin
Dancey, Charles Lohman *newspaper executive*
Frison, Rick *agricultural company executive*
Hupke, David R. *photographer*
Schurter, Richard Allen *secondary school history educator*

Peoria
Allen, Lyle Wallace *lawyer*
†Altenberger, William V. *federal judge*
Anglin, Linda Tannert *community health nurse, geriatrics nurse, educator*
†Atterbury, Robert Rennie, III *lawyer*
Ballowe, James *English educator, author*
Brill de Ramirez, Susan Berry *English educator*
Bussone, Frank Joseph *foundation executive, television broadcaster*
Chamberlain, Joseph Miles *retired astronomer, educator*
Christison, William Henry, III *lawyer*
Clough, Barry *marketing executive*
Coletta, Ralph John *lawyer*
Colvin, Connie Lou *administrative specialist, author*
Corso, Frank, Jr. *architect, educator*
Cunningham, Raymond Leo *research chemist, retired*
†Curtis, R. Craig *political science educator*
DuBois, Mark Benjamin *utilities executive*
Fites, Donald Vester *tractor company executive*
Freitag, Donna *head women's basketball coach*
Gard, Carol Lee *nurse educator*
Gross, Thomas Lester *obstetrician, gynecologist, researcher*
Hungate, Carolyn Wolf *health and public services administrator*
Kauffman, Robert Joseph *magistrate*
Kelly, Grace Dentino *secondary education educator*
Kenyon, Leslie Harrison *architect*
Kroehler, Ralph S. *association executive*
Kroll, Dennis Edwards *industrial engineering educator*
Laible-White, Sherry Lynne *welfare reform administrator*
Lund, Thomas C. *advertising executive*
McCollum, Jean Hubble *medical assistant*
McConnell, John Thomas *newspaper executive, publisher*
McDade, Joe Billy *federal judge*
McMullen, David Wayne *education educator*
Michael, Jonathan Edward *insurance company executive*
Mihm, Michael Martin *federal judge*
Miller, Rick Frey *emergency physician*
Miller, Wilma Hildruth *education educator*
Murphy, Sharon Margaret *educator*
Myers, John Joseph *bishop*
Nielsen, Eloise Wilma *elementary education educator*
Nielsen, Harald Christian *retired chemist*
Parsons, Donald James *retired bishop*
Polanin, W. Richard *engineering educator*
Price Boday, Mary Kathryn *choreographer, small business owner, educator*
Prusak, Maximilian Michael *lawyer*
Quanstrom, Roy Fred *non-profit organization executive*
Rankin, John Carter *consulting chemist*
Rushford, Eloise Johnson *land manager*
Ryan, Michael Beecher *lawyer, former government official*
Saha, Badal Chandra *biochemist*
Saxon, Randall Lee *pastor, author, educator*
Sheehan, Michael Gilbert *utilities executive*
Sprowls, Robert Joseph *energy company executive*
Stine, Robert Howard *pediatrician*
Strodel, Robert Carl *lawyer*
Thorstenson, Terry N. *construction equipment company executive*
Tondeur, Claire Lise *French educator*
Vaughan, David John *distribution company executive*
Viets, Robert O. *utilities executive*
Walker, Philip Chamberlain, II *health care executive*
Winget, Walter Winfield *lawyer*

Peoria Heights
Bergia, Roger Merle *educational administrator*
Bro, William Price *communications executive*

Percy
Rice, Charles Dale *labor relations specialist, writer*

Peru
Benning, Joseph Raymond *principal*
Carus, Andre Wolfgang *educational publishing firm executive*
Carus, Milton Blouke *publisher children's periodicals*
Kurtz, James Eugene *freelance writer, minister*
Lee, Wayland Sherrod *otolaryngologist*

Petersburg
Smith, Catherine Ann *principal*

Philo
Martin, Earl Dean *physical therapist*
Wood, Susanne Griffiths *environmental chemist, microbiologist*

Pinckneyville
Cawvey, Clarence Eugene *physician*
Johnson, Don Edwin *lawyer*

Plainfield
Chakrabarti, Subrata Kumar *marine research engineer*
Chase, Maria Elaine Garoufalis *publishing company executive*
Cook, Bruce Lawrence *research analyst, educator*
Diercks, Eileen Kay *educational media coordinator, elementary school educator*
Fichter, David Harry *conservationist, environmentalist*
Glenn, Gerald Marvin *marketing, engineering and construction executive*
Hofer, Thomas W. *landscape company executive*
Schinderle, Robert Frank *retired hospital administrator*

Pontiac
Glennon, Charles Edward *judge, lawyer*
Milanowski, Tanya Jane *school psychologist*

Princeton
Johnson, Watts Carey *lawyer*
Tillman, June Torrison *musician*

Prophetstown
Sanders, Gary Glenn *electronics engineer, consultant*

Prospect Heights
Byrne, Michael Joseph *business executive*
Clark, Donald Robert *retired insurance company executive*
Kosinski, Richard Andrew *public relations executive*
Leopold, Mark F. *lawyer*
Robinson, Martin (Marty) *television and radio broadcaster, media consultant*

Quincy
Adams, Beejay (Meredith Elisabeth Jane J. Adams) *sales executive*
Anderson, Peggy Joan *English educator*
Kallner, Norman Gust *management information systems manager*
†Klein, Mary Ann *English educator*
Mallory, Troy L. *accountant*
†Mejer, Robert Lee *art educator, curator*
Moritz, Betty Ann *retired editor*
Morrison, John Alexander *retired educator, foreign policy analyst*
†Preston, Ann Elizabeth *media and communication educator*
Randall, Robert Quentin *retired nursery executive*
Tyer, Travis Earl *library consultant*
Walters, Tom Frederick *manufacturing company official*

Rantoul
†Rosakopf, Arthur W. *artist*
Valencia, Rogelio Pasco *electronics engineer*

Richton Park
Burt, Gwen Behrens *elementary school administrator*
†Nevins, Patrick Fredrick *librarian*
Piucci, Virginio Louis *academic administrator*

River Forest
Li, Tze-chung *lawyer, educator*
Lund, Sister Candida *college chancellor*
Puthenveetil, Jos Anthony *laboratory executive*
Sloan, Jeanette Pasin *artist*
†Stadtwald, Kurt Werner *historian*
White, Philip Butler *artist*
Wirsching, Charles Philipp, Jr. *retired brokerage house executive, private investor*
†Zimbrakos, Paul William *editor*

River Grove
Hill-Hulslander, Jacquelyne L. *nursing educator and consultant*
†Jurkowski, Orion Lech *librarian*
Stein, Thomas Henry *social science educator*

Riverdale
Brown, Bruce Harding *naval officer*
Hoekwater, James Warren *treasurer*

Riverside
Dengler, Robert Anthony *professional association executive*
Gwinn, Robert P. *publishing executive*
Perkins, William H., Jr. *finance company executive*

Riverwoods
Douglas, Bruce Lee *oral and maxillofacial surgeon, medical director, educator, workplace health consultant, gerontology consultant*
Ferkenhoff, Robert J. *retail executive*
Kushner, Jeffrey L. *manufacturing company executive*
Smith, Carole Dianne *editor, writer, product developer*
Yarrington, Hugh *corporate lawyer, communications company executive*

Robbins
Fulson, Lula M. *educator*

Rochester
Petterchak, Janice A. *researcher, writer*
†Shaw, Linda K. *municipal official, librarian*

Rock Falls
Johnson, Virginia Gayle *secondary education educator*
Julifs, Sandra Jean *community action agency executive*

Rock Island
Abney, Stephen Douglas *civilian military employee*
Anderson, Richard Charles *geology educator*
Bradley, Walter James *emergency physician*
Cheney, Thomas Ward *insurance company executive*
Correll, Dan Eugene *physical education educator*
Crisp, Sandra Sue *contract specialist*
Forlini, Frank John, Jr. *cardiologist*
Hammer, William Roy *paleontologist, educator*
Hartsock, Jane Marie *nurse, educator*
Horstmann, James Douglas *college official*
Lardner, Henry Petersen (Peter Lardner) *insurance company executive*
Osborn, David Lee *engineer*
Sundelius, Harold W. *geology educator*
Telleen, John Martin *retired judge*
Tredway, Thomas *college president*
Wallace, Franklin Sherwood *lawyer*
Whitmore, Charles Horace *utility executive, lawyer, management consultant*

Rockford
Albert, Janyce Louise *business educator, banker*
Anderson, LaVerne Eric *lawyer*
Anderson, Max Elliot *television and film production company executive*
Apgar, Jean E. *artist, consultant*
Baptist, Errol Christopher *pediatrician, educator*
Barrick, William Henry *lawyer*
Bates, David Vliet *religious school administrator, minister*
Cadigan, Elise *social worker*
Canfield, Elizabeth Frances *lawyer*
Carlson, Allan Constantine *historian*
Casagranda, Robert Charles *industrial engineer*
Chitwood, Julius Richard *librarian*
Cohen, Phyllis Joanne *nurse*
Davit, Frank Torino *accountant*
Den Adel, Raymond Lee *classics educator*
Doran, Thomas George *bishop*
Eliason, Jon Tate *electrical engineer*

Faizone, John F. *association executive*
Fleming, Thomas J. *editor, publishing executive*
Frakes, James Terry *physician, gastroenterologist, educator*
†Gaziano, Mary J. *lawyer, educator*
Gloyd, Lawrence Eugene *diversified manufacturing company executive*
Green, Lisa R. *journalist*
Hanson, Murray Lynn *minister*
Hart, Jay Albert Charles *retired real estate broker*
Heerens, Robert Edward *physician*
Heinke, Warren E. *social services administrator*
Holder, Judith Anne *guidance counselor*
Hornby, Robert Ray *mechanical engineer*
Horst, Bruce Everett *manufacturing company executive*
Hoshaw, Lloyd *historian, educator*
Howard, John Addison *former college president, institute executive*
Hunsaker, Richard Kendall *lawyer*
Johnson, Elizabeth Ericson *retired educator*
Johnson, Thomas Stuart *lawyer*
†KC, Lisa Louise *school system administrator, jeweler*
Keating, Patricia Ann Stacy *retired physical education educator*
Kelleghan, Kevin Michael *writer, trainer*
Kimball, Donald Robert *food company executive*
Larsen, Steven *orchestra conductor*
Liebovich, Samuel David *warehouse executive*
Logli, Paul Albert *lawyer*
Mahlburg, Norine Elizabeth *retired nurse*
†Mahoney, Patrick M. *federal judge*
Marelli, Sister Sister Mary Anthony *secondary school principal*
Martas, Julia Ann *special education administrator*
Masters, Arlene Elizabeth *singer*
Matschullat, Dale Lewis *lawyer*
Maysent, Harold Wayne *hospital administrator*
McClelland, Patricia G. *minister*
Mc Nelly, Frederick Wright, Jr. *psychologist*
Moehling, Kathryn S. *mental health nurse, counselor*
O'Donnell, William David *retired construction firm executive*
O'Neill, Arthur J. *retired bishop*
Provo, Wade Arden *foreign language educator*
Rauch, Janet Melodie *elementary school educator*
Reinhard, Philip G. *federal judge*
Reno, Roger *lawyer*
Robinson, Donald Peter *musician, retired electrical engineer*
Rudy, Elmer Clyde *lawyer*
Seehausen, Richard Ferdinand *architect*
Shepler, John Edward *engineering executive*
Steele, Carl Lavern *academic administrator*
Steffan, Wallace Allan *entomologist, educator, museum director*
Sullivan, Peter Thomas, III *lawyer*
Sylvester, Nancy Katherine *speech educator, management consultant*
Walhout, Justine Simon *chemistry educator*
Weissbard, David Raymond *minister*
Wilke, Duane Andrew *educator*

Rolling Meadows
Brennan, Charles Martin, III *construction company executive*
Buchanan, Richard Kent *electronics company executive*
Cain, R. Wayne *sales, finance and leasing company executive*
Cash, Alan Sherwin *electronics assembly specialist*
†Cataldo, C. A. *hotel executive*
†Cataldo, Robert J. *hotel executive*
Giese, Robert James *minister*
Hassert, Elizabeth Anne *transportation executive*
Kuhar, June Carolynn *retired fiberglass manufacturing company executive*
†Medal, Carole Ann *library director*
Miles, Frank Charles *retired newspaper executive*
O'Connell, Edward Joseph, III *financial executive, accountant*
Padgitt, David G. *corporate executive*
Peekel, Arthur K. *secondary school educator*
Podgorski, Robert Paul *human resources executive*
Rahfeldt, Daryl Gene *minister*
Rebbeck, Lester James, Jr. *artist*
Strongin, Bonnie Lynn *English language educator*

Romeoville
Cizek, David John *sales engineer, small business owner*
Houlihan, James William *criminal justice educator*
Lifka, Mary Lauranne *history educator*
Nagel, Kurt E. *police officer*

Roscoe
Jacobs, Richard Dearborn *consulting engineering company executive*
Young, Larry Eugene *baseball umpire*

Roselle
Kao, William Chishon *dentist*
Laughlin, Terry Xavier *management consultant*
Lueder, Dianne Carol *library director*
Waite, Darvin Danny *accountant*

Rosemont
Aitken, Rosemary Theresa *financial planner, consultant*
Burkhardt, Edward Arnold *transportation company executive*
Currie, Earl James *transportation company executive*
Good, William Allen *professional society executive*
Isenberg, Howard Lee *manufacturing company executive*
Jenkins, Walter Donald *real estate executive*
Moster, Mary Clare *public relations executive*
Myers, Michael Charles *marketing executive*
Stabler, Nancy Rae *infosystems specialist*

Round Lake
Anderson, Ruth Nathan *syndicated columnist, TV news host, writer, recording artist, lyricist*
Breillatt, Julian Paul, Jr. *biochemist, biomedical engineer*
†Fejer, T. William *pianist, composer, architect, furniture designer*
Laskowski, Richard E. *retail hardware company executive*

Saint Anne
Heckman, Patricia A. *geriatrics nurse, educator*

Saint Charles
Carpenter, Mary Laure *hospital administrator*
Dowd, James Patrick *bookseller, writer*
Frank, Ruby Merinda *employment agency executive*
Markham, John Phillip, Jr. *research analyst*
McCartney, Charles Price *retired obstetrician-gynecologist*
Mc Kay, Thomas, Jr. *lawyer*
Nelson, Norman Augustine *minister*
Stone, John McWilliams, Jr. *electronics executive*
Urhausen, James Nicholas *real estate developer, construction executive*
Vance, Leslie Edwin *multimedia technologist*

Salem
Basnett, C. Jan *English educator*

Sauget
Baltz, Richard Arthur *chemical engineer*

Savanna
Kuk, Michael Louis *protective services official*

Savoy
Gauger, Randy Jay *minister*
Lane, Russell Watson *water treatment consultant retired, chemist*
Nelson, Clarence R. *writer*

Scales Mound
Lieberman, Archie *photographer, writer*

Schaumburg
Adrianopoli, Barbara Catherine *librarian*
Balasa, Mark Edward *investment consultant*
Barrett, Jeffrey Scott *real estate company executive*
†Cicarelli, James S. *college dean*
Dahn, Carl James *aerospace engineer*
Dibos, Dennis Robert *electronics industry executive*
Edmunds, Jane Clara *communications consultant*
Galvin, Christopher B. *electronics company executive*
Galvin, Robert W. *electronics executive*
Ghrist, John Russell *computer technician*
Hedke, Richard Alvin *gifted education educator*
Hill, Raymond Joseph *packaging company executive*
Hlousek, Joyce B(ernadette) *school system administrator*
Huff, Gayle Compton *advertising/marketing executive*
Kleppe, Joan Marie *entertainment executive*
Littel Zdon, Laura *communications executive*
Little, Bruce Washington *professional society administrator*
Meltzer, Brian *lawyer*
Otis, James, Jr. *architect*
Parker, Norman W. *scientist*
Patzke, Frank Thomas *investment advisor*
Sandler, Norman *business executive*
Schlossberg, Howard Barry *editor, freelance writer*
Shapiro, Edwin Henry *lawyer*
Silver, Bella Wolfson *daycare center executive, educator*
Stabej, Rudolph John *computer consultant*
Tompson, Marian Leonard *professional society administrator*
Tooker, Gary Lamarr *electronics company executive*
Tucker, Frederick Thomas *electronics company executive*
Uhrik, Steven Brian *clinical social worker, psychotherapist, employee assistance professional, behavioral science consultant*
†Williams, Kay Janene *elementary education educator*
Zhao, Jinsong Jason *engineer, researcher, administrator*

Schiller Park
Congalton, Christopher William *lawyer*

Scott Air Force Base
†Bridges, Clayton Gary *retired career officer*
†Coolidge, Charles H., Jr. *career officer*
†Floyd, Bobby O. *military officer*
†McNabb, Duncan J. *career officer*
†Regan, Gilbert J. *career officer*
Rehkop, John *career officer*
†Thompson, Roger G., Jr. *career military officer*
†Williams, George N. *military officer*
Young, Ben Farris *air force pilot*

Shabbona
†Prestegaard, Kathy Anne *secondary education educator*

Shelbyville
Storm, Sandy Lamm *secondary education educator*

Shorewood
Lombardo, David Albert *actor, writer, speaker, aviation educator*
Petrella, Mary Therese *community health and women's health nurse*
†Thomas, Mary Faith *library director*

Skokie
Alexander, John Charles *pharmaceutical company executive, physician*
Arandia, Carmelita S. *school administrator*
Becker, Daniel Paul *medicinal chemist, researcher*
Bellows, Randall Trueblood *ophthalmologist, educator*
Braun, Bennett George *psychiatrist*
Caldwell, Wiley North *retired distribution company executive*
Corley, William Gene *engineering research executive*
Fan, Tai-Shen Liu *dietitian*
Finkel, Bernard *public relations, communications and association management consultant, radio host*
Gershon, William I. *copywriter, voiceover actor, communications executive*
Gleason, John Patrick, Jr. *trade association executive*
Goldsmith, Barbara Cecile *sculptor, curator*
Greenspan, Jeffrey Dov *lawyer*
Haben, John William *funeral director*
Hedien, Wayne Evans *retired insurance company executive*
Johansson, Nils A. *information services executive*
Lass, Nancy Anne *physician*
Manos, John *editor-in-chief*
McCarthy, Michael Shawn *health care company executive, lawyer*
Plotnick, Paul William *lawyer*
Roemer, James Paul *data processing executive*
Salit, Gary *lawyer*
Seeder, Richard Owen *infosystems specialist*
Siegal, Burton Lee *product designer, consultant, inventor*
Siegal, Rita Goran *engineering company executive*
Sloan, Judi C. *physical education educator*
Wasik, John Francis *editor, writer, publisher*

Sleepy Hollow
†Galitz, Robert Walter *art broker, dealer*

South Barrington
Kissane, Sharon Florence *writer, consultant, educator*

South Holland
Capriglione, Ralph Raymond *geologist, educator*
Fota, Frank George *artist*

Sparta
Pritchett, Allen Monroe, III *healthcare administrator*

Spring Valley
Crowley, Michael Ryan *real estate appraiser/analyst, educator*

Springfield
Ballenger, Hurley René *electrical engineer*
Bell, John Perry *minister, religious organization administrator*
†Blake, William L. *airport company executive*
†Boozell, Mark Eldon *state official*
Campbell, Kathleen Charlotte Murphey *audiology educator, administrator, researcher*
Carroll, Howard William *state senator, lawyer*
Chen, Eden Hsien-chang *engineering consultant*
Cipfl, Joseph John, Jr. *university administrator*
Cluney, J(ohn) C(harles) (Jack Cluney) *minister*
Coss, John Edward *archivist*
†Coutrakon, Basil H. *federal judge*
Cowles, Ernest Lee *academic administrator, educator, consultant, researcher*
Craig, John Charles *educational researcher, consultant*
Currie, Barbara Flynn *state legislator*
Davis, George Cullom *historian*
Davis, Thomas Edward *prosecutor*
Dodge, Edward John *retired insurance executive*
Dodge, James William *lawyer, educator*
†Doyle, Rebecca Carlisle *state agency administrator*
Edgar, Jim *former governor*
Ellis, Michael Eugene *documentary film producer, writer, director, marketing executive*
†Evans, Charles H. *federal judge*
Evans, Marsha Jo Anne *nursing administrator*
Feldman, Bruce Alan *psychiatrist*
Ferguson, Mark Harmon *banker, lawyer*
Fischoff, Ephraim *humanities educator, sociologist, social worker*
Fleck, Gabriel Alton *electrical engineer*
Frank, Stuart *cardiologist*
Gallina, Charles Onofrio *nuclear scientist*
Gamble, Douglas Irvin *state official, educator*
Geo-Karis, Adeline Jay *state senator*
†Golemo, Timothy Franklin *urban planner*
Hahin, Christopher *metallurgical engineer, corrosion engineer*
Hallmark, Donald Parker *museum director, lecturer*
Harper, William Wayne *broadcast executive*
Heckenkamp, Robert Glenn *lawyer*
Herriford, Robert Levi, Sr. *army officer*
Holland, John Madison *family practice physician*
Hulin, Frances C. *prosecutor*
Immke, Keith Henry *lawyer*
Jackson, Jacqueline Dougan *educator, author*
Kaige, Alice Tubb *retired librarian*
Kerr, Gary Enrico *lawyer, educator*
Kuhn, Kathleen Jo *accountant*
Kwon, Ojoung *computer scientist, educator, consultant*
Lessen, Larry Lee *federal judge*
Lohman, Walter Rearick *banker*
Lynn, Naomi B. *academic administrator*
Lyons, J. Rolland *civil engineer*
Madigan, Michael Joseph *state legislator*
Malany, Le Grand Lynn *lawyer, engineer, bank executive*
Mathewson, Mark Stuart *lawyer, editor*
†Mayersdorf, Assa *neurologist*
Mazzotti, Richard Rene *pharmacist*
Mc Millan, R(obert) Bruce *museum executive, anthropologist*
Miller, Benjamin K. *state supreme court justice*
Mills, Jon K. *psychologist, educator, philosopher*
Mills, Richard Henry *federal judge*
Minocha, Anil *physician, educator, researcher*
Mogerman, Susan *state agency administrator*
Moore, Andrea S. *state legislator*
Moore, Robert *protective services official*
Morford, Lynn Ellen *state official*
Moy, Richard Henry *academic dean, educator*
Munyer, Edward A. *zoologist, museum administrator*
Myers, Phillip Ward *otolaryngologist*
Nanavati, Grace Luttrell *dancer, choreographer, instructor*
Narmont, John Stephen *lawyer*
†Nolen, Sam W. *protective services official*
Noyce, James Roger *chemist, consultant*
O'Connor, Sister Gertrude Theresa *clinical nurse specialist in surgery and anesthesia*
Penning, Patricia Jean *elementary education educator*
Philip, James (Pate Philip) *state senator*
Phillips, John Robert *political scientist, educator*
†Pilapil, Deborah Ann *legislative liaison*
Pistorius, Alvin William, Jr. (Bill Miller) *communications educator*
Poorman, Robert Lewis *education consultant, former college president*
Porter, William L. *electrical engineer*
Puckett, Carlissa Roseann *non-profit association executive*
Rabinovich, Sergio *physician, educator*
Reed, John Charles *chemical engineer*
Reyman, Jonathan Eric *archaeologist, anthropologist, researcher*
†Riedl, Stephen Thomas *state government official*
Rogers, James Allan *music director, hymnologist, author, editor*
Rowe, Max L. *lawyer, corporate executive, management and political consultant, writer, judge*
Ryan, Daniel Leo *bishop*
Ryan, James E. *state attorney general*
†Ryan, Jim *Illinois attorney general*
Schiller, William Richard *surgeon*
Schmidt, Mark James *state public health official*
Schroeder, Joyce Katherine *state agency administrator, research analyst*
Shahidian, Hammed *adult education educator*
Shim, Sang Koo *state mental health official*
†Sisneros, Anthony *political science educator*
†Skelton, Luther William, III *educator, consultant*
Stauffer, Edward Shannon *orthopedic surgeon, educator*
†Stephens, Norman L. *academic administrator*
Strow, Marcia Ann *critical care nurse*
Sumner, David Spurgeon *surgery educator*
Temple, Wayne Calhoun *historian*
Van Meter, Abram DeBois *lawyer, retired banker*
Voycheck, Gerald Louis *nursing home administrator, social worker*
†Washington, Odie *state agency administrator*
Wehrle, Leroy Snyder *economist, educator*
Weinhoeft, John Joseph *data processing executive*
†White, Jesse *state official*
Whitney, John Freeman, Jr. *political science educator*
†Wood, Corinne *state official*
Wood, Harlington, Jr. *federal judge*
Wynn, Nan L. *historic site administrator*
Yaffe, Stuart Allen *physician*
Zook, Elvin Glenn *plastic surgeon, educator*

Steger
Carpenter, Kenneth Russell *international trading executive*

Sterling
Albrecht, Beverly Jean *special education educator*
Attebury, Janice Marie *accountant*
Brooks, Terry *lawyer, author*
Conway, John Paul *retired steel executive*
Donahue, Shirley Ohnstad *elementary education educator*

Stockton
†Anderson, Leone Marie Castell *children's book author*

Stoy
Rhoten, Kenneth D. *writer*

Streamwood
Polkowski, Delphine Theresa *elementary education educator, speech therapist*
Samuelson, Rita Michelle *speech language pathologist*

Sugar Grove
Kanwar, Anju *English educator*

Sullivan
Hagen, Daniel Urban *editor, writer*
Harshman, Milton Moore *sales and marketing professional*

Summit Argo
Abramowicz, Alfred L. *retired bishop*

Sycamore
Johnson, Yvonne Amalia *elementary education educator, science consultant*
Young, Arthur Price *librarian, educator*

Table Grove
†Thomson, Helen Louise *artist*

Taylorville
Austin, Daniel William *lawyer*
Gardner, Jerry Dean *dentist, military officer*

Thornton
Braico, Carmella Elizabeth Lofrano *clergy member*

Tinley Park
Antia, Kersey H. *industrial and clinical psychologist, consultant*
Baker, Betty Louise *retired mathematician, educator*
Daniels, Kurt R. *speech and language pathologist*
Flanagan, John F. *publishing executive*
Freitag, Carol Wilma *state official*
Kostka, Elmer Bohumil *secondary school educator*
Leeson, Janet Caroline Tollefson *cake specialties company executive*

Tiskilwa
McCauley, Helen Nora *civic worker*

Toledo
Prather, William C. III *lawyer, writer*

Tonica
Ryan, Howard Chris *retired state supreme court justice*

Tremont
Luick, Barbara Jean *physical therapist assistant*

Union
Hilbert, Elroy E. "Buck" *retired airline pilot*
Perlick, Richard Allan *steel company executive*

University Park
Leftwich, Robert Eugene *oncological nursing educator*
McClellan, Larry Allen *educator, writer, minister*
Peterson, Kenneth Allen, Sr. *retired superintendent of schools*

Urbana
Addy, Alva Leroy *mechanical engineer*
†Ahmad, Irfan Saleem *agricultural engineer, researcher*
Aldridge, Alfred Owen *English language educator*
Antonsen, Elmer Harold *Germanic languages and literature educator*
Arnstein, Walter Leonard *historian, educator*
Austin, Jean Philippe *medical educator, radiologist*
Axford, Roy Arthur *nuclear engineering educator*
Baer, Werner *economist, educator*
Baker, David Hiram *nutritionist, nutrition educator*
Baker, Harold Albert *federal judge*
Balbach, Stanley Byron *lawyer*
†Banich, Marie T. *psychology educator*
Banwart, Wayne Lee *agronomy, environmental science educator*

Basar, Tamer *electrical engineering educator*
Bateman, John Jay *classics educator*
Baym, Nina *English educator*
Beak, Peter Andrew *chemistry educator*
Becker, Donald Eugene *animal science educator*
Bedford, Norton Moore *accounting educator*
Berenbaum, May Roberta *entomology educator*
Bergeron, Clifton George *ceramic engineer, educator*
†Bernthal, David G. *federal judge*
Birnbaum, Howard Kent *materials science educator*
Blahut, Richard Edward *electrical and computer engineering educator*
Bloomfield, Daniel Kermit *college dean, physician*
Boardman, Eunice *retired music educator*
Brems, Hans Julius *economist, educator*
Brichford, Maynard Jay *archivist*
Brown, Theodore Lawrence *chemistry educator*
Buetow, Dennis Edward *physiology educator*
Burger, Ambrose William *agronomy educator*
Burkholder, Donald Lyman *mathematician, educator*
Burton, Herbert *composer*
†Burton, Orville Vernon *history educator*
Carmen, Ira Harris *political scientist, educator*
Carroll, Robert Wayne *mathematics educator*
Chao, Bei Tse *mechanical engineering educator*
Chato, John Clark *mechanical and bioengineering educator*
Cheryan, Munir *agricultural studies educator, biochemical engineering educator*
Choldin, Marianna Tax *librarian, educator*
Chow, Poo *wood technologist, scientist*
Clausing, Arthur Marvin *mechanical engineering educator*
Coleman, Paul Dare *electrical engineering educator*
Conry, Thomas Francis *mechanical engineering educator, consultant*
Cook, Harry Edgar *engineering educator*
Crang, Richard Francis Earl *plant and cell biologist, research center administrator*
Cranston, Robert Earl *neurologist*
Crofts, Antony Richard *biophysics educator*
Cusano, Cristino *mechanical engineer, educator*
Dash, Leon DeCosta, Jr. *journalist*
Dawn, Clarence Ernest *history educator*
Dobrovolny, Jerry Stanley *engineering educator*
Doob, Joseph Leo *mathematician, educator*
Drickamer, Harry George *retired chemistry educator*
Due, Jean Margaret *agricultural economist, educator*
Dunn, Floyd *biophysicist, bioengineer, educator*
Dziuk, Philip John *animal scientist educator*
Edelsbrunner, Herbert *computer scientist, mathematician*
Eden, James Gary *electrical engineering and physics educator, researcher*
Ehrlich, Gert *science educator, researcher*
Endress, Anton G. *horticulturist, educator*
Fantini, Sergio *physical science researcher, educator*
Forbes, Richard Mather *biochemistry educator*
Fossum, Robert Merle *mathematician, educator*
Frazzetta, Thomas Henry *evolutionary biologist, functional morphologist, educator*
Friedman, Stanley *insect physiologist, educator*
Gabriel, Michael *psychology educator*
Gaddy, Oscar Lee *electrical engineering educator*
Garrigus, Upson Stanley *animal science and international agriculture educator*
Garrow, Timothy Alan *nutrition science educator*
Giertz, J. Fred *economics educator*
Giles, Eugene *anthropology educator*
Ginsberg, Donald Maurice *physicist, educator*
Glick, Karen Lynne *college administrator*
Goering, Carroll E. *agricultural engineering educator*
Goldberg, Samuel Irving *mathematics educator*
Goldwasser, Edwin Leo *physicist*
Goodman, David Gordon *Japanese, comparative literature educator, writer*
Gove, Samuel Kimball *political science educator*
Govindjee *biophysics and biology educator*
Gray, John Walker *mathematician, educator*
Greene, Laura Helen *physicist*
†Greene, Terry J. *legislative staff member*
Greenough, William Tallant *psychobiologist, educator*
Gruebele, Martin *chemistry educator*
†Guibbory, Achsah *English educator, writer*
Gutowsky, Herbert Sander *chemistry educator*
Hager, Lowell Paul *biochemistry educator*
Haile, H. G. *German language and literature educator*
†Haken, Rudolf *music educator*
Hale, Allean Lemmon *writer, educator*
Hall, William Joel *civil engineer, educator*
Hannon, Bruce Michael *engineer, educator*
Hanratty, Thomas Joseph *chemical engineer, educator*
Harper, James Eugene *plant physiologist*
Heath, James Edward *physiology educator, retired*
Hedlund, Barbara Smith *musician, educator, music publisher*
Hedlund, Ronald *baritone*
Heichel, Gary Harold *crop sciences educator*
Hendrick, George *English language educator*
Henson, C. Ward *mathematician, educator*
Herrin, Moreland *civil engineering educator, consultant*
Hess, Karl *electrical and computer engineering educator*
Hill, Lowell Dean *agricultural marketing educator*
Hixon, James Edward *physiology educator*
Hobgood, Burnet McLean *theater educator*
Hoeft, Robert Gene *agriculture educator*
Hoffmeister, Donald Frederick *zoology educator*
Holonyak, Nick, Jr. *electrical engineering educator*
Holt, Donald A. *university administrator, agronomist, consultant, researcher*
Horsfall, William Robert *educator*
†Hoxie, Frederick Eugene *history educator*
Huang, Thomas Shi-Tao *electrical engineering educator, researcher*
Hurt, James Riggins *English language educator*
Hymowitz, Theodore *plant geneticist, educator*
Iben, Icko, Jr. *astrophysicist, educator*
Isaacson, Richard Evan *microbiologist*
Jacobson, Howard *classics educator*
Jockusch, Carl Groos, Jr. *mathematics educator*
Jonas, Jiri *chemistry educator*
Jones, Benjamin Angus, Jr. *retired agricultural engineering educator, administrator*
Kang, Sung-Mo (Steve Kang) *electrical engineering educator*
Kaufman, Jerome Benzion *neurosurgeon*
Kaufmann, Urlin Milo *English literature educator*
Kirkpatrick, R(obert) James *geology educator*
Klein, Miles Vincent *physics educator*
Knight, Frank Bardsley *mathematics educator*
†Knott, Jack H. *political science educator, administrator*
Kocheril, Abraham George *physician, educator*
Kolodziej, Edward Albert *political scientist, educator*
Krock, Curtis Josselyn *pulmonologist*
Kumar, Panganamala Ramana *electrical and computer engineering educator*
Kushner, Mark Jay *physics and engineering educator*
Lasersohn, Peter Nathan *linguist, educator*
Lauterbur, Paul C(hristian) *chemistry educator*
Lazarus, David *physicist, educator*
Leuthold, Raymond Martin *agricultural economics educator*
Lieberman, Laurence *poet, educator*
Linowes, David Francis *political economist, educator, corporate executive*
Love, Joseph L. *history educator, cultural studies center administrator*
Makri, Nancy *chemistry educator*
Mall, Laurence S. *French language educator*
Malone, Paul Scott *writer, artist*
Manning, Sylvia *English studies educator*
Mapother, Dillon Edward *physicist, university official*
Marcovich, Miroslav *classics educator*
May, Walter Grant *chemical engineer*
Mayes, Paul Eugene *engineering educator, technical consultant*
McColley, Robert McNair *history educator*
McConkie, George Wilson *educational psychology educator*
Mc Glamery, Marshal Dean *agronomy, weed science educator*
McGlathery, James Melville *foreign language educator*
Melby, John B. *composer, educator*
Meyer, Richard Charles *microbiologist*
†Michelson, Bruce Frederic *academic administrator, educator*
Miley, George Hunter *nuclear engineering educator*
Miller, Robert Earl *engineer, educator*
†Mortimer, Armine Kotin *literature educator*
†Murdoch, H. Adlai *literature educator*
Nanney, David Ledbetter *genetics educator*
Nelson, Cary Robert *English educator*
Nelson, Ralph Alfred *physician*
Nettl, Bruno *anthropology and musicology educator*
Newman, John Kevin *classics educator*
O'Brien, Nancy Patricia *librarian, educator*
Oliphant, Uretz John *physician, surgeon*
O'Morchoe, Charles Christopher Creagh *administrator, anatomical sciences educator*
O'Morchoe, Patricia Jean *pathologist, educator*
Pai, Anantha Mangalore *electrical engineering educator, consultant*
Parker, Alan John *veterinary neurologist, educator, researcher*
†Picchietti, Daniel Leigh *neurologist*
Prosser, C. Ladd *physiology educator, researcher*
Raheel, Mastura *textile scientist, educator*
Rao, Nannapaneni Narayana *electrical engineer*
Rebeiz, Constantin A. *plant physiology educator*
Replinger, John Gordon *architect, retired educator*
Resek, Robert William *economist*
Rich, Robert F. *law and political science educator*
Ricketts, Gary Eugene *retired animal scientist*
Ridgway, Marcella Davies *veterinarian*
Rotzoll, Kim Brewer *advertising and communications educator*
Rowland, Theodore Justin *physicist, educator*
Salamon, Myron Ben *physicist, educator*
Satterthwaite, Cameron B. *physics educator*
Scanlan, Richard Thomas *classics educator*
Schacht, Richard Lawrence *philosopher, educator*
Schmidt, Stephen Christopher *agricultural economist, educator*
Schweizer, Kenneth Steven *physics educator*
Seigler, David Stanley *botanist, chemist, educator*
Shtohryn, Dmytro Michael *librarian, educator*
Siedler, Arthur James *nutrition and food science educator*
Siess, Chester Paul *civil engineering educator*
Simon, Jack Aaron *geologist, former state official*
Sinclair, James Burton *plant pathology educator, consultant*
Small, Erwin *veterinarian, educator*
Snyder, Lewis Emil *astrophysicist*
Solberg, Winton Udell *history educator*
Spence, Mary Lee *historian*
Spitze, Robert George Frederick *agricultural economics educator*
Stallmeyer, James Edward *engineer, educator*
Stout, Glenn Emanuel *retired science administrator*
Stukel, James Joseph *academic administrator, mechanical engineering educator*
Sturtevant, William T. *fundraising executive, consultant*
Sullivan, Zohreh T. *English educator*
Suslick, Kenneth Sanders *chemistry educator*
Swenson, George Warner, Jr. *electronics engineer, radio astronomer, educator*
Switzer, Robert Lee *biochemistry educator*
Talbot, Emile Joseph *French language educator*
Thompson, Margaret M. *physical education educator*
Tondeur, Philippe Maurice *mathematician, educator*
Trick, Timothy Noel *electrical and computer engineering educator, researcher*
Trigger, Kenneth James *mechanical and industrial engineering educator*
†Van Ness, Phillip R. *lawyer*
Visek, Willard James *nutritionist, animal scientist, physician, educator*
Voss, Edward William, Jr. *immunologist, educator*
Waldbauer, Gilbert Peter *entomologist, educator*
†Wallig, Matthew Alan *veterinary pathologist*
Wang, Shicai *research engineer*
Watson, Paula D. *library administrator*
Watts, Emily Stipes *English language educator*
Wedgeworth, Robert *dean, university librarian, former association executive*
Weir, Morton Webster *retired academic administrator, educator*
Welch, William Ben *emergency physician*
Wert, Charles Allen *metallurgical and mining engineering educator*
Westwater, James William *chemical engineering educator*
Whitt, Gregory Sidney *molecular phylogenetics, evolution educator*
Williams, Martha Ethelyn *information science educator*
Williamson, John Maurice *accountant*
Wirt, Frederick Marshall *political scientist*
Woese, Carl R. *biophysicist, microbiology educator*
Wolfe, Ralph Stoner *microbiology educator*
Wolynes, Peter Guy *chemistry researcher, educator*
†Woodard, Beth Stuckey *librarian, educator*
Yen, Ben Chie *water resources engineering educator*
Yoerger, Roger Raymond *agricultural engineer, educator*
Yu, George Tzuchiao *political science educator*
Zgusta, Ladislav *linguist, educator*

Vandalia
Sussenbach, Ward Virgil *minister*

Vernon Hills
Claassen, W(alter) Marshall *employment company executive*
Gnaedinger, John Phillip *structural engineer, consultant*
Keller, Richard Loran *physician*
Michalik, John James *legal educational association executive*

Villa Park
Peterson, Elaine Grace *technology director*
Smith, Barbara Ann *gifted education coordinator*
Tang, George Chickchee *investment company executive*
Taylor, Ronald Lee *school administrator*

Virden
McGartland, Steven Ross *secondary education music educator*

Wadsworth
Bannick, Janice Carol *automotive dealerships executive*

Waggoner
Matthews, Beverly J. *psychologist*

Warrenville
Symuleski, Richard Aloysius *chemical engineer*

Wasco
Bach, Jan Morris *composer, educator*

Washington
Blumenshine, Mahlon *banker*
Hallinan, John Cornelius *mechanical engineering consultant*

Waterloo
Coffee, Richard Jerome, II *lawyer*

Watseka
Neumann, Frederick Lloyd *plant breeder*
Tungate, James Lester *lawyer*

Wauconda
Kramer, Pamela Kostenko *librarian*

Waukegan
Bairstow, Richard Raymond *retired lawyer*
Bleck, Thomas Frank *architect*
Bleck, Virginia Eleanore *illustrator*
Brady, Terrence Joseph *judge*
Cherry, Peter Ballard *electrical products corporation executive*
Decker, David Alfred *lawyer*
Drapalik, Betty Ruth *civic worker, artist*
†Flanyak, Chrisann Marie *county court manager*
Hall, Albert L. *lawyer, retired*
Henrick, Michael Francis *lawyer*
†Jumisko, Marci Kay *economics educator*
Leibowitz, David Perry *lawyer*
Miller, Elaine Wilson *computer consultant*
Paulsen, Noreen *legal nurse consultant*

Waverly
†Stahr, Ellen Marie *secondary school educator*

West Chicago
Franzen, Janice Marguerite Gosnell *magazine editor*
Hauptmann, Randal Mark *biotechnologist*
Kieft, Gerald Nelson *mechanical engineer*
Paulissen, James Peter *retired physician, county official*

West Dundee
†Woltz, Kenneth Allen *consulting executive*

West Frankfort
Williams, Joseph Scott *energy and natural resources company executive, city commissioner*

West Peoria
McBride, Sharon Louise *counselor, technical communication educator*

Westchester
Anderson, Carol Lee *communications executive*
Brushwyler, Lawrence Ronald *minister*
Clarke, Richard Lewis *health science association administrator*
Crois, John Henry *local government official*
James, Joni *singer*
Kinney, Thomas J. *adult education educator*
Masterson, John Patrick *retired English language educator*
Pavelka, Elaine Blanche *mathematics educator*
Tutins, Antons *electrical and audio engineer*

Western Springs
Carroll, Aileen *retired librarian*
Carroll, Jeanne *public relations executive*
Frommelt, Jeffrey James *management consulting firm executive*
Hanson, Heidi Elizabeth *lawyer*
Rhoads, Paul Kelly *lawyer*
Tiefenthal, Marguerite Aurand *school social worker*

Westmont
Bajek, Frank Michael *career officer, retired, financial consultant*
Bellock, Patricia Rigney *state legislator*
†Kuhn, Robert Mitchell *rubber company executive*

Westville
Hammer, John Henry, II *hospital administrator*

Wheaton
†Abbott, Lenice C. *education educator, administrator*
Algeo, John Thomas *retired educator, association executive*
†Arasimowicz, George Zbigniew *composer, university dean*
Back, Robert Wyatt *investment executive, pharmaceutical company executive consultant*
Boudreau, Beverly Ann *health care professional*
Breckenfelder, Lynn E. *health and physical education educator*
Butt, Edward Thomas, Jr. *lawyer*
†Christensen, John Gary *urologic surgeon*
Estep, John Hayes *religious denomination executive, clergyman*
Fawell, Beverly Jean *state legislator*
†French, Talmadge L. *clergyman, educator*
Gill, Kenneth Duane *minister, missiologist*
Gow, Olivia Greco *public official, former English language educator*
Hamilton, Robert Appleby, Jr. *insurance company executive*
Harris, E(leanor) Lynn(e) *religious studies and literature educator*
Hollingsworth, Pierce *publishing executive*
Holman, James Lewis *financial and management consultant*
Koenigsmark, Joyce Elyn Sladek *geriatrics nurse*
Leston, Patrick John *judge*
Lowrie, Pamela Burt *educator, artist*
May, Frank Brendan, Jr. *lawyer*
O'Reilly, Roger Kevin *lawyer*
Pappas, Barbara Estelle *Biblical studies educator, author*
Pun, Pattle Pak Toe *microbiologist, educator*
Reszka, Alfons *computer systems architect*
Spedale, Vincent John *manufacturing executive*
Stein, Lawrence A. *lawyer*
Taylor, Mark Douglas *publishing executive*
Thompson, Bert Allen *retired librarian*
Tinder, Donald George *theology educator, lecturer*
Vest, R. Lamar *church administrator*
Williams, Susan DeVore *writer*
Wolfram, Thomas *physicist*

Wheeling
Ebeling, Arthur William *mechanical engineer*
Hammer, Donald Price *librarian*
Hestad, Bjorn Mark *metal distributing company executive*
†Johnson, Jeffrey Carl *elementary education educator*
Keats, Glenn Arthur *manufacturing company executive*
Klumpp, Stephen Paul *architect*
Kuennen, Thomas Gerard *journalist*
Long, Sarah Ann *librarian*
Mc Clarren, Robert Royce *librarian*
†Meehan, Tamiye Marcia *library director*
Ochsner, Othon Henry, II *importer, restaurant critic*
Raney, David Elliot *computer professional*
Tash, Suzan Sclove *child care center executive*

Willowbrook
†McCormack, Emily Anna *writer*
Walton, Stanley Anthony, III *lawyer*

Wilmette
Albright, Townsend Shaul *investment banker, government benefits consultant*
Barnett, Ralph Lipsey *engineering educator*
Barth, David Keck *industrial distribution industry consultant*
Blair, Virginia Ann *public relations executive*
Bowman, George Arthur, Jr. *judge*
Brill, Marlene Targ *writer*
Brink, Marion Francis *trade association administrator*
Bro, Kenneth Arthur *plastic manufacturing company executive*
Chiaro, A. William *management consultant*
Egloff, Fred Robert *manufacturers representative, writer, historian*
Eigel, Christopher John *real estate executive*
Ellis, Helene Rita *social worker*
Espenshade, Edward Bowman, Jr. *geographer, educator*
Frick, Robert Hathaway *lawyer*
Fries, Robert Francis *historian, educator*
Hansen, Andrew Marius *retired library association executive*
Hufnagel, Henry Bernhardt *financial advisor*
Klein, Robert Edward *publishing company executive, educator*
Lieberman, Eugene *lawyer*
Markus, Robert Michael *journalist, retired*
McCabe, Thomas James *civil engineer*
Mc Nitt, Willard Charles *business executive*
Merrier, Helen *actress, writer*
Miller, Frederick Staten *retired music educator, academic administrator*
Muhlenbruch, Carl W. *civil engineer*
Pearlman, Jerry Kent *electronics company executive*
Rhoad, Richard Arthur *secondary school educator, writer*
Rocek, Jan *chemist, educator*
Ryan, Mike *investment management consultant*
Schloss, Nathan *economist*
Simon, Thelma Brook *lawyer, educator*
Smutny, Joan Franklin *academic director, educator*
Snyder, Mary-Jane Ryan *communications executive*
Stockman, Robert Harold *religious organization administrator, educator*
Williams, Emory *former retail company executive, banker*

Winfield
McNutt, Kristen Wallwork *consumer affairs executive*

Winnetka
Abell, David Robert *lawyer*
Andersen, Kenneth Benjamin *retired association executive*
Barnard, Morton John *lawyer*
†Baule, Steven Michael *secondary education educator, author*
Bundy, Blakely Fetridge *early childhood educator, advocate*
Carrow, Leon Albert *physician*
Crowe, Robert William *lawyer, mediator*
Davis, Britton Anthony *retired lawyer*
Earle, David Prince, Jr. *physician, educator*
Fink, Eloise Bradley *educator, writer, editor*
Fraenkel, Stephen Joseph *engineering and research executive*
Gavin, James John, Jr. *diversified company executive*
Greenblatt, Ray Harris *lawyer*
Hartman, Robert S. *retired paper company executive*
Hausfeld, James Frank *executive director*
Huff, Stanley Eugene *dermatologist*

Huggins, Charlotte Susan Harrison *secondary school educator, author, travel speciali*
Kennedy, George Danner *chemical company executive*
Martin, Patrick Albert *investment adviser*
Mathers, Thomas Nesbit *financial consultant*
McCrea, Philip James *secondary school and college science educator*
Menke, Allen Carl *industrial corporation executive*
Nell, Janine Marie *metallurgical and materials engineer*
Owens, Luvie Moore *association consultant*
Person, Paula (Mrs. P. Barry Person) *social skills organization executive, entrepreneur*
Piper, Robert Johnston *architect, urban planner*
Plowden, David *photographer*
Puth, John Wells *consulting company executive*
Rossi, Ennio C. *physician, educator*
Schwartz, Daniel Joel *educational administrator*
Sick, William Norman, Jr. *investment company executive*

Winthrop Harbor
Getz, James Edward *legal association administrator*

Wonder Lake
McNamara, Joseph Burk *lawyer, corporate executive*

Wood Dale
Sorensen, Jimmy Louis *management consultant*

Wood River
Boger, Gena Cecile *school psychologist*
Copeland, Benny James *transportation agent*
Cox, Mary Linda *maintenance industry executive*
Stevens, Robert Edward *engineering company executive*

Woodridge
Conti, Lee Ann *lawyer*
Hedge, Jeanne Colleen *computer programmer*
Huffman, Sarilee Shesol *elementary school educator*
Stall, Alan David *packaging company executive*
Zucchero, Rocco *communications specialist*

Woodstock
Totz, Sue Rosene *secondary school educator*

Worth
Ammeraal, Robert Neal *biochemist*

Zion
†Gardner, Adrienne Moore *public relations specialist*
Hettich, Paul Joseph *theatre designer, technician, military officer*

INDIANA

Albany
Patrick, Alan K. *artist*

Albion
Hodson, Roy Goode, Jr. *retired logistician*

Alexandria
Irwin, Gerald Port *physician*

Anderson
Carrell, Terry Eugene *manufacturing company executive*
Case, Hank *wine importer, retired art educator, photographer*
Conrad, Harold August *retired religious pension board executive*
Cox, Archibald, Jr. *investment banker*
Grubbs, J. Perry *church administrator*
King, Charles Ross *physician*
Kufeldt, George *biblical educator*
Lambert, Lloyd Laverne *minister*
Leak, Arthur James *registrar*
Lyon, James Donald *minister*
Neidert, David Lynn *administrator*
Nicholson, Robert Arthur *college president*
Nuwer, Henry Joseph (Hank Nuwer) *journalist, educator*
Olson, Carol Lea *lithographer, educator, photographer*
Pleninger, Susan Elaine *women's health and pediatrics nurse*
Shank, Cheryl Lynn *university administrator*
Stohler, Michael Joe *dentist*
Whitaker, Audie Dale *hospital laboratory medical technologist*
Woodruff, Randall Lee *lawyer*

Angola
Bevington, Cindy *reporter*
†Dobbert, Duane Lloyd *forensic psychologist, educator, consultant*
Reynolds, R. John *acadmemic administrator*
Young, James E. *business executive, engineer*

Arcadia
Travison, John A. *English educator*

Attica
Harrison, Joseph William *state senator*

Auburn
Adair, Leslie Gayle *marketing professional*
Mountz, Louise Carson Smith *retired librarian*
Workman, Kenneth D. *school system administrator*

Avon
Shartle, Stanley Musgrave *consulting engineer, land surveyor*

Batesville
St. Pierre, William Edward *regional director*
Volk, Cecilia Ann *elementary education educator*

Beech Grove
Brown, Richard Lawrence *lawyer*
Clapper, George Raymond *retired accountant, computer consultant*

Bicknell
Risley, Gregory Byron *furniture company executive, interior designer*

Bloomington
Aman, Alfred Charles, Jr. *dean*
Anderson, Judith Helena *English language educator*
Arnove, Robert Frederick *education educator*
Bardzell, Jeffrey Scott *graphics designer*
Barnes, A. James *academic dean*
Barnstone, Willis (Robert Barnstone) *language literature educator, poet, scholar*
Belth, Joseph Morton *retired business educator*
Bent, Robert Demo *physicist, educator*
Bernhardt-Kabisch, Ernest Karl-Heinz *English and comparative literature educator*
Bishop, Michael D. *emergency physician*
Blankenfeld, Beverly (B. J. Blankenfeld) *real estate professional*
Boyd, Rozelle *university administrator, educator*
Braden, Samuel Edward *economics educator*
Brand, Myles *academic administrator*
†Brottman, Mikita *humanities educator, writer*
Browar, Lisa Muriel *librarian*
Brown, Keith *musician, educator*
Brown, Trevor *dean*
Buelow, George John *musicologist, educator*
Bundy, Wayne M. *retired geologist, consultant*
Burton, Philip Ward *advertising executive, educator*
Calinescu, Adriana Gabriela *museum curator, art historian*
Calinescu, Matei Alexe *literature educator*
Cameron, John M. *nuclear scientist, educator, science administrator*
Carroll, David Lee *museum administrator*
Chisholm, Malcolm Harold *chemistry educator*
†Choksy, Jamsheed *religious studies educator*
Choksy, Jamsheed Kairshasp *historian, religious scholar, language professional, humanities educator*
Clevenger, Sarah *botanist, computer consultant*
Cohen, William Benjamin *historian, educator*
Cole, Bruce Milan *art historian*
Collins, Dorothy Craig *retired educational administrator*
Conrad, Geoffrey Wentworth *archaeologist, educator*
Conway, Dennis *geography educator*
Counsilman, James Edward *physical education educator*
Crane, David Goodrich *psychiatrist, attorney, educator*
Crowe, James Wilson *university administrator, educator*
†Dalton, Dan R. *college dean*
Datcu, Ioana *visual artist*
Davidson, Ernest Roy *chemist, educator*
Davis, Charles Hargis *information scientist, educator*
Dawson, James Richard *fire and safety engineer*
Day, Harry Gilbert *nutritional biochemist, consultant*
DeHayes, Daniel Wesley *management executive, educator*
Dilts, Jon Paul *law educator*
Dinsmoor, James Arthur *psychology educator*
Dunn, Jon Michael *philosophy educator*
Edgerton, William B. *foreign language educator*
Edmondson, Frank Kelley *astronomer*
Engs, Ruth Clifford *health educator*
Estes, William Kaye *psychologist, educator*
Ferrell, Robert Hugh *historian, educator*
Frederick, Robert Allen *history educator*
Gealt, Adelheid Maria *museum director*
Gest, Howard *microbiologist, educator*
Glenn, G(eorge) Dale *principal*
Goodman, Charles David *physicist, educator*
Gordon, Paul John *management educator*
Gough, Pauline Bjerke *magazine editor*
Gros Louis, Kenneth Richard Russell *university chancellor*
Guth, Sherman Leon (S. Lee Guth) *psychologist, educator*
Haeberle, William Leroy *corporate director, business educator, entrepreneur*
Hammel, Harold Theodore *physiology and biophysics educator, researcher*
Hanson, Karen *philosopher, educator*
Harder, John E. *electrical engineer*
Hattin, Donald Edward *geologist, educator*
Hegeman, George Downing *microbiology educator*
Heiser, Charles Bixler, Jr. *botany educator*
Hendry, Archibald Wagstaff *physics educator*
Henson, Jane Elizabeth *information management professional, adult educati*
Hicks, Marilyn Sue *lay worker*
Hites, Ronald Atlee *environmental science educator, chemist*
Hopkins, Jack Walker *former university administrator, environmental educator*
Hustad, Thomas Pegg *marketing educator*
Jacobi, Peter Paul *journalism educator, author*
Johnson, Hollis Ralph *astronomy educator*
Johnson, Owen Verne *program director*
Johnson, Sidney Malcolm *foreign language educator*
Juergens, George Ivar *history educator*
Karkut, Richard Theodore *clinical psychologist*
Kibbey, Hal Stephen *science writer*
Klotman, Robert Howard *music educator*
Knight, Bob *college basketball coach*
Knudsen, Laura Georgia *linguist*
Kohr, Roland Ellsworth *retired hospital administrator*
Kravchuk, Robert Sacha *management educator, financial consultant*
Legler, April Arington *librarian, educator*
Long, John D. *retired insurance educator*
Lowe, Marvin *artist*
Macfarlane, Malcolm Harris *physics educator*
†Mack, P.A., Jr. *manager health network, state commissioner*
Mac Watters, Virginia Elizabeth *singer, music educator, actress*
Martin, Fenton Strickland *librarian, writer*
Martins, Heitor Miranda *foreign language educator*
Mathiesen, Thomas James *musicology educator*
Mc Clung, Leland Swint *microbiologist, educator*
McCluskey, John Asberry, Jr. *literature educator, writer*
Mehlinger, Howard Dean *education educator*
Mickel, Emanuel John *foreign language educator*
†Miller, Alyce *fiction writer, educator*
Mitchell, Bert Breon *literary translator*
Mobley, Tony Allen *university dean, recreation educator*
Moore, Ward Wilfred *medical educator*
Moran, Emilio Federico *anthropology and ecology educator*
Nelms, Charlie *academic administrator*
Nolan, Val, Jr. *biologist, lawyer*
O'Hearn, Robert Raymond *stage designer*
Ostrom, Vincent A(lfred) *political science educator*
Otteson, Schuyler Franklin *former university dean, educator*
Pagels, Jürgen Heinrich *balletmaster, dance educator, dancer, choreographer, author*
Palmer, Judith Grace *university administrator*
Parmenter, Charles Stedman *chemistry educator*
Patrick, John Joseph *social sciences educator*
Patterson, James Milton *marketing specialist, educator*
Peebles, Christopher Spalding *anthropologist, dean, academic administrator*
Peters, Dennis Gail *chemist*
Pfingston, Roger Carl *writer photographer, retired educator*
Phillips, Harvey *musician, soloist, music educator, arts consultant*
Pletcher, David Mitchell *history educator*
Pollock, Robert Elwood *nuclear physicist*
Preer, John Randolph, Jr. *biology educator*
Prosser, Franklin Pierce *computer scientist*
Purdom, Paul Walton, Jr. *computer scientist*
Puri, Madan Lal *mathematics educator*
Putnam, Frank William *biochemistry and immunology educator*
Rebec, George Vincent *neuroscience researcher, educator, administrator*
Rieselbach, Helen Funk *English educator*
Rink, Lawrence Donald *cardiologist*
Risinger, C. Frederick *social studies educator*
†Rodwin, Marc Andre *law educator*
Rosenberg, Samuel Nathan *French and Italian language educator*
Rousseau, Eugene Ellsworth *musician, music educator, consultant*
Rudolph, Lavere Christian *library director*
Ruesink, Albert William *biologist, plant sciences educator*
Ryan, John William *academic administrator*
Sanders, Steve *university official, political science educator*
Saunders, W(arren) Phillip, Jr. *economics educator, consultant, author*
Schaich, William L. *physics educator*
Schroeder, Judith Lois *editor, communications executive*
Schurz, Scott Clark *journalist, publisher*
Sears, Everett Maurice *personnel executive*
Sebeok, Thomas Albert *linguistics educator*
Shiffrin, Richard M. *psychologist, educator*
Shreve, Gene Russell *law educator*
Sinor, Denis *Orientalist, educator*
Smith, Carl Bernard *education educator*
Smith, Frederick Robert, Jr. *social studies educator*
Stirratt, Betsy *artist, gallery director*
Stolnitz, George Joseph *economist, educator, demographer*
Strickholm, Peter William *composer, environmentalist*
Stryker, Sheldon *sociologist, educator*
Sullivan, Michael Francis, III *executive*
Svetlova, Marina *ballerina, choreographer, educator*
†Timberlake, William David *psychology educator*
Torabi, Mohammad R. *health education educator*
Vincent, Jeffrey Robert *labor studies educator*
†Volkova, Bronislava *poet, scholar*
von Furstenberg, George Michael *economics educator, researcher*
Vontz, Thomas Scott *education educator*
Weaver, David Hugh *journalism educator, communications researcher*
Webb, Charles Haizlip, Jr. *retired university dean*
Weinberg, Eugene David *microbiologist, educator*
Wentworth, Jack Roberts *business educator, consultant*
Wilhoit, G. Cleveland *journalism educator*
Williams, Camilla *soprano, voice educator*
Williams, Edgar Gene *university administrator*
Wilson, Kathy Kay *foundation executive*
Wittlich, Gary Eugene *music theory educator*
†Yang, Seong-Deog *educator*

Bluffton
Brockmann, William Frank *medical facility administrator*
Elliott, Barbara Jean *librarian*
Lawson, William Hogan, III *electrical motor manufacturing executive*
Pitts, Neal Chase *rheumatologist*

Boonville
Campbell, Edward Adolph *judge, electrical engineer*

Brazil
Jones, Carole Moody-Anderson *retired outreach representative*

Brooklyn
Roach, Eleanor Marie *elementary education educator*

Brookville
†Ariens, Karla Rae *library director*

Brownsburg
Diasio, Richard Leonard *power transmission executive, sports facility executive*
Riggs, Anna Claire *metals company executive*
Weddell, Linda Anne *speech and language pathologist*

Brownstown
Robertson, Joseph Edmond *grain processing company executive*

Butler
Longardner, Craig Theodor *manufacturing executive*

Cambridge City
Slonaker, Mary Joanna King *columnist*

Carmel
Eden, Barbara Janiece *commercial and residential interior designer*
Gehring, Perry James *toxicologist, chemical company executive*
Goldberg, John Robert *information specialist, historian, advocate*
Hammond, Isaac William *physician, epidemiologist*
Hayashi, Tetsumaro *English and American literature educator, author*
Hilbert, Stephen C. *insurance company executive*
Kalwara, Joseph John *engineer*
Mahoney, Margaret Ellis *executive assistant*
Malik, Muhammad Iqbal *retired pathologist*
McCool, Richard Bunch *real estate developer*
Mc Laughlin, Harry Roll *architect*
Ong, James Shaujen *mechanical engineer*
Risdon, Michael Paul *manufacturing executive*
Sabl, John J. *lawyer*
Shoup, Charles Samuel, Jr. *chemicals and materials executive*
Stein, Richard Paul *lawyer*
Swartz, Paul Frederick *clergyman*
Walsh, John Charles *metallurgical company executive*
Watson, Ian Allen *chemist*

Cedar Lake
Loudermilk, Mary Ruth *local government volunteer*

Charlestown
†Bowen, Donna Darlyn *educator*
Fellows, Marilyn Kinder *elementary education educator*
Schmidt, Jakob Edward *medical and meaicolegal lexicographer, physician, author, inventor*

Chesterfield
Fry, Meredith Warren *civil engineer, consultant*

Chesterton
Brown, Gene W. *steel company executive*
†Calengas, Leonardo *writer*
Crewe, Albert Victor *physicist, artist, business executive*
Martino, Robert Salvatore *orthopedic surgeon*
Nelson, Paul James *educator*
Petrakis, Harry Mark *author*

Churubusco
Morgan, Gretna Faye *retired automotive executive*

Clinton
Keown, William Arvel *minister, educator*
Shew, Rose Jean *nurse*

Columbia City
Behrens, Diane R. *nursing educator*

Columbus
Abts, Henry William *banker*
Arthur, Jewell Kathleen *dental hygienist*
Berman, Lewis Paul *financial executive*
Boll, Charles Raymond *engine company executive*
Carter, Pamela Lynn *former state attorney general*
DeLorenzo, David W. J. *human resources manager, health consultant*
Fadarishan, Stephen Robert *systems engineer*
Fairchild, Raymond Francis *lawyer*
Flynn, Patrick Francis *engineering executive*
Garton, Robert Dean *state senator*
Hackett, John Thomas *economist*
Harrison, Patrick Woods *lawyer*
Henderson, James Alan *engine company executive*
Hollansky, Bert Voyta *stock brokerage executive*
Kirkpatrick, Robert Hugh *communications executive*
Miller, Joseph Irwin *automotive manufacturing company executive*
Nash, John Arthur *bank executive*
Spector, Judith Ann *English educator*
Tucker, Thomas Randall *public relations executive*

Connersville
Bischoff, Lawrence Joseph *farmer*
Herald, Sandra Jean *elementary education educator*
Kuntz, William Henry *lawyer, mediator*
Stanton, William Taylor *manufacturing engineer*

Corydon
Speth, Camille *engineer*

Crane
Waggoner, Susan Marie *electronics engineer*

Crawfordsville
Barnes, James John *history educator*
Boland, Joseph Anthony *state official*
Everett, Cheryl Ann *music educator, pianist*
Ford, Andrew Thomas *academic administrator*
Pribbenow, Paul P. *higher education administrator, consultant*
Servies, Richard L. *secondary education educator*
Simmons, Emory G. *mycologist*
Spurgeon, Nannette SuAnn (Susie Spurgeon) *special education educator*

Crown Point
Jones, Walter Dean *community program director*
Palmeri, Sharon Elizabeth *freelance writer, community educator*
Randazzo, Rebecca Ann *nursing administrator*
Retort, Valerie Carmel *public relations executive, educator*
Scheub, Richard Herman *photographer*

Culver
Manuel, Ralph Nixon *private school executive*

Dana
Bray, Rick *curator*

Danville
Baldwin, Jeffrey Kenton *lawyer, educator*

Dayton
Bomgarden, Stanley Ralph *minister*

DePauw
Baggett, Alice Diane *critical care nurse*

Dyer
DeGuilio, Jon E. *lawyer*

East Chicago
Platis, James George *secondary school educator*
Platis, Mary Lou *media specialist*
Psaltis, Helen *medical and surgical nurse*

Elkhart
Bryan, Norman E. *dentist*
Burns, B(illye) Jane *museum director*
Chism, James Arthur *information systems executive, business consultant*
Corson, Thomas Harold *manufacturing company executive*
Decio, Arthur Julius *manufacturing company executive*

Drexler, Rudy Matthew, Jr. *professional law enforcement dog trainer*
Free, Helen Mae *chemist, consultant*
Gassere, Eugene Arthur *lawyer, business executive*
Groom, Gary Lee *recreational vehicle manufacturing executive*
Harman, John Royden *lawyer*
Holtz, Glenn Edward *band instrument manufacturing executive*
Hunsberger, Ruby Moore *electronics manufacturing corporation executive, religious organization representative*
Kloska, Ronald Frank *manufacturing company executive*
Leader, Christopher Robert *manufacturing executive*
Martin, Rex *manufacturing executive*
Mathias, Margaret Grossman *manufacturing company executive, leasing company executive*
Mischke, Frederick Charles *manufacturing company executive*
Rand, Phillip Gordon *chemist*
Schreiber, David Raymond *reporter*
Shackle, Karen Ann *non-profit association executive*
Treckelo, Richard M. *lawyer*

Ellettsville
Matson, Donald Keith *genealogist*

Evansville
Able, Warren Walter *natural resource company executive, physician*
Alexander, Mary L. *historic site adminstrator*
Baugh, Jerry Phelps *lawyer*
Bennett, Kathi *women's basketball coach*
Bennett, Paul Edmond *engineering educator*
Berger, Charles Lee *lawyer*
Blandford, Dick *electrical engineering and communications educator*
Blesch, K(athy) Suzann *small business owner*
†Blevins, James Richard *English educator, academic administrator*
Brenner, Raymond Anthony *priest*
Brill, Alan Richard *entrepreneur*
Brown, William Fredrick *art educator*
Capshaw, Tommie Dean *judge*
Clouse, John Daniel *lawyer*
Cox, Vande Lee *critical care nurse*
Craig, Martha Ann *retail store owner*
Denner, Melvin Walter *retired life sciences educator*
Early, Judith K. *social services director*
Faw, Melvin Lee *retired physician*
Flowers, Glen Dale *minister*
Francis, Lorna Jean *nutritionist*
Fritz, Edward Lane *dentist*
Gerhart, Philip Mark *engineering educator*
Gettelfinger, Gerald Andrew *bishop*
Halterman, Martha Lee *social services administrator, counselor*
Hampel, Robert Edward *advertising executive*
Hoy, George Philip *clergyman, food bank executive*
Huff, Sheila Lindsey *secondary education educator, coach*
Humphrey, Lois M. *English educator*
†Hussmann, William G., Jr. *federal judge*
Jerrel, Bettye Lou *science educator*
Kiechlin, Robert Jerome *retired coal company executive, financial consultant*
Kitch, Frederick David *advertising executive*
Knight, Jeffrey Lin *lawyer, corporation executive*
Knott, John Robert *mathematics educator*
Koch, Robert Louis, II *manufacturing company executive, mechanical engineer*
Liberty, Arthur Andrew *judge*
Luckett, John Mills, III *construction company financial executive*
Mathews, Walter Garret *columnist*
Matthews, C(harles) David *real estate appraiser, consultant*
McCutchan, William Mark *banker*
McGuire, Brian Lyle *educator, health science facility consultant*
Muehlbauer, James Herman *manufacturing executive*
Penkava, Robert Ray *radiologist, educator*
Perkins, R. Wayne *philosophy, religion educator*
Ragsdale, Rex H. *health facility administrator, physician*
Raibley, Parvin Rudolph *dentist*
Roth, Carolyn Louise *art educator*
Rusche, Herman Frederick *gastroenterologist*
Ryder, Thomas Michael *newspaper editor*
Savia, Alfred *conductor*
†Schultz, John Edward *principal*
Streetman, John William, III *museum official*
Tilley, Sheryl J. (Sherry Tilley) *nonprofit organization executive*
Vinson, James Spangler *academic administrator*
Wallace, Keith M. *lawyer*
Williams, Jean Marie *religious organization administrator*
Wilson, Gregory Scott *kinesiology educator, coach*
Zion, Roger Herschel *consulting firm executive, former congressman*

Fairmount
Boswell, Larry Ray *electronics company executive*
Cowling, Judy Kathleen *historic preservation consultant, nurse*

Ferdinand
Bilskie, Kathy *religious order administrator, nun*

Fishers
Boegel, Nick Norbert *accountant, lawyer*
Chojnacki, Paul Ervin *pharmacist, pharmaceutical company official*
Gatto, Louis Constantine *educational authority executive*
Ruzbasan, Anthony *distribution executive*

Floyds Knobs
Vernia-Amend, Leah Nadine *counselor*

Fort Wayne
Aikman, Carol Chidester *education educator*
Anderson, Jim *zoo director*
Andorfer, Donald Joseph *university president*
Archer-Sorg, Karen S. *association coordinator*
Auburn, Mark Stuart *educator, administrator*
Baker, Carl Leroy *lawyer*
Balthaser, Linda Irene *academic administrator*
†Beckner, Walton Thomas (Tom) *adult education educator, academic administrator*
Beineke, Lowell Wayne *mathematics educator*
Bock-Tobolski, Marilyn Rose *artist, art educator*
Bunkowske, Eugene Walter *religious studies educator*
Burns, Thagrus Asher *manufacturing company executive, former life insurance company executive*
Carter, George Edward *education educator*
Cast, Anita Hursh *small business owner*
Chapman, Paula Anne *cultural organization administrator*
Clarke, Kenneth Stevens *insurance company executive*
Clay, Juanita Loundmon *mental health consultant*
Cole, Kenneth Duane *architect*
Collins, Linda Lou Powell *manager of contracts*
†Cooper, William Edgar *animal behaviorist, educator*
†Cosbey, Roger B. *federal judge*
Cox, David Jackson *biochemistry educator*
Cummings, William Robert, Jr. *business executive*
Curtis, Douglas Homer *small business owner*
Cutshall-Hayes, Diane Marion *elementary education educator*
D'Arcy, John Michael *bishop*
Detwiler, Susan Margaret *information brokerage executive*
Donesa, Antonio Braganza *neurosurgeon*
Dunsire, P(eter) Kenneth *insurance company executive*
Essig, Erhardt Herbert *English educator*
Fairchild, David Lawrence *philosophy educator*
Fink, Thomas Michael *lawyer*
Fleck, John R. *lawyer*
Flynn, Pauline T. *speech pathologist, educator*
†Fox, Linda Chodosh *Spanish educator*
Franklin, Al *artistic director*
†Frost, Helen Marie *writer*
Gaff, Alan Dale *writer*
Gehring, Ronald Kent *lawyer*
Goeglein, Gloria J. *state legislator*
Graf, Robert Arlan *retired financial services executive*
†Grant, Robert E. *federal judge*
Gretencord, David C. *tax consultant*
Grogg, Terrie Lynn *factory assembler*
Gutreuter, Jill Stallings *financial consultant, financial planner*
Hamrick, Linda L. *educator*
Helmke, (Walter) Paul *mayor, lawyer*
Hickey, Dixie Marie *school system administrator*
Hirschy, Gordon Harold *real estate agent, auctioneer*
†Inskeep, Richard Glenn *publishing executive*
Jarosh, Andrew T. *journalist*
Joffe, Benjamin *mechanical engineer*
†Jordan, Pamela Lee *educator*
Keefer, J(ames) Michael *lawyer*
Kennedy, Elizabeth *health facility administrator*
Kirkwood, Maurice Richard *banker*
Kline, Joel D. *pastor*
Klugman, Stephan Craig *newspaper editor*
Krull, Jeffrey Robert *library director*
Lair, Helen May *poet*
Latz, G. Irving, II *manufacturing company executive*
Lee, Shuishih Sage *pathologist*
Lee, Timothy Earl *international agency executive, paralegal*
Lee, William Charles *judge*
Lewark, Carol Ann *special education educator*
Lockwood, Robert Philip *publishing executive*
†Lucenta, Dominic A. *human resources executive*
Lyons, Jerry Lee *mechanical engineer*
Mann, David William *minister*
Marine, Clyde Lockwood *agricultural business consultant*
Mather, George Ross *clergy member*
Molfenter, David P. *electronics executive*
Moran, John *religious organization administrator*
Pease, Ella Louise *elementary education educator*
Pellegrene, Thomas James, Jr. *editor, researcher*
†Ramsey, Yvonne Akers *English language educator*
Rifkin, Leonard *metals company executive*
Robertson, Richard Stuart *insurance holding company executive*
Rolland, Ian McKenzie *insurance executive, retired*
Sandeson, William Seymour *cartoonist*
Scheetz, Sister Mary JoEllen *English language educator*
Schweickart, Jim *advertising executive, broadcast consultant*
Shaffer, Paul E. *retired banker*
Sims, Debbie Deann *psychotherapist*
Sipe, Roger Wayne *accountant, consultant*
†Skufca, Sherry Lee *newspaper editor*
Smith, Stephen Ralph *health facility administrator*
Stebbins, Vrina Grimes *retired elementary school educator, counselor*
Steiner, Paul Andrew *retired insurance executive*
Stevenson, Kenneth Lee *chemist, educator*
Taritas, Karen Joyce *telemarketing executive*
Tchivzhel, Edvard *music director*
Vachon, Marilyn Ann *retired insurance company executive*
†Wartell, Michael A. *academic administrator*
Waters, Wayne Arthur *conference and travel service agency executive*
Watkinson, Patricia Grieve *museum director*
Weicker, Jack Edward *educational administrator*
West, Thomas Meade *insurance company executive*
Wolf, Don Allen *hardware wholesale executive*

Fortville
Demegret, A. Jean Hughes *secondary education educator, artist*

Frankfort
Borland, Kathryn Kilby *author*
Stonehill, Lloyd Herschel *gas company executive, mechanical engineer*

Franklin
Bender, Larry Wayne *vocational educator*
Grossnickle, Ted Richard *non-profit consulting company executive*
Hamner, Lance Dalton *prosecutor*
Janis, F. Timothy *technology company executive*
Link, E.G. (Jay Link) *corporate executive, family wealth counselor*
Martin, William Bryan *chancellor, lawyer, minister*
Nugent, Helen Jean *history educator*
Taylor, Carla Marie *critical care nurse*

Fremont
Elliott, Carl Hartley *former university president*

Friendship
Miller, John *foundation administrator*

Ft Wayne
Spielman, Kim Morgan *lawyer, educator*

Garrett
Baker, Suzon Lynne *secondary education mathematics educator*

Gary
†Assibey-Mensah, George Ossei *political science educator*
Beamer, Laura *women's health and genetic health nurse*
Bennett, Richard Carl *social worker*
Davis, Venita Paula *elementary school educator*
Hall, James Rayford, III *adult educator*
Hull, Grafton Hazard, Jr. *social work educator*
Iatridis, Panayotis George *medical educator*
Kang, Young Woo *special education educator*
†LaGrand, James, Jr. *minister*
†Lindquist, Kent *federal judge*
Moran, Robert Francis, Jr. *library director*
Rosen, Kay *painter*
Smith, Vernon G. *education educator, state representative*
Stephens, Paul Alfred *dentist*
Szarleta, Ellen Jean *economics educator*
Washington, Wilma Jeanne *business executive*
Zunich, Janice *pediatrician, geneticist, educator, administrator*

Georgetown
Dailey, Donald Harry *adult education educator, volunteer*

Goshen
Chenoweth, Rose Marie *librarian*
Heap, James Clarence *retired mechanical engineer*
Lehman, Karl Franklyn *accountant*
Loomis, Norma Irene *marriage and family therapist*
Meyer, Albert James *educational researcher*
Mishler, John Joseph *sculptor, art educator*
Neterer, Christopher Dean *mural painter, manufacturing company official*
Schrock, Harold Arthur *manufacturing company executive*
Sterling-Hellenbrand, Alexandra Christina *language educator*
Stoltzfus, Victor Ezra *retired university president, academic consultant*
†Weaver, Henry David *retired educational administrator, consultant*

Granger
Engel, Brenda Bolton *controller*
Miller, Callix Edwin *manufacturing executive, consultant*
Skodras, Vicki Herring *banker*

Greencastle
Anderson, John Robert *retired mathematics educator*
Bottoms, Robert Garvin *academic administrator*
Cole, Joanne W. *women's health nurse, researcher*
Dittmer, John Avery *history educator*
Irwin, Stanley Roy *music educator, singer, conductor*
†Martin, Marilyn Mann *librarian*
Rosenberger, James Robert *counselor*
†Shumaker, Arthur Wesley *English educator*
Spicer, Harold Otis *retired English educator, communications educator*
Weiss, Robert Orr *speech educator*

Greenfield
Myerholtz, Ralph W., Jr. *retired chemical company executive, research chemist*
Saunders, James Kevin *principal*

Greensburg
†Porter, Kimberly Michelle *library director*
Ricke, David Louis *agricultural and environmental consultant*
Schilling, Don Russell *electric utility executive*

Greenwood
Calvano, Linda Sue Ley *insurance company executive*
Daniel, Michael Edwin *insurance agency executive*
†Du Bois, William, Jr. *retired public relations professional*
†Egold, Thomas A. *electronics company administrator*
Jacobs, Harvey Collins *newspaper editor, writer*
Saint-Pierre, Michael Robert *funeral director, consultant*
Smith, Donald Archie *retired religion and business executive, consultant*
Van Valer, Joe Ned *lawyer, land developer*

Griffith
Johnson, Mary Susan *transportation company professional*
†Wean, Charles Raymond, Jr. *retired secondary education educator*

Hagerstown
†Jones, Sarah Louise *principal*

Hammond
Ash, Frederick Melvin *manufacturing company executive*
Delph, Donna Jean (Maroc) *education educator, consultant, university administrator*
DeVaney, Cynthia Ann *elementary education educator, real estate broker*
Diamond, Eugene Christopher *lawyer, hospital administrator*
Dywan, Jeffery Joseph *judge*
Habzansky, Andrew Melvin *quality manager, maintenance manager, trainer*
Kadow, Cathi *academic counselor*
Lozano, Rudolpho *federal judge*
Moody, James T(yne) *federal judge*
Pierson, Edward Samuel *engineering educator, consultant*
Rodovich, Andrew Paul *lawyer, federal magistrate*
Ruman, Saul I. *lawyer*
Schroer, Edmund Armin *utility company executive*
†Springham, Theresa L. *federal judge*
Vojcak, Edward Daniel *metallurgist*
Yackel, James William *mathematician, academic administrator*
Yovich, Daniel John *educator*

Hanna
Stephenson, Dorothy Maxine *volunteer*

Hanover
Heck, Richard T. *tree farmer*
†Voris, David Clarence *retired neurosurgeon*

Hartford City
Ford, David Clayton *lawyer, Indiana state senator*

Highland
Forsythe, Randall Newman *paralegal, educator*
Lacera, Jana L. *critical care nurse, administrator*
Murovic, Judith Ann *neurosurgeon*
Purcell, James Francis *former utility executive, consultant*

Hobart
†Brandenburg, Jamie Enrico *elementary education educator*
Harrigan, Richard George *salesperson*
Mason, Earl James, Jr. *pathologist, educator*
McKee, Denise Arlene *neonatal intensive care nurse*
Seeley, Mark *agronomist*

Hope
Golden, Eloise Elizabeth *community health nurse*
Miller, David Kent *nursing administrator*

Howe
Bowerman, Ann Louise *author, genealogist, educator*

Huntington
†Brown, Robert Clark, Jr. *sales executive*
Doermann, Paul Edmund *retired surgeon*
Dowden, G. Blair *academic administrator*
Lahr, Beth M. *college administrator*
Seilhamer, Ray A. *bishop*
Smith, Mary Lou *librarian*

Indianapolis
Abbott, Verlin Leroy *sales executive*
Adkins, Derrick Ralph *Olympic athlete*
Ahlrichs, Nancy Surratt *marketing professional*
Albright, Terrill D. *lawyer*
Aliev, Eldar *artistic director, choreographer, educator*
Allen, David James *lawyer*
Allen, Stephen D(ean) *pathologist, microbiologist*
Altman, Joseph *author, neuroscientist*
Alvarez, Thomas *film/video producer, director, theater director, arts consultant*
Aprison, Morris Herman *biochemist, experimental and theoretical neurobiologist, emeritus educator*
Arburn, Jerry William *farmer, vice president Indiana Farm Bureau*
Aschen, Sharon Ruth *genetic counselor, psychotherapist, nurse*
Aschleman, James Allan *lawyer*
Ashford, Evelyn *former track and field athlete*
Atkins, Clayton H. *family physician, epidemiologist, educator*
Austin, Charles *Olympic athlete*
Badger, David Harry *lawyer*
Baetzhold, Howard George *English language educator*
Baird, John Michael *lawyer, non-profit organization executive*
†Balt, Christine Ann *family nurse practitioner*
Bannister, Geoffrey *university president, geographer*
Barcus, Robert Gene *educational association administrator*
Barker, Orel O'Brien *retired activity and social service director*
Barker, Sarah Evans *judge*
Barnes, Eric Randolph *Olympic athlete*
Bates, Gerald Earl *bishop*
Bates, Michael *Olympic athlete, track and field*
Batten, Jane Kimberly *olympic athlete*
Battle, Joe David *engineer*
Bauer, Dietrich Charles *medical educator*
†Bayt, Robert L. *federal judge*
Beazley, Hamilton Scott *volunteer health organization executive*
Beckwith, Lewis Daniel *lawyer*
Beeler, Virgil L. *lawyer*
Behner, Elton Dale *dentist*
Bennett, Cornelius *professional football player*
Bepko, Gerald Lewis *university administrator, law educator, lecturer, consultant, lawyer*
Bergstein, Jerry Michael *pediatric nephrology*
Be Sant, Craig *company executive*
Besch, Henry Roland, Jr. *pharmacologist, educator*
Beuter, Richard William *accountant*
Beyer, Werner William *retired English educator*
Biller, Jose *neurologist*
Bindley, William Edward *pharmaceutical executive*
Bird, Larry Joe *professional basketball coach, former professional basketball player*
Birky, Nathan Dale *publishing company executive*
Black, Elwood C. *councilman*
Blaydes, June Louise *volunteer*
Boggs, Christopher B. *accountant, auditor*
Boggs, John Steven *sales and development executive*
Boldt, Michael Herbert *lawyer*
Bolin, Daniel Paul *music educator*
Bonaventura, Leo Mark *gynecologist, educator*
Boner, Donald Leslie *information systems executive*
Borden, Amanda *gymnast, Olympic athlete*
Borman, Laurie D. *magazine editor-in-chief*
Born, Samuel Roydon, II *lawyer*
Borns, Robert Aaron *real estate developer*
Borst, Philip Craig *veterinarian, councilman*
Braddom, Randall L. *physician, medical educator*
Bradford, James *city official*
Brady, Mary Sue *nutrition and dietetics educator*
Braham, Delphine Doris *government accountant*
Brandt, Ira Kive *pediatrician, medical geneticist*
Brannon, Ronald Roy *minister*
Brannon-Peppas, Lisa *chemical engineer, researcher*
Braunstein, Ethan Malcolm *skeletal radiologist, paleopathologist, educator*
Bray, Donald Lawrence *religious organization executive, minister*
Brents, Maggie M. *city official*
Brickley, Richard Agar *retired surgeon*
Broadie, Thomas Allen *surgeon, educator*
†Brown, Daniel Stewart, Jr. *communications educator, university official*
Brown, Edwin Wilson, Jr. *physician, educator*
Brown, Freezell, Jr. *private school educator*
Broxmeyer, Hal Edward *medical educator*
Bryant, Maxine L(eona) *training consultant, entrepreneur*
Budniakiewicz, Therese *author*
Buechlein, Daniel Mark *archbishop*
Buford-Bailey, Tonja Yevette *track and field Olympic athlete*

Buhner, Byron Bevis health science facility administrator
Bulloff, Jack John physical chemist, consultant
Bundy, David Dale librarian, educator
Burkhart, John manufacturing company executive
Burr, David Bentley anatomy educator
Burrell, Leroy Russel track and field athlete
Buttrey, Donald Wayne lawyer
†Buzzetti, Lori Ebbers obstetrician and gynecologist
Caldwell, Howard Clay retired broadcast journalist, writer
Caldwell, John William pastor
Campbell, Judith Lowe child psychiatrist
Capehart, Craig Earl lawyer
Caperton, Albert Franklin newspaper editor
†Capone, Vince health system administrator
Caraher, Michael Edward systems analyst
Carlino, Guy Thomas construction executive
Carlock, Mahlon Waldo financial consultant, former high school administrator
Carney, Joseph Buckingham lawyer
Carr, William H(enry) A. public relations executive, author
†Carraway, Melvin J. protective services official
Carter, Jared poet
Castle, Howard Blaine religious organization administrator
Chase, Alyssa Ann editor
Chernish, Stanley Michael physician
Choplin, John M., II lawyer
Chow, Amy gymnast, Olympic athlete
Christen, Arden Gale dental educator, researcher, consultant
Christenson, Le Roy Howard insurance company officer
Christian, Joe Clark medical genetics researcher, educator
Chuang, Tsu-Yi dermatologist, epidemiologist, educator
Clark, Charles M., Jr. research institution adminstrator
Clary, Keith Uhl retired industrial relations executive
Cleary, Robert Emmet gynecologist, infertility specialist
Cliff, Johnnie Marie mathematics and chemistry educator
Coffey, Charles Moore communication research professional, writer
Cohen, Edward state official
Cohen, Gabriel Murrel editor, publisher
Collins, James Duffield marine engineer, editor
Comiskey, Nancy newspaper editor
Conley, Michael Alexander track and field athlete
Conour, William Frederick lawyer
Conway, Hollis track and field athletie, Olympic athlete
Cramer, Betty F. life insurance company executive
Crow, Paul Abernathy, Jr. clergyman, religious council executive, educator
Cunningham, Karen Lee marketing professional
Daily, Fay Kenoyer retired botany educator
Daly, Walter Joseph physician, educator
Damin, David E. technology integration company executive
Davis, Edgar Glenn science and health policy executive
Davis, Kenneth Wayne English language educator, business communication consultant
†Dawes, Dominique gymnast, Olympic athlete
Decker Slaney, Mary Teresa Olympic athlete
Dedert, Steven Ray marketing professional, consultant
Deer, Richard Elliott lawyer
Dere, Willard Honglen internist, educator
Dickeson, Robert Celmer retired university president, foundation executive, political science educator
Dickinson, Richard Donald Nye clergyman, educator, theological seminary administrator
Dickson, Brent E(llis) state supreme court justice
†Diehm, Jamie Renee company official
Dietz, William Ronald financial services executive
Dillin, S. Hugh federal judge
Dillon, Francis Xavier anesthesiologist
Dillon, Howard Burton civil engineer
Dimas, Trent Olympic athlete, gymnast
Dollens, Ronald W. pharmaceuticals company executive
Dorocke, Lawrence Francis lawyer
Dortch, Carl Raymond former association executive
Dowden, William councilman
Downs, Thomas K. lawyer
Due, Danford Royce lawyer
†Duncan, Dale A. publishing executive
Durbin, Robert Cain retired hotel executive
Dutton, Clarence Benjamin lawyer
Dutton, Stephen James lawyer
Dykstra, Clifford Elliot chemistry educator, researcher
†Edwards, Terri Michele special education educator
Eigen, Howard pediatrician, educator
Eisenberg, Paul Richard cardiologist, consultant, educator
Elkins, James Paul physician
Evans, Daniel Fraley college administrator, banker, retail executive
Evans, Daniel Fraley, Jr. lawyer
Evans, Richard James mechanical engineer
Evenbeck, Scott Edward university official, psychologist
Ewbank, Thomas Peters lawyer, retired banker
Ewick, Charles Ray librarian
Fadely, James Philip admission and financial aid director, educator
Farlow, Martin Rhys neurologist, researcher, educator
Faulk, Ward Page immunologist
Favor-Hamilton, Suzanne Marie track and field athlete, Olympian
Feigenbaum, Harvey cardiologist, educator
†Feldman, Richard David health commissioner
Felicetti, Daniel A. academic administrator, educator
Fellers, Frederick Paul librarian
Feng, Gen-sheng medical educator, researcher
†Fiers, John Robert business executive, police chaplain
Fife, Wilmer Krafft chemistry educator
Finley, Katherine Mandusic professional society administrator
Fisch, Charles physician, educator
Fisher, Gene Lawrence financial executive
Fisher, James R. lawyer
Fisher, Thomas Graham judge
FitzGibbon, Daniel Harvey lawyer
Fleming, Marcella journalist
Florestano, Dana Joseph architect
Forliti, Amy Marie reporter
†Foster, Kennard P. federal judge
Fox, Donald Lee mental health counselor, consultant
†Franken, Lynn English educator
Fredrickson, William Robert scientist, company executive
Friman, Alice Ruth poet, English educator
Frisch, Fred I. real estate executive
Fritz, Cecil Morgan investment company executive
Fruehwald, Kristin G. lawyer
Fuller, Samuel Ashby lawyer, mining company executive
Funk, David Albert retired law educator
Funk, James William, Jr. insurance agency administrator, business owner
Furlow, Mack Vernon, Jr. retired financial executive, treasurer
Gable, Robert William, Jr. aerospace engineer
Gagel, Barbara Jean health insurance administrator
Galvin, Matthew Reppert psychiatry educator
†Ganassi, Chip professional race car executive, owner
Gantz, Richard Alan museum administrator
Garmel, Marion Bess Simon journalist
Garrett, Deloris Brink (Dee) school psychologist, psychology educator
Gaunce, Michael Paul insurance company executive
Gaus, David Sheerin publisher
Gay, David Earl chemicals executive, chemist
Gentry, Marshall Bruce English educator
Gerdes, Ralph Donald fire safety consultant
Ghetti, Bernardino Francesco neuropathologist, neurobiology researcher
Gilman, Alan B. restaurant company executive
Gilmer, Gordon councilman
Gilroy, Sue Anne state official
Givan, Richard Martin state supreme court justice, retired
Glendenning, John Armand registered nurse
Gnat, Raymond Earl librarian
Godich, John Paul federal magistrate judge
Golc, Jeff councilman
Goldsmith, Stephen mayor
Goodwin, William Maxwell financial executive
Gooldy, Patricia Alice retired elementary education educator
Gooldy, Walter Raymond genealogist
†Goss, Rebecca O. lawyer, pharmaceutical company executive
Gray, Johnny track and field athlete, Olympic athlete
Gray, Monroe, Jr. councilman
Grayson, John Allan lawyer
Green, Morris physician, educator
Greenberg, Stephen S. publishing executive
Greene, Joe Olympic athlete, track and field
Greer, Charles Eugene company executive, lawyer
Greist, Mary Coffey dermatologist
Griffiths, David Neal utility executive
Griggs, Ruth Marie retired journalism educator, writer, publications consultant
Grosfeld, Jay Lazar pediatric surgeon, educator
Gutermuth, Scott Alan accountant, pharmaceutical company executive
Haddad, Freddie Duke, Jr. hospital development administrator
Haines, Lee Mark, Jr. religious denomination administrator
Hamilton, Cheryl Louise elementary education educator
Hamilton, David F. judge
Hamm, Richard L. church administrator
Hammack, Julia Dixon music educator
Hammel, John Wingate lawyer
Hancock, Joan Herrin retired executive search company executive
Handel, David Jonathan health care administrator
Hansell, Richard Stanley obstetrician, gynecologist, educator
Harmon, Tim James construction executive
Harness, David Keith pastor
†Harrison, Kenny Olympic athlete
Hayes, John Robert health care executive, psychiatrist
Heerens, Joseph Robert lawyer
Hegel, Carolyn Marie farmer, farm bureau executive
†Heise, Michael Richard law educator
Helveston, Eugene McGillis pediatric ophthalmologist, educator
Henderson, Bruce Wingrove insurance executive
Henning, Teresa Beth English educator
†Henry, Kenneth James, Jr. medicinal chemist, anti-infectives researcher
Hermann, Robert Bell physical chemist, consultant
Hetzner, Marc Andrew lawyer
Hicks, Allen Morley hospital administrator
Hill, Patricia Jo special education educator
Hillman, Charlene Hamilton public relations executive
Hingtgen, Joseph Nicholas psychologist, neuroscientist, educator
Ho, Thomas Inn Min computer scientist, educator
Hodes, Marion Edward genetics educator, physician
Holden, Robert Watson radiologist, educator, university dean
Holmberg, Sharon K. psychiatric mental health and geriatrics nurse, researcher, educator
Holt, John Manly retired corporate lawyer
Hoppe, David Rutledge writer
Horn, Brenda Sue lawyer
Horvath, Terri Lynn writer, publishing company executive
Houser, Nathan philosophy educator
Huffman, Rosemary Adams lawyer, corporate executive
Huffman-Hine, Ruth Carson adult education administrator, educator
Hunt, Robert Chester construction company executive
Husman, Catherine Bigot insurance company executive, actuary
Husted, Ralph Waldo former utility executive
Huston, Michael Joe lawyer
Irsay, James Steven professional football team owner
Irwin, Glenn Ward, Jr. medical educator, physician, university official
Israelov, Rhoda financial planner, writer, entrepreneur
Jackson, Valerie Pascuzzi radiologist, educator
Jacobs, Andrew, Jr. former congressman, educator
Jacobson, Marc Peter art educator
Jarrett, Leslie Joe video producer
Jegen, Lawrence A., III law educator
Jewett, John Rhodes real estate executive
Johnson, Allen Olympic athlete
Johnson, Dave Olympic athlete, track and field
Johnson, James P. religious organization executive
Johnson, Michael track and field Olympic athlete
Johnston, Cyrus Conrad, Jr. medical educator
Johnstone, Robert Philip lawyer
Johnting, Wendell law librarian
Jones, Paul councilman
Jones, Robert Brooke microbiologist, educator, associate dean
†Jones, Stanley state agency administrator
Joyner, John Erwin medical educator, neurological surgeon
Justice, Brady Richmond, Jr. medical services executive
Kacek, Don J. management consultant, business owner
Kahlenbeck, Howard, Jr. lawyer
Kappes, Philip Spangler lawyer
Kautzman, John Fredrick lawyer
Kaye, Gordon Israel pathologist, anatomist, educator
Kellison, Donna Louise George accountant, educator
Kemper, James Dee lawyer
Kempski, Ralph Aloisius bishop
Kerr, William Andrew lawyer, educator
King, J. B. medical device company executive, lawyer
King, J. Bradley lawyer
King, Kay Sue investment company executive
King, Lucy Jane psychiatrist, health facility administrator
†Kingdom, Roger olympic athlete
Kirk, Carol lawyer
Kirkham, James Alvin manufacturing executive
Klaper, Martin Jay lawyer
Kleiman, David Harold lawyer
Klinker, Sheila Ann J. state legislator, middle school educator
Klug, Michael Gregory scientist
Knapp, Madonna Faye property manager, administrator
Knebel, Donald Earl lawyer
Knoebel, Suzanne Buckner cardiologist, medical educator
Knutson, Roger Craig marketing and sales professional, inventor
Koch, Edna Mae lawyer, nurse
Koeller, Robert Marion lawyer
Krasean, Thomas Karl historian
Krauss, John Landers public policy, urban affairs consultant, mediator
Kressley, George John, Jr. financial analyst
Krueger, Alan Douglas communications company executive
Labsvirs, Janis economist, educator
La Crosse, James retail executive
Lacy, Andre Balz industrial executive
Lahiri, Debomoy Kumar molecular neurobiologist, educator
Lamkin, E(ugene) Henry, Jr. internist, medical management executive
Lamkin, Martha Dampf lawyer
Landis, Larry Seabrook marketing and communications consultant
Lanford, Luke Dean electronics company executive
Lee, Stephen W. lawyer
Lemberger, Louis pharmacologist, physician
Lenzi, Mark Olympic athlete, springboard diver
Leppard, Raymond John conductor, harpsichordist
Lobley, Alan Haigh retired lawyer
Lofton, Thomas Milton lawyer
Long, Clarence William accountant
Long, William Allan retired forest products company executive
Loveday, William John hospital administrator
Lovejoy, Kim Brian English educator
Lowe, Louis Robert, Jr. lawyer
Lumeng, Lawrence physician, educator
Lyst, John Henry newspaper editor
Lytle, L(arry) Ben insurance company executive, lawyer
MacDougall, John Duncan surgeon
Madura, James Anthony surgical educator
Manders, Karl Lee neurosurgeon
Manley, Karen Ann human resources director
†Manning, Peyton professional football player
Manworren, Donald B. church administrator
Marsh, Michael Lawrence track and field athlete
Marshall, Carolyn Ann M. church official, executive
Martindale, Larry Richard computer services company consultant
Mason, Thomas Alexander historian, educator, author
Mathioudakis, Michael Robert life insurance and estate planning executive
Maxwell, Florence Hinshaw civic worker
†Mays, William G. chemical company executive
McCarthy, Harold Charles retired insurance company executive
McCarthy, Kevin Bart lawyer
McClamroch, William Tobin councilman
McDonald, Clement J. biomedical engineer
McDonell, Edwin Douglas information systems executive, consultant, writer
Mc Farland, H. Richard food company executive
McGarvey, William K. otolaryngologist, surgeon
McKeand, Patrick Joseph newspaper publisher, educator
McKinney, Dennis Keith lawyer
McKinney, E. Kirk, Jr. retired insurance company executive
McKinney, Larry J. federal judge
†Metz, Anthony J., III federal judge
Metzner, Barbara Stone university counselor
Meyer, Fred William, Jr. memorial parks executive
Meyer, William Michael mortgage banking executive
Mihelich, Edward David chemist
Mikelsons, J. George air aerospace transportation executive
Miller, David W. lawyer
Miner, Susan K. special education administrator
Miniear, J. Dederick software company executive, consultant
Mirsky, Arthur geologist, educator
Mitchell, Dennis A. Olympic athlete, track and field
Miyamoto, Richard Takashi otolaryngologist
Modisett, Jeffrey A. state attorney general
Moffatt, Michael Alan lawyer
Molitoris, Bruce Albert nephrologist, educator
Moore, Brent Dale landscape architect, horticulturist
Moore, Judy Kay marketing communications consultant
Mora, James Ernest professional football coach, professional sports team executive
Morris, Greg James advertising executive
†Mosbaugh, Phillip George urologist, educator
Motsinger, Linda Sue university official
Mullen, Thomas Edgar real estate consultant
Mullin, Chris(topher) Paul professional basketball player
Mundell, John Anthony environmental engineer, consultant
Murray, Theresa Marie critical care nurse, nursing consultant
Nancrede, Sarah Elizabeth (Sally Nancrede) reporter
†Nass, Connie Kay state auditor
Natz, Jacques news director
†Neville, Susan S. writer, English educator
Ney, Michael Vincent university administrator
Nolan, Alan Tucker retired lawyer, labor artibrator, writer
Norins, Arthur Leonard physician, educator
Norman, LaLander Stadig insurance company executive
Norwalk, Kelli Curran retail executive, entrepreneur
†Nottingham, Theodore J. video producer, writer
Nurnberger, John I., Jr. psychiatrist, educator
O'Bannon, Frank Lewis governor, lawyer
O'Brien, Daniel Dion track and field athlete, Olympic athlete
Ochs, Sidney neurophysiology educator
O'Dell, Cory councilman
†Otte, Frank J. federal judge
Padgett, Gregory Lee lawyer
Page, Curtis Matthewson minister
Paul, Stephen Howard lawyer
†Pearce, Jason Alexander communications administrator, editor
Pettinga, Cornelius Wesley pharmaceutical company executive
Phelps, Jaycie gymnast, Olympic athlete
Pierce, Jack Olympic athlete, track and field
Plascak-Craig, Faye Dene psychology educator, researcher
Plaster, George Francis Roman Catholic priest
Plater, William Marmaduke English language educator, academic administrator
Poel, Robert Walter air force officer, physician
Poinsette, Donald Eugene business executive, value management consultant
Polston, Mark Franklin minister
Polston, Ronald Wayne law educator
Ponder, Lester McConnico lawyer, educator
Powdrill, Gary Leo production operations manager
Powell, Mike olympic athlete, track and field
Powlen, David Michael lawyer
Pratt, Arthur D. printing company executive
Price, Henry J. lawyer
Price, (John) Nelson author, journalist
Price, Thomas Allan entrepreneur
Pugh, Daniel Wilbert theatre educator
Pulliam, Eugene Smith newspaper publisher
Pyle, R. Michael wholesale distribution executive
†Quinn, Fran poet
Quiring, Patti Lee human resource consulting company executive
†Ramadan, Nabih M. medical director pharmaceutical company
Rati, Robert Dean data processing executive
Recker, Thomas Edward fraternal organization executive
†Reed, Suellen K. superintendent public instruction
Reese, Ted M. dentist
Reeve, Ronald Cropper, Jr. manufacturing executive
Reid, William Hill mathematics educator
Reuben, Lawrence Mark lawyer
Reynolds, Robert Hugh lawyer
Rhoades, Rodney Allen physiologist, educator
Richardson, Mildred Tourtillott retired psychologist
Richmond, James Ellis restaurant company executive
Riegsecker, Marvin Dean pharmacist, state senator
Riggin, Leh-daw Alice analytical chemist
†Rink, Richard Carlos pediatric urologist, educator
Robbins, N. Clay foundation administrator
Roberts, David airport executive
Roberts, William Everett lawyer
†Robertson, Jean Ellis art critic, art history educator
Robinson, Clifford Fossett human resources administrator
Robinson, Larry Robert insurance company executive
Rogers, Robert Ernest medical educator
Rose, Jalen professional basketball player
†Rosentraub, Mark S. educator
Ross, Edward cardiologist
Roth, Lawrence Max pathologist, educator
Ruben, Gary A. marketing and communications consultant
Russell, David Williams lawyer
Russell, Frank Eli retired newspaper publishing executive
Rust, Jo Ellen pediatric and neurosurgical nurse
Ryder, Henry C(lay) lawyer
Ryder, Kenneth William pathologist, educator
Salentine, Thomas James pharmaceutical company executive
Sales, Angel Rodolfo financial executive
Salewsky, Douglas Michael video producer
Sarbinoff, James Adair periodontist, consultant
Scaletta, Phillip Ralph, III lawyer
Scanlon, Thomas Michael lawyer
Schaad, Dee Edwin art educator
Schafer, Matthew T. English language educator, coach
Schilling, Emily Born editor, association executive
Schlegel, Fred Eugene lawyer
Schmetzer, Alan David psychiatrist
Schneider, William councilman
Scholer, Sue Wyant state legislator
Schreckengast, William Owen lawyer
Scism, Daniel Reed lawyer
Scriven, Eric Frank Vaughan chemist, researcher
Seitz, Melvin Christian, Jr. distributing company executive
Seneff, Smiley Howard business owner
SerVaas, Beurt Richard corporate executive
SerVaas, Cory health sciences association administrator
Shaffer, Alfred Garfield (Terry) service organization executive
Sharpnack, John Trent judge
Shaughnessy, Edward Lawrence English educator
Shepard, Randall Terry state supreme court justice
Sherman, Stuart internist, gastroenterologist
Shideler, Shirley Ann Williams lawyer
†Shields, V. Sue federal magistrate judge
Short, Frank T. councilman
Shula, Robert Joseph lawyer
Simmons, Roberta Johnson public relations firm executive
Simon, David real estate company officer
Simon, Herbert professional basketball team executive
Sindlinger, Verne E. bishop
Skvarenina, Joseph Lee development/public relations professional, editor
Slaymaker, Gene Arthur public relations executive
Small, Joyce Graham psychiatrist, educator
Smith, Donald Eugene healthcare facility management administrator owner

Smith, James Warren *pathologist, microbiologist, parasitologist*
Smith, K. Clay *machinery transport company executive*
Smith, Keith *protective services official*
Smits, Rik *professional basketball player*
Sokolov, Richard Saul *real estate company executive*
Solomon, Marilyn Kay *educator, consultant*
Spanogle, Robert William *marketing and advertising company executive, association administrator*
Speth, Gerald Lennus *education and business consultant*
Staff, Charles Bancroft, Jr. *music and theater critic*
Standish, Samuel Miles *oral pathologist, college dean*
Stayton, Michael Bruce *financial entrepreneur, corporate professional*
Stayton, Thomas George *lawyer*
Steger, Evan Evans, III *lawyer*
Stehman, Frederick Bates *gynecologic oncologist, educator*
Stewart, Judith A. *lawyer*
Stewart, Paul Arthur *pharmaceutical company executive*
Stieff, John Joseph *legislative lawyer, educator*
Stookey, George Kenneth *research institute administrator, dental educator*
Storhoff, Diana Carmack *research scientist*
Stout, William Jewell *department store executive*
Strain, Edward Richard *psychologist*
Strong, Amanda L. *community health nurse*
Stutz, Jay Francis *controller*
Sullender, Joy Sharon *elementary school educator*
Sutherland, Donald Gray *lawyer*
Sutton, Gregory Paul *obstetrician, gynecologist*
Suzuki, Hidetaro *violinist*
Sweezy, John William *political party official*
Tabler, Bryan G. *lawyer*
Tabler, Norman Gardner, Jr. *lawyer*
Talesnick, Stanley *lawyer*
Thomas, Jerry Arthur *soil scientist*
Thomas, John David *musician, composer, arranger, photographer, recording engineer, producer*
Thompson, Roland *marketing professional*
Tilford, Jody *councilwoman*
Tinder, John Daniel *federal judge*
†Tinkle, Carolyn J. *legislative staff member*
Tobias, Randall Lee *pharmaceutical company executive*
Todd, Zane Grey *retired utilities executive*
Tolliver, Kevin Paul *dentist*
Tomlinson, Joseph Ernest *manufacturing company executive*
Torrence, Gwen *Olympic athlete*
Towne, Edgar Arthur *theologian, educator*
Townsend, Earl C., Jr. *lawyer, writer*
†Tracy, Paul Anthony *race car driver*
Tuchman, Steven Leslie *lawyer, theatre critic*
Tucker, Dennis Carl *library executive*
Usher, Phyllis Land *state official*
†Van Lone Trieschman, Janet Anne *graphic arts educator*
†Vasser, Jimmy *professional race car driver*
Vereen, Robert Charles *retired trade association executive*
Vietor, John J. *audit manager*
Vlach, Jeffrey Allen *environmental specialist*
Walker, Frank Dilling *market research executive*
Walker, Steven Frank *management consultant*
Waller, Aaron Bret, III *museum director*
Walsh, Donnie *sports club executive*
Walther, Joseph Edward *health facility administrator, retired physician*
Wampler, Lloyd Charles *retired lawyer*
Wampler, Robert Joseph *lawyer*
Warstler, David John *auditor*
Watanabe, August Masaru *physician, scientist, medical educator, corporate executive*
Watkins, Harold Robert *minister*
Watkins, Sherry Lynne *elementary school educator*
Watts, Quincy Dushawn *track and field athlete*
Weber, George *oncology and pharmacology researcher, educator*
Weinberger, Myron Hilmar *medical educator*
Wellnitz, Craig Otto *lawyer, English language educator*
Welsh, Robert K. *relgious organization executive*
Westcott, April Sue Cook *landscape architect*
Whale, Arthur Richard *lawyer*
Wheeler, Daniel Scott *management executive, editor*
Whitchurch, Gail G. *communication educator*
White, Arthur Clinton *physician*
White, James Patrick *law educator*
Williams, Gregory Keith *accountant*
Willoughby, David Charles *photographer, forensics illustrator*
Wilson, Earle Lawrence *church administrator*
Wilson, Fred M., II *ophthalmologist, educator*
Wilson, Margaret L. *author, speaker*
Winemiller, James D. *accountant*
Wise, Rita J. *writer, poet*
Wishard, Gordon Davis *lawyer*
Wolsiffer, Patricia Rae *insurance company executive*
Wong, David T. *biochemist*
Wood, William Jerome *lawyer*
Woodard, Harold Raymond *lawyer*
Woodring, DeWayne Stanley *religion association executive*
Woollen, Evans *architectural firm executive*
Woolling, Kenneth Rau *internist*
Wright, David Burton *retired newspaper publishing company executive*
Yates, Robin Corriene *journalism instructor, freelance writer*
Yeager, Joseph Heizer, Jr. *lawyer*
Yee, Robert Donald *ophthalmologist*
Young, Katherine Tratebas *occupational health nurse*
Young, Kevin *track and field athlete*
Young, Philip Howard *library director*
Yovits, Marshall Clinton *computer and information science educator, university dean*
Yune, Heun Yung *radiologist, educator*
Zapapas, James Richard *pharmaceutical company executive*
Zipes, Douglas Peter *cardiologist, researcher*

Jamestown
Waymire, John Thomas *principal*

Jasper
Aronoff, Donald Matthew *mental health facility administrator*
Hayes, Mary Ann *social studies educator*
Kane, James Robert *financial executive*
Newman, Leonard Jay *retail jewel merchant, gemologist*

Jeffersonville
Barthold, Clementine B. *retired judge*
Hoehn, Elmer Louis *lawyer, state and federal agency administrator, educator, consultant*
Reisert, Charles Edward, Jr. *real estate executive*

Knox
Weiss, Randall A. *television producer, supermarket executive*

Kokomo
Coppock, Janet Elaine *mental health nurse*
Hall, Milton L. *bishop*
Highlen, Larry Wade *music educator, piano rebuilder, tuner*
Hill, Emita Brady *academic administrator*
Lopes, Dominic M. McIver *educator*
Lowther, Roberta Wynn *information security analyst*
Maugans, John Conrad *lawyer*
Miller, Robert Frank *retired electronics engineer, educator*
Nierste, Joseph Paul *software engineer*
Stein, Eleanor Bankoff *judge*
Ungerer, Walter John *minister*

Kouts
Miller, Sarabeth *secondary education educator*

La Porte
Hiler, John Patrick *former government official, former congressman, business executive*
Morris, Leigh Edward *hospital executive officer*

Lafayette
Achgill, Ralph Kenneth *retired research scientist*
Bement, Arden Lee, Jr. *engineering educator*
Branigin, Roger D., Jr. *lawyer*
Brewster, James Henry *retired chemistry educator*
Claflin, Robert Malden *retired veterinary educator, university dean*
de Branges de Bourcia, Louis *mathematics educator*
Etzel, James Edward *environmental engineering educator*
Feuer, Henry *chemist, educator*
Finch, Robert Jonathan *communications engineering consultant*
Fox, Robert William *mechanical engineering educator*
Frey, Harley Harrison, Jr. *anesthesiologist*
Gartenhaus, Solomon *physicist*
Geddes, LaNelle Evelyn *nurse, physiologist*
Geddes, Leslie Alexander *bioengineer, physiologist, educator*
Gerde, Carlyle Noyes (Cy Gerde) *lawyer*
Gordon, Irene Marlow *radiology educator*
Gustafson, Winthrop Adolph *aeronautical and astronautical engineering educator*
Hardin, Lowell Stewart *retired economics educator*
Harris, Donald Wayne *research scientist*
Helmuth, Ned D *financial planner*
Higi, William L. *bishop*
Judd, William Robert *engineering geologist, educator*
Kofmehl, Kenneth Theodore *political science educator*
Laczi, Deane Elizabeth *data control operator, poet*
Lazarus, Bruce I. *restaurant and hotel management educator*
Lindenlaub, J. C. *electrical engineer, educator*
Loeffler, Frank Joseph *physicist, educator*
Maickel, Roger Philip *pharmacologist, educator*
McBride, Angela Barron *nursing educator*
Messman, Bobette Marie (Harman) *nursing administrator*
Meyer, Brud Richard *retired pharmaceutical company executive*
Miller, Larry Joe *evangelist*
Nicholson, Ralph Lester *botanist, educator*
O'Callaghan, Patti Louise *court program administrator*
Ott, Karl Otto *nuclear engineering educator, consultant*
†Pfaff, Dana *urologist*
Porile, Norbert Thomas *chemistry educator*
Rubin, Jean Estelle *mathematics educator*
Schönemann, Peter Hans *psychology educator*
Shook, James Creighton *real estate executive*
Troutner, Joanne Johnson *school technology administrator, educator, administrator, consultant*
Whitsel, Robert Malcolm *retired insurance company executive*

Lagrange
Brown, George E. *judge, educator*
Glick, Cynthia Susan *lawyer*
Young, Rebecca Lee *special education educator*

Lawrenceburg
Dautel, Charles Shreve *retired mining company executive*
Dickey, Julia Edwards *aviation consultant*

Leesburg
Pryor, Dixie Darlene *elementary education educator*

Leo
Ridderheim, Mary Margaret *psychotherapist*

Ligonier
Sharp, Susan Gene *media educator*

Lincoln City
Blessinger, Timothy Louis *secondary school educator*

Linden
Eutsler, Mark Leslie *business services executive, real estate broker*

Logansport
Brewer, Robert Allen *physician*
†Mayfield, Kristina Sue *protective services administrator*
†Shih, Philip C. *library administrator*

Loogootee
Burcham, Eva Helen (Pat Burcham) *retired electronics technician*

Lowell
Reed, Gerald Wilfred *protective services official*

Madison
Cutschall, John Ray *hospital administrator*

Marion
Barnes, James Byron *university president*
Fisher, Pierre James, Jr. *physician*
Hall, Charles Adams *information systems specialist*
McIntyre, Robert Walter *church official*
Philbert, Robert Earl *secondary school educator*
Ryan, Patrick Nelson *lawyer*
Simons, Richard Stuart *retailer, owner*

Markle
†Hamilton, Rhonda Lynn *librarian*

Martinsville
Kendall, Robert Stanton *newspaper editor, journalist*

Merrillville
Adik, Stephen Peter *energy company executive*
†Birch-Vujovic, Judith Lee *writer, lecturer, educator*
Brenman, Stephen Morris *lawyer*
Collie, John, Jr. *insurance agent*
†Derner, Carol A. *librarian*
Kamanaroff, Charlene *elementary education educator*
Kinney, Richard Gordon *lawyer, educator*
Ledbetter, Brenda LaVerne *women's health nurse*
Lynn, Robert William *gas and electric utility official*
Miller, Richard Allen *lawyer*
Nguyen, Thach Ngoc *cardiologist*
Reitmeister, Noel William *financial planner, investment and insurance executive, author, consultant, columnist, television host and producer, educator*
White, Dean *advertising executive*

Michigan City
Blake, George Alan, Jr. *non-profit association executive, consultant*
Brockway, Lee J. *architect*
Brown, Arnold *physical therapy consultant*
Burgwald, Beryle Alan *political science educator*
Komp, Barbara Ann *marketing communications executive*
Mothkur, Sridhar Rao *radiologist*
Nasr, Suhayl Joseph *psychiatrist*
Pecze, David Emery *marketing professional*

Middlebury
Guequierre, John Phillip *manufacturing company executive*
Siegel, Harvey Robert *engineering and product development executive*

Milltown
Chapman, Sue Turner *artist*
†Pesek, James Robert *management consultant*

Mishawaka
Braunsdorf, James Allen *physics educator*
Brogan-Werntz, Bonnie Bailey *retired police officer, photographer*
Kapson, Jordan *automotive executive*
Ponko, William Reuben *architect*
Rubenstein, Pamela Silver *precision machinery executive*
Silver, Neil Marvin *manufacturing executive*
Troyer, LeRoy Seth *architect*
†Wilson, Rebecca Jo *dean, education educator*

Monroe City
Teverbaugh, Kerry Dean *television meteorologist, promotional consultant*

Monroeville
Ray, Annette D. *business executive*
Sorgen, Elizabeth Ann *retired educator*

Monrovia
Bennett, James Edward *retired plastic surgeon, educator*

Monticello
†Berry, Michael John *author, medical and dental management consultant*
Howarth, David H. *retired bank executive*

Morgantown
Boyce, Gerald G. *artist, educator*
Jones, Barbara Ewer *school psychologist, occupational therapist*

Morocco
Fernandez, Martin Andrew *secondary school educator*

Mount Vernon
Bach, Steve Crawford *lawyer*

Muncie
Adams, Thomas Wayne *chemistry educator*
Alford, Jeffrey Whitwam *university administrator*
Amman, E(lizabeth) Jean *university official*
Anderson, Stefan Stolen *bank executive*
Ball, Virginia Beall *investor*
Barber, Earl Eugene *consulting firm executive*
Bell, Stephen Scott (Steve Bell) *journalist, educator*
Bennon, Saul *electrical engineer, transformer consultant*
Bonneau, Sue Ellen *advancement researcher*
†Bowers-Bienkowski, Evelyn Joy *physical anthropologist, educator*
†Cambray-Nuñez, Rodrigo *mathematics educator, translator*
Carmin, Robert Leighton *retired geography educator*
Church, Jay Kay *psychologist, educator*
†Clark, Catherine Kay *human recources specialist*
Eddy, Darlene Mathis *poet, educator*
Ernstberger, Eric *architectural company executive*
Fisher, John Wesley *manufacturing company executive*
Freestone, Jeannette Warren *nurse practitioner*
Ghiglia, Oscar Alberto *classical guitarist*
Granger, Philip Richard *minister*
Hendrix, Jon Richard *biology educator*
Henzlik, Raymond Eugene *zoophysiologist, educator*
Hoffman, Mary Catherine *nurse anesthetist*
Holt, Gerald Wayne *retired counseling administrator*
Hozeski, Bruce William *English language and literature educator*
Ingelhart, Louis Edward *journalism educator, retired*
Irvine, Phyllis Eleanor *nursing educator, administrator*
Joyaux, Alain Georges *art museum director*
Kelly, Eric Damian *lawyer, educator*
Kuratko, Donald F. *business management educator, consultant*
Leitze, Annette Emily Ricks *mathematics educator*
Linson, Robert Edward *university administrator emeritus*
†Massé, Mark Henry *journalism educator*
†McAllister, Peter A. *music education educator*
McConnell, Sarah Stacey *film producer, French language educator*
McIntosh, David Eugene, Jr. *psychologist, educator*
Mertens, Thomas Robert *biology educator*
Norris, Tracy Hopkins *retired public relations executive*
Radcliff, William Franklin *lawyer*
Roch, Lewis Marshall, II *ophthalmic surgeon, medical entrepreneur*
Sargent, Thomas Andrew *retired political science educator*
Schaefer, Patricia *librarian*
Seymour, Richard Deming *technology educator*
Swartz, B(enjamin) K(insell), Jr. *archaeologist, educator*
Swetnam, Ruth E. Danglade *curriculum director*
Terrell, Pamela Sue *pharmacist*
†Trimmer, Joseph F. *English educator*
†Whitaker, Sandra Sue *soprano, educator*
Wiedmer, Terry Lynn *educational administration educator, consultant*
Yeamans, George Thomas *librarian, educator*

Munster
Amber, Douglas George *lawyer*
Colander, Patricia Marie *newspaper publisher*
Corsiglia, Robert Joseph *electrical construction company executive*
Fies, James David *elementary education educator*
Luerssen, Frank Wonson *retired steel company executive*
Moore, Carolyn Lannin *video specialist*
Nidetz, Myron Philip *health care delivery systems consultant, medical*
Palmer, Marcia Ann *healthcare management consultant, pharmacist*
Platis, Chris Steven *educator*
Shields, Robert Francis *stockbroker*
†Witting, Marie A. *management consultant*

Nappanee
Borger, Michael Hinton Ivers *osteopathic physician, educator*
Shea, James F. *manufacturing executive*

Nashville
Brown, Peggy Ann *artist*
Gurnack, Dean Hilton *artist*
Kriner, Sally Gladys Pearl *artist*
Rogers, Frank Andrew *restaurant, hotel executive*
Stackhouse, David William, Jr. *retired furniture systems installation contractor*
Walsh, Alan John *architect*

New Albany
Baker, Claude Douglas *biology educator, researcher, environmental activist*
Chowhan, Naveed Mahfooz *oncologist*
Estep, Lawrence Robert *videographer, video producer*
Johnson, John Edwin *orthodontist*
Kaiser, Michael Bruce *elementary education educator*
†Lorch, Basil H., III *federal judge*
Naville, Michael Gerard *lawyer*
Riehl, Jane Ellen *education educator*
Yeager, Lillian Elizabeth *nurse educator*

New Castle
Ford-Catron, Mary Elaine *nurse*
†Ratcliff, Richard Pickering *secondary education educator*

New Harmony
Koch, Jane Ellen *secondary school educator*

Newburgh
Feldbusch, Michael F. *engineering company executive*
Reavis, Hubert Gray, Jr. *metal products executive*
Tierney, Gordon Paul *real estate broker, genealogist*

Noblesville
Almquist, Donald John *retired electronics company executive*
Feigenbaum, Edward D. *legal editor, publisher, consultant*
Gatza, Louise Ruth *freelance medical writer, small business owner*
Monical, Robert Duane *consulting structural engineer*
Morrison, Joseph Young *transportation consultant*
Tank, Rod Gaillard *orthopaedic physical therapist*
Thacker, Jerry Lynn *school administrator*
Wilson, Norman Glenn *church administrator, writer*

North Liberty
Lowery, Joanne *English educator, writer, editor*

North Manchester
Harshbarger, Richard B. *economics educator*
Horn, Carol Garver *foundation administrator*
Myers, Anne M. *development director*
Seward, Steven Le Mar *optometrist*
Sponseller, Kay Lynn *secondary school educator, college educator*
Williams, Leonard A., Jr. *educator*

North Vernon
Hicks, Gregory Steven *marketing professional*
Williams, John Albert *developmental disabilities agency director*

Notre Dame
Arnold, Peri Ethan *political scientist*
Auriol, Yves *university women's head fencing coach*
Bartell, Ernest *economist, educator, priest*
Bass, Steven Craig *computer science educator*
Bender, Harvey A. *biology educator*
†Blantz, Thomas Edward *Roman Catholic priest, educator*
Blenkinsopp, Joseph *biblical studies educator*
Browne, Cornelius Payne *physics educator*
Castellino, Francis Joseph *university dean*
Craypo, Charles *labor economics educator*
Crosson, Frederick James *former university dean, humanities educator*

Delaney, Cornelius Francis *philosophy educator*
Despres, Leo Arthur *sociology and anthropology educator, academic administrator*
Dowty, Alan Kent *political scientist, educator*
Driscoll, Michael Stephan *priest, liturgy and theology educator*
Fallon, Stephen Michael *humanities educator*
Feigl, Dorothy Marie *chemistry educator, university official*
Ghilarducci, Teresa *economist, educator*
†Gleason, (John) Philip *history educator*
Goulet, Denis André *development ethicist, writer*
Gray, William Guerin *civil engineering educator*
Grazin, Igor Nikolai *law educator, state official*
Gunn, Alan *law educator*
Hatch, Nathan Orr *university administrator*
Hayes, Stephen Matthew *librarian*
Helquist, Paul M. *chemistry educator, researcher*
Hesburgh, Theodore Martin *clergyman, former university president*
Huber, Paul William *biochemistry educator, researcher*
Incropera, Frank Paul *mechanical engineering educator*
Jensen, Richard Jorg *biology educator*
Jerger, Edward William *mechanical engineer, university dean*
Johnstone, Joyce Visintine *education educator*
Klene, Mary Jean *English educator*
Kogge, Peter Michael *computer scientist, educator*
Kohn, James Paul *engineering educator*
Langford, James Rouleau *university press administrator*
Lanzinger, Klaus *language educator*
Leege, David Calhoun *political scientist, educator*
Malloy, Edward Aloysius *priest, university administrator, educator*
Marshalek, Eugene Richard *physics educator*
Matthias, John Edward *English literature educator*
McBrien, Richard Peter *theology educator*
McGraw, Muffet *women's basketball coach*
McInerny, Ralph Matthew *philosophy educator, author*
Mc Mullin, Ernan Vincent *philosophy educator*
Michel, Anthony Nikolaus *electrical engineering educator, researcher*
Moevs, Christian Robert *literature educator*
†Nordstrom, Carolyn Rebecca *anthropology and peace studies educator*
Nugent, Walter Terry King *historian*
O'Meara, Onorato Timothy *academic administrator, mathematician*
O'Meara, Thomas Franklin *priest, educator*
Payne, Lucy Ann Salsbury *law librarian, educator, lawyer*
Petrucelli, Chris *soccer coach*
Pilkinton, Mark C. *theater educator*
Pollak, Barth *mathematics educator*
Poulin, David James *hockey coach*
Quinn, Philip Lawrence *philosophy educator*
Reilly, Frank Kelly *business educator*
Rice, (Ethel) Ann *publishing executive, editor*
Rosenberg, Charles Michael *art historian, educator*
Sain, Michael Kent *electrical engineering educator*
Scheidt, W. Robert *chemistry educator, researcher*
Schmitz, Roger Anthony *chemical engineering educator, academic administrator*
Schuler, Robert Hugo *chemist, educator*
Shannon, William Norman, III *marketing and international business educator, food service executive*
Slabey, Robert McKeon *English educator*
Sommese, Andrew John *mathematics educator*
Sterling, Gregory Earl *religious studies educator*
Stoll, Wilhelm *mathematics educator*
Swartz, Thomas R. *economist, educator*
Szewczyk, Albin Anthony *engineering educator*
Thomas, John Kerry *chemistry educator*
†Trembath, Kern Robert *theology educator*
Varma, Arvind *chemical engineering educator, researcher*
Vasta, Edward *humanities educator*
Vecchio, Robert Peter *business management educator*
Wadsworth, Michael A. *athletic director, former ambassador*
Walicki, Andrzej Stanislaw *history of ideas educator*
Weigert, Andrew Joseph *sociology educator*
White, James Floyd *theology educator*
Wong, Warren James *mathematics educator*

Oakland City
Johnson, Ora J. *clergyman*
Schafer, Patricia Day *physical education educator*

Orleans
Mapes, Mary Etta *critical care and emergency room nurse*

Osceola
Tatum, Rita *communications executive*

Pendleton
Kischuk, Richard Karl *insurance company executive*
Phenis, Nancy Sue *educational administrator*

Peru
Davidson, John Robert *dentist*
Fager, Everett Dean *minister*
McMinn, William Lowell, Jr. *engineer*

Pittsboro
Hassfurder, Leslie Jean *principal*

Plainfield
Lucas, Georgetta Marie Snell *retired educator, artist*

Plymouth
Cardinal-Cox, Shirley Mae *education educator*
Jurkiewicz, Margaret Joy Gommel *secondary education educator*
Miller, Philip William *sales executive*
Nixon, William Rusty *sportswriter*
Sherwood, Lillian Anna *librarian, retired*

Portage
Cunningham, R. John *retired financial consultant*
Gasser, Wilbert (Warner), Jr. *retired banker*
Popp, Joseph Bruce *manufacturing executive*
Sullivan, Donna Dianne *accountant*
Zuick, Diane Martina *elementary education educator*

Portland
†Bisel, Marsha McCune *elementary education educator*
Martig, John Frederick *anesthesiologist*

Poseyville
Joos, Steven Lee *sports editor*

Purdue University
Bannatyne, Mark William McKenzie *technical graphics educator*
Beering, Steven Claus *academic administrator, medical educator*
Bernhard, Robert James *mechanical engineer, educator*
Brown, Herbert Charles *chemistry educator*
Guo, Peixuan *molecular virology educator*
Liley, Peter Edward *mechanical engineering educator*
Mobley, Emily Ruth *library dean, educator*
Schweickert, Richard Justus *psychologist, educator*
Zou, Zhen *English and Chinese educator, translator and critic, computer technologist*

Rensselaer
Ahler, Kenneth James *physician*
Slaby, Frank *financial executive*

Richmond
†Anderson, Claudia W. *oncology nurse*
Bennett, Douglas Carleton *academic administrator*
Farber, Evan Ira *librarian*
Kennedy, Barbara Ellen Perry *art therapist*
Kirk, Thomas Garrett, Jr. *librarian*
Maurer, Johan Fredrik *religious denomination administrator*
Robinson, Dixie Faye *school system administrator*
Southard, Robert Fairbairn *history educator*

Rochester
Neff, Kathy S. *swimming and water safety educator*
Willard, Shirley Ann Ogle *museum director, editor*

Rockport
Parker, Mary Anne *retired critical care nurse*

Rockville
Swaim, John Franklin *physician, health care executive*

Rolling Prairie
Eggleston, Alan Edward *musician, opera singer, Boy Scout executive*

Rosedale
George, Linda Olsen *mathematics educator, writer*

Rushville
Moore, Helen Elizabeth *reporter*
†Morrell, Douglas Wayne *family practice physician*

Russiaville
Knierim, Stephen Dale *minister*

Saint Meinrad
Cody, Aelred Joseph *editor, priest*
Daly, Simeon Philip John *librarian*

Sandborn
Hartsburg, Judith Catherine *computer web programmer*

Santa Claus
Edwards, James Dallas, III *consulting company executive*
Platthy, Jeno *cultural association executive*

Schererville
Griffin, Anita Jane *elementary education educator*
Hendricks, Stanley Marshall, II *executive recruiter, consultant*
Opacich, Milan *protective services official, musician*
Pettit, Wendy Jean *management company executive*

Scottsburg
Kho, Eusebio *surgeon*

Seymour
Bollinger, Don Mills *retired grocery company executive*
†Rust, Lois *food company executive*

Shelby
Kurzeja, Richard Eugene *professional society administrator*

South Bend
Agbetsiafa, Douglas Kofi *financial and management consultant*
Altman, Arnold David *business executive*
Anderson, Kenneth Paul *nephrologist, administrator*
Bellalta, Esmée Cromie *landscape architect, retired educator*
Brennen, William Elbert *management consultant*
Brueseke, Harold Edward *magistrate*
Carey, John Leo *lawyer*
†Carrington, Michael Davis *criminal justice administrator, educator, consultant*
Charles, Isabel *university administrator*
Cohen, Ronald S. *accountant*
Crowley, Joseph R. *bishop*
†Dees, Harry C., Jr. *federal judge*
Ford, George Burt *lawyer*
†Furlong, Patrick J. *historian, educator, university administrator*
Greenberg, Bruce Loren *health facility administrator*
Harriman, Gerald Eugene *retired business administrator, economics educator*
Horsbrugh, Patrick *architect, educator, environologist*
Hunt, Mary Reilly *organization executive*
Jorgensen, Robert William *product engineer*
Keen, Mike Forrest *sociologist, educator*
Kline, Syril Levin *writer, columnist, reporter, educational consultant, commentator, theatre critic*
Lambert, George Robert *lawyer, realtor*
Lampkin, Ralph, Jr. *vocalist, nightclub consultant, producer, writer, coach*
Littrell, Carl Paul *civil engineer*
Manion, Daniel Anthony *federal judge*
McGill, Warren Everett *lawyer, consultant*
Miller, Robert L., Jr. *federal judge*
Moore-Riesbeck, Susan *osteopathic physician*
Murphy, Christopher Joseph, III *financial executive*
Murphy, William Host *sales executive, retired*
†Owens, Ora Lee *elementary education educator*
Perrin, Kenneth Lynn *university chancellor*
†Pierce, Robin D. *federal judge*
Plunkett, Phyllis Jean *nursing administrator*
Reinke, William John *lawyer*
Ripple, Kenneth Francis *federal judge*
Rodgers, Grace Anne *university official*
Rodibaugh, Robert Kurtz *judge*
Schurz, Franklin Dunn, Jr. *media executive*
Seall, Stephen Albert *lawyer*
Shaffer, Thomas Lindsay *lawyer, educator*
Sharp, Allen *federal judge*
Shirley, Randall Delron *university dean*
Smith, E. Berry *television and radio executive*
Szigeti, Michelle Marie *critical care nurse*
van Inwagen, Peter Jan *philosophy educator*
Vogel, Nelson J., Jr. *lawyer*
Wensits, James Emrich *newspaper editor*
White, Robert Dennis *pediatrician*
Wrenn, Walter Bruce *marketing educator, consultant*

South Whitley
†Fox, Alan Hugo *musical instrument manufacturing company executive*

Spencer
Tucker, Mary Margaret *county government official*

Syracuse
Simmons, Frederick Harrison *retired otolaryngologist*

Tell City
Gebhard, Diane Kay *county administrator, political advisor*
Smith, Mary Katherine *banker*

Terre Haute
Aldridge, Sandra *civic volunteer*
Baker, Ronald Lee *English educator*
Bitzegaio, Harold James *retired lawyer*
Brennan, Matthew Cannon *English literature educator, poet*
Campbell, Judith May *physical education educator*
Carmony, Marvin Dale *linguist, educator*
Cary, Walter Ray *small business owner*
Coe, Michual William *physical therapist*
De Marr, Mary Jean *English language educator*
Drummond, Dorothy Weitz *geography education consultant, educator, author*
Dusanic, Donald Gabriel *parasitology educator, microbiologist*
Frank, Paula Elizabeth *nursing educator*
Guthrie, Frank Albert *chemistry educator*
†Hay, Dick *artist, educator*
Hulbert, Samuel Foster *college president*
Hunt, Effie Neva *former college dean, former English educator*
Jennermann, Donald L. *humanities educator*
Kesler, John A. *lawyer, land developer*
Kleiner, Elaine Laura *English literature educator*
Kunkler, Arnold William *retired surgeon*
Lamis, Leroy *artist, retired educator*
Landini, Richard George *university president, emeritus English educator*
Leach, Ronald George *educational administration educator*
†Lewis, Jordan D. *federal judge*
Malooley, David Joseph *electronics and computer technology educator*
Mansfield, Dianne Lynn *minister*
Montañez, Carmen Lydia *Spanish language educator, literature researcher, lawyer*
Moore, John William *university president*
†Myers, Andrea Lee *university administrator*
Ondish, Andrea *museum coordinator*
Perry, Eston Lee *real estate and equipment leasing company executive*
Pickett, William Beatty *history educator*
Pierard, Richard Victor *history educator*
Reeve, Cheryl Ann *basketball coach*
Roshel, John Albert, Jr. *orthodontist*
Siebenmorgen, Paul *physician, lay church worker*
Smith, Donald E. *banker*
Snow, Richard Kenneth *geographer, educator*
†Stephanian, Erick *neurosurgeon*
†Summers, Jerry Andy *education educator*
Taylor, Dean Alan *physicist*
Tió, Adrian Ricardo *artist, art educator*
Van Til, William *education educator, writer*

Union Mills
Johnson, Bruce Ross *elementary education educator*

Upland
Dayton, Nancy Cheryl *English educator*
Harbin, Michael Allen *religion educator, writer*
Kesler, Jay Lewis *academic administrator*
Kitterman, Joan Frances *education educator*
Koontz, Lisa Elaine *speech-language pathologist*

Valparaiso
Carr, Wiley Nelson *hospital administrator*
†Duvick, Randa Jane *French language educator*
Gaffney, Edward McGlynn *law educator, university administrator*
Harre, Alan Frederick *university president*
Johnson, Shelli Wright *lawyer*
Kobak, Alfred Julian, Jr. *obstetrician, gynecologist*
Koeppen, Raymond Bradley *lawyer*
Miller, John Albert *university educator, consultant*
Morgan, David A. *art history educator*
Mundinger, Donald Charles *college president retired*
Olson, Lynn *sculptor, painter, writer*
Persyn, Mary Geraldine *law librarian, law educator*
Peters, Howard Nevin *foreign language educator*
Schlender, William Elmer *management sciences educator*
Schnabel, Robert Victor *retired academic administrator*
Serpe-Schroeder, Patricia L. *elementary education educator*
Taylor, Kenard Lyle, Jr. *director training*
Zimmerman, Robert Gene *retired military officer, historian, lawyer*

Vincennes
Emison, Ewing Rabb, Jr. *lawyer*
Nead, Karen L. *university professor*
†Rogers, John Headley *educator*
Spurrier, James Joseph *theater educator*

Wabash
Leach, Elaine Kay *speech clinician*
Scales, Richard Lewis *sales representative*
Whitehead, Wendy Lee *special education educator*
Zimmerman, Philip L. *performing arts and foundation executive*

Walton
Chu, Johnson Chin Sheng *retired physician*

Warren
Pattison, Deloris Jean *retired counselor, university official*

Warsaw
Holbrook, Stephen Eugene *printing executive*
Stump, Christine Jo *daycare provider*
Walmer, James L. *lawyer*

Washington
Graham, David Bolden *food products executive*

Waterloo
Snyder, Joseph James *steel construction company executive*

West Lafayette
Abhyankar, Shreeram S. *mathematics and industrial engineering educator*
Adelman, Steven Allen *theoretical physical chemist, chemistry educator*
Albright, Jack Lawrence *animal science and veterinary educator*
Albright, Lyle Frederick *chemical engineering educator*
Altschaeffl, Adolph George *civil engineering educator*
Amstutz, Harold Emerson *veterinarian, educator*
Amy, Jonathan Weekes *scientist, educator*
Anderson, James George *sociologist, educator*
†Anderson, Kristine Jo *librarian*
Andres, Ronald Paul *chemical engineer, educator*
Andrews, Theodora Anne *retired librarian, educator*
Atallah, Mikhail Jibrayil *computer science educator*
Axtell, John David *genetics educator, researcher*
Barany, James Walter *industrial engineering educator*
Barnes, Virgil Everett, II *physics educator*
Baumgardt, Billy Ray *university official, agriculturist*
Belcastro, Patrick Frank *pharmaceutical scientist*
BeMiller, James Noble *biochemist, educator*
Bertolet, Rodney Jay *philosophy educator*
Bogdanoff, John Lee *aeronautical engineering educator*
Borch, Richard Frederic *pharmacology and chemistry educator*
Borgens, Richard *biologist*
Borowitz, Joseph Leo *pharmacologist*
†Brush, F(ranklin) Robert *psychobiology educator*
Chao, Kwang-Chu *chemical engineer, educator*
Chen, Wai-Fah *civil engineering educator*
Christian, John Edward *health science educator*
Cicirelli, Victor George *psychologist*
Cochrane, Thomas Thurston *tropical soil scientist, agronomist*
Cohen, Raymond *mechanical engineer, educator*
Connor, John Murray *agricultural economics educator*
Contreni, John Joseph, Jr. *humanities educator*
Cooper, Arnold Cook *management educator, researcher*
Cooper, James Albert, Jr. *electrical engineering educator*
Cosier, Richard A. *business educator, consultant*
Cox, Beverly E. *educational researcher, educator*
Cramer, William Anthony *biochemistry and biophysics researcher, educator*
Cutter, Charles Ross *historian, educator*
Delleur, Jacques William *civil engineering educator*
Diamond, Sidney *chemist, educator*
†DiGiulio, Cinzia *Italian language educator*
Drake, John Warren *aviation consultant*
Drnevich, Vincent Paul *civil engineering educator*
Eckert, Roger E(arl) *chemical engineering educator*
Edwards, Charles Richard *entomology and pest management educator*
Evanson, Robert Verne *pharmacy educator*
Farris, Paul Leonard *agricultural economist*
Ferris, Virginia Rogers *nematologist, educator*
Franzmeier, Donald Paul *agronomy educator, soil scientist*
Friedlaender, Fritz Josef *electrical engineering educator*
Gappa, Judith M. *university administrator*
Garfinkel, Alan *Spanish language and education educator*
Gennett, Timothy *academic administrator*
Gentry, Don Kenneth *academic dean*
Gottfried, Leon Albert *English language educator*
Greenkorn, Robert Albert *chemical engineering educator*
Grimley, Robert Thomas *chemistry educator*
Gruen, Gerald Elmer *psychologist, educator*
Hanks, Alan R. *chemistry educator*
Harmon, Bud Gene *animal sciences educator, consultant*
Hill, Rebecca Sue Helm *educator*
Hinkle, Charles Nelson *retired agricultural engineering educator*
Hoover, William Leichliter *forestry and natural resources educator, financial consultant*
Horwich, George *economist, educator*
Hunt, Michael O'Leary *wood science and engineering educator*
Ichiyama, Dennis Yoshihide *design educator, consultant, administrator*
Jagacinski, Carolyn Mary *psychology educator*
Johannsen, Chris Jakob *agronomist, educator, administrator*
Johns, Janet Susan *physician*
Kirby, John Thomas *comparative literature educator*
Kirksey, Avanelle *nutrition educator*
Koivo, Antti Jaakko *electrical engineering educator, researcher*
Lacci, John *chemical company executive*
Landgrebe, David Allen *electrical engineer*
Laskowitz, Kate *labor relations educator*
Laskowski, Michael, Jr. *chemist, educator*
Leap, Darrell Ivan *hydrogeologist*
Lechtenberg, Victor L. *agricultural studies educator*
Leimkuhler, Ferdinand Francis *industrial engineering educator*
Le Master, Dennis Clyde *natural resource economics and policy educator*
Lewellen, Wilbur Garrett *management educator, consultant*
Lin, Pen-Min *electrical engineer, educator*

Lipschutz, Michael Elazar *chemistry educator, consultant, researcher*
†Lyrintis, Anastasios Sotirios *engineering educator*
Lyrintzis, Anastasios Sotirios *aerospace engineering professor*
Margerum, Dale William *chemistry educator*
Markee, Katherine Madigan *librarian, educator*
Marshall, Francis Joseph *aerospace engineer*
Mc Bride, William Leon *philosopher, educator*
McFee, William Warren *soil scientist*
Mc Gillem, Clare Duane *electrical engineering educator*
Mc Laughlin, John Francis *civil engineer, educator*
McMillin, David Robert *chemistry educator*
Melhorn, Wilton Newton *geosciences educator*
Michael, Harold Louis *civil engineering educator*
Molnar, Donald Joseph *landscape architecture educator*
Moore, David Sheldon *statistics educator, researcher*
Mork, Gordon Robert *historian, educator*
Morrison, Harry *chemistry educator, university dean*
Moskowitz, Herbert *management educator*
Nelson, Philip Edwin *food scientist, educator*
Neudeck, Gerold Walter *electrical engineering educator*
Nichols, David Earl *pharmacy educator, researcher, consultant*
Nixon, Judith May *librarian*
†Oates, William Matthew *communication consultant*
Ohm, Herbert Willis *agronomy educator*
Ong, Chee-Mun *engineering educator*
Ortman, Eldon E. *entomologist, educator*
Overhauser, Albert Warner *physicist*
Pask, Judith Marie *librarian educator*
Peck, Garnet Edward *pharmacist, educator*
Peppas, Nikolaos Athanassiou *chemical engineering educator, consultant*
Perrucci, Robert *sociologist, educator*
Ramadhyani, Satish *mechanical engineering educator*
Rice, John Rischard *computer scientist, researcher, educator*
Richey, Clarence Bentley *agricultural engineering educator*
Ringel, Robert Lewis *university administrator*
Robinson, Farrel Richard *pathologist, toxicologist*
Rossmann, Michael George *biochemist, educator*
Rothenberg, Gunther Erich *history educator*
Rutledge, Charles Ozwin *pharmacologist, educator*
St. John, Charles Virgil *retired pharmaceutical company executive*
Salvendy, Gavriel *industrial engineer*
Saunders, James Robert *English educator*
Scaletta, Phillip Jasper *lawyer, educator*
Schendel, Dan Eldon *management consultant, business educator*
Schrader, Lee Frederick *agricultural economist*
Schreiber, Marvin Mandel *agronomist, educator*
Schwartz, Richard John *electrical engineering educator, researcher*
Shaw, Stanley Miner *nuclear pharmacy scientist*
Sherman, Louis Allen *biology educator*
Shertzer, Bruce Eldon *education educator*
†Sims-Curry, Kristy *women's college basketball coach*
†Smith, Robert Edward, Jr. *communication educator, writer*
Sozen, Mete Avni *civil engineering educator*
Steer, Max David *speech pathologist, educator*
Stevenson, Warren Howard *mechanical engineering educator*
Stob, Martin *physiology educator*
Stone, Beverley *former university dean, former dean of students*
Swensen, Clifford Henrik, Jr. *psychologist, educator*
Taber, Margaret Ruth *electrical engineering technology educator, electrical engineer*
Tacker, Willis Arnold, Jr. *medical educator, researcher*
Theen, Rolf Heinz-Wilhelm *political science educator*
Thursby, Jerry Gilbert *economics educator, consultant*
Tilton, Mark Campbell *educator*
Tomovic, Mileta Milos *mechanical engineer, educator*
Truce, William Everett *chemist, educator*
Tucker, John Mark *librarian, educator*
Tyner, Wallace Edward *economics educator*
Viskanta, Raymond *mechanical engineering educator*
Wankat, Phillip Charles *chemical engineering educator*
Watlington, Sarah Jane *community volunteer, retired military officer*
Weidenaar, Dennis Jay *college dean*
Weinstein, Michael Alan *political science educator*
White, Joe Lloyd *soil scientist, educator*
Williams, Theodore Joseph *engineering educator*
Woodman, Harold David *historian*
Wright, Alfred George James *band symphony orchestra conductor, educator*
Wright, Gordon Pribyl *management, operations research educator*
Wright, Jeff Regan *civil engineering educator*

Westville
Alspaugh, Dale William *university administrator, aeronautics and astronautics educator*
Van Cauwenbergh, Janice Topp *mental health and clinical nurse specialist, educator*

Whiting
Fies, Ruth Elaine *media specialist*

Winamac
Ligocki, Gordon Michael *artist, educator*

Winchester
Tanner, Judith Ann *retired speech-language pathologist*

Windfall
Cooper, Joyce Beatrice *medical/surgical nurse*

Winona Lake
Ashman, Charles H. *retired minister*
Davis, John James *religion educator*
Julien, Thomas Theodore *religious denomination administrator*
Lewis, Edward Alan *religious organization admnistrator*
†Plaster, David Roy *college executive*
†Soto, Mark Harrison *Biblical studies educator, pastor*
Williams, Ronald Eugene *minister, evangelist*

Yorktown
Downing, Barbara Kay *principal*
Stephenson, Julie *secondary school educator*

Zionsville
Bruess, Charles Edward *lawyer*
Hansen, Arthur Gene *former academic administrator, consultant*
Schlensker, Gary Chris *landscaping company executive*

IOWA

Ainsworth
Osterkamp-Sellars, Arlene Judy *gerontology nurse*

Akron
Hultgren, Dennis Eugene *farmer, management consultant*

Albia
Putnam, Bonnie Colleen *elementary education educator*

Algona
Andreasen, James Hallis *retired state supreme court judge*
Burrow, David Michael *mathematics educator, academic administrator*

Amana
Vorhies, Mahlon Wesley *veterinary pathologist, educator*

Ames
Ahmann, John Stanley *psychology educator*
Ahrens, Franklin Alfred *veterinary pharmacology educator*
†Ajax, Ernest Todd *neurologist*
Anderson, Lloyd Lee *animal science educator*
Anderson, Robert Morris, Jr. *electrical engineer*
Barnes, Richard George *physicist, educator*
Barton, Thomas Jackson *chemistry educator, researcher*
Basart, John Philip *electrical engineering and radio astronomy researcher, educator*
Baumann, Edward Robert *environmental engineering educator*
Beran, George Wesley *veterinary microbiology educator*
Berger, P(hilip) Jeffrey *animal science educator, quantitative geneticist*
Berry, Jay Robert, Jr. *English educator*
Black, James Robert *industrial engineer*
Bonomi, Ferne Gater *public relations executive*
Bourke, Kevin *coach*
Bowen, George Hamilton, Jr. *astrophysicist, educator*
Brown, Robert Grover *engineering educator*
Bruner, Charlotte Hughes *French language educator*
Buchele, Wesley Fisher *retired agricultural engineering educator*
Bullen, Daniel Bernard *mechanical engineering educator*
Burris, Joseph Stephen *agronomy educator*
Cao, Heping *biologist, researcher*
Cleasby, John LeRoy *civil engineer, educator*
Clem, John Richard *physicist, educator*
Colvin, Thomas Stuart *agricultural engineer, farmer*
Corbett, John Dudley *chemistry educator*
Crabtree, Beverly June *retired college dean*
Dahiya, Rajbir Singh *mathematics educator, researcher*
David, Herbert Aron *statistics educator*
Dial, Eleanore Maxwell *foreign language educator*
Dyrenfurth, Michael John *vocational technical and industrial technology educator, consultant*
Ebbers, Larry Harold *education educator*
Fennelly, William *basketball coach*
Finn, Brendan Peter *school psychologist*
Fox, Karl August *economist, eco-behavioral scientist*
Frederick, Lloyd Randall *soil microbiologist*
Freeman, Albert E. *agricultural science educator*
Fritz, James Sherwood *chemist, educator*
Fuller, Wayne Arthur *statistics educator*
Gartner, Michael Gay *editor, television executive*
Ghoshal, Nani Gopal *veterinary anatomist, educator*
Greve, John Henry *veterinary parasitologist, educator*
Gschneidner, Karl Albert, Jr. *metallurgist, educator, editor, consultant*
Hallauer, Arnel Roy *geneticist*
Harl, Neil Eugene *economist, lawyer, educator*
Hatfield, Jerry Lee *plant physiologist, biometeorologist*
Hill, Fay Gish *librarian*
Hobson, Keith Lee *civil engineer, consultant*
Horowitz, Jack *biochemistry educator*
Inger, George Roe *aerospace engineering educator*
Jacobson, Norman L. *retired agricultural educator, researcher*
Jacobson, Robert Andrew *chemistry educator*
†James, Patrick *political science educator*
Jischke, Martin C. *academic administrator*
Johnson, Howard Paul *agricultural engineering educator*
Johnson, Lawrence Alan *cereal technologist, educator, administrator*
Jones, Edwin Channing, Jr. *electrical engineering educator*
Kainlauri, Eino Olavi *architect*
Karlen, Douglas Lawrence *soil scientist*
Keeney, Dennis Raymond *soil science educator*
Kelly, James Michael *plant and soil scientist*
King, Michael Pearson *writer, English educator*
Klonglan, Gerald Edward *sociology educator*
Larsen, William Lawrence *materials science and engineering educator*
Manatt, Richard *education educator*
†Martin, Paul A. *veterinary educator and researcher*
McCarney, Dan *coach*
Mengeling, William Lloyd *veterinarian, virologist, researcher*
Mertins, James Walter *entomologist*
Mischke, Charles Russell *mechanical engineering educator*
Moon, Harley William *veterinarian*
Moore, Kenneth James *agronomy educator*
Moyer, James Wallace *physicist, consultant*
Mullen, Russell Edward *agricultural studies educator*
O'Berry, Phillip Aaron *veterinarian*
Okiishi, Theodore Hisao *mechanical engineering educator*
Orazem, Peter Francis *economics educator*
Palermo, Gregory Sebastian *architect*
Pearce, Robert Brent *agricultural studies educator*
Pearson, Phillip Theodore *veterinary clinical sciences and biomedical engineering educator*
Peterson, Francis *physicist, educator*
Rabideau, Peter Wayne *university dean, chemistry educator*
Riley, William Franklin *mechanical engineering educator*
Ross, Richard Francis *veterinarian, microbiologist, educator*
Ruedenberg, Klaus *theoretical chemist, educator*
Russell, Glen Allan *chemist, educator*
Sanders, Wallace Wolfred, Jr. *civil engineer*
Schuh, John Howard *adult education educator, academic administrator*
Seaton, Vaughn Allen *retired veterinary pathology educator*
Skarshaug, David Paul *industrial engineer*
Smiley, Jane Graves *author, educator*
Smith, Eugene D. *coach*
Smith, John Francis *materials science educator*
Smith, Kim Anthony *journalist, educator*
Snow, Joel Alan *research director*
Svec, Harry John *chemist, educator*
Tenek, Lazarus *mechanical engineer*
Thompson, Donald Oscar *physicist*
Thompson, Louis Milton *agronomy educator, scientist*
Topel, David Glen *agricultural studies educator*
Venkata, Subrahmanyam Saraswati *electrical engineering educator, electric energy and power researcher*
Voss, Regis Dale *agronomist, educator*
Wallin, Jack Robb *research plant pathology educator*
Wass, Wallace Milton *veterinarian, clinical science educator*
†Whitaker, Faye P. *education educator*
Wilder, David Randolph *materials engineer, consultant*
Willham, Richard Lewis *animal science educator*
Yeung, Edward Szeshing *chemist*
Young, Donald Fredrick *engineering educator*
Young, Jerry Wesley *animal nutrition educator*
Zimmerman, William *artist*
†Zimmerman, Zora Devrnja *dean, English language educator*

Anamosa
Haas, Lu Ann *counselor*

Anita
Everhart, Robert Phillip (Bobby Williams) *entertainer, songwriter, recording artist*

Ankeny
Boelens, Patricia Ann *accountant, nurse*
Creswell, Dorothy Anne *computer consultant*
Gilbert, Fred D., Jr. *college official*
Houghton, Myron James *theology educator*
Nash, John J(oseph) *real estate manager, computer programmer*
Rivers, Donald Lee *marketing professional*

Armstrong
†Jensen, Gertrude Eileen *librarian*

Arnolds Park
Ritzer, Karen Rae *executive secretary, office administrator*

Avoca
Hardisty, William Lee *English language educator*

Baxter
Edge, John Forrest *banker*

Belmond
Johnson, Roger Christie *environmental engineer*

Bettendorf
Edgerton, Winfield Dow *gynecologist*
Herdman, Susan *art educator, artist*
Heyderman, Arthur Jerome *engineer, civilian military employee*
Kucharo, Donald Dennis, Jr. *manufacturer's representative*
Rathje, James Lee *broker*
†Sandvick, Doris S. *elementary educator*

Birmingham
Goudy, James Joseph Ralph *electronics executive, educator*

Boone
Beckwith, F. W. *food products executive*
†Taylor, Sheila Marie *principal*

Britt
†Castillo, Leanne Marlow *artist, nurse*

Burlington
Brocket, Judith Ann *elementary education mathematics educator*
Hoth, Steven Sergey *lawyer*
Lundy, Sherman Perry *secondary school educator*
Paragas, Rolando G. *physician*
Trickler, Sally Jo *technical illustrator*

Carlisle
Berning, Robert William *librarian*

Carroll
De Moss, Lloyd G. *community service executive*
Neu, Arthur Alan *lawyer*

Cedar Falls
Clift, G.W. *critic*
Clohesy, William Warren *philosophy educator*
DiCecco, Tony *university head women's basketball coach*
†Edginton, Christopher R. *educator, academic administrator*
Fanelli, Michael Paul *music educator*
Gordon, Debra Gwen *music educator*
Greer, Willis Roswell, Jr. *accounting educator*
Hall, Teresa Joanne Keys *manufacturing engineer, educator*
Ishler, Margaret Fisher *education educator*
Johnson, Curtis Scott *engineer*
†Koob, Robert Duane *chemistry educator, educational administrator*
Kuethe-Strudthoff, Denise LaRae *librarian*
Oster, Merrill James *entrepreneur, publisher, author, lecturer*
Silverson, Rex *autos and homes builder, educator*
Sweet, Cynthia Rae *office administrator*
Wang, Jennie *literature educator*
Wilson, Robley Conant, Jr. *English educator, editor, author*
Wirth, David Eugene *software designer, consultant*

Cedar Rapids
Albright, Justin W. *lawyer*
Armitage, Thomas Edward *library director*
Baermann, Donna Lee Roth *property executive, retired insurance analyst*
Baker, Frank C. (Buzz Baker) *advertising executive*
Baldwin, George Koehler *retail executive*
Berry, Roberta Mildred *civic worker*
Blome, Dennis H. *United States marshal*
Boettcher, Norbe Birosel *chemist*
Damrow, Richard G. *marketing executive*
Dvorak, Clarence Allen *microbiologist*
Faches, William George *lawyer*
Feld, Thomas Robert *academic administrator*
Fick, E(arl) Dean *insurance executive*
Frangipane, Francis A. *minister, religious organization executive, writer*
Haines, Cathy Jean *elementary education educator*
Hansen, David Rasmussen *federal judge*
Healey, Edward Hopkins *architect*
Heller, Terry L(ynn) *English literature educator, writer*
Hensley, Robert Bruce *psychology educator*
Holder, Kathleen *elementary education educator*
Houmes, Blaine V. *emergency physician*
Hutton, Mary J. *guidance counselor*
†Jarvey, John A. *federal judge*
Keller, Eliot Aaron *broadcasting executive*
†Kilburg, Paul J. *federal judge*
Knapp, Barbara Allison *financial services, oncological nurse consultant*
Knepper, Eugene Arthur *realtor*
Krivit, Jeffrey Scot *surgeon*
Lisio, Donald John *historian, educator*
†McElmeel, Sharron Leila Hanson *author, editor*
Mc Manus, Edward Joseph *federal judge*
Melloy, Michael J. *federal judge*
Meyer, Curtis Ray *accountant*
Nazette, Richard Follett *lawyer*
Nebergall, Donald Charles *rural consultant*
Norris, Albert Stanley *psychiatrist, educator*
Novetzke, Sally Johnson *former ambassador*
Plagman, Ralph *principal*
Quarton, William Barlow *broadcasting company executive*
Reinertson, James Wayne *pediatrician*
Richardson, Robert Edward *data processing analyst*
Riley, Tom Joseph *lawyer*
†Ripma, Barbara Jean *realtor*
Rohlena, Robert Charles *retired real estate manager*
Rosberg, Merilee Ann *education educator*
†Schmidt, Joel Joseph *energy company executive*
Smith, Cindy Thompson *special education educator*
Speicher, Gary Dean *financial planner*
Stirler, Karen Sue *special education educator, adult education educator*
Stolte, Larry Gene *marketing executive, former computer and publishing company executive*
Stone, Herbert Marshall *architect*
Struthers, Eleanor Ann *writer, educator*
Sueppel, Carralee Ann *medical/surgical nurse*
†Tiemeyer, Christian *conductor*
Vanderpool, Ward Melvin *management and marketing consultant*
Whipple, William Perry *foundation administrator*
Wiese, Daniel Edward *marketing and communications researcher*
Williams, Colin Dale *school system administrator*
Wilson, Robert Foster *lawyer*
Wright, Walter Edward *county official, retired army officer*
Ziese, Nancylee Hanson *social worker*
†Zmolek, Gloria Jean *artist*

Center Junction
Antons, Pauline Marie *mathematics educator*

Centerville
Strube, Christopher William *pastor*

Chariton
Stuart, William Corwin *federal judge*

Charles City
†Krieger, Theodore Kent *poet*
Mc Cartney, Ralph Farnham *lawyer*

Cherokee
Simonsen, Robert Alan *marketing executive*

Clear Lake
Broshar, Robert Clare *architect*
Schultz, Patricia Ann *secondary education educator*

Clinton
Baker, Gilbert Jens *management consultant*
Hicok, Bethany Faith *English educator*
Unger, Gary Allen *recording industry executive, singer, lyricist*
Warner, Jean Lollich *poet*
Winkler, Joann Mary *secondary school educator*
Woodman, Grey Musgrave *psychiatrist*

Clive
Miller, Kenneth Edward *sociologist, educator*

Coggon
Hammer, Robert Eugene *psychologist*

Coon Rapids
Shirbroun, Richard Elmer *veterinarian, cattleman*

Coralville
Bell, Raymond Martin *retired physics educator*
†Lueder, Barbara Ann *school psychologist*

Corning
Rummer, Kenneth Dale *pastor*

Corydon
Hopkins, Theodore Mark *minister, guidance counselor*

Council Bluffs
Blum, Vicky Jolene *medical/surgical nurse*
Duquette, Diana Marie *company official*
†Godsey, James Mark *library director*
Johnson, Michael Randy *insurance company executive*
Kelly, Patricia Ann *communication arts educator*
Nelson, H. H. Red *insurance company executive*
Peterson, Richard William *magistrate judge, lawyer*
Roberts, Antonette *special education educator*

Dallas Center
McDonald, John Cecil *lawyer*
Snyder, Dana Renee Nelson *business executive*

Davenport
Asadi, Anita Murlene *business educator*
Bartlett, Peter Greenough *engineering company executive*
†Bradley, Ritamary *retired English educator*
Brocka, Bruce *editor, educator, software engineer*
Brocka, M. Suzanne *controller*
Brown, Colleen *broadcast executive*
Bush, Michael Kevin *lawyer*
Caffery, Lisa Kaye *nurse*
Dcamp, Charles Barton *educator, musician*
Dcamp, Richard Manley *secondary education educator*
Franklin, William Edwin *bishop*
Giudici, Michael Charles *cardiac electrophysiologist*
Gottlieb, Richard Douglas *media executive*
Halligan, Kevin Leo *lawyer*
Hudson, Celeste Nutting *education educator, reading clinic administrator, consultant*
Jecklin, Lois Underwood *art corporation executive, consultant*
Juckem, Wilfred Philip *manufacturing company executive*
Kruse, Rosalee Evelyn *accountant, auditor*
Lathrop, Roger Alan *lawyer*
Le Grand, Clay *lawyer, former state justice*
Melissano, Rita Rosaria *social work educator, marriage, family therapist*
†Mobley, William Clifford *urologist*
Monty, Mitchell *landscape company executive*
Neuman, Linda Kinney *state supreme court justice*
O'Keefe, Gerald Francis *bishop, retired*
Pedersen, Karen Sue *electrical engineer*
Potter, Corinne Jean *retired librarian*
Rogalski, Edward J. *university administrator*
Runge, Kay Kretschmar *library director*
Shammas, Nicolas Wahib *internist, cardiologist*
Shaw, Donald Hardy *lawyer*
Shaw, Elizabeth Orr *lawyer*
Skora, Susan Sundman *lawyer*
Stauff, Jon William *history educator*
†Stephans, Patrice Ann *dean*
Wilson, Frances Edna *protective services official*

Decorah
Barnes-Guzman, Beth Yvette *grants administrator*
Erdman, Lowell Paul *civil engineer, land surveyor*
Everman, Nancy Lidtke *farmer, organization executive*
Farwell, Elwin D. *minister, educational consultant*
Kalsow, Kathryn Ellen *library clerk*
Maurland, Anne Elisabeth *potter*
†Nelson, Harland Stanley *retired English educator*

Des Moines
Anderson, Eric Anthony *city manager*
†Anderson, James Donald *state official*
Arvidson, Robert Benjamin, Jr. *geneticist, consultant*
†Atchison, Christopher George *public health director*
Baybayan, Ronald Alan *lawyer*
Beisser, Sally Rapp *educator*
Bergman, Bruce E. *municipal official*
Bittle, Edgar H. *lawyer*
Blank, Myron Nathan *theater executive*
†Blazek, Steven Joseph *investment company executive, sales executive*
Bluder, Lisa *women's collegiate basketball coach*
†Bodensteiner, Carol A. *public relations executive*
Boyle, Bruce James *publisher*
†Brauch, William Leland *lawyer*
Bremer, Celeste F. *judge*
Brickman, Kenneth Alan *state lottery executive*
Brooks, Roger Kay *insurance company executive*
Brown, Loren Dennis *internist, educator*
Brown, Paul Edmondson *lawyer*
Bucksbaum, Matthew *real estate investment trust company executive*
Burgess, Donna Elaine *clinical social worker*
Burns, Bernard John, III *public defender*
Byal, Nancy Louise *food editor*
Campbell, Bruce Irving *lawyer*
Carroll, Frank James *lawyer, educator*
Carter, James H. *state supreme court justice*
Charron, Joseph L. *bishop*
Cherry, Linda Lea *federal agency official*
Claypool, David L. *lawyer*
†Cochran, Dale M. *state agency administrator*
Conlin, Roxanne Barton *lawyer*
Corning, Joy Cole *former state official*
Cortese, Joseph Samuel, II *lawyer*
†Culver, Chester J. *state official*
†Daniels, Preston A. *mayor*
Dawson, Armetta K. *mental health and geriatric nurse*
DeAngelo, Anthony James *media specialist, architect, writer, communication specialist*
Deluhery, Patrick John *state senator*
Doyle, Richard Henry, IV *lawyer*
Drake, Richard Francis *state senator*
Drury, David J. *insurance company executive*
Duckworth, Marvin E. *lawyer, educator*
Durrenberger, William John *retired army general, educator, investor*
Edwards, John Duncan *law educator, librarian*
Eichner, Kay Marie *mental health nurse*
†Eisenhower, Cynthia P. *state official*
Ellis, Mary Louise Helgeson *insurance company executive*
Elmets, Harry Barnard *osteopath, dermatologist*
Ely, Lawrence Orlo *retired surgeon*
Epting, C. Christopher *bishop*
Fagg, George Gardner *federal judge*
Ferrell, Lynn DuWayne *county official*
Fisher, Thomas George *lawyer, retired media company executive*
Fisher, Thomas George, Jr. *lawyer*
Fitzgerald, Michael Lee *state official*
Flynn, Thomas Lee *lawyer*
Foxhoven, Jerry Ray *lawyer*
Frederici, C. Carleton *lawyer*
†Gaines, Ruth Ann *educator*
Gardner, Richard Eugene *landscape architect*
†Giunta, Joseph *conductor, music director*
Graham, Diane E. *newspaper editor*
Graziano, Craig Frank *lawyer*
Grefe, Rolland Eugene *lawyer*
Grundberg, Betty *state legislator, property manager*
Hall, Donald Vincent *social worker*
Hansell, Edgar Frank *lawyer*
Hanusa, George Leonard *minister*
Harper, Patricia M. *state legislator*
Harris, Charles Elmer *lawyer*
Harris, K. David *state supreme court justice*
Henry, Barbara A. *publishing executive*
Henry, Phylliss Jeanette *United States Marshal*
Hill, Luther Lyons, Jr. *lawyer*
†Hill, Russell J. *federal judge*
Hill-Davis, Deborah Ann *school psychologist*
Hockenberg, Harlan David *lawyer*
Hoffmann, Michael Richard *lawyer*
Hyon, Won Sop *certified public accountant, auditor*
Isenstein, Laura *library director*
Israni, Kim *civil engineer*
†Jackwig, Lee M. *federal judge*
Jensen, Dick Leroy *lawyer*
Jeschke, Thomas *gifted education educator*
Jones, Floyd A. *municipal official*
Jordan, Charles Wesley *bishop*
Kalainov, Sam Charles *insurance company executive*
Kelley, Bruce Gunn *insurance company executive, lawyer*
Kerr, William T. *publishing and broadcasting executive*
Koehn, William James *lawyer*
Kramer, Mary Elizabeth *health services executive, state legislator*
Kruidenier, David *newspaper executive*
Langdon, Herschel Garrett *lawyer*
Larson, Jerry Leroy *state supreme court justice*
Lavorato, Louis A. *state supreme court justice*
Lawless, James L. *editor, columnist*
Lawyer, Vivian Jury *lawyer*
Leach, Dave Francis *editor, musician*
Lemmon, Jean Marie *editor-in-chief*
Leonard, George Edmund *real estate, bank, and consulting executive*
Lewis, Calvin Fred *architect, educator*
Longstaff, Ronald E. *federal judge*
Mattern, David Bruce *elementary education educator*
McGiverin, Arthur A. *state supreme court chief justice*
Miller, Thomas J. *state attorney general*
Molden, A(nna) Jane *retired counselor*
Moos, Pamela Sue *family development specialist*
Moulder, William H. *chief of police*
Myers, Mary Kathleen *publishing executive*
Narber, Gregg Ross *lawyer*
Neiman, John Hammond *lawyer*
Nelson, Charlotte Bowers *public administrator*
Nickerson, Don C. *lawyer*
Odell, Mary Jane *former state official*
†O'Donnell, Thomas Richard *reporter*
Peddicord, Roland Dale *lawyer*
†Pederson, Sally *state official*
Peterson, David Charles *photojournalist*
Peterson, Michael K. *Democrat party chairman*
Porter, Russell Mark *law enforcement executive, educator, trainer*
Powell, Sharon Lee *social welfare organization administrator*
Power, Joseph Edward *lawyer*
Proudfoot, James Mark *custodian*
Reece, Maynard Fred *artist, author*
Rhein, Dave *newspaper editor*
Richards, Riley Harry *insurance company executive*
Riper, Kevin *city official*
Rittmer, Elaine Heneke *library media specialist*
Rodgers, Louis Dean *retired surgeon*
Rood, Lee *newspaper editor*
Rosen, Matthew Stephen *botanist, consultant*
Rosenberg, Ralph *former state senator, lawyer, consultant, educator*
†Ryerson, Dennis *editor*
Schmidt, Barbara J. *educational consultant*
Schneider, William George *former life insurance company executive*
†Shao Collins, Jeannine *magazine publisher*
Shepherd, Tom Richard *financial executive*
Shors, John D. *lawyer*
Simpson, Lyle Lee *lawyer*
Smith, Sharman Bridges *state librarian*
Song, Joseph *pathologist, educator*
Speas, Raymond Aaron *retired insurance company executive*
†Stilwill, Ted *state agency administrator*
Stork, Frank James *lawyer*
Stubbs, David H. *vascular surgeon*
Szymoniak, Elaine Eisfelder *state senator*
Ternus, Marsha K. *state supreme court justice*
Thoman, Mark Edward *pediatrician*
†Truck, Frederick John *artist*
Vande Krol, Jerry Lee *architect*
Van Zante, Shirley M(ae) *magazine editor*
†Vaughan, Therese Michele *insurance commissioner*
Vietor, Harold Duane *federal judge*
†Vilsack, Thomas *governor*
Waldon, Marja Parker *mental health nurse*
†Walters, Ross A. *federal judge*
Wanek, Jerrold *lawyer*
Wannamaker, Mary Ruth *music educator*
Webb, Mary Christine *special education educator*
Wessendorf Knau, Suana Le *special education educator*
Westphal, Deborah Louise *retail executive, choreographer*
Williams, Carl Chanson *insurance company executive*
Wilson, Sally Ann *computer systems analyst, business executive*
Wine, Donald Arthur *lawyer*
Witke, David Rodney *newspaper editor*
Wolle, Charles Robert *federal judge*
Womack, Doug C. *labor union representative*
Yetmar, Scott Andrew *accountant, educator*

Dubuque
Barker, Barbara Yvonne *nursing home administrator*
Barker, Richard Alexander *organizational psychologist*
Barta, James Omer *priest, psychology educator, church administrator*
Beck, Robert Raymond *priest*
Bloesch, Donald George *theologian, writer, educator*
Brimeyer, James Leon *English educator*
Crahan, Jack Bertsch *manufacturing company executive*
Decker, Judith Ann *computer science educator*
Dunn, Frank M. (Francis Michael Dunn) *banker*
Dunn, M. Catherine *college administrator, educator*
Ernst, Daniel Pearson *lawyer*
Felderman, Robert John *real estate appraiser, realtor*
Fischer, Katherine Mary *English educator*
Gibbs, Robert T. (Tom) *sculptor, consultant*
Gifford, Thomas Eugene *writer*
Hammer, David Lindley *lawyer, author*
Hanus, Jerome George *archbishop*
Hemmer, Paul Edward *musician, composer, broadcasting executive*
Kolz, Beverly Anne *publishing executive*
Leblond, Jack James *multimedia executive*
†McAlpin, Sara Ann *English educator*
Nessan, Craig Lee *minister, educator*
Perry, E. Eugene *humanities educator*
Peterson, Walter Fritiof *academic administrator*
Phillips, Betty Joan *retired educator in student services*
†Stenberg, Michael Donald *physician*
Swiderski, Suzanne Marie *English educator*
Toale, Thomas Edward *school system administrator, priest*
Tully, Thomas Alois *building materials executive, consultant, educator*

Eldora
Kerns, Steve *geneticist*

Elliott
Hunt, Colleen A. *educational consultant*

Emmetsburg
Wells, Martha Johanna *elementary education educator*

Essex
Raynor, Patricia Ann Herbert *special education educator*

Estherville
Klepper, Robert Rush *plant physiologist*

Fairfield
Aubrey, Bryan *educator, writer, editor*
Hawthorne, Timothy Robert *direct response advertising and communications company executive*
†Joshi, Prabhakar G. *educator*
Schaefer, Jimmie Wayne, Jr. *agricultural company executive*
Wright, Max *information processing executive, consultant, youth leadership corporate training executive*

Fonda
Tamm, Eleanor Ruth *retired accountant*

Fort Dodge
DeLucca, Leopoldo Eloy *otolaryngologist, head and neck surgeon*
Hammar, David Bruce *clergyman*
Sutton, Melle Renee *laboratory technician*
Tursso, Dennis Joseph *business executive*
Walsh, Patrick R. *priest, school system administrator*
Wolf, Robert Charles *writer, news correspondent*

Fort Madison
Sallen, David Urban *lawyer*
Wallerich, Omer Kay *secondary education educator*

Garner
Mestad, Gary Allen *education educator*

George
†Martens-Rosenboom, Marcia Ann *secondary education educator*
Symens, Maxine Brinkert Tanner *restaurant owner*

Glenwood
Campbell, William Edward *mental hospital administrator*
Hoogestraat, Thomas John *human services professional*
Paul, Harva Hall *school psychologist*

Grinnell
Adelberg, Arnold Melvin *mathematics educator, researcher*
Campbell, David George *ecologist, researcher, author*
Ferguson, Pamela Anderson *mathematics educator, educational administrator*
Irving, Donald C. *English educator*
Kaiser, Daniel Hugh *historian, educator*
Kintner, Philip L. *history educator*
McKee, Christopher Fulton *librarian, naval historian, educator*
Michaels, Jennifer Tonks *foreign language educator*
Mitchell, Orlan E. *clergyman, former college president*
Osgood, Russell King *dean*
Schrift, Alan Douglas *philosophy educator*
†Smith, Don Alan *educator*
Walker, Waldo Sylvester *biology educator, academic administrator*

Harlan
Jacobsen, Linda Mary *county official*

Hiawatha
Merriam, Oliver Steven *city manager*
Pate, Paul Danny *secretary of state*
Robertson, Florence Winkler *advertising and public relations agency executive*

Honey Creek
Hansen, Cherry A. Fisher *special education educator*

Hopkinton
Pounds, Buzz R. *educator*

Hubbard
Cook, Lisle *farmer*

Ida Grove
Glisson, Melissa Ann *dietitian*

Indianola
Larsen, Robert LeRoy *artistic director*
Mace, Jerilee Marie *opera company executive*
Mapel, Patricia Jolene *farmer, consultant*
Ouderkirk, Mason James *lawyer*
Snyder, Arlen Dean *actor*

Inwood
Jacobs, Patricia Louise *geriatrics nurse*

Iowa City
Abboud, Francois Mitry *physician, educator*
Addis, Laird Clark, Jr. *philosopher, educator, musician*
Afifi, Adel Kassim *physician*
†Aikin, Judith Popovich *languages educator, academic administrator*
Albrecht, William Price *economist, educator, government official*
†Alford, Steve *college basketball coach*
Anderson, Eugene Harold *retired architect, sculptor*
Andreasen, Nancy Coover *psychiatrist, educator, neuroscientist*
Apicella, Michael Allen *physician, educator*
Arora, Jasbir Singh *engineering educator*
Bailey, Regenia Dee *non-profit executive*
Baird, Robert Dahlen *religious educator*
Baker, Richard Graves *geology educator, palynologist*
Banker, Gilbert Stephen *industrial and physical pharmacy educator, administrator*
Barkan, Joel David *political science educator, consultant*
Baron, Jeffrey *pharmacologist, educator*
†Baynton, Douglas Cameron *historian*
Bedell, George Noble *physician, educator*
Bell, Marvin Hartley *poet, English language educator*
Bentz, Dale Monroe *librarian*
Bishara, Samir Edward *orthodontist*
Bjorndal, Arne Magne *endodontist*
Blake, Darlene Evelyn *political worker, consultant, educator, author*
Block, Robert I. *psychologist, researcher, educator*
Bloom, Stephen G *journalist, educator*
Bonfield, Arthur Earl *lawyer, educator*
Bowden, Terry Wilson *coach*
Bowlsby, Bob *athletic director*
Boyd, Willard Lee *academic administrator, museum administrator, lawyer*
Brennan, Robert Lawrence *educational director, psychometrician*
Broffitt, James Drake *professor statistics and actuarial science*
Buckwalter, Joseph Addison *orthopedic surgeon, educator*
Burns, C(harles) Patrick *hematologist-oncologist*
Burton, Donald Joseph *chemistry educator*
Butchvarov, Panayot Krustev *philosophy educator*
Campion, Daniel Ray *editor*
†Caplan, Richard Melvin *retired medical educator, musician, author*
Clifton, James Albert *physician, educator*
†Coleman, Mary Sue *academic administrator*
Collins, Daniel W. *accountant, educator*
Colloton, John William *university health care executive*
Coolidge, Archibald Cary, Jr. *English language educator, literature researcher*
Cooper, Reginald Rudyard *orthopedic surgeon, educator*
Craft-Rosenberg, Martha Jane *nursing educator*
Cruden, Robert William *botany educator*
Cyphert, Stacey Todd *health facilities administrator*
Damasio, Antonio R. *physician, neurologist*
Daniels, Lacy *microbiology educator*
Davis, Julia McBroom *college dean, speech pathology and audiology educator*
Donelson, John Everett *biochemistry educator, molecular biologist*
Downer, Robert Nelson *lawyer*
Duck, Steve Weatherill *communications educator*
Duffy, William Edward, Jr. *retired education educator*
Eckstein, John William *physician, educator*
Elardo, Richard *psychology and education educator*
Erkonen, William E. *radiologist, medical educator*
Ertl, Wolfgang *German language and literature educator*
Eyman, Earl Duane *electrical science educator, consultant*
Feldt, Leonard Samuel *university educator and administrator*
Fellows, Robert Ellis *medical educator, medical scientist*
Ferguson, Richard L. *educational administrator*
Folsom, Lowell Edwin *English language educator*
Forell, George Wolfgang *religion educator*
Forsythe, Robert Elliott *economics educator*
Fumerton, Richard Anthony *philosopher educator*
Galask, Rudolph Peter *obstetrician and gynecologist*
Gantz, Bruce Jay *otolaryngologist, educator*
Gelfand, Lawrence Emerson *historian, educator*
Gerber, John Christian *English language educator*
Gergis, Samir Danial *anesthesiologist, educator*
Goldstein, Jonathan Amos *ancient history and classics educator*
Grabbe, Crockett Lane *physicist, researcher, writer*
Graham, Jorie *author*
Green, Peter Morris *classics educator, writer, translator*
Green, William *archaeologist*
Grose, Charles Frederick *pediatrician, infectious disease specialist*
Groves, William Arthur *industrial hygiene educator*
Gurnett, Donald Alfred *physics educator*
Haravon Collins, Leslea *women's studies educator*
Haug, Edward Joseph, Jr. *mechanical engineering educator, simulation research engineer*
Hausler, William John, Jr. *microbiologist, educator, public health laboratory administrator*
Hawley, Ellis Wayne *historian, educator*
Hein, Herman August *physician*
Heistad, Donald Dean *cardiologist*
†Helms, Charles Milton *medical educator, consultant*
Hines, N. William *dean, law educator, administrator*
Hogg, Robert Vincent, Jr. *mathematical statistician, educator*
Holstein, Jay Allen *Judaic studies educator*
Howell, Robert Edward *hospital administrator*
Husted, Russell Forest *research scientist*
Huttner, Sidney Frederick *librarian*
Johnson, Eugene Walter *mathematician, editor*
Johnson, Nicholas *writer, lawyer, lecturer*
Justice, Donald Rodney *poet, educator*
Kardon, Randy H. *ophthalmologist*
Keen, Ralph *religious studies educator*
Kelch, Robert Paul *pediatric endocrinologist*
Kennedy, Jack *secondary education journalism educator*
Kerber, Linda Kaufman *historian, educator*

Kerber, Richard E. *cardiologist*
Kessel, Richard Glen *zoology educator*
Kim, Chong Lim *political science educator*
Kinsey, Joni Louise *art history educator*
Kisker, Carl Thomas *physician, medical educator*
Kleinfeld, Erwin *mathematician, educator*
Knapp, Howard Raymond *internist, clinical pharmacologist*
Koch, Donald LeRoy *geologist, state agency administrator*
Kottick, Edward Leon *music educator, harpsichord maker*
Krause, Walter *retired economics educator, consultant*
Kurtz, Sheldon Francis *lawyer, educator*
Kusiak, Andrew *manufacturing engineer, educator*
Lamping, Kathryn G. *medical educator, medical researcher*
Lauer, Ronald Martin *pediatric cardiologist, researcher*
LeBlond, Richard Foard *internist, educator*
Lim, Ramon (Khe-Siong) *neuroscience educator, researcher*
Linhardt, Robert John *medicinal chemistry educator*
Loewenberg, Gerhard *political science educator*
Long, John Paul *pharmacologist, educator*
Lonngren, Karl Erik *electrical and computer engineering educator*
Marshall, Jeffrey Scott *mechanical engineer, educator*
Mason, Edward Eaton *surgeon*
Mather, Roger Frederick *music educator, writer*
McAndrew, Paul Joseph, Jr. *lawyer*
†McCarville, Sheila Ann *special education educator, elementary educator*
†McCloskey, Deirdre Nansen *economics and history educator*
†McDowell, Frederick Peter Woll *retired English educator*
Merkel-Hess, Mary Lynne *artist*
Milkman, Marianne Friedenthal *retired city planner*
Milkman, Roger Dawson *genetics educator, molecular evolution researcher*
Montgomery, Rex *biochemist, educator*
Morice, David Jennings *illustrator, writer*
Morriss, Frank Howard, Jr. *pediatrics educator*
Muir, Ruth Brooks *counselor, substance abuse service coordinator*
Nair, Vasu *chemist, educator*
Nathan, Peter E. *psychologist, educator*
Nelson, Herbert Leroy *psychiatrist*
Nelson, Richard Philip *medical educator, dean*
Nesbitt, John Arthur *recreation service educator, recreation therapy educator*
Neumann, Roy Covert *architect*
†Newman, Robert Preston *educator*
Noyes, Russell, Jr. *psychiatrist*
Ogesen, Robert Bruce *dentist*
Olin, William Harold *orthodontist, educator*
Osborne, James William *radiation biologist*
Patel, Virendra Chaturbhai *mechanical engineering educator*
Percas de Ponseti, Helena *foreign language and literature educator*
Pessin, Jeffrey E. *physiology educator*
Plapp, Bryce Vernon *biochemistry educator*
Pogue, Thomas Franklin *economics educator, consultant*
Ponseti, Ignacio Vives *orthopaedic surgery educator*
Porter, Nancy Lefgren *reading recovery educator*
Prokopoff, Stephen Stephen *art museum director, educator*
Raeburn, John Hay *English language educator*
Reynolds, David G(eorge) *retired physiologist, educator*
Richenbacher, Wayne Edward *cardiothoracic surgeon*
Richerson, Hal Bates *physician, internist, allergist, immunologist, educator*
Riesz, Peter Charles *marketing educator, consultant*
Rim, Kwan *biomedical engineering educator*
Ringen, Catherine Oleson *linguistics educator*
Robertson, Timothy Joel *statistician, educator*
Robinson, Robert George *psychiatry educator*
Roe, Gerald Bruce *director*
Routh, Joseph Isaac *biochemist*
Sayre, Robert Freeman *English language educator*
†Schlueter, Mary Sue *nurse*
Schmidt, Julius *sculptor*
See, William A. *urology educator*
Shannon, Lyle William *sociology educator*
Siebert, Calvin D. *economist, educator*
Skorton, David Jan *university official, physician, educator, researcher*
Smothers, Ann E. *museum director*
Snyder, Peter M. *medical educator, medical researcher*
Solbrig, Ingeborg Hildegard *German literature educator, author*
Soloski, John *journalism and communications educator*
Spies, Leon Fred *lawyer*
Steele, Oliver *English educator*
Stein, Robert A. *writer, educator*
Stern, Gerald Daniel *poet*
Strauss, John Steinert *dermatologist, educator*
Sulg, Madis *corporation executive*
Tallent, William Hugh *chemist, research administrator*
Taylor, Rachel Lee *pianist, educator*
Tephly, Thomas Robert *pharmacologist, toxicologist, educator*
Thompson, Herbert Stanley *neuro-ophthalmologist*
Titze, Ingo Roland *physics educator*
Tomkovicz, James Joseph *law educator*
Trank, Douglas Monty *rhetoric and speech communications educator*
Traynelis, Vincent Charles *neurosurgeon*
Turner, James Daniel *computer company executive*
Van Allen, James Alfred *physicist, educator*
Van Gilder, John Corley *neurosurgeon, educator*
Vaughan, Emmett John *academic dean, insurance educator*
Venzke, Kristina Lea *academic administrator*
Vernon, David Harvey *lawyer, educator*
Wachal, Robert Stanley *linguistics educator, consultant*
Wasserman, Edward Arnold *psychology educator*
Weinberger, Miles M. *physician, pediatric educator*
Weingeist, Thomas Alan *ophthalmology educator*
Weinstock, Joel Vincent *immunologist*
Weintraub, Neal L. *medical educator, cardiologist*
Whitmore, Jon Scott *university official, play director*
Widiss, Alan I. *lawyer, educator*
Wing, Adrien Katherine *law educator*
Woolson, Robert Francis *biostatistician*
Wunder, Charles C(ooper) *physiology and biophysics educator, gravitational biologist*
Wurster, Dale Eric *pharmacy educator*

Wurster, Dale Erwin *pharmacy educator, university dean emeritus*
Ziegler, Ekhard Erich *pediatrics educator*

Iowa Falls
Sessler, Donna Jean Hotz *secondary education educator*

Jesup
Loeb, DeAnn Jean *nurse*

Johnston
Duvick, Donald Nelson *plant breeder*
Leitner, David Larry *lawyer*
Schultz, Roger C. *career officer*
Schumacher, Larry P. *health facility administrator*

Kalona
†Skaden, Anne M. *library director*

Kellogg
Anderson, Dale C. *state agency professional, travel consultant*

Keokuk
Fecht, Lorene *surgical nurse*
Hoffman, James Paul *lawyer, hypnotist*

Keosauqua
Murphy, Donna Lee *retired dance school owner*

Knoxville
Joslyn, Wallace Danforth *retired psychologist*
Just, Jennie Martha *mental health nurse*
Ribar, Dixie Lee *marketing coordinator*
Taylor, Mary Kay *medical, surgical nurse*

Lake Mills
Knudtson, Nancy Ann *family nurse practitioner*
Thompson, Jeannine Lucille *community health nurse*

Lamoni
Wight, Darlene *retired speech educator, emerita educator*

Larchwood
Zangger, Russell George *organization executive, flying school executive*

Laurens
Barrett, Patricia Ruth *government official*

Madrid
Handy, Richard Lincoln *civil engineer, educator*

Mallard
Grethen, Cheryl Ann *artist*

Manchester
†Sherman, Jane Candace *nurse*

Maquoketa
Tubbs, Edward Lane *banker*

Marion
Prall, Barbara Jones *artist*
Starr, Dave *corporate executive*

Marshalltown
Brennecke, Allen Eugene *lawyer*
Brooks, Patrick William *lawyer*
Foote, Sherrill Lynne *retired manufacturing company technician*
Geffe, Kent Lyndon *lawyer, educator*
Packer, Karen Gilliland *cancer patient educator, researcher*
Reitenbaugh, Luann Rose *quality assurance professional*
Roe, Sue Lynn *journalist, free lance writer*
Shawstad, Raymond Vernon *retired business owner/computer specialist*

Mason City
Collison, Jim *business executive*
Dotson, John Ray *oil painter*
Heiny, James Ray *lawyer*
Iverson, Carol Jean *retired library media specialist*
Kuhlman, James Weldon *retired county extension education director*
Moneir, Tarek *community development administrator*
Murphy, David McGregor *manufacturing executive*
Olson, Paul Buxton *retired social studies, marketing, and business educator*

Mc Callsburg
Lounsberry, Robert Horace *former state government administrator*

Milford
Fontaine, Sue (Jeane Fontaine) *public relations professional*

Mount Etna
Sparks, (Theo) Merrill *entertainer, songwriter, translator, poet*

Mount Pleasant
Scarff, Hope Dyall *photographer*
Vance, Michael Charles *lawyer*

Mount Vernon
Ruppel, Howard James, Jr. *sociologist, sexologist, educator*
Will, Frederic *university president, writer*

Muscatine
Collins, Max Allan *writer*
Coulter, Charles Roy *lawyer*
Dahl, Arthur Ernest *former manufacturing executive, consultant*
Kautz, Richard Carl *chemical and feed company executive*
McMains, Melvin L(ee) *controller*
Nepple, James Anthony *lawyer*
Stanley, Richard Holt *consulting engineer*
Steinmaus, Mary Carol *foundation administrator*
Thomopulos, Gregs G. *consulting engineering company executive*

Nevada
Bilyeu, Gary Edward *government official*
Countryman, Dayton Wendell *lawyer*
Jamison, David Dwight *county treasurer*

New Hampton
Babcock, Judy Ann *auditor*
Boge, Arnold Joseph *builder, contractor*
Kennedy, Michael Kelly *attorney, state representative*

Newton
Cooper, Janis Campbell *public relations executive*
Hadley, Leonard Anson *appliance manufacturing corporation executive*
Ponder, Marian Ruth *retired mathematics educator*
Ward, Dean Morris *appliance manufacturing executive*
Ward, Lloyd D. *appliance company executive*

North Liberty
†Crowner, Dee Kay *library administrator*
Glenister, Brian Frederick *geologist, educator*

Oakdale
Spriestersbach, Duane Caryl *university administrator, speech pathology educator*

Okoboji
Pearson, Gerald Leon *food company executive*

Orange City
†Druliner, Marcia Marie *education educator*
Fynaardt, Tamara Dianne *public relations professional, educator*
Korver, Gerry R(ozeboom) *purchasing executive*
Schulte, Linda F. *faculty assistant, office manager*
Scorza, Sylvio Joseph *religion educator*

Osceola
Reynoldson, Walter Ward *state supreme court chief justice*
Vanderflught, Jack Ray *secondary educator, marketing professional*

Oskaloosa
Burrow, Paul Irving *educator*
Porter, David Lindsey *history and political science educator, author*

Ottumwa
†Dinsmore, Susan Marie *secondary education educator*
Krafka, Mary Baird *lawyer*
Lanman, Brenda Kay *operating room nurse*

Pacific Junction
Krogstad, Jack Lynn *accounting educator*

Pella
Baker-Roelofs, Mina Marie *retired home economics educator*
Farver, Mary Joan *building products company executive*
Racheter, Donald Paul *political science educator*
Rudd, Orville Lee, II *finance company executive*
Shimp, Karen Ann *accountant, municipal financial executive*

Peosta
Kelly, Kathleen Ann *humanities educator*

Pocahontas
Camp, Steven John *civil engineer*

Postville
Kozelka, Edward William *seed and feed company executive*

Saint Ansgar
Kleinworth, Edward J. *agricultural company executive*

Sergeant Bluff
†Moore, Daniel Alan *secondary school principal*

Shenandoah
Hanna, Suzanne Louise *nurse*

Sioux Center
Ringerwole, Joan Mae *music educator, recitalist*

Sioux City
Andersen, Leonard Christian *former state legislator, real estate investor*
Anderson, Paula D.J. *pharmacist*
Bennett, Mark Warren *lawyer, educator*
†Deck, Paul Wayne, Jr. *federal judge*
Dillman, Kristin Wicker *middle school educator, musician*
†Edmonds, William L. *federal judge*
Emmons, Jeanne Carter *English educator*
Giles, William Jefferson, III *lawyer*
Hatfield, Susan Williams *school psychologist, psychologist, consultant*
Knowler, Robert Gene *county treasurer*
Mack, Thomas Russell *foundation administrator, management consultant*
Marker, David George *university president*
Marks, Bernard Bailin *lawyer*
Mayne, Wiley Edward *lawyer*
Motz, Debra Sue *critical care nurse*
Mounts, Nancy *secondary education educator*
Nymann, P. L. *lawyer*
O'Brien, Donald Eugene *federal judge*
†Orwig, Timothy Thomas *academic administrator, writer*
Peterson, Delaine Charles *lawyer, bank executive*
Redwine, John Newland *physician*
†Schoenherr, Julie Ann *newspaper reporter*
Silverberg, David Stanley *financial consultant*
Soens, Lawrence Donald *bishop*
Tronvold, Linda Jean *occupational therapist*
Waller, Ephraim Everett *retired professional association executive*
Wharton, Beverly Ann *utility company executive*
Wick, Sister Margaret *college administrator*
Wilson, Kim Robin *reading educator*

Spencer
Franker, Stephen Grant *investment executive*

Lemke, Alan James *environmental specialist*
Martindale, Donald Patrick *elementary education educator*

Spirit Lake
Brett, George Wendell *retired geologist, philatelist*
van der Linden, John Edward *newspaper broker, consultant*

Springville
Nyquist, John Davis *retired radio manufacturing company executive*

Steamboat Rock
Taylor, Ray *state senator*

Storm Lake
†McDaniel, Timothy Elton *educator*
Miller, Curtis Herman *bishop*

Story City
Wattleworth, Roberta Ann *family practice physician, health facility administrator*

Stuart
Bump, Wilbur Neil *retired lawyer*

Tipton
Farwell, Walter Maurice *vocalist, educator*

Traer
Hulme, Darlys Mae *banker*

Treynor
†Guttau, Michael K. *state agency administrator, banker*

University Park
Rickman, W. Edward *college president*

Urbandale
Alumbaugh, JoAnn McCalla *magazine editor*
Lucas, Dale Adrian *grounds supervisor*

Vinton
Jorgensen, Ann *farmer*

Walford
Brooks, Debra Lynn *neuromuscular therapist, educator*

Walnut
Myers, Gloria Jean *elementary education educator*

Washington
Day, John Robert *lawyer*

Waterloo
Holub, Jeanne Helen *English language educator*
†Jaeger, Kathleen Grace *French educator*
Johannsen, Sonia Alicia *retired county official*
Newcomer, James Henry *government executive*
O'Rourke, Thomas Allan *county public health director*
Rapp, Stephen John *prosecutor*
Sass, Patricia Sharon *county official*
†Stewart, Margaret Faye *executive*

Waverly
Fredrick, David Walter *university administrator*
Juhl, Dorothy Helen *social worker, retired*
Kampfe, Doris Elaine *storyteller, folk artist, poet*
Schroeder, Randall Lee *librarian*

West Bend
Wuebker, Colleen Marie *librarian*

West Branch
Forsythe, Patricia Hays *development professional*
Kohan, Carol E. *historial site administrator*
Mather, Mildred Eunice *retired archivist*
Miller, Dwight Merrick *archivist, historian*
Walch, Timothy George *library administrator*

West Burlington
Polley, Michael Glen *mathematics educator*

West Des Moines
Alberts, Marion Edward *physician*
Bamford, Carol Marie *marketing executive*
Bobenhouse, Nellie Yates *insurance company executive*
Branstad, Terry Edward *former governor, lawyer*
Burnett, Robert A. *retired publisher*
Churchill, Steven Wayne *former state legislator, marketing professional*
Cunningham, Kevin James *internist*
Dooley, Donald John *retired publishing executive*
Hallagin, Janet Elaine *consultant, writer, editor*
Holderness, Susan Rutherford *at-risk educator*
Pearson, Ronald Dale *retail food stores corporation executive*
Pomerantz, Marvin Alvin *container corporation executive*
Reilly, Michael J. *stockbroker*
Shoafstall, Earl Fred *entrepreneur, consultant*
Zimmerman, Jo Ann *health services and educational consultant, former lieutenant governor*

West Union
Hansen, Ruth Lucille Hofer *business owner, consultant*

Westside
Stiles, Virginia Lee *newspaper editor, clergy*

Wever
Lodwick, Seeley Griffiths *agriculturist, consultant*

Williamsburg
Bruse, Kristy Dean *cardiovascular pharmacologist*

Wilton
Lenker, Floyd William *farmer*

Winfield
Carty, John Wesley *lawyer*

KANSAS

Andover
†Cost, Stephen James principal
Whiteside, Glenn G. aircraft design engineer

Anthony
Carr, Cynda Annette elementary education educator

Arkansas City
Kroeker, Lisa Dawn secondary education educator

Ashland
Lehman, Julie Aimée secondary education educator

Atchison
Bryan, Caroline Elizabeth nun
†Donaldson, Penny L. library director
McDonald, Joseph Andrew information services director, consultant, writer
Seago, Diana Marie college administrator
†Still, Vickye Sue elementary educator

Augusta
†Bolick, Jan Marie art educator
Richardson, Myrtle abstractor, former judge

Baldwin City
Lambert, Daniel Michael academic administrator

Basehor
Franklin, Shirley Marie marketing consultant

Baxter Springs
O'Neal, Vicki Lynn elementary education educator

Bonner Springs
Elliott-Watson, Doris Jean psychiatric, mental health and gerontological nurse educator

Caney
Barbi, Josef Walter engineering, manufacturing and export companies executive

Chanute
Dillard, Dean Innes English language educator

Cherryvale
Wood, Ruby Fern writer, retired elementary educator

Cimarron
Wiseman, susan J. English educator

Claflin
Burmeister, Paul Frederick farmer

Clay Center
Braden, James Dale former state legislator

Coffeyville
Garner, Jim D. state legislator, lawyer

Colby
Baldwin, Irene S. corporate executive, real estate investor
Finley, Philip Bruce retired state adjutant general
†Flanagin, Luetta Mae family and pediatric nurse practitioner

Coldwater
Adams, Elizabeth Herrington banker

Concordia
Fowler, Wayne Lewis, Sr. internist
†Raines, Louis Edward school administrator

Copeland
Birney, Walter Leroy religious administrator

Council Grove
Coffin, Bertha Louise telephone company executive
Grimsley, Bessie Belle Gates special education educator

Courtland
Johnson, Dorothy Phyllis retired counselor, art therapist

De Soto
Wilson, Darrell Glenn investment banker, software developer

Derby
Delamarter, Thelda Jean Harvey secondary education educator

Dighton
Stanley, Ellen May historian, consultant

Dodge City
Chaffin, Gary Roger business executive
Clifton-Smith, Rhonda Darleen art center director
Sapp, Nancy L. educational administrator

Downs
La Barge, William Joseph tutor, researcher

Durham
Curtis, Richard Lewis pastor

Easton
Rebarchek, Sherri Lynne reading educator

Effingham
Figgs, Linda Sue educational administrator

El Dorado
Adkins, William Lloyd state official
Cahalen, Shirley Leanore retired secondary education educator
Edwards, Alisyn Arden marriage and family therapist
Fangmann, Heather Ann secondary educator, English
Stone, Duane Snyder school psychologist, clergyman

Ellsworth
Aylward, Paul Leon lawyer, banker, rancher
†Thaemert, John C. farmer

Emporia
Hashmi, Sajjad Ahmad business educator, university dean
Hedstrom, Cora Zaletel public relations director
Heldrich, Philip Joseph English educator, academic administrator, writer
Hoy, James F. folklorist
†Mallein, Darla J. educator
Schallenkamp, Kay academic administrator
Sundberg, Marshall David biology educator
Woods, Warren Chip civil engineer

Enterprise
Wickman, John Edward librarian, historian

Eskridge
Taylor, Russell Benton mining executive

Eudora
Miller, David Groff political party executive

Fort Leavenworth
Brown, Richard Francis command and control systems engineer, military off
Burgess, Edwin Bond librarian, archivist
†Curran, John Mark military career officer
Oliver, Thornal Goodloe health care executive
†Steele, William M. career military officer
†Willbanks, James Hal educator, retired military officer

Fort Riley
†McFarren, Freddy E. military career officer
Spurrier-Bright, Patricia Ann executive director

Fort Scott
Emery, Frank Eugene publishing executive

Galena
Heistand, Anita May writer

Garden City
Reeve, Lee M. farmer

Gardner
Webb, William Duncan lawyer, mediator

Goddard
Peterman, Bruce Edgar aircraft company executive, retired
Picotte, Susan Gaynel geriatrics nurse, nursing educator, rehabilitation nurse

Goodland
Ross, Chester Wheeler retired clergyman
Warren, Janet Elaine librarian

Great Bend
Jones, Edward physician, pathologist
McLaughlin, Deborah Ann public relations and marketing executive
Nuss, Joanne Ruth sculptor, artist
Swan, James Albert library administrator, writer

Haven
Schlickau, George Hans cattle breeder, professional association executive

Hays
Boldra, Sue Ellen social studies educator, business owner
Champion, Michael Edward physician assistant, clinical perfusionist
Coyne, Patrick Ivan physiological ecologist
Curl, Eileen Deges nursing educator
Hammond, Edward H. university president
Harbin, Calvin Edward retired educator
Harman, Nancy June elementary education educator, principal
Hassett, Mary Ruth nursing educator
†Oiler, Dorilou Wemlinger artist
Talbott, Nancy Costigan science educator
Zerr, Dean A. family nurse practitioner

Hesston
Yost, Lyle Edgar farm equipment manufacturing company executive

Hiawatha
Pennel, Marie Lucille Hunziger retired elementary education educator

Hoyt
Lierz-Ziegler, Stacey Elizabeth educational consultant

Hugoton
Goering, Sherrill Anita newspaper editor
Nordling, Bernard Erick lawyer

Hutchinson
Baumer, Beverly Belle journalist
Buzbee, Richard Edgar newspaper editor
Dick, Harold Latham manufacturing executive
Dukelow, Samuel Griffith engineering consultant
Girst, Jack Alan computer graphic artist, writer, illustrator
Graves, Kathryn Louise dermatologist
Green, Thereasa Ellen elementary education educator
Harris, Bill Dean card services manager
Hayes, John Francis lawyer
Jaisinghani, Manish Kumar manufacturing engineer
Kerr, David Mills state legislator
Munger, Harold Hawley, II city engineer
O'Neal, Michael Ralph state legislator, lawyer
Schmidt, Gene Earl hospital administrator
Stevens, Leota Mae retired elementary education educator
Swearer, William Brooks lawyer
Wendelburg, Norma Ruth composer, pianist, educator

Independence
Swearingen, Harold Lyndon oil company executive

Iola
Lynn, Emerson Elwood, Jr. newspaper editor/publisher
Toland, Clyde William lawyer

Iuka
Bryan, Cynthia Joan emergency medical science educator, special education educator

Junction City
Lacey, Roberta Balaam emergency room nurse
Ling, Robert William, Jr. biologist, educator

Kansas City
Anderson, Harrison Clarke pathologist, educator, biomedical researcher
Arakawa, Kasumi physician, educator
Ardinger, Robert Hall, Jr. physician, educator
Baska, James Louis wholesale grocery company executive
Behbehani, Abbas M. clinical virologist, educator
Calkins, David Ross physician, medical educator
Campbell, Joseph Leonard trade association executive
Carolan, Douglas wholesale company executive
Case, Rosemary Podrebarac lawyer
Cheng, Chiachun medical educator
Cho, Cheng Tsung pediatrician, educator
Clifton, Thomas E. seminary president, minister
Cuppage, Francis Edward retired physician, educator
Damjanov, Ivan pathologist, educator
Davidson, Laura Janette nurse practitioner, educator
Dunn, Marvin Irvin physician
Ebner, Kurt Ewald biochemistry educator
†Flanagan, John T. federal judge
Forst, Marion Francis bishop
Freund, Ronald S. management consultant, marketing company executive
Gilliland, Marcia Ann nurse clinician, infection control specialist
Globoke, Joseph Raymond accountant
Godfrey, Robert Gordon physician
Godwin, Harold Norman pharmacist, educator
Goldberg, Ivan D. microbiologist, educator
Grantham, Jared James nephrologist, educator
Greenberger, Norton Jerald physician
Greenwald, Gilbert Saul physiologist
Hagen, Donald Floyd university administrator, former military officer
Holmes, Grace Elinor pediatrician
Horseman, Barbara Ann church musician, voice educator
Hudson, Robert Paul medical educator
Jerome, Norge Winifred nutritionist, anthropologist
Johnson, Joy Ann diagnostic radiologist
Jurcyk, John Joseph, Jr. lawyer
Keleher, James P. bishop
Kenyon, Elinor Ann social worker
Klingele, Janine Marie nursing administrator
Krantz, Kermit Edward physician, educator
Lee, Kyo Rak radiology educator
Lungstrum, John W. federal judge
Mathewson, Hugh Spalding anesthesiologist, educator
McCallum, Richard Warwick medical researcher, clinician, educator
Meyers, David George internist, cardiologist, educator
Mohn, Melvin Paul anatomist, educator
Noelken, Milton Edward biochemistry educator, researcher
Olofson, Tom William computer executive
Peddicord, Tom E. pharmacist
Pretz, James Bernard retired family physician
†Rushfelt, Gerald Lloyd magistrate judge
Samson, Frederick Eugene, Jr. neuroscientist, educator
Schloerb, Paul Richard surgeon, educator
Sciolaro, Charles Michael cardiac surgeon
Sharpe, Bobbie Mahon author
†Strecker, Ignatius J. archbishop
Suzuki, Tsuneo molecular immunologist
Taunton, Roma Lee nurse educator
Ternus, Jean Ann nursing educator
Tröster, Alexander Ivo neuropsychologist, educator
VanBebber, George Thomas federal judge
Voogt, James Leonard medical educator
Vratil, Kathryn Hoefer federal judge
Walaszek, Edward Joseph pharmacology educator
Waxman, David physician, university consultant
Whelan, Richard J. director special education and pediatrics programs, academic administrator
Ziegler, Dewey Kiper neurologist

Kinsley
Carlson, Mary Isabel (Maribel Carlson) county treasurer

Kiowa
Conrad, Melvin Louis biology educator
Drewry, Marcia Ann physician

Larned
Davis, Mary Elizabeth speech pathologist, educator, counselor
Linderer, Steve historic site executive
Zook, Martha Frances Harris retired nursing administrator

Lawrence
Alexander, John Thorndike historian, educator
Ammar, Raymond George physicist, educator
Angino, Ernest Edward retired geology educator
Armitage, Kenneth Barclay biology educator, ecologist
Ballard, Barbara W. state legislator
Beedles, William LeRoy finance educator, financial consultant
Benjamin, Bezaleel Solomon architecture and architectural engineering educator
Bovee, Eugene Cleveland protozoologist, emeritus educator
Bowman, Laird Price retired foundation administrator
Briscoe, Mary Beck federal judge
Byers, George William retired entomology educator
Casad, Robert Clair legal educator
Crowe, William Joseph librarian
Darwin, David civil engineering educator, researcher, consultant
Debicki, Andrew Peter foreign language educator
Devitt, Amy Joanne English educator
Dickinson, William Boyd, Jr. editorial consultant
†Dietz, Paul T. company executive
Dooley, Patrick John graphic designer, design educator
Dreschhoff, Gisela Auguste Marie physicist, educator
Duerksen, George Louis music educator, music therapist
Eldredge, Charles Child, III art history educator
Enos, Paul geologist, educator
Frederickson, Horace George former college president, public administration educator
Frick, John William health industry executive
Gay, Aleda Susan mathematician, educator
Gerhard, Lee Clarence geologist, educator
Gerner, Deborah Jeanne political scientist, educator
Gerry, Martin Hughes, IV federal agency administrator, lawyer
Ginn, John Charles journalism educator, former newspaper publisher
Grabow, Stephen Harris architecture educator
Green, Don Wesley chemical and petroleum engineering educator
Greenberg, Marc L. education educator
Gunn, James E. English language educator
Hanson, Anne Marie LaLonde speech and theatre educator
Harmony, Marlin Dale chemistry educator
Heller, Francis H(oward) law and political science educator emeritus
Hemenway, Robert E. academic administrator, language educator
Hermes, Marjory Ruth machine embroidery and arts educator
Hilding, Jerel Lee music and dance educator, former dancer
Himmelberg, Charles John, III mathematics educator, researcher
Hoeflich, Michael Harlan law school dean
Johnston, Richard Fourness biologist
Kautsch, M(ike) A. law educator
Koepp, Donna Pauline Petersen librarian
Kuntz, Dieter Kurt history educator, researcher, translator
Landgrebe, John Allan chemistry educator
Li, Chu-Tsing art history educator
Lichtwardt, Robert William mycologist
Locke, Carl Edwin, Jr. academic administrator, engineering educator
Loudon, Karen Lee physical therapist
Lucas, William Max, Jr. structural engineer, university dean
Mackenzie, Kenneth Donald management consultant, educator
McCabe, John Lee engineer, educator
McCabe, Steven Lee structural engineer
Mc Coin, John Mack social worker
†McCrea, Judith artist, educator
Meerson, Felix Zalmanovich cardiologist
Michener, Charles Duncan entomologist, researcher, educator
Miller, Don Robert surgeon
Mitscher, Lester Allen chemist, educator
Mona, Stephen Francis golf association executive
Moore, Richard Kerr electrical engineering educator
Muirhead, Vincent Uriel aerospace engineer
Murray, Thomas Veatch lawyer
Norris, Andrea Spaulding art museum director
O'Brien, William John ecology researcher
Olea, Ricardo Antonio mathematical geologist, petroleum engineer
Orel, Harold literary critic, educator
†Osness, Wayne H. physical education educator
Pasco, Allan Humphrey literature educator
Peterson, Nancy special education educator
Pickett, Calder Marcus retired journalism educator
Pilkington, Jeremy James graphic designer
Pinet, Frank Samuel former university dean
Pozdro, John Walter music educator, composer
Quinn, Dennis B. English language and literature educator
Roskam, Jan aerospace engineer
Rowland, James Richard electrical engineering educator
Saul, Norman Eugene history educator
Schiefelbusch, Richard Louis retired language educator, research administrator
Schnose, Linda Mae special education educator
Schoeck, Richard J(oseph) English and humanities scholar
Searles, Lynn Marie nurse
Secor, James L. editor
Shankel, Delbert Merrill microbiology and biology educator
Sheridan, Richard Bert economics educator
Simons, Dolph Collins, Jr. newspaper publisher
Smith, Glee Sidney, Jr. lawyer
Spires, Robert Cecil foreign language educator
Strauss, Eric James urban planning educator, lawyer, consultant
Tacha, Deanell Reece federal judge
†Thellman, Scott Thomas physician
†Thurmaier, Kurt Michael public administration educator
Turnbull, Ann Patterson special education educator, consultant
Turnbull, H. Rutherford, III law educator, lawyer
Tuttle, William McCullough, Jr. history educator
Vaccaro, Nick Dante painter, educator
Vossoughi, Shapour chemical and petroleum engineering educator
Washington, Marian women's basketball coach
Weiss, Thomas Joseph economics educator
Williams, Roy university athletic coach
Winter, Winton Allen, Jr. lawyer, state senator
Woelfel, James Warren philosophy and humanities educator
Worth, George John English literature educator

Leavenworth
Buselt, Clara Irene religious organization administrator
Camery, John William computer engineer
Hamilton, Mark Alan electrical engineer
Kansteiner, Beau Kent city official
McGilley, Sister Mary Janet nun, educator, writer, academic administrator
Meister, Kimberly Lenore Baltzer civil engineer, consultant
Mengel, Charles Edmund physician, medical educator
†Novak, Michael Paul English language educator
Pedigo, Sheila Denise dean
Poulose, Kuttikatt Paul neurologist
Stanley, Arthur Jehu, Jr. retired federal judge
Sumerall, Scott Wright psychologist
†Tillotson, John C. federal judge, lawyer
Zaretski, Ann Pikaart special education educator

Leawood
Ballard, John William, Jr. *banker*
Byers, Walter *athletic association executive*
Byrum, Judith Miriam *accountant*
Johnston, Jocelyn Stanwell *paralegal*
Karmeier, Delbert Fred *consulting engineer, realtor*
Kordash, Dorothy Mae *artist*
Linn, James Herbert *retired banker*
Marcy, Charles Frederick *food company executive*
McKay, Robert George *city official*
Tonkens, Rebecca Annette *maternal women's health nurse*
Vetter, James Louis *food research association administrator*

Lebanon
Colwell, John Edwin *retired aerospace scientist*

Lecompton
Conard, John Joseph *financial official*

Lenexa
Ascher, James John *pharmaceutical executive*
Barkley-Lueders, Elaine Kay *production art manager*
Fotopoulos, Sophia Stathopoulos *medical scientist, administrator*
Gressel, Gary Lee *telecommunications professional*
Laven, David Lawrence *nuclear and radiologic pharmacist, consultant*
Pierson, John Theodore, Jr. *manufacturer*
Scott, Robert Gene *lawyer*

Lewis
†Cross, David R. *farmer, livestock raiser*

Liberal
Rodenberg, Anita Jo *academic administrator*

Lindsborg
†Barbo, Beverly Ann *printing and publishing company executive*
Humphrey, Karen A. *college director*
Michael, Ronald Roy *registrar, librarian*

Louisburg
†Best, Pamela LaFeuer *secondary school educator*

Lyons
Hodgson, Arthur Clay *lawyer*

Macksville
Rohr, Brenda Ann *band and vocal director*

Manhattan
Ball, Louis Alvin *insurance company executive*
Chance-Reay, Michaeline K. *educator, psychotherapist*
Coffman, James Richard *academic administrator, veterinarian*
Davis, Kenneth Sidney *writer*
Durkee, William Robert *retired physician*
Erickson, Howard Hugh *veterinarian, physiology educator*
†Fedder, Norman J. *theatre educator, playwright*
Flaherty, Roberta D. *educational association administrator*
Foerster, Bernd *architecture educator*
Gillispie, Harold Leon *minister*
†Herspring, Dale R. *political science educator, consultant*
Higgins, James Jacob *statistics educator*
Hoyt, Kenneth Boyd *educational psychology educator*
Johnson, Terry Charles *biologist, educator*
Johnson, William Howard *agricultural engineer, educator*
Kaufman, Donald Wayne *research ecologist*
†King, Terry Scot *engineering educator*
Kirkham, M. B. *plant physiologist, educator*
Kremer, Eugene R. *architecture educator*
†Kremer, S. Lillian *English educator*
Lee, E(ugene) Stanley *engineer, mathematician, educator*
Lemire, David Stephen *school psychologist, educator*
†Mattson, Gary A. *city planning educator*
McCulloh, John Marshall *historian*
McKee, Richard Miles *animal studies educator*
Mengel, David Bruce *agronomy and soil science educator*
Moss, Larry W. *nursing administrator, quality management consultant*
Murray, John Patrick *psychologist, educator, researcher*
Nafziger, Estel Wayne *economics educator*
Oehme, Frederick Wolfgang *medical researcher and educator*
Paddock, Wesley Thomas *minister, educator*
Patterson, Deb *university women's head basketball coach*
Phares, E. Jerry *psychology educator*
Posler, Gerry Lynn *agronomist, educator*
Prins, Harald Edward Lambert *anthropologist, educator*
Richard, Patrick *science research administrator, nuclear scientist*
Richter, William Louis *university administrator*
Seaton, Edward Lee *newspaper editor and publisher*
Setser, Donald Wayne *chemistry educator*
Simons, Gale Gene *nuclear and electrical engineer, educator*
Spears, Marian Caddy *dietetics and institutional management educator*
Stolzer, Leo William *bank executive*
Streeter, John Willis *information systems manager*
Stunkel, Edith Leverenz *gerontologist, consultant*
Taketomi, Susamu *physicist, researcher*
†Tummala, Krishna Kumar *public administration educator*
Urick, Max *athletic director*
Walker Schlageck, Kathrine L. *museum educational administrator, educator*
Watt, Willis Martin *academic administrator, communications and leadership educator*
†Wefald, Jon *university president*

Marion
Bateman, Jeannine Ann *county official*

Mcpherson
Darting, Edith Anne *pharmaceutical company administrator*
Grauer, Douglas Dale *civil engineer*
Hull, Robert Glenn *retired financial administrator*
Steffes, Don Clarence *state senator*

Meade
Brannan, Cleo Estella *retired elementary education educator*

Mission Hills
Smith, DeLancey Allan *retired business executive*

Mulvane
George, Donald Richard *retired principal*

Neosho Falls
Bader, Robert Smith *biology, zoology educator and researcher*

Newton
Houser, Gordon Sinclair *editor*
Hymer, Martha Nell *elementary education educator*
Morford, Marie Arlene *insurance company executive*
†Newton, Jennifer Christine *newspaper reporter*
Westerhaus, Catherine K. *social worker*

North Newton
Fast, Darrell Wayne *minister*
Juhnke, James Carlton *humanities educator*
Quiring, Frank Stanley *chemist, educator*
Schroeder, Gregg LeRoy *critical care nurse*
Snider, Marie Anna *syndicated columnist*

Oakley
Wolfe, Mindy René *early childhood education educator*

Olathe
Bertrand, Robert Simeon *manufacturing engineer*
Bruski, Paul Steven *marketing executive*
Burke, Paul E., Jr. *governmental relations consultant*
Chipman, Marion Walter *judge*
Cordell, Steven Mark *small business owner*
Fraser, David Charles *investment banker*
Goodwin, Becky K. *secondary education educator*
Haskin, J. Michael *lawyer*
Jones, Robert Lyle *emergency medical services leader, educator*
Kamberg, Mary-Lane *writer, journalist*
Martin, Daniel James *university official, lawyer*
Mixer, Ronald Wayne *minister*
O'Connor, Kay *state legislator*
Shelton, Jody *school system administrator*
Smith, Katheryn Jeanette *music educator*
Snowbarger, Vince *congressman*
Stevens, Diana Lynn *elementary education educator*
Strieby, Douglas Hunter *law enforcement officer*

Osawatomie
Jimenez, Bettie Eileen *retired small business owner*

Ottawa
Howe, William Hugh *artist*
Tyler, Priscilla *retired English language and education educator*

Overbrook
Dale, Kenneth Ray *computer executive*

Overland Park
Benjamin, Janice Yukon *foundation development executive*
Bennett, Robert Frederick *lawyer, former governor*
Bleich, Michael Robert *healthcare administrator and consultant*
Bronaugh, Deanne Rae *home health care administrator, consultant*
Buchanan, William Murray *consulting actuary*
Burger, Henry G. *anthropologist, vocabulary scientist, publisher*
Callahan, Harry Leslie *civil engineer*
Callahan, Michael Thomas *construction consultant, lawyer*
Click, Marianne Jane *credit manager*
Cole, Elsa Kircher *lawyer*
Cole, Roland Jay *lawyer*
Dempsey, Cedric W. *sports association administrator*
Derr, Lee E. *chemical company executive*
Dunn, Robert Sigler *engineering executive*
FitzGerald, Thomas Joe *psychologist*
Golec, Jennifer Jane *insurance underwriter*
Hagemaster, Julia Nelson *nursing educator*
Hanson, Patti Lynn *human resources administrator*
Hudson, Tajquah Jaye *managed health care executive*
Hurcomb, Laura Grace *visual artist*
Intrater, Cheryl Watson Waylor *career marketing consultant*
Japp, Nyla F. *infection control services administrator*
Johnson, Sharon Denise *executive*
Jones, Charles Calhoun *estate and business planning consultant*
Keim, Robert Bruce *lawyer*
Keplinger, (Donald) Bruce *lawyer*
Kopac, Andrew Joseph *manufacturing executive*
Krauss, Carl F. *lawyer*
Lamb, Bill Henry *college administrator, educator*
Landry, Mark Edward *podiatrist, researcher*
McChesney, Samuel Parker, III *real estate executive*
†Molz, Philip Jack *management consultant*
Myers, A. Maurice *transportation executive*
Ostby, Frederick Paul, Jr. *meteorologist, retired government official*
Randolph, Scott Howard *chemical company executive*
Rayburn, George Marvin *business executive, investment executive*
Sampson, William Roth *lawyer*
Smith, Daniel Lynn *lawyer*
Smith, Edwin Dudley *lawyer*
Smith, Sidney Ted *environmental engineer, consultant*
Stein, Allison *media specialist*
Van Dyke, Thomas Wesley *lawyer*
Voska, Kathryn Caples *consultant, facilitator*
Waxse, David John *lawyer*
†Werner, Betty Jean *music educator*
Westerhaus, Douglas Bernard *lawyer*

Parsons
Lomas, Lyle Wayne *agricultural research administrator, educator*

Pittsburg
Beer, Pamela Jill Porr *writer, retired vocational school educator*
Behlar, Patricia Ann *political science educator*
Darling, John Rothburn, Jr. *university president, business educator*
†Emerson, Anne *state director*
Fish, David Carlton *architect*
Franklin, John Thomas Ikeda *English educator*
†Harmon, Stephen Albert *history educator*
Nettels, George Edward, Jr. *mining executive*
Washburn, Laura Lee *poet, English literature and writing educator*

Pomona
Gentry, Alberta Elizabeth *elementary education educator*

Prairie Village
Breidenbach, Monica Eileen *educator, career counselor*
Langworthy, Audrey Hansen *state legislator*
Stanton, Roger D. *lawyer*
Taylor, Ralph Orien, Jr. *real estate developer, investor*
†Trussell, Donna Laura *writer*

Pratt
DePew, Monette Evelyn *educator*
Jones, Debra K. *accountant*
Loomis, Howard Krey *banker*

Quinter
Brooks, Joyce Julianna *gerontological nurse*

Roeland Park
Morgan, Bruce Blake *banker*

Rose Hill
Chapman, Randell Barkley *family and emergency physician, medical educator*

Russell
Manion, Kay Daureen *newspaper executive*

Saint John
Hathaway, Michael Jerry *personal care assistant, editor, publisher*
Robinson, Alexander Jacob *clinical psychologist*
Wibright, Eddy Ann *secondary education educator*

Saint Marys
Latham, Dudley Eugene, III (Del Latham) *printing and paper converting executive*

Salina
Conner, Fred L. *lawyer*
Cosco, John Anthony *health care executive, educator, consultant*
Crawford, Lewis Cleaver *engineering executive*
†Delap, Joe Gene *educator*
Douglass, Mary Clement *retired curator, historian*
Dubuc, Deborah Jo *special education educator*
Entriken, Robert Kersey, Jr. *motorsport writer, retired newspaper editor*
Fitzsimons, George Kinzie *bishop*
Hansen, Donna Lauree *court reporting educator*
Horst, Deena Louise *state legislator*
Miller, Jeffery Dean *university admissions director, consultant*
Parker, Maryland (Mike Parker) *reporter, photographer*
Richards, Jon Frederick *physician*
Robb, David Dow *electrical engineer, consultant*
Ryan, Stephen Collister *funeral director*
Selm, Robert Prickett *engineer, consultant*

Shawnee
Bunch, Jolene Regina *educator*
Chaffee, Paul David *city official*
Delay, Susan Lyne *software trainer*
Eshelman, Enos Grant, Jr. *prosthodontist*
Goldberg, Nolan Hilliard *automotive company official*

Shawnee Mission
Arneson, George Stephen *manufacturing company executive, management consultant*
Badgerow, John Nicholas *lawyer*
Bartlett, Roger Danforth *engineering executive*
Bell, Deloris Wiley *physician*
Biggs, J. O. *lawyer, general industry company executive*
Billings, Patricia Jean *inventor*
Bond, Richard Lee *lawyer, state senator*
Bortko, Edward Joseph *retired city official*
Breen, Katherine Anne *speech and language pathologist*
Cahal, Mac Fullerton *lawyer, publisher*
Colgrove, Thomas Michael *landscape architect*
†Crossen, Shani Kathryn *secondary school educator, tax preparer*
Dougherty, Robert Anthony *manufacturing company executive*
Fairchild, Robert Charles *pediatrician*
Fuller, David Scott *construction and investment company executive*
Gamet, Donald Max *appliance company executive*
Goetz, Kenneth Lee *cardiovascular physiologist, research consultant*
Green, John Lafayette, Jr. *education executive*
Gregory, Lewis Dean *trust company executive*
Hagans, Robert Frank *industrial clothing cleaning company executive*
Hartzler, Geoffrey Oliver *retired cardiologist*
†Hayes, Colleen Ballard *writer, photographer*
Hays, Paul Lee, Jr. *insurance company executive*
Hill, W. Clayton *management consultant*
Hoffman, Alfred John *retired mutual fund executive*
Holliday, John Moffitt *insurance company executive*
Holter, Don Wendell *retired bishop*
Jones, George Humphrey *retired healthcare executive, hospital facilities and communications consultant*
Julien, Gail Leslie *model, public relations professional*
Kaplan, Marjorie Ann Pashkow *school district administrator*
Laing, Linda Jeanne *school counselor*
Landau, Mason Stephen *business broker, insurance professional*
Leifer, Loring *writer, information designer*
Lucas, James Raymond *author, business executive, management consultant*
Mandl, Herbert Jay *rabbi*
Martin, Donna Lee *publishing company executive, retired*
McEachen, Richard Edward *banker, lawyer*
Mealman, Glenn *corporate marketing executive*
Miller, Stanford *reinsurance executive, lawyer*
Minkoff, Jill S. *business owner, entrepreneur*
Mooney, Justin David *motel executive*
Nulton, William Clements *lawyer*
Olsen, Stanley Severn *minister*
Price, James Gordon *physician*
Putman, Dale Cornelius *management consultant, lawyer*
Rubin, Charles Elliott *lawyer, sports agent*
Sader, Carol Hope *former state legislator*
Schwartz, Lawrence Michael, Jr. *retired investment banker*
Shank, Suzanne Adams *lawyer*
Slater, William Adcock *retired social services organization executive*
Smith, Patricia Ann *religious organization administrator*
Sparks, Billy Schley *lawyer*
Stanton, Gary Charles *research chemist*
Stilwell, Connie Kay *secondary school educator*
Thomas, Christopher Yancey, III *surgeon, educator*
†Townley, Roderick Carl *writer*
Tucker, Keith A. *investment company executive*
Van Tuyl, Cecil L. *investment company executive*
Wallace, Sherry Lynn *speech-language pathologist*
Warren, Andrea Jean *writer*
Watson, Thomas Sturges *professional golfer*

Silver Lake
Nuzman, Carl Edward *retired hydrologist*
Rueck, Jon Michael *manufacturing executive*

Sterling
Kendall, Charles Terry *librarian*
Rogers, Rita Doris Luck *family nurse practitioner*

Stilwell
Keith, Dale Martin *management consultant*
Ledgin, Norman Michael *writer*
Snodgrass, Connie Sue *secondary education educator*

Sublette
Swinney, Carol Joyce *secondary education educator*

Tonganoxie
Torneden, Connie Jean *bank officer*

Topeka
Abbott, Bob *state supreme court justice*
Aleshire, Richard Joe *banker*
Allegrucci, Donald Lee *state supreme court justice*
Barton, Janice Sweeny *chemistry educator*
Beachy, William R. *non-profit executive*
Black, Kirk J. *television executive*
†Cann, Steven J. *political science educator*
Carlson, E. Dean *state official*
†Carlson, Scott Brandon *state agency administrator*
Cohen, Sheldon Hersh *chemistry educator, university official*
Concannon, James M. *law educator, university dean*
Cornish, Kent M. *television executive*
Covington-Kent, Dawna Marie *chemical dependency counselor, continuing care and outpatient coordinator, writer*
Cox, Joseph Lawrence *judge*
Crahan, Ann Teresa *magazine editor*
Crow, Sam Alfred *federal judge*
Davis, Robert Edward *state supreme court justice*
Dicus, John Carmack *thrift savings bank executive*
Dimmitt, Lawrence Andrew *lawyer*
Elrod, Linda Diane Henry *lawyer, educator*
Ferguson, Lewis LeRoy *senior correspondent*
†Findley, Troy R. *state legislator, bank officer*
†Fisk, Donald E. *air national guard officer*
Frahm, Sheila *association executive, former government official, academic administrator*
Freden, Sharon Elsie Christman *state education assistant commissioner*
Frogge, Beverly Ann *nurse, consultant*
Fyler, Carl John *dentist*
Gabbard, Glen Owens *psychiatrist, psychoanalyst*
Gatewood, Judith Anne *roofing company adminstrator*
Gatlin, Fred *agricultural program administrator, former state legislator*
†Glasscock, Joyce H. *public information officer*
Goetz, Roger Melvin *minister*
Gordon, Thelma Hunter *state official*
Graves, William Preston *governor*
Harwick, Dennis Patrick *lawyer*
Hedrick, Lois Jean *retired investment company executive, state official*
Heim, Dixie Sharp *family practice nurse clinician*
Hejtmanek, Danton Charles *lawyer*
Herd, Harold Shields *state supreme court justice*
Holmes, Richard Winn *lawyer, retired state supreme court justice*
Jacoby, Robert Edward, II *family practice physician*
Jervis, David Thompson *political science educator*
Johnson, Arnold William *mortgage company executive*
Karst, Gary Gene *architect*
Lacoursiere, Roy Barnaby *psychiatrist*
Lockett, Tyler Charles *state supreme court justice*
Lukert-Devoe, Linda Pauline *special education educator*
Lyon, Joanne B. *psychologist*
Macnish, James Martin, Jr. *judge*
Mara, John Lawrence *veterinarian, consultant*
Marquardt, Christel Elisabeth *judge*
Marshall, Herbert A. *lawyer*
Marvin, James Conway *librarian, consultant*
†Matson, Michael J. *press secretary*
Mays, M. Douglas *state legislator, financial consultant*
McClinton, James Alexander *stage agency administrator, councilman*
McFarland, Kay Eleanor *state supreme court chief justice*
Menninger, Roy Wright *medical foundation executive, psychiatrist*
Menninger, William Walter *psychiatrist*
Metzler, Dwight Fox *civil engineer, retired state official*
Miller, Robert Haskins *retired state chief justice*
†Mitchell, Gary R. *state official*
Moots, Jeffrey Alan *lawyer*
Morris, Michael Allen *insurance executive*
†Murray, Robert A. *state official*

Mutti, Albert Frederick minister
Navone, Edward William artist, educator
†Newman, Ronald C. federal judge
†Nichols, Rocky state representative, non-profit administrator
Pettijohn, Norma Agnes organist, educator
Plummer, Mary Elizabeth cosmetologist
Powers, Harris Pat retired broadcasting executive
Powers, Ramon Sidney historical society administrator, historian
Pusateri, James Anthony judge
Rainey, William Joel lawyer
†Rarrick, C. Steven state official
Reser, Elizabeth (Betty) May bookkeeper
Richardson, Jacqueline Sue school psychologist
Rivers, Julie Elaine concert pianist, composer, recording industry executive
†Robinson, Julie Ann federal judge
Rogers, Richard Dean federal judge
Rolley, Alan W. banker
Roy, William Robert physician, lawyer, former congressman
Saffels, Dale Emerson federal judge
Salisbury, Alicia Laing state senator
†Saville, Pat state senate official
Schroer, Gene Eldon lawyer
Sebelius, Kathleen Gilligan state commissioner
Sheffel, Irving Eugene psychiatric institution executive
Simmons, Charles E. state official
Simpson, William Stewart retired psychiatrist, sex therapist
Sipes, Karen Kay newspaper editor
Six, Fred N. state supreme court justice
Slemmons, Robert Sheldon architect
Smalley, William Edward bishop
†Smith, Loran Bradford educator
Spencer, William Edwin telephone company executive, engineer
Spohn, Herbert Emil psychologist
Spring, Raymond Lewis legal educator
Stauffer, Stanley Howard retired newspaper and broadcasting executive
Stoner, Leonard D. automotive parts company executive
Stovall, Carla Jo state attorney general
†Taylor, Glend Marie art educator
Thoms, Norman Wells cardiovascular and thoracic surgeon
Thornburgh, Ron E. state official
Uhler, William Grant, IV freight company administrator
Varner, Charleen LaVerne McClanahan (Mrs. Robert B. Varner) nutritionist, educator, administrator, dietitian
Vaughn, Ima Jean minister, educator
Vidricksen, Ben Eugene food service executive, state legislator
Volpert, Mary Katherine administrative assistant, revenue specialist
Wallace, Brett E. orthopedic surgeon
Webb, Marvin Russell former state agency director
Zerbe, Kathryn J. psychiatrist

Ulysses
Nordyke, Robyn Lee primary school educator

Uniontown
Conard, Norman Dale secondary education educator

Valley Center
Bryan, Paul Edward pharmacist

Valley Falls
†Wilson, Robert Eugene publisher

Wellington
Ferguson, William McDonald retired lawyer, rancher, author, banker, former state official
Willis, Robert Addison dentist
Winn, Robert Cheever rehabilitation services professional

Weskan
Okeson, Dorothy Jeanne educational association administrator

Westwood
Devlin, James Richard lawyer
Esrey, William Todd telecommunications company executive
Hart, Paul Vincent, Jr. emergency and family medicine physician, inventor
Ketter, James Patrick accountant
LeMay, Ronald T. telecommunications industry executive

Wichita
Aelmore, Donald K. systems engineer
Alvarez, Pablo aeronautical and aerospace engineer
Andrew, Kenneth L. research physicist, physics educator
Angel, Larry business professional
Arabia, Paul lawyer
Armstrong, Hart Reid minister, editor, publisher
Arnold, Donald Raymond addiction consultant
Ayres, Ted Dean lawyer, academic counsel
Barry, Donald Lee investment broker
†Beggs, Donald Lee university chancellor
Bell, Baillis F. airport terminal executive
Bell, Charles Robert, Jr. judge
Berner Harris, Cynthia Kay librarian
Brada, Donald Robert psychiatrist
Brown, Wesley Ernest federal judge
Burket, George Edward, Jr. retired family physician
Cadman, Wilson Kennedy retired utility company executive
Ceradsky, Shirley Ann psychiatric nursing
Chen, Zuohuang conductor
Clark, Susan Matthews psychologist
Cowdery, Robert Douglas consulting geologist
Cummings, Richard J. otologist
Curfman, Lawrence Everett retired lawyer
Curtright, Robert Eugene newspaper critic and columnist
Danuatmodjo, Cheryl Lynn home healthcare nurse
†Dietrich, Bryan David english educator, poet
Dill, Sheri publishing executive
†Dings, Fred poet
Docking, Thomas Robert lawyer, former state lieutenant governor
Dorr, Stephanie Tilden psychologist
Eby, Martin Keller, Jr. construction company executive
Ellington, Howard Wesley architect
†Elliott, Donald Harris utility executive
Essey, Basil bishop
Fink, Richard H. manufacturing company executive
Gates, Walter Edward small business owner
George, David Bruce hotel executive
Gerber, Eugene J. bishop
Getz, Robert Lee newspaper columnist
Goodpasture, Judy Gail Ashmore English language educator, administrator
Grace, Brian Guiles lawyer
Guthrie, Diana Fern nursing educator
Guthrie, Richard Alan physician
Hansen, Ole Viggo chemical engineer
Hatteberg, Larry Merle photojournalist
Hawley, Raymond Glen pathologist
Healy, Patricia Colleen social worker
Henry, Cecil James, Jr. insurance sales broker
Herr, Peter Helmut Friederich sales executive
Hicks, M. Elizabeth (Liz Hicks) pharmacist
Holland, Phillip Kent aerospace engineer
Hostetler, John Jay systems consultant
Humphreys, Karen M. judge
Janzen, Janet Lindeblad composer
Johnson, George Taylor training and manufacturing executive
Johnson, Guy Charles music educator, musician
Kennedy, Joseph Winston lawyer
Kice, John Edward engineering executive
Knight, Robert G. mayor, investment banker
Koch, Charles de Ganahl oil industry executive
Kruse, Wilbur Ferdinand architect
Lair, Robert Louis catering company executive
Lerman, Kenneth Barry marketing professional
Loux, Richard Charles retired research executive, accountant
Lowrey, Annie Tsunee retired cultural organization administrator
Lusk, William Edward real estate and oil company executive
†Marten, J. Thomas judge
McIntyre, Darla Jean sales executive, merchandiser
Menefee, Frederick Lewis advertising executive
Meyer, Russell William, Jr. aircraft company executive
†Moore, Tim J. lawyer
Nienke, Steven A. construction company executive
North, Doris Griffin retired physician, educator
Oxley, Dwight K(ahala) pathologist
Palmer, Ada Margaret systems accountant, computer consultant
Pottorff, Jo Ann state legislator
Rademacher, Richard Joseph librarian
†Reid, John T. federal judge
Rosenberg, Thomas Frederick physician
Rosendale, George William aircraft company executive
Rumisek, John David surgeon, medical educator
Sorensen, Harvey R. lawyer
Stark, Stephen M. lawyer
Stephenson, Richard Ismert lawyer
Stewart, John G., III health science association administrator
Thompson, (Morris) Lee lawyer
Trombold, Walter Stevenson supply company executive
Van Milligen, James M. health care administrator
Varner, Sterling Verl retired oil company executive
Watson, William M. chief of police
Wentz, William Henry, Jr. aerospace engineer, educator
Wilhelm, William Jean civil engineering educator
†Williams, Jackie N. prosecutor
Winkler, Dana John lawyer

Winfield
Andreas, Warren Dale lawyer
Gray, Ina Turner fraternal organization administrator
Hall, Lydia Jane geriatrics nurse
Hartzell, John Mason poet, service technician
Laws, Carolyn Marie Roderick medical surgical nurse, pediatrics nurse
Schul, Bill Dean psychological administrator, author
Willoughby, John Wallace former college dean, provost

KENTUCKY

Adairville
Lyne, Alison Davis illustrator

Arjay
Hoskins, Barbara R(uth) Williams elementary educator, elementary principal

Ashland
Carter, David Edward communications executive
Compton, Robert H. lawyer
Dansby, John Walter retired oil company executive
Maxwell, Donald Robert museum director
Mitchell, Maurice McClellan, Jr. chemist
Patterson, Peggy judge
Quin, Joseph Marvin oil company executive
Robinette, Anthony Edward military officer
Roth, Oliver Ralph radiologist
Touchton, Bobby Jay minister
Weaver, Carlton Davis retired oil company executive
Wilhoit, Henry Rupert, Jr. federal judge

Barbourville
Dabbagh, Mohamed Abdul-Hay financial economist, oil-capital flow researcher

Bardstown
Kibiloski, Floyd Terrance business and computer consultant, editor, educator

Bellevue
†Lemlich, Robert educator

Berea
Brosi, George Ralph small business owner
Schaffer, Susan D. nursing educator, family nurse practitioner
Stephenson, Jane Ellen educational association administrator

Bowling Green
†Bauer, David Christopher L. newspaper editor
Cangemi, Joseph Peter psychologist, consultant, educator
Carlock, Janet Lynne middle school educator
Cravens, Raymond Lewis retired political science educator
Dewhurst, William Harvey psychiatrist
†Dixon, John Morris, Jr. lawyer
Holland, John Ben clothing manufacturing company executive
Huddleston, Joseph Russell judge
Jhamb, Indar Mohan physician
Martin, Jerry W. family physician
Minton, John Dean historian, educator
Pannell, Patricia Gay independent living specialist, state official
Pierce, Verlon Lane pharmacist, small business owner
Quinn, Paula Miner publisher, healer, musician, educator
Rahim, M. Afzalur management educator, editor
†Rose, Ferrel Victoria humanities educator, translator
Russell, Josette Renee industrial engineer
Slocum, Donald Warren chemist
†Smith, Malcolm Mobutu art educator
Stewart, Harold Sanford real estate investment and supply executive
Wells, Jerry Wayne police official

Bronston
Mitchell, Steve Harold child development specialist

Burgin
†Bradshaw, Phyllis Bowman historian, historic site staff member

Calvert City
Butler, Sheila Morris occupational health nurse
Stice, Dwayne Lee broadcasting company executive

Campbellsburg
Mitchell, Mary Ann Carrico poet

Campbellsville
Dickens, Michele registered nurse, educator
Martin, Mary Lois nursing director, critical care nurse
Skaggs, Karen Gayle elementary school educator
Whitt, Marcus Calvin development and public relations executive

Carlisle
Wolf, John Howell retired publisher

Carrollton
Tatera, James Frank chemist, process analysis specialist

Catlettsburg
Fischer, Robert Lee engineering executive, educator

Corbin
Barton-Collings, Nelda Ann political activist, newspaper, bank and nursing home executive
Doby, John Thomas social psychologist
Mahan, Shirley Jean nursing educator
Steenbergen, Gary Lewis computer aided design educator

Covington
Bates, Patti Jean communications specialist in public safety
Boyd, James Robert oil company executive
Brothers, John Alfred oil company executive
Chellgren, Paul Wilbur industrial company executive
Elliot, Ernest Alexander retired naval rear admiral
†Hughes, William Anthony bishop
Michaels, Randy broadcast executive
Sampson, Susan J. marketing communications consultant, writer, television producer
Surber, David Francis public affairs consultant, syndicated television producer
Trimble, Vance Henry retired newspaper editor
†Wehrman, James Gregory federal judge
Wolnitzek, Stephen Dale lawyer

Crescent Springs
†Ott, James Daniel journalist, educator

Crestview Hills
Harper, Kenneth Franklin retired state legislator, real estate broker

Crestwood
Ray, Ronald Dudley lawyer
Roy, Elmon Harold minister

Cumberland
†Collins, Jenny Galloway poet, disc jockey, radio talk show host

Cynthiana
Dorton, Truda Lou medical, surgical and geriatrics nurse
Glascock, Robin secondary school educator
Harpel, Gerald Robert obstetrician-gynecologist

Danville
Breeze, William Hancock college administrator
Campbell, Stanley Richard library services director
†Frank, John editor
Muzyka, Jennifer Louise chemist, educator
Rowland, Robert E. secondary school principal
Ward, John Chapman academic affairs dean

Edgewood
Sansone, Susan Mary nursing administrator

Elizabethtown
Ball, Randall physician assistant, medical technologist
DeVries, William Castle surgeon, educator
Guthrie, Michael Steele magnetic circuit design engineer
Lee, William Christopher vocational school educator
Morgan, Mary Dan social worker
Phelps, Dennis Lane minister, educator, author
Rahman, Rafiq Ur oncologist, educator
Robey, John Dudley transportation executive

Erlanger
Cheser, Karen Denise school system administrator, writer
Cuneo, Dennis Clifford automotive company executive
Muench, Robert W. bishop

Falmouth
Mudd, Sheryl Kay secondary school educator, guidance counselor

Florence
Adams, Sandra Lynn principal
Frohlich, Anthony William lawyer, master commissioner
†Lawson, Harry Wilbur chemist, consultant, writer

Fort Campbell
†Clark, Robert T. career officer
†Hagenbeck, Franklin L. army officer
Swann, Steven Walter physician, army officer

Fort Knox
Barnes, Larry Glen journalist, editor, educator
†Carlile, Christopher Blake military officer, pilot
†Harmeyer, George H. military career officer

Fort Thomas
Gaston, Paul Lee academic administrator, English educator
Hill, Esther Dianne business education educator
Whalen, Paul Lewellin lawyer, educator, MEDIATOR

Fountain Run
Shanks, Gerald Robert retired insurance company executive

Frankfort
†Armstrong, David Love attorney general
Brown, John Y., III state official
Carroll, Julian Morton lawyer, former governor
Chadwell, James Russell, Jr. controller
Chadwick, Robert lawyer, judge
Chandler, Albert Benjamin III attorney general
Cody, Wilmer St. Clair educational administrator
Cross, Alvin Miller (Al Cross) political columnist, writer
Dringenburg, Duane Clinton social services executive
†Ellis, Normandi writer
†Ferguson, Barbara legislative staff member
Fletcher, Winona Lee theater educator
Freeman, Arthur L. state commissioner
Hamilton, John Kennedy state treasurer
Hatchett, Edward Bryan, Jr. state auditor, lawyer
Henry, Stephen Lewis state official, orthopedic surgeon, educator
†Herberg, Paul Thomas state agency administrator
Hestand, Joel Dwight minister, evangelist
Hood, Joseph M. federal judge
Lambert, Joseph Earl state supreme court chief justice
†Lanham, Sallie Clay artist, educator
McCarthy, Lynn Cowan professional genealogist
†McCloud, Ronald B. political organization executive
McDaniel, Karen Jean university library administrator, educator
Mosier, Jo Ann mathematics educator
Palmore, Carol M. state official
Palmore, John Stanley, Jr. retired lawyer
Patton, Paul E. governor
Richards, Jody state legislator, journalism educator, small business owner
†Rose, Gary protective services official
†Sapp, Wayne Douglass state official
†Smith, Billy Ray state commissioner
Smith, Sherri Long journalist, secondary education educator
Stephens, Robert F. state supreme court chief justice
Strong, Marvin E., Jr. state official
Stumbo, Janet Lynn state supreme court justice
Whaley, Charles E. state agency administrator
Wintersheimer, Donald Carl state supreme court justice

Franklin
Clark, James Benton railroad industry consultant, former executive

Ft Knox
†Gaddis, Evan R. career officer

Georgetown
Klotter, James C. historian, educator
Moffat, MaryBeth automotive company executive

Glasgow
Baker, Walter Arnold lawyer
Dickinson, Temple lawyer
Duvo, Mechelle Louise oil company executive, consultant
†Knicely, Carroll Franklin publishing executive
Lessenberry, Robert Adams retail executive

Goshen
McClinton, Donald George diversified holding company executive
Strode, William Hall, III photojournalist, publisher

Greenup
†Stuart, Jessica Jane writer, poet

Harlan
Greene, James S., III school administrator

Harrods Creek
Chandler, James Williams retired securities company executive

Harrodsburg
Lunger, Irvin Eugene university president emeritus, clergyman
Redwine, Donna J. middle school education educator

Henderson
Esser, James Mark cardiovascular and interventional radiologist
Wayne, Bill Tom secondary school educator, coach

Highland Heights
Boothe, Leon Estel university president emeritus, consultant

Brennan, Ronald Wesley *retired secondary school educator*
Brewer, Edward Cage, III *law educator*
Hopgood, James F. *anthropologist*
Jones, William Rex *law educator*
Littleton, Nan Elizabeth Feldkamp *psychologist, educator*
Maines, Leah *writer, business school director*
†Mauldin, Rosetta Johnson *dean, social work educator*
Redding, Rogers Walker *physics educator*

Hindman
Still, James *adult education educator, writer*

Hopkinsville
Birkhead, Thomas Larry *minister*
Cooley-Parker, Sheila Leanne *psychologist, consultant*
Neville, Thomas Lee *food service company executive*
†Satterwhite, Robert Lee *library director*

Inez
Duncan, Robert Michael *banker, lawyer, Republican national committeeman*

Irvine
†Carter, Jeffrey Scott *correctional officer*

La Grange
Livers, Thomas Henry *fundraiser for nonprofit organizations*

Lancaster
Arnold, Cecil Benjamin *former small business owner*
Hatton, Brenda Shirley (Linda Wellington) *writer, poet, songwriter*
Sea, Sherry Lynn *poet*

Lebanon
Benningfield, Troy Lee *language arts educator*

Lexington
†Abou-Khalil, Bassam Michael *cardiothoracic surgeon*
†Allen, John Jay *Spanish language educator*
Allison, James Claybrooke, II *broadcasting executive*
Anderson, James Wingo *physician*
Avant, Robert Frank *physician, educator*
Baesler, Scotty *lawyer, former congressman*
Bagby, William Rardin *lawyer*
Baker, Merl *engineering educator*
†Banning, Lance Gilbert *historian, educator*
Barnhart, Charles Elmer *animal sciences educator*
Baumann, Robert Jay *child neurology educator*
†Bell, Marcia Malone *marriage and family therapist, researcher*
Beshear, Steven L. *lawyer*
Bishop, Kay *media educator*
Blanchard, Richard Emile, Sr. *management services executive, consultant*
Bosomworth, Peter Palliser *university medical administrator*
Boucher, Larry Gene *sports association commissioner*
Breathitt, Edward Thompson, Jr. *lawyer, railroad executive, former governor*
Breckinridge, Scott Dudley, Jr. *author, government executive*
Brown, William Randall *geology educator*
Bryant, Joseph Allen, Jr. *English language educator*
Calvert, C(lyde) Emmett *state agency adminstrator, retired*
Cantrell, Donna Alexander *county commissioner finance*
Carney, Robert Arthur *restaurant executive*
Caroland, William Bourne *structural engineer*
Charley, Nancy Jean *communications professional*
Cheniae, George Maurice *plant biochemist*
Clawson, David Kay *orthopedic surgeon*
Coffman, Edward McKenzie *history educator*
Cole, Henry Philip *educational psychology educator*
Cremers, Clifford John *mechanical engineering educator*
Dalton, Waller Lisle *obstetrician and gynecologist*
Daniel, Marilyn S. *lawyer*
Davis, George A. *pharmacologist, medical researcher*
Davis, Vincent *political science educator*
DeLong, Lance Eric *physics educator, researcher*
DeLuca, Patrick Phillip *pharmaceutical scientist, educator, administrator*
Detjen, Ann L. *retired legal assistant*
†Dooley, Karla Jeanette *reporter*
Dorio, Martin Matthew *material handling company executive*
Drake, David Lee *electronics engineer*
Drake, Vaughn Paris, Jr. *electrical engineer, retired telephone company executive*
Elitzur, Moshe *physicist, educator*
Famularo, Joseph L. *prosecutor*
Farrar, Donna Beatrice *hospital official*
Fleming, Juanita W. *academic administrator*
Foree, Edward Golden *environmental engineer, consultant*
Forester, Karl S. *federal judge*
Frye, Wilbur Wayne *soil science educator, researcher, administrator*
Fryman, Virgil Thomas, Jr. *lawyer*
Gable, Robert Elledy *real estate investment company executive*
Garmer, William Robert *lawyer*
Glenn, James Francis *urologist, educator*
Gohde, Kurt R.D. *artist*
Goldman, Alvin Lee *lawyer, educator*
Goodman, Norman Loyal *microbiologist, educator*
Grabau, Larry J. *crop physiologist, educator*
Griffen, Ward O., Jr. *surgeon, educator, medical board executive*
Grimes, Craig Alan *electrical engineering educator*
Grimes, Dale Mills *physics and electrical engineering educator*
Hagen, Michael Dale *family physician educator*
Halley, Samuel Hampton, III *architect*
Hamburg, Joseph *physician, educator*
Hamilton-Kemp, Thomas Rogers *organic chemist, educator*
Hanson, Mark Tod *engineering mechanics educator*
Hinkle, Buckner, Jr. *lawyer*
Hochstrasser, Donald Lee *cultural anthropologist, community health and public administration educator*
Holsinger, James Wilson, Jr. *physician*
†Howard, William S. *federal judge*
Hughes, Carl Andrew *municipal construction executive*
Hultman, Charles William *economics educator*
Johnson, Jane Penelope *freelance writer*
†Johnson, Paul Brett *writer, illustrator*
Johnston, Patrick Richard *risk management specialist, county official*
Kang, Bann C. *immunologist*
Kaplan, Martin P. *allergist, immunologist, pediatrician*
Kasperbauer, Michael John *plant physiology educator, researcher*
Keeling, Larry Dale *journalist*
Kelly, Timothy Michael *newspaper publisher*
Kelso, Lynn A. *acute care nurse practitioner*
Kern, Bernard Donald *retired educator, physicist*
Kewin, Cynthia McLendon *secondary education educator*
Kissling, Fred Ralph, Jr. *publishing executive, insurance agency executive*
Krone, Julie *jockey*
Langford, Sheila Brandise *nurse*
Lawson, Frances Gordon *child guidance specialist*
Lee, Joe *federal judge*
Leukefeld, Carl George *researcher, educator*
Lewis, Kolb Kay, Jr. *fundraising executive*
Lewis, Thomas Proctor *law educator*
Liu, Keh-Fei Frank *physicist, educator*
†Lockard, Paula Lynn *human resources specialist*
Lodder, Robert Andrew *chemistry and pharmaceutics educator*
Loghry, Richard M. *architecture and engineering services executive*
†Love, Harold Gibson *agricultural economics educator*
Madden, Edward Harry *philosopher, educator*
Male, Alan Thomas *engineering educator, association executive*
Mason, Ellsworth Goodwin *librarian*
Matheny, Samuel Coleman *academic administrator*
Mattox, Bernadette *university head women's basketball coach*
Mayer, Lloyd D. *allergist, immunologist, physician, medical educator*
Meier, Mark Stephan *chemistry educator*
Millard, James Kemper *marketing executive*
Miller, Harry B(enjamin) *lawyer*
Miller, Pamela Gundersen *mayor*
Mitchell, George Ernest, Jr. *animal scientist, educator*
Mitchell, John Charles *business executive*
Monsen, Ronald Peter *musician, music educator, artist*
Mumme, Hal *coach*
Nasar, Syed Abu *electrical engineering educator*
Newberry, James Henry, Jr. *lawyer*
Ng, Kwok-Wai *physics educator*
Noonan, Jacqueline Anne *pediatrics educator*
Oberst, Paul *law educator*
Palmer, Brent David *environmental physiology educator, biologist*
Pirone, Thomas Pascal *plant pathology educator*
Poundstone, John Walker *preventive medicine physician*
†Prevel, Christopher Dean *plastic surgeon, hand surgeon*
Pruitt, Beth Anne *special education educator*
†Purcell, Marguerite Mary *diagnostic radiologist, consultant*
Ramsey, Robert *county official, retired career officer*
Rangnekar, Vivek Mangesh *molecular biologist, researcher*
Reed, Michael Robert *agricultural economist*
Romanowitz, Byron Foster *architect, engineer*
†Saha, Sibu Pada *surgeon, educator*
Sandoval, Arturo Alonzo *art educator, artist*
Savage, William Earl *bank executive, religious educator*
Schaeffer, Edwin Frank, Jr. *lawyer, finance company executive*
Scharlatt, Harold *management company executive*
Schwarcz, Thomas H. *surgeon*
†Scudder, Brooks Alfred *public administrator*
†Shannon, Susan G. *manufacturing company executive*
Sineath, Timothy Wayne *library educator, university dean*
Singletary, Otis Arnold, Jr. *university president emeritus*
Steele, Earl Larsen *electrical engineering educator*
Steensland, Ronald Paul *librarian*
Stevens, Gary *professional jockey*
Stockbridge, Richard H. *probability and statistics educator*
Straus, Robert *behavioral sciences educator*
Tauchert, Theodore Richmond *mechanical engineer, educator*
Thelin, John Robert *academic administrator, education educator, historian*
Thrift, Frederick A. *zoologist, educator*
Timoney, Peter Joseph *veterinarian, virologist, educator, consultant*
†Todd, James Black *federal judge*
Tollison, Joseph W. *family practice physician*
Turley, Robert Joe *lawyer*
Villaran, Yuri *physician, medical educator*
Wagner, Alan Burton *entrepreneur*
Walize, Reuben Thompson, III *health research administrator*
Warth, Robert Douglas *history educator*
Wesley, Robert Cook *dental educator*
Wethington, Charles T., Jr. *academic administrator*
Williams, James Kendrick *bishop*
Willis, Paul Allen *librarian*
Worell, Judith P. *psychologist, educator*
Yates, Isabel McCants *city council vice mayor*
Young, Paul Ray *medical board executive, physician*
Zinser, Elisabeth Ann *academic administrator*

Liberty
Wright, Rodney H. *architect*

London
Arekapudi, Kumar Vijaya Vasantha *compliance consultant, real estate agent*
Coffman, Jennifer B. *federal judge*
Giles, William Elmer *newspaper editor*
Gregory, Jerry *real estate agent*
Jensen, Tom *political party executive, lawyer*
Keller, John Warren *lawyer*
Siler, Eugene Edward, Jr. *federal judge*
Unthank, G. Wix *federal judge*

Louisa
Burton, John Lee, Sr. *banker*
†Compton, Hazel Louise *office administrator*

Louisville
Aberson, Leslie Donald *lawyer*
Adamkin, David Howard *pediatric medicine educator*
Adams, Christine Beate Lieber *psychiatrist, educator*
Adams, Robert Waugh *state agency administrator, economics educator*
Allen, Charles Ethelbert, III *lawyer*
Allen, Charles Mengel *federal judge*
Amin, Mohammad *urology educator*
Andrews, Billy Franklin *pediatrician, educator*
Apperson, Jeffrey A. *lawyer*
Ardery, Philip Pendleton *lawyer*
Arnold, Claire Groemling *health care analyst*
Atcher, Randy *musician, narrator, entertainer, retired realtor*
Ballantine, John Tilden *lawyer*
Baron, Martin Raymond *psychology educator*
Barr, James Houston, III *lawyer*
Bash, Lee *educational administrator*
Baxter, James William, III *investment executive*
Becker, Gail Roselyn *museum director*
Belanger, William Joseph *chemist, polymer applications consultant*
Benfield, Ann Kolb *lawyer*
Bentley, James Robert *association curator, historian, genealogist*
Berger, Barbara Paull *social worker, marriage and family therapist*
Berry, Phillip Reid *beverage distribution executive*
Bertolone, Salvatore J. *pediatric medicine educator*
Besser, Lawrence Wayne *corporate accountant*
Blaine, Steven Robert *lawyer*
Blaising, Craig Alan *religious studies educator*
Boggs, Danny Julian *federal judge*
Bradford, Gail Idona *minister*
Bratton, Ida Frank *secondary school educator*
Brones, Lisa Ann Mari *news anchorperson, reporter*
Brown, Bonnie Maryetta *lawyer*
Buckaway, William Allen, Jr. *lawyer*
Bujake, John Edward, Jr. *beverage company executive*
Bullard, Claude Earl *newspaper, commercial printing and radio and television executive*
†Cabal, Theodore James *dean, religious studies educator*
Callen, Jeffrey Phillip *dermatologist, educator*
Carr, Larry Dean *financial services executive*
Cecil, Bonnie Susan *elementary education educator*
Chauvin, Leonard Stanley, Jr. *lawyer*
Chien, Sufan *surgeon, educator*
Clapp, Martin *university co-head women's basketball coach*
Clark, John Hallett, III *consulting engineering executive*
Clayton, Marvin Courtland *engineering, manufacturing sourcing and health wellness consultant*
Coalter, Milton J, Jr. *library director, educator*
Cohn, David V(alor) *oral biology and biochemistry educator*
Collyer, George Stanley, Jr. *magazine editor*
Conner, Stewart Edmund *lawyer*
†Cook, Larry Norman *pediatrician, neonatologist, educator*
Cowan, Frederic Joseph *lawyer*
Crim, Gary Allen *dental educator*
Crum, Denny (Denzel Edwin Crum) *collegiate basketball coach*
Dale, Judy Ries *religious organization administrator*
Dalton, Jennifer Faye *accountant*
Danzl, Daniel Frank *emergency physician*
Davenport, Gwen (Mrs. John Davenport) *author*
Davidson, Gordon Byron *lawyer*
Deering, Ronald Franklin *librarian, minister*
DeKay, Barbara Ann *social worker*
DeLong, James Clifford *air transportation executive*
†Dickinson, Henry H. *federal judge*
Dolt, Frederick Corrance *lawyer*
Doyle, Billy Herman *film specialist, writer*
Draper, Charles William *religious studies educator*
Dudley, George Ellsworth *lawyer*
Duffy, Martin Patrick *lawyer*
Dunman, Leonard Joe, III *trucking company executive*
Early, Jack Jones *foundation executive*
Edgell, Stephen Edward *psychology educator, statistical consultant*
Edwards, Steven Alan *lawyer*
Egginton, Everett *educational administrator*
Elin, Ronald John *pathologist*
Everett, Elbert Kyle *marketing executive, consultant*
Faller, Rhoda Dianne Grossberg *lawyer*
Farman, Allan George *radiologist, oral pathologist, educator*
Fenton, Thomas Conner *lawyer*
Ferguson, Jo McCown *lawyer*
†Fitzpatrick, Joseph Lloveras *artist, art educator*
Fleming, Laura Elizabeth *non-profit executive*
Ford, Gordon Buell, Jr. *English language, linguistics, and medieval studies educator, author, retired hospital industry accounting financial management executive*
†Friedlander, Mitzi B. *artist*
Fuchs, Olivia Anne Morris *lawyer*
†Fullenlove, Carmen (Kit) Millay *public relations executive*
Furka, Árpád *organic chemist, educator*
Galandiuk, Susan *colon and rectal surgeon, educator*
Gall, Stanley Adolph *physician, immunology researcher*
†Gambill, C. Cleveland *federal judge*
Garcia, Rafael Jorge *retired chemical engineer*
Garfinkel, Herbert *university official*
Garretson, Henry David *neurosurgeon*
Gilman, Sheldon Glenn *lawyer*
Gist, William Claude, Jr. *dentist*
Gleis, Linda Hood *physician*
Gorman, Chris *lawyer*
Gott, Marjorie Eda Crosby *conservationist, former educator*
Granady, Juanita H. *retired religious organization administrator*
Gray, Laman A., Jr. *thoracic surgeon, educator*
Greaver, Joanne Hutchins *mathematics educator, author*
†Green, Catherine C. *foreign language educator*
Guethlein, William O. *lawyer*
Guillaume, Raymond Kendrick *banker*
Haddaway, James David *retired insurance company official*
Hallenberg, Robert Lewis *lawyer*
Hanley, Thomas Richard *engineering educator*
Hardy, Michael C. *performing arts administrator*
Harpring, Linda Jean *critical care and psychiatric nurse*
Harris, Patrick Donald *physiology educator*
Hawpe, David Vaughn *newspaper editor, journalist*
Hayes, William Meredith *pilot, retired career officer*
Haynes, Douglas Martin *physician, educator*
Heiden, Charles Kenneth *former army officer, metals company executive*
Heinicke, Ralph Martin *consultant*
Helm, Thomas Kennedy, Jr. *retired lawyer*
Heyburn, John Gilpin, II *federal judge*
Highland, Martha (Martie) *retired education educator, consultant*
Hobson, Douglas Paul *psychiatrist*
Holladay, James Franklin, Jr. *minister*
Holmes, Gary Lee *medical/surgical nurse*
†Holt, Homer A., Jr. *urologist, educator*
Hopson, Edwin Sharp *lawyer*
Hower, Frank Beard, Jr. *retired banker*
Hoye, Robert Earl *systems science educator*
Hughes, J. Deborah *quality management consultant*
Hunter, William Jay, Jr. *lawyer*
Ivory, Bennie *editor*
Jacob, Robert Allen *surgeon*
James, Virginia Lynn *contracts executive*
Jenkins, C(arle) Frederick *religious organization executive, minister, lawyer*
Jones, David Allen *health facility executive*
Karibo, John Michael *allergist, immunologist, pediatrician*
Keeney, Steven Harris *lawyer*
Kelly, Thomas Cajetan *archbishop*
King, William Bradley *emergency medicine physician*
Klotter, John Charles *retired legal educator*
Kmetz, Donald R. *retired academic administrator*
Lake, Nancy Jean *nursing educator, operating room nurse*
Landau, Herman *newspaperman retired*
La Rocca, Renato Vincenzo *medical oncologist, clinical researcher*
Lay, Norvie Lee *law educator*
Leightty, Sharon Howerton *artist, fine arts educator*
Lofton, Kevin Eugene *medical facility administrator*
Lumley, Thomas Dewey *travel professional, real estate investor*
Lunsford, W. Bruce *company executive*
Luvisi, Lee *concert pianist*
Lyndrup, Peggy B. *lawyer*
Macdonald, Lenna Ruth *lawyer*
Maddox, Robert Lytton *lawyer*
Maggiolo, Allison Joseph *lawyer*
Manassah, Edward E. *publisher*
Manly, Samuel *lawyer*
Maple, Mary Alice *lawyer*
Marsh, Virginia Jean *art educator*
Martin, Boyce Ficklen, Jr. *federal judge*
Martin, Janice Lynn *special education educator*
Martin, Shirley Bogard *maternal/women's health nurse administrator*
†McCall, John Richard *lawyer*
Mellen, Francis Joseph, Jr. *lawyer*
Melnykovych, Andrew O. *journalist*
Metzger, Gregory Scott *lawyer*
Miller, Marilee Hebert Slater *theatre administrator, producer, director, consultant*
Min, Hokey *business educator*
Mohler, Richard Albert, Jr. *academic administrator, theologian*
Moll, Joseph Eugene *chemical engineer, chemical company executive*
†Moore, Charles Damon, Jr. *technology educator*
Morreau, James Earl, Jr. *lawyer, entrepreneur*
Morrin, Peter Patrick *museum director*
Morris, Benjamin Hume *lawyer*
Morton, R. Meir *writer, editor*
Mountz, Wade *retired health service management executive*
Murrell, Deborah Anne *music educator, speaker, writer*
†Newby, Elizabeth Ann *elementary education educator*
Niblock, William Robert *manufacturing executive*
Nystrand, Raphael Owens *university dean, educator*
Oates, Thomas R. *university executive*
O'Bryan, Mary Louise *nursing administrator, consultant*
Olson, Walter Lewis, Jr. *neurology educator*
Osborn, John Simcoe, Jr. *lawyer*
Parker, Joseph Corbin, Jr. *pathologist*
Parkins, Frederick Milton *dental educator, university dean*
Peden, Katherine Graham *industrial consultant*
Pelfrey, D. Patton *lawyer*
Pelfrey, Deanna Kaye Wedmore *public relations and marketing executive, educator*
Pence, Hobert Lee *physician*
†Pennington, Royce Lee *English educator, writer*
Pepples, Ernest *tobacco company executive*
Pettyjohn, Shirley Ellis *lawyer, real estate executive*
Polk, Hiram Carey, Jr. *surgeon, educator*
Porter, Henry Homes, Jr. *investor*
Poston, Janice Lynn *librarian*
†Potter, Eugenia Kelly *state agency administrator, publisher*
Prough, Russell Allen *biochemistry educator*
Rapp, Christian Ferree *textile home furnishings company executive*
Reed, D. Gary *lawyer*
Reed, David Benson *bishop*
Reed, John Squires, II *lawyer*
Reinbold, Darrel William *energy engineering specialist*
†Richardson, J. David *surgeon*
†Roberts, J. Wendell *federal judge*
Roisen, Fred Jerrold *neurobiologist, educator, researcher, anatomy educator*
Rose, Judy Hardin *nursing administrator*
Rosky, Theodore Samuel *insurance company executive*
Rowe, Melinda Grace *public health service officer*
Royer, Robert Lewis *retired utility company executive*
Runyon, Keith Leslie *lawyer, newspaper editor*
Sanders, Russell Edward *protective services official*
Scheu, Lynn McLaughlin *scientific publication editor*
Schneider, Arthur *computer graphics specialist*
Schneider, Jayne B. *school librarian*
Schulman, Robert *journalist*
Schuster-Craig, John *music educator*
Schwab, John Joseph *psychiatrist, educator*
Scott, Lolita Jean *social worker*
Scott, Ralph Mason *physician, radiation oncology educator*
Shaikun, Michael Gary *lawyer*
†Shields, Christopher Brian *neurosurgeon*
Showalter, Robert Earl *banker*
Shumaker, John William *academic administrator*
Siewert, Robin Noelle *chemical engineer*
Simpson, Charles R., III *judge*
Skees, William Edward *lawyer*
Skees, William Leonard, Jr. *lawyer*
Slung, Hilton B. *surgeon*
Smith, Donald Ray *magazine dealer*

Smith, Mary Elinor retired dean, mathematics educator, counselor
Smith, Robert F., Jr. civil engineer
Spinnato, Joseph Anthony, II obstetrician
Spratt, John Stricklin surgeon, educator, researcher
Stewart, Arthur Van dental educator, geriatric health administrator
†Stone, Nancy Jon special education educator
Stosberg, David Thomas bankruptcy judge
Strachan, Gladys retired religious organization executive
Strause, Randall Scott judge, lawyer
Street, William May beverage company executive
†Sundine, Michael James plastic surgeon
Sutton, John Schuhmann, Jr. retired purchasing consultant
Swain, Donald Christie retired university president, history educator
Syed, Ibrahim Bijli medical educator and physicist, writer, philosopher, theologist, public speaker
Talbott, Ben Johnson, Jr. lawyer
Tasman, Allan psychiatry educator
Taylor, Kenneth Grant chemistry educator
Taylor, Robert Lewis academic administrator
Tinsley, Tuck, III book publishing executive
Towles, Donald Blackburn retired newspaper publishing executive
Tran, Long Trieu industrial engineer
Troop, (Walter) Michael prosecutor
†Truitt, Benjamin elementary education educator
Tsai, Tsu-Min surgeon
Tyrrell, Gerald Gettys banker
†Uhlenhuth, Eric R. urologist
VanMeter, Vandelia L. library director
†Villiger, Martha Ann English educator
Vincenti, Michael Baxter lawyer
Vogel, Werner Paul retired machine company executive
Waddell, William Joseph pharmacologist, toxicologist
Watts, Beverly L. civil rights executive
†Weiner, Leonard Jay surgery educator
Weisskopf, Bernard pediatrician, child behavior, development and genetics specialist, educator
Welsh, Alfred John lawyer, consultant
Weyland, C. William architect
White, Sara university co-head women's basketball coach
Willenbrink, Rose Ann lawyer
Wilson, Denise Watts secondary school educator
Wilson, Melissa Elizabeth artist, educator
Winland, Denise Lynn physician
Wren, Harold Gwyn arbitrator, lawyer, legal educator
Wright, Jesse Hartzell psychiatrist, educator
†Ziegler, Charles Edward political science educator
Zimmerman, Gideon K. minister
Zimmerman, Thom Jay ophthalmologist, educator
Zingman, Edgar Alan lawyer

Madisonville
Aubrey, Sherilyn Sue elementary school educator
†Hougland, Virginia Lee mathematics educator
May, Richard Warren writer, consultant, inventor
Monhollon, Leland lawyer
Ramsey, Frank retired basketball player
Veazey, Doris Anne state agency administrator, retired
†Werner, Mary Beth English educator

Maysville
Hunter, Nancy Donehoo education educator

Middlesboro
Potter, Karen Ann secondary school educator

Middletown
†O'Dell, Mary Ernestine poet, editor

Midway
Minister, Kristina speech communication educator

Morehead
†Bailey, Rebecca L. writer
†Barker, Garry Gene art center administrator
Besant, Larry Xon librarian, administrator, consultant
Huber, John Michael lumber executive
Johnson, Charlene Denise Logan medical/surgical and pediatric nurse
Litter, Laura women's basketball coach
Mann, James Darwin mathematics educator
Miller, Jon William emergency physician
†Newby, Earl Fernando educator
Thomas, Malayilmelathethil English language educator

Morganfield
†Edmondson, Austin Harold city manager

Mount Sterling
Moore, George William lawyer

Mount Vernon
Nielsen, Lu Ed retired community health nurse, civic worker

Munfordville
Lang, George Edward lawyer

Murray
†Aguiar, Sarah Appleton English language educator, writer
Boston, Betty Lee financial consultant, financial planner
Bumgardner, Cloyd Jeffrey school principal
Driskill, Charles Dwayne agriculture educator, researcher
Faihst, Michael Ernest plastics engineer
Fields, Eddie women's collegiate basketball coach
Keller, Randal Joseph toxicology educator
Loganathan, Bommanna Gounder environmental chemist, biologist, researcher, educator
Mateja, John Frederick science educator

Nancy
Watts, Brenda Sue elementary education educator, retired

Newport
Clinkenbeard, James Howard principal
Halloran, Brian Paul lawyer

Nicholasville
Bender, Betty Barbee food service professional
Crouch, Dianne Kay secondary school guidance counselor
McMullin, Shertina A. mathematics and English teacher

Olive Hill
Anderson, Melissa Eva small business owner

Owensboro
Bennett, Edith Lillian lay church worker, radio personality
Edge, Marianne Smith business owner
Ford, Steven Milton insurance agent
Hulse, George Althouse retired steel company executive
McRaith, John Jeremiah bishop
Miller, James Monroe lawyer
†Miller, Scott Bryan public administration specialist
†Schoenbachler, Matthew G. historian, educator

Paducah
Cloyd, Bonita Gail Largent rehabilitation nurse, educator
†Earles, Pat city administrator
Faoro, Victoria Anna museum director, magazine editor
Farr, Warren Earl artist
Johnstone, Edward Huggins federal judge
†King, W. David federal judge
Milford, Judy Gill author, poet
Nickell, Christopher Shea lawyer
Russell, Thomas B. judge
Westberry, Billy Murry lawyer
Wurth, Susan Winsett health facility manager

Paintsville
Wells, Zella Faye assistant school superintendent, consultant

Paris
Steffer, Robert Wesley clergyman

Pewee Valley
Gill, George Norman newspaper publishing company executive

Pikeville
Smith, Harold Hasken

Pineville
Miracle, Donald Eugene elementary school educator
Whittaker, Bill Douglas minister

Prestonsburg
Elliott, Myra Turner nursing educator
Mc Aninch, Robert Danford philosophy and government affairs educator
Pridham, Thomas Grenville retired research microbiologist

Princeton
Holt, Linda Fitzgerald elementary education educator

Propect
Shipley, Alden Peverly broadcaster, broadcasting executive

Radcliff
Cranston, John Welch historian, educator

Richmond
Beranek, Carla Tipton music educator
Branson, Branley Allan biology educator
Inman, Larry Joe coach
Kensicki, Peter Robert insurance, finance educator
King, Amy Cathryne Patterson mathematics educator, researcher
McQuaide, Benjamin Homer radiologist
Myers, Marshall Dean English educator
Shearon, Forrest Bedford humanities educator

Rineyville
Jackson, Charles Wayne food products executive, former telecommunications industry executive

Rousseau
Bach, Betty Jean health services educator

Russell
†Heck, Charles Ralph university dean

Russellville
Harper, Shirley Fay nutritionist, educator, consultant, lecturer

Salvisa
Lancaster, Clay architecture/design educator, writer

Scottsville
Porter, Charles Michael retail company executive
Secrest, James Seaton, Sr. lawyer
Wilcher, Larry K. lawyer

Shepherdsville
†Pike, Burlyn bank director, lawyer

Somerset
Caron, Anita Jo secondary education educator
Prather, John Gideon, Jr. lawyer

Southgate
Glenn, Jerry Hosmer, Jr. foreign language educator
Miller, Catherine Ann nursing administrator

Sturgis
Thornsberry, Willis Lee, Jr. chemist

Summer Shade
Smith, Ruby Lucille librarian

Union
Cook, Janice Eleanor Nolan retired elementary school educator
Hochstrasser, John Michael environmental engineer, industrial hygienist

Wiener, Kathleen Marie elementary education educator

Versailles
Humes, David Walker accountant
Preston, Thomas Lyter crisis management, anti-terrorism and workplace violence consultant
Stober, William John, II economics educator

Villa Hills
Celella, Jan Gerding retired legislative staff member

Vine Grove
Gray, Paul Clell secondary school educator
McNamara, Patricia Rae religious organization administrator, school system administrator

Warsaw
†LeGrand, William R. retired postmaster, insurance agent

Whitesburg
Smith, Roger Keith investment executive
Williams, Debbie Kaye optometrist

Wickliffe
Gray, Carol Hickson chemical engineer
Shadoan, William Lewis judge

Williamsburg
Burch, John Russell, Jr. technical services librarian
Faught, Jolly Kay English language educator
Fish, Thomas Edward English language and literature educator
†Johnson, J. B., Jr. federal judge
†Newquist, Lawrence Allen physics educator

Wilmore
Abbott, Edna Eleanor nurse, retired
Kinlaw, Dennis Franklin clergyman, society executive

Winchester
Book, John Kenneth (Kenny Book) retail store owner
Evans, William Halla minister
Farmer, Rebecca Anne educator
Hall, Bennett Freeman minister

LOUISIANA

Alexandria
Bolton, Robert Harvey banker
Bradford, Louise Mathilde social services administrator
Butler, Robert Moore, Jr. podiatrist
Gist, Howard Battle, Jr. lawyer
†Jones, Syble Thornhill dietitian
Little, F. A., Jr. federal judge
Maples, Mary Lou elementary education educator
Rogers, James Edwin geology and hydrology consultant
†Simon, John F. federal judge
Slipman, (Samuel) Ronald hospital administrator
Smith, Joe Dorsey, Jr. retired newspaper executive
Sneed, Ellouise Bruce nursing educator
Thevenot, Maude Travis retired home economist

Arabi
Stierwald, Marlene Lydia elementary school educator

Arcadia
Cummings, Kenneth Ila writer, retired dermatologist

Barksdale AFB
†Rider, Regner C. career officer
†Smoak, Andrew W. military officer

Baton Rouge
Anderson, George Hugo chemical engineer
†Anjier, Jennifer J.M. librarian
Arceneaux, William historian, educator, association official
Arman, Ara civil engineering educator
Baer, Michael Shellman, III lawyer, Louisiana Senate secretary
Baird, David Bryan architect
Bankston, Nathaniel D. city registrar
†Barkemeyer, Marsha D. artist, educator
Bedeian, Arthur George business educator
Besch, Everett Dickman veterinarian, university dean emeritus
Blackman, John Calhoun, IV lawyer
Blanco, Kathleen Babineaux lieutenant governor
Bohlinger, Lewis Hall state government official
Boyce, Bert Roy university dean, library and information science educator
Bray, George August physician, scientist, educator
†Breaux, Cindy Addison accountant
Brown, Raymond Jessie financial and insurance company executive
Brun, Judith principal
Burns, Paul Yoder forester, educator
Byrd, Warren Edgar, II lawyer
Caffey, H(orace) Rouse university official, agricultural consultant
Cahill, Marion Frances nursing and psychology educator
Calato, Damian television executive
Chastant, Ledoux J., III medical clinic administrator
Chen, Peter Pin-Shan electrical engineering and computer science educator, data processing executive
Cherry, William Ashley surgeon, state health officer
Cole, Luther Francis former state supreme court associate justice
Coleman, James Malcolm marine geology educator
Conerly, Evelyn Nettles educational consultant
Constant, William David chemical engineer, educator
Constantinides, Dinos Demetrios (Constantine Constantinides) music educator, composer, conductor
Cooper, William James, Jr. history educator
Corripio, Armando Benito chemical engineering educator
Costonis, John J. law educator, lawyer
†Crosby, Janice Celia language and literature educator
Crumbley, Donald Larry accounting educator, writer, consultant
Crusemann, F(rederick) Ross advertising agency official
†Czerwinski, Sally Huffman information systems manager
Davidge, Robert Cunninghame, Jr. hospital administrator
Desmond, John Jacob architect
DeVille, Donald Charles accountant
Dinardo, Gerry coach
Doty, Gresdna Ann education educator
D'Souza, Alan S. tax consultant, real estate agent, pianist, writer
Dunlap, Wallace Hart pediatrician
†E. Joseph, Savioe state education agency administrator
Estevens, Ellen Munsil healthcare professional
Finney, Clifton Donald publishing executive
Foster, M. J., Jr. (Mike Foster) governor
Francis, Michael G. political party official
†Frank, Juhan astrophysicist
Gammon, Malcolm Ernest, Sr. surveying and engineering executive
†Gay, Pamela Diane dance critic, historian
Giglio, Steven Rene lawyer
Gilmore, Clarence Percy writer, magazine editor
†Golsby, Marsanne press secretary
Granger, Frank, III assessor
Greer, Robert Stephenson insurance company executive
Gunter, Sue women's basketball coach
Hamilton, John Maxwell university dean, writer
Hansel, William biology educator
Hardy, John Edward English language educator, author
Harrelson, Clyde Lee secondary school educator
Hazel, Joseph Ernest geology educator, stratigrapher
Head, Jonathan Frederick cell biologist
†Hollman, Charlotte Anderson pediatric neurologist
Hughes, Alfred Clifton bishop
Hymel, L(ezin) J(oseph) prosecutor
Ieyoub, Richard Phillip state attorney general
Jaques, Thomas Francis librarian
Jeffers, Ben political organization executive
Jenkins, Louis (Woody) television executive, state legislator
Johnson, Joseph Clayton, Jr. lawyer
Karns, Barry Wayne lawyer
Kelley, Timothy Edward state judge
Kelly, Mary Joan librarian
Khonsari, Michael M. mechanical engineering educator
Kidd, James Marion, III allergist, immunologist, naturalist, educator
†Kisner, Wendell Howard, Jr. plastic surgeon
Klei, Thomas Ray parasitology educator
Lambremont, Edward Nelson, Jr. nuclear science educator
Lamonica, P(aul) Raymond lawyer, educator
Lane, Margaret Beynon Taylor librarian
†Lazzaro-Weis, Carol Marie foreign languages educator
LeBlanc, Hanson Paul, III communications educator, researcher
LeBlanc, J. Burton, IV lawyer
LeClere, David Anthony lawyer
Lee, Betty Redding architect
Lee, Jean Clarisse writer
Leonard, Paul Haralson retired lawyer
Le Vine, Jerome Edward retired ophthalmologist
Liuzzo, Joseph Anthony food science educator
†Loveland, Anne Carol history educator
Lucas, Fred Vance pathology educator, university administrator
Madden, David author
†Mainkar, Neeraj Arvind simulation modeler, physicist
†Mann, Robert Townley press secretary
Manship, Douglas broadcast and newspaper executive
Marino, Anthony airport commission
Markovich, Nicholas Charles architect, designer, educator
Marshak, Alan Howard electrical engineer, educator
Marvin, Wilbur real estate executive
Mathews, John William (Bill Mathews) insurance executive
Mc Cameron, Fritz Allen retired university administrator
Mc Clendon, William Hutchinson, III lawyer
McGarr, Charles Taylor accountant
Mc Glynn, Sean Patrick physical chemist, educator
McKeithen, Walter Fox secretary of state
Mohr, Jeffrey Michael real estate and insurance executive
Moore, Robert Wesley foundation administrator
Moreland, Richard Clayton English educator
Moyse, Hermann, III banker
†Nickel, James W. state director
Nijoka, Donald Wayne metropolitan council administrator
†Noland, Christine A. magistrate judge
Norem, Richard Frederick, Sr. musician, music educator
O'Connell, Robert Francis physics educator
†Odom, Bob state agricultural and forestry commissioner
Olney, James English language educator
Omoike, Isaac Irabor chemist, publisher, author
Palmer, Curtis Dwayne cardiopulmonary practitioner, microbiologist, researcher, builder
Parker, John Victor federal judge
Parks, James William, II public facilities executive, lawyer
Parra, Pamela Ann physician, educator
Pastorek, John news director
Patrick, William Hardy, Jr. wetland biogeochemist, educator, laboratory director
Patterson, Charles Darold librarian, educator
Perone, Thomas Patrick neurosurgeon
Phares, Greg protective services officer
Phillabaum, Leslie Ervin publisher
†Phillips, Louis M. federal judge
†Picard, Cecil state education agency administrator
Pike, Ralph Webster chemical engineer, educator, university administrator
Polozola, Frank Joseph federal judge
Porter, Gary Stephan minister
Prestage, James Jordan university chancellor
Pryor, William Austin chemistry educator
Pugh, George Willard law educator
Puyau, Francis Albert retired physician, radiology educator
†Pyle, Susan H. legal association official
Reible, Danny David environmental chemical engineer, educator
Reich, Robert Sigmund landscape architect
Ricapito, Joseph Virgil (Giuseppe) Spanish and comparative literature educator

Riddick, Winston Wade, Sr. *lawyer*
†Riedlinger, Stephen C. *federal judge*
Riopelle, Arthur Jean *psychologist*
Roberts, Harry Heil *geological research administrator*
Robichaux, Alfred Godfrey, III *obstetrician and gynecologist*
†Saccopoulos, Christos-Anastasios Argyriou *university dean, architect*
Sajo, Erno *nuclear engineer, physicist, consultant, educator*
Schroeder, Leila Obier *retired law educator*
Scimeca, Raymond C. *architect*
†Sheppard, John B., Jr. *state official*
Smith, David Jeddie *American literature educator*
Speier, Karen Rinardo *psychologist*
Stalder, Richard L. *corrections official*
Stopher, Peter Robert *civil and transportation engineering educator, consultant*
Swaggart, Jimmy Lee *evangelist, gospel singer*
†Thayer, Frederick Clifton *public policy educator*
Timmons, Edwin O'Neal *psychologist*
Tipton, Kenneth Warren *agricultural administrator, researcher*
Tolbert, Charles Madden, II *sociology educator*
Traynham, James Gibson *chemist, educator*
Triantaphyllou, Evangelos *industrial engineering educator*
Tumay, Mehmet Taner *geotechnical consultant, educator, academic administrator*
Turner, Bert S. *construction executive*
Unglesby, Lewis O. *lawyer*
Vaeth, Agatha Min-Chun Fang *clinical nurse, nursing administrator*
Valsaraj, Kalliat Thazhathuveetil *chemical engineering educator*
Walsh, Milton O'Neal *lawyer*
Warren, John William *professional society administrator*
West, Philip William *chemistry educator*
Wheeler, Otis Bullard *retired English educator and university official*
†Whittington, William R. *protective services official*
Willett, Anna Hart *composer*
Williams-Daly, Angelia Evette *marketing executive, small business owner*
Windhauser, John William *journalism educator*
Winkler, Steven Robert *hospital administrator*
Witcher, Robert Campbell *bishop*
Wittenbrink, Jeffrey Scott *lawyer*
†Yates, Marvin L. *retired academic administrator*
Young, Eugene A. *county official*
Zhu, Jianchao *computer and control scientist, engineer, educator*

Benton
†Charity, Nadine Ament *educator, poet*

Bogalusa
Henke, Shauna Nicole *police dispatcher, small business owner*

Bossier City
Bond, William Jennings, Jr. *air force officer*
Darling, Shannon Ferguson *special education educator*
Fry, Randy Dale *emergency medical technician, paramedic*
Guenther, Gordon P. *mechanical engineer*
Jaeger, Kathleen Rae *pediatrics nurse*
Johnson, Ruby LaVerne *retail executive*
Tice, William Fleet, Jr. *pastor*

Boutte
Breaux, Marion Mary *secondary education educator*

Boyce
Chilton, Alice Pleasance Hunter (Mrs. St. John Poindexter Chilton) *former state official, vocational counselor*
Chilton, St. John Poindexter *retired plant pathology educator, farm owner*

Calhoun
Robbins, Marion LeRon *agricultural research executive*
Roberts, Thomas Keith *minister*

Cecilia
†Girouard, Tina *artist, curator*

Chalmette
Crouchet, Kathleen Hunt *elementary educator, reading educator*
†Zelaya, Carlos Alberto, II *lawyer*

Chauvin
Sammarco, Paul William *ecologist, researcher*

Church Point
Romine, Donna Mae *middle school educator*

Columbia
Davis, (Shelton) Delane *petroleum engineer*

Covington
Blossman, Alfred Rhody, Jr. *banker*
†Ellis, Frederick Stephen *retired judge*
Files, Mark Willard *business and financial consultant*
Foil, Donald Carl *accountant*
Paddison, David Robert *lawyer*
Roberts, James Allen *urologist*
Stroup, Sheila Tierney *columnist*
Vercellotti, John Raymond *research chemist*

Crowley
†Foreman, Alfred G. *theologian, philosopher*
Harrington, Thomas Barrett *judge*
Martin, Edythe Louviere *business educator*

Cut Off
Adams, Laura Ann *critical care nurse*

Denham Springs
Kuhn, James E. *judge*
Perkins, Arthur Lee, Sr. *retired principal, real estate broker, insurance agent*

Deridder
Magee, Thomas Eston, Jr. *minister*
Mallory, Patricia Jody *museum curator*

Stailey, Janie Ruth *occupational health nurse*

Destrehan
Greene, Glen Lee *secondary school educator*

Donaldsonville
Watson, Stanley Ellis *clergyman, small business owner*

Dubach
Guin, Jeffery Keith *graphic designer*
Lindsay, Robby Lane *English educator*
Straughan, William Thomas *engineering educator*

Franklin
Fairchild, Phyllis Elaine *school counselor*
McClelland, James Ray *lawyer*

Franklinton
Alvarado, Luis Manuel *physician*

Golden Meadow
Strickland, Tara Lynn *elementary education educator*

Gonzales
Leake, Anita Robin *accountant, financial analyst*
Young, David Nelson *media and communications consultant*

Grambling
†El-Baghdadi, Mahdi Abbas *public administration educator*
Robinson, Eddie Gay *college football coach*

Gramercy
Deroche, Kathleen Samrow *elementary educator, mathematics consultant*

Grant
†Hahler, Gary Edwards *secondary school educator, coach*

Gretna
Calhoun, Milburn *publishing executive, rare book dealer, physician*
Simoneaux, Sandi Sue *veterinarian*
Wicker, Thomas Carey, Jr. *judge*

Hall Summit
Wimberly, Evelyn Louise Russell *nursing coordinator*

Hammond
Bender, Victor M. *educational administrator*
Broussard, Francis Peter *English educator*
Emerson, Peter Michael *counselor*
Hemberger, Glen James *university band director, music educator*
Matheny, Tom Harrell *lawyer*
Parker, Clea Edward *retired university president*
Shepherd, David Preston *biology educator, researcher*
Thorburn, James Alexander *humanities educator*

Harahan
Maclaren, Noel Keith *pathologist, pediatrician, educator*
Ryan, Teresa Weaver *obstetrical and clinical nurse specialist*

Harrisonburg
Alexander, Lisa D. *nursing administrator*

Harvey
Chee, Shirley *real estate broker*

Homer
Anglin, Walter Michael *minister, law enforcement professional$D*

Houma
Bordelon, Dena Cox Yarbrough *retired special education educator*
Conrad, Harold Theodore *psychiatrist*
Davis, Cheryl Suzanne *critical care nurse*
Ferguson, Thomas Glen *internist*
Gillespie, Betty Glover *critical care nurse*
†Jarrell, Charles Michael *bishop*
Lemoine, Pamela Allyson *principal*
Rhodes, Gene Paul *small business owner*

Independence
Camp, Cynthia M. *writer, consultant*

Iowa
†Guilbeau, Brian Gerald *sportswriter*
Leonard, Linda Faye *secondary education educator*

Jackson
Morrison, Francine Darlene *psychiatrist, massage therapist, herbal simplist*
Payne, Mary Alice McGill *behavior management healthcare quality consultant*

Jeanerette
Derise, Nellie Louise *nutritionist, educator, researcher*

Jefferson
Conino, Joseph Aloysius *lawyer*

Jennings
Patterson, Trudy Jenkins *librarian*

Kenner
Cook, Willie Chunn *retired elementary school educator*
deMonsabert, Winston Russel *chemist, consultant*
Kuebler, David Wayne *insurance company executive*
Levell, Edward, Jr. *city official*
Regan, Siri Lisa Lambourne *gifted education educator*
Scherich, Edward Baptiste *retired diversified company executive*
Siebel, Mathias Paul *mechanical engineer*
Valvo, Barbara-Ann *lawyer, surgeon*
White, Charles Albert, Jr. *medical educator, obstetrician-gynecologist*

La Place
Landry, Ronald Jude *lawyer, state senator*
Lodwick, Judith Lynne *nursing educator*
Outlaw, Kitti Kiattikunvivat *surgeon*

Lafayette
†Akin, Jonathan Andrew *educator*
Baudoin, Peter *family business consultant*
Boudreaux, Gloria Marie *nurse, educator*
Branch, Sonya Meyer *library director*
Breaux, Paul Joseph *lawyer, pharmacist*
Carstens, Jane Ellen *retired library science educator*
Cosper, Sammie Wayne *educational consultant*
Davidson, James Joseph, III *lawyer*
Davis, Ruth Louise-Weingartner *video company administrator, former military officer*
Davis, William Eugene *federal judge*
Doherty, Rebecca Feeney *federal judge*
Domingue, Emery *consulting engineering company executive, retired*
Duhe, John Malcolm, Jr. *federal judge*
Dur, Philip Francis *political scientist, educator, retired foreign service officer*
Fang, Cheng-Shen *chemical engineering educator*
Gaubert, Ronald Joseph *gas and oil industry executive, management consultant*
Guidry, Rodney-Lee Joseph *small business owner*
Haik, Richard T., Sr. *federal judge*
Hepguler, Gregory Gokhan *petroleum engineer*
Hermes, Mother Theresa Margaret *prioress*
Jolissaint, Stephen Lacy *pathologist*
Judice, Marc Wayne *lawyer*
Logan, Effie Tanner *mental health nurse*
Luppens, John Christian *petroleum engineer*
Mallet, Alexis, Jr. *construction company executive*
Mansfield, James Norman, III *lawyer*
Melançon, Tucker Lee *judge*
Methvin, Mildred E. *judge*
†Mizelle, William Donner *optometrist*
Moody, Janet Lynne *elementary education educator*
Myers, Stephen Hawley *lawyer*
O'Donnell, Edward Joseph *bishop, former editor*
Putnam, Richard Johnson *federal judge*
†Raffel, Burton Nathan *educator, poet, writer, translator*
Redding, Evelyn A. *dean, nursing educator*
Revels, Richard W., Jr. *lawyer*
Rieke, Herman Henry, III *petroleum engineering educator, consultant*
Saloom, Kaliste Joseph, Jr. *lawyer, retired judge*
Sides, Larry Eugene *advertising executive*
Stuart, Walter Bynum, III *banker*
Swift, John Goulding *lawyer*
Tynes, Pamela Anne *federal magistrate*
†Wyatt, Charles H. *cardiovascular surgeon*
Zuschlag, Richard Emery *small business owner*

Lake Charles
Beam, James C. (Jim Beam) *editor, newspaper*
Bradley, Judy Faye *elementary school educator*
Briggs, Arleen Frances *mental health nurse, educator*
Butler, Robert Olen *writer, educator*
Clements, Robert W. *lawyer*
Curol, Helen Ruth *librarian, English language educator*
†Daigle, Cynthia Coffey *speech and language pathologist*
Dilks, Sattaria S. *mental health nurse, therapist*
Drez, David Jacob, Jr. *orthopedic surgeon, educator*
Dronet, Virgie Mae *educational technology educator*
Earhart, Lucie Bethea *volunteer, former secondary school educator*
Everett, John Prentis, Jr. *lawyer*
Fields, Anita *dean*
Gunderson, Clark Alan *orthopedic surgeon*
Hanchey, James Clinton *lawyer*
Hebert, Robert D. *academic administrator*
Hunter, Edwin Ford, Jr. *federal judge*
Leder, Sandra Juanita *elementary school educator*
Leonard, Sherry Ann *critical care nurse*
Levingston, Ernest Lee *engineering company executive*
McLeod, William Lasater, Jr. *judge, former state legislator*
Middleton, George, Jr. *clinical child psychologist*
Mount, Willie Landry *mayor*
Ortego, Jim *lawyer, legal educator*
†Prater, Michael Albert *security executive*
Premeaux, Shane Richard *marketing educator*
Sanchez, Walter Marshall *lawyer*
Shaddock, William Edward, Jr. *lawyer*
Speyrer, Jude *bishop*
Stacey, Norma Elaine *farmer, civic worker*
Trimble, James T., Jr. *federal judge*
Veron, J. Michael *lawyer*
†Vincent, Amos Joseph, Jr. *priest*
†Wilson, Alonzo P. *federal judge*
Yadalam, Kashinath Gangadhara *psychiatrist*

Lecompte
Clark, Mary Machen *community health nurse*

Leesville
Farley, Michelle Renae *secondary school educator*
Norman, Paralee Frances *English language educator, researcher*
Wimberly, Beadie Reneau (Leigh Wimberly) *financial services executive*

Mandeville
Bartee, Roberta P. *nursing educator*
Christian, John Catlett, Jr. *lawyer*
Deano, Edward Joseph, Jr. *lawyer, state legislator*
Hruska, Francis John *marine surveyor and consultant*
Klein, Bernard Joseph *management specialist*
†Miller, Joseph Claude *principal*
Napier, William James, Jr. *marine oil and gas construction consultant*
Ray, Charles Jackson *retired surgeon*
Treuting, Edna Gannon *retired nursing administrator*
Wales, John Henry *physician, consultant*

Many
Byles, Robert Valmore *manufacturing company executive*
†Rains, Laura Jean Ponselle *special education educator, farmer*

Marksville
Riddle, Charles Addison, III *state legislator, lawyer*

Maurice
Larsen, Henrik Aslak *mechanical engineer*

Meraux
Broome, Randall *evangelist*

Metairie
Album, Jerald Lewis *lawyer*
Ales, Beverly Gloria Rushing *artist*
Ambrose, Ashley Avery *football player*
Baisier, Maria Davis *English language educator, theater director*
Benson, Tom *professional football executive*
Boazman, Franklin Meador *financial consultant*
Butcher, Bruce Cameron *lawyer*
Caruso, Kay Ann Pete *elementary education educator*
Conway, James Donald *internist, educator*
Derbes, Albert Joseph, III *lawyer, accountant*
Ditka, Michael Keller *professional football coach*
Doody, Louis Clarence, Jr. *accountant*
Edisen, Clayton Byron *physician*
Evans, Carol Rockwell *nursing administrator*
Falco, Maria Josephine *political scientist, academic administrator*
Feran, Russell G. *sales executive*
Friedman, Lynn Joseph *counselor*
Gereighty, Andrea Saunders *polling company executive, poet*
Goss, Donald Davis *consultant, author, lecturer*
Goyette, Geoffrey Robert *sales executive*
Grimm, John Lloyd *business executive, marketing professional*
Hardy, Ashton Richard *lawyer*
Harell, George S. *radiologist*
Hartman, James Austin *retired geologist*
Horkowitz, Sylvester Peter *chemist*
Johnson, Beth Michael *school administrator*
†Johnston, William J., Jr. *neurosurgeon*
Killeen, Edward Joseph *actor, designer*
Kramer, Helene G. *political and civic association executive*
Lake, Wesley Wayne, Jr. *internist, allergist, educator*
Mando, Wagih Rufaat *surgeon*
Martin, Shirley A. *physical education educator*
Mayo, Edwin M. *physical therapist*
McMahon, Robert Albert, Jr. *lawyer*
McShan, Clyde Griffin, II *financial executive*
McVay, Mary Ruth *speech pathologist*
Milam, June Matthews *life insurance agent*
Myers, Iona Raymer *real estate and property manager*
Nehrbass, Seth Martin *patent lawyer*
Newman, Claire Poe *corporate executive*
Nicoladis, Michael F. *engineering company executive*
N'Vietson, Tung Thanh *civil engineer*
Ochsner, Seymour Fiske *radiologist, editor*
Olivier, Jason Thomas *lawyer*
Ostendorf, Lance Stephen *lawyer, investor, financial consultant and planner*
Perlis, Sharon A. *lawyer*
Perrin, Roy Albert, Jr. *real estate developer, investor*
Reinike, Irma *writer, artist, poet*
Spruiell, Vann *psychoanalyst, educator, editor, researcher*
Whitehorn, W. Elizabeth Randazzo *accountant*

Monroe
Blondin, Joan *nephrologist educator*
Cage, Bobby Nyle *research and statistics educator*
Cooksey, John Charles *congressman, ophthalmic surgeon*
Ifediora, Okechukwu Chigozie *nephrologist, educator*
Sartor, Daniel Ryan, Jr. *lawyer*
Vankeerbergen, Bernadette Chantal *college educator*
Wolfe, Michael David *management educator*
†Zander, Arlen Ray *academic director*

Morgan City
†Denduluri, Ramarao M. *urologist*

Natchitoches
Egan, Shirley Anne *retired nursing educator*
Masson, Stephanie Reese *journalist*
Webb, Randall Joseph *mathematics educator, university president*
Wilkes, Charles Newton *sports administration and health and physical education educator*
Wolfe, George Cropper *retired private school educator, artist, author*

New Iberia
Gonsoulin Ghattas, Wendy Ann *choreographer, dancer*
Grubbs, Conway E. *marine company executive*
Henton, Willis Ryan *bishop*
Janssen, Christopher Frank *veterinarian*

New Orleans
Abaunza, Donald Richard *lawyer*
Abbott, Hirschel Theron, Jr. *lawyer*
Acomb, Robert Bailey, Jr. *lawyer, educator*
Adams, Darlene W. *computer services administrator*
†Africk, Lance M. *federal judge*
Agrawal, Krishna Chandra *pharmacology educator*
Alarcon, Terry Quentin *judge*
Allen, F(rank) C(linton), Jr. *lawyer, retired manufacturing executive*
Allerton, William, III *public relations executive*
Alsobrook, Henry Bernis, Jr. *lawyer*
Amoss, W. James, Jr. *shipping company executive*
Amoss, Walter James, III *editor*
Arshad, M. Kaleem *psychiatrist*
†Aymond, Gregory M. *academic administrator*
Bachmann, Richard Arthur *oil company executive*
Backstrom, William M., Jr. *lawyer*
Bacot, Marie *management consultant, researcher*
Bailey, Barry Stone *sculptor, educator*
Balée, William L. *anthropology educator*
Ball, Millie (Mildred Porteous Ball) *editor, journalist*
Baranovich, Diana Lea *music educator*
Barden, Janice Kindler *personnel company executive*
Barham, Mack Elwin *lawyer, educator*
Barker, Larry Lee *communications educator*
Barry, Francis Julian, Jr. *lawyer*
†Baudoin, Larry Anthony *academic administrator*
Bautista, Abraham Parana *immunologist*
Beahm, Franklin D. *lawyer*
Beard, Elizabeth Letitia *physiologist, educator*
Beck, David Edward *surgeon*
Beck, William Harold, Jr. *lawyer*
Beer, Peter Hill *federal judge*
Belsom, John Anton (Jack) *writer, researcher*
Benerito, Ruth Rogan (Mrs. Frank H. Benerito) *chemist*
Benjamin, Adelaide Wisdom *community volunteer and activist*
Benjamin, Edward Bernard, Jr. *lawyer*
Berrigan, Helen Ginger *federal judge*

Bertoniere, Noelie Rita research chemist
Bertrand, William Ellis public health educator, academic administrator
Best, Susan Marie artist, educator
Bieck, Robert Barton, Jr. lawyer
Birtel, Frank Thomas mathematician, philosopher, educator
Blitch, Ronald Buchanan architect
Boggs, Corinne Claiborne (Lindy Boggs) former congresswoman
†Boh, Robert Henry civil engineer, construction company executive
Boudreaux, Kenneth Justin economics and finance educator, consultant
†Brahney, Thomas J., III federal judge
Bricker, Harvey Miller anthropology educator
Bricker, Victoria Reifler anthropology educator
Bridges, Elizabeth Ann marketing consultant
Brody, Arnold Ralph research scientist, educator
Bronfin, Fred lawyer
Brosman, Catharine Savage French language educator, poet
†Brown, Jerry A. federal judge
†Brown, Mary Willoughby health facilities administrator
Bullard, Edgar John, III museum director
Burr, Timothy Fuller lawyer
Burton, Barbara Able psychotherapist
Butler, Shirley Ann social worker
Caldwell, Delmar Ray ophthalmologist, educator
Calogero, Pascal Frank, Jr. state supreme court chief justice
Carter, James Clarence university administrator
Casellas, Joachim art gallery executive
Chambers, Thomas Edward college president, psychologist
†Chasez, Alma L. federal judge
Cheatwood, Roy Clifton lawyer
Childress, Steven Alan law educator
Clancy, Thomas Hanley seminary administrator
Claverie, Philip deVilliers lawyer
Clement, Edith Brown federal judge
†Cohen, Rosalie civic worker
Cohn, Isidore, Jr. surgeon, educator
Coleman, James Julian lawyer
Coleman, James Julian, Jr. lawyer, industrialist, real estate executive
Collins, Harry David construction consultant, forensic engineering specialist, mechanical and nuclear engineer, retired army officer
†Collins, Richard Wayne English literature educator
Combe, John Clifford, Jr. lawyer
Connolly, Edward S. neurological surgeon
Cook, Victor Joseph, Jr. marketing educator, consultant
Correro, Anthony James, III lawyer
Corrigan, James John, Jr. pediatrician, dean
Cosenza, Arthur George opera director
Cospolich, James Donald electrical engineering executive, consultant
†Cowen, Scott S. university president
Creamer, German Gonzalo bank executive, educator
Creppel, Claire Binet hotel owner
Crumley, David Oliver publisher, author, foundation executive
Crumley, Martha Ann company executive
Crusto, Mitchell Ferdinand lawyer, educator
Curry, Dale Blair journalist
Cusimano, Cheryll Ann nursing administrator
Dahlberg, Carl Fredrick, Jr. entrepreneur
Danahar, David C. academic administrator, history educator
Daniels, Robert Sanford psychiatrist, administrator
Deasy, William John construction, marine dredging, engineering and mining company executive
Denegre, George lawyer
Dennery, Linda newspaper publishing executive
Dennis, James Leon federal judge
†Diaz, James Henry public health physician
Domingue, Gerald James medical scientist, microbiology, immunology and urology educator, researcher, clinical bacteriologist
Dribus, John Robert geologist
Dunbar, Prescott Nelson investment company executive
Duncan, Margaret Caroline physician
Duplantier, Adrian Guy federal judge
Duval, Stanwood Richardson, Jr. judge
Dwyer, Ralph Daniel, Jr. lawyer
Easson, William McAlpine psychiatrist
England, John David neurologist
Ensenat, Louis Albert surgeon
Epstein, Arthur William physician, educator
Esman, Marjorie Ruth lawyer
Espinoza, Luis Rolan rheumatologist
Eustis, Richmond Minor lawyer
Fagaly, William Arthur curator
Fallon, Eldon E. lawyer, educator, judge
Fantaci, James Michael lawyer
Favrot, Henri Mortimer, Jr. architect, real estate developer
Feldman, Martin L. C. federal judge
Ferguson, Charles Austin retired newspaper editor
Fertel, Ruth U. restaurant owner
Fierke, Thomas Garner lawyer
Filson, Ronald Coulter architect, educator, college dean
Fingerman, Milton biologist, educator
Fisher, James William medical educator, pharmacologist
Flower, Walter Chew, III investment counselor
†Fonseca, Ronald A. federal judge
Force, Robert law educator
Frantz, Phares Albert architect
Freudenberger, Herman retired economics educator
Friedman, Joel William law educator
Friedmann, Patricia Ann writer
Frohlich, Edward David medical educator
Fuselier, Harold Anthony, Jr. physician, urologist
Garcia, Patricia A. lawyer
Gatipon, Betty Becker medical educator, consultant
Gaubert, Lloyd Francis shipboard and industrial cable distribution executive
Gebauer, August William editor
†Gertjejansen, Doyle artist, educator
Ginsberg, Harley Glen pediatrician
Gordon, Joseph Elwell university official, educator
Gottlieb, A(braham) Arthur medical educator
Grace, Marcellus pharmacy educator, university dean
Grau, Jean Elizabeth retired insurance agent
Grau, Shirley Ann (Mrs. James Kern Feibleman) writer
Hackman, Gwendolyn Ann private duty nurse
Hamlin, James Turner, III university dean, physician
Handelsman, Walt cartoonist
Hannan, Philip Matthew bishop
Hansel, Stephen Arthur holding company executive
Hardy, Thomas Cresson insurance company executive
Harshfield, Neil Alan sculptor, educator
Hartz, Renee Semo cardiothoracic surgeon
Hassenboehler, Donalyn principal
Haygood, Paul M. lawyer
Healy, George William, III lawyer, mediator
Henderson, Helena Naughton legal association administrator
Hicks, Terrell Cohlman surgeon, educator, health facility administrator, academic administrator
Hoffman, Robert Dean, Jr. lawyer
Holditch, William Kenneth American literature educator
Howard, Richard Ralston, II medical health advisor, researcher, financier
Hudzinski, Leonard Gerard social worker
Huly, Jan C. career officer
Hunter, Sue Persons former state official
Hyman, Albert Lewis cardiologist
Hyman, Edward Sidney physician, consultant
Imig, John David medical educator
Incaprera, Frank Philip internist
Ingraham, Joseph Edwin financial officer
Ivens, Mary Sue microbiologist, mycologist
Jacobsen, Thomas Warren archaeologist, educator
Jaffe, Bernard Michael surgeon
Jeff, Morris F.X., Jr. muncipal or county official
Johnson, Arnold Ray public relations executive
Johnson, Bernette Joshua state supreme court justice
Johnson, Beth Exum lawyer
Johnson, Clifford Vincent college administrator
Johnson, Patrick, Jr. lawyer
Johnson, Peter Forbes transportation executive, business owner
Jones, Glenn Earle property management executive
Jones, John Anderson, Jr. school system administrator
Jones, Philip Kirkpatrick, Jr. lawyer
Jordan, Eddie J. prosecutor
†Jordan, Robert Smith political science educator
Judell, Harold Benn lawyer
†Jung, Rodney C. internist, academic administrator
Keller, Louis, Sr. municipal official
Keller, Thomas Clements lawyer
Kelly, Eamon Michael university president emeritus
Kemp, James Bradley, Jr. lawyer
Kewalramani, Laxman Sunderdas surgeon, consultant
Kilroy, James Francis educator
Kimball, Catherine D. state supreme court justice
†Kingsmill, T. Hartley, Jr. federal judge
Kline, David Gellinger neurosurgery educator
Klingman, John Philip architect, educator
Kolinsky, Michael Allen emergency physician
Kuerley-Schaffer, Dawn Renee medical/surgical nurse
Kukla, Jon (Keith) historian, museum director
Kuklok, Kevin B. career officer
Kupperman, Stephen Henry lawyer
Lang, Erich Karl physician, radiologist
Lannes, William Joseph, III electrical engineer
LaValle, Irving Howard decision analysis educator
Lavelle, Paul Michael lawyer
Le Blanc, Alice Isabelle public health educator, health program grants and contracts administrator
Ledbetter, Linda Carol pension fund executive, professional organization executive
Lee, Griff Calicutt civil engineer
Lee, Silas, III sociologist, public opinion research consultant
Leinbach, Philip Eaton retired librarian
Le Jeune, Francis Ernest, Jr. otolaryngologist
Lemann, Thomas Berthelot lawyer
†Lemelle, Ivan L.R. federal judge
Lemmon, Harry Thomas state supreme court justice
Levitzky, Michael Gordon physiology educator, researcher
Lewy, John Edwin pediatric nephrologist
†Liljeberg, Genevieve Brocato artist
Lind, Thomas Otto barge transportation company executive
Lingle, Sarah Elizabeth research scientist
Livaudais, Marcel, Jr. federal judge
Locke, William endocrinologist
Lopez, Manuel immunology and allergy educator
Lowe, Robert Charles lawyer
Lupberger, Edwin Adolph retired utility executive
Lupo, Robert Edward Smith real estate developer and investor
†Lupo, Thomas J.
Luza, Radomir Vaclav historian, educator
Lyall, Robert H. opera company executive
Mackin, Cooper Richerson university chancellor
Marcus, Bernard lawyer
Marcus, Walter F., Jr. state supreme court justice
Martin, David Hubert physician, educator
Martin, Gerald Wayne professional football player
Martin, Louis Frank surgery and physiology educator
Martof, Mary Taylor nursing educator
Masinter, Paul James lawyer
Massare, John Steve medical association administrator, educator
Mathes, Edward Conrad architect
McCall, John Patrick college president, educator
McDaniels, Warren fire official
McFarland, James W. academic administrator
†McFerren, Martha Dean writer, librarian
McGlone, Michael Anthony lawyer
McKinley, Kevin L. neurologist
McMahon, Maeve middle school administrator
McMillan, Lee Richards, II lawyer
McNamara, A. J. federal judge
Mentz, Henry Alvan, Jr. federal judge
Miller, Gary H. lawyer
Miller, Robert Harold otolaryngologist, educator
Millikan, Larry Edward dermatologist
Mintz, Albert lawyer
Mitchell, Kenneth D. physiologist, medical educator
Mitchell, Lansing Leroy federal judge
Mize, David M. military officer
Moely, Barbara E. psychology researcher, educator
Mogabgab, William Joseph physician, virologist, educator
Molony, Michael Janssens, Jr. lawyer
†Moore, Louis, Jr. federal judge
Morial, Marc Haydel mayor
Morrell, Arthur Anthony lawyer, state legislator
Murrish, Charles Howard oil and gas exploration company executive, geologist
Navar, Luis Gabriel physiology educator, researcher
Nelson, James Smith pathologist, educator
Nelson, Waldemar Stanley civil engineer, consultant
Nichols, Ronald Lee surgeon, educator
Norwood, Colvin Gamble, Jr. lawyer
Nuzum, Robert Weston lawyer
O'Brien, Gregory Michael St. Lawrence university official
Ochsner, John Lockwood thoracic-cardiovascular surgeon
O'Connor, Kim Claire chemical engineering and biotechnology educator
Oliver, Ronald retired medical technologist
Olson, Richard David psychology educator
O'Neal, Edgar Carl psychology educator
Orihel, Thomas Charles parasitology educator, research scientist
Ortique, Revius Oliver, Jr. city official
Owen, Kenneth Emerson museum director, retired librarian
Palmer, Vernon Valentine law educator
Pankey, George Atkinson physician, educator
Paolini, Gilberto literature and science educator
Paradise, Louis Vincent educational psychology educator, university official
Pearce, John Y. lawyer
Pedersen, Lynn Colton primary school educator
Pennington, Richard J. protective service official
Perdew, John Paul physics educator, condensed matter and density functional theorist
Perez, Luis Alberto lawyer
Pfister, Richard Charles physician, radiology educator
Phelps, Ashton, Jr. newspaper publisher
Phelps, Esmond, II lawyer
Plavsic, Branko Milenko radiology educator
Plymale, Ida Ruth Duffey journalist, educator
Poesch, Jessie Jean art historian
Poitevent, Edward Butts, II lawyer
Ponoroff, Lawrence law educator, legal consultant
Pope, John M. journalist
Porteous, G. Thomas, Jr. judge
†Postels, Douglas George neurologist
Price, Addie Marie Carter healthcare consultant
Pugh, William Whitmell Hill lawyer
Purvis, George Frank, Jr. life insurance company executive
Puschett, Jules B. medical educator, nephrologist, researcher
Qian, Zhaoming critic, literature educator
Quirk, Peter Richard engineering company executive
Rathke, Dale Lawrence community organizer and financial analyst
Rawls, John D. lawyer
Re, Richard Noel endocrinologist
Reck, Andrew Joseph philosophy educator
Regan, William Joseph, Jr. energy company executive
Remley, Theodore Phant, Jr. counseling educator, lawyer
Reyes, Raul Gregorio surgeon
Rice, Winston Edward lawyer
Riddick, Frank Adams, Jr. physician, health care facility administrator
Riess, George Febiger lawyer, educator
Rietschel, Robert Louis dermatologist
Rigby, Perry Gardner medical center administrator, educator, former university dean, physician
Roaf, William Layton professional football player
Robert, Phyllis Ann English educator
Roberts, Louise Nisbet philosopher
Robins, Robert Sidwar political science educator, administrator
Rodriguez, Antonio Jose lawyer
Rodriguez, Susan Miller nurse administrator
Roesler, Robert Harry city official
Rondeau, Clement Robert petroleum geologist
Rosen, Charles, II lawyer
Rosen, William Warren lawyer
Rosensteel, George Thomas physics educator, nuclear physicist
Roskoski, Robert, Jr. biochemist, educator, author
Ross, Kathleen elementary and secondary school educator, author
Rossowska, Magdalena Joanna physiology educator, research scientist
†Scelfo, Chris university football coach
Schaefer, Ralph municipal government official
Schally, Andrew Victor endocrinologist, researcher
Schleifstein, Mark Edwin newspaper reporter
Schmidt-Sommerfeld, Eberhard pediatrician
Schneider, George T. obstetrician-gynecologist
Schulte, Francis B. archbishop
Schwartz, Charles, Jr. federal judge
Scott, John Tarrell art educator, sculptor
Seab, Charles Gregory astrophysicist
Sear, Morey Leonard federal judge, educator
Sefcik, James Francis museum director
†Seibel, Klauspeter conductor
Sellin, Eric linguist, poet, educator
Serio, Charles V. United States marshal
Sexton, James Richard author, photographer
Simon, H(uey) Paul lawyer
Simoneaux, Catherine M. academic administrator
Simons, Dona artist
Sims, John William lawyer
Sinor, Howard Earl, Jr. lawyer
Skinner, Robert Earle university librarian, writer
Slater, Benjamin Richard, Jr. lawyer
Smith, John Webster retired energy industry executive, consultant
Snyder, Charles Aubrey lawyer
Solomonow, Moshe biomedical engineer, scientist, educator
Somers, Sally West librarian
Spurlock, Jimmie Paul, Jr. veterinarian, educator
Stansbury, Harry Case state commissioner
Stapp, Dan Ernest retired lawyer, utility executive
Steinmetz, Robert Charles architect
Stephens, Richard Bernard natural resource company executive
Stewart, Gregory Wallace physician
Straumanis, John Janis, Jr. psychiatry educator
†Strub, Richard Lester neurologist
Suber, Margaret Adele controller
Sullivan, Daniel Edmond fundraising executive
Superneau, Duane William geneticist, physician
Svenson, Ernest Olander psychiatrist, psychoanalyst
Sylvain, Vincent Todd Adams muncipal or county official
Tahir, Mary Elizabeth retail marketing and management consultant
Tarver, Michael Keith lawyer
Thomas, Robert Allen environmental communications educator
†Thompson, Michael Greenwood lawyer
Thornell, Jack Randolph photographer
Timmcke, Alan Edward physician and surgeon
Truehill, Marshall, Jr. minister
Usdin, Gene Leonard physician, psychiatrist
Vance, Robert Patrick lawyer
Vance, Sarah S. federal judge
Vanselow, Neal Arthur university administrator, physician
Vaudry, J. William, Jr. lawyer
Vella, Joseph Bayer portfolio manager
Ventura, Hector Osvaldo cardiologist
Waechter, Arthur Joseph, Jr. lawyer
Wakefield, Benton McMillin, Jr. banker
Waring, William Winburn pediatric pulmonologist, educator
Warren, William Frampton, Jr. religion educator
Washington, Robert Orlanda social policy educator, former university official
Webb, Watts Rankin surgeon
Wedig, Regina Scotto lawyer
Weeks, Lana Carol clinical social worker
Wegmann, Mary Katherine art director
Weiner, Roy Samuel medical educator, health facility administrator
Weinmann, John Giffen lawyer, diplomat
Weiss, Kenneth Andrew lawyer, law educator
Weiss, Susette Marie technical and photographic consultant, mass communications/media specialist
Weiss, Thomas Edward physician
Welden, Arthur Luna biology educator
Welsh, Ronald Arthur physician, educator
Whidden, Stanley John physiologist, physician
Wiener, Jacques Loeb, Jr. federal judge
Wild, Dirk Jonathan accountant
†Wilkie, Curtis Carter, Jr. journalist
Wilkinson, Joseph C. lawyer
Willems, Constance Charles lawyer
†Williams, Ronald David telecommunications executive
Winstead, Daniel Keith psychiatrist
Yates, Robert Doyle anatomy educator

New Roads
Christophe, Josita Lejuan special education educator

Norco
Marino, Ruche Joseph retired district court judge

Opelousas
Pinac, André Louis, III obstetrician, gynecologist
†Schiff, Gerald H. federal judge

Pineville
Adams, Jane Miller retired psychotherapist
Boswell, Bill Reeser religious organization executive
Cummings, Karen Sue corrections classification administrator
Howell, Thomas history educator

Plaquemine
Mc Cray, Evelina Williams librarian, researcher

Pride
Jones, LaCinda assistant principal

Ruston
Barmore, Leon head basketball coach
Barron, Randall Franklin mechanical engineer, educator, consultant
†Dodge Robbins, Dorothy Ellin English educator
Hale, Paul Nolen, Jr. engineering administrator, educator
Jordan, Carl David physical education educator
Marbury, Virginia Lomax insurance and investment executive
Marbury, William Ardis banker
Maxfield, John Edward retired university dean
Painter, Jack Timberlake civil engineer
Phillips, Kathye critical care, emergency nurse
Pullis, Joe Milton business administration educator, writer
Reneau, Daniel D. academic administrator
Sabin, Paul Edgar developer
Taylor, Foster Jay retired university president

Saint Bernard
Lee, Melvin Joseph minister

Saint Gabriel
Berggren, Gerard T. plant pathologist
Knight, Diane special education educator

Scott
Bergeron, Wilton Lee physician

Shreveport
Achee, Roland Joseph lawyer
Albright, James Aaron orthopedist, surgeon
Angermeier, Ingo hospital administrator, educator
Beaird, Charles T. publishing executive
Becker, Roger Vern information science educator
Bradley, Ronald James neuroscientist
Brock, Eric John urban planner, historian, consultant
Bryant, J(ames) Bruce lawyer
†Callaway, Stephen V. federal judge
Carmody, Arthur Roderick, Jr. lawyer
Carter, Louvenia McGee nursing educator
Colón, Carlos Wildo librarian
Conrad, Steven Allen physician, biomedical engineer, educator, researcher
Cox, John Thomas, Jr. lawyer
Dhanireddy, Ramasubbareddy neonatologist, researcher
Dickson, Markham Allen wholesale company executive
Dilworth, Edwin Earle retired obstetrician, gynecologist
Fort, Arthur Tomlinson, III physician, educator
Forte, Stephen Forrest interior designer
Freeman, Arthur Merrimon, III psychiatry educator, dean
Friend, William Benedict bishop
Ganley, James Powell ophthalmologist, educator
George, Ronald Baylis physician, educator
Goodman, Sylvia Klumok volunteer
Griffith, Robert Charles allergist, educator, planter
Haas, Lester Carl retired architect
Hall, Pike, Jr. lawyer
Harbuck, Edwin Charles insurance agent
Heacock, Donald Dee social worker
Hetherwick, Gilbert Lewis lawyer
Holt, Edwin Joseph psychology educator
Hughes, Mary Sorrows artist
Hummel, Kay Jean physical therapist
†Jacobs, Catherine Heriot financial advisor
Jamison, Richard Melvin virologist, educator
Jeter, Katherine Leslie Brash lawyer
Joshua, Percy English educator
Launius, Beatrice Kay critical care nurse, educator
Lazarus, Allan Matthew retired newspaper editor
Lenard, Lloyd Edgar financial consultant

Levy, Harold Bernard *pediatrician*
Lloyd, Cecil Rhodes *pediatric dentist*
Magness, Nan Jean *social services administrator*
Mancini, Mary Catherine *cardiothoracic surgeon, researcher*
McDonald, John Clifton *surgeon*
Nelson, George Dalman, Jr. *banker*
†O'Neal, Barron Johns *surgeon*
Payne, Roy Steven *judge*
Perlman, Jerald Lee *lawyer*
Politz, Henry Anthony *federal judge*
Politz, Nyle Anthony *lawyer*
Ragland, Preston Lamar *designer, small business owner*
Ramey, Cecil Edward, Jr. *lawyer*
Ratcliff, John Garrett *lawyer*
Rigby, Kenneth *lawyer*
Roberts, Robert, III *lawyer*
†Robinson, Edna Earle *publishing company executive*
Robinson, Garry Lewin *television news executive*
Rust, John McNeil *veterinarian*
Sandifer, Kevin Wayne *archival services executive*
Schneider, Thomas Richard *hospital administrator*
Shelby, James Stanford *cardiovascular surgeon*
†Shemwell, Robert H. *federal judge*
Simons, Dennis *performing company executive*
Skinner, Michael David *lawyer*
Smith, Brian David *lawyer, educator*
Smith, Harriet Gwendolyn Gurley *secondary school educator, writer*
Staats, Thomas Elwyn *neuropsychologist*
Stagg, Tom *federal judge*
Stewart, Carl E. *federal judge*
Stewart, James Joseph *minister, consultant*
†Sutton, Hal Evan *professional golfer*
Tenney, William Frank *pediatrician*
Thomas, Bessie *primary education educator*
Tullis, John Ledbetter *retired wholesale distributing company executive*
Walter, Donald Ellsworth *federal judge*
Webb, Donald Arthur *minister*
Williams, Patsy Ruth *poet*
Wray, Geraldine Smitherman (Jerry Wray) *artist*
Wright, Marie Beulah Battey *retired advertising executive*

Sicily Island
Dale, Sam E., Jr. *retired educational administrator*

Slidell
Dabdoub, Paul Oscar *academic administrator*
Dearing, Reinhard Josef *city official*
Eiermann-Wegener, Darlene Mae *paralegal*
Faust, Marilyn B. *middle school principal*
Grantham, Donald James *engineer, educator, author*
Hall, Ogden Henderson *retired allied health educator*
Hammond, Margaret *lawyer*
Hendricks, Donald Duane *librarian*
McBurney, Elizabeth Innes *physician, educator*
Muller, Robert Joseph *gynecologist*
Schexnayder, Manfred Jean *secondary education educator*
Schofield, Barbara Curtright *school administrator*
†Stroud, Robert Arlen *medical equipment company executive*
Tewell, Joseph Robert, Jr. *electrical engineer*

Sorrento
Welch, Joe Ben *academic administrator*

Springhill
Morgan, Larry Ronald *minister*

Sunset
Brinkhaus, Armand J. *lawyer*

Terrytown
Olson, Sandra Dittman *medical and surgical nurse*

Thibodaux
Bonin, Do *basketball coach*
Delahaye, Alfred Newton *retired journalism educator*
Delozier, Maynard Wayne *marketing educator*
Fairchild, Joseph Virgil, Jr. *accounting educator*
Hebert, Leo Placide *physician*
Howes, Michael *sculptor, educator*
Klaus, Kenneth Sheldon *choral conductor, vocalist, music educator*
Risch, Patricia Ann *critical care nurse, administrator*

Tioga
Tenney, Tom Fred *bishop*

Ville Platte
De Ville, Winston *genealogist*
†Saunders, Wesley Hugh *librarian*

Vivian
Collier, Samuel Melvin *aerospace engineer*

West Monroe
Reighney, Mary Kathryn *secondary education educator*
White, Karen Jo *nurse*
Williams, Sandra Ward *critical care nurse*

Westwego
Brehm, Loretta Persohn *secondary art educator, librarian, consultant*
Reyes, Shirley Norflin *computer learning center educator*

Zachary
Rogillio, Kathy June *musician, piano rebuilder, educator*

MAINE

Andover
Ellis, George Hathaway *retired banker and utility company executive*
Kaltsos, Angelo John *electronics executive, educator, photographer*

Arrowsic
Stone, Albert Edward *educator*

Ashland
Morrow, David Andrew *secondary education educator*

Auburn
Adams, Mark A. *city manager*
Clifford, Robert William *state supreme court justice*
†Lord, Michael Clark *executive secretary*
Rausch, Shanti Jo Vogell *mental health nurse*
Webb, Todd (Charles Clayton Webb) *photographer, writer*

Augusta
Adelberg, Arthur William *lawyer*
Ahearne, Douglas *state legislator*
Amero, Jane Adams *state legislator*
Asmussen, J. Donna *educational administrator, consultant*
†Bailey, Dennis *state official*
Barth, Alvin Ludwig, Jr. *state legislator*
Blais, Helen Christine *daycare operator*
Daggett, Beverly Clark *state legislator*
†Denaco, Parker Alden *state official*
Desmond, Mabel Jeannette *state legislator, educator*
Gervais, Paul Nelson *foundation administrator, psychotherapist, public relations executive*
Gwadosky, Dan A. *secretary of state*
†Hall, Christopher *political party official*
Hatch, Pamela H. *state legislator*
Ketterer, Andrew *state attorney general*
Kilkelly, Marjorie Lee *state legislator, community development official*
King, Angus S., Jr. *governor of Maine*
Martin, John L. *state legislator*
Moody, Stanley Alton *entrepreneur, financial consultant*
Nickerson, John Mitchell *political science educator*
Paradis, Judy *state legislator*
Phillips, Joseph Robert *museum director*
Roberts, Donald Albert *advertising, public relations, marketing and media consultant*
Sanders, Estelle Watson *school system adminstrator*
Saxl, Jane Wilhelm *state legislator*
†Schlenker, Jon Arlin *sociology and anthropology educator*
Sotir, Thomas Alfred *healthcare executive, retired shipbuilder*
Stevens, Kathleen *state legislator*
Townsend, Elizabeth *state legislator*
Trites, Donald George *human service consultant*
Waldron, Janet E. *state commissioner*
†Whitney, Carol F. *controller*

Bangor
Albrecht, Ronald Lewis *financial services executive*
Albrecht, Rondi Kim *financial services executive*
Ballesteros, Paula M. *nurse*
Beaupain, Elaine Shapiro *psychiatric social worker*
†Bequlieu, Eugene W. *federal judge*
Brody, Morton Aaron *federal judge*
Bullock, William Clapp, Jr. *banker*
Donnelly, James Owen *state legislator, bank executive*
Ebitz, Elizabeth Kelly *lawyer*
Foster, Walter Herbert, Jr. *real estate company executive*
Goss, Georgia Bulman *translator*
†Haines, James B., Jr. *federal judge*
Hsu, Yu Kao *aerospace scientist, mathematician, educator*
Johnson, Sharon Marguerite *social worker, clinical hypnotherapist*
King, Stephen Edwin *novelist, screenwriter, director*
McGuigan, Charles James *rehabilitation therapist*
McKinnon, Carolyn Ann *child care center director*
Moreau, James William *stuntman*
Rea, Ann W. *librarian*
Rudman, Paul Lewis *state supreme court justice*
†Shubert, Dennis L. *neurosurgeon, medical administrator*
Ward, Debora Elliott *psychologist*
Warren, Richard Jordan *newspaper publisher*
Warren, Richard Kearney *newspaper publisher*
Watt, Thomas Lorne *dermatologist*
Woodcock, John Alden *lawyer*
Ziegelaar, Bob W. *terminal executive*

Bar Harbor
Carman, John Herbert *elementary education educator*
Carpenter, William Morton *English educator, writer*
Dworak, Marcia Lynn *library director, library building consultant*
Hoppe, Peter Christian *biologist, geneticist*
Leiter, Edward Henry *scientist*
†Little, Carl von Kienbusch *academic director, writer*
Paigen, Kenneth *geneticist, research director*
Swazey, Judith Pound *institute president, sociomedical science educator*

Bar Mills
Buchanan, Bruce *metal artist, photographer*
Burns, Maryann Margaret *elementary education educator*

Bath
Dillon, Francis Richard *retired air force officer*
Simone, Gail Elisabeth *manfacturing administrator*
Stoudt, Howard Webster *biological anthropologist, human factors specialist, consultant*

Belfast
Aaron, Hugh *writer*
Worth, Mary Page *mayor*

Berwick
Bufithis, Cynthia Billings *media specialist*

Biddeford
Featherman, Sandra *university president, political science educator*
Ford, Charles Willard *university administrator, educator*
Konstantinovskaia, Valeria *puppeteer, puppet maker, sculptor, educator*

Blue Hill
Mills, David Harlow *psychologist, association executive*
Taylor, Samuel A. *playwright*
Wenglowski, Joyce *painter*

Blue Hill Falls
Stookey, Noel Paul *folksinger, composer*

Boothbay Harbor
Cavanaugh, Tom Richard *artist, antiques dealer, retired art educator*
Davison, Ruth Hilton *elementary education educator*
Eames, John Heagan *etcher*
Eriksen, Dan Oluf *film director*
Lenthall, Franklyn *theatre historian*

Brewer
Steele, Teresa Willett *psychiatric clinical nurse specialist, nursing educator*

Bristol
Sabin, William Albert *editor*
Schmidt, Thomas Carson *international development banker*

Brooklin
Schmidt, Klaus Dieter *management consultant, university administrator, marketing and management educator*
Yglesias, Helen Bassine *author, educator*

Brunswick
Ault, James Mase *bishop*
Cotton, Joyce E. Doherty *mental health nurse*
Edwards, Robert Hazard *college president*
Fuchs, Alfred Herman *psychologist, college dean, educator*
Geoghegan, William Davidson *religion educator, minister*
Greason, Arthur LeRoy, Jr. *university administrator*
Hodge, James Lee *German language educator*
Horton, Michael *public affairs executive, information specialist*
Morgan, Richard Ernest *political scientist, educator*
Owen, H. Martyn *lawyer*
Pfeiffer, Sophia Douglass *state legislator, lawyer*
Schwartz, Elliott Shelling *composer, author, music educator*
Tucker, Allen Brown, Jr. *computer science educator*
Watts, Helen Caswell *civil engineer*

Bryant Pond
Conary, David Arlan *investment company executive*

Bucksport
Ives, Edward Dawson *folklore educator*
Williams, Christine Hewes *elementary education educator*

Camden
Anderson, George Harding *broadcasting company executive*
†Keogh, Kevin *political party official*
Lavenson, Susan Barker *hotel corporate executive, consultant*
†Moran, Elizabeth Ames *library director*
†Rourke, Bradley Kevin *public affairs executive*

Canaan
Walker, Willard Brewer *anthropology educator, linguist*

Cape Eliz
Dalbeck, Richard Bruce *insurance executive*
Simonds, Stephen Paige *former state legislator*

Caribou
Bosse, Denise Frances *educational administrator, education educator*
Hutcheon, Wilda Vilene Burtchell *artist*
Swanson, Shirley June *registered nurse, adult education educator*

Castine
Berleant, Arnold *philosopher*
Davis, Peter Frank *filmmaker, author*
Hall, David *sound archivist, writer*
Hoople, Sally Crosby *retired humanities and communications educator*
Mancuso, Leni *artist, poet, educator*
Wiswall, Frank Lawrence, Jr. *lawyer, educator*

Center Lovell
Adams, Herbert Ryan *management consultant, retired clergyman, actor, director, educator, publishing executive*

Chebeague Island
Allen, Clayton Hamilton *physicist, acoustician*
Middleton, Elliott, Jr. *physician*
Traina, Albert Salvatore *publishing executive*

China
†Dwelley, Marilyn Joan *artist*

Cumb Foreside
Dill, William Rankin *college president*

Cumberland Center
Brewster, Linda Jean *family nurse practitioner*
Butland, Jeffrey H. *former state senator, retail company official*
Taylor, Joseph B. *former state legislator*
Thomas, Charles Carroll *investment management executive*

Cushing
Day, Giles William, Jr. (Bill Day) *religious studies educator*
Magee, A. Alan *artist*
Taylor, Roger Conant *writer*

Damariscotta
Blake, Bud (Julian Watson) *cartoonist*
Fuller, Melvin Stuart *botany educator*
Johnson, Arthur Menzies *retired college president, historian, educator*
Robinson, Walter George *arts management and funding consultant*
Waterman, Charles Albert *actor, director, retired sales executive*

Deer Isle
Smith, Gardner Watkins *physician*

Dover Foxcroft
Cross, Ruel Parkman *state legislator*

Dresden
Elvin, Peter Wayne *healthcare executive, consultant*
Turco, Lewis Putnam *English educator*

East Boothbay
Eldred, Kenneth McKechnie *acoustical consultant*
Peters, Andrea Jean *artist*
Smith, Merlin Gale *engineering executive, researcher*

Eastport
Kennedy, Robert Spayde *electrical engineering educator*

Edgecomb
Carlson, Suzanne Olive *architect*

Eliot
†Detgen, Amy Lynn *copywriter*

Ellsworth
Dudman, Richard Beebe *communications company executive, journalist*
Goodyear, Austin *electronics and retail company executive*
Remick, Oscar Eugene *academic administrator*
Wiggins, James Russell *newspaper editor*

Fairfield
†Carpenter, David Ronnie *artist*
Massaua, John Roger *retail executive*
Pratt, Loring Withee *otolaryngologist*

Falmouth
Cabot, Lewis Pickering *manufacturing company executive, art consultant*
Eno, Amos Stewart *natural resource foundation administrator*
Grondin, Jerry Rene *marriage and family therapist*
Nickerson, Bruce Donald *case manager*
Rohsenow, Warren Max *retired mechanical engineer, educator*
Sawyer, Wellington Oliver *radio announcer*

Farmington
Kalikow, Theodora June *university president*
Mueller, Lisel *writer, poet*

Fort Fairfield
Shapiro, Joan Isabelle *laboratory administrator, nurse*

Fort Kent
Taggette, Deborah Jean *special education educator*

Freeport
Gorman, Leon A. *mail order company executive*

Friendship
Du Bois, Clarence Hazel, Jr. *clergy member*
MacIlvaine, Chalmers Acheson *retired financial executive, former association executive*
Merrill, Mary Lee *professional society administrator*
Owen, Wadsworth *oceanographer, consultant*
Walker, Douglass Willey *retired pediatrician, medical center administrator*

Georgetown
Chapin, Maryan Fox *civic worker*

Gorham
Bearce, Jeana Dale *artist, educator*
Stump, Walter Ray *drama educator*

Gouldsboro
Eustice, Russell Clifford *consulting company executive, academic director*

Gray
Cahill, Richard Frederic *city planner*
Durgin, Scott Benjamin *radio frequency engineer, physics educator*

Greenville
Sommerman, Kathryn Martha *retired entomologist*

Guilford
Staley, Thomas Eugene *artist*

Hallowell
Crawford, Linda Sibery *lawyer, educator*

Hampden
Plowman, Debra D. *state legislator*
Stratton, Frances Ruth *retired bookkeeper*

Hancock
Silvestro, Clement Mario *museum director, historian*

Hartland
Larochelle, Richard C. *tanning company executive*

Hollowell
†Wormser, Baron Chesley *writer, educator*

Island Falls
Joy, Henry Lee *state legislator*

Islesboro
Maes, John Leopold *theologian, psychologist, educator*

Jackman
Thomas, Paulette Suzanne *holistic health practitioner, physician assistant*

Jefferson
Fiore, Joseph Albert *artist*

Jonesport
Radomski, Jack London *toxicology consultant*

Kennebunk
Betts, Edward *artist*

Damon, Edmund Holcombe *retired plastics company executive*
Escalet, Frank Diaz *art gallery owner, artist, educator*
Peterson, Karen Ida *marketing research company executive*
Schofield, John Emerson *consultant*
Sholl, John Gurney, III *physician*
Ward, Nina Gillson *jewelry store executive*

Kennebunkport
McLaughlin, Charles James, IV *social sciences scholar*

Kingfield
Collins, H(erschel) Douglas *retired physician*

Kittery
Clark, Sandra Ann *clinical social worker*
†Diggins, Dean Richard *dancer, artist*
McNally, James Henry *physicist, defense consultant*

Kittery Point
Burgard, Ralph *cultural/education planner*
Howells, Muriel Gurdon Seabury (Mrs. William White Howells) *volunteer*
Howells, William White *anthropology educator*

Lamoine
Becker, Ray Everett *management consultant*

Lewiston
Buckley, Paul Richard *insurance executive*
Christie, Donald Melvin, Jr. *physician*
Chute, Robert Maurice *retired biologist, educator, poet*
Cutter, David L. *advertising specialty executive*
Dennison, Gerard Francis *economic analyst*
Harward, Donald *academic official*
Murray, Michael Peter *economist, educator*
†Roy, Jean Ann *eduator*
Umpierre, Luz Maria *women studies educator, foreign language educator*
Williams, Linda F. *music educator, jazz musician, ethnomusicologist*

Liberty
Anderson, Alfred Oliver *mathematician, consultant*

Lincoln
Kneeland, Douglas Eugene *retired newspaper editor*

Lincolnville
Williams, Robert Luther *city planning consultant*

Lubec
Hudson, Miles *special education educator*
†Tanney, Rick Willard *philosophy educator, computer sciences educator*

Lyman
Reeves, Thomas William, Jr. *record label owner*

Machias
Hayes, Ernest M. *podiatrist*
Rosen, David Matthew *education educator*

Milbridge
Enslin, Theodore Vernon *poet*

Monhegan
Boehmer, Raquel Davenport *television producer, newsletter editor*

Mount Desert
Crawford, Richard Bradway *biologist, biochemist, educator*
Straus, Donald Blun *retired company executive*

New Gloucester
Kuhrt, Sharon Lee *nursing administrator*

New Harbor
Fradley, Frederick Macdonell *architect*
Lyford, Cabot *sculptor*

New Vineyard
Smith, Frederick Orville, II *wood products manufacturer, retired naval officer*
West, Arthur James, II *biologist*

North Haven
Pingree, Rochelle M. *state legislator*

North Yarmouth
Fecteau, Rosemary Louise *educational administrator, educator, consultant*

Norway
Skolnik, Barnet David *entrepreneur*

Ogunquit
†Nudelman, Stuart *artist, educator*

Old Orchard Beach
Bartner, Jay B. *school system administrator*

Old Town
†Alex, Joanne DeFilipp *educator Montesorri school*
Pajama, Helen *advocate*

Orono
Bennett, Carolyn L. *journalist, writer*
Borns, Harold William, Jr. *geologist, educator*
Boyle, Kevin John *economics educator, consultant*
Butterfield, Stephen Alan *education educator*
Campana, Richard John *retired plant pathology educator, writer, consultant*
Chute, Harold LeRoy *veterinary pathologist, former chemical company executive*
Cohn, Steven Frederick *sociology educator, consultant*
Cruikshank, Margaret Louise *humanities educator, writer*
Devino, William Stanley *economist, educator*
Erdley, Cynthia Anne *psychology educator*
Goldstone, Sanford *psychology educator*
Hartgen, Vincent Andrew *museum director, educator, artist*

Hatlen, Burton Norval *English educator*
Knight, Fred Barrows *forester, entomologist, educator*
Munson, Henry Lee, Jr. *anthropologist, educator*
Norton, Stephen Allen *geological sciences educator*
Radke, Margaret Hoffman *retired secondary school educator*
Rauch, Charles Frederick, Jr. *retired academic official*
Rogers, Deborah Dee *English language educator*
Ruthven, Douglas Morris *chemical engineering educator*
Weiss, Robert Jerome *psychiatrist, educator*
Whittington, Stephen Lunn *museum director*
Wiersma, G. Bruce *dean, forest resources educator*
Wilson, Dorothy Clarke *author*

Orrington
Snyder, Arnold Lee, Jr. *retired air force officer, research director*

Orrs Island
Lowndes, Janine Marie Herbert *journalist*
Porter, Maxiene Helen Greve *civic worker*

Pemaquid
Howell, Jeanette Helen *retired cultural organization administrator*

Pittsfield
†Cianchette, Alton E. *construction company executive*

Port Clyde
Thon, William *artist*

Portland
Anderson, Stephen Mills *investment broker*
Becker, Seymour *hazardous materials and wastes specialist*
Bohan, Thomas Lynch *lawyer, physicist*
Bradford, Carl O. *judge*
Bride, John W(illiam) *communications executive, entrepreneur*
Brigham, Christopher Roy *occupational medicine physician*
Brown, Andrea Lynn *executive recruiter*
†Brown, Linda M. *neurologist*
†Brownell, William S. *federal judge*
Candage, Howard Everett *insurance management consultant, agent, broker*
Carter, Gene *federal judge*
Caswell, Robert Stearns *public relations director*
Clark, Gordon Hostetter, Jr. *physician*
Coffin, Frank Morey *federal judge*
Coggeshall, Bruce Amsden *lawyer*
Cohen, David Michael *federal magistrate judge*
Concepción, David Alden *arbitrator, educator*
†Cote, Michael Richard *bishop*
Coughlan, Patrick Campbell *lawyer*
Culley, Peter William *lawyer*
Dana, Howard H., Jr. *state supreme court justice*
End, William Thomas *business executive*
Freilinger, James Edward *insurance and investments company executive*
Gerry, Joseph John *bishop*
†Gilbert, Laurent F., Sr. *state agency administrator*
Gilmore, Roger *college president*
Glassman, Caroline Duby *state supreme court justice*
Goodman, James A. *federal judge*
Graffam, Ward Irving *lawyer*
Hall, Christopher George Longden *management consultant*
Harte, Christopher McCutcheon *investment manager*
Hatem, Michael Thomas *child psychology educator*
Haynes, Peter Lancaster *utility holding company executive*
Hirshon, Robert Edward *lawyer*
Hornby, David Brock *federal judge*
Hull, William Floyd, Jr. *former museum director, ceramic consultant*
Kendrick, Peter Murray *communications executive, investor*
Konkel, Harry Wagner *civic volunteer, retired career officer*
Lancaster, Ralph Ivan, Jr. *lawyer*
LeBlanc, Richard Philip *lawyer*
Lipez, Kermit V. *federal judge, former state supreme court justice*
Louden, Robert Burton *philosopher, educator*
McCloskey, Jay P. *prosecutor*
†McDaniel, Dana Irene *linguistics educator*
McDowell, Donald L. *hospital administrator*
McKusick, Vincent Lee *former state supreme court justice, lawyer, arbitrator, mediator*
Morgan, Robin Evonne *poet, author, journalist, activist, editor*
Mullen, John Reagan *radiation oncologist*
†Munch, James C., Jr. *lawyer*
Neavoll, George Franklin *newspaper editor*
O'Leary, Edward Cornelius *former bishop*
Orr, James F., III *insurance company executive*
Pattenaude, Richard Louis *university executive*
Philbrick, Donald Lockey *lawyer*
Piombino, Alfred Ernest *law consultant, writer*
Raisbeck, Gordon *systems engineer*
Reid, Rosemary Anne *insurance agent*
Rundlett, Ellsworth Turner, III *lawyer*
Saufley, William Edward *banker, lawyer*
†Schultes, Jeffrey *transportation manager*
Schwanauer, Francis *philosopher, educator*
Scott, Aurélia Carmelita *non-profit organization executive, writer*
Shimada, Toshiyuki *orchestra conductor, music director*
†Sholl, Betsy *poet, English educator*
Smith, William Charles *lawyer*
Stauffer, Eric P. *lawyer*
†Sullivan, Mark *legislative staff member*
Tierney, Kevin Joseph *lawyer*
Ventimiglia, John Thomas *artist, art educator*
Weir, Anne *writer*
Whedon, Ralph Gibbs *manufacturing executive*
White, Jeffrey Munroe *lawyer*
Zarr, Melvyn *lawyer, law educator*

Presque Isle
Barrett, Paul J. *pharmacist*
Brown, James Walker, Jr. *city government planning and development administrator*
Huffman, Durward Roy *academic administrator, electrical engineer*

Rockland
Collins, Samuel W., Jr. *judge*

Rockport
Rohrbach, Lewis Bunker *investment company executive*

Rumford
Kent, Richard B. *secondary education educator*

S Portland
Harris, Penny Smith *fundraising consultant*

Saco
Queally, Christopher *secondary education educator, theatre director*

Saint Albans
†Clark, Raymond Leroy *singer*

Saint George
Bailey, Jonathan E. *photographer*

Sanford
†Allan, Jonathan David *autograph dealer, pop culture historian*
Nadeau, Robert Maurice Auclair *lawyer*
†Trask, James Stephen *artist, forester*

Scarborough
†Begert, Jerome Francis *writer*
Berardelli, Catherine Marie *women's health nurse, nurse educator*
Farrington, Hugh G. *wholesale food and retail drug company executive*
Hothersall, Loretta Anne *family nurse practitioner*
Martin, Harold Clark *humanities educator*
Sadik, Marvin Sherwood *art consultant, former museum director*
Warg, Pauline *artist, educator*

Searsport
Cagle, William Rea *librarian*

Sebago Lake
Murray, Wallace Shordon *publisher, educator*

Sedgwick
Becker, Robert Clarence *retired clergyman*
Donnell, William Ray *small business owner, communications executive*
Schroth, Thomas Nolan *editor*

South Berwick
Carroll, Gladys Hasty *author*

South Bristol
Wells, Arthur Stanton *retired manufacturing company executive*

South Paris
Barlow, Walter John, Jr. *utilities executive, consultant*
Creighton, Elizabeth Gaston *counselor*
Martin, Charles Seymour *middle school educator*

South Portland
Fetteroll, Eugene Carl, Jr. *human resources professional*
Huntoon, Abby Elizabeth *artist, teacher*
Martin, Joseph Robert *financial executive*
Townshend, Sharon *artist*

Spruce Head
Bird, Mary Alice *fund raising consultant*

Standish
†Balcomb, Scott Hull *mathematics educator*

Surry
†Doty, Maxene Stansell *psychologist, retired*
Kilgore, John Edward, Jr. *former petroleum company executive*
Pickett, Betty Horenstein *psychologist*
Sopkin, George *cellist, music educator*

Tenants Harbor
Quint-Rose, Marylin Iris *artist*

Togus
Hussey, John Francis *physician, geriatrician*

Topsham
Nulle, Christopher Reynolds *secondary education educator*
Palesky, Carol East *tax accountant*

Trevett
Mathias, Cordula *art dealer*

Union
†Perrin, Arnold Strong *writer, editor*

Vinalhaven
†Morton, Barbara Murphy *artist*

Waldoboro
Fassett, Frances Nicholas (Kitty Fassett) *pianist, record producer*
Hewett, David Edgar *journalist*

Waterford
Cutler, Cassius Chapin *physicist, educator*

Waterville
†Barnard, Bruce K. *academic administrator*
Bassett, Charles Walker *English language educator*
Cook, Susan Farwell *alumni relations director*
Cotter, William Reckling *college president*
Gemery, Henry Albert *economics educator*
Hudson, Yeager *philosophy educator, minister*
Mavrinac, Albert Anthony *political scientist, educator, lawyer*
Muehlner, Suanne Wilson *library director*
Nelson, Robert E. *geology professor*
Roisman, Hanna Maslovski *classics educator*
Sandy, Robert Edward, Jr. *lawyer*
Tormollan, Gary Gordon *health facility administrator, physical therapist*

Wells
Carleton, Joseph George, Jr. *lawyer, state legislator*
Hero, Barbara Ferrell *visual and sound artist, writer*
Neilson, Elizabeth Anastasia *health sciences educator, association executive, author, editor*

West Baldwin
Pierce, Elizabeth Gay *civic worker*
Simmonds, Rae Nichols *musician, composer, educator*

West Boothbay Harbor
Ryan, Marylou *education consultant*

Westbrook
Parks, George Richard *librarian*

Windham
Diamond, G. William *former secretary of state*
†Hiebert, Clement Arthur *surgeon, consultant, educator*
Mulvey, Mary Crowley *retired adult education director, gerontologist, senior citizen association administrator*
†Small, Richard Leroy *clergyman, sanctuary design consultant*
Walker, Steve Sweet *town official*

Winthrop
Saunders, Joseph Arthur *office products manufacturing company executive*

Wiscasset
Leslie, Seaver *artist*

Yarmouth
Bischoff, David Canby *retired university dean*
Bissonnette, Jean Marie *elementary school educator, polarity therapist*
†Clark, Gail Theroux *artist*
Grover, Mark Donald *computer scientist*
Hart, Loring Edward *academic administrator*
Smith, Gayle Muriel *medical/surgical nurse*
Webster, Peter Bridgman *lawyer*

York
Berlew, Frank Kingston *lawyer*
Hallam, Beverly (Beverly Linney) *artist*
Lauter, M. David *family physician*
Lyman, William Welles, Jr. *retired architect*
†Perry, Herbert Peter *newswriter*
Smart, Mary-Leigh Call (Mrs. J. Scott Smart) *civic worker*

MARYLAND

Aberdeen
Russell, William Alexander, Jr. *environmental scientist*

Aberdeen Proving Ground
†Andrews, Edward L. *career officer*
Cozby, Richard Scott *electronics engineer, reserve army officer*
Docken, Edsel Ardean, Sr. (Dean Docken) *urban planner*
†Doesburg, John C. *military career officer*
Evans, Edward Spencer, Jr. *entomologist*
Gibson, Annemarie *writer, editor*
†Jackson, Dennis K. *military career officer*
LaBar, Valerie Kulis *occupational health nurse*
Leonard, Virginia Kathryn *public financial manager*
Powers, Nelson Roger *entomologist*
Starnes, Edward Clinton *public relations executive*
Tobin, Aileen Webb *educational administrator*

Abingdon
Hosmer, Philip *writer, communications professional*
Moore, Brad Elliot *art educator, artist, printmaker*
Wolf, Martin Eugene *lawyer*

Adelphi
Langenberg, Donald Newton *academic administrator, physicist*
Mitchum, Cassandra *poet, writer*

Andrews Air Force Base
†Almquist, Theodore C. *retired military officer*
†Lichte, Arthur J. *career officer*
†Roudebush, James G. *career officer*
†Taylor, Francis X. *military officer*
Wong, Ruth Ann *nursing administrator*

Annapolis
†Achenback, Nancy Banks *pediatric nurse*
†Addison, William B.C., Jr. *state senate employee*
Alderdice, Cynthia Lou *artist*
†Anderson, William Carl *association executive, environmental engineer, consultant*
Astle, John Chandlee *state legislator*
Baldwin, John Ashby, Jr. *retired naval officer*
Barber, James Alden *military officer*
Bontoyan, Warren Roberts *chemist, state laboratories administrator*
Brady, Frank Benton *retired technical society executive*
Brown-Christopher, Cheryl Denise *physician*
Brunk, William Edward *astronomer*
Calabrese, Anthony Joseph *gastroenterologist*
Caldwell, Curtis Irvin *acoustical engineer*
Cann, Nancy Timanus *retail yacht sales executive*
Carman, Anne *management consultant*
Casey, Edward Dennis *newspaper editor*
Chambers, Ronald D. *book publishing executive*
Cheevers, James William *museum curator*
Clotworthy, John Harris *oceanographic consultant*
Cooper, Sherod Monroe, Jr. *retired English language educator*
Cordts, Thomas James *elementary education educator*
Corredor, Eva Livia *foreign language educator*
Coulter, James Bennett *state official*
Crosby, Ralph Wolf *communications executive*
Davis, Clarence *state legislator*
Dembrow, Dana Lee *lawyer*
Demler, Marvin Christian *air force officer*
DiAiso, Robert Joseph *civil engineer*
Dixon, Richard N. *state legislator*
Duncan, Charles Tignor *lawyer*
Eldridge, John Cole *judge*

Ellis, George Fitzallen, Jr. retired energy services company executive
Ferris, William Michael lawyer
†Fleming, Bruce E. English literature educator, writer
Fligsten, Ann M. historic foundation director
Florestano, Patricia Sherer state official
Glendening, Parris Nelson governor, political science educator
Good, Jane Elizabeth history educator
Granger, Robert Alan mechanical and aerospace engineering educator
Graze, Peter Robert physician
Gurlik, Philip John artist
Halpern, Joseph Alan physician
†Hamill, Peter VanVechten physician, epidemiologist, consultant
Hammer, Jacob Myer physicist, consultant
Heller, Austin Norman chemical and environmental engineer
Hixson, Sheila Ellis state legislator
Holtgrewe, Henry Logan urologist
Howard, Carolyn J. B. state legislator
Hyde, Lawrence Henry, Jr. industrial company executive
Iannoli, Joseph John, Jr. university development executive
Jason, Philip Kenneth English language educator
Jefferson, Ralph Harvey international affairs consultant
Johnson, Bruce engineering educator
Johnson, David Simonds meteorologist
†Johnson, Dean LaLander mayor
Jones, Sylvanus Benson adjudicator, consultant
Katz, Douglas Jeffrey naval officer, retired, consultant
Kelley, Delores Goodwin state legislator
Klima, Martha Scanlan state legislator
†Konkowski, Deborah Ann mathematics educator
Kozlowski, Ronald Stephan librarian
Kushlan, James A. biologist, research administrator, author, educator
Kushner, Jack physician executive
Larson, Charles Robert naval officer
Lee, T. Girard architect
Levin, David Alan lawyer
Levitan, Laurence lawyer, former state senator
Libby, Jane Elliott retired dietitian
Long, Robert Lyman John naval officer
Love, Mary Ann E. state legislator
Madden, Martin Gerard state legislator
Markman, Ronald artist, educator
McCabe, Christopher J. state legislator
McGuirk, Ronald Charles banker
Menes, Pauline H. state legislator
Michaelson, Benjamin, Jr. lawyer
Miller, John Grider magazine editor
Miller, Richards Thorn naval architect, engineer
Miller, Thomas V. Mike, Jr. state legislator
Moellering, John Henry aviation maintenance company executive
O'Toole, Tara Jeanne physician
Papenfuse, Edward Carl, Jr. archivist, state official
Parham, Carol Sheffey school system administrator
Perkins, Roger Allan lawyer
Pillsbury, Leland Clark service executive
Rapkin, Jerome defense industry executive
†Riddick, Major F., Jr.
Roesser, Jean Wolberg state legislator
Rosenthal, Michael Ross academic administrator, dean
Rowell, Charles Frederick chemistry educator
Ruben, Ida Gass state senator
Rubin, Samuel Bruce speech communication educator
Schleicher, Nora Elizabeth banker, treasurer, accountant
Schoenfeld, William Patton aerospace mechanical engineer
Smith, Robert Myron investment company executive
Smith Tarchalski, Helen Marie piano educator
Stahl, David Edward trade association administrator, retired
Taussig, Joseph Knefler, Jr. retired government official, lawyer
Teitelbaum, Leonard H. state legislator
Timperlake, Edward Thomas writer
Townsend, Kathleen Kennedy state official
Tuttle, Kenneth Lewis engineering educator, consultant
†Virts, Henry A. veterinarian, state agency administrator
Wasserman, Martin P. former state official
Werking, Richard Hume librarian, historian, academic administrator
Weyandt, Daniel Scott naval officer, engineer, physicist
Whitford, Dennis James naval officer, meteorologist, oceanographer
Wilkes, Joseph Allen architect
Willis, John T. state official

Annapolis Junction
Woodard, Mark Davis lawyer, association executive, lobbyist

Arbutus
Maloney, Charles Wayne gunsmith

Arnold
Barrett, John Anthony publishing and printing company financial executive
Brandimore, Wadie Miller retired pediatrics nurse
Harris, Roger Clark psychiatrist, consultant
†Kolb, Joyce Diana artist, educator
Powers, Tyrone criminal justice and sociology educator, writer

Ashton
Tabler, Shirley May retired librarian, artist

Baldwin
Decker, James Ludlow management consultant

Baltimore
Abeloff, Martin David medical administrator, educator, researcher
Achinstein, Peter Jacob philosopher, educator
†Achuff, Stephen Charles physician
Adams, Harold Lynn architect
Adkins, Edward James lawyer
Adkinson, N. Franklin, Jr. clinical immunologist
Ajmani, Ranjeet Singh educator
Albinak, Marvin Joseph chemistry educator
Albuquerque, Edson Xavier pharmacology educator
Alexander, Marcellus W., Jr. television station executive
Allen, Norma Ann librarian
Allen, Rodney Desvigne music educator
Allen, Ronald John astrophysics educator, researcher
Alpern, Linda Lee Wevodau health agency administrator
Ambler, Bruce Melville energy company executive
Anandarajah, Annalingam civil engineer, educator
†Anderson, Brady Kevin professional baseball player
Anderson, Gerard Fenton economist, university program administrator
Anderson, John William protective services official
Andres, Reubin gerontologist
Angelos, Peter G. professional sports team executive, lawyer
†Apfel, Kenneth S. federal government official
Applebaum, Gary E. medical director, executive
Archibald, James Kenway lawyer
Arnick, John Stephen lawyer, legislator
Arsham, Hossein operations research analyst
Asper, Samuel Philips medical administrator, educator
Ayres, Jeffrey Peabody lawyer
Bachur, Nicholas Robert, Sr. research physician
Bacigalupo, Charles Anthony brokerage company executive
Backas, James Jacob foundation administrator
Bailey, James (Jim Bailey) lawyer, professional football team executive
Baines, Harold Douglass professional baseball player
Bair, Robert Rippel lawyer
Baker, R. Robinson surgeon
Baker, Susan P. public health educator
Baker, Timothy Danforth physician, educator
Baldwin, Henry Furlong banker
Baldwin, John Wesley history educator
Ball, Marion J. health information professional
Balog, George G. city director of public works
Bard, James F., Jr. information systems professional
Bardaglio, Peter Winthrop humanities educator
Barnhouse, Robert Bolon lawyer
Barth, John Simmons writer, educator
Bartlett, John Gill infectious disease physician
Basile, Joseph John art history educator, archaeologist
Battaglia, Lynne Ann prosecutor
Baughman, Kenneth Lee cardiologist, educator
Baumgartner, William Anthony cardiac surgeon
Bausell, R. Barker, Jr. research methodology educator
Bayless, Theodore M(orris) gastroenterologist, educator, researcher
Beall, George lawyer
Beckenstein, Myron journalist
Beer, Alice Stewart (Mrs. Jack Engeman) retired musician, educator
Beilenson, Peter Lowell public health official
Bell, Lawrence A. city official
Bell, Robert M. state court chief judge
Bellack, Alan Scott clinical psychologist
Belle, Albert Jojuan professional baseball player
Benjamin, Thomas Edward music educator, composer, conductor
Benz, Edward John, Jr. physician, educator
Berlin, Fred Saul psychiatrist, educator
Bernhardt, Herbert Nelson law educator, labor arbitrator
Bett, Richard Arnot Home philosophy educator
Bever, Christopher Theodore, Jr. neurologist
Bhardwaj, Anish neuroscientist, medical educator
Bigelow, George E. psychology and pharmacology scientist
Black, Walter Evan, Jr. federal judge
†Blair, Timothy Daniel quality assurance specialist
Blake, Catherine C. judge
Blanton, Edward Lee, Jr. lawyer
Block, James A. hospital administrator, pediatrician
Blumberg, David Russell librarian
Boardman, John Michael mathematician, educator
Boone, Harold Thomas retired lawyer
Bor, Jonathan Steven journalist
Bordick, Michael Todd professional baseball player
Boston, Wallace Ellsworth, Jr. healthcare executive, financial consultant
Boughman, Joann Ashley dean
Bowe, Peter Armistead manufacturing executive
Bowen, Kit Hansel, Jr. chemistry educator
Bowen, Lowell Reed lawyer
Brace, Margaret Denise writer
Bradshaw, Cynthia Helene educational administrator
Brady, Joseph Vincent behavioral biologist, educator
Branch, Paula Johnson city councilwoman
Brewer, Nevada Nancy elementary education educator
Brewster, Gerry Leiper educator, lawyer
Brieger, Gert Henry medical historian, educator
Bright, Margaret sociologist
Brinkley, James Wellons investment company executive
Broadbent, J. Streett engineering executive
Brodie, M. J. (Jay Brodie) architect, city planner, government executive
Brody, Eugene B. psychiatrist, educator
Brody, William Ralph radiologist, educator
Broening, Walter Stephens, Jr. journalist, history educator
Brown, Donald David biology educator
Brumbaugh, John Maynard lawyer, educator
Bruner, William Gwathmey, III lawyer
Brunson, Dorothy Edwards broadcasting executive
Brusilow, Saul pediatrics researcher
Bryan, Thelma Jane university administrator, English educator
Bucher, Richard David sociology educator
Buggs, Elaine S. financial analyst
Bundick, William Ross retired dermatologist
Burch, Francis Boucher, Jr. lawyer
†Burnham, Gilbert Miracle physician, educator
Buser, Carolyn Elizabeth correctional education administrator
Byrd, Ronald Dicky lawyer
Cain, John L. city councilman
Cameron, Duke Edward cardiac surgeon, educator
Carbine, James Edmond lawyer
Carey, Anthony Morris lawyer
Carey, Jana Howard lawyer
Carmichael, Richard E. government official, financial manager, educator
Carroll, John Sawyer newspaper editor
Carroll, Karen art educator
Carson, Benjamin Solomon neurosurgeon
Cashman, Edmund Joseph, Jr. investment banker
Castro-Klaren, Sara Latin American literature educator
Catania, A(nthony) Charles psychology educator
Chang, Debbie I-Ju health services director
Chapelle, Suzanne Ellery Greene history educator
Chaplin, Peggy Fannon lawyer
Chen, Tar Timothy biostatistician
†Chen, Yu acupuncturist, Chinese herbologist
Chernow, Bart critical care physician
Chernow, Jeffrey Scott lawyer, educator, author
Chiarello, Donald Frederick lawyer
Chien, Chia-Ling physics educator
†Child-Olmsted, Gisèle Alexandra language educator
Childs, Barton retired, physician, educator
Chiu, Hungdah lawyer, legal educator
Chriss, Timothy D. A. lawyer
Clark, Patricia molecular biologist
Clark, Will (William Nuschler Clark, Jr.) professional baseball player
Clinger, William Floyd, Jr. former congressman
Cohen, Warren I. history educator
Cohn, Gary Dennis journalist
†Colvan, Carolyn W. federal agency administrator
Conine, Jeffrey Guy professional baseball player
Conley, Carroll Lockard physician, emeritus educator
Cook, Bryson Leitch lawyer
Cooper, Jerrold Stephen historian, educator
Cooper, Joseph political scientist, educator
Corn, Morton environmental engineer, educator
Coulston, Stephen Brett architect
Couper, William banker
Covi, Lino psychiatrist
Crawford, Edward E. psychologist
Crippen, Raymond Charles chemist, consultant
Crowe, Thomas Leonard lawyer
Cummings, Charles William physician, educator
Cunningham, Terence Thomas, III hospital administrator
Curley, John Francis, Jr. mutual fund executive
Curran, J. Joseph, Jr. state attorney general
Curran, Robert councilman
D'Adamo, Nicholas C. city councilman
Dagdigian, Paul Joseph chemistry educator
Dang, Chi Van hematology and oncology educator
†Daniels, Susan M. commissioner
Daniels, Worth Bagley, Jr. retired internist
Dannenberg, Arthur Milton, Jr. experimental pathologist, immunologist, educator
Davis, Andre Maurice judge, educator
Davis, Carole Joan psychologist
†Davish, William Martin priest, educator
DeAngelis, Catherine D. pediatrics educator
Deffenbaugh, Ralston H., Jr. immigration agency executive, lawyer
Degenford, James Edward electrical engineer, educator
DeKuyper, Mary Hundley non-profit consultant
DeLateur, Barbara Jane medical educator
DeLuna, D.N. literary educator
Deoul, Neal electronics company executive
Derby, Ernest Stephen federal judge
DeTolla, Louis James research veterinarian
Devan, Deborah Hunt lawyer
DeVito, Mathias Joseph retired real estate executive
Dicello, John Francis, Jr. physicist, educator
Dickey, George Edward water resources consultant, economics educator
Dickinson, Jane W. social services administrator
Dickler, Howard Byron biomedical administrator, research physician
Dietze, Gottfried political science educator
Digges, Edward S(imms), Jr. business management consultant
Dilloff, Neil Joel lawyer
Dishon, Cramer Steven sales executive
Dixon, Sheila councilwoman
Djordjevic, Borislav Boro materials scientist, researcher
Dolan, Jim broadcast executive
Donaldson, Sue Karen dean, nursing educator
Donkervoet, Richard Cornelius architect
Donovan, Sharon Ann educator
Dorsey, John Russell journalist
Douglass, Robert Lee electronics association executive, city councilman
Drachman, Daniel Bruce neurologist
Dubé, Lawrence Edward, Jr. lawyer
Dubner, Ronald neurobiologist, educator
Duke, George Wesley financial executive
Durham, J(ames) Michael retail executive
Eberwein, Granville Allen lay minister, civil servant
Edlund, Timothy Wendell management educator, consultant, researcher
Eichhorn, Gunther Louis chemist
Eisenberg, Gerson G. author, historian
Eisenberg, Howard Michael neurosurgeon
Eisner, Henry Wolfgang advertising agency executive
Eldefrawi, Amira Toppozada medical educator, toxicologist, pharmacologist
Ellin, Marvin lawyer
Ellingwood, Bruce Russell structural engineering researcher, educator
Ellis, Brother Patrick (H. J. Ellis) academic administrator
Ellsworth, Robert Fred investment executive, former government official
Elma, Bayani Borja physician
†Embry, Robert C. foundation administrator
Emerick, Norman Cooper consulting engineer
Engel, Paul Bernard lawyer
Englund, Paul Theodore biochemist, educator
Entwisle, Doris Roberts sociology educator
Ephross, Paul Hullman social work educator
Epstein, Daniel Mark poet, dramatist
Evans, Judy Anne health center administrator
Evans, Nolly Seymour lawyer
Eveleth, Janet Stidman law association administrator
Faden, Ruth R. medical educator, ethicist, researcher
Feldman, Deborah Karpoff nursing education consultant
Feldman, Gordon physics educator
Felsenthal, Gerald physiatrist, educator
Ferencz, Charlotte pediatrician, epidemiology and preventive medicine educator
Fergenson, Arthur Friend lawyer
Ferro, Elizabeth Krams lawyer
Fisher, Alan Hall guidebook writer
Fisher, Jack Carrington environmental engineering educator
Fisher, Morton Poe, Jr. lawyer
Fisher, Phoebe Gerber painter, antique dealer
Fitzgerald, Thomas Rollins university administrator
Fletcher, Sherryl Ann higher education administrator
Ford, John Gilmore interior designer
Forster, Robert history educator
Foster, Lester Anderson, Jr. retired steel company executive
Fowler, Bruce Andrew toxicologist
Fox, Harold Edward obstetrician, gynecologist, educator, researcher
Frazier, Elaine C. public health nurse
Frazier, Thomas C. protective services official
Freeman, John Mark pediatric neurologist
Freeze, James Donald administrator, clergyman
Freire, Ernesto biophysicist, educator
†Fried, Arthur lawyer
Fried, Herbert Daniel advertising executive
Friedman, Louis Frank lawyer
Friedman, Maria Andre public relations executive
Friedman, Marion internist, family physician, medical administrator, medical editor
Fuentealba, Victor William professional society administrator
Fulton, Thomas theoretical physicist, educator
Gall, Joseph Grafton biologist, researcher, educator
Gallups, Vivian Lylay Bess federal contracting officer
Gambert, Steven Ross geriatrician, internist
Garbis, Marvin Joseph judge
Gately, Mark Donohue lawyer
Gauvey, Susan K. judge
Gifford, Donald George academic dean
Gilbert, Blaine Louis lawyer
Gillece, James Patrick, Jr. lawyer
Gimenez, Luis Fernando physician, educator
Ginsberg, Benjamin political science educator
Girovich, Mark Jacob mechanical engineer
Gisriel-Bradford, Barbara Ann nurse administrator
Giuliano, Michael Philip arts journalist, educator
Glasgow, Jesse Edward newspaper editor
Glassgold, Israel Leon construction company executive, engineer, consultant
Glassman, Jon David business executive
Godenne, Ghislaine Dudley physician, psychoanalyst, educator
Goedicke, Hans archeology educator
Goetz, Clarence Edward retired judge, retired chief magistrate judge
Goldberg, Alan Marvin toxicologist, educator
Goldberg, Morton Falk ophthalmologist, educator
Goldman, Alan Joseph mathematician
Goldman, Brian Arthur lawyer, accountant
Goldman, Lynn Rose medical educator
Goodman, William Richard insurance adjusting company executive
Gordis, Leon physician
Graham, George Gordon physician
Grasmick, Nancy S. superintendent of schools
Graves, Charles C., III city planning director
Gray, Frank Truan lawyer
Gray, Oscar Shalom lawyer
Green, Bert Franklin, Jr. psychologist
Green, Robert Edward, Jr. physicist, educator
Greenough, William Bates, III medical educator
Griffin, Diane Edmund research physician, virologist, educator
Griffith, Lawrence Stacey Cameron cardiologist
Groenheim, Henri Arnold psychologist, consultant
Grollman, Sigmund Sidney physiology educator
Gross, Kathleen Albright interventional radiology nurse, educator
Grossman, Joel B(arry) political science educator
Grossman, Lawrence biochemist, educator
Grumbine, Francis gynecologic oncologist, educator
Habermann, Helen Margaret plant physiologist, educator
Hafets, Richard Jay lawyer
Haig, Frank Rawle physics educator, clergyman
Haines, Thomas W. W. lawyer
Hanks, James Judge, Jr. lawyer
Hansen, Barbara Caleen physiology educator, scientist
Hardiman, Joseph Raymond securities industry executive
Harrison, Michael opera company executive
Hart, John, Jr. behavioral neurologist, neuroscientist, educator
Hart, Robert Gordon federal agency administrator
Hartigan, Grace artist
Harvey, Alexander, II federal judge
Harvey, Curran Whitthorne, Jr. investment management executive
Harvey, Keiko Takeuchi telephone company executive
Hauser, Michael George astrophysicist
Hayden, Carla library director
†Hayes, John M. writer, sculptor, photographer
Hecht, Alan Dannenberg insurance executive
Hellmann, David Bruce medical educator
Helm, Donald Cairney hydrogeologist, engineer, educator
Henderson, Donald Ainslie public health educator
Henderson, Lenneal Joseph, Jr. political science educator
Henry, Richard Conn astrophysicist, educator
Henson, Daniel P., III housing and community development commissioner
Herr, Stanley Sholom law educator
Herschman, Jeffrey D. lawyer
Higgins, Kenneth Michael electrician
Higham, John history educator
†Hilgenberg, John Christian financial executive, corporate director, consultant
Hillers, Delbert Roy Near East language educator
Hillman, Sandra Schwartz public relations executive, marketing professional
Himelfarb, Richard Jay securities firm executive
Hinson, Karen Elizabeth secondary education educator
Hirsh, Theodore William lawyer
Hobbins, Thomas Eben physician
Hoch, David Allen physical education educator, athletic director
Hochberg, Bayard Zabdial lawyer
Hoffberger, Jerold Charles corporation executive
Hoffman, Barbara A. state legislator
Hofkin, Gerald Alan gastroenterologist
†Hollowak, Thomas Leo architist, historian
Holton, Helen Lara city official, marketing professional
Honemann, Daniel Henry lawyer
Hopkins, Samuel retired investment banker
Hopps, Raymond, Jr. film producer, lawyer
Houck, John Roland clergyman
Howard, Bettie Jean surgical nurse
Howard, J. Woodford, Jr. political science educator
Howell, Harley Thomas lawyer
Howland, Kristine Kay college administrator
Hrabowski, Freeman Alphonsa, III university president
Huang, Pien Chien biochemistry educator, scientist
Hubbard, Herbert Hendrix lawyer
†Huber, Jay D. state agency administrator
Hug, Richard Ernest environmental company executive
Hughes, Brenda Bethea state legislator
Hungerford, David Samuel orthopedic surgeon, educator
†Huse, James G. federal agency administrator
Igusa, Jun-Ichi mathematician, educator

Ihrie, Robert oil, gas and real estate company executive
Imboden, John Baskerville psychiatry educator
Immelt, Stephen J. lawyer
Ingle, Joan Marie nurse practitioner
Irwin, John Thomas humanities educator
Jackson, Harold journalist
Jackson, Stanley Edward retired special education educator
Jacobs, Richard James banker, educator
Jelinek, Frederick electrical engineer, educator
Jenkins, Louise Sherman nursing researcher
Jenkins, Robert Rowe lawyer
Johns, Richard James physician, educator
Johnson, Elaine McDowell retired federal government executive, educator
Johnson, Kenneth Peter neurologist, medical researcher
Johnson, Michael Paul history educator
Johnson, Richard T. neurology, microbiology and neuroscience educator, research virologist
Johnston, Edward Allan lawyer
Johnston, George W. lawyer
Jones, John Martin, Jr. lawyer
Jones, Raymond Moylan strategy and public policy educator
Judd, Brian Raymond physicist, educator
Judson, Horace Freeland history of science, writer, educator
Junck, Mary newspaper publishing executive
Kallina, Emanuel John, II lawyer
Kandel, Nelson Robert lawyer
Kandel, Peter Thomas lawyer
Karni, Edi economics educator
Karow, Charles Stanley computer consultant
Karp, Judith Esther oncologist, science administrator
Kastor, John Alfred cardiologist, educator
Katz, Joseph Louis chemical engineer, educator
Katz, Martha Lessman lawyer
Keller, George Charles higher education consultant, writer
Kellett, John M. museum director
Kelman, Gary F. environmental engineer
Kemp, Suzanne Leppart educator, clubwoman
Kent, Edgar Robert, Jr. investment banker
Kershaw, Robert Barnsley lawyer
Kessler, Herbert Leon art historian, educator, university administrator
Kessler, Wallace Frank school director, tour developer
Killebrew, Robert Sterling, Jr. investment manager
Kim, Lillian G. Lee retired administrative assistant
Kinnard, William James, Jr. retired pharmacy educator
Klarman, Herbert Elias economist, educator
†Klein, Daniel E., Jr. federal judge
Klitzke, Theodore Elmer former college dean, arts consultant
Knapp, David Allan pharmaceutical educator, researcher
Knight, Franklin W. history educator
Knoedler, Elmer L. retired chemical engineer
Kosaraju, S. Rao computer science educator, researcher
Koski, Walter S. chemistry educator, scientist
Kowarski, Allen Avinoam endocrinologist, educator
Kramer, Norma Domenica Andrea artist
Kramer, Paul R. lawyer
Krolik, Julian Henry astrophysicist, educator
Kroto, Joseph John secondary educator
Kruger, Jerome materials science educator, consultant
Kuppusamy, Periannan medical educator, medical researcher
Kurth, Lieselotte foreign language educator
Kuryk, David Neal lawyer
Kwon, Chul Soo psychiatrist
Lakatta, Edward Gerard biomedical researcher
Lamp, Frederick John museum curator
Lane, Malcolm Daniel biological chemistry educator
Larch, Sara Margaret chief operating officer
Larrabee, Martin Glover biophysics educator
Lashley, Mark Alan physician assistant
Lawrence, Robert Swan physician, educator, academic administrator
Lawson, Edward Earle neonatologist
Lazarus, Fred, IV college president
Lee, Carlton K. K. clinical pharmacist, consultant, educator
Lee, Denise Elizabeth editor
Lee, Yung-Keun physicist, educator
Legg, Benson Everett federal judge
Legum, Jeffrey Alfred automobile company executive
Lemer, Andrew Charles engineer, economist
Levin, Edward Jesse lawyer
Levin, Marshall Abbott judge, educator
Levine, Myron Max medical administrator
Levine, Richard E. lawyer
Lewis, Alexander Ingersoll, III lawyer
Lewison, Edward Frederick surgeon
Liberto, Joseph Salvatore retired banker
Lichtenstein, Lawrence Mark allergy, immunology educator, physician
Lidtke, Vernon LeRoy history educator
Liebmann, George W(illiam) lawyer
List, Douglass William management consultant, investment adviser, civil engineer
Litrenta, Frances Marie psychiatrist
Littlefield, John Walley geneticist, cell biologist, pediatrician
Livingstone, Harrison Edward writer, publisher
Lohr, Walter George, Jr. lawyer
Long, Donlin Martin surgeon, educator
Lowenthal, Henry retired greeting card company executive
Luck, Georg Hans Bhawani classics educator
Lundy, Audie Lee, Jr. lawyer
Lurie, Shelly Fern therapist
Maccini, Louis John economic educator
MacColl, J. A. lawyer
Machen, Arthur Webster, Jr. lawyer
Macleod, Donald clergyman, educator
Madansky, Leon particle physicist, educator
Magnuson, Nancy librarian
Maletz, Herbert Naaman federal judge
Malley, Martin councilman, lawyer
Mansfield, Carl Major radiation oncology educator
Manson, Paul Nellis plastic surgeon
Margalit, Shlomo educator
Marimow, William Kalmon journalist
Markey, Paul Victor videographer, videotape editor
Markowska, Alicja Lidia neuroscientist, researcher
Marriott, Salima Siler state legislator, social work educator
Marsh, Bruce David geologist, educator
Massof, Robert William neuroscientist, educator
Masson, Gerald M. computer science educator
Matheson, Nina W. medical researcher
†Mathison, Theodore E. air transportation executive
Matjasko, M. Jane anesthesiologist, educator
Maumenee, Irene H. ophthalmology educator
McCarter, P(ete) Kyle, Jr. Near Eastern studies educator
McCarty, Richard Earl biochemist, biochemistry educator
McCauley, H(enry) Berton retired public health dentist
McClung, A(lexander) Keith, Jr. lawyer
Mc Cord, Kenneth Armstrong consulting engineer
McGowan, George Vincent public utility executive
†McGuiness, Ilona Maria writing educator
McHugh, Paul R. psychiatrist, neurologist, educator
McKhann, Guy Mead physician, educator
McKinney, George K. protective services official
†McKusick, James Chase English educator
McKusick, Victor Almon geneticist, educator, physician
McManus, Walter Leonard investment executive
McPartland, James Michael university official
McPherson, Donald Paxton, III lawyer
McWilliams, John Michael lawyer
Meima, Ralph Chester, Jr. corporate execuitve, former foreign service officer
†Melville, Kraig Arthur emergency medicine physician
Melvin, Norman Cecil lawyer
Meny, Robert George medical research administrator
Messina, Bonnie Lynn lawyer
Meyer, Jean-Pierre Gustave mathematician, educator
Mfume, Kweisi former congressman
Mierzwicki, Anthony Joseph real estate executive
Migeon, Barbara Ruben pediatrician, geneticist
Migeon, Claude Jean pediatrics educator
Miliman, David Jay lawyer
Milio, Louis Romolo law educator (retired), social worker
Miller, Decatur Howard lawyer
Miller, Edward Doring anesthesiologist
Miller, Melvin Orville, Jr. artist
†Miller, Ray professional baseball team manager
Miller, Stanley Joseph dermatologic surgeon
Millspaugh, Martin Laurence real estate developer, urban development consultant
Milnor, William Robert physician
Mintz, Sidney Wilfred anthropologist
Mocko, George Paul minister
Mogilensky, Emma Sarah museum educator
Mohraz, Judy Jolley college president
Money, John William psychologist
Montgomery, Paula Kay publisher
Moorjani, Angela foreign languages educator
Moos, H. Warren physicist, astronomer, educator, administrator
Morrel, William Griffin, Jr. banker
Morris, David Michael insurance executive, lawyer
Moser, Hugo Wolfgang physician
Moser, M(artin) Peter lawyer
Mosley, Wiley Henry medical educator
Motz, Diana Gribbon federal judge
Motz, John Frederick federal judge
Mulholland, John Henry internist, educator
Munster, Andrew Michael medical educator, surgeon
Murnaghan, Francis Dominic, Jr. federal judge
Murphy, Philip Francis bishop
Murray, Joseph William banker
Mussina, Michael Cole baseball player
Mysko, William Kiefer emergency physician, educator
Myslinski, Norbert Raymond medical educator
Nagey, David Augustus physician, researcher
†Nammour, Henri Habib internist, pulmonologist, critical care physician
Nathans, Daniel molecular biology and genetics educator
Nathanson, Josef economist, urban planner, municipal official
Neil, Benjamin Arthur lawyer, educator
Newman, William C. bishop
Newman, William Louis geologist
†Newsome, Ozzie manager professional athletics
Nickerson, William Milnor federal judge
Nickon, Alex chemist, educator
Niemeyer, Paul Victor federal judge
Norman, Philip Sidney physician
Norris, Douglas Martin principal
Norris, Joseph, III computer engineer
Norris, Rebecca design firm executive
Northrop, Edward Skottowe federal judge
O'Melia, Charles Richard environmental engineering educator
Orman, Leonard Arnold lawyer
Orwig, Larry Gordon human resource professional
Ott, John Harlow museum administrator
Ourednik, Patricia Ann accountant
Owen, Stephen Lee lawyer
Palmucci Jr., John A. college administration executive
Palumbo, Francis Xavier Bernard pharmacy educator
Pappas, George Frank lawyer
Park, Mary Woodfill information consultant
Parsons, Ivy artist, sculptor, educator
Pass, Carolyn Joan dermatologist
Passano, E. Magruder, Jr. corporate philanthropist
Patz, Arnall ophthalmologist
Paulson, Ronald Howard English and humanities educator
Peacock, James Daniel lawyer
Peirce, Carol Marshall English educator
Permutt, Solbert physiologist, physician
Pettijohn, Francis John geology educator
Pimental, Laura emergency physician
Pinkard, Anne Merrick foundation administrator
Piotrow, Phyllis Tilson public health educator, international development specialist
Plant, Albin MacDonough lawyer
Plummer, Risque Wilson retired lawyer
Poehler, Theodore Otto university provost, engineer, researcher
Poindexter, Christian Herndon utility company executive
Pokempner, Joseph Kres lawyer
Pollak, Joanne E. lawyer
Pollak, Lisa columnist
Pollak, Mark lawyer
Popel, Aleksander S. engineering educator
Posner, Gary Herbert chemist, educator
Potra, Florian Alexander mathematics educator
Pratt, Joan M. comptroller
Preston, Mark I. investment company executive
Price, Debbie Mitchell journalist
Prince, Jerry Ladd engineering educator
Proctor, Donald Frederick otolaryngology educator, physician
Provost, Thomas Taylor dermatology educator, researcher
Purpura, Lia Rachel poet, educator
Putzel, Constance Kellner lawyer
†Rabin, Bruce Arlan neurologist
Radding, Andrew lawyer
Ranney, Richard Raymond dental educator, researcher
Ranum, Orest Allen historian, educator
†Rapoport, Morton I. medical educator, university administrator
Rauschenberg, Dale Eugene music educator
Rawlings, Stephanie city councilwoman
Rayson, Glendon Ennes internist, preventive medicine specialist, writer
Redden, Roger Duffey lawyer
Reed, Gregory lawyer
Reeder, Oliver Howard paint products manufacturing executive
Reinhart, Walter Josef educator
Rennels, Marshall Leigh neuroanatomist, biomedical scientist, educator
Reno, Russell Ronald, Jr. lawyer
Reynolds, William Leroy lawyer, educator
†Richardson, Sally Keadle state health care administrator
Ripken, Calvin Edwin, Jr. (Cal Ripken) professional baseball player
Ritter, Jeffrey Blake lawyer
Robinson, Alice Jean McDonnell drama and speech educator
Robinson, Brooks Calbert, Jr. former professional baseball player, TV commentator, business consultant
Robinson, Florine Samantha marketing executive
Robinson, Zelig lawyer
Rodowsky, Lawrence Francis state judge
Rodricks, Daniel John columnist, television commentator
Roland, Donald Edward printing company executive
Rolland, Donald F. printing company executive
Rose, Hugh retired economics educator
Rose, Noel Richard immunologist, microbiologist, educator
Rose, Rudolph L. lawyer
Roseman, Saul biochemist, educator
Rosen, Wendy Workman marketing professional
Rosenberg, Henry A., Jr. petroleum executive
†Rosenberg, Paul M. federal judge
Rosenthal, William J. lawyer
Ross, Richard Starr medical school dean emeritus, cardiologist
Roth, George Stanley research biochemist, physiologist
Rothschild, Amalie Rosenfeld artist
Rousuck, J. Wynn theater critic
Rubin, Robert Jay toxicologist
Rubinstein, Robert Lawrence anthropologist, gerontologist
†Ruknudin, Abdul biophysicist, researcher, educator
Russell-Wood, Anthony John R. history educator
Ryan, Judith W. geriatrics nurse, adult nurse practitioner, educator, researcher
Sachs, Murray B. audiologist, educator
Sack, George Henry, Jr. molecular geneticist
Sack, Sylvan Hanan lawyer
Safran, Linda Jacqueline fundraising consultant
Salamon, Lester Milton political science educator
Sallese, Paula Marie critical care, resuscitation nurse
Salters, Charles Robert biology educator, dean
Samet, Jonathan Michael epidemiologist, educator
Sanchez Alvarado, Alejandro embryologist, molecular biologist
Sanfilippo, Alfred Paul pathologist, educator
Santamaria, Barbara Matheny nurse practitioner
Scanlan, Robert Harris civil engineer, educator
Schaefer, Robert Wayne banker
Schaefer, William Goerman lawyer
Scheel, Paul Joseph, Jr. health facility administrator, physician
Scheeler, Charles construction company executive
Schilling, Franklin Charles, Jr. retail management professional
Schimpff, Stephen Callender internist, oncologist
Schmoke, Kurt L. mayor
Schneewind, Jerome Borges philosophy educator
†Schneider, James Frederick federal judge
Schnell, Eugene Richard, IV education director
Schochor, Jonathan lawyer
Schoenrich, Edyth Hull internal and preventive medicine physician
Schuster, Marvin Meier physician, educator
Scriggins, Larry Palmer lawyer
Sedlak, Valerie Frances English language educator, university administrator
Semans, Truman Thomas investment company executive
Sfekas, Stephen James lawyer, educator
Shabsin, Harry Stewart psychologist
Shaeffer, Charles Wayne investment counselor
Shamoo, Adil Elias biochemist, biophysicist, educator
Shaper, Christopher Thorne sales executive
Shapiro, Harry Dean lawyer
Shapiro, Sam health care analyst, biostatistician
Sharfstein, Steven Samuel health care executive, medical director
Sharkey, Robert Emmett lawyer
Sharpe, William Norman, Jr. mechanical engineer, educator
Shattuck, Mayo Adams, III investment bank executive
Sherman, Alan Theodore computer science educator
Shiffman, Bernard mathematician, educator
Short, Alexander Campbell lawyer
Shrestha, Shiva Kumar urban planner
Shuldiner, Alan Rodney physician, endocrinologist, educator
Siegel, Melvyn Harry financial consultant, securities company executive
Silbergeld, Ellen Kovner environmental epidemiologist and toxicologist
Silverstein, Arthur Matthew ophthalmic immunologist, educator, historian
Silverstone, Harris J. chemistry educator
Simpson, Thomas William physician
Sinno, Fady A. surgeon
Slepian, Paul mathematician, educator
Smalkin, Frederic N. federal judge
Smith, Hamilton Othanel molecular biologist, educator
Smith, Hoke LaFollette university president
Smith, Robert G. lawyer
Snead, James Arrington architect
Snyder, Solomon Halbert psychiatrist, pharmacologist
Somerville, Romaine Stec arts administrator
Sommer, Alfred medical educator, scientist, ophthalmologist
Southern, Hugh retired performing arts manager
Spector, Rochelle city councilwoman
Speed, Leslie Bokee lawyer
Spitznagel, John Keith periodontist, researcher
Stainrook, Harry Richard banker
Stalfort, John Arthur lawyer
Stanley, Julian Cecil, Jr. psychology educator
Stanley, Steven Mitchell paleobiologist, educator
Starfield, Barbara Helen physician, educator
Stark, Brian Alan nurse anesthetist, nursing administrator
Stein, Bernard Alvin business consultant
Steinbach, Alice journalist
Steinwachs, Donald Michael public health educator
Stenberg, Carl W(aldamer), III public administration educator, university dean
Sterne, Joseph Robert Livingston newspaper editor, educator
Stevens, Elisabeth Goss (Mrs. Robert Schleussner, Jr.) writer, journalist, graphic artist
Stewart, C(ornelius) Van Leuven lawyer
Stidman, Edith (Janet) Scales parliamentarian
Stolberg, Ernest Milton retired environmental engineer, consultant
Stolley, Paul David medical educator, researcher
Stone, Norman R., Jr. state legislator
Storrs, Alexander David astronomer
Strickland, George Thomas, Jr. physician, researcher, educator
Strickland, Marshall Hayward bishop
Strull, Gene technology consultant, retired electrical manufacturing company executive
Stukes, Melvin L. councilman
Sudia, Mary Eileen nurse
Sullam, Brian Eliot journalist
Suskind, Sigmund Richard microbiology educator
Swinson, Angela Anthony physician
Sykes, Melvin Julius lawyer
Talalay, Paul pharmacologist, physician
Talar, Charles John Thomas priest, educator
Talbot, Donald Roy consulting services executive
Tamminga, Carol Ann neuroscientist
Tatum, Arthur, III educator, lexicographer, pianist
Taylor, Carl Ernest physician, educator
†Temirkanov, Yuri music director
Tepper, Michael Howard publishing company executive
Terborg-Penn, Rosalyn Marian historian, educator
†Theda, Christiane pediatrics educator
Thomas, Jacqueline Marie journalist, editor
Thompson, Otho M. city solicitor
Tiefenwerth, William Philip university program director
Toomey, Sister Stephana designer liturgical architectural space, nun
Trimble, William Cattell, Jr. lawyer
Tringali, Joseph financial planner, accountant
Trpis, Milan vector biologist, scientist, educator
†Turner, Thomas Bourne retired microbiology educator
Tyler, Anne (Mrs. Taghi M. Modarressi) author
Uhl, Scott Mark state agency administrator
†Urick, Kevin lawyer
†Varga, Nicholas historian, archivist, retired educator
Vogelstein, Bert oncology educator
Wagner, Henry Nicholas, Jr. physician
Wainwright, Joan federal agency administrator
Walker, Erda Theresa nursing administrator
Walker, Irving Edward lawyer
Walker, Kenneth Adley aluminum fabricating company executive
Walker, Mack historian, educator
Walker, Wilbur Gordon physician, educator
Wallach, Edward Eliot physician, educator
Wallis, Sandra Rhodes educator
Walser, Mackenzie physician, educator
Walsh, Patrick Craig urologist
Walton, Kimberly Ann medical laboratory technician
†Warner, Christine Marie researcher
Wasserman, Richard Leo lawyer
Waterbury, Larry physician, educator
Weaver, Kenneth Newcomer geologist, state official
Weber, Nancy Walker charitable trust administrator
Weiss, James Lloyd cardiology educator
Welch, Agnes city councilwoman
Welch, Robert Bond ophthalmologist, educator
Weng, Han-Rong physiologist, researcher
Westerhout, Gart retired astronomer
Wheeler, Peter Martin federal agency administrator
White, Pamela Janice lawyer
White, William Nelson lawyer
Whitman, Marland Hamilton, Jr. lawyer
Wieczorek, Patricia Christine medical/surgical nurse
Wierman, John Charles mathematician, educator
Williams, Anna M. social worker
Williams, G(eorge) Melville surgeon, medical educator
Williams, Herman, Jr. protective services offical
Williams, Robert Eugene astronomer
Wilson, Donald Edward physician, educator
Wilson, Peter Mason computer programmer
Wilson, Thomas Matthew, III lawyer
Winn, James Julius, Jr. lawyer
Wist, Paul Gabriel accountant
Wolman, M. Gordon geography educator
Wong, Wing-Chun Godwin philosopher
Woods, William Ellis lawyer, pharmacist, association executive
Woodward, Theodore Englar medical educator, internist
†Wren, Frank professional baseball team executive
Wu, Albert W. medical educator
†Xiao, Yan science educator
Yantis, Steven George psychology educator
Yarmolinsky, Adam lawyer, educator
Ye, Shui Qing medical researcher
Yellin, Judith electrologist
Yossif, George psychiatrist
Young, Barbara psychiatrist, psychoanalyst, psychiatry educator, photographer
Young, Hobart Peyton economist, mathematician, educator
Young, Joseph H. federal judge
Zaiman, Joel Hirsh rabbi
Zaruba, Allen Scott Harmon sculptor
Zehler, Edward Joseph occupational safety and health consultant
Ziff, Larzer English language educator
Zinkham, W. Robert lawyer
†Zito, Julie Magno psychopharmacologist, pharmacist, educator
Zizic, Thomas Michael physician, educator

Bel Air

Baumgardner, Renee Elaine urban planner
Cash, (Cynthia) LaVerne physicist

Eichelberger, Robert John *retired government research and development administrator, consultant*
Kwetkauskie, John A. *medical technologist*
Lu, David John *history educator, writer*
Miller, Dorothy Eloise *education educator*
Phillips, Bernice Cecile Golden *retired vocational education educator*
Riley, Catherine Irene *former state senator, legislative staff member*

Beltsville

Abdul-Baki, Aref Asad *physiologist, researcher*
Andre, Pamela Q. J. *library director*
Collins, Anita Marguerite *research geneticist*
Ehrle, Raymond Albert *retired psychologist and university official*
Hackett, Kevin James *insect pathologist*
Johnson, Phyllis Elaine *chemist*
Levin, Gilbert Victor *health information, services and products*
Lewis, Bette Louise *school principal*
Little, R. Donald *architect, administrator*
Murrell, Kenneth Darwin *microbiologist, parasitologist*
Norman, H. Duane *dairy geneticist*
Palm, Mary Egdahl *mycologist*
Quirk, Frank Joseph *management consulting company executive*
Rupp, Monica Cecilia *nursing administrator*
Seyfried, Donna Marie *biomedical company executive*
Sickles, Carlton Ralph *employee benefit consultant*
Terrill, Clair Elman *animal scientist, geneticist, consultant*
Tso, Tien Chioh *federal agency official, plant physiologist*
Zarlenga, Dante Sam, Jr. *molecular biologist*

Berlin

Buchholz, Bernard *retired research manager*
Crawford, Norman Crane, Jr. *academic administrator, consultant*
Passwater, Richard Albert *biochemist, author*
Peters, Charity Nöel *health facility administrator*
Roche, Kathleen Anne *nursing administrator*

Berwyn Heights

†Kirchknopf, Matthew Bela *research laboratory manager*

Bethesda

Ahmad, Imad Aldean *astronomer, consultant*
Ahmed, S. Basheer *research company executive, educator*
Akin, Cem *internist*
Alexander, Duane Frederick *pediatrician, research administrator*
Allen, Toni K. *lawyer*
Alper, Jerome Milton *lawyer*
†Angelo, Robert M. *advertising executive*
Ashwell, G. Gilbert *biochemist*
Atkinson, Arthur John, Jr. *clinical pharmacologist, educator*
Atwell, Constance Woodruff *health services executive, researcher*
August, Diane L. *independent education consultant, policy researchr*
†Augustine, Hilton H., Jr. *computer company executive*
Augustine, Norman Ralph *industrial executive, educator*
Axelrod, Julius *pharmacologist, biochemist*
Azaryan, Anahit Vazgenovna *biochemist, researcher*
Backus, Robert Coburn *biophysical chemist*
Baird, Bruce Allen *lawyer*
Baird, Charles Fitz *retired mining and metals company executive*
Ballhaus, William Francis, Jr. *aerospace industry executive, research scientist*
Banik, Sambhu Nath *psychologist*
†Battey, James F. *federal agency administrator*
Bauersfeld, Carl Frederick *lawyer*
Beall, Robert Joseph *foundation executive*
Becker, Edwin Demuth *chemist, laboratory director*
†Begala, Kathleen *consumer safety organization administrator*
Belak, Michael James *information systems executive*
Bennink, Jack Richard *microbiologist, researcher*
Benson, Elizabeth Polk *Pre-Columbian art specialist*
Berendes, Heinz Werner *medical epidemiologist, pediatrician*
Blanchette, Robert Wilfred *business executive, lawyer*
Boshart, Edgar David *editor, journalist, photographer*
Bowsher, Charles Arthur *retired government official, business executive*
Brady, Roscoe Owen *neurogeneticist, educator*
Bregman, Jacob Israel *environmental consulting company executive*
Breman, Joel Gordon *epidemiologist, science administrator*
Briskman, Robert David *engineering executive*
Brodine, Charles Edward *physician*
Brown, Ann *federal agency administrator*
Brown, Dudley Earl, Jr. *psychiatrist, educator, health executive, former federal agency administrator, former naval officer*
Brown, Earle Palmer *advertising agency executive*
Brown, Thomas Philip, III *lawyer*
Brunell, Philip Alfred *physician*
Brunson, Burlie Allen *aerospace executive*
Buccino, Alphonse *university dean emeritus, consultant*
Buhler, Leslie Lynn *institute administrator*
Bunger, Rolf *physiology educator*
Burdeshaw, William Brooksbank *engineering executive*
Burg, Maurice Benjamin *renal physiologist, physician*
†Burkhalter, Susan Shively *music educator, organist*
Burt, Marvin Roger *financial advisor, investment manager*
Burton, Charles Henning *lawyer*
Calvert, Gordon Lee *retired legal association executive*
Cantoni, Giulio Leonardo *biochemist, government official*
Capaldini, Mark Laurence *online information service executive*
Carberry, Michael Glen *advertising executive*
Carney, William Patrick *medical educator*
Cassman, Marvin *biochemist*
Castelli, Alexander Gerard *accountant*
Chanock, Robert Merritt *pediatrician*
Chase, Thomas Newell *neurologist, researcher, educator*
Cheever, Allen Williams *pathologist*
Chen, Liping *molecular biologist, researcher, biochemist*
†Choquette, William H. *construction company executive*
Chretien, Jane Henkel *internist*
Chronister, Gregory Michael *newspaper editor*
Clark, A. James *real estate company executive*
Cleary, Timothy Finbar *professional society administrator*
Cody, Thomas Gerald *management consultant, writer*
Coelho, Anthony Mendes, Jr. *health science administrator*
†Coffman, Vance D. *aerospace company executive*
Cohen, Robert Abraham *retired physician*
Cohen, Sheldon Gilbert *physician, historian, immunology educator*
Cohn, Murray Steven *information technology administrator*
Collins, Francis S. *medical research scientist*
Comings, William Daniel, Jr. *mortgage banker, housing development executive*
Contreras, Thomas J., Jr. *naval officer*
Corn, Milton *academic dean, physician*
Cornelius, Maria G. *financial advisor*
Cornish, Edward Seymour *magazine editor*
Cotter, Dennis Joseph *health services company executive*
Craig, Douglas Warren *food service industry executive*
Crout, J(ohn) Richard *physician, pharmaceutical researcher*
Daly, John W. *chemistry research administrator*
Danforth, David Newton, Jr. *physician, scientist*
Daniel, Charles Dwelle, Jr. *consultant, retired army officer*
Day, Marylouise Muldoon (Mrs. Richard Dayton Day) *appraiser*
Day, Robert Dwain, Jr. *foundation executive, lawyer*
Dean, Jurrien *biomedical researcher, physician*
Dietrich, Robert Anthony *pathologist, medical administrator, consultant*
Dommen, Arthur John *agricultural economist*
Dox, Ida *author, medical illustrator*
Drazin, Lisa *real estate and corporate investment banker, financial consultant*
Dudley, Don *broadcast journalist, communications consultant*
Duncan, Constance Catharine *psychologist, educator, researcher*
Duncan, Francis *historian, government official*
Dyer, Doris Anne *nursing consultant*
Dyer, Frederick Charles *writer, consultant*
Dykstra, Vergil Homer *retired academic administrator*
Ehrenfeld, Ellie (Elvera Ehrenfeld) *health science association administrator*
Ehrenstein, Gerald *biophysicist*
Eisen, Eric Anshel *lawyer*
Elliott, George Armstrong, III *artist, journalist*
English, William deShay *lawyer*
Estrin, Melvyn J. *computer products company executive*
Eule, Norman L. *lawyer*
Evans, John Vaughan *communications satellite executive, physicist*
Fales, Henry Marshall *chemist*
Farmer, Richard Gilbert *physician, foundation administrator, medical advisor, health care consultant*
Fauci, Anthony Stephen *health facility administrator, physician*
Fefferman, Hilbert *lawyer, government official*
Feller, William Frank *surgery educator*
Felsenfeld, Gary *government official, scientist*
Ferris, Frederick Joseph *gerontologist, social worker*
†Ficca, Stephen A. *federal agency administrator*
Fischbach, Gerald D. *neurobiology educator*
†Flaherty, Barbara A. *marketing professional, artist*
Fleisher, Thomas Arthur *physician*
Fleming, Patricia Stubbs *federal official*
Fowler, Emil Eugene *nuclear technology consultant*
Frank, Martin *physiology educator, health scientist, association executive*
Frank, Richard Sanford *retired magazine editor*
Fraumeni, Joseph Francis, Jr. *scientific researcher, medical educator, physician, military officer*
Freedman, Joseph *sanitary and public health engineering consultant*
Fri, Robert Wheeler *museum director*
Friestedt, Amédée Chabrisson *medical genetics database manager*
†Frye, Robert Edward *federal agency administrator*
Funk, Sherman Maxwell *former government official, writer, consultant*
Gallagher, Hubert Randall *government consultant*
Galston, William Arthur *political scientist, educator*
†Garrison, Howard H. *public relations executive*
Gartland, William Joseph, Jr. *research institute administrator*
Gaston, Marilyn Hughes *health facility administrator*
Gelboin, Harry Victor *biochemistry educator, researcher*
Geller, Ronald Gene *health administrator*
Gellert, Martin Frank *biochemist*
Gerwin, Brenda Isen *research biochemist*
Gibson, Sam Thompson *internist, educator*
Gilbert, Daniel Lee *physiologist*
†Gilbert, Pamela *federal agency administrator*
Gilford, Dorothy Morrow *statistician, researcher*
Gilreath, Jerry Hollandsworth *community planner*
Gleazer, Edmund John, Jr. *retired education educator*
Goldschmidt, Peter Graham *physician executive, business development consultant*
Goldstone, Mark Lewis *lawyer*
Goodwin, Robert Cronin *lawyer, consultant*
†Gorden, Phillip *federal agency administrator*
Gordis, Enoch *science administrator, internist*
Grady, Patricia A. *health institute director, researcher*
Grandy, Fred *foundation administrator, former congressman, former actor*
Grau, John Michael *trade association executive*
Gray, James Gordon, Jr. *speech educator*
Green, Jerome George *federal government official*
Greenwald, Peter *physician, government medical research director*
Griffith, Robert Dean *military careerman, registered nurse*
Gruber, Jack *medical virologist, biomedical research administrator*
Guadagno, Mary Ann Noecker *social scientist, consultant*
Gude, Gilbert *former state and federal legislator, nurseryman, writer*
Guttman, Helene Nathan *biomedical research consultant, transpersonal counselor, regression therapist*
Haffner, William H.J. *obstetrician-gynecologist*
Hagberg, Viola Wilgus *lawyer*
Hallett, Mark *physician, neurologist, health research institute administrator*
Hallsted, Nancy Ruth Everett *pianist, music educator*
†Halpert, Stuart D. *real estate company executive*
Hancock, Charles Cavanaugh, Jr. *scientific association administrator*
Harney, Kenneth Robert *editor, columnist*
Harris, Curtis C. *physician*
Hartmann, Robert Trowbridge *author, consultant*
Hartnett, Elizabeth A. *trade association executive*
Haseltine, Florence Pat *research administrator, obstetrician, gynecologist*
Hauck, Frederick Hamilton *retired naval officer, astronaut, business executive*
Haugan, Gertrude M. *clinical psychologist*
Hausman, Steven Jack *health science administrator*
Heller, Daniel Robert *investment banker, portfolio manager*
Hemming, Val G. *university dean*
Hempstone, Smith, Jr. *diplomat, journalist*
Hendricks, John S. *broadcast executive*
Herman, Edith Carol *journalist*
Herman, Mary Margaret *neuropathologist*
Herman, Stephen Allen *lawyer*
Hershaft, Alex *organization executive*
Highfill, Philip Henry, Jr. *retired language educator*
Hill, Hugh Francis, III *lawyer, physician*
Himelfarb, Stephen Roy *lawyer*
Hodes, Richard J. *think tank executive, immunologist, researcher*
Hodgdon, Harry Edward *association executive, wildlife biologist*
Hoenack, August Frederick *architect*
Holland, Robert Carl *economist*
Hoover, Roland Armitage *publisher, printer*
Horakova, Zdenka Zahutova *retired toxicologist, pharmacologist*
†Howard, Frank Joseph, Jr. *public relations company executive*
Hoyer, Mary Louise *social worker, educator*
Hrynkow, Sharon Hemond *federal government administrator, researcher*
Huebner, John Stephen *geologist*
†Hughes, Gary L. *artist, sculptor*
Hundt, Reed Eric *federal agency administrator, lawyer*
†Hutchinson, David Michael *economist*
Hutton, John Evans, Jr. *surgery educator, retired military officer*
Hyman, Steven Edward *federal agency administrator, psychiatrist, educator*
Ikle, Doris Margret *energy efficiency company executive*
Ingraham, Edward Clarke, Jr. *foreign service officer*
†Jabbari, Bahman *neurologist, educator*
†Jabs, Arthur Dean *plastic surgeon*
Jackson, Michael John *physiologist, association executive*
Jameson, Sanford Chandler *education educator*
Javitt, Jonathan C. *physician, health policy analyst, writer*
Jayson, Lester Samuel *lawyer, educator*
†Jennings, Lane Eaton *futurist writer, editor, translator*
Jensen, Peter Scott *psychiatrist, public health service officer*
Jeppson, Lawrence Smith *publisher fine arts, consultant*
Jiang, He *biomedical scientist, entrepreneur*
John, Frank Herbert, Jr. *real estate appraiser, real estate investor*
Johnson, Eugene Clare *data processing company executive*
Johnson, Joyce Marie *psychiatrist, epidemiologist, public health officer*
Johnson, Richard Kent *publishing executive*
Jonas, Gary Fred *health care center executive*
Jones, John Courts *wildlife biologist*
Jordan, Elke *molecular biologist, government medical research institute executive*
Joy, Robert John Thomas *medical history educator*
Joyce, Bernita Anne *federal government agency administrator*
Katz, Stephen I. *dermatologist*
Katz, Stephen Ira *dermatologist*
Kaufman, Seymour *biochemist*
Keiser, Harry Robert *physician*
Kemelhor, Robert E(lias) *mechanical engineer*
Kibbe, James William *real estate broker*
Kidd, Charles Vincent *former civil servant, educator*
Kindt, Thomas James *chemist*
Kirby, Harmon E. *ambassador*
Kirschstein, Ruth Lillian *physician*
Klausner, Richard D. *federal agency administrator, cell biologist*
Klee, Claude Blenc *medical researcher*
Kleine, Herman *economist*
Knachel, Philip Atherton *librarian*
Koenig, Elizabeth Barbara *sculptor*
Koltnow, Peter Gregory *engineering consultant*
Korn, Edward David *biochemist*
Koslow, Stephen Hugh *science administrator, pharmacologist*
Kramer, Barnett Sheldon *oncologist*
Krause, Richard Michael *medical scientist, government official, educator*
Kruger, Gustav Otto, Jr. *oral surgeon, educator*
Kupfer, Carl *ophthalmologist, science administrator*
Laingen, Lowell Bruce *diplomat*
Larrabee, Barbara Princelau *retired intelligence officer*
Larrabee, Donald Richard *publishing company executive*
Law, Lloyd William *geneticist*
†Lee, Leamon M. *federal agency administrator*
Lee, Young Jack *federal agency administrator*
Leibowitz, Deborah Golub *early childhood, gifted and parent education consultant*
Lenfant, Claude Jean-Marie *physician*
Leonard, James Joseph *physician, educator*
Leonard, Sugar Ray (Ray Charles Leonard) *retired professional boxer*
Leppert, Phyllis Carolyn *obstetrician, gynecologist*
Leshner, Alan Irvin *science foundation administrator*
Levin, Carl *public and government relations consultant*
Lewis, James Histed *retired foreign service officer*
Lindberg, Donald Allan Bror *library administrator, pathologist, educator*
Linehan, William Marston *urologic surgeon, cancer researcher*
Liotta, Lance Allen *pathologist*
Lipkin, Bernice Sacks *computer science educator*
†Livermore, Arthur Hamilton *chemist, consultant*
London, Gary Wayne *neurologist*
Lorber, Mortimer *retired physiology educator*
Lu, Bai *neurobiologist*
Lystad, Mary Hanemann (Mrs. Robert Lystad) *sociologist, author*
MacLean, Paul Donald *government institute medical research official*
Macnamara, Thomas Edward *physician, educator*
Magrath, Ian Trevor *physician*
Manasse, Henri Richard, Jr. *academic administrator, pharmacy administration educator*
Mannix, Charles Raymond *law educator*
†Marini, Ann Marie *medical researcher, educator*
Marino, Pamela Anne *health sciences administrator*
Martino, Robert Louis *computational scientist and engineer, researcher*
Mastny-Fox, Catherine Louise *administrator, consultant*
Masur, Henry *internist*
McClure, Brooks *management consultant*
McCurdy, Harry Ward *otolaryngologist*
Mc Gurn, Barrett *communications executive, writer*
McMurphy, Michael Allen *energy company executive, lawyer*
Meakem, Carolyn Soliday *investment executive, financial planner, money manager, consultant*
Meier, Louis Leonard, Jr. *lawyer*
Metcalfe, Dean Darrel *medical research physician*
Metzenbaum, Howard Morton *former senator, consumer organization official*
Metzger, Henry *federal research institution administrator*
Miller, Judith Wolfe Cohen *consultant*
Miller, Louis Howard *biologist, researcher*
Mills, James Louis *medical researcher, pediatric epidemiologist*
Mineta, Norman Yoshio *aerospace transportation executive, former congressman*
Mirsky, Allan Franklin *psychologist, researcher*
Mishkin, Mortimer *neuropsychologist*
Monjan, Andrew Arthur *health science administrator*
Morgan, Jo Valentine, Jr. *lawyer*
Morgan, John Davis *consultant*
Moseley, Chris Rosser *marketing executive*
Moshman, Jack *statistical consultant*
Moss, Bernard *virologist, researcher*
Mullan, Fitzhugh *public health physician*
Murayama, Makio *biochemist*
†Murr, Thomas W., Jr. *federal agency administrator*
Nash, Howard Allen *biochemist, researcher*
Nason, Charles Tuckey *financial services executive*
Navarro, Joseph Anthony *statistician, consultant*
Naylor, Phyllis Reynolds *author*
Nee, Linda Elizabeth *social science analyst*
Neill, Denis Michael *international consultant*
Nejelski, Paul Arthur *retired judge, freelance writer*
Nelligan, William David *professional association executive*
Nelson, Stuart James *internist, medical informatician*
Nelson, William Eugene *lawyer*
Nessen, Ronald Harold *broadcast executive*
Neumann, Robert Gerhard *ambassador, consultant*
Neumann, Ronald Daniel *nuclear medicine physician, educator*
Neva, Franklin Allen *physician, educator*
Nimeroff, Phyllis Ruth *electronic engineer, visual artist*
Nirenberg, Marshall Warren *biochemist*
North, William Haven *foreign service officer*
Nyirjesy, Istvan *obstetrician, gynecologist*
Obrams, Gunta Iris *research administrator*
O'Callaghan, Jerry Alexander *government official*
Oddis, Joseph Anthony *associations executive*
Olmsted, Jerauld Lockwood *telephone company executive*
Ommaya, Ayub Khan *neurosurgeon*
Owen, Thomas Barron *retired naval officer, space company executive*
†Pakaluk, Debra Lorraine Behm *science educator*
Palmer, James Alvin *baseball commentator*
Pankopf, Arthur, Jr. *lawyer*
Papaioannou, Evangelia-Lilly *psychologist, researcher*
Paul, William Erwin *immunologist, researcher*
Peck, Edward Lionel *retired foreign service officer, corporate executive*
Perlin, Seymour *psychiatrist, educator*
Perry, Seymour Monroe *physician*
Peterson, Charles Marquis *medical educator*
Petty, John Robert *financier*
Piatigorsky, Joram Paul *research scientist, molecular biologist*
Pickerell, James Howard *photojournalist*
Pinn, Vivian W. *pathologist, federal agency administrator*
Pluta, Ryszard Marek *neurosurgeon, scientist*
Pollard, Harvey B. *physician, neuroscientist*
Poppleton, Miller John *lawyer*
Post, Robert Morton *psychiatrist*
Potter, Michael *genetics researcher, medical researcher*
Pratt, Dana Joseph *publishing consultant*
Pritchard, Wilbur *telecommunications engineering executive*
†Proctor, Sondra Goldsmith *musician*
Purcell, Robert Harry *virologist*
Quon, Michael James *medical scientist, physician*
Quraishi, Mohammed Sayeed *health scientist, administrator*
Rabson, Alan Saul *physician, educator*
Raffini, Renee Kathleen *foreign language professional, educator*
Rall, Joseph Edward *physician*
Rankin, James Patrick *financial services company executive*
Rapoport, Judith *psychiatrist*
Reed, Miriam Bell *legislative staff*
Reid, Clarice Delores *retired physician*
Rennert, Owen Murray *physician, educator*
Resnik, Harvey Lewis Paul *psychiatrist*
Rhim, Johng Sik *physician, educator, medical researcher*
Rice, Kenner Cralle *medicinal chemist*
Richardson, John *retired international relations executive*
Riley, Matilda White (Mrs. John W. Riley, Jr.) *sociologist*
Robbins, John Bennett *medical researcher*
Roberts, Doris Emma *epidemiologist, consultant*
Rooney, William Richard *magazine editor*
Rosenbaum, Greg Alan *merchant banker, consultant*
Rosenberg, Mark Louis *lawyer*

Rosenberg, Steven Aaron *surgeon, medical researcher*
Ross, William Warfield *lawyer*
Rowell, Edward Morgan *retired foreign service officer, lecturer*
Rubin, Allan Avrom *lawyer, regulatory agency consultant*
Rubin, William *editor*
Rymarcsuk, Jim Arthur *aerospace industry executive, consultant*
Safer, John *artist, lecturer, banker, real estate developer*
Saffiotti, Umberto *pathologist*
Salisbury, Tamara Paula *foundation executive*
Salmoiraghi, Gian Carlo *physiologist, educator*
Sammet, Jean E. *computer scientist*
Sams, James Farid *real estate development company executive*
†Sauer, Michael James *business consultant*
Saunders, Charles Baskerville, Jr. *retired association executive*
Saville, Thorndike, Jr. *coastal engineer, consultant*
†Sawhney, Roger Anu *consultant, physician*
†Scanlon, Thomas J. *consulting company executive*
Schambra, Philip Ellis *federal agency administrator, radiobiologist*
Schinski, Vernon David *retired navy officer*
Schmidt, Randall David *information technology and business consultant*
Schmidt, Raymond Paul *naval career officer, historian, government official*
Schoem, Alan Howard *lawyer*
Schwartz, Charles Frederick *retired economist, consultant*
Schwartz, Judy Ellen *cardiothoracic surgeon*
Scully, Roger Tehan *lawyer*
Serlin, David H. *history educator*
Sewell, Rodney Milton *biologist*
Shellow, Robert *management service company executive, consultant*
Sheridan, Philp Henry *pediatrician, neurologist*
Short, Elizabeth M. *physician, educator, federal agency administrator*
Shulman, Lawrence Edward *biomedical research administrator, rheumatologist*
Sich, Jeffrey John *health education analyst*
Silberberg, Rein *nuclear astrophysicist, researcher*
Silverman, Charlotte *epidemiologist, educator*
†Simon, Robert Isaac *psychiatrist*
Simonds, Peggy Muñoz *writer, lecturer, retired literature educator*
Sinclair, Warren Keith *radiation biophysicist, organization executive, consultant*
Skirboll, Lana R. *federal health policy director*
Slavkin, Harold Charles *biologist*
Smirnow, Virgil *publisher, consultant*
Smith, Kent Ashton *scientific and technical information executive*
Sober, Sidney *retired diplomat, education educator*
Soffer, Lowell Charles *financial executive*
Sokoloff, Louis *physiologist, neurochemist*
Solomon, Robert *economist*
Sontag, James Mitchell *cancer researcher*
Southwick, Paul *retired public relations executive*
Spangler, Miller Brant *science and technology analyst, planner, consultant*
Spector, Melbourne Louis *management consultant*
Spivak, Alvin A. *retired public relations executive*
Sponsler, George Curtis, III *research administrator, lawyer*
Sprott, Richard Lawrence *foundation administrator, researcher*
Stadtman, Earl Reece *biochemist*
Stetler-Stevenson, William George *pathologist*
Stokes, Arnold Paul *mathematics educator*
Stoner, Gerald Lee *neurovirologist, medical researcher*
Strickler, Scott Michael *lawyer*
Striner, Herbert Edward *economics educator*
Sturtz, Donald Lee *physician, naval officer*
Summers, Donald Fredrick *cancer research center administrator*
Tabor, Herbert *biochemist*
Talbot, Bernard *government medical research facility official, physician*
Tanenbaum, Jill Nancy *graphic designer*
Tape, Gerald Frederick *former association executive*
Taylor, John Darryl *computer scientist*
Taylor, William Jesse, Jr. *international studies educator, research center executive*
Terragno, Paul James *information industry executive*
Thursz, Daniel *retired service organization executive, consultant*
Tilley, Carolyn Bittner *technical information specialist*
Toomey, Thomas Murray *lawyer*
Trus, Benes Louis *structural chemist*
†Tuorkowski, Robert John *hydrogeologist*
Twiss, John Russell, Jr. *federal government agency executive*
Underwood, Brenda S. *microbiologist, grants administrator*
Ursano, Robert Joseph *psychiatrist*
Vaitukaitis, Judith Louise *medical research administrator*
van der Linden, Frank Morris *historian*
Van Dyke, Joseph Gary Owen *computer consulting executive*
Varmus, Harold Eliot *government health institutes administrator, educator*
Varricchio, Claudette Goulet *health science administrator, researcher*
Vaughan, Martha *biochemist*
Veniard, Jose M. *bank officer*
Vest, George Southall *diplomat*
Vigil, Eugene Leon *federal agency administrator, cell biologist*
Wagner, Cynthia Gail *editor, writer*
Waldmann, Thomas Alexander *medical research scientist, physician*
Walker, Mallory *real estate executive*
Walleigh, Robert Shuler *retired consultant*
Wasilewski, Vincent Thomas *retired lawyer*
Webster, Henry deForest *neuroscientist*
Weinberger, Alan David *corporate executive*
Weiss, George Herbert *mathematician, consultant*
Wente, Van Arthur *consultant, retired government official*
Wertheimer, Franc *retired corporate executive*
Western, Karl August *physician, epidemiologist*
Whaley, Storm Hammond *retired government official, consultant*
Wheeler, Porter King *economist*
Willner, Dorothy *anthropologist, educator*
Wimmel, Kenneth Carl *writer*
Wishart, Leonard Plumer, III *army officer*
Witkop, Bernhard *chemist*
Wolfbein, Seymour Louis *economist, educator*
Woolley, George Walter *biologist, geneticist, educator*
Work, Henry Harcus *physician, educator*
Wright, Helen Patton *professional society administrator*
Wright, James Roscoe *chemist*
Wu, Changyou *immunologist, educator*
Wurtz, Robert Henry *neuroscientist*
Wysocki, Annette B. *nurse scientist, educator*
Yaffe, Sumner Jason *pediatrician, research center administrator, educator*
Yager, Joseph Arthur, Jr. *economist*
Yamada, Kenneth Manao *cell biologist*
Young, Frank Edward *former federal agency administrator, religious organization administrator*
Zierdt, Charles Henry *microbiologist*
Zimmerberg, Joshua Jay *cellular biophysicist*
Zwanzig, Robert Walter *chemist, physical science educator*

Bladensburg
†Gordon, Pamela Ann Wence *piano teacher*

Bowie
Boland, Gerald Lee *health facility financial executive*
Cohn, Harvey *mathematician*
Lower, Philip Edward *lawyer*
Miller, M. Sammye *history educator*
Purcell, Steven Richard *international management consultant, engineer, economist*
Sterling, Richard Leroy *English and foreign language educator*
Stone, Edward Harris, II *landscape architect*
Stultz, Katherine Diane *genealogical society administrator*
Tobin, Charles Fulton, Jr. *information technology executive*
Towle, Laird Charles *book publisher*
Vidal, Pedro Jose *foreign language educator*

Bozman
Peterson, H(arry) William *chemicals executive, consultant*
Wyatt, Wilson Watkins, Jr. *communications and public affairs executive*

Brandywine
Jacob, Sharon Rose *accountant, consultant*
Jaffe, Morris Edward *insurance executive*

Brookeville
Johns, Warren LeRoi *lawyer*

Brooklandville
Azola, Martin Peter *civil engineer, construction manager*
Kolodny, Abraham Lewis *physician*
Miller, Paul George *computer company executive*

Brunswick
Quesada, Bernard *English educator*

Bryans Road
Boyer, Stephanie Ann *music educator*

Burkittsville
Aughenbaugh, Deborah Ann *mayor, retired educator*

Burtonsville
Covington, Marlow Stanley *retired lawyer*
Frederick, George Francis *manufacturing executive*
Kammeyer, Sonia Margaretha *real estate agent*
Peck, Carol Faulkner *poet, writer, publisher, educator*
Toussaint, Rose Marie *holistic physician, organ transplant surgeon*

Cabin John
Dragoumis, Paul *electric utility company executive*
Gallagher, Hugh Gregory *government affairs author, consultant*
Shropshire, Walter, Jr. *biophysicist emeritus, pastor*
Townsend, John William, Jr. *physicist, retired federal aerospace agency executive*

California
Avram, Henriette Davidson *librarian, government official*
Dobry, Aliki Calirroe *artist*
Jessup, Edwin Harley, III *aerospace engineering executive*

Cambridge
†Eckel, Grason John-Allen *lawyer*
Higgins, Michael Edward *finance executive*
Koch-Eilers, Evamaria Wysk *oceanographer, researcher*
Pierce, Nathaniel W. *minister*

Capitol Heights
McKinney-Ludd, Sarah Lydelle *middle school education, librarian*
Onyejekwe, Chike Onyekachi *physician, medical director*
Pressley, Denise M. *special education educator*

Catonsville
Ahalt, Mary Jane *management consultant*
Loerke, William Carl *art history educator*
Vanderlinde, Raymond Edward *clinical chemist*
Woolley, Alma Schelle *nursing educator*
Wynn, John Charles *clergyman, retired religion educator*
Zumbrun, Alvin John Thomas *law and criminology educator*

Centreville
Amos, James Lysle *photographer*
†Cupani, Jean Evelyn Morgan *elementary education educator*

Chesapeake City
Albert, Harry Francis *investments executive*
Smalley, Stephen Mark *priest*

Chester
Dabich, Eli, Jr. *insurance company executive*
Svahn, John Alfred *government official*

Chestertown
Clarke, Garry Evans *composer, educator, musician, administrator*
Mowell, George Mitchell *lawyer*
Parke, Jo Anne Mark *marketing executive*
Schreiber, Harry, Jr. *management consultant*
Sener, Joseph Ward, Jr. *securities company executive*
Trout, Charles Hathaway *historian, educator*
Wendel, Richard Frederick *economist, educator, consultant*
Williams, Henry Thomas *retired banker, real estate agent*

Cheverly
Murphy, Kathy Jean *nursing administrator*
Wilkes, Deborah Ann *neonatal intensive care nurse*

Chevy Chase
Adler, James Barron *publisher*
Albright, Raymond Jacob *government official*
Allison, Adrienne Amelia *voluntary organization administrator*
Auerbach, Seymour *architect*
Bacon, Donald Conrad *author, editor*
Beilenson, Anthony Charles *former congressman*
Bissinger, Frederick Lewis *retired manufacturing executive, consultant*
Bodman, Richard Stockwell *telecommunications executive*
Brenner, Marcella Siegel *retired education educator*
Broide, Mace Irwin *public affairs consultant*
Broumas, John George *retired banker, retired theatre owner*
Bruder, George Frederick *lawyer*
Bruno, Harold Robinson, Jr. *retired journalist, educator, writer*
Bush, Frederick Morris *federal official*
Chase, Nicholas Joseph *lawyer, educator*
Chaseman, Joel *media executive*
Choppin, Purnell Whittington *research administrator, virology researcher, educator*
Cody, Peter Malcolm *economics, development, management consultant*
Corrigan, Robert Foster *business consultant, retired diplomat*
Cowan, William Maxwell *neurobiologist*
Cron, Theodore Oscar *writer, editor, educator*
Delano, Victor *retired naval officer*
Dulin, Maurine Stuart *volunteer*
Duvall, Bernice Bettum *artist, exhibit coordinator, jewelry designer*
Edelson, Burton Irving *electrical engineer*
Elliott, R Lance *lawyer*
Ellis, Sydney *pharmacological scientist, former pharmacology educator*
Felton, Gordon H. *retired publishing executive*
Ferguson, James Joseph, Jr. *physician, academic administrator, researcher*
Freeman, Harry Louis *investment executive*
†Gaines, Michael Johnston *parole commissioner*
Gavin, James Raphael, III *biochemist*
Gottlieb, H. David *podiatrist*
Greenberg, Robert Milton *retired psychiatrist*
Harlan, William Robert, Jr. *physician, educator, researcher*
Harter, Donald Harry *research administrator, medical educator*
Hoffman, Kenneth Myron *mathematician, educator*
Holloway, William Jimmerson *retired educator*
Hudson, Anthony Webster *retired federal agency administrator, minister*
Hudson, Ralph P. *physicist*
Hunt, Frederick Talley Drum, Jr. *association executive*
Ikenberry, Henry Cephas, Jr. *lawyer*
Kainen, Jacob *artist, former museum curator*
Ketcham, Orman Weston *lawyer, former judge*
Kingsley, Nathan *journalist, consultant, educator*
Klain, Ronald Alan *lawyer*
Korth, Penne Percy *ambassador*
Kranking, Margaret Graham *artist*
Kriegsman, Alan M. *retired critic*
Krist, Gary Michael *writer*
Kullen, Shirley Robinowitz *psychiatric epidemiologist, consultant*
Lee, Edward Brooke, Jr. *real estate executive, fund raiser*
†Lewis, Jon Roderick *political advisor*
†Lubalin, Eve *legislative staff aide*
Lukens, Alan Wood *retired ambassador and foreign service officer*
Lyons, Ellis *retired lawyer*
Mansfield, Julian Peter *city manager*
Michaelis, Michael *management and technical consultant*
Montedonico, Joseph *lawyer*
Murphy, Robert Patrick *physician, ophthalmic researcher*
†Neiberger, Ami Dawn *public relations executive*
Norwood, Bernard *economist*
Norwood, Janet Lippe *economist*
†O'Leary, Hazel R. *former federal official, lawyer*
Ostar, Allan William *academic administrator, higher education consultant*
Oudens, Gerald Francis *architect, architectural firm executive*
Paul, Carl Frederick *lawyer, former judge*
Pitofsky, Robert *federal agency administrator, law educator*
Pogue, John Marshall *physician, editor, researcher*
Pogue, Mary Ellen E. (Mrs. L(loyd) Welch Pogue) *youth and community worker*
Posnick, Jeffrey Craig *plastic surgeon*
Prince, Julius S. (Bud Prince) *retired foreign service reserve officer*
Promisel, Nathan E. *materials scientist, metallurgical engineer*
Quinn, Eugene Frederick *government official, clergyman*
Riley, John Winchell, Jr. *consulting sociologist*
Roberts, Clyde Francis *business executive*
Rockwell, Theodore *nuclear engineer*
Romansky, Monroe James *physician, educator*
Rose, John Charles *physician, educator*
Rosenbaum, Alvin Robert *writer, regional planner*
Sampas, Dorothy Myers *government official*
Sapin, Burton Malcolm *political science educator, foreign policy analyst*
Sauer, Richard John *non-profit executive*
Saul, B. Francis, II *bank executive*
Schlegel, John Frederick *management consultant, speaker, trainer*
Shipler, David Karr *journalist, correspondent, author*
Short, Steve Eugene *engineer*
†Shosteck, Ruth Dub (Ruth Shosteck) *clinical social worker, educator*
Sinclair, Rolf Malcolm *retired physicist*
Smith, Peter Leonard *diversified financial services company executive*
†Sorenson, Roger A. *international relations consultant*
Toth, Robert Charles *retired polling consultant, journalist*
Walk, Richard David *retired psychology educator*
Weiss, Ernest *federal agency administrator*
Williams, Charles Laval, Jr. *physician, international organization official*
Willner, Ann Ruth *political scientist, educator*
Zurkowski, Paul George *information company executive*

Clarksburg
Gonano, J. Roland *technology research and development manager*

Clarksville
Brancato, Emanuel Leonard *electrical engineering consultant*
Hung, Mei-Jong Chow *social worker*

Clinton
Cruz, Wilhelmina Mangahas *nephrologist educator*
†Grace, René Earle *physician*
†Hamilton, Jaqueline Buckner *artist, landscaper*
Ives, Adriene Diane *real estate executive*
Kennedy, G. Alfred *retired federal agency administrator*
†Sauls, Carlton Rathele *academic administrator*
†Usher, Marcella Denise *management consultant*
Verge, Laurie *museum director, historian*
Ward, Sue Elleanore Fryer *social worker, state agency administrator*

Cobb Island
†Hedrick, Terry Elizabeth *psychologist, researcher*
Rudy, Linda Mae *secondary school educator*
Vanderslice, Joseph Thomas *chemist*

Cockeysville
Bart, Polly Turner *real estate developer*
Breitenecker, Rudiger *pathologist*
Cuninggim, Whitty Daniel *educator*
De Hoff, John Burling *physician, consultant*
Donaho, John Albert *consultant*
Hager, Louise Alger *retired chaplain*
Peirce, Brooke *English language educator*
Shepard, George Leo *sales and marketing executive, consultant*

Cockeysville Hunt Valley
Barr, Irwin Robert *retired aeronautical engineer*
Dans, Peter Emanuel *medical educator*
Edgett, William Maloy *lawyer, labor arbitrator*
Elkin, Lois Shanman *business systems company executive*
Futcher, Palmer Howard *physician, educator*
Simms, Charles Averill *environmental management company executive*
Somerville, Warren Thomas, II *management consultant*
Spinella, J(oseph) John *insurance company executive*
Whitehurst, William Wilfred, Jr. *management consultant*

Colesville
Peterson, William Frank *retired physician, administrator*

College Park
Anderson, John David, Jr. *aerospace engineer*
Anroman, Gilda Marie *assistant director, lecturer, educator*
Antman, Stuart Sheldon *mathematician, educator*
Ayyub, Bilal M. *civil engineering educator, researcher, executive*
Barbe, David Franklin *electrical engineer, educator*
Beasley, Maurine Hoffman *journalism educator, historian*
Benesch, William Milton *molecular physicist, atmospheric researcher, educator*
†Bento, Antonio Miguel R. *banking consultant*
†Berlinski, Edward Gerard *writing educator, writer*
Bouvier, Virginia Marie *foreign language educator, researcher, writer*
Briggs, Sue *academic administrator*
Broadnax, Walter D. *public policy educator*
Brodsky, Marc Herbert *physicist, research and publishing executive*
Burke, Frank Gerard *archivist*
Burns, James MacGregor *political scientist, historian*
†Bushrui, Suheil Badi *educator*
Carton, James Alfred *oceanographer, educator*
Clark, Eugenie *zoologist, educator*
†Collins, Merle *English educator*
Cunniff, Patrick Francis *mechanical engineer*
Czujko, Roman *psychologist, survey researcher*
De Lorenzo, William E. *foreign language educator*
DeMonte, Claudia Ann *artist, educator*
DeSilva, Alan W. *physics educator, researcher*
Diener, Theodor Otto *plant pathologist*
Dieter, George Elwood, Jr. *university official*
Dorsey, John Wesley, Jr. *university administrator, economist*
Dragt, Alexander James *physicist*
Ephremides, Anthony *electrical engineering educator*
Fago, David Paul *psychologist, educator*
Fanning, Delvin Seymour *soil science educator*
Feldman, Robert Harry *health psychology educator*
Fenselau, Catherine Clarke *chemistry educator*
Finkelstein, Barbara *education educator*
Fisher, Michael Ellis *mathematical physicist, chemist*
Fraistat, Neil Richard *English language educator*
†Frank, Howard *college dean*
Franz, Judy R. *physics educator*
Fretz, Thomas A. *agricultural studies educator*
Gantt, Elisabeth *plant biology educator, researcher*
Gass, Saul Irving *educator*
Gaylin, Ned L. *psychology educator*
Gentry, James Walter *chemical engineer, educator*
Geoffroy, Gregory L. *academic administrator*
George, Gerald William *author, administrator*
Gessow, Alfred *aerospace engineer, educator*
Gluckstern, Robert Leonard *physics educator*
Gomery, Douglas *communications educator, writer*
Gordon, Lawrence Allan *accounting educator*
Granatstein, Victor Lawrence *electrical engineer, educator*
Greenberg, Jerrold Selig *health education educator*
Greenberg, Oscar Wallace *physicist, educator*
Griem, Hans Rudolf *physicist, educator*
Grim, Samuel Oram *chemistry educator*

Grunig, James Elmer *communications educator, researcher, public relations consultant*
Gupta, Anil Kumar *management educator*
Gupta, Ashwani Kumar *mechanical engineering educator*
†Gurr, Ted Robert *political science educator, author*
Heath, James Lee *food science educator, researcher*
Helz, George Rudolph *chemistry educator, research center director*
Hiebert, Ray Eldon *educator, author, consultant*
Holder, Sallie Lou *training and meeting management consultant*
Holton, William Milne *English language and literature educator*
†Iozzi, Alessandra *mathematician, educator*
Irwin, George Rankin *physicist, mechanical engineering educator*
Jeffery, William Richard *developmental biology educator, researcher*
Johnson, Haynes Bonner *author, journalist, television commentator*
Just, Richard Eugene *agricultural and resource economics educator consultant*
†Kaplan, Barbara Beigun *university official, educator*
†Kasser, Joseph E. *educational administrator*
Kearney, Philip Charles *biochemist*
Kirk, James Allen *mechanical engineering educator*
Kolodny, Richard *finance educator*
Kundu, Mukul Ranjan *physics and astronomy educator*
Lamone, Rudolph Philip *business educator*
Lapinski, Tadeusz Andrew *artist, educator*
Lee, Chi Hsiang *electrical engineer, educator*
Levine, William Silver *electrical engineering educator*
Lewis, Roger Kutnow *architect, educator, author*
Lightfoot, David William *linguistics educator*
Lin, Hung C. *electrical engineer educator*
Locke, Edwin Allen, III *psychologist, educator*
Lubkin, Gloria Becker *physicist*
Marcus, Steven Irl *electrical engineering educator*
Massey, Thomas Benjamin *educator*
Mc Donald, Frank Bethune *physicist*
McGinnis, Scott Gary *language and linguistics educator*
Miller, Raymond Edward *computer science educator*
Miller, Raymond Jarvis *agronomy educator*
Minker, Jack *computer scientist, educator*
Misner, Charles William *physics educator*
Moss, Lawrence Kenneth *composer, educator*
Mote, Clayton Daniel, Jr. *mechanical engineer, educator, administrator*
Neal, Edward Garrison *lawyer*
Nerlove, Marc Leon *economics educator*
Newcomb, Robert Wayne *electrical engineer educator*
Olson, Keith Waldemar *history educator*
Olver, Frank William John *retired research educator*
Oster, Rose Marie Gunhild *foreign language professional, educator*
Pasch, Alan *philosopher, educator*
Peterson, David Frederick *government agency executive*
Piper, Don Courtney *political science educator*
Polakoff, Murray Emanuel *university dean, economics and finance educator*
Prentice, Ann Ethelynd *university dean*
Presser, Stanley *sociology educator*
Quester, George Herman *political science educator*
Rabin, Herbert *physics educator, university official*
Rasmusson, Eugene Martin *meteorology researcher*
Redish, Edward Frederick *physicist, educator*
Rosenfeld, Azriel *computer science educator, consultant*
Satin, Karen W. *university publications director*
Schelling, Thomas Crombie *economist, educator*
Schneider, Benjamin *psychology educator*
Schwab, Susan Carroll *university dean*
Sigall, Harold Fred *psychology educator*
Silverman, Joseph *chemistry educator, scientist*
Sims, Henry P., Jr. *management educator*
†Skroban, Stacy Brooke *criminology educator*
Skuja, Andris *physics educator*
Snow, George Abraham *physicist*
†Southerland, Wallace, III *academic administrator, consultant*
Spear, Richard Edmund *art history educator*
Sperling, Mindy Toby *social sciences and bilingual education educator*
Stark, Francis C(io), Jr. *horticulturist, educator*
Stehman, Betty Kohls *financial and management consultant*
Stewart, Teresa Elizabeth *elementary school educator*
Stover, Carl Frederick *foundation executive*
Struna, Nancy L. *social historian*
Szymanski, Edna Mora *rehabilitation psychology and special education educator*
Taylor, Leonard Stuart *engineering educator, consultant*
Thirumalai, Devarajan *physical sciences researcher, educator*
Toll, John Sampson *university president, physics educator*
Turner, Mark Bernard *English language educator*
Ulmer, Melville Jack *economist, educator*
Vandersall, John Henry *dairy science educator*
Wasserman, Paul *library and information science educator*
Weart, Spencer Richard *historian*
Webb, Richard Alan *physicist*
Weil, Raymond Richard *soil scientist*
White, Marilyn Domas *information science educator*
Whittemore, Edward Reed, II *poet, retired educator*
Williams, Aubrey Willis *anthropology educator*
Williams, Gary *collegiate basketball team coach*
Winik, Jay B. *writer, political scientist, consultant*
Winton, Calhoun *literature educator*
Yaney, George *history educator*
Yorke, James Alan *chaos mathematician*
Younger, Deirdre Ann *pharmacist*
Zen, E-an *research geologist, educator*

Columbia

†Arnold, Karen L. *writer, consultant*
Askew, Laurin Barker, Jr. *architect*
Bailey, John Martin *retired transportation planner, educator*
Bareis, Donna Lynn *biochemist, pharmacologist*
Barrow, Lionel Ceon, Jr. *communications and marketing consultant*
Beaudin, Christy Louise *health care administrator, consultant*
Bond, Gorman Morton *ornithologist, researcher*
Bruley, Duane Frederick *academic administrator, consultant, engineer*
Cargo, William Ira *ambassador, retired*
Carr, Charles Jelleff *pharmacologist, educator, toxicology consultant*
Clark, Billy Pat *physicist*
Cook, Stephen Bernard *homebuilding company executive*
Davis, Benjamin George *theologian, educator*
Davis, Janet Marie Gorden *secondary education educator*
Deutsch, Robert William *physicist*
Drummond, LaCreda Renee *journalist*
Fisher, Dale John *chemist, instrumentation and medical diagnostic device investigator*
Folkenberg, Lois Waxter *principal, educator, psychologist*
Franks, David A. *computer engineer*
Gottfeld, Gunther Max *retired urban mass transit official, consultant*
Gray, Kirk Lamond *social investment firm executive, anthropologist*
Gregorie, Corazon Arzalem *operations supervisor*
†Grill, Stephen Elliott *neuroscientist, neurologist, educator*
Hall, Wiley A. *columnist, journalist*
Harrison, Elza Stanley *medical association executive*
Hayes, Charles Lawton *insurance company executive, holding company executive*
Hilderbrandt, Donald Franklin, II *urban designer, landscape architect, artist*
Hill, Norma Louise *librarian*
Kasprick, Lyle Clinton *volunteer, financial executive*
Kendrick, John Lawrence *software engineer*
Khare, Mohan *chemist*
Kime, J. William *career officer, engineer, ship management executiv*
Klein, Sami Weiner *librarian*
Letaw, Harry, Jr. *technology corporation executive*
Levner, Louis Jules *contract administrator*
Lijinsky, William *biochemist*
†Mack, Kibibi Voloria *history educator*
Madison, Anne Conway *public relations and marketing professional*
Maier, William Otto *martial arts school administrator, educator, consultant*
Margolis, Vivienne O. *psychotherapist*
Marshall, Linda Murphy *linguist, government official*
Maseritz, Guy B. *lawyer*
May, John Raymond *clinical psychologist*
McCuan, William Patrick *real estate company executive*
McDaniel, John Perry *health care company executive*
Peck, Charles Edward *retired construction and mortgage executive*
Pounds, Moses Belt *medical anthropologist*
Queen, Sandy (Sandra Jane Queen) *psychologist, trainer*
†Quinter, Neil F. *legislative staff member*
†Ranasinghe, John Ananda *ecologist, researcher*
Riddle, Mark Alan *child psychiatrist*
Rovelstad, Gordon H. *dentist, researcher*
Scates, Alice Yeomans *former government official, consultant*
Slater, John Blackwell *landscape architect*
Sneck, William Joseph *counseling educator, researcher*
†Spicknall, Joan *music educator*
Spohn, William Gideon, Jr. *mathematician, musician*
Stanek, Gena Stiver *critical care clinical nurse specialist*
Straja, Sorin Radu *chemical engineer, mathematician, computer programmer*
Ulman, Louis Jay *lawyer*
Vassar, John Dixie, Jr. *environmental, radiological, and information technology consultant*
Vu, Cung *chemical engineer*
Whiting, Albert Nathaniel *former university chancellor*
Willging, Paul Raymond *trade association executive*

Crisfield

†Ryan, Jerome Francis *artist*

Crofton

Andrysiak, Frank Louis *videographer*
Harding-Clark, Jessica Rose *public affairs specialist, journalist*
Laurenson, Robert Mark *mechanical engineer*
Ross, E(dwin) Clarke *association executive, educator*
Watson, Robert Tanner *retired physical scientist*

Crownsville

Hanna, James Curtis *state official*
Wright, Harry Forrest, Jr. *retired banker*

Cumberland

†Decosta, Frank *artist*
Heckert, Paul Charles *sociologist, educator*
Jancuk, Kathleen Frances *educational administrator*
Johnson, Rex Ray *automotive education educator*
Mazzocco, Gail O'Sullivan *nursing educator*
Shelton, Bessie Elizabeth *school system administrator*
Wolford, Nancy Lou *medical and surgical nurse*

Damascus

Ventola, Dean Samuel *architect, architectural company executive*

Darnestown

Gottlieb, Julius Judah *podiatrist*
Hoffer, James Brian *physicist, consultant*

Davidsonville

Mahaffey, Redge Allan *movie producer, director, writer, actor, scientist*
Montague, Brian John *consulting company executive*

Dayton

Fischell, Robert Ellentuch *physicist*

Delmar

Ennis, Sharon Lynn *elementary education educator*

Denton

Camper, Michelle Gwen *community health nurse*
Doster, Rose Eleanor Wilhelm *artist*
†Jensen, Christian Edward *family practice physician*

Dowell

Reeves, Connie Lynn *writer, retired army officer*

Dunkirk

Vining, Pierre Herbert *real estate consultant*

Easton

Bronson, John Orville, Jr. *librarian*
Buescher, Adolph Ernst (Dolph Buescher) *aerospace company executive*
Burns, Michael Joseph *operations and sales-marketing executive*
Crowder, Jo Anne Corkran *certified public accountant*
Howard, Ann Hubbard *insurance agency executive*
Jacobs, Michael Joseph *lawyer*
Kehoe, Stephen H. *lawyer*
Maffitt, James Strawbridge *lawyer*
Peterson, James Kenneth *manufacturing company executive*
Schisler, Kenneth David *state legislator*
Snow, James Byron, Jr. *physician, research administrator*
†Wilson, Laura Ann *newspaper editor*

Edgewater

Hines, Anson H. *museum director*
Malley, Kenneth Cornelius *retired military officer, corporation executive*
Simons, Ross B. *environmental center director*

Edgewood

Tucker, Terry L. *critical care clinical nurse specialist*

Elkridge

Calton, Sandra Jeane *accountant*
Slatkin, Murray *paint sundry distribution executive*
Szilagyi, Sherry Ann *psychotherapist, lawyer*

Elkton

Harrington, Benjamin Franklin, III *retired business consultant*
Howe, Patricia Moore *adult education educator*
Jasinski-Caldwell, Mary L. *company executive*
Scherf, Christopher N. *trade association administrator*

Ellicott City

Alonso, Diane Lindwarm *cognitive psychologist*
Benton, Bill Browning *human services consultant*
Clive, Craig N. *compensation executive*
Closson, Walter Franklin *prosecutor*
†Cole, Deborah S. *psychologist*
Faulstich, Albert Joseph *banking consultant*
Gagnon, Robert Michael *engineering executive, educator*
Galinsky, Deborah Jean *county official*
Gleaves, Leon Rogers *marketing and sales executive*
Harding, John Walter *art critic*
Henry, Edwin Maurice, Jr. *lawyer, electrical engineer, consultant*
Huey, J(oseph) Wistar, III *import/export executive*
Leonard, Florence Jones *retired university graduate program director*
Longuemare, R. Noel, Jr. *former federal official*
Perry, Nancy Trotter *former telecommunications company executive*
Powell, Lillian Marie *retired music educator*
Raum, Bernard Anthony *lawyer, county court official, educator*
Robison, Susan Miller *psychologist, speaker, consultant*
Webster, Sharon B. *economist*
Zimmer, Janie Louise *school system administrator*

Elliott City

Morris, Stephen Brent *mathematician*

Emmitsburg

†Brown, Carrye Burley *federal agency administrator*
Collinge, William Joseph *humanities educator*
Houston, George R. *college president*
Stay, Byron Lee *rhetoric educator, college administrator*

Fallston

Lewis, Howard Franklin *chiropractor*

Finksburg

†Giuffre, Anthony T. *television producer, lighting director*
Konigsberg, Robert Lee *electrical engineer*

Forest Hill

†Ferretti, Kevin Michael *human resource director*
Klein, Michael Jeffrey *consumer products company executive*
Stuempfle, Arthur Karl *physical science manager*

Forestville

†Thompson, Elwood Ray *union executive, career consultant*

Fort George G Meade

Kwik-Kostek, Christine Irene *physician, air force officer*
Nobles, Danny Gene *army officer*
Schmitt, Robert Lee *computer scientist*

Fort Washington

Alexander, Gary R. *lawyer, state legislator, lobbyist*
Behrens, James William *physicist, administrator, author*
Cameron, Rita Giovannetti *writer, publisher*
Caveny, Leonard Hugh *mechanical engineer, aerospace scientist, consultant*
Coffey, Matthew B. *trade association executive*
Cross, Rita Faye *librarian, early childhood educator, writer*
Eddy, Elsbeth Marie *retired government official, statistician*
Gleason, John Thomas *consultant software development planner*
Hankerson, Charlie Edward, Jr. *music educator*
McCafferty, James Arthur *sociologist*
Miller, John Richard *interior designer*
Schlotzhauer, Virginia Hughes *parliamentary consultant*
Smoot, Burgess Howard *federal official*
Stiver, William Earl *retired government administrator*
Weaver, Frank Cornell *government agency administrator*
Wilcox, Richard Hoag *information scientist*

Frederick

Aiuto, Russell *science education consultant*
Alvord, W. Gregory *statistician*
Anderson, Arthur Osmund *pathologist, immunologist, army officer*
Archibald, Fred John *newspaper executive*
Boyd, Joseph Aubrey *communications company executive*
Byron, Beverly Butcher *congresswoman*
Carnochan, John Low, Jr. *retired aluminum company executive, consultant*
Carton, Robert John *environmental scientist*
Church, Martha Eleanor *retired academic administrator, scholar*
Cragg, Gordon Mitchell *government chemist*
Creasia, Donald Anthony *toxicologist, researcher*
Cuffie, Kevin Lamont *academic administrator, educational consultant*
Deale, Robert Elmer, Jr. *state official*
Delaplaine, George Birely, Jr. *newspaper editor, cable television executive*
Docksteader, Karen Kemp *marketing executive*
Duncan, Stephen Mack *lawyer*
Garver, Robert Vernon *research physicist*
Hamilton, Rhoda Lillian Rosen *guidance counselor, language educator, consultant*
Hein, David *religion educator*
Hindman, Margaret Horton *college administrator*
Hoff, Charles Worthington, III *banker*
Hogan, Ilona Modly *lawyer*
Klein, Elaine Charlotte *educational administrator*
Knisely, Ralph Franklin *retired microbiologist*
Kung, Hsiang-fu *health facility administrator*
Nayyar, Mohinder Lal *mechanical engineer*
†Offutt, Thomas Francis *insurance company executive*
†Pearson, Jennie Sue *retired government administrator*
Pyne, Frederick Wallace *genealogist, clergyman, retired civil engineer, retired mathematics educator*
Rock, Sandra Kaye *retail executive*
Schricker, Ethel Killingsworth *retired business management consultant*
Shackelford, Dan Elbert *federal procurement analyst*
Smith, Sharron Williams *chemistry educator*
Szeliga, Jan Stefan *chemist*
Wolf, Donald Joseph *industrial engineer*
†Zielinski, John Paul *archeologist, educator*

Friendship

Clagett, Diana Wharton Sinkler *museum docent*

Frostburg

Allen, Philip Mark *arts and humanities educator, dean, writer*
Coward, Patricia Ann *language educator*
Gira, Catherine Russell *university president*
Tam, Francis Man Kei *physics educator*

Fulton

Johnson, Virgil Evans, Jr. *research scientist*

Gaithersburg

Adams, James Michael *nuclear physicist*
Bingham, Raymond Joseph *newborn intensive care nurse*
Boddiger, George Cyrus *insurance corporate executive, consultant*
Cahn, John Werner *metallurgist, educator*
Caplin, Jerrold Leon *health physicist*
Carasso, Alfred Sam *mathematician*
Carey, John Edward *information services executive*
Carter, Kenneth Charles *geneticist*
Caswell, Randall Smith *physicist*
Celotta, Robert James *physicist*
Chi, Peter Howard *physicist*
Chin, James Ying *corporate executive*
Cookson, Alan Howard *electrical engineer, researcher*
Costrell, Louis *physicist*
Ehrlich, Clifford John *hotel executive*
Ewing, Frank Marion *lumber company executive, industrial land developer*
Flickinger, Harry Harner *organization and business executive, management consultant*
Fong, Jeffrey Tse-Wei *mechanical engineer*
French, Judson Cull *government official*
Frome, David Herman *dentist*
Gilsinn, David Edmund *mathematician, researcher*
Golden, Thomas Rutledge *psychotherapist, author*
Gravatt, Claude Carrington, Jr. *research and development executive*
Grecich, Daryl George *marketing communications executive*
Hall, Arthur Raymond, Jr. *minister*
Hamer, Walter Jay *chemical consultant, science writer*
Hansen, Paul Walden *conservation organization executive*
Harman, George Gibson *physicist, consultant*
Hegyeli, Ruth Ingeborg Elisabeth Johnsson *pathologist, government official*
Hertz, Harry Steven *government official*
Hoferek, Mary Judith *database administrator*
Horman, Karen Loeb *elementary education educator*
Hougen, Jon Torger *physical chemist, researcher*
Hsu, Stephen Ming *materials scientist, chemical engineer*
Hubbell, John Howard *radiation physicist*
Jacox, Marilyn Esther *chemist*
Jahanmir, Said *materials scientist, mechanical engineer*
Jefferson, David *computer scientist*
Johnson, Frederick Carroll *federal government executive*
Johnson, George H. *financial services company executive*
Johnson, W. Taylor *physician*
Kammer, Raymond Gerard, Jr. *government official*
†Keifer, Amy Jo *educator*
Kemmerer, Sharon Jean *computer systems analyst*
Levine, Robert Sidney *chemical engineer, consultant*
Liau, Gene *medical educator*
Mella, Gordon Weed *physician*
Nemecek, Albert Duncan, Jr. *retail company executive, investment banker, management consultant*
Nickle, Dennis Edwin *electronics engineer, church deacon*
Olejar, Paul Duncan *former information science administrator*
Peele, Roger *hospital administrator*
Phillips, Leo Harold, Jr. *lawyer*
Phillips, William Daniel *physicist*
Pierce, Daniel Thornton *physicist*
†Pine, Martin E. *management consultant, technology consultant*
Rabinow, Jacob *electrical engineer, consultant*
Reader, Joseph *physicist*
Rollence, Michele Lynette *molecular biologist*
Rosenblatt, Joan Raup *mathematical statistician*
Rosenstein, Marvin *public health administrator*
Ross, Sherman *psychologist, educator*

Rowe, Joseph Charles *elementary education educator, administrator*
Rupert, (Lynn) Hoover *minister*
Ruth, James Perry *financial planning executive*
Semerjian, Hratch Gregory *research and development executive*
Sengers, Johanna M. H. Levelt *thermophysicist*
Shull, Michael Slade *lecturer, writer, researcher*
Smith, Ruth Lillian Schluchter *librarian*
Snell, Jack Eastlake *federal agency administrator*
Stever, Horton Guyford *aerospace scientist and engineer, educator, consultant*
Taylor, Barry Norman *physicist*
Tenney, Lisa Christine Gray *healthcare administrator*
Tesk, John Aloysius *materials scientist*
Verkouteren, Robert Michael *chemist*
†Wang, Francis Wei-Yu *biomedical materials scientist, researcher*
Warshaw, Stanley Irving *government official*
Watanabe, Kyoichi A(loysius) *chemist, researcher, pharmacology educator*
Wicklein, John Frederick *journalist, educator*
Wiederhorn, Sheldon Martin *materials scientist engineer*
Wiese, Wolfgang Lothar *physicist*
Wisniewski, John William *mining engineer, bank engineering executive*
Wright, Richard Newport, III *civil engineer, retired government official*
Yang, Xiang Yang *engineer, entrepreneur*

Gambrills
Trimnal, Wanda Lee *secondary school educator*

Garrett Park
Baldwin, Calvin Benham, Jr. *retired medical research administrator*
Kornberg, Warren Stanley *science journalist*
Lincicome, David Richard *biomedical and animal scientist*
McDowell, Eugene Charles *systems analyst, bioethicist*
Melville, Robert Seaman *chemist*
Silbergeld, Sam *psychiatrist*

Germantown
Chambers, Helen McGraw *pianist*
Harris, William Norman *music educator*
Hill-Fessenden, Anne Lynn *multi-faceted food and beverage consultant*
Kirchner, Peter Thomas *nuclear medicine physician, educator, consultant*
Lee, Lin-Nan *communications engineer, engineering executive*
Nazarian, Ashot *chemical physicist, consultant, researcher*
Norcross, Marvin Augustus *veterinarian, retired government agency official*
Peratt, Anthony Lee *electrical engineer, physicist*
Searles, Thomas Daniel *society administrator*
Shaw, Jack Allen *communications company executive*
Singh, Braj Kumar *mechanical engineer*
Steadman, Stephen Geoffrey *physicist*
Stroud, Nancy Iredell *retired secondary school educator, freelance writer, editor*
†Taylor, Douglas Howard *translator*
Weiner, Claire Muriel *freelance writer*

Glen Arm
Harris, Benjamin Louis *chemical engineer, consultant*
Jackson, Theodore Marshall *retired oil company executive*
Lotz, George Michael *retired computer graphics executive, graphic designer, photographer*

Glen Burnie
Cole, Ronald Clark *lawyer*
Colvin, John Alexander *campus minister*
†Gaither, Nina Denise *special education educator*
Kirk, James Graham *pastor*
Oldfield, Allison Lee *physician, radiologist, educator*
Ruth, Shiela Grant *music educator*
Smalts, David H. *civil engineer*
Smith, John Stanley *lawyer, mediator*
Zabetakis, Thomas John *federal agency administrator*

Glen Echo
Stevenson, A. Brockie *retired artist*

Glencoe
Weeks, Anne Macleod *English language eductor, education director*

Glenelg
Williams, Donald John *research physicist*

Glenwood
Rossetti, Linda Elaine *special education educator*

Grasonville
Andrews, Archie Moulton *government official*
Prout, George Russell, Jr. *medical educator, urologist*

Greenbelt
Auerbach, Bob Shipley *librarian*
Boarman, Gerald L. *principal*
Brugger, George Albert *lawyer*
Chasanow, Deborah K. *federal judge*
Cooper, Robert Shanklin *engineering executive, former government official*
Degnan, John James, III *physicist*
Ervin, David Eugene *economist, educator, researcher*
Green, Patricia Pataky *school system administrator, consultant*
Greenwald, Andrew Eric *lawyer*
Häkkinen, Sirpa Marja Anneli *oceanographer*
Hill, Ben *broadcast executive*
Hogensen, Margaret Hiner *librarian, consultant*
Hollis, Jan Michael *astrophysicist, scientific computer analyst*
Holt, Stephen S. *astrophysicist*
Jascourt, Hugh D. *lawyer, arbitrator, mediator*
Kalnay, Eugenia *university administrator, meteorologist*
†Keir, Duncan W. *federal judge*
Krueger, Arlin James *physicist*
Ku, Jentung *mechanical and aerospace engineer*
Levitt, Gerald Steven *engineering services executive*
†Mannes, Paul *chief bankruptcy judge*
Maran, Stephen Paul *astronomer*
Mather, John Cromwell *astrophysicist*
Messitte, Peter Jo *judge*
Morris, Joseph Anthony *health science association administrator*
Mumma, Michael Jon *physicist*
Obamogie, Mercy A. *physician*
Ormes, Jonathan Fairfield *astrophysicist, science administrator, researcher*
Parkinson, Claire L. *climatologist*
Ramaty, Reuven Robert *physicist, researcher*
†Schulze, Jillyn K. *federal judge*
Simpson, Joanne Malkus *meteorologist*
Steiner, Mark David *engineering executive*
Stief, Louis John *chemist*
Thomas, Lindsey Kay, Jr. *research ecology biologist, educator, consultant*
Whitlock, Laura Alice *research scientist*
Williams, Alexander, Jr. *judge*
Wood, H(oward) John, III *astrophysicist, astronomer*

Hagerstown
Baer, John Metz *entrepreneur*
†Beachley, Donald E. *federal judge*
Berkson, Jacob Benjamin *lawyer, author, conservationist*
Bever, Melanie Sue *credit company manager*
Blickenstaff, Danny Jay *retired civilian military employee*
Coles, Robert Nelson, Sr. *religious organization administrator*
†Cost, Francis Howard, Jr. *physician*
Fisher, Charles Worley *editor*
†Foor, Jane A. *school counselor*
Harrison, Lois Smith *hospital executive, educator*
†Kelly, Philip A. *bank executive*
McCoy, Mildred Brookman *elementary eduation educator, retired*
†Monzur, Mohammed Ali *nephrologist*
†Noia, Alan James *utility company executive*
Paxton, Alice Adams *artist, architect and interior designer*
Peters, Marjorie Spanninger *historical society executive*
Rickard, Edythe *registered nurse, consumer advocate*
Shuttleworth, Rebecca Scott *English language educator*
Thomas, Yvonne Shirey *family and consumer science educator*
Warner, Harry Backer, Jr. *retired journalist, freelance writer*

Hancock
Popenoe, John *horticultural consultant, retired botanical garden administrator*

Hanover
Schmidt, Sandra Jean *financial analyst*

Havre De Grace
Huang, Yung-Hui *chemical engineer*
†Jay, Peter Augustus *writer, farmer*
Wetter, Edward *broadcasting executive*

Highland
Varga, Deborah Trigg *music educator, entertainment company owner*

Hollywood
Hertz, Roy *physician, educator, researcher*
Powledge, Fred Arlius *freelance writer*

Hughesville
Ignatavicius, Donna Dennis *geriatrics and case management consultant*

Hunt Valley
Kinstlinger, Jack *engineering executive, consultant*
Krotiuk, William John *mechanical engineer*
Moore, Jeffrey *chemical information scientist*
Tull, Willis Clayton, Jr. *librarian*

Huntingtown
†Emberland, Gorm Petter *software developer, computer programmer*

Hurlock
Bowens, Emma Marie *elementary education educator*

Hyattsville
Bell, Harriette Elizabeth *stock agency administrator*
Bender, Howard Jeffrey *software engineering educator*
Bender, Randi Laine *occupational therapist*
Dukes, Rebecca Weathers (Becky Dukes) *musician, singer, songwriter*
Embody, Daniel Robert *biometrician*
Ilogu, Edmund Christopher Onyedum *priest*
Moylan, John L. *secondary school principal*
Rodgers, Mary Columbro *academic administrator, English educator, author*
Rooney, Peggy Ann *executive secretary*
Rummel, Edgar Ferrand *retired lawyer*
Sindoris, Arthur Richard *electronics engineer, government official*
Smith, Irving *gerontologist*
Sondik, Edward J. *health science administrator*
Spiegel, Robert Alan *lawyer*

Ijamsville
Chen, Philip S., Jr. *government official*
Vickers, James Hudson *veterinarian, research pathologist*

Indian Head
Wamsley, Barbara Simborski *public administration educator*

Jefferson
Beall, James Robert *toxicologist*

Joppa
Bates, Charles Benjamin *elementary school administrator*
Kott, Beverly Parat *financial counselor*
Rehrig, William Harold *band and orchestra director*

Kensington
†Banner, Marilyn Ruth *artist, educator*
Daisley, William Prescott *lawyer*
Dauster, William Gary *lawyer, economist*
Glower, Raphael *personnel management administrator, program analyst*
Hayunga, Mary Ann *women's health nurse*
Hudson, Yvonne Morton *elementary education educator*
Hum, Vance York *technology consulting executive*
Hurt, Frank *labor union administrator*
Jackson, William David *research executive*
†Kelley, Patrick Alan *neurologist, educator*
Lisle, Martha Oglesby *retired mathematics educator*
Marienthal, George *telecommunications company executive*
Mathias, Joseph Marshall *lawyer, judge*
Rather, Lucia Porcher Johnson *library administrator*
Rosenthal, Alan Sayre *former government official*
Schmerling, Erwin Robert *counselor, retired physicist*
Suraci, Charles Xavier, Jr. *retired federal agency administrator, aerospace education consultant*

Kingsville
Pullen, Keats A., Jr. *electronics engineer*

La Plata
Firehock, Barbara A. *interior designer*
Fisher, Gail Feimster *government official*
†Johnson, Diane Jones *librarian*
†Wyman, Kenneth F. *construction executive*

Landover
Fortson-Rivers, Tina E. (Thomasena Elizabeth Fortson-Rivers) *information technology specialist*
†Strickland, Rodney *professional basketball player*
†Unseld, Westley Sissel *professional sports team executive, former professional basketball coach, former professional basketball player*

Lanham
Criscimagna, Ned Henry *mechanical engineer*
Hencke, Paul Gerard *editor, writer, broadcaster*
†Parker, William H., Jr. *telecommunications industry executive*

Lanham Seabrook
Banks, William Ashton *librarian*
Barnes, Margaret Anderson *business consultant*
Brasoveanu, Dan *systems analyst*
Cook, Linda Kay *critical care nurse*
Corrothers, Helen Gladys *criminal justice official*
Kari, Daven Michael *religion educator*
Littlefield, Roy Everett, III *association executive, legal educator*
Lyons, James Edward *publishing executive*
McCarthy, Kevin John *lawyer*
Yen, Wen Liang *aerospace engineer*

Largo
†Adams, Mark *retail executive*
Freeman, Ernest Robert *engineering executive*
Isom, Virginia Annette Veazey *nursing educator*
†Krauser, Peter B. *lawyer, political party executive*
†Schwartz, Mark *home improvement stores executive*
Wright, R. Russell *educator, musician*

Laurel
Avery, William Hinckley *physicist, chemist*
Babin, Steven Michael *atmospheric scientist, researcher*
Barcome, Marigail *special education educator*
Brandhorst, Wesley Theodore *information manager*
Brubaker, Lou Ann *advertising executive, consultant*
Chrismer, Ronald Michael *federal agency administrator*
Eaton, Alvin Ralph *aeronautical and systems engineer, research and development administrator*
Fox, Dawne Marie *safety scientist*
Gieszl, Louis Roger *mathematician*
Highman, Barbara *dermatologist*
Kossiakoff, Alexander *chemist*
Kuska, John Joseph, Jr. *accountant*
Landis, Donna Marie *nursing administrator, women's health nurse*
Lang, Colleen Anne *secondary education educator*
Lui, Anthony Tat Yin *physicist*
Maurer, Richard Hornsby *physicist*
Rorie, Conrad Jonathan *scientist, naval officer*
Sharpless, Joseph Benjamin *former county official*
†Spjut, Richard Wayne *botanist, consultant*
Wales, Patrice *school system administrator*
Zhang, Jun *pathologist, researcher*

Laytonsville
McDowell, Donna Schultz *lawyer*

Leonardtown
McIntosh, Heather Aileen *biologist*

Lexington Park
Donely, George Anthony Thomas, III *economist, consultant*
Lacer, Alfred Antonio *lawyer, educator*
Lineback, Harvey Lee *media specialist*
Sprague, Edward Auchincloss *retired association executive, economist*
†Swanson, Dane Craig *career officer*

Libertytown
Lindblad, Richard Arthur *retired health services administrator, drug abuse epidemiologist*

Linthicum
O'Brien, Sean Delaney *acoustical engineer*
Ramachandran, Anand *operations management executive*

Linthicum Heights
Fanseen, James Foster *lawyer*
Lavin, Charles Blaise, Jr. *association executive*
Skillman, William Alfred *consulting engineering executive*

Lusby
Eshelman, Ralph Ellsworth *maritime historian, educator, consultant*
Hutchins, Edith Elizabeth *payroll administrator*
Ladd, Culver Sprogle *secondary education educator*

Lutherville
†Buchholz, David W. *neurologist, headache specialist, educator*
Eisenberg, Joseph Martin *psychologist*
Goodman, Valerie Dawson *psychiatric social worker*
Mc Kenney, Walter Gibbs, Jr. *lawyer, publishing company executive*
†Moses, Howard *neurologist*
Revelle, Donald Gene *manufacturing and health care company executive, consultant*
Sagerholm, James Alvin *retired naval officer*

Lutherville Timonium
Cappiello, Frank Anthony, Jr. *investment advisor*
Cedrone, Louis Robert, Jr. *critic*
Kolker, Roger Russell *insurance executive*
Levasseur, William Ryan *lawyer*
Miller, John E. *cardiovascular surgeon*
Muuss, Rolf Eduard *retired psychologist, educator*
Park, Lee Crandall *psychiatrist*
Sternberger, Ludwig Amadeus *neurologist, educator*

Madison
Hoffman, Alicia Coro *retired federal executive*

Mechanicsville
Henderson, Madeline Mary (Berry) (Berry Henderson) *chemist, researcher, consultant*

Millersville
Martin, Donald William *psychiatrist*
†Schulmeyer, G(eorge) Gordon *information systems executive, consultant*
Vlavianos, John G. *retired federal agency administrator*

Mitchellville
Blough, Roy *retired economist*
Embree, Ainslie Thomas *history educator*
Hagans, Robert Reginald, Jr. *financial executive*
Spieth, Martha Maxwell *writer*

Monkton
Kernan, Pamela Lynne *critical care nurse*
Mountcastle, Vernon Benjamin *neurophysiologist*

Monrovia
Tokar, John Michael *retired oceanographer, ocean engineer*

Montgomery Village
Avedisian, Archie Harry *community organization executive*
Byrne, James Edward *international banking expert*
Kushner, Lawrence Maurice *physical chemist*
Malhotra, Deepak *accountant*

Mount Airy
Collins, Henry James, III *insurance company executive*
McCoskey, William L. *automotive executive*

Mount Lake Park
McClintock, Donna Mae *social worker*

New Market
Billig, Frederick Stucky *mechanical engineer*

Newark
Stidman, John Scales *school psychologist*

North Bethesda
Anderson, Owen Raymond *scientific and educational organization executive*
Halstead, Scott Barker *medical research administrator*
†McCarn, Davis Barton *computer company executive, mathematician*
Schwinn, Steven David *lawyer, mediator*
Sherman, Deane Murray *culture organization administrator*
Stearman, William Lloyd *military association executive, author*
Trachtenberg, Alan I. *public health physician*
White, Bonnie Havana *retired federal agency official*

North East
Marie, Linda *artist, photographer*

North Potomac
Dorsey, William Walter *aerospace engineer, engineering executive*
Kehoe, Patrick Emmett *law librarian, law educator*
Lide, David Reynolds *handbook and database editor*
Willis, Norman Hunt *new media writer, director, producer*

Ocean City
Skidmore, Linda Carol *science and engineering consultant*
Wimbrow, Peter Ayers, III *lawyer*

Odenton
Bridges, James D., Sr. *quality manager, former military officer*
Mucha, John Frank *information systems professional*

Olney
Brady, Anita Kelley *training and organizational development executive*
Delmar, Eugene Anthony *architect*
Lee, Daniel Kuhn *economist*
Michael, Jerrold Mark *public health specialist, former university dean, educator*
Weller, Jane Kathleen *emergency nurse*
Westerman, Rosemary Matzzie *nurse, administrator*

Owings Mills
Berg, Barbara Kirsner *health education specialist*
†Billick, Brian *professional football coach*
Burnett, Robert Barry *professional football player*
Disharoon, Leslie Benjamin *retired insurance executive*
Hirsh, Allan Thurman, Jr. *publishing executive*
Hoffman, Craig Allan *finance executive*
Holdridge, Barbara *book publisher*
Hubley, Carole Fierro *family nurse practitioner*
Kelly-Jones, Denise Marie *critical care nurse*
Kissel, William Thorn, Jr. *sculptor*
Modell, Arthur B. *professional football team executive*
Nes, David Gulick *retired diplomat*
Siegel, Bernard *foundation administrator*
Turner, Eric Ray *professional football player*
Walsh, Semmes Guest *retired insurance company executive*

Woodson, Roderick Kevin *professional football player*

Oxford
Radcliffe, George Grove *retired life insurance company executive*
Zachai, Dohrn Dorian *artist*

Oxon Hill
Dunleavy, Kristie Lyn *direct marketing and advertising executive*
Serrette, Cathy Hollenberg *lawyer*
†Shoap, Carla Shipman *community instructional educator*

Parkton
Cummins, Paul Zach, II *insurance company executive*
Fitzgerald, Edwin Roger *physicist, educator*

Parkville
Hill, Milton King, Jr. *lawyer*
Jensen, Arthur Seigfried *consulting engineering physicist*
Munson, Paul Lewis *pharmacologist*

Parsonsburg
Holley, Marie Theresa *medical/surgical nurse*

Pasadena
†Dalton, Frances Marlene *business consultant*
De Pauw, Linda Grant *history educator, publisher*
Yelton, Robert Foster *playwright, poet*
Young, Russell Dawson *physics consultant*

Patuxent River
Adams, Richard Eugene *aerospace engineer, project manager*
Fitzhugh, David Michael *lawyer*
Lockard, John Allen *naval officer*

Perry Point
Yackley, Luke Eugene *nursing administrator, mental health nurse*

Perryville
Ciampaglio, Jeff William *sculptor*

Phoenix
Byrd, Harvey Clifford, III *information management company executive*
Hairston, Walter Albert *school system administrator*
Lade, Poul Vestergaard *civil engineering educator, researcher, consultant*

Port Deposit
McMullen, Stanley Levon *author, composer*

Port Republic
Hanke, Byron Reidt *residential land planning and community associations consultant*
Karol, Eugene Michael *school system administrator*
Miller, Ewing Harry *architect*

Potomac
Baer, Ledolph *oceanographer, meteorologist*
Benton, Kay Myers *sales executive*
Bibby, Douglas Martin *mortgage association executive*
Brewer, Nathan Ronald *veterinarian, consultant*
Broderick, John Caruthers *retired librarian, educator*
Christian, John Kenton *organization executive, publisher, writer, marketing consultant*
Cohen, Trudy Ornstein *adult nurse practitioner, educator*
Conner, Troy Blaine, Jr. *retired lawyer, writer*
Cotton, William Robert *retired dentist*
Crowley, Mary Elizabeth (Mary Elizabeth Crowley-Farrell) *journalist, editor*
†Derricotte, Toi *poet, educator*
DiPentima, Renato Anthony *systems executive*
Dykewicz, Paul Gregory *journalist*
Engelmann, Rudolf Jacob *meteorologist*
Epstein, Edward S. *meteorologist*
Feinstein, Martin *performing arts consultant, art director*
Feldman, Myer *lawyer*
Fink, Daniel Julien *management consultant*
Fischetti, Michael *public administration educator, arbitrator*
Fox, Arthur Joseph, Jr. *editor*
Frey, James McKnight *government official*
Frieder, Gideon *computer science and engineering educator*
Gowda, Narasimhan Ramaiah *financial consultant*
Haddy, Francis John *physician, educator*
Hall, William Darlington *lawyer*
Heller, Peggy Osna *psychotherapist, poetry therapist*
Higgins, Nancy Branscome *management and counseling educator*
Jones, Sidney Lewis *economist, government official*
Jung, Richard Kieth *headmaster*
Karch, Karen Brooke *principal*
Karnow, Stanley *journalist, writer*
Keil, Marilyn Martin *artist*
Kernan, Barbara Desind *senior government executive*
Kessler, Ronald Borek *author*
Latham, Patricia Horan *lawyer*
Leva, Neil Irwin *psychotherapist, hypnotherapist*
Leva, Susan Mary *social worker*
Mapother, Margaret Loudermill *piano educator*
Mason, Dan *broadcast executive*
Meyer, Lawrence George *lawyer*
Millonig, Virginia Layng *health education and publishing company executive*
Mullenbach, Linda Herman *lawyer*
Muntzing, L(ewis) Manning *lawyer*
Neuman, Robert Henry *lawyer*
Newhouse, Alan Russell *retired federal government executive*
Noonan, Patrick Francis *conservation executive*
Pastan, Linda Olenik *poet*
Peter, Phillips Smith *lawyer*
Powell, Robert Dominick *lawyer*
Reynolds, Frank Miller *retired government administrator*
Rhode, Alfred Shimon *business consultant, educator*
Rosenberg, Sarah Zacher *institute arts administration executive, humanities administration consultant*
Rotberg, Iris Comens *social scientist*
Sceery, Beverly Davis *genealogist, writer, educator*
Schonholtz, Joan Sondra Hirsch *banker, civic worker*
Shapiro, Richard Gerald *retired department store executive, consultant*
Shepard, William Seth *government official, diplomat, writer*
Smallwood, Grahame Thomas, Jr. *genealogist*
Sowalsky, Patti Lurie *author*
Stetler, C. Joseph *retired lawyer*
Stupak, Ronald Joseph *dean, management educator, researcher, consultant*
Troffkin, Howard Julian *lawyer*
Vadus, Gloria A. *scientific document examiner*
Ventry, Paul Guerin *physician, government official*
Walker, Charls Edward *economist, consultant*
Wang, An-Ming *composer*
Wartofsky, William Victor *writer*
Waugaman, Richard Merle *psychiatrist, psychoanalyst, educator*
Weiss, Michael David *mathematician, mathematical economist*
Williams, Peter Maclellan *nuclear engineer*

Prince Frederick
Karol, Victoria Diane *educational administrator*

Princess Anne
Franklin, Robert Allen *broadcast executive, radio producer*
Joshi, Jagmohan *agronomist, consultant*
McKinney, Frances Hathaway *university program administrator*

Quantico
Scott, David Winfield *artist, consultant*

Queenstown
Bowie, Norman Ernest *university official, educator*
Denton, Lawrence Monette *consultant meteorologist, historian*
Kearns, Robert William *manufacturing inventor*
Ryans, Reginald Vernon *music education educator, special education educator*

Randallstown
Myers, Debra Taylor *elementary school educator, writer*
Ross, Norman Everett *cultural organization administrator*

Reisterstown
Bond, Nelson Leighton, Jr. *health care executive*
Clews, William Vincent *producer, writer*
Daley, Peter Edmund *business and human resources company executive*
Frank, Robert Louis *lawyer*
†Seth, Deepak *internist*
Tannenbaum, Harvey *defense technology consultant*

Riva
Barto, Bradley Edward *small business owner, educator*

Riverdale
Gonzalez Arias, Victor Hugo *management executive*
†Kumar, Shailendra *urologist, educator*
†Shah, Navic C. *urologist, educator*

Rockville
Aamodt, Roger Louis *federal agency administrator*
Adams, Mark David *molecular biologist*
Anderson, Walter Dixon *trade association management consultant*
Arons, Bernard S. *psychiatrist, educator, health services director*
Avery, Bruce Edward *lawyer*
Bainum, Stewart William, Jr. *health care and lodging company executive*
Barkley, Brian Evan *lawyer, political consultant*
Barr, Solomon Efrem *allergist*
Basinger, William Daniel *computer programmer*
Bayne, Kathryn Ann Louise *veterinarian*
Berger, Robert Lewis *retired biophysicist, researcher*
Birns, Mark Theodore *physician*
Bloch, Bobbie Ann *nurse, educator*
Boice, John Dunning, Jr. *epidemiologist, science administrator*
Bolle, Robert L. *lawyer, administrator*
Bollum, Frederick James *biotechnology executive*
Boyle, Lisa C. *marketing and communications executive*
Brown, David Harry *speech educator*
Brown, Martin Howard *physician*
Buchanan, John Donald *retired health physicist, radiochemist*
Burdick, William MacDonald *biomedical engineer*
Byrne, Olivia Sherrill *lawyer*
Cain, Karen Mirinda *musician, educator*
Calkins, Jerry Milan *anesthesiologist, educator, administrator, biomedical engineer*
Campbell, R. Nelson *financial executive*
Cannon, Grace Bert *immunologist*
Cantelon, Philip Louis *historian*
Caswell, Steven James *health care administrator*
Chavez, Nelba *federal agency administrator*
Chiogioji, Melvin Hiroaki *former government official, entrepreneur*
Conner, Susan Gordon *nurse, organization official, consultant*
Corley, Rose Ann McAfee *government official*
†Couig, Mary Patricia *federal agency administrator*
†Cyr, Karen D. *lawyer*
Decker, John Laws *physician*
De Jong, David Samuel *lawyer, educator*
Dicus, Greta Joy *federal commissioner*
Donahue, Mary Rosenberg *psychologist*
Eisenberg, John Meyer *physician, educator*
Elliott, Benjamin Paul *architect*
Epstein, Jay Stuart *medical researcher*
Erwin, Joseph Marvin *neurobiologist, primatologist*
Ewing, Blair Gordon *local government official*
Feingold, S. Norman *psychologist*
Finlayson, John Sylvester *biochemist*
Fouchard, Joseph James *retired government agency administrator*
Fox, Claude Earl *federal health official*
Fratantoni, Joseph Charles *medical researcher, hematologist, medical and regulatory consultant*
Freedman, Marc Allan *investment company executive*
Friedman, Michael A. *food and drug agency commissioner*
Frye, Roland Mushat, Jr. *lawyer*
Fthenakis, Emanuel John *diversified aerospace company executive*
Gabelnick, Henry Lewis *medical research director*
Gail, Mitchell H. *science foundation executive*
Galaty, Carol Popper *health policy administrator*
Gardner, David John *communications executive, recording engineer*
George, Kathryn Elaine *economist, financial writer*
Gillick, Betsy Brinkley *financial analyst*
Ginsberg, Harold Samuel *virologist, educator*
Gleich, Carol S. *health professions education executive*
Gluckstein, Fritz Paul *veterinarian, biomedical information specialist*
Goldenberg, Myrna Gallant *English language and literature educator*
Gordon, Joan Irma *lawyer*
Gougé, Susan Cornelia Jones *microbiologist*
Grady, Lee Timothy *pharmaceutical chemist*
Gulya, Aina Julianna *neurotologist, surgeon, educator*
†Guttman, Steven J. *real estate company executive*
Haas, Suzanne Newhouse *human resources generalist*
Halperin, Jerome Arthur *pharmaceutical executive*
Hanes, Donald Keith *cooperative executive*
Hanna, Michael George, Jr. *immunologist, institute administrator*
Haudenschild, Christian Charles *pathologist, educator, inventor*
Hazard, Robert Culver, Jr. *hotel executive*
Henderson, Harriet *librarian*
Hewlett, Richard Greening *historian*
†Holston, Sharon Smith *government official*
†Hoover, Carol Faith *publisher*
Horowitz, Harold *architect*
†Horton, Linda Rae *lawyer*
Howard, Lee Milton *international health consultant*
Hoyer, Leon William *physician, educator*
Hsia, David *health services researcher, administrator*
Hubbard, William Keith *government executive*
Hutchin, Nancy Lee *process engineering and change management consultant*
Hyde, Geoffrey *satellite communications research executive*
Isbister, James David *pharmaceutical business executive*
Jacques, Joseph William *investment advisor*
Jamieson, Graham A. *biochemist, organization official*
Johnson, Emery Allen *physician*
Kadish, Richard L. *lawyer*
Kafka, Marian Stern *neuroscientist*
Kalton, Graham *survey statistician*
Kamerow, Douglas Biron *epidemiologist, family physician, assistant surgeon general*
Kamerow, Norman Warren *business owner, financial services executive*
Katz, Steven Martin *lawyer, accountant*
Kelsey, Frances Oldham (Mrs. Fremont Ellis Kelsey) *government official*
Kerxton, Alan Smith *lawyer*
Kimzey, Lorene Miller *endocrinology nurse*
Kline, Raymond Adam *professional organization executive*
Kohlhorst, Gail Lewis *librarian*
Kohlmeier, Louis Martin, Jr. *newspaper reporter*
Krahnke, Betty Ann *county official*
Kusterer, Thomas *environmental planner*
Landon, John Campbell *medical research company executive*
Langley, Roger Richard *editor*
Leef, James Lewis *biology educator, immunology research executive*
†Leithauser, Lance *plastic surgeon*
Leslie, John Walter *development consultant*
Levine, Barbara Gershkoff *early childhood education educator, consultant*
Lewis, Andrew Morris, Jr. *virologist*
Lewis, Benjamin Pershing, Jr. *pharmacist, public health service officer*
Ley, Herbert Leonard, Jr. *retired epidemiologist*
Lin, Jonathan Chung-Shih *computer scientist*
Lloyd, Douglas Seward *physician, public health administrator*
Long, Cedric William *health research executive*
Luo, Ray *physical chemist, biochemist*
Luxemburg, Jack Alan *rabbi*
Macafee, Susan Diane *reporter*
MacGregor, James Thomas *toxicologist*
MacPhee, Martin James *medical researcher, immunologist*
Madle, Robert Albert *writer*
Maxwell, Robert James *trade association administrator*
McAuliffe, John F. *retired judge*
McClamroch, Donal Lee, Jr. *forensic chemist, educator*
McCormick, Kathleen Ann Krym *geriatrics nurse, computer information specialist, federal agency science administrator*
McDonald, Capers Walter *biomedical engineer, corporate executive*
McGaffigan, Edward, Jr. *federal agency administrator*
McGuire, Edward David, Jr. *lawyer*
McQuain, Jeffrey Hunter *writer, researcher*
Meade, Kenneth Albert *minister*
Mealy, J. Burke () *psychological services administrator*
Megan, Thomas Ignatius *retired judge*
Menkello, Frederick Vincent *computer scientist*
Mertz, Walter *retired government research executive*
Meyer, F. Weller *bank executive*
Milan, Thomas Lawrence *accountant*
Milner, Max *food and nutrition consultant*
†Mohan, Aparna Krishna *epidemiologist, researcher*
Molitor, Graham Thomas Tate *lawyer*
Moran, Sean Farrell *historian*
Moritsugu, Kenneth Paul *physician, government official*
Mount, G. Alan *architect*
Murphy, Gerard Norris *trade association executive*
Murray, Peter *metallurgist, manufacturing company executive*
Naunton, Ralph Frederick *surgeon, educator*
Nevin, Joseph Francis *computer systems engineer*
Niewiaroski, Trudi Osmers (Gertrude Niewiaroski) *social studies educator*
Nightingale, Stuart Lester *physician, public health officer*
Noll, Richard Dean, Jr. *psychologist, educator and historian*
O'Donnell, James Francis *retired health science administrator*
†Pappas, Gregory *health agency administrator*
Pensinger, John Lynn *lawyer*
Petzold, Carol Stoker *state legislator*
†Phillips, John K. *philosophy educator*
Phillips, Mark Douglas *information technology executive*
Pillote, Barbara Wiegand *volunteer*
Plaut, Thomas F.A. *psychologist*
Poljak, Roberto J(uan) *research director, biotechnology educator*
Porter, John Robert, Jr. *space technology company executive, geochemist*
Proffitt, John Richard *business executive, educator*
Rafajko, Robert Richard *medical research company executive*
Regeimbal, Neil Robert, Sr. *retired journalist*
Rheinstein, Peter Howard *government official, physician, lawyer*
Rosen, Saul Woolf *research scientist, health facility administrator*
Rosenberg, Judith Lynne *middle school educator*
Ryan, Kevin William *research virologist, educator, administrator*
Sacchet, Edward Michael *foreign service officer*
Saljinska-Markovic, Olivera T. *oncology researcher, educator*
Scardelletti, Robert A. *labor union administrator*
Schindler, Albert Isadore *physicist, educator*
Seagle, Edgar Franklin *environmental engineer, consultant*
Seltser, Raymond *epidemiologist, educator*
Shadoan, George Woodson *lawyer*
Sherman, Howard D. *financial consultant*
Shuren, Jeffrey Eliot *behavioral neurology researcher, lawyer*
Simpson, Lisa Ann *government agency administrator, physician*
Smith, Mark Alan *management consultant*
Smith, Raymond Douglas *management educator*
Smith, Shelagh Alison *public health educator*
Spahr, Frederick Thomas *association executive*
Sparks, David Stanley *university administrator*
Standing, Kimberly Anna *educational researcher*
Stano, Lester Paul *minister*
Stansfield, Charles W. *educational administrator*
Stenger, Judith Antoinette *middle school educator*
†Stoiber, Carlton Ray *government agency official*
Sumberg, Alfred Donald *professional association executive*
†Sundlof, Stephen Frederick *veterinary administrator*
Szabo, Daniel *government official*
Tabibi, S. Esmail *pharmaceutical researcher, educator*
Tabor, Edward *physician, researcher*
Taube, Herman *author, educator*
Thompson, Barry Hammond *medical geneticist*
Titus, Roger Warren *lawyer*
Trost, Carlisle Albert Herman *retired naval officer*
Trujillo, Michael H. *administrator*
Ulbrecht, Jaromir Josef *chemical engineer*
Van Grack, Steven *lawyer*
†Vietti-Cook, Annette *nuclear energy administrator*
Vincent, Michael Paul *plastic surgeon*
Waksberg, Joseph *statistical company executive, researcher*
Ward, Neil Anthony *corporate communications specialist*
Weiss, Stuart *government official*
Wolf, Marilyn *consumer safety officer*
Woodcock, Janet *federal official*
Yale, Kenneth P. *lawyer, dentist*
Yamazaki, Kazutami *journalist*
Yao, Andy Shunchi *computer science educator*
Zaphiriou, George Aristotle *lawyer, educator*
†Zoon, Kathryn Christine *biologics research administrator*
Zoon, Kathryn Egloff *biochemist*

Royal Oak
Israel, Lesley Lowe *political consultant*

Sabillasville
McCulloch, Anna Mary Knott *pharmacy technician*

Saint Inigoes
Masters, George Windsor *electrical engineer, educator*
Scruitsky, Robert Lee *senior project engineer*

Saint Leonard
Sugarman, Jule M. *children's services consultant, former public administrator*

Saint Marys City
Hill, Walter Watson, Jr. *political science educator*
Stabile, Donald Robert *economics educator, consultant economic history*

Saint Michaels
Brown, Omer Forrest, II *lawyer*
Jones, Raymond Edward, Jr. *brewing executive*
Marshall, Robert Gerald *language educator*
Meendsen, Fred Charles *retired food company executive*
Shipley, L. Parks, Jr. *banker*
Wilson, Jerry Vernon *criminology consultant, writer, educator*
Young, Donald Roy *pharmacist*

Salisbury
Booker, Betty Mae *poet*
†Buchness, Michael Patrick *cardiologist, surgeon*
Cubbage, Elinor Phillips *English language educator*
Ezell-Grim, Annette Schram *business management educator, academic administrator*
Hoffman, Richard Curzon, IV *business administration educator*
Houlihan, Hilda Imelio *physician*
House, Charletta *librarian*
Kettinger, David John *broadcast executive*
Leonard, Joseph Howard *association organization executive*
Merritt, Carole Anne *secondary school educator*
Moultrie, Fred *geneticist*
Mulligan, Joseph Francis *physicist, historian of science, educator*
Perdue, Franklin P. *retired poultry products company executive*
†Thursfield, Fred F. *foundation administrator*
Wanzer, Mary Kathryn *computer company executive, consultant*
Weber, Michael James *conductor*
Woolford, Dornell Larmont *academic administrator*

Sandy Spring
Cope, Harold Cary *former university president, higher education association executive*
Moulton, Phillips Prentice *religion and philosophy educator*

Savage
Filby, Percy William *library consultant*

Laurence, Robert Lionel chemical engineering educator
Lester, Julius B. author
Levine, Michael Lawrence financial planner
Liebling, Jerome photographer, educator
†Lowance, Mason I. American literature educator
MacKnight, William John chemist, educator
Manz, Charles C. management educator
Margulis, Lynn (Lynn Alexander) biologist
Marrett, Cora B. university educator, science educator
May, Ernest Dewey music executive, organist, choirmaster
Mazor, Lester Jay law educator
Mc Donagh, Edward Charles sociologist, university administrator
Mills, Patricia Jagentowicz political philosophy educator, writer
Nash, William Arthur civil engineer, educator
Oates, Stephen Baery history educator
Palmer, John Derry physiology educator
Palser, Barbara F. botany researcher, retired educator
Parkhurst, Charles retired museum director, art historian
Partee, Barbara Hall linguist, educator
Peterson, Gerald Alvin physics educator
Prince, Gregory Smith, Jr. academic administrator
Rabin, Monroe Stephen Zane physicist
Ralph, James R. physician
Ratner, James Henry dermatologist
Rohan, Virginia Bartholome college development director
Romer, Robert Horton physicist, educator
Rosbottom, Ronald Carlisle French, arts and humanities educator
Rossi, Alice S. sociology educator, author
Rupp, William John architect
Sandweiss, Martha A. author, American studies and history educator
Scott, David Knight physicist, university administrator
Skerrett, Joseph Taylor literature educator
Slakey, Linda Louise biochemistry educator
†Stavans, Ilan professor, writer
Stein, Otto Ludwig botany educator
Stein, Richard Stephen chemistry educator
Strickland, Bonnie Ruth psychologist, educator
Swift, Calvin Thomas electrical and computer engineering educator
Targonski, Stephen Donald electrical engineering researcher
Tate, James Vincent poet, English educator
Taubman, Jane Andelman Russian literature educator
Taubman, William Chase political science educator
Taylor, Robert Edward foreign language educator
Tenenbaum, Jeffrey Mark academic librarian
Tippo, Oswald botanist, educator, university administrator
Trahan, Elizabeth Welt retired comparative literature educator
Vogl, Otto polymer science and engineering educator
Watson, Ellen Doré poet, translator
Weems, Charles Chilton computer science educator
Wideman, John Edgar English literature educator, novelist
Wilcox, Bruce Gordon publisher
Wills, David Wood minister, educator
Wolff, Robert Paul philosophy educator
Woodbury, Richard Benjamin anthropologist, educator
Wyman, David Sword historian, educator
Yarde, Richard Foster art educator
†Zuniga, Ximena U. education educator, researcher

Andover
Africk, Steven Allen physicist
Boumil, Marcia Mobilia legal educator, mediator, writer
Chung, Tchang-Il engineer
Gaff, Brian Michael attorney, electrical engineer
†Harrison, Jeffrey Woods poet, educator
Jakes, William Chester electrical engineer
Lakin, John Francis lawyer
Lerch, Robert Bond cable television executive
Leyva, Christine Marie information specialist
Mac Neish, Richard Stockton archaeologist, educator
Maguire, Robert Edward retired public utility executive
Marsh, Robert Buford chemical engineer, consultant
Sampson, Robert Carl, Jr. psychiatrist
Seggev, Meir radiologist, educator
Simone, Joseph clergyman, educator
Wise, Kelly private school educator, photographer, critic

Arlington
Blinn, Cynthia Lees middle school educator
†Carver, Jeffrey A. writer
Corrigan, Terence Martin tax specialist, accountant
Fulmer, Vincent Anthony retired college president
Gumpertz, Werner Herbert structural engineering company executive
Keshian, Richard lawyer
Nahigian, Alma Louise technical documentation administrator
Nahigian, Russell Ara mathematician
Samuelson, Joan Benoit professional runner
†Van Orman, Jeanne planning consultant
Whitehead, George William retired mathematician

Ashfield
Cudnohufsky, Walter Lee landscape architect
Pepyne, Edward Walter lawyer, psychologist, former educator

Attleboro
Bischoff, Marilyn Brett clinical social worker
Hammerle, Fredric Joseph metal processing executive
Stahl, Robert Alan manufacturing executive, consultant
Stevens, E(lizabeth) Kathleen English language educator
†Tuniewicz, Mark Anthony political organization administrator

Auburn
Alexander, Judith Elaine psychologist, consultant
Bachelder, Robert Stephen minister
Baker, David Arthur small business owner, manufacturer
Donnelly, Carol Burns education educator
Hahn, Robert Simpson computer scientist, mechanical engineer

McDonald, Sean video professional

Auburndale
Lindgren, Charlotte Holt English language educator
Nahigian, Robert John real estate development broker
†Winslow, Donald James retired English educator, archivist

Ayer
Falter, Robert Gary correctional health care administrator, educator
†Namin, Reza chemistry educator, consultant

Babson Park
Genovese, Francis Charles (Frank Genovese) economist, consultant, editor, writer
Goldberg, Pamela Winer business manager
Higdon, Leo I., Jr. dean, finance educator
Jones, Kent Albert economist
Stephenson, Craig Allen financial educator

Barnstable
Langhans, Lester Frank, III construction company executive
Randolph, Robert Lee economist, educator
†Vila, Robert Joseph television host, designer, real estate developer

Barre
†Sullivan, James Edward poet

Bedford
Alarcon, Rogelio Alfonso physician, researcher
Brawley, Margaret Wacker communications executive
Carr, Paul Henry physicist
Castaldi, David Lawrence health care company executive
Chung-Welch, Nancy Yuen Ming biologist
Cronson, Harry Marvin electronics engineer
Elkinton, Joseph Russell medical educator
Ellenbogen, S. David electronics company executive
Fante, Ronald Louis engineering scientist
Goodman, William Beehler editor, literary agent
Griffin, Donald R(edfield) zoology educator
Hantman, Barry G. software engineer
†Hurwitz, Joshua Jacob physician
Kouyoumjian, Charles H. diversified financial services company executive
Lackoff, Martin Robert engineer, physical scientist, researcher
Letts, Lindsay Gordon pharmacologist, educator
Peiser, Robert Alan financial executive
Rudzinsky, David Michael information systems director
Schafer, Eva Cady elementary school teacher, musician
Sizer, Irwin Whiting biochemistry educator
Slechta, Robert Frank biologist, educator
Steinberg, James Jonah physician, medical administrator, educator
Volicer, Ladislav physician, educator
Wind, Herbert Warren writer

Belmont
Barsam, Joyce Lorna language educator, classicist
Bergson, Abram economist, educator
Bloch, Herbert classicist, medievalist, historian, educator
Bowen, H. Kent engineering educator
Buckley, Jerome Hamilton English language educator
Cavarnos, Constantine Peter writer, philosopher
Cohen, Bruce Michael psychiatrist, educator, scientist
Coyle, Joseph Thomas psychiatrist
de Marneffe, Francis psychiatrist, hospital administrator
†Dober, Richard Patrick campus and facility planner, writer
Durgin, Frank Herman, II aeronautical engineer
Ewing, Scott Edwin physician, psychiatrist, educator, researcher
Feldstein, Kathleen Foley economist, consultant
Haralampu, George Stelios electric power engineer, former engineering executive electric utility company
Harvey, Kenneth Richard middle education educator, writer
Hauser, George biochemist, educator
Hooker, Richard Arthur computer scientist
Junger, Miguel Chapero acoustics researcher
Kety, Seymour S(olomon) physiologist, neuroscientist
Klein, Martin Samuel management consulting executive
Lange, Nicholas Theodore biostatistician
Levendusky, Philip George clinical psychologist, administrator
Lewis, Henry Rafalsky manufacturing company executive
Luick, Robert Burns lawyer
Merrill, Edward Wilson chemical engineering educator
†Moore, Richard Thomas writer, poet
Onesti, Silvio Joseph psychiatrist
Ottenstein, Donald psychiatrist
†Pappas, Marilyn R. art educator
Pope, Harrison Graham, Jr. psychiatrist, educator
Rassulo, Donna Marie nurse, poet, writer, television producer
Reynolds, William Francis mathematics educator
Rich, Sharon Lee financial planner
Ronningstam, Elsa Frideborg psychologist
Scanlan, Robert theater director, writer
Sifneos, Peter Emanuel psychiatrist
Simpson, Russell Avington retired law firm administrator
Youngberg, Robert Lovett psychologist

Berkley
Mills, Carol Andrews mental health administrator

Bernardston
Fullerton, Albert Louis, Jr. bookstore owner
Harvey, Arthur John landscape architect, golf course architect

Beverly
Barger, Richard Wilson hotel executive
Harris, Miles Fitzgerald meteorologist
Manheim, Michael Philip photographer
McMahon, Joyce Arlene public information director

Roberts, Richard John molecular biologist, consultant, research director
Rose, Peter Henry nuclear physicist
Roy, Robert William artist, educator
Smith, Merelyn Elizabeth elementary and middle school educator
Wan, Zhimin physicist

Billerica
Gray, Charles Agustus chemical company research executive
Kolb, Charles Eugene research corporation executive
Kronick, Barry lumber company executive
McCaffrey, Robert Henry, Jr. retired manufacturing company executive
Miller, Dawn Marie meteorologist

Bolton
Langenwalter, Gary Allan manufacturing and management consulting company executive
Leighton, Charles Milton specialty consumer products executive

Boston
Aber, John William finance educator
Ablow, Joseph artist, educator
Aborn, Foster Litchfield insurance company executive
Abraham, Nicholas Albert lawyer, real estate developer
Abrams, Ruth Ida state supreme court justice
Achatz, John lawyer
Adams, Douglass Franklin radiologist, educator, medical ethicist
Adams, Phoebe-Lou journalist
Adelstein, S(tanley) James physician, educator
Aikman, William Francis venture capitalist
†Ainsworth, Kimberly E. federal employee
Aisenberg, Alan C. physician, educator, researcher
Akin, Steven Paul financial company executive
Alden, Vernon Roger corporate director, trustee
Aldrich, Bailey federal judge
Alexander, James Garth architect
Alexander, Joyce London judge
Alie, Alleyn A. construction and engineering company executive
†Allison, Jason professional hockey player
Allukian, Myron, Jr. government administrator, public health educator, dental educator
Alpert, Joel Jacobs medical educator, pediatrician
Alt, Frederick W. geneticist, pediatrician
Ames, James Barr lawyer
Amorello, Matthew John state senator
Amos, Harold retired biomedical researcher, educator
Ampola, Mary G. pediatrician, geneticist
Andre, Rae writer, organizational behavior educator
Andrews, Kenneth Richmond business administration educator
Andrews, Sally May healthcare administrator
Angelou, Maya author
Anselme, Jean-Pierre Louis Marie chemist
Anthony, Ethan architect
Aparicio, Luis Ernesto retired baseball player
Aresty, Jeffrey M. lawyer
Argyris, Chris organizational behavior educator
Arky, Ronald Alfred medical educator
Armstrong, Rodney librarian
Arnold, John David management counselor, catalyst
Aronow, Saul radiological physicist, consultant
Ashkin, Ronald Evan international executive
Atwan, Helene publishing executive
Auerbach, Arnold (Red Auerbach) professional basketball team executive
Auerbach, Joseph lawyer, educator
Austen, K(arl) Frank physician, educator
Austen, W(illiam) Gerald surgeon, educator
Avakian, Laura Ann hospital administrator
Avison, David photographer
Bacon, A(delaide) Smoki public relations consultant, television host
Bae, Frank S. H. law educator, law librarian
Bailey, Richard Briggs investment company executive
Baker, Brent dean
Baker, Charles Duane business administration educator, former management executive
Bangs, Will Johnston lawyer
Banks, Henry H. academic dean, physician
†Bannan, Patricia Mary nutrition specialist, public relations consultant
Barbee, George E. L. financial services and business executive
Bard, Terry Ross rabbi
Barnett, Guy Octo physician, educator
Bartley, Scott Andrew genealogist, archivist
†Bauer, Stuart Barry urologist
Baughman, James Carroll information and communication educator
Beal, Robert Lawrence real estate executive
Beard, Charles Julian lawyer
Beck, William Samson physician, educator, biochemist
Becker, Fred Ronald lawyer
Becker, James Murdoch surgeon, educator
Beckwith, Jonathan Roger geneticist
Beha, Ann Macy architect
Belin, Gaspard d'Andelot retired lawyer
Bellows, A. Robert ophthalmologist
Benacerraf, Baruj pathologist, educator
Benjamin, William Chase lawyer
Bennett, George Frederick investment manager
Benson, James M. investment company executive
Berenberg, William physician, educator
Berenson, Paul Stewart advertising executive
Berg, Gordon Hercher banker
Bergen, Kenneth William lawyer
Berger, Harvey Robert psychologist
†Berger, Jerome Morris communications executive
Berk, Lee Eliot college president
Berkey, Dennis D. mathematics educator
Berman, Lisa advertising executive
Bern, Murray Morris hematologist, oncologist
Bernfield, Merton Ronald pediatrician, scientist, educator
Bernhard, Alexander Alfred lawyer
Berson, Eliot Lawrence ophthalmologist, medical educator
†Bertino, Fred advertising executive
Bertonazzi, Louis Peter federal agency administrator
Berube, Margery Stanwood publishing executive
Bines, Harvey Ernest lawyer, educator, writer
†Biro, Kathy advertising executive
Black, Paul Henry medical educator, researcher
Blaisdell, Charmarie Jenkins historian, educator
Blendon, Robert Jay health policy educator
Bloch, Kurt Julius physician

Blodgett, Mark Stephen legal studies educator, author
Blout, Elkan Rogers biological chemistry educator, university dean
Bodman, Samuel Wright, III specialty chemicals and materials company executive
Bodoff, Joseph Samuel Uberman lawyer
Bohnen, Michael J. lawyer
Bok, Joan Toland utility executive
Bok, John Fairfield lawyer
Borenstein, Milton Conrad lawyer, manufacturing company executive
Bornheimer, Allen Millard lawyer
Boudin, Michael federal judge
Bougas, James Andrew physician, surgeon
Bourne, Katherine Day journalist, educator
Bourque, Ray professional hockey player
Bower, Joseph Lyon business administration educator
Bowler, Marianne Bianca judge
Bownes, Hugh Henry federal judge
Boyd, David Preston business educator
Brackett, Sharon (Elaine) medical/surgical nurse
Brain, Joseph David biomedical scientist
Brandt, Allan M. medical history educator
Braunwald, Eugene physician, educator
Brazelton, Thomas Berry pediatrician, educator
Brecher, Kenneth astrophysicist
Brenner, Barry Morton physician
Brody, Richard Eric lawyer
Bromsen, Maury Austin historian, bibliographer, antiquarian bookseller
Bronner, Michael advertising executive
Brountas, Paul Peter lawyer
†Brown, D. David performing company executive
Brown, Ellen Hynes nursing administrator
Brown, Judith Olans lawyer, educator
Brown, Lloyd David association executive, management educator
Brown, Matthew lawyer
Brown, Michael information technology executive
Brown, Michael Robert lawyer
Brown, Stephen Lee insurance company executive
Brown, William L. banker
Browne, Kingsbury lawyer
Brownell, Gordon Lee physicist, educator
Bruns, William John, Jr. business administration educator
Buchanan, Robert McLeod lawyer
Buchin, Stanley Ira management consultant, educator
Buckley, Mortimer Joseph physician
Budd, Eric Merrill company official, writer, consultant
Burack, Sylvia Kamerman editor, publisher
Burakoff, Steven James immunologist, educator
Burgess, John Allen lawyer
Burkhardt, Charles Henry professional society executive, author, lecturer, consultant
Burleigh, Lewis Albert lawyer
†Burnham, David Henderson management consultant
Burns, Pat professional hockey coach
Burns, Thomas David lawyer
Burr, Francis Hardon lawyer
Bursma, Albert, Jr. publishing company executive
Bustin, Edouard Jean political scientist, educator
Buxbaum, Robert C(ourtney) internist
Cabot, Charles Codman, Jr. lawyer
Cabot, Louis Wellington foundation trustee
Calderwood, Stanford Matson investment management executive
Caldwell, Ann Wickins academic administrator
Caldwell, Gail book critic
Callow, Allan Dana surgeon
Campbell, Levin Hicks federal judge
Canavan, Christine Estelle state legislator
Caner, George Colket, Jr. lawyer
Cantella, Vincent Michele stockbroker
Caplan, Louis Robert neurology educator
Cardona, Rodolfo Spanish language and literature educator
Carey, John Andrew investment company executive
Carliner, Geoffrey Owen economist, director
†Carlson, Neil Ryan computer scientist
Carr, Daniel Barry anesthesiologist, endocrinologist, medical researcher
Carr, Jay Phillip critic
Carr, Michael Leon professional sports team executive, former professional basketball player
Carr, Stephen W. lawyer
Carradini, Lawrence comparative biologist, science administrator
Carroll, James author
Carroll, James Edward lawyer
Carroll, Matthew Shaun reporter
Carter, Marshall Nichols banker
Casner, Truman Snell lawyer
Cass, Ronald Andrew dean
Cassandras, Christos George engineering educator, consultant
Cellucci, Argeo Paul state official
Chandler, Harriette Levy management consultant, educator, legislator
Chapin, Melville lawyer
Charnas, Fran Elka theatre director, educator, author
Chen, Ching-chih information science educator, consultant
Cherwin, Joel Ira lawyer
Chilvers, Derek insurance company executive
Chizauskas, Cathleen Jo manufacturing company executive
Chobanian, Aram Van medical school dean, cardiologist
Chow, Stephen Y(ee) lawyer
Christensen, Carl Roland business administration educator
Christenson, Charles John retired business educator
†Clark, Kim Bryce business educator
Clarke, Terence Michael public relations and advertising executive
Cleven, Carol Chapman state legislator
Clouse, Melvin E. radiologist
Coffin, John Miller molecular biologist, educator
Coffman, Jay Denton physician, educator
Cogan, John Francis, Jr. lawyer
Cohen, Alan Seymour internist
Cohen, Jonathan Brewer molecular neurobiologist, biochemist
†Cohen, Lawrence P. federal judge
Cohen, Rachelle Sharon journalist
Cohen, Robert Sonné physicist, philosopher, educator
Cohn, Andrew Howard lawyer
Colburn, Kenneth Hersey financial executive
Collier, R(obert) John biomedical researcher, academic dean

Lasser, Lawrence J. *investment company executive*
Last, Michael P. *lawyer*
Latham, James David *lawyer*
Lawner, Ron *advertising executive*
Lawrence, Mary Josephine (Josie Lawrence) *library official, artist*
Lawrence, Merloyd Ludington *editor*
Lawrence, Paul Roger *retired organizational behavior educator*
Lawson, Thomas Elsworth *advertising agency executive*
Leaman, J. Richard, Jr. *paper company executive*
Lee, Donald Young (Don Lee) *publishing executive, editor, writer*
Lee, Jonathan Owen *financial services company executive, lawyer*
Leeman, Susan Epstein *neuroscientist, educator*
Lees, Sidney *research facility administrator, bioengineering educator*
Leland, Timothy *newspaper executive*
†Leonard, James Patrick *writer, editor, communications consultant*
Le Quesne, Philip William *chemistry educator, researcher*
Lesser, Laurence *musician, educator*
Levenson, James William *physician*
Levine, Ruth Rothenberg *biomedical science educator*
Levinsky, Norman George *physician, educator*
Levitin, Lev Berovich *engineering educator*
Lewis, Anthony *newspaper columnist*
Lewis, Scott P. *lawyer*
Liang, Matthew H. *medical director*
Licata, Arthur Frank *lawyer*
Lichtin, Norman Nahum *chemistry educator*
Lieberman, Gail Forman *investment company executive*
Lindsay, Reginald Carl *lawyer*
Little, Arthur Dehon *investment banker*
Little, John Bertram *physician, radiobiology educator, researcher*
Liu, Brian Cheong-Seng *urology and oncology educator, researcher*
Livingston, David Morse *biomedical scientist, physician, internist*
†Lockhart, Keith Alan *conductor, musician, teacher*
Lockwood, Rhodes Greene *retired lawyer*
Lodge, George C(abot) *business administration educator*
Loeser, Hans Ferdinand *lawyer*
Loew, Brenda *publisher*
Logan, Lox Albert, Jr. *museum director*
Looney, William Francis, Jr. *lawyer*
Loria, Martin A. *lawyer*
Loring, Arthur *lawyer, financial services company executive*
Loscalzo, Joseph *cardiologist, biochemist*
Loughlin, Kevin Raymond *urological surgeon, researcher*
Lovejoy, George Montgomery, Jr. *real estate executive*
Lovell, Francis Joseph *investment company executive*
Lovett, Miller Currier *management educator, clergyman*
Lowe, Alfred Mifflin, III *advertising agency executive, writer*
Lowry, Bates *art historian, museum director*
Lowry, Lois (Hammersberg) *author*
Lucker, Jay K. *library education educator*
Lukey, Joan A. *lawyer*
Luongo, C. Paul *public relations executive*
Lyman, Henry *retired publisher, marine fisheries consultant*
Lynch, Francis Charles *lawyer*
Lynch, Neil L(awrence) *state supreme court justice*
Lynch, Sandra Lea *judge*
Lyons, David Barry *philosophy and law educator*
Lyons, Paul Vincent *lawyer*
MacArthur, Sandra Lea *financial services executive*
MacFarlane, Maureen Anne *lawyer*
Maciora, Joseph Gerard Vincent *reference librarian*
MacKay, Karel Lee *cancer institue administrator*
Macomber, John D. *construction executive*
Maher, Timothy John *pharmacologist, educator*
Malamy, Michael H(oward) *molecular biology and microbiology educator*
Malenka, Bertram Julian *physicist, educator*
†Malloy, William Francis, Jr. *lobbyist, navy officer*
Malt, Ronald Bradford *lawyer*
Mandel, David Michael *lawyer*
†Mandel, Jess *physician, educator*
Manfredi, David Peter *architect*
Mankin, Henry Jay *physician, educator*
Mannick, John Anthony *surgeon*
Manning, Robert Joseph *editor*
Manning, William Frederick *wire service photographer*
Mansfield, Christopher Charles *insurance company legal executive*
Margolis, Bernard Allen *library administrator*
Markel, Robert Thomas *mayor*
Markham, Jesse William *economist*
Markoff, Gary David *investment executive*
Markowitz, Phyllis Frances *mental health services administrator, psychologist*
Marks, Stephen Paul *law and international affairs educator, international official*
Marshall, Martin Vivan *business administration educator, business consultant*
Martin, Joseph Boyd *neurologist, educator*
Martin, Stanley A. *lawyer*
†Martinez, Pedro Jaime *professional baseball player*
Martinez, Ramon Jaime *professional baseball player*
Maso, Michael Harvey *theatre administrator*
Mason, Charles Ellis, III *magazine editor*
Mason, Emanuel Joel *psychology educator*
Mason, Herbert Warren, Jr. *religion and history educator, author*
†Matheson, Jean King *neurologist, educator*
Matthews, Roger Hardin *lawyer*
Maxwell, J. B. *financial and marketing consultant*
Mayer, Henri André Van Huysen *association executive*
Maynard, Kenneth Irwin *medical educator, researcher*
Mazzone, A. David *federal judge*
McArdle, Patricia Anne *security company executive*
McArthur, John Hector *business educator*
†Mc Carthy, Denis Michael *investment executive*
McChesney, S. Elaine *lawyer*
McCraw, Thomas Kincaid *business history educator, editor, author*
McCullen, Joseph T., Jr. *venture capitalist*
McDaniel, Joyce L. *artist, educator*
Mc Dermott, William Vincent, Jr. *physician, educator*
McDonald, John Barry, Jr. *lawyer*
McDougal, William Scott *urology educator*
McFarlan, Franklin Warren *business administration educator*
McGovern, Patrick J. *communications executive*
†McKain, Joshua Van Kirk *library director*
McKinnell, Noel Michael *architect, educator*
McKittrick, Neil Vincent *lawyer*
McLaughlin, John Joseph, Jr. *lawyer*
McLeod, Andrew Harvey *conservationalist*
McLinden, James Hugh *molecular biologist*
McNeil, Barbara Joyce *radiologist, educator*
McPhee, Jonathan *music director, conductor, composer, arranger*
Meenan, Robert Francis *academician, rheumatologist, researcher*
Meister, Mark Jay *museum director, professional society administrator*
Mellins, Harry Zachary *radiologist, educator*
Melnyczuk, Askold *writer*
Melton, David Van *dean, minister*
†Menard, Joan M. *state legislator*
Menino, Thomas M. *mayor*
Menzies, Ian Stuart *newspaper editor*
Merk, Frederick Bannister *biomedical educator, medical researcher*
Merrill, Stephen *former governor*
Merton, Robert C. *economist, educator*
Merullo-Boaz, Lisa Helen *marketing and fundraising executive*
Meserve, William George *lawyer*
Messerle, Judith Rose *medical librarian, public relations director*
Metcalfe, Robert *communications executive*
Metzer, Patricia Ann *lawyer*
Michel, Thomas Mark *internal medicine educator, scientist, physician*
Mikels, Richard Eliot *lawyer*
Milioria, Maria Teresa *chemist, psychotherapist, psychoanalyst, educator*
Millar, Sally Gray *nurse*
Miller, Bradley Adam *economist*
Miller, J. Philip *television producer, director, educator*
Minkel, Herbert Philip, Jr. *lawyer*
Mizel, Mark Stuart *orthopedic surgeon*
Moellering, Robert Charles, Jr. *internist, educator*
Mokriski, J. Charles *lawyer*
Monaco, Anthony Peter *surgery educator, medical institute administrator*
Moncreiff, Robert P. *lawyer*
Mongan, James John *physician, hospital administrator*
Montgomery, William Wayne *surgeon*
Mooney, Michael Edward *lawyer*
Moore, Francis Daniels *surgeon*
†Moore, Gregory L. *editor*
Moore, Richard Lawrence *structural engineer, consultant*
Moore, Richard Thomas *state legislator*
Morby, Jacqueline *venture capitalist*
Morgan, James Philip *pharmacologist, cardiologist, educator*
Morgentaler, Abraham *urologist, researcher*
Moriarty, George Marshall *lawyer*
Moriarty, John *opera administrator, artistic director*
Morris, Gerald Douglas *newspaper editor*
Morris, Robert *educator*
Morrison, Gordon Mackay, Jr. *investment company executive*
Morton, Edward James *insurance company executive*
Morton, William Gilbert, Jr. *stock exchange executive*
Moseby, LeBaron Clarence, Jr. *mathematics and computer science educator*
†Moses, Robert David *cardiothoracic surgeon*
Moyes, Norman Barr *journalism educator, writer, photographer*
Muldoon, Robert Joseph, Jr. *lawyer*
Mullare, T(homas) Kenwood, Jr. *lawyer*
Murphy, Evelyn Frances *economist*
Murray, Philip Edmund, Jr. *lawyer*
Murray, Terrence *banker*
Murray, Therese *state legislator*
Mutterperl, William Charles *lawyer*
Nadas, Alexander Sandor *pediatric cardiologist, educator*
Nanji, Amin Akbarali *biochemist, clinical pathologist, educator*
Nathan, David Gordon *physician, educator*
Neely, Cameron Michael *former professional hockey player*
Neely, Thomas Emerson *lawyer*
Nelson, David S. *federal judge*
†Nelson, Steven Ryerson *finance educator*
Ness, Arthur Joseph *musicologist*
Neumeier, Richard L. *lawyer*
Newbrander, William Carl *health economist, management consultant*
Newhouse, Joseph Paul *economics educator*
Newman, Richard Alan *publisher, editor and consultant*
Nichols, Guy Warren *retired institute executive, utilities executive*
Nissenbaum, Gerald L. *lawyer*
†Noble, Mildred M. *retired social worker*
Node, Koichi *cardiologist, researcher*
Norman, Dennis Keith *psychologist, educator*
Norment, Eric Stuart *newspaper editor*
Norris, Charles Head *lawyer, manufacturing executive*
Norris, Lonnie Harold *dean*
Nutt, Robert L. *lawyer*
Nuzzo, Anthony Gerald *banking executive*
Nyberg, Stanley Eric *cognitive scientist*
Nylander, Jane Louise *museum director*
Oates, William Armstrong, Jr. *investment company executive*
O'Block, Robert Paul *management consultant*
O'Brien, Shannon P. *state treasurer*
O'Brien, Thomas N. *city economic development officer*
†O'Byck, Robert William, Jr. *association administrator*
O'Connor, Francis Patrick *state supreme court justice*
O'Dell, Edward Thomas, Jr. *lawyer*
O'Donnell, Thomas Francis *vascular surgeon, health facility administrator*
O'Donnell, Thomas Lawrence Patrick *lawyer*
Oetheimer, Richard A. *lawyer*
Offerman, Jose Antonio Dono *professional baseball player*
O'Hern, Jane Susan *psychologist, educator*
O'Leary, Joseph Evans *lawyer*
Ondrechen, Mary Jo *chemistry educator, consultant, researcher*
O'Neill, Philip Daniel, Jr. *lawyer, educator*
O'Neill, Timothy P. *lawyer*
†Osei, Suzette Y. *endocrinologist*
O'Toole, George A., Jr. *judge*
Otten, Jeffrey *health facility administrator*
Packenham, Richard Daniel *lawyer*
Packer, Rekha Desai *lawyer*
†Paine, Lisa Lynn *university administrator*
Palter, Elizabeth Ann Schneck *dean*
†Pantano, Dick *advertising executive*
Papageorgiou, Panagiotis *medical educator*
Pardee, Arthur Beck *biochemist, educator*
Pardus, Donald Gene *utility executive*
Park, James Theodore *microbiologist, educator*
Park, William H(erron) *financial executive*
Park, William Wynnewood *law educator*
Parker, Christopher William *lawyer*
Parker, Olivia *photographer*
Partan, Daniel Gordon *lawyer, educator*
Patterson, John de la Roche, Jr. *lawyer*
Pauker, Susan Perlmutter *clinical geneticist, pediatrician*
Paul, Oglesby *cardiologist*
Paulsen, Anne M. *state legislator*
†Paxson, James Joseph, Jr. *sports team executive, former professional basketball player*
Pechilis, William John *lawyer*
Peek, Robin Patricia *library and information science educator*
Peirce, Georgia Wilson *public relations executive*
Penney, Sherry Hood *university president, educator*
Perera, Lawrence Thacher *lawyer*
Perkins, James Wood *lawyer*
Perkins, John Allen *lawyer*
Petersen, Robert Allen *pediatric ophthalmologist*
Petronella, Vincent F. *English educator, researcher*
Philbin, Ann Margaret *brokerage house executive*
Phillips, Daniel Anthony *trust company executive*
Phillips, William *English language educator, editor, author*
Pierce, Allan Dale *engineering educator, researcher*
Pierce, Donald Shelton *orthopedic surgeon, educator*
Pierce, Martin E., Jr. *fire commissioner*
Pinsky, Robert Neal *poet, educator*
Pitino, Richard *professional basketball coach, former collegiate basketball coach*
Pitts, James Atwater *financial executive*
Pochi, Peter Ernest *physician*
Pomeroy, Robert Corttis *lawyer*
Poser, Charles Marcel *neurology educator*
Poss, Stephen Daniel *lawyer*
Poussaint, Alvin Francis *psychiatrist, educator*
Prabakaran, Daniel *biochemist, researcher*
Previato, Emma *mathematics educator*
Prout, Curtis *internist, educator*
Puliafito, Carmen Anthony *ophthalmologist, healthcare executive*
Purcell, Patrick Joseph *newspaper publisher*
Pynchon, Thomas Ruggles, Jr. *author*
Rabkin, Mitchell Thornton *physician, hospital administrator, educator*
Radloff, Robert Albert *real estate executive*
Raeder, William Munro *publishing executive*
Raemer, Harold Roy *electrical engineering educator*
Raish, David Langdon *lawyer*
Rand, William Medden *biostatistics educator*
Ransil, Bernard J(erome) *research physician, methodologist, consultant, educator*
Rappaport, James Wyant *lawyer, real estate developer*
Ravid, Katya *medical educator*
Rawn, William Leete, III *architect*
Ray, William F. *banker*
Reardon, Frank Emond *lawyer*
Redlich, Marc *lawyer*
Reid, Lynne McArthur *pathologist*
Reiling, Henry Bernard *business educator*
†Reinertsen, James L. *healthcare executive*
Reinherz, Helen Zarsky *social services educator*
Relman, Arnold Seymour *physician, educator, editor*
Remis, Shepard M. *lawyer*
Reppert, Steven Marion *pediatrician, scientist, educator*
Rhinesmith, Stephen Headley *global management consultant*
Rhoads, Linda Smith *editor*
Riccelli, Richard Joseph *advertising agency executive*
Richie, Jerome Paul *surgeon, educator*
Richmond, Alice Elenor *lawyer*
Riely, John Cabell *english educator, art historian, consultant*
Ritt, Roger Merrill *lawyer*
Rivlin, Rachel *lawyer*
Rizzo, William Ober *lawyer*
†Robbins, Catherine *healthcare executive*
Rockoff, Mark Alan *pediatric anesthesiologist*
Roemer, Linda *educator, academic administrator*
Rogeness, Mary Speer *state legislator*
Rogers, Malcolm Austin *museum director, art historian*
Rohrer, Richard Jeffrey *surgeon, educator*
Ronayne, Michael Richard, Jr. *academic dean*
Rose, Alan Douglas *lawyer*
Rosen, Fred Saul *pediatrics educator*
†Rosen, Mark *management consultant*
Rosen, Stanley Howard *humanities educator*
Rosenberg, Irwin Harold *physician, educator*
Rosenberg, Manuel *retail company executive*
Rossell, Christine Hamilton *political science educator*
Roston, Arnold *information specialist, educator, advertising executive, artist, editor*
Rotenberg, Sheldon *violinist*
Roth, Alvin Eliot *economics educator*
Rouner, Leroy Stephens *religious studies educator, philosophy educator*
Rush, Sean Charles *higher education consultant*
Russell, Paul Snowden *surgeon, educator*
Rutstein, Stanley Harold *apparel retailing company executive*
Ryan, Kenneth John *physician, educator*
Ryser, Hugues Jean-Paul *pharmacologist, medical educator, cell biologist*
Sabbag, Douglas Walter *computer consultant company executive*
Saberhagen, Bret William *professional baseball player*
†Sacchetti, Dominic Vincent *school system administrator*
Sachs, David Howard *surgery and immunology educator, researcher*
Sadeghi-Nejad, Abdollah *pediatrician, educator*
Safe, Kenneth Shaw, Jr. *fiduciary firm executive*
Saleh, Bahaa E. A. *electrical engineering educator*
Sallan, Stephen E. *pediatrician*
Samaan, John George *nonprofit organization executive*
Sanborn, George Freeman, Jr. *genealogist*
Sand, Michael *industrial designer*
Sanders, Irwin Taylor *sociology educator*
Sant, Grannum Remy *urology educator*
Santos, Brenda Ann *community health clinical specialist*
Santos, Gilbert Antonio (Gil Santos) *radio and television sportscaster*
Saper, Clifford Baird *neurobiology and neurology educator*
Sapers, Carl Martin *lawyer*
Sargeant, Ernest James *lawyer*
Sargent, David Jasper *university official*
Saris, Patti Barbara *federal judge*
Sass, Steven Arthur *economist, editor*
Saunders, Roger Alfred *hotel group executive*
Sawyer, William C. *lawyer*
Sax, Daniel Saul *neurologist*
Say, Allen *children's writer, illustrator*
†Scanlan, Patrick Francis *legislative staff member*
Scanlon, Dorothy Therese *history educator*
†Schalick, Walton Orvyl, III *pediatrician*
Schaller, Jane Green *pediatrician*
Schifrin, Lalo *composer*
Schlossman, Stuart Franklin *physician, educator, researcher*
Schmelzer, Henry Louis Phillip *lawyer, financial company executive*
†Schneider, Joan *company executive*
Schnitzer, Iris Taymore *financial management executive, lawyer*
Schoenfeld, Barbara Braun *lawyer*
Schorr, Marvin G. *technology company executive*
Schottland, Edward Morrow *hospital adminstrator*
Schrager, Mindy Rae *business professional*
Schram, Ronald Byard *lawyer*
Schram, Stephen C. *professional basketball team executive*
Schribman, Shelley Iris *database engineer, consultant*
Schubel, Jerry Robert *marine science educator, scientist, university dean*
Schulz, John Joseph *communications educator*
Schwartz, Bernard *physician*
Schwartz, Lloyd *music critic, poet*
Schwister, Jay Edward *portfolio manager*
Scipione, Richard Stephen *insurance company executive, lawyer*
Scott, A. Hugh *lawyer*
Scott, James Arthur *radiologist, educator*
Scrimshaw, Nevin Stewart *physician, nutrition and health educator*
Sears, John Winthrop *lawyer*
Seddon, Johanna Margaret *ophthalmologist, epidemiologist*
Seely, Ellen Wells *endocrinologist*
Segal, Robert Mandal *lawyer*
Selkoe, Dennis Jesse *neurologist, researcher, educator*
Sexton, John Joseph *oral and maxillofacial surgeon*
Shader, Richard Irwin *psychiatrist, pharmacologist, educator*
Shafto, Robert Austin *retired insurance company executive*
Shames, Jeffrey *financial services company executive*
Shapiro, Jerome Herbert *radiologist, educator*
Shapiro, Sandra *lawyer*
Sharp, William Leslie *performing arts educator*
Shaw, M. Thomas, III *bishop*
Shaw, William Frederick *investment company executive*
Sheehan, Monica Mary *banker*
Shemin, Barry L. *insurance company executive*
†Shemin, Richard Jay *cardiothoracic surgeon, educator*
Shepard, Henry Bradbury, Jr. *lawyer*
Shields, Lawrence Thornton *orthopedic surgeon, educator*
Shirley, Dennis Lynn *education educator*
Shklar, Gerald *oral pathologist, periodontist, educator*
†Shore, Eleanor Gossard *university dean*
Sigman, Stuart J. *communications educator*
Silber, John Robert *university chancellor, philosophy and law educator*
Silberman, Robert A. S. *lawyer*
Silen, William *physician, surgery educator*
Silvey, Anita Lynne *editor*
Simard, Patricia Gannon *economic development finance administrator*
Simmons, Mary Jane *state legislator*
Simovic, Drasko *neurologist*
Sinai, Allen Leo *economist, educator*
Sinden, Harry *professional hockey team executive*
Singer, Thomas Eric *industrial company executive*
Sirkin, Joel H. *lawyer*
Skinner, Al *college basketball coach*
Skinner, Walter Jay *federal judge*
Skinner, Wickham *business administration educator*
Sklar, Holly L. *nonfiction writer*
Skrine, Bruce E. *lawyer*
Sledge, Clement Blount *orthopedic surgeon, educator*
Sloane, Carl Stuart *business educator, management consultant*
Smith, Edwin Eric *lawyer*
Smith, Kathy Delaney *basketball coach*
Smith, Philip Jones *lawyer*
Smith, Raoul Normand *computer science educator*
Smyth, Peter Hayes *radio executive*
Snyder, John Gorvers *lawyer*
Snydman, David Richard *infectious diseases specialist, educator*
Sobin, Julian Melvin *international consultant*
Soden, Richard Allan *lawyer*
Solet, Maxwell David *lawyer*
Solomon, Caren Grossbard *internist*
Sommerfeld, Nicholas Ulrich *lawyer*
Sonenshein, Abraham Lincoln *microbiology educator*
†Sonnabend, Roger Philip *hotel company executive*
Sonnenschein, Adam *lawyer*
Southard, William G. *lawyer*
†Spaienza, Tony *public relations executive*
Spelfogel, Scott David *lawyer*
Spellman, Mitchell Wright *surgeon, academic administrator*
Spiess, Gary A. *lawyer*
Spilhaus, Karl Henry *textiles executive, lawyer*
Sprague, Jo Ann *state legislator*
Stair, Thomas Osborne *physician, educator*
Stallman, Richard Matthew *software developer*
Stanley, H(arry) Eugene *physicist, educator*
Stare, Fredrick John *nutritionist, biochemist, physician*
Stearns, Richard Gaylore *judge*
Steere, Allen Caruthers, Jr. *physician, educator*
Steffian, John Ames, Jr. *architect*
Stein, Marshall David *lawyer*
Steinberg, Laura *lawyer*
Stepanian, Ira *banking executive*
Stern, Donald Kenneth *prosecutor*
Stevens, Marilyn Ruth *editor*
Stevenson, Howard Higginbotham *business educator*
Stevenson, Philip Davis *lawyer*

Stobaugh, Robert Blair *business educator, business executive*
Stokes, James Christopher *lawyer*
Stollar, Bernard David *biochemist, educator*
Stone, Arthur Harold *mathematics educator*
Storer, Jeffrey B. *lawyer*
Storer, Thomas Perry *lawyer*
Storey, James Moorfield *lawyer*
Storin, Matthew Victor *newspaper editor*
Story, Ellen *state legislator*
Stossel, Thomas Peter *medical educator, medical research director*
Streeter, Henry Schofield *lawyer*
Streilein, J. Wayne *research scientist*
Strickler, Gary *university athletic director*
Strominger, Jack Leonard *biochemist*
Strothman, Wendy Jo *book publisher*
Studds, Gerry Eastman *former congressman*
Sugarman, Paul Ronald *lawyer, educator, academic administrator*
Sullivan, Dorothy Rona *state official*
Sullivan, James Leo *organization executive*
Sullivan, John Louis, Jr. *retired search company executive*
†Sullivan, Megan Mary *English educator*
Surkin, Elliot Mark *lawyer*
Surman, Owen Stanley *psychiatrist*
Sutherland, John Edward *lawyer, educator*
Swaim, Charles Hall *lawyer*
Swartz, Morton Norman *medical educator*
Swift, Humphrey Hathaway *manufacturing executive*
Swift, Jane Maria *state official*
Swope, Jeffrey Peyton *lawyer*
Szep, Paul Michael *editorial cartoonist*
Tappé, Albert Anthony *architect*
Tarantino, Louis Gerald *business consultant, lawyer*
Tarlov, Alvin Richard *former philanthropic foundation administrator, physician, educator, researcher*
Tauber, Alfred Imre *hematologist, immunologist, philosopher of science*
Taubman, Martin Arnold *immunologist*
Tauro, Joseph Louis *federal judge*
Taveras, Juan Manuel *physician, educator*
Taylor, Benjamin B. *newspaper publishing executive*
Taylor, Edward Michael *insurance and risk management consultant*
Taylor, Stephen Emlyn *publishing executive*
Taylor, Thomas William *lawyer*
Taylor, William Osgood *newspaper executive*
Teich, Malvin Carl *electrical engineering educator*
Temkin, Robert Harvey *accountant*
Tempel, Jean Curtin *venture capitalist*
Terrill, Ross Gladwin *author, educator*
Testa, Richard Joseph *lawyer*
Thibedeau, Richard Herbert *environmental planner, administrator*
Thomas, Lee *professional sports team executive*
Thorn, George Widmer *physician, educator*
Thorndike, John Lowell *investment executive*
†Thys, Frederic Georges Rene *journalist*
†Tilchin, William Neal *educator*
Tilney, Nicholas Lechmere *surgery educator*
Tocco, Stephen *former airport administrator*
Tosteson, Daniel Charles *physiologist, medical school dean emeritus*
Totenberg, Roman *violinist, music educator*
Touster, Saul *law educator*
Towles, Stokley Porter *commercial and investment banking executive*
Trackman, Philip Charles *biochemist, researcher*
†Treacy, Michael Edmund Francis *venture capitalist*
Tremblay, Joan Louise *perishables administrator*
Trichopoulos, Dimitrios Vassilios *epidemiologist, educator*
Trier, Jerry Steven *gastroenterologist, educator*
Trimmier, Roscoe, Jr. *lawyer*
Tuchmann, Robert *lawyer*
†Tuchscherer, Konrad Timothy *anthropologist, historian, linguist*
Tucker, Louis Leonard *retired historical society administrator*
Tucker, Richard Lee *financial executive*
Turek, Sonia Fay *journalist*
Turillo, Michael Joseph, Jr. *management consultant*
Tyszkowski, Robert *business executive, cell biologist*
†Ullian, Elaine S. *health facility administrator*
Upshur, Carole Christofk *psychologist, educator*
Utiger, Robert David *medical editor*
Vachon, Louis *psychiatrist, educator*
Vaillant, George Eman *psychiatrist*
Valentin, John William *professional baseball player*
Vallee, Bert Lester *biochemist, physician, educator*
Van, Peter *lawyer*
Van Allsburg, Chris *author, artist*
Vance, Verne Widney, Jr. *lawyer*
Van Domelen, John Francis *academic administrator*
Vannasse, Dana Edward *corporation executive*
Vasaly, Ann Carol *classical studies educator*
Vatter, Paul August *business administration educator, dean*
Vaughan, Herbert Wiley *lawyer*
Vermeule, Cornelius Clarkson, III *museum curator*
Vermilye, Peter Hoagland *banker*
Vernon, Heidi *international business educator*
Verrochi, Paul M. *executive training company executive*
Volk, Kristin *advertising agency executive*
von Fettweis, Yvonne Caché *archivist, historian*
Wahlberg, Mark *actor*
†Walker, Antoine Devon *professional basketball player*
Walker, Gordon T. *lawyer*
Walrath, Patricia A. *state legislator*
Walsh, Christopher Thomas *biochemist, department chairman*
Wang, Helen Hai-ling *pathologist*
†Wardwell, Gerry E. *television producer, journalist*
Warga, Jack *mathematician, educator*
Warren, Rosanna *poet*
Warsh, David Lewis *economic journalist*
Warshaw, Andrew Louis *surgeon, researcher*
Washburn, Bradford (Henry B. Washburn, Jr.) *museum administrator, cartographer, photographer*
Webber, Stephen William *music educator, composer*
Weber, Georg Franz *immunologist*
Webster, Edward William *medical physicist*
Wechsler, Henry *research psychologist*
Weiner, Stephen Mark *lawyer*
Weinstein, Milton Charles *health policy educator*
†Weisberg, Bruce Steven *bank executive*
Weisman, Avery Danto *psychiatrist*
Weiss, Earle Burton *physician*
Weiss, James Michael *financial analyst, portfolio manager*
Weitzel, John Patterson *lawyer*
Weitzman, Arthur Joshua *English educator*
Welch, Garry William *psychologist, consultant, educator*
Wellington, Carol Strong *law librarian*
Weltman, David Lee *lawyer*
Wendorf, Richard Harold *library director, scholar*
†Weng, Zhiping *biomedical engineering educator*
Wentworth, Michael Justin *curator*
Wermuth, Paul Charles *retired English educator*
Westling, Jon *university administrator*
Wheatland, Richard, II *fiduciary services executive, museum executive*
Wheeler, W(illiam) Scott *composer, conductor, music educator*
White, Barry Bennett *lawyer*
White, George Edward *pedodontist, educator*
White, Jan Tuttle (Mrs. Benjamin Winthrop White) *information systems executive*
White, Morris Francis *biochemistry educator*
Whitlock, John L. *lawyer*
Whitters, James Payton, III *lawyer, university administrator*
Whitworth, William A. *magazine editor*
Wickenhiser, Sister Mary Mark *religious organization official, nun*
†Widmann, John Andrew *account administrator, musician*
Wiesel, Elie *writer, educator*
Wild, Victor Allyn *lawyer, educator*
Wilkes, Brent Ames *management consultant*
Williams, Charles Marvin *commercial banking educator*
Williams, Gordon Harold *internist, medical educator, researcher*
†Williams, Jimy *baseball team manager*
Williams, John Taylor *lawyer*
Williams, Rhys *minister*
Wilson, David Bruce *journalist*
Wilson, Robert Gould *management consultant*
Winkelman, James Warren *hospital administrator, pathology educator*
Winter, Donald Francis *lawyer*
Wirth, Dyann Fergus *public health educator, microbiologist*
Wiseman, James Richard *classicist, archaeologist, educator*
Woerner, Fred Frank *federal agency*
Woerner, Frederick Frank *international relations educator*
Wolf, David *lawyer*
Wolf, Dennis *university basketball coach*
Wolf, Gary Herbert *architect*
Wolf, Mark Lawrence *federal judge*
Wolfsdorf, Joseph Isadore *pediatrician, endocrinologist*
Wood, Henry Austin *architect*
Woodburn, Ralph Robert, Jr. *lawyer*
Woodlock, Douglas Preston *judge*
Woog, John J. *eye plastic surgeon*
Woolsey, John Munro, Jr. *lawyer*
Worthley, Harold Field *minister, educator*
Wu, Tung *curator, art historian, art educator, artist*
Yang, Zhen *research scientist, chemistry educator*
Yastrzemski, Carl Michael *former baseball player, public relations executive*
Young, Anne B. *neurologist, educator*
Young, Laura *dance educator, choreographer*
Young, Raymond Henry *lawyer*
Young, William Glover *federal judge*
Yu, Yong Ming *physiological biochemist, surgeon*
Yuan, Junying *medical educator, researcher*
Zabriskie, John L. *healthcare and agricultural products manufacturing company executive*
Zaldastani, Guivy *business consultant*
Zaldastani, Othar *structural engineer*
Zaleznik, Abraham *psychoanalyst, management specialist, educator*
Zarins, Bertram *orthopaedic surgeon*
Zeien, Alfred M. *consumer products company executive*
Zelen, Marvin *statistics educator*
Zervas, Nicholas Themistocles *neurosurgeon*
Zinner, Michael Jeffrey *surgeon, educator*
Zobel, Hiller Bellin *judge*

Bourne
Fantozzi-Pacheco, Peggy Ryone *environmental planner*
Roper, Burns Worthington *retired opinion research company executive*

Boxboro
Berry, Robert John *architect*
Lee, Shih-Ying *mechanical engineering educator*

Boxborough
Li, Yao Tzu *science educator*

Boxford
Glass, John Sheldon *manufacturing executive*
Hoover, Lynn Di Shong *psychotherapist, health care consultant*
Laderoute, Charles David *engineer, economist, consultant*

Bradford
†Murphy, Rich *educator in English language*

Braintree
Conlon, Eugene *artist, administrator*
Gittleman, Sol *university official, humanities educator*
Latham, Allen, Jr. *manufacturing company consultant*
Piraino, Thomas *writer, retired electrical engineer*
Salloway, Josephine Plovnick *school psychologist, marriage and family therapist, mental health counselor, psychology educator, college counselor*
Wilson, Blenda Jacqueline *foundation administrator*

Brewster
Hickok, Richard Sanford *retired accountant*
O'Brien, Gregory Francis *book publisher, writer, producer*

Bridgewater
Al-Obaidi, Jabbar A. *communication educator, film producer*
Casabian, Edward K., Jr. *secondary education educator*
Faiman-Silva, Sandra Lynne *anthropologist*
Hodge-Spencer, Cheryl Ann *orthodontist*
Hurley, Mike *English language educator*
Kreiling, Jean Louise *music educator*
Moses, Nancy Lee Heise *dance educator*
Nelson, Marian Emma *education educator*
Nicholeris, Carol Angela *music educator, composer, conductor*
Tinsley, Adrian *college president*
Zilonis, Mary Frances *information science educator, consultant*

Brighton
†Garrison, Jean Anne *social science educator*
Law, Bernard Francis Cardinal *archbishop*
Mahoney, Kathleen Mary *event planning company executive, consultant*
Murphy, William F. *priest, monsignor, religion educator*
†Novack, Sandy Alissa *social worker*
†Yurovich, Daniel J. *manufacturing company executive*

Brockton
Carlson, Desiree Anice *pathologist*
Clark, Carleton Earl *tax consultant*
Conboy, Martin Daniel *insurance broker, historian*
†Helfrich, Theodora Thompson *spanish educator, academic administrator*
Holland, David Vernon *minister*
Hyland, Douglas K. S. *museum administrator, educator*
Jellows, Tracy Patrick *software engineer*
Kligler, Roger Michael *physician*
Parcels, Burtis George *computer consultant, educator*
Park, Byiung Jun *textile engineer*
Sherman, Beverly Robin *medical/surgical, pediatric nurse*
Wiegner, Allen Walter *biomedical engineering educator, researcher*

Brookfield
Couture, Ronald David *art administrator, design consultant*

Brookline
Barron, Ros *artist*
Beaudoin, Carol Ann *psychologist*
Buchin, Jacqueline Chase *clinical psychologist*
Burnstein, Daniel *lawyer*
Caso, Adolph *publishing company executive*
Chryssavgis, John *theology educator, administrator*
†Cofield, Sherdena Dorsey *education director*
Creasey, David Edward *physician, psychiatrist, educator*
Cromwell, Adelaide M. *sociology educator*
Dubrovsky, Ben *communications executive*
Eden, Murray *electrical engineer, emeritus educator*
Epstein, Alvin *actor, director, singer, mime*
Erick, Miriam Anna *dietitian, medical writer*
Felsen, Leopold B. *engineering educator*
Ferrell, Robert Craig *computational physicist, consultant*
Frankel, Ernst Gabriel *shipping and aviation business executive, educator*
†Golden, Herbert Hershel *retired Romance languages educator*
Gray, Seymour *medical educator, author*
Jakab, Irene *psychiatrist*
Jordan, Ruth Ann *physician*
Kanin, Doris May *political scientist, consultant*
Keil, Alfred Adolf Heinrich *marine engineering educator*
Kibrick, Anne *nursing educator, university dean*
Koretsky, Sidney *internist, educator, paper historian*
Kraut, Joel Arthur *ophthalmologist*
Lown, Bernard *cardiologist, educator*
Lynton, Ernest Albert *physicist, educator, former university official*
Nadelson, Carol Cooperman *psychiatrist, educator*
Newman, Thomas Daniel *minister, school administrator*
Olenick, Arnold Jerome *accountant, financial management consultant*
†Ostfeld, Robert Jonathan *physician*
Rachlin, William Selig *surgeon*
Reedy, Harry Lee *financial services executive*
Reingardt, Ragnhild Sigrid Augusta *sculptor, artist*
Rubin-Katz, Barbara *sculptor, human services administrator*
Ruthchild, Rochelle Goldberg *education educator*
Saini, Gulshan Rai *soil physicist, agricultural hydrologist*
Schiller, Sophie *artist, graphic designer*
Shaw, Samuel Ervine, II *retired insurance company executive, consultant*
Strassler, Robert B. *investment professional*
Tuchman, Avraham *physicist, researcher*
Tuchman, Maurice Simon *library director*
Tyler, H. Richard *physician*
†Walter, Eugene Victor *writer*
Wax, Bernard *research and development consultant, lecturer*
Wertsman, Vladimir Filip *librarian, information specialist, author, translator*
Wilson, John *artist*
Zoll, Miriam Hannah *activist, writer, communication specialist*

Burlington
Bhathena, Firdaus *software company executive, consultant*
Birk, Lee (Carl Birk) *psychiatrist, educator*
Bright, Willard Mead *manufacturing company executive*
Clerkin, Eugene Patrick *physician*
DeCrosta, Susan Elyse *graphic designer*
Dubois, Cindy A. *guidance counselor*
Fager, Charles Anthony *physician, neurosurgeon*
Hampl, Mary Notermann *program manager*
Harding, Wayne Michael *sociologist, researcher*
Jones, Harvey Royden, Jr. *neurologist*
McLellan, Robert *gynecologist, oncologist, educator*
Moschella, Samuel L. *dermatology educator*
O'Brien, John Joseph *theology educator, priest*
Pettinella, Nicholas Anthony *financial executive*
Randall, Patricia Mary *consulting firm executive*
Reno, John F. *communications equipment company executive*
Schoetz, David John, Jr. *colon and rectal surgeon*
Seckel, Brooke Rutledge *plastic surgeon*
Smith, Derek Armand *consulting company executive*
Sproull, Robert Fletcher *research and development executive*
†Vlock, Deborah Michele *writer, public relations company executive*
Weatherby, David John *engineering company executive*
Wise, Robert Edward *radiologist*

Byfield
Kozol, Jonathan *writer*

Cambridge
Abban, Andrew Paul *laboratory coordinator*
Abelson, Harold *electrical engineer, educator*
Abernathy, Frederick Henry *mechanical engineering educator*
Abt, Clark C. *social scientist, executive, engineer, publisher, educator*
Ackerman, James Sloss *fine arts educator*
Ahmed, Leila Nadine *religious studies educator*
Alberty, Robert Arnold *chemistry educator*
Alcalay, Albert S. *artist, design educator*
Aldave, Barbara Bader *law educator, lawyer*
Alt, James Edward *political science educator*
Altshuler, David T. *software company executive*
Ancona, Henry *software company executive*
Anderson, Donald Gordon Marcus *mathematics educator*
Anderson, James Gilbert *chemistry educator*
Anderson, Stanford Owen *architect, architectural historian, educator*
Anderson, William Henry *psychobiologist, educator*
Andrews, William Dorey *lawyer, educator*
Anker, Peder Johan *historian of science*
Appley, Mortimer Herbert *psychologist, university president emeritus*
Argon, Ali Suphi *mechanical engineering educator*
Aronson, Michael Andrew *editor*
Artin, Michael *mathematics educator*
†Ascher, Maria Louise *translator, editor*
Aspinall, Mara Glickman *marketing and general management professional*
†Bacigalupo, Ana Mariella *anthropology educator*
Badian, Ernst *history educator*
Baggeroer, Arthur Bernard *electrical engineering educator*
Bailyn, Bernard *historian, educator*
Bakanowsky, Louis Joseph *visual arts educator, architect, artist*
Baker, Susan Lowell *psychologist*
Baldine, Joanne *academic administrator, researcher*
Bane, Bernard Maurice *publishing company executive*
Bane, Mary Jo *political science educator*
Barger, James Edwin *physicist*
Baron, Judson Richard *aerospace educator*
Baron, Sheldon *research and development company executive*
Bartee, Thomas Creson *computer scientist, educator*
Bartus, Raymond Thomas *neuroscientist, pharmaceutical executive, writer*
Bate, Walter Jackson *English literature educator*
Battin, Richard Horace *astronautical engineer*
Bazzaz, Fakhri A. *plant biology educator, administrator*
Beasley, David Muldrow *former governor*
Bedrosian, Edward Robert *investment management company executive*
Beér, János Miklós *engineering educator*
Ben-Akiva, Moshe Emanuel *civil engineering educator*
Benedek, George Bernard *physicist, educator*
Beranek, Leo Leroy *acoustical consultant*
Berg, Howard C. *biology educator*
Berliner, Joseph Scholom *economics educator*
Berlowitz, Leslie *cultural organization administrator*
Berndt, Ernst Rudolf *economist, educator*
†Berners-Lee, Tim *World Wide Web executive*
Biemann, Klaus *chemistry educator*
Birgeneau, Robert Joseph *physicist, educator*
Bishop, Robert Lyle *economist, educator*
Bizzi, Emilio *neurophysiologist, educator*
Blackmer, Donald Laurence Morton *political scientist*
Bloch, Konrad Emil *biochemist*
Bloembergen, Nicolaas *physicist, educator*
Bloom, Kathryn Ruth *public relations executive*
†Bloomfield, Steven B. *think-tank executive*
Boghani, Ashok Balvantrai *consulting firm executive*
Bogorad, Lawrence *biologist, educator*
Bok, Derek *law educator, former university president*
Bolster, Arthur Stanley, Jr. *history educator*
Bond, William Henry *librarian, educator*
Boorstein, Beverly Weinger *judge*
Borjas, George J(esus) *economics educator*
Bott, Raoul *mathematician, educator*
Bourneuf, Henri Joseph, Jr. *librarian*
Bouvier, Linda Fritts *publishing executive*
Boyle, Edward Allen *oceanography educator*
Bradt, Hale Van Dorn *physicist, x-ray astronomer, educator*
Brandt, John Henry *physician*
Branscomb, Lewis McAdory *physicist*
Branton, Daniel *biology educator*
Bras, Rafael Luis *engineering educator*
Brenner, Howard *chemical engineering educator*
Brockett, Roger Ware *engineering and computer science educator*
Brooks, Harvey *physics educator*
Brown, Edgar Cary *retired economics educator*
Brown, Robert Arthur *chemical engineering educator*
Bruce, James Donald *academic administrator*
Bruck, Phoebe Ann Mason *landscape architect*
Brusch, John Lynch *physician*
Brustein, Robert Sanford *English language educator, theatre director, author*
Brynjolfsson, Erik *management educator, researcher*
Buchwald, Jed Zachary *environmental health researcher, science history educator*
Buckler, Sheldon A. *energy company executive*
Buderi, Robert Bryan Hassan *author, journalist*
Bullock, Francis Jeremiah *pharmaceutical research executive*
Burchfiel, Burrell Clark *geology educator*
Burger, Todd Oliver *management consultant*
Burke, Bernard Flood *physicist, educator*
Burnham, Charles Wilson *mineralogy educator*
Burns, Carol J. *architect, educator*
Busch, Marc Lawrence *government educator*
Butler, James Newton *chemist, educator*
Cameron, Alastair Graham Walter *astrophysicist, educator*
Campbell, Robert *architect, writer*
Canizares, Claude Roger *astrophysicist, educator*
Carmichael, Alexander Douglas *engineering educator*
Carrier, George Francis *applied mathematics educator*
Carter, Ashton Baldwin *physicist, educator, government agency executive*
Caswell, Rex Ace *sales executive*
Ceyer, Sylvia T. *chemistry educator*
Chall, Jeanne Sternlicht *psychologist, educator*
Champion, (Charles) Hale *political science educator, former public official*
Chandler, Fay Martin *artist*

Chapin, Richard *arbitrator, consultant*
Chayes, Abram *law educator, lawyer*
Chen, Sow-Hsin *nuclear engineering educator, researcher*
Chernoff, Herman *statistics educator*
Cho, John Yungdo Nagamichi *atmospheric research scientist*
Chomsky, Avram Noam *linguistics and philosophy educator*
Clark, George Whipple *physics educator*
†Clark, Maynard Stephen *vegetarian resource center administrator*
Clark, Robert Charles *law educator, dean*
Clausen, Wendell Vernon *classics educator*
Cleary, David Michael *composer, library assistant*
Clifton, Anne Rutenber *psychotherapist*
Coatsworth, John Henry *history educator*
Cohen, Robert Edward *chemical engineering educator, consultant*
Cohn, Marjorie Benedict *curator, art historian, educator*
Cole, Heather Ellen *librarian*
Coleman, Sidney Richard *physicist, educator*
Coles, Robert *child psychiatrist, educator, author*
Collins, John William, III *librarian*
Colton, Clark Kenneth *chemical engineering educator*
Conley, Tom Clark *literature educator*
†Connaughton, David Michael *management consultant*
Connors, Frank Joseph *lawyer*
Conrades, George Henry *information systems company executive*
Cooper, Mary Campbell *information services executive*
Cooper, Richard Newell *economist, educator*
Corbato, Fernando Jose *electrical engineer and computer science educator*
Corey, Elias James *chemistry educator*
Coser, Lewis Alfred *sociology educator*
Covert, Eugene Edzards *aerophysics educator*
Cox, Archibald *lawyer, educator*
Crandall, Stephen Harry *engineering educator*
Cronin, Bonnie Kathryn Lamb *legislative staff executive*
Cross, Frank Moore, Jr. *foreign language educator*
Cummings-Saxton, James *chemical engineer, consultant, educator*
Cuno, James *art museum director*
Dame, Thomas Michael *radio astronomer*
Danheiser, Rick Lane *organic chemistry educator*
†D'Arbeloff, Alexander V. *electronics company executive*
Daukantas, George Vytautas *counseling practitioner, educator*
Davidson, Charles Sprecher *physician*
Davie, Joseph Myrten *physician, pathology and immunology educator, science administrator*
Davis, Paul Robert *investment manager, portfolio manager*
Demain, Arnold Lester *microbiologist, educator*
de Marneffe, Barbara Rowe *volunteer*
de Neufville, Richard Lawrence *engineering educator*
Dennis, Jack Bonnell *computer scientist*
Dershowitz, Alan Morton *lawyer, educator*
Dertouzos, Michael Leonidas *computer scientist, electrical engineer, educator*
Desai, Anita *writer*
Deshpandé, Rohit *marketing educator*
Deutch, John Mark *federal agency administrator, chemist, academic administrator*
Deutsch, Martin *emeritus physics professor*
de Varon, Lorna Cooke *choral conductor*
Dewart, Christopher *architectural educator, furniture maker*
Dewey, Clarence Forbes, Jr. *engineering educator*
DiCamillo, Gary Thomas *manufacturing executive*
Doering, William von Eggers *organic chemist, educator*
Dominguez, Jorge Ignacio *government educator*
Donahue, John David *public official, educator*
Donaldson, Peter Samuel *humanities educator*
Dorfman, Robert *economics educator*
Dornbusch, Rudiger *economics educator*
Doty, Paul Mead *biochemist, educator, arms control specialist*
Dowling, John Elliott *biology educator*
Downes, Gregory *architectural organization executive*
Drago-Severson, Eleanor Elizabeth *developmental psychologist, educator, researcher*
Drake, Elisabeth Mertz *chemical engineer*
Dresselhaus, Mildred Spiewak *physics and engineering educator*
Dryja, Thaddeus P. *opthalmologist, educator*
Dubowsky, Steven *mechanical engineering educator*
Dudley, Richard Mansfield *mathematician, educator*
Duffy, Robert Aloysius *aeronautical engineer*
Dugundji, John *aeronautical engineer*
Dunlop, John Thomas *economics educator, former secretary of labor*
Dunn, Charles William *Celtic languages and literature educator, author*
Dunn, Mary Maples *library director*
Durant, Graham John *medicinal chemist, drug researcher*
Dyck, Arthur James *ethicist, educator*
Dziewonski, Adam Marian *earth science educator*
Eagar, Thomas Waddy *metallurgist, educator*
Eagleson, Peter Sturges *hydrologist, educator*
Eckaus, Richard Samuel *economist, educator*
Edgerly, William Skelton *banker*
Edsall, John Tileston *biological chemistry educator*
Ehntholt, Daniel James *chemist*
†Ehrenfeld, John Roos *environmental policy educator*
Ehrenreich, Henry *physicist, educator*
Eisen, Herman Nathaniel *immunology researcher, medical educator*
Eisenberg, Carola *psychiatry educator*
Eldridge, Larry (William Lawrence Eldridge) *journalist*
Elias, Peter *electrical engineering educator*
Elkies, Noam D. *mathematics educator*
Ellwood, David Tabor *public policy educator*
Emanuel, Kerry Andrew *earth sciences educator*
Engell, James Theodore *English educator*
Epstein, David Mayer *composer, conductor, music theorist, educator*
Epstein, Henry David *electronics company executive*
Erdely, Stephen Lajos *music educator*
†Erdmann, Andrew Patrick Nicholas *historian*
Erikson, Raymond Leo *biology educator*
Eurich, Nell P. *educator, author*
Evans, Anthony Glyn *materials scientist*
Evans, David A(lbert) *chemistry educator*
†Evans, James Brian *geophysics educator*
†Everett, Thomas Gregory *musician, music educator*
Fallon, Richard H., Jr. *law educator*
Fanger, Donald Lee *Slavic language and literature educator*
†Fantone, Stephen D. *company executive*
Fay, James Alan *mechanical engineering educator*
Feininger, Theodore Lux *artist*
Feld, Michael Stephen *physics educator*
Feldstein, Martin Stuart *economist, educator*
Felman, Marc David *air force officer*
Feshbach, Herman *physicist, educator*
Field, George Brooks *theoretical astrophysicist*
Fineberg, Harvey Vernon *university official, physician, educator*
†Fiore, Lois Frances *editor, artist*
Fiorenza, Francis P. *religion educator*
Fischer, Kurt Walter *education educator*
Fisher, Franklin Marvin *economist*
Fisher, Roger Dummer *lawyer, educator, negotiation expert*
Flannery, Susan Marie *library administrator*
Fleming, Ronald Lee *urban designer, administrator, preservation planner, environmental educator*
Flier, Michael Stephen *Slavic languages educator*
Flowers, Woodie Claude *mechanical engineering educator and researcher, engineering director*
Fogelson, Robert Michael *history educator, writer, consultant*
Foley, James David *computer science educator, consultant*
Foner, Simon *research physicist*
Ford, Franklin Lewis *history educator, historian*
Ford, Patrick Kildea *Celtic studies educator*
Forman, Richard T. T. *ecology educator*
Forney, G(eorge) David, Jr. *retired electronics company executive*
Forrester, Jay Wright *management specialist, educator*
Fountain, Jane Ellen *public policy educator*
Fox, Ellen *academic administrator*
Fox, Gretchen Hovemeyer *staff assistant, freelance editor, genealogical consultant*
Fox, John Bayley, Jr. *university dean*
Fox, Maurice Sanford *molecular biologist, educator*
Frankel, Jeffrey Alexander *economist*
Freed, Lisa Ernestine *research scientist*
French, Anthony Philip *physicist, educator*
French, Kenneth Ronald *finance educator*
Frey, Frederick August *geochemistry researcher, educator*
Fried, Charles *law educator*
Friedman, Benjamin Morton *economics educator*
Friedman, Jerome Isaac *physics educator, researcher*
Friedman, Orrie Max *biotechnology company executive*
Frosch, Robert Alan *retired automobile manufacturing executive, physicist*
Fujimoto, James G. *electrical engineering educator*
Furman, Thomas D., Jr. *engineering company executive*
Gagliardi, Ugo Oscar *systems software architect, educator*
†Galbraith, John Kenneth *retired economist*
Gallager, Robert Gray *electrical engineering educator*
Gardner, Howard Earl *psychologist, author*
Garland, Carl Wesley *chemist, educator*
Garrelick, Joel Marc *acoustical scientist, consultant*
Gaskell, Ivan George Alexander De Wend *art museum curator*
Gates, Henry Louis, Jr. *English language educator*
Gatos, Harry Constantine *engineering educator*
Geller, Margaret Joan *astrophysicist, educator*
Gienapp, William Eugene *history educator*
Gilbert, Walter *molecular biologist, educator*
Gilligan, Carol F. *psychologist, writer*
Gilman, Todd Seacrist *language educator, musician*
Gingerich, Owen Jay *astronomer, educator*
Glaser, Peter Edward *mechanical engineer, consultant*
Glauner, Alfred William *lawyer, engineering company executive*
Glendon, Mary Ann *law educator*
Golay, Michael Warren *nuclear engineering educator*
Goldberg, Ray Allan *agribusiness educator*
Goldblith, Samuel Abraham *food science educator*
Goldfarb, Warren (David) *philosophy educator*
Goldstein, Mark Allan *pediatrician, adolescent medicine specialist*
Goldstone, Jeffrey *physicist*
Gomes, Peter John *clergyman, educator*
Gonson, S. Donald *lawyer*
Goodwin, Neva R. *economist*
Gordon, Roy Gerald *chemistry educator*
Gould, Stephen Jay *paleontologist, educator*
Graham, Loren Raymond *historian, educator*
Graham, William Albert *religion educator, history educator*
Graubard, Stephen Richards *history educator, editor*
Gray, Paul Edward *academic official*
Green, Richard John *architect*
Greenblatt, Stephen J. *English language educator*
Greene, Frederick D., II *chemistry educator*
Greenspan, Harvey Philip *applied mathematician, educator*
Greitzer, Edward Marc *aeronautical engineering educator, consultant*
Greyser, Linda Lorraine *education educator*
Griliches, Zvi *economist, educator*
Grindlay, Jonathan Ellis *astrophysics educator*
Grosz, Barbara Jean *computer science educator*
Grove, Timothy Lynn *geology educator*
Guerra, John Michael *optical engineer*
Guth, Alan Harvey *physicist, educator*
Guthke, Karl Siegfried *foreign language educator*
Halle, Morris *linguist, educator*
Halperin, Bertrand Israel *physics educator*
Hamilton, Malcolm Cowan *librarian, editor, indexer, personnel professional*
Hamner, W. Easley *architect*
Hanan, Patrick Dewes *foreign language professional, educator*
Handford, Martin John *illustrator, author*
Hansen, Kent Forrest *nuclear engineering educator*
Harleman, Donald Robert Fergusson *environmental engineering educator*
Harrington, Anne *science historian*
Harris, Wesley L. *aeronautics engineering educator*
Harris, William Wolpert *treasurer political action committee*
Hartl, Daniel Lee *genetics educator*
Hass, Michael Shepherdson *architect*
Hastings, John Woodland *biologist, educator*
Haus, Hermann Anton *electrical engineering educator*
Hauser, John Richard *marketing and management science educator*
Hausman, Jerry Allen *economics educator, consultant*
Havens, Leston Laycock *psychiatrist, educator*
Hax, Arnoldo Cubillos *management educator, industrial engineer*
Heaney, Seamus Justin *poet, educator*
Heimert, Alan Edward *humanities educator*
Helgason, Sigurdur *mathematician, educator*
Heney, Joseph Edward *environmental engineer*
Henninger, Polly *neuropsychologist, researcher and clinician*
Henrichs, Albert Maximinus *classicist, educator*
Hermes, Frank *marketing executive*
Herschbach, Dudley Robert *chemistry educator*
Heywood, John Benjamin *mechanical engineering educator*
Hilt, Mary Louise *artist*
Hoffman, Paul Felix *geologist, educator*
Holdren, John Paul *energy and resource educator, researcher, author, consultant*
Holm, Richard Hadley *chemist, educator*
Holton, Gerald *physicist, science historian*
Holzman, Philip Seidman *psychologist, educator*
Homburger, Freddy *physician, scientist, artist*
Horowitz, Morris A. *economist*
Horrell, Jeffrey Lanier *library administrator*
Horvitz, Howard Robert *biology educator, researcher*
Horwitz, Paul *physicist*
Houtchens, Robert Austin, Jr. *biochemist*
Howard, Jack Benny *chemical engineer, educator, researcher*
Howitt, Arnold Martin *university researcher, administrator, educator*
Hsiao, Jack Nai-Chang *physician*
Huang, Kerson *physics educator*
Hubbard, Ruth *biology educator*
Huchra, John Peter *astronomer, educator*
Hungness, Lisa Sue *English language educator, consultant*
Hunt, Swanee G. *public policy educator, former ambassador*
Huntington, Samuel Phillips *political science educator*
Hynes, Richard Olding *biology researcher and educator*
Ingard, Karl Uno *physics educator*
Ippen, Erich Peter *electrical engineering educator*
Iriye, Akira *historian, educator*
Jackiw, Roman *physicist, educator*
Jacoby, Henry Donnan *economist, educator*
Jaffe, Arthur Michael *physicist, mathematician, educator*
Jencks, Christopher Sandys *public policy educator*
Jensen, Klavs Flemming *chemical engineering educator*
John, Richard Rodda *transportation executive*
Johnson, Howard Wesley *former university president, business executive*
Johnson, Michael Lewis *psychiatrist*
Johnson, Willard Raymond *political science educator, consultant*
Jones, Christopher Prestige *classicist, historian*
Jordan, Thomas Hillman *geophysicist, educator*
Jorgenson, Dale Weldeau *economist, educator*
Joskow, Paul Lewis *economist, educator*
Joss, Paul Christopher *astrophysicist, atmospheric physicist, educator*
Kac, Victor G. *mathematician, educator*
Kagan, Jerome *psychologist, educator*
Kalb, Marvin *public policy and government educator*
Kalelkar, Ashok Satish *consulting company executive*
Kamentsky, Louis Aaron *biophysicist*
Kamm, Roger Dale *biomedical engineer, educator*
Kaplan, Benjamin *judge*
Kaplan, Justin *author*
Kaplow, Louis *law educator*
Karl, Barry Dean *historian, educator*
Karplus, Martin *chemistry educator*
Kassakian, John Gabriel *research electrical engineer, engineering director*
Kassman, Deborah Newman *university administrator, writer, editor*
Katz, Lawrence Francis *economics educator*
Kaufman, Andrew Lee *law educator*
Kaufman, Gordon Dester *theology educator*
Kaysen, Carl *economics educator*
Kazhdan, David *mathematician, educator*
Kazimi, Mujid Suliman *nuclear engineer, educator*
Keck, James Collyer *physicist, educator*
Keller, Evelyn Fox *history and philosophy educator*
Kelley, Albert Joseph *global management strategy consultant*
Kelman, Herbert Chanoch *psychology educator*
Kelman, Steven Jay *management educator*
Keniston, Kenneth *psychologist, educator*
Kennedy, David W. *law educator*
Kennedy, Stephen Dandridge *economist, researcher*
Kerman, Arthur Kent *physicist, educator*
Kerrebrock, Jack Leo *aeronautics and astronautics engineering educator*
Keyfitz, Nathan *sociologist, demographer, educator*
Keyser, Samuel Jay *linguistics educator, university official*
Khorana, Har Gobind *chemist, educator*
Khoury, Philip S. *social sciences educator, historian*
Kim, Peter Sungbai *biochemistry educator*
King, Ronold Wyeth Percival *physics educator*
Kirshner, Lewis A. *psychiatrist*
Kistiakowsky, Vera *physics researcher, educator*
Kleinman, Arthur Michael *medical anthropologist, psychiatrist, educator*
Klemperer, William *chemistry educator*
Kleppner, Daniel *physicist, educator*
Klibanov, Alexander Maxim *chemistry and biotechnology educator, researcher*
Knickrehm, Glenn Allen *management executive*
Knoll, Andrew Herbert *biology educator*
†Knox, Wendall J. *management consultant*
Kobus, Richard Lawrence *architect, designer, executive*
Koester, Helmut Heinrich *theologian, educator*
Kosslyn, Stephen M. *psychologist educator*
Kovach, Bill *educational foundation administrator*
Koyanis, Melinda T. *publishing executive, lawyer*
Krieger, Alex *architecture and design educator*
Kruger, Kenneth *architect*
Kulikovskaya, Svetlana Romanovna *artist, costume designer, self-employed*
Kung, Hsiang-Tsung *computer architect*
Kuttner, Robert Louis *editor, columnist*
Kyhl, Robert Louis *retired electrical engineering educator*
Ladd, Charles Cushing, III *civil engineering educator*
Ladjevardi, Habib *historian*
Laibinis, Paul Edward *chemical engineering educator*
Laiou, Angeliki Evangelos *history educator*
Lala, Jaynarayan Hotchand *computer engineer*
LaMantia, Charles Robert *management consulting company executive*
Lamberg-Karlovsky, Clifford Charles *anthropologist, archaeologist*
Lampson, Butler Wright *computer scientist*
Lander, Eric Steven *medical researcher*
Langer, Ellen Jane *psychologist, educator, writer*
Latanision, Ronald Michael *materials science and engineering educator, consultant*
Layton, Billy Jim *composer*
Lazarus, Maurice *retired retail executive*
Lee, Patrick A. *physics educator*
Leehey, Patrick *mechanical and ocean engineering educator*
LeMessurier, William James *structural engineer*
Leonard, Herman Beukema (Dutch Leonard) *public finance and management educator*
Lerman, Leonard Solomon *science educator, scientist*
Levi, Herbert Walter *biologist, educator*
Levy, Stephen Raymond *high technology company executive*
Lieberson, Stanley *sociologist, educator*
Light, Richard Jay *statistician, education educator*
Lightman, Alan Paige *physicist, writer, educator*
Lim, Jae Soo *engineering educator, information systems*
Lindzen, Richard Siegmund *meteorologist, educator*
Linsky, Martin Alan *public policy educator, consultant*
Lippard, Stephen James *chemist, educator*
Lipscomb, William Nunn, Jr. *retired physical chemistry educator*
Litster, James David *physics educator, dean*
Little, John Dutton Conant *management scientist, educator*
Littlefield, Paul Damon *management consultant*
Liu, Guosong *neurobiologist*
Livingston, James Duane *physicist, educator*
Lloyd, Boardman *investment executive*
Lodish, Harvey Franklin *biologist, educator*
Loeb, Abraham *astrophysics educator, researcher*
Lomon, Earle Leonard *physicist, educator, consultant*
London, Irving Myer *physician, educator*
Longwell, John Ploeger *chemical engineering educator*
Lorenz, Edward Norton *meteorologist, educator*
Low, Francis Eugene *physics educator*
Lunt, Horace Gray *linguist, educator*
Lusztig, George *mathematician*
Lynch, Harry James *biologist*
Lynch, Nancy Ann *computer scientist, educator*
Lyon, Richard Harold *physicist educator*
Maass, Arthur *political science and environmental studies educator*
MacDonald, Sandy *writer*
Mack, Robert Whiting *computer consultant*
Mackey, George Whitelaw *mathematician, educator*
MacMaster, Robert Ellsworth *historian, educator*
Magasanik, Boris *microbiology educator*
Magee, John Francis *research company executive*
Magnanti, Thomas L. *management and engineering educator*
Maher, Brendan Arnold *psychology educator, editor*
Maier, Charles Steven *history educator*
Maier, Pauline *history educator*
Makhoul, John Ibrahim *electrical engineer, researcher*
Malmstad, John Earl *Slavic languages and literatures, educator*
Maniatis, Thomas Peter *molecular biology educator*
Mann, Robert Wellesley *biomedical engineer, educator*
Mansbridge, Jane Jebb *political scientist, educator*
Mansfield, John H. *lawyer, educator*
Marder, William David *health economist*
Marini, Robert Charles *environmental engineering executive*
Markey, Winston Roscoe *aeronautical engineering educator*
Marolda, Anthony Joseph *management consulting company executive*
Marsden, Brian Geoffrey *astronomer*
Martin, Harry Stratton, III *law librarian*
Martin, Paul Cecil *physicist, educator*
Martino, Donald James *composer, educator*
Marvin, Ursula Bailey *geologist*
†Mason, Linda A. *social services administrator*
Masubuchi, Koichi *marine engineer, educator*
Mathews, Joan Helene *pediatrician*
Mayr, Ernst *retired zoologist, philosopher*
Mazur, Barry Charles *mathematician*
Mazur, Michael *artist*
McClintock, Frank Ambrose *mechanical engineer*
McElroy, Michael *physicist, researcher, educator*
McGarry, Frederick Jerome *civil engineering educator*
McKenna, Margaret Anne *college president*
McKenna, Martha Barry *college dean*
Mc Kie, Todd Stoddard *artist*
McMahon, Thomas Arthur *biology and applied mechanics educator*
†McMullen, Curtis T. *mathematics educator*
Mei, Chiang Chung *civil engineer, educator*
Melton, Douglas A. *molecular and cell biology educator*
Meltzer, Daniel J. *law educator*
Merrill, Dale Marie *lawyer*
Meselson, Matthew Stanley *biochemist, educator*
Metcalfe, Murray Robert *venture capitalist*
Meyer, John Edward *nuclear engineering educator*
Meyer, John Robert *economist, educator*
Michelman, Frank I. *lawyer, educator*
Milgram, Jerome H. *marine and ocean engineer, educator*
Miller, Arthur Raphael *law educator*
Miller, Chandra Marie *educator*
Miller, Rene Harcourt *aerospace engineer, educator*
Minsky, Marvin Lee *mathematician, educator*
Mitchell, William J. *dean, architecture educator*
Mitten, David Gordon *classical archaeologist*
Mnookin, Robert Harris *lawyer, educator*
Molina, Mario Jose *physical chemist, educator*
Moneo, José Rafael *architecture educator*
Montgomery, John Dickey *political science educator*
†Moore, Christine Palamidessi *writer*
Moore, Mark Harrison *criminal justice and public policy educator*
Moran, James Michael, Jr. *astronomer, educator*
Morris, Errol M. *filmmaker*
Moses, Joel *computer scientist, educator*
Mosteller, Frederick *mathematical statistician, educator*
Mueller, Robert Kirk *management consulting company executive*
Narayan, Ramesh *astronomy educator*
Nathanson, Larry *medical educator, physician*
Negele, John William *physics educator, consultant*

Keane, Thomas Edward *management consultant*
Kehoe, Dorrie Bonner *museum educator*
Liljestrand, James Stratton *physician administrator, internist*
Moore, Robert Lowell, Jr. (Robin Moore) *author*
Osepchuk, John Moses *engineering physicist, consultant*
Palay, Sanford Louis *retired scientist, educator*
Rarich, Anne Lippitt *management and organizational development consultant*
Schiller, Pieter Jon *venture capital executive*
Smith, Eric Parkman *retired railroad executive*
Smith, Peter Walker *finance executive*
Two Feathers, Morwen *event coordinating company executive*
Valley, George Edward, Jr. *physicist, educator*
Villers, Philippe *mechanical engineer*
White, James Barr *lawyer, real estate investor, consultant*
Wickfield, Eric Nelson *investment company executive*
Woll, Harry J. *electrical engineer*

Cotuit
Miller, Robert Charles *retired physicist*

Cummington
Smith, William Jay *author*
Wilbur, Richard Purdy *writer, educator*

Danvers
Baures, Mary Margaret *psychotherapist, author*
Dolan, John Ralph *retired corporation executive*
†Hodgin, Jean *English educator*
Keppler, Richard Rudolph *consultant, former oil company executive*
Langford, Dean Ted *lighting and precision materials company executive*
†Ronan, John J. *communications educator*
Rubinstein, Sidney Jacob *orthopedic technologist*
Traicoff, George *college president*
Waite, Charles Morrison *food company executive*

Dedham
Bachman, Carol Christine *trust company executive*
Daley, Charles Mike *vehicle recovery company executive*
Firth, Everett Joseph *timpanist*
†Hogan, Frances L. *executive*
Janson, Barbara Jean *publisher*
Magner, Jerome Allen *entertainment company executive*
Naughton, Marie Ann *corporate executive*
Nichols, Nancy Ruth *elementary educator*
Redstone, Sumner Murray *entertainment company executive, lawyer*
Spoolstra, Linda Carol *minister, educator, religious organization administrator*

Dennis
Weilbacher, William Manning *advertising and marketing consultant*

Dennis Port
Hebert, Donna Marie *food product executive*
Marcus, Marie Eleanor *pianist*
Singer, Myer R(ichard) *lawyer*

Devens
Anthony, Sylvia *social welfare organization executive*

Dorchester
†Boles, John P. *bishop*
Brelis, Matthew Dean Burns *journalist*
Bruzelius, Nils Johan Axel *journalist*
Daly, Charles Ulick *foundation executive*
Garrison, Althea *government official*
Goodman, Ellen Holtz *journalist*
Greenway, Hugh Davids Scott *journalist*
Lee, June Warren *dentist*

Dover
Aldrich, Frank Nathan *banker*
Bonis, Laszlo Joseph *business executive, scientist*
Craver, James Bernard *lawyer*
Crittenden, Gazaway Lamar *retired banker*
Edwards, Carl Normand *lawyer*
Kovaly, John Joseph *consulting engineering executive, educator*
Salhany, Lucille S. *broadcast executive*
Smith, William Henry Preston *writer, editor, former corporate executive*
Stockwell, Ernest Farnham, Jr. *banker*

Dracut
Brousseau, Catherine F. *school health services director*
Medor, Janice Elizabeth *healthcare administrator*
†Pieslak, Richard Alphonse *civil engineer*

Dudley
Carney, Roger Francis Xavier *retired army officer*
Van de Workeen, Priscilla Townsend *small business owner and executive*

Duxbury
Habgood, Robert P. *publishing executive*
McAuliffe, Eugene Vincent *retired diplomat and business executive*
†Meier, Carl William *retired educator*
Wangler, William Clarence *retired insurance company executive*

East Boston
Blute, Peter I. *transportation executive, former congressman*
Moore, Kerry Duane *mental health association administrator*

East Bridgewater
Farrell, Sharon Elaine *real estate broker*
Heywood, Anne *artist, educator*

East Dennis
†Ely, David (David E. Lilienthal, Jr.) *writer*
†Phillips, Clay Edison *surgeon*

East Longmeadow
Green, Frank Walter *industrial engineer*
Miller, Nancy Janet *insurance agent*
Skutnik, Bolesh J. *optics scientist, lay worker, lawyer*
Wald, Gloria Sue *educational consultant*

East Orleans
Burkert, Robert Randall *artist*

Eastham
Gross, Dorothy-Ellen *library director, dean*
Lynne-O'Brien, Vincent *director, actor*
McLaughlin, Richard Warren *retired insurance company executive*
Miller, Gabriel Lorimer *physicist, researcher*
Souther, Jean Lorraine *accounting and management educator, accountant*

Easthampton
†AAlfs, Janet Elizabeth *poet, writer, martial arts educator*
†Melnick, Ralph *library director, secondary school educator*
Perkins, Homer Guy *manufacturing company executive*

Easton
†Chichetto, James William *editor, educator*
Segersten, Robert Hagy *lawyer, investment banker*

Essex
Broome, Roger Greville Brooke, IV *fundraiser*
†Lawson, Judith Carroll *corporation executive, administrator*

Everett
Jenkins, Alexander, III *business executive*
Shedden, Kenneth Charles *fire department official, business owner*
Wright, Franz Paul *poet, writer, translator*

Fairhaven
Goes, Kathleen Ann *secondary education educator, choral director*
†Heskett, Robert Earl *psychologist*
Hotchkiss, Henry Washington *real estate broker and financial consultant*

Fall River
†Andrade, Manuela Pestana *art educator*
Connors, Robert Leo *city official*
Correia, Robert *state legislator*
†Dion, Marc Munroe *newspaper columnist*
†Guillemette, Mark Edgar *textile technologist*
Horvitz, Susan Smith *educator*
Ingles, James H. *community college dean*
King, Paula Jean *nursing administrator*
Lynds, Lucinda *music educator*
O'Malley, Sean *bishop*
Powers, Alan William *literature educator*
Sullivan, Ruth Anne *librarian*
†Tinberg, Howard *English educator*
Wolberg, Richard Allen *Cantor*

Falmouth
Goody, Richard Mead *geophysicist*
Litschgi, Richard John *computer manufacturing company executive*
Sato, Kazuyoshi *pathologist*
Schlesinger, Robert Walter *microbiologist, microbiology educator emeritus*

Feeding Hills
Norris, Pamela *school psychologist*

Fitchburg
Flinkstrom, Henry Allan *sales executive*
Jareckie, Stephen Barlow *museum curator*
Keough, William Richard *English language educator*
Mara, Vincent Joseph *college president*
Niemi, Beatrice Neal *social services professional*
Riccards, Michael Patrick *academic administrator*
Wieland, Paul Richard *broadcast executive*

Foxboro
Armstrong, Bruce Charles *professional football player*
Aubert, Kenneth Stephen *guidance and counseling administrator, educator*
Bledsoe, Drew *professional football player*
Bush, Raymond T. *accountant, corporate professional*
Carroll, Pete *professional football coach*
Coates, Ben Terrence *professional football player*
†Edwards, Robert *professional football player*
Hershman, Judith *advertising executive*
Kraft, Robert K. *professional sports team executive*
Pierce, Francis Casimir *civil engineer*
Ryskamp, Carroll Joseph *chemical engineer*
Savarese, Giovanni *professional soccer player*
†Zenga, Walter *professional soccer player*

Framingham
†Aronson, Benjamin *artist*
Austin, Sandra Ikenberry *nurse educator, consultant*
Bogard, Carole Christine *lyric soprano*
Bose, Amar Gopal *electrical engineering educator*
Cammarata, Bernard *retail company executive*
†Casselman, Frederick Lee *computer artist*
Crohan, Margaret Elizabeth *communications educator, consultant*
Crossley, Frank Alphonso *former metallurgical engineer*
Deutsch, Marshall E(manuel) *medical products company executive, inventor*
Donovan, R. Michael *management consultant*
Dube, Beatrice Dorothy *psychologist*
Feldberg, Sumner Lee *retired retail company executive*
Felper, David Michael *lawyer*
Finn, Gary *educator, entrepreneur*
Gatlin, Michael Gerard *lawyer, educator*
Goldman, Ralph Frederick *research physiologist, educator*
Harrington, Joseph Francis *educational company executive, history educator*
Heng, Gerald C. W. *lawyer*
Hillman, Carol Barbara *communications executive*
†Hillman, Reed V. *protective services official*
Hopkins, Esther Arvilla Harrison *retired chemist, patent lawyer*
Horn, Bernard *English language educator, writer*
Hunt, Samuel Pancoast, III *lawyer, corporate executive*
Jones, Clark Powell, Jr. *financial services executive*
Lavin, Philip Todd *biostatistician executive*
LeDuc, Karen Lorain Leacu *elementary and middle school education educator*
Leppo, Tamara Elizabeth Marks *account manager*

Levy, Joseph Louis *publishing company executive*
Lindsay, Leslie *packaging engineer*
Lipton, Leah *art historian, educator, museum curator*
Margolis, Bruce Lewis *human resources executive*
†McCarthy, Desmond Fergus *English literature educator*
Meador, Charles Lawrence *management and systems consultant, educator*
Meltzer, Jay H. *lawyer, retail company executive*
Merser, Francis Gerard *manufacturing company executive, consultant*
Munro, Meredith Vance *lawyer*
†Nolin, Anna Patricia *English language educator*
O'Bannon, Jacqueline Michele *geriatrics and mental health nurse*
Oleskiewicz, Francis Stanley *retired insurance executive*
Rosenberg, Victor Laurence *management educator, entrepreneur*
Scherr, Allan Lee *computer scientist, executive*
Silverman, Harold Irving *pharmaceutical executive*
Tischler, Henry Ludwig *sociology educator*
Vermette, Raymond Edward *clinical laboratories administrator*
Waters, James Logan *analytical instrument manufacturing executive*
Welte, A. Theodore *chamber of commerce executive*
Wishner, Steven R. *retail executive*
Wulf, Sharon Ann *management consultant*

Franklin
Lowrie, Kathryn Yanacek *high technology recruiter*
Pano, Gregory James *history educator*
Shastry, Shambhu Kadhambiny *scientist, engineering executive, consultant*

Gardner
Cosentino, Patricia Byrne *English educator, poet*
Coulter, Sherry Parks *secondary education educator*
Du Buske, Lawrence M. *immunologist, allergist, rheumotologist*
Hawke, Robert Douglas *retired state legislator*
Marceau, Judith Marie *elementary education educator*

Gloucester
Baird, Gordon Prentiss *publisher*
Birchfield, John Kermit, Jr. *lawyer*
†Brady, Patrick *advertising executive*
Donnelly, Barbara *artist, educator*
Hausman, William Ray *fund raising and management consultant*
Johnson, Anne Elisabeth *medical assistant*
Johnson, Janet Lou *real estate executive*
Lanzkron, Rolf Wolfgang *manufacturing company executive*
†Mammola, Dominic *advertising executive*
Means, Elizabeth Rose Thayer *financial consultant, lawyer*
White, Harold Jack *pathologist*
Zawinul, Josef *bandleader, composer, keyboardist, synthesist*

Grafton
Haggerty, John Edward *research center administrator, former army officer*
Hayes, Jacqueline M. *geriatrics nurse*
Tite, John Gregory *secondary school educator*

Great Barrington
Curtin, Phyllis *music educator, former dean, operatic singer*
Drew, Bernard Alger *writer*
Filkins, Peter Joel *English language educator*
Gilmour, Robert Arthur *foundation executive, educator*
Lane-Zucker, Laurie John *executive*
Lewis, Karen Marie *writer, editor*
Porteous, Skipp *private investigator, writer*
Rodgers, Bernard F., Jr. *academic administrator, dean*
Schenck, Benjamin Robinson *insurance consultant*
Stonier, Tom *theoretical biologist, educator*
Wampler, Barbara Bedford *entrepreneur*

Greenfield
Curtiss, Carol Perry *nursing consultant*
†Hassett, sulvia Ann *educator*
Lee, Marilyn (Irma) Modarelli *law librarian*
Robinson, John Alan *logic and computer science educator*
Ruiz, Lillian *English language educator*
Thidemann, Norman Ellis *town official*
†Young, Thomas Steven *artist, educator*

Groton
Searle, Andrew Barton *fund raising consultant*

Hamilton
†Ceballos, Ruben Alberto *nursing researcher*

Hanover
†Driscoll, Kathleen J *writer, research analyst*
Lonborg, James Reynold *dentist, former professional baseball player*
Mickunas, Nancy Ann *special education educator*

Hanscom AFB
Mailloux, Robert Joseph *physicist*
†McFarland, Ted M. *career officer*
Schmitt, Stephen Richard *electronics engineer*
Straka, Ronald Morris *physicist*

Hanson
Norris, John Anthony *health sciences executive, lawyer, educator*

Harvard
Evdokimoff, Merrily Weber *nursing administrator, community health nurse*
Larson, Roland Elmer *health care executive*
Matson, Stephen L. *technology industry executive*
Sutherland, Malcolm Read, Jr. *clergyman, educator*

Harwich
Bush, Richard James *engineering executive, lay worker*
Geberth, Frances White *painter*
†Steward, Aleta Joanna *artist*

Harwich Port
Staszesky, Francis Myron *independent energy consultant*

Hatfield
Yolen, Jane *author*

Haverhill
Dimitry, John Randolph *academic administrator*
†Hosman-Nelson, Jill Marie *special education educator*
Korinow, Ira Lee *rabbi*
MacMillan, Francis Philip *physician*
Morris, Robert *reinsurance analyst*
Niccolini, Drew George *gastroenterologist*
Ruiz-Rodriguez, Eduardo Antonio *psychology and sociology educator*
Walker, Robert Ross *social worker*

Hingham
Calnan, Arthur Francis *ophthalmologist*
Cooke, Gordon Richard *retail executive*
Hart, Richard Nevel, Jr. *financial exective, consultant*
†Kilroy, John Michael *artist, educator*
Lane, Frederick Stanley *lawyer*
†Larsen, Edward Lee *retail executive*
Reardon, Mary Agnes *painter, muralist, design consultant*
Zieper, Matthew Howard *policy analyst*

Holden
Cole, Theron Metcalf *engineer*
Gordon, Steven B. *chemist*
Jareckie, Gretchen Kinsman Fillmore *retired English language educator*
Owoc, CherylAnn Smith *geriatrics nurse, educator*

Holland
McGrory, Mary Kathleen *retired college president*

Holliston
O'Connor, Jude *special education educator, consultant*

Holyoke
Baker, David S. *architect*
Bilsky, Edward Gerald *clinical social worker*
Bluh, Cynthia Hubbard *insurance company executive*
Chapdelaine, Lorraine Elder *gerontology nurse*
†Dutcher, James Marshall *English language educator*
Dwight, William, Jr. *former newspaper executive, restaurateur*
Florek, Leona *nursing educator*
Lambert, Jean Marjorie *health care executive*
†O'Connor, Mary Ellen *principal*

Hopedale
Breault, Jean Winsor *nursing consultant*

Hopkinton
Harris, Jeffrey Sherman *technology company executive*
McGuire, Frank Joseph *accountant*
Nickerson, Richard Gorham *research company executive*
†Ruettgers, Michael C. *computer company executive*

Housatonic
Charpentier, Gail Wigutow *private school executive director*

Hudson
†Mixter, Jean E. *educational administrator*

Hull
Anderson, Timothy Christopher *consulting company executive*
Burgess, David Lowry *artist*

Hyannis
Makkay, Albert *broadcast executive*
Makkay, Maureen Ann *broadcast executive*
Miller, Timothy Alan *newspaper entertainment editor, film critic*
Nicholson, Ellen Ellis *clinical social worker*
White, Allen Jordan *nursing home adminstrator, consultant*

Hyde Park
†Clutz, Charles Nesbitt *architect*
Harris, Emily Louise *special education educator*
Riley, Lawrence Joseph *bishop*

Indian Orchard
†Daley, Veta Adassa *educational administrator*
Warren, Alice Louise *artist*

Ipswich
Barth, Elmer Ernest *wire and cable company executive*
Getchell, Charles Willard, Jr. *lawyer, publisher*
Hamilton, Donald Bengtsson *author*
Jennings, Frederic Beach, Jr. *economist, consultant, saltwater flyfishing guide*
Kennan, Elizabeth Topham *former university president and history educator*
†Moules, Deborah Ann *non-profit organization administrator*
Munro, Donald William, Jr. *non-profit organization executive*
Sturwold, Sister Rita Mary *educational administrator*
Wilson, Doris H. *volunteer*

Jamaica Plain
Arbeit, Robert David *physician*
Brown, Mary Jean *public health nurse*
Cook, Robert Edward *plant ecology educator, research director*
Florio, Christopher John *multimedia producer*
Hartley, Robert Milton *internist, rheumatologist, medical director*
Laudato, Gaetano Joseph, Jr. *retired locomotive engineer*
Lowenthal, Michael Francis *writer, editor*
Manzo, David William *human services administrator*
Murphy, Raymond Leo Harrington, Jr. *pulmonologist*
Nance, Marjorie Greenfield *educator*
Pierce, Chester Middlebrook *psychiatrist, educator*
Shapiro, Ascher Herman *mechanical engineer, educator, consultant*

Snider, Gordon Lloyd physician
Zahn, Carl Frederick museum publications director, designer, photographer

Kingston
Squarcia, Paul Andrew school superintendent

Lakeville
Colcord, Herbert Nathaniel, III food company executive
†Washburn, Stewart Alexander management consultant

Lancaster
McDowell, David Jamison clinical psychologist
Richter, Henry Andrew electrical engineer

Lanesboro
Wheeler, Kathleen Marie emergency nurse

Lawrence
Brophy, Susan Dorothy adapted physical education educator
Mosca, Anthony John substance abuse professional
Stanley, Malchan Craig school system administrator, psychologist

Lee
Rich, Philip Dewey publishing executive

Leeds
Baskin, Leonard sculptor, graphic artist
Grenz, Linda L. Episcopal priest

Leicester
Rogers, Randall Lloyd mechanical engineer

Lenox
Coffin, Louis Fussell, Jr. mechanical engineer
Collins, Oral Edmond theology educator, archaeologist
Curtis, William Edgar conductor, composer
Kochta, Ruth Martha art gallery owner
Meyer, Peter Barrett journalist
Vincent, Shirley Jones secondary education educator

Leominster
Cormier, Robert Edmund writer
Ford, John Stephen treasurer
Lorente, Roderick Dana optometrist
Marro, Matthew Shawn chemist

Leverett
Barkin, Solomon economist
†Pearson, Gayle Marlene writer, editor

Lexington
Aronin, Lewis Richard metallurgical engineer
Bailey, Fred Coolidge retired engineering consulting company executive
Bell, Carolyn Shaw economist, educator
Berstein, Irving Aaron biotechnology and medical technology executive
Bilow, Howard L. health care company executive
Bombardieri, Merle Ann psychotherapist
Brick, Donald Bernard consulting company executive
Brookner, Eli electrical engineer
Buchanan, John Machlin biochemistry educator
Burwen, Barbara R. painter
Cathou, Renata Egone chemist, consultant
Champion, Kenneth Stanley Warner physicist
Cooper, William Eugene consulting engineer
Davidson, Frank Paul retired macroengineer, lawyer
Davis, Barbara M(ae) librarian
Densmore, Ann speech pathologist, audiologist, writer
Dionne, Gerald Francis research physicist, educator, consultant
Drouilhet, Paul Raymond, Jr. science laboratory director, electrical engineer
Eaton, Allen Ober lawyer
Fillios, Louis Charles retired science educator
Fortmann, Thomas Edward research and development company executive
Fray, Lionel Louis management consultant
Freed, Charles engineering consultant, researcher
Freitag, Wolfgang Martin librarian, educator
Frey, John Ward landscape architect
Gibbs, Martin biologist, educator
Glovsky, Susan G. L. lawyer
Guivens, Norman Roy, Jr. mathematician, engineer
Holzman, Franklyn Dunn economics educator
†Hyde, Thomas D. lawyer
Jordan, Judith Victoria clinical psychologist, educator
Kanter, Irving mathematical physicist
Keicher, William Eugene electrical engineer
Kennedy, X. J. (Joseph Kennedy) writer
Kerr, Thomas Henderson, III electrical engineer, researcher
Kindleberger, Charles P., II economist, educator
Kingston, Robert Hildreth engineering educator
Kirkpatrick, Francis H(ubbard), Jr. biophysicist, intellectual property practitioner, consultant
Kluczynski, Janet computer company marketing executive
Levy, Steven Z. elementary education educator
Manganello, James Angelo psychologist
Melngailis, Ivars solid state researcher
Mollo-Christensen, Erik Leonard oceanographer
Monash, Curt Alfred software industry executive
Morrow, Walter Edwin, Jr. electrical engineer, university laboratory administrator
Muldowney, Michael Patrick finance executive
Nash, Leonard Kollender chemistry educator
Nason, Leonard Yoshimoto lawyer, writer, publisher
Nye, Joseph S(amuel), Jr. political science educator, administrator
Papanek, Gustav Fritz economist, educator
Paul, Norman Leo psychiatrist, educator
Perez, Carol Anne rehabilitation services professional
Picard, Dennis J. retired electronics company executive
Powers, Martha Mary nursing consultant, education specialist
Preve, Roberta Jean librarian, researcher
Ross, Douglas Taylor retired software company executive
Schafer, Alice Turner retired mathematics educator
Shapiro, Marian Kaplun psychologist
Shull, Clifford G. physicist, educator
Silverman, Sam Mendel physicist, lawyer
Smith, Robert Louis construction company executive
Spero, Rand Kevin management consultant
Stiglitz, Martin Richard electrical engineer
Strange, Donald Ernest health care company executive
Sussman, Martin Victor chemical engineering educator, inventor, consultant
Topalian, Naomi Getsoyan writer
Trainor, Bernard Edmund retired military officer
Washburn, Barbara Polk cartographer, researcher, explorer
White, Gary Francis investigation professional
Williamson, Richard Cardinal physicist
Wyss, David Alen financial service executive

Lincoln
Donald, David Herbert author, history educator
Gnichtel, William Van Orden lawyer
Green, David Henry manufacturing company executive
Holberton, Philip Vaughan entrepreneur, educator, professional speaker
Kulka, J(ohannes) Peter retired physician, pathologist
Langton, Jane Gillson writer, illustrator
LeGates, John Crews Boulton information scientist
Merrill, Vincent Nichols landscape architect
Mitchell, John Hanson writer, editor
Muirhead, Kevin James middle school administrator
Nenneman, Richard Arthur retired publishing executive
Payne, Harry Morse, Jr. architect
Payne, Roger Searle zoology researcher and administrator, conservationist
Schwartz, Edward Arthur lawyer
Tobin, James Robert biomedical device manufacturing company executive

Littleton
Crandall Hollick, Julian Bernard Hugh radio producer
Harland, William Robert, Sr. painter
Miller, Debra psychiatric nurse therapist
Patel, Mahendra Rambhai electronics executive
Pradas, Nanci Mara social worker

Longmeadow
Constance, Barbara Ann financial planner, small business owner, consultant
Ferris, Theodore Vincent chemical engineer, consulting technologist
Hopfe, Harold Herbert retired chemical engineer
Keady, George Cregan, Jr. judge
Leary, Carol Ann academic administrator
Lo Bello, Joseph David bank executive
Locklin, Wilbert Edwin management consultant
Skelton, Don Richard consulting actuary, retired insurance company executive
Stewart, Alexander Doig bishop
Wallace, Ruth Helpern special education educator

Lowell
Aste, Mario Andrea foreign language educator
Carr, George Leroy physicist, educator
Clark, Richard Paul electronics company executive
Coleman, Robert Marshall biology educator
Curtis, James Theodore lawyer
Dubner, Daniel William pediatrician
Hayes, Donald Paul, Jr. elementary and secondary education educator
Israel, Stanley C. chemistry educator
Martin, William Francis, Jr. lawyer
Mazur, Stella Mary former organization administrator
McNamara, John R. bishop
Natsios, Nicholas Andrew retired foreign service officer
Paikowsky, Samuel G. civil engineering educator
†Peters, Janice C. cable company executive
Richards, Constance Ellen nursing school administrator, consultant
Sakellarios, Gertrude Edith retired office nurse
Teague, Bernice Rita accountant
Tripathy, Sukant Kishore chemistry educator
†Wegman, David Howe health science educator, consultant

Ludlow
Budnick, Thomas Peter social worker
Roberge, Lawrence Francis neuroscientist, biotechnology consultant, writer, bioethicist, educator

Lunenburg
Pomeroy, Leon Ralph psychologist
†Tallman, Susan Porri library director

Lynn
Astuccio, Sheila Margaret educational administrator
D'Entremont, Edward Joseph infosystems engineer, educator
Denzler, Nancy J. artist
Farris, Robert Harold, Jr. artist, educator
Kercher, David Max mechanical engineer
McManus, Patrick J. mayor, lawyer, accountant
Ryder, Edward Francis secondary education educator
Zykofsky, Stephen Mark investment counselor

Lynnfield
Gianino, John Joseph retired insurance executive
Kerrigan, Nancy professional figure skater, former Olympic athlete
McGivney, John Joseph lawyer
Solomon, Jerry Lawrence sports marketing executive

Malden
Feeney, Lynda Jean secondary education educator
Fox, Bernard Hayman cancer epidemiologist, educator
Miller, Kenneth William, II research, development, engineering executive

Manchester
Arntsen, Arnt Peter engineer, consultant
Conley, Patrick clinic administrator
Moody, Marianna S. dietitian
†St. Clair, Lynn Owen artist, illustrator
Shepley, Hugh architect

Marblehead
Cohen, Merrill chemist
Ehrich, Fredric F. aeronautical engineer
Heins, Esther botanical artist, painter
Hoffman, Thomas Edgar mechanical engineer
Kennedy, Elizabeth Mae musician
Kleiman, Macklen manufacturing company executive
†Orlen, Gerald Lawrence secondary education educator
Petersen, Douglas W. state legislator
Plakans, Shelley Swift social worker, psychotherapist
Quigley, Stephen Howard executive editor
†Thompson, Michael Laurie food manufacturing executive
Zeo, Frank James health products company professional

Marion
McPartland, Patricia Ann health educator
Stone, David Barnes investment advisor
Verni, Mary L. medical/surgical and orthopedics nurse
Walsh, William Egan, Jr. electronics executive

Marlborough
Bennett, C. Leonard consulting engineer
Birstein, Seymour Joseph aerospace company executive
Brower, David Charles transportation executive
Carpenter, Elizabeth Jane communications executive
Lohr, Harold Russell bishop
†Moorman, Janet Elizabeth secondary education educator
Moran, James J., Jr. insurance executive
Otto, Jeffrey Bruce industrial research and development executive
Palihnich, Nicholas Joseph, Jr. retail executive
Petrin, John Donald town administrator
Shobert, Benjamin Andrew manufacturing executive
Wiedeman, Richard Lawrence electronics executive

Marshfield
Arapoff, John Richard artist
†Cunio, Maria T. Muñoz psychologist

Marshfield Hills
Krause, Dorothy Simpson fine artist, educator

Marstons Mills
Martin, Vincent George management consultant

Mashpee
LeBaron, Francis Newton biochemistry educator
Rockett-Bolduc, Agnes Mary nurse

Mattapoisett
Andersen, Laird Bryce retired university administrator
Perry, Blanche Belle physical therapist

Maynard
Gerroir, Richard Ernest retired computer industry executive
Holway, Ellen Twombly Hay primary education educator

Medfield
Heffernan, Peter John state official
Hein, John William dentist, educator
McQuillen, Jeremiah Joseph distribution executive
Woolston-Catlin, Marian psychiatrist

Medford
Anderson, Thomas Jefferson, Jr. composer, educator
Astill, Kenneth Norman mechanical engineering educator
Bedau, Hugo Adam philosophy educator
Berman, David lawyer, poet
Brooke, John L. history educator
Brosnan, David Patrick structural engineer
Burke, Edward Newell radiologist
Conklin, John Evan sociology educator
DeBold, Joseph Francis psychology educator
Dennett, Daniel Clement philosopher, author, educator
DeVoto, Mark Bernard music educator
DiBiaggio, John A. university president
DiPietro, Francis writer
Elkind, David psychology educator
Fyler, John Morgan English language educator
Galvin, John Rogers educator, retired army officer
Garrett, John R. communication executive
Giordano, Donna Langone foreign language and ESL educator
Greif, Robert mechanical engineering educator
Gunther, Leon physicist
Laurent, Pierre-Henri history educator
Luria, Zella Hurwitz psychology educator
Marcopoulos, George John history educator
Mc Carthy, Kathryn A. physicist
Miczek, Klaus Alexander psychology educator
Milburn, Richard Henry physics educator
Montgomery, Tommie Sue political scientist, educator
Mumford, George Saltonstall, Jr. former university dean, astronomy educator
Nelson, Frederick Carl mechanical engineering educator
O'Connell, Brian community organizer, public administrator, writer, educator
Quinto, Eric Todd mathematics educator
Salacuse, Jeswald William lawyer, educator
Schneps, Jack physics educator
Siegal, Kenneth Harvey editor
Sloane, Marshall M. banker
Thornton, Ronald physicist, educator
Ueda, Reed Takashi historian, educator
Uhlir, Arthur, Jr. electrical engineer, university administrator
Urry, Grant Wayne chemistry educator
†Wachman, Alan Michael educator

Medway
Hoag, David Garratt aerospace engineer
Yonda, Alfred William mathematician

Melrose
†Bond, Harold H. poet
Brown, Ronald Osborne telecommunications and computer systems consultant
Henken, Bernard Samuel clinical psychologist, speech pathologist
Maloney, Robert L. municipal official
Sullivan, Charles Irving polymer chemist

Methuen
Heron, Virginia Grace secondary education educator
Jean, Patricia Anne medical center administrator
Pollack, Herbert William electronics executive

Middleboro
†Judd, Marjorie Lois librarian, consultant
Llewellyn, John Schofield, Jr. food company executive
Sylvia, Constance Miriam family nurse practitioner, clinical specialist

Middleton
Daniels, William Albert food products executive
Stover, Matthew Joseph communications executive

Milford
Barrs, James Thomas linguistics educator
Carson, Charles Henry microwave engineer
Gliksberg, Alexander David engineering executive
Samojla, Scott Anthony accountant
Williams, Richard Charles computer programmer, consultant

Millbury
Noonan, Stephen Joseph accounting firm executive
Pan, Coda H. T. mechanical engineering educator, consultant, researcher

Millers Falls
Hutcheson, Thomas Worthington educational administrator
Ryan, Richard E. painter

Millis
Masterson, Patricia O'Malley publications editor, writer

Milton
Comeau, Lorene Anita Emerson real estate developer
Cooperstein, Paul Andrew lawyer, business consultant
Corcoran, Robert Joseph fund raising executive
Frazier, Marie Dunn speech educator, public relations and human resources specialist
†Gerring, Clifton, III corporate executive
Huban, Christopher M. retail buyer, manager
Randall, Lilian Maria Charlotte museum curator
Sgarlat, Mary Anne E. A. marketing, public relations professional
Warren, John Coolidge private school dean, history educator
Wengler, Marguerite Marie educational therapist

Monson
†De Santis, Sylvia library director
St. Louis, Paul Michael foreign language educator

Nantucket
Bartlett, Cheryl Ann public health service administrator
Devaney, John Goodwin painter, muralist
Ingram, George business executive
Lethbridge, Francis Donald architect
Lobl, Herbert Max lawyer
Louderback, Peter Darragh accountant, consultant
Mercer, Richard Joseph retired advertising executive, freelance writer
Pollard, Margaret Louise association administrator
Rorem, Ned composer, author
Sangree, Walter Hinchman social anthropologist, educator
†Sherry, William Joseph, III sculptor, gallery owner

Natick
Bensel, Carolyn Kirkbride psychologist
Bower, Kathleen Anne nurse consultant
Davis, Teresa Agnes school psychologist, educator
DeCosta, Peter F. chemical engineer
Geller, Esther (Bailey Geller) artist
Gregory, John C. artist, sculptor
Gregory, Thomas Raymond management consultant
Kushner, Harold Samuel rabbi
Lachica, R(eynato) Victor microbiologist
†Mangual, Jesus A. army officer
Marr, David E lawyer
Moler, Cleve Barry mathematician
Morgan, Betty Mitchell artist, educator
Nugent, John J. wholesale distribution executive
Rendell, Kenneth William rare and historical documents dealer, consultant
Sahatjian, Ronald Alexander science foundation executive
Schott, John William psychiatrist
Stack, Diane Virginia social service agency officer
Strayton, Robert Gerard public communications executive
Sutcliffe, Marion Shea writer
Wheeler, Mary Harrison (Mardy Wheeler) human resources development specialist, consultant
Zarkin, Herbert retail company executive

Needham
Bottiglia, William Filbert humanities educator
Carr, Iris Constantine artist, writer
Cogswell, John Heyland retired telecommunications executive, financial consultant
Coleman, Richard William lawyer
Criscenti, Joseph Thomas retired history educator
DerMarderosian, Diran Robert rug cleaning company executive
Di Domenica, Robert Anthony musician, composer
Donahue, Arthur Thomas television producer
Gormley, Gail F. mental health nurse
Kung, Patrick Chung-Shu biotechnology executive
La Camera, Paul A. television station executive
Mc Arthur, Janet Ward endocrinologist, educator
McEvoy, Michael Joseph economist
Meisner, Mary Jo editor
Mills, Elizabeth Ann librarian
Pucel, Robert Albin electronics research engineer
Walworth, Arthur author
Weller, Thomas Huckle physician, former educator
Zambone, Alana Maria special education educator

New Bedford
Anderson, James Linwood pharmaceutical sales official
Benoit, Richard Armand retired police chief, lawyer
Bullard, John Kilburn university administrator
Hartman, Barry David rabbi
Kellaway, Richard Allen minister, art association administrator
Koczera, Robert Michael state legislator
LaPorte, Adrienne Aroxie nursing administrator
Merolla, Michele Edward chiropractor, broadcaster
Messier, Gerald Roland genealogist
Murray, Robert Fox lawyer
Raposo, Deborah F. nursing administrator

Shapiro, Gilbert Lawrence *orthopedist*
Soares, Carl Lionel *quality control engineer, metrologist*

New Salem
Lenherr, Frederick Keith *neurophysiologist, computer scientist*

Newbury
Hamond, Karen Marie Koch *secondary education educator*

Newburyport
Allard, David Henry *judge*
Appleton, Daniel Randolph, Jr. *optometrist*
Berggren, Dick *editor*
MacWilliams, Kenneth Edward *investment banker*
Maslen, David Peter *lawyer*
Russell, David Francis *management consultant, utilities executive*
Vernon, Alexandra Reiss *artist*

Newton
†Avishai, Susan E. *artist, illustrator*
Balsamo, Salvatore Anthony *technical and temporary employment companies executive*
Barnet, Bruce *publishing executive*
Baron, Charles Hillel *lawyer, educator*
Bassuk, Ellen Linda *psychiatrist*
Benedict, Mary-Anne *educator*
Bernard, Michael Mark *lawyer, city planning consultant*
Blacher, Richard Stanley *psychiatrist*
Brilliant, Barbara *television host, producer, columnist, consultant, journalist, communications and media consultant*
Carton, Lonnie Caming *educational psychologist*
Chubb, Stephen Darrow *medical corporation executive*
Churchill, Daniel Wayne *management and marketing educator*
Clarkson, Cheryl Lee *healthcare executive*
Coquillette, Daniel Robert *lawyer, educator*
†Dangond, Fernando *neurologist, educator*
Dunlap, William Crawford *physicist*
Gerrity, J(ames) Frank, II *building materials company executive*
Glazer, Donald Wayne *lawyer, business executive, educator*
Glick-Weil, Kathy *library director*
Goldweitz, Julie *lawyer*
Havens, Candace Jean *planning consultant*
Heyn, Arno Harry Albert *retired chemistry educator*
Holbik, Karel *economics educator*
Huber, Richard Gregory *lawyer, educator*
Jarchow, Craig McHugh *technology manager*
Kardon, Brian *publishing company executive*
Knupp, Ralph *publishing company executive*
Korobkin, Barry Jay *architect*
Kosowsky, David I. *retired biotechnical company executive*
Lam, Thomas Manpan *architect*
†Lewis-Kausel, Cecilia *interior design educator*
Masi, Robin *artist, writer, educator*
Messing, Arnold Philip *lawyer*
Monahan, Marie Terry *lawyer*
Neth, Jerry *publishing company executive*
Norris, Melvin *lawyer*
Norton, (William) Elliot *retired drama critic*
Oles, Paul Stevenson (Steve Oles) *architect, perspectivist, educator*
Peterson, Osler Leopold *lawyer*
Rodman, Sumner *insurance executive*
Saffran, Kalman *engineering consulting company executive, entrepreneur*
Sasahara, Arthur Asao *cardiologist, educator, researcher*
Stein, Seymour *electronics scientist*
Sutherland, David Russell *filmmaker*
Svrluga, Richard Charles *entrepreneur*
Tuscher, Vincent James *author*
Weisskopf, Victor Frederick *physicist*
West, Doe *bioethicist, social justice activist*
White, Burton Leonard *educational psychologist, author*
Wilkins, Herbert Putnam *state supreme court chief justice, retired*
Zohn, Harry *author, educator*

Newton Center
Adams, F. Gerard *economist, educator*
†Everett, William Johnson *ethics educator, writer*
Mark, Melvin *consulting mechanical engineer, educator*
Sandman, Peter M. *communication educator, consultant*
Schuller, Gunther Alexander *composer*

Newton Hlds
Fanger, Mark *psychologist, psychotherapist, consultant*
Porter, Jack Nusan *writer, sociologist, educator, political activist*

Newtonville
Gomberg, Sydelle *dancer educator*
Monroe, Ramona Frey *nurse*
Polonsky, Arthur *artist, educator*
Zimmardi, James Anthony *musician, music educator*

North Adams
Conklin, Jack Lariviere *education educator*
Thurston, Donald Allen *broadcasting executive*

North Andover
Briggs, David Melvin *information systems executive*
Coleman, Daniel Eugene *physician*
Goldstein, Charles Henry *architect, consultant*
Holmes, Sue Ellen *library director*
†Jain, Anant Kumar *data communications and telecommunications consultant*
Jannini, Ralph Humbert, III *electronics executive*
Longsworth, Ellen Louise *art historian, consultant*
McCarthy, Albert Henry *executive search consultant*
Michaels, Patricia Palen *urban planner*
Riendeau, Theresa Frances *rehabilitation nurse*
†Wojtas, Susan A. *college administrator*

North Attleboro
Bordeleau, Lisa Marie *human services professional, consultant*
Inskeep, James R. *process control engineer*
Williams, Ruth L. *rehabilitation counselor, consultant*

North Billerica
Mellon, Timothy *transportation executive*
†Panditi, Surya
Witover, Stephen Barry *pediatrician*

North Brookfield
Neal, Avon *artist, author*
Parker, Ann (Ann Parker Neal) *photographer, graphic artist, writer*

North Chatham
O'Brien, Robert Emmet *insurance company executive*
Rowlands, Marvin Lloyd, Jr. *publishing and communications consultant*

North Chelmsford
Osenton, Thomas George *publisher*
†Trivers, Dianne H. *elementary educator*

North Dartmouth
†Ainscough, Thomas Lee, Jr. *business educator, internet marketing consultant*
Barrow, Clyde Wayne *political scientist, educator*
Cressy, Peter Hollon *university chancellor, retired naval officer*
Dace, Tish *drama educator*
†Hoagland, Everett H. *poet, English educator*
Law, Frederick Masom *engineering educator, structural engineering firm executive*
Sauro, Joseph Pio *physics educator*
Waxler, Robert Phillip *university educator, consultant*
Yoken, Mel B(arton) *French language educator, author*
Zuo, Yuegang *chemist, educator*

North Dighton
Cserr, Robert *psychiatrist, physician, hospital administrator*
Silvia, David Alan *insurance broker*

North Eastham
DeMuth, Vivienne Blake McCandless *artist, illustrator*
Masterson, Dianne Johnson *English language educator*
York, Elizabeth Jane *innkeeper*

North Easton
Dyer, Marsha Jean *critical care nurse*
Ratcliffe, Barbara Jean *special education educator*
†Wolf-Devine, Celia Curtis *philosophy educator*

North Falmouth
Bass, Norman Herbert *physician, scientist, university and hospital administrator, health care executive*
Morse, Robert Warren *research administrator*

North Grafton
Schwartz, Anthony *veterinary surgeon, educator*
†Stokowski, Leonard James *artist*

North Hatfield
†Moser, Arthur Barry *designer, illustrator, educator*

North Quincy
Segelman, Allyn Evan *dentist, researcher, insurance executive*

North Reading
Day, Ronald Elwin *consulting executive*
Green, Jack Allen *lawyer*

Northampton
Betlyon, John Wilson
Birkett, Mary Ellen *humanities educator*
Blumenfeld, Warren Jay *writer, educator*
Bowman, John Stewart *writer, editor*
Donfried, Karl Paul *minister, theology educator*
Elkins, Stanley Maurice *historian, educator*
Ellis, Frank Hale *English literature educator*
Fleck, George Morrison *chemistry educator*
Gardner, Thomas Neville *communications educator*
Hoyt, Nelly Schargo (Mrs. N. Deming Hoyt) *history educator*
Kaplan, James Lamport *writer, editor, publisher*
†Kitchen, Denis Lee *publisher, artist*
Lehmann, Phyllis Williams *archaeologist, educator*
Lightburn, Anita Louise *dean, social work educator*
Naegele, Philipp Otto *violinist, violist, music educator*
†Newman, Lesléa *writer*
Nickles, Herbert Leslie *college administrator*
Park, Beverly Goodman *lawyer*
Piccinino, Rocco Michael *librarian*
Pickrel, Paul *English educator*
Rice, Elisabeth Jane *volunteer*
Robinson, Donald Leonard *social scientist, educator*
Rose, Peter Isaac *sociologist, writer*
Rupp, Sheron Adeline *photographer, educator*
Russell, Joel Samuel *land use consultant*
Seelig, Sharon Cadman *English educator*
†Sherr, Richard J. *educator*
Simmons, Ruth J. *academic administrator*
Smith, Malcolm Barry Estes *philosophy educator, lawyer*
Unsworth, Richard Preston *minister, school administrator*
Vaget, Hans Rudolf *language professional, educator*
Volkmann, Frances Cooper *psychologist, educator*
von Klemperer, Klemens *historian, educator*

Northborough
Fulmer, Hugh Scott *physician, educator*

Norton
Dahl, Curtis *English literature educator*
Deekle, Peter Van *library director*
†Evans, Nancy Ann *classics educator*
Marshall, Dale Rogers *college president, political scientist, educator*
Taylor, Robert Sundling *English educator, art critic*

Norwell
Brett, Jan Churchill *illustrator, author*
Case, David Knowlton *management consultant*
O'Sullivan, James Michael *lawyer*
Rolnik, Zachary Jacob *publishing company executive*
Sostilio, Robert Francis *office equipment marketing executive*
Wentworth, Murray Jackson *artist, educator*

Norwood
Berliner, Allen Irwin *dermatologist*
Fuller, Samuel Henry, III *computer engineer*
Malay, Marcella Mary *nursing educator, administrator*
Mc Feeley, John Jay *chemical engineer*
Pence, Robert Dudley *biomedical research administrator, hospital administrator*
Pytka, Stephen Milton *office equipment executive*
Sheingold, Daniel H. *electrical engineer*
Tritter, Richard Paul *strategic planning consulting executive*
†Wolkovich-Valkaviciu, William Lawrence *priest*

Nutting Lake
Furman, John Rockwell *wholesale lumber company executive*

Oak Bluffs
Hardman, Della Brown Taylor *art educator, retired*

Oakham
Poirier, Helen Virginia Leonard *elementary education educator*

Orleans
Dessauer, John Phillip *publisher, financial management company executive*
Hiscock, Richard Carson *marine safety investigator*
Hughes, Libby *author*
Rappaport, Margaret M.W.E. *physician, psychologist, author, aviation consultant*

Osterville
Schwarztrauber, Sayre Archie *former naval officer, maritime consultant*
Silk, Alvin John *business educator*
Weber, Adelheid Lisa *former nurse, chemist*
Williams, Ann Meagher *retired hospital administrator*

Otis
Idzik, Daniel Ronald *lawyer*

Oxford
Stevens, D(onna) Lyn *preschool provider*

Palmer
Dupuis, Robert Simeon *sales executive*
Holland, Joseph Daniel *psychologist, counselor*
Roy, Alicia M. *secondary education educator*

Paxton
Kuklinski, Joan Lindsey *librarian*
†Locke, John R. *principal*

Peabody
Dee, Pauline Marie *artist*
Goldberg, Harold Seymour *electrical engineer, educator*
Gordon, Bernard M. *computer company executive*
†Hedrick, Hunt R(andolph), Jr. *sportswear company official*
Peters, Leo Francis *environmental engineer*
Torkildsen, Peter G. *consulting company executive*

Pembroke
Egan, Denise *home health nurse*
Khoylian, Carol J. *nurse*

Pepperell
Holmes, Jean Louise *real estate investor, Holocaust scholar, educator*
Osten, Patricia Ann *tax specialist*

Petersham
Chivian, Eric Seth *psychiatrist, environmental scientist, educator*

Pittsfield
Adams, Shelby Lee *photographer*
†Blodgett, Ruth *medical executive*
Bostley, Jean Regina *nun, library association administrator*
Cornelio, Albert Carmen *insurance executive*
Doyle, Anthony Peter *lawyer*
Fanelli, Robert Drew *surgeon*
Feigenbaum, Armand Vallin *systems engineer, systems equipment executive*
Gregware, James Murray *financial planner*
†Michaels, Basil M. *plastic surgeon, educator*
†Small, David J. *rabbi*
Watts, Dennis Lester *retired military officer*
Wenner, Gene Charles *arts management executive*
Wheelock, Kenneth Steven *chemist*

Plymouth
Baker, Peggy MacLachlan *cultural organization administrator*
Barreira, Brian Ernest *lawyer*
Forman, Peter *sheriff, former state legislator*
Freyermuth, Virginia Karen *secondary art educator*
Goggin, Joan Marie *school system specialist*
Gregory, Dick *comedian, civil rights activist*
Jones, Cheryl Bromley *English language and humanities educator*
Reid, Nanci Glick *health care professional*

Plympton
O'Connell, Philip Edward *retired retail business owner*

Provincetown
†Black, Constance Jane *artist*
Hutchinson, Peter Arthur *artist*
Oliver, Mary *poet*

Quincy
Adams, Ronald G. *middle school educator*
Bierman, George William *technical consulting executive, food technologist*
Cawthorne, Alfred Benjamin *education educator*
Chin, Jean Lau *health and mental health executive*
Chung, Cynthia Norton *communications specialist*
Colgan, Sumner *manufacturing engineer, chemical engineer*
Dunning, Thomas E. *newspaper editor*
Hagar, William Gardner, III *photobiology educator*
Hall, John Raymond, Jr. *fire protection executive*
Hayes, Bernardine Frances *computer systems analyst*
Hill, Kent Richmond *college president*
Kelley, James Francis *civil engineer*
Levin, Robert Joseph *retail grocery chain store executive*
Lippincott, Joseph P. *photojournalist, educator*
Markham, Charles Rinklin *financial executive, tax accountant*
Miller, George David *retired air force officer, marketing consultant*
Motejunas, Gerald William *lawyer*
O'Brien, John Steininger *clinical psychologist*
Spangler, Arthur Stephenson, Jr. *psychologist*
Tobin, Robert G. *supermarket chain executive*
Weischadle, David Emanuel, II *lawyer, literary agent*
Weischadle, Douglas Eric *lawyer, literary agent*
Werner, Joanne Loucille *financial executive*
Young, Richard William *corporate director*

Randolph
Cammarata, Richard John *financial advisor*
Margolin, Milton *sales and marketing professional*
Morrissey, Edmond Joseph *classical philologist*

Raynham
Jelley, Scott Allen *microbiologist*
Kaplan, Kenneth Barry *psychologist*

Reading
Burbank, Nelson Stone *investment banker*
Donald, John Hepburn, II *quality assurance professional, consultant*
Melconian, Jerry Ohanes *engineering executive*
White, Karen Ruth Jones *information systems executive*

Revere
Ferrante, Olivia Ann *retired educator, consultant*
Jay, Michael Eliot *radiologist*
Kirby, Brendan Timothy *security system specialist, entrepreneur*
†Recupero-Faiella, Anna Antonietta *poet*

Rockland
Bowes, Frederick, III *publishing executive*
†Crimi, Paul *artist*
Gauquier, Anthony Victor *special education counselor*
Pallai, David Francis *publishing executive*

Rockport
Bakrow, William John *college president emeritus*
Bissell, Phil (Charles P. Bissell) *cartoonist*
Calabro, Joanna Joan Sondra *artist*
Delakas, Daniel Liudviko *retired foreign language educator*
Fillmore, Laura *publisher*
Mosher, Donald Allen *artist*
Walen, Harry Leonard *historian, lecturer, author*
Wiberg, Lars-Erik *occupational compatibility consultant*

Roxbury
Berman, Marlene Oscar *neuropsychologist, educator*
Coleman, David Dennis, II *theater educator*
Franzblau, Carl *biochemist, consultant, researcher*
Kelley, Ruth M. *nurse, alcohol, drug abuse services professional*
MacNichol, Edward Ford, Jr. *biophysicist, educator*
Peters, Alan *anatomy educator*
Resnick, Oscar *neuroscientist*
Simons, Elizabeth R(eiman) *biochemist, educator*
Small, Donald MacFarland *biophysics educator, gastroenterologist*
Weeks, Clifford Myers *musician, educational administrator*

Salem
Brown, Walter Redvers John *physicist*
Ettinger, Mort *marketing educator*
Finamore, Daniel Robert *museum curator*
Flibbert, Joseph Thomas *English language educator*
Goss, Laurence Edward, Jr. *geographer, educator*
Gozemba, Patrica Andrea *women's studies and English language educator, writer*
Griffin, Thomas McLean *retired lawyer*
Gruhl, Suzanne Swiderski *accountant*
Harrington, Nancy D. *college president*
Loftis, Rebecca Hope *psychotherapist*
McLaughlin, Michael Angelo *mortgage consultant, author*
Moran, Philip David *lawyer*
Neel, Thomas Harris *museum director*
Piro, Anthony John *radiologist*
†Popkin, Nancy Popkin *financial planner*
Prokopy, John Alfred *government consultant*
Wathne, Carl Norman *hospital administrator*

Sandwich
Porter, John Stephen *retired television executive*
Terrill, Robert Carl *hospital administrator*

Saugus
Austill, Allen *dean emeritus*

Scituate
Keating, Margaret Mary *entrepreneur, business consultant*
Lane, Barbara Ann *environmental company official, systems analyst*
Ryan, George Edward *journalist*
†Spangler, Stanley Eugene *international relations educator*

Seekonk
Backes, Joan *artist*

Sharon
Douglas, Joanne M. Kaerwer *elementary education educator*
Dunham, Barbara Jean *administrator*
Paolino, Richard Francis *manufacturing company executive*
Reilley, Dennen *research agency administrator, educator*
Roberson, Kip Michael *library director, librarian*
†Smuts, R. Malcolm *historian, educator*
Wisotsky, Serge Sidorovich *engineering executive*

Sheffield
Velmans, Loet Abraham *retired public relations executive*

Shelburne Falls
McClatchy, Kate *political candidate*

Wellesley
Aall, Christian Bergengren *software company executive*
Aldrich, Richard Orth *lawyer*
†Allen, Michael W *management consultant*
Arnold, Peter Gordon *communications consultant*
Auerbach, Jerold S. *university educator*
Avery, Mary Ellen *pediatrician, educator*
Baum, Laura *educator*
Bidart, Frank *English educator, poet*
Carlson, Christopher Tapley *lawyer*
Castano, Elvira Palmerio *art gallery director, art historian*
Chandra, Rob S. *venture capitalist*
Charpie, Robert Alan *physicist*
Crane, Bonnie Loyd *art gallery owner, director, author*
Eilts, Hermann Frederick *international relations educator, former diplomat*
Fontaine, Eudore Joseph, Jr. *artist, art historian*
Freeman, Judi H. *curator, art historian*
Gailius, Gilbert Keistutis *manufacturing company executive*
Gerety, Robert John *microbiologist, pharmaceutical company executive, pediatrician, vaccinologist*
Giddon, Donald B(ernard) *psychologist, educator*
Gladstone, Richard Bennett *retired publishing company executive*
Goglia, Charles A., Jr. *lawyer*
Heartt, Charlotte Beebe *university official*
Henderson, Mary Louise *civic worker*
Hildebrand, Francis Begnaud *mathematics educator*
Jacobs, Ruth Harriet *poet, playwright, sociologist, gerontologist*
Jovanovic, Miodrag Stevana *surgeon, educator*
Kato, Walter Yoneo *physicist*
Kobayashi, Yutaka *biochemist, consultant*
Kottas, James Alan *computer scientist*
Landaw, Stephen Arthur *physician, educator*
Lazar, Jeffrey Bennett *rabbi, educator*
Marcus, William Michael *rubber and vinyl products manufacturing company executive*
McAlpine, Frederick Sennett *anesthesiologist*
McGibbon, Phyllis Isabel *artist, educator*
Merguerian, Arshag *architect*
Miller, Linda B. *political scientist*
Montague, Joel Gedney *public health consultant*
Murray, Joseph Edward *retired plastic surgeon*
Myers, Arthur B. *journalist, author*
Nagler, Leon Gregory *management consultant, business executive*
Numata, Nobuo *software company executive, consultant, engineer*
†Paarlberg, Robert L. *political science educator*
Parker, William H., III *federal official*
Ragone, David Vincent *former university president*
Rich, Wilbur Cornelius *political scientist, educator*
Riley, Michael Hylan *lawyer*
Samuels, Linda Sue *science educator*
Shea, Robert McConnell *lawyer*
Small, Parker Adams, III *investment banker*
Sutter, Linda Diane *health services administrator*
Tarr, Robert Joseph, Jr. *publishing executive, retail executive*
Tierney, Thomas J. *business management consultant*
Walsh, Diana Chapman *academic administrator, social and behavioral sciences educator*
Weil, Thomas Alexander *electronics engineer, retired*
Wilson, Elaine Louise *English language educator*
Wong, Bella Toy Funnd *secondary school educator, lawyer*

Wellesley Hills
Coco, Samuel Barbin *venture consultant*
Grimes, Howard Ray *management consultant*
Spierings, Egilius Leonardus Hendricus *pharmacologist, neurologist, headache specialist*

Wellfleet
Coughlin, Jack *printmaker, sculptor, art educator*
Coughlin, Joan Hopkins *artist, educator*
Limpitlaw, John Donald *retired publishing executive, clergyman*
Mc Feely, William Shield *historian, writer*
Piercy, Marge *poet, novelist, essayist*
†Wood, Ira *novelist*

Wenham
Baker, Ruth Holmes *retired secondary education educator*
Davis, Marjorie Alice *former city official*
Flint-Ferguson, Janis Deane *English language educator*
Herrmann, Robert Lawrence *biochemistry, science and religion educator*
Johnson, Alan B. *advertising executive*
Roberts, David E. *marketing professional*
†Sciola, Charlotte Ann *school system administrator*

West Barnstable
Field, Richard Albert *sales and marketing professional*
Kennedy, Michele Lyn *artist*

West Boylston
Cummings, Henry Savage Chase *manufacturing executive*

West Bridgewater
Worrell, Cynthia Lee *bank executive*
Wyner, Justin L. *laminating company executive*

West Brookfield
Higgins, Brian Alton *art gallery executive*

West Chatham
Rowley, Glenn Harry *lawyer*

West Falmouth
Carlson, David Bret *lawyer*
Holz, George G., IV *research scientist, medicine educator*
Vaccaro, Ralph Francis *marine biologist*

West Hyannisport
Devine, Nancy *postmaster*

West Newbury
Collins, John Joseph *communications consultant*
Dooley, Ann Elizabeth *freelance writers cooperative executive, editor*

West Newton
Elya, John Adel *bishop*
Morris, Glenn Louis *architect*

West Roxbury
Cohen, Carolyn Alta *health educator*
Goyal, Raj Kumar *medical educator*
Hedley-Whyte, John *anesthesiologist, educator*

West Springfield
Barrientos, Jane Ellen *art educator*
Desai, Veena Balvantrai *obstetrician and gynecologist, educator*
Dunphy, Maureen Ann *educator*
Engebretson, Douglas Kenneth *architect, interior designer*

West Stockbridge
Yanoff, Arthur Samuel *artist, art therapist*

West Tisbury
Logue, Edward Joseph *development company executive*
Méras, Phyllis Leslie *journalist*
Smith, Henry Clay *retired psychology educator*

Westborough
Badenhausen, John Phillips, II *mental health facility administrator*
Berthiaume, Wayne Henry *electrical engineer*
Crosby, Thomas W. *computer scientist*
Frank, Jacob *lawyer*
Gionfriddo, Maurice Paul *aeronautical engineer, research and development manager*
Gordon, Betty L. *health services administrator*
Horwitz, Eleanor Catherine *information and education official*
Houston, Alfred Dearborn *energy company executive*
Russell, John William *insurance executive*
Skates, Ronald Louis *computer manufacturing executive*
Staffier, Pamela Moorman *psychologist*
Tobias, Lester Lee *psychological consultant*
Young, Roger Austin *natural gas distribution company executive*

Westfield
Buckmore, Alvah Clarence, Jr. *computer scientist, ballistician*
Pollard, Frank Edward *lawyer*

Westford
Brady, Shelagh Ann *elementary education educator*
Geary, Marie Josephine *art association administrator*
Olsen, David Leslie *author, consultant*
Salah, Joseph Elias *research scientist, educator*
Selesky, Donald Bryant *software developer*
Stansberry, James Wesley *air force officer*

Weston
Alcock, George Lewis, Jr. (Peter Alcock) *investor, business strategist*
Aquilino, Daniel *banker*
Barry, William Anthony *priest, writer*
†Bines, Joan Paller *museum director*
Boothroyd, Herbert J. *insurance company executive*
Chu, Jeffrey Chuan *business executive, consultant*
Draskoczy, Paul R. *psychiatrist*
Fish, David Earl *insurance company executive*
Fleming, Nancy McAdam *landscape designer*
Haas, Jacqueline Crawford *lawyer*
Higgins, Sister Therese *English educator, former college president*
Ives, J. Atwood *financial executive*
Kendall, Julius *consulting engineer*
Kraft, Gerald *economist*
Landis, John William *engineering and construction executive, government advisor*
Lashman, L. Edward *arbitrator, mediator, consultant*
Oelgeschlager, Guenther Karl *publisher*
Raskin, Fred Charles *transportation and utility holding company executive*
Resden, Ronald Everett *medical devices product development engineer*
Rockwell, George Barcus *financial consultant*
Saad, Theodore Shafick *retired microwave company executive*
Sanzone, Donna S. *publishing executive*
Schloemann, Ernst Fritz (Rudolf August) *physicist, engineer*
Smick, Susan Schnee *tile designer and manufacturer, airline strategic, marketing planner*
Stambaugh, Armstrong A., Jr. *restaurant and hotel executive*
Sturgis, Robert Shaw *architect*
Thomas, Roger Meriwether *lawyer*
Valente, Louis Patrick (Dan) *business and financial executive*
Van Keuren, Korinne Suzanne *pediatrics and orthopedics nurse practitioner*
Vetterling, Mary-Anne *Spanish language and literature educator*
Walker, Marsha *lactation consultant*
Wang, Chia Ping *physicist, educator*
Wells, Lionelle Dudley *psychiatrist, educator*
†Wesley, Judith Ann *educational administrator*
Whitehouse, David Rempfer *physicist*
Wood, Jeremy Scott *architect, urban designer*

Westover AFB
Martin, Glenn Michael *mortgage banker*

Westport
Norcross, Alvin Watt *retired personnel administrator, consultant*

Westwood
Bernfeld, Peter Harry William *biochemist*
Bier, Louis Henry Gustav *minister*
Burrell, Sidney Alexander *history educator*
Donahue, Charles Lee, Jr. *health network executive*
Foster, Arthur Rowe *mechanical engineering educator*
Gillette, Hyde *retired investment banker*
†Jaillet, Michael André *town administrator*
Old, Bruce Scott *chemical and metallurgical engineer*
Philbrick, Margaret Elder *artist*
Riley, Henry Charles *banker*
Smith, Denis Joseph *mathematics educator*

Weymouth
Coughlin, H. Richard *real estate broker*
Crandlemere, Robert Wayne *engineering executive*
Iacovo, Michael Jamaal *medical consultant, small business owner*
Imbault, James Joseph *manufacturing company executive*
†Scott, Susan Shattuck *secondary education educator*

Whitinsville
DiVitto, Sharon Faith *mental health nurse, administrator*

Whitman
Anderson, Beth Ellen *English literature and composition educator*
Delaney, Matthew Michael *school administrator, fine arts educator*
Thompson, Andrew Ernest *secondary school educator*

Wilbraham
Dailey, Franklyn Edward, Jr. *electronic image technology company executive, analyst, consultant*
Gaudreau, Jules Oscar, Jr. *insurance and financial services company executive*
Nakashian, Craig Meran *sales professional*

Williamsburg
Cahillane, James Francis *writer*
Mazor, David S. *film distribution company executive*

Williamstown
†Beilin, Katarzyna Olga *educator*
Bell-Villada, Gene H. *literature educator, writer*
Birrell, Stephen Reynolds *college administrator*
Bolton, Roger Edwin *economist, educator*
Bundtzen, Lynda Kathryn *English and women's studies educator*
Burns, Joan Simpson *writer, editor*
Conforti, Michael Peter *museum director, art historian*
Cramer, Phebe *psychologist*
Crampton, Stuart Jessup Bigelow *physicist, educator*
Crider, Andrew Blake *psychologist*
Dalzell, Robert Fenton, Jr. *historian*
Dew, Charles Burgess *historian, educator*
Driscoll, Genevieve Bosson (Jeanne Bosson Driscoll) *management and organization development consultant*
Erickson, Peter Brown *librarian, scholar, writer*
Fuqua, Charles John *classics educator*
Graver, Lawrence Stanley *English language professional*
Hedreen, Guy Michael *art educator*
Horan, Patrick M. *English educator*
Kassin, Saul *psychology educator*
King, Anthony Gabriel *museum administrator*
Lee, Arthur Virgil, III *biotechnology company executive*
Markgraf, J(ohn) Hodge *chemist, educator*
McGill, Robert Ernest, III *retired manufacturing company executive*
McGill, Thomas Emerson *psychology educator*
Oakley, Francis Christopher *history educator, former college president*
Park, David Allen *physicist, educator*
Pasachoff, Jay Myron *astronomer, educator*
Payne, Harry Charles *historian, educator*
Payne, Michael Clarence *gastroenterologist*
Raab, Lawrence Edward *English educator*
Rudolph, Frederick *history educator*
Sabot, Richard Henry *economics educator, researcher, consultant, entrepreneur*
Scull, Christina *writer*
Shainman, Irwin *music educator, musician*
Sheahan, John Bernard *economist, educator*
Solomon, Paul Robert *neuropsychologist, educator*
Sprague, John Louis *management consultant*
Stamelman, Richard Howard *French and humanities educator*
Stuebner, Erwin August, Jr. *internist*
Wikander, Lawrence Einar *librarian*
Wilkins, Earle Wayne, Jr. *surgery educator emeritus*
Williams, Heather *neuroethologist, educator*
Wobus, Reinhard Arthur *geologist, educator*

Wilmington
Altschuler, Samuel *electronics company executive*
Bartlett, John Bruen *financial executive*
D'Alene, Alixandria Frances *human resources professional*
Faccini, Ernest Carlo *mechanical engineer*
Freeman, Donald Chester, Jr. *health care company executive*
Hayes, Carol Jeanne *physical education educator*
Patterson, William B. *occupational and environmental medicine physician*
Rosenzweig, Mark Richard *semiconductor equipment executive*

Winchendon
†Blair, C. Jackson *school administrator*

Winchester
Bigelow, Robert P. *lawyer, arbitrator, mediator, journalist*
Blackham, Ann Rosemary (Mrs. J. W. Blackham) *realtor*
Brennan, Francis Patrick *banker*
Brown, David A.B. *strategy consultant*
Cowgill, F(rank) Brooks *retired insurance company executive*
Dalton, Robert Edgar *mathematician, computer scientist*
Ewing, David Walkley *magazine editor*
Harris, Carole Ruth *educational consultant, researcher*
Hirschfeld, Ronald Colman *retired consulting engineering executive*
Ingari, Frank A. *communications executive*
Jabre, Eddy-Marco *architect*
Jackson, Francis Joseph *research and development company executive*
Meesa, Janet Jean *elementary educator*
Neuman, Robert Sterling *art educator, artist*
Ockerbloom, Richard C. *newspaper executive*
Shannon, Claude Elwood *mathematician, educator*
Smith, Robert Moors *anesthesiologist*
Taggart, Ganson Powers *management consultant*
Tisdale, Phebe Alden *cryptographer*

Winthrop
Brown, Alan Anthony *marketing executive*
Brown, Patricia Irene *lawyer, retired law librarian*
Costantino, Frank Mathew *architectural illustrator*
Lutze, Ruth Louise *retired textbook editor, public relations executive*
Vettel, Niki Marcia (Monica Marcia Scher) *broadcasting executive*

Woburn
By, Andre Bernard *engineering executive, research scientist*
Cox, Terrence Guy *manufacturing automation executive*
Curry, John Michael *investment banker*
Eddison, Elizabeth Bole *entrepreneur, information specialist*
Faro, Patricia Baker *school psychologist, consultant*
Gelb, Arthur *science association executive, electrical and systems engineer*
Goela, Jitendra Singh *researcher, consultant*
Hatch, Mark Bruce *software engineer*
McCulloch, James Callahan *corporate executive*
Mehra, Raman Kumar *data processing executive, automation and control engineering researcher*
Neville, Elisabeth *quality assurance professional*
Philbrook, Maureen *small business owner*
Reagan, Stevan Ray *cable company executive*
Smith, Judith Ann *retired geriatrics nurse*
Speerstra, Karen M. *publishing executive*
Tramonte, Michael Robert *education educator*

Woods Hole
Berggren, William Alfred *geologist, research micropaleontologist, educator*
Burris, John Edward *biologist, educator, administrator*
Butman, Bradford *oceanographer*
Cohen, Seymour Stanley *biochemist, educator*
Copeland, Donald Eugene *research marine biologist*
Ebert, James David *research biologist, educator*
Fofonoff, Nicholas Paul *oceanographer, educator*
Gagosian, Robert B. *chemist, educator*
Hart, Stanley Robert *geochemist, educator*
Inoué, Shinya *microscopy and cell biology scientist, educator*
Loewenstein, Werner Randolph *physiologist, biophysicist, educator*
Rafferty, Nancy Schwarz *anatomy educator*
Steele, John Hyslop *marine scientist, oceanographic institute administrator*
Uchupi, Elazar *geologist, researcher*
Von Herzen, Richard Pierre *research scientist, consultant*
Woodwell, George Masters *ecology research director, lecturer*

Worcester
Appelbaum, Paul Stuart *psychiatrist, educator*
Bagshaw, Joseph Charles *molecular biologist, educator*
†Balarajan, Yogarajah *electrophysiologist, cardiologist*
Banks, McRae Cave, II *management educator, consultant*
Bassett, Edward Caldwell, Jr. *lawyer*
Bernhard, Jeffrey David *dermatologist, editor, educator*
Billias, George Athan *history educator*
Binienda, John J. *state legislator*
†Boroff, Henry Jack *federal judge, educator*
Bowen, Alice Frances *school system administrator*
Brooks, John Edward *college president emeritus*
Camougis, George *health, safety and environmental consultant*
Candib, Murray A. *business executive, retail management consultant*
Capriole, Sister Carmen Maria *geriatric nurse*
Cary, Noel Demetri *history educator*
Cashman, Suzanne Boyer *health services administrator, educator*
Clarke, Edward Nielsen *engineering science educator*
Clifford, Jay *artist*
Covino, Paul Francis Xavier *religious executive, college chaplain, consultant*
Cowan, Fairman Chaffee *lawyer*
Davidson, Lee David *insurance executive*
DeFalco, Frank Damian *civil engineering educator*
†DeHoratius, Edmund Francis *secondary education educator*
Donnelly, James Corcoran, Jr. *lawyer*
Drachman, David Alexander *neurologist*
Dunlap, Ellen S. *library administrator*
Dunlop, George Rodgers *retired surgeon*
Gibbons, William Patrick *coach*
Goldberg, Marc Evan *biotechnology executive*
Gorton, Nathaniel M. *federal judge, lawyer*
†Grad, Bonnie L. *art historian, educator*
Greenberg, Nathan *accountant*
Grogan, William Robert *university dean*
Gurwitz, Arnold *city official, pediatrician*
Hanshaw, James Barry *physician, educator*
Hatstat, Judy Anne *nursing administrator*
Heman, Robert Jerome, Jr. *printing company executive, association executive*
Hohenemser, Christoph *physics educator, researcher*
Hunt, John David *retired banker*
Hunter, Richard Edward *physician*
Isaksen, Robert L. *bishop*
Johnson, Nancy Ann *education educator*
Kaplan, Melvin Hyman *immunology, rheumatology, medical educator*
Katz, Robert Nathan *ceramic engineer*
Koelsch, William Alvin *history educator*
Langevin, Edgar Louis *retired humanities educator*
Lanza, Robert Paul *medical scientist*
Laster, Leonard *physician, consultant, author*
Latham, Eleanor Ruth Earthrowl *neuropsychology therapist*
Lawrence, Walter Thomas *plastic surgeon*
Levine, Peter Hughes *physician, health facility administrator*
Loew, Franklin Martin *educational administrator, biologist, consultant*
Lougee, David Louis *lawyer*
Ludlum, David Blodgett *pharmacologist, educator*
Malone, Joseph James *mathematics educator, researcher*
†Maloney, Mary Elizabeth *dermatologist, educator*
Marcus, Elliott Meyer *neurologist, educator*
McCorison, Marcus Allen *librarian, cultural organization administrator*
†Merrill, Christopher Lyall *writer*
Moschos, Demitrios Mina *lawyer*
Nelson, John Martin *corporate executive*
Norton, Robert Leo, Sr. *mechanical engineering educator, researcher*
O'Brien, John F. *insurance company executive*
Och, Mohamad Rachid *psychiatrist, consultant*
Olson, Robert Leonard *retired insurance company executive*

Orringer, Mark Burton surgeon, educator
Owyang, Chung gastroenterologist, researcher
Paige, Jeffery Mayland sociologist, educator
†Palmer, Stephanie Candace English educator, literary critic
Parkinson, William Charles physicist, educator
Parsons, Jeffrey Robinson anthropologist, educator
Paul, Ara Garo university dean
Pedley, John Griffiths archaeologist, educator
Pehlke, Robert Donald materials and metallurgical engineering educator
Pepe, Steven Douglas federal magistrate judge
Perkins, Barbara M. English educator
Petrick, Ernest Nicholas mechanical engineer
Petty, Elizabeth Marie geneticist
Phillips, Daniel Miller lawyer
Pierce, Roy political science educator
Pitt, Bertram cardiologist, educator, consultant
Ploger, Robert Riis retired military officer, engineer
Pollack, Henry Nathan geophysics educator
Pollock, Stephen Michael industrial engineering educator, consultant
Porretta, Louis Paul education educator
Porter, John Wilson education executive
Potter, David Stone Greek and Latin educator
Powers, William Francis automobile manufacturing company executive
Pritts, Bradley Arthur, Jr. management systems consultant
Pulgram, Ernst linguist, philologist, Romance and classical linguistics educator, writer
Quinnell, Bruce Andrew retail book chain executive
†Rabe, Barry George natural resources and environment educator
Rea, David K. geology and oceanography educator
Reddy, Venkat Narsimha ophthalmologist, researcher
Reed, John Wesley lawyer, educator
Reese, James W. orthodontist
Reinarz, Alice G. academic administrator
Richardson, Rudy James toxicology and neurosciences educator
Roach, Thomas Adair lawyer
Robbins, Jerry Hal educational administration educator
Roe, Byron Paul physics educator
Romani, John Henry health administration educator
Root, William Lucas electrical engineering educator
Rosenthal, Amnon pediatric cardiologist
Rosseels, Gustave Alois music educator
Roush, William R. chemistry educator
Rumman, Wadi (Saliba Rumman) civil engineer
Rupp, Ralph Russell audiologist, educator, author
Rycus, Mitchell Julian urban planning educator, urban security and energy planning consultant
†Saddik, Annette Joy English literature educator
Samson, Perry J. environmental scientist, educator
Sandalow, Terrance law educator
Sasaki, Joseph Donald optometrist
Savageau, Michael Antonio microbiology and immunology educator
Sawyer, Charles Henry art educator, art museum director emeritus
Saxonhouse, Arlene W. political scientist, educator
Schacht, Jochen Heinrich biochemistry educator
Scharp-Radovic, Carol Ann choreographer, classical ballet educator, artistic director
Schmitt, Mary Elizabeth postal supervisor
Schneider, Carl Edward law educator
Schnitzer, Bertram hematopathologist
Schottenfeld, David epidemiologist, educator
Schwank, Johannes Walter chemical engineering educator
Schweitzer, Pamela Bifano psychiatric and mental health nurse practitioner
Scott, Norman Ross electrical engineering educator
Senior, Thomas Bryan A. electrical engineering educator, researcher, consultant
Shapiro, Matthew David economist
Shappirio, David Gordon biologist, educator
Shaw, Jiajiu chemist
Shayman, James Alan nephrologist, educator
Sheldon, Ingrid Kristina mayor
Simpson, A. W. B. law educator
Singer, Eleanor sociologist, editor
Singer, Joel David political science educator
Slavens, Thomas Paul library science educator
Sloan, Herbert Elias physician, surgeon
Smith, David John, Jr. plastic surgeon
Smith, Dean Gordon economist, educator
Smith, Donald Cameron physician, educator
Smith, Edward E. psychologist
Solomon, David Eugene engineering company executive
Sosnowski, David Joseph environmental protection specialist
Sparling, Peter David dancer, dance educator
Sprandel, Dennis Steuart management consulting company executive
Stafford, Frank Peter, Jr. economics educator, consultant
Stark, Joan Scism education educator
Steel, Duncan Gregory physics educator
Steiner, Peter Otto economics educator, dean
Steinhoff, William Richard English literature educator
Steiss, Alan Walter research administrator, educator
Stoermer, Eugene Filmore biologist, educator
Stolper, Wolfgang Friedrich retired economist, educator
Stolz, Benjamin Armond foreign language educator
Strang, Ruth Hancock pediatric educator, pediatric cardiologist, priest
Stross, Jeoffrey Knight physician, educator
Surovell, Edward David real estate company executive
Sussman, Alfred Sheppard university educator
Tai, Chen-To electrical engineering educator
Tamres, Milton chemistry educator
Tandon, Rajiv psychiatrist, educator
Thompson, Norman Winslow surgeon, educator
Tice, Carol Hoff middle school educator, consultant
Todd, Robert Franklin, III oncologist, educator
Townsend, LeRoy B. chemistry educator, university administrator, researcher
Trautmann, Thomas Roger history and anthropology educator
Turcotte, Jeremiah George physician, surgery educator
Ulaby, Fawwaz Tayssir electrical engineering and computer science educator, research center administrator
Upatnieks, Juris optical engineer, researcher, educator
Vakalo, Emmanuel-George architecture and planning educator, researcher
Vander, Judith Rose ethnomusicologist
Van der Voo, Rob geophysicist
Van Houweling, Douglas Edward university administrator, educator
Vining, (George) Joseph law educator
Wagner, Warren Herbert, Jr. botanist, educator
†Wahl, Richard Leo radiologist, educator, nuclear medicine researcher
Waldecker, Thomas Raymond social worker
Walker, Jack L. environmental scientist
Waller, Patricia Fossum transportation executive, researcher, psychologist
†Wang, Shixin research scientist
Ward, Peter Allan pathologist, educator
Ware, Richard Anderson foundation executive
Warner, Kenneth E. public health educator, consultant
Warner, Robert Mark university dean, archivist, historian
†Warren, Larry healthcare executive
Watkins, Paul B. academic research center administrator, medical educator
Weber, Wendell William pharmacologist
Weg, John Gerard physician
Weinreich, Gabriel physicist, minister, educator
Wharton, John James, Jr. research physicist
†White, B. Joseph university dean
White, James Boyd law educator
Whitehouse, Frank, Jr. microbiologist
Whitman, Marina Von Neumann economist, educator
Wiggins, Roger C. internist, educator, researcher
Williams, John Andrew physiology educator, consultant
Williams, John Troy librarian, educator
Willmarth, William Walter aerospace engineering educator
Wilson, Richard Christian engineering firm executive
Winbury, Martin Maurice pharmaceutical executive, educator
Wong, Victor Kenneth physics educator, academic administrator
Woo, Peter Wing Kee organic chemist
Woodcock, Leonard humanities educator, former ambassador
Wylie, Evan Benjamin civil engineering educator, consultant, researcher
Xie, Yu adult education educator
Yamada, Tadataka internist
Young, Edwin Harold chemical and metallurgical engineering educator
Zhang, Youxue geology educator
Zucker, Robert A(lpert) psychologist
†Zurier, Rebecca art history educator
Zwiep, Mary Nelva humanities educator

Arcadia
Ogilvie, Bruce Campbell financial consultant

Armada
Kummerow, Arnold A. superintendent of schools

Atlanta
†Francisco, Wayne H. criminalist, educator

Auburn
Gregory, Richard Joseph youth services professional

Auburn Hills
Abraham, Tajama basketball player
Brady, Michael John chemical engineer, automotive engineer
†Brondello, Sandy professional basketball player
Davidson, William M. diversified company executive, professional basketball executive
Drexler, Mary Sanford financial executive
Dumars, Joe, III retired professional basketball player
Eaton, Robert James automotive company executive
Etefia, Florence Victoria academic and behavior specialist
Farrar, Stephen Prescott glass products manufacturing executive
†Gentry, Alvin professional basketball coach
†Gerson, Ralph Joseph corporate executive
Hill, Grant professional basketball player
†Hlede, Korie professional basketball player
Kulesza, Chester Stephen (Bud Kulesza) finance executive
Laettner, Christian Donald professional basketball player
Lapadot, Sonee Spinner automobile manufacturing company official
Lieberman-Cline, Nancy professional basketball coach, former player
MacDonald, John marketing executive
Mandiberg, David Michael sculptor
Montross, Eric Scott professional basketball player
Mukundan, Gopalan information technologist
O'Brien, William J. lawyer
Stegmayer, Joseph Henry housing industry executive
Trebing, David Martin financial executive
Wagner, Bruce Stanley marketing communications executive
Williams, Calvin librarian, consultant
Wilson, Thomas S. professional basketball team administrator

Augusta
Barr, William Robert industrial engineer, consultant
Johnson, Wilbur Corneal (Joe Johnson) biologist

Bad Axe
Riegle, Karen Dewald communications educator
Sullivan, James Gerald business owner, postal letter carrier

Battle Creek
Andert, Jeffrey Norman clinical psychologist
Bishop, Joyce Ann special programs counselor
Cline, Charles William poet, pianist, rhetoric and literature educator
Davis, Laura Arlene retired foundation administrator
DeVries, Robert Allen foundation administrator
Fisher, James A. lawyer
Hazel, James R. C., Jr. small business owner, civic volunteer
Jagner, Ronald Paul financial administrator, consultant
Langbo, Arnold Gordon food company executive
Mawby, Russell George retired foundation executive
McKay, Eugene Henry, Jr. food company executive
McPhee, Paula Ann elementary education educator
Myer, Donna Gail writer, health researcher
Richardson, William Chase foundation executive
Wendt, Linda M. educational association administrator

Bay City
†Binder, Charles E. federal judge
Cleland, Robert Hardy federal judge
Greve, Guy Robert lawyer
Greve, Lucius, II metals company executive
†Hiner, John Patrick newspaper editor
Morrill, Geary Steven entrepreneur
Nicholson, William Noel clinical neuropsychologist
Rakowski, Barbara Ann principal
†Shapero, Walter federal judge
Spector, Arthur Jay federal judge
Van Dyke, Clifford Craig retired banker

Bellevue
Hamel, Louis Reginald systems analysis consultant

Benton Harbor
Atwood, Harold Ashley retired historian
Fernando, J. Anicetus P. manufacturing executive
Hopp, Daniel Frederick manufacturing company executive, lawyer
Whitwam, David Ray appliance manufacturing company executive
Wurz, Kevin Ross theater educator, director

Benzonia
Frostic, Gwen paper company executive

Berkley
Brewer, Garry Dwight social scientist, educator

Berrien Center
Dunbar, Mable Cleone counselor education, family

Berrien Springs
Ali, Muhammad (Cassius Marcellus Clay) retired professional boxer
Andreasen, Niels-Erik Albinus religious educator
Kis, Miroslav Mirko minister, religion educator
†Land, Gary Gene history educator
Lesher, William Richard retired academic administrator

Beulah
Auch, Walter Edward securities company executive
Edwards, Wallace Winfield retired automotive company executive

Beverly Hills
Edwards, Michael Gerard physician
Grey, Joseph Edward, II artist
Tolias, Linda Puroff music educator

Big Rapids
Barnes, Isabel Janet microbiology educator, college dean
Barnum, Robert Lyle artist, art educator
†Ding, Dan Xiong English educator
Lowther, Gerald Eugene optometry educator
Mathison, Ian William chemistry educator, academic dean
Mehler, Barry Alan humanities educator, journalist, consultant
Santer, Richard Arthur geography educator
Thapa, Khagendra survey engineering educator
Weber, Joseph Edwin librarian, educator

Bingham Farms
Fershtman, Julie Ilene lawyer
Gass, Gertrude Zemon psychologist, researcher
Gratch, Serge mechanical engineering educator
Harvey, Judith Gootkin elementary education educator, real estate agent
McKeen, Alexander C. engineering consulting company owner
†Mills, Helene Audrey education educator
Moffitt, David Louis lawyer, county and state official
Toll, Roberta Darlene (Mrs. Sheldon S. Toll) clinical psychologist
Toth, John Michael lawyer

Birmingham
Ashleigh, Caroline art and antiques appraiser
Bromberg, Stephen Aaron lawyer
Buczak, Douglas Chester financial advisor, lawyer
Buesser, Anthony Carpenter lawyer
Elsman, James Leonard, Jr. lawyer
Gold, Edward David lawyer
Harms, Deborah Gayle psychologist
Harms, Steven Alan lawyer
†Harter, Roger Karr retired telecommunications executive
†Kass, Evan J. pediatric urologist
Kienbaum, Thomas Gerd lawyer
La Plata, George federal judge
Lesser, Margo Rogers legal consultant
McDonald, Alonzo Lowry, Jr. business and financial executive
McIntyre, Bruce Herbert media and marketing consultant
Morganroth, Fred lawyer
Nicholson, Robert D. manufacturing executive
Ortman, George Earl artist
Park, Richard John value engineer
Sallen, Marvin Seymour investment company executive
†Schaefer, John Frederick lawyer
Shiener, Gerald Alan psychiatrist
Sweeney, Thomas Frederick lawyer
Van der Tuin, Mary Bramson headmistress
VanDeusen, Bruce Dudley company executive
Van Dine, Harold Forster, Jr. architect

Blissfield
†Thompson, Kenneth M. sculptor, educator

Bloomfield Hills
Abel Horowitz, Michelle Susan advertising executive
Adams, Charles Francis advertising and real estate executive
Allen, Maurice Bartelle, Jr. architect
Andrews, Frank Lewis lawyer
Baker, Robert Edward lawyer, retired financial corporation executive
Baumkel, Mark S. lawyer
†Beachum, James Curtis stockbroker
Belavek, Debra Louise school psychologist
Benton, William Pettigrew advertising agency executive
Berline, James H. advertising executive, public relations agency executive
Berlow, Robert Alan lawyer
Birkerts, Gunnar architect
Bissell, John Howard marketing executive
Brodhead, William McNulty lawyer, former congressman
Brown, Jack Wyman architect
Brown, Lynette Ralya journalist, publicist
Burnett, Patricia Hill artist, author, sculptor, lecturer
Chason, Jacob (Leon Chason) retired neuropathologist
Clippert, Charles Frederick lawyer
Coir, Mark Allen archivist
Colladay, Robert S. trust company executive, consultant
Cranmer, Thomas William lawyer
Cuffe, Stafford Sigesmund automotive engineer, consultant
Cunningham, Gary H. lawyer
Dawson, Stephen Everette lawyer
Dean, George Arthur physician, art educator
Doyle, Jill J. elementary school principal
Fauver, John William mayor, retired business executive
Frey, Stuart Macklin automobile manufacturing company executive
Gavin, Robert Michael, Jr. college president
Gelder, John William lawyer
Googasian, George Ara lawyer
Gossett, Kathryn Myers language professional, educator
Graff, Robert Alan computer consultant
Gulati, Vipin accountant
Hagenlocker, Edward E. retired automobile company executive
Haidostian, Alice Berberian concert pianist, civic volunteer and fundraiser
Halso, Robert real estate company executive
Hertz, Richard Cornell rabbi
Houston, E. James, Jr. bank officer
Hurlbert, Robert P. lawyer
Husband, William Swire computer industry executive
James, William Ramsay cable television executive
Janover, Robert H. lawyer
Jeffe, Sidney David automotive engineer
Jones, John Paul probation officer, psychologist
Kasischke, Louis Walter lawyer
Kaufman, Ira Gladstone judge
Kaufman, Jerome Seymour retired ophthalmologist
Kirk, John Mac Gregor lawyer
Lauer, Clinton Dillman automotive executive
Lehman, Richard Leroy lawyer
LoPrete, James Hugh lawyer
Marks, Craig management educator, consultant, engineer
Maxwell, Jack Erwin manufacturing company executive
McDonald, Patrick Allen lawyer, arbitrator, educator
McGarry, Alexander Banting lawyer
Meyer, George Herbert lawyer
Millsap, Barbara Ann clinical social worker
Nolte, Henry R., Jr. lawyer, former automobile company executive
Norris, John Hart lawyer
Nuss, Shirley Ann computer coordinator, educator
Pappas, Edward Harvey lawyer
Piliawsky, Monte Eddy college program director
Poth, Stefan Michael retired sales financing company executive
Rader, Ralph Terrance lawyer
Robinson, Jack Albert retail drug stores executive
Rosenfeld, Joel ophthalmologist, lawyer
Roy, Ranjit Kumar mechanical engineer
Rusin, Edward A. banker
Sandy, William Haskell training and communication systems executive
Schoenhals, Katherine Viola social worker
Simon, Evelyn lawyer
Snyder, George Edward lawyer
Solomon, Mark Raymond lawyer, educator
Stivender, Donald Lewis mechanical engineering consultant
Stunz, John Henry, Jr. retired physician
Syme, Daniel Bailey rabbi, institution executive
†Thompson, Richard Thomas academic administrator
Thurber, John Alexander lawyer
Victor, Richard Steven lawyer
Waller, Irene Bazan social services agency administrator
Weil, John William technology management consultant
Weinstein, William Joseph lawyer
Wermuth, Mary Louella secondary education educator
Williams, Walter Joseph lawyer
Wydra, Frank Thomas healthcare executive
Yamin, Joseph Francis lawyer, counselor
Ziegler, John Augustus, Jr. lawyer

Brighton
Bitten, Mary Josephine quality consultant, municipal official
Chrysler, Richard R. former congressman
Crabtree, John David manufacturing company executive
Darlington, Judith Mabel clinical social worker, Christian counselor
†Huget, Charlene Dorothy library director
Jensen, Baiba principal
Veno, Glen Corey management consultant

Brooklyn
Baumann, Gregory William physician, consultant

Bruce Crossing
Waara, Maria Esther artist

Buchanan
Falkenstein, Karin Edith elementary school principal
†Wade, Melvin Pitt principal

Burton
†Tabbaa, Abdul H. physician

Cadillac
Krafve, Allen Horton management consultant
Whitmer, Walter Glenn band director

Caledonia
Duren, Stephen D. artist

Canton
Kendall, Laurel Ann geotechnical engineer
Schulz, Karen Alice psychologist, medical psychotherapist, vocational case manager

Rajlich, Vaclav Thomas *computer science educator, researcher, consultant*
Rakolta, John, Sr. *construction company executive*
Rasmussen, Douglas John *lawyer*
Redman, Barbara Klug *nursing educator*
Reid, Irvin D. *academic official*
Reide, Jerome L. *social sciences educator, lawyer*
Rentenbach, Paul Robert *lawyer*
†Rhodes, Steven William *judge*
Roberts, Seymour M. (Skip Roberts) *advertising agency executive*
Roehling, Carl David *architect*
Rogers, Richard Lee *educator*
Rohr, Richard David *lawyer*
Rosen, Gerald Ellis *federal judge*
†Rosenblum, Mark L. *neurosurgeon*
Rozof, Phyllis Claire *lawyer*
Ruffner, Frederick G., Jr. *book publisher*
Ryan, James Leo *federal judge*
Salter, Linda Lee *security officer*
Santo, Ronald Joseph *lawyer*
Saxton, William Marvin *lawyer*
Saylor, Larry James *lawyer*
†Scheer, Donald A. *federal judge*
Schindler, Marvin Samuel *foreign language educator*
Schmidt, Robert *mechanics and civil engineering educator*
Schoenherr, Walter Joseph *bishop*
Scholler, Thomas Peter *lawyer, accountant*
Schreiber, Bertram Manuel *mathematics educator*
Schuster, Elaine *civil rights professional, state official*
Schwartz, Alan E. *lawyer*
Schweitzer, Peter *advertising agency executive*
Schwing, Mark David *artist*
Scott, Brenda M. *city official*
Scott, John Edward Smith *lawyer*
Sedler, Robert Allen *law educator*
Segel, Mark Calvin *diagnostic radiologist*
Semanik, Anthony James *instructional technology coordinator*
Semple, Lloyd Ashby *lawyer*
Sengupta, Dipak Lal *electrical engineering and physics educator, researcher*
Shaevsky, Mark *lawyer*
†Shaffrey, Christopher Ignatius *spinal surgeon*
Shah, Aashit K *neurologist*
Shanahan, Brendan Frederick *professional hockey player*
†Shankaran, Seetha *physician, educator, researcher, administrator*
Shannon, Margaret Anne *lawyer*
†Shannon, Timothy T. *educational adminstrator*
Shapiro, Michael B. *lawyer*
Shorter, Michelle Anne *secondary educator*
†Silverman, Mark *publisher*
Silverman, Norman Alan *cardiac surgeon*
Sima, Anders Adolph Fredrik *neuropathologist, neurosciences researcher, educator*
Simmons, John Franklin *writer*
Singh, Kameshwar Prasad *toxicologist, researcher*
Skoney, Sophie Essa *educational administrator*
Skutt, Richard Michael *lawyer*
Sloan, Andrew Edward *neurosurgeon*
Small, Melvin *history educator*
Smith, Gary Richard *technology educator*
†Smith, Jennette Helen *journalist*
Smith, John Francis, Jr. *automobile company executive*
Smith, Wilbur Lazear *radiologist, educator*
Smyntek, John Eugene, Jr. *newspaper editor*
Sokol, Robert James *obstetrician, gynecologist, educator*
Sott, Herbert *lawyer*
Spansky, Robert Alan *computer systems analyst, retired*
Sparrow, Herbert George, III *lawyer*
†Spearman-Leach, Anthony Maurice Paul *communications executive*
†Spickermann, Roland *history educator*
Spyers-Duran, Peter *librarian, educator*
†Stack, Steven John, Jr. *criminal justice educator*
Stark, Susan R. *film critic*
Stein, Paul David *cardiologist*
Stella, Frank Dante *food service and dining equipment executive*
Stewart, Melbourne George, Jr. *physicist, educator*
Stroud, Joe Hinton *newspaper editor*
Stynes, Stanley Kenneth *retired chemical engineer, educator*
Sullivan, Joseph B. *retired judge*
Sutton, Lynn Sorensen *librarian*
Talbert, Bob *newspaper columnist*
Tallet, Margaret Anne *theatre executive*
†Tan, Chin An *educator*
Taylor, Anna Diggs *judge*
Teagan, John Gerard *newspaper executive*
Thelen, Bruce Cyril *lawyer*
Thoms, David Moore *lawyer*
Thurber, Peter Palms *lawyer*
Timm, Roger K. *lawyer*
Tisdale, James Edward *pharmacy educator, pharmacotherapy researcher*
Tolia, Vasundhara K. *pediatric gastroenterologist, educator*
Toll, Sheldon Samuel *lawyer*
Trim, Donald Roy *consulting engineer*
Trout, Michael Gerald *airport administrator*
Tushman, J. Lawrence *wholesale distribution executive*
Uhde, Thomas Whitley *psychiatry educator, psychiatrist*
Uicker, Joseph Bernard *engineering company executive*
Ursache, Victorin (His Eminence The Most Reverend Archbishop Victorin) *archbishop*
Vaitkevicius, Vainutis Kazys *foundation administrator, medical educator*
van der Marck, Jan *art historian*
†Van Dyke, Daniel L. *geneticist*
Vega, Frank J. *newspaper publishing executive*
†Velick, Stephen H. *medical facility administrator*
†Vigneron, Allen Henry *theology educator, rector, auxiliary bishop*
Vincent, Charles Eagar, Jr. *sports columnist*
Volz, William Harry *law educator, administrator*
Voudoukis, Ignatios John *internist, cardiologist*
Waldmeir, Peter Nielsen *journalist*
Walsh, James Joseph *lawyer*
Warden, Gail Lee *health care executive*
Weiss, Mark Lawrence *anthropology educator*
Werba, Gabriel *public relations consultant*
Wheeler, Maurice B. *librarian*
White, Joseph B. *reporter*
Whitehouse, Fred Waite *endocrinologist, researcher*
Wiener, Joseph *pathologist*
Williams, J. Bryan *lawyer*
Wise, John Augustus *lawyer*
Wittlinger, Timothy David *lawyer*
Wood, R. Stewart *bishop*
Woods, George Edward *judge*
Worden, William Michael *city agency administrator, preservation consultant*
Yokich, Stephen P. *labor union administrator*
Yzerman, Steve *professional hockey player*
Zatkoff, Lawrence P. *federal judge*
Zoubareff, Kathy Olga *administrative assistant*

Dexter
†Sharp, Ronald Farrington *lawyer*

Dowagiac
Gourley, Everett Haynie *educator*
Mulder, Patricia Marie *education educator*
Ott, C(larence) H(enry) *citizen ambassador, accounting educator*

Durand
Cook, Bernadine Fern *book publisher, writer*

East Detroit
Cattaneo, Michael S. *heating and cooling company executive*

East Jordan
Donaldson, Robert Frost *minister*

East Lansing
Abbett, William S. *dean*
Abeles, Norman *psychologist, educator*
Abolins, Maris Arvids *physics researcher and educator*
Abramson, Paul Robert *political scientist, educator*
Allen, Bruce Templeton *economics educator*
Andersland, Orlando Baldwin *civil engineering educator*
Anderson, David Daniel *retired humanities educator, writer, editor*
Anderson, Donald Keith *chemical engineering educator*
Arens, Alvin Armond *accountant, educator*
Austin, Sam M. *physics educator*
Axinn, George Harold *rural sociology educator*
Bandes, Susan Jane *museum director, educator*
Benenson, Walter *nuclear physics educator*
Bitensky, Susan Helen *law educator*
Bladen, Edwin Mark *lawyer, judge*
Blosser, Henry Gabriel *physicist*
Brody, Theodore Meyer *pharmacologist, educator*
Brophy, Jere Edward *education educator, researcher*
Bukovac, Martin John *horticulturist, educator*
Burnett, Jean Bullard (Mrs. James R. Burnett) *biochemist*
Byerrum, Richard Uglow *college dean*
Case, Eldon Darrel *materials science educator*
Chapin, Richard Earl *librarian*
Chen, Kun-Mu *electrical engineering educator*
Cross, Aureal Theophilus *geology and botany educator*
Cutts, Charles Eugene *civil engineering educator*
Dennis, Frank George, Jr. *retired horticulture educator*
Dewhurst, Charles Kurt *museum director, curator, folklorist, English language educator*
D'Itri, Frank Michael *environmental research chemist*
Dye, James Louis *chemistry educator*
Eadie, John William *history educator*
Falk, Julia S. *linguist, educator*
†Fernandez, Ramona Esther *adult education educator*
Fischer, Lawrence Joseph *toxicologist, educator*
Fisher, Alan Washburn *historian, educator*
Fisher, Ronald C. *economics educator*
Foss, John Frank *mechanical engineering educator*
Francese, Joseph *Italian language and literature educator*
Freedman, Eric *journalist, educator, writer*
Fromm, Paul Oliver *physiology educator*
Gardner, Mary Adelaide *retired journalism educator*
Gelbke, Claus-Konrad *nuclear physics educator*
Gerhardt, Philipp *microbiologist, educator*
Goodman, Erik David *engineering educator*
Gottschalk, Alexander *radiologist, diagnostic radiology educator*
Granger, Bruce Ingham *retired English language educator*
Greenberg, Bradley Sander *communications educator*
Hackel, Emanuel *science educator*
Harrison, Jeremy Thomas *dean*
Harrison, Michael Jay *physicist, educator*
Hilbert, Virginia Lois *computer consultant and training executive*
Hollander, Stanley Charles *marketing educator*
Hollingworth, Robert Michael *toxicology researcher*
Honhart, Frederick Lewis, III *academic director*
Huzar, Eleanor Goltz *history educator*
†Hyndman, David William *geological sciences educator*
Ilgen, Daniel Richard *psychology educator*
Isleib, Donald R. *retired agricultural researcher*
†Izzo, Thomas *college basketball coach*
Johnson, John Irwin, Jr. *neuroscientist*
Kamrin, Michael Arnold *toxicology educator*
Kende, Hans Janos *plant physiology educator*
Kirk, Edgar Lee *musician, educator*
Knobloch, Irving William *retired biology educator, author*
Kreinin, Mordechai Eliahu *economics educator*
Kronegger, Maria Elisabeth *French and comparative literature educator*
†Labaree, David Fleming *eduator*
Langeland, Karen *basketball coach*
Lashbrooke, Elvin Carroll, Jr. *law educator, consultant*
Leepa, Allen *artist, educator*
Lenski, Richard Eimer *evolutionary biologist, educator*
Levy, Mark Robert *communication educator*
†Li, Tien-Yien *mathematics educator*
Liu, Jianguo *ecologist*
Lloyd, John Raymond *mechanical engineering educator*
Lockwood, John LeBaron *plant pathologist*
Lucas, Robert Elmer *soil scientist*
Luecke, Richard William *biochemist*
Mackey, Maurice Cecil *university president, economist, lawyer*
Macrakis, Kristie Irene *history of science educator*
Magen, Myron Shimin *osteopathic physician, educator, university dean*
Majors, Richard George *psychology educator*
Manderscheid, Lester Vincent *agricultural economics educator*
Manning, Peter Kirby *sociology educator*
Mansour, George P. *Spanish language and literature educator*
McKinley, Camille Dombrowski *psychologist*
McMeekin, Dorothy *botany, plant pathology educator*
McPherson, Melville Peter *academic administrator, former government official*
Mead, Carl David *retired educator*
Menchik, Paul Leonard *economist, educator*
Mitstifer, Dorothy Irwin *honor society administrator*
Moore, Kenneth Edwin *pharmacology educator*
Moran, Daniel Austin *mathematician*
Morton, Jerry Lee *journalist*
Mukherjee, Kalinath *materials science and engineering educator, researcher*
Munger, Benson Scott *professional society administrator*
Murray, Raymond Harold *physician*
Natoli, Joseph *English language educator*
Nelson, Ronald Harvey *animal science educator, researcher*
Netzloff, Michael Lawrence *pediatric educator, endocrinologist, geneticist*
Paananen, Victor Niles *English educator*
Palinski, Kay Marie *real estate broker*
Paneth, Nigel Sefton *epidemiologist, pediatrician*
Papsidero, Joseph Anthony *social scientist, educator*
Patterson, Maria Jevitz *microbiology-pediatric infectious disease educator*
Perrin, Robert *editorial consultant, writer*
Petrides, George Athan *ecologist, educator*
Pierre, Percy Anthony *university president*
Platt, Franklin Dewitt *retired history educator*
Poland, Robert Paul *business educator, consultant*
Pollack, Norman *history educator*
Potchen, E. James *radiology educator*
Preiss, Jack *biochemistry educator*
Press, Charles *retired political science educator*
Ricks, Donald Jay *agricultural economist*
Ristow, George Edward *neurologist, educator*
Robbins, Lawrence Harry *anthropologist*
†Robinson, Michael *protective services official*
Root-Bernstein, Robert Scott *biologist, educator*
Rosenman, Kenneth D. *medical educator*
Rovner, David Richard *endocrinology educator*
Rubner, Michael *international relations educator, university administrator*
Sato, Paul Hisashi *pharmacologist*
Schlesinger, Joseph Abraham *political scientist*
Silverman, Henry Jacob *history educator*
Simon, Lou Anna Kimsey *academic administrator*
Snell, John Raymond *civil engineer*
Snoddy, James Ernest *education educator*
Soffin, Stan *journalism educator*
Sommers, Lawrence Melvin *geographer, educator*
Soutas-Little, Robert William *mechanical engineer, educator*
Stanley, Kurt Edward *auto parts executive*
Stapleton, James Hall *statistician, educator*
Strassmann, W. Paul *economics educator*
Suits, Daniel Burbidge *economist*
Summitt, (William) Robert *chemist, educator*
Thomas, Franklin Richard *American studies and language educator, writer*
Thomas, Samuel Joseph *history educator*
Tien, H. Ti *biophysics and physiology educator, scientist*
Useem, John Hearld *sociologist, anthropologist*
Useem, Ruth Hill *sociology educator*
von Bernuth, Robert Dean *agricultural engineering educator, consultant*
Von Tersch, Lawrence Wayne *electrical engineering educator, university dean*
Waite, Donald Eugene *medical educator, consultant*
Wakoski, Diane *poet, educator*
Walker, Bruce Edward *anatomy educator*
Weng, John Juyang *computer science educator, researcher*
Whallon, William *literature educator*
Whiting, Lisa Lorraine Dobson *video production educator, producer, director*
Wilkinson, William Sherwood *lawyer*
Winder, Clarence Leland *psychologist, educator*
Witter, Richard Lawrence *veterinarian, educator*
Wolterink, Lester Floyd *biophysicist, educator*
Woodbury, Stephen Abbott *economics educator*
Wronski, Stanley Paul *education educator*
Yussouff, Mohammed *physicist, educator*

Eastpointe
Andrzejewski, Darryl Lee *clergyman*

Eastport
Tomlinson, James Lawrence *mechanical engineer*

Ecorse
†Williams, Reginald Bernard *library director*

Edwardsburg
Floyd, Alton David *cell biologist, consultant*

Escanaba
Schnesk, Elizabeth Ann *office manager, small business owner*

Evart
Fatum, Russ Allen *human resources professional, educator*

Farmington
Baker, Edward Martin *engineering and industrial psychologist*
Chou, Clifford Chi Fong *research engineering executive*
Ellens, J(ay) Harold *philosopher, educator, psychotherapist*
Ginsberg, Myron *computer scientist*
†Kadi, Osama
Moehlman, Ruth *historian, writer*
Neyer, Jerome Charles *consulting civil engineer*
Reddig, Walter Eduard *architect, master cabinet maker*
Torpey, Scott Raymond *lawyer*
Wine, Sherwin Theodore *rabbi*

Farmington Hills
Abrams, Roberta Busky *hospital administrator, nurse*
Birdsong, Emil Ardell *clinical psychologist*
Birnkrant, Sherwin Maurice *lawyer*
Blum, Jon H. *dermatologist*
Bricker, Gerald Wayne *marketing executive*
Bryfonski, Dedria Anne *publishing company executive*
Burns, Sister Elizabeth Mary *hospital administrator*
Cooper, Elaine Janice *physical therapist*
Dolan, Jan Clark *former state legislator*
Donald, Edward Milton, Jr. *marketing company executive*
Dragun, James *soil chemist*
Ebert, Douglas Edmund *banker*
Ellis, Robert William *engineering educator*
Ellmann, Sheila Frenkel *investment company executive*
Faxon, Jack *headmaster*
Fenton, Robert Leonard *lawyer*
Frederick, Raymond Joseph *sales engineering executive*
Gordon, Craig Jeffrey *oncologist, educator*
Haliw, Andrew Jerome, III *lawyer, engineer*
Hartman-Abramson, Ilene *adult education educator*
Harwell, William Earnest (Ernie Harwell) *broadcaster*
Hechler, Ellen Elissa *elementary education educator*
Heiss, Richard Walter *former bank executive, consultant, lawyer*
Helppie, Charles Everett, III *financial consultant*
Hodjat, Yahya *metallurgist*
Holmes, Tyrone Anthony *performance consulting company executive, educator*
Karniotis, Stephen Paul *computer scientist*
Karolak, Dale Walter *aerospace company executive*
Landry, Thomas Henry *construction executive*
Lewis, Barry Kent *cardiologist*
Mackey, Robert Joseph *business executive*
McQuiggan, Mark C. *urologist*
Michlin, Arnold Sidney *finance executive*
Papai, Beverly Daffern *library director*
Pargoff, Robert Michael *small business owner*
Plaut, Jonathan Victor *rabbi*
Sobczak, Judy Marie *clinical psychologist*
Theodore, Ares Nicholas *research chemist*
†Wiloch, Thomas *writer, editor*

Fenton
Anas, Julianne Kay *retired administrative laboratory director*
Manuel, Dennis Lee *real estate broker*

Ferndale
Baker, Elaine R. *radio station executive*
Gienapp, Helen Fischer *jewelry company owner*
Pence, Leland Hadley *organic chemist*

Fife Lake
Knecht, Richard Arden *family practitioner*

Flat Rock
Wright, Arthur Franklin *transportation executive, municipal official*

Flint
Alarie-Anderson, Peggy Sue *physician assistant*
Amy, Patricia Eleen *psychologist*
Becker, Michael Edward *police and emergency medical services executive*
Belcher, Max *social services administrator, college dean*
Dismuke, Leroy *special education educator, coordinator*
Duckett, Bernadine Johnal *retired elementary principal*
Edsall, David Leonard *councillor, religious educator*
Elieff, Lewis Steven *stockbroker*
Farrehi, Cyrus *cardiologist, educator*
Gadola, Paul V. *federal judge*
Germann, Steven James *museum director*
†Goldman, Marc L. *federal judge*
Goodstein, Sanders Abraham *scrap iron company executive*
Hart, Clifford Harvey *lawyer*
Hayes, Joyce Merriweather *secondary education educator*
Henneke, Edward George *lawyer*
Heymoss, Jennifer Marie *librarian*
Jayabalan, Vemblaserry *nuclear medicine physician, radiologist*
Johnson, Gary Keith *pediatrician*
Lorenz, John Douglas *college official*
McCartin, Brian James *mathematician, educator*
McClanahan, Connie Dea *pastoral minister*
Meissner, Suzanne Banks *pastoral associate*
Millon, Delecta Gay *nursing educator*
Novak, Jo-Ann Stout *chemical engineer*
Palinsky, Constance Genevieve *hypnotherapist, educator*
Pelavin, Michael Allen *lawyer*
†Phelps, Janet Ann *environmental health coordinator*
Piper, Mark Harry *retired banker*
Powers, Edward Herbert *lawyer*
Rappleye, Richard Kent *financial executive, consultant, educator*
Samuel, Roger D. *newspaper publishing executive*
†Sayyid, Samiullah N. *physician*
Soderstrom, Robert Merriner *dermatologist*
Spencer, Dianne S. *electronics executive, educator*
Stafford, Marjorie *emergency department nurse*
Stanley, Woodrow *mayor*
Stuckey, Janice Faith *English educator, sales executive*
Taeckens, Pamela Webb *banker*
Tauscher, John Walter *retired pediatrician, emeritus educator*
Tolbert-Bey, Gregory Lee *landscape architect and planner*
Tomblinson, James Edmond *architect*
White, William Samuel *foundation executive*
Wigston, David Laurence *biologist, university dean*
Williams, JoAnn Lucille *nurse*

Flushing
Barnes, Robert Vincent *elementary and secondary school art educator*
Gordon, Reva Jo *retired librarian*

Fort Gratiot
Mueller, Don Sheridan *retired school administrator*
Rowark, Maureen *fine arts photographer*
Salt, Alfred Lewis *priest*

Frankenmuth
Shetlar, James Francis *physician*

Frankfort
Acker, Nathaniel Hull *retired educational administrator*
†Bell, Sheila Sue *primary school educator*
Foster, Robert Carmichael *banker*
Gerberding, Miles Carston *lawyer*

Franklin
DeBrincat, Susan Jeanne nutritionist
†Reinhart, Anne Christine special education educator, consultant
Vanderlaan, Richard B. marketing company executive

Fruitport
Anderson, Frances Swem nuclear medical technologist
Collier, Beverly Joanne elementary education educator

Galesburg
Lawrence, John Warren business and broadcasting executive

Garden City
†Elmouchi, Joan Leslie library director

Gaylord
Cooney, Patrick Ronald bishop
Magsig, Judith Anne early childhood education educator, retired
Weiss, Debra S. bank commission official

Glen Arbor
Newblatt, Stewart Albert federal judge

Grand Blanc
Bell, Donald Lloyd retired engineer
Hicks, Susan Lynn Bowman small business owner
Lemke, Laura Ann foreign language educator, assistant principal
Riley, Ronald Jim inventor, consultant
Wasfie, Tarik Jawad surgeon, educator

Grand Haven
PreFontaine, Ronald Louis school psychologist, human resources consultant
Sabolcik, Gene manufacturing executive

Grand Ledge
Evert, Sandra Florence (Wheeler) medical/surgical nurse
Smith, Terry J. lawyer

Grand Rapids
Anderson, Roger Gordon minister
Auwers, Stanley John motor carrier executive
Baker, Hollis MacLure furniture manufacturing company executive
Bander, Thomas Samuel dentist
Barnes, Thomas John lawyer
Bartek, Gordon Luke radiologist
Beals, Paul Archer religious studies educator
Becker, Robert Joseph database consultant, computer science specialist, database software developer and educator
Bell, Robert Holmes federal judge
Bissell, Mark consumer products company executive
Blackwell, Thomas Francis lawyer
Borgdorff, Peter church adminstrator
Boyden, Joel Michael lawyer
Bradshaw, Conrad Allan lawyer
Bransdorfer, Stephen Christie lawyer
Brent, Helen Teressa school nurse
†Calkins, Richard W. college president
Canepa, John Charles banking consultant
Chase, Sandra Lee clinical pharmacist, consultant
Chester, Timothy J. museum director
Cline, Sister Barbara Jean educational administrator
†Crawford, Joseph Patrick editor
Curtin, Timothy John lawyer
Daniels, Joseph neuropsychiatrist
Davis, Henry Barnard, Jr. lawyer
Deems, Nyal David lawyer, mayor
DeLapa, Judith Anne business owner
DeVries, Robert K. religious book publisher
Diekema, Anthony J. college president emeritus, educational consultant
Dykstra, William Dwight business executive, consultant
Ehlers, Vernon James congressman
Engbers, James Arend lawyer
Foster, Linda Nemec poet, educator
Frankforter, Weldon DeLoss retired museum administrator
Garver, Frederick Merrill industrial engineering executive
†Gordon, Dan food service executive
†Gregg, James D. federal judge
†Grin, Oliver Daniel Woodhouse neurosurgeon
Hackett, James P. manufacturing executive
Hahn, H. Michael advertising executive
Hakala, Judyth Ann data processing executive
†Hardy, Lee Patrick humanities educator
Helder, Bruce Alan metal products executive
Hillman, Douglas Woodruff federal judge
Hofman, Leonard John minister
Hooker, Robert automotive executive
Hooker, William administrative services officer
†Howard, Lawrence E. federal judge
Hoyt, William city planner
Jackoboice, Sandra Kay artist
Jackson, Wendy S Lewis social worker
Jacobsen, Arnold archivist
Jansma, Theodore John, Jr. psychologist
Kaczmarczyk, Jeffrey Allen journalist, classical music critic
Kara, Paul Mark lawyer
Kemper, Donna Mae fine art and layoutartist
Kooistra, William Henry clinical psychologist
Kramer, Carol Gertrude marriage and family counselor
Kranz, Kenneth Louis human resources company executive, entrepreneur
Kregel, James R. publishing executive
Kuiper, Douglas Scott insurance executive
Lloyd, Michael Stuart newspaper editor
Logie, John Hoult mayor, lawyer
Lyons, David Eugene secondary education educator
Mauren, Kris Alan non-profit organization executive
Maurer, John Raymond internist, educator
Mayo, David Wayne sportswriter
†Mbah, Chris H.N. business educator
McGarry, John Everett lawyer
McNeil, John W. lawyer
Mears, Patrick Edward lawyer
Meijer, Douglas retail company executive
Meijer, Frederik retail company executive
Meijer, Hendrik retail company executive
Meijer, Mark retail executive
Messner, James W. advertising executive
Miles, Wendell A. federal judge
Miller, Barbara Jean nephrology home care nurse
Morin, William Raymond bookstore chain executive
†Murphy, Edward Thomas cardiothoracic surgeon
Oetting, Roger H. lawyer
Parrish, Kenneth Dale treasurer, accountant
Petersen, Jonathan William publishing executive, media consultant
Pew, Robert Cunningham, II office equipment manufacturing company executive
Portelli, Vincent George business consultant and executive
Quist, Gordon Jay federal judge
†Riley, Robert E. retail executive, lawyer
Rougier-Chapman, Alwyn Spencer Douglas furniture manufacturing company executive
Rozeboom, John A. religious organization administrator
Ryskamp, Bruce E. publishing executive
Sadler, David Gary management executive
Schwanda, Tom religious studies educator
Schwartz, Garry Albert advertising executive
†Scoville, Joseph G. federal judge
Sebastian, James Rae, Jr. management consultant
Smith, Bill advertising and marketing executive
Smith, Edgar Wright, Jr. editor religious books
Smith, H(arold) Lawrence lawyer
Sommers, Dana Eugene insurance agency executive
Spence, Brandon music director
Spies, Frank Stadler lawyer
Stadler, James Robert lawyer
†Stevenson, Jo Ann C. federal judge
Sytsma, Fredric A. lawyer
Tafelski, Michael Dennis psychologist
Thauer, Edwin William, Jr. financial services executive
Thompson, John Ross minister
Timpe, Michael Wayne systems analyst
Titley, Larry J. lawyer
Van Andel, Betty Jean retired direct selling company executive
†Vander Steen, Dirk Willem financial executive
VanderVorst, Mitchell S. writer
Van Haren, W(illiam) Michael lawyer
VanHarn, Gordon Lee college administrator and provost
VanScoy, Holly Carole educational researcher
Van't Hof, William Keith lawyer
Verdier, David D'Ooge ophthalmologist, educator
Welton, Michael Lee financial advisor
West, Terence Douglas furniture company design executive
Wilt, Jeffrey Lynn pulmonary and critical care physician
Wold, Robert Lee architect, engineer
Woodrick, Robert food products executive
Zimmerman, John public relations executive
Zuidervaart, Lambert Paul philosophy educator

Grawn
Clous, James M. electrical equipment company executive, engineer

Grayling
Davis, Alton Thomas judge, lawyer

Greenbush
Paulson, James Marvin engineering educator

Gregory
Frank, Richard Calhoun architect
Zarley, Karlta Rae nurse consultant

Grosse Ile
Kohn, Julieanne travel agent
Smith, Veronica Latta real estate corporation officer
Stump, M. Pamela sculptor

Grosse Pointe
Avant, Grady, Jr. lawyer
Axe, John Randolph lawyer, financial executive
Barrows, Ronald Thomas lawyer
Beierwaltes, William Henry physician, educator
Beltz, Charles Robert engineering executive
Blevins, William Edward management consultant
Brucker, Wilber Marion retired lawyer
Caldwell, John Thomas, Jr. communications executive
Cartmill, George Edwin, Jr. retired hospital administrator
Christian, Edward Kieren broadcasting station executive
Collinson, Vivienne Ruth education educator, researcher, consultant
Cross, Ralph Emerson mechanical engineer
DeVine, (Joseph) Lawrence drama critic
Dunlap, Connie Sue Zimmerman real estate professional
†Dzul, Paul J. physician, medical journal editor
Elsila, David August editor
Goss, James William lawyer
Hill, Draper editorial cartoonist
Holsapple, Linda Harris retired editor
Kerns, Gertrude Yvonne psychologist
King, John Lane retired lawyer
Knapp, Mildred Florence retired social worker
Krebs, William Hoyt company executive, industrial hygienist
Lane, James McConkey investment executive
Maleitzke, Kenneth Eugene automotive engineer, retired
McIntyre, Anita Grace Jordan lawyer
McWhirter, Glenna Suzanne (Nickie McWhirter) retired newspaper columnist
Mengden, Joseph Michael retired investment banker
Mogk, John Edward law educator, association executive, consultant
Obolensky, Marilyn Wall (Mrs. Serge Obolensky) metals company executive
Peters, Thomas Robert English language educator, writer
Powsner, Edward Raphael physician
Pytell, Robert Henry lawyer, former judge
Richardson, Dean Eugene retired banker
Robie, Joan elementary school principal
Simonds, Richard Kimball investment executive
Sphire, Raymond Daniel anesthesiologist
Surdam, Robert McClellan retired banker
Thurber, Cleveland, Jr. trust banker
Valk, Robert Earl corporate executive
Weingart, Robert Paul financial consultant
Whittaker, Jeanne Evans former newspaper columnist
Wilkinson, Warren Scripps manufacturing company executive

Grosse Pointe Farms
Allen, Lee Harrison industrial consultant, wholesale company executive

Grosse Pointe Park
Coe, John William management consultant
Wilson, Henry Arthur, Jr. management consultant

Grosse Pointe Shores
Smith, Frank Earl retired association executive

Grosse Pointe Woods
Darke, Richard Francis lawyer
†Sul, Yi Chul neurologist

Hancock
Dresch, Stephen Paul economist, state legislator
Puotinen, Arthur Edwin college president, clergyman

Harbert
Morrissette, Bruce Archer Romance languages educator

Harbor Springs
†Bailey, Thomas C. conservancy executive
Ketcham, Warren Andrew psychologist, educator
Turner, Lester Nathan lawyer, international trade consultant

Harper Woods
DeGiusti, Dominic Lawrence medical science educator, academic administrator
Havrilcsak, Gregory Michael history educator

Harrison Township
Childress, Janet Lynn logistician
McGregor, Theodore Anthony chemical company executive

Hartford
†Spriegel, John R. internist, medical association administrator

Hastings
Adrounie, V. Harry public health administrator, scientist, educator, environmentalist
Jones, Kensinger advertising executive
†Rahn, L. Joseph municipal official, business educator

Hickory Corners
Bristol, Norman lawyer, arbitrator, former food company executive
Lauff, George Howard biologist

Highland
Brown, Ray Kent biochemist, physician, educator

Highland Park
Crittenden, Mary Lynne science educator

Hillsdale
†Frudakis, Anthony Parker sculptor, educator
Kline, Faith Elizabeth college official
Roche, George Charles, III college administrator
Wolfram, Gary Lee economics educator, consultant

Holland
Brouwer, Wayne Allen clergyman, writer
Cook, James Ivan clergyman, religion educator
Foster, Glenn Kevin former christian relief agency executive, social service agency executive
Franken, Darrell counselor, writer, publisher
Haworth, Gerrard Wendell office systems manufacturing company executive
Haworth, Richard G. office furniture manufacturer
Hill, JoAnne Francis retired elementary education educator
Ingham, Mark Gordon physicist, educator
Jacobson, John Howard, Jr. college president
†Jelgerhuis, Jane Marie legislative staff member
Johanneson, Gerald Benedict office products company executive
Johnson, Robert Dale marketing technology administrator
Luchies, John Elmer religion educator
Mc Gurk, James Henry consultant company executive
Moritz, John Reid lawyer
Murphy, Max Ray lawyer
Nieuwsma, Milton John writer, journalist
Nyenhuis, Jacob Eugene college official
Spoelhof, John consumer products company executive
Van Voorst, Robert E. theology educator, minister
Van Wylen, Gordon John former college president
Witkowski, Kristen Ann academic administrator
Zick, Leonard Otto accountant, manufacturing executive, consultant
Zuidema, George Dale surgeon

Holly
Stolpin, William Roger artist, printmaker, retired engineer

Hopkins
Irish, Diana Maria wildlife rehabilitation agent

Houghton
Ex, Tom sculptor, gallery owner
Goel, Ashok Kumar electrical engineering educator
Heckel, Richard Wayne metallurgical engineering educator
Huang, Eugene Yuching civil engineer, educator
McGinnis, Gary David chemist, science educator
Tompkins, Curtis Johnston university president

Houghton Lake
Marra, Samuel Patrick retired pharmacist, small business owner

Howell
Cattani, Luis Carlos manufacturing engineer
Cotton, Larry ranching executive
†Eiss, Harry Edwin English educator
Heinel, Robert Steven social services administrator
Korsgren, Mary Louise home care nurse
Watkins, Curtis Winthrop artist

Hudson
Wollett, Eleanor Leigh general education curriculum coordinator

Huntington Woods
Gutmann, Joseph art history educator
†Hassig, Gordon L. automotive sales executive
Smith, Edwin Burrows language educator, academic administrator

Idlewild
Bullett, Audrey Kathryn retired public administrator
Wooley, Geraldine Hamilton writer, poet

Indian River
Heidemann, Mary Ann community planner

Inkster
Bullock, Steven Carl lawyer

Interlochen
Hanson, Byron Winslade music educator
Stolley, Alexander advertising executive

Ionia
Kunze, Linda Joye educator

Ironwood
Vanooyen, Amy Joy writer

Ishpeming
Cope, Robert Gary management educator, author, consultant

Jackson
Abbott, Mary Elaine photographer, lecturer, researcher
Collins, Dana Jon financial executive
Feldmann, Judith Gail language professional, educator
Haglund, Bernice Marion elementary school educator
Hildreth, Patricia Yvonne accounting executive
Jacobs, Wendell Early, Jr. lawyer
Kelly, Robert Vincent, Jr. metal company executive
Kendall, Kay Lynn interior designer, consultant
Marcoux, William Joseph lawyer
Nathaniel bishop
Osborn, Janet Lynn information systems executive
Richard, Lyle Elmore retired school social worker, consultant
Ross, Lorraine Sumiko mathematics and science educator, bookkeeper
Straayer, Carole Kathleen retired elementary education educator
Trap, Jennifer Josephine special education administrator
Vischer, Harold Harry manufacturing company executive
Weaver, Franklin Thomas newspaper executive

Jenison
Headley, Kathryn Wilma secondary education educator
Vunderink, Ralph William lay minister

Kalamazoo
Amdursky, Saul Jack library director
Arnold Hubert, Nancy Kay writer
Badra, Robert George philosophy, religion and humanities educator
Bannister, Brian retired organic chemist
Bennett, Arlie Joyce clinical social worker emeritus
Blickle, Peter German educator
Breisach, Ernst A. historian, educator
Callan, Edward Thomas English educator
Calloway, Jean Mitchener mathematician, educator
Carlson, Sharon Lee archivist
Carver, Joan Willson publishing executive, artist
Carver, Norman Francis, Jr. architect, photographer
Cheney, Brigham Vernon physical chemist
Chodos, Dale David Jerome physician, consumer advocate
Chou, Kuo-Chen biophysical chemist
Clarke, Allen Bruce mathematics educator, retired academic administrator
Cody, Frank Joseph secondary school administrator, education educator
Connable, Alfred Barnes retired business executive
Curry, John Patrick insurance company executive, management consultant
†Digby-Junger, Richard A educator in English
Donoghue, George Edward retired secondary educator
Donovan, Paul V. former bishop
†Dorner, Kenneth R. plastic surgeon
Dybek, Stuart English educator, writer
Edmondson, Keith Henry chemical company executive, retired
Engelmann, Paul Victor plastics engineering educator
Enslen, Richard Alan federal judge
Enyedi, Alexander Joseph plant physiologist, researcher
Fisher, George gerontological educator
Forsleff, Louise Stewart psychologist
Gilchrist, James A. communication educator
Gilmore, James Stanley, Jr. broadcast executive
Gladstone, William Sheldon, Jr. radiologist
†Gómez Lance, Betty Rita sciences and foreign language educator, writer
Gordon, Alice Jeannette Irwin secondary and elementary education educator
Greenfield, John Charles bio-organic chemist
Grotzinger, Laurel Ann university librarian
Haenicke, Diether Hans university president emeritus, educator
Halpert, Richard Lee lawyer
Heller, Janet Ruth English language, writing and literature educator
Hilboldt, James Sonnemann lawyer, investment advisor
Hite, Judson Cary retired pharmaceutical company executive
Holland, Harold Herbert banker
Hubbard, William Neill, Jr. pharmaceutical company executive
Hudson, Roy Davage retired pharmaceutical company executive
Jamison, Frank Raymond communications educator
Jones, Eugene Gordon pharmaceutical company executive
Jones, James Fleming, Jr. college president, Roman language and literature educator
†Kobrak, Peter Max educator

†Lacey, Bernardine M. *nursing administrator, educator*
Lander, Joyce Ann *nursing educator, medical/surgical nurse*
Lawrence, William Joseph, Jr. *retired corporate executive*
Light, Christopher Upjohn *writer, computer musician, photographer*
LoVerme, Charles *intermedia educator*
Markin, David Robert *motor company executive*
Marshall, Vincent de Paul *industrial microbiologist, researcher*
†Mingus, Matthew Scott *educator*
Muncey, Barbara Deane *university associate consultant*
Nassaney, Michael Shakir *anthropology educator*
Norris, Richard Patrick *museum director, history educator*
Ortiz-Button, Olga *social worker*
Raaberg, Gloria Gwen *literature educator*
Ransford, Sherry *secondary education educator*
Ritter, Charles Edward *lawyer*
Rowland, Doyle Alfred *federal judge*
†Sauret, Martine *French educator*
Schrier, Steven Robert *television producer, director*
Solomon, Paul Robert *artist, educator*
Strong, Russell Arthur *university administator*
Stufflebeam, Daniel LeRoy *education educator*
†Takeda, Yoshimi *music director*
Taylor, Duncan Paul *research neuropharmacologist*
Taylor, Joy Holloway *artist*
Tsai, Ti-Dao *electrophysiologist*
Van Vlack, Lawrence Hall *engineering educator*
Vescovi, Selvi *pharmaceutical company executive*
Welborn, John Alva *former state senator, small business owner*
Wilson, James Rodney *air equipment company executive*
Zupko, Ramon *composer, music professor emeritus*

Kalkaska
Batsakis, John George *pathology educator*

Kentwood
Kelly, William Garrett *judge*
†Scott, Helen Patricia *family physician*

Kincheloe
Light, Kenneth Freeman *college administrator*

Laingsburg
Scripter, Frank C. *manufacturing company executive*

Lake Angelus
Kresge, Bruce Anderson *retired physician*

Lake Linden
Campbell, Wilbur Harold *research plant biochemist, educator*

Lake Orion
Brewer, Judith Anne *special education educator*

Lanse
Butler, Patricia *protective services official*

Lansing
Baker, Frederick Milton, Jr. *lawyer*
Beardmore, Dorothy *state education official*
Bell Wilson, Carlotta A. *state official, consultant*
Billard, William Thomas *insurance company executive*
Blanchard, William Graham *film educator*
Brennan, Thomas Emmett *law school president*
Bretz, Ronald James *law educator*
Brewer, Mark Courtland *lawyer*
Brook, Susan G. *state agency administrator, horse farmer*
Brown, Nancy Field *editor*
Bullard, Willis Clare, Jr. *state legislator*
Burns, Marshall Shelby *retired judge, lawyer, arbitrator*
Butcher, Amanda Kay *retired university administrator*
Cannon, Patrick D. *federal offical, broadcaster*
Carlotti, Ronald John *food scientist*
Cavanagh, Michael Francis *state supreme court justice*
Croxford, Lynne Louise *social services administrator*
Demlow, Daniel J. *lawyer*
†Drake, Douglas Craig *university official*
Emmons, Joanne *state senator*
Feight, Theodore J. *financial planner*
Fink, Joseph Allen *lawyer*
Fitzgerald, John Warner *law educator*
†Fletcher, Mark Robert *political scientist*
Foster, Joe C., Jr. *lawyer*
Geake, Raymond Robert *state senator*
Geiger, Terry *state legislator*
†Granholm, Jennifer Mulhern *state attorney general*
Heater, William Henderson *retired psychology educator*
Hines, Marshall *construction engineering company executive*
Hollenshead, Robert Earl *judge*
†Huard, Jeffrey Scott *community planner*
Jellema, Jon *state legislator*
Kaza, Greg John *state representative, economist*
Klunzinger, Thomas Edward *writer, actor, director, township treasurer*
LaForge, Edward *state legislator*
LaHaine, Gilbert Eugene *retail lumber company executive*
Latovick, Paula R(ae) *lawyer, educator*
Lindemer, Lawrence Boyd *lawyer, former utility executive, former state justice*
Marvin, David Edward Shreve *lawyer*
McCoy, Bernard Rogers *television anchor*
†McGinnis, Kenneth L. *state official*
McKeague, David William *judge*
McManus, George Alvin, Jr. *state senator, cherry farmer*
Mee, Richard James *state agency administrator*
Miller, Candice S. *state official*
†Miller, Christine Ann *academic administrator*
Muchmore, Dennis C. *governmental affairs consultant*
Perricone, Charles *state legislator*
Piveronus, Peter John, Jr. *education educator*
Posthumus, Richard Earl *state official, farmer*
†Pruss, Stanley F. *consumer protection administrator*
Rasmusson, Thomas Elmo *lawyer*
Sauer, Harold John *physician, educator*
Schmidt, Thomas Walter *airport executive*
Schwarz, John J.H. *state senator, surgeon*
Shirtum, Earl Edward *retired civil engineer*
Sikkema, Kenneth R. *state legislator*
Spence, Howard Tee Devon *administrative law judge, arbitrator, lawyer, consultant, insurance executive, government official*
Suhrheinrich, Richard Fred *federal judge*
Svec, Sandra Jean *state official*
Terry, Russell, Jr. *home health aide*
Tieber, F. Martin *lawyer*
Tipton, James Alva *real estate agent, farmer*
†Trezise, Robert Lewis *economic development administrator*
†Truscott, John *state official*
Valade, Alan Michael *lawyer*
Venable, Robert Ellis *crop scientist*
Vincent, Frederick Michael, Sr. *neurologist, educational administrator*
Warren, J(ohn) Michael *lawyer*
Warrington, Willard Glade *former university official*
Wimmer, Billie Kops *association executive*
Winder, Richard Earnest *legal foundation administrator, writer, consultant*

Lapeer
Spray, Pauline Etha Mellish *retired elementary educator, writer*

Laurium
Pippenger, John Junior *fluid power engineer*

Lawrence
Fudge, Mary Ann *vocational school educator*

Lawton
†Bowman, Jerry Wayne *artist, research scientist*

Leland
Small, Hamish *chemist*

Lincoln Park
Bredell, Frank Fulston *public relations company executive*

Linden
†Piper, William Howard *banker*

Livonia
Babineau, Margaret Louise *music educator*
Borin, Jeffrey Nathan *real estate developer*
Borin, Ralph *real estate developer*
†Chowdhury, Subir *business executive, author, researcher*
Crundwell, Duncan James *electronics executive*
Davis, Lawrence Edward *church official*
Duffy, James Joseph *engineer*
Gaipa, Nancy Christine *pharmacist*
Hassan, Lois Mary *English language educator*
Hoffman, Barry Paul *lawyer*
Holtzman, Roberta Lee *French and Spanish language educator*
McCuen, John Francis, Jr. *lawyer*
Sobel, Howard Bernard *osteopath*
Thompson, Robert Rex *lawyer*
Valerio, Michael Anthony *financial executive*
Van de Vyver, Sister Mary Francilene *academic administrator*

Long Beach
Woodrome, Harvey Niles *education educator*

Ludington
Puffer, Richard Judson *retired college chancellor*

Macomb
Farmakis, George Leonard *education educator*
Schmeiser, Jerome Richard *landscape architect, city planner*

Madison Heights
Chapman, Gilbert Bryant *physicist*
Janke, Kenneth *investment consultant*
Kafarski, Mitchell I. *chemical processing company executive*
Koshy, Vettithara Cherian *chemistry educator, technical director and formulator*
†Metropoulos, George E. *occupational medicine physician*
Murphy, Donald Paul *research chemist*
O'Hara, Thomas Edwin *professional administrator executive*

Mancelona
Whelan, Joseph L. *neurologist*

Manchester
Nikoui, Hossein Reza *quality assurance professional*
Spencer, Mark Edward *management consultant*

Manistee
Behring, Daniel William *educational and business professional, consultant*

Maple City
Morris, Donald Arthur Adams *college president*

Marlette
Brabant, Lori Ann *nursing administrator*

Marquette
†Bailey, Judith Irene *university official, consultant*
Burt, John Harris *bishop*
Choate, Jean Marie *history educator*
Coleman, Patrick J. *urban planner*
Earle, Mary Margaret *marketing executive*
Garland, James H. *bishop*
†Greeley, Timothy P. *federal judge*
†Gupta, Pratap Chandra *neurologist, educator*
Heldreth, Leonard Guy *English educator, university official*
Hill, Betty Jean *nursing educator, academic administrator*
†LaJoie, James Alan *public relations professional*
Manning, Robert Hendrick *media consultant*
†Mitchell, David Thomas *humanities educator, filmmaker*
†Pentland, Karen Jean *mental health facility administrator*
Pesola, William Ernest *restaurant management executive*
Poindexter, Kathleen A. Krause *nursing educator, critical care nurse*
Ray, Thomas Kreider *bishop*
Roy, Michael Joseph *higher education administrator*
Sherony, Cheryl Anne *dietitian*
Skogman, Dale R. *bishop*
Suomi, Paul Neil *alumni association director*
Wellington, Rosemary *economic development coordinator*

Marshall
†Garypie, Rudolph Renwick *library director*

Marysville
Ledtke, Kathryn Ann *community health nurse*

Mason
Frappier, Cara Munshaw *school social worker*
Harrison, Michael Gregory *judge*
Toekes, Barna *chemical engineer, polymer consultant*

Mears
Binder, L(eonard) James *magazine editor, retired*

Midland
Barker, Nancy Lepard *university official*
Battle, Leonard Carroll *lawyer*
Birdsall, Arthur Anthony *chemical executive*
Buechner, Margaret *composer, music educator*
Bus, James Stanley *toxicologist*
Carson, Gordon Bloom *engineering executive*
Chao, Marshall *chemist*
Clarkson, William Morris *children's pastor*
Crummett, Warren Berlin *analytical chemistry consultant*
Cuthbert, Robert Lowell *product specialist*
Davidson, John Hunter *agriculturist*
†Doan, Herbert Dow *technical business consultant*
Dorman, Linneaus Cuthbert *retired chemist*
Dreyfuss, Patricia *chemist, researcher*
†Grzesiak, Katherine Ann *primary educator*
Hampton, Leroy *retired chemical company executive*
Hazleton, Richard A. *chemicals executive*
Huntress, Betty Ann *former music store proprietor, educator*
Leng, Douglas Ellis *chemical engineer, scientist*
Leng, Marguerite Lambert *regulatory consultant, biochemist*
Maneri, Remo R. *management consultant*
McCarty, Leslie Paul *pharmacologist, chemist*
Meister, Bernard John *chemical engineer*
Messing, Carol Sue *communications educator*
Nowak, Robert Michael *chemist*
Popoff, Frank Peter *chemical company executive*
Schmidt, William C. *chemical company executive*
†Scriven, John G. *lawyer, chemical company executive*
Seiler, Wallace Urban *chemical engineer*
Sira, Craig John *data coordinator*
Snyder, Robert Lee *anesthesiologist*
Sosville, Dick *sales and marketing executive*
Stavropoulos, William S. *chemical executive*
Thompson, Seth Charles *retired oral and maxillofacial surgeon*
Weiler, Scott Michael *machine tool manufacturing company executive*
Weisenberger, Elaine Sue *tax specialist, accountant*

Milford
Black, Denise Louise *secondary school educator*

Millersburg
Griffin, Richard Ray *minister*

Monroe
Costello, Joseph Anthony, Jr. *circuit court judge, educator*
Knezevich, Janice A. *critical care nurse*
Lipford, Rocque Edward *lawyer, corporate executive*
Mlocek, Sister Frances Angeline *financial executive*

Montague
Sirotko, Theodore Francis *priest, retired military officer*

Mount Clemens
Kolakowski, Diana Jean *county commissioner*
Robinson, Earl, Jr. *marketing and economic research executive, transportation executive, business educator, retired air force officer*

Mount Pleasant
Croll, Robert Frederick *economist, educator*
†Davenport, Richard W. *academic administrator*
Deromedi, Herb *athletic director*
Dietrich, Richard Vincent *geologist, educator*
Flynn, Dick *coach*
Justice-Malloy, Rhona Jean *educator, theatrical artist*
†Martin, Sue Ann *dean*
Novitski, Charles Edward *biology educator*
Petrick, Michael Joseph *journalism educator*
Plachta, Leonard E. *academic administrator*
Rubin, Stuart Harvey *computer science educator, researcher*
Tait, Alice Ann *journalism educator*
Traines, Rose Wunderbaum *sculptor, educator*
Voll, Fran *women's basketball coach university level*

Muskegon
Anderson, Harvey Gregg *pattern company executive*
Briggs, John Mancel, III *lawyer*
Butler, Mark Sherman *controller*
Delong, Donald R. *accountant*
Fauri, Eric Joseph *lawyer*
Heyen, Beatrice J. *psychotherapist*
Kuhn, Robert Herman *city and county official, engineer*
McKendry, John H., Jr. *lawyer, educator*
Mercer, Betty Deborah *electrologist, poet, writer, proofreader*
Nehra, Gerald Peter *lawyer*
†Opel, Patricia *counselor, artist*
Roy, Paul Emile, Jr. *county official*
Turner, Peter Merrick *retired manufacturing company executive*
Van Leuven, Robert Joseph *lawyer*

Naubinway
Beaudoin, Robert Lawrence *small business owner*
Smith, Richard Ernest *retired insurance company executive*

Negaunee
Friggens, Thomas George *state official, historian*
Matero, Janet Louise *counselor, educator*

New Haven
Shaw, Charles Rusanda *government investigator*

Newberry
Summersett, Kenneth George *psychiatric social worker, educator*

Niles
Metty, Michael Pierre *college dean*
Truesdell, Timothy Lee *financial consultant, real estate investor*

North Branch
†Mims, Sarah Patricia *English language educator*
Stevenson, James Laraway *communications engineer, consulting*

Northport
Munro, Roderick Anthony *quality assurance professional, human performance technologist*
Schultz, Richard Carlton *plastic surgeon*
Thomas, Philip Stanley *economics educator*

Northville
Abbasi, Tariq Afzal *psychiatrist, educator*
Hansen, Jean Marie *math and computer educator*
Hess, Bartlett Leonard *clergyman*

Novi
Chow, Chi-Ming *retired mathematics educator*
O'Mara, Marilyn Mae *communications executive*
Opre, Thomas Edward *magazine editor, film company executive, corporate travel company executive*

Oak Park
Borovoy, Marc Allen *podiatrist*
Brann, Donald Treasurer *manufacturing executive*
Kaplan, Randy Kaye *podiatrist*
Martin, Vivian *soprano*
Moilanen, Thomas Alfred *construction equipment distributor*
Novick, Marvin *investment company executive, former automotive supplier executive, accountant*
Piper, Annette Cleone *social services administrator, researcher*
Smith, Nelson David *artist educator*
Walker, Audrey Hope *business and finance executive*

Okemos
Berkman, Claire Fleet *psychologist*
Gast, Robert Gale *agriculture educator, experiment station administrator*
Giacoletto, Lawrence Joseph *electronics engineering educator, researcher, consultant*
Huddleston, Eugene Lee *retired American studies educator*
†Marcus, Harold G. *history educator*
Monson, Carol Lynn *osteopath, psychotherapist*
Montgomery, James Huey *state government administrator, consultant*
Schneider, Karen Bush *lawyer, educator*
Solo, Robert Alexander *economist, educator*
Velicer, Janet Schafbuch *elementary school educator*

Olivet
†Halseth, James A. *academic administrator*
Hubbel, Michael Robert *insurance company executive, educator*
Stevens, Charlotte Whitney *artist, retired art educator*

Ontonagon
Clark, Raymond John *Academic Administrator*

Orchard Lake
Casey, John Patrick (Jack Casey) *public relations executive, political analyst*
Maniscalco, Joseph *artist, educator*

Ortonville
Coffel, Patricia K. *retired clinical social worker*

Oscoda
Shackleton, Mary Jane *small business owner*

Otsego
Berneis, Kenneth Stanley *physician, educator*

Owosso
Bentley, Margaret Ann *librarian*
Hoddy, George Warren *electric company executive, electrical engineer*
Shulaw, Richard A. *lawyer*

Oxford
Hubbard, John Morris *golf course executive*

Paw Paw
Walker, Kay S. *geropsychiatric nurse*
Warner, James John *small business owner*

Petoskey
†Baird, Greg Ross *university program director, theater educator*
Hoshield, Susan Lynn *pediatric nurse practitioner*
Meyer, Catherine Lynn *elementary school educator*
Switzer, Carolyn Joan *artist, educator*
Vernon, Doris Schaller *retired writer*

Pigeon
Maust, Joseph J. *agricultural products supplier*

Plainwell
Flower, Jean Frances *art educator*

Pleasant Ridge
Krabbenhoft, Kenneth Lester *radiologist, educator*

Plymouth
Belobraidich, Sharon Lynn Goul *elementary education educator*
Champa, John Joseph *telecommunications engineer, consultant*
Clark, Kenneth William *mechanical engineer*
deBear, Richard Stephen *library planning consultant*
Garpow, James Edward *financial executive*
Heitman, Susan Marie *artist*
Hsi, Morris Yu *mechanical engineer, applied researcher*

Massey, Donald E. *automotive executiv*
McClendon, Edwin James *health science educator*
McNish, Susan Kirk *retired lawyer*
Merrill, Kenneth Coleman *retired automobile company executive*
Moore, Joan Elizabeth *human resources executive, lawyer*
Morgan, Donald Crane *lawyer*
Porter, Karen Collins *non-profit administrator, counselor*
Stewart, Katherine Hewitt *advanced practice nurse*
Vlcek, Donald Joseph, Jr. *food distribution company executive, consultant, business author*
Wroble, Lisa Ann *writer, educator*

Pontiac
†Auch, Fred H., Jr. *company executive*
†Brychtova, Jaroslava *sculptor*
Chamberlain, Jean Nash *county government department director*
Danielewicz, Claudia Anne *quality assurance engineer*
Decker, Peter William *academic administrator*
Grant, Barry M(arvin) *judge*
James, Reese Joseph *physician*
Mahone, Barbara Jean *automotive company executive*
Meldrum, Richard James *electrical engineer*
Moore, Herman Joseph *professional football player*
Pierson, William George *lawyer*
Popadak, Geraldine L. *organizational development consultant, educator*
Sanders, Barry *retired football player*
Schmidt, Chuck *professional football team executive*
Weeks, Timotheus *educational administrator*

Port Huron
Maraldo, Angela Marie *civil engineer*
Ragle, George Ann *accountant*
Thomson, Robert James *natural gas distribution company executive*
Wu, Harry Pao-Tung *retired librarian*

Portage
Brown, John Wilford *surgical/medical company executive*
Elliott, George Algimon *pathologist, toxicologist, veterinarian*
Lee, Edward L. *bishop*
Seely, Robert Eugene *management consultant*
†Toledo-Pereyra, Luis Horacio *transplant surgeon, researcher, historian educator*

Portland
Adams, Bill *principal*
Anesi, Michael Richard *restaurant executive*
Rainey, Derek Rexton *educator, sculptor*
Rich, Joseph John *accountant*

Rapid City
Coulson, John Selden *retired marketing executive*
Ring, Ronald Herman *lawyer*

Redford
Flint, H. Howard, II *printing company executive*
Gibbons, Gregory Dennis *minister*
Goslin, Gerald Hugh *concert pianist, educator*
Karpinski, Huberta Elaine *library trustee*
Krec, George Frank, Jr. *fundraiser*
Lamb, Michael John *librarian, consultant*
†Ravi Shankar, Suggan V. *software development engineer*

Reed City
Devendorf, Louise Marie *promoter, writer*
†Freeman, George Stanley *city manager, city and regional planner*

Richmond
Huvaere, Richard Floyd *auto dealer*

Riverdale
Kirby, Kent Bruce *artist, educator*

Rochester
Arrathoon, Leigh Adelaide *medievalist, editor, writer*
Bajor, James Henry *musician, jazz pianist*
†Connellan, William Wesley *higher education administrator*
Eberwein, Jane Donahue *English educator*
Giordano, Joseph, Jr. *financial planner, investment consulting firm executive*
Gouldey, Glenn Charles *manufacturing company executive*
Horwitz, Ronald M. *business administration educator*
Kienzle, William Xavier *author*
Maines, David Russell *sociology educator*
Nakao, Seigo *Japanese language, culture and literature educator*
Packard, Sandra Podolin *education educator, consultant*
Polis, Michael Philip *university dean*
†Rauch, Angelika Maria *psychoanalyst, educator*
Rossio, Richard Dominic *automobile company executive*
Russi, Gary D. *academic administrator*
†Shillor, Meir *mathematics educator*
Unakar, Nalin Jayantilal *biological sciences educator*

Rochester Hills
Akeel, Hadi Abu *robotics executive*
Badalament, Robert Anthony *urologic oncologist*
Bartunek, James Scott *psychiatrist*
Graves, Vashti Sylvia *computer analyst, EDP auditor, consultant*
Hicks, George William *automotive and mechanical engineer*
Matthews, George Tennyson *history educator*
Pfister, Karl Anton *industrial company executive*

Rockford
Boese, Ted C. *furniture designer*
Pappas, William John *principal, educator*
Westveld, Belinda Joyce *reliability and quality engineer, educator*

Romulus
Archer, Hugh Morris *consulting engineer, manufacturing professional*
Scannell, Thomas John *cold metal forming company executive*

Roseville
Geck, Francis Joseph *furniture designer, educator, author*

Royal Oak
Andrzejak, Michael Richard *insurance agent*
Bernstein, Jay *pathologist, researcher, educator*
†Beyerlein, Susan Carol *educational administrator*
Cook, Noel Robert *manufacturing company executive*
Corwin, Vera-Anne Versfelt *small business owner, consultant*
†Diokno, Ananias C. *urologic surgeon, educator*
Dworkin, Howard Jerry *nuclear physician, educator*
†Ernstoff, Raina Marcia *neurologist*
LaBan, Myron Miles *physician, administrator*
Lechner, Jon Robert *nursing administrator, educator*
Matzick, Kenneth John *hospital administrator*
O'Neill, William Walter *physician, educator*
Ryan, Jack *physician, retired hospital corporation executive*
Smith, John William Hugh *civil engineer*
Stanalajczo, Greg Charles *computer and technology company executive*

Saginaw
Blue, Robert Lee *secondary education educator*
Bosco, Jay William *optometrist*
Chaffee, Paul Charles *newspaper editor*
Cline, Thomas William *real estate leasing company executive, management consultant*
Evans, Harold Edward *banker*
Faubel, Gerald Lee *agronomist, golf course superintendent*
La Londe, Lawrence Lee *family practice physician*
†Maas, Norman Lewis *library director*
Martin, Walter *retired lawyer*
McGraw, Patrick John *lawyer*
Oesterling, Joseph Edwin *urologic surgeon*
Scharffe, William Granville *academic administrator, educator*
Shackelford, Martin Robert *social worker*
Sudhoff, Virginia Rae *retired elementary education educator*
Untener, Kenneth E. *bishop*
Wierzbicki, Jacek Gabriel *physicist, researcher*

Saint Clair Shores
Danielson, Gary R. *lawyer*
Doutt, Geraldine Moffatt *retired educational administrator*
Field, Thomas Lee *business executive, politician*
Hausner, John Herman *judge*
Seppala, Katherine Seaman (Mrs. Leslie W. Seppala) *retail company executive*
Shehan, Wayne Charles *lawyer*
Shine, Neal James *journalism educator, former newspaper editor, publisher*
Stanczyk, Benjamin Conrad *judge*
Walker, Frank Banghart *pathologist*
Weis, Lawrence Frederick *city official*
Woodford, Arthur MacKinnon *library director, historian*

Saint Ignace
Dodson, Bruce J. *funeral director*

Saint Joseph
Ahmad, Anwar *radiologist*
Anderson, Mary Jane *public library director*
Eversole, Gregory Charles *accountant*
Gleiss, Henry Weston *lawyer*
Hoyt, J. Brian *light manufacturing company logistics executive*
Keech, Elowyn Ann *interior designer*
King, George Raleigh *manufacturing company executive*
McCoy, Richard James *jeweler, real estate developer, broker*
Renwick, Ken *retail executive*
Skale, Linda Dianne *elementary education educator*
Wallace, Jon Robert *mortgage company executive, marketing professional*

Saline
Babcock, Leo Aloysius *architect, scenic designer*
Bender, Robert John *ceramic engineer*
Cornell, Richard Garth *biostatistics educator*
Low, Louise Anderson *consulting company executive*
†Niethammer, Leslee *library administrator*
†Ottum, Brian Douglas *research and marketing consulting executive*

Sandusky
Johnson, John Douglas *newspaper publisher*
Keeler, Lynne Livingston Mills *psychologist, educator, consultant*

Sanford
Wilmot, Thomas Ray *medical entomologist, educator*

Saranac
Herbrucks, Stephen *food products executive*
LaVean, Michael Gilbert *advertising agency executive, political consultant*

Saugatuck
Telder, Thomas Van Doorn *medical educator*

Sault Sainte Marie
Johnson, Gary Robert *political scientist, editor*

Shelby
Glerum, Sally Jane *English educator*

Shelby Township
Babar, Raza Ali *industrial engineer, utility consultant, futurist, management educator, marketing strategist, author, publisher*
Fillbrook, Thomas George *telephone company executive*
Kinkel, R. John *research company executive, educator*
Kortsha, Gene Xhevat *industrial hygienist*
Miller, Aileen Etta Martha *medical association administrator, consultant, metabolic nutritionist, therapeutic touch practitioner*

Shepherd
Herman, Mark Norman *translator*

Sidney
Tammone, William Whitmore *academic administrator, science educator*

South Haven
Nequist, John Leonard *retired food company executive*

Southfield
Anderson, Mark Brian *psychologist*
Antone, Nahil Peter *lawyer, civil engineer*
Arroyo, Rodney Lee *city planning and transportation executive*
Barnett, Marilyn *advertising agency executive*
Boyce, Daniel Hobbs *financial planning company executive*
Cantwell, Dennis Michael *finance company executive*
Chambers, Charles MacKay *university president*
Clayton, James A. *broadcast executive*
Colmery, Benjamin Herring, III *veterinarian*
Dawson, Dennis Ray *lawyer, manufacturing company executive*
Decerchio, John *advertising company executive*
Denes, Michel Janet *physical therapist, consultant in rehabilitation*
Dobritt, Dennis William *physician, researcher, pain management specialist*
Doctoroff, Martin Myles *judge*
Drebus, John Richard *financial consultant*
Dunlop, Michael *broadcast executive*
Duvernoy, Wolf F.C. *cardiologist*
Eagan, Catherine Bernice *financial executive*
Erickson, Garwood Elliott *computer consulting company executive*
Fennell, Christine Elizabeth *healthcare system executive*
Fleming, Mac Arthur *labor union administrator*
Gargaro, John Timothy *financial executive*
Gilchrist, Grace *television station executive*
Giles, Conrad Leslie *ophthalmic surgeon*
Gordon, Arnold Mark *arbitrator, lawyer*
Green, Henry Leonard *physician*
Gregory, Karl Dwight *economist, educator, consultant*
Gulda, Edward James *automotive executive*
Hanisko, John-Cyril Patrick *electronics engineer, physicist*
Hanket, Mark John *lawyer*
Hotelling, Harold *law and economics educator*
Howard, Michael Joseph *communications executive, real estate developer*
Ibrahim, Ibrahim N. *bishop*
Jackson, William Gene *computer company executive*
Jacobs, John Patrick *lawyer*
Kalter, Alan *advertising agency executive*
Kaplow, Robert David *lawyer*
Kippert, Robert John, Jr. *lawyer*
Leavell, Debbie Susann *secondary education educator*
†Liebold, William Henry *fundraiser*
†Liu, Huimin *engineering executive, consultant*
Lorenz, Sarah Lynne *secondary education educator*
Maibach, Ben C., Jr. *service executive*
Maibach, Ben C., III *construction company executive*
Makupson, Amyre Porter *television station executive*
Martin, Joseph Patrick *lawyer*
Mathog, Robert Henry *otolaryngologist, educator*
May, Alan Alfred *lawyer*
McAuley, Philip Christopher *audio engineer*
McClow, Roger James *labor lawyer*
McCuen, John Joachim *building company and financial company executive*
McDonald, Patricia Anne *professional society executive*
Morganroth, Mayer *lawyer*
Neiheisel, Stephen Walter *controller*
Newman, Steven E. *neurologist*
O'Hara, John Paul, III *orthopaedic surgeon*
Olsen, Douglas H. *superintendent*
Papazian, Dennis Richard *history educator, political commentator*
Plummer, Glenn Rodney *radio and television producer*
Ponka, Lawrence John *automotive executive*
Portnoy, Lynn A. *fashion retailer*
Raden, Louis *tape and label corporation executive*
Redstone, Daniel Aaron *architect*
Redstone, Louis Gordon *architect*
Ritchie, Alexander Buchan *lawyer*
Rosenzweig, Norman *psychiatry educator*
Ross, Dale Garand *therapist, programming consultant, speaker, writer*
Satovsky, Abraham *lawyer*
Schwartz, Robert H. *lawyer*
†Serra, Barbara Josephine *community relations administrator*
Shields, Robert Emmet *merchant banker, lawyer*
Smith, Nancy Hohendorf *sales and marketing executive*
Sullivan, Robert Emmet, Jr. *lawyer*
Swain, Melinda Susan *elementary education educator*
Swartz, William John *managed care company executive*
Taravella, Christopher Anthony *lawyer*
Thimotheose, Kadakampallil George *psychologist*
Tombers, Evelyn Charlotte *lawyer*
Washington, Anthony Nathaniel *mechanical engineer*
Way, Kenneth L. *seat company executive*
Willingham, Edward Bacon, Jr. *ecumenical minister, administrator*
Wisne, Lawrence A. *metal products executive*
Zubroff, Leonard Saul *surgeon*

Southgate
Jacob, Robert Edward *small business and non-profit tax consultant*

Sparta
Fairchild, Henry Brant, III *manufacturing executive*
Stevens, Richard *visual artist*

Spring Arbor
Dowley, Joel Edward *manufacturing executive, lawyer*
Thompson, Stanley B. *church administrator*

Stanton
Winchell, George William *curriculum and technology educator*

Stanwood
Cawthorne, Kenneth Clifford *retired financial planner*

Sterling Heights
†Chrzanowski, Winifred Helene *data management specialist*
Cutter, Jeffrey S. *secondary education educator, music educator*
Dipboye, Marilyn Joyce *publisher, editor, writer*
Frank, Michael Sanford *dermatologist*
Hammond-Kominsky, Cynthia Cecelia *optometrist*
Ice, Orva Lee, Jr. *history educator, retired*
Novak, Joseph Anthony *lawyer*
Pierson, Kathleen Mary *child care center administrator, consultant*
Smith, Gregory Robert *engineer, educator, marketing consultant*
Wilson-Pleiness, Christine Joyce *writer, poet, columnist*

Stockbridge
†Macdonald, Guy Allen *telecommunications company executive*

Sturgis
Cabansag, Vicente Dacanay, Jr. *medical association administrator*
Hair, Robert Eugene *editor, writer, historian*
Reiff, James Stanley *addictions, psychiatric, and osteopathic physician, surgeon*

Suttons Bay
Whitney, William Chowning *retired banker, financial consultant*

Tawas City
Jacob, Elizabeth Ann *elementary education educator*

Taylor
Beebe, Grace Ann *special education educator*
Hirsch, David L. *lawyer, corporate executive*
Leekley, John Robert *lawyer*
Manoogian, Richard Alexander *manufacturing company executive*
Pacynski, Rick Alan *corporation lawyer*
Rosowski, Robert Bernard *manufacturing company executive*

Tecumseh
†Herrick, Kenneth Gilbert *manufacturing company executive*
Herrick, Todd W. *manufacturing company executive*
Sackett, Dianne Marie *city treasurer, accountant*

Temperance
Jan, Colleen Rose *secondary school educator*
Kinney, Mark Baldwin *fellowship executive, educator*

Thompsonville
Perry, Margaret *librarian, writer*

Three Rivers
Boyer, Nicodemus Elijah *organic-polymer chemist, consultant*
Mackay, Edward *engineer*

Traverse City
Abeel, Samantha Lynn *juvenile fiction author*
Brickley, James H. *state supreme court justice*
Brown, Paul Bradley *architect*
Chang, Ching-I Eugene *insurance executive*
Childs, K. Ross *county administrator, consultant*
†Gillett, Ward Robert *urologist*
Howe, Gordon *former professional hockey player, sports association executive*
Keilitz, Gene Martin *retired association administrator*
McCafferty, John Martin *real estate executive, commodities trader*
Parsons, John Thoren *corporate executive, inventor*
Petersen, Evelyn Ann *education consultant*
Quandt, Joseph Edward *lawyer, educator*
†Sidor, Stanley *engineer*
Stepnitz, Susan Stephanie *special education educator*
Taylor, Donald Arthur *marketing educator*
Weaver, Elizabeth A. *state supreme court chief justice*
Williams, Madonna Jo *accountant*
Wolfe, Richard Ratcliffe *lawyer*
Zimmerman, Paul Albert *retired college president, minister*

Troy
Acton, David L(awrence) *automobile company executive*
Adderley, Terence E. *corporate executive*
Aksoy, Zeynel *manufacturing professional*
Alterman, Irwin Michael *lawyer*
Baker, Ernest Waldo, Jr. *advertising executive*
Baker, Michael Howard *sales executive*
Bautz, Jeffrey Emerson *mechanical engineer, educator, researcher*
Buschmann, Siegfried *manufacturing executive*
Cantor, Bernard Jack *patent lawyer*
Chapman, Conrad Daniel *lawyer*
†Cooper, Warren F. *retail executive*
Corace, Joseph Russell *automotive parts company executive*
Crane, Louis Arthur *retired labor arbitrator*
†Elder, Irma *automotive company executive*
Fritzsche, Hellmut *physics educator*
Given, Kerry Wade *plastics industry executive*
Golusin, Millard R. *obstetrician and gynecologist*
Grewell, Judith Lynn *computer services executive*
Gullen, Christopher Roy *lawyer*
Hall, Floyd *retail executive*
Hamilton, Edward Tedjasukmana *automotive executive, small business owner*
Haron, David Lawrence *lawyer*
Harrison, Christine Delane *company executive*
Hart, James Francis *civil engineer*
Hill, Richard A. *advertising executive*
Hirschhorn, Austin *lawyer*
†Horton, Gary J. *advertising executive*
Hunia, Edward Mark *foundation executive*
Hunter, Lorie Ann *women's health nurse*
Johnston, Timothy Sidney *computer engineer*
Kruse, John Alphonse *lawyer*
Kulich, Roman Theodore *healthcare administrator*
LaDuke, Nancie *lawyer, corporate executive*
Leach, Ralph F. *banker*
Lenihan, Robert Joseph, II *lawyer*
Lohrmann, David Kurt *curriculum director*
Lorencz, Mary *media relations administrator*
Maierle, Bette Jean *director nursery school*
Marshall, John Elbert, III *foundation executive*

Martin, Raymond Bruce *plumbing equipment manufacturing company executive*
McElmeel, Christopher John *writer*
McGinnis, Thomas Michael *lawyer*
McLaren, Karen Lynn *advertising executive*
Meyers, Christine Laine *marketing and media executive, consultant*
Moore, Oliver Semon, III *publishing executive, consultant*
Ovshinsky, Stanford Robert *physicist, inventor, energy and information company executive*
Parker, Richard E. *building products manufacturing company executive*
Ponitz, John Allan *lawyer*
Potts, Anthony Vincent *optometrist, orthokeratologist*
Ranney, Richard William *electronic data systems company official*
Schafer, Sharon Marie *anesthesiologist*
Serafyn, Alexander Jaroslav *retired automotive executive*
Sharf, Stephan *automotive company executive*
Sloan, Hugh Walter, Jr. *automotive industry executive*
Strome, Stephen *distribution company executive*
White, James, Jr. *psychiatric, mental health nurse, consultant*
Williams, David Perry *manufacturing company executive*
Wilson, Duane Isaac *executive search consultant*

Union Pier
Howland, Bette *writer*

Unionville
Othersen-Khalifa, Cheryl Lee *insurance broker, realtor*

University Center
†Boyse, Peter Dent *academic administrator*
Gilbertson, Eric Raymond *academic administrator, lawyer*
†Haynes, Margaret Elizabeth *English educator*
†Hill, Paul Christian *dean*
Hoerneman, Calvin A., Jr. *economics educator*

Utica
Olman, Gloria *secondary education educator*

Vicksburg
Garrett, Christopher Arthur *secondary education educator*

Walled Lake
Gillespie, J. Martin *sales and distribution company executive*
Peal, Christopher John *educational administrator*
Seglund, Bruce Richard *lawyer*
Williams, Sam B. *engineering executive*

Warren
Ableson, Donald William *automobile industry executive*
Arking, Lucille Musser *nurse epidemiologist*
Barr, David John *artist, educator*
†Beauchamp, Roy E. *career officer*
Belles, Christine Fugiel *office administration educator*
Bley, Ann *program analyst*
Bridenstine, Louis Henry, Jr. *lawyer*
Deak, Charles Karol *chemist*
Gallopoulos, Nicholas Efstratios *chemical engineer*
Gervason, Robert J *advertising executive*
Gilbert, Suzanne Harris *advertising executive*
Goldsmith, Aaron Clair *federal government executive*
Herbst, Jan Francis *physicist, researcher*
Heremans, Joseph Pierre *physicist*
Hopp, Anthony James *advertising agency executive*
Jacovides, Linos Jacovou *electrical engineering research manager*
†Johnson, Leonard Gustave *research mathematician, consultant*
Krygier, Michael Robert *mechanical engineer*
Lamb, David Alan *mathematician*
Lett, Philip Wood, Jr. *defense consultant*
Lorenzo, Albert L. *academic administrator*
Ludwig, William John *advertising executive*
Morelli, William Annibale, Sr. *aerospace manufacturing company executive*
Nagy, Louis Leonard *engineering executive, researcher*
Quay, Gregory Harrison *secondary school educator*
†Samra, Nicholas James *bishop*
Schultz, Louis Michael *advertising agency executive*
Schwartz, Shirley E. *chemist*
Smith, George Wolfram *physicist, educator*
Smith, John Robert *physicist*
Taylor, Kathleen (Christine) *physical chemist*
Viano, David Charles *automotive safety research scientist*
Wisz, Joseph A., Jr. *management consultant*
Woehrlen, Arthur Edward, Jr. *dentist*
Yakes, Barbara Lee *occupational and preventive medicine physician, former nurse*

Washington
Gothard, Donald Lee *retired auto company executive*

Waterford
Adler, Raphael *educator emeritus, speech pathologist*
†Anderson, Francile Mary *secondary education educator*
Blanchard, Danielle René *music educator*
Fontanive, Lynn Marie *special education educator*
Hampton, Phillip Michael *consulting engineering company executive*
Land, Robert Donald *business consultant*
Randall, Karl W. *aviation executive, lawyer*

Wayland
Willcox, William Brewster *minister*

Wayne
Carpenter, Arthur Lloyd *education educator*
†Cobbs, Alfred Leon *German language educator*

West Bloomfield
Barr, Martin *health care and higher education adminstrator*
Beck, Jerry Gunther *development company executive, consultant*
Ben, Manuel *chemist*
Considine, John Joseph *advertising executive*
Dvorkin, Louis *neuropsychologist*
Harwood, Julius J. *metallurgist, educator*
†Jones, Lewis Arnold *physician, radiologist*
Joseph, Ramon Rafael *physician, educator*
Mamut, Mary Catherine *retired entrepreneur*
Meyer, Philip Gilbert *lawyer*
Miller, Nancy Ellen *computer consultant*
†Montera, David John *lawyer*
Myers, Kenneth Ellis *hospital administrator*
Robbins, Norman Nelson *lawyer*
Romero, Josefino Tabernilla *nurse anesthetist*
Rosenfeld, Martin Jerome *executive recruiter, educator*
Sandler, Kevin Scott *education educator, film studies educator*
Sarwer-Foner, Gerald Jacob *physician, educator*
Sawyer, Howard Jerome *physician*
Seidman, Michael David *surgeon, educator*
Tobin, Bruce Howard *lawyer*
Williamson, Marilyn Lammert *English educator, university adminstrator*

Westland
Coates, Dianne Kay *social worker*
Mullinix, Barbara Jean *special services director*
Shaw, Randy Lee *human services administrator*

White Lake
Clyburn, Luther Linn *real estate broker, appraiser, ship captain*

Whitmore Lake
Stanny, Gary *infosystems specialist, rocket scientist*

Williamsburg
Harlan, John Marshall *construction company executive*

Williamston
Johnson, Tom Milroy *academic dean, medical educator, physician*

Wixom
Saussele, Charles William *marking systems company executive*

Wolverine Lake
†Arraf, Shreen *school system administrator*

Wyandotte
Aslam, Syed *chemist, research*
Beaudette, Robert Lee *transportation and logistics consultant*
Consiglio, Helen *nursing educator and consultant*
†Croci, Mary Ellen *artist, mental health specialist*
Dunn, Gloria Jean *artist*
Kirsch, Norman Maynard *clergyman*

Yale
Vuylsteke, Thomas A. *secondary education educator*

Ypsilanti
Barnes, James Milton *physics and astronomy educator*
Barr, John Monte *lawyer*
Boone, Morell Douglas *academic administrator, information and instructional technology educator*
Caswell, Herbert Hall, Jr. *retired biology educator*
Cere, Ronald Carl *languages educator, consultant, researcher*
deSouza, Joan Melanie *psychologist*
†Edwards, Gerald *plastics company executive*
Evans, Gary Lee *communications educator and consultant*
Fleming, Thomas A. *academic affairs assistant director, former special education educator*
†Friedman, Monroe *psychologist, educator*
Gerber, Lucille D. *elementary education educator*
Gledhill, Roger Clayton *statistician, engineer, mathematician, educator*
†Griffin, Carolyn Leigh *English educator, genealogist*
Gunasekera, Thilak Wijenayaka *mathematician, educator*
Hildebrandt, H(enry) M(ark) *pediatrician*
†Kirkpatrick, Garland Penn *pediatrician*
Lewis-White, Linda Beth *elementary school educator*
Lucy, Dlorah Rae *medical/surgical nurse*
Perkins, Bradford *history educator*
Ritter, Frank Nicholas *otolaryngologist, educator*
Sealy, Vernol St. Clair *scientist*
Shelton, William Everett *university president*
Staicar, Thomas Edward *writer*
Tobias, Tom, Jr. *elementary school educator*
Ullman, Nelly Szabo *statistician, educator*
Weinstein, Jay A. *social science educator, researcher*

MINNESOTA

Ada
†Sillerud, Arlen Roger *retired educator*

Adrian
Hanson, Jim Henry *veterinarian*

Aitkin
Morton, Craig Richard *real estate investor*

Albert Lea
Rechtzigel, Sue Marie (Suzanne Rechtzigel) *child care center executive*
Sturtz, William Rosenberg *retired judge*

Alexandria
Hultstrand, Donald Maynard *bishop*
Monahan, Edward Joseph, III *orthodontist*
Templin, Kenneth Elwood *paper company executive*

Annandale
Johnson, Jon E. *magazine editor and publisher*

Anoka
Hicken, Jeffrey Price *lawyer*
Nelson, Duane Juan *minister*
Quinn, R. Joseph *judge*
Sliefert, Paula Rhea *manufacturing company executive*
Ward, Bart James *investment executive*

Apple Valley
Doyle, O'Brien John, Jr. *emergency medical services consultant, lobbyist, writer*
Kettle, Sally Anne *consulting company executive, educator*

Appleton
Wilson, Orpha Hildred *writer*

Arden Hills
Alexander, Marjorie Anne *artist, hand papermaker, art consultant*
Hartsoe, James Russell *minister*
Van Houten, James Forester *insurance company executive*

Arnoka
Luther, Robert Alan *organist, educator*

Austin
Alcorn, Wallace Arthur *minister*
Anderson, Jeffrey Lynn *stone company executive*
Budd, Jim *communications manager*
Hodapp, Don Joseph *food company executive*
Holman, Ralph Theodore *biochemistry and nutrition educator*
Johnson, Joel W. *food products executive*
Leighton, Robert Joseph *state legislator*
Mauch, Matthew Douglas *poet, educator*
Morgan, Robert Ashton *minister, ethics and world religions educator*
Schmid, Harald Heinrich Otto *biochemistry educator, academic director*
Schneider, Mahlon C. *lawyer*

Babbitt
†Marks, Dawn Marie *excavating contractor*

Bayport
†Garofalo, Donald R. *window manufacturing executive*
†Johnson, Alan *retired window/patio door manufacturer*

Bemidji
Bridston, Paul Joseph *strategic consultant*
†Burg, Randall K. *federal judge*
Kief, Paul Allan *lawyer*
Logan, P. Bradley *music educator, church musician*
Woodke, Robert Allen *lawyer*

Benson
Wilcox, Donald Alan *lawyer*

Bertha
Peterson, Myra M. *special education educator*

Billings
†Schwidde, Jess T. *neurological surgeon*

Birchwood Village
Oliver, Marlys Mae *retired editor, writer*

Bloomington
Allen, Mary Louise Hook *secondary education educator*
Beckwith, Larry Edward *mechanical engineer*
Chadwick, John Edwin *financial counselor and planner*
Dahlberg, Burton Francis *real estate corporation executive*
Fellner, Michael Joseph *government executive, educator*
Hulbert, James Richard *health care educator, researcher*
Johnson, Leslie Carole *editor, publisher*
Lakin, James Dennis *allergist, immunologist, director*
Larson, Beverly Rolandson *elementary education educator*
McDill, Thomas Allison *minister*
Norris, William C. *engineering executive*
Powell, Christa Ruth *educational training executive*
Smith, Henry Charles, III *symphony orchestra conductor*
Thickins, Graeme Richard *marketing consultant*
Thomas, Margaret Jean *clergywoman, religious research consultant*
Ueland, Sigurd, Jr. *retired lawyer*
Wicker, Franklin Michael *financial consultant*

Brandon
Hansen, Richard Buddie *English educator, chef*

Brooklyn Center
Neff, Fred Leonard *lawyer*

Brooklyn Park
Rogers, David *apparel executive*

Buffalo
Hagen, Ione Carolyn *religion educator*
Swanson, Fern Rose *retired elementary education educator*

Burnsville
†Anderson, Eril W.L. *web designer*
Freeburg, Richard L. *elementary education educator*
Knutson, David Lee *lawyer, state senator*
Lai, Juey Hong *chemical engineer*
Larson, Doyle Eugene *retired air force officer, consultant*
Ringquist, Lynn Anne *micrographics company executive*

Byron
Nolting, Frederick William *dentist*

Cannon Falls
Bonde, Linda Merilyn *elementary school educator*

Castle Rock
Ericson, Harold Louis *communications executive*

Center City
Hammond, Bill *publishing executive*

Champlin
Hersch, Russell LeRoy *secondary education educator*

Chanhassen
Severson, Roger Allan *bank executive*
Thorson, John Martin, Jr. *electrical engineer, consultant*

Chaska
Knapp, Peggy Durda *international company administrator*

Chisholm
†Anderson, Brian Keith *editor*

Circle Pines
†Young, Jerry Francis *librarian*

Clarkfield
Richter, Franz Allbert *artist, historian*

Clear Lake
Casey, Daniel L. *school counselor*

Cloquet
Ellison, David Charles *special education educator*

Cokao
Weber, Rebecca Guenigsman *occupational health nurse*

Collegeville
Haile, Getatchew *archivist, educator*
Reinhart, Dietrich Thomas *university president, history educator*

Coon Rapids
Backes, Betty Lou *city clerk*
Elvig, Merrywayne *real estate manager*

Cottage Grove
Briggs, Robert Henry *infosystems specialist*
Glazebrook, Rita Susan *nursing educator*
Hudnut, Robert Kilborne *clergyman, author*
O'Gorman, Patricia Ann *lawyer*

Crookston
†Balke, Victor H. *bishop*
Shol, Kim Durand *accountant, computer program*

Crystal
Reske, Steven David *lawyer, writer*

Cushing
Perfetti, Robert Nickolas *educational consultant*

Dassel
Kay, Craig *principal*

Dent
Kosler, Sonja Raye *political consultant, artist*

Detroit Lakes
Remmen, Lawrence P. *city planner*
Super, William Alan *manufacturing executive*
†Sycks, Elaine Marie *deaconess*

Duluth
Aadland, Thomas Vernon *minister*
Andert, David August *minister*
Aufderheide, Arthur Carl *pathologist*
Bailey, Charles William *management consultant, researcher*
Bowman, Roger Manwaring *real estate executive*
Burns, Richard Ramsey *lawyer*
Chee, Cheng-Khee *artist*
Dillon, Herb Lester *critical care and emergency room nurse*
Eisenberg, Richard Martin *pharmacology educator*
Feroz, Ehsan Habib *accounting educator, researcher, writer*
Fischer, Roger Adrian *retired history educator*
Fryberger, Elizabeth Ann *financial consultant*
Hartley, Alan Haselton *lexicographer, stevedoring administrator*
Heaney, Gerald William *federal judge*
Heller, Lois Jane *physiologist, educator, researcher*
Hoffman, Richard George *psychologist*
Jankofsky, Klaus Peter *medieval studies educator*
Johnson, Arthur Gilbert *microbiology educator*
Kramer, Alex John *dentist*
Latto, Lewis M. *broadcasting company executive*
Madich, Bernadine Marie Hoff *savings and loan executive*
Morris, Katherine Lang *counseling psychologist*
Nelson, Dennis Lee *finance educator*
Nys, John Nikki *lawyer*
Ojard, Bruce Allen *photographer, educator*
Pearce, Donald Joslin *retired librarian*
Rapp, George Robert, Jr. (Rip Rapp) *geology and archeology educator*
Salmela, David Daniel *architect*
Schroeder, Fred Erich Harald *humanities educator*
Schwietz, Roger L. *bishop*
Sebastian, James Albert *obstetrician, gynecologist, educator*
Smith, Robert Francis *synthesist*
Stauber-Johnson, Elizabeth Jane *retired elementary mathematics education educator*
†Stender, Bruce William *business executive*
Stoddard, Patricia Florence Coulter *psychologist*
Wade, James Alan *lawyer*
Whiteman, Richard Frank *architect*
Whitmyer, Robert Wayne *soil scientist, consultant, researcher*
Whitney, Gwin Richard *brick distribution company executive*
†Wickstrom, Per Henrik *surgeon*
Zhdankin, Viktor Vladimirovich *chemistry educator*

Eagan
Clemens, T. Pat *manufacturing company executive*
Collier, Ken O. *editor*
Goh, Michael Pik-Bien *counseling, psychology educator, consultant*
Miller, Alan M. *editor, educator, writer*
Todd, John Joseph *lawyer*

Eden Prairie
Anderson, Gary Allan *professional football player*
Carlson, Kenneth George *data processing executive*
Carter, Cris *professional football player*
Cunningham, Randall *professional football player*
Degnan, Amy Marie *journalist*

Emison, James Wade *petroleum company executive*
†Erickson, Kim *consumer products company executive*
Green, Dennis *professional football coach*
Hanson, Dale S. *banker*
Harris, Jean Louise *physician*
Higgins, Robert Arthur *electrical engineer, educator, consultant*
Hoard, Leroy *professional football player*
Johnson, Howard Arthur, Jr. *corporate executive, operations analyst, financial officer*
†Joyce, Joseph M. *lawyer*
McClure, Alvin Bruce *information systems manager*
†McCombs, Billy Joe (Red McCombs) *professional football team executive*
McDaniel, Randall Cornell *professional football player*
†Moss, Randy *professional football player*
Nilles, John Michael *lawyer*
Nortwen, Patricia Harman *music educator*
Platt, Ann *animal care company executive*
†Reed, Cheryl Lynn *writer, journalist*
Roth, Thomas *marketing executive*
Schulze, Richard M. *consumer products executive*
Skeie, Philip *health plan administrator*
Svärd, N. Trygve *electrical engineer*
Thompsen, Joyce Ann *organizational consultant*
Verdoorn, Sid *food service executive*
†Woods, Gary *professional football team executive, former professional basketball team executive*

Edina
Boyle, Barbara Jane *insurance company executive*
Brown, Charles Eugene *retired electronics company executive*
Brown, Laurence David *retired bishop*
Burbank, John Thorn *entrepreneur*
Burdick, Lou Brum *public relations executive*
Burk, Robert S. *lawyer*
Cedar, Paul Arnold *church executive, minister*
Emmerich, Karol Denise *foundation executive, former retail executive*
†Fasching, Michael Cloud *plastic surgeon*
Foret, Mickey Phillip *air transportation company executive*
Gurstel, Norman Keith *lawyer*
Hunt, David Claude *sales and marketing executive*
Lillehaug, David Lee *lawyer*
Meyer, Warren George *vocational educator*
Polsfuss, Craig Lyle *leadership specialist, psychologist, social worker*
Prince, Robb Lincoln *manufacturing company executive*
Putnam, Frederick Warren, Jr. *bishop*
Sampson, John Eugene *consulting company executive*
Schwarzrock, Shirley Pratt *author, lecturer, educator*
Slocum, Rosemarie *physician management search consultant*
Trouten, Douglas James *journalist*
Weber, Gail Mary *lawyer*
Wurdeman, Lew Edward *data processing corporation consultant*

Elk River
Sandusky, Christine Ann *English language educator*

Ely
Swenson, L. Anne *publisher*

Elysian
Nickerson, James Findley *retired educator*
Thayer, Edna Louise *medical facility administrator, nurse*

Excelsior
Anderson, William Robert *pathologist, educator*
Bilka, Paul Joseph *physician*
Brekke, Judy Lynn *state agency administrator*
Fazio, Anthony Lee *investment company executive*
Fenske, Jerald Allan *minister*
Grathwol, James Norbert *lawyer*
Hoyt, Richard Comstock *economics consulting company executive*
Hugh, Gregory Joseph *finance company executive*
†Oas, Joan Margaret *artist*

Fairmont
McMurtry, Donna *multiarea nurse*
Rosen, Thomas J. *food and agricultural products executive*

Faribault
Strand, Melvin LeRoy *English educator*

Fergus Falls
Egge, Joel *clergy member, academic administrator*
Jahr, Armin N., II *clergy member, church administrator*
Lundburg, Paul Wesley *English educator*
MacFarlane, John Charles *utility company executive*
Overgaard, Robert Milton *religious organization administrator*
Rinden, David Lee *editor*

Finlayson
Luoma, Judy *ranching executive*

Forest Lake
Marchese, Ronald Thomas *ancient history and archaeology educator*

Fort Snelling
†Morris, Raymond Walter *state agency administrator*

Frazee
Ulmer, James Howard *potter*

Fridley
Savelkoul, Donald Charles *retired lawyer*

Gary
Anderson, Alden Alvin *music educator*

Georgetown
Thomas, Noreen Jo *healthcare system educator, writer*

Glenwood
Olson, Nancy Ann *artist, educator*

Golden Valley
Hagglund, Clarance Edward *lawyer, publishing company owner*
†Mindrum, Gerald Gene *physician*
Ng, Christine S. *chemical engineer*
Tracey, Timothy Neal *medical device, data processing executive*

Grand Marais
Cochrane, Tim *landmark administrator*

Grand Rapids
Crane, Faye *small business owner*
Johnson, Janis Kay *pharmacist*
Licke, Wallace John *lawyer*
†Nyvall, Robert Frederick *plant pathologist, educator*

Hackensack
Mentzer, Merleen Mae *retired adult education educator*

Hallock
Malm, Roger Charles *lawyer*

Harmony
Webster, Jeffrey Leon *graphic designer*

Hastings
†Avent, Sharon H. *consumer products company executive*
Blackie, Spencer David *physical therapist, administrator*
Bzoskie, James Steven *minister*

Hopkins
Hunter, Donald Forrest *lawyer*
Karls, Nicholas James *engineering executive*
Rappaport, Gary Burton *defense equipment and software company executive*
Zins, Martha Lee *elementary education educator, media specialist*

Houston
Euler, Diana Leone *nursing educator*

Hugo
Museus, Robert Allen *city manager*

International Falls
Westphal, Rolf Werner *sculptor, educator*

Inver Grove Heights
†Blaisdell, Elena Marie Marmo *artist, printer*
Evans, Roger Lynwood *scientist, patent liaison*
Kaner, Harvey Sheldon *lawyer, executive*
Koenig, Robert August *clergyman, educator*

Ivanhoe
Hoversten, Ellsworth Gary *insurance executive, producer*

Kelliher
Hughes, Patricia E. *secondary education educator*

Kenyon
Jacobson, Lloyd Eldred *retired dentist*
Peterson, Franklin Delano *lawyer*

Lake Crystal
Pawlitschek, Donald Paul *business consultant*

Lake Elmo
Schultz, Clarence John *minister*
Vivona, Daniel Nicholas *chemist*

Lakeland
Helstedt, Gladys Mardell *vocational education educator*

Lakeville
Krueger, Richard Arnold *technology executive*
Phinney, William Charles *retired geologist*

Le Roy
Erickson, Larry Alvin *electronics sales and marketing executive*

Lilydale
Kilbourne, Barbara Jean *health and human services consultant*

Lindstrom
Messin, Marlene Ann *plastics company executive*

Little Falls
Mottram, Richard Donald, Jr. *minister*

Long Lake
Lowthian, Petrena *college president*

Lutsen
Napadensky, Hyla Sarane *engineering consultant*

Madison
Husby, Donald Evans *engineering company executive*

Mahtomedi
Brainerd, Richard Charles *human resources executive, consultant, educator*

Mankato
Denn, Cyril Joseph *insurance agent*
Descy, Don Edmond *library media technology educator, writer, editor*
Dumke, Melvin Philip *dentist*
Gage, Fred Kelton *lawyer*
Hottinger, John Creighton *state legislator, lawyer*
Hustoles, Mary Jo *elementary education educator*
Hustoles, Paul John *theater educator*
Janavaras, Basil John *university business educator, consultant*
Johnson, William W. *dental educator*
Morrow, Steven Roger *computer scientist*
Orvick, George Myron *church denomination executive, minister*
Rush, Richard R. *academic administrator*
Taylor, Glen *professional sports team executive, printing and graphics company executive*

Maple Grove
Manthei, Robin Dickey *research technician*
Setterholm, Jeffrey Miles *systems engineer*

Mapleton
John, Hugo Herman *natural resources educator*

Maplewood
Gerber, Sandra Elaine *neonatal nurse practitioner*
Nemo, Anthony James *lawyer*

Marcell
Aldrich, Richard John *agronomist, educator*

Marshall
Schwan, Alfred *food products executive*

Mendota Heights
Frechette, Peter Loren *dental products executive*
Newman, Donald John *marketing executive*

Minneapolis
Ackerman, Eugene *biophysics educator*
Ackman, Lauress V. *lawyer*
Adams, John Stephen *geography educator*
Adamson, Oscar Charles, II *lawyer*
†Agler, Brian *professional basketball coach*
Aguilera, Richard Warren (Rick Aguilera) *baseball player*
Aldrich, Stephen Charles *lawyer, judge*
Allers, Marlene Elaine *legal administrator*
Amdahl, Douglas Kenneth *retired state supreme court justice*
Anderson, Alan Marshall *lawyer*
Anderson, Chester Grant *English educator*
Anderson, Davin Charles *business representative, labor consultant*
Anderson, Eric Scott *lawyer*
Anderson, John Edward *mechanical engineering educator*
Anderson, Laurence Alexis *lawyer*
Anderson, Ron *advertising executive*
Anderson, Tim *airport terminal executive*
Andreas, David Lowell *banker*
Andrews, Albert O'Beirne, Jr. *lawyer*
Anton, Frank Leland *insurance company executive*
Appel, John C. *investment company executive*
Appel, William Frank *pharmacist*
Aris, Rutherford *applied mathematician, educator*
Armitage, Shannon Lyn *editor-in-chief newspaper*
Arthur, Lindsay Grier *retired judge, author, editor*
Asp, William George *librarian*
Asplin, Edward William *retired packaging company executive*
Avella, Joseph Ralph *university executive*
Baker, John Stevenson (Michael Dyregrov) *writer*
Bakken, Earl Elmer *electrical engineer, bioengineering company executive*
Bales, Kent Roslyn *English language educator*
Bancroft, Ann *polar explorer*
†Barceló, Nancy Virginia (Rusty Barceló) *academic administrator*
Barnard, Allen Donald *lawyer*
Bashiri, Iraj *Central Asian studies educator*
Beardsley, John Ray *public relations firm executive*
Bearmon, Lee *lawyer*
Benson, Donald Erick *holding company executive*
Berens, William Joseph *lawyer*
Berg, Stanton Oneal *firearms and ballistics consultant*
Berg, Thomas Kenneth *lawyer*
Bergeson, James *advertising executive*
Berry, David J. *financial services company executive*
Berryman, Robert Glen *accounting educator, consultant*
Bileydi, Sumer *advertising agency executive*
Bird, Dick *sign painter*
Bisping, Bruce Henry *photojournalist*
Blackburn, Henry Webster, Jr. *retired physician*
Bland, J(ohn) Richard *lawyer*
Blanton, W. C. *lawyer*
Bleeker, Bernard Martin *designer, graphic*
Blomquist, Robert Oscar *insurance company executive*
Bly, Robert *poet*
Boelter, Philip Floyd *lawyer*
†Bogdan, Joann *retail executive*
Bolman, Ralph Morton, III (Chip Bolman) *cardiac surgeon*
†Bonnabeau, Raymond C. *physician*
Bonsignore, Michael Robert *electronics company executive*
Book, William Joseph *manufacturing executive*
Borger, John Philip *lawyer*
Bouchard, Thomas Joseph, Jr. *psychology educator, researcher*
Boudreau, Robert James *nuclear medicine physician, researcher*
†Bougie, Peter John *artist, educator*
Boyd, Belvel James *newspaper editor*
Boylan, Brian Richard *author, historian, director, photographer, literary agent*
Brand, Steve Aaron *lawyer*
Brasket, Curt Justin *systems analyst, chess player*
Brehl, James William *lawyer*
Breimayer, Joseph Frederick *patent lawyer*
Bress, Michael E. *retired lawyer*
Brink, David Ryrie *lawyer*
Bromelkamp, David John *investment officer*
Brooks, Gladys Sinclair *public affairs consultant*
Brosnahan, Roger Paul *lawyer*
Brown, David M. *physician, educator, dean*
Browne, Donald Roger *speech communication educator*
Bruner, Philip Lane *lawyer*
Buchwald, Henry *surgeon, educator, researcher*
Buggey, Lesley JoAnne *education educator, consultant*
Buoen, Roger *newspaper editor*
Buratti, Dennis P. *lawyer*
Burke, Martin Nicholas *lawyer*
Burns, Robert Arthur *lawyer*
Burton, Charles Victor *physician, surgeon, inventor*
Busdicker, Gordon G. *lawyer*
Bush, David H. *management consultant*
Campbell, James Robert *banker*
Campbell, Karlyn Kohrs *speech and communication educator*
Cardozo, Richard Nunez *marketing, entrepreneurship and business educator*
Carlson, Arne Helge *former governor*
Carlson, Curtis LeRoy *corporate executive*
†Carlson, Marilyn C. *travel service company executive*
Carlson, Thomas David *lawyer*
†Carlson-Nelson, Marilyn *advertising executive*
Carpenter, Norman Roblee *retired lawyer*
Carr, Robert Wilson, Jr. *chemistry educator*
Carson, Linda Frances *gynecologic oncologist*
Carter, Roy Ernest, Jr. *journalist, educator*
Cavert, Henry Mead *physician, retired educator*
Cerra, Frank Bernard *dean*
Chakravarthy, Balaji Srinivasan *strategic management educator, consultant*
Champlin, Steven Kirk *lawyer*
Chavers, Blanche Marie *pediatrician, educator, reseacher*
†Chemberlin, Peg *clergy, religious organization administrator*
Chen, William Shao-Chang *retired army officer*
Chester, Stephanie Ann *lawyer, banker*
Chester, Thomas Jay *physician*
Chipman, John Somerset *economist, educator*
Chisholm, Tague Clement *pediatric surgeon, educator*
Chou, Shelley Nien-chun *neurosurgeon, university official, educator*
Christensen, Nadia Margaret *writer, translator, editor, educator*
Christiansen, Jay David *lawyer*
Ciresi, Michael Vincent *lawyer*
Clary, Bradley G. *lawyer, educator*
†Clayton, Thomas Swoverland *English educator*
Clemence, Roger Davidson *landscape architect, educator*
Cohen, Arnold A. *electrical engineer*
Cohen, Earl Harding *lawyer*
Comstock, Rebecca Ann *lawyer*
Conn, Gordon Brainard, Jr. *lawyer*
†Cooper, William Allen *banking executive*
Cope, Lewis *journalist*
Cordova, Martin Keevin (Marty Cordova) *baseball player*
Corts, John Ronald *minister, religious organization executive*
Corwin, Gregg Marlowe *lawyer*
Cowles, John, Jr. *publisher, women's sports promoter*
Cowles, John, III *management consultant, investor*
†Cox, J. Allen *physicist*
Craig, James Lynn *physician, consumer products company executive*
Crawford, Bryce Low, Jr. *chemist, educator*
Crosby, Jacqueline Garton *newspaper editor, journalist*
Crosby, Thomas Manville, Jr. *lawyer*
†Cudd, J. Earl *federal judge*
†Cunningham, Bruce L. *plastic and reconstructive surgeon, educator*
Dahl, Gerald LuVern *psychotherapist, educator, consultant, writer*
Dale, John Sorensen *investment company executive, portfolio manager*
Danielson, James Walter *research microbiologist*
Davis, Howard Ted *engineering educator*
Davis, Michael J. *judge*
Dawis, René V. *psychology educator, research consultant*
Degenhardt, Robert Allan *architectural and engineering firm executive*
Degnan, John Michael *lawyer*
Deming, Frederick Lewis *banker*
Diemand, Kim Eugene *human resources executive*
DiGangi, Frank Edward *academic administrator*
DiPietro, Mark Joseph *lawyer*
Doepke, Katherine Louise Guldberg *choral director, former music educator*
Dommel, Darlene Hurst *writer*
Dooley, David J. *elementary school principal*
Doty, David Singleton *federal judge*
Drahmann, Brother Theodore *religious order official*
Drawz, John Englund *lawyer*
Dreher, Nancy C. *federal judge*
Du, Ding-Zhu *mathematician, educator*
Dunlap, William DeWayne, Jr. *advertising agency executive*
Dworkin, Martin *microbiologist, educator*
Dykstra, Dennis Dale *physiatrist*
Dyrud, Amos Oliver *minister, educator*
Eck, George Gregory *lawyer*
Eckberg, E. Daniel *secondary education educator*
Eckland, Jeff Howard *lawyer*
Ederer, Grace Mary *clinical laboratory scientist, retired*
Eich, Susan *public relations executive*
Eisenberg, Jay Lynn *marketing professional*
Eitingon, Daniel Benjamin *insurance consultant*
Erickson, Gerald Meyer *classical studies educator*
Erickson, Ronald A. *retail executive*
Erickson, W(alter) Bruce *business and economics educator, entrepreneur*
Erie, Gretchen Ann *cardiovascular clinician*
Erstad, Leon Robert *lawyer*
Fairhurst, Charles *civil and mining engineering educator*
Fallon, Patrick R. *advertising executive*
Farah, Caesar Elie *Middle Eastern and Islamic studies educator*
Faricy, John Hartnett, Jr. *lawyer*
Faricy, Richard Thomas *architect*
Farr, Leonard Alfred *hospital administrator*
Fauth, John J. *venture capitalist*
Fawcett, Marie Ann Formanek (Mrs. Roscoe Kent Fawcett) *civic leader*
Ferner, David Charles *non-profit management and development consultant*
Fetler, Paul *composer*
Feuss, Linda Anne Upsall *lawyer*
Fiedler, Robert Max *management consultant*
Findorff, Robert Lewis *retired air filtration equipment company executive*
†Fine, Pam *newspaper editor*
Fine, William Irwin *real estate developer*
Finzen, Bruce Arthur *lawyer*
Firchow, Evelyn Scherabon *German educator, author*
Firchow, Peter Edgerly *language professional, educator, author*
Fisch, Robert Otto *medical educator*
Fitch, Mary Killeen *salary design and human resources specialist*
Flanagan, Barbara *journalist*
Fleezanis, Jorja Kay *violinist, educator*
Fletcher, Edward Abraham *engineering educator*
Flom, Gerald Trossen *lawyer*
Floren, David D. *advertising executive*
Franklin, Robert Brewer *journalist*
Freeman, Orville Lothrop *lawyer, former governor of Minnesota, think tank executive*
Freeman, Todd Ira *lawyer*

French, John Dwyer *lawyer*
Frestedt, Joy Louise *scientist*
Friedman, Avner *mathematician, educator*
†Fritts, William D., Jr. *financial executive*
Gage, Edwin C., III (Skip Gage) *travel and marketing services executive*
Gagnon, Craig William *lawyer*
Gajl-Peczalska, Kazimiera J. *surgical pathologist, pathology educator*
Galambos, Theodore Victor *civil engineer, educator*
Gallagher, Gerald Raphael *venture capitalist*
Gandrud, Robert P. *fraternal insurance executive*
Gardebring, Sandra S. *academic administrator*
Gardner, William Earl *university dean*
Garfield, Joan Barbara *statistics educator*
Garon, Philip Stephen *lawyer*
Garton, Thomas William *lawyer*
Gavin, Sara *public relations executive*
Genia, James Michael *lawyer*
George, William Wallace *manufacturing company executive*
Gerberich, William Warren *engineering educator*
Gersemehl, William Terry *information systems manager*
Geweke, John Frederick *economics educator*
Gilbertson, Steven E(dward) Satyaki *real estate broker, guidance counselor*
Gill, Richard Lawrence *lawyer*
Gilpin, Larry Vincent *retail executive*
†Gilson, Gary *professional society administrator, journalist*
Gladhill, Bethany *community advocate, historic preservation consultant*
Gockel, John Raymond *construction executive*
Goldberg, Luella Gross *corporation executive*
Goldberger, Robert D. *food products company executive*
Goldman, Allen Marshall *physics educator*
Goldstein, Richard Jay *mechanical engineer, educator*
Goodman, Elizabeth Ann *lawyer*
Gordon, Corey Lee *lawyer*
Gorham, Eville *ecologist, biogeochemist*
Gorlin, Robert James *medical educator*
Gottschalk, Stephen Elmer *lawyer*
Graham, William Franklin (Billy Graham) *evangelist*
Grant, David James William *pharmacy educator*
Gray, Virginia Hickman *political science educator*
Grayson, Edward Davis *lawyer, manufacturing company executive*
†Grazzini, Gregory Paul *construction company executive*
Greener, Ralph Bertram *lawyer*
Griffith, G. Larry *lawyer*
Grundhofer, John F. *banking executive*
Gudeman, Stephen Frederick *anthropology educator*
Gudmundson, Barbara Rohrke *ecologist*
Gudorf, Kenneth Francis *business executive*
Gullickson, Glenn, Jr. *physician, educator*
Haase, Ashley Thomson *microbiology educator, researcher*
Hale, James Thomas *retail company executive, lawyer*
Hale, Roger Loucks *manufacturing company executive*
Halley, James Woods *physics educator*
Hallman, Gary L. *photographer, educator*
Hamel, William John *church administrator, minister*
Hamermesh, Morton *physicist, educator*
Hanson, A. Stuart *health facility administrator, physician*
Hanson, Bruce Eugene *lawyer*
Hanson, Kent Bryan *lawyer*
Harper, Donald Victor *transportation and logistics educator*
Harris, John Edward *lawyer*
Hauch, Valerie Catherine *historian, educator, researcher*
Hawkinson, Thomas Edwin *environmental and occupational health engineer*
Hawley, Sandra Sue *electrical engineer*
Hayward, Edward Joseph *lawyer*
Healton, Bruce Carney *data processing executive*
Heiberg, Robert Alan *lawyer*
Heller, Kenneth Jeffrey *physicist*
Hendrixson, Peter S. *lawyer*
Henson, Robert Frank *lawyer*
Hesslund, Bradley Harry *product manager*
Heston, Renate *nursing administrator*
Hetland, James Lyman, Jr. *banker, lawyer, educator*
Hibbs, John Stanley *lawyer*
Hillstrom, Thomas Peter *engineering executive*
Hippee, William H., Jr. *lawyer*
Hobbins, Robert Leo *lawyer*
Hodder, William Alan *fabricated metal products company executive*
Hoffmann, Thomas Russell *business management educator*
Hogenkamp, Henricus Petrus Cornelis *biochemistry researcher, biochemistry educator*
Holt, Robert Theodore *political scientist, dean, educator*
Hooke, Roger LeBaron *geomorphology and glaciology educator*
Horns, Howard Lowell *physician, educator*
Howe, Craig Walter Sandell *medical organization executive, internist*
Howland, Joan Sidney *law librarian, law educator*
Huang, Victor Tsangmin *food scientist, researcher*
Hudec, Robert Emil *lawyer, educator*
Humphrey, Hubert Horatio, III *state attorney general*
Hurwicz, Leonid *economist, educator*
Huston, Beatrice Louise *retired banker*
Innmon, (Tara) Arlene Katherine *artist, dancer, writer, storyteller, healer*
Ison, Christopher John *investigative reporter*
Jacob, Bernard Michel *architect*
Jacobs, Irwin Lawrence *diversified corporate executive*
Jarboe, Mark Alan *lawyer*
Jeffrey-Smith, Lilli Ann *biofeedback specialist, educator, administrator*
Jernberg, Sandra Kay *elementary education educator*
Jewell, H. Richard *English language educator*
Jirka, Brad Paul *sculptor, art educator*
Johnson, Badri Nahvi *sociology educator, real estate business owner*
Johnson, Carol R. *school system administrator*
Johnson, Cheryl (CJ) *newspaper columnist*
Johnson, David Wolcott *psychologist, educator*
Johnson, Donald Clay *librarian, curator*
Johnson, Gary LeRoy *publisher*
Johnson, Gary M. *lawyer*
†Johnson, Gary R. *corporate lawyer*
Johnson, John Warren *retired association executive*
Johnson, Larry Walter *lawyer*
Johnson, Lola Norine *advertising and public relations executive, educator*
Johnson, Margaret Ann (Peggy) *library administrator*
Johnson, Robert Glenn *geology and geophysics educator*
Johnson, Sankey Anton *manufacturing company executive*
Johnson, Walter Kline *civil engineer*
Jones, Thomas Walter *astrophysics educator, researcher*
Jones, Will(iam) (Arnold) *writer, former newspaper columnist*
†Jonsson, Egil Sigurd *artist*
Jorgensen, Daniel Fred *academic executive*
Joseph, Burton M. *retired grain merchant*
Joseph, Daniel Donald *aeronautical engineer, educator*
Joseph, Geri Mack (Geraldine Joseph) *former ambassador, educator*
Kahn, Donald William *mathematics educator*
Kain, Richard Yerkes *electrical engineer, researcher, educator*
Kalman, Marc *radio station executive*
Kane, Robert Lewis *public health educator*
Kaplan, Manuel E. *physician, educator*
Kaplan, Sheldon *lawyer*
Keane, William Francis *nephrology educator, research foundation executive*
Keets, John David, Jr. *insurance company executive*
Keller, Darla Lynn *financial manager, organization consultant*
Keller, Kenneth Harrison *engineering educator, science policy analyst*
Kelly, A. David *lawyer*
Kelly, Tom (Jay Thomas Kelly) *major league baseball club manager*
Kennedy, Adrienne Lita *playwright*
Kennedy, B(yrl) J(ames) *medicine and oncology educator*
Kennon, Rozmond Herron *physical therapist*
Keppel, William James *lawyer, educator, author*
Keyes, Jeffrey J. *lawyer*
Kilbourn, William Douglas, Jr. *law educator*
Kinderwater, Joseph C. (Jack Kinderwater) *publishing company executive*
King, Lyndel Irene Saunders *art museum director*
King, Reatha Clark *community foundation executive*
King, Robert Cotton *professional society consultant*
Kinney, Earl Robert *mutual funds company executive*
Kirschner, Ruth Brin *elementary education educator*
Klaas, Paul Barry *lawyer*
Klee, Carol Anne *foreign language educator*
Klemp, Harold *minister, writer*
Knoell, Nancy Jeanne *kindergarten educator*
Knoke, David Harmon *sociology educator*
Knopman, David S. *neurologist*
Kohlstedt, Sally Gregory *history educator*
Koneck, John Michael *lawyer*
Konieczny, Sharon Louise *insurance company executive*
Korotkin, Fred *writer, philatelist*
Koutsky, Dean Roger *advertising executive*
Kovacevich, Richard M. *banker*
Kozberg, Steven Freed *psychologist*
Kralewski, John Edward *health service administration educator*
Kramer, Joel Roy *journalist, newspaper executive*
Krause, Timothy Gilbert *English educator*
Kreiser, Frank David *real estate executive*
Krohnke, Duane W. *lawyer*
Kruegel, Patrick Ferdinand *purchasing agent*
Kruse, Paul Walters, Jr. *physicist, consultant*
Kudrle, Robert Thomas *economist, educator*
Kuhi, Leonard Vello *astronomer, university administrator*
Kukla, Edward Richard *rare books and special collections librarian, lecturer*
Kump, Warren Lee *diagnostic radiologist*
Kvalseth, Tarald Oddvar *mechanical engineer, educator*
Kvavik, Robert Berthel *university administrator*
Laing, Karel Ann *magazine publishing executive*
Lambert, Robert Frank *electrical engineer, consultant*
Landry, Paul Leonard *lawyer*
Lange, Katherine J. *writer*
†Lanyon, Scott Merrill *museum director, educator*
LaPrade, Robert F. *orthopedic surgeon, educator*
Lareau, Richard George *lawyer*
Larkin, Eugene David *artist, educator*
Larsen, Elizabeth B. (Libby Larsen) *composer*
Larson, Earl Richard *federal judge*
Lazar, Raymond Michael *lawyer, educator*
Lebedoff, David M. *lawyer, author, investment advisor*
Lebedoff, Jonathan Galanter *federal judge*
Lebedoff, Randy Miller *lawyer*
Ledin Moser, Debra Joan *occupational health nurse practitioner*
Lee, Robert Lloyd *pastor, religious association executive*
†Lehman, Tom *professional golfer*
Lemberg, Steven Floyd *electrical engineer*
Leon, Arthur Sol *research cardiologist, exercise physiologist*
Leppik, Ilo E. *neurologist, educator*
Lerner, Harry Jonas *publishing company executive*
Levitt, Seymour Herbert *physician, radiology educator*
Lindau, James H. *grain exchange executive*
Lindau, Philip *commodities trader*
Lindberg, Duane R. *minister, historian*
Lindell, Edward Albert *former college president, religious organization administrator*
Lindgren, D(erbin) Kenneth, Jr. *retired lawyer*
Linoff, Alan Lee *real estate development company executive*
Liszt, Howard Paul *advertising executive*
Littlejohn, Cherly *university head women's basketball coach*
Liu, Benjamin Young-hwai *engineering educator*
Lofstrom, Mark D. *lawyer, educator, communications executive*
Logan, Veryle Jean *retail executive, realtor*
Lucia, Donald J. *head coach men's ice hockey*
Luepker, Russell Vincent *epidemiology educator*
Lupient, James *automotive executive*
Luthringshauser, Daniel Rene *manufacturing company executive*
MacLaughlin, Harry Hunter *federal judge*
MacMillan, Whitney *food products and import/export company executive*
Magnuson, Roger James *lawyer*
Mammel, Russell Norman *retired food distribution company executive*
†Mandel, Jack Sheldon *epidemiologist, educator*
Manthey, Thomas Richard *lawyer*
Markus, Lawrence *retired mathematics educator*
Marling, Karal Ann *art history and social sciences educator, curator*
Marshak, Marvin Lloyd *physicist, educator*
Marshall, Sherrie *newspaper editor*
Marshall, Siri Swenson *corporate lawyer*
Martin, Phillip Hammond *lawyer*
Martin, Roger Bond *landscape architect, educator*
Matson, Wesley Jennings *educational administrator*
Matthews, James Shadley *lawyer*
Mazze, Roger Steven *medical educator, researcher*
McCune, Thomas *construction executive contractor*
McDaniel, Jan *television station executive*
McEnroe, Paul *reporter*
McErlane, Joseph James *insurance company executive*
†McGuire, Tim *editor*
McGuire, Timothy James *lawyer, editor*
McHale, Kevin Edward *former professional basketball player, sports team executive*
McQuarrie, Donald Gray *surgeon, educator*
Meador, Ron *newspaper editor, writer*
Meehl, Paul Everett *psychologist, educator*
Meese, Robert Allen *architect*
Meller, Robert Louis, Jr. *lawyer*
Mellum, Gale Robert *lawyer*
Meshbesher, Ronald I. *lawyer*
Meyer, Maurice Wesley *physiologist, dentist, neurologist*
Micek, Ernest S. *food products executive*
Michael, Alfred Frederick, Jr. *physician, medical educator*
Miller, John William, Jr. *bassoonist*
Miller, Robert Francis *physiologist, educator*
Miller, Willard, Jr. *mathematician, educator*
Minish, Robert Arthur *lawyer*
Mitau, Lee R. *bank executive*
Mitchell, James Austin *insurance company executive*
Mohr, L. Thomas *newspaper executive*
Moncharsh, Jane Kline *rehabilitation counselor, vocational specialist, mediator, case manager*
Mondale, Joan Adams *wife of former Vice President of United States*
Monson, Dianne Lynn *literacy educator*
Montgomery, Andrew Stuart *financial advisor*
Montgomery, Ann D. *judge, federal, educator*
Montgomery, Henry Irving *financial planner*
Moor, Rob *professional basketball team executive*
Moore, Tanna Lynn *business development executive*
Mooty, Bruce Wilson *lawyer*
Mooty, John William *lawyer*
Moraczewski, Robert Leo *publisher*
Morrison, Clinton *banker*
†Morrison, James Kent *higher education administrator*
Mouser, Les *broadcasting executive*
†Mowitt, John William *humanities educator*
Mulligan, Michael L. *sales and marketing executive*
Munic, Martin Daniel *lawyer*
Murphy, Diana E. *federal judge*
Murphy, Joseph Edward, Jr. *broadcast executive*
Myers, Howard Sam *lawyer*
Myers, Malcolm Haynie *artist, art educator*
Najarian, John Sarkis *surgeon, educator*
Nanne, Louis Vincent *professional hockey team executive*
Narvaez, Darcia Fe *educational psychologist*
Nee, Kay Bonner *advertising executive*
Nelson, Charles Alexander III *medical education educator*
Nelson, Gary Michael *lawyer*
Nelson, Glen David *medical products executive, physician*
Nelson, Richard Arthur *lawyer*
Nelson, Steven Craig *lawyer*
Nightingale, Edmund Joseph *clinical psychologist, educator*
Nitsche, Johannes Carl Christian *mathematics educator*
Noel, Franklin Linwood *federal chief magistrate judge*
Nolting, Earl *academic administrator*
Noonan, Thomas Schaub *history educator, Russian studies educator*
Norberg, Arthur Lawrence, Jr. *historian, physicist educator*
Nyrop, Donald William *airline executive*
O'Brien, Kathleen *muncipal or county official*
Ogata, Katsuhiko *engineering educator*
†Ohanian, Valerie Gay *homeopathic practitioner*
O'Keefe, Nancy Jean *real estate company executive*
Oliver, Edward Carl *state senator, retired investment executive*
Olson, Clifford Larry *management consultant, entrepreneur*
Olson, James Richard *retired transportation company executive*
Olson, Robert K. *police chief*
O'Neill, Brian Boru *lawyer*
Opperman, Dwight Darwin *publishing company executive*
Oriani, Richard Anthony *metallurgical engineering educator*
Ostrem, Walter Martin *librarian, educator, consultant*
Oue, Eiji *performing company executive*
Owens, Scott Andrew *sales executive*
Palahniuk, Richard John *anesthesiology educator, researcher*
Palmer, Brian Eugene *lawyer*
Palmer, Deborah Jean *lawyer*
Parker, Leonard S. *architect, educator*
Parsons, Charles Allan, Jr. *lawyer*
Paulu, Frances Brown *international center administrator*
Pazandak, Carol Hendrickson *liberal arts educator*
Perlman, Lawrence *business executive*
Persson, Erland Karl *electrical engineer*
Petersen, Douglas Arndt *financial development consultant*
Petersen, Maureen Jeanette Miller *management information consultant, former nurse*
Peterson, Douglas Arthur *physician*
†Peterson, Michael *business executive*
Peterson, Oliver H. *retired obstetrician/gynecologist*
†Peterson, Sandra Lynne *philosophy educator*
Pfender, Emil *mechanical engineering educator*
Phelps, Dorothy Rose *critical care nurse*
Phibbs, Clifford Matthew *surgeon, educator*
†Phillips, Carl Vincent *educator*
Pillsbury, George Sturgis *investment adviser*
Piper, Addison Lewis *securities executive*
Pluimer, Edward J. *lawyer*
Pohlad, Carl R. *professional baseball team executive, bottling company executive*
Pollock, Tony Joe *graphic designer, writer*
Porter, Philip Wayland *geography educator*
Portoghese, Philip Salvatore *medicinal chemist, educator*
Potuznik, Charles Laddy *lawyer*
Pour-El, Marian Boykan *mathematician, educator*
Prager, Stephen *chemistry educator*
Pratte, Robert John *lawyer*
Prem, Konald Arthur *physician, educator*
Preuss, Roger E(mil) *artist*
Price, Joseph Michael *lawyer*
Puckett, Kirby *professional baseball team executive, former player*
Quie, Paul Gerhardt *physician, educator*
Quinlan, C. Patrick *retired diplomat, educator*
†Rabinowitz, Paula *writer, educator*
Radmer, Michael John *lawyer, educator*
Rahman, Yueh-Erh *biologist*
Rahn, Alvin Albert *former banker*
Ramberg, Patricia Lynn *college president*
Rand, Peter Anders *architect*
Rand, Sidney Anders *retired college administrator*
Rauenhorst, Gerald *architectural, construction and development*
Ray, Charles Dean *neurosurgeon, spine surgeon, bioengineer, inventor*
Read, John Conyers *industrial management*
Redmon, Rose Marie *secondary school educator*
Reichgott Junge, Ember D. *state legislator, lawyer*
Reilly, George *lawyer*
Rein, Stanley Michael *lawyer*
Reinhart, Robert Rountree, Jr. *lawyer*
Reiss, Ira Leonard *retired sociology educator, writer*
Reister, Raymond Alex *retired lawyer*
Retzler, Kurt Egon *diversified management company merger and acquisition and financial executive, retired hospitality, travel and marketing company executive*
Reuss, Carl Frederick *sociologist*
Reuter, James William *lawyer*
Rich, David *visual artist*
Roberts, Katherine Erin *journalist*
Rockenstein, Walter Harrison, II *lawyer*
†Rockswold, Gaylan Lee *neurosurgeon*
Rockwell, Winthrop Adams *lawyer*
Roe, Roger Rolland *lawyer*
Rogers, William Cecil *political science educator*
†Rojas, Guillermo *educator*
Roloff, Marvin L. *publishing executive*
Rose, Thomas Albert *artist, art educator*
Rosenbaum, James Michael *judge*
Ross, Donald, Jr. *English language educator, university administrator*
†Rottenberg, David Allan *neurologist*
Rubens, Sidney Michel *physicist, technical advisor*
Rudelius, William *marketing educator*
Ruff, Dureen Anne *small business owner, operater*
Ryan, Terry *professional sports team executive*
Saeks, Allen Irving *lawyer*
Safley, James Robert *lawyer*
†Sagar, Michal *art educator, artist*
St. Germaine-Lattig, Charles Edwin *political writer*
Salyer, Stephen Lee *broadcast executive*
Sanger, Stephen W. *consumer products company executive*
Sanner, Royce Norman *lawyer*
Sarles, Harvey B. *humanities educator*
†Satkowski, Leon George *architecture educator*
Saunders, Philip D. *professional basketball coach*
Sawatsky, Ben *church administrator*
Sawchuk, Ronald John *pharmaceutical sciences educator*
Sayles Belton, Sharon *mayor*
Scallen, Thomas Kaine *broadcasting executive*
Schneider, Elaine Carol *lawyer, researcher, writer*
Schnell, Robert Lee, Jr. *lawyer*
Schnobrich, Roger William *lawyer*
Schoettle, Ferdinand P. *lawyer, educator*
Schreck, Robert *commodities trader*
Schreiner, John Christian *economics consultant, software publisher*
Schuh, G(eorge) Edward *university dean, agricultural economist*
Schultz, Alvin Leroy *retired internist, endocrinologist, retired university health science facility administrator*
Schultz, Louis Edwin *management consultant*
Schwartz, Howard Wyn *business/marketing educator, consultant*
Schwartzberg, Joseph Emanuel *geographer, educator*
Scott, Andrew *retired corporate executive*
Scott, Robert Lee *speech educator*
Scoville, James Griffin *economics educator*
Scriven, L. E(dward) *chemical engineering educator, scientist*
Seidel, Robert Wayne *science historian, educator, institute administrator*
Serrin, James Burton *mathematics educator*
Serstock, Doris Shay *retired microbiologist, educator, civic worker*
Severinsen, Doc (Carl H. Severinsen) *conductor, musician*
Shapiro, Burton Leonard *oral pathologist, geneticist, educator*
Shaughnessy, Thomas William *librarian, consultant*
Sheikh, Suneel Ismail *aerospace engineer, researcher*
Shively, William Phillips *political scientist, educator*
Shnider, Bruce Jay *lawyer*
Shulman, Yechiel *engineering educator*
Siepmann, Joern Ilja *chemistry educator*
†Silberfarb, Stephen Russell *lawyer*
Silverman, Robert Joseph *lawyer*
Simmer, Rita *public relations executive*
Sit, Eugene C. *investment executive*
Skare, Robert Martin *lawyer*
Skillingstad, Constance Yvonne *social services administrator, educator*
Skrowaczewski, Stanislaw *conductor, composer*
Slagle, James Robert *computer science educator*
Slorp, John S. *academic administrator*
Smith, Kevin H. *performing company executive*
Smyrl, William Hiram *chemical engineering educator*
Soland, Norman R. *corporate lawyer*
Sortland, Paul Allan *lawyer*
Southall, Francis Geneva *retired education educator music*
Spaeth, Nicholas John *lawyer, former state attorney general*
Speer, Nancy Girouard *educational administrator*
Spendlove, Steve Dale *vice president and general manager*
Spoor, William Howard *food company executive*
Staba, Emil John *pharmacognosy and medicinal chemistry educator*
†Stage, Brian *hotel facility executive*
Stageberg, Roger V. *lawyer*
†Staley, Warren *food products company executive*
Stark, Matthew *higher education and civil rights administrator*

†Nickerson, Ronald George *park planner*
Paschke, Jerry Bryan *lawyer*
Ramsey, Robert D. *writer*
Rothenberg, Elliot Calvin *lawyer, writer*
Schlutter, Lois Cochrane *psychologist*
†Stein, Steven David *neurologist*
Svendsbye, Lloyd August *college president, clergyman, educator*
Weisman, Herbert Neal *dentist, financial planner*
Wesselink, David Duwayne *finance company executive*

Saint Paul
Aggergaard, Steven Paul *journalist, musician*
Allison, John Robert *lawyer*
Alsop, Donald Douglas *federal judge*
Andersen, Elmer Lee *manufacturing and publishing executive, former governor of Minnesota*
Anderson, Charles S. *college president, clergyman*
Anderson, Clyde Bailey *musician, educator*
Anderson, Gordon Louis *foundation administrator*
Anderson, Gregory Shane *insurance executive*
Anderson, Kurt Lewis *artist*
Anderson, Paul Holden *state supreme court justice*
†Anton, Danilo Jose *geographer, writer*
Archabal, Nina M(archetti) *historical society director*
Ashton, Sister Mary Madonna *healthcare administrator*
Athans, Sister Mary Christine *church history educator*
Baker, Donald Gardner *retired soil science educator*
Barker-Nunn, Jeanne Beverly *English educator*
Barnwell, Franklin Hershel *zoology educator*
†Barry, Anne M. *public health officer*
Baukol, Ronald Oliver *company executive*
†Beers, Anne *protective services official*
Bell-Brown, Brenda Yvette *arts administrator*
Biery, Marilyn Ruth *organist, conductor, educator, composer*
Bingham, Christopher *statistics educator*
Blanchard, J. A. *publishing executive*
Boudreau, James Lawton *insurance company executive*
Bree, Marlin Duane *publisher, author*
†Broding, Marilyn A. *librarian*
Brudvig, Glenn Lowell *retired library director*
Bruener, James William *fundraiser*
Brushaber, George Karl *college-theological seminary president, minister*
Bry, Jeffrey Allen *auditor*
Burchell, Howard Bertram *retired physician, educator*
Burd, Francis John *packaging executive*
Burkart, Jeffrey Edward *communications educator*
Calvin, Rochelle Ann *development association adminstrator*
Carlson, Lyndon Richard Selvig *state legislator, educator*
Carruthers, Philip Charles *public official, lawyer*
Checchi, Alfred A. *airline company executive*
Cheng, H(wei) H(sien) *soil scientist, agronomic and environmental science educator*
Chiang, Huai Chang *entomologist, educator*
Clapp, C(harles) Edward *research chemist, soil biochemistry educator*
Clark, Ronald Dean *newspaper editor*
Clawson, John Thomas *government relations professional*
Close, Elizabeth Scheu *architect*
Cohen, Robert *medical device manufacturing-marketing executive*
Coleman, Norm *mayor*
Connors, William Edward *lawyer*
Crabb, Kenneth Wayne *obstetrician, gynecologist*
Dahl, Reynold Paul *applied economics educator*
D'Aurora, James Joseph *psychologist, consultant*
Davis, Margaret Bryan *paleoecology researcher, educator*
Davis, Richard Carlton *state agency administrator*
Dee, Scott Allen *veterinarian*
Desimone, Livio Diego *diversified manufacturing company executive*
Diesch, Stanley La Verne *veterinarian, educator*
Dietz, Charlton Henry *lawyer*
Doermann, Humphrey *economics educator*
Dykstra, Robert *retired education educator*
Ebert, Robert Alvin *retired lawyer, retired airline executive*
Edwards, Jesse Efrem *physician, educator*
Ek, Alan Ryan *forestry educator*
Engle, Donald Edward *retired railway executive, lawyer*
Esposito, Bonnie Lou *marketing professional*
Estenson, Noel K. *refining and fertilizer company executive*
†Eyunni, Vijay Raghavan *occupational medicine physician*
Failinger, Marie Anita *law educator, editor*
Feinberg, David Erwin *publishing company executive*
Feldman, Nancy Jane *health organization executive*
Ferkingstad, Susanne M. *cosmetics executive*
†Ferris, Paul Wayne, Jr. *religious studies educator*
Fesler, David Richard *foundation director*
Finney, William K. *police chief*
Fisk, Martin H. *lawyer*
Flynn, Harry Joseph *bishop*
Forshay, Steven R. *marketing professional, consultant*
Frederickson, Dennis Russel *senator, farmer*
Friel, Bernard Preston *lawyer*
†Galt, Margot Fortunato *writer*
Galvin, Michael John, Jr. *lawyer*
Garretson, Donald Everett *retired manufacturing company executive*
†Gehan, Mark William *lawyer*
Gehrz, Robert Gustave *retired railroad executive*
Geis, Jerome Arthur *lawyer, legal educator*
Gherty, John E. *food products and agricultural products company executive*
Gilgun, Jane Frances *social work educator*
Goff, Lila Johnson *historical society administrator*
Goodell, John Dewitte *electromechanical engineer*
Goodman, Lawrence Eugene *structural analyst, educator*
Graham, Charles John *university educator, former university president*
Greenfield, Lee *state legislator*
Hall, Beverly Joy *police officer*
Hansen, Robyn L. *lawyer*
†Hartford, Douglas Bennett *university administrator*
†Hatch, Mike *state attorney general*
Hays, Thomas S. *medical educator, medical researcher*
Hill, James Stanley *computer consulting company executive*
Hobbie, Russell Klyver *physics educator*
Hodgson, Jane Elizabeth *obstetrician and gynecologist, consultant*
Holt, Nancy Irene *elementary education educator*
Hopper, David Henry *religion educator*
Hoxmeier, Marlette Marie *nurse educator*
Hubbard, Stanley Stub *broadcast executive*
Huber, Sister Alberta *college president*
†Huffman, Douglas Scott *educator and administrator college level*
†Hugoson, Gene *state legislator, farmer*
Huntzicker, William Edward *journalism educator*
Hvass, Sheryl Ramstad *lawyer*
Jaberg, Eugene Carl *theology educator, administrator*
Jensen, James Robert *dentist, educator*
Jessup, Paul Frederick *financial economist, educator*
Johnson, Carolyn Jean *law librarian*
†Johnson, Feng-Ling Margaret *English educator*
Johnson, James Erling *insurance executive*
Johnson, Kenneth Harvey *veterinary pathologist*
Johnson, Paul Oren *lawyer*
Jones, C. Paul *lawyer, educator*
Jones, Charles Weldon *biologist, educator, researcher*
Kane, Lucile Marie *retired archivist, historian*
Kane, Stanley Phillip *insurance company executive*
Keillor, Garrison Edward *writer, radio host*
Kerr, Sylvia Joann *educator*
Kessler, Robert W. *director license, inspections, environmental rules*
Kielsmeier, James Calvin *nonprofit corporation executive*
†Kiffmeyer, Mary *state official*
Killorin Caswell, Mary Katherine *management consultant*
Kirchhoff, Frederick Thomas *academic administrator, dean*
Kirwin, Kenneth Francis *law educator*
Kiscaden, Sheila M. *state legislator*
Kishel, Gregory Francis *federal judge*
Kling, William Hugh *broadcasting executive*
Knoblach, James Michael *state represenative*
Kolehmainen, Jan Waldroy *professional association administrator*
Kommedahl, Thor *plant pathology educator*
Kuhrmeyer, Carl Albert *manufacturing company executive*
†Kuzer, Mindy Susan *educator*
Kyle, Richard House *federal judge*
Lambert, LeClair Grier *writer, lecturer, consultant, state government public information administrator*
Lampert, Leonard Franklin *mechanical engineer*
Larson, David Allen *law educator*
Lay, Donald Pomeroy *federal judge*
Leatherdale, Douglas West *insurance company executive*
Lehr, Lewis Wylie *diversified manufacturing company executive*
Lendt, Harold Hanford *manufacturing representative*
Leonard, Kurt John *plant pathologist, university program director*
Leppik, Margaret White *state legislator*
Levinson, Kenneth S. *lawyer, corporate executive*
†Ley, Carol Ann *preventative and occupational medicine physician*
Lineweaver, Joe Reherd *information scientist*
Ling, Joseph Tso-Ti *manufacturing company executive, environmental engineer*
†Litecky, Larry Paul *humanities educator, academic administrator*
Loken, James Burton *federal judge*
Lundy, Walker *newspaper editor*
Luther, Darlene *state legislator*
Lyubimov, Aleksandr Vladimirovich *toxicologist*
Maas, Duane Harris *distilling company executive*
Maclin, Alan Hall *lawyer*
Maffei, Rocco John *lawyer*
Magee, Paul Terry *geneticist and molecular biologist, college dean*
Magnuson, Norris Alden *librarian, history educator*
Mahoney, Kathleen Mary *lawyer*
Marini, John Joseph *medical scientist, educator, physician*
Martin, Steven S. *healthcare executive*
†Mason, John M. (Jack Mason) *federal judge*
Mason, John Milton (Jack Mason) *judge*
Mather, Richard Burroughs *retired Chinese language and literature educator*
Matteson, Clarice Chris *artist, educator*
†May, S. Rachel *Russian language educator, foundation executive*
McDonald, Malcolm Willis *real estate company executive*
McDougal, Stuart Yeatman *comparative literature educator, author*
McGuire, Mary Jo *state legislator*
McKinnell, Robert Gilmore *zoology, genetics and cell biology educator*
McMillan, Mary Bigelow *retired minister, volunteer*
McNamee, Sister Catherine *educator*
McNeely, John J. *lawyer*
McPherson, Michael Steven *academic administrator, economics educator*
Molnau, Carol *state legislator*
Munson, Robert Dean *agronomist, soil scientist, consultant*
Murphy, Edrie Lee *hospital laboratory administrator*
Murray, Peter Bryant *English language educator*
Myren, David James *aeronautical engineer*
Nash, Nicholas David *retailing executive*
Newmark, Richard Alan *chemist*
Nice, Pamela Michele *theatre director*
Nicholson, Morris Emmons, Jr. *metallurgist, educator*
†O'Brien, Dennis D. *federal judge*
Ofstedal, Paul Estrem *clergy member*
O'Keefe, Thomas Michael *government official*
Osman, Stephen Eugene *historic site administrator*
Osnes, Larry G. *academic administrator*
Ostby, Ronald *dairy and food products company executive*
Palmer, Roger Raymond *accounting educator*
Pampusch, Anita Marie *foundation administrator*
Parsons, Mark Frederick *college development officer*
Peterson, Willis Lester *economics educator*
Phillips, Ronald Lewis *plant geneticist, educator*
Pomeroy, Benjamin Sherwood *veterinary medicine educator*
Preus, David Walter *bishop, minister*
Pruzan, Irene *arts administrator, music educator, flutist, marketing and public relations specialist*
Rathburn, Robert Charles *retired educator*
Rebane, John T. *lawyer*
Renner, Robert George *federal judge*
Roach, John Robert *retired archbishop*
†Roberts, A(rthur) Wayne *organization administrator*
Robertson, Jerry Earl *retired manufacturing company executive*
Rogers, Karen Beckstead *gifted studies educator, researcher, consultant*
Rossmann, Jack Eugene *psychology educator*
Rothenberger, David Albert *surgeon*
Rothmeier, Steven George *merchant banker, investment manager*
Roy, Robert Russell *toxicologist*
Ruttan, Vernon Wesley *agricultural economist*
Sadowski, Richard J. *publishing executive*
†Sadowski, Rick *publisher*
Schultz, David A. *political science educator, editor, writer, lawyer*
†Schunk, Mae *state official*
Seagren, Alice *state legislator*
Senese, Dick *Democrat party chairman*
Sentz, James Curtis *agriculturist, agricultural developer*
Seymour, McNeil Vernam *lawyer*
Shaffer, Thomas Frederic *state official*
Shannon, Michael Edward *specialty chemical company executive*
Sher, Phyllis Kammerman *pediatric neurology educator*
Sinklar, Robert *insurance company executive*
Solberg, Loren Albin *state legislator, secondary education educator*
Southwick, David Leroy *geology researcher*
Spear, Allan Henry *state senator, historian, educator*
Spellmire, Sandra Marie *systems analyst, programmer*
Stadelmann, Eduard Joseph *plant physiologist, educator*
Stanek, Richard Walter *police captain, Minneapolis*
†Steenland, Douglas *lawyer*
Stewart, James Brewer *historian, author, college administrator*
Stringer, Edward Charles *state supreme court justice*
Stroud, Rhoda M. *elementary education educator*
Sullivan, Alfred Dewitt *academic administrator*
Swaiman, Kenneth Fred *pediatric neurologist, educator*
Swanson-Schones, Kris Margit *developmental adapted physical education educator*
Sykes, Philip Kimbark *retail executive*
Tecco, Romuald Gilbert Louis Joseph *violinist, concertmaster*
Thompson, Mary Eileen *chemistry educator*
Titus, Jack L. *pathologist, educator*
Tomljanovich, Esther M. *state supreme court justice*
Tordoff, Harrison Bruce *retired zoologist, educator*
Tylevich, Alexander V. *sculptor, architect, educator*
Uckun, Fatih *research scientist, pediatric medicine educator*
Ursu, John Joseph *lawyer*
†Varin, Jason Ashley *community pharmacist, educator*
Vellenga, Kathleen Osborne *former state legislator*
†Ventura, Jesse *governor*
Wagner, Mary Margaret *library and information science educator*
Walton, Matt Savage *retired geologist, educator*
†Washburn, Donald Arthur *business executive*
†Wedl, Robert J. *state agency commissioner*
Wehrwein, Austin Carl *newspaper reporter, editor, writer*
Wendt, Hans W(erner) *life scientist*
Weschcke, Carl Llewellyn *publishing executive*
Willis, Bruce Donald *judge*
Wilson, Leonard Gilchrist *history of medicine educator*
Winthrop, Sherman *lawyer*
Wolff, Hugh MacPherson *music director, conductor*
Wollner, Thomas Edward *manufacturing company executive*
Wruble, Bernhardt Karp *lawyer*
Zander, Janet Adele *psychiatrist*
Zenker, Paul Nicolas *epidemiologist, pediatrician, medical director*
Zeyen, Richard John *plant pathology educator*
Zietlow, Ruth Ann *reference librarian*
Zimmerman, Susan G. *sales executive*
Zylstra, Stanley James *farmer, food company executive*

Saint Peter
Conlon, Kathryn Ann *county official*
Jodock, Darrell Harland *minister, religion educator*
Kyoore, Paschal Baylon *foreign language educator*
Leitch, Richard *political science educator*
Mc Rostie, Clair Neil *economics educator*
Nelsen, William Cameron *foundation executive, former college president*
Ostrom, Don *political science educator*
Taylor, Scott Maxfield *sales and marketing executive*
Turnbull, Charles Vincent *retired real estate broker*
Voight, Phillip Anthony *forensics educator*

Saipan
†Camacho, Tomas Aguon *bishop*

Sandstone
†Laposky, James Edward *pastor*
Muth, William Henry Harrison, Jr. *medical/surgical nurse*

Sartell
Dominik, John Julius *retired advertising company executive*

Savage
Bean, Glen Atherton *entrepreneur*
Luth, James Curtis *systems consultant*

Scandia
Borchert, John Robert *geography educator*
Speer, David James *retired public relations executive*

Shoreview
O'Brien, Thomas E. *educator, priest*

Shorewood
Rotunda, Joseph L. *retail and service company executive*

South Saint Paul
Pugh, Thomas Wilfred *lawyer*

Spring Park
Haun, James William *retired food company executive, consultant, chemical engineer*

Springfield
Haseleu, Roseann Marie *medical/surgical nurse*

Starbuck
Rapp, Gregory Paul *physician assistant*

Stillwater
Carlson, Norman A. *government official*
Francis, D. Max *healthcare management executive*
Horsch, Lawrence Leonard *venture capitalist, corporate revitalization executive*
Rescigno, Aldo *pharmacokinetics educator*

Two Harbors
Carlson, Brian Jay *health facility executive*
McMillion, John Macon *retired newspaper publisher*

Ulen
Harmon, Kay Yvonne *elementary education educator*

Upsala
Piasecki, David Alan *social studies educator*

Vadnais Heights
Polakiewicz, Leonard Anthony *foreign language and literature educator*

Vergas
Joyce, Michael Daniel *personal resource management therapist and consultant, neurolearning therapist*

Victoria
Courtney, Eugene Whitmal *computer company executive*

Virginia
Knabe, George William, Jr. *pathologist, educator*

Walker
Collins, Thomas William *caterer, consultant*

Warren
Kruger, Virginia Joy *health facility administrator lecturer*

Waseca
Frederick, Edward Charles *university official*

Wayzata
Andrews, Dennis *customer service professional*
Bergerson, David Raymond *lawyer*
Blodgett, Frank Caleb *retired food company executive*
Bremel, Thomas John *biochemist, researcher*
Hoffman, Gene D. *food company executive, consultant*
Jamrogiewicz, Debra Lynn *educational consultant*
Johnson, Eugene Laurence *lawyer*
Reutiman, Robert William, Jr. *lawyer*
Rich, Willis Frank, Jr. *banker*
Shannon, James Patrick *foundation consultant, retired food company executive*
Swanson, Donald Frederick *retired food company executive*
†Tripp, Thomas William *monetary specialist*
Waldera, Wayne Eugene *crisis management specialist*
Wyard, Vicki Shaw *investment and insurance company executive*

West Saint Paul
Cento, William Francis *retired newspaper editor*
Sittard, Herman Joseph *public relations executive, editor, retired*

White Bear Lake
Goldin, Martin Bruce *financial executive, consultant*
Gutchë, Gene *composer*
Holmen, Reynold Emanuel *chemist*
Mulcahy, Greg *English educator, writer*

Willmar
Hulstrand, George Eugene *lawyer*
Norling, Rayburn *food service executive*
Vander Aarde, Stanley Bernard *retired otolaryngologist*

Winona
Beyer, Mary Edel *primary education educator*
Beyer, Susan Kelley *school psychologist*
Boseker, Barbara Jean *education educator*
DeThomasis, Brother Louis *college president*
Dill, Ellen Renée *minister*
Haugh, Joyce Eileen Gallagher *education educator*
Holm, Joy Alice *psychology educator, art educator, artist, goldsmith*
Krueger, Darrell William *university president*
Nasstrom, Roy Richard *education educator, consultant*
Ramos, Lilian Eva Maria *foreign language educator*
White, Marjorie Mary *elementary school educator*

Woodbury
Benforado, David M. *environmental engineer*
Bicking, Merlin Kim Lambert *consulting chemist, medical products executive*
Darr, John *insurance company executive*
Vaughn, John Rolland *auditor*

Zumbrota
Post, Diana Constance *retired librarian*

MISSISSIPPI

Aberdeen
Davidson, Glen Harris *federal judge*
Davis, Jerry Arnold *judge*
†Houston, David Winston *federal judge*
Senter, Lyonel Thomas, Jr. *federal judge*

Alcorn State
Mitchell, Jackie Williams *university administrator, consultant*

Amory
Bryan, Wendell Hobdy, II (Hob Bryan) *senator*

Batesville
Cook, William Leslie, Jr. *lawyer*
Neal, Joseph Lee *vocational school educator*

Bay Saint Louis
Bernstein, Joseph *lawyer*
†Fabian, Lori Foltz *grant consultant, singer, actress, producer*
Frey, Gerard Louis *retired bishop*
Torguson, Marlin F. *entertainment company executive*
Zeile, Fred Carl *oceanographer, meteorologist*

Belzoni
Halbrook, Rita Robertshaw *artist, sculptor*

Biloxi
Brown, Sheba Ann *elementary education educator*
Cadney, Carolyn *secondary education educator*
Crumbaugh, James Charles *psychologist*
Deegen, Uwe Frederick *marine biologist*
Erickson, Georganne Morris *nursing administrator, nursing educator, psychiatric-mental health consultant*
†Gaines, Edward R. *federal judge*
Gex, Walter Joseph, III *federal judge*
†Hastings, Stanley *librarian, organist*
†Howze, Joseph Lawson Edward *bishop*
Love, James Sanford, III *communications executive*
Manners, Pamela Jeanne *middle school educator*
O'Barr, Bobby Gene, Sr. *lawyer*
Roper, John Marlin, Sr. *federal magistrate judge*
Weeks, Roland, Jr. *newspaper publisher*
Zocchi, Louis Joseph *product designer, game company executive*

Brandon
Buckley, Frank Wilson *newspaper executive*
Burch, Sharron Lee Stewart *woman's health nurse*
McCreery, James Allan *retired business services company executive*
Nash, Jimmy Ray *life insurance sales executive*
Okojie, Felix A. *research administrator*

Brookhaven
†Ledet, Henry Joseph *librarian*
Parker, Michael (Mike Parker) *former congressman*
†Wells, Peggy Lynn *educator*

Calhoun City
†Spencer, Thomas M. *journalist*

Carriere
Woodmansee, Glenn Edward *employee relations executive*

Clarksdale
Cline, Beth Marie *school psychologist*
Curtis, Chester Harris *lawyer, retired bank executive*
Magdovitz, Lawrence Maynard *real estate executive, lawyer*
Walters, William Lee *accountant*
Williams, Kenneth Ogden *farmer*

Cleveland
Alexander, William Brooks *lawyer, former state senator*
Baker-Branton, Camille *counselor, educator*
Taylor, Donna Buescher *marriage and family therapist*
Wyatt, Forest Kent *university president*

Clinton
Bigelow, Martha Mitchell *retired historian*
Bryant, William Bruce *minister*
Eaves, Dorothy Ann Greene *music educator*
Eaves, Richard Glen *history educator, dean*
Jarnagin, Teresa Ellis *educator, nursing administrator*
McWilliams, Anne Washburn *retired journalist, writer*
Montgomery, Keith Norris, Sr. *insurance executive, state legislator*
Teague, Karen Lee Hawkins *nurse, administrator*
Whitlock, Betty *secondary education educator*

Columbia
Simmons, Miriam Quinn *state legislator*

Columbus
Davidson, Hubert James, Jr. *lawyer, educator*
Holt, Robert Ezel *data processing executive*
Hudnall, Jarrett, Jr. *management and marketing educator*
Kaye, Samuel Harvey *architect, educator*
†Labensky, Sarah Ross *culinary educator*
Rent, Clyda Stokes *academic administrator*

Diamondhead
Jones, Lawrence David *insurance and medical consultant*

Fayette
La Salle, Arthur Edward *historic foundation executive*

Gautier
Egerton, Charles Pickford *anatomy and physiology educator*

Greenville
†Bogen, Eugene M. *federal judge*
Keating, Bern *writer, journalist*
Martin, Andrew Ayers *lawyer, physician, educator*

Greenwood
Evans, Randall Dean, Jr. *interior designer*
Jones, Carolyn Ellis *publisher, retired employment agency and business service company executive*

Grenada
†Kincaide, Donald Lewis *political science educator*
Thomas, Ouida Power *music educator*

Gulfport
Branan, Bradley Thomas *journalist*
Dickerson, Monar Steve *city official*
Easton, Jill Johanna *state official*
Freret, René Joseph *minister*
Hash, John Frank *broadcasting executive*
Hewes, William Gardner, III *insurance executive, real estate agent, legislator*
Hopkins, Alben Norris *lawyer*
Mc Call, Jerry Chalmers *retired government official*
Olivier, Michael Joseph *economic development executive*
Perez, Jeffrey Joseph *optometrist*
Pickering, Shelbie Jean *mortgage loan executive*
Russell, Dan M., Jr. *federal judge*
Slade, Jeannye Zo *public relations executive*
Swetman, Glenn Robert *English language educator, poet*
Thatcher, George Robert *banker, columnist, author*
†Williams, Benjamin John *poet, playwright*

Hamilton
Ward, Robert Earl, Jr. *chemical engineer, chemical company administrator*

Hattiesburg
†Barthelme, Steven *English educator*
Bilbo, Linda Sue Holston *home health nurse*
Burrus, John N(ewell) *sociology educator*
Chain, Bobby Lee *electrical contractor, former mayor*
Culberson, James O. *retired rehabilitation educator*
Davis, Charles Raymond *political scientist, educator*
†Duhon, David Lester *business educator, management consultant*
Dyess, Joseph Dwight *commercial banker*
Fournier, Donald Joseph, Jr. *mechanical engineer, consultant, educator*
Giles, Michael Comer *physical education educator, aquatics consultant*
†Guirola, Louis, Jr. *federal judge*
Johnson, Ellen Randel *real estate broker*
Lucas, Aubrey Keith *retired academic administrator*
Martin, Matthew E. *advertising and marketing executive*
Noonkester, James Ralph *retired college president*
Pickering, Charles W., Sr. *federal judge*
Saucier, Gene Duane *state legislator*
Saucier Lundy, Karen *college dean, educator*
Taylor, David Neil *minister*
Watkins, Cathy Collins *corporate purchasing agent*

Hazlehurst
Nelson, Alberta Catchings *secondary education educator*

Hernando
Brown, William A. *lawyer*

Holly Springs
Beckley, David Lenard *academic administrator*

Houston
Griffin, T. David *family physician, pharmacist*

Hurley
Ross, Donald Paul, Jr. *robotics design executive*

Indianola
†Horton, W. Mike *financial company executive*
Matthews, David *clergyman*

Itta Bena
†Baral, Ram Chandra *educator, special education*
Harbor, Kingsley Okoro *communications and journalism educator, researcher*
Ware, William Levi *physical education educator, researcher*
Washington, Barbara J. *English educator*

Iuka
Crawford, Robert Roy *rail company executive*

Jackson
Achord, James Lee *gastroenterologist, educator*
†Anderson, James V. *state agency administrator*
†Balentine, William (Ray) *civil engineer*
Ball, Carroll Raybourne *anatomist, medical educator, researcher*
Barbour, William H., Jr. *federal judge*
Barksdale, Rhesa Hawkins *federal judge*
Barnett, Robert Glenn *lawyer*
Bennett, Marshall Goodloe, Jr. *state official, lawyer*
Black, D(eWitt) Carl(isle), Jr. *lawyer*
Bloom, Sherman *pathologist, educator*
Bobo, Len Davis *musician*
Boronow, Richard Carlton *gynecologist, educator*
Broome, Kathryn *secondary education educator*
Burrow, William Hollis, II *dermatologist*
Chambers-Mangum, Fransenna Ethel *special education educator*
Clark, David Wright *lawyer*
Clark, Eric C. *state official*
Conerly, Albert Wallace *academic administrator, dean*
Corlew, John Gordon *lawyer*
Creel, Sue Cloer *secondary education educator*
Cruse, Julius Major, Jr. *pathologist, educator*
Currie, Edward Jones, Jr. *lawyer*
Currier, Robert David *neurologist*
Duncan, Jennings Ligon *minister*
Durr, Eisenhower *protective services official*
Ebbers, Bernard J. *communications executive*
†Ellington, Edward *federal judge*
Elliott, Mitchell Lee *financial analyst*
Fordice, Kirk (Daniel Kirkwood Fordice, Jr.) *governor, construction company executive, engineer*
Freeland, Alan Edward *orthopedic surgery educator, physician*
Fuselier, Louis Alfred *lawyer*
Galloway, Patricia Kay *systems analyst, ethnohistorian*
†Garriga, Mark *state government administrator*
Gordon, Granville Hollis *church official*
Gray, Duncan Montgomery, Jr. *retired bishop*
Guyton, Arthur Clifton *physician, educator*
Hammond, Frank Jefferson, III *lawyer*
Harmon, George Marion *college president*
Hosemann, C. Delbert, Jr. *lawyer*
†Houck, William Russell *bishop*
Houston, Gerry Ann *oncologist*
Howard, William Percy *physician*
Hughes, Byron William *lawyer, oil exploration company executive*
†Ingram, James *state agency administrator*
Irby, Stuart Charles, Jr. *construction company executive*
†Johnson, Harvey, Jr. *mayor*
Jolly, E. Grady *federal judge*
Julian, Michael *grocery company executive*
Khansur, Tawfiq Iftekhar *physician, researcher, educator*
King, Kenneth Vernon, Jr. *pharmacist*
Larsen, Samuel Harry *minister, educator*
Laster, Rhonda Renée *juvenile probation/parole officer*
†Layzell, Thomas D. *academic administrator*
Lee, Tom Stewart *judge*
Leszczynski, Jerzy Ryszard *chemistry educator, researcher*
Lewis, Larry Lisle *human resources specialist company executive*
Lewis, Robert Edwin, Jr. *pathology immunology educator, researcher*
Lilley, Evelyn Lewis *operating room nurse*
Lilly, Thomas Gerald *lawyer*
†Lindsay, Susan Ruchti *school principal*
Malloy, James Matthew *managed care executive, health care consultant*
McKnight, William Edwin *minister*
McRae, Charles R. *state supreme court justice*
Mitchell, Dennis Jerrell *history educator, humanities consultant*
Moize, Jerry Dee *lawyer, government official*
Moore, Mike *state attorney general*
Musgrove, David Ronald *state official*
Musgrove, Ronnie *state official*
†Nicols, Alfred G., Jr. *federal judge*
Palmer, John N. *communications executive*
Payne, Mary Libby *judge*
Pearce, Colman Cormac *conductor, pianist, composer*
Pearce, David Harry *biomedical engineer*
Pennington, Andrew *women's basketball coach*
Petty, David *newspaper editor*
Phillips, George Landon *prosecutor*
Pigott, Brad *prosecutor*
Pittman, Edwin Lloyd *state supreme court justice*
Poole, Galen Vincent *surgeon, educator, researcher*
Prather, Lenore Loving *state supreme court chief justice*
Price, Alfred Lee *lawyer, mining company executive*
Ranck, Edward L. *state agency administrator*
†Rankin, William Duncan *theology educator*
Ray, H. M. *lawyer*
Read, Virginia Hall *biochemistry educator*
Risley, Rod Alan *education association executive*
Roberts, James L., Jr. *state supreme court justice*
Rogers, Oscar Allan, Jr. *college president*
Russell, Robert Pritchard *ophthalmologist*
Sardin, James Earl *school system administrator*
Sewell, Charles Haslett *banker*
†Shearin, Robert Patrick Noel *physician, medical administrator*
Shirley, Aaron *pediatrician*
†Simmons, Donna Addkison *political consultant*
Smith, Edgar Eugene *biochemist, university administrator*
Smith, James W., Jr. *state supreme court justice*
Sneed, Raphael Corcoran *physiatrist, pediatrician*
†Spell, Lester James *state agency administrator*
Stovall, Jerry (Coleman Stovall) *insurance company executive*
Suess, James Francis *retired psychiatry educator*
Sugg, Robert Perkins *former state supreme court justice*
Sullivan, John Magruder, II *government affairs administrator*
Sullivan, Michael David *state supreme court justice*
Sullivan, Scott D. *communications executive*
†Sumner, James C. *federal judge*
Tchounwou, Paul Bernard *environmental health specialist, educator*
Thigpen, James Tate *physician, oncology educator*
Thornton, Larry Lee *psychotherapist, author, educator*
Thrash, Edsel E. *educational administrator*
Tourney, Garfield *psychiatrist, educator*
Tuck, Amy *state senator, lawyer*
Vanderleest, Dirk *airport executive*
Walcott, Dexter Winn *allergist*
Welty, Eudora *author*
West, Carol Catherine *law educator*
Whitsett, Paul Timothy, Jr. (Tim Whitsett) *executive*
†Wilbur, Robert W. (Robbie) *state official*
Williams, Jerrie Sue Dockery *nurse, administrator*
Wilson, William Roberts, Jr. (Bob Wilson) *lawyer, apparel executive*
Wingate, Henry Travillion *federal judge*
Winter, William Forrest *former governor, lawyer*
Wise, Robert Powell *lawyer*
Wolfe, Mildred Nungester *artist*
Woodward, Wayne William *librarian, minister*

Keesler AFB
Linehan, Allan Douglas *prosthodontist*
†Locker, Dan L. *career officer*
†Pelak, Andrew J., Jr. *military officer*
Rigdon, David Tedrick *air force officer, geneticist, director*

Kosciusko
Kearley, F. Furman *minister, religious educator, magazine editor*
Shoemaker, William C. *journalist*

Laurel
Lacey, Peeler Grayson *diagnostic radiologist*

Long Beach
Burnham, Tom *state school system administrator*
Horton, Jerry Smith *minister*
Kanagy, Steven Albert *foundation administrator*
White, Edith Roberta Shoemake *elementary school educator*
Williams, James Orrin *university administrator, educator*

Lorman
Bristow, Clinton, Jr. *academic administrator*
Ezekwe, Michael Obi *animal science educator*
Walker, Shirley *university women's basketball coach*

Louisville
Hill, Wayne Thomas *school administrator, minister*

Lumberton
Tonry, Richard Alvin *lawyer, pecan farmer*

Macon
Johnson, Rolanda Lanetta *medical/surgical nurse, educator*

Madison
Dean, Jack Pearce *retired insurance company executive*
Hays, Mary Katherine Jackson *civic worker*
Hiatt, Jane Crater *arts agency administrator*
Morrison, Francis Secrest *physician*

Magnolia
Coney, Elaine Marie *English and foreign languages educator*
Lampton, Lucius Marion *physician, editor*

Mathiston
Hutchins, J. Mark *university administrator*
Maddox, Marilyn Coleman *literature and composition educator*

Mc Cool
Miller, Charlotte Faye *speech pathologist*

Meridian
Blackwell, Cecil *science association executive*
Church, George Millord *real estate executive*
Dear, Dana Lovorn *critical care nurse*
Eppes, Walter W., Jr. *lawyer*
Hoskins, Mable Rose *secondary education educator, English language educator*
Phillips, Patricia Jeanne *retired school administrator, consultant*
Thomas, Kenneth Eugene *auditor*

Mississippi State
Ahmad, Shair *mathematics educator*
Alley, Earl Gifford *chemist*
Bumgardner, Joel David *biomedical engineer, educator*
Cliett, Charles Buren *aeronautical engineer, educator, academic administrator*
Clynch, Edward John *political science educator, researcher*
Cooper, Robert Carl, Jr. *veterinary medicine educator*
Fanning, Sharon *university head basketball coach*
Gunter, John Edward *dean*
Hawkins, Merrill Morris, Sr. *college administrator*
Hughes, Patricia Newman *academic administrator*
Hutenstine, Marian Louise *journalism educator*
Jenkins, Johnie Norton *research geneticist, research administrator*
Lowery, Charles Douglas *history educator, academic administrator*
Mabry, Donald Joseph *university administrator, history educator*
Martin, Edward Curtis, Jr. *landscape architect, educator*
McGilberry, Joe Herman, Sr. *university administrator*
Nash, Henry Warren *marketing educator*
Nelson, Rachael Aine *mechanical engineering*
†Nybakken, Elizabeth *educator*
Reddy, Kambham Raja *plant physiology educator*
Taylor, Clayborne Dudley *engineering educator*
Thompson, Joe Floyd *aerospace engineer, educator*
Wall, Diane Eve *political science educator*
Watson, James Ray, Jr. *education educator*
White, Charles H. *food science and technology educator*
†Wilkinson, Dehlia Rae *educator*

Monticello
Allen, Frank Carroll *retired banker*

Moss Point
Reynolds, Margaret Jensen *quality assurance professional*

Myrtle
Pirkle, Estus Washington *minister*

Natchez
Barnett, James F., Jr. *historic properties and archives administrator*
Bramlette, David C., III *federal judge*
Dunnell, Robert Chester *archaeologist, educator*
Harris, W. D. *city housing inspector, small business owner*
Hutchins, Georgia Cameron *critical care nurse, nursing educator*

Nesbit
Berti, Phyllis Mae *health information management specialist*

Nettleton
Hairald, Mary Payne *vocational education educator, coordinator*
Newell, Harold Joe *quality assurance engineer*

Noxapater
Sumner, Margaret Elizabeth *elementary school educator*

Ocean Springs
Lee, Kathleen Mary *administration and nursing executive*
Lorenz, Ronald Theodore *manufacturing executive*
Luckey, Alwyn Hall *lawyer*
McNulty, Matthew Francis, Jr. *health sciences and health services administrator, educator, university administrator, consultant, horse and cattle breeder*
Parker, Rebecca Mary *special education facility administrator, educator*
Sims, Thomas Auburn *retired shipbuilding company executive*

Olive Branch
Frischenmeyer, Michael Leo *sales executive*

Oxford
Alexander, S. Allan *lawyer*
Biggers, Neal Brooks, Jr. *federal judge*
†Buchanan, Calvin D. (Buck Buchanan) *prosecutor*
Crews, David *protective services official*
Duke, Stephen Oscar *physiologist, researcher, educator*
†Fox, Elizabeth Talbert *writer, artist*
Johnson, Joyce Thedford *state agency administrator*
Lewis, Ronald Wayne *lawyer*
Moorhead, Sylvester Andrew *education educator retired*
Rayburn, S. T. *lawyer*
Walton, Gerald Wayne *retired university official*

Pascagoula
Chapel, Theron Theodore *quality assurance engineer*
Corben, Herbert Charles *physicist, educator*
†Horowitz, Michael Dory *cardiothoracic surgeon*

Irving, Thomas Ballantine *retired Spanish language educator, consultant*
Krebs, Robert Preston *lawyer*
McKee, Ronald Gene *vocational education educator*
Smith, Donald Vaughan *artist, educator*
†Touart, George F. *county official*

Pass Christian
Clark, John Walter, Jr. *shipping company executive*
McCardell, James Elton *retired naval officer*

Perkinston
†Mellinger, Barry Lee *community college president, vocational educator*

Philadelphia
Molpus, Dick H. *resource management company executive*

Picayune
Lowrie, Allen *geologist, oceanographer*

Pontotoc
Roberts, Rose Harrison *social services administrator, consultant*

Raleigh
Price, Tommye Jo Ensminger *community health nurse*

Ridgeland
Dye, Bradford Johnson, Jr. *lawyer, former state official*
O'Neill, Paul John *retired psychology educator*

Robinsonville
Askins, Arthur James *accountant, finance management and auditing executive*

Ruleville
Cosue, Lamberto Gutierrez, III *internist*

Southaven
†Flowers, Merle G. *legislative staff member*

Starkville
Carley, Charles Team, Jr. *mechanical engineer*
Ford, Robert MacDonald, III *architect, educator*
George, Ernest Thornton, III *financial consultant*
Gregg, Billy Ray *seed industry executive, consultant*
Jacob, Paul Bernard, Jr. *electrical engineering educator*
Knight, Aubrey Kevin *vocational education educator*
†Little, Randall Dean *agricultural economics educator, consultant*
Martin, Theodore Krinn *former university administrator (deceased)*
Rigsby, John Thomas, Jr. *accounting educator*
Roberts, Willard John *secondary school educator*
Thomas, Garnett Jett *accountant*
Townsend, John M. *education educator*
Wakeman, Olivia Van Horn *marketing professional*
Wolverton, Robert Earl *classics educator*
Yoste, Charles Todd *lawyer*

Stennis Space Center
Corbin, James H. *executive engineer, meteorologist, oceanographer*
Estess, Roy S. *federal agency administrator*
Hurlburt, Harley Ernest *oceanographer*
Sprouse, Susan Rae Moore *human resources specialist*

Stoneville
Ranney, Carleton David *plant pathology researcher, administrator*

Sunflower
Powell, Anice Carpenter *retired librarian*

Taylorsville
Dilmore, Cindy Corley *special education educator*
Windham, Velma Lee Ainsworth *writer, poet*

Thaxton
†Dean, Michael P. *dean*

Tishomingo
Poole, Wanda Sue *quality control inspector*

Tougaloo
Johnson, Richard Carl *philosophy educator, humanities educator*
†Ward, Jerry Washington *English language educator*

Tupelo
Armistead, John Grayson *journalist*
Bullard, Rickey Howard *podiatric physician, surgeon*
Bush, Fred Marshall, Jr. *lawyer*
Moffett, T(errill) K(ay) *lawyer*
Patterson, Aubrey Burns, Jr. *banker*
Ramage, Martis Donald, Jr. *banker*
Zurawski, Jeanette *rehabilitation services professional*

Tylertown
Mord, Irving Conrad, II *lawyer*

University
Aldy, Ron *women's basketball coach*
Bass, Jack *journalism educator*
Chen, Wei-Yin *chemical engineering educator, researcher*
Golding, Alan Charles *English educator*
Hall, J(ames) R(obert) *English educator*
Horton, Thomas Edward, Jr. *mechanical engineering educator*
Jordan, Winthrop Donaldson *historian, educator*
Keiser, Edmund Davis, Jr. *biologist, educator*
Khayat, Robert Conrad *chancellor*
Kiger, Joseph Charles *history educator*
Landon, Michael de Laval *historian, educator*
Lindgren, Carl Edwin *educational consultant, antiquarian, photographer, priest*
Martin, Jeanette St. Clair *adult education educator*
Meador, John Milward, Jr. *university dean*
Roach, David Giles *information technology administrator*
Shelnutt, Gregory William *sculptor, educator*
Smith, Allie Maitland *university dean*
Uddin, Waheed *civil engineer, educator*

Vicksburg
†Anderson, Phillip R. *career officer*
Bagby, Rose Mary *pollution control administrator, chemist*
Briuer, Elke Moersch *editor*
Hoover, Deborah *critical care, medical and surgical nurse*
Marcuson, William F. *research administrator*
Mather, Bryant *research administrator*
Mazzeo-Merkle, Linda Lou *legal administrator*
McRae, John Leonidas *civil engineer*
Richardson, Jeffrey Gunn *landscape architect*
Stafford, James Polk, Jr. *civil engineer*

Walls
Jones, Yvonne Dolores *social worker*

Waveland
Romagosa, Elmo Lawrence *retired clergyman, retired editor*

Waynesboro
Dickerson, Marie Harvison *nurse anesthetist*

Whitfield
Kliesch, William Frank *physician*
Morton, James Irwin *hospital administrator*
Whitehead, Zelma Kay *special education educator*

Yazoo City
Arnold, David Walker *chemical company executive, engineer*
Brown, Marion Lipscomb, Jr. *publisher, retired chemical company executive*

MISSOURI

Albany
Noble, Cheryl A. *library director*

Alton
Roe, Fredrick Evan *writer, farmer*

Arnold
Freukes, Patricia E. *pediatrics nurse, nursing supervisor*
†McGraw, Bryan Kelly *financial company executive*

Arrow Rock
Bollinger, Michael *artistic director*

Ash Grove
Johnson, Iver Christian *valuation company executive*

Ashland
Flink, Jane Duncan *publisher*

Ava
Murray, Delbert Milton *manufacturing engineer*

Ballwin
Ackerson, Charles Stanley *minister, social worker*
Anderson, James Donald *mining company executive*
Cornell, William Daniel *mechanical engineer*
Haller, Karen Sue *writer*
†Harris, Terry Allen *associate principal*
Marcus, Arthur H. *bank executive*
Sidoti, Daniel R. *food technologist*
Stevens, James Edward *chemistry educator*
Stevens, Julie Ann *peri-operative nurse*

Belton
Blim, Richard Don *retired pediatrician*

Bloomfield
Ferrell, Paul Cleveland *author*

Blue Springs
Accurso, Catherine Josephine *asset manager*
†Brock, Linda M. *educator*
Foudree, Charles M. *financial executive*
Heller, John L., II *food products executive*
Olsson, Björn Eskil *railroad supply company executive*
Reed, Tony Norman *aviation company executive*
†Rice, Durwin Dan *artist, art dealer*
†Snyder, James Robert *protective services official, educator*
Wood, Cynthia L. *secondary education educator*

Bolivar
Brown, Autry *psychology educator, clergyman*
†Coen, Cheryl Lynn *secretary*
Helton, Terry L. *city administrator*

Boonville
Gehm, David Eugene *construction and environmental management executive*
McVicker, Mary Ellen Harshbarger *museum director, art history educator*
Schuster, Joyce Anne *curriculum director*

Bourbon
Heitsch, Leona Mason *artist, writer*

Branson
Bradley, Leon Charles *musician, educator, consultant*
Burch, Lori Ann *obstetrics nurse*
Tillis, Mel(vin) *musician, songwriter*

Bridgeton
Asma, Lawrence Francis *priest*
Brauer, Stephen Franklin *manufacturing company executive*
Campbell, Anita Joyce *computer company executive*
Delaney, Robert Vernon *logistics and transportation executive*
Faulk, Marshall William *professional football player*
Hemming, Bruce Clark *microbiologist*
Johnson, Kevin Todd *physician*
Kenison, Raymond Robert *fraternal organization administrator, director*
†Piacentino, Marcia *advertising executive*
Shaw, John *sports association administrator*

Brookfield
Wild, Stacie Ann *vocational counselor*

Burlington Junction
McLaughlin, Lana Gale *business educator, office manager*

Camdenton
Clark, Mark Jeffrey *paralegal, researcher*
Decker, Malcolm Doyle *insurance agent*
DeShazo, Marjorie White *occupational therapist*
Hosman, Sharon *elementary education educator*

Cameron
Ervans, Mary Sue (Tripolino) *health facility administrator*

Canton
Glover, Albert Downing *retired veterinarian*
†Howe, Sandra Jo *library director*

Cape Girardeau
Bir, Michelle Marie *sales executive*
Blackwelder, Richard E(liot) *entomologist, zoology educator, archivist*
†Blanton, Lewis M. *federal judge*
Farrington, Thomas Richard *financial executive, investment advisor*
Gerber, Mitchel *political scientist, educator*
Hathaway, Ruth Ann *chemist*
Haugland, Susan Warrell *education educator*
†Hilty, Peter Daniel *retired English educator, poet*
Hoffman, Steven James *historian, educator*
†Jedan, Dieter *language educator*
Keys, Paul Ross *university dean*
Lowes, Albert Charles *lawyer*
McMahan, Gale Ann Scivally *education educator*
McManaman, Kenneth Charles *lawyer*
Nickell, Franklin Delano *historian*
†Raschlee, Debrah *English educator*
†Reinmann, Carol Sue *elementary educator*
†Schulte, Tom *public information officer*
Smallwood, Glenn Walter, Jr. *utility marketing management executive*

Carrollton
Lysne, Allen Bruce *laboratory director*

Carthage
Blackwood, Gary Lyle *author*
Coffield, Mary Eleanor *speech clinician, educator*
Jefferies, Robert Aaron, Jr. *diversified manufacturing executive, lawyer*

Caruthersville
Puangsuvan, Somporn *surgeon, consultant*

Cassville
Bates, Reitta Ione *retired mental health nurse*

Centralia
†Adams, Barbara Karen *special education teacher, real estate agent*
Harmon, Robert Wayne *electrical engineering executive*

Chaffee
Kitchen, Ellen Carleen *municipal official*

Charleston
Cassell, Lucille Richardson *small business owner*

Chesterfield
Allen, Linda Graves *air medical transport company executive*
Armstrong, Theodore Morelock *financial executive*
Baumann, Carol Kay *clinical nurse specialist*
Biebel, Curt Fred, Jr. *dentist*
Carpenter, Will Dockery *chemical company executive*
Coffin, Richard Keith *lawyer*
de Figueiredo, Mario Pacheco *food scientist*
Denneen, John Paul *lawyer*
Frawley, Thomas Francis *retired physician*
Hale, David Clovis *former state representative*
Handelman, Alice Samuels *public relations professional, writer, former social worker*
Henry, Roy Monroe *financial planner*
Hier, Marshall David *lawyer*
Higgins, Edward Aloysius *retired newspaper editor*
Hunter, Harlen Charles *orthopedic surgeon*
Johnston, Marilyn Frances-Meyers *physician, medical educator*
Kelly, James Joseph *printing company executive*
King, William Terry *retired manufacturing company executive*
Landram, Christina Louella *librarian*
Levin, Marvin Edgar *physician*
Liggett, Hiram Shaw, Jr. *retired diversified industry financial executive*
Malvern, Donald *retired aircraft manufacturing company executive*
Matros, Larisa Grigoryevna *medical philosophy researcher, writer*
McCarthy, Paul Fenton *aerospace executive, former naval officer*
Morse, Stacey Ann *art studio owner*
Palazzi, Joseph L(azarro) *manufacturing executive*
Pollihan, Thomas Henry *lawyer*
Pylipow, Stanley Ross *retired manufacturing company executive*
Robinson, Patricia Elaine *women's health nurse practitioner*
Schierholz, William Francis, Jr. *real estate developer*
Schwind, Wanda Ruth *retail executive*
Selfridge, George Dever *retired dentist, retired naval officer*
Willis, Frank Edward *retired air force officer*
Yardley, John Finley *aerospace engineer*

Chula
Murphy, Jenny Lewis *special education educator*

Clayton
Ball, Kenneth Leon *manufacturing company executive, organizational development consultant*
Belz, Mark *lawyer*
Beracha, Barry Harris *food company executive*
Buechler, Bradley Bruce *plastic processing company executive, accountant*
Christner, Theodore Carroll *architect*
Hall, Carl Loren *electrical distribution executive*
Heininger, S(amuel) Allen *retired chemical company executive*
Keyes, Marion Alvah, IV *manufacturing company executive*
Klarich, David John *lawyer, state senator*
Malnassy, Louis Sturges *public relations counselor*
Marcus, Larry David *broadcasting executive*
McCann-Turner, Robin Lee *psychoanalyst*
Mohrman, Henry J(oe), Jr. *lawyer, investment manager*
Nagelvoort, Charles Wendell *financial advisor*
Onken, Henry Dralle *plastic surgeon*
Preuss, James Eugene *human resources professional*
Ritter, Robert Thornton *lawyer*
Ross, E. Earl *small business owner*
Vecchiotti, Robert Anthony *management and organizational consultant*

Clinton
†Kelsay, David Roland *chemist*

Columbia
Adams, Algalee Pool *college dean, art educator*
Alexander, Martha Sue *librarian*
Alexander, Thomas Benjamin *history educator*
Allen, William Cecil *physician, educator*
Almony, Robert Allen, Jr. *librarian, businessman*
Anderson, Donald Kennedy, Jr. *English educator*
Archer, Stephen Murphy *retired theater educator*
Basu, Asit Prakas *statistician*
Bauman, John E., Jr. *chemistry educator*
Beem, John Kelly *mathematician, educator*
Biddle, Bruce Jesse *social psychologist, educator*
Bien, Joseph Julius *philosophy educator*
Blaine, Edward H. *health science administrator, educator*
Blevins, Dale Glenn *agronomy educator*
Boedeker, Ben Harold *anesthesiologist, educator*
Breimyer, Harold Frederick *agricultural economist*
Brenner, Donald John *journalism educator*
Brent, Ruth Stumpe *design educator, researcher, educator*
Brinegar, Elizabeth Anne *critical care nurse, educator*
Brouder, Gerald T. *academic administrator*
Brown, Olen Ray *medical microbiology research educator*
†Bumas, E. Shaskan *writer, educator*
Bunn, Ronald Freeze *political science educator, lawyer*
Colwill, Jack Marshall *physician, educator*
Constantinescu, Gheorghe M. *veterinarian*
†Cotton, Karen Theresa *audiologist*
Cunningham, Milamari Antoinella *anesthesiologist*
Darrah, Larry Lynn *plant breeder*
David, John Dewood *biology educator*
Davis, James O(thello) *physician, educator*
Decker, Wayne Leroy *meteorologist, educator*
DeJarnette, Shirley Shea *treasurer*
Dolliver, Robert Henry *psychology educator*
Duncan, Donald Pendleton *retired forestry educator*
Eggers, George William Nordholtz, Jr. *anesthesiologist, educator*
Ethington, Raymond Lindsay *geology educator, researcher*
Finkelstein, Richard Alan *microbiologist*
Fisch, William Bales *lawyer, educator*
Fluharty, Charles William *policy research institute director, consultant, researcher*
Frey, Jeffery Paul *internist, geriatrician*
Frisby, James Curtis *agricultural engineering educator*
George, Melvin Douglas *retired university president*
Goodrich, James William *historian, association executive*
Gysbers, Norman Charles *education educator*
Hardin, Christopher Demarest *medical educator*
Hensley, Elizabeth Catherine *nutritionist, educator*
Hess, Darla Bakersmith *cardiologist, educator*
Hess, Leonard Wayne *obstetrician gynecologist, perinatologist*
Hillman, Richard Ephraim *pediatrician, educator*
Horner, Winifred Bryan *humanities educator, researcher, consultant, writer*
Ignoffo, Carlo Michael *insect pathologist-virologist*
James, Elizabeth Joan Plogsted *pediatrician, educator*
Jones, James Wilson *physician, cell biologist, ethicist*
Jones, William McKendrey *language professional, educator*
Keith, Everett Earnest *educator, education administrator*
Khojasteh, Ali *medical oncologist, hematologist*
Kierscht, Marcia Selland *academic administrator, psychologist*
Kilgore, Randall Freeman *health information services administrator*
Knies, Paul Henry *former life insurance company executive*
†Koditschek, Theodore *historian, educator*
Lago, Mary McClelland *English language educator, author*
†Lambert, Edward Charles *journalism educator, broadcaster*
Larson, Sidney *art educator, artist, writer, painting conservator*
Longo, Daniel Robert *health services researcher, medical educator*
Loory, Stuart Hugh *journalist*
LoPiccolo, Joseph *psychologist, educator, author*
Lubensky, Earl Henry *diplomat, anthropologist*
Mays, William Gay, II *lawyer, real estate developer*
McDonald, Annette Howard *mental health nurse*
Miller, Kerby A. *history educator*
Miller, Paul Ausborn *adult education educator*
Mitchell, Roger Lowry *retired agronomy educator*
Morehouse, Georgia Lewis *microbiologist, researcher*
Morehouse, Lawrence Glen *veterinarian, educator*
†Morrison, Minion K. C. *political science educator*
Mullen, Edward John, Jr. *Spanish language educator*
Multon, Karen Diane *psychologist, educator*
†Muratore, Mary Jo *humanities educator*
†Nelson, C. Jerry *agronomy educator*
Nichols, Walter Kirt *surgeon*
Nikolai, Loren Alfred *accounting educator, author*
Nolan, Michael Francis *college program director*
Northway, Wanda I. *realty company executive*
O'Connor, John Thomas *civil engineering educator*
†Oro, John J. *neurosurgeon*
Overby, Osmund Rudolf *art historian, educator*
Pacheco, Manuel Trinidad *academic administrator*
Palo, Nicholas Edwin *professional society administrator*
Parrigin, Elizabeth Ellington *lawyer*
Payne, Thomas L. *university official*
Perkoff, Gerald Thomas *physician, educator*
Perry, Michael Clinton *physician, medical educator, academic administrator*
Petersen, George James *educational administration educator*
†Pierce, Glenn Palen *language educator*

Plummer, Patricia Lynne Moore chemistry and physics educator
Poehlmann, Carl John agronomist, researcher
Pringle, Oran Allan mechanical and aerospace engineering educator
Puckett, C. Lin plastic surgeon, educator
Rabjohn, Norman chemistry educator emeritus
Ratti, Ronald Andrew economics educator
†Reahr, Terrye Lee nurse
Rhyne, James Jennings condensed matter physicist
Robins, Betty Dashew antiques and arts dealer
Rowlett, Ralph Morgan archaeologist, educator
†Rueda, Ana M. Spanish literature educator
Salter, Christopher Lord geography educator
Sanders, Keith Page journalism educator
Schrader, Keith William mathematician
Schwabe, John Bennett, II lawyer
Schwartz, Richard Brenton English language educator, university dean, writer
See, William Mitchel (W. Mike See) cardiovascular and thoracic surgeon
Shelton, Kevin L. geology educator
Silver, Donald surgeon, educator
Southwick, Christopher Lyn anesthesiologist
Stack, Frank Huntington painter, educator
Staley, Marsha Lynn elementary school educator, principal
Stewart, Bobby Gene laboratory director
Stockglausner, William George accountant
Strickland, Arvarh Eunice history educator
Thompson, John Edward small appliance manufacturing company executive
Timberlake, Charles Edward history educator
Twaddle, Andrew Christian sociology educator
Unklesbay, Athel Glyde geologist, educator
Viswanath, Dabir Srikantiah chemical engineer
Vogt, Albert Ralph forester, educator, program director
Wagner, Joseph Edward veterinarian, educator
Wagner, William Burdette business educator
Wallach, Barbara Price classicist, educator
Weisman, Gary Andrew biochemist
Weiss, James Moses Aaron psychiatrist, educator
Welliver, Warren Dee lawyer, retired state supreme court justice
Westbrook, James Edwin lawyer, educator
Whitman, Dale Alan lawyer, law educator
Williams, Frederick statistics educator
Witten, David Melvin radiology educator
Woelfel, Stacey William news director
Wright, Farroll Tim statistics educator, researcher
Yanders, Armon Frederick biological sciences educator, research administrator
Yarwood, Dean Lesley political science educator
Yasuda, Hirotsugu Koge chemical engineering professor
†Yonker, John Joseph clergyman
Youmans, William Barton physiologist
Zemke, Deborah Esther illustrator
Zguta, Russell history educator

Conception
†Neenan, Benedict Thomas academic administrator, rector

Crane
Rose, Terri Kaye obstetrical gynecological nurse practitioner, forensic exam nurse

Creve Coeur
Bockserman, Robert Julian chemist
Helfrich, Thomas Stough healthcare company executive
Luzio, Timothy Joseph protective services official
Nicely, Constance Marie paralegal, physician recruiter, medical consultant

Crystal City
Parish, Brenda Louise telemetry nurse

Cuba
Work, Bruce Van Syoc business consultant

Des Peres
Mason, Jane Musselman artist

Dexter
Owens, Debra Ann chiropractor

Dittmer
Miller, Bertin priest, social administrator

Drexel
Williams, Shirley J. daycare provider, educator, writer

Eagleville
Hendren, Linda Sue secondary education educator

Earth City
Anderhalter, Oliver Frank educational organization executive
Frontiere, Georgia professional football team executive
Kroenke, Stan sports association administrator

Ellisville
Meiner, Sue Ellen Thompson gerontologist, nursing educator and researcher

Eureka
Lindsey, Susan Lyndaker zoologist
Warren, Kathryn Beckcom elementary school educator

Excelsior Springs
Berrey, Robert Wilson, III retired judge, lawyer
Loomis, Robert Arthur retired sales executive
Mitchell, Earl Wesley clergyman

Farmington
Lees, William Glenwood finance executive, retail executive
†Massie, Maureen Teresa elementary school educator
†Waters, David Lloyd principal, educator

Fayette
Burres, Carla Anne medical technologist
†Chaney, Sara Jo college official, clergywoman
Davis, H(umphrey) Denny publisher
Inman, Marianne Elizabeth college administrator
Keeling, Joe Keith religion educator, college official and dean
Melnyk, Julie Ann english educator
†Porneluzi, Paul A. biologist, educator

Fenton
Baer, Robert J. transportation and relocation services company executive
Greenblatt, Maurice Theodore transportation executive
Maritz, William E. communications company executive
Mix, GeGe Simmonds marketing professional
Stolar, Henry Samuel lawyer

Florissant
Ashhurst, Anna Wayne foreign language educator
Barnes, Rebecca Marie assistant principal
Bartlett, Robert James principal
Carman, Robert Eugene elementary school educator
James, Dorothy Louise King special education educator
Luebke, Martin Frederick retired curator
Owen, Robert Frederick internist, rheumatologist
Payuk, Edward William elementary education educator
Tomazi, George Donald retired electrical engineer
Ulrich, Janet M. retired elementary school educator
Ziemer, John Robert software engineer

Fordland
Fields, Samuel Preston, Jr. lay worker
Frazier, James Martell, Jr. retired insurance company official

Fort Leonard Wood
Combs, Robert Kimbal museum director
†Flowers, Robert B. military career officer
†Hewitson, William Craig physician, career officer
†Rhoades, M. Stephen career officer

Fortuna
Ramer, James LeRoy civil engineer

Franklin
Becker, Barbara Ann Stulac (Bobbie Becker) small business owner

Fulton
Archuleta, Laura Lynn marketing executive
Blair, Rebecca Sue English educator, lay minister
Garrett, Marilyn Ruth nurse
Geiger, Mark Watson management educator
Gish, Edward Rutledge surgeon
Jefferson, Kurt Wayne political science educator
†Mosley, Mary Ann Krehbiel freelance writer/editor, lobbyist
Roettger, Margaret Begley library director
Swiney, Doyle James principal

Gallatin
Smith, Joann Jewell retired educator
Wilsted, Joy elementary education educator, reading specialist, parenting consultant

Gladstone
†Hasty, Michael Joe protective services official

Grain Valley
Flora, Jairus Dale, Jr. statistician

Grandin
Wallace, Louise Margaret nurse

Grandview
Daugherty, Tonda Lou special education educator
Dietrich, William Gale lawyer, real estate developer, consultant
Justesen, Don Robert psychologist

Gravois Mills
Dunn, Floyd Emryl psychiatrist, neurologist, consultant

Greenwood
Klaus, Suzanne Lynne horticulturist, production specialist

Half Way
Graves, Jerrell Loren demographic studies researcher

Hannibal
Beshears, Brenda K. nursing educator
Carty, Raymond Wesley academic administrator
Coleman, Gloria Jean chemical manufacturing company professional
Galloway, Daniel Lee investment executive
Reinhard, James Richard retired judge
Sweets, Henry Hayes, III museum director
Welch, Joseph Daniel lawyer

Harrisonville
Hartzler, Vicky J. state legislator

Hazelwood
Bruns, Billy Lee electrical engineer, consultant
Rose, Joseph Hugh clergyman
Urshan, Nathaniel Andrew minister, church administrator

Hermann
Mahoney, Catherine Ann artist, educator

Higginsville
Allison, Sandy genealogist, appraiser, political consultant
Rhodes, Robert Charles cable company executive, consultant

Highlandville
Pruter, Karl Hugo bishop

Hillsboro
Adkins, Gregory D. higher education administrator
Howald, John William lawyer
†Russell, Brenda Carol technical educator

Holden
Martin, Laura Belle real estate and farm land owner and manager

Hollister
Head, Mary Mae elementary education educator
McCall, Edith Sansom writer

Houston
Ruckert, Rita E. retired elementary education educator

Imperial
Hughes, Barbara Bradford nurse, real estate manager
Usher, Mary Margaret special education educator

Independence
Booz, Gretchen Arlene marketing executive
Cady, Elwyn Loomis, Jr. medicolegal consultant, educator
Camper, Deniece Ann special education educator
Evans, Margaret Ann human resources administrator, business owner
†Farrington, Buford Lee lawyer
Francis, Mary Frances Van Dyke real estate executive, editor
Grover, Robert LaVern retired auto worker
Hackman, Larry J. program director
Henley, Robert Lee school system administrator
Hopkins, Earl Norris metallurgist
Johnson, Niel Melvin archivist, historian
Lambertson, John Mark museum director, historian
Lashley, Curtis Dale lawyer
Lindgren, A(lan) Bruce church administrator
Lundy, Sadie Allen small business owner
Marlow, Lydia Lou elementary education educator
Potts, Barbara Joyce retired historical society executive
Sturges, Sidney James pharmacist, educator, investment and development company executive
Tyree, Alan Dean clergyman
Vigen, Kathryn L. Voss nursing administrator, educator

Ironton
Douma, Harry Hein social service agency administrator

Jackson
Close, Edward Roy hydrogeologist, environmental engineer, physicist
Schott, Marilyn Job patient review auditor

Jefferson City
Bartlett, Alex lawyer
Bartman, Robert E. state education official
Beatty, Grover Douglas stockbroker
Benton, W. Duane judge
Blackmar, Charles Blakey state supreme court justice
Bray, Joan state legislator
Carnahan, Mel governor, lawyer
Clay, William Lacy, Jr. state legislator
Cook, Rebecca McDowell state official
Covington, Ann K. state supreme court justice
Craver, Charles Henry illustrator
Deutsch, James Bernard lawyer
Dey, Charlotte Jane retired community health nurse
Donnelly, Robert True retired state supreme court justice
Farnen, Ted William state legislator
Forbis, Bryan Lester state agency administrator
Gaw, Robert Steven lawyer, state representative
Gonder, Sharon special education educator
Greene, Thomasina Talley concert pianist, educator
Hanson, Richard A. state commissioner
Holden, Bob state official
Holstein, John Charles state supreme court judge
Karll, Jo Ann state agency administrator, lawyer
Kelley, Patrick Michael minister, state legislator
King, Robert Henry minister, church denomination executive, former educator
†Knox, William Arthur judge
Madison, Eddie Lawrence, Jr. public relations consultant, editor, writer
Mahfood, Stephen Michael governmental agency executive
Mc Auliffe, Michael F. retired bishop
McClelland, Emma L. state legislator
McDaniel, Sue Powell cultural organization administrator
Melton, June Marie nursing educator
Nixon, Jeremiah W. (Jay Nixon) state attorney general
Parker, Sara Ann librarian
Peeno, Larry Noyle state agency administrator, consultant
Price, William Ray, Jr. state supreme court judge
Reidinger, Russell Frederick, Jr. fish and wildlife scientist
Robertson, Edward D., Jr. state supreme court justice
†Saunders, John L. state agency administrator
Strifler, Vivian Elsie health facilities nursing consultant
Stroup, Kala Mays state higher education commissioner
Sugarbaker, Stephen Philip surgeon, educator
Tettlebaum, Harvey M. lawyer
Vieweg, Bruce Wayne mental health researcher
†Vincent, Trish state agency administrator
Westfall, Morris state legislator
†Wilnoit, W. L. protective services official
Wilson, Roger Byron lieutenant governor, school administrator

Jennings
Robards, Bourne Rogers elementary education educator

Joplin
Allman, Margaret Ann Lowrance counselor
†Boudreaux, Marjory Ann English language educator, consultant
Butler, Paul Thurman retired religious studies educator
Crumpacker, Rex K. anesthesiologist
Daus, Arthur Steven neurological surgeon
Ferson, Lu Ann medical and surgical nurse
Guillory, Jeffery Michael lawyer
Laas, Virginia Jeans historian
Logsdon, Cindy Ann small business owner
Massa, Richard Wayne communications educator
McReynolds, Allen, Jr. investment company executive
Merriam, Allen Hayes speech communication educator
Minor, Ronald Ray minister
Scott, Robert Haywood, Jr. lawyer
†Shaheen, Esber Ibrahim engineering consultant, writer
Singleton, Marvin Ayers otolaryngologist, senator
Weber, Maryann language educator
West, Diana D. freelance writer, social worker
Wilson, Aaron Martin religious studies educator, college executive

Kahoka
Huffman, Robert Merle insurance company executive

Kansas City
Abdou, Nabih I. physician, educator
Abele, Robert Christopher lawyer
Acheson, Allen Morrow retired engineering executive
Adam, Paul James engineering company executive, mechanical engineer
Adams, Beverly Josephine data processing specialist
Alarid, Leanne Fiftal criminal justice educator
†Allan, Clayton Paul publishing executive
Allen, Marcus retired professional football player
Anderson, Christopher James lawyer
Anderson, James Keith retired magazine editor
Andrews, Kathleen W. book publishing executive
Appier, (Robert) Kevin professional baseball player
Archer, J(ohn) Barry municipal official
†Arnold, Eric Daniell budget analyst
Arnold, Kathryn artist, educator
†Audy, Lynn editor
Ayers, Jeffrey David lawyer
†Bacon, Jennifer Gille lawyer
Baisden, Eleanor Marguerite airline compensation executive, consultant
Baker, John Russell utilities executive
Baker, Robert Thomas interior designer
Baker, Ronald Phillip service company executive
Baker, Roy E. accountant, retired educator
Ball, Owen Keith, Jr. lawyer
†Barnes, Kay mayor of Kansas City, Missouri
Bartlett, D. Brook federal judge
Bartlett, Paul Dana, Jr. agribusiness executive
Bartunek, Robert R(ichard), Jr. lawyer
Bass, Lee Marshall food products company executive
Bates, William Hubert lawyer
Batiuk, Thomas Martin cartoonist
Becker, Thomas Bain lawyer
Beckett, Theodore Charles lawyer
Beihl, Frederick lawyer
Bell, Wallace Edward minister
Belzer, Ellen J. negotiations and communications consultant
Benner, Richard Edward, Jr. management and marketing consultant, investor
Berkley, Eugene Bertram (Bert Berkley) envelope company executive
Berkowitz, Lawrence M. lawyer
Bernstein, Phyliss Louise psychologist
Bernstein, Robert advertising executive
Bevan, Robert Lewis lawyer
Bixby, Walter E. insurance company executive
Black, John Sheldon lawyer
Blackwell, Menefee Davis lawyer
Bloch, Henry Wollman tax preparation company executive
Boland, Raymond James bishop
Bolender, Todd choreographer
Borel, Steven James lawyer
Bowers, Curtis Ray, Jr. chaplain
Bowman, Pasco Middleton, II federal judge
Boyer, Helen King artist
Boysen, Melicent Pearl finance company executive
Bradbury, Daniel Joseph library administrator
Bradshaw, Jean Paul, II lawyer
Braude, Michael commodity exchange executive
Brett, George Howard baseball executive, former professional baseball player
Brisbane, Arthur Seward newspaper publisher
Brous, Thomas Richard lawyer
Brown, John O. banker
Brown, Zania Faye elementary education educator
Bruening, Richard P(atrick) lawyer
Buckner, William Claiborne real estate broker
Buford, Ronetta Marie music educator
Bugg, Leon Hayes music educator, performer, composer
Bugher, Robert Dean professional society administrator
Busby, Marjorie Jean (Marjean Busby) journalist
Butler, Alice Claire rehabilitation nurse
Butler, Merlin Gene physician, medical geneticist, educator
Canfield, Robert Cleo lawyer
Cantrell, (Thomas) Scott newspaper music critic
Ching, Wai Yim physics educator, researcher
Chisholm, Donald Herbert lawyer
†Christensen, Courtney Waide municipal administrator
Clark, Charles Edward arbitrator
Clarke, Milton Charles lawyer
Cleberg, Harry C. food products company executive
Collins, John W. nurse practitioner, lecturer
Conrad, William Merrill architect
Costin, James D. performing arts company executive
Courson, Marna B.P. public relations executive
Coveney, Raymond Martin, Jr. educator
Crawford, Howard Allen lawyer
Crayton, Billy Gene physician
Crockett, James Edwin physician, educator
Cross, William Dennis lawyer
Cruess, Leigh Saunders financial executive
Crumpley, Charles Robert Thomas journalist
†Cundiff, Jerry H. secondary music educator, church choir director
†Cunningham, Gunther professional football coach
Cunningham, Paul George minister
Dahl, Andrew Wilbur health services executive
Danner, Kathleen Frances Steele federal official
Davis, James Robert cartoonist
Davis, John Charles lawyer
Davis, Richard Francis city government official
Deacy, Thomas Edward, Jr. lawyer
Dees, Stephen Phillip agricultural finance executive, lawyer
De Vries, Robert John investment banker
Diehl, James Harvey church administrator
Dillingham, John Allen marketing professional
Dimond, Edmunds Grey medical educator
Dishman, Cris Edward professional football player
Dixon, George David radiologist
Doyle, Wendell E. retired band director, educator
Dumovich, Loretta real estate and transportation company executive
Durig, James Robert college dean
Eddy, Charles Alan chiropractor
Eddy, William Bahret psychology educator, university dean
Edgar, John M. lawyer

Edwards, Horace Burton *former state official, former oil pipeline company executive, management consultant*
Egan, Charles Joseph, Jr. *lawyer, greeting card company executive*
Eldridge, Truman Kermit, Jr. *lawyer*
English, R(obert) Bradford *marshal*
Estep, Michael R. *church administrator*
Eubanks, Eugene Emerson *education educator, consultant*
Fairchild, Sharon Elaine *corrections administrator*
†Faulwell, Bond R. *government executive*
†Federman, Arthur *federal judge*
Field, Lyman *lawyer*
Foster, Mark Stephen *lawyer*
Fox, Byron Neal *lawyer*
Frank, Eugene Maxwell *bishop*
Franke, Linda Frederick *lawyer*
Friedlander, Edward Robert *pathologist*
Fry-Wendt, Sherri Diane *psychologist*
Funkouser, Mark *auditor, municipal official*
Gaines, Robert Darryl *lawyer, food services executive*
Gaitan, Fernando J., Jr. *federal judge*
†Gansler, Robert *professional soccer coach*
Gardner, Brian E. *lawyer*
Garrison, Larry Richard *accounting educator*
Gibson, Floyd Robert *federal judge*
Gibson, John Robert *federal judge*
Gier, Audra May Calhoon *environmental chemist*
Gilbert, John Robert *advertising and public relations agency executive*
Glesner Fines, Barbara *law educator*
Godfrey, William Ashley *ophthalmologist*
Gorman, Gerald Warner *lawyer*
Graham, Charles *research psychologist*
Graham, Harold Steven *lawyer*
Graham, Robert *medical association executive*
Gray, Helen Theresa Gott *religion editor*
Green, Jerry Howard *investment banker*
Greer, Norris E. *lawyer*
Grossman, Jerome Barnett *retired service firm executive*
Gusewelle, Charles Wesley *journalist*
Hagan, John Charles, III *ophthalmologist*
Hall, Donald Joyce *greeting card company executive*
Handley, Gerald Matthew *lawyer*
Hanover, R(aymond) Scott *tennis management professional*
Hansen, Eric Lloyd *accountant*
Hanson, Phillip John *united way executive*
Hasan, Syed Eqbal *environmental geologist, educator*
Haw, Bill *association executive*
†Hays, Sarah W. *federal judge*
Hebenstreit, James Bryant *agricultural products executive, bank and venture capital executive*
Helder, Jan Pleasant, Jr. *lawyer*
†Hickok, Gloria Vando *publisher, editor, poet*
Hill, Stephen L., Jr. *prosecutor*
Hockaday, Irvine O., Jr. *greeting card company executive*
Hoffman, Gloria Levy *communications executive*
Hoffmann, Donald *architectural historian*
Howlett, Stephanie Ann *home care equipment sales representative, nurse*
Hubbell, Ernest *lawyer*
†Hunkeler, John Douglas *ophthalmologist*
Hunt, Lamar *professional football team executive*
Hunter, Elmo Bolton *federal judge*
Hunzicker, Warren John *research consultant, physician, cardiologist*
Jarka, Dale Elizabeth *surgeon*
†Jenkins, Melvin Lemuel *lawyer*
Jenkins, Orville Wesley *retired religious administrator*
Jennings, A. Drue *utility company executive*
†Johnson, Gregory Kent *dentist, educator*
Johnson, Leonard James *lawyer*
Johnson, Mark Eugene *lawyer*
Johnson, Richard Dean *pharmaceutical consultant, educator*
Johnson, Vicki Kristine *rehabilitation nurse*
Joyce, Michael Patrick *lawyer*
Juarez, Martin *priest*
Kagan, Stuart Michael *pediatrician*
Kahn, George Arnett *economist*
Kanaby, Robert F. *sports association administrator*
Kaplan, Harvey L. *lawyer*
Kaufman, Michelle Stark *lawyer*
Kendall, Earnest James *mental health nurse*
Kilroy, John Muir *lawyer*
Kilroy, William Terrence *lawyer*
King, Richard Allen *lawyer*
Kingsley, James Gordon *healthcare executive*
Kirila, Carol Elizabeth *osteopathic physician*
Knight, John Allan *clergyman, philosophy and religion educator*
Koger, Frank Williams *federal judge*
Krause, Heather Dawn *data processing executive*
Kroenert, Robert Morgan *lawyer*
Kronschnabel, Robert James *manufacturing company executive*
La Budde, Kenneth James *librarian*
Lalas, Alexi *professional soccer player*
Langworthy, Robert Burton *lawyer*
Lannigan, James William *voluntary service officer*
†Larsen, Robert Emmett *federal judge*
Larson, Gary *cartoonist*
Latshaw, John *entrepreneur*
Laughrey, Nanette K. *judge, federal*
Lee, Margaret Norma *artist*
Levi, Peter Steven *chamber of commerce executive, lawyer*
Lindsey, David Hosford *lawyer*
Lock, Robert Joseph *accountant*
Lofland, Gary Kenneth *cardiac surgeon*
Lolli, Don R(ay) *lawyer*
Lombardi, Cornelius Ennis, Jr. *lawyer*
Long, Edwin Tutt *surgeon*
Lotven, Howard Lee *lawyer*
Louis, William Joseph *theater educator, actor, director, artist, poet*
Lubin, Bernard *psychologist, educator*
Lynch, Bob David *retired business agent*
†Magee, Jon Dirk *health facility administrator, psychologist*
Magee, Thomas Mark *government official*
Malacarne, C. John *insurance company executive, lawyer*
Malecki, David Michael *airport manager*
Manka, Ronald Eugene *lawyer*
Margolin, Abraham Eugene *lawyer*
Martin, Deanna Coleman *university director*
Martin-Bowen, Lindsey *freelance writer*
Massey, Vickie Lea *radiologist*
Mast, Kande White *artist*
Matheny, Edward Taylor, Jr. *lawyer*
Matzeder, Jean Marie Znidarsic *lawyer*
Maughmer, John Townsend *federal judge*
Mazza, Biagio *religious studies educator*
Mazza-Deblauwe, Tania Sue *software engineer, technology educator*
Mazzetti, Timothy Alan *commercial real estate executive*
McCollum, Clifford Glenn *college dean emeritus*
McCoy, Frederick John *retired plastic surgeon*
McDermott, Alan *newspaper editor*
Mc Gee, Joseph John, Jr. *former insurance company executive*
†McGhee, Flin Cameron, III *chemistry educator, consultant*
McGlockton, Chester *professional football player*
McGuff, Joseph Thomas *professional sports team executive*
Mc Kelvey, John Clifford *research institute executive*
McKenna, George LaVerne *art museum curator*
McKinney, Janet Kay *law librarian*
McLendon, Jesse Lawrence *protective services official*
McManus, James William *lawyer*
Mc Meel, John Paul *newspaper syndicate and publishing executive*
McPhee, Mark Steven *medical educator, physician, gastroenterologist*
McSweeney, William Lincoln, Jr. *retired publishing executive*
Mebust, Winston Keith *surgeon, educator*
Meola, Tony *professional soccer player, actor*
Mick, Howard Harold *lawyer*
Miller, William Charles *theological librarian, educator*
Milton, Chad Earl *lawyer*
Molzen, Christopher John *lawyer*
Montgomery, Jeffrey Thomas *baseball player*
Moon, Harold Warren, Jr. *professional football player*
Moore, Dorsey Jerome *dentistry educator, maxillofacial prosthetist*
Moore, Stephen James *lawyer*
Mordy, James Calvin *lawyer*
Morrison, David Campbell *immunology educator*
†Muser, Tony *manager professional athletics*
Mustard, Mary Carolyn *financial executive*
Neely, Susanne J. *marketing professional, director*
Newcom, Jennings Jay *lawyer*
Newsom, James Thomas *lawyer*
Noback, Richardson Kilbourne *medical educator*
Northrip, Robert Earl *lawyer*
†O'Dell, Jane *automotive company executive*
Oliphant, Patrick *cartoonist*
Oliver, Pauline *community health and geriatrics nurse*
Otteson, Holly Carol Harvick-Ward *poet*
Owen, Loyd Eugene, Jr. *lawyer*
Owens, Stephen J. *lawyer*
Palmer, Cruise *newspaper editor*
Palmer, Dennis Dale *lawyer*
Parizek, Eldon Joseph *geologist, college dean*
Parker, Dennis Gene *former sheriff, karate instructor*
Peake, Candice K. Loper *data processing professional*
†Pearson, Donna Sutherland *lumber company executive*
Pedram, Marilyn Beth *reference librarian*
Pelofsky, Joel *lawyer*
Pemberton, Bradley Powell *lawyer*
Peterson, Carl *professional football team executive*
Petosa, Jason Joseph *publisher*
Piepho, Robert Walter *pharmacy educator, researcher*
Popper, Robert *law educator, former dean*
Potter, George William, Jr. *mining executive*
†Preki *professional soccer player*
Price, Charles H., II *former ambassador*
Price, James Tucker *lawyer*
Prince, William J. *church officer*
Prugh, William Byron *lawyer*
Ralston, Richard H. *lawyer*
Reaves, Charles William *insurance company executive, writer, educator, investment advisor*
Reed, Janice Moen *municipal employee*
Reiter, Robert Edward *banker*
Rengachary, Setti Subbiyer *neurosurgeon, educator*
Rison, Andre *football player*
Robertson, Leon H. *management consultant, educator*
Robinson, Spencer T. (Herk Robinson) *professional baseball team executive*
Rocha, Catherine T. *municipal official*
Rodman, Len C. *civil and communication engineering executive*
Roos, Kathleen Marie *special education educator*
Rost, William Joseph *chemist*
Roth, Lawrence Frederick, Jr. (Larry Roth) *writer*
Roush, Sue *newspaper editor*
Rove, Frances Ann *lawyer*
Rowden, A(lphro) J(ohn) *minister*
Rowland, Landon Hill *diversified holding company executive*
Rozell, Joseph Gerard *accountant*
†Ryan, William James *communication educator*
Sachs, Howard F(rederic) *federal judge*
Sader, Neil Steven *lawyer*
Salem, Lee *editor*
Sands, Darry Gene *lawyer*
Satterlee, Terry Jean *lawyer*
Sauer, Elisabeth Ruth *lawyer*
Sauer, Gordon Chenoweth *physician, educator*
Scarritt, Richard Winn *lawyer*
Schnell, Shirley Luke *art educator*
Schwab, Mark *marketing executive*
Scott, Deborah Emont *curator*
Scott, Ruth Lois *dental hygiene educator*
†See, Karen Mason *federal judge*
Seligson, Theodore H. *architect, interior designer, art consultant*
Sharp, Rex Arthur *lawyer*
Shaw, John W. *lawyer*
Shaw, Richard David *marketing and management educator*
Shay, David E. *lawyer*
Sheldon, Ted Preston *library director*
Sherwood, Joan Karolyn Sargent *career counselor*
Shields, Will Herthie *football player*
Shoemaker, Robert Shern *architect*
Shughart, Donald Louis *lawyer*
Shutz, Byron Christopher *real estate executive*
Simmonds, Corwin (Corey) Shawn *dean*
Smiley, David Bruce *administrative director*
Smith, Louis *sports association administrator*
Smith, Ortrie D. *judge*
†Smith, Ortrie Dale *judge*
Smith, R(onald) Scott *lawyer*
Solberg, Elizabeth Transou *public relations executive*
Spalty, Edward Robert *lawyer*
Sparks, Donald Eugene *interscholastic activities association executive*
Spencer, Richard Henry *lawyer*
Steadman, Jack W. *professional football team executive*
Steffens, John Howard *cytotechnologist*
Stelmach, Walter Jack *physician, medical education administrator*
Stevens, James Hervey, Jr. *retired financial advisor*
Stevens, Jane *advertising executive*
Stone, Jack *religious organization administrator*
Stoup, Arthur Harry *lawyer*
Stowers, James, III *data processing company executive*
Strain, Herbert Arthur, III *plastic surgeon*
Stueck, William Noble *small business owner*
Sullivan, Bill *church administrator*
Sullivan, Charles A. *food products executive*
Sullivan, John Joseph *bishop*
Suter, Carol J. *non-profit organization executive, lawyer*
Svadlenak, Jean Hayden *museum administrator, consultant*
Tadtman, Jeff *university head women's basketball coach*
†Takawira, Vitalis *professional soccer player*
Tammeus, William David *journalist, columnist*
Tansey, Robert Paul, Sr. *pharmaceutical chemist*
†Terry, Robert Brooks *lawyer*
Thompson, Catherine Rush *physical therapist, educator*
Thornton, Thomas Noel *publishing executive*
Todd, Stephen Max *lawyer*
Toll, Perry Mark *lawyer*
Townsend, Harold Guyon, Jr. *publishing company executive*
Truitt, Kenneth Ray *owner*
Ucko, David Alan *museum director*
Ulrich, Robert Gene *judge*
VanAuken, Alan Bradley *management consultant*
Van Buren, Abigail (Pauline Friedman Phillips) *columnist, author, writer, lecturer*
Vandever, William Dirk *lawyer*
Vaughan, Kirk William *banker*
Venable, William Ralph, III *marketing executive, banking executive*
Verbeek-Cowart, Pauline M. *textile designer, educator*
Vering, John Albert *lawyer*
Viani, James Lawrence *lawyer*
Vleisides, Gregory William *lawyer*
Vogel, Arthur Anton *clergyman*
Wade, Robert Glenn *engineering executive*
Wallis, Elizabeth Susan *air traffic control specialist*
Walsh, Rodger John *lawyer*
Ward, Todd Pope *educational resources executive*
Washington, Patricia Lane *retired school counselor*
Whipple, Dean *federal judge*
Whitener, William Garnett *dancer, choreographer*
Whittaker, Judith Ann Cameron *lawyer*
Wilkins, Arthur Norman *retired college administrator*
Wilkinson, Ralph Russell *biochemistry educator, toxicologist*
†Williams, Arthur Ross *health service administrator*
Williams, Thelma Jean *social worker*
†Willsie, Sandra K. *physician, educator*
Willy, Thomas Ralph *lawyer*
Wilson, Eugene Rolland *foundation executive*
Wilson, Marc Fraser *art museum administrator and curator*
Wingfield, Laura Allison Ross *fraternal organization executive*
Wirken, James Charles *lawyer*
Woods, Richard Dale *lawyer*
Woodson, Stephen William *collection agency executive*
Wright, Scott Olin *federal judge*
Wrobley, Ralph Gene *lawyer*
†Wu, William Quokan *neurologist, writer*
Zechman, David Mark *health system executive, educator*
Ziegenhorn, Eric Howard *lawyer, legal writer*
Zieman, Mark *newspaper editor*

Kearney
Shrimpton, James Robert *controller*

Keytesville
Wheeler, James Julian *lawyer*

Kimberling City
Docherty, Robert Kelliehan, II *minister*

Kirksville
Adkins, Dean Phillip *painter*
Davis, Adam Brooke *English educator*
Engber, Cheryl Ann *language educator, linguist*
Festa, Roger Reginald *chemist, educator*
French, Michael Francis *non-profit education agency administrator*
†Iles, Lawrence Irvine *liberal arts educator*
Kuchera, Michael Louis *osteopathic physician, educator, author*
Peterson, Donald Fred *physiologist, educator*
Siewert, Gregg Hunter *language professional educator*
†Tatro, Norbert *journalist, educator*
TenBrink, Terry Dean *academic administrator*

Kirkwood
†Black, Richard A. *community college president*
Holsen, James Noble, Jr. *retired chemical engineer*
Warner, Alvina (Vinnie Warner) *principal*
Wiecher, Delilah Lee *secondary school educator*

Knob Noster
†Corbett, Violet Jane *farmer, contracter*

Lake Lotawana
Heineman, Paul Lowe *consulting civil engineer*
Zobrist, Benedict Karl *library director, historian*

Lake Saint Louis
Dommermuth, William Peter *marketing consultant, educator*
German, John George *retired transportation consultant*

Lambert Airport
Griggs, Leonard LeRoy, Jr. *federal agency administrator*

Lampe
Linden, Paul Allen *optical engineer*

Lebanon
Beavers, Roy Lackey *retired utility executive, essayist, activist*
Caplinger, Patricia E. *family nurse practitioner*
Hutson, Don *lawyer*
Louderback, Kevin Wayne *business owner*

Lees Summit
Boehm, Toni Georgene *seminary dean, nurse*
Bond-Brown, Barbara Ann *musician, educator*
Couch, Daniel Michael *healthcare executive*
Demetreon, Daiboune Elayne *minister*
Ferguson, Julie Ann *physical education educator*
Griffith-Thompson, Sara Lynn *resource reading educator*
†Halsey, Joyce Leslie *secondary education educator*
Korschot, Benjamin Calvin *investment executive*
Letterman, Ernest Eugene *manufacturers representative company executive*
Mosley, Glenn Richard *religious organization administrator, minister*
†Rathbun, Katharine Cady *preventive medicine physician*
Reynolds, Tommy *secondary school educator*
St. John, Shay *fundraising executive*
Williams, Kenneth Eugene *advertising, marketing and sales professional*

Lewistown
Terpening, Virginia Ann *artist*

Lexington
Fuller, Janae *historic site administrator*

Liberty
†Bortko, Daniel John *photographer, educator*
Harriman, Richard Lee *performing arts administrator, educator*
McCaslin, WC *products and packaging executive*
Samuel, Robert Thompson *optometrist*
†Sizemore, William Christian *academic administrator*
Tanner, Jimmie Eugene *college dean*

Licking
White, Charles McBride *sculptor*

Macon
Parkinson, Paul K. *lawyer*

Maplewood
Schmidt, Skip Francis *writer*

Marceline
†Engelhard, Barbara Jo *education educator*

Marionville
Estep, Mark Randall *secondary education educator*

Marshall
Bunch, Albert William *minister*
Cox, Sandra Annette *economic developer*
Huff, Jane Van Dyke *secondary education educator*
Miller, Toni M. Andrews *critical care nurse, educator*
Peterson, William Allen *lawyer*

Marshfield
Gloe, Donna *nursing administrator*
Herren, Cline Champion *real estate agent*

Maryland Heights
Beumer, Richard Eugene *engineer, architect, construction firm executive*
Goldfarb, Marvin Al *retired civil engineer*
Marcus, John *wholesale distribution executive*
Sobol, Lawrence Raymond *lawyer*

Maryville
Heusel, Barbara Stevens *English scholar and educator*
Hubbard, Dean Leon *university president*
King, Terry Lee *statistician, mathematician*
Schultz, Patricia Bowers *vocal music educator*
†Trowbridge, William Leigh *writer*

Mexico
Hudson, Harold Don *veterinarian*
Rice, Marvin Elwood *dentist*
Stover, Harry M. *corporate executive*

Moberly
Ornburn, Kristee Jean *accountant*
Staley, Richard Lynn *school system administrator*

Monett
Block, Michael David *minister*

Mount Vernon
Pulliam, Frederick Cameron *educational administrator*
Witty, Thomas Ezekiel *psychologist, researcher*

Neosho
Guthery, Carolyn J. *pediatrics nurse*
Weber, Margaret Laura Jane *retired accountant*

Nevada
Brown, Fermon *photographer, advertising professional*
†Campbell, Catherine Ellen *French language educator*
Ewing, Lynn Moore, Jr. *lawyer*
Hornback, Joseph Hope *mathematics educator*

New Haven
Roth, Nancy Louise *former nurse, veterinarian*

Nixa
Aduddle, Larry Steven *marketing and sales executive, consultant*

North Kansas City
Conner, Leonard Wayne *banker, association administrator, layworker*
†Hartmetz, Walter Judson *library director*

Stout, Edward Irvin *medical manufacturing company executive*

O'Fallon
Lottes, Patricia Joette Hicks *foundation administrator, retired nurse*

Osage Beach
East, Mark David *physician*
Orr, Rita Hope *artist*

Osborn
Findley, Delpha Yoder *retired public health nurse*

Osceola
Dysart, Diana Marie *women's health nurse, medical/surgical nurse*
†Mathew, Stanley *physician*

Park Hills
Sebastian, Phylis Sue *real estate broker*

Parkville
Jacobs, Carl Eugene *printing company official*
Mitchell, Robert Lee, III *auditor*
Pettes, Robert Carlton *artist*
†Schultis, G. Ann *library director*

Perryville
Johnson, Charles Joseph *telecommunications executive, computer engineer*

Pierce City
†Hays, Otis Earl, Jr. *writer*

Pilot Kove
deCastro, Fernando Jose *pediatrics educator*

Plato
Wood, Joetta Kay *special education educator*

Platte City
Cozad, John Condon *lawyer*
Knight, Betty Ann *county commissioner*

Point Lookout
Anderson, Ruth G. *education educator, consultant*

Poplar Bluff
Black, Ronnie Delane *religious organization administrator, mayor*
Carr, Charles Louis *retired religious organization administrator*
Duncan, Leland Ray *retired mission administrator*
Lotuaco, Luisa Go *pathologist*
Piland, Donald Spencer *internist*

Portageville
†Dial, Marshall Reece *library director*

Potosi
Duing, Edna Irene *women's health nurse, nurse educator*

Raymore
DeLuca, John Richard, II *city planning administrator, geography educator*

Raytown
Blaine, Robert Virgil *principal*
Johnson, Sondra Lea *accountant*
Smith, Robert Francis *psychologist, consultant*

Rockville
McAvey, Maureen *municipal official*

Rogersville
Dowdy, Linda Katherine *psychiatric and geriatric nurse*
Hetherington, John Scott *principal*

Rolla
Adams, Craig David *environmental engineering educator*
Adawi, Ibrahim Hasan *physics educator*
Alexander, Ralph William, Jr. *physics educator*
Armstrong, Daniel Wayne *chemist, educator*
Barr, David John *civil, geological engineering educator*
Cohen, Gerald Leonard *foreign language educator*
Crosbie, Alfred Linden *mechanical engineering educator*
Dagli, Cihan Hayreddin *engineering educator*
Datz, Israel Mortimer *information systems specialist*
Finaish, Fathi Ali *aeronautical engineering educator*
Grimm, Louis John *mathematician, educator*
Irion, Arthur Lloyd *psychologist, educator*
Leventis, Nicholas *chemistry educator, consultant*
Mc Farland, Robert Harold *physicist, educator*
Munger, Paul R. *civil engineering educator*
Numbere, Daopu Thompson *petroleum engineer, educator*
O'Keefe, Thomas Joseph *metallurgical engineer*
Rueppel, Melvin Leslie *environmental research director and educator*
Sabnis, Ram Wasudeo *research chemist*
Saperstein, Lee Waldo *mining engineering educator*
Sarchet, Bernard Reginald *retired chemical engineering educator*
Sauer, Harry John, Jr. *mechanical engineering educator, university administrator*
Tsoulfanidis, Nicholas *nuclear engineering educator, university official*
Warner, Don Lee *dean emeritus*
Zobrist, George Winston *computer scientist, educator*

Saint Ann
Drury, Charles Louis, Jr. *hotel executive*
Farrow, Julie Anne *retired geriatrics nurse, administrator*
Johnson, Harold Gene *lawyer*

Saint Charles
Beste, Robert Culbertson *geologist*
Biggerstaff, Randy Lee *academic administrator, sports medicine rehabilitation consultant*
Brahmbhatt, Sudhirkumar *chemical company executive*
Castro, Jan Garden *author, arts consultant, educator*
Cox, Glenda Jewell *elementary school educator*
Dauphinais, George Arthur *import company executive*
Dieterich, Russell Burks *obstetrician, gynecologist*
Dorsey, Mary Elizabeth *lawyer*
Eckert, William Dean *retired educator, artist*
Evans, James Bruce *urban planner*
Frey, Laura Marie *special education administrator*
Gross, Charles Robert *personnel executive, legislator, appraiser*
Huckshold, Wayne William *elementary education educator*
Humphries, Pamela Jean *women's health nurse*
Izuchukwu, John Ifeanyichukwu *industrial and mechanical engineer*
Lang, Danny Robert *municipal development official*
Mager, Margaret Julia Eckstein *special education educator*
Nickisch, Willard Wayne *funeral director*
Pundmann, Ed John, Jr. *automotive company executive*
Radke, Rodney Owen *agricultural research executive, consultant*
Spencer, Richard Andrew *financial planner, investment advisor, artist*

Saint Joseph
Boor, Myron Vernon *psychologist, educator*
Brown, Jean Gayle *social worker*
Chelline, Warren Herman *English educator, clergy member*
Chilcote, Gary M. *museum director, reporter*
Huff, David Richard *funeral home executive*
Johnson, Robert Charles *medical administrator*
Kranitz, Theodore Mitchell *lawyer*
Miller, Lloyd Daniel *real estate agent*
Murphy, Janet Gorman *college president*
Rachow, Sharon Dianne *realtor*
Taylor, Michael Leslie *lawyer*
Tritten, Donald Michael *music educator*

Saint Louis
Abelov, Stephen Lawrence *uniform clothing company executive, consultant*
Adams, Albert Willie, Jr. *lubrication company executive*
†Adelman, Terry I. *federal judge*
Agrawal, Harish Chandra *neurobiologist, researcher, educator*
Ahrens, Clifford H. *judge*
Aldridge, Charles Ray *brokerage house executive, trade director*
Allen, Garland Edward *biology educator, science historian*
Allen, Renee *principal*
Alpers, David Hershel *physician, educator*
Amini, Amir Arsham *biomedical engineering researcher, educator*
†Anderson, Bruce John *foundation administrator*
Anderson, Odin Waldemar *sociologist, educator*
Antonacci, Anthony Eugene *controls engineer*
Appleton, R. O., Jr. *lawyer*
Arnold, John Fox *lawyer*
Arrington, Barbara *public health educator*
Arthur, Charles Gemmell, IV *accountant*
Asa, Cheryl Suzanne *biologist*
Atwood, Hollye Stolz *lawyer*
Austrin, Michael Steven *health care consultant, strategic planner*
Aylward, Ronald Lee *lawyer*
Babington, Charles Martin, III *lawyer*
Bachmann, John William *securities firm executive*
Bacon, Bruce Raymond *physician*
Badalamenti, Anthony *financial planner*
Baernstein, Albert, II *mathematician*
Baker, Martha Kaye *writer, editor*
Baker, Nannette A. *lawyer, city official*
Baker, Shirley Kistler *university administrator*
Baldwin, Edwin Steedman *lawyer*
Ballinger, Walter Francis *surgeon, educator*
Banks, Eric Kendall *lawyer*
Banstetter, Robert J. *lawyer*
Barken, Bernard Allen *lawyer*
Barksdale, Clarence Caulfield *banker*
Barmann, Lawrence Francis *history educator*
Barnes, Harper Henderson *movie critic, editor*
Barnett, William Arnold *economics educator*
Barney, Steven Matthew *human resources executive*
Barry, A. L. *church official*
Barta, James Joseph *judge*
Bascom, C. Perry *foundation administrator*
Baue, Arthur Edward *surgeon, educator, administrator*
Baum, Gordon Lee *lawyer, non-profit organization administrator*
Bauman, George Duncan *former newspaper publisher*
Beach, Douglas Ryder *lawyer, educator*
Bealke, Linn Hemingway *bank executive*
Bean, Bourne *lawyer*
Beare, Gene Kerwin *electric company executive*
Beck, Lois Grant *anthropologist, educator*
Becker, David Mandel *law educator, author, consultant*
Becker, Rex Louis *architect*
Bender, Carl Martin *physics educator, consultant*
Berendt, Robert Tryon *lawyer*
Berg, Leonard *neurologist, educator, researcher*
Berger, John Torrey, Jr. *lawyer*
Berland, David I. *psychiatrist, educator*
Bernstein, Donald Chester *brokerage company executive, lawyer*
Bernstein, Merton Clay *lawyer, educator, arbitrator*
Beuc, Rudolph, Jr. *architect, real estate broker*
Bextermiller, Theresa Marie Louise *architect, computer graphics*
Bickel, Floyd Gilbert, III *investment counselor*
Biondi, Lawrence *university administrator, priest*
Birman, Victor Mark *mechanical and aerospace engineering educator*
Blanke, Richard Brian *lawyer*
Bloemer, Rosemary Celeste *bookkeeper*
Blumenthal, Herman Theodore *physician, educator*
Boardman, Richard John *lawyer*
Bock, Edward John *retired chemical manufacturing company executive*
Boddie, Don O'Mar *recording company executive, producer, recording artist*
Bonacorsi, Mary Catherine *lawyer*
Boothby, William Munger *mathematics educator*
Borst, William Adam *educator, radio personality, writer*
Boyd, Robert Cotton *English language educator*
Brasunas, Anton de Sales *metallurgical engineering educator*
Breece, Robert William, Jr. *lawyer*
Breihan, Erwin Robert *civil engineer, consultant*
Brendle, Steven Michael *municipal official, accountant*
Brewer, Elizabeth *family therapist*
Briccetti, Joan Therese *theater manager, arts management consultant*
Brickey, Kathleen Fitzgerald *law educator*
Brickler, John Weise *lawyer*
Brickson, Richard Alan *lawyer*
Bridgewater, Bernard Adolphus, Jr. *footwear company executive*
Briggs, Cynthia Anne *educational administrator, clinical psychologist*
Briggs, William Benajah *aeronautical engineer*
Brodeur, Armand Edward *pediatric radiologist*
Brodsky, Philip Hyman *chemical executive, research director*
Brody, Lawrence *lawyer, educator*
Broeg, Bob (Robert William Broeg) *writer*
Browde, Anatole *electronics company executive, consultant*
Browman, David L(udvig) *archaeologist*
Brown, Frederick Lee *health care executive*
Brown, JoBeth Goode *food products executive, lawyer*
Brown, Melvin F. *corporate executive*
Brown, Stella Chaney *advertising agency executive*
Brown, Wendy Weinstock *nephrologist, educator*
Brownlee, Robert Hammel *lawyer*
Brubaker, James Clark *construction executive*
Brungs, Robert Anthony *theology educator, institute director*
Bryan, Henry C(lark), Jr. *lawyer*
Bryan, Jean Marie Wehmueller *nurse*
Bryant, Ruth Alyne *banker*
Bubash, Patricia Jane *special education educator*
Buck, Jack *sportscaster, broadcast executive*
†Buckles, Frederick R. *federal judge*
Burch, Stephen Kenneth *financial services company executive, real estate investor*
Burgess, James Harland *physics educator, researcher*
†Burgin, Richard Weston *writer, educator, editor*
Burke, James Donald *museum administrator*
Burke, Thomas Michael *lawyer*
Burkett, Randy James *lighting designer*
†Burkholder, Mark Alan *historian, educator*
Burleski, Joseph Anthony, Jr. *information technology executive*
Busch, August Adolphus, III *brewery executive*
Byrnes, Christopher Ian *academic dean, researcher*
Cabbabe, Edmond Bechir *plastic and hand surgeon*
Cahill, Clyde S. *retired federal judge*
Cain, James Nelson *arts school and concert administrator*
Cairns, Donald Fredrick *engineering educator, management consultant*
Callis, Clayton Fowler *research chemist*
Campbell, Cole C. *journalist, educator*
Carlson, Arthur Eugene *accounting educator*
Carp, Larry (Larry Carp) *lawyer*
Carpenter, Sharon Quigley *municipal official*
Carr, Gary Thomas *lawyer*
Carter, Carol *artist, educator*
Cawns, Albert Edward *computer systems consultant*
Chaplin, David Dunbar *medical research specialist, medical educator*
Chaplin, Hugh, Jr. *physician, educator*
Chism, Michelle *secondary education educator*
Chivetta, Anthony Joseph *architect*
Chole, Richard Arthur *otolaryngologist, educator*
Clark, Jeanenne Frances *community health nurse specialist*
Clear, John Michael *lawyer*
†Clemens, Robert *violin maker*
Cloninger, Claude Robert *psychiatric researcher, educator, genetic epdemiologist*
Coe, Rodney Michael *medical educator*
Cohen, Edwin Robert *financial executive*
Colagiovanni, Joseph Alfred, Jr. *lawyer*
†Combs, W. William *college administrator*
Conerly, Richard Pugh *retired corporation executive*
Conran, Joseph Palmer *lawyer*
Cooper, Robert James *purchasing consultant*
Corbett, James Joseph *retired computer programmer*
Corbett, Suzanne Elaine *food writer, marketing executive, food historian*
Cornfeld, Dave Louis *lawyer*
Costigan, Edward John *investment banker*
Cotton, W(illiam) Philip, Jr. *architect*
Cox, Jerome Rockhold, Jr. *electrical engineer*
Cramer, Michael William *insurance executive*
Crandell, Dwight Samuel *museum executive*
Crebs, P(aul) Terence *lawyer*
Crider, Robert Agustine *international financier, law enforcement official*
Critchlow, Donald Thomas *history educator*
Croat, Thomas Bernard *botanical curator*
Cryer, Philip Eugene *medical educator, scientist, endocrinologist*
Cullen, James D. *lawyer*
Cunningham, Charles Baker, III *manufacturing company executive*
Curran, Michael Walter *management scientist*
Curtiss, Roy, III *biology educator*
Dagogo-Jack, Samuel E. *medical educator, physician scientist, endocrinologist*
Danforth, William Henry *retired academic administrator, physician*
Davis, Christopher Kevin *equipment company executive*
†Davis, Eric Keith *professional baseball player*
Davis, Irvin *advertising, public relations, broadcast executive*
†Davis, Lawrence O. *federal judge*
Deal, Joseph Maurice *university dean, art educator, photographer*
†Demitra, Pavol *professional hockey player*
Devantier, Paul W. *communications executive, broadcaster*
Devers, Gail *track and field athlete*
Dewald, Paul Adolph *psychiatrist, educator*
†DeWitt, William O., Jr. *professional sports team executive*
Dezon-Jones, Elyane Agnes *French language educator, writer*
Dill, Charles Anthony *manufacturing and computer company executive*
Dill, John Francis *retired publishing company executive*
Dill, Virginia S. *accountant*
†DiTiberio, John Kesley *psychotherapist, educator, consultant*
Dodge, Paul Cecil *academic administrator*
Dodge, Philip Rogers *physician, educator*
Dodson, W(illiam) Edwin *child neurology educator*
Domahidy, Mary Rodgers *public policy educator*
Domjan, Laszlo Karoly *newspaper editor*
Donati, Robert Mario *physician, educational administrator*
Donohue, Carroll John *lawyer*
Donohue, Patricia Carol *academic administrator*
Dorwart, Donald Bruce *lawyer*
Dougherty, Charles Hamilton *pediatrician*
Dowd, Edward L., Jr. *prosecutor*
Drews, Robert Carrel *retired physician*
Driscoll, Charles Francis *financial services company executive, investment adviser*
Drucker, Barry Jules *environmental health specialist*
Dudukovic, Milorad P. *chemical engineering educator, consultant*
Duesenberg, Richard William *lawyer*
Duhme, Carol McCarthy *civic worker*
Duhme, H(erman) Richard, Jr. *sculptor, educator*
Dunivent, John Thomas *artist, educator*
Dunn, Jane Grace *retired educator*
Dunston, Shawon Donnell *professional baseball player*
Early, Gerald *writer*
Edison, Bernard Alan *retired retail apparel company executive*
Edwards, Benjamin Franklin, III *investment banker*
Ehrlich, Ava *television executive*
Eichhorn, Arthur David *music director*
Elkins, Ken Joe *broadcasting executive*
Elliott, Howard, Jr. *gas distribution company executive*
Ellis, Dorsey Daniel, Jr. *dean, lawyer*
†Engelhardt, Irl F. *coal company executive*
Engelhardt, Thomas Alexander *editorial cartoonist*
Epner, Steven Arthur *computer consultant*
Erickson, Robert Anders *optical engineer, physicist*
Etzkorn, K. Peter *sociology educator, author*
Evans, Pamela R. *marketing executive*
Evens, Ronald Gene *radiologist, medical center administrator*
Ezenwa, Josephine Nwabuoku *social worker*
Falk, William James *lawyer*
Farrell, John Timothy *hospital administrator*
Farris, Clyde C. *lawyer*
Faught, Harold Franklin *electrical equipment manufacturing company executive*
Ferguson, Gary Warren *retired public relations executive*
Filippine, Edward Louis *federal judge*
†Fink, Tracey Marks *chiropractor*
Finkel, Donald *poet*
Finnie, William C. *consulting company executive, educator*
Finnigan, Joseph Townsend *public relations executive*
†Fischer, Keith C. *nuclear medicine physician, radiology educator*
Fish, Michele Loyd *retailer*
Fitch, Coy Dean *physician, educator*
Fitch, Rachel Farr *health policy analyst*
Flanagan, Joan Wheat (Maggie Flanagan) *educational therapist*
†Flavin, D. Aeschliman *artist, lecturer, educator*
†Fleming, Susan *social worker*
Fletcher, James Warren *physician*
Floyd, Walter Leo *lawyer*
Flye, M. Wayne *surgeon, immunologist, educator, writer*
Fogle, James Lee *lawyer*
Fondaw, Ronald Edward *artist, educator*
Foster, Scarlett Lee *public relations executive*
Fowler, Marti *secondary education educator*
Fox, Richard Gabriel *anthropologist, educator*
Freese, Raymond William *mathematics educator*
Friedel, Helen Brangenberg *counselor, therapist*
Frieden, Carl *biochemist, educator*
Friedlander, Michael Wulf *physicist, educator*
Friedman, William Hersh *otolaryngologist, educator*
Fryer, Edwin Samuel *lawyer*
Fuhr, Grant *professional hockey player*
Gacem, Debra Ann *critical care nurse*
Gaertner, Gary M. *judge*
Gass, William H. *author, educator*
Gay, William Arthur, Jr. *thoracic surgeon, educator*
Geary, Daniel Patrick *postal service worker*
Geltman, Edward Mark *cardiologist, educator*
Gerard, Jules Bernard *law educator*
Gerdine, Leigh *retired academic administrator*
Gers, Harvey *marketing professional*
Gershenson, Harry *lawyer*
Gfeller, Donna Kvinge *clinical psychologist*
Ghosh, Soumitra Kumar *electrical engineer*
Gibbons, Patrick Chandler *physicist, educator*
Gilbert, Allan Arthur *manufacturing executive*
Gilhousen, Brent James *lawyer*
Gilligan, Sandra Kaye *private school director*
Gillis, John Lamb, Jr. *lawyer*
Gilroy, Tracy Anne Hunsaker *lawyer*
Ginsberg, Marvin A. *architect*
Gitner, Gerald L. *aviation and investment banking executive*
Gladding, Nicholas C. *lawyer*
Godiner, Donald Leonard *lawyer*
Goebel, John J. *lawyer*
Goldberg, Anne Carol *physician, educator*
Goldstein, Steven *lawyer*
Gomes, Edward Clayton, Jr. *construction company executive*
Goodenberger, Daniel Marvin *medical educator*
Goodman, Harold S. *lawyer*
Gottwald, George J. *bishop*
Gould, Phillip Louis *civil engineering educator, consultant*
Graff, George Stephen *aerospace company executive*
Graham, John Dalby *public relations executive*
Graham, Robert Clare, III *lawyer*
Gray, Charles Elmer *lawyer, rancher, investor*
Green, Darlene *comptroller, municipal official*
Green, Dennis Joseph *lawyer*
Green, Joyce *book publishing company executive*
Green, Maurice *molecular biologist, virologist, educator*
Greenbaum, Stuart I. *economist, educator*
Greenwalt, Mary Susan *counselor*
Grigsby, Perry Wayne *physician*
Grossberg, George Thomas *psychiatrist, educator*
Grubb, Robert L., Jr. *neurosurgeon*
Guerri, William Grant *lawyer*
Gupta, Surendra Kumar *chemical firm executive*
Guze, Samuel Barry *psychiatrist, educator*
Haberstroh, Richard David *insurance agent*
Hall, Homer L. *journalism educator*
Hall, Mary Taussig *volunteer*
Hall, William Kearney *retired dermatologist*
Hamburger, Viktor *retired biology educator*
Hamilton, Jean Constance *judge*
Hammerman, Marc Randall *nephrologist, educator*
Hanley, Thomas Patrick *obstetrician, gynecologist*
Hansen, Charles *lawyer*
†Hanser, Frederick O. *professional sports team executive*
†Hansman, Robert G. *art educator, artist*

Harmon, Clarence mayor
†Harris, Edwin B. educator, administrator
Harris, Roberta Lucas social worker
Harris, Whitney Robson lawyer, educator
Hartenbach, Stephen Charles small business owner
†Harvey, Richard Diamond psychology educator
Haskins, James Leslie mathematics educator
Hawkins, Pamela Leigh Huffman biochemist
Hays, Howard H. (Tim Hays) editor, publisher
Hays, Ruth lawyer
Heck, Debra Upchurch information technology, procurement professional
Hecker, George Sprake lawyer
Heiken, Jay Paul physician
Heiser, Walter Charles librarian, priest, educator
Hellmuth, George Francis architect
Hellmuth, Theodore Henning lawyer
Henderson, Ronald police chief
Hendricks, Flora Ann former case manager, former special education educator
Hernandez-Ledezma, Jose Juan laboratory administrator
Herzfeld-Kimbrough, Ciby mental health educator
Hetlage, Robert Owen lawyer
†Hickman, Charles Wallace educational association administrator
Hiles, Bradley Stephen lawyer
Hilgert, Raymond Lewis management and industrial relations educator, consultant, arbitrator
Hillard, Robert Ellsworth public relations consultant
Hirsch, Raymond Robert chemical company executive, lawyer
Hirsh, Ira Jean psychology educator, researcher
Hoblitzelle, George Knapp former state legislator
Hoessle, Charles Herman zoo director
Hofstatter, Leopold psychiatrist, researcher
Hogan, Michael Ray diversified company executive
Hollingsworth, Gary Mayes Internet access provider company
Holmes, Nancy Elizabeth pediatrician
Holt, Glen Edward library administrator
Holt, Leslie Edmonds librarian
Horwitz, Rita outpatient surgery nurse, educator
Horwitz, William J. treasurer
Howard, Walter Burke chemical engineer
†Huddleston, Charles B. surgeon, educator
Hundelt, Craig Thomas engineering executive, realtor
Hunt, Jeffrey Brian lawyer
Hunter, Earle Leslie, III professional association executive
Hyers, Thomas Morgan physician, biomedical researcher
†Hylton, John Baker music educator, university administrator
Inkley, John James, Jr. lawyer
Irwin, Hale S. professional golfer
Israel, Martin Henry astrophysicist, educator, academic administrator
Ittner, H. Curtis architect
Jackson, Carol E. federal judge
Jackson, Gayle Pendleton White venture capitalist, international energy specialist
Jackson, Paul Howard multimedia producer, educator
Jacobsen, Thomas H(erbert) banker
Jamison, Frederick William data processing executive
Jaudes, Richard Edward lawyer
†Jaudes, William E. retired lawyer
Jocketty, Walt professional sports team executive
Johnson, Gloria Jean counseling professional
Jones, Ellen Carol English educator
Jones, Ronald Vance health science association administrator
Joyner, Dee Ann bank official
Joyner Kersee, Jacqueline track and field athlete
Kaestner, John Thomas beverage company executive
Kagan, Sioma economics educator
Kaminski, Donald Leon medical educator, surgeon, gastrointestinal physiologist
Kang, Juan pathologist
Kanne, Marvin George newspaper publishing executive
Kaplan, Henry Jerrold ophthalmologist, educator
Karl, Michael M. endocrinology professor
Keller, Juan Dane lawyer
†Keller, Theodore G., Jr. real estate manager
Kelly, Ann Terese elementary education educator
Kelly, Daniel P. cardiologist, molecular biologist
Kemper, David Woods, II banker
Kempf, Kenneth Charles computer drafting professional
Key, Marcella Ann computer information specialist
Khinduka, Shanti Kumar university administrator, educator
Khoury, George Gilbert printing company executive, baseball association executive
Killenberg, George Andrew newspaper consultant, former newspaper editor
Kimmey, James Richard, Jr. medical educator, consultant
Kincaid, Marilyn Coburn medical educator
King, Joseph, Jr. government administrator, educator
Kinsella, Ralph Aloysius, Jr. physician
Kipnis, David Morris physician, educator
Kirby, Dianna Lea broadcast executive
Kiser, Karen Maureen medical technologist, educator
Kivikoski, Asko Ilmari obstetrician/gynecologist
Klahr, Saulo physician, educator
Kling, Merle political scientist, university official
Kling, S(tephen) Lee banker
Klobasa, John Anthony lawyer
Kniffen, Jan Rogers finance executive
Knutsen, Alan Paul pediatrician, allergist, immunologist
Kodner, Martin art dealer, consultant
Koehler, Harry George real estate executive
Koesterer, Larry J. pharmacist
Koff, Robert Hess foundation administrator
Kolar, Janet Brostron physician assistant, medical technologist
Kolker, Allan Erwin ophthalmologist
Komen, Leonard lawyer
Korando, Donna Kay journalist
Kornfeld, Rosalind Hauk research biochemist
Kornfeld, Stuart A. hematology educator
Kouchoukos, Nicholas Thomas surgeon
Krasney, Rina Susan school librarian
Krebs, Carol Marie architect, psychiatric therapist
Krehbiel, Robert John lawyer
Krukowski, Lucian philosophy educator, artist
Kuhlmann, Fred Mark lawyer
Kummer, Fred S. construction company executive
Kunc, Karen artist, educator
Kuss, Joseph municipal official
LaBruyere, Thomas Edward health facility administrator
Lackey, Kayle Diann elementary education educator
Lacy, Paul Eston pathologist
Lagunoff, David physician, educator
Lane, Frank Joseph, Jr. lawyer
†Langenberg, Oliver M. securities dealer, analyst
Langness, David Gordon manufacturing executive
Lankford, Raymond Lewis baseball player
La Russa, Tony, Jr. (Anthony La Russa, Jr.) professional baseball manager
Laskowski, Leonard Francis, Jr. microbiologist
Laster, Atlas, Jr. psychologist
Lause, Michael Francis lawyer
LeBlanc, Michael Stephen insurance and risk executive
Lebowitz, Albert lawyer, author
Leek, Diane Webb nurse
Leguey-Feilleux, Jean-Robert political scientist, educator
Lents, Peggy Iglauer marketing executive
Leonard, Eugene Albert banker
Leontsinis, George John lawyer
Lester, Jacqueline executive director city civil rights enforcement
Leven, Charles Louis economics educator
Levi, Hans Leopold artist, educator
Levin, Ronald Mark law educator
Le Vine, Victor Theodore political science educator
Lewis, Robert David ophthalmologist, educator
Liberman, Keith Gordon lawyer
Lickhalter, Merlin Eugene architect
Liddy, Richard A. insurance company executive
Lieberman, Edward Jay lawyer
Limbaugh, Stephen Nathaniel federal judge
Linder, Aaron Mark telelearning specialist, legal video specialist
Lipan, Petruta E. artist, curator, semiotician
Lipkin, David chemist
Loeb, Jerome Thomas retail executive
Loeb, Virgil, Jr. oncologist, hematologist
Logan, Joseph Prescott lawyer
Lovelace, Eldridge Hirst retired landscape architect, city planner
Lovin, Keith Harold university administrator, philosophy educator
Lowenhaupt, Charles Abraham lawyer
Loynd, Richard Birkett consumer products company executive
Lucy, Robert Meredith lawyer
†Luebbert, Karen M. academic administrator
Lustman, Patrick J. psychiatrist
Lutz, John Thomas author
Lyons, Gordon marketing executive
Macauley, Edward C. company executive
Macias, Edward S. chemistry educator, university official and dean
MacInnis, Al professional hockey player
Magill, Gerard health services educator
Maguire, John Patrick investment company executive
Mahan, David James university official
Mahsman, David Lawrence religious publications editor
Majerus, Philip Warren physician
Mandelker, Daniel Robert law educator
Mandelstamm, Jerome Robert lawyer
Mangelsdorf, Thomas Kelly psychiatrist, consultant
Manne, Marshall Stanley periodontist
Manske, Paul Robert orthopedic hand surgeon, educator
Mantovani, John F. pediatric neurologist
Marking, T(heodore) Joseph, Jr. transportation and urban planner
Marks, Murry Aaron lawyer
Marsh, James C., Jr. secondary school principal
Marshall, Garland Ross biochemist, biophysicist, medical educator
Martens, Patricia Frances adult education educator
Martin, Kevin John nephrologist, educator
Maschmann, Michael Wayne controller
Maupin, Stephanie Zeller educator, consultant
Maurer, Frederic George, III banker
Maxwell, Dorothea Bost Andrews civic worker
McCarter, Charles Chase lawyer
†McClain, Curtis Keith, Jr. religious studies educator, minister
†McCoole, Robert construction company executive
†McCracken, Ellis W., Jr. retired lawyer, corporation executive
McDaniel, James Edwin lawyer
McDonald, David P. federal judge
†McDonald, Josh William surgical pathologist
McDonnell, Sanford Noyes aircraft company executive
McFadden, James Frederick, Jr. surgeon
McGannon, John Barry university chancellor
McGee, William Dean (Willie McGee) professional baseball player
McGuinness, Barbara Sue food products executive
McGwire, Mark David professional baseball player
McKelvey, James Morgan chemical engineering educator
McKenna, William John textile products executive
McKinnis, Michael B. lawyer
McMillian, Theodore federal judge
†Medler, Mary Ann L. federal judge
Meisel, George Vincent lawyer
Meissner, Edwin Benjamin, Jr. retired real estate broker
Melman, Joy civic volunteer
Merrell, James Lee religious editor, clergyman
Merrill, Charles Eugene lawyer
Metcalfe, Walter Lee, Jr. lawyer
Meyer, John Strauch, Jr. lawyer
Meyersick, Sharon Kay nurse, insurance administrator
Michaelides, Constantine Evangelos architect, educator
Middelkamp, John Neal pediatrician, educator
Miller, Gary J. political economist
Miller, James Gegan research scientist, physics educator
Miller, Jo Ann education educator, college official
Mohan, John J. lawyer
Molloff, Florence Jeanine speech and language therapist
Monroe, Thomas Edward industrial corporation executive
Monteleone, Patricia academic dean
Montesi, Albert Joseph retired English educator
Mooradian, Arshag Dertad physician, educator
Moore, McPherson Dorsett lawyer
Moore, Patricia Kay investor, public relations director
Morales-Galarreta, Julio psychiatrist, child psychoanalyst
Morley, Harry Thomas, Jr. real estate executive
Morley, John Edward physician
Morris, John Carl neurologist, researcher
Morrison, Barton Douglas minister
Moseley, Marc Robards sales executive
Moten, John, Jr. gas industry executive, chemist
Mueller, Charles William electric utility executive
Muller, Lyle Dean retired religious organization administrator
Muller, Marcel W(ettstein) electrical engineering educator
Mulligan, Michael Dennis lawyer
†Mummert, Thomas C., III federal judge
Munger, George Howard, Jr. pastor, chaplain
Murray, Robert Wallace chemistry educator
Musial, Stan(ley) (Frank Musial) hotel and restaurant executive, former baseball team executive, former baseball player
Myerson, Robert J. radiation oncologist, educator
Nadeau, John marketing and corporate communications consultant
†Naunann, Joseph F. bishop
Needham, Carol Ann lawyer, educator
†Nelson, Barbara Jeanne sales executive
Neuefeind, Wilhelm economics educator, university administrator
Neville, James Morton lawyer, consumer products executive
Newman, Andrew Edison restaurant executive
Newman, Charles A. lawyer
Newman, Joan Meskiel lawyer
†Noce, David D. federal judge
Noel, Edwin Lawrence lawyer
Norman, Charles Henry broadcasting executive
North, Douglass Cecil economist, educator
Nussbaum, A(dolf) Edward mathematician, educator
O'Donnell, Mark Joseph accountant
O'Keefe, Michael Daniel lawyer
Olshwanger, Ron photojournalist
Olson, Clarence Elmer, Jr. newspaper editor
Olson, Robert Grant lawyer
O'Neill, Eugene Milton mergers and acquisitions consultant
O'Neill, John Robert airline executive
O'Neill, Sheila principal
Ong, Walter Jackson priest, English educator, author
Ortbals, Gerald Ray lawyer
Osborn, John David credit union executive
Osborn, Mark Eliot dentist
O'Shoney, Glenn church administrator
Ott, Sabina art educator
Owens, William Don anesthesiology educator
Ozawa, Martha Naoko social work educator
Palans, Lloyd Alex lawyer
†Pautrot, Jean-Louis Jacques educator
Payne, Meredith Jorstad physician
†Peck, Carol King physiologist, educator
Peck, William Arno physician, educator, university official and dean
Pennick, Paul Patrick newspaper editor
Penniman, Nicholas Griffith, IV newspaper publisher
Peper, Christian Baird lawyer
Perez, Carlos A. radiation oncologist, educator
Perlmutter, David H. physician, educator
Perotti, Rose Norma lawyer
Perry, Catherine D. judge
Perry, Lewis Curtis historian, educator
†Pertmutter, Joel S. physician
Peters, David Allen mechanical engineering educator, consultant
Pfefferkorn, Michael Gene, Sr. secondary school educator, writer
Pfefferkorn, Sandra Jo secondary school educator
Pickle, Robert Douglas lawyer, footwear industry executive
Pikaard, Craig Stuart biology educator
Pitelka, Linda Pacini history educator
Pittman, David Joshua sociologist, educator, researcher, consultant
Poellot, Luther minister
Pollack, Joe retired newspaper critic and columnist, writer
Pollack, Seymour Victor computer science educator
Pon-Salazar, Francisco Demetrio diplomat, educator, deacon, counselor
Poole, William bank executive
Pope, Robert E(ugene) fraternal organization administrator
Poscover, Maury B. lawyer
Powers, Pierce William, Jr. insurance specialist
Prensky, Arthur Lawrence pediatric neurologist, educator
Profeta, Salvatore, Jr. chemist
Provost, Cheryl Louise Winters account executive
Pulitzer, Michael Edgar publishing executive
Purdy, James Aaron medical physics educator
Purkerson, Mabel Louise physician, physiologist, educator
Quenon, Robert Hagerty retired mining consultant and holding company executive
Radentz, Michael Grey recording engineer, producer, composer, musician
Radford, Diane Mary surgeon, surgical oncologist
Raeuchle, John Steven computer analyst
Rao, Dabeeru C. epidemiologist
Rasche, Robert Harold banker, retired economics educator
Rataj, Edward William lawyer
Raven, Peter Hamilton botanical garden director, botany educator
Reeg, Kurtis Bradford lawyer
Regnell, Barbara Caramella retired media educator
Reid, Lorene Frances middle school educator
Reinert, Paul Clare university chancellor emeritus
Rich, Harry Earl financial executive
Richardson, Thomas Hampton design consulting engineer
Riddle, Veryl Lee lawyer
Rigali, Justin F. archbishop
Riner, Ronald Nathan cardiologist, business consultant
Ring, Lucile Wiley lawyer
Ritter, Robert Forcier lawyer
Ritterskamp, Douglas Dolvin lawyer
Roberts, Hugh Evan business investment services company executive
Robins, Lee Nelken medical educator
Robins, Marjorie McCarthy (Mrs. George Kenneth Robins) civic worker
Robinson, John Philip secondary educator
Rockwell, Hays Hamilton bishop
Rodenbaugh, Lisa Pyle nurse
Rodriguez, Katie Claire advocate disability awareness
Roediger, Henry L., III psychology educator
Rogers, John Russell manufacturing company executive, engineer
Rosenthal, Harold Leslie biochemistry educator
Rosenzweig, Saul psychologist, educator, administrator
Rosin, Walter L. retired religious organization administrator
Ross, Monte electrical engineer
Rowold, Henry Lawrence religious studies educator
Royal, Henry Duval nuclear medicine physician
Royce, Robert Killian physician
Rubenstein, Jerome Max lawyer
Ruland, Richard Eugene English and American literature educator, critic, literary historian
Russell-Davis, Valerie Sid Saint Louis executive director employment and training
Ruwitch, Ann Rubenstein urban planner executive
Sachs, Alan Arthur lawyer, corporate executive
Sage, Linda Catherine science writer, public relations professional
Sago, Janis Lynn photography educator
Sale, Llewellyn, III lawyer
Sale, Merritt classicist, comparatist, educator
Saligman, Harvey consumer products and services company executive
Salisbury, Robert Holt political science educator
Sandbach, Charlie Bernard accountant
Sandberg, John Steven lawyer
Sanders, Fred Joseph aerospace company executive
Sant, John Talbot lawyer
Sathe, Sharad Somnath chemical company executive
Scheffing, Donald George county government administrator
†Schermer, Barry S. federal judge
Schindler, Laura Ann piano teacher, accompanist
Schlafly, Phyllis Stewart author
Schlesinger, Milton J. virology educator, researcher
Schmidt, Clarence Anton financial consultant
Schmidt, Douglas Craig computer science educator, consultant
Schmidt, Gunter dentist
Schmidt, Robert Charles, Jr. finance executive
Schnuck, Craig D. grocery stores company executive
Schnuck, Scott C. grocery store executive
†Schoeffel, Georgia B. secondary education educator
Schoendienst, Albert Fred (Red Schoendienst) professional baseball coach, former baseball player
Schoene, Kathleen Snyder lawyer
Schoenhard, William Charles, Jr. health care executive
Schonfeld, Gustav medical educator, researcher
Schramm, Paul Howard lawyer
Schreiber, James Ralph obstetrics, gynecology researcher
Schwartz, Alan Leigh pediatrician, educator
Schwarz, Egon humanities and German language educator, author, literary critic
Schwier, Ann Stranquist economics educator
Searls, Eileen Haughey lawyer, librarian, educator
Seemann, Rosalie Mary international business and foreign policy association executive
Self, Larry Douglas architectural firm executive
Seligman, Joel dean
Sestric, Anthony James lawyer
Sexton, Owen James vertebrate ecology educator, conservationist
Shands, Courtney, Jr. lawyer
Shank, Robert Ely physician, preventive medicine educator, retired
Shapiro, Robert B. manufacturing executive
Shaw, Charles Alexander judge
Shaw, John Arthur lawyer
Shea, Daniel Bartholomew, Jr. English language educator, actor
Shell, Owen G., Jr. banker
Shepperd, Thomas Eugene accountant
†Shipman, Charles Andrew librarian
Shrauner, Barbara Wayne Abraham electrical engineering educator
Sibbald, John Ristow management consultant
Siegel, Barry Alan nuclear radiologist
Siemer, Paul Jennings public relations executive
†Sikic, Hrvoje mathematician
Sikorski, James Alan research chemist
Sincoff, Jerome J. architect
Sita, Michael John pharmacist, educator
†Slavin, Peter hospital administrator
Slavin, Raymond Granam allergist, immunologist
Sly, William S. biochemist, educator
Smith, Arthur E. counseling educator, vocational psychologist
Smith, Arthur Lee lawyer
Smith, Ozzie (Osborne Earl Smith) retired professional baseball player
Sneeringer, Stephen Geddes lawyer
Spector, Gershon Jerry physician, educator, researcher
Spindler, Michelle Lee accountant
Stann, John Anthony investment banker
Stanton, Frank Lawrence, Jr. graphic designer, illustrator, educator
Stearley, Robert Jay retired packaging company executive
Stephenson, Gwendolyn W. academic administrator
Stewart, John Harger music educator
Stiritz, William P. food company executive
Stodghill, Ronald school system administrator
Stoecker, David Thomas banker
Stohr, Donald J. federal judge
Stoneman, William, III physician, educator
Storandt, Martha psychologist
Stork, Donald Arthur advertising executive
Stratton, Sharon Elizabeth Spahn mental and women's health nurse, nurse supervisor
Stretch, John Joseph social work educator, management and evaluation consultant
Strevey, Tracy Elmer, Jr. army officer, surgeon, physician executive
Strunk, Robert Charles physician
Stumpf, Earlwayne Schwarze actor, advertising executive
Suhre, Walter Anthony, Jr. retired lawyer and brewery executive
Sullivan, Edward Lawrence lawyer
Suter, Albert Edward manufacturing company executive
Sutera, Salvatore Philip mechanical engineering educator
Sutter, Elizabeth Henby (Mrs. Richard A. Sutter) civic leader, management company executive
Sutter, Jane Elizabeth educator, writer
Sutter, Richard Anthony physician
Switzer, Frederick Michael, III lawyer, mediator
Szabo, Barna Aladar mechanical engineering educator, mining engineer
Takano, Masaharu physical chemist
Takes, Peter Arthur immunologist
Taylor, Andrew C. rental leasing company executive
Taylor, Jack C. rental and leasing company executive
Teasdale, Kenneth Fulbright lawyer
Teitelbaum, Steven Lazarus pathology educator
†Tempel, Lee W. neurologist
Templeton, Alan Robert biology educator
Ternberg, Jessie Lamoin pediatric surgeon
Thalden, Barry R. architect

Thomas, Pamela Adrienne *special education educator*
Thompson, Rodney Marlin *computer consultant*
Thompson, Vetta Lynn Sanders *psychologist, educator*
Throdahl, Monte Corden *former chemical company executive*
Tierney, Michael Edward *lawyer*
Tober, Lester Victor *shoe company executive*
Touhill, Blanche Marie *university chancellor, history-education educator*
†Triplett, Charles Lawrence *secondary education educator*
Trout, Keith William *electrical engineer*
Turley, Michael Roy *lawyer*
Turner, Harold Edward *education educator*
Tuten, Richard Lamar *professional football player*
Tyler, William Howard, Jr. *advertising executive, educator*
Ulett, George Andrew *psychiatrist*
Ullian, Joseph Silbert *philosophy educator*
Unanue, Emil Raphael *immunopathologist*
Upbin, Hal Jay *consumer products executive*
Van Cleve, William Moore *lawyer*
Van Dover, Donald *business owner, consultant*
Van Luven, William Robert *management consultant*
Virgo, John Michael *economist, researcher, educator*
Virgo, Katherine Sue *health services researcher*
Virtel, James John *lawyer*
Vonk, Hans *conductor*
Wagner, Raymond Thomas, Jr. *lawyer, corporation executive*
Walentik, Corinne Anne *pediatrician*
Walker, Robert Mowbray *physicist, educator*
Walsh, John E., Jr. *business educator, consultant*
Walsh, Joseph Leo, III *lawyer*
Walsh, Thomas Charles *lawyer*
Walz, Bruce James *radiation oncologist*
Ward, R. J. *bishop*
Ward, Richard Compton *management consultant*
†Ward-Brown, Denise *sculptor, educator*
Warner, Susan *loan specialist*
Wassell, Loren W. *public affairs administrator, writer*
Waters, Richard *retired publishing company executive*
Watkins, Hortense Catherine *middle school educator*
Watson, Patty Jo *anthropology educator*
Watson, Richard Allan *philosophy educator, writer*
Watters, Richard Donald *lawyer*
†Wayne, Jane Oxenhandler (Jane O. Wayne) *poet, writing educator*
Weaver, Charles Lyndell, Jr. *institutional and manufacturing facilities administrator, management and marketing systems consultant*
Weaver, William Clair, Jr. (Mike Weaver) *human resources development executive*
Webber, E. Richard, Jr. *judge*
†Weber, Mark F. *medical executive*
Weber, Morton M. *microbial biochemist, educator*
Weese, Cynthia Rogers *architect, educator*
Weidenbaum, Murray Lew *economics educator*
Weiss, Charles Andrew *lawyer*
Weiss, Robert Francis *former academic administrator, religious organization administrator, consultant*
Welch, David William *lawyer*
Welch, Michael John *chemistry educator, researcher*
Weldon, Virginia V. *university administrator*
Wellman, Carl Pierce *philosophy educator*
†Weppelman, Roger Michael *regulatory compliance officer*
Werner, Burton Kready *insurance company executive*
Whyte, Michael Peter *medicine, pediatrics and genetics educator, research director*
Wickline, Samuel Alan *cardiologist, educator*
Wiechart, Ralph *superintendent military memorial museum*
†Wielansky, Lee S. *real estate company executive*
Wiggins, Dewayne Lee *financial executive*
Wiley, Gregory Robert *publisher*
Wilke, LeRoy *church administrator*
Will, Clifford Martin *physicist, educator*
Willard, Gregory Dale *lawyer*
Williams, Mary Alice Baldwin *retired home economist, volunteer consultant*
Williams, Theodore Joseph, Jr. *lawyer*
Willman, Vallee Louis *physician, surgery educator*
Willmore, Luther James, Jr. *neurologist, academic administrator, educator*
Wilson, Edward Nathan *mathematician, educator*
Wilson, Margaret Bush *lawyer, civil rights leader*
Wilson, Michael E. *lawyer*
Winer, Warren James *insurance executive*
Winning, John Patrick *lawyer*
Winter, David Ferdinand *electrical engineering educator, consultant*
Winter, Mildred M. *educational administrator*
Winter, Richard Lawrence *financial and health care consulting company executive*
Winter, William Earl *retired beverage company executive*
Withers, W. Wayne *lawyer*
Witherspoon, William *investment economist*
Wold, William Sydney *molecular biology educator*
Wolfe, Charles Morgan *electrical engineering educator*
Wolff, Frank Pierce, Jr. *lawyer*
Wood, Denise P. *clinical nurse specialist*
Woodruff, Bruce Emery *lawyer*
Woodward, Robert Simpson, IV *economics educator*
Wrighton, Mark Stephen *chemistry educator*
Wu, Nelson Ikon *art history educator, author, artist*
Young, Marvin Oscar *lawyer*
Young, Paul Andrew *anatomist*
Zaborszky, John *electrical engineer, educator*
Zhuo, Min *neurobiology educator*
Zinner, Ernst K. *physics educator, earth and planetary science educator, researcher*
Zlobin, Nikolai V. *history educator*
Zurheide, Charles Henry *consulting electrical engineer*

Saint Paul
Unterreiner, C. Martin *financial advisor*

Saint Peters
†Brooks, Richard Eugene *cultural affairs administrator*
Krey, Mary Ann Reynolds *beer wholesaler executive*
Meier, Donald James *marketing executive*

Salem
Dent, Catherine Gale *secondary education educator*
†Jessen, Chris Michael *music educator*
Wood, Thomas Wesley *humanities educator, editor*

Salisbury
†Head, Shane Everett *animal nutrition company executive, consultant*

Savannah
Walker, Frances Morine *retired special education educator*

Sedalia
Hazen, Elizabeth Frances *retired special education educator*
Shelton, Thomas Alfred *Christian education director*

Sikeston
†Schuchart, Ann Murphy *artist, educator*

Smithville
Marzinski, Lynn Rose *oncological nurse*

Springfield
Allcorn, Terry Alan *principal, educator*
Archibald, Charles Arnold *holding company executive*
Ash, Sharon Kaye *real estate company executive*
Asher, Sandra Fenichel *author, playwright*
Baird, Robert Dean *mission director*
Berger, Jerry Allen *museum director*
Bohnenkamper, Katherine Elizabeth *library science educator*
Burgess, Ruth Lenora Vassar *speech and language educator*
Busch, Annie *library director*
Buschert, Jason Lee *accountant*
Byers, Thomas William *optometrist*
Carlson, Thomas Joseph *real estate developer, lawyer, former mayor*
†Carmichael, Joe *lawyer*
Champion, Norma Jean *communications educator, state legislator*
Clark, Russell Gentry *federal judge*
Clithero, Monte Paul *lawyer*
Condellone, Trent Peter *real estate developer*
Cooper, J. Michael *advertising executive*
Costabile-Heming, Carol Anne *humanities educator*
Denton, D. Keith *management educator*
†England, James C. *federal judge*
Feazell, Johnny Ray *physicians assistant*
Geter, Rodney Keith *plastic surgeon*
†Gillming, Kenneth *church administrator*
Glazier, Robert Carl *publishing executive*
Grams, Betty Jane *minister, educator, writer*
Green, David Ferrell *law enforcement official*
Groves, Sharon Sue *elementary education educator*
Gruhn, Robert Stephen *parole officer*
Hackett, Earl Randolph *neurologist*
†Hammons, John Q. *hotel executive*
Hansen, John Paul *metallurgical engineer*
Harris, Ralph William *religious journalist*
H'Doubler, Francis Todd, Jr. *surgeon*
Hignite, Michael Anthony *computer information systems educator, researcher, writer, consultant*
Hobus, Robert Allen *minister*
Horn, Kenneth Leroy *editor*
Hulston, John Kenton *lawyer*
Johnstone, Paula Sue *medical technologist*
Jones, Sheryl Leanne *retail sales executive*
Jura, James J. *electric utility executive*
†Keiser, John Howard *university president*
Kincaid, Paul Kent *public relations professional*
Leibrecht, John Joseph *bishop*
†Lin, Zhi *art educator*
Lowther, Gerald Halbert *lawyer*
Luttrull, Shirley JoAnn *protective services official*
Maltby, Florence Helen *library science educator*
McCartney, N. L. *investment banker*
McCorcle, Marcus Duane *obstetrician, gynecologist*
McCullough, V. Beth *pharmacist, educator*
McDonald, William Henry *lawyer*
Montgomery, Linda Stroupe *county official*
Moore, John Edwin, Jr. *college president*
†Moore, Neal Worden *archivist*
Morris, Ann Haseltine Jones *social welfare administrator*
Moulder, T. Earline *musician*
O'Block, Robert *behavioral scientist*
Ostergren, Gregory Victor *insurance company executive*
Ownby, Jerry Steve *landscape architect, educator*
Penninger, William Holt, Jr. *lawyer*
Prayson, Stephen Alexander *pharmacist*
†Qiao, Yuhua *public administration educator*
Quiroga, Ninoska *university official*
Roberts, Patrick Kent *lawyer*
Robertson, Ruth Ann *systems analyst, engineer*
Rogers, Roddy Jack *civil, geotechnical and water engineer*
Shealy, Michael Ivan *financial consultant, geologist*
Slye, Gail Lynn *educator*
Smith, Donald L. *social sciences educator*
Smith, Judith Ann *academic administrator*
Spicer, Holt Vandercook *speech and theater educator*
Starnes, James Wright *lawyer*
Staudte, Diane Elaine *medical-surgical, cardiac nurse*
Stern, Roy Dalton *manufacturing financial executive*
Stone, Allan David *economics educator*
Stovall, Richard L. *academic administrator*
Strickler, Ivan K. *dairy farmer*
Sylvester, Ronald Charles *newspaper writer*
Thompson, Clifton C. *retired chemistry educator, university administrator*
Thompson, Wade S. *artist, art and design educator*
Toste, Anthony Paim *chemistry educator, researcher*
Trask, Thomas Edward *religious organization administrator*
Van Cleave, William Robert *international relations educator*
Williams, Juanita (Tudie Williams) *home health care nurse, administrator*
†Wilson, Judith Ann *educator*
Wishard, Mary Lee *small business operator*
Witherspoon, John Thomas *water treatment company executive*
†Wooten, Rosalie *automotive company executive*

Steelville
Hagemeier, Juanita Elizabeth *human services administrator*

Stockton
Hammons, Brian Kent *lawyer, business executive*
Jackson, Betty L. Deason *real estate developer*

Sullivan
Penn, Ronald Hulen *manufacturing executive*

Sweet Springs
Long, Helen Halter *author, educator*

Tipton
Wazir, Tadar Jihad *chaplain, small business owner*

Town And Country
Lachenicht-Berkeley, Angela Marie *marketing professional*

Trenton
Myntti, Jon Nicholas *software engineer*

Troy
Simmons, Karen Elaine *secondary education educator*

Turners
Hone, Randolph Cooper *architect*

Unionville
Sparks, (Lloyd) Melvin *appraiser*

University City
Adams, Joseph Lee, Jr. *history educator, mayor*
Benson, Joseph Fred *journalist, legal historian*
Shen, Jerome Tseng Yung *retired pediatrician*

Verona
Jay, Jerry Leon, Sr. *retired publishing executive, industrial engineer*
Youngberg, Charlotte Anne *education specialist*

Viburnum
West, Roberta Bertha *writer*

Warrensburg
Adams, Wilburn Clifton *communication educator*
Allen, Densil E., Jr. *agricultural studies educator*
Carr, Richard Raymond *editor, public relations administrator*
Elliott, Eddie Mayes *academic administrator*
Lewis, Marcile Reneé *nursing educator*
Limback, E(dna) Rebecca *vocational education educator*
Robbins, Dorothy Ann *foreign language educator*
Stagg, David Lee *music educator*

Warson Woods
†Barnes, Walter C., Jr. *physician*

Washington
†Bauer, Carl Jonathan *public relations executive*
Chambers, Jerry Ray *school system administrator*

Waynesville
†Taylor, Lee Edward *quality control engineer*

Webb City
Nichols, Robert Leighton *civil engineer*

Webster Groves
Forry, John Emerson *retired aerospace company executive*
Kramer, Gerhardt Theodore *architect*
Osver, Arthur *artist*
Schenkenberg, Mary Martin *principal*

Wentzville
Garrett, Dwayne Everett *veterinary clinic executive*

West Plains
Dunlap, David Houston *judge*
Wilcoxson, Roy Dell *plant pathology educator and researcher*

Wheeling
†Roe, Mary Ann *postmaster*

Whiteman AFB
†Barnidge, Leroy, Jr. *military officer*

Wildwood
†Braun, David Joseph *financial executive*
Brawner, Patricia Ann *English educator*
Colletti, Teresa Ann *polymer chemist*
Crist, Lewis Roger *insurance company executive*

Windsor
Boarman, Marjorie Ruth *manufacturing company executive, consultant*

Windyville
Blosser, Pamela Elizabeth *metaphysics educator, counselor, minister*
Clark, Laurel Jan *adult education educator, author, editor, minister*
Condron, Barbara O'Guinn *metaphysics educator, school administrator, publisher*
Condron, Daniel Ralph *academic administrator, metaphysics educator*

Winigan
†Smith, Wayne Delarmie *veterinarian, farmer*

MONTANA

Antelope
Olson, Betty-Jean *retired elementary education educator*

Belt
Anderson, Harold Sterling *retired adult education educator*

Big Arm
†Dale, David Wilson *English educator, poet*

Bigfork
Shennum, Robert Herman *retired telephone company executive*

Billings
Aldrich, Richard Kingsley *lawyer*
†Anderson, Richard W. *federal judge*
Barnea, Uri N. *music director, conductor, composer, violinist*
Beiswanger, Gary Lee *lawyer*
†Cromley, Brent Reed *lawyer, legal association administrator*
Darrow, George F. *natural resources company owner, consultant*
DeRosier, Arthur Henry, Jr. *college president*
Fagg, Russell *judge, lawyer*
Gallinger, Lorraine D. *prosecutor*
Glenn, Guy Charles *pathologist*
Glenn, Lucia Howarth *retired mental health services professional*
Hanson, Norman *lawyer*
Haughey, James McCrea *lawyer, artist*
Kohler, William Curtis *sleep specialist, neurologist*
Larsen, Richard Lee *former mayor and city manager, business, municipal and labor relations consultant, arbitrator*
Malee, Thomas Michael *lawyer*
Matteucci, Sherry Scheel *prosecutor*
May, Michael Wayne *technical school executive*
McDaniel, Susan Roberta *academic administrator*
Nance, Robert Lewis *oil company executive*
Peterson, Arthur Laverne *foundation administrator*
Posey, Frederick Bruce *mortgage banker*
Reed, Kenneth G. *petroleum company executive*
Rich, Joseph David *psychiatrist*
Sample, Joseph Scanlon *foundation executive*
Shanstrom, Jack D. *federal judge*
†Thomas, Sidney R. *federal court judge*
Thompson, James William *lawyer*
Towe, A. Ruth *museum director*
Towe, Thomas Edward *lawyer*

Bozeman
Aig, Dennis Ira *writer, film producer*
Anacker, Edward William *retired chemistry educator*
Berg, Lloyd *chemical engineering educator*
Billau, Robin Louise *engineering and consulting executive*
Buck, John E. *sculptor, print maker, educator*
Cokelet, Giles Roy *biomedical engineering educator*
Conover, Richard Corrill *lawyer*
Costerton, John William Fisher *microbiologist*
Davis, Nicholas Homans Clark *finance company executive*
DeHaas, John Neff, Jr. *retired architecture educator*
Frohnmayer, John Edward *lawyer, legal scholar, ethicist, writer*
Goering, Kenneth Justin *college administrator*
Gray, Philip Howard *retired psychologist, educator*
Grieco, Paul Anthony *chemistry educator*
Harris, Christopher Kirk *lawyer*
Horner, John Robert *paleontologist, researcher*
Hovin, Arne William *agronomist, educator*
Lapeyre, Gerald J. *physics educator, researcher*
Lavin, Matthew T. *horticultural educator*
†Meister, Alice Marie *librarian*
Mentzer, Raymond Albert *history educator*
Mertz, Edwin Theodore *retired biochemist, emeritus educator*
Monaco, Paul *academic administrator, educator, artist, writer*
Nelson, Steven Dwayne *lawyer*
Sanddal, Nels Dodge *foundation executive, consultant*
Sanks, Robert Leland *environmental engineer, emeritus educator*
Savery, Matthew *music conductor, director, educator*
Selyem, Bruce Jade *photographer*
Sheehan, Tracey *basketball coach*
Spencer, Robert C. *retired political science educator*
Stanislao, Joseph *consulting engineer, educator*
Stroup, Richard Lyndell *economics educator, writer*
Todd, Kenneth S., Jr. *parasitologist, educator*
Wylie, Paul Richter, Jr. *lawyer*

Butte
Bishop, Robert Charles *architect, metals and minerals company executive*
Burke, John James *utility executive*
Mc Elwain, Joseph Arthur *retired power company executive*
Ouellette, Debra Lee *association administrator, consultant*
†Peterson, John Leonard *lawyer, judge*
†Reardon, Stephen James, Jr. *retired English speech educator*
Sherrill, Barbara Ann Buker *elementary school educator*
Shipham, Mark Roger *small business owner, artist*
Thompson, John *museum director*
van der Veur, Paul Roscoe *communication educator, researcher*
Zeihen, Lester Gregory *geology educator*

Circle
McDonough, Russell Charles *retired state supreme court justice*

Crow Agency
Deernose, Kitty *museum curator*
Pease-Pretty On Top, Janine B. *community college administrator*

Cut Bank
McCormick, Betty Leonora *accountant*

Dayton
Catalfomo, Philip *retired university dean*
Volborth, Alexis von *geochemistry and geological engineering educator*

Deer Lodge
McWright, Michael J. *historic site administrator*

Fairfield
Graf, Ervin Donald *municipal administrator*

Gardiner
Halfpenny, James Carson *scientist, educator, author*

Great Falls
Annau, Raymone Jeanine *cardiovascular nurse*
†Bobbitt, Curtis Wayne *English educator*
Booth Gilliam, Diane Lorraine *yoga instructor, former philosophy educator*
Coffman, Barbara LeAnn *environmentalist, state official*
Davidson, David Scott *architect*
Doherty, Steve *lawyer, state legislator*
Downer, William John, Jr. *retired hospital administrator*

Hatfield, Paul Gerhart *federal judge, lawyer*
†Heckel, James John *library director*
†Holter, Robert M. *federal judge*
Johnson, Gordon James *artistic director, conductor*
McKinnon, Robert Scott *swimming educator*
Milone, Anthony M. *bishop*
Paulson-Ehrhardt, Patricia Helen *sales executive*
Sletten, John Robert *construction company executive*
†Smith, Clayton Nowlin *academic administrator*
Stevens, George Alexander *realtor*
Walker, Leland Jasper *civil engineer*

Hamilton
Munoz, John Joaquin *research microbiologist*
Rudbach, Jon Anthony *biotechnical company executive*

Hardin
MacClean, Walter Lee *dentist*

Harrison
Jackson, Peter Vorious, III *retired association executive*

Havre
Clouse, Vickie Rae *biology and paleontology educator*
Gallus, Charles Joseph *journalist*
Mayer Lossing, Emily Ann *city official*
Moog, Mary Ann Pimley *lawyer*

Helena
Aleksich-Akey, Sue *Republican party chairman*
Brown, Jan Whitney *small business owner*
Cooney, Mike *state official*
Cordingley, Mary Jeanette Bowles (Mrs. William Andrew Cordingley) *social worker, psychologist, artist, writer*
†Cramer, Chuckie *state senate official*
Crofts, Richard A. *academic administrator*
Dorrance, Debra Ann *secondary school educator*
Ekanger, Laurie *state official*
Fitzpatrick, Lois Ann *library administrator*
Gray, Karla Marie *state supreme court justice*
†Guiliani, Marilyn Kay *educator*
Haines, John Meade *poet, translator, writer*
Hargrove, Don *state senator*
Harrison, John Conway *state supreme court justice*
Hart, John William *theology educator*
Hays, Rick F. *public policy executive*
Hunt, William E., Sr. *state supreme court justice*
†Hutchinson, Donald Wilson *state commissioner of financial institutions*
Johnson, David Sellie *civil engineer*
Johnson, Qulan Adrian *software engineer*
Jones, Charles Irving *bishop*
Kolstad, Allen C. *state official*
Leaphart, W. William *state supreme court justice*
†Lewis, Dave *state agency administrator*
Lovell, Charles C. *federal judge*
Malcolm, Andrew Hogarth *journalist, writer*
Manuel, Vivian *public relations company executive*
Mazurek, Joseph P. *state attorney general, former state legislator*
Meadows, Judith Adams *law librarian, educator*
Morrison, John Haddow, Jr. *engineering company executive*
Nelson, James C *state supreme court justice*
†O'Keefe, Mark David *state official*
†Peck, Ralph *state agency administrator*
Racicot, Marc F. *governor*
†Reap, Craig T. *protective services officer*
Scott, Joyce Alaine *university official*
Strickler, Jeffrey Harold *pediatrician*
Trieweiler, Terry Nicholas *state supreme court justice*
Turnage, Jean A. *state supreme court justice*
Warren, Christopher Charles *electronics executive*
†Watson, Thomas M. *civil engineer*

Hot Springs
Erickson, James Gardner *retired artist, cartoonist*

Kalispell
Lopp, Susan Jane *insurance underwriter*
Ormiston, Patricia Jane *elementary education educator*
Robinson, Calvin Stanford *lawyer*
Ruder, Melvin Harvey *retired newspaper editor*
von Krenner, Walther G. *artist, writer, art consultant and appraiser*

Lewistown
Edwards, Linda L. *elementary education educator*

Livingston
Clarke, Urana *writer, musician, educator*

Mc Leod
Hjortsberg, William Reinhold *author*

Miles City
Emilsson, Elizabeth Maykuth *special education educator*
Fraser, Mac Robert (Rob Fraser) *livestock auction owner, auctioneer*
Heitschmidt, Rodney Keith *rangeland ecologist*
†Larson, Gene L. *illustrator*
†Oberlander, Dale Eugene *college administrator*

Missoula
Barnett, Mary Louise *elementary education educator*
Brenner, Gerry *English educator*
Brown, Perry Joe *university dean*
Brown, Robert Munro *museum director*
Brumit, Lawrence Edward, III *oil field service company executive*
†Chacón, Hipólito Rafael *art historian, educator, art critic*
Dennison, George Marshel *academic administrator*
Egley, Thomas Arthur *computer services executive, accountant*
†Erickson, Leif B. *federal judge*
Fawcett, Don Wayne *anatomist*
Gallagher, Tonya Marie *family support specialist*
George, Alexander Andrew *lawyer*
Haddon, Sam Ellis *lawyer*
†Harlan, John W. *physician*
Jenni, Donald Alison *zoology educator*
Kemmis, Daniel Orra *cultural organization administrator, author*
Kindrick, Robert LeRoy *academic administrator, dean, English educator*
Knowles, William Leroy (Bill Knowles) *television news producer, journalism educator*
Listerud, (Lowell) Brian *choir director, music educator*
Lopach, James Joseph *political science educator*
Millin, Laura Jeanne *museum director*
Molloy, Donald William *lawyer, partner*
Morales, Julio K. *lawyer*
Morin, Paula Marie Yvette (Maryan Morin) *photographer, artist, photo researcher*
Mudd, John O. *lawyer*
Murray, Raymond Carl *forensic geologist, educator*
Osterheld, R(obert) Keith *chemistry educator*
Poore, James Albert, III *lawyer*
Power, Thomas Michael *economist, educator*
Renz, Jeffrey Thomas *lawyer, educator*
Rice, Steven Dale *electronics educator*
†Riggs, Thomas Jeffries, IV *editor*
Rippon, Thomas Michael *art educator, artist*
Selvig, Robin *basketball coach*
†Van Pelt, Peter J. *airport terminal executive*
Washington, Dennis *construction executive*
Williams, Pat *former congressman*
Wingenbach, Gregory Charles *priest, religious-ecumenical agency director*
Wolfe, Gary John *foundation administrator, wildlife biologist*
Wollersheim, Janet Puccinelli *psychology educator*
Yee, Albert Hoy *retired psychologist, educator*

Park City
Abrams, Ossie Ekman *fundraiser*

Philipsburg
Bauer, Robert Forest *petroleum engineer*

Polson
Stanford, Jack Arthur *biological station administrator*

Pony
Anderson, Richard Ernest *agribusiness development executive, rancher*

Poplar
Gabrielson, Shirley Gail *nurse*

Red Lodge
Kauffman, Marvin Earl *geoscience consultant*

Rollins
Zelezny, William Francis *retired physical chemist*

Savage
Thiessen, Dwight Everett *farmer*

Sidney
Beagle, John Gordon *real estate broker*

Stevensville
Derrick, William Dennis *physical plant administrator, consultant*
Laing-Malcolmson, Sally Anne *enrolled tax agent, tax consultant*

Superior
Schneider, Brenda Laureen *town official*
Tull, Steven Gerald *secondary education educator*

Troy
Sherman, Signe Lidfeldt *portfolio manager, former research chemist*

Utica
Stevenson, Sarah Schoales *rancher, business owner*

Whitefish
†Fielder, Maryann *artist, consultant*
Hemp, Ralph Clyde *retired reinsurance company executive, consultant, arbitrator, umpire*
James, Marion Ray *magazine founder, editor*
Miller, Ronald Alfred *family physician*

NEBRASKA

Alliance
Haefele, Edwin Theodore *political theorist, consultant*

Arlington
Boerrigter, Glenn Charles *educational administrator*

Atkinson
Martens, Helen Eileen *elementary school educator*

Beatrice
Coker, William B. *electrical engineer*

Bellevue
Elliott, Ronald Dean *minister*
Hightower, Pauline Patricia *elementary education educator*
James, Geneva Behrens *secondary school educator*
Moore, Alan Frank *management consultant*
Muller, John Bartlett *university president*
Nicholsen, James Therman *computer company executive*
Wright, John Charles *air force intelligence officer*

Benkelman
Whiteley, Rose Marie *city clerk, treasurer*

Blair
Christopherson, Myrvin Frederick *college president*

Boys Town
Lynch, Thomas Joseph *museum and historic house manager*

Callaway
Maring, Glady Marie *English educator, poet*

Chadron
Ayres, Elizabeth *educator*
Hazen, Vincent Allan *painter, printmaker*
Lecher, Belvadine (Reeves) *museum curator*
Winkle, William Allan *music educator*

Clay Center
Hahn, George LeRoy *agricultural engineer, biometeorologist*
Laster, Danny Bruce *animal scientist*

Columbus
Keller, Harry Allan *electronics technician*
Rieck, Janet Rae *special education educator*
Schumacher, Paul Maynard *lawyer*

Cozad
Peterson, Marilyn Ann Whitney *journalism educator*

Crete
Brakke, Myron Kendall *retired research chemist, educator*
†Martin, Gary John *art educator, artist*
Panec, William Joseph *lawyer*

Dalton
Swanson, Lauren A. *entrepreneur, educator, researcher*

Danbury
Drullinger, Leona Pearl Blair *obstetrics nurse*

Dickens
Rausch, Paul Matthew *financial executive*

Dodge
Inman, Mitchell Lee, Jr. *accountant*

Elkhorn
Welch, Vern A. *retired corn breeder*

Fort Calhoun
†Herman, Theresa Joan (Terri) *quality assurance professional*

Fremont
Deahl, William Evans, Jr. *minister*
Dunklau, Rupert Louis *personal investments consultant*
Gill, Lyle Bennett *retired lawyer*
Roesch, Robert Eugene *dentist*
Winans, Anna Jane *dietitian*

Friend
De Bevoise, Lee Raymond *editor, nurse, writer, photographer, webmaster*

Funk
Sjogren, Donald Ernest *farmer*

Gering
Weihing, John Lawson *plant pathologist, state senator*

Grand Island
Abernethy, Irene Margaret *civic worker, retired county official*
Buettner, Anne Ramona Wing-mui Yu *psychologist*
Busick, Denzel Rex *lawyer*
Etheridge, Margaret Dwyer *medical center director*
†Giddings, William Glenn *community college president*
†Mc Namara, Lawrence J. *bishop*
Ward, Kenneth Lee *recreation therapist*
Zichek, Melvin Eddie *retired clergyman, educator*
Zichek, Shannon Elaine *secondary school educator*

Gretna
Hintz, Norma A. *cardiac care nurse*
Riley, Kevin M. *principal*

Harrison
Coffee, Virginia Claire *civic worker, former mayor*
Knudson, Ruthann *environmental consultant*

Hastings
Bloyd, Beverly *nurse*
Bush, Marjorie Evelynn Tower-Tooker *educator, media specialist, librarian*
Dungan, John Russell, Jr. (Titular Viscount Dungan of Clane and Hereditary Prince of Ara) *anesthesiologist*
Freed, Donald Callen *vocal and choral musician, educator*
Kort, Betty *secondary education educator*
†Watts, James Washington *religion educator*

Hayes Center
Fornoff, Ann Lynette *secondary school educator*

Holdrege
Hendrickson, Bruce Carl *life insurance company executive*
Klein, Michael Clarence *lawyer*

Humboldt
Rumbaugh, Melvin Dale *geneticist, agronomist*

Inman
Keil, Holly Mae *elementary education educator*

Kearney
Fredrickson, Scott Alfred *instructional technology educator, consultant*
Glatter, Kathleen Mary *medical/surgical nurse*
Kelley, Michael Eugene *lawyer*
Kinsinger, Jack Burl *chemist, educator*
Luscher, Robert Michael *English educator, department chair*
Middleton, James G. *education educator, counselor*
Munro, Robert Allan *lawyer*
†Nabb, David Bruce *music educator*
Ramage, Jean Carol *former univesity dean, psychology educator*
Schuyler, Michael W. *historian, educator*
Voigt, Steven Russell *lawyer*
Wice, Paul Clinton *news director, educator*
Wittman, Connie Susan *oncology clinical nurse specialist*
Wubbels, Gene Gerald *chemistry educator*
Young, Ann Elizabeth O'Quinn *historian, educator*

Kilgore
Olsen, Lester Paul (Les Olsen) *minister*

Lincoln
Adams, Charles Henry *retired animal scientist, educator*
Allington, Robert William *instrument company executive*
Angle, John Charles *retired life insurance company executive*
Arth, Lawrence Joseph *insurance executive*
Auld, James S. *educational psychologist*
Bahar, Ezekiel *electrical engineering educator*
Ballinger, Royce Eugene *academic administrator, educator*
Beam, Clarence Arlen *federal judge*
Beermann, Allen J. *former state official*
†Bennie, Bob *investment company executive*
Blad, Blaine L. *agricultural meteorology educator, consultant*
Blankenau, Gail Shaffer *writer*
Bradley, Richard Edwin *retired college president*
†Brownson, E. Ramona Lidstone Brady *secretary*
Brownson, Elwyn James *artist, educator, art therapist*
Bruskewitz, Fabian W. *bishop*
Buhler, Stephen Michael *English educator*
Byrne, C. William, Jr. *athletics program director*
Campbell, John Dee *retired insurance executive*
Case, Sylvester Quezada *minister*
†Cavett, Dorcas C. *elementary educator*
Chisholm, George Nickolaus *dentist*
†Christensen, Douglas *state agency administrator*
Clifton, James K. *market research company executive*
Clyne, Dianna Marie *psychiatrist*
Colleran, Kevin *lawyer*
Connolly, William M. *state supreme court justice*
Connor, Carol J. *library director*
Cope, Thom K. *lawyer*
Curtis, Carl Thomas *former senator*
Davis, Fred *journalist, educator*
Deegan, Mary Jo *sociology educator*
Digman, Lester Aloysius *management educator*
Dittmer, Billie Spruill *school psychologist*
Dixon, Wheeler Winston *film and video studies educator, writer*
†Donovan, Gregory Stearn *human services administrator*
Dyer, William Earl, Jr. *retired newspaper editor*
Eckhardt, Craig Jon *chemistry educator*
Edison, Allen Ray *electrical engineer, educator*
Edwards, Donald Mervin *biological systems engineering educator, university dean*
Elias, Samy E. G. *engineering executive*
Engel, L. Patrick *state legislator*
Exon, J(ohn) James *former senator*
Fisher, Calvin David *food manufacturing company executive*
Fleharty, Mary Sue *secretary*
Foy, Edward Donald *financial planner*
Gardner, Charles Olda *plant geneticist and breeder, design consultant, analyst*
Genoways, Hugh Howard *systematic biologist, educator*
Gerrard, John M. *state supreme court justice*
Gonzalez, Jorge E. *psychologist, researcher*
Gray, Joni Nadine *state agency administrator*
Grew, Priscilla Croswell *university official, geology educator*
Hamilton, David Wendell *medical services executive*
Hanway, Donald Grant *retired agronomist, educator*
Hanway, Donald Grant *Episcopal priest*
Hastings, William Charles *retired state supreme court chief justice*
Heineman, David *state official*
Hendrickson, Kent Herman *university administrator*
Heng, Stanley Mark *national guard officer*
Hermance, Lyle Herbert *college official*
Hewitt, James Watt *lawyer*
Hirai, Denitsu *surgeon*
Hoffman, Glenn Jerrald *agricultural engineering educator, consultant*
Hubbard, Kenneth Gene *climatologist*
Hunhoff, Sister Phyllis *foundation administrator*
Janzow, Walter Theophilus *retired college administrator*
†Johanns, Michael O. *governor*
Johnson, Margaret Kathleen *business educator*
Johnson, Virgil Allen *retired agronomist*
Jones, Lee Bennett *chemist, educator, university official*
†Kathlene, Lyn *political science edcuator*
†Kilgarin, Karen *state official, public relations consultant*
†King, Robert Wandell *writer*
†Knoll, Robert Edwin *English educator*
Kopf, Richard G. *federal judge*
Landis, David Morrison *state legislator*
Laursen, Paul Herbert *retired university educator*
Leinieks, Valdis *classicist, educator*
Levin, Carole *history educator*
†Lewis, Michael Ray *book editor*
Lichty, Warren Dewey, Jr. *lawyer*
Lienemann, Delmar Arthur, Sr. *accountant, real estate developer*
Lingle, Muriel Ellen *retired elementary education educator*
Louda, Svata M. *ecologist, educator*
Luebke, Frederick Carl *retired humanities educator*
Luedtke, Roland Alfred *lawyer*
Lundstrom, Gilbert Gene *banker, lawyer*
Magorian, James *author, poet*
Manglitz, Marjorie Joan *religious education director*
Marsh, Frank (Irving) *former state official*
Massengale, Martin Andrew *agronomist, university president*
†Maurstad, David Ingolf *lieutenant governor, insurance agency executive*
McClurg, James Edward *research laboratory executive*
Metz, Philip Steven *surgeon, educator*
†Minahan, John C., Jr. *federal judge*
†Moeser, James Charles *university chancellor, musician*
Montag, John Joseph, II *librarian*
Moore, Scott *state official*
Morris, M(ary) Rosalind *cytogeneticist, educator*
Morrow, Andrew Nesbit *interior designer, business owner*
Moul, Maxine Burnett *state official*
Mulvaney, Mary Jean *physical education educator*
Mutunayagam, N. Brito *architecture and planning educator, associate dean*
Neal, Mo (P. Maureen Neal) *sculptor*
Nelson, Darrell Wayne *university administrator, scientist*
Nelson, W. Don *investment banker, lawyer*
†North, Christopher William *portfolio manager, securities analyst*
Ogle, Robbin Sue *criminal justice educator*

Gardnerville
Pyle, David *elementary education educator*

Glenbrook
Jabara, Michael Dean *investment banker, entrepreneur*

Hawthorne
Graham, Lois Charlotte *retired educator*

Henderson
Benson, James DeWayne *university administrator*
Bybee, Jay Scott *lawyer, educator*
Cohan, George Sheldon *advertising and public relations executive*
Creech, Wilbur Lyman *retired career officer*
Dobberstein, Eric *lawyer*
Freyd, William Pattinson *fund raising executive, consultant*
Gonyea, Bruce Edward *mortgage company executive*
Grembowski, Eugene *retired leasing company executive*
Hara-Isa, Nancy Jeanne *graphic designer, county official*
Hatfield, Samuel Fay, Jr. *retired military officer, construction consultant*
Henry, Philip Lawrence *marketing professional*
†Holdaway, Eric John *military officer*
Jackson, Robert Loring *science and mathematics educator, academic administrator*
Johnson, Joan Bray *insurance company consultant*
Martin, Donald Walter *author, publisher*
McCafferty, Steven Garth *English educator*
McKinney, Sally Vitkus *state official*
Perkins, Richard Dale *police official, state legislator*
Riske, William Kenneth *producer, cultural services consultant*
Trimble, Thomas James *retired utility company executive, lawyer*
Wills, Robert Hamilton *retired newspaper executive*

Incline Village
Diederich, J(ohn) William *internet publisher*
Groebli, Werner Fritz (Mr. Frick) *professional ice skater, realtor*
Henderson, Paul Bargas, Jr. *economic development consultant, educator*
Johnson, James Arnold *business consultant, venture capitalist*
Jones, Robert Alonzo *economist*
Kleinman, George *commodities executive*
Mitton, Michael Anthony *environmental technology company executive*
Moore, Patricia Ann *medical technology investor, consultant*
Strack, Harold Arthur *retired electronics company executive, retired air force officer, planner, analyst, author, musician*
Thompson, David Alfred *industrial engineer*
Wahl, Howard Wayne *retired construction company executive, engineer*
Yount, George Stuart *paper company executive*

Las Vegas
Adams, Charles Lynford *English language educator*
Alexander, John Bradfield *scientist, retired army officer*
Allen, Vicki Lynette *physical education educator*
Amirana, M. T. *surgeon*
Arce, Phillip William *hotel and casino executive*
Arum, Robert *lawyer, sports events promoter*
Basile, Richard Emanuel *retired management consultant, educator*
Beagles, Dorothy Boetticher *office administrator, homeopathic consultant*
Beglinger, Susan Marie *marriage and family therapist, rehabilitation counselor*
†Bein, Wolfgang Walter *computer science educator*
Benbow, Richard Addison *psychological counselor*
Bernard, Thelma Rene *property management professional*
Boehm, Robert Foty *mechanical engineer, educator, researcher*
Boyle, Carolyn Moore *public relations executive, marketing communications manager*
†Boynton, Peter G. *hotel executive*
Brebbia, John Henry *lawyer*
Broca, Laurent Antoine *aerospace scientist*
Brown, Lori Lipman *secondary school educator*
Capanna, Albert Howard *neurosurgeon, neuroscientist*
Capelle, Madelene Carole *opera singer, educator, music therapist*
Cardinalli, Marc Patrick *lawyer*
Carroll, Rossye O'Neal *college administrator*
Castro, Joseph Armand *music director, pianist, composer, orchestrator*
Chance, Patti Lynn *adult education educator*
Chesnut, Carol Fitting *lawyer*
Cinque, Thomas Joseph *dean*
†Ciski, Leslie A. *government official*
Close, Jack Dean, Sr. *physical therapist*
Cloud, Barbara Lee *adult education educator*
Collis, Kay Lynn *professional beauty consultant*
†Cooper, Matthew Marc *cardiothoracic surgeon*
Cram, Brian Manning *school system administrator*
Culp, Gordon Louis *consulting engineer*
Curran, William P. *lawyer*
Cwerenz-Maxime, Virginia Margaret *primary educator, secondary education educator*
Davidson, Joel *surgeon*
De La Hoya, Oscar *Olympic athlete, professional boxer*
DiOrio, Robert Joseph *psychotherapist, consultant*
Di Palma, Joseph Alphonse *investment company executive, lawyer*
Ecker, Howard *lawyer*
Eikenberry, Arthur Raymond *writer, service executive, researcher*
Ensign, John E. *former congressman*
Faiss, Robert Dean *lawyer*
Fennel, Peter J., Sr. *retired anesthesiologist*
Fernandez, Linda Flawn *entrepreneur, social worker*
Francis, Timothy Duane *chiropractor*
†Frederick, Sherman *publishing executive*
Fuller, Dolores Agnes *songwriter, actress*
Galane, Morton Robert *lawyer*
Gaspar, Anna Louise *retired elementary school teacher, consultant*
Gelfer, Jeffrey Ian *early childhood education educator*
George, Lloyd D. *federal judge*
Gideon-Hawke, Pamela Lawrence *fine arts small business owner*
Gilchrist, Ann Roundey *hospice nurse*
Gillespie, Marilyn *museum administrator*

Gold, Hyman *cellist*
Goldblatt, Hal Michael *photographer, accountant*
Goldstein, Morris *entertainment company executive*
Goldstein, Steven Edward *psychologist*
Goodall, Leonard Edwin *public administration educator*
Goodwin, Nancy Lee *corporate executive*
Grace, John William *electrical company executive*
Gray, Phyllis Anne *librarian*
Greene, Addison Kent *lawyer, accountant*
Gubler, John Gray *lawyer*
Haas, Robert John *aerospace engineer*
Hair, Kittie Ellen *secondary educator*
Hallas, Evelyn Margaret *physical therapist*
Hammargren, Lonnie *former lieutenant governor*
Han, Ittah *lawyer, political economist, high technology and financial strategist, computer engineer*
Hanson, Gerald Eugene *oral and maxillofacial surgeon*
Harter, Carol Clancey *university president, English language educator*
Havemann, Michael R. *court administrator*
Healy, Mary (Mrs. Peter Lind Hayes) *singer, actress*
Herzlich, Harold J. *chemical engineer*
Hess, John Warren *scientific institute administrator, educator*
Hilbrecht, Norman Ty *lawyer*
Hill, Judith Deegan *lawyer*
Hobbs, Guy Stephen *financial executive*
Holland, Robert Debnam, Sr. *investment company executive*
Holmes, David Leo *recreation and leisure educator*
Honsa, Vlasta *retired librarian*
Hudgens, Sandra Lawler *retired state official*
†Hunt, Roger Lee *judge*
Jackson, Barbara Patricia *city manager*
Jackson, Wilfried *banker*
Jaffe, Herb *retired newspaper editor, columnist*
Jagodzinski, Ruth Clark *nursing administrator*
Johnston, Robert Jake *federal magistrate judge*
Jones, Fletcher, Jr. *automotive company executive*
Jones, Jan Laverty *mayor*
†Jones, Robert Clive *judge*
Jost, Richard Frederic, III *lawyer*
Kaiser, Glen David *construction company executive*
Kalb, Benjamin Stuart *television producer, director*
Karau, Jon Olin *judge*
Kassouf, Esther Kay *middle school education educator*
Kelley, Michael John *newspaper editor*
Kennedy, Dennis L. *lawyer*
Kenny, Ray *geology and geochemistry educator, researcher*
Kielhorn, Richard Werner *chemist*
Klein, Freda *retired state agency administrator*
Knight, Gladys (Maria) *singer*
Komm, Kermit Matthew *software engineer*
Koon, Ray Harold *management and security consultant*
Kurlinski, John Parker *physician*
Lally, Norma Ross *federal agency administrator, retired*
Landau, Ellis *gaming company executive*
Landreth, Kathryn E. *prosecutor*
Latimer, Heather *writer*
Laub, William Murray *retired utility executive*
Law, Flora Elizabeth (Libby Law) *retired community health and pediatrics nurse*
Leake, Brenda Gail *enterostomal therapist nurse practitioner*
†Leavitt, Lawrence R. *federal judge*
Leibovit, Arnold L. *film producer, director*
Lewis, Jerry (Joseph Levitch) *comedian*
Lewis, Oli Parepa *curator*
Lovell, Carl Erwin, Jr. *lawyer*
Lukens, John Patrick *lawyer*
Magliocco, Peter Anthony *editor, writer*
Mahan, James Cameron *lawyer*
Maravich, Mary Louise *realtor*
Marcella, Joseph *information system administrator*
Marcovitz, Leonard Edward *retail executive*
Martin, Michael Albert *surveillance agent*
Martin, Myron Gregory *foundation administrator*
Mataseje, Veronica Julia *sales executive*
McAnelly, Robert D. *physiatrist, researcher*
McDonald, Malcolm Gideon *education educator*
Merkin, Albert Charles *pediatrician, allergist*
Messenger, George Clement *engineering executive, consultant*
Michel, Mary Ann Kedzuf *nursing educator*
Miller, Bobby W. *author*
Miller, Robert Joseph *governor, lawyer*
Mitchell, Guy *singer, entertainer, actor*
Moritz, Timothy Bovie *psychiatrist*
Mulvihill, Peter James *fire protection engineer*
Murray, Kevin Dennis *surgeon*
Nacht, Steve Jerry *geologist*
Naegle, Shirl R. *museum director*
Nold, Aurora R. *business educator*
Norman, Jean Reid *journalist*
Opfer, Neil David *construction educator, consultant*
Palmer, Lynne *writer, astrologer*
Peck, Gaillard Ray, Jr. *defense contractor, aerospace and business consultant, business owner*
Phillips, Karen *secondary education educator*
Pray, Donald Eugene *foundation administrator, lawyer*
Pringle, Thomas Hivick *sales executive*
Pro, Philip Martin *judge*
Pulliam, Francine Sarno *real estate broker and developer*
Regan, John Bernard (Jack Regan) *community relations executive, senator*
Regazzi, John Henry *retired electronic distributor executive*
Rich, Ray *human behavior educator*
Riddell, Richard Harry *retired lawyer*
Riegle, Linda B. *federal judge*
Ring, David C. *school administrator*
Rodgers, Steven Edward *tax practitioner, educator*
Rogers, David Hughes *finance executive*
Root, Alan Charles *diversified manufacturing company executive*
Rossin, Herbert Yale *business executive*
Rowe, Carl Osborn *business consultant*
Schaeffer, Glenn William *casino corporate financial executive*
Schneiter, George Malan *golfer, development company executive*
†Schwartz, Robert John *landscape contractor, landscape designer*
Segerblom, Sharon B. *social services administrator*
Shackelford, Ralph *municipal official*
†Shafe, Michele Wheeler *county administrator*
Shipper, Todd Jeffrey *communications executive*
Shires, George Thomas *surgeon, educator*

Shively, Judith Carolyn (Judy Shively) *contract administrator*
Shuman, R(obert) Baird *academic program director, writer, English language educator, educational consultant*
Singer, Michael Howard *lawyer*
†Sklar, Alan Curtis *lawyer*
Skoll, Pearl A. *retired mathematics and special education educator*
Smith, Mary B. *medical and surgical nurse*
Solomon, Mark A. *lawyer*
Speck, Eugene Lewis *internist*
Spencer, Carol Brown *association executive*
Steffen, Thomas Lee *lawyer, former state supreme court justice*
Stock, Lincoln Frederick *stockbroker, retired*
Strahan, Julia Celestine *electronics company executive*
Strauss, Paul Edward *English language educator*
Sullivan, Walter Gerard *plastic surgeon, lawyer*
Tate, Evelyn Ruth *real estate broker*
Thill, John Val *communications professional, writer, consultant*
Thomas, Keith Vern *bank executive*
Trevino, Mario H. *protective services official*
Troidl, Richard John *banker*
†Troncoso, Jose Gerardo *United States marshall*
†Unrue, Darlene Harbour *English educator, writer*
Vaccaro, Louis Charles *college president*
Vandever, Judith Ann *county official*
Van Noy, Terry Willard *health care executive*
†Vazquez, Jayme Jack *musician, songwriter, producer, technician*
Vucanovich, Barbara Farrell *former congresswoman*
Walker, Randall H. *air transportation executive*
Walsh, Daniel Francis *bishop*
Walter, Randall H. *county official*
Wax, Arnold *physician*
Weeks, Gerald *psychology educator*
Welter, William Michael *marketing and advertising executive*
Wendt, Steven William *business educator*
Wiemer, Robert Ernest *film and television producer, writer, director*
Wieting, Gary Lee *federal agency executive*
Wilson, Joseph Morris, III *lawyer*
Wood, Benjamin Carroll, Jr. *safety professional*
Wunstell, Erik James *non-profit organization administrator, communications consultant*
Zehm, Stanley James *education educator*
Zuspan, Frederick Paul *obstetrician, gynecologist, educator*

Logandale
Smiley, Robert William, Jr. *investment banker*

Lovelock
†Evenson, Steve Earle *lawyer*

Minden
Bently, Donald Emery *electrical engineer*
Jackson, John Jay *clergyman*
Muszynska, Agnieszka (Agnes Muszynska) *mechanical engineering research scientist*
Tyndall, Gaye Lynn *secondary education educator*
Zabelsky, William John *choral and band director*

Nellis A F B
†Lay, Theodore W., II *career officer*
†Moorhead, Glen W., III (Wally) *career officer*

North Las Vegas
Beachley, DeAnna Eileen *history educator*
Fiori, Frank Anthony *land use planner, historic preservation consultant*
Folden, Norman C. (Skip Folden) *information systems executive, consultant*
Green, Michael Scott *history educator, columnist*
Jacks, Roger Larry *secondary education educator*
Marchand, Russell David, II *fire chief*
Miller, Eleanor *English language and literature educator*
Moore, Richard *academic administrator*
Sullivan, Debra Kae *elementary education educator*
Williams, Mary Irene *business education educator*

Pahrump
Marsh, Mary Elizabeth Taylor *recreation administrator, dietician, nutritionist*
Nowell, Linda Gail *organization executive*

Park City
Milner, Harold William *hotel executive*

Rego Park
Manton, Thomas Joseph *former congressman*

Reno
Adams, Kenneth Robert *gaming analyst, writer, consultant, historian*
Albrecht, Carol Heath *artist, educator*
†Apassa, Cyril Omo-Osagie *clergyman, educator*
†Atkins, Phyllis Halsey *federal judge*
Bandurraga, Peter Louis *museum director, historian*
Barnet, Robert Joseph *cardiologist, ethicist*
Bigley, George Kim, Jr. *neurologist*
Binns, James Edward *retired banker*
Blake-Inada, Louis Michael *cardiologist, researcher*
Bohmont, Dale Wendell *agricultural consultant*
Bonham, Harold Florian *research geologist, consultant*
Bramwell, Marvel Lynnette *nurse, social worker*
Branch, Michael Paul *humanities educator*
Broili, Robert Howard *lawyer*
Brunetti, Melvin T. *federal judge*
Busig, Rick Harold *mining executive*
†Carrigan, Michael Andrew *journalism educator, journalist, writer*
Chapman, Samuel Greeley *political science educator, criminologist*
Chrystal, William George *minister*
Chu, Shih-Fan (George Chu) *economics educator*
Clark-Johnson, Susan *publishing executive*
Crowley, Joseph Neil *university president, political science educator*
Cummings, Nicholas Andrew *psychologist*
Daniels, Ronald Dale *conductor*
Danko, George *engineering educator*
Daugherty, Robert Melvin, Jr. *university dean, medical educator*
Davenport, Janet Lee *real estate saleswomen, small business owner*
Davis, Paul Bryan *political science educator*
Day, Kevin Thomas *banker, community services director*

Delaney, William Francis, Jr. *reinsurance broker*
Denham, Rena Belle *lawyer, educator*
†Eaton, John Monroe *neurologist, educator*
Feinhandler, Edward Sanford *writer, photographer, art dealer, sports mentor, consultant, educator*
Garcia, Katherine Lee *comptroller, accountant*
Gifford, Gerald Frederic *education educator*
Goin, Peter Jackson *art educator*
†Goldwater, Bert M. *federal judge*
Grady, Sean Michael *writer*
Graham, Denis David *marriage and family therapist, educational consultant*
Guild, Clark Joseph, Jr. *lawyer*
Guinn, Janet Martin *psychologist, consultant*
Hagen, David Warner *judge*
Haynes, Gary Anthony *archaeologist*
Hibbs, Loyal Robert *lawyer*
Hilts, Ruth *artist*
Horton, Robert Carlton *geologist*
Hug, Procter Ralph, Jr. *federal judge*
Hulse, James Warren *history educator, writer*
Humphrey, Neil Darwin *university president, retired*
†Iverson, Paul *government agency administrator*
Jarvis, Richard S. *academic administrator*
Jennison, Brian L. *environmental specialist*
Johnson, Arthur William, Jr. *planetarium executive*
Johnson, Richard Karl *hospitality company executive*
Kaylor, Andrea Lynn *secondary school counselor*
Kennedy, Jack Edward *lawyer*
King, Charles Thomas *retired school superintendent, educator*
Lee, David DeWitt *industrial hygienist*
Leipper, Dale Frederick *physical oceanographer, meteorologist, educator*
Leipper, Diane Louise *association administrator*
Leland, Joy Hanson *anthropologist, alcohol research specialist*
Lord, Jacklynn Jean *student services representative*
MacKintosh, Frederick Roy *oncologist*
Marshall, Robert William *lawyer, rancher*
Martinson, Julia Ellenor *health science administrator*
McDaniel, Susan Irene *nursing educator*
McKay, Alice Vitalich *academic administrator*
McKibben, Howard D. *federal judge*
†McQuaid, Robert A., Jr. *federal judge*
Middlebrooks, Deloris Jeanette *nurse, educator*
Miller, Newton Edd, Jr. *communications educator*
Newberg, Dorothy Beck (Mrs. William C. Newberg) *portrait artist*
Newberg, William Charles *stock broker, real estate broker, automotive engineer*
Ogle, James Richard, Jr. *news executive*
Perry, Anthony Frank *entertainment company executive, printing company executive, graphic designer*
Pierson, William Roy *chemist*
Pinson, Larry Lee *pharmacist*
†Poore, Coral Deane *educator*
Qualls, Robert Gerald *ecologist*
Raggio, William John *state senator*
Reddy, Rajasekara L. *mechanical engineer*
Reed, Edward Cornelius, Jr. *federal judge*
Ross, Robert Donald *librarian*
Salls, Jennifer Jo *secondary school educator*
Savoy, Douglas Eugene *bishop, religion educator, explorer, writer*
Scrimgeour, Gary James *writer, educator*
Shaffer, Wayne Alan *lawyer*
Shapiro, Leonard *immunologist, allergist*
Simonian, Lane Peter *history educator*
Sladek, Ronald John *physics educator*
Smith, Aaron *research director, clinical psychologist*
Straling, Phillip Francis *bishop*
Stratton, Bruce Cornwall *writer, landscape photographer, publisher*
Strauss, Judy *marketing educator, consultant, writer*
Taranik, James Vladimir *geologist, educator*
Von Bartheld, Christopher Stephen *neurobiologist*
Waddell, Theodore *painter*
Walen, Joanne Michele *secondary education educator, consultant*
Walrath, Harry Rienzi *minister*
Webster, Michael Anderson *experimental psychologist*
Weinberg, Leonard Burton *political scientist*
Weinbrenner, George Ryan *aeronautical engineer*
Weld, Roger Bowen *clergyman*
Westfall, David Patrick *academic administrator, educator*
White, Linda Louise *literture educator, writer*
White, Robert C. *air transportation executive*
Winzeler, Judith Kay *foundation administrator*

Silver City
Bloyd, Stephen Roy *environmental manager, educator, consultant*

Smith
Weaver, William Merritt, Jr. *investment banker*

Sparks
Corbin, Krestine Margaret *manufacturing company executive, fashion designer, columnist*
Kleppe, John Arthur *electrical engineering educator, business executive*
Kramer, Gordon Edward *manufacturing executive*
Lee, Richard Scott *neurologist*
Root, William Dixon *construction company executive*

Summerlin
Johnson, Mary Elizabeth *retired elementary education educator*

West Wendover
Psenka, Robert Edward *real estate developer, behavioral scientist*

Winnemucca
Clemons, Lynn Allan *land use planner*
Hesse, Martha O. *natural gas company executive*

Yerington
Dini, Joseph Edward, Jr. *state legislator*
Price, Thomas Munro *computer consultant*
Scatena, Lorraine Borba *rancher, women's rights advocate*

Zephyr Cove
Proctor, Robert Swope *retired petroleum company executive*

NEW HAMPSHIRE

Amherst
Collins, Paul Daniel principal
Willis, John Osgood educational evaluator, educator

Atkinson
Trotter, William John sales professional

Barrington
Lovejoy, George former state senator
Olivier, Julien L. translator, consultant

Bedford
Alderman, Walter Arthur, Jr. computer company and corporate rescue executive
Collins, Diana Josephine psychologist
Cronin, Timothy Cornelius, III computer manufacturing executive
Hall, Pamela S. environmental consulting firm executive
Khazei, Amir Mohsen surgeon, oncologist
Manocchi, James Charles marketing professional
Seidman, Alan educational administrator

Belmont
Bartlett, Gordon E. state legislator
†Donovan, Vicki A. elementary school teacher

Bennington
Verney, Richard Greville paper company executive
Willis, Barbara Florence artist
Willis, Sidney Frank artist, educator

Berlin
Doherty, Katherine Mann librarian, writer

Bethlehem
Worner, Theresa Marie physician

Bradford
Hersh, Burton David author
Lettvin, Theodore concert pianist

Brookline
Buff, Margaret Anne psychiatric nurse

Canterbury
Chamberlin, Robert West medical educator

Center Harbor
Shaw, Robert William, Jr. management consultant, venture capitalist

Center Sandwich
Booty, John Everitt historiographer
Simmons, Alan Jay electrical engineer, consultant

Claremont
Marashio, Paul William educational administrator, educator
Middleton, John Albert retired communications executive
Rich, Betty An early childhood educator

Colebrook
Peterson, John O.H. chemist, researcher

Concord
Arnold, Thomas Ivan, Jr. legislator
Bagan, Merwyn neurological surgeon
Barbadoro, Paul J. federal judge
Brock, David Allen state supreme court chief justice
Broderick, John T., Jr. state supreme court justice
Brown, Tom Christian newspaper publisher
Brunelle, Robert L. retired state education director
†Busselle, James A. educational administrator
Cann, William Francis judge
Caswell, William Stephen, Jr. civil engineer
Church, Gail Graham former television producer, consultant
Cote, David Edward state legislator
Crosier, John David trade association administrator
Day, Russell Clover state agency administrator
de Nesnera, Alexander Peter psychiatrist
Devine, Shane federal judge
DiClerico, Joseph Anthony, Jr. federal judge
Dunlap, Patricia C. state legislator
Fahey, Patricia Anne editor
Fields, Dennis H. state legislator
Franks, Suzan L. R. state legislator
Fraser, Marilyn Anne state legislator
Gagnon, Paul Michael lawyer, former county attorney
Gardner, William Michael state official
Hager, Elizabeth Sears state legislator, social services organization administrator
Hill, Donald S. commissioner, state
Hodes, Paul William record company executive, lawyer
Horton, Sherman D., Jr. state supreme court justice
Jacobson, Alf Edgar state legislator
Jean, Loren state legislator
Johnson, William R. state supreme court justice
Kalipolites, June Eleanor Turner rehabilitation professional
Lovejoy, Marian E. state legislator
Lozeau, Donnalee M. state legislator
Lundahl, Steven Mark musician, consultant
Mac Kay, James Robert psychiatric social worker, mayor
Mahon, Thomas James management consultant
†Maiola, Joel W. state official
McAuliffe, Steven James federal judge
McCracken, Linda librarian, commercial artist
McLaughlin, Philip T. state attorney general
McNamara, Wanda G. state legislator
Mekeel, Robert K. lawyer
Merritt, Deborah Foote state legislator, vocational coordinator
Mevers, Frank Clement state archivist, historian
Moore, Carol state legislator
†Muirhead, James R. federal judge
Pignatelli, Debora Becker state legislator
Porter, G. William education administrator
Pratt, Irene Agnes state legislator
†Raskin, Joy Lynn art educator, silversmith
Rath, Thomas David lawyer, former state attorney general
Richardson, Barbara Hull state legislator, social worker
Rines, Robert Harvey lawyer, inventor, educator, composer
Risley, Henry Brainard protective service official
Roberts, George Bernard, Jr. business and government affairs consultant, former state legislator
Rogers, Katherine Diane political consultant, commissioner
Shaheen, C. Jeanne governor
Slusser, Eugene Alvin electronics manufacturing executive
Smart, Melissa Bedor environmental consulting company executive
Snyder, Clair A. state legislator
Spear, Barbara L. state legislator
Stahl, Norman H. federal judge
†Taylor, Stephen H. state commissioner
Teschner, Douglass Paul mental health services executive
Thayer, W(alter) Stephen, III state supreme court justice
Theuner, Douglas Edwin bishop
Thomas, Georgie A. state official
Tomajczyk, S(tephen) F(rancis) communications company executive, author
†Twomey, Elizabeth Ann Molloy education commissioner
Wajenberg, Arnold Sherman retired librarian, educator
White, Jeffrey George healthcare consultant, educator
†Woodburn, Jeff political party official
Yates, Elizabeth (Mrs. William McGreal) author, editor
York, Michael Charest librarian

Contoocook
Payne, Paula Marie minister

Cornish
Allison, David C. state legislator
Duffy, Henry J. museum curator, consultant

Cornish Flat
Lawton, Jacqueline Agnes retired communications company executive, management consultant

Derry
Colantuono, Thomas Paul state legislator
Dowd, Sandra K. state legislator
Graff, David Austin chiropractor
Katsakiores, George Nicholas state legislator, retired restauranteur
Lazinsky, Jo Anne Marie advertising executive
MacDonald, Wayne Douglas fraud investigator
†Wixson, Kellie Donovan English educator

Dover
Bergeron, Tracey Anne mental health nurse, educator
Casey, Kimberlyn Lorettre artist, painter, educator
Catalfo, Alfred, Jr. (Alfio Catalfo) lawyer
Charos, Evangelos Nikolaou economics educator
†Handy, Carolyn newspaper editor
Mitchell, William Clark printmaker, graphic artist
Nelson, Michael Underhill association executive
Parks, Joe Benjamin entrepreneur, former state legislator
Pelletier, Arthur Joseph state legislator, educator
Pelletier, Marsha Lynn secondary school educator, state legislator
Wentworth, William Edgar journalist
†Winkler, Peter Alexander plastic surgeon

Dublin
Biklen, Paul retired advertising executive
Hale, Judson Drake, Sr. editor

Durham
Aber, John David global ecosystem research scientist
Appel, Kenneth I. mathematician, educator
DeMitchell, Todd Allan education educator
†Diller, Karl Conrad linguistics educator
Eggers, Walter Frederick academic administrator
Farrell, William Joseph university chancellor
Ford, Daniel (Francis) writer
Frankfurter, David Thomas Munro religious studies educator
Hapgood, Robert Derry English educator
Harter, Robert Duane soil scientist, educator
Leitzel, Joan Ruth university president
Mazzari, Louis W. program director
Palmer, Stuart Hunter sociology educator
Perry, Bradford Kent academic administrator
Pistole, Thomas Gordon microbiology educator, researcher
Romoser, George Kenneth political science educator
Rosen, Sam economics educator emeritus
Tischler, Herbert geologist, educator
Van Osdol, Donovan Harold mathematics educator
Wheeler, Douglas Lanphier history educator, author
Wheeler, Katherine Wells state legislator

East Alstead
Holloway, Robert Charles orchestrator, arranger, composer

East Rochester
Zemojtel, Alexander Michael corporate executive

East Sullivan
Hoffman, John Ernest, Jr. retired lawyer

Enfield
Gamache, Kathleen Smith retired psychotherapist
Gamache, Richard Donald retired business development executive

Epping
Boynton, James Robert educational institute professional

Etna
Copenhaver, Marion Lamson state legislator
Ferm, Vergil Harkness anatomist, embryologist
Mitrano, Peter Paul lawyer, engineer

Exeter
Beck, Albert manufacturing company executive
Dailey, Daniel Owen artist, educator, designer
DeLucia, Gene Anthony government administrator, computer company executive
Dunleavy, Janet Frank Egleson English language educator
Forrest, Douglas William banker
Gray, Christopher Donald software researcher, author, consultant
Harmon, Richard Wingate management consultant
Jackson, Patrick John public relations counsel, editor, author, public speaker
Kenick, Joseph Louis, III construction executive
Kozlowski, L. Dennis manufacturing company executive
Moroze, Marshall Brian lawyer
Sewitch, Deborah E. health science association administrator, educator, sleep researcher
Verzone, Ronald D. insurance brokerage executive, investment advisor
Vogelman, Lawrence Allen law educator, lawyer

Farmington
Meyers, James B. secondary education educator

Fitzwilliam
Cooper, Marshall information company executive

Franconia
Merwin, John David retired lawyer, former governor
Schaffer, David Edwin retired management systems executive

Franklin
†Dean, Shervin Christopher emergency medicine physician
Feuerstein, Martin state legislator

Freedom
Davidson, George Thomas, Jr. minister, educator
Keith, Barry Harold environmental scientist
Kucera, Henry linguistics educator
Stolz, Alan Jay youth camp executive

Fremont
Richardson, Artemas P(artridge) landscape architect

Georges Mills
Dulude, Richard glass manufacturing company executive

Gilmanton
Osler, Howard Lloyd controller

Glen
Zager, Ronald I. chemist, consultant

Goffstown
Engebretson, Kathleen Mary Murray women's health nurse, psychiatric nurse
Gillmore, Robert landscape designer, author, editor, publisher
Martel, Eva Leona accountant
Oktavec, Eileen M. anthropologist, artist

Gorham
Robitaille, Paul Réne photographer

Grantham
Behrle, Franklin Charles retired pediatrician and educator
Feldman, Roger Bruce government official
Goss, Richard Henry lawyer
Knights, Edwin Munroe pathologist
MacNeill, Arthur Edson physician, science consultant
Smith, Dudley Renwick retired insurance company executive

Greenfield
Wheelock, Major William, Jr. health care adminstrator

Greenland
Sargent, Douglas Robert air force officer, engineer

Hampstead
Bolton, (Margaret) Elizabeth artist, poet

Hampton
Morton, Donald John librarian
Prentiss, Barbara Ann principal
Russell, Richard R. chemicals executive

Hancock
Pollaro, Paul Philip artist

Hanover
Almy, Thomas Pattison physician, educator
Anthony, Robert Newton management educator emeritus
Arndt, Walter W. Slavic scholar, linguist, writer, translator
Baldwin, John Charles surgeon, researcher
Baumgartner, James Earl mathematics educator
†Bharucha, Jamshed dean
Bien, Peter Adolph English language educator, author
Boghosian, Varujan Yegan sculptor
Braun, Charles Louis chemistry educator, researcher
Brooks, H. Allen architectural educator, author, lecturer
Carfora, John Michael economics and political science educator
Clement, Meredith Owen economist, educator
Conley, Katharine language educator
Cook, William Wilbert English language educator
Crory, Elizabeth L. former state legislator
Daniell, Jere Rogers, II history educator, consultant, public lecturer
Danos, Paul dean, finance educator
Dean, Robert Charles, Jr. mechanical engineer, entrepreneur, innovator
Demko, George Joseph geographer
Doney, Willis Frederick philosophy educator
Ehrlich, David Gordon film director, educator
Fischel, William Alan economics educator
†Foelsche, Otmar Karl Ernst German language educator
Freedman, James Oliver university president, lawyer
Gardner, Peter Jaglom publisher
Garmire, Elsa Meints electrical engineering educator, consultant
Garthwaite, Gene Ralph historian, educator
Gert, Bernard philosopher, educator
Gilbert, John Jouett aquatic ecologist, educator
Green, Ronald Michael ethics and religious studies educator
Guest, Robert Henry state legislator, management educator
Hall, Raymond sociology educator
†Heatherton, Todd Frederick psychology educator
Heffernan, James Anthony Walsh English language and literature educator
Hennessey, John William, Jr. academic administrator
Howe, Harold, II academic administrator, former foundation executive, educator
Hunter, Marie Hope library media generalist
Hutchinson, Charles Edgar engineering educator
Kantrowitz, Arthur physicist, educator
Kemp, Karl Thomas insurance company executive
Kleck, Robert Eldon psychology educator
Koop, Charles Everett surgeon, educator, former surgeon general
Kritzman, Lawrence David humanities educator
Kurtz, Thomas Eugene mathematics educator
Lamperti, John Williams mathematician, educator
Logue, Dennis Emhardt financial economics educator, consultant
Long, Carl Ferdinand engineering educator
Low, Victor N. historian
Lyon, Bryce Dale historian, educator
Lyons, Gene Martin political scientist, educator
Mansell, Darrel Lee, Jr. English educator
Masters, Roger Davis government educator
Meadows, Donella environmentalist
Moeschler, John Boyer physician, educator
Montgomery, David Campbell physicist, educator
Moss, Ben Frank, III art educator, painter
Olcott, William Alfred magazine editor
Otto, Margaret Amelia librarian
Oxenhandler, Neal language educator, writer
Paganucci, Paul Donnelly banker, lawyer, former college official
Penner, Hans Henry historian
Perrin, Noel environmental studies educator
Prager, Susan Westerberg law educator, provost
Queneau, Paul Etienne metallurgical engineer, educator
Rawnsley, Howard Melody physician, educator
Riggs, Lorrin Andrews psychologist, educator
Rolett, Ellis Lawrence medical educator, cardiologist
Roos, Thomas Bloom biological scientist, educator
Rueckert, Frederic plastic and reconstructive surgeon
Russell, Robert Hilton Romance languages and literature educator
Rutter, Jeremy Bentham archaeologist, educator
Scher, Steven Paul literature educator
Scherr, Barry Paul foreign language educator
Sheldon, Richard Robert Russian language and literature educator
Shewmaker, Kenneth Earl history educator
Snell, James Laurie mathematician, educator
Spiegel, Evelyn Sclufer biology educator, researcher
Spiegel, Melvin retired biology educator
Sporn, Michael Benjamin cancer researcher
Staples, O. Sherwin orthopedic surgeon
Starzinger, Vincent Evans political science educator
Stockmayer, Walter H(ugo) chemistry educator
Sturge, Michael Dudley physicist
Wallace, Andrew Grover physician, educator, medical school dean
Wallis, Graham Blair engineer, educator
Wegner, Gary Alan astronomer
Wielgus, Chris women's basketball coach
Wood, Charles Tuttle history educator
Wright, James Edward college president, history educator
Zubkoff, Michael medical educator

Haverhill
†Brickner, Roger Kenneth secondary school educator

Henniker
Braiterman, Thea Gilda economics educator, state legislator, selectman
Cummiskey, J. Kenneth former college president
Currier, David P. retired state legislator

Hillsboro
Gibson, Raymond Eugene clergyman
Marsh, Richard J. strategic management consultant
Sargent, Maxwell D. state legislator

Holderness
Cutler, Laurence Stephan architect, urban designer, advertising executive, educator

Hollis
Litchfield, Barbara Mae Smith clergywoman
Lumbard, Eliot Howland lawyer, educator
Merritt, Thomas Butler lawyer

Hooksett
Gustafson, Richard Alrick college president
Rogers, David John lawyer

Hudson
Dumond, Robert Wilfred mental health consultant, lay pastoral worker
Rice, Annie Laura Kempton medical, surgical and rehabilitation nurse

Jackson
Johnson, Ned (Edward Christopher Johnson) publishing company executive
Synnott, William Raymond retired management consultant
Zeliff, William H., Jr. former congressman

Jaffrey
Foster, Walter Herbert, III mechanical and manufacturing engineer, executive
Royce, H. Charles state legislator
Schott, John (Robert) international consultant, educator
Schulte, Henry Frank journalism educator
Van Ness, Patricia Wood religious studies educator, consultant
Walling, Cheves Thomson chemistry educator

Jefferson
Leiper, Esther Mather writer

Keene
Ahern, Maureen Jeanne museum director, artist
Baldwin, Peter Arthur psychologist, educator, author, minister
Bell, Ernest Lorne, III lawyer

Burkart, Walter Mark *manufacturing company executive*
Fuld, Gilbert Lloyd *pediatrician*
Hickey, Delina Rose *education educator*
Long, Mark Chistopher *English educator*
Lowell, Janet Ann *nurse*
Martin, Vernon Emil *librarian*

Kingston
Welch, David A. *state legislator*
Weyler, Kenneth L. *state legislator*

Laconia
Heald, Bruce Day *English and music educator, historian*
Holbrook, Robert George *state legislator*
Mulloy, Paula Irene *nursing administrator*
Turner, Robert H. *state legislator*

Lancaster
Drapeau, Phillip David *banking executive*
Pratt, Leighton Calvin *state legislator*

Lebanon
Barney, Christine Anne *psychiatrist, educator*
Below, Clifton C. *state legislator*
Clendenning, William Edmund *dermatologist*
Cornwell, Gibbons Gray, III *physician, medical educator*
Cronenwett, Jack LeMoyne *vascular surgeon educator*
Emery, Virginia Olga Beattie *psychologist, researcher*
Fanger, Michael W. *medical educator*
Fiering, Steven *medical educator*
Foote, Robert Stephens *physician*
Galton, Valerie Anne *endocrinology educator*
Mc Cann, Frances Veronica *physiologist, educator*
McCollum, Robert Wayne *physician, educator*
Munck, Allan Ulf *physiologist, educator*
Nagy, Laura Lee *educator, writer, editor*
†Oseid, Mary M. *health facility administrator*
Ou, Lo-Chang *physiology educator*
Sadler, Barbara Ann *quality assurance professional*
Shorter, Nicholas Andrew *pediatric surgeon*
Silberfarb, Peter Michael *psychiatrist, educator*
Smith, Barry David *obstetrician-gynecologist, educator*
Sox, Harold Carleton, Jr. *physician, educator*
†Stommel, Elijah W. *neurologist*
Tinker, Averill Faith *special education educator*
Umling, David Arthur *urban planner*
Varnum, James William *hospital administrator*
von Reyn, C. Fordham *infectious disease physician*

Lee
Blidberg, D. Richard *marine engineer*
Young, James Morningstar *physician, naval officer*

Lincoln
Hogan, Lori Ann *finance director, accountant*

Lisbon
Trelfa, Richard Thomas *paper company executive*

Litchfield
Darlington, David William *management consultant*
Niccoli, Anne Marie *social sciences educator*

Littleton
Eaton, Stephanie *state legislator*

Londonderry
Kennedy, Ellen Woodman *elementary and home economics educator*
Michaud, Norman Paul *association administrator, logistics consultant*

Loudon
Moore, Beatrice *religious organization administrator*

Lyme
Darion, Joe *librettist, lyricist*
Dwight, Donald Rathbun *newspaper publisher, corporate communications executive*
McIntyre, Oswald Ross *physician*

Madbury
Bruce, Robert Vance *historian, educator*

Manchester
Ahern, Richard Favor *state legislator*
Angoff, Gerald Harvey *cardiologist*
Arnold, Barbara Eileen *state legislator*
Auclair, Louise A. *education educator*
†Burack, Thomas S. *lawyer*
Carkin, Gary Bryden *performing arts educator*
Christian, Francis Joseph *bishop*
Coleman, Linda Lee Devoe *museum educator*
Descoteaux, Carol J. *academic administrator*
Ehlers, Eileen Spratt *family therapist*
Feder, Robert Elliot *psychiatrist*
Gendron, Odore Joseph *retired bishop*
Horton, Joseph Matthew *college dean, humanities educator*
Jenkins, Margaret Constance *elementary education educator*
Keillor, Sharon Ann *electronics company executive*
Khouzam, Hani Raoul *psychiatrist, physician, educator*
Levins, John Raymond *investment advisor, management consultant, educator*
Mailloux, Raymond Victor *health services administrator*
McCarty, Winston H. *state legislator*
Mc Lane, John Roy *lawyer*
McQuaid, Joseph Woodbury *newspaper executive*
Millimet, Joseph Allen *retired lawyer*
Monson, John Rudolph *lawyer*
†Morse, Joshua Lin *advertising and communication executive*
Nardi, Theodora P. *former state legislator*
Perkins, Charles, III *newspaper editor*
Piotrowski, Thaddeus Marian *sociology educator*
Prew, Diane Schmidt *information systems executive*
Proulx, William John *producer*
Richards, Thomas H. *lawyer, arbitrator*
Stahl, Barbara J. *biologist, educator*
Turgeon, Roland M. *state legislator*
†Vaughn, Mark W. *federal judge*
Zachos, Kimon Stephen *lawyer*

Marlborough
Walton, Russell Sparey *foundation administrator*

Marlow
Lindholm, Ulric Svante *engineering research institute executive, retired*

Meredith
Hatch, Frederick Tasker *chemicals consultant*

Meriden
Demarest, Chris Lynn *writer, illustrator*

Merrimack
†Gallup, Patricia *computer company executive*
Kotelly, George Vincent *editor, writer, electrical engineer*
Uy, Philip M. *aeronautical engineer*

Milford
Morison, John Hopkins *casting manufacturing company executive*

Milton Mills
Kramer, Sherri Marcelle *business and community development consultant*
McKinley, Robert E. *state legislator, retired mechanical engineer*

Moultonborough
Foster, Robert W. *state legislator*

Nashua
Barry, William Henry, Jr. *federal judge*
Bergeron, Normand R. *retired state legislator*
Dowd, Karl Edmund *priest*
Fallet, George *civil engineer*
Garbacz, Gerald George *information services company executive*
Gregg, Hugh *former cabinet manufacturing company executive, former governor New Hampshire*
Hansen, Michele Simone *secondary education educator*
Hanson, Arnold Philip *retired lawyer*
Hargreaves, David William *communications company executive*
Hemming, Walter William *business financial consultant*
Hippauf, Georgette Laurin *company executive*
Holley, Sylvia A. *state legislator*
Jette, Ernest Arthur *lawyer*
Johnson, Arthur V., II *secondary education educator*
Light, James Forest *English educator*
MacPhail, Estelle R. *nursing administrator*
Meagher, Robert Michael *software engineer*
Mitsakos, Charles Leonidas *education educator, consultant*
Perkins, George William, II *financial services executive, film producer*
Piper, Linda Ammann *personnel consulting firm executive*
Purington, David W. *elementary education educator*
Smith, Thomas Raymond, III *software engineer*
Weinstein, Jeffrey Allen *consumer products company executive, lawyer*
Woodruff, Thomas Ellis *electronics consulting executive*

New Castle
Brink, Marion Alice *employee assistance professional*
Cohen, Burton Joseph *state senator*
Friese, George Ralph *retail executive*
Klotz, Louis Herman *structural engineer, educator, consultant*

New Durham
Herman, William George *municipal government executive*
Kosko, Susan Uttal *legal administrator*

New London
Bott, John Crist *artist, educator*
Gepfert, Alan Harry *management consultant, business educator, author*
Mc Laughlin, David Thomas *academic administrator, business executive*
Plant, David William *lawyer*
Sheerr, Deirdre McCrystal *architectural firm executive*
Thoma, Kurt Michael *business owner*
Vulgamore, Melvin L. *retired college president*
Wheaton, Perry Lee *management consultant*
Zuehlke, Richard William *technical communications consultant, writer*

Newfields
Wilson, Donald Alfred *land boundary consultant, surveyor*

Newmarket
Getchell, Sylvia Fitts *librarian*

Newport
Ruger, William Batterman *firearms manufacturing company executive*
Stamatakis, Carol Marie *state legislator, lawyer*

North Conway
Schmidt, Lynda Wheelwright *Jungian analyst*

North Hampton
Taylor, Donald *retired manufacturing company executive*
White, Ralph Paul *automotive executive, consultant*

North Haverhill
Charpentier, Keith Lionel *school system administrator*

North Salem
Stone, Robert Eldred *small business owner, museum director*

Northwood
Macri, Stephan Anthony *seafood export company executive*

Nottingham
Case, Margaret A. *state legislator*

Orford
Beale, Georgia Robison *historian, educator*
Karol, John J., Jr. *producer, filmmaker*

Ossipee
Bartlett, Diane Sue *clinical mental health counselor, family therapist*

Pelham
Holmes, Richard Dale *secondary education educator, historical consultant*

Penacook
Szoverffy, Joseph *educator, medieval scholar*

Peterborough
Alderman, Bissell *architect*
Dawes, Lyell Clark *publishing company executive*
Eppes, William David *civic worker, writer*
Farnham, Sherman Brett *retired electrical engineer*
Thomas, Elizabeth Marshall *writer*

Plaistow
Collins, James Francis *wildlife artist*
Senter, Merilyn P(atricia) *former state legislator and freelance reporter*

Plymouth
Drexel, Peter George *computer science educator*
Swift, Robert Frederic *music educator*

Portsmouth
Akridge, William David *hotel management company executive*
Balding, Bruce Edward *investment executive*
Baumann, Hans D. *engineering executive*
Brage, Carl Willis *genealogist*
Crossman, Harold G., Jr. *former state legislator*
DeGrandpre, Charles Allyson *lawyer*
Doleac, Charles Bartholomew *lawyer*
Greene, Douglas Edward *hotel executive*
Hopkins, Jeannette Ethel *book publisher, editor*
Lauzé, Karen Prudence *physician, neurologist*
Pearson, Timothy Alfred *sales executive, marketing professional*
Powers, Henry Martin, Jr. *oil company executive*
Silverman, George Alan *broadcasting executive*
Thornhill, Arthur Horace, Jr. *retired book publisher*
Tillinghast, John Avery *utilities executive*
Volk, Kenneth Hohne *lawyer*
Watson, Thomas Roger *lawyer*

Randolph
Bradley, Paula E. *retired state legislator*
Bradley, William Lee *retired foundation executive, educator*

Raymond
Reynolds, Debbie *educational administrator*

Rindge
Emerson, Susan *oil company executive*
†Forest, James Jared-Franzen *educator, reseacher*
†Gardenour, Diane Leslie *library director*
Killion, Richard Joseph *college official, political science educator*
White, Jean Tillinghast *former state senator*

Rochester
Dworkin, Gary Steven *insurance company executive*
Scott, Elaine Theresa *business development administrator*
Waterhouse, Trenton Dean *marketing director*

Rumney
King, Wayne Douglas *former state senator*
Smith, F(rederick) Dow(swell) *physicist, retired college president*

Rye
MacRury, King *management counselor*
Sullivan, James Ash *visitor information service executive*

Salem
Bonacorsi, Gregory James *mechanical engineer*
Simmons, Marvin Gene *geophysics educator*
Smith, Laurence Roger *journal editor*
Snierson, Lynne Wendy *communications executive*

Sanbornton
Weiant, Elizabeth Abbott *retired biology educator*

Sanbornville
Berg, Warren Stanley *retired banker*

Sandown
Densen, Paul Maximillian *former health administrator, educator*

Seabrook
McLean, James Nelson *structural engineer*

Silver Lake
Pallone, Adrian Joseph *research scientist*
Tregenza, Norman Hughson *investment banker*

Somersworth
Gow, Linda Yvonne Cherwin *travel executive*
Tully, Hugh Michael *music educator*
Vincent, Francis C. *state legislator*

Strafford
Simic, Charles *English language educator, poet*

Stratham
Bodine, John Jermain *pastor*

Sunapee
Cary, Charles Oswald *aviation executive*
Rauh, John David *manufacturing company executive*

Suncook
Weiss, Joanne Marion *writer*

Tilton
Schultz, Judith *educational administrator, consultant*
Stanley, George Joel *social services administrator*
Wolf, Sharon Ann *psychotherapist*

Walpole
Burns, Kenneth Lauren *filmmaker, historian*
Gooding, Judson *writer*

Warner
Face, Wayne Bruce *small business owner*

Webster
Blackey, Pamela Ann Conley *medical/surgical nurse*

West Chesterfield
Garinger, Louis Daniel *religion educator*

West Lebanon
Bower, Richard Stuart *economist, educator*
Isaacs, Robert Charles *retired lawyer*
MacAdam, Walter Kavanagh *consulting engineering executive*

Wilmot
Lambert, Elaine L. *surgical nurse, administrator*

Wilton
Potter, Robert Wallace, Jr. *educator*

Winchester
Tandy, Jean Conkey *art educator*

Windham
Arndt, Janet S. *state legislator*
Arvai, Ernest Stephen *consulting executive*
Hurst, Michael William *psychologist*

Winnisquam
Ricker, Frances Margaret *nursing administrator*

Wolfeboro
Bonin, Suzanne Jean *artist*
Pierce, Edward Franklin *retired academic administrator*
Varnerin, Lawrence John *physicist, retired educator*

Woodsville
†Page, Patti (Clara Ann Fowler) *vocalist*

Wyndham
Delahunty, Joseph Lawrence *state senator, business investor*

NEW JERSEY

Aberdeen
Stillwagon, Wesley William *corporate professional*

Absecon
Byrne, Shaun Patrick *law enforcement officer*
†Hiltner, Dawn Marie *elementary education educator*
Steinruck, Charles Francis, Jr. *management consultant, lawyer*
†Sweeten, E. Marshall *lighting designer*

Adelphia
Carter, Harry Robert *fire chief*

Allendale
Bai, Nina Beate *senior software engineer, consultant*
Bisanzo, Mark Thomas *sales executive*
Petersen, Martin Ross *public affairs executive*
Ruth, Rodney *musician, music consultant, contractor, educator*

Allenhurst
Hinson, Robert William *advertising executive, consultant*
Tognoli, Era M. *performing company executive, artistic director*

Allenwood
†Kerber, Beth-Ann *editor, reporter*

Alpine
†Farensbach, Mark August *banker, real estate executive*
Raasch, Ernest Martin *company executive*
Vandersteel, William *transportation executive*

Ancora
Valo, Martha Ann *hospital dietary executive, consultant*

Andover
Gioseffi, (Dorothy) Daniela *poet, performer, author, educator, jazz singer*

Annandale
Appelbaum, Michael Arthur *finance company executive*
Cohen, Morrel Herman *physicist, biologist, educator*
Drakeman, Donald Lee *biotechnology company executive, lawyer*
Drakeman, Lisa N. *biotechnology company executive*
Gorbaty, Martin Leo *chemist, researcher*
Sinfelt, John Henry *chemist*

Asbury
Gardner, Janette Lynn *critical care nurse, educator*
Konrad, Adolf Ferdinand *artist*

Asbury Park
Rosenthal, Robert Irwin *consultant*
Smith, Thomas S. *state legislator*

Atco
Conrad, George John *retired design engineer, planner*
Lowe, Thomas Joseph *history educator*

Atlantic City
Chambers, Robert Arthur *entertainment director*
Jacobson, Carole Renee *lawyer, educator*
Jamieson, John Edward, Jr. *social services administrator, minister, bioethicist*
Knight, Edward R. *judge, lawyer, educator, psychologist*
Mora, Kathleen Rita *state judicial administrator*

Atlantic Highlands
Corodemus, Steven James *state legislator, lawyer*

Crowley, Cynthia Johnson secondary school educator
Dellosso, Roy J. sales executive
Royce, Paul Chadwick medical administrator

Audubon
Montano, Arthur lawyer
Watson, Mark Henry lawyer, business writer

Avalon
Beatrice, Ruth Hadfield hypnotherapist, retired educator, financial administrator
Johnson, Adele Cunningham marina executive
Yochum, Philip Theodore retired motel and cafeteria chain executive

Avenel
†Appezzato, Marc Robert graphic artist
Berg, Louis Leslie investment executive
Sansone, Paul J. automotive executive

Avon By The Sea
Bruno, Grace Angelia accountant, retired educator
O'Neill, James Paul psychiatrist
Potter, Emma Josephine Hill language educator

Barnegat
Hawk, Frank Carkhuff, Sr. industrial engineer
Lowe, Angela Maria business owner

Barnegat Light
Gibbs, Frederick Winfield lawyer, communications company executive
Smith, Gail Hunter artist

Basking Ridge
Abeles, James David manufacturing company executive
Allen, Katherine Spicer writer, former chemist
Armstrong, C. Michael communications company executive
Atkyns, Robert Lee communications research professional
Collis, Sidney Robert retired telephone company executive
Conklin, Donald Ransford retired pharmaceutical company executive
Darrow, William Richard pharmaceutical company executive, consultant
Drewry, Don Neal fire protection engineer
Estes, Simon Lamont opera singer, bass-baritone
Giglio, William Vito secondary education educator
Grimes-Frederick, Dorothea D. communications executive
Medley, Marc Allen marketing executive
Munch, Douglas Francis pharmaceutical and health industry consultant
O'Neill, Adrienne academic administrator
Panzarino, Saverio Joseph physician
Probert, Edward Whitford foundation executive, volunteer
Riesenberger, John Richard pharmaceutical company executive
Schmidt, William Max management consultant, business executive
†Zeglis, John D. communications company executive, lawyer

Bay Head
O'Brien, Robert Brownell, Jr. investment banker, consultant, yacht broker, opera company executive

Bayonne
Blecher, Carol Stein oncology clinical nurse specialist
Doria, Joseph V., Jr. state legislator
†Goldman, Edward Merrill musician
Gorman, William David artist, graphic artist
†Lyndeck, Edmund actor
Martinez, Lisa Lynn elementary education educator
Masella, Robert Thomas political science educator, funeral service
McMahon, Eileen Marie artist's agent
Obernauer, Marne corporate executive
Rogow, Louis Michael oncologist, educator
Scudder, Carol Ann speech and language educator
Searle, Ronald artist
Wanko, Michael Andrew school system administrator
Zuckerman, Nancy Carol learning disabilities specialist, consultant

Beach Haven
†Houlihan, Gail Lanier child advocate, educator

Bedminster
Albert, Jack communications company executive
David, Edward Emil, Jr. electrical engineer, business executive
Hart, Terry Jonathan communications executive
Robinson, Paul Barry telecommunications executive
Vagelos, Pindaros Roy pharmaceutical company executive
Yannuzzi, Elaine Victoria food and home products executive

Belle Mead
Carroll, David Joseph actor
Sarle, Charles Richard health facility executive
Wilson, Nancy Jeanne laboratory director, medical technologist

Belleville
Caputo, Wayne James surgeon, podiatrist
Goldenberg, David Milton experimental pathologist, oncologist
Sales, Clifford M. surgeon

Bellmawr
Sibley, Robert Whitman printing company executive

Belmar
Branco, James Joseph estate planner
De Santo, Donald James psychologist, educational administrator

Bergenfield
Alfieri, John Charles, Jr. educational administrator
Clark, Fred legal writer, editor
Janow, Lydia Frances meeting planner
Knowles, John author
Kramer, Bernard physicist, educator
Phelan, Thomas Anthony private investigator

Berkeley Heights
Geusic, Joseph Edward physicist
Gottheimer, George Malcolm, Jr. insurance executive, educator
Mac Rae, Alfred Urquhart physicist, electrical engineer
Rabiner, Lawrence Richard electrical engineer
Shaffer, Gail Dorothy secondary education educator

Bernardsville
Baldwin, Frederick Stephen priest
Cooperman, Saul foundation administrator
Dixon, Richard Wayne retired communications company executive
Dixon, Rosina Berry physician, pharmaceutical development consultant
Lazor, Patricia Ann interior designer
Parker, Nancy Knowles (Mrs. Cortlandt Parker) publishing executive
Robinson, Maureen Loretta retired secondary school educator
Spofford, Sally (Hyslop) artist
Sullivan, Timothy Patrick ophthalmologist

Blackwood
Breve, Franklin Stephen pharmacist
Cloyd, Thomas Earl broadcast designer, consultant

Blairstown
Bean, Bennett artist
Martin, James Walter chemist, technology executive

Bloomfield
Conta, Richard Vincent actuary
Dickson, Geri Lenzen nursing educator, researcher
Dohr, Donald R. metallurgical engineer, researcher
Feldman, Max insurance executive
†Hemeleski, John Peter retired academic administrator
Lordi, Katherine Mary lawyer
Peizer, Maurice Samuel retired medical advertising consultant

Bloomingdale
Wanamaker, Ellen Ponce tax specialist

Bloomsbury
Clymer, Jerry Alan educational administrator

Bogota
Condon, Francis Edward retired chemistry educator
Oldenhage, Irene Dorothy elementary education educator

Boonton
Bona, Frederick Emil public relations executive
Walzer, James Harvey lawyer, author

Bordentown
Blackson, Benjamin F(ranklin) clinical social worker
Malone, Joseph R. state legislator

Bound Brook
Aloisi, Carol Ann marketing executive
Borah, Kripanath pharmacist
Karol, Frederick John industrial chemist

Brick
Alpiar, Hal management and marketing consultant, author
Cornblatt, Alan Jack lawyer
Godbold, Barbara Louise secondary education educator
Myers, Howard aerospace scientist, systems analyst
Pistolakis, Nicholas Stelios advertising executive
Roache, Patrick Michael, Jr. management consultant
Rusoff, Irving Isadore industrial food scientist, consultant
Shortess, Edwin Steevin marketing consultant
Tivenan, Charles Patrick lawyer

Bridgeport
Walters, Charles Joseph real estate developer

Bridgewater
Allen, Randy Lee corporate executive
†Chamorro, Juan Pablo financial analyst, marketing professional
Conroy, Robert John lawyer
Feldman, Arthur Edward urologist
Freeman, Henry McCall newspaper publisher
†Hassan, Fred pharmaceutical executive
Hirsch, Paul J. orthopedic surgeon, medical executive, educator
Hulse, Robert Douglas high technology executive
Kennedy, James Andrew chemical company executive
Kim, Soo-Ryong investment banker
Lewis, Donald Emerson banker
Mack, Robert William secondary school educator
Mencher, Stuart Alan sales and marketing executive
Mondadori, Cesare neurobiologist, researcher
Newman, Stephen Alexander chemical engineer, thermodynamicist
†Olson, Margaret Smith food services professional
Pedone, Joseph Lawrence advertising executive
Pickett, Doyle Clay employment and training counselor, consultant
Rothwell, Timothy Gordon pharmaceutical company executive
Skidmore, James Albert, Jr. management, computer technology and engineering services company executive
Wieschenberg, Klaus management consultant

Brielle
Christofi, Andreas finance educator

Brigantine
Holl, James Andrew prehospital care administrator
Kickish, Margaret Elizabeth elementary education educator

Brookside
†Keyes, Richard Paul small business owner

Browns Mills
Backman, Alan Gregory health sciences technologist
Cha, Se Do internist
Cholette, Maureen Theresa geriatrics nurse, nursing administrator
De Berardinis, Charles Anthony Joseph physician
DeWitt, Edward Frances artist
Di Nunzio, Dominick educational administrator
Lumia, Francis James internist
McNabb, Talmadge Ford religious organization administrator, retired military chaplain

Budd Lake
Bauer, Jean Marie accountant
Havens, Edwin Wallace manufacturing executive
Hilbert, Rita L. librarian
Khazen, Aleksandr Moiseyevich physicist
Pollack, Jordan Ellis pharmaceutical company executive

Burlington
Britt, Donna Marie school nurse
Gunn, Sandra Joyce musician and church lay leader
Kennedy, Christopher Robin ceramist
Rowlette, Henry Allen, Jr. social worker

Butler
Klaas, Nicholas Paul management and technical consultant
Wingert, Hannelore Christiane real estate sales executive, chemical company executive

Caldwell
Campbell, Sister Maura religious studies and philosophy educator
Chatlos, William Edward management consultant
Jennings, Sister Vivien Ann English language educator
Mann, Robert Christopher communications educator, television host, producer
†Mullaney, Marie Marmo history and political science educator
Werner, Patrice (Patricia Ann Werner) college president

Califon
Rosen, Carol Mendes artist

Camden
Abbott, Ann Augustine social worker, educator
Ances, I. G(eorge) obstetrician, gynecologist, educator
Beck, David Paul biochemist
Brotman, Stanley Seymour federal judge
Bryant, Wayne Richard state legislator
Burns, Gloria M. judge
Camishion, Rudolph Carmen physician
†Cummings, Melvin O'Neal educator elementary school, administrator
Dayer-Berenson, Linda adult and critical care nurse, educator
Elkind, Elizabeth C. perinatal clinical specialist
Fairbanks, Russell Norman law educator, university dean
Gans, Samuel Myer temporary employment service executive
Gerver, Joseph Leonide mathematics educator
Goldberg, Jack hematologist
Gordon, Walter Kelly retired provost, English language educator
Homan, Kenneth Lewis auditor
Irenas, Joseph Eron judge
Johnson, David Willis food products executive
Jones, Larry Darnell tax specialist
Kaden, Ellen Oran lawyer, consumer products company executive
†Kugler, Robert B. federal judge
Laskin, Lee B. laywer, state senator
Law, Robert finance director
Lewis, Michael Seth health care executive
Mandelbaum, Dorothy Rosenthal psychologist, educator
Meyers, Gilliard E. sales executive
†Miller, Audrey G. vice principal elementary school
†Morrison, Dale F. food company executive
Pomorski, Stanislaw lawyer, educator
Roberts, Thomas Andrew, II urban development executive
Rodriguez, Joseph H. federal judge
†Rosen, Joel B. federal judge
Scranton, Philip Brown history educator
Showalter, English, Jr. French language educator
Simandle, Jerome B. federal judge
Stahl, Gary Edward neonatologist
Wizmur, Judith H. federal judge
Wood, Martha Oakwell obstetrical and gynecological nurse practitioner
†Worrall, John D. economics educator, consultant, writer
†Zaontz, Mark Randall pediatric urologist

Cape May
Fox, Matthew Ignatius publishing company executive
Lassner, Franz George educator
Margolis, Jeffrey Allen guidance counselor

Cape May Court House
Cohen, Daniel Edward writer
Cohen, Susan Lois author
Foley, Eugene Arthur pastor

Carlstadt
Bonis, Joseph John financial executive

Carteret
Donald, James supermarket chain executive
Goldberg, Arthur M. gaming and fitness company executive, food products executive, lawyer
†Jemal, Lawrence retail executive
Strassler, Marc A. corporate lawyer

Cedar Grove
Carlozzi, Catherine L. corporate communications consultant, writer

Cedar Knolls
Blake, Richard F. transistor devices company executive
Stewart, Terry Gifford computer company executive

Chatham
Gormley, Robert John book publisher
Johnston, Dennis Roy computer systems integrator
Lax, Philip land developer, space planner
Lenz, Henry Paul management consultant
Leonett, Anthony Arthur banker
Manning, Frederick William retired retail executive
Murphy, Joseph James chiropractic physician

Cherry Hill
Adler, John Herbert lawyer, state legislator
Agasar, Ronald Joseph mortgage banker
Alexander, Eugene Morton electronics engineer
Amsterdam, Jay D. psychiatrist, educator
Ballas, Nadia S. writer, poet
Bashkin, Lloyd Scott marketing and management consultant
Baxter, Robert Theodore Stewart arts critic
Betchen, Stephen J. marital, family and sex therapist
Brenner, Lynnette Mary reading specialist, educator
Bryan, Henry Collier retired secondary school educator, clergyman
Burke, Linda Judith real estate broker
Callaway, Ben Anderson journalist
Chambers, Michele Denise technical writer
Clauser, Donald Roberdeau musician
Copsetta, Norman George real estate executive
Del Colliano, Gerard Anthony publisher
Doherty, Evelyn Marie data processing consultant
Dunfee, Thomas Wylie law educator
Erving, Julius Winfield, II (Dr. J. Erving) business executive, retired professional basketball player
Fuentevilla, Manuel Edward chemical engineer
Gardner, Joel Robert writer, historian
Garrigle, William Aloysius lawyer
Grado-Wolynies, Evelyn (Evelyn Wolynies) clinical nurse specialist, educator
Gutin, Myra Gail communications educator
Holfeld, Donald Rae railroad consultant
Israelsky, Roberta Schwartz speech pathologist, audiologist
Kahn, Sigmund Benham retired internist and dean
Keele, Lyndon Alan electronic company executive
Levin, Susan Bass lawyer
†Lipsius, Bruce David neurologist
Marsh, Robert Harry chemical company executive
McCormick, Donna Lynn social worker
McDonald, Mary Ellen retired nursing educator
Melick, George Fleury mechanical engineer, educator
Metzman, Frances Schuman gerontologist
Myers, Daniel William, II lawyer
Newell, Eric James financial planner, tax consultant, former insurance executive
Olearchyk, Andrew cardiothoracic surgeon, educator
Rose, Joel Alan legal consultant
Rudman, Solomon Kal magazine publisher
Sax, Robert Edward food service equipment company executive
Schelm, Roger Leonard information systems specialist
Stern, Howard S. chemistry educator
Tomar, William lawyer
Vaughan, Lynn Katherine insurance agent
Weinstein, Steven David lawyer
Werbitt, Warren gastroenterologist, educator

Chester
Cameron, Nicholas Allen diversified corporation executive
Fluker, Jay Edward middle school art educator

Cinnaminson
Johnson, Victor Lawrence banker
Kauffmann, Robert Fredrick software engineer

Clark
Burtnick, Ronald sales executive
Glatman-Stein, Marcia executive search company executive
Kinley, David physical therapist, acupuncturist
Kolaya, Margaret Helen Boutwell librarian
Meilan, Celia food products executive
Walsh, Daniel Stephen systems engineering consultant

Clayton
Bertenshaw, William Howard, III radio and television producer

Cliffside Park
Colagreco, James Patrick school superintendent
Diktas, Christos James lawyer
Ginos, James Zissis retired research chemist
Goldstein, Howard Bernard investment banker, advertising and marketing executive
†Hayes, Michael artist, editor
Perhacs, Marylouise Helen musician, educator

Clifton
Adelsberg, Harvey hospital administrator
Bronkesh, Annette Cylia public relations executive
Burke, Bruce Lowell consumer products company executive
Colflesh, Gertrude Patterson (Trudy Colflesh) psychotherapist, author
Epstein, William Eric health care executive
Held, George Anthony architect
Herman, Josh Seth actor, clown, magician
Kirrer, Ernest Douglas physician
Laskey, Frances M. secondary school educator
McCoy, Linda Korteweg media specialist
Meyer, John Anthony vice principal
Palma, Nicholas James lawyer
Ressetar, Nancy foreign language educator
Rodgers, John Joseph, III educational administration consultant
Rodimer, Frank Joseph bishop
Silber, Judy G. dermatologist
Stalbaum, Bernardine Ann English language educator
Svendsen, Joyce R. real estate company executive
Yau, Edward Tintai toxicologist, pharmacologist

Clinton
Acerra, Michele (Mike Acerra) engineering and construction company executive
DeGhetto, Kenneth Anselm engineering and construction company executive
Hansen, Arthur Magne engineering and manufacturing executive
Kennedy, Harold Edward lawyer
†Quandt, Michael T. manager systems analysis
Swift, Richard J. engineering company executive

Collingswood
Mohrfeld, Richard Gentel heating oil distributing company executive

Colonia
Wiesenfeld, Bess Gazevitz interior designer, real estate developer

Colts Neck
Gall, Michael Louis *educator*
Rode, Leif *retired real estate personal computer consultant*

Columbia
Timcenko, Lydia Teodora *biochemist, chemist*

Columbus
Litman, Bernard *electrical engineer, consultant*

Concordia
Reichek, Morton Arthur *retired magazine editor, writer*

Convent Station
Healy, Gwendoline Frances *controller*
Tintle, Carmel Joseph *public relations executive*

Cranbury
Barcus, Gilbert Martin *medical products executive, business educator*
Daoust, Donald Roger *pharmaceutical and toiletries company executive, microbiologist*
Hochreiter, Joseph Christian, Jr. *engineering company executive*
Iatesta, John Michael *lawyer*
Kemmerer, Peter Ream *financial executive*
Miller, Isadore *television executive, consultant*
Perhach, James Lawrence *pharmaceutical company executive*
Sofia, R. D. *pharmacologist*
Yoseloff, Julien David *publishing company executive*
Yoseloff, Thomas *publisher*

Cranford
Ascher, David Mark *lawyer*
Bardwil, Joseph Anthony *investments consultant*
†Casale, Paul Joseph *illustrator*
Cleaver, William Pennington *retired sugar refining company executive, consultant*
Crow, Lynne Campbell Smith *insurance company representative*
Herz, Sylvia Beatrice *clinical and community psychologist*
Jenssen, Warren Donald *microbiologist*
Mullen, Edward K. *paper company executive*
Schink, Frank Edward *electrical engineer*

Cresskill
Gardner, Richard Alan *psychiatrist, writer*
Smyth, Craig Hugh *fine arts educator*

Deal
Becker, Richard Stanley *music publisher*

Delmont
†Troyanovich, Stephen John *educational program director, poet*

Demarest
Brody, Saul Nathaniel *English literature educator*
Dornfest, Burton Saul *anatomy educator*

Denville
Breed, Ria *anthropologist*
Casper, Ephraim Saul *medical oncologist*
†Chung, Robert *dentist, educator*
Dudrow, Peter Warren *human resources executive, consultant*
Gangloff, Linda Lee *secondary education educator, underwater photographer, writer*
Husar, Walter Gene *neurologist, neuroscientist, educator*
Kirna, Hans Christian *lawyer, consultant*
Marfuggi, Richard Anthony *plastic surgeon*
Minter, Jerry Burnett *electronic component company executive, engineer*
Pan, Maria Weiyei *company executive*
Price, Robert Edmunds *civil engineer*
Trukenbrod, Sharon Lightbody *day care provider*

Dover
Byrnes, Robert William *secondary school educator*
Chung, Tae-Soo *physician*
†Geis, John P. *military career officer*
Hurwitz, David *entreprenuer, consultant*
Kassell, Paula Sally *editor, publisher*
Mc Donald, John Joseph *electronics executive*
†Michitsch, John F. *career officer*

Dumont
Sadock, Karen *editor, writer*

East Brunswick
Burns, Barbara *lawyer*
†Gawlikowski, Vladimir C. *organization executive*
Haupin, Elizabeth Carol *retired secondary school educator*
Hurst, Gregory Squire *artistic director, director, producer*
Kabela, Frank, Jr. *broadcast executive*
Karmazin, Sharon Elyse *library director*
Kupchynsky, Jerry Markian *orchestra conductor, educator*
Lachs, Annie *religious organization administrator*
Marshall, Keith *pharmaceutical consultant*
Meshowski, Frank Robert *business consultant*
†Miller, Andrew David *physician*
Mooney, William Piatt *actor*
Rosenberg, Norman *surgeon*
Todd, Edward Francis, Jr. *risk management consultant, insurance broker*
Yttrehus, Rolv Berger *composer, educator*

East Hanover
Anderson, Gary William *physician*
Baillie, Stuart Gordon *research technician*
Davidson, Anne Stowell *lawyer*
Elam, Karen Morgan *food company executive, consultant*
Foley, James Edward *scientist, pharmaceutical company executive*
Joseph, Jannan Marie *school social worker*
Kent, Bruce Jonathan *pharmaceutical executive*
Knight, Frank James *pharmaceutical marketing professional*
†Mogendovich-Lubin, Eugene Michael *scholar, writer*
Nemecek, Georgina Marie *molecular pharmacologist*
†Ori, Nancy Jean *video producer and director, photographer*

Tamburro, Peter James, Jr. *social studies secondary school educator*
Zhou, Honghui *clinical pharmacokineticist*

East Millstone
†Rodwell, Dean Edward *toxicologist*

East Newark
Huhn, Darlene Marie *county official, poet*

East Orange
Amadei, Deborah Lisa *librarian*
Anderson, Zina-Diane *real estate executive*
†Eldridge-Howard, Joyce *principal*
Fielo, Muriel Bryant *space engineer, interior designer*
Jones Gregory, Patricia *secondary art educator*
Oderman, Stuart Douglas *pianist, composer, playwright*
Wolff, Derish Michael *economist, company executive*
Yoo, James H. *radiation oncologist, nuclear medicine physician*

East Rutherford
Aufzien, Alan L. *professional sports team executive*
Brodeur, Martin *professional hockey player*
†Casey, Don *professional basketball coach*
†Fassel, Jim *head coach professional football*
Fetisov, Slava *hockey coach, former professional hockey player*
†Ftorek, Robbie Brian (Robert Brian Ftorek) *professional hockey coach*
Gerstein, David Brown *hardware manufacturing company executive, professional basketball team executive*
Golashesky, Chrysa Zofia *telecommunications company executive*
†Holik, Bobby *professional hockey player*
Kempner, Michael W. *public relations executive*
Kluge, John Werner *broadcasting and advertising executive*
Krockman, Arnold Francis *publisher, advertising executive*
Lamoriello, Louis Anthony *professional hockey team executive*
Mara, Wellington T. *professional football team executive*
†Marbury, Stephon *professional basketball player*
McMullen, John J. *professional hockey team executive*
Nash, John N. *professional basketball team executive*
Reed, Willis *professional basketball team executive, former head coach*
Singleterry, Gary Lee *investment banker*
Stevens, Scott *professional hockey player*
†Sykora, Peter *professional hockey player*
†Van Horn, Keith *professional basketball player*
Wadler, Arnold L. *lawyer*
†Williams, Jayson *basketball player*

Eatontown
Chomsky, Martin S. *county executive director*
DeMarinis, Bernard Daniel *engineering management consultant*
Granet, Kenneth M. *internist*
O'Hare-VanMeerbeke, Anne Marie *dietitian*
Orlando, Carl *medical research and development executive*

Edgewater
Karol, Cecilia Kalijman *psychiatrist, psychoanalyst*
Meier, August *historian, educator*
Virelli, Louis James, Jr. *lawyer*

Edison
Andreasen, Charles Peter *retired electronics executive*
Applebaum, Charles *lawyer*
†Arakawa, Peter Stanhope *artist, educator*
Avery, James Stephen *oil company executive*
Behr, Marion Ray *artist, author, business executive*
Blumengold, Jeffrey Gene *health care financial and reimbursement expert*
Comstock, Robert Ray *journalism educator, newspaper editor*
†Critchley, John J., Jr. *stock options trader*
Cronin, John Joseph *airline pilot, poet, author*
D'Agostino, Matthew Paul *bakery executive*
Doherty, Patricia Ann *computer systems analyst*
Donahue, John Edward *physician*
Duffy, James Patrick *writer*
Fink, Edward Murray *lawyer, educator*
Firstenberg, Donald Elliott *chemist*
Francis, Peter T. *gas and oil industry executive*
Frary, John Newton *history educator*
Haberman, Louise Shelly *consulting company executive*
Hecht, William David *accountant*
Hunter, Michael *publishing executive*
Hynes-Lasek, Nancy Ellen *secondary education educator*
Jacobey, John Arthur, III *surgeon, educator*
Jones, James Thomas, Jr. *tobacco company executive*
Kopidakis, Emmanuel G. *general surgeon*
Kumar, Krishan *management consultant company executive*
Maeroff, Gene I. *academic administrator, journalist*
Marash, Stanley Albert *consulting company executive*
McKiernan, Robert E. *career management consultant*
Neves, Paula *writer, editor*
Olszewski, Jerzy Adam *electrical engineer*
Provitera, Michael J. *investment company executive*
Pruden, Ann Lorette *chemical engineer, researcher*
Robinson, Donald Warren *educator, artist*
Tedesco, Richard Albert *minister*
Tyrl, Paul *mathematics educator, researcher, consultant*
†Visco, Nicholas *controller*
Wallerstein, Seth Michael *dentist*
Walters, Arthur Scott *neurologist, educator, clinical research scientist*
Wendel, Christopher Mark *exhibition designer*
Wexler, Annette Frances *writer*

Egg Harbor Township
Blee, Francis J. *municipal official*
Raftner, Thomas *airport terminal executive*
Reed, Frances Boogher *writer, actress*

Elizabeth
Aronowitz, Alfred Gilbert *writer*
Berger, Harold Richard *physician*
Finder, Robert Andrew *pharmaceutical company executive*

Gellert, George Geza *food importing company executive*
Kabak, Douglas Thomas *lawyer*
Layden, Thomas John *social services supervisor*
Morgan, Sister Ruth Zelena *educator*
Rosenstein, Neil *surgeon, genealogical researcher*
Verret, Joseph Marc *psychiatrist*
Watson, Rita Marie *internist, cardio vascular specialist*
Willis, Ben *writer, artist*

Elmer
†Magnan, Ruthann *registered nurse, social worker*
Slavoff, Harriet Emonds *learning disabilities teacher, consultant*
Ventrella, Gerard *physician*

Elmwood Park
Nadzick, Judith Ann *accountant*
Semeraro, Michael Archangel, Jr. *civil engineer*
Wygod, Martin J. *pharmaceuticals executive*

Emerson
Cheslik, Francis Edward *management consultant*
Finch, Carol Anne *former secondary education educator*
†Hannon, Patricia Ann *library director*

Englewood
Anuszkiewicz, Richard Joseph *artist*
Cherovsky, Erwin Louis *lawyer, writer*
Deresiewicz, Herbert *mechanical engineering educator*
Farrell, Patricia Ann *psychologist, educator*
Friedman, Emanuel *publishing company executive*
Griffin, Robert Douglas *publishing executive, genealogist*
Hertzberg, Arthur *rabbi, educator*
Hornblass, Bernice Miriam *educational evaluator, reading and learning disabilities specialist*
Khouri, Antoun *church administrator*
Koch, Randall Glory *hospital administrator*
Kreston, Martin Howard *advertising, marketing, public relations, and publishing executive*
Lapidus, Arnold *mathematician*
Masland, Richard Lambert *neurologist, educator*
Miles, Virginia (Mrs. Fred C. Miles) *marketing consultant*
Neis, Arnold Hayward *pharmaceutical company executive*
Orlando, George (Joseph) *union executive*
Rawl, Arthur Julian (Lord of Cursons) *retail executive, accountant, consultant, author*
Saliba, Philip E. *archbishop*
Schmidt, Ronald Hans *architect*
Schwartz, Howard Alan *periodontist*
Solomon, Edward David *consultant*
Wuhl, Charles Michael *psychiatrist*
Zwilich, Ellen Taaffe *composer*

Englewood Cliffs
Feuerstein, Herbert *food company executive*
Fredericks, Barry Irwin *lawyer*
†Haber, Barbara Fran *psychologist*
Haltiwanger, Robert Sidney, Jr. *book publishing executive*
†Heller, Hanes Ayres *lawyer*
†Kim, Jae Taik *educator*
Perry, Douglas Matthew *publishing executive, editor*
Saible, Stephanie Irene *magazine editor*
Shoemate, Charles R. *food company executive*
Shrem, Charles Joseph *metals corporation executive*
Vane, Dena *magazine editor-in-chief*

Ewing
Brown, Richard Alexander *chemist*
McGowan, Joan Yuhas *development researcher*
Sanders, Philip F., Jr. *artist, computer art educator*
Turner, Shirley K. *state legislator*

Fair Haven
Aumack, Shirley Jean *financial planner, tax preparer*
Derchin, Dary Bret Ingham *writer*
McKissock, David Lee *retired manufacturing company executive*

Fair Lawn
Felice, Nicholas R. *state legislator*
Hayden, Neil Steven *communications company executive*
Hirschklau, Morton *lawyer*
Mazel, Joseph Lucas *publications consultant*
Parker, Adrienne Natalie *art educator, art historian*
Wall, Mark Emanuel *banker, engineer, consultant*
Wallace, Mary Monahan *elementary and secondary schools educator*

Fairfield
Byer, Theodore Scott *accountant*
de Smet, Lorraine May *artist*
Guida, Pat *information broker, literature chemist*
Hower, Paul H. *hotel executive*
Johnson, David Blackwell *safety engineer*
Kull, Bryan Paul *business information/technology executive, real estate investor*
Mills, Gloria Adams *energy service company executive*
†Petrocelli, A. F. *hotel executive*
Stein, Robert Alan *electronics company executive*

Fairview
Anton, Bruce Norman *textile company executive*

Fanwood
Butler, Grace Caroline *medical administrator*
Butler, William Langdon *manufacturing company representative*
Whitaker, Joel *publisher*

Far Hills
Alexandre, Kristin Kuhns *public relations executive, writer*
Bruett, Karen Diesl *sales and fundraising consultant*
Corash, Richard *lawyer*
Fay, David B. *sports association executive*
McCall, David Warren *retired chemistry research director, consultant*

Farmingdale
†Edwards, Ann Concetta *human resources manager, writer*
Martin, Robert Francis *roof maintenance systems company executive*

Schluter, Peter Mueller *electronics company executive*

Flanders
Huang, Jacob Chen-ya *physician, city official*

Flemington
Bieri, Barbara Normile *systems analyst, consultant*
Castellanos, Diego Antonio *television personality, writer, educator*
Jackson, Ryno Marshall *forensic psychologist, consultant*
Kettler, Carl Frederick *airline executive*
Lance, Leonard *state legislator*
Miller, Louis H. *lawyer*
Salamon, Renay *real estate broker*
Schluter, William E. *state legislator*
Schneider, Kimberly Jane *special education educator*
†Thomas, Anne Moreau *newspaper owner*
Wiedl-Kramer, Sheila Colleen *biologist*

Florham Park
Atal, Bishnu Saroop *speech research executive*
Atkins, Richard Bart *film, television producer*
Bhagat, Phiroz Maneck *mechanical engineer*
Bossen, Wendell John *insurance company executive*
Brodkin, Adele Ruth Meyer *psychologist*
Calabrese, Arnold Joseph *lawyer*
Chase, Eric Lewis *lawyer*
Clayton, William L. *investment banking executive*
Gibson, William Ford *author*
Graham, Ronald Lewis *mathematician*
Hardin, William Downer *retired lawyer*
Henning, Neil Scott *financial consultant*
Katona, Bruce Richard *real estate company executive*
Kenney, William F. *process engineer, safety engineer, sports official*
Kovach, Andrew Louis *administrative executive*
Laulicht, Murray Jack *lawyer*
Lovell, Robert Marlow, Jr. *retired investment company executive*
MacMillan, David Paul *oil company executive*
Naimark, George Modell *marketing and management consultant*
Oths, Richard Philip *health systems administrator*
Rabinovich, Michael *computer scientist*
Russell, Jesse E. *communications executive*
Sloane, Neil James Alexander *mathematician, researcher*
Sniffen, Michael Joseph *hospital administrator*
Sperber, Martin *pharmaceutical company executive, pharmacist*
Stanton, Patrick Michael *lawyer*
Witman, Leonard Joel *lawyer*
Wright, Paul William *lawyer, oil company executive*

Fords
Blond, Stuart Richard *newsletter editor*
Kaufman, Alex *chemicals executive*

Forked River
Novak, Dennis E. *family practice physician*
Rudolph, Linda Louise *social worker, legal advocate*

Fort Dix
†Davis, Steven Michael *air force officer, test pilot*
Stankiewicz, John Jay *staff administrator*
†Welser, William, III *military officer*

Fort Lee
Abut, Charles C. *lawyer*
Bolster, William Lawrence *broadcast executive*
Chessler, Richard Kenneth *gastroenterologist, endoscopist*
†Cohn, Scott *television news correspondent*
Cox, Melvin Monroe *lawyer*
Fischel, Daniel Norman *publishing consultant*
Goldfischer, Jerome D. *cardiologist*
Houston, Whitney *vocalist, recording artist*
†Jamison, George Hill III *broadcast company executive, writer*
Kadish, Lori Gail *clinical psychologist*
Kiriakopoulos, George Constantine *dentist*
Levy, Valery *publisher*
Lippman, William Jennings *investment company executive*
†Murray, Brian Victor *investment banker*
†Nadeine, Vladimir *journalist, editor*
Schiessler, Robert Walter *retired chemical and oil company executive*
Screpetis, Dennis *nuclear engineer, consultant*
Seitel, Fraser Paul *public relations executive*
Sugarman, Alan William *educational administrator*
†Tesoriero, John Salvatore *physician*
Vignolo, Biagio Nickolas, Jr. *chemical company executive*
Welfeld, Joseph Alan *healthcare executive*
Yoo, Choon Wang *financial consultant*

Fort Monmouth
†Boutelle, Steven W. *army officer*
†Gust, David R. *military career officer*
Ignoffo, Matthew Frederick *English language educator, writer, counselor*
Perlman, Barry Stuart *electrical engineering executive, researcher*
Schwering, Felix Karl *electronics engineer, researcher*
Thornton, Clarence Gould *electronics engineering executive*
Washington, William Nicolai *government official*

Franklin Lakes
Baker, Cornelia Draves *artist*
†Baker, Philip Douglas *consultant, retired investment banker*
Castellini, Clateo *medical technology company executive*
Friedman, Martin Burton *chemical company executive*
Galiardo, John William *lawyer*
Hector, Bruce John *lawyer*
Kapr, John Robert *operations executive*
†Marcelina, Louis Alan *company executive*
Throdahl, Mark Crandall *medical technology company executive*

Franklin Park
Perry, Arthur William *plastic surgeon, educator*

Franklinville
DiGregory, Nicholas A. *secondary educator, coach*

Freehold
Avella, John Thomas principal, school administrator
Brown, Sanford Donald lawyer
Christ, Duane Marland computer systems engineer
Dillon, Patricia Harrington medical/surgical nurse
Farragher, Clare M. state legislator
Fisher, Clarkson Sherman, Jr. judge
Flynn, Pamela artist, educator
Foster, Eric Harold, Jr. retail executive
Hooper, John David coast guard officer
Kwon, Joon Taek retired chemistry researcher
Littman, Jules Sanford lawyer
Lomurro, Donald Michael lawyer
Newman, James Michael lawyer, judge
Nicholson, Henry Rexon county transportation director
Pofsky, Norma Louise interior designer, behavioral consultant
Prideaux, John Raymond, Jr. insurance company executive
Scarola, Susan Margaret lawyer
Schockaert, Barbara Ann operations executive
Schwartz, Perry Lester information systems engineer, consultant
Shapiro, Michael supermarket corporate officer
Stirrat, William Albert electronics engineer

Garfield
Herpst, Robert Dix lawyer, optics and materials technology executive
Kobylarz, Joseph Douglas secondary education educator
Kodaka, Kunio plastics company executive
Nickles, I. MacArthur librarian

Garwood
Smith, Joan Lowell syndicated columnist, feature writer

Gillette
Nathanson, Linda Sue publisher, author, technical writer
Pfafflin, Sheila Murphy psychologist

Gladstone
Caspersen, Finn Michael Westby diversified financial services company executive
Close, Donald Pembroke management consultant
Holt, Jonathan Turner public relations executive
Standish, Robert C. professional sports team executive

Glassboro
†DiBlasio, Denis musician, educator
Fails, Donna Gail mental health services professional
Holdcraft, Janet R. academic administrator
James, Herman Delano college administrator
†Johnson, Frances Swigon English educator
†Lewis, Phillip Allen business administration educator
†Libro, Antoinette C. university dean
Martin, Marilyn Joan library director
Mukhoti, Bela Banerjee economics educator
Robinette, Joseph Allen theater educator, playwright

Glen Gardner
Epstein, Edward Joseph textile company executive

Glen Ridge
Agnew, Peter Tomlin employee benefit consultant
Bracken, Eddie (Edward Vincent) actor, director, writer, singer, artist
Clemente, Celestino physician, surgeon
Drexel, John Frederick poet, writer, editor
Pendley, Donald Lee association executive
Swerdlow, Dave Baer surgeon
Zbar, Lloyd Irwin Stanley otolaryngologist, educator

Glen Rock
Krebs, Gary Michael editor, author
Markey, Brian Michael lawyer
Mc Elrath, Richard Elsworth retired insurance company executive
Winstead, Clint financial publisher

Green Brook
Bohanan, David John management consultant
Elias, Donald Francis environmental consultant
Hertzberg, Henry radiologist, educator
Spoeri, Randall Keith healthcare company executive

Green Village
Castenschiold, René engineering company executive, author, consultant
Riemer, Neal political scientist

Hackensack
Ahearn, James newspaper columnist
Angelakis, Manos G(eorge) filmmaker, communications executive
Baker, Andrew Hartill clinical laboratory executive
Borg, Malcolm Austin communications company executive
Caminiti, Donald Angelo lawyer
Carra, Andrew Joseph advertising executive
Cicchelli, Joseph Vincent secondary education educator
Ciccone, Joseph Lee criminal justice educator
†Comandini, Michele Louise newspaper reporter
Croland, Barry I. lawyer
Curtis, Robert Kern lawyer, physics educator
D'Alessandro, Dianne Marie public defender
Davies, Richard John oncologist
De Groote, Robert David general and vascular surgeon
Duus, Gordon Cochran lawyer
Ferguson, John Patrick medical center executive
Gallucci, Michael A. lawyer
Gingras, Paul Joseph real estate management company executive
Goldsamt, Bonnie Blume lawyer
Greenberg, Steven Morey lawyer
Heilborn, George Heinz investments professional
†Jones, Charles T. principal
Kestin, Howard H. judge
Latimer, Stephen Mark lawyer
Margulies, James Howard editorial cartoonist
Markey, Jonathan H. printing company executive
Masi, John Roger lawyer
Mavrovic, Ivo chemical engineer
Mehta, Jay financial executive
Michaelson, Richard Aaron health science facility administrator
Mullin, Patrick Allen lawyer
Navatta, Anna Paula lawyer
Parisi, Cheryl Lynn elementary school educator
Pollinger, William Joshua lawyer
Rauscher, Gregory E. plastic surgeon
Riegel, Norman physician
Shapiro, Sylvia psychotherapist
Shaw, Julie Ann addiction counselor
Spiegel, Linda F. lawyer
Stein, Gary S. state supreme court justice
Timmins, Michael Joseph communications services company executive
Waixel, Vivian journalist
Yagoda, Harry Nathan system engineering executive
Zimmerman, Marlin U., Jr. chemical engineer

Hackettstown
Brock, David Lawrence periodontist
Fremon, Richard C. retired infosystems specialist
Kays, Elena J. interior design educator
Kobert, Joel A. lawyer
Mulligan, Elinor Patterson lawyer
Passantino, Benjamin Arthur marketing executive
Scalza, Margaret T. publishing executive
†Sheninger, Arthur Wayne principal
Wiedemann, Charles Louis dentist

Haddon Heights
D'Alfonso, Mario Joseph lawyer
Gwiazda, Stanley John university dean

Haddonfield
Bauer, Raymond Gale sales professional
Capelli, John Placido nephrologist
Carter, Joan Pauline investment company executive
Cheney, Daniel Lavern retired magazine publisher
Chu, Horn Dean chemical engineer
Enfield, Ronald Lee Internet software company executive
Fuoco, Philip Stephen lawyer
Iavicoli, Mario Anthony lawyer
Kinee-Krohn, Patricia special education educator
Payne, Deborah Anne medical company officer
Siskin, Edward Joseph engineering and construction company executive
Suflas, Steven William lawyer

Hainesport
Sylk, Leonard Allen housing company executive, real estate developer

Hamburg
Buist, Richardson corporate executive, retired banker

Hamilton
Barclay, Robert, Jr. chemist
Holmes, Bradley Paul information technology management consultant
Inverso, Peter A. state legislator
Kane, Michael Joel physician

Hammonton
†Crawford, James A. transportation authority executive
Grefe, Bruce Paul art educator, artist
Pellegrino, Peter surgeon
Stephanick, Carol Ann dentist, consultant

Hampton
Lovejoy, Lee Harold investment company executive
Yates, Michael Francis management consultant

Hanover
†Von Moltke, Konrad environmental policy educator

Harrington Park
Covello, John Anthony water utility lobbyist
Grantuskas, Patricia Mary elementary education educator

Hasbrouck Heights
†Granoff, Michael investment agency manager
Kloepper, David Alan management consultant
Perham, Roy Gates, III industrial psychologist

Haworth
Posner, Roy Edward finance executive, retired
Stokvis, Jack Raphael urban planner, entrepreneur computer consultnt and developer, government agency administrator

Hawthorne
Cole, Leonard Aaron political scientist, dentist

Hazlet
Fisher, David Bruce land development executive
Miller, Duane King health and beauty care company executive
Wunsch, Anna Catherine Mary O'Brien Horton artist, consultant

Hewitt
Mollenkott, Virginia Ramey English language educator, author, guest lecturer
Selwyn, Donald engineering administrator, researcher, inventor, educator

Highland Lakes
Kiraly, Bèla Kàlmàn retired history educator, Hungarian army officer
Ludwig, Gregory Brian editor, writer

Highland Park
†Baker, Ross Kenneth political science educator, columnist
Brudner, Harvey Jerome physicist
Coughlin, Caroline Mary library consultant, educator
Feigenbaum, Abraham Samuel nutritional biochemist
†Kolodzei, Natalia A. art foundation administrator, art historian
Michaels, Jennifer Alman lawyer
Pane, Remigio Ugo Romance languages educator
Plaut, Eric Alfred retired psychiatrist, educator
Spencer, Herbert Harry structural engineering researcher, computer analyst

Highlands
Hansen, Christian Andreas, Jr. plastics and chemical company executive
Saad, Valerie Ann nursing administrator, naval officer

Hightstown
Brodman, Estelle librarian, retired educator
Bronner, William Roche lawyer
Decker, Christine Marie healthcare administrator
Fitch, Lyle Craig economist, administrator
Hart, Patricia Anne public health officer
Howard, Barbara Sue Mesner artist
Johnson, Walter Curtis electrical engineering educator
Moustafa, Fikry Sayed accountant
Smith, Datus Clifford, Jr. former foundation executive, publisher
†Viola, Albert T. arts center administrator, author, composer, actor
Wham, George Sims retired publishing executive

Hillsborough
Kenyhercz, Thomas Michael pharmaceutical company executive
Yuster-Freeman, Leigh Carol publishing company executive

Hillsdale
Copeland, Lois Jacqueline (Mrs. Richard A. Sperling) physician
DiBlasi, Dianne Clark editor
Kohan, Lois Rae community health nurse

Hillside
Fox, Sheldon retired radiologist, medical educator
†Jean-Mary, Joseph Belladere educator
Patell, Mahesh pharmacist, researcher
Webb, Joyce critical care nurse, educator, legal nurse consult

Ho Ho Kus
Munschauer, Robert Lloyd accountant
Van Slooten, Ronald Henry Joseph dentist

Hoboken
Abel, Kate researcher
Abel, Robert Berger science administrator
Boesch, Francis Theodore electrical engineer, educator
Bruno, Michael Stephen ocean engineering educator, researcher
†Einreinhofer, William Michael, Jr. television producer and director, educator
Fajans, Jack physics educator
Forman, Robert painter
Griskey, Richard George chemical engineering educator
Jurkat, Martin Peter management educator
Mintz, Kenneth Andrew librarian
Paradise, Paul Richard writer, editor
Regazzi, John James, III publishing executive
Rubin, Irvin I. plastics company executive
Sasso, Frank Sergio health officer
Savitsky, Daniel engineer, educator
Schmidt, George physicist
Shafran, Michael Wayne editor
Sisto, Fernando mechanical engineering educator
†Stohr, Katherine A. journalist
Widdicombe, Richard Palmer librarian
Woodward, Holly Lowell former educator, writer

Holmdel
Ayub, Yacub financial consultant
Boyd, Gary Delane electro-optical engineer, researcher
Burrus, Charles Andrew, Jr. research physicist
Erfani, Shervin electrical engineer, educator, scientist, writer
Gordon, James Power optics scientist
Hudson, Wendy Joy software manager
Kaminow, Ivan Paul physicist
†Kashyap, Satchitanand research scientis
Kogelnik, Herwig Werner electronics company executive
Lang, Howard Lawrence electrical engineer
Meadors, Howard Clarence, Jr. electrical engineer
Meyer, Robert Alan reinsurance company executive
Mollenauer, Linn Frederick physicist
Opie, William Robert retired metallurgical engineer
Ross, Ian Munro electrical engineer
†Samra, Said A. plastic surgeon
Smith, Sibley Judson, Jr. historic site administrator, educator
Vitullo, Anthony Joseph communications industry executive

Hopatcong
Bowen, Robert William publishing executive
Caddigan, Mary health facility administrator
Oken, Robert neuroscientist, researcher, consultant
Reese, Harry Edwin, Jr. electronics executive
Wolahan, Caryle Goldsack nursing educator

Hopewell
Halpern, Daniel poet, editor, educator
Pariso, Jean Brunner real estate professional
Wesselmann, Debbie Lee novelist, short story writer

Howell
Feinen, Cynthia Lucille pediatric nurse
Lance, Steven author

Irvington
Huber, Donald Mark protective services official
Paden, Harry municipal official
Steele-Hunter, Teresa Ann elementary education educator

Iselin
Accardi, Joseph Ronald accountant
Bragg, William David film producer, screenwriter
Clarke, David H. industrial products executive
De Rose, Louis John financial services executive
Dornbusch, Arthur A., II lawyer
Gupta, Rajat Kumar lawyer, accountant
Kalafsky, Kurt M. architect
Rosenthal, David Michael musician, songwriter, composer, producer, synthesizer programmer
Sangiuliano, Barbara Ann tax consultant
Smith, Orin Robert chemical company executive
Tice, George A(ndrew) photographer
Whelpley, William Albert management consultant, educator
Wolynic, Edward Thomas specialty chemicals technology executive

Island Heights
Noble, William Parker writer, educator

Jackson
Hagberg, Carl Thomas financial executive
†LaBollita, Sharon Ann retired executive secretary
Vacchiano, Julie Catherine special education educator

Jamesburg
Wolfe, Deborah Cannon Partridge government education consultant
Wright, Barbara W. state legislator, nurse
Zeigen, Spencer Steven architect

Jersey City
Adlershteyn, Leon naval architect, engineer, educator, researcher
Ashley, Willard Walden C., Sr. minister
Barrett, Kathleen Anne assistant principal
Bowen, Linda Florence pharmaceutical executive
Carmi, Giora illustrator
†Carter, Guy Christopher theologian
Catalano, James Anthony social worker
Christensen, Walter Frederick, Jr. information, telecommunications and financial systems specialist
†Coreil, Raymond Clyde English educator
Daane, Mary Constance English language educator
D'Alessandro, Daniel Anthony lawyer, educator
D'Amico, Thomas F. economist, educator
Degatano, Anthony Thomas educational association administrator
Demos, Nicholas John physician, surgeon, researcher
Dupey, Michele Mary communications specialist
Feder, Arthur A. lawyer
Frank, William Fielding computer systems design executive, consultant
Gallagher, Thomas M. city official Jersey City
Giorgio, Marilyn social worker
Giuffra, Lawrence John hospital administrator, medical educator
Goldberg, Arthur Abba merchant banker, financial advisor
Goria, Ellen Theresa professional society administrator
Gurevich, Grigory visual artist, educator
Hayes, Dennis Joseph library director
Ingrassia, Paul Joseph publishing executive
Johanson, Martha Cecilia elementary educator
Kahrmann, Robert George educational administrator
Kaplan, Ben Augustus financial services executive
Katz, Colleen publisher
Kollar, Mark Patrick newsletter editor
Koster, Emlyn Howard geologist, educator
Lane, Ted literacy education educator
Lang, Everett Francis, Jr. brokerage house executive
Larkins, Robert Joseph journal editor
Lawatsch, Frank Emil, Jr. lawyer
Leff, David lawyer
Levine, Richard James publishing executive
Maguire-Krupp, Marjorie Anne corporate executive
McFadden, Rosemary Theresa lawyer, mercantile exchange executive
Miller, Adele Engelbrecht educational administrator
Nakhla, Atif Mounir scientist, biochemist
Niemiec, Edward Walter professional association executive
Nissenbaum, Gerald physician, educator, inventor
Ortenzi, Regina (Gina Rae Ortenzi) home fashion products designer, educator
Owens, Dana (Queen Latifah) recording artist, actress
Pesce, Phyllis Anne elementary education educator
Pietrini, Andrew Gabriel automotive aftermarket executive
Poiani, Eileen Louise mathematics educator, college administrator, higher education planner
Râzim, William Wendell former radio broadcasting producer
†Rhodes, George Anthony plastic surgeon
Schundler, Bret Davis mayor
Signorile, Vincent Anthony lawyer
Smith, James Frederick securities executive
Stencer, Mark Joseph academic administrator, consultant
Wagner, Douglas Walker Ellyson journal editor
Wilzig, Siggi Bert banker
Winters, Robert Wayne medical educator, pediatrician
Zuckerberg, David Alan pharmaceutical company executive

Johnsonburg
Cioffi, Eugene Edward, III educational administrator

Kearny
†Antunes, Daniel L. sales consultant, camera operator
Badders, Rebecca Susanne military officer, educator, writer
Brady, Lawrence Peter lawyer
Perricci, Jeffrey Michael dentist

Keasbey
Hari, Kenneth Stephen painter, sculptor, writer

Kendall Park
Berger, Richard Stanton dermatologist
Cua, Florence consultant
Goldberg, Bertram J. social agency administrator
Hershenov, Bernard Zion electronics research and development company executive

Kenilworth
Cayen, Mitchell Ness biochemist
Evans, Charlie Anderson chemist
Gen, Martin corporate executive
Hoffman, John Fletcher lawyer
Johnson Velazco, Nancy Ruth marketing professional
Kravec, Cynthia Vallen microbiologist
Krishna, Gopal scientist, pharmacokineticist
Scott, Mary Celine pharmacologist

Keyport
Colmant, Andrew Robert lawyer

Kingston
Blank, Leonard psychologist
Gross, Steven medical marketing communications and device company executive

Kinnelon
†D'Arcy, Michael Patrick public relations professional
Haller, Charles Edward engineering consultant

Preston, Andrew Joseph *pharmacist, drug company executive*
Richardson, Joseph Blancet *former biology educator, educational facilities planning consultant*

Kirkwood Voorhees
Cohen, Mark N. *business executive*

Lake Hopatcong
Ollo, Michael Anthony *educational coordinator, educator*
Tomlinson, Gerald Arthur *writer, publisher, editor*

Lakehurst
Sherwood, Harold DeWitt *oil industry executive, consultant*

Lakeland
Connor, Wilda *government health agency administrator*

Lakewood
Biasini, Virginia *social worker*
Bielory, Abraham Melvin *lawyer, financial executive*
Bowers, John Zimmerman *physician, scientist, educator*
Brod, Morton Shlevin *oral surgeon*
Costanzo, Hilda Alba *retired banker*
Edwards, Francis Charles *municipal official*
Freitas, Elizabeth Frances *lawyer*
Gross, Michael Fred *biologist, educator, researcher*
Houle, Joseph E. *mathematics educator*
Levovitz, Pesach Zechariah *rabbi*
Nasr, Salah *sales executive*
Quinn, Evelyn Saul *social work educator*
Rodgers, Dianna Sue *private school educator*
Sloyan, Sister Stephanie *mathematics educator*
Taylor, Robert M. *minister*
†Valentino, Brian Joseph *public administrator*
Williams, Barbara Anne *college president*
Woodman, G. Roger *management consultant*

Lambertville
Batshaw, Marilyn Seidner *insurance professional*
Mackey, Philip English *non-profit organization consultant*

Laurel Springs
Cleveland, Susan Elizabeth *library administrator, researcher*

Laurence Harbor
Goodwin, Douglas Ira *steel trading company executive*

Lavallette
Tesoriero, Philip James *human resource consultant*

Lawrence Harbor
DeMatteo, Gloria Jean *insurance saleswoman*

Lawrenceville
Adams, Christine Hanson *advertising executive*
Baer, John Metz, Jr. *psychology educator*
Coleman, Wade Hampton, III *management consultant, mechanical engineer, former banker*
Cox, Teri P. *public relations executive*
Enegess, David Norman *chemical engineer*
Farrar, Donald Keith *retired financial executive*
Griffith, Barbara E. *social worker, political activist*
Hester, Kara-Lyn Annette *software engineer*
Hunt, Wayne Robert, Sr. *state government official*
Kihn, Harry *electronics engineer, manufacturing company executive*
Kline, Michael J. *lawyer*
Leonard, Patricia Louise *education educator, consultant*
Luedeke, J. Barton *academic administrator*
Moser, Rosemarie Scolaro *psychologist*
O'Brien, James Jerome *construction management consultant*
Onyshkevych, Larissa M. L. Zaleska *educator, editor*
O'Reilly, Mary Irby *literature educator, composition consultant*
Petronio, Bruce J. *librarian, writer*
Pouleur, Hubert Gustave *cardiologist*
Rudy, James Francis Xavier *lawyer*
Sheats, John Eugene *chemistry educator*
†Steele, Ryan Edward *chemical company executive*
Stockton, John Potter, III *retired state agency administrator*
Tharney, Leonard John *education educator, consultant*
†Tipton, June Frank *music educator*
†Wang, Minmin *communications educator*
Williams, Brown F *television media services company executive*

Lebanon
Barto, Susan Carol *writer*
Goulazian, Peter Robert *retired broadcasting executive*
Hakes, Thomas Brion *manufacturing company executive, physician*
Johnstone, Irvine Blakeley, III *lawyer*
O'Neill, Elizabeth Sterling *trade association administrator*
Svoboda, Joanne Dzitko *artist, educator*

Leonia
Armstrong, Edward Bradford, Jr. *oral and maxillofacial surgeon, educator*
Deutsch, Nina *pianist*

Liberty Corner
Bergeron, Robert Francis, Jr. (Terry Bergeron) *software engineer*
Edwards, Robert Nelson *lawyer*
McDermott, Frank Xavier *lawyer, lobbyist*

Lincroft
†Cody, James Patrick *writing educator*
Heirman, Donald Nestor *training engineering company executive, consultant*
Jones, Floresta D. *English educator*
Keenan, Robert Anthony *financial services company executive, educator, consultant*
Orost, Joseph Martin *computer scientist*

Linden
Banda, Geraldine Marie *chiropractic physician*
Bedrick, Bernice *retired science educator, consultant*
Covino, Charles Peter *chemicals executive*
Malec, Ruth Ellen *special services director*
Marconi, Dominic Anthony *clergyman*
Tamarelli, Alan Wayne *chemical company executive*

Lindenwold
†Farwati, Abdul Jalil *architect, civil engineer*

Linwood
Cohen, Diana Louise *private practice, consultation, psychology, educator, psychotherapist, consultant*
McCormick, Robert Matthew, III *newspaper executive*

Little Falls
Armellino, Michael Ralph *retired asset management executive*
Berra, Yogi (Lawrence Peter Berra) *professional baseball coach*
Birnberg, Jack *financial executive*
Blanton, Lawton Walter *retired dean*
Brophy, Debra Elisse *rehabilitation and orthopaedics nurse*
Draper, Daniel Clay *lawyer*
Glasser, Lynn Schreiber *publisher*
Glasser, Stephen Andrew *publishing executive, lawyer*

Little Silver
Finch, Rogers Burton *association management consultant*
Morrison, James Frederick *management consultant*
Turbidy, John Berry *investor, management consultant*

Livingston
Bertenshaw, Bobbi Cherrelle *producer*
Bottone, Frank Michael *secondary education educator*
Burns, Edward Charles *infosystems specialist*
†Candido, A. Michael *contracting company executive, real estate manager*
Cohn, Joseph David *surgeon*
Conde, Miguel A. *hematologist, oncologist*
Cone, Edward Christopher *newspaper publisher*
Daman, Ernest Ludwig *mechanical engineer*
DiGiovachino, John *special education educator*
Duberstein, Joel Lawrence *physician*
Eisenstein, Theodore Donald *pediatrician*
†Frankel, Jeffrey *neurologist*
Friedman, Merton Hirsch *retired psychologist, educator*
Grant, Daniel Gordon *information services company executive*
Greenberg, Aaron Rosmarin *public relations executive*
Harris, Brian Craig *lawyer*
Hill, George James *physician, educator*
Hock, Frederick Wyeth *lawyer*
Klein, Peter Martin *lawyer, retired transportation company executive*
Krieger, Abbott Joel *neurosurgeon*
Kuller, Jonathan Mark *lawyer*
Kurtz, Ellen R. *journalist*
Levine, Harry Bruce *stockbroker*
Machlin, Lawrence Judah *nutritionist, biochemist, educator*
Mandelbaum, Howard Arnold *marketing and management consultant*
Maron, Arthur *pediatrician, medical administrator*
Martin, Daniel Richard *pharmaceutical company executive*
Pantages, Louis James *lawyer*
Rickert, Robert Richard *pathologist, educator*
Rinsky, Joel Charles *lawyer*
Rommer, James Andrew *physician*
Schlesinger, Stephen Lyons *horticulturist*
Sethi, Deepak *leadership development/marketing executive*
Sikora, Barbara Jean *library director*
Templeton, Hilda B. *psychiatrist, educator*

Lodi
Melignano, Carmine (Emanuel Melignano) *video engineer*
Rozman, Francene Catherine *science educator*

Long Beach
Warren, Craig Bishop *flavor and fragrance company executive, researcher*

Long Branch
Barnett, Lester Alfred *surgeon*
Fox, Howard Alan *physician, medical educator*
Lagowski, Barbara Jean *writer, book editor*
†Manna, John C. *federal judge*
Nahavandi, Amir Nezameddin *retired engineering firm executive*
Pachman, Frederic Charles *library director*
Poch, Herbert Edward *pediatrician, educator*
Shine, Daniel I. *hospital administrator*
Stamaty, Clara Gee Kastner *artist*
Youssef, Nadine S. *secondary school educator*
†Zizzi, Catherine Sandra *metaphysical educator, counselor*

Long Valley
Cross, Thomas Gary *executive search consultant*
Ward, David F. *business executive*

Lyndhurst
Benschip, Gary John *manufacturing company executive*
Bunda, Stephen Myron *political advisor, consultant, lawyer, classical philosopher*
Herndon, John Laird *consulting firm executive*
Lasky, David *lawyer, corporate executive*
Ridenour, James Franklin *fund raising consultant*
Sieger, Charles *librarian*

Madison
Armstrong, Richard William *bank executive, management consultant*
Byrd, Stephen Fred *human resource consultant*
Calligan, William Dennis *retired life insurance company executive*
Campbell, William Cecil *biologist*
Connors, Joseph Conlin *lawyer*
Ellenbogen, Leon *nutritionist, pharmaceutical company executive*
Goodman, Michael B(arry) *communications educator*
Huettner, Richard Alfred *lawyer*
Kluck, Edward Paul *chief of police*
Kogan, Richard Jay *pharmaceutical company executive*
Leak, Margaret Elizabeth *insurance company executive*
Levy, Robert Isaac *physician, educator, research director*
Luciano, Robert Peter *pharmaceutical company executive*
Markowski, John Joseph *human resources executive*
Mc Mullen, Edwin Wallace, Jr. *English language educator*
Monte, Bonnie J. *performing company executive, director, educator*
O'Brien, Mary Devon *communications executive, consultant*
Parker, Henry Griffith, III *insurance executive*
Perriman, Wendy Karen *poet, educator*
Shelby, Bryan Rohrer *information systems consultant*
Siegel, George Henry *international business development consultant*
Somers, Sarah Pruyn *elementary school educator*
Stafford, John Rogers *pharmaceutical and household products company executive*
Tramutola, Joseph Louis *lawyer, educator*
Udenfriend, Sidney *biochemist*
†Van Story, Joseph Cleveland *facilities consultant, management consultant*
Weiner, Lowell B. *corporate communications executive*
Whitley, Arthur Francis *retired international consulting company executive, engineer, lawyer*
Woolley, Peter James *political scientist*
†Wright, Rosemary Ann *sociologist, consultant*
Yrigoyen, Charles, Jr. *church denomination executive*

Magnolia
Holt, James Theodore *nursing educator*
Warden, Karen Barbara *special education educator*

Mahwah
Boadt, Lawrence Edward *priest, religion educator*
Bryan, Thomas Lynn *lawyer, educator*
†Cevetillo, Gerri Marie *manufacturing company executive*
†Coley, Elliot Edward *delivery service executive*
Frundt, Henry John *sociologist, educator*
†Howenstein, Mark Stephen *law educator*
Hunt, Diana Dilger *university administrator, educator*
Inserra, Lawrence R. *retail executive*
Lynch, Kevin A. *book publishing executive*
Padovano, Anthony Thomas *theologian, educator*
Patten, Eileen Dunlevy *fine art consultant, public relations consultant*
Scott, Robert Allyn *college president*
Wagner, Susan Jane *sales and marketing consulting company executive*
Yeh, Lun-Shu Ray *electrochemist*

Manahawkin
†Aurner, Robert Ray *author, corporate executive*
†Harlan, Heather Gordon *reporter*
Logan, Ralph Andre *physicist*
Pulz, Gary Edward *psychologist*
Zalinsky, Sandra H. Orlofsky *school counselor*

Manalapan
Barratt, Donna Lee *elementary school educator*
Harrison-Johnson, Yvonne Elois *pharmacologist*
Stone, Fred Michael *lawyer*

Manasquan
†Giuffrida, Thomas S. *telecommunications executive*
Mangan, Judith Ann *English language educator*
Sbarbaro, Robert Arthur *banker*
Topilow, Arthur Alan *internist*

Mantoloking
Mehta, Narinder Kumar *marketing executive*

Maplewood
Bigelow, Page Elizabeth *public policy professional*
Hamburger, Mary Ann *medical management consultant*
Johnson, Dewey, Jr. *biochemist*
Joseph, Susan B. *lawyer*
Leeds, Norma Sterne *chemistry educator*
MacWhorter, Robert Bruce *retired lawyer*
Moore, Robert Condit *civil engineer*
Newmark, Harold Leon *biochemist, researcher, educator*
Rabadeau, Mary Frances *protective services official*
Safian, Gail Robyn *public relations executive*
Shuttleworth, Anne Margaret *psychiatrist*
Tatyrek, Alfred Frank *consultant, materials and environmental engineer, analytical and research chemist*

Margate City
Stoolman, Herbert Leonard *public relations executive*
Videll, Jared Steven *cardiologist*

Marlboro
Friedman, Howard Martin *financial executive*
Leveson, Irving Frederick *economist*

Marlton
†Arzt, Noam H. *academic administrator, consultant*
Benjamin, Leni Bernice *elementary education educator*
Farwell, Nancy Larraine *public relations executive*
Flacco, Elaine Germano *computer programmer*
Forbes, Gordon Maxwell *sports journalist, commentator*
Gorenberg, Charles Lloyd *financial services executive*
Gottfried, Benjamin Frank *retired manufacturing executive*
Haines, Lisa Ann *secondary education educator*
†Kimelman, Adam S. *journalist*
Klein, Gerhart Leopold *public relations executive*
McCullen, Michael John *advertising executive*
Samek, Edward Lasker *service company executive*
Singh, Krishna Pal *mechanical engineer*
Woods, Howard James, Jr. *civil engineer*

Marmora
Graves, Thomas Browning *investment banker*
Ingaglio, Diego Augustus *dentist*

Matawan
Amato, Vincent Vito *business executive*
Katz, Irwin *marketing executive*
Wubbenhorst, Clifford C. *financial analyst*

Mays Landing
Benner, Richard Byron *philosophy educator*
Doughty, Mark Edward *environmental consultant*
†May, John T. *college president*

Mc Afee
Fogel, Richard *lawyer*

Mc Guire AFB
Laramie, Regina Carol *career officer, writer*

Medford
Dunn, Roy J. *landscape architect*
Ferris, Violette Irene *nursing educator*
Galbraith, Frances Lynn *educational administrator*
Henderson, Rita Elizabeth *literary agent, journalist*
Hogan, Thomas Harlan *publisher*
Kesty, Robert Edward *chemical manufacturing company executive*
Klugman, Peter Jay *psychologist, consultant*
McGettigan, Katheryn Jones *curriculum and instruction coordinator*
Vereb, Michael Joseph *retired pharmaceutical and cosmetic executive*

Mendham
Chatfield, Mary Van Abshoven *librarian*
Hesselink, Ann Patrice *financial executive, lawyer*
Kirby, Allan Price, Jr. *investment company executive*
Pierson, Robert David *banker*
Skidmore, Francis Joseph, Jr. *securities company executive*
Smith, Elizabeth *artist*

Mercerville
Migliaccio, Patrick Frank *salesman*
Reiley, Matthew Canney *sculptor*
Yeager, Arthur Leonard *health company executive*

Merchantville
Wilson, H(arold) Fred(erick) *chemist, research scientist*

Metuchen
Breen, Vincent De Paul *bishop*
†D'Augustine, Robert *university administrator, lawyer*
Massey, Eleanor Nelson *school librarian, media specialist*
Rakov, Barbara Streem *marketing executive*
†Rodriguez-Laguna, Asela *Spanish educator*
Roma-Scott, Mary Lou *music educator*
Slobodien, Howard David *surgeon*
Smyth, David *editor, author*

Middlesex
McGuire, Catherine Frances *elementary education educator*

Middletown
Anania, William Christian *podiatrist*
Craney, Rose Stigliano *artist, sculptor*
Heng, Siang Gek *communications executive*
Jaros, Robert James *data processing executive*
Kyrillos, Joseph M. *state legislator*
Linker, Kerrie Lynn *systems engineer*
Lundgren, Carl William, Jr. *physicist*
Mannepalli, Yellamandeswara Rao *software engineer, consultant*
O'Neill, Eugene Francis *communications engineer*
Rosen, Beth Dee *travel agency executive*
Scott, Stephen Gregory *telecommunications company executive*
Shields, Patricia Lynn *educational broker, consultant*
Wyndrum, Ralph William, Jr. *communications company executive*

Midland Park
Dunn, Patricia Ann *school system administrator, English language educator*

Milford
Carter, Clarence Holbrook *artist*

Millburn
Corwin, Andrew David *physician*
Erenburg, Steven Alan *retired communications executive*
Grosman, Alan M. *lawyer*
Kuttner, Bernard A. *lawyer, former judge*
Tanguay, Anita Walburga *real estate broker*
Wernick, Jack Harry *chemist*

Millington
Glockmann, Walter Friedrich *physicist, consultant*

Milltown
Holland, Joseph John *financial manager*
Rickards, Cheryl Ann *counselor, minister, educator*
Sacharow, Beverly Lynn *gerontologist*
Sacharow, Stanley *chemist, consultant, writer*

Mine Hill
Nadeau, Michael Joseph *college service assistant*
Robertiello, Gina Marie *criminal justice educator*

Monmouth Beach
Herbert, LeRoy James *retired accounting firm executive*

Monmouth Junction
Carneiro, Mervyn Joseph *mechanical engineer*
Lancaster, Barbara Mae *management consulting company executive*
Lawton, Deborah Simmons *educational media specialist*
Olsen, Raymond T. *township official*

Montclair
Barnard, Kurt *retail trend/consumer spending forecaster, publisher*
Beerman, Miriam *artist, educator*
Bolden, Theodore Edward *denist, educator, dental research consultant*
Brown, Geraldine Reed *lawyer, consulting executive*
Campbell, Stewart Fred *foundation executive*
Chinard, Francis Pierre *physiologist, physician, preventive medicine consultant*
†Cioffi, Patrizia *soprano, voice educator, arts consultant*
Clech, Jean Paul Marie *mechanical engineer*

Coffin, Charlsa Lee Montessori school educator, writer, artist
DiGeronimo, Diane Mary nursing educator, psychotherapist
Dubrow, Marsha Ann high technology company executive, composer
Eager, George Sidney, Jr. electrical engineer, business executive
†Gaines Nelson, Tami Camari management consultant
Gogick, Kathleen Christine magazine editor, publisher
Haupt, Edward J. psychology educator
Hutchins, Carleen Maley acoustical engineer, violin maker, consultant
Jones, Rees Lee golf course architect
Kayser, Mary Ellen H. nursing consultant and educator
Kidde, John Lyon investment manager
Kowalski, Stephen Wesley chemistry educator
Leggett, Paul Arthur minister
Mason, Lucile Gertrude fundraiser, consultant
McMillan, Robert Lee psychology educator
Mullins, Margaret Ann Frances lawyer, educator
†Nirenberg, Nelson Marcio conductor, educator
O'Malley, Eileen (Ann) medical/surgical nurse
Schnitzer, Jeshaia rabbi, marriage and family therapist
Sierra, Roberto composer, music educator
Steiner, Roberta Dance not-for-profit organization executive
Tennen, Jane Savitt consultant to non-profit organizations, writer
Walker, George Theophilus, Jr. composer, pianist, music educator
Ward, Roger Coursen lawyer
Weisert, Kent Albert Frederick lawyer

Montvale
Baba, Thomas Frank corporate economist, economics educator
Brecht, Warren Frederick business executive
Corrado, Fred food company executive
Giambalvo, Vincent training and career development executive
Mackerodt, Fred public relations specialist
Politi, Beth Kukkonen publishing services company executive
Roob, Richard manufacturing executive
Showalter, David Scott accounting executive
Sifton, David Whittier magazine editor
Wood, James supermarket executive

Montville
Coleman, Earl Maxwell publishing company executive
Klapper, Byron D. financial company executive
Leeson, Lewis Joseph research pharmacist, scientist
Teubner, Ferdinand Cary, Jr. retired publishing company executive

Moonachie
Malley, Raymond Charles retired foreign service officer, industrial executive
Toscano, Samuel, Jr. wholesale distribution executive

Moorestown
Begley, Thomas D., Jr. lawyer
Benjamin, Milton Kemp computer scientist, engineer, physicist
Carson, William Charles sales and marketing executive
Cervantes, Luis Augusto neurosurgeon
Condax, Kate Delano (Kate Delano Condax Decker) marketing and public relations executive
†Dudley, Edward James retired news manager
Ewan, David E. lawyer
Kearney, John Francis, III lawyer
Margolis, Gerald Joseph psychiatrist, psychoanalyst
Rabil, Mitchell Joseph lawyer
Schwerin, Horace S. marketing research executive
Springer, Douglas Hyde retired food company executive, lawyer
Weeks, Maurice Richard, Jr. educational consultant, academic administrator

Morganville
†Choy-Kwong, Maria neurologist
Marder, Carol advertising specialist and premium firm executive
Sternfeld, Marc Howard investment banker

Morris Plains
Bruno, Anthony D. lawyer
Caveney, William John pharmaceutical company executive, lawyer
DeCroce, Alex state legislator
Fielding, Maralyn Joy principal, consultant
Fielding, Stuart psychopharmacologist
Goodes, Melvin Russell retired manufacturing company executive
†Johnson, Gregory L. lawyer
Korbman, Jack Soloman cantor, educator
Murphy, Carol J. state legislator
O'Neill, Robert Edward business journal editor
Otani, Mike optical company executive
Presslitz, Joseph Edwin biochemist

Morristown
Ahl, David Howard writer, editor
Aspero, Benedict Vincent lawyer
†Barpal, Isaac Ruben retired technology and operations executive
Bartkus, Robert Edward lawyer
Baughman, Ray Henry materials scientist
Berkley, Peter Lee lawyer
Bernson, Marcella Shelley psychiatrist
Bockian, James Bernard computer systems executive
Bossidy, Lawrence Arthur industrial manufacturing executive
Bromberg, Myron James lawyer
Campion, Thomas Francis lawyer
Casale, Alfred Stanley thoracic and cardiovascular surgeon
Cowles, Walter Curtis naval architect
Cregan, Frank Robert financial executive, consultant
Cucco, Judith Elene international marketing professional
de Mauret, Kevin John geologist
DiSerio, Frank Joseph pharmaceutical company executive, consultant
†Felsenstein, Frank Arjeh educator
Finkel, Marion Judith physician, pharmaceutical company administrator
Fishman, Richard Glenn lawyer, accountant
Freilich, Irvin M. lawyer
Geyer, Thomas Powick newspaper publisher
Gillen, James Robert lawyer, insurance company executive
Golecki, Ilan physicist, researcher, educator
Greenman, Jane Friedlieb lawyer
Hager, Mary Hastings nutritionist, educator, consultant
Handler, Lauren E. lawyer
Harbison, James Prescott research physicist
Haselmann, John Philip marketing executive
Heilmeier, George Harry electrical engineer, researcher
Herman, Robert Lewis cork company executive
Herzberg, Peter Jay lawyer
Hittinger, William Charles electronics company executive
Huck, John Lloyd pharmaceutical company executive
Humick, Thomas Charles Campbell lawyer
Hyland, William Francis lawyer
Jacobowitz, Walter Erwin obstetrician, gynecologist
Jolles, Ira Hervey lawyer
Kagan, Val Alexander engineer, researcher, educator
Kandravy, John lawyer
Kastner, Cynthia lawyer
Kearns, William Michael, Jr. investment banker
Kirby, Fred Morgan, II corporation executive
Klindt, Steven art museum director
Korf, Gene Robert lawyer
Kreindler, Peter Michael lawyer
Lavey, Stewart Evan lawyer
Levy, Joel Howard marketing research executive
Lieberman, Lester Zane engineering company executive
Lunin, Joseph lawyer
MacKinnis, Ann Phelps municipal government and land use management
Mammola, George Charles air pollution control executive
Mazur, Leonard L. pharmaceutical company executive
McClung, Kenneth Austin, Jr. training executive, performance consultant
McConnell, John Howard personnel management consultant, writer
McDonough, Joseph Richard lawyer
Mc Elroy, William Theodore lawyer
Moore, Milo Anderson banker
Morgan, Samuel P(ope) physicist, applied mathematician
Morse, Joyce Solomon nursing administrator
Munson, William Leslie insurance company executive
Murray, Charles Robert, charitable fundraiser, educator
Musa, John Davis computer and infosystems executive, software reliability engineering researcher and expert, independent consultant
Nadaskay, Raymond architect
Nalewako, Mary Anne corporate secretary
Newhouse, Robert J., Jr. insurance executive
Newman, John Merle lawyer
Nittoly, Paul Gerard lawyer
O'Connell, Daniel F. lawyer
O'Grady, Dennis Joseph lawyer
Pan, Henry Yue-Ming clinical pharmacologist
Pantel, Glenn Steven lawyer
Parr, Grant Van Siclen surgeon
Personick, Stewart David electrical engineer
Pollock, Stewart Glasson former state supreme court justice, lawyer
Prince, Leah Fanchon art educator and research institute administrator
Reid, Charles Adams, III lawyer
Robertson, William Withers lawyer
Rose, Robert Gordon lawyer
Rosenthal, Meyer L(ouis) lawyer
Ross, Thomas J., Jr. personal financial adviser
Scott, Susan lawyer
Sharkey, Vincent Joseph lawyer
Sherman, Sandra Brown lawyer
Smith, Richard C. Jr. public relations executive, quality assurance professional
Smith, Thomas J. surgeon, educator
Spence, Janet Blake Conley (Mrs. Alexander Pyott Spence) civic worker
Stephens, Jay B. lawyer
Sugahara, Byron Masahiko transportation company executive
Szuch, Clyde Andrew lawyer
Thornton, Yvonne Shirley physician, author, musician
Tullen, Colton (Skipp Tullen) recording engineer
Van Uitert, LeGrand Gerard retired chemist
Venezia, William Thomas school system administrator, counseling consultant
Watson, Esther Elizabeth medical/surgical and critical care nurse, retired
Weber, Joseph H. communications company executive
Whitmer, Frederick Lee lawyer
Williams, Joseph Dalton pharmaceutical company executive

Mount Arlington
Jacobs, Richard Moss consulting engineer
Krosser, Howard S. aerospace company executive, retired congressman

Mount Holly
Brown, Hershel M. retired newspaper publisher
†Holba, Annette M. county detective, educator
Hurlbut, Terry Allison pathologist
†Moffitt, Ronald James entrepreneur

Mount Laurel
Buchan, Alan Bradley rail transportation executive, consultant
Ciociola, Cecilia Mary science education specialist
Hart, Larry Edward communications company executive
Instone, John Clifford manufacturing company executive
Li, Pearl Nei-Chien Chu information specialist, executive
Moyer, Cheryl Lynn non-profit administrator
Rabbe, David Ellsworth oil company executive
Shoe, Margaret Ellen accountant
Stallings, Viola Patricia Elizabeth certified project manager, systems engineer, educational systems specialist
Torres, Robert Alvin dancer, singer, actor, sign language interpreter
Turner, John Carl internet development company executive
Vidas, Vincent George engineering executive

Mountain Lakes
Cook, Charles Francis insurance executive
King, Georgeann Camarda elementary education educator
LaForce, William Leonard, Jr. photojournalist, columnist

Mountainside
DiPietro, Ralph Anthony marketing and management consultant, educator
Glassman, Ronald Jay public health advocate
Jacobson, Gary Steven lawyer
Kozberg, Donna Walters rehabilitation administration executive
Lingle, Kathleen McCall consultant, marketing executive, entrepreneur
Lissenden, Carol Kay pediatrician
†Lombardi, Neil pediatric neurologist
Luckenbach, Edward Cooper chemical engineer
Newler, Jerome Marc accountant
†Sussman, Neil M(ark) neurologist
Weigele, Richard Sayre police officer

Mullica Hill
Demola, James, Sr. church administrator
Sparks, Barbara L. financial planner

Murray Hill
Adler, Nadia C. lawyer
Chu, Sung Nee George materials scientist
DiFrancesco, Jeffrey James telecommunication and media executive
Doescher, William Frederick communications executive
Kruskal, Joseph B. mathematician, statistician, researcher
†Li, Qi researcher
†McGinn, Richard A. telecommunications company executive
Potamianos, Alexandros electrical engineer, researcher
Taylor, Volney information company executive
White, Alice Elizabeth physicist, researcher

Neptune
Aguiar, Adam Martin chemist, educator
Amedu, Davis Jimoh industrial engineer
Baccarella, Theresa Ann primary school educator
Baro, Susan Marie surgeon
Boak, Joseph Gordon cardiologist
†Breen, Stephen P. editorial cartoonist
Clurfeld, Andrea editor, food critic
†Collins, Robert T. publisher
†Crosley, Powel A. physician
Harrigan, John Thomas, Jr. physician, obstetrician-gynecologist
Ollwerther, William Raymond newspaper editor
Plangere, Jules L., III newspaper company executive
†Rhee, Richard Sanchul physician, neurologist
Rice, Stephen Gary medical educator, sports medicine physician
†Siegel, Harris G. managing editor
Zurick, Jack electrical engineer

Neptune City
Axelrod, Glen Scott publishing company executive

Neshanic Station
Castellon, Christine New information systems specialist, real estate agent
Muckenhoupt, Benjamin retired mathematics educator

New Brunswick
Aisner, Joseph oncologist, physician
Alexander, Robert Jackson economist, educator
Amarel, Saul computer scientist, educator
Awan, Ahmad Noor civil engineer
Ballou, Janice Donelon research director
Becker, Ronald Leonard archivist
Bern, Ronald Lawrence consulting company executive
†Blumenthal, Eileen Flinder writer, theater educator
Boehm, Werner William social work educator
Bowden, Henry Warner religion educator
Burke, James Edward consumer products company executive
Burman, Sondra social work educator
Campbell, Robert Emmett retired health care products company executive
Cate, Phillip Dennis art museum director
Chambers, John Whiteclay, II history educator
Chasek, Arlene Shatsky academic director
Cheiten, Marvin Harold writer, hardware manufacturing company executive
Coakley, John Wayland theological historian, educator
Corbett, Siobhan Aiden surgeon
Corman, Randy lawyer
Day, Peter Rodney geneticist, educator
Day-Salvatore, Debra Lynn medical geneticist
Derbyshire, William Wadleigh language educator, translator
Dill, Ellis Harold university dean
Dougherty, Neil Joseph physical education educator, safety consultant
Dunn, Patricia C. social work educator
Durnin, Richard Gerry education educator
†Edson, Paul Lynwood quality assurance professional
Ehrenfeld, David William biology educator, author
Eisenreich, Steven John chemistry educator, environmental scientist
Ettinger, Lawrence Jay pediatric hematologist and oncologist, educator
Ferencz, Bradley judge
Fine, Roger Seth pharmaceutical executive, lawyer
Fisher, Hans nutritional biochemistry educator
Flaherty, Charles Foster, Jr. psychology educator, researcher
†Foley, Richard academic administrator
Funk, Cyril Reed, Jr. agronomist, educator
†Gambaccini, Louis John transportation executive, educational
Gardner, Lloyd Calvin, Jr. history educator
Garner, Charles William educational administration educator, consultant
†Gatta, Mary Lizabeth sociologist
Gillette, William historian, educator
Glasser, Paul Harold sociologist, educator, university administrator, social worker
Glickman, Norman Jay economist, urban policy analyst
Gocke, David Joseph immunology educator, physician, medical scientist
Goffen, Rona art educator
Graham, Alan Morrison surgeon
†Grassle, Judith Payne marine biology educator
Greco, Ralph Steven surgeon, researcher, medical educator
Griffin, Gary Arthur technological products executive
Grob, Gerald N. historian, educator
Haines, William Joseph pharmaceutical company executive
Hartman, Mary S. historian
Hayakawa, Kan-Ichi food science educator
Ho, Chi-Tang food chemistry educator
Horowitz, Irving Louis publisher, educator
Jaluria, Yogesh mechanical engineering educator
Kansfield, Norman J. seminary president
Karol, Reuben Hirsh civil engineer, sculptor
Katz, Carlos electrical engineer
Kelley, Donald Reed historian
Killingsworth, Mark R. economics educator, consultant
Kruskal, Martin David mathematical physicist, educator
Kulikowski, Casimir Alexander computer science educator
Lachance, Paul Albert food science educator, clergyman
Laraya-Cuasay, Lourdes Redublo pediatric pulmonologist, educator
Larsen, Ralph S(tanley) health care company executive
Lawrence, Francis Leo university president, language educator
Levine, George Lewis English language educator, literature critic
Lewis, David Levering history educator
Liao, Mei-June biopharmaceutical company executive
Lister, David Alfred healthcare administrator
Lynch, John A. lawyer, state senator
Lyons, Bridget Gellert English educator
Mandelbaum, David Ezra pediatric neurologist
Maramorosch, Karl virologist, educator
†Marder, Tod A. art historian, educator
McGuire, John Lawrence pharmaceuticals executive
Mechanic, David social sciences educator
Mills, Dorothy Allen investor
Mills, George Marshall insurance consultant
Momah, Ethel Chukwuekwe women's health nurse
†Mondschein, Lawrence Geoffrey medical products executive
Montville, Thomas Joseph food microbiologist, educator
Murray, Bertram George biology educator
Nash, Stanley Dana librarian
Nelson, Jack Lee education educator
Nosko, Michael Gerrik neurosurgeon
O'Neill, William Lawrence history educator
Ortiz, Raphael Montañez performance artist, educator
Ostriker, Alicia Suskin poet
Pallone, Nathaniel John psychologist, educator
Paz, Harold Louis internist and educator
Polelle, Mark Robert librarian, historian
Psuty, Norbert Phillip marine sciences educator
Reed, James Wesley social historian, educator
Reeling, Patricia Glueck library studies educator, educational consultant
Reock, Ernest C., Jr. retired government services educator, academic director
Robock, Alan meteorology educator
Rosen, Robert Thomas analytical and food chemist
Rosenberg, Seymour psychologist, educator
Ruben, Brent David communication educator, university administrator
Russell, Louise Bennett economist, educator
†Saidi, Parvin hematologist, medical educator
†Sapirman, Nadine Kadell university official
Saracevic, Tefko information science educator
Scanlon, Jane Cronin mathematics educator
Scott, David Rodick lawyer, legal educator
Scully, John Thomas obstetrician, gynecologist, educator
Seibold, James Richard physician, researcher
Serafini, Tina English and reading educator
Shirtz, Joseph Frank lawyer, consultant
Smith, Bonnie Gene historian, educator
Smith, Fredric Charles electronic technician, consultant
Solberg, Myron food scientist, educator
Somville, Marilyn F. dean
Spears, Marcia Hopp nursing educator, health facility administrator
Spencer, J. Ken artist
Stamato, Linda Ann Lautenschlaeger legal educator, mediator
Stewart, Ruth Ann public policy analyst, professor
Stich, Stephen Peter philosophy educator
Strauss, Ulrich Paul chemist, educator
Strawderman, William E. statistics educator
Strickland, Dorothy education educator
Taliaferro, James Hubert, Jr. communications educator
Tanner, Daniel curriculum theory educator
Tedrow, John Charles Fremont soils educator
Tiger, Lionel social scientist, anthropology consultant
Toby, Jackson sociologist, educator
Tripolitis, Antonia religion, classics and comparative literature educator
Turock, Betty Jane library and information science educator
Voos, Paula Beth economics educator
Walker, Steven F. comparative literature educator
Wang, Tsuey Tang science educator, venture capitalist
†Welsh, Andrew English educator
†Westermann, Martine Henriëtte art historian, educator, curator
Wilkinson, Louise Cherry psychology educator, dean
Wilson, Donald Malcolm publishing executive
Wilson, Robert Nathan health care company executive
Wolfe, Robert Richard bioresource engineer, educator
Yorke, Marianne lawyer, real estate executive

New Egypt
Erbe, Edward Robert social studies educator, music percussion educator

New Milford
Walsh, Joseph Michael magazine distribution executive

New Monmouth
Donnelly, Gerard Kevin marketing and retail executive

New Providence
Bishop, David John *physicist*
Boise, Audrey Lorraine *education educator*
Brinkman, William Frank *physicist, research executive*
Capasso, Federico *physicist, research administrator*
Chatterji, Debajyoti *manufacturing company executive*
Cho, Alfred Yi *electrical engineer*
Cohen, Melvin Irwin *communications systems and technology executive*
Cooper, Carol Diane *publishing company executive*
Dodabalapur, Ananth *electrical engineer*
†Esser, Joseph Allen *editor*
Gaylord, Norman Grant *chemical and polymer consultant*
Glass, Alastair Malcolm *physicist, research director*
Helfand, Eugene *chemist*
Hollister, Dean *publishing company executive*
Johnson, David Wilfred, Jr. *ceramic scientist, researcher*
Lanzerotti, Louis John *physicist*
Laudise, Robert Alfred *research chemist*
Longfield, William Herman *health care company executive*
MacChesney, John Burnette *materials scientist, researcher*
Manthei, Richard Dale *lawyer, health care company executive*
Miskiewicz, Susanne Piatek *elementary education educator*
Mumick, Inderpal Singh *computer scientist, engineer*
Murray, Cherry Ann *physicist, researcher*
Netravali, Arun N. *communications executive*
Passner, Albert *physicist, researcher*
Reynolds, Robert Webster *public relations executive*
Roycroft, Edward J. *publishing company executive*
†Russo, Patricia F. *communications executive*
Sivco, Deborah Lee *research materials scientist*
Stillinger, Frank Henry *chemist, educator*
Sundberg, Carl-Erik Wilhelm *telecommunications executive, researcher*
van Dover, Robert Bruce *physicist*
Westerland, Maureen A. *fundraiser*
Wilderotter, Peter Thomas *non-profit executive*

New Vernon
Dugan, John Leslie, Jr. *foundation executive*

Newark
Abrams, Roger Ian *law educator, arbitrator*
Ackerman, Harold A. *federal judge*
Alito, Samuel Anthony, Jr. *federal judge*
Apuzzio, Joseph J. *obstetrician-gynecologist*
Arabie, Phipps *marketing educator, researcher*
Aregood, Richard Lloyd *editor*
Askin, Frank *law educator*
Baer, Susan M. *airport executive*
Baker, Herman *medical educator, author*
Baldassarro, Anthony *human resources professional*
Bar-Ness, Yeheskel *electrical engineer, educator*
Barry, Maryanne Trump *federal judge*
Bartner, Martin *newspaper executive*
Bassler, William G. *federal judge*
Bergen, Stanley Silvers, Jr. *retired university president, physician*
Bissell, John W. *federal judge*
Bizub, Johanna Catherine *library director*
Blumrosen, Alfred William *law educator*
Blumrosen, Ruth Gerber *lawyer, educator, arbitrator*
Bohannon, Jean Andrea *research company executive*
Bradley, Bill *former senator*
Brescher, John B., Jr. *lawyer*
Cahn, Jeffrey Barton *lawyer*
†Caldwell, Toni L. *court official, charitable organization executive*
Callahan, Patrick Michael *lawyer*
Carroll, John Douglas *mathematical and statistical psychologist*
†Cavanaugh, Dennis M. *federal judge*
Chen, Chunguang *cardiologist*
Cheng, Mei-Fang *psychobiology educator, neuroethology researcher*
Cherniack, Neil Stanley *physician, medical educator*
Chesler, Stanley Richard *federal judge*
Clymer, Brian William *insurance company executive, former state official*
Cohen, Stanley *pathologist, educator*
Colli, Bart Joseph *lawyer*
Contractor, Farok *business and management educator*
Cook, Stuart Donald *physician, educator*
Cortez, Ricardo Lee *investment management executive*
Costenbader, Charles Michael *lawyer*
Creenan, Katherine Heras *lawyer*
Cummis, Clive Sanford *lawyer*
Cunningham, Glenn Dale *protective services official*
Darr, Walter Robert *financial analyst*
D'Astolfo, Frank Joseph *graphic designer, educator*
Debevoise, Dickinson Richards *federal judge*
Dee, Francis X. *lawyer*
Defeis, Elizabeth Frances *law educator, lawyer*
Del Tufo, Robert J. *lawyer, former US attorney, former state attorney general*
Dickson, Jim *writer, producer*
Diner, Steven Jay *history educator*
Donahoo, James Saunders *cardiothoracic surgeon*
Dubrovsky, Roman *engineering educator*
Eittreim, Richard MacNutt *lawyer*
English, Nicholas Conover *lawyer*
Evans, Hugh E. *pediatrician*
Everett, Richard G. *newspaper editor*
Ferland, E. James *electric utility executive*
†Fitzpatrick, Robert J. *transit company executive*
Flagg, E(loise) Alma Williams *educational administrator*
Fox, Sandra Gail *insurance marketing executive*
Franklin, H. Bruce *language educator, writer*
Friedland, Bernard *engineer, educator*
Fu, Shou-Cheng Joseph *biomedicine educator*
Gambardella, Rosemary *federal judge*
Garde, John Charles *lawyer*
Garner, Robert F. *bishop*
Garth, Leonard I. *federal judge*
Geskin, Ernest S(amuel) *science administrator, consultant*
Gironda, Marie Grace *English language educator*
Goldstein, Marvin Mark *lawyer*
Gordon, Jonathan David *psychologist, lawyer*
Gouraige, Hervé *lawyer*
Greenaway, Joseph Anthony, Jr. *judge*
Hadley, John Bart *financial analyst*
Hallard, Wayne Bruce *economist*
†Haneke, G. Donald *federal judge*
Hanesian, Deran *chemical engineer, chemistry and environmental science educator, consultant*
Haring, Eugene Miller *lawyer*
Harris, Carleina Hampton *muncipal or county official, educator*
Harrison, Roslyn Siman *lawyer*
Haycock, Christine Elizabeth *medical educator emeritus, health educator*
Healy, Phyllis M. Cordasco *school social worker*
†Hedges, Ronald J. *federal judge*
Herman, Steven Douglas *cardiothoracic surgeon, educator*
Hiltz, Starr Roxanne *sociologist, educator, computer scientist, writer, lecturer, consultant*
Hobson, Robert Wayne, II *surgeon*
Hochberg, Faith S. *prosecutor*
Hollander, Toby Edward *education educator*
Holzer, Marc *public administrator educator*
Hrycak, Peter *mechanical engineer, educator*
Hsu, Cheng-Tzu Thomas *civil engineering educator*
Iffy, Leslie *medical educator*
Jackson, Nancy Lee *geography educator*
James, Sharpe *mayor*
Kaltenbacher, Philip D(avid) *industrialist, former public official*
Kantor, Mel Lewis *dental educator, researcher*
Kanzler, George *journalist, critic*
Karp, Donald Mathew *lawyer, banker*
Khera, Raj Pal *civil and environmental engineering educator*
Knee, Stephen H. *lawyer*
Kott, David Russell *lawyer*
Labaj, Pamela Joan *Lawyer*
Laurino, Robert Dennis *prosecutor*
Lechner, Alfred James, Jr. *judge*
Leevy, Carroll Moton *medical educator, hepatology researcher*
Lenehan, Art *newspaper editor*
Leu, Ming Chuan *engineering educator*
Levin, Simon *lawyer*
Lifland, John C. *federal judge*
†Liman, Joan Pamela *university dean*
Linken, Dennis C. *lawyer*
Little, Alan Brian *obstetrician, gynecologist, educator*
Lourenco, Ruy Valentim *physician, educator*
Macal, Zdenek *conductor*
Martin, James Hanley *deputy state attorney general*
Martini, William J. *former congressman*
Materna, Thomas Walter *ophthalmologist*
Mc Carrick, Theodore Edgar *archbishop*
McGuire, William B(enedict) *lawyer*
McKelvey, Jack M. *bishop*
McKinney, John Adams, Jr. *lawyer*
Monty, Gloria *former television producer, film executive*
Morris-Yamba, Trish *educational and social service association director*
Murnick, Daniel Ely *physicist, educator*
Muscato, Andrew *lawyer*
Nelson, Douglas Lee *insurance company executive*
Neuer, Philip David *lawyer, real estate consultant*
Newhouse, Donald E. *newspaper publishing executive*
Newhouse, Mark William *publishing executive*
Norwood, Carolyn Virginia *business educator*
Oberdorf, John J. *lawyer*
O'Leary, Paul Gerard *investment executive*
†Oleske, James M. *pediatrician, allergist, immunologist, educator*
Patrick, Robert Herbert, Jr. *economist, educator*
Paul, James Caverly Newlin *law educator, former university dean*
Pfeffer, Edward Israel *educational administrator*
Pfeffer, Robert *chemical engineer, academic administrator, educator*
Pignataro, Louis James *engineering educator*
†Pisano, Joel A. *federal judge*
Politan, Nicholas H. *federal judge*
Rak, Lorraine Karen *lawyer*
Raveché, Elizabeth Scott *immunologist*
Reams, Bernard Dinsmore, Jr. *lawyer, educator*
Reddy, Gerard Anthony *corporate training executive*
Reichman, Lee Brodersohn *physician*
Reilly, William Thomas *lawyer*
Reynolds, Valrae *museum curator*
Rosato, Anthony Dominick *mechanical engineer, educator*
Rosenberg, Jerry Martin *business administration educator*
Roth, Allan Robert *lawyer, educator*
Rutan, Thomas Carl *nurse*
Ryan, Arthur Frederick *insurance company executive*
†Santiago, Joseph J. *protective services official*
Savage, Joseph George *hospital administrator*
Scales, John Thomas *state official*
Schweizer, Karl Wolfgang *historian, writer*
Scott, James Hunter, Jr. *investment executive*
Selover, R. Edwin *lawyer*
Shain-Alvaro, Judith Carol *physician assistant*
Sher, Richard B. *historian*
Siegal, Joel Davis *lawyer*
Siginer, Dennis A(ydeniz) *mechanical engineering educator, researcher*
Silipigni, Alfredo *opera conductor*
Simmons, Peter *law and urban planning educator*
Slutsky, Bruce *technical reference librarian*
Spillers, William Russell *civil engineering educator*
Spong, John Shelby *bishop*
Spruch, Grace Marmor *physics educator*
Stevenson, Joanne Sabol *older adults care provider, educator, researcher*
Stiller, Nikki *English language educator*
Storrer, William Allin *consultant*
Stoute, Gayle Casandra Tisdale *postal service official*
†Tamburri, Lawrence J. *artistic director*
Thomas, Gary L. *academic administrator*
Tischman, Michael Bernard *lawyer*
Tuohey, William F. *federal judge*
Vajtay, Stephen Michael, Jr. *lawyer*
Wachenfeld, William Thomas *lawyer, foundation executive*
Waelde, Lawrence Richard *chemist*
Walker, Linda Lee *lawyer*
Walls, William Hamilton *judge*
Wang, Jason Tsong-Li *computer science educator*
Weinshenker, Naomi Joyce *clinical psychiatrist, educator, researcher*
Weiss, Gerson *physician, educator*
Weiss, Stanley H. *physician, epidemiologist, educator, researcher, consultant*
Willse, James Patrick *newspaper editor*
Winfield, Novalyn L. *federal bankruptcy judge*
Wolin, Alfred M. *federal judge*
Wyer, James Ingersoll *lawyer*
Yamner, Morris *lawyer*
Young, Darlene *post office executive*
Yu, Yi-Yuan *mechanical engineering educator*
Zarbin, Marco Attilio *ophthalmologist, surgeon, educator*

Newfield
Hartman, Jeffrey Edward *pastor*

Newton
Ancona, Francesco Aristide *humanities and mythology educator, writer*
Cox, William Martin *lawyer, educator*
Cutshall, Janet Marie *educator*
Dagley, Mark *artist*
Koerber, Joan C. *retired educator*
MacMurren, Margaret Patricia *secondary education educator, consultant*
†Mielo, Gary John *journalism educator*

North Arlington
Borowski, Jennifer Lucile *corporate administrator*

North Bergen
†Choi, Jay Lee *women's apparel executive*
Karp, Roberta S. *wholesale apparel and accessories executive*
Marth, Fritz Ludwig *sports association executive*
Miller, Samuel Martin *apparel company finance executive*
Zondler, Joyce Evelyn *kindergarten educator*

North Branch
Gartlan, Philip M. *secondary school director*

North Brunswick
Kahrmann, Linda Irene *child care supervisor*
Livingston, Lee Franklin *recreation industry executive, real estate and finance consultant*
Sims, Gregory Michael *purchasing agent*

North Caldwell
Piel, Emil J. *retired science educator*
Siegel, Ira T. *publishing executive*
Stevens, William Dollard *consulting mechanical engineer*

North Haledon
Anstatt, Peter Jan *marketing services executive*
Dougherty, June Eileen *librarian*
Harrington, Kevin Paul *lawyer*
Onove, Daniel James *elementary educator*

Northfield
Pollock, Michael Jeffrey *periodical editor*

Northvale
Aronson, Jason *publisher*
Barna, Richard Allen *lighting company executive, broadcasting executive*
Di Mino, André Anthony *manufacturing executive, consultant*
Goodman, Stanley Leonard *advertising executive*
Kurzweil, Arthur *publisher, writer, educator*
Ruderman, Warren *chemist*
Seaman, Robert E., III *lawyer*

Nutley
Dennin, Robert Aloysius, Jr. *pharmaceutical research scientist*
English, Robert Joseph *electronic corporation executive*
Gordon, Robert Dana *transplant surgeon*
Mallard, Stephen Anthony *retired utility company executive*
McLellan, Kathleen Claire *speech therapist*
Mostillo, Ralph *medical association executive*
Olmsted, David John *capital management company executive*
Romanoski, Barbara Ann *neonatology nurse*
Seyffarth, Linda Jean Wilcox *corporate executive*
Tropiano, JoAnn Alma *librarian, library director*

Nyack
Flood, Diane Lucy *marketing communications specialist*

Oak Ridge
Sacerdote, Craig R. *management consultant, engineering consultant*

Oakhurst
Fasthuber-Grande, Traudy *financial services company executive*
Konvitz, Milton Ridbaz *law educator*
Widman, Douglas Jack *lawyer*

Oakland
†Brechtel, Unda Jurka *library director*
Butterfield, Charles Edward, Jr. *educational consultant*
†Dressel, Margaret Jane *artist, art educator*
Smith, Miranda Constance *writer, educator*

Ocean
Kreider, Clement Horst, Jr. *neurosurgeon*
†Marley, Melissa *educator*
Reich, Bernard *retired telecommunications engineer*

Ocean City
Altman, Brian David *pediatric ophthalmologist*
Gross, Kathleen Frances *parochial school mathematics educator*
Hughes, William John *former congressman, diplomat*
Reiter, William Martin *chemical engineer*
Speitel, Gerald Eugene *consulting environmental engineer*

Ocean Grove
Anderson, James Frederick *clergyman*

Ocean View
Gibson, John C. *state legislator*

Oceanport
Meibauer, Amery Filippone *special education educator*

Old Bridge
Downs, Thomas Edward, IV *lawyer*
Engel, John Jacob *communications executive*
Gulko, Edward *health care executive, consultant*
Swett, Stephen Frederick, Jr. *principal, educator*

Old Tappan
Dubnick, Bernard *retired pharmaceutical company administrator*
Gaffin, Joan Valerie *secondary school educator*
Howard, Clifton Merton *psychiatrist*
Terranova, Carl *real estate broker*

Oldwick
Griggs, Stephen Layng *management consultant*
Hitchcock, Ethan Allen *lawyer*
Kellogg, C. Burton, II *financial analyst*
Snyder, Arthur *publishing company executive*

Oradell
Nesoff, Robert *newspaper publisher*

Orange
Johnson, Anthony Peter *minister*
†Juliano, Kathryn Marie *artist*
Lewis, Peter Wayne *art educator, painter*
Monacelli, Jeffrey Paul *elementary education educator*

Palisades Park
†Chelariu, Ana Radu *library director*

Paramus
Balter, Leslie Marvin *business communications educator*
†Basuk, Richard *physician*
Blake, Mary Ellen *medical/surgical and home care nurse, educator*
Brissie, Eugene Field, Jr. *publisher*
DiGeronimo, Suzanne Kay *architect*
Dirr, John Charles (Jack Dirr) *television producer and director*
Fader, Seymour Jeremiah *management and engineering consulting company executive*
Fader, Shirley Sloan *writer*
Forman, Beth Rosalyne *specialty food trade executive*
Goldstein, Michael *retail executive*
Greenberg, William Michael *psychiatrist*
Lenk, Richard William, Jr. *history educator*
Levy, Joseph *lawyer*
Liva, Edward Louis *eye surgeon*
Maclin, Ernest *biomedical diagnostics company executive*
Nakasone, Robert C. *retail toy and game company executive*
†Ryan, Steven D. *English language educator*
†Schiffman, Erica Rae *psychiatrist*
Tumolo, Michael L. *corporate lawyer*
Weinstock, George David *financial services company executive*

Park Ridge
De Pol, John *artist*
Kennedy, Brian James *marketing executive*
Maurer, C(harles) F(rederick) William, III *museum director*
Olson, Frank Albert *car rental company executive*

Parlin
Chernow, Jay Howard *music industry executive*
Flick, Ferdinand Herman *surgeon, prevention medicine physician*
Gasparro, Madeline *banker*
†Griffin, Martin Edward *music educator*

Parsippany
Agostini, Rosemarie Coniglio *human services administrator*
Azzarone, Carol Ann *marketing executive*
Belmonte, Steven Joseph *hotel chain executive*
Berkowitz, Bernard Joseph *lawyer*
Brady, Philip T. *marketing professional*
†Buckman, James Edward *lawyer*
Bunin, Jeffrey Howard *manufacturing company executive*
Ceurvels, Warren Steven *school system administrator*
Chinitz, Jody Anne Kolb *data processing manager*
Chobot, John Charles *lawyer*
Deones, Jack E. *corporate executive*
Derr, Debra Hulse *advertising executive, publisher, editor*
Doherty, Robert Christopher *lawyer*
Donaghy, Christine Ann *English language educator*
Ferguson, Thomas George *retired healthcare advertising agency executive*
Fleisher, Seymour *manufacturing company executive*
Hafer, Frederick Douglass *utility executive*
Haney, James Kevin *lawyer*
Hansbury, Stephan Charles *lawyer*
Lezny, Christopher Adalbert *computer systems specialist*
†Mahoney, Mary *hotel executive*
Marscher, William Donnelly *engineering company executive*
McGirr, David William John *insurance executive*
McNicholas, David Paul *franchise company executive*
†Mistry, Yogesh Balubhai *architect*
Reiley, Thomas Phillip *consultant*
Shaw, Alan *lawyer, corporate executive*
Smay, Connie R. *educational media specialist, educator*
Wechter, Ira Martin *tax specialist, financial planner*
Weiner, Marian Murphy *insurance executive, consultant*
Weller, Robert N(orman) *hotel executive*
Winograd, Bernard *real estate and financial adviser*

Passaic
Haddad, Jamil Raouf *physician*
Lindholm, Clifford Falstrom, II *engineering executive, mayor*
Pino, Robert Salvatore *radiologist*
Stagen, Mary-Patricia Healy *marketing executive*

Paterson
Chiles, Lawton, III *non-profit organization executive*
Correa, Alonso Velez *neurosurgeon*
Daniels, Cheryl Lynn *pediatrics nurse, case manager*
Danziger, Glenn Norman *chemical sales company executive*
DeBari, Vincent Anthony *medical researcher, educator*
Greidanus, Ida *biology educator*
McEvoy, Lorraine Katherine *oncology nurse*
Sico, John Joseph *secondary education educator*
Welles, Ernest I. *chemical company executive*

Patterson
Murez, John *music education director, educator*

Paulsboro
Chang, Clarence Dayton *chemist*

Peapack
Gustafson, Robert Eric *artistic director*
Walsh, Philip Cornelius *retired mining executive*
Weiss, Allan Joseph *transport company executive, lawyer*

Pemberton
Witkin, Isaac *sculptor*

Pennington
†Bertone, Thomas Lee *management consultant*
Bracken, Thomas *bank executive*
Brandinger, Jay Jerome *electronics executive*
Calvo, Roque John *professional society administrator*
Dickerson, John Joseph, Jr. *airport manager*
Harris, Frederick George *publishing company executive*
Kluger, Richard *author, editor*
Mitchell, Janet Aldrich *fund raising executive, reference materials publisher*
Rodriguez, Noreen Barbara *occupational health nurse*

Penns Grove
Graham, Albert Darlington, Jr. *educational administrator*

Pennsauken
Helmetag, Steven Charles *recording industry executive*
Holman, Joseph S. *automotive sales executive*
†Kolb, John *automotive executive*
†Robinson, Mae F. *secondary education educator*

Perth Amboy
Richardson-Melech, Joyce Suzanne *music educator, singer*
Santiago, Theresa Marie *special education educator*

Phillipsburg
Cooper, Paul *mechanical engineer, research director*
Kim, Ih Chin *pediatrician*
King, Michael John *sanitarian*
Rosenthal, Marvin Bernard *pediatrician, educator*

Picatinny Arsenal
Janow, Chris *mechanical engineer*

Pilesgrove Township
Crouse, Farrell R. *lawyer*
Robinson, John Abbott *mechanical engineer*

Piscataway
Alderfer, Clayton Paul *organizational psychologist, educator, author, consultant, administrator*
Champe, Pamela Chambers *biochemistry educator, writer*
Colaizzi, John Louis *college dean*
Conney, Allan Howard *pharmacologist*
Coppola, Sarah Jane *special education educator*
Denhardt, David Tilton *molecular and cell biology educator*
Devlin, Thomas Joseph *physicist*
Essien, Francine B. *geneticist, educator*
Flanagan, James Loton *electrical engineer, educator*
Fogiel, Max *publishing executive*
Freeman, Herbert *computer engineering educator*
French, Kathleen Patricia *educational administrator*
Frenkiel, Richard Henry *systems engineer, consultant*
Gelfand, Israel Moseevich *mathematician, biologist*
Goldstein, Bernard David *physician, educator*
Gotsch, Audrey Rose *environmental health sciences educator, researcher*
Guo, Qizhong *engineering educator, researcher*
Hernandez, Prospero Medalla *book publisher, consultant*
Julesz, Bela *experimental psychologist, educator, electrical engineer*
Kalaher, Richard A. *company executive*
Kampouris, Emmanuel Andrew *corporate executive*
Kear, Bernard Henry *materials scientist*
Kelly, Robert Emmett *telecommunications company administrator*
Kenney, Mary R. *software engineer*
Kovach, Barbara Ellen *management and psychology educator*
Lebowitz, Joel Louis *mathematical physicist, educator*
Lee, Barbara Anne *educator, lawyer*
†Leibowitz, Michael J. *medical educator*
Lewis, Peter A. *energy consultant*
Lichtig, Leo Kenneth *health economist*
Lindenfeld, Peter *physics educator*
Liu, Alice Y. C. *biology educator*
Madey, Theodore Eugene *physics educator*
Mammone, Richard James *engineering educator*
Manowitz, Paul *biochemist, researcher, educator*
Martinez-Fernandez, Luis *history educator, writer*
Mc Cormick, Richard Patrick *history educator*
Mitchell, James Kenneth *geography educator*
Peterson, Donald Robert *psychologist, educator, university administrator*
Plano, Richard James *physicist, educator*
Pollack, Irwin William *psychiatrist, educator*
Pond, Thomas Alexander *physics educator, university official*
Pramer, David *microbiologist, educator, research administrator*
Rhoads, George Grant *medical epidemiologist*
Robbins, Allen Bishop *physics educator*
Rokhvarger, Anatoly Efim *materials science and ceramic technology scientist*
Rosalsky, Barbara Ellen *artist, home health aide*
Salkind, Alvin J. *electrochemical engineer, educator, dean*
Sannuti, Peddapullaiah *electrical engineering educator*
Schwebel, Milton *psychologist, educator*
Shatkin, Aaron Jeffrey *biochemistry educator*
Shea, Stephen Michael *physician, educator*
Smith, Bob *lawyer, assemblyman, educator*
Snitzer, Elias *physicist*
Strachan, William John *optical engineer*
Trivedi, Harsh Mahendra *research scientist, educator*
Upton, Arthur Canfield *experimental pathologist, educator*
Wagner-Westbrook, Bonnie Joan *management professional*
Wasserman, Marlie P(arker) *publisher*
†Waxman, Chain I. *educator in sociology, researcher*
Welkowitz, Walter *biomedical engineer, educator*
†Wernoski, Richard Scott *academic department administrator*
Williams, James Richard *human factors engineering psychologist*
Wilson, Abraham *lawyer*
Witkin, Evelyn Maisel *geneticist*
Witz, Gisela *chemist, educator*
Yacowitz, Harold *biochemist, nutritionist*
You, Aleta *education educator*
Zhao, Jian Hui *electrical and computer engineering educator*

Pitman
Carpenter, Hoyle Dameron *music educator emeritus*
Cloues, Edward Blanchard, II *lawyer*
Kephart, Wilmer Atkinson, Jr. *industrial management executive*

Pittsgrove
Burt, Diane Mae *women's health nurse*

Pittstown
Bell, Frank Joseph, III *architect*

Plainboro
†Stathatos, Peter Anthony *industrial psychologist*

Plainfield
Frost, David *former biology educator, medical editor, consultant*
Granstrom, Marvin Leroy *civil and sanitary engineering educator*
Green, Gerald B. *state legislator*
Limpert, John H., Jr. *fund raising executive*
Mattson, Joy Louise *oncological nurse*
Nierstedt, William James *planner*
Reilly, Michael Thomas *chemical engineer*

Plainsboro
Devine, Hugh James, Jr. *marketing executive, consultant*
Gorrin, Eugene *lawyer*
Holmes, Suzon Tropez *financial analyst*
Kozlowski, Thomas Joseph, Jr. *lawyer, trust company executive*
Royds, Robert Bruce *physician*
Schreyer, William Allen *retired investment firm executive*
Sorensen, Henrik Vittrup *electrical engineering educator*
Spiegel, Phyllis *public relations consultant, journalist*

Pleasantville
Andes, Derien Romaric *retired purchasing specialist*
Bennett, Eileen Patricia *copy editor, reporter*
Briant, Maryjane *newspaper editor*
Freeman, Lillie Brooks *communications company administrator*
London, Charlotte Isabella *secondary education educator, reading specialist*
Mento, Joseph Natale *guidance counselor*
†Peele, Thomas *journalist, writer*

Point Pleasant
Caponegro, Ernest Mark *stockbroker, financial planner*
Monaco, Robert Anthony *radiologist*
Woolley-Dillon, Barbara Allen *city planner*

Point Pleasant Beach
Beno-Clark, Candice Lynn *chemical company executive*

Pomona
Colijn, Geert Jan *academic administrator, political scientist*
Comfort, Priscilla Maria *college official, human resources professional*
Farris, Vera King *college president*
†Henderson, Dee Wursten *dean*
Krogh-Jespersen, Mary-Beth *academic administrator*
Lessie, Douglas Louis *physics educator*
Lyons, Paul Harold *social work educator*
†Mench, Fred Charles *classics educator*
Reid-Merritt, Patricia Ann *social worker, educator, author, performing artist*
Sharobeam, Monir Hanna *engineering educator*
Sharon, Yitzhak Yaakov *physicist, educator*
Sung, Edward *physician*

Pompton Plains
Costello, Gerald Michael *editor*
†Scroggs, Robin Jerome *theology educator*

Port Elizabeth
Ficcaglia, Leslie M. *psychologist, portrait artist*

Port Murray
Kunzler, John Eugene *physicist*
Stokes, Eileen Margaret *historic society administrator*

Port Norris
Canzonier, Walter Jude *shellfish aquaculturist*

Pottersville
Mellberg, James Richard *dental research chemist*

Princeton
Aarsleff, Hans *linguistics educator*
Ackourey, Peter Paul *lawyer*
Adler, Stephen Louis *physicist*
Aizenman, Michael *mathematics and physics educator, researcher*
Allen, Diogenes *clergyman, philosophy educator*
Altman, Robert Allen *educational assessment executive*
Altmann, Stuart Allen *biologist, educator*
Anderson, Bruce James *electrical engineer, consultant*
Anderson, Ellis Bernard *retired lawyer, pharmaceutical company executive*
Armstrong, Richard Stoll *minister, educator, writer, poet*
Ashenfelter, Orley Clark *economics educator*
Bahcall, Neta Assaf *astrophysicist*
Baker, Nancy Kassebaum (Nancy Kassebaum) *former senator, foundation official*
Balch, Stephen Howard *professional society administrator*
Barker, Richard Gordon *corporate research and development executive*
Barkocy, Andrew Bernard *executive search firm executive*
Barlow, Walter Greenwood *public opinion analyst, management consultant*
Bartolini, Robert Alfred *electrical engineer, researcher*
Becker, Ivan Endre *retired plastics company executive*
Beidler, Marsha Wolf *lawyer*
Belshaw, George Phelps Mellick *bishop*
†Benarde, Anita E. *artist*
Bergman, Edward Jonathan *lawyer, educator*
Bermann, Sandra Lekas *English language educator*
Berry, Charles Horace *economist, educator*
Billington, David Perkins *civil engineering educator*
Bishop, James Francis *executive search consulting company executive*
Blair, David William *mechanical engineer*
Bogan, Elizabeth Chapin *economist, educator*
Bogucki, Peter Ignatius *archaeologist*
Bombieri, Enrico *mathematician, educator*
Bonini, William Emory *geophysics educator*
Borel, Armand *mathematics educator*
Bowersock, Glen Warren *historian*
Boyd, John Howard *corporate location consultant*
Bradford, David Frantz *economist*
Brennan, William Joseph, III *lawyer*
Broad, Barbara Prentice *real estate agent*
Brombert, Victor Henri *literature educator, author*
Browder, William *mathematician, educator*
Brown, Leon Carl *history educator*
Bryan, Kirk, Jr. *research meteorologist, research oceanographer*
Bunnell, Peter Curtis *photography and art educator, museum curator*
Buttenheim, Edgar Marion *publishing executive*
Cahill, James Francis *retired art history educator*
Cakmak, Ahmet Sefik *civil engineering educator*
Carnes, James Edward *electronics executive*
Carver, David Harold *physician, educator*
Cavanaugh, James Henry *medical corporate executive, former government official*
Chamberlin, John Stephen *investor, former cosmetics company executive*
Champlin, Edward James *classics educator*
Chandler, James John *surgeon*
Chow, Gregory Chi-Chong *economist, educator*
Christie, David George *insurance company executive*
Christman, Edward Arthur *physicist*
Christodoulou, Demetrios *mathematics educator*
Cleary, Lynda Woods *financial advisor, consultant*
Coffey, Joseph Irving *international affairs educator*
Coffin, David Robbins *art historian, educator*
Cohen, Isaac Louis (Ike Cohen) *financial consultant*
Cole, Nancy Stooksberry *educational research executive*
Collins, Amy Amanda *research assistant*
Conn, Hadley Lewis, Jr. *physician, educator*
Connelly, John F. *communications executive*
Connor, Geoffrey Michael *lawyer*
Cook, Michael Allan *social sciences educator*
Cooke, R(ichard) Caswell, Jr. *architect*
Cooper, Joel *psychology educator*
Cooper, John Madison *philosophy educator*
Corngold, Stanley Alan *German and comparative literature educator, writer*
Cox, Douglas Lynn *financial corporation executive*
Crandall, David LeRoy *research scientist*
Crespi, Irving *public opinion and market research consultant*
†Cross, Richard James *physician, educator*
Cryer, Dennis Robert *pharmaceutical company executive, researcher*
Curschmann, Michael Johann Hendrik *German language and literature educator*
Curtiss, Howard Crosby, Jr. *mechanical engineer, educator*
Darnton, Robert Choate *history educator*
Davidson, Ronald Crosby *physicist, educator*
Debenedetti, Pablo Gaston *chemical engineering educator*
†de Grazia, Alfred *philosopher, behavioral scientist*
Deligne, Pierre René *mathematician*
De Lung, Jane Solberger *independent sector executive*
DeMarco, David G. *registered nurse, pharmaceuticals researcher*
Deneen, Patrick John *political scientist, educator*
Denlinger, Edgar Jacob *electronics engineering research executive*
Dickinson, Bradley William *electrical engineering educator*
†Diller, Elizabeth E. *artist, educator*
Doig, Jameson Wallace *political science educator*
Douglass, Jane Dempsey *theology educator*
Dovey, Brian Hugh *health care products company executive, venture capitalist*
†Doyle, Michael W. *think-tank executive*
Durbin, Enoch Job *aeronautical engineering educator*
Dyson, Freeman John *physicist*
Ehrenberg, Edward *executive, consultant*
Ermolaev, Herman Sergei *Slavic languages educator*
Estey, Audree Phipps *artistic director*
Etz, Lois Kapelsohn *architectural company principal*
†Evslin, Tom *internet telephone service executive*
Farley, Edward Raymond, Jr. *mining and manufacturing company executive*
Feder, John Nathan *molecular biologist*
Feeney, John Robert *banker*
Fefferman, Charles Louis *mathematics educator*
Fenske, Edward Charles *special education educator, consultant*
Feria, Bernabe Francis *linguist*
Fisch, Nathaniel Joseph *physicist*
Fitch, Val Logsdon *physics educator*
Florey, Klaus Georg *chemist, pharmaceutical consultant*
Ford, Jeremiah, III *architect*
Fox, Mary Ann Williams *librarian*
Friedberg, Aaron Louis *political science educator*
Fusillo, Thomas Victor *environmental engineer*
Ganoe, Charles Stratford *banker, consultant*
Gear, Charles William *computer scientist*
Geertz, Clifford James *anthropology educator*
Geertz, Hildred Storey *anthropology educator*
George, Robert Peter *educator, lawyer*
George, Thomas *artist*
Gibson, James John *electronics engineer, consultant*
Gillespie, Thomas William *theological seminary administrator, religion educator*
Gillham, John Kinsey *chemical engineering educator*
Gilpin, Robert George, Jr. *political science educator*
Glassman, Irvin *mechanical and aeronautical engineering educator, consultant*
Glucksberg, Sam *psychology educator*
Goheen, Robert Francis *classicist, educator, former ambassador*
Goldfarb, Irene Dale *financial planner*
Gomoll, Allen Warren *cardiovascular pharmacologist*
Gordenker, Leon *political sciences educator*
Gordon, Ernest *clergyman*
Gott, J. Richard, III *astrophysicist*
Gould, James L. *biology educator*
Grabar, Oleg *art educator*
Grafton, Anthony Thomas *history educator*
Graves, Michael *architect, educator*
Greenstein, Fred Irwin *political science educator*
Griffiths, Phillip A. *mathematician, academic administrator*
Grisham, Larry Richard *physicist*
Gross, Charles Gordon *psychology educator, neuroscientist*
Grossman, Allen Neil *publishing executive*
Groves, John Taylor, III *chemist, educator*
Gunning, Robert Clifford *mathematician, educator*
Gutmann, Amy *political science and philosophy educator*
Habicht, Christian Herbert *history educator*
Halpern, Manfred *political science educator*
Happer, William, Jr. *physicist, educator*
Harayda, Janice *newspaper book editor, author*
Harford, James Joseph *aerospace historian*
Harman, Gilbert Helms *philosophy educator*
Harvey, Norman Ronald *finance company executive*
Hawryluk, Richard Janusz *physicist*
Hawver, Dennis Arthur *psychological consultant*
Hayes, Edwin Junius, Jr. *business executive*
Haynes, William Forby, Jr. *retired internist, cardiologist, educator*
Hearn, Ruby Puryear *foundation executive*
Henbest, Jon Charles *accountant, consultant*
Hendrickson, Robert Frederick *pharmaceutical company executive*
Henkel, William *financial services executive*
Hill, James Scott *lawyer*
Hillier, James *technology management executive, researcher*
Hillier, J(ames) Robert *architect*
Hirschman, Albert Otto *political economist, educator*
Hitz, Frederick Porter *educator, lawyer*
†Hochschild, Jennifer L. *political scientist, educator*
Hochschwender, Karl Albert *international trade and government relations consultant*
Hollander, Lawrence Jay *marketing executive*
Hollander, Robert B., Jr. *Romance languages educator*
Holt, Philetus Havens, III *architect*
Hopfield, John Joseph *biophysicist, educator*
Hough, Robert Alan *civil engineer*
Howarth, William (Louis) *education educator, writer*
Hulse, Russell Alan *physicist*
Hut, Piet *astrophysics educator*
Hynes, Samuel *English language educator, author*
Issawi, Charles Philip *economist, educator*
Itzkowitz, Norman *history educator*
Jackson, Roy *chemical engineering educator*
Jacobs, William Paul *botanist, educator*
Jacobson, Herbert Leonard *licensing executive*
Jeffery, Peter Grant *musicologist, fine arts educator*
Jeffrey, Richard Carl *philosophy educator*
Jellinek, Paul S. *foundation executive, health economist*
Jenkins, Edward Beynon *research astronomer*
Jenson, Pauline Alvino *retired speech and hearing educator*
Johnson, Ernest Frederick *chemical engineer, educator*
Johnston, Robert Fowler *venture capitalist*
Jordan, William Chester *history educator*
Joyce, William Leonard *librarian*
Judge, Marty M. *lawyer*
Kassof, Allen H. *foundation administrator*
Kateb, George Anthony *political science educator*
Katz, Stanley Nider *law history educator*
Katzenbach, Nicholas deBelleville *lawyer*
Kauzmann, Walter Joseph *chemistry educator*
Kehrt, Allan William *architectural firm executive*
Kelble, William Francis *information services editor*
Kenen, Peter Bain *economist, educator*
Kenyon, Regan Clair *educational research executive*
Kerney, Thomas Lincoln, II *investments and real estate professional*
Kidd, Lynden Louise *healthcare consultant*
Knoepflmacher, Ulrich Camillus *literature educator*
Kohn, Joseph John *mathematician, educator*
Komunyakaa, Yusef (James Willie Brown, Jr.) *poet*
Kornhauser, Henry *advertising executive*
Kuebler, Christopher Allen *pharmaceutical executive*
Kuenne, Robert Eugene *economics educator*
Kyin, Saw William *chemist, consultant*
Labalme, Patricia Hochschild *educational administrator*
Langlands, Robert Phelan *mathematician*
Lazarus, Arnold Allan *psychologist, educator*
†Leaver, Robin A. *educator*
Lechner, Bernard Joseph *consulting electrical engineer*
Lemonick, Aaron *physicist, educator*
Lerner, Ralph *architect, university dean*
Levin, Simon Asher *mathematician, ecologist, educator*
Levy, Kenneth *music educator*
Lewis, Bernard *Near Eastern studies educator*
Lewis, David Kellogg *philosopher, educator*
Lewis, John Prior *economist, educator*
Liao, Paul Foo-Hung *electronics executive*
Lieb, Elliott Hershel *physicist, mathematician, educator*
Lincoln, Anna *company executive, foreign languages educator*
Linke, Richard A. *systems engineer, researcher*
Lippincott, Walter Heulings, Jr. *publishing executive*
Lo, Arthur Wu-nien *electrical engineering educator*
Lobo, Jennifer Helena *investment banker, venture capitalist*
Logue, Judith R. *psychoanalyst, educator*
Long, Frank Wesley, Jr. *chemist*
Loss, Stuart Harold *financial executive*
MacPherson, Robert Duncan *mathematician, educator*
Mahlman, Jerry David *research meteorologist*
Mahoney, Michael Sean *history educator*
Makadok, Stanley *management consultant*
Malkiel, Burton Gordon *economics educator*
Malkiel, Nancy Weiss *college dean, history educator*
Marks, John Henry *Near Eastern studies educator*
Matlock, Jack Foust, Jr. *diplomat*
May, Graham Stirling *physician*

Mayhew, Eric George *cancer researcher, educator*
McClure, Donald Stuart *physical chemist, educator*
McCullough, John Price *retired oil company executive*
McFarland, Thomas *English educator*
Mc Pherson, James Munro *history educator*
Meade, Dale Michael *laboratory director, researcher*
Merrill, Leland Gilbert, Jr. *retired environmental science educator*
Metzger, Bruce Manning *clergyman, educator*
Miles, Richard Bryant *mechanical and aerospace engineering educator*
Miller, George Armitage *psychologist, educator*
Miller, Patrick Dwight, Jr. *religion educator, minister*
Mills, Bradford *merchant banker*
Mills, Michael James *architect*
Miner, Earl Roy *literature educator*
Minton, Dwight Church *manufacturing company executive*
Montagu, Ashley *anthropologist, social biologist*
Moote, A. Lloyd *history educator*
Morgan, William Jason *geophysics educator*
Morris, Mac Glenn *advertising bureau executive*
Morrison, Simon Alexander *musicologist, educator*
Morrison, Toni (Chloe Anthony Morrison) *novelist*
Moynahan, Julian Lane *English language educator, author*
Mueller, Peter Sterling *psychiatrist, educator*
Mulder, Edwin George *retired minister, church official*
Muldoon, Paul *creative writing educator, poet*
Musinguzi, Hannington Rwabazaire *software engineer*
Nash, John Forbes, Jr. *research mathematician*
Neff, Robert Arthur *business and financial executive*
Nehamas, Alexander *philosophy educator*
Nied, Thomas H. *media company executive*
Nikain, Reza *civil engineer*
†Noble, Stephen Lloyd *information scientist*
Novotny, Jiri *biophysicist*
Oberg, Barbara Bowen *historian, educator, scholarly writer*
†Obi, Chinwe I *French language educator*
O'Connor, Neal William *former advertising agency executive*
O'Donnell, Laurence Gerard *editorial consultant*
Ondetti, Miguel Angel *chemist, consultant*
O'Neill, Harry William *survey research company executive*
Orphanides, Nora Charlotte *ballet educator*
Osei, Edward Kofi *financial analyst, educator, strategic planner*
Ostriker, Jeremiah Paul *astrophysicist, educator*
Page, Lyman Alexander, Jr. *physicist*
Palsho, Dorothea Coccoli *information services executive*
Paret, Peter *historian*
Parry, Scott Brink *psychologist*
Peebles, Phillip James E. *physicist, educator*
Picco, Steven Joseph *lawyer*
Pimley, Kim Jensen *financial training consultant*
Plaks, Livia Basch *foundation executive*
Platt, Judith Roberta *electrical engineer*
Poor, Harold Vincent *electrical engineering educator*
Potasek, Mary Joyce *physicist, researcher*
†Prodromou, Elizabeth Helen *political science educator*
Prud'homme, Robert Krafft *chemical engineering educator*
Rabb, Theodore K. *historian, educator*
Rebenfeld, Ludwig *chemist, educator*
Rigolot, François *French literature educator, literary critic*
Rodgers, Daniel Tracy *history educator*
Rodwell, John Dennis *biochemist*
Rosen, Arye *microwave, optoelectronics and medicine researcher*
Rosen, Marvin Abraham *music educator*
Rosenblatt, Louise Michel *emerita educator*
Rosenthal, Howard Lewis *political science educator*
Royce, Barrie Saunders Hart *physicist, educator*
Rozman, Gilbert Friedell *sociologist, educator*
Russel, William Bailey *engineering educator*
Rutherford, Paul Harding *physicist*
Sandy, Lewis Gordon *physician, foundation executive*
Sapoff, Meyer *electronics component manufacturer*
Saville, Dudley Albert *chemical engineering educator*
Scasta, David Lynn *forensic psychiatrist*
Schafer, Carl Walter *investment executive*
Schofield, Robert E(dwin) *history educator, academic administrator*
Schorske, Carl Emil *historian, educator*
Schroeder, Alfred Christian *electronics research engineer*
Schroeder, Steven Alfred *medical educator, researcher, foundation executive*
Seawright, James L., Jr. *sculptor, educator*
Seiberg, Nathan *physics educator*
Seman, Charles Jacob *research meteorologist*
Semrod, T. Joseph *banker*
Sethi, Shyam Sunder *management consultant*
Shapiro, Harold Tafler *academic administrator, economist*
Shear, Theodore Leslie, Jr. *archaeologist, educator*
Shenk, Thomas Eugene *molecular biology educator, academic administrator*
Shimizu, Yoshiaki *art historian, educator*
Shoemaker, Frank Crawford *physicist, educator*
Showalter, Elaine *humanities educator*
Simmons, Warren Hathaway, Jr. *retired retail executive*
Smagorinsky, Joseph *meteorologist*
Smith, Arthur John Stewart *physicist, educator*
Socolow, Robert Harry *engineering educator, scientist*
Souter, Sydney Scull *lawyer*
Spiro, Thomas George *chemistry educator*
Spitzer, T. Quinn *management consultant company executive*
Starr, Paul Elliot *sociologist, writer, editor, educator*
Steele, Marta F. Nussbaum *writer, editor, book*
Steinberg, Malcolm Saul *biologist, educator*
Stengel, Robert Frank *mechanical and aerospace engineering educator*
Stern, Gail Frieda *historical association director*
Sterzer, Fred *research physicist*
Stix, Thomas Howard *physicist, educator*
Sugerman, Abraham Arthur *psychiatrist*
Sutphin, William Taylor *lawyer*
Swenson, Christine Erica *microbiologist*
Tang, Chao *physicist*
Taylor, Joseph Hooton, Jr. *radio astronomer, physicist*
Thompson, Ellen Kubacki *microbiologist, medical writer, consultant*
Tierney, Bill *university athletic coach*
Tilghman, Shirley Marie *biology educator*
Torquato, Salvatore *civil engineering educator*
Treiman, Sam Bard *physics educator*
Tremaine, Scott Duncan *astrophysicist*
Treu, Jesse Isaiah *venture capitalist*
†Treves, George David *graphic artist*
Trussell, James *dean*
†Tsui, Daniel C. *electrical engineering educator*
Ufford, Charles Wilbur, Jr. *lawyer*
Ullman, Richard Henry *political science educator*
Umscheid, Ludwig Joseph *computer specialist*
Vahaviolos, Sotirios John *electrical engineer, scientist, corporate executive*
Van Houten, Franklyn Bosworth *geologist, educator*
VanMarcke, Erik Hector *civil engineering educator*
Villafranca, Joseph J. *pharmaceutical executive, chemistry educator*
Vincent, Emily (Jean Mulvey Friedmann) *book reviewer*
Vizzini, Carol Redfield *symphony musician, music educator*
†von der Schmidt, Edward, III *neurosurgeon*
Von Hippel, Frank Niels *public and international affairs educator*
Walter, Hugo Günther *humanities educator*
Walton, Clifford Wayne *chemical engineer, researcher*
Walzer, Michael Laban *political science educator*
Warren, Kay B. *anthropology educator*
Wavle, James Edward, Jr. *pharmaceutical company executive, lawyer*
Wei, Fong *nephrologist*
Wei, James *chemical engineering educator, academic dean*
Weimer, Paul K(essler) *electrical engineer, consultant*
Weinstein, Norman Jacob *chemical engineer, consultant*
Weinstein, Stephen Brant *communications executive, researcher, writer*
Weiss, Renée Karol *editor, writer, musician*
Weiss, Theodore Russell *poet, editor*
Welton, Donna Ann *curator, translator*
Wenglinsky, Harold Heidt *research scientist*
†Wentz, Sidney Frederick *insurance company executive, foundation executive*
West, Charles Converse *theologian, educator*
Westergaard, Peter Talbot *composer, music educator*
Westoff, Charles Francis *demographer, educator*
Wheeler, John Archibald *physicist, educator*
White, Morton Gabriel *philosopher, author*
Wieschaus, Eric F. *molecular biologist, educator*
Wightman, Arthur Strong *physicist, educator*
Wightman, Ludmilla G. Popova *language educator, foreign educator, translator*
Wilczek, Frank Anthony *physics educator*
Wildnauer, Richard Harry *pharmaceutical company executive*
Wiles, Andrew J. *mathematican, educator*
Wilkinson, David Todd *physics educator*
Williams, Robert H. *environmental scientist*
Willig, Robert Daniel *economics educator*
Willingham, Warren Willcox *psychologist, testing service executive*
Wilmerding, John *art history educator, museum curator*
Witten, Edward *mathematical physicist*
Wolf, Wayne Hendrix *electrical engineering educator*
Wood, Eric Franklin *earth and environmental sciences educator*
Woodward, Daniel Holt *librarian, researcher*
Woolf, Harry *historian, educator*
Yang, Hong *chemistry researcher*
Yao, Kuo Wei *biochemist*
Yun, Samuel *minister, educator*
Zatz, Irving J. *structural engineer*
Zierler, Neal *retired mathematician*
Zimmer, Richard Alan *lawyer*
Ziolkowski, Theodore Joseph *comparative literature educator*

Princeton Junction
Bair, William Alois *engineer*
Cohen, Florence Emery *financial services executive*
Lull, William Paul *engineering consultant*
Payne, Linda Cohen *business owner*
Pollard-Gott, Lucy *writer*

Rahway
Buckland, Barry C. *chemical engineer*
Dombrowski, Anne Wesseling *microbiologist, researcher*
Drew, Stephen Walker *chemical engineer*
Garcia, Maria Luisa *biochemist, researcher*
Kaczorowski, Gregory John *biochemist, researcher, science administrator*
Mandel, Lewis Richard *pharmaceutical company executive*
†McCoy, William Keith *library director*
Patchett, Arthur Allan *medicinal chemist, pharmaceutical executive*
Reynolds, Glenn Franklin *medicinal research scientist*
Shapiro, Bennett Michaels *biochemist, educator*
Strack, Alison Merwin *neurobiologist*
Tice, Kirk Clifford *health care facility executive*

Ramsey
Underwood, Steven Clark *publishing executive*

Randolph
Allen, B. Marc *managed care executive*
Capsouras, Barbara Ellen *college official*
Charm, Joel Barry *management consultant executive*
Chen, Kevin Sangone *corporate executive, consultant*
Femminella, Charles Joseph, Jr. *real estate appraiser, tax assessor, broker*
Stoskus, Joanna Jorzysta *computer information systems educator*
†Zulauf, Sander William *educator*

Raritan
Alatzas, George *delivery service company executive*
Frank, David Stanley *medical diagnostics company executive*
Hahn, Dowon *pharmaceutical researcher, educator*
Haller, William Paul *analytical chemist, robotics specialist*
Licetti, Mary Elizabeth *business analysis director*

Red Bank
Arnone, Michael J. *state legislator, dentist*
Auerbach, Philip Gary *lawyer*
Brown, Valerie Anne *psychiatric social worker, educator*
Cataldo, Patrick A., Jr. *corporate training executive*
Chynoweth, Alan Gerald *retired telecommunications research executive, consultant*
Dale, Madeline Houston McWhinney *banker*
Duggan, John Peter *lawyer*
Eiselt, Michael Herbert *optics scientist*
Fred, Rogers Murray, III *veterinary oncologist*
Gutentag, Patricia Richmand *social worker, family counselor, occupational therapist*
Haskell, Barry Geoffry *communications company research administrator*
†Hempstead, George H., III *lawyer, diversified company executive*
Hertz, Daniel Leroy, Jr. *entrepreneur*
Howson, Agnes Wagner *health educator*
Hughes, Barnard *actor*
Labrecque, Theodore Joseph *lawyer*
Lucky, Robert Wendell *electrical engineer*
Lukacs, Michael Edward *communications researcher*
McCann, John Francis *retired financial services company executive*
McWhinney, Madeline H. (Mrs. John Denny Dale) *economist*
Murray, Abby Darlington Boyd *psychiatric clinical specialist, educator*
Nucciarone, A. Patrick *lawyer*
Oberst, Robert John *financial analyst*
O'Hern, Daniel Joseph *state supreme court justice*
†Pohl, Anna Lise *executive*
Post, Barbara Joan *elementary education educator*
Reinhart, Peter Sargent *corporate executive, lawyer*
Rogers, Lee Jasper *lawyer*
Schneider, Sol *electronic engineer, consultant, researcher*
Sgaramella, Peter *chemical products executive, technical consultant*
†Stansbury, Kevin Bradley *English educator, educational consultant*
Tan, Nianxiong *electronics professional*
Weiant, William Morrow *investment banking executive*

Ridgefield
Aybar, Romeo *architect*
Goldman, Arnold Ira *biophysicist, statistical analyst*
†Riggs, Rory *pharmaceutical executive*
Shapira, Benjamin *cellist*

Ridgefield Park
D'Avella, Bernard Johnson, Jr. *publishing company executive, lawyer*
Hiemier, Paige Dana *nurse*
Jurasek, John Paul *mathematics educator, counselor*
Litwinowicz, Anthony *information specialist, researcher*

Ridgewood
Abplanalp, Glen Harold *civil engineer*
Baddoura, Rashid Joseph *emergency medicine physician*
Celentano, Linda Nancy *industrial designer*
†Ciannella, Joeen Moore *legislative staff member, small business owner*
Clements, Lynne Fleming *family therapist, programmer*
Ege, Hans Alsnes *securities company executive*
Haveliwala, Hozefa Y.A. *journalist, writer*
Healey, Frank Henry *retired research executive*
Herink, Richie *education company executive*
Hinckley, Deborah Clark *language services professional*
Kahlenberg, Jeannette Dawson *retired civic organization executive*
Kiernan, Richard Francis *publisher*
Lucca, John James *retired dental educator*
McBride, William Bernard *treasurer*
Mitgang, Lee David *journalist, author, lecturer*
Picozzi, Anthony *dentist*
Riccio-Sauer, Joyce *art educator*
Seigel, Jan Kearney *lawyer*
Sumers, Anne Ricks *ophthalmologist, museum director*
Tuthill, Jay Dean, II *investment executive*
Warner, John Edward *advertising executive*
Ziv, Pat Valentine *interior designer*

Ringwood
Edge, Thomas Leslie *minister*
Murphy, Gloria Walter *novelist, screenwriter*

River Edge
†Davis, Alison B. *company executive*
Gass, Manus M. *accountant, business executive*

River Vale
Becker, Murray Leonard *corporate financial consultant, consulting actuary*
Falcon, Raymond Jesus, Jr. *lawyer*
Lotito, Joseph Daniel *lawyer*
Moderacki, Edmund Anthony *music educator, conductor*
Peleg, Ephraim *sculptor*
Sommerhoff, Herrat H. *painter, educator*

Riverdale
Fremund, Zdenek Anthony *manufacturing company executive*

Robbinsville
†Buono, Frederick Joseph *secondary school educator*
Goldstein, Norman Robert *safety engineer*
Norback, Craig Thomas *writer*

Rochelle Park
Brandt, Robert Barry *lay worker*
Dadurian, Medina Diana *pediatric dentist, educator*
Knopf, Barry Abraham *lawyer*
Laskey, Richard Anthony *biomedical device executive*
Schapiro, Jerome Bentley *chemical company executive*

Rockaway
Allen, Dorothea *secondary education educator*
Kelsey, Ann Lee *library administrator*
Laine, Cleo (Clementina Dinah Dankworth) *singer*
Reeves, Marylou *financial planner*

Rockleigh
Heslin, Cathleen Jane *artist, designer, entrepreneur*
Heslin, John Thomas *entrepreneur, historic preservationist*
Siracusano, Louis H. *communications company executive*

Roosevelt
Herrstrom, David Sten *banking executive*
Landau, Jacob *artist*
Warren, Peter Beach *economist*

Roseland
Berkowitz, Bernard Solomon *lawyer*
Eakeley, Douglas Scott *lawyer*
Foster, M. Joan *lawyer*
Golden, Robert Charles *financial services executive*
Greenberg, Stephen Michael *lawyer, businesss executive*
Hochberg, Mark Stefan *foundation president, cardiac surgeon*
Kohl, Benedict M. *lawyer*
Lafer, Fred Seymour *data processing company executive*
Levithan, Allen B. *lawyer*
Lowenstein, Alan Victor *lawyer*
MacKay, John Robert, II *lawyer*
Malafronte, Donald *health executive*
Mitschele, Michael Douglas *concrete and aggregate company executive*
Newman, Gary *lawyer*
Rivero, Jose Antonio *computer company executive*
Schenkler, Bernard *lawyer*
Schneider, George *internist, endocrinoligist*
Smith, Wendy Hope *lawyer*
Sokalski, Debra Ann *computer systems developer, programming consultant*
Starr, Ira M. *lawyer*
Stern, Herbert Jay *lawyer*
Tarino, Gary Edward *lawyer*
Taub, Henry *retired computer services company executive*
Vanderbilt, Arthur T., II *lawyer*
Ventola, Elizabeth Eve *educational administrator*
Weinbach, Arthur Frederic *computing services company executive*
Wovsaniker, Alan *lawyer, educator*

Roselle
Bizub, Barbara L. *elementary school educator*
Di Marco, Barbaranne Yanus *multiple handicapped special education educator*
Mahadeshwar, Sanjay Sakharam *marine consultant*
Riley, Barbara Polk *retired librarian*

Roselle Park
Freeland, Herbert Thomas *minister*
Margolin, Michael Leonard *gastroenterologist*
Scarpelli, Vito *adult education educator, administrator*
Wilchins, Sidney A. *gynecologist*

Rumson
Brennan, William Joseph *manufacturing company executive*
Brenner, Theodore Engelbert *retired trade association executive*
Creamer, William Henry, III *insurance company executive*
Freeman, David Forgan *retired foundation executive*
Macdonald, Donald Arthur *publishing executive*
Pflum, William John *physician*
Rowe, Harrison Edward *electrical engineer*
Strong, George Hotham *private investor, consultant*
Topham, Sally Jane *ballet educator*

Rutherford
Aberman, Harold Mark *veterinarian*
Bertone, Andrew E. *biological scientist, environmental scientist*
Davis, Joe David *broadcast executive*
Gerety, Peter Leo *archbishop*
Liptak, Irene Frances *retired business executive*
Mongelli, Thomas Guy *broadcast executive, radio personality*
Petrie, Ferdinand Ralph *illustrator, artist*
†Rowe, Michael Richard *sports team executive, sports arena executive*
†Sawyer, Miriam *library director*
Suarez, Sally Ann Tevis *health care administrator, nurse, consultant*

Saddle Brook
Clifton, Nelida *social worker*
Donahoe, Maureen Alice *accounting consultant*
Pearlman, Peter Steven *lawyer*

Saddle River
Cappitella, Mauro John *architect*
Dowden, Carroll Vincent *publishing company executive*
Farmer, Martha Louise *retired college administrator*
Farrand, George Nixon, Jr. *marketing professional*
Giovannoli, Joseph Louis *entrepreneur, lawyer*
Lasser, Gail Maria *psychologist, educator*
McClelland, William Craig *paper company executive*
Noyes, Robert Edwin *publisher, writer*
O'Connor, Denise Lynn *marketing communications executive*
†Pak, Dongtak *business executive*
Roes, Nicholas A. *communications executive*

Salem
Crymble, John Frederick *chemical engineer, consultant*
Seabrook, John Martin *retired food products executive, chemical engineer*

Sayreville
†Rapp, Lea Bayers *author, journalist, show business consultant*

Scotch Plains
Bishop, Robert Milton *former stock exchange official*
Buckridee, Patricia Ilona *international marketing/strategy consultant*
†Dazzo, Nicholas John *economist*
Domeshek, Sol *aeronautical engineer*
Klock, John Henry *lawyer*
Palmer, Teresa Anne *nurse practitioner*
†Rebimbas, Lisa Vale *secondary foreign language educator*
Touretzky, Muriel Walter *nursing educator*
Ungar, Manya Shayon *volunteer, education consultant*

Sea Girt
Crispi, Michele Marie *lawyer*
Pace, Thomas *information services executive, lawyer*
Wyskowski, Barbara Jean *lawyer*

Rubin, Bernard *pharmacologist, biomedical writer, consultant*
Rusciano, Frank Louis *political science educator, consultant*
Russell, Joyce Anne Rogers *librarian*
Sakson, Robert George *artist*
Salgado, Luis José *state agency official*
Saraf, Komal C. *psychologist*
Scheiring, Michael James *college official*
Schirber, Annamarie Riddering *speech and language pathologist, educator*
Smallwood, Robert Albian, Jr. *secondary education educator*
†Soaries, DeForest B., Jr. *state official*
Sporn, Aaron Adolph *physician*
Sterns, Joel Henry *lawyer*
†Terhune, Jack *government administrator*
Terrill, Thomas Edward *health facility administrator*
Thompson, Anne Elise *federal judge*
Tolan, Robert Warren *pediatric infectious disease specialist*
Traier, John *state agency administrator*
Verniero, Peter *state attorney general*
Weinberg, Martin Herbert *retired psychiatrist*
Weld, Alison Gordon *artist, contemporary art curator*
Whitman, Christine Todd *governor*
Wolfson, Freda L. *judge*
†Yull, Peter Martin *state agency administrator*
Zanna, Martin Thomas *physician*

Tuckerton
Dinges, Richard Allen *entrepreneur*

Turnersville
Cammarota, Marie Elizabeth *nursing administrator, nursing educator*
DePace, Nicholas Louis *physician*
Matheussen, John J. *state legislator*

Union
Applbaum, Ronald Lee *academic administrator*
Darden, Barbara L. *library director*
Darden, Joseph Samuel, Jr. *health educator*
†David, Ivo A. *real estate broker, artist*
Donovan, Craig Poulenez *public administration educator*
Fabyanski, Mary Irene *nursing administrator*
Franks, Robert D. (Bob Franks) *congressman*
Hennings, Dorothy Grant (Mrs. George Hennings) *education educator*
Irwin, James Richard, Jr. *writer, editor*
Korbman, Meyer Hyman *rabbi, public school administrator*
Korn, Neal Mark *painter, art educator*
Kramer, Paula Lee *occupational therapist, educator*
Lapidus, Norman Israel *food broker*
Lederman, Susan Sturc *public administration educator*
Lewandowski, Andrew Anthony *utilities executive, consultant*
Muller, Gregory Alan *health facilities administrator, mayor*
Rokosz, Gregory Joseph *emergency medicine physician, educator*
Rosenberg, A. Irving *lawyer*
Sharp, Michele *women's basketball coach*
Sigmon, Scott B. *psychologist*
Stern, Marianne *advertising agency executive*
Wallerstein, Sheldon Melvin *mortgage company executive*
Weiger, Myra Barbara *educational administrator*
White, Robert L. G., Jr. *aerospace company executive*
Williams, Carol Jorgensen *social work educator*
Zois, Constantine Nicholas Athanasios *meteorology educator*

Union Beach
Gilmartin, Clara T. *volunteer*

Union City
Bull, Inez Stewart *special education and gifted music educator, coloratura soprano, pianist, editor, author*
Dulack, David Donald *retired city inspector*
Kaden, Lori Jill *school counselor*
Ortizio, Debra Louise *elementary education educator*
Rondon, Edania Cecilia *lawyer*
Sheehy, Janice Ann *elementary education educator, technology facilitator*
†Younan, Joseph *bishop*

Upper Montclair
Cordasco, Francesco *sociologist, educator, author*
†Courson, William A. *association administrator*
Delgado, Ramon Louis *educator, author, director, playwright, lyricist*
†Lynde, Richard A. *academic administrator*
†Narrett, Carla Marie *university administrator*
†Stock, Norman *librarian*
Zivari, Bashir *architect, industrial designer*

Upper Saddle River
Cullen, Thomas Joseph *history educator*
Dojny, Richard Francis *publishing company executive*
Marron, Darlene Lorraine *real estate development executive, financial and marketing consultant*
Ross, Deborah Ann *customer relations professional, philatelist*
Wallace, William, III *engineering executive*

Vauxhall
Ross, Mark Samuel *lawyer, educator, funeral director, writer*

Ventnor City
Bolton, Kenneth Albert *management consultant*
Mason, James Henry, IV *retired surgeon*
Panico, Elaine Hartman *nurse*
Robbins, Hulda Dornblatt *artist, printmaker*
Zuckerman, Stuart *psychiatrist, forensic examiner, educator*

Vernon
Megna, Steve Allan *elementary education educator*
Roche, Susan Lynn *elementary education educator*

Verona
Aronow, Edward *psychologist, educator*
Ayaso, Manuel *artist*
Brightman, Robert Lloyd *importer, textile company executive, consultant*
Greenwald, Robert *public relations executive*
McGinley, Daniel Joseph *association executive*
Meyer, Helen (Mrs. Abraham J. Meyer) *retired editorial consultant*

Vineland
DeVivo, Sal J. *newspaper executive*
†Gupta, Vipin K. *neurologist*
Hunt, Howard F(rancis) *psychologist, educator*
Kazam, Abdul Raoof *veterinarian*
Popp, Charlotte Louise *health development center administrator, nurse*
Steward, Mollie Aileen *mathematics and computer science educator*
†Warren, Corky *radio personality*

Voorhees
†Bailey, Linda A. *educator*
†Cohen, Gregory Leighton *computer operations executive*
Gottschalk, Milton Joe *management consultant*
†Kuchler, Joseph Albert *surgeon*
Layton, Amanda Emigh *non-profit organization fundraiser*
Picariello, Pasquale *lawyer*
†Siddiqi, Tariq Sifat *neurosurgeon*

Waldwick
Surdoval, Donald James *accounting and management consulting company executive*

Wall
Colford, Francis Xavier *gas industry executive*
Jost, Wesley William *automotive executive, mayor*

Wanaque
Jordan, Leo John *lawyer*

Warren
Biswas, Dhrubes *electrical engineer*
Blass, Walter Paul *consultant, management educator*
Chesney, Robert Henry *communications executive, consultant*
Chubb, Percy, III *insurance company executive*
Coleman, James H., Jr. *state supreme court justice*
Earle, Jean Buist *computer company executive*
Ellerbusch, Fred *environmental engineer*
Hartman, David Gardiner *actuary*
Hurley, Lawrence Joseph *lawyer*
Jackson, John Wyant *medical products executive*
Jaffe, Howard Lawrence *rabbi*
Kasper, Horst Manfred *lawyer*
Kozberg, Ronald Paul *health and human services administrator*
Mahecha, Juan Carlos, Jr. *financial services administrator*
Maull, George Marriner *music director, conductor*
O'Hare, Dean Raymond *insurance company executive*
Salem, Eli *chemical engineer*
Starr, Miriam Carolyn *telecommunications company executive*
†Wallace, Lorna H. *market strategy researcher*
Wildrick, Kenyon Jones *minister*

Washington
De Sanctis, Vincent *college president*
Drago, Joseph Rosario *urologist, educator*

Watchung
Grey, Ruthann E. *management consultant*
Knudson, Harry Edward, Jr. *retired electrical manufacturing company executive*
Kraus, Steven Gary *lawyer*
Michaelis, Paul Charles *engineering physicist executive*
Miller, John Ronald *minister*
Murphree, Henry Bernard Scott *psychiatry and pharmacology educator, consultant*
Schaefer, Jacob Wernli *military systems consultant*
Tornqvist, Erik Gustav Markus *chemical engineer, research scientist*

Wayne
†Ansari, Maboud *education educator*
Arturi, Anthony Joseph *engineering executive, consultant*
Bowles, Suzanne Geissler *history educator*
†Cetrulo, Jerry *sculptor*
Cheng, David Hong *mechanical engineering educator*
Cordover, Ronald Harvey *business executive, venture capitalist*
Donald, Robert Graham *retail food chain human resources executive*
Einreinhofer, Nancy Anne *art gallery director*
Eisenstein, Elliot Martin *pediatrician*
Freimark, Jeffrey Philip *retail supermarket executive*
Garcia, Ofelia *dean*
Gelman, Jon Leonard *lawyer*
Goldstein, Marjorie Tunick *special education educator*
Gollance, Robert Barnett *ophthalmologist*
Heyman, Samuel J. *chemicals and building materials manufacturing company executive*
Hochman, Naomi Lipson *special education educator, consultant*
Jeffrey, Robert George, Jr. *industrial company executive*
Katz, Leandro *artist, filmmaker*
Kolak, Daniel *philosopher*
Lang, William Charles *financial executive*
Laruccia, Stephen Dominic *university official*
Nicastro, Francis Efisio *defense electronics and retailing executive*
O'Connor, John Morris, III *philosophy educator*
Powell, Richard Cortland *advertising executive*
Rogoff, Paula Drimmer *English and foreign language educator*
Salloum, Salim George *sales executive*
Salny, Abbie Feinstein *psychologist*
Schwartz, Robert *automotive manufacturing company executive, marketing executive*
Sgroi, Donald Angelo *obstetrician, gynecologist*
Siepser, Stuart Lewis *cardiologist, internist*
Speert, Arnold *academic administrator, chemistry educator*
†Strasser, Janis Koeppel *education educator*
Tanzman-Bock, Maxine M. *psychotherapist, hypnotherapist, consultant*
Vaillancourt, Donald Charles *public affairs executive, lawyer*
White, Doris Gnauck *science educator, biochemical and biophysics researcher*
Younie, William John *special education educator, researcher*

Weehawken
Hayden, Joseph A., Jr. *lawyer*
Hess, Dennis John *investment banker*
Murphy, Barbara Ann *protective services official*

West Caldwell
Berenfeld, Mark M. *chemist*
Dixon, Jo-Ann Conte *management consultant*
Page, Frederick West *business consultant*
Reboli, John Anthony *publishing executive*
Schiff, Robert *healthcare consultancy company executive*
Trozzi, Patricia Lynn *graphic artist*
Wray, Gilbert Andrew *mechanical and civil engineer*

West Cape May
Cadge, William Fleming *gallery owner, photographer*

West Long Branch
Boronico, Jess Stephen *management science educator, academic dean*
Dvoichenko-Markov, Demetrius *history educator*
†Garvey, Brian Thomas *educator in English, university administrator*
Hedlund, Dennis M. *film company executive*
Holland, John Joseph, Jr. *economics educator*
Kovacs, Aimee *conference speaker, minister*
Lutz, Francis Charles *university dean, civil engineering educator*
Shagan, Bernard Pellman *endocrinologist, educator*
Stafford, Rebecca *academic administrator, sociologist*

West Milford
Ferguson, Harley Robert *service company executive*
Stelpstra, William John *minister*

West New York
Arias, David *bishop*
Gruenberg, Elliot Lewis *electronics engineer and company executive*
Kelly, Lucie Stirm Young *nursing educator*
Shapiro, Sandra Libby Rosenberg *dean, business education educator*

West Orange
†Aitchison, Kenneth W. *health facility administrator*
Askin, Marilyn *lawyer, educator*
Bearg, Esther Marilyn *school counselor*
Bornstein, Lester Milton *retired medical center executive*
†Bottitta, Joseph Anthony *lawyer*
Chin, Carolyn Sue *business executive*
De Lisa, Joel Alan *rehabilitation physician, rehabilitation facility executive*
Ficks, F. Lawrence *communications executive*
Ghali, Anwar Youssef *psychiatrist, educator*
Gordon, Harrison J. *lawyer*
Guthrie, William Anthony *minister*
Johnson, Clarice P. *materials procurement executive*
Katz, Alix Martha *respiratory care practitioner*
Kushen, Allan Stanford *retired lawyer*
Kushen, Betty Sandra *writer, educator*
Kyle, Corinne Silverman *management consultant*
Langsner, Alan Michael *pediatric cardiologist*
Laves, Benjamin Samuel *lawyer*
Nessel, Edward Harry *swimming coach*
Panagides, John *pharmacologist*
Petrokubi, Marilyn *film company executive, researcher, producer*
Rayfield, Gordon Elliott *playwright, political risk consultant*
Schreiber, Eileen Sher *artist*
Weiner, Mervyn *retired mergers and acquisitions executive*

West Paterson
†DeLouise, Tia Caputi *university executive*
King, Deborah Simpkin *music, voice educator*
Marren, Maryann Fahy *primary school educator*
†Pataki, Andrew *bishop*
St. John, Catherine *painter*
Seiffer, Neil Mark *photographer*

West Windsor
Giddings, Clifford Frederick *retired corporate executive*

Westfield
Bartok, William *environmental technologies consultant*
Besch, Lorraine W. *special education educator*
Connell, Grover *food company executive*
Cummin, Sylvia Esther *secondary education educator*
Cushman, Helen Merle Baker *retired management consultant*
†Decker, Mark Richard *lawyer*
DeMarco, Annemarie Bridgeman *telecommunications company manager*
Devlin, Wende Dorothy *writer, artist*
Dzury, Stephen Daniel *insurance company official*
Feret, Adam Edward, Jr. *dentist*
Frungillo, Nicholas Anthony, Jr. *accountant*
Kababik, Dana Lynne *health communications executive*
Keyko, George John *electronics company executive*
†Kozlowski, Dorothy *health center administrator*
Mazzarese, Michael Louis *executive coach, consultant*
McDevitt, Brian Peter *history educator, educational consultant*
Mc Fadden, G. Bruce *hospital administrator*
McLean, Vincent Ronald *former manufacturing company financial executive*
Phillips, John C. *lawyer*
Simon, Martin Stanley *commodity marketing company executive, economist*
Specht, Gordon Dean *retired petroleum executive*

Westville
Doughty, A. Glenn *minister*

Westwood
Bilz, Laurie S. *nursing educator*
Black, Theodore Halsey *retired manufacturing company executive*
Dorner-Andelora, Sharon Agnes Haddon *computer technical consultant, educator*
Schutz, Donald Frank *geochemist, environmental corporate executive*
Wright, Norman Albert, Jr. *middle school educator*

Whippany
Golden, John F. *packaging company executive*
Petitto, Barbara Buschell *artist*
Scroggs, Deb Lee *communications professional*

Whitehouse Station
Atieh, Michael Gerard *accountant*
Douglas, Robert Gordon, Jr. *physician*
Gilmartin, Raymond V. *health care products company executive*
Harvey Gibbs, Jane *graphic designer*
Lewent, Judy Carol *pharmaceutical executive*
McDonald, Mary M. *lawyer*
Nulman, Philip Roy *advertising executive*

Whiting
Husselman, Grace *retired innkeeper, educator*

Wildwood
Scully, Robert *museum director, curator*

Williamstown
†Bogis, Nana Eileen *librarian*
Morrison, Howard Irwin *computer services executive*

Willingboro
Bass, Joseph Oscar *minister*
Chagnon, Lucille Tessier *literacy and developmental learning specialist*
Collard, Thomas Albert *transportation executive*
Greene, Natalie Constance *protective services official*
Ingerman, Peter Zilahy *infosystems consultant*
Jackson, Wayne Samuel *university administrator, communications educator*

Winfield Park
James, Barbara Frances *school nurse, special education educator*

Woodbridge
Becker, Frederic Kenneth *lawyer*
Brauth, Marvin Jeffrey *lawyer*
Brown, Morris *lawyer*
Buchsbaum, Peter A. *lawyer*
Chesky, Pamela Bosze *school system administrator*
Cirafesi, Robert J. *lawyer*
Constantinou, Clay *lawyer, ambassador*
Galkin, Samuel Bernard *orthodontist*
Hoberman, Stuart A. *lawyer*
Kuchta, John Andrew *management consultant*
Lepelstat, Martin L. *lawyer*
McCarthy, G. Daniel *lawyer*
Mount, Karl A. *manufacturing executive*
†Nagy-Hartnack, Lois Ann *art educator*
Schaff, Michael Frederick *lawyer*
†Scolamiero, Peter *retired artist*

Woodbury
Adler, Lewis Gerard *lawyer*
Banks, Theresa Ann *retired elementary education educator*
Duffield-Myers, Arlene Anna *elementary education educator*
Gehring, David Austin *physician, administrator, cardiologist*
Lamey, Mary Cocove *elementary guidance counselor*
Stambaugh, John Edgar *oncologist, hematologist, pharmacologist, educator*
Stuhltrager, Gary W. *state legislator*
Zane, Raymond J. *state senator, lawyer*

Woodcliff Lake
Jacobs, Charles Nathan *editor, writer*
Morath, Max Edward *entertainer, composer, writer*
Morrione, Melchior S. *management consultant, accountant*
Nachtigal, Patricia *lawyer, equipment manufacturing company executive*
Perrella, James Elbert *manufacturing company executive*
Watson, Christopher D. *fundraising and communications consultant*

Woodstown
Tatnall, Ann Weslager *reading educator*

Wyckoff
Bauer, Theodore James *physician*
Brown, James Joseph *manufacturing company executive*
Bucko, John Joseph *investment corporation executive*
Butterfield, Bruce Scott *publishing, communications and education executive, consultant*
Cropper, Susan Peggy *veterinarian*
Eiger, Richard William *retired publisher*
Lane, Nathan *insurance agency executive*
Lavery, Daniel P. *management consultant*
Leedom, E. Paul *banker*
Marcus, Linda Susan *dermatologist*
Miller, Walter Neal *insurance company consultant*
Mirza, Muhammad Zubair *product development company executive, researcher, engineering consultant, inventor*
Stahl, Alice Slater *psychiatrist*

Yardville
Telencio, Gloria Jean *elementary education educator*

NEW MEXICO

Abiquiu
Martinez, Ray *museum director*

Alamogordo
Ashdown, Franklin Donald *physician, composer*
Black, Maureen *realty company executive*
Flanary, Kathy Venita Moore *librarian*
Lee, Joli Fay Eaton *elementary education educator*
Stapp, John Paul *flight surgeon, retired air force officer*

Albuquerque
Adams, Clinton *artist, historian*
Addis, Richard Barton *lawyer*
Anaya, Rudolfo *educator, writer*
Anderson, Lawrence Keith *electrical engineer*
Andrade, Joseph J., III *counselor, educator*
Antreasian, Garo Zareh *artist, lithographer, art educator*
Aubin, Barbara Jean *artist*
Aurbach, Robert Michael *lawyer, consultant, photographer*

Austin, Edward Marvin *retired mechanical engineer, researcher*
Baca, Jim *mayor*
Baca Archulata, Margie *city clerk*
Bardacke, Paul Gregory *lawyer, former attorney general*
Barnes, Donald Ray *writer, genealogical researcher*
Barrow, Thomas Francis *artist, educator*
Barry, Steve *sculptor, educator*
Basso, Keith Hamilton *cultural anthropologist, linguist, educator*
Baum, Carl Edward *electromagnetic theorist*
Baum, Marsha Lynn *law educator*
Beach, Arthur O'Neal *lawyer*
Beckel, Charles Leroy *physics educator*
Bell, Stoughton *computer scientist, mathematician, educator*
Benson, Sharon Stovall *primary school educator*
†Black, Bruce D. *judge*
Boshier, Maureen Louise *health facilities administrator*
Bova, Vincent Arthur, Jr. *lawyer, consultant, photographer*
Brown, James Randall *mechanical engineer*
†Button, Luella Mary Watkins (Lue) *retired physicist, dog trainer, coach rescue team*
Byrne, Raymond Harry *electrical engineer*
Campbell, C(harles) Robert *architect*
Caplan, Edwin Harvey *university dean, accounting educator*
Cargo, David Francis *lawyer*
Caruso, Mark John *lawyer*
Cass, Barbara Fay *elementary school educator*
Chronister, Richard Davis *physicist*
Cia, Manuel Lopez *artist*
Clark, Teresa Watkins *psychotherapist, clinical counselor*
Cobb, John Candler *medical educator*
†Colbert, James E. *writer, educator*
Cole, Terri Lynn *organization administrator*
Coleman, Barbara McReynolds *artist*
Constantineau, Constance Juliette *retired banker*
Conway, John E. *federal judge*
Cully, Suzanne Maria *modern language educator*
Culpepper, Mabel Claire *artist*
†Currey, Richard *writer*
†Cutchen, J. Thomas *physicist*
Dal Santo, Diane *judge, writer*
D'Anza, Lawrence Martin *marketing educator*
Danziger, Jerry *broadcasting executive*
Davidson, Juli *creativity consultant*
†Deaton, William W., Jr. *federal judge*
†DeGiacomo, Robert J. *federal judge*
DePalo, William Anthony, Jr. *Latin American studies educator*
DeWitt, Mary Therese *consultant*
Donovan, Leslie Ann *honors division educator, consultant*
Dorato, Peter *electrical and computer engineering educator*
Drummond, Harold Dean *education educator*
Dunn, Dennis Steven *artist, illustrator*
Durant, Penny Lynne Raife *author, educator*
Easley, Loyce Anna *painter*
Edwards, William Sterling, III *cardiovascular surgeon*
Elliott, Charles Harold *clinical psychologist*
Ellis, Willis Hill *lawyer, educator*
Emlen, Warren Metz *computer-related services company owner*
†Etulain, Richard Wayne *historian, educator*
Evans, Bill (James William Evans) *dancer, choreographer, educator, arts administrator*
Evans, Pauline D. *physicist, educator*
Falcon, Patricia *educator, health psychologist*
Farmer, Terry D(wayne) *lawyer*
†Fermin, John Enriquez *investor*
†Fisher, Don Carlton *toxicologist*
Flanagan, Don *coach*
Fleury, Paul Aimé *university dean, physicist*
Flournoy, John Charles, Sr. *training specialist, retired military officer*
Freeman, Patricia Elizabeth *library and education specialist*
Freiwald, David Allen *physicist, mechanical engineer*
Friberg, George Joseph *electronics company executive*
Frings, Manfred Servatius *philosophy educator*
Fuchs, Beth Ann *research engineer*
Fuller, Anne Elizabeth Havens *English language and literature educator, consultant*
Gaines, Barry Joseph *English literature educator*
Gander, John Edward *biochemistry educator*
Garcia, F. Chris *academic administrator, political science educator, public opinion researcher*
†Garcia, Lorenzo F. *federal judge*
Garland, James Wilson, Jr. *retired physics educator*
Gatlin, Karen Christensen *English language educator*
Geary, David Leslie *communications executive, educator, consultant*
George, Roy Kenneth *minister*
Godfrey, Richard George *real estate appraiser*
Golden, Julius *advertising and public relations executive, lobbyist, investor*
Gonzales, Stephanie *state official*
Gordon, Larry Jean *public health administrator and educator*
†Gordon, William C. *college administrator*
Gorham, Frank DeVore, Jr. *petroleum company executive*
Goss, Jerome Eldon *cardiologist*
Graff, Pat Stuever *secondary education educator*
Green, Mae Maera *artist*
Gregory, George Ann *writer, Native American educator*
Gross, William Allen *mechanical engineer*
Grossetete, Ginger Lee *retired gerontology administrator, consultant*
Gruchalla, Michael Emeric *electronics engineer*
Hadas, Elizabeth Chamberlayne *publisher*
Hadley, William Melvin *college dean*
Haertling, Gene Henry *ceramic engineering educator*
Hakim, Besim Selim *architecture and urban design educator, researcher*
Hale, Bruce Donald *retired marketing professional*
Hall, Jerome William *research engineering educator*
Hancock, Don Ray *researcher*
†Hansen, C. Leroy *judge*
Hansen, Curtis LeRoy *federal judge*
Harden, Clinton Dewey, Jr. *restaurant owner, state official*
Harris, Fred R. *political science educator, former senator*
Harrison, Charles Wagner, Jr. *applied physicist*
Hart, Frederick Michael *law educator*
Haulenbeek, Robert Bogle, Jr. *government official*
Hausner, Jerry *electronics engineer, consultant*
Hayo, George Edward *management consultant*
Heffron, Warren A. *medical educator, physician*
Henderson, Rogene Faulkner *toxicologist, researcher*
Hooker, Van Dorn *architect, artist*
Horner, Harry Charles, Jr. *sales executive, theatrical and film consultant*
Hovel, Esther Harrison *art educator*
Howard, Jane Osburn *educator*
Hsi, David Ching Heng *plant pathologist and geneticist, educator*
Huling, Morris *fire chief*
Hull, McAllister Hobart, Jr. *retired university administrator*
Humphries, Sandra Lee Forger *artist, teacher*
Hutton, Paul Andrew *history educator, writer*
Hylko, James Mark *health physicist, certified quality auditor*
Janis, Kenneth M. *physician*
Jaramillo, Mari-Luci *federal agency administrator*
Johnson, Ralph Theodore, Jr. *physicist*
Jorgensen, Gary C. *elementary and secondary education educator*
Karni, Shlomo *engineering and religious studies educator*
Keating, David *photographer*
Kelly, John J. *prosecutor*
Keyler, Robert Gordon *material handling company executive*
King, James Nedwed *construction company executive, lawyer*
King, Lowell Restell *pediatric urologist*
Knospe, William Herbert *medical educator*
Korman, Nathaniel Irving *research and development company executive*
Kotchian, Sarah *municipal government official*
Kroll, Paul Benedict *auditor*
Krostag, Diane Theresa Michaels *clinical informatics analyst*
Lamberson, Anna Weinger *state legislative finance director, economist*
Lang, Thompson Hughes *publishing company executive*
Lattman, Laurence Harold *retired academic administrator*
Leach, Richard Maxwell, Jr. (Max Leach, Jr.) *corporate professional*
Lederer, John Martin *retired aeronautical engineer*
Lee-Smith, Hughie *artist, educator*
Lind, Levi Robert *classics educator, author*
Liss, Norman Richard *insurance executive*
Lockington, David *conductor*
Loftfield, Robert Berner *biochemistry educator*
Loubet, Jeffrey W. *lawyer*
Lowrance, Muriel Edwards *program specialist*
Maestas, Alex Walter *state agency clerk*
†Malone, Henry Charles *writer, rare book dealer*
Manz, Bruno Julius *retired government agency executive*
Marsh, William David *government operations executive*
Mateju, Joseph Frank *hospital administrator*
Mauderly, Joe Lloyd *pulmonary toxicologist*
May, Gerald William *university administrator, educator, civil engineering consultant*
May, Philip Alan *sociology educator*
Mayes, Richard Adolphus *electronics executive*
McFeeley, Mark B. *federal judge*
†McGuire, Susan G. *state director*
McNeil, Mark Frasher *broadcast executive*
Messersmith, Lanny Dee *lawyer*
Miller, Gardner Hartmann *paralegal*
Miller, Michael *literary arts researcher, writer*
Miller, Mickey Lester *retired school administrator*
Minahan, Daniel Francis *manufacturing company executive, lawyer*
Mitchell, Lindell Marvin *financial planner*
Molzen, Dayton Frank *consulting engineering executive*
Moore, James C. *museum director*
Moore, Todd Allen *poet*
Mora, Federico *neurosurgeon*
Mueller, Diane Mayne *lawyer*
Multhaup, Merrel Keyes *artist*
Myers, Carol McClary *retired sales administrator, editor*
Nagatani, Patrick Allan Ryoichi *artist, art educator*
†Nagengast, Carole *anthropology educator*
Napolitano, Leonard Michael *anatomist, university administrator*
Nash, Gerald David *historian*
Navarro, Janyte Janine *environmental educator*
Nevin, Jean Shaw *artist*
Ofte, Donald *retired environmental executive, consultant*
Omer, George Elbert, Jr. *orthopaedic surgeon, hand surgeon, educator*
O'Neil, Daniel Joseph *science research executive, research educator*
Oppedahl, Phillip Edward *computer company executive*
Orman, John Leo *software engineer, writer*
Ortiz y Pino, Gerald *municipal official*
Papike, James Joseph *geology educator, science institute director*
Parker, James Aubrey *federal judge*
Parsley, Steven Dwayne *title company executive*
Paster, Janice Dubinsky *lawyer, former state legislator*
Peck, Ralph Brazelton *civil engineering educator, consultant*
Peck, Richard Earl *academic administrator, playwright, novelist*
Peña, Juan José *interpreter*
Perez-Castro, Ana Veronica *developmental biology researcher*
Pirkl, James Joseph *industrial designer, educator, writer*
†Pohl, Elizabeth *contracting company executive*
Prindle, Robert William *geotechnical engineer*
Pritchard, Betty Jean *art educator*
†Puglisi, Richard L. *federal judge*
Rael, Lawrence *city administrator*
Ramo, Roberta Cooper *lawyer*
Rice, Linda Angel *music educator*
†Rios, Phillip Peña *village administrator*
Roberts, Dennis William *association executive*
Rodriguez, William Joseph *vocational counselor, mental health professional*
Roehl, Jerrald J. *lawyer*
Romero, Jeff *lawyer*
Romig, Alton Dale, Jr. *materials scientist, educator*
†Rose, Stewart *federal judge*
Ross, Marie Heise *retired librarian*
†Roth, Frank J. *computer scientist*
Royle, Anthony William *accountant*
Rutherford, Thomas Truxtun, II *former state senator, county commissioner*
Sabatini, William Quinn *architect*
Saland, Linda Carol *anatomy educator, neuroscience researcher*
Samara, George Albert *engineer*
Sanchez, Robert Fortune *archbishop*
Sanderlin, Terry Keith *counselor*
Schoen, Stevan Jay *lawyer*
Schuler, Alison Kay *lawyer*
Schwerin, Karl Henry *anthropology educator, researcher*
Sedillo, Orlando Delano *city solid waste management director*
Seiler, Fritz Arnold *physicist*
Shaw, Mark Howard *lawyer, business owner, entrepreneur*
Sheehan, Michael Jarboe *archbishop*
Sickels, Robert Judd *political science educator*
Sisk, Daniel Arthur *lawyer*
Slade, Lynn Heyer *lawyer*
Smartt, Richard A. *museum director*
Smith, Katherine Theresa *human resources specialist, small business owner*
Smyer, Myrna Ruth *drama educator*
Snell, Patricia Poldervaart *librarian, consultant*
Sobolewski, John Stephen *computer scientist, consultant*
Solomon, Arthur Charles *pharmacist*
Stahl, Jack Leland *real estate company executive*
Stamm, Robert Jenne *building contractor, construction company executive*
Stevenson, James Richard *radiologist, lawyer*
†Stitelman, Leonard *educator*
Straus, Lawrence Guy *anthropology educator, editor-in-chief*
Stuart, Cynthia Morgan *university administrator*
Stuart, David Edward *anthropologist, author, educator*
Studer, James Edward *geological engineer*
Sullivan, Terry Brian *semiconductor plant executive*
†Svet, Don J. *federal judge*
Swenka, Arthur John *food products executive*
Tackman, Arthur Lester *newspaper publisher, management consultant*
Tainter, Joseph Anthony *archaeologist*
Thomas, Douglas Graham *technology company executive, communications consultant*
Thompson, Rufus E. *lawyer*
Thorson, James Llewellyn *English language educator*
Tinnin, Thomas Peck *real estate professional*
Townsend, Alvin Neal *artist*
Turner, William Joseph *retired psychiatrist*
Uhlenhuth, Eberhard Henry *psychiatrist, educator*
Vianco, Paul Thomas *metallurgist*
Vizcaino, Henry P. *mining engineer, consultant*
Wainio, Mark Ernest *insurance company consultant*
Waitzkin, Howard Bruce *physician, sociologist, educator*
Walch, Peter Sanborn *museum director, publisher*
Weems, Mary Ann *art gallery owner*
Weh, Allen Edward *airline executive*
White, Jennifer Phelps *counselor*
White, Robert Milton *lawyer*
Wilkinson, Frances Catherine *librarian, educator*
Winslow, Walter William *psychiatrist*
Witkin, Joel-Peter *photographer*
Wong, Phillip Allen *osteopathic physician*
Wood, Gerald Wayne *electrical engineer*
Worrell, Richard Vernon *orthopedic surgeon, college dean*
Zink, Lee Berkey *academic administrator, economist, educator*
Zumwalt, Ross Eugene *forensic pathologist, educator*

Alto
Thrasher, Jack Dwayne *toxicologist, researcher, consultant*
Zeitelhack, Gloria Jeanne *artist*

Arroyo Hondo
Davis, Ronald *artist, printmaker*

Artesia
Horner, Elaine Evelyn *secondary education educator*
Robinson, J. Kenneth *religious organization administrator, minister*
Sarwar, Barbara Duce *educational consultant*

Aztec
†Van Auken, Ginger Suzanne *mathematics educator*

Belen
Gutjahr, Allan Leo *mathematics educator, researcher*
Smith, Helen Elizabeth *retired career officer*
Toliver, Lee *mechanical engineer*

Bluewater
Marquez, Martina Zenaida *retired elementary education educator*

Bosque Farms
Kelly, Brian Matthew *industrial hygienist*

Cannon AFB
Chrisman, Lilly Belle *medical/surgical nurse, educator*

Carlsbad
Carpenter, Sheila H. *critical care and medical/surgical nurse*
D'Antonio, Kay Bishop *special education educator*
Deckert, Frank *park administrator*
Goldstein, Barry Bruce *biologist, food company executive, lawyer*
Gossett, Janine Lee *middle school educator*
†Kidd, Don *bank executive*
Markle, George Bushar, IV *surgeon*
Moore, Bobbie Fay *geriatrics nurse practitioner, nurse administrator*
Regan, Muriel *librarian*
Speed, Lynn Elizabeth *nurse practitioner*

Cebolla
Berryman, Donald Carroll *cattle rancher*

Cedar Crest
Rypka, Eugene Weston *microbiologist*
Sheppard, Jack W. *retired career officer*

Chama
Moser, Robert Harlan *physician, educator, writer*

Clovis
†Tharp, Fred C., Jr. *federal judge, lawyer*

Corrales
Adams, James Frederick *psychologist, educational administrator*
Eisenstadt, Pauline Doreen Bauman *investment company executive*
Page, Jake (James K. Page, Jr.) *writer, editor*

Crownpoint
Tolino, Arlene Becenti *elementary education educator*

Deming
Rogers, Alice Louise *retired bank executive, writer, researcher*
Sherman, Frederick Hood *lawyer*
Snyder, Charles Theodore *geologist*

Edgewood
Hamilton, Jerald *musician*

Embudo
Rogers, Benjamin Talbot *consulting engineer, solar energy consultant*

Farmington
Anderson, Mark Eugene *specialized truck driver, safety inspector*
Doig, Beverly Irene *systems specialist*
Finch, Thomas Wesley *corrosion engineer*
Garretson, Owen Loren *mechanical and chemical engineer*
Graham, Warren Kirkland *dentist*
Gurley, Curtis Raymond *lawyer*
Luttrell, Mary Lou *elementary educator*
MacCallum, (Edythe) Lorene *pharmacist*
Mathers, Margaret *charitable agency consultant, copy editor*
Neidhart, James Allen *physician, educator*
Plummer, Steven Tsosie, Sr. *bishop*
Thompson, Barbara Ann *retired physical education educator*
Webb, Marlo L. *automobile executive, banking executive*

Galisteo
Lippard, Lucy Rowland *writer, lecturer*

Gallup
Cattaneo, Jacquelyn Annette Kammerer *artist, educator*
Fellin, Octavia Antoinette *retired librarian*
Fuhs, Terry Lynn *emergency room nurse, educator*
†Ionta, Robert W. *federal judge, lawyer*
Miller, Elizabeth Heidbreder *dean instruction*

Grants
Lujan, John *landmark administrator*

Hobbs
Garey, Donald Lee *pipeline and oil company executive*
Garey, Patricia Martin *artist*
Reagan, Gary Don *state legislator, lawyer*

Jemez Springs
Bennett, Noël *artist, author*
Sigler, Marjorie Diane *computer programming executive, analyst*

Kirtland AFB
Anderson, Christine Marlene *software engineer*
†Cliver, Jeffrey G. *career officer*
†Gideon, Francis C., Jr. *military officer*
Henry, Gary Norman *air force officer, astronautical engineer*
Voelz, David George *electrical engineer*

La Plata
Kent, Mollie *writer, publishing executive, editor*

Las Cruces
Bell, M. Joy Miller *financial planner, real estate broker*
Bird, Mary Francis *secondary education educator*
Bloom, John Porter *historian, editor, administrator, archivist*
Borman, Frank *former astronaut, laser patent company executive*
Boykin, William Edward *principal*
Bratton, Howard Calvin *federal judge*
Coburn, Horace Hunter *retired physics educator*
Cochrun, John Wesley *financial consultant*
Colbaugh, Richard Donald *mechanical engineer, educator, researcher*
†Conroy, William B. *university administrator*
Constantini, Louis Orlando *financial consultant, stockbroker*
Easterling, Kathy *school system administrator*
†Erhard, Thomas Agnew *English educator*
Eriksson, Anne-Marie *social services executive, educator*
Ford, Clarence Quentin *mechanical engineer, educator*
Gale, Thomas Martin *university dean*
†Galvan, Joe H. *federal judge*
†Graham, Kenneth John Emerson *English language educator*
Jacobs, Kent Frederick *dermatologist*
Kemp, John Daniel *biochemist, educator*
Lease, Jane Etta *environmental science consultant, retired librarian*
Lease, Richard Jay *police science educator, former police officer*
Lovell, Charles Muir *museum curator, photographer*
Lutz, William Lan *lawyer*
Martin, Connie Ruth *lawyer*
Matthews, Larryl Kent *mechanical engineering educator*
Medoff, Mark Howard *playwright, screenwriter, novelist*
Morgan, John Derald *electrical engineer*
Myers, R. David *library director, dean*
†Nelson-Humphries, Tessa *writer, educator*
Neumann, Rita *lawyer*
Newman, Edgar Leon *historian, educator*
Pennington, Robert Michael *communications educator, consultant*
Perroni, Carol *artist, painter*
Peterson, Robin Tucker *marketing educator*
Pinnow, Timothy Dayne *theater educator, fight choreographer*
Ramirez, Ricardo *bishop*

Reeves, Billy Dean *obstetrics and gynecology educator emeritus*
Ritter, Sallie *painter, sculptor*
Roscoe, Stanley Nelson *psychologist, aeronautical engineer*
Schemnitz, Sanford David *wildlife biology educator*
Schweikart, Debora Ellen *lawyer*
Sharp, George Lawrence *counselor*
†Smith, Leslie C. *federal judge*
Talamantes, Roberto *developmental pediatrician*
Thayer, Michael J. *secondary education educator*
Ward, James D. *government educator, writer*
Welsh, Mary McAnaw *educator, family mediator*
Wilson, Keith Charles *retired English educator, poet, short story writer*

Las Vegas
Croxton, Dorothy Audrey Simpson *speech educator*
Riley, Carroll Lavern *anthropology educator*

Lordsburg
Renteria, Donna Jo Gonzales *elementary education educator*

Los Alamos
Becker, Stephen A. *physicist, designer*
Bell, George Irving *biophysics researcher*
Colgate, Stirling Auchincloss *physicist*
Engelhardt, Albert George *physicist*
Foryst, Carole *computer electronics executive*
Friar, James Lewis *physicist*
Garvey, Doris Burmester *environmental administrator*
Gibson, Benjamin Franklin *physicist*
Goldberg, David Charles *computer company executive*
Greene Lloyd, Nancy Ellen *infosystems specialist, physicist*
Gregg, Charles Thornton *research company executive*
Grilly, Edward Rogers *physicist*
Jackson, James F. *nuclear engineer*
Jagnow, David Henry *petroleum geologist*
Johnson, Mikkel Borlaug *physicist*
Judd, O'Dean P. *physicist*
Keepin, George Robert, Jr. *physicist*
Kellner, Richard George *mathematician, computer scientist*
Kubas, Gregory Joseph *research chemist*
†Lee, David Mallin *physicist*
Makaruk, Hanna Ewa *theoretical physicist*
Matlack, George Miller *radiochemist*
McComas, David John *science administrator, space physicist*
McDonald, Thomas Edwin, Jr. *electrical engineer*
Mendius, Patricia Dodd Winter *editor, educator, writer*
Mihalas, Dimitri Manuel *astronomer, educator*
Mitchell, Terence Edward *materials scientist*
Mjolsness, Raymond Charles *retired physicist, researcher*
Moore, Tom O. *program administrator*
Nekimken, Judy Marie *secondary school educator*
Nix, James Rayford *nuclear physicist, consultant*
O'Brien, Harold Aloysius, Jr. *nuclear chemist, physics researcher, consultant*
Orndoff, Elizabeth Carlson *retired reference librarian, educator*
Pack, Russell T. *theoretical chemist*
Penneman, Robert Allen *retired chemist*
†Pond, Daniel James *ergonomist*
Press, William Henry *astrophysicist, computer scientist*
Ramirez, Carlos Brazil *college administrator*
Redmond, Bill *former congressman, minister*
Rosen, Louis *physicist*
Sarracino, Margaret C. *artist*
Sayre, Edward Charles *librarian*
Seidel, Tammy Sue *secondary education educator*
Selden, Robert Wentworth *physicist, science advisor*
Smith, Fredrica Emrich *rheumatologist, internist*
Smith, James Lawrence *research physicist*
Snell, Charles Murrell *physicist, astrophysicist*
Stoddard, Stephen Davidson *ceramic engineer, former state senator*
Terrell, (Nelson) James *physicist*
Trewhella, Jill *biophysicist*
Van Tuyle, Gregory Jay *nuclear engineer*
Wadstrom, Ann Kennedy *retired anesthesiologist*
Wahl, Arthur Charles *retired chemistry educator*
Wallace, Jeannette Owens *state legislator*
Wallace, Terry Charles, Sr. *technical administrator, researcher, consultant*
†Weaver, Michael James *mechanical engineer*
Whitten, David George *chemistry educator*
Williams, Joel Mann *polymer material scientist*
WoldeGabriel, Giday *research geologist*
Zweig, George *physicist, neurobiologist*

Los Lunas
Behrend, Betty Ann *municipal official*
Graham, Robert Albert *research physicist*
Pope, John William *judge, law educator*

Milan
Kanesta, Nellie Rose *chemical dependency counselor*

Montezuma
Geier, Philip Otto, III *college president*

Mora
Hanks, Eugene Ralph *land developer, cattle rancher, forester, retired naval officer*
Mossavar-Rahmani, Bijan *oil and gas company executive*

Navajo
†Boomer, John D. *artist, sculptor*

Nogal
Moeller, Susan Elaine *artist*

Placitas
Bencke, Ronald Lee *financial executive*
Dunmire, William Werden *author, photographer*
Smith, Richard Bowen *retired national park superintendent*

Playas
Clifton, Judy Raelene *association administrator*

Portales
Agogino, George Allen *anthropologist, educator*
†Dixon, Steven Michael *university administrator*

Edwards, Carolyn Mullenax *public relations executive*
Goodwin, Martin Brune *radiologist*
Morris, Donald *tax specialist*
Overton, Edwin Dean *campus minister, educator*
†Poynor, Clifford Franklin *credit corporation owner, rancher*
Romo, Jose León *library consultant*
Williamson, Jack (John Stewart) *writer*

Questa
Sharkey, Richard David *architectural artisan, inventor, musician*

Ranchos De Taos
Marx, Nicki Diane *sculptor, painter*

Rio Rancho
†Belovarski, Borislav V. *scriptwriter, writer*
Duitman, Lois Robinson *artist, writer*
†Haney, Kevin Scott *administrator*
Meyerson, Barbara Tobias *elementary school educator*
Warder, William *artist*
Young, Frederic Hisgin *information systems executive, data processing consultant*

Rociada
Reed, Carol Louise *designer*

Rodeo
Scholes, Robert Thornton *physician, research administrator*

Roswell
Anderson, Donald Bernard *oil company executive*
Armstrong, Billie Bert *retired highway contractor*
Baldock, Bobby Ray *federal judge*
Bassett, John Walden, Jr. *lawyer*
Casey, Barbara A. Perea *state representative, school superintendent*
Haines, Thomas David, Jr. *lawyer*
Jennings, Emmit M. *surgeon*
Johnston, Mary Ellen *nursing educator*
†Kraft, Richard Lee *lawyer*
Miller, Candi *critical care nurse*
Miller, Nelson Alvin *retired army officer, public affairs administrator*
Olson, Richard Earl *lawyer, state legislator*
Pretti, Bradford Joseph *lay worker, insurance company executive, retired*
Robinson, Mark Leighton *oil company executive, petroleum geologist, horse farm owner*
Rosemire, Adeline Louise *writer, publisher*
Wiggins, Kim Douglas *artist, art dealer*

Ruidoso
Heger, Herbert Krueger *education educator*
Stover, Carolyn Nadine *middle school educator*
Thomsen, David Allen *lawyer*
Wade, Pamela Sue *women's health nurse*

Ruidoso Downs
Eldredge, Bruce Beard *museum director*

Sandia Park
Greenwell, Ronald Everett *communications executive*
Wilczynski, Janusz S. *packaging technology executive, physicist*

Santa Fe
Adams, Phoebe *sculptor*
Agresto, John *college president*
Allen, Page Randolph *artist*
Allen, Terry *artist*
Allio, Robert John *management consultant, educator*
Alsaker, Robert John *information systems specialist*
Ashman, Stuart *museum director*
Baca, Joseph Francis *state supreme court justice*
Baerwald, John Edward *traffic and transportation engineer, educator*
Ballard, Louis Wayne *composer*
Bauer, Betsy (Elizabeth Bauer) *artist*
Bergé, Carol *author*
Berne, Stanley *author*
Besing, Ray Gilbert *lawyer, writer*
Bienvenu, John Charles *lawyer*
Bradley, Walter D. *lieutenant governor, real estate broker*
Brandt, Richard Paul *communications and entertainment company executive*
Brown, Alan Whittaker *accountant*
Calloway, Larry *columnist*
Campos, Santiago E. *federal judge*
†Candelaria, Nash *writer*
Carpenter, Richard Norris *lawyer*
Cerny, Charlene Ann *museum director*
Charles, Cheryl *non-profit and business executive*
Clift, William Brooks, III *photographer*
Coffield, Conrad Eugene *lawyer*
Cowan, George Arthur *chemist, bank executive, director*
Crosby, John O'Hea *conductor, opera manager*
Culbert, Peter Van Horn *lawyer*
Davis, Shelby Moore Cullom *investment executive, consultant*
Dechert, Peter *photographer, writer, foundation administrator*
DiMaio, Virginia Sue *gallery owner*
Dirks, Lee Edward *newspaper executive*
Dodds, Robert James, III *lawyer*
Dreisbach, John Gustave *investment banker*
Enyeart, James L. *museum director*
Farber, Steven Glenn *lawyer*
Ferguson, Glenn Walker *consultant, writer, lecturer*
Fisher, Robert Alan *laser physicist*
Forsdale, (Chalmers) Louis *education and communication educator*
Franchini, Gene Edward *state supreme court justice*
Gaddes, Richard *performing arts administrator*
Gallenkamp, Charles *writer*
Gell-Mann, Murray *theoretical physicist, educator*
Gildzen, Alex *writer*
Gilmour, Edward Ellis *psychiatrist*
Giovanielli, Damon Vincent *physicist, consulting company executive*
Groseclose, Everett Harrison *retired editor*
Hanson, Cappy Love *writer, musician, singer, composer*
Harcourt, Robert Neff *educational administrator, journalist, genealogist*
Harding, Marie *ecological executive, artist*
Hatfield, Christian Andrew *lawyer*
Hice, Michael *editor, marketing professional*

Hickey, John Miller *lawyer*
Hoffmann, Louis Gerhard *immunologist, educator, sex therapist*
†Jackson, Polly *artist*
Johnson, Gary Earl *governor*
Johnson, William Hugh, Jr. *state official, hospital administrator*
Jones, Walter Harrison *chemist, educator*
†Kaiser, Don *media trainer*
Kelly, Paul Joseph, Jr. *judge*
Kennedy, Roger George *museum director, park service executive*
†Kinderwater, Diane *state official*
Kingman, Elizabeth Yelm *anthropologist*
Knapp, Edward Alan *retired government administrator, scientist*
Lamb, Elizabeth Searle *freelance writer, poet*
LaTourrette, Kathryn *family therapist, counselor, artist*
Lehmberg, Stanford Eugene *historian, educator*
Leibowitz, Jack Richard *physicist, educator*
Leon, Bruno *architect, educator*
LeRose, Thomas M. *photographer*
Lewis, James Beliven *state government official*
Lichtenberg, Margaret Klee *publishing company executive*
Lindsay, Richard Paul *artist, jewelry designer*
Livesay, Thomas Andrew *museum administrator, lecturer*
Longley, Bernique *artist, painter, sculptor*
Lukac, George Joseph *fundraising executive*
†Madrid, Patricia Ann *state attorney general, lawyer*
Maehl, William Henry *historian, university administrator, educational consultant*
†McCarthy, Laura Falk *forester*
McClaugherty, Joe L. *lawyer, educator*
Mc Kinney, Robert Moody *newspaper editor and publisher*
Melnick, Alice Jean (AJ Melnick) *counselor*
Mercer, James Lee *management consultant*
Merrin, Seymour *computer marketing company executive*
Miller, Dwight Richard *cosmetologist, corporate executive, hair designer*
Miller, Edmund Kenneth *retired electrical engineer, educator*
Minzner, Pamela B. *state supreme court justice*
Mitio, John, III *state agency administrator*
Moll, Deborah Adelaide *lawyer*
Montgomery, Michael Davis *real estate investor*
Montoya, Michael A. *state treasurer, accountant*
Moore, Jay Winston *director cytogenetics laboratory*
†Morris, Sidney Helen *educational administrator*
Myers, Charlotte Will *biology educator*
Noble, Merrill Emmett *retired psychology educator, psychologist*
Noland, Charles Donald *lawyer, educator*
†Noyes, Stanley Tinning *writer, educator, arts administrator*
Nuckolls, Leonard Arnold *retired hospital administrator*
Nurock, Robert Jay *investment analysis company executive*
Odell, John H. *construction company executive*
Pearson, Margit Linnea *development company executive*
Perkins, Linda Gillespie *real estate executive*
Perry, Nancy Estelle *psychologist*
Peterson, Harry Austin, Sr. *television producer, writer*
Phipps, Claude Raymond *research scientist*
Pickrell, Thomas Richard *retired oil company executive*
Pound, John Bennett *lawyer*
†Racuya-Robbins, Ann Elizabeth *artist*
Randolph, Somers *sculptor*
Ratliff, Floyd *biophysics educator, scientist*
Robinson, Charles Wesley *energy company executive*
Robinson, Richard Gary *management consultant, accountant*
Rogers, Jerry L. *federal agency administrator*
Romanowski, Thomas Andrew *physics educator*
Rubenstein, Bernard *orchestra conductor*
Ruybalid, Louis Arthur *social worker, community development consultant*
Saurman, Andrew (Skip Saurman) *state agency executive*
Schaafsma, Polly Dix *archaeologist, researcher*
Schoenborn, Benno P. *biophysicist, educator*
Schwartz, George R. *physician*
Schwarz, Michael *lawyer*
Sciame, Donald Richard *computer systems analyst, dentist, magician, locksmith*
Serna, Patricio *state supreme court justice*
Shubart, Dorothy Louise Tepfer *artist, educator*
Stedman, Myrtle Lillian *artist*
Stevens, Ron A. *lawyer, public interest organization administrator*
Stieber, Tamar *journalist*
Stringer, Gail Griffin *information systems consultant*
Struever, Stuart McKee *archaeologist*
Sumner, Gordon, Jr. *retired military officer*
Swartz, William John *retired transportation resources company executive*
Tarn, Nathaniel *poet, translator, educator*
Taylor, Beverly Lacy *stringed instrument restorer, classical guitarist*
Tenison, John Hughes *civil engineer, retired military officer*
Torres, Gilbert Vincent *elementary education educator*
Turney, Thomas Charles *civil engineer*
Vazquez, Martha Alicia *judge*
†Verant, William J. *state agency administrator*
Vigil-Giron, Rebecca *state official*
Watkins, Stephen Edward *accountant, newspaper executive*
Way, Jacob Edson, III *museum director*
Weckesser, Susan Oneacre *lawyer*
Wentz, Christopher James *state agency administrator*
†White, Darren *state agency administrator*
White, David Hywel *physics educator*
Williams, Ralph Chester, Jr. *physician, educator*
Williams, Stephen *anthropologist, educator*
Wilson, Bart Allen *media director, marketing consultant, educator*
Wise, Janet Ann *college official*
Wood, Nancy C. *author*
Yalman, Ann *lawyer*
Zorie, Stephanie Marie *lawyer*

Seneca
Monroe, Kendyl Kurth *retired lawyer*

Shiprock
Hill, Melodie Anne *special education educator*
West, Dorcas Joy *women's health nurse*

Silver City
Bettison, Cynthia Ann *museum director, archaeologist*
Foy, Thomas Paul *lawyer, retired state legislator, retired banker*
French, Laurence Armand *social science educator, psychology educator*
†Hall, Edward Payson, Jr. *communication educator*
Hall, Jean Quintero *communication educator*
Hamlin, Don Auer *financial executive*
†Hodges, Norman *retired district judge*
Snedeker, John Haggner *university president*
White, Don William *rancher, minister*

Smith Lake
Hansen, Harold B., Jr. *principal*

Socorro
Broadhead, Ronald Frigon *petroleum geologist, geology educator*
Kottlowski, Frank Edward *geologist*
†McKee, John DeWitt *retired English educator*

Sunspot
Altrock, Richard Charles *astrophysicist*
Beckers, Jacques Maurice *astrophysicist*

Taos
Bacon, Wallace Alger *speech communications educator, author*
Bell, Larry Stuart *artist*
Ebie, William D. *museum director*
†Grunthal, Donna Marie *art gallery executive, artist*
Holte, Debra Leah *investment executive, financial analyst*
Lackey, Marcia Ann *writer*
Lipscomb, Anna Rose Feeny *entrepreneur, arts organizer, fundraiser*
Manzo, Anthony Joseph *painter*
Martin, Agnes *artist*
Martin, Kena Sue *educator*
Pasternack, Robert Harry *school psychologist*
Scott, Doug *sculptor*
Witt, David L. *curator, writer*
Young, Jon Nathan *archeologist*

Tesuque
Gose, Celeste Marlene *writer*
Novak, Joe *artist*

Tijeras
Berry, Dawn Bradley *writer, lawyer*
Jager, Tom *Olympic athlete, swimmer*
Van Arsdel, Eugene Parr *tree pathologist, meteorologist*

Tucumcari
Woodard, Dorothy Marie *insurance broker*

Vaughn
Maes, Pat Julian *secondary education educator*

Watrous
Myers, Harry Charles *national monument administrator*

White Sands
†Gatanas, Harry D. *career officer*
Kestner, Robert Richard, II *engineering psychologist*
Molander, Glenn M. *human resources executive*

White Sands Missile Range
Arthur, Paul Keith *electronic engineer*

NEW YORK

Lipinsky de Orlov, Lucian Christopher *consultant*

Accord
Rivera, Beatriz *writer, educator*
Ryan, Michael Paul *artist*

Acra
Gaffney, Kathleen Mary *writer, videographer*

Adams Center
Hood, Thomas Gregory *minister*

Afton
Church, Richard Dwight *electrical engineer, scientist*
Rafter, Sandra Joy *special education educator*
Schwartz, Aubrey Earl *artist*

Akron
Greatbatch, Wilson *biomedical engineer*

Albany
Able, Kenneth Paul *biology educator*
Aceto, Vincent John *librarian, educator*
Alexander, Ellin Dribben *financial marketing company executive*
†Angelis, Janet Ives *executive*
Axelrod, Susan L. *fundraiser*
†Baaklini, Abdo Iskandar *educator*
Barron, Kevin Delgado *physician, educator*
Barsamian, J(ohn) Albert *lawyer, lecturer, educator, criminologist, arbitrator*
Bawa, Sukhdev Raj *biomedical researcher, educator, administrator*
Beach, John Arthur *lawyer*
Bee, Clair Francis Jr.
Bellacosa, Joseph W. *state supreme court justice*
Bennett, Edward Virdell, Jr. *surgeon*
Berman, Carol *commissioner*
Black, Robert Charles *author, lawyer*
Blount, Stanley Freeman *marketing educator*
Borys, Theodor James *state agency data center administrator*
Bowen, Mary Lu *ecumenical developer, community organizer*
Bradley, Edward James *state official, computer programmer and analyst*
Bradley, Wesley Holmes *physician*
Branigan, Helen Marie *educational administrator*
†Brown, David P. *public relations executive*
Brunner, Robert Vincent, Jr. *civil engineer*
Buldrini, George James *lawyer*
Burkart, Peter Thomas *hematologist*
Canestrari, Ronald *state legislator*
Capone, Robert Joseph *physician, educator*

Catalano, Jane Donna lawyer
Chretien, Margaret Cecilia public administrator
Clarey, Donald Alexander government affairs consultant
†Clifford, George W. college administrator
†Cohen, Tom F. critic
Cole, John Adam insurance executive
Cooke, Lawrence Henry lawyer, former state chief judge
†Corcoran, Colleen Marie grant and contract administrator
Cornell, Ralph Lawrence, Jr. publishing executive
Couch, Leslie Franklin lawyer
Creegan, Robert Francis philosophy educator, writer
†Croce, Alan J. government agency executive
Cross, Robert Francis city official
Csiza, Charles Karoly veterinarian, microbiologist
Davis, Paul Joseph endocrinologist
†DeBuono, Barbara Ann physician, state official
DeFelice, Eugene Anthony physician, medical educator, consultant, magician
D'Elia, Christopher Francis marine biologist
Demerjian, Kenneth Leo atmospheric science educator, research center director
DeNuzzo, Rinaldo Vincent pharmacy educator
Derderian, John A. systems analyst
Destito, RoAnn M. state legislator
†Doherty, Glen Patrick lawyer
†Donohue, Mary state official
Donovan, Robert Alan English educator
Dougherty, James orthopedic surgeon, educator, author
Doyle, Joseph Theobald physician, educator
Dulin, Thomas N. lawyer
Eckstein, Jerome philosopher, educator
Edmonds, Richard H. dean
Enemark, Richard Demeritt educational administrator
Fadeley, Eleanor Adeline secondary education educator
Fakundiny, Robert Harry geologist, educator, consultant
Fanuele, Frank John engineering executive
Farley, Eugene Joseph accountant
Farley, Hugh T. state senator, law educator
Faul, Karene Tarquin art department administrator
Favreau, Susan Debra management consultant
Ferrara, Donna state legislator
First, Tina Lincer writer
†Forsberg, Caroline Bernice acadamic administrator
Frank, Francine Harriet language educator, linguist
Frost, Robert Edwin chemistry educator
Garner, Doris Traganza educator
Gaw, James Richard corporate manager
†Glasel, David Paul lawyer
Glick, Deborah J. state legislator
Granderath, Walter Joseph tax administrator
Greene, Aurelia state legislator
Hahner, June Edith history educator
Hancox, David Robert audit administrator, educator
†Hancox, Steven J. auditor, state official
Hannon, Kemp state senator
Happ, Harvey Heinz electrical engineer, educator
Harenberg, Paul E. state legislator
Harris, Eric R. policy analyst, county official
†Hart, John P. archaeologist
Herman, Robert Samuel former state official, economist, educator
Herrick, Kristine Ford graphic design educator
Hill, Earlene Hooper state legislator
Hill, Mars Andrew writer, retired civil engineer
Hitchcock, Karen Ruth biology educator, university dean, academic administrator
Hobart, Thomas Yale, Jr. union president
Hochberg, Audrey G. state legislator
Hoffman, Nancy E. lawyer
Hoffmeister, Jana Marie cardiologist
Holmes, Walter John public relations consultant, author
Holstein, William Kurt business administration educator
†Homer, David Robert federal judge
Horn, Martin F. state agency administrator
Howard, Lyn Jennifer medical educator
Hsia, Franklin Wen-Hai computer programmer, systems analyst, consultant
Hubbard, Howard James bishop
Hudson, Paul Stephen lawyer, consumer advocate
Jacobs, Rhoda S. state legislator
Jakes, Lara Christine newspaper reporter
Kadamus, James Alexander educational administrator
†Kahn, Lawrence E. judge
Kahn, Lawrence Edwin judge
Katz, William A. library science educator
Kaye, Judith Smith state supreme court chief justice
Kekes, John philosopher, educator
†Kennedy, Debbie A. plastic surgeon
Kennedy, William Joseph novelist, educator
Kim, Jai Soo physics educator
Kim, Paul David emergency medical administrator
†King, Joshua Adam plastic surgeon
Koff, Howard Michael lawyer
Kuhl, John R., Jr. state legislator
Lack, James J. state senator, lawyer
Laird, Edward DeHart, Jr. lawyer
Lane, Nancy Lucille mental health and critical care nurse
Lawton, Nancy artist
Lefkowitz, Jerome lawyer
Leichman, Kenneth William investment executive
Leichter, Franz S. state senator
Levine, Louis David museum director, archaeologist
Ley, Ronald psychologist, educator
†Littlefield, Robert E., Jr. federal judge
†Loneck, Barry Martin social work researcher, educator
Long, David Russell academic program director
Macario, Alberto Juan Lorenzo physician
Mancuso, J(ohn) James librarian
Mastrangelo, Lisa Siobhan humanities educator
Matusow, Naomi C. state legislator
Matuszek, John Michael, Jr. environmental scientist, educator, consultant
Mayersohn, Nettie state legislator
McKay, Donald Arthur mechanical engineer
Meacham, Norma Grace lawyer
Meader, John Daniel judge
Miles, Christine Marie museum director
†Mills, Richard P. state agency administrator
Miner, Roger Jeffrey federal judge
Moore, Gwen Lova social sciences educator
Morris, Margretta Elizabeth conservationist
Mueller, I. Lynn strategic planning and communications consultant
Murphy, Thomas Joseph governmental official
Murray, Kevin Francis commissioner
Nathan, Richard P(erle) political scientist, educator
Naumann, Hans J. manufacturing company executive
Olmsted, Ruth Martin editor
O'Neil, Chloe Ann retired state legislator
Ortloff, George Christian, Sr. (Chris Ortloff) journalist, state legislator
†Pardo, Theresa Ann project director
Pataki, George E. governor
Paterson, David Alexander state senator
†Patton, Gerald Wilson state agency administrator
Paulson, Peter John librarian, publishing company executive
Peaslee, Maurice Keenan lawyer
†Peinovich, Paula E. academic administrator
†Perone, Filomena Maria university administrator
Philip, George Michael pension fund administrator
Piedmont, Richard Stuart lawyer
Pohlsander, Hans Achim classics educator
†Polan, David Ray public administrator
Powers, John Kieran lawyer
Proskin, Arnold W. state assemblyman, lawyer
Pryse, Marjorie Lee American literature educator, researcher
Quackenbush, Roger E. retired secondary school educator
Reese, William Lewis philosophy educator
Reichert, Leo Edmund, Jr. biochemist, endocrinologist
Reid, William James social work educator
Reynolds, Karl David state official
Reynolds, William Peter legislative aide
Richbart, Carolyn Mae mathematics educator
Risemberg, Herman Mario pediatrician, educator
Robbins, Cornelius (Van Vorse) education administration educator
Roberts, Louis William classics and humanities educator
Robinson, John Bowers, Jr. bank holding company executive
Rosenfeld, Harry Morris editor
Rosenkrantz, Daniel J. computer science educator
Roy, Rob J. biomedical engineer, anesthesiologist
Ruggeri, Robert Edward lawyer
Ruzow, Daniel Arthur lawyer
Salkin, Patricia E. law educator
†Sánchez-Murray, Rita Zunilda secondary Spanish language and culture educator
Santiago, Nellie state legislator
Santola, Daniel Ralph lawyer
Sbuttoni, Michael James orthodontist, building contractor
Schmidt, John Thomas neurobiologist
Schneider, Allan Stanford biochemistry neuroscience and pharmacology educator, biomedical research scientist
Schwartz, M. Myles neuropsychologist
Shadrick, Betty Patterson university administrator, consultant
Shankman, Gary Charles art educator
Shields, Robert Michael state agency administrator
Shubert, Joseph Francis librarian
Siegel, David Donald law educator
Smith, Michael Ernest archaeologist, educator
Smith, Ralph Wesley, Jr. federal judge
Smith, Rex William journalist
Spitze, Glenna D. sociology educator
†Spitzer, Eliot state attorney general
Sponsler, Thomas H. law educator, dean
Sprow, Howard Thomas lawyer, educator
Standish, John Spencer textile manufacturing company executive
Stevens, Gregory Irving university administrator, educator
Stevens, Roy W. microbiologist
Stewart, Margaret McBride biology educator, researcher
Sturman, Lawrence Stuart health research administrator
Sullivan, Frances Taylor state legislator
Swartz, Donald Percy physician
†Taber, Harry Warren research scientist
Teevan, Richard Collier psychology educator
Tepper, Clifford allergist, immunologist, educator
Thompson, Frank Joseph political science educator
Thornberry, Terence Patrick criminologist, educator
Thornton, Maurice retired academic administrator
Ting, Joseph K. mechanical engineer
Toombs, Russ William laboratory director
Treadwell, Alexander F. state official
Tyksinski, Eugene Kory broadcast executive
Uhl, Richard Laurence physician, medical educator
Unger, Gere Nathan physician, lawyer
Ushkow, Bruce Scott emergency physician
Van Nortwick, Barbara Louise library director
Velella, Guy John state legislator
Vitaliano, Eric Nicholas state legislator, lawyer
Volker, Dale Martin state senator, lawyer
von Schack, Wesley W. energy services company executive
Wallender, Michael Todd lawyer
Weiss, Linda Wolff health systems administrator
Welch, Janet Martin librarian
Williams, C(harles) Wayne education educator
Wilson, Brian Eugene computer scientist
Wright, Theodore Paul, Jr. political science educator
Wukitsch, David John lawyer
Zacek, Joseph Frederick history educator, international studies consultant, East European culture and affairs specialist
Zimmerman, Joseph Francis political scientist, educator

Albertson
Ferber, Samuel publishing executive
Michaels, Craig Adam psychologist

Albion
†Bannister, Richard D sculptor
Lyman, Nathan Marquis lawyer

Alfred
Billeci, Andre George art educator, sculptor
Coll, Edward Girard, Jr. university president
Higby, (Donald) Wayne artist, educator
†Keirn, Wendy Gay athletic trainer
Keith, Timothy Zook psychology educator
Ott, Walter Richard academic administrator
Pye, Lenwood David materials science educator, researcher, consultant
Rand, Joella Mae nursing educator, counselor
Rossington, David Ralph physical chemistry educator
Spriggs, Richard Moore ceramic engineer, research center administrator
†Tolhurst, Fiona English language educator

Alfred Station
Love, Robert Lyman educational consulting company executive

Amherst
Anisman, Martin Jay academic administrator
Braun, Kazimierz Pawel theatrical director, writer, educator
Brown, Stephen Ira mathematics educator
Chang, Ching Ming (Carl Chang) business executive, mechanical engineer, educator
Clark, Donald Malin professional association executive
Cohen, Herman Nathan private investigator
Coover, James Burrell music educator
Cramer, Stanley Howard psychology educator, author
Hartwick, Patrick James special education educator
Jen, Frank Chifeng finance and management educator
Jones, E. Thomas lawyer
Kibby, Michael William reading educator
Kurtz, Paul publisher, philosopher, educator
Levy, Gerhard pharmacologist
Murray, William Michael lawyer
†Ross-Stefanie, Bonnie Jean information systems company executive
†Schultz, Susan M. school principal
Sobolewski, Timothy Richard marketing executive
†Wickert, Max Albrecht English educator
Wiesenberg, Jacqueline Leonardi lecturer

Amityville
†Curri, Joanne M. pharmaceutical company executive
Gicola, Paul middle school science educator, administrator
Liang, Vera Beh-Yuin Tsai psychiatrist, educator
Serpe, Salvatore John internist
Upadhyay, Yogendra Nath physician, educator

Amsterdam
†Tasher, Jacob otolaryngologist

Ancramdale
Weinstein, Joyce artist

Andover
Witherow, Catherine Saslawsky secondary school educator

Angola
Green, Gerard Leo priest, educator

Annandale On Hudson
Achebe, Chinua writer, humanities educator
Botstein, Leon college president, music historian, conductor
Ferguson, John Barclay biology educator
Manea, Norman writer, educator
Mayo-Winham, Carolyn Ann development executive
Mullen, William Cocke classics educator
Papadimitriou, Dimitri Basil economist, college administrator

Appleton
Singer, Thomas Kenyon international business consultant, farmer

Ardsley
†Fasanella, Ralph P. artist
Kuntzman, Ronald pharmacology research executive
Mohl, Allan S. social worker
Sokolow, Isobel Folb sculptor
Utermohlen, Herbert Georg dermatologist

Ardsley On Hudson
Stein, Milton Michael lawyer

Argyle
Bruce, David Lionel retired anesthesiologist, educator

Armonk
Bergson, Henry Paul professional association administrator
Bolduc, Ernest Joseph association management consultant
Donofrio, Nicholas M. computer engineer
†Dunton, Gary C. insurance company executive
Elliott, David H. insurance company executive
Elson, Charles stage designer, educator
Gerstner, Louis Vincent, Jr. diversified company executive
Harreld, James Bruce computer company executive
Kohnstamm, Abby E. marketing executive
Korn, Steven Eric medical publisher
Levy, Kenneth James advertising executive
McGroddy, James Cleary retired computer company executive, consultant
Mellors, Robert Charles physician, scientist, educator
Moskowitz, Stuart Stanley lawyer
Quinn, James W. lawyer
Ricciardi, Lawrence R. lawyer
Sharpe, Myron Emanuel publisher, editor, writer
Sydney, Doris S. sports touring company executive, interior designer
Wood, Teri Wilford lawyer

Astoria
Davidson, Rex L. association executive
Fassoulis, Satiris Galahad communications company executive
Matheson, Linda retired clinical social worker
Morrow, Scott Douglas choreographer, educator
Salzberg, Russ sportscaster
Sheridan, Ruth Stewart business development consultant
Somers, Steve sportscaster

Athens
Lew, Roger Alan manufacturing company executive

Attica
Taylor, Karen Marie education educator

Auburn
†Bragger, Stacey Eileen elementary education educator
Eldred, Thomas Gilbert secondary education educator, historian
Long, Michael Howard landscape architect
†Ohl, Thomas Anthony school counselor
Patterson, John Edward language educator
Wolczyk, Joseph Michael lawyer

Aurora
Leybold-Taylor, Karla Jolene college official
†Schwab, Linda S. chemistry educator
Shilepsky, Arnold Charles mathematics educator, computer consultant

Averill Park
Costello, Amelia Fusco educator
Haines, Walter Wells retired economics educator
Traver, Robert William, Sr. management consultant, author, lecturer, engineer

Babylon
Collis, Charles aircraft company executive
Epstein, Jeffrey Mark neurosurgeon
Haley, Priscilla Jane artist, printmaker
Hennelly, Edmund Paul lawyer, oil company executive
Lopez, Joseph Jack oil company executive, consultant
Meirowitz, Claire Cecile editor, public relations executive

Bainbridge
Goerlich, Shirley Alice Boyce publisher, educator, consultant

Baldwin
Lister, Bruce Alcott food scientist, consultant
Nicoleau, Mireille patient service coordinator, nurse, case manager
Sarnoff, Paul metals consultant, author, editor

Baldwin Place
Kurian, George Thomas publisher

Baldwinsville
†Hansen, Beverly Anne environmental policy educator
Kline, Carole June special education educator
†Niemiec, Paul Wallace, Jr. artist, pharmacist

Ballston Lake
Cotter, William Donald state commissioner, former newspaper editor
Fiedler, Harold Joseph electrical engineer, consultant
McCann, Chris (Christian David McCann) software engineer, educator
Miller, Clark Alvin human resource and organization management consultant
Silverman, Gerald Bernard journalist

Ballston Spa
Barba, Harry author, educator, publisher
†MacDonald, Bonney English educator
Westbrook, Jack Hall metallurgist, consultant

Bardonia
†DiCarlo, Bernard telecommunication executive

Barrytown
Higgins, Dick (Richard Carter Higgins) writer, publisher, composer, artist
Shimmyo, Theodore Tadaaki seminary president

Batavia
Rigerman, Ruth Underhill mathematics educator
Saleh, David John lawyer
Small, Bruce Michael health facility administrator
Steiner, Stuart college president

Bath
Davidsen, Donald R. state legislator
†Latham, Joseph William judge
†Wu, Shiming materials scientist, researcher

Bay Shore
Pinsker, Tillene Giller special education administrator
Sampino, Anthony F. physician, obstetrician and gynecologist
Shreve, Sue Ann Gardner retired health products company administrator
Williams, Tonda entrepreneur, consultant

Bayport
Poli, Kenneth Joseph editor, writer, photographer

Bayside
Adoquei, Sam art educator, artist
Gavencak, John Richard pediatrician, allergist
Lee, Long Looi artist
Shainis, Murray Joseph management consultant
Testa, Lauren English educator
Yin, Henry Chih-Peng educator
Zinn, William violinist, composer, business executive

Beacon
Mc Keown, William Taylor magazine editor, author
Moreno, Zerka Toeman psychodrama educator
†Rosenfeld, Stephen S. dentist
Stokes, Catherine Ann elementary education educator

Bear Mountain
Smith, Andrew Josef historian, publishing executive, naturalist, writer

Bearsville
Sands, Martha Mercer (Nichole René) artist, musician, performing artist, poet
Szyszka, Roswita Evelyn artist

Bedford
Atkins, Ronald Raymond lawyer
Benedek, Armand landscape architect
Bowman, James Kinsey publishing company executive, rare book specialist
Chase, Chevy (Cornelius Crane Chase) comedian, actor, author
Chia, Pei-Yuan banker
Damora, Robert Matthew architect
Kluge, Steve secondary education educator
†Krensky, Harry F. fund manager, educator
Margolin, Carl M. psychotherapist

Philip, Peter Van Ness former trust company executive

Bedford Corners
Singer, Craig broker, consultant, investor

Bedford Hills
Jensen-Carter, Philip Scott advertising and architectural photographer, medical photographer
Ludlum, Robert author
Waller, Wilhelmine Kirby (Mrs. Thomas Mercer Waller) civic worker, organization official

Beechhurst
Cooke, Constance Blandy librarian

Bellmore
Andrews, Charles Rolland library administrator
†Bregman, Steven Howard library director
Harris, Ira Stephen secondary education educator, administrator

Bellport
†Baxter, Louise T. educational administrator
Moeller, Mary Ella retired home economist, educator, radio commentator
Regalmuto, Nancy Marie small business owner, psychic consultant, therapist
Roland, David Leonard broadcast production educator
Townsend, Terry publishing executive
†Trahan, Janet Marie artist, gallery owner

Berlin
Pelz, Caroline Duncombe retired educational administrator
Stephens, Donald Joseph retired architect

Bethpage
Brodie, Sheldon J. physician
Dolan, Charles Francis media, entertainment company executive
Dolan, James communications executive
Evers, Gene writer
Lemle, Robert Spencer lawyer
Lusgarten, Marc A. communications executive
Marrone, Daniel Scott business, production and quality management educator
Murphy, Susan Lynn Jaycox construction executive
Rolston, Richard Gerard industrial welding and heating company executive
Sapan, Joshua Ward cable TV executive
Sweeney, Daniel Thomas cable television company executive

Big Flats
Orsillo, James Edward computer systems engineer, company executive

Binghamton
Anderson, Warren Mattice lawyer
Axtell, Clayton Morgan, Jr. lawyer
Babb, Harold psychology educator
Beach, Beth elementary educator
Bearsch, Lee Palmer architect, city planner
Beck, Stephanie G. lawyer
Best, Robert Mulvane insurance company executive
Bethje, Robert retired general surgeon
Carrigg, James A. retired utility company executive
Chivers, James Leeds lawyer
Coates, Donald Robert geology educator, scientist
Coffey, Margaret Tobin education educator, county official
Cohen, William Mark publisher
Cornacchio, Joseph Vincent engineering educator, computer researcher, consultant
Dantini, Julie Ann educational administrator, director, counselor
DeFleur, Lois B. university president, sociology educator
Dublin, Thomas Louis history educator
Eisch, John Joseph chemist, educator, consultant
Farley, Daniel W. utility company executive, lawyer
Fay, Rowan Hamilton minister
Feisel, Lyle Dean university dean, electrical engineering educator
Florance, Douglas Allan wholesale distributor
Gaddis Rose, Marilyn comparative literature educator, translator
Gerhart, Eugene Clifton lawyer
Hilton, Peter John mathematician, educator
Isaacson, Robert Lee psychology educator, researcher
James, Gary Douglas biological anthropologist, educator, researcher
Kessler, Milton English language educator, poet
Kingsley, Robert Thomas developer
Klir, George Jiri systems science educator
Kunjukunju, Pappy insurance company financial executive
Levis, Donald James psychologist, educator
Libous, Thomas William state senator
Mac Lennan, Susan Mary performing company executive
Marella, Philip Daniel broadcasting company executive
McAvoy, Thomas James federal judge
Michael, Sandra Dale reproductive endocrinology educator, researcher
Michaels, Robert M. physician, medical educator
Murry, William Douglas human resource management educator, consultant
O'Neil, Patrick Michael political scientist, educator
Peterson, Alfred Edward family physician
Price, Paul Marnell lawyer
Quataert, Donald history educator
Shillestad, John Gardner financial services company executive
Sklar, Kathryn Kish historian, educator
Steffens, Martha Moutoux newspaper editor, civic journalism consultant
Stein, George Henry historian, educator, administrator
†Swain, Mary Ann Price university official
Wallerstein, Immanuel sociologist
Whittingham, M(ichael) Stanley chemist

Blasdell
Hope, Christopher Lawrence middle school educator
McNierney, Lisa Marie critical care nurse

Blauvelt
Citardi, Mattio H. business analyst, project manager, researcher

Gillespie, John Fagan mining executive

Bloomington
Ruffing, Anne Elizabeth artist

Blue Mountain Lake
Day, Jacqueline Frances museum director

Blue Point
†Daly, James Joseph bishop

Bohemia
Hausman, Howard electronics executive
Maccarone, Frances Mary publishing executive
Manley, Gertrude Ella librarian, media specialist
Ortiz, Germaine Laura De Feo secondary education educator, counselor
Rogé, Ronald William financial planner, investment management executive

Breesport
Peckham, Joyce Weitz foundation administrator, former secondary education educator

Brentwood
Connors, William Francis, Jr. psychology educator
Kelly, Margaret Frances English language educator
Manning, Randolph H. academic administrator

Brewster
Killackey, Dorothy Helen real estate professional, former educator
Neugroschl, Jill Paulette financial planning company executive
Shepard, Jean Heck publishing company consultant, author, agent
Simon, Andrew L. educational publishing executive
Vichiola, Christopher Michael educator, writer

Briarcliff Manor
Bates, Barbara J. Neuner retired municipal official
Bhargava, Rameshwar Nath physicist
Bingham, J. Peter electronics research executive
Cugnini, Aldo Godfrey electrical engineer
Del Colle, Paul Lawrence communications administrator, educator
Dolmatch, Theodore Bieley management consultant
Driver, Sharon Humphreys marketing executive
Glassman, Jerome Martin clinical pharmacologist, educator
Hopkins, Lee Bennett writer, educator
†Housman, Arno David urologist
Jepsen, Mary Lou optical scientist, business executive
Kennell, Richard Wayne recording artist, business manager
Leiser, Burton Myron philosophy and law educator
†Lowe, James Edward, Jr. plastic and reconstructive surgeon
Luck, Edward Carmichael professional society administrator
Maloney, Michael Patrick lawyer, mediator, arbitrator
Ostrofsky, Anna music educator, violinist
Pasquarelli, Joseph J. real estate, engineering and construction executive
Rinaldo, Peter Merritt publishing executive
Weintraub, Michael Ira neurologist

Briarwood
Takacs, Michael Joseph educator

Bridgehampton
Edwards, John W. school superintendent
Jackson, Lee artist
McMenamin, Joan Stitt headmistress
Needham, James Joseph retired financial services executive
Phillips, Warren Henry publisher

Bridgeport
Sheldon, Thomas Donald educational organization administrator

Brightwaters
†Kavanagh, Eileen J. librarian

Brockport
Bucholz, Arden Kingsbury historian, educator
Campbell, Jill Frost university official
Flanagan, Timothy James criminal justice educator, university official
Gemmett, Robert James university dean, English language educator
Herrmann, Kenneth John, Jr. social work educator
Leslie, William Bruce history educator
Ludwig, Kurt James residence director
Marcus, Robert D. historian, educator
Michaels, John G. mathematics educator

Bronx
Adams, Alice sculptor
Aldrich, Thomas Knight physician, scientist
Aronow, Wilbert Solomon physician, educator
Aronowitz, Julian management consultant
Asare, Karen Michelle Gilliam reading, math and English language educator
Balka, Sigmund Ronell lawyer
Behnken, William Joseph art educator, artist
Bennett, Keith George nurse
Bennett, Michael Vander Laan neuroscience educator
†Bernstein, Martin musicologist, bassist
Bingham, June author, playwright
Blake, Peter Jost architect
Blaufox, Morton Donald physician, educator
†Boon, Kevin Alexander English educator, writer
Bowers, Francis Robert literature educator
†Brickner, Alice painter, illustrator
†Brosius, Scott David professional baseball player
Bullaro, Grace Russo literature, film and foreign language educator, speaker
Burde, Ronald Marshall neuro-ophthalmologist
Buschke, Herman neurologist
Calamari, Andrew M. lawyer
Castora, Joseph Charles history educator
Chiaramida, Salvatore cardiologist, educator, health facility adminstrator
Clary, Roy hospital administration executive
Clemens, William Roger professional baseball player
Cohen, Herbert Jesse physician, educator
Cohen, Michael I. pediatrician
Cone, David Brian professional baseball player
†Conley, John Joseph philosophy educator, priest

Connor, Paul Eugene social worker
Conway, William Gaylord zoologist, zoo director, conservationist
Cornfield, Melvin lawyer, university institute director
Coupey, Susan McGuire pediatrician, educator
Cruz, Lucy city councilwoman
Damico, Debra Lynn college official, English and French educator
Davis, Charles Theodore baseball player
DeMartino, Anthony Gabriel cardiologist, internist
†Dent, Bucky (Russell Earl Dent) professional baseball coach, former player
†DeVivo, Darren Douglas broadcast executive, announcer
†DiFede, Joseph retired judge
Dobson, Joanne Abele English language educator
Draeger, Wayne Harold manufacturing company executive
Dulles, Avery priest, theologian
Dunn, Ann-Margaret pediatrics nurse
Dutcher, Janice Jean Phillips oncologist
Eder, Howard Abram physician
Eisland, June M. councilwoman
Elkin, Milton radiologist, physician, educator
Emanuel, Evelyn Louise nurse
Eng, Calvin cardiologist, researcher
Fahey, Charles Joseph priest, gerontology educator
Fast, Julius author, editor
Fernandez, Ricardo R. university administrator
Fernandez-Pol, Blanca Dora psychiatrist, researcher
Fishman, Joshua Aaron sociolinguist, educator
Fleischer, Norman Samuel director of endocrinology, medical educator
Foreman, Spencer pulmonary specialist, hospital executive
Foster, Wendell councilman
†Fox, Geoffrey E. educational administrator
Freeman, Leonard Murray radiologist, nuclear medicine physician, educator
Frenz, Dorothy Ann cell and developmental biologist
Friedman, Joel Matthew oral and maxillofacial surgeon, educator
Friedman, Ronald Marvin cellular biologist
Garance, Dominick (D. G. Garan) lawyer, author
George, Deinabo Dabibi writer, computer specialist, educator
Gerardi, Joan Lois art educator
Gerst, Paul Howard physician
Gillman, Arthur Emanuel psychiatrist
Girardi, Joseph Elliott baseball player
Gliedman, Marvin L. surgeon, educator
Goldberg, Marcia B. medical educator
†Goldstein, Robert David plastic surgeon, educator
Gonzalez, Rose A-Navarro artist
Goodrich, James Tait neuroscientist, pediatric neurosurgeon
Griffin, Kelly Ann public relations executive, consultant
Hadaller, David Lawrence dean
Hallett, Charles Arthur, Jr. English and humanities educator
Han, Timothy Wayne drug abuse professional, public health educator
Hatcher, Baldwin minister, educator
Hennessy, Thomas Christopher clergyman, educator, retired university dean
Herbert, Victor Daniel medical educator
Hilfstein, Erna science historian, educator
Hilliard, John Mauk university official
Himmelberg, Robert Franklin historian, educator
Hirano, Asao neuropathologist
Hodgson, W(alter) John B(arry) surgeon
Hooker, Olivia J. psychologist, educator
Humphry, James, III librarian, publishing executive
Hunt, George William priest, magazine editor
Hurwitz, Ted H. sports conference administrator
Hyman, Andrew M. lawyer
†Isaacs, Diane S. English educator
Jacobson, Harold Gordon radiologist, educator
Jaffé, Ernst Richard medical educator and administrator
Jeter, Derek baseball player
Joseph, Stephen nephrology and dialysis nurse
Kadish, Anna Stein pathologist, educator, researcher
Kahn, Thomas medical educator
Kanofsky, Jacob Daniel psychiatrist, educator
Karasu, T(oksoz) Byram psychiatry educator
Karkanias, George B. neurologist, educator
†Karwa, Gattu Lal urologist
Kassoy, Hortense (Honey Kassoy) artist, sculptor, painter, printmaker
Kaul, Dhananjaya Kumar physiologist
Kelly, Mary Susan psychologist, educator
Kirmse, Sister Anne-Marie Rose nun, educator, researcher
Kitt, Olga artist
Knoblauch, Edward Charles baseball player
Koranyi, Adam mathematics educator
Koss, Leopold G. physician, pathologist, educator
Kravath, Alan Wolfe education evaluator
Lane, Elizabeth Nilaja Hannah information analyst, educator
Lattis, Richard Lynn zoo director
†Leyritz, James Joseph professional baseball player
Lieber, Charles Saul physician, educator
Long, Gregory R. botanic garden administrator
Macklin, Ruth bioethics educator
†Marantz, Paul Russell medical educator
Martinez, Constantino professional baseball player
McCabe, James Patrick library director
McDonald, Mary pediatric nurse practitioner
Miller, Barry H. insurance company executive
Molloy, Joseph A. professional sports team executive
Mooney, Mary Ann early childhood educator
Moritz, Charles Fredric book editor
Morris, Kevin women's basketball coach
Morrow, Phillip Henry real estate development company executive
†Mottus, Jane E. college administrator, historian
Muschel, Louis Henry immunologist, educator
Nagler, Arnold Leon pathologist, scientist, educator
Nathanson, Melvyn Bernard university provost, mathematician
Nathenson, Stanley Gail immunology educator
Nitowsky, Harold Martin physician, educator
†Obioha, McLord Chinedum magazine editor
Okpalanma, Chika psychiatrist
O'Neill, Paul Andrew professional baseball player
Orkin, Louis Richard physician, educator
Orlando, Mary Jean community health and medical/surgical nurse
†Padnos, Mark reference librarian, literary translator
Parker, Everett Carlton clergyman
†Patel, Mahendrakumar P. plastic surgeon
Payson, Martin Saul secondary school educator, mathematician

Pettoello-Mantovani, Massimo pediatrician, educator, microbiologist, researcher
Pietarinen, George English language educator
Pita, Marianne D'Arcy English language educator
Pitchumoni, Capecomorin Sankar gastroenterologist, educator
Plimpton, Calvin Hastings physician, university president
Porter, Spence playwright
Posner, Bruce Frederick independent school administrator, consultant
Purpura, Dominick P. neuroscientist, university dean
Radel, Eva pediatrician, hematologist
Rapin, Isabelle physician
†Razani, Babak medical researcher
Regan, Harold James publishing executive
Reichert, Marlene Joy secondary school educator, writer
Reilly, Margaret Mary retired therapist
Reynolds, Benedict Michael surgeon
Riba, Netta Eileen secondary school educator
Richman, Arthur Sherman sports association executive
Rivera, Jose city councilman
Rivera, Mariano baseball player
Robinson, Bernard Pahl retired thoracic surgeon, educator
Robinson, John Gwilym conservationist
Romney, Seymour Leonard physician, educator
Rose, Israel Harold mathematics educator
Rosenbaum, David Herbert neurologist
Ruben, Robert Joel physician, educator
Rubinstein, Arye pediatrician, microbiology and immunology educator
Ruffing, Janet Kathryn spirituality educator
Sable, Robert Allen gastroenterologist
Satir, Birgit H. medical educator, medical researcher
Scanlan, Thomas Joseph college president, educator
Scharff, Matthew Daniel immunologist, cell biologist, educator
Schaumburg, Herbert Howard neurology educator
Scheuer, James physician, educator, researcher
†Schroth, Raymond Augustine university official, journalism educator, priest
Schwam, Marvin Albert graphic design company executive
Sedacca, Angelo Anthony police officer, scholar, philanthropist
†Segan, Scott Marshall neurologist
Seltzer, William statistician, social researcher, former international organization director
Senturia, Yvonne Dreyfus pediatrician, epidemiologist
Shafritz, David Andrew physician, research scientist
Shames, Jordan Nelson health care executive, consultant health services
Shamos, Morris Herbert physicist educator
Shapiro, David Joel poet, art critic, educator
Shapiro, Nella Irene surgeon
Shatin, Harry medical educator, dermatologist
Sherman, Judith Dorothy producer, recording company owner, recording engineer
Siddons, Sarah Mae chemist
Skurdenis, Juliann Veronica librarian, educator, writer, editor
Smith-Alhimer, Marie Margaret Cella mental health nurse
Somary, Johannes Felix conductor
Soulé, Charles Raymond, Jr. psychologist
Spitzer, Adrian pediatrician, medical educator
Sprecher, Baron William Gunther pianist, composer, conductor, diplomat
†Stein, Bernard L. publishing executive
Stein, Ruth Elizabeth Klein physician
Steinbrenner, George Michael, III professional baseball team executive, shipbuilding company executive
†Strauch, Berish plastic surgeon, hand surgeon
Strawberry, Darryl professional baseball player
Stuhr, David Paul business educator, consultant
Surks, Martin I. medical educator, endocrinologist
Sylvester, John Edward social worker
Tellis, Vivian Anthony transplant surgeon, administrator
Tetrokalashvili, Mikhail S. physician
Thysen, Benjamin biochemist, health science facility administrator, researcher
Tong, Hing mathematician, educator
Torre, Joseph Paul (Joe Torre) professional baseball team manager
Ultan, Lloyd historian
Waltz, Joseph McKendree neurosurgeon, educator
Warden, Lawrence A. councilman
Weiner, Richard Lenard hospital administrator, educator, pediatrician
Wiernik, Peter Harris oncologist, educator
Wigsten, Paul Bradley, Jr. computer and financial consultant
Wille, Rosanne Louise higher education administrator
Williams, Bernabe Figueroa professional baseball player
Williams, Marshall Henry, Jr. physician, educator
Yadeka, Theophilus Adeniyi administrator
Yalow, Rosalyn Sussman medical physicist
Zalaznick, Sheldon editor, journalist
Zimmer, Donald William coach professional athletics, former professional baseball manager

Bronxville
Auriemmo, Frank Joseph, Jr. financial holding company executive
Biscardi, Chester composer, educator
Broas, Donald Sanford hospital executive
Connola, Donald Pascal, Jr. management consultant, educator
Cook, Charles David international lawyer, arbitrator, consultant
Cutler, Kenneth Burnett lawyer, investment company executive
Dvorak, Roger Gran health facility executive
Ellinghaus, William Maurice communications executive
Falvey, Patrick Joseph lawyer
Farber, Viola Anna dancer, choreographer, educator
Franklin, Margery Bodansky psychology educator, researcher
Frost, A. Corwin architect, consultant
Fuller, David Otis, Jr. lawyer
Greenwald, Martin publishing company executive
Hutchison, Dorris Jeannette retired microbiologist, educator
Kaplan, Sanford Allen internist, allergist
Keller, LeRoy journalist, consultant
Knapp, George Griff Prather insurance consultant, arbitrator
Lawrence, Ruddick Carpenter public relations executive

Levitt, Miriam pediatrician
L'Huillier, Peter (Peter) archbishop
Lombardo, Philip Joseph broadcasting company executive
Martin, R. Keith business and information systems educator, consultant
Mau, Dwayne Holger minister
Myers, Michele Tolela college president
Peters, Sarah Whitaker art historian, writer, lecturer
Randall, Francis Ballard historian, educator, writer
Recabo, Jaime Miguel lawyer
Rizzo, Thomas Dignan orthopedic surgeon
Ryan, Frank James, Jr. advertising executive
Schneider, David Paul church administrator
Sharp, Donald Eugene bank consultant
Shuker, Gregory Brown publishing and production company executive
Sluberski, Thomas Richard international educator, journalist
†Solomon, Barbara Probst writer
Veneruso, James John lawyer
Wilson, John Donald banker, economist
Woodard, Komozi American history educator

Brookhaven
Reeves, John Drummond English language professional, writer

Brooklyn
Adasko, Mary Hardy speech pathologist
Ahrens, Thomas H. production company executive
Alfano, Edward Charles, Jr. elementary education educator
Alfonso, Antonio Escolar surgeon
Al-Hafeez, Humza minister, editor
Allen, George Desmond epidemiology nurse, surgical nurse
Allman, Avis Asiye artist, poet, Turkish and Islamic culture educator
Altura, Bella T. physiologist, educator
Altura, Burton Myron physiologist, educator
Alywahby, Nancy geriatric and adult nurse practitioner
Amendola, Sal John artist, educator, writer
Amon, Carol Bagley federal judge
Amy, Michaël Jacques art historian, educator, art critic
Anderson, James Noel (Jim Anderson) recording engineer, producer
Arcuri, Leonard Philip elementary education educator
Armenakas, Anthony Emmanuel aerospace educator
Aspenberg, Gary Alan personnel and labor relations professional
Astwood, William Peter psychotherapist
Azank, Roberto artist
Azrack, Joan M. judge
Bachman, George mathematics educator
Bakakos, Diana middle school educator
Balbi, Kenneth Emilio environmental lead specialist, researcher
Balogun, Joseph A. physical therapist, educator, researcher
Baltakis, Paul Antanas bishop
Banjoko, Alimi Ajimon financial planner
†Barbarito, Gerald Michael bishop
Barnes, John Wadsworth director, writer
Barth, Robert Henry nephrologist, educator
†Barton, Halbert Everett anthropology educator, consultant
Beaufait, Frederick W(illiam) civil engineering educator
Bergen, Christopher Brooke opera company administrator, translator, editor
Berger, David history educator
Bertoni, Henry Louis electrical engineering educator
Bianco, Anthony Joseph, III newswriter
Bigger, Philip Joseph judicial branch official
Birenbaum, William M. former university president
Biro, David Eric dermatologist
Biro, Laszlo dermatologist
Bisbee, Joyce Evelyn utility company manager
Blackman, Robert Irwin real estate developer and investor, lawyer, accountant
Blasi, Alberto Romance languages educator, writer
Block, Frederic judge
†Bloom, Leonard language educator
†Bofay, Fred university administrator
Boloker, Rose L. school psychologist
†Bordao, Rafael educator, writer, poet
Bottiglia, Frank Robert bank executive
Bowers, John Carl minister
Bowers, Patricia Eleanor Fritz economist
Bramwell, Henry federal judge
Brownstone, Paul Lotan retired speech communications and drama educator
Bugliarello, George university chancellor
Burlacu, Constantin journalist, educator
†Caden, John L. federal judge
†Cardinale, Drew Anthony language educator
Cardoza, Avery writer, publisher
Carlile, Janet Louise artist, educator
Carswell, Lois Malakoff botanical gardens executive, consultant
Carter, Zachary W. prosecutor
Castleman, Louis Samuel metallurgist, educator
Catell, Robert Barry gas utility executive
Charton, Marvin chemist, educator
†Cherin, Aaron Simon federal judge
Chernow, Ron writer, columnist
Chesler, Phyllis psychology educator
Choudhury, Deo Chand physicist, educator
†Chowdhury, Mohammed Shamsul educator
Clark, Luther Theopolis physician, educator, researcher
Cohen, Harris Saul dean
Cohn, Steven Lawrence internist, medical educator
Contino, Rosalie Helene drama educator, costume designer and historian, playwright
Corry, Emmett Brother librarian, educator, researcher, archivist
Courtice, Katie freelance writer and editor, office consultant
Cracco, Roger Quinlan medical educator, neurologist
Cranin, Abraham Norman oral and maxillofacial surgeon, researcher, implantologist
Crawford, Patricia Alexis Ann social justice and healthcare advocate, writer
†Creshevsky, Noah Ephriam music educator, composer
Critchlow, Edith Hope minister
Crum, Albert Byrd psychiatrist, consultant
Cullen-DuPont, Kathryn writer
†Cunningham, John Thomas science educator
†Cunningham, Joseph Newton, Jr. cardiothoracic and vascular surgeon
Curry, David guidance staff developer
Daily, Thomas V. bishop
Daley, Sandra retired artist, filmmaker, photographer
Daly, Joe Ann Godown publishing company executive
†Darrison, Cynthia R. political consultant
Davidson, Steven J. emergency physician
Dearie, Raymond Joseph federal judge
De Lisi, Joanne communications executive, educator
Del Rosario, Mariano Boras, Jr. artist
DeLustro, Frank Joseph financial executive, consultant
Del Valle, Cezar Jose artist, writer, theatre historian
Diamond, Jessica artist
Dibrienza, Stephen city councilman
Dimant, Jacob internist
Dinnerstein, Harvey artist
Dinnerstein, Simon Abraham artist, educator
†Doss, Amanda D. producer
Duberstein, Conrad B. federal judge
Duke-Masters, Velma Regina pediatrics and psychiatric-mental health nurse
†Dukes, Frank Ronald career military, collections investigator
Edemeka, Udo Edemeka surgeon
Eirich, Frederick Roland chemist, educator
Eisenberg, Karen Sue Byer nurse
El Kodsi, Baroukh gastroenterologist, educator
Engersgard, Jorgen architect
Erber, William Franklin gastroenterologist
Eriksen, Norman John librarian, research historian
Eschen, Albert Herman optometrist
Evans, Garth artist, educator
Everdell, William Romeyn humanities educator
Faison, Seth Shepard retired insurance broker
Fallek, Andrew Michael lawyer
Feinbaum, George internist, endocrinologist
†Feller, Jerome federal judge
Ferber, Linda S. museum curator
Fisher, Joel Anthony sculptor
Fisher, Kenneth K. councilman
Flam, Jack Donald art historian, educator
†Flateau, John academic administrator
Franco, Victor theoretical physics educator
Freijoso, Ricardo microbiologist
Friedman, Eli Arnold nephrologist
Friedman, Gerald Manfred geologist, educator
Friedman, Paul chemistry educator
Frisch, Ivan Thomas computer and communications company executive
Furchgott, Robert Francis pharmacologist, educator
Gabriel, Mordecai Lionel biologist, educator
Gabris, George Steven sculptor, welder
Garibaldi, Louis E. aquarium administrator
Gershon, Nina federal judge
Gintautas, Jonas physician, scientist, administrator
†Giusti, Karin F. artist, educator
Glasser, Israel Leo federal judge
Gleeson, John judge, educator
†Go, Marilyn D. federal judge
Golden, Howard municipal or county official
Goldstein, Brenda Iris retired elementary school educator
Goodman, Alvin S. engineering educator, consultant
Gotta, Alexander Walter anesthesiologist, educator
Grado, Angelo John artist
Grimblatov, Valentin physicist, biomedical engineer
Gross, Abraham rabbi, educator
Gross, Stephen Mark pharmacist, academic dean
Gura, Timothy James speech educator
Gustin, Mark Douglas hospital executive
Ham, Karen music educator
Hamm, Charles John banker
Harmon, Mary Carol writer
Harris, Fred orthotist, prosthetist
Harris, James Arthur, Sr. school system administrator, economist, consultant
Haum, Barbara Rose artist, researcher
Hazlitt, Donald Robert artist
Hechtman, Howard financial analyst
Helly, Walter Sigmund engineering educator
Henderson, Janice Elizabeth law librarian
Hendra, Barbara Jane public relations executive
Henry, Lloyd councilman
†Henschel, Milton G. church administrator
Herman, Allen Ian foundation administrator
Herzog, Lester Barry lawyer, educator
Hill, Elizabeth Anne academic administrator, lawyer
Hill, Isabel Thigpen urban planner
Hill, Leda Katherine librarian
Hird, Mary nursing administrator
†Hirsch, Charles Flynn writer, editor
Hoepfner, Karla Jean designer, artist
Hohenrath, William Edward retired banker
†Holland, Marvin A. federal judge
Hood, Ernest Alva, Sr. pharmaceutical company executive
Hopkins, Karen Brooks performing arts executive
Houston, Sandra Lee nurse educator, medical/surgical nurse, ambulatory surgical nurse
Huneke, John George minister
Hurley, Denis R. federal judge
Imperato, Pascal James physician, health administrator, author, editor, medical educator
Isaacson, Arline Levine association administrator
Jacobson, Barry Stephen lawyer, judge
Jaffe, Eric Allen physician, educator, researcher
Jaffe, Louise English language educator, creative writer
James, Milton Garnet economist
Jarman, Joseph jazz musician
Jenkins, Leroy violinist, composer
Jofen, Jean foreign language educator
Johnson, Sterling, Jr. federal judge
Jones, Susan Emily fashion educator, administrator, educator
Kaggen, Elias physician
Kamins, Barry Michael lawyer
Kaplan, Lawrence Rice psychologist
Kaplan, Mitchell Alan sociologist, researcher
Karkhanis, Sharad librarian, political science educator
Karmel, Roberta Segal lawyer, educator
Kazan, Basil Gibran religious music composer
Kemp, James William graphic artist
Kempner, Joseph aerospace engineering educator
King, Margaret Leah history educator
Kirshenbaum, Richard Irving public health physician
Kjeldaas, Terje, Jr. physics educator emeritus
Kjok, Solveig artist, art historian, linguist
Koppel, Audrey Feiler electrologist, educator
Korman, Edward R. federal judge
Kramer, Allan Franklin, II botanical garden official, researcher
Kramer, Meyer lawyer, editor, clergyman
Kurz, Irwin principal
LaCosta, Cosmo Joseph health facility administrator
Langiulli, Nino F. philosophy educator
Largo, Gerald Andrew academic adminstrator
Lattin, Vernon Eugene academic administrator
Lawrence, Deirdre Elizabeth librarian, coordinator research services
Lederman, Stephanie Brody artist
†Lee, Spike (Shelton Jackson Lee) filmmaker
Leff, Sanford Erwin cardiologist
Lehman, Arnold Lester museum official, art historian
†Lerner, Linda poet, English educator
Levendoglu, Hulya gastroenterologist, educator
Levi, Louise Landes poet, translator, musician
Levine, Nathan business educator
Levine, Neil small business owner
Levy, Norman B. psychiatrist, educator
†Levy, Robert Morris judge
Lewin, Ted Bert writer, illustrator
Lewis, Felice Flanery lawyer, educator
Leyh, Richard Edmund, Sr. retired investment executive
Lichtenstein, Harvey performing arts executive
Lieberman, Morris Baruch psychologist, educator, researcher
Lindo, J. Trevor psychiatrist, consultant
Lizt, Sara Enid Vanefsky lawyer, educator
Lobron, Barbara L. speech educator, writer, editor, photographer
Ma, Tsu Sheng chemist, educator, consultant
MacFarland, Craig George natural resource management professional
Magliocco, John wholesale distribution executive
Malave-Dilan, Martin councilman
†Mann, Roanne L. federal judge
Marcano, Soraya visual artist
Marcus, Harold retired physician, health facility administrator
Marcus, Leonard S. writer, book critic
Mark, Richard Kushakow internist
Markgraf, Rosemarie real estate broker
Marsala-Cervasio, Kathleen Ann medical/surgical nurse, administrator
Martinez-Pons, Manuel psychology educator
Matthews, Craig Gerard gas company executive
Mayer, Ira Edward gastroenterologist
†McCrary, Donald English language educator
McIntyre, John S. oral and maxillofacial surgeon
McLean, William Ronald electrical engineer, consultant
Mehlman, Ronald Walter sculptor, educator
Mendez, Hermann Armando pediatrician, educator
Mernyk, Ross Lou electronics engineer
Mesiha, Mounir Sobhy industrial pharmacy educator
Milhorat, Thomas Herrick neurosurgeon
Minkoff, Jack economics educator
Mirra, Suzanne Samuels neuropathologist, researcher
Moehring, Fred Adolf fastener distribution company executive
Mook, Sarah retired chemist
Morawetz, Herbert chemistry educator
Morgan, Mary Louise Fitzsimmons fund raising executive, lobbyist
†Morris, Sandra Winsome administrative assistant
†Morris, Traci D. poet, writer, educator
Morrison, Barbara Sheffield Japanese translator and interpreter, consultant
Morton, Marsha Lee art history educator
Mui, Jimmy Kun architect, network marketing executive
Mulvihill, Maureen Esther writer, educator, scholar
Murillo-Rohde, Ildaura Maria marriage and family therapist, consultant, educator, dean
†Neal, Florence Arthur artist
†Neill, Margaret Ann artist, writer
Nemser, Cindy writer
Newbauer, John Arthur editor
Nicholson, Michael lawyer
Nickerson, Eugene H. federal judge
Norstrand, Iris Fletcher psychiatrist, neurologist, educator
Nurhussein, Mohammed Alamin internist, geriatrician, educator
O'Connor, Sister George Aquin (Margaret M. O'Connor) college president, sociology educator
Oliner, Arthur Aaron physicist, educator
Olson, Robert Goodwin philosophy educator
Onken, George Marcellus lawyer
Orsini, Gail social worker
Ortiz, Mary Theresa biomedical engineer, educator
Ortner, Everett Howard magazine editor, writer
†Otterness, Tom artist
Oussani, James John stapling company executive
Pagala, Murali Krishna physiologist
†Palm, Marion educator
Pan, Huo-Hsi mechanical engineer, educator
Parker, Barbara L. educator
Pashman, Susan Ellen writer
Patel, Nagin Keshavbhai industrial pharmacy educator
Pearce, Eli M. chemistry educator, administrator
Pearlstein, Seymour artist
Peker, Elya Abel artist
Pelcyger, Iran retired principal
Pennisten, John William computer scientist, linguist, actuary
Pertschuk, Louis Philip pathologist
Peters, Mercedes psychoanalyst
Pine, Bessie Miriam social worker, editor, columnist
Pino, Richard Edmund financial analyst, financial planner
Pitynski, Andrzej Piotr sculptor
Plaut, Jane Margaret art educator
Plotz, Charles Mindell physician
Pollack, Bruce banker, real estate consultant
†Pollak, Cheryl L. federal judge
Poser, Norman Stanley law educator
Price, Ely dermatologist
Purdy, James writer
Rabinowitz, Simon S. pediatric gastroenterologist, scientist
Rabiu, Badru I.D. federal official
Raggi, Reena federal judge
Raskind, Leo Joseph law educator
Reich, Nathaniel Edwin physician, poet, artist, educator, explorer
Reinisch, June Machover psychologist, educator
Ressner, Philip editor
Reynolds, Nancy Remick editor, writer
Ricciardi, Christopher Gerard archaeologist, educator
Rice, John Thomas architecture educator
†Rittner, Leona Phyllis comparative literature scholar
Robinson, Annette councilwoman
Robles, Victor L. city councilman
Rocco, Ron artist
Roess, Roger Peter engineering educator
Ronn, Avigdor Meir chemical physics educator, consultant, researcher
†Rosario-Olmedo, Carmen Gloria principal
Rosen, Stuart Morris wholesale distributor
Ross, Allyne R. federal judge
Rothenberg, Mira Kowarski clinical psychologist and psychotherapist
Rucker, Bronwyn actress, writer, social worker
Ryan, Leonard Eames administrative law judge
Sage, Robert Ephram social service agency administrator
Sainer, Arthur writer, theater educator
†Salgado, Miran neurologist
Salzman, Eric composer, writer
Sanford, David Boyer writer, editor
Satterfield-Harris, Rita workers compensation representative
Savits, Barry Sorrel surgeon
Sawyer, Philip Nicholas surgeon, educator, health science facility administrator
Schaefer, Marilyn Louise artist, writer, educator
Schiffman, Gerald microbiologist, educator
Schneider, Adele Goldberg librarian, educator
Schwarz, Richard Howard obstetrician, gynecologist, educator
Seiden, Morton Irving humanities educator
Shalita, Alan Remi dermatologist
Sharify, Nasser educator, author, librarian
Shaw, Leonard Glazer electrical engineering educator, consultant
Shechter, Ben-Zion artist, illustrator
Shechter, Laura Judith artist
†Siegelman, Kenneth Barry social studies educator
Sifton, Charles Proctor federal judge
Silverstein, Louis art director, designer, editor
†Sinn, Jerry L. army officer
†Smith, John W(esley), Jr. data processing executive, consultant
Solan, Lawrence Michael lawyer
Soldo, John J. educator
†Solomon, Lyn S. art therapist
Solomon, Martin M. judge
Sonenberg, Jack artist
Sorscher, Marvin Loeb religious studies educator, rabbi
Spano, Robert performing company executive, conductor
†Sparrow, Jennifer Ruth English language educator
Spector, Robert Donald language professional, educator
Spivack, Frieda Kugler psychologist, administrator, educator, researcher
Steiner, Robert S. psychologist
Stern, Leon psychiatrist
Stracher, Alfred biochemistry educator
Strauss, Dorothy Brandfon marital, family, and sex therapist
Strohbehn, Edward Allen investment company executive
Sullivan, Joseph M. bishop
†Swain, Laura Taylor judge
Sweet, Marc Steven financial executive
†Templeton, Joan educator English
Thompson, Theodis healthcare executive, health management consultant
Thompson, William C., Jr. school system administrator
Trager, David G. federal judge
Traube, Charles internist, cardiologist
Tsai, Bor-sheng educator
Twining, Lynne Dianne psychotherapist, professional society administrator, writer
Vasisko, Gerard F. architect
Verma, Ram Sagar geneticist, educator, author, administrator
Vidal, Maureen Eris English language educator, actress
Viswanathan, Ramaswamy physician, educator
Von Essen, Thomas protective services official
von Rydingsvard, Ursula Karoliszyn sculptor
Walsh, George William publishing company executive, editor
Walz, Steven K. newspaper editor
Wapner, Myrna retired principal
Weill, Georges Gustave mathematics educator
Weiner, Anthony D. congressman
Weinstein, Jack Bertrand federal judge
Weinstein, Marie Pastore psychologist
†Weinstock, Deborah psychologist
Weston, I. Donald architect
†Whiting, Nathan poet, dancer
Wiener, Hesh (Harold Frederic Wiener) publisher, editor, consultant
Williams, Carl E., Sr. bishop
†Williams, Edward Frank poet, entertainment company executive
Williams, Emma Louise elementary education educator
Williams, Vida Veronica guidance counselor
Williams, William Magavern headmaster
Wilson, Veta Emily community health nurse
Wolf, Edward Lincoln physics educator
Wolfe, Ethyle Renee (Mrs. Coleman Hamilton Benedict) college administrator
Wolintz, Arthur Harry physician, neuro-ophthalmologist
Woolley, Margaret Anne (Margot Woolley) architect
Wooten, Priscilla A. councilwoman
Yeaton, Cecelia E(mma) healthcare administration executive
†Yin, Kenneth Joseph language educator
Zakanitch, Robert Rahway artist
Zawadi, Kiane musician
Zelin, Jerome retail executive
Zhang, Robert painter
†Zibrin, Michael academic administrator
Zisser, Martin Shepherd fur apparel manufacturer, investor and trader
Zuk, Judith botanic garden administrator
Zukowski, Barbara Wanda clinical social work psychotherapist
†Zweig, Janet artist, sculptor

Buffalo
Abrahams, Athol Denis geography researcher, educator
Ackerman, Philip Charles utility executive, lawyer
Alderdice, Douglas Alan secondary education educator
Allen, William Sheridan history educator
Amborski, Leonard Edward chemist
Ambrus, Clara Maria physician
Ambrus, Julian L. physician, medical educator
Anbar, Michael biophysics educator
Anderson, Wayne Arthur electrical engineering educator
Anderson, Wayne Keith dean
Ansar, Ahmad career counselor
Aquilina, Alan T. physician
Arcara, Richard Joseph federal judge
Aurbach, Herbert Alexander sociology educator

Bailey, Thomas Charles *lawyer*
Bardos, Thomas Joseph *chemist, educator*
Barney, Thomas McNamee *lawyer*
Batt, Ronald Elmer *gynecologist, scientist*
Bayles, Jennifer Lucene *museum education curator*
Bean, Edwin Temple, Jr. *lawyer*
Benenson, David Maurice *engineering educator*
Berlyn, Sheldon *art educator*
Bermingham, Joseph Daniel *lawyer*
Berner, Robert Frank *managerial statistics educator, administrator*
Biggs, Edmund Logan *college administrator*
Blaine, Charles Gillespie *retired lawyer*
Blane, Howard Thomas *research institute administrator*
Blessing, Gary Albert *technical communications executive*
Bobinski, George Sylvan *librarian, educator*
Brady-Borland, Karen *reporter*
Brock, David George *lawyer*
Brody, Harold *neuroanatomist, gerontologist*
Bromley, Hank J. *sociologist, educator*
Brooks, John Samuel Joseph *pathologist, researcher*
Bross, Irwin Dudley Jackson *biostatistician*
Brown, Jerrold Stanley *lawyer*
Brydges, Thomas Eugene *lawyer*
†Bucki, Carl L. *federal judge*
Calkins, Evan *physician, educator*
†Canfield, Holly Beth *legal nurse consultant*
Carmichael, Donald Scott *lawyer, business executive*
Casper, Bernadette Marie *critical care nurse*
†Choi, Namkee Gang *educator*
Chrisman, Diane J. *librarian*
Chu, Tsann Ming *immunochemist, educator*
Chutkow, Jerry Grant *neurologist, educator*
Ciancio, Sebastian Gene *periodontist, educator*
Clarkson, Elisabeth Ann Hudnut *civic worker*
Clemens, David Allen *lawyer*
Coburn, Lewis Alan *mathematics educator*
Coles, Robert Traynham *architect*
Coles, William Henry *ophthalmologist, educator*
Collins, Catherine *health administrator, educator*
Collins, J. Michael *public broadcasting executive*
Coppens, Philip *chemist*
Cozzi, Ronald Lee *antiquarian book seller, rare book appraiser*
Creaven, Patrick Joseph *physician, research oncologist*
Creeley, Robert White *author, English educator*
Curtin, John T. *federal judge*
Day, Donald Sheldon *lawyer*
Day, Richard *museum administrator*
Deasy, Jacqueline Hildegard *insurance consultant*
DeLisle, Alan H. *city commissioner*
Dewey, Henry S., Jr. *elementary education educator*
Dispenza, Joan Marie *ambulatory care nurse, administrator*
Doyno, Victor Anthony *literature educator*
Draper, Verden Rolland *accountant*
Drew, Fraser Bragg Robert *English language educator*
Drinnan, Alan John *oral pathologist*
Drury, Colin Gordon *engineering consultant, educator*
Duax, William Leo *biological researcher*
Durawa, Daniel T. *state commissioner*
Dwoskin, Joseph Y. *pediatric urologist*
Eberlein, Patricia James *mathematician, computer scientist, educator*
Elfvin, John Thomas *federal judge*
Enhorning, Goran *obstetrician, gynecologist, educator*
Fallavollita, James A. *cardiologist, educator, researcher*
Federman, Raymond *novelist, English and comparative literature educator*
Feldman, Irving *poet*
Feuerstein, Alan Ricky *lawyer, consultant*
Fiedler, Leslie Aaron *English educator, actor, author*
†Fisher, Jane Elizabeth *English educator*
Floss, Frederick George *economics and finance educator, consultant*
†Foschio, Leslie George *lawyer*
Freedman, Maryann Saccomando *lawyer*
Fryer, Appleton *publisher, sales executive, lecturer, diplomat*
Gallagher, Shaun Andrew *philosophy educator, writer*
Gardner, Arnold Burton *lawyer*
†Garland, Simon Greville *service technician*
Genco, Robert Joseph *scientist, immunologist, periodontist, educator*
Giambra, Joel Anthony *city comptroller*
Glanville, Robert Edward *lawyer*
Gogan, Catherine Mary *dental educator*
Goldhaber, Gerald Martin *communication educator, author, consultant*
Goldstein, Brian Alan *lawyer, physician*
Goodberry, Diane Jean (Oberkircher) *mathematics educator, tax accountant*
Goralski, Donald John *public relations executive, counselor*
Gort, Michael *economics educator*
Gracia, Jorge Jesus Emiliano *philosopher, educator*
Graham, (Lloyd) Saxon *epidemiology educator*
Grasser, George Robert *lawyer*
Gray, F(rederick) William, III *lawyer*
Greiner, William Robert *university administrator, educator, lawyer*
Gresham, Glen Edward *physician*
Grosz, Edward M. *bishop*
Gruen, David Henry *financial executive, consultant*
Gugino, Lawrence James *medical educator*
Hall, David Edward *lawyer*
Halpern, Ralph Lawrence *lawyer*
Halpert, Leonard Walter *retired editor*
Halt, James George *advertising executive, graphic designer*
†Hans, Mary Clare *aquatics director, red cross trainer*
Hare, Peter Hewitt *philosophy educator*
Hasek, Dominik *professional hockey player*
Hassett, Eva M. *city commissioner*
Hauptman, Herbert Aaron *mathematician, educator, researcher*
Hayes, J. Michael *lawyer*
He, Guang Sheng *research scientist*
Head, Christopher Alan *lawyer*
Head, Edward Dennis *bishop*
Headrick, Thomas Edward *lawyer, educator*
Heckman, Carol E. *judge*
Heilman, Pamela Davis *lawyer*
Henrich, Jean MacKay *painter, sculptor, educator*
Herdlein, Richard Joseph, III *college official and dean, educator*
Hershey, Linda Ann *neurology and pharmacology educator*
Hetzner, Donald Raymund *social studies educator, forensic social scientist*
Hida, George T. *chemical and ceramic engineer*
Hohn, David *physician*
†Hohn, David C. *healthcare executive*
Holzinger, Brian *professional hockey player*
Horoszewicz, Juliusz Stanislaw *oncologist, cancer researcher, laboratory administrator*
Hrycik, Pauline Emily *educator*
Hudson, Stanton Harold, Jr. *public relations executive, educator*
Hull, Elaine Mangelsdorf *psychology educator*
Hunter, Juanita K. *nurse, educator*
Iggers, Georg Gerson *history educator*
Irwin, Robert James Armstrong *investment company executive*
Jacobs, Jeremy M. *diversified holding company executive, hockey team owner*
Jain, Piyare Lal *physics educator*
Jasen, Matthew Joseph *state justice*
Jerge, Dale Robert *small business owner*
Jerge, Marie Charlotte *minister*
†Kaplan, Michael J. *federal judge*
Karwan, Mark Henry *engineering educator, dean*
Katz, Jack *audiology educator*
Kazmierczak, Elzbieta Teresa *graphic designer, illustrator, educator, semiotician*
Keane, Cornelius John *fire commissioner*
Kearns, John Thomas *philosophy educator*
Keem, Michael Dennis *veterinarian*
Kennedy, Bernard Joseph *utility executive*
Kinzly, Robert Edward *engineering company executive*
Kipping, Hans F. *dermatologist*
Kite, Joseph Hiram, Jr. *microbiologist, educator*
Koontz, Eldon Ray *management and financial consultant*
Kreuz, Daniel Edward *city engineer*
Kristoff, Karl W. *lawyer*
Krol, Nancy Ann *critical care nurse*
Krucenski, Leonard Joseph *secondary education educator*
LaHood, Marvin John *English educator*
Landi, Dale Michael *industrial engineer, academic administrator*
Layton, Rodney Eugene *controller, newspaper executive*
Lee, Genevieve Bruggeman *publishing company executive*
Lee, George C. *civil engineer, university administrator*
Lele, Amol Shashikant *obstetrician and gynecologist*
Levine, George Richard *English language educator*
Levine, Murray *psychology educator*
Levite, Laurence A. *communications executive*
Levy, Harold James *physician, psychiatrist*
Levy, Kenneth Jay *psychology educator, academic administrator*
Light, Murray Benjamin *newspaper editor*
Lippes, Gerald Sanford *lawyer, business executive*
Littlewood, Douglas Burden *business brokerage executive*
MacLeod, Gordon Albert *retired lawyer*
Maloney, Gail *women's basketball coach*
Manes, Stephen Gabriel *concert pianist, educator*
Mansell, Henry J. *bishop*
Masiello, Anthony M. (Tony Masiello) *mayor*
Mattar, Lawrence Joseph *lawyer*
†Maxwell, Edmund F. *federal judge*
Meredith, Dale Dean *civil engineering educator*
Merini, Rafika *foreign language and literature and women's studies educator*
Metz, Donald *art center director, musician*
Metzger, Ernest Hugh *aerospace engineer, scientist*
Mihich, Enrico *medical researcher*
Milgrom, Felix *immunologist, educator*
Miller, Kennon Sewall *urologist*
Milligan, John Drane *historian, educator*
Mindell, Eugene Robert *surgeon, educator*
Mirand, Edwin Albert *medical scientist*
Mitchell, William I. *historian, social studies educator*
Monaco-Hannon, Kelli Ann *secondary school educator*
†Moore, Muriel A. *college president*
Moss, Douglas G. *professional hockey league executive*
Mucci, Gary Louis *lawyer*
†Muir, Geraldine Marie *student affairs administrator*
Murray, Glenn Edward *lawyer*
Naughton, John Patrick *cardiologist*
†NeMoyer, Patrick H. *prosecutor*
Newman, Stephen Michael *lawyer*
Nichols, F(rederick) Harris *lawyer*
Nolan, James Paul *medical educator, scientist*
†Norvilitis, Jill Marie *psychology educator*
Novak, Mary Theresa *parochial school educator*
Nowak, Carol Ann *city official*
Oak, H(elen) Lorraine *academic administrator, geography educator*
O'Donnell, Denise Ellen *lawyer*
O'Donnell, William Edward *Spanish language educator*
Odza, Randall M. *lawyer*
Oliver, Dominick Michael *business educator*
O'Loughlin, Sandra S. *lawyer*
Oppenheimer, Randolph Carl *lawyer*
†Ousley, Laurie Marie *English educator*
Pajak, David Joseph *lawyer, consultant*
Patel, Mulchand Shambhubhai *biochemist, researcher*
Payne, Frances Anne *literature educator, researcher*
Pearson, Paul David *lawyer, mediator*
Pegels, C. Carl *management science and systems educator*
Pentney, Roberta Jean *neuroanatomist, educator*
Peradotto, John Joseph *classics educator, editor*
Perry, J. Warren *health sciences educator, administrator*
Pietruszka, Michael F. *judge*
Pincus, Stephanie Hoyer *dermatologist, educator*
Ping, Douglas Edward *food and beverage company executive*
Piver, M. Steven *gynecologic oncologist*
Priore, Roger L. *biostatistics educator, consultant*
Pruitt, Dean Garner *psychologist, educator*
Reboy, Diane L. *medical/surgical and community health nurse*
Regan, Peter Francis, III *physician, psychiatry educator*
Regier, Darcy John *professional hockey team coach*
Reismann, Herbert *engineer, educator*
Reitan, Paul Hartman *geologist, educator*
Rekate, Albert C. *physician*
Rice, Victor Albert *manufacturing executive, heavy*
Rich, Robert E., Jr. *food products company executive*
Richards, David Gleyre *German language educator*
Richmond, Allen Martin *speech pathologist, educator*
Riepe, Dale Maurice *philosopher, writer, illustrator, educator, Asian art dealer*
Robinson, David Clinton *reporter*
Rochwarger, Leonard *former ambassador*
Roehner, Linda Gail *claims consultant*
Rogovin, Milton *documentary photographer, retired optometrist*
Ross, Christopher Theodore *lawyer*
Rowell, David Benton *sales and marketing company executive, consultant*
Ruckenstein, Eli *chemical engineering educator*
†Ruff, Lindy *coach*
†Rusting, Cheryl Lenorre *psychology educator*
Ryan, Diane Phyllis *nurse*
†Salerno, Tomas A. *cardiothoracic surgeon*
Sampson, John David *lawyer*
Sanders, Wendy Lee *development professional*
Sarjeant, Walter James *electrical and computer engineering educator*
†Satan, Miroslav *professional hockey player*
Saveth, Edward Norman *history educator*
Schmidli, Keith William *vocational education administrator, educator, researcher*
Schroeder, Harold Kenneth, Jr. *lawyer*
†Schuetze, Pamela *psychology educator, researcher*
Schultz, Douglas George *art museum director*
†Scott, Hugh B. *federal judge*
Seitz, Mary Lee *mathematics educator*
Seller, Robert Herman *cardiologist, family physician*
Selman, Alan Louis *computer science educator*
Shaner, Bronwyn Marian *elementary education educator*
Shapiro, Stuart Charles *computer scientist, educator*
Shaw, David Tai-Ko *electrical and computer engineering educator, university administrator*
Shedd, Donald Pomroy *surgeon*
Sherwood, Arthur Morley *lawyer*
Shick, Richard Arlon *academic dean*
†Shimojo, Mitsuaki *linguist, educator*
Siedlecki, Peter Anthony *English language and literature educator*
Silver, Kathleen Frances *rehabilitation counselor*
Simpson, George True *surgeon, educator*
†Singer, Simon Isaac *sociology educator*
Skretny, William Marion *federal judge*
Smith, Bennett Walker *minister*
Snyder, Robert Carl *minister*
Southwick, Lawrence, Jr. *management educator*
Starks, Fred William *chemical company executive*
Stelzle, James Joseph *library administrator*
†Stinger, Charles L. *history educator*
Stoddard, Elizabeth Jane *physician assistant, artist*
Stoll, Howard Lester, Jr. *dermatologist*
Stone, Robert A. *airport administrator*
†Sullivan, Margaret M. *managing editor*
Tall, Emily *foreign language educator*
Tedlock, Barbara Helen *anthropologist, educator, academic administrator*
Tedlock, Dennis *anthropology and literature educator*
Thorpe, John Alden *academic administrator, mathematician*
Timmerman, Leon Bernard *pump industry consultant*
Toles, Thomas Gregory *editorial cartoonist*
Tomasi, Thomas B. *cell biologist, administrator*
Toohey, Philip S. *lawyer*
Tornatore-Morse, Kathleen Mary *pharmacy educator*
Treanor, Charles Edward *scientist*
Trevisan, Maurizio *epidemiologist, researcher*
Triggle, David John *university dean, consultant*
Trotter, Herman Eager, Jr. (Herman Trotter) *music critic*
Urban, Henry Zeller *newspaperman*
Vitagliano, Kathleen Alyce Fuller *secondary education educator*
Vogel, Michael N. *journalist, writer, historian*
Wang, Jui Hsin *biochemistry educator*
Weber, Thomas William *chemical engineering educator*
†Weisstein, Naomi *neuroscientist, psychology educator, writer*
Weller, Sol William *chemical engineering educator*
Wickser, John Philip *lawyer*
Wiesenberg, Russel John *statistician*
Wilbur, Barbara Marie *elementary education educator*
Wilmers, Robert George *banker*
Wisbaum, Wayne David *lawyer*
Woelfel, Joseph Donald *communications educator*
Wolck, Wolfgang Hans-Joachim *linguist, educator*
Wozniak, Richard Anthony *computer engineer*
Wright, John Robert *pathologist, educator*
†Zhitnik, Alexei *professional hockey player*
Zimmerman, Nancy Picciano *library science educator*

Buskirk
Johanson, Patricia Maureen *artist, architect, park designer*

Camillus
Caryl, William R., Jr. *orthodontist*
Davis, Lynn Harry *secondary education educator*
Endieveri, Anthony Frank *lawyer*

Campbell Hall
Greenly, Colin *artist*
Ottaway, James Haller, Jr. *newspaper publisher*
Stone, Peter George *lawyer, publishing company executive*

Canaan
Belknap, Michael H. P. *real estate developer*
†Knebel, Constance *potter, ceramicist*
Pennell, William Brooke *lawyer*
Rothenberg, Albert *psychiatrist, educator*
†Van Schaick, Laura *non-profit social service administrator*
Walker, William Bond *painter, retired librarian*

Canandaigua
Chappelle, Lou Jo *physical therapist assistant*
Innes, David George *environmental and safety engineer*
Lowther, Frank Eugene *research physicist*
Malinowski, Patricia A. *community college educator*
Read, Eleanor May *financial analyst*
Sands, Marvin *wine company executive*
†Stocker, Patricia Marilyn *library administrator*
Williams, Carolyn Woodworth *retired elementary education educator, consultant*

Canastota
Lawson, Eric Wilfred, Sr. *educator*

Canisteo
Florence, Sally A. *retired school nurse educator, nurse practitioner*

Canton
Goldberg, Rita Maria *foreign language educator*
O'Connor, Daniel William *retired religious studies and classical languages educator*
Pollard, Fred Don *finance company executive*
Romey, William Dowden *geologist, educator*
Thompson, Jean Alling *librarian*

Cape Vincent
Stiefel, Linda Shields *lawyer*

Carle Place
Seiden, Steven Jay *lawyer*
Smolev, Terence Elliot *lawyer, educator*

Carmel
Bardell, Paul Harold, Jr. *electrical engineer*
Carruth, David Barrow *landscape architect*
Iglehart, Patricia Ann *strategy and market planning executive*
Kinney, Harrison Burton *writer*
Laporte, Cloyd, Jr. *lawyer, retired manufacturing executive*
Shen, Chia Theng *former steamship company executive, religious institute official*

Caroga Lake
Nilsen, Richard H. *foundation administrator, consultant*

Carthage
Rishel, Kenn Charles *school superintendent*

Cassadaga
†Sack, Marianne Sorensen *career educator, counselor*

Castle Point
Laubscher, Leeann *medical and surgical nurse*
Mehta, Rakesh Kumar *physician, consultant*

Castleton
†Kienzle, John Fred *history educator*
VanVliet, Mary Lynne *English language educator, photographer's assistant*

Castleton On Hudson
Lanford, Oscar Erasmus, Jr. *retired university vice chancellor*

Catskill
Howie, Philip Wesley *sculptor*
Kingsley, John Piersall *lawyer*
Tompkins, Sharon Lee *primary education educator*
Wolfe, Geraldine *administrator*

Cazenovia
Bump, Karin Diann *animal scientist, educator*
Clarke, George Alton *chemist, acdemic administrator, retired*
Dillingham, Ruth Elaine *lawyer, nurse*
Fleming, William Sloan *energy, environmental and technology company executive*
Muschenheim, Frederick *retired pathologist*
Pavese, Jacqueline Marie *librarian*
Shattuck, George Clement *retired lawyer*

Cedarhurst
Cohen, David B. *optical company executive*
Cohen, Harris L. *diagnostic radiologist, consultant*
Cohen, Philip Herman *accountant*
Klein, Irwin Grant *lawyer*
Lipsky, Linda Ethel *business executive*
Seyfert, Wayne George *secondary education educator, anatomy educator*
Taubenfeld, Harry Samuel *lawyer*
Van Raalte, Polly Ann *reading and writing specialist, photojournalist*

Center Moriches
Cullen, Valerie Adelia *secondary education educator*

Centereach
Cutrone, Dee T. *retired elementary education educator*

Centerport
Carll, Elizabeth Kassay *psychologist*
Fischel, Edward Elliot *physician, educator*
McQueeney, Henry Martin, Sr. *publisher*
†Trotta, Ric Charles *aerospace company executive, consultant*
Tunick, Laraine Donisi *publishing executive*

Central Islip
Griffith, Philip Arthur *elementary school educator*
McGowan, Harold *real estate developer, investor, scientist, author, philanthropist*

Central Square
BuMann, Sharon Ann *sculptor*

Chappaqua
de Janosi, Peter Engel *research manager*
George, Jean Craighead *author, illustrator*
Glazer, Richard Basil *university program director*
Graham, Lawrence Otis *lawyer, writer, television personality*
Gstalder, Herbert William *publisher*
Howard, John Brigham *lawyer, foundation executive*
Laun, Louis Frederick *government official*
O'Neill, Robert Charles *inventor, consultant*
Pollet, Susan L. *lawyer*
Pomerene, James Herbert *retired computer engineer*
Ujifusa, Grant Masashi *editor*
Whittingham, Charles Arthur *publisher, library administrator*

Chatham
†DeGroodt, Jesse *municipal official, sports writer*

Chautauqua
Mackenzie, John Anderson Ross *educator*
†Yurth, Helene Louise *librarian*

Cheektowaga
Mruk, Eugene Robert *retired marketing professional, urban planner*
Woldman, Sherman *pediatrician*

Chenango Bridge
Fisher, Dale Dunbar *animal scientist, dairy nutritionist*

Cherry Valley
†Plymell, Charley Douglass *writer, educator*
Sapinsky, Joseph Charles *magazine executive, photographer*

Chestnut Ridge
Burns, Richard Owen *lawyer*
Day, Stacey Biswas *physician, educator*
Huntoon, Robert Brian *chemist, food industry consultant*

Chittenango
Baum, Peter Alan *lawyer*
Brady, Don Paul *school psychologist, therapist, consultant*
Cassell, William Walter *retired accounting operations consultant*

Cicero
Mirucki, Maureen Ann *academic administrator*

Circleville
Moore, Virginia Lee Smith *elementary education educator*

City Island
†George, James *retired diplomat, foundation executive*

Clarence
Bish, L. Ann *retired secondary education educator*
Hubler, Julius *artist*

Claverack
Haus, Ruthann Elizabeth *geriatrics, community health nurse*

Clayton
Schmidt, Karl M., Jr. *political science educator*

Clifton Park
Adomfeh, Charles N. *internist*
Buhac, Ivo *gastroenterologist*
de Colombi-Monguió, Alicia *poet, foreign language educator*
Farley, John Joseph *library science educator emeritus*
Fell, Samuel Kennedy (Ken Fell) *infosystems executive*
†Golden, David M. *educator*
Miller, Robert Carl *real estate developer*
Murphy, Mary Patricia *elementary education educator*
Panek, Jan *electrical power engineer, consultant*
Scher, Robert Sander *instrument design company executive*

Climax
Adler, Lee *artist, educator, marketing executive*

Clinton
Anthony, Donald Charles *librarian, educator*
Burns, Bernard O. *county legislator*
Couper, Richard Watrous *foundation executive, educator*
†Doubleday, Simon Richard *historian*
Fuller, Ruthann *principal*
Pagani, Albert Louis *aerospace system engineer*
Ring, James Walter *physics educator*
Rose, Alan Arthur *university administrator*
Stowens, Daniel *pathologist*
Tobin, Eugene Marc *academic administrator*
Wagner, Frederick Reese *language professional*

Clinton Corners
McDermott, Patricia Ann *nursing administrator*

Cobleskill
Ingels, Jack Edward *horticulture educator*
Wilson, Lewis Lansing *insurance executive*

Cohocton
Frame, Paul Sutherland *medical educator, physician*
Sarfaty, Wayne Allen *insurance agent, financial planner*

Cohoes
Kennedy, Kathleen Ann *faculty/nursing consultant*
Kreutz, Austin Thomas *clergyman*
Tabner, Mary Frances *secondary school educator*

Cold Spring
Brill, Ralph David *architect, real estate developer, venture capitalist*
Miller, Timothy Earl *planning company executive*
Pugh, Emerson William *electrical engineer*

Cold Spring Harbor
MacKay, Robert Battin *museum director*
Watson, James Dewey *molecular biologist, educator*
Wigler, Michael H. *molecular biologist*

College Point
Harvey, Joel *chaplain, educator*

Colonie
Mallory, Doris Ann *social worker, counselor*

Combria Heights
Davis-Jerome, Eileen George *principal*

Commack
Gittman, Elizabeth *educator*
Kruger, Barbara *audiologist, speech and language pathologist*
Steindler, Walter G. *retired lawyer*

Conesus
Dadrian, Vahakn Norair *sociology educator*

Congers
Commanday, Peter Martin *educator*
Nelson, Marguerite Hansen *special education educator*

Cooperstown
Bordley, James, IV *surgeon*
Deysenroth, Peter Albin *funeral director*
Franck, Walter Alfred *rheumatologist, medical administrator, educator*
Fullington, Cynthia Janette *pediatric nurse*
Harman, Willard Nelson *malacologist, educator*
Huntington, Robert Graham *environmental business consultant*
Irvin, Monte *retired baseball player*
Jenkins, Ferguson Arthur, Jr. (Fergie Jenkins) *former baseball player*
Lemon, Robert Granville *retired baseball player*
Mathews, Edwin Lee *retired baseball player*
Mays, Willie Howard, Jr. (Say Hey Kid) *former professional baseball player*
McCovey, Willie Lee *former professional baseball player*
Peters, Theodore, Jr. *research biochemist, consultant*
Reese, Harold Henry (Pee Wee Reese) *retired baseball player*
Rich, Walter George *railroad transportation executive*
Steinberg, Paul *allergist, immunologist*
Tilton, Webster, Jr. *contractor*
Tripp, Wendell *historian, publications director*
†Whelan, Mary Anne *pediatrician, neurologist, educator*
Wilhelm, James Hoyt *retired baseball player*
†Yount, Robin *retired professional baseball player*

Coram
Helmer, Carol A. *psychologist, school psychologist*

Corinth
Winslow, Norma Mae *elementary education educator*

Corning
Ackerman, Roger G. *ceramic engineer*
Behm, Forrest Edwin *glass manufacturing company executive*
Booth, C(hesley) Peter Washburn *manufacturing company executive*
Buechner, Thomas Scharman *artist, retired glass manufacturing company executive, museum director*
Davis, Francis Raymond *priest*
Ecklin, Robert Luther *materials company executive*
Hauselt, Denise Ann *lawyer*
Havewala, Noshir Behram *chemical engineer*
Houghton, James Richardson *retired glass manufacturing company executive*
Johnson, Janet LeAnn Moe *statistician, engineering professional*
Keck, Donald Bruce *physicist*
Lin, Min-Chung *obstetrician, gynecologist*
Maurer, Robert Distler *retired industrial physicist*
Miller, Roger Allen *physicist*
†Neubauer, Dean Veral *statistician*
Peck, Arthur John, Jr. *diversified manufacturing executive, lawyer*
Spillman, Jane Shadel *curator, researcher, writer*
Ughetta, William Casper *lawyer, manufacturing company executive*
Whitehouse, David Bryn *museum director*
Williams, Jimmie Lewis *research chemist*
Youst, David Bennett *career development educator*

Cornwall
Loeffel, Bruce *software company executive, consultant*

Cornwall On Hudson
Abrams-Collens, Vivien *artist*
Holstein, David *psychotherapist, management consultant, educator*

Corona
Afulezi, Uju N. *economic association administrator, professor, librarian, author, consultant*
Jackson, Andrew Preston *library director*
Levy, Barry Alan *technical writer, songwriter*
Little, Frederick Anton *landscape architect, municipal administrator*
Miele, Joel Arthur, Sr. *civil engineer*

Cortland
†Alsen, Eberhard *educator*
Anderson, Donna Kay *musicologist, educator*
Hischak, Thomas Stephen *theater educator, writer*
†Hurwitz, Mark Francis *filtration company executive, research engineer*
Kaminsky, Alice Richkin *English language educator*
Malakar, Jagadish Chandra *internist*
Miller, John David *manufacturing company executive*
Swartwood, Michie Odle *psychology educator*
†Wright, Donald R. *history educator*

Cortlandt Manor
Rosenberg, Marilyn Rosenthal *artist, visual poet*

Cranberry Lake
Glavin, James Edward *landscape architect*

Cross River
Kelsey, Sterett-Gittings *sculptor*

Croton On Hudson
Plotch, Walter *management consultant, fund raising counselor*
Rath, Bernard Emil *entrepreneur*
Rubinfien, Leo H. *photographer, filmmaker*
Shatzkin, Leonard *publishing consultant*
Straka, Laszlo Richard *publishing consultant*
Turner, David Reuben *publisher, author*
Werman, David Sanford *psychiatrist, psychoanalyst, educator*

Crown Point
Dajany, Innam *academic administrator*

Crugers
Norman, Jessye *soprano*
Walther, Zerita *paralegal*

Cutchogue
Aldcroft, George Edward *guidance counselor*
Bidwell, Robert Ernest *inventor*
O'Connell, Francis Joseph *lawyer, arbitrator*
Strimban, Robert *graphic designer*

Dansville
Vogel, John Walter *lawyer*

Davidson
†LeFauve, Linda Marie *college administrator*

De Witt
Pearl, Harvey *rehabilitation psychologist*

Dearby
Goodell, Joseph Edward *manufacturing executive*

Deer Park
D'Amore, Victor *director, choreographer, dance educator*
Maher, James Richard *protective services offical*
Sacco, Russell *community employment coordinator, clergyman*
Taub, Jesse J. *electrical engineering researcher*

Delhi
Hamilton, John Thomas, Jr. *lawyer*

Delmar
†Brewer, Floyd I. *history consultant*
Button, Rena Pritsker *public affairs executive*
†Campas, Anna Penelope *civil engineer, architect*
Eldridge, Douglas Alan *lawyer*
Erlich, Fredrick William *human services administrator*
Houghton, Raymond Carl, Jr. *computer science educator*
†LaFave, Cynthia S. *lawyer*
Mancuso, James Carmin *psychologist, educator*
Nitecki, Joseph Zbigniew *librarian*
Quackenbush, Cathy Elizabeth *secondary school educator*
Schwartz, Louise A. *musicologist*
Shen, Thomas To *environmental engineer*

Denver
Koutroulis, Aris George *artist, educator*

Depew
Koch, Ronald Peter *retired biologist*

Derby
Pordum, Francis J. *former state legislator, educator*

Dewitt
Stefano, Ross William *business executive*

Dix Hills
Braun, Ludwig *educational technology consultant*
Fisher, Fenimore *business development consultant*
†Ivy, Edward Joseph *plastic surgeon*
Katzberg, Jane Michaels *health care administrator, consultant, educator*
Kornhauser, Kenneth Richard *funeral director, executive*
Mastrogiannis, Dimitrios S. *obstetrician/gynecologist, perinatologist*
Meyers, George Edward *plastics company executive*
Pugliese, Paul Jones *cartographer*

Dobbs Ferry
Comizio-Assante, Delva Maria *nurse, clinical nurse specialist*
Downey, John Harold *publishing executive*
Grunebaum, Ernest Michael *investment banker*
Guggenheimer, Tobias Immanuel Simon *architect*
Holtz, Sidney *publishing company executive*
Juettner, Diana D'Amico *lawyer, educator*
Kapp, Richard P. *conductor, arts administrator*
LeRoy, Karen Leslie *English language educator*
Litwin, Burton Lawrence *entertainment industry executive, theatrical producer, lawyer*
Miss, Robert Edward *fundraiser*
Mooney, Vicki *playwright*
Poian, Edward Licio *historian*
Simon, Lothar *publishing company executive*
Sutton, Francis Xavier *social scientist, consultant*
Triplett, Kelly B. *chemist*
Weisman, Benjamin Brucker *finance educator, consultant*

Douglaston
†Hornick, Susan Florence *secondary education educator, fine arts educator*
Valero, René Arnold *clergyman*
Walsh, Sean M. *lawyer, audio-video computer forensics consultant*

Dover Plains
Arnold, Doris Foltz *minister, former health care administrator*

Dryden
Baxter, Robert Banning *insurance company executive*

Dundee
Pfendt, Henry George *retired information systems executive, management consultant*

Dunkirk
Bergmann, Dennis William *health facility administrator*
Huels, Steven Mark *laboratory analyst*
Woodbury, Robert Charles *lawyer*

Durham
Dearing, David Richard *secondary education educator*

East Amherst
Ernest, Welden Arenas *retired history educator*
†Haltam, Michael Patrick *medical device manufacturing executive*
Soong, Tsu-Teh *engineering science educator*

East Aurora
Birch, David William *college official*
Brott, Irving Deerin, Jr. *lawyer, judge*
Hawk, George Wayne *retired electronics company executive*
Hayes, Bonaventure Francis *priest*
Spahn, Mary Attea *retired educator*
Speller, Kerstin G. Rinta *psychologist*
Weidemann, Julia Clark *principal, educator*
Woodard, Carol Jane *educational consultant*

East Elmhurst
Marshall, Helen M. *city official*

East Fishkill
Poschmann, Andrew William *information systems and management consultant*

East Garden City
Baker, J. A., II *management consultant, monetary architect, financial engineer*

East Greenbush
Mucci, Patrick John *financial consultant, realtor, commercial loan broker*

East Hampton
Bruckmann, Donald John *investment banker*
Damaz, Paul F. *architect*
De Bruhl, Marshall *writer, editor, publishing consultant*
Dello Joio, Norman *composer*
†Duffy, Francis J. *public relations executive*
Ehren, Charles Alexander, Jr. *lawyer, educator*
Garrett, Charles Geoffrey Blythe *physicist*
Harmon, Marian Sanders *writer, sculptor*
Jaudon, Valerie *artist*
Karp, Harvey Lawrence *metal products manufacturing company executive*
Keagy, Dorothy (Dotti Keagy) *copywriter*
Merton, Robert K. *sociologist, educator*
Munson, Lawrence Shipley *management consultant*
Murbach, David Paul *horticulturist*
Paton, David *ophthalmologist, educator*
Petersen, Ellen Anne *artist*
Scott, Rosa Mae *artist, educator*
Stein, Ronald Jay *artist, airline transport pilot*
Swerdlow, Amy *historian, educator, writer*
†Thompson, William Irwin *humanities educator, author*
Vered, Ruth *art gallery director*

East Herkimer
Kroft, Glenn Vincent *painter*

East Islip
Delman, Michael Robert *physician*
Orsomarso, Don Frank *school system administrator*
Rogers, Jeanne Valerie *art educator, artist*
Somerville, Daphine Holmes *elementary education educator*

East Meadow
Adler, Ira Jay *lawyer*
Bergman, Bruce Jeffrey *lawyer*
Beyer, Norma Warren *secondary education educator*
Bunshaft, Marilyn Janosy *community services specialist*
Cymbler, Murray Joel *corporate professional*
De Santis, Mark *osteopathic physician*
†Fernandes, Carla Michelle *advertising assistant*
Fuchs, Jerome Herbert *management consultant*
Grassano, Thomas David *minister*
Hyman, Montague Allan *lawyer*
Mondello, John Paul *financial consultant*

East Northport
Haggerty, Arthur Daniel *stress and chronic pain management specialist*
†Meares, Elsi Junas *artist*

East Norwich
Rosen, Meyer Robert *chemical engineer*

East Quogue
Weiss, Elaine Landsberg *community development management official*

East Rochester
Murray, James Doyle *accountant*

East Setauket
Badalamenti, Fred Leopoldo *artist, educator*
Barcel, Ellen Nora *secondary school educator, free-lance writer, editor*
Briggs, Philip Terry *biologist*

East Syracuse
Wiley, Richard Gordon *electrical engineer*

Eastchester
†Weinberg, Dale G. *technical writer, consultant*

Eastport
Oliveri, Robert Peter *retired social worker*
Wruck, Michelle Mingino *pediatric nurse practitioner*

Elba
Kauffman, William Joseph *editor, writer*

Elizabethtown
Lawrence, Richard Wesley, Jr. *foundation executive*

Elizaville
Koeppel, Harry Saul *interior designer, educator*

Elmhurst
Barron, Charles Thomas *psychiatrist*
Byun, Hang S. *neurosurgeon, educator*
†Gregg-Mullings, Linda *educator*
Lester, Lance Gary *education educator, researcher*
Masci, Joseph Richard *medical educator, physician*
Matsa, Loula Zacharoula *social services administrator*
Maurer-Buterakos, Kathleen Ann *educational administrator, supervisor*
Schwartz, Evan Gary *orthopedist*
Wachsteter, George *illustrator*
Xu, Ying-Pei *artist*

Elmira
Amchin, Robert A. *music educator*
Graham, David Richard *orthopedic surgeon*

Henbest, Robert LeRoy *retired bank and insurance company executive*
Meier, Thomas Keith *college president, English educator*
Paul, Christopher Donald *carpenter, author*
Quintos, Elias Rilloraza *cardiac surgeon, thoracic surgeon*
Swartz, Melanie Lynn *nurse*

Elmont
Brancaleone Kenna, Laurie Ann *social worker*
Butera, Ann Michele *consulting company executive*
Cusack, Thomas Joseph *retired banker*

Elmsford
Clutter, Bertley Allen, III *management company executive*
De Nicola, Peter Francis *photographic manufacturer*
Fachnie, H(ugh) Douglas *film manufacturing company official*
Miranda, Robert Nicholas *publishing company executive*
Raymond, George Marc *city planner, educator*

Endicott
Englehart, Joan Anne *trade association executive*
Heide, Hans Dieter, Jr. *accountant*
Schwartz, Richard Frederick *electrical engineering educator*

Esopus
Tetlow, Edwin *author*

Fairport
Badenhop, Sharon Lynn *psychologist, educator, entrepreneur*
Carlton, Charles Merritt *linguistics educator*
Fisher, Jerid Martin *neuropsychologist*
Garg, Devendra *financial executive*
Germano, Mary Catherine *writer*
†Graham, Susette Ryan *retired English educator*
Herz, Marvin Ira *psychiatrist, educator*
Holtzclaw, Diane Smith *elementary school educator*
Lavoie, Dennis James *secondary education educator*
Oldshue, James Y. *chemical engineering consultant*
Paul, Thomas Wayne *psychotherapist*
Pearles, Linda Terry *secondary education educator*
Reidy, Thomas Michael *financial executive*
Talty, Lorraine Caguioa *accountant*
Wiener, David L. *secondary education educator*

Falconer
Ruhlman, Herman C(loyd), Jr. *manufacturing company executive*

Far Rockaway
Epstein, Samuel Abraham *stock and bond broker, petroleum consultant*
Farron, Robert *physician, family practice*
Kelly, George Anthony *clergyman, author, educator*
Madhusoodanan, Subramoniam *psychiatrist, educator*
†Mithcell, Lillian Adassa *educator*

Farmingdale
Blum, Melvin *chemical company executive, researcher*
Bolle, Donald Martin *retired engineering educator*
Bongiorno, Joseph John, Jr. *electrical engineering educator*
Cipriani, Frank Anthony *college president*
Doucette, David Robert *computer systems company executive*
Klosner, Jerome Martin *mechanical engineer, educator*
LaTourrette, James Thomas *retired electrical engineering and computer science educator*
Marcuvitz, Nathan *electrophysics educator*
Nolan, Peter John *physics educator*
Sandler, Gerald Howard *computer science educator, company executive*
Steckler, Larry *publisher, editor, author*
Thomas, Patrick N. *physical therapist*
Youla, Dante C. *electric engineer*

Farmingville
Di Marco, Anthony Sabatino *retired educational administrator*

Fayetteville
Chevli, Renate Naren *obstetrician, gynecologist*
Dosanjh, Darshan S(ingh) *aeronautical engineer, educator*
Hiemstra, Roger *adult education educator, writer, networker*
Pachter, Irwin Jacob *pharmaceutical consultant*
Paul, Linda Baum *geriatrics nurse, toy business owner*
Pirodsky, Donald Max *psychiatrist, educator*
Sager, Roderick Cooper *retired life insurance company executive*
Steele, Pamela Carey *artist, educator*
Wallace, Spencer Miller, Jr. *hotel executive*

Feura Bush
Byrne, Donn Erwin *psychologist, educator*

Fishkill
Brocks, Eric Randy *ophthalmologist, surgeon*
Stein, Paula Nancy *psychologist, educator*

Floral Park
Cardalena, Peter Paul, Jr. *lawyer, educator*
Chatoff, Michael Alan *lawyer*
Corbett, William John *government and public relations consultant, lawyer*
Dudek, Henry Thomas *management consultant*
Heyderman, Mark Baron *sales and marketing company executive*
Scricca, Diane Bernadette *principal*

Flushing
Amsterdam, David Erik *school psychologist*
†Ausubel, Hillel *librarian*
Belden, Ursula *set designer*
Bezrod, Norma R. *artist*
Bird, Thomas Edward *foreign language and literature educator*
Bonilla, Bobby (Roberto Martin Antonio Bonilla) *professional baseball player*
Brown, Kenneth Lloyd *lawyer*
Buell, Frederick Henderson *educator*
Capra, Linda Ann *elementary education educator*
Carlson, Cynthia Joanne *artist, educator*
Castro, Robert R. *retired surgeon*
Cathcart, Robert Stephen *mass media consultant*
Chang, Lee-Lee *lawyer*
Cheng, Sharon Goon *lawyer*
Chook, Paul Howard *publishing executive*
Coch, Nicholas Kyros *geologist, educator*
Commoner, Barry *biologist, educator*
†Dorn, Alfred *poet, retired English educator*
Doubleday, Nelson *professional baseball team executive*
Erickson, Raymond *academic dean, music historian, musician*
Erwin, Elizabeth Joy *early childhood and special education specialist*
Fichtel, Rudolph Robert *retired association executive*
Finks, Robert Melvin *paleontologist, educator*
Flechner, Roberta Fay *graphic designer*
Friedman, Alan Jacob *museum director*
Gafney, Harry D. *chemistry educator*
Georghiou, Michael *construction and development executive*
Givens, Janet Eaton *writer*
Goldman, Norman Lewis *chemistry educator*
Goldsmith, Howard *writer, consultant*
Goldstein, Milton *art educator, printmaker, painter*
Hacker, Andrew *political science educator*
Harrison, Julia *councilwoman*
†Henderson, Rickey Henley *professional baseball player*
Henshel, Harry Bulova *watch manufacturer*
†Hershiser, Orel Leonard, IV *professional baseball player*
Hirshson, Stanley Philip *history educator*
Hon, John Wingsun *physician*
Horowitz, Gayle Lynn *physical education educator*
Hui, William Man Wai *chiropractor*
Kiner, Ralph McPherran *sports commentator, former baseball player*
Kinsbruner, Jay *history educator*
Kobliner, Richard *secondary school educator*
Kresic, Eva *pediatrician*
Laderman, Gabriel *artist*
†Leiter, Alois Terry (Al) *professional baseball player*
†Liang, Zai *sociology educator*
Liccione, Alexander Anthony *artist*
Lonigan, Paul Raymond *language professional educator*
Lopez-Pumarejo, Tomas Alberto *communications educator, marketing consultant*
†Low, Frederick Emerson *English educator*
Madden, Joseph Daniel *trade association executive*
Matheis, Vickie Lynne *nurse*
Mendelson, Elliott *mathematician, educator*
Milone, James Michael *occupational health-safety forensic engineering technology executive, evironmental engineer*
Nori, Dattatreyudu *oncologist, researcher*
Nussbaum, Michel Ernest *physician*
Olerud, John Garrett *professional baseball player*
Overton, Rosilyn Gay Hoffman *financial services executive*
Parascos, Edward Themistocles *retired utilities executive*
†Parise, Frank Benjamin *dentist*
Piazza, Michael Joseph *professional baseball player*
Pillinger, James J. *lawyer, educator*
Psomiades, Harry John *political science educator*
Rabassa, Gregory *Romance languages educator, translator, poet*
Ranald, Margaret Loftus *English literature educator, author*
Richter, David Henry *English language educator, writer*
Ritchin, Barbara Sue *educational administrator, consultant*
Roberts, Kathleen Joy Doty *school administrator, educator*
Sanborn, Anna Lucille *pension and insurance consultant*
†Saylor, Bruce Stuart *composer, educator*
Seaver, Tom (George Thomas Seaver) *former professional baseball player*
Shen, Ronger *artist, educator*
Shirvani, Hamid *architect, educator, author, administrator*
Silver, Sheila Jane *composer, music educator*
†Sirowitz, Hal *poet, special education educator*
†Slatkes, Leonard Joseph *art history educator*
Smaldone, Edward Michael *composer*
Smith, Charles William *social sciences educator, sociologist*
Speidel, David Harold *geology educator*
Stahl, Frank Ludwig *civil engineer*
Stark, Joel *speech language pathologist*
Stavisky, Leonard Price *state legislator*
Tai, Emily Sohmer *history educator, writer*
†Taylor, Conciere Marlana *writer*
Tepper, Marvin B. *professional sports team executive*
Tytell, John *humanities educator, writer*
Uter, Carmenlita *secondary school educator, genealogist*
†Valentine, Robert John (Bobby Valentine) *professional baseball manager*
Ventura, Robin Mark *professional baseball player*
Viegas, Louis Paul *postmaster*
Weiss, George Arthur *orthodontist*
Wells, David I. *retired labor union administrator*
†Yeo, Kim Eng *artist*

Fly Creek
Dusenbery, Walter Condit *sculptor*

Forest Hills
Alsapiedi, Consuelo Veronica *psychoanalytic psychotherapist, consultant*
Baral, Lillian *artist, retired educator*
Crystal, Boris *artist*
†Dybman, Nick Nison *poet*
Eden, Alvin Noam *pediatrician, author*
†Gorbaty, Jan *pianist, music educator*
Grigorian, Marcos *artist, art gallery director*
Immerman, Mia Fendler *artist*
Kane, Sydell *elementary school principal*
Koslowitz, Karen *councilwoman*
Kra, Pauline Skornicki *French language educator*
Miller, Donald Ross *management consultant*
Narasimhan, Parthasarathy *physician*
Polakoff, Abe *baritone*
Povman, Morton *lawyer*
Prager, Alice Heinecke *music company executive*
Richard, Chava Wolpert *artist*
Tewi, Thea *sculptor*
Torrence-Thompson, Juanita Lee *public relations executive*
Van Westering, James Francis *management consultant, educator*

Forestville
†Adams, Lee Towne *lawyer*

Fort Drum
†Kuykendall, Benjamin Loren *military officer*
Magruder, Lawson William, III *military officer*

Fort Edward
Horn, Thomas Joseph, Jr. *educator*

Frankfort
Conigilaro, Phyllis Ann *retired elementary education educator*

Franklin
Young, William Donald, Jr. *bacteriologist, artist-blacksmith, photographer*

Franklin Square
Cohen, Carla Lynn *publisher*
Indiviglia, Salvatore Joseph *artist, retired naval officer*

Fredonia
Belliotti, Raymond Angelo *philosopher, educator, lawyer*
Benton, Allen Haydon *biology educator*
Browder, George Clark *history educator, writer*
Collingwood, Tracy Lynn *academic advisor, career counselor*
Klonsky, Bruce Gary *educator*
Krohn, Franklin Bernard *marketing specialist, educator*
Mac Vittie, Robert William *retired college administrator*
Mallory, George Wolcott *retired federal agency officer*
Sedota, Gladys Elizabeth *secondary education educator*
Sonnenfeld, Marion *linguist, educator*
†Steinberg, Theodore Louis *English educator*
Strauser, Jeffrey Arthur *public safety official*

Freeport
Burstein, Stephen David *neurosurgeon*
Dimancescu, Mihai D. *neurosurgeon, researcher, educator*
Halbfinger, Andrea Sue *journalist*
Martorana, Barbara Joan *secondary education educator*
†McCally, Daniel S. *urologist*
Pullman, Maynard Edward *biochemist*
Terris, Virginia R. *writer*

Fremont Center
Butter, Tom *sculptor, educator*

Fresh Meadows
Kaplan, Barry Hubert *physician*

Frewsburg
Burgeson, Joyce Ann *travel agency official*

Fulton
Long, Robert Emmet *author*

Gainesville
MacWilliams, Debra Lynne *primary reading specialist, consultant*

Garden City
†Anziano, Gale Mary *guidance counselor, social worker*
Atkins, William Allen *academic administrator*
Berka, Marianne Guthrie *health and physical education educator*
Campbell, James R. *transportation executive*
Caputo, Kathryn Mary *paralegal*
†Cohen, Harvey *lawyer*
Conlon, Brian Thomas *promotion executive*
Conlon, Thomas James *marketing executive*
Cook, George Valentine *lawyer*
Corleto, Raymond Anthony *lawyer*
Corsi, Philip Donald *lawyer*
Crom, James Oliver *professional training company executive*
Deane, Leland Marc *plastic surgeon*
Di Mascio, John Philip *lawyer*
Doucette, Mary-Alyce *computer company executive*
Egan, Frank T. *writer, editor*
Eickelberg, W. Warren Barbour *academic administrator*
†Falk, Patricia *English language educator*
†Fanelli, Sean A. *college president*
Festa, Jo Ann V. *nursing educator*
Fischoff, Gary Charles *lawyer*
Fishberg, Gerard *lawyer*
Fleisig, Ross *aeronautical engineer, engineering manager*
Good, Larry Irwin *physician, consultant*
Gordon, Barry Joel *investment advisor*
Gordon, Jay F(isher) *lawyer*
Harwood, Stanley *retired judge, lawyer*
Hinds, Glester Samuel *financier, program specialist, tax consultant*
Jenkins, Kenneth Vincent *literature educator, writer*
Kaplan, Joel Stuart *lawyer*
Kestenbaum, Harold Lee *lawyer*
†Koenig, Louis William *political science educator, author*
Korshak, Yvonne *art historian*
Kurlander, Neale *accounting and law educator, lawyer*
Lilly, Thomas Joseph *lawyer*
†Love, Douglas P. *editor*
Lovely, Thomas Dixon *banker*
McCann, Louise Mary *paralegal*
Minicucci, Richard Francis *lawyer, former hospital administrator*
Nicklin, George Leslie, Jr. *psychoanalyst, educator, physician*
Ohrenstein, Roman Abraham *economics educator, economist, rabbi*
Okulski, John Allen *principal*
Ostrow, Michael Jay *lawyer*
Podwall, Kathryn Stanley *biology educator*
Rhein, John Hancock Willing, III *publishing executive*
Shneidman, J. Lee *historian, educator*
Smith, Paul Thomas *financial services company executive*
Tucker, William P. *lawyer, writer*
Webb, Igor Michael *academic administrator*
†Zelman, Warren Henry *otolaryngologist, surgeon*

Gardiner
Mabee, Carleton *historian, educator*
Schneider, Evelyn Jean *educational consultant, English educator*

Garrison
Barnhart, Robert Knox *writer, editor*
Callahan, Daniel John *biomedical researcher*
Egan, Daniel Francis *priest*
Impellizzeri, Anne Elmendorf *insurance company executive, non-profit executive*
Murray, Thomas Henry *bioethics educator, writer*
Pierpont, Robert *fund raising executive, consultant*

Geneseo
Battersby, Harold Ronald *anthropologist, archaeologist, linguist*
Edgar, William John *philosophy educator*
†Lutkus, Alan H. *English educator*
†Nassif, Maggie N. *educator in English and literature, translator*
Olczak, Paul Vincent *psychology educator*
†Spicka, Edwin J. *biology educator*

Geneva
Coon, Penny K. *religious organization official*
Dickson, James Edwin, II *obstetrician, gynecologist*
Givelber, Harry Michael *pathologist*
Hersh, Richard H. *academic administrator*
Roelofs, Wendell Lee *biochemistry educator, consultant*
Singal, Daniel Joseph *historian*
Woodard, Richard Charles *college administrator*

Germantown
Callanan, Laura Patrice *foundation manager*
Linney, Romulus *author, educator*
Rollins, (Theodore) Sonny *composer, musician*

Getzville
†Schulman, Diane R. *chemistry educator*

Gilbertsville
Roos, Casper *actor*

Glen Cove
Burnham, Harold Arthur *pharmaceutical company executive, physician*
Chun, Arlene Donnelly *special education educator*
Conti, James Joseph *chemical engineer, educator*
Costa, Thomas Charles *priest*
Dehn, Joseph William, Jr. *chemist*
Makris, Constantine John *infosystems engineer*
Maxwell, J. Douglas, Jr. *chemical service company executive*
Mills, Charles Gardner *lawyer*
†Mulvihill, William Patrick *writer*
Petrovich, Peter Yurosh *English and foreign language educator, writer*
Tecce, Jacqueline *office manager*

Glen Falls
†Hall, Michael L. *business educator*

Glen Head
Boyrer, Elaine M. *principal*
Cohen, Lawrence N. *health care management consultant*
Huber, Don Lawrence *publisher*
Jamal, Moez Ahamed *banker*
Savinetti, Louis Gerard *lawyer*
Sutherland, Denise Jackson (Denise Suzanne Jackson) *ballerina*
Sutherland, Donald James *investment company executive*
Swift, Ronni *special education educator*

Glendale
Linekin, Patricia Landi *clinical nurse specialist*
Maltese, Serphin Ralph *state senator, lawyer*

Glenham
Douglas, Fred Robert *cost engineering consultant*

Glens Falls
Bartlett, Richard James *lawyer, former university dean*
†Brender, William Charles *plastic and reconstructive surgeon, artist*
Depan, Mary Elizabeth *civic volunteer, nurse*
Fawcett, Christopher Babcock *civil engineer, construction and water resources company executive*
Pearsall, Glenn Lincoln *brokerage house executive*
Trombley, Joseph Edward *insurance company executive, underwriter, financial planner*
Wurzberger, Bezalel *psychiatrist*

Glenville
Anderson, Roy Everett *electrical engineering consultant*
Pontius, James Wilson *foundation administrator*

Gloversville
†Casey, Kathleen Margaret *secondary education educator*
Rhodes, Alan Charles *minister*

Goshen
Goodreds, John Stanton *newspaper publisher*
Hawkins, Barry Tyler *author, mental health services professional*
Roncal, Rogelio *psychiatrist*
Seidman, A(bram) Alan *marketing representative, county official*
Ward, William Francis, Jr. *real estate investment banker*
†Warren, Sheila Deveney *nurse administrator, educator*

Gouverneur
Leader, Robert John *lawyer*

Grand Island
Backus, Kevin Michael *minister*
Beach, Sandra Marie Yudichak *secondary education educator*
Deutsch, Anne *clinical nurse specialist*
Hennigar, William Grant, Jr. *dentist*

Muck, Ruth Evelyn Slacer (Mrs. Gordon E. Muck) education educator
Schenck, Henry Paul telecommunications executive

Granville
†Stoddard, Andrea Louise special education educator, small business owner

Great Neck
Appel, Gerald investment advisor
Arlow, Jacob A. psychiatrist, educator
†Aronson, Margaret R. school psychologist
Blanda, Sandi artist
Blumberg, Barbara Salmanson (Mrs. Arnold G. Blumberg) retired state housing official, housing consultant
Bungarz, William Robert pediatrician
†Burghardt, Linda F. writer
Dantzker, David Roy health facility executive
Donenfeld, Kenneth Jay management consultant
†Epstein, Marc A. school system administrator
Feldman, Gary Marc nutritionist, consultant
Fiel, Maxine Lucille journalist, behavioral analyst, lecturer
Friedland, Louis N. retired communications executive
Gellman, Yale H. lawyer
Goldberg, Melvin Arthur communications executive
†Goldberger, Avriel Horwitz literary translator, retired French educator
†Goldes, Jordan legislative staff member
Goldman, Ira Steven gastroenterologist
Gross, Lillian psychiatrist
Hamovitch, William economist, educator, university official
Hampton, Benjamin Bertram brokerage house executive
Harris, Marilyn retired academic administrator
Hecht, Marie Bergenfeld retired educator, author
Hurwitz, Johanna (Frank) author, librarian
Joskow, Jules economic research company executive
Kahn, David editor, author
Katz, Edward Morris banker
Kawano, Arnold Hubert lawyer
Kechijian, Paul dermatologist, educator
†Keller, Alex Jay plastic and reconstructive surgeon
Kodsi, Sylvia Rose ophthalmologist
Lande, Ruth Harriet photographer, language educator
Lyons, Laurence securities executive, retired
†Means, Rosaline business executive, business educator
†Oberby, M. Chris physician, neurosurgeon
Panes, Jack Samuel publishing company executive
Pohl, Gunther Erich retired library administrator
Pollack, Paul Robert airline service company executive
Puttlitz, Donald Herbert medical microbiologist
Rockowitz, Noah Ezra lawyer
Rosegarten, Rory talent manager, television and theater producer
Rosenberg, Richard F. physician, radiologist
Rosenthal, Irving journalism educator
†Rossi, Ino anthropology educator
Roth, Harvey Paul publisher
Rubenstein, Stanley Ellis public relations consultant
Rubin, Karen Beth publishing, marketing and representation executive
Salzman, Stanley P. lawyer
Samanowitz, Ronald Arthur lawyer
Satinskas, Henry Anthony airline services company executive
†Schwartz, Alan Paul corporate executive
Seidler, Doris artist
Shaffer, Bernard William mechanical and aerospace engineering educator
Simon, Arthur pharmacologist, research laboratory executive
Simon, Seymour writer, photographer
Tosheff, Julij Gospodinoff psychiatrist
Turofsky, Charles Sheldon landscape architect
Vignola, Andrew Michael, Sr. systems management executive
Wachsman, Harvey Frederick lawyer, neurosurgeon
Wolff, Edward physician
†Zeiger, David poet, retired English educator
†Zeiger, Lila L. creative writing educator
Zirinsky, Daniel real estate investor and photographer

Greenfield Center
Conant, Robert Scott harpsichordist, music educator
Fonseca, John dos Reis writer, former law educator
Templin, John Leon, Jr. healthcare consulting executive

Greenlawn
Bachman, Henry Lee electrical engineer, engineering executive
Newman, Edward Morris engineering executive
†Roberts, Gloria Jean writer
Stevens, John Richard architectural historian

Greenport
†Cowley, Joseph Gilbert editor, writer
†Richland, Lisa library director

Greenvale
Cook, Edward Joseph college president
†Dinan, Susan Eileen history educator
Dircks, Phyllis Toal English language educator
Halper, Emanuel B(arry) real estate lawyer, developer, consultant, author
Leipzig, Arthur photographer, educator emeritus
Steinberg, David Joel academic administrator, historian, educator
Westermann-Cicio, Mary Louise academic administrator, library studies educator

Greenville
Overbaugh, Maryanne W. elementary educator

Greenwich
†Targan, Barry educator

Greenwood
Rollins, June Elizabeth elementary education educator

Greenwood Lake
†Shwiff, Kathy Joyce editor

Guilderland
†Bawa, Rubina pharmacist

Gordon, Leonard Victor psychologist, educator emeritus
†Reiff, Robert L. federal agency specialist
Yunich, Albert Mansfeld physician

Hamburg
Dor, Caplyn artist
Falkner, Noreen Margaret English language educator
Gaughan, Dennis Charles lawyer
Hargesheimer, Elbert, III lawyer
Keenan, John Paul management educator, consultant, psychologist
Kuhn, Merrily A. nursing educator
Markulis, Henryk John career military officer
Witt, Dennis Ruppert secondary school mathematics educator

Hamilton
†Balakian, Peter English educator
Berlind, Bruce Peter poet, educator
Blackton, Charles S(tuart) history educator
Busch, Briton Cooper historian, educator
Busch, Frederick Matthew writer, literature educator
Edmonston, William Edward, Jr. publisher, educator
Farnsworth, Frank Albert retired economics educator
Garland, Robert Sandford John classical studies educator
Hathaway, Robert Lawton Romance languages educator
Holbrow, Charles Howard physicist, educator
†Johnson, Anita Spanish language educator
Johnston, (William) Michael political science educator, university administrator
Jones, Howard Langworthy retired educational administrator, consultant
Kessler, Dietrich biology educator
Levy, Jacques educator, theater director, lyricist, writer
Soderberg, Dale LeRoy English language educator, drama director, producer
Staley, Lynn English educator
Tucker, Thomas William mathematics professor
Van Schaack, Eric art historian, educator
†Wilhelm, Simi Ruth college administrator

Hammond
Musselman, Francis Haas lawyer

Hampton Bays
Baker, Donald G. social sciences educator
Yavitz, Boris business educator, corporate director

Hancock
DeLuca, Ronald former advertising agency executive, consultant

Hannacroix
Schwebler, Stephen retired chemist

Harris
Buonanni, Brian Francis health care facility administrator, consultant

Harrison
Krantz, Melissa Marianne public relations company executive
McElwaine, Theresa Weedy academic administrator, artist
†O'Hare, Bernard F. lawyer
Paulli, Carla Nadene secondary education educator
Schulz, Helmut Wilhelm chemical engineer, environmental executive
Wadsworth, Frank Whittemore foundation executive, literature educator
†Wedge, Chris animation director
Wilson, William James marketing professional

Hartsdale
Aker, Susan K. elementary nursing education educator
Brozak-McMann, Edith May performing and visual artist
Cantor, Morton B. psychiatrist
Chait, Maxwell Mani physician
Jones, Donald Kelly state agency executive
Katz, John investment banker
Wallace, Arthur, Jr. retired college dean

Hastings On Hudson
Cooney, Patrick Louis writer
Cooper, Doris Jean market research executive
D'Antoni, Philip producer
Fischler, Steven Alan film producer
Goldstein, Eleanor artist, social worker
Landau, Peter Edward editor
Parrott, Billy James film director, communications executive
Reich, Herb editor
Weinstein, Edward Michael architect, consultant
Wolfe, Stanley composer, educator

Hauppauge
Amore, Michael Joseph financial and administrative executive
Arams, Frank Robert electronics company executive
Artzt, Russell M. computer software company executive
†Cyganowski, Melanie L. bankruptcy judge
de Lanerolle, Nimal Gerard process engineer
Graham, David Gregory preventive medicine physician, psychiatrist
Heller, Stanley Martin accountant
†Lindsay, Arlene Rosario federal judge
Reis, Don publishing executive
Wang, Chang Yi biomedical company executive
Wexler, Leonard D. federal judge

Haverstraw
Motin, Revell Judith retired data processing executive

Hawthorne
Batstone, Joanna L. physicist
Bisdikian, Chatschik electrical engineer
Carlucci, Marie Ann nursing administrator, nurse
Colmenares, Narses Jose electrical engineer
Frischmuth, Robert Alfred landscape planner, filmmaker
Green, Paul Eliot, Jr. communications scientist
Karnaugh, Maurice computer scientist, educator
Kiamie, Don Albert Najeeb accountant
Scheffler, Eckart Arthur publisher
Traub, Richard Kenneth lawyer

Turk, Stanley Martin advertising agency executive

Hemlock
Doty, Dale Vance psychotherapist, hypnotherapist

Hempstead
Agata, Burton C. lawyer, educator
Atwater, Stephen Dennis professional football player
Berliner, Herman Albert university provost and dean, economics educator
Block, Jules Richard psychologist, educator, university official
Blumenthal, Ralph Herbert natural science educator
Bowe, Frank G. educator
†Carty, Heidi Marlene educator, researcher
Cassidy, David C. science educator
Chapman, Ronald Thomas musician, educator
†Chrebet, Wayne professional football player
Comer, Debra Ruth management educator
Conway-Gervais, Kathleen Marie reading specialist, educational consultant
Danowski, John lacrosse coach
DiLuoffo, Santina chiropractor
Freese, Melanie Louise librarian, professor
Goldstein, Stanley Philip engineering educator
Graffeo, Mary Thérèse music educator, performer
Gutman, Steve professional football team executive
Hastings, Harold Morris mathematics educator, researcher, author
Haynes, Ulric St. Clair, Jr. university dean
†Johnson, Keyshawn professional football player
Laano, Archie Bienvenido Maaño cardiologist
Lee, Keun Sok business educator, consultant
Levinthal, Charles Frederick psychologist, psychology educator, writer
Lewis, Mo professional football player
Mahon, Malachy Thomas, Sr. lawyer, educator
Maier, Henry B. environmental engineer
Martin, Curtis professional football player
Masheck, Joseph Daniel art critic, educator
Montana, Patrick Joseph management educator
Parcells, Bill (Duane Charles Parcells) professional football coach
Pell, Arthur Robert human resources development consultant, author
†Pugliese, Stanislao history educator, researhcer
Schlegel-Danowski, Leslie university head basketball coach
Shuart, James Martin academic administrator
Sparberg, Esther B. chemist, educator
†Testaverde, Vincent Frank (Vinny) professional football player
Vissicchio, Andrew John, Jr. linen service company executive
Wattel, Harold Louis economics educator
Wilkes, David Ross therapist, social worker
Yndigoyen, Eloy guidance counselor

Henrietta
Carmel, Simon J(acob) anthropologist

Herkimer
Kirk, Patrick Laine lawyer
Martin, Lorraine B. humanities educator

Hewlett
Cohen, David Leon physician
Steinfeld, Philip Sheldon pediatrician
Wolff, Eleanor Blunk actress

Hicksville
Estrin, Morton pianist, music educator
Giuffré, John Joseph lawyer
Goldman, Donald Howard lawyer
Horowitz, Barry Allan music company executive
Rough, Herbert Louis insurance company executive
Ruiz, Gerard alcohol and drug abuse services professional
Stein, Melvin A. accountant
Tucci, Gerald Frank manufacturing company executive
Urschel, Effie Caroline Krogmann real estate broker, appraiser, poet, author
Walsh, Charles Richard banker
†Whitlock, Prentice Earle retired mathematics educator, clergyman
Yen, Henry Chin-Yuan computer systems programmer, software engineer, consulting company executive

Highland
Kurzdorfer, Peter John chess educator, writer
Rosenberger, David A. research scientist, cooperative extension specialist

Highland Mills
Gazzaniga, Antonette J. secondary school educator

Hillsdale
Dufault, Peter Kane writer, musician
Lunde, Asbjorn Rudolph lawyer
Richards, Joseph Edward artist

Hilton
Ratigan, Hugh Lewis middle school and elementary school educator

Holbrook
Jugueta, Eduardo Malubay mechanical engineer
Senholzi, Gregory Bruce secondary school educator

Holland
Pratt, David painter

Holtsville
Martin, Christopher Edward accountant, personal finance consultant
Miller, Ronald M. manufacturing executive
Musteric, Peter engineering director

Homer
Gustafson, John Alfred biology educator

Honeoye
Stone, Alan John manufacturing company executive, real estate executive

Hoosick Falls
Canedy, Nancy Gay comptroller, accountant, educator
Dodge, Cleveland Earl, Jr. manufacturing executive

Hopewell Junction
Anandan, Munisamy physicist
Cznarty, Donna Mae secondary education educator
Hayden, Spencer James management consultant

Horseheads
Huffman, Patricia Joan retired accounting coordinator
Josbeno, Larry Joseph physics educator
Tanner, David Harold professional roof consultant

Houghton
Chamberlain, Daniel Robert college president
Luckey, Robert Reuel Raphael retired academic administrator

Howard Beach
Iorio, John Emil retired education educator
Krein, Catherine Cecilia public relations professional, educator
Livingston, Barbara special education educator

Hudson
Artschwager, Richard Ernst artist
Avedisian, Edward artist
Dobson, Michael P. publishing executive
Isherwood, Jon sculptor
Miner, Jacqueline political consultant
Mustapha, Tamton gastroenterologist
Vile, Sandra Jane leadership training educator

Hudson Falls
Bronk, William writer, retail businessman
Leary, Daniel artist

Hunter
Jaeckel, Christopher Carol memorabilia company executive, antiquarian

Huntington
†Allis, Barbara A. physician
Augello, William Joseph lawyer
Brettschneider, Rita Roberta Fischman lawyer
Christiansen, Donald David electrical engineer, editor, publishing consultant
Connor, Joseph Robert editor
D'Addario, Alice Marie school administrator
DeMartin, Charles Peter lawyer
Emery, Howard Ivan, Jr. management consultant, telecommunications specialist
†Engstrand, Beatrice C. neurologist, educator
Fine, Barry Kenneth lawyer
German, June Resnick lawyer
Glickstein, Howard Alan law educator
Hochberg, Ronald Mark lawyer
†Israel, Steve town councilman
Jackson, Richard Montgomery former airline executive
Joseph, Richard Saul cardiologist
Levinthal, Beth Ellen (Kuby Levinthal) educator
Levitan, Katherine D. lawyer
Maglione, Lili fine artist, art consultant
Mandelbaum, Frank software company executive
Morris, Jeffrey Brandon law educator
Munson, Nancy Kay lawyer
Myers, Robert Jay retired aerospace company executive
Pettersen, Kevin Will investment company executive
Pratt, George Cheney law educator, retired federal judge
Robinson, Kenneth Patrick lawyer
Rosar, Virginia Wiley librarian
Ruppert, Mary Frances management consultant, school counselor
Salcedo-Dovi, Hector Eduardo anatomist, educator
Schulz, William Frederick human rights association executive
Sheil, Wilma Rohloff psychiatry, mental health nurse
Slutsky, Leonard Alan finance executive, consultant
Trager, Gary Alan endocrinologist, diabetologist
Twardowicz, Stanley Jan artist, photographer
Vale, Margo Rose physician
†Weissberg, David J. orthopaedic surgeon

Huntington Station
Agosta, Vito mechanical and aerospace engineering educator
Boxwill, Helen Ann primary and secondary education educator
Fouladvand, Hengameh artist
Lanzano, Ralph Eugene civil engineer
Miller, Sally public relations professional
Olson, Gary Robert banker
Pierce, Charles R. electric company consultant
Richardson, Charles Marsh electrical engineer, educator
Williams, Una Joyce psychiatric social worker

Hurley
Bedford, Brian actor
Opdahl, Viola Elizabeth secondary education educator

Hyde Park
Baker, Jennifer L. secondary education educator
Eastwood, D(ana) Alan author, publisher, consultant
Metz, Ferdinand chef, educator, academic administrator
Nihoff, John J. vocational educator, business owner
Pastrana, Ronald Ray Christian ministry counselor, theology and biblical studies educator, former school system administrator
Recchia, Susan Margaret artist, author
Smith, Lewis Motter, Jr. advertising and direct marketing executive

Interlaken
Bleiler, Everett Franklin writer, publishing company executive

Inwood
Jaiswal, Dinesh Kumar pharmaceutical scientist, educator

Irving
†Lee-Kwen, Peterkin physician, neurologist

Irvington
Bonomi, John Gurnee retired lawyer
Devons, Samuel educator, physicist
Elbaum, Marek electro-optical sciences executive, researcher
Goodkind, Louis William lawyer

Harris, Maria Loscutoff *special education educator, consultant*
Lyons, Michael Joseph *microbiologist, research, educator*
Massie, Robert Kinloch *author*
Peyser, Peter A. *former congressman, investment management company executive*
Trent, Bertram James *real estate executive*

Islandia
Davidow, Lawrence Eric *lawyer*
Wang, Charles B. *computer software company executive*

Islip
Baker, Lloyd Harvey *retired lawyer*
†Lombardi, Carlo *pianist, educator*

Islip Terrace
Mancuso, Elisa Alvarez *pediatrics nurse, educator, neonatal nurse practitioner*

Ithaca
Abrams, Meyer Howard *English language educator*
Adler, Kraig (Kerr) *biology educator*
Alexander, Martin *environmental toxicologist, consultant*
Ammons, Archie Randolph *poet, English educator*
Arntzen, Charles Joel *bioscience educator*
Ascher, Robert *anthropologist, archaeologist, educator, filmmaker*
Ashcroft, Neil William *physics educator, researcher*
Bail, Joe Paul *agricultural educator emeritus*
Barcelo, John James, III *law educator*
Barney, John Charles *lawyer*
Bassett, William Akers *geologist, educator*
Batterman, Boris William *physicist, educator, academic director*
Bauer, Simon Harvey *chemistry educator*
Bauman, Dale Elton *nutritional biochemistry educator*
Baylor, Harry Brooks *microbiologist*
Becherer, Richard John *architecture educator*
Ben Daniel, David Jacob *entrepreneurship educator, consultant*
Beneria, Lourdes *economist, educator*
Benson, Frances Goldsmith *editor-in-chief*
Berger, Toby *electrical engineer*
Berkelman, Karl *physics educator*
Bethe, Hans Albrecht *physicist, educator*
Blackler, Antonie William Charles *biologist*
Blau, Francine Dee *economics educator*
Boedo, Stephen *mechanical engineer, consultant*
Bourne, Russell *publisher, author*
Brown, Theodore Morey *art history educator*
Brownstein, Martin Lewis *political science educator*
Burns, Joseph Arthur *planetary science educator*
Calnek, Bruce Wixson *veterinary virologist*
Carlin, Herbert J. *electrical engineering educator, researcher*
Carpenter, Barry Keith *chemistry educator, researcher*
Clardy, Jon Christel *chemistry educator, consultant*
Clarkson, George Edward *theology educator, minister*
Colby-Hall, Alice Mary *Romance studies educator*
Conway, Richard Walter *computer scientist, educator*
Cornish, Elizabeth Turverey *stockbroker*
Craighead, Harold G. *physics educator*
Culler, Jonathan Dwight *English language educator*
Dacko, Marnie *coach*
Dalman, Gisli Conrad *electrical engineering educator*
Darlington, Richard Benjamin *psychology educator*
Davies, Peter John *plant physiology educator, researcher*
De Boer, Pieter Cornelis Tobias *mechanical and aerospace engineering educator*
Dick, Richard Irwin *environmental engineer, educator*
Dietert, Rodney Reynolds *immunology and toxicology educator*
Dobson, Alan *veterinary physiology educator*
Duhig, Susan C. *English language and literature educator*
Dyckman, Thomas Richard *accounting educator*
Dynkin, Eugene B. *mathematics educator*
Earle, Clifford John, Jr. *mathematician*
Earle, Elizabeth Deutsch *biology educator*
Easley, David *economics educator*
Eastman, Lester Fuess *electrical engineer, educator*
Eddy, Donald Davis *English language educator*
Ehrenberg, Ronald Gordon *economist, educator*
Eisner, Thomas *biologist, educator*
Elliott, John *accountant, educator, dean*
Farley, Jennie Tiffany Towle *industrial and labor relations educator*
Fay, Robert Clinton *chemist, educator*
Fick, Gary Warren *agronomy educator, forage crops researcher*
Finch, C. Herbert *retired archivist, library administrator, historian*
Fineman, Martha Albertson *law educator*
Firebaugh, Francille Maloch *university official*
Fireside, Harvey Francis *political scientist, educator*
Fitchen, Douglas Beach *physicist, educator*
Foote, Robert Hutchinson *animal physiology educator*
Forker, Olan Dean *agricultural economics educator*
Fox, Francis Henry *veterinarian*
Freed, Jack Herschel *chemist, educator*
Garrison, Elizabeth Jane *artist*
Germain, Claire Madeleine *law librarian, educator*
Gibian, George *Russian and comparative literature educator*
Gillett, James Warren *ecotoxicology educator*
Gold, Thomas *astronomer, educator*
Goldsmith, Paul Felix *physics and astronomy educator*
Goldsmith, William Woodbridge *city and regional planning educator*
Gottfried, Kurt *physicist, educator*
Grainger, Mary Maxon *civic volunteer*
Greenberg, Donald P. *engineering educator*
Greisen, Kenneth Ingvard *physicist, emeritus educator*
Grippi, Salvatore William *artist*
Groos, Arthur Bernhard, Jr. *German literature educator*
Grunes, David Leon *research soil scientist, educator, editor*
Haas, Jere Douglas *nutritional sciences educator, researcher*
Habicht, Jean-Pierre *public health researcher, educator, consultant*
Halpern, Bruce Peter *academic administrator, researcher, educator*
Haltom, Cristen Eddy *psychologist*
Hardy, Jane Elizabeth *communications educator*
Hart, Edward Walter *physicist*
Hartmanis, Juris *computer scientist, educator*
Hay, George Alan *law and economics educator*
Hess, George Paul *biochemist, educator*
Hester, Karlton Edward *composer, performer, music educator*
Hillman, Robert Andrew *law educator, former university dean*
Hockett, Charles Francis *anthropology educator*
Hoffmann, Roald *chemist, educator*
Hohendahl, Peter Uwe *German language and literature educator*
Holcomb, Donald Frank *physicist, academic administrator*
Hopcroft, John Edward *dean, computer science educator*
Howard, Rustin Ray *corporate executive*
Hudler, George *plant pathologist, educator*
Husa, Karel Jaroslav *composer, conductor, educator*
Isard, Walter *economics educator*
Jagendorf, Andre Tridon *plant physiologist*
Jarrow, Robert Alan *economics and finance educator, consultant*
†Johnson, Stephen Philip *educational administrator*
Kahin, George McTurnan *political science and history educator*
Kahn, Alfred Edward *economist, educator, government official*
Kallfelz, Francis A. *veterinary medicine educator*
Kammen, Carol Koyen *historian, educator*
Kendler, Bernhard *editor*
Kennedy, Kenneth Adrian Raine *biological anthropologist, forensic anthropologist*
Kennedy, Wilbert Keith, Sr. *agronomy educator, retired university official*
Kent, Robert Brydon *law educator*
†Kim, Youngmin *English educator*
Kingsbury, John Merriam *botanist, educator*
Kinoshita, Toichiro *physicist*
Kirsch, A(nthony) Thomas *anthropology and Asian studies educator, researcher*
†Kline, Ronald R. *history and technology educator*
Korf, Richard Paul *mycology educator*
Koschmann, J. Victor *history educator, academic program director*
Kramer, John Paul *entomologist, educator*
Kronik, John William *Romance studies educator*
Krueger, Charles Conrad *fishery science educator*
LaCapra, Dominick Charles *historian*
LaFeber, Walter Frederick *history educator, author*
Law, Gordon Theodore, Jr. *library director*
Lee, David Morris *physics educator*
Leibovich, Sidney *engineering educator*
Lengemann, Frederick William *physiology educator, scientist*
Lesser, William Henri *marketing educator*
Levitt, Bruce Allen *art educator*
Liboff, Richard Lawrence *physicist, educator*
Lopez, Jorge Washington *veterinary virologist*
Loucks, Daniel Peter *environmental systems engineer*
Lowi, Theodore J(ay) *political science educator*
Lumley, John Leask *physicist, educator*
Lund, Daryl Bert *food science educator*
Lurie, Alison *author*
Lynn, Walter Royal *civil engineering educator, university administrator*
Lyons, Thomas Patrick *economics educator*
Macey, Jonathan R. *law educator*
†Mackin, Jeanne Ann *writer, educator*
Mai, William Frederick *plant nematologist, educator*
Martin, Peter William *lawyer, educator*
Maxwell, William Laughlin *retired industrial engineering educator*
McCarroll, Earl *educator, director*
McConkey, James Rodney *English educator, writer*
McCue, Arthur Harry *artist, educator*
McDaniel, Boyce Dawkins *physicist, educator*
McGuire, William *civil engineer, educator*
McIsaac, Paul Rowley *electrical engineer, educator*
McLafferty, Fred Warren *chemist, educator*
McMurry, John Edward *chemistry educator*
Meinwald, Jerrold *chemist, educator*
Merle, H. Etienne *specialty foods broker, restaurateur*
Mermin, N. David *physicist, educator, essayist*
Meyburg, Arnim Hans *transportation engineer, educator, consultant*
Mikus, Eleanore Ann *artist*
Moon, Francis C. *mechanical engineer*
Moore, Charles Hewes, Jr. *industrial and engineered products executive*
Moore, Franklin Kingston *mechanical engineer, educator*
Morgenstern, Matthew *computer scientist*
Morrison, George Harold *chemist, educator*
Mortlock, Robert Paul *microbiologist, educator*
Mueller, Betty Jeanne *social work educator*
Murphy, Eugene Francis *retired government official, consultant*
†Najemy, John Michael *history educator*
Nation, John Arthur *electrical engineering educator, researcher*
Neisser, Ulric *psychology educator*
Nerode, Anil *mathematician, educator*
Nesheim, Malden C. *academic administrator, nutrition educator*
Norton, Mary Beth *history educator, author*
Novak, Joseph Donald *science educator, knowlege studies specialist*
Oliver, Jack Ertle *geophysicist*
O'Rourke, Thomas Denis *civil engineer, educator*
Pagliarulo, Michael Anthony *physical therapy educator*
Palmer, Larry Isaac *lawyer, educator*
Park, Roy Hampton, Jr. *advertising executive*
†Paul, John Lyon *artist*
Phelan, Richard Magruder *mechanical engineer*
Phemister, Robert David *veterinary medical educator*
Pimentel, David *entomologist, educator*
Pingali, Keshav Kumar *computer scientist*
Pohl, Robert Otto *physics educator*
†Polack, Evelyne Weber *veterinarian, pathologist*
Poleskie, Stephen Francis *artist, educator, writer*
Poppensiek, George Charles *veterinary scientist, educator*
Porte, Joel Miles *English educator*
†Pucci, Pietro *humanities educator*
Quimby, Fred William *pathology educator, veterinarian*
Radzinowicz, Mary Ann *language educator*
†Randel, Don M. *academic administrator*
Rasmussen, Kathleen Maher *nutritional sciences educator*
Rawlings, Hunter Ripley, III *university president*
Reppy, John David, Jr. *physicist*
Rhodes, Frank Harold Trevor *university president emeritus, geologist*
†Richardson, Robert Coleman *physics educator, researcher*
Robinson, Franklin Westcott *museum director, art historian*
Rodríguez, Ferdinand *chemical engineer, educator*
Rossi, Faust F. *lawyer, educator*
Rourke, Kathleen Elizabeth *editor*
Ruoff, Arthur Louis *physicist, educator*
Salpeter, Edwin Ernest *physical sciences educator*
Sass, Stephen Louis *education educator*
Scheraga, Harold Abraham *physical chemistry educator*
†Schettino, Leslie A. *program director*
Schlafer, Donald Hughes *veterinary pathologist*
Schwartz, Donald Franklin *communication educator*
Schwarz, Daniel Roger *English language educator*
Scott, Fredric Winthrop *veterinarian*
Scott, Norman Roy *academic administrator, agricultural engineering educator*
Seeley, John George *horticulture educator*
Shell, Karl *economics educator*
†Shepherd, Reginald *writer, educator*
Shoemaker, Sydney S. *philosophy educator*
Shore, Richard Arnold *mathematics educator*
Shuler, Michael Louis *biochemical engineering educator, consultant*
Silbey, Joel Henry *history educator*
Sims, William Riley *design and facility management educator, consultant*
Slate, Floyd Owen *chemist, materials scientist, civil engineer, educator, researcher*
Smith, Robert John *anthropology educator*
Smith, Robert Samuel *banker, former agricultural finance educator*
Stein, Irene Wald *social services administrator*
Steingraber, Sandra Kathryn *biologist, ecologist, writer*
Stevens, James Thomas *English educator*
Streett, William Bernard *retired university dean, engineering educator*
Stycos, Joseph Mayone *demographer, educator*
Sudan, Ravindra Nath *electrical engineer, physicist, educator*
Summers, Robert Samuel *lawyer, author, educator*
†Swieringa, Robert Jay *dean, accountant, educator*
Szasz, Suzy *librarian, writer*
Tang, Chung Liang *engineering educator*
Terzian, Yervant *astronomy and astrophysics educator*
Theisen, Henry William *lawyer*
Thomas, J. Earl *physicist*
Thoron, Gray *lawyer, educator*
Tigner, Maury *retired physicist, educator*
Tomek, William Goodrich *agricultural economist*
Trotter, Leslie Earl *operations research educator, consultant*
Turcotte, Donald Lawson *geophysical sciences educator*
Van Houtte, Raymond A. *financial executive*
Viands, Donald Rex *plant breeder and educator*
Walcott, Charles *neurobiology and behavior educator*
Wang, Kuo-King *manufacturing engineer, educator*
Wasserman, Robert Harold *biology educator*
Webb, Watt Wetmore *physicist, educator*
Weinstein, Leonard Harlan *institute program director, educator*
Welch, Ross Maynard *plant physiologist, researcher, educator*
Whalen, James Joseph *college president emeritus*
Whitaker, Susanne Kanis *veterinary medical librarian*
Whyte, William Foote *industrial relations educator, author*
Widom, Benjamin *chemistry educator*
Wilson, Robert Rathbun *retired physicist*
Wootton, John Francis *physiology educator*
†Yale-Loehr, Stephen William *lawyer, editor*
Zall, Robert Rouben *food scientist, educator*
Zilversmit, Donald Berthold *nutritional biochemist, educator*

Jackson Heights
Chang, Lydia Liang-Hwa *school social worker, educator*
Fischbarg, Zulema F. *pediatrician, educator*
Sabini, John D. *city councilman*
Schuyler, Jane *fine arts educator*
Sklar, Morty E. *publisher, editor*

Jamaica
Ahmed, Jimmie *health facility administrator*
Alberts, Alan Richard *rheumatologist*
Angione, Howard Francis *lawyer, editor*
†Barley, Linda R. *health education and gerontology educator*
Bartilucci, Andrew Joseph *university administrator*
Capellan, Angel *small business executive*
†Catanello, Ignatius Anthony *bishop*
†Cerny, Rosanne *librarian*
Connolly-Weinert, Francis David *theology educator*
Daubenas, Jean Dorothy Tenbrinck *librarian, educator*
Desser, Maxwell Milton *artist, art director, filmstrip producer*
Dircks, Richard Joseph *English language educator, writer*
†Donnelly, Anna *hospital administrator*
Ekbatani, Glayol *educator, program director, author*
Faust, Naomi Flowe *education educator, poet*
Fay, Thomas A. *philosopher, educator*
Feldman, Arlene Butler *aviation industry executive*
Flake, Floyd Harold *former congressman*
Grayshaw, James Raymond *judge*
Greenberg, Jacob *biochemist, educator, consultant*
Greenblatt, Fred Harold *data processing consultant*
Grilli, Cynthia Dyan *artist, educator*
Harmon, W. David *academic administrator*
Harmond, Richard Peter *historian, educator*
Harrington, Donald James *university president*
Heaney-Hunter, Joann Catherine *theology educator*
Jones, Cynthia Teresa Clarke *artist*
Keys, Martha McDougle *educational administrator*
Kitts, Thomas Michael *English language educator, writer*
Lassiter, Katrina Ann *medical/surgical nurse*
Lengyel, István *chemist, educator*
Maertz, Gregory *English language educator*
Mangru, Basdeo *secondary education educator*
McDuffie, Minnie *nursing administrator, community health nurse*
McGuire, William Dennis *health care system executive*
Mc Kinnon, Clinton Dan *aerospace transportation executive*
Morrill, Joyce Marie *social worker*
Mullen, Frank Albert *former university official, clergyman*
Prendergast, Thomas Francis *railroad executive*
Rose, Jodi *opera company founder and artistic director*
Rosner, Fred *physician, educator*
Sciame, Joseph *university administrator*
†Seliga, Charles G. *airport administrator*
Sossi, Anthony James *medical administrator*
Spigner, Archie *councilman*
Strong, Gary Eugene *librarian*
Sun, Siao Fang *chemistry educator*
Tschinkel, Andrew Joseph, Jr. *law librarian*
Vanora, Jerome Patrick *lawyer*
White, Thomas *city councilman*
Wintergerst, Ann Charlotte *language educator*
Wood, Stephen Douglas St. Elmo *designer*
Zenbopwe, (Walter Cade), III *artist, musician, singer, actor*
Zirkel, Patricia McCormick *theology educator, researcher*

Jamestown
Anderson, Raymond Quintus *diversified company executive*
†Bargar, Nancy Gay *real estate company executive*
Bargar, Robert Sellstrom *investor*
Benke, Paul Arthur *college president*
Elofson, Nancy Meyer *retired office equipment company executive*
Goldman, Simon *broadcasting executive*
Idzik, Martin Francis *lawyer*
Leising, David Michael *industrial engineer*
Leising, Mary Kathleen *manufacturing executive*
Martin, Margaret Gately *elementary education educator*
Seguin, David Gerard *community college official*
†Thompson, Birgit Dolores *civic worker, writer*
Wellman, Barclay Ormes *furniture company executive*

Jamesville
DeCrow, Karen *lawyer, author, lecturer*

Jefferson Valley
Huyghe, Patrick Antoine *science writer*

Jeffersonville
Craft, Douglas Durwood *artist*
Harms, Elizabeth Louise *artist*

Jericho
Astuto, Philip Louis *retired Spanish educator*
Axinn, Donald Everett *real estate investor, developer*
Blau, Harvey Ronald *lawyer*
Casem, Conrado Sibayan *civil, structural engineer*
Corso, Frank Mitchell *lawyer*
Faletra, Robert *editor*
Fialkov, Herman *investment banker*
Fitteron, John Joseph *real estate/petroleum products company executive*
Freedman, Mark *marketing executive*
Friedman, David Samuel *lawyer, law review executive*
Mandery, Mathew M. *principal*
Mannion, Kevin *publishing executive*
Rehbock, Richard Alexander *lawyer*
†Rosen, Robert Arnold *management company executive, real estate investor*
Schell, Norman Barnett *physician, consultant*
Shinners, Stanley Marvin *electrical engineer*

Johnson City
Barber, Kenneth W. *funeral director*
Bernardo, Aldo Sisto *foreign language educator, retired*
McGovern, Thomas Boardman *physician, pediatrician*

Johnstown
†Bell, Priscilla J. *academic administrator*

Katonah
†Baker, Ian Archbald *explorer, educator, writer, photographer*
Baker, John Milnes *architect*
Bashkow, Theodore Robert *electrical engineering consultant, former educator*
Crichton, (John) Michael *author, film director*
†Ferrarone, Teresa Lane *educational consultant*
Fry, John *magazine editor*
Hamilton, Kathryn Borys *marketing communications consultant*
Herbert, Marilynne *public relations executive, freelance photographer*
Kravitt, Martin Kenneth *architect*
Levine, Pamela Gail *business owner*
Raymond, Jack *journalist, public relations executive, foundation executive*

Keene Valley
Lanyon, Wesley Edwin *retired museum curator, ornithologist*
†Neville, Emily Tam Lin *writer, educator*

Keeseville
Turetsky, Aaron *lawyer*

Kendall
Rak, Linda Marie *elementary education educator, consultant*

Kenmore
Auerbach, Rita Argen *artist, educator*
Dumych, Daniel Martin *historian*
Elibol, Tarik *gastroenterologist*
Kenny, John Edward *computer analyst*

Keuka Park
Wilson, Levonne Baldwin *nurse*

Kew Gardens
Adler, David Neil *lawyer*
†Breslin, Jimmy *columnist, author*
Marks, Lillian Shapiro *secretarial studies educator, author*
Reichel, Aaron Israel *lawyer*
Schechter, Donald Robert *lawyer*
Schnakenberg, Donald G. *financial administrator*

Kinderhook
Benamati, Dennis Charles *law librarian, editor, consultant*

Kings Park
Greene, Robert William journalism educator, media consultant

Kings Point
Billy, George John library director
Mazek, Warren F(elix) academic administrator, economics educator

Kingston
Bruck, Arlene Lorraine secondary education educator
Ione, Carole psychotherapist, writer, playwright, director
Johnson, Marie-Louise Tully dermatologist, educator
McGuire, Thomas Peter show boat captain, secondary school educator
Petruski, Jennifer Andrea speech and language pathologist
Reis, Frank Henry insurance agency executive
Rypczyk, Candice Leigh employee relations executive
Salzmann, Richard Thomas protective services official
Soltanoff, Jack nutritionist, chiropractor
Stellar, Arthur Wayne educational administrator
Tsirpanlis, Constantine N. theology, philosophy, classics and history educator

Krumville
†Nagi, Catherine Raseh retired educational administrator, financial planner

Lackawanna
†Bordonaro, Salvatore librarian
McNair McAllister, Hazel pastor, educator, writer
Smith, Michael Joseph protective services official

Lagrangeville
Griffin, James V. artist

Lake George
Austin, John DeLong judge
Foulke, Robert Dana English educator, travel writer
Stafford, Dorothy Brooks private duty nurse

Lake Grove
Braff, Howard brokerage house executive, financial analyst
Brayson, Albert Aloysius, II educational association administrator

Lake Luzerne
Goldstein, Manfred retired consultant

Lake Placid
†Grimmette, Mark olympic athlete
†Martin, Brian olympic athlete
Reiss, Paul Jacob college president
Rossi, Ronald Aldo sports association administrator, Olympic athlete
†Sheer, Gordy olympic athlete
Strausbaugh, Scott David Olympic athlete, canoeist
†Thorpe, Chris olympic athlete

Lake Ronkonkoma
Delaney, Robert Patrick librarian, writer
Spahr, Clinton S., Jr. elementary education educator

Lake Success
Ponzi Kay, Marylou human resources specialist

Lakewood
McConnon, Virginia Fix dietitian

Lancaster
Kappan, Sandra Jean elementary education educator
Neumaier, Gerhard John environment consulting company executive
Scott, Harley Earle publisher, historian

Lansing
Gage, George H(enry) retired high technology company executive
Thomas, John Melvin retired surgeon

Larchmont
Berridge, George Bradford retired lawyer
Bloom, Lee Hurley lawyer, public affairs consultant, retired household products manufacturing executive
Engel, Ralph Manuel lawyer
Gould, Douglas C(hester) communications executive
Greenwald, Carol Schiro professional services marketing research executive
Guttenplan, Joseph B. biochemist
Hinerfeld, Ruth G. civic organization executive
Holleb, Arthur Irving surgeon
Levi, James Harry real estate executive, investment banker
Levy, Walter Kahn management consultant executive
Pelton, Russell Gilbert lawyer
Plumez, Jean Paul advertising agency executive, consultant
Quigley, Martin Schofield publishing company executive, educator
Rainier, Robert Paul publisher
Seton, Charles B. lawyer
Sklarew, Robert Jay biomedical research educator, consultant
Steinberg, Lois Saxelby marketing executive
Tobey, Alton Stanley artist
Vitt, Samuel Bradshaw communications media services executive
White, Thomas Edward lawyer
Wielgus, Charles Joseph information services company executive

Latham
Agard, Nancey Patricia nursing administrator
Caruso, Aileen Smith managed care consultant
Chase-Dooley, Johanna Anne medical/surgical and critical care nurse
Conway, Robert George, Jr. lawyer
Lvovsky, Yuri physicist, applied superconductivity engineer
Mathews, Susan McKiernan health care executive
McGoldrick, William Patrick educational consultant
Mitchell, Mark-Allen Bryant state government administrator
Rosner, Carl H. energy executive
Schwartz, Robert William management consultant
†Silverman, Warren physician

Stallman, Donald Lee corporate executive
Standfast, Susan J(ane) state official, researcher, consultant, educator

Laurelton
Watkins, Juanita city councilwoman

Laurens
Spoor, John Edward physician

Lawrence
†MacGuire, James P. broadcast executive
Sklarin, Ann H. artist
Sklarin, Burton S. endocrinologist
Wurzburger, Walter Samuel rabbi, philosophy educator

Le Roy
Ruekberg, David Remington secondary English educator
Smukall, Carl Franklin accountant

Levittown
Ahmad, Naseer pharmaceutical sales executive
Auteri, Rose Mary Patti school system administrator
Mader, Bryn John vertebrate paleontologist
Wieland, Thomas J. headmaster

Lewiston
Dexter, Theodore Henry chemist
Domzella, Janet library director
Gallo, Mark Allen microbiology educator
LoTempio, Julia Matild accountant
O'Neil, Mary Agnes health science facility administrator
Simonson, Lee J. small business owner
Waters, William Ernest microelectronics executive
Whitney, Stewart Bowman sociology educator and program director
Zavon, Mitchell Ralph physician

Liberty
Eisenberg, Bertram William lawyer
†Luckner-Smassanow, Lucille school system administrator

Lido Beach
Billauer, Barbara Pfeffer lawyer, educator
†Hoyt, James John educator

Lily Dale
Merrill, Joseph Hartwell religious association executive

Lincolndale
Morton, Mary Madeline family nurse practitioner

Lindenhurst
Boltz, Mary Ann aerospace materials company executive, travel agency executive
Farrell-Logan, Vivian actress
Hamilton, Daniel Stephen clergyman
Hungerford, Gary A. insurance executive, columnist, author, editor
Levy, (Alexandra) Susan construction company executive

Little Falls
Bunk, George Mark civil engineer, consultant
Feeney, Mary Katherine O'Shea retired public health nurse

Little Valley
Anastasia, David Jon state legislator
Himelein, Larry M. judge

Liverpool
Emmert, Roberta Rita health facility administrator
Greenway, William Charles electronics executive, design engineer
Miller, Eileen Renee counselor
Mitchell, John David journalism educator
Morabito, Bruno Paul machinery manufacturing executive
Munoz, Charlotte Marie English educator
†Schuehler, Kathleen H. biology educator
Trombley, Edward Francis, III educational administrator
Williams, John Alan secondary education educator, coach

Livingston Manor
Zagoren, Joy Carroll health facility director, researcher

Lockport
†Bontempi, Gail Diane small business owner
Carr, Edward Albert, Jr. medical educator, physician
Cull, John Joseph novelist, playwright
Godshall, Barbara Marie educational administrator
Hoyme, Chad Earl packaging company executive
Schultz, Gerald Alfred chemical company executive
Segarra, Tyrone Marcus pharmacist, medicinal chemist
Shah, Ramesh Keshavlal researcher, engineering educator

Lockwood
Keating, Keith Anthony English language educator

Locust Valley
Benson, Robert Elliott investment banker, consultant
Bentel, Frederick Richard architect, educator
Bentel, Maria-Luise Ramona Azzarone (Mrs. Frederick R. Bentel) architect, educator
DeRegibus, William artist
Lippold, Richard sculptor
†Mathews, Walter Michael university administrator
McGee, Dorothy Horton writer, historian
Schaffner, Charles Etzel consulting engineering executive
Schor, Joseph Martin pharmaceutical executive, biochemist
Webel, Richard Karl landscape architect
Zambito, Raymond Francis oral surgeon, educator
Zulch, Joan Carolyn retired medical publishing company executive, consultant

Long Beach
Bernstein, Lester editorial consultant
†Brontoli, Margreth J. ophthalmologist

Chaudhry, Humayun Javaid physician, medical educator, writer
Levine, Samuel Milton lawyer
Ostroy, Joseph education educator
Siegel, Herbert Bernard certified professional management consultant
Solomon, Robert H. lawyer

Long Eddy
Hoiby, Lee composer, concert pianist
Van Swol, Noel Warren secondary education educator and administrator

Long Island
Weiner, Alan E. lawyer

Long Island City
Alimaras, Gus lawyer
†Ard, Patricia English language educator
Bowen, Raymond Cobb academic administrator
Craig, Elizabeth Coyne marketing executive
Dillon, James Jude arts educator
Di Suvero, Mark sculptor
Donneson, Seena Sand artist
Goldstein, Katherine H. technology educator, computer consultant
Hoffman, Merle Holly political activist, social psychologist, author
Kane Hittner, Marcia Susan bank executive
Landau, Emily Fisher contemporary art collection, foundation executive
†Matsushita, Marimi educator, mathematician
McCoy, Ann artist
Pender, Karen Imelda humanities educator
Sadao, Shoji architect
Schoenberg, David Arthur business educator
Shyer, Christopher Dean optical company executive, writer
Theodoru, Stefan Gheorghe civil engineer, writer
Trent, James Alfred city official
Wanderman, Susan Mae lawyer
Weinberg, Louise J. artist, curator

Loudonville
Ferguson, Henry international management consultant
†Fiore, Peter Amadeus English educator, clergy
Haverly, Douglas Lindsay librarian, historian
†Mackin, Kevin Eugene academic administrator, clergyman
Ribley-Borck, Joan Grace medical/surgical rehabiliation nurse
Toal, James Francis academic administrator
Van Hook, John Edward philosophy educator

Lowville
Becker, Robert Otto orthopedic surgery educator
Daley, Laurana Bush elementary education educator

Lynbrook
Amorosi, Teresa artist
O'Malley, Edward Joseph, Jr. financial services administrator
Yee, David chemist, pharmaceutical company executive

Lyndonville
Bell, David Sheffield physician

Lyons
Olson, Daniel Anthony secondary education educator

Macedon
McGee, Dennis Emmett research technologist

Mahopac Falls
Travis, Alice Dimery journalist

Malone
Kelley, Sister Helen hospital executive
Premo, Angela Mary special education educator

Malverne
Benigno, Thomas Daniel lawyer
Freund, Richard L. communications company executive, consultant, lawyer
Gavalas, Alexander Beary artist
Knight, John Francis insurance company executive
Pollio, Ralph Thomas editor, writer, magazine publishing consultant
Ryan, Suzanne Irene nursing educator

Mamaroneck
Asher, Dana publishing executive
Flagg, Jeanne Bodin editor
Halpern, Abraham Leon psychiatrist
Hoffert, Paul Washington surgeon
Holz, Harold A. chemical and plastics manufacturing company executive
Korn, Barry Paul equipment and vehicle leasing company executive
Mazzola, Claude Joseph physicist, small business owner
Mizrahi, Abraham Mordechay retired cosmetics and health care company executive, physician
Nelson, Vita Joy editor, publisher
New, Anne Latrobe public relations, fund raising executive
Pugh, Grace Huntley artist
Randolph, Elizabeth writer
Rosenthal, Elizabeth Robbins physician
Topol, Robert Martin retired financial services executive

Manhasset
Anderson, Arthur N. retired utility company executive
Benewitz, Maurice Charles labor arbitrator, educator
Bialer, Martin George geneticist
Brackett, Ronald E. investment company executive, lawyer
Brand, Oscar folksinger, author, educator
Corva, Angelo Francis architect
Elkowitz, Sheryl Sue radiologist
Feinsilver, Steven Henry physician, educator
Fenton, Arnold N. obstetrician, gynecologist, educator
Grossi, Olindo architect, educator
Keen, Constantine retired manufacturing company executive
Kreis, Willi physician
Lipson, Steven Mark clinical virologist, educator

Lotruglio, Anthony F. financial consultant
†Lukash, Frederick Neil plastic surgeon
McGreal, Joseph A., Jr. publishing company executive
Mindin, Vladimir Yudovich information systems specialist, chemist, educator
Moran, Timothy newspaper editor
Nelson, Roy Leslie cardiac surgeon, researcher, educator
Pam, Eleanor behavioral sciences educator
Rostky, George Harold editor
Samuel, Paul cardiologist
Scherr, Lawrence physician, educator
Schiller, Arthur A. architect, educator
Sessler, Jane Virginia secondary school educator
†Vishnubhakat, Surya Murthy neurologist
Wachtler, Sol law educator, retired judge, arbitration corporation executive, writer
Wallace, Richard editor, writer

Manlius
Harriff, Suzanna Elizabeth Bahner advertising consultant
Jefferies, Michael John retired electrical engineer
Martonosi, Anthony Nicholas biochemistry educator, researcher
Omohundro, William Addison research marketing executive
Prior, John Thompson pathology educator
Vasile, Gennaro James health care executive

Manorville
Esp, Barbara Ann Lorraine research scientist, educator

Marcellus
Baker, Bruce Roy retired art educator, artist
DeForge, Katherine Ann secondary education educator
Moser, David John management consultant

Margaretville
Brockway-Henson, Amie producing artistic director

Marlboro
Pollak, Joel Michael school superintendent

Maryknoll
Ellsberg, Robert Boyd religious press editor
LaVerdiere, Claudette Marie sister, head religious order

Massapequa
Arbiter, Andrew Richard accountant
Batt, Alyse Schwartz technical officer
Bogorad, Barbara Ellen psychologist
Margulies, Andrew Michael chiropractor
†McCann, John W., III psychologist, consultant
Molitor, Michael A. entrepreneur, consultant
Odol, Marilyn Elaine accountant
Ting, Mark E. sex researcher, consultant
Witt, Denise Lindgren operating room nurse, educator
Zwanger, Jerome physician

Massapequa Park
Klein, Kenneth orchestra conductor, educator
Plotkin, Martin retired electrical engineer

Massena
DeLarm, Joan Sharon social worker, psychotherapist
Pellegrino, James Martin dentist
Perez, Loretta Ann Bronchetti secondary education educator, small business owner
Vazquez, Sue Ellen elementary education educator

Mastic Beach
Casciano, Paul school system administrator
Pagano, Alicia I. education educator

Mattituck
Marquardt, Ann Marie small business administrator

Medford
Barna, Douglas Peter collection agency executive
Brower, Robert Charles rehabilitation counselor, small business owner
Haig, Monica Elaine Nachajski special education educator
Snyder, Mark Jeffrey financial consultant, actuary
Tafuri, William sculptor

Medina
Berry, Cecilia Anne nephrology nurse practitioner
McAfee, Paul Hindman, III marketing professional

Melville
Bilenas, Jonas mechanical engineer, educator
Brandt, Robert Frederic, III newspaper editor, journalist
Carter, Sylvia journalist
Chan, Jack-Kang undersea warfare engineer, mathematician
Clinard, Joseph Hiram, Jr. securities company executive
Damadian, Raymond Vahan biophysicist
Donovan, Brian reporter, journalist
Dooley, James C. newspaper editor, director of photography
Feindler, Joan La Garde foreign language educator
Florea, Robert William real estate investment executive
Garrett, Laurie science correspondent
Grebow, Edward television company executive
Hall, Charlotte Hauch newspaper editor
Hildebrand, John Frederick newspaper columnist
Jagoda, Donald Robert sales promotion agency executive
Jansen, Raymond A., Jr. newspaper publishing executive
Kaufman, Stephen P. electronics company executive
Kennedy, Nancy Macri English language educator
Kissinger, Walter Bernhard automotive test and service equipment manufacturing executive
Klatell, Robert Edward lawyer, electronics company executive
Klurfeld, James Michael journalist
LaRocco, Elizabeth Anne management information systems professional
Lynn, James Dougal newspaper editor, journalist
Marro, Anthony James newspaper editor
McMillan, Robert Ralph lawyer
Moran, Paul James journalist, columnist

Niebuhr, Fred J(ohn) *real estate consultant*
Payne, Leslie *newspaper editor, columnist, journalist, author*
Pelle, Edward Gerard *biochemist*
Price, Howard Charles *chemist*
Rathkopf, Daren Anthony *lawyer*
Richards, Carol Ann Rubright *editor, columnist*
Robins, Marjorie Kaplan *newspaper editor*
Roel, Ron *newspaper editor*
Saul, Stephanie *journalist*

Merrick
Cariola, Robert Joseph *artist*
Cherry, Harold *insurance company executive*
Copperman, Stuart Morton *pediatrician*
Doyle, James Aloysius *retired association executive*
Garfinkel, Lawrence Saul *academic administrator, educator, television producer*
Kaplan, Steven Mark *accountant*
O'Brien, Kenneth Robert *life insurance company executive*
Poppel, Seth Raphael *entrepreneur*
Seader, Paul Alan *lawyer*

Mexico
Sade, Donald Stone *anthropology educator*

Middle Island
Crowder, Lillie Mae Brown *retired architectural engineer*
Linick, Andrew S. *direct marketing executive*

Middle Village
Heyd, Eva *photographer*
Kolatch, Alfred Jacob *publisher*
Ognibene, Thomas V. *councilman*
Thoering, Robert Charles *elementary education educator*
Walter, John Frederick *historical researcher, genealogist*

Middleport
Massaro, Joseph James *secondary school educator*
Travers, Carol *mathematics educator*

Middletown
†Aumick, Amalia *legislative staff member*
Bedell, Barbara Lee *journalist*
Blumenthal, Fritz *printmaker, painter*
Edelhertz, Helaine Wolfson *mathematics educator*
Sprick, Dennis Michael *critic, copy editor*
Teabo-Sandoe, Glenda Patterson *elementary education educator*

Milford
Seward, James L. *state legislator*

Mill Neck
Grieve, William Roy *psychologist, educator, educational administrator, researcher*
von Briesen, Edward Fuller *builder, real estate developer*

Millbrook
Hall, Penelope Coker *magazine editor*
Likens, Gene Elden *biology and ecology educator, administrator*
Nowak, Grzegorz *music educator*
Turndorf, Jamie *clinical psychologist*

Miller Place
Sanger, Eileen *gallery owner, artist*

Millerton
DeShields Brooks, DeLora, Sr. *medical technologist, medical writer*
Green, George Edward *surgeon*
Hastings, Donald Francis *actor, writer*
Paretsky, Sara N. *writer*

Mineola
Anana-Lind, Elenita M. *critical care and medical/ surgical nurse*
Bartlett, Clifford Adams, Jr. *lawyer*
Block, Martin *lawyer*
Braid, Frederick Donald *lawyer*
Brush, Louis Frederick *lawyer*
Burstein, Beatrice S. *judicial administrator, retired judge*
Cirker, Hayward *publisher*
Feinstein, Robert P. *dermatologist*
Hines, George Lawrence *surgeon*
Hinson, Gale Mitchell *social worker*
Hull, Magdalen Eleanor *reproductive medicine physician, educator*
Jones, Lawrence Tunnicliffe *lawyer*
Kelly, Edward Joseph *lawyer*
Klein, Arnold Spencer *lawyer*
Kral, William George *lawyer*
Lizardos, Evans John *mechanical engineer*
Mayer, Renee G. *lawyer*
Meyer, Bernard Stern *lawyer, former judge*
Miller, Loring Erik *insurance agent, broker*
Mofenson, Howard C. *pediatrician, toxicologist*
Molho, Laura *pathologist*
Monaghan, Peter Gerard *lawyer*
Newman, Malcolm *mechanical and civil engineering consultant*
Parola, Frederick Edson, Jr. *county comptroller*
Paterson, Basil Alexander *lawyer*
Pogrebin, Bertrand B. *lawyer*
Rossen, Jordan *lawyer*
Salten, David George *county agency administrator, academic administrator*
Sandback, William Arthur *lawyer*
Schaffer, David Irving *lawyer*
Stanisci, Thomas William *lawyer*
Tankoos, Sandra Maxine *court reporting services executive*
Twist, Paul Francis, Jr. *neonatologist*
Zuckerman, Richard Karl *lawyer*

Mohegan Lake
Ettinger, Jayne Gold *physical education educator*

Monroe
Karen, Linda Tricarico *fashion designer*
Lifshitz, Kenneth Bernard *computer programmer*
Werzberger, Alan *pediatrician*

Monsey
Erickson, Barbara Martha *historian, writer, florist*

Montauk
Butler, Thomas William *retired health and social services administrator*
First, Wesley *publishing company executive*
Lavenas, Suzanne *writer, editor, consultant*

Monticello
Lauterstein, Joseph *cardiologist*
Sorensen, Alan John *county official*

Montrose
Faden-Qureshi, Betsy Bruzzese *activity director, volunteer coordinator, recreation therapist*
Matthias, George Frank *educator*
Reber, Raymond Andrew *retired chemical engineer*

Mount Kisco
Curran, Maurice Francis *lawyer*
Godilo-Godlevsky, Eugene Alexandrovich *poet*
Goodhue, Mary Brier *lawyer, former state senator*
Gudanek, Lois Bassolino *clinical social worker*
Keesee, Thomas Woodfin, Jr. *financial consultant*
Laster, Richard *biotechnology executive, consultant*
Mann, Richard O. *public relations consulting company executive*
Marwell, Edward Marvin *instrument company executive*
Michael, Creighton *artist, educator*
Mooney, Robert Michael *ophthalmologist*
†Riechers, Roger Neil *urologist, surgeon*
Schneider, Robert Jay *oncologist*
Schwarz, Wolfgang *psychologist*
Stillman, Michael Allen *dermatologist*

Mount Sinai
†Bricka, Evelyn Chantel *educator*
Feinberg, Sheldon Norman *pediatrician*

Mount Vernon
Ben-Dak, Joseph David *political scientist, educator, consultant*
Richardson, W. Franklyn *minister*
Walters, Carolyn Maria *secondary school educator*
Williams, Patricia Helen *substance abuse services administrator*
Zucker, Arnold Harris *psychiatrist*

Mountainville
Johns, Margaret Bush *neuroendocrinologist, researcher, educator*

Munnsville
Carruth, Hayden *poet*

Nanuet
Andreen, Aviva Louise *dentist, researcher, academic administrator, educator*
†Faustino, Peter J. *school psychologist*
Magner, Martha Mary *education educator, consultant*
Miney, Maureen Elizabeth *middle school educator*
Rosenberg, Janice Carol Berman *principal, librarian, mentor*
Savitz, Martin Harold *neurosurgeon*

Naples
Beal, Myron Clarence *osteopathic physician*
†Flory, Sheldon *retired clergyman, poet*
Perreca, Michael Andrew *artistic director, freelance editor*

Neponsit
Re, Edward Domenic *law educator, retired federal judge*

Nesconset
Goldstein, Joyce *special education educator*

New City
Esser, Aristide Henri *psychiatrist*
Fenster, Robert David *lawyer*
†Golden, Gail K. *social worker*
Gromack, Alexander Joseph *state legislator*
†Karben, Ryan Scott *county legislator*
Mellon, Joan Ann *educator*
Spalding, Mary Branch *psychologist, psychotherapist*
Wechman, Robert Joseph *economist, educator*

New Hartford
†Arastu, Jameel Husain *neurologist*
Benzo-Bonacci, Rosemary Anne *health facility administrator*
Chapin, Mary Q. *arbitrator, mediator, writer, perfoming artist*
Eidelhoch, Lester Philip *physician, educator, surgeon*
Gupta, Subhash Chandra *metallurgical engineer*
Maurer, Gernant Elmer *metallurgical executive, consultant*

New Hyde Park
Armstrong, Denise Grace *medical association administrator*
Bocchino, Frances Lucia *retired oil company official*
Cooper, Milton *real estate investment trust executive*
Daley, John Terence *priest*
Eviatar, Lydia *pediatric neurologist*
Ezersky, William Martin *lawyer*
Grassi, Louis C. *accountant*
Hammer, Deborah Marie *librarian, paralegal*
Hinerfeld, Norman Martin *manufacturing company executive*
Hoffman, Maliza Mildred *interior designer*
Hyman, Abraham *electrical engineer*
Isenberg, Henry David *microbiology educator*
Jensen, Richard Currie *lawyer*
Lee, Won Jay *radiologist*
†McKinley, Matthew John *gastroenterologist*
Mealie, Carl A. *physician, educator*
Offner, Eric Delmonte *lawyer*
Prisco, Douglas Louis *physician*
Richards, Bernard *investment company executive*
Seltzer, Vicki Lynn *obstetrician, gynecologist*
Shenker, Ira Ronald *physician*
†Smith, Arthur David *urologist*
Wolf, Julius *medical educator*

New Lebanon
Baker, James Barnes *architect*

New Paltz
Cheng, Amy *artist*
Emanuel-Smith, Robin Lesley *special education educator*
Fakler, Mary Edith *English educator*
Fleisher, Harold *computer scientist*
Hathaway, Richard Dean *language professional, educator*
Hauptman, Laurence Marc *history educator*
Huth, Paul Curtis *ecosystem scientist, botanist*
Irvine, Rose Loretta Abernethy *retired communications educator, consultant*
†Lavallee, David Kenneth *chemistry educator, researcher*
Nyquist, Thomas Eugene *consulting business executive, mayor*
Ryan, Marleigh Grayer *Japanese language educator*
Schnell, George Adam *geographer, educator*
Smiley, Albert Keith *economist, resort executive*
Smith, Kathleen Tener *bank executive*
Whittington-Couse, Maryellen Frances *education administrator*

New Rochelle
†Balfe, Judith O'Hara *marketing professional, educator*
Beardsley, Robert Eugene *microbiologist, educator*
Berlage, Gai Ingham *sociologist, educator*
Black, Page Morton *civic worker*
Blotner, Norman David *lawyer, real estate broker, corporate executive*
Branch, William Blackwell *playwright, producer*
Capasso, Frank Louis *secondary school educator*
Cleary, James C. *audio-visual producer*
Donahue, Richard James *secondary school educator*
Fitch, Nancy Elizabeth *historian*
Gallagher, John Francis *education educator*
Gay, Elisabeth Feitler *actress*
Glassman, George Morton *dermatologist*
Golub, Sharon Bramson *psychologist, educator*
Goodman, Joan Frances *avionics manufacturing executive*
Gunning, Francis Patrick *lawyer, insurance association executive*
Hayes, Arthur Hull, Jr. *physician, clinical pharmacology educator, medical school dean, business executive, consultant*
Herzberg, Sydelle Shulman *lawyer, accountant*
Kelly, Sister Dorothy Ann *college chancellor*
Kelly, James Anthony *priest*
†Kleinman, Andrew Young *plastic surgeon*
Lin, Joseph Pen-Tze *retired neuroradiologist*
Lurie, Alvin David *lawyer*
Margolin, Harold *metallurgical educator*
Menzies, Henry Hardinge *architect*
Merrill, Robert *baritone*
Miller, Rita *personnel consultant, diecasting companyexecutive*
†Nodiff, David Marc *elementary education educator*
Noone, Katherine A. *English language educator*
†Pendleton, Thomas A. *English educator*
†Richard, St. Clair *Smith editor*
Rovinsky, Joseph Judah *obstetrician, gynecologist*
Saperstein, David *novelist, screenwriter, film director*
Saunders, Rubie Agnes *former magazine editor, author*
Shrage, Laurette *special education educator*
Slotnick, Mortimer H. *artist*
Tassone, Gelsomina (Gessie Tassone) *metal processing executive*
Thornton, Elaine Seretha *oncology nurse, clinical nurse specialist*
Wolf, Robert Irwin *psychoanalyst, art and art therapy educator*
Wolotsky, Hyman *retired college dean*

New Windsor
†Antony, Ajit Ivan *urologist*

New York
Aaron, Steven P. *publishing executive*
Abatemarco, Fred *editor in chief*
Abboud, Joseph M. *fashion designer*
Abdulezer, Susan Beth *communications educator*
Abeles, Sigmund M. *artist, printmaker*
Abelman, Arthur F. *lawyer*
Abelson, Alan *columnist*
Abernathy, James Logan *public relations executive*
Abish, Cecile *artist*
Ablow, Ronald Charles *hospital executive*
Abrams, Floyd *lawyer*
Abrams, George *type designer, executive*
Abrams, Pamela Nadine *magazine editor*
Abrams, Robert *lawyer, former state attorney general*
Abramson, Sara Jane *radiologist, educator*
Abramson, Stephanie W. *lawyer*
Abu-Lughod, Janet Lippman *sociologist, educator*
Acampora, Ralph Joseph *brokerage firm executive*
Achenbaum, Alvin Allen *marketing and management consultant*
Ackerman, Valerie B. *sports association executive*
Acrivos, Andreas *chemical engineering educator*
Adams, Alice *writer*
Adams, Barbara *English language educator, poet, writer*
Adams, Carl Fillmore, Jr. *finance company executive*
Adams, Dennis Paul *artist*
Adams, Edward A. *legal journalist*
Adams, Edward Thomas (Eddie Adams) *photographer*
Adams, George Bell *lawyer*
Adams, Jeffrey Alan *web developer, writer*
Adams, Joey *comedian, author*
Adams, John Brett *investment banker, company executive*
Adams, John Hamilton *lawyer*
†Adams, Rachel Elizabeth *English language educator*
Adams, Robert B. *financial services company executive*
Adams, Scott *cartoonist*
†Adcroft, Patrice Gabriella *editor*
Addison, Herbert John *publishing executive*
†Adenaike, Carolyn Keyes *historian, educator*
Adler, Edward I. *media and entertainment company executive*
Adler, Freda Schaffer (Mrs. G. O. W. Mueller) *criminologist, educator*
Adler, Karl Paul *medical educator, academic administrator*
Adler, Margot Susanna *journalist, radio producer*
Adler, Richard *composer, lyricist*
Adler, Robert *advertising executive*
Adri, (Adri Steckling Coen) *fashion designer*
†Adubato, Richard Adam (Richie Adubato) *professional basketball coach*
Aghassi, William J. *mechanical engineer, consultant*
Agisim, Philip *advertising and marketing company executive*
Agnew, William Harold *insurance company executive*
Agostinelli, Robert Francesco *investment banker*
Agranoff, Gerald Neal *lawyer*
Ahmad, Jameel *civil engineer, researcher, educator*
Ahmad, Kamal M. *lawyer*
Ahrens, Edward Hamblin, Jr. *physician*
†Ahrens, Lynn *lyricist*
Aibel, Howard J. *lawyer*
Aidinoff, M(erton) Bernard *lawyer*
†Aiello, Stephen *public relations executive*
Ailes, Roger Eugene *television producer, consultant*
Aisenbrey, Stuart Keith *trust company official*
†Aitken, Doug *artist*
Akingbemi, Benson Tokunbo *biomedical scientist, veterinarian, educator*
Aksen, Gerald *lawyer, educator, arbitrator*
Alabiso, Vincent *photojournalist*
Alafouzo, Antonia *marketing professional*
Alarcon, Raul, Jr. *broadcast executive*
Alazraki, Jaime *Romance languages educator*
Albee, Edward Franklin *author, playwright*
Albers, Charles Edgar *investment manager*
Albert, Garett J. *lawyer*
Albert, Marv *sportscaster, program director*
Albert, Neale Malcolm *lawyer*
Albertson, Christiern Gunnar (Chris Albertson) *broadcaster, music critic, writer*
Albertson, Gary David *marketing executive, consultant*
Albom, Michael Jonathan *surgeon, educator*
Alcantara, Theo *conductor*
Alden, Steven Michael *lawyer*
Alderson, Philip Otis *radiologist, educator*
Alenikoff, Frances *choreographer, performer, writer, dancer, artist*
Alessandroni, Venan Joseph *lawyer*
Alexander, Barbara Toll *investment banker*
Alexander, Jane *federal agency administrator, actress, producer*
Alexander, Roy *public relations executive, editor, author*
Alexander, Shana *journalist, author, lecturer*
Alfano, Michael Charles *dental school dean*
Alford, Robert Ross *sociologist*
Aliki, (Aliki Liacouras Brandenberg) *author, illustrator children's books*
Allard, Linda Marie *fashion designer*
Allen, Alice *communications and marketing executive*
Allen, Betty (Mrs. Ritten Edward Lee, III) *mezzo-soprano*
Allen, Claxton Edmonds, III *investment banker*
Allen, Jay Presson *writer, producer*
Allen, Leon Arthur, Jr. *lawyer*
Allen, Nancy *musician, educator*
Allen, Roberta *fiction and nonfiction writer, conceptual artist*
Allen, William Thomas *educator, lawyer, judge*
Allen, Woody (Allen Stewart Konigsberg) *actor, filmmaker, author*
Allentuck, Marcia Epstein *English language and art history educator*
Allison, David Bradley *psychologist*
Allison, Michael David *space scientist, astronomy educator*
Allmendinger, Paul Florin *retired engineering association executive*
Allner, Walter Heinz *designer, painter, art director*
Alonzo, Martin Vincent *mining and aluminum company executive, investor, financial consultant*
Alpert, Warren *oil company executive, philanthropist*
Alpert, William Harold *artist*
Alston, Alyce *publisher*
Alter, Andrew William *lawyer*
Alter, David *lawyer*
Alter, Eleanor Breitel *lawyer*
Alter, Jonathan Hammerman *journalist*
†Alterman, Barry *performing company executive*
Altfest, Lewis Jay *financial and investment advisor*
Altieri, Peter Louis *lawyer*
Altman, Harold *artist educator*
Altman, Lawrence Kimball *physician, journalist*
†Altman, Robert B. *film director, writer, producer*
Altman, Roy Peter *pediatric surgeon*
Altschul, Arthur Goodhart *investment banker*
Alvarado, Sandra Edga *nurse practitioner, psychotherapist*
†Alvarez-Babin, Carmen Maria *writer, retired educator*
†Alviggi, Christopher *insurance broker*
Amabile, John Louis *lawyer*
Amara, Lucine *opera and concert singer*
Amdur, Martin Bennett *lawyer*
Ames, George Joseph *investment banker*
Ames, Richard Pollard *physician, educator, lecturer*
Amhowitz, Harris J. *lawyer, educator*
Amitin, Mark Hall *cultural organization administrator, educator, writer*
Ammer, Bonnie *publisher*
Ammirati, Ralph *advertising agency executive*
Amster, Linda Evelyn *newspaper executive, consultant*
Amsterdam, Anthony Guy *law educator*
Amsterdam, Mark Lemle *lawyer*
Anagnost, Dino *artistic director*
Anbinder, Paul *publishing executive*
Anchlia, Than Mal *wholesale distribution executive*
Andersen, K(ent) Tucker *investment executive*
Andersen, Kurt Byars *writer*
Andersen, Marianne Singer *clinical psychologist*
Andersen, Richard Esten *lawyer*
Anderson, Arthur Allan *management consultant*
Anderson, David Poole *sportswriter*
Anderson, Eugene Robert *lawyer*
Anderson, Fred Richard *minister*
Anderson, Gavin *public relations consultant*
Anderson, Gloria Brown *publishing executive*
Anderson, Maxwell L. *museum director*
Anderson, O(rvil) Roger *biology educator, marine biology and protozoology, researcher*
Anderson, Poul William *author*
Anderson, Richard Theodore *urban planner, association executive*
Anderson, Robert Woodruff *playwright, novelist, screenwriter*
Anderson, Sydney *biologist, museum curator*
†Anderson, Timothy R. *investment banker*
Anderson, Walter Herman *magazine editor*
Andolsen, Alan Anthony *management consultant*
Andre, Carl *sculptor*
Andre, (Kenneth) Michael *editor, publisher, writer*
Andreopoulos, George John *history educator, lawyer, political science educator*
Andresen, Malcolm *lawyer*
Andrews, Benny *artist*

Andrews, Earl, Jr. commissioner, state and local
Andrews, Frederick Franck newspaper editor
Andrews, Gordon Clark lawyer
Andrulis, Dennis P. health policy analyst executive, researcher
Andrus, Roger Douglas lawyer
Angelakos, Evangelos Theodorou physician, physiologist, pharmacologist, educator
Angell, Roger writer, magazine editor
Angell, Wayne D. economist, banker
Angland, Joseph lawyer
Ankerson, Robert William management consultant
Annan, Kofi A. diplomat
Anspach, Ernst economist, lawyer
Antell, Darrick Eugene plastic surgeon
†Antezzo, Matthew J. artist
Anthoine, Robert lawyer, educator
Anthony, William Graham artist
Anton, Mace Damon loan officer
Antonakos, Stephen sculptor
Antonuccio, Joseph Albert hospitality industry executive
Apostolakis, James John shipping company executive
Appel, Albert M. lawyer
Appel, Marsha Ceil association executive
Appelbaum, Ann Harriet lawyer
Appelbaum, David Marc magazine editor, philosophy educator
Appelbaum, Judith Pilpel editor, consultant, educator
Applebaum, Stuart S. public relations executive
Applebroog, Ida artist
April, Max Michael otolaryngologist
Aptekar, Ken painter
Aquilino, Thomas Joseph, Jr. federal judge, law educator
Araiza, Francisco (José Francisco Araiza Andrade) opera singer
Archibald, Reginald Mac Gregor physician, chemist, educator
Arens, Nicholas Herman bank executive
Arenson, Gregory K. lawyer
Arizmendy, Helmer W. bank executive, lawyer
Arkin, Stanley S. lawyer
Arledge, Roone television executive
Arlow, Arnold Jack advertising agency executive, artist
Armenakas, Noel Anthony medical educator
Armstrong, James Sinclair foundation director, retired lawyer
Armstrong, Steven Holm lawyer
Arnett, Peter journalist
Arnold, Charles Burle, Jr. psychiatrist, writer
†Arnold, Dieter Karl Heinrich Egyptologist
†Arnone, William J. executive
Arnot, Andrew H. art gallery director
Aronin, Marc Jacob playwright, artistic director, director
Aronoff, Michael Stephen psychiatrist
Aronson, Donald Eric professional services firms consultant, value added tax consultant
Aronson, Edgar David venture capitalist
†Aronstam, Neil Lee media marketing firm executive
Arouh, Jeffrey Alan lawyer
Arquit, Kevin James lawyer
Arther, Richard Oberlin polygraphist, educator
Arvystas, Michael Geciauskas orthodontist, educator
Asahina, Robert James editor, publishing company executive
Asakawa, Takako dancer, dance teacher, director, choreographer
Asanuma, Hiroshi physician, educator
Asch, Arthur Louis environmental company executive
Ascher, Michael Charles transportation executive
†Ascherman, Jeffrey Alan plastic and reconstructive surgeon
†Aschheim, Eve Michele artist, educator
Aschoff, Lawrence Michael computer information scientist
Ascolese, Michael J. corporate communications executive
Asensi, Gustavo advertising executive, filmmaker
Ash, Herbert Leonard lawyer
Ashbery, John Lawrence language educator, poet, playwright
Ashdown, Marie Matranga (Mrs. Cecil Spanton Ashdown, Jr.) writer, lecturer
Ashen, Philip chemist
Asher, Aaron editor, publisher
†Ashkin, Michael artist
Ashkinazy, Larry Robert dentist
Ashley, Elizabeth actress
Ashton, Dore author, educator
Ashton, Jean Willoughby library director
Asmodeo Giglio, Ellen Theresa advertising executive
Asner, Edward actor
Assael, Henry marketing educator
Astor, David Warren journalist
Atigbi, Kofitunde Jolomi telecommunications professional
Atkins, Peter Allan lawyer
Atkinson, Holly Gail physician, journalist, business executive, author, lecturer, human rights activist
Atlas, James Robert magazine editor, writer
Atsada, Chaiyanam diplomat
Atwa, Salem Aldasouki entrepreneur
Atwater, Verne Stafford finance educator
Auchincloss, Kenneth magazine editor
Auchincloss, Louis Stanton writer
Auel, Jean Marie author
Auerbach, William lawyer
Aufses, Arthur H(arold), Jr. surgeon, medical educator
†Augenbraum, Harold library director, editor
Auld, Larry Elwood foundation executive
Auletta, Ken writer, columnist
Aurilia, Christine Marie administrative assistant
Auster, Paul writer
Austin, Danforth Whitley newspaper executive
Austin, Gabriel Christopher publisher
Austrian, Neil R. football league executive
Avedon, Richard photographer
†Avgerakis, George Harris video producer
Aviv, Jonathan Enoch otolaryngologist, educator
†Avlon, Helen Daphnis artist
Ax, Emanuel pianist
Axel, Richard pathology and biochemistry educator
Axelrod, Norman N(athan) technical planning and technology application consultant
Axinn, Stephen Mark lawyer
Ayotte, Richard L. architect
†Azrielant, Aya jewelry manufacturing executive
Azzoli, Val music company executive
Babyface, (Kenny Edmonds) popular musician
Bacall, Lauren actress
Bach, Thomas Handford lawyer, investor
Bachelder, Joseph Elmer, III lawyer
Backman, Gerald Stephen lawyer
Backstedt, Roseanne Joan artist
Bacot, John Carter retired banking executive
Badertscher, David Glen law librarian, consultant
Baechler, Donald painter
Baer, Harold, Jr. judge
Baer, Rudolf Lewis dermatologist, educator
Bagger, Richard Hartvig lawyer
Bahler, Gary M. lawyer
Bahr, Lauren S. publishing company executive
Bailey, Janet Dee publishing company executive
†Bain, Geri magazine editor
Bains, Harrison MacKellar, Jr. financial executive
Bains, Leslie Elizabeth banker
Bainton, J(ohn) Joseph lawyer
Baird, Dugald Euan oil field service company executive
Baird, Zoë lawyer, insurance company executive
Baity, John Cooley lawyer
Bakal, Carl writer, public affairs consultant, photojournalist
Baker, Deborah editor, writer
Baker, Elizabeth Calhoun magazine editor
Baker, James Estes foreign service officer
Baker, Jill Withrow artist, writer
Baker, Paul Raymond history educator
Baker, Russell Wayne columnist, author
Baker, Stephen advertising executive, author
Baker, Stuart David lawyer
Baker, William Franklin public broadcasting company executive
Baker-Riker, Margery television executive
†Bakinowski, Carol Ann journalist
Balaz, Beverly Ann publishing executive
Baldwin, David Allen political science educator
Baldwin, David Shepard physician
Baldwin, Stephen actor
Ball, Damon Howard investment management executive
Ball, John H(anstein) lawyer
Ball, Lillian sculptor, educator
Ball, Susan arts association administrator, art historian
Ballard, Charles Alan investment banker
Balliett, Whitney writer, critic
Balter, Bernice religious organization administrator
Bamberger, Michael Albert lawyer
Bancroft, Alexander Clerihew lawyer
Bancroft, Margaret Armstrong lawyer
Bandy, Mary Lea museum official
Banerjee, (Bimal) artist, educator
Banks, Helen Augusta singer, actress
Banks, Russell financial planner, consultant
Bankston, Archie Moore, Jr. lawyer
Baquet, Dean Paul newspaper editor
Bara, Jean Marc finance and communications executive
Baragwanath, Albert Kingsmill curator
Barandes, Robert lawyer
Baranski, Joan Sullivan publisher
Barasch, Clarence Sylvan lawyer
Barasch, Mal Livingston lawyer
Barbeosch, William Peter banker, lawyer
Barber, Ann McDonald physician
Barber, Russell Brooks Butler television producer
Barbera, Jose Eduardo international trade professional
Barchas, Jack David psychiatrist, educator
Bardach, Joan Lucile clinical psychologist
Bardos, Karoly television and film educator, writer, director
Barickman, Richard Bruce English educator, writer
Barie, Philip Steven surgeon, educator
Barish, Julian I. psychiatrist
Barist, Jeffrey A. lawyer
†Barkan, Leonard humanities educator
Barker, Barbara Ann ophthalmologist
Barker, Charles conductor
Barker, Edwin Bogue musician
Barker, Sylvia Margaret nurse
Barnabeo, Susan Patricia lawyer
Barnes, Duncan magazine editor, writer
Barnes, Edward Larrabee architect
Barnes, Jhane Elizabeth fashion design company executive, designer
Barnet, Will artist, educator
Barnett, Bernard accountant
Barnett, Henry Lewis pediatrician, medical educator
†Barnett, Larry R. umpire
Barnett, Vivian Endicott curator
Barnum, Barbara Stevens retired nursing educator
Barolini, Teodolinda literary critic
Baron, Carolyn editor, author, publishing executive
Baron, Robert folklorist
Baron, Sheri advertising agency executive
Barondess, Jeremiah Abraham physician
Barr, Michael Charles securities trader
Barr, Thomas D. lawyer
†Barrat, Martine photographer, videographer, filmmaker
Barrett, Bill sculptor
†Barrett, David J. broadcast company executive
Barrett, Elizabeth Ann Manhart nursing educator, psychotherapist, consultant
Barrett, Herbert artists management executive
Barrett, Loretta Anne publishing executive
Barrett, Martin Jay financial executive
Barrett, Paul journalist
Barrett, Paulette Singer public relations executive
Barrett, William Gary advertising executive
Barrie, Barbara actress
Barrios, Richard (John) writer, film historian
Barron, James Turman journalist
Barron, Susan clinical psychologist
Barry, David Earl lawyer
Barry, Desmond Thomas, Jr. lawyer
Barry, Edward William publisher
Barry, Thomas Corcoran investment counsellor
Barsalona, Frank Samuel theatrical agent
Barsamian, Khajag Sarkis primate
†Bart, Roger actor
Bartges, Hans investment company executive
Barth, Mark Harold lawyer
Barth, Richard pharmaceutical executive
Bartlett, Joseph Warren lawyer
Bartlett, Peter B. investment company executive
Bartlett, Thomas Foster international management consultant
Bartley, Robert LeRoy newspaper editor
Bartoli, Cecilia coloratura soprano, mezzo soprano
Barton, John Murray artist, appraiser, consultant, lecturer
Barton, Lewis consultant
Baruch, Ralph M. communications executive
Basilico, Claudio molecular biologist, educator
Bason, George R., Jr. lawyer
Bass, Hyman mathematician, educator
Bassen, Ned Henry lawyer
Bastidas, Hugo Xavier painter
Batchvarov, Alexander Ivanov financial analyst
Bates, Michael Lawrence curator
Batista, Alberto A. editor
Batscha, Robert Michael museum executive
Batts, Deborah A. judge
Bauer, Douglas F. lawyer
Bauer, Marion Dane writer
†Bauer, Peter publishing executive
Bauer, Ralph Glenn lawyer, maritime arbitrator
Baum, Richard Theodore engineering executive
Bauman, Martin Harold executive search firm executive
Baumgardner, John Ellwood, Jr. lawyer
Baumgardner, Matthew Clay artist
Baumgarten, Paul Anthony lawyer
†Baumgarten, Sidney lawyer, company executive
Baumrin, Bernard Stefan Herbert lawyer, educator
Bazell, Robert Joseph science correspondent
Bazerman, Steven Howard lawyer
Beach, Diana Lee psychotherapist, priest
Beal, Jack artist
Beale, Christopher William banker
Bear, Donald law firm executive director
Bear, Larry Alan lawyer, educator
Bearak, Corey B(ecker) lawyer
Beard, Eugene P. advertising agency executive
Beardsley, Theodore S(terling), Jr. professional society administrator
Beatie, Russel Harrison, Jr. lawyer
Beattie, Ann author
†Beatty, Prudence Carter federal judge
Beausoleil, Doris Mae federal agency administrator, housing specialist
Beck, Andrew James lawyer
Beck, Martha Ann art curator, director
Beck, Rosemarie artist, educator
†Becker, Glenn Adam plastic surgeon
Becker, Isidore A. business executive
Becker, Ivan advertising executive
Becker, Robert A. advertising executive
Becker, Susan Kaplan management consultant, educator
Becker-Roukas, Helane Renée securities analyst, financial executive
Beckhard, Herbert architect
Beckmann, John architect, designer, writer
Becofsky, Arthur Luke arts administrator, writer
Bederson, Benjamin physicist, educator
†Bederson, Joshua Benjamin neurosurgeon
Bedrij, Orest investment banker, scientist
Beerbower, John Edwin lawyer
Beerman, Joseph health educator
Beers, Charlotte Lenore advertising agency executive
Beeson, Jack Hamilton composer, educator, writer
Beeston, Paul professional baseball executive
Begell, William publisher
Begley, Evelyn Maria special education educator
†Begley, Louis lawyer, writer
Begley, Sharon Lynn journalist
Behr, Alan Andrew lawyer, writer
Behrens, Hildegard soprano
Behrens, Myles Michael neuro-ophthalmologist
Beim, David Odell investment banker, educator
Beim, Norman playwright, actor, director
Beinecke, Candace Krugman lawyer
Beinecke, Frederick William investment company executive
Beinecke, William Sperry corporate executive
Belag, Andrea Susan artist
Belden, David Leigh professional association executive, engineering educator
Bel Geddes, Joan writer
Belkin, Boris David violinist
Belknap, Norton petroleum company consultant
Belknap, Robert Lamont Russian and comparative literature educator
Bell, Charles A. hotel development and management executive
Bell, Derrick Albert law educator, author, lecturer
Bell, Jonathan Robert lawyer
Bell, Martin Allen investment company executive
Bell, Theodore Augustus advertising executive
Bell, Thomas Devereaux, Jr. advertising company executive
†Bell, Wally umpire
Bellamy, Carol international organization executive
Bellanger, Serge René banker
Bellas, Albert Constantine investment banker, advisor
Beller, Daniel J. lawyer
Beller, Gary A. lawyer, insurance company executive
Bellin, Howard Theodore plastic surgeon
Belliveau, Gerard Joseph, Jr. librarian
Bellows, Howard Arthur, Jr. marketing research executive
Belnick, Mark Alan lawyer
†Belok, Lennart C. neurologist
Bemis, Mary Ferguson magazine editor
Benakis, George James lawyer
Benchley, Peter Bradford author
Bender, John Charles lawyer
Bender, Thomas history and humanities educator, writer
Bendixen, Henrik Holt physician, educator, dean
Benedetto, M. William investment banker
Benedict, James Nelson lawyer
Benedikt, Michael poet, educator, author, editor, free-lance consultant
Benenson, Edward Hartley realty company executive
Benenson, Mark Keith lawyer
†Benfield, James Haines treasurer
Benglis, Lynda artist, sculptor
Ben-Haim, Zigi artist
†Benjamin, Ruth writer
Benjamin, Saragail Katzman writer, performer, composer
Benkard, James W. B. lawyer
†Benmosche, Robert H. insurance company executive
Bennett, James Marvin consulting company executive
Bennett, Joel Herbert construction company executive
Bennett, Scott Lawrence lawyer
Bennett, Tony (Anthony Dominick Benedetto) entertainer
Bentley, Anthony Miles lawyer
Benton, Donald Stewart publishing company executive, lawyer
Benton, Jack Mitchell management consultant
Benton, Nicholas theater producer
Ben-Zvi, Jeffrey Stuart gastroenterologist, internist
Berdick, Leonard Stanley insurance broker
Berenbeim, Ronald Everett business writer, educator
Berendt, John Lawrence writer, editor
Berenson, Robert Leonard advertising agency executive
Berg, Alan lawyer, government official
Berg, David author, artist
Bergan, Edmund Paul, Jr. lawyer
Bergen, John Donald communications, public affairs executive
Bergen, Polly actress
Berger, Frank Milan biomedical researcher, scientist, former pharmaceutical company executive
Berger, George lawyer
Berger, Ivan Bennett magazine editor, writer
Berger, Miriam Roskin creative arts therapy director, educator, therapist
Berger, Pearl library director
Berger, Thomas Louis author
Berghahn, Volker Rolf history educator
Bergman, Charles Cabe foundation executive
Bergreen, Bernard D. investment company executive
Bergreen, Morris Harvey lawyer, business executive, private investor
Bergstein, Daniel Gerard lawyer
Beringer, Stuart Marshall investment banker
Berk, Paul David physician, scientist, educator
Berkman, Lillian foundation executive, corporation executive, art collector
†Berkowitz, Alan Steven educator, poet
Berland, Sanford Neil lawyer
†Berley, Marc S. foundation administrator, English educator
Berlin, Howard Richard investment advisory company executive
Berlin, Jordan Stuart investment company executive
Berlind, Robert Elliot artist
Berliner, Barbara librarian, consultant
Berlowe, Phyllis Harriette public relations counselor
Berman, Ariane R. artist
Berman, Herbert E. councilman
Berman, Keith solicitor, lawyer
Berman, Philip Averill journalist, consultant
Berman, Richard Miles judge
Berman, Siegrid Visconti interior designer
Bernard, David George retired management consultant
Bernard, Richard Phillip lawyer
Bernard, Walter art director
Bernardi, Mario conductor
Bernbach, John Lincoln corporate strategies consultant
Berne, Bruce J. chemistry educator
Berner, Andrew Jay library director, writer
Berner, Mary publisher
†Bernikow, Leonard federal judge
†Bernikow, Louise writer
Bernstein, Alan Arthur oil company executive
Bernstein, Bernard lawyer, corporate executive
Bernstein, Daniel Lewis lawyer
Bernstein, Elliot Louis television executive
Bernstein, Jonine Lisa biometry researcher, epidemiologist, educator
Bernstein, Robert Louis publishing company executive
†Bernstein, Stuart M. federal judge
Bernstein, Theresa artist
Berris, Brian A. investment company executive
†Berry, Eliot Ward writer, appraiser
Berry, Halle actress
Berry, John Nichols, III publishing executive, editor
Berry, Joyce Charlotte university press editor
Berry, Loren Curtis lawyer, consultant
Berry, Nancy Michaels philanthropy consultant
Berthot, Jake artist
Bertino, Joseph Rocco physician, educator
Bertuccioli, Bruno petrochemical company executive
Berzow, Harold Steven lawyer
Beshar, Robert Peter lawyer
†Besterman, Douglas composer, orchestrator
Bettman, Gary Bruce lawyer
Betts, Richard Kevin political science educator
Beuchert, Edward William lawyer
Bewkes, Eugene Garrett, Jr. investment company executive, consultant
Bewkes, Jeff television broadcasting company executive
Beyer, Charlotte Bishop investment management executive
Beyer, Lisa journalist
Bezanson, Thomas Edward lawyer
Bhavsar, Natvar Prahladji artist
Bialkin, Kenneth Jules lawyer
Bialo, Kenneth Marc lawyer
Bible, Geoffrey Cyril tobacco company executive
Bickers, David Rinsey physician, educator
Bickford, Jewelle Wooten investment banker
Bicks, David Peter lawyer
Biddle, Flora Miller art museum administrator
Biderman, Mark Charles investment banker
Bidwell, James Truman, Jr. lawyer
Biederman, Barron Zachary (Barry Biederman) advertising agency executive
Biel, Leonard, Jr. urologist
Bielenstein, Hans Henrik August Oriental studies educator
Biggs, Barton Michael investment company executive
Biggs, John Herron insurance company executive
Bijur, Arthur William advertising executive
Bikel, Theodore actor, singer
Billington, Ken lighting designer
Bing, Jonathan Lloyd lawyer
Binger, Wilson Valentine civil engineer
Binkert, Alvin John hospital administrator
Biondi, Frank J., Jr. entertainment company executive
Birbari, Adil Elias physician, educator
Bird, Mary Lynne Miller professional society administrator
Birkelund, John Peter investment banking executive
Birkenhead, Thomas Bruce theatrical producer and manager, educator
Birnbaum, Edward Lester lawyer
Birnbaum, Henry librarian
†Birnbaum, Sheila L. lawyer, educator
†Birns, Nicholas Boe educator, editor
Birsh, Arthur Thomas publisher
Birsh, Philip S. publishing executive
Birstein, Ann writer, educator
Bishop, André artistic director, producer
Bishop, Susan Katharine executive search company executive
Bishop, Thomas Walter French language and literature educator
Bisson, Terry Ballantine author, editor
†Bitter, Shlomo Abraham systems integration company executive
Black, Barbara Aronstein legal history educator
Black, Cathleen Prunty publishing executive
Black, James Isaac, III lawyer
Black, Jerry Bernard lawyer
Blackford, John magazine editor
Blackman, Kenneth Robert lawyer

†Blackshear, Cornelius federal judge
Blair, Robin Elise Farbman financial and management consultant
Blair, William Granger retired newspaperman
Blakeslee, Edward Eaton lawyer, insurance executive
Blalock, Sherrill investment advisor
Blanc, Peter (William Peters Blanc) sculptor, painter
Blanc, Roger David lawyer
Bland, Frederick Aves architect
Bland, Teresa P. financial analyst, consultant
Blank, Matthew C. broadcast company executive
Blattmachr, Jonathan George lawyer
Blatz, Linda Jeanne marketing professional
†Blazejowski, Carol sports team executive, retired basketball player
Blechman, R. O. artist, filmmaker
Blinder, Albert Allan judge
Blinder, Richard Lewis architect
Blinken, Donald ambassador, investment banker
Blinken, Robert James manufacturing and communications company executive
†Blitzer, Judi Rappoport bank executive
Bliven, Bruce, Jr. writer
Bliven, Naomi book reviewer
Blobel, Günter cell biologist, educator
Bloch, Peter editor
Block, Francesca Lia writer
Block, John Douglas auction house executive
Block, Ned philosophy educator
Block, William Kenneth lawyer
Bloodworth, Sandra Gail artist, arts administrator
Bloom, Jack Sandler investment banker
Bloom, Robert H. advertising executive
Bloomberg, Michael Rubens finance and information services company executive
Bloomer, Harold Franklin, Jr. lawyer
Bloomfield, Louise Anne editor
Bloomgarden, Kathy Finn public relations executive
Blumberg, Gerald lawyer
Blume, Judy Sussman author
Blume, Lawrence Dayton lawyer
Blumkin, Linda Ruth lawyer
Blyth, Jeffrey journalist
Blyth, Myrna Greenstein publishing executive, editor, author
Blythe, William LeGette, II editor, writer
Boardman, Seymour artist
Bobbitt, Juanita Marilyn Crawford international organization executive
Boccardi, Louis Donald news agency executive
Bocchino, Lisa magazine editor
Bochner, Mel artist
Bock, Frank Joseph information systems specialist
Bock, Walter Joseph zoology educator
Bockstein, Herbert lawyer
Boddie, Reginald Alonzo lawyer
Bode, Walter Albert editor
Bodea, Andy S. bank executive
Bodovitz, James Philip lawyer
Boehm, David Alfred publisher, producer
Boehner, Leonard Bruce lawyer
Boelzner, Gordon orchestral conductor
Boes, Lawrence William lawyer
Bogdonoff, Morton David physician, educator
Bohrman, David Ellis television news producer
Boice, Craig Kendall management consultant
Boissevain, Benjamin Mathew investment banker
Bolan, Thomas Anthony lawyer
Bolanos, Michael Templeton new media executive
Boley, Bruno Adrian engineering educator
Bolotowsky, Andrew Ilyitch flutist, composer
Bolt, Dawn Maria real estate agent, financial adviser
Bolt, Thomas writer, artist
Bonacquist, Harold Frank, Jr. lawyer
Bonazzi, Elaine Claire mezzo-soprano
Bond, George Clement anthropologist, educator
Bonfante, Larissa classics educator
†Bonin, Gregory umpire
Bonino, Fernanda art dealer
Bonynge, Richard opera conductor
Boodey, Cecil Webster, Jr. political science educator
Bookhardt, Fred Barringer, Jr. architect
Boorstein, Laurence economist
Booth, Edgar Hirsch lawyer
†Booth, Margaret A(nn) communications company executive
Booth, Mitchell B. lawyer
Boothby, Willard Sands, III bank executive
Borders, William Alexander journalist
Bordiga, Benno automotive parts manufacturing company executive
Bordoff, Jason Eric consultant
Borecki, Kenneth Michael real estate investment consultant
†Borelli, Francis J(oseph) (Frank Borelli) insurance brokerage and consulting firm financial executive
Borer, Jeffrey Stephen cardiologist
Borge, Victor entertainer, comedian, pianist
Borisoff, Richard Stuart lawyer
Borkon, Doris educational administrator, entrepreneur
Bornstein, Steven M. broadcast executive
Boros, Jerome S. lawyer
Borowik, Ann writer
Borowitz, Sidney retired physics educator
Borrelli, John Francis architect
Borrone, Lillian C. transportation executive
Borsody, Robert Peter lawyer
Borst-Manning, Diane Gail management consultant
Borut, Josephine insurance executive
Bosco, Philip Michael actor
Bosman, Richard painter, printmaker
Bosses, Stevan J. lawyer
Bostock, Roy Jackson advertising agency executive
Bothmer, Dietrich Felix von museum curator, archaeologist
Boudreau, A. Allan historian, writer, educator
Bouloukos, Theodore, II writer, editor
Boultinghouse, Marion Craig Bettinger editor
Bourjaily, Vance novelist
Bourke, Thomas Anthony librarian, writer
Boutis, Tom artist, painter, print maker
Bouton, Marshall Melvin academic administrator
Bove, John Louis chemistry and environmental engineering educator, researcher
Bowden, Sally Ann choreographer, teacher, dancer
Bowden, William P., Jr. lawyer, banker
Bowen, Jean librarian, consultant
Bowen, William Gordon economist, educator, foundation administrator
†Bowles, Erskine White House staff member
Boxer, Leonard lawyer
Boyce, Joseph Nelson journalist
Boyer, Robert Allan business executive
Bozorth, Squire Newland lawyer
Brach, Paul Henry artist
Bradbury, Ray Douglas author
Brademas, John retired university president, former congressman
Braden, Martha Brooke concert pianist, educator
Bradford, Barbara Taylor writer, journalist, novelist
Bradford, Phillip Gnassi financial analytics developer
Bradford, Richard Roark writer
Bradley, E. Michael lawyer
Bradley, Edward R. news correspondent
Bradley, Lisa M. artist
Bradsell, Kenneth Raymond minister
Bradstock, John advertising executive
Braham, Randolph Lewis political science educator
Brainerd, Michael Charles international exchange organization executive
Brams, Steven John political scientist, educator, game theorist
Branch, Taylor writer
Brand, Leonard physician, educator
Brandrup, Douglas Warren lawyer
†Brandt-Rauf, Paul Wesley public health educator
Brant, Sandra J. magazine publisher
Braude, Robert Michael medical library administrator
Braudy, Susan Orr author
Braun, Jeffrey Louis lawyer
Braun, Neil S. communications executive
Braverman, Alan N. lawyer
Braverman, Robert Jay international consultant, public policy educator
Braxton, Toni popular musician
Braz, Evandro Freitas management consultant
Brazinsky, Irv(ing) chemical engineering educator
Brecher, Howard Arthur lawyer
Brechner, Stanley artistic director
Brecker, Jeffrey Ross lawyer, educator
Brecker, Michael saxophonist
Bredwell, Jo advertising executive
Breger, William N. architect, educator
Breglio, John F. lawyer
Bregman, Martin film producer
Breines, Simon architect
Breinin, Goodwin M. physician
Brendel, Alfred concert pianist
Brennan, Henry Higginson architect
Brennan, Murray Frederick surgeon, oncologist
Brennan, Terrence Michael publisher
Brenner, Beth Fuchs publishing executive
Brenner, Egon university official, education consultant
Brenner, Erma author
Brenner, Frank lawyer
Brenner, Howard Martin banker
Bresani, Federico Fernando business executive
Breslow, Esther May Greenberg biochemistry educator, researcher
Breslow, Jan Leslie scientist, educator, physician
Breslow, Ronald Charles chemist, educator
Bressler, Bernard lawyer
Bressler, Richard J. communications company executive
Brett, Nancy Heléne artist
Brewer, Karen librarian
Brewster, Robert Gene concert singer, educator
†Brian, Laura Anna freelance writer
Bridges, Linda Kay journalist
Briggs, Philip insurance company executive
Briggs, Taylor Rastrick lawyer
†Brill, Edward N. hotel executive
Brilliant, Richard art history educator
Brilliant, Robert Lee advertising agency executive
Brimelow, Peter journalist
Bring, Murray H. lawyer
Brinkley, Christie model, spokesperson, designer
†Brinkman, Joseph N. umpire
Briskman, Louis J. lawyer
Bristah, Pamela Jean librarian
Brittain, Willard W., Jr. (Woody Brittain) diversified financial services company executive
Brittenham, Raymond Lee investment company executive
Brittingham, Kimberly Anne magazine publisher
Britz Lotti, Diane Edward investment company executive
Broadwater, Douglas Dwight lawyer
Broches, Paul Elias architect
Brock, Charles Lawrence lawyer, business executive
Brockway, David Hunt lawyer
Broder, Douglas Fisher lawyer
†Brodsky, Beverly artist
Brodsky, Samuel lawyer
Brody, Alan Jeffrey investment company executive
Brody, Eugene David investment company executive
Brody, Jacqueline editor
Brody, Jane Ellen journalist
†Brohn, William David conductor, orchestrator
Brokaw, Thomas John television broadcast executive, correspondent
Brome, Thomas Reed lawyer
Bronfman, Edgar Miles beverage company executive
Bronstein, Richard J. lawyer
Brook, David William psychiatrist, researcher
Brook, Judith Suzanne psychiatry and psychology researcher and educator
Brooke, Paul Alan finance company executive
Brooks, Anita Helen public relations executive
Brooks, Diana B. auction house executive
†Brooks, Gary management consultant
Brooks, Jerome Bernard English and Afro-American literature educator
Brooks, Lorimer Page patent lawyer
Brooks, Paula advertising executive
Brooks, Steven R. architect
Brooks, Timothy H. media executive
Bross, Steward Richard, Jr. lawyer
Brosterman, Melvin A. lawyer
Brothers, Joyce Diane television personality, psychologist
Broude, Richard Frederick lawyer, educator
Broughton, Phillip Charles lawyer
Browdy, Joseph Eugene lawyer
Brown, Andreas Le book store and art gallery executive
Brown, Arnold management consultant
Brown, Carolyn Rice dancer, choreographer
Brown, Carroll diplomat, association executive
Brown, Charles Dodgson lawyer
Brown, Craig advertising agency executive
Brown, Darrell James publishing executive
Brown, David motion picture producer, writer
Brown, David Warfield management educator
Brown, Edward James, Sr. utility executive
Brown, Eric art gallery director, art dealer
Brown, Fred Elmore investment executive
Brown, Helen Gurley editor, writer
Brown, Hobson, Jr. executive recruiting consultant
Brown, James Nelson, Jr. accountant
Brown, Jason Walter neurologist, educator, researcher
Brown, Jonathan art historian, fine arts educator
Brown, Kenneth Charles manufacturing company executive
Brown, Les (Lester Louis) journalist
Brown, Meredith M. lawyer
Brown, Paul publishing executive
Brown, Paul M. lawyer
Brown, Ralph Sawyer, Jr. retired lawyer, business executive
Brown, Rita Mae author
Brown, Terrence Charles art association executive, researcher, lecturer
Brown, Tom publishing executive
Brown, Trisha dancer
Brown, Walter H. investment company executive
Brown, William Anthony (Tony) broadcast executive
Browne, Arthur newspaper editor
Browne, Jeffrey Francis lawyer
Browne, Joy psychologist
Browne, Malcolm Wilde journalist
Browning, John pianist
Brozman, Tina L. federal judge
Bruder, Harold Jacob artist, educator
Brumm, James Earl lawyer, trading company executive
Brun, Henry publishing executive
Brundige, Robert William, Jr. lawyer
Brunie, Charles Henry investment manager
Brusca, Robert Andrew economist
Brush, Craig Balcombe retired French language and computer educator
Brustein, Lawrence financial executive
Bruzs, Boris Olgerd management consultant
Bryan, Barry Richard lawyer
Bryan, Katherine Byram healthcare executive
Bryant, Coralie Marcus political science educator
Brzustowicz, Stanislaw Henry clinical dentistry educator
Buatta, Mario interior designer
Buchanan, Edna journalist
Buchbinder, Darrell Bruce lawyer
Buchwald, Art columnist, writer
Buchwald, Elias public relations executive
†Buchwald, Monita public relations executive
Buchwald, Naomi Reice judge
Buck, James E. financial exchange executive
Buck, Louise Zierdt psychologist
Buck, Robert Treat, Jr. gallery director, former museum director, educator
Buckles, Robert Howard retired investment company executive
†Buckley, Betty Lynn actress
Buckley, Christopher Taylor editor, author
Buckley, Kevin magazine editor
Buckley, Priscilla Langford magazine editor
Buckley, Virginia Laura editor
Buckley, William Frank, Jr. magazine editor, writer
Buckman, Thomas Richard foundation executive, educator
Buckwald, Joel David archivist
Budd, Thomas Witbeck lawyer
Budde, Neil Frederick publishing company executive, editor
Budig, Gene Arthur former chancellor, professional sports executive
Budnick, Ernest Joseph music industry executive
Buehler, Thomas psychotherapist, expressive therapist
Buford, Bill editor, writer
Buhagiar, Marion editor, author
Bujold, Lois McMaster science fiction writer
Bullen, Richard Hatch former corporate executive
Bulliet, Richard Williams history educator, novelist
Bulliner, P. Alan corporate lawyer
Bulow, George Mitchell entrepreneur
Bumbry, Grace soprano
Bungey, Michael advertising executive
Bunts, Frank Emory artist
Burak, H(oward) Paul lawyer
Burden, Donald Wesley publishing executive
Burenga, Kenneth L. publishing executive
Burge, Christopher auction house executive
Burger, Chester retired management consultant
Burgheim, Richard magazine editor
Burgweger, Francis Joseph Dewes, Jr. lawyer
Burke, James Joseph, Jr. investment banker
†Burke, Martin J. United States marshall
Burke, Mary Griggs (Mrs. Jackson Burke) art collector
Burke, Michael Desmond pathologist
Burkett, Newton Jones, III broadcast journalist
Burkhardt, Ann occupational therapist, clinical educator
Burkhardt, Ronald Robert advertising executive
Burleigh, A. Peter ambassador
Burnham, Lem psychologist
Burns, Arnold Irwin lawyer
Burns, John F. reporter
Burns, John Joseph, Jr. financial and insurance holding company executive
†Burns, Ralph conductor, orchestrator
Burnshaw, Stanley writer
Burrell, Orville Richard popular musician
Burrill, Kathleen R. F. (Kathleen R. F. Griffin-Burrill) Turkologist, educator
Burrows, Michael Donald lawyer
Bursky, Herman Aaron lawyer
Burson, Harold public relations executive
Burton, John Campbell university dean, educator, consultant
Burton, Peggy advertising executive
Bush, Harry Leonard, Jr. surgery educator
Bushnell, George Edward, III lawyer
Butler, Jay women's basketball coach
Butler, Jonathan Putnam architect
Butler, Robert Neil gerontologist, psychiatrist, writer, educator
Butler, Samuel Coles lawyer
Butler, Stephen Gregory accountant
Butler, Vincent Paul, Jr. physician, educator
Butler, William Joseph lawyer
Butowsky, David Martin lawyer
Buttenwieser, Lawrence Benjamin lawyer
Butterklee, Neil Howard lawyer
Buttner, Jean Bernhard publishing company executive
Button, Richard Totten television and stage producer, former figure skating champion
Byer, Diana performing arts company executive
Bylinsky, Gene Michael magazine editor
Byrd, Eva Wilson communications executive
Byron, Eric Howard sculptor, museum researcher and administrator
†Byron, Kim artist
Bystryn, Jean-Claude dermatologist, educator
Bystryn, Marcia Hammill city program administrator
Cabalquinto, Luis Carrazcal free-lance writer
Caggiano, Joseph advertising executive
Caginalp, Aydin S. lawyer
Cahan, William George surgeon, educator
Cahn, Steven Mark philosopher, educator
Cairns, AnneMarie public relations executive
Cajori, Charles Florian artist, educator
Calabrese, Rosalie Sue arts management consultant, writer
Calame, Byron Edward journalist
Calame, Kathryn Lee microbiologist, educator
Caliandro, Arthur minister
Calio, Vincent S. public relations executive
Calisher, Hortense (Mrs. Curtis Harnack) writer
Call, Neil Judson corporate executive
Callahan, Joseph Patrick lawyer
Callahan, Robert F., Jr. radio executive
Calovski, Naste diplomat
Calvillo, Ricardo C. communications executive
Camhy, Sherry Wallerstein painter
†Camins, Martin B. neurosurgeon
Cammisa, Frank P., Jr. surgeon, educator
Campbell, Colin Goetze foundation president
Campbell, Debra Lynn marketing and new venture consultant
Campbell, Douglass banker
Campbell, George, Jr. physicist, administrator
†Campbell, Margarette Monjoa interpreter, translator
Campbell, Maria Bouchelle lawyer, church executive
Campbell, Mary Schmidt dean art school
Campbell, Robert David minerals and metals executive
Campbell, Ronald Neil magazine designer
Campi, John G. newspaper publishing executive
Camps, Jeffrey Lowell financial services company general agent
Canada, Geoffrey social welfare administrator
Cancro, Robert psychiatrist, educator
Candido, Anthony Nicholas artist, educator
Canes, Brian Dennis professional services company official
Cannaliato, Vincent, Jr. investment banker, mathematician
Cannell, John Redferne lawyer
Cannistraro, Nicholas, Jr. newspaper executive
Cannon, James Anthony advertising agency executive
Cannon, John actor, performing arts association executive
Cannon, John J(oseph) real estate sales and marketing executive
†Cannon, Steve non-profit organization administrator
Canoni, John David lawyer
Canter, Stanley D. retired marketing consulting company executive
Cantilli, Edmund Joseph safety engineering educator, writer
Cantor, Melvyn Leon retired lawyer
Cantrell, Lana actress, singer, lawyer
Caouette, John Bernard insurance company executive
Capalbo, Carmen Charles director, producer
Capano, Edward Andrew publishing company executive
Caples, Richard James dance company executive, lawyer
Capolarello, Joe R. photojournalist
†Capozzi, Lou public relations executive
Cappiello, Angela church grants administrator
Cappon, Andre Alfred management consultant
Capriati, Jennifer Maria professional tennis player
Caputo, David Armand university president, political scientist educator
Caputo, Lucio trade company executive
Caputo, Philip Joseph author, journalist, screenwriter
Caraley, Demetrios James political scientist, educator, author
Carb, Stephen Ames lawyer
Cardew, William Joseph bank executive
Cardinali, Albert John lawyer
Cardozo, Benjamin Mordecai lawyer
Carey, Edward John utility executive
Carey, Ellen artist
Carey, Francis James investment banker
Carey, J. Edwin lawyer
Carey, James William university dean, educator, researcher
Carey, William Polk investment banker
Cargill, Ursula Bardot university official
Carling, Francis lawyer
Carlson, Marian Bille geneticist, researcher, educator
Carlson, Marvin Albert theater educator
Carlson, Mitchell Lans international technical advisor
Carlson, P(atricia) M(cElroy) writer
Carlson, Theodore Joshua lawyer, retired utility company executive
Carman, Gregory Wright federal judge
Carnase, Thomas Paul graphic designer, typographic consultant
Carnell, Richard Scott law educator
Carnella, Frank Thomas information executive
Carney, Michael orchestra leader
Caro, Robert Allan author
Caroff, Phyllis M. social work educator
Carpenter, Michael Alan financial services executive
Carpenter, Patricia music educator
Carr, Arthur Charles psychologist, educator
Carr, Gladys Justin publishing company executive, editor, writer
Carr, Maurice Kirk, Jr. publishing executive
Carr, Ronald Edward ophthalmologist, educator
Carro, Carl Rafael executive search consultant
Carroll, Kent book publishing executive
Carrus, Gerald broadcast executive
Carter, Edward Graydon editor
Carter, Elliott Cook, Jr. composer
Carter, James Hal, Jr. lawyer
Carter, John Mack publishing company executive
Carthay, R. Jon hand model, actor
Caruso, Rocco Andrew television producer
Casals-Ariet, Jordi physician
Case, Hadley oil company executive
Case, Stephen H. lawyer
Casebere, James Edward artist
Casella, Margaret Mary artist, photographer
Casey, Barbara Jeanne magazine marketing official
Casey, Karen Anne banker
†Casey, Richard Conway judge
Casey, Thomas Jefferson investment banker, venture capitalist
†Cassel, Christine Karen physician
Cassell, Eric Jonathan physician
Cassell, Kay Ann librarian
Cassella, William Nathan, Jr. organization executive
Castel, Nico tenor, educator
Castel, P. Kevin lawyer
Castellanos, Julio J(esus) banker
Castle, John Krob merchant banker

Castleberry, May Lewis *librarian, curator, editor*
Castoro, Rosemarie *sculptor*
Catanzaro, Daniel Frank *molecular biologist, educator*
Catley-Carlson, Margaret *professional organization administrator*
Catsimatidis, John Andreas *retail chain executive, airline executive*
Cavaglieri, Giorgio *architect*
Cavallo, Jo Ann *Italian language educator*
Cavanagh, Carroll John *business advisor, lawyer, principal art services company*
Cavanagh, Richard Edward *business policy organization executive*
Cavanagh-McKee, Kathryn *nurse*
Cavanna, Dino Francesco *chemicals executive*
Cavender, Catherine C. *magazine editor*
Cavior, Warren Joseph *communications executive*
Caws, Mary Ann *French language and comparative literature educator, critic*
Cayea, Donald Joseph *lawyer*
Cayne, James E. *investment banker*
Cazeaux, Isabelle Anne Marie *retired musicology educator*
Cecil, Donald *investment company executive*
Cedarbaum, Miriam Goldman *federal judge*
Celant, Germano *curator*
†Celmins, Vija *artist, photographer*
Cernuda, Paloma *artist*
Cesarani, Sal *fashion designer*
Chadick, Susan Linda *executive search consulting executive*
Chaganti, Raju S. *geneticist, educator, researcher*
Chaitman, Helen Davis *lawyer*
Chajet, Clive *communications consultant*
Chalsty, John Steele *investment banker*
Chamberlin, Ward Bryan, Jr. *public broadcasting executive*
†Chambers, Christopher Hart *artist*
Chambless, Anne Devon *wig and make-up artist*
Champion, Marge (Marjorie Celeste Champion) *actress, dancer, choreographer*
Chan, Lo-Yi Cheung Yuen *architect*
Chan, W. Y. *pharmacologist, educator*
Chandler, Kenneth A. *newspaper editor*
Chandler, Robert Leslie *public relations executive*
Chanes, Jerome Alan *non-profit organization administrator, public affairs analyst*
Chaney, Verne Edward, Jr. *surgeon, foundation executive, educator*
Chang, Jeannette *publishing executive*
Chang, Jenghwa *biomedical and electrical engineer, medical physicist*
Chang, Ling Wei *sales executive*
Chang, Marian S. *filmmaker, composer*
†Chanlatte, Lisandro Jose *consultant*
Channer, Harold Hudson *television producer, interviewer*
Channing, Stockard (Susan Stockard) *actress*
Chao, James S. C. *maritime executive*
Chapin, Schuyler Garrison *cultural affairs executive, university dean*
Chapman, James Albion *novelist, publisher*
Chapman, Max C. *investment company executive*
Chapman, Peter Herbert *investment company executive*
Chapnick, David B. *lawyer*
Chappell, John Charles *lawyer*
Charendoff, Mark Stuart *educator*
Chargaff, Erwin *biochemistry educator emeritus, writer*
Charney, Craig Russell *pollster, political scientist*
Charnin, Martin *theatrical director, lyricist, producer*
Charron, Paul Richard *apparel company executive*
Chase, Donald Jacob *film journalist, film producer*
Chase, Doris Totten *sculptor, video artist, filmmaker*
Chase, Edward Thornton *lawyer*
Chase, Merrill Wallace *immunologist, educator*
Chase, Norman Eli *radiologist, educator*
Chase, Sylvia B. *journalist*
Chasey, Jacqueline *lawyer*
Chatfield-Taylor, Adele *arts administrator, historic preservationist*
Chavers, Kevin G. *investment company executive*
Chaves, Jose Maria *diplomat, foundation administrator, lawyer, educator*
Chazen, Hartley James *lawyer*
Checketts, David Wayne *professional basketball team executive*
Cheesman, Frederick S. *editor*
Cheh, Huk Yuk *engineering educator, electrochemist*
Chell, Beverly C. *lawyer*
Chelstrom, Marilyn Ann *political education consultant*
Chen, Chi (Chen Chi) *artist*
Chen, Tak-Ming *civil engineer*
Chen, Wesley *lawyer*
Chenault, Kenneth Irvine *financial services company executive*
Cheney, Richard Eugene *public relations executive, psychoanalyst*
Cheng, Chuen Yan *biochemist, educator*
†Chenoweth, Kristin *actress*
Cherksey, Bruce David *physiology educator*
Chermayeff, Ivan *graphic designer*
Cherry, Vivian *photographer*
Chesnutt, Jane *publishing executive*
†Chess, William *public relations executive*
Chester, John E., III *financial services company executive*
Chester, Norman Charles *bank executive*
Chevray, Rene *physics educator*
Chia, Sandro *painter*
Chiang, Yung Frank *law educator*
Chiarchiaro, Frank John *lawyer*
Chichilnisky, Graciela *mathematician, economist, educator, consultant*
Childs, John Farnsworth *consultant, retired investment banker*
Chilstrom, Robert Meade *lawyer*
Chin, Denny *judge*
Chin, Sylvia Fung *lawyer*
Chinnis, Pamela P. *religion organization administrator*
Chirls, Richard *lawyer*
Chiu, David Tak Wai *surgeon*
Cho, Tai Yong *lawyer*
Chopey, Nicholas P. *editor*
Chou, Ting-Chao *pharmacology educator*
Chrisanthopoulos, Peter *advertising executive*
Christensen, Dieter *ethnomusicologist*
Christensen, Henry, III *lawyer*
Christian, Darrell L. *journalist*
Christo, (Christo Vladimirov Javacheff) *artist*
Christopher, Maurine Brooks *foundation administrator, writer, editor*
Christopher, Nicholas *poet, novelist*
Christophersen, Bill *editor, writer*
Christy, Arthur Hill *lawyer*
Chromow, Sheri P. *lawyer*
Chua, Nam-Hai *plant molecular biologist, educator*
Chung, Connie (Constance Yu-hwa Chung) *broadcast journalist*
Church, Frank Forrester *minister, author, columnist*
Church, George John *journalist*
Churgin, Amy *publishing executive*
Chwast, Seymour *graphic artist*
Chwatsky, Ann *photographer, educator*
Ciangio, Sister Donna Lenore *religious organization administrator*
Cicerchi, Eleanor Ann Tomb *fundraising executive*
Ciobanu, Niculae *oncologist, researcher*
Ciparick, Carmen Beauchamp *state judge*
Ciporen, Fred *publishing executive*
Cisneros, Sandra *poet, short story writer, essayist*
Clancy, John Patrick *real estate company executive*
Clancy, Thomas L., Jr. *novelist*
Clapman, Peter Carlyle *lawyer, insurance company executive*
Clapton, Eric *musician*
Clarens, John Gaston *investment executive*
†Clark, Alan Marshall *umpire*
Clark, Carolyn Cochran *lawyer*
Clark, Charles Alan *financial analyst*
†Clark, Harry Warren *public policy consultant*
Clark, Howard Longstreth, Jr. *finance company executive*
†Clark, Joan Hardy *retired journalist*
Clark, Matt *science writer*
Clark, Merrell Edward, Jr. *lawyer*
Clark, Robert Henry, Jr. *holding company executive*
Clark, Thomas Carlyle *banker*
Clark, William, Jr. *political advisor*
Clarke, Frank William *advertising agency executive*
Clarke, Garvey Elliott *educational association administrator, lawyer*
Clarke, Jerrold *architect*
Clarke, John M. *lawyer*
Clarke, Kenneth Kingsley *electrical equipment company executive*
Clarke, Marjorie Jane *environmental consultant, author, researcher*
Clary, Richard Wayland *lawyer*
Claster, Jill Nadell *university administrator, history educator*
Clayton, Joe Don *lawyer*
Clayton, Jonathan Alan *banker*
Clear, Todd *criminal justice educator*
Cleary, Beverly Atlee (Mrs. Clarence T. Cleary) *author*
Clemen, John Douglas *lawyer*
Clemente, Francesco *artist*
Clemente, Robert Stephen *lawyer*
Cliff, Walter Conway *lawyer*
Clifford, Stewart Burnett *banker*
†Clinton, Kathleen Ann *sales executive*
Close, Lanny Garth *otolaryngologist, educator*
Clovis, Donna Lucille *journalist, editor*
Cloward, Richard Andrew *social work educator*
Clutz, William (Hartman Clutz) *artist, educator*
Coane, James Edwin, III *information technology executive*
Cobb, Henry Nichols *architect*
†Coble, G. Drew *umpire*
Cochran, Raymond Martin *university financial administrator*
Cochrane, James Louis *economist*
Codding, Mitchell A. *cultural organization administrator*
Coffee, John Collins, Jr. *legal educator*
Coffin, Dwight Clay *grain company executive*
Cogan, Marshall S. *entrepreneur*
Cohane, Heather Christina *magazine publisher, editor*
Cohen, Abby Joseph *investment strategist*
Cohen, Arthur Morris *artist*
Cohen, Brian S. *public relations executive*
Cohen, Claire Gorham *investors service company executive*
Cohen, Claudia *journalist, television personality*
Cohen, Cora *artist*
†Cohen, Cynthia Price *institute administrator*
Cohen, David Harris *neurobiology educator, university official*
Cohen, Edmund Stephen *lawyer*
Cohen, Edward Herschel *lawyer*
†Cohen, Elliot L. *urologist, educator*
Cohen, Ezechiel Godert David *physicist, educator*
Cohen, Henry Rodgin *lawyer*
Cohen, Jeff *media critic, columnist*
Cohen, Joel Ephraim *scientist, educator*
Cohen, Joel J. *lawyer, investment banker*
Cohen, Jonathan Little *investment banker*
Cohen, Joseph M. *investment company executive*
Cohen, Michael *psychologist*
Cohen, Mildred Thaler *art gallery director*
†Cohen, Morton Norton *English educator, writer*
Cohen, Myron *lawyer, educator*
Cohen, Noel Lee *otolaryngologist, educator*
Cohen, Richard Gerard *lawyer*
Cohen, Richard Martin *journalist*
Cohen, Robert Stephan *lawyer*
Cohen, Samuel Israel *clergyman, organization executive*
Cohen, Saul Bernard *former college president, geographer*
Cohen, Selma *reference librarian, researcher*
Cohen, Selma Jeanne *dance historian*
Cohen, Stephen Frand *political scientist, historian, educator, author, broadcaster*
Cohen-Sabban, Nessim *auditor, accountant*
Cohn, Bertram Josiah *investment banker*
Cohn, David Herc *retired foreign service officer*
Colbath, Brian (Brian Colbath Watson) *actor, script and live performance writer*
Colby, Frank Gerhardt *scientific consultant*
Colby, Marvelle Seitman *business management educator, administrator*
Colby, Robert Alan *retired library science educator*
Cole, Ann Harriet *psychologist, communications consultant*
Cole, Carolyn Jo *brokerage company executive*
Cole, Charles Dewey, Jr. *lawyer*
Cole, Elma Phillipson (Mrs. John Strickler Cole) *social welfare executive*
Cole, Jonathan Richard *sociologist, academic administrator*
Cole, Lewis George *lawyer*
Cole, Max *artist*
Cole, Sylvan, Jr. *art dealer*
Cole, Vinson *tenor*
†Cole, Willie *artist*
Coleman, Cy *pianist, composer, producer*
Coleman, D. Jackson *ophthalmologist, educator*
Coleman, George Edward *tenor, alto and soprano saxophonist*
Coleman, Gregory G. *magazine publisher*
Coleman, John William *urologist*
Coleman, Lester Laudy *otolaryngologist*
Coleman, Martin Stone *retired office furniture company executive*
Coleman, Morton *oncologist, hematologist*
Colfin, Bruce Elliott *lawyer, video producer*
Coll, Jim *gallery director*
Coll, John Peter, Jr. *lawyer*
Collamore, Thomas Jones *corporate executive*
Collier, Zena *author*
Collins, J. Barclay, II *lawyer, oil company executive*
Collins, Timothy Clark *holding company executive*
Collinson, Dale Stanley *lawyer*
Collyer, Michael *lawyer*
Colman, John P. *publishing executive*
Colp, Norman Barry *photographic artist, curator*
Colson, Barbara *publishing executive*
Coltrin, Stephen Hugh *public relations, advertising and marketing executive*
Colvin, Shawn *recording artist, songwriter*
Coly, Lisette *foundation executive*
Combs, Sean *record company executive, producer*
Comfort, Jane *choreographer, director*
Comfort, William Twyman, Jr. *banker*
Comitas, Lambros *anthropologist*
Compagnon, Antoine Marcel *French language educator*
Conarroe, Joel Osborne *foundation administrator, educator, editor*
Conboy, Kenneth *lawyer, former federal judge*
Conde, Yvonne Menéndez *freelance journalist*
Condron, Christopher M. Kip *investment company executive*
Cone, James Hal *theologian, educator, author*
Conlon, James Joseph *conductor*
Connell, Evan Shelby, Jr. *author*
Connelly, Albert R. *lawyer*
†Connelly, Joan Breton *art educator*
Conner, Ruth Martha Edone *nonprofit executive*
Conniff, Richard *writer*
Connolly, Kevin Jude *lawyer*
Connor, John Thomas, Jr. *lawyer*
Connor, Joseph E. *accountant*
Conrad, Winthrop Brown, Jr. *lawyer*
Conroy, Catherine Martin *public relations executive*
Conroy, Pat (Donald Patrick Conroy) *writer*
Consagra, Sophie Chandler *academy administrator*
Constantine, Jan Friedman *lawyer*
Conston, Henry Siegismund *lawyer*
Conway, Kevin *actor, director*
Conway, Richard Francis *investment company executive*
Cook, Blanche Wiesen *history educator, journalist*
Cook, Ferris *writer, illustrator*
Cook, James *magazine editor*
Cook, John Wesley *foundation administrator*
Cook, Michael Lewis *lawyer*
Cook, Robert S., Jr. *lawyer*
Cook, Robin *author*
Cookson, Peter Willis, Jr. *sociologist, writer*
Coolio *popular musician*
Coombs, Janet *advertising executive*
†Coonelly, Francis X. *lawyer*
†Cooney, Joan Ganz *broadcasting executive*
Cooney, John Patrick, Jr. *lawyer*
Cooper, Arthur Martin *magazine editor*
Cooper, Gloria *editor, press critic*
Cooper, Michael Anthony *lawyer*
Cooper, Norman Streich *pathologist, medical educator*
Cooper, Paula *art dealer*
Cooper, Paulette Marcia *writer*
Cooper, R. John, III *lawyer*
Cooper, Stephen Herbert *lawyer*
Cooper, Steve Neil *art gallery owner, photographer*
Cooperman, Alvin *television and theatrical producer*
Corbin, Herbert Leonard *public relations executive*
Corbin, Sol Neil *lawyer*
Corcoran, David *newspaper editor*
Corigliano, John Paul *composer*
Corn, Alfred DeWitt *poet, fiction writer, critic, educator*
Cornell, Thomas Charles *peace activist, writer*
Cornwell, Patricia Daniels *author*
Corporon, John Robert *broadcasting executive*
Corrigan, E(dward) Gerald *investment banker*
Corry, James Michael *insurance executive, educator*
Corsaro, Frank Andrew *theater, musical and opera director*
Corso, Susan Falk *minister*
Cortor, Eldzier *artist, printmaker*
Cory, Jeffrey *television, film, stage, event and creative director*
Cose, Ellis *journalist, author*
Cosenza, Vincent John *accountant*
Costa, Max *health facility administrator, pharmacology educator, environmental medicine educator*
Costa, Victor Charles *fashion designer*
Costikyan, Edward N. *lawyer*
Cote, Denise Louise *federal judge*
Cotter, James Michael *lawyer*
Cotton, Richard *lawyer*
Coudert, Dale Hokin *real estate executive, marketing consultant*
Courant, Ernest David *physicist*
Couric, Katie (Katherine Couric) *broadcast journalist*
†Cousins, Derryl *umpire*
Cowan, Wallace Edgar *lawyer*
Cowen, Edward S. *lawyer*
Cowin, Stephen Corteen *biomedical engineering educator, consultant*
Cowles, Charles *art dealer*
Cowley, Robert William *editor, writer, lecturer*
Coyne, Frank J. *insurance industry executive*
Coyne, Nancy Carol *advertising executive*
†Craft, Terry *umpire*
Cramer, Edward Morton *lawyer, music company executive*
Crane, Benjamin Field *lawyer*
Crane, Roger Ryan, Jr. *lawyer*
Cranefield, Paul Frederic *physiology educator, physician, scientist*
Cranney, Marilyn Kanrek *lawyer*
Crary, Miner Dunham, Jr. *lawyer*
Craven, Wes *film director*
Crawford, Bruce Edgar *advertising executive*
†Crawford, Gerald J. (Jerry Crawford) *umpire*
Crawley, John Boevey *publisher*
Creech, Sharon *children's author*
Creel, Thomas Leonard *lawyer*
Cremer, Leon Earl *federal agent, lawyer*
Crews, Harry Eugene *author*
†Cripps, Kathy Hickey *public relations company official*
Crisona, James Joseph *lawyer*
Crist, Judith *film and drama critic*
Critchell, Simon James *corporate executive*
Critchlow, Charles Howard *lawyer*
Critchlow, Paul *marketing and communications executive*
Crittenden, Danielle Ann *writer, journalist*
Croce, Arlene Louise *critic*
Crocetti, Gino *elementary and secondary education educator*
Cromwell, Oliver Dean *investment banker*
Cronas, Peter Chris *company executive*
Cronholm, Lois S. *biology educator*
Cronkite, Walter *radio and television news correspondent*
Cronson, Caroline Mary *financial executive*
Crooke, Robert Andrew *media relations executive*
†Crosby, David *musician*
Cross, George Alan Martin *biochemistry educator, researcher*
Cross, Theodore Lamont *publisher, author*
Crow, Elizabeth Smith *publishing company executive*
Crowdus, Gary Alan *film company executive*
Crowell, Kenneth E. *lawyer, chemical engineer*
Crowley, M. Therese *broadcaster, singer, songwriter*
†Crumpacker, Margery Ann *educator*
Cryer, Gretchen *playwright, lyricist, actress*
Crystal, James William *insurance company executive*
Cubitto, Robert J. *lawyer*
Cuddihy, Robert Vincent, Jr. *marketing executive*
Cuiffo, Frank Wayne *lawyer*
Culligan, John William *retired corporate executive*
†Cullman, Joan *theatrical producer*
Culp, Michael Bronston *securities company executive, research director*
Cuming, Pamela *marketing professional, author*
†Cumming, Alan *actor*
Cummings, Josephine Anna *writer*
Cummins, Herman Zachary *physicist*
Cuneo, Donald Lane *lawyer, educator*
Cuneo, Jack Alfred *real estate investment executive*
Cunha, Mark Geoffrey *lawyer*
Cunningham, Jeffrey Milton *publishing executive*
Cunningham, Merce *dancer*
†Cunningham, Michael *author, educator*
†Cuomo, Mario Matthew *lawyer, former governor*
Cuozzo, Steven David *newspaper editor*
Cupolo, Joseph *periodical editor*
Curie, Eve *writer, lecturer*
Curley, Walter Joseph Patrick *diplomat, investment banker*
Curry, Ann *correspondent, anchor*
Curry, Jack *magazine editor*
Curry, Jane Louise *writer*
†Curry, Ravenel Boykin *investment manager*
Curtin, Jane Therese *actress, writer*
Curtis, Paul James *mime*
Curtis, Susan Grace *lawyer*
Curtis, Tony (Bernard Schwartz) *actor*
Cushing, Harry Cooke, IV *investment banker*
Cutler, Laurel *advertising agency executive*
Cutler, Ronnie *artist*
†Cutting, Court Baldwin *plastic surgeon, computer graphics researcher*
Czajka, James Vincent *architect*
Czerwinski, Edward Joseph *foreign language educator*
Dacey, Eileen M. *lawyer*
Daidone, Lewis Eugene *financial services company executive*
Dailey, Benjamin Peter *chemistry educator*
Dailey, Janet *novelist*
Daily, John Charles *executive recruiting company executive*
Dajani, Virginia *arts administrator*
Dakin, Christine Whitney *dancer, educator*
Dale, Jim *actor*
Dales, Samuel *microbiologist, virologist, educator*
Dallas, William Moffit, Jr. *lawyer*
Dallen, Russell Morris, Jr. *investment company executive, lawyer*
Dalton, Dennis Gilmore *political science educator*
Daly, Cheryl *broadcast executive*
Daly, George Garman *college dean, educator*
Daly, John Neal *investment company executive*
D'Amato, Alfonse M. *lawyer, former senator*
d'Amboise, Jacques Joseph *dancer, choreographer*
Dana, F(rank) Mitchell *theatrical lighting designer*
Danaher, Frank Erwin *transportation technologist*
Dane, Maxwell *former advertising executive*
D'Angelo, Ernest Eustachio *brokerage house executive*
D'Angelo, Joseph Francis *publishing company executive*
Dangue Rewaka, Denis *diplomat*
Daniel, Charles Timothy *transportation engineer, consultant*
Daniel, David Ronald *management consultant*
Daniel, Richard Nicholas *fabricated metals manufacturing company executive*
Danishefsky, Samuel J. *chemistry educator*
Danisi, John J. *philosopher, educator*
Dankner, Jay Warren *lawyer*
†Danley, Kerwin *umpire*
†Dannhauser, Stephen J. *lawyer*
Danto, Arthur Coleman *author, philosopher, art critic*
Danzig, Frederick Paul *newspaper editor*
Danziger, Jeff *political cartoonist, writer*
Danziger, Paula *author*
Daphnis, Nassos *artist*
Darcy, Keith Thomas *finance company executive, educator*
Darer, John David *insurance company executive*
Darling, Gary Lyle *carpet and furniture cleaning company executive*
†Darling, Gary R. *umpire*
D'Arms, John Haughton *association executive, classics educator*
Darnell, James Edwin, Jr. *molecular biologist, educator*
Darnton, John Townsend *journalist*
Darrell, Norris, Jr. *lawyer*
Darrow, Jill E(llen) *lawyer*
Darsin, Jose A. *transportation engineer*
Darst, David Martin *investment banking company executive, writer, educator*
Darvarova, Elmira *violinist, concertmaster*
Das, Kalyan *lawyer*
Dattner, Richard *architect, educator*
Daugherty, Marcus Vincent *mental health administrator*
Dauman, Philippe P. *telecommunications company executive*
Dauten, Dale Alan *newspaper columnist*
†Davenport, Ronald *lawyer*
David, Hal *lyricist*
David, Miles *association and marketing executive*
David, Reuben *lawyer*

David, Theoharis Lambros architect, educator
Davidson, Donald William advertising executive
Davidson, George Allan lawyer
Davidson, Mark Edward lawyer
Davidson, Nancy Brachman artist, educator
†Davidson, Robert Allan umpire
Davidson, Robert Bruce lawyer
Davidson, Sheila Kearney lawyer
David-Weill, Michel Alexandre investment banker
Davies, Dennis Russell conductor, music director, pianist
Davis, Clive Jay record company executive
Davis, Deborah Lynn lawyer
Davis, Douglas Matthew artist, educator, author
Davis, Evan Anderson lawyer
Davis, Florence Ann lawyer
Davis, George Linn banker
†Davis, Gerald umpire
Davis, Jerry Albert architect
Davis, Karen fund executive
Davis, Kathryn Wasserman foundation executive, writer, lecturer
Davis, Kenneth Leon psychiatrist, pharmacologist, medical educator
Davis, Leonard violist
Davis, Lisa Corinne artist
Davis, Lorraine Jensen writer, editor
Davis, Luane Ruth theatrical director, performer
Davis, Martin S. investment company executive
Davis, Michael S. lawyer
Davis, Peter Graffam music critic
Davis, Rece anchor, reporter
Davis, Richard Joel lawyer, former government official
Davis, Stephen Arnold artist, educator
Davis, Stephen Edward Folwell banker
Davis, Wendell, Jr. lawyer
Davison, Bruce actor
Davison, Daniel P. retired banking executive
Davoe, David communications executive
Dawson, Philip history educator
†Dawson, Stephanie Elaine city manager
Dawson, Thomas Cleland, II financial executive
Day, James television executive
Day, John W. international corporation executive
Dayson, Diane Harris superintendent, park ranger
Deak, Istvan historian, educator
Dean, Diane D. youth service agency executive, fund development consultant
De Angelis, Judy anchorwoman
de Bethmann, Heidi Elizabeth architect
Debo, Vincent Joseph lawyer, manufacturing company executive
DeBow, Jay Howard Camden public relations executive
DeBow, Thomas Joseph, Jr. advertising executive
Debs, Richard A. investment banker
DeBusschere, David Albert brokerage executive, retired professional basketball player and team executive
Decker, Dennis Dale industrial designer
DeCosta, Steven C. municipal official
de Duve, Christian René chemist, educator
Deem, George artist
Defendi, Vittorio medical research administrator, pathologist
De Ferrari, Gabriella curator, writer
De Forest, Roy Dean artist, sculptor
Degener, Carol Marie-Laure lawyer
De Gregorio, Anthony advertising executive
de Hartog, Jan writer
Deitz, Paula magazine editor
Dejammet, Alain diplomat
Dekker, Marcel publishing company executive
Delaney, Robert Vincent former gas company executive, economic development consultant
Delano, Lester Almy, Jr. advertising executive
de Lappe, Gemze dancer, educator, choreographer
de la Renta, Oscar fashion designer
DeLay, Dorothy (Mrs. Edward Newhouse) violinist, educator
Delbourgo, Joëlle Lily publishing executive
Delgado, George Ernest financial consultant
Della-Giustina, Jo-Ann Subotin lawyer
Demarest, Daniel Anthony retired lawyer
de Margitay, Gedeon acquisitions and management consultant
Demaria, Walter sculptor
deMause, Lloyd psychohistorian
de Menil, Lois Pattison historian, philanthropist
de Montebello, Philippe Lannes museum administrator
†DeMuth, Dana Andrew umpire
De Natale, Andrew Peter lawyer
Denby, David film critic
Dendy, Mark choreographer
†Denham, Alice writer
†Denison, Dwight Val educator
Denker, Henry playwright, author, director
†Denkinger, Donald Anton umpire
Denmark, Stanley Jay orthodontist
Dennis, Donna Frances sculptor, art educator
Dennis, Everette Eugene, Jr. foundation executive, journalism educator, writer
Denoon, David Baugh Holden economist, educator, consultant
DeNunzio, Ralph Dwight investment banker
DeOrchis, Vincent Moore lawyer
Derfner, Carol Ann management consultant, fundraising counsel
Derman, Cyrus mathematical statistician
Derow, Peter Alfred publishing company executive
Derwin, Jordan lawyer, consultant, actor
de Saint Phalle, Pierre Claude lawyer
De Sear, Edward Marshall lawyer
Desiato, Michael periodical editor-in-chief
DeSimone, Glenn J. advertising executive
Desnick, Robert John human geneticist
Despommier, Dickson Donald microbiology educator, parasitologist, researcher
Dessi, Adrian Frank marketing, communications executive
Detjen, David Wheeler lawyer
Deupree, Marvin Mattox accountant, business consultant
Deuschle, Kurt Walter physician, educator
Deutsch, Donny advertising executive
Deutsch, Martin Bernard Joseph editor, publisher
De Vido, Alfredo Eduardo architect
DeVita, M. Christine foundation administrator
De Vivo, Darryl Claude pediatric neurologist
†de Vries, Madeline public relations executive
DeWitt, Eula accountant
Dexheimer, Larry William advertising agency executive
Dhondt, Steven Thomas marketing consultant
Dhrymes, Phoebus James economist, educator
Diamond, Bernard Robin lawyer
Diamond, David Howard lawyer
Diamond, Harris corporate communications executive, lawyer
Diamond, Irene foundation administrator
Diamonstein-Spielvogel, Barbaralee writer, television interviewer/ producer
†Diawara, Manthia film and literature educator, writer, filmmaker
Diaz, Justino bass-baritone
Diaz, William Adams political scientist
Di Carlantonio, Martin publishing executive
DiCarlo, Dominick L. federal judge
Dichter, Barry Joel lawyer
Dichter, Misha concert pianist
Dick, Harold Michael orthopedic surgeon
†Dickinson, Nathan Kilmer writer
†Di Corcia, Philip-Lorca artist, photographer
di Cori, Pat Miller painter, sculptor
Didion, Joan author
Diehl, Stephen Anthony human resources consultant
Dienstag, Eleanor Foa corporate communications consultant
Dierdorf, Daniel Lee (Dan Dierdorf) football analyst, sports commentator, former professional football player
Dieterich, Douglas Thomas gastroenterologist, researcher
Diggins, John Patrick history educator
Diggins, Peter Sheehan arts administrator
†DiGiacinto, George Vincent neurosurgeon
DiGuido, Al publishing executive
Dikeman, May writer
Dill, Lesley sculptor
Dillard, Annie author
Diller, Barry entertainment company executive
Dillon, Clarence Douglas retired investment company executive
†Dillon, Laura White communications executive
†Dillon, Matt actor
DiMaggio, Frank Louis civil engineering educator
Di Meo, Dominick artist, sculptor, painter
Dimino, Sylvia Theresa elementary and secondary educator
Dimon, James financial services executive
Dimond, Thomas investment advisory company executive
Dinerman, Miriam social work educator
Ding, Chen investment banker
Dingle, Mark Edward management consultant
Dintenfass, Terry art dealer
†Dion, Celine musician
Dionne, Joseph Lewis publishing company executive
Di Paola, Robert Arnold mathematics and computer science educator
Dirks, Nicholas B. cultural research organization administrator/history educator
Di Salvo, Nicholas Armand dental educator, orthodontist
Discorfano, Sharon Marie English literature educator
Diskant, Gregory L. lawyer
Disney, Anthea publishing executive
Dissette, Alyce Marie television newsmedia and theatrical producer, non-profit foundation executive
Distenfeld, Ariel hematologist, educator
Dixon, Shirley Lee emergency physician
Djeddah, Richard Nissim investment banker
D'Lower, Del manufacturing executive
Dlugoszewski, Lucia artistic director
Dobbs, John Barnes artist, educator
Dobbs, Lou television executive, managing editor
Dobelis, Inge Nachman editor
Dobell, Byron Maxwell magazine consultant
Dobrinsky, Herbert Colman university administrator
Dobrof, Rose Wiesman professor
Dobrzynski, Judith Helen journalist, commentator
Doctorow, Edgar Lawrence novelist, English educator
Dodd, Lois artist, art professor
Dodge, Geoffrey A. magazine publisher
Dodson, Daryl Theodore ballet administrator, arts consultant
Doherty, Karen Ann corporate executive
†Doherty, Patrick William city official
Doherty, Thomas publisher
Dohrenwend, Bruce Philip psychiatric epidemiologist, social psychologist, educator
Dolan, Raymond Bernard insurance executive
Dole, Vincent Paul medical research executive, educator
Dolger, Jonathan editor, literary agent
Dolgin, Martin cardiologist
Dolice, Joseph Leo multimedia art publisher, exhibition director
†Dolinger, Michael H. federal judge
Doman, Nicholas R. lawyer
†Dombrowski, Bob artist, publisher
†Domingo, Placido tenor
Donald, Norman Henderson, III lawyer
Donaldson, James Neill banker
Donaldson, Stephen Reeder author
Donaldson, William Henry financial executive
Donati, Enrico artist
†Donegan, Cheryl artist
Donelian, Armen pianist, composer, author
Donnellan, Andrew B., Jr. lawyer
Donovan, Maureen Driscoll lawyer
Dooley, Thomas E. telecommunications company executive
Dooner, John Joseph, Jr. advertising executive
Doorish, John Francis physicist, mathematician, educator
Dopf, Glenn William lawyer
Dorado, Marianne Gaertner lawyer
Dore, Anita Wilkes English language educator
Dorfman, Howard David pathologist, educator
†Dorkey, Charles Edward, III lawyer
Dorn, Louis Otto minister, editor
Dorn, Sue Bricker consultant, retired hospital administrator
Dornemann, Michael book publishing executive
Dorsen, Norman lawyer, educator
Doty, Shayne Taylor organist
Douglas, Paul Wolff retired mining executive
Douglass, Robert Royal banker, lawyer
Dowling, Edward Thomas economics educator
Downey, John Alexander physician, educator
Downs, David Erskine television executive
Downs, Hugh Malcolm radio and television broadcaster
Doyle, Eugenie Fleri pediatric cardiologist, educator
Doyle, Joseph Anthony retired lawyer
Doyle, L. F. Boker retired trust company executive
Doyle, Paul Francis lawyer
Doyle, William Stowell venture capitalist
Drabkin, Catherine Lenore painter, educator
Drake, Laura director, performer
Drake, Owen Burtch Winters association administrator
Draper, James David art museum curator
Drasner, Fred newspaper publishing executive
Drebsky, Dennis Jay lawyer
†Dreckman, Bruce umpire
Dreifus, Claudia journalist
Dreikausen, Margret artist
Dreizen, Alison M. lawyer
Drescher, Jack psychoanalyst, psychiatrist
†Dressel, Henry Francis lawyer
Dressner, Howard Roy foundation executive, lawyer
Drexler, Joanne Lee art appraiser
Drexler, Michael David advertising agency executive
Driver, Martha Westcott English language educator, writer, researcher
Driver, Tom Faw theologian, writer, justice/peace advocate
Driver, William Raymond, Jr. banker
Drobis, David R. public relations company executive
Dropkin, Mary Jo nursing researcher, educator
†Druckenmiller, Robert Thompson public relations executive
Drucker, Jacquelin F. lawyer, arbitrator, mediator, educator, author
Drucker, Mort commercial artist
†Drucker, Stephen magazine editor-in-chief
Duane, Thomas K. councilman
Duberman, Martin historian
Dubin, James Michael lawyer
Duchin, Peter Oelrichs musician
Duff, John Ewing sculptor
Duffy, James Henry writer, former lawyer
Duffy, John Fitzgerald law educator
Duffy, Kevin Thomas federal judge
Dufour, Val (Albert Valery Dufour) actor
Dugan, Edward Francis investment banker
Dugan, Michael Joseph former air force officer, health agency executive
Duggan, Dennis Michael newspaper editor
†Duke, Anthony Drexel sociologist, educator, philanthropist
Duke, Robert Dominick mining executive, lawyer
Dulaine, Pierre ballroom dancer
DuLaux, Russell Frederick lawyer
Du Mont, Nicolas psychiatrist, educator
Duncan, Deborah L. bank executive
†Duncan, Pearl Rose writer, poet
Dunham, Corydon Busnell lawyer, broadcasting executive
Dunham, Wolcott Balestier, Jr. lawyer
Dunkelman, Loretta artist
Dunn, James Joseph magazine publisher
Dunn, Mignon mezzo-soprano
Dunn, M(orris) Douglas lawyer
Dunne, Diane C. marketing executive
Dunne, Gerard Francis lawyer
Dunne, John Gregory author
Dunst, Laurence David advertising executive
Duquesnay, Ann actress, singer
Durkin, Dorothy Angela university official
Durst, Carol Goldsmith educator
Dusenberry, Philip Bernard advertising executive
†Dutoit, Charles conductor
Dwek, Cyril S. banker
Dworetzky, Murray physician, educator
Dwyer, Jim reporter, columnist
Dylan, Bob (Robert Allen Zimmerman) singer, composer
†Dyson, Esther publisher, editor
Dyyon, Frazier Mario (LeRoy Frazier) artist
Eaker, Sherry Ellen entertainment newspaper editor
Ealy, Carleton Cato investment banker
Earle, Victor Montagne, III lawyer
Earls, Kevin Gerard insurance company executive
†Early, William Tracy journalist
Easum, Donald Boyd consultant, educator, former institute executive, diplomat
Eaton, Richard Gillette surgeon, educator
Ebersol, Dick television broadcasting executive
Ebin, Leonard Neil radiologist, educator, consultant
Eckel, Thomas Warne secondary education educator, musician
Eckman, Fern Marja journalist
Eckstut, Michael Kauder management consultant
Edelbaum, Philip R. lawyer
Edelman, Isidore Samuel biochemist and medical educator
Edelman, Judith H. architect
Edelman, Paul Sterling lawyer
Edelman, Richard Winston public relations executive
Edelson, Gilbert Seymour lawyer
Edelson, Mary Beth artist, educator
Edelstein, David Northon federal judge
Edelstein, Joan Erback physical therapy educator
Edelstein, Robert Glenn magazine editor
Edgar, Harold Simmons Hull legal educator
Edighoffer-Murray, Anna Barbel procurement officer, pharmacist, political scientist
Edinger, Lewis Joachim political science educator
Edlow, Kenneth Lewis securities brokerage official
Edmands, Susan Banks consulting company executive
Edmiston, Mark Morton publishing company executive
Edson, Andrew Stephen public relations executive
Edwards, Adrian L. medical educator
†Edwards, Christine Annette lawyer, securities firm executive
Edwards, Franklin R. economist, educator, consultant
Edwards, Harold Mortimer mathematics educator
Edwards, James D. accounting company executive
Edwards, Niloo Mario surgeon
Effel, Laura lawyer
Efrat, Isaac financial analyst, mathematician
Eger, Joseph conductor, music director
Egielski, Richard illustrator
Ehlers, Kathryn Hawes (Mrs. James D. Gabler) physician
Ehrenkranz, Joel S. lawyer
Eidsvold, Gary Mason physician, public health officer, medical educator
Eig, Norman investment company executive
Einach, Charles Donald advertising and publishing executive
Einhorn, David Allen lawyer
Einiger, Carol Blum investment executive
Eins, Stefan painter, conceptual artist, arts curator, sculptor
Eisenberg, Alan professional society administrator
Eisenberg, Sonja Miriam artist
Eisenman, Peter David architect, educator
Eisenstadt, G. Michael diplomat, author, lecturer, research scholar
Eisenthal, Kenneth B. physical chemistry educator
Eisert, Edward Gaver lawyer
Eisler, Colin Tobias art historian, curator
Eisner, Richard Alan accountant
Eitel, Antonius diplomat
Ekman, Richard foundation executive, educator
Elam, Leslie Albert museum administrator
Elaraby, Nabil A. Egyptian diplomat
Elder, Eldon stage designer, theatre consultant
Eldridge, Ronnie councilwoman
Elias, Rosalind mezzo-soprano
Elicker, Gordon Leonard lawyer
Elinson, Jack sociology educator
Eliot, Lucy artist
Elkes, Terrence Allen communications executive
Elkin, Jeffrey H. lawyer
Ellegard, Roy Whitney appraiser
Ellenbogen, Rudolph Solomon library curator
Ellerbee, Linda broadcast journalist
Ellig, Bruce Robert personnel executive
Elliman, Donald magazine company executive
Elliman, Donald M., Jr. magazine publisher and executive
Elliott, Dolores disabilities advocate, film producer
Elliott, Inger McCabe designer, textile company executive, consultant
Elliott, John, Jr. advertising agency executive
Elliott, Osborn journalist, educator, urban activist, former dean
Ellis, Albert clinical psychologist, educator, author
Ellis, Carolyn Terry lawyer
Ellis, Charles Richard publishing executive
Ellis, Judy broadcast executive
†Ellis, Ronald L. federal judge
Ellis, Scott theatrical director
†Ellroy, James writer
†Elmarsafy, Ziad Magdy educator
Elsen, Jon editor, columnist
Elsen, Sheldon Howard lawyer
Elster, Samuel Kase college dean, medical educator, physician
Elwin, Kevin Thomas broadcast engineering manager
Emanuel, Myron corporate communications specialist, consultant
†Embree, Catherine M. university official
Emek, Sharon Helene risk management consultant
Emerson, Andi (Mrs. Andi Emerson Weeks) sales and advertising executive
Emil, Arthur D. lawyer
Emmerich, Andre art gallery executive, author
Emmerman, Michael N financial analyst
Emrich, Edmund Michael lawyer
Enders, Elizabeth McGuire artist
Engelhardt, Sara Lawrence organization executive
Englander, Roger Leslie television producer, director
Engler, Robert political science educator, author
English, Joseph Thomas physician, medical administrator
Engstrom, Erik publishing company executive
Entremont, Philippe conductor, pianist
Epling, Richard Louis lawyer
Epstein, Barbara editor
Epstein, Cynthia Fuchs sociology educator, writer
Epstein, Jason publishing company executive
Epstein, Jeremy G. lawyer
Epstein, Melvin lawyer
Epstein, Seth Paul immunologist, infectious disease researcher
Erbsen, Claude Ernest journalist
Ercklentz, Alexander Tonio investment executive
Ercklentz, Enno Wilhelm, Jr. lawyer
Erdrich, (Karen) Louise fiction writer, poet
Ergas, Enrique orthopedic surgeon
Ericson, Robert Walter lawyer
Eristoff, Andrew S. councilman
Erlanger, Bernard Ferdinand biochemist, educator
†Eschenbach, Christoph conductor, pianist
Escobar, Marisol sculptor
Esiason, Boomer (Norman Julius Esiason) professional football player
Esman, Rosa Mencher art gallery executive
Esmerian, Ralph O. museum administrator
Espinoza, Galina magazine writer
†Espinoza, Noemi Ruth diplomat, researcher
Esposito, Richard Joseph journalist, executive
Espy, Willard Richardson author
†Essandoh, Hilda Brathwaite kindergarten educator
Esterow, Milton magazine editor, publisher
Estes, Richard artist
Estes, Richard Martin lawyer
Eswein, Bruce James, II human resources executive
Ethan, Carol Baehr psychotherapist
Eustice, James Samuel legal educator, lawyer
Evans, Alfred Lee, Jr. advertising executive
Evans, Douglas Hayward lawyer
†Evans, Eli Nachamson foundation adminstrator
Evans, James Bremond (Jim Evans) major league baseball umpire
Evans, James Hurlburt retired transportation and natural resources executive
Evans, John Thomas lawyer
Evans, Linda Kay publishing company executive
Evans, Martin Frederic lawyer
Evans, Mary Johnston corporate director
Evans, Van Michael advertising agency executive, consultant
Evarts, William Maxwell, Jr. lawyer
Eveillard, Jean-Marie financial company executive
Everly, Jack conductor
Evnin, Anthony Basil venture capital investor
Ewers, Patricia O'Donnell university administrator
Ewing, Anthony P. business consultant, lawyer
Ewing, Maria Louise soprano
Ewing, Patrick Aloysius professional basketball player
Ezrati, Milton Joseph investment manager, economist
Faber, Neil advertising executive
Faber, Peter Lewis lawyer
Fabian, Jeanne entrepreneur, executive recruiter
Fabian, Larry Louis university administrator
Fahey, James Edward financial executive
Fahmy, Ibrahim Mounir hotel executive
Fahn, Stanley neurologist, educator
Fairbairn, Ursula Farrell human resources executive
Fairbanks, Douglas Elton, Jr. actor, producer, writer, corporation director
Fairchild, John Burr publisher
Fales, Haliburton, II lawyer
Falk, Edgar Alan public relations consulting executive, author
Falk, Joan Frances public relations executive
Fallaci, Oriana writer, journalist
Falletta, Jo Ann musician
†Fallows, James Mackenzie magazine editor
Fan, Linda C. investment company executive
Fancher, Edwin Crawford psychologist, educator
Farah, Roger retail company executive
Faraone, Ted public relations executive, consultant
Faraone, Teri public relations executive

Genova, Joseph Steven *lawyer*
Geoghegan, Patricia *lawyer*
Georgakas, Dan *writer, educator*
George, Beauford James, Jr. *lawyer, educator*
Georges, Paul Gordon *artist*
Georgescu, Peter Andrew *advertising executive*
Georgis, William Theodore *architect*
†Geraci, Damiano *architect*
Gerard, Whitney Ian *lawyer*
Gerard-Sharp, Monica Fleur *communications executive*
Gerber, Gwendolyn Loretta *psychologist, educator*
Gerber, Robert Evan *lawyer*
Gerberg, Judith Levine *human resource company executive*
Gerdts, William Henry *art history educator*
Gerlach, Douglas Eldon *financial writer internet developer*
Germano, William Paul *publisher*
Gero, Anthony George *securities and commodities trader*
Gershengorn, Marvin Carl *physician, scientist, educator*
Gershon, Bernard *broadcast executive*
Gerson, Irwin Conrad *advertising executive*
Gerson, Kathleen *sociology educator*
Gerson, Robert Elisha *periodical editor-in-chief*
Gersoni-Edelman, Diane Claire *author, editor*
Gersony, Welton Mark *physician, pediatric cardiologist, educator*
Gerster, J. Alec *communications executive*
Gertler, Menard M. *physician, educator*
Gerzso, Gunther *painter, graphic artist*
Getnick, Neil Victor *lawyer*
Gewirtz-Friedman, Gerry *editor*
Gharib, Susie *television newscaster*
Ghebrehiwet, Berhane *immunologist, educator*
†Giacoponello, Joseph A. *hotel executive*
Giallo, Vito *antiques dealer*
Giancotti, Filippo Giusto *cell and molecular biologist*
Giannetti, Thomas Leonard *lawyer*
†Gibaldi, Joseph *publishing executive*
Gibb, Barry *vocalist, songwriter*
Gibbs, Jamie *landscape architect, interior designer*
Giblin, James Cross *author, editor*
†Gibson, Arlene Joy *headmaster*
Gibson, Charles DeWolf *broadcast journalist*
Gibson, Chip *publishing executive*
Gibson, Ralph H(olmes) *photographer*
Gibson, William Shepard *management consultant*
Giddins, Gary Mitchell *music critic, columnist*
Gifford, Steven *architect*
Gifford, William C. *lawyer*
Gilbert, Hamlin Miller, Jr. *publishing executive*
Gilbert, Rose Bennett *communications company executive*
Gilbert, Thomas Strong *Internet entrepreneur, venture capitalist*
†Gilbride, Joseph J. *advertising executive*
Giles, Robert Hartmann *journalist, educator*
Gilinsky, Stanley Ellis *department store executive*
Gill, Ardian C. *actuary, photographer*
Gill, E. Ann *lawyer*
Gillers, Stephen *law educator*
Gillespie, George Joseph, III *lawyer*
Gillespie, John Thomas *university administrator*
Gilliam, Paula Hutter *transportation company executive*
Gilliatt, Neal *advertising executive, consultant*
Gillies, Trent Donald *television producer*
Gilligan, Mary Ann *law librarian*
†Gillman, Johanna *artist*
†Gillman, Sarah Ann *management consultant*
Gilman, Richard H. *newspaper publishing executive*
Gilmore, Jennifer A.W. *computer specialist*
Giniger, Kenneth Seeman *publisher*
Ginsberg, David Lawrence *architect*
Ginsberg, Ernest *lawyer, banker*
Ginsberg, Frank Charles *advertising executive*
Ginsberg, Hersh Meier *rabbi, religious organization executive*
Ginsberg, Robert Jason *thoracic surgeon*
Ginsburg, Sigmund G. *museum administrator*
Ginter, Valerian Alexius *urban historian, educator*
Ginzberg, Eli *economist, emeritus educator, government consultant, author*
Ginzel, Andrew H. *artist*
Gioiella, Russell Michael *lawyer*
Giorlando, Jeanne A. *labor and delivery nurse*
Giorno, John *poet*
Giraldi, Robert Nicholas *film director*
Girard, Andrea Eaton *communication executive, consultant*
Girden, Eugene Lawrence *lawyer*
Giroux, Robert *editor, book publisher, author*
Gisondi, John Theodore *theater and television design*
Gissler, Sigvard Gunnar, Jr. *journalism educator, former newspaper editor*
Gitelson, Susan Aurelia *business executive, civic leader*
Gitter, Max *lawyer*
Gitterman, Alex *social work educator*
Gittis, Howard *holding company executive*
Gittler, Wendy *artist, art historian, writer*
Giuliani, Rudolph W. *mayor, former lawyer*
Gladstone, William Louis *accountant*
Glanstein, Joel Charles *lawyer*
Glasberg, Scot Bradley *plastic surgeon*
Glaser, Milton *graphic designer and illustrator*
Glass, David Carter *psychology educator*
†Glass, Philip *composer, musician*
Glassgold, Alfred Emanuel *physicist, educator*
Glassman, Alexander Howard *psychiatrist, researcher*
Glasson, Lloyd *sculptor, educator*
Glatt, Mitchell Steven *consumer products company executive*
Glaubinger, Lawrence David *manufacturing company executive, consultant*
Glekel, Jeffrey Ives *lawyer*
Glickstein, Steven *lawyer*
Glimcher, Arnold B. *art gallery executive*
†Glocer, Thomas Henry *lawyer*
Glover, Norman James *engineering executive*
Glover, Savion *actor, dancer*
Gluck, Andrew Lee *vocational economic analyst, counselor, philosopher*
Gluck, Carol *history educator*
Glusband, Steven Joseph *lawyer*
Glynn, Robert *lawyer, foundation chairman*
Gochberg, Thomas *real estate investor, financial executive*
Goddess, Lynn Barbara *commercial real estate broker*
Godman, Gabriel Charles *pathology educator*
Godoff, Ann *book editor*
Godwin, Ralph Lee, Jr. *real estate executive*
Goelet, Robert G. *investment executive*
Goertz, Augustus Frederick, III *artist*
Goetz, Maurice Harold *lawyer*
Goff, Robert Edward *health plan executive*
Gold, Albert *artist*
Gold, Jeffrey Mark *investment banker, financial adviser*
Gold, Lois Meyer *artist*
Gold, Mari S. *public relations executive*
Gold, Martin Elliot *lawyer, educator*
Gold, Sharon Cecile *artist, educator*
Gold, Simeon *lawyer*
Gold, William Elliott *health care management consultant*
Goldberg, David Alan *investment banker, lawyer*
Goldberg, Edward L. *financial services executive*
†Goldberg, Ira Jay *internist, educator*
Goldberg, Jane G. *psychoanalyst*
Goldberg, Jay *lawyer*
Goldberg, Michael *artist*
Goldberg, Richard W. *federal judge*
Goldberg, Sidney *editor*
Goldberg, Victor Paul *law educator*
Goldberger, Paul Jesse *architecture critic, writer, educator, editor*
Goldblatt, Eileen Witzman *foundation executive*
Golde, David William *physician, educator*
Golden, Arthur F. *lawyer*
Golden, Soma *newspaper editor*
Golden, William Theodore *trustee, corporate director*
Goldenberg, Charles Lawrence *real estate company executive*
Goldenberg, Marvin Manus *pharmacologist, pharmaceutical developer*
Goldfarb, Lisa Michele *psychiatrist*
Goldfrank, Lewis Robert *physician*
Goldin, Leon *artist, educator*
Goldman, James *playwright, screenwriter, novelist*
Goldman, Lawrence Saul *lawyer*
Goldman, Leo *psychologist, educator*
Goldman, Marvin Gerald *lawyer*
Goldrich, Stanley Gilbert *optometrist*
Goldschmidt, Charles *advertising agency executive*
Goldschmidt, Robert Alphonse *financial executive*
†Goldsmith, Barbara *author, social historian, journalist*
Goldsmith, Caroline L. *arts executive*
Goldsmith, Cathy Ellen *special education educator*
Goldsmith, Clifford Henry *former tobacco company executive*
Goldsmith, John H. *investment company executive*
Goldsmith, Lee Selig *lawyer, physician*
Goldsmith, Merwin *actor, theater director*
Goldsmith, Michael Allen *oncologist, educator*
Goldsmith, Robert Lewis *youth association magazine executive*
Goldsmith, Stanley Joseph *nuclear medicine physician, educator*
Goldstein, Alvin *lawyer*
Goldstein, Charles Arthur *lawyer*
Goldstein, Gary Sanford *executive recruiter*
Goldstein, Howard Sheldon *lawyer*
Goldstein, Howard Warren *lawyer*
Goldstein, Kenneth B. *lawyer*
Goldstein, Lisa Joy *writer*
Goldstein, Marc *microsurgeon, urology educator, administrator*
Goldstein, Marcia Landweber *lawyer*
Goldstein, Niles Elliot *rabbi, author*
Goldstein, Norm *editor, writer*
Goldstein, Richard A. *consumer products company executive*
†Goldstein, Walter *economics educator*
Goldstone, Steven F. *consumer products company executive*
Gollin, Albert Edwin *media research executive, sociologist*
Gollob, Herman Cohen *retired publishing company, editor*
Golomb, Frederick Martin *surgeon, educator*
Golson, George Barry *editor*
Golub, Gerald Leonard *accounting company executive*
Golub, Harvey *financial services company executive*
Gomory, Ralph Edward *mathematician, manufacturing company executive, foundation executive*
†Gonzalez, Arthur J. *federal judge*
Gonzalez, Eugene Robert *investment banker*
Gooch, Anthony Cushing *lawyer*
†Gooch, Brad *writer*
Goodale, James Campbell *lawyer, media executive, television producer/host*
Goodale, Toni Krissel *development consultant*
Goodfriend, Herbert Jay *lawyer*
†Goodman, Carol M. *lawyer*
Goodman, Gary A. *lawyer*
Goodman, George Jerome Waldo (Adam Smith) *author, television journalist, editor*
Goodman, Roger Mark *television director*
Goodman, Roy Matz *state senator, business executive*
Goodridge, Allan D. *lawyer*
Goodstein, Les *newspaper publishing executive*
Goodstone, Edward Harold *retired insurance company executive*
Goodwill, George Walton *hospital administrator*
Goodwin, Todd *banker*
Goott, Alan F(ranklin) *lawyer*
Gorchov, Ron *artist*
Gordevitch, Igor *publishing company executive*
Gordon, Alan Lee *psychiatrist*
Gordon, Alvin Joseph *cardiologist*
Gordon, Bridgette *professional basketball player*
Gordon, David *playwright, director, choreographer*
†Gordon, Douglas *artist*
Gordon, Frederick *marine engineer*
†Gordon, Leslie Peyton *executive recruiting consultant*
Gordon, Mark *actor, theater director, theater educator*
Gordon, Mary Catherine *author*
Gordon, Michael Mackin *lawyer*
Gorewitz, Rubin Leon *accountant, financial consultant*
†Gorman, Brian *umpire*
Gorman, Lawrence James *banker*
Gorup, Gregory James *marketing executive*
Goss, Mary E. Weber *sociology educator*
Gossage, Wayne *library director, management consultant, entrepreneur, executive recruiter*
Gossett, Robert Francis, Jr. *merchant banker*
Gotbaum, Betsy *historical society director*
†Gotian, Ruth *educational program administrator*
Gotschlich, Emil Claus *physician, educator*
Gottesman, David Sanford *investment executive*
Gotthoffer, Lance *lawyer*
Gottlieb, Jerrold Howard *advertising executive*
Gottlieb, Morton Edgar *theatrical and film producer*
Gottlieb, Paul *publishing company executive*
Gottlieb, Paul Mitchel *lawyer*
Gottlieb, Robert Adams *publisher*
Gotto, Antonio Marion, Jr. *internist, educator*
Gotts, Ilene Knable *lawyer*
Gottschall, Edward Maurice *graphic arts company executive*
Gould, Eleanor Lois (Eleanor Gould Packard) *editor, grammarian*
Gould, Harry Edward, Jr. *industrialist*
Gould, Jay Martin *economist, consultant*
Goulden, Joseph Chesley *author*
Goulianos, Konstantin *physics educator*
Gourevitch, Jacqueline *artist*
Gourgey, Karen Luxton *special education educator*
Gow, Christopher Radford Guthrie *sea shell and sculpture specialist*
Gowens, Walter, II *financial and business services executive*
Graber, Edward Alex *obstetrician, gynecologist, educator*
Grabois, Neil Robert *association executive, former college president*
Grace, Jason Roy *advertising agency executive*
Grad, Frank Paul *law educator, lawyer*
Grader, Patricia Alison Lande *editor*
Graf, Peter Gustav *accountant, lawyer*
Graff, George Leonard *lawyer*
Grafstein, Bernice *physiology and neuroscience educator, researcher*
Grafton, Sue *novelist*
Grafton, W. Robert *professional services company executive*
Graham, Jesse Japhet, II *lawyer*
Graham, Jul Eliot *lawyer, educator*
Graham, Robert *sculptor*
Gralla, Lawrence *publishing company executive*
Gramatte, Joan Helen *graphic designer, art director, photographer*
Grandizio, Lenore *social worker*
Granik, Russell T. *sports association executive*
Grann, Phyllis *publisher, editor*
Granoff, Gary Charles *lawyer, investment company executive*
Grant, Cynthia D. *writer*
Grant, James Deneale *health care company executive*
Grant, Stephen Allen *lawyer*
Grant, Susan Irene *lawyer*
Grant, William Packer, Jr. *banker*
Grashof, August Edward *lawyer*
Grasso, Richard A. *stock exchange executive*
Grau, Marcy Beinish *real estate broker, former investment banker*
Graves, Adam *professional hockey player*
Graves, Earl Gilbert *publisher*
Graves, Fred Hill *librarian*
Graves, Morris Cole *artist*
Graves, Thomas Vincent *sculptor*
Gray, Arthur, Jr. *investment counselor*
Gray, Bradford Hitch *health policy researcher*
Gray, Deborah Dolia *business writing consultant*
Gray, George *mural painter*
Gray, Glenn Oliver *lawyer*
Greco, Albert Nicholas *communications educator*
†Greco, Jose *choreographer*
Greeley, Sean McGovern *trust company executive*
Green, Adam Mitchell *investment banker*
Green, Alvin *lawyer, consultant*
Green, Dan *publishing company executive*
Green, David Edward *librarian, priest, translator*
Green, David O. *accounting educator, educational administrator*
Green, Eric Howard *lawyer*
Green, George Joseph *publishing executive*
Green, Jack Peter *pharmacology educator, medical scientist*
Green, Miriam Blau *psychologist*
Green, Robert S. *lawyer*
Greenawalt, Robert Kent *lawyer, law educator*
Greenawalt, William Sloan *lawyer*
Greenbaum, Maurice Coleman *lawyer*
Greenberg, Alan Courtney (Ace Greenberg) *stockbroker*
Greenberg, Carolyn Phyllis *anesthesiologist, educator*
Greenberg, Daniel Herbert *lawyer*
Greenberg, Daniel Lawrence *lawyer*
Greenberg, Gary Howard *lawyer*
Greenberg, Ira George *lawyer*
Greenberg, Irving *rabbi*
Greenberg, Jack *lawyer, law educator*
Greenberg, Maurice Raymond *insurance company executive*
Greenberg, Philip Alan *lawyer*
Greenberger, Howard Leroy *lawyer, educator*
Greene, Adele S. *management consultant*
Greene, Bernard Harold *lawyer*
Greene, Carl William *financial consultant, former utility company executive*
Greene, Ira S. *lawyer*
Greene, Kay C. *psychologist, author*
Greene, Richard H. *journalist*
Greenfield, Gordon Kraus *software company executive*
Greenfield, (Henry) Jeff *news analyst*
Greenfield, Scott H. *lawyer*
Greenfield, Seymour Stephen *mechanical engineer*
Greengard, Paul *neuroscientist*
Greenland, Leo *advertising executive*
Greenspon, Robert Alan *lawyer*
Greenstein, Abraham Jacob *mortgage company executive, accountant*
Greenwald, Harold *lawyer*
Greer, Allen Curtis, II *lawyer*
Grefé, Richard *graphic design executive*
†Gregg, Eric Eugene *umpire*
Gregori, Maria Isabel *critical care nurse*
Gregorian, Vartan *academic administrator*
Greig, Robert Thomson *lawyer*
Greilsheimer, James Gans *lawyer*
Grein, Richard Frank *bishop, pastoral theology educator*
Grenquist, Peter Carl *consultant*
Gretzky, Wayne Douglas *retired professional hockey player*
Grew, Robert Ralph *lawyer*
Griefen, John Adams *artist, educator*
Grier, David Alan *actor*
Griesa, Thomas Poole *federal judge*
Griffith, Alan Richard *banker*
Griffiths, Sylvia Preston *physician*
Grigonis, Richard William *technical editor*
Grigsby, Henry Jefferson, Jr. *editor*
Grijns, Laine *investment company executive*
Grimaldi, Nicholas Lawrence *social services administrator*
Grisham, John *writer*
Griswold, Frank Tracy, III *bishop*
Groban, Robert Sidney, Jr. *lawyer*
Groberg, James Jay *information sciences company executive*
Grodnick, Scott Randall *internet executive, music company executive*
Groh, Jennifer Calfa *law librarian*
Gromada, Thaddeus V. *historian, administrator*
Grooms, Red *artist*
Gropp, Louis Oliver *editor in chief*
Gropper, Allan Louis *lawyer*
Grose, William Rush *publishing executive*
Gross, Feliks *sociologist, educator, author*
Gross, Jonathan Light *computer scientist, mathematician, educator*
Gross, Michael Robert *writer, editor*
Gross, Richard Benjamin *lawyer*
Gross, Robert Emanuel *collateral loan broker*
Gross, Steven Ross *lawyer*
Grossman, Dan Steven *lawyer*
Grossman, Jack *advertising agency executive*
Grossman, Janice *magazine publishing company executive*
Grossman, Nancy *artist*
Grossman, Ruth Kostik *medical education company executive*
Grossman, Sanford *retired lawyer*
Groves, Ray John *accountant*
†Grubin, Sharon E. *federal judge*
Gruen, Michael Stephan *lawyer*
Grumbach, Doris *novelist, editor, critic, educator, bookseller*
Grunberger, Dezider *biochemist, researcher*
Grune, George Vincent *publishing company executive*
Grunstein, Leonard *lawyer*
Grunwald, Henry Anatole *ambassador, editor, writer*
Grusky, Robert R. *investor*
Gruson, Michael *lawyer*
Gruver, William Rolfe *investment banker*
Guare, John *playwright*
Guccione, Robert Charles Joseph Edward Sabatini *publisher*
Gudas, Lorraine Jean *biochemist, molecular biologist, educator*
Guenther, Paul Bernard *volunteer*
Guettel, Henry Arthur *retired arts executive*
Guggenheim, Martin Franklin *law educator*
Guida, Peter Matthew *surgeon, educator*
Guiher, James Morford, Jr. *publisher, writer*
†Guillaume, Juanita Connor *account clerk, minister*
Guillen, Michael Arthur *mathematical physicist, educator, writer, television journalist*
Guillot, Cyril Etienne *international organization administrator*
Guise, David Earl *architect, educator*
Gulati, Sunil *sports association administrator*
Gumbel, Greg *sportscaster*
†Gumpert, Lynn *gallery director*
Gunther, Jack Disbrow, Jr. *lawyer*
Guo, Chu *chemistry educator*
Gupta, Rajat *management consultant*
Gurfein, Richard Alan *lawyer*
†Gurganus, Allan *writer, educator*
†Gursky, Andreas *artist*
Gusberg, Saul Bernard *physician, educator*
Gussin, Arnold Marvin *lawyer*
Guth, Paul C. *lawyer*
Guthrie, Randolph Hobson, Jr. *plastic surgeon, consultant*
Gutman, Robert William *retired educator*
Guyot, James Franklin *political science educator*
Gwathmey, Charles *architect*
Gwertzman, Bernard *newspaper editor*
†Haac, Oscar Alfred *retired French educator*
Haacke, Hans Christoph Carl *artist, educator*
Haas, Eleanor A. (Mrs. Peter Ralph Haas) *investment banker*
Haas, Frederick Carl *paper and chemical company executive*
Habachy, Suzan Salwa Saba *development economist, non profit administrator*
Habecker, Eugene Brubaker *religious association executive*
†Habeeb, Gregory G. *hotel executive*
Haber, Ira Joel *artist, art educator*
Hackett, Buddy *actor*
Hackett, Kevin R. *lawyer*
Hacklin, Allan *artist, art educator*
Haddad, Heskel Marshall *ophthalmologist*
Haden, Charles *jazz bassist, composer*
Hadley, Leila Eliott-Burton (Mrs. Henry Luce, III) *author*
Haerer, Carol *artist*
Haessle, Jean-Marie Georges *artist*
Haffner, Alden Norman *university official*
Haffner, Alfred Loveland, Jr. *lawyer*
Hagen, Uta Thyra *actress*
Hagendorn, William *lawyer*
Hager, Charles Read *lawyer*
Hager, Larry Stanley *book editor, publishing executive*
Haggerty, Michael *advertising executive*
†Hagstrom, Jack Walter Carl Kling *retired pathology educator*
Hague, William Edward *editor, author*
Hahn, Fred *retired political science and history educator*
Haig, Robert Leighton *lawyer*
Haight, Charles Sherman, Jr. *federal judge*
†Haimes, Todd *artistic director*
Haims, Bruce David *lawyer*
Haines, Kathleen Ann *physician, educator*
Haire, Jack *magazine publisher*
Hajim, Edmund A. *financial services executive*
Hajjar, David Phillip *biochemist, educator*
Halaby, Samia Asaad *artist, educator, computer artist*
Halasz, Robert Joseph *editor*
Halberstam, Malvina *law educator, lawyer*
Hale, Stephen Michael *artist*
Hall, Abram *publishing production manager*
Hall, Nancy Christensen *publishing company executive, author, editor*
Hallberg, Bengt O. *systems strategy director, fiber optic specialist*
Hallett, E. Bruce, III *publishing executive*
Halley, Peter *painter, educator*
Halliday, Joseph William *lawyer*
Hallingby, Paul, Jr. *investment banker*
†Hallion, Thomas Francis *umpire*
Halloran, Leo Augustine *retired financial executive*
Halmi, Robert *film producer*
Halper, Thomas *political science educator*
Halperin, Richard E. *lawyer, holding company executive*
Halpern, Alvin Michael *physicist, educator*
†Halpern, Jeffrey *advertising company executive*
Halpern, Merril Mark *investment banker*

Isay, Richard Alexander *psychiatrist*
Iselin, John Jay *university president*
Iseman, Joseph Seeman *lawyer*
Isenberg, Steven Lawrence *publishing executive, retired*
Isnard, Arnaud *venture capitalist*
Isogai, Masaharu *women's apparel executive*
Isquith, Fred Taylor *lawyer*
Issler, Harry *lawyer*
Ivanick, Carol W. Trencher *lawyer*
Ivanovitch, Michael Steve *economist*
Ives, Colta Feller *museum curator, educator*
Ivory, James Francis *film director*
Ivy, Robert Adams, Jr. *architect, editor-in-chief*
†Iwamoto, Ralph Shigeto *artist*
Jacker, Corinne Litvin *playwright*
†Jackson, Ann Williams *publisher*
Jackson, Anne (Anne Jackson Wallach) *actress*
Jackson, Isaiah *conductor*
†Jackson, James Lewis Perdue, II *entertainment company executive*
Jackson, Kenneth Terry *historian, educator*
Jackson, Raymond Sidney, Jr. *lawyer*
Jackson, Reginald Martinez *former professional baseball player*
Jackson, Richard George *advertising agency executive*
Jackson, Thomas Gene *lawyer*
Jackson, Ward *artist*
Jackson, William Eldred *lawyer*
Jacob, Edwin J. *lawyer*
Jacob, Marvin Eugene *lawyer*
Jacobowitz, Harold Saul *lawyer*
Jacobs, Allan Joel *gynecologist, administrator*
Jacobs, Arnold Stephen *lawyer*
Jacobs, Dennis *federal judge*
†Jacobs, Elliot William *plastic surgery*
Jacobs, Jim *playwright, composer, lyricist, actor*
Jacobs, Mark Neil *financial services corporation executive, lawyer*
Jacobs, Robert Alan *lawyer*
Jacobsen, Theodore H. (Ted H. Jacobsen) *labor union official, educator*
†Jacobs-Furey, Marilyn Sandra *television director*
Jacobson, Gaynor I. *retired association executive*
Jacobson, Gilbert H. *association executive, lawyer*
Jacobson, Jeffrey Eli *lawyer, consultant*
Jacobson, Jerold Dennis *lawyer*
Jacobson, Lawrence Seymour *television executive producer*
Jacobson, Leslie Sari *biologist, educator*
Jacobson, Sandra W. *lawyer*
†Jacobson, Sibyl *insurance company executive*
Jacoby, A. James *securities brokerage firm executive*
†Jacoby, Coleman *scriptwriter*
Jacoby, Jacob *consumer psychology educator*
Jacoby, Robert Harold *management consulting executive*
Jacqueney, Stephanie A(lice) *lawyer*
Jacquette, Yvonne Helene *artist*
Jaeger, David Allen *economics educator*
Jaffe, Alan Steven *lawyer*
Jaffe, Andrew Mark *organization executive, editor, publisher, lecturer*
Jaffe, Mark M. *lawyer*
Jaffe, Susan *ballerina*
Jaffe, William J(ulian) *industrial engineer, educator*
Jaffin, Charles Leonard *lawyer*
Jaglom, Andre Richard *lawyer*
Jakacki, Diane Katherine *web production and marketing executive*
Jakes, John *author*
James-Dunston, Janet Renée *orchestral music teacher, composer, flutist*
Jameson, Richard *magazine editor, film critic*
Jamison, Jayne *magazine publisher*
Jamison, Judith *dancer*
Jander, Klaus Heinrich *lawyer*
Janeway, Elizabeth Hall *author*
Janiak, Anthony Richard, Jr. *investment banker*
Janney, Stuart Symington, III *investment company executive*
Janowich, Ron *artist*
Janssen, Peter Anton *magazine editor and publisher*
Jargalsaikhany, Enkhsaikhan *diplomat*
Jaroff, Leon Morton *magazine editor*
†Jasso, Guillermina *sociologist, educator*
Jassy, Everett Lewis *lawyer*
Javits, Eric Moses *lawyer*
Javitt, Norman B. *medical educator, researcher*
†Jay-Z (Jigga), (Sean Carter) *music company executive*
†Jeanson, Cedric *film company executive*
Jeffers, Kevin Allen *vocalist*
Jefferson, Margo L. *journalist*
Jelinek, Vera *university director*
†Jelks, Glenn William *plastic surgeon*
Jellinek, George *broadcast executive, writer, music educator*
Jenkin, James Thomas *videotape editor*
Jenkins, Anthony Charles *correspondent*
Jenkins, Paul *artist*
Jennings, Charles Robert *educator*
Jennings, Peter Charles *television anchorman*
Jensen, Dennis Mark *marketing executive*
Jensen, Michael Charles *journalist, lecturer, author*
Jepson, Hans Godfrey *investment company executive*
Jermain, Alan *advertising executive*
Jerome, Fred Louis *science organization executive*
Jervis, Robert *political science educator*
Jessup, John Baker *lawyer*
Jewler, Sarah *magazine editor*
Jeydel, Richard K. *lawyer*
Jeynes, Mary Kay *college dean*
Jhabvala, Ruth Prawer *author*
Jiménez, Emilio *corporate lawyer*
Jinnett, Robert Jefferson *lawyer*
Joffe, Robert David *lawyer*
Johansen, John MacLane *architect*
Johns, Jasper *artist*
Johnsen, Niels Winchester *ocean shipping company executive*
†Johnson, Angela *children's book author*
Johnson, Clarke Courtney *financial consultant, educator*
Johnson, Donald Raymond *lawyer*
Johnson, Douglas Wayne *church organization official, minister*
Johnson, Freda S. *public finance consultant*
Johnson, Harmer Frederik *art appraiser*
Johnson, Harold Earl *human resources specialist*
Johnson, Horton Anton *pathologist*
Johnson, J. Chester *financial executive, poet*
Johnson, James M. *orchestra executive*
Johnson, John *broadcast journalist*
Johnson, John H. *publisher, consumer products executive*
Johnson, John William, Jr. *executive recruiter*
Johnson, Johnnie Dean *investor relations consultant*
Johnson, Larry Demetric *professional basketball player*
Johnson, Lynne A. *lawyer*
†Johnson, Mark S. *umpire*
Johnson, Samuel Frederick *English and literature educator emeritus*
Johnson, Thomas Stephen *banker*
Johnson, Vickie *professional basketball player*
Johnsson, Hillary Crute *soloist, opera singer*
Johnston, Catherine V. *magazine publisher*
†Johnston, Ronald Charles *chemistry educator*
Jonas, Ruth Haber *psychologist*
Jonas, Saran *neurologist, educator*
Jones, Abbott C. *investment banking executive*
Jones, Alex S. *journalist, writer, broadcaster*
Jones, Anne *librarian*
Jones, Barclay Gibbs, III *investment banker*
Jones, Bill T. *dancer, choreographer*
Jones, Caroline Robinson *advertising executive*
†Jones, Christopher *advertising company executive*
Jones, David Milton *economist, educator*
Jones, David Rhodes *retired newspaper editor, consultant*
Jones, David R(ussell) *not-for-profit executive*
Jones, Diana Wynne *writer*
Jones, Douglas W. *lawyer*
Jones, Elaine R. *civil rights advocate*
Jones, Gwenyth Ellen *director publishing information systems/technology*
Jones, James Robert *ambassador, former congressman, lawyer*
Jones, Kristin Andrea *artist*
Jones, Laurie Lynn *magazine editor*
†Jones, Lawrence Worth *poet, editor, performance art producer, songwriter*
Jones, Ronald Arthur *physician, composer*
Jones, Thomas Owen *computer industry executive*
Jong, Erica Mann *writer, poet*
†Joo, Michael *artist, educator*
Jordan, John W., II *holding company executive*
Jordan, Michael Hugh *retired broadcasting and media company executive*
Jordan, Theresa Joan *psychologist, educator*
Joseph, Ellen R. *lawyer*
Joseph, Frederick Harold *investment banker*
Joseph, Gregory Paul *lawyer*
Joseph, L. Anthony, Jr. *lawyer*
Joseph, Leonard *lawyer*
Joseph, Michael Sarkies *accountant*
Josephs, Ray *public relations and advertising executive, writer, international relations consultant*
Josephson, Marvin *talent and literary agency executive*
Josephson, William Howard *lawyer*
†Joyce, James A., III (Jim Joyce) *umpire*
Juceam, Robert E. *lawyer*
Judson, Jeannette Alexander *artist*
Juliber, Lois *manufacturing executive*
Jung, Doris *dramatic soprano*
Juran, Sylvia Louise *editor*
Jurka, Edith Mila *psychiatrist, researcher*
Jurman, Elisabeth Antonie *economist*
Just, Gemma Rivoli *retired advertising executive*
Juszczyk, James Joseph *artist*
Kabat, Elvin Abraham *immunologist*
Kadar, Avraham *immunologist*
Kaden, Lewis B. *law educator, lawyer*
Kael, Pauline *film critic, author*
Kafka, Barbara Poses *author*
Kaggen, Lois Sheila *non-profit organization executive*
Kahan, Marlene *professional association executive*
Kahn, Alan Edwin *lawyer*
Kahn, Alfred Joseph *social worker and policy scholar, educator*
Kahn, Anthony F. *lawyer*
Kahn, Jim *magazine publisher*
Kahn, Laurence *communications executive*
Kahn, Leonard Richard *communications and electronics company executive*
Kahn, Nancy Valerie *publishing and entertainment executive, consultant*
Kahn, Norman *pharmacology and dentistry educator*
Kahn, Richard Dreyfus *lawyer*
Kahn, Wolf *artist*
Kailas, Leo George *lawyer*
†Kaiser, Kenneth J. *umpire*
†Kaiser, Michael *performing company, foundation administrator*
Kaiser, Suzanne Billo *investment banker*
Kaish, Luise Clayborn *sculptor, former educator*
Kaish, Morton *artist, educator*
Kaku, Michio *theoretical nuclear physicist, educator*
†Kakutani, Michiko *critic*
Kalajian-Lagani, Donna *publishing executive*
Kalayjian, Anie *psychotherapist, nurse, educator, consultant*
†Kalech, Marc *newspaper editor*
Kalikow, Peter Stephen *real estate developer, former newspaper owner, publisher*
Kalish, Arthur *lawyer*
Kalish, Myron *lawyer*
†Kallakis, Achilleas Michalis S. *shipping company executive*
Kallir, Jane Katherine *art gallery director, author*
Kalmanoff, Martin *composer*
Kalmus, Ellin *art historian, educator*
Kamali, Norma *fashion designer*
Kamarck, Martin Alexander *financial services executive*
Kamerman, Sheila Brody *educator, social worker*
Kamhi, Michelle Marder *editor, writer*
Kamin, Sherwin *lawyer*
Kaminsky, Arthur Charles *lawyer*
Kamlot, Robert *performing arts executive*
Kamm, Linda Heller *lawyer*
Kan, Diana Artemis Mann Shu *artist*
Kandel, Eric Richard *neuroscience educator*
Kandel, William Lloyd *lawyer, lecturer, author*
Kane, Alice Theresa *lawyer*
Kane, Daniel Hipwell *lawyer*
Kane, Edward K. *lawyer*
Kane, Siegrun Dinklage *lawyer*
Kane, Thomas Patrick *broadcast executive*
Kanick, Virginia *radiologist*
Kann, Peter R. *publishing executive*
Kann, Peter Robert *journalist, newspaper publishing executive*
Kanner, Frederick W. *lawyer*
Kanof, Norman B. *dermatologist*
Kanusher, Lawrence Allen *lawyer*
Kapelman, Barbara Ann *physician, educator*
Kaplan, Carl Eliot *lawyer*
Kaplan, Jay *cultural organization administrator, editor*
Kaplan, Jerry *magazine publisher*
Kaplan, Joseph Solte *lawyer*
Kaplan, Keith Eugene *insurance company executive, lawyer*
Kaplan, Leo Sylvan *social scientist, former college administrator*
Kaplan, Lewis A. *judge*
Kaplan, Peter James *lawyer*
Kaplan, Phyllis *computer artist, painter*
Kaplan, Theodore Norman *insurance company executive*
Kappas, Attallah *physician, medical scientist*
Karalekas, George Steven *advertising agency executive, political consultant*
Karan, Donna (Donna Faske) *fashion designer*
Karan, Paul Richard *lawyer*
Karatz, William Warren *lawyer*
Karcher, John Drake *textile and apparel company executive*
Karchin, Louis Samuel *composer, educator*
†Kardon, Dennis *artist,, educator*
Kardon, Janet *museum director, curator, educator*
Kardon, Peter Franklin *foundation administrator*
Karmali, Rashida Alimahomed *lawyer*
Karmazin, Mel *broadcast executive*
Karp, Barrie *artist*
Karp, Martin Everett *management consultant*
Karpel, Craig S. *journalist, editor*
Karr, Norman *trade association executive*
Karsen, Sonja Petra *retired American-Spanish literature educator*
†Kartiganer, Joseph *retired lawyer*
Kasakove, Susan *interior designer*
Kasinec, Edward Joseph *library administrator*
Kasinitz, Philip *sociologist*
Kaskell, Peter Howard *association executive, lawyer*
Kaslick, Ralph Sidney *dentist, educator*
Kasowitz, Marc Elliot *lawyer*
Kassel, Catherine M. *community and maternal-women's health nurse*
Kassel, Virginia Weltmer *television producer, writer*
Kastan, David Scott *university educator, writer*
†Kastrup, Dieter *United Nations official*
Katsh, Salem Michael *lawyer*
Katsoris, Constantine Nicholas *lawyer, consultant*
Katsoyannis, Panayotis George *biochemist, educator*
Katz, Abraham *retired foreign service officer*
Katz, Alex *artist*
Katz, Gregory *lawyer*
Katz, Jane *swimming educator*
Katz, Jerome Charles *lawyer*
Katz, Lois Anne *internist, nephrologist*
Katz, Marcia *public relations company executive*
Katz, Ronald Scott *lawyer*
Katz, Sidney *medical educator*
†Katz, Theodore H. *federal judge*
Katz, Thomas J. *chemistry educator*
Katzman, Herbert Henry *artist*
Kauffmann, Stanley Jules *author*
Kaufman, Arthur Stephen *lawyer*
Kaufman, Bel *author, educator*
Kaufman, David Marc *pediatric neurologist*
Kaufman, Lloyd *film director, producer*
Kaufman, Michele Beth *clinical pharmacist, educator*
Kaufman, Robert Max *lawyer*
Kaufman, Victor A. *broadcast executive, former film company executive*
Kaufmann, Charles Arthur *psychiatrist, educator*
Kaufmann, Ed *lawyer*
Kaufmann, Horacio Carlos *neurologist, educator*
Kaufmann, Jack *lawyer*
Kaufmann, Mark Steiner *banker*
Kauth, Benjamin *podiatrist consultant*
Kautz, James Charles *investment banker*
Kavaler, Thomas J. *lawyer*
Kavaler-Alder, Susan *clinical psychologist*
Kavesh, Robert A. *economist, educator*
Kavoukjian, Michael Edward *lawyer*
Kaye, Stephen Rackow *lawyer*
Kaye, Walter *financial executive*
Kaz, Nathaniel *sculptor*
Kazanjian, John Harold *lawyer*
Kazanjian, Shant *religious organization administrator*
Kazemi, Farhad *political science educator*
Kean, Hamilton Fish *lawyer*
Keane, Bil *cartoonist*
Keany, Sutton *lawyer*
Kearns, Richard P. *diversified financial services company executive*
Kearse, Amalya Lyle *federal judge*
†Keech, Pamela *artist, curator*
Keefe, Deborah Lynn *cardiologist, educator*
†Keegan, Leo Martin *plastic surgeon, educator*
Keenan, John Fontaine *federal judge*
Keenan, Michael Edgar *advertising executive*
Keene, Donald *writer, translator, language educator*
Kehret, Peg *writer*
Keigher, Sharon *physical education educator*
Keilin, Eugene Jacob *investment banker, lawyer*
Keill, Stuart Langdon *psychiatrist*
Keith, John Pirie *urban planner*
†Keller, Bill *journalist*
Keller, Martha Ann *artist, painter*
Kelley, Sheila Seymour *public relations executive, crisis consultant*
Kellogg, Cal Stewart, II *conductor, composer*
Kellogg, David *publisher*
Kellogg, Herbert Humphrey *metallurgist, educator*
†Kellogg, Jeffrey *umpire*
Kellogg, Peter R. *securities dealer*
Kelly, Brian *commodities trader*
Kelly, Daniel Grady, Jr. *lawyer*
Kelly, James *artist*
Kelly, Robert *airport executive*
Kelly, William Michael *investment executive*
Kelman, Charles D. *ophthalmologist, educator*
Kelman, Edward Michael *lawyer*
Kelmenson, Leo-Arthur *advertising executive*
Kemether, Eileen *psychiatrist*
Kende, Christopher Burgess *lawyer*
Kennedy, Daniel John *national and international public relations consultant, communications executive*
Kennedy, John Joseph *bank financial officer*
Kennedy, Marla Hamburg *publisher, gallery director*
Kennedy, Michael John *lawyer*
Kenney, John Joseph *lawyer*
Kenney, Thomas Michael *publisher*
Kenny, Roger Michael *executive search consultant*
Kent, Deborah Warren *hypnotherapist, consultant, lecturer*
Kent, Julie *ballet dancer, actress, model*
Kent, Linda Gail *dancer*
Kenyon, Kevin Bruce *insurance marketing executive*
Keogh, Kevin *lawyer*
Kepets, Hugh Michael *artist*
Keppler, Herbert *publishing company executive*
Kern, George Calvin, Jr. *lawyer*
†Kern, William Bliem, Jr. *minister*
†Kernis, Aaron Jay *composer*
Kernochan, John Marshall *lawyer, educator*
Kessel, Mark *lawyer*
Kesselman, Mark Jonathan *political science educator, writer*
Kessler, Fredric Lee *video producer, computer animation artist*
Kessler, Jeffrey L. *lawyer*
Kessler, Michael George *investigative consultant*
Kesting, Theodore *magazine editor*
Khan, Ahmed Kamal *ambassador*
†Khan, Sohail *investment banker*
Khanzadian, Vahan *tenor*
Khasday, Alyce Field *literary and film agent, psychic consultant, business owner*
Kheel, Theodore Woodrow *lawyer, arbitrator and mediator*
Khuri, Nicola Najib *physicist, educator*
Kiam, Victor Kermit, II *consumer products company executive*
Kidd, John Edward *lawyer, corporate executive*
Kiechel, Walter, III *editor*
Kiely, Garrett Paul *publishing executive*
Kieren, Thomas Henry *management consultant*
Kies, David M. *lawyer*
Kilburn, H(enry) T(homas), Jr. *investment banker*
Kill, Lawrence *lawyer*
Killeffer, Louis MacMillan *advertising executive*
Kim, Se Jung *civil engineer*
Kimball, Richard Arthur, Jr. *lawyer*
Kimmich, Christoph Martin *academic administrator, educator*
Kimsey, William L. *diversified financial services company executive*
†Kimura, Hiroshi *periodontist*
Kinberg, Judy *television producer, director*
Kind, Phyllis *art gallery owner*
King, B. B. (Riley B. King) *singer, guitarist*
King, Henry Lawrence *lawyer*
King, Lawrence Philip *lawyer, educator*
King, Marvin *research executive*
King, Roger M. *syndicated programs distributing company executive*
King, Sheldon Selig *medical center administrator, educator*
King, Thomas *physician, physiology educator*
Kingman, Dong *artist, educator*
†Kingon, Jacqueline Goldwyn (Jackie Kingon) *artist*
Kinnear, John Kenyon, Jr. *architect*
Kinnell, Galway *poet, translator*
Kinney, Stephen Hoyt, Jr. *lawyer*
Kinser, Richard Edward *management consultant*
Kinsman, Sarah Markham *investment company executive*
Kinsolving, Augustus Blagden *lawyer*
Kinsolving, Charles McIlvaine, Jr. *marketing executive*
Kinstler, Everett Raymond *artist*
Kinzler, Thomas Benjamin *lawyer*
Kirby, John Joseph, Jr. *lawyer*
Kirchner, Jake *publishing executive*
Kirk, Donald James *accounting educator, consultant*
Kirk, Susanne Smith *editor*
Kirsch, Arthur William *investment consultant*
Kirsch, Donald *financial consultant, author*
Kirschbaum, Myron *lawyer*
Kirsh, Michael Alan *financial estate planner*
Kirshbaum, Laurence J. *book publishing executive*
Kirshenbaum, Jerry *editor, journalist*
Kislik, Richard William *publishing executive*
Kismaric, Carole Lee *editor, writer, book packaging company executive*
Kisner, Jacob *poet, editor, publisher*
Kissane, Mary Elizabeth *communications executive, consultant*
Kissel, Howard William *drama critic*
Kito, Teruo *former international trading company executive*
Kivette, Ruth Montgomery *English language educator*
Kjellberg, Ann C. *editor*
Klamm de Betas, Ullrich *investor*
Klapper, Molly *lawyer, educator*
Klatell, Jack *dentist*
Klausen, Raymond *sculptor, television and theatre production designer*
Kleber, Herbert David *psychiatrist, educator*
Kleckner, Robert George, Jr. *lawyer*
Kleckner, Simone Marie *law librarian*
†Kleeblatt, Norman L. *museum curator*
Klein, Calvin Richard *fashion designer*
Klein, Donald Franklin *psychiatrist, scientist, educator*
Klein, Dyann Leslie *theater properties company executive*
Klein, Harvey *physician, educator*
Klein, Jeffrey Peter *advertising agency executive*
Klein, Joseph Michelman *musical director*
Klein, Morton *industrial engineer, educator*
Klein, Peter *theatrical producer*
Klein, T(heodore) E(ibon) D(onald) *writer*
Kleinbard, Edward D. *lawyer*
Kleinberg, Norman Charles *lawyer*
Kleinwald, Martin (Martin Littlefield) *book publishing executive*
Kligfield, Paul David *physician, medicine educator*
Kliment, Robert Michael *architect*
Kliment, Stephen Alexander *architect, editor, journalist*
Klinck, James William *insurance company executive*
Kline, Eugene Monroe *lawyer*
Kline, Kevin Delaney *actor*
Klingensmith, Mike *publishing executive*
Klingenstein, Frederick Adler *investment banking executive*
Klinghoffer, David *journalist*
Klingsberg, David *lawyer*
Klink, Fredric J. *lawyer*
Klinkenberg, Hilka Elisabeth *etiquette/protocol expert, author, speaker*
Klipstein, Robert Alan *lawyer*
Klopf, Gordon John *educational consultant, former college dean*
Klores, Dan *public relations executive*
Klotz, Florence *costume designer*
Kmiotek-Welsh, Jacqueline *lawyer*
†Knapp, Albert Bruce *gastroenterologist*
Knapp, Robert Charles *retired obstetrics and gynecology educator*
Knapp, Whitman *federal judge*
Kneller, John William *retired French language and literature educator*
Knepper, Ronald Alan *sculptor, educator*
Kner, Andrew Peter *art director*
Knight, (Charles) Ray *professional sports team executive*
Knight, Townsend Jones *lawyer*

Knobler, Alfred Everett ceramic engineer, manufacturing company executive, publisher
Knowles, Edward F(rank) architect
Knowlton, Alexander Whitney graphic designer
Knowlton, Leslie Brooks journalist
Knox, George L(evi), III consumer products company executive
Knutson, David Harry retired lawyer, banker
Kober, Jane lawyer
Koblenz, Michael Robert lawyer
Kobler, John writer
Kobrin, Lawrence Alan lawyer
Koch, David Hamilton chemical company executive
Koch, Edward I. former mayor, lawyer
Koch, Edward Richard lawyer, accountant
Koch, Kenneth poet, playwright
Koda-Callan, Elizabeth illustrator
Koegel, William Fisher lawyer
Koeltl, John George judge
Koenig, Marvin heavy manufacturing executive
Koenigsberg, Roberta Gale lawyer, non-profit organization administrator
Koeppel, Noel Immanuel financial planner, securities and real estate broker
Kohn, A. Eugene architect
Koke, Richard Joseph author, exhibit designer, museum curator
Kolatch, Myron magazine editor
Kolbe, Karl William, Jr. lawyer
Kolesar, Peter John business and engineering educator
Kolodny, Edwin Hillel neurologist, geneticist, medical administrator
Komansky, David H. financial services executive
Komar, Vitaly artist
Komaroff, Stanley lawyer
†Komisarjevsky, Christopher P.A. public relations executive
Kondylis, Costas Andrew architect
Koning, Hans (Hans Koningsberger) author
Konner, Joan Weiner university administrator, educator, publisher, broadcasting executive, television producer
Koob, Charles Edward lawyer
Koons, Jeff artist
Koontz, Dean Ray writer
Kopelman, Richard Eric management educator
Koplewicz, Harold Samuel child and adolescent psychiatrist
Koplik, Michael R. durable goods company executive
Koplik, Perry H. durable goods company executive
Koplovitz, Kay communication network executive
Kopp, Wendy teaching program administrator
Koppelman, Chaim artist
Koppelman, Dorothy Myers artist, consultant
Koppelman, Murray investment banker
Koppenaal, Richard John psychology educator
Koral, Alan Max lawyer
Korb, Lawrence Joseph government official
Korff, Phyllis G. lawyer
Korman, Jess J. advertising executive, writer, producer
Korman, Lewis J. entertainment/media company executive, lawyer
Kornberg, Alan William lawyer
Kornreich, Edward Scott lawyer
Korot, Beryl artist
Korotkin, Michael Paul lawyer
†Kosc, Greg umpire
Koshi, Annie K. education educator, researcher
Koslow, Sally editor-in-chief
Kosner, Edward A(lan) magazine editor and publisher
Kosovich, Dushan Radovan psychiatrist
Kostelanetz, Boris lawyer
Kostelanetz, Richard writer, media and visual artist
Kostelny, Albert Joseph, Jr. lawyer
Koster, Elaine Landis publishing executive
†Kostyra, Richard Joseph advertising executive
†Kotak, Marni marketing administrator, visual artist
Kotcher, Raymond Lowell public relations executive
Koteff, Ellen periodical editor
Kotlowitz, Robert writer, editor
Kotuk, Andrea Mikotajuk public relations executive, writer
Kourides, Ione Anne endocrinologist, researcher, educator
Kourides, Peter Theologos lawyer
Kozodoy, Neal magazine editor
Kra, Ethan Emanuel actuary
Kraemer, David C. theology educator
Kraemer, Lillian Elizabeth lawyer
†Krajick, Kevin Rudolph journalist
†Krakauer, David musician, educator
Kram, Shirley Wohl federal judge
Kramberg, Ross arts administrator
Kramer, Alan Sharfsin lawyer
Kramer, Daniel Jonathan lawyer
Kramer, Elissa Lipcon nuclear medicine physician, educator
Kramer, George P. lawyer
Kramer, Linda Konheim curator, art historian
Krane, Steven Charles lawyer
Kranwinkle, Conrad Douglas lawyer
Krasna, Alvin Isaac biochemist, educator
Krasner, Daniel Walter lawyer
Kraus, Norma Jean industrial relations executive
Kraushar, Jonathan Pollack communications and media consultant
Krauss, Alison country musician
Krauss, Herbert Harris psychologist
Krebsbach, Karen Anton journalist
Kreda, Allan Jay journalist
Kreek, Mary Jeanne physician
Kreisberg, Neil Ivan advertising executive
Kreitman, Benjamin Zvi rabbi, Judaic studies educator
Kreitzman, Ralph J. lawyer
Krementz, Jill photographer, author
Krenek, Debby newspaper editor
Krens, Thomas museum director
Krents, Milton Ellis broadcast executive
Kressel, Henry venture capitalist
Kretschmer, Keith Hughes investor
Krieger, Sanford lawyer
Krikorian, Van Z. lawyer
Krimendahl, Herbert Frederick, II investment banker
Krinsky, Carol Herselle art history educator
Krinsky, Robert Daniel consulting firm executive
Krinsly, Stuart Z. lawyer, manufacturing company executive
Kristof, Nicholas Donabet journalist
†Krizer, Jodi performing arts executive
Kroeber, Karl English language educator
Kroeger, Lin J. management consultant
Kroft, Steve news correspondent, editor
Kroll, Arthur Herbert lawyer, educator, consultant
Kroll, Sol lawyer
Krominga, Lynn cosmetic and health care company executive, lawyer
Krone, Irene product consultant
Kronen, Jerilyn psychologist
Kronish, Richard Mark sports association executive
Kronman, Carol Jane lawyer
Kropf, Susan J. cosmetics company executive
Krosnick, Joel cellist
Krouse, George Raymond, Jr. lawyer
Kruger, Barbara artist, art critic
Krupman, William Allan lawyer
Krupp, Fred D. lawyer, environmental agency executive
Krupska, Danya (Mrs. Ted Thurston) theater director, choreographer
†Kuby, Ronald L. lawyer
†Kuchment, Anna M. journalist
Kuchta, Ronald Andrew art museum director, magazine editor, curator
Kucic, Joseph management consultant, industrial engineer, network engineer, security specialist
Kufeld, William Manuel lawyer
Kuh, Joyce Dattel education administrator
Kuh, Richard Henry lawyer
Kuhbach, Robert Gerdes lawyer
Kuhl, William Bernard landscape architect
Kujawski, Elizabeth Szancer art curator, consultant
Kuklin, Anthony Bennett lawyer
Kulik, Lewis Tashrak dentist
Kulin, Keith David cinematographer
Kumble, Steven Jay lawyer
Kumin, Maxine Winokur poet, author
Kummerfeld, Donald David publisher
Kunitz, Stanley Jasspon poet, editor, educator
Kuntz, Lee Allan lawyer
Kuo, John Tsungfen geophysicist, educator, researcher
Kupferman, Theodore R. former state justice, lawyer
Kurnit, Shepard advertising agency executive
Kurnow, Ernest statistician, educator
Kurtz, Jerome lawyer, educator
Kury, Bernard Edward lawyer
Kurzweil, Harvey lawyer
Kushins, Joel communications executive
Kushner, Brian Harris pediatric oncologist
Kushner, Robert Ellis artist
Kusmin, Ellyn Sue music administrator
Kusturica, Emir film director
Kutosh, Sue artist
Kuyper, Joan Carolyn foundation administrator
Kvint, Vladimir Lev economist, educator, mining engineer
Labovitz, Deborah Rose Rubin occupational therapist, educator
Labrecque, Thomas G. bank executive
Labunski, Stephen Bronislaw professional society administrator
†LaChapelle, David photographer
Lachman, Marguerite Leanne real estate investment advisor
Lack, Andrew broadcast executive
Lacovara, Philip Allen lawyer
Lacy, Robinson Burrell lawyer
Lader, Lawrence writer
Laderman, Carol C. anthropologist, educator
Laderman, Michael Aaron flutist, music educator
Ladjevardi, Hamid fund manager
Lai, W(ei) Michael mechanical engineer, educator
†Laing, Jennifer advertising executive
Lakah, Jacqueline Rabbat political scientist, educator
Lakatos, Susan Carol artist, investment strategist
Lala, Dominick J. manufacturing company executive
Lambert, Abbott Lawrence retired accountant
Lambert, Eleanor (Mrs. Seymour Berkson) public relations executive, fashion authority, journalist
Lambert, Judith A. Ungar lawyer
Lambertsen, Eleanor C. nursing consultant
Lamensdorf, Sam Fielding, Jr. financial services company executive
Lamia, Thomas Roger lawyer
Lamirande, Arthur Gordon editor, author, musician, actor
Lamle, Hugh Roy investment advisor, consultant
Lamm, Donald Stephen publishing company executive
Lamm, Norman academic administrator, rabbi
Lammie, James L. financial planner, consultant
Lamont, Lansing journalist, public affairs executive, author
Lamont, Lee music management executive
Lamont, Rosette Clementine Romance languages educator, theatre journalist, translator
LaMotta, Connie Frances association executive
Lamparello, Patrick John surgeon, educator
Lampert, Zohra actress
Lancaster, Kelvin John economics educator
Lanchner, Bertrand Martin lawyer, advertising executive
Landa, Howard Martin lawyer, business executive
Landau, Ralph chemical engineer
Landau, Sidney I. publishing executive
Landau, Walter Loeber lawyer
Landegger, Carl Clement machinery and pulp manufacturing executive
Landrigan, Philip John epidemiologist
Landy, Joanne Veit foreign policy analyst
Landy, Rona broadcast executive
Lane, Alvin S. lawyer
Lane, Arthur Alan lawyer
Lane, Joseph M. orthopedic surgeon, educator, oncologist
Lane, Kenneth Robert producer, distributor
Lane, Lois N. artist
Lane, Louis musician, conductor
Lane, Nancy editor
†Lang, Christof television journalist
Lang, Daniel S. artist
Lang, Enid Asher psychiatrist
Lang, George restaurateur
Lang, John Francis lawyer
Lang, Pearl dancer, choreographer
Lang, Vera J. publishing company executive
Langan, Marie-Noelle Suzanne cardiologist, educator
Langbert, Mitchell Berke business educator
Lange, Marvin Robert lawyer
Lange, Phil C. retired education educator
Langer, Bruce Alden lawyer
Langford, Laura Sue ratings analyst
Langsam, Ida S. press agent, consultant
†Langstaff, Eleanor Marguerite library science educator
Langton, Cleve Swanson advertising executive
LaNicca, Ellen public relations executive
Lannamann, Richard Stuart executive recruiting consultant
La Noue, Terence David artist, educator
Lanquetot, Roxanne special education educator, writer
Lansbury, Edgar George theatrical producer
Lantier, Brendan John lawyer
Lapham, Lewis Henry editor, author, television host
Lapierre, Dominique writer, historian, philanthropist
Lapine, James Elliot playwright, director
La Pointe, Laurence Michael lawyer
Laragh, John Henry physician, scientist, educator
Larberg, John Frederick wine consultant, educator
Larkin, Leo Paul, Jr. lawyer
Larmore, Jennifer mezzo-soprano
Larose, Lawrence Alfred lawyer
La Rossa, James M(ichael) lawyer
Larsen, Robert Dhu lawyer
Larson, Steven Mark physician
La Rue, (Adrian) Jan (Pieters) musicologist, educator, author
Lascher, Alan Alfred lawyer
Lash, Stephen S. sales executive
Lash, Stephen Sycle auction company executive
Laskawy, Philip A. accounting and management consulting firm executive
Lasker, Jonathan Lewis artist
Lasker, Richard S. lawyer
Lassen, Robert Maurie graphic artist, photographer, editor
Lasser, Joseph Robert investment company executive
Last, Ruth Edith actress
Latimer, Hugh Scot healthcare consultant, architect
Lattin, Albert Floyd banker
Lauber, Patricia Grace writer
Lauder, Estee cosmetics company executive
Lauder, Leonard Alan cosmetic and fragrance company executive
Lauder, Ronald Stephen investor
Lauer, Eliot lawyer
Lauer, Matt broadcast journalist
Lauersen, Niels Helth physician, educator
Laufer, Beatrice composer
Laufer, Ira Jerome physician
Laufer, Jacob lawyer
Laufman, Harold surgeon
Laughlin, James Patrick lawyer
Laughlin, John Seth physicist, educator
Laughren, Terry marketing executive
Lauren, Ralph fashion designer
Laurence, Jeffrey Conrad immunologist
Laurence, Leslie journalist
Laurents, Arthur playwright
Laurus, (Laurus Skurla) archbishop
†Lavedan, Christiane artist, researcher
Laverge, Albert Johannes investment banker
Lavine, Lawrence Neal investment banker
La Vita, Roberto architect, art director, designer
Lavrov, Sergei Viktorovich ambassador
Lawrence, Bryan Hunt investment banking executive
Lawrence, Henry Sherwood physician, educator
Lawrence, Lauren psychoanalytical theorist, psychoanalyst
Lawry, Sylvia (Mrs. Stanley Englander) health association administrator
Lawson, William otolargyngologist, educator
Lawson-Johnston, Peter Orman foundation executive
Lax, Melvin theoretical physicist
Lax, Peter David mathematician, educator
†Laybourne, Geraldine broadcasting executive
†Layne, Jerry Blake umpire
Lazaroff, Shneur Zalmen stockbroker
Lazarus, Rochelle Braff advertising executive
Leach, Robin producer, writer, television host
Leaf, Robert Jay dental insurance consultant
Leahey, Lynn editor-in-chief
Leahey, Miles Cary economist
Leahy, Michael Joseph newspaper editor
Lear, Robert William holding company executive
Leavitt, Charles Loyal English language educator, administrator
Leavitt, David Adam writer
Leavitt, Michael P(aul) arts manager, concert producer, music industry record distributor
Lebec, Alain investment banker
Lebensohn, Jeremy sculptor
LeBlang, Skip Alan lawyer
LeBlond, Richard Knight, II banker
Lebouitz, Martin Frederick financial services industry executive, consultant
Lebow, Mark Denis lawyer
Lechay, James artist, emeritus art educator
Leckie, Gavin Frederick lawyer, banker
LeClerc, Paul library director
LeCompte, Elizabeth theater director
Lederberg, Joshua geneticist, educator
Lederer, Peter David lawyer
Lederman, Lawrence lawyer, writer, educator
Lederman, Sally Ann nutrition educator and researcher
Ledger, William Joe physician, educator
LeDoux, Harold Anthony cartoonist, painter
†LeDray, Charles Allan artist
†Lee, Alvin Yin-Hang financial risk management specialist
Lee, Bruce advertising executive
Lee, Catherine sculptor, painter
Lee, Clement William Khan trade association administrator
Lee, Dai-Keong composer
Lee, Frances Helen editor
†Lee, Iara filmmaker
Lee, In-Young lawyer
Lee, Jerome G. lawyer
Lee, Leslie Enders artist
Lee, Mathew Hung Mun physiatrist
Lee, Paul Lawrence lawyer
Lee, Robert Sanford psychologist
Lee, Sally A. editor-in-chief
Lee, Sidney Phillip chemical engineer, state senator
Lee, Tsung-Dao physicist, educator
Lee, Victor J. venture capitalist
Leebron, David Wayne law educator, dean
Leeds, Douglas Brecker advertising agency executive, theatre producer
Lees, Alfred William writer, former magazine editor
Leet, Mildred Robbins corporate executive, consultant
Leetch, Brian Joseph hockey player
Leff, Ilene J(oan) management consultant, corporate and goverment executive
Leff, Sandra H. gallery director, consultant
Lefferts, Gillet, Jr. architect
Lefkowitz, Howard N. lawyer
Lefkowitz, Jerry lawyer, accountant
Lefkowitz, Joel M. psychologist, educator
†Legg, Katharine Stewart executive director
Legrand, Michel Jean composer
Lehman, Edward William sociology educator, researcher
Lehman, Mark E. lawyer
Lehman, Orin retired state official
Lehmann-Haupt, Christopher Charles Herbert book reviewer
Lehodey, John Francois hotel company executive
Lehr, Janet art dealer, publisher, author
Lehrer, Leonard artist, educator
Leibovitz, Annie photographer
Leibow, David B. psychiatrist, writer
Leibowitz, Herbert Akiba English language educator, author
Leichtling, Michael Alfred lawyer
Leigh, Stephen industrial designer
Leighton, Lawrence Ward investment banker
Leiman, Joan Maisel university administrator
Leinwand, Freda photographer
Leisure, Peter Keeton federal judge
Leland, Richard G. lawyer
Lelchuk, Alan author, educator
Lelyveld, Joseph Salem newspaper editor, correspondent
Lemesh, Nicholas Thomas advertising executive
Lemisch, Jesse history educator, writer
Lemon, Ralph choreographer
Lencek, Rado Ludovik Slavic languages educator
L'Engle, Madeleine (Mrs. Hugh Franklin) author
Lenton, Roberto Leonardo research facility and environmental administrator
Leonard, Edwin Deane lawyer
Leonard, Elmore John novelist, screenwriter
Leonard, Rachel Rauh editor
†Leonard, Zoe artist
Leone, Rose Marie psychotherapist
†Lepor, Herbert urologist
Leritz, Lawrence R. choreographer, dancer, actor, producer, director, songwriter
Lerner, Martin museum curator
Lerner, Max Kasner lawyer
Lesch, Michael Oscar lawyer
Leslie, John Webster, Jr. communications company executive
Leslie, Seymour Marvin communications executive
Lesser, William Melville lawyer
Lessing, Brian Reid actuary
Lester, Pamela Robin lawyer
Letterman, David television personality, comedian, writer
Leubert, Alfred Otto Paul international business consultant, investor
Leung, Betty Brigid nursing administrator
Leung, Firman investment bank executive
Levai, Pierre Alexandre art gallery executive
Leval, Pierre Nelson federal judge
Levere, Richard David physician, academic administrator, educator
Levi, Isaac philosophy educator
Levie, Joseph Henry lawyer
Levin, Alan M. television journalist
Levin, Ezra Gurion lawyer
Levin, Gerald M. media and entertainment company executive
Levin, Herbert diplomat, foundation executive
Levin, Ira author, playwright
Levin, Martin P. publishing executive, lawyer
Levin, Michael Joseph lawyer
Levin, Michael Stuart steel company executive
Levin, Warren Mayer family practice physician
Levine, Alan lawyer
Levine, Arnold Jay molecular biology educator
Levine, Arthur Elliott academic administrator, educator
Levine, Charles Michael publishing company executive, consultant
Levine, Ellen R. magazine editor
Levine, James conductor, pianist, artistic director
Levine, Laurence William lawyer
Levine, Lawrence Steven lawyer
Levine, Mark Leonard lawyer
Levine, Melvin Charles lawyer
Levine, Naomi Bronheim university administrator
Levine, Robert Jay lawyer
Levins, Ilyssa public relations executive
Levinson, Paul Howard lawyer
Levinson, Rascha psychotherapist
Levinson, Robert Alan textile company executive
Levinson, Warren Mitchell broadcast journalist
Levison, Peggy Lee psychologist
†Levit, Mark S. marketing professional
Levitan, James A. lawyer
Levitan, Max Fishel geneticist, anatomy educator
Levitas, Mitchel Ramsey editor
Levitt, Mitchell Alan management consultant
Levitt, Norman Jay mathematician
Levitt, Sidney Mark author, illustrator, artist
Levitz, Paul Elliot publishing executive
†Levitz, Paul H. educator
Levoy, Myron author
Levy, Alan Joseph editor, journalist, writer
Levy, Albert family physician
†Levy, George Harold publishing company executive
Levy, Leon investment company executive
Levy, Matthew Degen investment company executive, consumer products executive, management consultant
†Levy, Owen writer
Levy, Stanley Herbert lawyer
Lewins, Steven security analyst, investment advisor, corporate executive, diplomatic advisor
Lewis, Donna Cunningham banker, communications consultant
†Lewis, Edward T. publisher
Lewis, Hylan Garnet sociologist, educator
Lewis, Jonathan Joseph surgical oncologist, molecular biologist, educator
Lewis, Loida Nicolas food products holding company executive
Lewis, Richard Warren advertising executive
Lewis, Russell T. newspaper publishing executive
Lewis, Sherman Richard, Jr. investment banker
Lewis, Sylvia Davidson association executive
†Lewis, W. Walker appraisal company executive
LeWitt, Sol artist
Lewy, Robert Max physician
Lewyn, Ann Salfeld English as a second language educator
Lewyn, Thomas Mark lawyer
Libby, John Kelway financial services company executive
Liberman, Alexander artist, editor
Libin, Paul theatre executive, producer
LiBretto, John Charles television director
Lichtblau, John H. economist
Liddell, Donald Macy, Jr. retired investment counsellor
Lidsky, Ella law librarian
Lieberman, Charles economist
Lieberman, James S. physiatrist, neurologist
Lieberman, Mark E. bank executive
Lieberman, Seymour biochemistry educator emeritus

Liebermann, Lowell composer, pianist, conductor
Liebman, Lance Malcolm law educator, lawyer
Liebman, Theodore architect
†Lifland, Burton R. federal judge
Lifland, William Thomas lawyer
Lifton, Robert Jay psychiatrist, author
Lifton, Robert Kenneth diversified companies executive
Lightman, Harold Allen marketing executive
Lilien, Mark Ira executive
†Limbaugh, Rush Hudson radio and talk show host
Lin, Maria C. H. lawyer
Linares, Guiller city councilman
Lincoln, Edmond Lynch investment banker
Lindheim, James Bruce public relations executive
Lindquist, Richard James portfolio manager
Lindsay, George Peter lawyer
Lindskog, David Richard lawyer
Lingeman, Richard Roberts editor, writer
Linsenmeyer, John Michael lawyer
Lipkin, Martin physician, scientist
Lipper, Kenneth investment banker, author, producer
Lipscomb, Thomas Heber, III information technology executive
Lipsey, Robert Edward economist, educator
Lipsky, Burton G. lawyer
Lipsky, Pat artist, educator
Lipson, Charles Barry finance company executive
Lipton, Charles public relations executive
Lipton, Charles Jules lawyer
Lipton, Joan Elaine advertising executive
Lipton, Lester ophthalmologist, entrepreneur
Lipton, Martin lawyer
Lipton, Robert Steven lawyer
Liss, Norman lawyer
Little, Robert David library science educator
Littleford, William Donaldson retired publishing executive
Liu, Si-kwang veterinary pathologist
†Livingston, Bernard author
Llinás, Rodolfo Riascos medical educator, researcher
Lloyd, Jean early childhood educator, television producer
†Lobo, Rebecca professional basketball player
Localio, S. Arthur retired surgeon, educator
†Lockhart, Sharon artist, photographer
Lockshin, Michael Dan rheumatologist
Lockwood, Helshi advertising executive
Loeb, John Langeloth, Jr. investment counselor
Loeb, Larry Morris communications company executive
Loeb, Marshall Robert journalist
Loeb, Peter Kenneth money manager
Loengard, John Borg photographer, editor
Loengard, Richard Otto, Jr. lawyer
Logan, Don publishing executive
Logan, Douglas George sports commissioner
Logue, Alexandra Woods higher education administrator, psychologist
Logue-Kinder, Joan investment brokerage firm executive
Lohf, Kenneth A. librarian, writer
Lois, George advertising agency executive
London, Herbert Ira humanities educator, institute executive
Loney, Glenn Meredith drama educator
Long, David L. magazine publisher
Long, Elizabeth Valk magazine publisher
Long, Lisa Valk communications company executive
Long, Rose-Carol Washton art historian
Long, Thomas Michael investment banker, private equity fund manager
Longley, Marjorie Watters newspaper executive
Longstreth, Bevis lawyer
Lonsford, Florence Hutchinson artist, designer, writer
Loo, Marcus H. physician, educator
Loomis, Carol J. journalist
Loomis, Robert Duane publishing company executive, author
Loprest, Frank James Jr. special assistant United States Attorney
Lorber, Barbara Heyman communications executive
Lorch, Ernest Henry lawyer
Lorch, Maristella De Panizza medieval and Renaissance scholar, writer
Lord, Barbara Joanni public official, lawyer
Lord, M. G. writer
Lord, Marvin apparel company executive
Lord, Richard Dennis photographer
Lord, Robert Wilder retired editor and writer
Lore, Martin Maxwell lawyer
Lorenz, Hilary S. artist
Loring, John Robbins artist
Loscalzo, Anthony Joseph lawyer
LoSchiavo, Linda Bosco library director
Losee, Thomas Penny, Jr. publisher
Loss, Margaret Ruth lawyer
Lotas, Judith Patton advertising executive
Loudon, Dorothy actress
Louganis, Greg E. former Olympic athlete, actor
†Louis, Murray dancer, choreographer, dance teacher
†Lovell, Whitfield artist
Low, Anthony English language educator
Low, Barbara Wharton biochemist, biophysicist
Low, Richard H. broadcasting executive, producer
Low, Setha Marilyn anthropology and psychology educator, consultant
Lowe, Ida Brandwayn library administrator, systems administrator
Lowe, Mary Johnson federal judge
Lowell, Stanley Edgar accountant
Lowell, Stanley Herbert lawyer
Lowenfeld, Andreas Frank law educator, arbitrator
Lowenfels, Fred M. lawyer
Lowenfels, Lewis David lawyer
Lowenstein, Louis legal educator
Lowenthal, Constance art historian
Lowry, Glenn David art museum director
Lowy, George Theodore lawyer
Lubell, David G. lawyer
Lubetski, Edith Esther librarian
Lubin, Carol Riegelman political scientist
Lubkin, Virginia Leila ophthalmologist
Lubovitch, Lar dancer, choreographer
Lubow, Nathan Myron accountant
Lucas, Christopher artist
Lucas, Henry Cameron, Jr. information systems educator, writer, consultant
Lucas, James E(vans) operatic director
Lucci, Susan actress
Luce, Charles Franklin former utilities executive, lawyer
Luce, Henry, III foundation executive
Lucht, John Charles management consultant, executive recruiter, writer
Luckman, Sharon Gersten arts administrator
Ludgin, Chester Hall baritone, actor
Luftglass, Murray Arnold manufacturing company executive
Luke, John Anderson, Jr. paper, packaging and chemical company executive
Luks, Allan Barry executive director
Lunardini, Christine Anne writer, historian, consultant
Lundquist, John Milton librarian, author, travel writer, photographer
Lunin, Lois F. information scientist, artist
Lunn, Kitty Elizabeth actress
Luntz, Maurice Harold ophthalmologist
Lupert, Leslie Allan lawyer
LuPone, Patti actress
Luria, Mary Mercer lawyer
Lurie, Ranan Raymond political cartoonist, political analyst, artist, lecturer
Lust, Herbert Cohnfeldt, II finance executive
Lustenberger, Louis Charles, Jr. lawyer
†Luthar, Suniya Sunanda psychologist, educator
Luther, Bruce Charles sound technician
Lutringer, Richard Emil lawyer
Lutzker, Elliot Howard lawyer
Lyall, Michael Rodney investment banker
Lynch, Gerald Weldon academic administrator, psychologist
Lynch, Gerard E. law educator
Lynn, Theodore Stanley lawyer
Lynne, Michael film company executive
Lynton, Michael publishing executive
Lyon, Carl Francis, Jr. lawyer
Lyon, Patty advertising executive, marketing professional
Lyons, John Matthew telecommunications executive, broadcasting executive
Maas, Peter writer
Maas, Werner Karl microbiology educator
†Mabrey, Vicki news correspondent, anchor
Macan, William Alexander, IV lawyer
Macchiarola, Frank Joseph academic administrator
MacDermott, Thomas Jerome investment banking executive
Macdonald, John Stephen oncologist, educator
Macdonald, Robert Rigg, Jr. museum director
MacDonald, Ronald Francis financial services company executive
Macer-Story, Eugenia Ann writer, artist
MacGowan, Sandra Firelli publishing executive, publishing educator
Machlin, Eugene Solomon metallurgy educator, consultant
Machlin, Milton Robert magazine editor, writer
MacIntyre, Steven Edmund investment banker, investor
Mack, Dennis Wayne lawyer
†Mack, John J. investment company executive
MacKay, Malcolm executive search consultant
Macken, Daniel Loos physician, educator
Mackey, Patricia Elaine university librarian
Mackie, Robert Gordon costume and fashion designer
MacKinnon, John Alexander lawyer
MacKinnon, Roger Alan psychiatrist, educator
MacLean, Babcock lawyer
MacLean, John professional hockey player
MacRae, Cameron Farquhar, III lawyer
Macri, Theodore William book publisher
Macris, Michael lawyer
MacTavish, Craig hockey coach, former hockey player
Macurdy, John Edward basso
Madden, Donald Paul lawyer
Madden, John television sports commentator, former professional football coach
Madden, Michael Daniel finance company executive
Madonna, Jon C. accounting firm executive
Madsen, Loren Wakefield sculptor
Madsen, Stephen Stewart lawyer
Mager, Ezra Pascal investment management company executive
Magnano, Joseph Sebastian lawyer
Mahon, Arthur J. lawyer
Mahon, John Joseph federal agency adminstrator
Mahoney, Margaret Ellerbe foundation executive
Mahoney, Thomas Henry, IV investment banker
Maidman, Richard Harvey Mortimer lawyer
Mailer, Norman author
Mailer-Howat, Patrick Lindsay Macalpine investment banker
Main, Patricia Englander investor
Mainieri, Mike vibraphonist, producer, arranger, composer
Maitland, Guy Edison Clay lawyer
Majda, Andrew J. mathematician, educator
Makovsky, Kenneth Dale public relations executive
Makrianes, James Konstantin, Jr. management consultant
Malamed, Seymour H. motion picture company executive
Malefakis, Edward E. history educator
Maleska, Martin Edmund publishing executive
Maletta, Lou broadcast executive
Malgieri, Nick chef, author, educator
Malin, Irving English literature educator, literary critic
Malina, Michael lawyer
Malitz, Sidney psychiatrist, educator, researcher
Malkin, Barry film editor, consultant
Malkin, Michael M. lawyer
Malkin, Peter Laurence lawyer
Mallet, Jacques Robert art dealer
Mallozzi, Cos M. public relations executive
Maloney, Elizabeth Mary psychiatric-mental health nurse
Maltby, Richard Eldridge, Jr. theater director, lyricist
Mamlok, Ursula composer, educator
†Manahan, Anna actress
Manassah, Jamal Tewfek electrical engineering and physics educator, management consultant
Mandel, Irwin Daniel dentist
Mandelbaum, Harold Neil accountant
Mandelstam, Charles Lawrence lawyer
Mandl, David architect
Mandracchia, Violet Ann Palermo psychotherapist, educator
Maneker, Morton M. lawyer
Maney, Michael Mason lawyer
†Manfred, Robert D. sports association executive
Mangan, Mona association executive, lawyer
Manger, William Muir internist
Manges, James Horace investment banker
Mangia, Angelo James lawyer
†Manglano-Ovalle, Inigo artist, sculptor
Mango, Wilfred Gilbert, Jr. real estate and construction company executive
Mann, Pamela A. lawyer
Mann, Sally photographer
Manning, Jack photographer, columnist, author
Manoff, Richard Kalman advertising executive, public health consultant, author
Mansi, Joseph Anneillo public relations company executive
Manski, Wladyslaw Julian microbiology educator, medical scientist
Mansouri, Lotfollah (Lotfi Mansouri) opera stage director, administrator
Mantegna, Joe Anthony actor, playwright
Mantle, Raymond Allan lawyer
†Manton, Edwin Alfred Grenville insurance company executive
Mapes, Glynn Dempsey newspaper editor
Mapp, Edward Charles speech educator
Maraynes, Allan Lawrence filmmaker, television producer
Marcosson, Thomas I. service company executive
Marcus, Eric Peter lawyer
Marcus, Eric Robert psychiatrist
Marcus, Gwen Ellen sculptor
Marcus, Hyman business executive
Marcus, Maria Lenhoff lawyer, law educator
Marcus, Norman lawyer
Marcusa, Fred Haye lawyer
Marcuse, Adrian Gregory academic administrator
Marden, Brice artist
Marder, John G. real estate investor, marketing consultant, corporate director
Marder, Michael Zachary dentist, researcher, educator
Marder, Samuel violinist
Mardin, Arif music industry executive, musician
Margolin, Jean Spielberg artist
Margolis, David I(srael) industrial manufacturing executive
Margulis, Howard Lee lawyer
†Mariam, Thomas Fred public relations executive, radio producer
Marinakis, Markos K. water transportation executive
Marincola, John association administrator
Marino, Michael Frank, III lawyer
†Marion, Cynthia Anne stage director
Marisol, (Marisol Escobar) sculptor
Mark, Laurence Peter anesthesiology educator
Mark, Reuben consumer products company executive
†Mark, Wendy artist
Markle, Cheri Virginia Cummins nurse
Markowitz, Robert insurance executive
Marks, Edward B. international relief administrator
Marks, Edwin S. investment company executive
Marks, Paul Alan oncologist, cell biologist, educator
†Markson, David Merrill writer, educator
Marlas, James Constantine holding company executive
Marlette, Douglas Nigel editorial cartoonist, comic strip creator
Marlin, John Tepper economist, writer, consultant
Marlin, Richard lawyer
†Maroney, Thomas Joseph lawyer
†Maroun, Mary advertising executive
Marrin, Albert history educator, writer
Marron, Donald Baird investment banker
Marsalis, Branford musician
Marsh, Jean Lyndsey Torren actress, writer
†Marsh, Randall Gilbert umpire
Marshak, Hilary Wallach psychotherapist, owner
Marshall, Alton Garwood real estate counselor
Marshall, Gary Charles mailing list company executive
Marshall, Geoffrey retired university official
Marshall, Michael Borden marketing executive
Marshall, Sheila Hermes lawyer
Marshall, Thomas Carlisle applied physics educator
Marston, Robert Andrew public relations executive
Martegani Luini, Micaela curator, art critic
Martin, Elliot Edwards theatrical producer
Martin, George J., Jr. lawyer
Martin, Glenn financial manager, consultant
†Martin, Jacqueline Briggs author juvenile prose
Martin, John Sherwood, Jr. federal judge
Martin, Judith Sylvia journalist, author
Martin, Linda Gaye demographer, economist
Martin, Malcolm Elliot lawyer
Martin, Mary-Anne art gallery owner
Martin, Michael Townsend racing horse stable executive, sports marketing executive
Martin, Paul Ross editor
Martin, Richard Harrison curator, art historian
†Martin, Ricky vocalist
Martinelli, Johnnie agent
Martini, Richard K. theatrical producer
Martino, Donna Frances newspaper sales administrator
Martins, Peter ballet master, choreographer, dancer
Martone, Patricia Ann lawyer
Martz, Lawrence Stannard periodical editor
†Marx, Herbert Lewis, Jr. arbitrator
Marx, Owen Cox lawyer
Marzulli, John Anthony, Jr. lawyer
Masey, Jack exhibition designer
Masi, Jane Virginia marketing and sales consultant
Masin, Michael Terry lawyer
Masinter, Edgar Martin investment banker
†Maslin, Janet film critic
Maslow, Will lawyer, association executive
Mason, Bobbie Ann novelist, short story writer
Masters, Jon Joseph corporate governance consultant, mediator
Masterson, James Francis psychiatrist
Masur, Kurt conductor
Matalon, Norma travel and public relations executive
Materna, Joseph Anthony lawyer
Mathers, William Harris lawyer
Mathews, Jack Wayne journalist, film critic
Mathisen, Harold Clifford portfolio management executive
Matteson, William Bleecker lawyer
Matthews, Edwin Spencer, Jr. lawyer
Matthews, Norman Stuart department store executive
Mattson, Francis Oscar retired librarian and rare books curator
Mattson, Marlin Roy Albin health facility administrator, psychiatry educator
Matus, Wayne Charles lawyer
Matyas, Charles Julian retired archivist
Matzner, Chester Michael writer
Maubert, Jacques Claude headmaster
Maughan, Deryck C. investment banker
Maulsby, Allen Farish lawyer
Maupin, Armistead Jones, Jr. writer
Maurer, Gilbert Charles media company executive
Maurer, Jeffrey Stuart finance executive
Mauskop, Alexander physician
Maxfield, Guy Budd lawyer, educator
Maxwell, Anders John investment banker
Maxwell, Carla Lena dancer, choreographer, educator
May, Elaine actress, theatre and film director
May, William Frederick manufacturing executive
Mayer, Martin Prager writer
Mayer, Rosemary artist
Mayer, William Emilio investor
Mayerson, Philip classics educator
Mayerson, Sandra Elaine lawyer
Mayesh, Jay Philip lawyer
Maynard, John Rogers English educator
Maynard, Virginia Madden charitable organization executive
Maysles, Albert H. filmmaker
Mazur, Jay J. trade union official
Mazza, Thomas Carmen lawyer
Mazzia, Valentino Don Bosco physician, educator, lawyer
Mazzilli, Paul John investment banker
Mazzola, Anthony Thomas editor, art consultant, designer, writer
Mazzola, John William former performing arts center executive, consultant
†McAleer, Edward Cornelius retired Englishliterature educator
McAniff, Nora P. publishing executive
McBride, Rodney Lester investment counselor
McBryde, Thomas Henry lawyer
†McCandless, Carolyn Keller human resources executive
McCarrick, Edward R. magazine publisher
McCarter, Thomas N., III investment counseling company executive
McCarthy, Denis artist, educator
†McCarthy, Jonathan Paul economist
McCarthy, Patrick magazine publishing executive
McCarthy, Robert Emmett lawyer
McCartin, Thomas Joseph advertising executive
McCarty, Maclyn medical scientist
†McCarty, V.K. publisher
McCaslin, Teresa Eve human resources executive
McCleary, Benjamin Ward investment banker
McClelland, Timothy Reid baseball umpire
McClimon, Timothy John lawyer
McClung, Richard Goehring lawyer
McCormack, Elizabeth J. foundation administrator
McCormack, Howard Michael lawyer
McCormack, John Joseph, Jr. insurance executive
McCormack, Thomas Joseph retired publishing company executive
McCormick, Donald E. librarian, archivist
McCormick, Hugh Thomas lawyer
†McCourt, Frank writer
McCourt, Robert D. marketing and creative services executive
†McCoy, Larry S. umpire
McCrary, Eugenia Lester (Mrs. Dennis Daughtry McCrary) civic worker, writer
McCredie, James Robert fine arts educator
McCrie, Robert Delbert editor, publisher, educator
Mc Crory, Wallace Willard pediatrician, educator
McCullough, Colleen author
McCullough, David author, educator
Mc Cullough, J. Lee industrial psychologist
McCurdy, Charles Gribbel publishing company executive
McCutchen, William Walter, Jr. management educator
McDarrah, Fred William photographer, editor, writer, photography reviewer
McDavid, William Henry lawyer
McDermott, Richard T. lawyer, educator
†McDonald, Audra Ann actress
McDonald, Gregory Christopher author
†McDonald, Joel Matthews lawyer
McDonald, Thomas Paul controller
McDonell, Robert Terry magazine editor, novelist
McDonough, Mamie public relations executive
McDonough, William J. banker
McDormand, Frances actress
McDowell, Edwin S. journalist, novelist
McEwen, James publishing executive
†McEwen, Mark anchor
McFadden, David Revere museum curator
McFadden, Mary Josephine fashion industry executive
McFadden, Robert Dennis reporter
McFeely, William Drake publishing company executive
McGanney, Thomas lawyer
McGarry, John Patrick, Jr. retired advertising agency executive
McGarvey, Mary Hewitt writer
McGeady, Sister Mary Rose religious organization administrator, psychologist
McGee, Henry broadcast executive
McGill, Frank media consulting firm specialist
McGill, Jay magazine publisher
Mc Gillicuddy, John Francis retired banker
McGinnis, Arthur Joseph publisher
†McGlynn, Brian public relations executive
†McGlynn, William Charles brokerage house executive
Mc Goldrick, John Gardiner retired lawyer
McGoldrick, John Lewis lawyer
McGovern, Maureen Ann curator
Mc Gowin, William Edward artist
McGrath, Charles Arthur editor, writer
McGrath, Christopher Thomas lawyer
McGrath, Eleanor Burns editor, writer
McGrath, Eugene R. utility company executive
McGrath, Judith broadcast executive
McGrath, Patrick J. advertising agency executive
McGrath, Thomas J. lawyer, writer, film producer
McGraw, Harold Whittlesey, Jr. publisher
McGraw, Harold Whittlesey, III (Terry McGraw) information company executive
McGuane, Thomas Francis, III author, screenwriter
McGuire, Eugene Guenard lawyer
McHugh, Caril Dreyfuss art dealer, gallery director, consultant
Mc Inerney, Denis lawyer
Mc Kay, Jim television sports commentator
McKean, Henry P. mathematics institute administrator
†McKean, James G. umpire
McKelvey, Andrew J. advertising executive
McKelvey, Gerald public relations executive
McKenna, Kevin Patrick newspaper editor
McKenna, Lawrence M. federal judge
McKenna, Malcolm Carnegie vertebrate paleontologist, curator, educator
McKenna, Peter Dennis lawyer
McKenna, William Michael advertising executive
McKenzie, Kevin Patrick artistic director

McKenzie, Mary Beth *artist*
McKesson, John Alexander, III *international relations educator*
Mc Kitrick, Eric Louis *historian, educator*
McLachlan, Sarah *composer, musician*
†McLaughlin, David *broadcast executive*
McLaughlin, Joseph *lawyer*
McLaughlin, Joseph Michael *federal judge, law educator*
McLaughlin, Michael John *insurance company executive*
McLean, Mora *institute administrator*
Mc Lendon, Heath Brian *securities investment company executive*
McMahon, James Charles *lawyer*
McMeen, Elmer Ellsworth, III *lawyer, guitarist*
McMorrow, Eileen *editor periodical*
McMullan, Alexander Joseph *municipal official*
McMullan, James Burroughs *illustrator, graphic designer*
McMullan, William Patrick, III *investment banker*
Mc Murtry, James Gilmer, III *neurosurgeon*
McMurtry, Larry Jeff *author*
McNally, John Joseph *lawyer*
†McNally, Terrence *playwright*
McNamara, J(ohn) Donald *retired lawyer, business executive*
McNamara, John Jeffrey *advertising executive*
McNamara, Mary E. *nonprofit executive, asset manager, minister*
McNamee, Louise *advertising agency executive*
Mc Nicol, Donald Edward *lawyer*
McPherson, James Lowell *writer*
McPherson, Mary Patterson *academic administrator*
Mc Pherson, Paul Francis *publishing and investment banking executive*
McQuown, Judith Hershkowitz *author, financial advisor*
McSherry, William John, Jr. *lawyer, consultant*
Mc Shine, Kynaston Leigh *curator*
McTeer, Janet *actress*
McVeigh, James Patrick *investment banker*
Meachin, David James Percy *investment banker*
Meade, Marion *author*
Meadow, Lynne (Carolyn Meadow) *theatrical producer and director*
Meagher, James Proctor *editor*
†Meals, Gerald *umpire*
Means Coleman, Robin Renee' *communication educator*
Medenica, Gordon *publisher*
Medina, Standish Forde, Jr. *lawyer*
Medney, Tania Levy *advertising agency executive*
Meehan, Robert Henry *human resources executive, business educator*
Meehan, Sandra Gotham *advertising executive, communications consultant*
Mehta, A. Sonny *publishing company executive*
Mehta, Julie Mahendra *editor, writer*
Meier, Richard Alan *architect*
Meigher, S. Christopher, III *communications and media executive, publisher*
Meigs, James B. *editor-in-chief*
Meiklejohn, Donald Stuart *lawyer*
†Meily, Rene S. *communications executive*
Meisel, Martin *English and comparative literature educator*
Meisel, Perry *English educator*
Meisel, Steven *advertising photographer*
†Meisel, Susan Pear *artist, antique dealer, real estate broker*
Meiselas, Susan Clay *photographer*
Mele, Gregg Charles *management consultant, attorney*
†Melendez, Louis *sports association executive*
Mellins, Robert B. *pediatrician, educator*
Mellins, Thomas Harrison *architectural historian*
Melloan, George Richard *editor, columnist, writer*
Melnik, Selinda A. *lawyer*
Melone, Joseph James *insurance company executive*
Meltzer, Milton *author*
Melvin, Russell Johnston *magazine publishing consultant*
Menack, Steven Boyd *lawyer, mediator*
Menaker, Ronald Herbert *bank executive*
Mencher, Melvin *journalist, retired educator*
Mendell, Oliver M. *banking executive*
Mendelson, Haim *artist, educator, art gallery director*
†Mendez, Ruben Policarpio *diplomat*
†Mendini, Douglas A. *publishing company executive, writer*
Menken, Alan *composer*
Menschel, Richard Lee *investment banker*
Mentz, Lawrence *lawyer*
Menuez, D. Barry *retired religious organization administrator*
Meranus, Arthur Richard *advertising agency executive*
Merchant, Ismail Noormohamed *film producer and director*
Mercorella, Anthony J. *lawyer, former state supreme court justice*
†Meriwether, Julius Edward (Chuck Meriwether) *umpire*
Meron, Theodor *law educator, researcher*
Merow, John Edward *lawyer*
Merrifield, Robert Bruce *biochemist, educator*
†Merrill, Edwin Durwood *umpire*
Merriss, Philip Ramsay, Jr. *banker*
Merritt, Bruce Gordon *lawyer*
Merritt, Michael Monroe *musician*
Mertens, Joan R. *museum curator, art historian*
Meserve, Mollie Ann *publisher*
Mesia, Augusto Fajardo *pathologist*
Mesnikoff, Alvin Murray *psychiatry educator*
Mesrop, Alida Yolande *academic administrator*
Messer, Thomas Maria *museum director*
Messinger, Ruth W. *borough president*
Messner, Thomas G. *advertising executive, copywriter*
Mestice, Anthony F. *bishop*
Mestres, Ricardo Angelo, Jr. *lawyer*
Metcalf, Karen *foundation executive*
Metcalf, William Edwards *museum curator*
Metsch-Ampel, Glenn Randy *lawyer, fundraiser*
Metz, Emmanuel Michael *investment company executive, lawyer*
Metz, Robert Roy *publisher, editor*
Mew, Calvin Marshall *advertising executive*
Meyaart, Paul Jan *distilling company executive*
Meyer, Edward Henry *advertising agency executive*
Meyer, Fred Josef *advertising executive*
Meyer, Karl Ernest *journalist*
Meyer, Melissa *artist*
Meyer, Pearl *executive compensation consultant*
Meyer, Pucci *newspaper editor*
Meyer-Bahlburg, Heino F. L. *psychologist, educator*
Meyerhoff, Erich *librarian, administrator*
Meyers, John Allen *magazine publisher*
Miano, Louis Stephen *arts advisor*
Michaels, Alan Richard *sports commentator*
Michaels, James Walker *magazine editor*
Michaels, Lorne *television writer, producer*
Michaelson, Arthur M. *lawyer*
Michals, Duane *photographer*
Michaud, Christopher *journalist*
Michel, Clifford Lloyd *lawyer, investment executive*
Michel, Henry Ludwig *civil engineer*
†Michel, Prakazrel (Pras) *musician, singer*
Michele, Robert Charles *investment management, portfolio manager*
Michels, Robert *psychiatrist, educator*
†Michels, William Charles *management consultant*
Michelsen, Christopher Bruce Hermann *surgeon*
Michelson, Gertrude Geraldine *retired retail company executive*
Michenfelder, Joseph Francis *public relations executive*
Midanek, Deborah Hicks *portfolio manager, director*
Middendorf, Henry Stump, Jr. *lawyer*
Middendorf, John Harlan *English literature educator*
†Middleberg, Don *company executive*
Middleton, David *physicist, applied mathematician, educator*
Mihailescu, Manuela *marketing executive*
Mikhail, Mona N. *education educator*
Mikita, Joseph Karl *broadcasting executive*
Milbank, Jeremiah *foundation executive*
Milder, Jay *artist*
Mildvan, Donna *infectious diseases physician*
Milgrim, Roger Michael *lawyer*
Miller, A. Gifford *city official*
Miller, Alan *software executive, management specialist*
†Miller, Andrew Kenneth *management consultant*
Miller, Arthur Madden *lawyer, investment banker*
Miller, B. Jack *investment company executive*
Miller, Caroline *editor-in-chief*
Miller, Charles Hampton *lawyer*
Miller, Darcy M. *publishing executive*
Miller, David *lawyer, advertising executive*
Miller, Douglas L. *stockbroker, money manager*
Miller, Edward Daniel *financial services executive*
Miller, Ernest Charles *management consultant*
Miller, Harry Brill *scenic designer, director, acting instructor, lyricist, interior designer*
Miller, Harvey R. *lawyer, bankruptcy reorganization specialist*
†Miller, Heidi G. *diversified financial company executive*
Miller, Israel *rabbi, university administrator*
Miller, John R. *accountant*
Miller, Lawrence *communications executive*
Miller, Linda Sarah *critical care, emergency room nurse*
Miller, Michael Jeffrey *editor, columnist*
Miller, Morgan Lincoln *textile manufacturing company executive*
Miller, Neil Stuart *financial officer, advertising executive*
Miller, Paul S(amuel) *lawyer*
Miller, Peggy A(nn) *lawyer*
Miller, Phebe Condict *lawyer, financial executive*
Miller, Philip Efrem *librarian*
Miller, Richard Allan *lawyer*
Miller, Richard Kidwell *artist, actor, educator*
Miller, Richard McDermott *sculptor*
Miller, Richard Steven *lawyer*
Miller, Robert *advertising executive*
Miller, Sam Scott *lawyer*
Miller, Steven Scott *lawyer*
Miller, Walter James *English and humanities educator, writer*
Miller, William Jacob *public relations executive*
Millett, Kate (Katherine Murray Millett) *political activist, sculptor, artist, writer*
Millstein, Ira M. *lawyer, lecturer*
Milmed, Paul Kussy *lawyer*
Milnes, Sherrill E. *baritone*
Milonas, Minos *artist, designer, poet*
Milton, Christian Michel *insurance executive*
Minard, Everett Lawrence, III *journalist, magazine editor*
Minarik, Else Holmelund (Bigart Minarik) *author*
Mincer, Jacob *economics educator*
Mines, Herbert Thomas *executive recruiter*
Minicucci, Robert A. *business executive*
Minkoff, Harvey Allen *English educator*
Minkowitz, Martin *lawyer, former state government official*
Minnelli, Liza *singer, actress*
Minotti, Diana Lynn *art appraiser, consultant*
Mintz, Donald Edward *psychologist, educator*
Mintz, Norman Nelson *investment banker, educator*
Mintz, Samuel Isaiah *English language educator, writer*
Mintz, Shlomo *conductor, violist, violinist*
Mintz, Walter *investment company executive*
Minuse, Catherine Jean *lawyer*
Mirante, Arthur J., II *real estate company executive*
Mirenburg, Barry Leonard *publisher, company executive, educator*
Misthal, Howard Joseph *accountant, lawyer*
Mitchell, Arthur *dancer, choreographer, educator*
Mitchell, Jerry *public affairs educator*
Mitchell, Richard Boyle *advertising executive*
Mitgang, Herbert *author, journalist*
Mitterand, Henri C. *education educator, writer*
†Mlynarczyk, Francis Alexander, Jr. *securities broker, investment manager*
Modlin, Howard S. *lawyer*
†Moed, Edward *company executive*
Moerdler, Charles Gerard *lawyer*
Moffett, Charles Simonton *museum director, curator, writer*
Mohler, Mary Gail *magazine editor*
Mohr, Jay Preston *neurologist*
Moise, Edwin Evariste *mathematician, educator*
Molho, Emanuel *publisher*
Mollica, Santo *percussionist, songwriter, performer*
Molnar, Lawrence *lawyer*
Moloney, Thomas Joseph *lawyer*
Molz, Redmond Kathleen *public administration educator*
†Mondello, Robert Charles *architect, writer*
Mondlin, Marvin *retail executive, antiquarian book dealer*
Monfasani, John *historian, educator*
Monge, Jay Parry *lawyer*
Monk, Debra *actress*
Monk, Meredith Jane *artistic director, composer, choreographer, film maker, director*
†Montague, Edward Michael *umpire*
Montgomery, Robert Humphrey, Jr. *lawyer*
Montorio, John Angelo *magazine editor*
Mooney, Richard Emerson *writer*
Moore, Andrew Given Tobias, II *investment banker, law educator*
Moore, Ann S. *magazine executive*
Moore, Anne *physician*
Moore, Donald Francis *lawyer*
†Moore, Frank Randolph *university official*
Moore, Franklin Hall, Jr. *lawyer*
Moore, Geoffrey Hoyt *economist*
Moore, Jane Ross *librarian*
Moore, John Joseph *lawyer*
Moore, Michael Watson *musician, string bass, educator*
Moore, Nicholas G. *finance company executive*
Moore, Paul, Jr. *bishop*
†Moore, Thomas A. *consumer products company executive*
Moore, Thomas Ronald (Lord Bridestowe) *lawyer*
Morales, Armando *artist*
†Moran, Kate *sculptor, photographer*
Moran, Martin Joseph *fundraising company executive*
Morath, Inge *photographer*
Morawetz, Cathleen Synge *mathematics educator*
Morehouse, Ward *human rights organization executive, publisher*
Moreira, Marcio Martins *advertising executive*
†Moreno, David *artist*
Morfopoulos, V. *metallurgical engineer, materials engineer*
Morgan, Frank Edward, II *lawyer*
Morgan, (George) Frederick *poet, editor*
Morgan, Jacqui *illustrator, painter, educator*
†Morgan, Jeffrey D. *publisher*
Morgan, Thomas Bruce *author, editor, public affairs executive*
Morgen, Lynn *public relations executive*
Morgenthau, Robert Morris *prosecutor*
†Mori, Mariko *video artist, photographer*
†Morillo, Mariano *journalist*
Morin, George Wilson *advertising agency executive*
Morley, Michael B. *public relations executive*
Moroz, Pavel Emanuel *research scientist*
Morphy, James Calvin *lawyer*
Morris, Clayton Leslie *priest*
Morris, Douglas Peter *recording company executive*
Morris, Edward William, Jr. *lawyer*
Morris, Eugene Jerome *lawyer*
Morris, James Peppler *bass*
Morris, John *composer, conductor, arranger*
Morris, Lynne Louise *psychotherapist*
Morris, Mark William *choreographer*
†Morris, Mary *writer, educator*
Morris, Stephen Burritt *marketing information executive*
Morris, Thomas Quinlan *hospital administrator, physician*
Morris, William Charles *investor*
†Morris, Wright *novelist, critic*
†Morrison, Dan G. *umpire*
Morrison, Patricia Kennealy *author*
Morrissey, Dolores Josephine *investment executive*
Morse, Edward Lewis *petroleum industry executive*
Morse, Stephen Scott *virologist, immunologist*
Mortimer, Peter Michael *lawyer*
Morton, Brian *writer, editor, educator*
Morton, Frederic *author*
Morton, James Parks *priest*
Moseley, Carlos DuPre *former music executive, musician*
Moses, Yolanda T. *academic administrator*
Moskin, John Robert *editor, writer*
Moskin, Morton *lawyer*
Moskovitz, Jim *radio, television and film producer, writer*
Moskowitz, Arnold X. *economist, strategist, educator*
†Mosley, Walter *writer*
Moss, Charles *advertising agency executive*
Moss, Lawrence Craig *lawyer*
Moss, Melvin Lionel *anatomist, educator*
Moss, William John *lawyer*
Moss-Salentijn, Letty (Aleida Moss-Salentijn) *anatomist*
Most, Jack Lawrence *lawyer, consultant*
Motley, Constance Baker (Mrs. Joel Wilson Motley) *federal judge, former city official*
Mottola, Thomas *entertainment company executive*
Motyl, Alexander John *political science educator*
†Mouchbahani, Christian Robert *banker*
†Mourad, Boaz Aaron *researcher, psychology educator*
Mow, Van C. *engineering educator, researcher*
Moy, Mary Anastasia *lawyer*
Moyer, David S. *executive search consultant*
Moyers, Bill D. *journalist*
Moyers, Judith Davidson *television producer*
Moyles, Philip Vincent, Jr. *financial services company executive*
Moyne, John Abel *computer scientist, linguist, educator*
Muccia, Joseph William *lawyer*
Muchnick, Richard Stuart *ophthalmologist*
Muckler, John *professional hockey coach, professional team executive*
Mueller, Shirley Anne *lawyer, real estate broker*
Mukamal, Steven Sasoon *lawyer*
Mukasey, Michael B. *federal judge*
†Muldow, Susan *publishing executive*
Mulhearn, Patrick F.X. *telecommunications company executive*
Mullaney, Thomas Joseph *lawyer*
†Mullen, Marie *actress*
Mullen, Peter P. *lawyer*
Muller, Charlotte Feldman *economist, educator*
Muller, Frank *mediator, arbitrator*
Muller, Henry James *journalist, magazine editor*
Muller, Jennifer *choreographer, dancer*
Mulligan, David Keith *consulting company executive, securities arbitrator*
Mulligan, Deanna Marie *management consultant*
Mulligan, Jeremiah T. *lawyer*
Mullman, Michael S. *lawyer*
Mulvihill, James Edward *periodontist*
Mundheim, Robert Harry *law educator*
Mundinger, Mary O'Neil *nursing educator*
Munhall, Edgar *curator, art history educator*
†Munro, Alice *author*
Munroe, George Barber *former mining and manufacturing company executive*
Munzer, Cynthia Brown *mezzo-soprano*
Munzer, Stephen Ira *lawyer*
Murase, Jiro *lawyer*
Murdoch, (Keith) Rupert *publisher*
Murdock, Robert Mead *art consultant, curator*
Murdolo, Frank Joseph *pharmaceutical company executive*
Murphy, Ann Pleshette *magazine editor-in-chief*
Murphy, Arthur William *lawyer, educator*
Murphy, Austin de la Salle *economist, educator, banker*
Murphy, Brian Stuart *internist, consultant*
Murphy, Charles Joseph *investment banker*
Murphy, Donna *actress*
Murphy, Elva Glenn *executive assistant*
Murphy, Helen *recording industry executive*
Murphy, James E. *public relations and marketing executive*
Murphy, James Gilmartin *lawyer*
Murphy, John Arthur *tobacco, food and brewing company executive*
Murphy, John Cullen *illustrator*
Murphy, John Joseph, Jr. *investment company executive*
Murphy, Mark Joseph *enterprise sales executive*
Murphy, Nora Sharkey *public relations executive*
Murphy, Peregine Leigh *priest*
Murphy, Ramon Jeremiah Castroviejo *physician, pediatrician*
Murphy, Richard William *retired foreign service officer, Middle East specialist, consultant*
Murphy, Rosemary *actress*
Murphy, Russell Stephen *dance company executive*
†Murphy, Tom *actor*
Murray, Allen Edward *retired oil company executive*
Murray, Bernard Joseph *former theology educator, former municipal government administrator*
Murray, Richard Maximilian *insurance executive*
Musgrave, R. Kenton *federal judge*
†Musham, Bettye Martin *consumer products executive*
Muskin, Victor Philip *lawyer*
Muslin, Lee *art gallery owner, artist*
Musser, Tharon *theatrical lighting designer, theatre consultant*
Muszynski, Cheryl Ann *neurosurgeon*
Muth, John Francis *newspaper editor, columnist*
Myers, Gerald E. *humanities educator*
Myerson, Toby Salter *lawyer*
Nabi, Stanley Andrew *investment executive*
Nachman, Ralph Louis *physician, educator*
Nadel, Elliott *investment firm executive*
Nadelberg, Eric Paul *brokerage house executive*
Nadich, Judah *rabbi*
Nadiri, M. Ishaq *economics educator, researcher, lecturer, consultant*
Naegle, Madeline Anne *mental health nurse, educator*
Naftalis, Gary Philip *lawyer, educator*
Nagler, Stewart Gordon *insurance company executive*
Nagourney, Herbert *publishing company executive*
Nahas, Gabriel Georges *pharmacologist, educator, writer*
Naiburg, Irving B., Jr. *publisher*
Nail, John Joseph *insurance company executive*
Nakamura, James I. *economics educator*
Nakanishi, Koji *chemistry educator, research institute administrator*
Nalls, Gayil Lynn *artist*
Nance, Allan Taylor *retired lawyer*
Nash, Edward L. *advertising agency executive*
†Nash, Graham William *singer, composer*
Nash, N. Richard *writer*
Nash, Paul LeNoir *lawyer*
Nassau, Michael Jay *lawyer*
Nathan, Andrew James *political science educator*
Nathan, Andrew Jonathan *lawyer, real estate developer*
Nathan, Frederic Solis *lawyer*
Nathan, Paul S. *editor, writer*
Natori, Josie Cruz *apparel executive*
Navasky, Victor Saul *magazine editor, publisher*
Nazem, Fereydoun F. *venture capitalist, financier*
Nazir, Tabinda *physician*
Neal, Patricia *actress*
Nebgen, Stephen Wade *stage producer*
Necarsulmer, Henry *investment banker*
Nederlander, James Morton *theater executive*
Needham, George Austin *investment banker*
Neff, Thomas Joseph *executive search firm executive*
Negroponte, John Dimitri *publishing company official, former diplomat*
†Neier, Aryeh *author, human rights organization administrator*
Neiman, LeRoy *artist*
Nelkin, Dorothy *sociology and science policy educator*
Nelson, Barbara Anne *judge*
Nelson, Barry *actor*
Nelson, Bruce Sherman *advertising agency executive*
Nelson, Edwin Stafford *actor*
Nelson, Iris Dorothy *retired guidance and rehabilitation counselor*
†Nelson, Roger R. *financial company executive*
Nelson, Wayne K. *advertising executive*
†Nemec, Yernita Ellen *artist, curator*
Nemser, Earl Harold *lawyer*
Nentwich, Michael Andreas Erhart *educator, consultant*
Nesbit, Robert Grover *management consultant*
Netzer, Dick *economics educator*
Neubauer, Peter Bela *psychoanalyst*
Neuberger, Roy R. *investment counselor*
Neuhaus, Richard John *priest, research institute president*
Neuspiel, Daniel Robert *pediatrician, epidemiologist*
Neuwirth, Alan James *lawyer*
Neuwirth, Robert Samuel *obstetrician, gynecologist*
Neveloff, Jay A. *lawyer*
Nevins, Arthur Gerard, Jr. *lawyer*
New, Maria Iandolo *physician, educator*
Newbold, Herbert Leon, Jr. *psychiatrist, writer*
Newcomb, Jonathan *publishing executive*
Newcombe, George Michael *lawyer*
Newell, Norman Dennis *paleontologist, geologist, museum curator, educator*
Newhouse, Nancy Riley *newspaper editor*
Newman, Alexander *psychologist*
Newman, Bernard *federal judge*
Newman, David Robert *magazine editor*
Newman, Elias *artist*
Newman, Frank Neil *bank executive*
Newman, Fredric Samuel *lawyer, business executive*
Newman, Howard Neal *lawyer, educator*
Newman, Lawrence Walker *lawyer*
Newman, Nancy *publishing executive*
Newman, Rachel *magazine editor*
Newman, Robert Gabriel *physician*
Newman, Samuel *trust company executive*
†Newman, William *real estate executive*
Ney, Edward N. *ambassador, advertising and public relations company executive*
Ng, Helen M. *financier, civil engineer*
Nibley, Andrew Mathews *editorial executive*
Niccolini, Dianora *photographer*

Nicholas, James A. surgeon, consultant, educator
Nicholls, Richard H. lawyer
Nichols, Carol D. real estate professional, association executive
Nichols, Edie Diane executive recruiter
Nicholson, Shelia Elaine senior print production manager
Nielsen, Nancy publishing executive
Nielsen Hayden, Patrick editor
Niemiec, David Wallace investment managment
Niesen, James Louis theater director
Niles, Nicholas Hemelright travel company executive
Nimetz, Gloria Lorch real estate broker, photographer
Nimetz, Matthew lawyer
Nimkin, Bernard William retired lawyer
Nirenberg, Louis mathematician, educator
Nisce, Lourdes radiologist
Nisenholtz, Martin Abram telecommunications executive, educator
Nivarthi, Raju Naga anesthesiology educator
Nixon, Agnes Eckhardt television writer, producer
Nixon, Shirnette pharmaceutical company administrator
Noback, Charles Robert anatomist, educator
Noddings, Nel education educator, writer
Nolan, Terrance Joseph, Jr. lawyer
Nolan, William Joseph, III banker
†Noman, Omar program manager, writer
Nonna, John Michael lawyer
Noonan, Susan Abert public relations executive
†Noonan, Tom playwright, actor, director
Norcia, Stephen William advertising executive
Nordquist, Stephen Glos lawyer
Norell, Mark Allen paleontology educator
Norfolk, William Ray lawyer
Norgren, William Andrew religious denomination administrator
Norman, Stephen Peckham financial services company executive
Norris, Floyd Hamilton financial journalist
North, Charles Laurence poet, educator
†North, Michael Jefferson librarian
North, Steven Edward lawyer
Norvell, Patsy artist
Norville, Deborah news correspondent
Norwick, Braham textile specialist, consultant, columnist
Notarbartolo, Albert artist
Novak, Gregory marketing professional
†Noveck, Madeline I. financial company executive
Novikoff, Harold Stephen lawyer
Novitz, Charles Richard television executive
Novogrod, Nancy Ellen editor
Nowick, Arthur Stanley metallurgy and materials science educator
Nugent, Nelle theater, film and television producer
Nusbacher, Gloria Weinberg lawyer
Nussbaum, Jeffrey Joseph musician
Nussbaumer, Gerhard Karl metals company executive
Nuzum, John M., Jr. banker
Nyren, Neil Sebastian publisher, editor
Oakes, John Bertram writer, editor
†Oakley, Charles professional basketball player
Oates, Joyce Carol author
Ober, Robert Fairchild, Jr. college president, retired government official
Oberly, Kathryn Anne lawyer
Oberman, Michael Stewart lawyer
Obermayer, Michael Erik Max management consultant
Obernauer, Marne, Jr. business executive
Obolensky, Ivan investment banker, foundation consultant, writer, publisher
O'Brien, Catherine Louise museum administrator
†O'Brien, Conan writer, performer, talk show host
O'Brien, Donal Clare, Jr. lawyer
O'Brien, Geoffrey Paul editor, writer
O'Brien, John Graham lawyer
O'Brien, Kevin J. lawyer
O'Brien, Patricia G. psychiatric clinical nurse, administrator
O'Brien, Tim writer
Ochoa, Manuel, Jr. oncologist
Ochs, Michael editor, librarian, music educator
O'Connell, Daniel S. private investments professional
†O'Connell, Jane B. school administrator
O'Connell, Margaret Ellen editor, writer
O'Connell, Margaret Sullivan lawyer
O'Connor, John Joseph Cardinal archbishop, former naval officer
O'Connor, Kevin computer programing executive
O'Connor, William Matthew lawyer
O'Dair, Barbara editor
O'Dea, Dennis Michael lawyer
Odenweller, Robert Paul philatelist, association executive, airline pilot
O'Doherty, Brian writer, filmmaker
O'Donnell, John Logan lawyer
O'Donnell, Rosie television personality, comedienne, actress
Oechler, Henry John, Jr. lawyer
Oettgen, Herbert Friedrich physician
Offit, Morris Wolf investment management executive
Offit, Sidney writer, educator
Ogden, Alfred lawyer
O'Grady, Beverly Troxler investment executive, counselor
O'Grady, John Joseph, III lawyer
O'Hara, Alfred Peck lawyer
O'Hare, Joseph Aloysius academic administrator, priest
Ohira, Kazuto theatre company executive, writer
Ohlson, Douglas Dean artist
O'Horgan, Thomas Foster composer, director
O'Keefe, Vincent Thomas clergyman, educational administrator
Okrent, Daniel magazine editor, writer
Okuhara, Tetsu artist, photographer
Okun, Herbert Stuart diplomat, educator
Okun, Melanie Anne venture capitalist
Olbrick, Valerie Lyn management consultant, information technologist
Oldenburg, Claes Thure artist
Oldenburg, Richard Erik auction house executive
Oldfield, Barney entertainment executive
Oldham, Joe editor
Oldham, John Michael physician, psychiatrist, educator
Oldham, Todd fashion designer
†O'Leary, Mary Louise television producer, educator
Olick, Philip Stewart lawyer
Oliensis, Sheldon lawyer
Olinger, Carla D(ragan) medical advertising executive
Olinger, Chauncey Greene, Jr. investment executive, editorial consultant
Olitski, Jules artist
Oliva, Lawrence Jay academic administrator, history educator
Olivares, Rene Eugenio translator
Olivere, Raymond Louis illustrator, artist, portrait painter
Olsen, David Alexander insurance executive
Olsen, David George executive search consultant
†Olson, Peter publishing executive
Olson, Thomas Francis, II communications company executive
Olsson, Carl Alfred urologist
†Oltion, Jerry author science fiction
Olyphant, David cultural, educational association executive
†Omolade, Barbara sociology educator
O'Neal, Hank entertainment producer, business owner
O'Neil, James Peter financial printing company executive
O'Neil, John Joseph lawyer
O'Neil Bidwell, Katharine Thomas fine arts association executive, performing arts executive
O'Neill, George Dorr business executive
O'Neill, Joseph J. futures market executive
O'Neill, June Ellenoff economist
O'Neill, Mary Jane health agency executive
O'Neill McGivern, Diane nursing educator
Ono, Yoko conceptual artist, singer, recording artist
Opel, John R. business machines company executive
Openshaw, Helena Marie investment company executive, portfolio manager
†Opie, Catherine photographer
Oppenheimer, Martin J. lawyer
Oppenheimer, Michael physicist
Oppenheimer, Paul English comparative literature educator, poet, author
Oppenheimer-Nicolau, Siobhan think tank executive
Orazi, Attilio anatomic pathologist, researcher, educator
Orben, Jack Richard investment company executive
Orden, Stewart L. lawyer
Ordorica, Steven Anthony obstetrician, gynecologist, educator
O'Reilly, Richard John pediatrician
Orell, Lawrence advertising executive
Oreskes, Irwin biochemistry educator
Oreskes, Susan private school educator
Orlov, Darlene management consultant
O'Rorke, James Francis, Jr. lawyer
Orovitz, Marcia Carol publishing executive
†Orozco, Gabriel artist
Orwoll, Mark Peter magazine editor
Osborn, Donald Robert lawyer
Osborn, Frederick Henry, III foundation executive
Osborn, June Elaine pediatrician, microbiologist, educator, foundation administrator
Osborne, Mary Pope writer
Osborne, Michael Piers surgeon, researcher, health facility administrator
Osborne, Richard de Jongh mining and metals company executive
Osborne, Stanley de Jongh investment banker
†Osgood, Charles news broadcaster, journalist
Osgood, Richard Magee, Jr. applied physics and electrical engineering educator, research administrator
Oshima, Michael W. lawyer
Osnos, Gilbert Charles management consultant
Osnos, Peter Lionel Winston publishing executive
†Osorio, Pepon artist
Oster, Martin William oncologist
Ostergard, Paul Michael bank executive
Ostling, Richard Neil journalist, author, broadcaster
Ostrager, Barry Robert lawyer
Ostrander, Thomas William investment banker
Ostrow, Joseph W. advertising executive
O'Sullivan, Eugene Henry retired advertising executive
O'Sullivan, John editor
O'Sullivan, Thomas J. lawyer
Ousley, John Douglas priest
Ovadiah, Janice cultural institute executive
Owen, Richard federal judge
Owen, Robert Dewit lawyer
Oxman, David Craig lawyer
†Oz, Frank (Frank Richard Oznowicz) puppeteer, film director
†Ozawa, Seiji conductor, music director
Ozick, Cynthia author
Paalz, Anthony L. beverage company executive
Paaswell, Robert Emil civil engineer, educator
Pace, Eric Dwight journalist
Pace, Stephen Shell artist, educator
Pacella, Bernard Leonardo psychiatrist
Pack, Leonard Brecher lawyer
Packard, George Randolph journalist, educator
Packard, Stephen Michael lawyer
Padberg, Manfred Wilhelm mathematics educator
Paddock, Anthony Conaway financial consultant
Pados, Frank John, Jr. investment company executive
Pagano, Michael Pro advertising executive
†Page, James Patrick (Jimmy Page) musician
Page, Jonathan Roy investment analyst
Pais, Abraham physicist, educator
Pakter, Jean medical consultant
Paladino, Daniel R. lawyer, beverage corporation executive
Palermo, Robert James architect, consultant, inventor
Paley, Alan H. lawyer
Palion, Peter Thaddeus financial planner
Palitz, Anka A. Kriser manufacturing and distributing company executive
Palitz, Bernard G. finance company executive
Palitz, Clarence Yale, Jr. commercial finance executive
Pall, Ellen Jane writer
Palmer, Edward Lewis banker
Palmer, John M. medical administrator
Palmer, Paul Richard librarian, archivist
Palmer, Robert Baylis librarian
Palmer, Wayne Lewis television director and producer
Palmeri, Marlaina principal
Palmiere, Catherine Emilia executive recruiter
Palmieri, Victor Henry lawyer, business executive
Paltos, Robert Nicholas sales executive
Paneth, Donald Joseph editor, writer
Panken, Peter Michael lawyer
Paolucci, Robert D. translator
Papa, Vincent T. insurance company executive
Papalia, Diane Ellen human development educator
†Papell, Gertrude Helen poet, retired librarian
Papernik, Joel Ira lawyer
Pappas, Michael financial services company executive
Paquette, Brian Christopher university administrator, dean
Paradise, Robert Richard publishing executive
Pardes, Herbert psychiatrist, educator
Paret, Dominique petroleum company executive
Parish, J. Michael lawyer, writer
Park, Chung painter, educator, computer software developer
Parker, Alice composer, conductor
Parker, James retired curator
Parker, Nancy Winslow artist, writer
Parkin, Gerard Francis Ralph chemistry educator, researcher
Parks, Gordon Roger Alexander film director, author, photographer, composer
Parlato, Charles advertising executive
Parnes, Robert Mark architect
Paro, Jeff publisher
Parseghian, Gene talent agent
Parsons, Estelle actress
†Parsons, Richard Dean communications company executive
Parver, Jane W. lawyer
Pasanella, Giovanni architect, architectural educator
Passage, Stephen Scott energy company executive
Passoff, Michelle writer
Paster, Howard G. public relations, public affairs company executive
Pastores, Gregory McCarthy physician, researcher
Paterson, Katherine Womeldorf writer
Paton, Leland B. investment banker
Patriarca, Silvana education educator
Patrick, Hugh Talbot economist, educator
Patterson, Ellmore Clark banker
Patterson, Perry William publishing company executive
Patterson, Robert Porter, Jr. federal judge
Patton, Joanna advertising agency owner
Paul, Andrew Mitchell venture capitalist
Paul, Eve W. lawyer
Paul, Herbert Morton lawyer, accountant, taxation educator
Paul, James William lawyer
Paul, Les entertainer, inventor
Paul, Robert David management consultant
Pauley, Jane television journalist
Pauley, Rhoda Anne communications and marketing executive
†Paulson, Henry Merritt, Jr. venture capitalist, investment banker
Paulus, Eleanor Bock professional speaker, author
Pavarotti, Luciano lyric tenor
Pavia, George M. lawyer
Pavone, Joseph Anthony designer, display
Paxton, Robert Owen historian, educator
Payton-Wright, Pamela actress
†Paz, Alberto advertising executive
Peacock, Molly poet
†Pearce, Carol Ann editor, writer
Pearlstine, Norman editor
†Pearson, Bruce artist
Pearson, Clarence Edward management consultant
Pearson, Henry Charles artist
Peasback, David R. recruiting company executive
Peaslee, James M. lawyer
Pechukas, Philip chemistry educator
†Peck, Andrew Jay federal judge
Peck, Richard Wayne novelist
Peck, Thomas newspaper publishing executive
Peckolick, Alan graphic designer
Pedersen, William architect
Pedley, Timothy Asbury, IV neurologist, educator, researcher
Peebler, Charles David, Jr. advertising executive
Peet, Charles D., Jr. lawyer
Pei, Chien Chung architect
Pei, Ieoh Ming architect
Peloso, John Francis Xavier lawyer
Pelster, William Charles lawyer
Pelz, Robert Leon lawyer
†Pendragon, Michael Malefica writer, poet
†Penland, Diane Robinson educator
Penn, Stanley William journalist
Pennebaker, Donn Alan film director, lecturer
Pennoyer, Paul Geddes, Jr. lawyer
Pennoyer, Robert M. lawyer
Peper, George Frederick editor
Pepper, Allan Michael lawyer
Peppers, Jerry P. lawyer
Peppet, Russell Frederick accountant
Perahia, Murray pianist
Percus, Jerome Kenneth physicist, educator
Perelman, Ronald Owen diversified holding company executive
Peress, Maurice symphony conductor, musicologist
Peretz, Eileen interior designer
Pérez-Rivera, Francisco writer
Peritz, Abraham Daniel business executive
Perkiel, Mitchel H. lawyer
Perkins, Lawrence Bradford, Jr. architect
Perkins, Leeman Lloyd music educator, musicologist
Perkins, Roswell Burchard lawyer
Perless, Ellen advertising executive
†Perlman, Cara Janet artist
Perlman, Itzhak violinist
Perlmuth, William Alan lawyer
Perlmutter, Alvin Howard television and film producer
Perlmutter, Diane F. communications executive
Perlmutter, Louis investment banker, lawyer
Perney, Linda newspaper editor
Perrette, Jean Rene investment banker
Perry, David priest
Perry, Douglas opera singer
Perry-Widney, Marilyn (Marilyn Perry) international finance and real estate executive, television producer
Perschetz, Martin L. lawyer
Persell, Caroline Hodges sociologist, educator, author, researcher, consultant
Pershan, Richard Henry lawyer
Pesin, Ella Michele journalist, public relations professional
Peskin, Charles physicist, educator
Pesner, Carole Manishin art gallery owner
Pesola, Helen Rostata nursing administrator
Petchesky, Rosalind Pollack political science and women's studies educator
Peters, Alton Emil lawyer
Peters, Robert Wayne organization executive, lawyer
Peters, Roberta soprano
Petersen, Barry Rex news correspondent
Peterson, Charles Gordon retired lawyer
Peterson, M. Roger international investment banker, retired manufacturing executive, retired air force officer
Peterson, Peter G. investment company executive
†Petito, Frank A. neurologist
Petkanics, Bryan G. lawyer
Petraro, Vincent L. lawyer
Petrella, Fernando Enrique diplomat
Petrie, Donald Joseph banker
Pettibone, Peter John lawyer
Pettit, William Dutton, Sr. investment executive, consultant
Petz, Edwin V. real estate executive, lawyer
Petzal, David Elias editor, writer
†Peyton, Elizabeth Joy writer
Pfaff, Donald W. neurobiology and behavior educator
Pfeffer, David H. lawyer
Pfeiffer, Jane Cahill former broadcasting company executive, consultant
Pfund, Niko publishing executive
Phelps, Edmund Strother economics educator
Philipp, Elizabeth R. manufacturing company executive, lawyer
Phillips, Anthony Francis lawyer
Phillips, Barnet, IV lawyer
Phillips, Charles Gorham lawyer
†Phillips, David Robert umpire
Phillips, Elizabeth Joan marketing executive
Phillips, Gerald Baer internal medicine scientist, educator
†Phillips, Graham Holmes retired advertising executive
Phillips, Joyce Martha human resources executive
Phillips, Pamela Kim lawyer
Phillips, Reneé magazine editor, author, public speaker
Phillips, Russell Alexander, Jr. retired foundation executive
Phillips, Stone newscaster
Phoon, Colin Kit-Lun pediatric cardiologist
Pickholz, Jerome Walter advertising agency executive
Piel, Gerard science editor, publisher
Piemonte, Robert Victor association executive
Pier, Gwen Marie art gallery director
Pierce, Charles Eliot, Jr. library director, educator
Pierce, Morton Allen lawyer
Pierpoint, Powell lawyer
Pierri, Mary Kathryn Madeline cardiologist, critical care physician, educator
Pietruski, John Michael, Jr. biotechnology company executive, pharmaceuticals executive
Pietrzak, Alfred Robert lawyer
Pigott, Irina Vsevolodovna educational administrator
Pike, Laurence Bruce retired lawyer
Pilcz, Maleta psychotherapist
Pilgrim, Dianne Hauserman art museum director
Pincus, Lionel I. venture banker
Pinczower, Kenneth Ephraim lawyer
Pinczuk, Aron physicist
Pinkard, Lee S. marketing and communications executive
Pinna, Michael Anthony financial consultant
Piombino, Nicholas psychotherapist
Piore, Emanuel Rueven physicist
Piper, Thomas Laurence, III investment banker
Pirani, Conrad Levi pathologist, educator
Pirsig, Robert Maynard author
Pisano, Ronald George art consultant
Pi-Sunyer, F. Xavier medical educator, medical investigator
Pitt, Jane medical educator
Pittman, Preston Lawrence executive assistant
Piven, Frances Fox political scientist, educator
Plain, Belva writer
†Plant, Robert Anthony singer, composer
Plaskitt, Piers sales and marketing executive
Platnick, Norman I. curator, arachnologist
Platt, Nicholas Asian affairs specialist, retired ambassador
Plavinskaya, Anna Dmitrievna artist
Plimpton, George Ames writer, editor, television host
Plottel, Jeanine Parisier foreign language educator
Plottel, Roland lawyer
Plum, Fred neurologist
Podd, Ann newspaper editor
Podracky, John Robert police and law enforcement historian, curator
Pogrebin, Letty Cottin writer, lecturer
†Pogue, Donald C. federal judge
Poirier, Richard English educator, literary critic
Polacco, Patricia children's author, illustrator
Polak, Werner L. lawyer
Polenz, Joanna Magda psychiatrist
Polevoy, Nancy Tally lawyer, social worker, genealogist
Polisar, Leonard Myers lawyer
Polisi, Joseph W(illiam) academic administrator
Polito, Robert writer
Poll, Robert Eugene, Jr. bank executive
†Pollack, Barbara Grace writer
Pollack, Milton federal judge
Pollack, Robert Elliot biologist, educator
Pollack, Stanley P. lawyer
Pollack, Stephen J. stockbroker
Pollak, Martin Marshall lawyer, training company executive
Pollan, Stephen Michael lawyer, personal finance expert, speaker, author
Pollard, Bobbie Jean librarian, educator
Pollitt, Katha writer, poet, educator
Pollock-O'Brien, Louise Mary public relations executive
Polonetsky, Jules city commissioner
Pomerantz, Charlotte writer
Pomeroy, Lee Harris architect
Pompadur, I. Martin communications executive
†Poncino, Larry umpire
Pool, Mary Jane design consultant, writer
Poole, William Daniel writer, editor
Poons, Larry artist
Poor, Peter Varnum producer, director
Pope, Albert Augustus financier
†Pope, Leavitt Joseph broadcast company executive
Pope, Liston, Jr. writer, journalist
Porizkova, Paulina model, actress
Portale, Carl publishing executive
Porter, Karl Hampton orchestra musical director, conductor
Porter, Liliana Alicia artist, photographer, painter, print and filmaker
Porter, Stephen Winthrop stage director
Porterfield, Christopher magazine editor, writer
Posamentier, Alfred Steven mathematics educator, university administrator
Posen, Susan Orzack lawyer
Poshni, Iqbal Ahmed microbiologist
Posin, Kathryn Olive choreographer
Posner, Donald art historian
Posner, Gerald author, lawyer
Posner, Jerome Beebe neurologist, educator
Posner, Louis Joseph lawyer, accountant

Rothfeld, Michael B. theatrical productions executive, investor
Rothholz, Peter Lutz public relations executive
Rothman, Bernard lawyer
Rothman, David J. history and medical educator
Rothman, Henry Isaac lawyer
Rothman, James Edward cell biologist, educator
Rothschild, Amalie Randolph filmmaker, producer, director, digital artist, photographer
Rothschild, Joseph political science educator
†Rothstein, Edward Benjamin writer, critic
Rothstein, Gerald Alan investment company executive
Rotstein, Andrew David lawyer
Rotter, Steven Jeffrey company executive
Roubos, Gary Lynn diversified manufacturing company executive
Roufa, Arnold gynecologist, obstetrician
Rouhana, William Joseph, Jr. business executive
Rover, Edward Frank lawyer
Rovine, Arthur William lawyer
Rovit, Richard Lee neurological surgeon
Rowan, John Patrick city official
Rowe, John Wallis university administrator, medical executive
Rowen, Ruth Halle musicologist, educator
Rowland, Esther E(delman) college dean, retired
Rowland, Lewis Phillip neurologist, medical editor, educator
Rozel, Samuel Joseph lawyer
Rozen, Jerome George, Jr. research entomologist, museum curator and research administrator
Ruben, William Samuel marketing consultant
Rubenfeld, Stanley Irwin lawyer
Rubenstein, Arthur Harold medical school official and dean, physician
Rubenstein, Howard Joseph public relations executive
Rubenstein, Joshua Seth lawyer
Rubin, Albert Louis physician, educator
Rubin, Harry Meyer entertainment industry executive
Rubin, Howard Jeffrey lawyer
Rubin, Jane Lockhart Gregory lawyer, foundation executive
Rubin, Joel Edward consulting company executive
Rubin, Richard Allan lawyer
Rubin, Robert Samuel investment banker
Rubin, Stephen Edward editor, journalist
Rubin, Theodore Isaac psychiatrist
Rubino, Victor Joseph academic administrator, lawyer
Rubinstein, Alina Anna psychiatrist
Rubinstein, Frederic Armand lawyer
Rudd, Nicholas marketing communications company executive
Rudel, Julius conductor
Ruder, William public relations executive
Rudin, Max Allen publishing executive
Rudin, Scott film and theatre producer
Rudman, Mark poet, educator
Rudoff, Sheldon lawyer
Ruebhausen, Oscar Melick lawyer
Ruegger, Philip T., III lawyer
Ruggie, John Gerard political science educator, diplomat
Rumore, Martha Mary pharmacist, educator
Rumschitzki, David Sheldon chemical engineering educator
Rupp, George Erik academic administrator
Rusch, William Graham religious organization administrator
Ruscha, Edward artist
Rushefsky, Steven graphic artist
Rusmisel, Stephen R. lawyer
Russo, Anthony Joseph public relations professional
Russo, Gregory Thomas lawyer
Russo, Thomas Anthony lawyer
Russotti, Philip Anthony lawyer
Rutishauser, Urs Stephen cell biologist
Ryan, J. Richard lawyer
Ryan, Michael E. newspaper publishing executive
Ryan, Regina Claire (Mrs. Paul Deutschman) editor, book packager, literary agent
Ryder, John George psychologist
Rylant, Cynthia author
Ryman, Robert Tracy artist
Rzewnicki, Janet C. state official
Sabat, Robert Hartman magazine editor
Sabatini, David Domingo cell biologist, biochemist
Sabel, Bradley Kent lawyer
Sabet, Hormoz entrepreneur
Sabino, Catherine Ann magazine editor
Sabosik, Patricia Elizabeth publisher, editor
†Sacca, Annalisa Italian literature educator
Sacerdote, Peter M. investment banker
Sachar, David Bernard gastroenterologist, medical educator
†Sachar, Louis writer prose
Sachdev, Ved Parkash neurosurgeon
Sachs, David lawyer
Sack, Robert David judge
Sacks, David G. retired distilling company executive, lawyer
Sacks, Ira Stephen lawyer
Sacks, Oliver Wolf neurologist, writer
Sacks, Temi J. public relations executive
Saddler, Donald Edward choreographer, dancer
Sadegh, Ali M. mechanical engineering educator, researcher, consultant
Sadock, Benjamin James psychiatrist, educator
Safer, Jay Gerald lawyer
Safer, Morley journalist
Safir, Howard police commissioner
Saft, Stuart Mark lawyer
Sager, Clifford J(ulius) psychiatrist, educator
Sahid, Joseph Robert lawyer
Saiman, Martin S. lawyer
St. Clair, Michael art dealer
Saint-Donat, Bernard Jacques finance company executive
†St. Pierre, Nakia Catherine consultant
Sakai, Hiroko trading company executive
Sakita, Bunji physicist, educator
Salans, Lester Barry physician, scientist, educator
Salant, Ari medical advertising writer
Sale, (John) Kirkpatrick writer
Salembier, Valerie Birnbaum publishing executive
Salerno, Frederic V. telecommunications company executive
Salerno-Sonnenberg, Nadja violinist
Salgo, Peter Lloyd internist, anesthesiologist, broadcaster, jounalist, lecturer, consultant
Salinger, Jerome David author
Salisbury, Nancy convent director
Salman, Robert Ronald lawyer
Salmans, Charles Gardiner banker
Salom, Roberto financial executive
Salonen, Esa-Pekka conductor
Salonga, Lea actress, singer
Salter, Kevin Thornton lawyer
Salter, Mary Jo poet
Saltz, Carole Pogrebin publisher
Samelson, Judy editor
Samet, Michael communications executive
Samman, Juan M. prosthodontist
Sampras, Pete tennis player
Samuel, Raphael lawyer
Samuels, Leslie B. lawyer
Sanchez, Miguel Ramon dermatologist, educator
Sand, Leonard B. federal judge
Sanders, Richard Louis executive editor
Sandler, Adam actor
Sandler, Kenneth Bruce advertising executive
Sandler, Lucy Freeman art history educator
Sandler, Robert Michael insurance company executive, actuary
Sandler, Ross law educator
Sands, Harry psychologist, health administrator, researcher
†Sandum, Howard E. literary agent
†Sanford, Eric lawyer
Sanseverino, Raymond Anthony lawyer
Santiago-Hudson, Ruben actor
Santlofer, Jonathan artist, educator
Santoro, Charles William investment banker
Saphir, Richard Louis pediatrician
Sappin, Edward Jonathan financial advisor
Sarachik, Myriam Paula physics educator
†Sargent, Herb writer, television producer
Sargent, Joseph Dudley insurance executive
Sargent, Pamela writer
Sarkis, J. Ziad management consultant
Sarnelle, Joseph R. electronic publishing specialist, magazine and newspaper editor
Sarnoff, Irving retired psychology educator, author
Sartori, Giovanni political scientist
Sassoon, Andre Gabriel lawyer
Sassoon, Countess Ingrid Anny von Siemering Shuenemann de Gehrs writer, illustrator, graphic artist, educator
Satine, Barry Roy lawyer
Sattan, William Daniel interior designer
Sauerhaft, Stan public relations executive, consultant
Saul, John Woodruff, III writer
Saunders, Arlene opera singer
Saunders, Mark A. lawyer
Saunders, Paul Christopher lawyer
†Savage, Tom poet, video librarian
Savas, Emanuel S. public management and public policy educator
Savell, Polly Carolyn lawyer
Savitt, Susan Schenkel lawyer
Savory, Mark management consultant, insurance company executive
Savrin, Louis lawyer
Sawyer, (L.) Diane television journalist
Saxe, Leonard social psychologist, educator
Saxena, Brij B. biochemist, endocrinologist, educator
Saxon, Wolfgang Erik Georg journalist
Sayre, Linda Damaris human resources professional
Scaffidi, Judith Ann school volunteer program administrator
Scammell, Michael writer, translator
Scannell, Herb broadcast executive
Scarborough, Charles Bishop, III broadcast journalist, writer
Scarola, John Michael dentist, educator
Scaturro, Philip David investment banker
Scelsa, Joseph Vincent sociologist
Schaap, Richard Jay journalist
†Schacht, Henry Brewer retired manufacturing executive
Schachter, Oscar lawyer, educator, arbitrator
Schade, Malcolm Robert lawyer
Schafer, Milton composer, pianist
Schaffer, Kenneth B. communications executive, satellite engineer, inventor, consultant
Schaffner, Bertram Henry psychiatrist
Schaffner, Cynthia Van Allen writer, curator, lecturer
Schain, Randy David computer software executive, venture capitalist
Schallert, Edwin Glenn lawyer
Schama, Simon historian, educator, author
Schapiro, Donald lawyer
Schapiro, Miriam artist
Schaub, Sherwood Anhder, Jr. management consultant
Schechner, Richard theater director, author, educator
†Scheck, Barry C. legal association administrator, educator
Scheeder, Louis theater producer, director, educator
†Scheer, Linda Canfield staff development specialist
Scheiman, Eugene R. lawyer
Schein, Gerald D. publishing executive
Scheindlin, Raymond Paul Hebrew literature educator, translator
Scheindlin, Shira A. federal judge
Scheler, Brad Eric lawyer
Scher, Irving lawyer
†Scherry, Howard Jay hotel reservation agent
Schick, Harry Leon investment company executive
Schickele, Peter composer
Schiff, Andrew Newman physician, venture capitalist
Schiff, David Tevele investment banker
Schiff, Marlene Sandler entrepreneur
Schiffrin, Andre publisher
Schilling, Warner Roller political scientist, educator
Schillinger, Liesl Katharine journalist
†Schimel, Lawrence David writer
Schindler, Alexander Moshe rabbi, organization executive
Schirmeister, Charles F. lawyer
Schiro, James J. brokerage house executive
Schisgal, Murray Joseph playwright
Schizer, Zevie Baruch lawyer
Schlang, David real estate executive, lawyer
Schlang, Joseph performing company executive
Schlein, Miriam author
Schlesinger, Arthur (Meier), Jr. writer, retired educator
Schlesinger, David Adam newspaper editor
Schlesinger, Sanford Joel lawyer
†Schlesinger, Yaffa sociology educator
Schless, Phyllis Ross investment banker
Schley, William Shain otorhinolaryngologist
Schlittler, Gilberto Bueno former UN official, political science educator
Schlosser, Herbert S. broadcasting company executive
Schmemann, Serge journalist
Schmertz, Eric Joseph lawyer, educator
Schmertz, Mildred Floyd editor, writer
Schmidt, Charles Edward lawyer
Schmidt, Daniel Edward, IV lawyer
Schmidt, Joseph W. lawyer
Schmidt, Stanley Albert editor, writer
Schmitter, Charles Harry electronics manufacturing company executive, lawyer
Schmolka, Leo Louis law educator
Schnall, David Jay management and administration educator
Schneck, Jerome M. psychiatrist, medical historian, educator
Schneider, Greta Sara economist, financial consultant
Schneider, Harold Lawrence lawyer
Schneider, Howard lawyer
Schneider, JoAnne artist
Schneider, Martin Aaron photojournalist, filmmaker, public advocate
Schneider, Mathieu hockey player
Schneider, Willys Hope lawyer
Schneiderman, Irwin lawyer
Schneier, Harvey Allen physician, pharmaceutical researcher
Schoell, William Robert editor, author
Schoen, Rem investment executive
Schoenfeld, Robert Louis biomedical engineer
Schonberg, Harold Charles music critic, columnist
Schoonmaker Powell, Thelma film editor
Schoonover, Jean Way public relations consultant
Schor, Laura Strumingher executive director, historian
Schorer, Suki ballet teacher
Schorr, Brian Lewis lawyer, business executive
Schorsch, Ismar clergyman, Jewish history educator
Schotter, Andrew Roye economics educator, consultant
Schrade, Rolande Maxwell Young composer, pianist, educator
Schrader, Michael Eugene columnist, editor
†Schrecker, Ellen Wolf historian, educator, editor
Schreiber, Paul Solomon lawyer
Schreyer, Leslie John lawyer
†Schrieber, Paul umpire
Schroeder, Aaron Harold songwriter
Schroeder, Edmund R. lawyer
Schubart, Mark Allen arts and education executive
Schueller, Thomas George lawyer
Schuhart, Anne Dashley (Susan Schuhart Zito) actress
Schuker, Eleanor Sheila psychiatrist, educator
Schulhof, Michael Peter entertainment, electronics company executive
Schulman, Mark Allen market research company executive
Schult, Frederick Charles, Jr. history educator
Schulte, Stephen John lawyer, educator
Schulz, Ralph Richard publishing consultant
Schumacher, Robert Denison banker
Schuman, Patricia Glass publishing company executive, educator
Schupak, Leslie Allen public relations company executive
Schur, Jeffrey advertising executive
Schur, Joan Brodsky secondary education educator, curriculum developer
Schuster, Carlotta Lief psychiatrist
Schuster, Karen Sutton administrator
Schwab, Frank, Jr. management consultant
Schwab, George David social science educator, author
Schwab, Terrance W. lawyer
Schwartz, Alan Victor advertising agency executive
Schwartz, Allen G. federal judge
Schwartz, Anna Jacobson economic historian
Schwartz, Barry Fredric lawyer, diversified holding company executive
Schwartz, Bernard Leon space and communications company executive
Schwartz, Carol Vivian lawyer
Schwartz, Daniel Bennett artist
Schwartz, Herbert Frederick lawyer
Schwartz, Irving Leon physician, scientist, educator
Schwartz, James Evan lawyer
Schwartz, Kenneth Ernst communications executive
Schwartz, Lois C. instructional technologist, consultant
Schwartz, Marvin lawyer
Schwartz, Melvin physics educator, laboratory administrator
Schwartz, Mischa electrical engineering educator
Schwartz, Renee Gerstler lawyer
Schwartz, Robert George retired insurance company executive
Schwartz, Roselind Shirley Grant podiatrist
Schwartz, Stephen Lawrence composer, lyricist
Schwartz, William lawyer, educator
Schwarz, Ekkehart Richard Johannes architect, urban designer
Schwarz, Frederick August Otto, Jr. lawyer
Schwarz, Ralph Jacques engineering educator
Schwed, Peter author, retired editor and publisher
Schwedler, Jillian Marie researcher
Schweitzer, George communications executive
Schwind, Michael Angelo law educator
†Sciarra, Daniel physician, consultant in neurology
†Sclafani, Anthony Paul plastic surgeon, educator, biomedical researcher
Scorsese, Martin film director, writer
Scott, Dale Allan major league umpire
Scott, Margaret Simon mortgage broker
Scott, Stanley DeForest real estate executive, former lithography company executive
†Scott, Willard Herman radio and television performer
Scott, William Clement, III entertainment industry executive
Scotti, Gavin A. advertising executive
Scotto, Renata soprano
Scribner, Charles, III publisher, art historian, lecturer
Scurry, Richardson Gano, Jr. investment management company financial executive
Seadler, Stephen Edward business and computer consultant, social scientist
Seal popular musician
Seaman, Alfred Jarvis retired advertising agency executive
Seaman, Barbara (Ann Rosner) author
Seary, Lawrence Anthony cinematographer, news assignment editor
Seave, Ava publishing executive
Seborovski, Carole artist
Secunda, Eugene marketing communications executive, educator
Sedaka, Neil singer, songwriter
Sederbaum, Arthur David lawyer
Sedgwick, Robert Minturn lawyer
Sedlin, Elias David physician, orthopedic researcher, educator
See, Saw-Teen structural engineer
Seegal, Herbert Leonard retired department store executive
†Seeger, Pete folk singer, songwriter
Seely, Robert Daniel physician, medical educator
Seff, Leslie S. securities trader
Segal, George actor
Segal, George sculptor
Segal, Jonathan Bruce editor
Segal, Lore writer
Segal, Martin Eli retired actuarial and consulting company executive
Segalas, Hercules Anthony investment banker
Segall, Harold Abraham lawyer
Seid, Lynne advertising agency executive
Seidel, Selvyn lawyer, educator
Seiden, Henry (Hank Seiden) advertising executive
Seiden, Steven Arnold executive search consultant
Seidenberg, Rita Nagler education educator
Seidler, Sheldon graphic designer, art director, inventor, educator, painter, sculptor
†Seidman, Hugh poet, technical writer
Seidman, Samuel Nathan investment banker, economist
Seifert, Thomas Lloyd lawyer
Seiff, Eric A. lawyer
Seigel, Jerrold Edward historian, writer
Seigel, Stuart Evan lawyer
Seitz, Frederick former university administrator
Selby, Cecily Cannan dean, educator, scientist
Selby, Frederick Peter investment banker
Seldes, Marian actress
Seldin, Penny G. creative director, artist
Selig, Karl-Ludwig language and literature educator
Seliger, Mark Alan photographer
Seligman, Daniel editor
Seligman, Delice lawyer
Seligson, Carl H. management consultant
Selkowitz, Arthur advertising agency executive
Sellers, Peter Hoadley mathematician
†Seltzer, Bob public relations executive
Seltzer, Jeffrey Lloyd investment banker
Seltzer, Joanne Lynn artist
Seltzer, Leo documentary filmmaker, educator, lecturer
Seltzer, Richard C. lawyer
Selver, Paul Darryl lawyer
Semaya, Francine Levitt lawyer
Semple, Robert Baylor, Jr. newspaper editor, journalist
Sendak, Maurice Bernard writer, illustrator
Sendax, Victor Irven dentist, educator, dental implant researcher
Sennett, Richard sociologist, writer
†Senouf, Yvonne Gabrielle art gallery administrator
Senzel, Martin Lee lawyer
Serbaroli, Francis J. lawyer, educator, writer
Serdans, Rebecca Sybille nurse
Serebrier, José musician, conductor, composer
Serota, Susan Perlstadt lawyer
Serrano, Andres artist
Servodidio, Pat Anthony broadcast executive
Sessions, Roy Brumby otolaryngologist, educator
†Setia, Rajiv Kumar research analyst
Setrakian, Berge lawyer
Settipani, Frank G. news correspondent
Seuk, Kook Jing (Joon Ho) foundation administrator
Severs, William Floyd actor
Seward, George Chester lawyer
Sexton, John Edward lawyer, dean, law educator
Seymore, James W., Jr. magazine editor
Seymour, Everett Hedden, Jr. lawyer
Seymour, Lesley Jane magazine editor-in-chief
Shaffer, Peter Levin playwright
Shaffer, Richard communications executive
Shaheen, George T. management consultant
†Shahid, Sam N. advertising executive
†Shaikh, Ayaz R. lawyer
Shaine, Frederick Mordecai newspaper executive, consultant
Shainess, Natalie psychiatrist, educator
Shair, David Ira human resources executive
Shalit, Hanoch imaging scientist, executive
Shallcross, Deanne investment company executive
Shamberg, Barbara A(nn) psychologist
†Shambroom, Paul artist, photographer
Shane, Rita opera singer, educator
Shanks, David publishing executive
Shanman, James Alan lawyer
Shapiro, Ellen M. graphic designer, writer, inventor
Shapiro, Harvey poet
Shapiro, Jerome Gerson lawyer
Shapiro, Joel Elias artist
Shapiro, Judith R. anthropology educator, academic administrator
Shapiro, Marvin Lincoln communications company executive
Shapiro, Mary J. writer, researcher, speech writer
Shapiro, Robert Frank investment banking company executive
Shapiro, Theodore psychiatrist, educator
Shapoff, Stephen H. financial executive
Sharp, Anne Catherine artist, educator
Sharp, Daniel Asher foundation executive
Sharp, J(ames) Franklin finance educator, investment portfolio manager
Sharpton, Alfred Charles minister, political activist
Shatan, Chaim Felix psychiatrist, medical educator, expert on Vietnam veterans, traumatic stress pioneer
Shaw, Alan Roger financial executive, educator
Shaw, (George) Kendall artist, educator
Shaw, Robert Bernard retired lawyer
Shays, Rona Joyce lawyer
Shea, Dion Warren Joseph university official, fund raiser
Shea, Edward Emmett lawyer, educator, author
Shea, James William lawyer
Shechtman, Ronald H. lawyer
Sheehan, Robert C. lawyer
Sheehan, Susan writer
Sheehy, Gail Henion author
Sheft, Peter Ian lawyer
Sheinman, Morton Maxwell editor, consultant, writer, photographer
Shelby, Jerome lawyer
Sheldon, Eleanor Harriet Bernert sociologist
Sheldon, Sidney author, producer
Shelley, Carole actress
Shelp, Ronald Kent non-profit business and trade association executive, author, lecturer, consultant
Shen, Michael lawyer
Shepard, Stephen Benjamin journalist, magazine editor
Shepard, Thomas Rockwell, III advertising sales executive
Shepherd, Gillian Mary physician
Shepherd, Kathleen Shearer Maynard television executive

Strum, Jay Gerson lawyer
Struve, Guy Miller lawyer
Stuart, Carole publishing executive
Stuart, Jane Elizabeth film and video executive
Stuart, Lori Ames public relations executive
Stuart, Lyle publishing company executive
Studin, Jan publishing executive
Stupin, Susan Lee investment banker
Stupp, Herbert William municipal official
Sturges, John Siebrand management consultant
Sturtevant, Peter Mann, Jr. television news executive
Stutman, Leonard Jay research scientist, cardiologist
Stutzmann, Nathalie classical vocalist
†Styblo Beder, Tanya financial engineer, educator
Subak-Sharpe, Gerald Emil electrical engineer, educator
Subin, Florence lawyer
Sucharipa, Ernst diplomat
Sugarman, Irwin J. lawyer
Sugarman, Robert Gary lawyer
†Sugden, Samuel M. lawyer
Sugihara, Kenzi publishing executive
Sugiyama, Kazunori music producer
Suhr, J. Nicholas lawyer
†Sui, Anna fashion designer
Sulcer, Frederick Durham advertising executive
Sulimirski, Witold Stanislaw banker
Sulkowicz, Kerry J. psychiatrist, psychoanalyst, consultant
Sullivan, Eugene John Joseph manufacturing company executive
Sullivan, Jim artist
Sullivan, Stephen Gene psychiatrist, pharmacologist, administrator
Sullivan, Timothy J. journalist
Sult, Jeffery Scot performing company executive, playwright, director, actor
Sultanik, Kalman professional society administrator
Sulzberger, Arthur Ochs newspaper executive
Sulzberger, Arthur Ochs, Jr. newspaper publisher
Summer, Sharon publisher
Summerall, Pat (George Allan Summerall) sportscaster
†Sun, Jeffrey C. legal educator
Sun, Ji research scientist
Sun, Tung-Tien medical science educator
†Sundukov, Alexei artist
Supino, Anthony Martin lawyer
Surrey, Milt artist
Suskind, Dennis A. investment banker
Sussman, Alexander Ralph lawyer
Sussman, David William lawyer
Sussman, George David academic administrator
Sussman, Gerald publishing company executive
Sussman, Jeffrey Bruce public relations and marketing executive
Sussman, Leonard Richard foundation executive
Sustendal, Diane consultant
Sutherland, Dame Joan retired soprano
Sutter, Laurence Brener lawyer
Sutton-Straus, Joan M. journalist
Svenson, Charles Oscar investment banker
Sverdlik, Samuel Simon physiatrist, physician
Svinkelstin, Abraham Joshua information technology executive
Swain, Robert artist
Swann, Brian writer, humanities educator
Swanson, David Heath agricultural company executive
Swanzey, Robert Joseph data processing executive
Swarz, Jeffrey Robert securities analyst, neuroscientist
Sweed, Phyllis publishing executive
Sweeney, Thomas Joseph, Jr. lawyer
Sweezy, Paul Marlor editor, publisher
Swensen, J. Scott investment manager
Swenson, Steven M. broadcast executive
Swid, Stephen Claar business executive
Swift, John Francis health care advertising company executive
†Swistel, Daniel George surgeon
Sykes, John communications company executive
Sykes, Jolene publishing executive
Sylla, Richard Eugene economics educator
Szenasy, Susan Selma magazine editor
Szer, Wlodzimierz biochemist, educator
Tabachuk, Emelia banker
Tabler, William Benjamin architect
Tafel, Edgar architect
Tagliabue, Paul John national football league commissioner
Talbot, Phillips Asian affairs specialist
Talese, Gay writer
Talese, Nan Ahearn publishing company executive
Talley, Truman Macdonald publisher
Tallmer, Margot Sallop psychologist, psychoanalyst, gerontologist
Talmi, Yoav conductor, composer
Tan, Amy Ruth writer
Tanaka, Patrice Aiko public relations executive
Tancredi, Laurence Richard law and psychiatry educator, physician
Tannenbaum, Bernice Salpeter religious organization executive
Tanner, Harold investment banker
Tanselle, George Thomas English language educator, foundation executive
Tapella, Gary Louis manufacturing company executive
Tàpies, Antoni painter, sculptor
Tapley, Donald Fraser university official, physician, educator
Taran, Leonardo classicist, educator
Tarantino, Dominic A. retired professional services firm executive
Tarnopol, Michael Lazar bank executive
Tarter, Fred Barry advertising executive
†Tata, Terry Anthony umpire
Tatum, Wilbert Arnold editor, publisher
Tavel, Mark Kivey money management company executive, economist
Tayar, Memduh Ali architect
Taylor, Barbara Alden public relations executive
Taylor, Clyde Calvin, Jr. literary agent
Taylor, Humphrey John Fausitt information services executive
Taylor, Job, III lawyer
Taylor, John Chestnut, III lawyer
Taylor, Lance Jerome economics educator
Taylor, Paul choreographer
Taylor, Richard Trelore retired lawyer
Taylor, Richard William investment banker, securities broker
Taylor, Sherril Wightman broadcasting company executive
Taylor, Susan L. editor, magazine
Taylor, Terry R. editor, educator
†Taymor, Julie theater, film and opera director and designer
Tayson, Richard Allan office management director, writer, educator
Teachout, Terry writer, critic
Teclaff, Ludwik Andrzej law educator, consultant, author, lawyer
Teich, Howard Bernard lawyer, activist, public affairs specialist
Teiman, Richard B. lawyer
Telang, Nitin T. cancer biologist, educator
Tello Macias, Manuel diplomat
Temin, Davia B. marketing executive
Tempelman, Jerry Henry investment funds trader
Temple, Donald Edward medical association executive
Temple, Wick journalist
Tendler, David international trade company executive
Tenenbaum, Bernard Hirsh entrepreneur, educator
Tengi, Frank R. lawyer, insurance company executive
Tenney, Dudley Bradstreet lawyer
Tepper, Lynn Marsha gerontology educator
Teran, Timothy Eric Alba marketing professional
Terrell, J. Anthony lawyer
Terris, Lillian Dick psychologist, association executive
Terry, Frederick Arthur, Jr. lawyer
Terry, James Joseph, Jr. lawyer
Tertzakian, Hovhannes bishop
Testa, Michael Harold lawyer
Tester, Leonard Wayne psychology educator
Thackeray, Jonathan E. lawyer
Thal, Steven Henry lawyer
Thalacker, Arbie Robert lawyer
Thaler, Richard Winston, Jr. investment banker
Tharoor, Shashi world organization official, writer
Thayer, Russell, III airlines executive
Themelis, Nickolas John metallurgical and chemical engineering educator
Thigpen, Lynne actress
Thomas, Brooks publishing company executive
Thomas, Isiah Lord, III former professional basketball player, basketball team executive
Thomas, Robert Morton, Jr. lawyer
Thomas, Roger Warren lawyer
Thomas, Stephen Jay anesthesiologist
Thomas, Violeta de los Angeles real estate broker
Thomashow, Byron Martin pulmonary physician
†Thomasos, Denyse artist
Thompson, Gary W. public relations executive
Thompson, Katherine Genevieve lawyer
Thompson, Martin Christian news service executive
Thompson, Page advertising executive
Thomson, Gerald Edmund physician, educator
Thorne, Francis composer
Thornton, Charles H. engineering executive
Thoyer, Judith Reinhardt lawyer
Thrall, Donald Stuart artist
Thurman, Robert theology, religious studies educator
Tierney, Paul E., Jr. investment company executive
Tierno, Philip Mario, Jr. microbiologist, educator, researcher
Tietjen, John Henry retired biology and oceanography educator
Tighe, Maria Theresa paralegal
Tilley, Shermaine Ann molecular immunologist, educator
Tillinghast, David Rollhaus lawyer
Tilson, Dorothy Ruth word processing executive
Tilson Thomas, Michael symphony conductor
†Tiravanija, Rirkrit sculptor
Tisch, James Solomon diversified holding company executive
Tisch, Jonathan Mark hotel company executive
Tisch, Laurence Alan diversified manufacturing and service executive
Tisch, Preston Robert finance executive
Tishman, John L. realty and construction company executive
Tisma, Marija Stevan artist
Titone, Vito Joseph state supreme court justice
Tizzio, Thomas Ralph brokerage executive
Tobach, Ethel retired curator
Tober, Barbara D. (Mrs. Donald Gibbs Tober) editor
†Tobon, Maria-Elena conductor, flutist
Todd, Ronald Gary lawyer
Tofel, Richard Jeffrey communication executive
Toff, Nancy Ellen book editor
Tognino, John Nicholas financial services executive
†Toguc, Nurhan economics educator, researcher
Tolchin, Joan Gubin psychiatrist, educator
Toll, Barbara Elizabeth art gallery director
†Tom, Howard S. company executive
Tomashefsky, Philip biomedical researcher, educator
Tomasz, Alexander cell biologist
Tomka, Peter Slovakian diplomat
Tomkins, Calvin writer
Tomlinson, James Francis retired news agency executive
Tondel, Lawrence Chapman lawyer
Tong, Kaity anchor
Toobin, Jeffrey Ross writer, legal analyst
Toohey, Edward Joseph financial services company executive
Tooker, George artist
Toote, Gloria E. A. developer, lawyer, columnist
Torn, Rip (Elmore Rual Torn, Jr.) actor, director
Torreano, John Francis painter, sculptor
Torrenzano, Richard public affairs executive
Torres, Louis editor, writer
Tortorello, Nicholas John public opinion and market research company executive
Touborg, Margaret Earley Bowers non-profit executive
Tourlitsas, John Constantine radiologist
Toussaint, Allen Richard recording studio executive, composer, pianist
Towbin, A(braham) Robert investment banker
Towers, Robert restaurant executive
Townsend, Alair Ane publisher, municipal official
Townsend, Charles H. publishing executive
Townsend-Butterworth, Diana Barnard educational consultant, author
Townshend, Peter musician, composer, singer
Tozer, Elizabeth Farran interior and floral designer, philanthropist
Tozer, W. James, Jr. investment company executive
Tracey, Margaret dancer
Trachtenberg, Matthew J. bank holding company executive
Tract, Marc Mitchell lawyer
Tracy, Janet Ruth legal educator, librarian
Trager, William biology educator
Train, John investment counselor, writer, government official
Trakas, George sculptor
Tramontine, John Orlando lawyer
Trapp, Peter Jarl Rudolf investment banker, farmer
Traub, J(oseph) F(rederick) computer scientist, educator
Traube, Victoria Gilbert lawyer
Traum, Jerome S. lawyer
Travers, Scott Andrew numismatist
Treadway, James Curran lawyer, investment company executive, former government official
Tree, Michael violinist, violist, educator
Tregellas, Patricia musical director, composer
Treitel, David Henry financial consultant
Trencher, Lewis advertising company executive
†Trent, Charles H., Jr. social work educator
Trigere, Pauline fashion designer
Trillin, Calvin writer, columnist
Trinkaus, John William management educator
Tronto, Joan Claire political science educator
Trost, J. Ronald lawyer
Trubin, John lawyer
Truesdell, Walter George minister, librarian
Tsai, Cynthia Ekberg entertainment executive
Tscherny, George graphic designer
†Tschida, Timothy J. (Tim Tschida) umpire
Tschumi, Bernard dean
Tse, Charles Yung Chang drug company executive
Tsividis, Yannis P. electrical engineering educator
Tsoucalas, Nicholas federal judge
Tuchman, Gary Robert television news correspondent
Tuchman, Phyllis critic
Tuck, Edward Hallam lawyer
Tucker, Alan David publisher
Tuckwell, Barry Emmanuel musician, music educator
Tudryn, Joyce Marie professional society administrator
Tulchin, David Bruce lawyer
Tune, Tommy (Thomas James Tune) musical theater director, dancer, choreographer, actor
Tung, Ko-Yung lawyer
Turino, Gerard Michael physician, medical scientist, educator
Turkel, Stanley hotel consultant, management executive
†Turnbaugh, Douglas Blair arts administration executive, author
Turndorf, Herman anesthesiologist, educator
Turner, Almon Richard art historian, educator
Turner, E. Deane lawyer
Turro, Nicholas John chemistry educator
Turso, Vito Anthony public relations executive
Turturro, John actor
Tusiani, Joseph foreign language educator, author
Tutun, Edward H. retired retail executive
Twiname, John Dean minister, health care executive
Tzimas, Nicholas Achilles orthopedic surgeon, educator
Ubell, Robert Neil editor, publisher, consultant
Uchitelle, Louis journalist
Udell, Richard lawyer
Udell Turshen, Rochelle Marcia publishing executive
Uehling, Judith Olson artist, painter, printmaker, sculptor
Uggams, Leslie entertainer
Uhry, Alfred Fox playwright
Ulanov, Alexander classics and comparative literature educator
Ule, Guy Maxwell, Jr. stockbroker
Ullman, Leo Solomon lawyer
Ulrey, Prescott David lawyer
Ulrich, Lars drummer
Underberg, Mark Alan lawyer
Underhill, Jacob Berry, III retired insurance company executive
Underweiser, Irwin Philip mining company executive, lawyer
Underwood, Joanna DeHaven environmental research and education organizations president
Ungaro, Susan Kelliher magazine editor
Unger, Irwin historian, educator
Unger, Peter Kenneth philosophy educator
Ungvarski, Peter J. nursing administrator
Upbin, Shari theatrical producer, director, agent, educator
Updike, Helen Hill investment manager, financial adviser
Uppman, Theodor concert and opera singer, voice educator
Upright, Diane Warner art dealer
Upshaw, Dawn soprano
Upson, Stuart Barnard advertising agency executive
Uram, Gerald Robert lawyer
Urdang, Alexandra book publishing executive
Uris, Leon Marcus author
Urkowitz, Michael banker
Urowsky, Richard J. lawyer
Urstadt, Charles Deane real estate executive
Vachss, Andrew Henry lawyer, author, juvenile justice and child abuse consultant
Valand, Theodore Lloyd media company executive
Valenti, Carl M. retired newspaper publisher
Valles, Jean-Paul manufacturing company executive
Van Allen, Barbara Martz marketing professional
Van Brunt, Albert Daniel advertising agency executive
VanBurkalow, Anastasia retired geography educator
Vance, Cyrus Roberts lawyer, former government official
Vander Heyden, Marsha Ann business owner
Van Dine, Vance investment banker
Vandross, Luther singer
Van Gorder, John Frederic lawyer
Van Gundy, Gregory Frank lawyer
Van Gundy, Jeff professional basketball coach
Van Halen, Eddie guitarist, rock musician
van Hengel, Maarten banker
†Vanover, Larry umpire
Van Sant, Peter Richard news correspondent
Van Setter, George Gerard lawyer
†Vant, Elizabeth D. health insurance company official
Varadhan, Srinivasa S. R. mathematics educator
Varet, Michael A. lawyer
Varnedoe, John Kirk Train museum curator
Varney, Carleton Bates, Jr. interior designer, columnist, educator
†Varone, Douglas Joseph choreographer
Vass, Joan fashion designer
Vassallo, Edward E. lawyer
Vassallo, John A. lawyer
†Vaughan, David George archivist
Vaughan, Edwin Darracott, Jr. urologist, surgeon
Vaughan, Linda publishing executive
Vaughan, Samuel Snell editor, author, publisher
Vecsey, George Spencer sports columnist
Vedder, Eddie singer
Vega, Marylois Purdy journalist
Vega, Matias Alfonso lawyer
Velayo, Richard Soriano psychologist, educator, researcher
Verdol, Joseph Arthur chemist
Vergilis, Joseph Semyon mechanical engineering educator
Vernon, Arthur educational administrator
Vernon, Darryl Mitchell lawyer
Versfelt, David Scott lawyer
Veru, Theodore advertising agency executive
Vessup, Jolene Adriel pastoral counselor
Vicente, Esteban artist
†Vick, Edward H. advertising executive
†Vickers, John A. hotel executive
Vidal, David Jonathan insurance company executive, journalist
Vidovich, Danko Victor neurosurgeon, neuroradiologist, researcher
Viener, John D. lawyer
Viertel, Jack theatrical producer, writer
Vig, Vernon Edward lawyer
Vilcek, Jan Tomas medical educator
†Villarreal, Raul artist, graphic designer
†Virga, Vincent Philip writer, picture editor, researcher, designer
Visconti, John C. financial consultant
Vitale, Alberto Aldo publishing company executive
Vitale, Dick commentator, sports writer
Vitale, Paul accountant
Vitkowsky, Vincent Joseph lawyer
Vitorovic, Nadezda artist, poet
Vittor, Kenneth Mark lawyer
Vittorini, Carlo publishing company executive
Vivera, Arsenio Bondoc allergist
Viviano, Sam Joseph illustrator
Vladeck, Bruce Charney health services administrator, policy educator
Vogel, Eugene Lewis lawyer
Vogelman, Joseph Herbert scientific engineering company executive
†Volchok, Susan writer
Volckhausen, William Alexander lawyer, banker
Volk, Norman Hans financial executive
Volk, Stephen Richard lawyer
Volpe, Joseph opera company administrator
Volpe, Thomas J. advertising executive
Von Brandenstein, Patrizia production designer
Von Foerster, Thomas physicist, editor
Von Fraunhofer-Kosinski, Katherina bank executive
von Mehren, Robert Brandt lawyer, retired
Vonnegut, Kurt, Jr. writer
Von Ringelheim, Paul Helmut sculptor
Voorhees, David William editor, historian
Voorsanger, Bartholomew architect
Vora, Ashok financial economist
†Vosloo, Paul public relations executive
Vuilleumier, François curator, biology and ornithology educator
†Vural, Volkan Turkish representative to UN
Vyskocil, Mary Kay lawyer
†Wachalter, Terry advertising executive
Wachner, Linda Joy apparel marketing and manufacturing executive
Wachtel, Norman Jay lawyer
Wachtel, Steven Edward social worker
Wachter, Susan Cohen advertising executive
Wacker, Susan Regina cosmetic design director
Wager, Walter Herman author, communications director
Wages, Robert Coleman equity investor
Wagner, Alan Cyril television and film producer
Wagner, Donald Arthur securities group executive
Wailand, George lawyer
Wainwright, Carroll Livingston, Jr. lawyer
Waite, David Allen software development executive
Wakefield, Dan author, screenwriter
†Wakeman, Thomas Herbert, III civil engineer, regional administrator
Waks, Jay Warren lawyer
Waksman, Byron Halsted neuroimmunologist, experimental pathologist, educator, medical association administrator
Waksman, Ted Stewart lawyer
Wald, Bernard Joseph lawyer
Wald, Richard Charles broadcasting executive
Wald, Sylvia artist
Walder, Eugene psychologist
Waldman, Robert Charles corporate entertainment executive
Walke, David Michael public relations executive
Walker, Alice Malsenior author
†Walker, Kara artist
Walker, Mort cartoonist
†Wall, Carolyn Raimondi communications executive
Wallace, G. David magazine editor
Wallace, Joyce Irene Malakoff internist
Wallace, Ken magazine publisher
Wallace, Mike television interviewer and reporter
Wallace, Nora Ann lawyer
Wallace, Patrick T. broadcast executive
Wallace, Stewart F. composer
Wallace, Thomas J. magazine editor-in-chief
Wallace, Walter C. lawyer, government official
Wallach, Eric Jean lawyer
†Wallach, Evan Jonathan judge, international law educator
Wallach, John Paul foundation administrator, author
Wallance, Gregory J. lawyer
Waller, Robert James writer
Waller, Tom marketing executive
Wallin, James Peter lawyer
Walman, Jerome psychotherapist, publisher, consultant, critic
Walpin, Gerald lawyer
Walsh, Annmarie Hauck research firm executive
†Walsh, James Francis, Jr. financial services executive
Walsh, Joseph Brennan ophthalmologist
Walsh, Thomas Gerard actuary
Walter, Ingo economics educator
Walters, Barbara television journalist
Walters, Milton James investment banker
Walters, Raymond, Jr. newspaper editor, author
Walton, Anthony John (Tony Walton) theater and film designer, book illustrator
†Walton, Kara Ann research and educational administrator
Walton, R. Keith academic administrator, lawyer
Walzer, Judith Borodovko academic administrator, educator
Wanek, William Charles public relations executive
Wang, Arthur Woods retired publisher
Wang, Frederick Mark pediatric ophthalmologist, medical educator
†Warbeck, Stephen composer
†Ward, Aileen retired humanities educator

Ward, Geoffrey Champion author, editor
Ward, Robert Joseph federal judge
Warden, John L. lawyer
Wareham, Raymond Noble investment banker
Waren, Stanley Arnold university administrator, theatre and arts center administrator, director
Warfield, Gerald Alexander composer, writer
Warner, Douglas Alexander, III banker
Warner, Edward Waide, Jr. lawyer
Warner, Miner Hill investment banker
Warner, Peter David publishing executive
Warner, Rawleigh, Jr. oil company executive
Warner, Scott Dennis investment banker
Warren, Irwin Howard lawyer
Warren, William Bradford lawyer
Warren, William Clements law educator
Warsawer, Harold Newton real estate appraiser and consultant
Warshauer, Irene Conrad lawyer
Warshaw, Leon J(oseph) physician
†Warshawsky, Stanford Seymour investment banker
Washburn, David Thacher lawyer
Washburn, Joan Thomas business owner, art gallery director
Washburn, Michael management consultant
Washington, Clarence Edward, Jr. insurance company executive
Wasser, Henry retired American literature and sociology educator
Wasserman, Albert film producer, writer, director
Wasserman, Louis Robert physician, educator
Watanabe, Roy Noboru lawyer
Waterhouse, Stephen Lee management consultant
†Waters, John film director, writer, actor
Waters, Michael Robert insurance management executive
Watkins, Charles Booker, Jr. mechanical engineering educator
Watson, James Lopez federal judge
Watson, Solomon Brown, IV lawyer, business executive
Watt, Douglas (Benjamin Watt) writer, critic
Wattleton, (Alyce) Faye educational association administrator
Watts, David Eide lawyer
Watts, Harold Wesley economist, educator
Waugh, Theodore Rogers orthopedic surgeon
Wax, Edward L. advertising executive
Waxenberg, Alan M. publisher
†Wayner, Richard A. investment banker, novelist
Wazen, Jack Joseph otolaryngologist, educator
Weathersby, George Byron association management executive
Weatherspoon, Teresa professional basketball player
Weaver, Richard Lindsay Newton financial services executive
Weber, Carol Martinez physician
Weber, Robert Maxwell cartoonist
Webster, John Kimball investment executive
Wechsler, Bradley J. film company executive
Wechsler, Gil lighting designer
Wechsler, Herbert retired legal educator
Wedgeworth, Ann actress
Weeks, David Frank foundation administrator
Weems, Carrie Mae photographer
Wehrmann, Renee Fainas french professor
Weida, Lewis Dixon marketing analyst, consultant
Weiksner, Sandra S. lawyer
Weil, Frank A. investment banker, lawyer
Weil, Gilbert Harry lawyer
†Weiland, Andrew J. orthopaedic surgeon
Weil-Garris Brandt, Kathleen (Kathleen Brandt) art historian
Weill, Sanford I. bank executive
Weinbaum, Sheldon biomedical engineer
Weinberg, H. Barbara art historian, educator, curator paintings and sculpture
Weinberg, Herschel Mayer lawyer
Weinberg, John Livingston investment banker
Weinberger, Harold Paul lawyer
Weiner, Andrew Jay lawyer
Weiner, Earl David lawyer
Weiner, Lawrence Charles artist
Weiner, Richard public relations executive
Weiner, Stephen Arthur lawyer
Weiner, Walter Herman banker, lawyer
Weingrow, Howard L. financial executive, investor
Weinschel, Alan Jay lawyer
Weinstein, Harvey film company executive
Weinstein, Herbert chemical engineer, educator
Weinstein, I. Bernard oncologist, geneticist, research administrator
Weinstein, Irving psychologist
Weinstein, Mark Michael lawyer
Weinstein, Martin aerospace manufacturing executive, materials scientist
Weinstein, Robert film company executive
Weinstein, Ruth Joseph lawyer
Weinstein, Sharon Schlein corporate communications executive, educator
Weinstein, Sidney university program director
Weinstock, Leonard lawyer
Weintraub, Daniel Ralph social welfare administrator
Weintz, Jacob Frederick, Jr. retired investment banker
Weintz, Walter Louis book publishing company executive
Weir, John Keeley lawyer
Weir, Peter Frank lawyer
Weisberg, Barbara writer, editor
Weisbrod, Carl lawyer, public official
Weisburd, Steven I. lawyer
Weiser, Martin Jay lawyer
Weisfeldt, Myron Lee physician, educator
Weisl, Edwin Louis, Jr. foundation executive, lawyer
Weiss, Donald L(ogan) retired sports association executive
Weiss, Lawrence N. lawyer
Weiss, Mark public relations executive
Weiss, Myrna Grace business consultant
Weiss, Paul Richard plastic surgeon
Weissman, Susan social services professional
Weissmann, Gerald medical educator, researcher, writer, editor
Weitz, Harvey lawyer
Weitz, John designer, writer
Weitzner, Harold mathematics educator
Weksler, Marc Edward physician, educator
Weld, Jonathan Minot lawyer
Weldon, Charles Jauverni actor
Welikson, Jeffrey Alan lawyer
†Welke, Timothy J. (Tim Welke) umpire
Welles, James Bell, Jr. lawyer
Wellin, Keith Sears investment banker
Welling, Kathryn Marie editor
Wellington, Harry Hillel lawyer, educator
Wellington, Sheila Wacks foundation administrator, psychiatry educator
Wellisz, Stanislaw economics educator
Wells, Linda Ann editor-in-chief
Wells, Patricia Trent auditor
Wells, Peter Scoville marketing executive
†Wels, D. (Deborah Wels) artist, educator
Welsh, Donald Emory publisher
Welt, Philip Stanley lawyer, consultant
Welts, Rick sports association executive
Wemple, William lawyer
Wender, Ira Tensard lawyer
Wender, Phyllis Bellows literary agent
Wenegrat, Saul S. arts administrator, art educator, consultant
Wenglowski, Gary Martin economist
Wenner, Jann Simon editor, publisher
Werfelman, William Herman, Jr. public relations executive
Werner, Andrew Joseph physician, endocrinologist, musicologist
Werner, Robert L. lawyer
Werthamer, N. Richard physicist
Weschler, Anita sculptor, painter
Wesely, Edwin Joseph lawyer
Wesley, John Mercer artist
Wessler, Sheenah Hankin psychotherapist, consultant
†West, Joseph Henry (Joe West) umpire
West, Paul Noden author
Westheimer, (Karola) Ruth Siegel psychologist, television personality
†Westhoff, John associate counsel
Westin, David broadcast executive
Westin, David Lawrence lawyer
Weston, Carol writer
Westwood, Donald C. opera executive
Wetschler, Ed editor
Wetterau, James Bernard electrical engineer
Wexelbaum, Michael lawyer
†Wexler, Allan architect, art educator
Wexler, Peter John producer, director, designer
Weyher, Harry Frederick lawyer
Wharton, Danny Carroll zoo biologist
Wharton, Ralph Nathaniel psychiatrist, educator
Wheeler, Michael broadcast executive
Whelan, Elizabeth Ann Murphy epidemiologist
Whelan, Stephen Thomas lawyer
Whelchel, Betty Anne lawyer
Whitaker, Mark Theis magazine editor
Whitcraft, Edward C. R. investment banker
White, Alexander William graphic designer, educator
White, Harry Edward, Jr. lawyer
White, John Patrick lawyer
White, Kate editor-in-chief
White, Keith Gordon bank executive
White, Lawrence J. economics educator
White, Mary Jo prosecutor
White, Russell publishing executive
White, Timothy Thomas Anthony writer, editor, broadcaster
Whitehead, Edgar Douglas urology educator
Whitehead, John Cunningham bank executive, diplomat, philanthropist
Whitehead, Robert theatrical producer
Whiteman, Douglas E. publisher
Whiteside, Duncan disability and child welfare foundation executive
†Whiting, Charles S(pencer), Jr. company executive, software consultant
Whiting, Gordon James investment banker
Whitman, Martin J. investment banker
Whitney, Edward Bonner investment banker
Whitney, Phyllis Ayame author
Whitsell, John Crawford, II retired general surgeon
Whittell, Polly (Mary) Kaye editor, journalist
Whittemore, Laurence Frederick private banker
Whoriskey, Robert Donald lawyer
†Wibisono, Makarim diplomat
Wicks, Sue basketball player
Widlund, Olof Bertil computer science educator
Wiegley, Roger Douglas lawyer
Wiener, Annabelle United Nations official
Wiener, Malcolm Hewitt foundation executive
Wiener, Marvin S. rabbi, editor, executive
Wiener, Solomon writer, consultant, former city official
Wiesel, Torsten Nils neurobiologist, educator
Wiggers, Charlotte Suzanne Ward magazine editor
Wigmore, Barrie Atherton investment banker
Wilbur, Melissa Ellen educator
Wilcox, John Caven lawyer, corporate consultant
†Wilcox, T.J. filmmaker
Wilder, Charles Willoughby lawyer, consultant
Wilds, Bonnie author, community volunteer
Wiley, Bradford publishing executive
Wilford, John Noble, Jr. news correspondent
Wilkinson, John Hart lawyer
Willett, Roslyn Leonore public relations executive, food service consultant, writer
Williams, Alun Gwyn publishing company executive
†Williams, Charles Herman (Charlie Williams) umpire
Williams, Charles Linwood (Buck Williams) retired professional basketball player
Williams, Dave Harrell investment executive
†Williams, James Edward musician, composer, author, producer, lecturer
Williams, Lowell Craig lawyer, employee relations executive
Williams, Michael lawyer, associate
†Williams, Sue artist
Williamson, Douglas Franklin, Jr. lawyer
†Williamson, Philemona artist
Willis, Beverly Ann architect
Willis, John Alvin editor
Willis, Thornton Wilson painter
Willis, William Ervin lawyer
Willkie, Wendell Lewis, II lawyer
Wilson, August playwright
Wilson, Basil academic administrator
Wilson, Christian Gideon portfolio manager
Wilson, F(rancis) Paul novelist, screenwriter
Wilson, James Reid, Jr. advertising executive
Wilson, Paul Holliday, Jr. lawyer
Wilson, Philip Duncan, Jr. orthopedic surgeon
Wilson, Robert M. theatre artist
†Wilson, Victor J. neuroscientist
Wimpfheimer, Michael Clark lawyer
Winawer, Sidney Jerome physician, clinical investigator, educator
Windelev, Claus engine manufacturing company executive
Windels, Paul, Jr. lawyer
Windhager, Erich Ernst physiologist, educator
Windsor, Patricia (Katonah Summertree) author, educator, lecturer
Winfrey, Carey Wells journalist, magazine editor
Wing, John Russell lawyer
Winger, Ralph O. lawyer
Winkleman, John Sandler public relations executive
Winship, Frederick Moery journalist
Winslet, Kate actress
†Winston, Stanley S. advertising executive
Winterer, Philip Steele lawyer
Winters, Mark Bennett personnel company executive
†Winters, Michael John umpire
†Winters, Terry artist
Wintour, Anna editor
Wirz, Pascal Francois trust company executive
Wise, Aaron Noah lawyer
Wise, David author, journalist
Wiseman, Cynthia Sue language educator
Wishnick, Marcia Margolis pediatrician, geneticist, educator
Wisner, Frank George insurance company executive, former ambassador
†Wisniewski, David author juvenile prose
Wit, David Edmund software and test preparation company executive
Wit, Harold Maurice investment banker, lawyer, investor
†Witherspoon, Roger academic administrator
†Witherspoon, Sophia professional basketball player
Witkin, Mildred Hope Fisher psychotherapist, educator
Witmeyer, John Jacob, III lawyer
Wittenberg, Kate editor
Wittman, Allan Henry publishing executive
Wittstein, Edwin Frank stage and film production designer
Wixom, William David art historian, museum administrator, educator
Wizen, Sarabeth Margolis compliance operations principal
Wogan, Robert broadcasting company executive
Wohl, Ronald Gene lawyer
Wojnilower, Albert Martin economist
Wolf, Gary Wickert lawyer
Wolf, James Anthony insurance company executive
Wolf, Peter Michael investment management and land planning consultant, educator, author
Wolfe, George C. theater director, producer, playwright
Wolfe, James Ronald lawyer
Wolfe, Thomas Kennerly, Jr. writer, journalist
Wolfert, Ruth Gestalt therapist
Wolff, Alexander Nikolaus writer
Wolff, Jesse David lawyer
Wolff, Kurt Jakob lawyer
Wolff, Richard Joseph public relations executive, consultant, historian
Wolff, Sanford Irving lawyer
Wolff, Virginia Euwer writer
Wolff, William F., III investment banker
Wolfson, Michael George lawyer
Wolins, Joseph artist
Wolitzer, Steven Barry investment banker
Wolkoff, Eugene Arnold lawyer
Wollman, Eric lawyer
Wolmer, Bruce Richard magazine editor
†Wolneki, Stephen S. church administrator
Wolson, Craig Alan lawyer
Wong, B.D. actor
†Wood, Frank actor
Wood, Kimba M. judge
Wood, Paul F. national health agency executive
Wood, Ronald musician
Woodcock, Les editorial director
Woodruff, Mark Reed magazine editor
Woodrum, Robert Lee executive search consultant
†Woods, Emily apparel executive
Woods, Ward Wilson, Jr. investment company executive
Woodward, Joanne Gignilliat actress
Worenklein, Jacob Joshua lawyer
Worgul, Basil Vladimir radiation scientist
Work, William H(enry) architect, consultant
Worman, Howard Jay physician, educator
Worth, Irene actress
Worthington, Lorne Raymond insurance executive
Wortman, Richard S. historian, educator
Wössner, Mark Matthias publishing company executive
Wray, Cecil, Jr. lawyer
†Wren, John advertising executive
Wright, Bob broadcasting executive
Wright, Faith-dorian artist
Wright, Gwendolyn art center director, writer, educator
Wright, Hugh Elliott, Jr. association executive, writer
Wright, Jane Cooke physician, educator, consultant
Wright, Joseph Robert, Jr. corporate executive
Wright, Michael Kearney retired public relations executive
Wright, Richard John business executive
Wright, Robert broadcast executive
Wriston, Walter Bigelow retired banker
Wrong, Dennis Hume sociologist, educator
Wruble, Brian Frederick private investor
Wu, Sarah Zheng investment banker
Wulf, Melvin Lawrence lawyer
Wunderman, Jan Darcourt artist
Wunderman, Lester advertising agency executive
Wuorinen, Charles Peter composer
Wurmfeld, Sanford artist, educator
Wyckoff, E. Lisk, Jr. lawyer
†Wyclef, Jean singer, record producer
Wyeth, James Browning artist
Wylie, James Malcolm educator
Wyn-Jones, Alun (William Wyn-Jones) software developer, mathematician
Wyse, Lois advertising executive, author
†Wyzner, Eugeniusz diplomat
Yablon, Leonard Harold publishing company executive
Yahr, Melvin David physician
Yalen, Gary N. insurance company executive
Yamin, Michael Geoffrey lawyer
Yancey, Richard Charles investment banker
Yao, David Da-Wei engineering educator
Yates, Marypaul textile company executive
Yeager, George Michael investment counsel executive
Yegulalp, Tuncel M. mining engineer, educator
Yeh, Hsu-Chong radiology educator
Yeh, Ming-Neng obstetrician, gynecologist
Yelenick, Mary Therese lawyer
Yellin, Victor Fell composer, music educator
Yerman, Fredric Warren lawyer
Yerushalmi, Yosef Hayim historian, educator
Yetman, Leith Eleanor academic administrator
Yoder, Patricia Doherty public relations executive
Yodowitz, Edward J. lawyer
†Yoffie, Erich H. (Rabbi) church administrator
Yorinks, Arthur children's author, writer, director
York, Alexandra writer, lecturer
York, Janet Brewster nurse, family and sex therapist, sculptor
York, Richard Travis art dealer
Young, Alice lawyer
Young, Ethan editor
Young, Genevieve Leman publishing executive, editor
Young, George Bernard, Jr. professional football team executive
Young, George Haywood, III investment banker
†Young, James R. corporate lawyer
Young, John Edward lawyer
Young, Jordan Marten cultural organization administrator, educator
Young, Michael Warren geneticist, educator
Young, Nancy lawyer
†Young, Neil musician, songwriter
Young, Paula Eva city official, journalist, writer
Young, Robert Craig banker
Young, Steve G. labor union administrator
Young, William F. legal educator
Youngerman, Jack artist, sculptor
Youngwood, Alfred Donald lawyer
Yuen, Janet financial analyst
Yunich, Peter B. publishing executive
Yurchenco, Henrietta Weiss ethnomusicologist, writer
Yurkiw, Mark Leo executive
Yurt, Roger William surgeon, educator
Zacharias, Thomas Elling real estate executive
Zackheim, Adrian Walter editor
Zahn, Paula newscaster
Zahn, Timothy writer
Zahnd, Richard H. professional sports executive, lawyer
Zaitzeff, Roger Michael lawyer
Zakim, David biochemist
Zakkay, Victor aeronautical engineering educator, scientist
Zaks, Jerry theatrical director, actor
Zammit, Joseph Paul lawyer
Zand, Dale Ezra business management educator
Zanetti, Richard Joseph publisher
Zara, Louis author, editor
Zarka, Albert Abraham author
Zarnowitz, Victor economist, educator
Zaslowsky, David Paul lawyer
Zatlin, Gabriel Stanley physician
Zauderer, Mark Carl lawyer
Zawistowski, Stephen Louis psychologist, educator
Zazula, Bernard Meyer physician administrator
Zedrosser, Joseph John lawyer
Zeldin, Richard Packer publisher
†Zelin, Madeleine think-tank executive
Zelnick, Strauss entertainment company executive
Zerin, Steven David lawyer
Zerman, Melvyn Bernard publishing company executive, author
Zeuschner, Erwin Arnold investment advisory company executive
Zevon, Susan Jane editor
Zhu, Ai-Lan opera singer
Zifchak, William C. lawyer
Zimand, Harvey Folks lawyer
Zimbalist, Efrem, III publishing company executive
Zimiles, Eric Ian government official
Zimmerman, Jean lawyer
Zimmerman, Kathleen Marie artist
Zimmerman, Sol Shea pediatrician
Zimmerman, William Edwin newspaper editor, publisher, writer
Zimmett, Mark Paul lawyer
Zinder, Norton David genetics educator, university dean
Zinn, Keith Marshall ophthalmologist, educator
†Zipay, Joanne Margaret theatre educator, director, dramaturge
Zirin, James David lawyer
Zirin, Ronald Andrew classics educator, psychoanalyst
Zirinsky, Bruce R. lawyer
†Zisfein, James physician
Zitrin, Arthur physician
Zlowe, Florence Markowitz artist
Zoeller, Donald J. lawyer
Zollar, Jawole Willa Jo art association administrator
Zolotow, Charlotte Shapiro author, editor
Zonana, Victor lawyer, educator
Zonszein, Joel endocrinologist
Zoogman, Nicholas Jay lawyer
Zornow, David M. lawyer
Zosike, Joanie Fritz theater director, actor
Zoullas, Deborah Anne auction company executive
Zucchi, Donna Marie insurance company executive
Zuck, Alfred Christian consulting mechanical engineer
Zucker, Howard lawyer
Zucker, Howard Alan pediatric cardiologist, intensivist, anesthesiologist
Zucker, Stefan tenor, writer, editor, radio broadcaster
Zuckerman, Mortimer Benjamin publisher, editor, real estate developer
Zukerman, Michael lawyer
Zuniga, Francisco sculptor, graphic artist
Zweibel, Joel Burton lawyer
Zwerling, Gary Leslie investment bank executive

New York Mills
Blank, William Russell mathematics educator

Newark
Hughes, Owen Willard artist

Newburgh
Copans, Kenneth Gary accountant
Cornell, Ryan Scott Michael communications company executive
Fallon, Rae Mary psychology educator, early childhood consultant
Flemming, Arlene Joan Dannenberg social worker, psychotherapist
Geiser, William Francis education educator
†Goldberg, Martin L. federal judge
Joyce, Mary Ann principal
Koskella, Lucretia C. real estate broker, appraiser
Liberth, Richard Francis lawyer
Milligram, Steven Irwin lawyer
†Ochs, Richard Wayne artist, gallery owner
Rubin, Jeffrey Michael psychologist
Saturnelli, Annette Miele school system administrator
Severo, Richard writer

Newport
Wilson, Eldon Ray minister

Newtonville
Apostle, Christos Nicholas *social psychologist*
†Conroy-LaCivita, Diane Catherine *city administrator*

Niagara Falls
Bharadwaj, Prem Datta *physics educator*
Dojka, Edwin Sigmund *civil engineer*
Gromosiak, Paul *historian, consultant, science and math educator*
Knowles, Richard Norris *chemist*
Laubaugh, Frederick *association executive, consultant*
Levine, David Ethan *lawyer*
Napolitano, Ralph E. *airport administrator*
Powers, Bruce Raymond *author, English language educator, consultant*
Shaghoian, Cynthia Lynne *accountant*

Niagara University
Martin, William Joseph *English language educator*
O'Leary, Daniel Francis *university dean*
Osberg, Timothy Michael *psychologist, educator, researcher*
Sarkees, Meredith Reid *political scientist, educator*

Nicksville
†Moshoyannis, Phillip Demetri Alexander *educator*

Niskayuna
Adler, Michael S. *control systems and electronic technologies executive*
Beharriell, Frederick John *German and comparative literature educator*
Billmeyer, Fred Wallace, Jr. *chemist, educator*
Burke, Joseph Eldrid *materials scientist*
Edelheit, Lewis S. *research physicist*
Fitzroy, Nancy deLoye *technology executive, engineer*
Huening, Walter Carl, Jr. *retired consulting application engineer*
Johnson, Ingolf Birger *retired electrical engineer*
Katz, Samuel *geophysics educator*
Lafferty, James Martin *physicist*
Mangan, John Leo *retired electrical manufacturing company executive, international trade and trade policy specialist*
Mihran, Theodore Gregory *retired physicist*
Omidvar, Bijan *structural engineer, researcher*
Stanard, Christopher Leon *statistician*
Whittingham, Harry Edward, Jr. *retired banker*
Zepp, Ann-Marie *rehabilitation nurse, adult nurse practitioner*

North Babylon
Löwenborg-Coyne, Kim *school administrator, musician*
Tipirneni, Tirumala Rao *metallurgical engineer*

North Bellmore
Klumpp, Barbara Anne *quality assurance and utilization review executive*

North Boston
Herbert, James Alan *writer*

North Point
Kohrt, Carl Fredrick *manufacturing executive, scientist*

North Salem
Burlingame, Edward Livermore *book publisher*
Larsen, Jonathan Zerbe *journalist*
Sloves, Marvin *retired advertising agency executive*

North Syracuse
Bragman, Michael J. *state legislator*
Brophy, Mary O'Reilly *industrial hygienist*
Kasouf, Joseph Chickery *lawyer*
Nilsen, Matthew Scott *computer programer*
Smith, Gail B. *small business owner*

North Tonawanda
Coleman, Kimberlee Michele *critical care nurse*
†Megahed, Mohamed Salah *neurologist, educator*
Rusin, Len M. *painter, educator*
†Whitbeck, Scott J. *business association executive*

North Woodmere
Aviles, Alice Alers *psychologist*

Northport
†Blume, Richard Stephen *medical company executive, physician*
Diamond, Stuart *educator, lawyer, business executive, consultant*
Gelfand, Andrew *software developer, consultant*
Hohenberger, Patricia Julie *fine arts and antique appraiser, consultant*
Krahel, Thomas Stephen *account executive*
Litchford, George B. *aeronautical engineer*
Reinertsen, Norman *retired aircraft systems company executive*
Weber, Ray Everett *engineering executive, consultant*

Norwich
†Broten, James M. *accountant*
Garzione, John Edward *physical therapist*
†Nassar, Elizabeth Fox *secondary educator*

Nyack
Borst, John Noble *television director, producer*
Bryant, Karen Worstell *financial advisor, investment company executive*
Degenshein, Jan *architect, planner*
Flood, (Hulda) Gay *editor, consultant*
Frawley-O'Dea, Mary Gail *clinical psychologist, psychoanalyst, educator*
Gaudy, Edward *landscape architect, consultant*
Hendin, David Bruce *literary agent, author, consultant, numismatist*
†Johnson, Judith Misner *educator*
Karp, Peter Simon *marketing executive*
Keil, John Mullan *advertising agency executive*
Mann, Kenneth Walker *retired minister, psychologist*
Oursler, Fulton, Jr. *editor, writer*
Paru, Marden David *fundraising executive*
Rossi, Harald Hermann *retired radiation biophysicist, educator, administrator*
Sandmeier, Harriet Virginia Heit *educational administrator*
Vaugel, Martine Olga *sculptor, educator*

Oakdale
Bragdon, Clifford Richardson *city planner, educator*
Lu, Yuxin *historian, linguist*
Meskill, Victor P. *college president, educator*

Oceanside
Hoffnung, Audrey Sonia *speech and language pathologist, educator*
Mills, James Spencer *author*
Reed, James William, Jr. *financial services, not for profit and injury prevention consultant*
Rubin, Hanan *retired insurance company executive*

Ogdensburg
Belgard, Stephen L. *airport administrator*
Krol, John Casimir *city manager, municipal planner*

Old Brookville
Fairman, Joel Martin *broadcasting executive*

Old Chatham
Teng, Juliet *artist*
Wright, Margaret Taylor *marketing consultant, publisher*

Old Westbury
Barbera, Anthony Thomas *accountant, educator*
DiGiovanna, Eileen Landenberger *osteopathic physician, educator*
†Ehrenreich, John Herman *psychologist*
Galatianos, Gus A. *computer executive, information systems consultant, educator*
Nelson, Edward Alan *electrical engineering educator*
O'Brien, Adrienne Gratia *communications educator*
Ozelli, Tunch *economics educator, consultant*
Schure, Matthew *college president*
van Wie, Paul David *secondary school educator, historian, educator*

Olean
Catalano, Robert Anthony *ophthalmologist, physician, hospital administrator, writer*
Gupta, Sanjay *psychiatrist*
Heyer, John Henry, II *lawyer*
Peters, Susan Mary *mental health nurse*

Olivebridge
Osborne, Seward Russell *writer*

Oneida
Hicks, Phyllis Ann *medical, surgical nurse*
Magee, William *state legislator*
Matthews, William D(oty) *lawyer, consumer products manufacturing company executive*
Moller, Jacqueline Louise *elementary education educator*
Pittner, Andrew Peter *landscape architect*
Stevens, James Walter *manufacturing representative*

Oneonta
Bergstein, Harry Benjamin *psychology educator*
Bucove, Arnold David *psychiatrist*
†Bulson, Christine E. *academic librarian*
Detweller, Richard Allen *college president, psychology educator*
Donovan, Alan Barton *college president*
†Falco, Gennaro Anthony *urologist, surgeon*
Gotsch, Susan D. *academic administrator, dean*
Grappone, William Eugene *clinical social worker, gerontologist, consultant*
Hill, Peter Waverly *lawyer*
Horner, Carl Matthew *chemistry educator*
Johnson, Richard David *retired librarian*
Lapidus, Patricia Jean *social worker*
†Lusins, John *neurologist*
Malhotra, Ashok Kumar *philosophy educator*
Matthews, Harry Bradshaw *dean*
Merilan, Michael Preston *astrophysicist, dean, educator*
†Michaelsen, Niels Henrik *painter, illustrator*
†Shrader, Douglas Wall, Jr. *philosophy educator*

Ontario
Loomis, Norman Richard *physician*
Nevil, Linda *nursing administrator*

Orangeburg
Adams, Barbara *artist, designer*
Furlong, Patrick Louis *health science association administrator*
Hennessy, James Ernest *academic administrator, telecommunications executive, retired*
Levine, Jerome *psychiatrist, educator*
Nixon, Ralph Angus *psychiatrist, educator, research neuroscientist*
Penney, Dixianne McCall *mental health services researcher, administrator*
†Seymour, James Craig *theater educator, actor, director*
Squires, Richard Felt *research scientist*
Stiles, Stephanie Johnson *English educator*
Ulrich, Max Marsh *executive search consultant*
Ye, Biqing *biomedical engineer, researcher*

Orchard Park
Bergmann, Cynthia *pediatrics nurse, lawyer*
Brown, Ruben Pernell *football player*
Butler, John *professional sports team executive*
†Flutie, Douglas Richard (Doug Flutie) *professional football player*
Fortunato, Pat Deakin *fine artist*
Franklin, Murray Joseph *retired steel foundry executive*
Fronckowiak, Felicia Ann *retired surgical services director*
Geiger, Loren Dennis *classical musician*
Holmes, Kathleen Marie *secondary education educator*
Lee, Richard Vaille *physician, educator*
†Moulds, Eric Shannon *professional football player*
†Phillips, Wade *professional football team coach*
Reed, Andre Darnell *professional football player*
Smith, Bruce *professional football player*
Thomas, Jimmy Lynn *financial executive*
Thomas, Thurman *professional football player*

Orient
Hanson, Thor *retired health agency executive and naval officer*

Ossining
Carter, Richard *publisher, writer*
Chervokas, John Vincent *town supervisor*
Daly, William Joseph *lawyer*
Getts, Nino *studio owner*
†Monroe, Stephen A. *educational administrator, financial consultant*
†Perlman, John Niels *educator, poet*
Pungello, Johanna Margaret *elementary education educator*
Reynolds, Calvin *management consultant, business educator*
Rothman, Barbara Schaeffer *speciali education educator*
Stein, Sol *publisher, writer, editor in chief*
Wolfe, Mary Joan *physician*

Oswego
Baitsell, Wilma Williamson *artist, educator, lecturer*
Fox, Michael David *art educator, visual imagist artist*
Gooding, Charles Thomas *psychology educator, retired college provost*
Gordon, Norman Botnick *psychology educator*
Greene, Stephen Craig *lawyer*
Jansen, Lambertus *judge*
Lisk, Edward Stanley *musician, educator, conductor*
Loveridge-Sanbonmatsu, Joan Meredith *communication studies educator*
Moody, Florence Elizabeth *education educator, retired college dean*
Nesbitt, Rosemary Sinnett *theatre educator*
Presley, John Woodrow *academic administrator*
†Sherman, Christopher Peter *customer service representative, musician*
Silveira, Augustine, Jr. *chemistry educator*
Smiley, Marilynn Jean *musicologist*
Thibault, Edward A. *criminology educator*
†Wallace, Jason Joseph *city official*

Owego
Davis, Joan *English language educator*
Kemp, Eugene Thomas *veterinarian*
McCann, Jean Friedrichs *artist, educator*
Smoral, Vincent J. *electrical engineer*

Oyster Bay
Amato, Camille Jean *manufacturing executive*
Bell, James Thomas *town official*
†Gambone, Kenneth F. *secondary education educator, English educator*
Ott, Gilbert Russell, Jr. *lawyer*
Robinson, Edward T., III *lawyer*
Russell, Mary Wendell Vander Poel *non-profit organization executive, interior*
Schwab, Hermann Caspar *banker*
Trevor, Bronson *economist*

Ozone Park
Catalfo, Betty Marie *health service executive, nutritionist*
Gebaide, Stephen Elliot *mathematics and computer science educator*

Palisades
Anderson, Margaret Tayler *real estate broker, career consultant*
Broecker, Wallace S. *geophysics educator*
Cane, Mark Alan *oceanography and climate researcher*
Davis, Dorothy Salisbury *author*
Hayes, Dennis Edward *geophysicist, educator*
Knowlton, Grace Farrar *sculptor, photographer, painter*
Krainin, Julian Arthur *film director, producer, writer, cinematographer*
Miller, Roberta Balstad *science administrator*
Polk, Milbry Catherine *media specialist*
Richards, Paul Granston *geophysics educator, seismologist*
Sykes, Lynn Ray *geologist, educator*

Palmyra
Frontuto, Penelope Kerr *mental health administrator*

Park Slope
Reisler, Helen Barbara *public relations consultant, publicity and product promotion*

Patchogue
Fogarty, James Vincent, Jr. *special education administrator, educator*
Gibbard, Judith R. *library director*
Gibbons, Edward Francis *psychobiologist*
Ihne, Edward Alan *railroad official, city official*
Lee-Valenti, Renee Ling Mee Bernadette *optometrist*
Orlowski, Karel Ann *elementary school educator*
Watkins, Linda Theresa *educational researcher*
Weisberg, David Charles *lawyer*

Patterson
Black, Charles Catus *industrial company executive*

Pawling
†Barbaro, Salvatore *educator*
Jones, James Earl *actor*
Peale, Ruth Stafford (Mrs. Norman Vincent Peale) *religious leader*
Stonesifer, John DeWitt *Episcopal priest, educator*
†Thomas, Cheryl Ann *educational administrator*
Wood, Christopher L. J. *consumer goods company executive*

Pearl River
Barik, Sudhakar *microbiologist, research scientist*
Caliendo, G. D. (Jerry Caliendo) *public utility executive*
Colman, Samuel *assemblyman*
Galante, Joseph Anthony, Jr. *computer programmer*
Griffith, Clark Dexter *consultant*
Jackson, Phillip Ellis *cause-related marketing executive, writer*
Projan, Steven Jay *microbiologist*

Peconic
Mitchell, Robert Everitt *lawyer*

Peekskill
Fishkind, Lawrence *marketing consultant*
Harte, Andrew Dennis *transportation company executive, travel agent*
Shea-Bergeron, Kevin Michael *artist, art therapist*
†Umland, James Frederick *painter*

Pelham
Gorman, Leo Joseph *priest*
Hanrahan, Michael G. *lawyer, business consultant*
Hearle, Douglas Geoffrey *public relations consultant*
Minick, Michael *publishing executive*
Niehoff, Karl Richard Besuden *financial executive*
Pough, Richard Hooper *conservationist*
Simon, Robert G. *lawyer*
Weiss, Stuart Lloyd *television and radio producer, tax attorney*

Penfield
Klose, Charlotte Ann *insurance agency owner*
†O'Kane, John Joseph *special education educator, administrator*
Perkins-Carpenter, Betty Lou *fitness company executive*

Penn Yan
Falvey, W(illiam) Patrick *judge*
Stiles, Leon Noble *genealogist*
Williams, Renee Arlene *secondary education educator*

Piermont
Berkon, Martin *artist*
Dusanenko, Theodore Robert *retired educator, county official*

Pine Bush
Wilson, David Palir *evangelist*

Pine Plains
†Finley, Madison K. *dean*

Pittsford
Benson, Warren Frank *composer, educator*
Cupini, Mariellen Louise *school district administrator*
Estin-Klein, Libbyada *advertising executive, medical writer*
Faloon, William Wassell *physician, educator*
Gallea, Anthony Michael *portfolio manager*
Green, Martin Lincoln *author, educator, publisher, consultant*
Herge, Henry Curtis, Jr. *consulting firm executive*
Hollingsworth, Jack Waring *mathematics and computer science educator*
Majchrzak, David Joseph *artist, printer*
Marshall, Joseph Frank *electronic engineer*
Saini, Vasant Durgadas *computer software company executive*
Snyder, Donald Edward *corporate executive*
Taub, Aaron Myron *healthcare administrator, consultant*
Thorndike, Elizabeth *educator*
Williams, Henry Ward, Jr. *lawyer*

Plainview
Butler, Alan M. *retired physical education educator*
Fein, Leona Moss *artist*
Feller, Benjamin E. *actuary*
Ginsberg, Carol Kerre *women's health nurse practitioner*
Kelemen, John *neurologist, educator*
Krauss, Leo *urologist, educator*
Lieberman, Elliott *urologist*
McCaffrey, John Anthony *brokerage house executive*
Newman, Edwin Harold *news commentator*
Rothenberg, Richard Lee *audio engineering executive*
†Shoen, Steven Lloyd *plastic surgeon*
Sidikman, David S. *state legislator*
Warrack, Maria Perini *psychotherapist*

Plandome
Williams, Morgan Lloyd *retired investment banker*

Plattsburgh
Bedworth, David Albert *health educator*
Bethlen, Francis R. *business and economics educator, food distribution engineering specialist*
†Carrino, Michael *writing educator*
Cooper, Richard Francis *computer company executive*
Dossin, Ernest Joseph, III *credit consulting company executive*
Hanton, E(mile) Michael *public and personnel relations consultant*
Helinger, Michael Green *mathematics educator*
Henning, Sylvie Debevec *French language educator*
Kuehl, Alexander Edward *physician, health facility administrator, medical educator, writer*
Lewis, Clyde A. *lawyer*
Medearis, Kenneth Robert *medical products manufacturing company executive*
Rech, Susan Anita *obstetrician, gynecologist*
Treacy, William Joseph *electrical and environmental engineer*
Virostek, Robert Joseph *physician*
Worthington, Janet Evans *academic director, English language educator*

Pleasant Valley
Marshall, Natalie Junemann *economics educator*
Odescalchi, Edmond Péry *international financial consultant, author*

Pleasantville
Ahrensfeld, Thomas Frederick *lawyer*
Annese, Domenico *landscape architect*
Antonecchia, Donald A. *principal*
Black, Percy *psychology educator*
†Bruckenstein, Joel P. *investment company executive, financial planner*
Keller, Mary Beth *consumer research consultant*
Krefting, Robert J(ohn) *publishing company executive*
Nelson, K. Bonita *literary agent*
Reps, David Nathan *finance educator*
Urban, Joseph Jaroslav *engineer, consultant*
Waletzky, Lucy R. *psychiatrist*
Willcox, Christopher Patrick *magazine editor*

Point Lookout
Stack, Maurice Daniel *retired insurance company executive*

Pomona
Brooks, Iris *writer, editor, musician*
Glassman, Lawrence S. *plastic surgeon*
Gordon, Edmund Wyatt *psychologist, educator*
Kapnick, Stewart *investment banker*
Masters, Robert Edward Lee *psychotherapist, neural researcher, human potential educator*
Zugibe, Frederick Thomas *pathologist*

Port Chester
Ailloni-Charas, Dan *marketing executive*
Oppenheimer, Suzi *state senator*
Penney, Linda Helen *music educator*

Port Ewen
Ausubel, David Paul *retired psychiatrist, author*

Port Jefferson
Arnaboldi, Joseph Paul *retired veterinarian*
Dranitzke, Richard J. *surgeon*
Hindin, Seymour *lawyer*
Lipitz, Elaine Kappel *secondary education fine arts educator*

Port Jefferson Station
Kaplan, Martin Paul *pediatrician, educator*
†Pepi, Vincent *artist*

Port Washington
Adler, Edward Andrew Koeppel *lawyer*
Aronstein, Jacqueline Bluestone *psychoanalyst, counselor, educator*
Brownstein, Martin Herbert *dermatopathologist*
Candido, Arthur Aldo *publishing and distribution company executive*
Ciccariello, Priscilla Chloe *librarian*
Feldman, Jay Newman *lawyer, telecommunications executive*
Futter, Joan Babette *former school librarian*
Gaddis, M. Francis *mechanical and marine engineer, environmental scientist*
Hackett, John Byron *advertising agency executive, lawyer*
Jay, Frank Peter *writer, educator*
Johnson, Tod Stuart *market research company executive*
Jones, Farrell *judge*
†Korez, John Joseph *chemical executive*
Kossin, Sanford Marshall *illustrator*
Phelan, Arthur Joseph *financial executive*
Read, Frederick Wilson, Jr. *lawyer, educator*
Sonnenfeldt, Richard Wolfgang *management consultant*
Tarleton, Robert Stephen *producer and distributor fine arts videos*
Williams, George Leo *retired secondary education educator*

Potsdam
Busnaina, Ahmed Ali *mechanical engineering educator*
Chin, Der-Tau *chemical engineer, educator*
Chugh, Ram L. *economics educator*
Cross, John William *foreign language educator*
DeGhett, Stephanie Coyne *writer, educator*
Fendler, Janos Hugo *chemistry educator*
Ha, Andrew Kwangho *education educator*
Harder, Kelsie Brown *retired language professional, educator*
†Henry, Richard Michael *educator*
Mackay, Raymond Arthur *chemist*
Matijevic, Egon *chemistry educator*
Mochel, Myron George *mechanical engineer, educator*
Pillay, Pragasen *engineering educator*
Rudiger, Lance Wade *secondary school educator*
Sarnoff, Joseph C. *academic administrator*
Sathyamoorthy, Muthukrishnan *engineering researcher, educator*
Siiman, Olavi *chemist*
Stevens, Sheila Maureen *teachers union administrator*
Stoltie, James Merle *academic administrator*
Stone, Irving Thomas *educator*

Poughkeepsie
Agerwala, Tilak Krishna Mahesh *computer company executive*
Bartlett, Lynn Conant *English literature educator*
Beck, Curt Werner *chemist, educator*
Bergon, Frank *English language educator, writer*
†Berk, Jeremiah E. *federal judge*
Berlin, Doris Ada *psychiatrist*
Borschel, Valerie Lynn *medical/surgical nurse*
Brakas, Nora Jachym *education educator*
Carino, Aurora Lao *psychiatrist, hospital administrator*
Chu, Richard Chao-Fan *mechanical engineer*
†Currie, Stephen *educator, writer*
Daniels, Elizabeth Adams *English language educator*
Davis, Harvey *commercial photographer, videographer*
Davis, Mary Lou *secondary education educator*
De Cusatis, Casimer Maurice *fiber optics engineer*
Deiters, Sister Joan Adele *psychotherapist, nun, chemistry educator*
DeMaria, Robert, Jr. *English language educator*
Dietz, Robert Barron *lawyer*
Dolan, Thomas Joseph *judge*
Fergusson, Frances Daly *college president, educator*
Filor, Anna May *secondary education educator*
Gennaro, Richard Francis, Jr. *chiropractor*
†Gesek, Thaddeus *artist*
Glasse, John Howell *retired philosophy and theology educator*
Gordon, Carolann *oncological nurse, community health nurse*
Griffen, Clyde Chesterman *retired history educator*
Handel, Bernard *accountant, actuarial and insurance consultant, lawyer*
Hansen, Karen Thornley *accountant*
Harmelink, Herman, III *clergyman, author, educator, ecumenist*
Heller, Mary Bernita *psychotherapist*
Henley, Richard James *health facility administrator*
Hytier, Adrienne Doris *French language educator*
†Johnson, Charles Colton *English educator, dean*
Johnson, M(aurice) Glen *political science educator*
†Joyce, Michael *educator*
†Kane, Paul *English language educator, poet*
Kelley, David Christopher *philosopher*
Kim, David Sang Chul *publisher, evangelist, retired seminary president*
Kranis, Michael David *lawyer, judge*
Lang, William Warner *physicist*
†Lewis, Richard Laurence *academic administrator, digital artist*
Logue, Joseph Carl *electronics engineer, consultant*
Mack, John Edward, III *utility company executive*
Maling, George Croswell, Jr. *physicist*
Mareth, Paul David *communications consultant*
McFadden, John Thomas *financial planner, insurance agent, investor*
Millman, Jode Susan *lawyer*
Opdycke, Leonard Emerson *retired secondary education educator, publisher*
Ostertag, Robert Louis *lawyer*
Pliskin, William Aaron *physicist*
Rosenblatt, Albert Martin *judge*
Skojec, William Charles *clinical psychologist*
Slade, Bernard Newton *electronics company executive*
Thomas, Sarah Rebecca *computer science educator*
VanBuren, Denise Doring *media relations executive*
Van Norden, Bryan William *Asian studies educator*
Van Zanten, Frank Veldhuyzen *retired library system director*
Wallace, Herbert Norman *lawyer*
Weiner, Marc V. *health services facility executive*
†Welker, William D. *dentist*
Willard, Nancy Margaret *writer, educator*
Wilson, Richard Edward *composer, pianist, music educator*

Poughquag
LaRussa, Joseph Anthony *optical company executive*

Pound Ridge
Abramovitz, Anita Zeltner Brooks (Mrs. Max Abramovitz) *writer*
Abramovitz, Max *architect*
Bennett, Edward Henry *reinsurance executive*
Ferro, Walter *artist*
Hart, Kenneth Nelson *lawyer*
Rubino, John Anthony *management and human resources consultant*
Schwebel, Renata Manasse *sculptor*
Throckmorton, Joan Helen *direct marketing consultant*
Webb, Richard Gilbert *financial executive*

Prt Jefferson
Strong, Robert Thomas *mayor, middle school educator*

Purchase
Alfredo, Joseph Albert *landscape architect*
Berman, Richard Angel *health and educational administrator*
Bowers, James W. *retired lawyer*
Casey, Gerard William *food products company executive, lawyer*
Cohen, Alan Norman *business executive*
Deering, Allan Brooks *soft drink company executive*
Dillon, John T. *paper company executive*
Ehrman, Lee *geneticist*
Enrico, Roger A. *soft drink company executive*
Finnerty, Louise Hoppe *beverage and food company executive*
Gedeon, Lucinda Heyel *museum director*
Guedry, James Walter *lawyer, paper corporation executive*
Kelly, Edmund Joseph *lawyer, investment banker*
Kornfeld, Lawrence *theatre director, educator*
Lacy, Bill *college president, architect*
Lytton, William B(ryan) *lawyer*
Magaziner, Elliot Albert *musician, conductor, educator*
Melican, James Patrick, Jr. *lawyer*
Muschio, Edward Charles *accountant*
Noonan, Frank Russell *business executive*
†Nooyi, Indra K. *food products company executive*
Papaleo, Louis Anthony *accountant*
Rainer, Renata Urbach *artist, photographer, educator*
Redkey, Edwin Storer *history educator*
Ryan, Edward W. *economics educator*
Sacco, John Michael *accountant*
Sandler, Irving Harry *art critic, art historian*
Sharpe, Robert Francis, Jr. *lawyer*
Siegel, Nathaniel Harold *sociology educator*
Staley, Harry Lee *fund raising executive*
Thomas, Dennis *paper company executive, former government official*
von der Heyden, Karl Ingolf Mueller *manufacturing company executive*
Wallach, Ira David *lawyer, business executive*
Wright, David L. *food and beverage company executive*

Putnam Valley
Amram, David Werner *composer, conductor, musician*

Queens Village
Cook, Michael Anthony *financial services executive*

Queensbury
Bitner, William Lawrence, III *retired banker, educator*
Mead, John Milton *banker*

Quogue
Lyons, Jude (Anne Lyons) *advertising agency executive*
Macero, Teo *composer, conductor*

Ransomville
Mayer, George Merton *retired elementary education educator*

Red Hook
Boretz, Benjamin Aaron *composer, music educator*

Rego Park
Brown, Kevin *writer*
Connington, Mary Ellen *health facility administrator*
Cortese, Edward *marketing and public relations executive*
Cronyn, Hume *actor, writer, director*
Gudeon, Arthur *podiatrist*
LeFrak, Samuel J. *housing and building corporation executive*
Meruelo, Raul Pablo *lawyer, mortgage brokerage executive*
Stumpf, Mary Rita *administrator, executive director*
†Weinstein, Gerald *housing and building corporation executive*

Remsenburg
Billman, Irwin Edward *publishing company executive*

Rensselaer
Hull, Raymond Whitford *public relations executive*
Kennedy, Linda Louise *secondary education educator*
Nack, Claire Durani *artist, author*
Semowich, Charles John *art historian, art dealer and appraiser, curator, artist*

Rensselaerville
Dudley, George Austin *architect, planning consultant, educator*

Rexford
Schmitt, Roland Walter *retired academic administrator*

Rhinebeck
Flexner, Josephine Moncure *musician, educator*
Flexner, Kurt Fisher *economist, educator*
Hellerman, Leo *retired computer scientist and mathematician*
Longden, Claire Suzanne *financial planner, investment advisor*
McGuire, John Francis, Jr. *construction company executive*
Rabinovich, Raquel *painter, sculptor*

Rhinecliff
Conklin, John Roger *retired electronics company executive*
Dierdorff, John Ainsworth *retired editor*

Richmond Hill
Hamroff, Michael Scott *archives executive*
†Sharif, Choudhry M. *secondary education educator*
Velazco, Julio E. *security specialist*

Ridgewood
Jones, Harold Antony *banker*

Riverdale
Chimsky, Mark Evan *publishing consultant*
De La Cancela, Victor *psychologist*
†Di Lascia, Alfred Paul *philosophy educator*
Ellentuck, Elmer *journal editor*
Greenberg, Arline Francine *artist, photographer*
Hauser, Bernice Worman *inter-campus director*
Itzkoff, Norman Jay *lawyer*
†Lee, Dong Hwan *business adminstration educator*
Lerner, Laurence M. *college administrator*
†Llena, Rey Lapiceros *secondary education educator, consultant*

Riverhead
Kent, Robert John *marine biologist*
Maggipinto, V. Anthony *lawyer*
Twomey, Thomas A., Jr. *lawyer*

Rochester
Abrams, Sam *humanities educator*
Adams, G. Rollie *museum executive*
Adiletta, Debra Jean Olson *business analyst consultant*
Akiyama, Toshio *cardiologist, educator, researcher*
†Albright, Daniel *English educator*
Alpert-Gillis, Linda Jayne *clinical psychologist*
Andolina, Lawrence J. *lawyer*
Angel, Allen Robert *mathematics educator, author, consultant*
Aydelotte, Myrtle Kitchell *nursing administrator, educator, consultant*
Baker, Bruce J. *lawyer*
Balch, Glenn McClain, Jr. *academic administrator, minister, author*
Bannon, Anthony Leo *museum director*
Baum, John *physician*
†Bauman, M. Garrett *English educator*
Belgiorno, John *career consultant, educator*
Bennett, John Morrison *medical oncologist*
Berg, Robert Lewis *physician, educator*
Bergeron, Ronald Jay *computer programmer, analyst*
Berman, Milton *history educator*
Bernstein, Paul *retired academic dean*
Bessey, Palmer Quintard *surgeon*
Bigelow, Nicholas Pierre *physicist, educator*
Billings, Ronald J. *dental research administrator*
Bluhm, William Theodore *political scientist, educator*
Boeckman, Robert Kenneth, Jr. *chemistry educator, organic chemistry researcher*
Bonfiglio, Thomas Albert *pathologist, educator*
Bouyoucos, John Vinton *research and development company executive*
Bowen, William Henry *dental researcher, dental educator*
†Braun, Wilhelm *retired educator*
Braunsdorf, Paul Raymond *lawyer*
Brideau, Leo Paul *healthcare executive*
Briggs, James T. *marketing executive*
Brody, Bernard B. *physician, educator*
Brooks, Walter S. *dermatologist*
Brovitz, Richard Stuart *lawyer*
Brown, Theodore M. *history educator, curator, historical consultant*
Burch, Bridgette *press secretary City of Rochester, New York*
Burgener, Francis André *radiology educator*
Burton, Richard Irving *orthopedist, educator*
Bushinsky, David Allen *nephrologist, educator, researcher*
Campbell, Alma Jacqueline Porter *elementary education educator*
Cantore Green, Jean *secondary education educator*
Carstensen, Edwin Lorenz *biomedical engineer, biophysicist*
Chang, Jack Che-man *imaging materials and media administrator*
Cherchi Usai, Paolo *film curator, film historian*
Chey, William Yoon *physician*
Chiarenza, Carl *art historian, critic, artist, educator*
Chiulli, Michael Richard *laboratory technician*
Clark, Matthew Harvey *bishop*
Clarkson, Thomas William *toxicologist, educator*
Clement, Thomas Earl *lawyer*
Clifford, Eugene Thomas *lawyer*
Cohen, Jules *physician, educator, former academic dean*
Cohen, Nicholas *immunologist, educator*
Coleman, Paul David *neurobiology researcher, educator*
†Condemi, John J. *physician*
Corio, Mark Andrew *electronics executive*
†Costanza, Marie *secondary education educator*
Crane, Irving Donald *pocket billiards player*
Crino, Marjanne Helen *anesthesiologist*
Cropper, André Dominic *research scientist*
Danforth-Morningstar, Elizabeth *obstetrician/gynecologist*
Deci, Edward Lewis *psychologist, educator*
Degraff, David Charles *purchasing executive*
DeMarco, Roland R. *foundation executive*
de Papp, Zsolt George *endocrinologist*
Diamond, David Leo *composer*
†Dill-Kocher, Laurie *textile artist*
Dohanian, Diran Kavork *art historian, educator*
Doty, Robert William *neurophysiologist, educator*
Dow, Ronald F. *librarian*
Doyle, Justin P *lawyer*
†Drepaul, Loris Omesh *infectious diseases physician*
Dreyfuss, Eric Martin *allergist*
Duarte, Francisco Javier *physicist, researcher*
DuBeshter, Brent *physician*
DuBrin, Andrew John *behavioral sciences, management educator, author*
†Duffy, Robert John *police chief*
Eaves, Morris Emery *English language educator*
Edson, Marian Louise *communications executive*
Eisenberg, Richard S. *chemistry educator*
Elder, Fred Kingsley, Jr. *physicist, educator*
Ernsthausen, Carol Knasel *educator*
†Fagan, Garth *choreographer, artistic director, educator*
†Fallesen, Elaine Gertrude *public relations professional*
Fallesen, Gary David *journalist*
†Farley, Susan Strack *elementary educator*
Farrar, James Martin *chemistry educator*
Fenno, Richard Francis, Jr. *political science educator*
Ferbel, Thomas *physics educator, physicist*
Feuerherm, Kurt Karl *artist, educator*
Fisher, George Myles Cordell *photographic imaging company executive, mathematician, engineer*
Fix, Meyer *lawyer*
Forbes, Gilbert Burnett *physician, educator*
Fowler, Robert Archibald *infosystems company executive*
Fox, Mary Maselli *psychologist*
Frazer, John Paul *surgeon*
Freeman, Leslie Jean *neuropsychologist, researcher*
†Ganley, Beatrice *English educator, writer*
Gans, Roger Frederick *mechanical engineering educator*
Gates, Marshall DeMotte, Jr. *chemistry educator*
Geiger, Alexander *lawyer*
George, Richard Neill *lawyer*
Goldberg-Schaible, Jocelyn Hope Schnier *market research consultant*
Golden, Reynold Stephen *geriatrician*
Goldman, Joel J. *retired lawyer*
Goldstein, Marvin Norman *physician*
Golisano, B. Thomas *finance company director, human resources director*
Gootnick, Margery Fischbein *lawyer*
Goyer, Virginia L. *accountant*
Griggs, Robert Charles *physician*
Gripe, Alan Gordon *minister*
Gustin, Carl E., Jr. *manufacturing company executive*
†Hacker, Robert Gordon *educator, consultant*
Hall, Dennis Gene *optics educator*
Hall, Donald S. *former planetarium administrator, pottery expert*
Hampson, Thomas Meredith *lawyer*
Hannon, Richard W. *director budget bureau*
Hanushek, Eric Alan *economics educator*
Harris, Diane Carol *merger and acquisition consulting firm executive*
Harris, Wayne Manley *lawyer*
Harrison, Daniel Gordon *music educator, musician*
Harter, Ralph Millard Peter *lawyer, educator*
Harvey, Douglass Coate *retired photographic company executive*
†Haschmann, Thomas Edwin *social services agency administrator*
Hauser, William Barry *history educator, historian*
Haywood, Anne Mowbray *pediatrics, virology, and biochemistry educator*
Heinle, Robert Alan *physician*
Herminghouse, Patricia Anne *foreign language educator*
Hickey, Dennis Walter *retired bishop*
Hilf, Russell *biochemist*
Hill, Edith Marie *medical/surgical nurse*
Hoch, Edward Dentinger *author*
Hoffberg, David Lawrence *lawyer*
Holcomb, Grant, III *museum director*
Holzbach, James Francis *civil engineer*
Hood, John B. *lawyer*
Howard, Hubert Wendell *English language educator, academic administrator, choral conductor*
Hoy, Cyrus Henry *language professional, educator*
Hunt, Roger Schermerhorn *healthcare administrator*
Hurlbut, Robert Harold *health care services executive*
Hurt, Davina Theresa *educator*
Hutchins, Frank McAllister *advertising executive*
Jackson, Thomas Humphrey *university president*
Jacobs, Laurence Stanton *physician, educator*
Jesserer, Henry L., III *lawyer*
John, Susan V. *state legislator*
Johnson, Bruce Marvin *English language educator*
Johnson, James William *English educator, author*
Johnson, Jean Elaine *nursing educator*
Johnson, William A., Jr. *mayor*
Johnston, Frank C. *psychologist*
Jones, Ronald Winthrop *economics educator*
Jones-Atkins, DeBorah Kaye *state official*
Joos, Felipe Miguel *mechanical engineer*
Joynt, Robert James *academic administrator*
Kampmeier, Jack August Carlos *chemist, educator*
Kehoe, L. Paul *state judge*
Kende, Andrew Steven *chemistry educator*
Kessler, Roslyn Marie *financial analyst*
†Kieburtz, Karl David *physician, educator, researcher*
Kingslake, Rudolf *retired optical designer*
Kingsley, Linda S. *corporation counsel*
Kinnen, Edwin *electrical engineer, educator*
Kirschenbaum, Howard *educator*
Knauer, James Philip *physicist*
Knox, Robert Seiple *physicist, educator*
Kowalke, Kim H. *music educator, musicologist, conductor, foundation executive*
Kraus, Sherry Stokes *lawyer*
Kreilick, Robert W. *chemist, educator*
Kurland, Harold Arthur *lawyer*
Langner, Andreas *chemistry educator, consultant*
Lank, Edith Handleman *columnist, educator*
Larimer, David George *federal judge*
Laschenski, John Patrick *accountant*
LaSpagnoletta, Benjamin Joseph *infosystems specialist*
LaSpagnoletta, Susan Ann *nurse*
Laties, Victor Gregory *psychology educator*
Law, Michael R. *lawyer*
Lawrence, Ruth Anderson *pediatrician, clinical toxicologist*
Lebman, Robert Richard *social services administrator*

Lessen, Martin engineering educator, consulting engineer
Lever, O. William, Jr. chemist
Levy, Harold David psycholinguist
Lewis, Charles Spencer professional business manager
Lichtman, Marshall Albert medical educator, physician, scientist
Loewen, Erwin G. precision engineer, educator, consultant
Lohouse, Dennis Elmer banker, investment manager
Long, John Broaddus, Jr. economist, educator
Lotta, (Anthony) Tom artist
Luckey, George William research chemist
Lundback, Staffan Bengt Gunnar lawyer
Macko, John lawyer, farmer
Makous, Walter Leon visual scientist, educator
Mandel, Leonard physics and optics educator, researcher
Mann, Alfred musicology educator, choral conductor
Marcellus, John Robert, III trombonist, educator
Margolis, Richard Martin photographer, educator
Marriott, Marcia Ann business educator, consultant
†Mattice, David Shane student affairs administrator
Matzek, Richard Allan library director
Mayka, Stephen Paul lawyer
McCaffrey, John P. protective services official
McCall, Thomas Donald marketing communications company executive
McClurg, Robert James emergency nurse practitioner
McCrory, John Brooks retired lawyer
McCrory, Robert Lee physicist, mechanical engineering educator
McCurdy, Gilbert Geier retired retailer
McDonald, Joseph Valentine neurosurgeon
Mc Kenzie, Lionel Wilfred economist, educator
†McKenzie, Stanley Don academic administrator, English educator
McKie, W. Gilmore human resources executive
McMeekin, Thomas Owen dermatologist
McQuillen, Michael Paul neurologist, educator
Meloni, Andrew P. protective services official
Merritt, Howard Sutermeister retired art educator
Metzler, Ruth Horton genealogical educator
Miller, Richard Bruce electronics company executive
Mittermeyer, Paul F. laser energetics technician, writer
Moore, Duncan Thomas optics educator
†Moore, James Conklin lawyer
Moore, Matthew Scott publisher, deaf advocate, author
Morgan, William Lionel, Jr. physician, educator
Morrison, Patrice B. lawyer
Morrow, Paul Edward toxicology educator
Moss, Arthur Jay physician
Muchmore, William Breuleux zoologist, educator
Mueller, John Ernest political science educator, dance critic and historian
Mundorff Shrestha, Sheila Ann cariologist
Munson, Harold Lewis education educator
Nace, Morton Oliver, Jr. human resources professional, performance consultant
Nazarian, Lawrence Fred pediatrician
Niemi, Richard Gene political science educator
†Ninfo, John C., II
†Nixon, David Michael poet
Nutter, David George urban planner
Oberlies, John William physician organization executive
Okunieff, Paul radiation oncologist, physician
O'Mara, Robert Edmund George radiologist, educator
Pacala, Leon retired association executive
Palermo, Anthony Robert lawyer
Paley, Gerald Larry lawyer
Palmer, Harvey John chemical engineering educator, consultant
Panner, Bernard J. pathologist, educator
Panz, Richard library director
Papadakos, Peter John critical care physician, educator
Parke, John Shepard marketing consultant
Parker, Kevin James electrical engineer educator
Parsons, George Raymond, Jr. lawyer
Pearse, Robert Francis psychologist, educator
Pearson, Thomas Arthur epidemiologist, educator
Phelps, Charles Elliott economics educator
Pincus, Patricia Hogan nurse
Pitoniak, Scott Michael sports columnist
Plosser, Charles Irving university dean, economics educator
Pollicove, Harvey Myles manufacturing executive
Powers, James Matthew neuropathologist
Prosser, Michael Hubert communications educator
Ramsey, Jarold William English language educator, author
Reed, James Alexander, Jr. lawyer
Regenstreif, S(amuel) Peter political scientist, educator
†Reynolds, Verne musician, retired music educator
Richards, Thomas Savidge utility company executive
Risher, William Henry cardiothoracic surgeon, educator
Robfogel, Susan Salitan lawyer
Rosenbaum, Richard Merrill lawyer
Rosenhouse, Michael Allan lawyer, editor, publishing executive
Rosett, Richard Nathaniel economist, educator
Rosner, Leonard Allen lawyer
Rothberg, Abraham author, educator, editor
Rothman-Marshall, Gail Ann psychology educator
Rouse, Christopher Chapman, III composer
Rowley, Peter Templeton physician, educator
Rulison, Joseph Richard investment advisor
Rustchenko, Elena geneticist
Sackett, David Harrison electrical engineer
Saisselin, Remy Gilbert fine arts educator
Salamone, Joseph Charles polymer chemistry educator
Sanders, John Theodore philosophy educator
Sawyer, William Curtis pest control company executive
Schaffner, Robert Jay, Jr. nurse practitioner
Schmidhammer, Robert Howard environmental executive, engineering consultant
Schmidt, John Gerhard neurologist, educator, researcher
Schumacher, Jon Lee lawyer
Schwantner, Joseph composer, educator
Schwartz, Seymour Ira surgeon, educator
Schwert, G(eorge) William, III finance educator
Scott, Joanna Jeanne writer, English language educator
Scutt, Robert Carl lawyer
Serrano, Rose Arlene vice principal
†Shahin, Raymond J. music educator, composer
Sharp, Alfred Jay retired personnel relations executive
Sherman, Charles Daniel, Jr. surgeon
Sherman, Fred biochemist, educator
†Shuffelton, Frank C. educator
Sieg, Albert Louis photographic company executive
Simon, Leonard Samuel banker
Simon, William biomathematician, educator
Simone, Albert Joseph academic administrator
†Siragusa, Charles J. judge
†Skinner-Linnenberg, Virginia English educator
Skupsky, Stanley laser fusion scientist
Smith, Harold Charles biochemistry educator, academic administrator
Smith, John Stuart lawyer
Smith, Jules Louis lawyer
Smith, Julia Ladd medical oncologist, hospice physician
Sparks, Charles Edward pathologist, educator
Speranza, Paul Samuel, Jr. lawyer
Spurrier, Mary Eileen investment advisor, financial planner
Stanley, Harold Watkins political science educator
Steamer, Robert Julius political science educator
Stewart, Sue S. lawyer
Stiller, Sharon Paula lawyer
Stone, Gail Ann elementary and secondary education educator
Stonehill, Eric lawyer
Strand, Marion Delores social service administrator
Swanton, Susan Irene library director
Telesca, Michael Anthony federal judge
Thomas, John Howard astrophysicist, engineer, educator
Thompson, Brian John university administrator, optics educator
Thorndike, Edward Harmon physicist
Toribara, Taft Yutaka radiation biologist, biophysicist, chemist, toxicologist
Trevett, Thomas Neil lawyer
Trueheart, Harry Parker, III lawyer
Turner, Scott MacNeely lawyer
Turri, Joseph A. lawyer
Twietmeyer, Don Henry lawyer
Tyler, John Randolph lawyer
Utell, Mark Jeffrey medical educator
Van Graafeiland, Ellsworth Alfred federal judge
Van Graafeiland, Gary P. lawyer
Vernarelli, Michael Joseph economics educator, consultant
Waite, Stephen Holden lawyer
Watanabe, Ruth Taiko music historian, library science educator
Watts, Ross Leslie accounting educator, consultant
†Waugh, Richard E. biomedical engineering educator
Wax, Paul Matthew emergency medicine physician, educator, medical toxicologist
†Wechsler, Harold Stuart history educator, consultant
Wegman, Robert B. food service executive
Wehner, Sister Mary B. pastoral counselor, spiritual director
Weiss, Howard A. violinist, concertmaster, conductor, music educator
Whitney, William Gordon investment management company executive
Wiedrick-Kozlowski, Jan Barbara communications executive
Wild, Robert Warren lawyer
Willett, Thomas Edward lawyer
Williams, Thomas Franklin physician, educator
Witmer, George Robert, Jr. lawyer
Wolf, Emil physics educator
Wynne, Lyman Carroll psychiatrist
Yager, William Stewart sculptor
Yarnall, Susanne Lusink elementary school educator
†Young, Cynthia Nason magazine editor, artist
Young, Deborah Schwind lawyer
Young, Mary Elizabeth history educator
Young, Thomas Paul lawyer
Zagorin, Perez historian, educator
Zamboni, Helen Attena lawyer, international telecommunications executive
Zax, Melvin psychologist, educator

Rock Hill
Lombardi, Kent Bailey insurance company administrator

Rockville Center
McHugh, James T. bishop

Rockville Centre
Bajaj, Celine Cosme medical/surgical and pediatric nurse
Becker, Nettie preschool administrator
Beyer, Suzanne advertising agency executive
Burton, Daniel G. insurance executive
†Cronacher, Warren William consulting engineer
Epel, Lidia Marmurek dentist
Erland, Shirley May nurse
Fassetta, Mary Elizabeth nursing educator
Fitzgerald, Sister Janet Anne philosophy educator, college president emeritus
Marohn, Ann Elizabeth health information professional
McFaul, Patricia Louise editor
McGann, John Raymond bishop
Rogers, Eugene Charles retired investment firm executive

Rome
Coppola, Anthony electrical engineer
†Dela Cruz, Pablito Sulit pediatrician, neurologist
Griffith, Emlyn Irving lawyer
†Kuhn, Jill Marie school psychologist
Romeu, Jorge Luis mathematics educator, writer
Simons, Richard Duncan lawyer, retired state judge
Waters, George Bausch newspaper publisher
Widrick, Lynn S. English language educator

Romulus
Ostrander, Robert Edwin retired United Nations interregional advisor, petroleum company executive

Ronkonkoma
Heiserer, Albert, Jr. automotive educator, small business owner
Pati, Christopher Martin musician, record company executive

Roscoe
DeFilippo, Dominic Joseph special effects inventor

Rosedale
Chan, Henry Albert minister

Roslyn
Arstark, Lester D. advertising agency executive
Damus, Paul Shibli cardiac surgeon
Epstein, Arthur Barry optometrist
Finke, Leonda Froehlich sculptor
Freedman, Joseph Mark optometrist
Kutscher, Eugene Bernard educational administrator
Risom, Ole Christian publishing company executive
Scollard, Patrick John hospital executive
Stein, Theodore Anthony biochemist, educator
Stracher, Dorothy Altman education educator, consultant
Ulanoff, Stanley M. communications executive
Zeitlan, Marilyn Labb lawyer

Roslyn Heights
Bauer, William Henry musician
†Bruder, Judith writer
Jaffe, Melvin securities company executive
Jordan, Patricia James secondary education educator
Newmark, Marilyn sculptor
Rogatz, Peter physician
Saridakis, Andrew Peter international trader and business consultant
Senft, Mason George musician

Rouses Point
†Van Acker, Henry C., Jr. federal judge
Weierstall, Richard Paul retired pharmaceutical chemist

Rushville
Carpenter, Florence Erika retired human services adminstrator

Rye
Anderson, Allan architectural firm executive
Barker, Harold Grant surgeon, educator
Beldock, Donald Travis financial executive
†Clyatt, Robert Lee executive distance learning firm
Davis, Samuel hospital administrator, educator, consultant
Dixon, Paul Edward lawyer, metal products and manufacturing company executive
Feinberg, Norman Maurice real estate executive
Finnerty, John Dudley investment banker, financial educator
Gambee, Robert Rankin investment banker
Goodenough, Andrew Lewis publishing executive
Gurfein, Stuart James data processing executive
Hopf, Frank Rudolph dentist
Hurwitz, Sol writer, consultant
Iakovos, (Demetrios A. Coucouzis) retired archbishop
Kaulakis, Arnold Francis management consultant
Lehman, Lawrence Herbert consulting engineering executive
Lehman, Myra Harriet sculptor, dental hygienist
Lerner, Frederic Howard financial executive, educator
Marcus, Joel David pediatrician
McDonnell, Mary Theresa travel service executive
Metzger, Frank management consultant
Mintz, Stephen Allan real estate company executive, lawyer
Mittelstadt, Charles Anthony advertising executive
Newburger, Howard Martin psychoanalyst
Reader, George Gordon physician, educator
Roberts, Thomas Alba lawyer
Stoller, Ezra photojournalist
Troller, Fred graphic designer, painter, visual consultant, educator
Vauclair, Marguerite Renée communications executive, sales executive
Vernon, Lillian mail order company executive
Wessler, Stanford physician, educator
Wilmot, Irvin Gorsage former hospital administrator, educator, consultant

Rye Brook
Garcia C., Elisa Dolores lawyer
Landegger, George F. engineering executive
Masson, Robert Henry paper company executive
McKenna, John computer company executive
†McKenna, John A., Jr. data processing executive
Smethurst, E(dward) William, Jr. brokerage house executive

Sackets Harbor
†Clancy, Michael Neville military officer

Sag Harbor
Baer, Jon Alan political scientist
Barry, Nada Davies retail business owner
Brathwaite, Harriet Louisa nursing educator
Cantor, Norman Frank history educator, writer
Pierce, Lawrence Warren retired federal judge

Sagaponack
Appleman, Marjorie (M. H. Appleman) playwright, educator, poet
Appleman, Philip poet, writer, educator
Butchkes, Sydney artist
Hagen-Stubbing, Yvonne Forrest writer

Saint Bonaventure
Doyle, Mathias Francis university president, political scientist, educator
Parikh, Rajeev Natvarlal educator, university administrator, accountant
Wood, Paul William language educator

Saint James
Bigeleisen, Jacob chemist, educator

Salamanca
Brady, Thomas Carl lawyer

Salt Point
Lackey, Mary Michele physician assistant

Sanborn
Schmidt-Bova, Carolyn Marie vocational school administrator, consultant
†Stoll, Marsal P. academic administrator

Sands Point
Busner, Philip H. retired lawyer
Cullinan, Bernice E(llinger) education educator
Goodman, Edmund Nathan surgeon, pain management consultant
Hoynes, Louis LeNoir, Jr. lawyer
Lear, Erwin anesthesiologist, educator
Tane, Susan Jaffe retired manufacturing company executive
Wurzel, Leonard retired candy manufacturing company executive
Zalben, Steven architect

Saranac
Smith, J. Kellum, Jr. foundation executive, lawyer

Saranac Lake
Caguiat, Carlos Jose health care administrator, episcopal priest
Jakobe, Virginia Ellis retired educator
†Kenny, Maurice Francis writer
North, Robert John biologist
Szwed, Beryl J. school system administrator, mathematics educator

Saratoga Springs
Dasgupta, Gautam theater educator, journal editor and publisher
Davis, John Eugene restaurant owner, disc jockey
De Vizzio, Nicholas Joseph violinist, educator, conductor
Dickinson, Richard Henry accountant
Dorsey, James Baker lawyer, surgeon
Higgins, Marika O'Baire registered nurse, philosophy educator, novelist, entrepreneur
Leary, Eileen Marie psychotherapist
Masie, Elliott training executive
†Myers, Philip Henry artist
Porter, David Hugh pianist, classicist, academic administrator, liberal arts educator
Ratzer, Mary Boyd secondary education educator, librarian
Rogoff, Jay poet, educator
Smith, Vincent De Paul realtor, real estate company executive
Stanley, Karen Francine Mary Lesniewski human resources professional
Studley, Jamienne Shayne lawyer
Upton, Richard Thomas artist
Wait, Charles Valentine banker

Sayville
Edelman, Hendrik library and information science educator
Lippman, Sharon Rochelle art historian, curator, art therapist, writer

Scarborough
Beglarian, Grant foundation executive, composer, consultant
†Byrne, Robert Eugene chess columnist
Parks, Robert Henry consulting economist, educator
Stigall, Phyllis Graham retired librarian
Wittcoff, Harold Aaron chemist

Scarsdale
Abbe, Colman investment banker
Angel, Dennis lawyer
Arond, Miriam magazine editor, writer
Blinder, Abe Lionel management consultant
Blitman, Howard Norton construction company executive
Bloomfield, Keith Martin management executive
Borg, Robert Frederic civil engineer
Breslow, Marilyn Ganon portfolio manager
Brooks, Lorraine Elizabeth music educator
Bruck Lieb Port, Lilly retired consumer advisor, broadcaster, columnist
Callaghan, Georgann Mary management consultant
Cohen, Irwin economist
Collins, Ann N. secondary school educator
Decaminada, Joseph Pio insurance company executive, educator
Del Duca, Rita educator
Edis, Gloria Toby pediatrician
Eforo, John Francis financial officer
Florman, Samuel Charles civil engineer
Fortune, Philip Robert retired metal manufacturing company executive
Frackman, Noel art critic
Frankel, Stanley Arthur columnist, educator, business executive
Gerber, Roger Alan lawyer, business consultant
†Gertler, Stephanie Jocelyn journalist
Goldberg, Harriet David urban planner
Gollin, Stuart Allen accountant
Goodwin, Everett Carlton minister
Graff, Henry Franklin historian, educator
Griffiths, Daniel Edward dean emeritus
Heese, William John music publishing company executive
Hemley, Eugene Adams trade association executive
Hershenson, Roberta Mantell writer, photographer
Hines, William Eugene banker
Hoffman, Richard M. lawyer
Johnson, Boine Theodore instruments company executive, mayor
†Johnson, Katharyn Price (Mrs. Edward F. Johnson) civic worker
Kanter, Carl Irwin lawyer
Kaufman, Robert Jules communications consultant, lawyer
Keeffe, John Arthur lawyer, director
King, Robert Lucien lawyer
Korzenik, Sidney S. lawyer
Liegl, Joseph Leslie lawyer
Macchia, Vincent Michael lawyer
Moser, Marvin physician, educator, author
Naughton, Ann Elsie educator
Newman, Fredric Alan plastic surgeon, educator
Newman, Stacey Clarfield artist, curator
O'Brien, Edward Ignatius lawyer, private investor, corporation director
O'Neill, Michael James editor, author
Paulin, Amy Ruth civic activist, consultant
Perez, Louis Anthony radiologist
Perko, Kenneth Albert, Jr. lawyer, real estate executive, mathematics researcher
Porosoff, Harold chemist, research and development director
Ries, Martin artist, educator
Rogalski, Lois Ann speech and language pathologist
Rosow, Jerome Morris institute executive
Rubenstein, Jacob Samuel rabbi
Sandell, Richard Arnold international trade executive, economist
Scheinberg, Labe Charles physician, educator
Schultz, Harley consulting company executive
Sheehan, Larry John lawyer

Sinsheimer, Warren Jack lawyer
Stamas, Stephen investment executive
Topping, Audrey Ronning photojournalist, author
Topping, Seymour publishing executive, educator
Wesely, Yolanda Thereza retired sociologist, marketing professional, researcher
Wile, Julius former corporate executive, educator
Winkler, Katherine Maurine management consultant, educator
Wolfzahn, Annabelle Forsmith psychologist

Schenectady
Alpher, Ralph Asher physicist
Anthony, Thomas Richard research physicist
Barber, Nicholas Carl tax specialist, real estate executive
Barthold, Lionel Olav engineering executive
Bedard, Donna Lee environmental microbiologist
†Bentrovato, Donald A. genito-urinary surgeon
†Blood, Robert Alvin sculptor
Board, Joseph Breckinridge, Jr. political scientist, educator
Bond, Michele Denise early childhood educator
Bucinell, Ronald Blaise mechanical engineer, educator
Cerne, Gerald John biology educator
Chestnut, Harold foundation administrator, engineering executive
Cline, Harvey Ellis metallurgist
Corcoran, Kevin James town planner
de la Rocha, Carlos A. retired physician
Demar-Salad, Geraldine real estate sales and development executive, management consultant
De Mello, F. Paul electrical engineer
Fleischer, Robert Louis physics educator
†Foley, Jeff freelance writer
Golub, Lewis supermarket company executive
Grant, Ian Stanley engineering company executive
Hebb, Malcolm Hayden physicist
Helmar-Salasoo, Ester Anette literacy educator, researcher
Hull, Roger Harold college president
Jonas, Manfred historian, educator
Kambour, Roger Peabody polymer physical chemist, researcher
Kliman, Gerald Burt electrical engineer
Levine, Howard Arnold state supreme court justice
Luborsky, Fred Everett research physicist
Matta, Ram Kumar aeronautical engineer
Morris, John Selwyn philosophy educator, college president emeritus
Murphy, William Michael literature educator, biographer
Murray, Edward Rock insurance broker
Oliker, David William healthcare management administrator
Pasquariello, Julius Anthony pharmacist
Ringlee, Robert James consulting engineering executive
Robb, Walter Lee retired electric company executive, management company executive
Roselli, Bart A. museum director
Sager, Robert Wendell retired social work administrator
Schenck, John Frederic physician
Sokolow, Lloyd Bruce lawyer, psychotherapist
Sternlicht, Beno research and development company executive
Terry, Richard Allan consulting psychologist, former college president
Thiele, Leslie Kathleen Larsen lawyer
Tiemann, Jerome J. physicist
Wallner, Ludwig John principal
Walsh, George William engineering executive
Wilson, Delano Dee consultant
Wolfe, Frederick Andrew engineering educator
Yamin-Garone, Mary Sultany writer, graphic designer
Zheng, Maggie (Xiaoci) materials scientist, turbine coating specialist

Schenevus
Fielder, Dorothy Scott postmaster
Green, Margaret Mildred English language educator

Schoharie
Decker, Cynthia J. Schafer community and occupational health nurse
Stiver, Patricia Abare elementary education educator

Sea Cliff
McGill, Gilbert William lawyer
Popova, Nina dancer, choreographer, director
Rich, Charles Anthony hydrogeologist, consultant

Seaford
Moore, Sister Mary Francis parochial school educator
Setzler, William Edward chemical company executive
Waage, Elaine community health nurse

Searington
†Byalick, Marcia author, columnist, reporter, educator

Seneca Falls
Nozzolio, Michael F. state legislator

Setauket
Gard, Richard Abbott religious institute executive, educator
Irving, A. Marshall marine engineer
Levine, Sumner Norton industrial engineer, educator, editor, author, financial consultant
Robinson, Richard M. technical communication specialist
Simpson, Louis Aston Marantz English educator, author

Shady
Ruellan, Andree artist

Shelter Island
Cerami, Anthony biochemistry educator
Culbertson, Janet Lynn artist
Gurevitz, Bernard Herman painter
†Moran, Daniel Thomas dentist

Shelter Island Heights
Slade, Roy artist, college president, museum director

Sherburne
Dodd, Jack Gordon, Jr. physicist, educator

Shoreham
Ciborowski, Paul John counseling psychology educator
Spier, Peter Edward artist, author

Sidney
Haller, Irma Tognola secondary education educator

Silver Bay
Parlin, Charles C., Jr. retired lawyer

Silver Creek
Schenk, Worthington George, Jr. surgeon, educator

Skaneateles
Huxford, J. David retired sales representative

Sleepy Hollow
Ferguson, Douglas Edward financial executive
Hershman, Jack Ira urologist
Maun, Mary Ellen computer consultant
Safian, Keith Franklin hospital administrator
Schippa, Joseph Thomas, Jr. psychologist, educational consultant, hypnotherapist
Schmidt, Klaus Franz advertising executive
Zegarelli, Edward Victor retired dental educator, researcher

Slingerlands
Carroll, Corlis Faith artist
Childs, Rhonda Louise motivational speaker, consultant
†Elliott, Ray Andrew, Jr. retired surgeon, consultant
Wilcock, Donald Frederick mechanical engineer

Smithtown
Dowis, Lenore lawyer
Dvorkin, Ronald Alan emergency physician
Friedlander, Gerhart nuclear chemist
Goldstein, Leonard Barry dentist, educator
†Guthrie, James Russell data system analyst
Jonassen, Gaylord D. computer company executive, new products and market development
Landau, Dorothy psychotherapist, consultant
†Nielsen-Jones, Ian Richard lottery and gaming executive
Pearl, Richard Alan neurologist, educator
Pruzansky, Joshua Murdock lawyer
Spellman, Thomas Joseph, Jr. lawyer
Sporn, Stanley Robert retired electronic company executive
Wertz, Robert Charles state legislator
†Zippin, Allen Gerald neurosurgeon

Snyder
Breverman, Harvey artist
Genrich, Willard Adolph lawyer

Somers
Banik, Douglas Heil marketing executive
Bauman, William Allen pediatrician, educator, health systems consultant
Boudreaux, John public relations/internet specialist
Chen, Shuang computer science professional
Cohn, Howard retired magazine editor
Cowles, Frederick Oliver lawyer
Davidson, Carl B. retired oil company executive
Elix, Douglas Thorne computer company executive
Gulick, Donna Marie accountant
Joerger, Jay Herman psychologist, entrepreneur
Lane, David Oliver retired librarian
†Newlin, George Christian writer
Rubin, Samuel Harold physician, consultant
†Siegel, Sarah Ellin electronics executive
Sora, Sebastian Antony business machines manufacturing executive, educator
Trzasko, Joseph Anthony psychologist
Wladawsky-Berger, Irving communications executive

Sound Beach
Everett, Graham English language educator, poet, publisher

South Dayton
Jones, Richard Allen horse breeder, educator

South Nyack
†Colsey, Alan Blair public safety executive
Leiser, Ernest Stern journalist
†Rumaker, Michael writer, English educator

South Salem
Moore, Raymond Lionel recording engineer, record producer
Saurwein, Virginia Fay international affairs specialist

Southampton
Atkins, Victor Kennicott, Jr. investment banker
Brokaw, Clifford Vail, III investment banker, business executive
Brophy, James David, Jr. humanities educator
Dublis, Raymond Anthony insurance executive
Ferrara-Sherry, Donna Layne education educator
Graham, Howard Barrett publishing company executive
Joel, Billy (William Martin Joel) musician
†Jones, Kaylie Ann writing educator, writer
Kanovitz, Howard artist
Lerner, Abram retired museum director, artist
Lieberman, Carol healthcare marketing communications consultant
Lopez, David lawyer
Platt, Harold Kirby lawyer
Platt, Jonathan James lawyer
Smith, Dennis (Edward) author, publisher

Southold
Bachrach, Howard L. biochemist
Callis, Jerry Jackson veterinarian

Sparkill
Dahl, Arlene actress, author, designer, cosmetic executive
Joyce, Ursula Mary psychologist
Myers, Adele Anna artist, educator, nun

Sparrow Bush
Murray, William Bruce opera singer

Speculator
Kelly, Paul John priest

Mulleedy, Joyce Elaine nursing service administrator, educator

Spencer
†Grunberg, Slawomir film and television producer and director, director of photography

Spencerport
Humphrey, Paul commercial writer
Vizy, Kalman Nicholas research physicist
Webster, Gordon Visscher, Jr. minister

Spencertown
Dunne, John Richard lawyer
Lieber, Charles Donald publisher

Spring Valley
†Ganchrow, Mandell I. surgeon
Stedge-Fowler, Joyce retired clergywoman

Springfield Gardens
†McFarquhar, Claudette Viviene nurse, educator

Springville
Loockerman, William Delmer educational administrator

Sprngfld Gdns
Bourne, John David city finance executive

Stamford
Bergleitner, George Charles, Jr. investment banker

Stanfordville
Zeyher, Mark Lewis real estate investor

Stanley
Jones, Gordon Edwin horticulturist

Staten Island
†Affron, Mirella Jona academic administrator
Auh, Yang John librarian, educational administrator
Banner, Burton pediatrician
Berman, Barbara educational consultant
†Bernardo, Susan Marie English educator
Bogholtz, William E. minister
Botwinick, Michael museum director
Brady, Christine Ellen education coordinator
Bruckstein, Alex Harry internist, gastroenterologist, geriatrician
Butler, Tyrone G. records manager
Camarda, Edith nurse educator
Chapin, Elliott Lowell retired bank executive
Connelly, Elizabeth Ann state legislator
Cross, Ronald musicologist, educator
Diamond, Richard Edward publisher
Dunne, Desma medical/surgical nurse
Fafian, Joseph, Jr. management consultant
Fernandes, Richard Louis retired advertising firm executive
Ferranti, Thomas, Jr. lawyer
Fishman, Brian Scott research assistant
Fried, Stephen William English language educator, poet
Friederwitzer, Fredda J(oy) mathematics educator
Garzi, John Joseph maintenance engineer
Gasteyer, Carlin Evans museum administrator, museum studies educator
Gavrity, John Decker insurance company executive
Gelbein, Jay Joel accountant
†Gordon, Benjamin physical therapist
Hardee, Lewis Jefferson, Jr. educator
†Herman, Robert John artist manager, author, music industry advisor
Hermus, Lance Jay art appraiser
Johansen, Robert John electrical engineer
Klingle, Philip Anthony law librarian
Landau-Crawford, Dorothy Ruth local social service executive
Locke Monda, Robin graphic designer, artist
Mastroianni, Armand director
Mayer, Andrew Mark librarian, journalist
McEwan, Gordon Francis archaeologist, educator
†McGee, Sean-Reed advertising official
Meeker, Susan Stewart economic development organization administrator
Miller, Wayne actor, designer, impresario
Minotti, Mark Anthony chemistry educator
Molinari, Guy Victor municipal official
Nelson, Carey Boone sculptor
Neuberger, Jerome M. lawyer
Newhouse, Samuel I., Jr. publishing executive
O'Connor, Robert James gynecologist, consultant
O'Donovan, Jerome councilman
Popler, Kenneth behavioral healthcare executive, psychologist
Popp, Lilian Mustaki writer, educator
†Popper, Deborah Epstein geography educator
Porter, Darwin Fred writer
Raz, Lois Katz speech-language pathologist, writer
Reing, Alvin Barry special education educator, psychologist
Robison, Paula Judith flutist
Sabido, Almeda Alice mental health facility administrator
Shullich, Robert Harlan systems analyst
†Silverstein, Arthur publishing executive
Singer, Edward Nathan radio engineer, consultant
Smith, Norman Raymond college president
Springer, Marlene university administrator, educator
Stathopoulos, Peter internist
†Stearns, Stephen Jerold history educator, writer
Storberg, Eric Philip financial planner
Straniere, Robert A. state legislator
Tessa, Marian Lorraine talk show host, writer, producer, educator
†Thomas, Charles Columbus educator, artist
Urbanc, Katica language educator
Winter, Steven internist, cardiologist
Wisniewski, Henryk Miroslaw pathology and neuropathology educator, research facility administrator, research scientist
Yang, Song-Yu research biochemist

Sterling
Seawell, Thomas Robert artist, retired educator

Stone Ridge
Terpening, Donald Lester science educator, medical technologist

Stony Brook
Alexander, John Macmillan, Jr. chemistry educator
Anderson, Michael Thomas mathematics researcher, educator
†Arens, William Edward social anthropology educator, writer
Aronoff, Mark H. linguistics educator, author, consultant
Bilfinger, Thomas Victor surgeon, educator
Bonner, Francis Truesdale chemist, educator, university dean
Booth, George cartoonist
Brandwein, Ruth Ann social welfare educator
Brown, Gerald Edward physicist, educator
Chen Ning Yang physicist, educator
Cochran, James Kirk dean, oceanographer, geochemist, educator
Cook, Jeannine Salvo library consultant
Cope, Randolph Howard, Jr. electronic research and development executive, educator
Cottrell, Thomas Sylvester pathology educator, university dean
†Coulehan, John Leo physician educator, poet
Crease, Robert Poole, Jr. philosopher, writer, educator
Davidson, Cynthia Ann English language educator, poet
Davis, James Norman neurologist, neurobiology researcher
Edelman, Norman Herman medical educator, university dean and official
†Epstein, Mark Daniel plastic surgeon
Erk, Frank Chris biologist, educator
Fritts, Harry Washington, Jr. physician, educator
Geyer, Dennis Lynn university administrator and registrar
Glimm, James Gilbert mathematician, educator
Goldberg, Homer Beryl English language educator
Goodman, Norman sociologist, researcher
†Grudens, Richard William retail executive, writer
Hanson, Gilbert Nikolai geochemistry educator
Harvey, Christine Lynn publishing executive
Herman, Herbert materials science educator
Ihde, Don philosophy educator, university administrator
Jasiewicz, Ronald Clarence anesthesiologist, educator
Jonas, Steven public health physician, medical educator, writer
Kahn, Peter B. physics educator
Katkin, Edward Samuel psychology educator
Katz, Victoria Manuela public relations executive, educator, consultant
Kenny, Shirley Strum university administrator
Koppelman, Lee Edward regional planner, educator
Krikorian, Abraham Der biochemistry and cell biology educator
Kuchner, Eugene Frederick neurosurgeon, educator
Kuspit, Donald Burton art historian, art critic, educator
Lane, Dorothy Spiegel physician
Laspina, Peter Joseph computer resource educator
Lawson, H(erbert) Blaine, Jr. mathematician, educator
Lennarz, William Joseph research biologist, educator
Levin, Richard Louis English language educator
Levinton, Jeffrey S. biology educator, oceanographer
Manvich, Donna multimedia copyright researcher, consultant, permissions specialist
Meyers, Morton Allen physician, radiology educator
Michelsohn, Marie-Louise mathematician, educator
Mignone, Mario B. Italian studies educator
Miller, Frederick pathologist
Mundie, Gene E. nursing educator
Neuberger, Egon economics educator
Ohannessian, Harry Haroutune travel agency executive
Ojima, Iwao chemistry educator
Pekarsky, Melvin Hirsch artist
Pindell, Howardena Doreen artist
Poppers, Paul Jules anesthesiologist, educator
Priebe, Cedric Joseph, Jr. pediatric surgeon
Rapaport, Felix Theodosius surgeon, editor, researcher, educator
†Richmond, Rollin C. academic administrator
Ricotta, John Joseph vascular surgeon, educator
Rohlf, F. James biometrician, educator
Scarlata, Suzanne Frances biophysical chemist
Schneider, Mark political science educator
Schoenfeld, Elinor Randi epidemiologist
Shamash, Yacov dean, electrical engineering educator
Silverman, Hugh J. philosophy educator
Spector, Marshall philosophy educator
Sreebny, Leo M. oral biology and pathology educator
Stalker, Dianne Sylvia librarian
Steigbigel, Roy Theodore infectious disease physician and scientist, educator
Steinberg, Amy Wishner dermatologist
Stolzberg, Mark Elliott psychologist
Stone, Elizabeth Caecilia anthropology educator
Swanson, Robert Lawrence oceanographer, academic program administrator
Tewarson, Reginald Prabhakar mathematics educator, consultant
Travis, Martin Bice political scientist, educator
Tucker, Alan Curtiss mathematics educator
Volkman, David J. immunology educator
Von Gonten, Kevin Paul priest, liturgist, theologian
†Waliser, Duane Edward atmospheric science educator, consultant
†Wang, Ban comparative literature educator, writer
Weidner, Donald J. geophysicist educator
Williams, George Christopher biologist, ecology and evolution educator
Wurster, Charles Frederick environmental scientist, educator
Zemanian, Armen Humpartsoum electrical engineer, mathematician

Stuyvesant
Tripp, David Enders numismatist, art historian, cartoonist
Tripp, Susan Gerwe museum director

Suffern
Codispoti, Andre John allergist, immunologist
Commanday, Sue Nancy Shair English language educator
Fogelman, Harold Hugo psychiatrist
Harvey, Emily Dennis art history educator
Harvuot, Cathleen Mary elementary education educator, principal
Jaffe, Elliot Stanley women's clothing retail chain founder, executive
Kromidas, Lambros cell biologist, physical scientist, toxicologist
Monahan, Frances Donovan nursing educator
Oppenheim, Jeffrey Sable neurosurgeon
Orazio, Paul Vincent financial planner

Stack, Daniel lawyer, financial consultant
Sutherland, George Leslie retired chemical company executive
Walsh, James Jerome philosophy educator

Sugar Loaf
Endico, Mary Antoinette artist
Rogers, James Tracy editor, author

Sunnyside
Giaimo, Kathryn Ann performing arts company executive
Turek, Charles Saul bookkeeper
Wallmann, Jeffrey Miner author

Syosset
Barry, Richard Francis retired life insurance company executive
Bermas, Stephen lawyer
†Collins, James Michael principal
Guthart, Leo A. electronics executive
Heller, Al marketing consultant, business journalist
Hull, Gretchen Gaebelein lay worker, writer, lecturer
Kniffin, Paula Sichel insurance sales executive
Lazor, Theodosius (His Beatitude Metropolitan Theodosius) archbishop
Nydick, David school superintendent
Roche, John Edward human resources management consultant, educator
Rudman, Michael P. publishing executive
Schiff, Peter Grenville venture capitalist
†Theodosius, (Most Blessed Theodosius) archbishop
Vermylen, Paul Anthony, Jr. oil company executive

Syracuse
Abbott, George Lindell librarian
Ackerman, Kenneth Edward lawyer, educator
Alston, William Payne philosophy educator
Andersen, Kristi Jean political scientist
Baker, Bruce Edward orthopedic surgeon, consultant
Baldwin, John Edwin chemistry educator
Barclay, H(ugh) Douglas lawyer, former state senator
Bellanger, Barbara Doris Hoysak biomedical research technologist
Berinstein, William Paul business executive
Birge, Robert Richards chemistry educator
Birkhead, Guthrie Sweeney, Jr. political scientist, university dean
Boeheim, Jim college basketball coach
Bogart, William Harry lawyer
Boghosian, Paula der computer business consultant
Braungart, Margaret Mitchell psychology educator
Braungart, Richard Gottfried sociology and international relations educator
Bunn, Timothy David newspaper editor
Burgess, Norma J. sociology educator
Burgess, Robert Lewis ecologist, educator
Butler, Richard John business educator
Carlson, William Clifford defense company executive
Carlton, Carole Gassett medical/surgical nurse
Charters, Alexander Nathaniel retired adult education educator
Cheng, David Keun engineering educator
Church, Philip Throop mathematician, educator
Cirando, John Anthony lawyer
Clausen, Jerry Lee psychiatrist
Cohen, William Nathan radiologist
Conan, Robert James, Jr. chemistry educator, consultant
Coppola, Elaine Marie librarian
Costello, Thomas Joseph bishop
Covillion, Jane Tanner mathematics educator
Crowley, John W(illiam) English language educator
Daly, Robert W. psychiatrist, medical educator
Davis, William E. utility executive
Delmar, Mario cardiac physiology educator
De Long, Jacob Edward real estate broker
Denise, Theodore Cullom philosophy educator
†DiBianco, Gustave J. federal judge, eductor
Drucker, Alan Steven mechanical engineer
Duerr, Dianne Marie physical education educator, professional sports medicine consultant
Dunham, Philip Bigelow biology educator, physiologist
Elms, Ben actor, director
Engel, Richard Lee lawyer, educator
Everett, Charles Roosevelt, Jr. airport executive
Farah, Fuad Salim dermatologist
Field, Daniel history educator
Fisher, Joseph V. retail executive
Fitzpatrick, James David lawyer
†Frank, Lawrence J. library administrator
Fraser, Henry S. lawyer
Frazier, J(ohn) Phillip manufacturing company executive
Frohock, Fred Manuel political science educator
Gaal, John lawyer
Gartner, Joseph Charles business systems administrator
Geisinger, Kurt Francis university administrator, psychometrician
Gerber, Edward F. lawyer, educator
Gilman, Karen Frenzel legal assistant
Gingold, Harlan Bruce lawyer
Gold, Joseph medical researcher
Graver, Jack Edward mathematics educator
Gray, Charles Augustus banker
†Gregory, Robert Granville historian
†Griffin, David mycologist
Grizanti, Anthony J. lawyer
Hamlett, James Gordon electronics engineer, management consultant, educator
Hancock, Stewart F., Jr. state judge
Hansen, Per Brinch computer scientist
Hayes, David Michael lawyer
Herzog, Peter Emilius legal educator
Higbee, Ann G. public relations executive, consultant
Hildebrandt, George Frederick lawyer
Hoffman, Arthur Wolf English language educator
Hole, Richard Douglas lawyer
Hollis, Susan Tower college dean
Honig, Arnold physics educator, researcher
Horn, Doreen T. critical care nurse
Horst, Pamela Sue medical educator, family physician
Hubbard, Peter Lawrence lawyer
Ikins, Rachael Zacov writer, illustrator, photographer
Irwin, Martin psychiatrist
Jensen, Robert Granville geography educator, university dean
Johnson, Marc Jay judge
Jump, Bernard, Jr. economics educator
Kelley, Johnnie L. mental health nurse
Kennedy, Samuel Van Dyke, III journalism educator
Kieffer, Stephen Aaron radiologist, educator
Konski, James Louis civil engineer
Kopp, Robert Walter lawyer
Krathwohl, David Reading education educator emeritus
Kriebel, Mahlon Edward physiology educator, inventor
Kriesberg, Louis sociologist, educator
Lambright, William Henry political science-public administration educator
LaRue, William David television critic
Lawton, Joseph J., Jr. retired lawyer
Lemon, Leslie Roy radar meteorologist
Levy, Hans Richard biochemistry educator
Lloyd, David Thomas writer, English educator
Luft, Eric v.d. librarian, educator
†Manke, Jeffrey Gerard college administrator
Marcoccia, Louis Gary accountant, university administrator
†Maroney, Thomas J. prosecutor
Mazur, Allan Carl sociologist, engineer, educator
McCoubrey, Sarah artist and art educator
McCurn, Neal Peters federal judge
McDonnell, Jeffrey John hydrology educator
Meinig, Donald William geography educator
Melnicoff, Joel Niesen lawyer, sports agent
Mesrobian, Arpena Sachaklian publisher, editor, consultant
Miller, Philip Charles lawyer
Monmonier, Mark geographer, graphics educator, essayist
Moses, Robert Edward lawyer
†Moynihan, James M. bishop
Mudrick, Nancy Ruth social work educator
Muller, Ernest H. geology educator
Munson, Howard G. federal judge
Murray, David George orthopedic surgeon, educator
Nafie, Laurence Allen chemistry educator
Nast, Edward Paul cardiac surgeon
Naum, Christopher John fire protection management and training consultant, educator
†Novelli, Cornelius educator, drama critic
†O'Keefe, Sean Charles public adminstration educator
Ortiz, Fernando, Jr. economic small business development consultant
Palmer, John L. social sciences researcher, educator
Pardee, Otway O'Meara computer science educator
Peters, Christopher Allen computer consultant
Pirozzi, Mildred Jean nursing administrator
Pooler, Rosemary S. federal judge
Powell, James Matthew history educator
Prucha, John James geologist, educator
Rabuzzi, Daniel D. medical educator
Ramsey, Dan Steven consultant, business executive
Ratner, Michael Harvey pediatric surgeon
Regan, Paul Michael lawyer
Robinson, Joseph Edward geology educator, consulting petroleum geologist
Rogers, Sherry Anne physician
Rogers, Stephen newspaper publisher
Rountree, Patricia Ann youth organization administrator
Rubin, David M. dean, educator
Russell-Hunter, Gus W(illiam) D(evigne) zoology educator, research biologist, writer
Sager, Jonathan Ward lawyer
Sagerman, Robert Howard radiation oncologist
Sargent, Robert George engineering educator
Scheinman, Steven Jay medical educator
Schiess, Betty Bone priest
†Schneider, Gerd Klaus German language educator
Schwartz, Richard Derecktor sociologist, educator
Scullin, Frederick James, Jr. federal judge
Shaw, Kenneth Alan university president
Shedlock, Kathleen Joan Petrouskie community health and research nurse
Skoler, Celia Rebecca art gallery director
Skoler, Louis architect, educator
Smith, Kenneth Judson, Jr. chemist, theoretician, educator
Smith, Robert L. medical research administrator
Stam, David Harry librarian
Steigerwald, Louis John, III corporate executive
Sternlicht, Sanford English and theater arts educator, writer
Sutton, Walter English educator
Szasz, Thomas Stephen psychiatrist, educator, writer
Tanenbaum, Stuart William biotechnologist, educator
Tatham, David Frederic art historian, educator
Thomas, Sidney fine arts educator, researcher
Threatte, Gregory Allen pathology educator, academic director
Turner, Christopher Edward cell biology educator
Verrillo, Ronald Thomas neuroscience educator, researcher
Waddy, Patricia A. architectural history educator
Wadley, Susan Snow anthropologist
Waite, Peter Arthur literacy educator, educational consultant
Ware, Bennie university administrator
Weiner, Irwin M. retired medical educator/ researcher, college dean,
Weiss, Volker university administrator, educator
Wellner, Marcel Nahum physics educator, researcher
Wells, Peter Nathaniel lawyer
Whaley, Ross Samuel academic administrator
Wiggins, James Bryan religion educator
Williams, William Joseph physician, educator
Wladis, Mark Neil lawyer
Wolff, Catherine Elizabeth opera company executive
Young, Douglas Howard lawyer
Zito, George Vincent sociologist, sociology educator

Syyosset
Gorenstein, Edward employment services executive

Tallman
Strasser, Joel A. public relations executive, engineer, producer

Tappan
Dell, Robert Christopher geothermal sculptor, scenic artist
Fox, Muriel public relations executive
Nickford, Juan sculptor, educator

Tarrytown
Anderson, John Erling chemical engineer
Ashburn, Anderson magazine editor
Bacaloglu, Radu chemical engineer
Baum, Carol Grossman physician
Bowen, Christopher Edward library director
Dobkin, John Howard art administrator
Farrell, Gregory Alan biomedical engineer
Ferrari, Robert Joseph business educator, former banker
Field, Barry Elliot internist, gastroenterologist
†Frisch, Albert T. composer
Fudge, Ann Marie marketing executive
Gross, Stanislaw environmental sciences educator, activist
Kane, Stanley Bruce food products executive
Kenney, Dion Patrick business strategist, entrepreneur
Kenney, John Michel architect
Kroll, Nathan film producer, director
LeGrice, Stephen magazine editor
Marcus, Sheldon social sciences educator
Neill, Richard Robert retired publishing company executive
Oelbaum, Harold lawyer, corporate executive
Panitz, Lawrence physician
Singer, Jeffrey Michael organic analytical chemist
Weiner, Max educational psychology educator
Whipple, Judith Roy book editor
Wood, Roger publishing executive

Thendara
Voce, Joan A. Cifonelli retired elementary school educator

Thornwood
Bassett, Lawrence C management consultant

Tillson
Giordano, Sondra nursing educator, medical and surgical nurse

Tivoli
Cary, Gregory J. dance center executive, dancer, choreographer, artist
Schade, Arthur George sculptor, educator

Tonawanda
Browning, James Franklin professional society executive
Dillman, Joseph John Thomas electric utility executive
Drozdziel, Marion John aeronautical engineer
Haller, Calvin John banker
Kulp, J. Robert metal company executive

Towson
Shriver, Pamela Howard retired professional tennis player, sports analyst

Troy
Abetti, Pier Antonio consulting electrical engineer, technology management and entrepreneurship educator
Ahlers, Rolf Willi philosopher, theologian
Belfort, Georges chemical engineering educator, consultant
Berg, Daniel science and technology educator
Bergles, Arthur Edward mechanical engineering educator
Block, Robert Charles nuclear engineering and engineering physics educator
Brazil, Harold Edmund political science educator
Breyman, Steve political science educator
Brunelle, Eugene John, Jr. mechanical engineering educator
Bunce, Stanley Chalmers chemist, educator
Burch, Mary Seelye Quinn law librarian, consultant
Carovano, John Martin not-for-profit adminstrator, conservationist
Daves, Glenn Doyle, Jr. science educator, chemist, researcher
Desrochers, Alan Alfred electrical engineer
Diwan, Romesh Kumar economics educator
Doremus, Robert Heward glass and ceramics processing educator
Drew, Donald Allen mathematical sciences educator
Duquette, David Joseph materials science and engineering educator
Dvorak, George J. mechanics and materials engineering educator
Ehrlich, Henry Lutz biology educator
Ferris, James Peter chemist, educator
Finkel, Sanford Norman lawyer
Fish, Jacob civil engineer, educator
Friedman, Sue Tyler technical publications executive
Gerhardt, Lester A. engineering educator, dean
Giaever, Ivar physicist
†Gil-Gomez, Ellen Marie English language educator
Gill, William Nelson chemical engineering educator
Glicksman, Martin Eden materials engineering educator
Goode, Jean publishing company executive
Gutmann, Ronald J. electrical engineering educator
Hampshire, John Carr, III artist, educator
Haviland, David Sands architectural educator, researcher, administrator
Hirsa, Amir H. aerospace engineer, educator
Hsu, Cheng decision sciences and engineering systems educator
Jones, E. Stewart, Jr. lawyer
Jordan, Mark Henry consulting civil engineer
Kahl, William Frederick retired college president
Krause, Sonja chemistry educator
Krempl, Erhard mechanics educator, consultant
Lahey, Richard Thomas, Jr. nuclear engineer, fluid mechanics engineer
Lemnios, Andrew Zachery aerospace engineer, educator, researcher
Levinger, Joseph Solomon physicist, educator
Littman, Howard chemical engineer, educator
McAllister, Edward William Charles educator
McDonald, John Francis Patrick electrical engineering educator
Medicus, Heinrich Adolf physicist, educator
Murarka, Shyam Prasad science educator, administrator
Nelson, John Keith electrical engineer
Oppenheim, Sheldon Frederick chemical engineer
Pascale, Ralph museum director
Phelan, Thomas clergyman, academic administrator, educator
Potts, Kevin T. emeritus chemistry educator
Romond, James principal
Rubens, Philip communications educator, technical writer
St. John, William Charles, Jr. business educator, administrator
Sanderson, Arthur Clark engineering educator
Saridis, George Nicholas electrical, computers and system engineering educator, robotics and automation researcher
Shuey, Richard Lyman engineering educator, consultant
Snyder, Patricia Di Benedetto theater director and administrator
Sperber, Daniel physicist
Stoloff, Norman Stanley materials engineering educator, researcher
Wait, Samuel Charles, Jr. academic administrator, educator
Watson, Edward Bruce science educator
Whitburn, Merrill Duane English literature educator
White, Frederick Andrew physics educator, physicist
Wilson, Jack Martin dean, scientific association executive, physics educator
Woods, John William electrical, computer and systems engineering educator, consultant
Zimmie, Thomas Frank civil engineer, educator

Truxton
Schultz, Helen Welkley marriage and family therapist, minister

Tuckahoe
Brecher, Bernd management consultant
Curtin, Brian Joseph ophthalmologist
Elliott, Dennis Dawson communications executive

Tupper Lake
Welsh, Peter Corbett museum consultant, historian

Tuxedo Park
Brown, Walston Shepard lawyer
Domjan, Joseph (Spiri Domjan) artist
Friedman, Rodger antiquarian bookseller, consultant
Groskin, Sheila Marie Lessen primary school educator
Hall, Frederick Keith chemist
Heusser, Calvin John biology educator, researcher
†Lippmann, Morton environmental health science researcher
Regan, Ellen Frances (Mrs. Walston Shepard Brown) ophthalmologist
Rossman, Toby Gale genetic toxicology educator, researcher

Unadilla
Compton, John Robinson rake company executive

Uniondale
Arbour, Alger professional hockey coach
†Boyle, E. Thomas federal judge
Cassidy, David Michael lawyer
Eilen, Howard Scott lawyer, mediator
Henning, Lorne Edward professional hockey coach
Milbury, Mike professional hockey coach
Mishler, Jacob federal judge
†Orenstein, Michael L. federal judge
Platt, Thomas Collier, Jr. federal judge
†Pohorelsky, Viktor Vaclav federal magistrate judge
Potvin, Felix professional hockey player
Seybert, Joanna federal judge
Spatt, Arthur Donald federal judge

Upper Nyack
†Seife, Agie information technologist

Upton
Blume, Martin physicist
Bond, Peter Danford physicist
Chrien, Robert Edward retired physicist
Fthenakis, Vasilis chemical engineer, consultant, educator
Goldhaber, Maurice physicist
Hamilton, Leonard Derwent physician, molecular biologist
Harbottle, Garman chemist
Hendrie, Joseph Mallam physicist, nuclear engineer, government official
Holroyd, Richard Allen research scientist
Lindenbaum, S(eymour) J(oseph) physicist
Lowenstein, Derek Irving physicist
Marr, Robert Bruce physicist, educator
McWhan, Denis Bayman physicist
Ozaki, Satoshi physicist
Pandey, Sanjeev Ulrich physicist
Petrakis, Leonidas research scientist, educator, administrator
Qian, Shinan optical engineer, researcher, educator
Radeka, Veljko electronics engineer
Rau, Ralph Ronald retired physicist
Ruckman, Mark Warren physicist
Samios, Nicholas Peter physicist
Setlow, Jane Kellock biophysicist
Setlow, Richard Burton biophysicist
Shutt, Ralph P. research physicist
Steinberg, Meyer chemical engineer
Studier, Frederick William biophysicist
Susskind, Herbert biomedical engineer, educator
Sutherland, John Clark physicist, researcher
Sutin, Norman chemistry educator, scientist

Utica
Antzelevitch, Charles research center executive
Austin, Michael Charles insurance company executive
Baller, William Warren school psychologist
Bowers, Roger Paul radiologist
Boyle, William Leo, Jr. educational consultant, retired college president
Brennan, John Joseph lawyer, legal administrator
Cardamone, Richard J. federal judge
Cuccaro, Ronald Anthony insurance adjusting company executive
Donovan, Donna Mae newspaper publisher
Ehre, Victor Tyndall insurance company executive
Fay, Nancy Elizabeth nurse
Gape, Serafina Vetrano decorative artist and designer
†Gerling, Stephen P. federal judge
†Hurd, David N. federal judge
Iodice, Arthur Alfonso biochemist
Jones, Hugh Richard lawyer
Labuz, Ronald Matthew design educator
Millet, John Bradford retired surgeon
Pribble, Easton artist
Schrauth, William Lawrence banker, lawyer
Schweizer, Paul Douglas museum director

Vails Gate
Fife, Betty H. librarian

Valhalla
Accardo, Pasquale J. pediatrician, educator
†Ahluwalia, Brij M. Singh neurologist, educator
Cimino, Joseph Anthony physician, educator
Couldwell, William Tupper neurosurgeon, educator
Czarnecki, Anthony J. correction administrator, educator

Del Guercio, Louis Richard Maurice *surgeon, educator, company executive*
Fink, Raymond *medical educator*
Frishman, William Howard *cardiology educator, cardiovasular pharmacologist, gerontologist*
Frost, Elizabeth Ann McArthur *physician*
†Hankin, Joseph Nathan *college president*
Hommes, Frits Aukustinus *biology educator*
Kilbourne, Edwin Dennis *virologist, educator*
Kline, Susan Anderson *medical school official and dean, internist*
Leone, Stephen Joseph *English language educator, computer technology consultant*
Madden, Robert Edward *surgeon, educator*
Masdeu, Jose Cruz *neurologist, medical school administrator*
McGiff, John C(harles) *pharmacologist*
Paik, John Kee *structural engineer*
Radeboldt-Daly, Karen Elaine *medical nurse*
Reed, George Elliott *surgery educator*
Smith-Young, Anne Victoria *health services coordinator*
Valsamis, Marius Peter *neuropathologist, educator*
Warakomski, Alphonse Walter Joseph, Jr. *sales executive*
Weisburger, John Hans *medical researcher*
Williams, Gary Murray *medical researcher, pathology educator*
Wolin, Michael Stuart *physiology educator*

Valley Cottage
Greene, Stephen *painter*
Shaderowfsky, Eva Maria *photographer, writer, computer specialist*
Stolldorf, Genevieve Schwager *media specialist*

Valley Stream
Blakeman, Royal Edwin *lawyer*
De Mita, Francis Anthony *mathematics educator*
Ellis, Bernice *financial planning company executive, investment advisor*
Ferares, Kenneth *automobile executive*
Haies, Evelyn S(olomon) *fundraiser, educator, writer*
Lehrer, Stanley *magazine publisher, editorial director, corporate executive*
Rachlin, Harvey Brant *author*
Rosenberg, Lee Evan *financial planner*
Wollman, June Rose *clothing executive*

Van Hornesville
†Durham, Ormonde George, III *manufacturing executive*

Vestal
Carpenter, Charles Albert *English language educator*
Piaker, Philip Martin *accountant, educator*

Victor
†Schmidt, Douglas Karl *elementary education educator*

Waccabuc
Reid, Mary Louise *educational consultant*

Wading River
Bolger, Virginia Joan *nursing administrator*
Budd, Bernadette Smith *newspaper executive, public relations consultant*
Marlow, Audrey Swanson *artist, designer*

Wainscott
Dubow, Arthur Myron *investor, lawyer*
Henderson, William Charles *editor*
Herzog, Arthur, III *author*
Russo, Alexander Peter *artist, educator*

Walden
Hraniotis, Judith Beringer *artist*
Konior, Jeannette Mary *elementary school educator*

Wallkill
Bittner, Ronald Joseph *computer systems analyst, magician*
Koch, Edwin Ernest *artist, interior decorator*
Leopold, Richard William *middle school educator*

Wantagh
Glaser, David *painter, sculptor*
†Kappenberg, Marilyn Lorrin *library director*
Kushner, Aileen *medical/surgical nurse*
Marcatante, John Joseph *educational administrator*
Ross, Sheldon Jules *dentist*
Smits, Edward John *museum consultant*
Urbaitis, Elena *artist*
Zinder, Newton Donald *stock market analyst, consultant*

Wappingers Falls
Engelman, Melvin Alkon *retired dentist, business executive, scientist*
Johnson, Jeh Vincent *architect*
Kells, Albert John *financial consultant*
Maissel, Leon Israel *physicist, engineer*
McCamy, Calvin Samuel *optics scientist*
Sucich, Diana Catherine *school psychologist, counselor*
Wolfson, Ann Helene *secondary school educator*

Warsaw
Dy-Ang, Anita C. *pediatrician*

Warwick
Franck, Frederick Sigfred *artist, author, dental surgeon*
Greenwood, John Edward Douglas *investment banker, lawyer*
†Kaminsky, Anatol *educator, writer*
Mack, Daniel Richard *furniture designer*
Sierra, Victor, Jr. *poet*
Simon, Dolores Daly *copy editor*

Washington Mills
†Wei, Wen Chen *neurosurgeon*

Washingtonville
Guarino, Louis Joseph *mechanical engineer, consultant*

Water Mill
D'Urso, Joseph Paul *interior designer*
Kreimer, Michael Walter *financial planner, investment company official*

Waterford
Glavin, A. Rita Chandellier (Mrs. James Henry Glavin, III) *lawyer*
Gold, James Paul *museum director*
†Madigan, Francis Vincent *English educator*

Watertown
Brett, James Clarence *retired journalism educator*
Coe, Benjamin Plaisted *retired state official*
Ebbels, Bruce Jeffery *physician, health facility administrator*
Fredriksen, Maryellen *physician assistant*
Henderson, Gladys Edith *retired social welfare examiner*
†Innes, George Michael *emergency medicine physician*
Johnson, John Brayton *editor, publisher*
Rankin, Bonnie Lee *insurance executive*
†Scanlon, Daniel, Jr. *federal judge*
Smith, Marcia Jeanne *secondary school educator*

Watervliet
Alber, Richard Lawrence *quality assurance professional*
Hilts, Earl T. *lawyer, government official, educator*

Waverly
Forest, Bob *author, poet*

Webster
Conwell, Esther Marly *physicist*
Dea, Donald Don *business executive*
Duke, Charles Bryan *research and development manufacturing executive, physics educator*
Herman, Richard Charles *educator*
Liebert, Arthur Edgar *retired hospital administrator*
McCormack, Stanley Eugene *financial consultant*
Nicholson, Douglas Robert *accountant*
Przybylowicz, Edwin Paul *chemical company executive, retired research director*
Shirkey, William Dan *writer*
Southard, Paul Raymond *financial executive*
Theis, Nancy Nichols *community activist, mental retardation specialist*
Witmer, G. Robert *retired state supreme court justice*

Weedsport
Cichello, Samuel Joseph *architect*

Wellsville
Tezak, Edward George *dean*

West Bloomfield
Charron, Helene Kay Shetler *retired nursing educator*

West Harrison
Verano, Anthony Frank *retired banker*

West Hempstead
Guggenheimer, Heinrich Walter *mathematician, educator*
Tartell, Robert Morris *retired dentist*

West Hurley
Martucci, Vincent James *composer, pianist*

West Islip
Cassell, Dean George *retired aerospace executive, management consultant*
Keller, Joyce *television and radio host, counselor, writer*
Softness, Donald Gabriel *marketing and manufacturing executive*

West Kill
Dwon, Larry *retired electrical engineer, educator, consultant*

West Leyden
Kornatowski, Susan Carol *elementary education educator*

West Nyack
†Cunneen, Sally McDevitt *English language educator, editor, writer*
Hornik, Joseph William *civil engineer*
†Katz, S. Sheldon *neurolosurgeon*
Oppenheim, Robert *beauty industry executive*
Pringle, Laurence Patrick *writer*

West Point
†Abizaid, John P. *career officer*
Barr, Donald Roy *statistics and operations research educator, statistician*
Burke, Michael Augustus *miliatary officer*
Christman, Daniel William *military officer*
Hilferty, Bryan Carey *English language educator*
Kingseed, Cole Christian *military officer, history educator*
Leupold, Herbert August *physicist*
Oldaker, Bruce Gordon *physicist, military officer*
Shoop, Barry LeRoy *electrical engineer, educator*
Watson, Georgianna *librarian*

West Sand Lake
Rogers, James Edwin *secondary school educator, retired*

West Seneca
Kelly, Anne Catherine *retired city official*
Krist, Betty Jane *mathematics educator, researcher*
Wolfgang, Jerald Ira *economic development educator*

West Shokan
Mackey, Jeffrey Allen *priest*

Westbury
Barboza, Anthony *photographer, artist*
†Bernstein, Stan *federal judge*
†Conrad, Francis G. *federal judge*
De Pauw, Gommar Albert *priest, educator*
Eisenberg, Dorothy *federal judge*
Ente, Gerald *pediatrician*
Fogg, Joseph Graham, III *investment banking executive*
†Krampitz, Barbara E.M. *library director*
Lelonek, David *optometrist*
†Mondello, Joseph N. *political party chairman*
Nogee, Jeffrey Laurence *lawyer*
O'Mara, Sharyn *advertising executive*
Rosenberg, Rudy *chemical company executive*
Sherbell, Rhoda *artist, sculptor*
Tulchin, Stanley *banker, lecturer, author, business reorganization consultant*
Zychick, Joel David *lawyer*

Westhampton Beach
Maas, Jane Brown *advertising executive*

White Plains
Alcena, Valiere *internist, hematologist, educator, television producer, broadcast journalist*
Alin, Robert David *lawyer*
Allen, Ralph Dean *diversified company corporate executive*
Araskog, Rand Vincent *diversified telecommunications multinational company executive*
Aron, Eve Glicka Serenson *personal care industry executive*
Barrow, Marie Antonette *elementary school educator*
Bartels, Juergen E. *hotel company executive*
Becker, Boris *professional tennis player*
Benjamin, Barbara Bloch *writer, editor*
Berlin, Alan Daniel *lawyer, international energy and legal consultant*
†Berliner, David C. *foundation administrator*
†Bernard, Robert William *plastic surgeon*
Bertles, John Francis *physician, educator*
Biers, Martin Henry *physician*
Bijur, Peter I. *petroleum company executive*
Blass, John Paul *medical educator, physician*
†Blau, Morocai *plastic surgeon*
Bloom, Adam I. *psychologist*
Bober, Lawrence Harold *retired banker*
Bodnar, Peter O. *lawyer*
Boeringer, Greta *librarian*
Boese, Geraldine Florence *nurse administrator*
Bostin, Marvin Jay *hospital and health services consultant*
Brazell, James Ervin *oil company executive, lawyer*
Brieant, Charles La Monte *federal judge*
Busch, Paul L. *engineering executive*
Canepa, Cathy *psychiatrist*
Carey, John *lawyer, judge*
Cheng, Alexander Lihdar *computer scientist, researcher*
Cobb, Vicki *writer*
Cohen, Joseph Michael *communications executive*
Colwell, Howard Otis *advertising executive*
†Connelly, John J. *federal judge*
Conner, William Curtis *judge*
Daraio, Robert Reid *technical/video engineer*
Davenport, Lindsay *professional tennis player*
DeMond, Jeffrey Stuart *cable television and telecommunications executive*
Engen, D(onald) Travis *diversified telecommunications company executive*
Erla, Karen *artist, painter, collagist, printmaker*
Feder, Robert *lawyer*
Fernandez, Gigi *professional tennis player*
Flanigen, Edith Marie *materials scientist, consultant*
Foster, John Horace *consulting environmental engineer*
Fowlkes, Nancy Lanetta Pinkard *social worker*
Fox, Mark D. *judge*
Frazier, Amy *professional tennis player*
†Gambill, Jan-Michael *professional tennis player*
Garrison-Jackson, Zina *retired tennis player*
Gilbert, Bradley *professional tennis coach, former professional tennis player, former Olympic athlete*
Gill, Patricia Jane *human resources executive*
Gillingham, Stephen Thomas *financial planner*
†Gimelstob, Justin *professional tennis player*
Gjertsen, O. Gerard *lawyer*
Goodman, Walter *author, editor*
†Gordon, Susan J. *writer*
Greene, Leonard Michael *aerospace manufacturing executive, institute executive*
Greenspan, Leon Joseph *lawyer*
†Greenup, Marion Teresa *not-for-profit health organization administrator*
Grossman, Ann *professional tennis player*
Halpern, Philip Morgan *lawyer*
Hardin, Adlai Stevenson, Jr. *judge*
Kabakoff, Jacob *retired religious studies educator*
Katz, Michael *pediatrician, educator*
Kaushik, Surendra Kumar *economist*
Keegan, Warren Joseph *business educator, consultant*
Klein, Paul E. *lawyer*
Kleisner, Fred *hotel executive*
Krasne, Charles A. *food products executive*
Lalli, Michael Anthony *lawyer*
Lapidus, Herbert *medical products executive*
Levine, Steven Jon *lawyer*
Liebert, Peter Selig *pediatric surgeon, consultant*
Lipsky, Leonard *merger, management and acquisition specialist, financial and marketing consultant*
Lukaszewski, James Edmund *communications executive*
Machover, Carl *computer graphics consultant*
Maffeo, Vincent Anthony *lawyer, executive*
Manville, Stewart Roebling *archivist*
Marano, Anthony Joseph *cardiologist*
Marrero, Vito Anthony *surgeon*
Martin, Thomas Rhodes *communications executive, writer*
Mattison, Donald Roger *dean, physician, educator, military officer*
McCarthy, John Robert *real estate firm officer*
McDowell, Fletcher Hughes *physician, educator*
McEnroe, Patrick *professional tennis player*
McMahon, Colleen *judge*
McNeil, Lori Michelle *professional tennis player*
Minsker, Eliot A. *publishing executive*
Mitchell, Robert Dale *consulting engineer*
Monteferrante, Judith Catherine *cardiologist*
Morello, Daniel Conway *plastic surgeon*
Morris, Robert Warren *physician assistant*
Munneke, Gary Arthur *law educator, consultant*
Mutz, Steven Herbert *lawyer*
Nesci, Vincent Peter *lawyer*
Nolletti, James Joseph *lawyer*
Orisek, Ivan *business executive, consultant*
Otten, Michael *data processing executive*
Papp, Laszlo George *architect*
Parker, Barrington D., Jr. *lawyer*
Patman, Jean Elizabeth *journalist*
Payson, Martin Fred *lawyer*
Peck, Alexander Norman *elementary education educator*
Peyton, Donald Leon *retired standards association executive*
Pfeffer, Cynthia Roberta *psychiatrist, educator*
†Raue, Patrick J. *psychologist*
†Raymond, Lisa *tennis player*
Reap, James B. *judge*
Reneberg, Richard (Richey Reneberg) *professional tennis player*
†Ritter, Robert W. *editor*
Roll, Irwin Clifford (Win Roll) *advertising, marketing and publishing executive*
Rosenberg, Michael *lawyer*
Rubin, Chanda *professional tennis player*
Ryan, Joseph F. *educator*
Ryan, Robert Davis *lawyer*
Ryan, Theresa Ann Julia *accountant*
Samii, Abdol Hossein *physician, educator*
Sanford, Linda S. *computer manufacturing executive*
†Sax, Boria *educator, writer*
†Schnyder, Patty *professional tennis player*
Scott, Nancy Ellen *psychologist*
Scott-Williams, Wendy Lee *information technology specialist*
Sedelmaier, J. J. *filmmaker*
Serchuk, Ivan *lawyer*
Silverberg, Steven Mark *lawyer*
Silverman, Al *editor*
Sive, David *lawyer*
Sloan, F(rank) Blaine *law educator*
Smith, Elizabeth Patience *oil industry executive, lawyer*
Smith, Gerard Peter *neuroscientist*
Smith, Lisa Margaret *lawyer*
Soley, Robert Lawrence *plastic surgeon*
Stalerman, Ruth *civic volunteer, poet*
Szolnoki, John Frank *special education educator, administrator*
Taft, Nathaniel Belmont *lawyer*
Taub, Larry Steven *education administrator*
Topol, Robin April Levitt *lawyer*
Triffin, Nicholas *law librarian, law educator*
Tsamis, Donna Robin *lawyer*
Vick, James Albert *publishing executive, consultant*
Vogel, Howard Stanley *lawyer*
Westerhoff, Garret Peter *environmental engineer, executive*
Wheaton, David *professional tennis player*
†Williams, Serena *professional tennis player*
†Williams, Venus *tennis player*
Winterton, Joseph Henry *computer software executive*
Woody, Carol Clayman *data processing executive*

Whitesboro
†Blake, Edward Stephens *secondary education educator*
Bulman, William Patrick *data processing executive*
Raymonda, James Earl *retired banker*

Whitestone
Caldwell, David Bruce *music store executive*
Dressler, Brenda Joyce *health educator, consultant, book and film reviewer*
Feinberg, Irwin L. *retired manufacturing company executive*
Juszczak, Nicholas Mauro *psychology educator*
Lodico, Cheryl Madeline *secondary education educator*
Rahr, Stewart *health medical products executive*
Rosmarin, Leonard Alan *dermatologist*

Williamson
Ross, Kathleen Marie Amato *secondary school educator*

Williamsville
Cloudsley, Donald Hugh *library administrator*
De Gasper, Edgar Eugene *food services consultant*
Jones, Robert Alfred *retired clergyman*
Krzyzan, Judy Lynn *automotive executive*
Mack, Gregory John *financial executive and consultant*
McDuffie, Michael Anthony *investment company executive*
Ogra, Pearay L. *physician, educator*
Reisman, Robert E. *physician, educator*
Stein, Alfred Marvin *hematologist*
Stoeckl, Shelley Joan *marketing professional*
Whitcomb, James Stuart *videographer, photographer, production company executive*

Williston Park
Segel, J. Norman *garment manufacturing company executive*

Willow
Bley, Carla Borg *jazz composer*
Cox, James David *art gallery executive*

Windsor
Decker, Susan Carol *elementary education educator*

Wolcott
Bartlett, Cody Blake *lawyer, educator*
Searle, Robert Ferguson *minister*

Woodbury
Bell, William Joseph *cable television company executive*
Doering, Charles Henry *research scientist, educator, editor, publisher*
Guttenplan, Harold Esau *retired food company executive*
Kitzis, Gary David *periodontist, educator*
McEnroe, Kate *broadcast executive*

Woodhaven
Bolster, Jacqueline Neben (Mrs. John A. Bolster) *communications consultant*
†Liu, Weihong *art critic*
Zizi *artist*

Woodmere
Bobroff, Harold *lawyer*
Cohen, Lawrence Alan *health facility administrator*
Levine, Solomon *clinical psychologist*
Natow, Annette Baum *nutritionist, author, consultant*

Woodside
Kekatos, Deppie-Tinny Z. *microbiologist, researcher, lab technologist*
VanArsdale, Diana Cort *social worker*
Vasilachi, Vasile Gheorghe *priest, vicar*
Wynne, Linda Marie *administrative assistant, artist*

Woodstock
Banks, Rela *sculptor*
Currie, Bruce *artist*
Dolamore, Michael John *physician*
Godwin, Gail Kathleen *author*
†Hahne Hofsted, Janet Lorraine *artist*
†Hamel, Manette C. *artist, writer*
Ober, Stuart Alan *investment consultant, book publisher*
Smith, Albert Aloysius, Jr. *electrical engineer, consultant*

Wyandanch
Barnett, Peter John *property development executive, educator*

Yonkers
Agli, Stephen Michael *English language educator, literature educator*
Alessi, George Anthony *financial advisor, consultant*
Alexander, Stanley F. *municipal agency administrator*
Alpert, Caroline Evelyn *nurse*
Baumel, Herbert *violinist, conductor*
†Baumel, Joan Patricia French *educator, writer, lecturer*
†Carman, Gary O. *hospital administrator*
Celli, Joseph *municipal government official*
Clark, Celia Rue *lawyer*
Connors, James Patrick *lawyer*
Daman, Harlan Richard *allergist*
Denver, Eileen Ann *magazine editor*
Eimicke, Victor W(illiam) *publishing company executive*
Farmer, Joe *municipal official*
Friend, Miriam Ruth *personnel company executive*
Goon, Gilbert *software consultant*
Hirschman, Shalom Zarach *physician*
Johansen, Robert Joseph *consulting actuary*
Kaiser, Ann *municipal agency administrator*
Karpatkin, Rhoda Hendrick *consumer information organization executive, lawyer*
Lamagna, Joseph *author*
LaPerche, James *municipal agency admimnstrator*
Leo, Jacqueline M. *television executive, editor*
Levatino, Thomas, Jr. *physics and chemistry educator*
Liggio, Jean Vincenza *adult education educator, artist*
Liszewski, John *municipal official*
Lukach, Arthur S., Jr. *manufacturing executive*
Lupiani, Donald Anthony *psychologist*
†Maritime, George *writer, photographer*
McGovern, Frank J. *municipal official*
Mennin, Gerald Stanley *ophthalmologist*
Miller, Karl A. *management counselor*
Monegro, Francisco *psychology educator, alternative medicine consultant*
Moonie, William M. *lawyer*
Neal, Leora Louise Haskett *social services administrator*
Newman, Suzanne Dinkes *web site development executive*
O'Donnell, Robert George *fine artist*
Pasquale, Terry *police department administrator*
†Rosch, Elliott Carl *internist*
Roth, Howard *chemist, engineer, consultant*
Saslow, Steve *television director, editor*
Sialiano, Salvatore *municipal agency administrator*
Singer, Cecile Doris *state legislator*
Smith, Aldo Ralston, Jr. *brokerage house executive*
Torrese, Dante Michael *prosthodontist, educator*
Tutoni, Mitchell A. *municipal official*
Varma, Baidya Nath *sociologist, broadcaster, poet*
†Wen, Sheree *computer compancy executive, president*
Weston, Francine Evans *secondary education educator*
Williams, Ted Vaughnell *physical education educator*
Wolfson, Irwin M. *insurance company executive*

York
Coleman, David Cecil *financial executive*

Yorktown Heights
Bennett, Charles H. *director programs*
Chaudhari, Praveen *materials physicist*
†Delmoro, Ronald Anthony *elementary school principal*
Dennard, Robert Heath *engineering executive, scientist*
d'Heurle, François Max *research scientist, engineering educator*
Dill, Frederick Hayes *electrical engineer*
Donovan, Andrew Joseph *financial consultant*
Fang, Frank Fu *physicist, electronics engineer*
Fowler, Alan Bicksler *retired physicist*
Garwin, Richard Lawrence *physicist*
Gutzwiller, Martin Charles *theoretical physicist, research scientist*
Hoffman, Alan Jerome *mathematician, educator*
Hong, Se June *computer engineer*
Jones, Lauretta Marie *artist, graphic designer, computer interface designer*
Kessler, Bernard Milton *organizational and human resources development specialist*
Keyes, Robert W. *physicist*
Kirkpatrick, Edward Scott *physicist*
Landauer, Rolf William *physicist*
Lang, Norton David *physicist*
Lavenberg, Stephen S. *electrical engineer, researcher*
†Masullo, Miriam Julia *computer scientist*
Ning, Tak Hung *physicist, microelectronic technologist*
Romankiw, Lubomyr Taras *materials engineer*
Rosenblatt, Stephen Paul *marketing and sales promotion company executive*
Sorokin, Peter Pitirimovich *physicist*
Spiller, Eberhard Adolf *physicist*
Terman, Lewis Madison *electrical engineer, researcher*
Troutman, Ronald R. *electrical engineer*
Wade, James O'Shea *publisher*
Wajda, Tadeusz *engineer*
Winograd, Shmuel *mathematician*

Youngstown
Alpert, Norman *chemical company executive*
Lamb, Charles F. *minister*
Micieli, Karen Krisher *geriatrics nurse*

NORTH CAROLINA

Aberdeen
Jacobson, Peter Lars *neurologist, educator*
Marcham, Timothy Victor *pharmacist*

Advance
Cochrane, Betsy Lane *state senator*
Herpel, George Lloyd *marketing educator*
Huber, Thomas Martin *container company executive*
Walser, Sandra Teresa Johnson *rehabilitation nurse, preceptor*

Andrews
Steinbronn, Richard Eugene *lawyer*

Angier
McClain, Gregory David *minister*

Apex
Ellington, John David *retired state official*
Liu, Andrew Tze Chiu *chemical researcher and developer*
Rawlings, John Oren *statistician, researcher*

Arden
Adams, Pamela Jeanne *nurse, flight nurse*

Asheboro
Davis, J. B. *furniture manufacturing executive*
Helsabeck, Eric H. *emergency physician*
Jones, David M. *zoological park director*
Talley, Doris Lanier *instructional technology specialist*

Asheville
Allen, Heather Lindsey *textile artist, art educator, writer*
Baldwin, Garza, Jr. *lawyer, manufacturing company executive*
Bissette, Winston Louis, Jr. *lawyer, mayor*
Born, Robert Heywood *consulting civil engineer*
Boyce, Emily Stewart *retired library and information science educator*
Branch, John Wells (Jack Twig) *lawyer*
Carver, M. Kyle *secondary education educator*
Cecil, William A.V. *landmark director*
†Chapman, Gary H. *artist, educator*
†Cogburn, Max Oliver *lawyer*
Coli, Guido John *chemical company executive*
Cragnolin, Karen Zambella *real estate developer, lawyer*
Damtoft, Walter Atkinson *editor, publisher*
Dickens, Charles Henderson *retired social scientist, consultant*
Edminster, Walter B. *protective services official*
Enriquez, Manuel Hipolito *physician*
Etter, Robert Miller *retired consumer products executive, chemist*
Haggard, William Henry *meteorologist*
Hyde, Herbert Lee *lawyer*
Johnson, John Andrew *construction executive*
Johnston, John Devereaux, Jr. *law educator, retired*
Jones, J. Kenneth *art dealer, former museum administrator*
King, Joseph Bertram *architect*
Korb, Elizabeth Grace *nurse midwife*
Levin, Robert Alan *glass artist*
Lowery, Douglas Lane *retired environmental engineer*
Meyerson, Seymour *retired chemist*
Murdock, William Joseph *foundation adminstrator, educator*
Neese, Heidi Sue *television news assignment editor*
Pickard, Carolyn Rogers *secondary school educator*
Pine, Charles *retail executive*
Quinn, Barbara Ann *athletics administrator, educator*
Ray, Ruth Alice Yancey *retired rancher, real estate developer*
Reed, Patsy Bostick *academic administrator*
Roberts, Bill Glen *retired fire chief, investor, consultant*
Scully, John Robert *oral and maxillofacial surgeon*
Sharpe, Keith Yount *retired lawyer*
Summers, Ruth T. *cultural organization executive*
Summey, Steven Michael *advertising company executive*
Thornburg, Lacy Herman *federal judge*
Turcot, Marguerite Hogan *innkeeper, medical researcher*
†Ulrey, Lee Williams *educator*
Vander Voort, Dale Gilbert *textile company executive*
Weber, Kathleen *basketball coach*
Weed, Maurice James *composer, retired music educator*
Weil, Thomas P. *health services consultant*
Weinhagen, Susan Pouch *emergency care nurse*
West, Michael J. *real estate developer, business owner*
White, Terry Edward *physician*

Atlantic Beach
Barnes, James Thomas, Jr. *aquarium director*

Ayden
Nobles, Lorraine Biddle *dietitian*

Balsam
†Merritt, Mark Francis *educator*

Banner Elk
Littlejohn, Mark Hays *radiologist*
Thomas, John Edwin *retired academic administrator*

Battleboro
Hardy, Linda Lea Sterlock *media specialist*

Beaufort
Cullman, Hugh *retired tobacco company executive*
Hardee, Luellen Carroll Hooks *school psychologist*
Mackenzie, James *fire protection and industrial safety executive*
Pagano, Filippo Frank *financial broker, commercial loan consultant*
Ramus, Joseph S. *marine biologist*

Belmont
Stowe, Robert Lee, III *textile company executive*

Benson
Taylor, Martha McClintock *marriage and family therapist, researcher*

Black Mountain
Cody, Hiram Sedgwick, Jr. *retired telephone company executive*
Hibbard, Carl Roger *social services administrator*
Lathrop, Gertrude Adams *chemist, consultant*

Blowing Rock
Barnebey, Kenneth Alan *food company executive*

Boiling Springs
Arnold, Ernest Woodrow *minister*
Hearne, Stephen Zachary *minister, educator*
Lamb, Robert Lee *religious studies educator*
Rainer, Jackson Patten *psychologist, educator*
Vaughan, Ted Wayne *music and communications educator, musician*
White, Martin Christopher *academic administrator*

Bolivia
Johnson, Melba Edwards *secondary education educator*

Boone
Aluri, Rao *book publisher*
Borkowski, Francis Thomas *university administrator*
Brown, Jane Comfort Brennan *educator, language and movement therapist*
Dean, James M. *investment adviser*
Domer, Floyd Ray *pharmacologist, educator*
Duke, Charles Richard *academic dean*
Durham, Harvey Ralph *academic administrator*
Falvo, Robert J. *music educator*
Greene, Melanie Anita Ward *education educator*
Johnson, Phillip Eugene *mathematics educator*
Jones, Dan Lewis *psychologist*
Land, Ming Huey *college dean*
Mackorell, James Theodore, Jr. *entrepreneur, small business owner*
†McCoy, Todd Edward *real estate appraiser*
Oelberg, Robert Nathan *landscape architect*
Parker, William Dale *management consultant, political adviser*
Pollard, William Barlow, III *university educator*
Pollitt, Phoebe Ann *school nurse*
Robinson, Linda *college program administrator*
†Simon, Stephen Joseph *history educator*
Williamson, Jerry Wayne *history educator, editor*
Woollcombe, Graham Douglas *dean*

Brevard
Bertrand, Annabel Hodges *civic worker, artist, calligrapher*
†Effron, David Louis *conductor, music director*
Flory, Margaret Martha *retired religious organization administrator*
Jones, Sandy (Sandra F.) *writer, speaker, parenting expert*
McDowell, Laura *music educator*
Murray, Douglas Timothy *sculptor, art educator*
Phillips, Euan Hywel *publishing executive*

Bryson City
Marr, Margaret Ann Lackey *writer*

Buies Creek
Whichard, Willis Padgett *law educator, former state supreme court justice*
Wiggins, Norman Adrian *university administrator, legal educator*

Bunn
Boblett, Mark Anthony *civil engineering technician*

Burlington
Buckley, J. Stephen *newspaper publisher*
†Clarke, Peter Randolph Hasche *neurologist*
Eddins, James William, Jr. *marketing executive*
Holt, Bertha Merrill *state legislator*
Kee, Walter Andrew *former government official*
Kernodle, Lucy Hendrick *school system nurse*
Knesel, Ernest Arthur, Jr. *diagnostic company executive*
Mason, James Michael *biomedical laboratories executive*
McCrickard, Eric Eugene *customer service representative*
Patterson, Robert Campbell, Jr. *civil engineer*
Powell, James Bobbitt *biomedical laboratories executive, pathologist*
Stafford, Kenneth Dean *architect*
Turanchik, Michael *research and development director*
Wilson, William Preston *psychiatrist, emeritus educator*

Burnsville
Bernstein, William Joseph *glass artist, educator*
Doyle, John Lawrence *artist*
Gouge, Ruby Lee *textiles company administrator*

Butner
Ostby, Sandra Josephine *dietitian*

Calabash
Colvin-Herron, Gayle Ann *mental health consultant, psychotherapist, health facility administrator, columnist writer*
Strunk, Orlo Christopher, Jr. *psychology educator*

Camden
Hammond, Roy Joseph *reinsurance company executive*

Camp Lejeune
Bedard, Emil R. *career officer*
Blackman, Robert R., Jr. *career officer*
Rollings, Wayne E. *military officer*

Candler
Crowder, Julian Anthony *optometrist*

Canton
Dixon, Shirley Juanita *restaurant owner*
Hooper, Carl Glenn *civil engineer, software author, contractor*

Cape Carteret
Mullikin, Thomas Wilson *mathematics educator*

Carrboro
Anderson, Arthur Lee *sculptor, writer*
Boggs, Robert Newell *editor*
†Brunet, James Robert *public administration research associate*

Cary
Alstadt, Donald Martin *business executive*
Bates, Roger Alan *entertainer*
Bat-haee, Mohammad Ali *educational administrator, consultant*
Conrad, Hans *materials engineering educator*
Glass, Fred Stephen *lawyer*
Goodnight, James *software company executive*
Hagan, John Aubrey *financial executive*
Harvey, Daniel Richard *minister*
Jones, James Arthur *retired utilities executive*
Khan, Masrur Ali *nuclear and chemical engineer, physicist*
Martin, William Royall, Jr. *retired association executive*
Mata, Elizabeth Adams *language educator, land investor*
McCarty, Thomas Joseph *publishing company executive*
†Meyer, William Eugene *marketing consultant*
Miranda, Constancio Fernandes *civil engineering educator*
Mochrie, Richard D. *physiology educator*
Montgomery, Charles Harvey *lawyer*
Nyce, David Scott *electronics company executive*
Saunders, Barry Wayne *state official*
Smith, Janet Sue *systems specialist*
Summers, Suzanne Frances Hememway *elementary education educator*
Sussenguth, Edward Henry *computer company executive, computer network designer*
Vick, Columbus Edwin, Jr. *civil engineering design firm executive*
Wait, George William *sales executive*

Cashiers
O'Connell, Edward James, Jr. *psychology educator, computer applications and data analysis consultant*
Runions, Sherman Curtis *landscape architect*
Yates, Linda Snow *communications, marketing executive*

Chapel Hill
†Adamson, Judy *theater educator*
Akin, John Stephen *economics educator*
Andrews, Richard Nigel Lyon *environmental policy educator, environmental studies administrator*
Arnold, Roland R. *dental educator and researcher*
Azar, Henry Amin *medical historian, educator*
Baerg, Richard Henry *podiatrist, surgeon*
Baker, Ronald Dale *dental educator, surgeon, university administrator*
Barker, Ben Dale *dentist, educator*
Baroff, George Stanley *psychologist, educator*
Baron, Samuel Haskell *historian*
Barton, Allen Hoisington *sociologist*
Bauer, Frederick Christian *motor carrier executive*
Bawden, James Wyatt *dental educator, dental scientist*
Betts, Doris June Waugh *author, English language educator*
Biles, Cindy Clemente *academic administrator*
Bister-Broosen, Helga *German linguistics educator*
Bland, Annie Ruth (Ann Bland) *nursing educator*
Blau, Peter Michael *sociologist, educator*
Bolas, Gerald Douglas *art museum administrator, art history educator*
Bondurant, Stuart *physician, educational administrator*
Boone, Franklin Delanor Roosevelt, Sr. *cardiovascular perfusionist, realtor*
Briggaman, Robert Alan *dermatologist, medical educator*
Brinkhous, Kenneth Merle *retired pathologist, educator*
Broad, Margaret (Molly) Corbett *university executive*
Brockington, Donald Leslie *anthropologist, archaeologist, educator*
Bromberg, Philip Allan *internist, educator*
Brookhart, Maurice S. *chemist*
Brooks, Frederick Phillips, Jr. *computer scientist*
Broun, Kenneth Stanley *lawyer, educator*
Brower, David John *lawyer, urban planner, educator*
Brown, Frank *social science educator*
Brown, Mark Walden *artist*
Brownlee, Robert Calvin *pediatrician, educator*
Buck, Richard Pierson *chemistry educator, researcher*
Bursey, Maurice M. *chemistry educator*
Campbell, B(obby) Jack *university official*
Campbell, William Aubrey *law educator*
Cance, William George *surgeon*
Carboni, Lisa Wilson *education educator*
Carroll, Roy *academic administrator*
Carson, Culley Clyde, III *urologist*
Cefalo, Robert Charles *obstetrician, gynecologist*
Churchill, Larry Raymond *ethics educator*
Clemmons, David Robert *internist, educator*
Cole, Richard Ray *university dean*
Collier, Albert M. *pediatric educator, child development center director*
Coulter, Elizabeth Jackson *biostatistician, educator*
Coulter, Norman Arthur, Jr. *biomedical engineering educator emeritus*
Crane, Julia Gorham *anthropology educator*
Crassweller, Robert Doell *retired lawyer, writer*
Crohn, Max Henry, Jr. *lawyer*
Cromartie, William James *medical educator, researcher*
Cunningham, James William *literacy education educator, researcher*
Dahlstrom, William Grant *psychologist, educator*
Davis, Morris Schuyler *astronomer*
Daye, Charles Edward *law educator*
Debreczeny, Paul *Slavic language educator, author*
De Friese, Gordon H. *health services researcher*
Denny, Floyd Wolfe, Jr. *pediatrician*
De Rosa, Guy Paul *orthopedic surgery educator*
Dickman, Catherine Crowe *retired human services administrator*
Dixon, Frederick Dail *architect*
Dixon, John Wesley, Jr. *retired religion and art educator*
Drutz, David Jules *biotechnology executive*
Earley, Laurence Elliott *medical educator*

Easterling, William Ewart, Jr. obstetrician, gynecologist
Edwards, Richard LeRoy academic dean, social work educator, non-profit management consultant
Eifrig, David Eric ophthalmologist, educator
Eliel, Ernest Ludwig chemist, educator
Falk, Eugene Hannes foreign language educator emeritus
Farber, Rosann Alexander geneticist, educator
Farmer, Thomas Wohlsen neurologist, educator
Fieleke, Norman Siegfried economist, educator
Fine, J(ames) Allen insurance company executive
Flora, Joseph M(artin) English language educator
Folda, Jaroslav Thayer, III art historian
Fordham, Christopher Columbus, III university dean and chancellor, medical educator
Forman, Donald T. biochemist
Fowler, Wesley Caswell, Jr. obstetrician, gynecologist
Fox, Ronald Ernest psychologist
Frampton, Paul Howard physics researcher, educator
Freund, Cynthia M. dean, nursing educator
Friday, William Clyde university president emeritus
Friedman, James Winstein economist, educator
Fuchs, Henry computer science educator
Fullagar, Paul David geology educator, geochemical consultant
Ganley, Oswald Harold university official
Garrett, Don James philosophy educator
Gilbert, Lawrence Irwin biologist, educator
Godschalk, David Robinson architect, urban development planner, educator
Gottlieb, Gilbert psychobiologist, educator
Goyer, Robert Andrew pathology educator
Graham, George Adams political scientist, emeritus educator
Graham, John Borden pathologist, writer, educator
Greganti, Mac Andrew physician, medical educator
Grendler, Paul Frederick history educator
Gressman, Eugene lawyer
Grisham, Joe Wheeler pathologist, educator
†Guthridge, Bill university basketball coach
Hackenbrock, Charles R. cell biologist, educator
Hammond, David Alan stage director, educator
Handy, Rollo Leroy philosopher, research executive
Harlan, Louis Rudolph history educator, writer
Haskell, Paul Gershon retired law educator
Hawkins, David Rollo, Sr. psychiatrist
Heninger, Simeon Kahn, Jr. English language educator
Henson, Anna Miriam otolaryngology researcher, medical educator
Henson, O'Dell Williams, Jr. anatomy educator
Hershey, H(oward) Garland, Jr. university administrator, orthodontist
Hill, Deborah Ann special education educator
Hill, Robert Folwell, Jr. information systems specialist
Hirsch, Philip Francis pharmacologist, educator
Hirschfield, Jim artist, educator
Hochbaum, Godfrey Martin retired behavioral scientist
Holley, Edward Gailon library science educator, former university dean
Hollister, William Gray psychiatrist
Hooker, Michael Kenneth university chancellor
Houpt, Jeffrey Lyle psychiatrist, educator
†Howes, Jonathan B. planning and public policy educator
Huang, Eng-Shang virology educator, biomedical engineer
Huang, Herman Fu transportation researcher
Huber, Evelyne political science educator
Hulka, Barbara Sorenson epidemiology educator
Hulka, Jaroslav Fabian obstetrician, gynecologist
Jackson, Blyden English language educator
Jerdee, Thomas Harlan business administration educator, organization psychology researcher and consultant
Johnson, Andrew Myron pediatric immunologist, educator
Johnson, George, Jr. physician, educator
Jones, Houston Gwynne history educator
Jones, Lyle Vincent psychology educator
Judd, Burke Haycock geneticist
Juliano, Rudolph L. medical educator
Karlin, Gary Lee insurance executive
Keagy, Blair Allen surgery educator
Kenan, Thomas Stephen, III philanthropist
Kilgour, Frederick Gridley librarian, educator
Kittredge, John Kendall retired insurance company executive
Kohn, Richard H. historian, educator
Konsler, Gwen Kline oncology and pediatrics nurse
Kuenzler, Edward Julian ecologist and environmental biologist
Kuhn, Matthew engineering company executive
Langenderfer, Harold Quentin accountant, educator
Lauder, Valarie Anne editor, educator
Lauterborn, Robert F. advertising educator, consultant
Lawrence, David Michael lawyer, educator
Lee, Kuo-Hsiung medicinal chemistry educator
Lee, Sherman Emery art historian, curator
Levine, Madeline Geltman Slavic literatures educator, translator
Ligett, Waldo Buford chemist
Lilley, Albert Frederick retired lawyer
Little, Loyd Harry, Jr. author
Loeb, Ben Fohl, Jr. lawyer, educator
Long, Douglas Clark philosophy educator
Lowman, Robert Paul psychology educator, academic administrator
Lucas, Carol Lee biomedical engineer
Ludington, Townsend English and American studies educator
Lunde, Anders Steen demographer
Macdonald, James Ross physicist, educator
MacGillivray, Lois Ann organization executive
Martikainen, A(une) Helen retired health education specialist
McBay, Arthur John toxicologist, consultant
†McGowan, John Patrick English language and literature educator
McKay, Kenneth Gardiner physicist, electronics company executive
McKay, Renee artist
McMillan, Campbell White pediatric hematologist
Melchert, Harold Craig adult education educator
Merzbacher, Eugen physicist, educator
Meyer, Thomas J. chemistry educator
Miller, C. Arden physician, educator
Miller, Daniel Newton, Jr. retired geologist, consultant
Mitchell, Earl Nelson physicist, educator
Moran, Barbara Burns librarian, educator
Morgan, Frank T. business educator, consultant
Morgan, G. Kenneth association executive
Munsat, Stanley Morris philosopher, educator
Munson, Eric Bruce hospital administrator
Murphy, Dan sculptor
Murphy, James Lee college dean, economics educator
Murray, Royce Wilton chemistry educator
Nebel, William Arthur obstetrician, gynecologist
Nelson, Philip Francis musicology educator, consultant, choral conductor
Neumann, Andrew Conrad geological oceanography educator
Newman, William Stein music educator, author, pianist, composer
Nolting, Mavis Williams critical care and pediatrics nurse
Okun, Daniel Alexander environmental engineering educator
Ontjes, David Ainsworth medicine and pharmacology educator
†Orsini, Peter F. graphics company executive
Pagano, Joseph Stephen physician, researcher, educator
Page, Ellis Batten psychologist, educator, corporate officer
Palmer, Gary Stephen health services administrator
Palmer, Jeffress Gary hematologist, educator
Parker, John Albert adult education educator
Parker, Scott Jackson theatre manager
Parr, Robert Ghormley chemistry educator
Perreault, William Daniel, Jr. business administration educator
Pfouts, Ralph William economist, consultant
Pillsbury, Harold Crockett, III otolaryngologist
Plow, Jean Osmann special education educator
Pollitzer, William Sprott anatomy educator
†Poock, Michael C. educator
Powell, Carolyn Wilkerson music educator
Prange, Arthur Jergen, Jr. psychiatrist, neurobiologist, educator
Prather, Donna Lynn psychiatrist
Price, David Eugene congressman, educator
Proffit, William Robert orthodontics educator
Pruett, James Worrell librarian, musicologist
Rabil, Albert, Jr. humanities educator
Reed, John Shelton, Jr. sociologist, writer
Reid, Jeffrey Paul higher education administrator, consultant
Richardson, Richard Judson political science educator
Riggs, Timothy Allan museum curator
Rindfuss, Ronald Richard sociology educator
Rogers, John James William geology educator
Rohe, William Michael urban planning educator
Rondinelli, Dennis A(ugust) business administration educator, research center director
Roper, William Lee dean, physician
Rosen, Benson business administration educator
Roth, Aleda Vender business educator
Runyan, Desmond Kimo medical educator, researcher
St. Jean, Joseph, Jr. micropaleontologist, educator
Sancar, Aziz research biochemist
Schier, Donald Stephen language educator
Schopler, John Henry psychologist, educator
Schoultz, Lars political scientist, educator
Scott, Tom Keck biologist, educator
Sheldon, George F. medical educator
Shelton-Scroggs, Karen hockey coach
Sheps, Cecil George physician
Simmons, Michael Anthony dean
Simpson, Richard Lee sociologist, educator
Singer, Philip Charles environmental engineer, educator
Slack, Lewis organization administrator
Slifkin, Lawrence Myer physics educator
Smith, Dean Edwards university basketball coach
Smith, Sidney Rufus, Jr. linguist, educator
Smithies, Oliver geneticist, educator
Snyder, Glenn Herald political science educator, writer
Sorenson, James Roger public health educator
Spencer, Elizabeth author
Spencer, Roger Felix psychiatrist, psychoanalyst, medical educator
Stadter, Philip Austin classicist, educator
Stamm, John William Rudolph dentist, educator, academic dean
Stanberry, D(osi) Elaine English literature educator, writer
Stasheff, James Dillon mathematics educator
Stephens, Laurence David, Jr. linguist, investor, oil industry executive
Steponaitis, Vincas Petras archaeologist, anthropologist, educator
Stewart, Richard Edwin insurance consulting company executive
Stidham, Shaler, Jr. operations research educator
Stipe, Robert Edwin design educator
Stiven, Alan Ernest population biologist, ecologist
Stockman, James Anthony, III pediatrician
Stumpf, Walter Erich cell biology educator, researcher
Suzuki, Kunihiko biomedical educator, researcher
Swanson, Michael Alan sales and marketing executive
Thakor, Haren Bhaskerrao manufacturing company executive
Tindall, George Brown historian, educator
Tolley, Aubrey Granville hospital administrator
Treml, Vladimir Guy economist, educator
Tunnessen, Walter William, Jr. pediatrician
Tyroler, Herman Alfred epidemiologist
Udry, Joe Richard sociology educator
Van Seters, John biblical literature educator
Van Wyk, Judson John endocrinologist, pediatric educator
Vogler, Frederick Wright French language educator
Waldon, Roger Stephen urban planner
Ware, William Brettel education educator
Warren, Donald William physiology educator, dentistry educator
Weinberg, Gerhard Ludwig history educator
Weiss, Charles Manuel environmental biologist
Weiss, Shirley F. urban and regional planner, economist, educator
Wheeler, Clayton Eugene, Jr. dermatologist, educator
White, Raymond Petrie, Jr. dentist, educator
Whybark, David Clay educational educator, researcher
Wicker, Marie Peachee civic worker
Wilcox, Benson Reid cardiothoracic surgeon, educator
Williams, John Trent public policy company executive
Williams, Roberta Gay pediatric cardiologist, educator
Williamson, Joel Rudolph humanities educator
Wilson, Glenn economist, educator
Wilson, Robert Neal sociologist, educator
Winfield, John Buckner rheumatologist, educator
Wogen, Warren Ronald mathematics educator
Wolfenden, Richard Vance biochemistry educator
Wright, Deil Spencer political science educator
York, James Wesley, Jr. theoretical physicist, educator
Zeisel, Steven H. nutritionist, scientist, educator
†Zenn, Michael Robert plastic and reconstructive surgeon
Ziff, Paul philosophy educator

Charlotte

Almond, Giles Kevin accountant, financial planner
Anderson, Gerald Leslie financial executive
†Andrews, David Scott thoracic and cardiovascular surgeon
Ayscue, Edwin Osborne, Jr. lawyer
Baldwin, Ed coach
Barrows, Frank Clemence newspaper editor
Beatty, Tina Marie legal assistant
Belk, Irwin retail executive
Belk, John M. retail company executive
Bernstein, Mark R. retired lawyer
†Blackburn, Richard Wallace lawyer
Bodine, Geoff professional race car driver
Boggs, Willene Graythen property manager, oil and gas broker, consultant
Bosse, Michael Joseph orthopedic trauma surgeon, retired medical officer
Bowden, James Alvin construction company financial executive
Brackett, Martin Luther, Jr. lawyer
Bradshaw, Howard Holt management consulting company executive
Brink, Arthur M. hospital administrator
Browning, Roy Wilson, III mortgage banking executive
Buchan, Jonathan Edward, Jr. lawyer
Buckley, Charles Robinson, III lawyer
Buckner, Jennie newspaper editor
Bullett, Vicky professional basketball player
Burke, Mary Thomas university administrator, educator
Burke, Steven Charles healthcare administration executive
Butler, Carol King advertising executive
Calloway, Mark T. prosecutor
Campbell, Hugh Brown, Jr. lawyer
Cannon, Robert Eugene librarian, public administrator, fund raiser
Carino, Linda Susan business consultant
Chaikin, Alyce artist
Clark, Ann Blakeney educational administrator
Coffey, Darren Kemper planner
Coleman, Derrick D. professional basketball player
Colvard, Dean Wallace emeritus university chancellor
Cornell, James Fraser, Jr. entomologist, educator
Cowell, Marion Aubrey, Jr. lawyer
Cox, Linda Smoak real estate broker
Crutchfield, Edward Elliott, Jr. banking executive
Curlin, William G. bishop
Curtis, Mary C. journalist
Dagenhart, Larry Jones lawyer
Dalton, Robert Issac, Jr. textile executive, consultant, researcher
Davis, Eric Wayne professional football player
Davis, William Maxie, Jr. lawyer
†DeForrest, Matthew McCoy educator, freelance writer
Diamond, Harvey Jerome machinery manufacturing company executive
Diemer, Arthur William real estate executive
Doherty, Barbara Whitehurst chemical purchasing manager
†Dorin, Dennis Daniel political science educator, researcher
Doyle, Esther Piazza critical care nurse, educator
Duffy, John Charles psychiatric educator
Ellis, Carolyn McClain educator
Eppes, Thomas Evans advertising executive, public relations executive
Eppley, Frances Fielden retired secondary education educator, author
Estes, Christopher J. landscape architect
Evans, Bruce Haselton art museum director
Evans, David Shawn financial executive
Ferebee, Stephen Scott, Jr. architect
Finley, Glenna author
Fortenberry, Carol Lomax real estate appraiser
Freeman, Tyler Ira physician
Fretwell, Elbert Kirtley, Jr. retired university chancellor, consultant
Gambrell, Sarah Belk retail executive
Gardner, Robert Charles systems analyst, administrator
Gay, David Braxton stockbroker
Georgius, John R. bank executive
Gerber, Charles M. sales and marketing executive
Gibbs, Joe Jackson former professional football coach, broadcaster, professional sports team executive
Goolkasian, Paula A. psychologist, educator
Graham, Sylvia Angelenia wholesale distributor, retail buyer
Greene, Kevin Darwin professional football player
Greene, William Henry L'Vel academic administrator
†Greer, Scott L. economist
Griep, Ann Marie education association education coordinator
Grier, Joseph Williamson, Jr. lawyer
Grigg, Eddie Garman minister, educator
Grigg, William Humphrey utility executive
Grimaldi, James Thomas investment fund executive
Haines, Kenneth H. television broadcasting executive
Halas, Paul Anthony, Jr. business appraisal and valuation specialist, consultant
Hall, Peter Michael physics educator, electronics researcher
Hallowell Schemmer, Shannon nurse anesthetist
Hance, James Henry, Jr. bank executive
Hanna, George Verner, III lawyer
Hardin, Elizabeth Ann academic administrator
Hardin, Thomas Jefferson, II investment counsel
Harris, Richard Foster, III lawyer
Hill, Ruth Foell language consultant
†Hodges, George R. federal judge
†Holbrook, Patricia Houston counselor, psychotherapist
†Horn, Carl, III federal judge
Horner, Bob broadcast executive
Huberman, Jeffrey Allen architect
Hudgins, Catherine Harding business executive
Hutcheson, J. Sterling allergist, immunologist, physician
Hutchinson, Olin Fulmer, Jr. transportation executive, data processing consultant
Ignozzi, Bryan K. management consultant
Irvan, Ernie (Swervin' Irvan) professional race car driver
Iverson, Francis Kenneth metals company executive
Jenkins, John Edward, Jr. electronics executive, engineering educator
Kallman, Kathleen Barbara marketing and business development professional
Keanini, Russell Guy mechanical engineering educator, researcher
Kidda, Michael Lamont, Jr. psychologist, educator
King, L. Ellis civil engineer, educator, consultant
Knox, Havolyn Crocker financial consultant
Labardi, Jillian Gay financial planner, insurance agent
Lapp, Charles Warren internal medicine physician, pediatrician
Latimer, Ben William healthcare executive
Lea, Scott Carter retired packaging company executive
Levinson, Eric Lee district court judge
†Lewis, Kenneth D. banker
Locke, Elizabeth Hughes foundation administrator
Loeffler, William George, Jr. advertising executive
Lowrance, Pamela Kay medical/surgical nurse
Lyerly, Elaine Myrick advertising executive
Maday, Clifford Ronald insurance professional
†Mager, Donald Northrop poet, educator
Manning, Sharon professional athlete
Mapp, Rhonda professional basketball player
Martin, James Grubbs medical research executive, former governor
Mascavage, Joseph Peter training executive
Mason, Anthony George Douglas professional basketball player
May, Benjamin Tallman securities specialist, administrator
McBryde, Neill Gregory lawyer
McCall, Billy Gene charitable trust executive
McCarley, DeWitt municipal official
McColl, Hugh Leon, Jr. bank executive
McConnell, David Moffatt lawyer
McCrory, Patrick mayor
McGill, John Knox lawyer
†McIntyre, Jane London healthcare administrator
†McKnight, H. Brent federal judge
McLanahan, Charles Scott neurosurgeon
McVerry, Thomas Leo manufacturing company executive
†Meadors, Marynell professional basketball coach
Melaragno, Michele architecture educator
Mendelsohn, Robert Victor insurance company executive
Michael, Caroline Marshall religious organization administrator
Miller, James Alfred Locke, Jr. (Jim Miller) aircraft maintenance technician
Misiek, Dale Joseph oral and maxillofacial surgeon
Montague, Edgar Burwell, III (Monty Montague) industrial designer
Mullen, Graham C. federal judge
Myers, Robert Manson English educator, author
Neel, Richard Eugene economics and business educator
Neill, Rolfe retired newspaper executive
Newitt, John Garwood, Jr. lawyer
Nicholson, Freda Hyams museum executive, medical educator
Nicholson, Henry Hale, Jr. surgeon
Oliver, John William Posegate minister
Orr, T(homas) J(erome) (Jerry Orr) airport terminal executive
Osborne, Richard Jay electric utility company executive
Owen, Kenneth Dale orthodontist, real estate broker
†Patrick, Timothy K. securities analyst
Peacock, A(lvin) Ward textile company executive
Perkins, Jim C. automotive executive
Perry, Barbara Ann museum curator
Phibbs, Garnett Ersiel engineer, educator, minister, religious organization administrator
Philippe, Scott Louis optometrist
Polking, Paul J. lawyer
Potter, Robert Daniel federal judge
†Powell, Dannye Romine news columnist
Preyer, Norris Watson history educator
Priory, Richard Baldwin electric utility executive
Prosser, Bruce Reginal, Jr. (Bo Prosser) minister, consultant
Prud'homme, Albert Fredric securities company executive, financial planner
Pyle, Gerald Fredric medical geographer, educator
Ragan, Robert Allison private investment executive, financial consultant
Rajani, Prem Rajaram transportation company financial executive
Rathke, Dieter B. construction company executive
Reed, Rita artist
Reeves, John Craig religious studies educator
Regelbrugge, Roger Rafael steel company executive
†Reid, Tracy professional basketball player
Richards, Craig M. wholesale distribution executive
†Ridder, Peter B. publishing executive
Risko, James Richard business executive
Rivenbark, Jan Meredith corporate executive
Roberts, Joyce Ann (Nichols) critical care nurse
Roels, Oswald Albert oceanographer, educator, business executive
Ross, David Edmond church official
Ruff, Edward Carr investment company executive
Rypien, Mark Robert professional football player
Schaffer, Eugene Carl education educator
Schenck, Sydney Neel writer
Schulz, Walter Kurt accountant, information technology consultant
Shah, Nandlal Chimanlal physiatrist
Sharits, Dean Paul motion picture company executive
Shaul, Roger Louis, Jr. health care consultant, executive, researcher
†Shaw, Ruth G. energy company executive
Shinn, George professional sports team executive
Shive, Philip Augustus architect
Shuford, Jill Renee museum educator, art educator
Siegel, Samuel metals company executive
†Silas, Paul professional basketball coach
Sintz, Edward Francis librarian
Smith, Edith Joan librarian, writer
Smith, Elizabeth Hegeman mental health therapist, hypnotherapist
Smylie, John Edwin education executive
Spangler, Clemmie Dixon, Jr. business executive
Spear, Andrea Ashford principal, educator
Squires, James Ralph development company executive
Stinson, Andrea professional basketball player

†Strawn, Martha Ann *art educator, photographer*
Sustar, T. David *college president*
Suter, George August *management and marketing consultant*
Swicegood, Steven Lloyd *reporter*
Thies, Austin Cole *retired utility company executive*
Thigpen, Richard Elton, Jr. *lawyer*
Thompson, David O'Neal *retired basketball player*
Thompson, John Albert, Jr. *dermatologist*
Tillett, Grace Montana *ophthalmologist, real estate developer*
Tolan, David Joseph *transportation executive*
Toth, James Joseph *power systems engineer*
Triplette, Laurance Daltroff *art advisor and appraiser*
Twisdale, Harold Winfred *dentist*
Van Allen, William Kent *lawyer*
Van Alstyne, Vance Brownell *arbitration management consultant*
Vinroot, Richard Allen *lawyer, mayor*
Visser, Valya Elizabeth *physician*
Voorhees, Richard Lesley *federal judge*
Waggoner, William Johnson *lawyer*
Walker, Clarence Wesley *lawyer*
Walker, Jewett Lynius *clergyman, church official*
Walker, Kenneth Dale *automotive service company executive*
Walls, Charles Wesley *football player*
Wallsh, Bonnie Elaine *meeting management consultant, educator*
Watkins, Carlton Gunter *retired pediatrician*
†Wayer, Glen Patrick *information and technology specialist*
Webster, Murray Alexander, Jr. *sociologist, educator*
Weisenburger, Randall *company executive*
Wheeler, Norman K. *consultant*
†Whitley, J. Craig *federal judge*
Wiggins, Jerome Meyer *apparel textile industry financial executive*
Wiggins, Nancy Bowen *real estate broker, market research consultant*
Williams, Edwin Neel *newspaper editor*
Wilson, Milner Bradley, III *retired banker*
Witzel, Barbara Binion *elementary education educator*
Wood, Donald Craig *retired marketing professional*
Wood, William McBrayer *lawyer*
Woodward, James Hoyt *academic administrator, engineer*
Woolard, William Leon *lawyer, electrical distributing company executive*
†Wooten, Marvin R. *federal judge*
†Zampieri, Robert P. *business consultant*
Zytkow, Jan Mikolaj *computer science educator*

Cherry Point
Braaten, Thomas A. *career officer*
Laviolette, Bruce Edward *industrial manufacturing management*
Wells, David Patrick *career officer*

Cherryville
Huffstetler, Palmer Eugene *lawyer*
Mayhew, Kenneth Edwin, Jr. *transportation company executive*

Chinquapin
Brown, Anita Lanier *women's health nurse*

Chocowinity
Castle, William Eugene *retired academic administrator*

Clarkton
Wuebbels, Theresa Elizabeth *visual art educator*

Clayton
Jenkins, Elaine Parker *secondary school educator*
Silberman, H. Lee *public relations executive*

Clemmons
†Church, Avery Grenfell *retired anthropology educator, poet*

Clinton
Faircloth, Duncan McLauchlin (Lauch Faircloth) *former senator, businessman, farmer*
Fetterman, Annabelle *packing company executive*
Friedman, Deborah Leslie White *educational administrator*

Clyde
Codd, Richard Trent, Jr. *computer scientist, educator*
Rogers, Garry Lee *minister, medical technician*

Columbus
Bell, Mildred Bailey *lawyer, educator*
Blate, Michael *author, lecturer*
†Sauvé, Carolyn Opal *writer, journalist, poet*

Concord
Sloop, Gregory Todd *clergyman*

Conover
Jarrett, Dale *professional race car driver*
Kundu, Debabrata *mechanical engineer*
†Wallace, Terri Goodman *communications executive, sales executive*

Cooperstown
Perry, Gaylord Jackson *former professional baseball player*

Corolla
Schrote, John Ellis *retired government executive*

Creedmoor
Cross, June Crews *retired music educator*

Cullowhee
Bardo, John William *university administrator*
Coulter, Myron Lee *retired academic administrator*
DuVall, Rick *education educator*
Farwell, Harold Frederick, Jr. *English language educator*
Gurevich, Robert *international development administrator*
Koons, Eleanor (Peggy Koons) *clinical social worker*
Reed, Alfred Douglas *university administrator*
Willis, Ralph Houston *mathematics educator*
Wilson, LeVon Edward *law educator, lawyer*

Davidson
Burnett, John Nicholas *retired chemistry educator*
Cole, Richard Cargill *English language educator*
Jackson, Herb *artist, educator*
Jones, Arthur Edwin, Jr. *library administrator, English and American literature educator*
Kuykendall, John Wells *academic administrator, educator*
†McMillen, Sally Gregory *history educator*
Mele, Alfred R. *philosophy educator*
Park, Leland Madison *librarian*
Plyler, John Laney, Jr. *retired healthcare management professional*
Spencer, Samuel Reid, Jr. *educational consultant, former university president*
†Toumazou, Michael K. *classics educator*
Williams, Robert Chadwell *history educator*
Zimmermann, T. C. Price *historian, educator*

Dobson
Atkins, Dixie Lee *critical care nurse*

Duck
Majewski, Theodore Eugene *chemist*

Dudley
Kelly, Edward John, V *counselor*

Dunn
Adams, Hoover *newspaper founder*
Blackman, Danny *religious organization administrator*
Davis, Dolly *religious organization administrator*
†Guldan, Janice Marie *librarian*
Heath, Preston *clergy member, religious organization administrator*
Robison, Frederick Mason *financial executive*
Spence, Othniel Talmadge *education minister, broadcast executive*

Durham
Abdel-Rahman, Mohamed *international agribusiness consultant*
†Adams, Rex *dean*
Aldrich, John Herbert *political science educator*
†Aldridge, Geoffrey *security consultant*
Alexander, C. Alex *physician*
Allard, William Kenneth *mathematician*
Althaus, David Steven *chemicals executive, controller*
Amos, Dennis B. *immunologist*
Anderson, Robert W. *surgeon*
Anderson, William Banks, Jr. *ophthalmology educator*
Anlyan, William George *surgeon, university administrator*
Barry, David Walter *infectious diseases physician, researcher*
Bartlett, Katharine Tiffany *law educator*
Beckum, Leonard Charles *academic administrator*
Behn, Robert Dietrich *public policy educator, writer*
Bejan, Adrian *mechanical engineering educator*
Bennett, Peter Brian *researcher, hyperbaric medicine*
Bettman, James Ross *management educator*
Bevan, William *retired foundation executive*
Blazer, Dan German *psychiatrist, epidemiologist*
Blazing, Michael August *internist*
Blum, Jacob Joseph *physiologist, educator*
Bolognesi, Dani Paul *virologist, educator*
Bond, Enriqueta Carter *science administrator*
Bradford, William Dalton *pathologist, educator*
Braibanti, Ralph John *political scientist, educator*
Brodie, Harlow Keith Hammond *psychiatrist, educator, past university president*
Brown, Patricia Anita *university official*
Buckley, Charles Edward, III *physician, educator*
Buckley, Rebecca Hatcher *physician, educator*
Budd, Louis John *English language educator*
Burger, Robert Mercer *semiconductor device research executive*
Burgess, Paula Lashenske *health facility administrator*
Burmeister, Edwin *economics educator*
Busse, Ewald William *psychiatrist, educator*
Butters, Ronald Richard *English language educator*
Byers, Garland Franklin, Jr. *private investigator, security firm executive*
Cady, Edwin Harrison *English language educator, author*
Caesar, Shirley *gospel singer, evangelist*
Canada, Mary Whitfield *librarian*
Carpenter, Charles Francis *lawyer*
Carrington, Paul DeWitt *lawyer, educator*
Carter, James Harvey *psychiatrist, educator*
Cartmill, Matt *anthropologist, anatomy educator*
Casey, H(orace) Craig, Jr. *electrical engineering educator*
Chafe, William Henry *history educator*
Chambers, Julius LeVonne *academic administrator, lawyer*
Chesnut, Donald Blair *chemistry educator*
Christie, George Custis *lawyer, educator, author*
Christmas, William Anthony *internist, educator*
Civello, Anthony Ned *retail drug company executive, pharmacist*
Clark, Arthur Watts *insurance company executive*
Cocks, Franklin Hadley *materials scientist*
Cohen, Harvey Jay *physician, educator*
†Cokgor, Ilkcan *neuro-oncologist, neurologist*
Coleman, Ralph Edward *nuclear medicine physician*
Collins, Bert *insurance executive*
Colton, Joel *historian, educator*
Colvin, O. Michael *medical director, medical educator*
Conner, James Leon, II *lawyer, mediator*
Cook, Clarence Edgar *research facility scientist*
Cooley, Jacob Alan *painter*
Cooper, Charles Howard *photojournalist, newspaper publishing company executive*
Cotten, Catheryn Deon *medical center international advisor*
Cox, James D. *law educator*
Cruze, Alvin M. *research institute executive*
Culberson, William Louis *botany educator*
Danner, Richard Allen *law educator, dean*
Davis, Calvin De Armond *historian, educator*
Dees, Susan Coons *physician, educator*
Dellinger, Walter Estes, III *lawyer, educator*
†Delucca, Robert Kenneth *adult education educator, writer, translator*
Dennehy, Leisa Jeanotta *company executive*
De Vone, James Milton *manufacturing company owner, entrepreneur*
Donker, Richard Bruce *health care administrator*
Dowell, Earl Hugh *university dean, aerospace and mechanical engineering educator*
Dunbar, Leslie Wallace *writer, consultant*
Efird, James Michael *theology educator*
Elliot, Jeffrey M. *political science educator, author*
Estes, Edward Harvey, Jr. *medical educator*
Evans, Ralph Aiken *physicist, consultant*
Fair, Richard Barton *electronics executive, educator*
Falletta, John Matthew *pediatrician, educator*
Feinglos, Susan Jean *library director*
Feldman, Jerome Myron *physician*
Fisher, Charles Page, Jr. *consulting geotechnical engineer*
Fisher, Stewart Wayne *lawyer*
Fiske, Edward Bogardus *editor, journalist, educational consultant*
Fogle, G. Lee *credit union executive, consultant*
Foreman, John William *pediatrician, educator*
Franklin, John Hope *historian, educator, author*
Frazier, Ann Lynette *medical/surgical nurse*
Freemark, Michael Scott *pediatric endocrinologist and educator*
Fridovich, Irwin *biochemistry educator*
Frothingham, Thomas Eliot *pediatrician*
Gaede, Jane Taylor *pathologist, educator*
Garg, Devendra Prakash *mechanical engineer, educator*
Georgiade, Nicholas George *plastic and oral surgeon, educator*
Gillham, Nicholas Wright *geneticist, educator*
Gittler, Joseph Bertram *sociology educator*
Gleckner, Robert Francis *English language professional, educator*
Goestenkors, Gail *head basketball coach*
Golding, Martin Philip *law and philosophy educator*
Greenfield, Joseph Cholmondeley, Jr. *physician, educator*
Gunter, Emily Diane *communications executive, marketing professional, real estate developer, author, educator*
†Guseh, James Sawalla *public administration educator*
†Hajcak, Catherine *geologist, consultant*
Hall, Conrad Alden *history educator*
Hamilton, Michael A. *medical educator*
Hammes, Gordon G. *chemistry educator*
Hammond, Charles Bessellieu *obstetrician, gynecologist, educator*
Han, Moo-Young *physicist*
Harman, Charles Morgan *mechanical engineer*
Harmel, Merel Hilber *anesthesiologist, educator*
Harrell, (Benjamin) Carlton *columnist, retired editor*
†Harrington-Austin, Eleanor Joyce *educator*
Harris, Jerome Sylvan *pediatrician, pediatrics and biochemistry educator*
Havighurst, Clark Canfield *law educator*
Hawkins, William E. N. *newspaper editor*
Heinz, E(dward) Ralph *neuroradiologist, educator*
Hochmuth, Robert Milo *mechanical and biomedical engineer, educator*
Holley, Irving Brinton, Jr. *historian, educator*
Holsti, Ole Rudolf *political scientist, educator*
Horowitz, Donald Leonard *lawyer, educator, researcher, political scientist, arbitrator*
†Houchin, Laura Braxton *oncology nurse clinician*
Huestis, Charles Benjamin *former academic administrator*
†Husain, Aatif Mairaj *neurologist*
Israel, Michael David *healthcare executive*
Jaszczak, Ronald Jack *physicist, researcher, consultant*
Jenkins, Richard Erik *patent lawyer*
Jennings, Robert Burgess *experimental pathologist, medical educator*
Joklik, Wolfgang Karl *biochemist, virologist, educator*
Kaprielian, Victoria Susan *medical educator*
Katz, Samuel Lawrence *pediatrician, scientist*
Kaufman, Russell Eugene *hematologist, oncologist*
Kay, Richard Frederick *paleontology and biological anthropology educator*
Keene, Jack Donald *molecular genetics and microbiology educator*
Kelley, Allen Charles *economist, educator*
Keohane, Nannerl Overholser *university president, political scientist*
Keohane, Robert Owen *political scientist, educator*
Kerckhoff, Sylvia Stansbury *mayor*
Kirshner, Norman *pharmacologist, researcher, educator*
Klitzman, Bruce *physiologist, plastic surgery educator, researcher*
Koepke, John Arthur *hematologist, clinical pathologist*
Krakauer, Thomas Henry *museum director*
Kreps, Juanita Morris *economics educator, former government official*
Krishnan, Krishnaswamy Ranga Rama *psychiatrist*
Krzyzewski, Mike *university athletic coach*
Kuniholm, Bruce Robellet *university administrator*
Lack, Leon *pharmacology and biochemistry educator*
Ladd, Marcia Lee *medical equipment and supplies company executive*
Land, Kenneth Carl *sociology educator, demographer, statistician, consultant*
Lange, David L. *law educator*
Langford, Thomas Anderson *retired theology educator, academic administrator*
Leach, Richard Heald *political scientist, educator*
Lee, Paul P. *physician, educator, consultant, lawyer*
Lefkowitz, Robert Joseph *physician, educator*
Lerner, Warren *historian*
Lindsey, Lydia *education educator, researcher*
Lockhead, Gregory Roger *psychology educator*
London, William Lord *pediatrician*
Loveland, Donald William *computer science educator*
Lozoff, Bo *nonprofit organization administrator*
Malindzak, George Steve, Jr. *cardiovascular physiology, biomedical engineer*
Marchuk, Douglas Alan *medical educator*
Markham, Charles Buchanan *lawyer*
Mauskopf, Seymour Harold *history educator*
Maxwell, Richard Callender *lawyer, educator*
McCarthy, David Bruce *minister*
†McDonald, Trevy Ann *communications educator, writer*
McKinney, Ross Erwin *civil engineering educator*
McMahon, John Alexander *law educator*
Menning, Karen Corinne *occupational therapist*
Meyer, Horst *physics educator*
Meyers, Eric Mark *religion educator*
Michener, James Lloyd *medical educator*
Mickiewicz, Ellen Propper *political science educator*
Modrich, Paul L. *biochemistry educator*
Moon, Samuel David *medical educator*
Moore, John Wilson *neurophysiologist, educator*
Mosteller, Robert P. *law educator*
Murphy, Barbara Anne *emergency physician, surgery educator*
Murphy, Thomas Miles *pediatrician*
Nakarai, Charles Frederick Toyozo *music educator, adjudicator*
Naylor, Aubrey Willard *botany educator*
Nevins, Joseph Roy *medical educator*
Nicklas, Robert Bruce *cell biologist*
Oakley, Wanda Faye *management consultant, educator*
Oates, John Francis *classics educator*
Odom, Guy Leary *retired physician*
Ogede, Ode *literature educator*
Opara, Emmanuel Chukwuemeka *biochemistry educator*
Osterhout, Suydam *physician, educator*
Otterbourg, Robert Kenneth *public relations consultant, writer*
Pearsall, George Wilbur *materials scientist, mechanical engineer, educator, consultant*
Pearsall, Samuel Haff, III *landscape ecologist, geographer, foundation administrator*
Perkins, Ronald Dee *geologist, educator*
Petroski, Henry *engineer educator*
Pinnell, Sheldon Richard *physician, medical educator*
Pizzo, Salvatore Vincent *pathologist*
Plonsey, Robert *electrical and biomedical engineer*
Porter, Joseph A. (Joe Ashby Porter) *English language educator, fiction writer*
Pratt, Philip Chase *pathologist, educator*
Preston, Richard Arthur *historian*
Putman, Charles E(d) *medical educator, clinician, academic administrator, radiologist*
†Radtke, Radney A. *neurologist*
Raetz, Christian R. H. *biochemistry educator*
Ramsay, Kerr Craige *architect*
Reif, John Henry *computer science educator*
Reves, Joseph Gerald *anesthesiology educator*
Richardson, Curtis John *ecology educator*
Richardson, Lawrence, Jr. *Latin language educator, archeologist*
Richardson, Stephen Giles *biotechnology company executive*
Richardson, Vanessa *education educator*
Roberson, Nathan Russell *physicist, educator*
Robertson, Horace Bascomb, Jr. *law educator*
Roland, Alex Frederick *history educator*
Rollins, Edward Tyler, Jr. *newspaper executive*
Rose, Donald James *computer science educator*
Rossiter, Alexander, Jr. *news service executive, editor*
Roulidis, Zeses Chris *medical educator*
Rouse, Doris Jane *physiologist, research administrator*
Rowe, Thomas Dudley, Jr. *law educator*
Sabiston, David Coston, Jr. *surgeon, educator*
Sanford, David Hawley *philosophy educator*
Schanberg, Saul Murray *pharmacology educator*
Schmalbeck, Richard Louis *university dean, lawyer*
Schmidt-Nielsen, Knut *physiologist, educator*
Schwarcz, Steven Lance *law educator, lawyer*
Scott, Anne Byrd Firor *history educator*
Scott, Lee Allen, Sr. *securities company executive*
Searles, Richard Brownlee *botany educator, marine biology researcher*
Semans, Mary Duke Biddle Trent *foundation administrator*
Serafin, Donald *plastic surgeon*
Severance, Harry Wells *emergency medicine educator*
Sheetz, Michael Patrick *cell biology educator*
Shelburne, John Daniel *pathologist*
Shetty, Ashok K. *neuroscientist*
Shimm, Melvin Gerald *law educator*
Simons, Elwyn LaVerne *physical anthropologist, primatologist, paleontologist, educator*
Sloan, Frank Allen *economics educator*
Smith, Grover C(leveland) *English language educator*
Smith, Harmon Lee, Jr. *clergyman, moral theology educator*
Smith, Peter *chemist, educator, consultant*
Snyderman, Ralph *medical educator, physician*
Somjen, George Gustav *physiologist*
Spach, Madison Stockton *cardiologist*
Squire, Alexander *management consultant*
Staddon, John Eric Rayner *psychology, zoology, neurobiology educator*
Staelin, Richard *business administration educator*
Stanley, Carol Jones *academic administrator, educator*
Stead, Eugene Anson, Jr. *physician*
Steinmetz, David Curtis *religion educator, publisher, minister*
Stiles, Gary Lester *cardiologist, molecular pharmacologist, educator*
Strauss, Harold Carl *cardiology educator*
Strohbehn, John Walter *engineering science educator*
Stroscio, Michael Anthony *physicist, educator*
Sum-Ping, Sam Thio *anesthesiologist, hospital administrator*
Surwit, Richard Samuel *psychology educator*
Swaim, Mark Wendell *hepatologist, molecular biologist, gastroenterologist, educator, photographer*
Taylor, James Francis *marketing professional*
Taylor, Martha Croll *nursing adminstrator*
Tedder, Thomas Fletcher *immunology educator, researcher*
Terborgh, John J. *natural science educator*
Thompson, John Herd *history educator*
Tiryakian, Edward Ashod *sociology educator*
Utku, Senol *civil engineer, computer science educator*
Vatavuk, William Michael *chemical engineer, author*
†Wallace, Maurice Orlando *educator, pastor*
Walter, Richard Lawrence *physicist, educator*
Ward, Robert *composer, conductor, educator*
Watts, Toni Eileen *actress*
Weiner, Richard David *psychiatrist*
Westbrook, Don Arlen *minister*
Wilder, Alma Ann *English educator*
Wilkins, Robert Henry *neurosurgeon, editor*
Williams, George Walton *English educator*
Williams, Redford Brown *medical educator*
†Wilson, Blake Shaw *electrical engineer, researcher*
Wilson, Ruby Leila *nurse, educator*
Woodbury, Max Atkin *polymath, educator, researcher*
Yancy, William Samuel *pediatrician*
Zaranka, Albert J. *musical director, pianist, educator*

Eden
Williams, Sue Darden *library director*

Edenton
Walklet, John James, Jr. *publishing executive*

Elizabeth City
Boyle, Terrence W. *federal judge*
Hall, Pamela Bright *school health nurse*
†Irvin, James Samuel *company executive*

Lewis, Tola Ethridge, Jr. retired state agency administrator, martial arts instructor

Elizabethtown
Taylor, David Wyatt Aiken retired clergyman

Elkin
Gillespie, James Davis lawyer
Sawyer, Michael E. library director

Ellenboro
Burgin, Max Edward minister, farmer

Elm City
Morris, Sharon Louise Stewart emergency medical technician

Elon College
Powell, William Council, Sr. service company executive
Tolley, Jerry Russell university administrator

Emerald Isle
†Gates, Herbert Stelwyn retired obstetrician-gynecologist

Fairmont
Byrne, James Frederick banker
Kemp, Charles E. secondary education educator, history

Fairview
Eck, David Wilson minister
Gaffney, Thomas Edward retired physician
Rhynedance, Harold Dexter, Jr. lawyer, consultant

Fayetteville
†Ayadi, Olusegun Felix finance educator
Baltz, Richard Jay health care company executive
Chipman, Martin neurologist, retired army officer
†Curtis, Marvin Vernell music educator
Dowd, John P., III academic administrator
Jansen, Michael John hospital administrator
Jones, James Curtiss surgeon
Kendrick, Mark Cleveland real estate executive
Lungu, Angela Maria career officer
Lydon, Kerry Raines school director
McMillan, Bettie Barney English language educator
Parish, James Riley lawyer
Resnick, Paul R. research chemist
Richardson, Emilie White manufacturing company executive, investment company executive, lecturer
Ross, Bernadette Marie-Teresa librarian
Ruppe, Arthur Maxwell lawyer
Schaefer, Lewis George physicians assistant
Smith, Karla Salge Jordan early childhood education educator
†Swain, Mary Margaret editor, marketing consultant
Townsend, William Jackson lawyer
Tyson-Autry, Carrie Eula legislative consultant, researcher, small business owner

Flat Rock
Demartini, Robert John textile company executive

Fort Bragg
Abreu, Sue Hudson physician, army officer
†Bergman, Mark non-commissioned officer
†Bowra, Kenneth R. career officer
†Boykin, William C. career officer
†Brown, Bryan D. career officer
†Dunkle, Keith Allen military officer
†Farage, Michael N. career officer
Juskowiak, Terry Eugene career military officer
†Kernan, William Frank lieutenant general United States Army
McMillan, William B. counselor, military science educator
†McNeill, Dan K. military career officer
Merritt, Roxanne Marie museum curator
Rinehart, James Forrest educator
†Ryneska, John Joseph military career officer
†Tangney, William Patrick military officer

Franklin
Earhart, Eileen Magie retired child and family life educator
Judernatz, Mary Seegers artist

Fremont
Overman, Betty Skeens critical care and pediatrics nurse
Whaley, Connie G. middle school educator

Garner
Barbour, Charlene management firm executive
†Monahan, Sherry Ann writer
Upchurch, Lisa Carole D. women's health nurse, clinical educator

Gastonia
Alala, Joseph Basil, Jr. lawyer, accountant
Eads, Ronald Preston management consultant
Kimbrell, Willard Duke textile company executive
Lawson, William David, III retired cotton company executive
Morris, Joseph Wesley physician assistant
Prince, George Edward retired pediatrician
Stott, Grady Bernell lawyer
Teem, Paul Lloyd, Jr. bank executive

Gibsonville
Crawford, Kathrine Nelson special education educator

Goldsboro
Barkley, Monika Johanna general contracting professional
Harper, Linda Ruth disabilities educator, consultant
Price, Eugene newspaper editor

Graham
Corbett, Lenora Meade community college educator
Walker, Daniel Joshua, Jr. lawyer

Granite Falls
Estes, Shirley Reid medical/surgical nurse
Humphreys, Kenneth King engineer, educator, association executive

Greenmountain
Smith, Kearney Isaac retired language educator

Greensboro
Adewuyi, Yusuf Gbadebo chemical engineering educator, researcher, consult
Agee, Lynne university head basketball coach
†Agesa, Richard Ugunzi economics educator
Allen, Jesse Owen, III management development and organizational behavior
Almeida, José Agustín romance languages educator
†Amponsah, William Appiah international economics educator
Ananian, Michael Fred artist
Bailey, William Nathan systems engineer
Baird, Haynes Wallace pathologist
Banegas, Estevan Brown environmental biotechnology executive
Bardolph, Richard historian, educator
Barker, Walter William, Jr. artist, educator
Barnett, Dorothy Prince retired university dean
Bell, Haney Hardy, III lawyer
Blackwell, William Ernest broadcast industry executive
Blanchet-Sadri, Francine mathematician
Brecht, Blaine Richard manufacturing company executive
†Bullock, Frank William, Jr. federal judge
Canipe, Stephen Lee educational administrator
Capone, Lucien, III lawyer
Carmichael, James Vinson, Jr. library and information science educator
Chappell, Fred Davis English language educator, poet
Clark, Clifton Bob physicist
Clark, David McKenzie lawyer
Conrad, David Paul business broker, retired restaurant chain executive
Cotter, John Burley ophthalmologist, corneal specialist
Covington, Gail Lynn nurse practitioner
Davidson, Gerard H., Jr. lawyer
Davis, Herbert Owen lawyer
Dziordz, Walter Michael priest
Elliott, Benny Lee, Jr. mechanical engineer
Englar, John David textile company executive, lawyer
Ertel, Ross Steven printing sales executive
Fenn, Ormon William, Jr. furniture company executive
Floyd, Jack William lawyer
Formo, Brenda Terrell travel company executive
Gabriel, Richard Weisner lawyer
†Gaucher, Kim Elizabeth artist, art director
†Gilbert, Marie Rogers poet
Gill, Diane Louise psychology educator, university official
Gill, Evalyn Pierpoint writer, editor, publisher
Goble, Alan Keith psychology educator
Goldman, Bert Arthur psychologist, educator
Gordon, Eugene Andrew judge
Goulder, Gerald Polster retail executive, management consultant, lawyer
Green, Jill I. dance educator, researcher
Gumbiner, Kenneth Jay lawyer
Hall, William Edward, Jr. insurance agency executive
Hazelton, Catherine Lynette elementary school educator
Herman, Roger Eliot professional speaker, consultant, futurist, writer
Hidore, John Junior geographer, educator
†Hilliard, Kelly McCollum employment manager
Hoffman, Lynn Renee elementary education educator
Holton, Walter Clinton, Jr. lawyer
Hopkins, John David lawyer
Hosier, Linda G. educator
Houston, Frank Matt dermatologist
Howard, Richard Turner construction company executive
Hull, James Ernest religion and philosophy educator
Hunter, Bynum Merritt lawyer
Jellicorse, John Lee communications and theatre educator
Johnson, Marshall Hardy investment company executive
Kennedy, Charles G. wholesale distribution executive
Kerley, Janice Johnson personnel executive
Kiser, Mose, III small business owner
Koonce, Neil Wright lawyer
Korb, William Brown, Jr. manufacturing company executive
Kornegay, Horace Robinson trade association executive, former congressman, lawyer
Kovacs, Beatrice library studies educator
Kurepa, Alexandra mathematician, educator
Lindemeyer, Nancy Jo public information officer
MacKenzie, David history educator, researcher, writer
Mann, Lowell Kimsey retired manufacturing executive
McKissick-Melton, S. Charmaine mass communications educator
McNemar, Donald William academic administrator
Mecimore, Charles Douglas retired accounting educator
Melvin, Charles Edward, Jr. lawyer
Middleton, Herman David, Sr. theater educator
Miller, Robert Louis university dean, chemistry educator
Moore, Beverly Cooper lawyer
†Moraru, Christian English educator
Murrelle, Ronald Kemp architectural designer
Nussbaum, V. M., Jr. former mayor
Orlowsky, Martin L. executive manager
Osteen, William L., Sr. federal judge
Peterson, John Edgar, Jr. retired agricultural executive, textile executive
†Porter, Thomas Earl history educator
Prodan, James Christian university administrator
Reed, William Edward government official, educator
Rights, Graham Henry minister
Ritter, Sandra Helen psychotherapist, counselor
Rogers, William Raymond college president emeritus, psychology educator
Rowlenson, Richard Charles lawyer
Russell, Peggy Taylor soprano, educator
Sadri, Fereidoon computer science educator
St. George, Nicholas James lawyer, manufactured housing company executive
Sanders, William Eugene marketing executive
Schell, Braxton lawyer
Schwenn, Lee William retired medical center executive
Sewell, Elizabeth author, English educator
†Sharp, Paul Trevor federal judge
Shelton, David Howard economics educator
Shivakumar, Kunigal Nanjundaiah aerospace engineer
Shotwell, Sheila Murray medical/surgical nurse
†Sitton, Larry Bruce lawyer
Smith, John McNeill, Jr. lawyer
Smith, Lanty L(loyd) lawyer, business executive
Soles, William Roger insurance company executive
Spears, Alexander White, III tobacco company executive
Staab, Thomas Robert consumer product company financial executive
Starling, Larry Eugene auditor
Stevens, Elliott Walker, Jr. allergist, pulmonologist
†Stocks, William L. federal judge
Styles, Teresa Jo producer, educator
Sullivan, Patricia A. academic administrator
Swan, George Steven law educator
Thompson, James Howard historian, library administrator
Tilley, Norwood Carlton, Jr. federal judge
Truesdale, Gerald Lynn plastic and reconstructive surgeon
Tugman, Stuart Grady, Jr. insurance executive
Turner, James Reginald lawyer
Wallace, Becky Whitley protective services official
Watson, Robert Winthrop poet, English language educator
Williams, Irving Laurence physics educator
†Wolfe, James B., Jr. retired federal judge
†Wood, Ellen Dianne drafting technician, artist
Wright, John Spencer school system administrator
Wright, Kieth Carter librarian, educator
Zopf, Paul Edward, Jr. sociologist

Greenville
Alexander, Samuel Rudolph retired concert manager, educational administrator
Bearden, James Hudson university official
Burti, Christopher Louis lawyer
Chauncey, Beatrice Arlene music educator
Clark, John Graham, III lawyer
Cunningham, Paul Raymond Goldwyn surgery educator
Drury, James Anthony Bartholomew psychiatrist, psychoanalyst
Eakin, Richard Ronald academic administrator, mathematics educator
†Eribo, Festus mass communication educator, journalist
†Fay, Julie writer
†Flanagan, Louise W. federal judge
Flanagan, Michael Perkins lawyer
Foley, Charles Bradford university dean, music educator
Hallock, James Anthony pediatrician, school dean
Hamrick, Mike Alan athletic director
Heath, Jeffrey Dale minister
Howard, Malcolm Jones federal judge
Howell, John McDade retired university chancellor, political science educator
Jackson, Bobby Rand minister
Lannin, Donald Rowe oncologist
Laupus, William Edward physician, educator
Lee, Tung-Kwang pathologist, cancer researcher
Leggett, Donald Yates academic administrator
Leggett, Nancy Porter university administrator
Meggs, William Joel internist, emergency physician, educator
Metzger, W. James, Jr. physician, researcher, educator
Norris, H. Thomas retired pathologist, academic administrator
Pakowski, Montie Early critical care nurse
Parks, Suzanne Lowry psychiatric nurse, educator
Pories, Walter Julius surgeon, educator
Runyan, Timothy Jack historian, educator
Schellenberger, Robert Earl management educator and department chairman
Shields, Edgar Thomson, Jr. American literature educator
Snyder, Harold Michael language educator
Thompson, Emerson McLean, Jr. retired clergyman
Thurber, Robert Eugene physiologist, researcher
Tingelstad, Jon Bunde physician
Tripp, Linda Lynn nutritition counselor
†Twardy, Charles A., Jr. writer
Volkman, Alvin pathologist, researcher, educator
Wallin, Leland Dean artist, educator
Webster, Raymond Earl psychology educator, director, psychotherapist
Williams, Melvin John sociologist, educator
Winn, Francis John, Jr. medical educator
Wood, Gerald David religious organization administrator
Workman, Lee DeWayne collegiate athletics administrator
Wortmann, Dorothy Woodward physician

Hampstead
McManus, Hugh F. principal
Solomon, Robert Douglas pathology educator
Unger, Stephen Allen publishing executive, editor

Harrisburg
Bell, Walter Clayton drag car racer, small business owner
Economaki, Chris Constantine (Christopher Economaki) publisher, editor
Ethridge, Mark Foster, III writer, publisher, media consultant
Helton, Max Edward minister, consultant, religious organization executive
Labonte, Terry professional race car driver
†Waltrip, Michael professional race car driver

Havelock
Lindblade, Eric Norman, Jr. minister
Lindelof, William Christian, Jr. financial company executive

Haw River
Poindexter, Richard Grover minister

Hayesville
Parch, Grace Dolores librarian

Hendersonville
Brittain, James Edward science and technology educator, researcher
Goehring, Maude Cope retired business educator
Halm, James Maurice retired chemist, poet
Hathorne, Gayle Gene musician, genealogical educator, writer
Haynes, John Mabin retired utilities executive
Heil, Mary Ruth former counselor
Hull, J(ames) Richard retired lawyer, business executive
Kehr, August Ernest geneticist, researcher
Kratz, Howard Russel physicist, researcher
Payne, Gerald Oliver retired elementary education educator
Reinhart, John Belvin child and adolescent psychiatrist, educator
Saby, John Sanford physicist
Schooley, Charles Earl electrical engineer, consultant
Schwarz, Richard William historian, educator
Sims, Bennett Jones minister, educator
Stepkoski, Robert John automobile dealership executive
Stokes, William Finley, Jr. insurance executive
Trexler, Edgar Ray minister, editor

Hertford
Guyer, Charles Grayson, II psychologist
Sutton, Louise Nixon retired mathematics educator

Hickory
George, Boyd Lee consumer products company executive
Hilton, Deanie Herman human resources executive, telecommunications manager
Kyker, Charles Clinton pastor
Lefler, Wade Hampton, Jr. ophthalmologist
Loehr, Arthur William, Jr. healthcare executive, nurse
†Luckadoo, Thomas D. legislative staff member
McDaniel, Michael Conway Dixon bishop, retired theology educator
Nye, John Robert furniture company executive, transportation consultant
Ryan Billingsley, Joanne medical/surgical and orthopedic nurse
Shuford, Harley Ferguson, Jr. furniture manufacturing executive

High Point
Bardelas, Jose Antonio allergist
Berrier, J. Alan transportation executive, entrepreneur
Blazek, F. Douglas surgeon
Bowman, Gray chemist, educator
†Burton, Ward professional race car driver
Culler, Robert Ransom furniture designing and product development company executive
Draelos, Zoe Diana dermatologist, consultant
Huston, Fred John retired automotive engineer
Kandt, Raymond S. neurologist
†Lyon, Wayne Barton manufacturing company executive
Marsden, Lawrence Albert retired textile company executive
Martinson, Jacob Christian, Jr. academic administrator
McCaslin, Richard Bryan history educator
Pate, William Patrick city manager
Phillips, Earl Norfleet, Jr. financial services executive
Smith, Michael Sterling insurance and financial services executive
Weatherford, Ronald Jeffrey minister
Winn, Walter Garnett, Jr. marketing strategist, advertising executive

Highlands
Bell, William Henry, Jr. banker
Shaffner, Randolph Preston shop owner, educator, writer
Tietze, Phyllis Somerville retired media specialist

Hillsborough
Bolduc, Jean Plumley journalist, education activist
Dula, Rosa Lucile Noell retired secondary education educator
†Fantazos, Henryk Michael painter, graphic artist
Goodwin, Craufurd David economics educator
Idol, John Lane, Jr. English language educator, writer, editor
Johnston, William Webb pathologist, educator
Martin, Harry Corpening lawyer, retired state supreme court justice
Marzluff, William Frank medical educator
Moore, Edward Towson electronics company executive, electrical engineer
Stephens, Brenda Wilson librarian
Williams, Virginia Parrott writer, company executive

Horse Shoe
Howell, George Washington lawyer, consultant

Hudson
Kincaid, Tina entertainer, producer

Huntersville
Brownlee, Sarah Hale elementary special education educator
†Church, John W. quality engineer
†Stewart, Tony professional race car driver

Indian Beach
Wiley, Albert Lee, Jr. physician, engineer, educator

Jacksonville
Hutto, James Calhoun retired financial executive
Kimball, Lynn Jerome historian
Taylor, Vaughan Edward lawyer, educator

Jefferson
Franklin, Robert McFarland book publisher
†Van Arnam, Mark Stephen sales executive

Jonas Ridge
Faunce, William Dale clinical psychologist, researcher, consultant

Kannapolis
Ridenhour, Joseph Conrad textile company executive
Thigpen, Alton Hill motor transportation company executive

Kernersville
Bruno, Frank A. film producer
Metcalf, Corwin Moore (Mickey) business educator, businessman, consultant

Kings Mountain
†Snow, Alice M. artist
Turner, Marguerite Rose Cowles library administrator

Kinston
Arcino, Manuel Dagan *microbiologist, consultant*
Baker-Gardner, Jewelle *interior designer*
Matthis, Eva Mildred Boney *college official*
Petteway, Samuel Bruce *college president*

Kitty Hawk
Sjoerdsma, Albert *research institute executive*

Kure Beach
Hoppe, Barbara G. *historic site administrator*
Lanier, James Alfred, III *aquarium administrator*

Lake Junaluska
Goodgame, Gordon Clifton *minister*
Hale, Joseph Rice *church organization executive*
Stanton, Donald Sheldon *academic administrator*
Tullis, Edward Lewis *retired bishop*

Lake Toxaway
Morgan, Marianne *corporate professional*

Landis
Lynch, Samuel Curlee, Jr. (Sir Sami Lynch) *painter, sculptor, writer*

Laurel Springs
Gilbert-Strawbridge, Anne Wieland *journalist*

Laurinburg
Bayes, Ronald Homer *English language educator, author*

Leasburg
Treacy, Sandra Joanne Pratt *art educator, artist*

Lenoir
Carswell, Jane Triplett *family physician*
Flaherty, David Thomas, Jr. *lawyer*
†Hicks, Cecilia Perkins *editor*
Michaux, Henry Gaston *art educator*
Moore, Mary Ellen *community health, hospice nurse*

Lewisville
Desley, John Whitney *medical illustrator*
Gould, Anne Austin *special education educator*

Lillington
Harrington, Anthony Ross *radio announcer, educator*
Overton, Elizabeth Nicole *elementary school educator, aerobics instructor*

Lincolnton
Hallman, Patricia Ann *music educator*

Linwood
Barnes, Melver Raymond *retired chemist*

Little Switzerland
Gross, Samson Richard *geneticist, biochemist, educator*

Louisburg
Davis, Sarah Irwin *retired English language educator*
†Fish, Hilda Jean Barker *library director*

Lumberton
Harding, Barry *school system administrator, educational consultant*

Maiden
Pruitt, Thomas P., Jr. *textiles executive*

Manteo
Berry, Russell W. *historic site administrator*
Miller, William Lee, Jr. *minister*

Marion
Burgin, Charles Edward *lawyer*

Marshall
Baker, James L. *judge*

Marshville
Steagald, Thomas Ray *minister*

Matthews
Rusho, Karen G. *critical care and community health nurse, educator*

Mebane
Langley, Ricky Lee *occupational medicine physician*

Mill Spring
Osborn, Christopher Raymoln, Jr. *minister*

Misenheimer
Smith, Thomas Harold, III *instrumental music educator, musician*

Mocksville
Smith, Mark Eugene *architectural engineering service company executive*

Mooresville
Benson, Johnny *professional race car driver*
†Cope, Derrike *professional race car driver*
Cox, Herbert Bartle *natural gas company executive*
†Earnhardt, Dale, Jr. *professional stock race car driver*
Herring, Ralph McNeely *nurse*
†Little, Charles Glen, Jr. (Chad) *professional race car driver*
Marlin, Sterling *professional race car driver*
Martin, Mark *professional race car driver*
Mayfield, Jeremy *professional race car driver*
Neill, Rita Jarrett *elementary school educator*

Morehead City
Graham, Gloria Flippin *dermatologist*

Morganton
Ervin, Samuel James, III *federal judge*
†Jones, Geraldine Mary Florence *journalist*

Morrisville
Cofer, John Isaac, IV *mechanical engineer*
Francis, Ron *professional hockey player*
Hardin, George Cecil, Jr. *petroleum consultant*
Karmanos, Peter, Jr. *professional sports team executive*
†Maurice, Paul *pro hockey coach*
†Peca, Michael *professional hockey player*
Rutherford, Jim *professional sports team executive*
Stokes, George Clive *healthcare administrator*

Mount Airy
Ratliff, Robert Barns, Jr. *mechanical engineer*
Rotenizer, R. Eugene *financial planner*
Short, Linda Matthews *elementary education educator*
Woltz, Howard Osler, Jr. *steel and wire products company executive*

Mount Olive
Raper, William Burkette *retired college president*
†Rigsbee, David E. *poet, educator*

Mount Ulla
Kluttz, Henry G. *principal*

Murfreesboro
Brett, Mauvice Winslow *retired educational administrator, consultant*
Burke, Marguerite Jodi Larcombe *writer, computer consultant*
Lott, Stanley G. *college president*
McLawhorn, Rebecca Lawrence *mathematics educator*
Whitaker, Bruce Ezell *college president*

Murphy
Bata, Rudolph Andrew, Jr. *lawyer*
Kerr, Walter Belnap *retired missile instrumentation engineer, English language researcher, consultant*
Khan, Rashid Hussain *physician, researcher*
Pezzella, Jerry James, Jr. *investment and real estate executive*

Nashville
Coggin, Michael Wright *insurance marketing and training executive*

New Bern
Antry, Ronald Virgel *county official*
Ash, William James *geneticist*
Baughman, Fred Hubbard *aeronautical engineer, former naval officer*
Davis, James Lee *lawyer*
Fegely, Eugene Leroy *retired humanities educator*
Finnerty, Frances Martin *medical administrator*
Forrester, Ann *nurse*
Futch, William Stewart, Jr. *gastroenterologist*
Hemphill, Jean Hargett *college dean*
Hunt, William B. *cardiopulmonary physician*
Kellum, Norman Bryant, Jr. *lawyer*
Love, Darryl Lewis *quality engineer*
Moeller, Dade William *environmental engineer, educator*
Overholt, Hugh Robert *lawyer, retired army officer*
Perdue, Beverly E. *state legislator, geriatric consultant*
Sinning, Mark Alan *thoracic and vascular surgeon*
Smith, Jean Lenora *music educator*
Smith, Larry Wayne *medical/surgical nurse*
Stoller, David Allen *lawyer*
Whitehurst, Brooks Morris *chemical engineer*

New Hill
Goncarovs, Gunti *radiation chemist*
Weber, Michael Howard *senior nuclear control operator*

Newland
Lustig, Susan Gardner *occupational therapist*
Singleton, Stella Wood *personal care supervisor*

Newport
Burge, Larry Brady *artist*
Williams, Winton Hugh *civil engineer*

Newton
Harris, Gerald Wayne *retired radio advertising sales executive*

North Wilkesboro
Ashworth, Robert Vincent *data processing executive*
Pardue, Dwight Edward *venture capitalist*
Parsons, Irene *management consultant*

Oak Ridge
Johnson, Mark Cyrus *financial planner, tax preparer*
Johnson, Willie Spoon *quality management consultant*

Oriental
Sutter, John Richard *manufacturer, investor*

Oxford
Burnette, James Thomas *lawyer*

Pembroke
Bukowy, Stephen Joseph *accounting educator*
Meadors, Allen Coats *health administrator, educator*
Sexton, Jean Elizabeth *librarian*

Penland
†Schulman, Norman *artist*

Pfafftown
Radford, Kathy Ann *veterinarian*

Pikeville
Sauls, Don *clergyman*

Pine Knoll Shores
Benson, Kenneth Victor *manufacturing company executive, lawyer*
Griffin, Thomas Lee, Jr. *industrial and federal government specialist*
Thatcher, Muriel Burger *mathematics education educator, consultant*

Pinehurst
Amspoker, James Mack *retired gas company executive*
Burris, Kenneth Wayne *biologist, educator*
Carroll, Kent Jean *retired naval officer*
Fleming, Doris Aven *mental health nurse*
Gilmore, Voit *travel executive*
Grantham, Joseph Michael, Jr. *hotel executive, management and marketing consultant*
Hopkins, Marjorie Johnson *writer*
Huizenga, John Robert *nuclear chemist, educator*
Nuzzo, Salvatore Joseph *defense, electronics company executive*
O'Loughlin, John Kirby *retired insurance executive*
O'Neill, John Joseph, Jr. *business consultant, former chemical company executive*
Paquette, Dean Richard *retired computer company executive, consultant*
Schneider, Donald Frederic *banker*

Pinetops
Robertson, Richard Blake *management consultant*

Pisgah Forest
Albyn, Richard Keith *retired architect*
Pulliam, Steve Cameron *business owner*

Pittsboro
Bailey, Herbert Smith, Jr. *retired publisher*
Doenges, Byron Frederick *economist, educator, former government official*
Hauser, Charles Newland McCorkle *newspaper consultant*
Magill, Samuel Hays *retired academic administrator, higher education consultant*
Noether, Emiliana Pasca *historian, educator*
Quinn, Jarus William *physicist, former association executive*
Shurick, Edward Palmes *television executive, rancher*

Polkton
Heilman, Thomas Lewis *educational administrator*

Pope AFB
Conley, Raymond Leslie *English language educator*
Vaughan, Clyde Vernelson *program director*

Princeton
Harrell, Michelle *special education educator*

Raleigh
Aldridge, Adrienne Yingling *accountant, business analyst*
†Ammon, John Richard *anesthesiologist*
Aronson, Arthur Lawrence *veterinary pharmacology and toxicology educator*
Arya, Satya Pal *meteorology educator*
Aspnes, David Erik *physicist, educator*
Atchley, William Reid *geneticist, evolutionary biologist, educator*
Baliga, Bantval Jayant *electrical engineering educator, research administrator*
Barish, Charles Franklin *internist, gastroenterologist, educator*
Beatty, Kenneth Orion, Jr. *chemical engineer*
Benson, D(avid) Michael *plant pathologist*
Berry, Joni Ingram *hospice pharmacist, educator*
Bitzer, Donald Lester *electrical engineering educator, retired research laboratory administrator*
Boone, Stephen Christopher *neurosurgeon*
Boyles, Harlan Edward *state official*
Britt, W. Earl *federal judge*
Buchanan, David Royal *associate dean*
Bull, Leonard S. *educational association administrator*
Burns, Robert Paschal *architect, educator*
Burris, Craven Allen *retired education administrator, educator*
Cameron, Christie Speir *lawyer*
Carlton, Alfred Pershing, Jr. *lawyer*
Carter, Jean Gordon *lawyer*
Case, Charles Dixon *lawyer*
Chou, Wushow *computer scientist, educator*
Church, Kern Everidge *engineer, consultant*
Ciraulo, Stephen Joseph *nurse, anesthetist*
Clarke, Lewis James *landscape architect*
Cohen, David Michael *newspaper editor, journalist*
Cole, Janice McKenzie *prosecutor*
Cook, Maurice Gayle *soil science educator, consultant*
Cook, Norma Baker *consulting company executive*
Cooper, Arthur Wells *ecologist, educator*
Corder, Billie Farmer *clinical psychologist, artist*
Cresimore, James Leonard *food broker*
Crisp, Fred *publishing executive*
Cummings, Ralph Waldo *soil scientist, educator, researcher*
Daniels, Frank Arthur, Jr. *newspaper publisher*
Daniels, Frank Arthur, III *publishing executive*
Dannelly, William David *lawyer*
Davis, Egbert Lawrence, III *lawyer*
Davis, Robin Reed *lobbyist, feminist advocate*
Davis, Thomas Hill, Jr. *lawyer*
DeJarnette, Fred Roark *aerospace engineer*
Denson, Alexander Bunn *federal magistrate judge*
Dixon, Daniel Roberts, Jr. *retired tax lawyer*
†Dixon, Wallace Wade *federal judge*
Dixon, Wright Tracy, Jr. *lawyer*
Doherty, Robert Cunningham *advertising executive, retired*
Dolce, Carl John *education administration educator*
Drew, Nancy McLaurin Shannon *counselor, consultant*
Droessler, Earl George *geophysicist educator*
Dudziak, Donald John *nuclear engineer, educator*
Dunphy, Edward James *crop science extension specialist*
Durant, Frederick Clark, III *aerospace history and space art consultant*
Eaddy, Paula Johnson *women's health nurse*
Eagles, Sidney Smith, Jr. *judge*
Easley, Michael F. *state attorney general*
Eberly, Harry Landis *retired communications company executive*
Ebisuzaki, Yukiko *chemistry educator*
Edwards, Charles Archibald *lawyer*
Effron, Seth Alan *editor, journalist*
Ellis, Lester Neal, Jr. *lawyer*
Ellis, Richard W. *lawyer*
Entman, Robert Mathew *communications educator, consultant*
Ferguson, Susan Katharine Stover *nurse, psychotherapist, consultant*
Fletcher, Oscar Jasper, Jr. *college dean*
Flournoy, William Louis, Jr. *landscape architect*

Foley, Gary J. *research chemical engineer, computer scientist, federal agency administrator*
Foley, Peter Michael *lawyer*
Fox, Marye Anne *university chancellor, chemistry educator*
Frye, Henry E. *state supreme court justice*
Gardner, Robin Pierce *engineering educator*
Garrett, Leland Earl *nephrologist, educator*
Garriss, Phyllis Weyer *music educator, performer*
Geller, Janice Grace *nurse*
†Gerlach, Daniel J. *budget and tax policy analyst*
Givens, George Franklin *lawyer*
Godwin, James Beckham *retired landscape architect*
Goldstein, Irving Solomon *chemistry educator, consultant*
†Gomez, Andrea Hope *artist*
Goodman, Major Merlin *botanical sciences educator*
Gordon, Morris Aaron *medical mycologist, microbiologist*
Gossman, Francis Joseph *bishop*
Graham, James A. *state commissioner*
Graham, Kent Hill *philanthropist, museum guide*
Graham, William Edgar, Jr. *lawyer, retired utility company executive*
Graham, William Thomas *lawyer*
Gremillion, David H(enry) *internist, educator*
Grubb, Donald Hartman *paper industry company executive*
Gulledge, Karen Stone *educational administrator*
Hall, John Thomas *lawyer*
Hansley, Lee *art gallery owner, curator*
Hanson, John M. *civil engineering and construction educator*
Hardin, Eugene Brooks, Jr. *retired banker*
Hardin, James W. *botanist, herbarium curator, educator*
Harper, Dixon Ladd *broadcast director*
Harvey, Glenn F. *association executive*
Hassan, Hosni Moustafa *microbiologist, biochemist, toxicologist and food scientist, educator*
Hauser, John Reid *electrical engineering educator*
Havlin, John Leroy *soil scientist, educator*
Havner, Kerry Shuford *civil engineering and solid mechanics educator*
Hayes, Charles Austin *economic development executive, consultant*
Hendricks, Chris *publisher*
Hensey, Charles McKinnon *retired lawyer*
Hiday, Virginia Aldigé *sociologist educator*
Hill, Hulene Dian *accountant*
Hinton, David Owen *retired electrical engineer*
Hodgson, Ernest *toxicology educator*
Holding, Lewis R. *banker*
Holton, William Coffeen *electrical engineering executive*
Homick, Daniel John *lawyer, financial executive*
Horton, Horace Robert *biochemistry educator*
Howell, Bruce Inman *academic administrator*
Huffman, David Curtis *minister*
Huggard, John Parker *lawyer*
Hughes, Francis P. *medical researcher*
Hunt, James Baxter, Jr. *governor, lawyer*
Hunter, Richard Samford, Jr. *lawyer*
James, Perry Edwin, III *director Raleigh finance department*
Jarrett, Polly Hawkins *secondary education educator, retired*
Jenkins, Clauston Levi, Jr. *college president*
Jessen, David Wayne *accountant*
Johnson, Charles Lavon, Jr. *clinical neuropsychologist, consultant*
Johnson, Marvin Richard Alois *architect*
Johnson, Peter Ray *minister*
Johnson, William Dean *power company executive*
Johnston, Linda Tidwell *municipal official*
Jolly, John Russell, Jr. *lawyer*
Jones, Frederick Claudius *English language and linguistics educator*
Joyner, Walton Kitchin *lawyer*
Kapp, Michael Keith *lawyer*
†Katz, Steven Barry *English educator, writer*
Kauffman, Terry *broadcast and creative arts communication educator, artist*
Kaufman, Sarah Hall *legal assistant*
Kelman, Arthur *plant pathologist, educator*
Keshk, Mamdouh M. (Mike Keshk) *design engineer*
Kimbrell, Odell Culp, Jr. *physician*
Kirkley, James Franklin *religion and ethics educator*
Kirkpatrick, Jayne F. *director public affairs*
Klein, Verle Wesley *corporate executive, retired naval officer*
Kriz, George James *agricultural research administrator, educator*
Kuhler, Renaldo Gillet *museum official, scientific illustrator*
Lancaster, H(arold) Martin *former congressman, former advisor to the President, academic administrator*
Larsen, Eric Lyle *information technology executive, writer, consultant, farmer*
Leak, Robert E. *economic development consultant*
†Leiter, Jeffrey Carl *sociologist, educator*
†Levine, Ronald H. *physician, state official*
Littleton, Isaac Thomas, III *retired university library administrator, consultant*
Lolley, William Randall *minister*
Maidon, Carolyn Howser *teacher education director*
Malecha, Marvin John *architect, academic administrator*
Malling, Martha Hale Shackford *clinical social worker, educator*
†Malone, Elmer Taylor, Jr. *religious organization administrator*
Maness, Edwin Clinton, III *highway patrol officer, video coordinator*
Mann, Thurston Jeffrey *academic administrator*
Marshall, Elaine Folk *state official*
Martin, John Charles *judge*
Maupin, Armistead Jones *lawyer*
McAllister, David Franklin *computer science educator*
McCormick, Thomas A., Jr. *city attorney*
McDowell, Timothy Hill *lobbyist*
McKinney, Charles Cecil *investment company executive*
McLaurin, Martha Regina *parking service company executive*
McNutt, James Charles *museum director*
McPherson, Samuel Dace, III *computer scientist, instructor, consultant*
Meelheim, Helen Diane *nursing administrator*
Meier, Wilbur Leroy, Jr. *industrial engineer, educator, former university chancellor*
Miller, Ralph Bradley *lawyer, state legislator*
Mitchell, Burley Bayard, Jr. *state supreme court chief justice*
Mitchell, Gary Earl *physicist, educator*
Monteith, Larry King *chancellor emeritus*

Moore, Thomas Lloyd *librarian*
Moreland, Donald Edwin *plant physiologist*
†Muddell, Jeffrey Allan *television news producer*
Nation, Philip David *financial planner*
Neely, Charles B., Jr. *lawyer*
Nelson, Cynthia Kaye *network engineer*
Nelson, Larry A. *statistics educator, consultant*
Newman, Slater Edmund *psychologist, educator*
Ofner, J(ames) Alan *management consultant*
Orr, Robert F. *state supreme court justice*
Owens, Tyler Benjamin *chemist*
Page, Anne Ruth *gifted education educator, education specialist*
Parker, Sarah Elizabeth *state supreme court justice*
Paschal, Beth Cummings *journalist, editor*
Payne, Harry Eugene, Jr. *state labor commissioner*
Peacock, Charles H. *agricultural studies educator*
Peacock, Erle Ewart, Jr. *surgeon, lawyer, educator*
Pinnix, John Lawrence *lawyer*
Poulton, Bruce Robert *former university chancellor*
Powell, Drexel Dwane, Jr. *editorial cartoonist*
Powell, Durwood Royce *lawyer*
Prior, William Allen *electronics company executive*
†Pruitt, Janet *state senate official*
Ragsdale, George Robinson *lawyer*
Redman, William Walter, Jr. *realtor*
Reeves, Ralph B., III *publisher, editor*
Renfrow, Edward *state auditor*
Rhodes, Donald Robert *musicologist, retired electrical engineer*
Roach, Wesley Linville *lawyer, insurance executive*
Robb, Nathaniel Heyward, Jr. *remote sensing company executive*
Robinson, Keith *sales and marketing executive*
Robinson, Prezell Russell *academic administrator*
Roisler, Glenn Harvey *quality assurance professional*
Russell, Thomas Lee *academic administrator*
Ryan, Bryan *language educator, writer, editor*
Sanders, Douglas Charles *horticulturist, researcher, educator*
Sapinsley, Elbert Lee *rabbi*
Sardi, Elaine Marie *special education educator*
Sasser, Jonathan Drew *lawyer*
Scandalios, John George *geneticist, educator*
Schwab, Carol Ann *law educator*
Scogin, Troy Pope *publishing company executive, accounts executive*
†Sean, Walsh *press secretary*
†Seater, John Joseph *economics educator*
Sederoff, Ronald Ross *geneticist*
Seiber, Frank *director information services*
Sharpe, Donald Charles *service manager*
Shaw, Robert Gilbert *restaurant executive, senator*
Shaw, Talbert O. *university president*
Simpson, Steven Drexell *lawyer*
†Singh, Munindar P. *adult education educator*
Skaggs, Richard Wayne *agricultural engineering educator*
Slaton, Joseph Guilford *social worker*
Sloan, O. Temple, Jr. *automotive equipment executive*
Small, Alden Thomas *judge*
Smith, Gail Grady *municipal official*
Smith, Sherwood Hubbard, Jr. *utilities executive*
Sneed, Ronald Ernest *engineering educator emeritus*
Stannett, Vivian Thomas *chemical engineering educator*
Stevens, Richard Yates *county official*
Stevenson, Denise L. *business executive, banking consultant*
Stewart, D. Jane *nursing educator, researcher*
Stewart, Debra Wehrle *university dean and official, educator*
Stiles, Phillip John *physicist, educator*
Stratas, Nicholas Emanuel *psychiatrist*
Stuber, Charles William *genetics educator, researcher*
Suhr, Paul Augustine *lawyer*
Sutton, Ronnie Neal *state legislator, lawyer*
Swaisgood, Harold Everett *biochemist, educator*
Tally, Lura Self *state legislator*
Taylor, Kaaryn Wilaine *civil engineer*
Taylor, Patricia Kramer *nurse*
Thomas, Mark Stanton *lawyer*
Thompson, Cleon F., Jr. *university administrator*
Timothy, David Harry *biology educator*
Triantaphyllou, H. H. *plant pathologist*
Turinsky, Paul Josef *nuclear engineer, educator*
Veenhuis, Philip Edward *psychiatrist, educator, administrator*
†Ward, Thomas Gregory *history and social science educator, curriculum developer and consultant*
Waschka, Rodney Anthony, II *composer, educator*
Webb, John *retired state supreme court justice*
Wesler, Oscar *mathematician, educator*
Wetsch, John Robert *information systems specialist*
Wetsch, Laura Johnson *lawyer*
†Wheeler, Dan *state commissioner*
Wheeler, Lawrence Jefferson *art museum director*
Whitehead, Ian *insurance company executive*
Whitten, Jerry Lynn *chemistry educator*
Wicker, Dennis A. *state official*
Willer, Edward Herman *real estate broker*
Williams, Hugh Alexander, Jr. *retired mechanical engineer, consultant*
Wilson, Robert Lee, Jr. *lawyer*
Winstead, Nash Nicks *university administrator, phytopathologist*
†Winston, Robert W., III *hotel facility executive*
Wollum, Arthur George, II *microbiologist, researcher, educator*
Wynne, Johnny Calvin *university dean, plant breeding researcher*
Zeng, Zhao-Bang *geneticist, educator*
†Zimmerman, Gerhardt *music director*

Randleman
Andretti, John *professional race car driver*
†Petty, Kyle *professional stock car driver*
Petty, Richard *retired professional race car driver*

Reno
†Seib, Kenneth Allen *English educator*

Research Triangle Park
Barrett, J. Carl *cancer researcher, molecular biologist*
Batey, Sharyn Rebecca *clinical research scientist*
Chao, James Lee *chemist*
Clark, Kevin Anthony *marketing executive, communications executive*
Connor, Walter Robert *classics educator, humanities center administrator*
de Serres, Frederick Joseph *genetic toxicologist*
Dunteman, George Henry *psychologist*
†Gaither, John Stokes *chemical company executive*
Golden, Carole Ann *immunologist, microbiologist*
Hamner, Charles *company executive*
Jarrell, Donald Ray *laboratory administrator*
Key, Karen Letisha *pharmaceutical executive*
Maar, Rosina *medical organization executive*
McClellan, Roger Orville *toxicologist*
Miller, Robert Reese *trade association executive*
Mumford, Stephen Douglas *population growth control research scientist*
Niedel, James E. *pharmaceuticals executive*
Olden, Kenneth *science administrator, researcher*
Panas, Raymond Michael *pharmaceutical researcher*
Qualls, Charles Wayne, Jr. *research pathologist*
Roses, Allen David *neurologist, educator*
Ross, Jeffrey Alan *research biologist*
Selkirk, James Kirkwood *biochemist*
Senzel, Alan Joseph *analytical chemistry consultant, music critic*
Wiener, Russell Warren *environmental scientist, researcher*
Wilson, Donald Hurst, III *biopharmaceutical industry executive*

Roanoke Rapids
Alves, Robert Mark *priest*

Robbins
Mac Kenzie, James Donald *clergyman*

Robbinsville
Ginn, Ronn *architect, urban planner, general contractor*

Rockingham
Robertson, Ralph S. *secondary school principal*

Rocky Mount
Jackson, Reed McSwain *educational administrator*
Polk, Ronald Thomas *marketing executive*
Rabon, Ronald Ray *retail jewelry store chain executive*
Smith, Preston *minister*
Sulfaro, Joyce A. *school program director*
†Watson, Elizabeth Anne *elementary education educator*
Weaver, James Paul *retired clergyman*
Wilkerson, William Holton *banker*
Wordsworth, Jerry L. *wholesale distribution executive*
Zipf, Robert Eugene, Jr. *legal medicine consultant, pathologist*

Ronda
Dobbins, Brenda Lorraine Adams *secondary school educator*

Rougemont
Cooney, M(uriel) Sharon Taylor *medical/surgical nurse, educator*
Nilsson, Mary Ann *music educator*

Roxboro
Daniel, Lori Edwards *assistant principal*
†Phillips, Mark T. *insurance agent*
†Woodall, Carolyn Glascoe *school counselor*

Rural Hall
Wager, Michael *company executive*

Rutherfordton
Conley, Katherine Logan *religious studies educator*
Metcalf, Ethel Edgerton *retired elementary school educator*

Salisbury
Baines, Rhunell (Nell Baines) *nurse*
Kiser, Glenn Augustus *retired pediatrician, investor*
Logan, David Bruce *health care administrator*
Lomax, Donald Henry *physician*
Post, Rose Zimmerman *newspaper columnist*
Shalkop, Robert Leroy *retired museum director*
Tseng, Howard Shih Chang *business and economics educator, investment company executive*

Saluda
Mc Cutcheon, John Tinney, Jr. *journalist*

Sanford
Higgins, George Edward *sculptor*
Hopkins, Cassandre' F. *land use planner*
Kilmartin, Joseph Francis, Jr. *business executive, consultant*
Raisig, Paul Jones, Jr. *lawyer*
Schneider, Steven L. *company executive*
Walker, Gary Linn *materials and logistics executive, consultant*
York, Carolyn Pleasants Stearns *English educator*

Semora
Williams, Pauline M. *psychiatric-mental and community health nurse*

Seymour Johnson AFB
†Bigum, Randall K. (Randy) *career officer*

Shelby
Arey, Robert Jackson, Jr. *small business owner*
Bolich, Gregory Gordon *humanities educator*
Cagle, Terry Dee *clergyman*

Smithfield
Schulz, Bradley Nicholas *lawyer*
Taylor, Ellen Borden Broadhurst *civic worker*
Wiggs, Shirley JoAnn *retired secondary school educator*

Smyrna
†Doble, Richard deGaris *editor, publisher, photographer*

Sneads Ferry
†LaMar, James Edward *preventive medicine physician, marine officer*

Southern Pines
Kaufmann, Rachel Norsworthy *educator*
Matney, Edward Eli *financial advisor*
Owings, Malcolm William *retired management consultant*
Toon, Malcolm *former ambassador*
Yarborough, William Pelham *writer, lecturer, retired army officer, consultant*

Southern Shores
Vander Myde, Philip Louis *architectural design firm executive*

Southport
Harrelson, Walter Joseph *minister, religion educator emeritus*

Sparta
Allen, Robert English *business development executive, consultant*

Spindale
Howard, Elizabeth Ann Blanton *courier service executive*
Trautmann, Patricia Ann *communications educator, storyteller*

Spring Creek
†Jones, Sara Sue Fisher *library director*

Spring Hope
Hildreth, James Robert *retired air force officer*

Stanfield
Dysart, John *historic site administrator*

Statesville
Deddens, Alan Eugene *otolaryngologist, head and neck surgeon*
Grogan, David R. *company executive*
Lawson, Willard Francis, Jr. *paper company owner, sales executive*
Lorentzen, James Clifford *radiologist*
Stewart, Patricia Canup *vocal music educator*

Steadman
Taylor, David *clergy member, religious administrator*

Supply
Pollard, Joseph Augustine *advertising and public relations consultant*

Swannanoa
Stuck, Roger Dean *electrical engineering educator*

Swansboro
Juhl, Harold Alexander *retired career officer, construction executive*

Tabor City
Jorgensen, Ralph Gubler *lawyer, accountant*

Tarboro
Andrews, Claude Leonard *psychotherapist*
Hopkins, Grover Prevatte *lawyer*

Thomasville
Sprinkle, Robert Lee, Jr. *podiatrist*

Trinity
Labonte, Bobby *professional race car driver*

Tryon
Flynn, Kirtland, Jr. *accountant*
McDermott, James Alexander *retired lawyer*
McDermott, Renée R(assler) *lawyer*
Stinson, George Arthur *lawyer, former steel company executive*

Tuckasegee
Lominac, Harry Gene *retired theater educator, designer*

Tyner
Sams, Robin Dahl *artist*

Valdese
Atkin, Andrew Scott *artist*

Vale
Miller, Barbara Sims *health promotion coordinator*

Vass
Glassman, Edward *public relations management creativity consultant*

Wake Forest
Blackmore, James Herrall *clergyman, educator, author*
Buchanan, Edward A. *education educator*
Delaney, Gary Louis *retired military officer, management consultant*

Wallace
Johnson, James Wilson *pastor*

Warrenton
Spence, Faye Yvonne *elementary school educator*

Washington
†Alligood, Lola Lurvey *educator*
Hackney, James Acra, III *industrial engineer, consultant, retired manufacturing company executive*
Heck, Henry D'Arcy *toxicologist*
Timour, John Arnold *retired librarian, medical bibliography and library science educator*

Waxhaw
Edwards, Irene Elizabeth (Libby Edwards) *dermatologist, educator, researcher*
Lamparter, William C. *printing and publishing consultant, digital printing and information systems specialist*

Waynesville
Lundy, Robert Fielden *minister*
McKinney, Alexander Stuart *neurologist, retired*
Nickerson, John Henry *artist, sculptor, designer*

Weaverville
Hauschild, Douglas Carey *optometrist*
Kledis, Jarel Emanuel *sculptor*
Parsons, Vinson Adair *retired computer software company executive*

Welcome
†Skinner, Mike *professional race car driver*

Weldon
Barringer, Paul Brandon, II *lumber company executive*

West End
Harman, Henry M., Jr. *accountant, educator*

West Jefferson
Merrion, Arthur Benjamin *mathematics educator, tree farmer*

Whisper Pines
Enlow, Donald Hugh *anatomist, educator, university dean*

Whiteville
Gilmore, Robin Harris *nursing administrator*
Scott, Stephen Carlos *academic administrator*

Whitsett
Fennell, Richard Arthur *artist*

Wilkesboro
Boyd, Robert Giddings, Jr. *health facility administrator*
†Carroll, Elizabeth Lee *educator English*
Thomas, David Lloyd *accountant, consultant*
Tillman, Robert L. *construction executive*
Waller, Jim D. *holding company executive*

Williamston
Hoggard, Minnie Coltrain *gifted education educator, consultant*

Wilmington
Bachman, David *neurologist, pediatric neurologist*
Bissette, Samuel Delk *astronomer, artist, financial executive*
Bolen, Eric George *biology educator*
Burton, Richard Greene *retired marketing executive*
Cahill, Charles L. *university administrator, chemistry educator*
Cameron, Kay *conductor, music director, arranger*
†Conser, Walter Hurley, Jr. *religion and philosophy educator*
Dewey, Ralph Jay *headmaster*
Dixon, N(orman) Rex *speech and hearing scientist, educator*
Flohr, Daniel P. *company executive*
†Foster, Amy Nicole *television station sales administrator*
Fox, James Carroll *federal judge*
Fulrath, Andrew Wesley *bank executive*
Funk, Frank E. *retired university dean*
Gillen, Howard William *neurologist, medical historian*
Graham, Otis Livingston, Jr. *history educator*
†Habibi, Don A. *philosophy educator*
Hansen, Steven Michael *fiber scientist, researcher*
Hucks, Cynthia Stokes *university finance officer, accountant*
Humphreys, Charles Raymond, Jr. *retired research chemist*
Israel, Margie Olanoff *psychotherapist*
Kaufman, James Jay *lawyer*
Kesler, James L. *ophthalmologist*
Lees, Anthony Philip *business consultant*
Leutze, James Richard *academic administrator, television producer and host*
†Mason, William Norton *federal judge*
Mc Cabe, Gerard Benedict *retired library administrator*
McCauley, Cleyburn Lycurgus *lawyer*
Medlock, Donald Larson *lawyer*
Oakley, Carolyn Cobb *library director, academic administrator*
Penick, George Dial *pathologist*
Perko, Mike A. *health education and health promotion educator*
Quin, Louis DuBose *chemist, educator*
Roer, Robert David *physiologist, educator*
Rorison, Margaret Lippitt *reading consultant*
Seagle, J. Harold *lawyer*
Seapker, Janet Kay *museum director*
Silloway, Benton, Jr. *food products executive*
Stokes, John Lemacks, II *clergyman, retired university official*
Thompson, Donald Charles *electronics company executive, former coast guard officer*
Watanabe, Wade Osamu *marine biologist*

Wilson
Bailey, Grace Daniel *retired secondary school educator*
Dean, Thomas A. *research laboratory executive*
†Hardy-Braz, Steven Thomas *psychologist*
Kushner, Michael James *neurologist, consultant*
Ladwig, Harold Allen *neurologist*
Lee, Jayne Frances Peacock *nursing administrator, critical care nurse, infection control practitioner*
†Lenard, Mary Jane *accounting and information systems educator*
†Leonard, J. Rich *federal judge, educator*
Mercer, Danny Thomas *sales representative*
Stewart, Burton Gloyden, Jr. *retired banker*
Wyatt, Edward Avery, V *city manager*

Wingate
Dodd, John Robert *non-profit organization administrator*

Winston Salem
Adams, Alfred Gray *lawyer*
Alexander, Eben, Jr. *neurological surgeon*
Atkinson, G. Douglas, Sr. *marketing executive, consultant*
Austell, Edward Callaway *banker*
Baker, Leslie Mayo, Jr. *banker*
Barnett, Richard Chambers *historian, educator*
Barnhardt, Zeb Elonzo, Jr. *lawyer, independent consultant*
Barnhill, Henry Grady, Jr. *lawyer*
Baxter, Lawrence Gerald *strategic analyst, law educator, business consultant*
Beach, Franklin Darrel *minister*
Beaty, James Arthur, Jr. *judge*
Berthrong, Merrill Gray *retired library director*
Blynn, Guy Marc *lawyer*
Boger, Richard Edwin, Jr. *minister*
†Brown, David G. *academic administrator*

Brunstetter, Peter Samuel *lawyer*
Buselmeier, Bernard Joseph *insurance company executive*
Butner, Fred Washington, Jr. *architect*
Capps, Richard Henry *minister*
Carney, Karen Rose *music educator, jazz, popular, classical pianist*
†Carruthers, Catharine *federal judge*
Carter, Henry Moore, Jr. *retired foundation executive*
Cawood, Hobart Guy *historic site administrator*
Cheng, Che Ping *cardiologist, researcher, educator*
Clarkson, Thomas Boston *comparative medicine educator*
Coffey, Larry B(ruce) *lawyer*
Copenhaver, W. Andrew *lawyer*
Cordell, A(lfred) Robert *cardiothoracic surgeon, educator*
Cowan, Robert Jenkins *radiologist, educator*
Cramer, John Scott *retired banker*
Crowder, Lena Belle *retired special education educator*
Davis, Linwood Layfield *lawyer*
Davis, Thomas Henry *airline executive*
Davis, William Allison, II *lawyer*
Dawson, Paula Dayl *oncological nurse*
Dean, Richard Henry *surgeon, educator*
Dobbins, James Talmage, Jr. *analytical chemist, researcher*
Dodd, Virginia Marilyn *veterinarian*
Doggett, Aubrey Clayton, Jr. *real estate executive, consultant*
Donofrio, Peter Daniel *neurology educator*
†Dykers, Carol Reese *communications educator*
Early, James H., Jr. *lawyer*
Ehle, John Marsden, Jr. *writer*
Eliason, Russell Allen *judge*
Erwin, Richard Cannon, Sr. *federal judge*
Evans, Lisbeth *business networking executive, political party official*
Ewing, Alexander Cochran *chancellor*
Faccinto, Victor Paul *artist, gallery administrator*
Farr, Henry Bartow, Jr. *lawyer*
Ferree, Carolyn Ruth *radiation oncologist, educator*
Fitzgerald, Ernest Abner *retired bishop*
Gallimore, Margaret Martin *poet*
Gallo, Vincent John *financial planner*
Ganz, Charles *laboratory executive*
Georgitis, John *allergist, educator*
Gitter, Allan Reinhold *lawyer*
Graybeal, Barbara *editor, writer*
Greason, Murray Crossley, Jr. *lawyer*
Griswold, George *marketing, advertising and public relations executive*
Gunzenhauser, Gerard Ralph, Jr. *management consultant, investor*
Hamlin, Edwin Cliburn *sales consultant*
Hanes, Ralph Philip, Jr. *former textiles executive, arts patron, cattle farmer*
Hardwick, James Carlton, Jr. *business and financial planner*
Hazzard, William Russell *geriatrician, educator*
Hearn, Thomas K., Jr. *academic administrator*
Henderson, Richard Martin *retired chemical engineer*
Hendricks, J(ames) Edwin *historian, educator, consultant, author*
Henrichs, W(alter) Dean *dermatologist*
Herring, Jerone Carson *lawyer, bank executive*
Hopkins, Judith Owen *oncologist*
Hopkins, Muriel-Beth Norbrey *lawyer*
Howell, Charles Maitland *dermatologist*
Howell, Julius Ammons *plastic surgeon*
Hutcherson, Karen Fulghum *healthcare executive*
Ibrahim, Mounir Labib *physician, psychiatrist*
Jackson, Mae Boger *executive administrative assistant, office manager*
James, Francis Marshall, III *anesthesiologist*
Janeway, Richard *university official*
Jarrell, Iris Bonds *elementary school educator, business executive*
Johnston, James Wesley *retired tobacco company executive*
Jorizzo, Joseph L. *dermatology educator*
Kaufman, Charlotte S. *communications executive*
Kaufman, William *internist*
Kelly, David Lee, Jr. *neurosurgeon, educator*
King, Wayne Edgar *educator, journalist*
Kohut, Robert Irwin *otolaryngologist, educator*
Lawless, Michael Rhodes *pediatrics educator*
Laxminarayana, Dama *geneticist, researcher, educator*
†Lee, Wei-Chin *political scientist*
Leonard, R. Michael *lawyer*
Loughridge, John Halsted, Jr. *lawyer*
Lu, Dan *systems analyst, mathematician, consultant*
†Lubin, David Martin *art and American studies educator*
MacKinnon, Sally Anne *retired fast food company executive*
Martin, James Alfred, Jr. *religious studies educator*
Maselli, John Anthony *food products company executive*
Maynard, Charles Douglas *radiologist*
McAllister, Kenneth Wayne *lawyer*
McNair, John Franklin, III *banker*
Medlin, John Grimes, Jr. *banker*
Meis, Paul Jean *obstetrics and gynecology educator*
Middaugh, Jack Kendall, II *management educator*
Mokrasch, Lewis Carl *neurochemist, educator*
Moskowitz, Jay *public health sciences educator*
Mueller-Heubach, Eberhard *medical educator*
†Oczkowicz, Edyta Katarzyna *English educator*
Osborn, Malcolm Everett *lawyer*
O'Steen, Wendall Keith *neurobiology and anatomy educator*
†Perret, Peter James *symphony conductor*
Petree, William Horton *lawyer*
Podgorny, George *emergency physician*
†Poston, William Roger, II *biomedical communications educator*
Rauschenberg, Bradford Lee *museum research director*
Ray, Michael Edwin *lawyer*
Rodgman, Alan *chemist, consultant*
Rogers, Lee Frank *radiologist*
Roth, Marjory Joan Jarboe *special education educator*
†Runde, Craig Eric *academic director*
Runnion, Howard J., Jr. *banker*
Sandridge, William Pendleton, Jr. *lawyer*
Schollander, Wendell Leslie, Jr. *lawyer*
Shapere, Dudley *philosophy educator*
Simon, Jimmy Louis *pediatrician, educator*
Smith, Zachary Taylor, II *retired tobacco company executive*
Smunt, Marsha Lynn Haeflinger *financial executive*
†Spach, John Thom *writer, educator*
Spach, Jule Christian *church executive*
Stein, Barry Edward *medical educator*
Sticht, J. Paul *retired food products and tobacco company executive*
Strickland, Robert Louis *corporations director*
Suttles, Donald Roland *retired academic administrator, business educator*
Talbert, Charles Harold *retired religion educator*
†Thrift, Ashley Ormand *lawyer*
Thrift, Julianne Still *academic administrator*
Toole, James Francis *medical educator*
Trautwein, George William *conductor*
Tursi, Frank Vincent *journalist*
Vance, Charles Fogle, Jr. *lawyer*
Veille, Jean-Claude *maternal-fetal medicine physician, educator*
Volz, Annabelle Wekar *learning disabilities educator, consultant*
Walker, George Kontz *law educator*
Walker, John Samuel *retired pediatrician*
Walker, Wendy K. *marketing executive*
Wallace, Roanne *hosiery company executive*
Wanders, Hans Walter *banker*
Ward, Hiram Hamilton *federal judge*
Ward, Marvin Martin *retired state senator*
Weeks, Sandra Kenney *healthcare facilitator*
Wells, Dewey Wallace *lawyer*
†Weyler, Karen Ann *English educator*
Winn, Albert Curry *clergyman*
Womble, William Fletcher *lawyer*
Woods, James Watson, Jr. *cardiologist*
Yeatts, Robert Patrick *ophthalmologist*

Wrightsville Beach
Block, Franklin Lee *retired lawyer*
Mc Ilwain, William Franklin *newspaper editor, writer*
Phull, Bopinder S. *research scientist*

Zebulon
Kirkland, Gerry Paul *sales executive*

NORTH DAKOTA

Amidon
Bergquist, Gene Alfred *farmer, rancher, county commissioner*

Ashley
Kretschmar, William Edward *state legislator, lawyer*

Bismarck
Bosch, Donna *home health nurse administrator*
†Brudvig, Jon Larsen *educator, historian*
Carlisle, Ronald Dwight *nursery owner*
Carmichael, Virgil Wesly *mining, civil and geological engineer, former coal company executive*
Christianson, James Duane *real estate developer*
Clairmont, William Edward *developer*
Clark, Tony *state agency administrator*
Conmy, Patrick A. *federal judge*
Edin, Charles Thomas *lawyer*
Erickstad, Ralph John *judge, retired state supreme court chief justice*
Evanson, Barbara Jean *middle school education educator*
Fry, Charles George *theologian, educator*
Gilbertson, Joel Warren *lawyer*
Gilmore, Kathi *state treasurer*
Heitkamp, Heidi *state attorney general*
†Hughes, James M. *protective services official*
Isaak, Larry A. *state agency administrator*
Jaeger, Alvin A. (Al Jaeger) *secretary of state*
†Kautzman, Dwight C.H. *federal judge*
Keeley, Ethel S. *secondary education program director*
†Keller, Kent Kyle *computer technician*
Klemin, Lawrence R. *lawyer*
Moritz, Florence Stolte *church official*
Murry, Charles Emerson *lawyer, official*
Myrdal, Rosemarie Caryle *state official, former state legislator*
†Ness, Gary Robert *administrator*
Neumann, William Allen *state supreme court justice*
Newborg, Gerald Gordon *state archives administrator*
Oldenburger, Norma Jane *medical surgical nurse*
†Ott, Doris Ann *librarian*
Pomeroy, Glenn *state insurance commissioner*
Sanstead, Wayne Godfrey *state superintendent, former lieutenant governor*
Schafer, Edward T. *governor*
Schuchart, John Albert, Jr. *utility company executive*
Severson, Lynn Kathleen *English educator*
Sperry, James Edward *anthropologist, retired state official*
Strutz, William A. *lawyer*
Thomas, John *communications technologist*
VandeWalle, Gerald Wayne *state supreme court chief justice*
Van Sickle, Bruce Marion *federal judge*

Bottineau
Gorder, Steven F. *business executive*

Cooperstown
Ratcliffe, Phyllis Ann *lawyer, antique dealer*

Devils Lake
Fixen, Randall Robert *academic director*
Tande, Teresa Lyn *secondary educator*

Dickinson
Brauhn, Richard Daniel *university administrator*
†Goetz, William G. *state legislator*

Edgeley
Schimke, Dennis J. *former state legislator*

Ellendale
Larson, Lavonne Fay *educator*

Fargo
Anderson, Gerald Dwight *history educator*
Bright, Myron H. *federal judge, educator*
†Cosgrove, William E. *English literature educator*
Danbom, David Byers *history educator*
†Ekberg, Susan Jane *writer, publisher*
Foss, Richard John *bishop*
Haakenson, Philip Niel *pharmacist, educator*
Hill, William A(lexander) *judge*
Hipschman, David *editor*
Kane, David Sheridan *insurance company executive*
†Klein, Karen K. *federal judge*
†Kloberdanz, Timothy J. *educator in social sciences, writer*
Li, Kam Wu *mechanical engineer, educator*
†Lipp, William Victor *secondary education educator*
Littlefield, Robert Stephen *communication educator, training consultant*
Magill, Frank John *federal judge*
Mathern, Tim *state senator, social worker*
†McCormick, Thomas Duncan *construction company executive*
Nelson, James Warren *architect, educator*
Ness, Gary Gene *accountant*
Nickel, Janet Marlene Milton *geriatrics nurse*
†O'Connor, Robert Harold *English educator*
Orr, Steven R. *health facility administrator*
Paulson, John Doran *newspaper editor, retired*
Peet, Howard David *English educator, writer*
Revell, Dorothy Evangeline Tompkins *dietitian*
Rice, Jon Richard *managed care administrator, physician*
Riley, Thomas Joseph *anthropologist, educational administrator*
Risher, Stephan Olaf *investment officer*
Rogers, David Anthony *electrical engineer, educator, researcher*
Schmidt, Claude Henri *retired research administrator*
Schneider, John Thomas *prosecutor*
Stone, Robert Rueben, Jr. *educational administrator*
Sullivan, James Stephen *bishop*
Tallman, Robert Hall *investment company executive*
Taylor, Doris Denice *physician, entrepreneur*
†Tharaldson, Gary *hotel executive*
Varma, Amiy *civil engineer, educator*
Wallwork, William Wilson, III *automobile executive*
Webb, Rodney Scott *judge*
Williams, Norman Dale *geneticist, researcher*

Fessenden
Streibel, Bryce *state senator*

Finley
Devlin, William Russell *newspaper owner*

Garrison
Gackle, Donald Christoph *publisher*

Gilby
McLean, Burton Neil *farmer, rancher*

Glenfield
Spickler, JoAnn Dorothy *secondary education educator*

Grand Forks
Anderson, Damon Ernest *lawyer*
Ashe, Kathy Rae *special education educator*
Baker, Kendall L. *academic administrator*
Berge, Scott Jerry *accountant*
Carlson, Edward C. *anatomy educator*
Clingan, Charles Edmund *historian*
Coleman, Joyce Kit *English literature educator, literary historian*
Davis, W. Jeremy *dean, law educator, lawyer*
DeMers, Judy Lee *state legislator, university dean*
Dixon, Kathleen Grace *English educator*
Ferraro, F. Richard *psychologist, educator*
Fox, Carl Alan *research executive*
Gjovig, Bruce Quentin *manufacturing consultant, entreprenuer*
Glassheim, Eliot Alan *program officer*
Jacobs, Christopher Paul *adult education educator, writer*
Jacobs, Francis Albin *biochemist, educator*
Lindseth, Paul Douglas *aerospace educator, flight instructor, farmer*
Long, William McMurray *physiology educator*
†Meek, Jay *educator, poet*
Nielsen, Forrest Harold *research nutritionist*
Nordlie, Robert Conrad *biochemistry educator*
Owens, Morgan Kasian *painter*
Page, Sally Jacquelyn *university official*
Penland, James Granville *psychologist*
Rolshoven, Ross William *legal investigator, art photographer*
Schmitz, Daniel Dean *mechanical engineer*
Senechal, Alice R. *judge, lawyer*
Skroch, Larry Eugene *railway conductor*
Sobus, Kerstin MaryLouise *physician, physical therapist*
Stenehjem, Wayne Kevin *state senator, lawyer*
Vogel, Robert *retired lawyer, educator*
Wambsganss, Jacob Roy *accounting educator, small business consultant*
Wilson, H. David *dean*
Wogaman, George Elsworth *insurance executive, financial consultant*

Jamestown
†Cox, Robert Ripley, Jr. *biology statistician*
†Cox, Sharon G. *art educator*
Kirby, Ronald Eugene *fish and wildlife research administrator*
†Lorenzo, David Joseph *history and political science educator*
Walker, James Silas *academic administrator*

Mandan
Bair, Bruce B. *lawyer*
Heick, Leon Joseph *data processing executive*
Hodge, Ann Linton *artist*
Novak, Laura J. *secondary school educator*
Paul, Jack Davis *retired state official, addictions consultant*

Mayville
Batesel, Billy Paul *English language educator*
Karaim, Betty June *librarian, retired*

Minot
Armstrong, Phillip Dale *lawyer*
Cederstrom, Gary Lynn *professional baseball umpire*
†Clark, Brandi M. *veterinary technician*
Iversen, David Stewart *librarian*
Jermiason, John Lynn *elementary school educator, farmer, rancher*
McQuarrie, Michelle Lee *accountant*
Mickelson, Stacey *state legislator*
Moe, Vida Delores *civic worker*
Mohler, Marie Elaine *nurse educator*
Morgan, Rose Marie *retired biology educator*
Rioux, Pierre August *psychiatrist*
Shaar, H. Erik *academic administrator*
Turner, Jane Ann *federal agent*

Minot AFB
Savage, Jeffrey Scott *military officer*

Northwood
Braaten, Linda Marie Skurdell *secondary education educator*

Regent
Krauter, Aaron Joseph *farmer, state senator*

Richardton
Miller, Jean Patricia Salmon *art educator*

Rolla
†Jacobsen-Theel, Hazel M. *historian*

Stanley
Patrick, Dennis M. *theology book dealer*

Turtle Lake
Lindteigen, Susanna *rancher, state official*

Valley City
Fischer, Mary Elizabeth *library director*

West Fargo
†Boutiette, Vickie Lynn *educator*
Cwikla, Rich I. *secondary education educator*
Parsley, Jamie Allen *writer*

Williston
Adducci, Joseph Edward *obstetrician, gynecologist*
Bekkedahl, Brad Douglas *dentist*
†Landes, Daniel Warren *English language educator*
Rennerfeldt, Earl Ronald *state legislator, farmer, rancher*
Yockim, James Craig *state senator*

Zeeland
Wolf, Trudy J. Fraase *music educator, librarian*

OHIO

Ada
Cooper, Ken Errol *management educator*
Elliott, Robert Betzel *retired physician*
Freed, DeBow *college president*
Herr, Sharon Marie *librarian*
†Keiser, Terry D. *biologist, educator*

Akron
Abraham, Tonson *chemist, researcher*
†Alexander, Anthony J. *electric power industry executive*
Auburn, Norman Paul *university president*
Barker, Harold Kenneth *former university dean*
Bartlo, Sam D. *lawyer*
Bell, Samuel H. *federal judge*
Blackstone, Patricia Clark *banker, psychotherapist*
Bohm, Georg G. A. *physicist*
Bonsky, Jack Alan *chemical company executive, lawyer*
†Borowiec, Andrew *art educator, photographer*
Bosley, Ronald Edmund *retired aircraft executive*
Brown, David Rupert *engineering executive*
Bryant, Keith Lynn, Jr. *history educator*
Cheng, Stephen Zheng Di *chemistry educator, polymeric material researcher*
Childs, James William *lawyer, legal educator*
Childs, Sally Johnston *elementary and secondary education administrator*
Chrisant, Rosemarie Kathryn *law library administrator*
Collier, Alice Elizabeth *retired community organization executive*
Contie, Leroy John, Jr. *federal judge*
Coyne, Thomas Joseph *economist, finance educator*
†Craig, Marci Lynne *insurance claims administrator*
Dotson, John Louis, Jr. *newspaper publisher*
Dowd, David D., Jr. *federal judge*
Evans, Douglas McCullough *surgeon, educator*
Fischer, Jennifer Welsh *English educator*
Fisher, James Lee *lawyer*
Fordyce, James Stuart *non-profit organization executive*
Frank, John V. *foundation executive*
Friedman, Richard Everett *librarian*
Fuentez, Tania Michele *copy editor, writer*
Gallagher, Mortimer Anthony *surgeon*
†Gallas, James S. *federal judge*
Gent, Alan Neville *physicist, educator*
Gibara, Samir S. G. *manufacturing executive*
Gippin, Robert Malcolm *lawyer*
Hackbirth, David William *aluminum company executive*
†Harvie, Crawford Thomas *lawyer*
Hochschwender, Herman Karl *international consultant*
Holland, Willard Raymond, Jr. *electric utility executive*
Hollis, William Frederick *information scientist*
Holloway, Donald Phillip *lawyer*
†Houston, Alma Faye *psychiatrist*
†Irvine, Edward D. *police chief*
Isayev, Avraam Isayevich *polymer engineer, educator*
Jasso, William Gattis *public relations executive*
Johnson, Joyce Marie *marketing and communications executive*
Kahan, Mitchell Douglas *art museum director*
Kaufman, Donald Leroy *building products executive*
Kazle, Elynmarie *producer, performing arts executive*
Keener, Polly Leonard *illustrator*
Kelley, Frank Nicholas *dean*
Kennedy, Joseph Paul *polymer scientist, researcher*
Kidder, Joseph P. *city service director*
Knepper, George W. *history educator*
Konkel, Mary Susan *library administrator*
Kraus, Henry *retired physician, educator*
Kreek, Louis Francis, Jr. *lawyer*
†Lalli, Anthony *insurance agent*
Lammert, Thomas Edward *lawyer*
Leach, Janet C. *publishing executive*
Lee, Brant Thomas *lawyer, federal official, educator*
Levy, Richard Philip *physician, educator*
Lombardi, Frederick McKean *lawyer*
Martino, Frank Dominic *union executive*
Maximovich, Michael Joseph *chemist, consultant*
Meeker, David Anthony *public relations executive*
Mettler, Gerald Phillip *reliability engineer*
Miller, Irving Franklin *chemical engineering educator, biomedical engineering educator, academic administrator*

Milsted, Amy *medical educator*
Molinari, Marco *marketing executive*
Moore, Walter Emil, Jr. *financial planner*
Moriarty, John Timothy *writer, transportation consultant*
Moss, Robert Drexler *lawyer*
Murphy, Bob *professional golfer*
Nolfi, Edward Anthony *lawyer*
Owens, Lee *coach*
Phillips, Dorothy Ormes *elementary education educator*
Piirma, Irja *chemist, educator*
†Plusquellic, Donald L. *mayor*
Powell, Robert Eugene *computer operator*
†Price, Susan Stem *primary education educator, antique dealer*
Quesada, Antonio Rettschlag *mathematics educator*
Rebenack, John Henry *retired librarian*
Richert, Paul *law educator*
Romanoski, George A. *municipal official*
Rooney, George Willard *lawyer*
Rothal, Max *director law department, lawyer*
Rothmann, Bruce Franklin *pediatric surgeon*
†Ruebel, Marion A. *university president*
Ruport, Scott Hendricks *lawyer*
†Sakezles, Priscilla Kathleen *philosophy educator*
Salkind, Michael Jay *technology administrator*
Sam, David Fiifi *political economist, educator*
Sancaktar, Erol *engineering educator*
Schrader, Alfred Eugene *lawyer*
Schubert, Barbara Schuele *performing company executive*
Seiberling, John Frederick *former congressman, law educator, lawyer*
Shaffer, Oren George *manufacturing company executive*
†Shea-Stonum, Marilyn *federal judge*
†Siebert, Loren J. *geography educator*
Sonnecken, Edwin Herbert *management consultant*
Spetrino, Russell John *retired utility company executive, lawyer*
†Su, Dongwei *economist, educator*
Symens, Ronald Edwin *electrical engineer, consultant*
Tan, James *physician*
Timmons, Gerald Dean *pediatric neurologist*
Tipping, Harry A. *lawyer*
Trotter, Thomas Robert *lawyer*
Walker, Debra May *marketing professional*
Weitendorf, Kurt Robert *lawyer*
West, Michael Alan *hospital administrator*
White, Harold F. *bankruptcy judge, retired federal judge*
Woolford, Warren L. *municipal official*
Zeno, Jo Ann *sales executive*
Zoeller, Fuzzy *professional golfer*

Alexandria
†Hannahs, Dorothy Gene *library director*

Alliance
Berthold, John William, III *physicist*
Brown, Elizabeth Anne *elementary educator*
Clem, Harriet Frances *library director*
Dunagan, Gwendolyn Ann *special education educator*
Fugelberg, Nancy Jean *elementary music specialist, educator*
†Henning, John Edward *secondary school educator in English, researcher*
Sheetz, Ernest Austin *academic administrator, educator*

Alpha
James, Francis Edward, Jr. *investment counselor*

Amelia
Hayden, Joseph Page, Jr. *company executive*
Thoman, Henry Nixon *lawyer*

Andover
Mole, Richard Jay *accounting company executive*

Archbold
Bergman, Jerry Rae *science educator*
McDougle, Larry George *academic administrator*

Ashland
Ford, Lucille Garber *economist, educator*
Kerr, Margaret Ann *elementary education educator*
Rogers, Robert P. *economist, educator*
Rueger, Daniel Scott *horticulture educator*
Waters, Ronald W. *educator, church executive, pastor*
Watson, JoAnn Ford *theology educator*

Ashley
Thomas, Annabel Crawford *writer*

Ashtabula
Hornbeck, Harold Douglas *psychotherapist*

Ashville
Brown, Edith Toliver *retired educator*

Athens
Ahrens, Kent *museum director, art historian*
†Baum, Edward *political science educator*
Booth, Alan Rundlett *history educator*
Boothe, Power *visual artist, filmmaker, set designer*
Borchert, Donald Marvin *philosopher, educator*
Brehm, Sharon Stephens *psychology educator, university administrator*
Bruning, James Leon *university official, educator*
Bugeja, Michael Joseph *educator, writer*
Chila, Anthony George *osteopathic educator*
Crowl, Samuel Renninger *former university dean, english language educator*
Dinos, Nicholas *engineering educator, administrator*
†Flaherty, Stephen Matthew *academic administrator*
Flannagan, Roy Catesby, Jr. *English literature educator, editor*
Glidden, Robert Burr *university president, musician, educator*
Hedges, Richard Houston *epidemiologist, lawyer*
Klare, George Roger *psychology educator*
Krendl, Kathy *dean*
Lee, Hwa-Wei *librarian, educator*
Matthews, Jack (John Harold Matthews) *English educator, writer*
Metters, Thomas Waddell *sports writer*
Moreno, Rosa-Maria *academic program coordinator*
†Parkinson, Sharran Fell *design educator*
Parmer, Jess Norman *university official, educator*
Perdreau, Cornelia Ruth Whitener (Connie Perdreau) *English as a second language educator, international exchange specialist*
Ping, Charles Jackson *philosophy educator, retired university president*
Rakes, Ganas Kaye *finance and banking educator*
Robe, Thurlow Richard *engineering educator, university dean*
Sanders, David *university press administrator*
Scott, Charles Lewis *photojournalist*
Stempel, Guido Hermann, III *journalism educator*
†Thorndike, John *writer*
Ungar, Irwin Allan *botany educator*
Wen, Shih-Liang *mathematics educator*
Werner, R(ichard) Budd *retired business executive*
Whealey, Robert Howard *historian*

Aurora
Braude, Edwin Simon *manufacturing company executive*
Hermann, Philip J. *lawyer*
Kirchner, James William *retired electrical engineer*
Lawton, Florian Kenneth *artist, educator*
Lefebvre, Gabriel Felicien *retired chemical company executive*
Nelson, Hedwig Potok *financial executive*
Rocco, James Robert *civil engineer*
Toomey, William Shenberger *retired wire manufacturing company executive*

Austintown
Gorcheff, Nick A. *controller*
Nithoo, Rovindranath *pharmacist*

Avon Lake
Gwiazda, Caroline Louise *school system administrator*
Kitchen, Charles William *lawyer*
†Zurcher, Vickie Lee *geneticist*

Bannock
Gentile, Anthony *coal company executive*

Barberton
Kitto, John Buck, Jr. *mechanical engineer*
Samples, Iris Lynette *elementary school educator*
Stevenson, Scot A. *lawyer, educator*
Zbacnik, Raymond Eric *process engineer*

Batavia
Bower, Kenneth Francis *electrical engineer*
†Dial, John Elbert *foreign language educator*
McDonough, James Francis *civil engineer, educator*
†Tissandier, Holly Jo *teacher of developmentally handicapped*

Bath
Bowman-Dalton, Burdene Kathryn *education testing coordinator, computer consultant*
Hoffer, Alma Jeanne *nursing educator*

Bay Village
Barney, Susan Leslie *academic administrator*
Berger, James (Hank) *business broker*
Stanbery, Robert Charles *veterinarian*

Beachwood
Boyle, Kammer *management psychologist*
Brandon, Edward Bermetz *retired banking executive*
Charnas, Michael (Mannie Charnas) *investment company executive*
Donnem, Roland William *board of directors, hotel owner, developer*
Sneiderman, Marilyn Singer *secondary and elementary school educator*
Van Aken, William J. *construction executive*
Weatherhead, Albert John, III *business executive*
Wilson, Sandra Lee *school nurse*
Wolf, Milton Albert *economist, former ambassador, investor*

Beavercreek
Bennett, Anna Dell *minister, religion educator, retired elementary school educator*
Busch, Sharon Lynne *elementary and secondary education educator*
Clarke, Cornelius Wilder *religious organization administrator, minister*
Gupta, Vijay Kumar *chemistry educator*
†McCullough, Margie Lu *artist*
Sivert, Sharon Lynn *critical care nurse*
Stadnicar, Joseph William *lawyer*

Bedford
Hodakievic, James Joseph *secondary education educator*

Bellbrook
McClelland, Herbert Lee *retired publisher, author*

Bellevue
Davenport, Thomas Herbert *small business owner*

Berea
Bersin, Susan Joyce-Heather (Reignbeaux Joyce-Heather Bersin) *critical care nurse, police officer*
Blumer, Frederick Elwin *philosophy educator*
Bonds, Georgia Anna *writer, lecturer*
Brannen, Daniel Jude *children's services administrator*
Brown, Lomas, Jr. *professional football player*
Harf, Patricia Jean Kole *syndicated columnist, educational consultant, lecturer, clinical psychologist, family therapist*
Jensen, Adolph Robert *former chemistry educator*
Jolles, Janet Kavanaugh Pilling *lawyer*
Lingswiler, Robert Dayton *philosophy educator*
Little, Richard Allen *mathematics and computer science educator*
Malicky, Neal *college president*
Martin, Terry Jon *English educator*
Matej, Elaine Diane *critical care nurse*
Miller, Dennis Dixon *economics educator*
Soppelsa, John Joseph *decal manufacturing company executive*

Bergholz
McElwain, Edwina Jay *elementary education educator*

Bexley
Maloney, Gerald P. *retired utility executive*

Blacklick
Doyle, Patrick Lee *retired insurance company executive*

Blue Creek
†Novakovich, Josip A. *writer, English educator*

Bluffton
Dudley, Durand Stowell *librarian*
Gundy, Jeffrey Gene *English educator*

Boardman
Donatelli, Daniel Dominic, Jr. *medical/surgical and oncological nurse*

Bowerston
McBride, Mildred Maylea *retired elementary school educator*
†Spencer, Dawn Joyce *librarian, educator*

Bowling Green
Anderson, Thomas Dale *retired geography educator, consultant, writer*
Blackney, Gary *university football coach*
†Blinn, John Robert *secondary school educator*
Brecher, Arthur Seymour *biochemistry educator*
Browne, Ray Broadus *popular culture educator*
Burnett, Frances *concert painist, teacher of piano*
Cadegan, Jaime B. *educational administrator*
†Cassara, Catherine *journalism educator*
Clark, Eloise Elizabeth *biologist, educator*
Clark, Jaci *women's collegiate basketball coach*
Clark, Robert King *communications educator emeritus, lecturer, consultant, actor, model*
Duling, Edward Burger *music education educator*
Fallon, L(ouis) Fleming, Jr. *public health consultant, researcher*
Foell, Kristie Ann *foreign language educator*
Gehring, Donald D. *education educator*
†Green, Cecilia Anne *humanities educator*
Guion, Robert Morgan *psychologist, educator*
Hakel, Milton Daniel, Jr. *psychology educator, consultant, publisher*
Hanna, Martin Shad *lawyer*
Heckman, Carol A. *biology educator*
Hernandez, Mark Alan *educator in Spanish*
†Hess, Gary Ray *historian*
Knight, William Edward *university administrator, educator*
Lavezzi, John Charles *art history educator, archaeologist*
Lunde, Harold Irving *management educator*
Marston-Scott, Mary Vesta *nurse, educator*
McCaghy, Charles Henry *sociology educator*
Newman, Elsie Louise *mathematics educator*
†Norton, Wayne Anderson *journalism educator, public relations specialist*
Ocvirk, Otto George *artist*
†Ribeau, Sidney A. *academic administrator*
Shehata, Said Ahmed *surgeon, researcher*
Steel, Steven Chesney *environmental scientist, educator*
Thomas, Marie Elena *newspaper editor*
Varney, Glenn Herbert *management educator*
Versteeg, Robert John *clergyman, dramatic artist, author*
Zwierlein, Ronald Edward *athletics director*

Bratenahl
Dunn, Horton, Jr. *organic chemist*
Jones, Trevor Owen *biomedical products and automobile supply company executive, management consultant*

Brecksville
Farkas, Julius *chemist*
Meyer, Karin Zumwalt *pharmacist*
Pappas, Effie Vamis *English and business educator, writer*
Usalis, George Jerome *metal processing executive*

Broadview Heights
Sternlieb, Lawrence Jay *marketing professional*

Brooklyn
Burns, Brenda Carolyn *retired special education administrator*

Brookpark
Wilson, Jack *aeronautical engineer*

Brookville
Howett, Mark William *kinesiotherapy*

Brunswick
Kuchynski, Marie *physician*
Reed, Jane Garson *accounting educator, consultant*
Rohlik, Harold Edward *engineer*

Bryan
Benedict, Gregory Bruce *business administration/finance professional, legal consultant*
Carrico, Virgil Norman *physician*
Mabus, Barbara Jean *secondary science educator*
Oberlin, Earl Clifford, III *securities brokerage company executive*
Stevens, Muriel Kay *elementary educator*

Bucyrus
Frey, Judith Lynn *elementary education educator*
Herold, Jeffrey Roy Martin *library director*
Neff, Robert Clark, Sr. *lawyer*
Solt, Robert Lee, Jr. *surgeon*

Burbank
Koucky, Frank Louis *geology educator, archeogeology researcher*

Burton
Snyder, Timothy H. *police officer, lawyer*

Cadiz
Hoffman, Barbara Jo *health and physical education educator, athletic director*
†Thompson, Sandra Lee *library administrator*

Cambridge
Dray, Dwight Leroy *retired school system administrator*
Tostenson, Beverly Ann *book store owner*

Canal Winchester
Bacus, Terrence Lee *labor relations consultant*
Burrier, Gail Warren *physician*

Canfield
Goldberg, Martin Stanford *lawyer*
Itts, Elizabeth Ann Dunham *psychotherapist, consultant, designer*
Mumaw, James Webster *lawyer*

Canton
†Ahmad, Mirza Nasir *plastic and reconstructive surgeon*
Barr, Dixie Lou *geriatrics nurse*
Bennington, Ronald Kent *lawyer*
Birkholz, Raymond James *metal products manufacturing company executive*
Brannen, John Howard *lawyer*
Brown, Larry R. *lawyer*
†Carp, Steven Scott *plastic surgery*
Carpenter, Noble Olds *banker*
Caswell, Linda Kay *insurance agency executive*
Ceroke, Clarence John *engineer, consultant*
Cummings, Carole Edwards *special education educator*
†Davis, Henry Arnold *healthcare company executive*
Dickens, Sheila Jeanne *family preservation educator*
Di Simone, Robert Nicholas *radiologist, educator*
Doriani, Beth Maclay *English language educator*
Elliott, Peter R. *athletic organization executive, retired*
Elsaesser, Robert James *retired manufacturing executive*
Goldwater, Leslie Rachel *business communications consultant*
Grant, Bud (Harry Peter Grant) *retired professional football coach*
Greene, Joe (Charles Edward Greene) *former professional football player, professional football coach*
Hoecker, David *engineering executive*
Howland, Willard J. *radiologist, educator*
Karabasz, Felix Francois "Sam" *engineering and manufacturing company executive*
Kellermeyer, Robert William *physician, educator*
Lindamood, John Beyer *lawyer*
†Mack, Tom *retired professional football player*
Maioriello, Richard Patrick *otolaryngologist*
Mason, Judith Snyder *fund development consultant*
Maxwell, John Alexander, Jr. *retired newspaper editor, consultant*
†McLaughlin, Joseph David *English educator, poet, writer*
Mokodean, Michael John *lawyer, accountant*
†Moorhouse, Linda Virginia *symphony orchestra administrator*
Nadas, John Adalbert *psychiatrist*
†Pahlau, Randi Christine *English language educator*
Pedoto, Gerald Joseph *supplier quality analyst*
Rodriques, Pamela S. *orthopedics nurse*
Rubin, Patricia *internist*
Schauer, Thomas Alfred *insurance company executive*
Selmon, Lee Roy *retired football player*
†Shaw, Billy *retired professional football player*
Sicard, Guillermo Rafael *dermatologist*
Smith, Jackie *former professional football player*
Stage, Richard Lee *consultant, retired utilities executive*
Strauss, John Leonard *artist*
Suarez, Benjamin *consumer products company executive*
Thomas, Suzanne Ward *public relations director, communications educator*
Traveria, Beth M. *mental health counselor*
Watson, Duane Frederick *religious studies educator*
†Williams, James H. *federal judge*

Cardington
Hart, Elizabeth Ann *surgical nurse supervisor*

Carrollton
Childers, John Charles *lawyer, engineer*

Cedarville
Firmin, Michael Wayne *counselor educator*
Gordin, Dean Lackey *retired agricultural products executive*

Celina
Fanning, Ronald Heath *architect, engineer*
Giesige, Mark Richard *county official, auditor*
Grapner-Mitchell, Pamela Kay *primary education educator*
Heinrichs, Timothy Arnold *family practice physician*
Wolfe, John Raymond *education educator*

Centerville
Baver, Roy Lane *retired protection services official, consultant*
Fulk, Paul Frederick *chiropractor*
Kelso, Harold Glen *family practice physician*
Shaffer, Jill *clinical psychologist*

Chagrin Falls
Brophy, Jere Hall *manufacturing company executive*
Brown, Jeanette Grasselli *university official*
Callahan, Francis Joseph *manufacturing company executive*
Church, Irene Zaboly *personnel services company executive*
Cordes, Loverne Christian *interior designer*
Cusumano, Philip Anthony *physician*
Downing, Cynthia Hurst *therapist, addiction and abuse specialist*
Eastburn, Richard A. *consulting firm executive*
Fisher, Will Stratton *illumination consultant*
Heckman, Henry Trevennen Shick *steel company executive*
Lange, David Charles *journalist*
Lingl, Friedrich Albert *psychiatrist*
Miller, Kimberly Clarke *human services manager*
Obert, Charles Frank *banker*
Ostendorf, Joan Donahue *fund raiser, volunteer*
Poza, Ernesto Juan *business consultant, educator*
Rawski, Conrad H(enry) *humanities educator, medievalist*
Sivak, Madeline Ann *nonprofit organization executive, nurse*
Streicher, James Franklin *lawyer*
Vail, Iris Jennings *civic worker*

Chandlersville
Herron, Janet Irene *industrial manufacturing engineer*

Chardon
Dietrich, Joseph Jacob retired chemist, research executive
Dobyns, Brown McIlvaine surgeon, educator
Jones, Sandra electronics executive
Karch, George Frederick, Jr. lawyer
Kellis, Michael John osteopathic physician
Langer, Edward L. trade association administrator
†O'Connor, Deborah Frances library director
Reinhard, Sister Mary Marthe educational organization administrator
Seidemann, Robert Simon manufacturing company executive
†Takacs, Cris Clair bookbinder
Uscheek, David Petrovich chemist

Chesapeake
Harris, Bob L(ee) retired educational administrator

Chesterland
Durn, Raymond Joseph lawyer
Kancelbaum, Joshua Jacob lawyer
Ruble, Bernard Roy educator, minister, labor relations consultant
Spitz, Arnoldt John international trade professional, consultant
Ullery, Richard Frank sales executive
†Wood, Kenneth Anderson artist, designer, consultant

Chillicothe
Basil, Brad L. technology education educator
Copley, Cynthia Sue Love insurance adjuster
Dickey, Phillip Nelson Theophilus (Philo Dickey) poet, playwright
†Jayne, Cristina Marsh retired elementary education educator
Leedy, Emily L. Foster (Mrs. William N. Leedy) retired education educator, consultant

Cincinnati
Ackermann, Russell Albert manufacturing company executive
Adams, Donald Scott engineer, pharmacist
Adams, Edmund John lawyer
Adams, Mendle Eugene minister
Adlard, Carole Rechtsteiner adoption educational agency executive
Adolph, Robert J. physician, medical educator
Agrawal, Dharma Prakash engineering educator
Alamin, Khosrow pathologist
Alexander, James Wesley surgeon, educator
Alexander, John J. chemistry educator
Anderson, James Milton lawyer
Anderson, Jerry William, Jr. technical and business consulting executive, educator
Anderson, Joan Balyeat religion educator, minister
Anderson, William Hopple lawyer
Aniskovich, Paul Peter, Jr. insurance company executive
Anthony, Thomas Dale lawyer
†Apanites, Jennifer Moore elementary educator
Arnett, Louise Eva information records management executive
Artzt, Edwin Lewis consumer products company executive
Ashdown, Charles Coster lawyer
†Aug, Jonathan Vincent federal bankruptcy judge
Avery, Steven Thomas professional baseball player
Azizkhan, Richard George pediatric surgeon, educator
Backherms, Kathryn Anne parochial school educator
Bahlman, William Thorne, Jr. retired lawyer
Bahr, Donald Walter chemical engineer
Bahrani, Al Sattar mechanical engineer
Baracskay, Daniel John political scientist, educator
Barr, Kevin Curtis poet
Baughman, Robert Phillip physician
Beamon, Mary Ann retired nursing administrator
Beary, John Francis, III physician, pharmaceutical executive
Beckwith, Barbara Jean journalist
Beckwith, Sandra Shank judge
Beggs, Patricia K. performing company executive
Belew, Adrian guitarist, singer, songwriter, producer
Benjamin, Lawrence retired research chemist
Benner, Charles Henry retired music educator
Bernish, Paul public relations executive, consultant
Berwanger, Kathleen A. secondary school educator
Bestehorn, Ute Wiltrud retired librarian
Bieliauskas, Vytautas Joseph clinical psychologist, educator
Biery, Charles John, Sr. accountant
Birmingham, Stephen writer
Bishop, George Franklin political scientist, educator
Bissinger, Mark Christian lawyer
Black, Robert L., Jr. retired judge
Black, Stephen L. lawyer
Blake, Jeff professional football player
Bleznick, Donald William Romance languages educator
Bluestein, Barbara Ann librarian
Bluestein, Venus Weller retired psychologist, educator
Boat, Thomas Frederick physician, educator, researcher
Bokenkotter, Thomas Stephen clergyman
Borgman, James Mark editorial cartoonist
Bostian, Harry Edward chemical engineer
Bowden, Jim professional sports team executive
Braman, Heather Ruth technical writer, editor, consultant, antiques dealer
Brestel, Mary Beth librarian
Bridenbaugh, Phillip Owen anesthesiologist, physician
Bridgeland, James Ralph, Jr. lawyer
Briggs, Henry Payson, Jr. headmaster
Brod, Evelyn Fay foreign language educator
Brod, Stanford graphic designer, educator
Broderick, Dennis John lawyer, retail company executive
Bromberg, Robert Sheldon lawyer
Brown, Dale Patrick retired advertising executive
Brown, Daniel independent art consultant, critic, writer
Brown, Mike professional sports team executive
Brumm, Paul Michael banker
Buchman, Elwood internist, pharmaceutical company medical director
†Buckley, Donald Charles cardiac thoracic surgeon
Buechner, Robert William lawyer, educator
Bull, Louis Antal (Tony) sales executive
Buncher, Charles Ralph epidemiologist, educator
Burleigh, William Robert newspaper executive
Byers, Kenneth Vernon insurance company executive
Carney, Robert Alfred health care administrator
Carothers, Charles Omsted retired orthopedic surgeon
Carr, George Francis, Jr. lawyer
Case, Douglas Manning lawyer
Chatterjee, Jayanta educator, urban designer
Chesley, Stanley Morris lawyer
Chin, Nee Oo Wong reproductive endocrinologist
Christensen, Paul Walter, Jr. gear manufacturing company executive
Christenson, Gordon A. law educator
Ciani, Alfred Joseph language professional, associate dean
Cioffi, Michael Lawrence lawyer
Cissell, James Charles lawyer
Clark, James Norman insurance executive
Cobey, John Geoffrey lawyer
Cody, Thomas Gerald lawyer
Coffey, Thomas William lawyer
Colwell, Christopher Scott telecommunications industry executive
Conaton, Michael Joseph financial service executive
Conley, Robert T. educational administrator
Constant, Anita Aurelia publisher
Coombe, V. Anderson valve manufacturing company executive
Coslet, Bruce N. professional football coach
Cowan, Jerry Louis lawyer
Crable, John V. chemist
Craig, L. Clifford lawyer
Cudkowicz, Leon medical educator
Curtin, Leah Louise publisher, editor, author, nurse
Dahmann, Rosemary Gaiser librarian
Daniels, Astar artist
Dehner, Joseph Julnes lawyer
DeLong, Deborah lawyer
Dember, William Norton psychologist, educator
Derstadt, Ronald Theodore health care administrator
Desmarais, Charles Joseph museum director, writer, editor
Desmond, William J. lawyer
Dickman, Gloria Joyce geriatrics nurse
Diller, Edward Dietrich lawyer
Dillon, David Brian retail grocery executive
Dooley, Jo Ann Catherine retired publishing company executive
Dornette, W(illiam) Stuart lawyer, educator
Dougherty, Charlotte Anne financial planner, insurance and securities representative
Draper, Sharon M. educator, author
Dunigan, Dennis Wayne real estate executive
Eager, William Earl information systems corporation executive
Ehrnschwender, Arthur Robert former utility company executive
Elleman, Lawrence Robert lawyer
Emmich, Linda L. secondary education educator, guidance counselor
Engel, Albert Joseph federal judge
Etges, Frank Joseph parasitology educator
Evans, Barry Craig financial services company exexutive
Evans, James E. lawyer
Everett, Karen Joan retired librarian, genealogy educator
Faller, Susan Grogan lawyer
Farmer, Richard T. uniform rental and sales executive
Fenoglio-Preiser, Cecilia Mettler pathologist, educator
Fink, Jerold Albert lawyer
Fischer, Carl G. anesthesiologist
Fischer, Patricia Ann middle school educator
Fitzgerald, James T. architect
Flanagan, John Anthony lawyer, educator
Fleming, Lisa L. lawyer
Flick, Thomas Michael mathematics educator, educational administrator
Foley, Cheryl M. company executive
Fontana, Michael educational foundation administrator, writer, poet
Ford, Emory A. chemist, researcher
Fowler, Noble Owen physician, university administrator
Francis, Marion David consulting chemist
Frantz, Robert Wesley lawyer
Frazier, Todd Mearl retired health science administrator, epidemiologist
Freedman, William Mark lawyer
Freshwater, Paul Ross consumer goods company executive
Fryxell, David Allen publishing executive
Galloway, Lillian Carroll modeling agency executive, consultant
Gardner, Leonard Burton, II retired industrial automation engineer
Garfinkel, Jane E. lawyer
†Garg, Prem K. civil engineer
Gelfand, Janelle Ann music critic
George, Allen Van manufacturing company executive
Gettler, Benjamin lawyer, manufacturing company executive
Gillespie, Anita Wright nursing administrator
Glendening, Everett Austin architect
Goetzman, Bruce Edgar architecture educator
Goin, Robert G. athletic director
Goldstein, Sidney pharmaceutical scientist
Goodman, Bernard physics educator
Goodman, Stanley lawyer
Gottschalk, Alfred college chancellor
Greenberg, David Bernard chemical engineering educator
Greenberg, Gerald Stephen lawyer
Greengus, Samuel academic administrator, religion educator
Greenwald, Theresa McGowan medical administrator, nurse
Greenwalt, Tibor Jack physician, educator
Groth, Jon Quentin management consultant
Halpert, Douglas Joshua immigration lawyer
Hardrick, Maria Darshell government official, tax examiner
Hardy, William Robinson lawyer
Harjo, Jeanne pediatrics nurse
Harmon, Patrick newspaperman
Harrell, Samuel Macy agribusiness executive
Harrington, Jeremy Thomas clergyman, publisher
Harris, Irving lawyer
Harrison, Donald Carey university official, cardiology educator
Harshman, Morton Leonard physician, business executive
Hawkins, Lawrence Charles management consultant, educator
Heaton, Charles Lloyd dermatologist, educator
Heekin, Mary Ann oncology social worker
Heimlich, Henry Jay physician, surgeon
Heinlen, Ronald Eugene lawyer
Heldman, James Gardner lawyer
Heldman, Paul W. lawyer, grocery store company executive
Henderson, Stephen Paul lawyer
Henry, Brian C. telephone company executive
Henry, J(ohn) Porter, Jr. sales consultant
†Henry, Laurie Jayne writer, educator
Hensgen, Herbert Thomas medical technologist
Herman, Donald Aloys radio station personality and official
Hermanies, John Hans lawyer, retired
Hess, Evelyn Victorine (Mrs. Michael Howett) medical educator
Hess, Marcia Wanda retired educator
Hessler, Gene Joseph retired musician, retired museum curator
Hiatt, Marjorie McCullough service organization executive
Hicks, Irle Raymond retail food chain executive
Hill, Thomas Clark lawyer
Hodge, Bobby Lynn mechanical engineer, manufacturing executive
Hodge, Robert Joseph retail executive
Hoff, James Edwin university president
Hoffheimer, Daniel Joseph lawyer
Hoffman, Donna Coy learning disabilities educator
Hoffman, Joel Harvey composer
Hogg, Stephen P. otolaryngologist
Hoke, Eugena Louise special education educator
Hollerman, Charles Edward pediatrician
†Holscher, Robert F. county official
Holschuh, John David, Jr. lawyer
†Hopkins, Jeffrey P. federal judge
Hornbaker, Alice Joy author
Horrell, Karen Holley insurance company executive, lawyer
Howe, John Kingman manufacturing, sales and marketing executive
Huenefeld, Thomas Ernst financial consultant, retired banker
†Huether, Carl A. biology educator
Huggins, Bob college basketball coach
Hust, Bruce Kevin lawyer
Hutton, Edward Luke diversified public corporation executive
Iachetti, Rose Maria Anne retired elementary education educator
†Ireland, Gene E. surgeon
Irwin, Miriam Dianne Owen book publisher, writer
Jackobs, Miriam Ann dietitian
†Jager, Durk I. marketing agency executive
Jennings, James Norbert, Jr. marketing executive, entrepreneur
Johnson, Betty Lou secondary education educator
Johnson, James J. lawyer
Johnson, K(enneth) O(dell) aerospace engineer
Johnson, Norma Louise accountant
Jones, Nathaniel Raphael federal judge
Kamp, Cynthia Lea elementary education educator
Katz, Robert Langdon human relations educator, rabbi
Kawahara, Fred Katsumi research chemist
Kelley, John Joseph, Jr. lawyer
Kenrich, John Lewis lawyer
Kiel, Frederick Orin lawyer
King, Margaret Ann communications educator
Kite, William McDougall lawyer
Klaserner, James publishing executive
Klein, Jerry Emanuel insurance and financial planning executive
Klinedinst, Thomas John, Jr. insurance agency executive
Knipschild, Robert artist, educator
Knowlton, Austin E. (Dutch Knowlton) professional football team executive
Knue, Paul Frederick newspaper editor
Koebel, Sister Celestia health care system executive
Kohl, David dean, librarian
Kollstedt, Paula Lubke communications executive, writer
†Kothari, Ravi science educator
Kowel, Stephen Thomas electrical engineer, educator
Krohn, Claus Dankertsen insurance company executive
Kunzel, Erich, Jr. conductor, arranger, educator
Lambert, Rebecca Jean secondary educator
Lang, Jackie Ann nursing consultant
Lange, Scott Leslie communications company executive, voice professional
Larkin, Barry Louis professional baseball player
Lawrence, James Kaufman Lebensburger lawyer
Lawson, Randall Clayton, II financial executive
Lemke, Judith A. lawyer
Levin, Debbe Ann lawyer
Levine, Aaron executive
Levinson, Charles Bernard architect
Levy, Sam Malcolm advertising executive
Lewis, Gene Dale historian, educator
Leyda, James Perkins retired pharmaceutical company executive
Lichtin, (Judah) Leon pharmacist
Lindner, Robert David finance company executive
†Lindquist, H.D. Alan parasitologist, restaurateur
Linsey, Nathaniel L. bishop
Lintz, Robert Carroll financial holding company executive
Lippincott, Jonathan Ramsay healthcare executive
Liss, Herbert Myron communications executive, educator, journalist
†Livingston, Mitchel Dean academic administrator, education educator
Lockhart, John Mallery management consultant
Loggie, Jennifer Mary Hildreth medical educator, physician
Long, Phillip Clifford museum director
Longenecker, Mark Hershey, Jr. lawyer
Lopez-Cobos, Jesus conductor
Lucas, Stanley Jerome radiologist, physician
Lucke, Robert Vito merger and acquisition executive
Luckner, Herman Richard, III interior designer
Lucky, Anne Weissman dermatologist
MacKnight, David Laurence dentist
Macpherson, Colin R(obertson) pathologist, educator
Maher, Terry Marina religious organization administrator
Maier, Craig Frisch restaurant executive
Maltz, Robert surgeon
Manley, Robert Edward lawyer, economist
Mann, David Scott lawyer
Mantel, Samuel Joseph, Jr. management educator, consultant
Margello, Frank Michael vocational educator
Marks, Jeffrey Alan writer
Martin, Daniel William acoustical physicist
Martin, John Bruce chemical engineer
Maruska, Edward Joseph zoo administrator
Mates, Lawrence A., II medical company executive, consultant
Maxfield, Anne M. sales executive
Maxwell, Robert Wallace, II lawyer
McClain, William Andrew lawyer
McDowell, John Eugene lawyer
McGavran, Frederick Jaeger lawyer
Mc Henry, Powell lawyer
†McInerney, Timothy P. city manager
McMullin, Ruth Roney publishing executive, trustee, management fellow
McNulty, John William retired public relations executive, automobile company executive
Meal, Larie chemistry educator, researcher, consultant
Mechem, Charles Stanley, Jr. former broadcasting executive, former golf association executive
Meese, Ernest Harold thoracic and cardiovascular surgeon
Meisner, Gary Wayne landscape architect
Meixner, Helmut consumer products company executive
Menyhert, Stephan retired chemist
Meranus, Leonard Stanley lawyer
Merchant, Mylon Eugene physicist, engineer
Meyer, Daniel Joseph machinery company executive
Meyer, Walter H. retired food safety executive, consultant
Michelini, Ann Norris classics educator
Million, Kenneth Rhea management consultant
Minter, Richard (Rick) football coach
Mital, Anil engineering educator
†Moeddel, Carl K. bishop
Molitor, Sister Margaret Anne nun, former college president, archivist
†Monder, Steven I. orchestra executive
Monroe, William Frederick marketing professional
Moore, John Edward marketing professional, freelance writer
Morgan, John Bruce hospital care consultant
†Morgan, Victoria artistic director
Morris, Margaret E. marketing professional
Mulholland-Spaulding, Catherine A. writer
Muntz, Ernest Gordon historian, educator
Neagle, Dennis Edward (Denny Neagle) professional baseball player
Neale, Henry Whitehead plastic surgery educator
Nebert, Daniel Walter molecular geneticist, research administrator
Nechemias, Stephen Murray lawyer
Nelson, David Aldrich federal judge
Nelson, Frederick Dickson lawyer
Nelson, Mary Ellen Dickson actuary
Nester, William Raymond, Jr. retired academic administrator and educator
Neumark, Michael Harry lawyer
Nielsen, George Lee architect
Norman, Eric Jesse laboratory director, medical researcher
Novak, Robert G. architect
†Oclander, Mónica Silvia women's health nurse practitioner
O'Connor, John Paul judge
O'Connor, Patricia Walker education educator
Oden, Fay Giles author, educator
Olson, Robert Wyrick lawyer
O'Reilly, Rosann Tagliaferro computer educator
Painter, Mark Philip judge
Pancheri, Eugene Joseph chemical engineer
Parker, R. Joseph lawyer
Patterson, Claire Ann vocational educator
Pedrick, Dwayne Ellis, Sr. information systems specialist
†Pendle, Karin music educator
Pepper, John Ennis, Jr. consumer products company executive
Perlman, Burton judge
Perry, Norman Robert priest, magazine editor
Petrie, Bruce Inglis lawyer
Petty, Priscilla Hayes writer, columnist, producer
Phillips, T. Stephen lawyer
Pichler, Joseph Anton food products executive
Pilarczyk, Daniel Edward archbishop
Pirtle, Laurie Lee women's basketball coach, university level
Porter, Robert Carl, Jr. lawyer
Powley, Elizabeth Ann health facility administrator
Preiser, Wolfgang Friedrich Ernst architect, educator, consultant, researcher
Price, Jay E. consumer products company executive
Price, Thomas Emile investment company executive
Proffitt, Kevin archivist
Puthoff, Francis Urban insurance salesman
Qualls, Roxanne mayor
Rand, Carolyn financial executive
Randman, Barry I. real estate developer
Randolph, Jackson Harold utility company executive
Rapoport, Robert Morton medical educator
Rashkin, Mitchell Carl internist, pulmonary medicine specialist
Ratliff, Thomas Asbury, Jr. retired engineer
Rebel, Jerome Ivo financial planner
Reeb, Patricia A. nursing educator, administrator
Reichert, David lawyer
Relyea, Carl Miller hydrologist
Rexroth, Nancy Louise photographer
Rice, Maurice Ainsworth management consultant
Rich, Robert Edward lawyer
Roche, Kevin R. architect, retail design, retail strategist
Rockwell, R(onald) James, Jr. laser and electro-optics consultant
Rogers, James Eugene electric and gas utility executive
Rogers, Millard Foster, Jr. retired art museum director
Roomann, Hugo architect
Rose, Donald McGregor retired lawyer
Rosenthal, Susan Leslie psychologist
Rubin, Stanley Gerald aerospace engineering educator
Ruthman, Thomas Robert manufacturing executive
Ryan, James Joseph lawyer
Saal, Howard Max clinical geneticist, pediatrician, educator
Safferman, Robert Samuel microbiologist
St. John, Maria Ann nurse anesthetist
Sanford, Wilbur Lee retired elementary education educator
Sawyer, John professional football team executive
Schaefer, Frank William, III microbiologist, researcher
Schaefer, George A., Jr. bank executive
Scheineson, Irwin Bruce insurance and investment company executive
Schmidt, Thomas Joseph, Jr. lawyer
Schmit, David E. lawyer
Schott, Marge professional baseball team executive
Schrantz, Donald Lee mechanical engineer
Schreiner, Albert William physician, educator

Schrier, Arnold historian, educator
Schuck, Thomas Robert lawyer, farmer
Schuler, Robert Leo appraiser, consultant
Schulman, Melvin Louis food processing company executive
Schutzius, Lucy Jean librarian
Scripps, Robert P. publishing executive
Semon, Warren Lloyd retired computer sciences educator
Senhauser, John Crater architect
†Shani, Hezekiah Gyunda Pyuza surgeon
Shea, Joseph William, III lawyer
Shenk, Richard Lawrence real estate developer, photographer, artist
Shepherd, Elsbeth Weichsel supply chain consultant
†Sherman, Jack, Jr. federal judge
Shoemaker, Hal Alan accountant
Shore, Thomas Spencer, Jr. lawyer
Siekmann, Donald Charles accountant
Silbersack, Mark Louis lawyer
Silvers, Gerald Thomas publishing executive
Simitses, George John engineering educator, consultant
Sims, Victor Dwayne lawyer
Skilbeck, Carol Lynn Marie elementary educator and small business owner
Smale, John Gray diversified industry executive
Smith, Beverly Ann community health nurse
Smith, C. LeMoyne publishing company executive
Smith, Gregory Allgire college administrator
Smith, Leroy Harrington, Jr. mechanical engineer, aerodynamics consultant
Smith, Roger Dean pathologist
Smittle, Nelson Dean artist
Sowder, Fred Allen foundation administrator, alphabet specialist
Sperelakis, Nicholas, Sr. physiology and biophysics educator, researcher
Sperzel, George E., Jr. personal care industry executive
Spiegel, S. Arthur federal judge
Stanberry, Lawrence Raymond virologist, vaccinologist, pediatrician, educator
Steger, Joseph A. university president
Steinberg, Janet Eckstein journalist
Steinbrunner, Sally Oyler dental consultant, hygienist
Stern, Joseph Smith, Jr. former footwear manufacturing company executive
Strauss, William Victor lawyer
Sullivan, Connie Castleberry artist, photographer
Sullivan, Dennis James, Jr. public relations executive
Sullivan, James F. physicist, educator
Suskind, Raymond Robert physician, educator
Swigert, James Mack lawyer
Terp, Thomas Thomsen lawyer
Thiemann, Charles Lee banker
Thompson, Herbert, Jr. bishop
Thompson, Morley Punshon textile company executive
Timpano, Anne museum director, art historian
Tobias, Charles Harrison, Jr. lawyer
Tobias, Paul Henry lawyer
†Tobler, William D. neurosurgeon
Tocco, James pianist
Toftner, Richard Orville engineering executive
Tolzmann, Don Heinrich curator, educator
Tomain, Joseph Patrick law educator, dean
Torbush, Robert Daniel transportation executive
Townsend, Robert J. lawyer
Vander Laan, Mark Alan lawyer
†van Lovern, Harry R. neurosurgeon
Victor, William Weir retired telephone company executive, consultant
Vilter, Richard William physician, educator
Vogel, Cedric Wakelee lawyer
Wagner, Thomas Edward academic administrator, educator
Wales, Ross Elliot lawyer
Wallace, Betty Louise Dollar retired religious educator
Walter, Gerry Henry rabbi
Wang, Charleston Cheng-Kung lawyer, engineer
Ward, Sherman Carl, III (Buzz Ward) theater manager
Watts, Barbara Gayle law academic administrator
Weber, Fredrick Louis, Jr. hepatologist, medical researcher
Weber, Herman Jacob federal judge
Weeks, Steven Wiley lawyer
Wehling, Robert Louis household products company executive
Weinrich, Alan Jeffrey occupational hygienist
Weiskittel, Ralph Joseph real estate executive
Weisman, Joel nuclear engineering educator, engineering consultant
Wellington, Jean Susorney librarian
Werner, Robert Joseph college dean, music educator
Weseli, Roger William lawyer
West, Clark Darwin pediatric nephrologist, educator
Weston, Phyllis Jean art gallery director
Whipple, Harry M. newspaper publishing executive
Whitaker, Glenn Virgil lawyer
White, Alfred Kenneth, Jr. lawyer
White, Joy Mieko communications executive
Williams, James Case metallurgist
Williams, Roy A. municipal official
Williamson, Vikki Lyn financial executive
Wilsey, Philip Arthur computer science educator
Wilson, Arthur Henry charitable institution executive
Wilson, Frederick Robert counselor educator
Wilson, James Miller, IV cardiovascular surgeon, educator
Winkler, Henry Ralph retired academic administrator, historian
Winternitz, Felix Thomas editor, educator, writer
Wiot, Jerome Francis radiologist
Witten, Louis physics educator
Wolford, Ronald Eugene computer operations professional
Wood, Robert Emerson pediatrics educator
Woodside, Frank C., III lawyer, educator, physician
Woodward, James Kenneth pharmacologist
Wright, Creighton Bolter cardiovascular surgeon, educator
Wulker, Laurence Joseph portfolio manager, educator, financial planner
Wygant, Foster Laurance art educator
†Yee, Leslie Mitchell physician executive, educator
Yurchuck, Roger Alexander lawyer
†Zabel, Rick writer
Zafren, Herbert Cecil librarian, educator
Zavatsky, Michael Joseph lawyer
Zealey, Sharon Janine lawyer
†Zimmerman, James M. retail company executive
Zimmerman, Sheldon college president, rabbi
Zola, Gary Phillip religious educational administrator, rabbi
†Zucker, David I. psychologist

Circleville

Ammer, William retired judge
Carpenter, Amy Lynn elementary education educator
Norman, Jack Lee church administrator, consultant
Strous, Allen poet
Tipton, Daniel L. religious organization executive

Clayton

Stutzman, L. Lee pastor

Cleveland

Abid, Ann B. art librarian
Abrams, Sylvia Fleck religious studies educator
Adamo, Kenneth R. lawyer
Adams, Leslie composer
Adler, Thomas William real estate executive
Agassi, Andre Kirk tennis player
Ainsworth, Joan Horsburgh university development director
Akers-Parry, Deborah lawyer
Aldrich, Ann federal judge
Alfidi, Ralph Joseph radiologist, educator
Alomar, Roberto Velazquez professional baseball player
Alomar, Sandy, Jr. (Santos Velazquez Alomar) professional baseball player
Altose, Murray David physician
Anders, Claudia Dee occupational therapist
Anderson, David Gaskill, Jr. Spanish language educator
Anderson, Harold Albert engineering and building executive
Anderson, Warren distribution company executive
Andorka, Frank Henry lawyer
Andrews, Oakley V. lawyer
Angus, John Cotton chemical engineering educator
Ashmus, Keith Allen lawyer
Asman, Robert Joseph
Austin, Arthur Donald, II lawyer, educator
†Auston, David Henry university administrator, educator
Awais, George Musa obstetrician, gynecologist
Ayers, Richard Wayne electrical company official
Bacon, Brett Kermit lawyer
Badal, Daniel Walter psychiatrist, educator
Baer, Eric engineering and science educator
Bahniuk, Eugene mechanical engineering educator
Bailey, Darlyne social worker, educator
Baker, Saul Phillip geriatrician, cardiologist, internist
Bambakidis, Peter neurologist, educator
Bamberger, David opera company executive
Bamberger, Richard H. lawyer
Barnett, Gene Henry neurosurgeon
Barrat-Gordon, Rene social worker
Bass, Jonathan dermatologist
Bassett, John E. dean, English educator
Bates, Walter Alan former lawyer
Baughman, R(obert) Patrick lawyer
Bause, George Stephen anesthesiologist
Baxter, Randolph judge
Beall, Cynthia anthropologist, educator
Beamer, Yvonne Marie psychotherapist, counselor
Beatie, Bruce Alan comparative and medieval studies educator
†Beckwith, Karen Danette artist, printer
†Begala, John Adelbert human service administrator
Behnke, William Alfred landscape architect, planner
Bell, Steven Dennis lawyer
Bella, Jonathan Noriega internist
Bender, Peggy Wallace fundraising consultant
Benghiat, Russell advertising agency executive
Benseler, David Price foreign language educator
Berger, Melvin allergist, immunologist
Berger, Sanford Jason lawyer, securities dealer, real estate broker
Bergholz, David foundation administrator
Bergman, Robert Paul museum administrator, art historian, educator, lecturer
Berick, James Herschel lawyer
Berry, Dean Lester lawyer
Bersoux, Henri Robert marketing executive
Bersticker, Albert Charles chemical company executive
Besse, Ralph Moore lawyer
Bidelman, William Pendry astronomer, educator
Bilchik, Gary B. lawyer
Binford, Gregory Glenn lawyer
Binstock, Robert Henry public policy educator, writer, lecturer
Birne, Kenneth Andrew lawyer
Bissett, Barbara Anne steel distribution company executive
Blackwell, John polymers scientist, educator
Blattner, Robert A. lawyer
Blodgett, Omer William electric company design consultant
Bloser, Dieter radiologist
Bluford, Guion Stewart, Jr. engineering company executive
Blum, Arthur social work educator
Bollenbacher, Herbert Kenneth steel company official
Boswell, Nathalie Spence speech pathologist
Bowen, Richard Lee architect
Bowerfind, Edgar Sihler, Jr. physician, medical administrator
Boyd, Arthur Bernette, Jr. surgeon, clergyman, beverage company executive
Boyko, Christopher Allan lawyer, judge
Brandt, John Reynold editor, journalist
Braverman, Herbert Leslie lawyer
Bravo, Kenneth Allan lawyer
Breen, John Gerald manufacturing company executive
Brennan, Maureen lawyer
Brentlinger, Paul Smith venture capital executive
Bronson, David Leigh physician, educator
Brooten, Dorothy dean, nursing educator
Brosilow, Coleman Bernard chemical engineering educator
Brown, Rushia basketball player
Brown, Seymour R. lawyer
Drucken, Robert Matthew lawyer
Buchstein, Frederick David public relations executive
Buescher, Thomas Paul labor market analyst
Buhrow, William Carl religious organization administrator
Burghart, James Henry electrical engineer, educator
Burke, John Francis, Jr. economist
Burke, Kathleen B. lawyer
Burke, Lillian Walker retired judge
Burns, Duffy women's basketball coach university level
Buzzelli, Laurence Francis lawyer
Byron, Rita Ellen Cooney travel executive, publisher, real estate agent, civic leader, photojournalist, writer
Cairns, James Donald lawyer
Calabrese, Leonard M. social services administrator
†Calcavecchia, Mark professional golfer
Calfee, John Beverly retired lawyer
Calfee, William Lewis lawyer
Calkins, Hugh foundation executive
Callsen, Christian Edward medical device company executive
Camden, Vera Jean psychoanalyst
Campbell, Paul Barton retired lawyer
Canary, Nancy Halliday lawyer
Carey, Paul Richard biophysicist
Cargile, Michael Edward advertising agency executive
Carlsson, Bo Axel Vilhelm economics educator
Carrick, Kathleen Michele law librarian
Carrol, Edward Nicholas psychologist
Carter, Daniel Paul lawyer, educator
Carter, James Rose, Jr. medical educator
Carter, John Dale organizational development executive
Cartier, Charles Ernest alcohol and drug abuse services professional
Cascorbi, Helmut Freimund anesthesiologist, educator
Cassill, Herbert Carroll artist
Castele, Theodore John radiologist
Cerone, David academic administrator
Chamis, Christos Constantinos aerospace scientist, educator
Chema, Thomas V. government official, lawyer
Cherchiglia, Dean Kenneth lawyer
Chester, Russell Gilbert, Jr. accountant, auditor
Clark, Dwight Edward sports team executive, former professional football player
†Clark, Gary R. newspaper editor
Clark, Robert Arthur mathematician, educator
Clarke, Charles Fenton lawyer
†Cleary, Martin Joseph real estate company executive
Cleary, Michael J. educational administrator
Clifton, Douglas C. newspaper editor
Cohen, Armond E. rabbi
Cole, Christopher Robert cardiologist
Cole, Monroe neurologist, educator
Coleman, George Michael chemical company executive
Collin, Thomas James lawyer
Collins, Duane E. manufacturing executive
Collis, John Stanley neurosurgeon
Connelly, Diane Cecile communications executive
Conrad, Loretta Jane educational administrator
Conrad, Robert David broadcast executive, educator
†Cook, Ron A. management company executive
Coon, Sharon Ann writer, public relations executive, educator
Cooper, James Clinton social services administrator, consultant
Coquillette, William Hollis lawyer
Cordero, Wilfredo Nieva professional baseball player
Coulman, George Albert chemical engineer, educator
Courier, Jim (James Spencer Courier, Jr.) tennis player
Cox, Clifford Ernest business executive former school administration
Coyle, Martin Adolphus, Jr. lawyer
Crist, Paul Grant lawyer
Crosby, Fred McClellan retail home and office furnishings executive
Cullis, Christopher Ashley dean, biology educator
†Curnow, Kathy art historian, educator
Currivan, John Daniel lawyer
Cutler, Alexander MacDonald manufacturing company executive
Daberko, David A. banker
Danco, Léon Antoine management consultant, educator
Daroff, Robert Barry neurologist
Daroff, William Clayton lawyer
Davidson, James Wilson clinical psychologist
Davis, David Aaron journalist
Davis, Pamela Bowes pediatric pulmonologist
de Acosta, Alejandro Daniel mathematician, educator
Deal, William Thomas school psychologist
Decker, John William steel company executive
Deissler, Robert George fluid dynamicist, researcher
DellaCorte, Christopher engineer, tribologist
Dell'Osso, Louis Frank neuroscience educator
De Marco, Thomas Joseph periodontist, educator
Deming, David Lawson art educator
Denihan, William M. city official
Denko, Joanne D. psychiatrist, writer
DesRosiers, Anne Booke performing arts administrator, consultant
Dipko, Thomas Earl minister, national church executive
Doershuk, Carl Frederick physician, professor of pediatrics
Dohnanyi, Christoph von musician, conductor
Doris, Alan S(anford) lawyer
Dossey, Richard Lee accountant
Dougherty, Ursel Thielbeule communications and marketing executive
Douglas, Janice Green physician, educator
Dowell, Michael Brendan chemist
Drinko, John Deaver lawyer
Dunbar, Mary Asmundson communications executive, investor and public relations consultant
Duncan, Ed Eugene lawyer
Duvin, Robert Phillip lawyer
Eakman, Mark chemist
Eaton, Henry Felix public relations executive
Eberhard, William Thomas architect
Edwards, Michelle Denise professional basketball player
Eiben, Robert Michael pediatric neurologist, educator
Eichhorn, Bradford Reese management consultant
Elewski, Boni Elizabeth dermatologist, educator
Ellis, Lloyd H., Jr. emergency physician
Elston, Robert C. medical educator
Erb, Donald composer
Everett, Ronald Emerson government official
Fabens, Andrew Lawrie, III lawyer
Fabris, James A. journalist
Faldo, Nick professional golfer
Faller, Dorothy Anderson international agency administrator
Falsgraf, William Wendell lawyer
Farone, Brigid Ann nursing administrator
Fay, Regan Joseph lawyer
Fay, Robert Jesse lawyer
Fay, Terrence Michael lawyer
Fazio, Victor Warren physician, colon and rectal surgeon
Feinberg, Paul H. lawyer
Ferguson, Suzanne Carol English educator
Fernandez, René aerospace engineer
Fijalkowski, Isabelle professional basketball player
Finn, Robert writer, lecturer, broadcaster
Fisher, Thomas Edward lawyer
Fitzmaurice, Catherine Theresa auditor
Fitzpatrick, Joyce J. nursing educator, former dean
Fountain, Ronald Glenn management consultant, finance/marketing executive
Frank, Robert Donald flight nurse
Freire, Gloria Medonis social worker
Friedman, Barton Robert English educator
Friedman, Ernest Harvey physician, psychiatrist
Friedman, Harold Edward lawyer
Friedman, James Moss lawyer
Frisman, Roger Lawrence industrial sales executive
Fritz, Dwain Eldon engineer
Gallagher, Patrick Francis Xavier public relations executive
Gallienne, Robert Lee nursing educator
Gardner, Richard Kent retired librarian, educator, consultant
Gardocki, Christopher football player
Garrison, William Lloyd cemetery executive
Gaughan, Patricia Anne judge
Geho, Walter Blair biomedical research executive
Gerhart, Peter Milton law educator
Gherlein, Gerald Lee lawyer, diversified manufacturing company executive
Giannetti, Louis Daniel film educator, film critic
Gibans, James David architect
Gillespie, Robert Wayne banker
Ginn, Robert Martin retired utility company executive
Gladden, Dean Robert arts administrator, educator, consultant
Glaser, Robert Edward lawyer
Gleisser, Marcus David author, lawyer, journalist
Glickman, Carl David banker
Goffman, William mathematician, educator
Goins, Frances Floriano lawyer
Gold, Gerald Seymour lawyer
Goldfarb, Bernard Sanford lawyer
Goldstein, Marvin Emanuel aerospace scientist, research center administrator
Goldstein, Melvyn C. anthropologist, educator
Goler, Michael David lawyer
Goll, Paulette Susan secondary education educator
Gonet, Judith Janu pediatric nurse, consultant
†Gooden, Dwight Eugene professional baseball player
Gould, Bonnie Marincic realtor
Grabow, Raymond John mayor, lawyer
Graham, David Browning lawyer
Graham, John W. advertising executive
Gray, James Patrick business executive, consultant, educator
Green, Barbara Buckstein political scientist, educator
Greer, Thomas H. newspaper executive
Greppin, John Aird Coutts philologist, editor, educator
Groetzinger, Jon, Jr. lawyer, consumer products executive
Grossman, Theodore Martin lawyer
Grundstein, Nathan David lawyer, management science educator, management consultant
Grundy, Kenneth William political science educator
Gund, Gordon advertising executive, sports team executive
Haiman, Irwin Sanford lawyer
Hamilton, Dorothy Jean acute care nurse practitioner in cardiology
Hamilton, Nancy Beth business executive
Hamilton, Thomas Woolman publishing company executive
Hamilton, William Milton manufacturing executive
Hanson, Richard Winfield biochemist, educator
Hardis, Stephen Roger manufacturing company executive
Hardman, Corlista Helena school system administrator
Hardy, Michael Lynn lawyer
Hargrove, Mike (Dudley Michael Hargrove) professional baseball team manager
Harkins, Richard Wesley marine engineer, naval architect
Harrington, Nancy Lynn tax accountant
Harris, Clayton police chief
Harris, John William physician, educator
Hart, John professional sports team executive
Hartley, Duncan fundraising executive
Hastie, Ronald Leslie sales executive
Hawkinson, Gary Michael financial services company executive
Heald, Morrell humanities educator
Hedrick, Hal Clemons company executive
Hellman, Peter Stuart technical manufacturing executive
†Hemann, Patricia A. federal judge
Henning, George Thomas, Jr. steel company executive
Henry, Edward Frank computer accounting service executive
Hermann, Robert Ewald surgeon
Heuer, Arthur Harold ceramics engineer, educator
Hill, Robert John aviation executive
†Hill-McDonald, Linda professional basketball coach
Hochman, Kenneth George lawyer
Hoerner, Robert Jack lawyer
Hokenstad, Merl Clifford, Jr. social work educator
Holck, Frederick H. George priest, educator
Hollington, Richard Rings, Jr. lawyer
Holzbach, Raymond Thomas gastroenterologist, author, educator
Hook, John Burney investment company executive
Horvitz, Michael John lawyer
Hulme, Mary Ann K. women's health nurse, administrator
Hunter, Sally Irene interior designer
Hushen, John Wallace manufacturing company executive
Huston, Samuel Richard health facility executive
Inglis, Patricia Marcus lawyer
Izant, Robert James, Jr. pediatric surgeon
Jackson, Edgar B., Jr. medical educator
Jackson, Marcia Lynette women's health, pediatrics and geriatrics nurse
Jackson, Michael Ray baseball player
Jacobs, Leslie William lawyer
Jacobs, Richard E. real estate executive, sports team owner
Jameson, J(ames) Larry chemical company executive
Janke, Ronald Robert lawyer
Jeavons, Norman Stone lawyer
Jenkins, Thomas Llewellyn physics educator
Jensen, Kathryn Patricia (Kit) public radio station executive
Jettke, Harry Jerome retired government official
Jindra, Christine editor

Jirkans, Maribeth Joie school counselor
Jones, Merlakia basketball player
Jones, Rosemary college official
Jones, Thomas F. protective services official
Jorgenson, Mary Ann lawyer
Judge, Nancy Elizabeth obstetrician, gynecologist
Juhlin, Doris Arlene French language educator
Justice, David Christopher baseball player
Kahrl, Robert Conley lawyer
Kamm, Christian Philip manufacturing company executive
Kanzeg, David George radio programming director
Kapp, C. Terrence lawyer
Kass, Lawrence hematologist, oncologist, hematopathologist
Katcher, Richard lawyer
Katz, Lewis Robert law educator
Katzman, Richard A. cardiologist, consultant
Kay, Albert Joseph textile executive
†Kay, Robert physician
Kelly, Dennis Michael lawyer
Kelly, John Terence architect
Kemp, Shawn T. professional basketball player
Kennedy, Frederick Morgan retired secondary education educator
†Khabeer, Beryl M.A. poet, playwright, educator
Kilbane, Catherine M. lawyer
Kilbane, Thomas Stanton lawyer
King, James Edward museum director
Kirchick, Calvin B. lawyer
†Klein, Eric Alan surgical oncologist, urologist
Klein, George Robert periodical distribution company executive
Klopman, Gilles chemistry educator
Knull, Erhard minister
Ko, Wen-Hsiung electrical engineering educator
Koch, Charles Joseph banker
Koenig, Jack L. chemist, educator
Kola, Arthur Anthony lawyer
Kolb, David Allen psychology educator
Konicek, Michael city official
†Konstan, Michael William pediatric pulmonologist, researcher
Kovacs, Rosemary newspaper editor
Kovel, Ralph M. author, antiques expert
Kovel, Terry Horvitz (Mrs. Ralph Kovel) author, antiques authority
Kowalski, Kenneth Lawrence physicist, educator
Kramer, Edward George lawyer
Kramer, Eugene Leo lawyer
Krieger, Irvin Mitchell chemistry educator, consultant
Krotinger, Myron Nathan lawyer
Krulitz, Leo Morrion financial executive
Krupansky, Robert Bazil federal judge
Kuehn, Richard Arthur telecommunications consultant
Kuerti, Rosi educator
Kundtz, John Andrew lawyer
Kurit, Neil lawyer
Lakshmanan, Mark Chandrakant physiologist, physician
Lamm, Michael Emanuel pathologist, immunologist, educator
Landau, Bernard Robert biochemistry educator, physician
†Landis, Dennis Michael Doyle neurologist, researcher
Lando, Jerome Burton macromolecular science educator
Lange, Frederick Edward, Jr. computer information systems architect
Langer, Carlton Earl lawyer
Langston, Mark Edward professional baseball player
†Latham, Deborah K. research nurse
Lawniczak, James Michael lawyer
Lawrence, Estelene Yvonne transportation executive, musician
Lazo, John, Jr. physician
Lease, Robert K. lawyer
Lebovitz, Harold Paul (Hal Lebovitz) journalist
†Lee, Inmoo business educator
†Lee, Jae-won journalism educator, political campaign consultant
Lee, Jinho research engineer, consultant
†Lee, Kenneth Young application engineer
Lefferts, William Geoffrey physician, educator
Leidner, Harold Edward lawyer
Leiken, Earl Murray lawyer
Lenkoski, Leo Douglas psychiatrist, educator
Lenn, Stephen Andrew lawyer
Lentz, Mary A. lawyer, educator
Lewis, John Bruce lawyer
Lewis, John Francis lawyer
Lewis, Peter Benjamin insurance company executive
Lewis, Robert Lawrence lawyer, educator
Litt, Morton Herbert macromolecular science educator, researcher
Little, Robert Andrews architect, designer, painter
Liu, Chung-Chiun chemical engineering educator
Long, Robert M. newspaper publishing executive
Loop, Floyd D. health, medical executive
Lopez, Nancy professional golfer
Lord, James Gregory organizational and philanthropic counsel to consultants
Lowry, Dennis Martin training executive
Lowry, Joan Marie Dondrea broadcaster
Luce, Priscilla Mark public relations executive
†Lucker, Andrew M. political science educator, computer consultant
Luke, Randall Dan retired tire and rubber company executive, lawyer
Lyatkher, Victor Mikhailovich seismology research, hydropower/windpower designer
Lytle, Bruce Whitney cardiovascular surgeon
Machaskee, Alex newspaper publishing company executive
Macklis, Roger Miton physician, educator, researcher
Mac Laren, David Sergeant manufacturing corporation executive, inventor
Madden, James Desmond forensic engineer
Madison, Robert Prince architect
Madsen, H(enry) Stephen retired lawyer
Mancuso, John H. lawyer, bank executive
Mandel, Jack N. manufacturing company executive
Manley, David Thomas employment benefit plan administration company executive
Manos, John M. federal judge
Mantzell, Betty Lou school health administrator
Marcus, Donald Howard advertising agency executive
Markey, Robert Guy lawyer
†Marks, Kenneth Edward orthopaedic surgeon
Markus, Richard M. judge
Marting, Michael G. lawyer
Mason, Marilyn Gell library administrator, writer, consultant
Mason, Thomas Albert lawyer
Matia, Paul Ramon federal judge, chief district judge
Mawardi, Osman Kamel plasma physicist
Mayland, Kenneth Theodore economist
Mayne, Lucille Stringer finance educator
McAndrews, James Patrick lawyer
McArdle, Richard Joseph academic administrator
†Mc Cartan, Patrick Francis lawyer
McCarthy, Mark Francis lawyer
McCormack, Mark Hume lawyer, business management company executive
McCrae, Keith R. medical educator, researcher
McCullough, Joseph college president emeritus
Mc Elhaney, James Wilson lawyer, educator
McFadden, John Volney retired manufacturing company executive
Mc Farlane, Karen Elizabeth concert artists manager
McGervey, John Donald physics educator, researcher
McHale, Vincent Edward political science educator
McHenry, Martin Christopher physician, educator
McKenna, Joseph Francis journalist, communications consultant
McLaughlin, Patrick Michael lawyer
McWhorter, John Francis manufacturing engineer
Medalie, Jack Harvey physician
Mehlman, Maxwell Jonathan law educator
Melsher, Gary W. lawyer
Melsop, James William architect
Meyer, G. Christopher lawyer
Milgrim, Franklin Marshall merchant
Miller, Arnold retired newspaper editor
Miller, Genevieve retired medical historian
Miller, John Robert environmental recycling company executive
Miller, Randal Howard health science association administrator
Millstone, David J. lawyer
Miyares, Benjamin David editor, publisher, consultant
Modic, Stanley John business editor, publisher
Mofflin, Lionel Hugh (Harry Mofflin) biomedical engineer, physician
Moll, Curtis E. manufacturing executive
Molyneaux, David Glenn newspaper travel editor
Montague, Drogo K. urologist
Moore, Karen Nelson judge
Moore, Kenneth Cameron lawyer
Moravec, Christine D. Schomis medical educator
†Morgenstern-Clarren, Pat federal judge
Morris, Thomas William symphony orchestra administrator
Morrison, Donald William lawyer
Moskowitz, Roland Wallace internist
Mullally, Pierce Harry retired steel company executive
Myeroff, Kevin Howard financial planner
Myers, David N. construction executive
Myers, Eddie Earl clinical psychologist
Nagel, William Lee management consultant
Najar, Leo Michael conductor, arranger, educator
Neal, Bennie F. school administrator, educator
Nelson, Richard Alan financial executive
Nemcova, Eva professional basketball player
Neuhauser, Duncan von Briesen health services educator
Newman, John M., Jr. lawyer
Nguyen, Pram engineer, consultant
Nickerson, Gary Lee secondary education educator
Noetzel, Arthur Jerome business administration educator, management consultant
Novick, Andrew Carl urologist
Nudelman, Sidney lawyer
Oakar, Mary Rose former congresswoman
Oberdank, Lawrence Mark lawyer, arbitrator
Oesterling, Thomas Ovid pharmaceutical company executive
Oliver, Solomon, Jr. judge
Ollinger, W. James lawyer
Olness, Karen Norma pediatrics and international health educator
Olson, Barry Gay advertising executive, creative director
Olszewski, Edward John art history educator
O'Malley, Kathleen M. federal judge
O'Shea, Lynne Edeen marketing executive, educator
Osvath, Ludovic Lajos minister
Pace, Stanley Dan lawyer
†Palmer, Chris professional football coach
Parker, Patrick Streeter manufacturing executive
Parker, Robert Frederic university dean emeritus
Pascarella, Perry James author, editor, speaker
Pavlovich, Donald educator, support person
Pearlman, Samuel Segel lawyer
†Perelman, David S. federal judge
Perez, Dianne M. medical researcher
Perkovic, Robert Branko international management consultant
Perry, Frederick John theater educator
Perry, George neuroscientist, educator
Petina, David Anthony private company analyst
Pierce, Mary professional tennis player
Pierson, Marilyn Ehle financial planner
Pike, Kermit Jerome library director
Pilla, Anthony Michael bishop
Podboy, Alvin Michael, Jr. lawyer, law library director
Policy, Carmen A. professional sports team executive
Pollack, Florence K.Z. management consultant
Pomeranz, Jerome Raphael dermatopathologist
Porter, James Morris judge
Powers, Richard Daniel banker
Prater-Fipps, Eunice Kay educational administrator
Preston, Robert Bruce retired lawyer
Pretlow, Thomas Garrett physician, pathology educator, researcher
Price, Charles T. lawyer
Pursell, Carroll Wirth history educator
Putka, Andrew Charles lawyer
Pyke, John Secrest, Jr. lawyer, polymers company executive
Pytte, Agnar academic administrator
Queen, Joyce Ellen elementary school educator
Quigney, Theresa Ann special education educator
Raaf, John Hart surgeon, health facility administrator, educator
Rains, M. Neal lawyer
Rakita, Louis cardiologist, educator
Ramirez, Manuel Aristides (Manny Ramirez) professional baseball player
Ransohoff, Richard Milton neurologist, researcher
Rapp, Robert Neil lawyer
Ratnoff, Oscar Davis physician, educator
Redus, Darrin Miguel banker
Reid, James Sims, Jr. automobile parts manufacturer
Rekstis, Walter J., III lawyer
Reppert, Richard Levi lawyer
Reshotko, Eli aerospace engineer, educator
Rich, Lawrence Vincent manufacturing and engineering company executive
Roberts, James Owen financial planning executive, consultant
Robertson, Edward Neil dentist
Robiner, Donald Maxwell federal official, lawyer
Rogers, Charles Edwin physical chemistry educator
Rogers, Douglas George endocrinologist
Roop, James John public relations executive
Rosegger, Gerhard economist, educator
Rosenbaum, Jacob I. lawyer
Rosenthal, Leighton A. aviation company executive
Ross, Harold Anthony lawyer
Roth, Jack Joseph historian, educator
†Rothner, A. David pediatric neurologist
Rothstein, Ronald professional basketball coach
Ruben, Alan Miles law educator
Rudy, Yoram biomedical engineer, biophysicist, educator
Ruf, H(arold) William, Jr. lawyer, corporation executive
Ruff, Robert Louis neurologist, physiology researcher
Rupert, John Edward retired savings and loan executive, business and civic affairs consultant
Rydzel, James A. lawyer
Saada, Adel Selim civil engineer, educator
Sabik, Joseph Andrew psycho-educational assessment specialist
Sabo, Richard Steven electrical company executive
Salomon, Roger Blaine English language educator
Samodelov, Leonid Feodor anesthesiologist
Samson, Gordon Edgar educator, consultant
Sandburg, Helga author
Sande, Theodore Anton architect, educator, foundation executive
Sanislo, Paul Steve lawyer
Satola, James William lawyer
Savinell, Robert Francis engineering educator
Sawyer, Raymond Terry lawyer
Scanlon, Thomas J. lawyer
Scarpa, Antonio medicine educator, biomedical scientist
Schiller, James Joseph lawyer
Schlotfeldt, Rozella May nursing educator
†Schmid, William Gregory bank executive
Schmidt, Patricia Jean medical lab technician
Schneider, Edward Martin retired physician
Schnell, Carlton Bryce lawyer
Schonberg, Alan Robert management recruiting executive
Schrott, Norman clinical social worker
Schuele, Donald Edward physics educator
Schultz, Jeffrey Eric optometrist
Schumacher, O. Peter physician, educator
Schutter, David John banker
Schwartz, Howard Julius allergy educator
Schwartz, Michael Alan physician
Seaton, Robert Finlayson retired planned giving consultant
Seles, Monica tennis player
Shakno, Robert Julian hospital administrator
Shapiro, Fred David lawyer
Sharp, Robert Weimer lawyer
Shaw, Scott Alan photojournalist
Sheffler, Dudley telecommunications industry executive
Shepard, Ivan Albert securities and insurance broker
Sherry, Paul Henry minister, religious organization administrator
Shrallow, Dale Phillip lawyer
Shuck, Jerry Mark surgeon, educator
Sibley, Willis Elbridge anthropology educator, consultant
Sicherman, Marvin Allen lawyer
Siefers, Robert George banker
Siegel, Robert heat transfer engineer
Sila, Cathy Ann neurologist
Simmons, Clinton Craig human resources executive
†Singh, Vijay professional golfer
Skolnik, David Erwin financial analyst
Skulina, Thomas Raymond lawyer
Slinger, Michael Jeffery law library director
Sloan, David W. lawyer
Smith, Barbara Jean lawyer
Smythe Zajc, M. Catherine library administrator, development officer
Sogg, Wilton Sherman lawyer
Solomon, Randall L. lawyer
Spencer, James Calvin, Sr. humanities educator
Spero, Keith Erwin lawyer
Spottsville, Sharon Ann counselor
Stanley, Hugh Monroe, Jr. lawyer
Stanton-Hicks, Michael D'Arcy anesthesiologist, educator
Stark, George Robert health science association administrator
†Starkman, Glenn David physicist, educator
Stavitsky, Abram Benjamin immunologist, educator
Stefunek, Paul Christopher executive search company executive
Stein, Herman David social sciences educator, past university provost
Steinberg, Arthur G(erald) geneticist
Steindler, Howard Allen lawyer
Stellato, Louis Eugene lawyer
Stern, Robert C. physician, educator
Stevens, Thomas Charles lawyer
†Stoller, Eleanor Palo sociology educator
Stone, Harry H. business executive
Strang, James Dennis editor
Stratton-Crooke, Thomas Edward financial consultant
Strauch, John L. lawyer
†Streepy, Jack B. federal judge
Streeter, Richard Edward lawyer
Striefsky, Linda A(nn) lawyer
Strimbu, Victor, Jr. lawyer
Strome, Marshall otolaryngologist, educator
Stuhan, Richard George lawyer
Sudow, Thomas Nisan marketing services company executive, broadcaster
Summers, William B. brokerage house executive
Swartzbaugh, Marc L. lawyer
Sweeney, Emily Margaret prosecutor
Swetland, David Wightman investment company executive
Szaller, James Francis lawyer
Szarek, Stanislaw Jerzy mathematics educator
Taft, Seth Chase retired lawyer
Taw, Dudley Joseph sales executive
Taylor, Margaret Wischmeyer retired English language and journalism educator
Taylor, Steve Henry zoologist
Thomas, Faye Evelyn J. elementary and secondary school educator
Thomas, Richard Stephen financial executive
Thompson, Stephen Arthur publishing executive
†Thornton, Jerry Sue community college president
Tomsich, Robert J. heavy machinery manufacturing executive
Toohey, Brian Frederick lawyer
Toomajian, William Martin lawyer
Topilow, Carl S. symphony conductor
Tracht, Allen Eric electronics executive
Trevor, Leigh Barry lawyer
Troiano, Alexander Robert metallurgist, educator
Troutman, David W. protective services official
Unger, Paul A. packaging executive
Utian, Wulf Hessel gynecologist, endocrinologist
Van Ummersen, Claire A(nn) academic administrator, biologist, educator
†Vayner, Ellen B. analyst
Vizquel, Omar Enrique professional baseball player
†von Dahnányi, Christoph music director
von Mehren, George M. lawyer
Wagner, James Warren engineering educator
Waldeck, John Walter, Jr. lawyer
Wallach, Mark Irwin lawyer
Walters, Farah M. hospital administrator
Wangermann, John Paul management consultant
Ward, William Edward museum exhibition designer
Wareham, Jerry broadcast executive
Waren, Allan David computer information scientist, educator
Warren, Russell James investment banking executive, consultant
Washington, John Augustine retired physician, pathologist
Waters, Gwendolyn human services administrator
Watson, Richard Thomas lawyer
Weber, Robert Carl lawyer
Webster, Leslie Tillotson, Jr. pharmacologist, educator
Weidenthal, Maurice David (Bud Weidenthal) educational administrator, journalist
Weiler, Jeffry Louis lawyer
Weinberger, Peter Henry lawyer
Weiner, George David medical association executive, researcher
Wells, Lesley B. judge
Wessel, Dennis James mechanical engineering administrator
White, George W. federal judge
White, Michael Reed mayor
Whiteman, Joseph David retired lawyer, manufacturing company executive
Whitney, Richard Buckner lawyer
Whittlesey, Diana surgeon
Williams, Arthur Benjamin, Jr. bishop
Williams, Clyde E., Jr. lawyer
Wish, Jay Barry nephrologist, specialist
†Withers, Carl Raymond lawyer
Wolfman, Alan medical educator, researcher
Wolinsky, Emanuel physician, educator
Wood, Kathleen Oliver writer, editor
†Woods, Jacqueline F. telecommunications industry executive
Woodson, Kevin writer
Woyczynski, Wojbor Andrzej mathematician, educator
Wright, Marshall retired manufacturing executive, former diplomat
Young, James Edward lawyer
Young, Jess Ray physician
Zambie, Allan John lawyer
Zangerle, John A. lawyer
Zdanis, Richard Albert academic administrator
Zheng, Yao computational scientist
†Zollinger, Robert Milton, Jr. surgery educator
Zubal, John Thomas book exchange executive, publisher, bibliographer
Zung, Thomas Tse-Kwai architect
Zupancic, Anthony English and communication educator
Zurawski, Dale L. art director, graphic designer, illustrator

Cleveland Heights
Bruhn, Paul Robert principal
Drane, Walter Harding publishing executive, business consultant
Gutfeld, Norman E. lawyer
Jackson, Cedric Douglas Tyrone, Sr. minister
King, George academic administrator
Shorey, Amy Guy fundraiser
Travis, Frederick Francis academic administrator, historian
†Zierler, Lawrence Stephen rabbi, community leader

Coldwater
Bladen, Laurie Ann women's health nurse

College Corner
Gilmore, Robert Witter foundation administrator

Columbia Station
Pingatore, Sam Robert systems analyst, consultant, business executive

Columbiana
†Geary, Amy Jo librarian
Richman, John Emmett architect

Columbus
†Abel, Mark R. federal judge
Acker, Frederick Wayne lawyer
Ackerman, John Henry health services consultant, physician
Adams, John Marshall lawyer
Alban, Roger Charles construction equipment distribution executive
Alexander, Carl Albert ceramic engineer, educator
Alger, Chadwick Fairfax political scientist, educator
Altan, Taylan engineering educator, mechanical engineer, consultant
Amatos, Barbara Hansen accounting executive
Anderson, Carole Ann nursing educator
Anderson, Jon Mac lawyer
Anderson, Kerrii B. construction company executive
Arnold, Kevin David psychologist, educational researcher
Arps, David Foster electronics engineer
Aukland, Duncan Dayton lawyer
Austin, David George dentist
Babcock, Charles Luther classics educator
Bachman, Sister Janice health care executive
Bailey, Cecil Dewitt aerospace engineer, educator
Bailey, Daniel Allen lawyer
†Baishanski, Jacqueline Marie foreign language educator
Baker, Gregory Richard mathematician
†Baker, John electronics executive
Ballou, Charles Herbert financial executive

Banasik, Robert Casmer *nursing home administrator, educator*
Barker, Llyle James, Jr. *management consultant, journalism educator*
Barnes, Wallace Ray *retired lawyer*
Barry, James P(otvin) *writer, editor*
Barth, Rolf Frederick *pathologist, educator*
Barthelmas, Ned Kelton *investment and commercial real estate banker*
Battersby, James Lyons, Jr. *English language educator*
Bechtel, Stephen E. *mechanical engineer, educator*
Beck, Paul Allen *political science educator*
Becker, Ralph Leonard *psychologist*
Beckholt, Alice *clinical nurse specialist*
Bedford, Keith Wilson *civil engineer, atmospheric science educator*
Behrman, Edward Joseph *biochemistry educator*
Beja, Morris *English literature educator*
Bell, George Edwin *retired physician, insurance company executive*
Beller, Stephen Mark *university administrator*
Belton, John Thomas *lawyer*
Bennett, Robert Thomas *lawyer*
Bergstrom, Stig Magnus *geology educator*
Berndt, Ellen German *company executive*
Berry, William Lee *business administration educator*
Beversdorf, David Quentin *neurologist, researcher*
Bhushan, Bharat *mechanical engineer*
Bianco, Don Christopher *civil servant, retired*
Bibart, Richard L. *lawyer*
Bilderback, George Garrison, III *chemical dependency counselor*
Billings, Charles Edgar *physician*
Black, David Evans *sculptor, painter*
Black, Larry David *library director*
Blackwell, J. Kenneth *state official*
Blankenship, Dolores Moorefield *principal, music educator, retired*
Blickenstaff, Kathleen Mary *lawyer, mental health nurse, nursing educator*
Boerner, Ralph E. J. *forest soil ecologist, plant biology educator*
Boh, Ivan *philosophy educator*
Bohm, Friedrich (Friedl) K.M. *architectural firm executive*
Booker, James Douglas *retired lawyer, government official*
Bosworth, Jeffrey Willson *emerging technologies consultant, client/server specialist*
Boudoulas, Harisios *physician, educator, researcher*
Boué, Daniel Robert *pathologist*
Boulger, Francis William *metallurgical engineer*
Bourguignon, Erika Eichhorn *anthropologist, educator*
Bowen, John Wesley Edward, IV *lawyer*
Bowman, Louis L. *emergency physician*
Branscomb, Lewis Capers, Jr. *librarian, educator*
Bridgman, G(eorge) Ross *lawyer*
Brierley, Gerald P. *physiological chemistry educator*
Brinkman, Dale Thomas *lawyer*
Brodkey, Robert Stanley *chemical engineering educator*
Brooks, Richard Dickinson *lawyer*
Brown, Herbert Russell *lawyer, writer*
Brown, Philip Albert *lawyer*
Brown, Rowland Chauncey Widrig *information systems, strategic planning and ethics consultant*
Brown, Susan Thomas *research scientist*
Brubaker, Robert Loring *lawyer*
Buchenroth, Stephen Richard *lawyer*
Bullock, Joseph Daniel *pediatrician, educator*
Burke, Kenneth Andrew *advertising executive*
Burnham, John Chynoweth *historian, educator*
Burns, Beth *women's collegiate basketball coach*
Burns, Robert Edward *lawyer*
†Burton, Barry Alan *county official*
†Caldwell, Charles M. *federal judge*
Calhoun, Donald Eugene, Jr. *federal judge*
Callander, Kay Eileen Paisley *business owner, retired gifted talented education educator, writer*
Campbell, Richard Rice *retired newspaper editor*
Capen, Charles Chabert *veterinary pathology educator, researcher*
Carlson, Larry Vernon *insurance company executive*
Carnahan, John Anderson *lawyer*
Carpenter, Jot David *landscape architect, educator*
Carpenter, Michael H. *lawyer*
Carter, Christine Sue *cardiac recovery nurse*
Carter, Melinda *municipal official*
Castlen, Peggy Lou *insurance company executive*
Chandrasekaran, Balakrishnan *computer and information science educator*
Chapman, John William, Jr. *marketing executive*
Charles, Bertram *radio broadcasting executive*
Chesley-Lahm, Diane *lawyer*
Chesser, Kerry Royce *financial director*
Chester, John Jonas *lawyer*
Chovan, John David *biomedical engineer*
Christensen, John William *lawyer*
Christoforidis, A. John *radiologist, educator*
Chu, Roderick Gong-Wah *educational administrator*
Clark, Robert Wesley *neurologist*
Cline, Richard Allen *lawyer*
Colburn, Julia Katherine Lee *volunteer, educator*
Cole, Clarence Russell *college dean*
Cole, Ransey Guy, Jr. *judge*
†Cole Wardell, Kirstin *television news anchor*
Collins, Michael Edward *religious newspaper editor*
Conley, Sarah Ann *health facility administrator*
Cook, John Roscoe, Jr. *insurance executive*
†Cooper, John *university football coach*
Copeland, William Edgar, Sr. *physician*
Corbato, Charles Edward *geology educator*
Cornwell, David George *biochemist, educator*
Cottingham, Richard Sumner *paper company executive*
Cottrell, David Alton *school system administrator*
Cox, Mitchel Neal *editor*
Cramblett, Henry Gaylord *pediatrician, virologist, educator*
Crane, Jameson *plastics manufacturing company executive*
Cross, April Lee *geriatrics nurse, nursing educator*
Cruz, Jose Bejar, Jr. *engineering educator*
Culbertson, Jack Arthur *education educator*
Curtin, Michael Francis *editor*
Curtis, Loretta O'Ellen *retired construction executive*
Cvetanovich, Danny L. *lawyer*
Daab-Krzykowski, Andre *pharmaceutical and nutritional manufacturing company administrator*
Daehn, Glenn Steven *materials scientist*
Darling, George Curtis *minister, administrator*
Dawson, Virginia Sue *newspaper editor*
Dederer, William Bowne *music educator, administrator*
de la Chapelle, Albert *education educator*
De Lucia, Frank Charles *physicist, educator*
Denniss, Juliet Dawn *environmental specialist, geologist*
DeRousie, Charles Stuart *lawyer*
Dervin, Brenda Louise *communications educator*
DeSando, John Anthony *humanities educator*
DeVassie, Terry Lee *newspaper executive*
Dietrich, Carol Elizabeth *educator, former dean*
Dillon, Merton Lynn *historian, educator*
Di Lorenzo, John Florio, Jr. *lawyer*
Disinger, John Franklin *natural resources educator*
Donovan, Dennis Dale *priest*
Donovan, Maureen Hildegarde *librarian, educator*
Douglas, Andrew *state supreme court justice*
Dowling, Thomas Allan *mathematics educator*
Draghi, Raymond Amadea *retired postal worker*
Draper, E(rnest) Linn, Jr. *electric utility executive*
Draper, Gerald Linden *lawyer*
Dreher, Darrell L. *lawyer*
Dresser, Karen Kerns *state agency administrator*
Drvota, Mojmir *cinema educator, author*
Duckworth, Winston Howard *retired ceramic engineer*
†Duff, Steven Barron *cardiovascular surgeon*
Duryee, Harold Taylor *insurance executive*
Elam, John Carlton *lawyer*
Elliot, David Hawksley *geologist*
Ellison, Edwin Christopher *physician, surgeon*
Emanuelson, James Robert *retired insurance company executive*
Ensminger, Dale *mechanical engineer, electrical engineer*
Evans, Daniel E. *sausage manufacturing and restaurant chain company executive*
Fahey, Richard Paul *lawyer*
Falcone, Robert Edward *surgeon*
Faure, Gunter *geology educator*
Fausey, Norman Ray *soil scientist*
Fawcett, Sherwood Luther *research laboratory executive*
†Fechtor, Steve *advertising executive*
Feck, Luke Matthew *utility executive*
Fenton, Robert Earl *electrical engineering educator*
Ferguson, Gerald Paul *lawyer*
Ferguson, Ronald Morris *surgeon, educator*
Fidler, Carol Ann *accountant*
Filipic, Matthew Victor *state official*
Firestone, Richard Francis *chemistry educator*
Fisher, Lawrence L. *lawyer*
Fisher, Lloyd Edison, Jr. *lawyer*
†Fitzgerald, Tom *professional soccer coach*
Flanagan, Harry Paul *publishing executive*
Floyd, Gary Leon *plant cell biologist*
Foland, Kenneth A. *geological sciences educator*
Fornshell, Dave Lee *educational broadcasting executive*
†Franano, Susan Margaret Ketteman *orchestra administrator, soprano*
Francis, John Wayne *educator*
Frasier, Ralph Kennedy *lawyer, banker*
Fried, Samuel *lawyer*
Fry, Donald Lewis *physiologist, educator*
Frye, Richard Arthur *lawyer*
Fu, Paul Shan *law librarian, consultant*
Fullerton, Charles William *retired insurance company executive*
Fultz, Robert Edward *lawyer*
Furney, Linda Jeanne *state legislator*
Furste, Wesley Leonard, II *surgeon, educator*
†Gall, Linda Lee *artist, administrator*
Gardner, Robert Meade *retired building contractor*
†Garner, Carol Lynn *executive*
Gartner, Daniel Lee *computer information executive*
Gibson, Rankin MacDougal *lawyer*
Gilliom, Bonnie Lee *arts educator, consultant*
Gilliom, Morris Eugene *social studies and global educator*
Gillmor, Karen Lako *state agency administrator, strategic planner*
Glaser, Gary A. *bank executive*
Glaser, Ronald *microbiology educator, scientist*
†Glass, Amy Jocelyn *economist*
Glenn, John Herschel, Jr. *former senator*
†Glimcher, David J. *real estate executive*
†Glimcher, Herbert *real estate company executive*
Goerler, Raimund Erhard *archivist*
†Goff, John *state agency administrator*
Goff, Wilmer Scott *photographer*
Goldsmith, Jocelyn Stone *state employment professional*
Goodridge, Alan Gardner *research biochemist, educator*
Gordon, Sydney Michael *research chemist*
Gower, Cindy Elaine Lones *electronic technician*
Graham, James Lowell *federal judge*
Grant, Michael Peter *electrical engineer*
Greek, Darold I. *lawyer*
Gribble, Charles Edward *editor, Slavic languages educator*
Gross, James Howard *lawyer*
Grossberg, Michael Lee *theater critic, writer*
Hadipriono, Fabian Christy *engineering educator, researcher*
†Hagerman, James Brien *speech and drama educator*
Hahm, David Edgar *classics educator*
Hamilton, Harold Philip *fund raising executive*
Hanrahan, Barbara *university press executive*
Hansen, Thomas Nanastad *pediatrician, health facility administrator*
Hardymon, David Wayne *lawyer*
Hare, Robert Yates *music history educator*
Harris, Donald *composer*
Harris, Ronald David *chemical engineer*
Hart, Mildred *counselor*
†Haskell, Brenton Ernest *health facility administrator*
Hedrick, Larry Willis *airport executive*
Heinlen, Daniel Lee *alumni organization administrator*
Herbst, Eric *physicist, astronomer*
Herron, Holly Lynn *flight nurse, educator*
Hewitt, William Harley *investment and marketing executive*
Hilliker, Grant Gilbert *writer, former diplomat and educator*
Hoffmann, Charles Wesley *retired foreign language educator*
Hollenbaugh, H(enry) Ritchey *lawyer*
Hollis-Allbritton, Cheryl Dawn *retail paper supply store executive*
Hollister, Nancy *state legislator*
Holschuh, John David *federal judge*
Horowitz, Stanley H. *electrical engineer*
Horton, John Edward *periodontist, educator*
Hottinger, Jay *state legislator*
Houser, Donald Russell *mechanical engineering educator, consultant*
Huber, Joan Althaus *sociology educator*
Huheey, Marilyn Jane *ophthalmologist*
Hutson, Jeffrey Woodward *lawyer*
Iammartino, Nicholas R. *corporate communications executive*
Ichiishi, Tatsuro *economics and mathematics educator*
Inglis, William Darling *internist, health facility administrator*
Jackson, David Gordon *religious organization administrator*
Jackson, G. James *protective services official*
Jackson, Janet Elizabeth *city attorney, association executive*
Jackson, Randall W. *geography educator*
Jacox, John William *mechanical engineer and consulting company executive*
Jarvis, Gilbert Andrew *humanities educator, writer*
Jenkins, George L. *lawyer, fast food company executive*
Jenkins, John Anthony *lawyer*
Johnson, Mark Alan *lawyer*
Johnston, Jeffery W. *publishing executive*
Jolly, Daniel Ehs *dental educator*
Jung, Diana Lynn *graphic designer*
Kakos, Gerard Stephen *thoracic and cardiovascular surgeon*
Kanwar, Deepak Vineet *telecommunications company executive*
Kapral, Frank Albert *medical microbiology and immunology educator*
Kasper, Larry John *accountant, litigation support consultant*
Kasulis, Thomas Patrick *humanities educator*
Kearns, Merle Grace *state senator*
Kefauver, Weldon Addison *publisher*
Keith, Barry Allen *clinical social worker*
Keller, Kenneth Christen *advertising executive*
†Kemp, Terence P. *federal judge*
Kessel, John Howard *political scientist, educator*
Ketcham, Richard Scott *lawyer*
Kidder, C. Robert *food products executive*
Kiefer, Gary *newspaper editor*
Kindig, Fred Eugene *statistics educator, arbitrator*
King, G. Roger *lawyer*
King, Norah McCann *federal judge*
Kingseed, Wyatt *city official*
Kirk, Ballard Harry Thurston *architect*
Kirwan, William English, II *mathematics educator, university official*
†Kissel, John Thomas *neurologist*
Knilans, Michael Jerome *supermarkets executive*
Knisely, Douglas Charles *accountant*
Koblentz, Robert Alan *lawyer*
Koehn, Susan Michele *accountant*
Koenigsknecht, Roy A. *education administrator*
Kolattukudy, Pappachan Ettoop *biochemist, educator*
Kouyoumjian, Robert G. *electrical engineering educator*
Kreager, Eileen Davis *administrative consultant*
Ksienski, Aharon Arthur *electrical engineer*
Kucinich-Horn, Sandra Lee McCarthy *secondary education educator*
Kuehnle, Kenton Lee *lawyer*
Kuhn, Albert Joseph *English educator*
Kurtz, Charles Jewett, III *lawyer*
Kusma, Kyllikki *lawyer*
Kyte, Susan Janet *lawyer*
Ladman, Jerry R. *economist, educator*
Lal, Rattan *soil scientist, researcher*
LaLonde, Bernard Joseph *educator*
Lander, Ruth A. *medical group and association administrator*
Larzelere, Kathy Lynn Heckler *paralegal*
Lashutka, Gregory S. *mayor, lawyer*
Laufman, Leslie Rodgers *hematologist, oncologist*
Lazar, Theodore Aaron *retired manufacturing company executive, lawyer*
Leach, Russell *judge*
Lebow, Richard Ned *political science, history and psychology educator*
Lee, Anne Beatrice *archaeologist, forensic anthropologist*
Lehman, Harry Jac *lawyer*
Leier, Carl Victor *internist, cardiologist*
Leissa, Arthur William *mechanical engineering educator*
Leiter, William C. *banking executive*
Leong, G. Keong *operations management educator*
Lewis, Richard Phelps *physician, educator*
†Lewis, Sharon Kay *artist, craftsman*
Lindsay, Dianna Marie *educational administrator*
Lindsey, Thomas Kenneth *lawyer, administrator*
Ling, Ta-Yung *physics educator*
Litvak, Ronald *psychiatrist*
Liu, Ming-Tsan *computer engineering educator*
†Lomax, Howard *security officer*
Lombardi, Adolph Vincent, Jr. *orthopaedic surgeon*
Long, Sarah Elizabeth Brackney *physician*
Long, Thomas Leslie *lawyer*
Lowe, Clayton Kent *photography, cinema, and video educator*
Lowry, Bruce Roy *lawyer*
Lucier, P. Jeffrey *publishing executive*
Luck, James I. *foundation executive*
Lundstedt, Sven Bertil *behavioral and social scientist, educator*
Lux, Kathleen Mary *community health educator, nurse*
Lynn, Arthur Dellert, Jr. *economist, educator*
†Madia, William Juul *chemist*
Magliocca, Larry Anthony *education educator*
Maloon, Jerry L. *trial lawyer, physician, medicolegal consultant*
Mangum, Stephen L. *business educator*
Marble, Duane Francis *geography educator, researcher*
Markus, Kent Richard *lawyer*
†Marshall, Kenneth B. *protective services agency administrator*
Martin, William Giese *lawyer*
Marushige-Knopp, Yuka *food scientist*
Marzluf, George Austin *biochemistry educator*
Mason, Raymond E., Jr. *distributing company executive*
Massey, Robert John *telecommunications executive*
Massie, Robert Joseph *publishing company executive*
Mathis, Lois Reno *retired elementary education educator*
†Matkovic, Velimir *physical medicine and rehabilitation educator*
†Matthews, Terina Joann *human resources specialist*
Mayer, Victor James *earth system science educator*
Maynard, Robert Howell *lawyer*
Mazzaferri, Ernest Louis *physician, educator*
McAlister, Robert Beaton *lawyer*
McBride, Brian *soccer player*
McCloud, Laurie *critical care nurse*
McConnaughey, George Carlton, Jr. *lawyer*
Mc Cormac, John Waverly *judge*
McCoy, William Earl, Jr. *economic development training consultant*
McCurdy, Kurt Basquin *real estate corporation officer*
McCutchan, Gordon Eugene *lawyer, insurance company executive*
McDermott, Kevin R. *lawyer*
McFerson, Diamond Richard *insurance company executive*
McGrath, Barbara Gates *city manager*
McGuire, Mark Joseph *graphic designer, art educator*
McInturff, Floyd M. *retired state agency administrator*
McKenna, Alvin James *lawyer*
McLin, Rhine Lana *state senator, funeral service executive, educator*
McMahon, John Patrick *lawyer*
McNealey, J. Jeffrey *lawyer, corporate executive*
McNennamin, Michael J. *bank executive*
Mead, Priscilla *state legislator*
Meites, Samuel *clinical chemist, educator*
Meredith, Meri Hill *reference librarian, educator*
Metzler, Eric Harold *retired state agency administrator, researcher*
Meuser, Fredrick William *retired seminary president, church historian*
Meyer, Patricia Morgan *neuropsychologist, educator*
†Milenthal, David *advertising executive*
†Milenthal, Rick *advertising executive*
Milford, Frederick John *retired research company executive*
Miller, Don Wilson *nuclear engineering educator*
Miller, Malcolm Lee *retired lawyer*
Miller, Michael Stratton *lawyer*
Miller, Terry Alan *chemistry educator*
Miller, Terry Morrow *lawyer*
Miller, Wayne Clayton *student services director*
Millett, Stephen Malcolm *futurist, consultant, historian*
Milligan, Glenn Wesley *business educator*
Minor, Charles Daniel *lawyer*
Minor, Robert Allen *lawyer*
Mirman, Joel Harvey *lawyer*
Mitchell, Carol Elaine *publishing executive, writer, educator*
Moloney, Thomas E. *lawyer*
Mone, Robert Paul *lawyer*
Montgomery, Betty Dee *state's attorney general, former state legislator*
Moore, Margaret Docherty *educator*
Morgan, Dennis Richard *lawyer*
Morrison, Joel Lynn *cartographer, geographer*
Morrow, Grant, III *medical research director, physician*
Moser, Debra Kay *medical educator*
Moul, William Charles *lawyer*
Moulton, Edward Quentin *civil engineer, educator*
Moyer, Thomas J. *state supreme court chief justice*
Mueller, Charles Frederick *radiologist, educator*
Muller, Mervin Edgar *information systems educator, consultant*
Murphy, Andrew J. *managing news editor*
Myers, William C. *city commissioner*
Nakayama, Mineharu *language professional/educator Japanese*
Namboodiri, Krishnan *sociology educator*
†Nappi, James Francis *hand surgeon, educator*
Nasrallah, Henry Ata *psychiatry researcher, educator*
Nathan, Jerry E. *lawyer*
Naylor, James Charles *psychologist, educator*
Needham, Glen Ray *entomology and acarology educator, researcher*
Neely, Scott Hays *legislative liaison*
Newman, Barbara Miller *psychologist, educator*
Newman, Diana S. *development consultant*
Newman, Philip Robert *psychologist*
Newsom, Gerald Higley *astronomy educator*
Newton, William Allen, Jr. *pediatric pathologist*
Nikias, Anthony Douglas *accountant, educator*
†Nobrega, Fred Thomas *hospital executive*
Noe, Fred J. *sports association administrator*
Norris, Alan Eugene *federal judge*
†O'Brien, Jim *university basketball coach*
Ockerman, Herbert W. *agricultural studies educator*
†O'Connor, Maureen *state official, lawyer*
O'Donnell, F. Scott *banker*
†Olesen, Doug *think tank executive*
Olesen, Douglas Eugene *research institute executive*
Oliphant, James S. *lawyer*
Olson, Carol Ann *librarian*
Oman, Richard Heer *lawyer*
O'Reilly, Michael Joseph *lawyer, real estate investor*
Osipow, Samuel Herman *psychology educator*
Otte, Paul John *academic administrator, consultant, trainer*
Owsiany, David James *lawyer, lobbyist*
Oxley, Margaret Carolyn Stewart *elementary education educator*
Ozkan, Umit Sivrioglu *chemical engineering educator*
Page, Linda Kay *banking executive*
Paquette, Leo Armand *chemistry educator*
†Patel, Vipinchandra Natwarlal *computer engineer*
Patrick, George Milton *dentist*
Patterson, Samuel Charles *political science educator*
Penn, Gerald Melville *pathologist*
Peterle, Tony John *zoologist, educator*
Peters, Leon, Jr. *electrical engineering educator, research administrator*
Peterson, Gale Eugene *historian*
Petricoff, M. Howard *lawyer, educator*
Petro, James Michael *lawyer, politician*
Petty, Richard Edward *psychologist, educator, researcher*
Pfeifer, Paul E. *state supreme court justice*
Pfening, Frederic Denver, III *manufacturing company executive*
Phillips, James Edgar *lawyer*
Pieper, Heinz Paul *physiology educator*
Pitzer, Martha Seares *nursing educator*
Plagenz, George Richard *minister, journalist, columnist*
Pointer, Peter Leon *investment executive*
Post, Natalie Jenkins *recreational vehicle executive*
Pressley, Fred G., Jr. *lawyer*
Pritchard, Kristiane *history educator*
Quigley, John Bernard *law educator*
Quinn, Robert David *research institute executive*
Radnor, Alan T. *lawyer*
Ramey, Denny L. *bar association executive director*
Rapp, Robert Anthony *metallurgical engineering educator, consultant*
Ray, Edward John *economics educator, administrator*
Ray, Frank Allen *lawyer*
Ray, Frank David *government agency official*

Reasoner, Willis Irl, III *lawyer*
Redmond, Robert Francis *nuclear engineering educator*
Reed, Constance Louise *materials management and purchasing consultant*
Reeve, John Newton *molecular biology and microbiology educator*
Reibel, Kurt *physicist, educator*
Reichwein, Jeffrey Charles *archaeologist*
Reilly, Joy Harriman *theatre educator, playwright, actress, director*
Relle, Ferenc Matyas *chemist*
Rennick, Kyme Elizabeth Wall *lawyer*
Resnick, Alice Robie *state supreme court justice*
Ress, Charles William *management consultant*
Rice, Thomas W. *city public safety official*
Richardson, Laurel Walum *sociology educator*
Ridgley, Thomas Brennan *lawyer*
†Riede, David George *English educator*
Roberts, William Eric *investment company executive*
Robinson, Barry R. *lawyer*
Robol, Richard Thomas *lawyer*
Rohrbaugh, Wayne Joseph *chemical company executive*
Rose, Michael Dean *lawyer, educator*
Rosenberg, Paul *physicist, consultant*
Rosenstock, Susan Lynn *orchestra manager*
Roth, Robert Earl *environmental educator*
Roth, Susan King *design educator*
Ruberg, Robert Lionel *surgery educator*
Rubin, Alan J. *environmental engineer, chemist*
Rudmann, Sally Vander Linden *medical technology educator*
Ruhlin, Peggy Miller *investment adviser, financial planner*
Rule, John Corwin *history educator*
Rund, Douglas Andrew *emergency physician, educator*
†Russell, William Fletcher, III *opera company director*
Ryan, Joseph W., Jr. *lawyer*
Ryan, Robert *consulting company executive*
Sahai, Yogeshwar *engineering educator*
St. Pierre, George Roland, Jr. *materials science and engineering administrator, educator*
St. Pierre, Ronald Leslie *anatomy educator, university administrator*
Sargus, Edmund A., Jr. *judge*
†Saunders, Mary L. *military officer*
Sawyers, Elizabeth Joan *librarian, administrator*
Sayers, Martin Peter *pediatric neurosurgeon*
Scanlan, James Patrick *philosophy and Slavic studies educator*
Schafer, William Harry *loss prevention consultant*
Schoedinger, David Stanton *funeral director*
Schottenstein, Jay L. *retail executive*
Schrag, Edward A., Jr. *lawyer*
Schuller, David Edward *cancer center administrator, otolaryngology*
Selby, Diane Ray Miller *fraternal organization administrator*
Sellers, Barbara Jackson *federal judge*
Senhauser, Donald A(lbert) *pathologist, educator*
Shamansky, Robert Norton *lawyer*
†Shea, Mary Pharo *health education program administrator*
Shepard, Kirk Van, Sr. *physician, researcher*
Sherrill, Thomas Boykin, III *retired newspaper publishing executive*
Shikina, Seiji *educator, consultant*
Shook, Robert Louis *business writer*
†Siciliani, Alessandro Domenico *conductor*
Sidman, Robert John *lawyer*
Silbajoris, Frank Rimvydas *Slavic languages educator*
Simms, Lowelle *synod executive*
Sims, Richard Lee *hospital administrator*
Simson, Bevlyn *artist*
Singh, Rajendra *mechanical engineering educator*
Skillman, Thomas Grant *endocrinology consultant, former educator*
Slivka, Andrew Paul Jr. *neurologist, physician*
Smail, Harry E(ugene) *environmental planner and administrator*
Smith, Ann Marie *rehabilitation nurse*
Smith, Eric Craig *construction executive*
Smith, George Curtis *judge*
Smith, George Leonard *industrial engineering educator*
Smith, Linda Sue *special education educator*
Smith, Marion Leroy *college dean emeritus, mechanical engineer*
Smith, Norman T. *lawyer*
Smith, Philip John *industrial and systems engineering educator*
Smith, R(obert) Michael *lawyer*
Soloway, Albert Herman *medicinal chemist*
Speck, Samuel Wallace, Jr. *academic administrator*
Speicher, Carl Eugene *pathologist*
Stallworth, Sam *television executive*
Steckel, Richard Hall *economist*
Stein, Jay Wobith *legal research and education consultant, mediator arbitrator*
Stephens, Sheryl Lynne *family practice physician*
Stephens, Thomas M(aron) *education educator*
Stephenson, David D. *journalist*
Stern, Geoffrey *lawyer, disciplinary counsel*
Stevenson, Robert Benjamin, III *prosthodontist, writer*
Stewart, Mac A. *educator*
Stinehart, Roger Ray *lawyer*
Stoner, Gary David *cancer researcher*
Stratton, Evelyn Lundberg *state supreme court justice*
Stratton, James Edward *construction educator*
Strode, George K. *sports editor*
Studer, William Joseph *library director*
Sullivan, Ernest Lee *human resources director*
Sully, Ira Bennett *lawyer*
Sunami, John Soichi *designer*
Sweeney, Asher William *state supreme court justice*
Sweeney, Francis E. *state supreme court justice*
Taaffe, Edward James *geography educator*
Tabor, Mary Leeba *literary magazine editor, author*
Taft, Bob *governor*
Taft, Sheldon Ashley *lawyer*
Taggart, Thomas Michael *lawyer*
Taiganides, E. Paul *agricultural and environmental engineer, consultant*
Tait, Robert E. *lawyer*
Tarpy, Thomas Michael *lawyer*
Taylor, Celianna Isley *information systems specialist*
Taylor, Joel Sanford *lawyer*
Teater, Dorothy Seath *county official*
Thomas, Duke Winston *lawyer*
Thompson, James W., Jr. *state official*
Tipton, Clyde Raymond, Jr. *communications and resources development consultant*
Todd, William Michael *lawyer*
Tornes, Virginia L. *retired nurse*
Traver, Noel Allen *small business owner, creative director*
Treneff, Craig Paul *lawyer*
Triplehorn, Charles A. *entomology educator, insects curator*
Tripp, Thomas Neal *lawyer, political consultant*
†Tsao, Chang Yong *pediatric neurologist*
Tuckman, Bruce Wayne *educational psychologist, educator, researcher*
Turano, David A. *lawyer*
Turchi, Peter John *aerospace and electrical engineer, educator*
Tzagournis, Manuel *physician, educator, university administrator*
Ultes, Elizabeth Cummings Bruce *artist, retired art historian and librarian*
Unverferth, Barbara Patten *small business owner*
Uotila, Urho Antti Kalevi *geodesist, educator*
†Upchurch, Carl Douglass *lecturer, consultant, columnist*
Vassell, Gregory S. *electric utility consultant*
Ventresca, Joseph Anthony *energy coordinator*
Vermilyea, Stanley George *prosthodontist, educator*
Viezer, Timothy Wayne *economist*
Vogel, Thomas Timothy *surgeon, health care consultant, lay church worker*
von Recum, Andreas F. *veterinarian, bioengineer*
Vorys, Arthur Isaiah *lawyer*
Voss, Anne Coble *nutritional biochemist*
Voss, Jerrold Richard *city planner, educator, university official*
Wagner, Robert Walter *photography, cinema and communications educator, media producer, consultant*
Wagoner, Robert Hall *engineering educator, researcher*
Waldron, Kenneth John *mechanical engineering educator, researcher*
Wali, Mohan Kishen *environmental science and natural resources educator*
Walker, Jewel Lee *health facility administrator, consultant*
Ware, Brendan John *retired electrical engineer and utility executive*
Warmbrod, James Robert *agriculture educator, university administrator*
Warner, Charles Collins *lawyer*
Watson, John Allan *clergyman*
Weaver, Leah Ann *journalist, speech writer*
†Webb, Kevin Roger *executive*
Webb, Thomas Evan *biochemistry educator*
Weinhold, Virginia Beamer *interior designer*
Weisberg, Herbert Frank *political science educator*
Weisgerber, David Wendelin *editor, chemist*
Wexner, Leslie Herbert *retail executive*
Whipps, Edward Franklin *lawyer*
Whitacre, Caroline Clement *immunologist, researcher*
Whitlatch, Elbert Earl, Jr. *engineering educator*
Wightman, Alec *lawyer*
Wigington, Ronald Lee *retired chemical information services executive*
Wilkins, John Warren *physics educator*
Williams, Gregory Howard *law educator, dean*
Willke, Thomas Aloys *university official, statistics educator*
Wiseman, Randolph Carson *lawyer*
Wojcicki, Andrew Adalbert *chemist, educator*
Wolf, John Steven *construction executive, land developer*
†Wong, Albert Y. *artist*
Wood, Jackie Dale *physiologist, educator, researcher*
Woods, Jo Ellen *medical technologist*
Wright, Harry, III *retired lawyer*
Yashon, David *neurosurgeon, educator*
Yeazel, Keith Arthur *lawyer*
Yenkin, Bernard Kalman *coatings and resins company executive*
†Yeo, Augustus C. *business and systems consultant*
Yohn, David Stewart *virologist, science administrator*
†Young, Thomas Beetham *writer*
Zakin, Jacques Louis *chemical engineering educator*
Zande, Richard Dominic *civil engineering firm executive*
Zapp, David Edwin *infosystems specialist, investment consultant*
Zartman, David Lester *animal sciences educator, researcher*

Concord
Conway, Neil James, III *title company executive, lawyer, writer*
Schremp, Pamela S. *nurse, risk manager, lawyer*

Conneaut
Strawbridge, Mary Elizabeth *English educator*

Continental
Dranchak, Lawrence John *retired mechanical engineer*

Copley
Pasini, Debbie Dobbins *nutrition support nurse*

Cortland
Lane, Sarah Marie Clark *elementary education educator*

Coshocton
Havelka, Thomas Edward *secondary education educator*
Parkhill, Harold Loyal *artist*

Crestline
Brouwer, Mark Nicholas *publisher, newspaper, retired*
Maddy, Janet Marie *retired educator, dean of students*

Cumberland
Reece, Robert William *zoological park administrator*

Cuyahoga Falls
Barsan, Robert Blake *dentist*
Haag, Everett Keith *architect*
Hamilton, Donald Dow Webb *publisher, freelance writer*
Hessler, William Gerhard *tax consultant*
Jones, John Frank *retired lawyer*
Moses, Abe Joseph *international financial consultant*
Ohm, Joseph Ronald *industrial designer*
Rothkin, Marilyn Mae *psychotherapist*
Thomas, Carol Todd *law firm administrator*

Dayton
Alexander, Roberta Sue *history educator*
Allen, Rose Letitia *special education educator*
Battino, Rubin *chemistry educator, retired*
Berra, P. Bruce *computer educator*
Betz, Eugene William *architect*
Bowman, Ed *school administrator*
Burick, Lawrence T. *lawyer*
†Carollo, Russell *journalist*
Cawood, Albert McLaurin (Hap Cawood) *newspaper editor*
Chait, William *librarian, consultant*
Chang, Jae Chan *hematologist, oncologist, educator*
Chernesky, Richard John *lawyer*
Chuck, Leon *materials scientist*
Clamme, Marvin Leslie *recording engineer, electronic engineer*
†Clark, William Alfred *federal judge*
Coil, Carolyn Chandler *educational consultant*
Conway, Mark Allyn *lawyer*
Cordasco, Martha Ann *therapist, social worker, consultant*
Cowden, Roger Hugh, II *systems engineer*
Crowe, Shelby *educational specialist, consultant*
Croyle, Barbara Ann *health care management executive*
Cruikshank, Stephen Herrick *physician, consultant*
Daley, Robert Emmett *foundation executive, retired*
Daoud, George Jamil *hotel and motel consultant*
DeWall, Richard Allison *retired surgeon*
Diggs, Matthew O'Brien, Jr. *air conditioning and refrigeration manufacturing executive*
Duncan, Richard Leo *communications educator*
Dunn, Margaret M. *general surgeon*
Duval, Daniel Webster *manufacturing company executive*
Elliott, Daniel Whitacre *surgeon, retired educator*
Enouen, William Albert *paper corporation executive*
Escalón Delgado, Clara S. *English language education specialist*
Fang, Zhaoqiang *research physicist*
Faruki, Charles Joseph *lawyer*
Finn, Chester Evans *lawyer*
Fitz, Brother Raymond L. *university president*
†Flack, Harley E. *university president*
Frydman, Paul *real estate broker and developer*
Garcia, Oscar Nicolas *computer science educator*
Gardner, Charles Clifford, Jr. *colorectal surgeon*
†Garrison, David Lee *language educator*
Gillen, Patrick Bernard *flight nurse*
Gittleman, Neal *orchestra conductor*
Goldenberg, Kim *university president, internist*
Gottschlich, Gary William *lawyer*
Hadley, Robert James *lawyer*
Halki, John Joseph *retired military officer, physician*
Hamlin, Tom *radio and television sportcaster, realtor*
Harden, Oleta Elizabeth *English educator, university administrator*
Harlan, Norman Ralph *construction executive*
Hayes, Stephen Kurtz *author*
Heath, Mariwyn Dwyer *writer, legislative issues consultant*
Heller, Abraham *psychiatrist, educator*
Henley, Terry Lew *computer company executive*
Hewes, Robert Charles *radiologist*
Heyman, Ralph Edmond *lawyer*
Hill, William E. *director technology services city government*
Hines, Jeff G. *environmental protection administrator*
Houpis, Constantine Harry *electrical engineering educator*
Isaacson, Milton Stanley *research and development company executive, engineer*
Jacobs, Richard E. *lawyer*
Janning, John Louis *research scientist, consultant*
†Jelus, Susan Crum *writer, editor*
Jenks, Thomas Edward *lawyer*
Johnson, C. Terry *lawyer*
Jones, Reginald Lorrin *clinical psychologist, consultant*
Kankey, Roland Doyle *academic administrator*
Kegerreis, Robert James *management consultant, marketing educator*
Kinlin, Donald James *lawyer*
Kinsey, Douglas Paul *insurance agent, financial planner*
Klinck, Cynthia Anne *library director*
Knapp, James Ian Keith *judge*
Koeller, Lynn Garver *public defender*
†Koubek, Richard John *engineering educator*
Ladehoff, Leo William *metal products manufacturing executive*
Laird, John *photographer*
Lamont, Gary Byron *electrical engineer*
Lashley, William Bartholomew *county official*
Lasley, Thomas J., II *education educator*
Lechner, George William *surgeon*
Lentz, Linda Kay *school psychologist, learning disability educator*
Lockhart, Gregory Gordon *lawyer*
†Lowe, Ronald, Sr. *chief of police*
Macklin, Crofford Johnson, Jr. *lawyer*
Maher, Frank Aloysius *research and development executive, psychologist*
Mandal, Anil Kumar *nephrologist, medical educator*
†Martin, Herbert Woodward *English educator, poet*
Martin, James Gilbert *university provost emeritus*
Matheny, Ruth Ann *editor*
Mathews, David *foundation executive*
Mathile, Clayton Lee *corporate executive*
†McCormick, Patti Leona *holistic health educator, nurse*
McCutcheon, Holly Marie *accountant*
McIntosh, Linda Clair *special education program specialist*
McSwiney, Charles Ronald *lawyer*
Mc Swiney, James Wilmer *retired pulp and paper manufacturing company executive*
Merz, Michael *federal judge*
Miles, Alfred Lee *real estate broker, educator*
Mohler, Stanley Ross *physician, educator*
Monk, Susan Marie *physician, pediatrician*
Morris, John Steven *marketing professional*
†Mullins, Robert P. *educator*
Nanagas, Maria Teresita Cruz *pediatrician, educator*
Nevin, Robert Charles *information systems executive*
Nicholson, Mark William *lawyer*
Nielsen, Philip Edward *physicist, research manager*
Nixon, Charles William *bioacoustician*
Nyberg, Lars *company executive*
Nyerges, Alexander Lee *museum director*
Paden, Kimbra Lea Kahle *medical/surgical nurse*
Pajak, Michael E. *mechanical engineer*
Peterson, Skip (Orley R. Peterson, III) *newspaper photographer*
Pflum, Barbara Ann *pediatric allergist*
Phillips, Chandler Allen *biomedical engineer*
Ponitz, David H. *academic administrator*
Poseidon, Pantelis Lee *marketing and product executive*
Posey, Terry Wayne *lawyer*
†Pringle, Mary Beth *educator, writer*
Randall, Vernellia *lawyer, nurse, educator*
Rapp, Gerald Duane *lawyer, manufacturing company executive*
Reading, Anthony John *business executive, accountant*
Reid, Marilyn Joanne *state legislator, lawyer*
Repperger, Daniel William *electrical engineer*
Riley, David Richard *management consultant, retired military officer*
Roberts, Brian Michael *lawyer*
Robinson, Gregory Alan *practice management executive*
Rogers, Richard Hunter *lawyer, business executive*
Rucker, Richard Sim *information systems executive*
Ruffer, David Gray *museum director, former college president*
Saul, Irving Isaac *lawyer*
Savage, Joseph Scott *physician*
Schmitt, George Frederick, Jr. *materials engineer*
Schnier, David Christian *marketing executive, author*
Schwartzhoff, James Paul *foundation executive*
Sessler, Albert Louis, Jr. *lawyer*
Shaw, George Bernard *consulting engineer, educator*
Shuey, John Henry *diversified products company executive*
†Sifferlen, Ned *university president*
Singhvi, Surendra Singh *finance and strategy consultant*
Staker, Robert Dale *cost analyst, computer scientist, biologist, educator*
Stefanics, Charlotte Louise *clinical nurse specialist, retired*
Stout, Donald Everett *real estate developer, environmental preservationist*
Sweeney, James Lee *retired government official*
Tan, Seng C. *research scientist, materials research executive*
Taronji, Jaime, Jr. *lawyer*
Tatar, Jerome F. *business products executive*
Taylor, Elisabeth Coler *secondary school educator*
Thomas, Marianna *volunteer community activist, writer, speaker*
Tillson, John Bradford, Jr. *newspaper publisher*
Twale, Darla Jean *education educator*
Uphoff, James Kent *education educator*
Vaughan, David Kirk *aviation educator*
Vice, Roy Lee *history educator*
Von Gierke, Henning Edgar *biomedical science educator, former government official, researcher*
†Waldron, Thomas F. *federal judge*
Walters, Jefferson Brooks *musician, retired real estate broker*
Walusis, Eric M. *product developer, consultant*
Watts, Steven Richard *lawyer*
Weathington, Billy Christopher *analytical chemist*
Weinberg, Sylvan Lee *cardiologist, educator, author, editor*
Wertz, Kenneth Dean *real estate executive*
Whitlock, David C. *retired military officer*
Wichman, Edna Carol *media specialist, librarian*
Wightman, Ann *lawyer*
Wilkins, John *graphic designer*
Williams, Charles Vernon, III *education administrator*
Williams, Clarence E. *muncipal official*
Williams, Michael Alan *psychologist*
Wilson, Jack *advertising executive*
Wilson, Robert M. *financial executive*
Wilson, William C.M. *gastroenterologist*
Yeager, Tamara Layne *educational association executive*
Yerkeson, Douglas Alan *lawyer*
Zahner, Mary Anne *art educator*

Defiance
Harris, James Thomas, III *college administrator, educator*
Kane, Jack Allison *physician, county administrator*
Slocum, Lori Sue *secondary school educator*

Delaware
Courtice, Thomas Barr *academic administrator*
Eells, William Hastings *retired automobile company executive*
Faerber, Abigail Hobbs *physician, farm manager*
Fry, Anne Evans *zoology educator*
Gierhart, Mary Kelbley *school psychologist*
Hamre, Gary Leslie William *entrepreneur*
Jamison, Roger W. *pianist, piano educator*
Kraus, John D. *electrical engineer, educator*
Lattimore, Vergel Lyronne *minister, educator, counselor*
Lewes, Ulle Erika *English educator*
Pettigrew, Carolyn Landers *theological school official, minister*
Schlichting, Catherine Fletcher Nicholson *librarian, educator*

Delphos
Clark, Edward Ferdnand *lawyer*
Staup, John Gary *safety engineer*

Delta
Miller, Beverly White *past college president, education consultation*
Monahan, Leonard Francis *musician, singer, composer, publisher*
Rees, Erica Sue *insurance company executive*

Dover
Hamilton, Beverly Edith *former nurse educator*
Miller, Mary Katherine *management consultant*

Dublin
Baker, Mary Evelyn *church librarian, retired academic librarian*
†Bennett, George H., Jr. *lawyer, healthcare company executive*
Bennett, Steven Alan *lawyer*
Bordelon, Carolyn Thew *elementary school educator*
Borror, Donald A. *construction company executive*
Borror, Douglas G. *construction company executive*
Brooks, Keith *retired speech communication educator*
Childress, Eric Rogers *librarian, consultant, metadata specialist*
Clement, Henry Joseph, Jr. *diversified building products executive*
Conrad, Marian Sue (Susan Conrad) *special education educator*

Cornwell, Paul M., Jr. *architect*
Dugan, Charles Francis, II *lawyer*
Freytag, Donald Ashe *management consultant*
Hagar, Jack *mathematics and science educator*
Heneman, Robert Lloyd *management educator*
Inzetta, Mark Stephen *lawyer*
Lamp, Benson J. *tractor company executive*
Madigan, Joseph Edward *financial executive, consultant, director*
Major, Coleman Joseph *chemical engineer*
McCauley, William Albert *business executive*
McCormick, William Edward *environmental consultant*
Miller, Charles *business management research and measurements consultant*
†Mullen, Thomas J. *mortgage company executive*
Needham, George Michael *association executive*
Smith, K(ermit) Wayne *computer company executive*
Spies, Phyllis Bova *information services company executive*
Tenuta, Luigia *lawyer*
Walter, Robert D. *wholesale pharmaceutical distribution executive*

Duncan Falls
Cooper, April Helen *nurse*

East Cleveland
Soule, Lucile Snyder *pianist, music educator*

East Liverpool
Ash, Thomas Phillip *superintendent of schools*
Feldman, Marvin Herschel *financial consultant*

East Palestine
Patterson, Paula Jeanne *secondary education educator*

Eastlake
Kerata, Joseph J. *secondary education educator*
Spohn, Wayne Robert *mechanical engineer*

Eaton
Bennett, Herd Leon *lawyer*
Thomas, James William *lawyer*

Edgerton
Wu, Lawrence Mg Hla Myin *physician*

Elmore
†Huizenga, Georgiana R. *public library director, storyteller*

Elyria
Burrell, Joel Brion *neurologist, researcher, clinician*
Dunaevsky, Valery *mechanical engineer, researcher*
Eady, Carol Murphy (Mrs. Karl Ernest Eady) *retired medical association administrator*
Hughes, Kenneth G. *elementary school educator*
Patton, Thomas James *sales and marketing executive*
Schrott, Janet Ann *human resources specialist, consultant*
Stefanik, Janet Ruth *realtor*
Wood, Jacalyn Kay *education educator, educational consultant*

Englewood
Shearer, Velma Miller *clergywoman*

Euclid
Arko, John David *transportation company driver*
Convery, Patrick George *orthopedic surgeon*
Taylor, Theresa Evereth *registered nurse, artist*

Fairborn
Beer, Daniel Jackson *sales executive*
Byczkowski, Janusz Zbigniew *toxicologist*
Conklin, Robert Eugene *electronics engineer*
Davis, Kathy *critical care nurse*
Lawlis, Patricia Kite *air force officer, computer consultant*
Miller, Kenneth Gregory *retired air force officer*
Nowak, John Michael *retired air force officer, company executive*
Roach, B. Randall *lawyer, city council member*
Workman, John Mitchell *chemist*

Fairfield
Cutter, John Michael *dentist*
Rafalowski, Raymond Victor *printing and publishing executive*
Robertson, Oscar Palmer (Big O Robertson) *chemical company executive, former professional basketball player*
Royer, Thomas Jerry *financial planner*

Fairlawn
Brubaker, Karen Sue *manufacturing executive*

Fairview Park
Bellamy, John Stark, II *librarian*
Condon, George Edward *journalist*

Findlay
Jetton, Girard Reuel, Jr. *lawyer, retired oil company executive*
Kostyo, John Francis *lawyer*
Moore, Nick Alan *information systems specialist, consultant*
Musser, Saundra Jeanne (Berry) *music educator, composer*
Peters, Milton Eugene *educational psychologist*
Resseguie, James Lynn *theology educator*
Sipes, Theodore Lee *educator*
Stephani, Nancy Jean *social worker, journalist*
Wallen, Raeburn Glenn *religion educator*
Wilkin, Richard Edwin *clergyman, religious organization executive*
Yammine, Riad Nassif *retired oil company executive*

Fostoria
Howard, Kathleen *computer company executive*

Franklin
Foley, Harriet Elizabeth Fealy *retired school librarian*
Murray, Thomas Dwight *advertising agency executive*
Wilkey, Mary Huff *investor, writer, publisher*
Withrow, Sheila Kay *school nurse*

Fremont
Bridges, Roger Dean *historical agency administrator*
Johnson, Laurence F. *college executive*
Recktenwald, Fred William *financial executive*
Sattler, Nancy Joan *educational administrator*
Smith, Bradley Jason *lawyer, recreational facility owner*

Fulton
McCloskey, Katherine Mary *retired office manager*

Gahanna
†Douglas, James (Buster) *boxer*
Kaye, Gail Leslie *healthcare consultant, educator*
Robbins, Darryl Andrew *pediatrician*

Galion
Butterfield, James T. *small business owner*
Cobey, Ralph *industrialist*
Ross, Shirley S. *retired English educator*

Gallipolis
Clarke, Oscar Withers *physician*
Cremeans, Frank A. *former congressman*
Medley, William S. *municipal judge*
†Mingus, Deborah Lynn *treasurer*
Niehm, Bernard Frank *mental health center administrator, retired*
Senthil Nathan, Selvaraj *internist, geriatrician*

Gambier
†Daugherty, Craig A. *college financial aid director*
Guiney, Mortimer Martin *French educator*
Macionis, John Johnston *professor, writer*
†Oden, Robert A., Jr. *college president*
Sharp, Ronald Alan *English literature educator, author*
†Will, Katherine H. *university administrator*

Garfield Heights
Chamberlin, Joan Mary *assistant principal, academic services director*
De Piero, Nicholas Gabriel *anesthesiologist*

Garrettsville
Diskin, Michael Edward *plastics industry executive*

Gates Mills
Abbott, James Samuel, III *marketing executive*
Altman, Leslie Joan *secondary school educator*
Enyedy, Gustav, Jr. *chemical engineer*
†Lazos, Stergios John *secondary education educator*
Obloy, Leonard Gerard *priest*
O'Malley, Mary Kay *elementary education educator*
Pace, Stanley Carter *retired aeronautical engineer*
Reitman, Robert Stanley *manufacturing and marketing executive*
Veale, Tinkham, II *former chemical company executive, engineer*

Geneva
Foote, David Ward, Jr. *insurance agency executive*
†Reed, Roger Duane *maintenance technician*

Georgetown
Conway, Dorothy Jean Williams *economist*
Frame, Lawrence Milven, Jr. *inventor*

Germantown
Lansaw, Charles Ray *sales industry executive*

Girard
Gaylord, Sanford Fred *physician*

Gnadenhutten
McKeown, Barbara *curator*

Grand River
Abel, Mary Ellen Kathryn *quality control executive, chemist*

Granville
†Bonar, Daniel Donald *mathematics educator*
Haubrich, Robert Rice *biology educator*
Lisska, Anthony Joseph *humanities educator, philosopher*
†Oliva, Maurizio *computer technologist*
Pollard, Jeffrey Wallace *college counseling, health services director*
Santoni, Ronald Ernest *philosophy educator*
†Sinsabaugh, Joseph Charles *airline pilot*
†Townsend, Ann C. *poet, English educator*
Woodyard, David Oliver *religious studies educator, clergy member*

Greenville
Franz, Daniel Thomas *financial planner*
King, Charles Homer *manufacturing executive*

Grove City
Jackson, Steven Donald *English educator*
Kilman, James William *surgeon, educator*
Lok, Silmond Ray *pharmaceutical executive*
Purdy, Dennis Gene *insurance company executive, education consultant*

Groveport
Keck, Vicki Lynn *special education educator*
Ricart, Fred *automotive company executive*

Hamilton
Earley, Kathleen Sanders *municipal official*
Fein, Linda Ann *nurse anesthetist, consultant*
Fein, Thomas Paul *software support specialist*
Ferng, Douglas Ming-Haw *infosystems executive*
James, Ronald Bruce *journalist*
†Jones, Rick H. *arts administrator*
†Krafft, John M. *English educator, editor*
Marcum, Joseph LaRue *insurance company executive*
New, Rosetta Holbrock *home economics educator, nutrition consultant*
Pontius, Stanley N. *bank holding company executive*
Royer, Diana Amelia *educator*
Sebastian, Sandra Mary Thompson *clinical counselor, social worker*
†Zahner, Anne Colette *preschool educator*

Harrison
Coakley, Janet Marie *English educator, consultant creative arts theater*

†Cron, Marc C. *secondary education educator*
Kocher, Juanita Fay *retired auditor*
Stoll, Robert W. *principal*
Wuest, Larry Carl *tax examiner*

Heath
Gregorich, Penny Denise *purchasing agent*

Hebron
Slater, Wanda Marie Worth *rental property manager*

Helena
Moss, Clifton Michael *factory laborer, small business owner*

Highland Hills
Brathwaite, Ormond Dennis *chemistry educator*
Zahs, David Karl *secondary school educator, educational administrator*

Hilliard
Cash, Francis Winford *hotel industry executive*
Cupp, David Foster *photographer, journalist*
†Herta, Bryan *race car driver*
Price, Virginia Ashbaugh *technical service director, workers compensation c*
Rahal, Robert W. *automotive company executive*
Relle, Attila Tibor *dentist, geriodontist*

Hillsboro
Snyder, Harry Cooper *retired state senator*

Hiram
Jagow, Elmer *retired college president*
Oliver, G(eorge) Benjamin *educational administrator, philosophy educator*
Rose, Jane Preston *dean*

Holland
D'Anniballe, Priscilla Lucille *contracting company executive*
Hirsch, Carl Herbert *retired manufacturing company executive*
Sippo, Arthur Carmine *occupational medicine physician*

Holmesville
Bolender, James Henry *tire and rubber manufacturing executive*

Howard
Lee, William Johnson *lawyer*

Hubbard
Ehrlich, Lawrence *retired cantor, educator*
Vukovich, Ruth Ann *secondary educator*

Hudson
Antonucci, Ron *librarian, editor*
Ashcroft, Richard Carter *controller*
Bell, Harry Edward *quality consulting company executive*
Duchon, Roseann Marie *business owner, consultant*
Ellis, Christine Jo *middle school educator*
Galloway, Ethan Charles *technology development executive, former chemicals executive*
Gardiner, Stephanie Joann *staff office nurse, endoscopy nurse*
Giffen, Daniel Harris *lawyer, educator*
Kempe, Robert Aron *venture management executive*
Ong, John Doyle *retired lawyer*
Shaw, Doris Beaumar *film and video producer, executive recruiter*
Sorgi, Mercedes Prieto *psychologist*
Stec, John Zygmunt *real estate executive*
Wilfong, Brenda A. *telecommunications executive*
Wooldredge, William Dunbar *health facility administrator*

Huron
†Brownlow, Wilfred J. *retired physician*
†Herdendorf, Charles Edward, III *retired oceanographer, limnologist, consultant*
Ruble, Ronald Merlin *humanities and theater communications educator*

Independence
Jenson, Jon Eberdt *association executive*
Pesec, David John *data systems executive*
Schwallie, Daniel Phillip *legal consultant*

Ironton
Cremeans, James L. *minister*
Murnahan, Vera Mae *elementary school educator*
Nourse, Michael Duane *special education educator*

Jackson
Benson, Steven Clark *man ment and engineering executive*

Jackson Center
Thompson, Wade Francis Bruce *manufacturing company executive*

Jacksontown
Schultz, Charles Edward *state official*

Jefferson
Gibbs, Arland LaVerne *retired real estate agent*
Macklin, Martin Rodbell *psychiatrist*

Kent
Aleman, Mindy R. *advertising and public relations consultant, marketing and development executive, newspaper columnist, freelance writer*
Bancik, Steven Charles *information specialist, researcher*
Beer, Barrett Lynn *historian, educator*
Bissler, Richard Thomas *mortician*
Buttlar, Rudolph Otto *retired college dean*
Byrne, Frank Loyola *history educator*
Cartwright, Carol Ann *university president*
Centuori, Jeanine Gail *architecture educator*
Cooperrider, Tom S. *botanist*
Cummins, Kenneth Burdette *retired science and mathematics educator*
Doane, J. William *physics educator and researcher, science administrator*
Dzeda, Bruce Michael *history educator*
Feinberg, Richard *anthropologist, educator*
†Floyd, Kevin R. *English educator*

Fontes, Manuel Da Costa *foreign language educator*
†Hakutani, Yoshinobu *English educator*
Hassler, Donald Mackey, II *English language educator, writer*
Heimlich, Richard Allen *geologist, educator*
Hilliard, Bonnie Jean *writer, editor*
James, Patricia Ann *philosophy educator*
†Keller, John David *earth science educator*
Kline, Vicki Ann *investment consultant*
Kwong, Eva *artist, educator*
Lindsay, Bob *basketball coach*
McKee, David Lannen *economics educator*
Myers, R(alph) Thomas *chemist, educator*
Nguyen, Phong Thuyet *ethnomusicologist, musician, educator*
Nome, William Andreas *lawyer*
Pees, Russell Dean *coach*
†Prioleau, Darwin E. *dance educator, choreographer*
Reid, Sidney Webb *English educator*
†Remley, R. Dirk *English educator, consultant*
Schwartz, Michael *university president, sociology educator*
Sommers, David Lynn *architect*
Stevenson, Thomas Herbert *management consultant, writer*
Thapar, Neela *geographer*
Tuan, Debbie Fu-Tai *chemistry educator*
Varga, Richard Steven *mathematics educator*
Williams, Harold Roger *economist, educator*

Kenton
Petty, Sue Wright

Kettering
Clark, Leland Charles, Jr. *biochemist, medical products executive*
Denlinger, Vicki Lee *secondary school physical education educator*
Horn, Charles F. *state senator, lawyer, electrical engineer*
Kwiatek, Kim David *emergency physician*
Mantil, Joseph Chacko *nuclear medicine physician, researcher*
Porter, Walter Arthur *retired judge*
Purdy, John Edgar *manufacturing company executive*
Seto, Ken Hon *consultant, small business owner*

Kimbolton
†Thomas, Richard Duane *artist*

Kingston
Mathew, Martha Sue Cryder *retired education educator*

Kirtland
Johnston, Stanley Howard, Jr. *curator of rare books, bibliographer*
Munson, Richard Howard *horticulturist*
Rebolj, Joan Kaletta *language educator*
Ryan, William Joseph *multimedia and distance education designer*

LaGrange
Kaatz, Lynn Robert *artist, graphic designer*

Lakeside
Mead, Millard Wilmer *retired minister*

Lakewood
Bradley, J. F., Jr. *retired manufacturing company executive*
Brodhead, Thomas McCourtney *music engraver, computer programmer*
Chabek, Daniel James *journalist, writer, public relations professional*
Schultz, Joann Thomas *clinical nurse specialist*
Smith, Marvin D. *artist*

Lancaster
Burns, Glenn Richard *dentist*
Fox, Robert Kriegbaum *manufacturing company executive*
Hurley, Samuel Clay, III *investment management company executive*
Katlic, John Edward *management consultant*
Libert, Donald Joseph *lawyer*
Phillips, Edward John *consulting firm executive*
Phillips, Karen Ann *psychiatric-mental health nurse*
Rusk, Karla Marie *nurse practitioner*
Sulick, Robert John *general contractor*
Varney, Richard Alan *medical office manager*
Voss, Jack Donald *international business consultant, lawyer*
Young, Nancy Henrietta Moe *retired elementary education educator*

Lebanon
Hollett, Grant T. *career officer*
Osborne, Quinton Albert *psychiatric social worker, inspector of institutional services*

Lewis Center
Strip, Carol Ann *gifted education specialist, educator*

Liberty Center
Jones, Marlene Ann *family and consumer sciences educator*

Liberty Township
Bartlett, Shirley Anne *accountant*
Conditt, Margaret Karen *scientist, policy analyst*

Lima
Becker, Dwight Lowell *physician*
Collins, William Thomas *retired pathologist*
Couts, Rose Marie *medical radiographer, sonographer*
Cupp, Robert Richard *state senator, attorney*
Fisher, Glenn Duane *small business executive*
Jacobs, Ann Elizabeth *lawyer*
Johnson, Patricia Lyn *mathematics educator*
†Lucente, Thomas John, Jr. *editor*
Miller, Roy Raymond *optician, ocularist*
Palmer, Arthur Eugene *nursing home administrator*
Pranses, Anthony Louis *retired electric company executive, organization executive*
Robenalt, John Alton *lawyer*

Lisbon
Dailey, Coleen Hall *lawyer, judge*

Lodi
Berry, Beverly A. *real estate investment executive*
Bock, Carolyn A. *author, consultant, trainer, small business owner*
Cox, Hillery Lee *primary school educator*

Logan
Carmean, Jerry Richard *broadcast engineer*
Conner, Leland Lavon *Indian lorist*

London
Hughes, Clyde Matthew *religious denomination executive*
Wiley, Jerold Wayne *environmental services executive, retired air force officer*

Lorain
Bado, Kenneth Steve *automotive company administrator*
Buzas, John William *hospital administrator, surgical nurse*
Quinn, Alexander James *bishop*
Shimandle, Sharon Anne *critical care nurse*

Loveland
Dalambakis, Christopher A. *workplace performance consultant*
Glover, Robert Caldwell *computer graphics specialist, artist*
Grimmet, Alex J. *clergyman, school administrator, elementary and secondary education educator*
McCoy, John Joseph *lawyer*
Newton, Baldwin Charles *artist, educator*
Reynolds, Robert Gregory *toxicologist, management consultant*

Lucasville
Reno, Ottie Wayne *former judge*

Lyndhurst
Kastner, Christine Kriha *newspaper correspondent*
Sevin, Eugene *engineer, consultant, educator*

Lynx
Watters, Cora Tula *musician*

Macedonia
Szczurek, Thomas Eugene *marketing executive*

Madison
Stafford, Arthur Charles *medical association administrator*

Magnolia
Zimmerman, Judith Rose *elementary art educator*

Maineville
Collins, Larry Wayne *small business owner, information systems specialist*
Laybourne, George Thomas *scientist, quality control engineer, consultant*

Mansfield
Adair, Charles Valloyd *retired physician*
Amadio-Backowski, Therese Marie *small business owner*
Beiter, Thomas Albert *crystallographer, research scientist, consultant*
Benham, Lelia *small business owner, social/political activist*
Bogart, Keith Charles *neurologist*
Capaldo, Guy *obstetrician, gynecologist*
Crittenden, Sophie Marie *communications executive*
†Dominick, Raymond Hunter, III *history educator*
Ellison, Lorin Bruce *management consultant*
Gorman, James Carvill *pump manufacturing company executive*
Granter, Sharon Savoy *restaurateur, caterer*
Gregory, Deirdre Dianne *secondary educator*
Gregory, Thomas Bradford *mathematics educator*
Haldar, Frances Louise *business educator, accountant, treasurer*
Hartman, Ruth Ann *educator*
Hooker, James Todd *manufacturing executive*
Houston, William Robert Montgomery *ophthalmic surgeon*
Nordstrom, Walter Erick *communications consultant*
Prater, Willis Richard *county government agency official*
Reese, Wina Harner *speech pathologist, consultant*
Reynolds Westerfelt, Debra Kay *education educator, consultant*
Riedl, John Orth *university dean*
Shah, James M. *actuarial consultant*
Stander, Richard Ramsay, Sr. *retired civil engineer and construction engineer*
†Wheeler, Joyce Nadine *child care company professional*

Mantua
Ray, James Allen *research consultant*

Marblehead
Haering, Edwin Raymond *chemical engineering educator, consultant*

Marietta
†Dixon, Carol Ann *writer, educator*
Fields, William Albert *lawyer*
O'Connor, Ginger Hobba *speech pathologist*
Wilbanks, Jan Joseph *philosopher*
Wilson, Lauren Ross *academic administrator*

Marion
Badertscher, Doris Rae *elementary education educator*
Lim, Shun Ping *cardiologist*
Rogers, Richard Michael *judge*
Rowe, Lisa Dawn *computer programmer/analyst, computer consultant*
Tozzer, Jack Carl *civil engineer, surveyor*

Marysville
Baik-Kromalic, Sue S. *metallurgical engineer*
Berger, Charles Martin *food company executive*
Covault, LLoyd R., Jr. *retired hospital administrator, psychiatrist*
Jones-Morton, Pamela *human resources specialist*

Mason
Clements, Michael Craig *health services consulting executive, retired renal dialysis technician*
Colson, Anny-Odile *chemist*
Drees, Stephen Daniel *financial services executive, strategy, marketing and product development executive*
Erbe, Janet Sue *medical surgical, orthopedics and pediatrics nurse*
Leusch, Mark Steven *microbiologist*
Liedhegner, Barbara Griffin *pediatrics and surgical nurse*
†Meyer, Joan M. *drug researcher*
Nichols, Dennis Arnold *newspaper editor*
Roemer, John Alan *financial executive*

Masonnnati
Wilson, Frederic Sandford *pharmaceutical company executive*

Massillon
Dawson, Robert Earle *utilities executive*
Fogle, Marilyn Louise Kiplinger *hospital administrator*
Lawrence, Alice Lauffer *artist, educator*
Snyder, Rachel Ann *manufacturing company specialist*
Vaughn, Lisa Dawn *physician, educator*
Walker, James William *secondary education educator, freelance writer*

Masury
Wagner, Julie Ann *newspaper designer*

Materials Park
Putnam, Allan Ray *association executive*

Maumee
Anderson, Richard Paul *agricultural company executive*
Kline, James Edward *lawyer*
Marsh, Benjamin Franklin *lawyer*
Mohler, Terence John *psychologist*
Musa, Mahmoud Nimir *psychiatry educator*
Nowak, Patricia Rose *advertising executive*
Oakes, Frank Leslie, Jr. *retired insurance agency executive*
Pauken, Stephen J. *mayor*
Sacksteder, Thomas M. *corporate executive, entrepreneur, writer*
Seymour, Dale Joseph *insurance company executive*
Tigges, Kenneth Edwin *retired financial executive*
Yeager, Robert Julius *priest, financial consultant*

Mayfield Heights
Newman, Joseph Herzl *advertising consultant*
Rankin, Alfred Marshall, Jr. *business executive*

Mechanicsburg
Maynard, Joan *education educator*

Medina
Ballard, John Stuart *retired educator, former mayor, former lawyer*
Batchelder, Alice M. *federal judge*
†Foster, David Ben *creative writing educator, freelance writer*
Meacher, Earl Robert *vocational educator*
Noreika, Joseph Casimir *ophthalmologist*
Prakup, Barbara Lynn *communications executive*
Smith, Richey *chemical company executive*
Steinmetz, Robert Francis *lawyer*
Sullivan, Thomas Christopher *coatings company executive*
Walcott, Robert *healthcare executive, priest*

Mentor
Andrassy, Timothy Francis *trade association executive*
Core, Harry Michael *psychiatric social worker, mental health therapist and administrator*
Driggs, Charles Mulford *lawyer*
Miller, Frances Suzanne *historic site curator*
Russell, Brenda Sue *critical care nurse*
Towns, Gregory Wayne *elementary educator*
Traub, Ronald Matthew *municipal administrator*

Miamisburg
†Brown, Paul William *publishing executive*
Byrd, James Everett *lawyer*
Dalrymple, Cheryl *online information company executive*
Davies, Tim *online information company executive*
Gieskes, Hans *information services and publishing executive*
Lucius, Mary Albus *dietitian*
Michaelis, Betty Jane *sculptor, retired small business owner*
Peterson, George P. *mechanical engineer, research and development firm executive*
Tozer, Theodore William *mortgage company executive*
Yakura, Thelma Pauline *retired library director, consultant, writer*

Middleburg Heights
Hazlett, Paul Edward *realtor, information systems executive*
Maciuszko, Kathleen Lynn *librarian, educator*

Middletown
†Combopiano, Charles Angelo *opera company executive*
Gilby, Steve *metallurgical engineering researcher*
Gordon, Sandy Gale Combs *medical surgical nurse, community health nurse*
Kohler, Edith A. *senior citizen's organization executive*
Marine, Susan Sonchik *analytical chemist, educator*
McClain, Michael H. *writer*
Newby, John Robert *metallurgical engineer*
Powell, Stephen Walter *judge*
Rathman, William Ernest *lawyer, minister*
Rhein, Thomas Anthony *recreational facility administrator*
Schaefer, Patricia Ann *retired librarian*

Milan
Henry, Joseph Patrick *chemical company executive*

Milford
Comstock, Walter *biologist, educator*
Conover, Nellie Coburn *retail furniture company executive*
Creath, Curtis Janssen *pediatric dentist*
Donahue, John Lawrence, Jr. *paper company executive*
Fite, Myra J. Cropper *critical care nurse*
Humbert, Cheryl Ann *field nurse*
Kenner, Carole Ann *nursing educator*
Klosterman, Albert Leonard *technical development business executive, mechanical engineer*
Shipley, Tony L(ee) *software company executive*
Vorholt, Jeffrey Joseph *lawyer, software company executive*
Zimov, Bruce Steven *software engineer*

Miller City
Raudabaugh, James Eugene *secondary education educator*

Millersport
Thogmartin, Mark Bruce *elementary education educator, writer*

Minerva
Martin, Robert Dale *lawyer*

Mogadore
Kelly, Janice Helen *elementary school educator*

Montpelier
Deckrosh, Hazen Douglas *retired state agency educator and administrator*

Moreland Hills
Hardie, James Carl *college administrator*
Tolchinsky, Paul Dean *organization design psychologist*

Mount Gilead
Gress, Allen E. *newspaper editor*

Mount Vernon
†Bennett, Marguerite M. *college administrator, mathematics educator*
Meharry, Ronald Lee *real estate investor, inn keeper*
Nease, Stephen Wesley *college president*
Shriver, William Russell *secondary education educator*
Turner, Harry Edward *lawyer*

Munroe Falls
Stahl, Steve Allen *protective services official*

Navarre
Monroe, Kevin Anthony *municipal official*

New Albany
Brown, Michael Richard *minister*
Kessler, John Whitaker *real estate developer*

New Bremen
Dicke, James Frederick, II *manufacturing company executive*
Wierwille, Marsha Louise *elementary education educator*

New Carlisle
Bowlin, Gloria Jean *artist*
Hansford, Larry Clarence *computer consultant company executive*
Leffler, Carole Elizabeth *mental health nurse, women's health nurse*

New Concord
Brown, Karen Rima *orchestra manager, Spanish language educator*
Van Tassel, Daniel Ellsworth *academic administrator, consultant, educator*

New Middletown
Ade, Barbara Jean *secondary education educator*

New Philadelphia
Goforth, Mary Elaine Davey *secondary education educator*
Lazar, Mary Diane *English educator*
Mears, Orum Glenn, III *automotive executive*
Robinson, Scott Alan *social services administrator*

New Richmond
Menke, William Charles *lawyer*
Reynolds, Ronald Davison *family physician*
Scott, Michael Lester *artist, educator*

New Vienna
Howell, Michelle Elane Davis *educator*

Newark
Fortaleza, Judith Ann *school system administrator*
Green, John David *engineering executive*
Hopson, James Warren *publishing executive*
Manning, Ronald Lee *banker*
Mantonya, John Butcher *lawyer*
McConnell, William Thompson *commercial banker*
Paul, Rochelle Carole *special education educator*
Reidy, Thomas Anthony *lawyer*
Van Dervort, Sharyn L. *secondary education educator*

Newton Falls
Old, Thomas Leigh *judge*

Niles
Cornell, William Harvey *clergyman*
Markovich-Lytle, Darlene A. *author*
Rizer, Janet Marlene *city tax administrator*

North Canton
Foster, James Caldwell *academic dean, historian*
Jackson, David Lee *real estate executive*
Lynham, C(harles) Richard *foundry company executive*
Malcolm, Douglas Raymond *insurance agent, business consultant*
Patton, June G. *oncology nurse, educator*
Rodriguez, Irene Tobias *artist, art educator*
Watkins, Carolyn A. *retired nursing administrator, nursing educator*

North Olmsted
Brady, Michael Cameron *investment consultant*
Galysh, Robert Alan *information systems analyst*
Lundin, Bruce Theodore *engineering and management consultant*
Middleton, Mary *secondary education educator*
Smolen, Cheryl Hosaka *special education educator*

North Ridgeville
Baughman, Dennis John *director of operations service*
Rehm, John Edwin *manufacturing company executive*

North Royalton
Iacobelli, Mark Anthony *dentist*
Jungeberg, Thomas Donald *lawyer*

Northfield
Buzzelli, Charlotte Grace *educator*

Norton
Kun, Joyce Anne *secondary education educator, small business owner*

Norwalk
Germann, Richard Paul *pharmaceutical company chemist, executive*
Gutowicz, Matthew Francis, Jr. *radiologist*
Holman, William Baker *surgeon, coroner*

Norwood
Tubbs, Robin Lee *secondary education educator*

Oberlin
Blodgett, Geoffrey Thomas *history educator*
Boe, David Stephen *musician, educator, college dean*
Brown, John Lott *educator*
Care, Norman Sydney *philosophy educator*
Carlton, Terry Scott *chemist, educator*
Cartier, Brian Evans *association executive*
Colish, Marcia Lillian *history educator*
Collins, Martha *English language educator, writer*
Cooke, Lloyd Miller *former organization executive*
Dye, Nancy Schrom *academic administrator, history educator*
English, Ray *library administrator*
Friedman, William John *psychology educator*
†Hernton, Calvin Coolidge *African American studies educator, artist, writer*
Layman, Emma McCloy (Mrs. James W. Layman) *psychologist, educator*
MacKay, Alfred F. *dean, philosophy educator*
MacKay, Gladys Godfrey *adult education educator*
Polivnick, Paul *conductor, music director*
Reinoehl, Richard Louis *artist, scholar, martial artist*
Simonson, Bruce Miller *geologist, educator*
Taylor, Gail Richardson *civic worker, lawyer, former university official*
Taylor, Richard Wirth *political science educator*
†Vujavic, Veljko *sociology educator*
Warner, Robert Edson *physics educator*
Weinstock, Robert *physics educator*
Young, David Pollock *humanities educator, author*
Zinn, Grover Alfonso, Jr. *religion educator*

Okeana
Bloch, Rosemarie *artist, musician*

Olmsted Falls
Kiessling, Ronald Frederick *retired federal government executive*

Oregon
Crain, John Kip *school system administrator*

Oregonia
†McCollister, Cynthia A. *minister*

Orrville
Warner, Patricia Ann *secondary school educator*

Owensville
Davis, Valerie Jeanne *physical education educator*
Seifert, Caroline Hamilton *community health nurse, school nurse*

Oxford
†Bauer, Steven Albert *English educator, writer*
Becker, Stephen Bradbury *fraternal organization administrator*
Brown, Edward Maurice *retired lawyer, business executive*
Eshbaugh, W(illiam) Hardy *botanist, educator*
†Ewing, Susan R. *artist, educator*
†Finch, Annie R(idley) C(rane) *poet*
†Garland, James C. *college president*
Goodman, Eric Keith *writer, educator*
Gordon, Gilbert *chemist, educator*
Jeep, John Michael *German studies educator*
MacKenzie, Ann Haley *science educator*
Macklin, Philip Alan *physics educator*
Miller, Robert James *educational association administrator*
Parks, John Gordon *English educator*
Pearson, Paul Guy *academic administrator emeritus*
Pont, John *football coach, educator*
†Powell, Myrtis H. *university administrator*
Pringle, Lewis Gordon *marketing professional, educator*
†Reiss, James *poet, English educator, editor*
Rejai, Mostafa *political science educator*
Sanders, Gerald Hollie *communications educator*
Sessions, Judith Ann *librarian, university library dean*
Shriver, Phillip Raymond *academic administrator*
Siatra, Eleni *English educator*
Snavely, William Brant *management educator and consultant*
Stevens, Brenda Anita *psychologist, educator*
Wagenaar, Theodore Clarence *sociology educator*
Ward, Roscoe Fredrick *engineering educator*
Williamson, Clarence Kelly *microbiologist, educator*
Wilson, James Ray *international business educator*
Wortman, William Allen *librarian*
Yen, David Chi-Chung *management information systems educator*

Painesville
Davis, Barbara Snell *college educator*
Humphrey, George Magoffin, II *plastic molding company executive*

Jayne, Theodore Douglas *technical research and development company executive*
Luhta, Caroline Naumann *airport manager, flight educator*
Scozzie, James Anthony *chemist*
†Spencer, Elden A. *retired manufacturing company executive*
Taylor, Norman Floyd *computer educator, administrator*

Pandora
Stucky, Ken *clergy member, church organization administrator, foundation executive*

Parma
Bate, Brian R. *psychologist*
Krise, Jack Cloyde, Jr. *treasurer*
McFadden, Nadine Lynn *secondary education Spanish educator*
Moskal, Robert M. *bishop*
Pisarchick, Sally *special education educator*
Shirey, Connie Mae *secondary school educator*
Tener, Carol Joan *retired secondary education educator*
Verba, Betty Lou *real estate executive, investor*
Wells Bradley, Charlena Renee *editor, writer*
Yanda, Timothy George *cable television engineer*

Parma Heights
Cook, Jeanne Garn *historian, genealogist*
†Konchan, Kenneth Joseph *humanities educator*

Pataskala
†Caw, Thomas William *retired publisher and editor*

Pemberville
King, Laura Jane *librarian, genealogist*

Peninsula
Brobeck, David George *middle school administrator*
Ludwig, Richard Joseph *ski resort executive*

Pepper Pike
Bray, Pierce *business consultant*
Fallon, Pat *artist, art educator*
Fredrickson, Sharon Wong *accountant*
Grabner, George John *manufacturing executive*
Hauserman, Jacquita Knight *electricity company executive*
Leech, John Dale *lawyer, health care/corporate consultant*
Mc Call, Julien Lachicotte *banker*
O'Neill, Katherine Templeton *journalist, museum administrator, former nursing educator*
Rule-Hoffman, Richard Carl *art therapist, educator, counselor*
Solomon, Glen David *physician, researcher*

Perrysburg
Autry, Carolyn *artist, art history educator*
Carpenter, J. Scott *vocational school educator*
Eastman, John Richard *retired manufacturing company executive*
Khan, Amir U. *agricultural engineering consultant*
King, John Joseph *manufacturing company executive*
Kovacik, Neal Stephen *hotel and restaurant executive*
Lieder, W. Donald *chemical engineer*
Reider, Marlyn *nursing educator*
Scherer, Clarene Mae *occupational health nurse*
Weaver, Richard L., II *writer, speaker, educator*
Williamson, John Pritchard *utility executive*
Yager, John Warren *retired banker, lawyer*
Zuchowski, Beverly Jean *chemistry educator*

Pettisville
Switzer, Stephen Stuart *school superintendent*

Pickerington
Basinger, Cheryl Kathryn Ricketts *organizational development executive*
Rana-Collins, Arlene *secondary education educator*
Young, Glenna Asche *elementary education educator*
Zacks, Gordon Benjamin *manufacturing company executive*

Piketon
Manuta, David Mark *research chemist, consultant*

Piqua
Disbrow, Michael Ray *aerospace supplier company executive*

Plain City
Brown, D. Robin *elementary school educator*
Kinman, Gary *company executive*

Poland
Carlin, Clair Myron *lawyer*

Polk
Welch, Karen Joan *secondary education educator*

Pomeroy
Brockert, Joseph Paul *government executive, writer, editor, designer*
Edwards, John David *investment executive*

Port Clinton
Ewersen, Mary Virginia *retired educator*
Subler, Edward Pierre *advertising executive*

Portsmouth
Billiter, Freda Delorous *elementary education educator, retired*
†Cain, Beverly Lynn *library director*
Chapman, James Paul *university official*
Christensen, Margaret Anna *nurse, health management educator*
Deaterla, Michael Franklin *journalist, publicity specialist*
Gerlach, Franklin Theodore *lawyer*
Horr, William Henry *lawyer*

Powell
Borin, Gerald W. *zoological park administrator*
Funk, John William *emergency vehicle manufacturing executive, packaging company executive, lawyer*
Schwab, Glenn Orville *retired agricultural engineering educator, consultant*

Spangler, Edra Mildred *clinical psychologist*

Randolph
Pecano, Donald Carl *truck trailer manufacturing executive*

Ravenna
Turcotte, Margaret Jane *retired nurse*

Reynoldsburg
Boiman, Donna Rae *artist, art academy executive*
†Daily, Fred L.
Gunnels, Lee O. *retired finance and management educator, manufacturing company executive*
Odor, Richard Lane *mental health administrator, psychologist*
Woodward, Greta Charmaine *construction company executive*

Richfield
Buzzelli, Michael John *critical care nurse*
Feola, David Craig *secondary school administrator*
Schulz, Mary Elizabeth *lawyer*
Tobler, D. Lee *retired chemical and aerospace company executive*

Richmond
Martin, Clara Rita *elementary education educator*

Richmond Heights
Acheampong, Robert Kwabena *investment consultant*

Rio Grande
†Hart, Jack Wayne *English language educator*
Shibley, Ralph Edwin, Jr. *special education, vocational education educator*

Riverside
Wyllie, Stanley Clarke *retired librarian*

Rockford
Thompson, Robert Douglas *computer science educator, banker, consultant*

Rocky River
Grmek, Dorothy Antonia *accountant*
Hosek, John Jude *planning organization executive*
Masters, Albert Townsend *mechanical engineer*
Montgomery, Gary *dentist*
O'Brien, John Feighan *investment banker*
Riedthaler, William Allen *risk management professional*
Schoun, Mila *mechanical engineer*
Shively, Daniel Jerome *retired transportation executive*

Rootstown
Blacklow, Robert Stanley *physician, medical college administrator*
†Boex, James Richard *academic administrator, medical researcher*
Brodell, Robert Thomas *internal medicine educator*
Campbell, Colin *obstetrician, gynecologist, school dean*
†Jamison, James Mark *cell biologist*

Rossford
Salmon, Stuart Clive *manufacturing engineer*

Russell
Spring, Nicole Marie *legal nurse consultant*

Sagamore Hills
Consilio, Barbara Ann *legal administrator, management consultant*

Saint Clairsville
Dankworth, Margaret Anne *management consultant*
Fisher, Sandra Irene *English educator*
Sidon, Claudia Marie *psychiatric and mental health nursing educator*

Saint Marys
Kemp, Barrett George *lawyer*

Salem
†Babb, Elizabeth *artist, graphic artist*
Barcey, Harold Edward Dean (Hal Barcey) *real estate counselor*
Bowman, Scott McMahan *lawyer*
Fehr, Kenneth Manbeck *retired computer systems company executive*
Rice, Douglas Francis *English educator*

Sandusky
Amos, Janice Rae *automotive executive*
Bailey, K. Ronald *lawyer*
Behrens, Ellen Elizabeth Cox *writer, counselor, educator*
Freehling, Harold George, Jr. *respiratory therapist, consultant*
†Rothermel, Joan Ashley *artist*
Sokol, Dennis Allen *hospital administrator*
Stacey, James Allen *retired judge*

Seven Hills
Kuznik, Susan Marie *management consultant*
Stanczak, Julian *artist, educator*

Seville
Webb, Adele Ann *pediatric nurse practitioner*

Shaker Heights
Donnem, Sarah Lund *financial analyst, non-profit and political organization consultant*
Ekelman, Daniel Louis *lawyer*
Feuer, Michael *office products superstore executive*
Gellert, Edward Bradford, III *architect, consultant*
Held, Lila M. *art appraiser*
Kaplan, Norman Charles *industrialist, philanthropist*
Lichtman, Lillian Margaret Yaeger *special education educator*
†Mendel, Roberta *editor, publisher, writer*
Messinger, Donald Hathaway *lawyer*
Provan, Carol McLaughlin *fundraising executive*
Solganik, Marvin *real estate executive*
Tubbs Jones, Stephanie *prosecuting attorney*
Winter, John Alexander *realtor, real estate appraiser*

Shauck
Garvick, Kenneth Ryan *broadcast engineer, announcer, educator*

Sheffield Lake
Friend, Helen Margaret *chemist*

Shelby
Moore, Florian Howard *electronics engineer*

Sidney
Laurence, Michael Marshall *magazine publisher, writer*
Lawrence, Wayne Allen *publisher*
Seitz, James Eugene *retired college president, freelance writer*
Stevens, Robert Jay *magazine editor*

Solon
Gallo, Donald Robert *retired English educator*
Johnson, Madeline Mitchell *retired administrative assistant*
†Layman, Martin W. *dentist*
Rosica, Gabriel Adam *corporate executive, engineer*

South Euclid
Janson, Patrick *singer, actor, conductor, educator*
Mehok, Edward Eugene *priest, English and theology educator*

South Lebanon
Campbell, David Rogers *engineer*

Spencer
Snyder, Teresa Ann *medical surgical nurse*

Springboro
Mishler, Mark David *financial executive, educator*
Ramey, Rebecca Ann *elementary education educator*
Saxer, Richard Karl *metallurgical engineer, retired air force officer*

Springfield
Berridge, Paul Thomas *minister*
Browne, William Bitner *lawyer*
Cantrell, John L. *language educator*
Dobson, Janet Louise *writer*
Dominick, Charles Alva *college official*
Fullmer, Lee Wayne *minister*
Hobbs, Horton Holcombe, III *biology educator*
Kinnison, William Andrew *retired university president*
Kurian, Pius *nephrologist, educator*
Lagos, James Harry *lawyer*
Maddex, Myron Brown (Mike Maddex) *broadcasting executive*
Mauriello, Tracie Lynn *journalist*
Moon, Farzana *author*
Moose, Elton LeRoy *minister, counselor, senior center executive*
Parks, Brenda K. *geriatrics nurse*
Patterson, Martha Ellen *artist, art educator*
Rowland-Raybold, Roberta Rae *insurance agent, music educator*
Ryu, Kyoo-Hai Lee *physiologist*
Whaley-Buckel, Marnie *social service administrator*
Wood, Dirk Gregory *surgeon, physician, forensic consultant*

Steubenville
Cummiskey, Raymond Vincent *academic administrator*
Hall, Alan Craig *library director*
†Ottenweller, Albert Henry *bishop*
Sheldon, Gilbert Ignatius *clergyman*
White, Vicki Lee *bank service representative*

Streetsboro
Drugan, Cornelius Bernard *school administrator, psychologist, musician*
Kearns, Warren Kenneth *business executive*
Weiss, Joseph Joel *consulting company executive*

Strongsville
Nekola, Louis William *utility line clearance executive*
Oltman, C. Dwight *conductor, educator*
Shambaugh, Catherine Anne *elementary education educator*

Struthers
Sugden, Richard Lee *pastor*

Sunbury
Griffin, Larry Allen *minister, evangelist*

Sylvania
Bergsmark, Edwin Martin *mortgage bank executive*
Lock, Richard William *packaging company executive*
Rabideau, Margaret Catherine *media center director*
Ring, Herbert Everett *management executive*
Sampson, Wesley Claude *auditor, software inventor*
Verhesen, Anna Maria Hubertina *counselor*

Tallmadge
Starcher-Dell'Aquila, Judy Lynn *special education educator*

The Plains
†Carsey, Tamara *paralegal*

Tiffin
Davison, Kenneth Edwin *American studies educator*
Einsel, David William, Jr. *retired army officer and consultant*
Galipeau, Peter Armand *video producer, advertising account executive*
Hillmer, Margaret Patricia *library director*
Kramer, Frank Raymond *classicist, educator*
†Norton, Holly Louise *English literature educator*
Talbot-Koehl, Linda Ann *dancer, ballet studio owner*

Tipp City
†Hogan, John Terry *investment company executive*
Panayirci, Sharon Lorraine *textiles executive, design engineer*
Tighe-Moore, Barbara Jeanne *electronics executive*

Toledo
†Abeln, Maura *plastics company executive*
Al-Marayati, Abid A. *political science educator*
†Armstrong, Vernelis K. *federal magistrate judge*
Baker, Richard Southworth *lawyer*
†Barden, Thomas Earl *English literature educator*
Barrett, Michael John *anesthesiologist*
Batt, Nick *property and investment executive*
†Baumgartner, Holly Lynn *educator in English language and literature*
Bedell, Archie William *family physician, educator*
Benham, Linda Sue *civil engineer*
Bernieri, Frank John *social psychology educator*
Billups, Norman Fredrick *college dean, pharmacist*
Block, Allan James *communications executive*
Block, John Robinson *newspaper publisher*
Block, William K., Jr. *newspaper executive*
Boesel, Milton Charles, Jr. *lawyer, business executive*
Boggs, Ralph Stuart *retired lawyer*
Boller, Ronald Cecil *glass company executive*
Braithwaite, Margaret Christine *elementary education educator*
†Brass, Alan W. *healthcare executive*
Brower, James Calvin *graphic artist, painter*
Brown, Charles Earl *lawyer*
Brown, James Edward *safety engineer*
Cardwell, Larry *executive director Toledo Youth Commission*
Carr, James Gray *judge*
Carson, Samuel Goodman *retired banker, company director*
Cave, Alfred Alexander *history educator, writer*
Chilton, Bradley Stewart *law educator*
Cousino, Joe Ann *sculptor*
Cummings, Erwin Karl *information technology executive*
Dalrymple, Thomas Lawrence *retired lawyer*
Dane, Stephen Mark *lawyer*
Davis-Hartenstein, Sharon Lynne *juvenile parole officer, human services program consultant*
Doner, Gary William *lawyer*
Donnelly, Robert William *bishop*
Dukkipati, Rao Venkateswara *engineering educator, researcher, scientist*
Eberly, William Somers *financial consultant*
Ferguson-Rayport, Shirley Martha *psychiatrist*
Finkbeiner, Carlton S. (Carty Finkbeiner) *mayor*
Fisher, Donald Wiener *lawyer*
Flaskamp, Ruth Ehmen Staack *retired elementary education educator*
Fuhrman, Charles Andrew *country club proprietor, real estate management executive, lawyer*
Geisler, Nathan David *financial consultant*
Hartung, James H. *airport authority executive*
Heintz, Carolinea Cabaniss *retired home economics educator*
†Heritage, Lee Morgan *music educator, composer*
Hiett, Edward Emerson *retired lawyer, glass company executive*
Hills, Arthur W. *architectural firm executive*
Hiner, Glen Harold, Jr. *materials company executive*
Hoffman, James R. *bishop*
Holmes, Debbie *nurse*
Horton, Frank Elba *university official, geography educator*
Jackson, Reginald Sherman, Jr. *lawyer*
James, William Morgan *bishop*
Kastner, Michael James *dentist*
Katz, David Allan *judge, former lawyer, business consultant*
Khan, Munawwar Jehan (Meena) *librarian, investor*
Kim, E. Kitai *pathologist*
Kimble, James A. *management consultant, accountant*
Kneen, James Russell *health care administrator*
Knorr, John Christian *entertainment executive, bandleader, producer*
Knotts, Frank Barry *physician, surgeon*
Koppus, Betty Jane *retired savings and loan association executive*
Kovacik, Thomas L. *chief operating officer and safety director Toledo*
Kozbial, Richard James *elementary education educator*
Kuhlman, Kimberly Ann *clinical dietician*
Kunze, Ralph Carl *retired savings and loan executive*
La Rue, Carl Forman *lawyer*
Lawrence, Edmund Pond, Jr. *neurosurgeon*
Leech, Charles Russell, Jr. *lawyer*
Lemieux, Joseph Henry *manufacturing company executive*
Machin, Barbara E. *lawyer*
Martin, John Thomas *physician, author, educator*
Martin, Robert Edward *architect*
Massey, Andrew John *conductor, composer*
Matthews, Christian William, Jr. *minister*
McCormick, Edward James, Jr. *lawyer*
McGlauchlin, Tom *artist*
Moon, Henry *academic administrator*
Morcott, Southwood J. *automotive parts manufacturing company executive*
Morgan, James Edward *lawyer*
Mulrow, Patrick Joseph *medical educator*
Nicholson, Brent Bentley *lawyer, educator*
Nitschke, Shaun Michael *bank officer*
Nordin, Phyllis Eck *sculptor, painter, consultant*
Nowatzki, Robert Carl *English educator*
Nycz, Joseph Donald *engineer*
O'Connell, Maurice Daniel *lawyer*
Oh, Keytack Henry *industrial engineering educator*
Paquette, Jack Kenneth *management consultant, antiques dealer*
Pawelczak, Mark A. *health department investigator*
Pletz, Thomas Gregory *lawyer*
Potter, John William *federal judge*
†Puligandla, Ramakrishna *educator*
Raczkowski, Dale Peter *city government administrator*
Reams, Anthony L. *director Toledo public service department*
Rejent, Marian Magdalen *pediatrician*
Rice, Kollin Lawrence *lawyer*
Rickus, Mary Ann *school nurse*
Romanoff, Marjorie Reinwald *education educator*
Romanoff, Milford Martin *building contractor*
Root, David Leigh *advertising company executive*
Rosenbaum, Kenneth E. *journalist, editor*
Royhab, Ronald *journalist, newspaper editor*
Saffran, Murray *biochemist*
St. Clair, Donald David *lawyer*
Senour, Connie Lee *internist*
†Shelley, E. Dorinda *dermatologist*
Shelley, Walter Brown *physician, educator*
Shoffer, Jeffrey David *financial planner*
Smith, Robert Nelson *former government official, anesthesiologist*
Speer, Richard Lyle *federal judge*
Spitzer, John Brumback *lawyer*
Stankey, Suzanne M. *editor*
Steadman, David Wilton *museum official*

Strobel, Martin Jack *lawyer, motor vehicle and industrial component manufacturing and distribution company executive*
Talmage, Lance Allen *obstetrician/gynecologist, career military officer*
Thomas, Lewis Edward *laboratory executive, retired petroleum company executive*
Toczynski, Janet Marie *oncological nurse*
Tuschman, James Marshall *lawyer*
Vicary, William Charles, Jr. *director sales and marketing*
Webb, Thomas Irwin, Jr. *lawyer*
Weikel, Malcolm Keith *health care company executive*
West, Ann Lee *clinical nurse specialist, educator, trauma nurse coordinator*
White, Polly Sears *religious organization administrator*
Wicklund, David Wayne *lawyer*
Willey, John Douglas *retired newspaper executive*
Wolfe, Robert Kenneth *engineering educator*
Wolff, Edwin Ray *retired construction engineer, consultant*
Woods, Doris A. *kinesiotherapist*
Yonke, David Arthur *music critic, journalist, writer*
Zychowicz, Ralph Charles *lawyer*

Trotwood
Caldwell, Ronald DeWitt, Sr. *industrial engineer, consultant*

Troy
Bazler, Frank Ellis *retired lawyer*
Davies, Alfred Robert *physician, educator*
Enright, Georgann McGee *mental health nurse*
Szoke, Joseph Louis *psychologist, mental health facility administrator*

Twinsburg
Hill, Thomas Allen *lawyer*
Morris, Jeffrey Selman *orthopedic surgeon*
Novak, Harry R. *manufacturing company executive*
Rose, Brendan J. *accountant*
†Spagg, Jim *artist*

Uniontown
Allison, Dianne J. Hall *insurance company official*
Krabill, Robert Elmer *osteopathic physician*
Lucas, Jeffrey A. *computer analyst*
Naugle, Robert Paul *dentist*

University Heights
Aggor, Francis Komla *language educator*
Cook, Alexander Burns *museum curator, artist, educator*
Epstein, Marvin Morris *retired construction company executive*
Gatto, Katherine Gyékényesi *modern languages and literatures educator*
†Klema, Mary Kulifay *nurse*
Rothschild, Beryl Elaine *mayor*

Upper Arlington
†Evans, David Charles *elementary education educator*
Holcomb, Dwight A. *city chief of police*
Snyder, Susan Leach *science educator*
Williams, Cathy Lynn *nurse*

Upper Sandusky
Baker, Harrison Scott *computer consultant*

Urbana
Bronkar, Eunice Dunalee *artist, art educator*

Valley View
Miller, Susan Ann *school system administrator*

Van Wert
Greve, Diana Lee *community health nurse*
McCune, Barry Lynn *minister*
Walters, Sumner J. *former judge, lawyer*

Vandalia
†Schear, Peggy Simmons *educator*
Smith, Marjorie Aileen Matthews *museum director*

Vermilion
Bersche, James H. *secondary education educator*

Vincent
Meek, Barbara Susan *elementary education educator*

Wadsworth
Brumbaugh, John A., Jr. *electrical engineer*
Hughes, Karen Sue *geriatrics nurse*
Neumann, Jeffrey Jay *photographer, minister*
†Nichols, C. Allen *librarian*
Rastok, Stacie Lynn *elementary school principal*

Wakeman
Krupp, Barbara D. *artist*

Walbridge
†Rudolph, Frederick William *contractor*

Warren
Dennison, David Short, Jr. *lawyer*
†Dudley, Joseph Michael *English educator*
Gianakos, Patricia Ann *social services supervisor*
Nader, Robert Alexander *judge, lawyer*
Perera, Vicumpriya Sriyantha *mathematics educator*
Platthy, Terrance Lee *accountant*
Rizer, Franklin Morris *physician, otolarynogologist*
Robbins, Robert Marvin *accountant*
Rossi, Anthony Gerald *lawyer*
Rush, William John *newspaper executive*
Storozuk, Barbara Sue *obstetric and pediatric nurse*
Thompson, Eric Thomas *manufacturing company executive*
Westman, Robert Allan *management consultant*
Yoke, Carl Bernard *English language educator, critic*

Wauseon
Boyers, Janeth Mauree *interior designer*

Waverly
Carlson, Carolin McCormick Furst *civic worker*
Hays, Richard Secrest *minister*

Waynesville
Parks, Janice Jean *critical care nurse, legal nurse consultant*

West Alexandria
†Sappington, Lynda Louisa Burton *artist*
Scoville, George Richard *marketing professional*

West Chester
Loughman, Barbara Ellen *immunologist researcher*
Mack, Mark Philip *chemical company executive*
Neiheisel, Thomas Henry *marketing research consultant*

West Farmington
Hardesty, Hiram Haines *ophthalmologist, educator*

West Jefferson
Puckett, Helen Louise *tax consulting company executive*

West Milton
Dallura, Sal Anthony *physician*

West Union
Young, Vernon Lewis *lawyer*

Westerville
Anderson, Jane Ellsworth *secondary school educator*
Barr, John Michael *investor, training and management consultant*
Dadmehr, Nahid *neurologist*
DeVore, Carl Brent *college president, educator*
Diersing, Carolyn Virginia *educational administrator*
Ellis, E. Addison, III *publishing executive*
Goh, Anthony Li-Shing *business owner, consultant*
Hoyt, Rosemary Ellen *tax accountant*
Husarik, Ernest Alfred *educational administrator*
Kerner, Joseph Frank, Jr. *management consultant, educator*
Kerr, Thomas Jefferson, IV *academic official*
Lattimore, Joy Powell *preschool administrator*
Min, Linda Lou *elementary education educator*
O'Meara, John Richard *park district director*
Rummell, Helen Mary *critical care and pediatrics nurse*
Schultz, Arthur LeRoy *clergyman, educator*
Strapp, Naomi Ann *women's health nurse*
Tiefel, Virginia May *librarian*
VanSant, Joanne Frances *academic administrator*
Williams, John Michael *physical therapist, sports medicine educator*

Westfield Center
Blair, Robert Cary *insurance company executive*
Spinelli, Anne Catherine *elementary education educator*

Westlake
†Coeling, Harriet V. *nursing educator, editor*
Connelly, John James *retired oil company technical specialist*
Distelhorst, Garis Fred *trade association executive*
Huff, Ronald Garland *mechanical engineer*
Loehr, Marla *spiritual care coordinator*
Peterson, Amy *Olympic athlete*
Whitehouse, John Harlan, Jr. *systems software consultant, diagnostician*

Wheelersburg
Hulse, Dexter Curtis *manufacturing executive*

Whipple
Carney Stalnaker, Lisa Ann *gerontological and home health nurse*

Whitehall
Pieri, Sharon Ann *rehabilitation nurse administrator*

Whitehouse
Howard, John Malone *surgeon, educator*

Wickliffe
Anthony, Donald Barrett *engineering executive*
†Fisher, Nancy DeButts *library director*
Kidder, Fred Dockstater *lawyer*
Kornbrekke, Ralph Erik *colloid chemist*
Pevec, Anthony Edward *bishop*

Willard
Fritz, Melissa Jane *English educator*

Willoughby
Abelt, Ralph William *bank executive*
Baker, Charles Stephen *music educator*
Campbell, Talmage Alexander *newspaper editor*
Carter, John Robert *physician*
Combs, Steven Paul *orthopedic surgeon*
Corrigan, Faith *journalist, educator*
Grossman, Mary Margaret *elementary education educator*
Hassell, Peter Albert *electrical and metallurgical engineer*
†Krause, Marjorie N. *biochemist, computer scientist*
Lillich, Alice Louise *retired secondary education educator*
Manning, William Dudley, Jr. *retired specialty chemical company executive*
Oldham, Lea Leever *business owner, author*
O'Toole, Thomas J. *journalist, photographer*
Sherman, Francis George Harry *advertising agency executive*
Stern, Michael David *dentist*
Trennel, Lawrence William *accountant*

Willshire
Myers, Janet L(ouise) *geriatrics nurse, educator*

Wilmington
Brindle, David Lowell *minister*
Buckley, Frederick Jean *lawyer*
Hackney, Howard Smith *retired county official*
Hodapp, Larry Frank *accountant*
Lundblad, John Ladd *airline pilot, flight instructor*
Mongold, Sandra K. *corporate executive*
Schutt, Walter Eugene *lawyer*

Wooster
Albright, Mindy Sue *college health and geriatrics nurse*
August, Robert Olin *journalist*
Basford, James Orlando *container manufacturing company executive*
Degnan, Martin J. *rubber products corporation executive, lawyer*
Ferree, David Curtis *horticultural researcher*
Grewal, Parwinder S. *biologist, researcher*
Hickey, Damon Douglas *library director*
Kennedy, Charles Allen *lawyer*
Kuffner, George Henry *dermatologist, educator*
Lafever, Howard Nelson *plant breeder, geneticist, educator*
Madden, Laurence Vincent *plant pathology educator*
Schmitt, Wolfgang Rudolf *consumer products executive*
Shepherd, Mary Anne *elementary education educator*
Shostak, Debra Beth *English educator*

Worthington
Browning, Robert Lynn *educator, clergyman*
Castner, Linda Jane *instructional technologist, nurse educator*
Compton, Ralph Theodore, Jr. *electrical engineering educator*
Craig, Judith *bishop*
Giannamore, David Michael *electronics engineer*
Lentz, Edward Allen *consultant, retired health administrator*
Meyer, Betty Jane *former librarian*
Newkirk, Peggy Rose Wills *civic volunteer*
Stone, Linda Chapman *physician, consultant, medical educator*
Trevor, Alexander Bruen *computer company executive*
Wasserman, Karen Boling *clinical psychologist, nursing consultant*
Winston, Janet Margaret *real estate professional, civic volunteer*
Winter, Chester Caldwell *physician, surgery educator*

Wright Patterson AFB
Agnes, Gregory Stephen *engineering educator, military officer*
†Babbitt, George T. *career officer*
Boff, Kenneth Richard *engineering research psychologist*
Bohanon, Kathleen Sue *neonatologist, educator*
Caudill, Tom Holden *governmental policy and analysis executive*
†Courter, Robert J., Jr. *career officer*
D'Azzo, John Joachim *electrical engineer, educator*
Eastwood, DeLyle *chemist*
Fernelius, Nils Conard *physicist*
Frazier, John W. *physiologist, researcher*
Garscadden, Alan *physicist*
Haritos, George Konstantinos *engineer, educator, military officer*
†Herrelko, David A. *career officer*
†Johnson, Charles L., II *military officer*
†Kelley, Joseph E. *career officer*
Maguire, Frank Edward *military officer*
Metcalf, Charles David *museum director, retired military officer*
Mitchell, Philip Michael *aerospace engineer, consultant, educator*
†Mushala, Michael C. *career officer*
†Nielsen, Paul Douglas *Air Force officer, engineering manager*
†Parr, Sharon E. *purchasing executive*
†Paul, Richard R. *military officer*
†Pearson, Wilbert D. *career officer*
†Samic, Dennis R. *career officer*
†Sieg, Stanley A. *military official*
†Stewart, Todd I. *military officer*
Szucs, Andrew Eric *training manager*
Voevodin, Andrey Aleksejevich *material scientist*

Wyoming
Cooley, William Edward *regulatory affairs manager*

Xenia
Chappars, Timothy Stephen *lawyer*
Richey, William Keith *secondary education educator*
Zellner, Sharon Michelle *special education educator*

Yellow Springs
Economos, Nikkiann *physical therapist*
Fogarty, Robert Stephen *historian, educator, editor*
Graham, Jewel Freeman *social worker, lawyer, educator*
Hamilton, Virginia (Mrs. Arnold Adoff) *author*
Hudson, Jon Barlow *sculptor*
Keyes, Ralph Jeffrey *writer*
†Moinzadeh, Sadie *institutional researcher, educator*
Schulsinger, Michael Alan *data processing executive*
Spokane, Robert Bruce *biophysical chemist*
Trolander, Hardy Wilcox *engineering executive, consultant*
Webb, Paul *physician, researcher, consultant, educator*

Youngstown
Ausnehmer, John Edward *lawyer*
Blair, Richard Bryson *lawyer*
†Bodah, William T. *federal judge*
Bowers, Bege K. *English educator*
Briach, George Gary *lawyer, consultant*
Brothers, Barbara *English language educator*
Buckley, John Joseph *obstetrician, gynecologist*
Byrd, Swettie Lee *minister*
Camacci, Michael A. *commercial real estate broker, development consultant*
Catoline-Ackerman, Pauline Dessie *small business owner*
Cochran, Leslie Herschel *university administrator*
Coleman, Esther Mae Glover *educator*
Courtney, William Francis *food and vending service company executive*
DeBartolo, Edward John, Jr. *professional football team owner, real estate developer*
Economus, Peter Constantine *judge*
†Flick, James Dennis *journalist, free lance writer*
Fok, Thomas Dso Yun *civil engineer*
Franzetta, Benedict C. *bishop*
Gottron, Francis Robert, III *small business owner*
Howe, Kimberly Palazzo *critical care nurse*
Lacivita, Michael John *safety engineer*
Loch, John Robert *educational administrator*
Matune, Frank Joseph *lawyer*
Melnick, Robert Russell *lawyer*
Mossman, Robert Gillis, IV *civil and environmental engineer*
Murcko, Donald Leroy *architect*
Nadler, Myron Jay *lawyer*
Powers, Paul J. *manufacturing company executive*
Przelomski, Anastasia Nemenyi *retired newspaper editor*
Roth, Daniel Benjamin *lawyer, business executive*
Rubin, Jeffrey Reed *vascular surgeon*
Stahl, Joel Sol *plastic and chemical engineer*
Stevens, Paul Edward *lawyer*
†Sweeney, Christopher John *psychology educator, consultant*
†Thomas, James D. *federal judge*
Tierno, Edward Gregory *insurance company executive*
Tucker, Don Eugene *retired lawyer*
†Villani, Jim Nicholas *publisher, English educator*
Ward, Linda V. *nursing administrator*
†Wathen, Norman Daniel *athletic trainer*
Wellman, Thomas Peter *lawyer*
Westenbarger, Don Edward *retired association executive*
Zitto, Richard Joseph *physics educator*
Zona, Louis A. *art institute director*
Zordich, Steve *retired art educator, artist*
Zorn, Robert Lynn *education educator*

Zanesfield
Tetirick, Jack E. *retired surgeon*

Zanesville
Camma, Albert John *neurosurgeon*
Hartman, Julie Marie *school psychologist*
Jones, Marlene Wiseman *elementary education educator, reading specialist*
Koncar, George Alan *secondary education educator*
Kopf, George Michael *ophthalmologist*
Micheli, Frank James *lawyer*
O'Sullivan, Christine *executive director social service agency*
Ray, John Walker *otolaryngologist, educator, broadcast commentator*
Westgerdes, Gerald Lee *sculptor, art educator*
Whitacre, Vicki Ann *emergency physician*
Workman, James E. *retired school psychologist*

Zoar
Fernandez, Kathleen M. *cultural organization administrator*

OKLAHOMA

Ada
Anoatubby, Bill *governor*
Daniel, Arlie Verl *speech education educator*
Davison, Victoria Dillon *real estate executive*
Dennison, Ramona Pollan *special education educator*
Reese, Patricia Ann *retired editor, columnist*
Stafford, Donald Gene *chemistry educator*
Van Burkleo, Bill Ben *osteopath, emergency physician*
Wilkin, Richard Thomas *geochemist*

Altus
Muse, John Scott *video and animation producer*
†Smith, Donna Jean *librarian*
Wilcoxen, Joan Heeren *fitness company executive*

Altus AFB
†Kelly, Christopher A. *brigadier general United States air force*

Alva
Hardaway, Roger Dale *historian, educator*
Yates, James Newton *English educator*

Anadarko
†Kidd, Lovetta Monza *music educator*

Antlers
Caves, Peggy *medical/surgical nurse*
Stamper, Joe Allen *lawyer*

Ardmore
Aldridge, Charles Douglas *veterinarian*
Mynatt, Cecil Ferrell *psychiatrist*
Thompson, John E. *principal*

Atoka
Gabbard, (James) Douglas, II *judge*

Bartlesville
Allen, W. Wayne *oil industry executive*
Cox, Glenn Andrew, Jr. *petroleum company executive*
Doty, Donald D. *retired banker*
Dwiggins, Claudius William, Jr. *chemist*
Hedrick, Kirby L. *petroleum company executive*
Hogan, J(ohn) Paul *chemistry researcher, consultant*
Huchteman, Ralph Douglas *lawyer*
Johnson, Marvin Merrill *chemical engineer, chemist*
Lai, Young-Jou *industrial engineer*
Mihm, John Clifford *chemical engineer*
Risner, Anita Jane *career planning administrator*
Roff, Alan Lee *lawyer, consultant*
†Sanders, Jan W. *librarian*
Silas, Cecil Jesse *retired petroleum company executive*
Tayrien, Dorothy Pauline *retired nurse educator*
Welch, M. Bruce *research chemist*
†Whitworth, J. Bryan, Jr. *oil company executive, lawyer*

Bethany
Johnson, John Randall, Sr. *religious organization administrator*
Keeth, Betty Louise *geriatrics nursing director*
Leggett, James Daniel *bishop*
†Powell, Cynthia Diane *finance educator*
Wire, Teddy Kermit *psychotherapist*

Big Cabin
Stinson, Marion Dennis *regional association administrator*

Bixby
Brown, James Roy *retail executive*
Garrett, James Lowell *contractor*

Broken Arrow
†Byarse, Anthony *artist*
Hale, Richard Lee *magazine editor*
Janning, Sister Mary Bernadette *nun, retired association executive*
Miller, Robert Elmer *management consultant*
Roberson, Deborah Kay *secondary school educator*

GEOGRAPHIC INDEX 5691 OKLAHOMA

Checotah
Mann, Patsy Sue *secondary education educator*

Chickasha
Beets, Freeman Haley *retired government official*
Brown, Steven L. *art educator*
Good, Leonard Phelps *artist*
Meredith, Howard Lynn *American Indian studies educator*

Choctaw
†Linduff, James Virgil *criminologist*

Claremore
Cesario, Sandra Kay *women's health nurse, educator*

Clinton
Askew, Penny Sue *choreographer, artistic director, ballet instructor*

Collinsville
Councilman, Richard Robert *product development engineer*

Cushing
Cruzan, Clarah Catherine *dietitian*
†Evans, Cheryl Lynn *elementary school principal*
Kyker, James Charles *engineering executive, computer programmer*
Olesen, Sylvia Lawrence *educator, administrator*

Disney
Hamilton, Carl Hulet *retired academic administrator*

Drummond
Harris, Joyce Faye *elementary education educator*

Duncan
Adams, Brenda Kay *publications administrator, consultant*

Durant
Christy, David Hardacker *secondary school educator, music educator*
Craige, Danny Dwaine *dentist*
England, Dan Benjamin *accountant*
Gumm, Jay Paul *association executive*
Kennedy, Elizabeth Carol *psychologist, educator*
Rice, Stanley Arthur *biology educator*

Edmond
Aclin, Keith Andrew *technicial service executive, educator*
Bailey, Elizabeth Anne *middle school education educator*
Brown, William Ernest *dentist*
Caire, William *biologist, educator*
French, Dana Lewis *computer consultant*
†Hamilton, Carol Jean *English educator, writer, storyteller*
Harryman, Rhonda L. *education educator*
Keckel, Peter J. *advertising executive*
Lester, Andrew William *lawyer*
Loman, Mary LaVerne *retired mathematics educator*
Loving, Susan Brimer *lawyer, former state official*
McCoy, William Ulysses *journalist*
Morgan, Ralph Rexford *manufacturing company executive*
Nelson, John Woolard *neurology educator, physician*
Nelson, Laurence Clyde *pastoral psychotherapist*
Pydynkowsky, Joan Anne *journalist*
Schader, Billy Wayne *oil company executive*
Smock, Donald Joe *governmental liaison, political consultant*
Tucker, Leslie Ray *accountant, historian*

El Reno
Buendia, Imelda Bernardo *clinical director, physician*
Phillips, William Allison *research animal scientist*

Elgin
Gault, Jeannie Farmer *gerontological nurse, nursing home administrator*

Enid
Berry, Robert Bass *construction executive*
Dandridge, William Shelton *orthopedic surgeon*
Deunk, N. Howard, III *flying educator*
Dolezal, Leo Thomas *telecommunications executive*
Dyche, Kathie Louise *secondary school educator*
Jones, Stephen *lawyer*
Lopez, Francisco, IV *health care administrator*
Mabry, Betsy *elementary education educator*
Martin, Michael Rex *lawyer*
McNaughton, Alexander Bryant *lawyer*
Musser, William Wesley, Jr. *lawyer*
Taylor, Donna Lynne *adult training coordinator*
Ward, Llewellyn Orcutt, III *oil company executive*
Wyatt, Robert Lee, IV *lawyer*

Erick
Chittum, Jamey Eve *principal*

Fairview
†Swearingen, David Eugene *oil industry executive*

Fort Sill
†Adair, Lawrence R. *army officer*
†Baxter, Leo J. *career officer*
Livingston, Douglas Mark *lawyer*
Massey, Ronald Florian, Jr. *career officer*
Spivey, Towana *museum director*

Fort Towson
Pike, Thomas Harrison *plant chemist*

Frederick
Stone, Voye Lynne *women's health nurse practitioner*

Goodwell
Goldsmith, Dale Campbell *university official*

Guthrie
†Cleek, Clifford R. *power assembly company executive*
Dowdy, Fredella Mae *secondary school educator*
Scott-Christian, Tres Mali *employment counselor, consultant*

Guymon
Wood, Donald Euriah *lawyer*

Healdton
Eck, Kenneth Frank *pharmacist*

Hinton
Pasby, Garry Edward *assistant principal*

Hobart
Ball, William James *pediatrician*

Hodgen
Brower, Janice Kathleen *library technician*

Jones
Dean, Bill Verlin, Jr. *lawyer*
Jones, Jeffery Lynn *software engineer*

Keota
Davis, Thomas Pinkney *secondary school educator*

Kingfisher
Buswell, Arthur Wilcox *physician, surgeon*

Konawa
Rains, Mary Jo *banker*

Langston
Mallik, Muhammad Abdul-Bari *soil microbiologist*

Lawton
Brooks, (Leslie) Gene *cultural association administrator*
Buckley, Gary Steven *science educator*
Calaway, James *elementary education educator*
Cates, Dennis Lynn *education educator*
Davis, Don Clarence *university president*
Ellenbrook, Edward Charles *county official, small business owner*
†Erwin, Shon T. *federal judge*
Gardner, Carol Elaine *elementary school educator*
Hensley, Ross Charles *dermatologist*
Hooper, Roy B. *home health consultant, insurance broker, lobbyist*
Mayes, Glenn *social worker*
McKellips, Terral Lane *mathematics educator, university administrator*
Moore, Roy Dean *judge*
Sparkman, Mary M. *medical, surgical and rehabilitation nurse*
Spencer, Mark Morris *creative writing educator*
Stanley, George Edward *writer*
Webb, O(rville) Lynn *physician, pharmacologist, educator*
Young, J. A. *bishop*

Marlow
†Bannister, Lois Ann *library director*

Mcalester
Cornish, Richard Pool *lawyer*

Miami
Dicharry, James Paul *company official, retired air force officer*
Vanpool, Cynthia Paula *special education educator, special services consultant*

Midwest City
Bogardus, Carl Robert, Jr. *radiologist, educator*
Gonzalez, Richard Theodore *photographer*
Smith, Wayne Calvin *chemical engineer*

Moore
Grider, John Anthony *child and family therapist, consultant*
Harrington, Gary Burnes *retired controller*

Mounds
Fellows, Esther Elizabeth *musician, music educator*
Halsey, James Albert *international entertainment impressario, theatrical producer, talent manager*

Muskogee
Barrage, Billy Michael *judge*
Burrage, Billy Michael *judge, federal*
†Green, Bruce *lawyer*
Kendrick, Thomas Rudolph *chemist*
Kent, Bartis Milton *physician*
†Payne, James H. *federal judge*
Seay, Frank Howell *federal judge*
Williams, Betty Outhier *lawyer*

Mustang
Laurent, J(erry) Suzanna *technical communications specialist*

Newcastle
Mudroch, Kimberly Ann *veterinarian*

Newkirk
Mullin, Melissa Yvonne *secondary English educator*
Newport, L. Joan *consultant, retired psychotherapist*

Norman
Affleck, Marilyn *sociology educator*
Atkinson, Gordon *chemistry educator*
Bell, Robert Eugene *anthropologist educator*
Bert, Charles Wesley *mechanical and aerospace engineer, educator*
Bluestein, Howard Bruce *meteorology educator*
Boren, David Lyle *academic administrator*
Budai, William H. *music educator*
Campbell, John Morgan *retired chemical engineer*
Carey, Thomas Devore *baritone, educator*
Carpenter, Charles Congden *zoologist, educator*
Christian, Sherril D. *chemistry educator, administrator*
Ciereszko, Leon Stanley, Sr. *chemistry educator*
Coale, Sherri *university women's basketball coach*
Cochran, Gloria Grimes *pediatrician, retired*
Corr, Edwin Gharst *ambassador*
Crane, Robert Kendall *engineering educator, researcher, consultant*
Dalton, Deborah Whitmore *dean*
Dary, David Archie *journalism educator, author*
Day, Adrienne Carol *artist, art educator*
Denison, Gilbert Walter *chemical engineer, administrator*
Dille, John Robert *physician*
Donahue, Patricia Toothaker *retired social worker, administrator*
Drayton, John N. *publishing executive*
†Dyer, Suzette Morales *higher education administrator*
Eilts, Michael Dean *research meteorologist, manager*
Fairbanks, Robert Alvin *lawyer*
Fears, Jesse Rufus *historian, educator, academic dean*
†Gaddie, Ronald Keith *political science educator, writer*
Gaskins-Clark, Patricia Renae *dietitian*
Gilje, Paul Arn *history educator*
Hagan, William Thomas *history educator*
Hammon, Norman Harold *fundraising counsel and development consultant*
Haring, Kathryn Ann *special education educator, research scientist*
Hassrick, Peter Heyl *art historian*
Henderson, Arnold Glenn *architect, educator*
Henderson, George *educational sociologist, educator*
Henkle, James L. *industrial designer*
Hiner, Gladys Webber *psychologist*
Hobbs, Catherine Lynn *English language and literature educator*
Hodgell, Murlin Ray *university dean*
Hodges, Thompson Gene *librarian, retired university dean*
Hufnagel, Glenda Ann Lewin *human relations educator and administrator*
Hutchison, Victor Hobbs *biologist, educator*
Kaid, Lynda Lee *communications educator*
Kemp, Betty Ruth *librarian*
Kessler, Edwin *meteorology educator, consultant*
Lakshmivarahan, Sivaramakrishnan *computer science educator*
Lamb, Peter James *meteorology educator, researcher, consultant*
Lee, Sul Hi *library administrator*
Lester, June *library information studies educator*
Lis, Anthony Stanley *retired business administration educator*
Lowitt, Richard *history educator*
MacFarland, Miriam Katherine (Mimi) (Mimi MacFarland) *computer science consultant, writer*
Mallinson, Richard Gregory *chemical engineering educator*
Mankin, Charles John *geology educator*
Morgan, Elizabeth Anne *foundation consultant, writer*
Morton, Linda P. *journalism educator*
Muraleetharan, Kanthasamy Kadirgamar *civil engineering educator*
†Olasiji, Thompson Dele *educator*
O'Rear, Edgar Allen, III *chemical engineering educator*
Owens, Rochelle *poet, playwright*
Pain, Betsy M. *lawyer*
Palmer, Marilyn Joan *English composition educator*
Pappas, James Pete *university administrator*
Perkins, Edward J. *diplomat*
Petersen, Catherine Holland *lawyer*
Pigott, John Dowling *geologist, geophysicist, geochemist, educator, consultant*
Price, Linda Rice *community development administrator*
†Raadschelders, Jozef Cornelis Nicolaas *political science educator*
Roberts, Raymond Url *geologist*
Ross, Allan Anderson *music educator, university official*
Scaperlanda, Maria d *writer, journalist, author*
Schindler, Barbara Francois *education educator*
Sharp, Paul Frederick *former university president, educational consultant*
Sorey, Thomas Lester, Jr. *architect, educator*
Stover, Curtis Sylvester *retired vocational school educator*
†Stroud, Clarke *university official*
Talley, Richard Bates *lawyer*
Trimble, Preston Albert *retired judge*
Tuttle, Arthur Norman, Jr. *architect, university administrator, educational facilities planner*
Van Horn, Richard Linley *academic administrator*
Wallis, Robert Ray *psychologist*
Weber, Jerome Charles *education and human relations educator, former academic dean and provost*
†Xue, Ming *meteorologist, researcher*
Zaman, Musharraf *civil engineering educator*
Zapffe, Nina Byrom *retired elementary education educator*
Zelby, Leon Wolf *electrical engineering educator, consulting engineer*
Zelby, Rachel *realtor*

Nowata
Osborn, Ann George *retired chemist*

Ochelata
Hitzman, Donald Oliver *microbiologist*

Oklahoma City
†Abbamondi, John Gabriel *lawyer*
Acers, Patsy Pierce *financial seminars company executive*
Ackerman, Raymond Basil *advertising agency executive*
Adams, Warren Lynn *publisher, business consultant*
Alaupovic, Alexandra Vrbanic *artist, educator*
Alaupovic, Petar *biochemist, educator*
Alexander, Patrick Byron *zoological society executive*
Allbright, Karan Elizabeth *psychologist, consultant*
Allen, Robert Dee *lawyer*
Alley, Wayne Edward *federal judge, retired army officer*
Almond, David Randolph *lawyer, company executive*
Angel, Arthur Ronald *lawyer, consultant*
Arbuckle, Averil Dorothy (Cookie Arbuckle) *healthcare facility administrator*
†Argo, Doyle W. *federal magistrate*
Bahr, Carman Blocdow *internist*
Bailey, Clark Trammell, II *public relations/public affairs professional*
Batenic, Mark K. *manufacturing company executive*
Beech, Johnny Gale *lawyer*
Bell, Thomas Eugene *psychologist, educational administrator*
Bell, Tony Cliffton *radio show host, producer*
Beltran, Eusebius Joseph *archbishop*
Benson, Travis Theo "Doc" *minister, association administrator*
†Blount, James Robert *military career officer*
Bogle, Ronald E. *academic administrator*
Bohanon, Luther L. *federal judge*
Bohanon, Richard Lee *federal judge*
Boston, Billie *costume designer, costume history educator*
Boston, William Clayton *lawyer*
Bozalis, John Russell *physician*
Bradford, Dennis Doyle *real estate broker, developer*
Bradford, Reagan Howard, Jr. *ophthalmology educator*
Brandt, Edward Newman, Jr. *physician, educator*
Brawner, Lee Basil *librarian*
Brooks, Norma Newton *legal assistant*
Brown, Kenneth Ray *banker*
Browne, John Robinson *banker*
Brown-Kuykendall, Donita *early childhood educator*
Brumback, Roger Alan *neuropathologist, researcher*
†Buchanan, Rick *press secretary*
Buckley, Stephanie Denise *health care executive*
Butkin, Robert *state treasurer*
Campbell, David Gwynne *petroleum executive, geologist*
Cassel, John Elden *accountant*
Cauthron, Robin J. *federal judge*
Champlin, Richard H. *lawyer, insurance company executive*
Christiansen, Mark D. *lawyer*
Claflin, James Robert *pediatrician, allergist*
Clark, Gary Ray *licensing board executive*
Clark, Robert Lloyd, Jr. *librarian*
Coats, Andrew Montgomery *lawyer, former mayor, dean*
Coleman-Portell, Bi Bi *women's health and high risk perinatal nurse*
Collins, William Edward *aeromedical administrator, researcher*
Comp, Philip Cinnamon *medical researcher*
Conison, Jay *lawyer*
Cooper, George *superintendent animal welfare Oklahoma City*
Couch, James Russell, Jr. *neurology educator*
Court, Leonard *lawyer, educator*
Craig, George Dennis *economics educator, consultant*
Craig, Jon Lee *state environmental program administrator*
Crow, Charles Delmar *human resources manager, consultant*
Cunningham, Stanley Lloyd *lawyer*
Davis, Emery Stephen *wholesale food company executive*
Daxon, Tom *state agency administrator*
Decker, Michael Lynn *lawyer, judge*
Derrick, Gary Wayne *lawyer*
Dungan, Paul Barnes *director city-county health department*
Dunn, Parker Southerland *retired chemical company consultant*
Durland, Jack Raymond *lawyer*
Edmondson, William Andrew *state attorney general*
Elder, James Carl *lawyer*
Ellis, Robert Smith *allergist, immunologist*
Enis, Thomas Joseph *lawyer*
Everett, Mark Allen *dermatologist, educator*
Fallin, Mary Copeland *state official*
Featherly, Henry Frederick *lawyer*
Felton, Warren Locker, II *surgeon*
Fernandez, Lisa *softball player*
Filley, Warren Vernon *allergist, immunologist*
Ford, Charles Reed *state senator*
Forni, Patricia Rose *dean, nursing educator*
Foster, Victor Lynn *translator*
Garrett, Sandy Langley *school system administrator*
Gavaler, Judith Ann Stohr Van Thiel *bio-epidemiologist*
Gaylord, Edward Lewis *publishing company executive*
George, James Noel *hematologist-oncologist, educator*
Gilchrist, John Mark *otolaryngologist*
Gonzales, Sam C. *protective service official*
Gordon, Kevin Dell *lawyer*
Gourley, James Leland *editor, publishing executive*
Grupe, Robert Charles *corporate training consultant*
Gumerson, Jean Gilderhus *health foundation executive*
Halverstadt, Donald Bruce *urologist, educator*
Hamilton, Thomas Allen *independent insurance agent*
Hanna, Terry Ross *lawyer, small business owner*
Harbour, Robert Randall *state agency administrator*
Hargrave, Rudolph *state supreme court justice*
†Harlan, Ross Edgar *retired utility company executive, writer, lecturer, consultant*
Haywood, B(etty) J(ean) *anesthesiologist*
Hemry, Jerome Eldon *lawyer*
Hendrick, Howard H. *state government administrator*
Henry, Robert Harlan *federal judge, former attorney general*
Hight, Joe Irvin *editor*
Hill, Robert Fred *medical educator*
Hodges, Ralph B. *state supreme court justice*
Hofener, Steven David *civil engineer*
Holder, Lee *educator and university dean emeritus*
Holloway, Othelle June *elementary school educator*
Holloway, William Judson, Jr. *federal judge*
Horner, Russell Grant, Jr. *energy and chemical company executive*
Hough, Jack Van Doren *otologist*
Howeth, Lynda Carol *small business owner*
†Howland, Ronald L. *federal judge*
Hulseberg, Paul David *financial executive, educator*
Humphreys, Kirk *mayor*
†Hunter, Michael James *state government official, lawyer, educator*
Hurley, Thomas P. *city clerk*
Ille, Bernard Glenn *insurance company executive*
Irwin, Pat *federal magistrate judge*
Jennings, Stephen Grant *academic administrator*
Johnson, B(ruce) Connor *biochemist, educator, consultant*
Johnson, James Terence *college chancellor*
Johnson, Robert Max *lawyer*
Jones, Charles Edwin *historian, bibliographer, chaplain*
Jones, Renee Kauerauf *health care administrator*
Jonsson, Skuli *construction company executive*
Keating, Francis Anthony, II *governor, lawyer*
Kimerer, Neil Banard, Sr. *retired psychiatrist, educator*
Kinasewitz, Gary Theodore *medical educator*
Kirkpatrick, John Elson *oil company executive, retired naval reserve officer*
Kline, David Adam *lawyer, educator, writer*
Kline, Timothy Deal *lawyer*
Kraker, Deborah Schovanec *special education educator*
Kuner, Charles Michael *minister*

Lambird, Mona Salyer *lawyer*
Lambird, Perry Albert *pathologist*
LaMotte, Janet Allison *retired management specialist*
Lavender, Robert Eugene *state supreme court justice*
Lee, Ellen Faith *insurance company associate*
Legg, William Jefferson *lawyer*
Leonard, Timothy Dwight *judge*
Lestina, Roger Henry *English language educator*
Levine, Joel *music director, conductor*
†Lindsey, Paul L. *federal judge*
Lovelace, George David, Jr. *quality engineer*
Lowell, Jeanne *nursing educator, psychiatric-mental health nurse*
†Luebbert, Stephen P. *career officer*
Macer, Dan Johnstone *retired hospital administrator*
Magarian, Robert Armen *medicinal chemist, researcher, educator, inventor*
Mardis, Richard Lyle *television producer and director, production manager*
Mason, Betty G(wendolyn) Hopkins *school system administrator*
Mather, Ruth Elsie *writer*
Mather, Stephanie J. *lawyer*
Matsumoto, Hiroyuki *biochemistry educator, researcher*
Maxey, Wanda Jean *geriatrics nurse practitioner, consultant*
McCampbell, Robert Garner *lawyer*
McClellan, Mary Ann *pediatrics nurse, educator*
McCoy, Wesley Lawrence *musician, conductor, educator*
McEwen, Irene Ruble *physical therapy educator*
McFadden, Robert Stetson *hepatologist*
McKenzie, Clif Allen *Indian tribe official, accountant*
McLaughlin, Lisa Marie *educational administrator*
McNitt, Susan *municipal official*
Mikkelson, Dean Harold *geological engineer*
Mildren, Jack *oil/gas company executive, former state official*
Miles-La Grange, Vicki *judge*
Miller, Herbert Dell *petroleum engineer*
Milsten, Robert B. *lawyer*
Mitrovgenis, James William, Jr. *journalist*
Mock, Randall Don *lawyer*
Moler, Edward Harold *lawyer*
Moody, Robert M. *bishop*
Moore, Billy Don *video scriptwriter, producer*
Moore, Joanne Iweita *pharmacologist, educator*
Mosby, Lee Emerson *writer*
Mulvihill, John Joseph *medical geneticist*
Munhollon, Samuel Clifford *investment brokerage house executive*
Murphy, Deborah Hill *education cosultant, psychotherapist*
Neaves, Norman Earl *minister*
Necco, Alexander David *lawyer, educator*
Nesbitt, Charles Rudolph *lawyer, energy consultant*
Neuenschwander, Pierre Fernand *medical educator*
Nichols, J. Larry *energy company executive, lawyer*
Noakes, Betty LaVonne *retired elementary school educator*
Norick, Ronald J. *former mayor*
Opala, Marian P(eter) *state supreme court justice*
O'Steen, Randy A. *nursing administrator*
Owens, Barbara Ann *English educator*
Paden, Larry J. *electronics engineer, lawyer*
Paris, Wayne *social worker, researcher*
Parke, David Wilkin, II *ophthalmologist, educator, healthcare executive*
†Parr, Royse Milton *lawyer, writer, book reviewer*
Parrott, Nancy Sharon *lawyer*
Paul, William George *lawyer*
Payne, Gareld Gene *vocal music educator, medical transcriptionist*
Peace, H. W., II *oil company executive*
Perez-Cruet, Jorge *physician, psychiatrist, psychopharmacologist, psychophysiologist, educator*
Philipp, Anita Marie *computer sciences educator*
Porter, Don E. *sports administrator*
†Purcell, Gary M. *federal judge*
†Quaid, Gloria J. *school administrator*
Rahhal, Donald K. *obstetrician, gynecologist*
Randall, Mike *urban planner, municipal official*
†Raulston, Robert Owen *urologist, educator*
†Reynolds, Charles Lee, Jr. *urologist*
Reynolds, Norman Eben *lawyer*
Richardson, Dot *softball player*
Ricks, Bob Alonzo *state official*
Ridley, Betty Ann *educator, church worker*
†Rix, Robert Alvin, Jr. *retired neurosurgeon*
†Roberts, Bana Blasdel *federal judge*
Robison, Clarence, Jr. *surgeon*
Rockett, D. Joe *lawyer*
Ross, William Jarboe *lawyer*
Rundell, Orvis Herman, Jr. *psychologist*
Rush, Richard P. *chamber of commerce executive*
Russell, David L. *federal judge*
Ryan, Patrick M. *prosecutor*
†Sauer, Brian *molecular geneticist, researcher*
Schwabe, George Blaine, III *lawyer*
Schwemin, Joseph *retired pharmacist*
Scott, Lawrence Vernon *microbiology educator*
Shaw, William James *psychologist*
Sheldon, Eli Howard *minister*
Shillingburg, Herbert Thompson, Jr. *dental educator*
Shirey, Margaret (Peggy Shirey) *elementary school educator*
Shurley, Jay Talmadge *psychiatrist, medical educator, administrator, behavioral sciences researcher, polar explorer, author, genealogist*
Simmons, Jesse Doyle *retired minister, educator*
Simms, Robert D. *state supreme court justice*
Simpson, Jerome Dean *librarian*
Smith, Michele *softball player*
Smith, Robert Walter *food company executive*
Sookne, Herman Solomon (Hank Sookne) *retirement services executive*
Sowers, Wesley Hoyt *lawyer, management consultant*
Spencer, Melvin Joe *hospital administrator, lawyer*
Srouji, Elias Salim *retired pediatrician, educator*
Steinhorn, Irwin Harry *lawyer, educator, corporate executive*
Stringer, L.E. (Dean Stringer) *lawyer*
Summers, Hardy *state supreme court justice*
Taliaferro, Henry Beauford, Jr. *lawyer*
Taylor-White-Grigsby, Queen Delores *minister, consultant*
Terrell, Danny *director general svcs*
†TeSelle, John *federal judge*
Thadani, Udho *physician, cardiologist*
Thomas, Gary Wayne *actor*
Thompson, Carolyn Stallings *lawyer*
Thompson, Guy Thomas *safety engineer*
Thompson, Ralph Gordon *federal judge*
Thurman, William Gentry *medical research foundation executive, pediatric hematology and oncology physician, educator*
†Tillinghast, Jon Dalton *public health physician*
Todd, Joe Lee *historian*
Tolbert, James R., III *financial executive*
Tompkins, Raymond Edgar *lawyer*
Towery, Curtis Kent *lawyer, judge*
Trent, Luther E. *airport executive, state agency executive*
Trent, Richard O(wen) *financial executive*
Triplett, E. Eugene *editor*
Trost, Louis Frederick, Jr. *banker, financial planner*
Tuck-Richmond, Doletta Sue *prosecutor*
Turner, Eugene Andrew *manufacturing executive*
Turpen, Michael Craig *lawyer*
Twyman, Nita (Venita) *music educator*
†Tyndall, Robert James *neurologist*
Tytanic, Christopher Alan *lawyer*
Van Rysselberge, Charles H. *organization administrator*
Vaughn, James Eldon *retired military officer, civic volunteer*
Waldo, Catherine Ruth *private school educator*
Walsh, Lawrence Edward *lawyer*
†Ward, Lance D. *state senate official*
Watt, Joseph Michael *state supreme court justice*
Welden, Mary Clare *nurse*
Werries, E. Dean *food distribution company executive*
West, Lee Roy *federal judge*
Wheat, Willis James *retired university dean, management educator*
Wheeler, Albert Lee, III *lawyer, legal consultant*
†Wheeler, Jane Frances *protective services official*
White, James Robert *minister*
Whitener, Carolyn Raye *commercial artist*
Wickens, Donald Lee *engineer executive, consultant, rancher*
Wilkerson, Matha Ann *oil company executive*
Williams, Richard Donald *retired wholesale food company executive*
Williams, William Ralston *retired bank and trust company executive*
Wilson, Alma *state supreme court justice*
†Wisdom, Peggy J. *neurologist*
Wood, Paula Davidson *lawyer*
Woods, Harry Arthur, Jr. *lawyer*
Woods, Pendleton *retired college official, author*
Woody, Mark Edward *financial planner*
Worsham, Bertrand Ray *psychiatrist*
Worthington, J.B. *chemical company executive*
Zevnik-Sawatzky, Donna Dee *litigation coordinator*
Zuhdi, Nabil (Bill) *lawyer, litigator, consultant, producer*
Zuhdi, Nazih *surgeon, administrator*

Okmulgee
Doan, Patricia Nan *librarian*
Turner, Michael Dan *university administrator*

Owasso
Reed, Walter George, Jr. *osteopathic physician*

Paden
Adams, Darlene Agnes *secondary education educator*

Park Hill
Mankiller, Wilma Pearl *tribal leader, retired*

Pauls Valley
Pesterfield, Linda Carol *school administrator, educator*

Pawhuska
Strahm, Samuel Edward *veterinarian*

Perkins
Sasser, William David *advertising company executive*

Perry
Doughty, Michael Dean *insurance agent*

Ponca City
Bolene, Margaret Rosalie Steele *bacteriologist, civic worker*
Collins, Walter Lloyd George *editor*
Leonard, Samuel Wallace *oil company and bank executive*
Northcutt, Clarence Dewey *lawyer*
Raley, John W., Jr. *lawyer*
Surber, Joe Robert *assistant superintendent of schools*
Tatum, Betty Joyce *secondary school educator*
Wann, Laymond Doyle *retired petroleum research scientist*

Poteau
†Kerr, Robert Samuel, III *state official*

Prague
Stefansen, Peggy Ann *special education educator*

Pryor
Burdick, Larry G. *school system administrator*

Purcell
Lucas, Roy Edward, Jr. *minister*

Sallisaw
Mayo, James Watie (Jim Mayo) *publishing executive*

Sand Springs
Ackerman, Robert Wallace *steel company executive*
Ray, Eddye Robert *occupational safety and health professional*

Sapulpa
Gardner, Dale Ray *lawyer*
Lane, Tom Cornelius *lawyer*

Seminole
Moran, Melvin Robert *oil industry executive*
Wantland, William Charles *retired bishop, lawyer*

Shawnee
Hicks, Steve L. *artist, art educator*
Hill, Bryce Dale *school administrator*
Wilks, Jacquelin Holsomback *educational counselor*
Wilson, Robert Godfrey *radiologist*
†Windel, Frank E., Jr. *writer*

Zuhdi, Omar *secondary school educator*

Skiatook
Hoy, Charles William, III *electrical controls company executive*

Spiro
Aishman, Sharon Kay *science educator*

Stillwater
Agnew, Theodore Lee, Jr. *historian, educator*
Barfield, Billy Joe *agricultural engineer, educator*
Berlin, Kenneth Darrell *chemistry educator, consultant, researcher*
Boger, Lawrence Leroy *university president emeritus*
Browning, Charles Benton *retired university dean, agricultural educator*
Brusewitz, Gerald Henry *agricultural engineering educator, researcher*
Campbell, John Roy *animal scientist educator, academic administrator*
Case, Kenneth Eugene *industrial engineering educator*
Confer, Anthony Wayne *veterinary pathologist, educator*
Cooper, Donald Lee *physician*
Curl, Samuel Everett *university dean, agricultural scientist*
Ewing, Sidney Alton *veterinary medical educator, parasitologist*
Fischer, LeRoy Henry *historian, educator*
Fischer, Richard Samuel *lawyer*
Gorin, George *retired chemistry educator*
Grischkowsky, Daniel Richard *research scientist, educator*
Halligan, James Edmund *university administrator, chemical engineer*
Hayes, Kevin Gregory *university administrator*
Hoberock, Lawrence Linden *mechanical engineer, educator*
Holder, Mike *coach*
Hughes, Michael *civil engineer*
Johnson, Edward Roy *library director*
Langwig, John Edward *retired wood science educator*
Lawson, F. D. *bishop*
Leider, Charles L. *landscape architect*
Luebke, Neil Robert *philosophy educator*
Mc Collom, Kenneth Allen *retired university dean*
Mize, Joe Henry *industrial engineer, educator*
†Mowen, John C. *business educator*
Noyes, Ronald Tacie *agricultural engineering educator*
Provine, Lorraine *mathematics educator*
Quinn, Art Jay *veterinarian, retired educator*
†Rooney, John F., Jr. *geography educator, researcher*
Sandmeyer, Robert Lee *university dean, economist*
Shirley, Glenn Dean *writer*
Smeyak, Gerald Paul *telecommunication educator*
Thompson, David Russell *engineering educator, academic dean*
Trennepohl, Gary Lee *finance educator*
Whitcomb, Carl Ervin *horticulturist, researcher*
Wilkinson, J(anet) Barbara *psychologist, educator*

Stonewall
McDonald, Mary Elizabeth *singer, songwriter*

Tahlequah
Campbell, Jane Turner *former educator and realtor*
Carment, Thomas Maxwell *accounting educator, consultant, researcher*
†Clark, Mark William *dean, educator*
Edmondson, Linda Louise *optometrist*
Hare, Jerry Wayne *communications executive*
Howard, James Kenton *university administrator, journalist*
Wickham, M(arvin) Gary *optometry educator*
Williams, Larry Bill *academic administrator*

Tinker AFB
Goodman, Ernest Monroe *air force officer*
†McFann, Maurice L., Jr. *career officer*
†Perez, Charles H. *military officer*
Scott, Carol Lee *child care educator*

Tulsa
Abbott, William Thomas *claim specialist*
Abrahamson, A. Craig *lawyer*
Allen, Thomas Wesley *medical educator, dean*
Anderson, Peer LaFollette *lawyer, petroleum corporation executive*
Arrington, John Leslie, Jr. *lawyer*
Bailey, Keith E. *petroleum pipeline company executive*
Ball, Rex Martin *urban designer, architect*
†Bartmann, Kathryn *collections management executive*
Beasley, William Rex *judge*
Belsky, Martin Henry *law educator, lawyer*
Bender, John Henry, Jr. (Jack Bender) *editor, cartoonist*
Bennison, Allan Parnell *geological consultant*
Berlin, Steven Ritt *business educator*
†Berry, Charles Miles *cardiac surgeon*
Biolchini, Robert Fredrick *lawyer*
Bishop, Mary Fern *editor*
Blackstock, LeRoy *lawyer*
Blackstock, Virginia Lee Lowman (Mrs. LeRoy Blackstock) *civic worker*
Blais, Roger Nathaniel *physics educator*
Blanton, Roger Edmund *mechanical engineer*
Blenkarn, Kenneth Ardley *mechanical engineer, consultant*
Bowman, David Wesley *lawyer*
Boyle, Lester Joseph *marketing and broadcast executive*
Braumiller, Allen Spooner *oil and gas exploration company executive, geologist*
Brett, Thomas Rutherford *federal judge*
Brewster, Clark Otto *lawyer*
Brightmire, Paul William *retired judge*
Brill, James P. *petroleum engineer, educator*
Brolick, Henry John *energy company executive*
Brunk, Samuel Frederick *oncologist*
Bryant, Hubert Hale *lawyer*
Buckley, Thomas Hugh *historian, educator*
Buthod, Mary Clare *school administrator*
Cadieux, Chester *gas industry executive*
Calvert, Delbert William *chemical company executive*
Calvert, Jon Channing *family practice physician*
Candreia, Peggy Jo *financial analyst*
Clark, Gary Carl *lawyer*
Clark, Wendell W. *lawyer*
Cobbs, James Harold *engineer, consultant*
Collins, John Roger *transportation company executive*
Cook, Harold Dale *federal judge*
Cooke, Marvin Lee *sociologist, consultant, urban planner*
Cooper, Richard Casey *lawyer*
Council, Terry Ray *military officer*
Cox, William Jackson *bishop*
†Crawford, Carol I. *opera company artistic director*
Davenport, Gerald Bruce *lawyer*
Davis, Annalee Ruth Conyers *clinical social worker*
Davis, G. Reuben *lawyer*
Davis, Lourie Irene Bell *computer education and information systems specialist*
Dearmon, Thomas Alfred *automotive industry and life insurance executive*
Deihl, Michael Allen *federal agency administrator*
Dotson, George Stephen *drilling company executive*
Duncan, Maurice Greer *accountant, consultant*
Eagan, Claire Veronica *magistrate judge*
Earlougher, Robert Charles, Sr. *petroleum engineer*
Eaton, Leonard James, Jr. *aerospace executive*
Eldridge, Richard Mark *lawyer*
Ellison, James Oliver *federal judge*
Ezechukwu, Bonnie Ok. *author, educator, counselor, poet, storyteller, multiculturalist, anti-drug and violence speaker*
Faingold, Eduardo Daniel *language and linguistics educator, researcher*
Farrell, John L., Jr. *lawyer, business executive*
Friedman, Mark Joel *cardiologist, educator*
Frizzell, Gregory Kent *judge*
Gaberino, John Anthony, Jr. *lawyer*
Gable, G. Ellis *retired lawyer*
Gentry, Bern Leon, Sr. *minority consulting company executive*
Goodman, Jerry L(ynn) *judge*
Gottschalk, Sister Mary Therese *nun, hospital administrator*
Graham, Tony M. *lawyer*
Gregg, Lawrence J. *physician*
Gustavson, Cynthia Marie *social worker, writer*
Hannah, Barbara Ann *nurse, educator*
Haring, Robert Westing *newspaper editor*
Hatfield, Jack Kenton *lawyer, accountant*
Hatfield, William Keith *minister*
Hawkins, Francis Glenn *banker, lawyer*
Haynie, Tony Wayne *lawyer*
Healey, David Lee *investment company executive*
Helmerich, Hans Christian *oil company executive*
Henderson, James Ronald *industrial real estate developer*
Hill, Delinda Jean *medical/surgical nurse, enterostomal therapy nurse*
Hill, Josephine Carmela *realtor*
Hoe, Richard March *insurance and securities consultant, writer*
Holmes, Sven Erik *federal judge*
Hood, William Wayne, Jr. *lawyer*
Horkey, William Richard *retired diversified oil company executive*
Horn, Myron Kay *consulting petroleum geologist, author, educator*
Howard, Gene Claude *lawyer, former state senator*
Huber, Fritz Godfrey *physical education educator, excercise physiologist*
Huffman, Robert Allen, Jr. *lawyer*
Hulings, Norman McDermott, Jr. *energy consultant, former company executive*
Imel, John Michael *lawyer*
Imhoff, Pamela M. *marketing educator*
Ingram, Charles Clark, Jr. *energy company executive*
†Irvin, Mary Eleanor Yturria *artist*
†Jensen, Joli *communicatons educator*
Johnson, Gerald, III *cardiovascular physiologist, researcher*
Joice, Nora Lee *clinical dietitian*
Jones, Jenk, Jr. *editor, educator*
Jones, Jenkin Lloyd *retired newspaper publisher*
Jones, Michael Lynn *financial consultant, operations manager*
Jones, Robert Lawton *architect, planner, educator*
Joyner, John Brooks *museum director*
†Joyner, Sam A. *federal judge*
Kalbfleisch, John McDowell *cardiologist, educator*
Kellough, William C. *lawyer*
Kennedy, Nancy Louise *retired draftsman*
Kern, Terry C. *judge*
Kihle, Donald Arthur *lawyer*
Killin, Charles Clark *lawyer*
King, Peter Cotterill *former utilities executive*
Kitchen, Brent A. *airport executive*
Klein, Deborah Rae *health facility administrator*
Knaust, Clara Doss *retired elementary school educator*
Korstad, John Edward *biology educator*
Kothe, Charles Aloysius *lawyer*
Kruse, David Louis, II *transportation company executive*
Kukura, Rita Anne *elementary school educator*
Lafitte, Bobby Gene *radio announcer*
Langenkamp, Sandra Carroll *retired healthcare policy executive*
La Sorsa, William George *lawyer, educator*
Lawless, Robert William *academic administrator*
Lewis, Stephen C. *prosecutor*
Luthey, Graydon Dean, Jr. *lawyer*
Mahoney, Jack *real estate broker, software developer*
Major, John Keene *radio broadcasting executive*
Manhart, Marcia Y(ockey) *art museum director*
Marlar, Donald Floyd *lawyer, partner*
Martin, Edward Thomas *cardiologist*
Matthews, Dane Dikeman *urban planner*
Matthies, Mary Constance T. *lawyer*
†McCarthy, Frank H. *federal judge*
McGee, Glorea Hooks *religious organization adminstrator, minister*
†Michael, Terrence L. *federal judge*
Miller, Gerald Cecil *immunologist, laboratory administrator, educator*
Mojtabai, Ann Grace *author, educator*
Moore, David Arthur *composer, music educator*
Murphy, Patrick Gregory *real estate company executive*
Narwold, Lewis Lammers *paper products manufacturer*
†Neal, E(verett) G(ilbert) *sculptor, clown, small business owner*
Neas, John Theodore *investment company executive*
Nettles, John Barnwell *obstetrics and gynecology educator*
Nigh, Robert Russell, Jr. *lawyer*
Okada, Robert Dean *cardiologist*
Osborn, La Donna Carol *clergywoman*
O'Toole, Allan Thomas *electric utility executive*
Owens, Jana Jae *entertainer*
Palmer, Ronald *police chief*

Parker, Robert Lee, Sr. *petroleum engineer, drilling company executive*
Parker, Robert Lee, Jr. *drilling company executive*
Plunket, Daniel Clark *pediatrician*
Prayson, Alex Stephen *drafting and mechanical design educator*
Preston, Kenneth Marshall *computer and business educator*
Price, Alice Lindsay *writer, artist*
Primeaux, Henry, III *automotive executive, author, speaker*
†Rasure, Dana L. *federal judge*
Reddicliffe, Steven *periodical editor-in-chief*
Repasky, Mark Edward *oil and gas company executive*
Rex, Lonnie Royce *religious organization administrator*
Riggs, David Lynn *company executive*
Rippley, Robert *wholesale distribution executive*
Roberson, Jerry Donn *urban planner*
Roberts, (Granville) Oral *clergyman*
Saferite, Linda Lee *library director*
Saied, James Guy *conductor, consultant*
Sanditen, Edgar Richard *investment company executive*
Savage, Susan M. *mayor*
Say, Burhan *physician*
Schaechterle, Gordon Everett *retail propane executive*
Scott, John Prosser *television program producer, management consultant*
Seymour, Stephanie Kulp *federal judge*
Shane, John Marder *endocrinologist*
Slattery, Edward J. *bishop*
Slicker, Frederick Kent *lawyer*
†Smith, Edwin Bernard *journalism and advertising educator*
Smothers, William Edgar, Jr. *geophysical exploration company executive*
Spencer, Laurie Lee *sculptor, art educator*
Spencer, Winifred May *art educator*
Stearns, Frederic William *dermatologist*
Steltzlen, Janelle Hicks *lawyer*
Stephens, C. Michael *service executive*
Stewart, Murray Baker *lawyer*
Stone, William Charles *surgeon*
Taylor, Joe Clinton *judge*
Thomas, Robert Eggleston *former corporate executive*
Thompson, Carla Jo Horn *mathematics educator*
Thompson, Harold Jerome *counselor, mental retardation professional*
Tomer, Mark John *manufacturing/research and development executive*
Tompkins, Robert George *retired physician*
Undernehr, Laura Lee *elementary education educator*
Upton, Howard B., Jr. *management writer, lawyer*
Vaughn, Rosalind Nzinga *artist*
Vincent, Carl G., Jr. *real estate portfolio manager*
Wagner, Ann Louise *management consultant, public relations executive*
Wagner, Clarence H., Jr. *charitable organization administrator*
Walker, Floyd Lee *lawyer*
Walton, Corinne Hemeter *psychotherapist, educator*
Warren, W. K., Jr. *oil industry executive*
Wesenberg, John Herman *professional society administrator*
Williams, David Rogerson, Jr. *engineer, business executive*
Williams, John Horter *civil engineer, oil, gas, telecommunications and allied products distribution company executive*
Williams, Patricia *financial analyst*
Wood, Emily Churchill *educator, educational consultant*
Worley, Joe *editor*
Wyckoff, Lydia Lloyd *art curator*

Vici
McCoy, Carroll Pierce *retired minister*

Vinita
Castor, Carol Jean *artist, teacher*
Gray, Donald Lyman *orchard owner*
Johnston, Oscar Black, III *lawyer*
Neer, Charles Sumner, II *orthopedic surgeon, educator*

Wanette
Thompson, Joyce Elizabeth *retired state education official*

Warr Acres
Weir, Richard Dale *elementary education educator*

Weatherford
Schwartz, John Charles *chemical engineer*

Welling
Varner, Joyce Ehrhardt *librarian*

Wetumka
Hughes, Steven Bryan *gas measurement company executive*

Woodward
Fisher, Deena Kaye *social studies education, administrator*
Keith, Howard Barton *surgeon*
Selman, Minnie Corene Phelps *elementary school educator*

Yale
Berger, Billie David *corrosion engineer*

Yukon
Morgan, Robert Steve *mechanical engineer*

OREGON

Albany
Chowning, Orr-Lyda Brown *dietitian*
Dooley, George Joseph, III *metallurgist*
Wood, Kenneth Arthur *retired newspaper editor, writer*
Yu, Kitson Szewai *computer science educator*

Aloha
Jones, Charles J. *transportation executive, firefighter*

Amity
†Skloot, Floyd *writer*

Applegate
Boyle, (Charles) Keith *artist, educator*
Pursglove, Betty Merle *computer-software quality assurance tester*
Pursglove, Laurence Albert *technical writer, computer quality tester*

Ashland
Addicott, Warren Oliver *retired geologist, educator*
Berkman, James L. *bicycle builder, publisher*
Bornet, Vaughn Davis *former history and social science educator, research historian*
Chatfield, Michael *accounting educator*
Christianson, Roger Gordon *biology educator*
Farrimond, George Francis, Jr. *management educator*
Fine, J. David *lawyer*
Grover, James Robb *chemist, editor*
Jackson, Elizabeth Riddle *writer, translator, educator*
Kirschner, Richard Michael *naturopathic physician, speaker, author*
Kreisman, Arthur *higher education consultant, humanities educator emeritus*
Levy, Leonard Williams *history educator, author*
MacMillen, Richard Edward *biological sciences educator, researcher*
Mularz, Theodore Leonard *architect*
Shaw, Arthur E. *conductor*
Smith, G(odfrey) T(aylor) *academic administrator*
Weeks, Roger Wolcott, Jr. *retired German and Russian language educator*

Astoria
Bainer, Philip La Vern *retired college president*
Holcom, Floyd Everett *international business consultant*
†Lee, Kristen Kae *education professional*

Athena
Mengis, Chris Ludwig *retired internist*

Azalea
Massy, Patricia Graham Bibbs (Mrs. Richard Outram Massy) *social worker, author*

Baker City
Graham, Beardsley *management consultant*

Bandon
Lindquist, Louis William *artist, writer*
Millard, Esther Lound *foundation administrator, educator*

Beavercreek
Filener, Millard Lee *wholesale and retail distribution company executive*
Lawler, Alice Bonzi (Mrs. Oscar T. Lawler) *retired college administrator, civic worker*

Beaverton
Barnes, Keith Lee *electronics executive*
Bilow, Steven Craig *computer and video systems specialist*
Bruce, John Allen *foundation executive, educator*
Chartier, Vernon Lee *electrical engineer*
†Dinh, Thin Van *electronics specialist*
Donahue, Richard King *athletic apparel executive, lawyer*
Fulsher, Allan Arthur *lawyer*
Hammond, George Simms *chemist, consultant*
Hill, Wilmer Bailey *administrative law judge*
Ivester, (Richard) Gavin *industrial designer*
Knight, Philip H(ampson) *shoe manufacturing company executive*
Little, Gayle Anne *neonatal nurse, educator*
Machida, Curtis A. *research molecular neurobiologist, educator*
Murray, Jean Rupp *communications executive, author, speaker*
†Overlund, Ervin Kenneth *pastor*
Palau, Luis *evangelist*
Parrish, Stanley Glenister *real estate broker*
Pond, Patricia Brown *library science educator, university administrator*
Sanford, David Roy *journalist, educator*
Stewart, Kirk T. *public relations executive*
Stewart, Lindsay D. *corporate lawyer*
Strobeck, Ken Leslie *state legislator, healthcare organization executive*
Swank, Roy Laver *physician, educator, inventor*
†Wilskey, Mike *marketing professional*

Bend
Acosta, Cristina Pilar *artist*
Connolly, Thomas Joseph *bishop*
Cooley, Wes *former congressman*
Donohue, Stacey Lee *English language and literature educator*
Evers-Williams, Myrlie *cultural organization administrator*
Fain, Jay Lindsey *brokerage house executive, consultant*
†Gaston, Michael *library director*
Goodman, Susan Kathleen *charitable organization administrator, educator*
Gustafson, Lewis Allan *engineering geologist*
Moore, Jerry N. *museum director*
Taylor, Gene Raymond *computer and information systems educator*
Thompson, Mari Hildenbrand *medical, legal and administrative consultant*
Wonser, Michael Dean *retired public affairs director*

Boring
Robinson, Jeanne Louise *lecturer, writer*

Brookings
Maxwell, William Stirling *retired lawyer*
Nolan, Benjamin Burke *retired civil engineer*

Camas Valley
Lounsbury, Steven Richard *lawyer*

Canby
Drummond, Gerard Kasper *lawyer, retired minerals company executive*
Flinn, Roberta Jeanne *management, computer applications consultant*
Thalhofer, Paul Terrance *lawyer*

Cannon Beach
Greaver, Harry *artist*
Hillestad, Charles Andrew *lawyer*

Central Point
Richardson, Dennis Michael *lawyer, educator*

Chiloquin
Siemens, Richard Ernest *retired metallurgy administrator, researcher*

Clackamas
Cole, June Ann *safety, health and emergency manager*
Merrill, William Dean *retired architect, medical facility planning consultant*

Coos Bay
†Wright, Deborah George *dean, author*

Coquille
Potter, Kenneth Roy *retired minister*
Taylor, George Frederick *newspaper publisher, editor*

Corvallis
†Arnold, Roy *provost, university administrator*
Arp, Daniel James *biochemistry educator*
Baird, William McKenzie *chemical carcinogenesis researcher, biochemistry educator*
Borg, Marcus Joel *theologian, theology educator*
Brown, George *research forester and educator*
Byrne, John Vincent *higher education consultant*
Castle, Emery Neal *agricultural and resource economist, educator*
Cerklewski, Florian Lee *human nutrition educator, nutritional biochemistry researcher*
Chambers, Kenton Lee *botany educator*
Coffin, Chris *managing editor*
Dalrymple, Gary Brent *research geologist*
Davis, John Rowland *university administrator*
Dennis, John Davison *minister*
Drake, Charles Whitney *physicist*
Engelbrecht, Rudolf *electrical engineering educator*
Engle, Molly *program evaluator, preventive medicine researcher, medical educator*
Evans, Harold J. *plant physiologist, biochemist, educator*
Farkas, Daniel Frederick *food science and technology educator*
Frakes, Rod Vance *plant geneticist, educator*
Gillis, John Simon *psychologist, educator*
Hafner-Eaton, Chris *health services researcher, educator*
Hall, Don Alan *editor, writer*
Hansen, Hugh Justin *agricultural engineer*
Harter, Lafayette George, Jr. *economics educator emeritus*
Healey, Deborah Lynn *education administrator*
Ho, Iwan *research plant pathologist*
Huyer, Adriana *oceanographer, educator*
Johnson, Duane P. *academic administrator*
Knudsen, James George *chemical engineer, educator*
†Lafrance, Richard Arthur *neurologist*
Landers, Teresa Price *librarian*
Liegel, Leon Herman *soil scientist, research forester*
Lumpkin, Margaret Catherine *retired education educator*
McCarthy, William Robert *minister*
Miner, John Ronald *bioresource engineer*
Mohler, Ronald Rutt *electrical engineering educator*
Moore, George W(illiam) *geologist*
Moore, Thomas Carrol *botanist, educator*
Morita, Richard Yukio *microbiology and oceanography educator*
Oldfield, James Edmund *nutrition educator*
Parker, Donald Fred *college dean, human resources management educator*
Parks, Harold Raymond *mathematician, educator*
Rapier, Pascal Moran *chemical engineer, physicist*
Risser, Paul Gillan *academic administrator, botanist*
Rounds, Donald Edwin *retired cell biologist*
Schmidt, Bruce Randolph *science administrator, researcher*
Shoemaker, Clara Brink *retired chemistry educator*
Sleight, Arthur William *chemist*
Steele, Robert Edwin *orthopedic surgeon*
Steiner, Kenneth Donald *bishop*
†Stephens, Kay Kuipers *education educator*
Storvick, Clara Amanda *nutrition educator emerita*
Temes, Gabor Charles *electrical engineering educator*
Thomas, Thomas Darrah *chemistry educator*
Trappe, James Martin *mycologist*
Van Holde, Kensal Edward *biochemistry educator*
Westwood, Melvin Neil *horticulturist, pomologist*
Wilkins, Caroline Hanke *consumer agency administrator, political worker*
Yeats, Robert Sheppard *geologist, educator*
Young, J. Lowell *soil chemist, biologist*
Young, Roy Alton *university administrator, educator*

Cottage Grove
Miller, Joanne Louise *middle school educator*
Nordin, Donald Marion *manufacturing industry executive*

Cove
Kerper, Meike *family violence, sex abuse and addiction educator, consultant*

Creswell
Briggs, Bonnie Jean *secondary school educator*

Culver
Siebert, Diane Dolores *author, poet*

Dallas
Calkins, Loren Gene *church executive, clergyman*

Dayton
Gilhooly, David James, III *artist*
Purcell, Kevin Brown *director of special services*

Depoe Bay
Fish, Barbara Joan *investor, small business owner*

Eugene
Acker, Martin Herbert *psychotherapist, educator*
Aikens, C(lyde) Melvin *anthropology educator, archaeologist*
Albert-Galtier, Alexandre *literature and language educator*
Algra, Ronald James *dermatologist*
†Alley, Frank R. *federal judge*
Ambrose, Daniel Michael *publishing executive*
Andrews, Fred Charles *mathematics educator*
Bailey, Exine Margaret Anderson *soprano, educator*
Baker, Alton Fletcher, III *newspaper editor, publishing executive*
Baker, Bridget Downey *newspaper executive*
Baker, Edwin Moody *retired newspaper publisher*
Bascom, Ruth F. *retired mayor*
Bassett, Carol Ann *journalism educator, writer*
Bennett, Robert Royce *engineering and management consultant*
Bergquist, Ed Peter, Jr. *music educator emeritus*
Biglan, Anthony *medical educator*
†Blonigen, Bruce Aloysius *economics educator*
Boekelheide, Virgil Carl *chemistry educator*
Burris, Vallon Leon, Jr. *sociologist, educator*
Calvert, Leonard James *editor, writer*
Camp, Delpha Jeanne *counselor*
Chambers, Carolyn Silva *communications company executive*
Clark, Chapin DeWitt *law educator*
†Coffin, Thomas M. *federal magistrate judge*
Cox, Joseph William *academic administrator*
Crasemann, Bernd *physicist, educator*
Davis, Richard Malone *economics educator*
Diwu, Zhenjun *chemist*
Donnelly, Marian Card *art historian, educator*
Donnelly, Russell James *physicist, educator*
Drennan, Michael Eldon *banker*
DuPriest, Douglas Millhollen *lawyer*
Edwards, Ralph M. *librarian*
†Frank, David Anthony *educator*
Frohnmayer, David Braden *university president*
Gall, Meredith Damien (Meredith Mark Damien Gall) *education educator, author*
†Gersten, Russell Monroe *educational foundation administrator*
Gillespie, Penny Hannig *business owner*
Girardeau, Marvin Denham *physics educator*
†Goins, Steven Carter *pediatric neurologist*
Griffith, Osbie Hayes *chemistry educator*
Grossen, Bonnie Joy *education research scientist*
Gwartney, Patricia Anne *sociology educator*
Hale, Dean Edward *social services administrator*
Hamren, Nancy Van Brasch *bookkeeper*
Harth-Bedoya, Miguel *conductor*
Henner, Martin E. *arbitrator, mediator*
Hess, Suzanne Harriet *newspaper administrator, photographer*
Hildebrand, Carol Ilene *librarian*
Hildenbrand, Donald Gerald *editor*
Hogan, Michael R(obert) *judge*
Hoy, Harold Henry *artist*
Khang, Chulsoon *economics educator*
Lande, Russell Scott *biologist, educator*
Leeds, Elizabeth Louise *miniature collectibles executive*
Li, David Leiwei *English and Asian American studies educator*
Lindholm, Richard Theodore *economics and finance educator*
Littman, Richard Anton *psychologist, educator*
Loescher, Richard Alvin *gastroenterologist*
Martin, John Stewart *software engineer*
Matthews, Brian W. *molecular biology educator*
Mazo, Robert Marc *chemistry educator, retired*
†McMillen, Shannon M. *urologist*
Miner, John Burnham *industrial relations educator, writer*
†Mohr, Debbie (Doris Elaine) *author*
Morrison, Perry David *librarian, educator*
Moseley, John Travis *university administrator, research physicist*
Mumford, William Porter, II *lawyer*
Pascal, C(ecil) Bennett *classics educator*
Peterson, Donna Rae *marketing professional*
†Radcliffe, Albert E. *bankruptcy judge*
Retallack, Gregory John *geologist educator*
Richards, James William *electromechanical engineer*
Roe, Thomas Leroy Willis *pediatrician*
Runge, Jody *coach*
Sahlstrom, E(lmer) B(ernard) *retired lawyer*
Sanders, Jack Thomas *religious studies educator*
Schellman, John A. *chemistry educator*
Schroeder, Donald J. *orthopedic surgeon*
Scoles, Eugene Francis *law educator, lawyer*
Sherriffs, Ronald Everett *communication and film educator*
Stahl, Franklin William *biology educator*
Starr, Grier Forsythe *retired pathologist*
Tykeson, Donald Erwin *broadcasting executive*
von Hippel, Peter Hans *chemistry educator*
Watson, Mary Ellen *ophthalmic technologist*
Wickes, George *English language educator, writer*
Wilhelm, Kate (Katy Gertrude) *author*
Winnowski, Thaddeus Richard (Ted Winnowski) *bank executive*
Wood, Daniel Brian *educational consultant*
Youngquist, Walter Lewellyn *consulting geologist*

Florence
Corless, Dorothy Alice *nurse educator*
Day, John Francis *city official, former savings and loan executive, former mayor*
Ericksen, Jerald Laverne *educator, engineering scientist*
Gray, Augustine Heard, Jr. *computer consultant*
Serra, Robert Emmett *newspaper editor*

Forest Grove
Boersema, David Brian *philosopher, educator*
Carson, William Morris *manpower planning and development advisor*
Gibby-Smith, Barbara *psychologist, nurse*
Moeller, Bonnie Jean *elementary school educator*
Randolph, Harry (Randy) Franklin, III *health facility administrator, educator, physician assistant*
Singleton, Francis Seth *dean*

Gold Beach
Dillon, Robert Morton *retired association executive, architectural consultant*
Gores, Gary Gene *credit union sales manager*

Grand Junction
Van Horn, O. Frank *retired counselor, consultant*

Grants Pass
Boling, Judy Atwood *civic worker*
Comeaux, Katharine Jeanne *realtor*
Davis, Maxine Mollie *nurse*
Marchini, Claudia Cilloniz *artist*
Petersen, Michael Kevin *internist,endoscopist, osteopathic physician*
Remington, Mary *artist, author*

Smith, Barnard Elliot *management educator*
Stafford, Patrick Purcell *poet, writer, management consultant*

Gresham
Davis Lash, Cynthia *public health nurse*
Light, Betty Jensen Pritchett *former college dean*
Nicholson, R. Stephen *organization administrator*
†Vela, Joel E. *college president*
Webb, Donna Louise *academic director, educator*

Hermiston
Ortiz, James George *educator*

Hillsboro
Bhagwan, Sudhir *computer industry and research executive, consultant*
Carruthers, John Robert *scientist*
Cleveland, Charles Sidney *secondary education educator*
Curry, Everett William, Jr. *minister*
Matlock, John Hudson *science administrator, materials engineer*
Rice, Richard Lee, Jr. *minister, office manager*
Rotithor, Hemant Govind *electrical engineer*
Yang, Lin *chemist*
Yates, Keith Lamar *retired insurance company executive*

Hood River
Browning, Edmond Lee *retired bishop*

Hubbard
Hick, Kenneth William *business executive*

Jacksonville
Lowe, Barbara Annette *retired elementary education educator*

Joseph
Gilbert, David Erwin *retired academic administrator, physicist*

Junction City
Humphry, Derek *association executive, writer*
Sharples, Thomas Davy *retired mechanical engineer*

Keizer
Null, Paul Bryan *minister*

Klamath Falls
Bohnen, Robert Frank *hematologist, oncologist, educator*
Hunsucker, Robert Dudley *physicist, electrical engineer, educator, researcher*
Klepper, Carol Herdman *mental health therapist*
Leonhardt, Thomas Wilburn *librarian, library director*
Pastega, Richard Louis *retail specialist*
Wendt, Richard L. *manufacturing executive*

Lake Oswego
†Bullivant, Rupert Reid *lawyer*
Byczynski, Edward Frank *lawyer, financial executive*
Campbell, Colin Herald *former mayor*
Cooper, Rachel Bremer *accountant*
Gawf, John Lee *foreign service officer*
Kovtynovich, Dan *civil engineer*
Ladehoff, Robert Louis *bishop*
Le Shana, David Charles *retired academic administrator*
McPeak, Merrill Anthony *business executive, consultant, retired officer*
Meltebeke, Renette *career counselor*
Morse, Lowell Wesley *banking and real estate executive*
Mylnechuk, Larry Herbert *financial executive*
Silbert, Amy Foxman *clinical art therapist*
Stewart, Thomas Clifford *trading and investment company executive*
Thong, Tran *biomedical company executive*
†Waggener, Melissa *public relations executive*

Lebanon
Girod, Frank Paul *retired surgeon*
Kuntz, Joel Dubois *lawyer*
Pearson, Dennis Lee *optometrist*

Lincoln City
Gehrig, Edward Harry *electrical engineer, consultant*

Madras
Brooks, Marian *retired comptroller and credit manager*
Hillis, Stephen Kendall *secondary education educator*

Mcminnville
Naylor-Jackson, Jerry *public relations consultant, retired, entertainer, broadcaster*
Roberts, Michael Foster *biology educator*
Walker, Charles Urmston *retired university president*

Medford
Barnes, Joseph Curtis *aircraft development executive*
Bouquet, Francis Lester *physicist*
Cole, Richard George *public administrator*
Davenport, Wilbur Bayley, Jr. *electrical engineering educator*
Deatherage, William Vernon *lawyer*
Hannum, Gerald Luther (Lou Hannum) *retired tire manufacturing company official*
Hennion, Carolyn Laird (Lyn Hennion) *investment executive*
Hennion, Reeve Lawrence *communications executive*
Horton, Lawrence Stanley *electrical engineer, apartment developer*
Johnson, Morgan Burton *artist, writer*
Keener, John Wesley *management consultant*
Kent, Roberta B. *literary consultant*
Lantis, Donna Lea *retired banker, art educator, artist*
Linn, Carole Anne *dietitian*
Mansfield, William Amos *lawyer*
O'Connor, Karl William (Goodyear Johnson) *lawyer*
†Ryder, Stephen Willis *newspaper publisher*
Shinn, Duane K. *music publisher*
Skelton, Douglas H. *architect*
Smith, Robert F. (Bob Smith) *rancher, congressman*
Sours, James Kingsley *association executive, former college president*
Stong, John Elliott *retail music and electronic company executive*
Straus, David A. *architectural firm executive*
Tevis, Barry Lee *television producer, marketing executive*
Vinyard, Roy George, II *hospital administrator*
†Worland, Ronald Glenn *plastic surgeon*

Merrill
Porter, Roberta Ann *counselor, educator, school system administrator*

Milwaukie
Michael, Gary Linn *architect, artist*
Staver, Leroy Baldwin *banker*

Monmouth
Forcier, Richard Charles *information technology educator, computer applications consultant*
White, Donald Harvey *physics educator emeritus*

Myrtle Creek
Hull, Tom Allan *mechanics educator*
Shirtcliff, John Delzell *business owner, oil jobber*

Myrtle Point
Walsh, Don *marine consultant, executive*

Newberg
Adams, Wayne Verdun *pediatric psychologist, educator*
†Austin, Joan D. *personal care industry executive*
Keith, Pauline Mary *artist, illustrator, writer*
McMahon, Paul Francis *finance company executive*

Newport
Kennedy, Richard Jerome *writer*
Weber, Lavern John *marine science administrator, educator*

North Bend
de Sá e Silva, Elizabeth Anne *secondary school educator*
Shepard, Robert Carlton *English language educator*
†Vendler, Zeno *retired philosophy educator*

Oakland
Smelt, Ronald *retired aircraft company executive*

Oceanside
Wadlow, Joan Krueger *academic administrator*

Ontario
Edwards, Dale Leon *library director*
Tyler, Donald Earl *urologist*

Oregon City
Hill, Gary D. *lawyer*
Lareau, Virginia Ruth *counselor*

Otis
Haralson, Linda Jane *communications executive*
King, Frank William *writer*

Otter Rock
Eaton, Leonard Kimball *retired architecture educator*
Kassner, Michael Ernest *materials science educator, researcher*

Pendleton
Bedford, Amy Aldrich *public relations executive, corporation secretary*
†Bloom, Stephen Michael *magistrate judge, lawyer*
Harper, Gloria Janet *artist, educator*
Jensen, Judy Dianne *psychotherapist*
Klepper, Elizabeth Lee *physiologist*
Nichols, Albert Myron *minister*
†Reeder, Clinton Bruce *farmer*
Smiley, Richard Wayne *research center administrator, researcher*

Philomath
Stensvad, Allan Maurice *minister*

Phoenix
Blackman, David Lee *research scientist*
Dodd, Darlene Mae *nurse, retired air force officer*

Pleasant Hill
Kesey, Ken *writer*

Port Orford
Drinnon, Richard *history educator*

Portland
Abbott, Robert Carl *management company executive*
Abrams, Marc *lawyer, state political party executive*
Abravanel, Allan Ray *lawyer*
Ace, Katherine *artist*
Achterman, Gail Louise *lawyer*
Ahuja, Jagdish Chand *mathematics educator*
Anderegg, Karen Klok *management and marketing consultant*
Anderson, Herbert Hatfield *lawyer, farmer*
Arthur, Michael Elbert *lawyer*
†Ashmanskas, Donald C. *federal judge*
Bacon, Vicky Lee *lighting services executive*
Bailey, Robert C. *opera company executive*
Baker, Diane R.H. *dermatologist*
Baker, Timothy Alan *healthcare administrator, educator, consultant*
Bakkensen, John Reser *lawyer*
Baldwin-Halvorsen, Lisa Rogene *community health and critical care nurse*
Balmer, Thomas Ancil *lawyer*
Barmack, Neal Herbert *neuroscientist*
Barnes, Lynne Hanawalt *nurse, educator*
Bauer, Louis Edward *retail bookstore executive, educator*
Beatty, John Cabeen, Jr. *judge*
Becker, Bruce Douglas *mechanical engineer*
Bennett, Charles Leon *vocational and graphic arts educator*
Bennett, William Michael *physician*
Benson, John Alexander, Jr. *physician, educator*
Berentsen, Kurtis George *music educator, choral conductor*
Berger, Leland Roger *lawyer*
Bernstine, Daniel O'Neal *law educator, university president*
Bhatia, Peter K. *editor, journalist*
Bither, Marilyn Kaye *emergency nurse, educator*
Blodgett, Forrest Clinton *economics educator*
Blumberg, Naomi *symphony musician, educator*
Blumel, Joseph Carlton *university president*
Bosch, Samuel Henry *computer company executive*
Boston, Gretha *mezzo-soprano, actress*
Bowyer, Joan Elizabeth *medical technologist, realtor*
Boyle, Gertrude *sportswear company executive*
Boynton, Robert Granville *computer systems analyst*
Brenneman, Delbert Jay *lawyer*
†Brockley, John P. *state agency executive, airport executive*
Broughton, Ray Monroe *economic consultant*
Brown, Deborah Elizabeth *television producer*
Browne, Joseph Peter *retired librarian*
Bruechert, Beverly Ann *interior design consultant, recording artist, pianist*
Buchanan, John E., Jr. *museum director*
Burton, Mike *regional government officer*
Butler, Leslie Ann *advertising agency owner, artist, writer, editor*
Button, Jerry Edward *biologist*
Cable, John Franklin *lawyer*
Campbell, John Richard *pediatric surgeon*
Canaday, Richard A. *lawyer*
Canfield, James *art director*
Cantelon, John Edward *academic administrator*
†Carlile, Henry David *poet, writer, educator*
Cassidy, Richard Arthur *environmental engineer, governmental water resources specialist*
Cereghino, James Joseph *health facility administrator, neurologist*
Chevis, Cheryl Ann *lawyer*
Cichoke, Anthony Joseph, Jr. *chiropractor, writer, health consultant, researcher, lecturer*
Clarke, J(oseph) Henry *dental educator, dentist*
Claycomb, Cecil Keith *biochemist, educator*
Cohen, Norm *chemist*
Collins, Maribeth Wilson *foundation president*
Collins, Michael Sean *obstetrician and gynecologist, educator*
Conkling, Roger Linton *consultant, business administration educator, retired utility executive*
Connor, William Elliott *physician, educator*
†Cooke, Roger Anthony *lawyer*
Cooper, Ginnie *library director*
Crabbs, Roger Alan *publisher, consultant, small business owner, educator*
Crawshaw, Ralph *psychiatrist*
Crowell, John B., Jr. *lawyer, former government official*
Dahl, Joyle Cochran *lawyer*
Dailey, Dianne K. *lawyer*
Daly, Donald F. *engineering company executive*
Davis, James Allan *gerontologist, educator*
Day, L. B. *management consultant*
Deering, Thomas Phillips *lawyer*
DeMots, Henry *cardiologist*
†DePreist, James Anderson *conductor*
De Roest, Jan Marie *mental health counselor*
Dickinson, Janet Mae Webster *relocation consulting executive*
Dotten, Michael Chester *lawyer*
Dow, Mary Alexis *auditor*
Dryden, Robert D. *engineering educator*
†Dunleavy, Michael Joseph *professional basketball coach*
†Dunn, Randall L. *federal judge*
Eberwein, Barton Douglas *construction company executive, consultant*
Edwards, Richard Alan *lawyer*
Eichinger, Marilynne H. *museum administrator*
Eighmey, George V. *lawyer, state legislator*
Englert, Walter George *classics and humanities educator*
English, Stephen F. *lawyer*
Epperson, Eric Robert *financial executive, film producer*
Epstein, Edward Louis *lawyer*
Erickson, Pamela Sue *state agency administrator*
Eshelman, William Robert *librarian, editor*
Fell, James F. *lawyer*
Ferrua, Pietro Michele Stefano *foreign language educator, writer*
Feuerstein, Howard M. *lawyer*
Finley, Lewis Merren *financial consultant*
Flowerree, Robert Edmund *retired forest products company executive*
Foehl, Edward Albert *chemical company executive*
Foley, Ridgway Knight, Jr. *lawyer, writer*
Forsberg, Charles Alton *computer, information systems engineer*
Foster, Mark Edward *lawyer, consultant, international lobbyist*
Franzke, Richard Albert *lawyer*
Frasca, Robert John *architect*
Fraunfelder, Frederick Theodore *ophthalmologist, educator*
Frisbee, Don Calvin *retired utilities executive*
Fritz, Barbara Jean *occupational health nurse*
Frye, Helen Jackson *judge*
Furse, Elizabeth *former congresswoman, small business owner*
Galbraith, John Robert *insurance company exeuctive*
Georges, Maurice Ostrow *retired lawyer*
Giffin, Sandra Lee *nursing administrator*
Gilkey, Gordon Waverly *curator, artist*
Gillette, Richard Gareth *neurophysiology educator, researcher*
Glasgow, William Jacob *lawyer, venture capitalist, business executive*
Glass, Laurel Ellen *gerontologist, developmental biologist, physician, retired educator*
Glickman, Harry *professional basketball team executive*
Goldfarb, Timothy Moore *hospital administrator*
Graber, Susan P. *judge*
Grant, Brian Wade (General Grant) *professional basketball player*
Grappe, Harold Hugo *civil engineer*
Gray, John Delton *retired manufacturing company executive*
Greene, Herbert Bruce *lawyer, investor*
Greenlick, Merwyn Ronald *health services researcher*
Greer, Monte Arnold *physician, educator*
†Griffin, Robert H. *army officer*
Griggs, Gail *marketing executive*
Grimsbo, Raymond Allen *forensic scientist*
Gunnels, Mary Dahlgren *trauma coordinator*
Gunsul, Brooks R. W. *architect*
Hacker, Thomas Owen *architect*
Hagenstein, William David *forester, consultant*
Haggerty, Ancer Lee *judge*
Hagmeier, Clarence Howard *retired anesthesiologist*
†Hall, Mike Burt (Marshall B.) *artist, educator*
Hanna, Harry Mitchell *lawyer*
Harrell, Gary Paul *lawyer*
Harris, Frederick Philip *retired philosophy educator*
†Hart, Jack Robert *newspaper editor*
Hart, John Edward *lawyer*
Hatfield, Mark Odom *former senator*
Heart, Tracy *therapist, counselor*
Helmer, M(artha) Christie *lawyer*
†Hemstreet, Mark S. *hotel executive*
Henderson, George Miller *foundation executive, former banker*
Henry, Samuel Dudley *educator*
Hergenhan, Kenneth William *lawyer*
Higdon, Polly Susanne *federal judge*
Hill, James Edward *insurance company executive*
Hill, Mary Lou *accountant, business consultant*
Hinckley, Gregory Keith *financial executive*
Hinkle, Charles Frederick *lawyer, clergyman, educator*
Holman, Donald Reid *lawyer*
Howorth, David Bishop *lawyer*
Hubel, Dennis James *judge*
Hudson, Jerry E. *foundation administrator*
Huggett, Monica *performing company executive*
Hurd, Paul Gemmill *lawyer*
Hutchens, Tyra Thornton *physician, educator*
Jacob, Stanley Wallace *surgeon, educator*
Janzen, Timothy Paul *family practice physician*
†Jelderks, John A. *federal judge*
Jenkins, Donald John *art museum administrator*
Jensen, Edmund Paul *retired bank holding company executive*
Jensen, Marion Pauline *singer*
Jernstedt, Kenneth Elliott *lawyer*
†Johnson, Mark Andrew *lawyer*
Johnson, Martin Clifton *physician*
Johnson, Thomas Floyd *former college president, educator*
Johnston, Virginia Evelyn *editor*
Jones, Richard Theodore *biochemistry educator*
Jones, Robert Edward *federal judge*
Josephson, Richard Carl *lawyer*
Julien, Robert Michael *anesthesiologist, author*
Jungers, Francis *oil consultant*
Kafoury, Marge *city official*
Katz, Vera *mayor, former college administrator, state legislator*
Kendall, John Walker, Jr. *medical educator, researcher, university dean*
Kennedy, Jack Leland *lawyer*
Kennedy, R. Evan *engineering executive, consultant, retired structural engineer*
Kester, Randall Blair *lawyer*
Khalil, Mohammad Aslam Khan *environmental science and engineering educator, physics educator*
Kilbourn, Lee Ferris *architect, specifications writer*
Kimbrell, Leonard Buell *retired art history educator, art appraiser*
King, Garr Michael *federal judge*
Kinley, Loren Dhue *museum director*
Kleim, E. Denise *city official*
Knoll, James Lewis *lawyer*
Koblik, Stevens S. *academic administrator*
Kohler, Peter Ogden *physician, educator, university president*
Kolde, Bert *professional basketball team executive*
Krahmer, Donald Leroy, Jr. *lawyer*
Kristof, Ladis Kris Donabed *political scientist, author*
Lacrosse, Patrick *museum administrator*
Lambert, Richard William *mathematics educator*
Lang, Philip David *former state legislator, insurance company executive*
Langrock, Karl Frederick *former academic administrator*
Larpenteur, James Albert, Jr. *lawyer*
Larson, Wanda Z(ackovich) *writer, poet*
Lawrence, Sally Clark *academic administrator*
Leavy, Edward *judge*
†Lee, Susan E. *public affairs coordinator*
Leedy, Robert Allan, Sr. *retired lawyer*
Leineweber, Peter Anthony *forest products company executive*
Lewis, Kenneth *shipping executive*
Leyden, Norman *conductor*
Lilly, Elizabeth Giles *mobile park executive*
Lindley, Thomas Ernest *environmental and trial lawyer, law educator*
Linstone, Harold Adrian *management and systems science educator*
Loewenthal, Nessa Parker *communications educator*
†Lorenz, Nancy *artist*
Love, William Edward *lawyer*
Lynch, Nita Marie Smith *vocational curriculum developer, ballroom dancer*
Maclean, Charles (Bernard Maclean) *philanthropy researcher, consultant, coach*
Maloney, Robert E., Jr. *lawyer*
Mapes, Jeffrey Robert *journalist*
Marsh, John Harrison *environmental planner, lawyer*
Marsh, Malcolm F. *federal judge*
Marshall, David Brownell *biologist, consultant*
Martin, Ernest Lee *academic administrator, historian, theologian, writer*
Martinez-Maldonado, Manuel *medical service administrator, physician*
Mason, Sara Smith *managed healthcare consultant*
Matarazzo, Harris Starr *lawyer*
Matarazzo, Joseph Dominic *psychologist, educator*
McClave, Donald Silsbee *professional society administrator*
McCoy, Eugene Lynn *civil engineer*
McDaniel, Rickey David *senior living executive*
McDonald, Robert Wayne *cardiac sonographer*
McKay, Laura L. *banker, consultant*
McKennon, Keith Robert *chemical company executive*
Meighan, Stuart Spence *hospital consultant, internist, writer*
Miller, Robert G. *retail company executive*
Miller, William Richey, Jr. *lawyer*
Mooney, Michael Joseph *college president*
Moose, Charles A. *state official*
Morgan, Gwendolyn Jean *minister, writer*
Morgan, James Earl *librarian, administrator*
Mowe, Gregory Robert *lawyer*
Murphy, Francis Seward *journalist*
Nagel, Stanley Blair *retired construction and investment executive*
Nash, Frank Erwin *lawyer*
Noonan, William Donald *physician, lawyer*
Nunn, Robert Warne *lawyer*
Olson, Roger Norman *health service administrator*
Orloff, Chet *cultural organization administrator*
O'Scannlain, Diarmuid Fionntain *judge*
Palmer, Earl A. *ophthalmologist, educator*
Pamplin, Robert Boisseau, Sr. *textile manufacturing executive, retired*
Pamplin, Robert Boisseau, Jr. *manufacturing company executive, minister, writer*

Archbald
Drozdis, Lori *medical/surgical nurse*

Ardmore
Beebe, Leo Clair *industrial equipment executive, former educator*
Gerbner, George *communications educator, university dean emeritus*
Ginsburgh, Brook *association executive*
Gutwirth, Marcel Marc *French literature educator*
Kline, George Louis *author, translator, retired philosophy and literature educator*
Lockett-Egan, Marian Workman *advertising executive*
Luther, Judy *management consultant*
†Maginnis, Robert P. *bishop*
Mirick, Henry Dustin *architect*
Noone, Kathleen Mary *art educator*
Stanley, Edward Alexander *geologist, forensic scientist, technical and academic administrator*
Winsor, Eleanor Webster *dispute resolution company executive*

Ashland
Lucas, Harry David *secondary education educator*

Aston
Cadorette, Lisa Roberts *medical, surgical nurse*
Gambescia, Stephen Francis *higher education administrator*
Horvath, David Bruce *computer consultant, writer, educator*

Auburn
Johnson, Barbara Jean *rehabilitation nurse, gerontology nurse*
Ruof, Richard Alan *clergyman*

Audubon
†Palmer, Christine M. *mathematics educator*

Avoca
Centini, Barry J. *airport administrator*
†Keelan, Hugh *music director*

Avondale
Foster, Paul *playwright*
Friel, Daniel Denwood, Sr. *manufacturing executive*

Baden
Hodge, Daniel Ray *auditor*
†Stuban, Michael L. *management professional*

Bairdford
Lewetag, Bonita Louise *education manager*

Bala Cynwyd
Albertini, Stephen Anthony *public relations and advertising executive*
Bausher, Verne C(harles) *banker*
Begley, Dennis *radio station executive*
Bentivegna, Peter Ignatius *architectural company executive*
Bersh, Philip Joseph *psychologist, educator*
Blumberg, June Beth *artist*
Cades, Stewart Russell *lawyer, communications company executive*
Cander, Leon *physician, educator*
Cawthorn, Robert Elston *health care executive*
Chiu, Helen Lienhard *educator*
Chiusano, Michael Augustus *urologic surgeon, mechanical engineer*
Chovanes, Eugene *lawyer*
Corliss, John Ozro *zoology educator*
Driscoll, Edward Carroll *construction management firm executive*
DuBois, Ruth Harberg *human service agency executive*
Ezold, Nancy O'Mara *lawyer*
Field, Joseph Myron *broadcast executive*
Frankel, Andrew Joel *management consultant*
Furey, Susan Mary *elementary education educator*
Furlong, Edward V., Jr. *paper company executive*
Garrity, Vincent Francis, Jr. *lawyer*
Gerber, Albert B. *lawyer, former legal association executive*
Hosey, Sheryl Lynn Miller *editor*
Isdaner, Lawrence Arthur *accountant*
Kane-Vanni, Patricia Ruth *lawyer, production consultant, educator*
Kates, Gerald Saul *printing executive*
Lasak, John Joseph *lawyer*
Lee, Jerry *broadcast executive*
Lotman, Herbert *food processing executive*
Manko, Joseph Martin, Sr. *lawyer*
Marden, Philip Ayer *physician, educator*
McGill, Dan Mays *insurance business educator*
Miller, L. Martin *accountant, financial planning specialist*
Odell, Herbert *lawyer*
Oswald, James Marlin *education educator*
Peret, Karen Krzyminski *health service administrator*
Rines, John Randolph *automotive company executive*
†Robinson, James Alfred *retired educator*
Shepard, Geoffrey Carroll *insurance executive*
Sutnick, Alton Ivan *dean, educator, researcher, physician*
Wiener, Thomas Eli *lawyer*

Bally
Kelsch, Joan Mary *elementary education educator*

Bangor
Spry, Donald Francis, II *lawyer*
Wolf, Stewart George, Jr. *physician, medical educator*

Bart
Scaccia, Leo Ralph, III *nurse*

Barto
Isett, Deborah Michele Gunther *elementary education educator*
†Knight, Cheryl DuBois *library director*

Bath
Smith, Cathy Dawn *administrator*

Beaver
James, Robert Brandon *social service agency administrator*
Ledebur, Linas Vockroth, Jr. *retired lawyer*
Price, Ronald James *electrical products company executive*
Sefton, Mildred McDonald *retired educator*

Beaver Falls
Copeland, Robert Marshall *music educator*
†Focer-Richards, Linda Jean *library director*
Lambert, Lynda Jeanne *humanities, arts educator, artist*
Mulhollen, Phyllis Marie *special education educator, instructional support coordinator*

Bedford
Koontz, Brad Matthew *accountant*

Belle Vernon
Kline, Bonita Ann *middle school guidance counselor, educator*
Wapiennik, Carl Francis *manufacturing firm executive, planetarium and science institute executive*

Bellefonte
Betz, William Robert *chemist*

Bensalem
Bevan, Norman Edward *religious organization executive*
Burtt, James *humanities educator*
Graf, William J. *entrepreneur*
Kang, Benjamin Toyeong *writer, clergyman*
Klingerman, Karen Nina *elementary school educator, teacher consultant, course coordinator*
Sergey, John Michael, Jr. *distribution company executive*

Berwick
Crake, Roger F. *general surgeon*
Michael, Phyllis Callender *composer*

Berwyn
Base, Carol Cunningham *occupational health nurse, clinical research scientist*
Burch, John Walter *mining equipment company executive*
Ewing, Joseph Neff, Jr. *lawyer*
Fry, Clarence Herbert *retail executive*
Gadsden, Christopher Henry *lawyer*
Gockley, Barbara Jean *corporate professional*
Greene, Ronald D. *advertising executive*
Guenther, George Carpenter *travel company executive, retired*
Huffaker, John Boston *lawyer*
Ledwith, James Robb *lawyer*
Markle, John, Jr. *lawyer*
Mauch, Robert Carl *service industry executive, venture capitalist*
McIntyre, James Owen *insurance executive*
Reed, Clarence Raymond *retired association executive*
Silverman, Stanley Wayne *chemical company executive*
Swank, Annette Marie *software designer*
Watters, Edward McLain, III *lawyer*
Weinberg, Michael *psychologist*
Whittington, Cathy Dee *chemist*
Wood, Thomas E. *lawyer*

Bethel Park
Bohn, James Francis *physical education educator*
Buyny, Marianne Jo *eating disorders therapist, addictions counselor*
Douds, Virginia Lee *elementary education educator*
Funka, Thomas Howard *minister*
Korchynsky, Michael *metallurgical engineer*
Marrs, Sharon Carter *librarian*
O'Donnell, William James *engineering executive*
Willard, John Gerard *consultant, author, lecturer*

Bethlehem
Alhadeff, Jack Abraham *biochemist, educator*
Allen, Beatrice *music educator, pianist*
Anderson, David Martin *environmental health engineer*
Aronson, Jay Richard *economics educator, researcher, academic administrator*
Barnette, Curtis Handley *steel company executive, lawyer*
Barsness, Richard Webster *management educator, administrator*
Beedle, Lynn Simpson *civil engineering educator*
Beidler, Peter Grant *English educator*
Benz, Edward John *clinical pathologist*
Bergethon, Kaare Roald *retired college president*
†Caldwell, Douglas W. *clergyman*
Chen, John C. *chemical engineering educator*
Church, Thomas Trowbridge *former steel company executive*
Cole, Jack Eli *physician*
Corriere, Julie Anne *family therapist*
Dorward, Judith A. *association executive*
Dowling, Joseph Albert *historian, educator*
Durkee, Jackson Leland *civil engineer*
Eades, J. A. *electron microscopist, physicist, consultant*
Erdogan, Fazil *mechanical engineer*
Evenson, Edward Bernard *geology educator*
†Farrington, Gregory C. *university administrator*
Felix, Patricia Jean *steel company purchasing professional*
Filipos, Xenia Elizabeth Lychos *political scientist*
Fisher, John William *civil engineering educator*
Friedman, Sharon Mae *science journalism educator*
Georgakis, Christos *chemical engineer educator, consultant, researcher*
Ghosh, Bhaskar Kumar *statistics educator, researcher*
Graham, William Henry *lawyer*
Gunton, James Douglas *physics educator*
Hartmann, Robert Elliott *manufacturing company executive, retired*
Haynes, Thomas Morris *philosophy educator*
Heath, Douglas Edwin *geography educator*
Heindel, Ned Duane *chemistry educator*
†Herrenkohl, Roy Cecil *psychology educator*
Hertzberg, Richard Warren *materials science and engineering educator, researcher*
Hobbs, James Beverly *business administration educator, writer*
Karakash, John J. *engineering educator*
†Lasker, Judith N. *sociologist, educator*
Levy, Edward Kenneth *mechanical engineering educator*
Lewis, Andrew Lindsay, Jr. (Drew Lewis) *former transportation and natural resources executive*
Lindgren, John Ralph *philosophy educator*
Lyman, Charles Edson *materials scientist, educator*
†Markley, Nelson G. *academic administrator*
McAulay, Alastair D. *electrical and computer engineer, educator*
Mraz, John Stephen *Roman Catholic priest*
Penny, Roger Pratt *management executive*
Pense, Alan Wiggins *metallurgical engineer, academic administrator*
Rivlin, Ronald Samuel *mathematics educator emeritus*
Roberts, Leonard Robert *English language educator, poet*
Rokke, Ervin Jerome *college president*
Rushton, Brian Mandel *chemical company executive*
†Scanlon, Edward Charles *clinical psychologist*
Schattschneider, Doris Jean *mathematics educator*
Schumacher, Susan Louise *underwriter*
Schwartz, Eli *economics educator, writer*
Smyth, Donald Morgan *chemical educator, researcher*
†Spengler, Mark Glenn *educator*
Spillman, Robert Arnold *architect*
Steffen, Lloyd Howard *minister, religion educator*
Stella, John Anthony *investment company executive*
Styer, Jane M. *computer consultant*
Troyan, Sue *university head coach women's basketball*
Tuzla, Kemal *mechanical engineer, scientist*
Watkins, George Daniels *physics educator*
Weidner, Richard Tilghman *physicist, educator*
Wenzel, Leonard Andrew *engineering educator*
†Zerkle, Paula Ring *music educator*

Birdsboro
Lewars, James A. *historic site director*
Mengle, Tobi Dara *mechanical engineer, consultant*
†Shipe, Susan Louise *librarian*

Bloomsburg
†Holdren, Murray F. *municipal official*
Lowthert, William Hughes, III *utility company executive*
Miller, David Jergen *insurance executive*
Salas Elorza, Jesús *language educator*
Stropnicky, Gerard Patrick *theater director, consultant*
Ulloth, Dana Royal *communications educator*

Blue Bell
Baine, Richard Joseph *vocational rehabilitation counselor*
Barron, Harold Sheldon *lawyer*
Barry, Lei *medical equipment manufacturing executive*
Bell, Michael G. *trade association administrator*
Brendlinger, LeRoy R. *college president*
Cartlidge, Edward Sutterley *mechanical engineer*
Cherry, John Paul *science research center director, researcher*
Drye, William James *business owner*
Elliott, John Michael *lawyer*
Faden, Lee Jeffrey *technical advisory service executive*
Flaherty, Lois Talbot *psychiatrist, educator*
Giordano, Nicholas Anthony *stock exchange executive*
Gleklen, Donald Morse *investment company executive*
Halas, Cynthia Ann *business information specialist*
Miniutti, John Roberts *software services executive*
Nichols, James Lee *advertising executive*
Scheuring, David Keith, Sr. *financial services company executive*
Settle, Eric Lawrence *lawyer*
Siedzikowski, Henry Francis *lawyer*
Simon, David Frederick *lawyer*
Swansen, Samuel Theodore *lawyer*
Teklits, Joseph Anthony *lawyer*
Theis, Steven Thomas *executive safety director*
Villwock, Kenneth James *procurement executive*
Weinbach, Lawrence Allen *business executive*
Young, Charles Randall *software professional*

Boalsburg
Gettig, Martin Winthrop *retired mechanical engineer*
Rashid, Kamal A. *program director, researcher*

Boothwyn
Bagley, Mark Joseph *investment analyst*

Boswell
Straw, Gary Lee *construction company executive*

Boyertown
Slider, Dorla Dean (Freeman) *artist*
Thomas, Richard Earl, Jr. *biologist*

Brackney
Carlson, Paul Robins *Presbyterian minister, author*

Braddock
Slack, Edward Dorsey, III *financial systems professional, consultant*

Bradford
Cox, J. Arthur *minister*
Hauser, Christopher George *lawyer*
Rice, Lester *electronics company executive*
Ross, Jean Louise *physical education educator*

Bradfordwoods
Allardice, John McCarrell *coatings manufacturing company executive*

Breinigsville
Brady, Jeffrey Kevin *photographer*

Brentwood
Swanson, Fred A. *retired communications designer, former councilman*

Bridgeport
Kevis, David Ernest *author*

Bridgeville
Andersen, Theodore Selmer *engineering manager*
Keddie, Roland Thomas *physician, hospital administrator, lawyer*

Bristol
Atkinson, Susan D. *producing artistic director, theatrical consultant*
Bush, Harold Ehrig *computer consultant*
Shenefelt, Arthur B. *transportation executive, consultant*

Brodbecks
McMenamin, Helen Marie Foran *home health care, pediatric, and maternal nurse*

Brodheadsville
†Smith, Wanda Lou *English educator*

Brookhaven
DiRosa, Steven Joseph *primary and secondary school educator*

Brookville
Smith, Sharon Louise *lawyer, consultant*

Broomall
Cohen, Philip D. *book publishing executive*
Czuj, Chester Francis, Jr. *food service professional*
Emplit, Raymond Henry *electrical engineer*
Narin, Stephen B. *lawyer*
Saunders, Sally Love *poet, educator*

Brownsville
†Blaine, Barry Richard *library director*
†Martin, Richard H. *principal*

Bryn Mawr
Ackoff, Russell Lincoln *systems sciences educator*
†Applegate, Jeffrey Scott *social work educator*
Ballam, Samuel Humes, Jr. *retired corporate director*
Beck, Christine Safford *photographer, publisher, volunteer*
Bober, Phyllis Pray *humanities educator, art historian*
Braha, Thomas I. *business executive*
Brand, Charles Macy *history educator*
Broido, Arnold Peace *music publishing company executive*
Cannon, John *investment consultant*
Cooney, Patricia Ruth *civic worker*
Crawford, Maria Luisa Buse *geology educator*
Dostal, Robert Joseph *philosophy educator*
Dudden, Arthur Power *historian, educator*
Fletcher, Marjorie Amos *librarian*
Gaisser, Julia Haig *classics educator*
Goutman, Lois Clair *retired drama educator*
Gruenberg, Alan Mark *psychiatrist*
Hankin, Mitchell Robert *lawyer*
Harkins, Herbert Perrin *otolaryngologist, educator*
Hermann, George Arthur *pathologist, educator*
Hoffman, Howard Stanley *experimental psychologist, educator*
Hoopes, Janet Louise *educator, psychologist*
Huth, Edward Janavel *physician, editor*
King, Willard Fahrenkamp (Mrs. Edmund Ludwig King) *Spanish language educator*
Kline, John Charles *painter, educator*
Kraftson, Raymond Harry *business executive*
Krausz, Michael *philosopher, educator*
Lane, Barbara Miller (Barbara Miller-Lane) *humanities educator*
Lang, Mabel Louise *classics educator*
Levitt, Robert E. *gastroenterologist*
Lewis, James Earl *financier*
Mallory, Frank Bryant *chemistry educator*
Mani, Korah Thattunkal *engineer, consultant*
Mc Lean, William L., III *publisher*
Moll, Robin Bitterlich *fundraising executive, consultant*
Moyer, F. Stanton *financial executive, advisor*
†Nast, Philip Robert *gastroenterologist*
†Neeleman, Carolyn Emerson *sociology educator, researcher*
Noone, Robert Barrett *plastic surgeon*
Porter, Judith Deborah Revitch *sociologist, educator*
Richards, Rhoda Root Wagner *civic worker*
Salisbury, Helen Holland *education educator*
Segal, Donald Henry Gilbert *real estate developer*
Smith, Nona Coates *academic administrator*
Stucky, Steven (Edward) *composer*
Tanis, James Robert *library director, history educator, clergyman*
†Vickers, Nancy J. *academic administrator*
Widzer, Steven J. *pediatric gastroenterologist*
Worrall, Charles Harrison *elementary education educator*
Wright, James Clinton *dean, archaeology educator*

Buckingham
Altier, William John *management consultant*

Buffalo Mills
Braendel, Douglas Arthur *healthcare executive*
Housel, Donna Jane *artist*

Bushkill
Ellwood, Edith Muesing *free-lance writer*
Muesing Ellwood, Edith Elizabeth *writer, researcher, publisher, editor*

Butler
Artz, Frederick James *diversified manufacturing company executive*
Bashline, Aryl Ann *photographer, fiber artist*
Coleman, Arthur Robert *retired accountant*
Kay, George Paul *environmental engineer*
Kendall, George Jason *accountant, financial planner, computer consultant*
Kosar, John E. *architectural firm executive*
†Meals, Cynthia *management analyst*
Rettig, Carolyn Faith *educator*
Rickard, Dennis Clark *sheriff, educator*
†Simms, Donald Ray *engineer*

California
Langham, Norma *playwright, educator, poet, composer, inventor*

Cambridge Springs
Learn, Richard Leland *corrections school principal*
Youngblood, Constance Mae *elementary school principal*

Camp Hill
Crist, Christine Myers *consulting executive*
Custer, John Charles *investment broker*
Grass, Alexander *retail company executive*

Gunn, G. Greg insurance executive
Holliday, Albert Edwards publisher
Johnston, Thomas McElree, Jr. church administrator
McGeary, Clyde Mills artist, educator, advisor
McNutt, Charlie Fuller, Jr. retired bishop
Mead, James Matthew insurance company executive
Nowak, Jacquelyn Louise administrator, realtor, consultant, artist
Parry-Solá, Cheryl Lee critical care nurse
Roach, Ralph Lee human services and rehabilitation consultant
Rowe, Michael Duane artist
Wagner, Tanya Suzanne health facility administrator

Canonsburg
Harker, Joseph Edward construction, industrial and steel company executive
Mascetta, Joseph Anthony principal
Piatt, Jack Boyd manufacturing executive
Prado, Gerald M. investment banker

Cape May Point
Jordan, Joe J. architect

Carlisle
Blackledge, David William academic administrator
Davenny, Ward Leslie artist, educator
Fish, Chester Boardman, Jr. retired publishing consultant, writer
Fox, Arturo Angel Spanish language educator
Freund, Roland Paul farm management extension agent
Gorby, William Guy anesthesiologist
Graham, William Patton, III plastic surgeon, educator
†Grier, Philip Todd philosophy educator
Jacobs, Norman G(abriel) sociologist, educator
Jones, Oliver Hastings consulting economist
Kilgore, Joe Everett, Jr. army officer
Laws, Kenneth L. physics educator, author
Long, Howard Charles physics educator emeritus
Mentzer, Marsha Lee secondary school educator
†Moffat, Wendy English educator
Nichols, Brooks Ashton English language educator
Powell, Mary Arthur adult and family nurse practitioner, administrator
Reed, David LaRue minister
†Rhoads, Philip R., Sr. safety director
Russell, Theodore Emery diplomat
Schiffman, Joseph Harris literary historian, educator
Shrader, Charles Reginald historian
Streidl, Isabelle Roberts Smiley economist
Talley, Carol Lee newspaper editor
†Tilford, Earl Hawkins, Jr. defense analyst

Carlisle Barracks
†Scales, Robert H., Jr. army officer

Carnegie
Chambers, Lisa M. psychiatric and mental health nurse
†Whitfield, Tammy J. educator

Cashtown
Saliu, Ion software developer, computer programmer

Castle Shannon
Selkowitz, Lucy Ann security officer

Catasauqua
Fogelson, Brian David educational administrator

Center Valley
Smillie, Douglas James lawyer

Central City
Brown, Robert Alan retired construction materials company executive

Centre Hall
Rudy, Ruth Corman former state legislator

Chadds Ford
Cohen, Felix Asher lawyer
Duff, James Henry museum director, environmental administrator
Isakoff, Sheldon Erwin chemical engineer
King, M. Jean association executive
Reddish, John Joseph management consulting company executive
Sanford, Richard D. computer company executive
Swensson, Evelyn Dickenson conductor, composer, librettist
Webster, Owen Wright chemist
Witcher, Phyllis Herrmann secondary education educator

Chalfont
Hauber, Patricia Anne educator
Schott, Jeffrey Brian software engineer

Chambersburg
Boretz, Naomi Messinger artist, educator
Fleming, Steven Robert minister
LaBorde, Terrence Lee small business owner, negotiator
Lesher, Richard Lee association executive, retired
Neilson, Winthrop Cunningham, III communications executive, financial communications consultant
Ross, Larry Michael county economic development official
Rumler, Robert Hoke agricultural consultant, retired association executive

Charleroi
Kravec, Frances Mary elementary education educator
Savona, Michael Joseph lawyer

Cheltenham
Hart, William C. insurance underwriter, educator, writer
Oflazian, Paul Sarkis small business owner
Shmukler, Herman William retired biochemist, consultant
Skaler, Robert Morris architect, forensic architect
Weinstock, Walter Wolfe systems engineer

Chester
Bruce, Robert James university president
Buck, Lawrence Paul academic administrator
DiAngelo, Joseph Anthony, Jr. management educator, academic dean
Fisher, M. Janice hospital administrator
Jackson, Cynthia Marie elementary school educator
Kornfield, Nathaniel Richard computer engineer educator
Leach, Lynne E. nursing educator
Moll, Clarence Russel retired university president, consultant
Wepner, Shelley Beth education educator, software developer

Chester Springs
Scheer, R. Scott physician
Simms, Amy Lang writer, educator

Cheswick
Dermody, Frank state legislator, lawyer

Cheyney
Bagley, Edythe Scott theater educator

Churchill Borough
Aronson, Mark Berne consumer advocate

Claridge
Perich, Terry Miller secondary school educator

Clarion
Foreman, Thomas Alexander dentist
Siddiqui, Dilnawaz Ahmed communications educator, international communication planning advisor, consultant
Thomas, Joe Alan art historian

Clarks Summit
Alperin, Irwin Ephraim clothing company executive
Beemer, John Barry lawyer
Ross, Adrian E. drilling manufacturing company executive

Clarksville
Ankrom, Barbara Burke journalist

Clearfield
Falvo, Mark Anthony lawyer
Grippo, James Joseph writer, educator
Haag, Harvey Eugene physics educator
Reighard, Edward Buzard retired education executive director
Ulerich, William Keener publishing company executive
Wriglesworth, Vicki Lee nurse

Cleona
Carpenter, Roxanne Sue realtor

Clifton Heights
Bonaduce, Judith medical/surgical nurse, community health nurse
Rothermel, Rodman Schantz manufacturing company executive

Coatesville
Ainslie, George William psychiatrist, behavioral economist
Burton, Mary Louise Himes computer specialist
Copeland, W(illiam) Joel, Jr. clergyman
Fitzgerald, Susan Helena elementary educator
Smith, Patricia Anne special education educator

Cochranton
Baldwin, Anthony Blair systems theoretician, agricultural executive

Cochranville
Procyson, Mary G. Walton critical care nurse
Sazegar, Morteza artist

Collegeville
De Rosen, Michel pharmaceutical company executive
Fago, George Clancy psychology educator
Holder, Neville Lewis chemist
Howard, Michael Earl clinical research specialist
Kun, Kenneth A. business executive
Maco, Teri Regan accountant, engineer
McCairns, Regina Carfagno pharmaceutical executive
Mellanby, Ian John publisher
Richter, Richard Paul academic administrator
Strassburger, John Robert academic administrator

Colmar
Taylor, Robert Morgan electronics executive
Weber-Roochvarg, Lynn English second language adult educator, communications consultant

Columbia
Gillmore, Vicki Longenecker health care administrator
McTaggart, Timothy Thomas secondary education educator

Conestoga
Fritz, Eugene Earl university administrator
Gochnauer, Elisa Anne marketing executive

Confluence
Bower, Roy Donald minister, counselor

Conneaut Lake
Piroch, Joseph Gregory internist, cardiologist

Connellsville
Benzio, Donna Marie cardiopulmonary rehabilitation nurse, educator

Conshohocken
Bramson, Robert Sherman lawyer
Cheung, Peter Pak Lun investment company executive, chemistry educator
Cunningham, James Gerald, Jr. transportation company executive
Fletcher, Jeffrey Edward editor, biochemist, medical writer
Gibson, Thomas Richard automobile import company executive
Kirkpatrick, John Alger organic chemist, food scientist
Naples, Ronald James manufacturing company executive
Rippel, Harry Conrad mechanical engineer, consultant
Spaeth, Karl Henry retired chemical company executive, lawyer

Conway
Krebs, Robert Alan lawyer

Coopersburg
Kohler, Deborah Diamond dietitian, food service executive
Peserik, James E. electrical, controls and computer engineer, consultant, forensics and safety engineer, fire cause and origin investigator
Siess, Alfred Albert, Jr. engineering executive, management consultant
Spira, Joel Solon electronics company executive
Winters, Arthur Ralph, Jr. chemical and cryogenic engineer, consultant

Cooperstown
Hogg, James Henry, Jr. retired education educator

Coraopolis
Al-Qudsi, Hassan Shaban engineer, project manager
Bacher, Lutz film, video and photography educator
Giliberti, Michael Richard financial planner
Koepfinger, Joseph Leo utilities executive
†Luffy, Robert H. construction company executive
Moretti, Edward Charles environmental engineer, consultant
Skovira, Robert Joseph information scientist, educator

Cornwall
McGill, William James, Jr. academic administrator, writer

Corry
Rathinavelu, Madi manufacturing executive

Coudersport
Rigas, John broadcast executive

Cranberry Township
Bashore, George Willis bishop
Conti, Carolyn Ann elementary school educator
Hogberg, Carl Gustav retired steel company executive
Lorenz, John George librarian, consultant
Tiller, Olive Marie retired church worker
Walsh, Arthur Campbell psychiatrist

Cresco
Reinhardt, Susan Joan writer

Cresson
Griffith, Madlynne Veil controller
†Strange, Russell Littlejohn school system administrator

Dallas
Johnson MacDowell, Tina elementary education educator
Moran, Michael Lee physical therapist, computer consultant
Rockensies, Kenneth Jules physicist, educator

Danielsville
Billings, Johanna Schmidt journalist, antiques consultant

Danville
Cochran, William John physician, pediatrician, gastroenterologist, nutritionist, consultant
Coffman, David Ervin accountant, valuation analyst
Dirienzo, Margaret Helen nursing administrator
Kazem, Ismail radiation oncologist, educator, health science facility administrator
Kleponis, Jerome Albert dentist
Knouse, Brenda Lee (Weikel) critical care, medical/surgical nurse
Lessin, Michael Edward oral-maxillofacial surgeon
Pierce, James Clarence surgeon
Randall, Neil Warren gastroenterologist
Wert, Barbara J. Yingling special education consultant

Dayton
Patterson, Madge Lenore elementary education educator

Delaware Water Gap
Woods, Philip Wells (Phil Woods) jazz musician composer

Delmont
Thompson, Paul A. business consultant, performance improvement expert

Devon
Burget, Dean Edwin, Jr. plastic surgeon
Garbarino, Robert Paul retired administrative dean, lawyer
Heebner, Albert Gilbert economist, banker, educator

Dickson City
Carluccio, Sheila Cook psychologist

Dillsburg
Bowers, Glenn Lee retired professional society administrator
Jackson, George Lyman nuclear medicine physician

Donora
Todd, Norma Jean Ross retired government official

Downingtown
Glitz, Donald Robert insurance underwriting executive
Kovach, George Daniel writer
Newman, Richard August psychiatrist, educator
Skrajewski, Dennis John health care informatics executive

Doylestown
Blewitt, George Augustine physician, consultant
Brink, Frank, Jr. biophysicist, former educator
Carson, John Thompson, Jr. environmental consultant
Cooke, Chantelle Anne writer
Elliott, Richard Howard lawyer
Gathright, Howard T. lawyer
Ginsberg, Barry Gavrille psychologist, consultant, trainer
King, Robert Edward retired pharmacy educator
Kohlhepp, Edward John financial planner
Marino, Paul Michael science education educator
Maser, Frederick Ernest clergyman
McNulty, Carrell Stewart, Jr. retired manufacturing company executive, architect
McNutt, Richard Hunt manufacturing company executive
Miller, Lynne Marie critical care nurse, administrator
Mishler, John Milton (Yochanan Menashsheh ben Shaul) natural sciences educator, administrator, artist
Morgnanesi, Lanny M. journalist
Murray, Karen Lee special education educator
Rubenstein, Alan Morris district attorney
Rufe, Cynthia Marie judge
Shaddinger, Dawn Elizabeth medical researcher
Smith, Charles Paul newspaper publisher
Tabachnick, Michael Neil physicist, educator
Wolfinger, Audrey Jane retired librarian

Drexel Hill
Alexander, Lloyd Chudley author
Bomberger, John Henry Augustus pediatrician
Heilig, Margaret Cramer nurse, educator
Ligenza, Andrea Angela nurse
Martino, Michael Charles entertainer, musician, actor
Schiazza, Guido Domenic (Guy Schiazza) educational association administrator
Thompson, William David minister, homiletics educator
West, Kenneth Edward lawyer

Drums
†Frask, Robin Ann Kostanesky secondary school educator

Du Bois
Blakley, Benjamin Spencer, III lawyer
Donahue, Ross Donald state official
Kearney, Linda Lee secondary education educator
Nye, George N secondary school educator
Pyle, Debora L. critical care nurse
Williams, Kathryn Blake librarian

Duncansville
Huntley-Speare, Anne language educator

Dunmore
Culliney, John James radiologist, educator
Pencek, Carolyn Carlson treasurer, educator
Sebastianelli, Mario Joseph internist, nephrologist, health services administrator
†Zawistowski, Theodore L. sociology educator, editor

Dushore
Getz, Mary E. medical/surgical nurse

Eagles Mere
Sample, Frederick Palmer former college president

East Berlin
Greer, Robert Bruce, III orthopedic surgeon, educator

East Earl
Kass, Howard R. information systems consultant

East Norriton
O'Connor, Sheryl Ann medical services administrator

East Petersburg
Stuempfle, Catherine Diane secondary education educator
Whare, Wanda Snyder lawyer

East Stroudsburg
Bishop, Gerald Iveson pharmaceutical executive
Brackbill, Nancy Lafferty elementary education educator
†Cohen, Beth Ann neurologist
Crackel, Theodore Joseph historian
Dillman, Robert John academic administrator
Kratz, Charles E., Jr. library director
†Lane, Miharu Qualkinbush artist, educator
Rosenblum, Stewart Irwin recording industry executive

Easton
†Bartolocci, Paulette E Marie elementary school educator, aerobic instructor
Bonanni, Marc A. English language educator, newscaster
Brown, Robert Carroll lawyer
Burkhart, Glenn Randall corporate internal auditor
Danjczek, Michael Harvey social service administrator
DiMatteo, Rhonda Lynn speech-language pathologist, audiologist
†Engler, Brian Keith radio broadcast personality
Grunberg, Robert Leon Willy nephrologist
Hagar, Susan Mack school psychologist, school counselor
Holmes, Larry, Jr. retired professional boxer
Kaye, Daniel Barnett secondary education educator, consultant
Kincaid, John political science educator, editor
Lear, Floyd Raymond, III entrepreneur
†Lusardi, James Proctor English language and literature educator
Moore, Joyce Kristina financial planner
Noel, Nicholas, III lawyer
Rothkopf, Arthur J. college president
Schlueter, June Mayer English educator, author
Snyder, Charles Terry director
Stipe, Edwin, III mechanical contracting company executive
Stitt, Dorothy Jewett journalist
Sun, Robert Zu Jei inventor, manufacturing company executive
Tomaino, George Peter, Jr. pharmacist
Van Antwerpen, Franklin Stuart federal judge
Yost, Robert R. social services agency administrator

Ebensburg
Ramsdell, Richard Adoniram *marine engineer*
Rolt, Holly Lavonne *nursing educator, geriatrics nurse*

Edinboro
Antley, Eugene Brevard *sociology and religion educator*
†Brown, Lisa Rochell *academic administrator*
Cox, Clifford Laird *university administrator, musician*
Curry-Carlburg, Joanne Jeanne *elementary education educator*
Jones, Jean Grace *speech educator*
Kemenyffy, Steven *artist, art educator*
Miller, G(erson) H(arry) *research institute director, mathematician, computer scientist, chemist*
Paul, Charlotte P. *nursing educator*
Tramontano, John Patrick, Jr. *electrical products company executive*
Weinkauf, David *film, animation, and photography educator*

Eighty Four
Capone, Alphonse William *retired industrial executive*
Hardy, Joseph A., Sr. *wholesale distribution executive*
†Magerko, Maggie Hardy *lumber company executive*

Elizabeth
Levdansky, David Keith *state legislator*

Elizabethtown
Brown, Dale Weaver *clergyman, theologian, educator*
Johnson, Clarence Ray *minister*
Madeira, Robert Lehman *professional society administrator*
Ritsch, Frederick Field *academic administrator, historian*
†Winpenny, Thomas Reese, III *history educator*
Woodward, Vern Harvey *retired engineering sales executive*

Elizabethville
Romberger, John Albert *scientist, historian*

Elkins Park
Davidson, Abraham Aba *art historian, educator, photographer*
Dickstein, Joan Borteck *arbitrator, conflict management consultant*
Erlebacher, Martha Mayer *artist, educator*
Glijansky, Alex *psychiatrist, psychoanalyst*
Goode, Paul *psychologist, educator, consultant*
Havir, Bryan Thomas *urban planner*
Maslin, Simeon Joseph *rabbi*
Prince, Morton Bronenberg *physicist*
Rosen, Rhoda *obstetrician and gynecologist*
Schatz, Charlotte Asness *artist, educator*
Serber, William *radiation oncologist, educator*
Shedinger, Robert Frederick *religious studies educator*
Yun, Daniel Duwhan *physician, foundation administrator*

Emmaus
Beldon, Sanford T. *publisher*
Bowers, Klaus D(ieter) *retired electronics research development company executive*
Bricklin, Mark Harris *magazine editor, publisher*
Caton, Timothy Charles *marketing professional*
Daniels, Jonathan Paul *web developer*
Greenslade, Kathryn Elizabeth *art director*
Lafavore, Michael J. *magazine editor*
Rodale, Ardath *publishing executive*
Zahradnik, Fredric Douglas *marketing professional*

Ephrata
Sager, Gilbert Landis *investment company executive*
Young, David Samuel *minister*

Eranheim
Murphy, Mary Marguerite *artist*

Erie
Adovasio, J. M. *anthropologist, archeologist, educator*
Allshouse, Robert Harold *history educator*
Barber, Michele A. *title one educator*
†Baxter, Susan Paradise *federal judge, lawyer*
†Bentz, Warren Worthington *federal bankruptcy judge*
Boyes, Karl W. *state legislator*
Bracken, Charles Herbert *banker*
Brunner, Kirstin Ellen *pediatrician, psychiatrist*
†Chorazy, Zdzislaw J. *surgeon*
Chrisman, Marlene Santia *special education educator*
Cocco, Karen Jean *school psychologist*
Crankshaw, John Hamilton *mechanical engineer*
†Dempsey, Jennifer Camille *art educator, artist*
Diefenbach, William Paul *neurosurgeon*
Drexler, Nora Lee *retired educator, writer, illustrator*
Duval, Albert Frank *paper company executive*
Eberlin, Richard D. *education educator*
Egan, Corrine Halperin *trade association administrator*
Faulkner, Bonita Louise *enrichment education educator*
†Flamini, John Anthony *physician*
Gottschalk, Frank Klaus *real estate company executive*
Gray, Robert Beckwith *electrical engineer, consultant*
Hagen, Thomas Bailey *business owner, former state official, former insurance company executive*
Kalkhof, Thomas Corrigan *physician*
Karlson, Eskil Leannart *biophysicist*
Kish, George Franklin *thoracic and cardiovascular surgeon*
Lilley, John Mark *academic administrator, dean*
Lund, Edwin Harrison *business accounting systems executive*
Mainzer, Francis Kirkwood *neurosurgeon, health facility administrator*
Mason, Gregg Claude *orthopedic surgeon, researcher*
McDyer, Susan Spear *academic administrator*
†McLaughlin, Sean J. *judge*
McMahon, Patricia Pasky *family nurse practitioner*
Mencer, Glenn Everell *federal judge*
Michaelides, Doros Nikita *internist, medical educator*
Minot, Walter S. *English language educator*
Monahan, Thomas Andrew, Jr. *accountant*
Nihill, Karen Bailey *nursing home executive, nurse clinician*
Nygaard, Richard Lowell *federal judge*
Rowley, Robert Deane, Jr. *bishop*
Ryan, Gerald Anthony *financial advisor, venture capitalist*
Savocchio, Joyce A. *mayor*
Sensor, Mary Delores *hospital official, consultant*
Trautman, Donald W. *bishop*
Vanco, John L. *art museum director*

Essington
Piasecki, Frank Nicholas *aircraft corporation executive, aeronautics engineer*

Evans City
Zellers, Robert Charles *materials engineer, consultant, speaker*

Everett
Gibbons, Janet M. *home health services admininstrator*
Weaver, E(lvin) Paul *minister*

Exeter
Stocker, Joyce Arlene *retired secondary school educator*

Export
Colborn, Harry Walter *electrical engineering consultant*
Hampton, Edward John *engineering company executive*
Robinette, Teresa Louise *oncology nurse*
Wagner, Charles Leonard *electrical engineer, consultant*

Exton
Amichetti, Dennis Joseph *advertising executive*
Ashton, Mark Randolph *lawyer*
Bush, Joanne Tadeo *financial consultant, corporate executive*
Dorsey, Jeremiah Edmund *pharmaceutical company executive*
Hedges, Donald Walton *lawyer*
Lewis, Thomas B. *specialty chemical company executive*
Molloy, Christopher John *molecular/cellular biologist, pharmacist*
Newhall, John Harrison *non profit company executive*
Penrose, Charles, Jr. *professional society administrator*
†Romeo, Joseph Anthony *computer programmer*
Shollenberger, Sharon Ann *secondary school educator*

Fairfield
†Freund, John Richard *former English educator*

Fairless Hills
Marable, Simeon-David *artist*
Rosella, John Daniel *clinical psychologist, educator*

Fairview
Graziani, Linda Ann *secondary education educator*
Krider, Margaret Young *art educator*
Weckesser, Elden Christian *surgery educator*
Wondra, Norbert Francis *accountant, controller*

Feasterville Trevose
Dickstein, Jack *chemist*
Liberati, Maria Theresa *fashion production company executive*
Osterhout, Richard Cadwallader *lawyer*

Ferndale
Folk, James *sales executive*

Fleetwood
Buckalew, Robert Joseph *psychologist, consultant*
†Zucco, Doug *artist*

Flourtown
Christy, John Gilray *financial company executive*
Di Maria, Charles Walter *mechanical and automation engineer, consultant*
Lambert, Joan Dorety *elementary education educator*
Lee, Adrian Iselin, Jr. *journalist*
Moore, Sandra Kay *counselor, administrator*

Fogelsville
Young, Richard Robert *logistics and transportation educator*

Folsom
White, Barbara Cloud *principal, educator*

Ford City
†Smits, Ronald Francis *English educator, poet*
Ursiak, David Allen *operations executive, consultant*

Forest City
Kameen, John Paul *newspaper publisher*

Fort Washington
Blumberg, Donald Freed *management consultant*
Cassel, Neil Jonathon *business owner*
Fulton, Cheryl Lynn *customer service administrator*
Lewis, Richard Arnold *architect*
Meyer, Andrew R. *manufacturing executive*
†Minniti, Martha Jean *home healthcare company executive*
Pappas, Charles Engelos *plastic surgeon*
Pillai, Raviraj Sukumar *chemical engineer, researcher*
Ross, Roderic Henry *insurance company executive*
Urbach, Frederick *physician, educator*
Visek, Albert James *retired computer engineer*
Wint, Dennis Michael *museum director*

Forty Fort
Henderson, Robb Alan *minister*
Meeker, Robert Gardner *English language educator*

Franklin
Lytle, Elizabeth Ann *secondary education educator, writer*
Miller, John Karl *protective services official*
Moore, Mary Julia *educator*

Frazer
Stirling, Douglas Bleecker, Jr. *human resources specialist*

Frederick
†Sekellick, Ronald E. *special education educator*

Freeland
Rudawski, Joseph George *educational administrator*

Freeport
Chvala, Kathleen Ann *administrative assistant*

Gaines
Beller, Martin Leonard *retired orthopaedic surgeon*

Germansville
Vittorio Phillips, Mary Lou *pediatric nurse practitioner, educator*

Gettysburg
†Birkner, Michael J. *history educator*
Cisneros, Jose A. *historical site administrator*
Coughenour, Kavin Luther *career officer, military historian*
Gritsch, Ruth Christine Lisa *editor*
Hallberg, Budd Jaye *management consulting firm executive*
Heisler, Barbara Schmitter *sociology educator*
Hendrix, Sherman Samuel *biology educator, researcher*
Latschar, John A. *historic site administrator*
Nelson-Small, Kathy Ann *foundation administrator*
Ozag, David *human resources executive*
Roach, James Clark *government official*
Schmoyer, Richard Harvey *county official*

Gibsonia
Haas, Eileen Marie *homecare advocate*
Heilman, Carl Edwin *lawyer*
Pochapin, Jay Frank *marketing executive*
Shoub, Earle Phelps *engineer, industrial hygienist, educator*
Szymanski, George Joseph *school administrator*

Girardville
Dempsey, Thomas Joseph *postmaster*

Gladwyne
Acton, David *lawyer*
Booth, Harold Waverly *lawyer, finance and investment company executive*
Cathcart, Harold Robert *hospital administrator*
Geisel, Cameron Meade, Jr. *investment professional*
Gilbert, Robert Pettibone *retired physician, educator*
Gonick, Paul *retired urologist*
Murray, William D.G. *publishing executive*
Patten, Lanny Ray *industrial gas industry executive*

Glassport
Lippard, Thomas Eugene *lawyer*

Glen Mills
Churchill, Stuart Winston *chemical engineering educator*
Turner, Janet Sullivan *painter*

Glen Rock
Hortman, David Jones *secondary education educator*

Glenmoore
DeGuatemala, Joyce *sculptor*
Walish, Geralyn Rose *business consultant, analyst*

Glenside
†Adelsberger, Donna L. *lawyer, educator*
Bardliving, Clifford Lee, Jr. *graphic designer*
Carter, Ruth B. (Mrs. Joseph C. Carter) *foundation administrator*
Frudakis, Zenos Antonios *sculptor, artist*
†Grady, Hugh H. *English educator*
Hargens, Charles William, III *electrical engineer, consultant*
Johnson, Waine Cecil *dermatologist*
Mazzucelli, Colette Grace Celia *author, university adminstrator, educator*
Mee, Carolyn Jean *education educator*
Mermelstein, Jules Joshua *lawyer, township official*
Reiss, George Russell, Jr. *physician*
†Sacks, Robert D. *educational administrator, fund raiser*
Splawn, P. Jane *English language educator*
Taylor, Judith Ann *art educator, artist*

Gouldsboro
Duricko, Erma O. *stage director, educator*
West, Daniel Jones, Jr. *hospital administrator, rehabilitaton counselor, health care consultant, educator*

Grantham
†Eby, John W. *sociology educator*
Falk, Noel Wesley *biology educator, radio and television program host, horticultural consultant*
Kraybill, Donald Brubaker *college provost*
Sider, E(arl) Morris *English language and history educator, archivist*

Gratz
Herb, Jane Elizabeth *banker*

Greenock
†Swift, James *minister*

Greensburg
Anderson, Linda D. *psychologist*
Boyd, Robert Wright, III *lamp company executive*
†Cassell, Frank Alan *university president, history educator*
†Dorsey, John Victor *poet, screenwriter, editor*
Duck, Patricia Mary *librarian*
Foreman, John Daniel *financial executive*
Galloway, Richard H. *lawyer*
Gounley, Dennis Joseph *lawyer*
Guyker, William Charles, Jr. *electrical engineer, researcher*
Lisowitz, Gerald Myron *neuropsychiatrist*
Ramm, Douglas Robert *psychologist*

Greentown
Forcheskie, Carl S. *former apparel company executive*
Schumaker, William Thomas *insurance company executive*

Greenville
Lillie, Marshall Sherwood *college safety and security director, educator*
Rugen, Richard Hall *college administrator*
Stuver, Francis Edward *former railway car company executive*

Grove City
McBride, Milford Lawrence, Jr. *lawyer*
Smith, Gary Scott *historian, educator, clergyman*
Wentworth, Theodore Oscar, Jr. *Spanish language educator*

Grover
†Shedden, Lynette Karen *small business owner*

Gwynedd Valley
Duclow, Donald Francis *philosophy educator, researcher*
Feenane, Sister Mary Alice *principal*
Giordano, Patricia J. *radiation therapist*
O'Connell, Antoinette Kathleen *training executive, consultant, artist*
†Strasburg, William Edward *retired newspaper publisher*

Halifax
Stauffer, Joanne Rogan *steel company official*

Hamburg
Schappell, Abigail Susan *speech, language, hearing and massage therapist*
Weiss, Gerald Francis, Jr. *secondary education educator, coach*

Hanover
Antonaccio, Mario Americo *retired manufacturing executive*
Barnhart, Nikki Lynn Clark *elementary school educator*
Clark, Sandra Marie *school administrator*
Davis, Ruth Carol *pharmacy educator*
Hazel, Marianne Elizabeth *educational administrator*
Martin, Levona Ann *women's health nurse*
Stevenson, Paul J. *bank executive, bank officer*
Toft, Thelma Marilyn *secondary school educator*
Wallen, Carol Stonesifer *social worker*

Harleysville
Daller, Walter E., Jr. *banking executive*
†Johnson, Andrew W. *secondary education educator*
Ritchings, Frances Anne *priest*

Harmony
Baldwin, Carla Suzann *psychologist*

Harrisburg
Allen, Heath Ledward *lawyer*
Armstrong, Gibson E. *state senator*
Armstrong, Thomas Errol *state legislator*
†Baehre, Edna Victoria *college president*
Baird, Irene Cebula *educational administrator*
Banks, Albert Victor, Jr. *government administrator*
Barasch, David M. *prosecutor*
Barley, John E. *state legislator*
Barto, Charles O., Jr. *lawyer*
Bebko-Jones, Linda *state legislator*
Bello, Shere Capparella *foreign language educator*
Blittenbender, Robert A. *state official*
Boswell, William Douglas *lawyer*
Breslin, Michael Joseph, III *social services administrator, educator*
Britton, Wesley Alan *English language educator*
Brown, John Walter *vocational education supervisor*
Burcat, Joel Robin *lawyer*
Burns, Rebecca Ann *educator, librarian*
Cadieux, Roger Joseph *physician, mental health care executive*
Caldwell, William Wilson *federal judge*
Campbell, Carl Lester *banker*
Cate, Donald James *mechanical engineer, consultant*
Cauley, Alvin Paul *state government administrator*
Chambers, Clarice Lorraine *clergy, educational consultant*
Chernicoff, David Paul *osteopathic physician, educator*
Cline, Andrew Haley *lawyer*
Cohen, Lita Indzel *state legislator*
Comoss, Patricia B. *cardiac rehabilitation nurse, consultant*
Cramer, John McNaight *lawyer*
Dattilo, Nicholas C. *bishop*
Dean, Eric Arthur *auditor, accountant*
DeKok, David *writer, reporter*
Diehm, James Warren *lawyer, educator*
Dietz, John Raphael *consulting engineer executive*
Dodge, Clifford Howle *geologist*
Drachler, Stephen Edward *press secretary*
DuBrock, Calvin William *wildlife program administrator*
Dunn, Kenneth Ralph *insurance company executive*
Ebaugh, David Paul *minister, school system administrator*
Edmiston, Guy S., Jr. *bishop*
Edwards, JoAnn Louise *human resources executive*
†Evanko, Paul J. *commissioner, colonel Pennsylvania state police*
Farrell, Kelly Jean *health and physical education educator*
Fisher, D. Michael *state attorney general*
Forcier, Teresa Elaine *state legislator*
Fox, Miriam Annette *state legislative fiscal analyst*
Frye, Mary Catherine *prosecutor*
Gallaher, William Marshall *dental laboratory technician*
Gardner, Judith Sturgen *nursing administrator, educator*
Goell, James Emanuel *electronics company executive*
Gover, Raymond Lewis *newspaper executive*
†Granzow, Robert Frederick, III *security firm executive*
Gruitza, Michael *state legislator, lawyer*
Hafer, Barbara *state official*
Hafer, Joseph Page *lawyer*
Hamory, Bruce Hill *health facility administrator*
Hanson, Robert DeLolle *lawyer*
Hart, Melissa A. *state senator*
†Hayes, Samuel E., Jr. *state agency administrator*

†Snyder, Wayne L. *real estate company executive*
Volpe, Ralph Pasquale *insurance company executive*
Wachs, David V. *retired apparel executive*
†Wagenmann, Ronald George *township manager*
Wang, Xin-Min *molecular biologist*
Winkhaus, Hans-Dietrich *chemicals executive*

Kingston
Evanofski, Bernard Peter *Roman Catholic priest*
Fierman, Gerald Shea *electrical distribution company executive*
Friedman, Pauline Poplin *civic worker, consultant*
Godlewski, James Bernard *elementary school educator, principal, consultant*
Kopen, Dan Francis *surgeon, consultant*
Meyer, Martin Jay *lawyer*
Weisberger, Barbara *artistic director, educator, choreographer*

Kittanning
†Sehring, Frederick Albert *dean*

Knox
Rupert, Elizabeth Anastasia *retired university dean*
†Schwab, Joyce Lynn *educator*

Kulpsville
Pavlov, Gregory Charles *engineer*

Kutztown
Coyle, Charles A. *marketing educator*
†Dewey, Sylvie Pascale *French and Spanish language educator*
Johnson, Nils, Jr. *minister*
Laub, Mary Lou *elementary education educator*
McFarland, David E. *university official*
Ogden, James Russell *marketing educator, consultant, lecturer, trainer*
Spencer, JoAnn Nora *education educator*
Watrous, Robert Thomas *academic director*

La Plume
Boehm, Edward Gordon, Jr. *university administrator, educator*

Lafayette Hill
Green, Raymond Ferguson St. John *marketing and advertising executive*
†King, Diane Averbach *education educator*
King, Leon *financial services executive*
†Leomporra, Tullio Gene *federal judge*
Slagle, Robert Lee, II *elementary and secondary education educator*

Lake Ariel
Casper, Marie Lenore *middle school educator*

Lake Harmony
Polansky, Larry Paul *court administrator, consultant*

Lampeter
Schuler, Jere W. *state legislator*

Lancaster
Andrew, John Alfred, III *history educator*
Ashby, Richard James, Jr. *bank executive, lawyer*
Augsburger, Aaron Donald *clergyman*
Auster, Carol Jean *sociology educator*
Baker, Mark Allen *author, historian, consultant*
†Barnett, Elizabeth Lucinda (Lucy) *television news producer*
Brod, Roy David *ophthalmologist, educator*
Brunner, Lillian Sholtis *nurse, author*
Buchanan, Lovell *entertainer*
Byler, Vickie Lynne Jennifer *educator, athletic director*
Carlisle, James Patton *clergyman*
Case, Edward Ralph *manufacturing executive*
Dodge, Arthur Byron, Jr. *business executive*
Drum, Alice *college administrator*
Dunlap, Hallowell *data processing executive*
Duroni, Charles Eugene *retired lawyer, food products executive*
Ebersole, J. Glenn, Jr. *engineering, marketing, management and public relations executive*
Ebersole, Mark Chester *emeritus college president*
Falk, Robert Barclay, Jr. *anesthesiologist, educator*
Filler, Mary Ann *librarian*
Freeman, Clarence Calvin *financial executive*
Fritsch, Richard Elvin *trust company executive*
Gingerich, Naomi R. *emergency room nurse*
Glick, Garland Wayne *retired theological seminary president*
†Grochowski, Jelsia *music educator*
†Harman, Mark *English educator*
Hess, Donald F. *retired manufacturing executive, accountant*
High, S. Dale *diversified company executive*
Hoover, Donald Leroy *construction executive*
Kelly, Robert Lynn *advertising agency executive*
†Kenien, Nicholas N. *psychologist*
Kneedler, Alvin Richard *college president*
Liddell, W. Kirk *specialty contracting company executive*
Linton, Joy Smith *primary school educator*
Lorch, George A. *manufacturing company executive*
Lu, Milton Ming-Deh *plastic surgeon, consultant*
Minney, Michael Jay *lawyer*
†Mongia, Padmini *English language educator*
Nast, Dianne Martha *lawyer*
†Needleman, Alvin D. *research and development company executive*
Pyfer, John Frederick, Jr. *lawyer*
Rothermel, Joan Marie *occupational health nurse*
Rupp, Theodore Hanna *retired French language educator*
Schuyler, David P. *historian, educator*
Shaw, Charles Raymond *journalist*
Shenk, Willis Weidman *newspaper executive*
Simmons, Deidre Warner *performing company executive*
Spatcher, Dianne Marie *finance executive*
Steiner, Robert Lisle *language consultant, retired*
Sware, Richard Michael, Jr. *electric company executive*
Taylor, Ann *business consultant, human resource educator*
Veitch, Boyer Lewis *printing company executive*
Zeager, Lloyd *librarian*
Zimmerman, D(onald) Patrick *lawyer*

Langhorne
Babb, Wylie Sherrill *college president*
Barbetta, Maria Ann *health information management consultant*
Byrne, Jeffrey Edward *pharmacology researcher, educator, consultant*
†Fitzgerald, Dorothy Stickle *librarian*
Hillje, Barbara Brown *lawyer*
Lamonsoff, Norman Charles *psychiatrist*
Touhill, C. Joseph *environmental engineer*

Lansdale
Campman, Christopher Kuller *consulting company executive*
Cusimano, Adeline Mary Miletti *educational administrator*
Fawley, John Jones *retired banker*
Habecker, Sandra K. *retired nurse*
Ladman, A(aron) J(ulius) *anatomist, educator*
Lafredo, Stephen *systems associate*
Lovelace, Robert Frank *health facility administrator, researcher*
Reast, Deborah Stanek *ophthalmology center administrator*
Rosen, Bonnie *elementary school principal, consultant*
Schwartz, Louis Winn *ophthalmologist*
Strohecker, Leon Harry, Jr. *orthodontist*
Sultanik, Jeffrey Ted *lawyer*
Wittreich, Warren James *psychologist, consultant*

Lansdowne
Kyriazis, Arthur John (Athanasios Ioannis Kyriazis) *lawyer*
Nolan, Barbara Lee *critical care nurse*
Popovics, Sandor *civil engineer, educator, researcher*

Large
Allen, David Woodroffe *computer scientist*
Dick, Douglas Patrick *construction company executive*

Latrobe
Berardi, Ronald Stephen *pathologist, educator*
Daughenbaugh, Terry Lee *steel industry executive*
Hager, Edward Paul *development executive*
Watson, Bradley Charles Stephen *political science educator, lawyer, writer*
Zanotti, Marie Louise *hospital admininstrator*

Laverock
Block, Isaac Edward *professional society administrator*

Lebanon
Bard, Judy Kay *librarian*
Brightbill, David John *state senator, lawyer*
McMindes, Roy James *aggregate company executive*
Parrott, Charles Norman *bank executive*
Paul, Herman Louis, Jr. *valve manufacturing company executive*
Synodinos, John Anthony *academic administrator*

Lederach
Hallman, H(enry) Theodore, Jr. *artist, textile designer*

Leesport
Jackson, Eric Allen *philatelist*

Lehigh Valley
Kocsis, James Paul *artist*

Lehighton
Levis, Cynthia Ann *English language educator, German language educator*

Lehman
Williams, Thomas Alan *secondary education educator, coach*

Lemoyne
Deeg, Emil Wolfgang *manufacturing company executive, physicist*
Kirkwood, James Mace *pharmaceutical benefit management company executive*
Klein, Michael Elihu *physician*
Powell, Fredrick Charles *business executive*
†Vickery, Jon Livingstone *neurologist*

Lenhartsville
Adams, Faye Ann *musician, educator*

Leola
McElhinny, Wilson Dunbar *banker*
Wedel, Paul George *retired hospital administrator*

Lester
DiGiamarino, Marian Eleanor *realty administrator*

Levittown
Halberstein, Joseph Leonard *retired associate editor*
McAllister, Sally L. *learning center administrator*
Oppenheimer, Sanford (Sandy Oppenheimer) *newspaper editor*
Wolverton, Carolyn Patricia *English language educator*

Lewisberry
Smith, Bruce I. *state legislator*

Lewisburg
Adams, William D. *university president*
Bannon, George *retired economics educator, department chairman*
Blair, Harry Wallace *political science educator, consultant*
Candland, Douglas Keith *educator*
Fedorjaka, Kathy *university basketball coach*
Hetherington, Bonita Elizabeth *elementary education educator*
Jump, Chester Jackson, Jr. *clergyman, church official*
Kim, Jai Bin *civil engineering educator*
Lenhart, Lorraine Margaret *county official*
Little, Daniel Eastman *philosophy educator, university program director*
Lowe, John Raymond, Jr. *mechanical engineer*
Main, A. Donald *bishop*
Ondrusek, David Francis *discount store chain executive*
Orbison, James Graham *civil engineer, educator*
Rote, Nelle Fairchild Hefty *business consultant*
Sojka, Gary Allan *biologist, educator, university official*

Lewistown
Levin, Allen Joseph *lawyer*

Library
Kokowski, Palma Anna *nurse consultant*

Ligonier
Mattern, Gerry A. *engineering consultant*
Mellon, Seward Prosser *investment executive*
Pilz, Alfred Norman *manufacturing company executive*
Walters, Gomer Winston *lawyer*

Lima
Newett, Edward J., Jr. *accountant*

Limerick
Monte, Wendy Houser *rehabilitation services professional, counselor*

Lincoln University
Favor, Kevin Eli *psychology educator*
Jackson, Katherine Church *former elementary school educator, reading educator*
Racine, Linda Jean *college health nurse*
Roberts, Lynn Ernest *theoretical physicist, educator*
Williams, Willie, Jr. *physicist, educator*

Lititz
Bolinger, Robert Stevens *banker*
Koch, Bruce R. *diplomat*
Lord, Kathleen Virginia Anderson *fundraising executive, educator*

Littlestown
Plunkert, Donna Mae *business owner*

Lock Haven
Almes, June *retired education educator, librarian*
†Chang, Shirley Lin (Hsiu-Chu Chang) *librarian*
Hanna, Michael K. *state legislator*
†Little, Robert Owens *administration and technology executive*
Podol, Peter L. *foreign language educator*
Snowiss, Alvin L. *lawyer*
Sweeny, Charles David *chemist*
Willis, Craig Dean *academic administrator*

Long Pond
Mattioli, Joseph Reginald, Jr. *raceway executive, former dentist*

Loretto
Sackin, Claire *emerita social work educator*
Wilson, David Patrick *academic administrator*
Woznak, John Francis *English language educator*

Lower Burrell
Kinosz, Donald Lee *quality consultant*
Rose, Robert Henry *arts education administrator*

Lower Gwynedd
Pendleton, Robert Grubb *pharmacologist*
Torok, Raymond Patrick *steel and aluminum company executive*

Lumberville
Fallon, Robert Thomas *English language educator*
Katsiff, Bruce *artist*

Lyon Station
Breidegam, DeLight Edgar, Jr. *battery company executive*

Macungie
Gavin, Austin *retired lawyer*
Nikischer, Frank William, Sr. *retired restaurant owner and operator*
†Paulson, Michael George *foreign language educator*
Rubin, Arthur Herman *university administrator, consultant*

Madison
Nair, Bala Radhakrishnan *engineer*

Malvern
Bedrosian, Gregory Ronald *investment banker*
Brighton, Ruth Louise *lay worker, educator*
Cameron, John Clifford *lawyer, health science facility administrator*
Everhart, Rodney Lee *software industry executive*
Figaniak, Laura Mary Ann *poet, executive assistant*
Fisher, Sallie Ann *chemist*
Fitch, Mary Jane Early *lawyer, computer consultant, writer*
Hendrix, Stephen C. *financial executive*
Moulton, Hugh Geoffrey *lawyer, business executive*
Quay, Thomas Emery *lawyer*
Swymer, Stephen *principal*
Weisman, Harlan Frederick *pharmaceutical company executive*
†Yost, R. David *healthcare manufacturing company administrator*

Manheim
Geib, Violet M. *elementary education educator*

Marietta
†Lawrence, James David *principal*
Shumaker, Harold Dennis *lawyer*

Marion Center
Bomboy, John David *mathematics educator*

Martinsburg
Clemens, Tammy Leah *geriatrics nurse*
Stern, Jerry Allen *state legislator*

Matamoras
Linden, Harold Arthur *interior designer, consultant*

Mc Donald
Craig, Trisha Ann Varish *secondary school teacher*
Maurer, Karen Ann *special education educator*
Tannehill, Norman Bruce, Jr. *consultant, educator*

Mc Kean
Chitester, Robert John *television producer*

Mc Keesport
Kaufer, Virginia Gross *family therapist, mental health program, manager*
Kessler, Steven Fisher *lawyer*

Mc Murray
Brzustowicz, John Cinq-Mars *lawyer*
Langenberg, Frederick Charles *business executive*

McConnellsburg
Taylor, Margaret Uhrich *professional society administrator*

McKees Rocks
Butala, Anthony Francis *vocalist, entertainer, small business owner*

Meadowbrook
Baeckstrom, Marianne *actuary*
Kiesel, Harry Alexander *internist*

Meadville
Adams, Earl William, Jr. *economics educator*
Cable, Charles Allen *mathematician*
Cable, Mabel Elizabeth *urban planner, artist*
Dixon, Armendia Pierce *school program administrator*
Foster, Catherine Rierson *manufacturing company executive*
Helmreich, Jonathan Ernst *history educator*
Irwin, Melinda Kay *physical education educator*
Katope, Christopher George *English language educator*
Wharton, William Polk, Jr. *consulting psychologist, retired educator*

Mechanicsburg
†Boughter, Ronald Edward *video specialist*
Clousher, Fred Eugene (Freddie Cee Clousher) *entertainment producer, booking agent, musician*
†Davis, Frank Daniel *retired journalist*
Kinney, Linford Nelson *retired army officer*
Pearsall, Gregory Howard *naval officer*
Rudolph, Robert Norman *secondary school educator, adult education educator*
Scher, David Lee *cardiac electrophysiologist*
†Van Zile, Susan J.

Mechanicsville
Bye, Ranulph DeBayeux *artist, author*

Media
Baitzel, Gregory Wilson *accounting executive*
Beeman, Richard Roy *historian, educator*
Bettner, Betty Lou *psychotherapist*
Comeforo, Jean Elizabeth *hearing-impaired educator*
Cooke, M(erritt) Todd *banker*
Coyle, Edward J. *physical education coordinator*
Dunion, Celeste Mogab *consultant, township official*
Dunlap, Richard Frank *school system administrator*
Elman, Gerry Jay *lawyer*
Emerson, Sterling Jonathan *lawyer*
Ewing, Robert Clark *lawyer*
Garrison, Susan Kay *lawyer*
Garrison, Walter R. *corporate executive*
Garvin, Florence Ward *management consultant*
Hemphill, James S. *investment management executive, financial advisor*
Kessler, Woodrow Bertram *family practice physician, geriatrician, educator*
Leonard, Vincent Albert *music composer*
Lewandowski, Theodore Charles *psychology educator*
Resnick, Stewart Allen *diversified company executive*
Smith, David Gilbert *political science educator*
Smith, Eleanor Cowan *social worker*
†Sorkin, Adam J. *English educator*
Tomlinson, Herbert Weston *lawyer*
Valdes-Dapena, Marie Agnes *retired pediatric pathologist, educator*
Voltz, Sterling Ernest *physical chemist, researcher*
Wood, Richard D., Jr. *retail executive*
Zicherman, David L. *lawyer, educator, financial consultant*

Melrose Park
Steinlauf, Michael Charles *historian*

Mendenhall
Lee, Virginia Diane *lay worker*
Reinert, Norbert Frederick *patent lawyer, retired chemical company executive*

Mercer
Brady, Wray Grayson *mathematician, educator*

Mercersburg
Coffman, Patricia JoAnne *school nurse, counselor*
Fegan, Martina Kriner *secondary education educator*

Merion
Laddon, Warren Milton *lawyer, arbitrator*

Merion Station
Amado, Ralph David *physics educator*
Camp, Kimberly N. *museum administrator, artist*
Jacobs, Suzanne *author*
Kulp, Jonathan B. *elementary school educator*
Littell, Franklin Hamlin *theologian, educator*
Littell, Marcia Sachs *Holocaust educator*
Mayer, Charles Arthur *management consultant, musician*
Pearcy, Lee Theron *secondary education educator, writer*
Ueland, Elizabeth Pritchard *English language educator*

Meyersdale
Cober, Kay Ann *secondary school educator*

Middletown
Dhir, Krishna Swaroop *business administration educator*
Jordan, Lois Wenger *university official*
Pannebaker, James Boyd *lawyer*
†Richards, Winston Ashton *mathematics educator, statistician*
South, James Dawson, II *university administrator*
Yucelt, Ugur *marketing professional, educator*

Midland
Vosler Petrella, Brenda Gayle *family nurse practitioner, educator, researcher*

Mifflintown
Lauver, Nelson Charles *narrator, voice-over, small business owner*

Milford
Eckert, Allan Wesley *writer*
Le Guin, Ursula Kroeber *author*
Reynolds, Edwin Wilfred, Jr. *retired secondary education educator*

Millersville
Caputo, Joseph Anthony *university president*
Craven, Roberta Jill *educator in literature and film*
Kabacinski, Stanley Joseph *health and physical education educator, consultant, speaker*
Kendall, Leigh Wakefield *surgeon*
†Renfroe, Aubrey Vance *company executive*
Suskie, Linda Anne *academic administrator*

Millerton
Lyon, Berenice Iola Clark *civic worker*

Millville
Shoup, Michael C. *newspaper reporter, editor*

Milton
†Brandau, Susan Carol *library director*

Mohnton
Bowers, Richard Philip *manufacturing executive*
Hart, LeRoy Banks *financial software executive, real estate developer*
Hildreth, Eugene A. *physician, educator*

Monaca
Jaskiewicz, David Walter *optometrist*
Nutter, James Randall *management educator*

Monongahela
Brandon, John Mitchell *physician*
Fisher Prutz, Mary Louise *coronary care nurse*
†Yovanof, Silvana *physician*

Monroeville
Campbell, Donald Acheson *nuclear engineer, consultant*
Edelstein, Jason Zelig *rabbi, psychologist*
Jacobi, William Mallett *nuclear engineer, consultant*
Maclay, William Nevin *retired manufacturing and construction company executive*
Moenich, David Richard (D.R.M. Johnston) *writer*
Sehring, Hope Hutchison *library science educator*
Stanger, Robert Henry *psychiatrist, educator*
Valentine, Ruthann Loretta *counseling company executive*

Mont Alto
Caldwell, Corrinne Alexis *academic administrator*
Russo, Peggy Anne *English language educator*
Sourbier, James Henry, IV *police chief*
Toothacker, William Sanford, III *physics educator*

Montgomeryville
Seal, John S., Jr. *manufacturing company executive*

Montoursville
Woolever, Naomi Louise *retired editor*

Moon Township
Alstadt, Lynn Jeffery *lawyer*
†Farley, Glen David *English educator*
†Kiliany, Mary Catherine *program director, communications educator*
Lipson, Barry J. *lawyer, columnist*
Rabosky, Joseph George *engineering consulting company executive*

Moosic
Owens, Evelyn *elementary education educator*

Morrisville
Glosser, Harry John, Jr. *lawyer*
Heefner, William Frederick *lawyer*
Robinson, Lorna Jane *marketing executive*

Mount Joy
D'Agostino, Raymond *city manager*
Lodde, Gordon Maynard *health physics consultant*

Mount Pleasant
Dangelo, Eugene Michael *elementary education educator*
Juriga, Raymond Michael *dentist*

Moylan
Eberl, James Joseph *physical chemist, consultant*
Peabody, William Tyler, Jr. *retired paper manufacturing company executive*

Murrysville
McWhirter, James Herman *consulting engineering business executive, financial planner*
Schlabach, Leland A. *electrical engineer*

Myerstown
Heiser, Janet Dorothy *physical education educator*
Schwenk, James Lee *minister, educator*

Nanticoke
McHale, Maureen Bernadette Kenny *controller*
Shelton, Elisabeth Nesbitt *pediatric nurse and educator*
†Stankovich, Joseph George, Jr. *social science researcher*

Narberth
Fenichel, Richard Lee *retired biochemist*
Grenald, Raymond *architectural lighting designer*
Luscombe, Herbert Alfred *physician, educator*
Madow, Leo *psychiatrist, educator*
Mezvinsky, Edward M. *lawyer*
Nathanson, Neal *virologist, epidemiologist, educator*
Strom, Brian Leslie *internist, educator*

Narvon
High, Linda Oatman *author*

Natrona Heights
Baldassare, Louis J. *school superintendent*

Nazareth
†Ferraro, Margaret Louise (Peg Ferraro) *educator*
Rayner, Robert Martin *financial executive*

New Alexandria
Ackerman, Robert Lloyd *chemical engineer, environmental tree farmer*

New Brighton
Baldwin, Clarence Jones, Jr. *electrical engineer, manufacturing company executive*
Rodney, Claudette Cecilie *hospital program director*

New Castle
Blair, Phyllis E. *artist, sculptor, illustrator*
Denniston, Marjorie McGeorge *retired elementary education educator*
Flannery, Harry Audley *lawyer*
Flannery, Wilbur Eugene *health science association administrator, internist*
Grzebieniak, John Francis *psychologist*
Halm, Nancye Studd *private school administrator*
Mangino, Matthew Thomas *lawyer*
Moore, Janet Marie *accountant, state official*
Peterson, Janet Ruth *medical/surgical and rehabilitation nurse*
Roux, Mildred Anna *retired secondary school educator*
Sands, Christine Louise *English educator*

New Cumberland
Peters, Ralph Edgar *architectural and engineering executive*
Rose, Bonnie Lou *state official*
Scheiner, James Ira *engineering company executive*

New Holland
Amor, James Michael *dentist, actor*
Cox, James Michael *school district administrator, psychologist*
Kermes, Constantine John *artist, industrial designer*
Papadakis, Emmanuel Philippos *physicist, consultant*
West, Daniel Charles *lay worker, dentist*

New Hope
Bertele, William *environmental engineer*
Connolly, Janet Elizabeth *retired sociologist and criminal justice educator*
Knight, Douglas Maitland *educational administrator, optical executive*
Lee, Robert Earl *retired physician*
Patterson, Donald William *painter*
Purpura, Peter Joseph *museum curator, exhibition designer*
Raabe, Gerhard Karl *epidemiologist*
Stahl, Stephen Lee *theater director, writer, producer*
Williamson, Frederick Beasley, III *rubber company executive*

New Kensington
Blair, Karen Elaine *respiratory care practitioner, health educator*
Bonzani, Renée Marie *anthropologist, researcher*
Demmler, Albert William, Jr. *retired editor, metallurgical engineer*
Hahn, William Orr *psychologist, consultant*
Jarrett, Noel *chemical engineer*
†Krochalis, Jeanne Elizabeth *English language educator*
Lederman, Frank L. *scientist, research center administrator*
Miller, Albert Jay *retired library and information sciences director*
Pien, Shyh-Jye John *mechanical engineer*

New Stanton
Black, Cora Jean *evangelist, wedding consultant*

New Tripoli
Fiedler, Kathy Lou *library media specialist*
Fritzinger, Rebecca Ann *English language educator*

New Wilmington
Deegan, John, Jr. *academic administrator, researcher*
Perkins, James Ashbrook *English language educator*
Pitman, Grover Allen *music educator*

Newton Square
Sacks, Susan Bendersky *mental health clinical specialist, educator*

Newtown
Brennan, Thomas John *city and state official, consultant, educator*
†Bursk, Christopher I. *educator*
Coale, Ansley Johnson *economics educator*
Duncan, Stephen Robert *elementary education educator*
Fiore, James Louis, Jr. *public accountant, educator, professional speaker, trainer consultant*
Godwin, Robert Anthony *lawyer*
Henshaw, Jonathan Cook *manufacturing company executive*
Keenan, Terrance *foundation executive*
Luo, Nianzhu *mechanical engineer*
Palmer, Robert Roswell *historian, educator*
Pfeiffer, John Edward *author*
Richard, James Thomas *psychologist, educator*
Ross, Edwin William *rubber company executive*
Scull, Charles D. *insurance company executive*
Simkanich, John Joseph *lawyer, engineer*
Smith, Karen Ann *visual artist*
Somers, Anne Ramsay *medical educator*
Wurster, Julie Anne *financial executive*

Newtown Square
Benenson, James, Jr. *manufacturer*
Bower, Ward Alan *management consultant, lawyer*
Graf, Arnold Harold *employee benefits executive, financial planner*
Klein, Mark Paul *real estate developer*
Pacini, Renee Annette *consulting company executive*
Perrone, Nicholas *mechanical engineer, business executive*
Staats, Dean Roy *retired reinsurance executive*
Steinman, Robert Cleeton *accountant*
Tomlinson, Charles Wesley, Jr. *advertising executive*
Traynor, Sean Gabrial *manufacturing executive*
Turner, George Pearce *consulting company executive*
Yeh, George Chiayou *engineering company executive*

Newville
Rand, Sharon Kay *elementary education educator*

Norristown
Aman, George Matthias, III *lawyer*
Breckenridge, Betty Gayle *management development consultant*
Clemens, Alvin Honey *insurance company executive*
Del Collo, Mary Anne Demetris *school administrator*
Feeny, Margaret A. *English language educator, real estate agent*
Genuardi, Charles A. *retail executive*
Gerdes, Michelle Ann *designer*
Gregg, John Pennypacker *lawyer*
Heyser, William H. *landscape contractor*
Hunter, Patricia Phelps *physician assistant*
Leigh, Nanette Marie *psychologist*
Nelson, Dawn Marie *middle school science and math educator*
Rounick, Jack A. *lawyer, company executive*
Scheffler, Stuart Jay *lawyer*
Steinberg, Arthur Irwin *periodontist, educator*
Tornetta, Frank Joseph *anesthesiologist, educator, consultant*
Tsou, Walter Hai-tze *physician*
Williamson, Ronald Thomas *lawyer*
†Woolf, Steven *principal*

North Andover
†Walker, Lawrence Gordon *technology company executive*

North Wales
Dorney, Paulette Sue *critical care nurse, consultant, educator*
Kleiman, Keith Jeffrey *computer consultant*
Rayevsky, Robert *illustrator*
Szabo, Joseph George *publisher, journalist, cartoonist, editor*

Northampton
Greenleaf, Janet Elizabeth *principal*

Nottingham
White, Richard Edmund *marketing executive*

Oakdale
Gilden, Robin Elissa *elementary education educator*

Oakmont
DeFazio, John Lorenzo *retired manufacturing executive*
Medonis, Robert Xavier *lawyer*
Ockershausen, Jane Elizabeth *journalist*

Oaks
Lenfest, Harold Fitz Gerald *cable television executive, lawyer*

Oil City
Loring, Richard William *psychotherapist*

Old Forge
Rakauskas, Matthew *vice-principal*

Olyphant
Paoloni, Virginia Ann *insurance company executive*

Orefield
Tannery, Charles N. *language educator*
†Yost, Brenda Ann *therapist*

Orwigsburg
Bemiller, C. Richard, II *consultant*
Garloff, Samuel John *psychiatrist*
Ketchledge, Kathleen A. *nurse*
Troutman, E. Mac *federal judge*

Ottsville
Hughes, Charles Martin *retired educator*

Oxford
Palser, Beth Anne *painter*

Palmyra
Miller, John Patrick *secondary education educator*
Singer, William Harry *interactive multimedia architect, software engineer, expert systems designer, consultant, entrepreneur*

Paoli
Agnew, Christopher Mack *minister, historian*
Blankley, Walter Elwood *manufacturing company executive*
Denny, William Murdoch, Jr. *investment management executive*
Emory, Hugh Mercer *lawyer*
Gallagher, Terrence Vincent *editor*
LeWitt, Michael Herman *physician, educator*

Peach Glen
Carey, Dean Lavere *fruit canning company executive*

Peckville
Mellow, Robert James *state senator*

Pen Argyl
Cali-Ascani, Mary Ann *oncology nurse*

Penn Hills
†D'Alesandro, Paul J. *legislative staff member*

Penn Valley
Berman, Phillip Lee *religious institute administrator, author*
Pedersen, Darlene Delcourt *health science publishing consultant, psychotherapist*

Pennsburg
Shuhler, Phyllis Marie *physician*

Perkasie
Ferry, Joan Evans *school counselor*
Laincz, Betsy Ann *nurse*
Ritter, Paul Revere *retired minister*

Philadelphia
Aaron, Kenneth Ellyot *lawyer*
Abbott, Frank Harry *lawyer*
Abraham, Lynne M. *district attorney*
Abrahm, Janet Lee *hematologist, oncologist, educator*
Abramowitz, Robert Leslie *lawyer*
Ackerman, Franklin Kenneth *health services administrator*
Adams, Arlin Marvin *lawyer, arbitrator, mediator, retired judge*
Agus, Zalman S. *physician, educator*
Aiken, Linda Harman *nurse, sociologist, educator*
Ajzenberg-Selove, Fay *physicist, educator*
Albertini, William Oliver *telecommunications industry executive*
Alexander, John Dewey *internist*
†Alexander, Marcellus W. *television station executive*
Alexander, William Herbert *business educator, former construction executive*
Amexo, Kwaku *internist*
Anders, Jerrold P. *lawyer*
Anderson, Barbara Graham *philanthropic resources development consultant*
Anderson, Jerry Allen *financial analyst*
Anderson, Rolph Ely *marketing educator*
Andrisani, Paul *business educator, management consultant*
Angelini, Eileen Marie *foreign languages educator*
Angell, M(ary) Faith *federal magistrate judge*
†Anzalone, Frank Michael *stage manager*
Arce, A. Anthony *psychiatrist*
Armstrong, Clay *physiology educator*
Arnold, Lee *library scientist*
Aronstein, Martin Joseph *lawyer, educator*
Arrastia, Javier Armando *administrative law judge*
Asbury, Arthur Knight *neurologist, educator*
Atkinson, Barbara Frajola *pathologist*
Austrian, Robert *physician, educator*
Auten, David Charles *lawyer*
Avery, William Joseph *packaging manufacturing company executive*
Azoulay, Bernard *chemicals company executive*
Azzolina, David Sean *librarian*
Babbel, David Frederick *finance and insurance educator*
Baccini, Laurance Ellis *lawyer*
Bachman, Arthur *lawyer*
Backman, Robert Marc *television and radio station executive*
Bacon, Edmund Norwood *city planner*
Badler, Norman Ira *computer and information science educator*
Baessler, Christina A. *medical/surgical nurse*
Baker, Lester *physician, educator, research administrator*
Baldino-Gloster, Tara *critical coronary care nurse*
Baldwin, Harold Scott *pediatrician*
Bales, John Foster, III *lawyer*
Ballengee, James McMorrow *lawyer*
Bamberger-Herrmann, Julia Kathryn *social worker*
Banerji, Ranan Bihari *mathematics and computer science educator*
Bantel, Linda Mae *museum curatorial consultant*
Barchi, Robert Lawrence *clinical neurologist, neuroscientist, educator*
Barker, Clyde Frederick *surgeon, educator*
Barnett, Jonathan *architect, city planner*
Barnett, Samuel Treutlen *international company executive*
Barrett, James Edward, Jr. *management consultant*
Barrett, John J(ames), Jr. *lawyer*
Barrett, Thomas Leon Francis *information technology software executive*
Bartle, Harvey, III *federal judge*
Bartlett, Allen Lyman, Jr. *retired bishop*
Basora, Adrian Anthony *ambassador*
Bates, James Earl *academic administrator*
Batterman, Steven Charles *engineering mechanics and bioengineering educator, forensic engineering and biomechanics consultant*
Baum, E. Harris *lawyer*
Baum, Stanley *radiologist, educator*
Baxt, William G. *medical educator*
Beard, Richard Burnham *engineering educator emeritus, researcher*
Bearn, Alexander Gordon *physician scientist, former pharmaceutical company executive*
Beasley, James Edwin *lawyer*
Bechtle, Louis Charles *federal judge*
Becker, Edward Roy *federal judge*
Bergelson, Jeffrey Michael *pediatrician , educator*
Berger, David *lawyer*
Berger, Harold *lawyer, engineer*
Berkley, Emily Carolan *lawyer*
Berkman, Richard Lyle *lawyer*
Bernard, John Marley *lawyer, educator*
Bernstein, Joseph *orthopedic surgeon, philosopher*
Bershad, Jack R. *lawyer*
Berwind, C. G., Jr. *manufacturing executive*
Best, Franklin Luther, Jr. *lawyer*
Beukers, Karen Viola (Karen Viola) *cardiac nurse*
Bevilacqua, Anthony Joseph Cardinal *archbishop*
Bianchi, Carmine Paul *pharmacologist*
Bibbo, Marluce *physician, educator*
Biddle, Daniel R. *editor, reporter*
Bildersee, Robert Alan *lawyer*
Binder, David Franklin *lawyer, author*
Binzen, Peter Husted *columnist*
Birchard, Bruce *religious organization administrator*
Bischoff, Kenneth Bruce *chemical engineer, educator*
Black, Allen Decatur *lawyer*
Black, Creed C., Jr. *lawyer*
Black, Perry *neurological surgeon, educator*
Blades, Herbert William *diversified consumer products company executive*
Blavat, Jerry (Gerald Joseph Blavat) *radio and television personality, actor*
Bloom, Michael Anthony *lawyer*
Blumberg, Baruch Samuel *academic research scientist*
Blume, Marshall Edward *finance educator*
Blumstein, Edward *lawyer*
Boasberg, Leonard W. *reporter*
Bochetto, George Alexander *lawyer*
Boda, Veronica Constance *lawyer*
Boden, Guenther *endocrinologist*
Bodine, James Forney *retired civic leader*
Bodner, Susan R. *marketing and communications executive*
Boehne, Edward George *banker*
Bogutz, Jerome Edwin *lawyer*
Boldt, David Rhys *journalist*
Bonett, Edward Joseph, Jr. *law clerk, public housing manager*
Bookspan, Michael Lloyd *musician*

Booth, Anna Belle accountant
Borer, Edward Turner investment banker
Borislow, Alan Jerome hospital dental department chairman
Borovik, Alexei Peter ballet dancer, educator
Boss, Amelia Helen law educator, lawyer
Botwinick, Milton Edward genealogist, researcher
Bove, Alfred Anthony medical educator
Bowles, L. Thompson medical executive
Boyd, Larry Chester recruitment manager
Bracey, Cookie Frances Lee minister
†Brader, William R. engineer, architectural firm executive
Bradley, Kevin J. publishing company executive
Bradley, Raymond Joseph lawyer
Brady, Luther W., Jr. physician, radiation oncology educator
†Brady, Thomas Geoffrey artist
Brantley, Jeffrey Hoke professional baseball player
Breitman, Joseph B. prosthodontist, dental educator
Bressler, Barry E. lawyer
Bridger, Wagner H. psychiatrist, educator
Brighton, Carl Theodore orthopedic surgery educator
Brind'Amour, Rod Jean professional hockey player
Brinster, Ralph Lawrence biologist
Brobeck, John Raymond physiology educator
Broderick, Raymond Joseph federal judge
Brodsky, Julian A. broadcasting services, telecommunications company executive
Brody, Anita Blumstein judge
Brott, M. Paul architectural firm executive
Brown, Betty Marie government agency administrator
Brown, Denise Scott architect, urban planner
Brown, Lawrence Harvey (Larry Brown) basketball coach
Brown, Richard P., Jr. lawyer
Brown, Ronald Rea software engineer, artist
Brown, Stephen D. lawyer
Brown, William Hill, III lawyer
Browne, Stanhope Stryker lawyer
Brown-Gatta, Linda Marion women's health nurse
Brucker, Paul C. academic administrator, physician
Brunner, Janet Lee physician assistant
†Buchheit, William A. neurosurgeon, educator
Buckwalter, Ronald Lawrence federal judge
Buerkle, Jack Vincent sociologist, educator
Burbank, Stephen Bradner law educator
Burch, Francis Floyd clergyman, English educator
Burgess, Ann Wolbert nursing educator
Burns, Rosalie Annette neurologist, educator
Burstein, Elias physicist, educator
Butz, Geneva Mae pastor
Byer, Harold George environmental engineer
Bykofsky, Stuart Debs newspaper columnist
Byrd, Malcolm Todd public health administrator
Cabot, Diana Marie marketing professional, travel and transportation executive
Cabot, Stephen Jay lawyer
Calabi, Eugenio mathematician, educator
Callé, Craig R.L. packaging executive
Calman, Robert Frederick mining executive
Calvert, Jay H., Jr. lawyer
Camp, Donald Eugene experimental photographer, educator
Cannon, John, III lawyer
Capizzi, Robert Lawrence physician
Caputo, Richard Kevin social work educator, researcher
Carey, Arthur Bernard, Jr. editor, writer, columnist
Carnecchia, Baldo M., Jr. lawyer
†Carpenter, Amy Tacy architect
Carroll, Thomas Colas lawyer, educator
Carter, Irene Lavenia greeting card company owner, poet
Carter, John Swain museum administrator, consultant
Carter, Richard E(itel) legal association executive
Casey, Kenneth G. neurosurgeon, educator
Casey, Rita Jo Ann nursing administrator
Casper, Charles B. lawyer
Cass, David economist, educator
Chait, Arnold radiologist
Chance, Britton biophysics and physical chemistry educator emeritus
Chance, Henry Martyn, II engineering executive
Chang, Howard Fenghau law educator, economist
Cherken, Harry Sarkis, Jr. lawyer
Cheston, George Morris lawyer
Chiacchiere, Mark Dominic lawyer
Childress, Scott Julius medicinal chemist
Chimples, George lawyer
Cho, Young Il mechanical engineering educator
Chu, Mon-Li Hsiung dermatology educator
Chung, Edward Kooyoung cardiologist, educator, author
Clark, John Arthur lawyer
Clark, John J. economics and finance educator
†Clark, Paul J. management consultant
Clark, William H., Jr. lawyer
Clarke, John Rodney surgeon
Clarke, Robert Earle (Bobby Clarke) hockey executive
Clarkin, John Francis health care management executive
Clearfield, Harris Reynold physician
Clothier, Isaac H., IV lawyer
Coché, Judith psychologist, educator
†Cohen, Betsy Z. bank executive
Cohen, David councilman
Cohen, David Louis lawyer
Cohen, David Walter academic administrator, periodontist, educator
Cohen, Ira Myron aeronautical and mechanical engineering educator
Cohen, Marc cardiologist
Cohen, Sidney medical educator
Cohen, Sylvan M. lawyer
Cohn, Herbert Edward surgeon, educator
Cohn, Mildred biochemist, educator
Coleman, Robert J. lawyer
Collings, Robert L. lawyer
Collons, Rodger Duane decision sciences educator
Colman, Robert Wolf physician, medical educator, researcher
Comer, Nathan Lawrence psychiatrist, educator
Comerota, Anthony James vascular surgeon, biomedical researcher
Comfort, Robert Dennis lawyer
Comisky, Hope A. lawyer
Comisky, Marvin retired lawyer
Conn, Rex Boland, Jr. physician, educator
Connor, Joseph Patrick, III lawyer
Cook-Sather, Scott Douglas pediatric anesthesiology educator
Cooney, John Gordon lawyer
Cooney, J(ohn) Gordon, Jr. lawyer
Cooper, Edward Sawyer cardiovascular internist, educator
Cooper, Jane Todd (J. C. Todd) poet, writer, educator
Cooper, Richard Lee newspaper editor, journalist
Cooper, Wendy Fein lawyer
Cooperman, Barry S. educational administrator, educator, scientist
Coppock, Ada Gregory theatre executive
Cornelius, Jeffrey Michael music educator
Cortes, Ron reporter
Cortner, Jean Alexander physician, educator
Coulson, Zoe Elizabeth retired consumer marketing executive
Cowles, Roger E. computer consultant
Cox, Roger Frazier lawyer
Coyne, Charles Cole lawyer
Cramer, Harold lawyer
Cramer, Richard Charles artist, educator
Crawford, James Douglas lawyer
Creech, Hugh John chemist
†Croce, Pat sports team executive
Crough, Daniel Francis lawyer, insurance company executive
Crumb, George Henry composer, educator
Dabrowski, Doris Jane lawyer
Dagit, Charles Edward, Jr. architect, educator
Dalinka, Murray Kenneth radiologist, educator
Daly, Donald Francis investment counsel
Dalzell, Stewart federal judge
Damsgaard, Kell Marsh lawyer
D'Angio, Giulio John radiologist, educator
Danzon, Patricia M. medical educator
Darby, Karen Sue legal education administrator
Darling, Pamela Ann Wood religious consultant, educator
Davidson, Stuart West lawyer
Davis, Alan Jay lawyer
Davis, Allen Freeman history educator, author
Davis, C. VanLeer, III lawyer
Davis, Howard Jeffrey lawyer
Davis, Raymond, Jr. physical chemistry researcher
Davis, Robert Harry physiology educator
DeBunda, Salvatore Michael lawyer
de Cani, John Stapley statistician, educator
DeHoratius, Raphael Joseph rheumatologist
De La Cadena, Raul Alvarez physician, physiology and thrombosis educator
Delacato, Carl Henry education educator
DeLaura, David Joseph English language educator
†DeLong, David G. architect, urgan planner, educator
Del Raso, Joseph Vincent lawyer
Deming, Frank Stout lawyer
Dennis, Edward S(pencer) G(ale), Jr. lawyer
Denworth, Raymond K. lawyer
Depp, (O.) Richard, III obstetrician-gynecologist, educator
De Simone, Louis A. bishop
D'Este, Mary Ernestine investment group executive
Detweiler, David Kenneth veterinary physiologist, educator
de Vassal, Vladimir investment management executive
Devlin, John Gerard lawyer, author
Devlin, Thomas McKeown biochemist, educator
d'Harnoncourt, Anne museum director, executive
Diamond, Paul Steven lawyer
Diaz, Nelson Angel lawyer
DiBerardino, Marie Antoinette developmental biologist, educator
Di Bernadinis, Michael commissioner recreation Philadelphia
Dichter, Mark S. lawyer
DiCiccio, Frank J. city official
Dickerson, Rita M. human resources professional
Dilks, Park Bankert, Jr. lawyer
Dinoso, Vicente Pescador, Jr. physician, educator
DiPalma, Joseph Rupert pharmacology educator
Ditter, J. William, Jr. federal judge
Diver, Colin S. law educator, dean
Djerassi, Isaac physician, medical researcher
Donahue, John M(ichael) lawyer
Donohue, James J. lawyer
Donohue, John Patrick lawyer
Doran, William Michael lawyer
Dorfman, John Charles lawyer
Doty, Richard Leroy medical researcher
Drake, Donald Charles journalist
Drake, William Frank, Jr. lawyer
Driscoll, Lee Francis, Jr. corporate director, lawyer
Druckrey, Inge Heide graphic designer, educator
Dubin, Leonard lawyer
Dubin, Stephen Victor lawyer, holding company executive
DuBois, Jan Ely federal judge
Dubrow-Eichel, Steve Kenneth psychologist
Duclow, Geraldine historian, theatre and film librarian
Durant, Marc lawyer
Dutton, Peter Leslie biochemist, educator
Dworetzky, Joseph Anthony lawyer, city official
Dymicky, Michael retired chemist
Dyson, Robert Harris museum director emeritus, archaeologist, educator
Eastwood, James W. naval officer
Ecker, Paul Gerard physician, educator
Eddy, Julia Veronica educator
Ehrlich, George Edward rheumatologist, international pharmaceutical consultant
Eisen, Howard Joel physician, researcher
Eisenstein, Bruce Allan electrical engineering educator
Eisenstein, Toby K. microbiology educator
Eiswerth, Barry Neil architect, educator
Elkins, S. Gordon lawyer
El-Sherif, Mahmoud A. electrical engineering educator
Engheta, Nader electrical engineering educator, researcher
Epstein, Alan Bruce lawyer
Erdmann, James Bernard educational psychologist
Erichsen, Peter Christian university official, lawyer
Erickson, Ralph O. botany educator
Ernst, Calvin Bradley vascular surgeon, surgery educator
Eskin, Bernard Abraham obstetrics and gynecology educator, medical researcher
Esser, Carl Eric lawyer
Esterhai, John Louis, Jr. surgeon, medical educator
Estrin, Deborah Perry human resources executive
Evan, William Martin sociologist, educator
Evangelista, Allan clergy member, medical researcher
Evans, Audrey Elizabeth physician, educator
Fabbri, Anne R. art museum director, curator
Faber, Donald Stuart neurobiology and anatomy educator
Fader, Henry Conrad lawyer
Fagin, Claire Mintzer nursing educator, administrator
Fala, Herman C. lawyer
Falcao, Linda Phyllis lawyer, former screenwriter
Falkie, Thomas Victor mining engineer, natural resources company executive
Faraghan, George Telford photographer
Farber, Emmanuel pathology and biochemistry educator
†Farrar, John T. physician, researcher
Fegley, Kenneth Allen systems engineering educator
Feirson, Steven B. lawyer
Feldman, Albert Joseph lawyer
Feninger, Claude industry management services company executive
Fernandez, Happy Craven (Gladys Fernandez) city council member
Ferrick, Thomas Jerome, Jr. journalist
Ferst, Walter B. lawyer
Fickler, Arlene lawyer
Fiebach, H. Robert lawyer
Fielding, Allen Fred oral and maxillofacial surgeon, educator
Finney, Graham Stanley management consultant
Fioretti, Michael D. lawyer
Fish, Elizabeth Ann physical education educator
Fisher, Allan Campbell railway executive
Fisher, Aron Baer physiology and medicine educator
Fisher, Marshall Lee operations management educator
Fisher, Robert gastroenterologist, health facility administrator
Fishman, Alfred Paul physician
Fitts, Donald Dennis chemist, educator
Fitts, Michael Andrew law educator
FitzGerald, Garret Adare medical educator
Fitzgerald, Robert Hannon, Jr. orthopedic surgeon
Flanagan, Joseph Patrick, Jr. lawyer
Flaster, Richard Joel lawyer
Fleetwood, Rex Allen insurance company executive
Flores, J. Terry accountant
†Flynn, Kevin healthcare company executive
Fonseca, Raymond J. dental medicine educator
Foster, David John journalist
Foti, Margaret Ann association executive, publisher, editor
Foulke, William Green retired banker
†Fox, Bruce I. federal judge
Fox, Renée Claire sociology educator
Francescone, John Bernard accountant
†Francona, Terry Jon manager professional athletics
Frank, Barry H. lawyer
Frank, Harvey lawyer, author
†Frank, Leonard Arnold physician
Frankel, Francine Ruth political science educator
Frankl, William Stewart cardiologist, educator
Franklin, Harold Leroy graphic artist, filmmaker
Franzini-Armstrong, Clara biologist
Fraser, David William epidemiologist
Freedman, Robert Louis lawyer
Freese, Andrew neurosurgeon, educator, scientist
French, Jeffrey Stuart architect
Freyd, Peter John mathematician, computer scientist, educator
Friedman, Harvey Michael infectious diseases educator
Friedman, Murray civil rights official, historian
Friedman, Sidney A. financial services executive
Fritton, Karl Andrew lawyer
Frohlich, Kenneth R. insurance executive
Fullam, John P. federal judge
Fuller, John Garsed Campbell food and drug company executive
Furth, John Jacob molecular biologist, pathologist, educator
Fussell, Paul author, English literature educator
Gabrielson, Ira Wilson physician, educator
Gaither, William Samuel civil engineering executive, consultant
Gant, Ron (Ronald Edwin Gant) professional baseball player
Garcia, Celso-Ramón obstetrician and gynecologist
Garcia, Richard Raul major league umpire
Garcia, Rudolph lawyer
Gardiner, Geoffrey Alexander, Jr. radiologist, educator
Garonzik, Sara Ellen stage director
Gartland, John Joseph physician, writer
Gary, Nancy Elizabeth nephrologist, academic administrator
Gault, Janice Ann ophthalmologist, educator
Gawthrop, Robert Smith, III federal judge
Gelles, Richard James sociology and psychology educator
Gendron, Michèle Marguerite Madeleine librarian
Genkin, Barry Howard lawyer
Gerber, Jack artist
Gerbino, Philip Paul university president, consultant
German, Edward Cecil lawyer
Gerner, Edward William medical educator
Gerrity, Thomas P. dean
Giegengack, Robert university administrator
Gilberg, Kenneth Roy lawyer
Gilbert, Harry Ephraim, Jr. hotel executive
Giles, James T. federal judge
Gilmour, D(avid) James strategic planner, systems analyst
Ginsberg, Phillip Carl physician
Giordano, Antonio medical educator
Glanton, Richard H. lawyer
Glassman, Howard Theodore lawyer
Glassmoyer, Thomas Parvin lawyer
Glazer, Ronald Barry lawyer
Glazer, Tom (Thomas Zacariah Glazer) folksinger, writer, composer
Glick, Jane Mills biochemistry educator
Glick, John H. oncologist, medical educator
†Glickman, Edward A. real estate investment executive
Glusker, Jenny Pickworth chemist
†Glusman, David H. healthcare consultant
Glusman, David Howard accountant
Goldberg, Martin physician, educator
Goldberg, Marvin Allen lawyer, business consultant
Golden, Gerald Samuel national medical board executive
Goldfarb, Stanley internist, educator
Goldhamer, David J. medical educator, researcher
Goldin, Judah Hebrew literature educator
†Goldin, Paul Rakita history educator
Goldman, Gary Craig lawyer
Goldman, Jerry Stephen lawyer
Goldman, Richard Paul educational administrator
Goldstein, William Marks lawyer
Golomb, Richard Moss lawyer
Gonnella, Joseph Salvator medical educator, university dean and official, consultant, researcher
Gonzalez-Scarano, Francisco Antonio neurologist
Goodenough, Ward Hunt anthropologist, educator
Goodman, Charles Schaffner marketing educator
Goodman, David Barry Poliakoff physician, educator
Goodman, Stephen Murry lawyer
Goodrich, Herbert Funk, Jr. lawyer
Gordon, Anne Kathleen editor
Gough, John Francis lawyer
Gozum, Marvin Enriquez internist
Graessle, William Rudolf pediatrician, educator
Graffman, Gary pianist, music educator
Graham, Walter S. environmental engineer
Granoff, Gail Patricia lawyer
Grant, M. Duncan lawyer
Grant, Richard W. lawyer
Graziani, Leonard Joseph pediatric neurologist, researcher
Green, Clifford Scott federal judge
Green, Tyler Scott professional baseball player
Greenfield, Bruce Harold lawyer, banker
Greenfield, Val Shea ophthalmologist
Greenstein, Jeffrey Ian neurologist
Gross, Larry Paul communications educator
Grossman, Sanford Jay economics educator
Grove, David Lavan lawyer
Groves, Dorothy Frances nursing education specialist
Gruliow, Rebecca Agnes Lindsay editor, translator, artist
Gueson, Emerita Torres obstetrician, gynecologist
Gusoff, Patricia Kearney elementary education educator
Gustafson, Sandra Lynne secondary education educator
†Guyer, Hedy-Ann Klein special education educator
Hack, Gary Arthur dean
Hackney, Francis Sheldon university president
Hackney, Sheldon federal agency administrator, academic administrator
†Hadlock, Philip G. French language educator
Haignere, Clara Sue health education educator
Hairston, Harold B. protective services official
Haley, Vincent Peter lawyer
Hall, Robert J. newspaper executive
Halpern, Eric Franklin university publishing director
†Halpern, Marcia Lynn neurologist
Hameka, Hendrik Frederik chemist, educator
Hamme, David Codrington architect
Hammond, Benjamin Franklin microbiologist, educator
Hammond, Charles Ainley clergyman
Hand, Peter James neurobiologist, educator
Hand, Virginia Saxton home health nurse
Hanks, Gerald E. oncologist
Hanle, Paul Arthur museum administrator
Hanselmann, Fredrick Charles lawyer
Hansen-Flaschen, John Hyman medical educator, researcher
Harbater, David mathematician
Harkins, John Graham, Jr. lawyer
Harmelin, Stephen Joseph lawyer
Harris, Raymond Jesse retired government official
Harvey, Colin Edwin veterinary medicine educator
Harvey, John Adriance psychology and pharmacology educator, researcher, consultant
Harvey, Rebecca Suzanne accountant, management consultant
Harvey, William J. religious service organization, religious publication editor
Haugaard, Niels pharmacologist
Hauptfuhrer, George Jost, Jr. lawyer
Havard, Bernard theater producer
Havas, Peter physicist, educator
Haviland, Bancroft Dawley lawyer
Haydanek, Ronald Edward lawyer and consultant
Hayes, John Freeman architect
Hayllar, Ben city finance director
Haynes, Gary Allen photographer, journalist, newspaper editor
Heilig, William Wright coal and manufacturing company executive
Heitz, James W. anesthesiologist, internist
Henrich, William Joseph, Jr. lawyer
Henry, Rene Arthur, Jr. environmental agency administrator
Hess, Hans Ober lawyer
Hextall, Ron professional hockey player
Hickey, Gregory Joseph priest, educational administrator
Hildebrand, David Kent statistics educator
Hill, Tyrone professional basketball player
Hillgren, Sonja Dorothy journalist
Hillman, Alan L. internist, educator, researcher
Hines, Susan Carol English language educator
Hinshaw, Keith C. veterinarian
Hochstrasser, Robin M. chemist, educator
Hoelscher, Robert James lawyer
Hoenigswald, Henry Max linguist, educator
Hoffman, Alan Jay lawyer
Hoffman, Daniel (Gerard) literature educator, poet
Holmgren, Paul professional hockey coach
†Holod, Renata historian
Holzbaur, Erika L. medical educator
Hoskins, Alexander L. (Pete Hoskins) zoological park administrator
Hossain, Murshed physicist
Hsu, Samuel music history educator, concert pianist
†Huang, Peter Henry law educator
Hunter, Jack Duval lawyer
Hunter, James Austen, Jr. lawyer
Hussain, M. Mahmood medical educator
Hussar, Daniel Alexander pharmacy educator
Hutton, Herbert J. federal judge
Hyder, Frank J. artist, educator
Iannotti, Joseph Patrick orthopedic surgeon
Iglewicz, Boris statistician, educator
†Ingram, George Herschel university administrator, writer
Intemann, Robert Louis physics educator, researcher
Iverson, Allen basketball player
Izenour, Steven architect
Jackson, Laird Gray physician, educator
Jacobs, Eugene Gardner, Jr. psychiatrist, psychoanalyst, educator
Jacoby, Thomas S. school system administrator
Jamieson, Kathleen Hall dean, communications educator
Jaron, Dov biomedical engineer, educator
Jarvis, J. Andrew architectural firm executive
Jellinek, Miles Andrew lawyer
Jensh, Ronald Paul anatomist, educator
Jimenez, Sergio A. internist, science educator
Joglekar, Prafulla Narayan information systems management educator, consultant
Johns, Michael Douglas government relations executive, policy analyst, health care consultant
Johnson, Craig Norman investment banker
Johnson, Joseph Eggleston, III physician, educator

Schneider, Carl William *lawyer*
Schneider, Jan *obstetrics and gynecology educator*
Schneider, Richard Graham *lawyer*
Scholl, David Allen *federal judge*
Schotland, Donald Lewis *retired medical educator, neurologist*
Schultz, Jane Schwartz *health research administrator*
Schumacher, H(arry) Ralph *internist, rheumatologist, medical educator*
Schwan, Herman Paul *electrical engineering and physical science educator, research scientist*
Schwartz, Gordon Francis *surgeon, educator*
Schwartz, Robert M. *lawyer*
Scirica, Anthony Joseph *federal judge*
Scott, Donald Allison *lawyer*
Scott, Joseph C. *professional hockey team executive*
Scott, William Proctor, III *lawyer*
†Scuderi, Peter B. *federal judge*
Searcy, Jarrell D. (Jay Searcy) *sportswriter*
Sebold, Russell Perry, III *Romance languages educator, author*
Segal, Bernard Louis *physician, educator*
Segal, Irving Randall *lawyer*
Segal, Robert Martin *lawyer*
Seligman, Martin E. P. *psychologist*
Selles, Robert Hendrikus *actuary, consultant*
Seltzer, Vivian Center *clinical psychologist, educator*
Sevy, Roger Warren *retired pharmacology educator*
†Shachmurove, Yochanan *economics educator*
Shapiro, Howard *newspaper editor*
Shapiro, Raymond L. *lawyer*
Shatz, Stephen Sidney *mathematician, educator*
Sheehan, Donald Thomas *academic administrator*
Sheils, Denis Francis *lawyer*
Shelkrot, Elliot L. *library director*
Shen, Benjamin Shih-Ping *scientist, engineer, educator*
Shestack, Jerome Joseph *lawyer*
Shiekman, Laurence Zeid *lawyer*
†Shils, Edward B. *management educator, lawyer*
Shipman, Lynn Karen *lawyer*
Shmukler, Stanford *lawyer*
Shockman, Gerald David *microbiologist, educator*
Shoemaker, Innis Howe *art museum curator*
Showers, Ralph Morris *electrical engineer educator*
Siderer, Jack Philip *engineering executive*
Siegel, Bernard Louis *lawyer*
Sigmond, Richard Brian *lawyer*
Sigmund, Diane Weiss *judge*
Silberberg, Donald H. *neurologist*
Silvers, Willys Kent *geneticist*
Simpkins, Henry *medical educator*
Simpson, Carol Louise *investment company executive*
Siskind, Ralph Walter *lawyer*
Sitarski, Stephen *historic site administrator*
Sivin, Nathan *historian, educator*
Slavitt, David Rytman *writer*
Sloviter, Dolores Korman *federal judge*
Sloviter, Henry Allan *medical educator*
†Smith, Charles Boyd *federal judge*
Smith, David Stuart *anesthesiology educator, physician*
Smith, Frederick Samuel, Jr. *accountant*
Smith, Jonathan M. *computer science educator*
Smith, Lloyd *musician*
Smith, Randall Norman *orthopedist*
Smith, Robert Rutherford *university dean, communication educator*
Snider, Edward Malcolm *professional hockey club executive*
Solano, Carl Anthony *lawyer*
Solmssen, Peter *academic administrator*
Solomon, Phyllis Linda *social work educator, researcher*
Somers, Hans Peter *lawyer*
Sorgenti, Harold Andrew *petroleum and chemical company executive*
Soslow, Arnold *quality consultant*
Sotnick, M.J. *architectural firm executive*
Souders, Deryl V. *medical/surgical and rehabilitation-detox nurse*
Sovie, Margaret Doe *nursing administrator, educator, clinician, researcher*
Spaeth, Edmund Benjamin, Jr. *lawyer, law educator, former judge*
Spaeth, George Link *physician, ophthalmology educator, writer*
Spandorfer, Merle Sue *artist, educator, author*
Sparrow, Ruth S. *lawyer*
Spector, Martin Wolf *lawyer, business executive*
Speyer, Debra Gail *lawyer*
Spolan, Harmon Samuel *banker*
Sprague, James Mather *medical scientist, educator*
Stabenau, Walter Frank *systems engineer*
Stalberg, Zachary *newspaper editor*
Staloff, Arnold Fred *financial executive*
Steinberg, Laurence *psychology educator*
Steinberg, Marvin Edward *orthopaedic surgeon, educator*
Steinberg, Robert Philip *lawyer*
†Steiner, Wendy Lois *English educator*
Stern, Joan Naomi *lawyer*
Stetson, John Batterson, IV *construction executive*
Stevens, Rosemary A. *public health and social history educator*
Stevenson, Josiah, IV *cultural arts administrator*
Stewart, Robert Forrest, Jr. *lawyer*
Stick, Thomas Howard Fitchett *corporate architect, construction litigation consultant*
Stiles, Michael *prosecutor*
Stiller, Jennifer Anne *lawyer*
Strasbaugh, Wayne Ralph *lawyer*
Strauss, Jerome Frank, III *physician, educator*
Strickler, Matthew M. *lawyer*
Strong, Ann Louise *planning educator*
Stunkard, Albert James *psychiatrist, educator*
Stuntebeck, Clinton A. *lawyer*
Subak, John Thomas *lawyer*
Sudak, Howard Stanley *physician, psychiatry educator*
Sulyk, Stephen *archbishop*
Summers, Anita Arrow *public policy and management educator*
Summers, Clyde Wilson *law educator*
Summers, Robert *economics educator*
Sun, Hun H. *electrical engineering and biomedical engineering educator*
Sunderman, Frederick William *physician, educator, author, musician*
Sutman, Francis Xavier *university dean*
Swan, Ralph Edward *higher education educator*
Sztandera, Les Mark *computer science educator*
Taichman, Norton Stanley *pathology educator*
Takashima, Shiro *biophysics educator*
Tammen, James F. *plant pathologist, educator*
Tasco, Marian B. *councilwoman*
Tasman, William Samuel *ophthalmologist, medical association executive*
Tawyea, Edward Wayne *university administrator, librarian*
Taylor, Jeffrey Matthew *principal*
Taylor, Robin Lynn *anchorperson, reporter*
Taylor, Wilson H. *diversified financial company executive*
Teacher, Stuart *book publishing company executive*
Temin, Michael Lehman *lawyer*
Terry, John Joseph *transportation investor*
Terzian, Karnig Yervant *civil engineer*
Thomas, Carmen Christine *physician, consultant administrator*
Thomas, Lowell Shumway, Jr. *lawyer*
Thomas, William Harrison *professional football player*
Thompson, Sheldon Lee *refining company executive*
†Thomson, Sharon Anne *writer, performer, director*
Tierney, Brian Patrick *advertising and public relations executive*
Tigay, Jeffrey H(oward) *foreign language, literature, religion educator*
Tiger, Ira Paul *lawyer*
Toll, Seymour Irving *lawyer, writer, educator*
Tominaga, Masatoshi *anthropologist, consulting company executive*
Tomiyasu, Kiyo *consulting engineer*
†Tomlinson, Gary Alfred *music educator*
Torg, Joseph Steven *orthopaedic surgeon, educator*
Tortella, Bartholomew Joseph *trauma surgeon*
Tourtellotte, Charles Dee *physician, educator*
Tractenberg, Craig R. *lawyer*
Tremonte Spigonardo, Ada Mary *interior architect*
Trulear, Harold Dean *minister, theological educator, social researcher*
Tsykalov, Eugene *neuroscientist, researcher*
Tucker, Cynthia Delores Nottage (Mrs. William M. Tucker) *political party official, former state official*
Tumola, Thomas Joseph *lawyer*
†Turchi, Ralph P. Ray, Jr. *retired labor union administrator*
Turner, Evan Hopkins *retired art museum director*
Turner, Franklin Delton *bishop*
Tyng, Anne Griswold *architect*
Uhler, Walter Charles *government official, writer, reviewer*
†Uhlhorn, Ray *healthcare executive*
Vaira, Peter Francis *lawyer*
†Van Arsdalen, Keith Norman *urologist*
Van Artsdalen, Donald West *federal judge*
Vanbiesbrouck, John *professional hockey player*
Van der Spiegel, Jan *engineering educator*
Van De Walle, Etienne *demographer*
Vargus, Ione Dugger *university administrator*
Varkonyi, Istvan Laszlo *language educator*
Velos Weiss, Joan Claire *adult/geriatric nurse practitioner*
Venturi, Robert *architect*
Veon, Dorothy Helene *educational consultant*
Verna, Anna Cibotti *city council official*
Vinh, Binh *architect*
Visconto, Anthony J. *small business owner*
Vitek, Vaclav *materials scientist*
Vitez, Michael *reporter*
Vogel, Robert Philip *lawyer*
Wachman, Marvin *university chancellor*
Wachs, Saul Philip *Jewish education educator*
Wadden, Thomas Antony *psychologist, educator*
Wagner, Daniel A. *human developement educator, academic administrator*
Wagner, Thomas Joseph *lawyer, insurance company executive*
Waite, Helen Eleanor *funeral director*
Waldman, Jay Carl *judge*
†Waldron, Arthur Nelson *international relations educator*
Wales, Walter D. *physicist, educator*
Walinsky, Paul *cardiology educator*
Walker, Allen Lyon *logistics analyst*
Walker, Douglas C. *banker*
Walker, Kent *lawyer*
Walker, Valaida Smith *university administrator*
Wallace, Anthony Francis Clarke *anthropologist, educator*
Walsh, Patricia Regina *trauma nurse, coordinator, educator*
Walters, Donald Lee *education educator*
Warner, Frank Wilson, III *mathematics educator*
Warner, Theodore Kugler, Jr. *lawyer*
Warnick, Patricia Ann *healthcare consultant, nurse ethicist*
Watson, Bernard Charles *foundation administrator*
Watt, David Harrington *history educator*
Webber, John Bentley *orthopedic surgeon*
Webber, Ross Arkell *management educator*
Weber, Janet M. *retired nurse*
Weese, James Leighton *surgical oncologist*
Weigley, Russell Frank *history educator*
Weil, Jeffrey George *lawyer*
Wein, Alan Jerome *urologist, educator, researcher*
Weiner, Charles R. *federal judge*
†Weinraub, Marsha A. *psychology educator*
Weisberg, Morris L. *retired lawyer*
Weiss, William *retired pulmonary medicine and epidemiology educator*
Welch, Charles Edgar, Jr. *retired English language educator, writer*
Weller, Elizabeth Boghossian *child and adolescent psychiatrist*
†Wells, Carol Sandra Moore *federal judge*
Welsh, Diane M. *judge*
Wengert, Timothy *church history educator, clergyman*
Wernick, Richard Frank *composer, conductor*
Wert, Robert Clifton *lawyer*
Whelan, Daniel J. *communications company executive*
Whelan, Gerald Patrick *emergency physician*
Whitaker, Linton Andin *plastic surgeon*
White, Howard D. *information science educator*
Whiteside, William Anthony, Jr. *lawyer*
Wiksten, Barry Frank *communications executive*
Wilcots, David N. *consulting and environmental geologist, artist*
Wild, Richard P. *lawyer*
Wilde, Norman Taylor, Jr. *investment banking company executive*
Wilder, Robert George *advertising and public relations executive*
Wilf, Frederic Marshal *lawyer*
Wilkinson, Signe *cartoonist*
Willet, E(verett) Crosby *artist*
Williams, James Boughton *artist, art educator*
Williams, Robert Benjamin *convention center executive*
†Williams, Ronald Leander *English educator*
Williams, Sankey Vaughan *health services researcher, internist*
†Williams-Witherspoon, Kimmika Lyvette *anthropology educator*
Wilson, James Lawrence *chemical company executive*
Winfrey, Marion Lee *television critic*
Winkler, Sheldon *dentist, educator*
Wittels, Barnaby Caesar *lawyer*
Wivel, Nelson Auburn *physician, medical researcher, educator*
Woestendiek, (William) John, Jr. *columnist*
Wolf, Bruce *lawyer*
Wolf, Nelson Marc *cardiologist*
Wolf, Robert B. *lawyer*
Wolfe, J. Matthew *lawyer*
Wolff, Deborah H(orowitz) *lawyer*
Wolitarsky, James William *securities industry executive*
Woods, Teri *paralegal, writer*
Woosnam, Richard Edward *venture capitalist, lawyer*
Wright, Minturn Tatum, III *lawyer*
Wright, Yvette V. *termination contracting officer*
Wrobleski, Jeanne Pauline *lawyer*
Xin, Li *physiologist*
Xu, Gang *medical educator*
Yaffe, Peter Marc *public policy executive*
Yanoff, Myron *ophthalmologist*
Yohn, William H(endricks), Jr. *federal judge*
Young, Andrew Brodbeck *lawyer*
Young, Donald Stirling *clinical pathology educator*
Young, Robert Crabill *medical researcher, science facility administrator, internist*
Yunginger, John W. *allergist*
Zalecky, Donna Michelle *land use planner, landscape architect*
Ziegler, Donald Robert *accountant*
Zivitz, Stephen Charles *lawyer*
Zuchman, Philip Abrim *artist, educator*
Zucker, William *retired business educator*
Zweiman, Burton *physician, scientist, educator*

Philadephia

Kumanyika, Shiriki K. *nutrition epidemiology researcher, educator*

Phildelphia

Wiesner, David *illustrator, children's writer*

Philipsburg

†Genesi, Susan Petrovich *educator*

Phoenixville

Allen, Carol Linnea Ostrom *art educator*
Bretz, Connie *poet, storyteller*
Brundage, Russell Archibald *retired data processing executive*
Gillie, Michelle Francoise *industrial hygienist*
Koenig, Michael Edward Davison *information science educator*
Lukacs, John Adalbert *historian, retired educator*

Pipersville

Erickson, Edward Leonard *biotechnology company executive, consultant*
Sigety, Charles Edward *lawyer, family business consultant*

Pittsburgh

Aaron, Marcus, II *lawyer*
Aderson, Sanford M. *lawyer*
Alexander, Andrew James *commercial lender*
Ambrose, Donetta W. *federal judge*
Anderson, Edwyna Goodwin *lawyer*
Anderson, John Leonard *chemical engineering educator*
Anderson, John Robert *psychology and computer science educator*
Anthony, Edward Mason *linguistics educator*
Apone, Carl Anthony *journalist*
Arbutina, Petra *advertising executive*
Archer, David Horace *process engineer, consultant*
Arnett, Ronald Charles *communication educator*
†Artz, John Curtis *lawyer*
Badics, Zsolt *electrical engineer, researcher*
Balada, Leonardo *composer, educator*
Balas, Egon *applied mathematician, educator*
Baldauf, Kent Edward *lawyer*
†Banerjee, Sujata *telecommunications educator*
†Barazzone, Esther Lynn *academic administrator, educator*
Bardyguine, Patricia Wilde *ballerina, ballet theatre executive*
Barry, Herbert, III *psychologist*
Bartlett, Byron Robert *consumer products company marketing executive*
Bartley, Burnett Graham, Jr. *oil company and manufacturing executive*
Basinski, Anthony Joseph *lawyer*
Bauccio, Lisa Ruth *obstetric nurse, high-risk perinatal nurse*
Bell, Lori Jo *crisis counselor, psychiatric nurse*
†Bellinger, Mark F. *urology educator*
Bellisario, Domenic Anthony *lawyer*
Bender, Charles Christian *retail home center executive*
†Benson, Kenneth J. *federal judge, educator*
Bentz, Michael Lloyd *plastic and reconstructive surgeon*
Berga, Sarah Lee *women's health physician, educator*
Bergmann, Carl Adolf *chemical engineer, researcher*
Berman, Malcolm Frank *health facility administrator*
Bernt, Benno Anthony *financial executive, entrepreneur and investor*
Berry, Guy Curtis *polymer science educator, researcher*
Bettis, Jerome Abram *professional football player*
Bickel, Minnette Duffy *artist*
Biondi, Manfred Anthony *physicist, educator*
Birks, Neil *metallurgical engineering educator, consultant*
Bleier, Carol Stein *writer, researcher*
Bleier, Michael E. *lawyer*
Bleil, Walter G. *lawyer*
Blenko, Walter John, Jr. *lawyer*
Bloch, Alan Neil *federal judge*
Blumstein, Alfred *urban and public affairs educator*
Bly, James Charles, Jr. *financial services executive*
Boczkaj, Bohdan Karol *structural engineer*
†Bolster, Ronald Hugh *company executive*
Bonessa, Dennis R. *lawyer*
Bonner, Shirley Harrold *business communications educator*
Boocock, Stephen William *lawyer*
Boswell, William Paret *lawyer*
Bothner-By, Aksel Arnold *chemist, horseman*
Boyce, Alfred Warne *analytical laboratory executive*
Boyce, Doreen Elizabeth *lecturer, civic development foundation executive*
Boyd, William, Jr. *business advisor, banker*
Brauner, Ronald Allan *religion educator*
Breault, Theodore Edward *lawyer*
Brennan, Carey M. *lawyer*
Brennen, Carole J. *researcher in human services*
†Brignano, Russell Carl *English educator, research specialist*
Broker, Jeffrey John *accountant*
Brown, Bobby R. *retired coal company executive*
Brown, Kevin James *real estate broker, consultant*
Brown, Ronald James *lawyer, political consultant*
†Bruckner, Lynne Dickson *English educator*
Brunson, Kenneth Wayne *cancer biologist*
Bryant, Randal Everitt *computer science educator, consultant*
Buchanan, James Junkin *classics educator*
Burger, Herbert Francis *advertising agency executive*
Burke, Leah Weyerts *physician*
Burke, Linda Beerbower *lawyer, aluminum manufacturing company executive, mining executive*
Burke, Timothy Francis, Jr. *lawyer*
Burnham, Donald Clemens *manufacturing company executive*
Burston, Daniel *psychology educator*
Byrnes, Paul David *software engineer, consultant*
Caginalp, Gunduz *mathematician, educator, researcher*
Cahouet, Frank Vondell *banking executive*
†Caiazza, Francis X. *federal judge*
Candris, Laura A. *lawyer*
Capobianco, Tito *opera director*
Carbo, Toni (Toni Carbo Bearman) *information scientist, university dean*
Cardenes, Andres Jorge *violinist, music educator*
Caretto, Albert Alexander *chemist, educator*
Carney, David John *computer scientist, music theorist*
Carr, Walter James, Jr. *research physicist, consultant*
Carroll, Holbert Nicholson *political science educator*
Carter, Donald K. *architectural firm executive*
Casasent, David Paul *electrical engineering educator, data processing executive*
Cassidy, William Arthur *geology and planetary science educator*
Casturo, Don James *venture capitalist*
Charap, Stanley Harvey *electrical engineering educator*
Charochak, Dale Michael *county official*
Cheever, George Martin *lawyer*
Cheever, Meg *non-profit organization administrator*
Cherna, Marc Kenneth *human services executive*
Chigier, Norman *mechanical engineering educator*
Chipman, Debra Decker *paralegal*
Choyke, Wolfgang Justus *physicist*
Christiano, Paul P. *academic administrator, civil engineering educator*
Chrysanthis, Panos Kypros *computer science educator, researcher*
Chu, Deh-Ying *chemist, researcher*
Cindrich, Robert James *judge*
Clack, Jerry *classics educator*
Clemence, Bonnie J. *pediatrics nurse*
Clyde, Larry Forbes *banker*
Cockerham, Kimberly Peele *ophthalmologist*
Cohen, Henry Bruce *mathematics educator*
Cohen, Henry C. *lawyer*
Cohen, Jacqueline *university researcher, sociology educator*
Cohill, Maurice Blanchard, Jr. *federal judge*
†Cohon, Jared L. *university administrator*
Colen, Frederick Haas *lawyer*
Collins, Rose Ann *minister*
†Colosimo, Steven Francis *counselor*
Coltman, John Wesley *physicist*
†Colwell, Denis *music director*
Coney, Aims C., Jr. *lawyer, labor-management negotiator*
Connolly, Ruth Carol *urological nurse practitioner*
Connors, Eugene Kenneth *lawyer, educator*
Conti, Joy Flowers *lawyer*
Conti, Ronald Samuel *electronics engineer, fire prevention engineer*
Cooper, Thomas Louis *lawyer*
Cooper, William Marion *physician*
Corbett, Thomas Wingett, Jr. *lawyer*
Cosetti, Joseph Louis *federal judge*
Costa, Guy *city official*
Courtsal, Donald Preston *manufacturing company executive, financial consultant*
Cowan, Barton Zalman *lawyer*
Cowher, Bill *professional football coach*
Croan, Robert James *music critic, singer*
†Crumrine, Patricia K. *physician, educator*
Cunningham, Leah Vota *medical/surgical nursing educator*
Curry, Nancy Ellen *educator, psychoanalyst, psychologist*
Cutler, John Charles *physician, educator*
Czuszak, Janis Marie *former credit company official, researcher*
Damianos, Sylvester *architect, sculptor*
Daniel, Robert Michael *lawyer*
Dannenberg, Roger Berry *computer scientist*
D'Appolonia, Elio *civil engineer, educator*
Dato, Virginia Marie *public health physician*
Daube, Patricia Barrett *health facility administrator*
Davidson, George A., Jr. *utility company executive*
Davis, John Phillips, Jr. *lawyer*
Davis, Otto Anderson *economics educator*
Dawes, Robyn Mason *psychology educator*
Dawson, Dermontti Farra *professional football player*
Dawson, Mary Ruth *curator*
DeForest, Walter Pattison, III *lawyer*
deGroat, William Chesney *pharmacology educator*
DeKosky, Steven Trent *neurologist*
Dell, Ernest Robert *lawyer*
Demmler, John Henry *lawyer*
Dempsey, Jacqueline Lee *special education director*
Dempsey, Jerry Edward *retired service company executive*
Denys, Sylvia *lawyer*
Deskins, Wilbur Eugene *mathematician, educator*
Detre, Katherine Maria *physician*
Detre, Thomas *psychiatrist, educator*
Diamond, Gustave *federal judge*
Dick, David E. *construction company executive*
Dieter, Richard Charles *marketing and management professional*
Di Medio, Gregory Lawrence *writer, English language educator, information analyst*
Dinman, Bertram David *consultant, retired aluminum company executive*

Rosenkranz, Herbert S. environmental toxicology educator
Ross, Madelyn Ann newspaper editor
Roth, Loren H. psychiatrist
Rubin, Robert Terry physician, researcher, educator
Ruddock, Ellen Sylves business consultant
Rudy, Ellen Beam nursing educator
Russell, Alan James chemical engineering and biotechnology educator
Rust, William James retired steel company executive
Sandman, Dan D. lawyer
Sanfilippo, Joseph Salvatore physician, reproductive endocrinologist, educator
Sanzo, Anthony Michael health care executive
Sarraf, Roberta Jean planning consultant
Sashin, Donald pet physicist, radiological physicist, educator
Scarlata, Charles Francis lawyer
Schade, Robert Richard medical educator, researcher
Schaub, Marilyn McNamara religion educator
Scheinholtz, Leonard Louis lawyer
Schliebs, Charles Allan lawyer
Schmidt, Edward Craig lawyer
Schmidt, Thomas Mellon lawyer
Schorr-Ribera, Hilda Keren psychologist
Schultz, Jerome Samson biochemical engineer, educator
Schulze, Karen Joyce clinical psychologist
Schwab, Arthur James lawyer
Schwalb, Harry artist
Schwendeman, Paul William lawyer
Sciannameo, Franco Ludovico Orlando music educator
Scully, Erik Vincent lawyer, accountant
Sees, Kay Anne accountant, healthcare consultant
Sekerka, Robert Floyd physics educator, scientist
Seligson, Mitchell A. Latin American studies educator
Sell, William Edward legal educator
Sensenich, Ila Jeanne magistrate judge
Shaffer, Terry George pastor
Shane, Charles William communication company executive, marketing consultant
Shaw, Mary M. computer science educator
Sheehan, Robert James, II management and market research consultant
Sheon, Aaron art historian, educator
Sherry, John Sebastian lawyer
Shuman, Joseph Duff lawyer
Siker, Ephraim S. anesthesiologist
Silverman, Arnold Barry lawyer
Simaan, Marwan electrical engineering educator
Simmermon, James Everett credit bureau executive
Simmons, Richard L. surgeon
Simmons, Richard P. steel company executive
†Simms, Michael Arlin poet, publishing executive
Simon, Herbert A(lexander) social scientist
Simonds, John Ormsbee landscape architect
Sinclair, Glenn Bruce mechanical engineering educator, researcher
Siporin, David human resources specialist
Skwaryk, Robert Francis judge
Slayton, Val Warren health services executive
Slifkin, Malcolm clincal microbiologist, educator
Smartschan, Glenn Fred school system administrator
Smrekar, Karl George, Jr. financial planner
Sokol, Stephen M. lawyer
Sorensen, Raymond Andrew physics educator
Spalding, Rita Lee artist
Spanovich, Milan retired civil engineer
Stahl, Laddie L. electrical engineer, manufacturing company executive
Standish, William Lloyd judge
Stargell, Willie (Wilver Dornel Stargell) professional sports team coach, former baseball player
Stearns, Peter Nathaniel history educator
Steele, Cheryl A. oncology nurse
Stein, Arland Thomas lawyer
Stella, Janet Louise special education educator
Stephenson, Robert Clay real estate company executive
Stern, Theodore electric company executive
Stevens, William Talbert financial services executive
†Stewart, Kordell professional football player
Stiff, Robert Henry dentist, educator
Stirewalt, John Newman coal company executive
†Stoner, Eugenia Chambers lawyer, corporation secretary
Strader, James David lawyer
†Straka, Martin professional hockey player
Strauss, Robert Philip economics educator
Sullivan, Dorothy Louise nurse
Sullivan, Loretta Roseann elementary education educator
Sussna, Edward economist, educator
Suzuki, Jon Byron dean, periodontist, educator
Swain, William Grant landscape architect
Swann, Lynn Curtis sportscaster, former professional football player
Sweeney, Clayton Anthony lawyer, business executive
Symons, Edward Leonard, Jr. lawyer, educator, investment advisor
Tarasi, Louis Michael, Jr. lawyer
Tarr, Joel Arthur history and public policy educator
Taylor, D. Lansing cell biology educator
Taylor, Mark Chandlee choreographer
Thomas, Richard Irwin lawyer
Thomas, W(illiam) Bruce retired steel, oil, gas company executive
Thompson, Gerald Luther operations research and applied mathematics educator
Thompson, Thomas Martin lawyer
Thorne, John Reinecke business educator, venture capitalist
Thorner, John professional society administrator
Thurman, Andrew Edward lawyer
Tierney, John William chemical engineering educator
Toeplitz, Gideon symphony society executive
Toker, Franklin K. art history educator, archaeologist, foundation executive
Totten, Mary Anne internist
Tripodi, Tony social worker, educator
Troen, Philip physician, educator
Tucker, Richard Blackburn, III lawyer
Turnbull, Gordon Keith metal company executive, metallurgical engineer
Turner, Harry Woodruff lawyer
Ubinger, John W., Jr. lawyer
Usher, Thomas James steel executive, energy executive
Van Dusen, Albert Clarence university official
Van Kirk, Thomas L. lawyer
Vater, Charles J. lawyer
Vater, David Joseph architect
Veeder, Peter Greig lawyer
Verlich, Jean Elaine writer, public relations consultant
Victor, Ronald Joseph, Jr. banking professional
†Vincent, Timothy C. secondary school educator
Vogel, Victor Gerald medical educator, researcher
Vogeley, Clyde Eicher, Jr. engineering educator, artist, consultant
von Waldow, Arnd N. lawyer
Vrscak, William Martin artist, art educator
Wald, Niel public health educator
Wallace, Richard Christopher, Jr. school system administrator, educator
Wallenberger, Frederick T. materials scientist
Walton, James M. investment company executive
Walton, Jon David lawyer
Walton, Joseph Carroll investor
Wang, Allan Zuwu cell biologist, pharmacologist
Ward, Thomas Jerome lawyer
Warsaw, Rand A. energy/financial services company executive
Weidman, John Carl, II education educator, consultant
Weingartner, Rudolph Herbert philosophy educator
†Weinstein, Mark Jay opera general director
Weis, Joseph Francis, Jr. federal judge
†Welch, William Charles neurosurgeon
Welfer, Thomas, Jr. utility company executive
West, Michael Davidson English educator
Westerberg, Arthur William chemical engineering educator
White, Robert Marshall physicist, government official, educator
Wilde, Patricia retired artistic director
Wilkins, David George fine arts educator
Will, James Fredrick steel company executive
Williams, John Wesley fine arts educator
†Williams, Stephen Edward corporate lawyer
Wilson, George David school administrator
Wilson, Wanda Lee Davis entertainment promotions professional, casting director
Wink, John Joseph project manager
Winnie, Glenna Barbara pediatric pulmonologist
Winter, Peter Michael physician, anesthesiologist, educator
Wishart, Alfred Wilbur, Jr. foundation administrator
Wohleber, Lynne Farr archivist, librarian
Woo, Savio Lau-Yuen bioengineering educator
Woodward, Thomas Aiken lawyer
†Wright, Michelle Maria English language educator
Wuerl, Donald W. bishop
Wycoff, William Mortimer lawyer
Yang, Wen-Ching chemical engineer
Yates, John Thomas, Jr. chemistry educator, research director
Yorsz, Stanley lawyer
Young, Hugh David physics educator, writer, organist
Youngner, Julius Stuart microbiologist, educator
Yourison, Karola Maria information specialist, librarian
Zanardelli, John Joseph healthcare services executive
Zappala, Stephen A. state supreme court justice
Ziegler, Donald Emil federal judge
Ziegler, Janet Cassaro holistic health nurse
†Zimmerman, Richard Kent family physician, preventive medicine specialist

Plains
Pugliese, Frank Anthony, Jr. health executive

Plymouth Meeting
Andes, Charles Lovett direct marketing executive
Britt, Earl Thomas lawyer
Delacato, Janice Elaine learning consultant, educator
Friedman, Philip Harvey psychologist
Levinson, Gary Howard real estate investor
Litman, Raymond Stephen financial services consultant
Mitchell, Matthew Dunlap medical research analyst
Nobel, Joel J. biomedical researcher
Shindledecker, Joseph Gregory programmer, analyst
Siegal, Jacob J. management and financial consultant
†Silver, Louis Edward investment banker, management consultant
Thomsen, Thomas Richard retired communications company executive

Pocono Pines
Hardiman, Therese Anne lawyer

Pocopson
Mulligan, James Francis retired business executive, lawyer

Port Matilda
Henshaw, Beverly Ann Harsh women's health nurse, consultant

Port Royal
Wert, Jonathan Maxwell, II management consultant

Portland
Hutton, William Michael manufacturing company owner

Pottstown
Hergert, Herbert Lawrence consultant
Hylton, Thomas James author
Kelly, Thomas Joseph, III photojournalist
Prowant, Gregory E. township manager
White, Thomas David, II academic administrator

Pottsville
Boran, Robert Paul, Jr. orthopedic surgeon
Jones, Joseph Hayward lawyer
Steffan, Nancy Marie cardiothoracic/intensive care nurse
Tamulonis, Frank Louis, Jr. lawyer
Walsh, James William mental health professional

Punxsutawney
Graffius, Richard Stewart, II middle school educator
Klohr, Joanne Carol nurse

Quakertown
Ambrus, Lorna medical, surgical and geriatrics nurse
de Limantour, Clarice Barr food scientist
†Hauff, Sara Jeannette newspaper editor
McDaniel, Robert Stephen technical professional

Quarryville
Schreiner, Helen Ann special education educator

Radnor
Baxter, John Michael editor
Buck, James Mahlon, Jr. venture capital executive
Castle, Joseph Lanktree, II energy company executive, consultant
Eagleson, William Boal, Jr. banker
Fisher, Ellen Roop librarian, educator
†Harper, Charles Little, Jr. foundation administrator, planetary scientist
Harrison, Robert Drew management consultant
Humes, Graham investment banker
Merchenthaler, Istvan Jozsef anatomist, neuroscientist
Paier, Adolf Arthur computer software and services company executive
Stearns, Milton Sprague, Jr. financial executive
Templeton, John Marks, Jr. pediatric surgeon, foundation executive
Vanarsdall, Robert Lee, Jr. orthodontist, educator
Zucker, Herbert publishing executive

Reading
Beaver, Howard Oscar, Jr. retired alloys manufacturing company executive
Bell, Frances Louise medical technologist
Boscov, Albert retail executive
Bowles, Patricia Mary secondary education educator
Buckendorff, Rosemary Hauseman secondary education educator
Decker, Kurt Hans lawyer, educator, author
Dersh, Rhoda E. management consultant, business executive
De Syon, Guillaume Paul Sam history educator
Dietrich, Bruce Leinbach planetarium and museum administrator, astronomer, educator
Ehlerman, Paul Michael industrial battery manufacturing company executive
Erdman, Carl L. N. retired banker
Feeman, James Frederic chemist, consultant
Fiore, Nicholas Francis special alloys and materials company executive
Gebbia, Robert James tax executive
Hackenberg, Barbara Jean Collar retired advertising and public relations executive
Hard, Brian truck leasing company executive
Hollander, Herbert I. consulting engineer
Kline, Sidney DeLong, Jr. lawyer
Kraras, Gust C. hotel executive
Lusch, Charles Jack oncologist
Lysakowski, Linda Suzanne fund raising consulting company executive
Mattern, Donald Eugene retired association executive
Millar, Robert James social science educator
†Miller, Regina Dancull Gouger artist, designer, educator
Moriarty, John Klinge electronics engineer, consultant
Morrill, Michael William consumer activist
Murphy, Kevin Keith foundation executive
Pugliese, Anthony Paul construction company executive, educator
Richart, Douglas Stephen chemist
Rochowicz, John Anthony, Jr. mathematician, mathematics and physics educator
Roesch, Clarence Henry banker
Rohrer, Samuel Edward state legislator
Rothermel, Daniel Krott lawyer, holding company executive
Stevens, Jennifer Roehl critical care nurse
†Twardowski, Thomas M. federal judge
Unser, Alfred, Jr. professional race car driver
Welty, John Rider lawyer
White, Timothy Paul brokerage house executive

Rebersburg
Kuhns, Nancy Evelyn minister

Red Lion
Hartman, Charles Henry nonprofit management consultant
Keener, Wayne B. interior designer
Saylor, Stanley E. state legislator
Van Kouwenberg, Martha Nester secondary education educator

Reynoldsville
Wheeler, Mark Andrew, Sr. lawyer

Richboro
Burtt, Larice A.R. artist
Higginbotham, Kenneth James financial services executive

Ridgway
Aiello, Gennaro C. insurance company executive

Ridley Park
Brittell-Whitehead, Diane Peeples secondary education educator, addiction counselor
Logan, Thomas Joseph molecular biologist, pharmaceutical researcher
Walls, William Walton, Jr. management consultant

Riegelsville
Banko, Ruth Caroline retired library director

Roaring Spring
Dell, Linda Treese gifted and talented education educator

Robesonia
Evaul, Charleen McClain education educator
†Fuhrman, Gwendolyn Sue secondary school educator

Rochester
Garlathy, Frank Bryan minister

Roscoe
O'Hara, Paul Anthony, Jr. retired art educator, artist

Rosemont
Bolger, Stephen Garrett English and American studies educator
Connally, Andrew David historian, educator

Royersford
Zearfoss, Herbert Keyser lawyer

Russell
†Thomas, Bryan Valentine secondary school educator, artist

Russellton
Curtis, Paula Annette elementary and secondary education educator

Rydal
Bacon, George Hughes, Jr. systems analyst, consultant
Black, Thomas Donald retired religious organization administrator
Roediger, Janice Anne artist, educator

Saint Davids
Baird, John Absalom, Jr. college official
Bertsch, Frederick Charles, III business executive
Denenberg, Herbert Sidney journalist, lawyer, former state official
Gage, (Leonard) Patrick research company executive
McCarthy, Justin Milton marketing professional
Pollard, Edward Ellsberg banker
Rogers, James Gardiner accountant, educator
Sauer, James Leslie librarian, educator
Sheftel, Roger Terry merchant bank executive
Shurkin, Lorna Greene writer, publicist, fund raiser
Smalley, Christopher Joseph pharmaceutical company professional

Saint Marys
Johnson, J. M. Hamlin manufacturing company executive

Saltsburg
Kyle, Diane Wagman librarian
Pidgeon, John Anderson headmaster

Salunga
Landis, Paul Groff bishop, mission executive

Saxonburg
†Howell, Cherie Ann volunteer recruitment coordinator, educator

Saxton
†Curfman, Walter L. school system administrator

Sayre
May, Lisa Gregory cell biologist, researcher
Moody, Robert Adams neurosurgeon

Scenery Hill
Schaltenbrand, Philip Edward art educator

Schnecksville
Kiechel, Barbara Bernadette vocational school educator

Schuylkill Haven
Sarno, Patricia Ann biology educator
Vickers, Anita Marissa English language and literature educator

Scottdale
Lee, John Lawrence, Jr. educational administrator
Miller, Levi publishing administrator
Schrock, Paul Melvin editor

Scranton
†Alexander, Steven artist, educator
†Blewitt, Thomas M. federal judge
Bourcier, Richard Joseph French language and literature educator
†Caputo, A. Richard judge
Cimini, Joseph Fedele law educator, lawyer, former magistrate
Clymer, Jay Phaon, III science educator
Conaboy, Richard Paul federal judge
Denaro, Anthony Thomas psychiatrist
†Dougherty, John Martin bishop
Eckersley, Richard Laurence accountant
Farrell, Marian L. nursing educator
Gougeon, Len Girard literature educator
Haggerty, James Joseph lawyer
Howley, James McAndrew lawyer
Janoski, Henry Valentine banker, former investment counselor, realtor
†Lepore, Marie Ann home care nurse
Lynett, George Vincent newspaper publisher
Lynett, William Ruddy publishing, broadcasting company executive
Maislin, Isidore hospital administrator
McShane, Joseph Michael priest, academic administrator, theology educator
Meredick, Richard Thomas podiatrist
Morse, Terry Wayne clergyman
Myers, Morey Mayer lawyer
Nealon, William Joseph, Jr. federal judge
Nee, Sister Mary Coleman college president emeritus
O'Hora, Eileen Rita emergency care nurse
O'Leary, Robert Thomas physiatrist
O'Malley, Carlon Martin judge
Ostrowski, Thomas John accountant
Parente, William Joseph political science educator
Passon, Richard Henry academic administrator
Powell, Robert Ellis mathematics educator, college dean
Reap, Sister Mary Margaret college administrator
Rhiew, Francis Changnam physician
Rogers, Edwin Earl newspaper editor
Sebastianelli, Carl Thomas clinical psychologist
Shovlin, Joseph P. optometrist, consultant
Singleton, David Earl newspaper reporter
Sokolowski, Walter D. protective services official
Timlin, James Clifford bishop
Turel, Joan Marie religious program director
Turock, Jane Parsick nutritionist
Vanaskie, Thomas Ignatius judge
Volk, Thomas accountant
Walsh, Denise Ann Jessup critical care nurse
†Whitman, Roy Eric television specialist
†Wiese, Marjorie Ann administrative assistant
Williams, Holly Thomas business executive
†Zaboski, Gerald Christopher academic administrator
Zaydon, Jemille Ann English language and communications educator

Selinsgrove
Clark, Beth minister
Connolly, Elma Troutman artist, contractor, designer
Cunningham, Joel Luther university president
†Fincke, Gary W. educator
Kolbert, Jack foreign language educator, French literature educator, humanities educator

†Richard, David Seward *biology educator*
Whitman, Jeffrey Paul *philosophy educator*

Sellersville
Fluck, J. Stephen *disability issues information specialist, writer, educator, poet*
Loux, Norman Landis *psychiatrist*
Rilling, David Carl *surgeon*

Seneca
Spring, Paull E. *bishop*

Sewickley
Bouchard, James Paul *steel manufacturing and planning executive*
Chaplin, James Crossan, IV *securities firm executive*
Jehle, Michael Edward *financial executive*
Newell, Byron Bruce, Jr. *Episcopalian pastor, director pastoral services*
Ostern, Wilhelm Curt *retired holding company executive*
Rastogi, Anil Kumar *medical device manufacturer executive*
Ryan, George H. *foundation administrator*
Snyder, William Penn, III *manufacturing company executive*
Thorbecke, Willem Henry *international company executive, consultant*

Sharon
Chaudhri, Amin Qamar *film company executive*
Edwards, Patricia Ann *poet*
Epstein, Louis Ralph *retired wholesale grocery executive*
Myers, Ronald Kosty *manufacturing executive, inventor*
Rosenblum, Harold Arthur *grocery distribution executive*

Sharpsville
Durek, Dorothy Mary *retired English language educator*

Shickshinny
Luksha, Rosemary Dorothy *art educator*

Shippensburg
Blair, Margaret Whitman *writer, researcher*
Ceddia, Anthony Francis *university administrator*
Collier, Duaine Alden *manufacturing and distribution company executive*
Gay, Mathew Frank *secondary education educator*
Grim, Patricia Ann *banker*
Kaluger, George *clinical psychologist, educator*
Kujawa, Lorraine Frances *elementary educator*
Luhrs, H. Ric *toy manufacturing company executive*
Stone, Susan Ridgaway *marketing educator*
Sturtz-Davis, Shirley Zampelli *retired arts administrator/educator, fashion archivist*
Thompson, Elizabeth Jane *small business owner*

Shiremanstown
Denison, Richard Eugene *retired agricultural services company executive*
Nesbit, William Terry *small business owner, consultant*

Shoemakersville
Graeff, David Wayne *maintenance executive, consultant*

Shohola
Harding, Linda Otto *gerontological nurse*

Silverdale
Grande, Alexander, IV *artist*

Skippack
Rothenberger, Jack Renninger *clergyman*
Stonehouse, Daniel *municipal officer*

Slippery Rock
Bickel, Nora Kathryn *elementary education educator*
†Boggs, William O. *English educator*
Gordon, Tom Lee *education educator*
Smith, Grant Warren, II *university administrator, physical sciences educator*

Solebury
Anthonisen, George Rioch *sculptor, artist*
Cross, Robert William *lawyer, venture capital executive*
Gart, Herbert Steven *communications executive, producer*
Hulko, Robert Lee *recording studio executive*
Sellers, Susan Taylor *principal*
Valentine, H. Jeffrey *legal association executive*

Somerset
Barkman, Annette Shaulis *real estate management executive*
Barkman, Jon Albert *lawyer*
†Kappel, David A. *lawyer*
†Minarik, John Paul *engineer, writer*
Nair, Velupillai Krishnan *cardiologist*
Thomas, Darlene Jean *state employee*
Watson, Frances Margaret *critical care nurse, case manager*

Souderton
†Delp, R. Lee *meat packing company executive*
Hoeflich, Charles Hitschler *banker*
Lapp, James Merrill *clergyman, marriage and family therapist*
Moyer, June Faye *critical care nurse*

Southampton
Bendiner, Robert *writer, editor*
DaCosta, Edward Hoban *plastics and electronics manufacturing company executive*
†Levin, Lynn Ellen *poet*
Zocholl, Stanley Ernest *electronics executive*

Southeastern
Hawley, Linda Donovan *advertising executive*
Zlotolow-Stambler, Ernest *real estate executive, architectural executive*

Spring City
Mayerson, Hy *lawyer*

Spring Grove
Alcon, Sonja Lee de Bey Gebhardt Ryan *retired medical social worker*
Helberg, Shirley Adelaide Holden *artist, educator*

Spring House
†Canavan, Christophe R. *municipal manager*
Herb, Samuel Martin *manufacturing company executive*
Klotz, Wendy Lynnett *analytical chemist*
Payn, Clyde Francis *technology company executive, consultant*
Reitz, Allen Bernard *organic chemist*
Rosoff, William A. *lawyer, executive*
van Steenwyk, John Joseph *health care plan consultant, educator*

Springfield
Berenato, Anthony Francis *financial executive*
Blazek, Wayne Joseph *auditor*
Carter, Frances Moore *educator, writer*
Gordon, Robert Bruce *mechanical engineer*
Linker, Frank Vincent, II *manufacturing executive, consultant*
Meahl, Barbara *occupational health nurse*
Reeves, Thomas A. *naturalist*
Wilkinson, William Durfee *museum director*

Springtown
Hunt, John Wesley *English language educator*

State College
Asbell, Bernard *author, English language educator*
Atchley, Anthony Armstrong *physicist, educator*
Barnoff, Robert Mark *civil engineering educator*
†Cabrera, Alberto F. *education educator*
Darnell, Doris Hastings *storyteller, antique costume collector*
DeVoss, James Thomas *community foundation administrator, retired*
Foderaro, Anthony Harolde *nuclear engineering educator*
Forth, Stuart *librarian*
Garrett, Steven Lurie *physicist*
German, Randall Michael *materials engineering educator, consultant*
Ginoza, William *retired biophysics educator*
Gould, Peter Robin *geographer, educator*
Haas, John C. *architect*
Heldman, Louis Marc *newspaper publisher and executive*
†Henisch, Heinz Kurt *retired physics educator*
Hettche, L. Raymond *research director*
Hoffa, Harlan Edward *retired university dean, art educator*
Kowalczyk, Kim Jan *editor, writer*
Lamb, Robert Edward *diplomat*
La Porte, Robert, Jr. *political science educator, researcher*
Maneval, David Richard *mineral engineering consultant*
Max, Elizabeth *educator*
Mills, Rilla Dean *university administrator, consultant*
Morrow, David Austin, III *veterinary medical educator*
Nollau, Lee Gordon *lawyer*
Olson, Donald Richard *mechanical engineering educator*
Phillips, Janet Colleen *educational association executive, editor*
Plut, Richard Robert *psychologist, psychometrician*
Redford, Donald Bruce *historian, archaeologist*
Remick, Forrest Jerome, Jr. *former university official*
Robinett, Betty Wallace *linguist*
Santavicca, Pamela Ferguson *social welfare administrator*
†Shaner, Frederick J. *hotel company executive*
†Shaner, Lance T. *hotel executive*
Spencer, Priscilla James *physical education educator*
Strasser, Gerhard Friedrich *German language and comparative literature educator*
Toombs, William Edgar *professor*
†Watson, Jennifer Annette *urban planner, landscape architect*
Wysk, Richard A. *engineering educator, researcher*
Zhao, Hequan *chemist, researcher*

Strasburg
Dun, David W. *museum director*
Lindsay, George Carroll *former museum director*
Ware, Marilyn *water company executive*
Ware, Paul W. *gas industry executive*

Stroudsburg
Batistoni, Ronald *educational association administrator*
Miller, Nancy A. *nursing administrator*

Summerdale
Young, James Alan *academic administrator*

Summerhill
McCoy, Patrick J. *family therapist, educator*

Sunbury
Ely, Donald J(ean) *clergyman, secondary school educator*
Fernsler, John Paul *lawyer*
Hetrick, Theodore Lewis, Jr. *emergency medicine physician*
Saylor, Charles Horace *lawyer*
Weis, Robert Freeman *supermarket company executive*

Swarthmore
Anderson, Margaret Lavinia *history educator*
Bannister, Robert Corwin, Jr. *history educator*
Berger, Dianne Gwynne *educator*
Bilaniuk, Oleksa Myron *physicist, educator*
Blackburn, Thomas Harold *English language professional, educator*
Bloom, Alfred Howard *college president*
Carey, William Bacon *pediatrician, educator*
Devin, (Philip) Lee *dramaturg, theater educator*
Frost, Jerry William *religion and history educator, library administrator*
Gelzer, David Georg *English educator, missionary*
Gilbert, Scott Frederick *biologist, educator, author*
Hammons, James Hutchinson *chemistry educator, researcher*
Heaps, Marvin Dale *food services company executive*
Hopkins, Raymond Frederick *political science educator*

Kaufman, Antoinette D. *business services company executive*
Kaufman, John Robert *marketing and information management consultant*
Keith, Jennie *anthropology educator and administrator, writer*
Kelemen, Charles F. *computer science educator*
Kitao, T. Kaori *art history educator*
Krattenmaker, Thomas John *public relations executive*
Krendel, Ezra Simon *systems and human factors engineering consultant*
Lacey, Hugh Matthew *philosophy educator*
North, Helen Florence *classicist, educator*
Oneal, Glen, Jr. *retired physicist*
Ostwald, Martin *classics educator emeritus*
Pasternack, Robert Francis *chemistry educator*
Saffran, Bernard *economist, educator*
Sawyers, Claire Elyce *arboretum administrator*
Sing, Robert Fong *physician*
Swearer, Donald Keeney *Asian religions educator, writer*
Ullman, Roger Roland *lawyer, realtor*

Sweet Valley
Aldrow-Liput, Priscilla R. *elementary education educator*

Swiftwater
Melling, Jack *biotechnologist*
Six, Howard R. *microbiologist*
Woods, Walter Earl *biomedical research and development executive*

Tamaqua
Seifert, William Norman *priest, religion educator*

Tannersville
Love, Mark Steven *lawyer*
Moore, James Alfred *ski company executive, lawyer*

Telford
Hagey, Walter Rex *retired banker*

Temple
Stump, Richard Carl *environmental services administrator, consultant*
VonNieda, Jean Lorayne *medical/surgical nurse*

Thorndale
Hodess, Arthur Bart *cardiologist*

Titusville
Campasino, Ellen Marie *elementary education educator*
Hall, Mary Ann *English language educator*
Peaslee, Margaret Mae Hermanek *zoology educator*

Tobyhanna
Weinstein, William Steven *technical engineer*

Topton
Allison, Robert Harry *school counselor*
Bloom, Ruth Elsa *educator, administrator*
Haskell, Ellery Bickford *retired philosophy educator*

Towanda
Hulslander, Marjorie Diane *auditor*

Transfer
Larson, Sharon Lynn *oncological nurse*

Trevose
Faulkner, Henry, III *automotive executive*
Gerace, Diane *journalist*
McEvilly, James Patrick, Jr. *lawyer*

Trout Run
McKissick, Michael Landon *transportation consultant*

Tylersport
Raub, Donald Wilmer *minister, author*

Tyrone
Lewis, Kathryn Huxtable *pediatrician*
Shaw, Marilyn Margaret Mitchell *artist, photographer*
Stoner, Philip James *hospital administrator*

Uniontown
Carder, Mary Alice *dietitian*
Curry, Kimberly M. *communications consultant*
Eberly, Robert Edward *oil and gas production company executive*
Fox, Susan E. *legal assistant*

Unionville
De Marino, Donald Nicholson *international business executive, former federal agency administrator*
Forney, Robert Clyde *retired chemical industry executive*
Irwin, Robert Hugh Crawford *manufacturing company executive*

University Park
Allcock, Harry R. *chemistry educator*
Ameringer, Charles D. *history educator*
Anderson, John Mueller *retired philosophy educator*
Andrews, George Eyre *mathematics educator*
Antle, Charles Edward *statistics educator*
Aplan, Frank Fulton *metallurgical engineering educator*
Askov, Eunice May *adult education educator*
†Ayoub, Raymond George *mathematics educator*
Badding, John Victor *chemistry educator*
Baisley, Robert William *music educator*
Barnes, Hubert Lloyd *geochemistry educator*
Barron, Eric *earth scientist*
Benkovic, Stephen James *chemist*
Benson, Thomas Walter *rhetoric educator, writer*
Biederman, Edwin Williams, Jr. *petroleum geologist*
Blackadar, Alfred Kimball *meteorologist, educator*
Bollag, Jean-Marc *soil biochemistry educator, consultant*
Bose, Nirmal Kumar *electrical engineering, mathematics educator*
†Brandt, William Nielsen *astronomer*
Brault, Gerard Joseph *French language educator*
Brenchley, Jean Elnora *microbiologist, researcher*
†Brighton, John *academic administrator*

Brown, John Lawrence, Jr. *electrical engineering educator*
Buskirk, Elsworth Robert *physiologist, educator*
Buss, Edward George *geneticist*
Cahir, John Joseph *meteorologist, educational administrator*
Castleman, Albert Welford, Jr. *physical chemist, educator*
Cavanagh, Peter Robert *science educator, researcher*
†Clothiaux, Eugene Edmund *climate research scientist, meteorology educator*
Coleman, Michael Murray *polymer science educator*
Cross, Leslie Eric *electrical engineering educator*
Davids, Norman *engineering science and mechanics educator, researcher*
De Armas, Frederick Alfred *foreign language educator*
Domowitz, Ian *economics educator*
Duda, John Larry *chemical engineering educator*
Dupuis, Victor Lionel *retired curriculum and instruction educator*
Dutton, John Altnow *meteorologist, educator*
Eaton, Nancy Ruth Linton *librarian, university dean*
Elliott, Herschel *agricultural engineer, educator*
Epp, Donald James *economist, educator*
Erickson, Rodney Allen *dean, educator*
Fedoroff, Nina Vsevolod *research scientist, consultant, educator*
Feller, Irwin *think-tank executive, economics educator*
Feng, Tse-yun *computer engineer, educator*
Ford, Donald Herbert *psychologist, educator*
Fowler, H(oratio) Seymour *retired science educator*
Frank, Robert Worth, Jr. *English language educator*
Frankl, Daniel Richard *physicist, educator*
Friedman, Robert Sidney *political science educator*
Gannon, Robert Haines *writing educator, writer*
Geselowitz, David Beryl *bioengineering educator*
Golany, Gideon Salomon *urban designer*
Goldschmidt, Arthur Eduard, Jr. *history educator, author*
Gouran, Dennis Stephen *communications educator*
†Grosholz, Emily Rolfe *philosophy educator, poet*
Hagen, Daniel Russell *physiologist, educator*
Halsey, Martha Taliaferro *Spanish language educator*
Ham, Inyong *industrial engineering educator*
Hammond, J. D. *university dean, insurance executive*
Herr, Edwin Leon *educator, academic administrator*
Hogg, Richard *mineral/particle process engineering educator*
Holl, John William *engineering educator*
†Holmes, Charlotte Amalie *English educator*
Hood, Lamartine Frain *agriculture educator, former dean*
Hosler, Charles Luther, Jr. *meteorologist, educator*
Howell, Benjamin Franklin, Jr. *geophysicist, educator*
Jackman, Lloyd Miles *chemistry educator*
†Jackson, Ronald Lee, II *communications educator*
Jaffe, Austin Jay *business administration educator*
Jordan, Bryce *retired university president*
Junker, Edward P., III *retired diversified financial services company executive*
Kabel, Robert Lynn *chemical engineering educator*
Kaidanov, Emmanuil Gregory *coach*
Kasting, James Fraser *research meteorologist, physicist*
Klein, Philip Alexander *economist*
Knott, Kenneth *engineering educator, consultant*
Koopmann, Gary Hugo *educational center administrator, mechanical engineering educator*
Kuhns, Larry J. *horticulturist, educator*
Kulakowski, Bohdan Tadeusz *mechanical engineering educator*
Lakshminarayana, Budugur *aerospace engineering educator*
Lampe, Frederick Walter *chemistry educator, consultant*
†Lantolf, James Paul *linguistics educator*
Larson, Daniel John *physics educator*
Larson, Russell Edward *university provost emeritus, consultant agriculture research and development*
Lee, Robert Dorwin *public affairs educator*
Leslie, Donald Wilmot *landscape architecture educator*
Levin, James *education educator*
Lima, Robert *Hispanic studies and comparative literature educator*
Lindsay, Bruce George *statistics educator*
†Liu, Zi-Kui *materials science and engineering educator*
Ma, Hong *plant molecular biologist, educator*
MacCarthy, Stephen Justin *university amdinistrator, consultant*
Manbeck, Harvey B. *agricultural and biological engineer, wood engineer, educator*
Mansfield-Richardson, Virginia Dell *communications educator, researcher*
Marshall, Robert Clifford *economics educator*
Martorana, Sebastian Vincent *educator, educational consultant*
Mathews, John David *electrical engineering educator, research director, consultant*
Matthews, Berry *ceramic engineer*
Mayers, Stanley Penrose, Jr. *public health educator*
McCormick, Barnes Warnock *aerospace engineering educator*
McDonnell, Archie Joseph *environmental engineer*
McKeown, James Charles *accounting educator, consultant*
McWhirter, John Ruben *chemical engineering educator*
Mentzer, John Raymond *electrical engineer, educator*
Muhlert, Jan Keene *art museum director*
Neff, Robert Wilbur *academic administrator, educator*
Nelsen, Hart Michael *sociologist, educator*
Newnham, Robert Everest *materials scientist, educator, research director*
Nicely, Robert Francis, Jr. *education educator, administrator*
Nisbet, John Stirling *electrical engineering educator*
Pazur, John Howard *biochemist, educator*
Porterfield, Neil Harry *landscape architect, educator*
Portland, Rene *university athletic coach*
Ramani, Raja Venkat *mining engineering educator*
Rao, Calyampudi Radhakrishna *statistician, educator*
Ray, William Jackson *psychologist*
†Robinson, Joyce Henri *museum curator, art history educator*
Rolls, Barbara Jean *nutrition educator, laboratory director*
Rose, Adam Zachary *economist, educator*
Rosenberger, James Landis *statistician, educator, consultant*
Roy, Rustum *interdisciplinary educator, materials researcher*
Rusinko, Frank, Jr. *fuels and materials scientist*

Ruud, Clayton Olaf *engineering educator*
†Sanchez, Victoria E. *English educator*
Scanlon, Andrew *structural engineering educator*
Schaie, K(laus) Warner *human development and psychology educator*
Schmalstieg, William Riegel *Slavic languages educator*
Snow, Dean Richard *anthropology educator, archaeologist*
Song, Chunshan *chemist, chemical engineer, educator*
Spanier, Graham Basil *academic administrator, family sociologist, demographer, marriage and family therapist*
Spanier, Sandra Whipple *English language educator*
Stern, Robert Morris *gastrointestinal psychophysiology researcher, psychology educator*
Stinson, Richard Floyd *retired horticulturist, educator*
Taleff, Michael James *chemical dependency educator, consultant*
Tavossi, Hasson M. *process engineering educator, consultant*
Taylor, William Daniel *biophysics educator, university dean*
Thatcher, Sanford Gray *publishing executive*
Thompson, William, Jr. *engineering educator*
Tittmann, Bernhard Rainer *engineering science and mechanics educator*
Tukey, Loren Davenport *pomology educator, researcher*
Vannice, M. Albert *chemical engineering educator, researcher*
Walden, Daniel *humanities and social sciences educator*
Webb, Ralph Lee *mechanical engineering educator*
Weintraub, Stanley *arts and humanities educator, author*
Weiss, Beno *Italian language educator*
Wheeler, C. Herbert *architect, consultant, educator*
White, William Blaine *geochemist, educator*
Whitko, Jean Phillips *academic administrator*
Williams, Edward Vinson *music history educator*
Williams, Julie *coach*
Williams, Lisa Rochelle *logistics and transportation educator*
Willumson, Glenn Gardner *curator, art historian*
Winograd, Nicholas *chemist*
Witzig, Warren Frank *nuclear engineer, educator*
Yoder, Edgar Paul *education educator*

Upland
Graves, Maxine *medical and surgical nurse*
Green, Lawrence *neurologist, educator*

Upper Darby
Clemens, David Allen *minister*
†Fleitz, John *legislative administrator*
Gasparro, Frank *sculptor*
Hudiak, David Michael *academic administrator, lawyer*
Hurley, Harry James, Jr. *dermatologist*
Leiby, Bruce Richard *secondary education educator, writer*
Livingston, Margery Elsie *missionary, clinical psychologist*

Upper Saint Clair
Anderson, Catherine M. *consulting company executive*
Dunkis, Patricia B. *school system administrator*

Valencia
Hill, Ellen Brown *emergency medicine/gerontology professional, nurse*

Valley Forge
Bogle, John Clifton *investment company executive*
Boreen, Henry Isaac *computer company executive*
Bovaird, Brendan Peter *lawyer*
Dachowski, Peter Richard *manufacturing executive*
Erb, Doretta Louise Barker *polymer applications scientist*
Erb, Robert Allan *physical scientist*
Kunin, Richard H. *educational association administrator, artist*
LaBoon, Lawrence Joseph *personnel consultant*
Miller, Betty Brown *freelance writer*
Polli, G. Patrick *publishing executive*
Rassbach, Herbert David *marketing executive*
Sundquist, John A. *religious organization executive*
Walters, Bette Jean *lawyer*
Weiss, Daniel Edwin *clergyman, educator*
Wright-Riggins, Aidsand F., III *religious organization executive*

Valley View
Shankweiler, Carl David *minister*

Vandergrift
Bullard, Ray Elva, Jr. *retired psychiatrist, hospital administrator*
Kulick, Richard John *computer scientist, researcher*
Quader, Patricia Ann *elementary education educator*

Venetia
Breslin, Elvira Madden *tax lawyer, educator*

Villanova
Beck, Robert Edward *computer scientist, educator*
Beletz, Elaine Ethel *nurse, educator*
Bergquist, James Manning *history educator*
Bersoff, Donald Neil *lawyer, psychologist*
Caputo, John David *philosophy educator*
Cerino, Angela Marie *lawyer, educator*
Clement, Barbara Koltes Sadtler *academic administrator*
Dobbin, Edmund J. *university administrator*
Edwards, John Ralph *chemist, educator*
Fitzpatrick, M. Louise *dean, nursing educator*
Friend, Theodore Wood, III *foundation executive, historian*
Gould, Lilian *writer*
Hafkenschiel, Joseph Henry, Jr. *cardiologist, educator*
Hunt, John Mortimer, Jr. *classical studies educator*
Johannes, John Roland *political science educator, academic administrator*
Lesch, Ann Mosely *political scientist, educator*
Lewis, Wayne H. *investment company executive*
Malik, Hafeez *political scientist, educator*
Maule, James Edward *law educator, lawyer*
McDiarmid, Lucy *English educator, author*
Mullins, James Lee *library director*
Mulroney, Michael *lawyer, law educator, graduate program director*
Nolan, Patrick Joseph *screenwriter, playwright, educator*
Palmer, Donald Curtis *interdenominational missionary society executive*
Phares, Alain Joseph *physicist, educator*
Ricks, Thomas Miller *university administrator, historian*
Salmon, John Hearsey McMillan *historian, educator*
Scheffler, Barbara Jane *statistician, business executive*
Scott, Robert Montgomery *museum executive, lawyer*
Smith, Standish Harshaw *non-profit company executive*
Steele, Robert Dennis *radio producer, announcer*
Steg, Leo *research and development executive*
Tepper, Lloyd Barton *physician*
Termini, Roseann Bridget *lawyer, educator*
Tomlinson, J. Richard *engineering services company executive*
Vander Veer, Suzanne *aupair business executive*

Wallingford
Cook, Harvey Carlisle *law enforcement official*
Cruz-Sáenz, Michèle Frances Schiavone de *educator, researcher*
Daly, Charles Arthur *health services administrator*
Maull, Ethel Mills *retired special education educator*
McCarthy, Carol A. *pediatric nurse practitioner*
Morrison, Donald Franklin *statistician, educator*
Parker, Jennifer Ware *chemical engineer, researcher*

Warminster
†Bodkin, Thomas William *architectural engineer*
Jesberg, Robert Ottis, Jr. *science educator*
Koch, Nancy Joy *music educator, choral director, vocal coach*
Tatnall, George Jacob *aeronautical engineer*

Warren
Crone, John Rossman *pharmacist*
Ristau, Mark Moody *lawyer, petroleum consultant*

Warrendale
Buckley, Deborah Jeanne Morey *manager of process*
Cooper, Eric *multimedia executive*
†Mullig, Michael Brendan *systems administrator*
Rumbaugh, Max Elden, Jr. *professional society administrator*
Scott, Alexander Robinson *engineering association executive*
Snyder, Linda Ann *book editor*

Warrington
Moneghan, John Edward *aerospace engineer*
Shaw, Milton Herbert *conglomerate executive*
Walker, Edwin Stuart, III *retired missionary organization executive*
Ward, Hiley Henry *journalist, educator*

Washington
Allison, Jonathan *retired lawyer*
Burnett, Howard Jerome *college president*
Curran, M(ichael) Scot *lawyer*
Diamond, Daniel Lloyd *surgeon*
†Gleason, James Edward, Jr. *mining engineer*
Grimm, Donald Lee *executive*
Kastelic, Robert Frank *aerospace company executive*
†Longo, James McMurtry *college administrator*
Mc Cune, Barron Patterson *retired federal judge*
Posner, David S. *lawyer*
Richman, Stephen I. *lawyer*
Robinson, Jennifer Lynn *nursing educator*
†Starek, John T. *banker*
Troost, Linda Veronika *English language educator*

Washington Crossing
Castle, Eric F. *administrator historic site*

Waterford
Kelley, Betty Marie *office manager*

Waymart
Willis, Ellen Debora *psychiatric nurse*

Wayne
Agersborg, Helmer Pareli K. *pharmaceutical company executive, researcher*
Annenberg, Leonore A. *foundation administrator*
Baldwin, Frank Bruce, III *lawyer*
Carroll, Robert W. *retired business executive*
Carter, Edward Carlos, II *librarian, historian*
Cavitt, Lorraine DiMino *reading specialist, elementary educator*
Churchill, Winston John *lawyer, investment firm executive*
Curry, Thomas James *manufacturers representative*
de Rivas, Carmela Foderaro *psychiatrist, hospital administrator*
†DiPietro, Michele A. *insurance underwriter*
Donnella, Michael Andre *lawyer*
Etris, Samuel Franklin *trade association administrator*
Frye, Roland Mushat *literary historian, theologian*
Garrison, Guy Grady *librarian, educator*
Grace, Thomas Lee *healthcare administrator, nurse*
Griffith, Edward, II *lawyer*
Grigg, William Clyde *electrical engineer*
Guernsey, Louis Harold *retired oral and maxillofacial surgeon, educator*
†Higgs, Jon Scott *computer company executive, researcher*
Horwitz, Orville *cardiologist, educator*
Kalogredis, Vasilios J. *lawyer, health care management consultant*
Kopelman, Joshua Marc *information company executive*
Krutsick, Robert Stanley *retired science center executive*
Lefevre, Thomas Vernon *retired utility company executive, lawyer*
Lief, Harold Isaiah *psychiatrist*
Mackey, Betty Barr *writer*
MacNeal, Edward Arthur *economic consultant*
†Manas, Gerald Bennett *systems consultant*
McArdle, Joan Terruso *parochial school mathematics and science educator*
Mestre, Oscar Luis *financial consultant*
Murray, Pamela Alison *business executive*
†Perrott, Lenore Catherine *psychologist*
Rabii, Patricia Berg *church administrator*
Rolleri, Denise Marie *business owner, radiation therapist*
Rubley, Carole A. *state legislator*
Sims, Robert John *financial planner*
†Smedley, David Robert *college official, educator*
Thelen, Edmund *research executive*
Townsend, Philip W., Jr. *library director*
Wang, Stephen *oil company executive*
Wheatley, William Arthur *architect, musician*
Wilson, Bruce Brighton *retired transportation executive*
Wolcott, Robert Wilson, Jr. *consulting company executive*
Woodbury, Alan Tenney *lawyer*
Yoskin, Jon William, II *insurance company executive*
Youman, Roger Jacob *editor, writer*

Waynesboro
Benchoff, James Martin *manufacturing company executive*
Christopher, Michael Anthony *township manager*
Punt, Terry Lee *state legislator*
Stefenelli, George Edward *physician*

Waynesburg
Visser, Richard Edgar *minister*

Wellsboro
Baker, Matthew Edward *state legislator*
Driskell, Lucile G. *artist*

Wernersville
Panuska, Joseph Allan *academic administrator*
Worley, Jane Ludwig *lawyer*

Wescosville
Rienzo, Robert James *radiologist*

West Aliquippa
Peya, Prudence Malava *retired gifted and talented education educator*

West Chester
Adler, Madeleine Wing *academic administrator*
Aiken, Robert McCutchen *retired chemical company executive, management consultant*
Begley, Kathleen A. *communications trainer and writer*
Benzing, Cynthia Dell *economics educator*
Blasiotti, Robert Vincent *accountant, consultant*
Bove, Patrice Magee *elementary education educator*
Briggs, Douglas D. *communications executive*
Burton, John Bryan *music educator*
Casellas, Gilbert F. *lawyer, business executive*
Dinniman, Andrew Eric *county commissioner, history educator, academic program director, international studies educator*
Dong, Gangyi *acupunturist, medical researcher*
Dunlop, Edward Arthur *computer company executive*
Flood, Dorothy Garnett *neuroscientist*
Gadsby, Robin Edward *chemical company executive*
Gougher, Ronald Lee *foreign language educator and administrator*
Green, Andrew Wilson *economist, lawyer, educator*
Handzel, Steven Jeffrey *accountant*
Hanna, Colin Arthur *county official, management and computer consultant*
Hanson, Diane Charske *management consultant*
Harrington, Anne Wilson *medical librarian*
Hickman, Janet Susan *college administrator, educator*
†Kim, James Joo-Jin *electronics company executive*
Lamm, Sharon Lea *corporate educator, consultant*
Mahoney, William Francis *editor/author*
McMeen, Albert Ralph, Jr. *investment advisor*
Merion, Richard Donald *retired onstruction company executive*
Morgan, John David *middle school educator*
Murphy, Stephan David *electrical engineer*
Murray, Lawrence *management consultant*
Pettigrew, Claire Rudolph *music educator*
St. Landau, Norman *lawyer*
Schickling, Barry *editor, newspaper*
Segel, Joseph M. *broadcasting executive*
Swope, Charles Evans *bank president, lawyer*
Taylor, Bernard J., II *banker*
†Van Liew, Maria Christina *adult education educator*
Villella, John William *music education educator*
Weston, Roy Francis *environmental consultant*

West Conshohocken
†Ball, John H. *construction executive*
Boenning, Henry Dorr, Jr. *investment banker*
Ceccola, Russ *electrical engineer, writer*
Ivanov, Vladimir Gennadievich *biomedical engineer*
Miller, Paul Fetterolf, Jr. *retired investment company executive*
Mullen, Eileen Anne *human resources executive*
Newman, Sandra Schultz *state supreme court justice*
Richard, Scott F. *portfolio manager*
Sharp, M. Rust *lawyer*
Teillon, L. Pierre, Jr. *lawyer*

West Grove
Allman, Margo Hutz *sculptor, painter*
Allman, William Berthold *musician, engineer, consultant*

West Mifflin
Ardash, Garin *mechanical engineer*
Carneal, Pamela Lynn *technical recruiter, technical, freelance writer*
Clayton, John Charles *scientist, researcher*
DiCioccio, Gary Francis *secondary education educator*
Goldstein, Keith Stuart *family practice physician, emergency physician*
Starmack, John Robert *mathematics educator*

West Nanticoke
†Gardner, Judith Ann *secondary school and university educator*

West Newton
Sever, Tom *labor union administrator*

West Point
Ball, William Austin *health facility director, researcher*
Caskey, Charles Thomas *biology and genetics educator*
Chen, I-Wu *pharmaceutical researcher*
Hilleman, Maurice Ralph *virus research scientist*
Keyser, Janet Marie *pharmaceutical industry executive*
Scolnick, Edward Mark *science administrator*
Sherwood, Louis Maier *physician, scientist, pharmaceutical company executive*
Vickers, Stanley *biochemical pharmacologist*

West Sunbury
Stewart, Mark Thomas *compressed gas company executive*

Wexford
DoVale, Fern Louise *civil engineer*
Efaw, Cary Ross *manufacturing company executive*
Hutchinson, Barbara Winter *middle school educator*
Myers, Renée Leslie *school system administrator, educator*
Osby, Larissa Geiss *artist*

White Haven
Phillips, David George *financial planner*

White Oak
Lebovitz, Charles Neal *surgeon*
Pribanic, Victor Hunter *lawyer*

Whitehall
Collina, Kathleen Alice *corrugated box company executive*

Wilkes Barre
Bali, Ajay Kumar *cardiologist*
Brady, Patricia Marie *nurse*
Curry, Dianne Swetz *school nurse*
Dewey, George Willis, III *non-profit corporation executive*
†Durkin, Raymond J. *federal judge*
Hayes, Wilbur Frank *biology educator*
†Hupchick, Dennis Paul *history educator, writer*
Joyce, Ann Iannuzzo *art educator*
Mech, Terrence Francis *library director*
Ogren, Robert Edward *biologist, educator*
Olerta, Leslie Anne *nuclear medicine technologist*
Reilly, Michael James *law librarian*
Rosenn, Max *federal judge*
Roth, Eugene *lawyer*
Schwartz, Roger Alan *judge*
†Thomas, John J. *federal judge*
Ufberg, Murray *lawyer*
Yarmey, Richard Andrew *portfolio manager*

Williamsport
Bellmore, Lawrence Robert, Jr. *financial planner*
Douthat, James Evans *college administrator*
Ertel, Allen Edward *lawyer, former congressman*
Feinstein, Sascha *English language educator*
Griffith, Stephen Ray *philosophy educator*
Kingery, Sandra Lynn *Spanish language educator, translator*
Knecht, William L. *lawyer*
Largen, Joseph *retailer, furniture manufacturer, book wholesaler*
Lattimer, Gary Lee *physician*
Madigan, Roger Allen *state legislator*
McClure, James Focht, Jr. *federal judge*
McDonald, Peyton Dean *brokerage house executive*
Meyers, Judith Ann *education educator*
Muir, Malcolm *federal judge*
Pittman-Schulz, Kimberley C. *foundation executive*
Rosebrough, Carol Belville *cable television company executive*
Waggaman, John Floyd, II *photographer*

Willow Grove
Asplundh, Christopher B. *tree service company executive*
Duff, Donald James *religious organization administrator*
Emory, Thomas Mercer, Jr. *data communications equipment manufacturing executive*
Kulicke, C(harles) Scott *business executive*
Moore, Norma Jean *real estate associate broker*
Schiffman, Louis F. *management consultant*
Suer, Marvin David *architecture, consultant*

Windber
Baltzer, Patricia Germaine *elementary school educator*

Woolrich
Himes, Kenneth Alan *retired marketing executive*

Worcester
Curtis, Alton Kenneth *film company executive, clergyman*
McAdam, Will *electronics consultant*

Wormleysburg
Cherewka, Michael *lawyer*

Wrightsville
†Burkhart, Dennis Lloyd *artist, illustrator*
Sonneborn, Sylvia Lou Hott *secondary school educator*

Wyncote
Ciao, Frederick J. *educational administrator, educator*
Webb, Frances Moore *writer, educator*

Wyndmoor
Pfeffer, Philip Elliot *biophysicist*
Uemura, Teruki *child brain developmentalist*

Wynnewood
Alter, Milton *neurologist, educator*
Belinger, Harry Robert *business executive, retired*
Brady, John Paul *psychiatrist*
Carbine, Sharon *lawyer, corporation executive*
Connor, James Edward, Jr. *retired chemical company executive*
Freeman, Morton S. *former bar association executive, retired lawyer*
Hodges, John Hendricks *physician, educator*
Khouri, Fred John *political science educator*
Koprowska, Irena *cytopathologist, cancer researcher*
†Martino, Joseph F. *bishop*
McNally, Michael James *priest*
Meyers, Mary Ann *writer, consultant*
Phillips, Almarin *economics educator, consultant*
Schmaus, Siegfried H. A. *engineering executive, consultant*

Sider, Ronald J. *theology educator, author*
Singer, Samuel L(oewenberg) *journalist*
Squires, Bonnie Stein *fundraising consultant*
Weinhouse, Sidney *biochemist, educator*

Wyomissing
Blessing, Scott Francis *marketing executive*
Cellucci, Peter T. *principal*
Cottrell, G. Walton *manufacturing executive*
Garr, Carl Robert *manufacturing company executive*
Hampton, Richard Clinton, Jr. *clergy member, therapist*
Henry, John Martin *urologist*
Kessler, Leona Hanover *interior designer*
Moll, Lloyd Henry *banker*
Moran, William Edward *academic administrator*
Stephen, Dennis John *financial planner*
Williams-Wennell, Kathi *human resources consultant*

Yardley
Ahrens, Henry William *art educator, consultant, puppeteer*
Breitenfeld, Frederick, Jr. *educational consultant, former public broadcasting executive*
Elliott, Frank Nelson *retired college president*
Kaska, Charles Powers *psychologist*
Kubilus, Norbert John *information technology executive*
Lynch, Sister Francis Xavier *nun, development director*
Metzger, Mary Catherine *special education educator*
Minter, Philip Clayton *retired communications company executive*
Newsom, Carolyn Cardall *management consultant*
Somma, Beverly Kathleen *medical and marriage educator*
Soultoukis, Donna Zoccola *library director*
Spector, Ira Charles *pharmaceutical research executive, consultant*
Thomas, Nora R. *neonatal critical care nurse*
Zulker, Charles Bates *broadcasting company executive*

Yeadon
Logan, Thomas Wilson Stearly, Sr. *priest*

York
Aarestad, James Harrison *retired educational administrator, army officer*
Bartels, Bruce Michael *health care executive*
Barton, Dawn Kanani *elementary school educator*
Binder, Mildred Katherine *retired public welfare agency executive*
Burness, James Hubert *chemistry educator*
Cassimatis, Emanuel Andrew *judge*
Chronister, Virginia Ann *school nurse, educator*
Davis, Jane G. *corporate lawyer*
Day, Ronald Richard *financial executive*
Fontanazza, Franklin Joseph *accountant*
Greisler, David Scott *healthcare executive*
Grossman, Robert Allen *transportation executive*
Hake, Theodore Lowell *auction house owner, writer*
Hamilton, Shirley Ann *nursing administrator*
Hoffmeyer, William Frederick *lawyer, educator*
Horn, Russell Eugene *engineering executive, consultant*
Horn, Russell Eugene, Jr. *business executive*
Jackson, Renée Bernadette *English language educator*
Keiser, Paul Harold *hospital administrator*
†Kroh, Mark Sinclair *educational administrator*
†Liberante, Carrie A. *reporter*
Link, Rebecca Clagett *registrar*
Livingston, Pamela Anna *corporate image and marketing management consultant*
Macdonald, Andrew *entrepreneur*
Madama, Patrick Stephen *academic official*
Markowitz, Lewis Harrison *lawyer*
McMillan, Wendell Marlin *agricultural economist*
Miller, Donald Kenneth *engineering consultant*
Moore, Christine Helen *nurse anesthetist*
Moore, Walter Calvin *retired chemical engineer*
Owens, Marilyn Mae *elementary school educator, secondary school educator*
Page, Sean Edward *emergency medical care provider, educator*
Paraskevakos, Kelly Diane *secondary education educator*
Perry, Ronald *lawyer*
Pokelwaldt, Robert N. *manufacturing company executive*
Rebert, Jephrey Lee *transportation planner, musician*
†Rhoads, Jonathan Evan, Jr. *surgeon, medical educator*
Roetenberg, Aaron David *retail implementation specialist*
Rosen, Raymond *health facility executive*
Russell, Stephen Speh *lawyer*
Schmitt, Ralph George *manufacturing company executive*
Springer, Joel Henry *artist, educator*
Stetler, Stephen H. *state legislator*
Strayer, Gene Paul *lay worker, educator*
Thornton, George Whiteley *investment company executive*

Youngstown
Palmer, Arnold Daniel *professional golfer*

Zelienople
Moyer, Christina Beth *elementary education educator, reading specialist*

Zionsville
Fleming, Richard *chemical company executive*

RHODE ISLAND

Adamsville
Quick, Joan B. *state legislator*

Barrington
Carpenter, Charles Colcock Jones *physician, educator*
Deakin, James *writer, former newspaperman*
Graser, Bernice Erckert *elementary school principal*
Mihaly, Eugene Bramer *corporate executive, consultant, writer, educator*
O'Toole, John Dudley *retired utility executive, consultant*
Paolino, Ronald Mario *clinical psychologist, consultant, psychopharmacologist, pharmacist*
Soutter, Thomas Douglas *retired lawyer*

Block Island
Coxe, Weld *management consultant*
Gasner, Walter Gilbert *retired dermatologist*

Bristol
Bogus, Carl Thomas *law educator*
†Boulé, Denise Marguerite *educational administrator*
Esty, David Cameron *marketing and communications executive*
Parella, Mary A. *state legislator*
Schipper, Michael *university official*

Central Falls
Leclerc, Leo George *guidance counselor*
Lyle, John William, Jr. *former state senator, lawyer, social studies educator*
Tajrá, Harry William Michael *theologian, religious writer*

Charlestown
Ungaro, Joseph Michael *newspaper publishing executive, consultant*

Coventry
Traficante, Daniel Dominick *chemist*

Cranston
Ahlgren, Charles Stephen *business and public policy consultant*
Cervone, Anthony Louis *lawyer*
†Dillon-Marcotte, Kathryn Anne *Lawyer*
Fang, Pen Jeng *engineering executive and consultant*
Feinstein, Alan Shawn *writer, financial adviser*
Ferguson, Christine C. *lawyer, state agency administrator*
†Gallo, Adrienne Arline *librarian*
Kane, Steven Michael *psychotherapist, educator*
Langlois, Michael A(rthur) *brokerage house executive*
Lanzi, Beatrice A. *state legislator*
MacGunnigle, Bruce Campbell *manufacturing company executive*
Morrissey, Elizabeth A. Schwimer *language educator, writer*
Mruk, Charles Karzimer *agronomist*
Parravano, Amelia Elizabeth (Amy Beth Parravano) *recording industry executive*
Thielsch, Helmut John *engineering company executive*

Cumberland
LaFlamme-Zurowski, Virginia M. *secondary school special education educator*
Rossi, Joseph Anthony *film and television make-up artist, educator*

East Greenwich
Dence, Edward William, Jr. *lawyer, banker*
Hunter, Garrett Bell *investment banker*
Juechter, John William *retired mechanical engineer, consultant*
Soderberg, Clarence Harold, Jr. *surgeon, artist*
†Weiss, Alan *management consultant, author*
†White, Sidney Howard *English educator*

East Providence
Horton, Debbi-Jo *accountant*
McGee, Mary Alice *health science research administrator*
†Spaught, Maureen Whalen *primary educator*
Tripp, Michael Windsor *accountant*

Foster
Sawyer, Mildred Clementina *real estate agent*

Harrisville
Jubinska, Patricia Ann *ballet instructor, choreographer*

Hope Valley
Devin, Carl Eric *artist*

Jamestown
Logan, Nancy Allen *library media specialist*
Prip, Janet *metalsmith*
Todd, Thomas Abbott *architect, urban designer*
Worden, Katharine Cole *sculptor*

Johnston
†Castellone, Natalie Lynné *accountant*
MacDonald, Cindy Marie *publisher, consultant*

King Hou
Sundlun, Bruce *former governor*

Kingston
Alexander, Lewis McElwain *geographer, educator*
†Aronian, Suna *Russian and women's studies educator*
Carothers, Robert Lee *academic administrator*
Gaulin, Lynn *experiential education educator*
Goos, Roger Delmon *mycologist*
Harlin, Marilyn Miler *marine botany educator, researcher, consultant*
Harrison, Robert William *zoologist, educator*
Katzanek, Robin Jean *physical therapy educator*
Kim, Yong Choon *philosopher, theologian, educator*
MacLaine, Allan Hugh *English language educator*
Mazze, Edward Mark *marketing educator, consultant*
McKinney, William Lynn *education educator*
Nixon, Scott West *oceanography science educator*
Polk, Charles *electrical engineer, educator, biophysicist*
Roxin, Emilio Oscar *mathematics educator*
Schmidt, Charles T., Jr. *labor and industrial relations educator*
†Schroeder, Jonathan Edward *business administration educator*
Schwegler, Robert Andrew *English language educator*
Seifer, Marc Jeffrey *psychology educator*
Sharif, Mohammed *economics educator, researcher*
Stark, Dennis Edwin *finance executive*
Sullivan, Richard Ernest *educator*
Tufts, Donald Winston *electrical engineering educator*
Turnbaugh, William Arthur *archeologist, educator*
Youngken, Heber Wilkinson, Jr. *former university administrator, pharmacy educator*

Lincoln
Barlow, August Ralph, Jr. *minister*
Brites, José Baptista *secondary education educator, writer, artist*
Carter, Wilfred Wilson *financial executive, controller*
Magendantz, Henry Guenther *physician*

Little Compton
Caron, Wilfred Rene *lawyer*
MacKowski, John Joseph *retired insurance company executive*

Middletown
Demy, Timothy James *military chaplain*
Jackson, John Edward *educator, logistician, retired naval officer*
Ponte, Stephen Carl *school system administrator*
Watkins, William, Jr. *electric power industry executive*

Narragansett
Apperson, Jack Alfonso *retired army officer, business executive*
Bentley-Scheck, Grace Mary *artist*
Loontjens, Maurice John, Jr. *town manager*
Pierson, Douglas H. *special education educator*
Pilson, Michael Edward Quinton *oceanography educator*
Sullivan, Paul Joseph *artist*

Newport
Bergstrom, Albion Andrew *army officer, federal official*
Brennan, Joseph Gerard *philosophy educator*
Burgin, William Lyle *architect*
Cicilline, J. Clement *state legislator*
Clark, Cathy Ann *mathematician*
Flowers, Sandra Joan *elementary education educator*
Haas, William Paul *humanities educator, former college president*
Holloway, Jerome Knight *publisher, former military strategy educator, retired foreign service officer*
Koch, Robert Michael *senior research scientist, consultant, educator*
Levie, Howard S(idney) *lawyer, educator, author*
MacLeish, Archibald Bruce *museum administrator*
Malkovich, Mark Paul, III *musician, artistic director, scientist, sports agent*
McConnell, David Kelso *lawyer*
Michael, Dorothy Ann *nursing administrator, naval officer*
Mullaney, Joann Barnes *nursing educator*
Mulrooney, Melissa Hutchens *museum director*
Nash, Karen Marsteller Myers *sculptor, designer, systems analyst*
Nelligan, Kenneth Egan *lawyer*
Piepgrass, Daniel James *logistics manager*
Piquette, Jean Conrad *physicist*
†Rogers, Rita *artist, conservator*
Scheck, Frank Foetisch *retired lawyer*
Schnare, Robert Edey, Jr. *library director*
Scoll, Eulalie Elizabeth *writer, researcher*
Scott, Gerald Wesley *American diplomat*
Smith, Bernard J. *military officer*
Stone, Edward Luke *private equity investor, realtor*
Tarpgaard, Peter Thorvald *naval architect*
Tuchman, Adam Michael *federal contract negotiator*
Turner, Numa Fletcher, III *family physician, military officer*
Wood, Berenice Howland *educator*
Wurman, Richard Saul *architect*

North Kingstown
Kenty, Janet Rogers *nursing educator*
Kilguss, Elsie Schaich *artist, gallery owner*
Kullberg, Gary Walter *advertising agency executive*
Resch, Cynthia Fortes *secondary education educator*
Sharpe, Henry Dexter, Jr. *retired manufacturing company executive*

North Providence
Maciel, Patricia Ann *development professional*
Mollis, A. Ralph *mayor*
Stankiewicz, Andrzej Jerzy *physician, biochemistry educator*

North Scituate
Dupree, Thomas Andrew *forester, state official*

North Smithfield
Muratori, Janice Anne *nurse*

Pawtucket
Baum, Herbert Merrill *toy company executive*
Carleton, Richard Allyn *cardiologist*
Davison, C. Hamilton *greeting card executive*
Davison, Charles Hamilton *financial executive*
DeWerth, Gordon Henry *management consultant*
Glicksman, Arvin S(igmund) *radiation oncologist*
Gordon, Harold P. *manufacturing executive*
Hassenfeld, Alan Geoffrey *toy company executive*
Hoffman, Andrew Jay *writer*
Kiessling, Louise Sadler *pediatrician, medical educator*
Kranseler, Lawrence Michael *lawyer*
Metivier, Robert Emmett *retired mayor*
O'Neill, John T. *toy company executive*
Reed, Cynthia S. *manufacturing ecutive*
†Riches, Wendy *advertising executive*
Roy, Gail Florine *nursing administrator*
Tarpy, Eleanor Kathleen *social worker*

Peace Dale
Brennan, Noel-Anne Gerson *anthropology educator, writer*

Portsmouth
Becken, Bradford Albert *engineering executive*
Hostetler, Dean Bryan *industry environmental compliance consultant*
Mello, Michael William *educational administrator*
Needham, Richard Lee *magazine editor*

Providence
Aflague, John M. *mental health nurse, educator, administrator*
Ajello, Edith H. *state legislator*
Algiere, Dennis Lee *state senator*
Almeida, Onésimo Teotónio *foreign language educator*
Almond, Lincoln *governor, lawyer*
Ames, Robert San *retired manufacturing company executive*
Anderson, James Arthur *humanities educator, academic director*
Andrews, Sue E. *park director*
Anton, Thomas Julius *political science and public policy educator, consultant*
Arant, Patricia *Slavic languages and literature educator*
Aronson, Stanley Maynard *physician, educator*
Avery, Donald Hills *metallurgist, educator, ethnographer*
Baar, James A. *public relations and corporate communications executive, author, consultant, internet publisher, software developer*
Banchoff, Thomas Francis *mathematics educator*
Barnhill, James Orris *theater educator*
Barnum, William Milo *architect*
Bensmaia, Reda *French studies educator, researcher*
Berenson, Stephen *actor, educator*
Biron, Christine Anne *medical science educator, researcher*
Blish, John Harwood *lawyer*
Block, Stanley Hoyt *pediatrician, allergist*
Boegehold, Alan Lindley *classics educator*
Boekelheide, Kim *pathologist*
Bogan, Mary Flair *stockbroker*
Borod, Richard Melvin *lawyer*
Borts, George Herbert *economist, educator*
†Boudewyns, Timothy M. *federal judge*
Bourcier, John Paul *state supreme court justice*
Bray, Philip James *physicist*
Briant, Clyde Leonard *metallurgist, educator*
†Brown, William Douglas *pediatric neurologist*
Bryan, Elizabeth Johnson *English language educator*
Burns, Robert E. *bank executive*
Burr, Jean Marie *university women's basketball coach*
Calabresi, Paul *oncologist, educator, pharmacologist*
Caldwell, Naomi Rachel *library media specialist*
Cambio, Bambilyn Breece *state legislator*
†Cao, Weibiao *physiologist, researcher*
†Carey, Russell Christopher *university administrator, lawyer*
Carlotti, Stephen Jon *lawyer*
Carpenter, Gene Blakely *crystallography and chemistry educator*
Cassill, Ronald Verlin *author*
Charniak, Eugene *computer scientist, educator*
Chauvin, Charlotte Ann *computer science educator*
Choquette, Paul Joseph, Jr. *construction company executive*
Church, Russell Miller *psychology educator*
Clifton, Rodney James *engineering educator, civil engineer, consultant*
Conway, Paul Gary *neuropharmacologist*
Cook, Albert Spaulding *comparative literature and classics educator, writer*
Cooper, Caroline Ann *hospitality faculty dean*
Cooper, Leon N. *physicist, educator*
Coover, Robert *writer, scriptwriter, educator*
Courage, Thomas Roberts *lawyer*
Crowley, James Patrick *hematologist, medical educator*
Curran, Joseph Patrick *lawyer*
Dafermos, Constantine Michael *applied mathematics educator*
Dahlberg, Albert Edward *biochemistry educator*
Davis, Philip J. *mathematician*
Davis, Robert Paul *physician, educator*
Dempsey, Raymond Leo, Jr. *radio and television producer, moderator, writer*
Dewing, Linda Thimann *sculptor*
Donnelly, Kevin William *lawyer*
Donovan, Bruce Elliot *classics educator, university dean*
Dowben, Robert Morris *physician, scientist*
Dujardin, Richard Charles *journalist*
Easton, J(ohn) Donald *neurologist, educator*
Edens, Myra Jim *health facility nursing administrator*
Elbaum, Charles *physicist, educator, researcher*
Enteman, Willard Finley *philosophy educator*
Erikson, G(eorge) E(mil) (Erik Erikson) *anatomist, archivist, historian, educator, information specialist*
†Esolen, Anthony Michael *English educator*
Esposito, Dennis Harry *lawyer*
Ewing, John Harwood *mathematics educator*
†Farmer, Richard Edward *college dean*
Farmer, Susan Lawson *broadcasting executive, former secretary of state*
Farrell, Margaret Dawson *lawyer*
†Faxon, Brad *professional golfer*
Feldman, Walter Sidney *artist, educator*
Feng, William Ching-lih *cardiothoracic surgeon*
Field, Noel Macdonald, Jr. *lawyer*
Filomeno, Linda Jean Harvey *elementary education educator*
Fleming, Wendell Helms *mathematician, educator*
Fogarty, Charles Joseph *state official*
Fogarty, Edward Michael *lawyer*
Fornara, Charles William *historian, classicist, educator*
Freiberger, Walter Frederick *mathematics educator, actuarial science consultant, educator*
Frerichs, Ernest Sunley *religious studies educator*
Freund, Lambert Ben *engineering educator, researcher, consultant*
Furness, Peter John *lawyer*
Gale, Edwin John *prosecutor*
Gardner, Thomas Earle *investment banker, managment/financial consultant*
Gasbarro, Pasco, Jr. *lawyer*
Geckle, Robert Alan *manufacturing company executive*
Gee, Elwood Gordon *university administrator*
Geisser, Peter James *artist, educator for hearing impaired*
Gerritsen, Hendrik Jurjen *physics educator, researcher*
Gibbs, June Nesbitt *state senator*
Gilbane, Jean Ann (Mrs. Thomas F. Gilbane) *construction company executive*
†Gilbane, William James *construction executive*
Gilmore, Judith Marie *physician*
Gleason, Abbott *history educator*
Glicksman, Maurice *engineering educator, former dean and provost*
Goldstein, Sidney *sociology educator, demographer*
Goodman, Elliot Raymond *political scientist, educator*
Goodwin, Maryellen *state legislator*
Gottschalk, Walter Helbig *mathematician, educator*
Grasso, James Anthony *public relations executive, educator*
Graziano, Catherine Elizabeth *retired nursing educator*
Greene, Edward Forbes *chemistry educator*
Greer, David S. *university dean, physician, educator*

Grimaldi, Vince *artist*
Groden, Gerald *psychologist*
Grossman, Herschel I. *economics educator*
Gurland, Joseph *engineering educator*
Hagopian, Jacob *federal judge*
Hamerly, Michael T. *librarian, historian*
Hamolsky, Milton William *physician*
Hardymon, James Franklin *retired diversified products company executive*
Harleman, Ann *English educator, writer*
Harris, Richard John *diversified holding company executive*
Hastings, Edwin H(amilton) *lawyer*
Hay, Susan Stahr Heller *museum curator*
Hazeltine, Barrett *electrical engineer, educator*
†Head, James W., III *geological sciences educator*
Heath, Dwight Braley *anthropologist, educator*
Henseler, Suzanne Marie *state legislator, social studies educator, majority whip*
Hermance, John Francis *geophysics educator, environmental geophysics and hydrology consultant*
Heyman, Lawrence Murray *printmaker, painter*
Honig, Edwin *comparative literature educator, poet*
Houghton, Anthony *physics educator, research scientist*
Howes, Lorraine de Wet *fashion designer, educator*
†Hoyas, Raymond T. *state senate official*
Hsieh, Din-Yu *applied mathematics educator*
†Hulbert, Stephen *state agency administrator*
Hurt, Robert Howard *chemical engineering educator*
Hutchinson, Park William, Jr. *theatre educator*
Iannitelli, Susan B. *state legislator*
Imbrie, John *oceanography educator*
†Iven, Chris *journalist*
Jackson, Benjamin Taylor *retired surgeon, educator, medical facility administrator*
Johnson, Vahe Duncan *lawyer*
Jones, Ferdinand Taylor, Jr. *psychologist, educator*
†Jones, Lauren Evans *lawyer*
Joukowsky, Artemis A. W. *private investor*
Juchatz, Wayne Warren *lawyer*
Kacir, Barbara Brattin *lawyer*
Kahn, Douglas Marc *osteopath*
Kane, Agnes Brezak *pathologist, educator*
†Kaufman, Joel M. *physician executive, neurologist*
Kean, John Vaughan *retired lawyer*
Kim, Jaegwon *philosophy educator*
†Kirschenbaum, Blossom S. *educator of English language*
Klyberg, Albert Thomas *historical society administrator*
Kniesche, Thomas Werner *German language educator*
Konstan, David *classics and comparative literature educator, researcher*
Krech, Shepard, III *anthropology educator*
Kushner, Harold Joseph *mathematics educator*
Lagueux, Ronald Rene *federal judge*
Langevin, James R. *state official*
Lanou, Robert Eugene, Jr. *physicist, educator*
Lederberg, Seymour Samuel *molecular biologist, educator*
Lederberg, Victoria *judge, former state legislator, lawyer*
Lesko, Leonard Henry *Egyptologist, educator, publisher*
Levin, Frank S. *physicist, educator*
Leviten, Riva Shamray *artist*
Lewis, David Carleton *medical educator, university center director*
Leyden, John James *protective services official*
Licht, Richard A. *lawyer*
Lima, Charlene *state legislator*
†Lindstrom, David Philip *sociology educator*
Lisi, Mary M. *federal judge*
Long, Beverly Glenn *lawyer*
Long, Nicholas Trott *lawyer*
†Lovegreen, Robert W. *federal judge*
Lynch, William Joseph *lawyer*
Manchester, Robert D. *venture capitalist*
†Mandel, Peter Bevan *writer, columnist*
Mandle, Earl Roger *design school president, former museum executive*
Marchant, Douglas Jeffery *surgeon, obstetrician, gynecologist, educator*
Marot, Lola *accountant*
Marsh, Donald Jay *medical school dean, medical educator*
Marsh, Robert Mortimer *sociologist, educator*
Marshall, Jean McElroy *physiologist*
Mates, Susan Onthank *physician, medical educator, writer, violinist*
McCann, Gail Elizabeth *lawyer*
Mc Donald, Charles J. *physician, educator*
McEleney, Brian *actor*
McIntyre, Jerry L. *lawyer*
McMahon, Eleanor Marie *education educator*
McNeil, Paul Joseph, Jr. *employment security interviewer*
†McWalters, Peter *state agency administrator*
Medeiros, Matthew Francis *lawyer*
Merlino, Anthony Frank *orthopedic surgeon*
Metrey, George David *social work educator, academic administrator*
Metts, Harold M. *state legislator*
Milhaven, John Giles *religious studies and ethics educator*
Modell, John *social sciences educator*
Monteiro, George *English educator, writer*
Monteiro, Lois Ann *medical science educator*
Motte, Sister Mary Margaret *missionary*
Mulvee, Robert Edward *bishop*
Mumford, David Bryant *mathematics educator*
Naughton, Eileen Slattery *state legislator*
Nazarian, John *academic administrator, mathematics educator*
Needleman, Alan *mechanical engineering educator*
Nelson, Ron *composer, conductor, educator*
Neu, Charles Eric *historian, educator*
Neumann, Dietrich *architectural historian*
Nichols, David Harry *gynecologic surgeon, obstetrics and gynecology educator, author*
Ockerse, Thomas *graphic design educator*
Oh, William *physician*
Olmsted, Audrey June *communications educator*
Olsen, Hans Peter *lawyer*
†Ortega, Julio *humanities educator, writer*
Paiva Weed, M(arie) Teresa *state legislator*
Parks, Albert Lauriston *lawyer*
Parks, Robert Emmett, Jr. *medical science educator*
Parmentier, E. M. (Marc) *geophysics educator*
Parris, Thomas Godfrey, Jr. *medical facility administrator*
Paster, Benjamin G. *lawyer*
Patinkin, Terry Allan *physician*
Pearce, George Hamilton *archbishop*
Pendergast, John Joseph, III *lawyer*
Perkins, Whitney Trow *political science educator emeritus*
Perry, Rhoda E. *state legislator*
Pierce, Richard Hilton *lawyer*
Pieters, Carle McGetchin *geology educator, planetary scientist, researcher*
Pine, Jeffrey Barry *state attorney general*
Pivin, Jeanette Eva *psychotherapist*
Plotz, Richard Douglas *pathologist*
Preparata, Franco Paolo *computer science and engineering educator*
Pueschel, Siegfried M. *pediatrician, educator*
Putnam, Michael Courtney Jenkins *classics educator*
Rachleff, Larry *performing company executive*
Ragosta, Vincent A.F. *judge*
Reilly, Charles James *lawyer, educator, accountant*
Resnik, David Alan *manufacturing company executive*
Ribbans, Geoffrey Wilfrid *Spanish educator*
Richman, Marc Herbert *forensic engineer, educator*
Rieger, Philip Henri *chemistry educator*
Risen, William Maurice, Jr. *chemistry educator*
Robinson, William Philip, III *lawyer*
Rohr, Donald Gerard *history educator*
Rosenberg, Alan Gene *newspaper editor*
Rosenberg, Bruce Alan *English language educator, author*
Rothman, Frank George *biology educator, biochemical genetics researcher*
Roussel, Normand Lucien *advertising executive*
Rueschemeyer, Dietrich *sociology educator*
Saint-Amand, Pierre Nemours *humanities educator*
Salter, Lester Herbert *lawyer*
Sanderson, Edward French *state official*
Sasso, Eleanor Catherine *state senator*
Satterthwaite, Franklin Bache, Jr. *management educator, executive coach*
Savage, John Edmund *computer science educator, researcher*
Scharf, Peter Mark *Sanskrit and Indian studies educator*
Schevill, James Erwin *poet, playwright*
Schmitt, Johanna Marie *plant population biologist, educator*
Schulz, Juergen *art history educator*
Selya, Bruce Marshall *federal judge*
Shapiro, Raquel *school psychologist, counselor*
Shepp, Bryan Eugene *psychologist, educator*
Sherman, Deming Eliot *lawyer*
Silverman, Joseph Hillel *mathematics educator*
Siqueland, Einar *psychology educator*
Smith, Robert Leslie *journalist*
Sosa, Ernest *philosopher, educator*
Souney, Paul Frederick *pharmacist*
Spilka, Mark *retired English language educator*
Staples, Richard Farnsworth *lawyer*
Stein, Jerome Leon *economist, educator*
Stout, Robert Loren *psychologist*
Stultz, Newell Maynard *political science educator*
†Sullivan, Patrick K. *surgeon*
†Sutton, Howard G. *publishing executive*
Suuberg, Eric Michael *chemical engineering educator*
Svengalis, Kendall Frayne *law librarian*
Sweeney, Judith Kiernan *secondary education educator*
Swift, Robert Michael *psychiatrist, educator*
Symonds, Paul Southworth *mechanical engineering educator, researcher*
Tabenkin, Alexander Nathan *metrologist*
Tauc, Jan *physics educator*
Taylor, Richard Henry *minister*
Terras, Victor *Slavic languages and comparative literature educator*
Thayer, Walter Raymond *internist*
Torres, Ernest C. *federal judge*
Trueblood, Alan Stubbs *former modern language educator*
van Dam, Andries *computer scientist, educator*
Vezeridis, Michael Panagiotis *surgeon, educator*
†Vogel, Paula Anne *playwright*
†Volpe, Stephen *agency administrator*
Votolato, Arthur Nicholas, Jr. *judge*
Walker, Howard Ernest *lawyer*
Wang, Ping *biomedical researcher, medical educator*
Watkins, John Chester Anderson *newspaper publisher*
Weaver, Barbara Frances *librarian*
Webb, Thompson *geological sciences educator, researcher*
Weiner, Jerome Harris *mechanical engineering educator*
Weisberger, Joseph Robert *state supreme court chief justice*
Whitcomb, Robert Bassett *journalist, editor*
Widgoff, Mildred *physicist, educator*
Williams, Anastasia P. *state legislator*
Williams, Lea Everard *history educator*
Wood, Gordon Stewart *historian, educator*
Wrenn, James Joseph *East Asian studies educator*
Wunderlich, Alfred Leon *artist, art educator*
†Younkin, Richard Ambrose *state official, air quality specialist*

Prudence Island
†McEntee, Grace Hall *writer, writing and education consultant*

Riverside
Lekas, Mary Despina *retired otolaryngologist*

Rumford
Findley, William Nichols *mechanical engineering educator*
Irons, William V. *state legislator*
Sullivan, Stephanie *information services professional*

Saunderstown
Carter, Kenneth *state legislator, restauranteur*
Donovan, Gerald Alton *retired academic administrator, former university dean*
Leavitt, Thomas Whittlesey *museum director, educator*

Scituate
Gorham, Bradford *lawyer*

Slatersville
Pannullo, Deborah Paolino *lawyer, training and consulting company executive*

Smithfield
Baker, Ruth Sharon *nurse*
Fischman, Burton Lloyd *communications educator, management consultant*
Morahan-Martin, Janet May *psychologist, educator*
Ready, Christopher James *accountant*

South Kingstown
Zarrella, Arthur M. *superintendent schools*

Wakefield
Boothroyd, Geoffrey *industrial and manufacturing engineering educator*
†Coffin, Tristram Potter *retired English educator, writer*
Doody, Agnes G. *communications educator, management and communication consultant*
†Fair, Charles Maitland *neuroscientist, author*
Garvey, Eugene Francis *state legislator*
Lanni, Lorette Marie *nursing manager*
Leete, William White *artist*
Moore, George Emerson, Jr. *geologist, educator*
Morrison, Fred Beverly *real estate consultant*
Rothschild, Donald Phillip *lawyer, arbitrator*
Wyman, James Vernon *newspaper executive*

Warwick
Baffoni, Frank Anthony *biomedical engineer, consultant*
Charette, Sharon Juliette *library administrator*
Florio, David Peter *probation and parole counselor*
Ginaitt, Peter Thaddeus *state legislator*
Goldman, Steven Jason *lawyer, accountant*
Groh, Susan Laurel *public relations consultant*
Halperson, Michael Allen *publishing company executive*
Izzi, John *educator, author*
Knowles, Charles Timothy *lawyer, state legislator*
Lachapelle, Cleo Edward *real estate broker*
†L'Europa, Gary A. *neurologist*
Pagliarini, John Raymond *public affairs executive*
Patchis, Pauline *handwriting expert, consultant*
Revens, John Cosgrove, Jr. *state senator, lawyer*
Roberts, Elaine *airport terminal executive*
†Russo, James Michael *legislative staff member*
Sholes, David Henry *lawyer, former state senator*
Sloan, Robert Hood, Jr. *insurance agent*
Worthington, Samuel Andrew *social welfare administrator*

West Greenwich
Anderson, Theodore Robert *physicist*

West Kingston
Haring, Howard Jack *newsletter editor*
†Sullivan, Nancy *retired educator, poet*

West Warwick
Galkin, Robert Theodore *company executive*
†Lancellotta, John Jerry-Louis *public service administrator*
Pollock, Bruce Gerald *lawyer*

Westerly
Algier, Angela Jane *newspaper editor*
Bachmann, William Thompson *dermatologist*
Day, Chon *cartoonist*
Devault, David V. *bank executive*
Hence, Jane Knight *designer*
Hirsch, Larry Joseph *retail executive, lawyer*
Looper, George Kirk *religious society executive*

Wood River Junction
Carlson-Pickering, Jane *gifted education educator*

Woonsocket
Dubuc, Mary Ellen *educational administrator*
Gauvey, Ralph Edward, Jr. *writer, poet*
Goldstein, Stanley P. *retail company executive*
†Ryan, Thomas M. *drug store chain executive*

SOUTH CAROLINA

Aiken
Alexander, Robert Earl *university chancellor, educator*
Cutting, Robert Thomas *army officer, physician*
Ely, Duncan Cairnes *non profit/human services executive, civic leader*
Groce, William Henry, III *environmental engineer, consultant*
Hanna, Carey McConnell *securities and investments executive*
Hootman, Harry Edward *retired nuclear engineer, consultant*
Johnston, Carolyn Judith *construction engineer*
Maxwell, Ronald A. *lawyer, state political party executive*
Murphy, Edward Thomas *engineering executive*
Noah, John Christopher *scientist, planner, educator*
Perdunn, Richard Francis *management consultant*
Ristow, Gail Ross *art educator, paralegal, children's rights advocate*
Rudnick, Irene Krugman *lawyer, former state legislator, educator*
Salter, David Wyatt *secondary school educator*
Simons, Charles Earl, Jr. *federal judge*
Smith, Gregory White *writer*
Tully, Susan Sturgis *adult education educator*
Voss, Terence J. *human factors scientist, educator*
Williamson, Thomas Garnett *nuclear engineering and engineering physics educator*
Wood, Susan *applied technology center executive*

Anderson
Anderson, George Ross, Jr. *federal judge*
Burks, Robert Edward *minister, educator*
Cheatham, Valerie Meador *clinical dietitian*
Elzerman, Alan William *environmental chemistry educator*
George-Lepkowski, Sue Ann *echocardiographic technologist*
Harllee, Mary Beth *social worker, educator*
Howard, Gerald Kelly *county official*
Norris, Joan Clafette Hagood *educational administrator*
Pflieger, Kenneth John *architect*
Urakami, Akio *manufacturing company executive*
Watkins, William Law *retired lawyer*
Wisler, Darla Lee *pastor*

Arcadia
Dent, Frederick Baily *mill executive, former ambassador, former secretary of commerce*

Barnwell
Loadholt, Miles *lawyer*
Miller, Elizabeth Jane *secondary education educator*

Batesburg
Covington, Tammie Warren *elementary education educator*

Beaufort
Chambers, Henry Carroll *realty broker*
Day, John Sidney *management sciences educator*
Harvey, William Brantley, Jr. *lawyer, former lieutenant governor*
McCaslin, F. Catherine *consulting sociologist*
Pinkerton, Robert Bruce *mechanical engineer*
Plyler, Chris Parnell *dean*
Richards, Charlene Anna *computer manufacturing company executive*
Rowland, Lawrence Sanders *history educator*
Shaw, Nancy Rivard *museum curator, art historian, educator*
Sheldon, Jeffrey Andrew *college official*
Wise, Stephen Robert *museum director and curator, educator*

Bennettsville
Best, Carolyn Anne Hill *middle school education educator*
Kinney, William Light, Jr. *newspaper editor, publisher*

Bethune
Ogburn, Thomas Willis *artist*

Bishopville
Cox, Jamson L. *historic site director*

Bluffton
Brown, Dallas Coverdale, Jr. *retired army officer, retired history educator*
Pendley, William Tyler *naval officer, international relations educator*

Blythewood
Moore, Edward Raymond, Jr. *pastor, chaplain, campaign consultant*

Camden
Craig, Joanna Burbank *historic site director*
Daniels, John Hancock *agricultural products company executive*
Davis, Paul Michael *sales executive, transportation company executive*
Jacobs, Rolly Warren *lawyer*
Reich, Merrill Drury *intelligence consultant, writer*

Cayce
McElveen, William Lindsay *broadcasting executive, lecturer*
McGill, Cathy Broome *gifted and talented education educator*

Central
Smith-Cox, Elizabeth Shelton *art educator*

Chapin
†McNinch, Michel Cottingham *artist, educator*

Charleston
Abbott-Lyon, Frances Dowdle *journalist, civic worker*
Addlestone, Nathan Sidney *metals company executive*
Anderson, Ivan Verner, Jr. *newspaper publisher*
Austin, Charles John *health services educator*
Barclay, James Ralph *psychologist, educator*
Barker, Douglas Alan *lawyer*
Baron, Seymour *engineering and research executive*
Basler, Thomas G. *librarian, administrator, educator*
Beale, Mark Douglas *psychiatrist, educator*
Bell, Norman Howard *physician, endocrinologist, educator*
Blatt, Solomon, Jr. *federal judge*
Branham, C. Michael *lawyer*
Brewerton, Timothy David *psychiatrist*
Brown, Linda Meggett *reporter*
Burrell, Victor Gregory, Jr. *marine scientist*
Buvinger, Jan *library director*
Calhoun, Deborah Lynn *emergency room nurse, consultant*
Cannon, Hugh *lawyer*
Carek, Donald J(ohn) *child psychiatry educator*
†Carr, Robert S. *federal judge*
Carter, James Folger *obstetrician-gynecologist, consultant*
†Chambers, Joe Carroll *physician, consultant, educator*
Chapin, Fred *airport executive*
Chaplin, George *newspaper editor*
†Chen, Mei-Qin *mathematics educator*
Cheng, Kenneth Tat-Chiu *pharmacy educator*
Cheng, Thomas Clement *parasitologist, immunologist, educator, author*
Clement, Robert Lebby, Jr. *lawyer*
†Coates, Timothy Joel *historian*
Coleman, Dorothy Zipper *retired educational administrator*
Conrad, Thomas *basketball coach*
Cuddy, Brian Gerard *neurosurgeon*
Daniell, Herman Burch *pharmacologist*
Darling, Stephen Edward *lawyer*
De Wolff, Louis *management consultant*
Dobson, Richard Lawrence *dermatologist, educator*
Donehue, John Douglas *interdenominational ministries executive*
Dowell, Richard Patrick *technology company executive*
Duffy, Patrick Michael *judge, federal*
Dulaney, William Marvin *history educator, curator*
Edwards, James Burrows *university president, oral surgeon*
Falsetti, Sherry Ann *psychologist, medical educator*
Favaro, Mary Kaye Asperheim (Mrs. Biagino Philip Favaro) *pediatrician*
Finn, Albert Frank, Jr. *physician*
French, Kenneth Wayne *radio station executive, consultant*
Gaillard, John Palmer, Jr. *former government official, former mayor*
Geentiens, Gaston Petrus, Jr. *former construction management consultant company executive*
Gettys, Thomas Wigington *medical researcher*
Gilbreth, Frank Bunker, Jr. *retired communications executive, writer*
Goff, R. Garey *architect*
Good, Joseph Cole, Jr. *lawyer*
Greenberg, Raymond Seth *academic administrator, educator*

Grimball, William Heyward *retired lawyer*
Grush, Owen Charles *psychiatry educator*
Gunn, Morey Walker, Jr. *secondary school educator, choir director, organist*
Haines, Stephen John *neurological surgeon*
Harding, Enoch, Jr. *clothing executive*
Hawkins, Falcon Black, Jr. *federal judge*
Hinman, Eve Caison *academic administrator*
Hoffman, Brenda Joyce *gastroenterology educator*
Hogan, Edward Leo *neurologist*
Hollis, Bruce Warren *experimental nutritionist, industrial consultant*
Hood, Robert Holmes *lawyer*
Hughes, Blake *retired architectural institute administrator, publisher*
Hunter, Jairy C., Jr. *academic administrator*
Infinger, Gloria Altman *nursing administrator*
Jacobs, Walter Darnell *political scientist, educator*
Jaffa, Ayad A. *medical educator, medical researcher*
Jaffe, Murray Sherwood *surgeon, retired*
Jenrette, Joseph Malphus, III *radiation oncologist*
Johnson, Dewey E(dward), Jr. *dentist*
Johnston, Stephen Edward *clinical information systems coordinator, educator*
Kahn, Ellis Irvin *lawyer*
Kaplan, Allen P. *physician, educator, researcher*
Karesh, Janice Lehrer *special education consultant*
Keating, Thomas Patrick *health care administrator, educator*
Kent, Harry Ross *construction executive, lay worker*
Key, Janice Dixon *physician, medical educator*
Kreese, John L. *basketball coach*
†Kuzenski, John C. *educator*
Lally, Margaret Mates *English educator, poet*
Langdale, Emory Lawrence *physician*
Langley, Lynne Spencer *newspaper editor, columnist*
LeRoy, Edward Carwile *rheumatologist*
Lovinger, Sophie Lehner *child psychologist*
Lucas, Frank Edward *architect*
Lutz, Myron Howard *obstetrician, gynecologist, surgeon, educator*
Mackaness, George Bellamy *retired pharmaceutical company executive*
†Maize, John Christopher *dermatology educator*
Manigault, Peter *media executive*
Margolius, Harry Stephen *pharmacologist, physician*
†Markland, Alan Colin *medical educator*
Martin, Roblee Boettcher *retired cement manufacturing executive*
McCallum, Corrie *painter, printmaker*
McCurdy, Layton *medical educator*
Mesic, Harriet Lee Bey *medical support group administrator*
Mohr, Lawrence Charles *physician*
†Nielsen, Barbara Stock *state educational administrator*
Norton, David C. *federal judge*
O'Brien, Paul Herbert *surgeon*
Ogawa, Makio *physician*
Ogier, Alton L. *lawyer*
Othersen, Henry Biemann, Jr. *pediatric surgeon, physician, educator*
†Parker, James H. *business reporter*
†Parson, Jack *academic administrator, political science educator*
Patrick, Charles William, Jr. *lawyer*
Plichta, Thomas Edward *software engineering company executive*
President, Toni Elizabeth *guidance counselor, former elementary educator*
Prewitt, William Chandler *financial executive*
Redden, Nigel A. *performing company executive*
Reed, Stanley Foster *editor, author, publisher, lecturer*
†Rennhack, Joan Lee *safety enforcement official*
Robinson, Jakie Lee *human services administrator*
Roof, Betty Sams *internist*
Rustin, Rudolph Byrd, III *physician*
Salinas, Carlos Francisco *dentist, educator*
Salmon, Edward Lloyd, Jr. *bishop*
Sanders, Tence Lee Walker *elementary education educator*
Sarasohn, Evelyn Lois Lipman *principal*
Schreadley, Richard Lee *writer, retired newspaper editor*
Schuman, Stanley H. *epidemiologist, educator*
Shealy, Ralph McKeetha *emergency physician, educator*
Siewicki, Jean Ann *middle school educator*
Simms, Lois Averetta *retired secondary education educator, musician*
Smith, W. Stuart *strategic planning director*
Spitz, Hugo Max *lawyer*
Stewart, Brent Allen *business educator*
Sutusky, John Charles *higher education educator*
Tarleton, Larry Wilson *newspaper editor*
Thompson, David B. *bishop*
Thompson, William Birdsall *journalist*
Thompson, W(ilmer) Leigh *pharmaceutical company executive, physician, pharmacologist*
Underwood, Paul Benjamin *obstetrician, educator*
Warren, John Hertz, III *lawyer*
Watts, Claudius Elmer, III *retired air force officer*
Whelan, Wayne Louis *higher education administrator*
Willi, Steven Matthew *physician, educator, researcher*
Wilson, Frederick Allen *medical educator, medical center administrator, gastroenterologist*

Charleston AFB
Gillespie, Shawn Paul *military pilot*

Charlotte
†Seifert, George *professional football coach*

Chesnee
Saunders, J. Farrell *historic site director*

Chester
Driggers, Edward Rosemond *city administrator*

Clemson
Adair, Trevor *soccer coach*
Birrenkott, Glen P., Jr. *poultry science educator*
Boykin, Joseph Floyd, Jr. *librarian*
Bunn, Joe Millard *retired agricultural engineering educator*
Byars, Betsy (Cromer) *author*
Caldwell, Judith *horticultural educator*
Cheatham, Harold Ernest *university dean, counselor, educator*
Clayton, Donald Delbert *astrophysicist, nuclear physicist, educator*
Cox, Headley Morris, Jr. *lawyer, educator*
Curris, Constantine William *university president*
Davies, Brian Ewart *environmental sciences educator*
†Davis, Jim *university basketball coach*
Gangemi, J(oseph) David *microbiology educator, biomedical researcher, research administrator, hospital administrator*
Golan, Lawrence Peter *mechanical engineering educator, energy researcher*
Grant, H(arry) Roger *history educator*
Griffin, Villard Stuart, Jr. *geology educator*
Halfacre, Robert Gordon *landscape architect, horticulturist, educator*
Han, Young Jo *agricultural engineer, educator*
Hare, Eleanor O'Meara *computer science educator*
Kelly, John William, Jr. *university adminstrator*
Kishimoto, Yuji *architect, educator*
Krause, Lois Ruth Breur *chemistry educator*
Kriese, Charles (Chuck) *tennis coach*
Leonard, Michael Steven *industrial engineering educator*
Mabry, Rodney Hugh *economics and finance educator*
Moran, Ronald Wesson *retired English educator, dean, writer*
Morrissey, Lee *language educator*
†Nicholas, Davis M. *history educator*
Nilson, Linda Burzotta *director center for teaching*
Pursley, Michael Bader *electrical engineering educator, communications systems research and consulting*
Sheriff, Jimmy Don *accounting educator, academic dean*
Underwood, Richard Allan *English language educator*
Underwood, Sandra Jane *planning and management director*
Vogel, Henry Elliott *retired university dean and physics educator*
Wehrenberg, William Busse *agricultural studies educator*
Wiley, Byron Anthony *state official*
Wilkinson, T. Ross *microbiologist, educator*
Williamson, Robert Elmore *agricultural engineering educator*
Young, Joseph Laurie *architecture educator*
Zumbrunnen, David Arnold *mechanical engineering educator, consultant*

Cleveland
†Sinclair, Bennie Lee *English educator*

Clinton
Cornelson, George Henry, IV *retired textile company executive*
†Cox, Kevin Monterey *school administrator*
Franklin, Larry Brock *publishing executive*
Griffith, John Vincent *academic official*
Vance, Robert Mercer *textile manufacturing company executive, banker*

Clio
McLeod, Marilynn Hayes *educational administrator, farmer*

Columbia
Abel, Anne Elizabeth Sutherland *pediatrician*
Abel, Francis Lee *physiology educator*
Adams, John Hurst *bishop*
Adams, Weston *diplomat, lawyer*
Adcock, David Filmore *radiologist, educator*
Aelion, C. Marjorie *adult education educator*
†Akhavi, Shahrough *educator*
Almond, Carl Herman *surgeon, physician, educator*
Amidon, Roger Lyman *health administration educator*
Anderson, Joseph Fletcher, Jr. *federal judge*
Ashley, Perry Jonathan *journalism educator*
Aull, James Stroud *retired bishop*
Averyt, Gayle Owen *insurance executive*
Babcock, Keith Moss *lawyer*
Bailey, George Screven *lawyer*
Baird, Davis W. *philosophy educator*
Baker, Carleton Harold *physiology educator*
†Barton, Rayburn *educational administrator*
Baskin, C(harles) R(ichard) *retired civil engineer, physical scientist*
Belasco, Simon *French language and linguistics educator*
Bell, Ronald Mack *university foundation administrator*
Best, Robert Glen *geneticist*
†Bishop, William Thurmond *federal judge*
Bjontegard, Arthur Martin, Jr. *foundation executive*
Blachman, Morris J. *dean, management consultant*
Blanton, Hoover Clarence *lawyer*
Boggs, Jack Aaron *banker, municipal government official*
Booth, Hilda Earl Ferguson *clinical psychologist, Spanish language educator*
Bradham, Tamala Selke *audiologist*
†Breedin, Berryman Brent *journalist, public relations, historian, consultan*
Bristow, Walter James, Jr. *retired judge*
Brooks, Israel, Jr. *protective services official*
Broome, Michael Cortes *college administrator*
Brubaker, Lauren Edgar *minister, educator*
Bruccoli, Matthew Joseph *English educator, publisher*
†Brugh, Rex *urologist*
Bryant, Douglas E. *public health service official*
†Buchanan, Robert L., Jr. *federal judge, lawyer*
Buchanan, William Jennings *lawyer, judge*
Carpenter, Charles Elford, Jr. *lawyer*
Chapman, Robert Foster *federal judge*
Cilella, Mary Winifred *director*
Cilella, Salvatore George, Jr. *museum director*
Clark, David Randolph *wholesale grocer*
Cleveland, Elbin L. *theatre design and technology educator*
†Cobbs, Charlene Rene' *parent educator*
Condon, Charles Molony *state attorney general*
Conrad, Paul Ernest *transportation consultant*
Corey, David Thomas *invertebrate zoology specialist*
Courson, John Edward *state senator, insurance company executive*
da Silva, Ercio Mario *physician*
Davidson, Janine Anne *military officer*
Davis, Barbara Langford *financial advisor*
†Davis, Bertha L. *dean women, Bible educator*
†Davis, J. Bratton *federal judge*
Davis, Keith Eugene *psychologist, educator, consultant*
Dawson, Wallace Douglas, Jr. *geneticist*
Day, Richard Earl *lawyer, educator*
†DePass, William Brunson, Jr. *commercial and industrial real estate broker*
Donald, Alexander Grant *psychiatrist, educator*
Duffie, Virgil Whatley, Jr. *state agency administrator*
Duggan, Carol Cook *research director*
Eastman, Caroline Merriam *computer science educator*
Edgar, Walter Bellingrath *historian*
Edge, Ronald Dovaston *physics educator*
Edwards, James Benjamin *accountant, educator*
†Edwards, Kathryn A. *history educator*
Elkins, Toni Marcus *artist, art association administrator*
Ernst, Edward Willis *electrical engineering educator*
Feinn, Barbara Ann *economist*
Ferillo, Charles Traynor, Jr. *public relations executive*
Finkel, Gerald Michael *lawyer*
Finney, Ernest Adolphus, Jr. *state supreme court chief justice*
Fischer, Robert Andrew *computer executive*
Flanagan, Clyde Harvey, Jr. *psychiatrist, psychoanalyst, educator*
Floyd, Timothy Sherwood *graphic designer*
Flynn, Cheryl Dixon *accountant*
Friedman, Myles Ivan *education educator*
Fry, Catherine Howard *publishing executive*
Gantt, Michael David *business executive*
Gasque, (Allard) Harrison *disc jockey, volunteer*
Geckle, George Leo, III *English language educator*
Gibbes, William Holman *lawyer*
Ginsberg, Leon Herman *social work educator*
Goble, Robert Thomas *planning consultant*
Gore, David Curtiss *investment banker, consultant*
Gressette, Lawrence M., Jr. *utilities executive*
Griffin, Mary Frances *retired library media consultant*
Grimball, Caroline Gordon *sales professional*
Hamilton, Clyde Henry *federal judge*
Handel, Richard Craig *lawyer*
Hansen, Harold John (Harry) *artist, educator*
Hardin, James Neal *German and comparative literature educator, publisher*
†Harpootlian, Richard Ara *lawyer, political party official*
Harrison, Faye Venetia *anthropologist, educator*
Harvin, Charles Alexander, III *state legislator, lawyer*
Hatch, David Lincoln *sociology educator*
Hatch, Mary Gies *German language educator*
Helsley, Alexia Jones *archivist*
Henderson, Robert Edward *research institute director*
†Hodges, James H. *governor*
Hollis, Charles Eugene, Jr. *savings and loan association executive*
Horger, Edgar Olin, III *obstetrics and gynecology educator*
Howard-Hill, Trevor Howard *English language educator*
Hultstrand, Charles John *architect*
Humphries, John O'Neal *physician, educator, university dean*
Inkley, Scott Russell, Jr. *state agency administrator*
Jennings, William R. *state agency administrator*
Jervey, Harold Edward, Jr. *medical education consultant, retired*
Johnson, Herbert Alan *history and law educator, lawyer, chaplain*
Johnson, James Bek, Jr. *library director*
Johnson, Lawrence Wilbur, Jr. *lawyer*
Joiner, Elizabeth Garner *French language educator*
Jones, Donald Lee *religious studies educator*
†Josey, Jon Rene *prosecutor*
Kay, Carol McGinnis *literature educator*
Kiker, Billy Frazier *economics educator*
King, John Ethelbert, Jr. *education educator, former academic administrator*
†King, Sam B., III *legislative staff member*
Krantz, Palmer E., III *parks and recreation director*
Lander, James Albert *retired military officer, comptroller*
Leatherman, Hugh Kenneth, Sr. *state senator, business executive*
LeClair, Betty Jo Cogdill *special education and early childhood educator*
Lin, Tu *endocrinologist, educator, researcher, academic administrator*
†Lolas, Anthony Joseph, Sr. *health and environmental business executive*
Long, Eugene Thomas, III *philosophy educator, administrator*
Luckes, Mary Helen B. *mental health nurse*
Luna, Gene Irving *academic administrator, education educator*
Luoma, Gary A. *accounting educator*
Ma, Fashang *mechanical engineering educator*
Mackey, Peter Francis *English educator, university official*
Madden, Norman Edward, Jr. *English educator*
Marchant, Bristow *lawyer*
Marchant, Trelawney Eston *retired national guard officer, lawyer*
Matthews, Steve Allen *lawyer*
McAbee, Thomas Allen *psychologist*
†McCrorey, Joseph R. *federal judge*
McCrory, Sarah Graydon *church lay leader, retired lawyer*
McCulloch, Anne Merline Jacobs *college dean*
McCullough, Ralph Clayton, II *lawyer, educator*
McGill, Jennifer Houser *non-profit association administrator*
McMaster, Henry Dargan *lawyer*
Melton, Gary Bentley *psychology and law educator*
Meriwether, James Babcock *retired English language educator*
Miles, Jim *state official*
Miller, Johnny Vincent *academic administrator*
†Mitchell, J. Joseph, Jr. *educator, administrator, consultant*
Mohr, Laura Lee *school system administrator*
Monahan, Thomas Paul *accountant*
Muzekari, Thomasine Dabbs *adult education educator*
Myerson, Joel Arthur *English language educator, researcher*
†Nance, Robert M. *legislative staff member*
Neff, Linda Joy *epidemiologist, researcher*
Nexsen, Julian Jacobs *lawyer*
Nolte, William Henry *English language educator*
†Norman, George Buford, Jr. *foreign language educator*
Olsgaard, John Newman *library science educator, university official*
Paleologos, Evangelos *hydrologist, educator*
Palms, John Michael *academic administrator, physicist*
Patterson, Grady Leslie, Jr. *state treasurer*
Peeler, Bob *state official*
Perrin, K(arl) Eric *minister*
Perry, Matthew J., Jr. *federal judge*
Petty, Donna Matthews *middle school educator*
Powell, J(ohn) Key *estate planner, consultant*
Quinn, Michael William *public affairs educator*
Ramsey, Bonnie Jeanne *mental health facility administrator, psychiatrist*
Rawlinson, Helen Ann *librarian*
Reeves, George McMillan, Jr. *comparative literature educator, educational administrator*
Reisz, Howard Frederick, Jr. *seminary president, theology educator*
Resch, Mary Louise *social services administrator*
Rhoades, Donald Scott *zoo and botanical park curator, biology educator*
Richardson, Gwendolyn E. *medical/surgical nurse*
Rippeteau, Bruce Estes *archaeologist, administrator*
Robinson, Robert Earl *chemical company executive*
Rouse, LeGrand Ariail, II *retired lawyer, educator*
Rowland, Thomas C., Jr. *obstetrician/gynecologist*
†Schramm, Susan Lynn *education educator*
Schuette, Oswald Francis *physics educator*
Schwarz, Ferdinand (Fred Schwarz) *ophthalmologist, ophthalmic plastic surgeon*
Secor, Donald Terry, Jr. *geologist, educator*
Shabazz, Aiysha Muslimah *social work administrator*
Shedd, Dennis W. *federal judge*
Sheppe, Joseph Andrew *surgeon*
Shmunes, Edward *dermatologist*
†Siebert, Donald Tate, Jr. *English educator*
Sloan, Frank Keenan *lawyer, writer*
Smith, Debra Marie *special education educator*
Smith, Susan Arlene *nursing educator*
Sproat, John Gerald *historian*
Starr, Harvey *political scientist*
†Starrett, William *dancer, artistic director*
Stewart, Nathaniel Johnson *emergency medicine physician*
Still, Charles Neal *neurologist, consultant*
Strom, J. Preston, Jr. *lawyer*
Strong, Franklin Wallace, Jr. *lawyer*
Tate, Harold Simmons, Jr. *lawyer*
Timmons, Judith Herring *English educator*
Toal, Jean Hoefer *state supreme court justice, lawyer*
Toombs, Kenneth Eldridge *librarian*
Turk, John Cobb *architect, educator*
Unger, Richard Mahlon *lawyer*
Vernberg, Frank John *marine and biological sciences educator*
Waites, Candy Yaghjian *former state official*
†Waites, John E. *federal judge*
Walker, Richard Louis *former ambassador, educator, author*
Wallace, Edwin Ruthven, IV *psychiatrist, neuropsychiatrist psychotherapist*
Walters, Rebecca Russell Yarborough *medical technologist*
Warren, Charles David *library administrator*
Watabe, Norimitsu *biology and marine science educator*
Wilder, Ronald Parker *economics educator*
Witherspoon, Walter Pennington, Jr. *orthodontist, philanthropist*
Wright, Harry Hercules *psychiatrist*
Zaepfel, Glenn Peter *psychologist*

Conway
LeForce, Alan *women's basketball coach*
Nale, Julia Ann *nursing educator*
Sarvis, Elaine Magann *assistant principal*
Saxena, Subhash Chandra *mathematics educator, researcher, administrator*
Squatriglia, Robert William *university dean, educator*
Talbert, Roy, Jr. *history educator*
Wiseman, Dennis Gene *university dean*

Darlington
†Rainey, Nettie Sue *library director*

Dataw Island
Scoville, Laurence McConway, Jr. *arbitrator, mediator*

Denmark
Crum, Henry Hayne *lawyer*

Dillon
Chandler-Walton, Marcia Shaw Barnard *farmer*

Due West
Farley, Benjamin Wirt *religious studies educator, writer*
Koonts, Jones Calvin *retired education educator*

Easley
Cole, Lois Lorraine *retired elementary school educator*
Failing, George Edgar *editor, clergyman, educator*
Henderson, Stephen Keith *academic administrator*
Leith, John Haddon *clergyman, theology educator*
Spearman, David Hagood *veterinarian*
Spearman, Patsy Cordle *real estate broker*

Edgefield
Allen, Jerry Wayne *organization executive*

Edisto Island
Van Metre, Margaret Cheryl *artistic director, dance educator*

Elgin
Peake, Frank *middle school educator*

Fair Play
Apinis, John *chemist*

Florence
Baroody, Albert Joseph, Jr. *pastoral counselor*
Currie, Cameron McGowan *judge*
Dixon, Gale Harllee *drug company executive*
Dupre, Judith Ann Neil *real estate agent, interior decorator*
†Fisher, Christine S. *music educator*
Hardouin, Bernard Michael, III *fitness specialist*
Houck, Charles Weston *federal judge*
Imbeau, Stephen Alan *allergist*
Isgett, Donna Carmichael *critical care nurse, administrator*
†Jiang, Longzhi *mechanical engineer*
Rutherford, Vicky Lynn *special education educator*
Smith, Walter Douglas *retired college president*
†Swearingen, Ervin S. *federal judge*
Thigpen, Neal Dorsey *political science educator*
Whitaker, Wilma Neuman *mathematics instructor*
White, Victor Daniel, III *English educator*
Windham, Nancy Quintero *obstetrician, gynecologist*

Folly Beach
Shutrump, Mary Jill *writer, editor, photographer, educator*

Fort Mill
Fogle O'Keefe, Maureen Ann *nursing administrator*
Honeycutt, Brenda *secondary education educator*
Horten, Carl Frank *textile manufacturing company executive*
Morris, John *trading company executive*

Gaffney
Davis, Lynn Hambright *culinary arts educator*
Griffin, Walter Roland *college president, educator, historian*
Harrison, Richard Dean *minister, counselor*
Jones, Nancy Gale *retired biology educator*
Lawrence, Daniel Thomas *architect*
Suttle, Helen Jayson *retired education educator*
Wheeler, William Earl *general surgeon*
Wilde, Edwin Frederick *mathematics educator*

Georgetown
Allison, Christopher FitzSimons *bishop*
Bowen, William Augustus *financial consultant*
Hopkins, Linda Ann *school psychologist*
Isbell, Robert *writer*
McGrath, James Charles, III *financial services company executive, lawyer, consultant*
Moore, Albert Cunningham *lawyer, insurance company executive*
Terhune, Jane Howell *legal assistant, educator*
†Walters, Alan Wayne *police officer*
Williams, Rynn Mobley *community health nurse*

Goose Creek
Johnson, Johnnie *bishop*

Green Pond
Ittleson, H(enry) Anthony *foundation executive*

Greenville
Alberga, Alta Wheat *artist*
Alford, Robert Wilfrid, Jr. *elementary school educator*
Armstrong, Joanne Marie *clinical and consulting psychologist, business advisor, mediator*
Barash, Anthony Harlan *lawyer*
Bauknight, Clarence Brock *consultant*
Becker, Cheri A(nn) *marketing professional, business consultant*
Belk, F. Norman *librarian*
Bell, Robert Daniel *religious studies educator*
Bonner, Jack Wilbur, III *psychiatrist, educator, administrator*
Carter, Sherry *women's basketball coach*
†Catoe, William M., Jr. *federal judge*
Clark, Elizabeth Annette *retired insurance company administrator*
Crawford, William David *real estate broker, consultant*
†Cundiff, Kathleen Jean *business executive*
Cureton, Claudette Hazel Chapman *biology educator*
Davis, Joan Carroll *museum director*
Day, Angela Riddle *occupational health nurse, educator*
DeLoache, William Redding *pediatrician*
Dobson, Robert Albertus, III *lawyer, executive, volunteer*
Dobson, Robert Albertus, IV *corporate executive*
†Dorsey, Benjamin William *engineering/construction company executive*
Earle, Patricia Nelson *artist*
Edwards, Harry LaFoy *lawyer*
Eskew, Rhea Taliaferro *newspaper publisher*
Fernandez, Miguel Angel *process safety, design engineer, energy consultant*
Fitzgerald, Eugene Francis *management consultant*
Foulke, Edwin Gerhart, Jr. *lawyer*
Friedman, Steven M. *textile company executive*
Gardner, Donald Angus *architect*
Gerretsen, Gilbert Wynand (Gil Gerretsen) *marketing consultant, coach*
Gresham, James Steve *health service administrator*
Hardin, Frankie Creamer *elementary education educator*
Hendrix, Susan Clelia Derrick *civic worker*
Herlong, Henry Michael, Jr. *federal judge*
Hill, Grace Lucile Garrison *education educator, consultant*
Hipp, William Hayne *insurance and broadcasting executive*
Hortis, Athena Maria *physical education educator*
Horton, James Wright *retired lawyer*
Inglis, Robert D. (Bob Inglis) *former congressman, lawyer*
†Khandke, Kailash *economics educator*
Kilgore, Donald Gibson, Jr. *pathologist*
Kline, David Jonathan *video producer*
LaFleur, Karen Meredith *science educator*
LeBlanc, L(ouis) Christian *architect*
Lloyd, Wanda Smalls *newspaper editor*
Manly, Sarah Letitia *state legislator, ophthalmic photographer, angiographer*
Mann, James Robert *congressman*
Mauldin, John Inglis *public defender*
McKinney, Ronald W. *lawyer*
McKnight, Edgar Vernon *religion educator*
Mitchell, William Avery, Jr. *orthodontist*
Neal, James Austin *architect*
Oxner, G. Dewey *lawyer*
Oxner, Glenn Ruckman *financial executive*
Payne, George Frederick *educational administrator*
Phillips, Joseph Brantley, Jr. *lawyer*
Price, Thomas M. *reproductive endocrinologist*
Robinson, Benjamin Pierce *theater director, coach, actor*
Roe, Thomas Anderson *building supply company executive*
Rogers, Jon Martin *financial consultant, financial company executive*
Schneider, George William *retired aircraft design engineer*
Selvy, Barbara *dance instructor*
Simmons, David Jeffrey *real estate executive*
Smith, Philip Daniel *academic administrator, education educator*
Smith, Willie Tesreau, Jr. *retired judge, lawyer*
Thompson, Robert Thomas *lawyer*
Todd, John Dickerson, Jr. *lawyer*
Townes, Bobby Joe *travel agency executive*
Traxler, William Byrd, Jr. *federal judge*
†Turner, Barbara F. *elementary educator*
Walker, Wesley M. *lawyer*
Walters, Johnnie McKeiver *lawyer*
Weimer, Tonja Evetts *author, recording artist, consultant*
Whitmire, John Lee *daycare provider*
Wilkins, William Walter, Jr. *federal judge*
Wyche, Cyril Thomas *lawyer*
Wyche, Madison Baker, III *lawyer*

Greenwood
Abercrombie, Stoney Alton *family physician*
Armfield, Fred Munger *minister*
Bateman, Carol Vaughan *pharmacist*
Jackson, Larry Artope *retired college president*
Mecca, Thomas Vincent *college administrator*
Moore, James E. *state supreme court justice*
Morgan, John Augustine *university executive, consultant*
Nexsen, Julian Jacobs, Jr. *lawyer*
Scales, Carol Jean *nursing educator*
Self, W. M. *textile company executive*
Smith, Sara Elizabeth Cushing *English language educator, writer*
Townsend, Catherine Anne Morgan *information specialist*

Greer
Baldwin, Leroy Franklin *minister*
Fantry, John Joseph *chemist*
Gallman, Clarence Hunter *textile executive*
Gregg, Marie Byrd *retired farmer*
Lane, James Garland, Jr. *diversified industry executive*
Poore, Timothy Shawn *elementary educator*

Hampton
Platts, Francis Holbrook *plastics engineering manager*

Hartsville
Browning, Peter Crane *packaging company executive*
Coker, Charles Westfield *diversified manufacturing company executive*
Daniels, James Douglas *academic administrator*
Menius, Espie Flynn, Jr. *electrical engineer*
†Shelley, James Herbert *lawyer, paper company executive*
Stallings, Frank, Jr. *industrial engineer*

Heath Springs
Feagin, Eugene Lloyd *pastor*

Hilton Head Island
Adams, William Hensley *ecologist, educator*
Ballantine, Todd Henry *environmental scientist*
Baumgardner, Barbara Borke *publishing consultant*
Becker, Karl Martin *lawyer*
Birk, Robert Eugene *retired physician, educator*
Brown, Arthur Edmon, Jr. *retired army officer*
Coble, Paul Ishler *advertising agency executive*
Cox, Albert Harrington, Jr. *economist*
Cramer, Laura Schwarz *realtor*
Cross, Wilbur Lucius *writer, editorial consultant*
Cunningham, William Henry *retired food products executive*
Engelman, Karl *physician*
Exley, Winston Wallace *middle school educator*
Fleischman, Kathryn Agnes *secondary education educator*
Flemister, Launcelot Johnson *physiologist, educator*
Gruchacz, Robert S. *real estate executive*
Gui, James Edmund *architect*
Hagoort, Thomas Henry *lawyer*
Haley, Cain Calmes *computer consultant*
Harty, James D. *former manufacturing company executive*
†Hill, Courtney King *marketing professional*
Huckins, Harold Aaron *chemical engineer*
Humphrey, Edward William *surgeon, medical educator*
Ink, Dwight A. *government agency administrator*
Kadar, Karin Patricia *librarian*
Kemp, Mae Wunder *real estate broker, consultant*
Lindner, Joseph, Jr. *physician, medical administrator*
Little, Thomas Mayer *public relations executive*
Love, Richard Emerson *equipment manufacturing company executive*
Male, Roy Raymond *English language educator*
Margileth, Andrew Menges *physician, former naval officer*
Martin, Donald James *marketing professional*
McDowell, Theodore Noyes *public relations consultant*
McKay, John Judson, Jr. *lawyer*
McKeldin, William Evans *management consultant*
McKinney, Donald Lee *magazine editor*
Mersereau, Hiram Stipe *wood products company consultant*
Mirse, Ralph Thomas *former college president*
Patton, Joseph Donald, Jr. *management consultant*
Pritchard, Dalton Harold *retired electronics research engineer*
Pustilnik, Jean Todd *elementary education educator*
Rapp, Fred *virologist*
Rose, William Shepard, Jr. *lawyer*
Rulis, Raymond Joseph *manufacturing company executive, consultant*
Russell, Allen Stevenson *retired aluminum company executive*
Santos, George Wesley *physician, educator*
Scarminach, Charles Anthony *lawyer*
†Shepard, Steven Louis *graphic artist, painter*
Simpson, John Wistar *energy consultant, former manufacturing company executive*
Stoll, Richard Edmund *retired manufacturing executive*
Thompson, David Charles, Sr. *retired management executive*
Tucker, Frances Laughridge *civic worker*
Wesselmann, Glenn Allen *retired hospital executive*
Windman, Arnold Lewis *retired mechanical engineer*
†Wolf, Dona *management consultant*

Holly Hill
Niemeyer, Sandra Kay *secondary education educator*

Irmo
Gandy, James Thomas *meteorologist, entrepreneur*
Hric, Joan Esther *English educator, writer*
Stewart, Alexander Constantine *medical technologist*

Isle Of Palms
Elliott, Larry Paul *cardiac radiologist, educator*
McKinley, Debra Lynn McKinney *dog show judge*
Wohltmann, Hulda Justine *pediatric endocrinologist*

Jenkinsville
Loignon, Gerald Arthur, Jr. *nuclear engineer*

Johns Island
Behnke, Wallace Blanchard, Jr. *consultant, engineer, retired utility executive*
Cameron, Thomas William Lane *investment company executive*
Rhea, Marcia Chandler *accountant*

Kershaw
Lucas, Dean Hadden *retired educator*

Kiawah Island
Bernard, Lowell Francis *academic administrator, educator, consultant*
Norton, Norman James *exploration geologist*
Reed, Rex Raymond *retired telephone company executive*

Ladson
Cannon, Major Tom *special education educator*
Diamond, Michael Shawn *science and math educator, computer consultant*

Lake City
Hawkins, Linda Parrott *school system administrator*
TruLuck, James Paul, Jr. *dentist, vintner*

Lake Wylie
Buggie, Frederick Denman *management consultant*

Lancaster
Bundy, Charles Alan *foundation executive*
Carter, Richard Bonner *systems specialist*

Landrum
Wyche, Samuel David *sportscaster*

Langley
Bell, Robert Morrall *lawyer*

Laurens
Bost, John Rowan *retired manufacturing executive, engineer*
†Cooper, William Copeland *public library director*
Dixon, Albert King, II *retired university administrator*
Martin, Margaret McNeill *home economist, educator*
Williams-Tims, Lillie Althea *distribution administrator, genealogist*

Leesville
Crumley, James Robert, Jr. *retired clergyman*

Lexington
Dubé, Richard Lawrence *landscape specialist, consultant*
Gatch, Charles Edward, Jr. *academic administrator*
Maranville, June Kimberly *speech language pathologist*
Morris, Earle Elias, Jr. *retired state official, business executive*
Wilkins, Robert Pearce *lawyer*

Little River
Ehrlich, John Gunther *writer*

Loris
Logan, Alexander C., III *pathologist*

Manning
DuBose, James Daulton *dentist*

Marion
Inabinet, Lawrence Elliott *retired pharmacist*
Waller, John Henry, Jr. *state supreme court justice*

Mauldin
Frank, Myra Linden *consultant*
Phillips, James Oscar *minister*

Mc Cormick
Clayton, Verna Lewis *retired state legislator*

Moncks Corner
Deavers, James Frederick *optometrist*

Mount Pleasant
Ayres, Paul Erdman *artist*
Bennett, Janet Sandhoff *physical education educator*
Cantwell, John Dalzell, Jr. *management consultant*
Gilbert, James Eastham *academic administrator*
Hill, Larkin Payne *real estate company data processing executive*
Krupa, Patricia Ann *retired nurse, consultant*
Laddaga, Lawrence Alexander *lawyer*
McConnell, John William, Jr. *lawyer*

Mullins
Stonesifer, Richard James *humanities and social science educator*

Murrells Inlet
†Flannery, Joseph Edward *retired education association executive*
Lillemoen, Henry Daniel *retired writer*

Myrtle Beach
Breen, David Hart *lawyer*
Harwell, David Walker *retired state supreme court chief justice*
Madory, James Richard *hospital administrator, former air force officer*
Schwartz, Steve Wendelin *physician*
Uzenda, Jara Carlow *technical writer, residential contractor*

Newberry
Martell, Denise Mills *lay worker*
Pollard, Wendy Higgins *counselor*
Pope, Thomas Harrington, Jr. *lawyer*

North
Moran, John Bernard *government official*

North Charleston
Fei, James Robert *engineer*
Reilly, David Henry *university dean*
Zucker, Jerry *energy systems manufacturing executive*

North Myrtle Beach
Kantner, Helen Johnson *church education administrator*

Orangeburg
Briggman, Jessie B. *secondary education educator*
Caldwell, Rossie Juanita Brower *retired library service educator*
Champy, William, Jr. *mathematician, educator, researcher, scientist*
Clark, Paul Buddy *management information systems educator, consultant*
Creekmore, Verity Veirs *media specialist*
Graule, Raymond (Siegfried) *metallurgical engineer*
Hampton, Raymond *painter*
Isa, Saliman Alhaji *electrical engineering educator*
Johnson, Alex Claudius *English language educator*
†Sandrapaty, Ramanchandra Rao *engineering educator*
Sims, Edward Howell *editor, publisher*
Williams, Karen Johnson *federal judge*

Patrick
Privette, Rosa Lee Millsaps *county official*

Pawleys Island
Alexander, William D., III *civil engineer, consultant, former army air force officer*
Daniel, J. Reese *lawyer*
Ford, Anna Marie *language professional*
Hudson-Young, Jane Smither *investor*
Kay, Thomas Oliver *agricultural consultant*
Noble, Joseph Veach *fine arts administrator*
Proefrock, Carl Kenneth *academic medical administrator*
Tarbox, Gurdon Lucius, Jr. *retired museum executive*

Pendleton
Fehler, Polly Diane *neonatal nurse, educator*
Kline, Priscilla Mackenzie *nursing educator*
†Owens, Gwendolyn Billups *education educator*
Spain, James Dorris, Jr. *biochemist, educator*

Pickens
Gilman, Nancy Ellen Helgeson *medical and surgical nurse*
†Shields, William George *elementary education educator*

Piedmont
Davis, Robert Barry *technician, religious studies educator*

Pineland
Centgraf, Damian Louis *broadcast engineer*

Port Royal
Wilson, Thomas David, Jr. *urban planner*

Prosperity
Hause, Edith Collins *college administrator*
†Jennings, Wirt Holman, Jr. *retired marketing executive*

Reidville
Armstrong, Thomas Gliem *steel company executive*

Ridgeland
Gardner, James *recreational management executive, personal care industry executive*

Rock Hill
Bristow, Robert O'Neil *writer, educator*
Click, John William *communication educator*
Di Giorgio, Anthony J. *college president*
Du Bois, Paul Zinkhan *library director*
Hardin, William Beamon, Jr. *electrical engineer*
Hull, William Martin, Jr. *ophthalmologist*
†Milstead, John David *newspaper editor*
Prus, Joseph Stanley *psychology educator, consultant*
†Sweet, Robert Michael *plastic surgeon, dentist*
†Tarvers, Josephine Koster *English language educator*
Viault, Sarah Underhill *civic volunteer*
Wilson, Melford Alonzo, Jr. *secondary education educator*

Salem
Everett, C(harles) Curtis *retired lawyer*
Harbeck, William James *real estate executive, lawyer, international consultant*
Jones, Charles Edward *mechanical engineer*

Saluda
Nussbaumer, Melany Hamilton *program director*

Seneca
Caperton, Richard Walton *automobile repair company executive, educator, consultant*
Clausen, Hugh Joseph *retired army officer*
Curry, Mary Earle Lowry *poet*
Fleming, Mack Gerald *lawyer*
Uden, David Elliott *cardiologist, educator*

Shaw A F B
†Cameron, Hugh C. *career officer*

Simpsonville
Gilstrap, Leah Ann *media specialist*
Hall, Marilyn Margaret *occupational health nurse*
Maguire, D.E. *electronics executive*

Society Hill
King, Amanda Arnette *elementary school educator*

Spartanburg
Adamson, James B. *business executive*
Agnew, Janet Burnett *secondary education educator*
Bullard, John Moore *religion educator, church musician*
Burnett, E. C., III *state supreme court justice*
Chauhan, Suneet Bhushan *medical educator*
Clark, Elizabeth Adams (Liz Clark) *genealogy educator*
Codespoti, Daniel Joseph *computer science educator*

Deku, Afrikadzata *Afrikan-scholar, researcher, writer, educator*
Dillard, Richard *director of public affairs*
Ely, Elizabeth Wickenberg *priest*
Feinstein, Marion Finke *artistic director, dance instructor*
Fogartie, James Eugene *retired clergyman*
Fowler, Paul Raymond *physician, lawyer*
†Fudenberg, Herman Hugh *immunologist, educator*
Gray, Gwen Cash *real estate broker*
Gray, Nancy Ann Oliver *college administrator*
Gregg, Paula Ann *middle school educator*
Hilton, Theodore Craig *computer scientist, computer executive*
†Jackson, Tracey Leigh *health care organization administrator*
King, David Steven *quality control executive*
King, Henry Spencer, III *lawyer*
Kuhn, Hans Heinrich *chemist*
Lambert, Kurt *marketing executive*
Leonard, Walter Raymond *retired biology educator*
Lesesne, Joab Mauldin, Jr. *college president*
Mahaffey, James Perry *education educator, consultant*
Mahanes, Michael Wayne *audio-visual electronics company executive*
McGehee, Larry Thomas *university administrator*
Milliken, Roger *textile company executive*
Moore, Charles Gerald *educational administrator*
Patterson, Elizabeth Johnston *former congresswoman*
Richards, Marty Grover *university foundation director*
Schultz, Warren Robert *manufacturing administrator*
Sovenyhazy, Gabor Ferenc *surgeon*
Stephens, Barbara Jane *academic administrator*
Stephens, Bobby Gene *college administrator, consultant*
Stewart, James Charles, II *insurance agent*
White, Robert Bruce *keyboard instruments company acoustical consultant*

Sullivans Island
Humphreys, Josephine *novelist*
Romaine, Henry Simmons *investment consultant*

Summerville
†Christie, Joseph Francis *city planner*
Orvin, George Henry *psychiatrist*
Reisman, Rosemary Moody Canfield *writer, humanities educator*
Sexton, Donald Lee *retired business administration educator*
Vorwerk, E. Charlsie *artist*
Young, Margaret Aletha McMullen (Mrs. Herbert Wilson Young) *social worker*

Sumter
Abbott, Vicky Lynn *educational administrator*
Arl, Ellen Marie *English educator, television producer and host*
Dawson-August, Annie Lee *state official*
†Eberl, James J. *consultant*
Justus, Adalu *writer, designer*
†Maness, Dinford Gray *English educator*
†McDougall, John Olin *lawyer*
Olsen, Thomas Richard, Sr. *air force officer*
Van Bulck, Hendrikus Eugenius *accountant*

Taylors
Dean, Cheryl Ann *urban planner*
†Frederes, Marshall *stockbroker*
Smith, Morton Howison *religious organization administrator, educator*
Vaughn, John Carroll *minister, educator*

Townville
Wright, George Cullen *electronics company executive*

Union
Berry, Peter DuPre *real estate executive*
Denton, David Thomas *small business owner*
Dineen, Joseph Lawrence *legal compliance professional, consultant*
Lorenz, Latisha Jay *elementary education educator*

Walhalla
Watson, Jean Vaughn *critical care nurse, ambulatory surgery nurse*

Walterboro
Boensch, Arthur Cranwell *lawyer*

Ware Shoals
Webb, Patricia Dyan W. *speech and language pathologist, sign language educator*

Wedgefield
McLaurin, Hugh McFaddin, III *military officer, historian consultant*

West Columbia
Brown, Opal Diann *medical technologist, nurse*
Jedziniak, Lee Peter *lawyer, educator, state insurance administrator*
Ochs, Robert David *history educator*
Palmer, Susan Smith *dietitian*
Parker, Harold Talbot *history educator*
Wilson, Addison Graves (Joe Wilson) *state senator, lawyer*

West Union
Klutz, Anthony Aloysius, Jr. *health, safety and environmental manager*

Williamston
Alewine, James William *financial executive*

Winnsboro
King, Robert Thomas *editor, free-lance writer*
McCants, Clyde Taft *retired clergyman*
McMaster, Mary Rice *civic worker*

Woodruff
Childers, Bob Eugene *educational association executive*

Yemassee
Olendorf, William Carr, Jr. *small business owner*

York
Blackwell, Paul Eugene, Sr. *army officer*
Huffman, Mervin Nicky *educator*

SOUTH DAKOTA

Aberdeen
†Akkerman, Charlotte Ann *principal*
Eldredge, Robert John *social services administrator, psychologist*
Gruca, Pawel Piotr *neuroradiologist*
Hastings, Albert Waller *English and journalism educator, consultant*
Hedges, Mark Stephen *clinical psychologist*
Markanda, Raj Kumar *mathematics educator*
Richards, Carlyle Edward *magistrate judge*
Stoia, Viorel G. *life underwriter*
Tebben, Sharon Lee *education educator*

Belle Fourche
†Crabill, Mark Clare *agricultural specialist*

Bison
Wishard, Della Mae *newspaper editor*

Black Hawk
Maicki, G. Carol *former state senator, consultant*

Britton
Farrar, Frank Leroy *lawyer, former governor*

Brookings
Duffey, George Henry *physics educator*
Elliott, Peggy Gordon *university president*
Hamidzadeh, Hamid Reza *mechanical engineer, educator, consultant*
Jamerson, Patricia Ann Locandro *pediatrics nurse, nursing educator*
Janssen, Larry Leonard *economics educator, researcher*
Jensen, William Phelps *chemistry educator*
†Landau, Enita Ann *library director*
Marquardt, Steve Robert *library director*
McClure-Bibby, Mary Anne *former state legislator*
Miller, John Edward *history educator*
Moore, Raymond A. *consultant, retired agriculture educator*
Nass, James Charles *utilities engineering manager*
Ryder, Mary Ruth *English language educator*
Singh, Yadhu Nand *pharmacology educator, researcher*
Spease, Loren William *chiropractor*
Sword, Christopher Patrick *microbiologist, university dean*
Williams, Elizabeth Evenson *writer*

Burbank
Simmons, Joseph Thomas *accountant, educator*

Canton
Perkinson, Robert Ronald *psychologist*

Centerville
Thomson, John Wanamaker *bank executive*

Dakota Dunes
Healy, William Charles *electrical engineer*
Peterson, Robert L. *meat processing executive*
Putney, Mark William *lawyer, utility executive*

Elk Point
Chicoine, Roland Alvin *farmer, state official*
Gille, John Paul *agricultural extension educator*

Fort Pierre
Hoyt, Irvin N. *judge*

Freeman
†Koller, Berneda Joleen *library administrator*
Roussos, Stephen Bernard *minister*

Gettysburg
†Williams, Peggy A. *library director*

Huron
Bryant, James Arthur *painter*
Kuhler, Deborah Gail *grief therapist, former state legislator*

Kadoka
Stout, Maye Alma *educator*

Keystone
Wagner, Mary Kathryn *sociology educator, former state legislator*

Kyle
Davies Silcott, Loma Geyer *freelance writer, English educator*

Lake City
Daberkow, Dave *historic site director*

Lennox
Brendtro, Larry Kay *psychologist, organization administrator*
Courey, Fred Samuel *management consultant, former mayor*

Madison
†Talley, Daniel Alfred *economics educator*
Tunheim, Jerald Arden *academic administrator, physics educator*

Miller
Morford, JoAnn (JoAnn Morford-Burg) *state senator, investment company executive*

Mission Hill
Karolevitz, Robert Francis *writer*

Mitchell
Gaede, James Ernest *physician, medical educator*
Schilling, Katherine Lee Tracy *retired principal*
Swigart Johnson, Mary Colleen *special education educator*
Widman, Paul Joseph *insurance agent*

Mobridge
Lucek, Donald Walter *surgeon*

Parker
Zimmer, John Herman *lawyer*

Parkston
Coleman, Gary William *elementary school educator*

Philip
†Cook, Andrea Jenelle *newspaper editor, rancher*

Pierre
†Adam, Patricia A. *state legislator*
Amundson, Robert A. *state supreme court justice*
Barnett, Mark William *state attorney general*
Benson, Bernice LaVina *elementary education educator*
Dunn, James Bernard *mining company executive, state legislator*
Gilbertson, David *state supreme court justice*
Hazeltine, Joyce *state official*
Hillard, Carole *state official*
†Hurd, Paula *state official*
Janklow, William John *governor*
Johnson, Julie Marie *lawyer/lobbyist*
Miller, Robert Arthur *state supreme court chief justice*
Miller, Suzanne Marie *law librarian, educator*
†Moreno, Mark A. *federal judge*
Pederson, Gordon Roy *state legislator, retired military officer*
Perry, Robert Tad *educational official*
Sabers, Richard Wayne *state supreme court justice*
Templeton, Barbara Ann *civil engineering technologist*
Thompson, Charles Murray *lawyer*

Platte
Pennington, Beverly Melcher *financial services company executive*

Rapid City
Battey, Richard Howard *judge*
Bogue, Andrew Wendell *federal judge*
Buum, Mary Kay *dialysis nurse*
Corwin, Bert Clark *optometrist*
Croyle, Robert Harold *physician assistant*
Erickson, John Duff *retired educational association administrator*
Foye, Thomas Harold *lawyer*
Gowen, Richard Joseph *electrical engineering educator, academic administrator*
Han, Kenneth *dean*
Hughes, William Lewis *former university official, electrical engineer*
Johnson, William Jennings *marketing consultant, entrepreneur, estate planner*
Kennedy, Judith Mary *school psychologist*
Klock, Steven Wayne *engineering executive*
Lee, Jamie Lee *video specialist*
Lefevre, Donald Keith *electrical engineer*
Lien, Bruce Hawkins *minerals and oil company executive*
Mabon, William Clarence *photographer, sales executive*
†Ochse, Ann *special education educator, consultant*
Riemenschneider, Albert Louis *retired engineering educator*
Schleusener, Richard August *college president*
Scofield, Gordon Lloyd *mechanical engineer, educator*
Sykora, Harold James *military officer*
Wells-Johnson, Vesta Lynn *audio/video production company executive*
†Young, Marshall P. *federal judge*

Redfield
†Morrison, Janet Kay *county treasurer*

Saint Lawrence
Lockner, Vera Joanne *farmer, rancher, legislator*

Selby
Akre, Donald J. *school system administrator*

Sioux Falls
Aldern, Robert Judson *architectural, liturgical and landscape artist*
Allmendinger, Betty Lou *retired bank employee*
Ashworth, Julie *elementary education educator*
Balcer, Charles Louis *college president emeritus, educator*
Brandt, David Dean *accountant, financial planner, valuation analyst*
Brown, Sue *foundation executive*
Carlson, Robert James *bishop*
Carpenter, Paul Lynn *cardiologist*
Christensen, David Allen *manufacturing company executive*
Cowles, Ronald Eugene *church administrator*
Danielson, David Gordon *health science facility administrator, general legal counsel*
Dertien, James LeRoy *librarian*
Ecker, Peder Kaloides *former judge*
Ellis, Peter *editor*
Engen, Lee Emerson *savings and loan executive*
†Erpenbach, Steve W. *state director*
Fenton, Lawrence Jules *pediatric educator*
Flora, George Claude *retired neurology educator, neurologist*
Garson, Arnold Hugh *newspaper publisher*
Grupp, Carl Alf *art educator, artist*
Haas, Joseph Alan *court administrator, lawyer*
Huseboe, Arthur Robert *American literature educator*
Jaqua, Richard Allen *pathologist*
Johnson, Richard Arlo *lawyer*
Jones, John Bailey *federal judge*
Kilian, Thomas Randolph *rural economic developer, consultant*
†Kolb, John Joseph *art educator*
Kontos, George John, Jr. *cardiothoracic surgeon*
Layton, Jean C. *non-profit association administrator*
†Marshall, Mark F. *federal judge*
Morse, Peter Hodges *ophthalmologist, educator*
Nygaard, Lance Corey *nurse, data processing consultant*
Olson, Gary Duane *history educator*
Paisley, Keith Watkins *state senator, small business owner, retired*
Peters, John Henry *artist*
Piersol, Lawrence L. *federal judge*
Reynolds, Leo Thomas *electronics company executive*
†Richards, George Alvarez *psychiatrist, educator*
Richards, LaClaire Lissetta Jones (Mrs. George A. Richards) *social worker*
†Rosenthal, Joel *manufacturing executive*
Schreier, Karen Elizabeth *prosecutor*
Smith, Murray Thomas *transportation company executive*
†Srstka, William J., Jr. *judge*
Staggers, Kermit LeMoyne, II *history and political science educator, state senator*
Talley, Robert Cochran *medical school dean and administrator, cardiologist*
†Thompson, Harry Floyd, II *curator, managing editor*
Thompson, Ronelle Kay Hildebrandt *library director*
Trujillo, Angelina *endocrinologist*
Tucker, William Vincent *vocational evaluator, former college president*
VanDemark, Michelle Volin *critical care, neuroscience nurse*
VanHeerde, Carolyn Kay *program manager*
Viste, Arlen Ellard *chemistry educator*
Wagoner, Ralph Howard *academic administrator, educator*
Weeks, M. J. *international management consultant*
Wegner, Karl Heinrich *physician, educator*
Williams, W. Vail *psychologist*
Wollman, Roger Leland *federal judge*
Zawada, Edward Thaddeus, Jr. *physician, educator*

Spearfish
Anderson, Thomas Caryl *financial and administrative systems professional*
Erickson, Richard Ames *physicist, emeritus educator*
Hood, Earl James *lawyer, state legislator*
Termes, A. Dick *artist*
Thie, Genevieve Ann *retired secondary school educator*

Sturgis
Baldwin, Judy *critical care nurse*
Daane, Kathryn D. *retired nursing administrator*
Ingalls, Marie Cecelie *former state legislator, retail executive*
†Musilek, Betty Marie *elementary education educator*

Timber Lake
Flynn, Peggy Lou *county official*

Vermillion
Carlson, Loren Merle *political science educator*
Clem, Alan Leland *political scientist*
Cunningham, Frank Robert *humanities educator, researcher*
Dahlin, Donald C(lifford) *academic administrator*
Freeman, Jeffrey Vaughn (Jeff Freeman) *art educator, artist*
Gasque, Thomas James *English educator*
Klein, Dennis Allan *language educator, writer*
Korte, Leon Lee *accountant, educator*
Langworthy, Thomas Allan *microbiologist, educator*
Neuhaus, Otto Wilhelm *biochemistry educator*
Rotert, Denise Anne *occupational therapist, army officer, educator*
†Sanford, Geraldine Agnes *editor, retired English educator*

Volga
Moldenhauer, William Calvin *soil scientist*

Watertown
Schumacher, Ervin *retired social services administrator*
Witcher, Gary Royal *minister, educator*

Yankton
Crandall, Terrence Lee *counselor*
Piper, Kathleen *Democrat party chairwoman*

TENNESSEE

Alamo
Finch, Evelyn Vorise *financial planner*
Raines, Irene Freeze *real estate broker*

Alcoa
Disney, Karen C. *critical care nurse*

Antioch
Ely, Joe *singer and songwriter*
Morris, Jeannine Eddings *administrative assistant*
Nelson, Richard Alver *contractor*
Sandlin, Debbie Crowe *critical care nurse*
Worthington, Melvin Leroy *minister, writer*

Arnold AFB
Davis, John William *government science and engineering executive*

Ashland City
†Hall, Steve Harris *educator*

Athens
†Pfeifer, Diane M. *dean*
Stevenson, Jean Myers *education educator*

Big Sandy
Chastain, Kenneth Duane *retired foreign language educator*

Blountville
Grau, Garry Lee *business educator*

Bolivar
Buchanan, Bennie Lee Gregory *special education educator*
Wingate, Robert Lee, Jr. *internist*

Brentwood
†Banks, Halbert Jay *real estate executive*
Bennett, Harold Clark *clergyman, religious organization administrator*
Cline, Judy Butler *human resources executive*
Dalton, James Edgar, Jr. *health facility administrator*
Flanagan, Van Kent *journalist*

German, Ronald Stephen health care facility administrator
Goodwin, William Dean consulting company executive
Martin, William Edwin government official
McClary, Jim Marston accounting executive, consultant
McNamara, Kevin Michael accountant
Porch, James Milton religious organization administrator
Power, Elizabeth Henry consultant
Provine, John C. lawyer
Pruett, James William psychotherapist
Raskin, Edwin Berner real estate executive
Schreiber, Kurt Gilbert lawyer
Tucker, Tanya Denise singer
Wood, Stephen Fletcher mortgage banker, software executive

Brighton
King, James Andrew protective services educator and administrator

Bristol
Anderson, Jack Oland retired college official
Cauthen, Charles Edward, Jr. retail executive, business consultant
Macione, Beatriz Huarte-Irujo Spanish language educator
McIlwain, William Anthony orthopedic surgeon
Moore, Marilyn Patricia community counselor
Mueller, Roy Clement graphic arts company executive
Patel, Ashvin Ambalal psychiatrist
Sessoms, Stephanie Thompson accountant

Brownsville
Kalin, Robert retired mathematics educator
Stevenson, William Edward chemical engineer

Buchanan
Frensley, Joe Thomas elementary education educator

Camden
Brown, John Robert computer company executive
Burchum, Jacqueline Rosenjack family nurse practitioner

Chapel Hill
Christman, Luther Parmalee retired university dean, consultant

Chattanooga
Adams, Morgan Goodpasture lawyer
Akers, Samuel Lee lawyer
Anderson, Lee Stratton newspaper publisher, editor
Beach, Hazel Elizabeth nurse
Callahan, North author, educator
Campbell, Paul, III lawyer
Chandler, J. Harold insurance company executive
Clapp, David Foster library administrator
Clark, Jeff Ray economist
Collier, Curtis Lynn lawyer
Cooper, Gary Allan lawyer
Copeland, Floyd Dean lawyer
Cox, Ronald Baker engineering and management consultant, university dean
De Riemer, Daniel Louis leasing company executive
Derthick, Alan Wendell architect
Eason, Marcia Jean lawyer
Ebiefung, Aniekan Asukwo mathematics educator and researcher
Edgar, R(obert) Allan federal judge
Elder, Thomas Woodrow real estate consultant
Fody, Edward Paul pathologist
Franks, Herschel Pickens judge
†Hendrick, Diane Goza psychiatric nurse
Holmberg, Albert William, Jr. publishing company executive
Holmberg, Ruth Sulzberger publishing company executive
†Kelley, Ralph Houston judge
Kiser, Thelma Kay analytical chemist
Knight, Ralph H. consumer products company executive
Lutgen, Robert Raymond newspaper editor
MacManus, Yvonne Cristina editor, videoscripter, writer, consultant
Maloney, J. Patrick minister, educator, seminary administrator
Manaker, Arnold Martin mechanical engineer, consultant
Martin, Chester Y. sculptor, painter
Matherley, Steve Allen cost accountant
McFarland, Jane Elizabeth librarian
Milburn, Herbert Theodore federal judge
Miles, Bradley James athletic trainer
Mills, Olan, II photography company executive
Mohney, Nell Webb religion educator, speaker, author
Moore, Hugh Jacob, Jr. lawyer
Obear, Frederick Woods academic administrator
Parker, Christine Wright medical director
Phillips, John Bomar lawyer
Porter, Dudley, Jr. environmentalist, foundation executive, lawyer
Powers, John Y. federal judge
Proctor, John Franklin lawyer
Quinn, Patrick tranportation executive
Rabin, Alan Abraham economics educator
Ragan, Charles Oliver, Jr. lawyer
Ragon, Robert Ronald clergyman
Randall, Kay Temple accountant, real estate agent, retired
Russe, Conrad Thomas Campbell accountant
Saeger, Dixie Forester dietitian
St. Goar, Herbert retired food corporation executive
Sargeant, Jonathan Douglas professional organization administrator
†Scalice, John A. nuclear energy executive
Scarbrough, Cleve Knox, Jr. museum director
Scott, Mark Alden hospital network executive
Shuck, Edwin Haywood, III surgeon
Stacy, Bill Wayne academic administrator
†Stinnett, R. Thomas federal judge
Summitt, Robert Murray circuit judge
Thow, George Bruce surgeon
Tosteson, Heather communications specialist, writer
†Trew, Reba C. artist
Tucker, Stanley R. headmaster
Vital, Patricia Best lawyer
Weinmann, Judy Munger nurse
Williams, Robert Carlton electrical engineer
Williams, Rosemary Helen paralegal
Wilson, Richard Lee political science educator
Young, Michael J. secondary education educator, pastor
Young, Sandra Joyce nursing administrator, consultant
Zimmerman, Ray Arthur naturalist

Chuckey
Casteel, DiAnn Brown principal

Church Hill
Faulk, Michael Anthony lawyer

Clarksville
Eaves, Arthur Joseph English literature educator
Gardner, Susanne women's basketball coach
Hester, Bruce Edward library media specialist, lay worker
Love, Michael Joseph lawyer
Manson, Tony James education educator
Shelton, William Scott former city official
Smith, Gregory Dale lawyer, judge

Cleveland
Albert, Leonard religious organization executive
Alford, Delton Lynol religious organization executive
Baker, Michael Lyndon minister
Breuer, William Bentley writer
Callais, Elaine Denise Rogers accountant
Gillum, Perry Eugene religious organization administrator, minister
Johnson, Beverly Phillips chairman, bank officer
Knight, Sandra Norton civil engineer
Laws, Charles George mathematics educator, quality engineer
Lawson, Billie Katherine elementary school educator
Lockhart, Madge Clements educational organization executive
Nicol, Jessie Thompson librarian
Owens, Kelly Ann elementary education educator
Rayburn, Billy J. Church administrator
Reyes, Jose Antonio, Sr. minister
†Rhodes, Arthur Delano benefits administrator
Suttles, David Clyde educator
Taylor, William Al church administrator
Vaughan, Roland church administrator
Walker, Donald Murray minister
†Washick, James Stewart English educator
Watson, S. Michele home health nurse
Wood, George Ambos city manager

Clinton
Birdwell, James Edwin, Jr. retired banker
Seib, Billie McGhee Rushing nursing administrator, consultant

Collegedale
Bennett, Peggy Elizabeth librarian, library director, educator
Crosby, Ellen Louise counselor
McKee, Ellsworth R. food products executive
†Perumal, John biologist, educator

Collierville
†Beaudette, Michele J. language educator
Bentley, Sheila Carver communication consultant, education educator
Golden, Eddie Lee optometrist
Ludwig, Charles T. technical company executive
Ratzlaff, David Edward minister
Schmidt, Ronald R. academic administrator
Springfield, James Francis retired lawyer, banker

Columbia
Cantrell, Sharron Caulk secondary school educator
Curry, Beatrice Chesrown retired English educator
Loper, Linda Sue learning resources center director

Cookeville
Adkisson, Randall Lynn minister
Alfred, Suellen English education educator
Campana, Phillip Joseph German language educator
Chowdhuri, Pritindra electrical engineer, educator
†Coe, Felix Gilmore science educator
Day, David Owen lawyer
Elkins, Donald Marcum dean, agronomy educator
Forest, Herman Silva biology educator
Gentry, Ricky Glyn accountant
Harris, John Wallace biology educator
Kumar, Krishna physics educator
Musacchio, Marilyn Jean nurse midwife, educator
Peters, Ralph Martin education educator
Richards, Melinda Lou speech and language pathologist
Sissom, Leighton Esten engineering educator, dean, consultant
Ting, Kwun-Lon engineer, educator, consultant
Underwood, Lucinda Jean poet, playwright, small business owner, researcher
Volpe, Angelo Anthony university administrator, chemistry educator

Copperhill
Jacobi, Joe Olympic athlete, canoeist

Cordova
Colbert, Robert B., Jr. apparel company executive
Dean, Jimmy meat processing company executive, entertainer
Echols, James agricultural products supplier
Hamilton, David John business systems/technology manager
Lieberman, Phillip Louis allergist, educator
McKinney, William Douthitt, Jr. sales and engineering company executive

Cornersville
Caulfield, Henry John physics educator

Cowan
Yates, Patricia England human resources company executive

Crossville
Hovmand, Svend chemical engineer, engineering executive
Lansford, Edwin Gaines accountant
Lawrence, Ralph Waldo manufacturing company executive
Moser, Michael R. newspaper editor
Pitt, Woodrow Wilson, Jr. engineering educator
Roe, Michael Henry computer specialist, business manager
Sweetland, Loraine Fern librarian, educator

Dandridge
Comer, Evan Philip manufacturing company executive
†Menzel, William Clarence, Jr. nuclear engineer
Trent, Wendell Campbell business owner
Weatherly-McWaters, Barbara Cannon artist

Dickson
Auchterlonie, David Thomas quality assurance professional
Thomas, Janey Sue elementary school principal

Dresden
McWherter, Ned Ray government administrator, farmer, investor
Powell, Wanda Garner librarian
†Swearington, Sheila Holt parole board official

Dunlap
†Nelson, Roger T. surgeon

Dyersburg
Scearce, Janna Luebkemann sales professional

East Brainerd
Swanger, Daniel A.I. artist

Elizabethton
Claussen, Lisa Renee engineering executive
Taylor, Wesley Alan accountant, consultant

Fayetteville
Dickey, John Harwell lawyer
Dickey, Nancy Eagar social worker
Wolfhard, Hans Georg research scientist

Franklin
Awalt, Marilene Kay principal
Bransford, Helen M. writer, jewelry designer
Bull, Sandy (Alexander Benjamin Bull) musician, composer
Daniel, Cathy Brooks tutor, educational consultant
Dorland, John Howard international management consultant
Guthrie, Glenda Evans educational company executive
Moessner, Harold Frederic allergist
Schuerer, Paula Ann veterinarian, biology educator
Smotherman, Carolyn mathematics educator
Stafford, Clay film producer, director, writer, actor, educator, public speaker
Woodside, Donna J. nursing educator
Young, William Edgar religious organization official

Gallatin
Bradley, Nolen Eugene, Jr. personnel executive, educator
Crutcher, Dimetrec Artez electronics technician
Ellis, Joseph Newlin retired distribution company executive
†Flynn, John David writer, educator
Whiteside, Ann Birdsong university public relations director

Gatlinburg
Cave, Kent R. national park ranger
Flanagan, Judy marketing specialist, entertainment manager, university official
Hooper, William Edward broadcast journalist
Wade, Karen national parks administrator

Germantown
Allison, Beverly Gray seminary president, evangelism educator
†Koerber, Robert Conrad company executive
Lensch, Kristin Marie organist, recitalist
†Mills, William Barney municipal official
†Mitchell, Sheila Lankford pharmacy executive
Nolly, Robert J. hospital administrator, pharmaceutical science educator
Nottingham, Edgar Jameson, IV clinical psychologist
Stevens, Colleen Newport artist
†Vastagh, George Frederick physician

Goodlettsville
Stickel, Lisa Mays accountant
Tongate, Darrel Edwin accountant
Vatandoost, Nossi Malek art school administrator

Gray
Bailey, Donovan Olympic athlete
Combs, Stephen Paul pediatrician, health facility administrator
Terry, Glenn A. retired nuclear chemist

Greenback
†Rollins, Freddie Wayne artist, graphic design
Weeks, Robet Andrew materials science researcher, educator

Greenbrier
Newell, Paul Haynes, Jr. engineering educator, former college president

Greeneville
†Carter, William Randall educator, administrator
Corey, Mark historic site director
Hull, Thomas Gray federal judge
†Inman, Dennis H. federal judge
Parsons, Marcia Phillips judge
Renner, Glenn Delmar agricultural products executive
Smith, Myron John, Jr. librarian, author
Starks, Charles Wiley minister

Hampton
McClendon, Fred Vernon real estate professional, business consultant, equine and realty appraiser, financial consultant

Harrogate
Money, Max Lee family nurse practitioner
Robertson, Edwin Oscar banker

Hartsville
Linville, Mary Todd family nurse practitioner

Henderson
England, Richard C., Jr. special education educator
†Schwartz, Robert Marc psychology educator

Hendersonville
Ambrose, Charles Stuart sales executive
†Buttolph, John company executive
Cash, June Carter singer
Davis, Robert Norman hospital administrator
†Morgan, Gerald Lee artist

Hermitage
Axton, Hoyt Wayne singer, composer
Chambers, Curtis Allen clergyman, church communications executive
†Greenleaf, Douglas A. information specialist
†Kreegel, Drew A. plastic and reconstructive surgeon
Quaintance, Alice Lynn elementary school media specialist

Humboldt
Lynch, Elizabeth Humphreys artist, educator

Huntingdon
Spain, Joyce Hicks nurse

Huntsville
Boardman, Maureen Bell community health nurse
Ellis, Lonnie Calvert educator
Galloway, John W., Jr. lawyer

Jackson
Agee, Bob R. university president, educator, minister
Bailey, James Andrew middle school educator
Barefoot, Hyran Euvene academic administrator, educator, minister
Benson, Aaron Lee art educator
†Boswell, G(eorge) Harvey federal judge
†Breen, J. Daniel federal judge
Garner, Jeffrey L. accountant
Hazlehurst, George Edward physician
Holt, Michael Kenneth management and finance educator, consultant
†Lovett, Marilyn Denise social services educator
Maynard, Terrell Dennis minister
McMillin, Barbara Ann English educator
Misulis, Karl Edward physician
Smith, Geri Garrett nurse educator
†Spruill, James H. neurologist
Stutts, Gary Thomas clinical analyst auditor
Taylor, Ronald Fulford physician
Tims, Ramona Faye medical and surgical nurse
Todd, James Dale federal judge
Torstrick, Robert Frederick hand surgeon, orthopaedic surgeon
Woodall, Gilbert Earl, Jr. medical administrator

Jefferson City
Baumgardner, James Lewis history educator
Huff, Cynthia Owen nursing educator, nurse practitioner
Krug, John Carleton (Tony Krug) college administrator, library consultant
Maddox, Jesse Cordell academic administrator
Milligan, Karen Little education educator

Jellico
Hausman, Keith Lynn hospital administrator, physical therapist

Johnson City
Adebonojo, Festus O. medical educator
Alfonso, Robert John university administrator
Bradford, Michael Lee religious organization administrator, clergyman
Coogan, Philip Shields pathologist
†Cupp, Horace Ballard surgeon, educator
Epps, James Haws, III lawyer
Franks, Ronald Dwyer university dean, psychiatrist, educator
Hendricks, Miriam Joan English educator
Jenrette, Thomas Shepard, Jr. music educator, choral director
Kemp, Karen women's basketball coach
Kiener, John Leslie judge
Kostrzewa, Richard Michael pharmacology educator
Larkin, Donald Wayne clinical psychologist
†Lucas, R. Robert finance engineer, corporate tax planner
Phillips, Dorothy Alease lay church worker, educator, freelance writer
†Pumariega, Andres Julio medical educator, administrator
Pumariega, JoAnne Buttacavoli mathematics educator
Schneider, Valerie Lois speech educator
Schueller, William Alan dermatologist
Sell, Joan Isobel mobile home company owner
Shurbaji, M. Salah pathologist
Skalko, Richard Gallant anatomist, educator
†Spritzer, Allan D. business educator
Stanley, Isabel Bonnyman English educator
Surface, James Louis, Sr. trust officer, lawyer
Wilkes, Clem Cabell, Jr. stockbroker
†Wozniak, James Lawrence reporter
Wyatt, Doris Fay Chapman English language educator
Zayas-Bazan, Eduardo foreign language educator

Jonesborough
Kozsuch, Mildred Jeannette librarian, archivist

Kingsport
Coffman, Wilma Martin women's health nurse, educator
Coover, Harry Wesley manufacturing company executive
Davis, Tammie Lynette music educator, director
Deavenport, Earnest W., Jr. chemical executive
Findley, Don Aaron manufacturing company executive
Gibson, David Allen civil engineer
Head, William Iverson, Sr. retired chemical company executive
Hyder, Betty Jean art educator
Ice, Billie Oberta retail executive
Messamore, Michael Miller pharmacist
Quillen, James Henry (Jimmy Quillen) former congressman
Reasor, Roderick Jackson industrial engineer
Robelot, Milton Paul deacon, architect
Siirola, Jeffrey John chemical engineer

Kingston
Manly, William Donald metallurgist
Worden, Marny artist, musician

Knoxville
Acker, Joseph Edington retired cardiology educator
Adams, David Parrish historian, educator
Adams, Linas Jonas gastroenterologist
Alexeff, Igor physicist, electrical engineer, educator emeritus
Anderson, Edward Riley state supreme court chief justice
Anderson, Ilse Janell clinical geneticist
Armistead, Willis William university administrator, veterinarian
Arnett, Foster Deaver lawyer
Bales, William Joseph academic administrator
Barker, Keith Rene investment banker
Barrett, Lida Kittrell mathematics educator
Beam, Richard Kenneth college administrator
Bly, Robert Maurice lawyer
Bodenheimer, Sally Nelson reading educator
Boling, Edward Joseph university president emeritus, educator
Borie, Bernard Simon, Jr. physicist, educator
Bose, Bimal Kumar electrical engineering educator
Brady, Patrick French literature educator, novelist
Bressler, Marcus N. consulting engineer
Brown, Billy Charlie secondary school educator
Burkhart, John Henry retired physician
Campbell, William Buford, Jr. materials engineer, chemist, forensic consultant
Caponetti, James Dante botany educator
Carcello, Joseph Vincent accounting educator
Carroll, Roger Clinton medical biology educator
Chapman, Jefferson museum director
Chen, James Pai-fun biology educator, researcher
Christenbury, Edward Samuel lawyer
Cliff, Steven Burris engineering executive
Cloud, Gary Lynn food and nutrition services administrator
Cole, William Edward economics educator, consultant
Conger, Bob Vernon plant and soil science educator
Cossé, R. Paul realty company executive
Cottrell, Jeannette Elizabeth retired librarian
Cox, Anna Lee retired administrative assistant
Creekmore, David Dickason lawyer, educator
Cremins, William Carroll lawyer
Crowell, Craven H., Jr. federal agency administrator
Dean, John Aurie chemist, author, chemistry educator emeritus
DePersio, Richard John otolaryngologist, plastic surgeon
Dillard, W. Thomas lawyer
Drinnon, Janis Bolton artist, poet, author, volunteer
Ensor, Allison Rash English language educator
Faires, Ross Norbert manufacturing company executive
Filston, Howard Church pediatric surgeon, educator
Fisher, John Hurt English language educator
Ford, Harriet-Lynn English educator
Fowler, Joseph Clyde, Jr. protective services official
Froula, James DeWayne national honor society director, engineer
Gallo, Louis historian, educator
Garrison, Arlene Allen engineering executive, engineering educator
Giordano, Lawrence Francis lawyer
Gonzalez, Rafael Ceferino electrical engineering educator
Gotcher, Jack Everett, Jr. oral and maxillofacial surgeon
Gould, Howard Richard physician
Griffin, Mary Jane Ragsdale educational consultant, writer, small business owner
Grubb, Rick secondary education educator
Hagood, Lewis Russell lawyer
Harris, Charles Edgar retired wholesale distribution company executive
Harris, Roland Arsville, Jr. college official
Harris, William Franklin, III biologist, environmental science director and educator
Haslam, James A., III petroleum sales executive
Heizer, Ruth Bradfute philosophy educator
Henderson, R(ichard) Winn physician
Herndon, Anne Harkness sales executive
Hohenberg, John journalist, educator
Holton, Raymond William botanist, educator
Howard, George Turner, Jr. retired surgeon
Howard, Lewis Spilman lawyer
Hung, James Chen engineer, educator, consultant
Igoe, Terence B. airport terminal executive
Jarvis, James Howard, II judge
Jenkins, Frances Owens retired small business owner
Jordan, Robert Leon federal judge
Kirkpatrick, Carl Kimmel prosecutor
Klein, Milton Martin history educator
Kliefoth, A(rthur) Bernhard, III neurosurgeon
Klingerman, Robert Harvey manufacturing company executive
LeVert, Francis Edward nuclear engineer
Lloyd, Francis Leon, Jr. lawyer
Lobins, Christine Marie accounts sales administrator
London, James Harry lawyer
Mahan, Gerald Dennis physics educator, researcher
Mankel, Francis Xavier former principal, priest
Martin, James Robert identification company executive
Mayfield, T. Brient, IV media and computer executive
Mazur, Peter cell physiologist, cryobiologist
McCall, Jack Humphreys, Jr. lawyer
Mc Dow, John Jett agricultural engineering educator
McGuire, Sandra Lynn nursing educator
Mc Hargue, Carl Jack research laboratory administrator
Menefee-Greene, Laura S. psychiatric nurse
Midkiff, Kimberly Ann paralegal
Mise, Jesse Sherden structural engineer, consultant
†Mooney, Wanda school administrator
Moran, James D., III child development educator, university administrator
Moser, Harold Dean historian
Murphree, Sharon Ann lawyer, mediator
Murphy, Deborah Jane lawyer
Murrian, Robert Phillip magistrate, judge, educator
Ownby, Jere Franklin, III lawyer
Parker-Conrad, Jane E. occupational health nurse consultant
Pearce, James Walker electronics engineer
Penland, Barbara Hubbard multi media publishing company executive
Penn, Dawn Tamara entrepreneur
†Perrin, Robert George sociology educator
Phillips, Jerry Juan law educator
Phillips, Kenneth D. nursing educator
Phillips, Thomas Wade judge, lawyer
Plaas, Kristina Maria neonatal nurse specialist, registered nurse
†Prosser, George T. utilities executive
Pulliam, Walter Tillman newspaper publisher
Ratliff, Eva Rachel elementary education educator
Rayson, Edwin Hope lawyer
Reynolds, Marjorie Lavers nutrition educator
Richards, Stephen Harold engineering educator
Richardson, Don Orland agricultural educator
Roach, Jon Gilbert lawyer
Roddy, Patrick zoological park administrator
Rodgers, Ralph Emerson lawyer
Roth, J(ohn) Reece electrical engineer, educator, researcher-inventor
Routh, John William lawyer
Rukeyser, William Simon journalist
Sansom, William E. consumer products executive
Schuler, Theodore Anthony retired civil engineer, retired city official
Schumann, Jane Anne education educator
Schweitzer, George Keene chemistry educator
Sickles, Helma-Jane museum director
Siler, Jennifer university press administrator
Siler, Susan Reeder communications educator
†Sitton, Ronald William editor
Smith, Leonard Ware lawyer
Smith, Vicky Lynn nurse, geriatrics nurse
†Snyder, William T. university chancellor
South, Stephen A. academic administrator
†Stair, Richard, Jr. federal judge
Stooksbury, William Claude minister
Stringfield, Hezz, Jr. contractor, financial consultant
Sublett, Carl Cecil artist
Swanson, Lorna Ellen physical therapist, athletic trainer, researcher
Swingle, Homer Dale horticulturist, educator
Taylor, Lee organization development practitioner
Teeter, Dwight Leland, Jr. journalism educator
Tenopir, Carol information science educator
†Thomas, Laurel Lynn educational administrator, consultant
Trevor, Kirk David Niell orchestra conductor, cellist
Trout, Monroe Eugene hospital systems executive
Turner, John Charles physician
Turner, Peggy Ann graphic designer, visual artist, educator
Uhrig, Robert Eugene nuclear engineer, educator
Vaughan, Gary David governmental and public relations executive
†Velazquez, Sheila Synnott writer, newspaper columnist
Walsh, Joanne Elizabeth retired educator, librarian
Ward, Robert Cleveland computer science researcher, administrator
Watson, Patricia L. library director
Wesley, Stephen Harrison pharmaceutical company executive
White, David Cleaveland microbial ecologist, environmental toxicologist
White, Edward Gibson, II lawyer
Wier, Allen english educator
Williams, Thomas Ffrancon chemist, educator
Woodard, H. Tom entertainment company executive
Worthington, Carole Yard Lynch lawyer
Wunderlich, Bernhard physical chemistry educator
Young, Peter Bernhart neuropsychologist
Zimmer, Willie Mae medical/surgical nurse

Kodak
Kreider, Sandra Anne Miller medical/surgical nurse

La Follette
Eads, Ora Wilbert clergyman, church official
Justice, Melissa Morris family nurse practitioner

La Vergne
†Ingram, David entertainment company executive

Lafayette
Crowder, Bonnie Walton small business owner, composer

Lebanon
Davis, Julie Kramer communications executive
Howard, Lounita Cook nonprofit executive director

Lenoir City
Brown, Donald Vaughn technical educator, engineering consultant

Lewisburg
Gonzalez, Raquel Maria pharmacist

Linden
Mitchell, Elizabeth Marelle nursing educator, medical, surgical nurse

Livingston
†Roberts, John M. law educator, former prosecutor

Lookout Mountain
Aplin, James Granger artist
Cavett, Van Andrew retired journalist
Leitner, Paul Revere lawyer
Rymer, S. Bradford, Jr. retired appliance manufacturing company executive
Wyeth, Andrew artist

Loudon
Jones, Robert Gean religion educator
†Puckett, Robert Marion clergyman
Wilks, Kimberly Susan occupational health nurse, educator

Louisville
McReynolds, David Hobert hospital administrator
Wheeler, George William university provost, physicist, educator

Lynchburg
Logan, Debora Joyce elementary and special education educator

Madison
North, Jo Ann McLendon county assessor
Prince, Anna Lou composer, music publisher, construction company executive
Simmons, Gary M. writer, small business owner
Spillers, James Andrew Bible and history educator, minister
Williams, Edward Macon poet

Manchester
Woodworth, Gene Boswell educational writer, educator

Martin
Black, Ruby L. nursing educator
†Depta, Victor Marshall English educator, editor
Gathers, Emery George computer science educator
†Norton, Dorotha Oliver speech educator
†Petty, James Alan mathematics educator, consultant

Maryville
Crisp, Polly Lenore psychologist
Davis, William Walter recruiter, trainer
Forster, Frederick Harwood air force officer
Hall, Marion Trufant botany educator, arboretum director
Hendren, Jo Ann small business owner
Howard, Cecil Byron pediatrician
Lawson, Fred Raulston banker
†Lewis, Wallace L. history educator
Lucas, Melinda Ann pediatrician, educator
Oakes, Lester Cornelius retired electrical engineer, consultant
†Wright, Nathalia retired English educator

Mascot
Roberts, Sharon gifted and talented education educator

Mc Ewen
Williams, John Lee lawyer

Mc Minnville
Gammon, James Edwin, Sr. clergyman
Henry, Mary Lou Smelser elementary education educator
Martin, Ron editor, superintendent of schools, consultant, minister

Memphis
Abston, Dunbar, Jr. management executive
Adsit, Russell Allan landscape architect
Agrawal, Surendra P. accountant, educator
Allen, James Henry magistrate
Allen, Newton Perkins lawyer
Andrews, William Eugene construction products manufacturing executive
Ballou, Howard Burgess commercial plumbing designer
Barnes, Janice Bryant elementary educator
†Bigelow, Gordon Stinson English educator
†Blake, Norman hotel executive
Blake, Norman Perkins, Jr. finance company executive
Booth, Robert Lee, Jr. banker
†Bracken, Bruce A. psychologist, educator
Brandon, Elvis Denby, III financial planner
Broadhurst, Jerome Anthony lawyer
Brooks, Kathleen journalist
Brown, Bailey federal judge
†Brown, William Houston lawyer
Brownell, Blaine Allison university administrator, history educator
Buchignani, Leo Joseph lawyer
†Butler, Darel Anthony neurologist
Butts, Herbert Clell dentist, educator
†Call, M. Douglas university administrator
Carr, Oscar Clark, III lawyer
Carter, Michael Allen college dean, nursing educator
Casey, Paula F. writer, speaker
Chesney, Russell Wallace pediatrician
Ching, James Michael artistic director opera company
Christopher, Robert Paul physician
Chung, King-Thom microbiologist, educator
Cicala, Roger Stephen physician, educator
Cody, Walter James Michael lawyer, former state official
Coker, Georgina Harris elementary education educator
Coleman, Veronica Freeman prosecutor
Collins, Earline Brown medical and surgical and nephrology nurse
Connolly, Matthew B., Jr. conservationist
Cook, August Joseph lawyer, accountant
Cooper, Irby real estate development company executive
Copper, John Franklin Asian studies educator, consultant
Cox, Clair Edward, II urologist, medical educator
Cox, Larry D. airport terminal executive
Crain, Frances Utterback retired dietitian
Crane, Laura Jane research chemist
Crisman, D'Etta Marie nursing administrator, chemical dependency and psychiatric nurse
Curran, Thomas molecular biologist, educator
Czestochowski, Joseph Stephen museum administrator
Daniel, Coldwell, III economist, educator
Dann, Alexander William, Jr. lawyer
De Mere-Dwyer, Leona medical artist
Depperschmidt, Thomas Orlando economist, educator
†De Saussure, Richard Laurens, Jr. retired neurosurgery educator
Desiderio, Dominic Morse, Jr. chemistry and neurochemistry educator
deWitt, Charles Benjamin, III lawyer, educator
Diggs, Walter Whitley health science facilty administrator
Doherty, Peter Charles immunologist
Donald, Bernice B. judge
Drescher, Judith Altman library director
Dreyfus, Susan Kahn elementary education educator
Drinkard, D(onald) Dwight, Sr. sports event director
Duke, Gary James electronics executive
Dunathan, Harmon Craig college dean
Dunavant, William Buchanan, Jr. textiles executive
Dunnigan, T. Kevin electrical and electronics manufacturing company executive
Edwards, Doris Porter computer specialist
Edwards, William Harold, Jr. nursing administrator, consultant
Elfervig, Lucie Theresa Savoie independent ophthalmic nursing consultant
Ellis, Stephen Walker corporate executive
Emery, Sue McHam bulletin editor, owner bridge studio
Evans, James Mignon architect
Fain, John Nicholas biochemistry educator
Foote, Shelby author
Ford, Kimball Sudderth middle school educator
Forell, David Charles financial executive
Fountain, Robert Allen organizational management executive
Franklin, Stanley Phillip computer scientist, cognitive scientist, mathematician, educator
Freeman, Bob A. retired microbiology educator, retired dean
Friedman, Robert Michael lawyer
Fussell, Keith Baugus minister
Gagne, Ann Marie special education educator
Garland, Linda M. nursing case manager
Gaskins, Linda Carol educator
Gawehn-Frisby, Dorothy Jeanne retired freelance technical writer
Gerald, Barry radiology educator, neuroradiologist
Gibbons, Julia Smith federal judge
Gilman, Ronald Lee judge
Glasgow, Agnes Jackie social welfare administrator, therapist
Godsey, William Cole physician
Goldstein, Jerome Arthur mathematics educator
Gourley, Dick R. college dean
Graham, Tina Tucker psychiatric and pediatrics nurse
†Gray, Bruce F(rank) lawyer
Green, Joseph Barnet neurologist, educator
Haight, Scott Kerr lawyer
Haizlip, Henry Hardin, Jr. real estate consultant, former banker
Hale, Danny Lyman financial executive
Hamada, Omar Louis physician
Harpster, James Erving lawyer
Harris, Edward Frederick orthodontics educator
Harvey, Albert C. lawyer
Hathcock, John Edward vocalist
Head, Willis Stanford music educator, performer
Heimberg, Murray pharmacologist, biochemist, physician, educator
Herenton, Willie W. mayor
Herrod, Henry Grady, III allergist, immunologist
Hofmann, Polly A. physiology educator
Horn, Ralph bank executive
Howe, Martha Morgan microbiologist, educator
Hughes, Walter Thompson physician, pediatrics educator
Hunt, James Calvin academic administrator, physician
Hurley, Jeffrey Scott fabric company administrator
Iannaccone, Alessandro ophthalmologist, clinical scientist
Iles, Roger Dean accountant
Ingram, Alvin John surgeon
Jacobson, Gerald psychologist
Jarvis, Daphne Eloise laboratory administrator
Jenkins, Ruben Lee chemical company executive
Johnson, Robert Lewis, Jr. retail company executive
Jolly, William Thomas foreign language educator
Jones, Teresa A. college official
Jurand, Jerry George periodontology educator, researcher
Kaplan, (Claudia) Claudette S. volunteer, professional leader, philanthropist
Kellogg, Frederic Hartwell civil engineer, educator
†Kemme, David Michael economics educator
Kennedy, David Stewart federal judge
Kitabchi, Abbas Eqbal medical educator
Kitts, Judith Pate English educator
Knight, H. Stuart law enforcement official, consultant
Knox, Roger zoological park administrator
Korones, Sheldon Bernarr physician, educator
Krieger, Robert Lee, Jr. human resource/ management consultant, educator, writer, travel/ meeting planner, political analyst
Kudsk, Kenneth Allan surgeon
Kushma, David William journalist
Lang, Lillian Owen accountant
Lasslo, Andrew medicinal chemist, educator
Latta, George Haworth, III neonatologist
Latta, Jennie Davidson lawyer
Lawson, Virginia King nutritionist, consultant
Lazar, Rande Harris otolaryngologist
†Leal, Gumersindo R. physician
Ledbetter, Paul Mark lawyer, writer
Legg, J. Ivan academic administrator
†Lovelace, J. William hotel executive
Lowery, F(loyd) Lynn, Jr. insurance executive
Magrill, Joe Richard, Jr. religious organization administrator, minister
Maksi, Gregory Earl engineering educator
Manire, James McDonnell lawyer
Mann, Donald Cameron marketing company executive
Mantey, Elmer Martin food company executive
Masterson, Kenneth Rhodes lawyer
Mauer, Alvin Marx physician, medical educator
†Maxwell, Martha Ellen performing company executive
McBride, Juanita Loyce oncological nurse
McCalla, Jon P. federal judge
†McCarthy, David Patterson art educator
McCullar, Bruce Hayden oral and maxillofacial surgeon
McEachran, Angus newspaper editor
McIntosh, John Osborn engineering consultant
McLean, Robert Alexander lawyer
McPherson, Larry E(ugene) photographer, educator
McRae, Robert Malcolm, Jr. federal judge
McRee, Celia composer
Mendel, Maurice audiologist, educator
Meredith, Donald Lloyd librarian
Miller, Beverly McDonald geriatric nurse practitioner
Mirvis, David Marc health administrator, cardiologist, educator
Monypeny, David Murray lawyer
Morgan, Colby Shannon, Jr. lawyer
Morreim, E. Haavi medical ethics educator
Mulholland, Kenneth Leo, Jr. health care facility administrator
Neely, Charles Lea, Jr. retired physician
Nesin, Jeffrey D. academic administrator
Newman, Charles Forrest lawyer
Nichols, William Howard, Jr. minister
Nienhuis, Arthur Wesley physician, researcher
Noble, Douglas Ross museum administrator
†Parish, Barbara Shirk writer, educator
Patton, Charles Henry lawyer, educator
Piazza, Marguerite opera singer, actress, entertainer
Pohlmann, Marcus D. political science educator
Pourciau, Lester John librarian
†Pruitt, Stephen Wallace finance educator
Pugh, Dorothy Gunther artistic director ballet company
Ranta, Richard Robert university dean
Rawlins, V. Lane university president
Riely, Caroline Armistead physician, medical educator
Risner, Paul Edward lawyer
Riss, Murray photographer, educator
Romanoff, Stanley M., Jr. human resource specialist
Rutledge, Roger Keith lawyer

†Satre, Philip Glen *casino entertainment executive, lawyer*
Schaefgen, Philip P. *business owner, consultant, accountant*
Seidman, Phillip Kenneth *lawyer*
Shanklin, Douglas Radford *physician*
Sharpe, Robert F., Sr. *writer, lecturer, educator, consultant, publisher*
Shochat, Stephen Jay *pediatric surgeon*
Simpson, Art *agricultural products supplier*
Smith, Frederick Wallace *transportation company executive*
†Smith, Kimberly Ann *art educator*
Smith, Whitney Bousman *music and drama critic*
Smolenski, Lisabeth Ann *family practice physician*
†Solmson, Robert M. *hotel executive*
Sossaman, William Lynwood *lawyer*
Spore, Richard Roland, III *lawyer, educator*
Stagg, Louis Charles *English language and literature educator*
Steib, James Terry *bishop*
Steinhauer, Gillian *lawyer*
Stokes, Henry Arthur *journalist*
Sullivan, Eugene Joseph *food service company executive*
Sullivan, Jay Michael *medical educator*
Summers, James Branson *lawyer*
Tate, Stonewall Shepherd *lawyer*
Terry, Joseph Ray, Jr. *lawyer*
Tibbs, Martha Jane Pullen *civic worker*
Todd, Virgil Holcomb *clergyman, religion educator*
Tuggle, Gloria Harris *school system administrator*
Tuggle, Melvin *philosophy educator, publisher*
Turner, Bernice Hilburn *recording industry executive*
Turner, Jerome *federal judge*
Tutko, Robert Joseph *radiology administrator, law enforcement officer*
†Vescovo, Diane K. *federal judge*
Vinson, Mark Alan *English language and literature educator*
Waddell, Phillip Dean *lawyer*
Waller, Robert Rex *ophthalmologist, educator, foundation executive*
Wallis, Carlton Lamar *librarian*
Ward, Jeannette Poole *psychologist, educator*
Watson, Ada *secondary education educator*
Wellford, Harry Walker *federal judge*
Wheeler, Orville Eugene *university dean, civil and mechanical engineering educator*
Whitesell, Dale Edward *retired association executive, natural resources consultant*
Wilcox, Harry Hammond *retired medical educator*
Wilder, James Sampson, III *lawyer, judge*
Wildman, Gary Cecil *chemist*
Williams, David Russell *retired music educator*
Williams, Edward F(oster), III *environmental engineer*
Williams, J. Maxwell *lawyer, arbitrator and mediator*
Williamson, James F. *architect, educator*
Wilson, Charles Glen *zoo administrator*
Winters, Darcy LaFountain *medical management company executive*
Woodson, Gayle Ellen *otolaryngologist*
Yawn, David McDonald *journalist*
Yeates, Zeno Lanier *retired architect*
Yoakum, Barry Alan *architect*

Millington
Lee, Diane *obstetrics/gynecology nurse practitioner*
Melcher, Jerry William Cooper *clinical psychologist, army officer*
Reed, Erbie Loyd *dentist*

Milton
Coaker, George Mack *minister*

Morristown
Culvern, Julian Brewer *retired chemist, educator*
Harmon, David Eugene *optometrist, geneticist*
Hopper, Peggy F. *education educator*
Johnson, Evelyn Bryan *flying service executive*

Mount Juliet
Beeman, Bob Joe *minister*
Masters, John Christopher *psychologist, educator, writer*
Varallo, Deborah Garr *marketing executive*

Mountain City
Tilley, Charles H. *interior designer*

Mountain Home
McCoy, Sue *surgeon, biochemist*

Murfreesboro
Doyle, Delores Marie *elementary education educator*
†Fitzgerald, Sharon Holt *writer, consultant*
Ford, William F. *banker*
†Gilbert, Linda Arms *music educator*
Hayes, Janice Cecile *education educator*
Lasater, Sandra Jo *nurse*
Leaming, Deryl Ray *dean*
Lee, John Thomas *finance educator, financial planner*
Lowe, Larry Veazey *retired speech educator, consultant*
Marshall, John David *retired librarian, author*
Mitchell, Jerry Calvin *environmental company executive*
Rupprecht, Nancy Ellen *historian, educator*
Walker, David Ellis, Jr. *educator, minister, consultant*
Walker, James E. *academic administrator, educator*

Nashville
Adams, Kenneth Stanley, Jr. (Bud Adams) *energy company executive, football executive*
Allen, George Sewell *neurosurgery educator*
Allison, Fred, Jr. *physician, educator*
Anderson, Charles Hill *lawyer*
Armstrong, Jeanette *education director*
Babbitt, Robert T. *municipal official*
†Baggett, Janet Rosalind *secondary education educator*
Baines, Gwendolyn L. *university office manager*
Baker, Cosette Marlyn *religion writer, editor*
Barnett, Joey Victor *pharmacologist, educator, researcher*
Barton, Neal, Jr. *meteorologist*
Bass, James Orin *lawyer*
Bates, George William *obstetrician, gynecologist, educator*
Battle, William Robert (Bob Battle) *retired newspaper executive*
Bayuzick, Robert J. *materials scientist*
†Beasley, John Snodgrass, II *university administrator*
Beck, Robert Beryl *real estate executive*
Belton, Robert *law educator*
Benbow, Camilla Persson *psychology educator, researcher*
Bender, Harvey W., Jr. *cardiac and thoracic surgeon*
Benson, Edwin Welburn, Jr. *trade association executive*
Bernard, Louis Joseph *surgeon, educator*
Berry, William Wells *lawyer*
Birch, Adolpho A., Jr. *state supreme court justice*
Blair, Joyce Allsmiller *computer science educator*
Bloch, Frank Samuel *law educator*
Blumstein, James Franklin *legal educator, lawyer, consultant*
Bolian, George Clement *health care executive, physician*
Boorman, Howard Lyon *history educator*
Bostick, Charles Dent *lawyer, educator*
Bottorff, Dennis C. *banker*
Boucher, Pamela Kay *church consultant, editor*
†Bourne, John R. *educator*
Boyd, Theophilus Bartholomew, III *publishing company executive*
†Bracks, Lean'tin LaVerne *African-American literature educator*
Bradford, James C., Jr. *brokerage house executive*
Bramlett, Paul Kent *lawyer*
Bredesen, Philip Norman *mayor*
Brigham, Kenneth Larry *medical educator*
Brill, Aaron Bertrand *nuclear medicine educator*
Brodersen, Arthur James *electrical engineer*
Brophy, Jeremiah Joseph *financial company official, former army officer*
Brown, Joe Blackburn *judge*
Brown, Norman James *financial manager*
Brown, Tony Ersic *record company executive*
Browning, T. Jeff *commissioner, state and local*
Buckles, Stephen Gary *economist, educator*
Burch, John Christopher, Jr. *investment banker*
Burish, Thomas Gerard *psychology educator*
Burk, Raymond Franklin, Jr. *physician, educator, researcher*
Burkett, Gerald Arthur *lawyer, musician*
Burnett, Lonnie Sheldon *obstetrics and gynecology educator*
Burt, Alvin Miller, III *anatomist, cell biologist, educator, writer*
Butler, Javed *cardiologist*
Byrd, Andrew Wayne *investment company executive*
Byrd, Benjamin Franklin, Jr. *surgeon, educator*
Cadzow, James Archie *engineering educator, researcher*
†Campbell, Donal *state official*
Carpenter, Janet Sharkey *nursing researcher*
Carpenter, Mary Chapin *singer, songwriter*
Carr, Davis Haden *lawyer*
†Carson, Paul Eugene *insurance examiner*
Cawthon, William Connell *operations management consultant*
Chambers, Carol Tobey *elementary school educator*
Chaney, Sharon Henderson *secondary education educator, consultant*
†Chapdelaine, Perry Anthony, Jr. *public health physician, educator*
Chapman, John Edmon *university dean, pharmacologist, physician*
Chapman, Morris Hines *denominational executive*
Chappell, Charles Richard *space scientist*
Cheek, James Howe, III *lawyer, educator*
Chytil, Frank *biochemist*
†Claverie, Roy E. *water transportation executive, transportation exec*
Clinton, Barbara Marie *university health services director, social worker*
Clouse, R. Wilburn *education educator*
Cobb, Stephen A. *lawyer*
Cohen, Stanley *biochemistry educator*
Collier, Simon *history educator*
Collins, Jerry Clayton *biomedical engineering educator*
Compton, John Joseph *philosophy educator*
Conkin, Paul Keith *history educator*
Conner, Lewis Homer, Jr. *lawyer*
Conway-Welch, Colleen *dean, nurse midwife*
Cook, Ann Jennalie *English language educator*
Cook, Charles Wilkerson, Jr. *banker, former county official*
Cook, George Edward *electrical engineering educator, consultant*
Cordaro, Matthew Charles *utility executive, energy developer, engineer*
Covington, Robert Newman *law educator*
Crabtree, Bruce Isbester, Jr. *architect*
Culbertson, Katheryn Campbell *lawyer*
Cunningham, Leon William *biochemist, educator*
Cupit, Jim (Thomas) *county official*
Daane, James Dewey *banker*
Dale, Kathy Gail *rehabilitation rheumatology nurse*
Dalzell, Jeffrey Alexander *agent, musician*
†Daniel, George Emmett *academic administrator*
Darnell, Riley Carlisle *state government executive, lawyer*
Daughtrey, Martha Craig *federal judge*
Davis, James Verlin *insurance brokerage executive*
Davis, Terry L. *historical association executive*
Day, John Arthur *lawyer*
Dean, Karl *public defender*
Dettbarn, Wolf-Dietrich *neurochemist, pharmacologist, educator*
Dickerson, Dennis Clark *history educator*
Diller, John C. *professional athletics executive*
Dobbs, George Albert *funeral director, embalmer*
Dohrmann, Richard Martin *computer software publishing executive*
Doody, Margaret Anne *English language educator*
Doyle, Don Harrison *history educator*
Draper, James Thomas, Jr. (Jimmy Draper) *clergyman*
Driscoll, Joseph Francis *real estate executive*
Drowota, Frank F., III *state supreme court justice*
Du Bois, Tim *recording industry executive*
Dupont, William Dudley *biostatistician, educator*
†Dye, Henry C. *public relations firm executive*
Dykes, Archie Reece *financial services executive*
Echols, Robert L. *federal judge*
Edwards, Mark E. *healthcare company lawyer*
Elberry, Zainab Abdelhaliem *insurance company executive*
Emans, Robert LeRoy *academic administrator, education educator*
Estes, Moreau Pinckney, IV *real estate executive, lawyer*
Farris, Frank Mitchell, Jr. *retired lawyer*
Faust, A. Donovan *communications executive*
Fazio, Sergio *medical educator, researcher*
Fenichel, Gerald Mervin *neurologist, educator*
Fischer, Patrick Carl *computer scientist, retired educator*
†Fisher, Jack *medical educator, plastic surgeon*
Fisher, Jeff *professional football coach*
Fitzgerald, Edmund Bacon *electronics industry executive*
Fleck, Bela *country musician*
Fleming, Samuel M. *banker*
Fort, Tomlinson *chemist, chemical engineering educator*
Foster, Henry Wendell *medical educator*
Fox, Edward Inman *education administrator and Spanish educator*
†Foxworthy, Jeff *comedian, actor, writer*
Franks, John Julian *anesthesiology educator, medical investigator*
Freeman, James Atticus, III *lawyer, insurance and business consultant*
Freudenthal, Ernest Guenter *technology and business educator*
Frey, Herman S. *publishing company executive*
†Frist, Thomas Fearn, Jr. *hospital management company executive*
Fryd, Vivien Green *art history educator, researcher*
Fyke, James H. *city official*
Galloway, Kenneth Franklin *engineering educator*
Gannon, John Sexton *lawyer, management consultant, arbitrator/mediator*
Gaultney, John Orton *life insurance agent, consultant*
Geisel, Martin Simon *college dean, educator*
George, Alfred L., Jr. *medical educator, researcher*
†George, Eddie *professional football player*
Gibbs, Brian J. *behavioral scientist, business educator*
Gill, Vince *country musician, singer*
Gillmor, John Edward *lawyer*
Girgus, Sam B. *English literature educator*
Gove, Walter R. *sociology educator*
Graham, George J., Jr. *political scientist, educator*
Graham, Hugh Davis *history educator*
Graham, Thomas Pegram, Jr. *pediatric cardiologist*
Grantham, Dewey Wesley *historian, educator*
Graves, Rebecca O. *public health nurse, consultant*
Green, Lisa Cannon *business editor*
Greene, Lydia Abbi Jwuan *elementary education educator*
Greer, Herschel Lynn, Jr. *real estate broker*
†Griffen, Juliet E. *federal judge*
Griffith, James Leigh *lawyer*
Griffith, Jerry Lynn *physical education educator*
Guinsburg, Philip Fried *alcohol and substance abuse counselor*
Gulmi, James Singleton *apparel manufacturing company executive*
Guy, Sharon Kaye *state agency executive*
Hahn, George Thomas *materials engineering educator, researcher*
Hall, Douglas Scott *astronomy educator*
Hall, Richard Clyde, Jr. *religious educational administrator*
Halperin, John William *English literature educator*
†Hamberg, Marcelle Robert *retired urologist*
Hamilton, Russell George, Jr. *academic dean, Spanish and Portuguese language educator*
Hancock, M(arion) Donald *political science educator*
Hanselman, Richard Wilson *entrepreneur*
Hardin, Hal D. *lawyer, former United States attorney, former judge*
†Hargrave, James Lee *editor, consultant*
Hargrove, Erwin Charles, Jr. *political science educator*
Harrawood, Paul *civil engineering educator*
Harris, Alice Carmichael *linguist, educator*
Harris, J(acob) George *health care company executive*
Harris, James Harold, III *lawyer, educator*
Harris, Thomas Raymond *biomedical engineer, educator*
Harrison, Clifford Joy, Jr. *banker*
Harrison, Connie Day *cardiovascular clinical nurse specialist, nursing administrator, consultant*
Harrod, Howard Lee *religion educator*
Hart, Richard Banner *lawyer*
Hass, Joseph Monroe *automotive executive*
Hassel, Rudolph Christopher *English language educator*
Hauk, Gary H. *associate director, discipleship and family group*
Heard, (George) Alexander *retired educator and chancellor*
Hefner, James A. *academic administrator*
Heiser, Arnold Melvin *astronomer*
Henderson, Milton Arnold *professional society administrator*
Hercules, David Michael *chemistry educator, consultant*
Higgins, Thomas A. *federal judge*
Hofstead, James Warner *laundry machinery company executive, lawyer*
Hogan, Brigid L. *molecular biologist*
Holovak, Mike *sports association executive*
Holsen, Robert Charles *accountant*
Horton, Teresa Evetts *municipal official*
Houk, Benjamin Noah *artistic director, choreographer*
House, Robert William *technology management educator*
†Houston, Bill *state commissioner*
Howell, John Floyd *insurance company executive*
Huffman, William Raymond *emergency physician*
Hunt, Walter *county government official*
Hutchison, Barbara Bailey *singer, songwriter*
Infante, Ettore Ferrari *mathematician, educator, university administrator*
Ingram, Martha Rivers *company executive*
Ingram, Orrin Henry, II *transportation executive*
James, Hugh Neal *video, record, movie producer, director*
James, Kay Louise *management consultant, healthcare executive*
Jamison, Connie Joyce *sociology educator*
Jennings, Henry Smith, III *cardiologist*
Johnson, David *medical administrator*
Johnson, Hollis Eugene, III *foundation executive*
Jones, Evelyn Gloria *medical technologist, educator*
Jones, Kathryn Cherie *pastor*
Jonsson, Bjarni *mathematician, educator*
Judd, Wynonna *vocalist, musician*
Kaas, Jon H. *psychology educator*
Kaplan, Peter Robert *cardiologist*
Kisber, Matthew Harris *state legislator*
Klein, Christopher Carnahan *economist*
Kmiec, Edward Urban *bishop*
Kono, Tetsuro *biochemist, physiologist, educator*
Konrad, Peter Erich *neurosurgeon*
Krantz, Sanford Burton *physician*
Kuhn, Paul Hubert, Jr. *investment counsel*
Kulinski, Stephen Edward *interior designer*
Kurek, Michael Henry *music educator*
Land, Rebekah Ruth *marriage and family therapist*
†Land, Richard Dale *minister, religious organization administrator*
Lane, William Arthur *lawyer*
Lange, Robert John (Mutt Lange) *producer*
Lawrence, Thomas Patterson *public relations executive*
Lawton, Alexander Robert, III *immunologist, educator*
Ledyard, Robins Heard *lawyer*
Lee, Douglas A. *music educator*
Leftwich, Russell Bryant *allergist, immunologist, consultant*
Levinson, L(eslie) Harold *lawyer, educator*
Levy, Bruce P. *muncipal or county official*
Lodowski, Charles Alan *business association executive*
Lombardy, Anthony Michael *classics educator*
Lowe, Harold Gladstone, Jr. *photojournalist, small business owner, farmer*
†Lubinski, David John *psychologist, educator*
Lukehart, Charles Martin *chemistry educator*
†Lundin, Keith M. *federal judge*
Lyle, Virginia Reavis *retired archivist, genealogist*
Lynch, John Brown *plastic surgeon, educator*
Lyon, Philip K(irkland) *lawyer*
Madu, Leonard Ekwugha *lawyer, human rights officer, newspaper columnist, politician, business executive*
Mahanes, David James, Jr. *retired distillery executive*
Maier, Harold Geistweit *law educator, lawyer*
Maihafer, Harry James *retired banker, former army officer, writer*
Manning, David Lee *health care executive*
Marney, Samuel Rowe, Jr. *physician, educator*
Martin, Peter Robert *psychiatrist, pharmacologist*
Martin, Theodore Halliwell *minister*
†Mathews, Robert C.H. *state agency executive*
May, James M. *medical educator, medical researcher*
May, Joseph Leserman (Jack) *lawyer*
Mayden, Barbara Mendel *lawyer*
Mayhew, Aubrey *music industry executive*
Mc Creary, James Franklin *lawyer, mediator*
McInteer, Jim Bill *minister, publishing executive, farmer*
McMurry, Idanelle Sam *educational consultant*
†McNair, Steve *professional football player*
McNamee, Dennis Patrick *lawyer*
McPhee, Scott Douglas *occupational therapist, academic administrator*
Medwedeff, Fred M(arshall) *dentist*
Meltzer, Herbert Yale *psychiatry educator*
Meredith, Owen Nichols *public relations executive, genealogist*
Merritt, Gilbert Stroud *federal judge*
Miller, Richard L. *architectural executive*
Mills, Liston Oury *theology educator*
Mizell, Yolanda Mattei *ornamental plaster company executive*
Montgomery, Dillard Brewster *musician, educator*
Moore, William Grover, Jr. *management consultant, former air freight executive, former air force officer*
Morrow, Jason Drew *medical and pharmacology educator*
Mosely, Marcella-M. *speech pathology educator*
Murphy, James L., III *muncipal or county official*
Murray, Richard Keith *marketing executive*
†Murrell, Henry James *principal*
Neilson, Eric Grant *physician, educator, health facility administrator*
Nelson, Edward Gage *merchant banking investment company executive*
Niedergeses, James D. *bishop*
Nixon, John Trice *judge*
Nolan, Eugene F. *municipal or county official*
†Nzabatsinda, Anthere *French language educator*
Oates, John Alexander, III *medical educator*
Oates, Sherry Charlene *portraitist*
O'Day, Denis Michael *ophthalmologist, educator*
Oldfield, Russell Miller *lawyer*
O'Neill, James Anthony, Jr. *pediatric surgeon, educator*
Orgebin-Crist, Marie-Claire *biology educator*
Ossoff, Robert Henry *otolaryngological surgeon*
†Paine, George C., II *federal judge*
Palmer-Hass, Lisa Michelle *state official*
Parker, Mary Ann *lawyer*
Partain, Clarence Leon *radiologist, nuclear medicine physician, educator, administrator*
Partlett, David F. *law educator*
†Patterson, Paige *church administrator, former seminary president*
Pellegrino, James William *college dean, psychology educator*
Pendergrass, Henry Pancoast *physician, radiology educator*
Pennington, Harold Thomas *graphic designer*
Penny, William Lewis *lawyer*
Penterman, Carol A. *opera company executive*
†Perrey, Ralph Martin *state government administrator*
Person, Curtis S., Jr. *state senator, lawyer*
†Petrie, William Marshall *psychiatrist*
Petty, Paula Gail *freelance writer, volunteer*
†Phillips, Clyde M. *accounting executive*
Phillips, John A(tlas), III *geneticist, educator*
Phillips, W. Alan *entertainment lawyer, educator*
Pincus, Theodore *microbiologist, rheumatologist, educator*
Pinson, Charles Wright *transplant surgeon, educator*
†Pitts, J. Kenneth *information systems specialist*
Potter, John Leith *mechanical and aerospace engineer, educator, consultant*
Purcell, William Paxson, III *university policy center administrator*
Pursell, Cleo Wilburn *church official*
Ragsdale, Richard Elliot *healthcare management executive*
Ramsaur, Allan Fields *lawyer, lobbyist*
Ray, Wayne Allen *epidemiologist*
Rayburn, Ted Rye *newspaper editor*
Reeves, Robert Grant *artist manager*
Reid, Donna Joyce *small business owner*
Reid, Lyle *former state supreme court justice*
Reuther, Rosann White *advertising agency executive*
†Richard G., Rhoda *educational administrator*
Richmond, Samuel Bernard *management educator*
Ridley, Carolyn Fludd *social studies educator*
Riley, Harris DeWitt, Jr. *pediatrician, medical educator*
Roberts, Kenneth Lewis *investor, lawyer, foundation administrator*
Roberts, Sandra *editor*
Robertson, David *physician, scientist, educator*
Robinson, Roscoe Ross *nephrologist, educator*

Roden, Dan Mark cardiologist, medical educator
Rogers, Barbara Jean (B.J. Rogers) writer, editor
Rose, Don Garry social worker
Ross, Joseph Comer physician, educator, academic administrator
Russell, Clifford Springer economics and public policy educator
Russell, Fred McFerrin journalist, author, lawyer
Ryan, Sean Patrick physician
†Saltsman, John B. political party executive
Sanders, Jay William audiology educator
Saunders, Ted Elliott accountant
Scheffman, David Theodore economist, management educator, consultant
Schermerhorn, Kenneth music director
Schnelle, Karl Benjamin, Jr. chemical engineering educator, consultant, researcher
Schoggen, Phil H(oward) psychologist, educator
Seigenthaler, John Lawrence retired newpaper executive
Sekwat, Alex Sube public administration educator
Shack, R. Bruce plastic surgeon
Sharp, Bert Lavon retired education educator, retired university dean
Sharp, Vernon Hibbett psychiatrist
Shaw, Carole editor, publisher
Shaw-Cohen, Lori Eve magazine editor
Sherborne, Robert editor
Shipley Biddy, Shelia artist management executive
Shockley, Ann Allen librarian
Siegfried, John association officer
Silberman, Enrique physics researcher and administrator
Sims, Wilson lawyer
Sircy, Bob C., Jr. accountant, financial executive
†Sizemore, Douglas M. state commerce and insurance commissioner
†Skaggs, Ricky country musician
Skoney, Bob municipal official
Sloan, Reba Faye dietitian, consultant
Smith, Charles Edward state agency administrator
Smith, Dani Allred sociologist, educator
Smith, Joseph A. urologic surgeon
Smith, Michael W. popular musician
Smith, Samuel Boyd history educator
Smith, William Barney allergist
Snyders, Dirk Johan electrophysiologist, biophysicist, educator
Soderquist, Larry Dean lawyer, educator, consultant, writer
Speece, Richard Eugene civil engineer, educator
Speller-Brown, Barbara Jean pediatric nurse practitioner
Spengler, Dan Michael orthopedic surgery educator, researcher, surgeon
Stahlman, Mildred Thornton pediatrics and pathology educator, researcher
Stewart, David Marshall librarian
Stockell, Albert W., III information systems analyst, accountant
Stone, Lawrence Mynatt publishing executive
Stringfield, Charles David hospital administrator
Strupp, Hans Hermann psychologist, educator
Strupp, John Allen oncologist
Stuart, Marty country music singer, musician, songwriter
Stubbs, Gerald biochemist, educator
Sullivan, Allen Trousdale securities company executive
†Summers, Paul state attorney general
Sumner, Rachel Diane vocalist, educator
Sundquist, Don governor, former congressman, sales corporation executive
Surowiec, Andrew Julius biophysicist, researcher
Sutcliffe, James Sheldon human genetics educator, researcher
Sutherland, Frank publishing executive, editor
Sweeney, Mark Owen publisher
Swensson, Earl Simcox architect
Swing, Marilyn S. metropolitan clerk
†Taylor, Richard Kevin magazine editor
Thackston, Edward Lee engineer, educator
Thompson, Anthony retired corporate executive
Thornton, Spencer P. ophthalmologist, educator
Tillis, Pam country singer, songwriter
Tippin, Aaron country music singer, songwriter
Trauger, Aleta Arthur judge
Trautman, Herman Louis lawyer, educator
Tuke, Robert Dudley lawyer, educator
Turk, Thomas Liebig cultural organization administrator
Twain, Shania country musician
Ullestad, Merwin Allan tax services executive
Urmy, Norman B. hospital administrator
Valentine, Alan Darrell symphony orchestra executive
Van, George Paul international money management consultant
van Eys, Jan retired pediatrician, educator, administrator
†Van Mol, Louis John public relations firm executive
Van Mol, Louis John, Jr. public relations executive
Voegeli, Victor Jacque history educator, dean
von Raffler-Engel, Walburga (Walburga Engel) linguist, cross-cultural communications specialist, lecturer, writer
Wadley, Fredia Stovall state commissioner
Walkup, John Knox state attorney general
†Walters, Jane state agency administrator
Wang, Taylor Gunjin science administrator, astronaut, educator
Wasserman, David H. medical educator, researcher
†Waters, Raymond hotel executive
Watts, Carolyn Sue nurse
Weingartner, H(ans) Martin finance educator
Wert, James Junior materials scientist, educator
Westfield, Fred M. economics educator
Wetenhall, John museum director
Whetsell, William Otto, Jr. neuropathologist
Whitaker, Evans Parker academic administrator
White, Bruce David law and ethics educator
White, Michael James healthcare facilities administrator
Whitten-Frickey, Wendy Elise entertainer
Wilder, John Shelton state official, former state legislator
Wilkinson, Grant Robert pharmacology educator
Williams, Lester Frederick, Jr. general surgeon
Williams, Marsha Rhea computer scientist, educator, researcher, consultant
Williams, Mary Helen elementary education educator
Winstead, Elisabeth Weaver poet, writer, English language educator
Winstead, George Alvis law librarian, biochemist, educator, consultant
Wire, William Shidaker, II retired apparel and footwear manufacturing company executive
Wise, Bill school system administrator
Wiseman, Thomas Anderton, Jr. federal judge
Wolraich, Mark Lee pediatrician
Wray, Harmon Lee religious organization administrator, religious studies educator
Wyatt, Joe Billy academic administrator
Yearwood, Trisha country music singer, songwriter
Yuspeh, Alan Ralph lawyer, healthcare company executive
Zibart, Michael Alan wholesale book company executive
Zierdt, John Graham, Jr. transportation company executive
Zimmerman, Raymond retail chain executive

Newport
Ball, Travis, Jr. educational consultant, editor
Bell, John Alton lawyer, judge
Dykeman, Wilma writer, lecturer
Kridler, Jamie Branam children's advocate, social psychologist
Runnion, Cindie J. elementary school educator

Normandy
Stockton, Kim Welch nurse practitioner

Oak Ridge
Arnold, Jamie K. program management, safety and health, and training professional
Auerbach, Stanley Irving ecologist, environmental scientist, educator
Boyle, William R. science administrator
Brown, Robert Frederick industrial systems engineer, technology applications, industrial systems and management systems consultant
Bugg, Keith Edward computer software developer, software company executive
Carlsmith, Roger Snedden chemistry and energy conservation researcher
Clapp, Neal Keith experimental pathologist
†Cragle, Donna Lynne university administrator, researcher
Dickens, Justin Kirk nuclear physicist
Fontana, Mario H. nuclear engineer
Foust, Donna Elaine Marshall women's health nurse
Fricke, Martin Paul science company executive
Gifford, Franklin Andrew, Jr. meteorologist
Horak, James Albert materials scientist, nuclear engineer, educator
Huff, Dale Duane hydrologist, educator
Hurt, Nathan Hampton, Jr. mechanical engineer
Jasny, George Roman retired energy company executive
Johnson, Ruth Crumley economics educator
Jones, Virginia McClurkin social worker
Kasten, Paul Rudolph nuclear engineer, educator
Kliewer, Kenneth Lee computational scientist, research administrator
Krause, Manfred Otto physicist
Larson, Bennett Charles solid state physicist, researcher
Luxmoore, Robert John soil and plant scientist
Maienschein, Fred C. physicist
Penniman, W. David information scientist, educator, consultant
Pinnaduwage, Lal Ariyaritna physicist, educator
Plasil, Franz physicist
Postma, Herman physicist, consultant
Poutsma, Marvin L. chemical research administrator
Raridon, Richard Jay computer specialist
Rosenthal, Murray Wilford chemical engineer, science administrator
Runtsch, Clarence Frederick artist, sculptor
Russell, Liane Brauch geneticist
Satchler, George Raymond physicist
Slusher, Kimberly Goode researcher
Spray, Paul Ellsworth surgeon
Stevens, George M., III surgeon
Totter, John Randolph biochemist
Trauger, Donald Byron nuclear engineering laboratory administrator
Trivelpiece, Alvin William physicist, corporate executive
Weinberg, Alvin Martin physicist
Whealton, John H. physicist, educator
Wise, Edmund Joseph physician assistant, industrial hygienist
Young, Jack Phillip chemist
†Yzadi, Kay Tisko artist
Zucker, Alexander physicist, administrator

Old Hickory
Brett, John Brendan, Jr. corporate advertising and public relations executive
Davis, Fred Donald, Jr. optometrist

Ooltewah
Ratz, Kathy Ann Farmer secondary education educator

Palmyra
Davidson, Robert Donald civilian military employee

Paris
McNutt, Gwyn Bellamy archivist

Parsons
Franks, Hollis B. retired investment executive

Pickwick Dam
Casey, Beverly Ann postmaster

Pigeon Forge
Brackett, Colquitt Prater, Jr. judge, lawyer

Portland
†Ryan, Hans Thomas government official, political consultant

Powell
Gentry, Robert Vance physicist, researcher, writer
Hyman, Roger David lawyer

Pulaski
Baker, Kerry Allen management consultant
Croft, Janet Brennan library director, fiber artist, costume designer

Puryear
Stephenson, Jerry Coleman mail carrier

Rockvale
Ferguson, Piete Jackson home health nurse

Rogersville
Fairchild, Dorcas Sexton English educator

Sevierville
Koff, Shirley Irene writer, church administrator
Stone, Mary Overstreet newspaper editor
Waters, John B. lawyer

Sewanee
Chitty, (Mary) Elizabeth Nickinson university historian
Croom, Frederick Hailey college administrator, mathematics educator
Dunkly, James Warren theological librarian
Flynn, John Francis historian, educator
Hughes, Robert Davis, III theological educator
Lorenz, Anne Partee special education educator, consultant
Lytle, Guy Fitch, III priest, educator, dean
Mohiuddin, Yasmeen Niaz economics educator
Patterson, William Brown university dean, history educator
Puckette, Stephen Elliott mathematics educator, mathematician
Williamson, Samuel Ruthven, Jr. historian, university president
Yeatman, Harry Clay biologist, educator

Seymour
Garren, Lisa Ann veterinarian
Steele, Ernest Clyde retired insurance company executive

Shelbyville
Nelson, Clara Singleton human resources consultant

Shiloh
Hawke, Paul Henry historian

Signal Mountain
Cook, Arthur John David labor arbitrator
Cooper, Robert Elbert state supreme court justice
Hall, Thor religion educator
Howe, Lyman Harold, III chemist

Smyrna
†Moore, Wesley Boyd occupational physician

Soddy Daisy
Dall, Peter Andrew management and organizational consultant
Frazier, Douglas Almeda McRee former energy facility analyst
Swafford, Douglas Richard corporate credit executive

Somerville
†Cross, Rose Marie school administrator

South Pittsburg
Cordell, Francis Merritt instrument engineer, consultant

Sparta
Pearson, Margaret Donovan former mayor

Springfield
Fagan, A. Rudolph minister
Nutting, Paul John city manager
Wilks, Larry Dean lawyer

Summertown
Emanuel, William Gilbert electrical engineer

Tazewell
Herrell, Virgil Lee secondary education educator, English educator

Toone
Slaughter, Phillip Howard computer company executive

Trenton
Harrell, Limmie Lee, Jr. lawyer
McCullough, Kathryn T. Baker social worker

Trezevant
Blanks, Naomi Mai retired English language educator

Tullahoma
Baucum, William Emmett, Jr. electrical research engineer
Butler, R. W. engineering company executive
Collins, S(arah) Ruth Knight education educator
Dahotre, Narendra Bapurao materials scientist, researcher, educator
Garrison, George Walker, Jr. mechanical and industrial engineering educator
Gossick, Lee Van consultant, executive, retired air force officer
Hill, Susan Sloan safety engineer
Majors, Betty-Joyce Moore genealogist, writer
McCay, Thurman Dwayne university official
Scalf, Jean A. Keele medical/surgical, geriatrics and home health nurse

Unicoi
Hatcher, James Mitchell principal

Union City
Graham, Hardy Moore lawyer
Graham, R(ichard) Newell soft drink bottling company executive
†Hill, Joe H. legislative staff member

Vonore
Lownsdale, Gary Richard mechanical engineer

Waverly
Doyle, Lloyd Allen, III minister

White House
Boyd, Becky M. secondary school educator

Whiteville
Traylor, Sharon Elain writer, school food service staff member

Williamsport
Dysinger, Paul William physician, educator, health consultant

Winchester
Cashion, Joe Mason home health care administrator

TEXAS

Abilene
Anderson, John Thomas librarian, historian
Baird, Larry Don minister, nurse
Bentley, Clarence Edward savings and loan executive
Boone, Billy Warren lawyer, judge
Boone, Celia Trimble lawyer
Boyll, David Lloyd broadcasting company executive
Bridges, Julian Curtis sociologist educator, department head
Crymes, Mary Cooper secondary school educator
Hennig, Charles William psychology educator
Hobbs, Karen French development officer
Hunter, Robert Dean (Bob Hunter) state legislator, retired university official
Kyker, Christine White (Chris Kyker) human services consultant
Marler, Charles Herbert journalism educator, historian, consultant
McCaleb, Gary Day university official
Morgan, Clyde Nathaniel dermatologist
Owen, Dian Grave investment corporation executive
Pickens, Jimmy Burton earth and life science educator, military officer
Richert, Harvey Miller, II ophthalmologist
Robinson, Vianei Lopez lawyer
Russell, Byron Edward physical therapy educator
Shimp, Robert Everett, Jr. academic administrator, historian
Surovik, Bob J. lawyer
Suttle, Stephen Hungate lawyer
Tindell, William Norman oil company executive, petroleum geologist
†Tippens, Darryl L. educator in English, writer
Weatherl, Charles Rick architect
Whitten, C. G. lawyer
Wilson, Stanley P. retired lawyer
Zachry, Juanita Daniel writer, bookkeeper

Addison
†Anderson, Jack Roy health care company executive
Grote, Richard Charles management consultant, educator, radio commentator
Kline, J. Peter hotel executive
Parr, Richard Arnold, II lawyer
Smith, Cece venture capitalist
Tull, C. Thomas investment advisor
Turner, Bruce Edward lawyer
Waldrep, Alvis Kent, Jr. non-profit foundation administrator

Alamo
Fellenstein, Cora Ellen Mullikin retired credit union executive
Pritchett, Thomas Ronald retired metal and chemical company executive

Aledo
Barton, Charles David religious studies educator, author, researcher, historian
Lindsay, John, IV principal

Alice
†Shalhoub, Issam Toufic urologist

Alpine
†Baker, Katherine H. federal judge
Morgan, Raymond Victor, Jr. university administrator, mathematics educator
Ortego y Gasca, Felipe de education educator

Alvarado
Evans, Garen Lee laboratory director, regulatory compliance officer

Alvin
Crider, Allen Billy English educator, novelist

Amarillo
Anderson, Allan Curtis pharmaceuticals researcher
Arnold, Winnie Jo retired mental health nurse, nursing administrator
†Averitte, Clinton E. federal judge
Ayad, Joseph Magdy psychologist
Berry, Rita Kay medical technologist
Borchardt, Paul Douglas recreational executive
Bowling, Joyce Blankenchip retired critical care nurse
Bull, Walter Stephen police officer
Burgess, C(harles) Coney bank executive
Burrows, Emily Ann nurse
Dunn, Jim Edward sales executive
Elkins, Lloyd Edwin, Sr. petroleum engineer, energy consultant
Johnson, Philip Wayne judge
Keaton, Lawrence Cluer safety engineer, consultant
†Kelleher, John Charles, Jr. plastic surgeon
Klein, Jerry Lee, Sr. religion educator, minister
Laur, William Edward retired dermatologist
Madden, Wales Hendrix, Jr. lawyer
Malcolm, Steven Bryan chemist, laboratory manager
Martin, Luan accountant, payroll and timekeeping supervisor
Marupudi, Sambasiva Rao surgeon, educator
Matthiesen, Leroy Theodore retired bishop
McDuff, Lightnin sculptor
McGaughy, Rebecca Lynn nursing administrator, consultant
Myers, Terry Lewis clinical geneticist, educator
Norrid, Henry Gail osteopathic physician and surgeon, biologist, researcher, human anatomy and physiology educator
Parker, Gerald M. physician, researcher
Peck, Kay Chandler resource development consultant
Pratt, Donald George physician
Robinson, Mary Lou federal judge
Saadeh, Constantine Khalil internist, health facility administrator, educator
St. Clair, Shelley music therapist
†Smith, John Paul counselor, university official
Smithee, John True lawyer, state legislator
Sowers, Thomas Edwin accountant, auditor
Spies, Dennis J. editor

Sprowls, Robert Wayne veterinarian, laboratory administrator
Streu, Raymond Oliver financial planner, securities executive
Stubben, Dolus Jane (D. J. Stubben) advertising executive
Sutterfield, Deborah Kay special education educator
Taylor, Wesley Bayard, Jr. retired army officer
Utterback, Will Hay, Jr. labor union administrator
White, Sharon Elizabeth lawyer
Williams, Jerry Don bank executive
Woods, John William retired lawyer

Anahuac
Fontenot, Jackie Darrel safety and health consultant

Andrews
Scarbrough, Glenda Judith elementary education educator

Angleton
Handy, Robert Truman association administrator

Anson
Godsey, Martha Sue speech-language pathologist

Aransas Pass
Hamilton, Kathleen Allen secondary education educator
Stehn, Lorraine Strelnick physician

Argyle
Merritt, Joe Frank industrial supply executive
Pettit, John Douglas, Jr. management educator

Arlington
Alicea, Luis Rene professional baseball player
Anderson, Dale Arden aerospace engineer, educator
Anguizola, Gustav (Antonio) historian, educator, writer, consultant
†Baldwin, Donald James, II software developer
Burkart, Burke geology educator, researcher
Burkett, John David professional baseball player
Burnett, Paul David small business owner
Burson, Betsy Lee librarian
Chen, Mo-Shing electrical engineering educator
Chong, Vernon surgeon, physician, Air Force officer
Clark, Dayle Meritt civil engineer
Cole, Richard Louis political scientist, educator
Damuth, John Erwin marine geologist
Deaver, Pete Eugene civil and aeronautical engineer
Dickinson, Roger Allyn business administration educator
English, Marlene Cabral management consultant
Ericson, Phyllis Jane psychologist, psychotherapist, consultant
Ferrier, Richard Brooks architecture educator, architect
Fields, Valerie Daralice journalist
Fung, Adrian Kin-Chiu electrical engineering educator, researcher
Gates, Richard Daniel retired manufacturing company executive
Gonzalez, Juan (Alberto Vazquez) professional baseball player
Gorski, Timothy N. obstetrician-gynecologist, educator
Greenspan, Donald mathematician, educator
Hammond, Karen Smith marketing professional, paralegal
Han, Chien-Pai statistics educator
Harris, Vera Evelyn personnel recruiting and search firm executive
Hawkins, Robert A. college administrator
Henderson, Arvis Burl data processing executive, biochemist
Jensen, John Robert lawyer
†Kelly, Roberto Conrado (Bobby Kelly) professional baseball player
Kemp, Thomas Joseph electronics company executive
Kendall, Jillian D. information systems specialist, program developer, educator, consultant
†Kunkle, David M. police chief
Lewis, Frank Leroy electrical engineer, educator, researcher
Lingerfelt, B. Eugene, Jr. minister
Lombard, Mitchell Monte marketing professional
Machle, Edward Johnstone emeritus educator
Mansen, Steven Robert manufacturing company executive
McCuistion, Peg Orem hospice administrator
McCuistion, Robert Wiley lawyer, hospital administrator, management consultant
Mc Elroy, John Harley electrical and industrial engineering educator
McNairn, Peggi Jean speech pathologist, educator
Melvin, Robert Douglas professional sports team executive
Mullendore, Walter Edward economist
Munoz, Celia Alvarez artist
Oates, Johnny Lane professional baseball team manager
Odom, Elzie D. mayor
Otto, Ludwig director, publisher, educator
Palmeiro, Rafael Corrales professional baseball player
Pickard, Myrna Rae dean
Pierson, Grey lawyer
Pomerantz, Martin chemistry educator, researcher
Ptaszkowski, Stanley Edward, Jr. civil engineer, structural engineer
Qasim, Syed Reazul civil and environmental engineering educator, researcher
Quant, Harold Edward financial services company executive, rancher
Raisinghani, Mahesh (Mike) Sukhdev software consultant
Rajeshwar, Krishnan chemist, educator
Ramsey, Charles Eugene sociologist, educator
Reilly, Michael Atlee financial company executive, venture capital investor
Reyes, Arthur Alexander computer science educator
Rodriguez, Ivan Torres professional baseball player
Rollins, Albert Williamson civil engineer, consultant
Rosenberry, William Kenneth lawyer, educator
†Ryan, Nolan former professional baseball player
Sambaluk, Nicholas Wayne auditor
†Samuels, Harold D. legislative staff member
Satterlee, Warren Sanford, II retail management professional
Savage, Ruth Hudson poet, writer, speaker
Sawyer, Dolores motel chain executive
†Schieffer, J. Thomas professional baseball team executive

Smatresk, Neal Joseph physiologist, biology educator, science education consultant
Smith, Charles Isaac geology educator
Sobol, Harold retired dean, manufacturing executive, consultant
Sorensen, Jeff Merwyn university director
Spears, Georgann Wimbish marketing executive
Stevens, Gladstone Taylor, Jr. industrial engineer
Swanson, Peggy Eubanks finance educator
Watkins, Ted Ross social work educator
Wetteland, John Karl professional baseball player
Wiig, Elisabeth Hemmersam speech language pathologist, educator
Wiig, Karl Martin knowledge management expert and consultant
Witt, Anne Cleino musician, education educator
Witt, Robert E. marketing educator
Wright, James Edward judge
†Zeile, Todd Edward baseball player

Athens
Geddie, Thomas Edwin retired small business owner
Hawkins, Audrey Denise academic administrator, educator
Malcom, Carl Ray secondary education educator

Aubrey
Pizzamiglio, Nancy Alice performing company executive

Austin
Acker, Virginia Margaret nursing educator
Adair, Dwight Rial film director, educator
Adcock, Willis Alfred electrical engineer, educator
†Albright, Alan D. federal judge
Alexander, Drury Blakeley architectural educator
Allday, Martin Lewis lawyer
†Allen, Glenn T. manufacturing executive
Alpert, Mark Ira marketing educator
Ancker-Johnson, Betsy physicist, engineer, retired automotive company executive
Anderson, David Arnold law educator
Anderson, Urton Liggett accounting educator
Antokoletz, Elliott Maxim music educator
Armbrust, David B. lawyer
Armstrong, Neal Earl civil engineering educator
Ashworth, Kenneth Hayden public affairs specialist, educator
Attal, Gene (Fred Eugene Attal) hospital executive
Austin, David Mayo social work educator
Auvenshine, Anna Lee Banks school system administrator
Avant, Patricia nursing educator
Ayres, Robert Moss, Jr. retired university president
Baade, Hans Wolfgang legal educator, law expert
Baird, Charles F. state supreme court justice
Baker, James A. state supreme court justice
Baker, Lee Edward biomedical engineering educator
Banks, Virginia Anne (Ginger Banks) association administrator
Bard, Allen Joseph chemist, educator
Barnes, James Randal state official
Barnes, Jay William, Jr. architect, rancher
Barnes, Thomas Joseph migration program administrator
Barr, Howard Raymond architect
Bash, Frank Ness astronomer, educator
Baumgartner, Robert consultant
†Bay, Peter orchestra conductor
Baysinger, Stephen Michael quality assurance professional
Beaman, Margarine Gaynell scrap metal broker
Beard, Leo Roy civil engineer
†Beckner, William mathematician
Belle-Isle, David Richard organization and management consultant
Benavides, Fortunato Pedro (Pete Benavides) federal judge
Bengtson, Roger Dean physicist
Bernard, David Kane minister, writer, editor
Bernstein, Robert retired physician, state official, former army officer
Biesele, John Julius biologist, educator
Billings, Harold Wayne librarian, editor
Bishop, Amelia Morton freelance writer
Blake, Robert Rogers psychologist, behavioral science company executive
Blankenbeker, Joan Winifred communications, computer, and information management executive
Blodgett, Warren Terrell public affairs educator
†Blumenthal, Michael Charles writer, educator
Bobbitt, Philip Chase lawyer, educator, writer
†Boehm, P. Diann elementary education educator
Boggs, James Ernest chemistry educator
†Bomer, Elton state official
Bona, Jerry Lloyd mathematician, educator
Bonevac, Daniel Albert philosopher, author
Bonjean, Charles Michael foundation executive, sociologist, educator
Bordie, John George linguistics educator
Box, John Harold architect, educator, academic dean
Boyd, Carolyn Patricia history educator
Brager, Walter S. retired food products corporation executive
Branch, Brenda Sue library director
Breen, John Edward civil engineer, educator
Brender, Jean Diane epidemiologist, nurse
Breunig, Robert G. botanical facility administrator
Brewer, Thomas Bowman retired university president
Brock, James Rush chemical engineering educator
Brockett, Oscar Gross theatre educator
Bronaugh, Edwin Lee electromagnetic compatibility engineer, consultant
Bronson, Franklin H. zoology educator
Brown, Frank Beverly, IV lawyer
Brown, J. E. (Buster Brown) state senator, lawyer
Brown, Norman Donald history educator
Brown, Stephen Neal computer engineer
Buchanan, Bruce, II political science educator
Bullock, Robert D. (Bob Bullock) lawyer, lieutenant governor, state legislator
Bunten, William Daniel retired banker
Burnham, Walter Dean political science educator
Burns, Ned Hamilton civil engineering educator
Bush, George W. governor
Byrd, Linward Tonnett lawyer, rancher
Caldwell, William McNeilly insurance agent
Calhoun, Frank Wayne lawyer, former state legislator
Campbell, Grover Stollenwerck university official
Campion, Alan chemistry educator
Cannon, William Bernard retired university educator
†Canter, Jamie A. web designer, marketing consultant
Cantilo, Patrick Herrera lawyer
†Capelle, Stephen H. federal judge
Cardozier, Virgus Ray higher education educator

Carey, Graham Francis engineering educator
Carleton, Don Edward history center administrator, educator, writer
Carlton, Donald Morrill research, development and engineering executive
Carpenter, Elizabeth Sutherland journalist, author, equal rights leader, lecturer
Carrasquillo, Ramon Luis civil engineering educator, consultant
Casabonne, Richard J. publishing company executive
Casey, James Francis management consultant
Castaldi, Frank James environmental engineer, consultant
Caudle, Ben Hall petroleum engineering educator
Causey, Robert Louis philosopher, educator, consultant
Chavarria, Ernest Montes, Jr. international trade, business and finance consultant, lecturer
†Cheng, Michelle Mei-Hsue lawyer
Churgin, Michael Jay law educator
Clark, Charles T(aliferro) retired business statistics educator
Clark, Roy Thomas, Jr. chemistry educator, administrator
Cleaves, Peter Shurtleff university and foundation official
Cleland, Charles Carr psychologist, educator
†Combs, Susan commissioner of agriculture
Conine, Ernest newspaper commentator, writer
Cook, Chauncey William Wallace retired food products company executive
Cook, J. Rowland lawyer
Cooke, Carlton Lee, Jr. mayor
Cornyn, John state attorney general
Cragon, Harvey George computer engineer
Craig, James Norman marketing executive, Internet consultant
Crenshaw, Ben professional golfer
†Crowley, Robert Kenan radio station executive
Crum, Lawrence Lee banking educator
Culp, Joe C(arl) electronics executive
Cundiff, Edward William marketing educator
Cunningham, Judy Marie lawyer
Cunningham, William Hughes academic administrator, marketing educator
Curle, Robin Lea computer software industry executive
Cywar, Adam Walter management engineer
Dabbs Riley, Jeanne Kernodle retired public relations executive
Dalton, Caryl school psychologist
Dalton, Don principal
Danielson, Wayne Allen journalism and computer science educator
Davis, Donald Gordon, Jr. librarian, educator
Davis, Donald Robert nutritionist, researcher, consultant
Deal, Ernest Linwood, Jr. banker
Deisler, Paul Frederick, Jr. retired oil company executive
Delevoryas, Theodore botanist, educator
Denny, Mary Craver state legislator, rancher
DeWitt-Morette, Cécile physicist
Dicus, Duane A. physicist, educator
Dijkstra, Edsger Wybe computer science educator, mathematician
Divine, Robert Alexander history educator
Doenges, Rudolph Conrad finance educator
Doerr, Barbara Ann health facility director
Doluisio, James Thomas pharmacy educator
Dougal, Arwin Adelbert electrical engineer, educator
Dougherty, John Chrysostom, III lawyer
Drake, Stephen Douglas clinical psychologist, health facility administrator
Drew, Aubrey Jay accountant
Drummond Borg, Lesley Margaret clinical geneticist
Dulles, John Watson Foster history educator
Duncombe, Raynor Lockwood astronomer
Dupuis, Russell Dean electrical engineer, research scientist
Durbin, Richard Louis, Sr. healthcare administration consultant
Dusansky, Richard economist, educator
Dyer, Cromwell Adair, Jr. lawyer, international organization official
Easley, Christa Birgit nurse, researcher
†Edgecomb, Virginia real estate broker
Edwards, Wayne Forrest paper company executive
Elequin, Cleto, Jr. retired physician
Ellis, Glen Edward, Jr. insurance agent, financial planner
Enoch, Craig Trively state supreme court justice
Epstein, Jeremiah Fain anthropologist, educator
Ersek, Robert Allen plastic surgeon, inventor
Erskine, James Lorenzo physics educator
Eyre, Pamela Catherine retired army officer
Fair, James Rutherford, Jr. chemical engineering educator, consultant
Falola, Toyin history educator
Farrell, Edmund James retired English language educator, author
†Faulkner, Larry Ray chemistry educator, university official
†Favor, Lesli Joanna writer, researcher
Fearing, William Kelly art educator, artist
Fehle, Frank Rudolf finance educator
Feiner, Robert Franklin petroleum and mechanical engineer
Felsted, Carla Martindell librarian, travel writer
Fisher, William Lawrence geologist, educator
Fishkin, Shelley Fisher English language educator
Flawn, Peter Tyrrell businessman, retired university president, educator
Fleeger, David Clark colon and rectal surgeon
Folk, Robert Louis geologist, educator
Fonken, Gerhard Joseph retired chemistry educator, academic administrator
†Fonté, Richard W. university administrator
Ford, Davis L. sanitary & environmental engineer
Fowler, David Wayne architectural engineering educator
Fox, Beth Wheeler library director
Franklin, Billy Joe international higher education specialist
Franklin, G(eorge) Charles academic administrator
Friedman, Alan Warren humanities educator
Fuller, John William lawyer
Fults, Kenneth Wyatt civil engineer, surveyor
Furman, James Housley lawyer
Galinsky, Gotthard Karl classicist, educator
Gambrell, James Bruton, III lawyer, educator
Gammage, Robert Alton (Bob Gammage) lawyer
Gangstad, John Erik lawyer
Gans, Carl zoologist, educator
Gardiner, William Cecil, Jr. chemist, educator
Gardner, Dan Nobles deacon, church official
Gardner, David Walton educational administration educator

Gardner, Joan medical, surgical nurse
Garner, Harvey Louis computer scientist, consultant, electrical engineering educator
Garrido, Augie university athletic coach
Garwood, William Lockhart federal judge
Gates, Charles W., Sr. city official
Gavenda, J(ohn) David physicist
†Gazzaway, Kenneth M. information systems consultant, educator
Gentle, Kenneth William physicist
George, Walter Eugene, Jr. architect
Getman, Julius Gerson law educator, lawyer
Gibbins, Bob lawyer
Gibson, William Willard, Jr. law educator
Gill, Clark Cyrus retired education educator
Gillman, Leonard mathematician, educator
Gimble, Johnny country musician
Girling, Bettie Joyce Moore home health executive
Girling, Robert George William, III business owner
Glade, William Patton, Jr. economics educator
Gloyna, Earnest Frederick environmental engineer, educator
Golden, Edwin Harold insurance company executive
Golden, Kimberly Kay critical care, flight nurse
Goldstein, E. Ernest lawyer
Goldstein, Peggy R. sculptor
Golemon, Ronald Kinnan lawyer
Gonzalez, Raul A. state supreme court justice
Goodenough, John Bannister engineering educator, research physicist
Gracy, David Bergen, II archivist, information science educator, writer
Graglia, Lino Anthony lawyer, educator
Graham, Seldon Bain, Jr. lawyer, engineer
Grangaard, Daniel Robert psychologist
Granof, Michael H. accounting educator
Grant, Verne Edwin biology educator
Graves, Howard Dwayne army officer, academic administrator, educator
Graydon, Frank Drake retired accounting educator, university administrator
Green, Shirley Moore public affairs and communications executive
Greene, John Joseph lawyer
Greenhill, Joe Robert former chief justice state supreme court, lawyer
Greig, Brian Strother lawyer
Grifel, Stuart Samuel management engineer, consultant
Griffy, Thomas Alan physics educator
Guerin, John William artist
Gurasich, Stephen William, Jr. advertising executive
Gustafsson, Lars Erik Einar writer, educator
Gutiérrez, Elisa de León languages educator
Guzma'n, Ana Margarita university administrator
Haas, Joseph Marshall petroleum consultant
Hall, Beverly Adele nursing educator
Hamermesh, Daniel Selim economics educator
Hamilton, Dagmar Strandberg lawyer, educator
Hammer, Katherine Gonet software company executive
Hampton, Charles Edwin lawyer, mathematician, computer programmer
Hancock, Ian Francis (O Yanko le Redžosko) linguistics educator
Haneke, Dianne Myers education educator
Hansen, Niles Maurice economics educator
Harms, Robert Thomas linguist, educator
Harris, Ben M. education educator
Harris, Richard Lee engineering executive, retired army officer
Harrison, Richard Wayne lawyer
Hart, Roderick P. communications educator, researcher, author
Hatgil, Paul Peter artist, sculptor, educator
Hayes, Patricia Ann health facility administrator
Hazel, Joseph Patrick law educator
Hecht, Nathan Lincoln state supreme court justice
Heffley, James Dickey nutrition counselor
Helburn, Isadore B. arbitrator, mediator, educator
Heller, Adam chemist, researcher
Helman, Stephen Jody lawyer
Henderson, George Ervin lawyer
†Hess, Peter Andreas German language educator
Hester, Thomas Roy anthropologist
Hetzler, Susan Elizabeth Savage educational administrator
High, Timothy Griffin artist, educator, writer
Hilburn, John Charles geologist, geophysicist
Himmelblau, David Mautner chemical engineer
Hinkley Thompson, Carol Joyce philanthropy consultant, motivational speaker, writer
Hinojosa-Smith, Roland English language educator, writer
Hitchcock, Joanna publisher
Hixson, Elmer L. engineering educator
Ho, Paul Siu-Chung physics educator
Holtzman, Joan King musician, composer
Holtzman, Wayne Harold psychologist, educator
Holz, Robert Kenneth geography educator
Horton, Claude Wendell physicist, educator
Howard, John Loring retired trust banker
Howell, John Reid mechanical engineering educator
Hubbs, Clark zoologist, researcher
Hudspeth, Emmett LeRoy physicist, educator
Huff, David L. geography educator
†Hughes, Cynthia L. festival director, writer, editor
Hull, David George aerospace engineering educator, researcher
†Hull, Richard Thompson retired philosophy educator, non-profit executive
Hunter, Brother Eagan education educator
Hurley, Laurence Harold medicinal chemistry educator
Huston, Ted Laird psychology educator
Ikard, Frank Neville, Jr. lawyer
Inman, Bobby Ray investor, former electronics executive
Iscoe, Ira psychology educator
Ivins, Molly columnist, writer
Ivy, John L. medical educator, researcher
Jackson, Eugene Bernard librarian
Jackson, William Vernon library science and Latin American studies educator
Jacobson, Antone Gardner zoology educator
Jazayery, Mohammad Ali foreign languages and literature educator emeritus
Jeffrey, Robert Campbell university dean
Jennings, Coleman Alonzo theatre educator
Jennings, John Cecil lawyer, minister, career officer
Jentz, Gaylord Adair law educator
Jirsa, James Otis civil engineering educator
Johnson, Corwin Waggoner law educator
Johnson, Lady Bird (Mrs. Lyndon Baines Johnson) widow of former President of United States
Johnson, Mildred Snowden retired nursing educator
Johnson, Sam D. federal judge
Johnson, Sandra Lynn education consultant

Jordan-Bychkov, Terry Gilbert *geography educator*
Jorgeson, Brent Wilson *management executive*
Justice, William Wayne *United States district judge*
Kam, Mitchell M.T. *international career specialist*
†Kelly, Larry E. *federal judge*
Kendall, Dorothy Helen *retired art historian*
Kendrick, David Andrew *economist, educator*
Kennamer, Lorrin Garfield, Jr. *retired university dean*
Kennan, Kent Wheeler *composer, educator*
Kimberlin, Sam Owen, Jr. *financial institutions consultant*
†King, Betty D. *state senate employee*
†King, Carole *songwriter, singer*
Knapp, Mark Lane *communications educator, consultant*
†Knee, Stanley La Moyne *protective services official*
Knight, Gary *lawyer, educator, publisher, trader*
†Knowles, Harry *communications executive*
†Knowles, Harry Jay *internet personality*
Knudsen, John Roland *retired mathematics educator, consultant*
Koen, Billy Vaughn *mechanical engineering educator*
Koros, William John *chemical engineering educator*
Kozmetsky, George *computer science educator*
Krueger, William Wayne, III *lawyer*
Laine, Katie Myers *communications consultant*
Lake, Larry Wayne *petroleum engineering educator, researcher*
Lam, Simon Shin-Sing *computer science educator*
Lamb, Jamie Parker, Jr. *mechanical engineer, educator*
Lariviere, Richard Wilfred *Asian studies educator, university administrator, consultant*
Larkam, Beverley McCosham *clinical social worker, family therapist*
Larkam, Peter Howard *electric utility executive, entrepreneur*
Larson, James W. *architect*
Larson, Kermit Dean *accounting educator*
Lary, Banning Kent *video producer, publisher*
Laycock, Harold Douglas *law educator, writer*
Lehmann, Ruth Preston Miller *literature educator*
Lehmann, Winfred Philipp *linguistics educator*
Lehmann-Carssow, Nancy Beth *secondary school educator, coach*
Lemens, William Vernon, Jr. *banker, finance company executive, lawyer*
Lenoir, Gloria Cisneros *small business owner, educator*
Lewis, Nancy Louine Lambert *school counselor*
Ling, Frederick Fongsun *mechanical engineering educator*
Little, Emily Browning *architect*
Livingston, Ann Chambliss *lawyer*
Livingston, William Samuel *university administrator, political scientist*
Lochridge, Lloyd Pampell, Jr. *lawyer*
Lockett, Landon Johnson *retired linguistic educator, researcher*
Loehlin, John Clinton *psychologist, educator*
Loehr, Raymond Charles *engineering educator*
Long, Bert Louis, Jr. *artist*
Lopreato, Joseph *sociology educator, author*
Louis, William Roger *historian, educator, editor*
Luedecke, William Henry *mechanical engineer*
†Lund, Jeffrey Nelson *university official, human resources consultant*
Lundgren, Clara Eloise *public affairs administrator, journalist*
Mackey, Louis Henry *philosophy educator*
Maguire, Kevin *travel management consultant*
Malcolm, Mollybeth *political party official, counselor*
Maloney, Frank *judge, lawyer*
Manosevitz, Martin *psychologist*
Mansfield, Stephen W. *state supreme court justice*
Marcus, Leah S. *English educator*
Martin, Earin Miller *program director, educator, trainer*
Martin, Frederick Noel *audiology educator*
Martinez, Ernesto, III *sales professional*
Mathews, Steven Conrad *educational company executive*
Mathias, Reuben Victor (Vic Mathias) *real estate executive, investor*
†Matwiczak, Kenneth Matthew *university educator, consultant*
Mauzy, Oscar Holcombe *lawyer, retired state supreme court justice*
Maxwell, Arthur Eugene *oceanographer, marine geophysicist, educator*
Mayer, Susan Martin *art educator*
Mayes, Wendell Wise, Jr. *broadcasting company executive*
McBee, Frank Wilkins, Jr. *industrial manufacturing executive*
Mc Carthy, John Edward *bishop*
McCarty, Sally F. *educational consultant, entrepreneur*
McCormick, Michael Jerry *judge*
McCoy, John Denny *artist*
McCullough, Frank Witcher, III *lawyer*
McDaniel, Myra Atwell *lawyer, former state official*
McElroy, Maurine Davenport *financier, educator*
McFadden, Dennis *experimental psychology educator*
Mc Ketta, John J., Jr. *chemical engineering educator*
Mc Kinney, Michael Whitney *trade association executive*
McReynolds, Mary Maureen *municipal environmental administrator, consultant*
Megaw, Robert Neill Ellison *English educator*
†Mennell Putman, T. Elizabeth *anthropologist, researcher*
Mersky, Roy Martin *law educator, librarian*
Meyers, Lawrence Edward *state judge*
Middleton, Christopher *Germanic languages and literature educator*
Middleton, Harry Joseph *library administrator*
†Miller, Charles (Chuck) E. *judge*
Misra, Jayadev *computer science educator*
Moag, Rodney Frank *language educator, country music singer*
†Molina, Eduardo *state agency administrator*
†Monroe, Frank R. *federal judge*
Moore, Rebecca Ann Rucker *marketing executive*
Morales, Dan *state attorney general*
†Moses, Mike *commissioner*
Moss, Bill Ralph *lawyer*
Moyers, Robert Charles *systems analyst, state official, microcomputer consultant*
Mullen, Ron *insurance company executive*
Mullins, Charles Brown *physician, academic administrator*
Nelson, Steven Douglas *construction company executive*
Nevola, Roger Paul *lawyer*
†Newburger, Caryn Lason *English educator*
Newton, Charles Chartier *architect*
Nguyen, Truc Chinh *analytical chemist*
Nicastro, David Harlan *forensic engineer, consultant, author*
Nichols, Steven Parks *mechanical engineer, university official*
Nolen, William Lawrence, Jr. *insurance agency owner, real estate investor*
Nowlin, James Robertson *federal judge*
Oden, John Tinsley *mathematician, theoretical mechanics consultant*
O'Geary, Dennis Traylor *contracting and engineering company executive*
Onstead, Randall *consumer goods company executive*
Oppel, Richard Alfred *newspaper executive*
Oram, Robert W. *library administrator*
Osborne, Duncan Elliott *lawyer*
Overstreet, Morris L. *state supreme court justice*
Owen, Priscilla Richman *state supreme court justice*
Painter, Theophilus Shickel, Jr. *physician*
†Parker, Randall Martin *educator*
Passons, Donna Janelle *academic administrator*
Patman, Philip Franklin *lawyer*
Patterson, Donald Eugene *research scientist*
Paul, Donald Ross *chemical engineer, educator*
Paulsgrove, Robin *fire chief*
Payne, Eugene Edgar *insurance company executive*
Payne, John Ross *rare books and archives appraisal consulting company executive, library science educator*
Payne, Tyson Elliott, Jr. *retired insurance executive*
†Pena, Richard *lawyer*
Perkins, Richard Burle Jamail, II *chemical engineer, international consultant*
†Perry, Rick *state official*
†Peters, Gregory A. *technology company executive*
Peterson, Robert Allen *marketing educator*
Phelps, Gerry Charlotte *economist, minister*
Phillips, Thomas Royal *state supreme court chief justice*
Pickens, Franklin Ace *lawyer*
Pingree, Dianne *sociologist, educator, mediator, consultant*
Pixley, Carl Preston *mathematician*
Polomé, Edgar Charles *foreign language and linguistics educator*
Pope, Andrew Jackson, Jr. (Jack Pope) *retired judge*
Posey, Daniel Earl *analytical chemist*
Poulsen, Lawrence LeRoy *research scientist*
Pradzynski, Andrzej Henryk *chemist*
Prentice, Norman Macdonald *clinical psychologist*
Probus, Michael Maurice, Jr. *lawyer*
Prosperi, Wayne Joseph *lawyer, mediator*
Quinn, Mike *dean*
Raina, Rajesh *computer engineer*
Rascoe, Paul Stephen *librarian, researcher*
Ray, Cread L., Jr. *retired state supreme court justice*
Reavley, Thomas Morrow *federal judge*
Rebhorn, Wayne Alexander *literature educator*
Rector, Clark Ellsworth *advertising executive*
Reed, Lester James *biochemist, educator*
Reese, Lymon Clifton *civil engineering educator*
Reid, Jackson Brock *psychologist, educator*
Rich, John Martin *humanities educator, researcher*
Richards, Ann Willis *former governor*
Richards-Kortum, Rebecca Rae *biomedical engineering educator*
Richardson, Betty Kehl *nursing educator, administrator, counselor, researcher*
Richardson, Freda Leah *state agency executive*
Ricks, Patricia Wynn *author, publisher*
Rider, Brian Clayton *lawyer*
Riggs, Deborah Kay *critical care, pediatrics nurse*
Roach, James Robert *retired political science educator*
Roan, Forrest Calvin, Jr. *lawyer*
Robertson, Jack Clark *accounting educator*
†Robinson, Priscilla *artist*
†Roe, Emily Matthews *recruiting coordinator*
Rogers, Lorene Lane *university president emeritus*
Rostow, Elspeth Davies *political science educator*
Rostow, Walt Whitman *economist, educator*
Roueche, John Edward, II *education educator, leadership program director*
Royal, Darrell K. *university official, former football coach*
Rylander, Henry Grady, Jr. *mechanical engineering educator*
Sadun, Lorenzo Adlai *mathematician*
Sager, Thomas William *statistics research administrator*
Saltmarsh, Sara Elizabeth *lawyer*
Sandberg, Irwin Walter *electrical and computer engineering educator*
Sansom, Andrew *state agency administrator*
Saunders, Jimmy Dale *aerospace engineer, physicist, naval officer*
Sawyer, Margo Lucy *artist, educator*
Sayrak, Akin *economics educator*
Schapery, Richard Allan *engineering educator*
Schechter, Robert Samuel *chemical engineer, educator*
Schleuse, William *psychiatrist, psychoanalyst*
†Schmandt, Jurgen Augustinus *public affairs educator*
Schmandt-Besserat, Denise *archaeologist, educator*
Schmidt, Philip S. *mechanical engineering educator*
Schmitt, Karl Michael *retired political scientist*
Schwartz, Leonard Jay *lawyer*
Sciance, Carroll Thomas *chemical engineer*
Seung, Thomas Kaehao *philosophy educator*
Shaffer, Roberta Ivy *law librarian*
Shapiro, Sander Wolf *lawyer*
Sharir, Yacov *artistic director, choreographer*
Shaw, Frederic Elijah *epidemiologist*
†Shepperd, Jerry Wayne *sociology educator*
Shipley, George Corless *political consultant*
†Shumway, Nicolas *Spanish American literature educator*
Simpson, Beryl Brintnall *botany educator*
Sims, Robert Barry *lawyer*
Smith, Alfred Goud *anthropologist, educator*
Smith, Barry Alan *hotel executive*
Smith, Dorothy Brand *retired librarian*
†Smith, Jeffrey Chipps *art educator*
Smith, Todd Malcolm *political consultant*
Snell, Esmond Emerson *biochemist*
Sohie, Guy Rose Louis *electrical engineer, researcher*
Sparks, Sam *federal judge*
†Sparrow, Bartholomew Huntington *political scientist, educator*
Speck, Lawrence W. *architect*
Spector, Rose *state supreme court justice*
Spence, Roy *advertising executive*
Spielman, David Vernon *retired insurance, finance and publications consultant*
Staley, Thomas Fabian *language professional, academic administrator*
Steinfink, Hugo *chemical engineering educator*
Stephen, John Erle *lawyer, consultant*
Stewart, Kent Kallam *analytical biochemistry educator*
Stokoe, Kenneth H., II *civil engineer, educator*
Stone, Leon *banker*
Stoner, James Lloyd *retired foundation executive, clergyman*
Stout, Patricia A. *communications educator*
Straiton, Archie Waugh *electrical engineering educator*
Strauser, Robert Wayne *lawyer*
Streetman, Ben Garland *electrical engineering educator*
Sturdevant, Wayne Alan *computer executive*
Sturley, Michael F. *law educator*
Su, Jie *researcher, engineer*
†Sullivan, Charlotte Ann *educator*
Sullivan, Jerry Stephen *electronics company executive*
Sullivan, Teresa Ann *law and sociology educator, academic administrator*
Sutherland, William Owen Sheppard *English language educator*
Sutton, Harry Eldon *geneticist, educator*
Sutton, John F., Jr. *law educator, dean, lawyer*
Swartzlander, Earl Eugene, Jr. *engineering educator, former electronics company executive*
Swinney, Harry Leonard *physics educator*
Tate, John T. *mathematics educator*
†Taute, Barbara Ehli *telecommunications company official*
†Taylor, Joseph Arthur *internation communication educator*
Taylor, Mildred Lois *nursing home administrator*
Teague, Hyman Faris *former publishing company executive*
Temple, Larry Eugene *lawyer*
Terry, Craig Robert *lawyer*
Tesar, Delbert *machine systems and robotics educator, researcher, manufacturing consultant*
Thiessen, Delbert Duane *psychologist*
Thomajan, Robert *lawyer, management consultant*
Thompson, G. Gaye *lawyer*
Thompson, Larry Flack *semiconductor equipment company executive*
Thornton, Joseph Scott *research institute executive, materials scientist*
Thurston, George Butte *mechanical and biomedical engineering educator*
Tinsley, Anna Melissa *reporter*
Todd, Bruce M. *public affairs executive, former mayor*
Toubin, Charles Irving *commercial real estate executive, writer*
Townsend, Richard Marvin *government insurance executive, city manager, consultant*
Trabulsi, Judy *advertising and marketing executive*
Trafton, Laurence Munro *astronomer*
Tucker, Richard Lee *civil engineer, educator*
Turner, Billie Lee *botanist, educator*
Turner, Sylvester *state legislator, lawyer*
Turney, James Edward *computer scientist*
Tyler, Noel *geological researcher and educator*
Tyler, Ronnie Curtis *historian*
Udagawa, Takeshi *physicist, educator*
Uhlenbeck, Karen Keskulla *mathematician, educator*
†Ulibarri, River Cecilia *construction company executive*
Umeadi, Albert Nkuni *civil engineer, consultant*
Van Buren, William Benjamin, III *retired pharmaceutical company executive*
Vande Hey, James Michael *corporate executive, former air force officer*
Vandel, Diana Geis *performance consultant*
Vliet, Donna Love *educator*
Vliet, Gary Clark *mechanical engineering educator*
Vykukal, Eugene Lawrence *wholesale drug company executive*
Wadlington, Warwick Paul *English language educator*
Wahlberg, Philip Lawrence *former bishop*
Walker, James Roy *microbiologist*
Walls, Carl Edward, Jr. *communications company official*
Walton, Charles Michael *civil engineering educator*
Watkins, Sarah Frances Ashford *electronic manufacturing company executive*
Watson, Kirk *mayor*
Weddington, Sarah Ragle *lawyer, educator, speaker, writer*
Wehring, Bernard William *nuclear engineering educator*
Weinberg, Louise *law educator, author*
Weintraub, Russell Jay *lawyer, educator*
Weismann, Donald Leroy *art educator, artist, filmmaker, writer*
Welch, Ashley James *engineering educator*
Wellborn, Olin Guy, III *law educator*
Werbow, Stanley Newman *language educator*
West, Glenn Edward *business organization executive*
Westbrook, Jay Lawrence *law educator*
Wheeler, John Craig *astrophysicist, writer*
Whitbread, Thomas Bacon *English educator, author*
White, Alice Virginia *volunteer health corps administrator*
White, John Michael *chemistry educator*
White, Tom Martin *playwright, music publisher*
Williams, Diane Elizabeth *architectural historian*
Williams, Mary Pearl *judge, lawyer*
Williamson, Hugh Jackson *statistician*
Willson, C. Grant *chemistry educator, engineering educator*
Wilson, James William *retired lawyer*
Wilson, Margaret Scarbrough *retail executive*
Winegar, Albert Lee *computer systems company executive*
Winters, J. Sam *lawyer, federal government official*
Wolf, Harold Arthur *finance educator*
†Woods, Charles Thomas *public service executive*
Woodson, Herbert Horace *retired electrical engineering educator*
Wright, Charles Alan *law educator, author*
Wright, Stephen Gailord *civil engineering educator, consultant*
Zager, Steven Mark *lawyer*
Ziegler, Daniel Martin *chemistry educator*
†Ziegler, Sharon Northrud *educational administrator*
Zimmerman, Louis Seymour *lawyer*

Baird
Rodenberger, Charles Alvard *aerospace engineer, consultant*

Bastrop
Eskew, Benton *judge*

Batson
Johnston, Maxine *retired librarian*

Bay City
Aylin, Elizabeth Twist Pabst *real estate broker, developer*
Peden, Robert F., Jr. *retired lawyer*

Bayou Vista
Schlotfeldt, William (Bill) West *real estate investor*

Baytown
Black, Sarah Joanna Bryan *secondary school educator*
Coker, Mary Shannon *surgical nurse*
Coker, Sally Jo *sociology educator*
Culp, Barbara June *secondary school educator*
Leiper, Robert Duncan *local government official*
Mendelson, Robert Allen *polymer scientist, rheologist*
Williams, Drew Davis *surgeon*

Beaumont
Alter, Nelson Tobias *jewelry retailer and wholesaler*
Alter, Shirley Jacobs *jewelry store owner*
Black, Robert Allen *lawyer*
†Bradford, J. Michael *prosecutor*
Brentlinger, William Brock *college dean*
Brooks, Jack Bascom *congressman*
Cobb, Howell *federal judge*
Everett, John Howard *diving business owner, paramedic*
Fisher, Joseph Jefferson *federal judge*
Gagne, Mary *secondary school principal*
†Galante, Joseph A. *bishop*
Hawkins, Emma B. *humanities educator*
Heartfield, Thad *judge*
†Hines, Earl S. *federal judge*
Long, Alfred B. *former oil company executive, consultant*
Lord, Evelyn Marlin *former mayor*
Lozano, Jose *nephrologist*
Mueller, Lisa Maria *process engineer*
†Radford, Wendell C. *federal judge*
Roth, Lane *communications educator*
Saur, Pamela S. *English and German educator*
Schell, Richard A. *federal judge*
Scofield, Louis M., Jr. *lawyer*
Smith, David Ryan *museum director*
Smith, Floyd Rodenback *retired utilities executive*
Ware, John David *valve and hydrant company executive*

Bedford
Champney, Raymond Joseph *advertising and marketing executive, consultant*
Collins, Stephen Barksdale *retired health care executive*
Donnelly, Barbara Schettler *medical technologist, retired*
Flaherty, Carole L. *medical, surgical and mental health nurse*
Lentz, Luther Eugene *graphic arts technical specialist*
Lieber, David Leslie *journalist*
Rosene, Linda Roberts *organizational consultant, researcher*
Rosene, Ralph Walfred *consulting company executive*
Walther, Richard Ernest *psychology educator, library administrator*

Beeville
Lamm, Harriet A. *mathematics educator*
Myers, Patricia Louise *college administrator*

Bellaire
Ballanfant, Kathleen Gamber *newspaper executive, public relations company executive*
Haywood, Theodore Joseph *physician, educator*
Holmquest, Donald Lee *physician, astronaut, lawyer*
Jacobus, Charles Joseph *lawyer, title company executive, author*
Knolle, Mary Anne Ericson *psychotherapist, business communications consultant*
Lundy, Victor Alfred *architect, educator*
Moore, Pat Howard *engineering and construction company executive*
Pokorny, Alex Daniel *psychiatrist*
Richardson, William Wightman, III *personnel and employee benefits consultant*
Smeal, Janis Lea *operating room nurse, health facility administrator*
Teas, John Frederick *small business owner*
Thorne, Lawrence George *allergist, immunologist, pediatrician*
Wisch, David John *structural engineer*

Bellville
Neely, Robert Allen *ophthalmologist*

Belton
Andreason, George Edward *university administrator*
Harrison, Benjamin Leslie *retired army officer*
Miller, Richard Joseph *lawyer*
Parker, Bobby Eugene, Sr. *college president*
Shoemaker, Robert Morin *retired army officer, county government official*

Bertram
Albert, Susan Wittig *writer, English educator*

Big Lake
†McCarson, Roberta Joan *educator in English, art, theatre*

Big Spring
Fryrear, Donald William *agricultural engineer*
Simmons, Lorna Womack *elementary school educator*
†Walker, John Hester *newspaper editor, author*

Blanco
Evett, Philip John *sculptor, educator*
Holmes, Darrell *travel consultant*

Boerne
Daugherty, Linda Hagaman *private school executive*
Mitchelhill, James Moffat *civil engineer*

Morton, Michael Ray *retail company consultant*
Price, John Randolph *writer*
Wittmer, James Frederick *preventive medicine physician, educator*

Bonham
Phillips, Don Lee *nursing administrator*
Seale, Mary Louise *medical, surgical and geriatrics nurse*
Youree, Cheryl Ann *secondary education educator*

Borger
Allen, Bessie Malvina *music educator, church organist*
Brown, Roger Dale *college dean*
Chisum, Matthew Eual *laboratory manager*
Edmonds, Thomas Leon *lawyer, management consultant*

Brazoria
Jones, Lawrence Ryman *retired research chemist*

Breckenridge
†Fox, Grady Harrison *library director*
†Rominger, James Corridon *political party administrator*

Brenham
Dalrymple, Christopher Guy *chiropractor*
Lubbock, Mildred Marcelle (Midge Lubbock) *former small business owner*
Pipes, Paul Ray *county commissioner*
Rothermel, James Douglas *retired finance educator*

Bridge City
Smith, Phillip Carl *marine and ship pilot, rancher*

Brooks AFB
Balldin, Ulf Ingemar *medical researcher*
Corrigan, Paula Ann *military officer, internist*
†Jernigan, John G. *career officer*
Monk, Richard Francis *air force officer, health care administrator*
Patterson, John C. *clinical psychology researcher*
Wilde, James Dale *archaeologist, educator*

Brookshire
Utley, Jane B. *poet*

Brownfield
Cameron, Glenda Faye *secondary education educator*
Moore, Bradford L. *lawyer*
Swoopes, Sheryl *professional basketball player*

Brownsville
†Black, John W. *federal judge*
Boze, Betsy Vogel *university dean, marketing educator*
Caballero, Bertha Lucio *gifted and talented education educator*
Cohen, Barry Mendel *financial executive, educator*
Farst, Don David *zoo director, veterinarian*
Fitzpatrick, John J. *bishop*
Fleming, Tommy Wayne *lawyer*
†Garza, Fidencio C., Jr. *federal judge*
Garza, Reynaldo G. *federal judge*
Godinez, Magdalena *cardiology nurse*
Marz, Loren Carl *environmental engineer, chemist, meteorologist*
Pena, Raymundo Joseph *bishop*
Ray, Mary Louise Ryan *lawyer*
Vela, Filemon B. *federal judge*
Walss, Rodolfo J. *obstetrician-gynecologist, artist*
Weisfeld, Sheldon *lawyer*
Xu, Zhong Ling *mathematician, educator*

Brownwood
Bell, Mary E. Beniteau *accountant*
Bell, William Woodward *lawyer*
Murphy, Justin Duane *history educator*
Roby, Annie Beth Brian *librarian*
Smith, Robert Leonard *pastor, religious studies educator*
Tumlinson, Michael Ray *educational administrator*

Bryan
Bear, Robert Emerson *secondary education art educator*
Bement, Jill Leigh *occupational therapist*
†Borden, Robert Christian *editor*
Dirks, Kenneth Ray *pathologist, medical educator, army officer*
Hill, Henry Carl *college administrator*
Hubert, Frank William Rene *retired university system chancellor*
Lusas, Edmund William *food processing research executive*
Michel, C. Randall *judge, lawyer*
Owens, Harold B. *former state agency consultant*
Pearce, Stephen Lamar *management consultant*
Samson, Charles Harold, Jr. (Car Samson) *retired engineering educator, consultant*
Smith, Elouise Beard *restaurant owner*
Smith, Steven Lee *lawyer, judge*
Strong, Stephen Andrew *lawyer*
Sulik, Edwin (Pete Sulik) *health care administrator*

Buda
Levinson, Joseph *computer company executive, marketing and sales consultant*

Bullard
Buckner, John Hugh *retired real estate broker, retired construction company executive, retired air force officer*

Burleson
Godbey, Helen Kay *city official*
Johnstone, Deborah Blackmon *lawyer*
Manning, Walter Scott *accountant, former educator, consultant*
Prior, Boyd Thelman *management consultant*

Bushland
Howell, Terry Allen *agricultural engineer*
Unger, Paul Walter *soil scientist*

Calvert
Alemán, Marthanne Payne *environmental planner, consultant*

Camp Wood
Triplett, William Carryl *physician, researcher*

Candelaria
Chambers, Johnnie Lois (Tucker) *retired elementary school educator, rancher*

Canyon
†Dudt, Charmazel *classics educator*
Kirby, Brenda Jean *critical care nurse*
Long, Russell Charles *academic administrator*
†Teichmann, Sandra Gail *English educator*

Canyon Lake
Phelan, Charlotte Robertson *journalist, book critic*
Reinhardt, Linda Kay *minister*

Carrizo Springs
†Myers, Jay Scott *cattle rancher*

Carrollton
Goodman, Thomas Blackburn, III *regional processor specialist*
Heath, Jinger L. *cosmetics executive*
Hulbert, Paul William, Jr. *paper, lumber company executive*
Kelly, Ralph Whitley *emergency physician, health facility administrator*
Maher, Sheila *secondary school principal*
Plummer, Paul James *software company executive*
Primas, Vinson Bernardi *management consultant*
Riggs, Arthur Jordy *retired lawyer*
Schulz, Richard Burkart *electrical engineer, consultant*
Sherman, Lisa Le Ellen *pharmacist*
†Strockbine, Richard Lewis *athletics administrator*
Wang, Peter Zhenming *physicist*
Withrow, Lucille Monnot *nursing home administrator*

Carthage
Cooke, Walta Pippen *automobile dealership owner*

Castroville
Strickland, Sandra Jean Heinrich *nursing educator*

Cedar Creek
Akins, Vaughn Edward *retired engineering company executive*

Cedar Hill
Findley, Milla Jean *nutritionist*
Garrett, C. Lynn *researcher, business consultant*
Hickman, Traphene Parramore *library director, storyteller, library and library building consultant*
Kilgore, Janice Kay *musician, educator*
Kincaid, Sherrie Lynn *clinical research and surgical intensive care unit nurse*
Lang, James Devore, Jr. *ministry executive*
Shower, Robert Wesley *financial executive*

Cedar Park
Albin, Leslie Owens *biology educator*
Dorsch, Jeffrey Peter *journalist*
†Vela, Wesley James *finance director*

Chandler
Jacobsen, Shirley Marie *editor, songwriter, artist*
Sanders, Sharon Raye (Sharri Sanders) *telecommunications executive, educator*

Channelview
Gower, Bob G. *gas and oil industry executive*
Wallace, Betty Jean *elementary school educator, lay minister*

Chillicothe
Brock, Helen Rachel McCoy *retired mental health and community health nurse*

China Spring
Weaver, Donna Kay *writer, genealogist*

Cibolo
Jensen, Andrew Oden *retired obstetrician, gynecologist*
Newsom, Melvin Max *retired research company executive*
Smith, Harry Leroy *securities firm executive*

Clarendon
Chamberlain, William Rhode *county official*

Cleburne
MacLean, John Ronald *lawyer*
Palmer, Lynn Landry *conductor, musician*

Cleveland
Campbell, Selaura Joy *lawyer*
Rice, J. Andrew *management consultant, tree farmer*
Surls, James *sculptor*
White, Cecile Renee Kingsbury *dance educator*

Coldspring
Bunch, Robert Craig *librarian*

College Station
Adkisson, Perry Lee *university system chancellor*
Armstrong, Robert Beall *physiologist*
Arnold, J(ames) Barto, III *marine archaeologist*
Arnowitt, Richard Lewis *physics educator, researcher*
†Balfour, Stephen Paul *educational analyst*
Baskharone, Erian Aziz *mechanical and aerospace engineering educator*
Bass, George Fletcher *archaeology educator*
Beaver, Bonnie Veryle *veterinarian, educator*
Berg, Robert Raymond *geologist, educator*
Berner, Leo De Witte, Jr. *retired oceanographer*
Bhattacharyya, Shankar Prashad *electrical engineer, educator*
Black, Samuel Harold *microbiology and immunology educator*
Bond, Jon Roy *political science educator*
Borlaug, Norman Ernest *agricultural scientist*
†Burk, James Steven *sociologist*
Buth, Carl Eugene *civil engineer*
Calhoun, John C., Jr. *academic administrator*
Cannon, Garland *English language educator*
†Cantrell, Carol Whitaker *educational administrator*
Carpenter, Delbert Stanley *educational administration educator*
†Christensen, Paul Norman *English educator, writer*
Christiansen, James Edward *agricultural educator*
Chui, Charles K. *mathematics educator*
Cocanougher, Arthur Benton *university dean, former business administration educator*
Cochran, Robert Glenn *nuclear engineering educator*
Cockroft, Jeannette Wimmer *historian educator*
Cohen, Aaron *aerospace engineer*
Conway, Dwight Colbur *chemistry educator*
Copp, James Harris *sociologist, educator*
Cotton, Frank Albert *chemist, educator*
Davenport, Manuel Manson *philosophy educator*
Dethloff, Henry Clay *history educator*
Duce, Robert Arthur *atmospheric chemist, university administrator*
Ehsani, Mehrdad (Mark Ehsani) *electrical engineering educator, consultant*
Erlandson, David Alan *education administration educator*
Evans, Carol Ann Butler *consultant, lecturer*
Ewing, Richard Edward *mathematics, chemical and petroleum engineering educator*
Fackler, John Paul, Jr. *chemistry educator*
Fisher, Richard Forrest *soils educator*
Fletcher, Leroy Stevenson *mechanical engineer, educator*
Furubotn, Eirik Grundtvig *economics educator*
Galloway-McQuitter, Liz *university head basketball coach*
Godbey, Luther David *architectural and engineering executive*
Goode-Haddock, Celia Ross *title company executive*
Goodman, David Wayne *research chemist, educator*
Greenhut, Melvin Leonard *economist, educator*
Gunn, Clare Alward *travel consultant, writer, retired educator*
Haden, Clovis Roland *university administrator, engineering educator*
Hall, Kenneth Richard *chemical engineering educator, consultant*
Hall, Timothy Couzens *biology educator, consultant*
Hardy, John Christopher *physicist, educator*
Heidelbaugh, Norman Dale *veterinary medicine educator, consultant, author, inventor*
Hiler, Edward Allan *agricultural and engineering educator*
Howe, Lisa Marie *veterinarian, educator*
Huang, Chang-Shan *landscape architect, educator*
Isdale, Charles Edwin *chemical engineer*
Jansen, Dennis William *economics educator, consultant*
Junkins, John Lee *aerospace engineering educator*
†Kainthla, Ramesh Chand *manufacturing company executive*
Kallendorf, Craig William *English, speech and classical languages educator*
Kennedy, Robert Alan *educational administrator*
Knobel, Dale Thomas *history educator, university administrator*
Knutson, Ronald Dale *economist, educator, academic administrator*
Kohel, Russell James *geneticist*
Kunze, Otto Robert *retired agricultural engineering educator*
Kuo, Lih *medical educator*
Kuo, Way *industrial engineer, researcher*
Laane, Jaan *chemistry educator*
Lee, William John *petroleum engineering educator, consultant*
Lemanski, Larry Fredrick *medical educator, university administrator*
Lowery, Lee Leon, Jr. *civil engineer*
Luepnitz, Roy Robert *psychologist, consultant, small business owner, entrepreneur*
Mason, Stephanie Jo *writer*
Mathewson, Christopher Colville *engineering geologist, educator*
McCrady, James David *veterinarian, educator*
McIntyre, John Armin *physics educator*
McIntyre, Peter Mastin *physicist, educator*
Meier, Kenneth John *political science journal editor*
Milford, Murray Hudson *soil science educator*
Monroe, Haskell Moorman, Jr. *university educator*
Murphy, Kathleen Jane *psychologist, educator*
Nachman, Ronald James *research chemist*
Natowitz, Joseph B. *chemistry educator, research administrator*
Neill, William Harold, Jr. *biological science educator and researcher*
Nightingale, Arthur E. *retired horticulture sciences educator*
O'Connor, Rod *chemist, consultant, inventor*
Page, Robert Henry *engineer, educator, researcher*
Painter, John Hoyt *electrical engineer*
Parlos, Alexander George *systems and control engineering educator*
Parzen, Emanuel *statistical scientist*
Patton, Alton DeWitt *electrical engineering educator, consultant, research administrator*
Perrone, Ruth Ellyn *university administrator*
Plum, Charles Walden *retired business executive and educator*
Prescott, John Mack *biochemist, retired university administrator*
Reed, Raymond Deryl *architect*
Reid, Robert Osborne *oceanographer*
Reinschmidt, Kenneth Frank *engineering and construction executive*
Richardson, Herbert Heath *mechanical engineer, educator, institute director*
Roesset, Jose M. *civil engineering educator*
Rosberg, David William *plant sciences educator*
Rotell, Thomas M. *publishing executive*
Sanchez, David Alan *mathematics educator*
†Schultz, Roger Herman *theater educator*
Scott, Alastair Ian *chemistry educator*
†Shepley, Mardelle McCuskey *architect, educator*
Sis, Raymond Francis *veterinarian, educator*
Slater, Robert Owen *education educator*
Slocum, Richard Copeland (R.C.) *university athletic coach*
Solecki, R. Stefan *anthropologist, educator*
Stanton, Robert James, Jr. *geologist, educator*
Steffy, John Richard *nautical archaeologist, educator*
Stipanovic, Robert Douglas *chemist, researcher*
†Stone, Mary Elizabeth *artist*
Storey, J. Benton *horticulturalist, educator*
Unterberger, Betty Miller *history educator, writer*
Urbanik, Thomas, II *research civil engineer*
Vandiver, Frank Everson *institute administrator, former university president, author, educator*
Vandiver, Renee Lillian Aubry *interior designer, architectural preservator*
Van Riper, Paul Pritchard *political science educator*
Wagner, John Philip *safety engineering educator, science researcher*
Weese, John Augustus *mechanical engineer, educator*
Wichern, Dean William *business educator*
Wild, James Robert *biochemistry and genetics educator*
Wilding, Lawrence Paul *pedology educator, soil science consultant*
Wilson, Don Whitman *retired archivist, historian*
Woodcock, David Geoffrey *architect, educator*
Wu, Guoyao *animal science, nutrition and physiology educator*
Yao, James Tsu-Ping *civil engineer*

Colleyville
†Berges, Juneria Parr *middle school principal*
Compo, Lawrence Judd *sales and marketing executive*
Jones, Pamela Susan *middle school educator*
Love, Ben Howard *retired organization executive*
Maddox, Roger Wayne *minister*
Thompson, James Richard *human resources management consultant*

Comanche
Droke, Edna Faye *elementary school educator, retired*

Commerce
Avard, Stephen Lewis *finance educator*
Linck, Charles Edward, Jr. *English language educator*
†Linck, Ernestine Porcher *English educator, writer*
Perry, Thomas Amherst *English literature and language educator*
Ridgeway, Glenda S. *mental health nurse, educator*
Schmidt, L. Lee, Jr. *university official*

Conroe
Bruce, Rachel Mary Condon *nurse practitioner*
Cecil, Linda Marie *obstetrician/gynecologist*
Judge, Dolores Barbara *real estate broker*
Marsh, Sue Ann *special education educator*
Parle, Bertha Ibarra *writer short stories, poetry*
Shepherd, Elizabeth Poole *health science facility administrator*
†Vinson, Judith Paull *veterinarian*

Converse
Droneburg, Nancy Marie *geriatrics nurse*
Hulsey, Rachel Martinez *secondary education educator*
Vontur, Ruth Poth *elementary school educator*

Coppell
Foster, William Edwin (Bill Foster) *nonprofessional basketball coach*
Minyard, Liz *food products executive*
Owen, Cynthia Carol *sales executive*
Smothermon, Peggi Sterling *middle school educator*
†Williams, Gretchen Minyard *food store executive*

Copperas Cove
London, David Tshombe *military officer*
Sullivan, Theresa Maria *maternal and child health care nurse*
Wright, David Ray *secondary school educator*

Corinth
Church, Jo Hall *educator*

Corpus Christi
Abdelsamad, Moustafa Hassan *dean*
Alberts, Harold *lawyer*
Allin, Bonnie A. *city official*
Allison, Joan Kelly *music educator, pianist*
Alvarez, Peter, Jr. *police chief*
Appel, Truman Frank *surgeon*
Azopardi, Korita Marie *secondary school educator*
Benn, Douglas Frank *information technology and computer science executive*
Benner, Richard Walter *oil company executive, geologist, engineer*
Berkebile, Charles Alan *geology educator, hydrogeology researcher*
Branscomb, Harvie, Jr. *lawyer*
Brazell, Ida Hernandez *judge*
Brown, Marguerite Johnson *music educator*
Carnahan, Robert Narvell *lawyer*
Chodosh, Robert Ivan *retired middle school educator, coach*
Clark, Joyce Naomi Johnson *nurse*
Cox, William Andrew *cardiovascular thoracic surgeon*
Cutlip, Randall Brower *retired psychologist, college president emeritus*
Davis, Martin Clay *lawyer, professor*
Doty, James Edward *pastor, psychologist*
Duarte, Eduardo Adolfo *nursing home administrator*
DuVall, Lorraine *recreation center owner*
Early, William James *education educator*
Finley, George Alvin, III *wholesale executive*
Fleischer, Daniel *minister, religious organization administrator*
Furgason, Robert Roy *university president, engineering educator*
Haas, Paul Raymond *petroleum company executive*
Hamrick, Bill Allen *principal, retired*
Harper, Sandra Stecher *university administrator*
Harrison, William Oliver, Jr. *lawyer, small business owner*
Head, Hayden Wilson, Jr. *judge*
Heinz, Walter Ernst Edward *retired chemical executive*
Jack, Janis Graham *judge*
Jones, Audrey Beyer *dietitian*
Jones, Rebecca Alvina Patronis *nurse*
Kane, Sam *meat company executive*
Kemmerer, Dennis Allen *artist, educator*
Kylstra, Johannes Arnold *physician*
Laws, Gordon Derby *lawyer*
Leon, Rolando Luis *lawyer*
Locke, William Henry *lawyer*
Lowe, J. Allen *minister*
Morey, Jeri Lynn Snyder *architect*
Muniz, Eva Vera *English educator*
†Murray, E'Lane Carlisle *freelance writer*
Norman, Wyatt Thomas, III *landman, consultant*
Parker, Roy Denver, Jr. *entomologist*
Paulson, Bernard Arthur *oil company executive, consultant*
Peterson, Harold R. *municipal official*
Pinkel, Donald Paul *pediatrician*
Pivonka, Leonard Daniel *priest*
Salem, Joseph John *jeweler, real estate developer*
Schake, Lowell Martin *animal science educator*
Schmidt, Richard S. *federal judge*

Stone-Magner, Rose Marie *vocational educator*
Ullberg, Kent Jean *sculptor*
Umfleet, Lloyd Truman *electrical engineering technology educator*
Vargas, Joe Flores *insurance claims executive*
Vaughan, Alice Felicie *accountant, real estate executive, tax consultant*
Wood, James Allen *retired lawyer*
Wooster, Robert *history educator*
Worden, Elizabeth Ann *artist, comedy writer, singer, playwright*

Corrigan
Murphy, Linda Marie *school district administrator*

Corsicana
Batchelor, J. Casey *career military officer*
Carroll, Ray Dean, Sr. *veterinarian*
Dyer, James Mason, Jr. *investment company executive*
Orsak, Charlie George *community college administrator*
Roberts, Nancy Mize *retired librarian, composer, pianist*
Sodd, Glenn *lawyer*

Cotulla
Gonzales, Pablo *pharmacist*

Crane
Crawford, Judy Carol *energy services company executive*
Dohlman, Dennis Raye *oil company executive*

Crockett
Jones, Don Carlton *insurance agent*
LaClair, Patricia Marie *physical education director, medical technician*

Crosby
Griffin, John Joseph, Jr. *chemist, video producer*

Crystal Beach
Dunn, Glennis Mae *retired writer, lyricist*

Cuero
Stubbs, Janine LaVelle *social science educator*

Cypress
Day, Robert Michael *oil company executive*
Drennan, Harry Joseph *minister*
Hamilton, Phyllis *principal*
Peck, Edwin Russell *real estate management executive*
Sorrell, Adrian Lloyd *education educator*

Dallas
Abney, Frederick Sherwood *lawyer*
†Abramson, Harold C. *federal judge*
Acker, Rodney *lawyer*
Adams, James R. *electronics company executive*
Adriance, Brenda *broadcast executive*
Agnich, Richard John *lawyer, electronics company executive*
Al-Hashimi, Ibtisam *oral scientist, educator*
Allen, John Carlton *minister*
Allen, Terry Devereux *urologist, educator*
Alvey, David Lynn *advertising executive, artist, curator, poet*
Anderson, Barbara McComas *lawyer*
Anderson, E. Karl *lawyer*
Anderson, Robert Theodore *music educator, organist*
Anderson, Ron Joe *hospital administrator, physician, educator*
Anglin, Michael Williams *lawyer*
Ardoin, John Louis *author*
Armour, James Lott *lawyer*
Arnold, George Lawrence *retired advertising company executive*
Ash, Mary Kay *cosmetics company executive*
Atkinson, Bill *artistic director*
Attanasio, John Baptist *law educator*
Augur, Marilyn Hussman *distribution executive*
†Azcarraga, Gaston *hotel executive*
Baggett, Steven Ray *lawyer*
Baggett, W. Mike *lawyer*
Bailon, Gilbert *newspaper editor*
†Baker, Robert Woodward *airline executive*
Barbee, Linton E. *lawyer*
Barnes, Robert Vertreese, Jr. *masonry contractor executive*
Barnett, Peter Ralph *health science facility administrator, dentist*
Barr, Richard Stuart *computer science and management science educator*
Bartlett, Richard Chalkley *business executive, writer, conservationist*
Bartley, David Anthony *electronics executive*
†Barton, Fritz Engel *plastic surgeon, educator*
Bartos, Jerry Garland *corporate executive, mechanical engineer*
Bashour, Fouad Anis *cardiology educator*
Bateman, Giles Hirst Litton *finance executive*
†Bates, Barry D. *career officer*
Bearden, Fred B(urnette), Jr. *marketing executive*
Beck, Luke Ferrell Wilson *insurance specialist*
Beidel, John Michael *headmaster, pastor*
Bell-Tolliver, LaVerne *social worker*
Bennett, Paul William *lawyer*
Bennett, Verna Green *employee relations executive*
Berkeley, Betty Life *gerontology educator*
Berkeley, Marvin H. *management educator, former university dean*
Bersano, Bob *newspaper editor*
Betts, Dianne Connally *economist, educator*
Beuttenmuller, Rudolf William *lawyer*
Bick, Rodger Lee *hematologist, oncologist, researcher, educator*
Bickel, John W., II *lawyer*
Birkeland, Bryan Collier *lawyer*
Blachly, Jack Lee *lawyer*
Blackistone, Kevin *sports columnist*
Blattner, Wolfram Georg Michael *meteorologist*
Blessen, Karen Alyce *free lance illustrator, designer*
Bliss, Robert Harms *lawyer*
Blomqist, Carl Gunnar *cardiologist*
Blount, Charles William, III *lawyer*
Blow, Steve *newspaper columnist*
Blue, J(ohn) Ronald *evangelical mission executive*
Blumenthal, Karen *newspaper executive*
Blumer, Donna *councilwoman*
Bollinger, Pamela Beemer *health facilities administrator*
Bolton, Kevin Michael *human resources executive*
Bond, Myron Humphrey *investment executive*
Bonelli, Anthony Eugene *former university dean*
Bonesio, Woodrow Michael *lawyer*
Bonney, Samuel Robert *lawyer*
Bonte, Frederick James *radiology educator, physician*
Boswell, George Marion, Jr. *orthopedist, health care facility administrator*
Bounds, Donald Leroy *landscape architect, educator*
†Boyle, Jane J. *federal judge*
Brachman, Malcolm K. *oil company executive*
Bradford, William Edward *oil field equipment manufacturing company executive*
Bradley, John Andrew *hospital management company executive*
Bradshaw, Lillian Moore *retired library director*
Brewer, David Madison *lawyer*
Brin, Royal Henry, Jr. *lawyer*
†Brinson, Barbara Ann *music educator*
Bromberg, John E. *lawyer*
Brooks, E. R. (Dick Brooks) *utility company executive*
Brooks, James Elwood *geologist, educator*
Brown, Gloria Vasquez *banker*
Brown, Michael Stuart *geneticist, educator, administrator*
Brown, Phillip James *systems engineer*
Brown, Ronald Lee *lawyer*
Brown, Stephen Bryan *real estate editor*
†Brown, Timothy Allen *executive search consulting company executive*
Browne, Richard Harold *statistician, consultant*
Bruene, Warren Benz *electronic engineer*
Bryant, John Wiley *former congressman*
Bryant, L. Gerald *health care administrator*
Buchholz, Donald Alden *stock brokerage company executive*
Buchmeyer, Jerry *federal judge*
Buickerood, Richard W. *park and recreation director*
Bumpas, Stuart Maryman *lawyer*
Burke, William Temple, Jr. *lawyer*
Burns, Sandra *lawyer, educator*
Burns, Scott *columnist*
Burnside, John Wayne *medical educator, university official*
Busbee, Kline Daniel, Jr. *law educator, lawyer, retired*
Caetano, Raul *psychiatrist, educator*
Cain, David *state senator, lawyer*
Calado, Miguel Maria *food company executive*
Caldwell, Thomas Howell, Jr. *accountant, financial management consultant*
Callahan, Rickey Don *business owner*
Cameron, Glenn Nilsson *loan executive*
Cansler, Denise Ann *real estate executive*
†Caramia, Philip Dominick *government official*
Carl, Robert E. *retired marketing company executive*
Carlton, Dean *lawyer*
Carman, George Henry *retired physician*
†Carnes, Joseph Sydney *clergyman*
Carpenter, Gordon Russell *lawyer, banker*
Carson, Virginia Hill *oil and gas executive*
Carter, Donald J. *wholesale distribution, manufacturing executive*
Carty, Donald J. *airline company executive*
Case, Thomas Louis *lawyer*
Cavanagh, Harrison Dwight *ophthalmic surgeon, medical educator*
Cave, Skip *company executive*
Chadbourne, John Frederick, Jr. *engineering executive*
Champion, Michael Ray *health facility administrator*
Chatterjee, Pal *electrical engineer, manufacturing executive*
Chawner, Lucia Martha *English educator*
Chen, Zhangxin John *mathematics educator*
Cheney, Dick (Richard Bruce Cheney) *former secretary of defense, former congressman*
Clardy, Thelma Sanders *lawyer*
Clark, John W. *lawyer*
Clark, Robert Murel, Jr. *lawyer*
Click, Bennie R. *protective services official*
Cline, Bobby James *insurance company executive*
Closser, Patrick Denton *radio evangelist, artist*
Cloud, Robert Royce *surgeon*
Cochran, George Calloway, III *retired bank executive, lawyer*
†Coggins, Paul Edward, Jr. *prosecutor*
Coldwell, Philip Edward *financial consultant*
Coleman, Lester L. *corporate lawyer*
Coleman, Robert Winston *lawyer*
Collins, Lynn M. *oncology clinical nurse specialist*
Collins, Michael James *investment company executive*
Comini, Alessandra *art historian, educator*
Conant, Allah B., Jr. *lawyer*
Conger, Sue Ann *computer information systems educator*
Cook, Gary Raymond *university president, clergyman*
Copley, Edward Alvin *lawyer*
Corman, Jack Bernard *lawyer, investment manager*
†Cortese, Anthony Joseph *sociologist*
Countryman, Edward Francis *historian, educator*
Courtney Westfall, Constance *lawyer*
Cox, James William *newspaper executive*
Cox, Richard D. *lawyer*
Cox, Rody P(owell) *medical educator, internist*
Coy, Christopher Hartmann *finance executive*
Crain, Gayla Campbell *lawyer*
Crain, John Walter *historian*
Creany, Cathleen Annette *television station executive*
Creel, Luther Edward, III *lawyer*
Crockett, Dodee Frost *brokerage firm executive*
Cromartie, Eric Ross *lawyer*
Crotty, Robert Bell *lawyer*
Crowley, James Worthington *retired lawyer, business consultant, investor*
Cruikshank, Thomas Henry *energy services and engineering executive*
Cullum, Colin Munro *psychiatry and neurology educator*
Cummins, James Duane *correspondent, media executive*
Curran, David Bernard, Jr. *real estate executive*
Curran, Geoffrey Michael *lawyer*
Dao, Khanh Phuong Thi *automotive executive, sales professional*
Davis, Clarice McDonald *lawyer*
Davis, Daisy Sidney *history educator*
Davis, Elise Miller (Mrs. Leo M. Davis) *writer*
Davis, Gregory T. *radio station executive*
Davis, Maria Teresa *architect*
Davis, Patricia M. *literacy educator*
Dawson, Edward Joseph *merger and acquisition executive*
Day, Maurice Jerome *automobile parts distributing company executive*
Decherd, Robert William *newspaper and broadcasting executive*
Dedman, Robert Henry *sales executive*
Dees, Tom Moore, II *internist*
Demarest, Sylvia M. *lawyer*
Denur, Jack Boaz *scientific researcher, scientific consultant*
DeOre, Bill *editorial cartoonist*
DeSpain, Becky Ann *dental educator*
Dicus, Brian George *lawyer*
Dillard, Robert Lionel, Jr. *lawyer, former life insurance executive*
Dillon, David Anthony *journalist, lecturer*
Dillon, Donald Ward *management consultant*
†Dir, Dave *professional soccer coach*
Dodson, George Wayne *computer company executive, consultant*
Doke, Marshall J., Jr. *lawyer*
Doran, Mark Richard *real estate financial executive*
Dorris, Carlos Eugene *chemicals executive*
Douglass, Frank Russell *lawyer*
Dozier, David Charles, Jr. *marketing public relations and advertising executive*
Drumm, David Gary *lawyer*
Dufner, Edward Joseph *business newswriter*
Dugger, Joe E. *accountant*
Duncan, Larry Edward *councilman*
Durham, Michael Jonathan *information technology company executive*
Durkee, Joe Worthington, Jr. *nuclear engineer*
Dutta, Paritosh Chandra *immunologist*
Dutton, Diana Cheryl *lawyer*
Dyer, Paul D. *municipal official*
Dyess, Bobby Dale *lawyer*
Dykeman, Alice Marie *public relations executive*
Eagar, Stephen Wade *television news anchor, reporter*
†Eatenson, Ervin Theodore *retired librarian*
Eaton, Michael William *lawyer, educator*
Eddleman, William Roseman *lawyer*
†Edmondson, James Howard *former insurance executive, investor*
Edwards, George Alva *physician, educator*
Eichenwald, Heinz Felix *physician*
Einspruch, Burton Cyril *psychiatrist*
Elder, Sheri Lynne *symphony orchestra official*
Elkins-Elliott, Kay *law educator*
Ellis, Alfred Wright (Al Ellis) *lawyer*
Ellis, James Alvis, Jr. *lawyer*
Ellis, June B. *human resource consultant*
Ellison, Luther Frederick *oil company executive*
Emerson, Walter Caruth *artist, educator*
Emery, Herschell Gene *lawyer*
Emmett, Michael *physician*
Engels, Lawrence Arthur *metals company executive*
Engleman, Donald James *lawyer, corporate executive*
Estabrook, Ronald Winfield *chemistry educator*
Etgen, Ann *ballet educator*
Evans, Linda Perryman *foundation adminstrator*
†Evans, William Will *hospitality executive*
Everbach, Otto George *lawyer*
Fagan, Peter Gail *occupational medicine physician*
Fanning, Barry Hedges *lawyer*
Farquhar, Robert Michael *lawyer*
Farrar, Beverly Jayne *psychologist*
Farrington, Bertha Louise *nursing administrator*
Farrington, Jerry S. *utility holding company executive*
†Fearon, Jeffrey Archer *surgeon*
Fegan, Jeffrey P. *airport executive*
Feld, Alan David *lawyer*
Feldman, H. Larry *lawyer*
Fenner, Suzan Ellen *lawyer*
Ferguson, Hugh W., III *lawyer*
Fielder, Charles Robert *oil industry executive*
Fifield, William O. *lawyer*
Finn, Peter Michael *television production executive*
Fish, A. Joe *federal judge*
Fitzwater, Sidney Allen *federal judge*
Fix, Douglas Martin *electrical engineer*
Flanagan, Christie Stephen *lawyer*
Flanary, Donald Herbert, Jr. *lawyer*
Flatt, Adrian Ede *surgeon*
Flegle, Jim L. *lawyer*
Flournoy, John Craig *newspaper reporter*
Fogelman, Evan Marr *literary agent, entertainment consultant, lawyer*
Fontana, Robert Edward *electrical engineering educator, retired air force officer*
Forêt, Randy Blaise *insurance executive*
Fortado, Michael George *lawyer*
Forward, Gordon E. *manufacturing executive*
Foster, Daniel W. *medical educator*
Foutch, Michael James *actor, dancer, lighting designer, producer*
France, Newell Edwin *former hospital administrator, consultant*
Frank, Steven Neil *chemist*
†Frano, Ronald A. *non-profit executive*
Free, Mary Moore *biological and medical anthropologist*
Freiberger, Katherine Guion *composer, retired piano educator*
French, Joseph Jordan, Jr. *lawyer*
Frenkel, Eugene Phillip *physician*
Freytag, Sharon Nelson *lawyer*
Friedberg, Errol Clive *pathology educator, researcher*
Friedheim, Stephen Bailey *public relations executive*
Fritze, Julius Arnold *marriage counselor*
Fry, Edward Irad *anthropology educator*
Fullingim, John Powers *consulting firm executive*
Fyfe, Alistair Ian *cardiologist, scientist, educator*
Gage, Tommy Wilton *pharmacologist, dentist, pharmacist, educator*
Gajewski, Ronald S. *consulting and training company executive*
Galloway, Randy *newspaper sports columnist*
Galt, John William *actor, writer*
Gant, Norman Ferrell, Jr. *obstetrician, gynecologist*
Gantt, James Raiford *thoracic surgeon*
†Gardner, Ricki *retail store official, minister*
Garison, Lynn Lassiter *real estate executive*
Garner, Paul Trantham *data services administrator*
Geddie, Tom *business communications consultant*
Gensheimer, Elizabeth Lucille *software specialist*
†Gentry, Jerry L. *manufacturing executive*
Gibbs, James Alanson *geologist*
Gidel, Robert Hugh *real estate investor*
Gifford, Porter William *retired construction materials manufacturing company executive*
Gilchrist, Henry *lawyer*
Gilder, Richard Earl *clinical information system administrator, data analyst*
Gilman, Alfred Goodman *pharmacologist, educator*
Gilmore, Jerry Carl *lawyer*
†Ginsberg, Carl Haralson *lawyer*
Glancy, Walter John *lawyer*
Glass, Carson McElyea *lawyer*
Glatstein, David *investment company executive*
Glendenning, Don Mark *lawyer*
Glines, Carroll Vane, Jr. *magazine editor*
Godfrey, Cullen Michael *lawyer*
Goldmann, James Allen *healthcare consultant*
Goldstein, Joseph Leonard *physician, medical educator, molecular genetics scientist*
Gonwa, Thomas Arthur *nephrologist, transplant physician*
Goodell, Sol *retired lawyer*
Goodson, Shannon Lorayn *behavioral scientist, author*
Goodstein, Barnett Maurice *lawyer*
Gores, Christopher Merrel *lawyer*
Goss, James Walter *oil company executive*
Gossen, Emmett Joseph, Jr. *motel chain executive, lawyer*
Gouge, Betty Merle *family therapist*
Govett, Brett Christopher *lawyer*
†Grahmann, Charles V. *bishop*
Grant, Joseph Moorman *finance executive*
Gratton, Patrick John Francis *oil company executive*
Graves, Deidra Nicole *international tax consultant*
Gray, James Larry *metals company executive*
Grayson, Walton George, III *retired lawyer*
Green, Cecil Howard *geophysicist, consultant, educator*
Griffith, Dotty (Dorothy Griffith Stephenson) *journalist, speaker*
Griffith, Rachel *neonatologist*
Griffitts, Keith Loyd *oil industry executive*
Grissom, Gerald Homer *lawyer, mediator, arbitrator*
Gross, Gary Neil *allergist, physician*
Gross, Harriet P. Marcus *religious studies and writing educator*
Grundy, Scott Montgomery *physician, medical educator*
Guerin, Dean Patrick *executive*
Guthrie, M. Philip *insurance company executive*
Haayen, Richard Jan *university official, insurance company executive*
Hall, Cheryl *newspaper editor*
Hallam, Robert G. *wholesale distribution executive*
Halpin, James *retail computer stores executive*
Hamilton, David Lee *retired environmental company executive*
Hammerlindl, Donald James *petroleum consultant*
Hammond, Herbert J. *lawyer*
Hamon, Richard Grady *lawyer*
Harbaugh, Lois Jensen *secondary education educator*
Hare, John *radio station executive*
Harkness, R. Kenneth *restaurant chain executive*
Harper, John Frank *cardiologist*
Harrell, Roy Harrison, Jr. *minister*
Harrington, Marion Ray *ophthalmologist*
Harris, Leon A., Jr. *writer*
Harris, Lucy Brown *accountant, consultant*
Harrison, Frank *former university president*
Hart, David Royce *structural engineer*
Hartnett, Thomas Robert, III *lawyer, author*
Hartnett, Will Ford *lawyer*
Haworth, Charles Ray *lawyer*
Hay, Betty Jo *civic worker*
Hay, Jess Thomas *retired finance company executive*
†Haydar, Ziad Rafic *geriatrician*
†Haydel, Raymond *computer animation artist*
Haynes, J. Neauell *clergyman, bishop*
Heatherley, Melody Ann *nursing administrator*
†Helfman, Carolyn Rae *middle school educator*
Helm, Phala Aniece *physiatrist*
†Henderson, Michael Howard *artist, educator*
Henkel, Kathryn Gundy *lawyer*
Hennessy, Daniel Kraft *lawyer*
Hensell, Linda Marie *environmental scientist*
Herbener, Mark Basil *bishop*
Hewlett, Gloria Louise *rancher, retired educator, civic volunteer*
Heydrick, Linda Carol *consulting company executive, editor*
Hicks, Donald W., Sr. *councilman*
Hicks, Marion Lawrence, Jr. (Larry Hicks) *lawyer*
†Hicks, Thomas O. *buyout firm executive, professional baseball team executive*
Higginbotham, Patrick Errol *federal judge*
Hilgemann, Donald William *medical educator*
Hill, Jesse Hoyt *training specialist, economics & business educator*
Hinshaw, Chester John *lawyer*
Hirsch, Laurence Eliot *construction executive, mortgage banker*
Hirsh, Bernard *supply company executive, consultant*
Hitt, David Hamilton *retired hospital executive*
Hogan, Thomas Victor *insurance company executive*
Holleman, Sandy Lee *religious organization administrator*
Holl-Matthews, Dee Lynn *career counselor, psychotherapist, personal development and success coach*
Holman, James *allergist, immunologist*
Holmes, Bert Otis E., Jr. *retired newspaperman*
Holmes, James Hill, III *lawyer*
Honea, Floyd Franklin *lawyer*
Honkanen, Jari Olavi *electrical engineer*
Horchow, S(amuel) Roger *marketing consultant*
Horton, Paul Bradfield *lawyer*
Howell, Bradley Sue *librarian*
Howie, John Robert *lawyer*
Hranitzky, Rachel Robyn *lawyer*
Hudgins, Louise Nan *art educator*
Huey, Ward L(igon), Jr. *media executive*
Huffman, Gregory Scott Combest *lawyer*
Hughes, Keith William *banking and finance company executive*
Hughes, Vester Thomas, Jr. *lawyer*
Hughes, Waunell McDonald (Mrs. Delbert E. Hughes) *retired psychiatrist*
Humble, Monty Garfield *lawyer*
Hunt, Ray L. *petroleum company executive*
Hunter, Kermit *writer, former university dean*
Hunter, Robert Grams *retired English language educator*
Hurd, Eric Ray *rheumatologist, internist, educator*
Ibach, Robert Daniel, Jr. *library director*
Ingram, Osmond Carraway, Jr. *minister*
Jackson, Alphonso *utility company executive*
Jaffe-Blackney, Sandra Michelle *special education educator*
†Jaksa, David M. *wireless network company official*
Jayson, Melinda Gayle *lawyer*
Jennings, Dennis Raymond *accountant*
Jennings, Susan Jane *lawyer*
Jialal, Ishwarlal *medical educator*
Jobe, Larry Alton *financial company executive*
Johnson, Alonzo Bismark *city official, court administrator*
†Johnson, David W. (Dave) *hotel facility executive*

Johnson, James Joseph Scofield *lawyer, judge, educator, author*
Johnson, Kevin Orlin *publisher, writer*
Johnson, Murray H. *optometrist, researcher, consultant, lecturer*
Johnson, Robert Lee, Jr. *physician, educator, researcher*
Jones, Everett Riley, Jr. *oil company executive*
Jones, Rosemarie Frieda *service executive*
Joplin, Julian Mike *lawyer*
Jordan, Karen Leigh *newspaper travel editor*
†Jordan, Matt *professional soccer player*
Jordan, William Davis *lawyer*
Juergens, Bonnie Kay *not-for-profit company executive*
†Kaplan, Jeffrey A. *federal judge*
Karayanis, Plato Steven *opera company executive*
Kearney, Douglas Charles *lawyer, journalist*
Keath, (Martin) Travis *business valuation consultant*
Keck, Philip Walter *transportation executive*
Keiser, Robert Lee *gas and oil industry executive*
Keithley, Bradford Gene *lawyer*
Kelleher, Herbert David *airline executive, lawyer*
Kelly, Robert Vincent, III *transportation executive*
Kemper, Robert Van *anthropologist, educator*
Kendall, Joe *federal judge*
Kennedy, Marc J. *lawyer*
Kent, David Charles *lawyer*
Kilby, Jack St. Clair *electrical engineer*
Killam, Jill Minervini *oil and gas company executive*
Kindberg, Shirley Jane *pediatrician*
King, Clarence Carleton, II *healthcare executive*
Kinnebrew, Jackson Metcalfe *lawyer*
Kinser, Katherine Anne *lawyer*
Kirby, James Edmund, Jr. *theology educator*
Kirby, Le Grand Carney, III *lawyer, accountant*
Kirk, Ron *mayor, lawyer*
†Kirk, Ronald *mayor*
Kitner, David N. *lawyer*
Klehfoth, Jay Gordon *publisher, writer, consultant*
Kline, George William, II *television producer*
Kneipper, Richard Keith *lawyer*
Knight, Gary Charles *mechanical engineer*
Kobdish, George Charles *lawyer*
Kohl, Kathleen Allison Barnhart *lawyer*
Kolb, Nathaniel Key, Jr. *architect*
Kollmeyer, Kenneth Robert *surgeon*
Korba, Robert W. *communications executive*
Kruse, Ann Gray *computer programer*
Kuhn, Willis Evan, II *lawyer, mediator*
Kutner, Janet *art critic, book reviewer*
Lacy, John Ford *lawyer*
Lafving, Brian Douglas *lawyer*
Lake, Joseph Edward *ambassador*
Lakhanpal, Sharad *physician*
Lam, Chun Hung *finance educator, consultant*
Lan, Donald Paul, Jr. *lawyer*
Lancaster, John Lynch, III *lawyer*
Land, Geoffrey Allison *science administrator*
Landry, Tom (Thomas Wade Landry) *former professional football coach*
Lane, Alvin Huey, Jr. *management consultant*
Lane, Shawn Lanard *journalist, motivational speaker*
Lang, Douglas Stewart *lawyer*
†Langdale, Mark *hotel executive*
Langer, Ralph Ernest *journalist, newspaper executive and editor*
Lang-Miers, Elizabeth Ann *lawyer*
Laramore, Evelyn K. *nursing supervisor*
Laves, Alan Leonard *lawyer*
†Lawrence, Annette *artist*
Lebos, Richard Jesse *lawyer*
Lee, Jimmy Che-Yung *city planner*
Leedom, John Nesbett *distribution company executive, state senator*
Leeper, Harold Harris *arbitrator*
Leigh-Manuell, Robert Allen *training executive, educator*
Levenson, Stanley Richard *public relations and advertising executive*
Levin, Hervey Phillip *lawyer*
Levin, Richard C. *lawyer*
Levine, Harold *lawyer*
Levinson, Mark Bradley *corporate professional*
Lewis, Jerry M. *psychiatrist, educator*
Lichliter, Warren Eugene *surgeon, educator*
†Lippe, George L. *company executive*
Litton, Andrew *musical director*
London, W(illiam) Boyd, Jr. *investment company executive*
Long, Joann Morey *publishing company executive, editor*
Lotzer, Gerald Balthazar *lawyer*
Lowe, John Stanley *lawyer, educator*
Lumry, William Raymond *physician, allergist*
Lutes, Benjamin Franklin, Jr. *investor*
†Mackenzie, Nanci *gas company executive*
Mackey, Stacy Leigh *accounting assistant*
MacMahon, Paul *advertising executive*
Maddoux, Marlin *broadcast executive, journalist, author*
Maddrey, Willis Crocker *medical educator, internist, academic administrator, consultant, researcher*
Maguire, Kevin Jerome *lawyer*
Mahadeva, Manoranjan *financial executive, accountant*
Mahr, George Joseph *financial service executive, real estate developer*
Mallory, Barbara Len *councilwoman*
Maloney, Robert B. *federal judge*
Malorzo, Thomas Vincent *lawyer*
Malouf, Edward Wayne *lawyer*
Mandeville, Hubert Turner, Jr. *oil company executive*
Mankoff, Ronald Morton *lawyer*
Margerison, Richard Wayne *diversified industrial company executive*
Margolin, Solomon Begelfor *pharmacologist*
Maris, Stephen S. *lawyer, educator*
Marshall, John Harris, Jr. *geologist, oil company executive*
Martin, Carol Jacquelyn *educator, artist*
Martin, Jack *physician*
Martin, Richard Kelley *lawyer*
Mason, Barry Jean *retired banker*
Massman, Richard Allan *lawyer*
Matthews, Clark J(io), II *retail executive, lawyer*
May, William Francis *ethicist, educator*
†Mayo, Thomas William *law educator*
†Mays, Edwin David *technical consulting company executive*
Maza, Michael William *newspaper editor, columnist*
McCally, Charles Richard *construction company executive*
McCarthy, Michael Joseph *communications company executive*
Mc Clelland, Robert Nelson *surgeon, educator*
McClure, Frederick Donald *investment banker, lawyer*
McCurley, Mary Johanna *lawyer*
McDonald, Michael Scott *lawyer*
Mc Elhaney, John Hess *lawyer*
McElvain, David Plowman *retired manufacturing company financial executive*
McElyea, Jacquelyn Suzanne *accountant, real estate consultant*
McGarry, Charles William *lawyer*
McGowan, Patrick Francis *lawyer*
†McGuire, Robert C. *federal judge*
McKnight, Joseph Webb *law educator, historian*
McKnight, Steven Lanier *molecular biologist*
McLane, David Glenn *lawyer*
†McNamara, Anne H. *lawyer, corporate executive*
McNamara, Lawrence John *lawyer*
McNamara, Martin Burr *lawyer, oil and gas company executive*
McTeer, Robert D., Jr. *banker*
McWilliams, Mike C. *lawyer*
Mears, Rona Robbins *lawyer*
Mebus, Robert Gwynne *lawyer*
Megredy, Millard Howard *retired aviation director, realtor, consultant*
Melton, Robert W. *city auditor*
†Meltzer, Larry Alan *public relations executive*
Menges, John Kenneth, Jr. *lawyer*
Menter, M(artin) Alan *dermatologist*
Meyer, Ferdinand Charles, Jr. *lawyer*
Mighell, Kenneth John *lawyer*
Miles, Ray *telecommunications executive, educator*
Miller, Dodd *protective services official*
Miller, Jo Carolyn Dendy *family and marriage counselor, educator*
Millican, Chestella Alvis Hudel *athletics educator*
Mills, Jerry Woodrow *lawyer*
Mitchell, Teddy Lee *physician*
†Mittlestet, Stephen *academic administrator*
Mong, Robert William, Jr. *media executive*
†Monk, Cody James *writer*
Montgomery, Kathy MacLean *international business consultant*
Montgomery, Philip O'Bryan, Jr. *pathologist*
Moore, Stanley Ray *lawyer*
Moore, Thomas Joseph *financial company executive*
Morse-McNeely, Patricia *poet, writer, middle school educator*
Moss, Robert Williams *real estate developer*
Mow, Robert Henry, Jr. *lawyer*
Mueller, Mark Christopher *lawyer*
Mullinax, Otto B. *retired lawyer*
Murphy, John Joseph *manufacturing company executive*
Murphy, Randall Kent *training consultant*
Murray, John William, Jr. *writer, legal investigator*
Murrell, William Ivan *accountant*
Naor, Daniel *management consultant*
Neaves, William Barlow *cell biologist, educator*
Nelson, Donald Arvid (Nellie Nelson) *professional basketball coach*
Nelson, Jill E. *health care consultant, health facility administrator, researcher*
New, William Neil *physician, retired naval officer*
Nichols, Henry Louis *lawyer*
Novack, Lynne Dominick *academic and international programs administrator*
†Nussbaum, Paul A. *hospitality executive*
Nye, Erle Allen *utilities executive, lawyer*
O'Bannion, Mindy Martha Martin *nurse*
O'Brien, George Aloysius, Jr. *paper company executive*
Oden, William Bryant *bishop, educator*
Odom, Floyd Clark *surgeon*
Osborn, Jacqueline Elizabeth *water treatment systems company executive*
Osborne, Burl *newspaper publisher, editor*
Osen, Gregory Alan *water conditioning company executive*
Owens, Rodney Joe *lawyer*
Page, Richard Leighton *cardiologist, medical educator, researcher*
Palmer, Christine (Clelia Rose Venditti) *operatic singer, performer, pianist, vocal instructor, lecturer, entertainer*
Palmer, Philip Isham, Jr. *lawyer*
Parent, David Hill *investment company executive*
Parker, James Francis *lawyer, airline executive*
Parkey, Robert Wayne *radiology and nuclear medicine educator, research radiologist*
Parmerlee, Mark S. *food service executive*
Patterson, Ronald Paul *publishing company executive, clergyman*
Pauley, Shirley Stewart *religious organization executive*
Pearce, Ronald *retired cosmetic company executive*
†Pearson, Robert Lawrence *executive recruiter*
Pederson, Rena *newspaper editor*
Pell, Jonathan Laurence *artistic administrator*
†Perkins, Judson W. *real estate company executive*
Perot, H. Ross, Jr. *real estate developer, sports team executive*
Perry, Anne Gordon *arts and humanities educator, writer*
Perry, Edward Gordon, III *record production executive*
Perry, George Wilson *oil and gas company executive*
Perry, Malcolm Oliver *vascular surgeon*
Peterson, Edward Adrian *lawyer*
Pettey, Walter Graves, III *lawyer*
Pew, John Glenn, Jr. *lawyer*
Phelan, Robin Eric *lawyer*
Phelps, Robert Frederick, Jr. *lawyer*
Philipson, Herman Louis, Jr. *investment banker*
Phillips, Betty Lou (Elizabeth Louise Phillips) *author, interior designer*
Phillips, Margaret A. *pharmacology educator*
Pike, Kenneth Lee *linguist, educator*
Pingree, Bruce Douglas *lawyer*
Pinson, William Meredith, Jr. *pastor, writer, administrator*
Pippin, John Joseph *cardiologist*
Pistor, Charles Herman, Jr. *former banker, academic administrator*
Pleasant, James Scott *lawyer*
Poindexter, Barbara Glennon *secondary school educator*
Portman, Glenn Arthur *lawyer*
Poss, Mary *mayor*
Powell, Boone, Jr. *hospital administrator*
Powell, Larry Randall *columnist*
Powell, Michael Vance *lawyer*
†Preston, Donna Joan *dietitian, consultant*
Price, John Aley *lawyer*
Price, Robert Eben *judge*
†Price, Steve *advertising executive*
Pride, Charley *singer*
Prothro, Jerry Robert *lawyer*
Pruitt, Brad Alexander *business executive*
Pruzzo-Hawkins, Judith Josephine *office manager*
Pryor, Richard Walter *telecommunications executive, retired air force officer*
†Puente-Brancato, Gina I. *concession company executive*
Purkey, Thomas Eugene *social worker*
Purnell, Charles Giles *lawyer*
Purnell, Maurice Eugene, Jr. *lawyer*
Qualls, June Carol *elementary education educator*
Race, George Justice *pathology educator*
Raggio, Kenneth Gaylord *lawyer, mediator*
Raggio, Louise Ballerstedt *lawyer*
Rainey, William E., II *medical educator*
Ray, Bradley Stephen *petroleum geologist*
Read, James Carroll *geneticist educator*
Reagan, Barbara Benton *economics educator*
Rees, Frank William, Jr. *architect*
Reid, Langhorne, III *merchant banker*
Reinert, James A. *entomologist, educator*
Reinganum, Marc Richard *finance educator*
Rice, Darrel Alan *lawyer*
Richards, Jeanne Herron *artist*
Richards, Stanford Harvey *advertising agency executive, design studio executive*
Richardson, Dennise Marie *physician assistant*
Ries, Edward Richard *petroleum geologist, consultant*
Rinne, Austin Dean *insurance company executive*
Roach, John D. C. *manufacturing company executive*
Roach-Reeves, Catharyn Petitt *librarian, educator*
Robb, Aaron David *child protective services investigator*
Robbins, Jane Lewis *elementary school educator*
Robbins, Ray Charles *manufacturing company executive*
Roberts, Harry Morris, Jr. *lawyer*
Robertson, Beverly Carruth *retired steel company executive*
Robertson, Calvin Coolidge, Sr. *pastor*
Robertson, Herbert Chapman, Jr. *geoscience consulting company executive*
Robertson, Jane Ryding *marketing executive*
Robertson, Ted Zanderson *judge*
Robinson, Edgar Allen *retired oil company executive*
Robinson, Hugh Granville *consulting management company executive*
Rochon, John Philip *cosmetics company executive*
Rohrich, Rodney James *plastic surgeon, educator*
†Rollins, Richard A. *religious association administrator*
Roman, Patricia Ann *sculptor*
†Romero, John *computer game company executive*
Romero, Jorge Antonio *neurologist, educator*
Rosenberg, Roger Newman *neurologist, educator*
Ross, Elliott M. *pharmacology, researcher, educator*
Rosson, Glenn Richard *building products and furniture company executive*
Routman, Daniel Glenn *business development executive, lawyer*
Roy, Clarence Leslie *landscape architect*
†Rubin, Warren Lloyd *retail sales executive*
Rubottom, Roy Richard, Jr. *retired diplomat and educator, consultant*
Rushton, Lynn Noelle *artist*
Rutherford, Paris *planning and urban development executive*
Ryan, Timothy Christopher *anchor, reporter*
St. John, Bill Dean *diversified equipment and services company executive*
Salazar, Ramiro S. *library administrator*
Salazar, Steve *lawyer*
Salerno, Philip Adams *information systems specialist*
Sammons, Elaine D. *corporate executive*
†Samson, Duke Staples *neurosurgeon*
Sanders, Harold Barefoot, Jr. *federal judge*
Sanderson, William Fletcher, Jr. *federal judge*
Santamaria, Rose Faye *real estate agent*
Savage, Wallace Hamilton *lawyer*
Schecter, Arnold Joel *preventive medicine educator*
Schenkel, Pete *food company executive*
Schmid, Frances M. *lawyer, law librarian, nurse*
Schreiber, Sally Ann *lawyer*
Schulze, Richard Hans *engineering executive, environmental engineer*
Schwartz, Irving Donn *architect*
Schwartz, Marilyn *columnist*
Scuro, Joseph E., Jr. *lawyer*
Sealander, John Arthur *writer, educator*
See, Robert Fleming, Jr. *lawyer*
Seldin, Donald Wayne *physician, educator*
Selinger, Jerry Robin *lawyer*
Shahsavari, Darius *oil and gas company executive*
Sharp, William Wheeler *geologist*
Shaw, Don Wayne *physical chemist*
†Sheffield, Cinnamon *coach, dance educator, choreographer*
Sheinberg, Israel *computer company executive*
Sherwood, Rhonda Griffin *playwright, writer, designer*
Shimer, Daniel Lewis *corporate executive*
Shoup, Andrew James, Jr. *oil company executive*
Sides, Jack Davis, Jr. *lawyer*
Siegel, Mark Jordan *lawyer*
Siegel, Thomas Louis *lawyer*
Siegfried, Tom *newspaper editor*
Silcox, Frances Eleanor *museum and exhibits planning consultant*
Silverman, Alan Kenneth *dermatologist, consultant*
Simmang, Clifford Liles *surgeon*
Simon, Theodore Ronald *physician, medical educator*
Sizer, Phillip Spelman *consultant, retired oil field services executive*
Skaggs, Ronald Lloyd *architect*
Sloman, Marvin Sherk *lawyer*
Smiles, Ronald *management educator*
Smith, Barry Samuel *physiatrist*
Smith, Brian *lawyer*
Smith, David Lee *newspaper editor*
Smith, Frank Tupper *lawyer*
Smith, James G. *minister, educator*
Smith, Milton Clark, Jr.
Smith, Sue Frances *newspaper editor*
Smith, Valerie Gay *school counselor*
Smith, William Randolph (Randy Smith) *health care management executive*
Smither, Edward Murray *art consultant, appraiser*
Snead, Richard Thomas *restaurant company executive*
Solender, Robert Lawrence *financial executive*
Solis, Jorge Antonio *federal judge*
Solomon, William Tarver *general construction company executive*
Spears, Robert Fields *lawyer*
†Spencer, Mary Helen *interior designer*
Spiegel, Lawrence Howard *advertising executive*
Staber, Dorothee Beatrice *administrative assistant*
Stacy, Dennis William *architect*
Stage, Key Hutchinson *urologist*
Stalcup, Joe Alan *lawyer, clergyman*
Steinberg, Lawrence Edward *lawyer*
Stembridge, Vernie A(lbert) *pathologist, educator*
Stepherson, Karen Evette *administrative assistant*
†Stern, Andrew Milton *public relations executive*
Stewart, Wesley Holmgreen *judge, lawyer*
Stilwell, John Quincy *lawyer*
Stinnett, Mark Allan *lawyer*
Stockard, James Alfred *lawyer*
Stone, Donald James *retired retail executive*
Stone, Marvin Jules *physician, educator*
Storey, Charles Porter *lawyer*
Stratton, Robert *financial company executive, physicist*
Stump, Ann Louise B. *nurse*
Sudhof, Thomas C. *molecular genetics educator, neuroscientist*
Sullivan, Thomas Patrick *lawyer*
Sundgaard, Arnold Olaf *playwright*
Talmadge, John Mills *physician*
Tannebaum, Samuel Hugo *accountant*
Taylor, Herman Ivan, Jr. *defense company manager*
Taylor, Martha Ellen *private school educator*
Terry, Marshall Northway, Jr. *English language educator, author*
Thau, William Albert, Jr. *lawyer*
Thomas, Chester Wiley *special agent*
Thomas, Paul Lindsley *composer, organist, music director*
†Thomas, Philip Robinson *management consulting company executive*
Thomas, Sarah Elaine *elementary music educator*
Thompson, Charles Kerry *company executive*
Thompson, Jesse Eldon *vascular surgeon*
†Tolle, John B. *federal judge*
Tong, Alex Waiming *immunologist*
Treasure, Suzanne Marie *marketing and sales professional, writer, poet*
Trevino, Lee Buck *professional golfer*
True, Roy Joe *lawyer*
Tubb, James Clarence *lawyer*
Tucker, John Edward *architect, consultant*
Tucker, L. Dan *lawyer*
Turner, Ralph James *obstetrician-gynecologist*
Turner, Robert Gerald *university president*
Tygrett, Howard Volney, Jr. *lawyer*
Uhr, Jonathan William *immunologist, educator, researcher*
Ussery, Terdema L. *professional sports team executive*
Valentine, Foy Dan *clergyman*
Vanderveld, John, Jr. *international business development specialist*
Vega, Roberto *physics educator*
Verner, Jimmy Lynn, Jr. *lawyer, expert witness*
Vetter, James George, Jr. *lawyer*
Vitetta, Ellen Shapiro *microbiologist educator, immunologist*
Vogel, Donald Stanley *gallery executive, artist*
†Walker, Robert Martin *writer, minister*
Walkowiak, Vincent Steven *lawyer*
Walne, Alan *councilman*
Wasserman, Richard Lawrence *pediatrician, educator*
Waters, Rollie Odell *management consultant*
†Waterston, Judy C. *healthcare administrator*
Weakley, Clare George, Jr. *insurance executive, theologian, entrepreneur*
Weaver, Betsy Dianne *elementary school educator*
Weeks, Jerome Christopher *writer, drama, book critic*
Weinberger, Blanche Raphael *public relations executive*
Weinkauf, William Carl *instructional media company executive*
Wells, Leonard Nathaniel David, Jr. *lawyer*
Wenrich, John William *college president*
Werner, Seth Mitchell *advertising executive*
White, Irene *insurance professional*
White, James Richard *lawyer*
Whitehead, Michael Richard *painter*
Whitson, James Norfleet, Jr. *retired diversified company executive*
Wilber, Robert Edwin *corporate executive*
Wilde, Patrick Joseph *administrator*
Wildenthal, C(laud) Kern *physician, educator*
Wiles, Charles Preston *minister*
Williams, Bryan *university dean, medical educator*
Williams, Charles Edward *engineer*
Williams, James Alexander *lawyer*
Williams, Martha Spring *psychologist*
†Williams, Sterling L. *computer software executive*
Willingham, Clark Suttles *lawyer*
Wilson, Claude Raymond, Jr. *lawyer*
Wilson, Jean Donald *endocrinologist, educator*
Winters, J. Otis *oil industry consultant*
†Wise, Kurt Alan *educator*
Wise, Marvin Jay *lawyer*
†Wood, Rodney W. *military officer*
†Woolley, (Lowell) Bryan *author, journalist*
Wuntch, Philip Samuels *journalist, film critic*
Wyly, Charles Joseph, Jr. *corporate executive*
Yanagisawa, Samuel Tsuguo *electronics executive*
Yarbrough, Fletcher Leftwich *lawyer*
Yeslow, Rosemarie *real estate professional*
Young, Barney Thornton *lawyer*
Young, Julia Anne *librarian, elementary education educator*
Young, Kay Lynn *dance educator, small business owner*
Ziff, Morris *internist, rheumatologist, educator*
Zimmerman, S(amuel) Morton (Mort Zimmerman) *electrical and electronics engineering executive*
Zumwalt, Richard Dowling *flour mill executive*

De Soto

Aars, Rallin James *management, business development, marketing communications executive, consultant*
Ball, Millicent Joan (Penny Ball) *multimedia developer*
Harrington, Betty Byrd *entrepreneur*
Jackson, Johnny W. *minister*
Lewis, Paul Wesley *minister*
Tyrer-Ferraro, Polly Ann *music instructor, software developer*

Decatur

Jordan, Linda Susan Darnell *elementary school educator*

Deer Park

Deutsch, Lawrence Ira *minister*
Sandstrum, Steve D. *engineering executive*

Simpson, Dennis Dwayne *psychologist, educator*
Smaistrla, Jean Ann *family therapist*
†Smith, Gene A. *history educator, writer*
Smith, William Burton *retired chemist, educator*
Strength, Danna Elliott *nursing educator*
Suggs, Marion Jack *minister, college dean*
Tatum, Stephen Lyle *lawyer*
Teegarden, Kenneth Leroy *clergyman*
Thompson, Carson R. *retail and manufacturing company executive*
Thornton, Charles Victor *metals executive*
Tillman, Massie Monroe *federal judge*
Tinsley, Jackson Bennett *newspaper editor*
Tobey, Martin Alan *cardiologist*
Toulouse, Mark Gene *religion educator*
Tracy, J. David *lawyer, educator*
Treviño, Fernando Manuel *medical educator*
Tucker, William Edward *academic administrator, minister*
Turner, Loyd Leonard *advertising executive, public relations executive*
Turner, R(alph) Chip *public relations and telecommunications executive, religious studies educator*
Turner, Wesley R. *publishing executive*
Underwood, Harvey Cockrell *real estate executive*
Von Rosenberg, Gary Marcus, Jr. *parochial school educator*
Wallach, David Michael *lawyer*
Walwer, Frank Kurt *dean, legal educator*
Warren, Peter Gigstad *financial consultant, investment advisor*
Watson, Robert Francis *lawyer*
Wayland, Sharon Morris *law librarian*
Webb, James Robert *strategic management consultant*
Webb, Theodore Stratton, Jr. *aerospace scientist, consultant*
Weekley, Frederick Clay, Jr. *lawyer*
Wertz, Spencer K. *philosophy educator*
Weyandt, Linda Jane *anesthetist, physician*
Whillock, David Everett *film and television educator, consultant*
White, Warren Travis *educational consultant firm executive*
Whitney, William Bernard *lawyer*
Wilkie, Valleau, Jr. *foundation executive*
Williams, Billie Barron *architect*
Williamson, Philip *apparel executive*
Willis, Doyle Henry *state legislator, lawyer*
Wilson-Webb, Nancy Lou *adult education administrator*
Windham, Thomas *protective services official*
Woodward, Ralph Lee, Jr. *historian, educator*
Worcester, Donald Emmet *history educator, author*
Wynn, Susan Rudd *physician*
Yanni, John Michael *pharmacologist*
Zahn, Donald Jack *lawyer*

Fredericksburg
Malec, William Frank *utilities company executive*
Thompson, Glenn Judean *retired library science educator*

Freeport
Baskin, William Gresham *counselor, music educator, vocalist*
Tsai, Tom Chunghu *chemical engineer*

Friendswood
Kennedy, Priscilla Ann *elementary school educator*
†White, John Albert *retired history educator*
Wood, Loren Edwin *aerospace engineering administrator, consultant*

Frisco
Bloskas, John D. *financial executive*
Larsen, David Wayne *telecommunications industry executive*
Wicker, James Robert *minister*

Gainesville
Dietz, David W. *elementary education educator*
Killian, Lawrence Harding (Larry H.), II (Larry H. Killian) *sculptor*

Galena Park
Price, Joe Sealy *law enforcement officer*

Galveston
Arens, James F. *anesthesiologist, educator*
†Avery, A. Nelson *physician, medical educator*
Bailey, Byron James *otolaryngologist, medical association executive*
Baker, Robert Ernest, Jr. *retired foundation executive*
Banet, Charles Henry *academic administrator, clergyman*
Barratt, Ernest Stoelting *psychologist, educator*
Bernier, George Matthew, Jr. *physician, medical educator, medical school dean*
Bonchev, Danail Georgiev *chemist, educator*
Brasier, Allan R. *medical educator*
Bryan, George Thomas *pediatrician, academic administrator*
Bungo, Michael William *physician, educator, science administrator*
Burns, Chester Ray *medical history educator*
Cabanas, Elizabeth Ann *nutritionist*
Caldwell, Garnett Ernest *lawyer*
Calverley, John Robert *physician, educator*
Carrier, Warren Pendleton *retired university chancellor, writer*
Chonmaitree, Tasnee *pediatrician, educator, infectious disease specialist*
Clayton, William Howard *retired university president*
Darst, Mary Lou *elementary education educator*
Dawson, Earl Bliss *obstetrics and gynecology educator*
Ewing, George H. *pipeline company executive*
Fisher, Seymour *psychologist, educator*
†Frederickson, Christopher John *neuroscientist*
†Froeschner, John R. *federal judge*
Giam, Choo-Seng *marine science educator*
Goodwin, Jean McClung *psychiatrist*
Goodwin, Sharon Ann *academic administrator*
Gorenstein, David G. *chemistry and biochemistry educator*
†Hargraves, Martha Ann *health services administrator, educator*
Harrison, Dony *poet, writer, journalist, lecturer*
Heins, Sister Mary Frances *educational administrator, nun*
Herndon, David N. *surgeon*
Hillman, Gilbert Rothschild *medical educator*
Hilton, James Gorton *pharmacologist*
Ivy, Berrynell Baker *critical care nurse*
James, Thomas Naum *cardiologist, educator*
Kent, Samuel B. *federal judge*
Kurosky, Alexander *biochemist, educator*
LaGrone, Lavenia Whiddon *chemist, real estate broker*
Lawrence, Kathy *medical, surgical, and radiology nurse*
Levin, William Cohn *hematologist, former university president*
Luo, Hong Yuan *biomedical scientist, educator*
Luthra, Gurinder Kumar *osteopath*
May, Joy Elaine *recreational facility executive*
Monts, Elizabeth Rose *insurance company executive*
Newman, Frances Moody *foundation executive*
Otis, John James *civil engineer*
Pearl, William Richard Emden *pediatric cardiologist*
Phillips, Linda Goluch *plastic surgeon, educator, researcher*
Prakash, Satya *biology educator*
†Rice, James Carter *medical educator*
Ryan, James Gilbert *historian, educator, writer*
Sandstead, Harold Hilton *medical educator*
Schreiber, Melvyn Hirsh *radiologist*
Schwartz, Aaron Robert *lawyer, former state legislator*
Selig, Oury Levy *financial consultant*
Shannon, Mary Lou *adult health nursing educator*
Sheppard, Louis Clarke *biomedical engineer, educator*
Shope, Robert Ellis *epidemiology educator*
Short, James Ferebee *portfolio manager*
Smith, Edgar Benton *physician*
Smith, Eric Morgan *virology educator*
Stobo, John David *physician, educator*
Suzuki, Fujio *immunologist, educator, researcher*
Thompson, Edward Ivins Brad *biological chemistry and genetics educator, molecular endocrinologist, department chairman*
Valentine, John Henry, Jr. *foundation president, secondary education educator*
Vie, George William, III *lawyer*
Welch, Ronald J. *actuary*
Wells, Robert Louis *priest*
White, Robert Brown *medical educator*
Willis, William Darrell, Jr. *neurophysiologist, educator*
Würsig, Bernd Gerhard *marine biology educator*
Zimmerman, Roger Joseph *fishery biologist*

Ganado
†Sanford, Annette Amelia *writer*

Garland
Baker, John *director engineering*
Bickerstaff, Jeffery Wayne *municipal official*
Bohli, Harry John, Jr. *structural engineer, consultant*
Brockles, Arge James *pastor, educator*
Christensen, Allan Robert *electrical engineer, enrolled agent*
Driver, Joe L. *state legislator, insurance agent*
Duren, Michael *cardiologist*
Foster, Rebecca Anne Hodges *secondary school educator*
Goheen, Debra Elaine *secondary education educator*
Haynsworth, Robert F., Jr. *anesthesiologist*
Hinton, Charles *lawyer*
Hughes, Arthur Hyde *accountant, consultant*
Irby, Holt *lawyer*
Kauffman, George *financial administrator*
Lord, Jacqueline Ward *accountant, photographer, artist*
McGill, Maurice Leon *financial executive*
McGrath, James Thomas *real estate investment company executive*
Sims, Judy *software company executive*
Spence, Jim *mayor*
Tabor, Beverly Ann *retired elementary school educator*

Georgetown
Aadnesen, Christopher *railroad company executive, consultant*
Bryce, William Delf *lawyer*
Busfield, Roger Melvil, Jr. *retired trade association executive, educator*
Camp, Thomas Harley *economist*
Elder, John Blanton *psychologist, clergyman*
Girvin, Eb Carl *biology educator*
Graham, Charles Passmore *retired army officer*
Manning, Robert Thomas *physician, educator*
Sawyer, William Dale *physician, educator, university dean, foundation administrator*
Shilling, Roy Bryant, Jr. *academic administrator*
Weyrauch, Paul Turney *retired army officer, educator*
Wilkerson, James Neill *lawyer*

Graham
Cagle, Paulette Bernice *mental health administrator and psychologist*

Granbury
Almy, Earle Vaughn, Jr. (Buddy Almy) *real estate executive*
Carder, Thomas Allen *nuclear energy industry emergency planner, educator*
Garrison, Truitt B. *architect*
†Jones, Collette Ann *artist*
Mainord, William Ronald *pilot*
McWilliams, Chris Pater Elissa *elementary school educator*

Grand Prairie
Loo, Maritta Louise *military officer, nurse*
Rose, Douglas Raymond *minister*

Grapevine
Carter, Terri Gay Manns *Latin language educator*
Gibbons, Michael Lawrence *software engineer*
Hirsh, Cristy J. *school counselor*
Holley, Cyrus Helmer *management consulting service executive*
Ketter, Ronald George *political science educator, consultant*
Killebrew, James Robert *architectural engineering firm executive*
Kraft, Karen Ann *secondary school educator*
Stack, George Joseph *philosopher, writer*

Greenville
Johnston, John Thomas *engineering executive*
Rice, Melva Gene *retired education educator*

Groesbeck
Gilbert, Edith Harmon *medical, surgical and occupational health nurse*

Gun Barrel City
Smith, Thelma Tina Harriette *gallery owner, artist*

Hallettsville
Baber, Wilbur H., Jr. *lawyer*

Hallsville
†Dunlap, James Elvie *school superintendent, educator*
Hutcherson, Donna Dean *retired music educator*

Haltom City
Rickett, Carolyn Kaye Master *artist, criminologist*

Hamilton
†Freeman, Michael Lee *veterinarian*

Harker Heights
Hughes, William Foster *career officer, surgeon, obstetrician, gynecologist*

Harlingen
Dittman, Kathryn Anne *veterinarian*
Godfrey, Aline Lucille *music specialist, church organist*
Johnson, Orrin Wendell *lawyer*
Klein, Garner Franklin *cardiologist, internist*
Martin, Leland Morris (Pappy Martin) *history educator*
Matz, James Richard *county official*
Zaslavsky, Robert *secondary school educator*

Hawkins
Scott, Thomas Gordon *chemistry educator, writer*

Hearne
Helpert-Nunez, Ruth Anne *clinical social worker, psychotherapist*
Moore, Loretta Westbrook *retired banker*

Helotes
Kuba, John Albert *mortician*

Hemphill
Dutton, Frank Elroy *data processing executive*

Hempstead
Propst, Catherine Lamb *biotechnology company executive*

Hewitt
Pickens, Lee *history educator*
Watson, Jessica Lewis *writer*

Hico
Blankenship, Jenny Mary *public relations executive, publisher, editor-in-chief*
Rice, James W. *author, illustrator*

Hidalgo
McKelvy, Nicole Andrée *librarian*

Highland Village
Coogan, Melinda Ann Strank *chemistry educator*
Richardson, K. Scott *sales executive*
Wiedemann, Ramona Diane *occupational therapist*

Hillsboro
Auvenshine, William Robert *academic administrator*

Hitchcock
†Lampl, Lee A. *small business owner*
Shaffer, Richard Paul *business owner, retired career military officer*
Teague, Mary Kay *realtor*

Hochheim
Redman, Violet Jane *printer, writer, genealogist*

Hockley
Sweeney, George Bernard *petrochemical industry executive, investor, broadcast executive, travel agency executive*

Hollywood Park
Smith, Richard Thomas *electrical engineer*

Horseshoe Bay
Anderson, Kenneth Ward *investor, consultant*
Jorden, James Roy *oil company engineering executive, consultant*
Ramey, James Melton *chemist*

Houston
Aarons-Holder, Charmaine Michele *lawyer*
Abbey, George W. S. *space center executive*
Abbott, Lawrence E. *lawyer*
Abbruzzese, James Lewis *medical oncologist*
Acree, G. Hardy *airport executive*
Adams, C. Lee *marketing executive*
Adams, Daniel Clifford *music educator*
Adams, Elaine Parker *college administrator*
Adams, James Mervyn, Jr. *pediatrician, neonatologist, educator*
Adamson, Janice Lynne *fundraiser, grant writer, event coordinator*
Aguilar, Melissa Ward *newspaper editor*
Aguilar-Bryan, Lydia *medical educator, medical researcher*
Ahart, Jan Fredrick *electrical manufacturing company executive*
Ahmad, Salahuddin *nuclear scientist*
Alexander, Harold Campbell *insurance consultant*
Alexander, Leslie Lee *professional sports team executive*
Alexanian, Raymond *hematologist*
Alford, Bobby Ray *physician, educator, university official*
Allen, Don Lee *dentistry educator*
Allender, John Roland *lawyer*
†Alou, Moises *professional baseball player*
Anderson, Eric Severin *lawyer*
Anderson, Richard Carl *geophysical exploration company executive*
Anderson, Thomas Dunaway *retired lawyer*
Anderson, William (Albion), Jr. *investment banker*
Andrews, Lavone Dickensheets *architect*
Antalffy, Leslie Peter *mechanical engineer*
Appel, Stanley Hersh *neurologist*
Arbuckle, Kurt *lawyer*
Arcain, Janeth *professional athlete*
Arledge, David A. *business executive*
Armentrout, Debra Catherine *neonatal nurse practitioner*
Arnold, Daniel Calmes *finance company executive*
Arnold, James Phillip *religious studies educator, history educator*
Aslam, Muhammed Javed *physician*
Atlas, Nancy Friedman *judge*
Austin, Harry Guiden *engineering and construction company executive*
Bagwell, Jeff (Jeffrey Robert Bagwell) *professional baseball player*
Bahl, Saroj Mehta *nutritionist, educator*
Baig, Mukarram *internist*
Bailey, Harold Randolph *surgeon*
Bair, Royden Stanley *architect*
Baker, Stephen Denio *physics educator*
Ballantyne, Christie Mitchell *medical educator*
†Ballard, Linda C. *director financial aid*
Bambace, Robert Shelly *lawyer*
Banks, Evelyn Yvonne *middle school educator*
Barkley, Charles Wade *professional basketball player*
Barlow, Jim B. *newspaper columnist*
Barnett, Edward William *lawyer*
Barracano, Henry Ralph *retired oil company executive, consultant*
Barrere, Clem Adolph *business brokerage company executive*
Barrere, Jamie Newton *real estate executive*
Barrett, Bernard Morris, Jr. *plastic and reconstructive surgeon*
Barrett, Michael Joseph *priest*
Barron, Andrew Ross *chemistry educator, consultant*
Barrow, Thomas Davies *oil and mining company executive*
Baskin, David Stuart *neurosurgeon, educator*
Bass, Daniel Thomas *banker*
Bast, Robert Clinton, Jr. *medical researcher, medical educator*
Battin, R(osabell) Ray (Rosabell Harriet Ray) *audiologist, neuropsychologist*
Baughn, Robert Elroy *microbiology educator*
Baysal, Edip *executive*
Baysal, Fatih Dogan *trading company executive*
Bazelides, Diane *public relations executive*
Beasley, Robert Palmer *epidemiologist, dean, educator*
Bech, Douglas York *lawyer, resort executive*
Becher, Andrew Clifford *lawyer*
Beck, John Robert *pathologist, information scientist*
Becker, Frederick Fenimore *cancer center administrator, pathologist*
Beirne, Martin Douglas *lawyer*
Bell, Chris *city councilman*
†Bell, Derek *baseball player*
Bellatti, Lawrence Lee *lawyer*
Bellinger, Patricia McHugh *oncology and adult nurse practitioner*
Bennett, George Nelson *biochemistry educator*
Bentsen, Kenneth Edward *architect*
Berg, David Howard *lawyer*
Berger, Sidney L. *theater educator, director*
Berry, Michael A. *physician, consultant*
Berti, Margaret Ann *early childhood education educator*
Bethea, Louise Huffman *allergist*
Bethune, Gordon *airline executive*
Bevers, Therese Bartholomew *physician, medical educator*
Bickel, Stephen Douglas *insurance company executive*
Biggio, Craig *professional baseball player*
Bilger, Bruce R. *lawyer*
Bischoff, Susan Ann *newspaper editor*
Bishop, Calvin Thomas *landscape architect, educator*
Bistline, F. Walter, Jr. *lawyer*
Black, David Charles *astrophysicist*
Blackburn, Sadie Gwin Allen *executive*
Blackmon, Willie Edward Boney *lawyer*
Blackshear, A. T., Jr. *lawyer*
Blair, Graham Kerin (Kerry Blair) *lawyer*
Bland, John L. *lawyer*
Blanton, Jack Sawtelle *oil company executive*
Bliss, Ronald Glenn *lawyer*
Bluestein, Edwin A., Jr. *lawyer*
Bodner, Emanuel *industrial recycling company executive*
Bollich, Elridge Nicholas *investment executive*
Bomba, John Gilbert *civil engineer, consultant*
Boney, Jew Don *councilman*
Bonner, Billy Edward *physics educator*
Bonneville, Richard Briggs *retired petroleum exploration and production executive*
Booker, Ronald Joseph *physician practice management*
Boren, William Meredith *manufacturing executive*
Botley, Calvin *lawyer, magistrate judge*
Bottoms, Barbara Ann *nurse*
Boudreaux, Bob *broadcast journalist*
Bovay, Harry Elmo, Jr. *retired engineering company executive*
Bowden, Nancy Butler *school administrator*
Bowen, W. J. *retired gas company executive*
Bowersox, Thomas H. *lawyer*
Bowman, Jeffrey Neil *podiatrist*
Bowron, Edgar Peters *art museum curator, administrator*
Bozeman, Ross Elliot *engineering executive*
Braden, John Alan *accountant*
Bradford, C.O. *protective services officer*
Bradie, Peter Richard *lawyer, engineer*
Brandenstein, Daniel Charles *astronaut, retired naval officer*
Brandt, I. Marvin *chemist, engineer*
Brann, Richard Roland *lawyer*
Brantley, John Randolph *lawyer*
Brents, Daniel Rugel *architectural firm executive*
Bridges, David Manning *lawyer*
Brinsmade, Lyon Louis *lawyer*
Brinson, Gay Creswell, Jr. *lawyer*
Brito, Dagobert Llanos *economics educator*
Brooks, Philip Russell *chemistry educator, researcher*
†Brosh, Rita *performing company executive*
Brotzen, Franz Richard *materials science educator*
Brown, Benjamin A. *gas, oil industry executive*
Brown, Dale, Jr. *obstetrician, educator, health facility administrator*
Brown, Glenda Ann Walters *ballet director*
Brown, Jack Harold Upton *physiology educator, university official, biomedical engineer*
†Brown, Karen K. *federal judge*

Brown, Lee Patrick *federal official, law enforcement educator*
Brown, Patricia Tilley *pharmacist*
Brown, Sharon Elizabeth *software engineer*
Brucker, Janet Mary *nurse*
Brunson, John Soles *lawyer*
Bryan, James Lee *oil field service company executive*
Bryant, John Bradbury *economics educator, consultant*
Buchanan, Dennis Michael *manufacturing and holding company executive*
Buckingham, Edwin John, III *lawyer*
Bue, Carl Olaf, Jr. *retired federal judge*
Bui, Long Van *church custodian, translator*
Bunch, Fred *newspaper picture editor*
Burch, Voris Reagan *retired lawyer, mediator, arbitrator*
Burden, Rhea Ann *athletic trainer*
Burdette, Walter James *surgeon, educator*
Burdine, John A. *hospital administrator, nuclear medicine educator*
†Burgos-Sasscer, Ruth *chancellor*
Burke, Kevin Charles Antony *geologist*
Burke, Michael Donald *oil and gas company executive*
Burroughs, Jack Eugene *dentist, management consultant*
Burzynski, Stanislaw Rajmund *internist*
Busch, Harris *medical educator*
Bush, George Herbert Walker *former President of the United States*
Buster, John Edmond *gynecologist, medical researcher*
Butel, Janet Susan *virology educator*
Butler, Ian John *neurologist*
Butler, William Thomas *college chancellor, physician, educator*
Bux, William John *lawyer*
Buyse, Leone Karena *orchestral musician, educator*
†Cabello, J. David *lawyer*
Caddy, Michael Douglas *lawyer*
Caldwell, Rodney Kent *lawyer*
Calhoun, Harold *architect*
†Callender, David L. *medical educator, administrator*
Callender, Norma Anne *psychology educator, counselor*
Camerino, Pat W. *medical college official*
Cameron, William Duncan *plastics company executive*
Camfield, William Arnett *art educator*
Campbell, Andrew William *immunotoxicology physician*
Campbell, Bert Louis *lawyer, mediator, arbitrator*
Campbell, Carl David *oil industry executive*
Cantrell, William Allen *psychiatrist, educator*
Cantwell, Thomas *geophysicist, electrical engineer*
Capps, Ethan LeRoy *oil company executive*
Carabello, Blase Anthony *cardiology educator*
Caram, Dorothy Farrington *educational consultant*
Carameros, George Demitrius, Jr. *natural gas company executive*
Cardus, David *physician*
Carmody, James Albert *lawyer*
Carpenter, Dana Lynn *elementary educator*
Carr, Edward A. *lawyer*
Carroll, Michael M. *academic dean, mechanical engineering educator*
†Carson, Arch Irwin *toxicology educator, preventive medicine physician*
Carter, Daniel Roland *lawyer*
Carter, James Sumter *oil company executive, tree farmer*
Carter, John Boyd, Jr. *oil operator, bank executive*
Carter, John Francis, II *lawyer*
Carter, John Loyd *lawyer*
Casscells, Samuel Ward, III *cardiologist, educator*
Castañeda, James Agustin *Spanish language educator, university golf coach*
Castillo, John E. *councilman*
Catlin, Francis Irving *physician*
Cesario, Robert James *music educator, performer*
Chalmers, David B. *petroleum executive*
Chance, Jane *English literature educator*
†Chancellor, Van *professional basketball coach*
Chandler, George Francis, III *lawyer, naval architect*
Chavez, John Anthony *lawyer*
Cheatham, John Bane, Jr. *retired mechanical engineering educator*
Chiquelin, David Bryan *mechanical engineer*
Christie, Richard Joel *studio executive*
Chu, Paul Ching-Wu *physicist*
Chu, Wei-Kan *physicist, educator*
Cizek, John Gary *safety and fire engineer*
Cizik, Robert *manufacturing company executive*
Claridge, Elmond Lowell *retired engineering educator, consultant*
Clark, John William, Jr. *electrical engineer, educator*
Clark, Judith Redmond *editor, writer*
Clark, Letitia Z. *federal judge*
Clark, Pat English *lawyer*
Clark, Ron D(ean) *cosmetologist*
Clark, Scott *newspaper editor*
Clarke, Jeff *television station executive*
Clarke, Robert Logan *lawyer*
Clemenceau, Paul B. *lawyer*
Clore, Lawrence Hubert *lawyer*
Coffey, Clarence W. *treasurer*
Cofran, George Lee *telecommunication consultant*
Coghlan, Kelly Jack *lawyer*
Colaco, Joseph P. *civil engineer*
Coleman, Bryan Douglas *lawyer, educator, arbitrator, mediator*
Collins, Vincent Patrick *radiologist, physician, educator*
Collipp, Bruce Garfield *ocean engineer, consultant*
Combs, Janet Louise *sales and advertising company executive*
Concilio, Charles Bennett *retired chemist, educator*
Condit, Linda Faulkner *economist*
Conlon, Michael William *lawyer*
Cook, B. Thomas *lawyer*
Cook, Eugene Augustus *lawyer*
Cooley, Denton Arthur *surgeon, educator*
Cooper, Cynthia *professional basketball player*
†Cooper, Timothy Robert *neonatologist, pediatrician, educator, consultant*
Corral, Edward Anthony *fire marshal*
Corrallo, Carl Anthony *lawyer*
Corriere, Joseph N., Jr. *urologist, educator*
Couch, Jesse Wadsworth *retired insurance company executive*
Couch, Robert Barnard *physician, scientist, educator*
Cox, Frank D. (Buddy Cox) *oil company executive, exploration consultant*
Cox, James Talley *lawyer*
Craig, Robert Mark, III *lawyer, educator*
Crain, Richard Charles *school district music director*
Crimmins, Sean T(homas) *oil company executive*
Crisp, Jennifer Ann Clair *neurosurgical nurse*
Crispin, Andre Arthur *international trading company executive*
Crist, Lynda Lasswell *editor, historian*
Criswell, Ann *newspaper editor*
Crooker, John H., Jr. *lawyer*
Crutchfield, Robert Alan *computer scientist*
Crystal, Jonathan Andrew *executive recruiter*
Cunningham, R. Walter *venture capitalist*
Curl, Robert Floyd, Jr. *chemistry educator*
Currie, John Thornton (Jack Currie) *retired investment banker*
Curry, Alton Frank *lawyer*
Cuthbertson, Gilbert Morris *political science educator*
Cutler, John Earl *landscape architect*
D'Agostino, James Samuel, Jr. *financial executive*
Daily, James L., Jr. *retired financial executive*
Daily, Louis *ophthalmologist*
Darby, Anita Loyce *secondary school educator*
Dasgupta, Amitava *chemist, educator*
†Davenport, Bill *sculptor*
Davidson, Chandler *sociologist, educator*
Davis, Bruce Gordon *retired principal*
Davis, Michael Jordan *civil engineer, natural gas company executive*
Davis, Rex Lloyd *insurance company executive*
Dawood, Mohamed Yusoff *obstetrician, gynecologist*
Dean, Robert Franklin *insurance company executive*
Dean, Warren Michael *construction company executive*
DeAtley, James Harry *prosecutor*
DeBakey, Lois *science communications educator, writer, editor*
DeBakey, Michael Ellis *cardiovascular surgeon, educator, scientist*
DeBakey, Selma *science communications educator, writer, editor, lecturer*
de Castro, Jimmy *radio station executive*
de Kanter, Ellen Ann *English language professional, educator*
DeLeön, John Joseph *city agency executive*
Delpassand, Ebrahim Seyed *pathologist, nuclear medicine physician*
DeMent, James Alderson, Jr. *lawyer*
DeMoss, Harold Raymond, Jr. *federal judge*
Dent, Leanna Gail *secondary education educator*
†Derrick, James V., Jr. *lawyer*
desVignes-Kendrick, Mary *municipal official*
DeVault, John Lee *oil company executive, geophysicist*
Devlin, Robert Manning *financial services company executive*
de Vries, Douwe *oil company executive*
Dewing, Henry Woods, Sr. *telecommunications executive*
De Wree, Eugene Ernest *manufacturing company executive*
Diaz-Arrastia, George Ravelo *lawyer*
Dice, Bruce Burton *exploration company executive*
DiCorcia, Edward Thomas *oil industry executive*
Dierker, Larry *professional baseball team manager*
Dillon, Clifford Brien *retired lawyer*
†Dimachkie, Mazen Mohammad *health care educator*
Dinkins, Carol Eggert *lawyer*
Dirks, Mike *golf coach*
Disher, David Alan *lawyer, geophysical research consultant*
†Djerejian, Edward Peter *institute administrator, former diplomat*
Dobbs, Rita Marie *travel company executive*
Dodson, D. Keith *engineering and construction company executive*
Donie, Scott *Olympic athlete, platform diver*
Doubleday, Charles William *dermatologist, educator*
Dougan, Deborah Rae *neuropsychology professional*
Douglas, Frank Fair *architect, graphic designer*
Douglas, James M. *universtiy president*
Douglas, P C *producer, director, reporter, editor*
Downing, Margaret Mary *newspaper editor*
Downs, Hartley H., III *chemist*
Doyle, Joseph Francis, III *art educator*
Drew, Katherine Fischer *history educator*
Driscoll, Ray F. *city official*
†Driver, Larry C. *medical educator*
Drury, Leonard Leroy *retired oil company executive*
Drutz, Jan Edwin *pediatrics educator*
Duerr, David *civil engineer*
Duke, Michael B. *aerospace scientist*
Dumont, Edward Abdo *architect, interior designer*
Duncan, Charles William, Jr. *investor, former government official*
Duncan, Cheryl L. *critical care/cardiac catherization nurse*
Duncan, Dan L. *gas company executive*
Dunlop, Fred Hurston *lawyer*
Dunn, James Randolph *corporate executive*
DuPont, Herbert Lancashire *medical educator, researcher*
Dykes, Osborne Jefferson, III *lawyer*
Eastin, Keith E. *lawyer*
Ebaugh, Helen Rose *sociology educator, researcher*
Edens, Donald Keith *oil company executive*
Edwards, Victor Henry *chemical engineer*
†Eggen, Svein *company executive*
Ehlinger, Janet Ann Dowling *elementary school educator*
†Ehsani, Michael *quality assurance executive*
Eichberger, LeRoy Carl *mechanical engineer, consultant, stress analyst*
Eisner, Diana *pediatrician*
Elkins, James Anderson, Jr. *banker*
Elkins, James Anderson, III *investment banker*
Elliot, Douglas Gene *chemical engineer, engineering company executive, consultant*
Elwood, William Norelli *medical researcher*
Engel, James Harry *computer company executive*
England, Rudy Alan *lawyer*
Englesmith, Tejas *actor, producer, curator*
Epright, Charles John *aerospace engineer*
Essmyer, Michael Martin *lawyer*
Estle, Thomas Leo *physicist, educator*
Eubank, J. Thomas *lawyer*
Eusibio, Raul Antonio *baseball player*
Evans, Harry Launius *pathology educator*
Ewoh, Andrew Ikeh Emmanuel *political science educator*
Farenthold, Frances Tarlton *lawyer*
†Farley, Claire S. *petroleum company executive*
Feigin, Ralph David *medical school president, pediatrician, educator*
Feldcamp, Larry Bernard *lawyer*
Fellers, Rhonda Gay *lawyer*
Fenn, Sandra Ann *programmer, analyst*
Ferguson, Arlen Gary *human resources specialist*
Ferrand, Jean C. *oil company executive*
Ferrendelli, James Anthony *neurologist, educator*
†Fiorenza, Joseph A. *bishop*
Fischer, Craig Leland *physician*
Fisher, Janet Warner *secondary school educator*
Fishman, Marvin Allen *pediatrician, neurologist, educator*
Flack, Joe Fenley *county and municipal official, former insurance executive*
Fladung, Richard Denis *lawyer*
Flato, William Roeder, Jr. *software development company executive*
Fleming, Michael Paul *lawyer*
Focht, John Arnold, Jr. *geotechnical engineer*
Folk, Katherine Pinkston *English language educator, writer, journalist*
Forbes, Arthur Lee, III *lawyer*
Foreman, George *boxer, minister, boxing broadcaster*
Foster, Dale Warren *political scientist, educator, management consultant, real estate*
Foster, Joe B. *oil company executive*
Fowler, Robert Asa *diplomat, consultant, business director*
Foyt, A(nthony) J(oseph), Jr. *auto racing crew chief, former professional auto racer*
Fraga, Felix *councilman*
Frankhouser, Homer Sheldon, Jr. *engineering and construction company executive*
Freeman, John Clinton *meteorologist, oceanographer*
Freeman, Marjorie Schaefer *mathematics educator*
Freireich, Emil J *hematologist, educator*
Frieden, Kit *newspaper editor*
Friedkin, Thomas H. *automotive executive*
Fritsch, Derek Adrian *nurse anesthetist*
Fromm, Eva Maria *lawyer*
Frost, John Elliott *minerals company executive*
Fullenweider, Donn Charles *lawyer*
Fulwiler, Robert Neal *oil company executive*
Galvani, Christiane Mesch *English as a second language educator, translator*
Ganter, Garland *radio station executive*
Garcia, Hector David *toxicologist*
Gardner, Everette Shaw, Jr. *information sciences educator, consultant, author*
Garten, David Burton *lawyer*
Gaucher, Donald Holman *public opinion research company executive*
†Gaucher, Jane Heyck *retail executive*
Gauer, William Keith *accountant*
Gause, Val Hollis *middle school educator*
Gayle, Gibson, Jr. *lawyer*
Geer, Ronald Lamar *mechanical engineering consultant, retired oil company executive*
Geis, Duane Virgil *retired investment banker*
George, Deveral D. *editor, journalist, advertising consultant*
Georgiades, William Den Hartog *educational administrator*
Gerhart, Glenna Lee *pharmacist*
Gernon, George Owen, Jr. *civil engineer*
Gerraughty, David R. *newspaper editor*
Getz, Lowell Vernon *financial advisor*
Giacalone, Frank Thomas *energy and environmental company executive*
Gibbs, Mary Bramlett *banker*
Gibson, Everett Kay, Jr. *space scientist, geochemist*
Gibson, Jerry Leigh *oil company executive*
Gibson, Rex Hilton *lawyer*
Giddens, Paul Joseph *human resources executive*
Gidley, John Lynn *engineering executive*
Giesecke, Noel Martin *cardiovascular anesthesiologist*
Gigli, Irma *physician, educator, academic administrator*
Gilbert, Harold Stanley *warehousing company executive*
Gildenberg, Philip Leon *neurosurgeon*
Gillis, (Stephen) Malcolm *academic administrator, economics educator*
Gilmore, Vanessa D. *federal judge*
Girouard, Peggy Jo Fulcher *ballet educator*
Gissel, L. Henry, Jr. *lawyer*
Glassell, Alfred Curry, Jr. *investor*
Glassman, Armand Barry *physician, pathologist, scientist, educator, administrator*
Glowinski, Roland *mathematics educator*
Gockley, (Richard) David *opera director*
Goff, Robert Burnside *retired food company executive*
Goins, William C., Jr. *engineering executive*
Goldberg, William Jeffrey *accountant*
Goldman, Stanford Milton *medical educator*
Goldsmith, Billy Joe *real estate broker*
Goldstein, Margaret Ann *biologist*
Goloby, George William, Jr. *environmental scientist, ornithologist, aviculturist*
Gonynor, Francis James *lawyer*
Goodman, Herbert Irwin *petroleum company executive*
Gordon, William Edwin *physicist, engineer, educator, university official*
Gorry, G. Anthony *medical educator*
Gorski, Daniel Alexander *art educator*
Gos, Michael Walter *English educator, author*
Gover, Alan Shore *lawyer*
Grace, Priscilla Anne *labor union executive*
Graham, David Yates *gastroenterologist*
Graham, Michael Paul *lawyer*
Gray, Robert Steele *publishing executive, editor*
Green, Gene *congressman*
†Greenberg, Stephen Baruch *physician, educator*
†Greendyke, William R. *federal judge*
Griffin, Oscar O'Neal, Jr. *writer, former oil company executive*
Griffith Fries, Martha *controller*
Grossberg, Marc Elias *lawyer*
Grossett, Deborah Lou *psychologist, behavior analyst, consultant*
Grossman, Herbert Barton *urologist, researcher*
Grossman, Robert George *physician, educator*
Gruber, Ira Dempsey *historian, educator*
Guilliouma, Larry Jay, Jr. *performing arts administrator, music educator*
Guillory, Curtis J. *bishop*
Gunn, Albert Edward, Jr. *internist, educator, lawyer, administrator*
Gunn, Joan Marie *health care administrator*
Gupta, Kaushal Kumar *internist*
Guynn, Robert William *psychiatrist, educator*
Haas, Merrill Wilber *geologist, oil company executive*
Hackerman, Norman *chemist, academic administrator*
Hafner, Joseph A., Jr. *food company executive*
Halbouty, Michel Thomas *geologist, petroleum engineer, petroleum operator*
Hale, Leon *newspaper columnist*
Hall, Charles Washington *lawyer*
Hall, Robert Joseph *physician, medical educator*
Halyard, Raymond James *aerospace engineer, mathematics educator*
Hamilton, Carlos Robert, Jr. *internist, endocrinologist*
Hamilton, Jacqueline *art consultant*
Hamilton, Lorraine Rebekah *adult education consultant*
Hammond, Ken *newspaper magazine editor*
Hammond, Michael Peter *music educator, dean*
Hanania, Nicola Alexander *physician*
Hargrove, James Ward *financial consultant*
Harman, Angela Diane *construction company executive*
Harmon, Melinda Furche *federal judge*
Harper, Alfred John, II *lawyer*
Harrell, James Earl, Sr. *radiologist, educator*
†Harrell, Michael V. *hospitality company executive*
Harrington, Bruce Michael *lawyer, investor*
†Harris, Courteney Franchelle *program manager*
Harris, John H. *radiologist*
Harris, Lyttleton Tazwell, IV *property management-investment company executive*
Harris, Richard Foster, Jr. *insurance company executive*
Harris, Warren Wayne *lawyer*
Hart, James Whitfield, Jr. *retired corporate public affairs executive, lawyer*
Hartrick, Janice Kay *lawyer*
Hartsfield, Henry Warren, Jr. *electronics company executive, retired astronaut*
Harvey, F. Reese *mathematics educator*
Harvin, David Tarleton *lawyer*
Haskell, Thomas Langdon *history educator*
†Hawes, William Kenneth *communication educator*
Haymond, Paula J. *psychologist, diagnostician, hypnotherapist*
Haynie, Thomas Powell, III *physician*
†Hearne, Barbra M. *foundation administrator*
Heath, Frank Bradford *dentist*
Heggen, Ivar Nelson *lawyer*
†Heiker, Vincent Edward *information systems executive*
Heilman, Robert Edward *mechanical engineer*
Heinrich, Randall Wayne *lawyer, investment banker*
Heinsen, Lindsay *newspaper editor*
Helland, George Archibald, Jr. *management consultant, manufacturing executive, former government official*
Hellums, Jesse David *chemical engineering educator and researcher*
Helton, Kim *coach*
Hempel, John P. *mathematics educator*
Henderson, Nathan H. *bishop*
Henington, David Mead *library director*
†Henley, Ernest Justus *chemical engineering educator, consultant*
Henry, Randolph Marshall *company executive, real estate broker*
Hermann, Robert John *lawyer, corporate executive*
Herrington, James Benjamin, Jr. *job recruiting executive*
Hewitt, Lester L. *lawyer*
Hicks, John Bernard *internist*
Hightower, Joe Walter *chemical engineering educator, consultant*
Hinton, Paula Weems *lawyer*
Hipps, Larry Clay *clergyman, evangelistic association executive*
Hirasaki, George Jiro *chemical engineer, educator*
Hirsch, Edward Mark *poet, English language educator*
Hitchman, Cal McDonald, Sr. *secondary education educator*
Hittner, David *federal judge*
Hlozek, Carole Diane Quast *financial services company officer*
Ho, Yhi-Min *university dean, economics educator*
Hoang, Hung Manh *information systems analyst, consultant*
Hobby, William Pettus *broadcast executive, retired*
Hodge, Etta Lee *director of surgical services, nurse*
Hodo, Edward Douglas *university president*
Hoffman, Philip Guthrie *former university president*
Hoglund, Forrest Eugene *petroleum company executive*
Holcomb, William A. *retired oil and gas exploration, pipeline executive, retired real estate broker, consultant*
Holderness, Algernon Sidney, Jr. *lawyer*
Hollister, Leo Edward *physician, educator*
Holloway, Gordon Arthur *lawyer*
Hollyfield, John Scoggins *lawyer*
Holmes, Ann Hitchcock *journalist*
Holmes, Cecile Searson *religion editor*
Holmes, Harry Dadisman *health facility administrator*
Holmes, Roscette Yvonne Lewis *organizational development and training consultant*
Holstead, John Burnham *lawyer*
Honeycutt, George Leonard *photographer, retired*
Hong, Waun Ki *medical oncologist, clinical investigator*
Hook, Harold Swanson *management consulting executive*
Hornak, Anna Frances *library administrator*
Horvitz, Paul Michael *finance educator*
Howell, Paul Neilson *oil company executivе*
Hoyt, Kenneth M. *federal judge*
Hoyt, Mont Powell *lawyer*
Hrna, Daniel Joseph *pharmacist, lawyer*
Hsu, Thomas Tseng-Chuang *civil engineer, educator*
Huck, Lewis Francis *lawyer*
Hudson, W. Gail *social worker*
Hudspeth, Chalmers Mac *lawyer, educator*
Huffington, Roy Michael *business executive, former ambassador*
Hughes, James Baker, Jr. *retail executive, consultant*
Hughes, Lynn Nettleton *federal judge*
Hughes, William Joseph *management consultant*
Hulce, Durward Philip *theatrical lighting designer*
Hult, Susan Freda *history educator*
Hunsicker, Gerry *professional sports executive*
†Hurwitz, Charles Edwin *manufacturing company executive*
Huston, John Dennis *English educator*
Hutcheson, Thad Thomson, Jr. *international executive*
Hyman, Harold M. *history educator, consultant*
Ifft, Lewis George, III *company administrator*
Ignatiev, Alex *physics researcher*
Iliev, Milko Nikolov *physicist, researcher*
Ilin, Andrew V. *software engineer*
Irwin, John Robert *oil and gas drilling executive*
Ivins, Marsha S. *aerospace engineer, astronaut*
Jackson, Ernest, Jr. *broadcasting executive*
Jackson, Gilchrist L. *surgeon*
Jackson, R. Graham *architect*

Jackson, Susanne Leora *creative placement firm executive*
Jackson, Tammy *basketball player*
Jacobson, Charles Allen *aerospace company executive*
Jamail, Joseph Dahr, Jr. *lawyer*
Janes, Joseph Anthony, Jr. *optometrist*
Jankovic, Joseph *neurologist, educator, scientist*
Jansen, Donald Orville *lawyer*
Jeanneret, Paul Richard *management consultant*
Jenkins, Linda Faye *executive secretary*
†Jenkins, Margie Little *human relations specialist, psychotherapist*
Jennings, Debra Vera *lawyer*
Jeske, Charles Matthew *lawyer*
Jetton, Steve *newspaper editor*
Jewell, George Hiram *lawyer*
Jhin, Michael Kontien *health care executive*
Jimmar, D'Ann *elementary education educator, fashion merchandiser*
Johnson, James Harold *lawyer*
Johnson, Judy Dianne *elementary education educator*
Johnson, Kenneth Oscar *oil company executive*
Johnson, Nancy K. *judge*
Johnson, Richard James Vaughan *newspaper executive*
†Johnson, Sandra Ann *elementary educator educator*
Johnson, Thomas David *pharmacologist*
Johnson, Wayne D. *gas industry executive*
Johnston, Marguerite *journalist, author*
Jones, Dan Brigman *ophthalmologist, educator*
Jones, Edith Hollan *federal judge*
Jones, Edith Irby *physician*
Jones, Florence M. *music educator*
Jones, Frank Griffith *lawyer*
Jones, Larry Leroy *oil company executive*
Jones, Sonia Josephine *advertising agency executive*
Jordan, David Thomas *financial analyst, consultant*
Jordon, Robert Earl *physician*
Joyce, James Daniel *clergyman*
Jurtshuk, Peter, Jr. *microbiologist*
Justice, (David) Blair *psychology educator, author*
Kahan, Barry Donald *surgeon, educator*
Kaplan, Alan Leslie *gynecology educator, oncologist*
Kaplan, Lee Landa *lawyer*
Kaptopodis, Louis *supermarket chain executive*
Karff, Samuel Egal *rabbi*
†Kastely, James Louis *English language educator*
Kaufman, Raymond Henry *physician*
Kaup, David Earle *law enforcement officer*
Kavanagh, John Joseph *medical educator*
Kay, Joel Phillip *lawyer*
Kelber, Werner Heinz *religious educator*
Kellar, William Henry *university official, history educator*
Kellaway, Peter *neurophysiologist, researcher*
Keller, Robert Bounds *marketing professional, consultant, inventor*
Kellison, Stephen George *insurance executive*
Kelly, Hugh Rice *lawyer*
Kelly, Margaret Elizabeth *financial analyst, planner*
Kendall, Kay L. Orth *university official*
Kendrick, Robert Warren *county administrator, superindendent*
Kennedy, Ken *computer science educator*
Kerr, Baine Perkins *oil company executive*
Kershaw, Carol Jean *psychologist*
Ketchand, Robert Lee *lawyer*
Kevan, Larry *chemistry educator*
Key, James Everett *ophthalmologist*
Kientz, Renee *newspaper editor*
Kim, Pyung-Soo *martial arts educator*
Kimbrell, Deborah Ann *geneticist, educator*
Kimmel, Herbert David *psychology educator*
Kimmel, Marek *biomathematician, educator*
King, Carl Edward *employee screening executive*
King, Carolyn Dineen *federal judge*
King, Kay Wander *design educator, fashion designer, consultant*
Kinnaird, Susan Marie *special education educator*
Kinsey, James Lloyd *chemist, educator*
Kirby, Sarah Ann Van Deventer *aerospace engineer*
Kirkland, John David *oil and gas company executive, lawyer*
Kit, Saul *biochemist, educator*
Kitowski, Vincent Joseph *medical consultant, former physical medicine and rehabilitation physician*
Klausmeyer, David Michael *scientific instruments manufacturing company executive*
Klein, George D. *geologist, executive*
Kline, Allen Haber, Jr. *lawyer*
Kline, John William *retired air force officer, management consultant*
Knapp, David Hebard *banker*
Knauss, Robert Lynn *international business educator, corporate executive*
Knight, J. Vernon *medicine and microbiology educator*
Knotts, Glenn R(ichard) *foundation administrator*
Kobayashi, Riki *chemical engineer, educator*
Koch, Douglas Donald *ophthalmologist*
Kochi, Jay Kazuo *chemist, educator*
Koenig, Rodney Curtis *lawyer, rancher*
Kollaer, Jim C. *real estate executive, architect*
Konisky, Jordan *microbiology educator*
Kors, R. Paul *search company executive*
Kouri, Donald Jack *chemist, educator*
Kraft, Irvin Alan *psychiatrist*
Krakower, Terri Jan *biochemist, researcher*
Kramm, Deborah Ann *data processing executive*
Kratochvil, L(ouis) Glen *lawyer*
Krause, William Austin *engineering executive*
Krebs, Arno William, Jr. *lawyer*
Krueger, Artur W. G. *international business consultant*
Kruse, Charles Thomas *lawyer*
Kuntz, Hal Goggan *petroleum exploration company executive*
Kurz, Thomas Patrick *lawyer*
Kutka, Nicholas *nuclear medicine physician*
LaBoon, Robert Bruce *lawyer*
Lacey, David Morgan *lawyer, school administrator*
Lackey, S. Allen *lawyer, petroleum company executive*
Lake, Kathleen Cooper *lawyer*
Lake, Sim *federal judge*
Lamb, Sydney MacDonald *linguistics and cognitive science educator*
†Lanier, Bob *mayor*
Lanier, Robert C. (Bob Lanier) *real estate owner, developer, former mayor*
Larkin, Lee Roy *lawyer*
Larkin, William Vincent, Jr. *service company executive*
Larks, Jack *forensic engineer, consultant*
Larrey, Inge Harriette *jazz and blues freelance photographer*
Larson, Peter L. *legal assistant, investigator*
Lassiter, James Morris, Jr. *real estate investment executive*
Latimer, Roy Truett *museum executive*
†Laurent, John Paul *neurosurgeon*
Lawson, Ben F. *lawyer, international legal consultant*
Lay, Kenneth Lee *diversified energy company executive*
†Leal, Manuel D. *federal judge*
Lechago, Juan *pathologist, educator*
Lechner-Fish, Teresa Jean *chemical engineer, analytical chemist*
Lee, Janie C. *curator*
Lee, Robert Leyne *plantation company executive, consultant*
Lee, William Gentry *lawyer*
†Lehne, Kathy Prasnicki *gas industry executive*
Lehrer, Kenneth Eugene *real estate advisor, economic consultant*
Leonard, Gilbert Stanley *oil company executive*
Lerup, Lars G. *architecture educator, college dean*
Lestin, Eric Hugh *real estate investment banking executive*
Levin, Bernard *physician*
Levit, Max *food service executive*
Levit, Milton *grocery supply company executive*
Levy, Robert Edward *management consultant*
Lewis, Carl (Frederick Carlton Lewis) *Olympic track and field athlete*
Lewis, Richard D. *municipal official*
Lewis, Wanda Howell *health facility administrator*
Liang, Edison Parktak *astrophysicist, educator, researcher*
Lienhard, John Henry, IV *mechanical engineering educator*
Lindig, Bill M. *food distribution company executive*
Lindsey, John Horace *insurance agency executive*
Ling, Lily Hsu-Chiang *real estate executive, accountant*
†Linn, Heather *neurologist*
Little, Jack Edward *petroleum company executive*
Locke, Gene L. *lawyer*
Loftis, Jack D. *newspaper editor, newspaper executive*
Long, William Everett *retired utility executive*
Looper, Donald Ray *lawyer*
Lopez, David Tiburcio *lawyer, educator, arbitrator, mediator*
Loro, Antonio *artist*
Louck, Lisa Ann *lawyer*
Louderback, Truman Eugene *environmental project manager*
Loveland, Eugene Franklin *petroleum executive*
Low, Morton David *physician, educator*
Lucid, Shannon W. *biochemist, astronaut*
†Luckner, Robert Clark *oil industry executive*
Luigs, Charles Russell *gas and oil drilling industry executive*
Lukens, Max L. *manufacturing company executive*
Luss, Dan *chemical engineering educator*
Lynch, Bob (Robert Wayne Lynch, Jr.) *newspaper editor, educator*
Lynch, John Edward, Jr. *lawyer*
Lyons, Phillip Michael, Sr. *insurance accounting and real estate executive*
Maligas, Manuel Nick *metallurgical engineer*
Malone, Lisa R. *accountant, scheduler*
Maloney, James Edward *lawyer*
Malorzo Waller, Amy Lynn *physician assistant in pediatric neurosurgery*
Mamedov, Edouard Akhmed *chemist, researcher*
Manero, Joseph Anthony *political consultant, lobbyist*
Maness, Darrell Ray *television producer, editor*
Mangapit, Conrado, Jr. *manufacturing company executive*
Mansell, Joyce Marilyn *special education educator*
Marcus, Jerry *broadcasting executive*
Margotta, Maurice Howard, Jr. *management consultant*
Margrave, John Lee *chemist, educator, university administrator*
Marion, Suzanne Margaret *music educator*
Marley, Everett Armistead, Jr. *lawyer*
Marsel, Robert Steven *law educator, mediator, arbitrator*
Marshall, Jane Pretzer *newspaper editor*
Marshall, Thom *columnist*
Marston, Edgar Jean, III *lawyer*
Martin, James Kirby *historian, educator*
Martin, Kenneth Frank *insurance company executive*
Martin, Randi Christine *psychology educator*
†Martin, Raymond Anthony *neurologist, educator*
Martin, William C. *sociology educator, writer*
Marzio, Peter Cort *museum director*
Mason, Franklin Rogers *retired automotive executive*
Mateker, Emil Joseph, Jr. *geophysicist*
Mathis, James Forrest *retired petroleum company executive*
Mathis, Sharon Ann *home health nurse, mental health nurse, consultant, columnist, entrepreneur*
Matney, William Brooks, VII *electrical engineer, marine engineer*
Matthews, Charles Sedwick *petroleum engineering consultant, research advisor*
Matthews, Kathleen Shive *biochemistry educator*
Mauck, William M., Jr. *executive recruiter, small business owner*
Max, Ernest *surgeon*
Mayo, Marti *art historian, curator*
Mayor, Richard Blair *lawyer*
McCleary, Beryl Nowlin *civic worker, travel agency executive*
McCleary, Henry Glen *geophysicist*
McClure, Daniel M. *lawyer*
McCollam, Marion Andrus *consulting firm executive, educator*
†McCollum, Charles H. *surgeon*
McComas, Marcella Laigne *marketing educator*
McCormack, David Richard *lawyer*
McDaniel, Jarrel Dave *lawyer*
McDavid, George Eugene (Gene Mc David) *retired newspaper executive*
†McDonald, Scott *real estate company executive*
Mc Fadden, Joseph Michael *history educator*
McGary, Betty Winstead *minister, counselor, individual, marriage, and family therapist*
Mc Ginty, John Milton *architect*
McGuire, Dianne Marie *psychotherapist*
McIntire, Larry Vern *chemical engineering educator*
McIntire, Mary Beth *university dean and official*
McIntosh, Susan Keech *anthropology educator*
McKechnie, John Charles *gastroenterologist, educator*
McKim, Paul Arthur *management consultant, retired petroleum executive*
McLane, Drayton, Jr. *professional baseball team executive*
McPherson, Alice Ruth *ophthalmologist, educator*
Mease, Robert B. *architect*
Meeks, Herbert Lessig, III *pastor, former school system administrator*
Mehra, Jagdish *physicist*
Meinke, Roy Walter *electrical engineer, consultant*
Melamed, Richard *lawyer*
†Mendelsohn, John *oncologist, hematologist, educator*
Menscher, Barnet Gary *steel company executive*
Metyko, Michael Joseph *owner, manager development company*
Metzger, Lewis Albert *brokerage house executive, financial consultant*
Meyer, Dianne Scott Wilson *secondary school educator, librarian*
Meyer, John Stirling *neurologist, educator*
Miele, Angelo *engineering educator, researcher, consultant, author*
Milam, John Daniel *pathologist, educator*
Miles, Ruby A. Branch *librarian, consultant*
Millar, Jeffery Lynn *columnist*
Miller, Charles Rickie *thermal and fluid systems analyst, engineering manager*
Miller, Gary Evan *psychiatrist, mental health services administrator*
†Miller, Geoffrey *child neurologist*
Miller, Harry Freeman *university administrator*
Miller, Janel Howell *psychologist*
Miller, John Pendleton (Jack) *publishing company executive*
Miller, Michael Jaye *energy executive*
Miller, Mike *mechanical engineer*
Milloy, Maryrose *judge*
Miner, Michael E. *neurosurgery educator*
Minter, David Lee *English literature educator*
Minton, Melanie Sue *neuroscience nurse*
Mithoff, Richard Warren *lawyer*
Moehlman, Michael Scott *lawyer*
Moncure, John Lewis *lawyer*
Montgomery, Cleothus *minister*
Montgomery, Denise Karen *nurse*
Moore, Lois Jean *health science facility administrator*
Moorhead, Gerald Lee *architect*
Morehead, James Caddall, Jr. *architect, educator*
Morgan, Richard Greer *lawyer*
Morgenstern, Lewis B. *medical educator*
Morris, (William) Carloss *lawyer, insurance company executive*
Morris, David Hargett *broadcast executive, rancher*
Morris, Owen Glenn *engineering corporation executive*
Morris, Seth Irwin *architect*
Mueller, Carl Gustav, Jr. *lawyer*
Munisteri, Joseph George *construction executive*
Munk, Zev Moshe *allergist, researcher*
Murad, Ferid *physician*
Murphy, Calvin Jerome *professional sports team executive*
Murphy, Ewell Edward, Jr. *lawyer*
Murphy, William Alexander, Jr. *diagnostic radiologist, educator*
†Murray, Frank *heating, air conditioning manufacturing executive*
Myers, Franklin *lawyer, oil service company executive*
Myers, James Clark *advertising and public relations executive*
Myers, Norman Allan *marketing professional*
Nacol, Mae *lawyer*
Nanz, Robert Hamilton *petroleum consultant*
Nasser, Moes Roshanali *optometrist*
Nations, Howard Lynn *lawyer*
Nelson, David Loren *geneticist, educator*
Nelson, John Robert *theology educator, clergyman*
Neuhaus, Philip Ross *investment banker*
Neuhaus, William Oscar, III *architect*
Newbold, Benjamin Millard, Jr. *library manager, education consultant*
Newton, Jon P. *lawyer*
Nicandros, Constantine Stavros *retired oil company executive*
Nielsen, Niels Christian, Jr. *theology educator*
Nimmer, Raymond T. *lawyer, law educator*
Nolen, Roy Lemuel *lawyer*
Nollen, Margaret Roach *financial administrator*
Nordgren, Ronald Paul *engineering educator, researcher*
†Nordlander, Peter Jan Arne *physics educator, researcher*
Northington, David Knight, III *research center director, botanist, educator*
Nuss, Eldon Paul *casket manufacturer*
Nyberg, Donald Arvid *oil company executive*
Obiora, Chris Sunny *architect*
O'Brient, David Warren *sales executive, consultant*
O'Connor, Ralph Sturges *investment company executive*
†O'Donnell, Lawrence, III *lawyer*
Olajuwon, Hakeem Abdul *professional basketball player*
Oldham, Darius Dudley *lawyer*
O'Malley, Bert William *cell biologist, educator, physician*
O'Neil, John *artist*
Onstead, Robert R. *consumer goods company executive*
Ordonez, Nelson Gonzalo *pathologist*
Oren, Bruce Clifford *newspaper editor, artist*
Orner, Linda Price *family therapist*
Orr, Carole *artist*
Orton, John Stewart *lawyer*
Osgood, Christopher Mykel *radio account executive*
†Oshman, Marilyn *retail executive*
Osterberg, Susan Snider *communications educator, farmer*
Ostrow, Stuart *theatrical producer, educator*
O'Toole, Austin Martin *lawyer*
†Pace, Allan Jay *financial advisor*
Page, Ann *stock brokerage executive*
Palmer, James Edward *public relations executive*
Park, Cheryl Antoinette *women's health nurse, educator*
Parker, Dallas Robert *lawyer*
Parker, Norman Neil, Jr. *software systems analyst, mathematics educator*
Parsons, Edmund Morris *investment company executive*
Pate, James Leonard *oil company executive*
Pate, Patricia Ann *women's health nurse*
Patten, Robert Lowry *English language educator*
Patterson, Ronald R(oy) *health care systems executive*
Patterson, Steve *professional football team executive*
Paul, Alida Ruth *secondary school educator*
Paul, Gordon Lee *behavioral scientist, psychologist*
Paul, Thomas Daniel *lawyer*
Paulsen, James Walter *law educator*
Pearson, James Boyd, Jr. *electrical engineering educator*
Pearson, Michael P. *lawyer*
Pederson, Tony Weldon *newspaper editor*
Pendergraft, Roy Daniel *medical educator, physician*
Peng, Liang-Chuan *mechanical engineer*
Perrot, Kim *basketball player*
Peterkin, George Alexander, Jr. *marine transportation company executive*
Petit, Brenda Joyce *credit bureau sales executive*
†Petrovich, Alisa Vladimira *historian, educator*
Pham, Cuong Huy *chemical engineer*
Phillippi, Elmer Joseph, Jr. *data communications consultant*
Phillips, Joseph Daniel *geomagneticist, oceanographer*
Phung, Nguyen Dinh *medical educator*
Pickering, James Henry, III *academic administrator, educator*
Piech, Ruth Diane *nursing administrator*
Pippen, Scottie *professional basketball player*
Pitts, Gary Benjamin *lawyer*
Plaeger, Frederick Joseph, II *lawyer*
Plunkett, Jack William *writer, publisher*
Poats, Lillian Brown *education educator*
Pognonec, Yves Maurice *steel products executive*
Polhemus, Mary Ann *elementary school principal, educator*
†Pomerantz, James Robert *psychology educator, academic administrator*
Pomeroy, Carl Fredrick *petroleum engineer*
Portman, Ronald Jay *pediatric nephrologist, researcher*
Poston, Walker Seward, II *medical educator, researcher*
Poulos, Michael James *insurance company executive*
Powell, Alan *engineer-scientist*
Powell, Michael Robert *biophysicist, physicist, chemist*
Powers, Hugh William *newspaper executive*
†Powers, William Edward *emergency physician, educator*
Prather, Rita Catherine *psychology educator*
Prats, Michael *petroleum engineer, educator*
Pravel, Bernarr Roe *lawyer*
Prentice, James Stuart *energy company executive, chemical engineer*
Prestridge, Pamela Adair *lawyer*
Price, Mark Eldredge *lawyer*
†Priwin, Daniel *finance company executive*
Prokurat, Michael *religious studies educator, pastor*
Pruitt, Robert Randall *lawyer*
Pryor, William Daniel Lee *humanities educator*
Pugsley, Frank Burruss *lawyer*
Pyle, Jerry *automotive executive*
Raber, Martin *health facility administrator, medical educator*
Radoff, Leonard Irving *librarian, consultant*
Raia, Carl Bernard *commercial real estate executive and developer*
Raijman, Isaac *gastroenterologist, endoscopist, educator*
Rainey, John David *federal judge*
Ranck, Bruce E. *waste management executive*
Rasbury, Julian George *financial services company executive*
Rawson, Jim Charles *accountant, executive*
Ray, Hugh Massey, Jr. *lawyer*
Ray, Priscilla *physician*
Raymer, Warren Joseph *retired allergist*
Read, Michael Oscar *editor, consultant*
Reasoner, Harry Max *lawyer*
Reed, Kathlyn Louise *occupational therapist, educator*
Reif, Louis Raymond *lawyer, utilities executive*
Reiff, Patricia Hofer *space physicist, educator*
Rendon, Josefina Muniz *judge, mediator, arbitrator*
Reso, Anthony *geologist, earth resources economist*
Reynolds, John Terrence *oil industry executive*
Rhodes, Allen Franklin *engineering executive*
Ribble, Anne Hoerner *communications executive*
Ribble, John Charles *medical educator*
Rice, Emily Joy *retired secondary school and adult educator*
Richards, Leonard Martin *investment executive, consultant*
Richardson, Deborah Kaye *clinical nurse specialist, educator*
Riedel, Alan Ellis *retired manufacturing company executive, lawyer*
Riesser, Gregor Hans *arbitrage investment advisor*
Rigsby, Carolyn Erwin *music educator*
Riley, Harold John, Jr. *business executive*
Riley, William John *neurologist*
Roach, Joe *councilman*
Robbins, Earl L. *oil operator*
Robertson, James Woolsey *lawyer*
Robins, W. Ronald *lawyer*
Robison, Buena Chambers, III *environmental scientist*
Rock, Douglas Lawrence *manufacturing executive*
Rockwell, Elizabeth Dennis *retirement specialist, financial planner*
†Rodgers, James Turner *petroleum engineer, oil industry executive*
Roff, J(ohn) Hugh, Jr. *energy company executive*
Rogers, Arthur Hamilton, III *lawyer*
Röller, Herbert Alfred *biology and medical scientist, educator*
Romsdahl, Marvin Magnus *surgeon, educator*
Roorda, John Francis, Jr. *business consultant*
Roos, Sybil Friedenthal *retired elementary school educator*
Rosenthal, Lee H. *federal judge*
Rosenthal, Morris William *pediatrician*
†Ross, Michael Wallis *public health educator*
Rossler, Willis Kenneth, Jr. *petroleum company executive*
Rozzell, Scott Ellis *lawyer*
Rudolph, Andrew Henry *dermatologist, educator*
Rudolph, Frederick Byron *biochemistry educator*
Runge, Barbara Kay *lawyer, arbitrator, mediator*
Ruppert, Susan Donna *critical care nursing educator, family adult nurse practitioner*
Russell, Anna *city administrator*
Russell, John Francis *retired librarian*
Ryan, Thomas William *lawyer*
Ryan, Vince *lawyer*
Rypien, David Vincent *engineering executive*
Salch, Steven Charles *lawyer*
Sales, James Bohus *lawyer*
†Salzer, John Richard *shipyard designer and company executive*
Sampson, Franklin Delano *minister*
Sanchez, Orlando *city councilman*
Sapp, Walter William *lawyer, energy company executive*

Sass, Ronald Lewis biology and chemistry educator
Saunders, Charles Albert lawyer
Saunders, William Arthur management consultant
Sayer, Coletta Keenan gifted education educator
Schachtel, Barbara Harriet Levin epidemiologist, educator
Scharold, Mary Louise psychoanalyst, educator
Schechter, Arthur Louis lawyer
Schier, Mary Jane science writer
Schiflett, Mary Fletcher Cavender retired health facility executive, researcher, educator
Schmeal, Jacqueline Andre art store owner
Schneider, David J. psychology educator, academic administrator
Schneider, Karen Lee psychotherapist
†Schneider, Pamela Jean psychotherapist
Schoolar, Joseph Clayton psychiatrist, pharmacologist, educator
Schultz, Stanley George physiologist, educator
Schwartz, Brenda Keen lawyer
Schwartz, Charles Walter lawyer
Scott, David Warren statistics educator
Scott, Ronald lawyer
Scuseria, Gustavo Enrique theoretical chemist
Seaton, Alberta Jones biologist, educator, consultant
Secrest, Ronald Dean lawyer
Segner, Edmund Peter, III natural gas company executive
Selke, Charles Richard real estate lawyer
Selke, Oscar O., Jr. physiatrist, educator
Seymour, Barbara Laverne lawyer
Shaddock, Carroll Sidney lawyer
Shankel, Gerald Marvin professional society administrator
Shapiro, Carrie Kimberly epidemiologist, researcher
Sharp, Douglas Andrew secondary school educator
Shearer, William Thomas pediatrician, educator
Sheehan, Linda Suzanne educational administrator
Shelley, Clyde Burton artist
Shen, Liang Chi electrical engineer, educator, researcher
Sher, George Allen philosophy educator
Sheriff, Robert geophysicist, educator, consultant
†Shook, Barbara Rhines journalist, consultant
Shulman, Robert Jay physician
Shurn, Peter Joseph, III lawyer
Siekman, Thomas Clement lawyer
Sill, Gerald de Schrenck hotel executive
Simmons, Stephen Judson lawyer
Simpson, Joe Leigh obstetrics and gynecology educator
Sims, Rebecca Gibbs accountant, certified fraud examiner, journalist, editor
Sing, William Bender lawyer
Singleton, John Virgil, Jr. retired federal judge, lawyer
Sirbasku, David Andrew medical educator
Sisson, Virginia Baker geology educator
Skalla, John Lionell insurance agent
Skov, Arlie Mason petroleum engineer, consultant
Slack, Karen Kershner advertising agency executive
Slaugh, Lynn H. chemist
Sloan, Harold David chemical engineering consultant
Smalley, Arthur Louis, Jr. engineering and construction company executive
Smalley, Richard Errett chemistry and physics educator, researcher
Smith, Arthur Kittredge, Jr. academic administrator, political science educator
Smith, Brooke Ellen lawyer
Smith, David Kingman retired oil company executive, consultant
Smith, J. Thomas mental health consultant
Smith, Jerry Edwin federal judge
Smith, Ken A. physicist
Smith, Michael William construction and consulting company executive
Smith, Richard Joseph history educator
†Smith, Roland Blair university administrator
Smith, Tal sports association administrator
Smith, William Randolph lawyer
Smythe, Cheves McCord dean, medical educator
Soileau, Kerry Michael aerospace technologist, researcher
Soliz, Joseph Guy lawyer
Solomon, Marsha Harris draftsman, artist
Solymosy, Edmond Sigmond Albert international marketing executive, retired army officer
Sonfield, Robert Leon, Jr. lawyer
†Southwell, Samuel Beall English educator
Souza, Marco Antonio civil engineer, educator
Spalding, Andrew Freeman lawyer
Spanos, Pol Dimitrios engineering educator
Spellman, Oliver B., Jr. city official
Sperber, Matthew Arnold direct marketing company executive
Spincic, Wesley James oil company executive, consultant
Spira, Melvin plastic surgeon
†Stacy, Frances H. judge
Staine, Ross lawyer
Stankiewicz, Bogdan Artur geologist
Starkey, Elizabeth LaRuffa accountant
Steele, James Harlan former public health veterinarian, educator
†Steen, Wesley Wilson bankruptcy judge, lawyer
Stehlin, John Sebastian, Jr. surgeon
Stephens, Carson Wade minister
Stephens, Delia Marie Lucky lawyer
Stevenson, Ben artistic director
†Storey, Gail Donohue writer, editor
Stradley, William Jackson lawyer
Streng, William Paul lawyer, educator
Strong, George Walter political consultant
Stryker, Daniel Ray adult education educator
Stryker, Steven Charles lawyer
Sullivan, Neil Maxwell oil and gas company executive
Summers, Joseph Frank author, publisher
Sun, Wei-Joe aerospace engineer, consultant
Susman, Morton Lee lawyer
Susman, Stephen Daily lawyer
Suter, Jon Michael academic library director, educator
Swanson, Charles Richard accountant, oil and gas consultant
Sweet, Christopher William computer company executive
Sweet, James Brooks oral and maxillofacial surgeon
Swezey, Christopher Stephen geologist
Sydow, Michael David lawyer
Szalkowski, Charles Conrad lawyer
Talwani, Manik geophysicist, educator
Tanous, Helene Mary physician
Tatarinov, Kirill computer software company executive
Tatham, Robert Haines geophysicist
†Taylor, William Lansing geologist
Temkin, Larry Scott philosopher, educator
Temple, Robert Winfield chemical company executive
Templeton, Robert Earl engineering and construction company executive
Thacker, Shannon Stephen financial advisor
Thomas, Edred broadcast executive
†Thomas, Larry Dee poet
Thomas, Lavon Bullock interior designer
Thomas, Marilyn Jane insurance agent, agency owner
Thomas, Orville C. physician
Thompson, Ewa M. foreign language educator
Thompson, Tina professional basketball player
†Thompson-Draper, Cheryl L. electronics executive, real estate executive
Thorn, Terence Hastings international energy industry executive
Tice, Pamela Paradis scientific editor, writer
Tidwell, Mary Ellen loss control coordinator
Tilney, Elizabeth A. marketing executive
Tiras, Herbert Gerald engineering executive
Toedt, D(ell) C(harles), III lawyer
Tomjanovich, Rudolph professional athletic coach
Tong, Louis Lik-Fu information scientist
Tooker, Carl E. department store executive
Touchy, Deborah K. P. lawyer, accountant
Travis, Andrew David lawyer
Tripp, Karen Bryant lawyer
Tucker, Gary Wilson nurse educator
Tucker, Randolph Wadsworth engineering executive
Tulloch, Brian Robert endocrinologist
Tullos, Hugh Simpson orthopedic surgeon, educator
Turner, Kelley Bailey volunteer program administrator
Untermeyer, Charles Graves (Chase) computer company executive
Urbina, Manuel, II legal research historian, history educator
Vacar, Richard M. airport executive
Vallbona, Carlos physician
Van Caspel, Venita Walker retired financial planner
Vance, Carol Stoner lawyer
van Cleave, Kirstin Dean (Kit van Cleave) martial arts educator, writer, educator, publishing executive
Vanderploeg, James M. preventive medicine physician
Van Doesburg, Hans chemical engineer, management consultant
Van Dusen, Glenn T. controller, secretary, treasurer
Van Fleet, George Allan lawyer
Van Kerrebrook, Mary Alice lawyer
Vassilopoulou-Sellin, Rena medical educator
Veletsos, A(nestis) civil engineer, educator
Vest, G. Waverly, Jr. lawyer
†Vindekilde, Soren John physician
†Wade, Freddie, III program director
Waggoner, James Virgil chemicals company executive
Wagner, Charlene Brook small business owner, retired middle school educator, consultant
Wagner, Donald Bert health care consultant
Wakil, Salih Jawad biochemistry educator
Walbridge, Willard Eugene broadcasting executive
Walker, William Easton surgeon, educator, lawyer
Wall, Kenneth E., Jr. lawyer
Wall, Matthew J., Jr. surgeon, scientist
Wallace, Mark Allen hospital executive
Wallis, Olney Gray lawyer
Walls, Martha Ann Williams (Mrs. B. Carmage Walls) newspaper executive
Walton, Conrad Gordon, Sr. architect
Wang, Chao-Cheng mathematician, engineer
Ward, Bethea artist, small business owner
Ward, David Henry (Dave Ward) television news reporter, anchorman
Warren, J(oseph) E(mmet) petroleum engineer
Waska, Ronald Jerome lawyer
Wasserman, Steve broadcast executive
†Watson, Chuck electric power industry executive
Watson, John Allen lawyer
Watson, Max P., Jr. computer software company executive
Waycaster, Bill chemicals executive
Webb, Jack M. lawyer
Webb, Marty Fox principal
Weber, Fredric Alan lawyer
Weber, Owen broadcast executive
Weber, Wilford Alexander education educator
Weberpal, Michael Andrew lawyer
Weinstein, Roy physics educator, researcher
Welch, Byron Eugene communications educator
Welch, Kathy Jane information technology executive
Welch, Robert Morrow, Jr. lawyer
Wells, Benjamin Gladney lawyer
Wells, Damon, Jr. investment company executive
Wells, Raymond O'Neil, Jr. mathematics educator, researcher
Werlein, Ewing, Jr. federal judge
Wesse, David Joseph higher education consultant
†Westberry, John Elliott mathematics educator
Westby, Timothy Scott lawyer
Wheelan, R(ichelieu) E(dward) lawyer
Wheless, James Warren neurologist
†Wheless, Randolph F. federal judge
Whitaker, Gilbert Riley, Jr. academic administrator, business economist
White, Craig Alan history educator, consultant
White, David Alan, Jr. manufacturing company executive
Wickliffe, Jerry L. lawyer
Wieber, Sandra Jean pediatric critical care nurse
Wiemer, David Robert plastic surgeon
Wiener, Martin Joel historian
Wike, D. Elaine business executive
Wilcox, Barbara Montgomery accountant
Wilde, Carlton D. lawyer
Wilde, William Key lawyer
Wilkinson, Harry Edward management educator and consultant
Williames, Lee John university official, history educator
Williams, Edward Earl, Jr. entrepreneur, educator
Williams, James Lee financial industries executive
Williams, Robert Henry oil company executive
Williams, Robert Lyle corporate executive, consultant
Williams, Temple Weatherly, Jr. internist, educator
Williams, Wright psychologist, educator
Williamson, Peter David lawyer
Wilsmann, Edward Charles chemical company executive, educator
Wilson, Carl Weldon, Jr. construction company executive, civil engineer
Wilson, Edward Converse, Jr. oil and natural gas production company executive
Wilson, Patricia Potter library science and reading educator, educational and library consultant
Wilson, Rick Keith political science educator
Wilson, Thomas Leon physicist
Wilson, Walter Clinton gas, oil industry executive
Winzeler, Ted J. geologist
†Wise, Linda marketing executive, consultant
Wise, William Allan oil company executive, lawyer
Wisecup, Barbara Jean retired medical/surgical nurse
Wnuk, Wade Joseph manufacturing and service company executive
Wolinsky, Ira nutritionist
Woo, Walter computer systems consultant
Woodhouse, John Frederick food distribution company executive
Woods, Stephanie Elise computer professional
Woodson, Benjamin Nelson, III insurance executive
Woodward, Clifford Edward chemical engineer
Worthington, William Albert, III lawyer
Wray, Thomas Jefferson lawyer
Wren, Robert James aerospace engineering manager
Wuensche, Vernon Edgar construction company executive
Wyatt, Oscar Sherman, Jr. retired energy company executive
Wyschogrod, Edith philosophy educator
Yang, Chao Yuh chemistry educator
Yang, Zhong-Jing physician assistant
Yarbrough, Michael city councilman
Yetter, R. Paul lawyer
Yokubaitis, Roger T. lawyer
York, James Martin judge
Young, Jeanette Cochran corporate planner, reporter, analyst
Young, John Watts astronaut
Yu, Aiting Tobey engineering executive
Yuen, Benson Bolden airline management consultant, software executive
Zeff, Stephen Addam accounting educator
Zeigler, Ann dePender lawyer
Zlatkis, Albert chemistry educator
†Zoghbi, Huda Y. pediatric neurology and genetics educator
Zorn Pickens, Caroline Mae social services administrator

Howe
Jarma, Donna Marie secondary education educator

Hughes Springs
Koelker, Gail family nurse practitioner

Humble
Brinkley, Charles Alexander geologist
Fields, Jack Milton, Jr. former congressman
†Gruman, Robert Richard energy management consultant
Hahne, C. E. (Gene Hahne) computer services executive
St. Pé, Carolyn Ann elementary education educator
Trowbridge, John Parks physician

Hunt
Price, Donald Albert veterinarian, consultant

Huntsville
Bowers, Elliott Toulmin university president
Budge, Marcia Charlene family nurse practitioner
Conwell, Halford Roger physician
†Gratz, Cindy Carpenter dance educator, choreographer
Hoffmann, Frank William library science educator, writer
Jenkin, Douglas Alan computer consultant
Lea, Stanley E. artist, educator
LeBlanc, Jacob D. vice principal
Marks, Bobby Kees academic administrator, educator
Payne, David Emer university administrator
Payne, Richard Harold political science educator
†Policarpo, Alcibiades G. educator Spanish language and literature
Raymond, Kay E(ngelmann) Spanish language educator, consultant
Russell, George Haw video production company executive
Schwetman, John William English language professional educator
Smyth, Joseph Philip travel industry executive
Stowe, Charles Robinson Beecher management consultant, educator, lawyer
Vick, Marie retired health science educator
Ward, Richard Hurley university administrator, writer
Warner, Laverne education educator

Hurst
Bennett, Lori Jayne elementary school educator
Bishara, Amin Tawadros management and consulting firm executive, technical services executive
Buford, Evelyn Claudene Shilling jewelry specialist, merchandising professional
Dooley, Lena Rose (Nelson) writer, editor
Mc Keen, Chester M., Jr. business executive

Industry
Huitt, Jimmie L. rancher, oil, gas, real estate investor

Ingram
Hughes, David Michael oil service company executive, rancher

Irving
Aikman, Troy professional football player
Allen, Larry Christopher football player
Anastasi, Richard Joseph computer software consultant
Anderson, Greg R. communications company executive
Anderson, Michael Curtis computer industry analyst
Appel, John C. communications company executive
Armey, Richard Keith (Dick Armey) congressman
Attwood, James Albert, Jr. telecommunications industry executive
Barber, Jerry Randel medical device company executive
Basinger, Lawrence Edwin real estate executive
Bayne, James Elwood oil company executive
†Belfour, Ed professional hockey player
Bielss, Otto William, Jr. secondary school educator
†Caldwell, James D. hospitality company executive
Cannon, Francis V., Jr. academic administrator, electrical engineer, economist
Chase, Pearline adult education educator
Clinton, Tracy Peter, Sr. financial executive, systems analyst
Cooper, Alcie Lee, Jr. insurance executive
Cooper, Kathleen Bell economist
Corcoran, Thomas Joseph hotel executive
Cox, David Leon telecommunications company executive
Dinicola, Robert consumer products company executive
Dykstra, Ronald Joseph military officer
Forson, Norman Ray controller
Fukui, George Masaaki microbiology consultant
†Gailey, Thomas Chandler professional football coach
Garcia, Raymond Lloyd dermatologist
Geisinger, Janice Allain accountant
Gibson, Colvin Donald human resources specialist
†Gilbert, Glen Stuart marketing executive
Glober, George Edward, Jr. lawyer
Gorman, MaureenU. foundation administrator
Gretzinger, Ralph Edwin, III management consultant
Halter, Jon Charles magazine editor, writer
Helm, Terry Allen telecommunications consultant
Hendrickson, Constance Marie McRight chemist, consultant
†Hitchcock, Ken professional hockey coach
Holdar, Robert Martin chemist
Hull, Brett A. professional hockey player
Irvin, Michael Jerome professional football player
Ismail, Raghib (Rocket Ismail) professional football player
Jones, Jerry (Jerral Wayne Jones) professional football team executive
Jorns, Steven D. hotel executive
Kaufman, Sanders computer programmer
Kuckelman, Brian Thomas architect
Lett, Leon professional football player
Lieberman, Mark Joel lawyer
Lifson, Kalman Alan management consultant, retail executive
Lites, James R. professional hockey team executive
Longwell, H.J. petroleum engineer, executive
Lutz, Matthew Charles oil company executive, geologist
Martin, Stacey accountant
Martin, Thomas Lyle, Jr. university president
Masterton, Craig William management consultant
Matthews, Charles W. lawyer
McClain, Dennis Douglas advertising executive
†McClinton, Travis Victor, II mathematics educator
†McCormack, Grace Lynette civil engineering technician
McVay, Barbara Chaves secondary education mathematics educator
Meredith, Karen Ann accountant, financial executive
Messina, Paul Francis education consultant
Milgrim, Samuel G. television producer
Mobley, William Hodges management educator, researcher
†Modano, Michael professional hockey player
Norris, Richard Anthony accountant
Nugent, John Hilliard communications executive
Olson, Herbert Theodore trade association executive
†Owen, Joe David editor
Pitts, Joe W., III (Chip Pitts) lawyer, law educator
Plaskett, Thomas G. transportation company executive
Potter, Robert Joseph technical and business executive
Rainwater, R. Steven systems engineer
Rethore, Bernard Gabriel diversified manufacturing and mining company executive
†Roig, Daniel G. finance company executive
†Rowling, Robert B. hotel executive
Sanders, Deion Luwynn football player
Sasseen, Robert Francis university educator
Savage, Richard Mark quality manager
Sensabaugh, Mary Elizabeth financial consultant
†Sidu, Sanjiv computer software executive
Siefkin, William Charles investor, Internet sales executive, consultant
Skinner, John Vernon retail credit executive
Smith, Emmitt J., III professional football player
Sommerfeldt, John Robert historian
Sparrow, Larry J. telecommunications executive
Stepnoski, Mark Matthew professional football player
Stern, Ilene executive fund raiser
Stevens, Dennis Max audit director
Sweat, Jason Ellis government official, consultant
Wahlstrom, Paul Burr television producer
Warren, Christopher Collins professional football player
Whitaker, Heidi Sue accountant, systems developer, project manager
White, Thomas W. telecommunications company executive
Wicks, William Withington retired public relations executive
Williams, Erik George professional football player
Woodson, Darren Ray professional football player
Young, J. Warren magazine publisher

Jacksboro
Webb, Michael Alan city manager

Jacksonville
Blaylock, James Carl clergyman, librarian
Brewer, Brett lawyer
Pruitt, William Charles, Jr. minister, educator
Thrall, Gordon Fish lawyer

Jefferson
Lawrence, Sharon Orleans publishing executive, writer

Jonesville
Vaughan, Martha Louise agency administrator

Joshua
Hoggard, William Zack, Jr. amusement park executive

Junction
Evans, Jo Burt communications executive

Karnes City
Davis, Troy Arnol reflexologist, hypnotherapist

Katy
Bradshaw, Melissa Webb librarian
†Coleman, Curtis H. financial executive
Gibert, Charlene West gifted education educator

Harbour, Patricia Ann Monroe poet
Huffaker, E. Wayne artist
Hughes, Sandra Michelle education administrator, educator
Paden, Carolyn Eileen Belknap dietitian
Thorne, Melvin Quentin, Jr. managed healthcare executive

Kaufman
Legg, Reagan Houston lawyer

Keene
Smith, Pamela Sue mid-management educator

Keller
White, Lee Alvin mechanical engineer, engineering executive

Kelly A F B
†Bielowicz, Paul L. career officer
†Murdock, Robert M. career officer
Murdock, Robert McClellan air force officer
Stringer, Jerry Ray magazine editor

Kemp
Wurlitzer, Fred Pabst surgeon

Kempner
Parker, Catharine Janet education administrator, consultant, entrepreneur

Kermit
Gremmel, Gilbert Carl family physician

Kerrville
Frudakis, Evangelos William sculptor
Matlock, (Lee) Hudson civil engineer, educator
Parmley, Robert James lawyer, consultant
Rhodes, James Devers psychotherapist
Shaw, Alan Bosworth geologist, paleontologist, retired
†Tran, Qui-Phiet English educator
Williams, William Henry, II publisher

Kilgore
Carter, Michael Wayne electrical engineer
Garvin, Wilford L. sales and marketing manager
†Holda, William Michael academic administrator
Pipkin, Wade Lemual, Jr. reference librarian
Rorschach, Richard Gordon lawyer

Killeen
†Anderson, James Raymond academic administrator
Beck, Barbara Nell elementary school educator
Crawford, Norma Vivian nurse
Montgomery, Marietta H. (Bunnie Montgomery) secondary education educator
Reid, Sharon Lea educational facilitator
Reid, Thomas Michael middle school educator
Vancura, Stephen Joseph radiologist

Kingsland
Johnson, Vicki Valeen paramedic, technical advisor movie studios

Kingsville
Cecil, David Rolf mathematician, educator
†Cortazar, Alejandro educator
Ibanez, Manuel Luis university official, biological sciences educator
Robins, Gerald Burns education educator
Stanford, Jane Herring business administration educator
Wiley, Millicent Yoder retired secondary school educator, realtor

Kingwood
Bowman, Stephen Wayne quality assurance engineer, consultant
Burghduff, John Brian mathematics educator
Hawk, Phillip Michael service corporation executive
Romere, Mary Elaine public health services manager
†Wigglesworth, David Cunningham business and management consultant

Klein
Esmond, Cheri Sue secondary school educator

Knippa
†Gracia, Brenda Lee poet

La Feria
Philip, Sunny Koipurathu municipal official

La Porte
Darby, Barbara Ann-Lofthouse chemical technician
Davenport, C. W. historic site director
Yoder, Nelson Brent oil company executive

Lackland A F B
Rodgers, Robert Aubrey physicist

Lackland AFB
†Barksdale, Barry W. career officer
Burghardt, Walter Francis, Jr. veterinarian
Charlip, Ralph Blair career officer
Lydic, Garry Keith producer
Winn, Vicki Elaine nurse, consultant

Lago Vista
Garcia y Carrillo, Martha Xochitl pharmacist

Laguna Park
Folkens, Alan Theodore clinical and pharmaceutical microbiologist

Lake Creek
Smith, Shirley Ann Nabors secondary school educator

Lake Jackson
Elbert, James Peak independent insurance agent, minister
Tasa, Kendall Sherwood college administrator

Lake Whitney
Lawson, Carole Jean religious educator, author, poet

Lakeway
Boswell, Gary Taggart investor, former electronics company executive

Lampasas
Harvey, Leigh Kathryn lawyer

Lancaster
Goelden-Bowen, Michelle Marie occupational therapist
Pratt, John Edward law educator
Wendorf, Denver Fred, Jr. anthropology educator

LaPorte
†Defee, Vicki Jean elementary education educator

Laredo
Barrett, Bryan Edward prosecutor
Black, Clifford Merwyn academic administrator, sociologist, educator
Colón, Phyllis Janet city official
Fierros, Ruth Victoria retired secondary school educator
Kazen, George Philip federal judge
Knapp, Thomas Edwin sculptor, painter
Lakshmana, Viswanath computer and information systems executive
†Mitchell, Thomas Reagan English educator
Nixon-Mendez, Nina Louise urban planner
†Notzon, Marcel C. federal judge
Qualey, Thomas Leo, Jr. human services administrator
Reuthinger, Georgeanne special education educator
Watson, Helen Richter educator, ceramic artist
Weber, Janice Ann library director, grant writer
Zaffirini, Judith state senator, small business owner

League City
Burns, Richard Robert chemicals executive
Ellis, Walter Leon minister
Moore, Walter D., Jr. retired pathologist
Senyard, Corley Price, Jr. engineering executive, consultant
Williams, Richard Robert artist, educator

Leander
Erickson, Ralph D. retired physical education educator, small business owner, consultant
Reed, Carol Brady Summerlin secondary education educator

Levelland
Harrell, Wanda Faye retail executive
Pearson, Dana Bart librarian
Sears, Edward L. English language educator, real estate investor
†Taylor, James Lynn college administrator
Walker, James Kenneth judge

Lewisville
Browne, M. Lynne artist, optician
Ferguson, R. Neil computer systems consultant
Mebane, Barbara Margot service company executive, studio owner
Myers, Madeleine Becan secondary school educator
Tucker, Phyllis Anita sales representative, guidance counselor
Vacca, John Joseph, Jr. television executive

Liberty
Hughes, Paul Anthony minister, musician, songwriter, author, publisher
Wheat, John Nixon lawyer

Liberty Hill
Adams, Christopher Steve, Jr. retired defense electronics corporation executive, former air force officer
West, Felton retired newspaper writer

Lindale
Bockhop, Clarence William retired agricultural engineer
Carter, Thomas Smith, Jr. retired railroad executive

Livingston
Horner, Jennie Linn retired educational administrator, nurse
Jones, Janet Valeria psychiatric nurse, clinical nurse educators
Oliver, Debbie Edge elementary education educator
Perkins, Sue Dene editor
Wolter, John Amadeus librarian, government official

Llano
Walter, Virginia Lee psychologist, educator

Longview
Cromer-Campbell, Tammy commercial and fine art photographer
Fouse, Anna Beth education educator
Harper, Verne Jay petroleum landman
Hearne, Carolyn Fox art, history educator, artist, art museum director
LeTourneau, Richard Howard retired college president
Mann, Jack Matthewson bottling company executive
Martin, John Foster university official
Martin, Ulrike Balk laboratory technician
Pursley-Davis, Alice Janet elementary school educator
Sonnier, David Joseph wholesale distributing executive
Turner, Ellis Dale clergyman, paint manufacturing executive
Welge, Jack Herman, Jr. lawyer

Lorena
Mc Call, Charles Barnard health facility executive, educator

Los Fresnos
†Sterling, William Carlisle physician assistant

Lubbock
†Akard, John C. federal judge
Archer, James Elson engineering educator
Askins, Billy Earl education educator, consultant
Aykal, Gürer conductor
Beck, George Preston anesthesiologist, educator
Bricker, Donald Lee surgeon
Bronwell, Nancy Brooker writer
Broselow, Linda Latt medical office technician, aviculturist
Buesseler, John Aure ophthalmologist, management consultant
†Burns, John Mitchell academic administrator
Butterworth, Daniel Drew humanities educator, consultant
Chavarria, Dolores Esparza financial service executive
Cochran, Joseph Wesley law librarian, educator
Connor, Seymour Vaughan historian, educator, writer
Conover, William Jay statistics educator
Cooke, Alex "Ty", Jr. mayor
Crowson, James Lawrence lawyer, financial company executive, academic administrator
Cummings, Sam R. federal judge
†Davis, Alvin G. company executive
Davis, Jimmy Frank assistant attorney general
Dersch, Charette Alyse marriage and family therapist
Dudek, Richard Albert engineering educator
Edson, Gary Francis museum director
Elder, Bessie Ruth pharmacist
Fontenot, Andrea Dean communications executive
Gibbons, Connie Sue art association administrator
Gibson, David Roger optometrist
Giesselmann, Michael Guenter electrical engineer, educator, researcher
Gilliam, John Charles economist, educator
Haragan, Donald Robert university administrator, geosciences educator
Havens, Murray Clark political scientist, educator
Hennessey, Audrey Kathleen computer researcher, educator
Hentges, David John microbiology educator
Hester, Ross Wyatt retired business forms manufacturing executive
Hisey, Lydia Vee educational administrator
†Homan, Richard Warren physician, educator
Huggins, Cannie Mae Cox Hunter retired elementary school educator
Hurst, Mary Jane English language educator
Ishihara, Osamu electrical engineer, physicist, educator
Jackson, Francis Charles physician, surgeon
Jackson, Raymond Carl cytogeneticist
Johnson, Ronda Janice professional not-for-profit fundraiser
Kaye, Alan David anesthesiologist, researcher
Kelsey, Clyde Eastman, Jr. philosophy and psychology educator
†Kennedy, Linda Carol art and art educator
Ketner, Kenneth Laine philosopher, educator
Kimbrough, Robert Cooke, III infectious diseases physician
King, Linda Carol music educator
Kristiansen, Magne electrical engineer, educator
Kurtzman, Neil A. medical educator
Laing, Malcolm Brian geologist, consultant
Lucas, Don John music educator
†Martinez-Flores, Sylvia Alicia management consultant
May, Donald Robert Lee ophthalmologist, retina and vitreous surgeon, educator, farmer
McBeath, Don B. health administrator
Miller, Stephen Laurence responsive services executive
†Mitchell, Gary W. molding company executive
Mittemeyer, Bernhard Theodore urology and surgery educator
Montford, John Thomas state legislator, academic administrator, lawyer
Murrah, David J. archivist, historian
Nelson, Toza elementary school educator
Nugent, Connie elementary education educator
Pelley, Patricia Marie Asian history specialist
Pike, Douglas Eugene educator
Portnoy, William Manos electrical engineering educator
Purdom, Thomas James lawyer
Purinton, MarJean D. English language educator, researcher
Reeves, A. Sue Windsor healthcare administrator
Robinson, G. Wilse molecular physicist, educator
Rodriguez, Placido bishop
Sabatini, Sandra physician
Schiffer, Randolph Brenton physician
Schmidly, David J. academic administrator, dean, biology educator
Sharp, Marsha basketball coach
Sitton, Windy mayor of Lubbock, Texas
Skoog, Gerald Duane science educator
Smith, Doris Corinne Kemp retired nurse
Snell, Robert retail executive
Stein, William Warner anthropology educator
Stem, Carl Herbert business educator
Stoll, Mark Richard humanities educator
van Appledorn, Mary Jeanne composer, music educator, pianist
Walker, Warren Stanley English educator
Wall, Betty Jane real estate consultant
Wampler, Richard Scotten marriage and family therapy educator
†Warnick, J.Q., Jr. federal judge
Warren, Jennifer Elizabeth neonatal nurse
Way, Barbara Haight dermatologist
Wendt, Charles William soil physicist, educator
Willingham, Mary Maxine fashion retailer
Wilson, Margaret Eileen retired physical education educator
Wolfe, Verda Nell pension consultant, financial planner
Wolpmann, Michael Joseph physician
Wood, Richard Courtney library director, educator
Woodworth, Margo Deane religious organization administrator
Woolam, Gerald Lynn surgeon
Young, Teri Ann Butler pharmacist
Zhang, Hong-Chao manufacturing engineer, educator

Lufkin
Billingsley, Shirley Ann writer, poet
Garrison, Pitser Hardeman lawyer, mayor emeritus
Hannah, John Henry, Jr. judge
Perry, Lewis Charles emergency medicine physician, osteopath
†Shaw, Dianne Elizabeth school administrator
Strohschein, Helen Frances educational administrator

Mansfield
Icenhower, Della Maude retired school librarian
Parnell, Charles L. speechwriter
†Simeus, Dumas food products executive

Marathon
Kurie, Andrew Edmunds mining geologist

Marble Falls
Simpson, H. Richard (Dick Simpson) retailer

Marfa
Meyer, Ellen Adams arts consultant

Marshall
Magrill, Rose Mary library director
Sudhivoraseth, Niphon pediatrician, allergist, immunologist

Mason
Johnson, Rufus Winfield lawyer
Ponder, Jerry Wayne historian

Mc Dade
Carson, David Costley psychologist, health care administrator

Mc Kinney
Brewer, Ricky Lee investment broker, estate planner
Dickinson, Richard Raymond retired oil company executive
Fairman, Jarrett Sylvester retail company executive
Goldstein, Lionel Alvin personal financial and investment advisor
Hoffmann, Manfred Walter consulting company executive
Kessler, John Paul, Jr. financial planner
Kincaid, Elsie Elizabeth educational therapist
Merritt, Linda Ann neonatal nurse
Roessler, P. Dee lawyer, former judge, educator

Mc Queeney
Gunter, Edwin Dale, Jr. pilot

Mcallen
Cox, George Sherwood computer science educator
†Garcia, David P. construction company executive
Gonzalez, Rolando Noel secondary school educator, religion educator, photographer
Hinojosa, Ricardo H. federal judge
McGee, William Howard John library system coordinator
Mohner, Carl Martin Rudolf movie actor, artist
†Ormsby, Peter E. federal judge
Ramirez, Leo Armando secondary school educator
Ramirez, Mario Efrain physician
†Rebuelta, Avelino Luis public administration educator
Sands, Norman Earl elementary school educator, composer
Sutton, William Blaylock pastor
Troester, Waltraud artist, graphic designer, consultant
Whisenant, B(ert) R(oy), Jr. insurance company executive

Meadows Place
Greco, Janice Teresa psychology educator

Mercedes
Alaniz, Theodora Villarreal elementary education educator

Mesquite
Montgomery, Marvin musical producer
Williamson, Barbara Jo retired community health nurse, educator

Mico
Shockey, Thomas Edward real estate executive, engineer

Midland
Arizaga, Lavora Spradlin retired lawyer
Best, Alynda Kay conflict resolution mediator
Bullock, Maurice Randolph lawyer
Coombs, Kerry Leland veterinarian, educator
Craddick, Thomas Russell state representative, investor
Franklin, Robert Drury oil company executive
Furgeson, William Royal federal judge
Groce, James Freelan financial consultant
Grover, Rosalind Redfern oil and gas company executive
Helms, Micky engineering executive
Lankford, Jill elementary school principal
Lohmann, George Young, Jr. neurosurgeon, hospital executive, artist
McAfee, John Wilson, Sr. retired principal
Powers, Patricia Kennett piano and organ educator
Roberts, David Glen regional marketing director, investor
Roomberg, Susan Kelly management consultant
Roper, Eddie Joe energy company executive
Stoltz, Michael Rae lawyer
Sullivan, Patricia G. maternal, child and women's health nursing educator
Tom, James Robert accountant
Truitt, Robert Ralph, Jr. lawyer
Wade, Margaret Gaston real estate property manager, educator

Midlothian
†Davis, Brenda D. journalist

Mineral Wells
Reedy, Thomas Wayne minister, theologian, educator
Scott, Geneva Lee Smith nursing educator

Mission
McClendon, Maxine artist
Rapp, Joanna A. retired geriatrics nurse, mental health nurse

Missouri City
Chang, Jeffrey Chai dentist, educator, researcher
Hodges, Jot Holiver, Jr. lawyer, business executive

Montgomery
Falkingham, Donald Herbert oil company executive
Gooch, Carol Ann psychotherapist consultant
Snider, Robert Larry management consultant
Tharp, Benjamin Carroll, Jr. architect

Mount Pleasant
Caskey, Judith Ann educational director
O'Donnell, Robert Patrick priest

Cloud, Bruce Benjamin, Sr. *construction company executive*
Colyer, Kirk Klein *insurance executive, real estate investment executive*
†Cook, Harold Rodney *military officer, medical facility administrator*
Corrales, Frank Campa *composer, writer, guitarist*
Cory, William Eugene *retired consulting company executive*
Cottingham, Stephen Kent *real estate development executive, researcher*
Crabtree, Ben C. *home health care agency administrator*
Crabtree, Tania Oylan *home health nurse, administrator, consultant*
Croft, Harry Allen *psychiatrist*
Culver, John Blaine *minister*
Cummings Persellin, Diane Y. *music education educator*
Cutshall, Jon Tyler *aerospace engineer, researcher*
Davenport, Pamela Beaver *rancher, small business owner*
†Davila, Rodolfo G. *pharmaceutical company executive*
Davis, George Edward *industrial designer*
Davis, Jolene Bryant *magazine publishing executive consultant*
Davis, Steven Andrew *dermatologist*
Davis, Walter Barry *quality assurance professional*
Davis, Yolette Marie Toussaint *home nursing administrator, parish nurse, camp nurse*
Dazey, William Boyd *retired lawyer*
Dean, Jack *protective services official*
Deviney, Marvin Lee, Jr. *research institute scientist, program manager*
Dobie, Robert Alan *otologist*
Donaldson, Willis Lyle *research institute administrator*
Dudley, Brooke Fitzhugh *educational consultant*
Duncan, A. Baker *investment banker*
†Duncan, Tim *professional basketball player*
†Dunkelberg, Lee *journalist*
Durbin, Richard Louis, Jr. *lawyer*
†Elaydi, Saber Nasr *educator*
Elliot, Sean Michael *professional basketball player*
Ellis, James D. *communications executive, corporate lawyer*
Emerson, Arthur Rojas *broadcast executive*
Emick, William John *real estate investor, retired federal executive*
Estep, Myrna Lynne *systems analyst, philosophy educator*
Evans, Michelle Lee *lawyer, educator*
Fasano, Anthony John *marketing consultant*
Fawcett, Leslie Clarence, Jr. *accountant*
Fecher, Vincent John *priest*
Fehrenbach, T(heodore) R(eed) *author, businessman*
Ferrin, Marshall Sims *telecommunications executive*
Field, Charles Twist *artist, art educator*
Firestone, Juanita Marlies *sociology educator*
Fite, Patricia Paulette *English educator*
Flores, Patrick F. *archbishop*
Flores, Roger *city official*
Flynn, Robert Lopez *writer*
Fogg, Ernest Leslie *minister, retired*
Fornos, Peter Secundino *pulmonary medicine physician*
Foster, Charles F. *communications executive*
Fox, Michael W. *lawyer*
Fraley, Debra Lee *critical care nurse*
Franklin, Larry Daniel *communications company executive*
Frazer, Robert Lee *landscape architect*
Freeman, Theodore Monroe *physician*
Frigerio, Charles Straith *lawyer*
Frith, Lynda Kathryn *principal*
Garcia, Henry Frank *finance and administration executive*
Garcia, Hipolito Frank (Hippo Garcia) *federal judge*
Garcia, Orlando Luis *judge*
Garza, Emilio M(iller) *federal judge*
†Garza, Jaime Ruperto *plastic/reconstructive surgeon*
Gates, Mahlon Eugene *applied research executive, former government official, former army officer*
Gaulin, Jean *gas distribution company executive*
Gibbons, Robert Ebbert *university official*
Giust, Steve *television station executive*
Gladstone, George Randall *planetary scientist*
Glueck, Sylvia Blumenfeld *writer*
Goelz, Paul Cornelius *university dean*
Gomes, Norman Vincent *retired industrial engineer*
Gonzalez, Efren *airport executive*
Gonzalez, Hector Hugo *nurse, educator, consultant*
Gonzalez, Henry Barbosa *former congressman*
Greehey, William Eugene *energy company executive*
Greenberg, Nat *orchestra administrator*
Griffin-Thompson, Melanie *accounting firm executive*
†Groff, James Edward *education educator, academic administrator*
Guenther, Jack Egon *lawyer*
Guerrero, Debra Ann *council woman*
Guess, James David *lawyer*
Gwathmey, Joe Neil, Jr. *broadcasting executive*
Hall, Brad Bailey *orthopaedic surgeon, health care administrator*
Hall, Douglas Lee *computer science educator*
Hamm, William Joseph *retired physics educator*
Hammond, Weldon Woolf, Jr. *hydrogeologist*
Hanahan, Donald James *biochemist, educator*
Hannah, John Robert, Sr. *accountant*
Hardberger, Phillip Duane *judge, lawyer, journalist*
Hardy, Harvey Louchard *lawyer*
Hargrave, Robert Warren *hair styling salon chain executive*
Harris, Richard John *social sciences educator*
Harte, Houston Harriman *marketing executive*
Hawken, Patty Lynn *retired nursing educator, dean of faculty*
Haywood, Norcell Dan *architect*
Hazuda, Helen Pauline *sociologist, educator*
Hemminghaus, Roger Roy *energy company executive, chemical engineer*
Henderson, Connie Chorlton *city planner, artist and writer*
Henderson, Dwight Franklin *dean, educator*
Henington, C. Dayle *retired economist*
Henry, Peter York *lawyer, mediator*
Herres, Robert Tralles *financial services executive*
Hill, William Victor, II *retired army officer, secondary school educator*
Hollin, Shelby W. *lawyer*
†Holt, Peter M. *sports team executive*
Hopper, Vanessa J. *oncological nurse*
Horton, Granville Eugene *occupational medicine physician, retired air force officer*
Hubbard, Walter Bryan *engineer, consultant*
Huff, Robert Whitley *obstetrician, gynecologist, educator*
Iglehart, T. D. *bishop*
Irving, George Washington, III *veterinarian, research director, consultant*
Jackson, Brenda S. *nursing educator*
Jackson, Earl, Jr. *medical technologist, retired*
Jackson, Steve Glen *health services administrator*
Jacobson, David *rabbi*
Jacobson, Helen Gugenheim (Mrs. David Jacobson) *civic worker*
†Jansen-Brown, Angelika Charlotte *art museum director*
Javore, Gary William *lawyer*
Jensen-White, Teresa Elaine *financial planner*
Jiménez, Leonardo *popular accordionist*
Johnson, Katherine Anne *health research administrator, lawyer*
Johnson, Sammye LaRue *communications educator*
Joiner, Lorell Howard *real estate development and investment executive*
Jones, James Richard *business administration educator*
Jones, Jay, II *radio station executive*
Jorgensen, James H. *pathologist, educator, microbiologist*
Joslyn, James *television station executive*
Kalkwarf, Kenneth Lee *academic dean*
Kalter, Seymour Sanford *virologist, educator*
Kamada-Cole, Mika M. *allergist, immunologist, medical educator*
Kehl, Randall Herman *executive, consultant, lawyer*
Keyser-Fanick, Christine Lynn *banking executive, marketing and strategic planning professional*
King, Ronald Baker *federal judge*
Kittle, Joseph S. *science administrator, consultant*
Klaerner, Curtis Maurice *former oil company executive*
Knox, Robert Burns *religious organization administrator*
Knue, Joseph *writer, historian*
Kossaeth, Tammy Gale *intensive care nurse*
Kotas, Robert Vincent *research physician, educator*
Koym, Zala Cox *elementary education educator*
Kozuch, Julianna Bernadette *librarian, educator*
Kreisberg, Jeffrey I. *medical educator, researcher*
Krier, Joseph Roland *chamber of commerce executive, lawyer*
Kutchins, Michael Joseph *aviation consultant, former airport executive*
Labay, Eugene Benedict *lawyer*
Labenz-Hough, Marlene *dispute resolution professional*
Langlinais, Joseph Willis *educator, chaplain*
Laurence, Dan H. *author, literary and dramatic specialist*
Leal, Barbara Jean Peters *fundraising executive*
Leal, J. Terri *academic facility administrator*
†Lebras, Paul J. *career officer*
LeCoeur, Jo *adult education educator*
Ledvorowski, Thomas Edmund *secondary education educator*
Leies, John Alex *theology educator, clergyman*
Leighton, Albert Chester *history educator*
Le Maistre, Charles Aubrey *internist, epidemiologist, educator*
Lenke, Joanne Marie *publishing executive*
Leon, Robert Leonard *psychiatrist, educator*
Lloyd, Susan Elaine *middle school educator*
Lowe, Douglas Howard *architect*
Lowry, A. Robert *federal government railroad arbitrator*
Lussky, Warren Alfred *librarian, educator, consultant*
Lutter, Charles William, Jr. *lawyer*
Lyle, Robert Edward *chemist*
Macon, Jane Haun *lawyer*
Madrid, Olga Hilda Gonzalez *retired elementary education educator, association executive*
Maloney, Marynell *lawyer*
Marbut, Robert Gordon *communications and broadcast executive, investor*
Maring, Michael William *property management company executive*
Markwell, Dick R(obert) *retired chemist*
Marrou, Chris René *television newscaster*
Marshall, Joyce Ramsey *elementary education educator*
Martinez, Ruben *critical care nurse*
Masoro, Edward Joseph, Jr. *physiology educator*
Masters, Bettie Sue Siler *biochemist, educator*
Matthews, Rebecca Jan *English educator*
Mayo, Sandra Marie *college dean*
Mays, L. Lowry *radio station executive*
Mc Allister, Gerald Nicholas *retired bishop, clergyman*
†McBee, Lucy A. *elementary education educator, administrator*
McClane, Robert Sanford *former bank holding company executive, entrepreneur*
McCoy, Reagan Scott *oil company executive, lawyer*
McDonald, Mary Helen *special education educator*
McFee, Arthur Storer *physician*
McGill, Henry Coleman, Jr. *physician, educator, researcher*
McIntosh, Dennis Keith *veterinary practitioner, consultant*
Mercado, Mary Gonzales *cardiologist*
Michaels, Willard A. (Bill Michaels) *retired broadcasting executive*
Migachyov, Valery *mechanical engineer*
Mills, Linda S. *public relations executive*
Mitchell, George Washington, Jr. *physician, educator*
Moder, John Joseph *academic administrator, priest*
Montecel, Maria Robledo (Cuca Robledo Montecel) *educational association administrator*
Montemayor, Carlos Rene *advertising executive*
Montgomery, James Edward, Jr. *lawyer*
Moore, Kurt W. *pharmaceuticals company executive*
Moore, Steve *executive director San Antonio convention bureau*
Morales, Rolando *city official San Antonio*
Moss, Betty Harris *secondary education educator*
Moynihan, John Bignell *lawyer*
Neel, Spurgeon Hart, Jr. *physician, retired army officer*
New, Pamela Zyman *neurologist*
Nix, Robert Lynn *minister*
Nowak, Nancy Stein *judge*
†O'Connor, Robert B. *federal judge*
Ognibene, Andre J(ohn) *physician, army officer, educator*
†Oliver, Beverly *secondary school principal, administrator*
Orr, Joseph Newton *recreational guide, outdoor educator*
Owens, Amelia Anne *elementary education educator*
Palmer, Hubert Bernard *dentist, retired military officer*
Palmer, J(ohn) David *politcal science educator*
Paloczy, Susan Therese *elementary school principal*
Paris, Karen Marie *nurse, educator*
Parker, Warren Andrew *public health dentist, consultant*
Passty, Jeanette Nyda *English language educator*
Patrick, Dane Herman *lawyer*
Peak, Howard W. *mayor*
Pena, Octavio *director city internal revenue department*
Persellin, Robert Harold *physician*
Pestana, Carlos *physician, educator*
Petty, Scott, Jr. *rancher*
Pfanstiel Parr, Dorothea Ann *interior designer*
Philippus, Al A. *protective services official*
Pigno, Mark Anthony *prosthodontist, educator, researcher*
Pina, Alberto Buffington *trust company official*
Pixley, Beryl Kay *nursing educator*
Polan-Curtain, Jodie Lea *physiologist researcher*
†Popovich, Gregg *professional basketball coach*
Post, Gerald Joseph *retired banker, retired air force officer*
Potts, Martha Lou *elementary education educator*
Prado, Edward Charles *federal judge*
†Primono, John W. *federal judge*
Pruitt, Basil Arthur, Jr. *surgeon, retired army officer*
†Puckett, Terry Gay *art educator, artist*
Putman, (James) Michael *lawyer*
Rafelson, Max Emanuel, Jr. *biochemist, medical school administrator*
Ramos, Raul *surgeon*
Ramsey, Sara Annette *elementary education educator*
Randall, Charles Wilson *gastroenterologist*
†Rankin, Karen S. *retired career officer*
Reesman, Jeanne Campbell *English language educator*
Reuter, Stewart Ralston *radiologist, lawyer, educator*
Rhodes, Linda Jane *psychiatrist*
Ribble, Ronald George *psychologist, educator, writer*
†Ricks, Philip L., II *legislative director*
Rivard, Robert *editor*
Robinson, David Maurice *professional basketball player*
Rogers, Frances Evelyn *author, retired educator and librarian*
Rogers, William *psychologist, behavior specialist, writer, lecturer, journalist*
Rosenow, Doris Jane *critical care nurse, nursing consultant*
Ross, James Ulric *lawyer, accountant, educator*
Roth-Roffy, Paul William *accountant*
Rowe, Reginald *artist*
Ruttenberg, Frank Z. *lawyer*
Sablik, Martin John *research physicist*
Sakai, Peter A. *lawyer*
Sarangapani, Jagannathan *intelligent systems and controls engineer, educator*
Sauer, James Benson *philosopher, educator*
Schenker, Steven *physician, educator*
Schlueter, David Arnold *law educator*
Schonhoff, Robert Lee *marketing and advertising executive*
Schuk, Linda Lee *legal assistant, business educator*
Schultz, Marilyn Ann *medical/surgical nurse*
Schultz, Steven T. *hotel executive*
†Schurr, Theodore George *molecular anthropologist, human geneticist*
Sessions, William Steele *lawyer, former government official*
†Shelton-Colangelo, Sharon *English educator*
Shipman, Ross Lovelace *petroleum executive*
Shirley, Graham Edward *management executive*
Silva, Aurelia Davila *education educator*
Simmons, Cecelia E. *quality improvement, infection control and employee health nurse, researcher*
Simpson, Andrea Lynn *energy communications executive*
Singer, Merton *engineer*
Singh, Yesh Pal *mechanical engineering educator, consultant*
Sinkin, Fay Marie *environmentalist*
Smith, Reginald Brian Furness *anesthesiologist, educator*
†Solomon, Diane Hurst *neurologist*
Soucy, Mark D. *psychiatric-mental health clinical nurse specialist, educator*
Spannagel, Alan Wayne *physiologist*
Spears, Diane Shields *art academy administrator*
Spears, Sally *lawyer*
Spiro, Herbert John *political scientist, politician, educator, ambassador*
Springer, Karl Josef *science administrator*
Steen, John Thomas, Jr. *lawyer*
Stone, William Harold *geneticist, educator*
Summers, Barbara June *artist*
Sutherland, Berry *geologist, educator*
Suttle, Dorwin Wallace *federal judge*
Swansburg, Russell Chester *medical administrator educator*
Swiggett, Harold E. (Hal Swiggett) *writer, photographer*
Synek, Miroslav *physicist, chemist, world affairs consultant, researcher*
Teran, Sister Mary Inez *retired nun, educator*
Terracina, Roy David *private investor*
Terry, James Crockett *school system administrator, mediator*
Tomkewitz, Marie Adele *elementary school educator*
Townsend, Frank Marion *pathology educator*
Traylor, Donald Reginald *mathematics educator*
Tsin, Andrew Tsang Cheung *biochemistry educator*
Tucker, Stephen Lawrence *health administration educator, consultant*
Ullmer, (R.) John *computer company executive, retired educator*
Von Honts, Jacqueline Jay *artist*
Wachsmuth, Robert William *lawyer*
Walker, Mary Erline *critical care nurse*
Wallace, James Oldham *retired librarian*
Wallis, Ben Alton, Jr. *lawyer*
†Walsh, Nicolas Eugene *rehabilitation medicine physician, educator*
†Ware, Joseph Milton *military officer, public administration educator*
Weatherston, George Douglas, Jr. *food service executive*
Wellberg, Edward Louis, Jr. *insurance company executive*
Welmaker, Forrest Nolan *lawyer*
Whitacre, Edward E., Jr. *telecommunications executive*
†White, Charles B. *academic administrator*
White, Mary Ruth Wathen *social services administrator*
Whitesell, Stephen Ernest *parks and recreation director*
Wickstrom, Jon Alan *telecommunications executive, consultant*
Wiedeman, Geoffrey Paul *physician, air force officer*
†Wilkinson, Kenton Todd *communications educator*
Williams, James David *history educator*
Williamson, Deborah Daywood *lawyer*
Wilson, Bennie James, III *human resource executive, educator*
Wilson, Janie Menchaca *nursing educator, researcher*
Wimpee, Mary Elizabeth *elementary school educator*
Wimpress, Gordon Duncan, Jr. *corporate consultant, foundation executive*
Windham, Janice Gay *principal*
Winik, Joanne *broadcast executive*
†Wolff, Hugh Lipman *urologist, educator*
Woodson, Linda Townley *English educator, writer*
Yates, Norris William, Jr. *lawyer*
Yerkes, Susan Gamble *newspaper columnist*
Young, James Julius *university administrator, retired army officer*
Young, Olivia Knowles *retired librarian*
Zachry, Henry Bartell, Jr. *construction company executive*
Zehner, William Melville *network executive*
Zilveti, Carlos B. *preventive medicine physician, pediatrician*

San Diego
Pena, Modesta Celedonia *retired principal*

San Juan
Shelby, Nina Claire *special education educator*

San Marcos
Barragán, Celia Silguero *elementary education educator*
Beebe, Susan Jane *English language educator*
Bullock, Jerry McKee *retired military officer, consultant, educator*
Fite, Kathleen Elizabeth *education educator*
Fletcher, John Lynn *psychology educator*
Longley, Glenn *biology educator, research director*
Miloy, Leatha Faye *university program director*
Mooney, Robert Thurston *health care educator*
Moore, Patsy Sites *food service consultant*
Nguyen, Philong *electrical engineer*
Schiflett, Peggy L. Kucera *secondary school educator, consultant*
Supple, Jerome H. *academic administrator*
Taylor, Ruth Arleen Lesher *marketing educator*
Wetter-Kubeck, Daisy Fisher *dietitian, consultant*
†Wilson, Steven Michael *English educator, poet*

Sanger
Foote, Ruth Annette *business executive, land developer*
Head, Gregory Alan *mechanical engineer, consultant*

Seabrook
†Niksich, Peggy Linda *elementary education educator*
Patten, Bernard Michael *neurologist, writer, educator*

Sealy
Young, Milton Earl *retired petroleum company executive*

Seguin
Moline, Jon Nelson *philosopher, educator, college president*

Selma
†Lee, Allen Scott *protective services official*

Sheppard AFB
Daskal, Paul Linn *psychiatric and mental health professional*

Sherman
Brown, Paul Neeley *federal judge*
†Evans, Sarah Nell *information technology administrator*
†Faulkner, Robert W. *federal judge*
Jordan, David William *college administrator, faculty dean*
Page, Oscar Cletice *academic administrator*
†Swamy, Ponnuswámy T. *plastic surgeon*
†Tonelli, Mary Jo *public health physician*
†Williams, Ruby Jo *retired principal*

Skidmore
Barnes, Patricia Ann *art teacher*

Snyder
Anderson, Elsie Miners *mathematics educator*

Sonora
Earwood, Barbara Tirrell *artist*

Southlake
Alford, Stephen Clark *communications executive, multi image programmer*
Allen, Eleanor Kathleen (Missy Allen) *elementary education educator*
Gelinas, Marc Adrien *healthcare administrator*
George, David Webster *architect*
Herrmann, Debra McGuire *chemist, educator*
Roth, Robert William *technical consultant*
Sorge, Karen Lee *commercial printing company executive, consultant*

Spearman
Jarvis, Billy Britt *lawyer*

Spicewood
Carrell, Hammel Lee *jewelry designer*
Robbins, Eugene Weldon *genealogist*

Spring
Cooley, Andrew Lyman *corporation executive, former army officer*
Coy, Elba Boone *retired real estate developer*
Hearn-Haynes, Theresa *lawyer*
Hendricks, Randal Arlan *lawyer*
Ho, Hwa-Shan *engineering executive, civil engineer, consultant, drilling engineer*
Hunt, T(homas) W(ebb) *retired religion educator*
Jones, Katharine Jean *research physicist*

Kerr, Alva Rae *writer, editor, association executive, playwright*
Mackay, Cynthia Jean *music educator*
Maxfield, Mary Constance *management consultant*
McGregor, Martin Luther, Jr. *lawyer*
Moceanu, Dominique *gymnast, Olympic athlete*
Mohalley, Patricia JoAnn *library media specialist*
Templeton, Randall Keith *insurance company executive*

Springtown
Marrs, James F., Jr. (Jim Marrs) *author, journalist, educator*

Stafford
Franks, Charles Leslie *investments executive*
Friedberg, Thomas Harold *insurance company executive*
Herrera, Mary Cardenas *education educator, music minister*
†Lindsey, Dawn S. *legislative staff member*
Orman, Helen Belton *humanities educator, artist*
Polinger, Iris Sandra *dermatologist*

Stephenville
Christopher, Joe Randell *English language educator*
Levisay, Leesa Dawn *music educator, composer*
Simpson, Charles Edmond *crop science educator*
Sims, Larry Kyle *secondary school educator*

Stonewall
Betzer, Roy James *retired national park service ranger*

Sugar Land
Duvall, Cathleen Elaine *elementary school educator, consultant*
Hosley, Marguerite Cyril *volunteer*
Keefe, Carolyn Joan *tax accountant*
Kempner, Isaac Herbert, III *sugar company executive*
†Lin, Norman C.C. *project controls manager*
Odegard, Mark Erie *geophysicist, consultant*
Preng, David Edward *management consultant*
Romero, Mario H. *engineering executive*
Weispfennig, Klaus *chemical engineer, educator*
Westphal, Douglas Herbert *engineering company executive*

Sugarland
†DeVere, Ronald *neurologist*

Sulphur Springs
Gibson, Jannette Poe *educator, consultant*
McKenzie, Michael K. *wholesale executive*
Tiegiser, Donald P. *business owner*

Sweeny
Griffin, Stanley Ray *machinist*

Sweetwater
Jones, Charles Eric, Jr. *lawyer*

Temple
Aldrich, C. Elbert *real estate broker*
Bailey, William Harold *medical educator*
Brasher, George Walter *physician*
Chamlee, Ann Combest *music educator*
Cone, Thomas Conrad *communications executive*
Frost, Juanita Corbitt *retired hospital foundation coordinator*
Knudsen, Kermit Bruce *physician*
Mathis, Marsha Debra *software company executive*
Moore, Joanna Elizabeth *real estate professional*
Odem, Joyce Marie *human resources specialist*
Patureau, Arthur Mitchell *chemical engineer, consultant*
Rajab, Mohammad Hasan *biostatistician, educator*
Skelton, Byron George *federal judge*
Stoebner, John Martin *physician*
Swartz, Jon David *psychologist, educator*
Tobin, Margaret Ann *cardiac medical critical care nurse*
Van Ness, James Samuel *academic administrator, historian*
Watson, Linley Everett *cardiologist*
†Waxman, Jeffrey Alan *urologist*

Terrell
Makowski, John Jaroslaw, Jr. *psychiatrist*
†Perry, Lanny Joseph *secondary education educator, clergyman*
Wolfe, Tracey Dianne *distributing company executive*

Texarkana
Bertrand, Betty Harleen *nurse*
Folsom, David *judge*
Harrison, James Wilburn *gynecologist*
Hines, Betty Taylor *women's center administrator*
Selby, Roy Clifton, Jr. *neurosurgeon*
Turner, Paige Lea *cardiac telemetry nurse*

Texas City
Chen, Yuan James *chemical company executive*
Legan, Robert William *securities analyst*

The Woodlands
Frison, Paul Maurice *health care executive*
Jones, Lincoln, III *army officer*
Jones, Susan Chafin *management consultant*
Lewis, Daniel Edward *systems engineer, computer company executive*
Logan, Mathew Kuykendall *journalist*
Manson, Lewis Auman *energy research executive*
Martineau, Julie Peperone *social worker*
Norton, David Jerry *mechanical research engineer*
†Oubari, Dalal *pharmaceutical executive*
Schlacks, Stephen Mark *lawyer, educator*
Sharman, Diane Lee *secondary school educator*
Sudbury, John Dean *religious foundation executive, petroleum chemist*
Thompson, John Kenton *energy company executive, natural gas engineer*
Ulin, Samuel Alexander *computer systems developer*
Wortham, James Mason *gas supply representative*

Thorndale
Fish, Howard Math *aerospace industry executive*

Tiki Island
Kahn, Kathleen Pica *photojournalist, journalist, mediator, arbitrator*

Tomball
†Burgoyne, Mojie Adler *clinical social worker*

Tow
Shepherd, Donald Ray *pathologist*

Trophy Club
Caffee, Virginia Maureen *executive administrative associate*
Haerer, Deane Norman *marketing and public relations executive*

Tyler
†Abel, C. Houston *federal judge*
Albertson, Christopher Adam *librarian*
Arps, Joyce Ann *librarian*
Baker, Deborah Kay *secondary education educator*
Bell, Henry Marsh, Jr. *banking executive*
Berry, David Val *newspaper editor*
Brock, Dee Sala *television executive, educator, writer, consultant*
Carmody, Edmond *bishop*
Cleveland, Mary Louise *librarian, media specialist*
Davidson, Jack Leroy *academic administrator*
Deardorff, Kathleen Umbeck *nursing educator, researcher*
Edwards, D. M. *retail, wholesale distribution and commercial real estate investment executive*
Ellis, Donald Lee *lawyer*
Frankel, Donald Leon *retired oil service company executive*
Gann, Benard Wayne *air force officer*
Guthrie, Judith K. *federal judge*
Hardin, James *retail food company executive*
Hardy, William McDonald, Jr. *clergyman, physician assistant*
Hatfield, James Allen *theater arts educator*
Kronenberg, Richard Samuel *physician, educator*
†Lewis, Linda Katherine *elementary education educator*
†McKee, Harry W. *federal judge*
Moore, David L. *financial consultant*
Morgan, Freeman Louis, Jr. *engineer, consultant*
Ott, Wendell Lorenz *art museum director, artist*
Parker, Robert M. *federal judge*
Patterson, Donald Ross *lawyer, educator*
Pinkenburg, Ronald Joseph *ophthalmologist*
Ramirez, Enrique Rene *social sciences educator*
Resnik, Linda Ilene *marketing and information executive, consultant*
Rogers, Cheryl Lynn *music and dance educator*
Seeber, Joseph Oliver, IV *small business owner, lawyer*
Smith, Howard Thompson *business executive*
Smith, Janna Hogan *nursing administrator, surgical nurse*
Steger, William Merritt *federal judge*
†Turman, Judith Jenkins *English educator*
Waller, Wilma Ruth *retired secondary school educator and librarian*
Walsh, Kenneth Albert *chemist*
Warner, John Andrew *foundry executive*
Winskie, Richard Clay *retail executive, songwriter*

Universal City
Atchley, Curtis Leon *mechanical engineer*
McElveen-Combs, Gail Marie *middle school educator*
Smith, James Earlie, Jr. *financial services auditor*

Uvalde
Ramsey, Frank Allen *veterinarian, retired army officer*
Wilson, Benjamin Franklin, Jr. *education educator*
Wood, James Albert *foreign language educator*

Valley View
Wallace, Donald John, III *rancher, former pest control company executive*

Van Alstyne
Daves, Don Michael *minister*
†Hazelton, Juanita Louise *librarian*

Van Horn
Dodson, Hersha Rhee *psychiatric-mental health nurse*

Vega
Cook, Clayton Henry *rancher*

Vernon
Bearden, Jeff R. *hospital official*
Casimir, Kenneth Charles *adolescent forensic psychiatrist, educator*
Cook, Marcella Kay *drama educator*
Slosser, Jeffery Eric *research entomologist*
Streit, Gary Bernard *judge*

Victoria
Craft, Sheryl McArthur *rehabilitation nurse*
†Fellhauer, David E. *bishop*
Haynes, Karen Sue *university president, social work educator*
Logan, Mary Calkin *development and public relations consultant*
Lorenzen, Janice Ruth *physician*
Satava, David Richard *accountant, educator*
Spicak, Doris Elizabeth *health services company executive*
Stubblefield, Page Kindred *banker*

Vidor
Stokely, Joan Barbara *elementary school educator*

Waco
Andrist, Debra Diane *Spanish language educator*
Baird, Robert Malcolm *philosophy educator, researcher*
Belew, John Seymour *academic administrator, chemist*
Bonnell, Pamela Gay *library administrator*
Bracken, William Earl, Jr. *lawyer*
Brooks, Roger Leon *university president*
Cavanaugh, Joseph Thomas *museum director*
Chewning, Richard Carter *religious business ethics educator*
Collins, Robert Craig *business educator*
Collmer, Robert George *English language educator*
Colvin, (Otis) Herbert, Jr. *musician, educator*
Corley, Carol Lee *school nurse*
Davis, Mary Duesterberg (Mimi) *librarian, publisher*
Dow, David Sontag *retired ophthalmologist*
Dow, William Gould *electrical engineer, educator*
Farison, James Blair *electrical biomedical engineer, educator*
Flanders, Henry Jackson, Jr. *religious studies educator*
†Fulmer, Phillip *university football coach*
Goode, Clement Tyson *retired English language educator*
†Green, Dennis G. *federal judge*
Herring, Jack William *retired English language educator*
Hillis, William Daniel *biology educator*
Hogg, Sonja *university athletics coach*
Hollingsworth, Martha Lynette *secondary school educator*
†Hunt, Maurice Arthur *English educator, researcher*
Kagle, Joseph Louis, Jr. *artist, arts administrator*
Kahn, Alan Harvey *therapist, administrator, consultant*
†Lahaie, Ute S. *language educator*
Lindsey, Jonathan Asmel *development executive, educator*
Mathews, Cameron Anthony *internet design consultant*
Morrison, Michael Dean *lawyer, law educator*
Moseley, Mary Prudence *education educator*
Moshinskie, James Francis *educational technology educator*
Odell, Patrick Lowry *mathematics educator*
Osborne, Harold Wayne *sociology educator, consultant*
Page, Jack Randall *lawyer*
Pedrotti, Leno Stephano *physics educator*
Progar, Dorothy *retired library director*
Rapoport, Bernard *life insurance company executive*
Reynolds, Herbert Hal *academic administrator*
Richie, Rodney Charles *critical care and pulmonary medicine physician*
Rolf, Howard Leroy *mathematician, educator*
Rose, John Thomas *finance educator*
Rusling, Barbara N(eubert) *real estate executive, state commisioner*
Russell, Inez Snyder *non-profit organization executive*
†Sloan, Robert B. *university president*
Smith, Cullen *lawyer*
Smith, Walter S., Jr. *federal judge*
†Tomey, Dick *university football coach*
†Veselka, Nancy C. *entrepreneur*
†Walbesser, Henry Herman *computer science educator*
Wendorf, Hulen Dee *law educator, author, lecturer*
Wilson, John Ross *retired law educator*
Wood, James E., Jr. *religion educator, author*

Warda
Kunze, George William *retired soil scientist*

Waxahachie
Cockerham, Sidney Joe *professional society administrator*
Hastings, Ronnie Jack *secondary school educator*
McLane, William Delano *mechanical engineer*
†Speed, Randall Sherman *engineering consultant*
Tschoepe, Thomas *bishop*

Weatherford
Bergman, Anne Newberry *civic activist*
Buckner-Reitman, Joyce *psychologist, educator*
Estes, Carolyn Ann Hull *retired elementary school educator*
McMahon, Robert Lee, Jr. (Bob McMahon) *information systems executive*
Trigg, George Leon *construction executive*

Webster
Farnam, Jafar *allergist, immunologist, pediatrician*
Kobayashi, Herbert Shin *electrical engineer*
Shaffer, Anita Mohrland *counselor, educator*

Weslaco
Jordan, Timothy Edward *secondary education educator*

West
Eisma, Jose A. *physician*
Smith, George Norvell *physician*

Wharton
Gonzalez, Antonio *academic administrator, mortgage company executive*
Jackson, Larry C. *publishing executive*
†Johnson, Alan Gerhard *English educator*
Schulze, Arthur Edward *biomedical engineer, researcher*

Whitehouse
Baker, Rebecca Louise *musician, music educator, consultant*
Stansell, Aiszeleen *secondary school educator*

Whitewright
Watkins, Regina Gail *elementary education educator*

Wichita Falls
Altman, William Kean *lawyer*
Bourland, D(elphus) David, Jr. *linguist*
Cates, Sue Sadler *educational diagnostician*
Cleary, Thomas J. *social worker, administrator*
Harvey, Peter Marshall *podiatrist*
Harvill, Melba Sherwood *university librarian*
Hoggard, Lynn *French and English language educator*
Pemberton, Merri Beth Morris *educator*
Peterson, Holger Martin *electrical engineer*
†Roach, Robert K. *federal judge*
Rodriguez, Louis Joseph *university president, educator*
†Schaffer, Candler Gareld *conductor, hornist, educator*
Silverman, Gary William *financial planner*
Uzzell-Baggett, Karon Lynette *career officer*

Willis
McCrary, Linda Hulon *elementary school educator*

Wimberley
Ellis, John *small business owner*
Skaggs, Wayne Gerard *financial services company executive, retired*

Winnsboro
Fairchild, Raymond Eugene *oil company executive*

Woodway
Mulholland, Barbara Ann *school director*

Yoakum
Williams, Walter Waylon *lawyer, pecan grower*

UTAH

Alpine
Tanner, Jordan *state legislator*

American Fork
Reinhold, Allen Kurt *graphic design educator*

Bingham Canyon
Callender, Jonathan Ferris *environmental geologist, consultant*

Boulder
Davis, Larry *park director*

Bountiful
Burningham, Kim Richard *former state legislator*
Carter, Richard Bert *retired church official, retired government official*
Dowling, Lona Buchanan *nurse*
Powell, Ted Ferrell *micrographics specialist*
Rawlins, Jan *principal*
Rowland, Ruth Gailey *retired hospital official*

Brigham City
†Adams, J. Phillip *oil industry executive*
Huchel, Frederick M. *historian, writer, consultant, speaker, educator*
Krejci, Robert Henry *aerospace engineer*
McCullough, Edward Eugene *patent agent, inventor*
Pflug, Andrew Knox *aerospace company executive*

Cedar City
†Bostick, Curtis Van *history educator*
Hunter, R. Haze *former state legislator*
Morrison, Craig Somerville *physical education educator*
Stauffer, Gregory L(ynn) *program director*
†Templin, Carl Ross *college dean, educator*

Clearfield
Daniels, Robert Paul *special education administrator*

Clinton
Johnson, Charles N. *elementary education educator*

Corinne
Ferry, Miles Yeoman *state official*

Draper
Mecham, Lee *real estate director*
Schutz, Roberta Maria (Bobbi) *social worker*

Farmington
Gutzman, Philip Charles *aerospace executive, logistician*

Fort Duchesne
Cameron, Charles Henry *petroleum engineer*

Heber City
Day, Gerald W. *wholesale grocery company executive*
McLean, Hugh Angus *management consultant*

Hill Air Force Base
†Oriordan, Thomas A. *career officer*
†Roellig, Richard H. *military officer*

Holladay
Reinkoester, Robert William, Jr. *critical care nurse*

Hooper
Atwater, Julie Demers *critical care nurse*

Hurricane
Christensen, Steven J. *foreign language educator*

Kaysville
Ashmead, Allez Morrill *speech, hearing, and language pathologist, orofacial myologist, consultant*

Layton
Gregson, Garry Evan *network administrator, information consultant*
Yates, Jay Reese *physician*

Logan
†Ahlstrom, Callis Blythe *university official*
Aust, Steven Douglas *biochemistry, biotechnology and toxicology educator*
Bowles, David Stanley *engineering educator, consultant*
Burke, Lee Hall *administrative assistant*
Crumbley, Paul James *English language educator*
Drozdeck, Steven Richard *management consultant*
Eldredge, Garth Melvin *rehabilitation counseling educator*
Emert, George Henry *biochemist, academic administrator*
Hargreaves, George Henry *civil and agricultural engineer, researcher*
Hillyard, Lyle William *lawyer*
Honaker, Jimmie Joe *lawyer, ecologist*
Hunsaker, Scott Leslie *gifted and talented education educator*
Keller, Jack *agricultural engineering educator, consultant*
McKell, Cyrus M. *retired college dean, plant physiologist*
Milner, Clyde A., II *historian*
Rasmussen, Harry Paul *horticulture and landscape educator*
Schunk, Robert Walter *space physics research administrator*

Scouten, William Henry chemistry educator, academic administrator
Sharik, Terry Lane forest resources educator
Shaver, James Porter education educator, university dean
Vest, Hyrum Grant, Jr. horticultural sciences educator
Watterson, Scott home fitness equipment manufacturer

Magna
McDonough, Karel Joy Doop secondary education educator, musician

Manti
Petersen, Benton Lauritz paralegal

Midvale
Kitto, Franklin Curtis computer systems specialist
Teerlink, J(oseph) Leland real estate developer

Midway
Zenger, John Hancock training company executive

Monroe
Kirby, Orville Edward potter, painter, sculptor

Monticello
†Redd, F. Bennion federal judge

Mount Pleasant
Schade, Wilbert Curtis educational administrator

Murray
†Haun, Henry Lamar corrections department executive
Webster, Linda Jane clinical social worker, consultant

North Logan
Chen, Li computer scientist, software engineer
Sunderland, Norman Ray (Norm Sunderland) health physicist, nuclear engineer educator

North Salt Lake
Barden, Robert Christopher lawyer, psychologist, educator, analyst, author

Ogden
Bailey, Charles Richard political consultant
Browning, Roderick Hanson banker
Buckner, Elmer La Mar insurance executive
Davidson, Thomas Ferguson chemical engineer
Dilley, William Gregory aviation company executive
Draper, Richard Nelson banker
Eisler, David Lee provost
†Fullerton, Douglas B. sports association administrator
Graff, Darrell Jay physiology educator
Harrington, Mary Evelina Paulson (Polly Harrington) religious journalist, writer, educator
Holt, Ronald Lawrence anthropologist, educator
Jones, Galen Ray physician assistant
Klepinger, John William trailer manufacturing company executive
Manning, Donna banker
Maughan, Willard Zinn dermatologist
Mecham, Glenn Jefferson lawyer, mayor
Mecham, Steven Ray school system administrator
Montgomery, Robert F. state legislator, retired surgeon, cattle rancher
Nickerson, Guy Robert lumber company executive
†Ogden, Melvin J. retire purchaser
Palmer, Kim Michaele mental health counselor, consultant
Richards, Richard lawyer, political consultant
Ritchey, Harold W. retired chemical engineer
Smith, Robert Bruce college administrator
Southwick, James Albert realtor
Spencer, LaVal Wing physician
Sullivan, Kevin Patrick lawyer
Thompson, Paul Harold university president
Trundle, W(infield) Scott publishing executive newspaper
Warner, Frank Shrake lawyer
Welch, Garth Larry chemistry educator, retired

Orderville
Goddard, David Benjamin physician assistant, clinical perfusionist

Orem
Green, John Alden university director study abroad program
Hall, Blaine Hill retired librarian
Harris, Michael James software engineer
Moore, Hal G. mathematician, educator
Morey, Robert Hardy communications executive
Nordgren, William Bennett engineering executive
Peterson, Craig Anton former state senator
Sauter, Gail Louise speech pathologist
Sawyer, Thomas Edgar management consultant
Schulz, Raymond Alexander medical marketing professional, consultant
Snow, Marlon O. trucking executive, state agency administrator

Paradise
Bremer, Ronald Allan genealogist, editor

Park City
†Bergoust, Eric olympic athlete
†Dunn, Shannon olympic athlete
Edwards, Howard Lee retired petroleum company executive, lawyer
Kennicott, James W. lawyer
McIntyre, Elizabeth Geary United States downhill skier
Moe, Tommy (Thomas Sven Moe) skier, former Olympic athlete
Montgomery, James Fischer savings and loan association executive
†Moseley, Jonny olympic athlete, free style skier
†Powers, Ross olympic athlete
Roffe-Steinrotter, Diann Olympic athlete
Solomon, Dorothy Jeanne Allred writer, communications executive
†Stone, Nikki retired olympic athlete
Street, Picabo Olympic athlete
Wardell, Joe Russell, Jr. retired pharmacologist
Weight, Alec Charles retired management consultant
Zaharia, Eric Stafford developmental disabilities program administrator

Price
†Donaldson, Rebecca S. elementary education educator, reading specialist

Provo
Abbott, Charles Favour lawyer
Anderson, Mark T. business developer, entrepreneur, financier
Bahr, Howard Miner sociologist, educator
Bangerter, Vern secondary education educator
Bartlett, Leonard Lee communications educator, retired advertising agency executive, advertising historian
Bateman, Merrill Joseph university president
Bennett, Bill publishing company executive
Blake, George Rowland soil science educator, water resources research administrator
Bullock, J(ames) Robert judge
Christensen, Bruce LeRoy academic administrator, former public broadcasting executive
Christiansen, John Rees sociologist, educator
Clark, Bruce Budge humanities educator
Cracroft, Richard Holton English literature educator
Crookston, R. Kent agronomy educator
Densley, Colleen T. elementary education educator, curriculum facilitator
Diepholz, Daniel R. real estate consultant, accountant
Fleming, Joseph Clifton, Jr. dean, law educator
Forster, Merlin Henry foreign languages educator, author, researcher
Fry, Earl Howard political scientist, educator
Hall, Howard Tracy chemist
Hansen, H. Reese dean, educator
Harding, Ray Murray, Jr. judge
Hatch, Steven Graham publishing company executive
Herrera, Shirley Mae personnel and security executive
Hill, Richard Lee lawyer
Huber, Clayton Shirl university dean
Hunt, H(arold) Keith business management educator, marketing consultant
†Jaccard, Jerry-Louis music educator, translator
Jensen, Richard Dennis librarian
Jonsson, Jens Johannes electrical engineering educator
Keele, Alan Frank adult education educator
Kimball, Edward Lawrence law educator, lawyer
Kunz, Phillip Ray sociologist, educator
Lang, William Edward mathematics educator
†Lawrence, Keith American literature educator
Lee, Blaine Nelson executive consultant, educator, author
Lyon, James Karl German language educator
Manning, Richard L economics educator
McArthur, Eldon Durant geneticist, researcher
Merritt, LaVere Barrus engineering educator, civil engineer
†Murphy, John Joseph educator in English literature, critic, editor
Newitt, Jay construction management educator
Porter, Blaine Robert Milton sociology and psychology educator
Pratt, Rosalie Rebollo harpist, educator
Roberts, Stanley Dwayne physician, medical educator
Shippen, Trent university head women's basketball coach
Smith, H(oward) Duane zoology educator
Smith, Nathan McKay library and information sciences educator
Soter, Nicholas Gregory advertising agency executive
Stahmann, Robert F. education educator
Tata, Giovanni publishing executive
Thomas, David Albert law educator
Todd, Sally McClay teacher gifted and talented, psychologist
Valentine, John Lester state legislator, lawyer
Whatcott, Marsha Rasmussen elementary education educator

Richfield
†Fields, Linda Jean library director

Riverside
Reveal, Arlene Hadfield librarian, consultant

Riverton
Gaustad, Richard Dale financier
Rockwood, Linn Roy retired recreation executive, educator

Saint George
Beesley, H(orace) Brent savings and loan executive
Chilow, Barbara Gail social worker
Day, John Denton retired company executive, cattle and horse rancher, trainer, wrangler, actor, educator
Day, Steven M. accounting educator, accountant
Gallian, Russell Joseph lawyer
Hauenstein, Karen physician's assistant, critical care nurse
Martin, George Wilbur trade association administrator
†Nuffer, David O. federal judge
Terry, Gary A. lawyer, former trade association executive
Violet, Woodrow Wilson, Jr. retired chiropractor

Salem
Hahn, Joan Christensen retired drama educator, travel agent

Salt Lake City
Abildskov, J. A. cardiologist, educator
Adams, Joseph Keith lawyer
†Alba, Samuel federal judge
†Allen, Joi Lin government official
Allen, Roy Verl life insurance company executive
Alter, Edward T. state treasurer
Anderson, Joseph Andrew, Jr. retired apparel company executive, retail consultant
Anderson, Kent Taylor lawyer
Anderson, Robert Monte lawyer
Anderson, Stephen Hale federal judge
Anspaugh, Lynn Richard research biophysicist
Atkin, Gary Eugene lawyer
Ballard, Melvin Russell, Jr. investment executive, church official
Baranova, Elena basketball player
Barney, Kline Porter, Jr. retired engineering company executive, consultant
Barusch, Lawrence Roos lawyer
Baucom, Sidney George lawyer
Bauer, A(ugust) Robert, Jr. surgeon, educator
Beall, Burtch W., Jr. architect
Benjamin, Lorna Smith psychologist
Bennett, Janet Huff legislative staff member
Benson, Dee Vance federal judge
Berman, Daniel Lewis lawyer
Bishop, Rob political party executive
Black, Rosa Vida writer, educator
Black, Wilford Rex, Jr. state senator
Blackner, Boyd Atkins architect
Bouley, Joseph Richard pilot
†Bowen, Melanie state official
†Boyce, Ronald N. federal judge
Brady, Rodney Howard holding company executive, broadcast company executive, former college president, former government official
Brems, David Paul architect
†Brown, Rulon Spilsbury agricultural consultant
Buchi, Mark Keith lawyer
†Bulkeley, Brooke healthcare administratrator, small business owner
Burdette, Robert Soelberg accountant
Burkle, Ronald W. food service executive
Buttars, Gerald Anderson librarian
Campbell, Stewart Clawson retired sales executive, artist
Campbell, Tena judge
Cannell, Cyndy Michelle elementary school principal
Capecchi, Mario Renato genetecist, educator
Carey, John Clayton pediatrician
Carnahan, Orville Darrell retired state legislator, retired college president
Cash, R(oy) Don gas and petroleum company executive
Chase, Randal Stuart communication educator, consultant
Chivers, Laurie Alice state educational administrator
Chong, Richard David architect
Christensen, Patricia Anne Watkins lawyer
Christensen, Ray Richards lawyer
Christopher, James Walker architect, educator
Clark, Deanna Dee civic leader and volunteer
†Clark, Glen Edward judge
Clark, Jeffrey Raphiel research and development company executive
Clark, Robert Stokes lawyer
Clark, Scott H. lawyer
†Clinesmith, Frederick Clinton business executive
Cofield, Philip Thomas educational association administrator
Colessides, Nick John lawyer
Corley, Jean Arnette Leister infosystems executive
Cornaby, Kay Sterling lawyer, former state senator
Corradini, Deedee mayor
Cousins, Richard Francis diversified financial services company executive
Crawford, Kevan Charles nuclear engineer, educator
Curtis, LeGrand R., Jr. lawyer
Dahlstrom, Donald Albert former chemical-metallurgical engineering educator
Davis, Brian Adam physician
Davis, Roy Kim otolaryngologist, health facility administrator
De Vries, Kenneth Lawrence mechanical engineer, educator
Dick, Bertram Gale, Jr. physics educator
†DiPadova, Laurie Newman educator
Drew, Clifford James university administrator, special education and educational psychology educator
Durham, Christine Meaders state supreme court justice
†Dydek, Malgorzata professional basketball player
Eccles, Spencer Fox banker
Elkins, Glen Ray service company executive
Emerson, Sharon B. biology researcher and educator
Engar, Richard Charles insurance executive, dentist, educator
Epperson, Vaughn Elmo civil engineer
Erickson, David Belnap lawyer
Evans, Max Jay historical society administrator
Evensen, Jay Douglas newspaper editor
†Ewers, Anne opera company director
Eyring, Henry Bennion bishop
Faust, James E. church official
Fehr, J. Will newspaper editor
Fink, Kristin Danielson secondary education educator
Foltz, Rodger Lowell chemistry educator, mass spectroscopist
†Fowler, James Raymond surgeon
†Foxley, Cecelia Harrison commissioner
Fujinami, Robert Shin neurology educator
Gallivan, John William publisher
Gandhi, Om Parkash electrical engineer
Gardiner, Lester Raymond, Jr. lawyer
Garn, Edwin Jacob (Jake Garn) former senator
Gold, Rick L. federal government executive
Goldstein, Michael L. neurologist
Good, Rebecca Mae Wertman learning and behavior counselor, grief and loss counselor, hospice nurse, therapeutic touch practitioner, educator
Goodey, Ila Marie psychologist
Gortatowski, Melvin Jerome retired chemist
Gough, Eugene V. vocational education educator
Grabarz, Donald Francis pharmacist
Graham, Jan state attorney general
Grant, Raymond Thomas arts administrator
Greene, Enid former congresswoman
Greene, John Thomas judge
†Greenwood, Richard A. protective services official
Gregory, Herold La Mar chemical company administrator
†Griggs, John Bronson technology executive
Grosser, Bernard Irving psychiatry educator
†Haight, David B. church official
Hall, Gordon R. retired state supreme court chief justice
Hamill, Mark Richard actor
Hansen, Kent public relations professional, consultant
Harpending, Henry Cosad anthropologist, educator
Harrie, Daniel Andrew newspaper reporter
Hartley, Elise Moore theatrical milliner, costume designer
Hatch, George Clinton television executive
Hatch, Wilda Gene broadcast company executive
Hembree, James D. retired chemical company executive
Hemingway, W(illiam) David banker
Hereth, Lyle George electrical engineering technologist
Hilbert, Robert Backus county water utility administrator
Hill, George Richard chemistry educator
Hill, Kenneth O. performing company executive
Hinckley, Gordon B. church official
Holbrook, Donald Benson lawyer
Holbrook, Meghan Zanolli fundraiser, public relations specialist, state pol
Holding, R. Earl oil company executive
†Holland, Jeffrey R. religious organization administrator
Holtkamp, James Arnold lawyer, educator
Hornacek, Jeffrey John professional basketball player
Howe, Richard Cuddy state supreme court chief justice
Howell, Kevin L. hotel executive
Howells, R. Tim professional sports team executive
Hunt, George Andrew lawyer
Huntsman, Jon Meade chemical company executive
Iverius, Per-Henrik physician, biochemist, educator
†Jacobs, Johann performing arts company executive
Jacobsen, Stephen C. biomedical engineer
Jenkins, Bruce Sterling federal judge
Jensen, Dallin W. lawyer
Jensen, Rodney H. hotel executive
Johanson, Orin William social worker, school counselor, consultant
Johnson, Frank retired state official, educator
Johnson, Jon L. advertising executive
Johnson, Mary Perrine musician, educator
Joklik, Günther Franz mining company executive
Joseph, Kevin Mark financial services executive
Judd, Thomas Eli electrical engineer
†Kåge, Jonas ballet company artistic director
Kanes, William Henry geology educator, research center administrator
Kelen, Joyce Arlene social worker
Kelm, Linda opera singer
Kenison, Lynn T. chemist
King, R. Peter science educator, academic center director
Kraus, Peter Leo librarian
Lamborn, W. John bank executive
Layden, Francis Patrick (Frank Layden) professional basketball team executive, former coach
Lazzi, Gianluca electronics engineer, researcher
†Leary, G. Edward state finance commisioner
Lease, Ronald Charles financial economics educator
Leavitt, Michael Okerlund governor, insurance executive
Lee, Glenn Richard medical administrator, educator
Leonard, Glen Milton museum administrator
Linardakis, Nikos Michalis physician, publisher
Lindsay, Elena Margaret nurse
Lloyd, Ray Dix health physicist, consultant
Lochhead, Robert Bruce lawyer
Loh, Eugene C. physicist, educator
Losse, John William, Jr. mining company executive
Lund, Victor L. retail food company executive
Lustica, Katherine Grace marketing executive, artist, consultant
Mabey, Ralph R. lawyer
Magleby, Florence Deming special education educator
Maher, David L. drug store company executive
Majerus, Rick collegiate basketball team coach
Malone, Karl professional basketball player
Mangum, Garth Leroy economist, educator
Manning, Brent V. lawyer
Martineau, Holly Low dietitian
†Martinez, Art L. legislative staff member
Mason, James Ostermann public health administrator
Masters, Lorraine Susanne religious organization administrator
Matsen, John Martin academic administrator, pathologist
Matsumori, Douglas lawyer
Matsuo, Fumisuke physician, educator
Matthews, Patricia Deneise special education educator
Maxwell, Neal A. church official
McCleary, Lloyd E(verald) education educator
McConkie, Oscar Walter lawyer
McDermott, Kathleen E. retail executive
McIntosh, James Albert lawyer
McIntosh, Terrie Tuckett lawyer
McIntyre, Jerilyn Sue academic administrator
McKay, Monroe Gunn federal judge
Meldrum, Peter Durkee venture capital/biotechnology company executive
Melich, Doris S. public service worker
Middleton, Anthony Wayne, Jr. urologist, educator
Miller, Jan Dean metallurgy educator
Miller, Larry H. professional sports team executive, automobile dealer
Miller, Lorraine business owner
†Miller, Susan Jane Passler English and writing educator
Miller, William Charles college dean, architect
Mills, Carol Margaret business consultant, public relations consultant
Mills, Lawrence lawyer, business and transportation consultant
†Minson, Dixie L. state director
Mock, Henry Byron lawyer, writer, consultant
Moe, Scott Thomas chemist
Mogren, Paul Andrew librarian
Monson, Thomas Spencer church official, former publishing company executive
†Moore, Annette B. state senate employee
Moore, Carrie A. journalist
Moore, James R. lawyer
Moore, Larry Gale lawyer
Morey, Charles Leonard, III theatrical director
Morris, Sylvia Marie university official
Mortimer, William James newspaper publisher
Moser, Royce, Jr. physician, medical educator
Motter, Thomas Franklin medical products executive
Murphy, Michael R. federal judge
Nelson, Roger Hugh management educator, business executive
Nelson, Russell Marion surgeon, educator
Newell, Clayton Coke media professional, writer
Nicolatus, Stephen Jon financial consultant
Niederauer, George H. bishop
Nielsen, Greg Ross lawyer
Nixon, Carol Holladay park and recreation director
Norton, Delmar Lynn candy company executive, video executive
Oaks, Dallin Harris lawyer, church official
Odell, William Douglas physician, scientist, educator
O'Halloran, Thomas Alphonsus, Jr. physicist, educator
Olpin, Robert Spencer art history educator
Olson, Ferron Allred metallurgist, educator
Orton, William H. (Bill Orton) former congressman, lawyer
Ottley, Jerold Don choral conductor, educator
Packer, Boyd K. church official
Palmer, Wendy professional basketball player
Parry, Robert Walter chemistry educator
†Perry, L. Tom church official, merchant

Pershing, David Walter *chemical engineering educator, researcher*
Petersen, Finn Bo *oncologist, educator*
Peterson, Chase N. *university president*
Pickering, AvaJane *specialized education facility executive*
Pierce, Diane Jean *artist*
Porter, Bruce Douglas *federal agency administrator, educator, writer*
Poulter, Charles Dale *chemist, educator, consultant*
†Purdie, Tonya Marie Thomas *college academic counselor*
Purser, Donald Joseph *lawyer*
Rasmussen, Thomas Val, Jr. *lawyer, small business owner*
†Raucci, Francis Joseph *lawyer, business executive*
Reeder, F. Robert *lawyer*
Reeves, Bruce *social worker*
Renzetti, Attilio David *physician*
Rigtrup, Kenneth *state judge, arbitrator, mediator*
Roberts, Jack Earle *lawyer, ski resort operator, wood products company executive, real estate developer*
Robison, Barbara Ann *retired newspaper editor*
Roth, John Roger *geneticist, biology educator*
Russon, Leonard H. *state supreme court justice*
†Sajé, Natasha *educator, poet*
Salisbury, Frank Boyer *plant physiologist, educator, author*
Sam, David *federal judge*
Schmitt, Gary A. *energy company director*
Scofield, David Willson *lawyer*
†Scott, Richard G. *church official*
Seader, Junior DeVere (Bob) *chemical engineering educator*
Shelledy, James Edwin, III *editor*
Shepherd, Karen *former congresswoman*
Sillars, Malcolm Osgood *communication educator*
Silver, Barnard Joseph Stewart *mechanical and chemical engineer, consultant, inventor*
Silverstein, Joseph Harry *conductor, musician*
Simmons, Lynda Merrill Mills *educational administrator*
Simmons, Roy William *banker*
Sinclair, Sara Voris *health facility administrator, nurse*
Skurzynski, Gloria Joan *writer*
Sloan, Jerry (Gerald Eugene Sloan) *professional basketball coach*
Smith, Donald E. *broadcast engineer, manager*
Smith, Eldred Gee *church leader*
Smith, J(ames) Scott *elementary education educator*
Sohn, Hong Yong *chemical and metallurgical engineering educator*
†Sorensen, Parry Daniel *educator*
†Spalding, Barbara *small business owner*
Steiner, Richard Russell *company executive*
Stewart, Isaac Daniel, Jr. *state supreme court justice*
Stock, Peggy A(nn) *college president, educator*
Stockton, John Houston *professional basketball player*
Straight, Richard Coleman *photobiologist, natural philosopher*
Stringfellow, Gerald B. *engineering educator*
Sullivan, Claire Ferguson *retired marketing educator*
Swaner-Smoot, Paula Margetts *clinical psychologist*
Talbot, Steven Richards *vascular technologist, consultant, writer*
Tateoka, Reid *lawyer*
Teitelbaum, Lee E. *law educator, dean*
Terry, David Thames *government administrator*
Thatcher, Blythe Darlyn *assistant principal*
†Thorne, Kim S. *state official*
Todd, Jay Marlyn *editor*
Tremitiere, Chantel *basketball player*
Vanderhooft, Jan Eric *orthopedic surgeon, educator*
Van Wagenen, Sterling *film producer, director*
Vardeny, Zeev Valy *physicist educator*
†Varela, Vicki *deputy chief of staff Governor of Utah*
Velick, Sidney Frederick *research biochemist, educator*
†Verdoia, Kenneth Louis *documentary producer*
Wadsworth, Harold Wayne *lawyer*
Walker, Olene S. *lieutenant governor*
Wall, Lloyd L. *geological engineer*
Wallace, Matthew Walker *retired entrepreneur*
Ward, John Robert *physician, educator*
Warner, Homer R. *physiologist, educator*
Weigel, Richard George *psychologist, educator*
Weiss, Loren Elliot *lawyer, law educator*
Welch, Dominic *publishing executive*
White, Raymond Leslie *geneticist*
Wikstrom, Francis M. *lawyer*
Winder, David Kent *federal judge*
†Wirthlin, Joseph B. *church official*
Wolf, Harold Herbert *pharmacy educator*
Wong, Kuang Chung *anesthesiology and pharmacology educator*
Wyness, Steven Charles *illustrator*
Young, Scott Thomas *business management educator*
†Zemmels, David Russell *theatre educator, lighting designer*
Zimmerman, Michael David *state supreme court justice*

Sandy
Bush, Rex Curtis *lawyer*
Fullmer, Timothy Shawn *printing company executive*
†Jayne, Fred Eugene *financial planner*
Jorgensen, Leland Howard *aerospace research engineer*
Kille, Willard Bronson, III *business executive*
Liddle, Jacqueline S. *secondary education educator*
Littleton, Gaye Darlene *nonprofit executive director*
Macumber, John Paul *insurance company executive*
Pierce, Ilona Lambson *educational administrator*
Sabey, J(ohn) Wayne *academic administrator, consultant*
Skidmore, Joyce Thorum *public relations and communication executive*
Smith, Willard Grant *psychologist*
Volpe, Ellen Marie *middle school educator*

Smithfield
Rasmuson, Brent (Jacobsen) *photographer, graphic artist, lithographer*

South Jordan
Rowley, Maxine Lewis *home economics educator, writer*

Spanish Fork
Ashworth, Brent Ferrin *lawyer*

Spring City
Bennion, Joseph Wood *potter*

Tooele
Lawrence, Stephen Lee *elementary school principal, mechanic*
Rice, Stuart Evan *researcher, author*

Tremonton
Eakle, Arlene Haslam *genealogist*
Kerr, Kleon Harding *former state senator, educator*

Vernal
Judd, Dennis L. *lawyer*

Wendover
Arnoldson, Earl Randon *educator*

West Jordan
Carter, Paul Edward *publishing company executive*
Shepherd, Paul H. *elementary school educator*

West Valley City
Mickelson, Elliot Spencer *quality assurance professional*
Wright, Gearld Lewis *mayor, retired educator*

Woods Cross
Ingles, Joseph Legrand *social services administrator, political science educator*

VERMONT

Alburg
DiSipio, Rocco Thomas *writer*
Schallert, Patrick James *bed and breakfast owner, importer*

Arlington
Nowicki, George Lucian *retired chemical company executive*
Pentkowski, Raymond J. *superintendent*

Barnard
Larson, John Hyde *retired utilities executive*

Barre
Milne, James *former secretary of state*

Bennington
Adams, Pat *artist, educator*
†Burkhardt, Frederick Henry *editor*
Coleman, Elizabeth *college president*
Cooper, Charleen Frances *special and elementary education educator*
†DeBey, Mary *educator*
Glazier, Lyle *writer, educator*
Killen, Carroll Gorden *electronics company executive*
Miller, Steven H. *museum director*
Perin, Donald Wise, Jr. *former association executive*
Sternberg, Rolf Max *lawyer*
Wallace, Harold James, Jr. *physician*

Bethel
Obuchowski, Raymond Joseph *lawyer*

Bradford
Kaplow, Leonard Samuel *pathologist, educator*
Mallary, Gertrude Robinson *civic worker*

Brattleboro
Akins, Zane Vernon *association executive*
Ames, Adelbert, III *neurophysiologist, educator*
Brofsky, Howard *musician, music educator*
Cohen, Richard B. *grocery company executive*
Cole, Stephen Adams *psychiatrist*
Cramer, Walter Elwood, II *educational administrator*
Edgerton, Brenda Evans *soup company executive*
Gorman, Robert Saul *architect*
Gregg, Michael B. *health science association administrator, epidemiologist*
Kotkov, Benjamin *clinical psychologist*
Milkey, Virginia A. *state legislator*
Murtha, J. Garvan *federal judge*
Oakes, James L. *federal judge*

Bridgewater
Bramhall, Peter *artist, sculptor, designer, craftsman*

Bridport
Wagner, Barbara Anne Beebe *critical care nurse*

Brookfield
Gerard, James Wilson *book distributor*

Brownsville
Olderman, Gerald *retired medical device company executive*

Burlington
Allard, Judith Louise *secondary education educator*
Anderson, Richard Louis *electrical engineer*
Angell, Kenneth Anthony *bishop*
Bartlett, Richmond Jay *soil chemistry educator, researcher*
Bergesen, Robert Nelson *transportation company executive*
Brandenburg, Richard George *university dean, management educator*
Chiu, Jen-Fu *biochemistry educator*
Ciongoli, Alfred Kenneth *neurologist*
†Comey, Rachel Mickyla *gallery curator and director, sculptor*
Cooper, Sheldon Mark *medical educator, immunology researcher, rheumatologist*
Craighead, John Edward *pathology educator*
Cram, Reginald Maurice *retired air force officer*
Critchlow, Dale *electrical engineer*
Crouse, Roger Leslie *information analyst, quality consultant, facilitator*
Cutler, Stephen Joel *sociologist*
Daniels, Robert Vincent *history educator, former state senator*
Davis, Christopher Lee *lawyer*
Davis, John Herschel *surgeon, educator*
Della Santa, Laura *principal*
Dinse, John Merrell *lawyer*
Ferrari, Dennis M. *secondary education educator*
Flores, Yolanda *literature educator*
Forcier, Lawrence Kenneth *natural resource educator*
Frymayer, John W. *dean*
Galbraith, Richard Anthony *physician, hospital administrator*
Glitman, Maynard Wayne *foreign service officer*
Hall, Robert William *philosophy and religion educator*
Haugh, Larry Douglas *statistics professor*
Hearon, Shelby *writer, lecturer, educator*
Heffernan, Patricia Conner *management consultant*
Heinrich, Bernd *biologist, educator*
Hendley, Edith Di Pasquale *physiology and neuroscience educator*
Hoff, Philip Henderson *lawyer, former state senator, former governor*
Hong, Richard *pediatrician, educator*
LaRue, S. Renee *middle level educator*
Lawson, Robert Bernard *psychology educator*
LeWinter, Martin M. *cardiologist*
Lidofsky, Steven David *medical educator*
Liley, Elizabeth Ellen *journalist, educator*
Lucey, Jerold Francis *pediatrician*
Martin, Allen *lawyer*
Martin, Luther Howard *religious studies educator*
Mead, Philip Bartlett *healthcare administrator, physician*
Metcalfe, William Craig *retired history educator*
Miller, Jane Cutting *elementary education educator*
Milliard, Aline *social worker*
Neale, Gail Lovejoy *non-profit organization management consultant*
†Niedermeier, Jerome J. *federal judge*
Nunley, Gayle Roof *language educator*
Nyborg, Wesley Lemars *physics educator*
Parker, Fred I. *federal judge*
Pinder, George Francis *engineering educator, scientist*
Ramaley, Judith Aitken *university president, endocrinologist*
Richardson, Gail Marguerite *community services agency executive*
Riddick, Daniel Howison *obstetrics and gynecology educator, priest*
Ross, Donald Savage *soil chemist, laboratory director*
Sampson, Samuel Franklin *sociology educator*
Sessions, William K., III *judge, federal*
Shattuck, Gary G. *lawyer*
Smallwood, Franklin *political science educator*
Sobel, Burton Elias *physician, educator*
Tampas, John P. *radiologist*
Tetzlaff, Charles Robert *prosecutor*
Thimm, Alfred Louis *management educator*
Varricchio, Louis *radio producer, science writer, personality, public relations executive*
Waterman, Gerald Scott *psychiatrist, physician educator*
Weed, Lawrence L. *biochemist, educator*
White, William North *chemistry educator*
Wick, Hilton Addison *lawyer*

Castleton
†Lavin, Stuart Roy *writer, adult education educator*
†Miller, Judith *adult education educator*

Cavendish
Shapiro, David *artist, art historian*

Charlotte
Harris, Kathleen McKinley *writer*
Melby, Edward Carlos, Jr. *veterinarian*
Monsarrat, Nicholas *newspaper editor, writer, educator*
Pricer, Wilbur David *electrical engineer*

Chester
Coleman, John Royston *newspaper publisher*
Parsons, Cynthia *writer, educational consultant*

Colchester
Danielson, Ursel Rehding *psychiatrist*
Fellows, Diana Potenzano *educational administrator*
Hazelett, S(amuel) Richard *mechanical engineer*
Lawton, Lorilee Ann *pipeline supply company owner, accountant*
Moore, Mitchell Steven *computer consultant*
Thompson, Ellen Ann *elementary education educator*

Concord
Norsworthy, Elizabeth Krassovsky *lawyer*

Danby
Rudy, Kathleen Vermeulen *small business owner*

Dorset
Bamford, Joseph Charles, Jr. *gynecologist, obstetrician, educator, medical missionary*
Ketchum, Richard Malcolm *editor, writer*
†Pember, John Scott *poet*

East Burke
Burnham, Patricia White *consultant advocate, writer on aging, business executive, author*
Burnham, Robert Alan *educator, academic administrator*

East Calais
Gahagan, James Edward, Jr. *artist*
Gahagan, Patricia de Gogorza *sculptor*
Harding, John Hibbard *insurance company executive*

East Fairfield
Long, Joan Hazel *accountant*

East Middlebury
†Gavin, Thomas Michael *retired English educator, writer*

East Montpelier
Christiansen, Andrew P. *Internet consulting business executive*

East Ryegate
Martland, T(homas) R(odolphe) *philosophy educator*

Enosburg Falls
Svendsen, Alf *artist, art educator*

Essex Junction
Coffey, Jean Sheerin *pediatric nurse, educator*
Davignon, Charles Philias *priest*
Dietzel, Louise A. *psychologist*
Dustan, Harriet Pearson *former physician, educator*
†Ishaq, Mousa Hanna *materials engineer*
Lampert, S. Henry *dentist*
Lee, Mankoo *device engineer/scientist, design engineer*
Parizo, Mary Ann *state legislator*
†Pillsbury, Penelope DeLaire *library director*
Sweetser, Gene Gillman *quality assurance professional, state legislator*

Fair Haven
Barnouw, Erik *broadcasting educator, writer*

Flushing
Krasner, Michael Alan *political science educator*

Hardwick
Holtz, Laurence *artisan, photographer*

Hartland
Dunne, Matthew Bailey *state legislator*
Oort, Abraham Hans *meteorologist, researcher, educator*

Hartland Four Corners
Brady, Upton Birnie *editor, literary agent*

Hinesburg
Forauer, Robert Richard *elementary education educator*

Huntington
Spear, Robert Newell, Jr. *museum director*

Johnson
Whitehill, Angela Elizabeth *artistic director*

Killington
Laing, David *natural science educator*

Lincoln
Kompass, Edward John *consulting editor*

Ludlow
Davis, Vera *elementary school educator*

Lyndonville
James, Bruce Allan *radio station owner, general manager*

Manchester
Carey, James Henry *banker*
Gagliardi, Lee Parsons *federal judge*
Kouwenhoven, Gerrit Wolphertsen *museum director*

Manchester Center
Dunning, Steven *painter*

Marlboro
†Dudley, Ellen Revie *writer, editor, publisher*
Poster, Lauren Olitski *art administrator, artist*

Middlebury
Blair, Patricia Wohlgemuth *economics writer*
Ferm, Robert Livingston *religion educator*
Gibson, Eleanor Jack (Mrs. James J. Gibson) *retired psychology educator*
Jacobs, Travis Beal *historian, educator*
Katz, Michael Ray *Slavic languages educator*
Kunin, Madeleine May *ambassador to Switzerland, former governor*
Lamberti, Marjorie *history educator*
Landgren, Craig Randall *academic administrator*
McCardell, John Malcolm, Jr. *college administrator*
†Napolitano, Peter Joseph *academic administrator*
Nunley, Charles Arthur *language educator*
O'Brien, George Dennis *retired university president*
Palmer, Michael Paul *lawyer, mediator, educator*
Rader, Rhoda Caswell *academic program director*
Robison, Olin Clyde *political science educator, former college president*
Saul, George Brandon, II *biology educator*
Vail, Van Horn *German language educator*
Winkler, Paul Frank, Jr. *astrophysicist, educator*
Wonnacott, (Gordon) Paul *economics educator*
Wright, Nancy Means *author, educator*

Middletown Springs
Asch, Frank *writer children's books, illustrator*
Lloyd, Robert Andrew *art educator*

Montpelier
Barbieri, Christopher George *professional society administrator*
Brock, James Sidney *lawyer*
Costle, Elizabeth Rowe *commissioner*
Dean, Howard *governor*
Diamond, M. Jerome *lawyer, former state official*
Diamond, Rickey Gard *writer, educator*
Dooley, John Augustine, III *state supreme court justice*
Dumville, John P. *historic site director*
Facos, James Francis *English language educator, author*
Fitzhugh, William Wyvill, Jr. *printing company executive*
Gibson, Ernest Willard, III *retired state supreme court justice*
Good, Jeffrey *journalist*
Griswold, David James *therapist and physician's assistant*
Guild, Alden *retired lawyer*
Johnson, Denise Reinka *state supreme court justice*
†LaClair, Jolinda *legislative staff member*
†Markowitz, Deborah L. *state government official*
May, Edgar *former state legislator, nonprofit administrator*
Morse, James L. *state supreme court justice*
Paquin, Edward H., Jr. *state legislator*
†Pelham, Tom *commissioner, state*
†Peterson, Julie *public information officer*
Racine, Doug *state official*
Ready, Elizabeth M. *state legislator*
Rivers, Cheryl P. *state legislator*
Ross, Frederick W., III *transportation engineer*
Sorrell, William H. *state attorney general*
Steele, Karen Kiarsis *state legislator*

Stevens, Allyssa Elizabeth *retail executive*
Valsangiacomo, Oreste Victor *state legislator*

Morrisville
Lechevalier, Hubert Arthur *microbiology educator*
Lechevalier, Mary Pfeil *retired microbiologist, educator*
Simonds, Marshall *lawyer*

Newark
Van Vliet, Claire *artist*

Newbury
McGarrell, James *artist, educator*

Newfane
Farber, Lillian *retired photography equipment company executive*
Reed, John Addison Jr. *European studies educator*

Newport Center
MacKellar, James Marsh *minister*

North Bennington
Adler, Irving *mathematician*
Belitt, Ben *poet, educator*

North Pomfret
Crowl, John Allen *retired publishing company executive*

North Troy
Rosenberger, Janice Whitehill *speech and language pathologist*
Weingart, Carol Jayne *university administrator, educator, psychotherapist*

Northfield
†Batra, N.D. *communications educator*
†Chevalier, Frances Sikola *French language educator*
Wick, William Shinn *clergyman, chaplain*

Norwich
Chapman, Robert James *clinical psychiatrist, educator*
Lamperti, Claudia Jane McKay *editor*
Lundquist, Weyman Ivan *lawyer*
Naumann, Robert Bruno Alexander *chemistry and physics educator*
Post, Avery Denison *retired church official*
Stetson, Eugene William, III *film producer*
White, Cleveland Stuart, Jr. *architect*

Orleans
Floersheim, Sandra Kelton *community health nurse*

Pawlet
Buechner, Carl Frederick *minister, author*

Peacham
Engle, James Bruce *ambassador*

Perkinsville
Freeburg, Richard Gorman *financial derivatives company executive*
Harris, Christopher *publisher, designer, editor*

Plymouth
Crandell, Sarah Allen *dean*

Poultney
Edwards, Charles Arthur *college administrator*

Pownal
Gibson, Sarah Ann Scott *art librarian*

Putney
Darrow, Steve *state legislator*
†Hunt, Bill *artist, educator*

Quechee
Baney, John Edward *insurance company executive*
DeRouchey, Beverly Jean *investment company executive*

Randolph
Angell, Philip Alvin, Jr. *lawyer*
Calter, Paul Arthur *mathematics educator, mechanical engineer*

Randolph Center
Casson, Richard Frederick *lawyer, travel bureau executive*

Rochester
Schenkman, Joseph *publishing executive*
†Weisfeld, Jay Stanley *public health physician*

Rutland
†Corbett, Joseph Edward *neurosurgeon*
Faignant, John Paul *lawyer, educator*
Ferraro, Betty Ann *corporate administrator, state senator*
Haley, John Charles *financial executive*
Keyser, Frank Ray, Jr. *lawyer, former governor*
Marro, Charles John *retired bankruptcy judge*
Stafford, Robert Theodore *lawyer, former senator*
Taylor, A. Jeffry *lawyer*
Wiles, William Patrick *English language educator*
Wright, William Bigelow *retired financial executive*

Saint Johnsbury
Crosby, George Miner *former state legislator*
Mayo, Bernier L. *secondary school principal*
Toll, David *pediatrician*

Saxtons River
Aho, Eric *artist*

Shelburne
Carpenter, Donald Blodgett *real estate appraiser*
Kurrelmeyer, Louis Hayner *retired lawyer*
Little, George Thomas *international relations educator, retired*
Lynch, Peter *biology educator*
Ross, Charles Robert *lawyer, consultant*
Rovner, Lisa Jane *architect*
Ryerson, William Newton *non profit organization executive*

Sawabini, Wadi Issa *retired dentist*
Weiger, John George *foreign language educator*

South Burlington
Hamilton, John J., Jr. *airport executive*
Johnson, Robert Eugene *physiologist*
Kebabian, Paul Blakeslee *librarian*
Perrine, Mervyn William Bud *alcohol center director, forensic consultant*
Pizzagalli, James *construction executive*

South Hero
Bisson, Roger *middle school educator*

South Londonderry
Coleman, Wendell Lawrence *former state legislator*
Spiers, Ronald Ian *diplomat*

South Pomfret
Arkin, William Morris *military and political analyst, writer, consultant*

South Royalton
Chang, David Ping-Chung *business consultant, architect*
Doria, Anthony Notarnicola *college dean, educator*
Foose, Robert A. *higher education administrator*
Jones, Timothy Mark *graphic designer, painter*
Powers, Thomas Moore *author*
Wroth, L(awrence) Kinvin *lawyer, educator*

Springfield
Putnam, Paul Adin *retired government agency official*
Thayer, Rosealyce Cullen *artist*

Stowe
Fagan, William Thomas, Jr. *urologist*
Fiddler, Barbara Dillow *sales and marketing professional*

Thetford
Hoagland, Mahlon Bush *biochemist, educator*
Morgan, Susan McGuire McGrath *psychotherapist*
Paley, Grace *author, educator*

Tunbridge
Stewart, Donald George *musician, music industry executive, composer*

Underhill
Danforth, Elliot, Jr. *medical educator*

Vergennes
Sinkewicz, Robert William *financial analyst, accountant*

Waitsfield
Parrish, Thomas Kirkpatrick, III *marketing consultant*
Raphael, Albert Ash, Jr. *lawyer*

Washington
Brynn, Edward Paul *former ambassador*

Waterbury
Bunting, Charles I. *academic administrator*
Recchia, Christopher *state agency environmental administrator*

Waterbury Center
Amestoy, Jeffrey Lee *state supreme court chief justice*

West Dover
Humphreys, George H., II *surgery educator*

West Glover
Hadash, Brendan Douglas *minister*

Weston
Kasnowski, Chester Nelson *artist, educator*
Stettler, Stephen F. *performing company executive*

Weybridge
Berens, Betty Kathryn McAdam *community program administrator*

White River Junction
Barton, Gail Melinda *psychiatrist, educator*
Bohi, Lynn *state legislator*
Linnell, Robert Hartley *environment, safety consultant*
Myers, Warren Powers Laird *physician, educator*
Rous, Stephen Norman *urologist, educator*
Rutter, Frances Tompson *publisher*

Williamstown
Dickinson, Charles Arthur *manufacturing company executive*

Williston
Adams, Charles Jairus *lawyer*
†Coleman, Dale Lynn *health facility administrator, educator*

Windsor
Furnas, Howard Earl *business executive, educator, retired government official*
Hydrisko, Stanley Joseph *financial company executive*

Woodstock
Billings, Franklin Swift, Jr. *federal judge*
Blackwell, David Jefferson *retired insurance company executive*
Chiefsky, Susan Justine *secondary education educator*
Hoyt, Coleman Williams *postal consultant*
Killian, Edward James *pediatrician*
Lash, James William (Jay Lash) *embryology educator*
Sincerbeaux, Robert Abbott *lawyer, preservationist, foundation executive*
Wollman, Harry *health care and executive search consultant*

VIRGINIA

Abingdon
Graham, Howard Lee, Sr. *corporate executive*
†Hamilton, Bobby *professional race car driver*
Jones, James Parker *federal judge*
Jones, Mary Trent *endowment fund trustee*
Mashburn, Donald Eugene *educator*
Ramos-Cano, Hazel Balatero *caterer, chef, innkeeper, entrepreneur*
Roberts, John Bennett, Jr. *veterinarian*
Taylor, Alfred Raleigh *geologist*
Widener, Hiram Emory, Jr. *federal judge*
Williams, Glen Morgan *federal judge*

Accomac
Manter, Sandra *county planner*
Plonk, William McGuire *retired minister*

Aldie
Weaver, Kitty Dunlap *author*

Alexandria
Abell, Richard Bender *lawyer, federal judicial official*
Adams, Ranald Trevor, Jr. *retired air force officer*
†Akukwe, Chinua *public health physician, health service executive*
Alberger, William Relph *lawyer, government official*
Aller, John Cosmos *diplomat*
Alloway, Robert Malcombe *computer consulting executive*
Amiri, Afsaneh *computer professional*
Ancell, Robert Manning *leadership organization executive*
Bachus, Walter Otis *retired army general, former association executive*
Baker, George Harold, III *physicist*
Ball, Robert M(yers) *social security, welfare and health policy specialist, writer, lecturer*
Ballard, Edward Brooks *landscape architect*
Barbato, Joseph Allen *writer*
†Barker, Charles Oliver *military officer*
Baroody, Michael Elias *trade association executive*
Battle, Timothy Joseph *lawyer*
Battocletti, Elizabeth Carmel *marketing executive*
Beach, Barbara Purse *lawyer*
†Benchoff, Dennis L. *career officer*
Berger, Patricia Wilson *retired librarian*
Berman, Alan *physicist*
Bernsen, Harold John *marketing executive, political affairs consultant, retired naval officer*
Bezold, Clement *think tank executive*
Biberman, Lucien Morton *physicist*
Birely, William Cramer *investment banker*
Bolger, Robert Joseph *retired trade association executive*
Borden, Enid A. *public relations executive*
Bowman, Richard Carl *defense consultant, retired air force officer*
Bozell, L. Brent, III *communications executive*
Brenner, Alfred Ephraim *physicist*
Brickhill, William Lee *international finance consultant*
Brinkema, Leonie Milhomme *federal judge*
Brown, Frederic Joseph *army officer*
Brown, Quincalee *professional society administrator*
Brownfeld, Allan Charles *columnist*
Bryan, Albert V., Jr. *federal judge*
Budde, Mitzi Marie Jarrett *librarian*
Buhain, Wilfrido Javier *medical educator*
Burch, Michael Ira *public relations executive, former government official*
Burke, Kelly Howard *former air force officer, business executive*
Bussler, Robert Bruce *management consultant*
Byrd, Barbara A. *professional society administrator*
Byrne, John Edward (JEB Byrne) *writer, retired government official*
Byrnside, Oscar Jehu, Jr. *professional society administrator*
Cacheris, James C. *federal judge*
†Caldwell, John S. *career officer*
Campbell, Francis James *retired chemist*
Campbell, Thomas Douglas *lawyer, consultant*
Carlson, J(ohn) Philip *lawyer*
Carpenter, Stanley Hammack *retired military aviation organization executive*
Carter, Gene R. *professional society administrator*
Carvalho, Julie Ann *psychologist*
Casey, Michael Kirkland *business executive, lawyer*
Chapman, Anthony Bradley *psychiatrist*
Christie, Thomas Philip *federal agency administrator, research manager*
Cicolani, Angelo George *research company executive, operating engineer*
Clower, William Dewey *trade association executive*
Clubb, Bruce Edwin *retired lawyer*
†Coburn, John G. *career officer*
Cohen, Bernard S. *lawyer*
Collins, Cardiss *former congresswoman*
Comeau, Kathy Darr *publishing executive*
Connally, Ernest Allen *retired federal agency administrator*
Connell, John Gibbs, Jr. *former government official*
Cook, Charles William *aerospace consultant, educator*
Cooney, David Martin *organization administrator, retired naval officer*
Cooper, B. Jay *public relations executive*
Cooper, David E.K. *foundation executive*
Cooper, Kenneth Banks *business executive, former army officer*
Cooper, Roger Merlin *information technology executive,federal government official, school administrator*
Corson, Walter Harris *sociologist*
Coryell, Glynn Heath *financial service executive*
Costagliola, Francesco *former government official, macro operations analyst*
Costello, Daniel Brian *lawyer, consultant*
Coyne, James Kitchenman, III *association executive, congressman, aviator*
Crane, Stephen Charles *professional society administrator*
Cross, Eason, Jr. *architect*
Culkin, Charles Walker, Jr. *trade association administrator*
Curtin, Gary Lee *air force officer*
D'Amours, Norman Edward *lawyer, former congressman*
Danaher, James William *retired federal government executive*
Daniel, Dorothy Isom *nurse specialist, consultant*
Darling, Thomas, Jr. *retired rural electrification specialist*
David, Joseph Raymond, Jr. *writer, periodical editor*
Davis, Ruth Margaret (Mrs. Benjamin Franklin Lohr) *technology management executive*
De Barbieri, Mary Ann *nonprofit management consultant*
Deel, Frances Quinn *retired librarian*
De Graf, William Bradford *career officer*
Del Fosse, Claude Marie *aerospace software executive*
†DePiro, Michael Francis *program analyst*
Devine, Donald J. *management and political consultant*
Dietrich, Laura Jordan *international policy advisor*
Dillman, Grant *journalist*
Dokurno, Anthony David *lawyer*
Downs, Michael Patrick *retired marine corps officer*
Duggan, Ervin S. *federal agency administrator*
Dunn, Bernard Daniel *former naval officer, consultant*
DuVall, Jack *television executive, fund raiser, speechwriter*
Dyer, Joseph Wendell *career officer*
Ellis, Thomas Selby, III *federal judge*
Emery, Vicki Morris *school library media specialist*
Engler, Brian David *systems operations executive*
Ensslin, Robert Frank, Jr. *retired association executive and military officer*
Erion, Carol Elizabeth *music educator*
Evans, Grose *former curator, retired educator*
Evans, H(arold) Bradley, Jr. *lawyer*
Fahey, Helen F. *prosecutor*
Fairchild, Lillie McKeen *nurse, educator*
Fairey, Chad Christopher *secondary education educator*
Farrell, William Christopher *lobbyist*
Fichenberg, Robert Gordon *newspaper editor, consultant*
Fisher, Donald Wayne *medical association executive*
Fisher, Joseph Allen *retired government official*
Fitton, Harvey Nelson, Jr. *former government official, publishing consultant*
Fleming, Douglas Riley *journalist, publisher, public affairs consultant*
Foster, Robert Francis *communications executive*
Foxwell, Elizabeth Marie *editor, writer*
Francis, Samuel Todd *columnist*
Fugate, Wilbur Lindsay *lawyer*
Furash, Edward E. *investment company executive, writer, lecturer*
†Garrett, Thomas W. *career officer*
Georges, Peter John *lawyer*
Gilchrist, Richard Irwin *real estate developer*
Girouard, Shirley Ann *nurse, policy analyst*
Gould, Phillip *defense planner, engineer*
Graham, John H. IV *health science association administrator*
Gray, Dorothy Louise Allman Pollet *librarian*
Greenstein, Ruth Louise *research institute executive, lawyer*
Haas, Ward John *research and development executive*
†Hammad, Alam E. *international business consultant, educator*
Harris, David Ford *management consultant, retired government official*
Hartsock, Linda Sue *educational and management association executive*
Harwood, Matthew David *artist*
Hathaway, Fred William *lawyer*
Havens, Harry Stewart *former federal assistant comptroller general, government consultant*
Hazard, Christopher Wedvik *international business executive*
Heacock, Phillip Kaga *aerospace executive*
†Heath, Ross Bradley *consulting company executive*
Helman, Gerald Bernard *government official*
Henton, Melissa Kaye *strategic technology and arms control analyst*
Hewitt, Charles C. *broadcast executive*
Hilton, Claude Meredith *federal judge*
Hilton, Robert Parker, Sr. *national security affairs consultant, retired naval officer*
Hirsch, Robert Louis *energy research-development-management consultant*
Hobbs, Michael Edwin *broadcasting company executive*
Holland, Dianna Gwin *real estate broker*
Huckabee, Harlow Maxwell *lawyer, writer*
Hughes, Grace-Flores *former federal agency administrator, consultant*
†Huh, Jae Young *finance company executive*
†Hunter, Henley A. *federal judge*
Hurtado, Rodrigo Claudio *allergist, immunologist*
Hussey, Ward MacLean *lawyer, former government official*
Hutzelman, Martha Louise *lawyer*
Jarrard, James Paul *school program administrator*
Johnson, Edgar McCarthy *psychologist*
Johnson, William David *retired university administrator*
Jokl, Alois Louis *electrical engineer*
Jolly, Bruce Overstreet *retired newspaper executive*
†Jones, Thomas Rawles, Jr. *federal judge*
Kelly, Nancy Frieda Wolicki *lawyer*
Klewans, Samuel N. *lawyer*
Kolar, Mary Jane *trade and professional association executive*
Kopp, Eugene Paul *lawyer*
Kotok, Alan *publishing association executive*
Kroesen, Frederick James *retired army officer, consultant*
LaMarca, Mary Margaret *elementary education educator*
†Lane, Debra Elizabeth *principal*
Langstaff, David Hamilton *aerospace industry executive*
Lantz, Phillip Edward *corporate executive, consultant*
Latson, Richard Charles *audio visual manager*
Laurent, Lawrence Bell *communications executive, former journalist*
Le, Thuy Xuan *financial control systems developer, consultant, metaphysics scientist*
Leach, Debra Ann *alcohol beverage association executive*
Leestma, Robert *federal agency administrator, educator*
Lenz, Edward Arnold *trade association executive, lawyer*
†Lightner, Candace Lynne *management consultant*
Locigno, Paul Robert *public affairs executive*
Losey, Michael Robert *professional society administrator*
Lovejoy, Bret D. *vocational association administrator*
Loving, William Rush, Jr. *public relations company executive, consultant*
Lundeberg, Philip Karl Boraas *curator*
Luttig, J. Michael *federal judge*

Lytle, Michael Allen *criminologist, consultant*
Mackay, James Cobham *museum director*
MacLaren, William George, Jr. *engineering executive*
Magazine, Alan Harrison *association executive, consultant*
Mandil, I. Harry *nuclear engineer*
Mann, Seymour Zalmon *political science and public administration educator emeritus, union official*
Mar, Eugene *lawyer, financial consultant*
Marschall, Albert Rhoades *engineer*
Marshall, Maryann Chorba *office administrator*
Masterson, Kleber Sanlin, Jr. *physicist*
Mathis, William Lowrey *lawyer*
Matthews, Sir Stuart *aviation industry executive*
Maves, Michael Donald *medical association executive*
McClure, Roger John *lawyer*
McCulloch, William Leonard *trade association administrator*
McDowell, Charles Eager *lawyer, retired military officer*
McKinney, James Clayton *electronics executive, electrical engineer*
Mc Lucas, John Luther *aerospace company executive*
McMillan, Charles William *consulting company executive*
McMiller, Anita Williams *entrepreneur, management consultant, public*
Mc Mullen, Thomas Henry *retired air force officer*
McNair, Carl Herbert, Jr. *army officer, aeronautical engineer*
Merrick, Roswell Davenport *educational association administrator*
Milling, Marcus Eugene, Sr. *geologist*
Minor, Mary Ellen *civilian military employee*
†Mitchell, Howard J. *career officer*
†Mitchell, Stephen Scott *federal judge*
Molinari, Susan *former congresswoman*
Molseed, Robert Basil *architect, specifications consultant*
Montague, Robert Latane, III *lawyer*
Montgomery, Gillespie V. (Sonny Montgomery) *former congressman*
Morrison, Tiffany L. *cable television executive*
Morse, Burnham Spottswood *broadcast executive*
Muir, Warren Roger *chemist, toxic substances specialist*
Murray, Robert John *think-tank executive*
Murray, Russell, II *aeronautical engineer, defense analyst, consultant*
Murtagh, William John *preservationist, educator*
Nelson, David Leonard *process management systems company executive*
Noland, Royce Paul *association executive, physical therapist*
O'Brien, Patrick Michael *library administrator*
O'Hara, John Patrick *lawyer, accountant*
Pabarcius, Algis *investment executive*
Parsons, Henry McIlvaine *psychologist*
Pastin, Mark Joseph *association executive*
†Patrick, Erline M. *federal agency administrator*
Patterson, Lillian Stanton *museum specialist*
Paturis, E. Michael *lawyer*
Paul, Andrew Robert *trade association executive*
Perchik, Benjamin Ivan *operations research analyst*
Phillips, Karen Borlaug *economist, association executive*
†Poretz, Barry R. *federal judge*
Powell, Colin Luther *retired military officer, author*
Price, James Edward *federal government executive*
Pringle, Robert Maxwell *diplomat*
Puscheck, Herbert Charles *social sciences educator*
Radewagen, Fred *publisher, organization executive*
Rainwater, Joan Lucille Morse *investment company executive*
Rasmus, John Charles *trade association executive, lawyer*
Ray, Terrill Wylie *physical scientist*
Rector, John Michael *association executive, lawyer*
Reed, Leon Samuel *policy analyst, writer, photographer*
Revere, Virginia Lehr *clinical psychologist*
Richards, Darrie Hewitt *investment company executive*
Riggs, Frank *former congressman*
Ritter, James William *architect, educator*
Rossi, Eugene Joseph *federal prosecutor, law educator*
Rubin, Burton Jay *lawyer, editor*
Sauer, H. Arthur *legislative staff member*
†Schanzer, Steven T. *defense security director*
Scheibel, James Allen *volunteer service executive*
†Schmidt, Elaine Melotti *assistant principal*
Schultz, Franklin M. *retired lawyer*
Schwartz, Richard *consumer association executive*
Sciulla, Michael Garri *association executive*
Scurlock, Arch Chilton *chemical engineer*
Sczudlo, Walter Joseph *lawyer*
Seale, William *historian*
Searle, Willard F., Jr. *marine and salvage engineer*
Senese, Donald Joseph *former government official, research administrator*
†Sewell, W. Curtis *federal judge*
Shapiro, Maurice Mandel *astrophysicist*
Sherk, George William *lawyer*
Simmons, Richard De Lacey *mass media executive*
Skoug, Kenneth Nordly, Jr. *diplomat*
Smith, Jeffrey Greenwood *industry executive, retired army officer*
†Smith, Larry G. *career military officer*
Smith, Robert Luther *management educator*
Snyder, Jed C. *foreign affairs specialist*
†Sogoian, Mikael F. *artist*
Southworth, R. Morrison *fundraising counsel*
Spadin, Gaile Luanne *association administrator*
Spar, Edward Joel *demographer*
†Starr, James Edward *logistics management executive*
Stempler, Jack Leon *government and aerospace company executive*
Stout, Mary Webb *supervisory educational services specialist, educator*
Straub, Peter Thornton *lawyer*
Strickland, Nellie B. *library program director*
Studebaker, John Milton *utilities engineer, consultant, educator*
Sturtevant, Brereton *retired lawyer, former government official*
Sulick, Joseph Edward *military communications administrator*
Swinburn, Charles *lawyer*
Tatham, Julie Campbell *writer*
Taylor, William Brockenbrough *engineer, consultant, management consultant*
†Tesler, Diane Elaine *artist*
Thomas, William Griffith *lawyer*
Thompson, LeRoy, Jr. *radio engineer, military reserve officer*
Ticer, Patricia *state senator*
Toulmin, Priestley *geologist*
Trent, Darrell M. *academic and corporate executive*
Triefeldt, Rein *sculptor, educator*
Tucker, John Robert *financial executive*
Turner, Mary Jane *educational administrator*
Van Cleve, Ruth Gill *retired lawyer, government official*
Vander Myde, Paul Arthur *technology and engineering services executive*
†Vollrath, Frederick E. *military officer*
Von Drehle, Ramon Arnold *lawyer*
Walkup, Charlotte Lloyd *lawyer*
Wallace, Barbara Brooks *writer*
Walton, Thomas Edward *research scientist, educator, administrator*
Wasko-Flood, Sandra Jean *artist, educator*
Watkins, Birge Swift *government contractor*
Weiler, Todd Alan *army official*
Weiner, Robert Michael *engineering design company executive, retired consulting engineer*
Weisberg, Leonard R. *retired research and engineering executive*
Weiser, John Conrad *photography administrator*
Wells, Fay Gillis *writer, lecturer, broadcaster, aviation historian*
Wendel, Charles Allen *lawyer*
†Whelden, Craig B. *army officer*
Widner, Ralph Randolph *civic executive*
Wieder, Bruce Terrill *lawyer, electrical engineer*
Wilding, James Anthony *airport administrator*
Williams, Jody *political organization administrator*
Williams, Justin W. *government official*
†Williams, Norman E. *army officer*
Wilner, Morton Harrison *retired lawyer*
Wilson, Charles H(arrison) *retired air force officer, financial planner, human resource development professional*
†Wilson, Johnnie Edward *military officer*
Woelflein, Kevin Gerard *banker*
Wolicki, Eligius Anthony *nuclear physicist, consultant*
Woolley, Mary Elizabeth *research administrator*
Wright, Mary James *managing editor*
Wurzel, Mary V. *past association executive*
Wynn, Robert E. *electronics executive, retired career officer*
Yaworsky, George Myroslaw *physicist, technical and management consultant*
Yoder, Edwin Milton, Jr. *columnist, educator, editor, writer*
Zook, Theresa Fuetterer *gemologist, consultant*

Amelia Court House

Wallace, John Robert *county administrator*

Amherst

Armstrong, Gregory Timon *religious studies educator, minister*
Campbell, Catherine Lynn *elementary and middle school educator*
Herbert, Amanda Kathryn *special education educator*

Amissville

Coutu, Charles Arthur *deacon*

Annandale

Abdellah, Faye Glenn *retired public health service executive*
Binder, Richard Allen *hematologist, oncologist*
Christianson, Geryld B. *government relations consultant*
Clayton, William E. *naval officer*
Connair, Stephen Michael *financial analyst*
Downen, Robert Lynn *international affairs analyst and consultant, editor, writer*
†Ernst, Richard James *academic administrator*
†Evenson, Eric Todd *army officer, public health physician*
Gaberman, Harry *lawyer, economic analyst*
Greinke, Everett Donald *corporate executive, international programs consultant*
Hedrick, Floyd Dudley *retired government official, author*
Henretty, Donald Bruce *history educator*
Herbst, Robert LeRoy *organization executive*
Hollis, Daryl Joseph *judge*
Hollis, Linda Eardley *urban planning consultant*
Hovis, Robert Houston, III *lawyer*
Jarvis, Elbert, II (Jay Jarvis) *employee benefits specialist*
Jones, David Charles *international financial and management consultant*
Khim, Jay Wook *high technology systems integration executive*
Kiernan, Paul Darlington *thoracic surgeon, educator*
Lefrak, Edward Arthur *cardiovascular and thoracic surgeon*
Matuszko, Anthony Joseph *research chemist, administrator*
McCaffree, Burnham Clough, Jr. *retired naval officer*
McKee, Fran *retired naval officer*
Nowak, Jan Zdzislaw *writer, consultant*
Rogers, Stephen Hitchcock *former ambassador*
Samuelson, Douglas Alan *information systems company executive*
Scott, Hugh Patrick *physician, naval officer*
Shamburek, Roland Howard *physician*
Simonian, Simon John *surgeon, scientist, educator*
Tontz, Robert L. *government official*
Watts, Helena Roselle *military analyst*
Williams, James Arthur *retired army officer, information systems company executive*

Arlington

Adams, Donald Edward *biotechnology and pharmaceutical patent examiner*
Adams, John Hanly *retired magazine editor, writer, consultant*
Adreon, Beatrice Marie Rice *pharmacist*
Adreon, Harry Barnes *architect*
Aggrey, Orison Rudolph *former ambassador, university administrator*
Akkara, Joseph Augustine *biochemist*
Alford, Paula N. *federal agency administrator*
Allard, Dean Conrad *historian, retired naval history center director*
Allard, Scott Morgan *cost, benefit analyst, information professional*
Allen, David *government official*
†Amlin, Gary W. *finance administrator*
Anderson, Steven Hunter *media relations professional*
Anthony, Robert Armstrong *lawyer, educator*
†Banks, Willie J. *orthopaedic surgeon, educator*
Bartlett, Elizabeth Susan *audio-visual specialist*
Bast, James Louis *trade association executive*
Basu, Sunanda *scientific administrator, researcher in space physics*
†Baum, Robert L. *federal agency executive*
Bautz, Laura Patricia *astronomer*
Behney, Clyde Joseph *health services researcher*
Bennett, John Joseph *professional services company executive*
Berg, John Richard *chemist, former federal government executive*
Berg, Sister Marie Majella *university chancellor*
Bertenthal, Bennett Ira *foundation administrator*
Beyer, Barbara Lynn *aviation consultant*
Bianchi, Charles Paul *technical and business executive, money manager, financial consultant*
Bird, Caroline *author*
Blankinship, Henry Massie *management consultant*
Bloomer, William Arthur *security industry executive*
Bodley, Harley Ryan, Jr. *editor, writer, broadcaster*
Bolster, Archie Milburn *retired foreign service officer*
Bordogna, Joseph *engineer, educator*
Bossman, David A. *trade association administrator*
†Boster, Davis Eugene *retired ambassador*
Bowman, Frank Lee *admiral and director naval nuclear propulsion*
Boyle, Robert Patrick *retired government agency consultant, lawyer*
Brandt, Werner William *federal agency official*
Brazeal, Aurelia Erskine *former ambassador*
Brenner, Edgar H. *legal administrator*
Bridgewater, Albert Louis *science foundation administrator*
Brown, Gardner Russell *engineering executive*
Brown, Robert Lyle *foreign affairs consultant*
Bruck, William *business executive*
Bullard, Marcia *publishing executive*
Bune, Karen Louise *criminal justice official*
†Bussman, Charles Haines *publisher*
Bussmann, Charles Haines *publisher*
Cameron, Maryellen *science association administrator, geologist, educator*
Carbaugh, John Edward, Jr. *lawyer*
Carr, Kenneth Monroe *naval officer*
Carter, William Harold, Sr. *physicist, researcher, electrical engineer*
Cavanaugh, Margaret Anne *chemist*
Chapman, Donald D. *retired naval officer, lawyer*
Chapple, Thomas Leslie *lawyer*
Chipman, Susan Elizabeth *psychologist*
†Chung, Caroline *airline executive, aerobics instructor*
Ciment, Melvyn *mathematician*
Clarke, Frederic B., III *risk analysis consultant*
Clayton, James Edwin *journalist*
Clema, Joe Kotouc *computer scientist*
Clutter, Mary Elizabeth *federal official*
Coady, Philip James, Jr. *retired naval officer*
Cocolis, Peter Konstantine *business development executive*
Cole, Benjamin Richason *newspaper executive*
Coleman, Howard S. *engineer, physicist*
Coleman, Rodney Albert *government affairs consultant*
Coles, Bertha Sharon Giles *visual information specialist*
Collins, Philip Reilly *lawyer, educator*
Colwell, Rita Rossi *microbiologist, molecular biologist, educator, federal agency administrator*
Contis, George *medical services company executive*
Cooper, Jon Charles *environmental science educator, lawyer*
Corell, Robert Walden *science administration educator*
Corley, Sarah Taylor *physician*
Covington, James Edwin *government agency administrator, psychologist*
Cox, Henry *research company executive, research engineer*
Cullen, James G. *telecommunications industry executive*
Cummings, John William, Jr. *logistician, systems analyst*
Curley, John J. *diversified media company executive*
Curley, Thomas *newspaper executive*
D'Alessio, Frederick D. *telecommunications company executive*
Davis, John P. *career officer*
Davis, Maynard Kirk *accountant*
Davis, Ruth A. *ambassador*
†Davison, Michael S., Jr. *military officer*
Del Duca, Betty Spahr *association executive*
Dentzer, Susan *journalist*
Dickman, Robert Laurence *physicist, researcher*
Dolan, William David, Jr. *physician*
Doles, John Henry, III *retired telecommunications company manager*
Dorman, Craig Emery *oceanographer, academic administrator*
Doyle, Gerard Francis *lawyer*
Drayton, William *lawyer, social entrepreneur, management consultant*
Dunn, Loretta Lynn *lawyer*
Edmondson, William Brockway *retired foreign service officer*
Ehrman, Madeline Elizabeth *federal agency administrator*
Elam, Fred Eldon *retired career army officer*
Ensminger, Luther Glenn *chemist*
Erwin, Frank William *personnel research and publishing executive*
Everett, Warren Sylvester *consultant, former government official*
Fabian, John McCreary *non-profit company executive, former astronaut, former air force officer*
Fazio, Vic *former congressman*
Feller, Mimi *newspaper publishing executive*
Ferguson Kennedy, Barbara Brownell *journalist*
Fernandez, Fernando Lawrence *aeronautical engineer, research company executive*
Ferraz, Francisco Marconi *neurological surgeon*
Fleishman, Phil *radio news executive*
Fowler, David Lucas *corporate lawyer*
Frame, Nancy Davis *lawyer*
Frantz, Cecilia Aranda *psychologist*
†Fredericks, Michael Edwin *criminal investigator*
Freeman, Neal Blackwell *communications corporation executive*
French, Mary B. *English educator*
Fuchs, Roland John *geography educator, university science official*
Funseth, Robert Lloyd Eric Martin *international consultant, lecturer, retired senior foreign service officer*
Gaffney, Paul Golden, II *military officer*
†Garfinkel, Patricia Gail *speech writer, policy analyst, poet*
Garner, Jay Montgomery *career officer*
Gauvin, Charles F. *professional society administrator*
Gianturco, Delio E. *management consultant*
Gibbons, Miles J., Jr. *foundation administrator*
Gniewek, Raymond Louis *newspaper editor*
Goforth, Wayne Reid *research administrator, biologist*
Golden, James Leslie *information technology executive*
Golladay, Mary Jean *statistician*
Gonzalez, Eduardo *federal agency administrator*
Gooding, Robert C. *engineering administrator*
Goodman, Mark *journalist, educator*
Goodwin, Richard Clarke *military analyst*
Gracey, James Steele *corporate director, retired coast guard officer, consultant*
Grandmaison, J. Joseph *federal agency executive*
Gregg, David, III *investment banker*
Gunderson, Steve Craig *consultant, former congressman*
Guruswamy, Dharmithran *urban planner*
Hagn, George Hubert *electrical engineer, researcher*
Hall, Carl William *agricultural and mechanical engineer*
Hamed, Martha Ellen *government administrator*
Hansen, Kenneth D. *lawyer, ophthalmologist*
Haq, Bilal Ul *national science foundation program director, researcher*
Harper, Michael John Kennedy *obstetrics and gynecology educator*
Harris, William James, Jr. *research administrator, educator*
Harrison-Jones, Virginia M. *federal government agency employee*
†Hassett, Valerie Jane *interior architect*
Healy, Bernadine P. *physician, educator, federal agency administrator, scientist*
Heineken, Frederick George *biochemical engineer*
Held, Joe Roger *veterinarian, epidemiologist*
Henderson, John Brown *economist*
Henderson, Robert Earl *mechanical engineer, educator, consultant*
Hendrickson, Jerome Orland *trade association executive, lawyer*
Henle, Peter *retired economic consultant, arbitrator*
Hickman, Elizabeth Podesta *retired counselor, educator*
Highsmith, Wanda Law *retired association executive*
Hill, Donald Wain *education accreditation commission executive*
Hill, Donna Marie *communications executive*
Hittle, James Donald *writer, business consultant*
Hochstein, Anatoly Boris *maritime ports and waterways educator, researcher, consultant*
Hogue, Dale Curtis, Sr. *lawyer*
Houston, Paul David *school association administrator*
Hunkele, Lester Martin, III *retired federal agency administrator*
Hunter, J(ohn) Robert *insurance consumer advocate*
Ingrassia, Anthony Frank *human resource specialist*
Iqbal, Zafar *biochemist, neurochemist*
Itoh, William H. *former ambassador*
Jackson, William Paul, Jr. *lawyer*
Jankowski, John Edward, Jr. *government administrator*
Johnson, Charles Nelson, Jr. *physicist*
Johnson, John A. *communications company executive*
Johnson, Rosemary Wrucke *personnel management specialist*
Junker, Bobby Ray *research and development executive, physicist*
Jurgensen, Karen *newspaper editor*
Kanter, L. Erick *public relations executive*
Katona, Peter Geza *biomedical engineer, educator*
Keel, Alton Gold, Jr. *ambassador*
Keeve, Jack Philip *physician, educator, retired*
†Kelley, David J. *military officer*
Kelley, Paul Xavier *retired marine corps officer*
Kelley, Virginia (Judy) Wiard *dance educator*
Kelly, John James *lawyer*
Kem, Richard Samuel *retired army officer*
†Kenne, Leslie F. *military officer*
Kent, Jill Elspeth *academic healthcare adminstrator, lawyer*
†Kern, Paul John *army officer*
Kerns, Wilmer Lee *social science researcher*
Kilduff, Bonnie Elizabeth *director of expositions*
Kirtley, Jane Elizabeth *professional society administrator, lawyer*
Klosk, Russell Martin *human resources executive*
Knipling, Edward Fred *retired research entomologist, agricultural administrator*
Knowlton, William Allen *political and military consultant, educator*
Korman, James William *lawyer*
Kostoff, Ronald Neil *aerospace scientist*
Kotler, Wendy Illene *art educator, social studies educator, grants coordinator*
Koury, Agnes Lillian *real estate owner and manager*
Krys, Sheldon Jack *retired foreign service officer, career minister*
Kuelbs, John Thomas *lawyer*
Kull, Joseph *government administrator*
Lampe, Henry Oscar *stockbroker*
Lampe, Margaret Sanger *community activist*
Langworthy, Everett Walter *association executive, natural gas exploration company executive*
Larsen-Basse, Jorn *mechanical and materials engineering educator, researcher, consultant*
†Lash, William Henry *law educator*
†Lasowski, Anne-Marie F. *federal agency administrator*
Lau, Clifford *electrical engineer, researcher*
Lazich, Daniel *aerospace engineer*
Leibensperger, Philip Wetzel *secondary education educator*
Leland, Marc Ernest *trust advisor, lawyer*
Lester, Barnett Benjamin *editor, foreign affairs officer*
Levinson, Lawrence Edward *lawyer, corporation executive*
Lewis, Hunter *financial advisor, publisher*
Lieberman, Robert J. *federal agency administrator*
Lisanby, James Walker *retired naval officer*
Litman, Richard Curtis *lawyer*
Long, Madeleine J. *mathematics and science educator*
Lorell, Monte *newspaper editor*
Loverde, Paul S. *bishop*
Lowe, Jeanne Catherine *pastor*
Luffsey, Walter Stith *transportation executive*
Lynch, John Thomas *science foundation administrator, physicist*
Lynch, Patricia Gates *broadcasting organization executive consultant, former ambassador*
MacDougall, William Lowell *magazine editor*

MacNeil, Robert Breckenridge Ware retired broadcast journalist, writer
Makonnen, Sophia Mehret international development/Africa specialist
Malone, William Grady retired lawyer
Maness, Stephen Ray manufacturing engineer, retired army officer
Marcuccio, Phyllis Rose association executive, editor
Marini, Elizabeth Ann civilian military executive
Marshall, Charles Burton political science consultant
Marzetti, Loretta A. government agency executive, policy analyst
Mason, Phillip Howard aircraft company executive, retired army officer
Mathews, Linda McVeigh newspaper editor
Mathis, Mark Jay lawyer
Mazzarella, David newspaper editor
McCaskill, James H. secondary education educator, consultant
McClure, William Earl financial advisor
McCorkindale, Douglas Hamilton lawyer, publishing company executive
McCoy, Timothy John naval officer
McDermott, Francis Owen lawyer
McFarland, Walter Gerard management consultant
McGann, Barbara E. career officer
McKinley, Sarah Elizabeth journalist
McLeer, Laureen Dorothy drug development, pharmaceutical professional
McMasters, Paul Kenneth foundation executive
McNamara, Tom newspaper editor
McShane, Michael John lobbyist
McWethy, John Fleetwood journalist
McWethy, Patricia Joan educational association administrator
Merrifield, Dudley Bruce business educator, former government official
Merritt, Jack Neil retired army officer
Meyers, Sheldon engineering company executive
Mirrielees, James Fay, III publishing executive
Morgan, Bruce Ray international consultant
Morgan, Robert Peter engineering educator
Morris, John Woodland, II businessman, former army officer
Mossinghoff, Gerald Joseph patent lawyer, educator
Muris, Timothy Joseph law educator
Murray, Jeanne Morris computer scientist, educator, consultant, researcher
Mylonakis, Stamatios Gregory chemicals company executive
Nanos, George P. career officer, physicist
†Nash, Henry G. company executive
Neikirk, William Robert journalist
Neuharth, Allen Harold newspaper publisher
Norris, James Arnold federal agency administrator
Obermayer, Herman Joseph newspaper publisher
O'Neill, Brian research organization administrator
Ordway, Frederick Ira, III educator, consultant, researcher, author
†Osterholz, John Louis information administrator
Otstott, Charles Paddock company executive, retired army officer
Page, Carolyn Ann writer
Pan, Gary George information technology executive, consultant
Papadopoulos, Patricia Marie healthcare professional
Patrick, Michele Mary government official
Paynter, Harry Alvin retired trade association executive
Pensmith, Sharyn Elaine communications executive
Perry, Bill photojournalist
Peterson, Paul Quayle retired university dean, physician
Plevyak, Thomas Joseph communications executive
Poehlein, Gary Wayne chemical engineering educator
Pollock, Neal Jay electronics executive
†Pugliese, Frank P., Jr. federal agency administrator
Putnam, George W., Jr. retired army officer
Quinn, John Collins publishing executive, newspaper editor
Quinn, William Wilson army officer, manufacturing executive
Reagan, Lawrence Paul, Jr. systems engineer
Reed, Paul Allen artist
Reeder, Franklin S. retired federal agency administrator
Rees, Clifford Harcourt, Jr. (Ted Rees) association executive, retired air force officer
Reiss, Susan Marie editor, writer
Reynik, Robert John materials scientist, research and education administrator
Reynolds, Peter James physicist
Rhodes, Alice Graham lawyer
Richtol, Herbert Harold science foundation program director
Riegel, Kurt Wetherhold environmental protection executive
Ritter, Hal newspaper editor
Roach, Arthur Hudgins fund raising consultant
Roberts, James Milnor, Jr. professional society administrator
Rockefeller, Sharon Percy broadcast executive
Rogers, James Frederick banker, management consultant
Romney, Carl F. seismologist
Rosenker, Mark Victor trade association executive
Rousselot, Peter Frese consultant
Saalfeld, Fred Erich naval researcher
†Salisbury, Gary LeRoy corporate information manager, military officer
Samburg, A. Gene security company executive
Samsot, Robert Louis newspaper editor, consultant
Sands, Frank Melville investment manager
Sargent, David Putnam, Jr. career officer
Sawhill, John Crittenden conservationist, economist, university president, government official
Scarborough, Robert Henry, Jr. enterpreneur
Schneider, Clara Garbus dietitian, nursing consultant
Schreurs, Brian Frederick editor, publisher
Schrock, Philip John army officer
Schwartz, Lyle Howard materials scientist, science administrator
Seely, James Michael defense consultant, retired naval officer, small business owner
Sewell, William George, III electronics engineer
Shaker, William Haygood marketing professional, public policy reformer
Shannon, Thomas Alfred retired educational association administrator emeritus
Shipway, John Francis career officer
Shortal, Terence Michael systems company executive
Shrier, Stefan mathematician, educator
†Siegel, Laurence C. real estate investment executive
Simonson, David C. retired newspaper association executive
Simpson, John Mathes newspaper editor
Singstock, David John military officer
Smerdon, Ernest Thomas academic administrator
Smith, Elise Fiber international non-profit development agency administrator
Smith, Ellen Elisabeth publisher, journalist
Smith, Myron George former government official, consultant
Spooner, Richard Edward aerospace company executive
Stackpole, Kerry Clifford association executive
Stevens, Donald King retired aeronautical engineer, consultant
Stewart, Gordon Mead architect
Stokes, B. R. retired transportation consultant
Stolgitis, William Charles professional society executive
Stover, David Frank lawyer
Sutton, George Walter research laboratory executive, mechanical engineer, physicist
Swartz, Roger Donald computer scientist
Taggart, G. Bruce government program executive
Tanzer, Lester editor
†Tarbell, David S. federal agency administrator
Taylor, Robert William professional society administrator
Teem, John McCorkle retired association executive
Terzian, Grace Paine publisher
Tyrrell, Robert Emmett, Jr. periodical editor, writer
Umminger, Bruce Lynn government official, scientist, educator
Uncapher, Mark Elson lawyer, trade association administrator
Van Horn, Hugh M. physicist, astronomer
Van Lare, Wendell John lawyer
Vaught, Wilma L. foundation executive, retired air force officer
Verburg, Edwin Arnold federal agency administrator
Vernon, Anthony Cliffe financial systems support specialist
Verville, Elizabeth Giavani federal official
Vesper, Carolyn F. newspaper publishing executive
Violand-Sanchez, Emma Natividad school administrator, educator
Volkmer, Harold L. former congressman
Walker, Cecil L. broadcast executive
Walker, Woodrow Wilson lawyer, cattle and timber farmer
Wall, Barbara Wartelle lawyer
Watson, Alexander Fletcher organization executive, former ambassador
Webb, David Owen petroleum engineer, association executive
Weber, Alfons physicist
Weidemann, Celia Jean social scientist, international business and financial development consultant
Weiss, Susan newspaper editor
Welch, Jasper Arthur, Jr. retired air force officer
Wells, Christine foundation executive
Welsford, James Joseph secondary school educator
Werbos, Paul John neural net research director
Wesberry, James Pickett, Jr. financial management consultant, auditor, international organization executive
Whitcomb, James Hall geophysicist, foundation administrator
White, Dale Timothy (Tim White) television journalist, producer
Wilcox, Shirley Jean Langdon genealogist
Wilkie, Julia Bullard government affairs representative
Williams, Luther Steward science foundation administrator
Wilson, Minter Lowther, Jr. retired officers association executive
Wodarczyk, Francis John chemist
Wolf, Stephen M. airline executive
†Woods, Willie E. information specialist
Yankwich, Peter Ewald chemistry educator
Yarymovych, Michael Ihor retired manufacturing company executive
Yount, George R. admiral commander
Zakheim, Dov Solomon economist, government official
Zgonc, Janice Ann technical information specialist
Zirkind, Ralph physicist, educator
Zirkle, William Vernon philanthropist
Zorthian, Barry communications executive
Zumwalt, Elmo Russell, Jr. retired naval officer

Aroda
Nisly, Loretta Lynn medical and surgical nurse, geriatrics nurse

Ashburn
Bennett, Lawrence Herman physicist
Boyne, Walter James writer, former museum director
Cooke, John Kent professional sports management executive
Cuteri, Frank R., Jr. automotive executive
Gold, George Myron lawyer, editor, writer, consultant
Pavsek, Daniel Allan banker, educator
Tice, Raphael Dean army officer
Turk, Matt football player
Turner, Norv professional football coach
Waetjen, Daniel G. information technology executive
Walsh, Geraldine Frances nursing administrator
Weyman, Steven Aloysius military officer

Ashland
Chandler, Kimberley Lynn gifted education resource specialist
d'Evegnee, Charles Paul lawyer
Henshaw, William Raleigh middle school educator
Inge, Milton Thomas American literature and culture educator, author
Martin, Roger Harry college president

Baskerville
Simmons, Barry William university official, consultant

Bedford
Henry, Nancy Sinclair middle school educator

Big Island
Durham, Betty Bethea therapist
Durham, John I. retired religious studies educator

Blacksburg
†Archer, Vanessa education program director
Ash, Philip psychologist
Baehr, Stephen Lessing Russian langauge educator, researcher
Batra, Romesh Chander engineering mechanics educator, researcher
Bauer, Henry Hermann chemistry and science educator
Blackwell, William Allen electrical engineering educator
Bliznakov, Milka Tcherneva architect
Boardman, Gregory Dale environmental engineer, educator
Brown, Gary Sandy electrical engineering educator
Brown, Gregory Neil university administrator, forest physiology educator
Brozovsky, John A. accounting educator
Bryant, Clifton Dow sociologist, educator
Buhyoff, Gregory J. forestry specialist, educator
Burkhart, Harold Eugene forestry educator
Byers, Albert Samuel aerospace education specialist
Cairns, John, Jr. environmental science educator, researcher
Calvera, Jorge artist
Campbell, Joan Virginia Loweke secondary school educator, language educator
Cannell, Robert Quirk agricultural sciences educator
Carlisle, Ervin Frederick university provost, educator
Cheramie, Lesley Goyette veterinarian
Cowles, Joe Richard biology educator
Crawford, Peggy Smith design educator
Davis, Carole Carrera watercolor artist
De Datta, Surajit Kumar soil scientist, agronomist, educator
de Wolf, David Alter electrical engineer, educator
Doswald, Herman Kenneth German language educator, academic administrator
Edwards, Patricia K. dean
Fabrycky, Wolter Joseph engineering educator, author, industrial and systems engineer
†Falco, Edward writer, English educator
Gablik, Suzi art educator, writer
Glasser, Wolfgang Gerhard wood science and chemical engineering researcher, educator
Good, Irving John statistics educator, mathematician, philosopher of science
†Goodsell, Charles T. educator
Gray, Festus Gail electrical engineer, educator, researcher
Graybeal, Jack Daniel chemist, educator
Grover, Norman LaMotte theologian, philosopher
Haney, Harry L., Jr. forestry specialist, educator
Harris, Sally Lee public relations coordinator
Haugh, Clarence Gene agricultural engineering educator
†Henrickson, Bonnie college basketball coach
Hibbard, Walter Rollo, Jr. retired engineering educator
†Hirt, Joan B. education educator
Kincade, Doris Helsing apparel marketing educator
Landen, Robert Geran retired historian, educator, university administrator
Langel, Robert Allan, III geophysicist
Lee, Fred C. electrical engineering educator
Lynch, Sherry Kay counselor
McGrath, James Edward chemistry educator
McKenna, James Richard agronomy educator
†Meszaros, Peggy academic administrator
Minckler, Leon Sherwood forestry and conservation educator, author
Mitchell, James Kenneth civil engineer, educator
Mo, Luke Wei physicist, educator
Moore, Laurence John business educator
Morgan, George Emir, III financial economics educator
†Muffo, John Anthony administrator
Murray, Thomas Michael civil engineering educator, consultant
Ogliaruso, Michael Anthony chemist, educator
Olin, Robert Floyd mathematics educator and reseacher
Patterson, Douglas MacLennan finance educator
Perumpral, John Verghese agricultural engineer, administrator, educator
Phadke, Arun G. electrical engineering educator
†Poirier-Bures, Simone Thérèse composition and creative writing educator, writer
Poole, Calvert King elementary school educator
Price, Dennis Lee industrial engineer, educator
Randall, Clifford Wendell civil engineer
Rodriguez-Camilloni, Humberto Leonardo architect, historian, educator
Sgro, Joseph Anthony psychologist, educator
Shepard, Jon Max sociologist
Smith, Robert McNeil university dean
Squires, Arthur Morton chemical engineer, educator
Steger, Charles William university administrator
Stutzman, Warren Lee electrical engineer, educator
†Sullivan, Ernest Walter, II English educator
Sweeney, Lucy Graham psychologist
Swiger, L. A. agricultural studies educator
Terhune, Robert William optics scientist
Tillar, Thomas Cato, Jr. university alumni relations administrator, consultant
Torgersen, Paul Ernest academic administrator, educator
Warren, William Kermit media company executive

Blackstone
Allen, Jeffrey Rodgers lawyer

Blue Ridge
Elmore, Walter A. electrical engineer, consultant

Bluefield
Spracher, John C. banking executive

Bluemont
Kobetz, Richard William criminologist, consultant

Boones Mill
Oyler, Amy Elizabeth medical/surgical nurse
Sumpter, James Hardee, III sales executive

Boston
Engle, Reed Laurence landscape architect

Bowling Green
Long, Clarence Dickinson, III lawyer

Boyd Tavern
Darden, Donna Bernice special education educator

Bridgewater
Armstrong, Martha Susan accountant, educator
Bittel, Muriel Helene managing editor
Geisert, Wayne Frederick educational consultant, retired administrator

Bristol
Creger, David Lee financial planner, insurance executive
Macione, Joe television station executive
McGlothlin, James W. wholesale distribution executive
Muller, William Albert, III library director
Shean, Timothy Joseph manufacturing company executive

Broad Run
Hinkle, Barton Leslie retired electronics company executive
Kube, Harold Deming retired financial executive
Peters, William Nelson physicist

Broadway
Keeler, James Leonard food products company executive

Brookneal
Elson, James Martin historic foundation director, college music educator, fine arts administrator

Burgess
Towle, Leland Hill retired government official

Burke
Daski, Robert Steven federal civil servant
Forster, William Hull aerospace executive
Holmes, Stephanie Eleanor music educator, violinist
Lynch, Charles Theodore, Sr. materials science engineering researcher, consultant, educator
O'Connor, Edward Cornelius army officer
Pfister, Cloyd Harry consultant, former career officer
Smeeton, Thomas Rooney governmental affairs consultant
White, Terry Joe writer, editor
†Zelasko, Nancy Faber education association manager

Burkeville
Stiles, Anne Plum healthcare specialist

Burlington
†Kete, Mary Louise English and American Literature educator

Cape Charles
Brookshire, James Knox, Jr. transportation facility administrator

Castleton
Hahn, James Maglorie former librarian, farmer

Catlett
Broderick, Anthony James air transportation executive
Scheer, Julian Weisel business executive, author

Centreville
†Amerault, James F. military officer
Bucciero, Joseph Mario, Jr. executive consulting firm
Hanson, Lowell Knute seminar developer and leader, information systems consultant
James, Louis Meredith personnel executive

Chantilly
†Chrzanowski, Leye Jeanette publisher
Harris, Paul Lynwood aerospace transportation executive
†Matthews, Stephen Philip association executive
Miller, Donald Eugene aerospace electronics executive
Priem, Richard Gregory writer, information systems executive, entertainment company executive
Sroka, John Walter trade association executive
Willner, Larry Elliott telecommunications company executive, consultant

Charlotte Court House
Hoffman, William author
Prophett, Andrew Lee political science educator

Charlottesville
Abbot, William Wright history educator
Abraham, Henry Julian political science educator
†Adams, Lawrence Earl educator
Alford, Neill Herbert, Jr. retired law educator
Anderson, Robert Barber architect
Arnold, Albert James foreign language educator
Barnett, Benjamin Lewis, Jr. physician
Barolsky, Paul art history educator
Battestin, Martin Carey English language educator
Bednar, Michael John architecture educator
Beller, George Allan medical educator
Berkeley, Edmund, Jr. retired archivist, educator
Berkeley, Francis Lewis, Jr. retired archivist
Berne, Robert Matthew physiologist, educator
Biltonen, Rodney Lincoln biochemistry and pharmacology educator
Bloomfield, Louis Aub physicist, educator
Bly, Charles Albert nuclear engineer, research scientist
Bonnie, Richard Jeffrey legal educator, lawyer
Bouchard, Ronald A. health care administrator
Bovet, Eric David economist, consultant
Bradbeer, Clive biochemistry and microbiology educator, research scientist
Brandt, Richard Martin education educator
Breneman, David Worthy dean, educator
Brill, Arthur Sylvan biophysics educator
Broome, Oscar Whitfield, Jr. accounting educator, administrator
Brownrigg, Walter Grant cartoonist, corporate executive
Bull, George Albert retired banker
Bunker, Linda Kay dean, physical education educator
Cano-Ballesta, Juan Spanish language educator
Cantrell, Robert Wendell otolaryngologist, head and neck surgeon, educator
Carey, Robert Munson university dean, physician
Casey, John Dudley writer, English language educator
Casteen, John Thomas, III university president
Catlin, Avery engineering and computer science educator, writer
Chandler, Lawrence Bradford, Jr. lawyer
Chapel, Robert Clyde stage director, theater educator
Cherno, Melvin humanities educator
Chevalier, Robert Louis pediatric nephrologist, educator, researcher
Chevalier, Roger Alan astronomy educator, consultant

Beckler, David Zander government official, science administrator
Bennett, James Thomas economics educator
Bloomquist, Dennis Howard lawyer
Bluitt, Karen software engineering director
Boerner-Nilsen, Jo M. real estate trainer
Boneau, C. Alan psychology educator, researcher
Bowden, Howard Kent accountant
Bradunas, John Joseph marine corps officer
Brehm, William Keith information systems company executive
Buchanan, James McGill economist, educator
Cahill, Anne Pickford economist, demographer
Carr, Patricia Warren adult education educator
Carretta, Albert Aloysius lawyer, educator
Censer, Jack Richard history educator
Cicala, Jac soccer coach
Codding, Frederick Hayden lawyer
Cook, Gerald electrical engineering educator
Coulter, David Creswell research engineer
Cullison, Alexander C. (Doc Cullison) mediator, arbitrator
Dawalt, Kenneth Francis former army officer, former aerospace company executive
Denning, Peter James computer scientist, engineer
Dettinger, Garth Bryant surgeon, physician, retired air force officer, county health officer
DuRocher, Frances Antoinette physician, educator
Edwards, James Owen engineering and construction company executive
Elieff, Richard George energy industry consultant
Emely, Charles Harry trade association executive, consultant
Emely, Mary Ann association executive
Field, David Ellis lawyer
Fisher, Mary Maurine federal agency official, retired
†Fleishman, Edwin Alan psychologist, author
Folk, Thomas Robert lawyer
†Gillespie, Samuel H., III lawyer, oil company executive
Ginn, Richard Van Ness retired army officer, health care executive
Gollobin, Leonard Paul chemical engineer
Goode, William Josiah sociology educator
Gray, William H., III association executive, former congressman
Gross, Patrick Walter business executive, management consultant
Groves, Hurst Kohler lawyer, oil company executive
Grunder, Fred Irwin program administrator, industrial hygienist
Harper, Doreen C. nursing educator
Hatch, Ross Riepert weapon system engineering executive
Havlicek, Sarah Marie educator, artist, small business owner
Hess, Milton Siegmund computer company executive
Hilbrink, William John violinist
Hill, Christopher Thomas administrator, educator
Hollans, Irby Noah, Jr. retired association executive
Howard-Peebles, Patricia N. clinical cytogeneticist
Isbister, Jenefir Diane Wilkinson microbiologist, researcher, educator, consultant
Jackman, Thomas M. newspaper reporter, columnist
Jamieson, John Anthony engineering consulting company executive
†Johnson, Clarion Ellis physician
Johnson, George William retired academic administrator
†Johnson, Kelly Hal performance analyst
Johnson, Wallace retired army officer
Kash, Don Eldon political science educator
Kautt, Glenn Gregory financial planner
Kear, Maria Martha Ruscitella lawyer
Khoury, Riad Philip corporation executive, financial consultant
King, James Cecil Medievalist, educator
Krupinski, Christine Margaret artist
Langley, Rolland Ament, Jr. retired engineering technology company executive
Larsen, Phillip Nelson electrical engineer
Lavine, Thelma Zeno philosophy educator
†Lehman, Elyse Brauch psychology educator
Levis, Alexander Henry systems engineer, educator, consultant
Lott, Wayne Thomas systems engineer
Madison-Colmore, Octavia Dianne adult education educator
Maiwurm, James John lawyer
Malouff, Frank Joseph health care association executive
Maul, Kevin Jay financial consultant
McCormick, Robert Junior company executive, former government official
McCrohan, Kevin Francis business educator
†Merrick, Phillip technology company executive
Merten, Alan Gilbert academic administrator
Miller, Linda Karen educator
Molino, Michael Anthony trade association executive
Morowitz, Harold Joseph biophysicist, educator
Mund, Richard Gordon foundation executive
Nidiffer, Sheri Lynn medical/surgical nurse
Noto, Lucio A. gas and oil industry executive
O'Leary, Robert J. oil industry executive
Palmer, James Daniel information technology educator
Parrish-St. John, Florence Tucker writer, retired government official
Peters, Esther Caroline aquatic toxicologist, pathobiologist, consultant
†Pfiffner, James Price political science educator
†Potter, David L. academic administrator
Powell, Karan Hinman university program administrator, consultant
Priesman, Elinor Lee Soll family dynamics administrator, mediator, educator
Pugh, Arthur James (Jay Pugh) retired department store executive, consultant
Pyatt, Everett Arno government official
Ramage, Michael P. petroleum company executive
Robertson, Patricia Aileen adult and geriatric nurse
Rogers, Alan Victor former career officer
Rosenburgh, Stephen Aruthur executive
Rosenkranz, Robert Bernard military officer
Rowley, Charles Kershaw economics educator
Rubin, Robert Joseph physician, health care consultant
Sage, Andrew Patrick, Jr. systems information and software engineering educator
Sanderson, Douglas Jay lawyer
Saverot, Pierre-Michel nuclear waste management company executive
Schneck, Paul Bennett computer scientist
Schrock, Simon retail executive
Sheehan, Edward James technical consultant, former government official
Sheehy, Vincent automotive executive
Singer, S(iegfried) Fred geophysicist, educator
Smith, J. Daniel maritime association administrator
Southern, Lonnie Steven minister
Spage, Catherine Marie budget analyst
Spitzberg, Irving Joseph, Jr. lawyer, corporate executive
Stage, Thomas Benton psychiatrist
Stearns, Frank Warren lawyer
Steele, Howard Loucks economic development consultant, author
Stitt, David Tillman judge
Stone, Gregory Michael law enforcement and public safety consultant
†Stringfellow, Charles automotive executive
Sullivan, Penelope Dietz computer software development company executive
Tobin, Paul Edward, Jr. naval officer
Tompros, Andrew Elias financial analyst
Tringale, Anthony Rosario insurance executive
Tucker, Dewey Duane systems analyst
Turjanica, Mary Ann clinical nurse specialist, consultant
Vance, Mary Lee academic administrator
Wan, Ming political scientist, educator
Ward, George Truman architect
Warfield, John Nelson engineering educator, consultant
†Weiss, Joshua Noah political science educator, consultant, researcher
Whitcomb, Darrel Dean pilot
Williams, Marcus Doyle judge
Witek, James Eugene retired public relations executive
Wood, C(harles) Norman association executive
Woodruff, C(harles) Roy professional association executive
Wu, Chien-yun (Jennie Wu) nursing educator
Ziff, Irwin (Irv Ziff) actor

Fairfax Station
Abuzaakouk, Aly Ramadan publishing executive
Bishop, Alfred Chilton, Jr. lawyer
Coaker, James Whitfield mechanical engineer
Johansen, Eivind Herbert special education services executive, former army officer
Kaminski, Paul Garrett federal agency administrator, investment banker
Ross, Jimmy Douglas army officer
Sielicki-Korczak, Boris Zdzislaw political educator, investigative consultant
Starry, Donn Albert former aerospace company executive, former army officer
Taylor, Eldon Donivan government official

Falls Church
Anderson, George Kenneth physician, foundation executive, retired air force officer
Bankson, Marjory religious association administrator
Barkley, Paul Haley, Jr. architect
Benson, William Edward (Barnes) geologist
Benton, Nicholas Frederick publisher
Berg, Lillian Douglas chemistry educator
Beyer, Donald Sternoff, Jr. state official
Bingman, Charles Franklin public administration educator
Blanck, Ronald Ray hospital administrator, internist, career officer
Blaydes, Stephanie Anne policy analyst
Block, John Rusling former secretary of agriculture
Bonzagni, Vincent Francis lawyer, program administrator, analyst, researcher
Boyd, Lynne Kaplan software company executive
Brown, Gerald Curtis retired army officer, engineering executive
Cain, David Lee corporate executive
†Cain, Eddie army officer
Calkins, Gary Nathan lawyer, retired
Calkins, Susannah Eby retired economist
Carney, Daniel L. program and financial management consultant
Cetron, Marvin Jerome management executive
Chabraja, Nicholas D. lawyer
Christman, Bruce Lee lawyer
Cleland, Sherrill college president
Clizbe, John Anthony psychologist, organization administrator
Conde, Carlos Danache journalist
Conklin, Kenneth Edward lawyer, industry executive
Cromley, Allan Wray journalist
Diamond, Robert Michael lawyer
Drake, Diana Ashley financial planner
Duesenberg, Robert H. lawyer
Ehrlich, Bernard Herbert lawyer, association executive
Elderkin, Helaine Grace lawyer
Elliott, Virginia F. Harrison retired anatomist, kinesiologist and educator, investment advisor, publisher, philanthropist
Evans, Peter Yoshio ophthalmologist, educator
Ezard, Gary Carl video editor
Fischer, Dennis James government official
Flory, Robert Mikesell computer systems analyst, personnel management specialist
Flynn, Patrick designer, programmer, consultant
Frazier, Walter Ronald real estate investment company executive
Geithner, Paul Herman, Jr. banker
Glass, Lawrence business executive
Golomb, Herbert Stanley dermatologist
Gorges, Heinz August retired research engineer
Gray, D'Wayne retired marine corps officer
Greigg, Ronald Edwin lawyer
Gruggel, John Stuart, Jr. judge
Hahn, Thomas Joonghi accountant
Hamor, Kathy Virginia consultant
Han, Syung D. international trade consultant, financier
Hart, C(harles) W(illard), Jr. zoologist, curator
Ho, Hien Van pediatrician
Holthausen, Martha Anne interior designer, painter
Honigberg, Carol Crossman lawyer
Inglefield, Joseph T., Jr. allergist, immunologist, pediatrician
Isaac, William Michael investment firm executive, former government official
Jennings, Thomas Parks lawyer
†John, Sarah A. emergency medicine physician
Jones, Russel Cameron civil engineer
Kaplan, Jocelyn Rae financial planning firm executive
Kaplow, Herbert Elias journalist
Kling, William economist, retired foreign service officer
Kondracki, Edward John lawyer
Layman, Lawrence naval officer
Leighton, Frances Spatz writer, journalist
Lindholm, Lori Ann program manager, naval officer
Lorenzo, Michael engineer, government official, real estate broker
May, Carol Lee mechanical engineer
Miller, Mary Jeannette office management specialist
†Montero, Mario F., Jr. military career officer
Morrison, H. Robert writer, editor, politician
Morse, Marvin Henry judge
Mortensen, Robert Henry landscape architect, golf course architect
Mushtaq, Ednan physician
Nashman, Alvin Eli computer company executive
Orben, Robert editor, writer
Orkand, Donald Saul management consultant
Padden, Anthony Aloysius, Jr. federal government official
Padgett, Gail Blanchard lawyer
Perkins, Jack Edwin lawyer
†Pischke, Vail W. lawyer, Judge
Purvis, Ronald Scott financial counselor, real estate executive
Redmond, Robert lawyer, educator
Rice, Sue Ann dean, industrial and organizational psychologist
Rooney, Kevin Davitt lawyer
Rosenberg, Theodore Roy financial executive
Schmidt, Paul Wickham lawyer
†Sculley, Patrick David army officer
Seifert, Patricia Clark cardiac surgery nurse, educator, consultant
Simokaitis, Frank Joseph air force officer, lawyer
Simpson, John Arol retired government executive, physicist
†Singleton, John Knox hospital executive
Sowell, Dale Anthony civil engineer
Spector, Louis retired federal judge, lawyer, arbitrator, consultant
†Spencer, Ralph Edwin federal government official
Spindel, William chemist, consultant
Stone, Marvin Lawrence journalist, government official
Tamondong, Susan Daet international social scientist
Theismann, Joseph Robert former professional football player, announcer
†Thompson, Carol S. artist
Thomsen, Samuel Borron non-profit executive, consultant
Villarreal, Carlos Castaneda engineering executive
Ward, George Frank, Jr. ambassador
Ward, Joe Henry, Jr. retired lawyer
Waud, Roger Neil economics educator
Weiss, Armand Berl economist, association management executive
Whitehead, Kenneth Dean author, translator, retired federal government official
†Willison, Kimberly Schumaker gifted education educator
Winzer, P.J. lawyer
Wise, Thomas Nathan psychiatrist
†Withers, Benjamin G. preventive medicine physician, career officer

Farmville
Boyer, Calvin James librarian
Dorrill, William Franklin political scientist, educator
Moon, William Arthur, Jr. petroleum geologist, consultant
Whaley, Michael David graphic designer

Farnham
Durham, James Michael, Sr. marketing consultant

Ferrum
†Obiechina, Emmanuel Nwanonye humanities educator
Sandidge, June Carol physical education educator

Fincastle
Cummings, Kevin Bryan minister

Fishersville
Matthews, Judith Nygaard nursing administrator, home health nurse
Ward, Kathryn Elizabeth Kurek nursing case manager

Flint Hill
Dietel, William Moore former foundation executive

Floyd
Clemens, Donald Faull chemistry educator
Cosby, John Canada lay professional church worker, retired

Fort Belvoir
Barnholdt, Terry Joseph chemical, industrial, and general engineer
†Chamberlin, Edward Robert career officer, educator
Clarke, Frederick James civil engineer
Daverede, Heidi Marianne government official
Diercks, Frederick Otto government official
†Foley, David W. career officer
Frizzelle, Charles Delano, Jr. military officer, educator
†Glisson, Henry T. director
Humphreys-Heckler, Maureen Kelly nursing home administrator
Molholm, Kurt Nelson federal agency administrator
†Noonan, Robert W., Jr. career officer
Raymond, George Edward, Jr. (Chip Raymond) operations research analyst
†Reed, William H. federal agency administrator
St. John, Adrian, II retired army officer
Severin, Scott Robert veterinarian
Smith, Margherita writer, editor
Suycott, Mark Leland naval flight officer

Fort Defiance
Livick, Malcolm Harris school administrator

Fort Eustis
Brown, Daniel G. military officer

Fort Lee
Johnson, Harry Watkins defense analyst
Sterling, Keir Brooks historian, educator

Fort Monroe
†Abrams, John N. career officer
†Bolt, William J. military officer
†Buckley, Edward T., Jr. career officer
†Goff, Leroy R. (Rob), III career officer
†Morehouse, James W. career officer
†Wallace, Stewart S. career military officer

Fort Myer
†Costello, John military officer

Fort Story
Smail, Leslie Anne librarian

Franklin
Atkinson, Sandra Miller marketing educator
Cobb, G. Elliott, Jr. lawyer
Culpepper, Jo Long librarian
Feldt, Glenda Diane educational administrator
Minor, Edward Colquitt paper company executive, lawyer

Fredericksburg
Bailey, Amos Purnell clergyman, syndicated columnist
Billingsley, Robert Thaine lawyer
Bourdon, Roger Joseph history educator
Craig, N(orvelle) Wayne secondary education educator
†Daniel, James Richard surgeon, oncologist
Dennis, Donald Daly retired librarian
Detwiler, Joseph Alden artist
Dorman, John Frederick genealogist
Dyal, William M., Jr. federal agency administrator
Geary, Patrick Joseph naval security administrator
Glessner, Thomas Allen lawyer
Hajek, Otomar mathematics educator
Herndon, Cathy Campbell artist, art educator
Hickman, Richard Lonnie advertising executive
Jenks-Davies, Kathryn Ryburn retired daycare provider and owner, civic worker
Jones, Julia Pearl elementary school educator
Karpiscak, Linda Sue pediatrics nurse
Lipscomb, Stephen Leon mathematics educator, researcher
Medding, Walter Sherman environmental engineer
Mercer, Monique Yvette social sciences researcher
Moorman, William Jacob agronomist, consultant
Nails, Debra philosophy educator
Nichols, Mary Reid community and parent-child health nursing educator
Schmutzhart, Berthold Josef sculptor, educator, art and education consultant
Speirs, Carol Lucille nurse, naval officer
†Strahan, Bradley Russel publisher, poet, educator
Westebbe, Barbara Liebst writer, sculptor

Front Royal
Andes, Larry Dale minister
Dengel, Ottmar Hubert physicist
Douglas, J(ocelyn) Fielding toxicologist, consultant
Greco, Barbara Ruth Gomez literacy organization administrator
Marx, Paul Benno author, social service administrator, missionary
Stanley, Douglas Parnell county planner

Gainesville
Austin, James Grover, Jr. theologian, pastor, telecommunications manager
Steger, Edward Herman chemist

Galax
Sense, Karl August physicist, educator

Glen Allen
Alves, Constance Dillenger special education educator
Batzli, Terrence Raymond lawyer
Bennett, Donald Dalton grocery stores executive
Carneal, Drew St. John lawyer
Collier, Roger Malcolm minister
Fairbank, Richard diversified financial services company executive
Fife, William Franklin retired drug company executive
†Hinkle, Douglas Paddock retired languages educator
Lloyd, Christopher Donald consultant
Minor, George Gilmer, III drug and hospital supply company executive
Murphey, Robert Stafford pharmaceutical company executive
Reed, Austin F. lawyer
†Vaughn, Ann Marie art educator, artist
Weaver, Mollie Little lawyer
Wright, Sylvia Hoehns computer systems specialist

Gloucester
Powell, Bolling Raines, Jr. lawyer, educator

Great Falls
Benen, Elaine Carol educational administrator
Crook, Frederick W. economist
DiBona, Charles Joseph retired trade association executive
Garrett, Wilbur (Bill) magazine editor
Neidich, George Arthur lawyer
Preston, Charles George lawyer
Railton, William Scott lawyer
Savage, Michael Thomas federal executive
Schreiner, George E. nephrologist, educator, writer
Schwartz, Robert Terry professional association executive
Skeen, David Ray systems engineer, consultant
Wallman, Steven Mark Harte lawyer
Whipple, David Doty retired professional society administrator
Zimmermann, Warren former foreign service officer

Gwynn
Pickle Beattie, Katherine Hamner real estate agent

Halifax
Anderson, Howard Palmer former state senator
Greenbacker, John Everett retired lawyer

Hampden Sydney
Bagby, George Franklin, Jr. English language educator
Kniffen, Donald Avery astrophysicist, educator, researcher
†Weese, Katherine Jane English educator
Wilson, Samuel V. college president

Hampton
Adeyiga, Adeyinka A. engineering educator
Barnes, Myrtle Sue Snyder editor
Bartels, Robert Edwin aerospace engineer
Beauregard, Leslie Michelle budget analyst, legislative liaison

Bhuiyan, Mohammad Ali university administrator, educator, consultant
Brauer, Harrol Andrew, Jr. broadcasting executive
Brown, Loretta Ann Port physician, geneticist
Cage-Bibbs, Patricia coach
Creedon, Jeremiah F. aeronautical research laboratory administrator
Daniels, Cindy Lou space agency executive
Deepak, Adarsh meteorologist, aerospace engineer, atmospheric scientist
Dennis, Walter Decoster suffragan bishop
Drummond, James Everman defense technology transfer consultant, former army officer
Duberg, John Edward retired aeronautical engineer, educator
Dwoyer, Douglas Leon engineering executive
Erck, Walter W. air force officer
Farrukh, Usamah Omar electrical engineering educator, researcher
Fox, Margaret Louise retired secondary education educator
Henderson, Salathiel James minister, clergy
Houbolt, John Cornelius physicist
Joshi, Suresh Meghashyam research engineer
Kelly, Jeffrey Jennings mechanical engineer
Krueger, Ronald aerospace engineer
Kulp, Eileen Bodnar social worker
Maher, Kim Leverton museum administrator
McNider, James Small, III lawyer
Mehrotra, Sudhir C. engineering company executive
Meyers, James Frank electronics engineer
Phillips, William H. aeronautical engineer
Saqib, Mohammad materials scientist
Schauer, Catharine Guberman public affairs specialist
Schon, Alan Wallace lawyer, actor
Singleterry, Robert Clay, Jr. aerospace technologist, material research engineer
Sobieski, Jaroslaw aerospace engineer
Steele, James Eugene school system administrator, educator
Tessler, Alexander aerospace engineer
Wagstaff, Deborah A. geriatrics and mental health nurse, family nurse practitioner
Whitesides, John Lindsey, Jr. aerospace engineering educator, researcher
Whittenburg, Carolyn Sparks history educator

Hardy
Harriett, Rebecca park director

Harrisonburg
Aley, Shelley B. composition and rhetoric educator
Alotta, Robert Ignatius historian, educator, writer
Burkholder, Owen Eugene religious organization administrator
Carrier, Ronald Edwin university administrator
Childers, Bud university head basketball coach
Davis, Melodie Miller writer, editor
Geary, Robert Francis, Jr. English educator
Gill, Gerald Lawson librarian
Hedrick, Joyce Ann Coryell educational support services professional
Helmuth, Les N. fund raising executive, non-profit consultant
Ivory, Ming Marie political scientist
†Krumm, Ross W. federal judge
Maxfield, Sandra Lynn librarian, educator
McNamara, Joseph Gerard physician
Morey, Ann-Janine English educator
Morgan, Christy university head field hockey coach
†Nickels, Cameron Charles English educator
Richardson, John MacLaren, Jr. clergyman
Rollman, Steven Allan communication educator
Wallinger, M(elvin) Bruce lawyer
White, Larry Hartford chemistry educator
Zehr, Howard social sciences educator

Hartfield
Lovell, Robert R(oland) engineering executive

Haymarket
Crafton-Masterson, Adrienne real estate executive, writer, poet
Doolittle, Warren T. retired federal official
Douglas, Clarence James, Jr. corporation executive, management consultant
Katz, Alan Charles toxicologist
Phillips, Robert Benbow financial planner

Haysi
Deel, George Moses elementary school educator

Heathsville
McKerns, Charles Joseph lawyer
Stubbs, Susan Conklin statistician
Winkel, Raymond Norman aerospace industry consultant, avionics manufacturing executive

Herndon
Abbott, Gayle Elizabeth human resources consultant
Abdullah, Nina Junaina psychologist
Cope, Laurence Brian utilities company executive, economic consultant
Crossfield, Albert Scott aeronautical science consultant, pilot
Dodd, Steven Louis systems engineer
†Etcheverry, Marco professional soccer player
Guerreri, Carl Natale electronic company executive
Guirguis, Raouf Albert health science executive
†Harkes, John professional soccer player
Harris, Shelley Follansbee proposal manager
Hermansen, John Christian computational linguist
Kunkel, David Nelson lawyer
Lassiter, Roy soccer player
Lynch, George Michael family practice physician
Mandine, Salvador G. insurance executive
†Moreno, Jaime professional soccer player
Payne, Fred J. physician, educator
Payne, Kevin professional soccer organization executive
Polemitou, Olga Andrea accountant
†Rongen, Thomas professional soccer coach
†Ross, Barbara Ann gifted/talented education educator
Schrader, William communications company executive
Snyder, Franklin Farison hydrologic engineering consultant
Spragens, William Clark public policy educator, consultant
Stanton, Patricia Lynn Noboa management and consulting executive
Ulvila, Jacob Walter management consultant
Vakerics, Thomas Vincent lawyer

Hillsboro
Farwell, Byron Edgar writer

Hot Springs
Trotter, Susan Collins artist

Huddleston
Kopp, Richard Edgar electrical engineer

Hudgins
Story, Martha vanBeuren librarian

Independence
Craig, James Hicklin fine arts consultant
Hurst, John Emory, Jr. retired airline executive

Ivy
Wilcox, Harvey John lawyer

Kenbridge
Walton, G. Clifford family practice physician

Keswick
Ackell, Edmund Ferris university president
Fletcher, John Caldwell bioethicist, educator
Massey, Donald Wayne Disciples of Christ minister, Episcopal minister, small business owner
Norgren, C. Neil retired manufacturing company executive
Nosanow, Barbara Shissler art association administrator
Pochick, Francis Edward financial consultant

Keysville
Carwile, Nancy Ramsey educational administrator

Kilmarnock
Maxwell, W(ilbur) Richard management consultant
Moore, William Black, Jr. retired aluminum company executive
Parrett, Sherman O. lawyer
Smith, Raymond Francis company executive

King George
Hoglund, Richard Frank research and technical executive
Newhall, David, III former government official
Revercomb, Horace Austin, III judge

Kingstowne
Hixson, Stanley G. speech, language and computer technology educator

Lake Ridge
Englert, Helen Wiggs writer
Hinnant, Hilari Anne educator, educational consultant

Lancaster
Beane, Judith Mae psychologist
Rowden, William Henry naval officer

Lanexa
Green, Richard Bertram sculptor

Langley AFB
Dawson, Robert A. physician assistant
†Dylewski, Gary R. military officer
†Haines, Dennis G. military officer
†Hawley, John W. military officer
†Johnston, Lawrence D. career officer
†MacGhee, David F. military officer
†Meyerrose, Dale William career officer
†Modica, Edward S., Jr. air force officer
†Moorman, William A. career officer
†Peck, William A., Jr. career officer
†Rayburn, Bentley B. career officer
†Robbins, Earnest O., II career officer
†Schafer, Klaus O. military officer

Leesburg
Davidson, Noreen Hanna financial services company executive
Ecker, G. T. Dunlop hospital administration executive
McDonough, Joseph Corbett former army officer, aviation consultant
Mims, William Cleveland state legislator, lawyer
Minchew, John Randall lawyer
Mitchell, Russell Harry dermatologist
Mokhtarzadeh, Ahmad Agha agronomist, consultant
Rader, Toni Christine secondary education educator

Lexington
Beveridge, Albert Jeremiah, III lawyer
Brooke, George Mercer, Jr. historian, educator
DeVogt, John Frederick management science and business ethics educator, consultant
Dunlap, Kathleen Jane public relations executive
Elmes, David Gordon psychologist, educator
Elrod, John William university president, philosophy and religion educator
Gaines, James Edwin, Jr. retired librarian
Hickman, Cleveland Pendleton, Jr. biology educator
Hodges, Louis Wendell religion educator
Jarrard, Leonard Everett psychologist, educator
John, Lewis George political science educator
Kirgis, Frederic Lee law educator
Knapp, John Williams retired college president
†Krantz, Linda Law librarian
†Lyle, Katie Letcher writer, educator
Lynn, Michael A. historic site director
McCloud, Anece Faison academic administrator
Phillips, Charles Franklin, Jr. economist, educator
†Pierpaoli, Paul George educator
Ryan, Halford Ross speech educator
Sessions, William Lad philosophy educator, administrator
†Solod, Lisa writer
Spencer, Edgar Winston geology educator
Stuart, Dabney, III poet, author, English language educator
Sullivan, Barry law educator
Sundby, Scott Edwin law educator
Tierney, Michael John mathematics and computer science educator
Tyree, Lewis, Jr. retired compressed gas company executive, inventor, technical consultant
Wiant, Sarah Kirsten law library director, educator
Winfrey, John Crawford economist, educator
Young, Kenneth Evans educational consultant

Lightfoot
Morris, Robert Louis management consultant

Linden
Cole, Crystal Lynn artist
Poulin, Claude R. actuarial consultant

Locust Grove
Sjogren, Robert William internist

Lorton
Francis, Richard Haudiomont government administrator
Sun, Li-Teh economics educator

Lottsburg
Kohler, Karl Eugene architect

Louisa
Black, James David woodcarver, English educator, editor, poet
Small, William Edwin, Jr. association and recreation executive

Luray
Burzynski, Norman Stephen editor

Lynchburg
†Anderson, William E. federal judge
Barkley, Henry Brock, Jr. research and development executive
Burnette, Ralph Edwin, Jr. lawyer
†Carwile, Billie Newman history educator
Cooper, Alan Michael psychiatrist
†Cushman, Valerie Jean athletic director
Davenport, James Robert retired city official, retired utility executive
Falwell, Jerry L. clergyman
Fulcher, Hugh Drummond author
Gilmore, Philip Nathanael finance educator, accountant
Healy, Joseph Francis, Jr. lawyer, arbitrator, retired airline executive
Hudson, Walter Tiree artist
Johnson, Robert Bruce historic preservationist
†Kimball, Anne Spofford French language educator
Lane, Richard Allan physician, health sciences educator
Latimer, Paul Jerry non-destructive testing engineer
Luck, Ray Egan pianist, music educator
McRorie, William Edward life insurance company executive
†Moon, Norman K. judge
Moorman, Steve Thomas systems analyst
Morgan, Evan chemist
Morland, John Kenneth sociology and anthropology educator
†Morrison, John Douglas theology and philosophy educator
Packert, G(ayla) Beth lawyer
Quillian, William Fletcher, Jr. retired banker, former college president
Shircliff, James Vanderburgh communications executive
Simms, Alice Jane secondary school educator
Snead, George Murrell, Jr. army officer, scientist, consultant
Stephens, Bart Nelson former foreign service officer
Stewart, George Taylor insurance executive
Sullivan, Gregory Paul secondary education educator
Swain, Diane Scott principal
Weimar, Robert Henry clinical hypnotherapist
Westenburger, Linda Santner lawyer
Whittemore, Linda Genevieve clinical psychologist
Womack, Edgar Allen, Jr. energy executive

Machipongo
Bonniwell, Ann Glenn educational administrator

Madison
Brewer, Philip Warren civil engineer
Coates, Frederick Ross lawyer
McGhee, Kenneth Hamilton civil engineer, consultant

Maidens
Adams, Jimmy Wayne osteopath

Manakin Sabot
Bright, Craig Bartley lawyer
Thompson, Walter David, Jr. systems analyst

Manassas
†Adamson, Heidi Beth English educator
Archer, Chalmers, Jr. education educator
Bahner, Sue (Florence Suzanna Bahner) radio broadcasting executive
†Beirne-Patey, Marian Josephine secondary educator
Cypess, Raymond Harold bioscience organization executive
Edwards, Peter educator, writer
Foote, John Holland lawyer
Geerdes, James D(ivine) chemical company executive
Gustavson, Brandt religious association executive
Houston, Caroline Margaret editor
Jakub, Paula Sue association administrator
Lumpkin, Vicki G. minister
Lytton, Linda Rountree marriage and family therapist, test consultant
McCormick, Ferris Ellsworth computer technology consultant
McGolrick, J. Edward, Jr. lawyer
Mitchell, William Graham Champion lawyer, business executive
Parrish, Frank Jennings food company executive
Sehn, James Thomas urological surgeon
Slayton, Gus foundation administrator
Smith, Todd Lawrence computer scientist
Sutton, Robert K. park administrator
Thompson, Sandy Maria health and staff development coordinator
Tidman, Derek Albert physics researcher
Twitchel, Nancy Lou medical/surgical and emergency room nurse
Webb, Dennis Wayne protective services official
Weimer, Peter Dwight mediator, lawyer, corporate executive
Wilson, Robert Spencer magazine editor

Marion
Armbrister, Douglas Kenley surgeon
Elledge, Glenna Ellen Tuell journalist
†Grinstead, Paul Lee materials company official
Pratt, Mark Ernest mechanical engineer

Marshall
Han, Nong artist, sculptor, painter
Rose, Charles Grandison, III (Charlie Rose) former congressman

Martinsville
Eller, M. Edward, Jr. physician
McCann, Thomas Ryland, Jr. minister
Shackleford, William Alton, Sr. minister
Torrence, Billy Hubert minister

Mason Neck
Heiberg, Elvin Ragnvald, III civil engineer, army officer
Mc Curdy, Patrick Pierre editor, consultant
Randall, Ross Gilbert, II museum administrator

Mc Lean
Adler, Larry marketing executive
Alberts, Henry Celler real estate company executive
Allison, George Burgess systems analyst
Anthony, Joan Caton lawyer, writer
Appler, Thomas L. lawyer
†Armistead, William Spencer communications executive, political organization executive, political writer
Armstrong, C(harles) Torrence lawyer
Aucutt, Ronald David lawyer
Baldassari, Robert Gene accountant
Bardack, Paul Roitman lawyer, consultant
Bartlett, John Wesley consulting firm executive
Bingaman, Anne K. lawyer
Bivins, Susan Steinbach systems engineer
†Blair, Bonnie former professional speedskater, former Olympic athlete
Blanchard, Townsend Eugene retired service companies executive
Braddock, Joseph Vincent physicist
Brendsel, Leland C. federal mortgage company executive
Brown, Thomas Cartmel, Jr. lawyer
Buck, Alfred Andreas physician, epidemiologist
Burke, Sheila P. legislative staff member
Byrnes, William Joseph lawyer
Cahill, Harry Amory diplomat, educator
Calio, Anthony John scientist, business executive
Callahan, Vincent Francis, Jr. state legislator, publisher
Cannon, Mark Wilcox government official, business executive
Capone, Lucien, Jr. management consultant, former naval officer
Carnicero, Jorge Emilio aeronautical engineer, business executive
Carter, William Walton physicist
Chang, Michael tennis player
Church, Randolph Warner, Jr. lawyer
Cohn, Herbert B. lawyer
Connelly, Mary Creedon insurance company executive
Corson, J. Jay, IV lawyer
Cowhill, William Joseph retired naval officer, consultant
Cuffe, Robin Jean nursing educator
Dean, Lydia Margaret Carter (Mrs. Halsey Albert Dean) nutrition coordinator, author, consultant
Deardourff, John D. political consultant
De Lauder, Roy Allen business administrator
Dempsey, James Raymon industrial executive
Dobson, Donald Alfred retired electrical engineer
Domeyko, Cecilia television producer
Donahue, Timothy M. communications executive
Doyle, Frederick Joseph retired government research scientist
Drew, K financial advisor, management consultant
Duncan, Robert Clifton retired government official
†Early, Gregg Steven executive editor
Eckman, Dianne Ingeborg critical care nurse
Estren, Mark James business and media consultant, TV producer, author
Fedorochko, William, Jr. retired army officer, policy analyst
Felts, William Robert, Jr. physician
Filerman, Gary Lewis health education executive
Franklin, Jude Eric electronics executive
Freyer, Victoria C. fashion and interior design executive
Friedlander, Jerome Peyser, II lawyer
Fromm, Joseph retired magazine editor, foreign affairs consultant
Frostic, Frederick Lee strategic planning and defense policy consultant
Gallagher, Anne Porter business executive
Gammon, James Alan lawyer
García-Godoy, Cristián historian, educator
Garnes, Ronald Vincent marketing executive, finance broker, consultant
Gerson, Elliot Francis health care executive
Gladeck, Susan Odell social worker
Glenn, David Wright mortgage company executive
Goolrick, Robert Mason lawyer, consultant
Graf, Dorothy Ann business executive
Greene, Timothy Geddes lawyer
Haddock, Raymond Earl career officer
Hagar, James Thomas retail executive
Halaby, Najeeb E. financier, lawyer
Harmon, Robert Gerald health company administrator, educator
Harrison, Carol Love fine art photographer
Hathaway, William Dodd federal agency administrator
Healy, Theresa Ann former ambassador
Herge, J. Curtis lawyer
Hjort, Howard Warren consultant, economist
Hopkins, Thomas Matthews former naval officer
Horowitz, Barry Martin systems research and engineering company executive
James, Daniel J. management consultant
Jennings, Jerry D. communications company executive
Johnson, Mary Zelinda artist
Kennedy, Cornelius Bryant retired lawyer
Kimberly, William Essick investment banker
Klinedinst, Duncan Stewart lawyer
Klopfenstein, Rex Carter electrical engineer
Krugman, Stanley Liebert science administrator, geneticist
Landfield, James Seymour financial manager
Lane-Maher, Maureen Dorothea marketing educator, consultant
Laning, Robert Comegys retired physician, former naval officer
Larson, Arvid Gunnar electrical engineer
Layson, William McIntyre research consulting company executive

Levy, Michael Howard *environmental management professional*
Linville, Ray Pate *logistics analyst, editor*
Loatman, Robert Bruce *computer scientist*
Lotz, Denton *minister, church official*
Loven, Andrew Witherspoon *environmental engineering company executive*
Mahan, Clarence *retired govenment official, writer*
Maloof, Farahe Paul *lawyer*
Mars, Forrest E., Jr. *candy company executive*
Mars, John F. *candy company executive*
Mars, Virginia Cretella *civic worker*
Martin, Marsha Pyle *federal agency administrator*
Martin, Todd *professional tennis player*
Mater, Maud *lawyer*
McCormack, Richard Thomas Fox *government official, former ambassador*
McIlwain, Clara Evans *agricultural economist, consultant*
McInerney, James Eugene, Jr. *trade association executive*
McLean, Robert, III *real estate company executive*
McLennan, Barbara Nancy *management consultant*
McNichols, Gerald Robert *consulting company executive*
Mehuron, William Otto *electronics company executive*
Michalowicz, Karen Dee *secondary education educator*
Miller, Christine Marie *marketing executive, public relations executive*
Molino, Thomas Michael *retired military officer*
Morris, James Malachy *lawyer*
Murphy, Thomas Patrick *lawyer*
Neel, Samuel Ellison *lawyer*
Newman, William Bernard, Jr. *telecommunications executive*
Norris, Genie M. *senior government official*
O'Brien, Francis Anthony *retired lawyer*
O'Brien, Morgan Edward *communications executive, lawyer*
Okay, John Louis *telecommunications company executive*
Oren, John Birdsell *retired coast guard officer*
Parshall, Gerald *journalist*
Paschall, Lee McQuerter *retired communications consultant*
Peet, Richard Clayton *lawyer, consultant*
Perry, Stephen Clayton *manufacturing executive*
Prichard, Edgar Allen *lawyer*
Ramsey, Lloyd Brinkley *retired savings and loan executive, retired army officer*
Rau, Lee Arthur *lawyer*
Reswick, James Bigelow *former government official, rehabilitation engineer, educator*
Rhyne, Charles Sylvanus *lawyer*
Roellig, Paul David *publishing executive*
Rogers, Thomas Francis *foundation administrator*
Rosenbaum, David Mark *engineering executive, consultant, educator*
Rugala, Karen Francis (Karen Francis) *artist, television producer*
Russo, Anthony Sebastian *telecommunications executive*
St. Germain, Fernand Joseph *congressman*
Salzinger, Mark Alan *editor, violinist*
Schmeidler, Neal Francis *engineering executive*
Schools, Charles Hughlette *banker, lawyer*
Schweiker, Richard Schultz *trade association executive, former senator, former cabinet secretary*
Searles, Dewitt Richard *retired investment firm executive, retired air force officer*
Shank, Fred Ross *food scientist*
Shepard, Julian Leigh *lawyer, humanitarian*
†Skantze, Lawrence A. *retired military officer*
†Skantze, Pat *model, consultant*
Smith, Dorothy Louise *pharmacy consultant, author*
Smith, Esther Thomas *communications executive*
Smith, Russell Jack *former intelligence official*
Smith, Thomas Eugene *investment company executive, financial consultant*
Somers, James Wilford *information management company executive*
Sonnemann, Harry *electrical engineer, consultant*
Sowle, Donald Edgar *management consultant*
Sparks, Robert Ronold, Jr. *lawyer*
Spaulding, Wallace Holmes *retired federal agency professional*
Stasior, William F. *engineering company executive*
Stephens, William Theodore *lawyer, business executive*
Steventon, Robert Wesley *marketing executive*
Strean, Bernard M. *retired naval officer*
Stump, John Sutton *lawyer*
Talbot, Lee Merriam *ecologist, educator, association executive*
Tansill, Frederick Joseph *lawyer*
Theon, John Speridon *meteorologist*
Tomeh, Osama Adnan *civil engineer*
Toole, John Harper *lawyer*
Topping, Eva Catafygiotu *writer, lecturer, educator*
Traver, Courtland Lee *lawyer*
Trotter, Haynie Seay *lawyer*
Turner, Stansfield *former government official, lecturer, writer, teacher*
Tuttle, William G(ilbert) T(ownsend), Jr. *research executive*
Vandemark, Robert Goodyear *retired retail company executive*
Vazsonyi, Balint *concert pianist, television producer*
Verhalen, Robert Donald *consultant*
Waesche, R(ichard) H(enley) Woodward *combustion research scientist*
Wallace, Robert Bruce *surgeon, retired*
Walsh, John Breffni *aerospace consultant*
Walsh, Marie Leclerc *nurse*
Walton, Edmund Lewis, Jr. *lawyer*
Watt, William Stewart *physical chemist*
†Whitehead, Clay Thomas *business executive*
Wong, Andrew *telecommunications company executive*
Wright, William Evan *physician*
Wümpelmann, Knud Aage Abildgaard *clergyman, religious organization administrator*
Yancik, Joseph John *government official*
Youngs, William Ellis *motion picture engineer, projectionist*
Zeleny, Marjorie Pfeiffer (Mrs. Charles Ellingson Zeleny) *psychologist*

McLean
Alexander, Fred Calvin, Jr. *lawyer*
Brady, Phillip Donley *lawyer*
†Houle, Jeffrey Robert *lawyer*
†Metters, Samuel *engineering executive*
Singley, George T., III *mechanical engineer, federal agency administrator*
†Somogyi, Maria M. *artist*

Mechanicsville
Bock, John Louis *architect*
Jones, Stuart Cromer *mechanical engineer*
Mann, Stephen Ashby *financial counselor*
Peterson, William Canova *architect*

Melfa
†Hickman, John Norwood *marketing executive*

Merrifield
Earner, William Anthony, Jr. *naval officer*
Miller, Emilie F. *former state senator, consultant*
Nelson, Ruth Naomi *marketing professional*
Scott, James Martin *state legislator, healthcare system executive*

Middleburg
Coven, Robert Michael *secondary school educator, researcher, writer*
Evans, John Derby *telecommunications company executive*
Heckler, John Maguire *stockbroker, investment company executive*
Larmore, Catherine Christine *university official*
†Luco, Wende *artist*
Parkinson, James Thomas, III *investment consultant*
Robinson, Michael Francis *private art dealer and appraiser*

Middletown
Ibach, Douglas Theodore *minister*

Midlothian
Alligood, Mary Sale *special education educator*
Andrako, John *health sciences educator*
Chapman, Gilbert Whipple, Jr. *publishing company executive*
Coleman, Ronald Lee *insurance claims executive*
Doumlele, Ruth Hailey *communications company executive, broadcast accounting consultant*
Jones, John Evan *medical educator*
Lee, Jerome Odell *minister*
Pearson, Gregory David *publisher, media specialist*
Shands, William Ridley, Jr. *lawyer*
Stringham, Luther Winters *economist, administrator*
Wadsworth, Robert David *advertising agency executive*

Mineral
Donald, James Robert *federal agency official, economist, outdoors writer*
Schelling, John Paul *lawyer, consultant*
Speer, Jack Atkeson *publisher*
Whitlock, Willie Walker *lawyer*

Moneta
Pfeuffer, Robert John *musician*
Singleton, Samuel Winston *physician, pharmaceutical company executive*
Ulmer, Walter Francis, Jr. *consultant, former army officer*

Monroe
Sandidge, Oneal Cleaven *academic administrator, educator*

Monterey
Kirby, Mary Weeks *elementary education educator, reading specialist*
Tabatznik, Bernard *retired physician, educator*
†Woodson, Albert Tarleton *retired navy enlisted man*

Montpelier Station
Mullins, Kathleen Stiso *historic site director*

Montross
Fountain, Elizabeth Bean *home economist, musician, philanthropist*
Fountain, Robert Roy, Jr. *farmer, industrial executive, naval officer*

Mosman
Barusch, Ronald Charles *lawyer*

Mount Crawford
Creswell, Norman Bruce *minister*
German, Lynne Cummings *music educator*

Mount Jackson
Cohen, Lewis Isaac *lawyer*
Sylvester, George Howard *retired air force officer*

Mount Vernon
Brownson, Anna Louise Harshman *publishing executive, editor*
Rees, James Conway, IV *historic site administrator*
Saadian, Javid *accountant, consultant*
Spiegel, H. Jay *lawyer*

Nellysford
Sims, John Rogers, Jr. *lawyer*

Newington
Bowen, Harry Ernest *management consultant*
Sebastian, Richard Lee *physicist, executive*

Newport News
Abbott, Beverly Stubblefield *artist*
Banks, Charles Augustus, III *manufacturing executive*
Beach, Harry Lee, Jr. *mechanical engineer, aerospace engineer*
Behlmar, Cindy Lee *business manager, consultant*
Benedict, Jeffery West *planner, estimator*
†Bobbitt, John Maxwell *surgeon, medical educator*
†Bradberry, James E. *federal judge*
Buranelli, Vincent John *writer*
Corlett, William Albert *retired aerospace engineer*
Cuthrell, Carl Edward *lawyer, educator, clergyman*
Donaldson, Coleman duPont *aerodynamics and aerospace consulting engineer*
Edmonds, Michael Darnell *music educator*
Evans, Robert August, Jr. *newspaper reporter, editor*
Fisher, Denise Butterfield *marketing executive*
Fricks, William Peavy *shipbuilding company executive*
Gies, Robert Jay *mechanical engineer*
Goldberg, Ivan Baer *real estate executive*
Goldberg, Stanley Irwin *real estate executive*
Guastaferro, Angelo *company executive*
†Han, D(ongyeon) Peter *urologist*
Hawkins, J. Michael *housing development administrator*
Hightower, John Brantley *arts administrator*
Hubbard, Harvey Hart *aeroacoustician, noise control engineer, consultant*
Isgur, Nathan Gerald *physicist, educator*
Kamp, Arthur Joseph, Jr. *lawyer*
Keator, Margaret Whitley *legislative aide*
†Keeling, Kara Kay *English literature educator*
Laroussi, Mounir *electrical engineer*
Le Mons, Kathleen Ann *portfolio manager, investment officer*
Martin, Terrence Keech *lawyer, city councilor*
Mazur, Rhoda Himmel *community volunteer*
Miller, W. Marshall, II *insurance consultant*
Noblitt, Nancy Anne *aerospace engineer*
Perry, Donald A. *cable television consultant*
Phillips, Denise *critical care nurse*
Phinazee, Henry Charles *systems analyst, educator*
Powell, Jouett Lynn *college dean, philosophy and religious studies educator*
Ray, Randy *state agency administrator*
Salvatori, Vincent Louis *corporate executive*
Santoro, Anthony Richard *history educator*
Segall, James Arnold *lawyer*
†Smith, James Robert *airport terminal executive*
Summerville, Richard M. *mathematician, retired academic administrator*
†Thomas, Lawsey Shyrone *safety and training administrator*
Tracy, Tracy Faircloth *special education educator*
Trible, Paul Seward, Jr. *former United States senator*
Warren, Daniel Churchman *health facility administrator*
Wiatt, Carol Stultz *elementary education educator*
Williamson, Jack *city official*
Yacavone, David William *military officer, consultant, researcher*

Norfolk
Achampong, Francis Kofi *law educator, consultant*
Addis, Kay Tucker *newspaper editor*
Ahrari, M. Ehsan *political science educator, researcher, consultant*
Andrews, Mason Cooke *mayor, obstetrician, gynecologist, educator*
Andrews, William Cooke *physician*
Baird, Edward Rouzie, Jr. *lawyer*
Baker, Stephen H. *career officer*
Barry, Richard Francis, III *publishing executive*
Batten, Frank *newspaper publisher, cable broadcaster*
Berent, Irwin Mark *writer, software executive*
Bland, Gilbert Tyrone *foodservice executive*
Blount, Robert Haddock *corporate executive, retired naval officer*
Boland, James Francis, Jr. *naval officer, helicopter pilot*
Bonko, Larry Walter *columnist, writer, radio personality*
Bonney, Hal James, Jr. *federal judge*
Boyd, Robert Friend *lawyer*
Breit, Jeffrey Arnold *lawyer*
Bullington, James Richard *business educator, former ambassador*
Clark, Morton Hutchinson *lawyer*
Clarke, J. Calvitt, Jr. *federal judge*
Corcoran, Andrew Patrick, Jr. *lawyer*
Cranford, Page Deronde *lawyer, educator, executive*
Crenshaw, Francis Nelson *lawyer*
Curry, Robert Furman, Jr. *educator, academic advisor*
Cutchins, Clifford Armstrong, III *banker*
Dandoy, Suzanne Eggleston *physician, academic administrator, educator*
Daughtrey, R. Breckenridge *city clerk*
Davies, George Patrick *city official*
Denyes, James Richard *industrial engineer*
DeVenny, Lillian Nickell *trophy company executive*
†Devine, Patrick Campbell *urologist, educator*
Doumar, Robert George *judge*
Drescher, John Webb *lawyer*
Dungan, William Joseph, Jr. *insurance broker, economics educator*
Faulconer, Robert Jamieson *pathologist, educator*
Ferriter, Edward Chadwick *naval officer*
Filer, Emily Symington Harkins *social services administrator*
Fitzpatrick, William Henry *retired journalist*
Florer, Hayward Stanley *career officer*
Fox, Thomas George *health science educator*
Frieden, Jane Heller *art educator*
Giambastiani, Edmund P., Jr. *military officer, federal agency administrator*
†Gile, Greg L. *military career officer*
Glickman, Albert Seymour *psychologist, educator*
Goode, David Ronald *transportation company executive*
†Gora, JoAnn M. *academic administrator*
†Greene, Douglas George *humanities educator, author, publisher*
Griffith, Charles Dee, Jr. *state official*
Hailstork, Adolphus Cunningham *composer*
Herrera, Henry Francis *career officer*
High, Melvin C. *protective services official*
Hines, Dean Howard *military officer*
Jackson, Raymond A. *federal judge*
Jones, Franklin Ross *education educator*
Jones, Leon Herbert, Jr. (Herb Jones) *artist*
†Keane, John M. *career officer*
Keifer, John M. *director Norfolk public works department*
†Kimbrough, Walter Mark *university activities director*
Knapp, Roland B. *rear admiral United States Navy*
Knox, Richard Douglas, Jr. *healthcare executive*
Koch, James Verch *academic administrator, economist*
Larry, Wendy *head coach women's basketball*
Lester, Richard Garrison *radiologist, educator*
Lidstrom, Peggy Ray *mental health administrator, psychotherapist*
Lind, James Forest *surgeon, educator*
Maly, Kurt John *computer science educator*
Marchello, Joseph Maurice *mathematics and physical science educator*
Mark, Peter *director, conductor*
Martin, Roy Butler, Jr. *museum director, retired broker*
Martin, Wayne A. *clinical social worker*
McCarthy, Dennis M. *deputy director*
†McElwee, Jerry W. *military career officer*
Mc Gaughy, John Bell *civil engineer*
McKee, Timothy Carlton *taxation educator*
McKinnon, Arnold Borden *transportation company executive*
McMurray, Jennifer Lee *pediatric nurse practitioner*
†Miller, John F. *military officer*
†Miller, Tommy Eugene *federal judge*
Miller, Yvonne Bond *state senator, educator*
Mobley, Joseph S. *military officer*
Morgan, Henry Coke, Jr. *judge*
Morrison, Ashton Byrom *pathologist, medical school official*
Musgrave, Thea *composer, conductor*
Myers, Donald Allen *university dean*
Oelberg, David George *neonatologist, educator, researcher*
Parker, Richard Wilson *lawyer*
Pearson, John Y., Jr. *lawyer*
Pedone, Mary Ann Garcia *adult and geriatric nurse practitioner*
†Peppe, Timothy A. *career officer*
Perkins, Annie Suite *adult education educator*
Peterson-Vita, Elizabeth Ann *psychologist*
Pettigrew, Kenneth W. *career officer*
Pope, Stephanie Marie *classicist, educator*
Powell, Stephen Kenneth *financial planner*
Prince, William Taliaferro *federal judge*
Reed, Sally Gardner *library director*
Rendin, Robert Winter *environmental health officer*
Rephan, Jack *lawyer*
Richard, Ronald Gene *career officer*
Ritter, Alfred Francis, Jr. *communications executive*
Ritz, John Michael *education educator*
Rohrer, Susan Earley *film producer, writer, director*
†Ruckdeschel, Susan *writing educator*
Ruehlmann, William John *communications educator*
Rump, Kendall E. *air transportation executive*
Russell, C. Edward, Jr. *lawyer*
Rutyna, Richard Albert *history educator*
Ryan, John M. *lawyer*
†St. John, Stephen C. *federal judge*
Sanders, James Grady *biogeochemist*
Schellenberg, Karl Abraham *biochemist*
Schneider, Daniel Scott *pediatric cardiologist*
†Scott, Karen Cain *vice educator, soprano*
Scott, Kenneth R. *transportation executive*
Shannon, John Sanford *retired railway executive, lawyer*
Sizemore, William Howard, Jr. *newspaper editor*
Smith, Rebecca Beach *federal judge*
Smith, Richard Muldrow *lawyer*
Stallings, Valerie A. *health director*
Sutton, William G. *military officer*
Tolmie, Donald McEachern *lawyer*
†Tonelson, Stephen W. *special education educator*
Train, Harry Depue, II *retired naval officer*
Vaughan, Linda Ann *hospital administrator, nurse*
Wakeham, Ronald T. *protective services official*
Waldo, Joseph Thomas *lawyer*
Washington, Ann S. *city official*
West, Roger Seiker, III *finance executive*
Wheeler, Jock Rogers *dean, medical educator*
White, Ira Beauregard, III *pro audio company executive*
Williamson, Jean Elizabeth *office manager*
Wilson, Angela Saburn *nursing educator*
Wilson, Lloyd Lee *organization administrator*
Wiltse, James Clark *civil engineer*
Wolcott, Hugh Dixon *obstetrics and gynecology educator*
Wooldridge, William Charles *lawyer*
Ziemer, Robert T. *career officer*

North Garden
Moses, Hamilton, III *medical educator, hospital executive, management consultant*

North Tazewell
Oldham, William Edward *minister, accountant, educator*

Norton
Kennedy, J. Jack, Jr. *court administrator, bank director, lawyer*
Shortridge, Judy Beth *lawyer*
Vest, Gayle Southworth *obstetrician and gynecologist*
Vest, Steven Lee *gastroenterologist, hepatologist, internist*

Oak Hill
†Adler, Dale Ann *artist*
Hubbard, Carl Aubrey *aerospace engineer, management consultant*

Oakton
Anderson, William Robert *career naval officer*
Curry, Thomas Fortson *electronics engineer, defense industry executive*
Entzminger, John Nelson, Jr. *federal agency administrator, electronic engineer, researcher*
Hough, Edythe S. Ellison *dean*
Hu, Sue King *elementary and middle school educator*
Mosemann, Lloyd Kenneth, II *business executive*

Onancock
Verrill, John Howard *museum director*

Ophelia
Simonsen, August Henry *education director*

Orange
†Burke, Robert Lawrence *consultant*

Orlean
Kulski, Julian Eugeniusz *architect, planner, educator*

Palmyra
Leslie, William Cairns *metallurgical engineering educator*
Ramsey, Forrest Gladstone, Jr. *retired engineering company executive*
Sahr, Morris Gallup *financial planner*
White, Luther Wesley *retired lawyer*

Pearisburg
Morse, F. D., Jr. *dentist*

Pennington Gap
†Kinser, Cynthia D. *state supreme court justice*

Petersburg
Baskervill, Charles Thornton *lawyer*
Calkins, Christopher Miles *historian*
†Challa, Chandrashekar Dutt *business educator*
†Davis, Louise Minnie *writer*

Edmunds, Cecelia Powers health facility administrator
Hart, Donald Purple bishop
Isom, Rebecca Jayne newspaper editor, newspaper columnist
Northrop, Mary Ruth mental retardation nurse
Shell, Louis Calvin lawyer
Spero, Morton Bertram lawyer
Stronach, Carey Elliott physicist, educator
Watkins, Sherry Ligon medical facility data executive, nurse

Phenix
Davis, Peggy Hamlette banking executive

Poquoson
Holloway, Paul Fayette retired aerospace executive
†Tai, Elizabeth Shi-Jue Lee library director

Portsmouth
Agricola, Dianne G. secondary education educator, tutor
Bangel, Herbert K. lawyer
Barnes, Judith P. nursing administrator
Blachman, Michael Joel lawyer
Brown, James Andrew naval architect
†Clare, Frank Brian neurosurgeon, neurologist
Cox, William Walter dentist
DaMoude, Denise Ann postal worker
Dudley, Delores Ingram secondary education educator, poet, writer
Glasson, Linda hospital security and safety official
†Hoggard, Sharon Riddick public relations executive
Jackson, Cheryl K. English educator
Mapp, Alf Johnson, Jr. writer, historian
Thomas, Ted, Sr. bishop
Williams, Lena Harding English language educator
Wolf, Jeffrey Stephen physician

Potomac Falls
Payne, Roger Lee geographer

Powhatan
Unison, Wendy Jane critical care nurse

Preston
Biddle, A. G. W., III (Jack Biddle) venture capitalist

Prince George
Farrar, Andrew Lockett agricultural education educator

Pulaski
Cox, David Alan superintendent of schools

Purcellville
Kok, Frans Johan investment banker
Mainwaring, Thomas Lloyd motor freight company executive
Sharples, Winston Singleton automobile importer and distributor

Quantico
Downey, Gary Neil marine corps officer
†Howard, Patrick Gene marine corps officer
Klimp, Jack W. military officer
LeDoux, John Clarence law enforcement official
Mangan, Terence Joseph retired police chief
Palm, Leslie M. military officer

Radford
†Camphouse, Mark David music educator, dean, composer, conductor
James, Clarity (Carolyne Faye James) mezzo-soprano
Jervey, Edward Drewry retired history educator
Phelps, George Graham computer systems engineer, consultant
Reed, Helen Inez medical-clinical resource nurse
Shell, Robert Edward Lee photographer, writer
Southern, Ann Gayle nurse, educator
Thomas, Robert Wilburn media and advertising executive
Turk, James Clinton, Jr. lawyer
Wille, Lois Jean retired newspaper editor

Rapidan
Grimm, Ben Emmet former library director and consultant

Reston
†Backus, John Carlton, Jr. venture capitalist
Bredehoft, Elaine Charlson lawyer
Brennan, Norma Jean professional society publications director
Brooker, Susan Gay employment consulting firm executive
Brown, James Robert retired air force officer
Burton, James Samuel physical chemist
Cerf, Vinton Gray telecommunications company executive
Chattman, Raymond Christopher foundation executive
Choi, Michael Kamwah aerospace engineer, mechanical engineer, thermal engineer, researcher
Christ, Thomas Warren electronics research and development company executive, sociologist
Clapp, Stephen Caswell journalist
Cornette, William Magnus scientist, technical advisor
Crawford, Lawrence Robert aviation and aerospace consultant
Curry, John Joseph professional organization executive
Davis, James E. professional association executive
†DeFrantz, Anita physical education educator
Duscha, Lloyd Arthur engineering executive
Easton, Glenn Hanson, Jr. management and insurance consultant, federal official, naval officer
Foster, William Anthony management consultant, educator
Fox, Edward A. business executive
†Fusco, Barbara Leigh communications executive, editor
Gates, James David retired association executive, consultant
Gemma, Peter Benedict, Jr. political, public relations and fund raising consultant
Gorog, William Francis corporate executive
†Groat, Charles geologist
Harvey, Aubrey Eaton, III industrial engineer
Heginbotham, Jan Sturza sculptor
Hope, Samuel Howard accreditation organization executive
Humphreys, David John lawyer, trade association executive
Jaynes, Robert Henry, Jr. retired military officer
†Johnson, Thea Jean internet and intranet security service provider
Kader, Nancy Stowe nurse, consultant, bioethicist
Keefe, James Washburn educational writer, researcher, consultant
†Keler, Marianne Martha lawyer
Kramish, Arnold physicist, historian, author
Kreyling, Edward George, Jr. railroad executive
Lynch, Daniel C. multimedia executive
Madry-Taylor, Jacquelyn Yvonne educational administrator
Mahlmann, John James music education association administrator
Mallette, Malcolm Francis newspaper editor, educator
Mendelsohn, Stuart management consultant, environmental engineer, lawyer
Miller, Donald Lane publishing executive
Miller, John Edward army officer, educational administrator
Miller, Lynne Marie environmental company executive
Minton, Joseph Paul retired safety organization executive
Mogge, Harriet Morgan educational association executive
Mowbray, Robert Norman natural resource management consultant
Mumzhiu, Alexander optical and imaging processing engineer, researcher
Naylon, Michael Edward retired army officer
Ovissi, Nasser artist
Peck, Dallas Lynn retired geologist
Powell, Anne Elizabeth editor
Pyle, Thomas Alton instructional television and motion picture executive
Ross, Malcolm mineralogist, crystallographer
Ryan, Mary Catherine pediatrician
Salisbury, Alan Blanchard information systems executive
Scharff, Joseph Laurent lawyer
Scheeler, James Arthur architect
Schleede, Glenn Roy energy market and policy consultant
Seiberlich, Carl Joseph retired naval officer
Sherwin, Michael Dennis government official
†Sikes, Arthur D. military officer
Smith, Ralph Lee author, musician
Spath, Gregg Anthony lawyer
Watson, William Downing, Jr. economist, educator
Wilkinson, Edward Anderson, Jr. retired naval officer, business executive

Richmond
Ackerly, Benjamin Clarkson lawyer
Ackman, Paul Jeffrey wholesale distribution executive, researcher
Addison, David Dunham lawyer
Adiele, Nkwachukwu Moses state official
Aigner, Emily Burke lay worker
Allen, George Felix lawyer
Aron, Mark G. lawyer, transportation executive
†August, Albert T., III publishing executive
Ayres, Stephen McClintock physician, educator
Baar, Diane advertising executive
Baker, Donald Parks journalist, educator
Baliles, Gerald L. lawyer, former governor
Balster, Robert Louis pharmacologist
Barker, Thomas Carl retired health care administration educator, executive
Barton, Jonathan Miller clergyman
Bates, Hampton Robert, Jr. pathologist
Bates, John Wythe, III lawyer
Belcher, Dennis Irl lawyer
Berry, William Willis retired utility executive
Bing, Richard McPhail lawyer
Binns, Walter Gordon, Jr. investment management executive
Black, Robert Perry retired banker, executive
Blank, Florence Weiss literacy educator, editor
Blumberg, Michael Zangwill allergist
Blumberg, Peter Steven manufacturing company executive
Boadle-Biber, Margaret Clare physiology educator
Booker, Lewis Thomas lawyer
Boyd, B(everley) Randolph lawyer
Brasfield, Evans Booker lawyer
Brissette, Martha Blevins lawyer
Broaddus, John Alfred, Jr. bank executive, economist
Brockenbrough, Henry Watkins lawyer
Brooks, Robert Franklin, Sr. lawyer
Bryan, John Stewart, III newspaper publisher
Bunzl, Rudolph Hans retired diversified manufacturing company executive
Burke, Arthur Wade retired physician
Burke, John K(irkland), Jr. lawyer
Burrus, Robert Lewis, Jr. lawyer
Bush, Thomas Norman lawyer
Bustard, Clarke music critic, newswriter, radio producer
Campbell, Neal Franklin musician, educator
Campbell, Thomas Corwith, Jr. economics educator
Capps, Thomas Edward utilities company executive, lawyer
Capps, Thos E. diversified financial services company executive
Carr, David Turner physician
Carrell, Daniel Allan lawyer
Carrico, Harry Lee state supreme court chief justice
Carter, Joseph Carlyle, Jr. lawyer
Catlett, Richard H., Jr. retired lawyer
Charlesworth, Arthur Thomas mathematics and computer science educator
Chmura, Christine economist
Ciulla, Joanne Bridgett business ethics educator
Clinard, Robert Noel lawyer
Cohn, David Stephen lawyer
Combs, Sandra Lynn state parole board official
Compton, Asbury Christian state supreme court justice
Compton, Olin Randall consulting electrical engineer, researcher
Cooper, William Edwin university president, educator
Cullen, Richard lawyer, former state attorney general
Dabney, H. Slayton, Jr. lawyer
Daniel, Beth professional golfer
David, Ronald Brian child neurologist
Deekens, Elizabeth Tupman writer
Denny, Collins, III lawyer
Dent, Edward Eugene manufacturing company specialist
Dessypris, Emmanuel Nicholas hematologist-oncologist
De Vries, Dawn Ann theology educator
DeWitt, Brydon Merrill development consultant
DeWitt, Michele Mixner community planner
Dickinson, Alfred James realtor
Dilworth, Robert Lexow career military officer, adult education educator
Dombalis, Constantine Nicholas minister
Dray, Mark S. lawyer
†Dunn, Leo James obstetrician, gynecologist, educator
Earley, Mark Lawrence state attorney general
Edloe, Leonard Levi pharmacist
Edmonds, Thomas Andrew state bar executive director
Effinger, Steven Craig state agency administrator
Ellis, Andrew Jackson, Jr. lawyer
Ellis, Anthony John education educator
Elmore, Edward Whitehead lawyer
Epps, Augustus Charles lawyer
Estes, Gerald Walter newspaper executive
†Eutsler, R(alph) Kern retired bishop, church finance consultant
Farrell, Thomas Francis energy company executive
†Fischer, Carl R. hospital executive
Fischer, Carl Robert health care facility administrator
Fisher, Todd Rogers transportation executive
Fitzsimmons, Ellen Marie lawyer
Forbes, J. Randy state senator
Franko, Bernard Vincent pharmacologist
Freed, David Clark artist
Freund, Emma Frances medical technologist
†Fuhr, Edward J. lawyer
†Fuller, Kathryn Helgesen historian, educator
Gary, Richard David lawyer
Geraghty, Patrick James organ transplant coordinator
Gerrish, Brian Albert theologian, educator
Gilchrist, Eunice Bass nursing educator
Gilmore, James Stuart, III governor
Goodpasture, Philip Henry lawyer
Goodykoontz, Charles Alfred newspaper editor, retired
Gordon, John L., Jr. historian, educator
Gordon, Thomas Christian, Jr. former justice
Gorr, Louis Frederick investment consultant
Gottwald, Bruce Cobb chemical company executive
Gottwald, Bruce Cobb, Jr. treasurer analyst
Gottwald, Floyd Dewey, Jr. chemical company executive
†Graham, Sam Dixon urologist
Graves, H. Brice lawyer
Gray, Clarence Jones foreign language educator, dean emeritus
Gray, Francis Campbell bishop
Gray, Frank C. bishop
Gresham, Ann Elizabeth retailer, horticulturist executive, consultant
Grover, Peter Dun cultural organization administrator
Hackney, Virginia Howitz lawyer
Hager, John Henry state official
Hall, Stephen Charles lawyer
Hamel, Dana Bertrand academic administrator
Hamlett, Robert Barksdale systems engineer
Hanzak, Gary A. John credit and leasing executive
Hardy, Richard Earl rehabilitation counseling educator, clinical psychologist
Harris, Louis Selig pharmacologist, researcher
Hassell, Leroy Rountree, Sr. state supreme court justice
Heilman, E. Bruce academic administrator
Heiss, Frederick William political science educator, public administrator, policy researcher
Helwig, Arthur Woods chemical company executive
Henley, Vernard William banker
Hettrick, George Harrison lawyer
Hicks, C. Flippo lawyer
Hintz, Robert Louis transportation company executive
Holcomb, Richard D. state commissioner
Hong, James Ming industrialist, venture capitalist
Horsley, Waller Holladay lawyer
Horwitz, Marcia J. fundraiser, writer
Hoskie, Lorraine consumer products representative, poet
Howell, George Cook, III lawyer
Howell, Talmadge Rudolph radiologist
†Huggins, M. Wayne protective services agency administrator
Hughes, Mike advertising executive
Hull, Rita Prizler accounting educator
James, Allix Bledsoe retired university president
Jandl, Henry Anthony architect, educator
Jarrard Mahayni, Mary Melissa psychiatric nurse
Joel, William Lee, II interior and lighting designer
Johnston, Francis Claiborne, Jr. lawyer
Jones, Catesby Brooke retired banker
Jones, Jeanne Pitts director early childhood school
Jones, Jerry Lee computer educator
Jordan, Henry Preston, Jr. manufacturer's representative
Kaplowitz, Lisa Glauser physician, educator
Kearfott, Joseph Conrad lawyer
Keenan, Barbara Milano state supreme court justice
Kendig, Edwin Lawrence, Jr. physician, educator
Kennedy, James Bruce operations administrator
Kevorkian, Richard artist
King, Allen B. company executive
†King, Robert Bruce federal judge
King, Robert Leroy business administration educator
King, Ronald L. state official, English educator
Kinsey, David Jonathan state official, meteorologist
Kline, Robert H. foundation administrator
Kontos, Hermes Apostolou dean
Kronzer, Lance city auditor, Richmond, Virginia
†Landsidle, William Edward comptroller
Laskin, Daniel M. oral and maxillofacial surgeon, educator
Laverge, Jan tobacco company executive
Lawrence, Walter, Jr. surgeon
Leary, David Edward university dean
Ledbetter, David Oscar lawyer
Lee, Peter James bishop
Levit, Heloise B. (Ginger Levit) art dealer, art consultant
Levit, Jay J(oseph) lawyer
Linkonis, Suzanne Newbold community corrections case manager, counselor
Lockhart, Mack L. Richmond City Assessor
†Lowe, David G. federal judge
Mackenzie, Ross newspaper editor
Macleod, Cynthia Ann national park service official, historian
Mallory, Jean Long paralegal
Malone, Nicholas Sherlon systems analyst, consultant
†Marcus, M. Boyd, Jr. state official
Marshall, Wayne Keith anesthesiology educator
Martin, Bernard Murray painter, educator
Mattauch, Robert Joseph electrical engineering educator
Mauck, Henry Page, Jr. medical and pediatrics educator
McClard, Jack Edward lawyer
McDonough, Reginald Milton religious organization executive
McElligott, James Patrick, Jr. lawyer
McGee, Henry Alexander, Jr. university official
McKee, Paul Vincent advertising agency executive
McLees, Ainslie Armstrong secondary education educator
McVey, Henry Hanna, III lawyer
†Mehrhof, Austin Irving plastic surgery educator
Mellette, M. Susan Jackson physician, educator, researcher
Merhige, Robert Reynold, Jr. lawyer
Mezzullo, Louis Albert lawyer
Miller, Stephen Wiley lawyer
Milmoe, Patrick Joseph lawyer
Minardi, Richard A., Jr. lawyer
†Miner, Mark Aaron state official
Minor, Marian Thomas elementary and secondary school educational consultant
Mollen, Edward Leigh pediatrician, allergist and clinical immunologist
Moore, Andrew Taylor, Jr. banker
Moore, John Sterling, Jr. minister
Moore, Thurston Roach lawyer
Morrill, Richard Leslie university administrator
Morris, James Carl architect
Mullinax, Perry Franklin rheumatologist, allergist, immunologist
Murdoch-Kitt, Norma Hood clinical psychologist
Musick, Robert Lawrence, Jr. lawyer
Neal, Gail Fallon physical therapist, educator
†Nelson, Robert McDowell English educator
Neman, Daniel Louis movie critic
Newbrand, Charles Michael advertising firm executive
O'Keeffe, Charles B. pharmaceutical executive
O'Neal, Robert Steven criminologist, consultant
Oulton, Richard James lawyer, entrepreneur
Owen, Duncan Shaw, Jr. physician, medical educator
Owen, Howard Wayne journalist, writer
Palik, Robert Richard mechanical engineer
Palmore, Fred Wharton, III lawyer
Pasco, Hansell Merrill retired lawyer
Pauley, Stanley Frank manufacturing company executive
Payne, Robert E. federal judge
Payne, William Sanford insurance company executive
†Petera, Anne P. state official
Peters, David Frankman lawyer
Phillips, Elizabeth Jason lawyer
Phillips, Thomas Edworth, Jr. financial advisor, senior consultant
Pinckney, Charles Cotesworth lawyer
†Plum, Kenneth political organization administrator
Poff, Richard Harding state supreme court justice
Pollard, Overton Price state agency executive, lawyer
Pope, Robert Dean lawyer
Powell, Kenneth Edward investment banker
Powell, Lewis Franklin, III lawyer
Rada, Heath Kenneth social service organization executive
Rainey, Gordon Fryer, Jr. lawyer
Reveley, Walter Taylor, III dean
Richardson, David Walthall cardiologist, educator, consultant
Rigsby, Linda Flory lawyer
Rilling, John Robert history educator
Roach, Edgar Mayo, Jr. lawyer
Robert, Joseph Clarke historian, consultant
Robertson, William Franklin publishing executive
Rogers, Isabel Wood religious studies educator
Rogers, James Edward paper company executive
Rolfe, Robert Martin lawyer
Roop, Ralph Goodwin retired oil marketing company executive
Roper, Hartwell H. tobacco company executive
Rosenblum, John William dean
Rowe, Mae Irene investment company executive
Rowley, Frank Selby, Jr. artist
Rubinstein, Phyllis M. lawyer
Rucker, Douglas Pendleton, Jr. lawyer
Rudlin, David Alan lawyer
Rudnick, Alan A. management company executive, corporate lawyer
Sasser, Ellis A. gifted and talented education educator
Saunders, Dero Ames writer, editor
Savedge, Anne Creery artist, photographer
Schaar, Susan Clarke state legislative staff member
Scott, George Cole, III investment advisor
Scott, Sidney Buford financial services company executive
Seals, Margaret Louise newspaper editor
Sgro, Beverly Huston head of collegiate school, state official, educator
Shapiro, Gary Michael philosophy educator
Sharer, John Daniel lawyer
Sharp, Richard L. retail company executive
Sheehan, Jeremiah J. metal company executive
†Shelley, Blackwell N. federal judge
Showalter, J. Kirk general registrar, Richmond, Virginia
Simmons, S. Dallas former university president
Sirica, Alphonse Eugene pathology educator
Slater, Thomas Glascock, Jr. lawyer
Slaughter, Alexander Hoke lawyer
Smith, R. Gordon lawyer
Smith, Russell Edward priest
Smith, Ted Jay, III mass communications educator
Smoker, Wendy Rue Kartinos neuroradiologist, consultant, educator
Smolla, Rodney Alan lawyer, educator
Sniffin, John Harrison retail executive
Spahn, Gary Joseph lawyer
Spain, Jack Holland, Jr. lawyer
Spencer, James R. federal judge
Spitzer, William John healthcare social work administrator
Sprinkle, William Melvin engineering administrator, audio-acoustical engineer
Stallard, Hugh R. telephone company executive
Starke, Harold E., Jr. lawyer
Stoyko, William Nelson lawyer
Strickland, William Jesse lawyer
Suleymanian, Mirik biophysicist
Sullivan, Walter Francis bishop
Sweeney, Arthur Hamilton, Jr. metal manufacturing executive, retired army officer
Sydnor, Charles Wright broadcast executive, historian

Talley, Charles Richmond commercial banking executive
Thomas, John Charles lawyer, former state supreme court justice
Thompson, Francis Neal financial services consultant
Thompson, Paul Michael lawyer
Thornhill, Barbara Cole marketing executive
Tice, Douglas Oscar, Jr. federal judge
Tilghman, Richard Granville banker
†Tillet, Ronald state official
Torrence, Rosetta Lena educational consultant
Totten, Arthur Irving, Jr. retired metals company executive, consultant
Towne, Alan Raymond neurologist, educator
Trani, Eugene Paul academic administrator, educator
Trott, Sabert Scott, II marketing professional
Troy, Anthony Francis lawyer
Trumble, Robert Roy business educator
Tuck, Grayson Edwin real estate agent, former natural gas transmission executive
Tunner, William Sams urological surgeon
Turner, Elaine S. allergist, immunologist
Tuszynski, Daniel J., Jr. sales, management and marketing consultant
Ukrop, James E. retail executive
Upton, David Edward finance educator
Urofsky, Melvin Irving historian, educator, director
Vallentyne, Peter Lloyd philosophy educator
Vartanian, Isabel Sylvia dietitian
Waite-Franzen, Ellen Jane academic administrator
Wakeham, Helmut Richard Rae chemist, consulting company executive
Walsh, William Arthur, Jr. lawyer
Ward, John Wesley retired pharmacologist
Warthen, Harry Justice, III lawyer
Washburn, John Rosser entrepreneur
Washington, James MacKnight former chemical engineer
Watkins, Hays Thomas retired railroad executive
Watts, Robert Glenn retired pharmaceutical company executive
Watts, Stephen Hurt, II lawyer
Weis, Laura Visser lawyer
Wender, Herbert title company executive
White, Hugh Vernon, Jr. lawyer
White, James M., III lawyer
White, Kenneth Ray health administration educator, consultant
†White, Shelley Reaves educator, counselor
Whiting, Henry H. state supreme court justice
Wilder, Eunice city official
Williams, Deborah Yvonne secondary education educator
Williams, Richard Leroy federal judge
†Williams, Steven Robert lawyer
Winslett, Stoner artistic director
Winter, Joan Elizabeth psychotherapist
Wist, Abund Ottokar biomedical engineer, radiation physicist, educator
Witt, Walter Francis, Jr. lawyer
Wolf, Barry genetics, pediatric educator
Wood, Jeanne Clarke charitable organization executive
Young, Estelle Irene dermatologist
Yu, Robert Kuan-jen biochemistry educator

Riner
Foster, Joy Via library media specialist

Roanoke
Al-Zubaidi, Amer Aziz physicist, educator
Ayyildiz, Judy Light writer, poet, educator
Barnhill, David Stan lawyer
Bates, Harold Martin lawyer
Beagle, Benjamin Stuart, Jr. columnist
Berry, John Coltrin insurance executive
Butler, Manley Caldwell retired lawyer
Coar, Richard John mechanical engineer, aerospace consultant
Coleman, Sallye Terrell retired social studies educator
†Conrad, Glen E. federal judge
Crouch, Robert P., Jr. prosecutor
Dagenhart, Betty Jane Mahaffey nursing educator, administrator
Dillard, Richard Henry Wilde English language professional, educator, author
Duff, Doris Eileen (Shull) critical care nurse
Easterling, Eddie Jean publisher
Enright, Michael Joseph radiologist
Fishwick, John Palmer lawyer, retired railroad executive
Gardner, Marvin Allen, Jr. pastoral and clinical psychologist
Hale, Lance Mitchell lawyer
Harding, Margaret Tyree minister
Harris, Bayard Easter lawyer
†Harrison, John Todd social studies teacher
Hudick, Andrew Michael, II finance executive
Hutcheson, Jack Robert hematologist, medical oncologist
Jackson, Daniel Wyer electrical engineer
Jiang, John Jianzhong materials engineer
†Journiette, Melvin Diago civil engineer
†Karnes, Daniel Elmo clinical social worker
Keesee, Roger Neal, Jr. lawyer
Kennedy, Stephen Smith hematologist, oncologist, educator
Lemon, William Jacob lawyer
MacLean, Iain Stewart religion educator
Marmion, William Henry retired bishop
McGarry, Richard Lawrence lawyer
†Miles, Sherry Celestine disabilty determinatin analyst
Mitchell, Sharon Stanley supply analyst, accountant
Moore, Richard Carroll, Jr. family physician
Moriarty, Marilyn Frances English educator, writer
Mundy, Gardner Marshall lawyer
Nickens, Harry Carl academic administrator
Reiley, John Echols writer
Rugaber, Walter Feucht, Jr. newspaper executive
Schlegel, Beverly Faye private club administrator
Shaffner, Patrick Noel retired architectural engineering executive
Shaftman, Fredrick Krisch telephone communications executive, lawyer
Stadler, Donald Arthur management engineer
Turk, James Clinton federal judge
†Wiley, David music director
Wilson, Samuel Grayson federal judge
Woodrum, Clifton A., III lawyer, state legislator
Woods, Walter Ralph retired agricultural scientist, administrator
Zomparelli, Wendy newspaper executive

Rockbridge Baths
Patteson, Roy Kinneer, Jr. retired clergyman, administrator

Rockville
Smith, Lucy Anselmo mental health nurse

Roseland
Arey, William Griffin, Jr. former government official
Stemmler, Edward Joseph physician, retired association executive, retired academic dean
Wood, Maurice medical educator

Round Hill
Pugh, Marion Stirling archaeologist, author

Rustburg
Hughes, Deborah Enoch circuit court clerk

Ruther Glen
Bush, Mitchell Lester, Jr. retired federal agency administrator

Saint Charles
Matlock, Anita Kay family nurse practitioner

Saint Paul
Gregory, Ann Young editor, publisher

Salem
Bansemer, Richard Frederick bishop
Brand, Edward Cabell retail executive
Burkart, Francis William, III lawyer
Chakravorty, Ranes Chandra surgeon, educator
Gring, David M. academic administrator
Koontz, Lawrence L., Jr. state supreme court justice
Pearson, Henry Clyde judge
Willett, Roy Baldwin judge

Schuyler
Mastromarino, Mark Anthony historian

Seaford
Jenkins, Margaret Bunting human resources executive

Shawsville
Murray, Lynda Beran counselor

Smithfield
Baxter, Raoul meat packing company executive
Lauder, Robert Scott health education coordinator
†Luter, Joseph Williamson, III meat packing and processing company executive
Wynne, John Boyce performing company executive

South Hill
Clay, Carol Ann family nurse practitioner

Sperryville
Armor, David J. sociologist

Spotsylvania
Arnhoff, Franklyn Nathaniel psychologist, sociologist, educator
Hardy, Dorcas Ruth business and government relations executive
Kozloski, Lillian Terese D. history of aerospace technology educator
Orsini, Eric Andrew army official
†Todd, Deborah Kathleen library media specialist
Westwood, Geraldine E. elementary school educator

Springfield
Bartlow, Gene Steven association executive, retired air force officer
Borum, Olin Henry realtor, former government official
Broome, Paul Wallace engineering research and development executive
Bruen, John Dermot business management consultant
Casazza, John Andrew electrical engineer, business executive, educator
Chatelier, Paul Richard aviation psychologist, training company officer
Dake, Marcia Allene retired nursing educator, university dean
Dean, John Wilson, Jr. business consultant, retired army officer
Duff, William Grierson electrical engineer
Eastman, Donna Kelly composer, music educator
Edwards, Renee Camille logistics engineer, public relations professional
Englert, Roy Theodore lawyer
Finnegan, Philip journalist
†Gaffney, Theresa Adcock nursing administrator
Gallagher, Matthew Philip, Jr. advertising agency executive
Gresham, Dorothy Ann operating room nurse, educator
†Ha, Dinh Trong retired air force officer, computer sepcialist
Hastings, Melanie (Melanie Jean Wotring) television news anchor
Hillis, John David television news executive, producer, writer
Hunt, Robert Gayle former government official
Hyland, Patricia Ann (Pat Hyland) writer
Jones, Bonnie Damschroder special education specialist
Larson, Reed Eugene foundation administrator
Lautzenheiser, Marvin Wendell computer software engineer
Leavitt, Mary Janice Deimel special education educator, civic worker
Luisada, Paul Victor psychiatrist
†Malmberg, Kenneth Brian environmentalist
Meikle, Philip G. engineer, retired government agency executive
Minetree, James Lawrence, III military officer, educator
Nodeen, Janey Price company executive
Quick, Danny Richard computer systems engineer
Ray, Carol Lynn special education educator
†Rothschild, Susy Schaflander data analyst
Schlegelmilch, Reuben Orville electrical engineer, consultant
Stottlemyer, David Lee government official

Stafford
Brown, Harold Eugene magistrate

Collins, Vicki Tichené critical care and emergency room nurse
†Humphrey, Matthew Cameron computer scientist, consultant
Kline, Denny Lee hazardous devices and explosives consultant
Sedlak, James William organization administrator
Tallent, Robert Glenn chemical and environmental engineer, entrepreneur
Weselin, Mary Lou interior designer

Stanardsville
Anns, Arlene Eiserman publishing company executive
Anns, Philip Harold international trading executive, former pharmaceutical company executive

Staunton
Balsley, Philip Elwood entertainer
†Carter, Sandra Jo art therapist, costume designer, consultant
†Fultz, Sara Spitler art educator
Hammaker, Paul M. retail executive, business educator, author
Kopp, George Philip, Jr. minister
Lossing, Wallace William inventor, minister
Tyson, Cynthia Haldenby academic administrator

Sterling
Bennett, William Leo, Jr. management consultant
Bockwoldt, Todd Shane nuclear engineer
Friedheim, Jerry Warden museum consultant
Heberling, Timothy Alan information systems engineer
Henshaw, Barbara Louise Hanby retired psychology tester, counselor
Howard, Angela Kay lawyer, accountant
Jaffe, Russell Merritt pathologist, research director
Jefferson, Sandra Traylor choreographer, ballet coach
Lewis, Gene Evans retired medical equipment company executive
McBarnette, Bruce Olvin lawyer, corporate executive
Moulton, James Roger small business owner
Munger, Paul David educational administrator
Oller, William Maxwell retired energy company executive, retired naval officer
Paraskevopoulos, George aerospace engineer
Piper, Thomas Samuel minister, consultant
Pittman, Robert Warren entertainment executive
Port, Arthur Tyler retired government administrator, lawyer
Sanfelici, Arthur H(ugo) editor, writer

Suffolk
Berndt, Martin R. career officer
Birdsong, George Yancy manufacturing company executive
Carroll, George Joseph pathologist, educator
Derby, Shelah Ann Novak English language educator
†English, Betty Jo Boone programming educator
Gray, Marcia Lanette health, physical education and recreation educator
Hines, Angus Irving, Jr. petroleum marketing executive
Hope, James Franklin mayor, civil engineer, consultant
Matson, Virginia Mae Freeberg (Mrs. Edward J. Matson) retired special education educator, author
Tritten, James John national security educator

Sugar Grove
Greer, Carole Kilby reading specialist

Sumerduck
McCamy, Sharon Lynn English educator

Surry
Wachsmann, Elizabeth Rideout reading specialist

Susan
Ambach, Dwight Russell retired foreign service officer

Sweet Briar
Grubbs, Judith Evans classical studies educator
McClenon, John Raymond chemistry educator
Miller, Reuben George economics educator
Piepho, (Edward) Lee humanities educator
Shea, Brent Mack social science educator
Wassell, Stephen Robert mathematics educator, researcher

Swoope
Avery, Robert Newell sculptor

Tazewell
Garner, June Brown journalist
Weeks, Ross Leonard, Jr. museum executive

Thaxton
Buchanan, Ray Allen clergyman

The Plains
Gibbons, John Howard (Jack Gibbons) government official, physicist
Rose, Henry lawyer

Toano
Carlson, David Emil physicist

Topping
Willett, Albert James, Jr. family historian

Tysons Corner
Hicks, C. Thomas, III lawyer

University Of Richmond
Hall, James H(errick), Jr. philosophy educator, author
Terry, Robert Meredith foreign language educator

Upperville
di Zerega, Thomas William former energy company executive, lawyer
Smart, Edith Merrill civic worker
Smart, Stephen Bruce, Jr. business and government executive

Urbanna
Hudson, Jesse Tucker, Jr. financial executive
Salley, John Jones university administrator, oral pathologist

Vienna
†Baity, William F. federal agency administrator
Browning, Charles publishing executive
Cantus, H. Hollister government relations consultant
Chandler, Hubert Thomas former army officer
†Colosi, Thomas R. educator
Cramer, Roxanne Herrick gifted and talented education educator
Croog, Roslyn Zeporah senior systems engineer
de Planque, Emile, III computer consultant
DeWitt, Charles Barbour federal government official
†Feld, Kenneth performing company executive
Feld, Kenneth J. entertainment executive
†Frakes, Ronald LaVerne, Jr. systems analyst
Giovacchini, Robert Peter toxicologist, manufacturing executive, retired
Hatch, Harold Arthur retired military officer
Higginbotham, Wendy Jacobson political adviser, writer
Jackson, Dempster McKee retired naval officer
Jahn, Laurence Roy retired biologist, institute executive
Jandreau, James Lawrence information systems executive
Jayne, Edward Randolph, II executive search consultant
Jenkins, Robert Gordon retired air force officer, technology executive
Keiser, Bernhard Edward engineering company executive, consulting telecommunications engineer
Kim, Jay former congressman
Kinsolving, Sylvia Crockett musician, educator
Lawing, Charles William retired naval officer, consultant
Leonard, Edward Paul naval officer, dentist, educator
Lillard, Mark Hill, III computer consulting executive, former air force officer
Mandl, Alex J(ohann) telecommunications company executive
Marinelli, Ada Santi retired government official, real estate broker
Mc Arthur, George journalist
McCabe, Thomas Edward lawyer
Miller, Claire Ellen periodical editor
Mitchell, John David ophthalmologist
Moen, Ahmed Abdul national and international health educator
Molineaux, Charles Borromeo lawyer, arbitrator, columnist, poet
Mulvihill, John Gary retired information services administrator
Oleson, Ray Jerome computer service company executive
Olshaker, Mark Bruce author, film-maker
Palmer, Stephen Eugene, Jr. government official
Penrose, Cynthia C. health plan administrator, consultant
†Poulos, Stephen Paul information systems specialist
Price, Ilene Rosenberg lawyer
Razzano, Frank Charles lawyer
Rothery, Chet business executive
Rovis, Christopher Patrick clinical social worker, psychotherapist
Salah, Sagid retired nuclear engineer
Schneider, Peter Raymond political scientist
Schwartz, Richard Harvey pediatrician
Seidman, Paul Joseph lawyer
Sheinbaum, Gilbert Harold international management consultant
Spiro, Robert Harry, Jr. foundation and business executive, educator
Steele, Carol D. information processing coordinator
Syence Kennedy, Karen advertising agency executive
Titus, Bruce Earl lawyer
Tordiff, Hazel Midgley education director
Tucker, Alvin Leroy retired government official
Urbanas, Alban William estate planner
Vachher, Sheila Ann information systems consultant
Van Putten, Mark environmentalist
Van Stavoren, William David investor, retired government official
Walker, Edward Keith, Jr. business executive, retired naval officer
Webb, William Loyd, Jr. army officer
West, Richard Luther defense consultant, retired army officer
Whitaker, Thomas Patrick lawyer
Witman, Kim Pensinger opera company executive
Woodward, Kenneth Emerson retired mechanical engineer
Yarborough, William Glenn, Jr. military officer, forest farmer, defense and international business executive
Zehl, Otis George optical physicist
Zeitlin, Gerald Mark electrical engineer
Zoeller, Jack Carl financial executive

Virginia Beach
Abbott, Regina A. neurodiagnostic technologist, consultant, business owner
Alexander, Christina Anamaria translator, performing company executive
Alexander, William Powell business advisor
Allen, Elizabeth Maresca marketing and telecommunications executive
Atkinson, John T. treasurer City of Virginia Beach
Barriskill, Maudanne Kidd primary school educator
Brennan, Patrick Jeremiah software developer
Bryant, Jacqueline Eola educational consultant, urban specialist
Budd, Richard Wade university official, communications scientist
Burgess, Marvin Franklin human resources, management specialist, consultant
Burke, Thomas Joseph accountant
Caplan, Helene Moses psychologist
Carlston, John A. allergist
Carter, James Walton fire chief
Christy, Larry Todd publisher
Corbat, Patricia Leslie special education educator
Cowart, Gwen municipal official
Dantone, Joseph John, Jr. naval officer
Dean, Edwin Becton business owner
DiCarlo, Susanne Helen financial analyst
Dixon, John Spencer international executive
Ellis, John Carroll, Jr. life insurance sales executive
Fischer, Daniel Edward psychiatrist
Freyss, David producer, director
Friedman, Andrew director housing and neighborhood preservation
Fruit, J. Curtis municipal court clerk

Gallagher, Vicki Smith real estate agent
Gibbs, Jordan Smith music educator, artist
Glenn, Joe Davis, Jr. retired civil engineer, consultant
†Godsey, James Paul (J.P. Godsey) security firm executive
Goffigan, Christopher Wayne research associate
Goodwin, Robert human resources specialist
Grochmal, David municipal government official
Gunn, S. Jeanne writer, artist, Reiki educator
Hajek, Francis Paul lawyer
Halpin, Timothy Patrick former air force officer
Harrison, William Wright retired banker
Heuser, George Kelly physician
Hilgers, John Jack William management and transportation consultant
Jones, Robert Clair middle school educator
Kawczynski, Diane Marie elementary and middle school educator, composer
†King, Stephen Miles public administration educator
Kodis, Mary Caroline marketing consultant
Kornylak, Harold John osteopathic physician
Layton, Garland Mason lawyer
Lowe, Cameron Anderson dentist, endodontist, educator
†MacDonald, Douglas Alexander educator
Mann, Harvey Blount retired banker
Maxwell, Donald L. municipal official
McDaniel, David Henry physician
Merchant, Donald Joseph retired microbiologist and educator
Morgan, Raymond Franklin education educator
Newsome, Moses social work educator
Oberndorf, Meyera E. mayor
O'Brien, Robert James financial consultant, business owner
Onsanit, Tawachai physician
Pefley, Charles Saunders real estate broker
Phillips, Joey Heyward special education educator
Polley, John Edward military officer
Price, Alan Thomas business and estate planner
Quicke, Andrew Charles cinema-television educator, consultant, writer
Radford, Gloria Jane retired medical/surgical nurse
Richardson, Daniel Putnam director
Ricketts, James municipal official
Robertson, Pat (Marion Gordon Robertson) religious broadcasting executive
Ruben, Leonard retired art educator
Sekulow, Jay Alan lawyer
Selig, William George university official
Seward, William W(ard), Jr. author, educator
Simmons, Marsha Thrift science and reading educator, musician
Smith, A. Robert editor, author
Smith, Ruth Hodges city clerk
Spitzli, Donald Hawkes, Jr. lawyer
Stanton, Pamela Freeman interior designer, writer
Stevens, Suzanne Duckworth artist, educator
Stockard, Joe Lee public health service officer, consultant
Sullivan, David C. municipal agency administrator
Swope, Richard McAllister retired lawyer
Szto, Mary Christine law educator
Toth, Stephen Michael electronics specialist
Turner, Susan Victoria architect intern, interior designer
Vita, James Paul software engineer
Von Mosch, Wanda Gail middle school educator
Warnstaff, Clarence O. municipal utilities executive
†White, Stephen James city planner, educator
Wick, Robert Thomas retired supermarket executive
Wicker, Richard Fenton, Jr. editor
Wiggins, Samuel Paul education educator
Williams, John Rodman theologian, educator
†Windsor, Michael Harold clergyman, educator
Zimmerman, Solomon dentist, educator

Wachapreague
Wilkins, (Ira) Guy painter, art teacher

Warm Springs
Orem, Henry Philip retired chemist, chemical engineer, consultant

Warrenton
Estaver, Paul Edward writer, poet
Fox, Raymond Graham educational technologist
Gullace, Marlene Frances information engineer, systems analyst, consultant
Henricson, Beth Ellen microbiologist
Howard, Blair Duncan Lawyer
Lutz, Elaine Elizabeth veterinarian
Malmgren, Harald Bernard economist
Norskog, Eugenia Folk elementary education educator
Rodgers, Lynne Saunders women's health nurse
Sass, Arthur Harold educational executive
Smith, William Raymond farmer, thoroughbred owner, breeder and trainer, retired history educator, philosophy educator

Washingtons Birthplace
Donahue, John Joseph park and recreation director

Waterford
Harper, James Weldon, III finance consultant
Harris, Caspa, Jr. lawyer, educator, association administrator

Waynesboro
Clark, Olive Iola retired secondary and elementary education educator
McNair, John William, Jr. civil engineer
Prye, Ellen Ross graphic designer

Weems
LaPrade, Carter lawyer

White Stone
Wroth, James Melvin former army officer, computer company executive

Williamsburg
Aaron, Bertram Donald corporation executive
Ackerman, Lennis Campbell management consultant retired
†Andrews, Timothy William public relations executive
Axtell, James Lewis history educator
Ball, Donald Lewis retired English language educator
Becker, Lawrence Carlyle philosopher, educator, author
Bernhardt, John Bowman banker
Birney, Robert Charles retired academic administrator, psychologist
Blouet, Brian Walter geography educator
Cell, Gillian Townsend historian, educator
Chappell, Miles Linwood, Jr. art history educator
Christison, Muriel Branham retired art museum director emeritus, fine arts educator
Church, Dale Walker lawyer
Coffman, Orene Burton hotel executive
Coleman, Henry Edwin art educator, artist
Connell, Alastair McCrae physician
Crapol, Edward P. history educator
Davis, Richard Bradley internal medicine, pathology educator, physician
Dhillon, Avtar Singh psychiatrist
Drum, Joan Marie McFarland federal agency administrator
Dunn, Ronald Holland civil engineer, management executive, consultant
Emerson, Philip G. historic site director
Esler, Anthony James historian, novelist, educator
Farrar, John Thruston health facility adminstrator
Fisher, Chester Lewis, Jr. retired lawyer
Fulmer, Robert M. business educator, management consultant
Garrison, George Hartranft Haley curator
Geddy, Vernon Meredith, Jr. lawyer
Gentry, James William retired state official
Goodwin, Bruce Kesseli retired geology educator, researcher
Gordon, Baron Jack stockbroker
Griffith, Melvin Eugene entomologist, public health official
Gross, Robert Alan history educator
Herbert, Albert Edward, Jr. interior and industrial designer
Herrmann, Benjamin Edward former insurance executive
Hoegerman, Stanton Fred cytogeneticist
Hoffman, Ronald historical institute administrator, educator
Holmes, David L. religion educator
Holt, Paul deCourcy, III city planner
Hornsby, Bruce Randall composer, musician
Hughes, George Farant, Jr. retired safety engineer
Humphreys, Homer Alexander former principal
Jacoby, William Jerome, Jr. internist, retired military officer
Johnston, Robert Atkinson psychologist, educator
Jones, David Proctor academic administrator
Kelm, Bonnie G. art museum director, educator
Kossler, William John physics educator
Kottas, John Frederick business administration educator
Lambert, Stephen Robert electrical engineer, consultant
Lange, Carl James psychology educator
Longsworth, Charles R. foundation administrator
Lorenz, Hans Ernest photographer
Lund, Wendell Luther retired lawyer
Lynn, Larry (Verne Lauriston Lynn) engineering executive
Maloney, Milford Charles retired internal medicine educator
Marcus, Paul law educator
McBeth, Elaine Susan university administrator
McGiffert, Michael retired history educator, editor
Mc Kean, John Rosseel Overton university dean
McLane, Henry Earl, Jr. philosophy educator
Messmer, Donald Joseph business management educator, marketing consultant
†Mills, Joan Elizabeth educator
Montgomery, Joseph William finance company executive
Muller, Julius Frederick chemist, business administrator
Nettels, Elsa English language educator
Oakley, John Howard humanities educator
O'Connell, William Edward, Jr. finance educator
Parham, Annette Relaford librarian
Pearson, Roy Laing business administration educator
Pipes, Robert Byron retired academic administrator, mechanical engineer
Price, Richard anthropologist, author
Regan, Donald Thomas financier, artist, lecturer
Roberson, Robert S. investment company executive
Robinson, Jay (Thurston) artist
Rodman, Leiba mathematics educator
Rogers, Leo P. deputy county attorney, educator
Rosche, Loretta G. medical, surgical nurse
Roseberg, Carl Andersson sculptor, educator
Rosen, Ellen Freda psychologist, educator
Scholnick, Robert J. college dean, English language educator
Schwartz, Miles Joseph cardiologist
Siegel, Robert Ted physicist
Sisk, Albert Fletcher, Jr. retired insurance agent
Smith, James Brown, Jr. secondary school educator
Smith, Roger Winston political theorist, educator
Spitzer, Cary Redford avionics consultant, electrical engineer
Stanley, Shirley Davis artist
Starnes, William Herbert, Jr. chemist, educator
Strong, John Scott finance educator
Sullivan, Timothy Jackson law educator, academic administrator
Sutton, Karen nurse, historian
Tate, Thaddeus W(ilbur), Jr. (Thad Tate) history educator, historical institute executive, historian
Van Tassel-Baska, Joyce Lenore education educator
Voorhess, Mary Louise pediatric endocrinologist
Wallach, Alan art historian, educator
Warren, William Herbert business administration educator
Webster, Robert Louis insurance company executive
Wehrly, Jack R. chemical company executive
Whitehead, James Madison law librarian
Whyte, James Primrose, Jr. former law educator
Wilburn, Robert Charles institute executive
Wilson, Paul Lowell lawyer, mortgage company executive
Winstead, Joy journalist, consultant
Zhang, Xiaodong computer scientist, educator, researcher

Winchester
Bechamps, Gerald Joseph surgeon
Bonometti, Robert John technology management and strategy executive
Braswell, Gary Joseph secondary school educator, military officer
Butler, Scot economist, researcher
Byrd, Harry Flood, Jr. newspaper executive, former senator
Engelage, James Roland business executive, consultant
Gaither, George Manney marketing consultant
Holland, James Tulley plastic products company executive
Hughes, Donna Jean librarian
Jamison, Richard Bryan airport consultant
Jolly, Bruce Dwight manufacturing company executive
Kohl, Harold missionary, educator
Ludwig, George Harry physicist
Meschutt, David Randolph historian, curator
Murtagh, John Edward alcohol production consultant
Pleacher, David Henry secondary school educator
Proe, John David business educator, consultant, administrator
†Sample, Travis Lamar business educator
Smith, Lanna Cheryl secondary school educator
Tisinger, Catherine Anne college dean
Wagner, Carolyn A(nn) adult and gerontological nurse practitioner

Wise
Lemons, L. Jay academic administrator
Smiddy, Joseph Charles retired college chancellor

Woodberry Forest
Campbell, Dennis Marion educator, university administrator, theologian

Woodbridge
Derrickson, Denise Ann secondary school educator
Dillaber, Philip Arthur budget and resource analyst, economist, consultant
Flori, Anna Marie DiBlasi nurse anesthetist, educational administrator
Garon, Richard Joseph, Jr. chief of staff, political worker
Graham, Reina Lynn rehabilitation counselor
Hood, Ronald Chalmers, III historian, writer
Packard, Mildred Ruth middle school educator
Richardson, Sharon Young marketing professional
Rose, Marianne Hunt business educator
†Soyer, Aysegul neurologist
Townsend, Kenneth Ross retired priest
Woods, Barbara A. Shell psychotherapist

Woodstock
Duceman, Mark Eugene county zoning administrator, planner
Hull, Linda Weaver outreach coordinator
Kabriel, Marcia Gail psychotherapist
Walker, Charles Norman retired insurance company executive
Walton, Morgan Lauck, III lawyer

Woodville
Mc Carthy, Eugene Joseph writer, former senator

Wytheville
†DiYorio, John Salvatore chemistry educator
McConnell, James Joseph internist
Wright, Donald Gene accountant

Yorktown
Forrest, Kay V. educator, editor, writer
Gross, Leroy sugar company executive
Rogers, Sheila Wood elementary and secondary school educator
Stinnette, Timothy Earl minister

WASHINGTON

Anacortes
Higgins, Robert (Walter) military officer, physician
Holtby, Kenneth Fraser manufacturing executive
Kuure, Bojan Marlena operating room nurse
Mc Cracken, Philip Trafton sculptor
Randolph, Carl Lowell chemical company executive

Auburn
†Anderson, Brian Lynn urologist
Blum, Sarah Leah nurse psychotherapist
Colburn, Gene Lewis insurance and industrial consultant
Dillon, Joseph Neil pastor
Duhnke, Robert Emmet, Jr. retired aerospace engineer
Eaton, Edgar Eugene retird educator, writer
Howard, George Harmon management consultant
Ketchersid, Wayne Lester, Jr. medical technologist
Maier, Anthony Alvin pastor, counselor
Sata, Lindbergh Saburo psychiatrist, physician, educator
Sims, Marcie Lynne English language educator, writer
Westbo, Leonard Archibald, Jr. electronics engineer
Willson, David Allen reference librarian, writer

Bainbridge Island
Blumenthal, Richard Cary construction executive, consultant
Bowden, William Darsie retired interior designer
Carlson, Robert Michael artist
Cioc, Charles Gregory information systems executive
Eber, Lorenz aeronautical engineer, civil engineer, inventor
Glosten, Lawrence Robert engineering executive
Huntley, James Robert government official, international affairs scholar and consultant
Milander, Henry Martin educational consultant
Moyemont, Terry Walter video producer, videographer
Schmidt, Karen Anne travel company executive, state legislator
†Snydal, James Matthew poet

Battle Ground
Fineran, Diana Lou association administrator
Hansen, James Lee sculptor
Morris, William Joseph paleontologist, educator

Bellevue
Abboud, G. Jason telecommunications executive, consultant, engineer
Akutagawa, Donald psychologist, educator
Andersen, James A. retired state supreme court justice
Arnold, Robert Lloyd investment broker, financial advisor
Arnold, Ronald Henri nonprofit organization executive, consultant
Benveniste, Jacob retired physicist
Bergstrom, Marianne Elisabeth program coordinator, special education educator
Berkley, James Donald clergyman
Boespflug, John Francis, Jr. lawyer
†Bondarook, Nina public relations consultant
†Burleson, Hugh Latimer, II retired foreign service officer, translator
Clay, Orson C. insurance company executive
Davidson, Robert William merchant banker
Dickerson, Eugenie Ann writer, journalist
Dow, Daniel Gould electrical engineering educator
Edde, Howard Jasper retired engineering executive
Edwards, Kirk Lewis real estate company executive
Erickson, Virginia Bemmels chemical engineer
Evans, Robert Vincent sales and marketing executive
Flom, Robert Michael interior designer
†Frei, Brent R. computer software executive
Fremouw, Edward Joseph physicist
Graham, John Robert, Jr. financial executive
Groten, Barnet energy company executive
Gulick, Peter VanDyke lawyer
Hackett, Carol Ann Hedden physician
Hall, Eleanor Williams public relations executive
Hibbard, Richard Paul industrial ventilation consultant, lecturer
Hoag, Paul Sterling architect
Hovind, David J. manufacturing company executive
Johnson, Gary Kent management education company executive
Jones, John Wesley entrepreneur
Kiest, Alan Scott social services administrator
Kimball, Mark Douglas lawyer
Landau, Felix lawyer
Lauver, Lydia Monserrat Ollis public relations executive
Matsumoto, Shinichi surgeon, researcher
Meeker, Milton Shy manufacturing company executive
Morie, G. Glen lawyer, manufacturing company executive
Mutschler, Herbert Frederick retired librarian
Nowik, Dorothy Adam medical equipment company executive
†Otterholt, Barry L. technology management consultant
Parks, Donald Lee mechanical engineer, human factors engineer
†Passage, James Thompson engineering executive
†Pastore, Michael Anthony college administrator
Phillips, Zaiga Alksnis pediatrician
Pigott, Charles McGee transportation equipment manufacturing executive
Pigott, Mark C. automotive executive
†Pool, David software executive
Rossi, Amadeo Joseph chemist
Salerno, Joseph Michael retired air cargo company executive
Schairer, George Swift aeronautical engineer
Schuiski, Larry Leroy information scientist
Sebris, Robert, Jr. lawyer
Smith, Lester Martin broadcasting executive
Speer, Paul Alan record producer, recording artist
Treacy, Gerald Bernard, Jr. lawyer
Warren, James Ronald retired museum director, author, columnist
Warsinke, Norman George interior designer, sculptor
Weaver, William Schildecker electric power industry executive
Wells-Henderson, Ronald John investment counselor
Williams, Jerald Arthur mechanical engineer
Wright, Theodore Otis forensic engineer

Bellingham
Albrecht, Albert Pearson electronics engineer, consultant
Anderson, David Bowen lawyer
Becker, Michael Kelleher university administrator, consultant
Bestwick, Warren William retired construction company executive
Burdge, Rabel James sociology educator
Doerper, John Erwin publisher, editor
Fiero, Petra Schug language professional educator
Haensly, Patricia Anastacia psychology educator
Haggen, Donald E. food products executive
Hoover, Kenneth Ray political science educator, writer
Howe, Warren Billings physician
Jansen, Robert Bruce consulting civil engineer
Johnson, Jennifer Lucky psychotherapist
Johnstone, Kenneth Ernest electronics and business consultant
Larner, Daniel M. theater educator, playwright, author
Little, Marie Ann ESL educator, program facilitator
Morse, Joseph Grant chemistry educator
Morse, Karen Williams academic administrator
Nugent, Frank Anthony psychology educator
Olsen, Mark Norman small business owner
Packer, Mark Barry lawyer, financial consultant, foundation official, mediator
Parker, Diana L. nurse, consultant
Raas, Daniel Alan lawyer
Uhrig, Ira John attorney, court commissioner
Wayne, Marvin Alan emergency medicine physician
Whisenhunt, Donald Wayne history educator

Biemerton
McClung, J(ames) David corporate executive, lawyer

Black Diamond
Morris, David John mining engineer, consultant, mining executive

Blaine
James, Herb Mark (Jay James) foundation and insurance executive, free trade consultant

Bothell
Alvi, Khisal Ahmed chemist
Banks, Cherry Ann McGee education educator
Cao, Thai-Hai industrial engineer
Cothern, Barbara Shick county official
Hoffman, Marianne Macina corporate relations administrator
Icenhower, Rosalie B. retired elementary school principal
Jacobs, Harold Robert mechanical engineering educator, practitioner
McDonald, Michael Lee clinic administrator, retired naval officer
Sakkal, Mamoun architect, interior designer

Bremerton
Garrison, Eva Heim school counselor
Genuit, David Walter podiatrist

Hanf, James Alphonso *poet, government official*
Joseph, James Edward *mechanical engineering technician*
Rickerson, Jean Marie *video producer, journalist, photographer*
Schuyler, Michael Robert *librarian*
†Shephard, Deane Anthony *mechanical and design engineer*

Buckley
Christensen, Doris Ann *antique dealer, researcher, writer*

Burlington
Herbaugh, Roger Duane *computer and software company executive*

Camano Island
Blair, Edward Payson *theology educator*
de Vries, Rimmer *economist*

Camas
Liem, Annie *pediatrician*

Carnation
Beshur, Jacqueline E. *pet training consultant, writer*

Centralia
Brunswig, Jessie *executive assistant*
Buzzard, Steven Ray *lawyer*
Kirk, Henry Port *academic administrator*
Kyte, Lydiane *retired botanist*
Miller, James McCalmont *pediatrician*

Chehalis
Burrows, Robert Paul *optometrist*
Detrick, Donald Howard *minister*
Neal-Parker, Shirley Anita *obstetrician and gynecologist*

Cheney
†Jordan, Stephen M. *university president*
Pfeifer, Jocelyn *women's collegiate basketball coach*

Chimacum
Hollenbeck, Dorothy Rose *special education educator*

Clarkston
McCullough, Yvonne *counselor, educator*

Clinton
Forward, Robert L(ull) *physicist, businessman, consultant, writer*

Clyde Hill
Condon, Robert Edward *surgeon, educator, consultant*

Colfax
Beckmann, Michele Lillian *secretary*
Webster, Ronald B. *lawyer*

Colton
†Straughan, Gene Thomas *educator*

Colville
Higginbotham, Edith Arleane *radiologist, researcher*

Concrete
Mincin, Karl John *nutritionist, educator*

Coupeville
Canfield, Stella Stojanka *artist, art gallery owner*
Eaton, Gordon Pryor *geologist*
Lotzenhiser, George William *music educator, university administrator, composer*
Warren, Patricia J. *arts association executive*

Dayton
McFarland, Jon Weldon *retired county commissioner*

Deer Park
Griffin, Leslie Dee *educational administrator*

Des Moines
Brandmeir, Christopher Lee *hospitality and food service consultant*
Ortmeyer, Carl Edward *retired demographer*
Tuell, Jack Marvin *retired bishop*

Dupont
Pettit, Ghery St. John *electronics engineer*

Eastsound
Anders, William Alison *aerospace and defense manufacturing executive*
Fowles, George Richard *physicist, educator*

Edmonds
Bell, Nancy Lee Hoyt *real estate investor, middle school educator, volunteer*
†Bell, Ralph Rogers *retired superintendent schools, genealogist*
Brinton, Richard Kirk *marketing executive*
Crone, Richard Allan *cardiologist, educator*
Decker, Sharyn Lynn *newspaper reporter*
Deering, Anne-Lise *artist, real estate salesperson*
DeForeest, Joanne Marie *educator*
Dunbar, R. Allan *college administrator, clergyman*
Galster, Richard W. *engineering geologist*
Johnson, d'Elaine Ann Herard *artist*
Johnson, LuAn *disaster management consultant*
Kim, Sang U. *gastroenterologist*
Monroe, James Walter *retired organization executive*
Owen, John *retired newspaper editor*
Parrish, John Brett *business executive*
Paul, Ronald Stanley *research institute executive*
Peckol, James Kenneth *consulting engineer*
Schmit, Lucien André, Jr. *structural engineer*
Terrel, Ronald Lee *civil engineer, business executive, educator*
Yoon, Jay Myoung *oncologist, hematologist, internist*

Ellensburg
Cadello, James Peter *philosopher, educator*
Collins, Fuji *mental health professional*
Comstock, Dale Robert *mathematics educator*
Housner, Jeanette Ann *artist, jeweler*
†Janke, John Eric *secondary educator*
†Kline, Celeste Marie *librarian*
Nelson, Ivory Vance *academic administrator*
Parker-Fairbanks, Dixie *artist*
Paul, Virginia Otto *writer, administrator*
Rosell, Sharon Lynn *physics and chemistry educator, researcher*
Shults, Mary J. *retail store owner*
Yu, Roger Hong *physics educator*

Enumclaw
Vernier, Richard *educator, author*

Ephrata
Aiken, Michael DeWayne *lawyer*
Fitterer, Richard Clarence *judge*

Everett
Adams, Victoria Eleanor *retired realty company executive*
Beegle, Earl Dennis *family physician*
Hundley, Ronnie *academic administrator*
Krahn, Thomas Frank *photographer*
Labayen, Louie Anthony Lopez *information analyst, consultant*
Mestel, Mark David *lawyer*
Miller, Robert Scott *mental health administrator, social worker*
Nelson, Gary *county councilman, engineer*
Oliver, William Donald *orthodontist*
Valentine, Mark Conrad *dermatologist*
Van Ry, Ginger Lee *school psychologist*
Waldron, Richard Frederick *musician, educator*

Everson
McGulpin, Elizabeth Jane *nurse*

Federal Way
Boling, Joseph Edward *numismatist, retired military officer*
Cunningham, John Randolph *systems analyst*
Dorman, Thomas Alfred *internist, orthopaedist*
Duggan, Edward Martin *secondary education educator*
Mail, Patricia Davison *public health specialist*
Mast, Robert F. *structural engineer*
Muzyka-McGuire, Amy *marketing professional, nutrition consultant*
Studebaker, Irving Glen *mining engineering consultant*

Ferndale
Jordan, Marvin Evans, Jr. *record company executive*

Fircrest
Martin, Robert Joseph *dermatologist*

Fort Lewis
†Edwards, Warren Chappelle *military career officer*
Maher, Cornelius Creedon, III *neurologist, toxicologist, army officer*
†Smith, Zannie O. *army officer*

Freeland
Freehill, Maurice F. *retired educational psychology educator*

Friday Harbor
Agosta, William Carleton *chemist, educator*
Brookbank, John W(arren) *retired microbiology educator*
Buck, Robert Follette *retired banker, lawyer*
Gonser, Thomas Howard *lawyer, former bar association executive*
Waite, Ric *cinematographer*

Gig Harbor
Bratrud, Linda Kay *secondary education educator*
Canter, Ralph Raymond *psychology educator, research director*
Cuzzetto, Charles Edward *accountant, financial analyst, educator*
Hedman, Janice Lee *business executive*
McGill, Charles Morris *physician, consultant*
McMahan, Lois Grace *former state legislator*
†Nelson, Jo Ann *writer, educator*
Robinson, James William *retired management consultant*
Thompson, Ronald Edward *lawyer*
Wissmann, Carol Reneé *sales executive*

Goldendale
Musgrave, Lee *artist, museum administrator*
Nygaard, Mary Payne *primary school education*
Watson, Darrell Valentine, Jr. *church administrator*

Greenacres
Panter, Sara Jane *medical/surgical nurse*

Hamilton
Anderson, Duwayne Marlo *earth and polar scientist, university administrator*

Hansville
Blalock, Ann Bonar *policy analyst, evaluation researcher*

Hoquiam
Kessler, Keith Leon *lawyer*

Independence
Feng, Xiangdong Shawn *chemist*

Index
Davis, Peter (Peter Pathfinder Davis) *priest*

Issaquah
Barchet, Stephen *physician, former naval officer*
Benoliel, Joel *lawyer*
Brotman, Jeffrey H. *variety stores executive*
Hunt, Robert William *theatrical producer, data processing consultant*
Newbill, Karen Margaret *elementary school educator, education educator*
Reid, John Mitchell (Jack Reid) *biomedical engineer, researcher*
Sinegal, James D. *variety store wholesale business executive*
Stanley, James Gordon *retired engineering marketing executive, writer*
Tenenbaum, Michael *steel company executive*
Trask, Robert Chauncey Riley *author, lecturer, foundation executive*
Wainwright, Paul Edward Blech *construction company executive*

Kenmore
Guy, Arthur William *electrical engineering educator, researcher*

Kennewick
Hames, William Lester *lawyer*
Knight, Janet Ann *elementary education educator*
Stevens, Henry August *insurance agent, educator*

Kent
Bangsund, Edward Lee *former aerospace company executive, consultant*
†Brannen, George Elsdon *surgeon*
Goo, Abraham Meu Sen *retired aircraft company executive*
Hebeler, Henry Koester *retired aerospace and electronics executive*
Hickey, Shirley Louise Cowin *elementary education educator*
Irwin, Deborah Jo *secondary education educator, flutist*
Johnson, Dennis D. *elementary school principal*
†Klennert, Daniel Charles *artist*
O'Bara, Kenneth J. *physician*
Pettigrew, Dana Mary *musician, insurance agent*
Pierce, Danny Parcel *artist, educator*
Schneider, Eugene Saul *microbiologist, laboratory administrator*
†White, Dana Eileen *public health research and evaluation assistant*
Williams, Max Lea, Jr. *engineer, educator*

Kirkland
Barto, Deborah Ann *physician*
Biggs, Thomas Wylie *chemical company executive*
Boxleitner, Warren James *electrical engineer, researcher*
Brown, Chadwick Everett *football player*
Clarkson, Lawrence William *airplane company executive*
Collins, Mark *professional football player*
Dorkin, Frederic Eugene *lawyer*
Dunn, Jeffrey Edward *neurologist*
Glover, Kevin *football player*
Goldman, Ralph Morris *political science educator*
Holden, Fred Stephen *industrial tree farmer*
Holmgren, Mike *professional football coach*
Hooper, Steven W. *communications executive*
Kennedy, Cortez *professional football player*
Ladd, James Roger *international business executive and consultant*
Look, Janet K. *psychologist*
McDonald, Joseph Lee *insurance broker*
Melby, Orville Erling *retired banker*
Puckett, Allen Weare *health care information systems executive*
Rich, Clayton *retired university official and educator*
Ryles, Gerald Fay *private investor, business executive*
Steinmann, John Colburn *architect*
Szablya, Helen Mary *author, language professional, lecturer*
Szablya, John Francis *electrical engineer, consultant*
Tyllia, Frank Michael *university official, educator*
Watters, Richard James *professional football player*
Wenk, Edward, Jr. *civil engineer, policy analyst, educator, writer*
Wolff, Joel Henry *human factors engineer, lawyer*

La Center
Holley, Lawrence Alvin *retired labor union official*

La Conner
Knopf, Kenyon Alfred *economist, educator*
†Mack, James Willard *artist, educator*
Robbins, Thomas Eugene *author*

Lacey
Edwards, Margaret H. *English as second language instructor*
Jones, Kelley Simmons *therapist, social worker*
Kuniyasu, Keith Kazumi *secondary education educator*
†Reilich, Eileen *education educator*
Shkurkin, Ekaterina Vladimirovna (Katia Shkurkin) *social worker*
Spangler, David Robert *college administrator, engineer*
Wells, Roger Stanley *software engineer*

Lake Forest Park
Favorite, Felix *oceanographer*

Lake Stevens
Quigley, Kevin Walsh *state legislator, lawyer*

Lakewood
Buchanan, Enid Jane *healthcare professional, housing administrator*
Monk, Gordon Ray *recreation therapist*
Oakes, DuWayne Earl *retired principal*

Langley
Kenny, Robert Martin *organizational development consultant*

Leavenworth
Bergren, Helen Duffey *retired nurse*
Wadlington, William Jewell *principal, secondary education educator*

Liberty Lake
Anderson, Gregory Martin *medical company representative*

Lilliwaup
McGrady, Corinne Young *design company executive*

Littlerock
Gunderson, Cleon Henry *management consultant corporation executive*

Longview
Campbell, Kristine Koetting *academic administrator*
Kirkpatrick, Richard Alan *internist*
Moosburner, Nancy *nutritionist*
Natt, Theodore McClelland *newspaper editor, publisher*
Sandstrom, Robert Edward *physician, pathologist*
Williamson, Debra Faye *performing arts educator*
Wollenberg, Richard Peter *paper manufacturing company executive*

Lopez Island
Whetten, John Theodore *geologist*

Lummi Island
Ewing, Benjamin Baugh *environmental engineering educator, consultant*

Lynnwood
Bear, Gregory Dale *writer, illustrator*
Jenes, Theodore George, Jr. *retired career officer*
Krause, Thomas Evans *record promotion and radio consultant*
Moore, Susan Lynn *writer, television producer*
†Oharah, Jack *academic administrator*
Olsen, Kenneth Harold *geophysicist, astrophysicist*
Stocking, Sherl Dee *retail executive*
Woodruff, Scott William *cosmetic, reconstructive and maxillofacial surgeon*

Malaga
Nanto, Roxanna Lynn *marketing professional, management consultant*

Manson
Hackenmiller, Thomas Raymond *writer, publisher*
Stager, Donald K. *construction company executive, retired*

Maple Valley
Brown, Thomas Andrew *retired aircraft/weaponry manufacturing executive*

Marysville
Bartholomew, Shirley Kathleen *municipal official*
McClure, Allan Howard *materials engineer, space contamination specialist, space materials consultant*

Mazama
Hogness, John Rusten *physician, academic administrator*

Medical Lake
Grub, Phillip Donald *business educator*

Medina
Schlotterbeck, Walter Albert *manufacturing company executive, lawyer*
Waldmann, Raymond John *aerospace executive*
Ward, Marilyn Beeman *commissioner*
Wong, Janet Siu *writer*

Mercer Island
Adams, Belinda Jeanette Spain *nursing administrator*
Berman, Gizel *sculptor*
Coe, Robert Campbell *retired surgeon*
Dykstra, David Charles *management executive, consultant, accountant, author, educator*
Elgee, Neil Johnson *retired internist and endocrinologist, educator*
Francis, Carolyn Rae *music educator, musician, author, publisher*
Gould, Alvin R. *international business executive*
Herres, Phillip Benjamin *computer software executive*
Langhout-Nix, Nelleke *artist*
Porad, Francine Joy *poet, painter*
Spitzer, Jack J. *banker*
Steinhardt, Henry *photographer*

Mill Creek
Bacon, Vinton Walker *civil engineer*
Corbally, John Edward *foundation director*
Larson, Mary Bea *elementary education educator*
†Nelson, Elinor S. *human resources consultant, labor mediator*

Monroe
Kirwan, Katharyn Grace (Mrs. Gerald Bourke Kirwan, Jr.) *retail executive*
Nguyen-Ely, Darlene *sculptor*

Montesano
Clausel, Nancy Karen *minister*

Mount Vernon
Bogensberger, Joan Helen Hess *school administrator, consultant*
Cline, Pauline M. *educational administrator*
Garcia, John *psychologist, educator*
Gaston, Margaret Anne *retired business educator*
Hall, David Ramsay *architect*
Havist, Marjorie Victoria *librarian, educator*
Klein, Henry *architect*
Meyer, John Michael *judge*
Moser, C. Thomas *lawyer*
Poppe, Patricia Lee *clinical social worker, consultant*

Mountlake Terrace
English, Donald Marvin *loss control representative*
Rapp, Nina Beatrice *financial company executive*

Mukilteo
Bohn, Dennis Allen *electrical engineer, executive*

Napavine
Morgan-Fadness, Corrina May *staff charge nurse*

Newcastle
†Meshke, Paul John *business consultant*

Nine Mile Falls
Payne, Arlie Jean *parent education administrator*

North Bend
Kaplan, Donna Elaine *artist, educator*

Oak Harbor
Corey, Stuart Merton *minister*
Crampton, George Harris *neuroscientist, retired army officer*

Diggs, Bradley C. lawyer
Dillard, Marilyn Dianne property manager
Dimmick, Carolyn Reaber federal judge
Dively, Dwight Douglas finance director
Dolan, Andrew Kevin lawyer
Dorpat, Theodore Lorenz psychoanalyst
Drew, Jody Lynne secondary education educator
Dubes, Michael John insurance company executive
Duckworth, Tara Ann insurance company executive
Dunner, David Louis medicine educator
Duryee, David Anthony management consultant
Dworkin, Samuel Franklin dentist, psychologist
Dwyer, William L. federal judge
Dyer, Philip E. insurance company executive
†Eastham, John D. business executive
Ebell, C(ecil) Walter lawyer
Edmondson, W(allace) Thomas retired limnologist, educator
Eigsti, Roger Harry insurance company executive
Ellegood, Donald Russell publishing executive
Ellings, Richard James political and economic research institution executive
Elliott, Clifton Langsdale lawyer
Ellis, James Reed lawyer
Ellis, John W. professional baseball team executive, utility company executive
Ellison, Herbert Jay history educator
Elyn, Mark retired opera singer, educator
Emory, Meade lawyer
Erdmann, Joachim Christian physicist
Eschbach, Joseph Wetherill nephrology educator
Etcheson, Warren Wade business administration educator
Euster, Joanne Reed retired librarian
Evans, Bernard William geologist, educator
Evans, Charles Albert microbiology educator
Evans, Daniel Jackson former senator
Evans, Ellis Dale psychologist, educator
Evans, Richard Lloyd financial services company executive
Everett, Virginia Sauerbrun counselor
Fadden, Delmar McLean electrical engineer
Fancher, Michael Reilly newspaper editor, newspaper publishing executive
†Farbanish, Thomas sculptor
Farrell, Anne Van Ness foundation executive
Farrington-Hopf, Susan Kay plumbing and heating contractor
Farris, Jerome federal judge
Faulstich, James R. retired bank executive
Fay, Christopher Wayne mechanical engineer, consultant
Feiss, George James, III financial services company executive
Felton, Samuel Page biochemist
Figley, Melvin Morgan radiologist, physician, educator
Fine, James Stephen physician
Finlayson, Bruce Alan chemical engineering educator
Fischer, Edmond Henri biochemistry educator
Fischer, Fred Walter physicist, engineer, educator
Fischer, Mary E. special education educator
Fitzpatrick, Thomas Mark lawyer
Fix, Wilbur James department store executive
Fletcher, Betty B. federal judge
Floss, Heinz G. chemistry educator, scientist
Forbes, David Craig musician
Fortson, Edward Norval physics educator
Freedman, Bart Joseph lawyer
Freeny, Patrick Clinton radiology educator, consultant
Gabbe, Steven Glenn physician, educator
Galvan, Elias Gabriel bishop
Gandara, Daniel lawyer
Gardiner, John Jacob leadership studies educator, author, philosopher
Gardiner, T(homas) Michael artist
Gartz, Paul Ebner systems engineer
Garvens, Ellen Jo art educator, artist
Gaskill, Herbert Leo accountant, engineer
Gates, Mimi Gardner museum administrator
Gates, Theodore Allan, Jr. database administrator
Geballe, Ronald physicist, university dean
Gerberding, William Passavant retired university president
Gerhart, James Basil physics educator
Gerrodette, Charles Everett real estate company executive, consultant
Gerstenberger, Donna Lorine humanities educator
Gerwick-Brodeur, Madeline Carol marketing and timing professional
Geyman, John Payne physician, educator
Gibaldi, Milo dean
Giblett, Eloise Rosalie hematology educator
Gilbert, Paul H. engineering executive, consultant
Gilder, George communications executive, writer
Giles, Robert Edward, Jr. lawyer
Gillispie, Steven Brian systems analyst, researcher
Gist, Marilyn Elaine organizational behavior and human resource management educator
Gittinger, D. Wayne lawyer
Givan, Boyd Eugene aircraft company executive
Glaser, Rob communications company executive
†Glass, Stephen Tolman pediatric neurologist
†Glover, Thomas T. federal judge
Godden, Jean W. columnist
Goeltz, Thomas A. lawyer
Golston, Joan Carol psychotherapist
Goodlad, John Inkster education educator, author
Gordon, Milton Paul biochemist, educator
Gore, William Jay political science educator
Gores, Thomas C. lawyer
Gormezano, Keith arbitrator, writer, marketer
Gottlieb, Daniel Seth lawyer
Gouldthorpe, Kenneth Alfred Percival publisher, state official
Gouterman, Martin Paul chemistry educator
Govedare, Philip Bainbridge artist, educator
Graham, Stephen Michael lawyer
Gray, Marvin Lee, Jr. lawyer
Grayston, J. Thomas medical and public health educator
Green, Joshua, III banker
Greenan, Thomas J. lawyer
Greene, John Burkland lawyer
Greene, Martin Lee internist
Greenwood, W. R., III investment banker
Gregory, Norman Wayne chemistry educator, researcher
Griffey, Ken, Jr. (George Kenneth Griffey, Jr.) professional baseball player
Griffin, William R. consulting company executive
Grimley, Janet Elizabeth newspaper editor
Grinstein, Gerald transportation executive
Groff, David Clark, Jr. lawyer
Groman, Neal Benjamin microbiology educator
Gross, Catherine Mary (Kate Gross) writer, educator
Gross, Edward retired sociologist, educator, lawyer
Grossman, Robert James architect
Gunter, Laurie M. retired nurse educator
Guntheroth, Warren Gaden physician
Guskin, Alan E. university president
Gustafson, Alice Fairleigh lawyer
Guy, Andrew A. lawyer
Guzak, Karen Jean Wahlstrom artist
Gwinn, Mary Ann newspaper reporter
Hackett, John Peter dermatologist
Hall, Stanton Harris dental educator, orthodontist
Halver, John Emil nutritional biochemist
Haman, Raymond William lawyer
Hampton, Shelley Lynn hearing impaired educator
Han, Mao-Tang surgeon, researcher
Hansen, Wayne W. lawyer
Hanson, William Lewis lawyer
Haralick, Robert Martin electrical engineering educator
Harder, Virgil Eugene business administration educator
Hargiss, James Leonard ophthalmologist
Harmon, Daniel Patrick classics educator
Harrington, LaMar curator, museum director
Harrison, Don Edmunds oceanographer, educator
Hartl, John George film critic
Hartwell, Leland Harrison geneticist, educator
Hastings, L(ois) Jane architect, educator
Hazelton, Penny Ann law librarian, educator
Heath, George Ross oceanographer
Hecht, Irene Margret lawyer
Heer, Nicholas Lawson Arabist and Islamist educator
Hegyvary, Sue Thomas nursing school dean
†Helgath, Sheila Fay environmental company executive
†Helgerson, Steven Dale epidemiologist, educator
Henderson, Maureen McGrath medical educator
†Henderson, Scottie Yvette researcher
Hendrickson, Anita Elizabeth biology educator
Henley, Ernest Mark physics educator, university dean emeritus
Herman, Lloyd Eldred curator, consultant, writer
Herring, Susan Weller dental educator, oral anatomist
Hertzberg, Abraham aeronautical engineering educator, university research scientist
Hill, G. Richard lawyer
Hille, Bertil physiology educator
Hills, Regina J. journalist
Hilpert, Edward Theodore, Jr. lawyer
Hinshaw, Mark Larson architect, urban planner
Hirondelle, Anne Elizabeth ceramic artist
Hirschman, Charles, Jr. sociologist, educator
Hodge, Paul William astronomer, educator
Hoffman, Allan Sachs chemical engineer, educator
Holm, Vanja Adele developmental pediatrician, educator
Holmes, King Kennard medical educator
Hom, Richard Yee research engineer
Hood, Leroy Edward molecular biologist, educator
Hornbein, Thomas Frederic anesthesiologist
†Horsey, David editorial cartoonist
Hough, John Dennis public relations executive
†Hsiang, John neurosurgeon
Huchthausen, David Richard sculptor, real estate developer
Hudson, Leonard Dean physician
Huey, Constance Anne Berner mental health counselor
Huff, Gary D. lawyer
Hunthausen, Raymond Gerhardt archbishop
†Huntsman, Lee university provost, academic administrator
Huston, John Charles law educator
Hutcheson, Mark Andrew lawyer
Ii, Jack Morito aerospace engineer
Ingalls, Robert Lynn physicist, educator
Isaki, Lucy Power Slyngstad lawyer
Ishimaru, Akira electrical engineering educator
Israel, Allen D. lawyer
Jackson, Dillon Edward lawyer
Jacobson, Phillip Lee architect, educator
Jenkins, Speight opera company executive, writer
Jennerich, Edward John university official and dean
Johnson, Bruce Edward Humble lawyer
Johnson, Wayne Eaton writer, editor, former drama critic
Johnston, Norman John architecture educator
Johnston, William Frederick emergency services administrator
Jonassen, James O. architect
Jones, Edward Louis historian, educator
Jones, Grant Richard landscape architect, planner
Jones, Samuel conductor
Jonsen, Albert R. retired medical ethics educator
Joppa, Robert Glenn aeronautics educator
Judson, C(harles) James (Jim Judson) lawyer
Kahn, Steven Emanuel medical educator
Kalina, Robert Edward physician, educator
Kane, Alan Henry lawyer
Kane, Christopher lawyer
Kaplan, Barry Martin lawyer
Kapur, Kailash Chander industrial engineering educator
Karr, James Richard ecologist, educator, research director
Kasama, Hideto Peter accountant, business advisor, real estate consultant
Katz, Charles J., Jr. lawyer
Keegan, John E. lawyer
Kelley, John F. airline executive
Kellogg, Kenyon P. lawyer
Kelly, Dennis Ray sales executive
Kenney, Richard Laurence poet, English language educator
Keyt, David philosophy and classics educator
Kibble, Edward Bruce insurance-investment advisory company executive
Killinger, Kerry Kent bank executive
King, Mary-Claire geneticist, educator
Kippenhan, Charles Jacob mechanical engineer, retired educator
Klebanoff, Seymour Joseph medical educator
Klee, Victor La Rue mathematician, educator
Klein, Otto G., III lawyer
Knox, Venerria L. municipal or county official
Kobayashi, Albert Satoshi mechanical engineering educator
Koehler, Reginald Stafford, III lawyer
Koerber, Linda René Givens educator, counselor
Kohn, Alan J. zoology educator
Kolb, Keith Robert architect, educator
Korg, Jacob English literature educator
Korn, Jessica Susan education educator, researcher, ambassador
Kraft, Donald Bowman advertising agency executive
Kraft, Elaine Joy community relations and communications official
Kraft, George Howard physician, educator
Krebs, Edwin Gerhard biochemistry educator
Krochalis, Richard F. municipal government official
Krohn, Kenneth Albert radiology educator
Kruckeberg, Arthur Rice botanist, educator
Kruse, Paul Robert retired librarian, educator
Kuhl, Patricia K. science educator
Kuhrau, Edward W. lawyer
Kunkel, Georgie Bright writer, retired school counselor
Kwiram, Alvin L. physical chemistry educator, university official
Lacitis, Erik journalist
Lackie, Kenneth William physical scientist
Laing, Thomas Dallas, Jr. marine surveyor, salvage consultant
Lang, Kurt sociologist, educator, writer
†Langford, Jean Marie cultural anthropologist
LaPoe, Wayne Gilpin retired business executive
Lauritzen, Peter Owen electrical engineering educator
Lawrence, Jacob artist, educator
Leale, Olivia Mason import marketing company executive
Lee, John Marshall mathematics educator
Lee, Qwihee Park plant physiologist
Leitzell, Terry Lee lawyer
Lemly, Thomas Adger lawyer
Liljebeck, Roy C. transportation company executive
Lindsey, Gina Marie airport executive
Lingafelter, Edward Clay, Jr. chemistry educator
Livingston, Patricia Ann marine biologist, researcher
Loftus, Thomas Daniel lawyer
Lombard, David Norman lawyer
Lord, Jere Johns retired physics educator
Lovett, Wendell Harper architect
Lubatti, Henry Joseph physicist, educator
Lundgren, Gail M. lawyer
MacDonald, Andrew Stephen management consulting firm executive
Mackenzie, Donald Matthew, Jr. minister
MacLachlan, Douglas Lee marketing educator
Mah, Feng-hwa economics educator
Malcolm, Garold Dean architect
Maleng, Norm prosecuting attorney
Malins, Donald Clive biochemistry, researcher
Mallory, V(irgil) Standish geologist, educator
Malone, Thomas William lawyer
Mankoff, David Abraham nuclear medicine physician
Margon, Bruce Henry astrophysicist, educator
Marshall, David Stanley lawyer
†Martensen, Keith Charles cattle company executive
Martin, George Coleman aeronautical engineer
Martin, George M. pathologist, gerontologist, educator
Martinez, Edgar professional baseball player
Matchett, William H(enry) English literature educator
Mathis, Teresa Gale association executive
Matsen, Frederick Albert, III orthopedic educator
Matthews, Donald Rowe political scientist, educator
McAleer, William Harrison software venture capitalist
McCann, Richard Eugene lawyer
McConnell, J. Daniel sports marketing professional
McCormick, Richard Levis academic administrator
McFarland, Lynne Vernice pharmaceutical executive
Mc Feron, Dean Earl mechanical engineer
Mc Govern, Walter T. federal judge
McHugh, Heather poet
†Mc Intyre, Vonda Neel author
McKay, Michael Dennis lawyer
†McKeown, Mary Margaret judge
McKinnon, James Buckner real estate sales executive, writer, researcher
McKinstry, Ronald Eugene lawyer
McMahon, John Joseph college official
McReynolds, Neil Lawrence management consultant
Meditch, James Stephen electrical engineering educator
Medved, Michael film critic, author, talk show host
†Melendez, Rosa Maria United States marshall
Mennella, Vincent Alfred automotive manufacturing and airplane company executive
Merendino, K. Alvin surgical educator
Merkle, Alan Ray lawyer
Michael, Ernest Arthur mathematics educator
Miller, Paige port executive
Miller, Robert Carmi, Jr. microbiology educator, university administrator
Mines, Michael lawyer
Mitchum, Beth bookstore manager
Miyata, Keijiro culinary arts educator
Moch, Robert Gaston lawyer
Mohai, Peter internist, rheumatologist, research administrator
Monsen, Elaine Ranker nutritionist, educator, editor
Moore, Benjamin theatrical producer
Moore, Daniel Charles physician
Moore, Judith Ann educational administrator
Moore, Ronald Melville Philosophy educator
Morrill, Richard Leland geographer, educator
Morse, John Moore architect, planner
Mottet, Norman Karle pathologist, educator
Motulsky, Arno Gunther geneticist, physician, educator
Muilenburg, Robert Henry hospital administrator
Mulally, Alan R. aerospace company executive
†Murakami, Christine Sybil university official, educational technologist
Murray, James Dickson mathematical biology educator
Murray, Michael Kent lawyer
Mussehl, Robert Clarence lawyer
Nalder, Eric Christopher investigative reporter
Narver, John Colin business administration educator
Nash, Cynthia Jeanne journalist
Nellermoe, Leslie Carol lawyer
Nelson, Allen F. investor relations company executive
Nelson, James Alonzo radiologist, educator
Nelson, Walter William computer programmer, consultant
Nester, Eugene William microbiology educator
Neurath, Hans biochemist, educator
Newmeyer, Frederick Jaret linguist, educator
Niemi, Janice lawyer, former state legislator
Nijenhuis, Albert mathematician, educator
Ning, Xue-Han (Hsueh-Han Ning) physiologist, researcher
Nishitani, Martha dancer
Noble, Phillip D. lawyer
Oehler, Richard William lawyer
Oldknow, Constantina W. art historian
Oles, Stuart Gregory lawyer
Oliver, Donny Glen electronics engineer
Olmstead, Marjorie Ann physics educator
Olsen, Harold Fremont lawyer
Olson, David John political science educator
Olson, James William Park architect
Olstad, Roger Gale science educator
O'Mahony, Timothy Kieran writer
O'Malley, Robert Edmund, Jr. mathematics educator
Oman, Henry retired electrical engineer, engineering executive
Orcutt, James Craig ophthalmologist
Orians, Gordon Howell biology educator
Ostrom, Katherine Elma retired educator
Overstreet, Karen A. federal bankruptcy judge
Page, Roy Christopher periodontist, scientist, educator
†Palais, James B. educator
Palm, Gerald Albert lawyer
Palmer, Douglas S., Jr. lawyer
Palmer, Hollis Marie public relations executive
Parker, Omar Sigmund, Jr. lawyer
Parks, Gerald Thomas, Jr. lawyer, business executive
†Parks, Michael James publisher, editor
Parks, Patricia Jean lawyer
Parsons, A. Peter lawyer
Patrick, Donald Lee social scientist, health services researcher
Patten, Richard E. personnel company owner
Patterson, Beverley Pamela Grace accountant
Pawula, Kenneth John artist, educator
Payne, Ancil Horace retired broadcasting executive
Payton, Gary Dwayne professional basketball player
Pearce, Ann Ruble minister
Pearce, Jeannie writer, real estate agent
Peddy, Julie Ann admininstrative officer
Peden, Irene Carswell electrical engineer, educator
Pekelis, Rosselle judge
Perey, Ron lawyer
Perkin, Gordon Wesley international health agency executive
Perrin, Edward Burton health services researcher, biostatistician, public health educator
Petersdorf, Robert George physician, medical educator
Peterson, Jan Eric lawyer
Petrie, Gregory Steven lawyer
Pettigrew, Edward W. lawyer
Pflauer, Katrina Campbell lawyer
†Pflaumer, Katrina C. lawyer
Phillips, William Robert physician
Piniella, Louis Victor professional baseball team manager
Piven, Peter Anthony architect, management consultant
Plorde, James Joseph physician, educator
Pocker, Yeshayau chemistry, biochemistry educator
Porad, Laurie Jo jewelry company official
Porter, Stephen Cummings geologist, educator
Porter, Walter Thomas, Jr. bank executive
Portuesi, Donna Rae psychotherapist, consultant
Prentke, Richard Ottesen lawyer
Pressly, Thomas James history educator
Price, John Richard lawyer, law educator
Prins, David speech pathologist, educator
Pritchard, Llewelyn G. lawyer
Pyke, Ronald mathematics educator
Pyle, Kenneth Birger historian, educator
Pym, Bruce Michael lawyer
Rabinovitch, Benton Seymour chemist, educator emeritus
Raisbeck, James David engineering company executive
Ramsey, Paul Glenn internist
Ratner, Buddy Dennis bioengineer, educator
Ravenholt, Reimert Thorolf epidemiologist
Ray, Charles Kendall retired university dean
Ray, Marianne Yurasko social services administrator
Ray, Sankar communication network research and development professional
Read, Charles Raymond, Sr. business executive
Reardon, Mark William lawyer
Redman, Eric lawyer
Reed, Richard John retired meteorology educator
Reinhardt, William Parker chemical physicist, educator
Reis, Jean Stevenson administrative secretary
Rhines, Peter Broomell oceanographer, atmospheric scientist
†Rho, Jong Min physician, educator
Rice, Norman B. bank executive, former mayor
Rieke, Paul Victor lawyer
Rimel, Linda June writer
Rinearson, Peter Mark journalist, author, software developer
Ritter, Daniel Benjamin lawyer
Robb, Bruce former insurance company executive
Robb, Candace novelist
Robb, John Wesley religion educator
Robertson, Robert Graham Hamish physicist
Rose, Carol Ann air transportation executive
Rosen, Jon Howard lawyer
Rosenblatt, Roger Alan physician, educator
†Ross, David Lawrence broadcaster
Ross, Russell pathologist, educator
Rothstein, Barbara Jacobs federal judge
Royal, Richard artist
Ruckelshaus, William Doyle investment group executive
Ruddy, James W. lawyer
Rudolph, Thomas Keith aerospace engineer
Ruff, Lorraine Marie public relations executive
Rullkoetter, Jill E. museum education administrator
Rummage, Stephen Michael lawyer
Russell, Francia ballet director, educator
Russell, Willie historic site director
Ryder, Hal theater educator, director
Sale, George Edgar physician
Samuel, Gerhard orchestra conductor, composer
Sander, Susan Berry environmental planning engineering corporation executive
Sandman, Irvin W(illis) lawyer
Sandstrom, Alice Wilhelmina accountant
†Sarachik, Edward S. atmospheric sciences educator
Sarason, Irwin G. psychology educator
Sasaki, Tsutomu (Tom Sasaki) real estate company executive, international trading company executive, consultant
Sateren, Terry theater technical production
Saxberg, Borje Osvald management educator
Schall, Lawrence Delano economics educator, consultant
Schell, Paul E. S. mayor
Schilling, John Albert surgeon
Schimmelbusch, Werner Helmut psychiatrist
Schmidt, Peter Gustav shipbuilding industry executive
Schoenfeld, Walter Edwin manufacturing company executive
Scott, Brian David lawyer

Scott, Patrick broadcast executive
Scribner, Belding Hibbard medical educator, nephrologist
Segal, Jack mathematics educator
Shepard, Thomas Hill physician, educator
Shipman, Keith Bryan sportscaster
Shrontz, Frank Anderson airplane manufacturing executive
Sidran, Mark H. lawyer
Siegel, Shepherd education administrator
Silbergeld, Jerome Leslie art historian, educator
Silver, Michael school superintendent
Simkin, Peter Anthony physician, educator
Singer, Sarah Beth poet
Sizemore, Herman Mason, Jr. newspaper executive
Skidmore, Donald Earl, Jr. government official
Skilling, John Bower structural and civil engineer
Skoor, John Brian art educator, art consultant
Sleicher, Charles Albert chemical engineer
Slocumb, Heathcliff professional baseball player
Smith, Andrew Vaughn telephone company executive
Smith, Gerald R. molecular geneticist
Smith, Jeffrey L. (The Frugal Gourmet) cooking expert, television personality, author
Smith, Le Roi Matthew-Pierre, III municipal administrator
Smith, Mara A. small business owner, artist
Smith, Orville Auverne physiology educator
Smith, Teresa Ann computer consultant
Snow-Smith, Joanne Inloes art history educator
Soden, John P. publishing executive
Soltys, John Joseph lawyer
Sonnenfeld, Sandi writer
Spafford, Michael Charles artist
Spindel, Robert Charles electrical engineering educator
Spinrad, Bernard Israel physicist, educator
Spitzer, Hugh D. lawyer
Sprague, Dale Joseph writer
Squires, William Randolph, III lawyer
Stamper, Norman H. police chief
Stanton, Michael John newspaper editor
Startz, Richard economist
Staryk, Steven Sam violinist, concertmaster, educator
Stearns, Susan Tracey lighting design company executive, lawyer
Steele, Cynthia literary critic, translator, educator
Steers, George W. lawyer
Steinberg, Jack lawyer
†Steiner, Samuel J. bankruptcy judge
Stenchever, Morton Albert physician, educator
Stern, Edward Abraham physics educator
Stevens, Robert William church denomination administrator
Stewart, Thomas J. wholesale distribution executive
Stoebuck, William Brees law educator
Stolov, Walter Charles physician, rehabilitation educator, physiatrist
Stonecipher, Harry Curtis manufacturing company executive
Stowell, Kent ballet director
Strahilevitz, Meir inventor, researcher, psychiatry educator
Strandjord, Paul Edphil physician, educator
Strandness, Donald Eugene, Jr. surgeon
Strichartz, James Leonard lawyer
Stringer, William Jeremy university official
Strombom, Cathy Jean transportation planner, consultant
Strombom, David Glen designer
Stroup, Elizabeth Faye librarian
Stubbs, Christopher W. physics educator
Stumbles, James Rubidge Washington multinational service company executive
Sugar, Peter Frigyes historian
Swain, Robert Edson architect
Swanson, August George physician, retired association executive
Swanson, Phillip Dean neurologist
Sweeney, David Brian lawyer
†Sweigert, Philip K. federal judge
Swift, William Charles professional baseball player, Olympic athlete
Szeto, Hung publisher
Szkody, Paula astronomy educator, researcher
Tallman, Richard C. lawyer
Talvi, Ilkka Ilari violinist
Tapper, David pediatric surgeon
Terrell, W(illiam) Glenn university president emeritus
Tessier, Dennis Medward paralegal, lecturer, legal advisor, consultant
Thiel, Arthur Warren journalist
Thomas, Edward Donnall physician, researcher
Thomas, Karen P. composer, conductor
Thompson, Arlene Rita nursing educator
Thompson, Dwight Alan vocational rehabilitation expert
Thorne, David W. lawyer
Thornton, Dean Dickson retired airplane company executive
Thorson, Lee A. lawyer
Thouless, David James physicist, educator
Tift, Mary Louise artist
Todaro, George Joseph pathologist
Tollett, Glenna Belle accountant, mobile home park operator
Tousley, Russell Frederick lawyer
Towne, David L. zoological park administrator
Treiger, Irwin Louis lawyer
Trimpin artist
Tschernisch, Sergei P. academic administrator
Tsutakawa, Deems Akihiko musician, composer, record producer
Tucker, Gary Jay physician, educator
Tukey, Harold Bradford, Jr. horticulture educator
Turner, Wallace L. reporter
Turnovsky, Stephen John economics educator
VanArsdel, Rosemary Thorstenson English studies educator
Van Citters, Robert Lee medical educator, physician
van den Berg, Sara Jane English educator
van den Berghe, Pierre Louis sociologist, anthropologist
Varanasi, Usha environmental scientist
Veblen, John Elvidge lawyer
Vesper, Karl Hampton business and mechanical engineering educator
Vestal, Josephine Burnet lawyer
Voget, Jane J. city official, lawyer
Wagner, Patricia Hamm lawyer
Wagoner, David Everett lawyer
Wagoner, David Russell author, educator
Walker, Walter Frederick professional basketball team executive
Wallerstein, George astronomer, educator
Walsh, Kenneth Andrew biochemist
Walter, Michael Charles lawyer
†Warlum, Michael Frank rraining, consulting and writing company executive
Warner, Vincent W. bishop
Washington, James Winston, Jr. artist, sculptor
Wayne, Robert Jonathan lawyer, educator
Webb, Eugene English language educator
Wechsler, Mary Heyrman lawyer
Wegelin, Jacob Andreas statistician
Weinberg, John Lee federal judge
Weiss, Dick Joseph artist
Weiss, Noel S. epidemiologist
Weissman, Eugene Yehuda chemical engineer
Weitkamp, William George retired nuclear physicist
Wells, Christopher Brian lawyer
Wenick, Dean photographer
Wesley, Virginia Anne real estate property manager
West, Richard Vincent art museum official
†Westphal, Paul professional basketball coach
Whalen, Jerome Demaris lawyer
†Wheeler, Deborah Lynn educator
Whitacre, John apparel executive
White, Rick lawyer, former congressman
White, Thomas S. lawyer
Whitehead, James Fred, III lawyer
Whitford, Joseph P. lawyer
Whitson, Lish lawyer
Wilets, Lawrence physics educator
Williams, J. Vernon lawyer
Williams, Kenneth A. food service executive
Williams, Robert Walter physics educator
Wilske, Kenneth Ray internist, rheumatologist, researcher
Wilson, David Eugene magistrate judge
Wilson, Emily Marie sales executive
Winn, H. Richard surgeon
Wolfle, Dael Lee public affairs educator
Wood, Stuart Kee retired engineering manager
Woodruff, Gene Lowry nuclear engineer, university dean
Woods, James Sterrett toxicologist
Woods, Nancy Fugate dean, women's health nurse
Woods, Ronald Earl foreign policy educator
Wooster, Warren S(criver) marine science educator
Wott, John Arthur arboretum and botanical garden executive, horticulture educator
Wright, Eugene Allen federal judge
Yee, Kuo Chiang neuroscientist, neurologist
Yue, Agnes Kau-Wah otolaryngologist
Zehr, Clyde James church administrator
Ziadeh, Farhat J. Middle Eastern studies educator
Zilly, Thomas Samuel federal judge

Seaview
McNeil, Helen Jo Connolly nursing educator, administrator

Sedro Woolley
Hinckley, Ted C. historian, educator, writer

Sequim
Barton, Jay university administrator, biologist
Beaton, Roy Howard retired nuclear industry executive
Huston, Harriette Irene Otwell (Ree Huston) retired county official
Laube, Roger Gustav retired trust officer, financial consultant
Mc Hugh, Margaret Ann Gloe psychologist
McMahon, Terrence John retired foreign service officer
Meacham, Charles Harding government official
Walker, Raymond Francis business and financial consulting company executive

Shelton
Mullen, Cathryne Anne civic worker
St. George, Laura Mae retired middle school educator

Shoreline
Hanson, Kermit Osmond business administration educator, university dean emeritus
Privat, Jeannette Mary librarian
Reddecliffe, Karin Linnae Ellis educator
Treseler, Kathleen Morrison retired nursing educator

Silverdale
Walcott, William Oliver family practice physician
Walske, M(ax) Carl, Jr. physicist

Snohomish
Hill, Valerie Charlotte nurse
Meister, John Edward, Jr. consultant, technical educator, systems analyst
Philpott, Larry La Fayette horn player
Reese, Kerry David minister

South Bend
Heinz, Roney Allen civil engineering consultant

Spanaway
Campbell, Thomas J. chiropractor, legislator
Loete, Steven Donald pilot
Paris, Kathleen secondary school educator
Roberts-Dempsey, Patricia E. secondary school educator

Spokane
Adolfae, Michael H. municipal government official
Bakker, Cornelis B. psychiatrist, educator
Ballinger, Charles Kenneth information specialist
Barnes, Steve James elementary education educator
Barney, Kellee university athletics coach
Bender, Betty Wion librarian
Blewett, Stephen Douglas journalism educator, public relations consultant
Bonuccelli, Dominic Arizona photographer
Bray, R(obert) Bruce music educator
†Brock, Randall J. poet
Burkhead, Virginia Ruth rehabilitation nurse
Burr, Robert Lyndon information services specialist
Burton, Robert Lyle accounting firm executive
Campbell, Harry Woodson geologist, mining engineer
Carriker, Robert Charles history educator
Cohen, Arnold Norman gastroenterologist
Coker, Charlotte Noel political activist
†Connelly, James P. prosecutor
Connolly, K. Thomas lawyer
Coughlin, Bernard John university chancellor
Cowles, William Stacey publisher
Dashiell, G. Ronald marshal
Durham, Warren John television and radio producer
Eliassen, Jon Eric utility company executive
Falkner, James George foundation executive
Fosseen, Neal Randolph business executive, former banker, former mayor
Foster, Ruth Mary dental association administrator
Fowler, Walton Berry franchise developer, educator
Garrett, Paul Edgar insurance executive, writer, poet
Genung, Sharon Rose pediatrician
George, Aubrey Westmoreland director Spokane public library
Geraghty, John Vincent public relations consultant
Gray, Alfred Orren retired journalism educator, communications specialist
Green, Dale Monte retired judge
Greenwood, Collette P. municipal official, finance officer
Harbaugh, Daniel Paul lawyer
Harden, Harvey director civil service department, Spokane
Hendershot, Carol Miller physical therapist
Higgins, Shaun O'Leary media executive
Hoyt, Bradley James financial advisor
†Imbrogno, Cynthia magistrate judge
Kafentzis, John Charles journalist, educator
Kirschbaum, James Louis real estate company administrator
Kobluk, Michael D. municipal official
Koegen, Roy Jerome lawyer
Kossel, Clifford George retired philosophy educator, clergyman
Kremers, Carolyn Sue writer, musician, educator
Krueger, Larry Eugene import export company executive, lawyer
Kunkel, Richard Lester public radio executive
Ladd, Dean mechanical engineer
Lee, Hi Young physician, acupuncturist
†Lee, Richard Francis James evangelical clergyman, media consultant
Leighton, Jack Richard small business owner, former educator
Lengyel, Larry director employment and training, Spokane
Lindsay, Donald Parker former savings bank executive
Matters, Clyde Burns former college president
Maus, John Andrew computer systems engineer
Mayer, Herbert Carleton, Jr. computer consultant
McClellan, David Lawrence physician
McManus, Patrick Francis educator, writer
McWilliams, Edwin Joseph banker
Mechetti, Fabio orchestra conductor
†Minkler, James Elton humanities educator, academic administrator
†Monson, Dan college basketball coach
Murphy, Mary Ann human services administrator
Nielsen, William Fremming federal judge
Novak, Terry Lee public adminstration educator
Nyman, Carl John, Jr. university dean and official
Paulsen, Richard Wallace counselor
Paulsen, Susan Steenbakkers counselor
Peck, Christopher editor
Perry, Lois Wanda safety and health administrator
Pfister, Terri city clerk
†Phillips, John (Jack) Grant theatre director
Pontarolo, Michael Joseph lawyer
Powell, Sandra Theresa timber company executive
Quackenbush, Justin Lowe federal judge
Rice, Michael John psychiatric mental health nurse
Riherd, John Arthur lawyer
Rimbach, Evangeline Lois retired music educator
Robinson, William P. academic administrator, consultant, speaker
Schlicke, Carl Paul retired surgeon
Sciuchetti, Dale municipal government official
Segal, Vladimir M. metallurgist, researcher
Shaw, Brenda Carol cardiac nurse
Shaw, Margery Wayne Schlamp geneticist, physician, lawyer
Siegel, Louis Pendleton forest products executive
Sines, Randy Dwain business executive
Skylstad, William S. bishop
Stackelberg, John Roderick history educator
Steadman, Robert Kempton oral and maxillofacial surgeon
Steele, Karen Dorn journalist
Storey, Francis Harold business consultant, retired bank executive
Teets, Walter Ralph accounting educator
Tsutakawa, Edward Masao management consultant
Twohig, Kevin foundation administrator
Van Sickle, Frederick L. federal judge
Wagner, Teresa Ann business owner
Walsdorf, Donald Peter art show producer, gallery director
Weatherhead, Leslie R. lawyer
Whaley, Robert Hamilton judge
Williams, Robert Stone protective services official
Wirt, Michael James library director
†Woodbury, Sara Jean poet

Sumas
Hemry, Larry Harold former federal agency official, writer

Sumner
Olson, Ronald Charles aerospace executive

Sunnyside
Capener, Regner Alvin electronics engineer, minister, author, inventor

Tacoma
†Arnold, J. Kelley federal judge
Baldassin, Michael Robert secondary school educator
Barnett, Suzanne Wilson history educator
Bartlett, Norma Thyra retired administrative assistant
†Beckett, Kurt A. legislative staff member
†Brandt, Philip H. federal judge
Brevik, J. Albert communications consultant
Browning, Christopher R. historian, educator
Bryan, Robert J. federal judge
Burgess, Franklin Douglas judge
Burns, Robin C(arol) mathematics theoretician, accountant
Champ, Stanley Gordon scientific company executive
Chiappinelli, Eric Andrew law educator
Collier, Richard Bangs philosopher, foundation executive
†Collins, George J., Jr. surgeon
Crisman, Mary Frances Borden librarian
Davis, Albert Raymond secondary education educator
Douglas, Robert Owen writer
†Ebersole, Brian mayor
Ernst, John Allan clinical neuropsychologist
Fetters, Norman Craig, II banker
Garner, Carlene Ann fundraising consultant
Gates, Thomas Edward civil engineer, waste management administrator
George, Nicholas criminal defense lawyer, entrepreneur
Gilbert, Ben William retired newspaper editor
Gordon, Joseph Harold lawyer
Graves, Ray lawyer
Graybill, David Wesley chamber of commerce executive
Habedank, Gary L. brokerage house executive
Hendley, Ashley Preston, Jr. clinical social worker
†Hill, Mack career officer
Holman, Kermit Layton chemical engineer
Holt, William E. lawyer
Hostnik, Charles Rivoire lawyer
Hudson, Edward Voyle linen supply company executive
Hutchings, George Henry food company executive
Ingram, Artonyon S. psychology educator
Jensen, Mark Kevin foreign language educator
King, Gundar Julian retired university dean
Krueger, James A. lawyer
Le Roy, Bruce Murdock historian
Lewis, Jan Patricia education educator
Liddle, Alan Curtis architect
Luttropp, Peter C. director of finance, Tacoma
Maloney, Patsy Loretta university official, nursing educator
Maynard, Steven Harry writer
McLaughlin, Peter Donald staff scientist, program manager
Metsker, Thomas Charles map company executive
Miller, Judson Frederick lawyer, former military officer
†Mladenich, Ronald E. publishing executive
Mohler, Georgia Ann geriatrics nurse practitioner
Mungia, Salvador Alejo, Jr. lawyer
Nance, John Joseph lawyer, writer, air safety analyst, broadcaster, consultant
Nazaire, Michel Harry physician
Neff Balch, Betty Marie nursing educator
Noll, Anna Cecilia curator
Norwood, Paula Kay medical and surgical nurse
Odlin, Richard Bingham retired banker
Otten, Thomas zoological park director
Owen, Thomas Walker banker, broker
†Parikh, Neel library director
Peterson, Thomas Charles minister, pastoral counselor and therapist
Rieke, William Oliver foundation director, medical educator, former university president
Robinson, Richard Allen, Jr. human resources development trainer, consultant
Rogel, Steven R. forest products company executive
Sackmann, Margaret E. geriatric nurse practitioner
Schauss, Alexander George psychologist, researcher
Sloane, Sarah Jane English educator
†Snyder, Paul federal judge
Stailey, Heather Ann health facility administrator
Steele, Anita Martin (Margaret Anne Martin) law librarian, legal educator
Sterbick, Peter Lawrence lawyer
Strege, Timothy Melvin economic consultant
Tanner, Jack Edward federal judge
Vlasak, Walter Raymond state official, management development consultant
Waldo, James Chandler lawyer
Wang, Arthur Ching-li administrative law judge, law educator
Warren, Dale Andrew publishing company executive
Wiegman, Eugene William minister, former college administrator
Wold, David C. bishop
Wolf, Frederick George environmentalist

Tenino
Orsini, Myrna J. sculptor, educator

Toppenish
Hefflinger, LeRoy Arthur agricultural manager
Ross, Kathleen Anne college president

Tracyton
Pliskow, Vita Sari anesthesiologist

Tukwila
Gouras, Mark Steven lawyer
Lamb, Ronald Alfred editor

University Place
Bourgaize, Robert G. economist
Flemming, Stanley Lalit Kumar family practice physician, mayor, state legislator

Vancouver
Congdon, Roger Douglass theology educator, minister
Craven, James Michael economist, educator
Ferguson, Larry Emmett educational administrator
Gordon, Ingrid Thorngren gerontology, home health nurse
Guenther, Sheila Walsh sales and promotion executive
Hamby, Barbara Jean writer, poet
Hixon, Robin Ray food service executive, writer
Hulburt, Lucille Hall artist, educator
Kleweno, Gilbert H. lawyer
Middlewood, Martin Eugene technical communications specialist, writer, consultant
Ogden, Daniel Miller, Jr. government official, educator
Ovens, Mari Camille school system administrator, dietitian
Power, Margaret Rae (Margo Power) publisher
Simontacchi, Carol Nadine nutritionist
Simpson, Carolyn Marie critical care nurse
Smith, Linda A. former congresswoman
Smith, Milton Ray computer company executive, lawyer
Smith, Sam Corry retired foundation executive, consultant
Taylor, Carson William electrical engineer
Tehrani, Diane Hawke English as a second language educator
†Vogel, Ronald Bruce food products executive
Wiita, Kathryn Carpenter public relations company executive

Vashon
Biggs, Barry Hugh lawyer
Mann, Claud Prentiss, Jr. retired television journalist, real estate agent
†Vallarta, Josefina M. retired child neurologist

Vaughn
Schottland, Robert Milton *secondary school educator*

Walla Walla
†Apostolidis, Paul C. *political science educator*
Carlsen, James Caldwell *musicologist, educator*
Edwards, Glenn Thomas *history educator*
Hayner, Herman Henry *lawyer*
Hedine, Kristian Einar *lawyer*
Johnson, Robert Arnold *physician, cardiologist, poet*
Jonish, Arley Duane *retired bibliographer*
Perry, Louis Barnes *retired insurance company executive*
Potts, Charles Aaron *management executive, writer*
Stratton, Jon *philosophy educator*
Yaple, Henry Mack *library director*
Zipf, Teri M. *poet, writer*

Wallula
Hodge, Ida Lee *physical therapist assistant*

Wenatchee
Elfving, Don C. *horticulturist*
Foreman, Dale Melvin *lawyer, state official*
Knecht, Ben Harrold *surgeon*
Krebs, Sherry Lynn *elementary education educator*
Montague, Gary Leslie *county commissioner, retired newspaper advertising executive*
Schrader, Lawrence Edwin *plant physiologist, educator*
Sorom, Terry Allen *ophthalmic surgeon*
Williams, Keith Roy *museum director*

White Salmon
Verry, William Robert *retired mathematics researcher*

Woodinville
Herron, Sidney Earl *sales executive*
Lanter, Sean Keith *software engineer*
Manevich, Leonard A. *cultural organization administrator, composer*
McGavin, Jock Campbell *airframe design engineer*
Newlands, Sheila Ann *consumer products company executive, controller*
Sanders, Richard Kinard *actor*

Woodland
Mairose, Paul Timothy *mechanical engineer, consultant*

Yakima
Dorsett, Judith A. *elementary education educator*
Eng, Joan Louise *retired special education educator*
Jensen, Cherryl Kay *writer, public relations consultant*
Landreau, Anthony Norman (Tony Landreau) *anthropologist, museologist*
Larson, Paul Martin *lawyer*
McDonald, Alan Angus *federal judge*
Meshke, George Lewis *drama and humanities educator*
Myers, Elizabeth Rouse *management consultant*
Nelson, Bryan H(erbert) *non-profit agency administrator*
Newland, Ruth Laura *small business owner*
Newstead, Robert Richard *urologist*
†Rossmeissl, John A. *federal judge*
Simonson, Susan Kay *hospital administrator*
Suko, Lonny Ray *judge*
Sveinsson, Johannes *former city and county government official*
†Ullas, Yvonne L.
Vujovic, Mary Jane *education and employment training planner*
†Williams, Patricia C. *federal judge*
Wolf, John Arthur, Jr. *urologist*

WEST VIRGINIA

Alloy
Wymer, Robert Ernest *metals company executive*

Arthurdale
Hall, Marilee Alice *elementary education educator*

Athens
Beasley, Jerry Lynn *academic administrator*
Marsh, Joseph Franklin, Jr. *emeritus college president, educational consultant*

Barboursville
Lucas, Carol McCann *vocational education educator*
Vance, Charles Randall *minister*

Beaver
Baligar, Virupax C. *research soil scientist*
Voigt, Paul Warren *research geneticist*

Beckley
Dinh, Anthony Tung *internist*
Kennedy, David Tinsley *retired lawyer, labor arbitrator*

Berkeley Springs
†Thorman, Richard Kahn *editor, writer*

Bethany
Cooey, William Randolph *economics educator*
Cummins, Delmer Duane *academic administrator, historian*

Bluefield
Auville, Frances Carter *educational administrator*
Blevins, Thomas E. *college administrator, educator*
Davenport, Dorothy Dean *retired nurse*
Evans, Wayne Lewis *lawyer*
Faber, David Alan *federal judge*
Feinberg, Mary Stanley *judge*
Haag, Mark Waldo, II *director network operations*
Hager, Donald Wayne *secondary education educator*
Patsel, E. Ralph, Jr. *registrar*
†Pujari, Bhasker Rao *physician*

Buckhannon
Ifert, Danette Eileen *communication educator*
McCauley, David W. *lawyer, educator*

Caldwell
Diem, Debra R. *elementary school educator*

Charles Town
McDonald, Angus Wheeler *farmer*
Na, (Terry) Tsung Shun *Chinese studies educator, writer*

Charleston
†Adkins, Charles M., Jr. *United States marshall*
Arrington, Carolyn Ruth *education consultant*
Bennett, Robert Menzies *retired gas pipeline company executive*
Betts, Rebecca A. *lawyer*
Bhasin, Madan Mohan *chemical research scientist*
Brown, James Knight *lawyer*
Brown, Kathryn Elizabeth *development director*
Bryant, George Macon *chemist*
Chapman, John Andrew *association executive*
Chilton, Elizabeth Easley Early *newspaper executive*
†Clark, Hanley C. *state insurance commissioner*
Cline, Michael Robert *lawyer*
Conlin, Thomas (Byrd) *conductor*
Copenhaver, John Thomas, Jr. *federal judge*
Davis, Billie Johnston *school counselor*
Davis, James Hornor, III *lawyer*
Douglass, Gus Ruben *state agency administrator*
†Etter, Alan Yancy *legal administration executive*
Gage, Charles Quincey *lawyer*
Gillespie, William Harry *forestry executive, geology educator*
Goodwin, Claude Elbert *lawyer, former gas utility executive*
Goodwin, Joseph R. *judge*
Goodwin, Phillip Hugh *hospital administrator*
Grimes, Richard Stuart *editor, writer*
Gunnoe, Nancy Lavenia *food executive, artist*
Haden, Charles Harold, II *federal judge*
Hallanan, Elizabeth V. *federal judge*
Haught, James Albert, Jr. *journalist, newspaper editor, author*
Hechler, Ken *state official, former congressman, political science educator, author*
Heck, Albert Frank *neurologist*
†Hogg, Jerry D. *federal judge*
Ilar, Craig Scott *audio engineer*
Isabella, Mark Douglas *communication consultant*
Ives, Samuel Clifton *minister*
Kizer, John Oscar *lawyer*
Knapp, Dennis Raymond *federal judge*
Koleske, Joseph Victor *chemical engineer, consultant*
Maddox, Timothy Dwain *natural gas company manager*
†Manning, Sherry Fischer *college president emerita, business executive*
Marland, Melissa Kaye *judge*
†Marockie, Henry R. *state school system administrator*
Maroney, Thomas P. *lawyer, political party executive*
Martin, Jerry Harold *bank examiner*
McClaugherty, John Lewis *lawyer*
Mc Gee, John Frampton *communications company executive*
Mc Graw, Darrell Vivian, Jr. *state attorney general*
McHugh, Thomas Edward *state supreme court justice*
Melton, G. Kemp *former mayor*
Michael, M. Blane *federal judge*
†Miles, Jill Leone *state official*
Minear, Alana Wilfong *development director*
Morton, Mark Edward *accountant, clothing store executive*
Neely, Richard *lawyer*
†Pearson, Ronald G. *federal judge*
Prichard, John David *minister*
†Rader, John B. *state agency administrator*
Simmons, Virginia Gill *educational administrator*
†Small-Plante, Susan *legislative administrator*
†Smith, Ingrid L. *librarian*
Stacy, Charles Brecknock *lawyer*
Teare, John Richard, Jr. *lawyer*
Tomblin, Earl Ray *state official*
Tyson, David Richard *lawyer, political party official*
Ukoha, Ozuru Ochu *surgeon, educator*
Underwood, Cecil H. *governor, company executive*
Welch, Edwin Hugh *academic administrator*
Whittington, Bernard Wiley *electrical engineer, consultant*
Workman, Margaret Lee *state supreme court justice*
Zak, Robert Joseph *lawyer*

Clarksburg
Highland, Cecil Blaine, Jr. *newspaper publisher, lawyer, banker*
Huber, Clayton Lloyd *marketing professional, engineer*
Jarvis, John Cecil *lawyer*
Keeley, Irene Patricia Murphy *federal judge*
Ona-Sarino, Milagros Felix *physician, pathologist*
Reynolds, Lewis Dayton *pastor*
Sarino, Edgardo Formantes *physician*
†Trupo, Leonard Joseph *United States marshall*

Clay
Gillespie, Larry *secondary school principal*

Crab Orchard
Janney, Patra Ellen *principal*

Dailey
Kolsun, Bruce Alan *special education educator*

Dunbar
Russell, James Alvin, Jr. *college administrator*

Elkins
†Core, David L. *federal judge*
Maxwell, Robert Earl *federal judge*
Reed, Elizabeth May Millard *mathematics and computer science educator, publisher*
Spears, Jae *state legislator*

Fairmont
Fulda, Michael *political science educator, space policy researcher*
Goodwin, Andrew Wirt, II *radiologist*
Hardway, Wendell Gary *former college president*
O'Connor, John Edward *theater educator, director*
Saunders-Starn, Rose *elementary education educator*
Stanton, George Patrick, Jr. *lawyer*
Stevens, Earl Patrick *minister*
York, Linda Kay *real estate appraiser, executive*

Fairview
Bunner, Patricia Andrea *lawyer*

Falling Waters
Schellhaas, Linda Jean *toxicologist, consultant*

Farmington
Lambert, Delores Elaine *secondary education educator*

Glen Jean
Beverly, Laura Elizabeth *special education educator*

Glenville
Tubesing, Richard Lee *library director*

Grafton
Knotts, Robert Lee *insurance executive*

Great Cacapon
Chapple, Abby *consumer communications consultant*

Greenville
Warner, Kenneth Wilson, Jr. *editor, association and publications executive*

Harpers Ferry
Cooley, Hilary Elizabeth *county official*
Startzell, David N. *sports association executive*

Hillsboro
Pierce, William Luther *association executive, writer*

Hinton
Glaser, Robert Harvey, Sr. *pastor*

Huntington
Baber, Ralph King *writer, publisher*
Bagley, Charles Frank, III *lawyer*
Bateman, Mildred Mitchell *psychiatrist*
Cocke, William Marvin, Jr. *plastic surgeon, educator*
Davis, Donald Eugene *real estate management executive*
deBarbadillo, John Joseph *metallurgist, management executive*
Edwards, Roy Alvin *physician, psychiatrist, educator*
Engle, Jeannette Cranfill *medical technologist*
Gilley, James Wade *university president*
Gould, Alan Brant *academic administrator*
Hayes, Robert Bruce *former college president, educator*
Hooper, James William *educator*
Justice, Franklin Pierce, Jr. *oil company executive*
Kent, Calvin Albert *university administrator*
Leppla, David Charles *pathology educator*
McKown, Charles H. *dean*
McSorley, Danny Eugene *sales executive*
Miller, Jerry Brian *radio broadcaster*
†Molina, Rafael Evencio *urologist*
Morabito, Rocco Anthony *urologist*
Morgan, Linda Rice *secondary education educator*
Mufson, Maurice Albert *physician, educator*
Reynolds, Marshall Truman *printing company executive*
Ritchie, Garry Harlan *television broadcast executive*
†Rule, Judy K. *library director*
St. Clair, James William *lawyer*
Simpson, Juliene *university head women's basketball coach*
Stultz, Patricia Adkins *health care risk administrator*
†Taylor, Maurice G., Jr. *federal judge*

Hurricane
Nance, Martha McGhee *rehabilitation nurse*

Institute
DasSarma, Basudeb *chemistry educator*
Garrett, Naomi Mills *foreign language educator, retired*

Inwood
Cloyd, Helen Mary *accountant, educator*
Rizzetta, Carolyn Teresa *musical instrument, sound recording entrepreneur*

Kearneysville
Biggs, Alan Richard *plant pathologist, educator*

Kingwood
Moyers, Sylvia Dean *retired medical record librarian*
Rock, Gail Ann *obstetrical/gynecological nurse*

Lahmansville
Harman, Jo Ann Snyder *secondary school educator*

Lewisburg
Ford, Richard Edmond *lawyer*
Fowler, Linda McKeever *hospital administrator, management educator*
Galyean, Tag *architect*
Hooper, Anne Dodge *pathologist, educator*
Mazzio-Moore, Joan L. *radiology educator, physician*
Willard, Ralph Lawrence *surgery educator, physician, former college president*

Logan
Galya, Thomas Andrew *geologist*

Mabscott
Gangopadhyay, Nirmal Kanti *mining company executive*

Man
Saunders, Brenda Rhea *secondary education educator*

Mannington
Peterson, Kristina J. *religious organization executive*
Schumacher, Theresa Rose (Terry Schumacher) *singer, musician, legal assistant*

Martinsburg
Coyle, Geraldine Anne *nursing administrator*
Hoffmaster, Beverly Ann *elementary education educator*
Malin, Howard Gerald *podiatrist*
Rice, Lacy I., Jr. *lawyer*
†Slaven, Chip *district director*

Yoe, Harry Warner *retired agricultural economist*

Montgomery
Gourley, Frank A., Jr. *engineering educator*

Moorefield
Hedrick, John O. *railroad executive*

Morgantown
Allamong, Betty D. *academic administrator*
Bajura, Richard Albert *university administrator, engineering educator*
Barba, Roberta Ashburn *retired social worker*
Beattie, Diana Scott *biochemistry educator*
Bergstein, Jack Marshall *surgeon*
Biddington, William Robert *university administrator, dental educator*
Blaydes, Sophia Boyatzies *English language educator*
Brisbin, Richard A., Jr. *political scientist, educator*
Brooks, Dana D. *dean*
†Bruner, Jeffrey Benham *foreign language educator*
Bucklew, Neil S. *educator, past university president*
Bunner, William Keck *lawyer*
Butcher, Fred R. *biochemistry educator, university administrator*
Cayton, Mary Evelyn *minister*
†Claar, Victor Vyron *economics educator*
Cleckley, Franklin D. *law educator*
Cochrane, Robert Lowe *biologist*
D'Alessandri, Robert M. *dean*
Das, Kamalendu *chemist*
Davis, Leonard McCutchan *speech educator*
De Vore, Paul Warren *technology educator*
Ducatman, Alan Marc *physician*
†Fisher, John Welton, II *law educator, magistrate judge, university official*
Fleming, William Wright, Jr. *pharmacology educator*
Fodor, Gábor Béla *chemistry educator, researcher*
Fusco, Andrew G. *lawyer*
Gagliano, Frank Joseph *playwright*
Gladfelter, Wilbert Eugene *physiology educator*
Guthrie, Hugh Delmar *chemical engineer*
Haggett, Rosemary Romanowski *dean*
Hardesty, David Carter, Jr. *university president*
Hill, Ronald Charles *surgeon, educator*
Hudson, David M. *minister*
Iammarino, Richard Michael *pathologist, student support services director*
Kent, James A. *consulting chemical engineer, author, consultant*
Leslie, Nan S. *nursing educator, womens' health nurse*
Mansmann, Paris Taylor *medical educator*
Martin, James Douglas *neurologist*
Massey, W(ilmet) Annette *nurse, former educator*
Maxwell, Robert Haworth *agricultural consultant*
McAvoy, Rogers *educational psychology educator, consultant*
Mili, Jude Joseph *priest, religious organization administrator*
Moore, Mark Tobin *museum curator, director, art educator*
Morris, William Otis, Jr. *lawyer, educator, author*
Nath, Joginder *genetics and biology educator, researcher*
Pearce, Meredith *graphic designer*
Peterson, Sophia *international studies educator*
Poland, Alan Paul *oncology educator*
Ponte, Charles Dennis *pharmacist, educator*
Pyles, Rodney Allen *archivist, county official*
Reese, Hayne Waring *psychologist*
Schlunk, Jurgen Eckart *German language educator*
Schroder, John L., Jr. *retired mining engineer*
Seehra, Mohindar Singh *physics educator, researcher*
Sikora, Rosanna Dawn *emergency physician, educator*
Singer, Armand Edwards *foreign language educator*
Stewart, Guy Harry *university dean emeritus, journalism educator*
Warden, Herbert Edgar *surgeon, educator*
Wiedebusch, Mary Kathryne *dance educator*
Witt, Tom *economics researcher, educator*
Yanero, Lisa Joyce *medical and surgical nurse*

New Cumberland
†Mehaffey, Oplas Jane *librarian*

Newell
Spayth, Ann Schuyler *poet*

Nitro
Atkinson, Tommy Ray *sportscaster, sportswriter*
Lucas, Panola *elementary education educator*

Oak Hill
Janney, Sally Baggs *civic worker*

Parkersburg
Aebi, Charles Jerry *minister, educator*
Brum, Brenda *state legislator, librarian*
Burdette, Jane Elizabeth *nonprofit association executive, consultant*
Crooks, Dorena May (Dee Crooks) *administrative assistant, social worker*
Fahlgren, H(erbert) Smoot *advertising agency executive*
Gilbert, Kenneth G. *art educator*
Robinson, Robert Joseph *elementary school educator, art educator*

Petersburg
Garber, Harold David *school system superintendent, columnist*

Philippi
Lambert, Olivia Sue *commercial artist, writer*

Pratt
Terrell-McDaniel, Robin F. *cardiac rehabilitation and critical care nurse*

Princeton
Knowles, Virginia Lynn *gerontology services educator*

Rainelle
Scott, Pamela Moyers *physician assistant*

Ranson
Rudacille, Sharon Victoria *medical technologist*

Ravenswood
Hamrick, Leslie Wilford, Jr. *metallurgy supervisor*

Reedsville
Williford, Drury Fisher, Jr. *historical researcher*

Ridgeley
Unger, Roberta Marie *special education educator*

Romney
Saville, Royce Blair *lawyer*

Saint Albans
Alderson, Gloria Frances Dale *rehabilitation specialist*
Smith, Robert Carlisle *department administrator, welding educator*

Salem
Frasure, Carl Maynard *political science educator*
Ohl, Ronald Edward *academic administrator*
Raad, Virginia *pianist, lecturer*

Shady Spring
Reed, Cathy Lorraine *elementary education educator*

Shepherdstown
Elliott, Jean Ann *librarian emeritus*
Parmesano, Vincent, III *construction executive, mayor*
Snyder, Joseph John *editor, historian, author, lecturer, consultant*
Wilson, Miriam Janet Williams *publishing executive*

Sistersville
Archer, Joseph Neale *industrial designer*

South Charleston
Britton, Laurence George *research scientist*
Drummond, Patrica Ferguson *secondary education educator*
Garnett, Susan Ellen *special education educator*
Nielsen, Kenneth Andrew *chemical engineer*

Spencer
Chapman, William Ervin *elementary education educator*
Kosowicz, Francis John *concert organist*
Parker, Theresa Ann Boggs *special education educator*

Sprague
Rhoades, Marye Frances *paralegal*

Summersville
Yeager, Charles William *lawyer, newspaper publisher*

Summit Point
Taylor, Harold Allen, Jr. *industrial mineral marketing consultant*
Woods, David Lyndon *publishing and broadcast executive, former federal agency executive*

Sutton
Hopen, William Douglas (Bill Hopen) *sculptor*

Sylvester
Mace, Mary Alice *coal company administrator*

Triadelphia
McCullough, John Phillip *management consultant, educator*

Union
Sprouse, James Marshall *retired federal judge*

Vienna
Acree, Wilma Katheryn *retired secondary school educator*

Wardensville
Vance, Dama Lee *obstetrical/gynecological nurse, ultrasound sonographer*

Wayne
Crockett, Patricia Jo Fry *psychiatric-mental health nurse*

Weirton
Robinson, Charles Warren *controller*

Wellsburg
Bell, Charles D. *lawyer*
Viderman, Linda Jean *paralegal, corporate executive*

West Liberty
†Gold, Jonathan M. *philosophy and religion educator*

West Union
Howes, Melinda Sue *marketing executive*

Weston
†Billeter, Robert James *newspaper publisher*

Westover
Trythall, Harry Gilbert *music educator, composer*

Wheeling
Campbell, Clyde Del *academic administrator*
Clarke, S. Bruce *paper company executive*
Exley, Ben, III *retired pharmaceutical company executive*
†Friend, L. Edward *federal judge*
Good, Laurance Frederic *office director*
Hughes, Mary Elizabeth *interior designer*
Phillips, John Davisson *retired lawyer*
Phillis, Marilyn Hughey *artist*
Poland, Michelle Lind *medical-surgical and critical care nurse, educator*
Recht, Arthur *former state supreme court justice*
Riley, Arch Wilson, Jr. *lawyer*
Schmitt, Bernard W. *bishop*
Seibert, James E. *lawyer, magistrate judge*
Stidd, Linda Marie *rehabilitation nurse*
Urval, Krishna Raj *health facility administrator, educator*
Wilmoth, William David *lawyer*
Worby, Rachael Beth *conductor*

White Sulphur Springs
Kleisner, Ted J. *museum director*

WISCONSIN

Algoma
Golomski, William Arthur *consulting company executive*

Altoona
James, Henry Thomas *former foundation executive, educator*

Amherst
Reed, Penny Rue *special education educator, administrator*

Appleton
Amm, Sophia Jadwiga *artist, educator*
Barlow, F(rank) John *mechanical contracting company executive*
Bayorgeon, James Thomas *judge*
†Biringer, Gene Douglas *music educator, theorist*
Boldt, Oscar Charles *construction company executive*
Boren, Clark Henry, Jr. *general and vascular surgeon*
Brehm, William Allen, Jr. *urban planner*
Chaney, William Albert *historian, educator*
Crowley, Geoffrey Thomas *airline executive*
†Damp, George Edward *music educator*
†Dintenfass, Mark *writer, English educator*
Drescher, Kathleen Ebben *lawyer*
Drescher, Park Morris *lawyer*
†Eno, Woodrow E. *lawyer*
Froehlich, Harold Vernon *judge, former congressman*
Goldgar, Bertrand Alvin *literary historian, educator*
Harrington, Beverly *museum director*
Houk, Margaret *writer*
Leahy, Patricia M. *speech-language pathologist*
Lillge, Eugene Francis *county official*
Lonergan, Kevin *lawyer*
Luther, Thomas William *retired physician*
McManus, John Francis *association executive, writer*
Petinga, Charles Michael *transportation executive*
Rankin, Arthur David *paper company executive*
Rice, Ferill Jeane *writer, civic worker*
†Schaphorst, Kenneth W. *music educator, composer*
Spiegelberg, Harry Lester *retired paper products company executive*
Tincher, Barbara Jean *university official*
Warch, Richard *academic administrator*

Argyle
Daley, Ron (Ronald Eugene Daley) *playwright, poet, director, producer*
Davis, Jane Strauss *business owner*

Ashland
Smith, Jane Schneberger *retired city administrator*

Baraboo
Baymiller, Lynda Doern *social worker*
Smith, Walter DeLos *accountant, professional speaker*

Barneveld
†Welsh, Randy N. *writer*

Bayfield
Gallinat, Michael Paul *fisheries biologist*
Wilhelm, Sister Phyllis *principal*

Bear Creek
Schleicher, Susan Lea *critical care nurse*

Beaver Dam
Butterbrodt, John Ervin *real estate executive*
Manthe, Cora De Munck *real estate and investment company executive*

Belgium
Slater, John Greenleaf *financial consultant*

Belleville
†Tomlin, Nicholas John *chief of police*

Beloit
Davis, Harry Rex *political science educator*
Ferrall, Victor Eugene, Jr. *college administrator, lawyer*
Green, Harold Daniel *dentist*
Hendricks, Kenneth *wholesale distribution executive*
Kaplan, Kenneth Franklin *manufacturing company financial executive*
Kreider, Leonard Emil *economics educator*
Melvin, Charles Alfred, III *superintendent of schools*
Rodeman, Frederick Ernest *accountant*
Savage, Christine Dadez *women's health nurse, educator*
Simon, Michael Alexander *photographer, educator*
Tubbs, Charles Allan *protective services official*

Berlin
Martin, Rebecca Ann *artist, graphic designer*

Black River Falls
†Lahmayer, Albert T. *optometrist*
Michaels, Marion Cecelia *writer, editor, news syndicate executive*

Bloomer
Prenzlow, Elmer John-Charles, Jr. *minister*

Blue Mounds
Winner, Scott *company executive*

Boulder Junction
†Russell, John Robert *neurosurgeon*

Brodhead
O'Neil, J(ames) Peter *computer software designer, educator*

Brookfield
Bader, Ronald L. *advertising executive*
Bauer, Chris Michael *banker*
Breu, George *accountant*
Brown, Edward Sherman *computer company executive*
Gia-Russo, A(nthony) Paul *retired minister, lawyer*
Gradeless, Donald Eugene *secondary education educator*
Grove, Richard Charles *power tool company executive*
Hardman, Harold Francis *pharmacology educator*
Hundt, Paul Anthony *financial planner*
Huss, William Lee *computer consultant*
Kortebein, Stuart Rowland *orthopedic surgeon*
Krueger, John Anthony *biomedical engineer, musician*
Lessiter, Frank Donald *magazine editor*
Murphy, Josephine Mancuso *critical care nurse, adult nurse practitioner*
Nickerson, Greg *public relations executive*
Robles, Ted Canillas *electrical engineering educator*
Roder, Ronald Ernest *accountant*
Saam, Robert Harry *human resources consultant*
Scheving, Lawrence Einar *anatomy educator, scientist*
Thomas, John *mechanical engineer, research and development*
Trytek, David Douglas *insurance company executive*
Welnetz, David Charles *human resources executive*
Wenzler, Edward William *architect*
Zimmerman, Jay *secondary education educator*

Cadott
Blair, David Chalmers Leslie *composer, writer*

Cambria
Bronson, Martha Ann *secondary education educator*

Cambridge
Stevens, Chester Wayne *real estate executive*

Cascade
Baumann, Carol Edler *retired political science educator*

Cedar Grove
Feider, Gary Joseph *newspaper editor*

Cedarburg
Cass, Richard Eugene *English language educator*
King, Frederic *health services management executive, educator*
Schaefer, Gordon Emory *food company executive*

Chetek
Erspamer, Peter Roy *humanities educator, writer*

Chippewa Falls
Copeland, Christine Susan *therapist*
†Schmider, Mary Ellen Heian *American studies educator, academic administrator*

Columbus
Brinkman, Michael Owen *health care consultant, educator*
Schellin, Patricia Marie Biddle *educator*

Cottage Grove
Hesse, Thurman Dale *welding and metallurgy educator, consultant*

Darien
Miller, Malcolm Henry *manufacturing sales executive, real estate developer*

De Pere
†Frechette, Bonnie L. *secondary education educator*
Manion, Thomas A. *college president*
†Mori, Kyoko *writer, educator*
Rueden, Henry Anthony *accountant*
†Tepe, Judith Mildred *vocal music teacher, choral director*

Deerfield
†Banaszynski, Carol Jean *educator*
Pappas, David Christopher *lawyer*

Delafield
Behrendt, David Frogner *journalist*
Hausman, C. Michael *lawyer, judge*
Kurth, Ronald James *university president, retired naval officer*
Roberts, Thomas Blair *retired insurance broker*

Delavan
Armstrong, Kevin William *marketing executive, researcher*
Lepke, Charma Davies *musician, educator*

Denmark
Martens, Lyle Charles *state education administrator*

Dodgeville
Dentinger, Ronald Lee *comedian, speaker, freelance writer*
Dyke, William Daniel *circuit court judge*
Eisenberg, Lee B. *communications executive, author*
Rux, Paul Philip *management consultant, educator*

Dunbar
†Horn, Samuel Edgar *academic administrator*

Eagle River
Nieuwendorp, Judy Lynell *special education educator*

Eau Claire
Biegel, Eileen Mae *hospital executive*
Brill, Donald Maxim *educator, writer, researcher*
Cunningham, Michael Gerald *composer, music educator*
Dick, Raymond Dale *psychology educator*
Frank, John LeRoy *lawyer, government executive, educator*
†Hart, Holly Joy *educational administrator*
Hugo, Miriam Jeanne *educator, counselor*
Kirby, H(arry) Scott *priest*
Larson, Brian Foix *architect*
Lawler, John Griffin *graphic designer, educator*
Leary, Robin Janell *administrative secretary, county government official*
Mash, Donald J. *college president*
Menard, John R. *lumber company executive*
Patterson, Donald Lee *music educator*
Richards, Jerry Lee *academic administrator, religious educator*
†Sen, Asha *English educator*
†Utschig, Thomas S. *federal judge*
Weil, D(onald) Wallace *business administration educator*

Edgerton
Everson, Diane Louise *publishing executive*

Elcho
Doran, Kay JoAnn *Spanish language educator*

Elkhorn
Dunn, Walter Scott, Jr. *writer, former museum director, consultant*
Eberhardt, Daniel Hugo *lawyer*
O'Brien, Francis Joseph *environmental services company executive*
Reinke, Doris Marie *retired elementary education educator*
Sweet, Lowell Elwin *lawyer, writer*

Elm Grove
Barth, Karl Luther *retired seminary president*
Bielke, Patricia Anne *psychologist*
Gorske, Robert Herman *retired lawyer*
Halvorsen, Morrie Edward *trade association administrator*

Ferryville
Tedeschi, John Alfred *historian, librarian*

Fish Creek
Abegg, Martin Gerald *retired university president*

Fitchburg
Hill, Michael John *newspaper editor*

Fond Du Lac
Bespalec, Dale Anthony *clinical psychologist*
Hayes, Elizabeth Lamb *biology educator*
Kaufman, Harvey Isidore *neuropsychology consultant*
Kraus, Michael John *English language and literature educator*
Lambert, Eugene Kent *oncologist, hematologist*
Mailer, Kathleen *academic administrator*
Reed, Jeffrey Garth *organizational psychologist, educator*
Stein, Michael Alan *cardiologist, medical educator*
Treffert, Darold Allen *psychiatrist, author, hospital director*
†Ward, JoAnn Boettner *convention and tourist bureau administrator*

Fort Atkinson
Albaugh, John Charles *hospital executive*
Jones, Alan Porter, Jr. *food manufacturing executive*
†Knox, Brian Victor *newspaper publisher and editor*
Knox, William David *publishing company executive*
Meyer, Eugene Carlton *retired editor*
Sager, Donald Jack *publisher, former librarian*

Fox Point
†Robertson, Susan Elendra *municipal government administrator*
Stahl, Mary Gail *elementary educator*

Franklin
Bui, Ty Van *computer programmer, systems analyst*
Czaplewski, Lynn Marie *intravenous nurse, educator*
Roark, Barbara Ann *librarian*

Frederic
Rudell, Milton Wesley *aerospace engineer*

Freedom
Moscinski, David Joseph *educational administrator, school psychologist*

Germantown
Fischer, Roberta Jane *accountant*
Hargan, Charles James *lithographer, village official*
Statkus, Jerome Francis *lawyer*
Tietyen, David Earl *marketing professional*

Glendale
Chait, Jon Frederick *corporate executive, lawyer*
Moeser, Elliott *principal*
Schenker, Eric *university dean, economist*

Grafton
Kacmarcik, Thomas *manufacturing company executive*
Yarger, James Gregory *chemical company executive*

Green Bay
†Baek, Paul *neurological surgeon*
Banks, Robert J. *bishop*
Bush, Robert G. *food service executive*
Butler, Robert Andrews *clinical psychologist*
Daley, Arthur James *retired magazine publisher*
Day, Douglas Eugene *public information officer*
Favre, Brett Lorenzo *professional football player*
Finesilver, Alan George *rheumatologist*
Fisher, Robert Warren *accountant*
†Freeman, Antonio Michael *professional football player*
Geisendorfer, James Vernon *author*
Harlan, Robert Ernest *professional football team executive*
Justen, Ralph *museum director*
Kraft, Michael Eugene *political science educator*
Kress, William F. *manufacturing company executive*
Kuehne, Carl W. *food products executive*
†Levens, (Herbert) Dorsey *professional football player*
Manske, Lynn Darlene *surgical nurse*
Martens, Donald Mathias *orthodontist*
Meng, Jack *food products executive*
Mervilde, Michael John *clinical social worker*
Morneau, Robert Fealey *bishop*
Noel, Donald Claude *clergyman, sculptor*
Pearson, Carol Ann *chemistry educator*
Poppenhagen, Ronald William *advertising agency executive*
Promis, Brenda *parks director*
Rhodes, Raymond Earl *professional sports team executive*
Schneider, Donald J. *trucking company executive*
Sehring, Frederick George *obstetrician/gynecologist*

†Sickel, James *federal judge*
†Style, Christine L. *art educator, curator*
Swetlik, William Philip *orthodontist*
Taillon, James Howard *orthotist*
Toonen, Linda Marie *composition educator*
Vesta, Richard V. *meat packing company executive*
von Heimburg, Roger Lyle *surgeon*
Weidner, Edward William *university chancellor, political scientist*
Weyers, Larry Lee *energy executive*
White, Reggie (Reginald Howard White) *retired professional football player*

Greendale
†Kaiser, Ann Christine *magazine editor*
Kuhn, Roseann *sports association administrator*

Greenfield
Havey, Francis Powers *fund raising executive, lawyer*
Helland, Sherman M. *author*
McKillip, Patricia Claire *operatic soloist*
Neal, Jon C(harles) *accountant, consultant*

Hales Corners
Case, Karen Ann *lawyer*
Kuwayama, S. Paul *physician, allergist, immunologist*
Michalski, (Żurowski) Wacław *adult education educator*

Hartford
Babbitt, Donald Patrick *radiologist*

Hartland
Burrus, Daniel Allen *research company executive, consultant*
†Moses, D. James (Jim) (Jim Moses) *public library director*
Stamsta, Jean F. *artist*
Vitek, Richard Kenneth *scientific instrument company executive*

Hatley
Bartholomaus, Brett William *small business owner*

Hayward
Peterson, Louis Robert *retired consumer products company executive*

Highland
Kreul, Carol Ann *nurse*

Hollandale
Colescott, Warrington Wickham *artist, printmaker, educator*
Myers, Frances *artist*

Holmen
Meyer, Karl William *retired university president*

Hudson
Benson, Sandra Jean *media specialist*
Christenson, Garth Neil *optometrist*
Dahle, Johannes Upton *academic administrator*

Hurley
Nicholls, Thomas Maurice *business owner*

Iola
Krause, Chester Lee *publishing company executive*
Mishler, Clifford Leslie *publisher*
Rosenberger, Carolyn Ann *art educator*
Van Ryzin, Robert Richard *magazine editor*

Jackson
Brunner, Elizabeth King *health facility administrator, consultant*

Janesville
Butters, John Patrick *educator, tour director*
Fitzgerald, James Francis *cable television executive*
†Fuiks, Kimball Sands *neurosurgeon*
Gianitsos, Anestis Nicholas *surgeon*
Neumann, Mark W. *former congressman*
Steil, George Kenneth, Sr. *lawyer*
Taylor, Timothy Leon *college dean*
Thomas, Margaret Ann *educational administrator, art educator*
Wood, Wayne W. *state legislator*

Jefferson
Morgan, Gaylin F. *public relations consultant*
†Myers, Gary *public relations executive*

Juneau
Ebert, Dorothy Elizabeth *county clerk*
Fitzgerald, Scott *state legislator*

Kenosha
Adler, Seymour Jack *social services administrator*
Akalin, Roberta Ann *education counselor*
Baker, Douglas Finley *library director*
Brown, Howard Jordan *newspaper publisher*
Campbell, F(enton) Gregory *college administrator, historian*
Cyr, Arthur I. *political science and economics educator*
Huml, Donald Scott *manufacturing company executive*
Infusino, Achille Francis *construction company executive*
†Kummings, Donald Dale *English educator*
†Lenard, Mary Kathleen *English educator*
Levis, Richard George *secondary school educator*
†Lindgren, Scott Arthur *athletic educator*
Potente, Eugene, Jr. *interior designer*
Seitz, Florian Charles *retired banker*
Statham, Anne Adele *sociology educator*
Steigerwaldt, Donna Wolf *clothing manufacturing company executive*
†Tobin, Daniel Eugene *poet, English language educator*
Wright, David Jonathan *finance educator*

Keshena
Kussel, William Ferdinand, Jr. *lawyer*

Kewaunee
Allen, Gerald Campbell Forrest *management consulting company owner*

Kimberly
Van Boxtel, Randall Anthony *secondary education educator*

Kohler
Kohler, Herbert Vollrath, Jr. *diversified manufacturing company executive*
Kohler, Laura E. *public relations executive*

La Crosse
Albrechtson, Rick *psychologist*
Boudreau, Richard Owen *retired English educator, freelance writer*
Burke, Raymond L. *bishop*
Corser, David Hewson *pediatrician, retired*
Gelatt, Charles Daniel *manufacturing company executive*
Kastantin, Joseph Thomas *accounting educator*
Klos, Jerome John *lawyer*
Lindesmith, Larry Alan *physician, administrator*
Medland, William James *college president*
Nix, Edmund Alfred *lawyer*
Novotney, Donald Francis *superintendent of schools*
†Polodna, David Lee *library director*
†Provencher, Denis Michael *French language educator*
Rausch, Joan Mary *art historian*
Rozelle, Lee Theodore *physical chemist*
Ruyle, Kim Ernest *training and software development executive*
Schroth, John Henry *associate lawyer*
Schumacher, Philip Gerard *fundraising executive*
Schute, Valentine Joseph, Jr. *architect*
Silva, Paul Douglas *reproductive endocrinologist*
Sleik, Thomas Scott *lawyer*
Smith, Martin Jay *physician, biomedical research scientist*
Webster, Stephen Burtis *physician, educator*
†White-Parks, Annette *English educator*

Lake Geneva
Braden, Berwyn Bartow *lawyer*
Liebman, Monte Harris *retired psychiatrist*
†Nelson, Dawn Lynelle *secondary education educator*
Petersen, Edward Schmidt *retired physician*
Slocum, Robert Boak *minister, educator*
Weed, Edward Reilly *marketing executive*
Williams, Joanne Molitor *elementary education educator, retired*

Lake Mills
Lazaris, Pamela Adriane *community planning and development consultant*
Quest, Kristina Kay *art educator*
Roselle, Paul Lucas *material scientist*

Laona
†Sturzl, Alice A. *school district administrator*

Lodi
Schereck, William John *retired historian, consultant*

Madison
†Aberle, Elton David *dean*
Abrahamson, Shirley Schlanger *state supreme court chief justice*
Abualsamid, Ahmad Zuhair *software scientist, researcher*
Abubakr, Said Mohammed *chemical engineering educator*
Adler, Julius *biochemist, biologist, educator*
Albert, Daniel Myron *ophthalmologist, educator*
Aldag, Ramon John *management and organization educator*
Ammerman, Robert Ray *philosopher, educator*
Anderson, Louis Wilmer, Jr. *physicist, educator*
Andreano, Ralph Louis *economist, educator*
Armstrong, Gregory Davenport *arboretum administrator*
Askey, Richard Allen *mathematician*
Atkinson, Richard Lee, Jr. *internal medicine educator*
Bablitch, William A. *state supreme court justice*
Baldwin, Gordon Brewster *lawyer, educator*
Baldwin, Janice Murphy *lawyer*
†Baldwin, Robert Edward *economics educator*
†Baldwin, Tammy *congresswoman*
Banks, Aubrey *architect, educator*
Barger, Vernon Duane *physicist, educator*
Barish, Lawrence Stephen *nonpartisan legislative staff administrator*
Barnes, Robert F. *agronomist*
Barnhill, Charles Joseph, Jr. *lawyer*
Barnick, Helen *retired judicial clerk*
Baron, Alma Fay S. *management educator*
Barr, James, III *telecommunications company executive*
Barrows, Richard Lee *economics educator, academic administrator*
Bartell, Jeffrey Bruce *lawyer*
Bass, Paul *pharmacology educator*
Bauman, Susan Joan Mayer *lawyer, mayor of Madison, Wisconsin*
Beachley, Norman Henry *mechanical engineer, educator*
Beck, Anatole *mathematician, educator*
Becker, David *artist, educator*
Behrend, William Louis *electrical engineer*
Beinert, Helmut *biochemist*
†Beissinger, Margaret Hiebert *educator*
†Beissinger, Mark Richard *political scientist, educator*
Bennett, Kenneth Alan *retired biological anthropologist*
†Benson, John T. *state agency administrator*
Bentley, Charles Raymond *geophysics educator*
Berg, William James *French language educator, writer, translator*
Berghahn, Klaus Leo *German and Jewish studies educator*
Berthouex, Paul Mac *civil and environmental engineer, educator*
Beyer-Mears, Annette *physiologist*
Bielinski, Daniel Walter *management consultant*
Bird, Robert Byron *chemical engineering educator, author*
Bisgard, Gerald Edwin *biosciences educator, researcher*
Bloodworth, J(ames) M(organ) Bartow, Jr. *physician, educator*
Bochert, Linda H. *lawyer*
Bogue, Allan George *history educator*
Bohnhoff, David Roy *agricultural engineer, educator*
Botez, Dan *physicist*
Boucher, Joseph W(illiam) *lawyer, accountant, educator, writer*
Boutwell, Roswell Knight *oncology educator*
Boyle, William Charles *civil engineering educator*
Brachman, Richard John, II *financial services consultant, banking educator*
Bradley, Ann Walsh *state supreme court justice*
†Brancel, Ben *state agency administrator*
Brann, Edward R(ommel) *editor*
Bremer, Howard Walter *consulting patenting and licensing lawyer*
Bretherton, Francis P. *atmospheric and oceanic sciences educator*
Brock, Thomas Dale *microbiology educator*
Brock, William Allen, III *economics educator, consultant*
Brown, Arnold Lanehart, Jr. *pathologist, educator, university dean*
Bryson, Reid Allen *earth sciences educator*
Bubenzer, Gary Dean *agricultural engineering educator, researcher*
Buchholz, Ronald Lewis *architect*
Budzak, Kathryn Sue (Mrs. Arthur Budzak) *physician*
Bugge, Lawrence John *lawyer*
Bula, Raymond J. *agronomist*
Bullock, William Henry *bishop*
Bunge, Charles Albert *library science educator*
Burgess, James Edward *newspaper publisher, executive*
Burgess, Richard Ray *oncology educator, molecular biology researcher, biotechnology consultant*
Burke, Brian B. *state senator, lawyer*
Burkholder, Wendell Eugene *retired entomology educator, researcher*
Burns, Elizabeth Murphy *media executive*
Burris, Robert Harza *biochemist, educator*
Busby, Edward Oliver *retired dean*
Callen, James Donald *nuclear engineer, plasma physicist, educator*
Carbon, Max William *nuclear engineering educator*
Carbone, Paul Peter *oncologist, educator, administrator*
Cassinelli, Joseph Patrick *astronomy educator*
Chang, Y. Austin *materials engineer, educator*
Chapman, Loren J. *psychology educator*
Christensen, Nikolas Ivan *geophysicist, educator*
Chu, Hsien Ming *investment company executive*
Churchwell, Edward Bruce *astronomer, educator*
Ciplijauskaite, Birute *humanities educator*
Clark, David Leigh *marine geologist, educator*
Clay, Clarence Samuel *acoustical oceanographer*
Cleland, W(illiam) Wallace *biochemistry educator*
Cohen, Bernard Cecil *political scientist, educator*
Cohen, Marcus *allergist, immunologist*
Connors, Kenneth Antonio *retired chemistry educator*
Converse, James Clarence *agricultural engineering educator*
Corcoran, Mary Alice *retired medical surgical nurse, educator*
Crabb, Barbara Brandriff *federal judge*
Craddock, (John) Campbell *geologist, educator*
Cravens, Stanley H. *software development manager*
†Crocker, Stephen L. *federal judge*
Cronin, Patti Adrienne Wright *state agency administrator*
Cronon, William *history educator*
Crow, James Franklin *retired genetics educator*
Curry, Robert Lee *lawyer*
Curtiss, Charles Francis *chemist, educator*
Dahl, Lawrence Frederick *chemistry educator*
Dahlberg, James E(ric) *biochemist, molecular biologist*
Davis, Erroll Brown, Jr. *utility executive*
Davis, Richard *musician, music educator*
de Boor, Carl *mathematician*
Deininger, David George *judge*
Dembo, Lawrence Sanford *English educator*
Dembski, Stephen Michael *composer, university music composition professor*
Denton, Frank M. *newspaper editor*
Derzon, Gordon M. *hospital administrator*
Deutsch, Harold Francis *biochemist, researcher, educator*
DeWerd, Larry Albert *medical physicist, educator*
Dick, Elliot Colter *virologist, epidemiologist, educator*
Dietmeyer, Donald Leo *retired electrical engineer, educator*
Dodson, Vernon Nathan *physician, educator*
Dott, Robert Henry, Jr. *geologist, educator*
Downs, Donald Alexander, Jr. *political scientist, educator*
Doyle, James E(dward) *state attorney general*
Drechsel, Robert Edward *journalism educator*
Dubrow, Heather *English educator*
Duffie, John Atwater *chemical engineer, educator*
Dunham, Michael Herman *human services executive*
DuRose, Stanley Charles, Jr. *insurance executive*
Earl, Anthony Scully *former governor of Wisconsin, lawyer*
Easterday, Bernard Carlyle *veterinary medicine educator*
Ebben, James Adrian *college president*
Ediger, Mark D. *chemistry educator*
Eisler, Millard Marcus *financial executive*
Ellis, Arthur Baron *chemist, educator*
Emmert, Gilbert Arthur *engineer, educator*
Ensign, Jerald C. *bacteriology educator*
Enslin, Jon S. *bishop*
Evans, Donald LeRoy *real estate company executive*
Evenson, Merle Armin *chemist, educator*
Fahien, Leonard August *physician, educator*
Farrar, Thomas C. *chemist, educator*
Farrow, Margaret Ann *state legislator*
Fennema, Owen Richard *food chemistry educator*
Ferry, John Douglass *retired chemist, educator*
Fiedler, Patrick James *circuit court judge*
Field, Henry Augustus, Jr. *lawyer*
Filipowicz, Halina *literature educator*
Finman, Ted *lawyer, educator*
Fitchen, Allen Nelson *publisher*
Flanagan, David Thomas *lawyer, attorney general*
Fleischman, Stephen *art center director*
Ford, Charles Nathaniel *otolaryngologist, educator*
Forster, Francis Michael *physician, educator*
Fowler, Barbara Hughes *classics educator*
Fox, Michael Vass *Hebrew educator, rabbi*
Freudenburg, William R. *sociology educator*
Frykenberg, Robert Eric *historian*
†Gamble, Vanessa N. *historian*
Garver, Thomas Haskell *curator, art consultant, writer*
Goldberger, Arthur Stanley *economics educator*
Goodkin, Richard Elliot *French educator, writer*
Goodman, Robert Merwin *microbiologist, plant biologist, educator*
Googins, Louise Paulson *financial planner*
Gorski, Jack *biochemistry educator*
Govier, Gordon Oliver *radio news broadcaster, consultant*
Graf, Truman Frederick *agricultural economist, educator*
Graham, James Miller *physiology researcher*
Graziano, Frank Michael *medical educator, researcher*
Greaser, Marion Lewis *science educator*
Greenfield, Norman Samuel *psychologist, educator*
Greenwald, Caroline Meyer *artist*
Guillery, Rainer Walter *anatomy educator*
Gurney, Mary Kathleen *pharmacist*
Gwynne, Robert Harold *minister*
Hachten, William Andrews *journalism educator, author*
Hagedorn, Donald James *phytopathologist, educator, agricultural consultant*
Hall, David Charles *zoo director, veterinarian*
Haller, Archibald Orben *sociologist, educator*
Hamalainen, Pekka Kalevi *historian, educator*
Hamerow, Theodore Stephen *history educator*
Hamers, Robert J. *chemistry educator, researcher*
Hansen, James John *accountant*
Hansen, W. Lee *economics educator, author*
Hanson, David James *lawyer*
Hardie, Anthony D. *legislative staff member, social welfare administrator*
Harkness, Donald Richard *retired hematologist, educator*
Harvey, John Grover *mathematics educator*
Haslanger, Philip Charles *journalist*
Hedden, Gregory Dexter *environmental science educator, consultant*
Heffernan, Nathan Stewart *retired state supreme court chief justice*
Helgeson, John Paul *plant physiologist, researcher*
Helstad, Orrin L. *lawyer, legal educator*
Hester, Donald Denison *economics educator*
Heymann, S. Richard *lawyer*
Hickman, James Charles *business and statistics educator, business school dean*
Higby, Gregory James *historical association administrator, historian*
Hildebrand, Daniel Walter *lawyer*
Hill, Charles Graham, Jr. *chemical engineering educator*
Hofeldt, John W. *lawyer*
Hokin, Lowell Edward *biochemist, educator*
Holbrook, John Scott, Jr. *lawyer*
Hopen, Herbert John *horticulture educator*
Houghton, David Drew *meteorologist, educator*
Hoyt, James Lawrence *journalism educator, athletic administrator*
Hutchison, Jane Campbell *art history educator, researcher*
Iltis, Hugh Hellmut *plant taxonomist-evolutionist, educator*
Jackson, Marion Leroy *agronomist, soil scientist*
Jacobs, Eleanor R. *retired volunteer*
Jarrell, Wesley Michael *soil and ecosystem science educator, researcher*
Javid, Manucher J. *retired neurosurgery educator*
Jeanne, Robert Lawrence *entomology educator*
Jefferson, James Walter *psychiatry educator*
Johnson, Millard Wallace, Jr. *mathematics and engineering educator*
Johnson, Richard Arnold *statistics educator, consultant*
Jones, James Edward, Jr. *retired law educator*
Kaesberg, Paul Joseph *virology researcher*
Kepecs, Joseph Goodman *physician, educator*
Kimble, Judith E. *molecular biologist, cell biologist*
Kindig, David A. *medical educator*
Kirk, Thomas Kent *research scientist*
Klein, Sheldon *computational linguist, educator*
Kleinhenz, Christopher *foreign language educator, researcher*
Kleinmaier, Judith Marie Raddant *journalist*
Klodt, Gerald Joseph *office product development executive*
Klug, Scott Leo *former congressman*
Knowles, Richard Alan John *English language educator*
Kore, Anita Maureen *veterinary toxicologist*
Kreuter, Gretchen V. *academic administrator*
Krusick, Margaret Ann *state legislator*
Kulcinski, Gerald LaVerne *nuclear engineer, educator*
Kutler, Stanley Ira *history and law educator, author*
Laessig, Ronald Harold *preventive medicine and pathology educator, state official*
La Follette, Douglas J. *secretary of state*
Lagally, Max Gunter *physics educator*
†Lakes, Diana Mary *artist*
Langer, Richard J. *lawyer*
Lardy, Henry A(rnold) *biochemistry educator*
Larson, John David *life insurance company executive, lawyer*
†Larson, Ronald Jon *library director*
Lasseter, Robert Haygood *electrical engineering educator, consultant*
Latimer, James Harold *percussionist, conductor, composer, educator*
Launder, Yolanda Marie *graphic design director*
Lautenschlager, Peggy Ann *prosecutor*
Lawler, James Edward *physics educator*
Lawson, David E. *architect*
Leavitt, Judith Walzer *history of medicine educator*
Leavitt, Lewis A. *pediatrician, medical educator*
Lemanske, Robert F., Jr. *allergist, immunologist*
Lemberger, August Paul *university dean, pharmacy educator*
Lightfoot, Edwin Niblock, Jr. *chemical engineering educator*
Lillesand, Thomas Martin *remote sensing educator*
Link, O(gle) Winston *photographer*
Linstroth, Tod Brian *lawyer*
Lipo, Thomas A. *electrical engineer, educator*
†Litscher, Jon E. *protective services official*
Little, George Daniel *clergyman*
Littlefield, Vivian Moore *nursing educator, administrator*
Long, Willis Franklin *electrical engineering educator, researcher*
Lonnebotn, Trygve *battery company executive*
Loper, Carl Richard, Jr. *metallurgical engineer, educator*
Lovell, Edward George *mechanical engineering educator*
Luening, Robert Adami *agricultural economics educator emeritus*
Lyall, Katharine C(ulbert) *academic administrator, economics educator*
Mack, Kirbie Lyn *municipal official*
Mackie, Frederick David *retired utility executive*
MacKinney, Archie Allen, Jr. *physician*

Magnuson, John Joseph zoology educator
Maher, Louis James, Jr. geologist, educator
Maki, Dennis G. medical educator, researcher, clinician
Malkus, David Starr mechanics educator, applied mathematician
Maloney, Thomas Peter library services professional
Malter, James Samuel pathologist, educator
Marks, Elaine French language educator
Martin, Robert David judge, educator
Marton, Laurence Jay clinical pathologist, educator, researcher
Mathwich, Dale F. insurance company executive
McBeath, Andrew Alan orthopedic surgery educator
McCallum, Laurie Riach lawyer, state government
McCallum, Scott state official
McMillan, Reed John sales executive
McNelly, John Taylor journalist, educator
Melli, Marygold Shire law educator
Mertens, Diane K. secondary education educator
Miller, Frederick William publisher, lawyer
Miller, James Alexander oncologist, educator
Mitby, Norman Peter college president
Moen, Rodney Charles state senator, retired naval officer
Moore, Edward Forrest computer scientist, mathematician, former educator
Moore, John Ward chemistry educator
Morton, Stephen Dana chemist
Moss, Richard L. physiology educator
Mtalika Banda, Kelekeni university soccer coach
Mueller, Willard Fritz economics educator
Mukerjee, Pasupati chemistry educator
Mullins, Jerome Joseph real estate developer, consulting engineer
Murphy, Robert Brady Lawrence lawyer
Myers, Franklin Lewis, II ophthalmologist
Nelson, Oliver Evans, Jr. geneticist, educator
Nevin, John Robert business educator, consultant
Newcomb, Eldon Henry retired botany educator
Nichols, Donald Arthur economist, educator
Niederhuber, John Edward surgical oncologist and molecular immunologist, university educator and administrator
Nisbet, Thomas Klein architect
Nora, Wendy Alison lawyer
Novotny, Donald Wayne electrical engineering educator
O'Brien, James Aloysius foreign language educator
Odden, Allan Robert education educator
†Ohnuki-Tierney, Emiko social sciences educator
Olien, David William academic administrator
Olson, Norman Fredrick food science educator
Onsager, David Ralph cardiothoracic surgeon, educator
Opitz, David Wilmer corporate executive, state political party executi
Owens, Robert George psychologist, researcher
Pariza, Michael Willard research institute executive, microbiology and toxicology educator
Parrino, Cheryl Lynn federal agency administrator
Pella, Milton Orville retired science educator
Peters, Henry Augustus neuropsychiatrist
Peterson, David Maurice plant physiologist, research leader
Pitot, Henry Clement, III physician, educator
Pitzner, Richard William lawyer
Policano, Andrew J. university dean
Pondrom, Lee Girard physicist, educator
Porter, Andrew Calvin educational administrator, psychology educator
Porter, Cloyd Allen state representative
Potter, Kevin former United States attorney
Potter, Van Rensselaer cancer researcher, author
Powell, Barry Bruce classicist
Prange, Roy Leonard, Jr. lawyer
Pray, Lloyd Charles geologist, educator
Prieve, E. Arthur arts administration educator
†Racette, Elizabeth Anne artist
Ragatz, Thomas George lawyer
Ray, Willis Harmon chemical engineer
Reynolds, Ernest West retired physician, educator
Rice, Joy Katharine psychologist, educational policy studies and women's studies educator
Rich, Daniel Hulbert chemistry educator
Richards, Hugh Taylor physics educator
Richter, Pat university athletic director
Rideout, Walter Bates English educator
Ring, Gerald J. real estate developer, insurance executive
Ris, Hans zoologist, educator
Robertson, James Magruder geological research administrator
Robins, H(enry) Ian medical oncologist
Robinson, Arthur Howard geography educator
Robinson, Stephen Michael applied mathematician, educator
Roessler, Carol Ann state senator
Rogers, Katherine Kuelbs artist, writer
Rosser, Annetta Hamilton composer
Rowe, George Giles cardiologist, educator
Rowe, John Westel retired organic chemist
Rude, Brian David state legislator
Rueckert, Roland Rudyard retired virologist, educator
Russell Harrsch, Patricia Eileen healthcare rules writer
Satter, Larry Dean biochemist, scientific research administrator
Sauer, Jeff university hockey coach
Saunders, Charles David state official
Savage, Blair deWillis astronomer, educator
Scheidler, James Edward business executive
Schmidt, Cheryl A. Zeise acute care nurse
Schmidt, John Richard agricultural economics educator
Schmidt, Martha Bubeck educator, counselor
Schoeller, Dale Alan nutrition research educator
Schutta, Henry Szczesny neurologist, educator
Seireg, Ali A(bdel Hay) mechanical engineer
Sewell, Richard Herbert historian, educator
Sewell, William Hamilton sociologist
Shabaz, John C. federal judge
Shain, Irving retired chemical company executive and university chancellor
Sharkey, Thomas David educator, botanist
Sih, Charles John pharmaceutical chemistry educator
Sims, Terre Lynn insurance company executive
Skiles, James Jean electrical and computer engineering educator
Skinner, James Lauriston chemist, educator
Skoog, Folke Karl botany educator
†Skupniewitz, Joseph W. federal judge
Slesinger, Doris Peyser sociology educator
Smalley, Eugene Byron plant pathology educator, forest pathologist, mycologist
Smith, Morton Edward ophthalmology educator, dean
Sobkowicz, Hanna Maria neurology researcher
Sondel, Paul Mark pediatric oncologist, educator
Sonnedecker, Glenn Allen pharmaceutical historian, pharmaceutical educator
Spear, Thomas Turner history educator
†Spencer, C. Stanley insurance executive
†Spring, Terri political organization executive
Steinmetz, Donald Walter state supreme court justice
Stewart, Warren Earl chemical engineer, educator
Stites, Susan Kay human resources consultant
Stoddard, Glenn McDonald lawyer
Stone, John Timothy, Jr. writer
Strasma, John Drinan economist, educator
Strier, Karen Barbara anthropology educator
Sunde, Milton Lester retired poultry science educator
Susman, Millard geneticist, educator
Suttie, John Weston biochemist
Swoboda, Lary Joseph state legislator
Szybalski, Waclaw molecular geneticist, educator
Taylor, Fannie Turnbull social education and arts administration educator
Temkin, Harvey L. lawyer
Thesen, Arne industrial engineering educator
Thiesenhusen, William Charles agricultural economist
Thomas, J. Mark research fellow, sociology educator
Thompson, Tommy George governor
Tishler, William Henry landscape architect, educator
Tomar, Russell Herman pathologist, educator, researcher
Turner, Robert Lloyd state legislator
Uyehara, Otto Arthur mechanical engineering educator emeritus, consultant
Valdivia, Hector Horacio medical educator
Vandell, Kerry Dean real estate and urban economics educator
Vaughan, Michael Richard lawyer
Vaughan, Worth Edward chemistry educator
Voight, Jack C. state official
Vowles, Richard Beckman literature educator
Wade, Royce Allen financial services representative
Wagner, Burton Allan lawyer
Waldo, Robert Leland retired insurance company executive
Walker, Duard Lee medical educator
Walsh, David Graves lawyer
Wanek, Ronald Melvin orthodontist
Ward, David academic administrator, educator
Webster, John Goodwin biomedical engineering educator, researcher
Wegenke, Rolf educational association administrator
Weinbrot, Howard David English educator
Welker, Wallace Irving neurophysiologist, educator
Wenger, Ronald David surgeon
Wermers, Donald Joseph registrar
West, Robert Culbertson chemistry educator
Westman, Jack Conrad child psychiatrist, educator
Westphal, Klaus Wilhelm university museum director
Whiffen, James Douglass surgeon, educator
White, William Fredrick lawyer
Whitford, Albert Edward astronomer
Whitney, Robert Michael lawyer
Wilcox, Jon P. state supreme court justice
Wilcox, Michael Wing lawyer
Wilson, Franklin D. sociology educator
Wilson, Jacquelyn writer
Wilson, Pamela Aird physician
Wineke, William Robert reporter, clergyman
Wirz, George O. bishop
Wolman, J. Martin retired newspaper publisher
Young, Merwin Crawford political science educator
Young, Raymond Allen chemist, educator
Young, Rebecca Mary Conrad state legislator
Yuill, Thomas MacKay academic administrator, microbiology educator
Zedler, Joy Buswell ecological sciences educator
Zimmerman, Howard Elliot chemist, educator
Zografi, George pharmacologist, educator
Zweifel, David Alan newspaper editor

Manitowish Waters
Laidig, William Rupert retired paper company executive

Manitowoc
Butler, Robin Erwin retired vocational technical educator, consultant
Schuh, Martha Schuhmann mathematics educator
Shimek, Rosemary Geralyn medical/surgical nurse
Trader, Joseph Edgar orthopedic surgeon

Marathon
Natzke, Paulette Ann manufacturing executive

Marinette
†Lawton, Robert Cushman county official
Staudenmaier, Mary Louise banker, lawyer

Marion
Simpson, Vinson Raleigh manufacturing company executive

Markesan
Chamberlain, Robert Glenn retired tool manfacturing executive

Marshfield
†Carter, Alden Richardson writer
David, Barbara Marie medical, surgical nurse
Fye, W. Bruce, III cardiologist
Gardner, Ella Haines artist
Jaye, David Robert, Jr. retired hospital administrator
Stueland, Dean Theodore emergency physician

McNaughton
Bradshaw, Glenn Raymond art educator

Menasha
Mills, Laurel poet

Menomonee Falls
Chicorel, Ralph composer, lyricist, playwright
Griswold, Paul Michael clinical psychologist, consultant
Hinnrichs-Dahms, Holly Beth middle school educator
Kellogg, William S. retail executive
Walters, Ronald Ogden mortgage banker

Menomonie
†Asthana, Rajiv engineering educator, researcher
Cutnaw, Mary-Frances emeritus communications educator
Hecker, Margo Joan editor, writer
Levy, Michael Marc English educator
Naland, Patricia Mae psychotherapist
Steans, Phillip Michael lawyer

Mequon
Berry, William Martin financial consultant
Burroughs, Charles Edward lawyer
Diesem, John Lawrence business executive
Dohmen, Frederick Hoeger retired wholesale drug company executive
Dohmen, Mary Holgate retired primary school educator
Elias, Paul S. marketing executive
Ellis, William Grenville academic administrator, management consultant
Miller, Scott Joseph software executive
†Rapkin, Stephanie G. lawyer, educator
Ratcliffe, Kermit Herman theology educator
Ryan, Mary Nell H. training consultant
Smith, Leila Hentzen artist
Tolan, David J. lawyer, insurance company official
Watson-Boone, Rebecca A. library & information studies educator, researcher
Woessner, William Craig school psychologist

Merrill
Gravelle, John David secondary education educator
Rogers, James Thomas lawyer
Whitburn, Gerald insurance company executive
Wulf, William Arthur lawyer

Middleton
Berman, Ronald Charles lawyer, accountant
Ferry, James Allen physicist, electrostatics company executive
Foss, Karl Robert auditor
Hinsdill, Ronald Dwight bacteriology educator, immunotoxicologist
Lee, Leslie Warren marketing executive, public speaker
Lobeck, Charles Champlin, Jr. pediatrics educator
McDermott, Molly lay minister
Ostrom, Meredith Eggers retired geologist
†Rowland, Pleasant publisher, toy company executive
Senn, Richard Allan environmental safety professional

Milton
Hosler, Russell John retired education educator

Milwaukee
Abraham, William John, Jr. lawyer
Adamson, John William hematologist
Alexander, Janice Hoehner physician, educator
Alverson, William H. lawyer
Aman, Mohammed Mohammed university dean, library and information science educator
Arbit, Bruce direct marketing executive, consultant
Armstrong, Douglas Dean journalist
Atlee, John Light physician
Auer, James Matthew art critic, journalist
Babler, Wayne E., Jr. lawyer
Bader, Alfred Robert chemist
Baker, John Edward cardiac biochemist, educator
Balbach, George Charles technology company executive
Ballweg, Mary Lou nonprofit association administrator and founder, writer, consultant
Bannen, John T. lawyer
Barbee, Lloyd Augustus lawyer
Barnes, Paul McClung lawyer
Bartel, Fred Frank consulting engineer executive
Basquin, Mary Smyth (Kit Basquin) independent curator, writer
Bateman, C. Barry airport terminal executive
Battocletti, Joseph Henry electrical engineer, biomedical engineer, educator
Beals, Vaughn Le Roy, Jr. retired motorcycle manufacturing executive
Beaudry, Diane Fay Puta quality management executive
Beckwith, David E. lawyer
Bergmann, Linda J. marketing professional
Berkman, Dave mass communications educator
Berkoff, Marshall Richard lawyer
Besharse, Joseph Culp cell biologist, researcher
Bicha, Karel Denis historian, educator
Biehl, Michael Melvin lawyer
Biller, Geraldine Pollack curator
Biller, Joel Wilson lawyer, former foreign service officer
Bishop, Charles Joseph manufacturing company executive
Blain, Peter Charles lawyer
Blankenship, Jay Randall social services executive
†Blumberg, Sherry Helene Jewish education educator
Boese, Gilbert Karyle cultural organization executive
†Boese, Lillian R. performing company executive
Boettcher, Harold Paul engineer, educator
Bogdon, Glendon Joseph orthodontist
Bovée, Warren Gilles retired journalism educator
Bowen, Michael Anthony lawyer, writer
Bremer, John M. lawyer
Brever, Michael Stephen non-profit executive director, alderman
†Brookman, Adam L. lawyer
Bruce, Jackson Martin, Jr. lawyer
Busch, John Arthur lawyer
†Callahan, William E., Jr. federal judge
Cannon, David Joseph lawyer
Carballo, Fernando Anthony gastroenterologist, hepatologist
Carozza, Davy Angelo Italian language educator
Casey, John Alexander lawyer
Casper, Richard Henry lawyer
Chan, Carlyle Hung-lun psychiatrist, educator
Chan, Shih Hung mechanical engineering educator, consultant
†Choban, Glenwood T. business owner
Christiansen, Keith Allan lawyer
Clark, James Richard lawyer
Cleary, John Washington lawyer
Coffman, Terrence J. academic administrator
Cohn, Lucile psychotherapist, nurse
Colbert, Virgis William brewery company executive
Connelly, Mark writer, educator
Connolly, Gerald Edward lawyer
Constable, John advertising executive
Coogan, Frank Neil health and social services administrator
Cooper, Richard Alan hematologist, college dean, health policy analyst
Corby, Francis Michael, Jr. manufacturing company executive
Counsell, Paul S. advertising executive
Curran, Thomas J. federal judge
Cutler, Richard Woolsey lawyer
Daily, Frank J(erome) lawyer
Dallman, Robert E. lawyer
Davis, Thomas William computer company executive
Davis, Walter Stewart lawyer
†Deacon, John Stanley Raymond physician
Delfs, Andreas performing company executive
Demerdash, Nabeel Aly Omar electrical engineer
Dionisopoulos, George Allan lawyer
Donahue, John Edward lawyer
Downey, John Wilham composer, pianist, conductor, educator
Drummond, Robert Kendig lawyer
Duback, Steven Rahr lawyer
Dunn, Michael J. dean
Dupuis, Kateri Theresa elementary education educator
Ehlinger, Ralph Jerome lawyer
Einhorn, Stephen Edward mergers and acquisitions executive, consultant, investment banker
†Eisenberg, Russell A. federal judge
Ericson, James Donald lawyer, insurance executive
Ertel, Gary Arthur accountant
Esterly, Nancy Burton physician
Evans, Terence Thomas federal judge
Farris, Trueman Earl, Jr. retired newspaper editor
Felde, Martin Lee advertising agency executive, accountant
Fiorelli, Karen Lynn nurse
Fitzsimonds, Roger Leon bank holding company executive
Florsheim, Richard Steven lawyer
Foster, Richard journalist
Fournelle, Raymond Albert engineering educator
Frautschi, Timothy Clark lawyer
Friday, Gerald Edmund biologist, educator
Friedman, James Dennis lawyer
Fromstein, Mitchell S. temporary office services company executive
Fuller, Howard education educator, academic administrator
Gaggioli, Richard Arnold mechanical engineering educator
Gaines, Irving David lawyer
Gallagher, Richard S. lawyer
Gallop, Jane (Anne) women's studies educator, writer
Garbaciak-Bobber, Joyce Katherine news anchor
†Garner, Phil professional baseball manager
Gefke, Henry Jerome lawyer
Gemignani, Joseph Adolph lawyer
Gerlach, Frederick Herman international business consultant
Geyer, Sidna Priest business education educator
Ghiardi, James Domenic lawyer, educator
Giese, Heiner lawyer, real estate investor
Gjerdset, Kristin Anne art educator, artist
Glazer, Gerald Sherwin real estate broker
Goetsch, John Hubert consultant and retired utility company executive
Gonnering, Russell Stephen ophthalmic plastic surgeon
Goodkind, Conrad George lawyer
Goodstein, Aaron E. federal magistrate judge
Gordon, Myron L. federal judge
†Grebe, Michael W. lawyer
Green, Edward Anthony museum director
Greenberg, Martin Jay lawyer, educator, author
Greenler, Robert George physics educator, researcher
Greenstreet, Robert Charles architect, educator
Griffith, Owen Wendell biochemistry educator
†Grissom, Marquis Dean professional baseball player
Grochowski, Mary Ann psychotherapist
Groethe, Reed lawyer
Groiss, Fred George lawyer
Haberman, F. William lawyer
Habush, Robert Lee lawyer
Hachey, Thomas Eugene British and Irish history educator, consultant
Handelman, Howard political scientist, educator
Hansen, John Herbert university administrator, accountant
Hansen-Rachor, Sharon Ann conductor, choral music educator
Hanthorn, Dennis Wayne performing arts association administrator
Harrington, John Timothy lawyer
Harvieux, Anne Marie psychotherapist
Hase, David John lawyer
†Hatch, Michael Ward lawyer
Hatton, Janie R. Hill principal
Hawkins, Brett William political science educator
Haworth, Daniel Thomas chemistry educator
Hay, Robert Pettus history educator
Hazelwood, John A. lawyer
Headlee, Raymond psychoanalyst, educator
Heiloms, May (Mrs. Samuel Heiloms) artist
Heim, Kathryn Marie psychiatric nurse, author
Heinen, James Albin electrical engineering educator
Helbert, Clifford L. graphic designer, journalism educator
Hendee, William Richard medical physics educator, university official
Henry, Julietta commissioner, state and local
Henry, Rick broadcast executive
Herr, Richard Joseph sculptor, educator
†Hill, James Warren college dean
Hinkley, Gerry newspaper editor
Hinshaw, Edward Banks broadcasting company executive
Hirsch, June Schaut chaplain
Hoffman, Nathaniel A. lawyer
Hoffmann, Gregg J. journalist, author
Horvat, Sarah Kobs museum adminstrator
Hosenpud, Jeffrey cardiovascular physician
Hudson, Katherine Mary manufacturing company executive
Huf, Carol Elinor tax service company executive
Huff, Marsha Elkins lawyer
Hunter, Victor Lee marketing executive, consultant
Hur, Su-Ryong physician, anesthesiologist
Huston, Kathleen Marie library administrator
Huston, Margo journalist
Iding, Allan Earl lawyer
Jache, Albert William retired chemistry educator, scientist
James, Charles Franklin, Jr. engineering educator
†Jansen, Daniel Ervin professional speedskater, marketing professional, former Olympic athlete
Janzen, Norine Madelyn Quinlan medical technologist
Jaques, Damien Paul theater critic
Johannes, Robert J. lawyer

Joseph, Jules K. retired public relations executive
Jost, Lawrence John lawyer
Joyce, Michael Stewart foundation executive, political science educator
Kaiser, Martin newspaper editor
Kampine, John P. anesthesiologist
Kamps, Charles Q. lawyer
Karkheck, John Peter physics educator, researcher
Kasten, G. Frederick, Jr. investment company executive
Kelley, Lyle Ardell insurance company executive
Kelly, Francis Daniel retired lawyer
Kendall, Leon Thomas finance and real estate educator, retired insurance company executive
Kennedy, John Patrick lawyer, corporate executive
†Kessler, Frederick Philip labor arbitrator
Kessler, Joan F. lawyer
Keuler, Roland Leo retired shoe company executive
Keyes, James Henry manufacturing company executive
Killian, William Paul industrial corporate executive
King, William Stewart, II public relations executive
Kirby, Russell Stephen epidemiologist, statistician, geographer
Kircher, John Joseph law educator
Kloehn, Ralph Anthony plastic surgeon
Kochar, Mahendr Singh physician, educator, administrator, scientist, writer, consultant
†Koelpin, Daniel Herbert religious association administrator
Krausen, Anthony Sharnik surgeon
Kringel, Jerome Howard lawyer
Kritzer, Paul Eric media executive, communications lawyer
Krueger, Raymond Robert lawyer
Kubale, Bernard Stephen lawyer
Kuchan, Anthony Mark psychologist, educator
Kupst, Mary Jo psychologist, researcher
Kurtz, Harvey A. lawyer
LaBudde, Roy Christian lawyer
LaMalfa, Joachim Jack clinical psychologist
Landis, Fred mechanical engineering educator
Lange, Marilyn social worker
Langley, Grant F. municipal lawyer
Lanier, Bob former professional sports team executive, former basketball player
Larson, David Lee surgeon
Larson, Marlene Louise educator, hotel consultant
Laughlin, Steven L. advertising executive
Leonard, Richard Hart journalist
Lesniewski, Christine Veronica special education educator, consultant
Levine, Herbert lawyer
Levit, William Harold, Jr. lawyer
Levy, Alan M. lawyer
†Lickel, Robin L. editor
Liddy, James Daniel Reeves English educator
Lietz, Jeremy Jon educational administrator, writer
Long, Robert Eugene banker
Lubar, Sheldon Bernard venture capitalist
Lueders, Wayne Richard lawyer
MacGregor, David Lee lawyer
MacIver, John Kenneth lawyer
Mahler, Stephanie Irene executive assistant
Maio, F. Anthony lawyer
Mancuso, Joseph Edward medical psychotherapist
Manko, Wesley Daniel insurance advisor
Manning, Kenneth Paul food company executive
Marcus, Richard Steven lawyer
Marcus, Stephen Howard hospitality and entertainment company executive
Marquis, William Oscar lawyer
Marringa, Jacques Louis manufacturing company executive
Martin, Vincent Lionel manufacturing company executive
Masland, Susan Wistar retired education educator
Maynard, John Ralph lawyer
McCanles, Michael Frederick English language educator
McCann, Dennis John columnist
McGaffey, Jere D. lawyer
†McGarity, Margaret Dee federal judge
†McGinnity, Thomas G. university administrator
†McIntyre, Virginia Ann poet
†McNally, Joel Douglas newspaper editor, columnist
McSweeney, Maurice J. (Marc) lawyer
Medved, Paul Stanley lawyer
Meldman, Robert Edward lawyer
Melin, Robert Arthur lawyer
Melton, Margaret Mary telecommunications specialist
Michaels-Paque, Joan M. artist, educator
Michelstetter, Stanley Hubert lawyer
Miller, David Hewitt environmental scientist, writer
Miller, Edward Carl William physician
Moberg, David Oscar sociology educator
Morris, G. Ronald industrial executive
Moynihan, William J. museum executive
Mulcahy, Robert William lawyer
Muñoz, Amalia biochemical researcher
Noelke, Paul lawyer
Nomo, Hideo professional baseball player
Norquist, John Olof mayor
Nortman, M. Judith Haworth geriatrics nurse
Obenberger, Thomas E. lawyer
Olson, Frederick Irving retired history educator
Orzel, Michael Dale lawyer
O'Shaughnessy, James Patrick lawyer
Ovitsky, Steven Alan musician, symphony orchestra executive
Papas, George Nick bakery company executive
Parker, Charles Walter, Jr. consultant, retired equipment company executive
Paul, Mary Melchior human resources professional
Peckerman, Bruce Martin lawyer
Pelisek, Frank John lawyer
Penman, Julie A. commissioner, state and local
Phillips, Thomas John lawyer
Pindyck, Bruce Eben lawyer, corporate executive
Pisciotta, Anthony Vito physician, educator
Powell, Edmund William lawyer
Puerner, Paul Raymond lawyer
Quade, Quentin Lon political science educator
Quereshi, Mohammed Younus psychology educator, consultant
Rader, I. A. electronic components manufacturing company executive
Radke, Dale Lee religious organization administrator, deacon, editor, pastor
Randa, Rudolph Thomas judge
Randall, William Seymour leasing company executive
Read, Sister Joel academic administrator
Reed, John Kennedy Emanuel elementary school teacher
Reid, Margaret Kathleen literature educator
Reid, Robert Lelon mechanical engineering educator
Reynolds, John W. federal judge
Rheams, Annie Elizabeth education educator
Rhoten, Juliana Theresa retired school principal
Rich, Robert C. manufacturing executive
Richman, Stephen Erik lawyer
Riemer, David R. lawyer
Rinnemaki, William Allen transportation executive
Ritz, Esther Leah civic worker, volunteer, investor
Rivero, Albert J. English educator
Robertson, Michael Swing church administrator
Robinson, Richard Russell lawyer
Roeming, Robert Frederick foreign language educator
Roozen, Mary Louise public relations executive
Rosenblatt, Suzanne Maris performance artist, poet, visual artist
Rosenblum, Martin Jack historian
Ryan, Patrick Michael lawyer
Samson, Allen Lawrence bank executive
Samson, Richard Max investments and real estate executive
Sandler, Lawrence newspaper reporter
Sanfilippo, Jon Walter lawyer
Sankovitz, James Leo retired development director, lobbyist
Sante, William Arthur, II electronics manufacturing executive
Scarvie, Walter Bernard clergyman
Schaleben, Arville newspaper editor, writer, educator
Scheinfeld, James David travel agency executive
†Schmidt, Christian E. bank executive
Schneider, Thomas Paul prosecutor
Schnoll, Howard Manuel investment banking and managed asset consultant
Schnur, Robert Arnold lawyer
Schrader, Thomas F. utilities executive
Schroeder, John H. university chancellor
Schultz, Richard Otto ophthalmologist, educator
Schwartz, Joseph English language educator
Scrivner, Thomas William lawyer
Selig, Allan H. (Bud Selig) professional baseball team executive
†Selig-Prieb, Wendy sports team executive
Shapiro, James Edward judge
Shapiro, Robert Donald management consultant
Shetty, Kaup Rajmohan endocrinologist, educator
Shields, James Richard alcohol and drug counselor, consultant
Shiely, John Stephen company executive, lawyer
Shindell, Sidney medical educator, physician
Shriner, Thomas L., Jr. lawyer
Siegesmund, Kenneth August retired forensic scientist, anatomist, consultant, and educator
Silverman, Franklin Harold speech pathologist, educator
†Sklba, Richard J. bishop
Smith, David Bruce lawyer
†Smith, James John physiologist
Smith, John Allen English educator
Soergel, Konrad Hermann physician
Solomon, Donald William mathematics and computer science educator, consultant
Spann, Wilma Nadene educational administrator
Sporc, Keith Kent newspaper executive
Stadtmueller, Joseph Peter federal judge
Steinmiller, John F. professional basketball team executive
Stephenson, Robert Baird energy company executive
Sterner, Frank Maurice industrial executive
Stokes, Kathleen Sarah dermatologist
Stratton, Bradley Jon magazine editor
Stubbe, Ray William minister, chaplain, author
Sturm, William Charles lawyer
Sullivan, Edward periodical editor
Swanson, Roy Arthur classicist, educator
Szallai, Kenneth J. muncipal or county official
Szmanda, Lucille Marie retired vocational school educator
Taylor, Allen M. community foundation executive
Taylor, Robert oncologist
Terry, Leon Cass neurologist, educator
Terschan, Frank Robert lawyer
Teuschler, Michael Alexander computer consultant
Theis, William Harold lawyer, educator
†Thompson, Basil F. ballet master
Thrall, Arthur Alvin artist
Titley, Robert L. lawyer
Towne, Jonathan Baker vascular surgeon
Trindal, Joseph William federal law enforcement official
Tweddell, James Scott surgeon
Uecker, Bob actor, radio announcer, former baseball player, TV personality
Valance, Marsha Jeanne library director, story teller
Van Grunsven, Paul Robert lawyer
Vice, Jon Earl hospital executive
Viets, Hermann college president, consultant
Vos, Theresa Carmella nurse
Wagner, Diane M(argaret) theology educator
Wagner, Marvin general and vascular surgeon, educator
Wake, Madeline Musante nursing educator, university dean
Waldbaum, Jane Cohn art history educator
Waller, Mary Bellis psychotherapist, education educator, consultant
Walmer, Edwin Fitch lawyer
Walthers, Bruce Julius hobby industry executive
Warren, Richard M. experimental psychologist, educator
Weakland, Rembert G. archbishop
†Weening, Richard William, Jr. banker, finance and communications executive, venture capitalist
Weifbecker, Robert T. healthcare administrator
Weinhauer, Bob professional sports team executive
White, Jill Mary nursing educator
Whyte, George Kenneth, Jr. lawyer
Widera, Georg Ernst Otto mechanical engineering educator, consultant
†Wild, Robert Anthony university president
Wilde, Anne Marie sales executive, artist
Wiley, Edwin Packard retired lawyer
Wilkenhauser, Charles zoological park administrator
Will, Trevor Jonathan lawyer
Williams, Clay Rule lawyer
Wilsdon, Thomas Arthur product development engineer, administrator
Winsten, Saul Nathan lawyer
Winston, Maxine Spears social worker
†Witty, Christine (Chris Witty) speed skater
Wolfe, Christopher political science educator
Wucherer, Ruth Marie small business owner
Wynn, Stanford Alan lawyer
Yontz, Kenneth Fredric medical and chemical company executive
Youker, James Edward radiologist
Zeidler, Frank P. former association administrator, mayor, arbitrator, mediator, fact-finder
Zelazo, Nathaniel K. engineering executive
Zore, Edward John insurance company executive

Mineral Point
Olson, John W. advocate

Minocqua
Pickert, Robert Walter accountant
Utt, Glenn S., Jr. motel investments and biotech industry company executive
Van Howe, Robert Storms pediatrician

Monona
Fritz, Bruce Morrell photographer

Monroe
Bean, Virginia Ann marketing executive
Bishop, Carolyn Benkert public relations counselor
Kindschi, George William pathologist
Kittelsen, Rodney Olin lawyer
Wilcox, Winton Wilfred, Jr. computer specialist, consultant

Montello
Burns, Robert Edward editor, publisher
Dufour, Richard Joseph district attorney
Wissbaum, Donna Cacic lawyer

Mukwonago
†Adelman, Lynn S. United States district judge

Muskego
Stefaniak, Norbert John business administration educator

Nashotah
Kriss, Gary W(ayne) Episcopal priest
Vincent, Norman L. retired insurance company executive

Neenah
Bergstrom, Dedric Waldemar retired paper company executive
Bero, R.D. manufacturing executive
Crouch-Smolarek, Judith Ann community health nurse
Hanson, Charles R(ichard) manufacturing company executive
Stanton, Thomas Mitchell lawyer, educator
Tsai, Fu-Jya polymer scientist and engineer
Workman, Jerome James, Jr. chemist

Neshkoro
Eiche, Candace Rose journalist

New Berlin
Fishburn, Kay Maurine nurse
Kuglitsch, Maureen Rose maternal/child health nurse
Peck, Curtiss Steven organization development consultant, author
Weinzierl, Thomas Allen data processing and data communications manager
Winkler, Dolores Eugenia retired hospital administrator

New Glarus
Etter, Peter Erich school district administrator
Marsh, Robert Charles writer, music critic
Sippy, David Dean dentist

New London
Fitzgerald, Laurine Elisabeth university dean, educator

New Richmond
Schwan, LeRoy Bernard artist, retired educator

Oak Creek
Harris, R(ichard) Steven data processing executive, consultant, educator
Kim, Zaezeung allergist, immunologist, educator
†Rivera, Mario Angelo anthropologist, consultant, researcher
Semmes, Sally Peterson dance educator, performer, speech educator, choreographer
Thomae, Mary Joan Pangborn special education educator

Oconomowoc
Luedke, Patricia Georgianne microbiologist
Schacht, Ruth Elaine nursing educator
Vespa, Ned Angelo photographer

Oconto Falls
Leifker, Dale Alan accountant
Schlieve, Hy C. J. principal

Onalaska
†Pertzsch, Evelyn Maria civic worker
Waite, Lawrence Wesley osteopathic physician

Oregon
Dorner, Peter Paul retired economist, educator

Osceola
Finster, James Robert library media specialist

Oshkosh
Barwig, Regis Norbert James priest
Blake, Frank Burgay librarian, writer
Cooper, Janelle Lunette neurologist, educator
Curtis, George Warren lawyer
Deniston-Trochta, Grace Marie educator, artist
Drebus, Richard William pharmaceutical company executive
Gruberg, Martin political science educator
Herzog, Barbara Jean secondary school educator, administrator
Hu, Li art educator
Hulsebosch, Charles Joseph truck manufacturing company executive
Jones, Norma Louise librarian, educator
Kerrigan, John E. academic administrator
†Larson, Vicki Lord communication disorders educator
McWilliams, Robert Lindsay music educator, musician, conductor
Mocker, Donald W. dean
†Rojahn, Elizabeth J. diplomat
Schoenrock, Tracy Allen airline pilot, securities trader
†Siepmann, James Patrick family practice physician
Sutter-Olson, Linda Kristine minister
Zuern, Rosemary Lucile manufacturing executive, treasurer

Palmyra
Hammiller, Ruth Ellen school psychologist

Pelican Lake
Martin, Mary Wolf newspaper editor

Pewaukee
Dupies, Donald Albert retired civil engineer
Jasiorkowski, Robert Lee real estate broker, computer consultant
Lee, Jack (Jim Sanders Beasley) broadcast executive
Lestina, Gerald F. wholesale grocery executive
Quadracci, Harry V. printing company executive, lawyer
Schaefer, Mark Donald mechanical engineer

Phillips
Peterson, Catherine Lois newspaper reporter

Pleasant Prairie
Knudtson, Diane Marie elementary education educator
Morrone, Frank electronic manufacturing executive
Pollocoff, Michael R. village administrator
Schutte, Richard David financial officer
Ziccarelli, Joan Mary secretary

Plymouth
Gentine, Lee Michael marketing professional
Woythal, Constance Lee psychologist

Portage
†Jensen, Hans William library director

Prescott
†Kees, Mary Adele school psychologist

Racine
†Bray, Charles William, III foundation executive
Campbell, Edward Joseph retired machinery company executive
Coates, Glenn Richard lawyer
Doll, David Michael journalist
Du Rocher, James Howard lawyer
Dye, William Ellsworth lawyer
†Engelman, John Herrick chemist
Fouse, Sarah Virginia geriatrics nurse
Gasiorkiewicz, Eugene Anthony lawyer
Gunnerson, Robert Mark manufacturing company executive, accountant, lawyer
Henley, Joseph Oliver manufacturing company executive
Hodges, Lawrence H. agricultural engineer
Hoelzel, Sally Ann lawyer
Johnson, Samuel Curtis wax company executive
Klein, Gabriella Sonja retired communications executive
Konz, Gerald Keith retired manufacturing company executive
Kunz, Charles Alphonse farm machinery manufacturing executive
McPheron, JoAnn Marie B. music educator, poet
Miller, Yolanda publisher, writer
Moles, Randall Carl orthodontist
†Perez, William D. chemical company executive
Petrie, Marie Rose educational specialist
†Phillips, Robert Derrick psychiatrist
Rosser, Richard Franklin higher education consultant
†Rosso, Jean-Pierre electronics executive
Rudebusch, Alice Ann lawyer
Schoening, Ruth Irene music educator, retired, musician
Sikora, Suzanne Marie dentist
Singh, Susan Marie critical care, maternal, women's health nurse
Stewart, Richard Donald internist, educator
Swanson, Robert Lee lawyer
†Vinakmens, Andris manufacturing executive
Wright, Betty Ren children's book writer

Randolph
Belongie, Michael Eugene English language educator, poet

Rhinelander
Cohen, Nancy L. high school teacher
Kovala, Kathleen Ann small business owner, educator
Newman, Linnaea Rose interior horticulturist consultant
Van Brunt, Marcia Adele social worker

Rice Lake
Alho, Sister Bonnie Kathleen religion educator

Richland Center
Gollata, James Anthony library director

Rio
Kohlwey, Heather Louise landscape architect, artist

Ripon
Miller, George H. historian, educator
Prissel, Barbara Ann paralegal, law educator
Steinbring, John Henry (Jack Steinbring) archaeologist

River Falls
Karolides, Nicholas J. English educator
Thibodeau, Gary A. academic administrator

River Hills
Silverman, Albert A. retired lawyer, manufacturing company executive

Saint Croix Falls
Finster, Diane L. Stelten secondary educator, media specialist, home economics educator

Saint Francis
Grade, Jeffery T. manufacturing company executive

GEOGRAPHIC INDEX 5753 WYOMING

Schofield
Adams, James William *retired chemist*
Gettelman, Robin Claire *media specialist*
Gontarz, Michael Joseph *school psychologist*

Shawano
Heikes, Keith *science administrator*
Lyon, Thomas L. *agricultural organization administrator*
Wilson, Douglas *genetics company executive*

Sheboygan
Buchen, John Gustave *retired judge*
Cecil, Louis Anton *mathematics educator*
†Dussault, Nicholas F. *educator*
Fritz, Kristine Rae *secondary education educator*
Gore, Donald Ray *orthopedic surgeon*
Hanson, Paul Anthony *publisher*
Marr, Kathleen Mary *biologist, educator*

Shorewood
Cataldi, Phyllis Jean *writer, publisher of genealogies*
Surridge, Stephen Zehring *lawyer, writer*

Soldiers Grove
Zimmer, Paul Jerome *publisher, editor, poet, retired*

Solon Springs
Robek, Mary Frances *business education educator*

South Milwaukee
Kitzke, Eugene David *research management executive*
Knoll, Gregg A. *artist, printmaker, educator*
Thibaudeau, May Murphy *writer*

Spooner
Frey, Paul Howard *chemical engineer, engineering consultants company executive*

St Francis
Schaubel, Harry Albert *volunteer*

Stevens Point
Ackley, Katherine Anne *English educator, writer*
Copps, Michael William *retail and wholesale company executive*
Doherty, Patricia Anne *psychologist*
George, Thomas Frederick *chemistry educator*
Morrison, Clifford August *history educator*

Stone Lake
Voss, William Charles *retired oil company executive*

Stoughton
Brenz, Gary Jay *publishing executive*
Huber, David Lawrence *physicist, educator*
†McEvoy, James H. *artist*

Suamico
Roddan, Ray Gene *chiropractor*

Sun Prairie
Berkenstadt, James Allan *lawyer*
†Ford, Dorothy Mary *principal*
Rollette, Harold Henry *insurance company executive*

Superior
Billig, Thomas Clifford *publishing and marketing executive*
Bischoff, Joan *English educator*
Ciccone, Margaret *mayor*
Fliss, Raphael M. *bishop*
Jordan, Robert Earl *business educator*
Peterson, Charlene Marie *educational administrator*

Sussex
Dantzman, Gregory Peter *design engineer*
Losee, John Frederick, Jr. *manufacturing executive*
Stromberg, Gregory *printing ink company executive*

Thiensville
Dickow, James Fred *management consultant*
Hobbs, Walter Clarence *retired educator*
Kostecke, B. William *utilities executive*
Roselle, William Charles *librarian*

Tomah
Due, James M. *pharmacist*
Johnson, Linda Arlene *petroleum and flatbed semi-freight transporter*
Odiet, Fred Michael *family practice physician assistant*

Union Grove
Stern, Walter Wolf, III *lawyer*
Swanson, William Fredin, III *manufacturing executive*

Verona
Hartjes, Laurie Beth *pediatric nurse practitioner, woman's health nurse*
Schroeder, Henry William *publisher*
Waldron, Ellis Leigh *retired political science educator*

Viroqua
†Possehl, Robert *visual artist*

Walworth
Rowland, David Kenneth *religious organization executive*

Warrens
Potter, June Anita *small business owner*

Washington Island
Raup, David Malcolm *paleontology educator*
Schweikert, Norman Carl *musician*

Waterford
Gunderson, Scott Lee *state legislator*
Karraker, Louis Rendleman *retired corporate executive*

Waterloo
Burke, Richard A. *manufacturing executive*

Watertown
Cech, Joseph Harold *chemical engineer*
Degnitz, Dorothy Elsie *nurse*
Henry, Carl Ferdinand Howard *theologian*
Peebles, Allene Kay *manufactured housing company executive*
Thompson, Richard Lloyd *pastor*
Williams, Edward Allen *religious educator, minister*

Waukesha
Dreyfus, Lee Sherman *international speaker*
Dukes, Jack Richard *history educator*
Falcone, Frank S. *academic administrator*
Garrot, Patricia Mary *secondary education educator*
Gesler, Alan Edward *lawyer*
Gruber, John Edward *editor, railroad historian, photographer*
Hanson, Jason David *lawyer*
Larson, Russell George *magazine publisher*
Leatherberry, Anne Knox Clark *interior designer, architectural designer*
Macy, John Patrick *lawyer*
Mielke, William John *civil engineer*
†Wallace, Stan W. *minister*

Waunakee
Kronschnabel, Gerald Leo *sales executive*

Waupaca
Moerschel, Blanche Lenore *pianist, composer, educator*
Schoofs, Gerald Joseph *pilot*

Waupun
Norman, Steve Ronald *librarian*
Wendt, Thomas Gene *controller*

Wausau
Ament, Richard Rand *psychologist*
Bartells, James L. *lawyer*
Builer, Dorothy Marion *business owner*
Connor, Mary Roddis *foundation administrator*
Fleming, Thomas Michael *artist, educator*
Huebner, Suzanne Marie *insurance company executive*
Krause, Steven Albert *writer*
Orr, San Watterson, Jr. *lawyer*
Slayton, John Arthur *electric motor manufacturing executive*
†Whitney, John Denison *English educator, writer*

Wauwatosa
Bub, Alexander David *acoustical engineer*
Fibich, Howard Raymond *retired newspaper editor*
Hollister, Winston Ned *pathologist*
Ladd, Louise Elizabeth *investments company executive*
Wellumson, Douglas R. *religious organization administrator*
Wright, Isaac Wilson, Jr. *quality assurance professional*

West Allis
Aderman, Ralph Merl *English educator*
Mayer, Anthony John *investment company executive*

West Bend
Fabian, Thomas Robert *superintendent of schools*
Fraedrich, Royal Louis *magazine editor, publisher*
Lenz, Dave N. *safety administrator*
Rodney, Joel Morris *dean, campus executive officer*

Weyauwega
Hanneman, Elaine Esther *salesperson*

Whitefish Bay
McInerny, Paul Michael *educational administrator*

Whitehall
Nordhagen, Hallie Huerth *nursing home administrator*

Whitewater
Culbertson, Frances Mitchell *psychology educator*
Gauger, Michele Roberta *photographer, studio administrator, corporate executive*
Greenhill, H. Gaylon *academic administrator*
Gulgowski, Paul William *German language, social science, and history educator*
Kirk, Constance Carroll *health educator*
Kolda, Thomas Joseph *non-profit organization executive*
Ritterbusch, Dale E. *English educator*
Thatcher, Janet Solverson *finance educator*
Ulbricht, Walter Louis *university public affairs administrator*

Williams Bay
Hobbs, Lewis Mankin *astronomer*
Morava, Alice Jean *corporate executive*

Windsor
Baumer, Martha Ann *minister*

Winnebago
Hable, Steven James *recreational therapist, track coach*

Wisconsin Rapids
Engelhardt, LeRoy A. *retired paper company executive*
Gignac, James E. *municipal fire chief, consultant*
Kenney, Richard John *paper company finance executive*
Knuteson, Miles Gene *advertising executive*
Mead, George Wilson, II *paper company executive*
Welland, Teri Ann *principal*

Woodruff
Agre, James Courtland *physical medicine and rehabilitation educator*
DeBauche, Jacqueline Jean *wildlife rehabilitator*

Zenda
Sills, William Henry, III *investment banker*

WYOMING

Afton
Hoopes, Farrel G. *secondary education educator*
Hunsaker, Floyd B. *accountant*

Aladdin
Brunson, Mabel (Dipper) *researcher*

Alpine
Cittone, Henry Aron *hotel and restaurant management educator*

Bonduant
Ellwood, Paul Murdock, Jr. *health policy analyst, consultant*

Buffalo
†Kirven, Timothy J. *lawyer*
Urruty, Katherine Jean *secondary school educator*
Watkins, Eugene Leonard *surgeon, educator*

Casper
Bostwick, Richard Raymond *retired lawyer*
Combs, W(illiam) Henry, III *lawyer*
Day, Stuart Reid *lawyer*
Donley, Russell Lee, III *former state representative*
Downes, William F. *judge*
Durham, Harry Blaine, III *lawyer*
Gray, Jan Charles *lawyer, business owner*
Hinchey, Bruce Alan *environmental engineering company executive*
Hjelmstad, William David *lawyer*
Jozwik, Francis Xavier *agricultural business executive*
Keim, Michael Ray *dentist*
Lowe, Robert Stanley *lawyer*
Meenan, Patrick Henry *state legislator*
Reed, James Earl *fire department commander*
Seese, William Shober *chemistry educator*
Stroock, Thomas Frank *oil and gas company executive*
True, Diemer D. *trucking company executive, former state senator*
Wilkes, Shar (Joan Charlene Wilkes) *elementary education educator*
Wold, John Schiller *geologist, former congressman*

Centennial
Nord, Thomas Allison *healthcare consultant*
Russin, Robert Isaiah *sculptor, educator*

Cheyenne
Argeris, George John *lawyer*
Barrett, James Emmett *federal judge*
†Beaman, William C. *federal judge*
Brimmer, Clarence Addison *federal judge*
†Brooks, John C. *federal judge*
Brorby, Wade *federal judge*
Carlson, Kathleen Bussart *law librarian*
†Catchpole, Judy *state agency administrator*
Ferrari, David Guy *auditor*
Freudenthal, David D. *prosecutor*
Freudenthal, Steven Franklin *lawyer*
Geringer, James E. *governor*
Golden, T. Michael *state supreme court justice*
Grothaus, Pamela Sue *marketing professional*
Hanes, John Grier *lawyer, state legislator*
Hardway, James Edward *vocational and rehabilitative specialist*
†Hart, Joseph H. *bishop*
Hathaway, Stanley Knapp *lawyer*
†Helart, August Marvin *state agency administrator*
Hill, William U. *state supreme court justice*
†Houston, Janice Lynn *employment counselor*
Johnson, Alan Bond *federal judge*
Johnson, Wayne Harold *librarian, county official*
Knight, Robert Edward *banker*
Lehman, Larry L. *state supreme court justice*
Macy, Richard J. *state supreme court justice*
†McBride, John P. *state insurance commissioner*
Mc Clintock, Archie Glenn *lawyer*
†McNiff, Peter J. *federal judge*
Milton, Wayne Alvin *health services administrator*
Moore, Mary French (Muffy Moore) *potter, community activist*
Myers, Rolland Graham *investment counselor*
Noe, Guy *retired social services administrator*
Ohman, Diana J. *state official, former school system administrator*
Price, Keith Glenn *accountant*
Richardson, Earl Wilson *elementary education educator, retired*
†Rodekohr, Diane E. *state official*
Rounds, Linnea Paula *library administrator*
Schliske, Rosalind Routt *journalism educator, journalist*
Schrader, Robert Wesley *judge*
Schuman, Gerald Eugene *soil scientist*
Scorsine, John Magnus *lawyer*
Smith, Stanford Sidney *state treasurer*
Taylor, William Al *state supreme court justice*
Thomson, Thyra Godfrey *former state official*
†Wagner, Samuel Albin Mar *records management executive, educator*
Weeks, William Rawle, Jr. *oil company executive*
†Woodhouse, Gay Vanderpoel *state attorney general*

Cody
Fees, Nancy Fardelius *special education educator*
Grimes, Daphne Buchanan *priest, artist*
Housel, Jerry Winters *lawyer*
Keenan, Beverly Owen *entrepreneur*
Patrick, H. Hunter *lawyer, judge*
Riley, Victor J., Jr. *financial services company executive*
Shreve, Peg *state legislator, retired elementary educator*
Stradley, Richard Lee *lawyer*

Douglas
Harrop, Diane Glaser *shop owner, mayor*
†Willox, James Hugh *rancher*

Fort Laramie
Mack, James A. *parks director*

Francis E Warren AFB
†Neary, Thomas H. *career officer*

Gillette
Brown, Toni Cyd *elementary, middle, and secondary school educator*
Garry, James B. *historian, storyteller, researcher, writer*
Mathers, Earl Frank *economic developer*
Naramore, James Joseph *family practice physician, educator*
Sharp, Pamela Ann *quality assurance engineer*

Glenrock
Bennington, Leslie Orville, Jr. *insurance agent*

Green River
Marty, Lawrence A. *magistrate*
Thoman, Mary E. *business and marketing educator, rancher*

Hulett
†Nuckolls, J. W. *rancher*

Jackson
Bommer, Timothy J *lawyer*
Davis, Randy Lee *soil scientist*
Gordon, Stephen Maurice *manufacturing company executive, rancher*
Herrick, Gregory Evans *technology corporation executive*
LaLonde, Robert Frederick *state senator, retired*
Law, Clarene Alta *innkeeper, state legislator*
Massy, William Francis *education educator, consultant*
†Sandlin, Tim Bernard *author, screenwriter*
Schuster, Robert Parks *lawyer*
Shockey, Gary Lee *lawyer*
Spence, Gerald Leonard *lawyer, writer*

Jackson Hole
Farkas, Carol Garner *nurse, administrator*

Kemmerer
Sundar, Vijendra *lawyer educator*

Lander
†Gist, Richard D. *federal judge*
†Price, Raymond E. *state agency administrator*
†Thompson, Douglas Lynn *rancher*
Tipton, Harry Basil, Jr. *state legislator, physician*

Laramie
Bantjes, Adrian Alexander *history educator*
Bellamy, John Cary *civil engineer, meteorologist*
Boresi, Arthur Peter *author, educator*
Chai, Winberg *political science educator*
Chisum, Emmett Dewain *historian, archeologist, researcher*
Christensen, Martha *mycologist, educator*
Cottam, Keith M. *librarian, educator, administrator*
Crocker, Thomas Dunstan *economics educator*
Darnall, Roberta Morrow *association executive*
Dickman, Francois Moussiegt *former foreign service officer, educator*
†Forsling, Peter J. *defense analyst*
Forster, Bruce Alexander *dean*
Frye, Susan Caroline *English literature educator*
Gill, George Wilhelm *anthropologist*
Gowdy, Curtis *sportscaster*
Grandy, Walter Thomas, Jr. *physicist, educator*
Hansen, Matilda *state legislator*
Hanson, Mary Louise *retired social services administrator*
Hardy, Deborah Welles *history educator*
Harkin, Michael Eugene *anthropologist, educator, writer*
Hausel, William Dan *economic geologist, martial artist*
Kelley, Robert Otis *medical science educator*
Kinney, Lisa Frances *lawyer*
Laman, Jerry Thomas *mining company executive*
Lewis, Randolph Vance *molecular biologist, researcher*
Maxfield, Peter C. *state legislator, law educator, lawyer*
McBride, Judith *elementary education educator*
Meyer, Edmond Gerald *energy and natural resources educator, resources scientist, entrepreneur, former chemistry educator, university administrator*
Meyer, Joseph B. *state official, former academic administrator*
Mingle, John Orville *engineer, educator, lawyer, consultant*
†Pell, Kynric Martin *engineering educator*
Rechard, Paul Albert *civil engineering consulting company executive*
Reif, (Frank) David *artist, educator*
Roark, Terry Paul *astronomer, educator*
Roberts, Philip John *history educator, editor*
Schmitt, Diana Mae *elementary education educator*
Shaffer, Sherrill Lynn *economist*
Stewart, Larry Ray *engineer, financial director, quality consultant*
Williams, Roger Lawrence *historian, educator*

Mills
Kennerknecht, Richard Eugene *marketing executive*

Moose
Craighead, Frank Cooper, Jr. *ecologist*
Schreier, Carl Alan *writer, publisher*

Newcastle
Sample, Bette Jeane *elementary educator*

Pinedale
Barlow, John Perry *writer*

Powell
Brophy, Dennis Richard *psychology and philosophy educator, administrator, clergyman*
Voege, Jean *nursing educator*

Riverton
Bebout, Eli Daniel *oil executive*
Clark, Stanford E. *accountant*
Girard, Nettabell *lawyer*
Hudson, Gary Michael *corporate executive*
Peck, Robert A. *newspaper publisher*
Pursel, Harold Max, Sr. *mining engineer, civil engineer, architectural engineer*

Rock Springs
Blackwell, Samuel Eugene *state legislator*
Kathka, David Arlin *director educational services*
Magnuson, Dennis Duane *secondary education educator*
Schumacher, Jon Walter *accountant, educator*

Saratoga
†Palen, Jerry artist

Sheridan
Aguirre-Batty, Mercedes Spanish and English language and literature educator
Cannon, Kim Decker lawyer
†Connor, Robert W., Jr. federal judge
Goodwin, Doris Helen Kearns history educator, writer
Ryan, Michael Louis controller
Schatz, Wayne Ardale district technology coordinator, computer educator

Story
Mc Ewan, Leonard former judge

Thermopolis
†Krisko, Mary Ellen primary school educator

Wapiti
Sowerwine, Elbert Orla, Jr. chemist, chemical engineer

Wheatland
Bunker, John Birkbeck cattle rancher, retired sugar company executive
Hunkins, Raymond Breedlove lawyer, rancher
Morrison, Samuel Ferris secondary school educator
Whitney, Ralph Royal, Jr. financial executive

Wilson
Chrystie, Thomas Ludlow investor
Fritz, Jack Wayne communications and marketing company executive
Lawroski, Harry nuclear engineer
Sage, Andrew Gregg Curtin, II corporate investor, manager

Worland
Foster, William Silas, Jr. minister
Wise, Kathryn Ann middle school educator
Woods, Lawrence Milton airline company executive

Yellowstone National Park
†Cole, Stephen E. federal judge
Finley, Michael national park administrator

TERRITORIES OF THE UNITED STATES

AMERICAN SAMOA

Pago Pago
Lutali, A. P. senator
†Mailo, Toetagata Albert territory attorney general
Sunia, Tauese governor
Tulafono, Togiola T.A. state official
Weitzel, John Quinn bishop

FEDERATED STATES OF MICRONESIA

Chuuk
Neylon, Martin Joseph retired bishop
†Samo, Amando bishop

Pohnpei
King, Edward C. judge

GUAM

Agana
Apuron, Anthony Sablan archbishop
Bordallo, Madeleine Mary (Mrs. Ricardo Jerome Bordallo) lieutenant governor
Espaldon, Ernesto Mercader former senator, plastic surgeon
Gutierrez, Carl T. C. governor
Lamorena, Alberto C., III supreme court justice guam
Maraman, Katherine Ann judge
San Agustin, Joe Taitano Guamanian senator, financial institution executive, management researcher
Unpingco, John Walter Sablan federal judge
Weeks, Janet Healy supreme court justice

Hagatna
Alano, Ernesto Olarte secondary education educator

Mangilao
Colfax, Richard Schuyler business management and human resources educator
Lee, Chin-Tian academic administrator, agricultural studies educator

Santa Rita
Bradner, Diana Jean psychiatric and pediatric nurse

Talofofo
Taylor, James John academic administrator

Tamuning
Cahinhinan, Nelia Agbada retired public health nurse, administrator

Yigo
Kio, Stephen Hre minister

NORTHERN MARIANA ISLANDS

Saipan
Dela Cruz, Jose Santos retired state supreme court chief justice
Munson, Alex Robert judge
†Tenorio, Pedro Pangelinan government official

PUERTO RICO

Aguadilla
Jaramillo, Juana Segarra dean

Bayamon
Berio, Blanca editor
Bonilla, Daisy Rose parochial school English language educator
Herrans-Perez, Laura Leticia psychologist, educator, research consultant
Ortiz, William composer, music educator

Caguas
Corrada del Rio, Alvaro bishop
Rivera-Urrutia, Beatriz Dalila psychology and rehabilitation counseling educator

Ceiba
DeMaio, Dorothy Walters tutorial school administrator, consultant

Dorado
Ortiz-Quiñones, Carlos Ruben electronics engineer, educator
Spector, Michael Joseph agribusiness executive

Guayama
Febres-Santiago, Samuel F. university chancellor

Guaynabo
Barquin, Ramón Carlos, III political scientist, consultant
Gonzalez, Edgardo Antonio lawyer

Hato Rey
Cerezo, Carmen Consuelo federal judge
†DeJesus-Kellogg, Sara E. federal judge
Ferrer, Miguel Antonio brokerage firm and investment bank executive
Laffitte, Hector Manuel federal judge
†Lamoutte, Enrique S. federal judge
Vilches-O'Bourke, Octavio Augusto accounting company executive
Wirshing, Herman protective services official

Hormigueros
Acosta, Ursula psychologist

Humacao
Castrodad, Felix A. university administrator
Delgado-Rodriguez, Manuel secondary school educator

Luquillo
Pinney, Frances Bailey art therapist, artist, consultant

Mayaguez
Casiano Vargas, Ulises Aurelio bishop
Collins, Dennis Glenn mathematics educator
Sahai, Hardeo medical statistics educator
Souto Bachiller, Fernando Alberto chemistry educator

Ponce
Cummings, Luis Emilio anesthesiologist, consultant
Surinach Carreras, Ricardo Antonio bishop
Torres Oliver, Juan Fremiot bishop

Rio Piedras
†Arrillaga, Maria foreign language educator
Davila, Norma developmental psychologist and program evaluator
López de Mendez, Annette Giselda education educator

Sabana Seca
Sierra Millán, Daniel school administrator

San German
Mojica, Agnes academic administrator

San Juan
Abella, Marisela Carlota business executive
Acevedo-Vila, Anibal state legislator, lawyer
Acosta, Raymond Luis federal judge
Andreu-Garcia, Jose Antonio territory supreme court chief justice
Aponte Martinez, Luis Cardinal archbishop
†Arenas, Justo federal judge
Basols, Jose Andres school director, priest
Bonilla-Felix, Melvin A. pediatrician, educator
Burgos, Norma secretary of state
†Callen, Tarquin M. hotel executive
†Carlo-Altieri, Gerardo A. federal judge
Carreras, Francisco José retired university president, foundation executive
Casellas, Salvador E. judge
†Castellanos, Jesus Antonio federal judge
Corrada del Rio, Baltasar supreme court justice
Cortes, Ivette elementary education educator
†Delgado-Colon, Aida M. federal judge
del Toro, Ilia retired education educator
de Rodon, Miriam Naveira supreme court justice
de Taboas, Hilda Rivera occupational health nurse
Díaz de Gonzalez, Ana María psychologist, educator
Dominguez, Daniel R. judge
Febo, Nilda Luz pediatrics and psychiatric-mental health nurse
Fernández-Coll, Fred microbiologist, food technology laboratory director
Fusté, José Antonio federal judge
Fuster, Jaime B. supreme court justice
Ghaly, Evone Shehata pharmaceutics and industrial pharmacy educator
Gierbolini-Ortiz, Gilberto federal judge
Gil, Guillermo prosecutor
Hernandez-Denton, Federico supreme court justice
Irizarry-Yunque, Carlos Juan lawyer, educator
Maldonado, Norman I. academic administrator, physician educator
Marvel, Thomas Stahl architect
Matheu, Federico Manuel university chancellor
Muñoz-Solá, Haydeé Socorro library administrator
Ocasio Belén, Félix E. real estate development company executive
Ocasio-Melendez, Marcial Enrique history educator
Orkand, Richard Kenneth neurobiologist, researcher, educator
Pabon-Perez, Heidi medical physicist, educator
Pierluisi, Pedro R. lawyer
Ramos, Carlos E. law educator
Rodriguez, Agustin Antonio surgeon
Rodriguez Arroyo, Jesus gynecologic oncologist
Rodriguez-Diaz, Juan E. lawyer
Rosario-Guardiola, Reinaldo dermatologist
Torruella, Juan R. federal judge
Uribe, Javier Miguel investment executive
Vallone, Ralph, Jr. lawyer
†Velez Silva, Xenia Puerto Rican government official
Weinstein-Bacal, Stuart Allen lawyer, educator

Yauco
Artiles, Nemuel Othniel hospital executive

REPUBLIC OF MARSHALL ISLAND

Majuro
Plaisted, Joan M. diplomat

TRUST TERRITORY OF PACIFIC ISLANDS

Palau
Barden, Kenneth Eugene lawyer, educator

VIRGIN ISLANDS

Charlotte Amalie
Aubain, Joseph F. municipal official
†Barnard, Geoffrey W. federal judge
Bolt, Thomas Alvin Waldrep lawyer
Feuerzeig, Henry Louis lawyer
Hurd, James A., Jr. prosecutor
†James, Gerard Amwur, II lieutenant governor
Stapleton, Marylyn Alecia diplomat
Thomas, Elliott G. bishop

Christiansted
Finch, Raymond Lawrence judge
Hart, Thomas Hughson, III lawyer
Resnick, Jeffrey Lance federal magistrate judge

Saint John
Walker, Ronald R. writer, newspaper editor, educator

Saint Thomas
Caffee, Lorren Dale judge
Duarte, Patricia M. real estate and insurance broker
Hodge, Verne Antonio judge
Mabe, Hugh Prescott, III prosecutor
Mattsson, Ake psychiatrist, physician
Moore, Thomas Kail chief judge supreme court VI
†O'Bryan, James A. communications specialist
Schneider, Roy former US Virgin Islands government official
†Simmonds, Ruby government official
†Turnbull, Charles W. governor

MILITARY ADDRESSES OF THE UNITED STATES

ATLANTIC

APO
Alexander, Leslie M. ambassador
Baltimore, Richard Lewis, III foreign service officer
Carner, George foreign service executive, economic strategist
Creagan, James Francis diplomat
Gutierrez, Lino diplomat
Jett, Dennis Coleman foreign service officer
Kamman, Curtis Warren ambassador
Maisto, John F. ambassador

EUROPE

APO
Adams, Ronald Emerson army officer
Barry, William Patrick military officer
†Begert, William J. lieutenant general United States Air Force
†Bell, Burwell Baxter, III major general United States Army
Benedict, John Anthony, II army officer
Bikales, Norbert M. chemist, science administrator
†Brady, Roger A. brigadier general United States Air Force
Cook, Frances D. diplomat
†Croom, Charles Edward, Jr. brigadier general United States Air Force
†Deptula, David A. United States Air Force general
Fowler, Wyche, Jr. ambassador
Gibbs, Oscar Keith physician assistant
†Hendrix, John Walter lieutenant general United States Army
Johnson, Melissa Ann early childhood educator
King, Daniel Carleton physician assistant, air force officer, consultant
Kornblum, John Christian ambassador
Lederer, Max Donald, Jr. lawyer
Lino, Marisa Rose diplomat
Meigs, Montgomery Cunningham, Jr. military officer
Milam, William Bryant diplomat, economist
Niles, Thomas Michael Tolliver university administrator
†Paddock, John Francis, Jr. rear admiral United States Navy Reserve
Ray, Norman Wilson career officer
Scholes, Edison Earl army officer
Scriggins, Alan Lee developmental pediatrician
Thon, Patricia Frances pediatrics nurse, medical and surgical nurse
Wakefield, Marie Annette librarian
Walker, Edward S., Jr. diplomat

FPO
Bailey, Steven Scott operations research analyst
Bryant, Stanley W. career officer
Metzger, James W. military officer
Murphy, Daniel J., Jr. military officer
Naughton, Richard J. military officer
Shirk, Keith Byron US Navy weather specialist

London
Bartholomew, Reginald diplomat

PPO
Loren, Donald Patrick naval officer

PACIFIC

APO
Beeman, Josiah Horton diplomat
Calder, Kent Eyring political science educator, diplomat
†Dallager, John R. career officer
Gordon, Carey Nathaniel lawyer, federal agency administrator
Hobbs, Roy Jerry military career officer, health services administrator
Holmes, Genta Hawkins diplomat
Murray, Terrence P. career officer
Ormes, Ashton Harrison career officer
Pulaski, Lori Jaye career officer
Turner, David Lowery system safety engineer

FPO
Boucher, Richard A. ambassador
Haskins, Michael Donald naval officer
†Murphy, Dennis John military officer

CANADA

Hamilton
Collins, John Alfred obstetrician-gynecologist, educator

Sherbrooke
Deslongchamps, Pierre chemistry educator

Toronto
†Sharp, Isadore hotel facility executive

Winnipeg
†Barwinsky, Jaroslaw cardiac surgeon
†Hodgkins, William F. career officer

ALBERTA

Alberta
Nissinen, Mikko Pekka dancer

Calgary
Armstrong, David Anthony physical chemist, educator
Bartlett, Grant A. professional sports team executive
Campbell, Finley Alexander geologist
Caron, Ernie Matthew airport executive
Cumming, Thomas Alexander stock exchange executive
Curtis, John Barry archbishop
Edwards, N. Murray professional sports team owner
†Epton, Gregg performing company executive
Forbis, Richard George archaeologist
Furnival, George Mitchell petroleum and mining consultant
Gish, Norman Richard oil industry executive
Glockner, Peter G. civil and mechanical engineering educator
Graf, Hans conductor
Hagerman, Allen Reid mining executive
Haskayne, Richard Francis petroleum company executive
Heidemann, Robert Albert chemical engineering educator, researcher
Holman, J(ohn) Leonard retired manufacturing corporation executive
Horton, William Russell retired utility company executive
Hotchkiss, Harley N. professional hockey team owner
Hriskevich, Michael Edward oil and gas consultant
Hughes, Margaret Eileen law educator, former dean
Hume, James Borden corporate professional, foundation executive
Hyne, James Bissett chemistry educator, industrial scientist, consultant
Izzo, Herbert John language and linguistics educator, researcher
Janes, Robert Roy museum executive, archaeologist
Jones, Geoffrey Melvill physiology research educator
Kelley, Jane Holden archaeology educator
Lederis, Karolis Paul (Karl Lederis) pharmacologist, educator, researcher
Libin, Alvin G. business executive
†Lipton, Jeffrey M. chemical company executive
Little, Brian Frederick oil company executive
Lougheed, Peter lawyer, former Canadian official
MacDonald, Alan Hugh librarian, university administrator
Maclagan, John Lyall retired petroleum company executive
†MacNeill, Brian F. oil and natural gas company executive
Maher, Peter Michael management educator
Maier, Gerald James corporate executive
Malik, Om Parkash electrical engineering educator, researcher
McCaig, Jeffrey James transportation company executive
McCaig, John Robert transportation executive
McDaniel, Roderick Rogers petroleum engineer
McEwen, Alexander Campbell cadastral studies educator, former Canadian government official, surveying consultant
McIntyre, Norman F. petroleum industry executive
Mc Kinnon, F(rancis) A(rthur) Richard utility executive
Melvill-Jones, Geoffrey physician, educator
Milavsky, Harold Phillip real estate executive
Monk, Allan James baritone
Mossop, Grant Dilworth geological institute director
Neale, E(rnest) R(ichard) Ward retired university official, consultant
O'Brien, David Peter business executive
Peltier, John Wayne (Jack Peltier) oil and gas industry executive
Pick, Michael Claude international exploration consultant
Pierce, Robert Lorne petrochemical, oil and gas company executive
Raeburn, Andrew Harvey performing arts association executive, record producer
Rasporich, Anthony Walter university dean

†McFeetors, Raymond L. *insurance company executive*
Morrish, Allan Henry *electrical engineering educator*
Naimark, Arnold *medical educator, physiologist, educator*
Oberman, Sheldon Arnold *writer, educator*
Persaud, Trivedi Vidhya Nandan *anatomy educator, researcher, consultant*
Poettcker, Henry *retired seminary president*
Praznik, Darren Thomas *provincial legislator*
Ronald, Allan Ross *internal medicine and medical microbiology educator, researcher*
Ross, Robert Thomas *neurologist, educator*
Schacter, Brent Allan *oncologist, health facility administrator*
Schaefer, Theodore Peter *chemistry educator*
Schnoor, Jeffrey Arnold *lawyer*
Seifert, Blair Wayne *clinical pharmacist*
Smith, Ian Cormack Palmer *biophysicist*
Spohr, Arnold Theodore *artistic director, choreographer*
Suzuki, Isamu *microbiology educator, researcher*
Thorfinnson, A. Rodney *hospital administrator*
Tovey, Bramwell *conductor, composer*
Turner, Robert Comrie *composer*
Wall, Leonard J. *bishop*
Watchorn, William Ernest *venture capitalist*
†Wilhelm-Boyles, Andrew *performing company executive*
Wolfart, H.C. *linguistics scholar, author, editor*
Wreford, David Mathews *magazine editor*

NEW BRUNSWICK

Campbellton
Blanchard, Edmond P. *Canadian government official*

Charters Settlement
Easterbrook, James Arthur *psychology educator*

Douglas
Cogswell, Frederick William *English language educator, poet, editor, publisher*

Fredericton
Faig, Wolfgang *survey engineer, engineering educator*
Grotterod, Knut *retired paper company executive*
Kenyon, Gary Michael *gerontology educator, researcher*
LeBreton, Paul M. *government official*
Lemmon, George Colborne *bishop*
Lewell, Peter A. *international technology executive, researcher*
Lumsden, Ian Gordon *art gallery director*
McGreal, Rory Patrick *educational administrator*
Parr-Johnston, Elizabeth *academic administrator*
Strange, Henry Hazen *judge*

Moncton
McKenna, Frank Joseph *Canadian government official, lawyer*

Rothesay
Fairweather, Robert Gordon Lee *lawyer*
Troy, J. Edward *bishop*

Saint Andrews
Anderson, John Murray *operations executive, former university president*

Saint John
Condon, Thomas Joseph *university historian*
Mowatt, E. Ann *women's voluntary leader, lawyer*

Sussex
Secord, Lloyd Douglas *healthcare administrator*

Westfield
Logan, Rodman Emmason *retired jurist*

NEWFOUNDLAND

Corner Brook
Payne, Sidney Stewart *retired archbishop*

Saint John's
Clark, Jack I. *civil engineer, researcher*
Davis, Charles Carroll *aquatic biologist, educator*
Grattan, Patricia Elizabeth *art gallery director*
Harvey, Donald Frederick *bishop*
May, Arthur W. *university president*
Rochester, Michael Grant *geophysics educator*
Russell, Frederick William *travel company executive, former Canadian provincial official*
Williams, Harold *geology educator*

Saint Johns
Gibbons, Rex Vincent *geologist*

NORTHWEST TERRITORIES

Yellowknife
Croteau, Denis *bishop*
LeBlanc, Pierre Gabriel *military officer*

NOVA SCOTIA

Antigonish
Gillis, John William *retired geologist, retired provincial government legislator*

Bedford
Hennigar, David John *investment broker*

Dartmouth
Elliott, James A. *oceanographer, researcher*
Horrocks, Norman *library science educator, editor*
Keen, Charlotte Elizabeth *marine geophysicist, researcher*
Mann, Kenneth Henry *marine ecologist*
Platt, Trevor Charles *oceanographer, scientist*

Elmsdale
Shrieves, Janet *airport terminal executive*

Halifax
Birdsall, William Forest *librarian*
Borgese, Elisabeth Mann *political science educator, author*
Carrigan, David Owen *history educator*
Casson, Alan Graham *thoracic surgeon, researcher*
Cosman, Francene Jen *government official*
Dahn, Jeff Raymond *physics educator*
Dexter, Robert Paul *lawyer*
†Dunnel, Leslie B. *conductor*
Dykstra Lynch, Mary Elizabeth *library and information science educator*
Fillmore, Peter Arthur *mathematician, educator*
Fowler, Charles Allison Eugene *architect, engineer*
Glube, Constance Rachelle *Canadian chief justice*
Gold, Edgar *marine affairs educator, mariner, lawyer*
Gold, Judith Hammerling *psychiatrist*
Goldbloom, Richard Ballon *pediatrics educator*
Gratwick, John *management consulting executive, writer, consultant*
Gray, James *English literature educator*
Hall, Brian Keith *biology educator, author*
Kinley, John James *government official*
Langley, George Ross *medical educator*
Mingo, James William Edgar *lawyer*
Murray, Thomas John (Jock Murray) *medical humanities educator, medical researcher, neurologist*
O'Dor, Ron *physiologist, marine biology educator*
Ozmon, Kenneth Lawrence *university president, educator*
Pincock, Douglas George *electronics company executive*
Renouf, Harold Augustus *business consultant, retired*
Shaw, Timothy Milton *political science educator*
Smith, Ronald Emory *telecommunications executive*
Sparling, Mary Christine *foundation executive*
Stairs, Denis Winfield *political science educator*
Stevenson, Candace J. *museum director*
Stewart, Ronald Daniel *medical educator, government official*
Tonks, Robert Stanley *pharmacology and therapeutics educator, former university dean*
Winham, Gilbert Rathbone *political science educator*

Hammonds Plains
Wilson, Frank Henry *retired electrical engineer*

Kentville
Baker, George Chisholm *engineering executive, consultant*

Lawrencetown
Pottie, Roswell Francis *Canadian federal science and technology consultant*

Lower Sackville
Ortlepp, Bruno *marine navigation educator, master mariner*

North Sydney
Nickerson, Jerry Edgar Alan *manufacturing executive*

Parrsboro
Hatfield, Leonard Fraser *retired bishop*

Stellarton
Rowe, Allan Duncan *company executive*
Sobey, David Frank *food company executive*
Sobey, Donald Creighton Rae *real estate developer*

Tatamagouche
Roach, Margot Ruth *retired biophysicist, educator*

Timberlea
Verma, Surjit K. *retired school system administrator*

Toronto
Tolmie, Kenneth Donald *artist, author*

Truro
Mac Rae, Herbert Farquhar *retired college president*

Wallace
Boyle, Willard Sterling *physicist*

Waverley
Grady, Wayne J. *government official*

Wolfville
Bishop, Roy Lovitt *physics and astronomy educator*
Colville, David Alexander *artist*
Elliott, Robbins Leonard *consultant*
Ogilvie, Kelvin Kenneth *university president, chemistry educator*
Toews, Daniel Peter *zoologist*
Zeman, Jarold Knox *history educator*

Yarmouth
Wingle, James Mathew *bishop*

ONTARIO

Agincourt
Lutgens, Harry Gerardus *food company executive*

Almonte
Morrison, Angus Curran *aviation executive*

Ancaster
Brockhouse, Bertram Neville *physicist, retired educator*

Aurora
Lanthier, Ronald Ross *retired manufacturing company executive*
Stronach, Frank *automobile parts manufacturing executive*

Blenheim
Thompson, Wesley Duncan *grain merchant*

Bracebridge
Evans, John David Daniel *judge*
MacKenzie, Lewis Wharton *military officer*

Brampton
Allen, Clive Victor *lawyer, communications company executive*
Bastian, Donald Noel *bishop, retired*
Greenhough, John Hardman *business forms company executive*
Malhi, Gurbax Singh *legislator*
Savoie, Leonard Norman *transportation company executive*
Toole, David George *pulp and paper products executive*

Brantford
Inns, Harry Douglas Ellis *optometrist*
Woodcock, Richard Beverley *health facility administrator*

Brockville
McLeod, Philip Robert *publishing executive*
Spalding, James Stuart *retired telecommunications company executive*

Burlington
Harris, Philip John *engineering educator*
Karsten, Albert *religious organization administrator*
McGeorge, Ronald Kenneth *hospital executive*
McMulkin, Francis John *retired steel company executive*

Caledon East
Fallis, Albert Murray *microbiology educator*

Cambridge
Eldred, Gerald Marcus *retired performing arts association executive*
MacBain, William Halley *minister, theology educator, seminary chancellor*
Turnbull, Robert Scott *manufacturing company executive*
White, Joseph Charles *manufacturing and retailing company executive*

Campbellville
Georgije, Djokic *bishop*

Chalk River
Allan, Colin James *research and development manager*
Milton, John Charles Douglas *nuclear physicist*
Torgerson, David Franklyn *chemist, research facility administrator*

Chatham
McKeough, William Darcy *investment company executive*

Cornwall
La Rocque, Eugene Philippe *bishop*

Deep River
Davies, John Arthur *physics and engineering educator, scientist*
Newcombe, Howard Borden *biologist, consultant*

Don Mills
Applebaum, Louis *composer, conductor*
Atwood, Margaret Eleanor *author*
Budrevics, Alexander *landscape architect*
French, William Harold *retired newspaper editor*

Downsview
Burton, Ian *environmentalist, consultant, scholar, writer*
Endler, Norman Solomon *psychology educator*
Forer, Arthur H. *biology educator, researcher, editor*
Ribner, Herbert Spencer *physicist, educator*
Tennyson, Roderick C. *aerospace scientist*
Thomas, Clara McCandless *retired English language educator, biographer*

Dundas
Shaw, John Firth *orchestra administrator*

Elgin
Lafave, Hugh Gordon John *medical association executive, psychiatrist, educator, consultant*

Etobicoke
Coleman, K. Virginia *diaconal minister*
†Cooper, Simon F. *hotel executive*
Howe, James Tarsicius *retired insurance company executive*
Hyland, Geoffrey Fyfe *energy service company executive*

Fort Erie
Watson, Stewart Charles *construction company executive*

Freelton
Sonnenberg, Hardy *data processing company research and development executive, engineer*

Galt
Dobbie, George Herbert *retired textile manufacturing executive*

Gloucester
Boisvert, Laurier Joseph *communications executive*
MacFarlane, John Alexander *former federal housing agency administrator*
Marsters, Gerald Frederick *retired aerospace science and technology executive*

Greely
Smith, Stuart Lyon *psychiatrist, corporate executive*

Grimsby
Morgan, Wayne Philip *curator, writer, researcher*

Guelph
Benn, Denna M. *veterinarian*
Beveridge, Terrance James *microbiology educator, researcher*
Bewley, John Derek *botany researcher, educator*
Dickinson, William Trevor *hydrologist, educator*
Jorgensen, Erik *forest pathologist, educator, consultant*
Karl, Gabriel *physics educator*
Kasha, Kenneth John *agriculturist, educator*
Land, Reginald Brian *library administrator*
Oaks, B. Ann *plant physiologist, educator*
Sells, Bruce Howard *biomedical sciences educator*

Hamilton
Banaschewski, Bernhard *mathematics educator*
Bandler, John William *electrical engineering educator, consultant*
Basinski, Zbigniew Stanislaw *metal physicist, educator*
Basmajian, John Varoujan *medical scientist, educator, physician*
Bienenstock, John *physician, educator*
Blewett, David Lambert *English literature educator*
Campbell, Colin Kydd *electrical and computer engineering educator, researcher*
Crowe, Cameron Macmillan *chemical engineering educator*
Datars, William Ross *physicist, educator*
Garland, William James *engineering physics educator*
George, Peter James *economist, educator*
Gillespie, Ronald James *chemistry educator, researcher, writer*
Hill, Graham Roderick *librarian*
Johnston, Malcolm Carlyle *bank executive*
King, Leslie John *geography educator*
Lee, Alvin A. *literary educator, scholar, author*
Lipton, Daniel Bernard *conductor*
MacLean, David Bailey *chemistry educator, researcher*
McKay, Alexander Gordon *classics educator*
Mueller, Charles Barber *surgeon, educator*
Parnas, David Lorge *engineering educator, computer scientist*
Roland, Charles Gordon *physician, medical historian, educator*
Ryan, Ellen Bouchard *psychology educator, gerontologist*
Schwarcz, Henry Philip *geologist, educator*
Shaw, Denis Martin *university dean, former geology educator*
Spenser, Ian Daniel *chemist educator*
Sprung, Donald Whitfield Loyal *physics educator*
Stanbury, Robert Douglas George *lawyer, executive*
Telmer, Frederick Harold *steel products manufacturing executive*
Tonnos, Anthony *bishop*
Uchida, Irene Ayako *cytogenetics educator, researcher*
Welch, Douglas Lindsay *physics educator*

Hanover
Adams, John David Vessot *manufacturing company executive*

Islington
White, Adrian Michael Stephen *financial executive*

Kanata
Dudley, Rick *professional hockey coach*
†Martin, Jacques *professional hockey coach*
†Rhodes, Damian *professional hockey player*
†Yashin, Alexei *hockey player*

Keswick
Macdonald, John Barfoot *research foundation executive*

Kingston
Akenson, Donald Harman *historian, educator*
Bacon, David Walter *chemical engineering educator*
Batchelor, Barrington de Vere *civil engineer, educator*
Campbell, L(ouis) Lorne *mathematics educator*
Dick, Susan Marie *English language educator*
Ewan, George Thomson *physicist, educator*
Glynn, Peter Alexander Richard *hospital administrator*
Hamilton, Albert Charles *English language educator*
Kaliski, Stephan Felix *economics educator*
Kaufman, Nathan *pathology educator, physician*
Leggett, William C. *biology educator, academic administrator*
Low, James A. *physician*
McDonald, Arthur Bruce *physics educator*
McGeer, James Peter *research executive, consultant*
Meisel, John *political scientist*
Read, Allan Alexander *minister*
Riley, Anthony William *German language and literature educator*
Sayer, Michael *physics educator*
Spence, Francis John *archbishop*
Spencer, John Hedley *biochemistry educator*
Stewart, Alec Thompson *physicist*
Szarek, Walter Anthony *chemist, educator*
Turpin, David Howard *biologist, educator*
Wyatt, Gerard Robert *biology educator, researcher*

Kitchener
Coles, Graham *conductor, composer*
Huras, William David *bishop*
MacDonald, Wayne Douglas *publisher*
Pollock, John Albon *broadcasting and manufacturing company executive*
Winger, Roger Elson *church administrator*

Kleinburg
Tyler, Barbara A. *museum director*

Lions Bay
Bartholomew, Gilbert Alfred *retired physicist*

London
Allan, Ralph Thomas Mackinnon *insurance company executive*
Baker, Steve J. *airport executive*
Bancroft, George Michael *chemical physicist, educator*
Bauer, Michael Anthony *computer scientist, educator*
Borwein, David *mathematics educator*
†Brian, Jackson *artistic director*
Buck, Carol Kathleen *medical educator*
Carruthers, S. George *medical educator, physician*
Collins, Thomas Joseph *English language educator*
Cornies, Larry Alan *journalist, educator*
Crncich, Tony Joseph *retired pharmacy chain executive*
Davenport, Alan Garnett *civil engineer, educator*
Davenport, Paul *university administrator, economics educator*
Dreimanis, Aleksis *emeritus geology educator*
Ehrman, Joachim Benedict *mathematics educator*
Fyfe, William Sefton *geochemist, educator*

Gerber, Douglas Earl *classics educator*
Groden, Michael Lewis *English literature educator*
Haskett, Dianne Louise *mayor, lawyer*
Inculet, Ion I. *electrical engineering educator, research director, consultant*
Laidler, David Ernest William *economics educator*
Lala, Peeyush Kanti *medical scientist, educator*
Livick, Stephen *fine art photographer*
Locke, Michael *zoology educator*
Marotta, Joseph Thomas *medical educator*
McMurtry, Robert Y. *academic dean*
McWhinney, Ian Renwick *physician, medical educator*
Osbaldeston, Gordon Francis *business educator, former government official*
Pearson, Norman *urban and regional planner, administrator, academic and planning consultant, writer*
Peterson, Leslie Ernest *bishop*
Poole, Nancy Geddes *art gallery curator*
Reaney, James Crerar *dramatist, poet, educator*
Scott, W. Peter *bishop*
Sherlock, John Michael *bishop*
Stafford, Earl *conductor*
Stewart, Harold Brown *biochemist*
Stillman, Martin J. *physical science research administrator, bioinorganic chemist*
Stothers, John B. *chemistry educator*
William, David *director, actor*
Wilson, Gerald Einar *mechanical and industrial engineer, business executive*
Wonnacott, Ronald Johnston *economics educator*

Manitowaning
Hamilton, Donald Gordon *religious association administrator*

Manotick
Hobson, George Donald *retired geophysicist*
Prince, Alan Theodore *former government official, engineering consultant*

Markham
Burns, H(erbert) Michael *corporate director*
Calkin, Joy Durfée *healthcare executive, consultant, educator*
Dayment, David *airport executive*
Nelson, William George, IV *software company executive*
Ten Cate, Arnold Richard *dentistry educator*

Mississauga
Barkin, Martin *pharmaceutical company executive, physician*
Beckley, Michael John *hotel executive*
Burrell, Carol Ann *trade association executive*
Davies, Michael Norman Arden *lawyer, business executive*
Farrell, Craig *hotel executive*
Gaston, Cito *former professional baseball manager*
Griffin, William Arthur *clergyman, religious organization executive*
†Jackson, Michael I. *hospitality company executive*
Lewis, William Leonard *food products executive*
Mills, Donald McKenzie *librarian*
Peterson, Oscar Emmanuel *pianist*
Roth, John Andrew *communications executive*
Ryan, Noel *librarian, consultant*
Thibault, J(oseph) Laurent *service company executive*
Tobias, Kal *transportation executive*
Turnbull, Adam Michael Gordon *financial executive, accountant*

Nepean
Beare-Rogers, Joyce Louise *former research executive*
Bishop, Claude Titus *retired biological sciences research administrator, editor*
Cornell, Peter McCaul *economic consultant, former government official*
Kallmann, Helmut Max *music historian, retired music librarian*
Stanford, Joseph Stephen *diplomat, lawyer, educator*

Newmarket
Wood, Neil Roderick *real estate development company executive*

Niagara-on-the-Lake
Olley, Robert Edward *economist, educator*
Scott, Campbell *artist*

Nobleton
Embleton, Tony Frederick Wallace *retired Canadian government official*

North York
Adelman, Howard *philosophy educator*
Buzacott, John Alan *engineering educator*
Carrothers, Gerald Arthur Patrick *environmental and city planning educator*
Cumming, Glen Edward *art museum director*
Davey, Kenneth George *biologist, university official*
Denham, Frederick Ronald *management consultant*
Hanna, William Brooks *book publisher*
Harris, Sydney Malcolm *retired judge*
Jacob, Ellis *entertainment company executive*
MacKenzie, Donald Murray *hospital administrator*
Regan, David *brain researcher, psychology and biology educator*
Richmond, Anthony Henry *sociologist, emeritus educator*
Turnbull, John Cameron *pharmacist, consultant*

Nova Scotia
Hooper, Wayne Nelson *clergy member*

Oakville
Barlow, Kenneth James *management consultant*
Holmes, James *investment company executive*

Ontario
McNally, Joseph Lawrence *retired space agency executive*

Orleans
Murray, Larry *government agency administrator*

Ottawa
Abbott, Jim *member of Canadian parliament*
Ablonczy, Diane *member Canadian parliament*
Adams, John L. *retired career officer, federal agency administrator*
Alper, Howard *chemistry educator*
Anderson, David *Canadian government official*
Andrew, Bryan Haydn *astronomer*
Archambault, Pierre Guy *judge*
Armstrong, Henry Conner *former Canadian government official, consultant*
Assadourian, Sarkis *member of parliament*
Augustine, Jean *member of parliament*
Austin, Jacob (Jack Austin) *Canadian senator*
Axworthy, Lloyd *Canadian government official*
Baril, Maurice *career officer*
Barnes, Susan Carol *member of parliament*
Batra, Tilak Raj *research scientist*
Beatty, Perrin *broadcasting company executive*
Beaudoin, Gérald-A(rmand) *lawyer, educator, senator*
Beaumier, Colleen *member Canadian Parliament*
Beehan, Cathy *government official, lawyer*
Bélair, Réginald *Canadian government official*
Bélisle, Paul C. *Canadian government official*
Bell, Phillip Michael *curator*
Bellemare, Eugene *member of parliament*
Bernier, Gilles *member of parliament*
Bevilacqua, Maurizio *member of Canadian parliament*
Bhartia, Prakash *defense research management executive, researcher, educator*
Bigras, Bernard *Canadian government official*
Bisby, Mark Ainley *physiology educator*
Blaikie, William *government official*
Bonin, Raymond *member of Canadian parliament*
Borotsik, Rick *member of Canadian parliament*
Boudria, Don *Canadian government official*
Breitkreuz, Garry *member of parliament*
Bright, M. W. A. *physical science administrator*
Brooks, David Barry *resource economist*
Brown, Bonnie *Canadian parliamentarian*
Buchanan, John MacLennan *Canadian provincial official*
Cameron, Christina Stuart *government official*
Cappe, Melvin Samuel *economist*
Carroll, M(argaret) Aileen *member of Canadian parliament*
Carty, Arthur John *science policy advisor, research administrator*
Casson, Rick *member of Canadian parliament*
Catterall, Marlene *Canadian legislator*
Cauchon, Martin *Canadian government official*
Chamberlain, Brenda Kay *member of Canadian parliament*
Chan, Raymond *Canadian government minister*
Charbonneau, Yvon *member of parliament*
Chatters, Dave *member of parliament*
Chrétien, (Joseph Jacques) Jean *prime minister of Canada, lawyer*
Clever, W(arren) Glenn *editor, publishing executive, poet, writer, educator*
Clouthier, Hector *member of Canadian parliament*
Cockshutt, E(ric) Philip *engineering executive, research scientist, energy consultant*
Coleman, John Morley *transportation engineering executive*
Collenette, David M. *Canadian government official*
Copps, Sheila *Canadian government official*
Csörgö, Miklós *mathematics and statistics educator*
Cullen, Jack Sydney George Bud *federal judge*
Dalphond-Guiral, Madeleine *member of Canadian parliament*
d'Aquino, Thomas *lawyer, business council chief executive*
Davey, Clark William *newspaper publisher*
Davies, Gareth John *lawyer, trade executive*
Davis, John Christopher *zoologist, aquatic toxicologist*
Dawson, Mary E. *government official*
de Bold, Adolfo J. *pathology and physiology educator, research scientist*
Décary, Robert *judge*
de Chastelain, A(lfred) John G(ardyne) D(rummond) *Canadian army officer, diplomat*
†Decker, Franz Paul *symphony conductor, educator*
Dence, Michael Robert *retired research director*
DeVillers, Paul *member of parliament*
Dhaliwal, Herb *Canadian government official*
Dingwall, David C. *Canadian government official*
Dion, Stéphane *federal official*
Discepola, Nunzio (Nick) *Canadian government official*
Dlab, Vlastimil *mathematics educator, researcher*
Doyle, Norman E. *member of Canadian parliament*
Doyle, Richard James *retired Canadian senator, former editor*
Dray, William Herbert *philosophy educator*
Dromisky, Stan *Canadian government official*
Duhamel, Ronald J. *Canadian government official*
Duncan, John M. *Canadian government official*
Easter, Wayne Arnold *Parliament member*
Ecroyd, Lawrence Gerald *trade association administrator*
Eggleton, Arthur C. *Canadian government official, member of Parliament*
Elley, Reed *member of parliament*
Fairbairn, Joyce *Canadian government official*
Fallis, Alexander Graham *chemistry educator*
Fellegi, Ivan Peter *statistician*
Finestone, Sheila *Canadian government official*
Finlay, John Baird *government official*
Finn, Gerard *federal government official*
Forseth, Paul *member of parliament*
Franca, Celia *ballet director, choreographer, dancer, narrator*
Freedman, Charles *bank executive*
†Fry, Hedy *government minister*
Gagliano, Alfonso *Canadian government official*
Georganas, Nicolas D. *electrical engineering educator*
Gillingham, Bryan Reginald *music educator*
Gilmour, William *government official*
Giroux, Robert-Jean-Yvon *retired Canadian government official*
Gold, Lorne W. *Canadian government official*
Gonthier, Charles Doherty *Canadian supreme court justice*
Goodale, Ralph E. *Canadian government minister*
Gouk, James William *government official*
†Graham, B. Alasdair *government official*
Gray, Herbert Eser *Canadian government official*
Grey, Deborah Cleland *Canadian government official*
Griller, David *economics and technology consultant*
Grose, Ivan *member of parliament*
Gusella, Mary Margaret *commissioner*
Gussow, William Carruthers *petroleum engineer, geologist*
Hagen, Paul Beo *physician, medical scientist*
Halliday, Ian *astronomer*
Hamelin, Marcel *historian, educator*
Harb, Mac *Canadian government official*
Harder, V. Peter *government official*
Harington, Charles Richard *vertebrate paleontologist*
Hart, James *member of Canadian parliament*
Harvie, James Duncan *nuclear regulator*
Haworth, Richard Thomas *geophysicist, science director*
Heald, Darrel Verner *retired Canadian federal judge*
Hill, Jay *member of parliament*
Himms-Hagen, Jean Margaret *biochemist*
Holmes, John Leonard *chemistry educator*
Hoyles, John D.V. *company executive*
Hugessen, James K. *judge*
Hughes, Stanley John *mycologist*
Hurteau, Gilles David *retired obstetrician, gynecologist, educator, dean*
Iacobucci, Frank *lawyer, educator, jurist*
Ianno, Tony *member of Canadian parliament*
Ingold, Keith Usherwood *chemist, educator*
Ingstrup, Ole Michaelsen *Canadian government agency official*
Ives, John David (Jack Ives) *geography and environmental sciences educator*
Jackson, Ovid *member of parliament*
Jackson, W. Bruce *ophthalmology educator, researcher*
Jaffer, Rahim *parliamentarian*
Johnston, Dale *member of parliament*
Kates, Morris *biochemist, educator*
Kerpan, Allan *government official*
Kilgour, David *Canadian member of parliament*
Kingsley, Jean-Pierre *government official*
Kirkwood, David Herbert Waddington *Canadian government official*
Kroeger, Arthur *university chancellor, former government official*
Labarge, Margaret Wade *medieval history educator*
Lalonde, Francine *member of parliament*
Lamer, Antonio *Canadian supreme court chief justice*
Landriault, Jacques Emile *retired bishop*
Langill, George Francis *hospital administrator, educator*
Lapointe, Lucie *government agency executive*
LaRocque, Judith Anne *federal official*
Lavoie, Lionel A. *physician, medical executive*
LeBlanc, Roméo *Canadian Governor General*
Lee, Derek *member of parliament*
L'Heureux-Dubé, Claire *judge*
Lincoln, Clifford *member of parliament*
Lister, Earle Edward *animal science consultant*
Losos, Joseph Zbigniew *epidemiologist*
Lowther, Eric *member of parliament*
Lunn, Janet Louise Swoboda *writer*
Lynch-Staunton, John *Canadian senator*
MacAulay, Lawrence A. *Canadian government official*
MacDonald, Flora Isabel *Canadian government official*
MacEachen, Allan Joseph *retired parliamentarian*
MacKay, William Andrew *judge*
Macklem, Michael Kirkpatrick *publisher*
MacNeill, James William *international environment consultant*
Macphail, Moray St. John *mathematics educator emeritus*
Maheu, Shirley *Canadian legislator*
Major, John Charles *judge*
Maloney, John *member of parliament*
Malouin, Jean-Louis *university dean, educator*
Manley, John *Canadian government official*
Margeson, Theodore Earl *judge*
Marleau, Diane *Canadian government official*
Marmet, Paul *physicist*
Martin, Keith Philip *member of parliament, physician*
Martin, Paul *Canadian government official*
Massé, Marcel *Canadian government minister*
Mayfield, Philip *member of parliament*
McAvity, John Gillis *museum director, association executive, museologist*
McCormick, Larry *member of parliament*
McGuire, Joe *federal official*
McKeown, William Philip *judge*
McLachlin, Beverley *supreme court judge*
McLaren, Digby Johns *geologist, educator*
McLellan, A. Anne *Canadian government official*
McLure, John Douglas *government relations*
McNally, Grant *member of parliament*
Mifflin, Fred John *Canadian government official*
Milliken, Peter Andrew Stewart *legislator*
Mills, Bob *member of parliament*
Mills, Dennis J. *member of parliament*
Mills, Russell Andrew *newspaper publisher*
Minna, Maria *member of parliament*
Mitchell, Andy *Canadian federal official*
Moore, William John Myles *electrical engineer, researcher*
Morand, Peter *investment company executive*
Morrison, Lee *member of parliament*
Muise, Mark *member of parliament*
Muldoon, Francis Creighton *Canadian federal judge*
Murray, Ian *member of parliament*
Murray, Joseph Philip Robert *Canadian protective services official*
Murray, Lowell *Canadian senator*
†Normand, Gilbert *government official*
Nunziata, John *member of parliament*
O'Brien, Lawrence *member of parliament*
Ouellet, André *business executive*
Paradis, Denis *member of parliament*
Parent, Gilbert *member Canadian House of Commons*
Penner, Keith *Canadian government official*
Penson, Charlie *member of parliament*
Perić, Janko *government official*
Perry, Malcolm Blythe *biologist*
Peterson, Jim *member of parliament*
Pettigrew, Pierre S. *politician, member of parliament*
Philogene, Bernard J. R. *academic administrator, science educator*
Picard, Pauline *Canadian goverment official*
Pickard, Jerry *member of parliament*
Pilliteri, Gary *member of parliament*
Poulin, Marie-Paule *Canadian government official*
Proud, George *member of parliament*
Ramsay, Donald Allan *physical chemist*
Ramsay, Jack *federal official*
Redhead, Paul Aveling *physicist*
Richardson, John *member of parliament*
Riis, Nelson *member of parliament*
Rip, Gerald J. *federal judge*
Robertson, Robert Gordon *retired Canadian government official*
Robichaud, Fernand *Canadian government official*
Robichaud, Louis Joseph *Canadian senator*
Robillard, Lucienne *federal official*
Robinson, Svend J. *member of parliament*
Rock, Allan Michael *Canadian government official*
Roland, Anne *registrar Supreme Court of Canada*
Ryan, William Francis *priest*
St. Denis, Brent *member of parliament*
St-Hilaire, Caroline *member of parliament*
St-Onge, Denis Alderic *geologist, research scientist*
Saucier, Guylaine *broadcast executive*
Schmidt, Werner *member of parliament*
Schneider, William George *chemist, research consultant*
Scott, Andy *government official*
Scott, Marianne Florence *librarian, educator*
Seely, John F. *dean*
Serré, Ben *member of parliament*
Sharp, Mitchell William *advisor to prime minister*
Sheflin, Michael John Edward *environment and transportation official*
Shepherd, Alex *member of parliament*
Silverman, Ozzie *consulting strategist*
Sinha, Ramesh Chandra *plant pathologist*
Soloman, John *member of parliament*
Squire, Anne Marguerite *religious leader*
Staines, David McKenzie *English educator*
Steckle, Paul *federal official*
Storey, Kenneth Bruce *biology educator*
Strayer, Barry Lee *federal judge*
Sylvestre, Jean Guy *former national librarian*
Tait, John Charles *Canadian government official*
Tassé, Roger *lawyer, former Canadian government official*
Telegdi, Andrew *member of parliament*
Templeton, Ian Malcolm *retired physicist*
Thomson, Shirley Lavinia *museum director*
Topp, George Clarke *soil physicist*
Torsney, Paddy Ann *member of parliament*
Ur, Rose-Marie *member of parliament*
Urie, John James *lawyer, retired Canadian federal judge*
Valeri, Tony *member of parliament*
Vanclief, Lyle *federal official*
Varshni, Yatendra Pal *physicist*
Veizer, Ján *geology educator*
Wallot, Jean-Pierre *archivist, historian*
Wappel, Tom *member of parliament*
Whelan, Susan *member of parliament*
White, Randy *member of parliament*
White, Ted *member of parliament*
Whitehead, J. Rennie *science consultant*
Wilson, Lois M. *minister*
Withers, Ramsey Muir *government consultant, former government official*
Wood, Bob *member of parliament*
Yalden, Maxwell Freeman *Canadian diplomat*
Yeomans, Donald Ralph *Canadian government official, consultant*

Owen Sound
Bradford, Karleen *writer*
Jones, Phyllis Edith *nursing educator*
Morley, Lawrence Whitaker *geophysicist, remote sensing consultant*

Palgrave
Kieffer, Susan Werner *research geologist and development consultant*

Peterborough
Doyle, James Leonard *bishop*
Hutchinson, Thomas Cuthbert *ecology and environmental educator*
Kristensen, John *church organization administrator*
Theall, Donald Francis *retired university president*

Pickering
Irwin, John Wesley *publisher*

Port Hope
Mowat, Farley McGill *writer*

Port Rowan
Francis, Charles MacKenzie *wildlife biologist*

Richmond Hill
Carson, Edward John *book publisher*
Fernie, John Donald *astronomer, educator*
Garrison, Robert Frederick *astronomer, educator*
Tushingham, (Arlotte) Douglas *museum administrator*

Rockcliffe
Marchi, Sergio Sisto *Canadian government official*

Rockwood
Eichner, Hans *German language and literature educator*

Saint Catharines
O'Mara, John Aloysius *bishop*
Picken, Harry Belfrage *aerospace engineer*

Sault Sainte Marie
Calce, Brenda V. *airport executive*
Ferris, Ronald Curry *bishop*
Kondo, Edward Shinichi *plant pathologist, researcher*

Scarborough
Bassnett, Peter James *retired librarian*
Besse, Ronald Duncan *publishing company executive*
Hunter, Bernice Thurman *writer*
Knycha, Josef *journalist*
Mikloshazy, Attila *bishop*
Mitchell, Arthur Harris *newspaper columnist*
White, Calvin John *zoo executive, financial manager, zoological association executive*

Schumacher
Lawrence, Caleb James *bishop*

Stittsville
MacLeod, Robert Angus *microbiology educator, researcher*
Tellier, Henri *retired Canadian military officer*

Sudbury
Havel, Jean Eugène Martial *author, educator*

Thornbury
Keyes, Gordon Lincoln *history educator*

Thornhill
Nimmons, Phillip Rista *composer, conductor, clarinetist, educator*

Thunder Bay
Locker, J. Gary *university official, civil engineering educator*

Toronto
Aberman, Arnold *dean*
Akazawa-Eguchi, Miyuki Rei Real *landscape architect, environmental artist*
Alberti, Peter William *otolaryngologist*
Alcock, Charles Benjamin *materials science consultant*
Alvarez, Frank *radio station executive*
Apple, B. Nixon *lawyer*
Armstrong, Robin Louis *university official, physicist*
Arthur, James Greig *mathematics educator*
Arthurs, Harry William *legal educator, former university president*
Ash, Gordon Ian *professional sports team executive*
Astman, Barbara Ann *artist, educator*
Athanassoulas, Sotirios (Sotirios of Toronto) *bishop*
Atwood, Harold Leslie *physiology and zoology educator*
Augustine, Jerome Samuel *merchant banker*
†Bachand, Stephen E. *retail company executive*
Baillie, Alexander Charles, Jr. *banker*
Baines, Andrew DeWitt *medical biochemist*
Balmain, Keith George *electrical engineering educator, researcher*
Bandeen, Robert Angus *management corporation executive*
Barrett, Matthew W. *banker*
Beckwith, John *musician, composer, educator*
†Berezin, Sergei *professional hockey player*
Berton, Pierre *journalist, author*
Bickford, James Gordon *banker*
Black, Conrad Moffat *publishing corporate executive*
Blissett, William Frank *English literature educator*
Bloomberg, Lawrence S. *securities executive, art collector*
†Bloomberg, Lawrence S. *securities executive, art collector*
Blundell, William Richard Charles *electric company executive*
Bodsworth, Fred *author, naturalist*
Bohme, Diethard Kurt *chemistry educator*
Boland, Janet Lang *judge*
Boswell, Philip John *opera administrator*
Boultbee, John Arthur *publishing executive*
Bradshaw, Richard James *conductor*
†Braithwaite, J(oseph) Lorne *real estate executive*
Braswell, Paula Ann *artist*
Bregg, Peter *photojournalist*
Bristow, David Ian *lawyer*
Brook, Adrian Gibbs *chemistry educator*
Brooks, Robert Leslie *bank executive*
Brown, Gregory Michael *psychiatrist, educator, researcher*
Browning, Kurt *figure skating champion*
Bruce, William Robert *physician, educator*
Bryant, Josephine Harriet *library executive*
Cahill, Catherine M. *orchestra executive*
†Cahill, Chris J. *hotel executive*
Carlen, Peter Louis *neuroscientist educator, science administrator*
Carswell, Allan Ian *physics educator*
†Carter, Butch *professional basketball coach, former sports team executive*
Carter, Gerald Emmett *retired archbishop*
†Carter, Vince *professional basketball player*
Chamberlain, Wilton Norman *retired professional basketball player*
Chan Hon Goh *ballerina*
Chester, Robert Simon George *lawyer*
†Cieszkowski, Edward D. *marketing and management professional*
Cinader, Bernhard *immunologist, gerontologist, scientist, educator*
Clancy, Louis John *newspaper editor, journalist*
Clark, Samuel Delbert *sociology educator*
Cleghorn, John Edward *bank executive*
Cockwell, Jack Lynn *financial executive*
Colgrass, Michael Charles *composer*
Colombo, John Robert *poet, editor, writer*
Connell, Philip Francis *food industry executive*
Cook, Stephen Arthur *mathematics and computer science educator*
Cooper, Marsh Alexander *mining company executive*
Cowan, Charles Gibbs *lawyer, corporate executive*
Coxeter, Harold Scott Macdonald *mathematician*
Cullingworth, Larry Ross *residential and real estate development company executive*
Cunningham, Gordon Ross *financial executive*
Curlook, Walter *management consultant*
Dale, Robert Gordon *business executive*
†D'Alessandro, Dominic *financial executive*
Davis, William Grenville *lawyer, former Canadian government official*
Davison, Edward Joseph *electrical engineering educator*
Dawson, Donald Andrew *mathematics educator, researcher*
Dean, William George *geography educator*
DeMone, Robert Stephen *hotel company executive*
Diamond, Abel Joseph *architect*
Dickens, Bernard Morris *law educator*
Dimma, William Andrew *real estate executive*
Downing, John Henry *columnist, journalist*
Drabinsky, Garth Howard *entertainment company executive*
†Dryden, Ken *sports team executive*
Dryer, Douglas Poole *retired philosophy educator*
Dubin, Charles Leonard *lawyer*
Dunlop, David John *geophysics educator, researcher*
Eagles, Stuart Ernest *business executive*
Egan, Vincent Joseph *journalist, newspaper columnist*
Egoyan, Atom *film director*
Eisenberg, Howard Edward *physician, psychotherapist, educator, consultant, author*
Eklof, Svea Christine *ballet dancer*
Elkhadem, Saad Eldin Amin *foreign language and literature educator, author, editor, publisher*
Elliott, R(oy) Fraser *lawyer, holding and management company executive*
Endrenyi, Janos *research engineer, educator*
Evans, John Robert *former university president, physician*
Eyton, John Trevor *senator, business executive*
Farquharson, Gordon MacKay *lawyer*
†Fatt, William R. *hospitality company executive*
Ferguson, Kingsley George *psychologist*
Fernandez, Tony (Octavio Antonio Castro Fernandez) *baseball player*
Fierheller, George Alfred *corporate director*
Fife, Edward H. *landscape architecture educator*
Finlay, Terence Edward *bishop*
Flanagan-Eguchi, Barbara L. *landscape architect, theme park designer*
Fletcher, Darrin Glen *baseball player*
Flood, A. L. (Al Flood) *retired bank executive*
Foster, John Stanton *nuclear engineer*
Frank, Roberta *English language educator*
Fraser, Donald Alexander Stuart *mathematics educator*
Fraser, William Neil *government official, retired*
Freedman, Harry *composer*
Freedman, Theodore Jarrell *healthcare executive*
Fregosi, James Louis *professional baseball team manager*
Friedlander, John Benjamin *mathematics educator*
Fullerton, R. Donald *banker*
Galloway, David Alexander *publishing company executive*
Ganczarczyk, Jerzy Jozef *civil engineering educator, wastewater treatment consultant*
†Gasque, Laurel *educator*
Gee, Gregory Williams *lawyer*
Gillespie, Alastair William *former Canadian government official*
Girard, Francois *film director*
Glasco, Kimberly *ballet dancer*
Godfrey, John Morrow *lawyer, retired Canadian government official*
Godfrey, Paul *publisher*
Godfrey, Paul Victor *communications company executive*
†Godsoe, Peter Cowperthwaite *banker*
Goffart, Walter André *history educator*
Goldberg, David Meyer *biochemistry educator*
Goldfarb, Martin *sociologist*
Goodenow, Robert W. *labor union administrator*
Goring, David Arthur Ingham *chemical engineering educator, scientist*
Gotlieb, Allan E. *former ambassador*
Gotlieb, Calvin Carl *computer scientist, educator*
Graham, Victor Ernest *French language educator*
Granatstein, Jack Lawrence *history educator*
Grayson, Albert Kirk *Near Eastern studies educator*
Greenwood, Lawrence George *banker*
Gregor, Tibor Philip *management consultant*
Greig, Thomas Currie *retired financial executive*
Greiner, Peter Charles *mathematics educator, researcher*
Grier, Ruth *environmentalist*
Grinspun, Ricardo *economist, educator*
Halperin, John Stephen *mathematics educator*
Harris, Nicholas George *publisher*
Harvey, George Edwin *communications company executive*
Hayes, Derek Cumberland *banking executive, lawyer*
Hayhurst, James Frederick Palmer *career and business consultant, inspirational speaker, writer*
Heath, Michele Christine *botany educator*
Helleiner, Gerald Karl *economics educator*
Hentgen, Patrick George *baseball player*
Herbert, Stephen W. *hospital executive*
Hirst, Peter Christopher *consulting actuary*
Hodgson, Chris *Canadian provincial official*
Hofmann, Theo *biochemist, educator*
Hollander, Samuel *economist, educator*
Hollins, David Michael *professional baseball player*
Holyday, Douglas Charles *city councillor*
Honderich, John Allen *newspaper publisher*
Hore, John Edward *commodity futures educator*
Hudson, Alan Roy *neurosurgeon, medical educator, hospital administrator*
Innanen, Larry John *lawyer, food products executive*
Irwin, Samuel Macdonald *toy company executive*
Israelievitch, Jacques H. *violinist, conductor*
Ivey, Donald Glenn *physics educator*
Janischewskyj, Wasyl *electrical engineering educator*
Jay, Charles Douglas *religion educator, college administrator, clergyman*
Jervis, Robert E. *chemistry educator*
Johnson, Robert Eugene *historian, academic administrator*
Joseph, Curtis Shayne *professional hockey player*
Kalant, Harold *pharmacology educator, physician*
Kalow, Werner *pharmacologist, toxicologist*
Karp, Allen *motion picture company executive*
Kelly, Patrick Franklin *baseball player*
Kerr, David Wylie *natural resource company executive*
King, John Charles Peter *newspaper editor*
King, Kris *professional hockey player*
Kluge, Holger *retired bank executive*
Knowlton, Thomas A. *retired food products executive*
Korey-Krzeczowski, George J. M. Kniaz *university administrator, management consultant*
Kossuth, Selwyn Barnett *trade association consultant*
Krajicek, Mark Andrew *lawyer*
Kramer, Burton *graphic designer, educator*
Kresge, Alexander Jerry *chemistry educator*
Kudelka, James *choreographer, artistic director*
Kuerti, Anton Emil *pianist, composer*
Kunov, Hans *biomedical and electrical engineering educator*
Kushner, Donn Jean *microbiologist, children's author*
Kushner, Eva *academic administrator, educator, author*
†Lamon, Jeanne *music director, concertmaster, educator*
Landsberg, Michele *journalist*
Lasker, David Raymond *newspaper editor, musician*
Lastman, Melvin D. *mayor*
Lawson, Jane Elizabeth *bank executive*
Leech, James William *technology company executive*
Lewis, Robert *periodical editor, journalist*
Lindsay, Roger Alexander *investment executive*
Lindsay, William Kerr *surgeon*
List, Roland *physicist, educator, former UN official*
Litherland, Albert Edward *physics educator*
Liversage, Richard Albert *cell biologist*
Lombardi, John Barba-Linardo *broadcasting executive*
Lowe, Donald Cameron *consulting company executive*
Lowe, Robert Edward *financial company executive*
Macdonald, Donald Stovel *lawyer*
Macdonald, Hugh Ian *university president emeritus, economist, educator*
MacDougall, Hartland Molson *corporate director, retired bank executive*
Mackiw, Vladimir Nicholaus *metallurgical consultant*
MacLennan, David Herman *research scientist, educator*
MacRae, Donald Alexander *astronomy educator*
Mann, George Stanley *real estate and financial services corporation executive*
Mann, Susan *history educator*
Marshall, Donald Stewart *computer systems company executive*
Martin, Robert William *corporate director*
McAuliffe, Jane Dammen *religious studies and Islamic studies educator*
McCoubrey, R. James *advertising and broadcast executive*
Mc Culloch, Ernest Armstrong *physician, educator*
McKenna, Marianne *architect*
McMurtry, R. Roy *chief justice*
McNeill, John *botanist*
McWilliam, Joanne Elizabeth *retired religion educator*
Meadows, George Lee *communications company executive*
Meagher, George Vincent *mechanical engineer*
Mercier, Eileen Ann *management consultant*
Miller, Anthony Bernard *physician, medical researcher*
Miller, Kenneth Merrill *computing services company executive*
Millgate, Jane *language professional*
Millgate, Michael (Henry) *retired English educator*
Moens, Peter B. *biology researcher and educator*
Moffat, John William *physics educator*
Montgomery, Donald Russell *labor consulting firm executive*
Moore, Carole Irene *librarian*
Moore, Christopher Hugh *writer*
Morden, John Reid *security-business intelligence company executive*
Morey, Carl Reginald *musicologist, academic administrator*
Munk, Peter *mining executive*
Munro, John Henry Alexander *economics educator, writer*
Naldrett, Anthony James *geology educator*
Nesbitt, Mark *management consultant*
Norris, Geoffrey *geology educator, consultant*
Novak, David *Judaic studies educator, rabbi*
Ogilvie, Richard Ian *clinical pharmacologist*
Oliphant, Betty *ballet school director*
Osler, Gordon Peter *retired utility company executive*
Ostry, Sylvia *academic administrator, economist*
Ottmann, Peter *choreologist, ballet master*
Packer, Katherine Helen *retired library educator*
Packham, Marian Aitchison *biochemistry educator*
Page, Linda Jewel *mental health care educator*
Parr, James Gordon *writer*
Pawson, Anthony J. *molecular biologist*
Payton, Thomas William *corporate finance consultant executive*
Pedersen, Paul Richard *composer, educator*
Peterson, David Robert *lawyer, former Canadian government official*
Peterson, Robert B. *petroleum company executive*
Petrillo, Leonard Philip *corporate securities executive, lawyer*
Pilliar, Robert Mathews *metallurgy educator, materials scientist*
Plaut, Wolf Gunther *minister, author*
Polanyi, John Charles *chemist, educator*
†Pollock, Samuel *diversified financial services company executive*
Poprawa, Andrew *financial services executive, accountant*
Pratt, Robert Cranford *political scientist, educator*
Prichard, John Robert Stobo *academic administrator, law educator*
Pritchard, Huw Owen *chemist, educator*
Prugovecki, Eduard *mathematical physicist, educator, author*
†Quinn, Pat (John Brian Patrick Quinn) *professional sports team manager*
Rakoff, Vivian Morris *psychiatrist, writer*
Rapoport, Anatol *peace studies educator, mathematical biologist*
Rasky, Harry *producer, director, writer*
Rauhala, Ann Elaine *reporter*
Rimrott, Friedrich Paul Johannes *engineer, educator*
Roberts, William D. *broadcasting executive*
Rogers, Edward Samuel *communications company executive*
Rooney, Paul George *mathematics educator*
Rose, Jeffrey Raymond *economist, educator, negotiator*
Ross, Murray George *social science educator, university president emeritus*
Rowe, David John *physics educator*
Runnalls, (Oliver) John (Clyve) *nuclear engineering educator*
Runte, Roseann *academic administrator*
Ryan, James Franklin *retail executive*
Salama, C. Andre Tewfik *electrical engineering educator*
Saunderson, William *Canadian provincial official*
Schogt, Henry Gilius *foreign language educator*
Scholefield, Peter Gordon *health agency executive*
Schramek, Tomas *ballet dancer, educator*
†Schwartz, Gerald Wilfred *financial executive*
Seaquist, Ernest Raymond *astronomy educator*
Sedra, Adel Shafeek *electrical engineering educator, academic administrator*
Semak, Michael William *photographer, educator*
Semlyen, Adam *electrical engineering educator*
†Sharpe, John L. *hotel executive*
Shaw, Ian Alexander *mining company executive, accountant*
Shearing, George Albert *pianist, composer*
Shields, Carol Ann *writer, educator*
Sigal, Israel Michael *scientist*
Silk, Frederick C.Z. *financial consultant*
Silverman, Melvin *medical research administrator*
Siminovitch, Louis *biophysics educator, scientist*
Singleton-Wood, Allan James *communications executive*
Skinner, Alastair *accountant*
Skvorecky, Josef Vaclav *English literature educator, novelist*
Slaight, Gary *broadcasting executive*
Slemon, Gordon Richard *electrical engineering educator*
Sloan, David Edward *retired corporate executive*
Smith, Peter William Ebblewhite *electrical engineering educator, scientist*
Sole, Michael Joseph *cardiologist*
Sopko, Michael D. *mining company executive*
Spooner, Ed Thornton Casswell *geology educator and researcher*
Stadelman, William Ralph *chemical institution executive*
Staines, Mavis Avril *artistic director, ballet principal*
Stavro, Steve A. *professional hockey team executive*
Stefanschi, Sergiu *dancer*
†Steinberg, Gregg Martin *financial and management consultant, investment banker*
Stoicheff, Boris Peter *physicist, educator*
Styles, Richard Geoffrey Pentland *retired banker*
†Sundin, Mats Johan *professional hockey player*
Tall, Franklin David *mathematics educator*
Tanaka, Ron S. *hotel executive*
Taylor, Allan Richard *retired banker*
Thall, Burnett Murray *newspaper executive*
Thomas, Kenneth Glyndwr *mining executive*
†Thomas, Steve *professional hockey player*
Thomson, Richard Murray *retired banker*
Thornley, Shirley Blumberg *architect*
Tidwell, Thomas Tinsley *chemistry educator*
Till, James Edgar *medical educator, researcher*
Tindal, Douglas Lorne *religious organization administrator*
Tobe, Stephen Solomon *zoology educator*
Tory, John A. *newspaper publishing executive*
Troubetzkoy, Alexis Serge *foundation administrator, educator*
Tsubouchi, David H. *Canadian provincial official*
Tsui, Lap-Chee *molecular genetics educator*
Tulving, Endel *psychologist, educator*
Turner, Gerald Phillip *hospital administrator*
Turner, John Napier *former prime minister of Canada, legislator*
Turner, Robert Edward *psychiatrist, educator*
Turpen, Louis A. *airport terminal executive*
van Ginkel, Blanche Lemco *architect, educator*
Van Houten, Stephen H. *manufacturing company executive*
Venetsanopoulos, Anastasios Nicolaos *electrical engineer, educator*
Volpé, Robert *endocrinologist, researcher, educator*
Wadenberg, Marie-Louise Gertrud *psychopharmacologist, researcher*
Webb, Anthony Allan *banker*
Webster, Jill Rosemary *historian, educator*
Weldon, David Black *company director*
Wells, David Lee *professional baseball player*
Weston, Sr., W. Galen *diversified holdings executive*
Wetzel, Heinz *foreign language educator*
Wevers, John William *retired Semitic languages educator*
Whittington, Stuart Gordon *chemistry educator*
Wicks, Frederick John *research mineralogist, museum curator*
Wilder, Valerie *ballet company administrator*
Wildman, Charles Jackson *political organization official*
Wilkins, Ormsby *music director, conductor, pianist*
Willis, Kevin Alvin *professional basketball player*
Wilson, Ian Edwin *cultural organization administrator, archivist*
Wilson, Jim *Canadian provincial official*
Wilson, Lynton Ronald *telecommunications company executive*
Wilson, Thomas Arthur *economics educator*
Winter, Frederick Elliot *fine arts educator*
Wleugel, John Peter *manufacturing company executive*
Wonham, Walter Murray *electrical engineer, educator*
Yarlow, Loretta *art museum director*
Yip, Cecil Cheung-Ching *biochemist, educator*
†Zimmerman, Adam Hartley *retired mining and forest industries executive*

Unionville
Gulden, Simon *lawyer, investment company executive*
Nichols, Harold Neil *corporate executive, former pipeline company executive*

Waterloo
Aczél, János Dezsö *mathematics educator*
Berczi, Andrew Stephen *academic administrator, educator*
Cowan, Donald Douglas *mathematician, educator, computer scientist*
Falding, Harold Joseph *sociology educator*
Gladwell, Graham Maurice Leslie *mathematician, civil engineering educator*
Haworth, Lawrence Lindley *philosophy educator*
Hynes, Hugh Bernard Noel *biology educator*
Kay-Guelke, Jeanne *dean, educator*
Mills (Kutz-Harder), Helga *religious organization executive*
Morgan, Alan Vivian *geologist, educator*
Nelson, J. Gordon *geography educator*
Paldus, Josef *mathematics educator*
Penlidis, Alexander *chemical engineering educator*
Rempel, Garry Llewellyn *chemical engineering educator, consultant*
Rosehart, Robert George *university president, chemical engineer*
Sherbourne, Archibald Norbert *civil engineering educator*
Smith, Rowland James *educational administrator*
Sprott, David Arthur *statistics and psychology educator*
Stewart, Cameron Leigh *mathematics educator*
Urquhart, Tony *artist, educator*
Vlach, Jiri *electrical engineering educator, researcher*
Warner, Barry Gregory *geographer, educator*
Wright, Douglas Tyndall *business executive, university executive emeritus*

Weston
McIntyre, John George Wallace *real estate development and management consultant*

Willowdale
Binder, Herbert R. *drug store chain executive*
Bloom, David Ronald *retail drug company executive*
Bulloch, John Frederick Devon *foundation administrator*
Dean, Geoffrey *book publisher*
Kerner, Fred *book publisher, writer*
MacDonald, Brian Scott *management consultant*
McDonald, William Henry *financial executive*

Windsor
Auld, Frank *psychologist, educator*
Drake, Gordon William Frederic *physics educator*
Ferguson, John Duncan *medical researcher*
Hackam, Reuben *electrical engineering educator*
†Haig, Susan *conductor*
Jones, William Ernest *chemistry educator*
Minton, Henry Lee *psychology educator*
Thibert, Roger Joseph *clinical chemist, educator*

Yarker
Smallman, Beverley N. *biology educator*

PRINCE EDWARD ISLAND

Charlottetown
Carruthers, Norman Harry *Canadian province supreme court justice*
Severance, Christopher Churchill *museum director*

QUEBEC

Beaconsfield
Harder, Rolf Peter *graphic designer, painter*

Beauport
Parent, André *neurobiology educator, researcher*

Charlesbourg
Paradis, Andre *librarian*

Chelsea
Warren, Jack Hamilton *former diplomat and trade policy adviser*

Chicoutimi
Couture, Jean Guy *bishop*

Dollard
Des Roches, Antoine *retired newspaper executive*

Hull
Blondin-Andrew, Ethel *Canadian government official*
Ebacher, Roger *archbishop*
Stewart, Christine Susan *Canadian government official*
Stewart, Jane *Canadian federal official*

Ile des Soeurs
Dagenais, Marcel Gilles *economist, educator*

Ile Perrot
Tomlinson, George Herbert *retired industrial company research executive*

Laval
Adrian, Donna Jean *librarian*
David, Michel Louis *geostatistician, consultant*
Kluepfel, Dieter *microbiologist*
Pavilanis, Vytautas *microbiology educator, physician*
Pichette, Claude *former banking executive, university rector, research executive*

Leclercville
Morin, Pierre Jean *retired management consultant*

Longueuil
Caplan, L(azarus) David *manufacturing company executive*
St. Jean, Guy *electric power industry consultant*
Smith, Elvie Lawrence *retired corporate director*

Montpellier
Poirier, Louis Joseph *neurology educator*

Montreal
Aguayo, Albert Juan *neuroscientist*
Alain, Robert *foundation administrator*
Alepian, Taro *engineering and construction executive*
Alou, Felipe Rojas *professional baseball manager*
Audet, Henri *retired communications executive*
Baxter, Donald William *physician, educator, retired*
Beardmore, Harvey Ernest *retired physician, educator*
Beattie, James Louis *professional sports team executive*
Beaubien, Philippe de Gaspe, II *communications executive*
Beaudoin, François *financial institution president, chief executive officer*
Beaudoin, Laurent *industrial, recreational and transportation company executive*
Beauregard, Luc *public relations executive*
Becklake, Margaret Rigsby *physician, educator*
Bentley, Kenneth Chessar *oral and maxillofacial surgeon, educator*
Berard, André *bank executive*
Beugnot, Bernard Andre Henri *French literature educator*
Bisson, Claude *retired chief justice of Quebec*
Black, William Gordon *pension consultant*
Bougie, Jacques *aluminum company executive*
Bourgeault, Jean-Jacques *air transportation executive*
Bourque, Pierre *mayor*
Bouthillier, André *public relations executive, consultant*
Braide, Robert David *broadcast executive*
Brecher, Irving *economics educator*
Brecher, Michael *political science educator*
Brierley, John E. C. *legal educator, former university dean*
Brisebois, Marcel *museum director*
Brochu, Claude Renaud *professional baseball team executive*
Brown, Peter Gilbert *philosopher, educator, tree farmer*
Bruemmer, Fred *writer, photographer*
Burgess, John Herbert *physician, educator*
Burns, James William *business executive*
Caillé, André *public service company executive*
Cameron, Alastair Duncan *engineering consultant*
Carreau, Pierre *chemical engineering educator*
Carroll, Robert Lynn *biology educator, vertebrate paleontologist, museum curator*
†Cavell, Charles G. *printing company executive*
Cedraschi, Tullio *investment management company executive*
Chan, Tak Hang *chemist, educator*
Chang, Thomas Ming Swi *medical scientist, biotechnologist*
Charney, Melvin *artist, architect, educator*
Clermont, Yves Wilfrid *anatomy educator, researcher*
Cloutier, Gilles Georges *academic administrator, research executive*
Corinthios, Michael Jean George *electrical engineering educator*
Corson, Shayne *professional hockey player*
Crowston, Wallace Bruce Stewart *management educator*
Cruess, Richard Leigh *surgeon, university dean*
Cuello, Augusto Claudio Guillermo *medical research scientist, author*
Cyr, J. V. Raymond *telecommunications company executive*
Daly, Gerald *accountant*
†Dancyger, Alain *performing company executive*
Dansereau, Pierre *ecologist*
Das Gupta, Subal *physics educator, researcher*
Davidson, Colin Henry *architect, educator*
Dealy, John Michael *chemical engineer, educator*
Derome, Jacques Florian *meteorology educator*
Desmarais, Paul *holding company executive*
Des Marais, Pierre, II *communications holding company executive*
de Takacsy, Nicholas Benedict *physicist, educator*
Dubuc, Serge *mathematics educator*
Dufour, Jean-Marie *economics researcher, educator*
Duquette, Jean-Pierre *French language and literature educator*
Edward, John Thomas *chemist, educator*
Eisenberg, Adi *chemist*
Elie, Jean André *investment banker*
Feindel, William Howard *neurosurgeon, consultant*
Freedman, Samuel Orkin *university official*
Freeman, Carolyn Ruth *radiation oncologist*
French, Stanley George *university dean, philosophy educator*
Fridman, Josef Josel *telecommunications company executive*
Gabbour, Iskandar *city and regional planning educator*
Gaudry, Roger *chemist, university official*
Genest, Jacques *physician, researcher, administrator*
Gibbs, Sarah Preble *biologist, educator*
Gillespie, Thomas Stuart *lawyer*
Gold, Alan B. *former Canadian chief justice*
Gold, Phil *immunologist, educator, researcher*
Goldstein, Sandu *biotechnology executive, researcher*
Goltzman, David *endocrinologist, educator, researcher*
Gouin, Serge *corporate executive*
Granger, Luc Andre *university dean, psychologist*
†Gratton, Robert *diversified financial services company executive*
†Guerrero, Vladimir *professional baseball player*
Guindon, Yvan *science administrator, research scientist*
Gulkin, Harry *arts administrator, film producer*
Haccoun, David *electrical engineering educator*
Hakim, Michel *religious leader*
Hay, Allan Stuart *chemist, educator*
Herling, Michael *steel company executive*
Hoffmann, Peter Conrad Werner *history educator*
Hutchison, Andrew Sandford *bishop*
Ikawa-Smith, Fumiko *anthropologist, educator*
Ivanier, Paul *steel products manufacturing company executive*
Jacobs, Peter Daniel Alexander *architecture and landscape architecture educator*
Jasmin, Gaetan *pathologist, retired educator*
Johnston, David Lloyd *academic administrator, lawyer*
Johnstone, Rose Mamelak (Mrs. Douglas Johnstone) *biochemistry educator*
Jolicoeur, Paul *molecular biologist*
Jonassohn, Kurt *sociologist, educator*
Juneau, Pierre *broadcasting company executive*
Karpati, George *neurologist, neuroscientist*
Kearney, Robert Edward *biomedical engineering educator*
Kinsley, William Benton *literature educator*
Kirkpatrick, John Gildersleeve *lawyer*
Kramer, Michael Stuart *pediatric epidemiologist*
Labelle, Eugene Jean-Marc *airport director general*
Lacoste, Paul *lawyer, educator, university official*
Ladanyi, Branko *civil engineer*
Lajeunesse, Marcel *university administrator, educator*
Lalonde, Marc *lawyer, former Canadian government official*
Lamarre, Bernard *engineering, contracting and manufacturing advisor*
Landry, Roger D. *publishing company executive*
Langleben, Manuel Phillip *physics educator*
Large, John Andrew *library and information service educator*
Laurin, Pierre *finance company executive*
Leblond, Charles Philippe *anatomy educator, researcher*
Lemaire, Jacques *professional hockey coach*
Lowy, Frederick Hans *university president, psychiatrist*
Maag, Urs Richard *statistics educator*
MacDonald, R(onald Angus) Neil *physician, educator*
Mac Lean, Lloyd Douglas *surgeon*
Mailhot, Louise *judge*
Martel, Jacques G. *engineer, adminstrator*
McEwen, Jean *painter*
McGregor, Maurice *cardiologist, medical educator*
Melzack, Ronald *psychology educator*
Menard, Louis Jacques *professional sports team executive*
Mercier, Francois *lawyer*
Messier, Pierre *lawyer, manufacturing company executive*
Messing, Karen *occupational health researcher*
Michaud, Georges Joseph *astrophysics educator*
Milic-Emili, Joseph *physician, educator*
Milner, Brenda Atkinson Langford *neuropsychologist*
Milner, Peter Marshall *psychology educator*
Mintzberg, Henry *management educator, researcher, writer*
Molson, Eric H. *beverage company executive*
Montcalm, Norman Joseph *lawyer*
†Monty, Jean C. *communications executive*
Monty, Jean Claude *telecommunications company executive*
Moore, Sean *pathologist, educator*
Morin, Yves-Charles *linguistics educator, researcher*
Moser, William Oscar Jules *mathematics educator*
Mulder, David S. *cardiovascular surgeon*
Mulroney, (Martin) Brian *former prime minister of Canada*
Mysak, Lawrence Alexander *oceanographer, climatologist, mathematician, educator*
Nadeau, Bertin Felix *diversified company executive*
Nadeau, Reginald Antoine *medical educator*
Nattel, Stanley *cardiologist, research scientist*
Nayar, Baldev Raj *political science educator*
Neveu, Jean *company executive*
Normandeau, Andre Gabriel *criminologist, educator*
Olivella, Barry James *financial executive*
Orban, Edmond Henry *political science educator*
Ormsby, Eric Linn *educator, researcher, writer*
Osmond, Dennis Gordon *medical educator, researcher*
†O'Toole, Tess *English educator*
Paidoussis, Michael Pandeli *mechanical engineering educator*
Paikowsky, Sandra Roslyn *art historian*
Pal, Prabir Kumar *aluminium company executive*
Panneton, Jacques *librarian*
Pelletier, Louis Conrad *surgeon, educator*
Pendleton, Mary Catherine *foreign service officer*
Pépin, Marcel *broadcast executive*
Perlin, Arthur Saul *chemistry educator*
Picard, Laurent A(ugustin) *management educator, administrator, consultant*
Pinard, Raymond R. *pulp and paper executive*
Plourde, Gerard *company executive*
Podgorsak, Ervin B. *medical physicist, educator, administrator*
Popovici, Adrian *law educator*
Pound, Richard William Duncan *lawyer, accountant*
Purdy, William Crossley *chemist, educator*
Ramachandran, Venkatanarayana Deekshit *electrical engineering educator*
Raynauld, Andre *economist, educator*
Redfern, John D. *manufacturing company executive*
Régnier, Marc Charles *lawyer, corporate executive*
Rhodes, Lawrence *artistic director*
Richler, Mordecai *writer*
Robb, James Alexander *lawyer*
Rolland, Lucien Gilbert *paper company executive*
Romanelli, G. Jack *journalist*
Rothman, Melvin L. *judge*
Saint-Jacques, Madeleine *advertising agency executive*
Saint-Pierre, Guy *engineering executive*
Saumier, Andre *finance executive*
Sauvageau, Philippe *library director*
Schwartz, Roy Richard *holding company executive*
Scraire, Jean-Claude *lawyer, investment management executive*
Scriver, Charles Robert *medical scientist, human geneticist*
Selvadurai, Antony Patrick Sinnappa *civil engineering educator, applied mathematician, consultant*
Sheppard, Claude-Armand *lawyer*
Silverthorne, Michael James *classics educator*
Sirois, Charles *communications executive*
Sirois, Gerard *pharmacy educator*
Smith, Philip Edward Lake *anthropology educator*
†Snell, Linda S. *physician, medical educator*
Solomon, Samuel *biochemistry educator, administrator*
Sourkes, Theodore Lionel *biochemistry educator*
Speirs, Derek James *diversified corporation financial executive*
Stangel, Ivan *biomaterials scientist, educator*
Stanners, Clifford Paul *molecular and cell biologist, biochemistry educator*
Stewart, Jane *psychology educator*
Stoneman, William Hambly, III *professional baseball team executive*
Suen, Ching Yee *computer scientist and educator, researcher*
Sykes, Stephanie Lynn *library director, archivist, museum director*
Szabo, Denis *criminologist, educator*
Taddeo, Dominic *transportation executive*
Taras, Paul *physicist, educator*
Tellier, Paul M. *Canadian railway transportation executive*
Thompson, John Douglas *financier*
Torrey, David Leonard *investment banker*
Tousignant, Jacques *human resources executive, lawyer*
Tremblay, Andre Gabriel *lawyer*
Tremblay, Rodrigue *economics educator*
Trigger, Bruce Graham *anthropology educator*
Trogani, Monica *ballet mistress*
Trudeau, Pierre Elliott *lawyer, former Canadian prime minister*
Turcotte, Jean-Claude Cardinal *archbishop*
Turmel, Jean Bernard *banker*
†Turovsky, Yuli *conductor*
Uzan, Bernard *general and artistic director*
Vaillancourt, Jean-Guy *sociology educator*
Vennat, Michel *lawyer*
Vikis-Freibergs, Vaira *psychologist, educator*
Vinay, Patrick *university dean*
Waller, Harold Myron *political science educator*
Webster, Norman Eric *journalist, charitable foundation administrator*
Weir, Stephen James *financial executive*
Whitehead, Michael Anthony *chemistry educator*
†Widger, Chris *professional baseball player*
Woszczyk, Wieslaw Richard *audio engineering educator, researcher*

Mount Royal
Chauvette, Claude R. *building materials company administrator*
Glezos, Matthews *consumer products and services company executive*

Nemaska
Coon Come, Matthew *Native American tribal chief*

North Hatley
Jones, Douglas Gordon *retired literature educator*

Outremont
Derderian, Hovnan *church official*
Domaradzki, Theodore Felix *Slavic studies educator, editor*
Larose, Roger *former pharmaceutical company executive, former university administrator*
Letourneau, Jean-Paul *business association executive and consultant*
Levesque, Rene Jules Albert *retired physicist*

Pointe Claire
Bachynski, Morrel Paul *physicist*
Bolker, Henry Irving *retired chemist, research institute director, educator*

Quebec
Belanger, Gerard *economics educator*
Bouchard, Lucien *Canadian government official*
Bourget, Edwin Robert *marine ecologist, educator*
Courtois, Bernard Andre *communications executive*
Couture, Jean G. *retired surgeon, educator*
Engel, Charles Robert *chemist, educator*
Fortier, Jean-Marie *retired archbishop*
Gervais, Michel *academic administrator*
Labrie, Fernand *physician, researcher*
Lecours, Michel *electrical engineering educator*
LeMay, Jacques *lawyer*
Migue, Jean Luc *economics educator*
Morin, Louis *judge*
Page, Michel *biochemist*
Potvin, Pierre *physiologist, educator*
Pronovost, Jean *government official*
Saint-Pierre, Michel R. *financial services executive*
Stavert, Alexander Bruce *bishop*
Tavenas, François *civil engineer, educator*
Theodorescu, Radu Amza Serban *mathematician, educator*
Tremblay, Marc Adélard *anthropologist, educator*
Trudel, Marc J. *botanist*
Verge, Pierre *legal educator*

Quebec City
Marchand, Jean-Paul *government official*
Noel, Laurent *bishop, educator*

Rimouski
Blanchet, Bertrand *archbishop*
Larivée, Jacques *conservationist*

Rosemere
Hopper, Carol *meeting and trade show administrator*

Rouyn
Hamelin, Jean-Guy *bishop*

Saint Anne Des Lacs
Rochette, Louis *retired shipowner and shipbuilder*

Saint Jerome
Valois, Charles *retired bishop*

Saint Lambert
Archambault, Louis *sculptor*
Terreault, Charles *engineer, management educator, researcher*

Saint Lazare
Fanning, William James *professional baseball team executive, radio and television broadcaster*

Saint Sauveur
Dunsky, Menahem *retired advertising agency executive, communications consultant, painter*
Hanigan, Lawrence *retired railway executive*

Sainte Anne de Bellevue
Broughton, Robert Stephen *irrigation and drainage engineering educator, consultant*
Buckland, Roger Basil *university dean, educator, vice principal*
Grant, William Frederick *geneticist, educator*
Steppler, Howard Alvey *agronomist*

Sainte Foy
Dussault, Jean H. *endocrinologist, medical educator*
Legendre, Louis *biological oceanography educator, researcher*
Maranda, Guy *oral maxillofacial surgeon, Canadian health facility executive, educator*
Murray, Warren James *philosophy educator*
Normand, Robert *lawyer*
Pasquier, Joël *music educator*

Sherbrooke
Bureau, Michel André *pediatrician, pulmonologist*
Tremblay, André-Marie *physicist*

Sillery
Couture, Maurice *archbishop*
Dinan, Robert Michael *lawyer*
La Rochelle, Pierre-Louis *civil engineering educator*

Trois Rivieres
Lavallee, H.-Claude *chemical engineer, researcher*

Valleyfield
Lebel, Robert *bishop*

Varennes
Bartnikas, Raymond *electrical engineer, educator*

Verdun
Ferguson, Michael John *electronics and communications educator*
Gauthier, Serge Gaston *neurologist*
Lessard, Michel M. *finance company executive*

Wakefield
Roots, Ernest Frederick *scientific advisor emeritus*

Westmount
Fortier, L. Yves *barrister*

SASKATCHEWAN

Muenster
Novecosky, Peter Wilfred *abbot*

Prince Albert
Burton, Anthony John *bishop*
Morand, Blaise E. *bishop*

Regina
Atkinson, Patricia *minister of health*
Balfour, Reginald James *retired lawyer*
Bayda, Edward Dmytro *judge*
Clayton, Raymond Edward *government official*
Dalla-Vicenza, Mario Joseph *steel company executive*
Davis, Gordon Richard Fuerst *retired biologist, translator*
Holm, Roy K. *church administrator*
Hughes, Robert Lachlan *newspaper executive*
Laschuk, Roy Bogdan *lawyer*
MacKay, Harold Hugh *lawyer*
Mallon, Peter *archbishop*
Mollard, John Douglas *engineering and geology executive*
Phillips, Roger *steel company executive*
Powell, Trevor John David *archivist*
Romanow, Roy John *provincial government official, barrister, solicitor*
Shillington, Edward Blain *government official*
Sonntag, Bernard H. *agrologist, public service executive*
Teichrob, Carol *Canadian provincial official*
Wiebe, J. E. N. *province official*

Regina Beach
Barber, Lloyd Ingram *retired university president*

Saskatoon
Babiuk, Lorne Alan *virologist, immunologist, research administrator*
Billinton, Roy *engineering educator*
Blakeney, Allan Emrys *Canadian government official, lawyer*
Bornstein, Eli *artist, sculptor*
Carr, Roy Arthur *agricultural products applied research, development and commercialization processing organization executive*
Childers, Charles Eugene *mining company executive*
Epp, Menno Henry *clergyman*
Harvey, Bryan Laurence *crop science educator*
Hirose, Akira *physics educator, researcher*
Houston, C(larence) Stuart *radiologist, educator*
Huang, Pan Ming *soil science educator*
Irvine, Vernon Bruce *accounting educator, administrator*
Ish, Daniel Russell *law educator, academic administrator*
Jacobson, Sverre Theodore *retired minister*
Kennedy, Marjorie Ellen *librarian*
Knott, Douglas Ronald *college dean, agricultural sciences educator, researcher*
Kumar, Surinder *electrical engineering educator, consultant*
Kupsch, Walter Oscar *geologist*
Morgan, Thomas Oliver *bishop*
Popkin, David Richard *academic dean, obstetrician, gynocologist*
Randhawa, Bikkar Singh *psychologist, educator*
Sachdev, Mohindar Singh *engineering educator*
Shokeir, Mohamed Hassan Kamel *medical geneticist, educator*
Steck, Warren Franklin *chemical company executive, former biochemistry researcher*
Stewart, John Wray Black *college dean*

YUKON TERRITORY

Whitehorse
Lobsinger, Thomas *bishop*

MEXICO

Aguascalientes AGS
Godinez Flores, Ramon *auxiliary bishop*

Cabo San Lucas
Morrow, James Thomas *investment banker, financial executive*

Coahuila
Whelan, James Robert *communications executive, international trade and investment consultant, author, educator, mining executive*

Cuernavaca
†Bolivar Zapata, Francisco *biochemist*
Illich, Ivan *educator, researcher*

Guadalajara
Sandoval Iñiguez, Juan Cardinal *archbishop*

Jalisco
Wolf, Charlotte Elizabeth *sociologist*

La Noria
Campos, Jorge *professional soccer player*

Mexico City
Baer, George Martin *veterinarian, researcher*
Bruton, John Macaulay *trade association executive*
Cervantes Aguirre, Enrique *Mexican government official*
Chavez, Julio Cesar *professional boxer*
†Davidow, Jeffrey *ambassador to Mexico*
de la Fuente Ramirez, Juan Ramon *Mexican government official*
del Conde, Teresa *museum director, art historian, researcher*
de Maria y Campos, Mauricio *United Nations official*
†Friedeberg, Pedro *painter, sculptor, designer*
Green Macias, Rosario *United Nations official*
Joppy, William *professional boxer*
Kim, Earnest Jae-Hyun *import and export company executive*
Leon-Portilla, Miguel *historian, educator*
†Nicholas, Ronald Wayde *business consultant*
Peimbert, Manuel *astronomer*
Ruiz Sacristán, Carlos *Mexican government official*
Zedillo Ponce de León, Ernesto *president of Mexico*

Mexico DF
†Rivera Carrera, Norberto Cardinal *archbishop*

Morelia
Warren, J. Benedict *retired history educator*

Morelos
Cauduro, Rafael *painter, muralist*

Puebla
Zehe, Alfred Fritz Karl *physics educator*

San Luis Soyatlan
Sizemore, Deborah Lightfoot *writer, editor*

San Nicolas de Garza
Suarez Rivera, Adolfo Antonio *archbishop*

Santiago Colima
Williams, Wayne De Armond *lawyer*

Veracruz
Janssens, Joe Lee *controller*

ARGENTINA

Buenos Aires
Bergel, Meny *physician, researcher*
Sacerdote, Manuel Ricardo *banker*

AUSTRALIA

Avalon
West, Morris Langlo *novelist*

Belair
Briggs, Geoffrey Hugh *retired librarian*

Brisbane Queensland
Chang, Weilin Parrish *construction and engineering educator, administrator, researcher*

Canberra
Gani, Joseph Mark *statistics educator, administrator, researcher*
Philip, John Robert *physicist, mathematician, researcher*
Sargeson, Alan McLeod *chemistry educator*
Taylor, Stuart Ross *geochemist, author*

Kings Cross
Davis, Judy *actress*

Melbourne
Metcalf, Donald *biomedical researcher*
†Stark, Janice Ann *elementary education educator*

Mona Vale
Seale, John Clement *director, cinematographer*

Nedlands
Oxnard, Charles Ernest *anatomist, anthropologist, human biologist, educator*

Parkville
Denton, Derek Ashworth *medical researcher, foundation administrator*

Randwick
Hall, Peter Francis *physiologist*

Richmond
Conomikes, Melanie Remington *marketing executive*

Ringwood
Base, Graeme Rowland *illustrator, author*

Stirling, ACT
Keith, Leroy Allen *aviation safety executive*

Subiaco Perth
Newnham, John Phillipps *obstetrician*

Surry Hills
†Blanchett, Cate *actress*

Sydney
Albinski, Henry Stephen *academic research center director, writer*
Guerin, Didier *magazine executive*
Melkonian, Harry G. *insurance executive, rancher*
†Miller, George *film director*
Norman, Gregory John *professional golfer*
Olsen, Robert John *savings and loan association executive*
Rayward, Warden Boyd *librarian, educator*

AUSTRIA

Graz
Weisstein, Ulrich Werner *English literature educator*

Laxenburg
MacDonald, Gordon James Fraser *geophysicist*

Vienna
Pohl, Adolf Leopold *clinical chemist, quality assurance consultant*
Steinbruckner, Bruno Friedrich *foreign language educator*

BAHAMAS

Nassau
Dingman, Michael David *industrial company executive, international investor*
Templeton, John Marks *investment counsel, financial analyst*

BAHRAIN

Manaman
†Young, Johnny *foreign service officer*

BELGIUM

Brussels
Barnum, John Wallace *lawyer*
Bustin, George Leo *lawyer*
Glazer, Barry David *lawyer*
Jadot, Jean Lambert Octave *clergyman*
Kempe, Frederick Schumann *newspaper editor, author*
Labio, Catherine Marie Bernadette Henriette *humanities educator, researcher, international organization administrator*
Liebman, Howard Mark *lawyer*
†Moschetta, Philippe *financial executive*
Oberreit, Walter William *lawyer*
Prigogine, Vicomte Ilya *physics educator*

Drongen
Charlier, Roger Henri *oceanography, geography, and geology educator*

Lens
Peat, Randall Dean *defense analysis company executive, retired air force officer*

Liège
Mosora, Florentina Ioana *physics educator*

Strombeek Bever
Mancel, Claude Paul *household product company executive*

BERMUDA

Hamilton
Beerbower, Cynthia Gibson *lawyer*
Kramer, Donald *insurance executive*

Pembroke
Stempel, Ernest Edward *insurance executive*

Tuckers Town
Heizer, Edgar Francis, Jr. *venture capitalist*

BRAZIL

Brasilia
†Lopes Borio, Pedro Henrique *diplomat*

Rio Claro
Christofoletti, Antonio *geography educator*

Rio de Janeiro
Lin, Frank Chiwen *computer science educator*
Sales, Eugenio de Araujo Cardinal *archbishop*

São José dos Campos
Berman, Marcelo Samuel *mathematics and physics educator, cosmology researcher*

Sao Paulo
Leighton, Robert Bruce *investment company executive*
Reigrod, Robert Hull *manufacturing executive*

Sorocaba
Martins, Nelson *physics educator*

BRITISH WEST INDIES

Grand Cayman Island
Ronald, Pauline Carol *retired art educator*

BULGARIA

Sofia
Franken, Martin *public relations company executive*

CAPE VERDE

Praia
McNamara, Francis T. *ambassador*

Santa Catarina
Kern, Jean Glotzbach *elementary education educator, gifted education educator*

CAYMAN ISLANDS

Grand Cayman
Crockett, James Grover, III *musician, former music publisher*

CHILE

Concepcion
Trzebiatowski, Gregory L. *education educator*

Santiago
†O'Leary, John Joseph, Jr. *ambassador*
Wilkey, Malcolm Richard *retired ambassador, former federal judge*

CHINA

Beijing
Melville, Richard Allen *investment company executive*
Ni, Jun *physics educator*
Pinoli, Burt Arthur *airline executive*
Shu, Wenlong *environmental engineer, educator*
Xue, Lan *engineering educator*
Zhou, Zhigang *materials scientist, educator*

Chengdu
Zeng, Xuegang *telecommunications engineer, engineering educator*
Zhou, Kang-Wei *physics educator*

Guangzhou
Mundorf, Nancy Knox *early childhood educator*

Hong Kong
Chang, H. K. *biomedical engineer, educator*
Chang, Shu Ting *fungal geneticist, mushroom biologist*
Chu, Franklin Dean *lawyer*
Chun, Wendy Sau Wan *investment company executive*
Gundersen, Mary Lisa Kranitzky *finance company executive*
Kung, Shain-dow *molecular biologist, academic administrator*
Laurie, James Andrew *journalist, broadcaster*
Lehner, Urban Charles *journalist*
Li, Victor On-Kwok *electrical engineering educator*
Liou, Ming-Lei *electrical engineer*
O'Brien, Timothy James *lawyer*
Pisanko, Henry Jonathan *command and control communications company executive*
Scown, Michael John *lawyer*
Tanner, Douglas Alan *lawyer*
Tse, Edmund Sze-Wing *insurance company executive*
Wang, Jun *engineering educator*
Xu, Lei *computer scientist, educator*

Jiangsu
Xia, Jiding *chemical engineering educator*

Kowloon
†Woo, John *film director*

Shanghai
Jackson, Robert Keith *manufacturing company executive*
Ng, Lorenz K. *neurologist, educator*

COLOMBIA

Cali
Keppel, Timothy Anderson *humanities educator, writer*

COSTA RICA

San José
Hoffman, Irwin *orchestra conductor*

CZECH REPUBLIC

Prague
Dine, Thomas Alan *foreign policy expert*
Kalkus, Stanley *librarian, administrator, consultant*
Shattuck, John *diplomat, civil rights lawyer, university administrator*

DEM REPUBLIC OF CONGO, AFRICA

Kinshasha
†Musafiri, Ngongo Elongo *import-export executive, agricultural consultant*

DENMARK

Copenhagen
Alsted, Peter *lawyer*
Benjamin, David Nicholas *architect, researcher*
Bohr, Aage Niels *physicist, educator*
Bundesen, Claus Mogens *psychologist, educator*
Hansen, Ole *physicist*
Larsen, Poul Steen *library educator*
†Mottelson, Ben R. *physicist*
Pethick, Christopher John *physicist*

Hoersholm
Sørensen, Erik *international company executive*

Vedbaek
Nordqvist, Erik Askbo *shipping company executive*

DOMINICAN REPUBLIC

Santo Domingo
Marichal Sanchez, Juan Antonio *retired baseball player, agency administrator*

ECUADOR

Quito
Sanbrailo, John A. *mission director*

EGYPT

Cairo
Boutros-Ghali, Boutros *former United Nations official*
Callison, Charles Stuart *retired foreign service officer, development economist*
Miller, Harry George *education educator*
†Sullivan, Earl Le Roy *political science educator, academic administrator*

ENGLAND

Ascot Berkshire
Grubman, Wallace Karl *chemical company executive*

Askett Bucks
Irons, Jeremy John *actor*

Balcombe
Scofield, Paul *actor*

Beverley
Edles, Gary Joel *lawyer*

Birmingham
Fry, Maxwell John *economist, educator*

Simpson, Michael Kevin *university president, political science educator*
Ungaro, Emanuel Matteotti *fashion designer*
Williams, C(harles) K(enneth) *poet, literature and writing educator*
Yuechiming, Roger Yue Yuen Shing *mathematics educator*

Ramatuelle
Collins, Larry *author, journalist*

Sannois
Cornell, Robert Arthur *retired international government official, consultant*

Strasbourg
Shea, William Rene *historian, science philosopher, educator*

Toulouse
Courtés, Joseph Jean-Marie *humanities educator, writer, semiotician*

Vence
Polk, William Roe *historian*

Villeneuve d'Ascq
Allain, Louis *literature educator, scientific advisor*

GERMANY

Aachen
Pischinger, Franz Felix *engineer, researcher*

Berlin
Abbado, Claudio *conductor*
Freudenheim, Tom Lippmann *museum administrator*
Goodman, Alfred *composer, musicologist*
Saloom, Joseph A., III *diplomat*

Bonn
Selten, Reinhard *retired economist, educator*
Wohlleben, Rudolf *microwave and antenna researcher*

Bremen
Fahle, Manfred *ophthalmology researcher*

Cologne
Sabatini, Gabriela *retired tennis player*
Ungers, Oswald M. *architect, educator*

Darmstadt
Hofmann, Karl Heinrich *mathematics educator*

Dortmund
Freund, Eckhard *electrical engineering educator*

Dresden
Schreier, Peter *tenor*

Düsseldorf
Stuhl, Oskar Paul *scientific and regulatory consultant*

Erlangen
Gladysz, John Andrew *chemistry educator*
Lips, H. Peter *systems engineer director*

Eschborn
Fozzati, Aldo *automobile manufacturing company executive*

Finning
English, Charles Brand *retired lawyer*

Forst
DeVol, Luana *dramatic soprano, consultant, arts administrator*

Frankfurt
Ammann, Jean-Christophe *art director*
Michel, Hartmut *biochemist*
Simitis, Spiros *legal educator*

Garching
Fischer, Ernst Otto *chemist, educator*
Mössbauer, Rudolf Ludwig *physicist, educator*

Göttingen
Eigen, Manfred *physicist*
Neher, Erwin *biophysicist*
Sheldrick, George Michael *chemistry educator, crystallographer*

Groebenzell
Chandrasekhar, B(ellur) S(ivaramiah) *physics educator*

Gütersloh
†Middelhoff, Thomas *publishing executive*

Halle
Schmoll, Hans Joachim *internal medicine, hematology, oncology educator*

Hamburg
Lehne, Pascal Horst *chemistry educator, consultant*
Neumeier, John *choreographer, ballet company director*

Mannheim
Henn, Fritz Albert *psychiatrist*

Moglingen
Meyberg, Bernhard Ulrich *entrepreneur*

Münster
Spevack, Marvin *English educator*

Munich
Hein, Fritz Eugen *engineer, consultant, architect*
Huber, Robert *biochemist, educator*
Saur, Klaus G. *publisher*
Schell, Maximilian *actor, director*

Whetten, Lawrence Lester *international relations educator*

Nuremberg
Doerries, Reinhard René *modern history educator*

Salzwedel
Nowack, Nicolas Sebastian *psychotherapist, psychiatrist*

Schleusingen-Gethles
Frank, Dieter *technical consultant, retired chemical company executive*

Schwerte
Rosenberg, Alex *mathematician, educator*

Stuttgart
Anderson, Reid Bryce *ballet company artistic director*
Bettisch, Johann *linguist, researcher*
Cardona, Manuel *physics educator*
Klitzing, Klaus von *research facility administrator, physicist*

Tübingen
Nüsslein-Volhard, Christiane *medical researcher*

Witten
Gaengler, Peter Wolfgang *dentist, researcher*

Würzburg
Hölldobler, Berthold Karl *zoologist, educator*

Wuppertal
Schubert, Guenther Erich *pathologist*

GREECE

Athens
Arnis, Efstathios Constantinos *space naval designer*
Hatzakis, Michael *retired electrical engineer, research executive*
Kalamotousakis, George John *economist*
Larounis, George Philip *manufacturing company executive*
Ligomenides, Panos Aristides *electrical and computer engineering educator, consultant*

Thessaloniki
Angelides, Demosthenes Constantinos *civil engineer*

GRENADA

Saint George's
Barrett, James Thomas *immunologist, educator*
Helgerson, John Walter *lawyer*

GUATEMALA

Antigua
Rodgers, Frank *librarian*

Guatemala
Loesener, Otto Robert *aerospace engineer*

HONG KONG

Causeway Day
Ignatius, Alan (Adi) *magazine editor*

Clear Water Bay
Tang, Wilson Hon-chung *engineering educator*

Hong Kong
Smale, Stephen *retired mathematics educator*

Kowloon
Banister, Judith *demographer, educator*
Chang, Leroy L. *physicist*

Pokfulam
McNaughton, William Frank *translator, educator*
†Wang, Aihe *educator*

Wan Chai
Kao, Charles Kuen *electrical engineer, educator*

HUNGARY

Budapest
Evans, Myron Wyn *physicist*

Dunaharszti
Hope, Mark Alan *soft drink company executive*

INDIA

Bahadurgarh
Garg, Ajay *systems administrator*

New Delhi
Mehta, Ravi Ravinder Singh *banking trainer and researcher, trade specialist*

INDONESIA

Jakarta
Roy, J(ames) Stapleton *ambassador*

IRAN

Tehran
Dinkha, Mas Kh'nanya, IV *church administrator*

IRELAND

Ballyvaughan
Wicks, Eugene Claude *college president, art educator*

Donegal
Friel, Brian (Bernard Patrick Friel) *author*

Dublin
Montle, Paul Joseph *entrepreneur*
Sheridan, Jim *director, screenwriter*
Voss, Katherine Evelyn *international management consultant*

Galway
†Hynes, Garry *theatre director*

Mullingar
Donleavy, James Patrick *writer, artist*

Wicklow
McCaffrey, Anne Inez *author*

ISRAEL

Herzliyya
Warshavsky, Eli Samuel *media company chief executive*

Jerusalem
Kornel, Ludwig *medical educator, physician, scientist*
Masri, Jane Martyn *finance and operations administrator*
Rosenne, Meir *lawyer, government agency administrator*

Ra'ananna
Hayon, Elie M. *chemist, educator*

Rehovot
Sachs, Leo *geneticist, educator*
Sharon, Nathan *biochemist*

Savyon
Bushinsky, Jay (Joseph Mason) *journalist, radio/TV correspondent, columnist*

Tel Aviv
Jortner, Joshua *physical chemistry scientist, educator*
Manheim, Alan A. *rehabilitation agency executive, psychologist*
Mehta, Zubin *conductor, musician*
Rubin, Barry Mitchel *foreign policy analyst, writer*

ITALY

Assergi
Berezinsky, Veniamin Sergeevich *physicist*

Bosisio Parini
Buttram, Debra Doris *dog trainer, apparel executive*

Florence
Cecil, Charles Harkless *artist, educator*
Kaiser, Walter *English language educator*

Frascati
Hàegi, Marcel *scientist, physicist*

Milan
Bolognesi, Giancarlo *linguist, orientalist, educator*
Bruno, E. *bank company executive*
Dulbecco, Renato *biologist, educator*

Naples
Tarro, Giulio *virologist*

Pisa
Settis, Salvatore *archaeologist, art historian*

Ravello
Vidal, Gore *writer*

Rome
Alegi, Peter Claude *lawyer*
Audet, Leonard *theologian*
Barbanti, Sergio *diplomat*
Baum, William Wakefield Cardinal *archbishop*
†Benigni, Roberto *actor, writer, director, producer*
Bertini, Catherine Ann *United Nations official*
Cassiers, Juan *diplomat*
†Gagnon, Edouard Cardinal *ecclesiastic*
†Levi-Montalcini, Rita *neurobiologist, researcher*
Loren, Sophia *actress*
Meyers, William Henry *economics educator*
†Piovani, Nicola *composer*
Westley, John Richard *economist*
Wilson, George Peter *international organization executive*
Wynn, Coy Wilton *journalist*

Sestri Levante
Barlascini, Cornelius Ottavio, Jr. *physician*

Turin
Agnelli, Giovanni *industrial executive*

Venice
Pasinetti, Pier Maria *author*

MASSACHUSETTS

Rome
Murray, Pius Charles William *priest, librarian, educator*

JAPAN

Aichi
Abe, Yoshihiro *ceramic engineering educator, materials scientist*

Bunkyo
Kobayashi, Seiei *English literature educator*

Chiba
Arai, Toshihiko *retired microbiology and immunology educator*
Yamada, Shinichi *mathematician, computer scientist, educator*

Fukuoka
Fukumoto, Yasunobu *American history educator*

Gummaken
Okada, Ryozo *educator, clinician and researcher*

Gyoda
Shibasaki, Yoshio *chemistry educator, researcher*

Hachioji
Kojima, Takeshi *law educator, arbitrator, writer*

Hiroshima
Kasami, Tadao *information science educator*

Hiyoshicho Tkorozawa
Nakamura, Hiroshi *urology educator*

Irumagun
Kobayashi, Noritake *business educator*

Ishikawa
Mukawa, Akio *pathology educator*

Izumi
Hagiwara, Naoyuki *English language and literature educator*

Kanagawa
Okui, Kazumitsu *biology educator*
Shimazaki, Yoji *civil engineering educator*
Swarz, Sahl *sculptor*

Kanagawa-ken
Fukatsu, Tanefusa *retired Chinese classics educator*
Hoshino, Yoshiro *industrial technology critic*

Kitakyushu
Mine, Katsutoshi *instrumentation educator*

Kobe
Tochikura, Tatsurokuro *applied microbiologist, home economics educator*

Koganei
Akiyama, Masayasu *chemistry educator*

Kumamoto
Fukuda, Shohachi *English language educator*

Kyoto
Miki, Arata *law educator*
Shima, Hiromu *management educator*

Meguroku
Miura, Akio *quality assurance management professional*

Minato-ku Tokyo
Manz, Johannes Jakob *Swiss diplomat*
Scullion, Tsugiko Yamagami *non-profit organization executive*

Mito
Kobayashi, Susumu *supercomputer company executive*

Miyazaki
Meyer, Ruth Krueger *museum administrator, educator, art historian*

Nagano-ken
Wahl, Thomas Peter *priest, monk, educator*

Nagasaki
Lorenz, Loretta Rose *English language educator*

Nago
Senaha, Eiki *English literature educator, university administrator*

Nagoya
Hayashi, Mitsuhiko *retired physics educator*
Kaneyoshi, Takahito *physicist*
Kato, Masanobu *lawyer, educator*
Kimura, Miyoshi *statistics educator, researcher*
Maeda, Kenji *medical educator*
Sendo, Takeshi *mechanical engineering educator, researcher, author*
Tanaka, Harumi *linguist, educator*
Tasaka, Shuji *engineering educator*

Nara
Miyata, Gen *history of religion educator*

Nishi ku
Nakagawa, Koji *endocrinologist, educator*

Oita
Ishibashi, Eiichi *engineering researcher and educator*

Okayama
Ubuka, Toshihiko *biochemistry educator, dean*

Okazaki
Ebashi, Setsuro *scientist, educator*

Omiya
Hozumi, Motoo *medical educator, medical researcher*

Osaka
Ikeda, Kazuyosi *physicist, poet*
Solberg, Norman Robert *lawyer*

Sakyo
Ueno, Hiroshi *biochemist*

Shimizu
Anma, So *engineering consultant*
Uyeda, Seiya *geophysics educator*

Shinjuku
Shimada, Haruo *physical chemistry educator*

Suita
Ohashi, Shoichi *business administration educator*

Tochigi
Hyodo, Haruo *radiologist, educator*

Tokyo
Akera, Tai *pharmacologist*
Akutsu, Yoshihiro *communications educator*
Aoyama, Hiroyuki *structural engineering educator*
Azuma, Takamitsu *architect, educator*
Baba, Isamu *construction company executive*
Eto, Hajime *information scientist, educator*
Fuketa, Toyojiro *physicist*
Ginkel, Johannes Auguste van *geographer, educator*
Hunter, Larry Dean *lawyer*
Iida, Shuichi *physicist, educator*
Inoue, Akira *law educator*
Ishii, Akira *medical parasitologist, malariologist, allergologist*
Ishii, Yoshinori *geophysics educator*
Kaneko, Hisashi *engineering executive*
Krisher, Bernard *foreign correspondent*
Kusama, Yayoi *sculptor, painter*
Lunding, Christopher Hanna *lawyer*
Makino, Shojiro (Mike Makino) *chemicals executive*
Manabe, Syukuro *climatologist*
Nagata, Akira *publishing executive*
Nakamura, Hideo *law educator*
Nishi, Osamu *law educator*
Nishiyama, Chiaki *economist, educator*
Ohga, Norio *electronics and entertainment executive*
Owada, Hisashi *diplomat*
Saba, Shoichi *manufacturing company executive*
Saito, Shuzo *electrical engineering educator*
Sakai, Akiyoshi *urban redevelopment consultant*
Sakuta, Manabu *neurologist, educator*
Sakuta, Masaaki *engineering educator, consultant*
Shirai, Shun *law educator, lawyer*
Taguchi, Yoshitaka *architect*
Terao, Toshio *physician, educator*
Ueno, Tomiko F. *forestry company executive*
Wada, Yutaka *patent information executive*
Wakumoto, Yoshihiko *electronics company executive, grants executive*
Wright, William H., IV *military officer, federal official*
WuDunn, Sheryl *journalist, correspondent*
Yagyu, Kuniyoshi *surgeon*
Yamasaki, Yukuzo *lawyer*
Yasufuku, Sachio *electrical engineer, educator*
Yates, Ronald Eugene *newspaper editor, journalist*

Toyota
Toyoda, Shoichiro *automobile company executive*

Tsukuba Ibaraki
Esaki, Leo *physicist, foundation executive*

Yamaguchi
Suzuki, Nobutaka *chemistry educator*

Yokohama
Ito, Noboru *electric power industry executive*
Kaneko, Yoshihiro *cardiologist, researcher*

KOREA

Seoul
Kim, Geun-Eun *surgeon, educator*

LEVERKUSEN

Tannenberg
Reyna, Claudio *soccer player*

LUXEMBOURG

Luxembourg
Kasperczyk, Jürgen *business executive, government official, educator*

MADAGASCAR

Antananarivo
†Rajaonarivony, Narisoa *program chief, researcher*

MALAYSIA

Kuala Lumpur
Chee, Chee Pin *neurosurgeon, consultant*
Looi, Lai-Meng *pathology educator*

Penang
†Ang, Hooi Hoon *pharmaceutical educator*

MONACO

Monte Carlo
†Marton, Eva *opera singer*

MONGOLIA

Ulaanbaatar
Mandel, Leslie Ann *investment advisor, business owner, author*

THE NETHERLANDS

Aerdenhout
Vinken, Pierre Jacques *publishing executive, neurosurgeon*

Amsterdam
Averill, Bruce Alan *chemistry educator*
Baer, Jo *painter*
Bal, Mieke *literature educator, cultural critic and theorist*
Bruggink, Herman *publishing executive*
Dornbush, K. Terry *former ambassador, consulting company executive*
Kolko, Gabriel *historian, educator*

Goor
Bonting, Sjoerd Lieuwe *biochemist, priest*

Groningen
Gips, Christiaan Hendrik *medical educator*

Hengelo
†Cruz, Wilfredo Vargas *software safety and reliability consultant*

Leiden
Banta, Henry David *physician, researcher*

Maastricht
Van Praag, Herman Meir *psychiatrist, educator*

Noordwijk
†van der Lugt, Robert Jan *development consultant*

Roosendaal
van Deventer, Arie Pieter *agricultural engineer*

Sittard
van Raalte, John A. *research and engineering management executive*

The Hague
Herkströter, Cornelius *retired oil industry executive*
Van Wachem, Lodewijk Christiaan *petroleum company executive*

NEW ZEALAND

Wellington
Paquin, Anna *actress*

NIGERIA

Abuja
†Milutinovic, Bora *soccer coach*

Lagos
†Omole, Gabriel Gbolabo *international venture capitalist*

Sagamu
†Adetoro, Olalekan Olayiwola *obstetrician, gynecologist, educator*

NORWAY

Kolbotn
†Skow, Rune *telecommunication specialist*

Österås
Löe, Harald *retired dentist, educator, researcher*

Oslo
Fleischer, Carl August *law educator, consultant*
Haavelmo, Trygve *economics educator*
†Jansons, Mariss *orchestra conductor*

Sandvika
Christensen, Hans Christian *retired chemist*

PAKISTAN

Faisalabad Punjab
†Siddique, Muhammad *poultry pathobiologist*

Lahore
Geoffrey, Iqbal (Mohammed Jawaid Iqbal Jafree) *artist, lawyer*

Multan
†Khan, Abdul Rahim *mathematics educator, researcher and author*

PANAMA

Panama
Fletcher Arancibia, Pablo Enrique *internal medicine endocrinology physician, educator*
Roussel, Lee Dennison *economist*

PERU

Lima
Castro-Pozo, Talia *dancer, educator*
French, Edward Ronald *plant pathologist*

THE PHILIPPINES

Makati City
Aramian, Marc *composer, music producer*

Manila
Siguion-Reyna, Leonardo *lawyer, business executive*
Stepanich, Fred Charles *civil and water resources engineer*

Pasay
Lim, Sonia Yii *minister*

POLAND

Warsaw
Koscielak, Jerzy *scientist, science administrator*
Romney, Richard Bruce *lawyer*

PORTUGAL

Coimbra
dos Reis, Luciano Sérgio Lemos *surgeon*
Holm, John Alexander *linguist, educator*

Funchal
Mayda, Jaro *lawyer, educator, author, consultant*

Lisbon
†Berger, Jason *artist, printmaker*
Thore, Sten Anders *economics and aerospace engineering educator*

Oeiras
Howe, Marvine Henrietta *newspaper reporter*

REPUBLIC OF CHINA

Taipei
Lin, Yeou-Lin *engineer, consultant*

REPUBLIC OF KOREA

APO AE
Tille, James Eugene *army chaplain*

Inchon
McNaughton, William John *bishop*

Kuri
Kim, Kwang-Iel *psychiatrist, educator*

Kyung
†Kim, Doohie *public health educator*

Pohang
Choi, Sang-il *physics educator, researcher*

Pusan
Ha, Chang Sik *polymer science educator*

Seoul
Rhi, Sang-Kyu *lawyer, educator*
Surh, Young-Joon *medical educator*

Taegu
Park, Soong-Kook *internist, researcher*

RUSSIA

Moscow
Arnold, Vladimir Igorevich *mathematics researcher*
Basov, Nikolai Gennadievich *physicist*
Ginzburg, Vitaly Lazarevich *physicist*
Goldanskii, Vitalii Iosifovich *chemist, physicist*
Knaus, Jonathan Charles *manufacturing executive*
Solzhenitsyn, Aleksandr Isayevich *author*

Novosibirsk
Aleksandrov, Leonid Naumovitsh *physicist, educator, researcher*

RWANDA

Kigali
Gribbin, Robert E., III *former ambassador*

SAINT LUCIA

Castries
Felix, Kelvin Edward *archbishop*

SAUDI ARABIA

Abha
Gedebou, Messele *microbiologist, educator*

Riyadh
Olayan, Suliman Saleh *finance company executive*
Palmer, Leslie Ellen *registered nurse*
Taylor, Frederick William, Jr. (Fritz Taylor) *lawyer*
Uygur, Mustafa Eti *materials and mechanical engineering educator*

SCOTLAND

Aberdeen
Rice, Charles Duncan *university official*

Cellardyke
Roff, William Robert *history educator, writer*

Dundee
Black, Sir James (Whyte) *pharmacologist*

Edinburgh
Atiyah, Sir Michael Francis *mathematician*
Macneil, Ian Roderick *lawyer, educator*
McMaster, Brian John *artistic director*
Miller, James *construction company executive*

Gullane
Collins, Jeffrey Hamilton *research facility administrator, electrical engineering educator*

Peebles
Hooper, John Edward *retired physicist, researcher*

Saint Andrews
Lenman, Bruce Philip *historian, educator*

SINGAPORE

Singapore
†Doctoroff, Mark Gunther *bank officer*
Ho, Yik Hong *colon and rectal surgeon*
McDonough, Richard Michael *philosophy educator*
†Umehara, Ichigo *hotel executive*

SLOVAKIA

Bratislava
Lankford, Richard Oliver *diplomat*

SOUTH AFRICA

Arcadia
Berry, Ann Roper *diplomat*

Auckland Park
Koekemoer, Carl Lodewicus *university official, business consultant*

Capetown
Benatar, Solomon Robert *internist*

Gauteng Province
Ntlola, Peter Makhwenkwe *retired translator*

Johannesburg
Berk, Philip Woolf *journalist*
Crockett, Noluthando Phyllis *communications executive*

Klippoortjie
Els, Theodore Ernest *professional golfer*

Marshalltown
Chen, Philip Minkang *investment banker, corporate executive, lawyer, engineer*

SPAIN

Barcelona
de Larrocha, Alicia *concert pianist*

Madrid
Feltenstein, Harry David, Jr. *chemical executive*
Frühbeck de Burgos, Rafael *conductor*
Muniain, Javier P. *computer company executive, theoretical physicist, researcher*

Santander
Ballesteros, Severiano *professional golfer*

Santiago de Compostela
Balseiro Gonzalez, Manuel *management executive, consultant*

Seville
Sanchez, Leonedes Monarrize Worthington (His Royal Highness Duke de Leonedes of Spain Sicily Greece) *fashion designer*

SRI LANKA

Colombo
Smyth, Richard Henry *foreign service officer*
Spain, James William *political scientist, writer, investor*

SWEDEN

Bralanda
Emilson, Henry Bertil *artist*

Göteborg
Bona, Christian M. *dentist, psychotherapist*
Carlsson, Per Arvid Emil *pharmacologist, educator*
Norrby, Klas Carl Vilhelm *pathology educator*

Huddinge
Jensen, Elwood Vernon *biochemist*

Lerum
Borei, Sven Hans Emil *translator*

Österskär
Bolin, Bert Richard Johannes *atmospheric physicist, research meteorologist*

Stockholm
Hillert, Mats *materials scientist, educator*
Johnson, Antonia Axson *corporate executive*
Peskov, Vladimir Dmitrievich *physicist, educator, consultant*
Schröder, Harald Bertel *aerospace industry executive*
Soederstrom, Elisabeth Anna *opera singer*

Uppsala
Ahlstedt, N. Staffan immunologist

SWITZERLAND

Arzier
Wilson, Ronald Gene physician

Bäch
Rohrer, Heinrich physicist

Basel
Arber, Werner microbiologist
Gehring, Walter Jakob biology and genetics educator
Rosenthal, David lawyer, publicist

Bern
Braun, Reto computer systems company executive
Leavey, Thomas Edward international organization administrator
Reuter, Harald pharmacologist

Busingen
Friede, Reinhard L. neuropathologist, educator

Cologny
Maglacas, A. Mangay nursing researcher, educator

Fribourg
Gurley, Franklin Louis lawyer, military historian

Geneva
Abram, Morris Berthold lawyer, educator, diplomat
Amorim, Celso Luiz Nunes government official
Barenboim, Daniel conductor, pianist
Berger, Andrew L. investment banker, lawyer
Brown, Kent Newville ambassador
Charpak, Georges physicist, nuclear scientist
Farman-Farmaian, Ghaffar investment company executive
Hearn, John Patrick biologist, educator
Henderson, Ralph Hale physician
Kessinger, Tom G. academic administrator
Overseth, Oliver Enoch physicist, educator
Peterson, Trudy Huskamp archivist
Piot, Peter United Nations official, public health official
Purcell, James Nelson, Jr. international organization administrator
Rohrer, Maurice Pierre journalist
Schweitzer, Theodore Gottlieb, III United Nations administrator
Steinberger, Jack physicist, educator
Twarog, Sophia Nora economist, international civil servant
Weber, George international social welfare administrator

Küsnacht
Eschenmoser, Albert chemist

Lausanne
Bloemsma, Marco Paul investor

Lyss
Scheftner, Gerold marketing executive

Signy
Murphy, Edmund Michael federal agency administrator, demographer

Staad
Moore, Roger George actor

Versoix
Mahler, Halfdan Theodor physician, health organization executive

Zurich
Bailey, James Edwin chemical engineer
Barnevik, Percy Nils electrical company executive
Binnig, Gerd Karl physicist
Diederich, Francois Nico chemistry educator
Dunitz, Jack David retired chemistry educator, researcher
Ernst, Richard Robert chemist, educator
Fitzpatrick, John Henry insurance company executive
Gut, Rainer E. banker
Jones, Gwyneth soprano
Kalman, Rudolf Emil research mathematician, system scientist
Lanford, Oscar Erasmus, III mathematics educator
Morari, Manfred chemical engineer, educator
Moser, Jürgen Kurt mathematician, educator
Nievergelt, Jurg computer science educator
Papadakis, Panagiotis Agamemnon banker, international business executive
†Siegenthaler, Walter Ernst internal medicine educator
Wüthrich, Kurt molecular biologist, biophysical chemist
Zinkernagel, Rolf Martin immunology educator

TAIWAN

Chungli
†Chen, Hsin-Hwa education educator, researcher

Hsinchu
Huang, Jia-Hong materials science educator

Hualien
Lin, Jung-Chung microbiologist, researcher
Shieh, John Ting-chung economics educator

Taichung
Lu, Shih-Peng history educator

Tainan
Huang, Ting-Chia chemical engineering educator, researcher
Shih, Tso Min mining engineering educator

Taipei
Chang, Parris Hsu-cheng law-maker, political science educator, writer
Ho, Low-Tone physician, researcher, educator
Lee, Yuan Tseh chemistry educator
O'Hearn, James Francis chemical company executive
Pao, Yih-Hsing engineer, educator
Yeh, Kuo Hsing bank executive
Yin, Shih-Jiun biochemist
Young, Der-Liang Frank civil engineering educator, researcher

THAILAND

Bangkok
McInerney, Joseph Aloysius hotel executive

Nakorn Pathom
†Chanthanom-Good, Suvajee science educator

TRINIDAD AND TOBAGO

Diego Martin
Walcott, Derek Alton poet, playwright

TUNISIA

Tunis
Raphel, Robin ambassador

TURKEY

Ankara
Camlibel, Dizdar marketing professional, advertising consultant

Camkaya
Wales, Gwynne Huntington lawyer

UNITED ARAB EMIRATES

Abu Dhabi
Preska, Margaret Louise Robinson education educator, administrator

Al Ain
Voth, Douglas W. academic dean

URUGUAY

Montevideo
†Dodd, Thomas J. ambassador, educator

VATICAN CITY

Vatican City
Foley, John Patrick archbishop
John Paul, His Holiness Pope, II (Karol Jozef Wojtyla) bishop of Rome
†Stafford, James Francis archbishop
Szoka, Edmund Casimir Cardinal archbishop

VENEZUELA

Caracas
Mendelovici, Efraim Eliahu materials chemistry and earth sciences researcher

Turmero
†Botha, Francois (Frans) professional boxer

VIETNAM

Hanoi
Peterson, Douglas Pete (Pete Peterson) ambassador, former congressman

Ho Chi Minh City
Ray, Charles Aaron foreign service officer

WALES

Aberystwyth
Walters, Kenneth applied mathematics educator

Gwynedd
Owen, Walter Shepherd materials science and engineering educator

Powys
Seaton, Michael John physicist

Wiltshire
Sherwin, James Terry lawyer

WEST INDIES

Grenada
†Taylor, Keith Breden physician, educator

Roseau
Jeffries, Charles Dean microbiology educator, scientist

ZAMBIA

Lusaka
Hipple, Walter John English language educator

Mumbwa
Hansen, Florence Marie Congiolosi (Mrs. James S. Hansen) social worker

ZIMBABWE

Borrowdale
Rooney, John Patrick company executive

ADDRESS UNPUBLISHED

Aaroe, Paul Morris retired superior court judge
†Aaron, Melissa D. education educator
Aaron, Roy Henry entertainment company executive
†Aarstol, Michael Patrick economics educator
Aasen-Hull, Audrey Avis music educator
Aaslestad, Halvor Gunerius college dean, retired
Abadi, Fritzie artist, educator
Abate, Frank Salvatore, Jr. mental health services professional
Abbe, Elfriede Martha sculptor, graphic artist
Abbott, Edward Leroy finance executive
Abbott, Gregory Andrew lawyer
Abbott, Rebecca Phillips museum director, art consultant
Abel, Harold psychologist, educator, academic administrator
Abeles, Kim Victoria artist
Abell, Murray Richardson retired medical association administrator
Abels, Robert Frederick tax consultant
Abercrombie, Stanley magazine editor
Ablin, Richard Joel immunologist, educator
Abramowicz, Janet painter, print-maker
Abramowitz, Morton I. former ambassador
Abromson, Irving Joel financial services professional
Achorn, Robert Comey retired newspaper publisher
Acker, Woodrow Louis (Lou Acker) security and protection professional
Ackerman, Jack Rossin investment banker
Ackerman, Melvin investment company executive
†Ackerman, Robert Keith journalist
Ackermann, Karen publishing executive
Ackerson, Barry James social worker
Adam, John, Jr. insurance company executive emeritus
Adam, Orval Michael retired financial executive, lawyer
Adams, Alfred Hugh college president
Adams, Bryan vocalist, composer
Adams, Christopher Paul journalist
Adams, Corlyn Holbrook nursing facility administrator
Adams, David Gray lawyer
Adams, Edwin Melville former foreign service officer, actor, author, lecturer
Adams, Harlene speech communications educator
†Adams, Hilary Shiels theater director
Adams, James Blackburn former state government official, former federal government official, lawyer
Adams, James Thomas surgeon
Adams, John Andrew physicist, engineering company executive
Adams, John Quincy economist, educator
†Adams, Marilyn Kay music educator
Adams, Michael John air force non-commissioned officer
Adams, Renee Bledsoe elementary school educator
Adams, Robert McCormick anthropologist, educator
Adams, Sharon Farrell financial analyst
Adams, Thomas Lawrence lawyer
Adams, Thomas Lynch, Jr. lawyer
Adams, William White retired manufacturing company executive
Adaskin, Murray composer
Adato, Perry Miller documentary producer, director, writer
Adcock, Richard Paul lawyer
Adducci, Regina Marie medical/surgical nurse
Addy, Frederick Seale retired oil company executive
Addy, Jan Arlene clinical nurse, educator
Adelman, Richard Charles gerontologist, educator
Adelman, Robert Paul retired construction company executive, lawyer
Adelman, Rodney Lee federal agency administrator
Adelson, Merv Lee entertainment and communication industry executive
Adkins, Terry R. artist
Adkins, Thomas Samuel library director
Adkisson, Gregory Hugh anesthesiologist
Adler, Richard Melvin architect, planner
Adler, Samuel Hans retired conductor, composer
Aehlert, Barbara June health services executive
Agar, John Russell, Jr. school district administrator
Agarwal, Suman Kumar editor
Agrios, George Nicholas plant pathology educator
Aharonov, Yakir physicist, educator
Ahearne, John Francis scientific research administrator, researcher
Ahlgren, Gibson-Taylor real estate broker
Ahlquist, Paul Gerald molecular biology researcher, educator
Ahmed, Syed Z. anthropologist
Aikman, Albert Edward lawyer
Ainsworth, Harriet Crawford journalist, public relations consultant
†Ajax, Ernest Theodore neurology educator
Akasofu, Syun-Ichi geophysicist
Akel, Ollie James oil company executive
Akiyama, Carol Lynn motion picture industry executive
Alagem, Beny former electronics executive
Albagli, Louise Martha psychologist
Alberghetti, Anna Maria singer, actress
Albers, Edward James, Sr. retired secondary school educator
Albert, Margaret Cook communications executive
†Albert, Sarah Cathleen public policy specialist
Alberternst, Judith Ann pension administrator
Alberts, David artistic director, mime
Albertson, Susan L. retired federal government official
Albino, George Robert business executive
Alda, Alan actor, writer, director
Aldredge, Theoni Vachliotis costume designer
Aldrich, Franklin Dalton research physician
Aldrich, Patricia Anne Richardson retired magazine editor
Alexakos, Frances Marie business owner, psychology educator, researcher, producer, editor
†Alexander, Andrew Lamar (Lamar Alexander) lawyer, former secretary of education, former governor
Alexander, Edward Russell retired disease research administrator, educator
Alexander, Jonathan cardiologist, consultant
Alexander, Melvin Taylor quality assurance engineer, statistician
Alexander, Peter Houston artist
Alfonso, Roberta Jean emergency room nurse
Alford, Joyce Wray educational administrator
Alfred, Stephen Jay lawyer
Alig, Frank Douglas Stalnaker retired construction company executive
Aljian, James Donovan investment company executive
Alker, Hayward Rose political science educator
Allaire, Gloria Kaun Italian language educator
Allen, Anna Marie financial executive
Allen, Charles Eugene college administrator, agriculturist
Allen, Danny Eugene writer, naturalist, activitist
Allen, Donald Merriam editor, publisher
Allen, Edgar Burns records management professional
Allen, Eric Andre professional football player
†Allen, Herbert investment banker
Allen, Jane Ingram artist, educator
Allen, John Lyndon social studies educator
Allen, Leatrice Delorice psychologist
Allen, Lew, Jr. laboratory executive, former air force officer
Allen, Marilyn Myers Pool theater director, video producer
Allen, Paul computer executive, professional sports team owner
Allen, Ralph Gilmore dramatist, producer, drama educator
Allen, Thomas B. writer
Allerton, John Stephen association executive
Alley, Kirstie actress
Alligood, Elizabeth Ann Hiers retired special education educator
Allington, Richard Lloyd literacy studies educator
Allinson, Carl radiologist
Allison, Andrew Marvin church executive
Allison, John McComb retired aeronautical engineer
Allison, Mary Moon Southwell community health nurse, nursing administrator
Allison, Robert Clyde business and computers consultant
Allred, Michael Sylvester lawyer
Allums, James A. retired cardiovascular surgeon
†Alm, Alvin Leroy retired technical services executive
Almond, Joan retired chemist
Aloff, Mindy writer
Aloisio, Maria Theresa tax accountant
Alonso, Maria Conchita actress, singer
Alper, Merlin Lionel financial executive
Alpern, Andrew lawyer, architect, architectural historian
Alpert, Ann Sharon insurance claims examiner
Alpher, Victor Seth retired clinical psychologist, consultant,
Al-Qadi, Imad Lutfi civil engineering educator, researcher
Alstat, George Roger special education educator
Altekruse, Joan Morrissey retired preventive medicine educator
Altheide, Phyllis Sage computer scientist, software engineer
Altman, Adele Rosenhain radiologist
Altman, Irwin psychology educator
Altshuler, Alan Anthony political scientist
Altshuler, Kenneth Z. psychiatrist
Altstock, Marsha Marie pediatrics nurse
Alvarez, Barry university football coach
Alvord, Joel Barnes retired bank executive
Amancio, Ruth Carson safety professional
Amann, Charles Albert mechanical engineer
Amar, Akhil Reed law educator
Ambrose, James Richard consultant, retired government official
Ambrose, Thomas Cleary communications executive
Ambrosio, Deborah Ann critical care nurse
Ambrozic, Aloysius Matthew (His Eminence Aloysius Cardinal Ambrozio) cardinal archbishop
Amdahl, Byrdelle John business consulting executive
Ames, Donald Paul retired aerospace company executive, researcher
Ames, Steven Reede financial planner
Ammeraal, Brenda Ferne secondary school educator
Ammon, R. Theodore food products executive
Ammons, Barbara Ellen gerontological, oncological, medical/surgical nurse
Amparado, Keith D. communications company executive
Amstutz, Daniel Gordon international trade association administrator, former grain dealer, government and intergovernment official
Anaple, Elsie Mae medical, surgical and geriatrics nurse
Anastasi, William Joseph artist
Anastole, Dorothy Jean retired electronics company executive
Ancheta, Caesar Paul software developer
Ancona, George E. photographer, film producer, author
Anderer, Joseph Henry textile company executive
Anders, Brenda Michelle communications professional
Anders, Edward chemist, educator
Anderson, Bernard E. economist
Anderson, Carolyn Harvey retired pediatrician
Anderson, Charles Lee Royal retired academic administrator
Anderson, Donald Lloyd weapon systems consultant
†Anderson, Eric David electrical engineer
Anderson, Fletcher Neal chemical executive
Anderson, Geoffrey Allen retired lawyer
Anderson, Iris Anita retired secondary education educator
Anderson, John Firth church administrator, librarian
Anderson, John Gaston electrical engineer
Anderson, Jon Eric lawyer
Anderson, Joseph Norman executive consultant, former food company executive, former college president
Anderson, Karl Peter controller
Anderson, Keith retired lawyer, retired banker
Anderson, Lois D. nursing administrator, mental health nurse
Anderson, Louise Stout crime analyst
Anderson, Mark Robert data processing executive, biochemist
Anderson, Mary Theresa investment manager
Anderson, Nils, Jr. former government official, retired business executive, industrial historian
Anderson, Paul Milton steel company executive
Anderson, Philip Warren physicist

GEOGRAPHIC INDEX 5765 ADDRESS UNPUBLISHED

Anderson, Robert Orville oil and gas company executive
Anderson, Shalor Maria medical/surgical and pediatrics nurse
Anderson, Sparky (George Lee Anderson) broadcast analyst, former baseball team manager
Anderson, Susan Elaine Mosshamer education and organizational consultant
Anderson, Thomas Patrick mechanical engineer, educator
Anderson, Vernon Russell technology company executive, entrepreneur
Anderson, Wayne Carl public information officer, former corporate executive
Anderson-Spivy, Alexandra writer, editor
Andersson, Craig Remington retired chemical company executive
Andes, Phoebe Cabotaje women's health nurse, educator
Andrade, Edna artist, art educator
Andrau, Maya Hedda physical therapist
Andreas, Dwayne Orville business executive
Andreozzi, Louis Joseph lawyer
Andretti, Mario race car driver
Andretti, Michael Mario professional race car driver
Andrews, Carol primary education educator
Andrews, David Ralph lawyer
Andrews, Jean artist, writer
Andrews, Julie actress, singer
Andrews, Richard Vincent physiologist, educator
Andrews, William Frederick manufacturing executive
Andringa, Patricia Perkins fundraiser, consultant
Andriole, Stephen John information systems executive
Andrisani, John Anthony editor, author, golf consultant
Andruzzi, Ellen Adamson nurse, marital and family therapist
Angel, Armando Carlos rheumatologist, internist
†Angeline, Mary poet
Angell, Richard Bradshaw philosophy educator
Angelov, George Angel pediatrician, anatomist, teratologist
Angst, Karen K. mental health nurse
Anguiano, Lupe business executive
Angulo, Gerard Antonio publisher, investor
Angus, Robert Carlyle, Jr. health facility administrator
Anker, Robert Alvin retired insurance company executive
Annenberg, Walter H. philanthropist, diplomat, editor, publisher, broadcaster
Annus, John Augustus artist
Ansley, Shepard Bryan lawyer
Anspach, Herbert Kephart retired appliance company executive, patent attorney
†Anspacher, Stephen J. university official
†Antioco, John F. entertainment company executive
Anton, Barbara writer
Antonellis, Patricia Annette community health nurse
Apel-Brueggeman, Myrna L. entrepreneur
†Appel, Robert A. urologist
Appell, Kathleen Marie management consultant, legal administrator
Appell, Louise Sophia consulting company executive
Appenzeller, Otto neurologist, researcher
Applegate, Christina actress
Apted, Michael David film director
Aptheker, Herbert historian, lecturer
Aquino-Kaufman, Florence (Florence Anglin) actress, playwright
Arango, Richard Steven architect, graphic and industrial designer
Arat, Metin retired psychiatrist
Arbelbide, C(indy) L(ea) historian, author
†Archambault, George Francis editor, pharmaceutical consultant
†Archer, Mary Kathryn elementary education educator
Archer, Sarah Ellen public health consultant
Archibald, Nolan D. household and industrial products company executive
Archuleta, Walter R. educational consultant, language educator
Arden, Bruce Wesley computer science and electrical engineering educator
Arden, Sherry W. publishing company executive
Ardire, Linda Lea critical care nurse
Areen, Judith Carol dean
Arenal, Julie (Mrs. Barry Primus) choreographer
Arenberg, Julius Theodore, Jr. retired accounting company executive
Arenstein, Walter Alan environmental scientist
Aretz, Barbara Jane reading specialist, educator
†Argraves, Hugh Oliver poet, artist, playwright
†Arias, Incencio F. diplomat
Ark, Laurine writer
Arledge-Benko, Patricia retired minister
Arlen, Michael J. writer
Arlidge, John Walter utility company executive
Armacost, Mary-Linda Sorber Merriam former college president, educational consultant
Armistead, Katherine Kelly (Mrs. Thomas B. Armistead, III) interior designer, travel consultant, civic worker
Armocida, Patricia Anne managed health care official
Armour, David Edward Ponton trade association administrator
Armstrong, Anne Legendre (Mrs. Tobin Armstrong) former ambassador, corporate director
Armstrong, F(redric) Michael retired insurance company executive, consultant
Armstrong, (Arthur) James educator, consultant, lecturer, writer
Armstrong, John Allan business machine company research executive
Armstrong, Michael David investment banker
Armstrong, Neil A. former astronaut
†Armstrong, Terry Lee publishing executive, carpenter
Armstrong, Thomas Newton, III American art and garden specialist, consultant
Armstrong-Law, Margaret school administrator
Arnaud, Claude Donald, Jr. physician, educator
Arnett, Edward McCollin chemistry educator, researcher
Arnold, Deborrah Ann human services director
†Arnold, Gloria Malcolm artist, educator
Arnold, Henri cartoonist
Arnold, Jerome Gilbert lawyer
Arnold, Leslie Ann special education educator
Arnold, P. A. special education educator
Arnold, Robert Jeffrey musician
Arnold, Ruth Ann elementary education educator
Arnold, William Howard retired nuclear fuel executive
Arnott, Howard Joseph biology educator, university dean
Aron, Peter Arthur charitable foundation executive, private investor
Aronson, Luann Marie actress
Aronson, Marc artist
Aronson, Norman Leonard publishing executive, consultant
Arp Lotter, Donna investor, venture capitalist
Arrott, Patricia Graham artist, art instructor
Arthur, Beatrice actress
Arthur, John Morrison retired utility executive
Arthur, Rochelle Linda creative director
Artinian, Nancy Trygar critical care nurse, researcher
†Arumugham, Gayathri Shakthi healthcare activist, educator
Arveson, Raymond Gerhard retired state official
Arvisais, Kari Lynn marriage and family therapist
Aschauer, Charles Joseph, Jr. corporate director, former company executive
Ashcraft, Kimberly M. nursing administrator
Ashe, Bernard Flemming arbitrator, educator, lawyer
Ashkin, Rajasperi Maliapen marketing executive
Ashman, Alicia Koninska civic activist
Ashton, Betsy Finley broadcast journalist, author, lecturer
Ashton, Harris John business executive
Askew, Dennis Lee poet
Askey, William Hartman magistrate, lawyer
Askins, Wallace Boyd manufacturing company executive
Asokan, Unisa information professional
Aspen, Alfred William international trading company executive
Assael, Michael lawyer, accountant
Assante, Armand actor
Assunto, Richard Anthony payroll executive
Astaire, Carol Anne Taylor artist, educator
Ataie, Ata Jennati oil products marketing executive
Ataie, Judith Garrett middle school educator
Atcheson, Sue Hart business educator
Atchison, Richard Calvin trade association director
Atherton, William actor
†Atkinson, Donna Durant research and evaluation consultant
Atlas, Randall Ivan architect, criminologist
Atsberger, Deborah Brown clinical nurse specialist
Auberjonois, René Murat actor
Aubrey, James Reynolds English educator
Audet, Paul Andre retired newspaper executive
Auerbach, Jonathan Louis securities trader
August, Louise artist, illustrator, educator
August, Robert William designer, educator
Augustus, Susan J. nurse anesthetist
Aulbach, George Louis property investment company executive
Aurin, Robert James entrepreneur
Ausburn, Lynna Joyce vocational and technical curriculum developer, consultant
Auslander, Marc Alan computer scientist
Austin, Janet Hays artist
Austin, Robert Clarke naval officer
Aved, Barry retail executive, consultant
Avery, James Thomas, III lawyer, management consultant
Avery, Stephen Goodrich marketing professional, consultant
Avian, Bob choreographer, producer
Avnet, Jonathan Michael motion picture company executive, film director
Axilrod, Stephen Harvey global economic consultant, economist
Azarnoff, Daniel Lester pharmaceutical company consultant
†Azhar, Rubaina Shameem journalist
†Azrael, Judith Anne educator
Babb, Frank Edward lawyer, executive
Babb, Roberta Joan educational administrator
Babbitt, Samuel Fisher retired university official
Babitzke, Theresa Angeline health facility administrator
†Bach, Jean Enzinger filmmaker
Bach, Mária-Cathérine writer, researcher, translator
†Bacharach, Burt composer, conductor
Bacharach, Melvin Lewis retired venture capitalist
Bachtel, Ann Elizabeth educational consultant, researcher, educator
Bacon, Benjamin B. title designer
Bacon-Smith, Camille educator, writer
Badalamenti, Angelo composer, conductor
Baddour, Anne Bridge pilot
Baddour, Raymond Frederick chemical engineer, educator, entrepreneur
Bade, Carl August retired secondary education educator
Badeaux, Diane Marie mental health nurse
Bader, Lorraine Greenberg textile stylist, designer, consultant
Badham, John MacDonald motion picture director
Baehr, Theodore religious organization administrator, communications executive
Baggett, Donnis Gene journalist, editor
Bagley, Steven Robert food bank organization executive, consultant
Bagley, William Thompson lawyer
Baglio, Vincent Paul management consultant
Bahbah, Bishara Assad editor
†Bahr, Jane Marie writer, retired English educator
Bahr, Sheila Kay physician
Bahre, Jeannette English language educator, education educator, librarian
Baier, Edward John former public health official, industrial hygiene engineer, consultant
Baigis, Wendy Sue probation and parole officer
Bailar, Benjamin Franklin academic administrator, administration educator
Bailey, Charles-James Nice linguistics educator
Bailey, David Roy Shackleton classics educator
Bailey, Donnis Aaron David county official
Bailey, Francis Lee lawyer
Bailey, Rita Maria investment advisor, psychologist
Bailey, William Waddell writer, communications executive
Bain, Diane Martha D'Andrea clinical nurse specialist in critical care
Bain, William Donald, Jr. lawyer, chemical company executive
Baiocco, Sharon A. college administrator
Baird, Alan C. screenwriter
Baird, William David retired anesthesiologist
Bajcsy, Ruzena Kucerova computer science educator
Baker, C. B. retired day care director, organizer, communicator
Baker, Carol Ann elementary school educator
Baker, Charles DeWitt research and development company executive
Baker, Donald lawyer
Baker, Edward Kevin retail executive
Baker, Henry S., Jr. retired banker
Baker, Howard Henry, Jr. former senator, lawyer
Baker, Joseph Roderick, III aviculturist
Baker, Judith J. nurse manager
Baker, Nadine Lois medical technician
Baker, Ronald James English language educator, university administrator
Baker, Susan Marie Victoria, Rev. writer, artist
Baker, William Thompson, Jr. lawyer
Baker, Zachary Moshe librarian
Bakht, Baidar civil engineer, researcher, educator
Balaban, Bob actor, director
Balder, James Ellsworth infosystems specialist
Balderston, William, III retired banker
Baldrige, Letitia writer, management training consultant
Baldwin, Alec (Alexander Rae Baldwin, III) actor
Baldwin, Deanna Louise dietitian
Baldwin, DeWitt Clair, Jr. physician, educator
Baldwin, George Curriden physicist, educator
†Baldwin, Miles Arnold air force officer
Baldwin, William Russell optometrist, foundation executive
Balick, Kenneth D. international real estate finance executive
Balkcom, Carol Ann insurance agent
Balke, Robert Roy architect
Ball, Howard Guy education specialist educator
Ball, John Robert healthcare executive
Ballantine, John Wallis retired banker
Ballard, Diane E. nursing administrator
Balog, Rita Jean retired librarian
Balsamello, Joseph Vincent information services manager
Balser, Robert Edward animation film producer, director
Baltazzi, Evan Serge engineering research consulting company executive
Balter, Alan conductor, music director
Balter, Frances Sunstein civic worker
Baltz, Antone Edward, III journalist, writer, academic administrator
Bamberger, Gerald Francis plastics marketing consultant
Bamberger, Joseph Alexander mechanical engineer, educator
Bambrick, James Joseph labor economist, labor relations executive
Bandeen, William Reid retired meteorologist
Bandy, Jack D. lawyer
Baney, Richard Neil physician, internist
†Bang, Mary Jo poet
Bangs, John Kendrick lawyer, foundation executive, former chemical company executive
Bank, Marji D. actress
Banks, Robert Sherwood lawyer
Bannister, Dan R. professional and technical services company executive
Bansak, Stephen A., Jr. investment banker, financial consultant
Bantry, Bryan entrepreneur, producer, director
†Bapst, Donald Joseph, Jr. writer
Barabino, William Albert science and technology researcher, inventor
Baranski, Christine actress
Barber, James David political scientist, retired educator
Barber, Kimberly Lisanby elementary education educator
Barber, Laura Elizabeth medical/surgical nurse
Barber, Marsha company executive
Bar-Cohen, Avram mechanical engineering educator
Bardin, Clyde Wayne biomedical researcher
Bardin, Rollin Edmond electrical engineering consultant
Bare, Bruce retired life insurance company executive
Barger, William James management consultant, educator
Barham, Charles Dewey, Jr. electric utility executive, lawyer
Barhydt, Sally J. publishing company executive
†Barkai, Ornit television producer, broadcast journalist
Barker, Clive artist, screenwriter, director, producer, writer
Barker, Judy foundation executive
Barker, Lisa Ann aerospace engineer
Barker, Verlyn Lloyd retired minister, educator
Barker, Virginia Lee nursing educator
Barkey, Brenda technical writer, publications manager
Barkley, Richard Clark ambassador
Barlow, Jean art educator, artist
Barlow, John Sutton neurophysiologist, electroencephalographer, lexicographer
Barner, John L. radiologist
Barnes, Joanna author, actress
Barnes, Judith Anne communications executive
†Barnes, Kate poet
Barnes, Rosemary Lois minister
Barnes, Wesley Edward energy and environmental executive
Barnett, James Monroe rector, author
Barnett, Linda Kay Smith vocational guidance counselor
Barnett, Margaret Edwina nephrologist, researcher, business consultant
Barney, Austin Dunham, II estate planner
Barnhart, Jo Anne B. government official
Barone, Janine Mason foundation administrator
Barone, John Anthony university provost emeritus
Barone, Stephanie Lynn academic administrator, psychology researcher
Barr, John Baldwin chemist, research scientist
Barrack, William Sample, Jr. petroleum company executive
Barrett, Barbara McConnell ranch owner, community leader, lawyer
Barrett, Christine Khan engineering project management coordinator
Barrett, Evelyn Carol retired secondary education educator
Barrett, Izadore retired fisheries research administrator
Barrett, Janet Tidd academic administrator
†Barrett, Katherine writer, multimedia producer
Barrett, Linda L. real estate executive
Barrett, Lisa Marie acupuncture physician, herbologist
†Barrett, Tina professional golfer
Barrett, William Joel investment banker
Barrett, Yvonne Laughlin retail manager
Barrickman, Les L. psychiatrist
Barricks, Michael Eli retinal surgeon
Barron, Charles Elliott retired electronics executive
Barron, Peggy Pennisi management consultant
Barron, Sara nurse manager
†Barry, Camille T. health and human services director
Barselou, Paul Edgar actor, writer
Bartel, Arthur Gabriel educational administrator, city official
Bartels, Betty J. nurse
Barth, Frances Dorothy artist
Bartholomew, Charles R. advertising executive
Bartizal, Robert George computer systems company executive, business consultant
Bartlett, David journalist
Bartlett, Desmond William engineering company executive
Bartlett, James Williams psychiatrist, educator
†Barton, Glen A. manufacturing company executive
Barton, Joe Linus congressman
Barton, Nancy Shover nursing administrator
Barton, Peter Richard, III communications executive
†Barton, Tina Roxanne technical information specialist, writer
Bartoo, Richard Kieth chemical engineer, consultant
Bartrem, Duane Harvey retired military officer, designer, building consultant
Baruch, Monica Lobo-Filho psychological counselor
Barville, Rebecca Penelope elementary school educator
Barzun, Jacques author, literary consultant
Basch, Reva information services company executive
Bascom, Willard Newell engineer, scientist, underwater archaeologist
Basford, Robert Eugene retired biochemistry educator, researcher
Bashore, Irene Saras research institute administrator
Baskin, Stuart Jay lawyer
Bass, Lynda D. medical/surgical nurse, educator
Bass, Robert Olin manufacturing executive
Bassett, Elizabeth Ewing (Libby Bassett) writer, editor
Bassist, Donald Herbert retired academic administrator
Bast, Kenneth George healthcare executive
Batalden, Paul Bennett pediatrician, health care educator
†Batchelder, Jennifer Jo legislative staff member
Bateman, David Alfred lawyer
Bateman, Robert McLellan artist
Bates, Charles Turner lawyer, educator
Bates, Richard Mather dentist
†Batsell, Jacob Paul journalist
Batt, Philip E. former governor
Batterden, James Edward business executive
Battistelli, Joseph John electronics executive
Battle, Dolores Elaine speech, language pathologist, educator
Battle, Emery Alford, Jr. sales executive
Battle, Frank Vincent, Jr. lawyer
Batts, Warren Leighton retired diversified industry executive
Bauer, Barbara Ann marketing consultant
Bauer, Caroline Feller author
Bauer, Elaine Louise ballet dancer
Bauer, Judy Marie minister
Bauer, Richard Carlton nuclear engineer
Baugh, John Frank wholesale company executive, retired
Baughman, J. Ross photographer, writer, educator
Baum, Stanley David lawyer
Bauman, Richard Arnold coast guard officer
Bauman, Robert Patten diversified company executive
Baumann, Michelle Renae editor, writer
Baumann-Sinacore, Patricia Lynn nursing administrator
Baumgartner, John H. refining and petroleum products company executive
Bautista, Anthony Hernandez biomedical company executive
Baxter, Cecil William, Jr. retired college president
Baxter, Stephen Bartow retired history educator
Baxter-Smith, Gregory John shareholder
Bayard, Susan Shapiro educator, small business owner
†Bayer, Gregory D. historian, researcher
Bayer, Robert Edward retired defense department official, consultant
Baym, Gordon Alan physicist, educator
Bayne, David Cowan priest, legal scholar, law educator
Beach, Edward Latimer writer, retired naval officer
Beadle, John Grant retired manufacturing company executive
Beal, Merrill David conservationist, museum director
Beals, Nancy Farwell state legislator
Beamish, Mary Kathryn copy editor
Beasley, Barbara Starin sales executive, marketing professional
Beasley, James W., Jr. lawyer
Beattie, Charles Robert, III lawyer
Beattie, Edward James surgeon, educator
Beattie, Nora Maureen insurance company executive, actuary
Beatts, Anne Patricia writer, producer
Beaumont, Richard Austin management consultant
Bechtol, Larry Owen pastor
Becich, Raymond Brice healthcare consultant, mediator, trainer, educator
Beck, Andrew Robert accountant
Beck, Karen Portsche elementary education educator
Beck, Mary Virginia lawyer, public official
Beck, Stuart Edwin lawyer
Beck, Timothy Daniel human resources specialist, consultant
Becker, Bruce Carl, II physician, educator
Becker, Jon Andrew arts and education consultant
Becker, Richard Charles retired college president
Becker, Walter Heinrich vocational educator, planner
Becker, William Watters lawyer
Beckjord, Eric Stephen nuclear engineer, energy researcher
†Beckwith, Marlin aeronautics program manager
Beckwith, Sidney Johnson director special programs, curriculum administrator
†Bedford, Danielle public relations specialist
Beebe, Hank composer
Beebe, John Eldridge financial service executive
Begley, Ed, Jr. actor
Behlmer, Rudy H., Jr. director, writer, film educator
Behrendt, John Charles research geophysicist
†Behrouz, Elizabeth J. service director
Beighey, Lawrence Jerome packaging company executive
Beitz, Alexandra Grigg political activist
Belafonte, Harry singer, concert artist, actor
Belanger, Cherry Churchill elementary school educator
Belanger, Luc oncologist
Belay, Brenda May emergency room nurse
Belco, Karen Marie cardiology nurse

Beldock, Myron *lawyer*
Bell, Clarence Deshong *state senator, lawyer*
†Bell, Gary M. *college dean*
Bell, P. Jackson *computer executive*
Bell, Scott Lee *pastor*
Bell, Susan Jane *nurse*
Bellamy, James Carl *insurance company executive*
Beller, Luanne Evelyn *accountant*
Belles, Donald Arnold *pastoral therapist, mental health counselor*
Bellow, Donald Grant *mechanical engineering educator*
Bellow, Saul C. *writer*
Belluomini, Frank Stephen *accountant*
Belmont, Larry Miller *retired public health executive*
Belmont, Madra Alvis *lawyer*
Belnap, Nuel Dinsmore, Jr. *philosophy educator*
†Beloff, Zoe *artist, educator*
Belonick, Cynthia Ann *psychiatric-mental health nurse*
Belton, Deborah Carolyn Knox *state information systems administrator*
†Belton, John *English educator*
Benc, Tamara Susan *reading and language arts educator*
Bencini, Sara Haltiwanger *concert pianist*
Bender, Hy *writer*
Bender, Ross Thomas *minister*
†Bender, Sheila Sue *essayist, poet, author*
Benenson, Claire Berger *investment and financial planning educator*
Benford, Anne Michele *pediatric nurse practitioner, clinical nurse specialist*
Benjamin, Georges Curtis *emergency physician, consultant*
Benn, Julie Eve Arend *writer, communications specialist*
Bennack, Frank Anthony, Jr. *publishing company executive*
Bennett, Jay Brett *medical device company executive*
Bennett, Michele Margulis *women's health nurse*
Bennett, Peter Dunne *retired marketing educator*
Bennett, Richard Thomas *retired manufacturing executive*
Bennett, Robert LeRoy *computer software development company executive*
Bennett, Saul *public relations agency executive*
Bennett, Sharon Kay *music educator*
Benowitz, Roy *composer, orchestrator, copyist, organist, pianist*
Benson, Joanne E. *former lieutenant governor*
Benson, Sharon Joan *mathematics educator*
†Benson, Stephen Edward *writer*
Bensoussan, Abraham *rabbi*
Benton, Fletcher *sculptor*
Benton, Robert *film director, screenwriter*
Benton, Robert Dean *educational organization executive*
†Bentsen, Lloyd *former government official, former senator*
Ben-Veniste, Richard *lawyer*
Benzel, Ilona Fran *artist*
Benzle, Curtis Munhall *artist, art educator*
Bercel, Nicholas Anthony *neurologist, neurophysiologist*
Bercovitch, Sacvan *English language professional, educator*
†Beresford, Bruce *film director*
Beresford, Wilma *elementary and gifted education educator*
Berezin, Tanya *acting coach, actress*
Berg, Alfred Oren *epidemiology and famiy practice medicine educator*
†Berg, A(ndrew) Scott *author, biographer*
Berg, Peter *actor*
Bergan, William Luke *lawyer*
Bergen, Candice *actress, writer, photojournalist*
Berger, Anita Hazel *psychotherapist, adult educator, organizational consultant*
Berger, Frank Stanley *management executive*
Berger, Frederick Jerome *electrical engineer, educator*
Berger, Linda Fay *writer*
Berger, Marleda Carter *student health nurse practitioner*
Berger, Stephen *financial services company executive*
Bergeron, Earleen Fournet *actress*
Bergey, John M. *retired technology executive*
Bergin, Allen Eric *clinical psychologist, educator*
Bergin, Colleen Joan *medical educator*
Berglund, Robin G. *child psychiatrist, former corporate executive*
Bergman, Hermas John (Jack Bergman) *retired college administrator*
Bergmann, Donald Gerald *pharmaceutical company executive*
Bergmann, Meredith Gang *sculptor*
Bergquist, Sandra Lee *medical and legal consultant, nurse*
Bergstein, Stanley Francis *horse racing executive*
Bering, Eva *healthcare executiver*
Beringer, William Ernst *mediator, arbitrator, lawyer*
Berke, Sarah Ballard *geriatrics nurse, mental health nurse*
Berkhofer, Robert Frederick, Jr. *retired history educator*
Berkholtz, Nicholas Evald *engineering manager, consultant*
Berkofsky, Martin *concert pianist*
†Berkowitz, Robert *psychiatrist*
Berkowitz, Steve *publishing company executive*
Berle, Milton (Milton Berlinger) *actor*
Berle, Peter Adolf Augustus *lawyer, media director*
Berlincourt, Marjorie Alkins *government official, retired*
Berlind, Roger Stuart *stage and film producer*
Berlinger, Warren *actor*
†Berloff, Andrea *performing arts company official*
Berlowitz Tarrant, Laurence *biotechnologist, university administrator*
Bermack, Elaine *speech educator*
Berman, Aaron *art appraiser, director, consultant*
Berman, Eleanore *artist*
Berman, Harry J. *educator, college administrator*
Berman, Joshua Mordecai *lawyer, manufacturing company executive*
Berman, Lori Beth *legislative staff member*
Berman, Richard Bruce *lawyer*
Berman, Sanford Solomon *motion picture sound designer, composer, arranger, artist*
Berman, William H. *publishing company executive*
†Bermard, Theodore G. *marketing executive*
Bern, Lynda Kaplan *women's health and pediatric nurse*
Bernard, Richard Lawson *geneticist, retired*
Bernath, Mary Therese *special education educator*
†Bernbeck, Volkert Joachim *retired plastic surgeon*
Berndt, Jane Ann *writer, researcher, educator*
Bernhardt, Jean Louise *special education educator*
Bernheimer, Martin *music critic*
Bernstein, George L. *lawyer, accountant*
Bernstein, I(rving) Melvin *university official and dean, materials scientist*
Bernstein, Jane *writer*
Bernstein, Peter Walter *publisher*
Bernstein, Richard Allen *company executive*
Berra, Robert Louis *human resources consultant*
Berresford, Susan Vail *philanthropic foundation executive*
Berrey, Robert Forrest *lawyer*
†Berridge, Mary *photographer*
Berry, Laurie Ann *critical care nurse*
Berry, Leora Mary *school nurse*
Berry, Richard Lewis *author, magazine editor, lecturer, programmer*
Berry, Richard Stephen *chemist*
Berry, Robert Vaughan *retired electrical manufacturing company executive*
Berry, Robert Worth *lawyer, educator, retired army officer*
Bers, Abraham *electrical engineering and physics educator*
Bers, Donald Martin *physiology educator*
Bersin, Richard Lewis *physicist, plasma process technologist*
Bersin, Ruth Hargrave *priest, social services administrator*
Bertelsman, William Odis *federal judge*
Bertin, John Joseph *aeronautical engineer, educator, researcher*
Bertman, Skip *baseball coach*
Bertram, Manya M. *lawyer*
Bertram, Susan *rehabilitation counselor*
Bertrand, Frederic Howard *retired insurance company executive*
Bertucelli, Robert Edward *accountant, educator*
Beston, Rose Marie *retired college president*
Bethlen, Ilona R. *designer, educator*
Betsinger, Peggy Ann *oncological nurse*
Betti, John Anso *federal official, former automobile manufacturing company executive*
Beukema, John Frederick *lawyer*
Beutler, Arthur Julius *manufacturing company executive*
Bey, Joan S. *retired public information specialist, writer*
Beyer, Gordon Robert *foreign service officer*
†Bhargava, Dinesh *plastic and reconstructive surgeon*
†Bhattacharya, Nandini *English educator, researcher, writer*
Biagi, Richard Charles *retail executive, real estate consultant*
Bice, Michael David *retail and wholesale executive, marketing consultant, insurance consultant*
Bick, Katherine Livingstone *scientist, international liaison, consultant*
Bickford, Shirley Verna Williams *retired English educator*
Bicofsky, David Marc *public relations executive*
†Biddle, Albert G. W. *trade association executive*
Bidwell, Roger Grafton Shelford *biologist, educator*
Bieber-Roberts, Peggy Eilene *communications educator, editor, journalist, researcher*
†Biedermann, Paul Frederick *graphic designer*
Biegel, David Eli *social worker, educator*
Bierley, Paul Edmund *musician, author, publisher*
Bierwirth, John Cocks *retired aerospace manufacturing executive*
Bigbee, Ivy Cave *photographer, author*
Biggers, Joan Nevill *social services organization administrator*
Biggers, William Joseph *retired manufacturing company executive*
Biggs, Arthur Edward *retired chemical manufacturing company executive*
Bigham, James George *structural engineer*
Biklen, Stephen Clinton *retired student loan company executive*
Bilbray, James Hubert *former congressman, lawyer, consultant*
Bilezikjian, Edward Andrew *architect*
Biljetina, Richard *natural gas industry executive*
Bill, Karen S. *actress*
Billingsley, Florence Ilona *nurse, case manager*
Billman, Larry Edward *writer, director*
Binch, Caroline Lesley *illustrator, photographer*
Binder, James Kauffman *computer consultant*
Binder, Madeline Dotti *retail professional*
Binks, Rebecca Anne *communications executive*
Bino, Marial Desolyn *librarian, educator, psychologist*
Binoche, Juliette *actress*
Binsfeld, Connie Berube *former state official*
Birch, Patricia *choreographer, director*
Bird, Harrie Waldo, Jr. *psychiatrist, educator*
Bird, Phillip Craig *mortgage company executive*
Birk, John R. *marketing/financial services consultant*
Birkenstock, James Warren *business machine manufacturing company executive*
Birkmayer, Donald Tefft *college official*
Birman, Linda Lee *elementary education educator*
Birnbaum, Stevan Allen *investment company executive*
Birne, Cindy Frank *business owner*
Bishop, Blaine Elwood *football player*
Bishop, Budd Harris *retired museum administrator, artist*
Bishop, Charles Edwin *university president emeritus, economist*
Bishop, Gordon Bruce *journalist*
Bishop, J. Joe *social studies educator*
Bishop, June A. *secondary education educator*
Bishop, Linda Baxter *critical care nurse*
Bishop, Maureen E. *critical care nurse, clinical nurse specialist*
Bishop, Nancy Stephanie *nurse, health educator*
Bishop, (Ina) Sue Marquis *dean, psychiatric and mental health nurse educator, researcher*
Bisnette, Dena Lynn *journalist*
Bissell, Allen Morris *engineer, consultant*
Bissell, James Dougal, III *motion picture production designer*
Bitner, John William *banker*
Bivans, Maurita W. *school administrator*
Bivens, Lynette Kupka *elementary education educator*
Bixler, Margaret Triplett *former manufacturing executive*
Biziou, Peter *cinematographer*
Bjerknes, Michael Leif *dancer*
Bjorndahl, David Lee *electrical engineer*
Black, Barbara Ann *publisher*
Black, Georgia Ann *educational administrator*
Black, Karen *actress*
Black, Rhonda Stout *special education educator*
Black, Richard Bruce *business executive, consultant*
Black, Rilla Alma *violinist, library assistant, poet*
Black, Susan *public relations consultant*
Blackbourn, David Gordon *history educator*
Blacker, Harriet *public relations executive*
Blackston, Brenda Joyce *computer software company manager*
†Blackstone, Dara *music educator*
Blaine, Davis Robert *valuation consultant executive*
Blair, Charlie Lewis *elementary school educator*
Blair, Fred Edward *social services administrator*
Blair, Robert Noel *artist*
Blair, Sandra Jean *author, publisher*
Blake, John Edward *retired car rental company executive*
Blake, Ran *jazz pianist, composer*
Blanchard, Cary *football player*
Blanchard, David Lawrence *aerospace executive, real estate developer, consultant*
Blanchard, George Samuel *retired military officer*
Blanchard, Louis A. *medical/surgical nurse, educator*
Blanchard, Richard Frederick *construction executive*
Blanco, Laura *film producer*
Blaschke, Renee Dhossche *alderman*
Blasco, Alfred Joseph *business and financial consultant*
Blatt, Harold Geller *lawyer*
Blatt, Philip Mark *hematologist, educator*
Blattner, Florence Anne *music educator*
Blazey, Judith Leiston *school district administrator*
Blazina, Janice Fay *transfusion medicine physician*
Blazzard, Norse Novar *lawyer*
Blecke, Arthur Edward *principal*
Blethen, Shirley E. *dialysis nurse, administrator*
Blevins, Jeffrey Alexander *lawyer*
Bliley, Thomas Jerome, Jr. *congressman*
Blinder, Janet *art dealer*
Bliss, William Stanley, Jr. *corporate financial and marketing consultant*
Blitt, Rita Lea *artist*
Bloch, Erich *retired electrical engineer, former science foundation administrator*
Bloch, Julia Chang *foundation administrator, former bank executive, educator*
Block, Barbara Ann *biology educator*
Block, Dennis Jeffrey *lawyer*
Block, Emil Nathaniel, Jr. *military officer*
Block, Lawrence *author*
Block, Paul Alan *novelist, editor*
Block, Richard Raphael *lawyer, economic development arbitrator*
Block, William *newspaper publisher*
Blomgren, Ronald Walter *business executive*
Blomstrom, Bruce A. *healthcare executive*
Blood, Archer Kent *retired foreign service officer*
Bloodworth, Gladys Leon *educator*
Bloomquist, Kenneth Gene *music educator, university bands director*
Blossom, Beverly *choreographer, dance educator*
Blount, Kerry Andrew *defense analyst*
Bloustein, Peter Edward *entertainment management consultant, producer*
Blow, George *lawyer*
Bluestein, Steve Franklin *comedian, writer*
Bluhm, Gene Elwood *trade journal editor and publisher*
Blum, Barbara Davis *investor*
†Blum, Betty Ann *footwear company executive*
Blumberg, Mark Stuart *consultant*
Blumenau, Iris Warech *nursing consultant*
Blumenfeld, Rochelle S. Reznik *artist*
†Blumenfeld-Kosinski, Renate *French educator*
Blummer, Kathleen Ann *counselor*
†Blumstein, Susan Bender *fundraiser*
Blum-Veglia, Cheryl Ann *accountant*
Blush, Steven Michael *nuclear scientist, safety consultant*
Boal, Dean *retired arts center administrator, educator*
Boatman, Deborah Ann *hospice nurse*
Boatwright, Charlotte Jeanne *hospital marketing and public relations executive*
Bobbie, Walter *theatrical director*
Bochner, Hart *actor*
Bock, Jerry (Jerrold Lewis) *composer*
Bockius, Ruth Bear *nursing educator*
†Bocskor, Nancy Leah *political consultant*
†Boczko, Stanley *urologist*
Bodanszky, Miklos *chemist, educator*
Boddie, Lewis Franklin *obstetrics and gynecology educator*
Bodey, Richard Allen *minister, educator*
Bodnar, Elisabeth M. *occupational health consultant*
Boeker, Paul Harold *non-profit organization official, diplomat*
Bogart, Carol Lynn *writer, media consultant*
Bogart, Judith Saunders *public relations executive*
Bogart, Rebecca A. *musician, educator*
Boge, Walter Edward *retired army civilian official, private consultant*
Boggs, Robert Wayne *healthcare administrator*
†Bogner, Norman *novelist, screenwriter, playwright*
Bogosian, Eric *actor, writer*
Bohannan, Jules Kirby *printing company executive*
Bohannan, Paul James *anthropologist, writer, former university administrator*
Bohle, Robert Henry *journalism educator*
Boho, Dan L. *lawyer*
Bohoskey, Bernice Fleming *mineral-land owner, writer*
Bok, Sissela *philosopher, writer*
Boland, Catherine A. Benning *quality assurance specialist*
Boldosser, Randy Richard *management consultant, communications equipment company executive*
Boles, Thomas Lee *medical technician*
Bolie, Victor Wayne *engineering educator emeritus*
Boling, Patricia Ann *political science educator, researcher, writer*
Boling, Robert Bruce *physical education educator*
Bollback, Anthony George *minister*
Bolles, Susan *production designer*
Bolliger, Eugene Frederick *retired surgeon*
Bollinger, Kenneth John *aerospace engineer, computer and space scientist*
†Bolluyt, Linda Beth *library director*
Bolotin, Lora M. *retired business owner, electronics executive*
Bolsterli, Margaret Jones *English educator, farmer*
Boltz, Christine *community health and emergency nurse*
Bond, Audrey Mae *real estate broker*
Bond, Victoria Ellen *conductor, composer*
Bondar, Richard Jay Laurent *biochemist*
Bondarenko, Hesperia Aura Louis *entrepreneur*
Bonds, Sophia Jane Riddle *geriatrics, medical/surgical nurse*
Bonerz, Peter *actor, director*
Boniey, Emily Ann *critical care nurse, anesthesist nurse*
Bonifay, Cam *professional sports team executive*
Bonn, Ethel May *psychiatrist, educator*
Bonnard, Raymond *theater director*
Bonner, Jack *public relations company executive*
Bonner, John Tyler *biology educator*
†Bonner, William P. *physician*
Bonnet, John David *physician, medical facility administrator*
Bonsack, Rose Mary Hatem *state legislator, physician*
Bonutti, Alexander Carl *architect, urban designer*
Booker, Michael James *philosophy educator*
Booker, Nana Laurel *public relations executive*
Boone, John Lewis *religious organization administrator*
Boone, Karen *nutritionist, oriental medicine physician*
Booth, Bonnie Nelson *human resources consultant*
Booth, George Geoffrey *finance educator*
Bootle, William Augustus *retired federal judge*
Boozer, Howard Rai *retired state education official*
Borchardt, Donald Arthur *visual and performing arts educator*
Borda, Richard Joseph *management consultant*
Bordy, Bill (William James Bordy) *publisher*
Borecky, Isidore *bishop*
Borg, Ruth I. *home nursing care provider*
Borger, Gloria *journalist, editor*
Borgnine, Ernest *actor*
Borgstahl, Kaylene Denise *health facility administrator*
Bork, Robert Heron *lawyer, author, educator, former federal judge*
Borleis, Melvin William *management consultant*
Bormann, Frederick Herbert *forestry and environmental science educator*
Bornhorst, Kenneth Frank *electromagnetics and systems engineer*
†Bornstein, David Neil *writer*
Borntrager, John Sherwood *principal*
Borowitz, Albert Ira *lawyer, author*
Borsick, Marlin Lester *data processing executive*
Borst, Philip West *academic administrator*
Borten, William H. *research company executive*
†Borum, Bradford R. *policy analyst*
Borum, Rodney Lee *financial business executive*
Borwein, Jonathan Michael *mathematics educator*
Borysewicz, Mary Louise *editor*
Bosco, Anthony Gerard *bishop*
Bose, Anjan *electrical engineering educator, academic administrator*
Boslaugh, Leslie *retired judge*
Bosmajian, Haig Aram *speech communication educator*
Bosse, Malcolm Joseph, Jr. *professional language educator, author*
Bost, Raymond Morris *retired college president*
Bost, Thomas Glen *lawyer*
Bothwell, John Charles *archbishop*
Bottone, JoAnn *health services executive*
Bougalis, Katherine G. *medical surgical nurse, educator*
†Boulden, Judith Ann *bankruptcy judge*
Bourke, William Oliver *retired metal company executive*
Bourrie, Sally Ruth *writer*
Bova, Benjamin William *author, editor, educator*
†Bowe, Riddick Lamont *professional boxer*
Bowen, James Ronald *banker*
Bowen-Forbes, Jorge Courtney *artist, author, poet*
Bower, Jean Ramsay *lawyer, writer*
†Bower, Marilyn Kay *landscape artist*
Bower, Shelley Ann *business management consultant*
Bowie, E(dward) J(ohn) Walter *hematologist, researcher*
Bowlby, Richard Eric *retired computer systems analyst*
Bowles, Barbara Landers *investment company executive*
Bowman, Charles Hay *petroleum company executive*
Bowman, Patricia Lynn *lawyer*
Bowne, James DeHart *museum official*
Bowne, Shirlee Pearson *finance and housing consultant*
Box, George Edward Pelham *statistics educator*
Boxer, Stanley Robert *artist, sculptor*
Boyatt, Thomas David *former ambassador*
Boyd, Danny Douglass *financial counselor, marriage and family counselor*
Boyd, Edward Lee *financial executive*
Boyd, Francis Virgil *retired accounting educator*
Boyd, Julianne Mamana *theater director*
Boyd, Liona Maria *musician*
Boyd, Thomas Marshall *lawyer*
Boyenga, Cindy A. *secondary education educator*
Boyer, Heidi Hild *public policy consultant*
Boyes, Stephen Richard *hydrogeologic consultant*
Boyett, Dorothy Eleanor Anderson *dietitian, educator*
Boykin, Robert Heath *banker*
Boyle, Dennis Joseph, III *computer company executive*
Boyle, Francis Joseph *retired federal judge*
†Boyle, Kathleen Marie *English educator, soccer coach*
Boyle, Peter *actor*
Boyle, R. Emmett *metal products executive*
Boyle, Richard James *banker*
Boyles, James Kenneth *retired banker*
Boysen, Thomas Cyril *state school system administrator*
Bozzolo, Donna Louise *family nurse practitioner*
Brabec, Rosemary Jean *retail executive*
Bracco, Lorraine *actress*
Bracey, Earnest Norton *political science educator*
Bracken, Peg *author*
Brackenhoff, Lonnie Sue *principal*
Brackett, Tracy Ann *science journalist, consultant*
Braden, Charles Hosea *physicist, university administrator*
Braden, George Walter, II (Barron of Carrigaline) *company executive*
Braden, Thomas Wardell *news commentator*
Bradford, Barbara Reed *lawyer*
Bradley, Kathryn *health facility administrator*
Bradley, Marilynne Gail *advertising executive, advertising educator*
Bradley, Patricia Ellen *professional golfer*
Bradley, Sandra Lynn Grant *nursing administrator*
Bradley, William Bryan *cable television regulator*
Bradshaw, Dove *artist*
†Bradshaw, John Robert *internet service company executive*
Brady, George Moore *real estate executive, mortgage banker*

Brady, Jean Stein retired librarian
Braen, Bernard Benjamin psychology educator
Brafford, William Charles lawyer
Bragdon, Paul Errol educator
Bragenzer, June Anna Ruth Grimm community health nurse
†Braid, Bernice program director, dean
Brain, George Bernard university dean
Braisted, Madeline Charlotte financial planner
Bram, Leon Leonard publishing company executive
†Bramlett, David A. retired military officer
Branagan, James Joseph lawyer
Brancato, Leo John manufacturing company executive
Branch, Anne Heather fund raiser
Brand, John Charles chemistry educator
Brandauer, Klaus Maria actor
Brando, Marlon, Jr. actor
†Brandon, Tabitha A. health service administrator
Brandt, Ronald Stirling writer
Brannick, Ellen Marie management consultant
Brantz, George Murray retired lawyer
Branyan, Robert Lester retired university administrator
†Branyan, W. David novelist
Brashears, Sumner funeral director
Bratsch, Steven Gary chemistry educator
Bratt, Nicholas investment management and research company executive
Bratton, William Edward electronics executive, management consultant
Bratzler, Mary Kathryn desktop publisher
Brauchli, Marcus Walker foreign correspondent
Brauer, Rhonda Lyn lawyer
Braugher, Andre actor
Braun, Jerome Irwin lawyer
†Braunworth, Brent Taylor firefighter, paramedic, police officer
Bravo, Rose Marie retail executive
Brawer, Catherine Coleman foundation executive, curator
Brawner, Sharon Lee bilingual education educator, researcher
Bray, Sharon Ann management company executive
Braye, Rubye Howard army officer
Brazier, Don Roland retired railroad executive
Breathed, Berkeley cartoonist
Brechbill, Susan Reynolds lawyer, educator
Brecht, Sally Ann quality assurance executive
Brecker, Randal Edward musician, arranger
Bredfeldt, John Creighton economist, financial analyst, retired air force officer
Breen, Janice DeYoung health services executive, community health nurse
Breidenbach, Cherie Elizabeth lawyer, accountant
Brekke, Gail Louise broadcasting administrator
Bremer, Victor John broadcasting executive
Bremner, John McColl agronomy and biochemistry educator
Brennan, Donna Lesley public relations company executive
Brennan, Maryann business consulting executive
Brennen, Stephen Alfred international business consultant
Brenner, Jane Segrest former city council member
Brent, Robert Leonard radiology and pediatrics educator
Breslin, Elizabeth Walker biological scientist, biomedical consultant
Breslin, Evalynne Louise Wood-Robertson retired psychiatric nurse
Brettell, Richard Robson art historian, museum consultant, educator
Bretthauer, Erich Walter chemist, educator
Brewer, Carey retired academic administrator
Brewer, Gail Lee pre-cast concrete company executive, banker
†Brewer, Keith F. plastic surgeon
Brewer, Stanley R. wholesale grocery executive
Brewster, Elizabeth Winifred English language educator, poet, novelist
Brezzo, Steven Louis museum director
†Briare, John M. business official
Brickell, Charles Hennessey, Jr. marine engineer, retired military officer
Bricker, William Rudolph organization executive
†Bridenbaugh, Peter Reese industrial research executive
†Bridge, Andrew theatrical lighting designer
Bridger, Baldwin, Jr. electrical engineer
Bridgewater, Brad Olympic athlete
Brigance, Marcelena critical care nurse
Brigeois, Evelyne Brigitte artist, publisher
†Briggle, Gary Lee singer, actor, director
Briggs, James Henry, II engineering administrator
Briggs, Janet Marie Louise nurse practitioner
Brigham, John Allen, Jr. financial executive, environmentalist, polition
Brill, Winston Jonas microbiologist, educator, research director, publisher and management consultant
Brim, Orville Gilbert, Jr. former foundation administrator, author
Brimley, Wilford actor
Brinberg, Herbert Raphael information management, publishing company executive
Brinckerhoff, Richard Charles retired manufacturing company executive
Brink, Richard Edward lawyer
Brinkley, Glenda Willis medical/surgical nurse, women's health nurse
Britt, John Roy banker
†Britt, Lois G. farming executive
Broadbent, Amalia Sayo Castillo graphic arts designer
Broadhurst, Norman Neil foods company executive
Broadwater, James E. publisher
Broberg, Merle retired social worker
Brock, John Morgan, Jr. composer, synthesist
Brock, Russell Ernest educational administrator
Brockway, Laurie Sue editor, journalist, author, minister
Broderson, Thelma Sylvia marketing professional
Brodhead, David Crawmer lawyer
Brodie, Alice Velma health and ethics advocate
Brodsky, David M. lawyer
Brody, Jacob Jerome art history educator
Brody, Martin food service company executive
Broedling, Laurie Adele human resources consultant, psychologist, educator
†Brogan, Frank T. lieutenant governor
Broggini, Carolyn orthopedics and neuroscience nurse
Brohammer, Richard Frederic psychiatrist
†Brondizio, Eduardo Sonnewend ecological researcher, consultant
†Bronsdon, Robert Lawrence acoustical engineer, artist
†Bronstein, Lynne writer
Brooke, Ralph Ian dental educator
Brooker, Robert Elton, Jr. retired manufacturing company executive
Brookman, Carol Joyce writer
Brookner, Anita writer, educator
Brooks, Albert (Albert Einstein) actor, writer, director
Brooks, Babert Vincent publisher
Brooks, Dennis Mark secondary education educator
Brooks, Garth (Troyal Garth Brooks) country music singer
Brooks, Kenneth N. forestry educator
Brooks, Mark Hunter systems engineering manager, consultant
Brooks, Michael Paul urban planning educator
Brooks, Thomas Aloysius, III retired naval officer, telecommunications company executive
Brooks Shoemaker, Virginia Lee volunteer, librarian
†Broomes, Shelly Lori human resources professional
Brosda, Alexander Christian investment banker
Brosnan, Peter Lawrence documentary filmmaker
Brosnan, Pierce actor
Brosz, Margaret Headley pediatrics nurse
Broth, Ray retail executive
Brotman, Stuart Neil management consultant, lawyer, educator
Broude, Ronald music publisher
Broughton, Carolyn Miles public relations executive
Brouillette, Yves insurance company executive
Broussard, Carol Madeline writer, literary consulting agent, photographer
Browder, Felix Earl mathematician, educator
Brower, Charles Nelson lawyer, judge
Brower, Forrest Allen retired health facility administrator
†Brower, Sara E. Maskell elementary education educator
Brown, Alice Elste artist
Brown, Ann Barton museum director
Brown, Ann Lenora community economic development professional
Brown, Anne Rhoda Wiesen civic worker
Brown, Barbara June hospital and nursing administrator
Brown, Barbara S. environmental scientist
Brown, Billye Jean retired nursing educator
Brown, Britt retired publishing company executive
Brown, Carol (Rose) artist
Brown, David Grant university president
†Brown, David R. think-tank executive
Brown, Donald Douglas transportation company executive, retired air force officer, consultant
Brown, Dorothy Howard medical practice administrator
Brown, Eli Matthew anesthesiologist
Brown, Geraldine nurse, freelance writer
Brown, Hardin occupational health nurse
†Brown, Henry surgeon
Brown, Henry Bedinger Rust financial management company executive
†Brown, James H., Jr. state insurance commissioner, lawyer
Brown, Jim (James Nathaniel Brown) film actor, former professional football player
†Brown, Joseph W., Jr. (Jay Brown) insurance company executive
Brown, Marcia Joan author, artist, photographer
Brown, Michael Robert finance specialist
Brown, Rhonda Rochelle chemist, health facility administrator, lawyer
Brown, Richard Carlos journalism educator, editor
Brown, Richard E. state legislator
Brown, Robert Laidlaw state supreme court justice
Brown, Ronald Malcolm engineering corporation executive
Brown, Rosanna Sofia landscape architect
Brown, Samuel retired corporate executive
Brown, Suzanne Wiley museum director
Brown, Tina magazine editor
Browne, Diana Gayle artist, social services
Browne, Edmund John Phillip oil company executive
Browne, Thomas Reed neurologist, researcher, educator
Browning, Colin Arrott retired banker
Brownlee, Paula Pimlott educational consultant, former academic administrator
Brubaker, Crawford Francis, Jr. government official, aerospace consultant
Bruce, James Edmund retired utility company executive
Brugioni, David Michael graphic designer, illustrator, artist
Bruinsma, Theodore August retired business executive
Brumberg, G. David history bibliographer
Brune, David Hamilton financial corporation executive, lawyer
Brune, Eva fundraiser
Brunnett, Kathleen Shannon secondary educator
Bruno, Barbara Altman social worker
Bruno, Cathy Eileen management consultant, former state official
Brunt, Harry Herman, Jr. psychiatrist
Bryan, Lawrence Dow college president
Bryan, Sukey artist
Bryant, Bertha Estelle retired nurse
Bryant, Daryl Leslie painter, educator
Bryant, John author, publisher
Bryant, Paul Thompson English language educator
Bryant, Roy, Sr. bishop
Bryant, Winston former state attorney general
Bryer, Lena Dorothy nursing educator
Bubar, Joseph Bedell, Jr. church official
Bubrick, Melvin Phillip surgeon
Buchanan, Patrick Joseph journalist
Buchanan, William Hobart, Jr. lawyer, publishing company executive
Buchbinder, Sharon Bell health care management educator
Buchin, Jean psychologist
Buchmann, Alan Paul lawyer
Buck, Alison Jennifer computer programmer
Buck, Earl Wayne insurance investigator, private detective
Buck, Linda Dee civic worker
Buck, William Joseph theatrical designer, educator
Buckels, Marvin Wayne savings and loan executive
Buckler, Marilyn Lebow school psychologist, educational consultant
Buckley, William Elmhirst publishing consultant
Buckman, Frederick W. gas utility executive
Buckstein, Caryl Sue writer
†Budnick, Lawrence David physician, medical educator
Budoff, Penny Wise physician, author, researcher
Budzinski, James Edward interior designer
Buechel, William Benjamin lawyer
†Buell, Dexter artist, sculpture
Buell, Diana E. nursing administrator, special education professional
Buenaventura, Milagros Paez psychiatrist
Bueno, Ana healthcare marketing and public relations executive, writer
Buffkins, Archie Lee public television executive
Bugbee, Joan Barthelme retired corporate communications executive
Bujold, Tyrone Patrick lawyer
Buker, Robert Hutchinson, Sr. army officer, thoracic surgeon
Bulcken, Carolyn Anne Brooks retired special education educator
Bull, Bergen Ira retired equipment manufacturing company executive
Bulla, Clyde Robert writer
Bullard, Sharon Welch librarian
Bullins, Ed author
Bullock, Molly retired elementary education educator
Bullock, Theodore Holmes biologist, educator
Bullough, Vern LeRoy nursing educator, historian, sexologist, researcher
Bumbery, Joseph Lawrence diversified telecommunications company executive
Bunch, Franklin Swope architect
Bunch, Jennings Bryan, Jr. electrical engineer
Bundi, Renee art director, graphic designer
Bundy, Hallie Flowers biochemist, educator
Bundy, Mary Lothrop retired clinical social worker
Bunim, Mary-Ellis television producer
Bunker, Debra J. elementary education educator
Bunning, Jim senator, former professional baseball player
Bunton, Lucius Desha, III federal judge
Bunyan, Ellen Lackey Spotz chemist, educator
Burbridge, Ann Arnold elementary school educator, music educator
Burch, Hamlin Doughty, III retired sheet metal professional
Burch, Robert Emmett retired physician, educator
Burcham, Randall Parks lawyer, farmer
Burchiel, Susan Marguerite nurse educator
Burchman, Leonard government official
Burczyk, Mary Elizabeth corporate communications executive
Burd, Shirley Farley clinical specialist, mental health nurse
Burden, Ordway Partridge investment banker
†Burfeindt, Douglas Glenn civilian military official
Burgdoerfer, Jerry J. marketing and distribution executive
Burge, John Wesley, Jr. management consultant
Burger, Leslie Morton physician, army officer
Burger, Robert Eugene author, chess expert
†Burger, Werner Carl retired art educator
Burgess, Diane Glenn real estate broker, paralegal
Burgess, Hayden Fern (Poka Laenui) lawyer
Burgess, Marjorie Laura protective services official
Burgess, Michael H. management consultant
Burke, Bill art educator
Burke, Doug author, director, producer, inventor
Burke, Edmond Wayne retired judge, lawyer
Burke, Joseph C. former university official
†Burkett, Robert L. investment company executive
Burkett, Thomas O. manufacturing executive
Burkholder, Timothy James religious organization administrator
Burki, Fred Albert labor union official
Burks, Jack D. investment executive
†Burlingame, Anson Hollyday retired engineer
Burlingame, John Hunter lawyer
Burlingame, Lloyd Lamson retired design instructor
Burnett, Glenda Morris community health nurse
Burnham, J. V. sales executive
Burns, Bebe Lyn journalist
Burns, Donald Snow registered investment advisor, financial and business consultant
†Burns, Ellen Jean arts educator
Burns, James Milton retired educator
Burns, Kitty playwright
Burns, Marie T. retired secondary education educator
Burns, Richard Francis mechanical engineer
Burns, Ward textile company executive
Burnside, Orvin Charles agronomy educator, researcher
Burr, Laurie Diane information technology consultant
Burris, Frances White retired state official
Burris-Schnur, Catherine medical/surgical nurse, educator, minister, pastoral psychologist
Burroughs, Pamela Gayle information systems specialist
Burrows, E. Michael art educator, artist
†Burrows, Edwin Gladding retired broadcaster, writer, poet
Burton, Al producer, director, writer
†Burton, Jeff professional race car driver
Burton, Joseph Alfred state legislator
Büsch, Annemarie retired mental health nurse
Busch, Joyce Ida small business owner
Busch, Noel Henry banker
Bush, Barbara Pierce volunteer, wife of former President of the United States
Bush, Larry sportswriter
Bush, Richard Clarence, III federal government executive
Bush, Sarah Lillian historian
Bushnell, Prudence former diplomat, management consultant, trainer
Busse, Leonard Wayne banker, financial consultant
Bussey, George Davis psychiatrist
Bussgang, Julian Jakob electronics engineer
Bussman, John Wood physician, health care administrator
Butcher, Vanessa Jean critical care nurse
Butler, George Frank editor, literary historian
Butler, Jack Fairchild semiconductors company executive
Butler, Robert Leonard sales executive
Butler, Robert Thomas retired advertising executive
†Butrimovitz, Gerald Paul financial planner, securities analyst, investment advisor
Butterfield, Deborah Kay sculptor
Buttrick, Harold architect
Butts, Virginia corporate public relations executive
Butzner, John Decker, Jr. federal judge
Buxton, Winslow Hurlbert manufacturing company executive
Buzard, James Albert healthcare management consultant
Byard, Vicki Faye English educator
Byford, Emma rancher
Bynes, Frank Howard, Jr. physician
†Byrd, Joan Eda film librarian
Byrd, Lloyd Garland civil engineer
Byrd, Lorenda Sue nursing administrator
Byrne, Catherine swimmer
Byrne, David musician, composer, artist, director
Byrne, Jamie Maria communications educator
Byrne-Dempsey, Cecelia (Cecelia Dempsey) journalist
Cachia, Pierre Jacques Middle East languages and culture educator, researcher
Caddeo, Maria Elizabeth critical care nurse
Caesar, Sid actor, comedian
Caffee, Marcus Pat publishing company executive
Cahn, Robert Nathan physicist
Cain, Patricia Jean accountant
Caine, Raymond William, Jr. retired public relations executive
Cairns, Diane Patricia motion picture executive
†Calabrese, Karen Ann artist, educator
Calcaterra, Edward Lee construction company executive
Calder, Iain Wilson publishing company executive
Caldwell, Elwood Fleming food scientist
Caldwell, Judy Carol advertising executive, public relations executive
Caldwell, Karin D. biochemist educator
Caldwell, Sarah opera producer, conductor, stage director and administrator
Caldwell, William Edward educational administration educator, arbitrator
Calegari, Maria ballerina
Califano, Joseph Anthony, Jr. lawyer, public health policy educator, writer
†Call, Elizabeth Ann mental health counselor
Callan, John Garling entrepreneur, management executive, business consultants
Callander, Bruce Douglas journalist, free-lance writer
Callard, David Jacobus private equity investor
Calleo, David Patrick political science educator
Callison, Nancy Fowler nurse administrator
Callow, Keith McLean judge
Callow, William Grant retired state supreme court justice
Calvano-Smith, Rita journalist, small business owner
Calvert, James Francis manufacturing company executive, retired admiral
Calvert, William Preston radiologist
Camacho, Hector boxer
Camayd-Freixas, Yoel management, strategy & planning consultant
Camdessus, Michel (Jean) federal agency administrator, international organization executive
Cameron, Daniel Forrest communications executive
Cameron, David Brian health service administrator
Cameron, J. Elliot retired parochial educational system administrator
Cameron, JoAnna actress, director
†Cameron, Kirk MacGregor Drummond statistician
Cameron, Lucille Wilson retired dean of libraries
Caminiti, Kenneth Gene professional baseball player
Camm, Gertrude Elizabeth physician, writer
Camp, Alethea Taylor executive and organizational design consultant
Camp, Clifton Durrett, Jr. newspaper consultant, rancher
Camp, Kristin Mary primary school educator
Camp, Virginia Ann medical/surgical nurse
Campanelli, Pauline Eble artist
Campbell, Addison James, Jr. writer
Campbell, Arthur Andrews retired government official
Campbell, Brian Scott army officer
Campbell, Byron Chesser publishing company executive
Campbell, Clarence Bowen retired educator, real estate developer, columnist
Campbell, Demarest Lindsay artist, designer, writer
Campbell, Donald Alfred retired government official
Campbell, Edwin Denton consultant
Campbell, Henry Cummings librarian
Campbell, Jean retired human services organization administrator
Campbell, Margaret M. retired social work educator
Campbell, Patton stage designer, educator
Campbell, Richard Alden electronics company executive
Campbell, Susan Carrigg secondary education educator
Campbell, Will Davis writer
†Campbell, William research analyst, educator
Campbell, William Yates investment banker
†Campbell-ray, Kecia Lynn elementary school teacher
Camper, John Saxton public relations and marketing executive
†Campion, Jane director, screenwriter
Campos-Orrego, Nora Patricia lawyer, consultant
Canan, Michael James lawyer, author
†Canavan, Patrick Joseph artist
Candlish, Malcolm manufacturing company executive
Cane, David E. chemistry educator
Canjar, Patricia McWade psychologist
Cannon, Dyan actress
Cannon, Isabella Walton mayor
Canoff, Karen Huston lawyer
Cantliffe, Jeri Miller artist, art educator
Cantrell, Stephanie Ann nurse
Cantril, Albert H(adley) public opinion analyst
Capice, Philip Charles television production executive
Caples, Anne L. healthcare consultant, former nursing educator
Capobianco, Anna Theresa retired patient education specialist
Capon, Edwin Gould church organization administrator, clergyman
Caporaso, Pat Marie art dealer
Capps, James Leigh, II lawyer, reserve military career officer
Caputo, Salvatore critic
Caras, Roger Andrew author, motion picture company executive, television correspondent, radio commentator
Carbajal, Michael boxer
Carder, Paul Charles advertising executive
Cardman, Lawrence Santo physics educator, research administrator
Cardone, Bonnie Jean photojournalist
Cardwell, Nancy Lee editor, writer
Cardy, Andrew Gordon hotel executive
Carew, Rodney Cline batting coach, former professional baseball player
Carey, John Jesse academic administrator, religion educator
Carey, Ronald former labor union leader
Carillo, Mary broadcaster, tennis analyst
Carlin, Betty educator
Carlquist, Sherwin biology and botany educator
Carls, Alice Catherine history educator
Carlsen, Mary Baird clinical psychologist
†Carlson, Donald Otto magazine publisher, editor

†Carlson, Elizabeth Anne library director
Carlson, Freda Ellen educator, consultant
Carlson, Gustav Gunnar anthropology educator
Carlson, Janet Frances psychologist, educator
Carlson, Marguerite T. science educator
Carlson, Natalie Traylor publisher
Carlucci, Gino Dominic, Jr. urban planner, policy analyst
Carlucci, Joseph P. lawyer
Carmack, Mildred Jean retired lawyer
Carman, Susan Hufert nurse coordinator
Carmichael, Judy Lea record industry executive, concert jazz pianist
Carner, Charles Robert, Jr. screenwriter, director
Carney, Arthur William Matthew actor
†Carney, Timothy Michael diplomat
Caro, Anthony (Alfred Caro) sculptor
Carpenter, Anne Betts pathologist, physician, immunologist
Carpenter, Derr Alvin landscape architect
Carpenter, Edward Kearney writer, editor
†Carpenter, James Farlin consultant
Carpenter, Myron Arthur manufacturing company executive
Carpenter, Patricia Lynn author
Carpenter, Phyllis Jean medical/surgical nurse
Carpenter-Mason, Beverly Nadine health care and quality assurance nurse consultant
Carper, James David magazine editor
Carr, Albert Anthony retired organic chemist
Carr, Bessie retired middle school educator
Carr, Harold Noflet investment corporation executive
Carr, Jesse Metteau, III lawyer, engineering executive
Carr, Paul Wallace actor
Carradine, Keith Ian actor, singer, composer
Carreker, John Russell retired agricultural engineer
Carrera, Rodolfo nuclear engineer, physicist
Carrison, Dale Mitchell emergency medicine physician
Carroll, Brenda Sandidge retired civic worker
Carroll, Joanne Zlate elementary education educator
Carroll, Joseph J(ohn) lawyer
Carroll, Marie-Jean Greve educator, artist
Carroll, Marshall Elliott architect
Carroll, Philip Joseph engineering company executive
Carruthers, Claudelle Ann occupational and physical therapist
Carson, Margaret Marie gas and electric industry executive, marketing professional
Carson, Mary Silvano career counselor, educator
Carta, Franklin Oliver retired aeronautical engineer
Carter, David LaVere soil scientist, researcher, consultant
†Carter, Gale Boatwright hotel services executive
Carter, Herbert Edmund former university official
Carter, (William) Hodding, III foundation executive, former journalist, public official and educator
Carter, Jaine M(arie) human resources development company executive
Carter, Joseph Edwin former nickel company executive, writer
Carter, Nanette Carolyn artist
†Carter, Paul Milton, Jr. federal agency administrator
Carter, Richard Duane business educator
Carter, Rosalynn Smith wife of former President of United States
Carter, Thomas Allen retired engineering executive, consultant
Carter, William George, III career officer
Cartier, Celine Paule librarian, administrator, consultant
Cartland, Barbara author
Caruana, Joan educator, psychotherapist, nurse
Carver, Calvin Reeve public utility company director
Carver, Kendall Lynn insurance company executive
Carvey, Dana actor, stand up comedian
Cary, Anne O. retired diplomat
†Casa, Douglas James sports medicine educator
Casadesus, Penelope Ann advertising executive, film producer
Casei, Nedda mezzo-soprano
Casella, Peter F(iore) patent and licensing executive
Casey, Robert J. international trade association executive
Casey, Robert Reisch lawyer
Casey, Thomas Warren graphic design company executive, architect
Cash, Deanna Gail nursing educator, retired
Cash, Johnny entertainer
Cashatt, Charles Alvin retired hydro-electric power generation company executive
Caso, Philip Michael financial services company executive, educator
Cason, Nica Virginia nursing educator
Casoni, Richard Albert marine technologist, educator
Casper, Gerhard academic administrator, law educator
Cassano, Valerie women's health nurse
Cassel, Seymour actor
Cassell, William Comyn retired college president
Casselman, William E., II lawyer
Cassidy, Esther Christmas retired government official
Cassidy, James Mark construction company executive
Cassidy, John Harold lawyer
Cassidy, Kevin Andrew retired engineering company executive
Cassin, James Richard broadcast educator
Castagna, William John federal judge
Castberg, Eileen Sue construction company owner
Castel, Jean Gabriel lawyer
Castile, Rand (Jesse Randolph, III) retired museum director
Castle, James Cameron information systems executive
Castle, Sandie writer, playwright, artist
Caston, J(esse) Douglas medical educator
Castor, Betty academic administrator
Castor, Christina Pelayo critical care nurse
Castro, Amuerfina Tantiongco geriatrics nurse
Caswell, Frances Pratt retired English language educator
Catacosinos, William James retired utility company executive
Cates, Phoebe actress
Cather, Phyllis Baker pediatrics nurse
Cattani, Maryellen B. lawyer
Catuzzi, J(erome) P(rimo), Jr. lawyer
Caulder, Jerry Dale weed scientist
Causey-Jeffery, Tracy Ann art dealer, art historian
Cauthorne-Burnette, Tamera Dianne family nurse practitioner, healthcare consultant
†Cavalcante-Fleming, Maria A. preschool educator, language educator, translator
Cavender, Michael Charles broadcast news executive
†Cavender, Patricia Patten director program
Cavill, Karen A. writer, editor
Cavin, Susan Elizabeth sociologist, writer
Cavins, William Robert deacon, educator
Cawood, Charles David urologist
Cazalas, Mary Rebecca Williams lawyer, nurse
Ceasor, Augusta Casey medical technologist, microbiologist
Ceci, Louis J. former state supreme court justice
Cecil, Maxine critical care nurse
Celentano, Francis Michael artist, art educator
†Celentino, Victor Gerard special education educator
Centafont, Lucy Ann Alexander occupational therapy consultant
Centner, Christopher Martin intelligence analyst, writer
†Centofanti, Joyce Michelina artist, educator
Ceraso, Chris dramatist, actor
Cercelle, Audrey Lynn school psychologist
Cerny, Louis Thomas civil engineer, association executive
Cerveny, Kathryn M. educational administrator
Cesnik, James Michael union official, newspaperman, printer, consultant
Chafkin, Rita M. physician, dermatologist
Chaikin, A. Scott public relations executive
Chaikof, Elliot Lorne vascular surgeon
Chaim, Robert Alex dean, educator
Challela, Mary Scahill maternal, child health nurse
Chaloner, Alice Brainerd mathematics educator
Chamberlain, George Arthur, III manufacturing company executive, venture capitalist
Chamberlain, William Edwin, Jr. management consultant
Chamberlin, Michael Meade lawyer
Chambers, Judith Tarnpoll speech pathologist, audiologist
Chamings, Patricia Ann nurse, educator
Champlin, William Glen clinical microbiologist-immunologist
Chance, Kenneth Donald engineer
Chandler, Alfred Dupont, Jr. historian, educator
Chandler, Alice higher education consultant, university president
Chandra, Abhijit engineering educator
Chandra, Pramod art history educator
†Chang, David Woosuk medical educator
Chang, Helen Chung-Hung piano pedagogy specialist
Chang, T. Susan book editor
Chao, James Min-Tzu architect
Chapanis, Alphonse human factors engineer, ergonomist
Chapin, Deborah artist
Chapman, Richard LeRoy public policy researcher
Chapman, William baritone
Charles, Walter actor
Charlton, Betty Jo retired state legislator
Charlton, Gordon Taliaferro, Jr. retired bishop
Charlton, Jesse Melvin, Jr. management educator, lawyer
Charlton, Shirley Marie educational consultant
Charnin, Jade Hobson magazine executive
Charron, Susan E. mental health nurse
Charry, Michael R(onald) musician, conductor
Chase, Alison M. adult nurse practitioner
Chase, Clinton Irvin psychologist, educator, business executive
Chase, Edith Newlin preschool educator, poet
Chase, James Richard retired college president
Chase, Seymour M. lawyer
Chassin, Mark R. health policy educator
Chastain-Knight, Denise Jean process engineer
Chater, Shirley Sears health educator
Chattin, Gilbert Marshall financial analyst
Chave, Carolyn Margaret lawyer, arbitrator
Chaykin, Robert Leroy manufacturing and marketing executive
Chciuk, Zofia women's health nurse, neonatal nurse
Cheeger, Jeff education educator
Cheek, Arthur Lee administrative professional
Chelberg, Bruce Stanley holding company executive
Chelberg, Robert Douglas army officer
Chellas, Brian Farrell retired philosophy educator, author
Chelle, Robert Frederick electric power industry executive
Chemla, Daniels S. director, adult education educator
Chen, Di electro-optic company executive, consultant
†Chen, Stephen S. F. diplomat
Chen, Stephen Shau-tsi retired psychiatrist, physiologist
Cheney, Lois Sweet infection control nurse
Cheng, Liangsheng engineer, researcher, educator
Chenhall, Robert Gene former museum director, consultant, author
Chercover, Murray television executive
Cherenzia, Bradley James radiologist
Chernish, Lelia Margaret fundraiser
Chernoff, Amoz Immanuel hematologist, consultant
Cherry, Carol Jean health educator
Cherryh, C. J. writer
†Cheser, Raymond Norris, III medical devices company executive
Chesler, Doris Adelle real estate professional
Chesney, Susan Talmadge writer, developer
Chesson, Michael Bedout history educator
Cheston, Theodore C. electrical engineer
Chevalier, Paul Edward retired retail executive, lawyer
Chew, Margaret Sarah geography educator, retired
†Child, Abigail artist, educator
Child, Carroll Cadell research nursing administrator
Child, Judith artist
Child, Julia McWilliams (Mrs. Paul Child) cooking expert, television personality, author
Childress, Dudley Stephen biomedical engineer, educator
Childress, Walter Dabney, III insurance executive, financial planner
Chin, Cindy Lai accountant
Chin, Janet Sau-Ying data processing executive, consultant
†Chin, Paul L. human resources professional
Chin, Robert Allen engineering graphics educator
†Chin, Tanya Jade policy analyst
Ching, Julia philosophy and religion educator
Chinitz, Benjamin economics educator
Chinni, Peter Anthony artist
†Chiswick, Barry Raymond economics educator
Chiu, William Chien-Chen surgeon
†Chizeck, Howard Jay engineering educator
Chmielarz, Sharon Lee writer, educator
Chmielinski, Edward Alexander retired electronics company executive
Choi, Man-Duen mathematics educator
Choukas-Bradley, Melanie writer, photographer
Chow, John Lap Hong physician, biomedical engineer
Chow, Rita Kathleen nurse consultant
Christen, Paul Richert financial company executive
Christensen, Caroline vocational educator
Christensen, Maria emergency room nurse
Christenson, Gregg Andrew bank executive
Christenson, William Newcome retired physician
Christian, James Wayne economist
Christie, Walter Scott retired state official
Christina, Greta book and film critic, writer, editor
Christman, Robert Alan podiatric radiologist
Christoffersen, Ralph Earl chemist
Christopher, Russell Lewis baritone
Christopher, Sharon A. Brown bishop
Christy, Thomas Patrick human resources executive, educator
Chrysostomos, (González-Alexopoulos) archbishop, clergyman, psychologist, educator
Chu, Benjamin Thomas Peng-Nien chemistry educator
Chu, Ellin Resnick librarian, consultant
Chu, Steven physics educator
Church, Eugene Lent physicist, consulting scientist
Churchill, Robert Wilson state legislator, lawyer
Cibbarelli, Pamela Ruth information executive
Ciccone, F. Richard retired newspaper editor
Cimino, Ann M. education educator
Cimino, James Ernest physician
Cimino, Michael film director, writer
Cioczek, Henryk Antoni medical oncologist, internist
Cipparone, Josephine Magnino medical/surgical and community health nurse
Ciullo, Rosemary psychologist
Clabaugh, Elmer Eugene, Jr. lawyer
Claes, Gayla Christine writer, editorial consultant
†Claiborne, Liz (Elisabeth Claiborne Ortenberg) fashion designer
Clapp, Beverly Booker accountant
Clapper, Lyle Nielsen magazine publisher
Clarizio, Josephine Delores corporate services executive, former manufacturing and engineering company executive, foundation executive
Clark, Barbara Walsh nurse educator, administrator, clinical specialist
Clark, Candy actress
Clark, Carolyn Archer aerospace technologist, life scientist
†Clark, Don Alan journalist, reporter
Clark, James Covington journalist, historian
Clark, James Milford college president, retired
Clark, Jeffrey Ray surgeon
Clark, Joyce Lavonne receptionist
Clark, Larry photographer
Clark, Margaret Pruitt education and advocacy executive administrator
Clark, Mary Higgins author, business executive
Clark, Maxine retail executive
Clark, Patricia Ryan crisis intervention specialist
Clark, Peter Bruce newspaper executive
Clark, Raymond Oakes banker
Clark, Sharon Jackson private school administrator
Clark, Steven Marston film producer, real estate licensee
†Clark, Sue Janet business owner
Clark, Thomas Alonzo federal judge
Clark, Thomas Ryan retired federal agency executive, business and technical consultant
Clarke, Edward Owen, Jr. lawyer
Clarke, Henry Lee foreign service officer, former ambassador
Clarke, John Clem artist
Clarke, Lambuth McGeehee retired college president
Clarke, Una city official
Clarke, Walter Sheldon military consultant, educator
Claus, Carol Jean small business owner
Clauser, Angela Frances medical surgical, pediatrics and geriatrics nurse
Clauser, Kenneth Alton professional photographer, banjo player
Claver, Robert Earl television director, producer
Clawson, Roxann Eloise college administrator, computer company executive
†Clayson, Susan Hollis art historian, educator
Clayton, Bruce David pharmacology educator
Clayton, David A(lvin) biology educator
Clayton, Paul Douglas medical facility director
Clayton, Richard Reese retired holding company executive
Clayton-Townsend, JoAnn aerospace analyst
Claytor, Richard Anderson retired federal agency executive, consultant
Cleary, Sue Ellen secondary school educator
Cleaver, Emanuel, II former mayor, minister
Cleaver, James Edward radiologist, educator
Clecak, Dvera Vivian Bozman psychotherapist
Clemendor, Anthony Arnold obstetrician, gynecologist, educator
Clement, Alain Gérard photographer
Clement, Hope Elizabeth Anna librarian
Clement, Robert Alton retired chemist
Clemetson, Charles Alan Blake physician
Cleveland, Ashley musician
Cleveland, Charlene S. community health nurse
Clevenger, Mark Thomas communications executive, writer
†Clifford, Edward R. municipal official
Clifford, Maurice Cecil physician, former college president, foundation executive
Clifford, Brother Peter academic administrator, religious educator
†Clifton, Lucille Thelma author
Clifton, Russell B. banking and mortgage lending consultant, retired mortgage company executive
Cline, Carolyn Joan plastic and reconstructive surgeon
Cloonan, Clifford B. electrical engineer, educator
Cloonan, Patrick Michael radio news producer, writer
Cloud, Stanley Wills journalist, editor, writer
Clough, Lauren C. retired special education educator
Clouston, Ross Neal retired food and related products company executive
Clum, Debra Sue elementary education educator
Cluxton, Joanne Genevieve elementary school educator
Clymer, Wayne Kenton bishop
†Coates-Shrider, Lisa Nicole psychology educator
Cobb, John Boswell, Jr. clergyman, educator
Cobb, Miles Alan retired lawyer
Cobb, Ruth artist
Cobb, Virginia Horton artist, educator
Coble, Howard congressman, lawyer
Coble, Hugh Kenneth engineering and construction company executive
Coburn, D(onald) L(ee) playwright
Coburn, James actor
Cochran, Carolyn library director
Cochran, George Moffett retired judge
Cochran, Jacqueline Louise management executive
†Cochran, Johnie Faye registrar
Cochran, Thad senator
Cochrane, Walter E. education administrator, writer
Cockrum, Bob city official
Cockrum, William Monroe, III investment banker, consultant, educator
Coffee, Joseph Denis, Jr. retired college chancellor
Coffey, Dennis James performance technology consultant
Coffey, Joanne Christine dietitian
Coffey, John Louis federal judge
Coffey, Nancy Ann commercial real estate broker
Coffman, Stanley Knight, Jr. English educator, former college president
Cogan, John Dennis artist
Cogan, Karen Elizabeth author, educator
Cohen, Alexander H. theatrical and television producer
Cohen, Allan Richard broadcasting executive
†Cohen, Barbara L. clinical neuropsychologist
Cohen, Evelyn L. nursing educator, author
Cohen, Henry historian, retired educator
Cohen, Larry film director, producer, screenwriter
†Cohen, Mark D. social service admnistrator
Cohen, Mark Herbert broadcasting company executive
Cohen, Philip retired hydrogeologist
Cohen, Roberta Jane government executive
Cohen, Seymour lawyer
Cohen, Sharleen Cooper interior designer, writer
Cohen, Sherry Suib writer
Cohen, Shirley Mason educator, writer, civic worker
Cohn, Avern Levin federal judge
Cohn, Leonard Allan retired chemical company executive
Cohn, Martin advertising executive, consultant
Coil, Charles Ray printing executive, managed healthcare executive
Coke, Frank Van Deren museum director, photographer
Colaianni, Joseph Vincent judge
Colangelo, James Joseph psychotherapist
Colburn, Harold Lewis dermatologist, state legislator
Cole, Betty Lou McDonel Shelton (Mrs. Dewey G. Cole, Jr.) judge
Cole, Brady Marshall retired naval officer
Cole, Clifford Adair clergyman
Cole, Jerome Foster research company executive
Coleman, Claire Kohn public relations executive
Coleman, Dabney W. actor
Coleman, Jean Black nurse, physician assistant
Coleman, John Michael lawyer, consumer products executive
Coleman, Leon Horn real estate investor
Coleman, Lewis Waldo bank executive
Coleman, Malcolm James, Jr. band director, music educator, flute educator
Coleman, Robert Elliott retired secondary education educator
Coleman, Robert Lee retired lawyer
†Coleman, Robert Wayne airline company executive
Coleman, Ronald D. (Ron Coleman) former congressman
Coleson, Sarrah Lynn women's health nurse, critical care nurse
†Colgan, Ann K. educator
Colgate, Stephen small business owner
Colgate-Lindberg, Catharine Pamella educator
Colker, Edward artist, educator
Coll, Kathleen M. home care manager
Collett, Merrill Judson management consultant
Collette, Frances Madelyn retired tax consultant, lawyer
Collier, Herman Edward, Jr. retired college president
Collier, Robert Steven broadcast technician
Collins, Allen Howard psychiatrist
Collins, Barbara-Rose former congresswoman
Collins, Eileen Marie astronaut
Collins, Frank Charles, Jr. industrial and service quality specialist
Collins, Harker economist, manufacturing executive, publisher, marketing, financial, business and legal consultant
Collins, James Francis lawyer, financial consultant
Collins, Jean Katherine English educator
Collins, Joan Henrietta actress
Collins, John Francis landscape architect, educator
Collins, Kathleen Anne artistic director
Collins, Mary Ellen human resources executive
Collins, Melissa Ann oncological nurse
Collyer, Robert B. trade association administrator
Colodny, Edwin Irving lawyer, retired airline executive
Cologne, Gordon Bennett lawyer
Colonnier, Marc Leopold neuroanatomist, educator
Colton, Sterling Don lawyer, business executive, missionary
Coluccio, Josephine Catherine primary and elementary school educator
Colvin, Burton Houston mathematician, government official
†Colwell, David Russell software engineer
†Combs, Roy James, Jr. analyst, researcher
Compton, Norma Haynes retired university dean, artist
Compton, W. Dale physicist
Conant, Steven George psychiatrist
Conaway, Mary Ann behavioral studies educator
†Concannon, Matthew Jerome plastic surgeon
Condayan, John retired foreign service officer, consultant
Condie, Vicki Cook nurse, educator
Condry, Robert Stewart retired hospital administrator
Cone, Edward Toner composer, emeritus music educator
Conerly-Perks, Erlene Brinson retired chemist
†Conklin, Sarah C. health education educator
Connell, George Edward former university president, scientist
Connell, Shirley Hudgins public relations professional
Connelly, Margery Annette research pathologist, educator
Connelly, Patricia Lorraine travel executive
Connelly, Sharon Rudolph lawyer, federal official
Connes, Alain education educator
Connolly, John Joseph health care company executive
†Connors, Christopher geology educator
Conole, Clement Vincent business administrator
†Conover, Jill M. freelance writer
Conover, Mona Lee retired adult education educator
Conrad, Richard A. opera singer, educator
Conrad-England, Roberta Lee pathologist

Conrader, Constance Ruth artist, writer, librarian
Conroy, Tamara Boks artist, special education educator, former nurse
Consoli, Marc-Antonio composer
†Constable, Burt Wilson newspaper columnist
Constantine, Michael actor
Conte, Andrea retail executive, health care consultant, community activist
Contillo, Lawrence Joseph financial and computer company executive
Conto, Aristides advertising agency executive
Convery, Fredrick Richard retired surgeon, orthopedist
Conway, Gene Farris cardiologist
Conway, James Valentine Patrick forensic document examiner, former postal service executive
Conway, Richard Ashley environmental engineer
Conyers, Claude Brunson retired publishing executive
Cook, Charles William, Jr. manufacturing executive
Cook, Fielder producer, director
Cook, Gary L. management professional
Cook, Gloria Jean writer
†Cook, James Anthony artist, educator
Cook, Julian Abele, Jr. federal judge
Cook, M(elvin) Garfield chemical company executive
Cook, Michelle Jo marketing professional
†Cook, Pamela Margaret French educator
Cook, Quentin LaMar lawyer, healthcare executive, church leader
Cook, Stephen Champlin retired shipping company executive
Cooke, Eileen Delores retired librarian
Cooke, Thomas Paul education educator
Cookson, Albert Ernest telephone and telegraph company executive
Cooley, James William retired executive researcher
†Coolidge, Anne R. investment company executive
Cooney, John Thomas retired banker
Coonts, Stephen Paul novelist
Coop, Frederick Robert retired city manager
Cooper, Austin Morris chemist, chemical engineer, consultant, researcher
Cooper, Bobbie (Minna Louise Morgan Cooper) volunteer
Cooper, Charles Donald association executive, editor, retired career officer
Cooper, Charles Gordon insurance consultant, former executive
Cooper, Diann Caryn critical care nurse, staff development specialist
Cooper, Eugene Bruce speech, language pathologist, educator
Cooper, Francis Loren advertising executive
Cooper, Hal television director
Cooper, Hal Dean lawyer
Cooper, James Hayes Shofner (Jim Cooper) investment company executive, former congressman, lawyer
Cooper, James Robert, III computer software company executive, mobile communications consultant
Cooper, John Milton, Jr. history educator, author
Cooper, Norton J. (Sky Cooper) liquor, wine and food company executive
Cooper, Rebecca art dealer
Cooper, Sarah Jean nursing educator
Cooper-Avrick, Anita Beverly television stage manager
Coover, Doris Dimock artist
†Coover, Roderick Luis anthropologist
Copeland, Henry Jefferson, Jr. former college president
Coplans, John Rivers artist
Coplin, Mark David lawyer
†Copperfield, David (David Kotkin) illusionist, director, producer, writer
Coppie, Comer Swift state official
Coppola, Francis Ford film director, producer, writer
Coppolecchia, Rosa internist
†Corbin, Tracy Dianne researcher
†Corcoran, Philip E. wholesale distribution executive
†Cordova, Denise A. foreign language educator
Corey, Jeff actor, director, educator
Corey, Kenneth Edward geography and urban planning educator, researcher
Cork, Edwin Kendall business and financial consultant
Corkery, James Caldwell retired Canadian government executive, mechanical engineer
Corle, Frederic William, II government relations executive
Corley, Charles J. middle school educator
Cormia, Frank Howard industrial engineering administrator
†Corn, Lovick P. retired foundation executive
Cornell, David Roger health care executive
Cornell, Thomas Browne artist, educator
Cornett, Gregg newspaper publisher, newspaper editor, computer company executive
Cornish, Richard Joseph international affairs consultant, retired diplomat
†Cornwell, Marguerite Kelsey college administrator
Corr, Robert Mark computer company executive
Correnti, John David steel company executive
†Corripio Ahumada, Ernesto Cardinal retired archbishop
Cortes, Dennis Alfredo internist
Cortese, Richard Anthony computer company executive
Cortlund, Joan Marie educator
†Corto, Diana Maria lyric-coloratura, producer, educator
Corvino, Ernesta ballet dancer
Corwell, Ann Elizabeth public relations executive
Cory, Angelica Jo author, spiritual consultant
Cory, Peter de Carteret retired Canadian supreme court justice
Cosby, Bill actor, entertainer
†Cosmatos, George Pan film director
Cosnotti, Richard Louis development director
Cossa, Dominic Frank baritone
Costa, Albert Bernard retired science history educator
Costa, Michael F. multimedia communications executive
Costa-Gavras, (Konstaninos Gavras) director, writer
Costantini, Mary Ann C. writer, editor, retired elementary educator
Costas, Bob (Robert Quinlan Costas) sportscaster
Costello, Daniel Walter retired bank executive
Costello, James Joseph retired electrical manufacturing company executive
Cotrubas, Ileana opera singer, lyric soprano, retired
Cotsonas, Nicholas John, Jr. physician, medical educator
Cotter, Lawrence Raffety management consultant
Cotting, James Charles manufacturing company executive
Couchman, Robert George James human services consultant
Coughlan, William David professional society administrator
Cougill, Roscoe McDaniel mayor, retired air force officer
Coukis, Peter George musician, composer
Counsil, William Glenn electric utility executive
†Courbis, Sarah Shelby marine biologist
Courtheoux, Richard James management consultant
Couto, Nancy Vieira poet, literary consultant
Covell, Christopher Greene management executive
Covin, Carol Louise computer consultant
†Covington, Faith Henrietta health educator
Covino, William Anthony English language educator
Covintree, George E. retired physician
Cowan, Andrew Glenn television writer, producer, performer
Cowan, Mark Douglas government relations executive, lawyer
Cowles, Elizabeth Hall program consultant
Cox, Carol A. oncological nurse
Cox, J. William retired physician, health services administrator
Cox, John Curtis healthcare and educational administrator
Cox, John Francis retired cosmetic company executive
Cox, John Michael cardiologist
Cox, Marshall lawyer
Cox, Pat artist
Cox, Wilford Donald retired food company executive
Cox, William Frederick hospital executive
Coyle, Francis Sylvester, III management consultant
Cozan, Lee clinical research psychologist
Cozen, Lewis orthopedic surgeon
Crabtree, Davida Foy minister
Crabtree, Gerald R. pathology and biology educator
Craft, Edmund Coleman automotive parts manufacturing company executive
Craiglow, James Hawkins graduate school official
Craine, Diane M. nursing educator
Cramer, John Sanderson health care executive
Cramer, Robert Vern retired college administrator, consultant
Crampton, Esther Larson sociology and political science educator
Crane, Stacey Lynn association executive
Cranford, James Blease retired real estate executive
Craw, Freeman (Jerry Craw) graphic artist
Crawford, Harold Bernard publisher
Crawford, Kenneth Charles educational institute executive, retired government official
Crawford, Marc professional hockey coach
Crawford, Margaret Jean Barnes physical education educator, consultant
Crawford, Muriel Laura lawyer, author, educator
Crawford, Pamela J. critical care nurse
Crawford, William David office equipment company executive
Crawford, William Walsh retired consumer products company executive
Craymer, Helen Stoughton educator
Crecente, Brian David writer, journalist
Creech, John Lewis retired scientist, consultant
Creigh, Thomas, Jr. utility executive
Cremer, Richard Eldon marketing professional
†Crenshaw, Barclay MacBride film producer, writer
Crews, Esca Holmes, Jr. utility company executive
Crews, Mara Lynne writer
Crilley, Joseph James artist
Criscuolo, Wendy Laura lawyer, interior design consultant
Crisler, Paul Richard retired auditor
Crisman Carlson, Ruth Marie writer
Crispo, Richard Charles artist, ethnologist, minister
Critoph, Eugene retired physicist, nuclear research company executive
Crocker, Barbara Jean infection control practitioner
†Crocker, George A. career officer
Croft, Kathryn Delaine business executive, consultant
Cromwell, Florence Stevens occupational therapist
Cromwell, Ronald R. educator
Cronkite, Eugene Pitcher physician, retired
Cronson, Robert Granville lawyer
Crook, Barbara Coenson marketing and sales professional
Crook, Donald Martin lawyer
Crosby, Julie Lynne theater industry executive, educator
Crosby, (Claire) Marena Lienhard retired college administrator
Crosby, Norman Lawrence comedian
Cross, Alexander Dennis business consultant, former chemical and pharmaceutical executive
Cross, Betty Felt small business owner
Cross, Brian Gregory internist
Cross, Charlotte Lord social worker
Cross, Dolores Evelyn university administrator, educator
Cross, Harold Dick physician
Cross, Harold Zane agronomist, educator
Cross, Robert Lawrence retired surgeon
Crossland, Ann Elizabeth retired psychotherapist
Crosson, John Albert advertising executive
Croteau, Joan M. nursing administrator, educator
Crouse, Carol K. Mavromatis elementary education educator
Crouse, Lindsay actress
Crowder, Richard Morgan pilot
Crowe, James Joseph lawyer
Crowley, Joseph Michael electrical engineer, educator
†Crowley-Kiggins, Margaret Louise artist
Crown, Nancy Elizabeth lawyer
Crowther, James Earl radio and television executive, lawyer
Crowther, Richard Layton architect, consultant, researcher, author, lecturer
Crozier, William Marshall, Jr. bank holding company executive
Cruise, Tom (Tom Cruise Mapother, IV) actor
Crump, Lisa M. rehabilitation nurse
Cruse, Denton W. marketing and advertising executive, consultant
Crutzen, Paul Josef research meteorologist, chemist
Cruz-Romo, Gilda soprano
Cuatrecasas, Pedro Martin research biochemist, pharmaceutical executive
Cuetter, Albert Cayetano neurologist
Culberson, Gary Michael hotel manager
Culbertson, Philip Edgar, Sr. aerospace company executive, consultant
Culkin, Macaulay actor
Cull, Robert Robinette electric products manufacturing company executive
†Cullen, Paula Bramsen author
Cullen, Robert John publishing executive, financial consultant
Culley, June Elizabeth clinical reviewer, quality improvement specialist
Cullingford, Hatice Sadan chemical engineer
Culp, Faye Berry former state legislator
Culp, Gordon Calvin retired lawyer
Culverwell, Albert Henry historian
Culwell, Charles Louis retired manufacturing company executive
Cumber, Sherry G. psychotherapist, research consultant
Cummer, William Jackson former oil company executive, investor
Cumming, Robert Hugh artist, photographer
Cummings, Brian Thomas public relations company executive
Cummings, Constance actress
Cummings, David William artist, educator
Cummings, Lucille Maud geriatrics, psychiatric mental health nurse
Cunningham, Andrea Lee public relations executive
†Cunningham, Ron choreographer, artistic director
Cunningham, William Francis, Jr. English language educator, university administrator
†Cuppo Csaki, Luciana foreign language educator, writer
Currie, Fergus Gardner performing arts educator
Currie, Steven Ray artist
Currier, Ruth dancer, choreographer and educator
Curry, Carlton E. corporate executive, city councilman
Curry, Hugh Robert tennis player
Curson, Theodore musician
Curtis, Arnold Bennett lumber company executive
Curtis, Mary Ellen (Mary Curtis Horowitz) publishing company executive
Cushing, Ralph Harvey chemical company executive
Cushwa, William Wallace retired machinery parts company executive
Cutler, Maxine Gordon French language and literature educator
Cyr, Conrad Keefe federal judge
Czarnecki, Gerald Milton investment banking and venture capital
Dabbs, Henry Erven television and film producer, educator
Dackow, Orest Taras insurance company executive
Daddario, Diane Kay nurse, educator
Dafoe, Willem actor
Daga, Andrew William architect, inventor, space technology researcher
Dageforde, Mary L. technical writer, software designer
D'Agostino, Stephen Ignatius bottling company executive
D'Agusto, Karen Rose lawyer
Dahlgren, Carl Herman Per educator, arts administrator
Dahse, Kenneth William educator, photojournalist
Dailey, Irene actress, educator
Dailey, Thomas Hammond retired surgeon
Dale, Wesley John chemistry educator
Dale Riikonen, Charlene Boothe international health administrator
D'Alesandro, Philip Anthony parasitologist, immunologist, retired educator
D'Alessio, David Wesley communications educator
Dallas, Donald Edward, Jr. corporate executive
†Dallenbach, Wally professional race car driver
Dallmann, Daniel F. artist, educator
Dallwein, Edward K. controller
Dally, James William mechanical engineering educator, consultant
Dalton, John Howard Former Secretary of the Navy, financial consultant
Daly, Chuck (Charles Jerome Daly) sports commentator, professional basketball coach
Daly, Tyne actress
Daly, William James retired health industry distributing company executive
Damaska, Mirjan Radovan law educator
D'Amato, Anthony Roger recording company executive
†D'Ambrosio, Vinni Marie writer
Dane, Steven Howard neurologist, educator
Danforth, John Claggett former senator, lawyer, clergyman
D'Angelo, Beverly actress
Dangoor, David Ezra Ramsi consumer goods company executive
Danhof, Vicki Spicher maternal/women's health nurse
Daniel, Elbert Clifton journalist
Daniels, Arlene Kaplan sociology educator
Daniels, James Maurice physicist
Daniels, Jeff actor
Daniels, Ronald George theater director
Danilowicz, Delores Ann pediatric cardiologist, pediatrics educator
Dannenberg, Martin Ernest retired insurance company executive
Danner, Paul Kruger, III telecommunications executive
D'Antonio, William Vincent sociology educator
†Danza, Tony actor
Danziger, Gertrude Seelig metal fabricating executive
†Dar, Huma Bashir computer scientist, researcher, educator
D'Arbanville-Quinn, Patti actress
Dargan, Pamela Ann systems and software engineer
Darien, Steven Martin management consulting company executive
Darkovich, Sharon Marie nurse administrator
Darling, Robert Edward designer, stage director
†Darlow, Andrew J. photographer
Darr, Carol C. lawyer
†Darton, Eric writer
Dasburg, John Harold airline executive
Daugherty, Frederick Alvin federal judge
Daus, Victoria Lynn nurse midwife
Davatzes, Nickolas broadcast executive
Davenport, Lawrence Franklin school system administrator
Davenport, William Harold mathematics educator
Daves, Donald Rae entertainment industry executive
David, Marilyn Hattie lawyer, retired military officer
Davidovsky, Mario composer
Davidow, Jenny Jean counselor, writer
Davidson, Bonnie Jean gymnastics educator, sports management consultant
Davidson, James Melvin academic administrator, researcher, educator
Davidson, Mayer B. medical educator, researcher
Davies, Michael S. security analyst
†Davies, Peter Ho writer, educator
Davies-McNair, Jane retired educational consultant
Davila, Rebecca Tober health and physical education educator
Davion, Ethel Johnson school system administrator, curriculum specialist
Davis, Anna Jane Ripley elementary education educator
Davis, Anthony composer, pianist, educator
Davis, Bobby Eugene business owner
Davis, Carolyne Kahle health care consultant
Davis, Christina artist
Davis, Crystal Michelle oil company administrator
Davis, Danny (George Joseph Nowlan) musician
Davis, Darrell L. automotive executive
Davis, Deborah Cecilia auditor
Davis, Debra Greer music educator, pianist
Davis, Dempsie Augustus former air force officer, educator
†Davis, Don D., III author, lawyer
Davis, Frances Kay lawyer
Davis, Gay Ruth psychotherapist, social welfare educator, author, researcher, consultant
Davis, Gloria Jean gerontology clinical specialist
Davis, Henry Jefferson, Jr. former naval officer
Davis, Joseph Lloyd educational administrator, consultant
Davis, Keigh Leigh aerospace engineer
Davis, Kristin W. periodical editor
Davis, Luther writer, producer
Davis, Margaret Thacker critical care, medical and surgical nurse
Davis, Mary Byrd conservationist, researcher
Davis, Mary Christine artist, art educator
†Davis, Nathan actor
Davis, Robert H. financial executive, arbitrator, mediator, educator
†Davis, Robert Scott criminal justice educator
Davis, Roger Edwin lawyer, retired discount chain executive
Davis, Russell Haden pastoral psychotherapist
Davis, Susanne Marie writer, educator
Dawkins, Marva Phyllis psychologist
Dawson, Gerald Lee engineering company executive
Dawson, Horace Greeley, Jr. former diplomat, government official
Dawson, Karen Oltmanns school health nurse, womens health nurse, educator
Day, Anthony newspaper writer
Day, Charlotte Ellen education administrator
Day, Neil McPherson trade association executive
Day, Roland Bernard retired chief justice state supreme court
Day, Rosalee P. probation officer
Deacon, David Emmerson advertising executive
Dealy, Janette Diane marketing consultant
Deam, Connie Marie school nurse
Dean, Dearest (Lorene Glosup) songwriter
Dean, Francis Hill landscape architect, educator
Dean, Leesa Jane musician
Dean, Leslie Alan (Cap Dean) economic and social development consultant
Dean, Michael M. lawyer
Dean, Walter Jeryl Jerry newswriter
De Antoni, Edward Paul cancer control research scientist
DeBello, Marguerite Catherine oncological nurse
Debevoise, A. Clay artist
De Blasi, Tony (Anthony Armando De Blasi) artist
de Blasis, James Michael artistic director, producer, stage director
de Blij, Harm Jan geography educator, editor
DeBock, Ronald Gene real estate company executive
Debreu, Gerard economics and mathematics educator
Debs, Barbara Knowles former college president, consultant
Debus, Eleanor Viola retired business management company executive
DeCamp, Graydon journalist
Dechar, Peter Henry artist
Deck, Judith Z. adult nurse practitioner
Decker, Gilbert Felton manufacturing company executive
Decker, Oscar Conrad, Jr. retired army officer
Decker, Walter Johns toxicologist
De Concini, Dennis lawyer, former United States senator, consultant
†Deconinck, Isabelle F. marketing and promotion specialist, writer
†DeConti, Robert W. plastic surgeon
Dedman, Bill journalist
Deely, Maureen Cecelia community health nurse
Deere, Don U. civil engineer
Deering, Fred Arthur retired insurance company executive
De Felitta, Frank Paul producer, writer, director
DeFlorio, Mary Lucy physician, psychiatrist
†DeFrancisco, Joseph E. military officer
†De Fronzo, Joseph Michael village manager
Degann, Sona Irene obstetrician-gynecologist, educator
DeGeest, Elaine Beck artist
de Grazia, Sebastian political philosopher, author
De Herrera, Juan Abran United States marshal
Deisenhofer, Johann biochemistry educator, researcher
Deitz, Susan Rose newspaper advice columnist
De Jong, Arthur Jay education consultant, former university president
DeLaFuente, Charles lawyer, educator, journalist
de la Garza, Kika (Eligio de la Garza) former congressman
Delahanty, Rebecca Ann school system administrator
De Laney, Allen Young retired surgeon
de la Piedra, Jorge orthopedic surgeon
†de la Torre Falzon, Alicia Maria Spanish language educator
de Leon, Lidia Maria magazine editor
Delgado, Gloria Eneida medical nurse
Deli, Steven Frank financial services executive
Deligiorgis, Stavros G. retired literature educator
Dell, Thomas Charles nurse anesthetist
†Dellaportas, George physician, medical facility administrator
Dellere, Diana Marie school psychologist
Dellis, Frédy Michel travel exchange company executive
De Loach, Bernard Collins, Jr. retired physicist
DeLoach, (Elise) Debra critical care nurse, administrator
DeLong, Janice Ayers education educator
De Long, Katharine retired secondary education educator
De Looper, Willem Johan artist, museum curator
DeLoyht-Arendt, Mary I. artist

Del Rosario, Rose Marie *clinical sociologist, educator, consultant*
Delson, Sidney Leon *architect*
†DeLuca, Kristin Leigh *graphic designer*
†Del Valle, Irma *protective services official, poet*
Delwiche, Patricia Ellen *family nurse practitioner*
Dely, Steven *aerospace company executive*
Dema-ala, Relie L. *medical/surgical nurse*
Demenchonok, Edward Vasilevich *philosopher, linguist, researcher, educator*
De Metz, Della Christine *executive, writer, social consultant, food worker*
†De Mille, Barbara Munn *writer, former English literature educator*
DeMillion, Julianne *health and fitness specialist, personal trainer, rehabilitation therapist, consultant*
†DeMint, James Warren *congressman, marketing executive*
†Demissie, Yemane I. *filmmaker*
DeMitchell, Terri Ann *law educator*
†De Mornay, Rebecca *actress*
De Moss, Robert George *religious foundation executive*
Dempsey, David Allan *company official, small business owner*
†Dench, Judith Olivia *actress*
Dendrinos, Dimitrios Spyros *urban planning educator*
Denegall, John Palmer, Jr. *construction company executive*
Denevan, William Maxfield *geographer, educator, ecologist*
Denham, Caroline Virginia *retired college official*
Denise, Robert Phillips *consultant*
Denneny, James Clinton, Jr. *business consultant*
Denney, Lucinda Ann *retired relocation services executive*
Dennis, Kimberly Ohnemus *philanthropy consultant*
†Dennis, Rodney L. *physician*
Denton, David Edward *retired education educator*
Denton, Joan Cameron *reading consultant, former educator*
†Denzler, James Wyatt *pharmacist*
Deoul, Kathleen Boardsen *executive*
DePalma, Ralph George *surgeon, educator*
Depkovich, Francis John *retired retail chain executive*
de Planque, E. Gail *physicist*
Derchin, Michael Wayne *financial analyst*
De Reineck, Marie *interior designer*
Deric, Arthur Joseph *lawyer, management consultant, health coop trustee*
Derickson, Stanley Lewis *minister, writer*
Dermanis, Paul Raymond *architect*
†DeRosa, David Francis *finance educator, trading company executive*
†de Russy, Candace Uter *education reformer*
†DeSanto, William Allan *marketing professional*
Desbarats, Peter Hullett *journalist, academic administrator*
Desjardins, Eric *professional hockey player*
Desloge, Christopher Davis, Sr. *real estate and merchant banking executive*
Desmarais, Maurice *trade association administrator*
Desmond, Patricia Lorraine *psychotherapist, writer, publisher*
Detert, Miriam Anne *chemical analyst*
Deutsch, David Allan *artist*
Deutsch, Herbert Arnold *music educator*
DeVaney, Carol Susan *management consultant*
Devers, Susan Marie *clinical nurse specialist, researcher*
DeVita, Vincent Theodore, Jr. *oncologist*
DeVivo, Ange *former small business owner*
Devlin, Michael Coles *bass-baritone*
†DeVore, Daun Aline *lawyer*
DeVore, Kimberly *business executive*
DeVos, Elisabeth *political association executive*
Dewey, Donna *director, actress*
Dewhurst, William George *psychiatrist, educator, research director*
DeWitt, Sallie Lee *realtor*
Dey, Carol Ruth *secondary education educator*
Dey, Marlene Melchiorre *nursing educator, critical care nurse*
de Zoeten, Gustaaf Adolf *plant pathologist*
Diamond, Fred I. *electronic engineer*
Diamond, Susan Zee *management consultant*
Dias, Kathleen R. Bruni-Kerrigan *foreign language educator*
Diaz, Cameron *actress*
Diáz, Elena R. *community health nurse*
†Diaz, Javier Vicente *bank executive*
DiBattiste, Carol A. *lawyer*
Dibner, David Robert *architect*
DiCarlo, Laurette Mary *nurse*
Dick, James Cordell *concert pianist*
Dickens, Charles Allen *petroleum company executive*
Dickerman, John Melvin *lawyer*
†Dickerson, Justin Brandt *financial and telecommunications policy analyst*
Dickes, Robert *psychiatrist*
Dickey, Robert Marvin (Rick Dickey) *property manager*
Dickinson, Donald Charles *library science educator*
Dickinson, Gail Krepps *educational administrator, educator*
Dickinson, Peter *composer*
Dickinson, William Richard *retired geologist and educator*
Dickman, Bernard Harold *statistics educator*
Dickman, James Bruce *photojournalist*
Dickson, Eva Mae *credit manager*
Dickson, James Francis, III *surgeon*
Dickson, Max Charles *retired career counselor, coordinator*
Dickstein, Cynthia Diane *international professional exchange specialist*
Didich, Jan *hospice consultant*
Didlo, Larry L. *security officer, educator*
DiDomenico, Mauro, Jr. *communication executive*
†DiEdwardo, Mary Ann Pasda *artist, writer*
Diehl, Carol Lou *library director, retired, library consultant*
Diehl, Deborah Hilda *lawyer*
Diehl, Harry Alfred *chemist, genealogist*
Diehl, Louis F. *hematologist*
Diemer, Emma Lou *composer, music educator*
Diener, Erwin *immunologist*
Diener, Royce *corporate director, retired healthcare services company executive*
Dietel, James Edwin *lawyer, consultant*
Dietrich, William Alan *author, journalist*
Dietz, Janis Camille *business educator*
Dietz, Patricia Ann *engineering administrator*
Dietz, William *retired aeronautics engineer, consultant*
Diffrient, Niels *industrial designer*
Di Giovanni, Anthony *retired coal mining company executive*
DiGirolamo, Glen Francis *actor*
†DiLeo, Daniel *social sciences educator*
Dill, Laddie John *artist*
Dille, Earl Kaye *utility company executive*
Dillon, Robert Sherwood *retired government official*
Dillon-McHugh, Cathleen Theresa *librarian, consultant*
Dills, James Arlof *retired publishing company executive*
Dilts, David Michael *management researcher, university facility director*
DiMaria, Rose Ann *nursing educator*
DiMauro, Nancy Marion *nursing administrator*
Dimitry, Theodore George *retired lawyer*
Dini, Joseph J. *aircraft leasing and finance executive*
Diorio, Eileen Patricia *medical technologist, retired, philosophy educator*
Di Paolo, Maria Grazia *language educator, writer*
DiPasquale, Paul Albert *sculptor*
DiPiazza, Michael Charles *insurance company executive*
Dirks, Leslie Chant *communications and electronics company executive*
Dirksen, Richard Wayne *canon precentor, organist, choirmaster*
Dirvin, Gerald Vincent *retired consumer products company executive*
DiSalle, Michael Danny *secondary education educator*
Disch, Thomas M(ichael) *author*
Dishong, Diane Elizabeth *medical/surgical nurse, rehabilitation nurse*
Dishy, Bob *actor*
Dittenhafer, Brian Douglas *banker, economist*
Dittmer, Linda Jean *retired photojournalist, photographer, computer artist*
Divine, Theodore Emry *electrical engineer*
†Divon, Michael Y. *obstetrician and gynecologist*
Dixon, Ann Renee *writer*
Dixon, Gordon Henry *biochemist*
Dixon, Marguerite Anderson *retired nursing educator*
Dixon, Michael Wayne *designer, writer, researcher*
Dixon, William Robert *musician, composer, educator*
Djordjevic, Dimitrije *historian, educator*
Dmochowski, Jan Rafal *surgeon, researcher*
Doane, Woolson Whitney *internist*
Dobelis, George *manufacturing company executive*
Dobler, Donald William *retired college dean, consultant, corporate executive*
†Dobson, James Lane *bank executive*
Dockery, J. Lee *retired medical school administrator*
Dodd, Joe David *safety engineer, consultant, administrator*
Dodd, Sara Mae Palmer *executive assistant*
Dodds, Brenda Kay *nurse*
Dodds, Christine J. *nursing administrator*
Dodds, Lawrence Donald *lawyer*
Dodds, Linda Carol *insurance company executive*
Doderer, Minnette Frerichs *state legislator*
Dodson, Donald Mills *restaurant executive*
Dodson, Samuel Robinette, III *investment banker*
Dogançay, Burhan C. *artist, photographer, sculptor*
Doherty, Charles Vincent *investment counsel executive*
Doherty, John L. *lawyer*
Doherty, Thomas Joseph *financial services industry consultant*
Dohrmann, Russell William *manufacturing company executive*
Dolan, Edward Francis *writer*
†Dolan, Ellen Marie *library director*
Dolan, June Ann *health facility administrator*
Dolan, Peter Brown *lawyer*
†Dolan, Peter J. *corporate financial consultant*
Dolan, Peter Robert *company executive*
Dolbin, Steven Michael *sculptor, educator*
Dole, Arthur Alexander *psychology educator*
Dole, Robert Paul *retired appliance manufacturing company executive*
Dolgen, Jonathan L. *motion picture company executive*
Dolich, Andrew Bruce *sports marketing executive*
Dolin, Samuel Joseph *composer, educator*
Dolliver, James Morgan *retired state supreme court justice*
Dolman, John Phillips (Tim), Jr. (Tim Dolman) *communications company executive*
Dolnick, Irene *financial services company official*
Dominguez, Eddie *artist*
Donaldson, Wilma Crankshaw *elementary education educator*
Donath, Therese *artist, author*
Dondanville, John Wallace *lawyer*
Dong, Zhaoqin *materials and testing engineer, researcher*
Donnelly, Leslie Faye Harris *psychologist, psychology educator*
Donnelly-Kempf, Moira Ann *nursing administrator*
D'Onofrio, Mary Ann *medical transcription company executive*
Donohue, George L. *federal aviation educator, former government official, mechanical engineer*
Donohue, Marc David *chemical engineering educator*
Donovan, Dorothy Diane *adult nurse practitioner*
Donovan, Marion Conran *school social worker*
†Dooley, Timothy Kevin *retail professional*
Dooling, Richard Patrick *writer, lawyer*
Doolittle, James H. *retired cable television systems company executive*
Doran, Charles Edward *textile manufacturing executive*
Dorland, Dodge Oatwell *investment advisor*
Dorman, Richard Frederick, Jr. *association executive, consultant*
Dorn, Dolores *actress*
Dorn, Natalie Reid *consultant*
Dorros, Irwin *consultant, retired telecommunications executive*
Dorsey, Loraine *English educator*
Dorsey, Rhoda Mary *retired academic administrator*
†Dorsky, Nathaniel *filmmaker*
Dosé, Frederick Philip, Jr. *art historian, art and antiques appraiser, consultant, liquidator*
Dosti, Rose *newspaper columnist, author*
Doty, James Robert *lawyer*
Doty, Philip Edward *accountant*
Doucette, Betty *public and community health and geriatrics nurse*
Doud, Wallace C. *retired information systems executive*
Dougherty, Floyd Wallace *design engineer*
Douglas, Robert Lee *lawyer*
Douglass, Betty Jean *executive secretary*
Douglass, Ellen Heather *humanities educator*
Douglass, Laura Lee *pharmaceutical company official*
Douty, Robert Watson *minister, educator*
Dove, Lorraine Faye *gerontology nurse*
Dow, Peter Anthony *advertising agency executive*
Dowd, Morgan Daniel *political science educator*
Dowie, Ian James *management consultant*
Dowling, Paul Dennis *bilingual special education educator*
Downes, Rackstraw *artist*
Downey, Deborah Ann *systems specialist*
Downey, Michael Peter *public television executive*
Downey, Roma *actress*
Downing, Kathryn M. *publishing executive, lawyer*
Downing, M. Scott *budget systems analyst*
Doyle, Gillian *actress*
Doyle, Irene Elizabeth *electronic sales executive, nurse*
Doyle, John Laurence *manufacturing company executive*
Doyle, Judith Stovall *real estate executive, retired*
Doyle, Tom *sculptor, retired educator*
Dozier, James Lee *former army officer*
Dozier, Nancy Kerns *retired geriatrics nurse*
Drabek, Doug (Douglas Dean Drabek) *baseball player*
Dracker, Robert Albert *physician*
Dragon, William, Jr. *footwear and apparel company executive*
†Drake, Barbara Ruth *writer*
Drake, Ervin Maurice *composer, author*
Drake, George Albert *college president, historian*
Drake, Robert Alan *state legislator, animal nutritionist, mayor*
Drake, Rodman Leland *investment company executive, consultant*
Dransite, Brian Robert *product manager*
Draper, Edgar *psychiatrist*
Drasler, Gregory John *artist*
Draznin, Jules Nathan *journalism and public relations educator, consultant*
Drennen, William Miller, Jr. *cultural administrator, film executive, producer, director, mineral resource executive*
†Drennon-Gala, Donney Thomas *correctional treatment specialist, sociologist*
Dresbach, Mary Louise *state educational administrator*
Dressel, Barry *museum administrator*
Dressel, Irene Emma Ringwald *alcoholism and family therapist*
Dressler, David Charles *retired aerospace company executive*
Drew, Elizabeth Heineman *publishing executive*
Drew, Walter Harlow *retired paper industry executive*
Drews, Jürgen *pharmaceutical researcher*
†Drexler, Clyde *retired professional basketball player*
Dreyfuss, Joel Philippe *magazine editor*
Driggers, L. Eley *clinical metaphysicist*
Driscoll, Garrett Bates *retired telecommunications executive*
Driver, Lottie Elizabeth *librarian*
Drooyan, John Neal *visual artist, photographer, fine artist*
Droukas, Ann Hantis *management executive*
Droullard, Steven Maurice *jewelry company executive*
Drucker, Peter Ferdinand *writer, consultant, educator*
Druzinsky, Edward *musician*
†Drymon, David E. *investigative consultant, background investigator*
Duarte, Cristobal G. *nephrologist, educator*
Dubesa, Elaine J. *biotechnology company executive*
Dubois, Nancy Q. *elementary school educator*
Du Boise, Kim Rees *artist, photographer, art educator*
†Dubroff, Susanne *poet, former social worker*
Dubuc, Carroll Edward *lawyer*
Dudash, Karen Shreffler *community health nurse*
†Dudick, Michael Joseph *retired bishop*
Dudics-Dean, Susan Elaine *interior designer*
Dudycha, Anne Elizabeth *retired special education educator*
Dudzik, Carol Joanne *lawyer, art educator*
Duecker, Robert Sheldon *retired bishop*
Duerr, Herman George *retired publishing executive*
Duff, John Bernard *college president, former city official*
Duffy, Brian Francis *immunologist, educator*
Duffy, John Joseph *retired academic administrator, history educator*
Duffy, Martin Edward *management consultant, economist*
Duffy, Mary Kathleen *neonatal nurse*
Dugan, Patrick Raymond *microbiologist, university dean*
Duguid, Dorothy Ann Ramseyer *artist*
Duigan, John *film director*
Duke, Bill *film director, actor*
†Dula, Brett M. *retired military officer*
Dull, William Martin *engineering executive*
Dumont, Allan Eliot *retired physician, educator*
Dunbar, Bruce Stephen *photographer, gallery administrator*
Dunbar, Patricia Lynn *new product development consultant*
Duncan, Carol Greene *art historian, educator*
Duncan, Donald William *lawyer*
Duncan, Elizabeth Charlotte *marriage and family therapist, educational therapist, educator*
Duncan, James Richard *systems administrator*
Duncan, Nora Kathryn *lawyer*
Dunford, David Joseph *foreign service officer, ambassador*
Dungan, Gloria Kronbeck *critical care nurse*
Dunham, Benjamin Starr *editor, arts administrator*
Dunham, Rebecca Betty Beres *school administrator*
Dunkelberger, Steve Walter *journalist*
Dunlap, James Riley, Sr. *former financial executive, credit manager*
Dunlap, Richard Donovan *artistic director*
Dunmeyer, Sarah Louise Fisher *retired health care consultant*
Dunn, Deborah Dechellis *special education educator*
Dunn, John Raymond, Jr. *stockbroker*
Dunn, Margaret Ann *religious studies educator, administrator, minister*
Dunn, Michael V. *federal agency administrator*
Dunn, Suzanne Lynne *media company executive*
Dunn, Warren Howard *retired lawyer, brewery executive*
Dunning, Kenneth Owen *mental health counselor*
Dunton-Downer, Leslie Linam *writer*
Dunworth, John *retired college president*
Durant, John Ridgeway *physician*
Durell, Jack *psychiatrist*
Durham, Thena Monts *microbiologist, researcher, management executive*
Durning, Charles *actor*
Durr, Robert Joseph *construction firm executive, mechanical engineer*
Durrani, Sajjad Haidar *retired space communications engineer*
Durst, Roberta J. *accountant, healthcare consultant*
†Dusan, Makavejev *film director, film producer*
Dutson, Thayne R. *university dean*
Dutton, Karen Vander Wall *critical care nurse*
Duva, Lou *boxing promoter, manager*
Duval, Michael Raoul *investment banker*
†Duval-Carrié, Edouard *artist*
DuVall, Patricia Arlene *secondary education educator*
Dwan, Dennis Edwin *broadcast executive, photographer*
Dwight, Harvey Alpheus *retired small business owner*
Dwinell, Ann Jones *special education educator*
Dwyer, Charles Breen *arbitrage and Eurobond specialist*
Dwyer, Gerald Paul, Jr. *economist, educator*
Dye, Robert Harris *retired manufacturing company executive*
Dye, Sharon Elizabeth Herndon *speech pathologist*
Dyer, Arlene Thelma *retail company owner*
Dyer, Geraldine A. (Geri A. Dyer) *artist, poet*
Dyer, Ira *ocean engineering educator, consultant*
Dyer, L. Keith *entertainment company producer*
Dyer, Rita Frances *medical/surgical and oncology nurse*
Dyer, Wayne Walter *psychologist, author, radio and television personality*
Dyrstad, Joanell M. *former lieutenant governor, consultant*
Dysart, Richard A. *actor*
Eacho, Esther MacLively *special education educator*
Eagle, Jack *commercial actor, comedian*
Eaglet, Robert Danton *electrical engineer, aerospace consultant, retired military officer*
Eaker, Ira *publishing executive*
Earle, Arthur Percival *textile company executive, airport executive*
Earle, Timothy Keese *anthropology educator*
Easley, Mack *retired state supreme court chief justice*
Easterling, Charles Armo *lawyer*
Easterly, Susan *music and humanities educator*
†Easterson, Sam *artist*
Eastman, Francesca Marlene *volunteer, art historian*
Eastman, Wilfred W. *retired surgeon*
Easton, Charles Clement, Jr. *corporate executive*
Easton, Michelle *foundation executive*
Eastup, Lavonda Jo *writer, poet, songwriter*
Eastwood, Clint *actor, director, former mayor*
Eaton, Curtis Howarth *banker, state agency administrator*
Eaton, Joe Oscar *federal judge*
Eaton, Larry Ralph *lawyer*
Eaton, Merrill Thomas *psychiatrist, educator*
Eaves, Sandra Austra *social worker*
Ebb, Fred *lyricist, librettist*
Ebbert, Arthur, Jr. *retired university dean*
Eberle, Charles Edward *paper and consumer products executive*
Eberly, Joseph Henry *physics educator, consultant*
Eberstein, Arthur *former biomedical engineering educator, researcher*
†Eby, Carl Peter *English educator*
Eby, Cecil DeGrotte *English language educator, writer*
†Eckert, Tom W. *artist, educator*
Economou-Pease, Bessie Carasoulas *city planner, consultant*
Ecton, Donna R. *business executive*
Eddy, David Maxon *health policy and management administrator*
Eddy, Don *artist*
Edel, Abraham *philosophy educator*
†Edelmann, Carolyn Foote *author, poet, editor*
Edelstein, Rosemarie *nurse educator, medical-legal consultant*
Edens, Betty Joyce *reading recovery educator*
Edgar, Gilbert Hammond, III *business administrator*
Edgar, Thomas Flynn *chemical engineering educator*
Edgerton, Richard *restaurant and hotel owner*
Edgren, Gretchen Grondahl *magazine editor*
Edington, Robert Van *university official*
Edmonds, Anne Carey *librarian*
Edmunds, (Arthur) Lowell *philology educator*
Edmundson, Charles Wayne *mechanical engineer, communications executive*
Edrington, Sue Ellen *critical care nurse*
Edwards, Anthony *actor*
Edwards, Ardis Lavonne Quam *retired elementary education educator*
Edwards, Charles *neuroscientist, educator*
Edwards, Daniel Paul *lawyer, educator*
Edwards, Elwood Gene *mathematician, educator*
Edwards, Geoffrey Hartley *newspaper publisher*
Edwards, Helen Thom *physicist*
Edwards, Jerome *lawyer*
Edwards, Larry David *internist*
Edwards, Ninian Murry *judge*
Edwards, Patricia Burr *small business owner, counselor, consultant*
Edwards, Patrick Ross *former retail company executive, lawyer, management consultant*
Edwards, Ryan Hayes *baritone*
Edwards, Ward Dennis *psychology and industrial engineering educator*
Edwards, William Henry Von, III *United States marshal*
Edwards, William Pearson *retail company executive*
Efros, Leonid *computer software scientist and developer*
Egan, John Frederick *retired electronics executive*
Egan, Wesley William, Jr. *ambassador*
Eggers, Jennifer Christine *management consultant*
Eggleston, G(eorge) Dudley *management consultant, publisher*
†Eggleton, Elizabeth *gerontologist, educator*
Eglee, Charles Hamilton *television and movie writer, producer*
Egnor, Joanne McClellan *psychology educator*
Ehrlich, Amy *editor, writer*
Ehrlich, Grant C(onklin) *business consultant*
Ehrling, Sixten *orchestra conductor*
Ehrman, John *federal agency official, historian*
Eicher, George John *aquatic biologist*
Eichhorn, Frederick Foltz, Jr. *retired lawyer*
Eischen, Michael Hugh *retired railroad executive*
Eisen, Leonard *food and retail company executive*
Eisenberg, Albert Charles *federal agency administrator*
†Eisenberg, Daniel *filmmaker*

†Ford, S. Theodore, Jr. academic administrator
Ford, Victoria author, educator
Ford, Wendell Hampton former senator
†Ford, William D. English educator
Ford, William Francis retired bank holding company executive
Forest, Eva Brown songwriter, producer
Forest, Philip Earle housing finance consultant
Forester, Russell artist
Forman, Paula advertising agency executive
Forman-Mason, Monica N. speech and language pathologist
Formo, Jerome Lionel chemist
Forney, Ronald Dean elementary school educator, consultant, educational therapist
Forney, Virginia Sue educational counselor
Foronda, Elena Isabel secondary school educator
Forsgren, John H., Jr. financial executive
†Forsman, Catherine Anne poet, webmaster
†Forster, Robert actor, speaker
Forsythe, Henderson actor
Foss, Charles R. transportation operations specialist
Foss, Lukas composer, conductor, pianist
Fossier, Mike Walter consultant, retired electronics company executive
†Fossum, Judy Kaye radio news reporter
Foster, Charles Henry Wheelwright former foundation officer, consultant,author
Foster, Martha Tyahla educational administrator
†Foster, Michele educator
Foster, Robert Lawson retired judge, deacon
Foster, Stephen Kent banker
†Foulkes, Julia Lawrence historian
Fountain, Andre Ferchaud academic program director
Fountain, Linda Kathleen health science association executive
Fowler, Flora Daun lawyer
†Fox, Anne C. state agency administrator
Fox, Eleanor Mae Cohen lawyer, professor, author
Fox, John David educator, physicist
Fox, Kelly Diane financial advisor
Fox, Michael Wilson veterinarian, animal behaviorist
†Fox, Terry Lynn art psychotherapist
Fox, Warren Halsey academic administrator, consultant
Fox, William Richard retired physician
Foy, Charles Daley retired soil scientist
Fradkin, David Milton physicist, educator
Frailey, Stephen A. photographer
France, Richard William finance executive
Franchini, Roxanne banker
Franciosa, Anthony (Anthony Papaleo) actor
Franciosa, Joseph Anthony health care consultant
Francke, Linda Bird journalist
Frank, Edgar Gerald retired financial executive
Frank, Judith Ann (Jann Frank) retired entrepreneur, small business owner
Frank, Leona Veda artist
†Frank, Mikel R. art museum manager, artist
Franke, Wayne Thomas retired government affairs director, consultant
Frankel, Charles James, III banker
Frankel, Glenn journalist
Frankel, Judith Jennifer Mariasha clinical psychologist, consultant
Franken, Al humorist, actor, writer
Frankenberger, Bertram, Jr. investor, consultant
†Frankenheimer, John Michael film and stage director
Franklin, Bonnie Selinsky federal agency administrator
Franklin, Jon Daniel writer, journalist, educator
Franklin, Michael Harold arbitrator, lawyer, consultant
†Franklin, Raymond A. medical facility administrator
Franklin, William Emery international business educator
Franks, Gary Alvin former congressman, real estate professional
Franz, John E. bio-organic chemist, researcher
Frappia, Linda Ann management executive
Fraser, Campbell business consultant
Fraser, Donald C. engineering executive, educator
Fraser, Donald MacKay former mayor, former congressman, educator
Fraser, Kathleen Joy poet, creative writing educator
†Fratkin, Leslie photographer
Frauenfelder, Hans physicist, educator
Fravel, Elizabeth Whitmore accountant
Frazier, Henry Bowen, III retired judge, government official, lawyer
Fréchette, Louise Canadian diplomat
Frederich, Kathy W. social worker
†Frederick, Craig Matthew sculptor
Frederick, Lizetta Mary educator, counselor
Frederick-Mairs, T(hyra) Julie administrative health services official
Fredrickson, Donald Sharp physician, scientist
Freed, Melvyn Norris writer, retired higher education educator
Freedman, Monroe Henry lawyer, educator, columnist
Freedman, Russell Bruce author
Freeman, Arthur veterinarian, retired association administrator
Freeman, Meredith Norwin former college president, education educator
Freeman, Peter A. computer science educator, dean
Freeman, Ralph Carter management consultant
Freeman, Russell Adams lawyer
Freese, Barbara T. nursing educator
Freilicher, Jane artist
Freitag, Harlow retired computer scientist and corporate executive
Fremont-Smith, Thayer judge
French, Clarence Levi, Jr. retired shipbuilding company executive
French, Marilyn author, critic
Freston, Thomas E. cable television programming executive
Freter, Mark Allen marketing and public relations executive, consultant
Frey, Glenn songwriter, vocalist, guitarist
Frey, Katie Manciet educational administrator
Frick, Ivan Eugene college president emeritus, education consultant
Fricklas, Anita Alper religious organization administrator
Friday, Katherine Orwoll artist
Friedlander, Charles Douglas space consultant
Friedman, Eugene Warren surgeon
Friedman, Frances Wolf political fund raiser
Friedman, Howard W. retired real estate company executive
Friedman, Marla Lee creative services company executive, author
Friedman, Martin museum director, arts adviser
Friedman, Mildred designer, educator, curator
Friedman, Paul Richard lawyer
Friedman, Richard Burtram journalist
Friedman, Richard Lee lumberyard owner
Friedman, Victor Allen linguist, eduator
Frieling, Gerald Harvey, Jr. specialty steel company executive
Fries, Raymond Sebastian manufacturing company executive
Frisco, Louis Joseph retired materials science company executive, electrical engineer
Frison, George C. education educator
Fritcher, Earl Edwin civil engineer, consultant
Fritschler, A. Lee retired college president, public policy educator
Fritz, Charles John artist
Fritz, Ethel Mae Hendrickson writer
Fritz, Jan Marie planning educator
Fritz, Mark Francis journalist
Fritz, Rene Eugene, Jr. manufacturing executive
Froberg, Brent Malcolm classics educator
Froehlke, Robert Frederick financial services executive
Frohock, Sylvanus E. food company executive
†Fromm, Peter Francis author
Frost, Anne real estate broker, author, publisher
Frost, Ellen Louise political economist
Frost, Everett Lloyd academic administrator
Frost, J. Ormond otolaryngologist, educator
Frost, James Hamner health facility administrator
Frost, Linda Gail clergyman, hospital chaplain
Fry, Malcolm Craig retired clergyman
Fry, Shirley Ann Mills nursing administrator, educator
Fryburger, Lawrence Bruce lawyer, mediator, writer
Fryer, Thomas Waitt, Jr. writer and editor
Fuchs, Joseph Louis retired magazine publisher
Fuchs, Michael Joseph television executive
Fuenning, Esther Renate adult education educator
Fuentes, Carlos writer, former ambassador
Fuerstner, Fiona Margaret Anne ballet company executive, ballet educator
Fujita, Beverly Yumi advertising copywriter
Fulbright-Brock, Vivian supervisory probation officer
Fulco, Paula artist
Fuld, Richard Severin, Jr. investment banker
Fuller, Charles H, Jr playwright
Fuller, Elizabeth L. writer, playwright
Fuller, James Chester Eedy retired chemical company executive
Fuller, Margaret Jane medical technologist
Fuller, Maxine Compton retired secondary school educator
Fuller, Nancy MacMurray mathematics educator, tutor
†Fuller, Norine L. lobbyist, educational administrator
Fuller, Robert Ferrey lawyer, investor
Fuller, Stephen Herbert business administration educator
Fullerton, Gail Jackson university president emeritus
Fullerton, Jymie Luie pharmaceutical company executive, consultant
Funk, Vicki Jane librarian
†Furlow, Thomas William, Jr. neurologist
†Furst, E. Kenneth accountant
†Furth, Karen J. artist, art educator
Fusciardi, Katherine nursing administrator
Futter, Victor lawyer
Gabel, Creighton retired anthropologist, educator
Gabel, Katherine academic administrator
Gable, Carl Irwin business consultant, private investor, lawyer
Gabria, Joanne Bakaitis health and education volunteer, former information processing systems equipment company executive
Gabriel, Ethel Mary entertainment executive
Gabriel, Rennie financial planner
†Gabriele, Mark David policy analyst
†Gac-Artigas, Priscilla foreign language educator publisher
Gaddis, John Lewis history educator
Gaede, Ruth Ann nursing manager
Gaertner, Donell John retired library director
Gaffney, Thomas banker
Gagen, J. Wilfrid business owner, marketing and public relations executive, consultant
Gagnon, Edith Morrison ballerina, singer, actress
Gaiber, Lawrence Jay financial company executive
Gaillard, George Siday, III architect
Gainey, Robert Michael professional hockey coach, former player
Gainor, Thomas Edward banker
Galbraith, John Semple history educator
Galbraith, Nanette Elaine Gerks forensic and management sciences company executive
Galbraith, William Bruce physician, educator
Galdi-Weissman, Natalie Ann secondary education educator
Galison, Peter Louis history of science educator
Gallagher, Cynthia artist, educator
Gallagher, John Paul association administrator
Gallagher, Lindy Allyn banker, financial consultant
Gallagher, Peter actor
†Gallert, Barbara Lynn communications executive
Gallo, Robert Charles research scientist
Gallucci, Robert Louis diplomat, federal government official
†Gallucci, Robert R. librarian
Galvao, Louis Alberto import and export corporation executive, consultant
Galvin, Thomas John retired information science policy educator, retired librarian, retired information scientist
Gamble, E. James lawyer, accountant
Gamble, Harry T. professional football team executive
Gamble, Mary G(race) marketing and quality professional
Gambone, Philip Arthur English language educator
Gammon, Samuel Rhea, III association executive, former ambassador
Gamroth, Arthur Paul small business owner
Gamsky, Neal Richard university administrator, psychology educator
Gandolfo, Lucian John minister, federal official
Gandy, Bonnie Sergiacomi oncological and intravenous therapy nurse
Gangarosa, Raymond Eugene epidemiologist, engineer
Gannon, James Patrick newspaper editor
Gantz, Carroll Melvin industrial design consultant, consumer product designer
Garahan, Peter Thomas software company executive
Garbacz, Patricia Frances school social worker, therapist
Garbacz, Stephen Lawrence financial director
Garcia, Alexander orthopedic surgeon
†Garcia-Guzman, Barbara Mari secondary education educator
Garcia-Mely, Rafael retired education educator
Gard, Judy Richardson artist, educator
Gardner, Anne Lancaster lawyer
Gardner, Barbara Rogers humanities educator, writer
Gardner, Clyde Edward healthcare executive, consultant, educator
Gardner, Guy S. government official
Gardner, John Howland, III neurologist
Gardner, Lee Robbins psychiatrist
Gardner, Nancy Bruff writer
Gardner, Richard Hartwell oil company executive
Gardner, Warner Winslow lawyer
Gardner, Wilford Robert physicist, educator
Garell, Paul Charles family practice physician
Garfield, Nancy Ellen marketing and advertising professional
Garfield, Robert Edward newspaper columnist
Garibaldi, Marie Louise state supreme court justice
Garmendia, Francisco bishop
Garner, James (James Scott Bumgarner) actor
Garner, Mary Martin lawyer
Garnett, Linda Kopec nurse, researcher
Garnick, Jerry Jack periodontist, educator
Garniss, Joan Brewster musician, educator
Garrett, Cheryl Gay secondary education educator, writer
Garrett, Roberta Kampschulte nurse
Garriott, Owen Kay astronaut, scientist
Garrison, Paul Cornell retired office products company executive
Garruto, Ralph Michael research anthropologist, educator, biologist
Garry, John Thomas, II lawyer
Gartenberg, Seymour Lee retired recording company executive
Gartner, Lawrence Mitchel pediatrician, medical college educator
†Garza, Fernando Raul small business owner
Gasper, Jo Ann consulting firm executive
Gasper, Ruth Eileen real estate executive
Gass, Arthur Edward, Jr. chemist
Gassert, Richard Adam engineering company executive
Gatch, Milton McCormick, Jr. library administrator, clergyman, educator
Gates, Donna Marie special education educator
Gates, Laura Jean Cummings journalist
Gates, Martina Marie food products company executive
Gates, Susan Inez magazine publisher
Gatewood, Barbara J. medical legal consultant, lawyer
Gathright, John Byron, Jr. colon and rectal surgeon, educator
Gati, William Eugene architect, designer and planner
Gaugler, Robert Walter retired career military officer
Gaunt, Janet Lois arbitrator, mediator
Gause, Charles Marvin artist
Gauthier, Mary Elizabeth librarian, researcher, secondary education educator
Gay, Susan Matthews publishing professional
†Gay, Tito (Virginia Lewis Gray Findlay) artist, educator
Gay, William Ingalls veterinarian, health science administrator
Gayle, Margot preservationist, writer
Gaylor, Barbara Gail Davis geriatric nurse
Geary, Pamela Blalack community health and medical/surgical nurse
Gechtoff, Sonia artist
Geddes, Jane professional golfer
Geddes, Robert architect, educator
Gee, Irene food products executive, school administrator
Geer, James Hamilton, Jr. counselor, consultant
Gehm, Denise Charlene ballerina, arts administrator
Geis, Bernard book publisher
Geiselhart, Lorene Annetta English language educator
Geissinger, Frederick Wallace investment banking executive
Geist, Kathe Sternbach art history, cinema and English educator, writer
Geitgey, Doris Arlene retired nursing educator, dean
Geller, Lisa Michele copy editor
Geller, Norman Harvey music arranger, conductor
Geller, Seymour retired educator, researcher
Gellman, Isaiah environmental consultant
Gelman, Larry actor, director
Gelotte, Bob Gunnar musician
Gelpi, Armand Philippe internist
Gemell, Nicholas I. retired radiologist
Gemignani, Michael Caesar clergyman, retired educator
Gendell, Gerald Stanleigh retired public affairs executive
Gendre, Michael philosophy educator
Gendreau, Bernice Marie retired women's health nurse
Gennaro, Antonio L. biology educator
Genovese, Lawrence Matthew secondary education educator
Genovese, Philip William civil engineer
Gens, Ralph Samuel electrical engineering consultant
Gentilcore, John C. school principal
Gentry, Francis G. German language educator
Genung, Norman Bernard computer consultant
Geoffroy, Charles Henry retired business executive
†George, Anna book designer, artist
George, Carole Schroeder computer company executive
George, Joyce Jackson judge emeritus, lawyer
†George, Linda Shumaker writer, educator
George, Sharon A. nurse educator, nurse practitioner
George, Susan E. Gould health facility administrator
George, William Douglas, Jr. retired consumer products company executive
†Georgiades, Aristotle artist, educator
Gerald, Michael Charles pharmacy educator, college dean
Gerard, Gary neurologist
Gerard, Roy Dupuy oil company executive, retired
Gerbehy, Christine Petric medical/surgical and mental health nurse
Gerber, Seymour retired publishing company executive
Gere, Richard actor
Gerhardt, Heinz Adolf August aircraft design engineer
Gerhardt, Jon Stuart mechanical engineer, engineering educator
Gericke, Shane William writer
Gerlach, Jeanne Elaine English language educator
Gerlach, Luther Paul anthropologist
Germanotta, Jeffrey Steven investment banker
Germany, Daniel Monroe aerospace engineer
Gerou, Phillip Howard architect
Gerry, Debra Prue psychotherapist, recording artist, writer
†Gershman, John Jeremy research analyst, consultant
Gerstner, Mary Jane nurse
Gertenbach, Robert Frederick medical research organization executive, accountant, lawyer
†Gervits, Leonid art educator, artist
Getting, Ivan Alexander physicist, former aerospace company executive
Ghymn, Esther Mikyung English educator, writer
Giannella, Susanne R. maternal/women's health nurse, medical/surgical nurse
Gibbons, Doria Desaix gastroenterology nurse
Gibbons, Erin secondary education educator
Giblett, Phylis Lee Walz middle school educator
Gibson, Beatrice Ann retired systems analyst, artist
Gibson, Benjamin F. federal judge
Gibson, Scott Russell nurse
†Giddings, Paula Jane author, educator
Gidwitz, Gerald retired hair care company executive
Giebel, Miriam Catherine librarian, genealogist
Gifford, Frank Newton sportscaster, commentator, former professional football player
Gifford, Heidi editor, writer
Gifford, John Irving retired agricultural equipment company executive
Gilb, Corinne Lathrop history educator
Gilberg, Margot D. secondary school Spanish educator
Gilbert, Frederick E. development planner, Africanist, consultant
Gilbert, Nancy Louise librarian
Gilbertson, Susan nurse manager
Gilbride, William Donald lawyer
Gilchrest, Thornton Charles retired association executive
Gilchrist, Ellen Louise writer
Gilchrist, James Beardslee banker
Giles, James Francis financial executive
Giles, Walter Edmund alcohol and drug treatment executive
Gilinsky, Victor physicist
Gill, Henry Herr photojournalist
Gill, Richard Thomas opera singer, economic analyst
Gill, Thomas James, III physician, educator
Gill, William Robert soil scientist
Gillespie, Gerald Ernest Paul comparative literature educator, writer
Gillespie, Helen Davys marketing/industry consultant, analyst, author
Gillespie, Robert James manufacturing company executive
Gillett, Mary Caperton military historian
Gillette, W. Michael state supreme court justice
Gilliam, Terry Vance film director, actor, illustrator, writer
Gillice, Sondra Jupin (Mrs. Gardner Russell Brown) sales and marketing executive
Gillin, Carol Ann middle school educator
Gilman, Richard drama educator, author
Gilman, Steven A. management consultant
Gilmore, Gail Pearsall consultant, writer
Gilmour, David Patton economic and community planner
Gilreath, Warren Dean retired packaging company executive
Gilroy, Frank Daniel playwright
Gilster, Peter Stuart lawyer
Gimbolo, Aleksei Frank Charles (Cimbolo) artist, philosopher, author
†Gingher, Marianne B. English educator
Gingras, John Richard lawyer, consultant
Gingrich, Newt(on Leroy) former congressman
Giordano, James Joseph neuroscientist, aeromedical engineer, educator
†Gipson, Shelley R. artist, educator
†Girton, Marcy athletic director
Girvin-Quirk, Susan nursing administrator
Gischlar, Karen Lynn elementary education educator
Giuffrida, Tom A. publisher
Giusti, Joseph Paul retired
Giusti, Robert George artist, educator
Givens, Richard Ayres lawyer
Gladstone, Carol Lynn assistant principal
Glancy, Diane English educator
Glasauer, Franz Ernst neurosurgeon
Glasberg, Laurence Brian private investor, business executive
Glashow, Sheldon Lee physicist, educator
Glass, Dorothea Daniels physiatrist, educator
Glass, Kenneth Edward management consultant
Glasser, Ira Saul civil liberties organization executive
Glatzer, Robert Anthony marketing and sales executive
Glaze, Lynn Ferguson development consultant
Gleach, Frederic Wright anthropologist
Gleason, Carol Ann rehabilitation nurse
Gleason, John James theatrical lighting designer
Gleaton, Harriet E. retired anesthesiologist
†Gleba, Beth Ann (Beth Ann Coleman) communications executive
Gleijeses, Mario holding company executive
Glenn, Jules psychiatrist
Glenn, Richard Alan adult education educator
Glennen, Robert Eugene, Jr. retired university president
Glennon, Harrison Randolph, Jr. retired shipping company executive
†Glenz, Nancy L. educator
Glesk, Ivan physicist, educator, researcher
Gleue, Lorine Anna elementary education educator
Glick, J. Leslie biotechnology entrepreneur
Glick, Ruth Burtnick author, lecturer
Gloeckler, George physics educator
†Gloman, David J. artist
Glosser, Jeffrey Mark lawyer
†Glover, Asia Wong communications services executive
Glover, Crispin Hellion actor
Glover, Lisa Marie research analyst
Glover, William Harper theater critic
Glower, Donald Duane university executive, mechanical engineer
Glück, Louise Elisabeth poet
Gluys, Charles Byron retired marketing management consultant
Glynn, Carlin (Carlin Masterson) actress
†Glynn, Edward college dean
Gobel, John Henry lawyer
Goble, Paul author, illustrator, artist
†Godbee, Gary Russell artist
Goddard, James Russell producer, writer, actor
Goddard, Thelma Taylor critical care nurse, nursing educator

Godfrey, Margaret Ann *educator*
Godo, Einar *computer engineer*
Godwin, Naomi Nadine *editor*
Goellner, Jack Gordon *publishing executive*
Goen, Bob *television show host*
Goerke, Glenn Allen *university administrator*
Goetzel, Claus Guenter *metallurgical engineer*
Goewey, Gordon Ira *university administrator*
Goff, Jane E. *secondary school educator*
Goffman, Thomas Edward *radiation oncologist, researcher*
Gogarty, William Barney *oil company executive, consultant*
Gold, Leonard Singer *librarian, translator*
†Gold, Matea Jenny *journalist, educator*
Gold, Sylviane *entertainment editor, writer, critic*
Goldberg, Bradley Jay *artist*
†Goldberg, Gerald Jay *writer, educator*
Goldberg, Lee Winicki *furniture company executive*
Goldberg, Mark Arthur *neurologist*
Goldberg, Maxwell Henry *retired humanities educator*
Goldberg, Norma Lorraine *retired public welfare administrator*
Goldberg, Samuel *retired mathematician, foundation officer*
Goldberg, Victor Joel *retired data processing company executive*
Goldberg, Whoopi (Caryn Johnson) *actress*
Goldberger, Blanche Rubin *sculptor, jeweler*
Goldberger, Marvin Leonard *physicist, educator*
Golden, Beth *Special Olympics administrator*
Golden, David Edward *physicist*
Golden, Elliott *judge*
Golden, Judith Greene *artist, educator*
Goldfarb, Muriel Bernice *marketing and advertising consultant*
Goldin, Jacob Isaak *software executive*
Goldin, Marion Freedman *television news producer, reporter*
Golding, Carolyn May *former government senior executive, consultant*
Goldinger, Shirley Anne *elementary education educator*
Goldman, Alan Ira *investment banking executive*
Goldman, Alfred Emanuel *marketing research consultant*
Goldman, Barbara Deren *film and theatrical producer*
Goldman, Charles Norton *retired corporate lawyer*
Goldman, Gerald Hillis *beverage distribution company executive*
Goldman, Joseph Elias *advertising executive*
Goldman, Mia *film editor*
Goldman, Rachel Bok *civic volunteer*
Goldman, Robert David *cell biologist, educator*
Goldman, Sherry Robin *public relations executive*
Goldner, Sheldon Herbert *export-import company executive*
Goldoff, Anna Carlson *public administration educator*
Goldsmith, Arthur Austin *magazine editor*
Goldspiel, Arnold Nelson *real estate executive*
Goldstein, Alfred George *retail and consumer products executive*
Goldstein, Bernard *transportation and casino gaming company executive*
Goldstein, Joseph *law educator*
Goldstein, Naomi *psychiatrist*
Goldstein, Norman Ray *international trading company executive, consultant*
Goldstein, Phyllis Ann *art historian, educator*
Goldston, Stephen Eugene *community psychologist, educator, consultant*
Goldstone, James *film, television and stage director*
Goldwater, John Leonard *publisher, writer*
Gollings, Ruth Erickson *community health nurse*
Golomb, Myra J. *nurse*
Gomez, David Frederick *lawyer*
Gonzalez-Vales, Luis Ernesto *historian, educational administrator*
Good, Linda Lou *elementary education educator*
Good, Walter Raymond *investment executive*
Goodby, Jeffrey *advertising agency executive*
Goode, Stephen Hogue *publishing company executive*
Goodkin, Michael Jon *publishing company executive*
Goodman, Erika *dancer, actress*
Goodrich, Kenneth Paul *retired college dean*
Goodrich, Leon Raymond *lawyer*
Goodrich, Robert Lawrence, Jr. *educator, accountant*
Goodson, Raymond Eugene *business educator, former automotive executive*
Goodwin, Felix Lee *retired educational administrator, retired army officer*
Goolsby, Charles William *artist, educator*
Goonrey, Charles W. *retired lawyer*
Gootee, Tara Renee *educational counselor, family therapist*
Gora, Daniel Martin *lawyer*
†Gorbell, Michael Randall *federal agency and business management executive*
Gordan, Gilbert Saul *physician, educator*
Gordimer, Nadine *author*
Gordis, David Moses *academic administrator, rabbi*
Gordly, Avel Louise *senator, community activist*
Gordon, Ann Marie *pharmacist*
Gordon, Cyrus Herzl *Orientalist, educator*
Gordon, David Zevi *retired lawyer*
Gordon, Ezra *architect, educator*
†Gordon, Fran diLustro *writer*
†Gordon, Kenneth Antony *publisher*
Gordon, Marjorie *lyric coloratura soprano, opera producer, teacher*
Gordon, Peter Lowell *immigration and naturalization administrator*
Gordon, Ruby Daniels *retired nursing educator, counselor*
Gordon-Spearman, Florida Lee *nursing educator*
Gorenberg, Norman Bernard *aeronautical engineer, consultant, retired*
Gorence, Patricia Josetta *judge*
Gorham, George H. *playwright, lyricist*
Gorman, Cliff *actor*
Gorman, Joseph Tolle *corporate executive*
Gorman, Michael Stephen *construction executive*
Gorr, Elaine Gray *therapist, elementary education educator*
Gorsline, Stephen Paul *security firm executive*
Goslawski, Violet Ann *nurse, substance abuse counselor*
Goss, J.B. *psychopharmacologist*
Goss, Joel Francis *writer*
Goss, Porter J. *congressman*
Gossett, Louis, Jr. *actor*
Gottfried, Eugene Leslie *physician, educator*
Gottlieb, Alan Merril *advertising, fundraising and broadcasting executive, writer*
Gottlieb, Sherry Gershon *author, editor*
Gottschalk, Charles M. *international energy consultant*
Gould, Harold *actor*
Gould, Martha Bernice *retired librarian*
†Gould, Ronald *lawyer*
Gounaris, Anne Demetra *biochemistry educator, researcher*
Gouse, S. William, Jr. *engineering executive, scientist*
Govan, Gladys Vernita Mosley *retired critical care and medical/surgical nurse*
†Gowen, Kay S. *communications educator*
Goyan, Jere Edwin *business executive, former university dean*
Goyan, Michael Donovan *stockbroker, investment executive*
Goz, Harry G. *actor, singer*
Grab, Frederick Charles *lawyer*
Grabemann, Karl W. *lawyer*
Grace, Helen Kennedy *retired foundation administrator*
Grace, Marcia Bell *advertising executive*
Grady, James Thomas *novelist*
Grady, Maureen Frances *lawyer*
Graebner, James Herbert *transportation executive*
Graessley, William Walter *retired chemical engineering educator*
Graeve, Peter John *county official*
Graf, Steffi *professional tennis player*
Graff, Randy *actress*
Graffis, Julie Anne *entrepreneur, retail consultant, interior designer*
Graham, Brenda J. *nurse*
Graham, Cynthia Armstrong *banker*
†Graham, Heather *actress*
Graham, James Herbert *dermatologist*
Graham, Kathleen Margaret (K. M. Graham) *artist*
Graham, Parker Lee, II *computer systems manager*
Gralla, Milton *publisher*
Grandinetti, Micheal Lawrence *marketing executive*
Grandstrand, Ruth Helena *retired community health and gerontology nurse*
Granger, Kay *congresswoman*
Grant, Alexander Marshall *ballet director*
†Grant, D(oris) Jean *writer*
Grant, Eileen Gerard *medical/surgical nurse*
†Grant, Gretchen Gullicksen *artist*
Grant, James Colin *banker*
†Grant, Joseph D. *business administrator, executive director*
Grant, Lee (Lyova Haskell Rosenthal) *actress, director*
Grant, Leonard Tydings *clergyman*
Grant, Linda Susan *nursing consultant*
Grant, Merrill Theodore *producer*
Grantham, Shonnette Denise *mental health nurse, care facility supervisor*
Grass, George Mitchell, IV *pharmaceutical executive*
Grassmuck, George Ludwig *political science educator*
Grasso, Anthony Robert *priest, educator*
Graupner, Sheryll Ann *elementary education educator*
Graves, Denyce Antoinette *mezzo-soprano*
Graves, Lorraine Elizabeth *dancer, educator, coach*
Graves, Sid Foster, Jr. *retired library and museum director*
Graves, Wallace Billingsley *retired university executive*
Gray, Darlene Agnes *nurse*
Gray, David Lawrence *retired air force officer*
Gray, Deborah Mary *wine importer*
Gray, Diane *dancer, choreographer*
Gray, Francine du Plessix *author*
Gray, Gordon L. *communications educator*
Gray, Harry Joshua *electrical engineer, educator*
Gray, John Lathrop, III *retired advertising agency executive*
Gray, Richard Alexander, Jr. *retired chemical company executive*
Gray, Susanne Marie Hartman *ambulatory care nurse*
Gray, Thomas Stephen *newspaper editor*
Gray, Vicki Lou Pharr *music educator*
†Graybill, Guy Oldt *writer*
†Grayson, Richard Steven (Lord of Mursley) *foreign correspondent, international legal and political management consultant, educator*
Graziani, N. Jane *communications executive, publisher*
Greaves, James Louis *art conservator*
Greaves, William Webster *chemist, patent analyst*
Grebb, Michael D. *systems analyst*
Grebstein, Sheldon Norman *university administrator*
Greeff, Adele Montgomery Burcher *artist*
Green, Bennett Donald *biotechnologist*
Green, Beth Ingber *intuitive practitioner, counselor, musician, composer*
Green, Carol H. *lawyer, educator, journalist*
Green, Daphne Kelly *mental health nurse*
Green, Karen Danielle *psychotherapist*
Green, Mark Joseph *lawyer, author*
Green, Nancy Loughridge *academic administrator*
Green, Richard Calvin, Jr. *utility company executive*
Greenberg, Albert *art director*
Greenberg, Arnold Elihu *water quality specialist*
Greenberg, Bonnie Lynn *music industry executive*
Greenberg, Hinda Feige *library director*
Greenberg, Ina Florence *retired elementary education educator*
Greenberg, Joshua F. *lawyer, educator*
Greenberg, Milton *corporation executive*
Greenberg, Nancy Ward *school health consultant*
Greenburg, Dan *author*
Greene, Barnett Alan *anesthesiologist*
Greene, Beverly Ann *clinical psychologist*
Greene, Elinore Aschah *speech and drama professional, writer*
Greene, Frank Sullivan, Jr. *investment management executive*
Greene, John Colton *retired history educator*
Greene, Laurence Whitridge, Jr. *surgical educator*
Greenemeier, Cheryl S. *women's health nurse*
Greenfield, Sanford Raymond *architect*
†Greenhouse, Carol Joan *editor, writer, educator*
Greenman, David Lewis *consultant physiologist and toxicologist*
Greenwald, Gerald *air transportation executive*
Greenwald, John Edward *newspaper and magazine executive*
Greenwood, Janet Kae Daly *psychologist, educational administrator*
Greenwood, Janet Kingham *sanitarian, county official*
Greer, Carl Crawford *petroleum company executive*
Greer, Germaine *author*
Greer, K. Gordon *banker*
†Greer, Kathleen E. *college registrar*
Greever, Margaret Quarles *retired mathematics educator*
Gregg, Walter Emmor, Jr. *financial corporation executive, accountant, lawyer*
Gregoire, Christine O. *state attorney general*
Gregor, Dorothy Deborah *librarian*
Gregory, Mary Sharon *educator*
Gregory, Myra May *religious organization administrator, educator*
Greider, John Calhoun *English educator*
Grejtak, Gena Renee *critical care nurse*
Grenander, Ulf *mathematics educator*
Gretser, George Westfall *publisher*
Greve, Sally Doane *English educator*
Grey, Elizabeth K. *critical care nurse, retired*
Grey, Jennifer *actress*
Grier, Dorothy Ann Pridgen *secondary education specialist*
Grier, Pamela *actress, writer, singer*
Griesbauer, Michele Elaine *newspaper official*
†Grieve, Pierson MacDonald *retired specialty chemicals and services company executive*
Griffie, Gayle G. *retired principal*
Griffin, Annette L. *critical care nurse, educator*
Griffin, Campbell Arthur, Jr. *lawyer*
Griffin, Carleton Hadlock *accountant, educator*
Griffin, Christopher Oakley *hospital professional, humanities educator*
Griffin, Eren G. *retired nursing educator*
Griffin, James Anthony *bishop*
Griffin, John Henry *medical researcher*
Griffin, Myrna McIntosh *critical care nurse*
Griffin, Robert Paul *former United States senator, state supreme court justice*
Griffith, B(ezaleel) Herold *physician, educator, plastic surgeon*
Griffith, Carl Leslie *protective services official*
Griffith, David L. *protective services official*
Griffith, Dewey Maurice *mechanical engineer, investor*
Griffith, James Lewis *lawyer*
Griffith, Katherine Scott *communications executive*
Griffith, Melanie *actress*
†Griffith, Patricia Browning *writer, educator*
Griffith, Steven Franklin, Sr. *lawyer, real estate title insurance agent and investor*
Griggs, Bobbie June *civic worker*
Griggs, Emma *management executive*
Griggs, John Robert *financial and consumer credit services executive*
Grimes, Hugh Gavin *physician*
Grimes, William Alvan *retired state supreme court chief justice*
Grimm, Roberta Pauline Johnson *performing arts company director*
Grindal, Mary Ann *former sales professional*
Grindea, Daniel *international economist*
Grine, Florence May *secondary education educator*
Grinnell, Helen Dunn *musicologist, arts administrator*
Griswold, Gary Norris *engineering company executive*
Groat, Pamela Ferne *school media specialist*
Groban, Lee David *artist*
†Grobel, Michael Lawrence *writer, editor*
Grodsky, Jamie Anne *lawyer*
Grody, Donald *actor, judge, lawyer, arbitrator*
Grody, Mark Stephen *public relations executive*
Groening, Matthew *writer, cartoonist*
Groezinger, Leland Becker, Jr. *investment professional*
Grogan, Debby Elaine *geriatric and intensive care nurse*
Gromen, Richard John *historian, educator*
Groome, Reginald Kehnroth *company executive, consultant*
Gros, Francisco Roberto André *banker*
Groskopf, Aubrey Bud *motion picture television executive*
Grosland, Emery Layton *banker*
Gross, Gil *radio talk show host, columnist*
Gross, Laura Ann *marketing and communications professional, acupuncturist, herbalist*
Gross, Ruth Taubenhaus *physician*
†Gross, Steven Jay *education educator*
Gross, Terry R. *radio producer, host*
Grosset, Anne Marie *biophysicist, researcher*
Grossman, Jerrold B. *pharmaceutical executive*
Grossman, Marc *diplomat*
Grotta, Sandra Brown *interior designer*
Grove, Myrna Jean *elementary education educator*
Groves, Bernice Ann *educator*
Groves, Michael *banker*
Groves, Sheridon Hale *orthopedic surgeon*
Grow, Robert Theodore *economist, association executive*
Growe, Joan Anderson *former state official*
Grubbs, Christopher Andrew *electronics company executive*
Gruber, Fredric Francis *financial planning and investment research executive*
Grunbaum, Marianne Hettner *artist*
Grundlehner, Conrad Ernest *information company executive, economic consultant*
Grutman, Jewel Humphrey *lawyer, writer*
Gschwind, Donald *management and engineering consultant*
Gudenberg, Harry Richard *arbitrator, mediator*
Gudnitz, Ora M. Cofey *secondary education educator*
Guerber, Howard P. *retired electrical engineer*
Guerra, Armando J. *corporate professional*
Guerrero, Lilia *school nurse*
Gugel, Craig Thomas *advertising and new media executive*
Guild, Nelson Prescott *retired state education official*
Guiliano, Francis James *office products manufacturing company executive*
Guillemette, Gloria Vivian *dressmaker, designer*
Guimond, John Patrick *retired financial consultant*
Guinness, Sir Alec *actor*
Guittar, Lee John *retired newspaper executive*
Gulcher, Robert Harry *aircraft company executive*
†Guldner, Joel Raymond *librarian*
†Gumbel, Bryant Charles *broadcaster*
Gumen, Murad *artist, writer, film director and producer*
Gummel, Hermann Karl *retired physicist, laboratory administrator*
Gummere, John *insurance company executive*
Gumpel, Liselotte *German language educator*
Gumppert, Karella Ann *federal government official*
Gundersen, Allison Maureen *management consultant*
Gundersen, Wayne Campbell *management consultant, oil and gas consultant*
Gunderson, Judith Keefer *golf association executive*
†Gunderson, Keith Robert *philosophy educator*
Gunderson, Ted Lee *security consultant*
Gundlach, Robert William *retired physicist*
†Guo, Sheng Ming *retired history educator*
Gupta, Ramesh Chandra *geotechnical engineer, consultant*
Gurney, Daniel Sexton *race car manufacturing company executive, racing team executive*
Gurvis, Sandra Jane *writer*
Gurwitch, Arnold Andrew *communications executive*
Gurwitz-Hall, Barbara Ann *artist*
Gusdon, John Paul, Jr. *obstetrics and gynecology educator, physician*
Gustafson, Denise Krupka *special education educator*
Gustavson, Mark Steven *lawyer*
Guthman, Sandra Polk *foundation executive*
Guthrie, Janet *professional race car driver*
Guthrie, Robert Val *retired psychologist and educator*
Guthrie, Timothy Sean *art educator, artist*
Guthrie, Wallace Nessler, Jr. *naval officer*
Gutierrez, Gerald Andrew *theatrical director*
Gutman, Richard Edward *lawyer*
Gutmann, Reinhart Bruno *clergyman, social worker*
Gutsch, William Anthony, Jr. *astronomer*
Gutstein, Carol Feinhandler *realtor*
Guttenberg, Steve *actor*
Guttentag, Joseph Harris *lawyer, educator*
†Guttman, Irving Allen *opera stage director*
Guy, Eleanor Bryenton *writer*
Guyer, Bernard *maternal and child health educator*
Guyon, John Carl *retired university administrator*
Haag, Walter M(onroe), Jr. *philatelist*
Haas, Charlie *screenwriter*
Haber, Ralph Norman *psychology consultant, researcher, educator*
Haber, Warren H. *investment company executive*
Haberer, John Henry, Jr. *minister*
Haberl, Judy Ann *artist, educator*
Haberl, Valerie Elizabeth *physical education educator, company executive*
Haberman, Charles Morris *mechanical engineer, educator*
†Habich, Elizabeth Chamberlain *librarian*
Habkirk, Sue Ann *education educator*
Hackel-Sims, Stella Bloomberg *lawyer, former government official*
Hackett, Robert John *lawyer*
Hackett, Wesley Phelps, Jr. *lawyer*
Hackstadt, Chiquita Darleen *medical/surgical nurse*
Hadas, Julia Ann *social services administrator*
Haddock, Harold, Jr. *retired accounting firm executive*
Hadley, Jane Byington *psychotherapist*
Haeberle, Rosamond Pauline *retired educator*
Haegele, John Ernest *business executive*
Haft, Gail Klein *pediatrician*
Hagan, Joseph Henry *university administrator*
Hage, George Campbell *social studies educator, minister, and counselor*
Hagel, Raymond Charles *publishing company executive, educator*
Hagelston, Karman Weatherly *speech pathologist*
Hagemier, Herman Frederick *chemist*
Hagen, Edna Mae *retired medical nurse*
Hager, Paula Michele *critical care nurse*
Hager, Robert Worth *retired aerospace company executive*
Hagerman, Michael Charles *lawyer, arbitrator, mediator*
Haggerty, Robert Johns *physician, educator*
Hahn, Helene B. *motion picture company executive*
Hahn, Lucille Denise *paper company executive, retired*
Hahn, Mary Downing *author*
Haining, Jeane *psychologist*
Hairston, James Christopher *airline catering and distribution executive*
Hajek, Robert J., Sr. *lawyer, real estate broker, commodities broker, nursing home owner*
Hakala, Karen Louise *retired real estate adminstrator*
Hakimoglu, Ayhan *electronics company executive*
Halberstam, Heini *mathematics educator*
Halbert, Ronald Joel *preventive medicine physician, educator*
Haldeman, Joe William *novelist*
Halden, Martha Ann *pediatrics nurse, educator*
Hale, Christy *illustrator, designer, art educator*
Hale, Kenneth Byron *retired law enforcement officer, eudcator*
†Hales, Robert D. *church official*
Haley, George Brock, Jr. *lawyer*
Haley, Richard Edward, Jr. *computer scientist*
Halfen, David *publishing executive*
Hall, Arsenio *actor, comedian*
Hall, Conrad L. *cinematographer*
Hall, David *newspaper editor*
Hall, Grace Rosalie *physicist, educator, literary scholar*
Hall, Hansel Crimiel *communications executive*
Hall, J. Tillman *physical education educator, administrator, writer*
Hall, James Stanley *jazz guitarist, composer*
Hall, Jay *social psychologist*
Hall, John Hopkins *retired lawyer*
Hall, Julie Jane *community health nurse, administrator*
Hall, Keith R. *federal official*
Hall, Kendra Jean *neuroscience nurse, researcher, educator*
Hall, Milton Reese *retired oil company executive*
Hall, Monty *television producer, actor*
Hall, Ralph Carr *lawyer, real estate consultant*
Hall, Susan Laurel *artist, educator, writer*
Hall-Barron, Deborah *lawyer*
Halleck, Charles White *lawyer, former judge*
Halleck, Lois Renee *critical care and emergency room nurse*
Hallett, William Jared *nuclear engineer*
Halliday, William Ross *retired physician, speleologist, writer*
†Halmer, Judith R. *writing and literature educator*
Halper, June Ann *human resource development consultant*
Halpin, Daniel William *civil engineering educator, consultant*
Halsey, Gary *illustrator*
Haltom, Elbert Bertram, Jr. *retired federal judge*
Halushynsky, George Dobroslav *systems engineer*
Hambidge, Douglas Walter *archbishop*
Hambrecht, William R. *retired venture capitalist*
Hamill, Dorothy Stuart *professional ice skater*
Hamill, (William) Pete *newspaper columnist, author, editor*
Hamilton, Allan Corning *retired oil company executive*

Hamilton, David Eugene minister, educator
Hamilton, Lyman Critchfield, Jr. telecommunications industry executive
Hamilton, Nancy Richey critical care nurse, educator
Hamilton, Thomas Michael marketing executive
Hamilton, William Eugene, Jr. electrical engineer
Hamilton, William Howard laboratory executive
Hamit, Francis Granger freelance writer
Hamlisch, Marvin composer, conductor, pianist, entertainer
Hamm, Vernon Louis, Jr. management and financial consultant
Hammam, M. Shawky electrical engineer, educator
Hammer, Wade Burke retired oral and maxillofacial surgeon, educator
Hammerschmidt, John Paul retired congressman, lumber company executive
Hammond, Glenn Barry, Sr. lawyer, electrical engineer
Hammond, Judith Anne family nurse practitioner
Hammond, Robert Lee retired feed company executive
Hammond, Vernon Francis school administrator
Hampton, Rex Herbert former mining executive, director
Hamrock, Margaret Mary retired educator, writer
Hanan, Laura Molen artist
Hancock, John Coulter telecommunications company executive
Hand, Janet L. medical, surgical and critical care nurse, educator
Handler, Harold Robert lawyer
Handy, Edward Otis, Jr. financial services executive
Hanford, George Hyde retired educational administrator
Hankin, Charles Edward sculptor
Hanks-DeCrescenzo, Jame Melisse insurance company executive
Hanman, Ted E. music educator, choral conductor
Hanmer, Stephen Read, Jr. retired government executive
Hanna, Lee Ann critical care nurse
Hanna, Noreen Anelda retired adult education administrator, consultant
†Hannah, Gregg S. business educator
Hanneken, David William advertising executive
Hanneman, Rodney Elton metallurgical engineer
Hannewald, Norman Eugene secondary school educator
Hanrahan, Lawrence Martin healthcare consultant
Hansell, John Royer retired physician
Hansen, Alan Edward mental health nurse
Hansen, Donald Curtis retired manufacturing executive
Hansen, Enid Eileen secondary education educator
Hansen, Hal T. investment company executive
Hansen, Leland Joe communications executive
Hansen, Wendell Jay clergyman, gospel broadcaster
†Hanser, Russell P. lawyer
Hanson, Ann M. women's health care nurse practitioner
Hanson, Carl Malmrose financial company executive
Hanson, David Gordon otolaryngologist, surgeon
Hanson, Dennis Michael medical imaging executive
Hanson, Erik Brian professional baseball player
Hanson, Janice Crawford artist, financial analyst
Hanson, Jo artist
Hanson, Wendy Karen chemical engineer
Hanzlik, Rayburn DeMara lawyer
†Hapka, Catherine M. internet executive
Hapner, Mary Lou securities trader and dealer
†Haque, Akhlaque Ul educator, researcher
Harari, Hananiah artist
Harden, Patrick Alan journalist
Harder, Robert Clarence state official
Hardin, Clifford Morris retired university chancellor, cabinet member
Hardin, Paul, III law educator
Harding, John T. journalist
Hardison, Diane Sorrell Parker special education educator
Hardman, Joel Griffeth pharmacologist
Hardy, Bridget McColl screenwriter
Hardy, Clarence Earl, Jr. human resources executive
Hardy, James Chester speech pathologist, educator
Hardy, Ralph W. F. biochemist, biotechnology executive
Hardy De Jesus, Georgette Marilyn university administrator
Hare, Frederick Kenneth geography and environmental educator, university official
Hare, LeRoy, Jr. pharmaceutical company executive
†Harenza, Brian James international banker
Hargadon, Bernard Joseph, Jr. retired consumer goods company executive
Hargrove, Erwin C. political scientist, educator
Harkness, Peter Anthony editor, publisher
Harlan, Jack Rodney geneticist, emeritus educator
Harlan, Kathleen Troy (Kay Harlan) business consultant, professional speaker and seminar leader
Harlow, Charles Vendale, Jr. finance educator, consultant
Harlow, Joan Beverley writer
Harman, Wallace Patrick lawyer
Harmon, Debra Mae journalist
Harmon, James Allen federal agency administrator
Harmston, Robert Albert secondary education educator
Harnack, Don Steger lawyer
Harp, Solomon, III former airport executive
Harper, Christine Johnson psychiatric clinical nurse, administrator
Harper, Harlan, Jr. lawyer
Harper, Henry H. military officer, retired
Harper, James Robert graphic designer
Harper, Richard Henry film producer, director
Harper, W(alter) Joseph financial consultant
Harrell, Henry Howze tobacco company executive
Harrell, Ina Perry maternal/women's and medical/surgical nurse
Harrigan, Anthony Hart author
Harrigan, Rosanne Carol dean, nursing educator
Harriman, John Howland lawyer
Harriman, Philip Darling geneticist, science foundation executive
Harrington, Jean Patrice college president
Harrington, Michael Ballou health economist, systems engineer
Harris, Annie Rene elementary school teacher
Harris, Burton H. surgeon
Harris, Delmarie Jones elementary education educator
Harris, Ed Jerome retired judge
Harris, Elaine K. medical consultant
Harris, Elliott Stanley toxicologist
Harris, Gretchen Elizabeth treasury analyst, consultant
Harris, Harry H. television director
Harris, Howard Hunter oil company executive
†Harris, Jana writer, educator
Harris, Jeanette Marianne writer
Harris, John M. historian
Harris, Louis public opinion analyst, columnist
Harris, Marcelite Jordan retired air force officer
Harris, Margaret pianist, conductor, composer
Harris, Merle Wiener college administrator, educator
Harris, Pamela Sue rehabilitation physician
Harris, Patricia Lee engineering executive
†Harris, Richard Eugene Vassau lawyer
Harris, Robert Norman advertising and communications educator
Harris, Rogers Sanders bishop
Harris, Roy Hartley electrical engineer
Harris, Thelma Lee data processing executive
Harris, Theodore Clifford songwriter, music publisher
Harris, William John retired management holding company executive, consultant
Harrison, Alonzo construction company executive
Harrison, Charles Maurice lawyer, former communications company executive
Harrison, Deborah Lynn human service executive
Harrison, Earl Grant, Jr. educational administrator
Harrison, Gregory actor
†Harrison, Jonathan Edward accountant, law enforcement consultant
Harrison, William Burwell, Jr. banker
†Harrod, Lois Marie secondary school educator, poet
Harsha, Amy Beth elementary education educator
†Harshman, Marc writer, poet, consultant
Hart, Arthur Alvin historian, author
Hart, Dorothy actress, international affairs speaker
Hart, Howard Roscoe, Jr. retired physicist
Hart, Sharown educator
†Harter, Hugh Anthony foreign language educator
Hartford, Shaun Alison pediatrics nurse, educator
Hartley, Craig Sheridan mechanical and materials engineering educator
Hartman, Elizabeth Diane retired elementary education educator
Hartman, James Theodore physician, educator
Hartman, Margaret J. biologist, educator, university official
Hartmann, George Herman retired manufacturing company executive
Hartness, Sandra Jean venture capitalist
Harton, John James utility executive, consultant
Hartsell, Samuel David insurance agent
Hartwick, Thomas Stanley technical management consultant
Hartzell, Irene Janofsky psychologist
†Hartzog, William W. retired military officer
Harvey, Birt retired pediatrician, educator
Harvey, Joseph Emmett construction executive
Harvey, Virginia Isham curator, fiber artist
Harvey, Willard Albertson, Jr. writer, distribution company executive
Harville Smith, Martha Louise special education educator
Harvitt, Adrianne Stanley lawyer
Harwood, Vanessa Clare ballet dancer
Hashimi, Caren Sue food service manager
Haskell, Margaret Howard writer, psychotherapist
Haskin, Larry Allen earth and planetary scientist, educator
†Hassell, Mark Joseph counselor
Hasselmeyer, Eileen Grace medical research administrator
Hasselmo, Nils university official, linguistics educator
Hasson, Raymond Edward, III artist, writer
Hast, Adele editor, historian
†Hastaacca, Alfredo Xavier medical researcher
Hatch, Orrin Grant senator
Hatchell, Sylvia basketball coach
Hatcher, Herbert John biochemist, microbiologist
Hathaway, David Roger physician, medical educator, scientist
Hauenstein, George Carey life insurance executive
Haug, Marilyn Ann reading and mathematics educator
Hauptli, Barbara Beatrice program administrator
Hausman, Arthur Herbert electronics company executive
Hausman, Bruce retired lawyer
Hauver, Constance Longshore lawyer
Havens, Keith Cornell artist
Havice, Pamela Ann maternal/women's health nurse, nurse educator
Havran, Martin Joseph historian, educator, author
Hawes, Sue lawyer
Hawk, Carole Lynn insurance company executive, research analyst
Hawk, Robert Dooley wholesale grocery company executive
†Hawke, Simon Nicholas writer, educator
Hawkes, Kevin Cliff illustrator, author
Hawkins, Armis Eugene former state supreme court chief justice
Hawkins, John writer
Hawkins, Mary Ellen Higgins (Mary Ellen Higgins) former state legislator, public relations consultant
Hawkins, Michael Daly federal judge
Hawkins, Roberta Rosenthal theater educator
Hawkins, Willis Moore aerospace and astronautical consultant
Haworth, Dale Keith art history educator, gallery director
Hawryluk, Christine Joanne school nurse
Hayashi, Teru zoologist, educator
Haydock, Michael Damean building and code consultant, writer
Hayek, Carolyn Jean retired judge, former church administrator
†Hayek, Salma actress
Hayes, Charles religious organization executive, clergyman
Hayes, David Vincent sculptor
Hayes, George J. retired neurosurgeon
Hayes, Janet Gray retired business manager, former mayor
Hayes, John Patrick retired manufacturing company executive
Hayes, Judy Diane medical/surgical and ophthalmological nurse, nursing administrator
Hayes, Mary Phyllis savings and loan association executive
Hays, John Alan military officer, construction company executive
Hays, Robert actor
Hays, Thomas Chandler holding company executive
Hayward, Charles Winthrop retired railroad company executive
Hazard, Geoffrey Cornell, Jr. law educator
Hazard, Margaret Louise (Peggy Hazard) management consultant
Hazekamp, Phyllis Wanda Alberts library director
Head, Henry Buchen physician
Healey, Myron Daniel actor
Healy, Sonya Ainslie health facility administrator
Heap, Sylvia Stuber civic worker
†Heard, James Henry lawyer, educator
Heard, Ronald Roy motion picture producer
Hearn, Charles Lee petroleum reservoir engineer
Hearn, Joyce Camp retired state legislator, educator, consultant
†Hearst, George Randolph, Jr. publishing executive, diversified ranching and real estate executive
Heath, Alice Privé women's health nurse, educator
Heath, Charles Dickinson lawyer, telephone company executive
†Heath, Jerome Bruce information systems educator
Heath, Richard Eddy lawyer
Heath, Richard Murray retired hospital administrator
Heath, Roger Charles state senator, writer
†Heatherley, James Lawrence psychologist, educator
Heaton-Marticorena, Jean early childhood educator
Hebert, Christine Anne educator
†Heche, Anne actress
Hechler, David Samuel journalist
Hecht, Harold Arthur orchidologist, chiropractor
Heckart, Eileen actress
Heckel, John Louis (Jack Heckel) aerospace company executive
Hecker, Michael Hanns Louis retired electrical engineer, speech scientist
†Heckerling, Amy film director
Heckley, Teresa JoAnn health facility administrator
Hedahl, Gorden Orlin theatre educator, university dean
Hedien, Colette Johnston lawyer
Hedler, Kenneth Bruce journalist
Hedrick, Basil Calvin state agency administrator, ethnohistorian, educator, museum and multicultural institutions consultant
Heeschen, David Sutphin astronomer, educator
Heestand, Diane Elissa educational technology educator, medical educator
Hefferan, Colien Joan economist
Heffron, Howard A. lawyer
Hegarty, George John university president, English educator
Heider, Jon Vinton retired lawyer, corporate executive
Heidt-Dunwell, Debra Sue vocational education educator
Heilmann, Christian Flemming corporate executive
Heiman, Deborah Reid medical and legal consultant, rehabilitation consultant
Heiman, Grover George, Jr. magazine editor, author
Heimburger, Irvin LeRoy retired surgeon
Heine, Leonard M., Jr. investment executive
Heiney, John Weitzel former utility executive
Heinicke, Peter Hart computer consultant
Heit, Ivan packaging equipment company executive
Heitz, Edward Fred freight traffic consultant
Helander, Bruce Paul artist
Held, Barbara Kay pediatric nurse
Held, Nancy B. perinatal nurse, lactation consultant
Heldrich, Eleanor Maar publisher
†Helfen, Spencer Jon lawyer
Helfgott, Roy B. economist, educator
Heller, Arthur advertising agency executive
Heller, Dorothy artist
Heller, Richard H. writer, editor, book critic, publisher
Heller, Ronald Gary manufacturing company executive, lawyer
Hellerstein, Alvin Kenneth judge
Hellman, Martin Edward retired electrical engineering educator
Hellmers, Norman Donald historic site director
Hellwig, Eileen Marie critical care nurse
Helm, DeWitt Frederick, Jr. consultant, professional association administrator
Helm, Lewis Marshall public affairs executive
Helman, Alfred Blair retired college president, education consultant
Helms, J. Lynn former government agency administrator
Helms Guba, Lisa Marie nursing administrator
Helprin, Mark author
Hemlow, Joyce language and literature educator, author
Hemmer, James Paul lawyer
Hemperly, Rebecca Sue publishing manager
Hempleman, Barbara Florence archivist
Henderson, Charles Brooke research company executive
Henderson, Deirdre Healy interior decorating, leasing company executive
Henderson, Douglas museum director
Henderson, Gary Allen computer scientist, educator, consultant
Henderson, Melford J. epidemiologist, molecular biologist, chemist
Henderson, Scott jazz guitarist
Hendl, Walter conductor, pianist, composer
Hendrick, Arnold J. game designer
Hendricks, Deborah J. medical/surgical and oncological nurse
Hendricks, Gilbert L., III physiologist, researcher
Hendricks, Leonard D. emergency medicine physician, consultant
Hendrickson, William George business executive
Henes, Donna celebration artist, ritualist, writer
Henig, Robin Marantz journalist
Henigson, Ann Pearl freelance writer, songwriter, lyricist
Henkel, Cynthia Leigh elementary education educator
Henne, Andrea Rudnitsky business educator
Henneman, Stephen Charles counselor
Henner, Marilu actress
Hennessey, William Joseph physician
Henricks, Roger Lee retired social services administrator
Henry, Charles Jay library director
Henry, Frances Ann journalist, educator
Henry, Joanne Landers writer
Henry, John Raymond sculptor
Henry, Olga Elaine nursing educator, health care trainer
Henselmeier, Sandra Nadine retired training and development consulting firm executive
Hensley, Mary Susan Mask emergency room nurse
Hensley, Stephen Allan insurance executive
Henson, Ralph Eugene sheriff, retired
Hentic, Yves Frank Mao investment banker, industrial engineer
Hepburn, Valerie Ann state agency administrator
Heppe, Karol Virginia lawyer, educator
Heptinstall, Robert Hodgson physician
Herbel, LeRoy Alec, Jr. telecommunications engineer
†Herbers, Joan Marie biology educator
Herbert, Carol Sellers farming executive, lawyer
Herbert, Mary Katherine Atwell freelance writer
Herbig, Günther conductor
Herbst, Jurgen history and education educator
Herd, Joanne May Beers intravenous therapy nurse, educator
Herdeck, Donald Elmer publishing executive, retired humanities educator
Herguth, Robert John columnist
Hering, Doris Minnie dance critic
Herkner, Bernadette Kay occupational health nurse
Herman, Chester Joseph physician
Herman, David Henry artist, violin restorer and dealer
Herman, David Jay orthodontist
†Herman, Deborah Ann secondary education educator
Herman, George Adam writer
Herman, Hank writer
Herman, Martin Neal neurologist, educator
Herman, William Arthur engineering and physics laboratory administrator
Hernandez, Ramon Robert retired clergyman and librarian
Heronen, Marie F. nursing administrator, medical/surgical nurse
Herrin, Frances E. critical care nurse
Herrmann, Walter retired laboratory administrator
Herron, Edwin Hunter, Jr. energy consultant
Hershberger, Steven Kaye controller
Herson, Arlene Rita producer, journalist, television program host
Herstein, Howard Joseph author
Hertz, Kenneth Theodore health care executive
Herzberg, Thomas artist, illustrator
Herzfeld, Charles Maria physicist
Herzig, Julie Esther designer
Hess, David Willard journalist
Hess, Jeanette Ruth county official
Hess, Sidney Wayne management consultant
Hesse, Christian August mining and underground construction consultant
Hester, Nancy Elizabeth county government official
Hett, Joan Margaret civic administrator
†Hetzmark, Abby M. secondary education educator
Heuer, Margaret B. retired microcomputer laboratory coordinator
Hewes, Laurence Ilsley, III lawyer, management, development, legal consultant
Hewlett-Kierstead, Nancy Carrick psychologist
Heyman, Ira Michael federal agency administrator, museum executive, law educator
Heymann, C(lemens) David author
Heymann, Philip Benjamin law educator, academic director
Heyssel, Robert Morris physician, retired hospital executive
Heyward, Harold financial consultant
Hiatt, Arnold shoe manufacturer, importer, retailer
Hibner, Rae A. insurance company official, nurse
Hickerson, Glenn Lindsey leasing company executive
Hickey, Joseph Michael investment banker
Hickey, Sharon Marie middle school educator
Hickey, Winifred E(spy) former state senator, social worker
†Hickman, Patricia artist, craftswoman
Hickman, Terrie Taylor administrator
Hicks, Dolores Kathleen (De De Hicks) association executive
Hicks, Jack Alan library director
Hidalgo, Miguel transportation company executive
Hieb, Mario Kirk broadcast engineer, inventor, writer, consultant
Hiebel, William Raymond writer, artist, composer, retired English educator
Higby, Edward Julian safety engineer
Higdon, Shirley A. medical/surgical nurse
Higginbotham, John Taylor lawyer
Higgins, Dorothy Marie academic dean
†Higgins, Margaret Christie photographer
Higginson, Jerry Alden, Jr. bank executive
†Higginson, Karen Ann Dorothy librarian
Hightower, Jack English former state supreme court justice, congressman
Higman, Sally Lee company executive
Hijuelos, Oscar novelist
Hilborn, Michael G. lawyer, real estate development executive
†Hilburn, Hedwig Alison electrician
Hilker, Helen-Anne journalist
Hill, Anita Carraway retired state legislator
†Hill, Carol DeChellis writer, novelist
Hill, Harold Nelson, Jr. lawyer
Hill, Raymond Heit management consultant
Hill, Shirley Ann mathematics educator
Hill, Steven John journalist, political reformer
Hill, Virgil professional boxer
Hill, William Frank history educator
Hille, Robert Arthur healthcare executive
Hillerman, Tony writer, former journalism educator
Hilli, Mary Elizabeth rehabilitation nurse, administrator
Hilliard, Sam Bowers geography educator
Hilsman, Roger government educator
Himes, John Harter medical researcher, educator
Himmelfarb, Milton editor, educator
Hinds, Edward Dee insurance and investment professional, financial planner
Hiner, Elizabeth Ellen pharmacist
Hines, Anthony Loring automotive executive
Hines, Gregory Oliver actor, dancer
Hines, JoAnn R. professional association executive and consultant
Hines, Voncile special education educator
Hingle, Pat actor
Hinkley, Everett David, Jr. physicist, business executive
Hinson, Claudia Burns elementary school educator
Hinson, Howard Houston petroleum company executive
Hinson, Sue Ann legal assistant, orthopedic nurse
Hintz, Charles Bradley diversified financial executive
Hirahara, Patti public relations executive
Hires, William Leland psychologist, consultant
Hirose, Teruo Terry surgeon, educator
Hirsch, Bruce Elliot anatomy educator
Hirsch, Horst Eberhard business consultant in metals and semiconductors
†Hirsch, Stuart orthopaedic surgeon
Hirsch, Walter economist, researcher
Hirschberg, Vera Hilda writer

Hirsh, Norman Barry management consultant
Hirst, Heston Stillings former insurance company executive
Hirst, Joanne Flip community health nurse
Hitchborn, James Brian telecommunications executive
Hitchcock, Walter Anson educational consultant, retired educational administrator
Hite, Catharine Leavey orchestra manager
Hixon, Allen Wentworth landscape architect, land planner
Hladky, William George protective service official
Hlywa, Jennifer Lyn secondary educator
Ho, Chih-Ming physicist, educator
Ho, John Wing-Shing biochemistry educator, researcher
Hoaglund, Leora Mae emergency nurse, radiology nurse
Hoart, Gladys Gallagher English language educator
Hoban, Lillian author, illustrator
Hobbs, Avaneda Dorenza publishing company executive, minister, singer
Hobday, John Charles foundation administrator
Hobson, Alesa medical/surgical nurse
Hoch, Frederic Louis medical educator
†Hoch, Scott Mabon professional golfer
Hochheimer, Frank Leo brokerage executive
†Hochreiter, John Allen computer company owner, firefighter
Hochschild, Carroll Shepherd medical equipment and computer company executive, educator
Hock, Morton entertainment advertising executive
Hockeimer, Henry Eric business executive
Hodge, Mary Gretchen Farnam manufacturing company distributor, manager and executive
Hodge, Patricia Marie Cascio nurse practitioner in psychiatry
Hodges, Ann actress, singer, dancer
Hodges, Judith Anne artist, art educator
Hodges, Kenneth Stuart controlller
Hodnicak, Victoria Christine pediatric nurse
Hodsoll, Francis Samuel Monaise government official
Hodson, Nancy Perry real estate agent
Hoeg, Donald Francis chemist, consultant, former research and development executive
Hoeprich, Paul Daniel physician educator
Hoerig, Gerald Lee retired chemical company executive
Hoffer, Roy Daniel forensic electrical engineer
Hoffheimer, Minette Goldsmith community service volunteer
Hoffman, Ira Eliot lawyer
Hoffman, Jerry Irwin dental educator
Hoffman, John D. engineering educator
Hoffman, Judy Greenblatt preschool director
Hoffman, N.M. poet
Hoffman, S. David lawyer, engineer, educator
Hoffmann, Christoph Ludwig lawyer
Hofmann, Paul Bernard healthcare consultant
Hoft, Lynne Ann educator, remedial specialist, educational consultant
Hogan, Neville John mechanical engineering educator, consultant
Hogan, Robert Henry trust company executive, investment strategist
Hogan, Thomas Francis federal judge
Hoggard, Lara Guldmar conductor, educator
Hogstel, Mildred Onelle gerontology nursing consultant
†Hohl, Craig Stephen risk management executive
Hoke, Martin Rossiter former congressman
Hoke, Sheila Wilder retired librarian
Holbrook, Hal (Harold Rowe Holbrook, Jr.) actor
Holden, Mary Gayle Reynolds lawyer
Holden, Rebecca Lynn artist
Holden, William Hoyt, Jr. lawyer
Holder, Richard Gibson retired metal products executive
Holder, Trudy H. accounting director
Holiday, Edith Elizabeth former presidential adviser, cabinet secretary
Holland, Charles Edward medical products corporate executive
Holland, David Thurston former editor
Holland, Henry Norman marketing and management consultant
Holland, James Paul lawyer
Holland, Robert Campbell anatomist, educator
Holland, Robert Stevens advertising executive, graphic designer
Holland, Rosemary Sheridan program evaluation consultant
Hollander, Anne writer
Hollandsworth, Todd Mathew baseball player
Holle, Reginald Henry retired bishop
Holleb, Doris B. urban planner, economist
Holler, Rita Atwell photojournalist
Holliday, Robert Kelvin retired state senator, former newspaper executive
Hollis, Mary Fern Caudill nurse educator, music educator
Holloran, Thomas Edward business educator
Holloway, Hiliary Hamilton retired lawyer, banker
Holloway, Julia Bolton professor emerita, theologian
Holloway, Richard Lawrence marriage-family therapist, college official
Holly, Lauren actress
Holmes, Charles Everett lawyer
Holmes, Doloris Grant (Doloris Schwerner) writer, social worker, theater director
Holmes, Erline Morrison retired educational administrator, consultant
Holmes, Jerry Dell retired organic chemist
Holmes, Keith professional boxer
Holmes, Marjorie Rose author
Holmes, Michael Gene lawyer
Holmes, Robert Wayne service executive, consultant, biological historian
Holoubek, Joe physician
Holt, Marjorie Sewell lawyer, retired congresswoman
Holtkamp, Susan Charlotte elementary education educator
Holtmeier, Robert J. accountant
Holton, Grace Holland accountant
Holton, Robert Page publishing executive
†Holton, William artist
Holtz, Carolyn A. medical/surgical nurse
Holtzmann, Howard Marshall lawyer, judge
Holway, James Michael regional planner, state agency administrator
Holzer, Jenny artist
Holzman, D. Keith record company executive, producer, arts consultant
†Holzman, Sandra artist, educator
Homb, Scott Michael rehabilitation services professional
Homestead, Susan (Susan Freedlender) psychotherapist
Honea, Joyce Clayton critical care nurse
Honeystein, Karl lawyer, entertainment company executive
Honnold, John Otis law educator
Honour, Lynda Charmaine research scientist, educator, psychotherapist
Hood, Luann Sandra special education educator
Hood, William Boyd, Jr. cardiologist, educator
Hook, Vivian Yuan-Wen Ho biochemist, neuroscientist
Hooper, Billy Ernest retired medical association administrator
Hooper, Gerry Don information systems specialist, consultant
Hooper, Josh screen actor, director, producer, writer
Hooper, Marcia Sarita pediatric critical care nurse
†Hooper, Patricia writer
Hooper, Roger Fellowes architect, retired
Hoopes, Townsend Walter business consultant, former government official
Hoops, William James clergyman
Hoover, Davonna Maria primary education educator
Hoover, John Elwood former military officer, consultant, writer
†Hoover, Oliver D. classics scholar
Hope, Thomas Walker marketing professional
Hopkins, Bernard (The Executioner Hopkins) professional boxer
Hopkins, Robert Elliott music educator
Horan, Mary Jo adult education educator, consultant
Horisberger, Don Hans conductor, musician
Horn, Andrew Warren lawyer
Horn, Vickie Lynn medical/surgical nurse, educator
Hornak, Thomas retired electronics company executive
Hornby-Anderson, Sara Ann metallurgical engineer, marketing professional
Horner, Matina Souretis retired college president, corporate executive
Horovitz, Zola Philip pharmaceutical company executive
Horsch, Kathleen Joanne social services administrator, educator, consultant
Horton, Odell federal judge
Horton, Patricia Mathews artist, violist and violinist
Horton, Sir Robert Baynes railroad company executive
Horton, Wilfred Henry mathematics educator
Horwitz, Donald Paul lawyer
Hosea, Julia Hiller communications executive, paralegal
Hosek, James Robert economist
Hoskins, John Howard urologist, educator
Hosman, Sharon Lee music educator
Hostettler, Stephen John naval officer
Houchin, Susan Kay social services administrator
Hough, Janet Gerda Campbell research scientist
Hough, M. Catherine nursing educator
Houghtaling, Pamela Ann technology writer, consultant
Houghton, Katharine actress
Houlihan, Patrick Thomas museum director
House, Kay Seymour editor
House, Stephen Eugene information systems consultant
Houser, Thomas Henri voice educator
Hoving, Raymond Howard consultant
Howard, Charlene community health nurse, administrator
Howard, Clarice Hardee special education educator
Howard, David ballet school administrator
Howard, Dean Denton electrical engineer, researcher, consultant
Howard, Donald Searcy banker
Howard, Edward Francis lawyer
Howard, George, Jr. federal judge
Howard, James Joseph, III utility company executive
Howard, James Webb investment banker, lawyer, engineer
Howard, Joseph Harvey retired librarian
Howard, Michael Eliot historian, educator
Howard, Robert Elliott former federal official, consultant, educator
Howard, Stephen Wrigley telecommunications executive
Howe, John Prentice, III health science center executive, physician
Howe, Wesley Jackson medical supplies company executive
Howell, Christopher Allen technical writer
Howell, Connie Rae critical care nurse
Howell, Donald Lee lawyer
Howell, Embry Martin researcher
Howell, Joel DuBose physician, educator
Howell, Mary Ellen Helms nursing educator, neonatal nurse
Howell, William Robert retail company executive
Howes, Sophia DuBose writer
Hoy, Harold Joseph marketing educator, retail executive, management consultant, author, military officer
Hoyle, William Vinton, Jr. lawyer
Hoyt, Mary Finch author, editor, media consultant, former government official
Hoyt, William Lloyd chief justice
Hsiao, Kwang-Jen genetics and biochemistry educator
Hubbard, Elizabeth actress
Hubbard, Michael James lawyer
Hubbard, Paul Leonard company executive
Hubbard, Stevan Ralph biophysicist, educator
Hubbe, Henry Ernest financial forecaster, funds manager
Hubbell, Elizabeth Wolfe English language educator
Huber, Ann Cervin nurse
Huber, Colleen Adlene artist
Huber, Douglas Crawford pathologist
Huber, Vida S. nursing educator
Hubley, Reginald Allen publisher
Huckaby, Mark Anson paramedic, educator, emergency medical services specialist
†Huckman, Michael Andrew reporter
Hudak, Thomas F(rancis) finance company executive
Hudson, Donald J. retired stock exchange executive
Hudson, Ernie actor
Hudson, Franklin Donald diversified company executive, consultant
Hudson, Jacqueline artist
Hudson, Jerry Charles communications educator
Hudson, Julie Danielle newspaper editor
Huenemann, Rodney Karl state administrator, executive
Huff, Janet House special education educator
†Huffington, Anita sculptor
†Huffington, Arianna writer
Huffman, Carol Koster retired middle school educator
Huffman, James Thomas William oil exploration company executive
Hufschmidt, Maynard Michael resources planning educator
Huggins, Charles Edward obstetrician-gynecologist, educator
Huggins, Robert Brian nonprofit organization official
Hughes, Ann Hightower retired economist, international trade consultant
Hughes, Charles R., Jr. health facility administrator
Hughes, Edward T. retired bishop
Hughes, Michaela Kelly actress, dancer
Hughes, Thomas Parke history educator
Huibregtse, Jayne Lynnor medical surgical nurse
Hukins-Rodrigue, Dana Ann community health nurse
Hull, Louise Knox retired elementary educator, administrator
Hull, Margaret Ruth artist, educator, consultant
†Hume, Beverly Ann English and linguistics educator
Humke, Ramon Lyle utility executive
Hummel, Gene Maywood retired bishop
Humphrey, Arthur Earl university administrator, retired
Humphrey, Doris Davenport publishing company executive, consultant, educator
Humphreys, Robert Russell lawyer, consultant, arbitrator
Hungerford, Edward Arthur humanities professional educator
Huning, Devon Gray actress, dancer, audiologist, photographer, video producer and editor
Hunsberger, Robert Earl mechanical engineer, manufacturing executive
Hunt, Donald Edward planning and engineering executive
Hunt, Donnell Ray retired agricultural engineering educator
Hunt, George Nelson bishop
Hunt, Helen actress
Hunt, Martha sales executive, researcher
Hunt, Ronald Duncan veterinarian, educator, pathologist
Hunt, Ronald Forrest lawyer
Hunt, William Edward neurosurgeon, educator
Hunt-Clerici, Carol Elizabeth academic administrator
Hunte, Beryl Eleanor mathematics educator, consultant
Hunter, Duncan Lee congressman
Hunter, Kim (Janet Cole) actress
Hunter, Mattie Sue (Moore) health facility administrator
Hunter, Rebecca Kathleen accountant, personnel administrator
Hunter, Sarah Ann community health nurse
†Hunter, Tanya Antoinette insurance biller
Hunter-McLean, Elana M. critical care and trauma nurse
Huntington, Irene Elizabeth special education educator
Huntley, Robert Ross physician, educator
Hurd, Byron Thomas newspaper executive, retired
Hurd, Richard Nelson pharmaceutical company executive
Hurd, Suzanne Sheldon federal agency health science director
Hurd, Veronica Terez career soldier
Hurn, Raymond Walter minister, religious order administrator
Huron, Roderick Eugene small business owner
Hurst, Kenneth Thurston publisher
Hurst, Leland Lyle natural gas company executive
Hurtado, Eduardo soccer player
Husain, Taqdir mathematics educator
Huse, Johna Kathleen secondary school educator
†Hussman, Lawrence Eugene writer, retired educator
Huston, Nancy Louise writer, educator
Hutcheon, Linda Ann English language educator
Hutchins, Robert Ayer architectural consultant
Hutchinson, John Woodside applied mechanics educator, consultant
Hutchinson, Joseph Candler retired foreign language educator
Hutchison, Deborah L. critical care nurse
Hutchison, Kay Bailey senator
Huttenback, Robert Arthur academic administrator, educator
Huttner, Richard M. publishing executive
Hutzler, Lisa Ann mental health nurse, adult clinical psychologist
Huyler, Jean Wiley media and interpersonal communications consultant, hypnotherapist
Hyatt-Smith, Ann Rose non-profit organization executive, consultant
Hybl, William Joseph lawyer, foundation executive
Hyde, James A. service executive
Hyman, Seymour C(harles) arbitrator
Iadipaolo, Donna Marie educator, writer, director, artist, performer
Iaquinto, Joseph Francis electrical engineer
Iceman, Sharon Lorraine elementary education educator
Ichaporia, Pallan R. pharmaceutical marketing executive
Ichino, Yoko ballet dancer
Idaszak, Jerome Joseph economic journalist
Ierardi, Eric Joseph school system administrator
Igbineweka, Andrew Osabuohien public administration/political science educator
Ihde, Daniel Carlyle health science executive
Ihlanfeldt, William investment company executive, consultant
Ikeda, Tsuguo (Ike Ikeda) social services center administrator, consultant
Iklé, Richard Adolph lawyer
†Imhof, Susan Anne Poet
Imlah, MaryPat sales, advertising and marketing executive
Impellizeri, Monica pension fund administrator, consultant
Imtiaz, Kauser Syed aerospace engineer
Inbody, Dale Dewayne farmer
Infante-Ogbac, Daisy Inocentes sales and real estate executive, marketing executive
Ingersoll, Paul Mills banker
Ingham, Charles Andrew literature and English language educator
Ingle, James Chesney, Jr. geology educator
Inglett, Betty Lee retired media services administrator
Inglis, James telecommunications company executive
Ingraham, Jeanne pediatric nurse practitioner
Inlow, Rush Osborne chemist
Innerst, Carol Jean journalist
Intihar-Hogue, Cynthia Ann nursing administrator
Inui, Thomas Spencer physician, educator
Irey, Charlotte York dance educator
Irizarry, Michael Carl neurologist, neuroscientist, educator
Irvine, John Alexander lawyer
Irvine, William Burriss management consultant
Irving, George Steven actor
Irwin, Anna Mae English language educator
Irwin, Byron management executive
†Irwin, Kenny professional race car driver
Irwin, Lamour Mitch real estate developer
Irwin, Linda Belmore marketing consultant
Irwin, Peter John orthopaedic surgeon
Isaac, Steven Richard communications executive
†Isaacs, Anne Elizabeth writer
Isaacs, Susan novelist, screenwriter
Isaacson, Edith L. civic leader
Isbell, Harold M(ax) writer, investor
Ismach, Arnold Harvey retired journalism educator
Isom, Harriet Winsar ambassador
Isom, Lloyd Warren management consultant
Israel, Robert Allan statistician
†Issel, Daniel Paul sports team executive, former professional basketball coach
†Ita, John Bradley history educator
Ivry, Alfred Lyon history of, Jewish and Islamic philosophy educator
Izenstark, Joseph Louis radiologist, physician, educator
Jablonski, Robert Leo architect
Jabs, Carolyn R. writer
Jackman, Jay M. psychiatrist
Jackson, Bart educator, game developer
Jackson, Carmault Benjamin, Jr. physician
Jackson, Charles Ian writer, consultant
Jackson, Elmer Joseph lawyer, oil and gas company executive
Jackson, Erin Denise speech therapist
†Jackson, Jeanne Pellegren apparel executive
Jackson, Lambert Blunt academic administrator
Jackson, M. Dorothy medical surgical nurse, researcher
†Jackson, Michelle A. artist
Jackson, Miles Merrill retired university dean
Jackson, Nagle stage director, playwright
Jackson, Robbi Jo non-hazardous agricultural products company executive, lawyer
Jackson, Robert William utility company executive, retired
Jackson, Rudolph Ellsworth pediatrician, educator
Jackson, Samuel L. actor
Jackson, Victor Louis retired naturalist
Jacob, Rosamond Tryon librarian
Jacob, Ted Manas biomedical and forensic photographer
Jacobi, Veronica Ann community health nurse, educator
Jacobowitz, Ellen Sue museum and temple curator, administrator
Jacobs, Arthur Dietrich educator, researcher, health services executive
Jacobs, Delores Hamm secondary education educator
Jacobs, Eleanor art consultant, retired art administrator
Jacobs, Ferne Kent artist
Jacobs, Hyde Spencer soil chemistry educator
Jacobs, Linda Rotroff elementary school educator
Jacobs, Sister Margaret Mary nurse
Jacobs, William Jay historian, writer
Jacobsen, Egill Lars dentist, educator
Jacobson, James Bassett insurance executive
Jacobson, Richard Lee lawyer, educator
Jacques, Andre Charles financial consultant
Jaenike, William F. retired investment company executive
†Jaffee, Annette Williams novelist
Jakubauskas, Edward Benedict college president
Jallins, Richard David lawyer
James, Harold L(loyd) geologist
James, Michael Andrew lawyer
James, Nadine H. psychiatric nurse, occupational health and home care nurse, nursing administrator, educator
James, Tracey Faye screenwriter
James, William W. banker
Jamieson, Michael Lawrence lawyer
Jamison, John Callison business educator, investment banker
Jan, Yuh Nung biochemistry and physiology educator
Janis, Conrad actor, jazz musician, art dealer, film producer, director
Janis, Ronald H. lawyer
Janko, May graphic artist
Jannuzi, F. Tomasson economics educator
Janowitz, Henry David gastroenterologist, researcher, medical educator
Jansen, Angela Bing artist, educator
†Janzen, Jean Wiebe poet, educator
†Jaren, Courtney Bates historian, lawyer, consultant
Jarmie, Nelson physicist, consultant
Jarmusch, Jim director, actor
Jarrett, Keith pianist, composer
Jarvis, Barbara Ann conference planner, conference manager
Jarvis, William Esmond retired Canadian government official
Jaskula, Janet pediatrics nurse, educator
Jaszarowski, Kelly Ann nurse, enterostomal therapy specialist
Jaw, Andrew Chung-Shiang software analyst
Jay, Norma Joyce artist
Jayne, Cynthia Elizabeth psychologist
Jefferies, William McKendree internist, educator
Jeffers, Ida Pearle management consultant, volunteer
Jenkins, Anthony Curtis sales executive
Jenkins, Billie Beasley film company executive
Jenkins, Brenda Gwenetta early childhood/special education specialist
Jenkins, Darrell Lee librarian
Jenkins, James William osteopath, medical consultant
†Jenkins, Marie P. art educator
Jenkins, Royal Gregory manufacturing executivve
Jenkins, William E. business executive
Jenks, Tom writer
Jennings, Carol marketing executive
Jennings, Joseph Ashby banker
†Jennings, La Vinia Delois educator
Jennings, Reba Maxine critical care nurse
Jensen, Anne Turner automobile service company executive
†Jensen, Edward Charles forestry educator
Jensen, Erik Hugo pharmaceutical quality control consultant
Jensen, Jack Michael publishing executive
Jensen, Marvin Eli retired agricultural engineer

Jensen, Robert Travis *physician, educator, researcher*
Jensen, Robert Trygve *lawyer*
Jepson, Robert Scott, Jr. *international investment banking specialist*
Jerace, Charlotte Louise *writer, consultant*
Jernigan, Madeleine Annetta *medical/surgical nurse*
Jerrytone, Samuel Joseph *trade school executive*
†Jett, Terri Renee *educator*
Jew, Henry *pharmacist*
Jiang, Bai-Chuan *optical educator*
Jiler, William Laurence *publisher*
Jimenez, Luis Alfonso, Jr. *sculptor*
†Jiménez, Onilda A. *Spanish educator*
Jimmink, Glenda Lee *retired elementary school educator*
Jinks, Robert Larry *retired newspaper publisher*
Jirousek, Charles Edward *small business owner*
Jobson, Kathleen Miller *nurse midwife*
Jochner, Michele Melina *lawyer*
Jochum, Lester H. *dentist*
Joelson, Mark Rene *lawyer*
Johansen, Karen Lee *retired sales executive*
John, Gerald Warren *hospital pharmacist, educator*
†John, Judith A. *literature educator*
John, Mertis, Jr. *record company executive*
John, Ralph Candler *retired college president, educator*
Johnson, Albert Wesley *consultant on governance*
Johnson, Alice Elaine *retired academic administrator*
Johnson, Arnold Ivan *civil engineer*
Johnson, Beth Ann *pediatric nurse, gerontology nurse*
Johnson, Bruce Alan *financial company executive*
Johnson, Byron Jerald *retired state supreme court judge*
Johnson, Claudia Anderson *psychologist*
Johnson, Cyrus Edwin *grain farmer, former food products executive*
Johnson, Deborah Crosland Wright *mathematics educator*
Johnson, Don Robert *religious organization leader, administrator*
Johnson, E. Scott *lawyer*
Johnson, Eydith G. Ivory *poet*
Johnson, Glendon E. *retired insurance company executive*
Johnson, Gordon Gilbert *religion educator, minister*
†Johnson, Henry Breavoid *occupational therapist, career officer*
Johnson, Irving Stanley *pharmaceutical company executive, scientist*
Johnson, Jennie *chaplain, social worker*
Johnson, John Prescott *philosophy educator*
†Johnson, Jone E. *clergy member*
Johnson, Karla Ann *county official*
Johnson, Katherine Holthaus *health care marketing professional*
Johnson, Kay Durbahn *real estate manager, consultant*
Johnson, Kenneth Lance *baseball player*
Johnson, Kevin Rogers *systems analyst, journalist*
Johnson, Kirsten Denise *elementary education educator*
Johnson, LaVerne St. Clair *retired elementary school educator*
Johnson, Laymon, Jr. *management analyst*
Johnson, Leonard Hjalma *lawyer*
Johnson, Leonard Morris *pediatric surgeon*
†Johnson, Leonard R. *industrial engineer, educator*
Johnson, Malcolm Clinton, Jr. *publishing consultant*
Johnson, Marlene M. *nonprofit executive*
Johnson, Mary Elizabeth Susan *consulting engineer*
Johnson, Mary Murphy *social services administrator, writer*
Johnson, Michael Warren *international relations specialist*
Johnson, Naomi Bowers *nurse*
Johnson, Olin Chester *education educator*
Johnson, Patricia Mary *publisher*
†Johnson, Paul Eugene *telecommunications engineer, consultant*
Johnson, Philip *investment banking executive*
Johnson, Ralph Raymond *ambassador, federal agency administrator*
Johnson, Richard Turner *television producer, consultant*
Johnson, Robert Walter *marine engineer, priest*
Johnson, Rodney Dale *retired law enforcement officer, photographer*
Johnson, Rogers Bruce *retired chemical company executive*
Johnson, Scott Loren *sales executive*
Johnson, Silas R., Jr. *air force officer*
Johnson, Stewart Willard *civil engineer*
Johnson, Sylvia Sue *university administrator, educator*
Johnson, Theodore *retired physician*
Johnson, Vernon Eugene *history educator, educational administrator*
Johnson, Warren Donald *retired pharmaceutical executive, former air force officer*
Johnson, William Ray *insurance company executive*
Johnson-Brown, Hazel Winfred *nurse, retired army officer*
Johnston, F. Bruce, Jr. *educator*
Johnston, James Monroe, III *air force officer*
Johnston, William Medford *artist, retired educator*
Johnstone, John William, Jr. *retired chemical company executive*
Johnstone, Stowell *former state agency administrator*
Joiner, Charles Wycliffe *judge*
Jolly, Charles Nelson *lawyer, pharmaceutical company executive*
Jones, Anita Katherine *computer scientist, educator*
Jones, Billy Ernest *dermatology educator*
Jones, Brenda K. *health facility administrator*
Jones, Carleton Shaw *information systems company executive, lawyer*
†Jones, Catherine Elaine *educational administrator*
Jones, Christine Massey *retired furniture company executive*
Jones, Claire Burtchaell *artist, teacher, writer*
Jones, Clifford Aaron, Sr. *lawyer, international businessman*
Jones, Cynthia Rector *artist*
Jones, Dale Cherner *marketing executive, consultant*
Jones, Daniel Hamilton *optometrist*
Jones, David Charles *retired air force officer, former chairman Joint Chiefs of Staff*
Jones, Dean Carroll *actor*
Jones, Deanna Elaine *mathematics educator*
Jones, Donna Lee Noble *emergency nurse*
Jones, Dorothy Joanne *social services professional*
Jones, Elizabeth Selle *minister*
Jones, Jack Dellis *oil company executive*
Jones, Joan Megan *anthropologist*
Jones, Kacy Douglas *accountant*
Jones, Keith Alden *lawyer*
Jones, Lawrence Neale *university dean, minister*
Jones, Leonade Diane *media publishing company executive*
Jones, Norman Thomas *retired agricultural products company executive*
Jones, Peter d'Alroy *historian, writer, retired educator*
Jones, Phyllis Gene *judge*
Jones, Richard Melvin *bank executive, former retail executive*
†Jones, Robert A. *equity finance company executive*
Jones, Roy *professional boxer*
Jones, Shirley *actress, singer*
†Jones, Taylor Burnett *cartoonist*
Jones, Ted C(ooke) *distance learning educator*
Jones, Therese M. *special education educator*
Jones, Thornton Keith *research chemist*
Jones, Tommy Lee *actor*
Jones, Walton Linton *internist, former government official*
Jones, William Augustus, Jr. *retired bishop*
Jordan, Carrie Grayson *writer, poet, drama designer*
Jordan, Fred *publishing company executive*
Jordan, Howard Emerson *retired engineering executive, consultant*
Jordan, Jeffrey Guy *marketing and marketing research consultant*
Jordan, Joseph Louis *education educator, government official*
Jordan, Michael Jeffrey *retired professional basketball player, retired baseball player*
Jordan, Thomas Fredrick *physics educator*
Jordan, William Bryan, Jr. *art historian*
†Jordania, Vakhtang *conductor, educator*
Jorden, William John *writer, retired diplomat*
Jorgensen, Erik Holger *lawyer*
†Joseph, Jofi John *policy analyst*
Joseph, Shirley Troyan *retired executive*
Josephson, Kenneth Bradley *artist, retired educator*
Joslin, David Bruce *bishop*
Joustra, Barbara Lynn *nurse*
†Joyce, Stephen Thomas *occupational and preventive medicine physician*
Joyce, William Robert *textile machinery company executive*
Judell, Cynthia Kolburne *craft company executive*
Judelson, David N. *company executive*
Judge, Rosemary Ann *oil company executive*
Juenemann, Sister Jean *hospital executive*
Jumper, John Phillip *career officer*
June, Roy Ethiel *lawyer*
Jungbluth, Kirk E. *real estate appraiser, mortgage banking executive*
Jurasek, Randall John *educational consultant*
Juredine, David Graydon *insurance company executive*
Just, Ward Swift *author*
Juviler, Peter Henry *political scientist, educator*
Kabat, Linda Georgette *civic leader*
Kachuba, John Barrie *writer, editor*
Kachur, Betty Rae *elementary education educator*
Kacprowicz, Donna Marie (Leonetti) *staff nurse*
Kacur, Lois Marie *obstetric and pediatric nurse*
Kadota, Takashi Theodore *mathematician, electrical engineer*
Kagan, Constance Henderson *philosopher, educator, consultant*
Kagan, Julia Lee *magazine editor*
Kahan, Rochelle Liebling *lawyer, concert pianist*
Kahana, Eva Frost *sociology educator*
Kahl, David Burr *artist*
†Kahlenberg, Susan Gale *communications educator*
Kahn, Charles Howard *architect, educator*
Kahn, Herta Hess (Mrs. Howard Kahn) *retired stockbroker*
Kahn, James Steven *retired museum director*
Kahn, Pauline Gitman *volunteer*
Kahn, Susan Beth *artist*
Kain, Rikki Floyd *investment company executive*
Kalick, Laura Joy *lawyer, exempt organization tax speciality*
Kalin, D(orothy) Jean *artist, educator*
Kalina, Richard *artist*
Kalkwarf, Leonard V. *minister*
Kamen, Martin David *physical biochemist*
Kamenar, Elizabeth *neurologist, neuropathologist*
†Kamin, Blair Douglass *newspaper critic*
Kaminsky, Phyllis *international consulting executive*
Kampe, Carolyn Jean *elementary art and special education educator*
Kampf, Marilyn Jeanne *medical analyst*
Kampmeier, Curt *management consultant*
Kamstra, Bettye Maurice *secondary education educator*
†Kamuf, Rachael L. *reporter*
Kander, John Harold *composer*
Kane, Loana *foreign language educator*
Kane, Patricia Lanegran *language professional, educator*
Kane, Ryan Thomas *corporate executive*
Kanin, Fay *screenwriter*
Kannenstine, Margaret Lampe *artist*
Kanter, Jerome Jacob *insurance company executive*
†Kanter, Lynn *writer*
†Kantrowitz, Melanie Kaye *writer*
Kantrowitz, Susan Lee *lawyer*
Kapcsandy, Louis Endre *building construction and manufacturing executive, chemical engineering consultant*
Kapitan, Mary L. *retired nursing administrator, educator*
Kaplan, Candia Post *psychologist*
Kaplan, Erica Lynn *typing and word processing service company executive, pianist*
Kaplan, Helene Lois *lawyer*
Kaplan, Leonard Eugene *accountant*
Kaplan, Ozer Benjamin *environmental health specialist, consultant*
Kaplan, Richard James *producer, director, writer, educator, consultant*
Kaplan, Robert B. *linguistics educator, consultant, researcher*
Kaplan, Steven F. *business management executive*
Kapnick, Richard Bradshaw *lawyer*
Kapor, Mitchell David *venture capitalist*
Kappner, Augusta Souza *academic administrator*
Kaprielian, Walter *advertising executive*
Karakey, Sherry JoAnne *financial and real estate investment company executive, interior designer*
Karalekas, Anne *media executive*
Karalis, John Peter *computer company executive, lawyer*
Karam, Naji E. *cardiologist*
Karawina, Erica *artist, stained glass designer*
Karben, Shelley Valerie *elementary and special education school educator*
Karber, Johnnie Faye *elementary education educator*
Karczmar, Mieczyslaw *economist*
Kares, Robin Lee *English educator*
†Karl, George *professional basketball coach*
Karnilova, Maria *actress*
Karnofsky, Mollyne *artist, poet, art educator*
Karol, Michael Alan *editor*
Karp, David *communications executive, writer*
Karp, Rosanne *medical/surgical nurse*
Karpilow, Craig *physician*
Karpinos, Robert Douglas *anesthesiologist*
Karr, Gerald Lee *agricultural economist, state senator*
Karrh, Bruce Wakefield *retired industrial company executive*
Karson, Emile *international business executive*
Karson, Samuel *psychologist, educator*
†Karwacki, Jerome John *physician*
Karwacki, Robert Lee *judge*
Kasberger-Mahoney, Elvera A. *educational administrator*
Kaschak, Virginia Ruth *elementary education educator*
Kaser, David *retired librarian, educator, consultant*
Kash, Wyatt Keith *publishing executive*
Kashani, Javad Hassan-Nejad *physician*
Kaskey, Baylen *communications corporate executive*
Kaskowitz, Edwin *social services executive*
Kaslow, Florence Whiteman *psychologist, educator*
†Kasper, Victor, Jr. *economics educator*
Kaspin, Jeffrey Marc *floor covering professional*
Kaspin, Susan Jane *child care specialist*
Kass, Jerome Allan *writer*
Kassulke, Natasha Marie *reporter*
Kaster, Laura A. *lawyer*
Kastner, Marc Aaron *physics educator*
Kastor, Frank Sullivan *English language educator*
Katayama, Toshihiro *artist, educator*
Kates, Robert William *geographer, educator, independent scholar*
Kathan, Joyce C. *social worker, administrator*
Kather, Gerhard *retired air force base administrator*
Katz, Anne Harris *biologist, educator, writer, aviator*
Katz, Martin Howard *lawyer*
Katz, Phyllis Alberts *developmental research psychologist*
Katz, Richard Jon *marketing and advertising company executive*
Katz, Robert David *architecture educator*
Katz, Roberta R. *lawyer*
Katz, Sanford Noah *lawyer, educator*
Katz, William Loren *author*
Katzenbach, John Strong Miner *author*
Katznelson, Ira Isaac *social sciences educator, writer*
Kauffman, Dagmar Elisabeth *writer, researcher*
Kauffman, Kaethe Coventon *art educator, artist, author*
Kaufman, Charles David *controller*
Kaufman, Paula T. *librarian*
Kaufman, Raymond L. *energy company executive*
Kaufmann, Caroline Elizabeth *surgical technologist, critical care nurse*
Kauger, Yvonne *state supreme court chief justice*
Kavalek, Lubomir *chess expert*
Kawano, James Conrad *investment analyst*
Kay, Patricia Kremer *business owner*
Kayfetz, Victor Joel *writer, editor, translator*
Kaylan, Howard Lawrence *musical entertainer, composer*
Kazan, Elia *theatrical, motion picture director and producer, author*
Kazmarek, Linda Adams *secondary education educator*
Keach, Stacy, Sr. *producer, director*
Keala, Francis Ahloy *security executive*
Kearns, James Joseph *artist*
Keaton, Michael *actor, comedian*
Kebblish, John Basil *retired coal company executive, consultant*
Keegan, Kenneth Donald *financial consultant, retired oil company executive*
Keehner, Michael Arthur Miller *investment bank executive*
Keeler, William Henry *cardinal*
Keena, J. Bradley *political commentator*
†Keenan, Joseph Michael *military officer*
Keene-Burgess, Ruth Frances *army official*
Keeter, Lynn Carpenter *English educator*
Keffer, Charles Joseph *consultant*
Keil, M. David *retired international association executive*
Keim, Betty Adele T. *mayor*
Keiser, Carol Jane *artist*
Keister, Jean Clare *lawyer*
Keith, Brian Thomas *automobile executive*
Keith, Carol Jean *writer, regional historian*
Keller, Jami Ann *special education educator*
Keller, Paul *advertising agency executive*
Kellerman, Faye Marder *novelist, dentist*
Kellerman, Jonathan Seth *pediatric psychologist, writer*
Kelley, A. Benjamin *author, consultant*
Kelley, Mary Elizabeth (LaGrone) *computer specialist*
Kelley, Patricia Colleen *educator, researcher*
Kelley, Wayne Plumbley, Jr. *retired federal official*
Kellgren, George Lars *manufacturing company executive*
Kellner, Irwin L. *economist*
Kelly, Anthony Odrian *flooring manufacturing company executive*
Kelly, Aurel Maxey *retired judge*
Kelly, Douglas Elliott *retired biomedical researcher, association administrator*
Kelly, Ellsworth *painter, sculptor*
Kelly, Michael Joseph, Jr. *publishing executive*
Kelly, Nancy Folden *arts administrator*
Kelso, Frank Benton, II *naval officer*
Kelso, John Hodgson *former government official*
Kelts, David William *elementary education educator*
†Kemmett, William Joseph *poet, educator*
Kemper, John Dustin *mechanical engineering educator*
Kempf, Cecil Joseph *naval officer*
Kempner, Maximilian Walter *law school dean, lawyer*
Kendall, Christopher (Christopher Wolff) *conductor, lutenist, educator, university official*
Kendall, Harry Ovid *internist*
Kendig, William Lamar *retired government official, accountant*
Kendrick, Budd Leroy *psychologist*
Kendrick, Joseph Trotwood *former foreign service officer, writer, consultant*
Kendzior, Robert Joseph *marketing executive*
†Kennedy, Charles *retired medical educator*
Kennedy, Debra Joyce *marketing professional*
Kennedy, Earle James *retired steel manufacturing company executive*
Kennedy, Harvey Edward *science information publishing executive*
Kennedy, Jerrie Ann Preston *public relations executive*
Kennedy, John Fitzgerald, Jr. *lawyer, magazine editor*
Kennedy, Kathleen *film producer*
Kennedy, Marla Catherine *psychologist*
Kennedy, Orin *film company executive*
Kennedy, Thomas J. *lawyer*
Kennedy, Thomas Patrick *financial executive*
Kennel, Charles Frederick *physics educator, government official*
Kenny, Patrick Edward *publishing executive*
Kent, Betty Dickinson *horsemanship educator*
Kent, E(verett) Allen *performing arts administrator*
Kent, Howard Lees *obstetrician, gynecologist*
Kenyon, Daphne Anne *economics educator*
Kepes, Gyorgy *author, painter, photographer, educator*
Kepner, Jane Ellen *psychotherapist, educator, minister*
Kerber, Ronald Lee *industrial corporation executive*
Kerbs, Wayne Allan *transportation executive*
Kerins, Francis Joseph *college president*
Kern, Charles William *retired university official, chemistry educator*
Kern, Donald Michael *internist*
Kern, Irving John *retired food company executive*
Kern, Jerome H. *lawyer*
Kernan, Joseph E. *state official*
Kernodle, Robert Gary *dance and exercise ecucator*
Kerr, Deborah Jane *actress*
Kerr, Donald MacLean, Jr. *physicist*
Kerr, Forrest David *actor, writer, producer*
Kerrigan, Mabel Baisley *retired peri-operative nurse, educator*
Kerstetter, Michael James *retired manufacturing company executive*
Kersting, Edwin Joseph *retired university dean*
Kerwin, Larkin *retired physics educator*
Kerwin, Walter Thomas, Jr. *career officer, consultant*
Kesend, Michael *publishing executive*
Kessler, Pete William *dentist*
Kessler, Stephen James *writer, editor*
Kessler-Harris, Alice *historian, educator*
Ketch, Tina *writer*
Ketron, Carrie Sue *secondary school educator*
Kettel, Edward Joseph *oil company executive, retired*
Kettelkamp, Donald Benjamin *retired surgeon and educator*
Key, Dana Lynn *English education and biology educator*
Key, Ted *cartoonist*
Keyes, Joan Ross Rafter *education educator, author*
Keyes, Margaret Naumann *home economics educator*
Keyes, Saundra Elise *newspaper editor*
Keyser, Charles Lovett, Jr. *bishop*
Kezer, Pauline Ryder *state government executive*
Kezlarian, Nancy Kay *social services administrator, family counselor*
Khachadurian, Avedis *physician*
Khalid, Samy *writer*
Khan, Arfa *radiologist, educator*
†Khinoy, Andrew *journalist*
†Khoury, Jehad *research scientist*
Kiang, Barbara Norris *scientific research assistant*
†Kidd, Feda Sutton *elementary education educator*
Kidd, James Lambert *retired minister*
Kidd, Robert Hugh *financial executive, accountant*
Kidde, Geoffrey Carter *composer, flutist, music educator*
Kidder, (John) Tracy *writer*
Kiefer, Helen Chilton *neurologist, psychiatrist*
Kiefer, Robert Harry *real estate broker*
Kieffer, Joyce Loretta *health science facility administrator, educator*
Kiehlbauch, Sheryl Lynn *elementary education educator*
Kiel, Brenda Kay *medical/surgical nurse*
Kielt, Raymond John *naval officer, dentist*
Kile, Carol Ann *lawyer*
Killeen, Michael John *lawyer*
Killgore, Le *journalist, political columnist*
Kilpatrick, James Jackson, Jr. *columnist, author*
Kimbriel-Eguia, Susan *engineering planner*
Kimbrough, Lorelei *elementary education educator*
Kimes, Beverly Rae *editor, writer*
Kincaid, Jamaica *writer*
Kindness, Thomas Norman *former congressman, lawyer, consultant*
King, Algin Braddy *marketing educator*
King, Charles Benjamin *minister*
King, Charolette Elaine *retired career officer*
King, Chris Allen *military officer*
King, Edward William *retired transportation executive*
King, (Lenard) Glen *broadcasting educator, composer*
King, John Quill Taylor *science center administrator, college administrator emeritus*
King, Joy Rainey *poet, retired medical secretary*
†King, Karen Kay *petroleum company executive*
King, Larry L. *playwright, actor*
King, Philip Gordon *public relations consultant*
King, Rosalyn Mercita *social science researcher*
King, Rosemary Ann *air force officer*
King, Rosemary Kranyak *pediatrics nurse*
King, Susan Bennett *retired glass company executive*
King, William Collins *oil company executive*
King-Garner, Miria *elementary education educator*
Kingsbery, Walton Waits, Jr. *retired accounting firm executive*
Kinnear, Greg *actor, producer*
Kinslow, Margie Ann *volunteer worker*
Kinzer, James Raymond *retired pipeline company executive*
†Kinzer, Joseph W. *military officer*
Kinzie, Daniel Joseph *biomedical engineer*
Kinzley, Colleen Elizabeth *zoological park curator*
Kipnis, Nahum S. *science educator*
Kipniss, Robert *artist*
Kippur, Merrie Margolin *lawyer*
†Kirby, Carol Bingham *Spanish language educator*
Kirby, Priscilla Crosby *dietitian*
Kirchner, Lisa Beth *vocalist, actress*
Kirk, Colleen Jean *retired conductor, educator*
†Kirk, Rea Helene (Rea Helene Glazer) *special education educator*
Kirkby, Maurice Anthony *oil company executive*
Kirkland, Geoffrey Alan *motion picture production designer*

Lee, Ginger discharge planning supervisor, administrator
Lee, Harrison Hon naval architecture librarian, consultant
Lee, J. Daniel, Jr. retired insurance company executive
Lee, James Matthew Canadian politician
†Lee, James Wade humanities educator, writer, actor
Lee, Jeanne Kit Yew administrative officer
Lee, Joseph William sales executive
Lee, Marianna retired editor
Lee, Michele actress
Lee, Nancy T. healthcare administrator, educator
Lee, Peter Bernard marketing executive
Lee, Sarah Tomerlin design executive
Lee, Susan Ann social worker, therapist
Lee, W. Bruce management consultant
Lee, Warren Weilun marketing analyst
Lee, William Franklin, III association administrator, musician, composer
Leeds, Nancy Brecker sculptor, lyricist
†Leeves, Jane actress
Leff, Joseph Norman yarn manufacturing company executive
Lefferts, George producer, writer, director
Legal, Kenneth Joseph control systems engineer
Légaré, Henri Francis archbishop
Leger, Richard Roubine public relations executive, writer
†Legere, Kathy Ann artist
Legere, Phoebe Hemenway composer, artist
Leggett, Roberta Jean (Bobbi Leggett) social services administrator
Legington, Gloria R. middle school educator
Lehman, John F., Jr. industrialist
Lehman, Todd Wilson artist
Lehner-Quam, Alison Lynn library administrator
Lehrman, Nat magazine editor
Lehtinen, Merja Helen Kokkonen journalist, researcher, publisher
Leiber, Jerry songwriter
Leiber, Judith Maria designer, manufacturer
Leibowitz, Ann Galperin lawyer
Leigh, Vincenta M. health administrator
Leihgeber, Katherine L. retired nursing administrator
Leirer, Jennifer Lea journalist, beauty consultant
Leis, Henry Patrick, Jr. surgeon, educator
Leistner, Mary Edna retired secondary education educator
Leith, Karen Pezza psychologist, educator
†Leiva, Nicolas artist
†Leivy, David Mayer neurosurgeon
Lekan, Briana Marker photographer
Leland, David J. political association executive
Lembark, Connie Wertheimer art consultant
Le Mehaute, Bernard Jean marine physics educator
LeMense, Fay Ann special education educator
Lemke, James Underwood physicist
Lemon, Sharon Kay rehabilitation nurse
LeMonnier, Daniel Brian small business owner, entertainer
Lenahan, Walter Clair retired foreign service officer
Lenard, Lisa H. writer, educator
Lenhart, Gary Alan poet
Lennon, Joseph Luke college official, priest
Lennox, Donald D(uane) automotive and housing components company executive
Lentz, Sandra M. family nurse practitioner
León, Tania Justina composer, music director, pianist
Leonard, Guy Meyers, Jr. international holding company executive
Leonetti, Evangeline Phillips retired nursing educator
Leoni, Tea (Elizabeth Tea Pantleoni) actress
Lepage, Robert actor, director, playwright
Lepkowski, Wil (Wilbert Charles Lepkowski) journalist
L'Eplattenier, Nora Sweeny Hickey nursing educator
Lerit, Delia Tumulak school nurse
†Lerner, Ilya artist
Lerner, Vladimir Semion computer scientist, educator
Lerner-Lam, Eva I-Hwa transportation executive
LeRoy, G. Palmer art dealer
Lesher, John Lee, Jr. consulting services company executive
Lesko, Harry Joseph transportation company executive
Leslie, Cynthia mental health nurse
Leslie, Gerrie Allen immunologist
†Lessy, Harriet Gail columnist
Lester, Robin Dale educator, author, former headmaster
Lester, Virginia Laudano education administrator
Letcher, Naomi Jewell quality engineer, educator, counselor
Leva, James Robert retired electric utility company executive
LeVay, Simon neuroscientist, writer, educator
Leveille, Gilbert Antonio food products executive
Levenson, Marc David optics and lasers specialist, scientist, editor
Leventhal, Ellen Iris portfolio manager, financial services executive
Leventhal, Nathan performing arts executive, lawyer
†Levering, Judy A. sports association executive
Levi, Barbara Goss physicist, editor
Levi, Josef Alan artist
Levi, Maurice David economics educator
Levien, David Harold surgeon
Levin, Gerald Henry English educator
†Levin, Judith Maria consultant to non-profit organizations
Levin, Morton D(avid) artist, printmaker, educator
Levin, Richard Charles academic administrator, economist
†Levin, Robert Barry motion picture company executive
Levin, William Edward lawyer
Levine, Alan J. entertainment company executive
Levine, Benjamin lawyer
Levine, David M. newspaper editor
Levine, Ellen (Sunni) Silverberg pediatric nurse practitioner
Levine, Gerald Richard investment stockbroker, mortgage banker
Levine, Israel E. writer
Levine, Jack artist
Levine, Maita Faye mathematics educator
Levine, Michael Joseph economic development executive
Levinson, Herbert Sherman civil and transportation engineer
Levinson, Kenneth Lee lawyer
Levinson, Stephen Eliot engineering educator, electrical engineer
Levin-Wixman, Irene Staub librarian
Levitsky, Melvyn ambassador
Levitt, Irene Hansen sales associate, writer, artist
Levy, Andrew Alan literature educator, curator, editor
Levy, David lawyer, insurance company executive
Levy, Debra S. humanities educator
Levy, Leah Garrigan federal official
Levy, Leslie Ann business researcher, consultant, professor, software producer
Levy, Louis Edward retired accounting firm executive
Lewin, K(atherine) Tamar reporter
Lewis, Alexander, Jr. oil company executive
Lewis, Arthur Dee corporation executive
Lewis, Arthur Orcutt, Jr. retired English language educator, dean
†Lewis, Carla S. retired psychology educator
Lewis, Ceylon Smith, Jr. physician, educator
Lewis, Charles Leonard psychologist
Lewis, Claudia Jean marketing professional
Lewis, Dale Kenton retired lawyer, mediator
Lewis, Dennis Carroll writer, publisher, educator
Lewis, Emanuel Raymond historian, psychologist, retired librarian
Lewis, Floyd Wallace former electric utility executive
Lewis, Gordon Carter auditor
Lewis, Jacquelyn Rochelle nursing consultant
Lewis, Josephine Victoria retired marketing executive
Lewis, L(inda) Maureen publishing executive
Lewis, Lois A. health services administrator
Lewis, Martin Edward shipping company executive, foreign government concessionary
Lewis, Martin R. paper company executive, consultant
Lewis, Robert Alan physiologist, environmental toxicologist
Lewis, Robert Turner retired psychologist
Lewis, Russell Carl, Jr. family nurse practitioner
Lewis, Samuel Winfield retired government official, former ambassador
Lewis Mill, Barbara Jean school psychologist, educator
Lewitzky, Bella choreographer
Leybourn, Carol musician, educator
Leys, Sue Ellen Rohrer designer, costume
Li, Tingye electrical engineer
Liacos, Paul Julian retired state supreme judicial court chief justice
Libava, Jerry Ronald franchise consultant
†Libensky, Stanislav art educator
Liberman, Gail Jeanne editor
Libertiny, Thomas Gabor mechanical engineer, administrator
Lichtenberg, Byron K. futurist, manufacturing executive, space flight consultant, pilot
Lichtenstein, Sarah Carol lawyer
†Lichterman, Paul R. educator
Liddell, Jane Hawley Hawkes civic worker
Lie, Yu-Chun Donald electrical engineer
Liebeler, Susan Wittenberg lawyer
Lieberman, Anne Marie financial executive, retired
Lieberman, Louis (Karl Lieberman) artist
Liebler, Arthur C. automotive executive
Lief, Thomas Parrish sociologist, educator
Liffers, William Albert retired chemical company executive
Liftin, John Matthew lawyer
Light, Arthur Heath bishop
Light, Pamela Delamaide interior designer
Lightburn, Faye Marie genealogist
Lightstone, Ronald lawyer
Liles, Frank professional boxer
Liljegren, Frank Sigfrid artist, art association official
Lilley, William, III information and communications business consultant
Lillibridge, John Lee retired airline executive
Lilly, Edward Guerrant, Jr. retired utility company executive
Liman, Ellen painter, writer, arts advocate
Lin, Ping mechanical engineer
Lincoln, Harry B. musicologist
Linda, Gerald advertising and marketing executive
Lindars, Laurence Edward retired health care products executive
Lindberg, Francis Laurence, Jr. management consultant
Linde, Hans Arthur state supreme court justice
Linde, Maxine Helen lawyer, business executive, private investor
Lindegren, Jack Kenneth elementary and secondary education educator
Lindenberger, Herbert Samuel writer, literature educator
Lindenmeyer, Mary Kathryn secondary education educator
Lindgren, William Dale librarian
†Lindner, Carl Martin English educator
Lindquist, Michael Adrian career military officer
Lindsay, Dale Richard research administrator
Lindsay, Franklin Anthony business executive, author
Lindsay, John Vliet former mayor, former congressman, author, lawyer
LIndsey, Mack Clay computer programmer
Lindsey, Roberta Lewise music researcher, historian
Lindstedt-Siva, (Karen) June marine biologist, environmental consultant
Line, Diane Jer'i writer
†Linenger, Jerry Michael astronaut
Lingenfelter, Andrea Diane translator, writer
Lingle, Marilyn Felkel freelance writer, columnist
Linhares, Judith Yvonne artist, educator
Link, William Theodore television writer, producer
Linklater, Richard film director
Linto, Nancy medical unit director
Lipkin, David Lawrence physician
Lipman, Carol Koch designer
Lipman, David multimedia consultant
Lipman, Ira Ackerman security service company executive
Lippert, Christopher Nelson dentist, consultant
Lippes, Richard James lawyer
Lippincott, James Andrew biochemistry and biological sciences educator
Lippincott, Philip Edward retired paper products company executive
Lipschutz, Marian Shaw secondary education educator, writer
Lipscomb-Brown, Edra Evadean retired childhood educator
Lipsey, John C. (Jack Lipsey) insurance company executive
Lipsitt, Lewis Paeff psychology educator
Lipsky, Stephen Edward engineering executive, electronic warfare engineer
†Lipton, Eunice art history, writer
Lipton, Judith Eve psychiatrist
Lipton, Nina Anne healthcare executive
†Lisi, Anthony Salvatore police officer
Liskamm, William Hugo architect, urban planner, educator
Liskov, Barbara Huberman software engineering educator
Lisovskaya, Elena Borisovna sociologist, educator
Lithgow, John Arthur actor, director
Little, Brian W. pathology educator, administrator
Little, Loren Everton musician, ophthalmologist
Littler, Gene Alec professional golfer
Littleton, Harvey Kline artist
Littlewood, Thomas Benjamin retired journalism educator
Littman, Earl advertising and public relations executive
Liu, Alan Fong-Ching mechanical engineer
Liu, Ernest K. H. international banking executive, international financial consultant
Liu, Shengzhong (Frank) chemist, researcher
Liu, Young King biomedical engineering educator
Lively, Edwin Lester retired oil company executive
Lively, Pierce federal judge
Livezey, Mark Douglas physician
Livingston, Alan Wendell communications executive
Livingston, Gideon (Guy) Eleazar food and nutrition scientist, consultant
Livingston, Margaret Gresham civic leader
Livingstone, Susan Morrisey management consultant
Livingstone, Trudy Dorothy Zweig dancer, educator
Livingston-MacIrelan, Joan Persilla artist
Livo, Norma Joan writer
Lloyd, David Nigel song writer, poet, performer
Lloyd, Joseph Wesley physicist, researcher
Lloyd, Michael Jeffrey recording producer
Lloyd, Michael L. nursing administrator, educator
Loach, Paul Allen biochemist, biophysicist, educator
Lobanov-Rostovsky, Oleg management consultant
Lobdell, Kevin Wallace cardiothoracic surgeon
Lober, Lionel M. screenwriter, producer
Localio, Marcia Judith medical/surgical nurse
Lockart, Barbetta fabric designer, artist, jeweler, art educator
Locke, John Howard lawyer
Locke, Norton hotel management and construction company executive
Lockhart, Aileene Simpson retired dance, kinesiology, physical education educator and editor
Locklear, Heather actress
Lockwood, Robert W. management consultant
Lockwood, Theodore Davidge former academic administrator
Lodge, Arthur Scott mechanical engineering educator
Loeffler, James Joseph lawyer
Loeks, Barrie Lawson theater company executive
Lofton, Kenneth professional baseball player
Logan, James Kenneth lawyer, former federal judge
Logan, John Francis electronics company executive, management consultant
Loggins, Bobby Gene meat company executive
Lohmuller, Martin Nicholas bishop
Lohrer, Richard Baker investment consultant
Loiello, John Peter diplomat
Loludice, Thomas Anthony gastroenterologist, researcher
Lokmer, Stephanie Ann public relations/business development consultant
Lombard, Marjorie Ann financial officer
Long, Carl Dean management consultant
Long, Charles William child and adolescent psychiatrist
Long, (Lotus) Elaine writer, editor
Long, Jennifer L. elementary educator
†Long, Patricia A. librarian
Long, Robert Livingston retired photographic equipment executive
Longobardo, Anna Kazanjian engineering executive
Longstreet, Stephen (Chauncey Longstreet) author, painter
Looser, Donald William academic administrator
Loper, James Leaders broadcasting executive
Lopez, Barry Holstun writer
Lopez, Constance R. mental health facility administrator
Lopez, Ricardo professional boxer
Lopez-Boyd, Linda Sue geriatrics nurse, educator, consultant
†Lopez-Cuenca, Victor emergency medicine physician
Loppnow, Milo Alvin clergyman, former church official
Lord, Roy Alvin retired publisher
Lord, Walter author
Lorelli, Michael Kevin consumer products and services executive
Loren, Mary Rooney controller
Lorente, Rafael journalist
†Lorenzo, Francisco A. airline companies executive
Lorenzo Franco, José Ramón Mexican government official
Loring, Gloria Jean singer, actress
Loring, Mildred Rogers elementary educator, reading specialist
Los, Marinus retired agrochemical researcher
Loser, Joseph Carlton, Jr. dean, retired judge
Losten, Basil Harry bishop
Lotz, Joan Theresa public relations company executive
Lotz, Linda Ann religious organizer
Loube, Samuel Dennis physician
Loucks, Ralph Bruce, Jr. investment company executive
Loughran, James Newman philosophy educator, college administrator
Love, Laurie Miller science editor
Love, Miron Anderson retired judge
Love, Sara Elizabeth retired educator
Lovelace, Rose Marie Sniegon federal space agency administrator
Lovell, Mary Ann secondary education educator
Lovetri, Jeannette Louise voice educator
Lovinger, Warren Conrad emeritus university president
Lovitz, Jon actor, comedian
Lovy, Andrew osteopathic physician, psychiatrist
Low, Emmet Francis, Jr. mathematics educator
Low, Harry William judge
†Low, Lisa Elaine English educator
Low, Robert Teh-Pin educator
Lowden, John L. retired corporate executive
Lowe, John, III consulting civil engineer
Lowe, Rob actor
Lowenthal, Susan artist, designer, retired finance executive
Lowndes, Jeffrey Dennis auto mechanic
Lowrie, Walter Olin management consultant
Lowry, Marilyn Jean horticultural retail company executive
Lu, Ming Liang software company executive, educator
†Luban, David Jay law educator
Lubbers, Alice Dianne operating room nurse
Lubell, Ellen writer
Lubic, Ruth Watson association executive, nurse midwife
Lubin, Steven concert pianist, musicologist
Lubinsky, Menachem Yechiel communications executive
Lucas, Bert Albert pastor, social services administator, consultant
Lucas, Rebecca Leigh community health nurse
Lucas, Rhett Roy mediator, arbitrator, lawyer, chemical engineer, artist, photographer
Lucas, Wayne Lee sociologist, educator
Lucas, William Ray aerospace consultant
Lucchese, Eugene Frank EMS educator, emergency medicine/critical care
Lucentini, Mauro journalist
Luciano, Roselle Patricia advertising executive, editor
Luckey, Doris Waring civic volunteer
Ludwig, Allan Ira photographer, artist, author
Ludwig, Christa mezzo-soprano
Lueke, Donna Mae yoga instructor, reiki practitioner
Luetkehoelter, Gottlieb Werner (Lee) retired bishop, clergyman
†Luft, Gary Alan secondary education educator
Lugenbeel, Edward Elmer publisher
Luger, Donald R. engineering company executive
Lugt, Hans Josef physicist
Luhn, Robert Kent writer, magazine editor
Luke, David Lincoln, III retired paper company executive
Luke, Douglas Sigler business executive
Lumpkin, Anne Craig retired television and radio company executive
Lumpkin, John Henderson retired banker
Lund, David Nathan artist
Lundgren, Leonard, III retired secondary education educator
†Lundquist, James Harold lawyer
Lungren, John Howard law educator, oil and gas consultant, author
†Luo, Li-Shi physics scientist
Lupu, Radu pianist
Lurix, Paul Leslie, Jr. chemist
Lusk, Harlan Gilbert national park superintendent, business executive
Luttner, Edward F. consulting company executive
Lutz, Lawrence Joseph family practice physician
LyListon, William Phillip writer, poet
Lyman, Ruth Ann psychologist
Lynch, Charles Andrew chemical industry consultant
Lynch, Charlotte Andrews communications executive
Lynch, Florence Jones real estate counselor, property manager
Lynch, Jair Olympic athlete
Lynch, John Daniel secondary education educator, state legislator
Lynch, Laura Ellen elementary education educator
Lynch, Michael Edward medical facility administrator
Lynch, Peter George artist
Lynch, Robert Emmett mathematics educator
Lynch, Robert Martin lawyer, educator
Lynch, Thomas Peter securities executive
Lynch, Thomas Wimp lawyer
Lynds, Beverly Turner retired astronomer
Lyne, Dorothy-Arden educator
Lyngbye, Jørgen hospital administrator, researcher
†Lynn, Bonnie Jane music educator
Lyon, Mary Kuehlewind childbirth educator
Lyons, John W(inship) retired government official, chemist
†Lyons, Michelle Cherie journalist
Lyons, Natalie Beller family counselor
Lyshak-Stelzer, Frances artist
†Lyttle, Kim Eugene bank officer
Maas, Anthony Ernst pathologist
Maatman, Gerald Leonard insurance company executive
Mabson, Robert Langley clergyman, librarian
MacArthur, Diana Taylor advanced technology executive
Macaulay, David (Alexander) author, illustrator
MacCarthy, Talbot Leland civic volunteer
Macdonald, James Kennedy, Jr. executive search consultant
MacDonald, Robert Taylor newspaper executive
Macdonald, Sheila de Marillac transaction management company executive
MacDougall, Ingeborg Reibling mental health nurse
MacDougall, Peter lawyer
MacFarlane, Andrew Walker media specialist, educator
†MacFarquhar, Larissa journalist
Machado, Paulo Almeida art educator
Machen, Ethel Louise Lynch retired academic administrator
†Macinskas, Wendy Lasser secondary education educator
Mack, Rebecca Ann primary education educator
Mackenzie, Linda Alice alternative medicine and awareness company executive, entertainer, educator, hypnotherapist, motivational speaker
Mackety, Carolyn Jean laser medicine and nursing consultant
MacLachlan, Patricia author
MacLean, John Angus former premier of Prince Edward Island
MacLennan, Beryce Winifred psychologist
MacLeod, Donald William secondary school educator
Macleod, Normajean writer
†Macmillan, Carol neurologist
Macmillan, William Hooper university dean, educator
MacMullen, Jean Alexandria Stewart nurse, administrator
Macnee, (Daniel) Patrick actor
Macon, Carol Ann Gloeckler micro-computer data base management company executive
Macormic, William Dean railway company executive
MacPhee, Donald Albert academic administrator
MacQueen, Robert Moffat solar physicist
†Madden, John Philip motion picture director
Madden, Richard Blaine forest products executive
Maddin, Robert metallurgist educator
Madeira, Francis King Carey conductor, educator
Madera, Joseph J. bishop
Madlang, Rodolfo Mojica retired urologic surgeon
Madrick, Jeffrey G. writer, economic consultant
Maehl, William Harvey historian, educator
Maehr, Martin Louis psychology educator

Maestrone, Frank Eusebio *diplomat*
Maffia, Roma *actress*
Magafas, Diania Lee *geriatrics nurse consultant, administrator*
Magee, Karen Strope *nurse, health facility administrator*
Magid, Lee *video and recording producer, manager, composer, lyricist*
Magill, Rosalind May *psychotherapist*
Maginnis, Tara Michele *costume designer, educator*
Maglich, Bogdan Castle *physicist*
Magnabosco, Louis Mario *chemical engineer, researcher, consultant*
Magnano, Salvatore Paul *retired financial executive, treasurer*
Magnuson, Paul Arthur *federal judge*
Magnuson, Robert Martin *retired hospital administrator*
Magor, Louis Roland *conductor*
Maguire, Robert Francis, III *real estate investor*
Magurno, Richard Peter *lawyer*
Maher, Jan Colleen *artist, educator*
Mahfouz, Ilham Badreddine *artist*
Mahle, Christoph Erhard *electrical engineer*
Mahoney, John *actor*
Mahoney, Linda Kay *mathematics educator*
Mahoney, Michael Robert Taylor *art historian, educator*
Mai, Chao Chen *engineer*
Maier, Robert Hawthorne *biology educator*
Maier, Robert Henry *real estate executive*
Maiman, Theodore Harold *physicist*
Main, Myrna Joan *mathematics educator*
Main, Robert Gail *communications educator, training consultant, television and film producer, former army officer*
Mair, Douglas Dean *medical educator, consultant*
Maisel, Herbert *computer science educator*
Major, Patrick Webb, III *principal*
Mak, Ben Bohdan *engineer*
Makepeace, Coline M. *computer scientist*
Makins, James Edward *retired dentist, dental educator, educational administrator*
Makowski, Edgar Leonard *obstetrician and gynecologist*
Malach, Monte *physician*
Malakhov, Vladimir *dancer*
†Maldonado-Mendez, Nilsa B. *language educator*
Malek, Marlene Anne *cultural organization, foundation executive*
Malhotra, Pulin *financial infrastructure consultant*
Mali, Bradley James Michael *geriatrics service professional*
Malis, Leonard Irving *neurosurgeon*
Malkinson, Frederick David *dermatologist*
Mallis, Sophia G. *nurse, educator*
Mallo-Garrido, Josephine Ann *advertising agency owner*
Mallory, Arthur Lee *university dean, retired state official*
Mallory, William Barton, III *lawyer*
Malloy, Craig Riggs *physician, educator*
Malloy, John Richard *lawyer, chemical company executive*
Malloy, Johnn Edward *performing artist, aerospace historian*
Malloy, Michael Terrence *journalist, newspaper editor*
Malone, James William *retired bishop*
†Malone, Kevin *sports team executive*
Maloney, Diane Marie *legal nurse consultant*
†Maloney, James Henry *congressman*
Maloney, Therese Adele *insurance company executive*
Malott, Adele Renee *editor*
Malouf-Cundy, Pamela Bonnie *visual arts editor*
Malti-Douglas, Fedwa *educator*
Maltin, Freda *retired university administrator*
†Mameli, Peter Angelo *city official, public management educator*
Mamet, David Alan *playwright, director, essayist*
Manahan, Joan Elsie *health and physical education educator*
Mañas, Rita *educational administrator*
Manasse, Arlynn H. *pediatric nurse practitioner*
Mancher, Rhoda Ross *federal agency administrator, strategic planner*
Manchester, Carol Ann Freshwater *psychologist*
Manchester, Kenneth Edward *electronics executive, consultant*
Manchester, William *writer*
Mand, Martin G. *financial executive*
Mandel, Jack Kent *marketing and advertising educator, publishing consultant*
Maness, Diane Mease *pediatrics nurse*
Mangan, Patricia Ann Pritchett *statistician*
Manganaro, Francis Ferdinand *naval officer*
Manganiello, Janice Marie *peri-operative nurse*
Mangham, R. Harold *retired church administrator*
Mangione, Chuck (Charles Frank Mangione) *jazz musician, composer*
Mangler, Robert James *lawyer*
Mangold, Sylvia Plimack *artist*
†Manika, John Francis *computer information systems analyst*
Maniloff, Jack *biophysicist, educator*
Manley, Joan A(dele) Daniels *retired publisher*
Mann, Clarence Charles *real estate company official*
Mann, Emily Betsy *writer, artistic director, theater director*
Manne, Henry Girard *lawyer, educator*
Mannering, Jerry Vincent *agronomist, educator*
Mannes, Elena Sabin *film and television producer, director*
Manning, John Joseph *retired physician, healthcare administrator*
Manning, Richard Dale *writer*
Mano, D. Keith *novelist*
Manogue, Ralph Anthony *English language educator*
Mans, Thomas Charles *dean*
Mansell Mayo, Catherine *writer, editor, economist*
†Manso, Leira A. *Latin American literature educator*
Mansour, Stephen Malik *software developer, mathematician*
Maradona, Remigio Martin *international delegate, poet*
Marbach, Diane *food service executive*
Marceau, Yvonne *ballroom dancer, educator*
March, Jacqueline Front *retired chemist*
Marchand, Nancy *actress*
Marchant, JoAnn Reviczky *English language educator, actress*
†Marchman, Frederick Alan *artist*
†Marcille, Lorraine May *finance company executive, accountant*
Marcus, Greil Gerstley *critic*
Marcuse, Dietrich *retired physicist*
Margolis, Harold Stephen *epidemiologist*
Marietta, Elizabeth Ann *industrial engineer*
Marin, Cheech (Richard Anthony Marin) *actor, writer, director*
Marinetti, Guido V. *biochemistry educator*
Marini, Frank Nicholas *political science and public administration educator*
Marinis, Thomas Paul, Jr. *lawyer*
Marino, Joseph Anthony *retired publishing executive*
Marion, John Louis *fine arts auctioneer and appraiser*
Marion, Marjorie Anne *English language educator, education consultant*
Mark, Alan Samuel *lawyer*
Mark, Mary Ellen *photographer*
Mark, Michael Laurence *retired music educator*
Mark, Saralyn *endocrinologist*
Marker, Marc Linthacum *lawyer, investor*
Markham, Richard Glover *research executive*
Markle, Roger A(llan) *retired oil company executive*
Markovic, Nenad S. *internist, hematologist, oncologist, educator*
Markovitz, Alvin *molecular biologist, geneticist, educator*
Marks, Bruce *artistic director, choreographer*
Marks, James Frederic *pediatric endocrinologist, educator*
Marks, Leonard, Jr. *retired corporate executive*
Marks-DeMourelle, Karen *diabetes nurse*
Marky, William Bernard *motion picture sound engineer, mixer*
Marlar, Janet Cummings *retired public relations officer*
Marlatt, Dorothy Barbara *university dean*
Marler, Larry John *private investor, leadership consultant*
Marlow, Edward A. *retired career officer*
Marlowe, Willie *fine arts educator, artist*
Marmer, Nancy *editor*
Maroon, Mickey *clinical social worker*
Maropis, Nicholas *engineering executive*
Marquardt, Sandra Mary *activist, lobbyist, researcher*
Marquis, Harriet Hill *social worker*
Marr, Carmel Carrington *retired lawyer, retired state official*
Marsalis, Wynton *musician*
Marsee, Susanne Irene *lyric mezzo-soprano*
Marsh, Denise A. *critical care and medical/surgical nurse*
Marsh, Joan Knight *educational film, video and computer software company executive, publisher children's books*
Marsh, Merrilyn Delano *sculptor, painter*
Marsh, Michael L.H. *trade association administrator*
Marshak, Robert Reuben *former university dean, medical educator, veterinarian*
Marshall, Brenda Lebowitz *health educator*
Marshall, Charles Noble *railroad executive*
Marshall, Donald Thomas *medical technologist*
Marshall, George Dwire *retired supermarket chain executive*
Marshall, Gerald Francis *optical engineer, consultant, physicist*
Marshall, John Crook *internal medicine educator, researcher*
Marshall, Kathryn Sue *lawyer*
Marshall, Odessa Josephine *mental health nurse*
Marshall, Richard *art historian, curator*
Marshall, Robert Charles *computer company executive*
Martarella, Franc David *television executive*
†Marti, Virgil *artist*
Martin, Alan Edward *gasket company executive*
Martin, Albert Charles *manufacturing executive, lawyer*
Martin, Andrea Louise *actress, comedienne, writer*
Martin, Archer John Porter *retired chemistry educator*
Martin, Catherine Elizabeth *anthropology educator*
Martin, Cheri Christian *health services administrator*
Martin, Christy *professional boxer*
Martin, Ione Edwards *social worker*
Martin, James Kay *government official*
Martin, James Victor, Jr. *foreign service officer, writer*
Martin, James William *lawyer*
Martin, John Swanson *retired educator*
Martin, John William *educator, antiquarian bookseller*
Martin, John William, Jr. *retired lawyer, automotive industry executive*
†Martin, Keith Mitchel *state ageny administrator*
Martin, Lee *mechanical engineer*
Martin, Marta *learning disability specialist, educator*
Martin, Mary *secondary education educator*
Martin, Noel *graphic design consultant, educator*
†Martin, Patricia A. *musician*
Martin, Paul Raymond *writer*
Martin, Raymond Edward *management consultant*
Martin, Sally S. *family studies educator*
Martin, William Collier *hospital administrator*
Martindale, Nancy Elaine *writer, publisher, editor*
Martini, Robert Edward *wholesale pharmaceutical and medical supplies company executive*
Martino, Joseph Paul *research scientist*
Martino, Rocco Leonard *computer systems executive*
Martino, Silvana *osteopath, medical oncologist*
Martyl, (Mrs. Alexander Langsdorf, Jr.) *artist*
Martz, Judy Helen *state official*
Marvel, Andrew Scott *producer, songwriter, record company executive*
Marvel, Wanda Faye *home health clinical consultant*
Marvin, Roy Mack *retired foundry executive*
Marvin, William Glenn, Jr. *former foreign service officer*
Marx, Anne (Mrs. Frederick E. Marx) *poet*
Mascheroni, Eleanor Earle *investment company executive*
Masiello, Rocco Joseph *airlines and aerospace manufacturing executive*
Masket, Edward Seymour *television executive*
Maslansky, Carol Jeanne *toxicologist*
Mason, Connie Jeanne *writer*
Mason, Frank Henry, III *automobile company executive, leasing company executive*
†Mason, Gloria *secondary education educator*
Mason, J. Day *painter, poet, actress, educator*
Mason, James Albert *retired museum director, former university dean*
Mason, Johanna Hendrika Anneke *retired secondary education educator*
Mason, John E. *political association executive*
Mason, John Latimer *engineering executive*
Mason, John Oliver *free-lance journalist*
Mason, Linda *physical education educator, softball and basketball coach*
Mason, Marsha *actress, director, writer*
Mason, Martha *elementary education consultant, former educator*
Mason, Robert Lester *engineer, small business computer consultant*
Massa, Salvatore Peter *psychologist*
Massad, Stephen Albert *lawyer*
Massaro, Linda P. *science foundation executive*
Massey, Kathleen Marie Oates *lawyer*
Massey, Stephen Charles *auctioneer*
Mast, Stewart Dale *retired airport manager*
Masterson, Peter *actor, director*
Mastin, Wayne Alan *consumer education administrator*
Matasovic, Marilyn Estelle *business executive*
Matelic, Candace Tangorra *museum studies educator, consultant, museum director*
Matera, Frances Lorine *elementary educator*
Materson, Richard Stephen *physician, educator*
Mates, Robert Edward *mechanical engineering educator*
Mathay, Mary Frances *marketing executive*
Matheny, Adam Pence, Jr. *child psychologist, educator, consultant, researcher*
Matherlee, Thomas Ray *health care consultant*
Matheson, Scott Milne, Jr. *law educator*
Mathews, Barbara Jean *genealogist*
Mathews, Harry Burchell *poet, novelist, educator*
Mathews, Mary Kathryn *retired government official*
Mathis, Harry *city official*
Mathis, John Bernard *employee training company executive*
Mathis, Sharon Bell *author, retired elementary educator and librarian*
Matlow, Linda Monique *photographic agency executive, publishing executive*
Matsuda, Fujio *technology research center administrator*
Matterson, Joan McDevitt *physical therapist*
Matthau, Charles Marcus *film director*
Matthew, Lyn *sales and marketing executive consultant*
Matthews, Gail Thunberg *marketing executive*
Matthews, L. White, III *railroad executive*
Matthews, Warren Wayne *state supreme court justice*
Matthews, Wendy Schempp *psychologist, researcher*
Matthiesen, David Karl *consultant*
Mattingly, Mack Francis *former ambassador, former senator, entrepreneur*
Mattis, Olivia *musicologist*
†Mattson, Harold Frazyer, Jr. *mathematics educator*
Mattson, Richard Henry *neurologist, educator*
†Matzky, Karl Frederick, Jr. *history educator*
Mauldin, Jean Ann *controller*
Maulding, Barry Clifford *lawyer*
Maunder, Addison Bruce *agronomic research company executive*
Mauney, Thomas Lee *theater designer*
Maurer, Beverly Bennett *school administrator*
Maurer, Geraldine Marie *perinatal nurse, consultant*
Maxwell, Barbara Sue *systems analyst consultant, educator*
Maxwell, Linda Jeanne *newspaper reporter, photographer*
†Maxwell, Mark S. *secondary education educator, novelist*
Maxwell, Ruth Elaine *artist, interior designer, decorative painter*
May, Henry Stratford, Jr. *lawyer*
May, Kenneth Nathaniel *food industry consultant*
May, Robert M. *retired obstetrician, gynecologist, educator*
Maybury, Greg J *academic administrator*
Maycock, Ian David *retired oil executive*
Mayer, Allan *media consultant, writer*
Mayer, Patricia Lynn Sorci *mental health nurse, educator*
Mayerson, Peter *psychiatrist, educator*
Mayfield, Robert Charles *university official, geography educator*
†Maymind, Ilana *accountant*
Mayo, Robert Porter *banker*
Mayoras, Donald Eugene *corporate executive, writer, consultant, educator*
Mayron, Melanie *actress, writer*
Mazankowski, Donald Frank *Canadian government official*
Mazur, Deborah Joan *counselor*
Mazzarella, Rosemary Louise *business administration executive*
Mazzarelli, Marc F. *landscape architect*
Mazzatenta, Rosemary Dorothy *retired school administrator*
Mazzetti, Robert F. *real estate manager, retired orthopedic surgeon*
McAlmond, Russell Wayne *bank executive*
McAndrews, Daryl Lynn *community health nurse*
McBee, Robert Levi *retired federal government official, writer, consultant*
McBride, Jack J. *financial services executive*
McBride, Sandra Teague *psychiatric nurse*
†McBryde, Daphne Michelle *government official*
McBurney, Margot B. *librarian*
McCabe, Charles Law *retired manufacturing company executive, management consultant*
McCabe, Patricia *medical/surgical and intensive care nurse*
McCaffrey, Phillip *English language educator*
McCall, Patricia Alene *secondary music education educator*
McCallister, Duane *newspaper executive*
McCann, Elizabeth Ireland *theater, television and motion picture producer, lawyer*
McCann, Joseph F. *retired public relations executive*
McCarthy, Carolyn *congresswoman*
McCarthy, Daniel William *management consultant*
McCarthy, J. Thomas *lawyer, educator*
McCarthy, Jean Jerome *retired physical education educator*
†McCarthy, Jeffrey Mathes *English educator*
McCarthy, Joanne Mary *reading specialist*
McCarthy, Vincent Paul *lawyer*
Mc Carthy, Walter John, Jr. *retired utility executive*
McCartney, James Robert *psychiatrist*
McCartney, (James) Paul *musician*
McCaskill, Dean Morgan *manufacturing industry executive*
†McCaslin, Robert Brian *educator*
McCaw, Craig O. *communications executive*
McClain, Richard Stan *cinematographer*
McClanahan, Rue (Eddi-Rue McClanahan) *actress*
†McClean, Karen Leslie *photographer*
Mc Clellan, Catharine *anthropologist, educator*
McClellan, Robert Edward *civil engineer*
McClelland, Richard Lee *dentist*
McClintock, George Dunlap *lawyer*
McClinton, James Leroy *city administrator*
McClinton, Wendell C. *religious organization administrator*
McCloskey, J(ohn) Michael *retired association administrator*
McClosky, Barbara Henneberger *voice educator, therapist*
McClurg, Patricia A. *minister*
McCluskey, Jean Ashford *nursing educator, retired*
McCobb, John Bradford, Jr. *lawyer*
McCone, Michael F. *retired cultural organization administrator*
McConnaughey, Bayard Harlow *retired biology educator*
McConnell, Albert Lynn *educational official*
McConnell, Calvin Dale *retired clergyman*
McConnell, Edward Bosworth *legal organization administrator, lawyer*
McCorkle, Michael *electrical engineer*
McCormack, Marjorie Guth *psychology educator, career counselor, communications educator, public relations consultant*
McCormick, David Arthur *lawyer*
McCormick, Elaine Alice *former nurse, retired fundraising executive*
McCormick, Homer L., Jr. *lawyer*
McCormick, John Owen *retired comparative literature educator*
McCormick, Kenneth L. *pediatrics educator, researcher*
†McCormick, Michael D. *lawyer*
McCown, Hale *retired judge*
McCoy, David Brion *middle school educator*
McCoy, Georgia Sideris *magazine editor, writing consultant*
McCoy, Mary Ann *state official*
†McCoy, Nancy Jeanne *history educator, writer*
McCoy, Patricia A. *clinical special educator, writer, art critic*
Mc Coy, Tidal Windham *former government official*
McCrary, Sharon Hash *medical and surgical nurse*
McCready, Kenneth Frank *past electric utility executive*
McCue, Howard McDowell, III *lawyer, educator*
McCullough, David L. *urologist*
McCully, Emily Arnold *illustrator, writer*
McCurdy, Michael Charles *illustrator, author*
McCurley, Robert Lee, Jr. *lawyer*
McDade, Joseph Michael *former congressman*
McDaniel, Mike *political association executive*
McDarrah, Gloria Schoffel *editor, author*
McDermott, Agnes Charlene Senape *philosophy educator*
McDermott, Kevin J. *engineering educator, consultant*
McDonagh, Thomas Joseph *physician*
McDonald, Barbara Jean *real estate broker*
McDonald, Bradley G. *lawyer*
†McDonald, Peter Jeffrey *journalist*
McDonald, Tanny *actress*
Mc Donnell, Loretta Wade *lawyer*
Mc Donough, John Richard *lawyer*
McDougall, Donald Blake *retired government official, librarian*
McDougall, Jacquelyn Marie Horan *therapist*
McDowell, Malcolm *actor*
McDowell, W. Stuart *producer, playwright, university department chair*
McElveen, William Henry *minister*
McElwee, Doris Ryan *psychotherapist*
McEvoy-Jamil, Patricia Ann *English language educator*
McEwen, Bruce S. *neuroendocrinology educator*
McEwen, Joan Grace (Joanie Lawrence) *actress, recording company executive*
†McFadden, Dorothy Irene *piano and music theory educator*
Mc Fadden, George Linus *retired army officer*
McFadden, Irene Frances *medical/surgical nurse, educator*
McFadden, Millidene Kathleen *nurse educator*
McFadden, Nancy Elizabeth *lawyer*
McFadden, Peter William *retired mechanical engineering educator*
McFall, Catherine Gardner *poet, critic, educator*
McFarland, Constance Anne *nursing educator*
McFarland, Robert Edwin *lawyer*
McFarland, Victor Alan *toxicologist*
McFate, Patricia Ann *foundation executive, scientist, educator*
Mc Fee, Thomas Stuart *retired government agency administrator*
McGann, Lisa B. Napoli *language educator*
McGarry, Kevin Vincent *retired newspaper executive*
McGaughy, Richard Wayne *nuclear consultant*
McGaw, Kenneth Roy *wholesale distribution executive*
†McGee, Carrie L. *artist*
McGee, Patrick Edgar *postal service clerk*
McGhee, Lori Jean Vote *medical/surgical nurse*
Mc Gill, Archie Joseph *venture capitalist*
McGill, Karleen A. *family nurse practitioner*
McGillis, Kelly *actress*
McGillivray, Donald Dean *seed company executive, agronomist*
McGinty, Brian Donald *lawyer, author*
†McGlaughlin, William *symphony conductor*
McGonigle, John Leo, Jr. *civil engineer*
McGough, Duane Theodore *economist, retired government official*
McGovern, Frances *retired lawyer*
Mc Govern, George Stanley *former senator*
†McGrail, Christopher W. *aerospace machinist*
McGrath, Anna Fields *retired librarian*
McGregor, Darren James *counselor, researcher, mediator*
McGuire, Hunter Holmes, Jr. *surgeon, educator*
McGuire, John W., Sr. *advertising executive, marketing professional, author*
McGuirk, Terrence *former broadcasting company executive*
McHale, Paul *former congressman, lawyer*
McHenry, Robert (Dale) *editor*
McHugh, Elizabeth Ann *infection control occupational health nurse*
McInnis, Susan Musé *corporate communications manager*
McIntosh, Calvin Eugene *retired small business owner*
McIntyre, Carol Chrisman *social services administrator*
McIntyre, Douglas Alexander *magazine publisher*
Mc Isaac, George Scott *business policy educator, government official, former management consultant*
McKay, John *lawyer*
†McKean, Barbara Jane *theatre educator*
McKean, Robert Jackson, Jr. *retired lawyer*

McKee, Adele Dieckmann *retired church music director, educator*
McKee, Roger Curtis *retired federal magistrate judge*
McKegan, Nicholas *music director*
†McKelton, Drue-Marie *academic director*
McKelway, Alexander Jeffrey *religion studies educator*
McKenna, Terence Patrick *insurance company executive*
McKeown, Lorraine Laredo *travel company executive, writer*
McKey, Thomas J. *lawyer*
McKinley, Ellen Bacon *priest*
McKinney, John Gage *purchasing agent, writer*
†Mc Kinney, Joseph Crescent *retired bishop*
McKinney, Louise Chestnut *volunteer*
McKinnon, Daniel Wayne, Jr. *naval officer*
McKinstry, Lydia *chemistry educator*
McKnight, Patricia Marie *elementary education educator*
McKnight, Thomas Frederick *artist*
McLain, Thelma Louise *retired college librarian, artist*
McLaren, Susan Smith *therapist, healing touch practitioner, instructor*
McLaughlin, Audrey *Canadian government official*
McLaughlin, Jean Wallace *art director, artist*
McLaughlin, Michael Rob *secondary school educator, coach*
†McLaughlin, Patricia Ann *writer*
McLaughlin, Robert Bruce *software designer*
McLaughlin, William Irving *space technical manager*
†McLaurin, Cathy Reneé *small business owner, artist, educator*
McLean, Amy C. *secondary school educator*
McLean, Walter Franklin *international consultant, pastor, legislator*
McLellon, Richard Steven *aerospace engineer, consultant*
McLendon, George Leland *chemistry educator, researcher*
McLennan, Robert Gordon *asset management company executive*
McLeskey, Charles Hamilton *anesthesiology educator*
†Mc Mahon, Barbara A. *teacher*
Mc Mahon, George Joseph *academic administrator*
McManus, Jason Donald *editor, retired*
McManus, Joseph Warn *urban planner, architect*
McManus, Richard Philip *lawyer, agricultural products company executive*
†McMillan, Gloria L. *writing educator*
McMillan, Stephen Walker *artist*
McMillan, Terry L. *writer, educator*
McMillen, Elizabeth Cashin *artist*
McMorrow, Margaret Mary (Peg McMorrow) *retired educator*
McMullin, Joyce Anne *general contractor*
McMurray, Ron *political association executive*
McMurtry, Florence Jean *educational administrator*
McNabb, Robert Henry *minister*
McNamara, David Joseph *financial and tax planning executive*
†McNamee, Gregory Lewis *writer, editor*
McNeeley, Donald Robert *steel company executive*
McNeil, Edward Warren *real estate executive*
McNeill, Douglas Arthur *priest*
McNeill, Robert Patrick *investment counselor*
McNeil Staudenmaier, Heidi Loretta *lawyer*
McNulty, Kathleen Anne *clinical social worker, psychotherapist, business consultant*
McPeak, Allan *career services director, educator, lawyer, consultant*
McPeters, Sharon Jenise *artist, writer*
McPhearson, Geraldine June *medical and surgical nurse*
Mc Phee, John Angus *writer*
Mc Pheeters, Edwin Keith *architect, educator*
Mc Pherson, Frank Alfred *retired manufacturing corporate executive*
McPherson, James Alan *writer, educator*
Mc Pherson, Peter *university president*
Mc Pherson, Robert Donald *retired lawyer*
Mc Quade, Lawrence Carroll *lawyer, corporate executive*
McQuarrie, Terry Scott *technical director*
McQueen-Gibson, Ethlyn *diabetes clinical nurse specialist*
McQuilkin, John Robertson *religion educator, academic administrator, writer*
McRae, Thomas Kenneth *retired investment company executive*
McSain, Tara Jacqueline *medical/surgical nurse, oncological nurse, infusion nurse*
McShefferty, John *retired research company executive, consultant*
McSpadden, Katherine Frances *English language educator*
McSweeny, William Francis *petroleum company executive, author*
McTague, John Paul *automobile manufacturing company executive, chemist*
McVeigh-Pettigrew, Sharon Christine *communications consultant*
McVicker, Jesse Jay *artist, educator*
Mead, Beverley Tupper *physician, educator*
Mead, Loren Benjamin *writer, consultant*
Meaders, Nobuko Yoshizawa *therapist, psychoanalyst*
Meadows, Lois *mental health nursing clinician and educator*
Meads, Donald Edward *management services company executive*
Meaker, Marijane Agnes *author*
Means-Enoch, Barbara Ann *critical care nurse*
†Mear, Annie M. *communications educator*
Meara, Anne *actress, playwright, writer*
Medavoy, Mike *motion picture company executive*
Medina, Kathryn Bach *book editor*
Medinger, C. Wynn *design and branding consultant*
Medley, Donald Matthias *education educator, consultant*
Mednick, Robert *accountant*
Meehan, John Joseph, Jr. *hospital administrator*
Meek, Forrest Burns *trading company executive*
Meek, Paul Derald *oil and chemical company executive*
Meeks, Linda Mae *women's health nurse, educator*
Mehdizadeh, Parviz *insurance company executive*
Mehlman, Benjamin *psychologist, educator*
Mehne, Paul Randolph *associate dean, medical educator*
Mehta, Peshotan Rustom *magnetotherapist and holisticologist*
Meidav, Edie Emanuela *writer, educator*
Meier, Enge *preschool educator*
Meier, George Karl, III *pastor, lawyer*
Meier, Henry George *architect*
Meil, Kate *sculptor*
Meiling, Gerald Stewart *materials scientist*
Meilman, Edward *physician*
Meinert, Bobbi Irene *college program administrator*
Meintsma, Peter Evans *history and political science educator*
Meis, Nancy Ruth *marketing and development executive*
Melady, Thomas Patrick *academic administrator, ambassador, author, public policy expert, educator*
Melamid, Alexander *artist*
Melanson, Susan C. *herbalist*
Melczek, Dale J. *bishop*
Mele, Jim *writer*
Mele, Joanne Theresa *dentist*
Meli, Salvatore Andrew *lawyer*
Melillo, Joseph Vincent *producer, performing arts*
Mellanby, Scott Edgar *professional hockey player*
Mellema, Donald Eugene *retired radio news reporter and anchor*
Mellendorf, Patricia Jean *retired personnel professional*
Melman, Cynthia Sue *special education educator*
Melnikoff, Sarah Ann *gem importer, jewelry designer*
Melody, Michael Edward *publishing company executive*
Melsheimer, Mel P(owell) *consumer products business executive*
†Melville, R. Jerrold *mental health services professional*
Melvin, Ben Watson, Jr. *petroleum and chemical manufacturing executive*
Melvin, Billy Alfred *clergyman*
Melzer, Barbara Evelyn *minister*
Mench, John William *retail store executive, electrical engineer*
Mende, Robert Graham *retired engineering association executive*
Mendels, Joseph *psychiatrist, educator*
Mendez, Albert Orlando *industrialist, financier*
Mendez, C. Beatriz *obstetrician, gynecologist, educator*
Mendonsa, Arthur Adonel *retired city official*
Mendoza, George *poet, author*
†Mendoza, Nydia *language arts educator*
Meneeley, Edward Sterling *artist*
Menhall, Dalton Winn *lawyer, insurance executive, professional association administrator*
Menn, Julius Joel *scientist*
Meo, Roxanne Marie *critical care nurse*
Mercer, Edwin Wayne *lawyer*
Mercuri, Joan B. *foundation executive*
Mercurio, Renard Michael *real estate corporation executive*
Meredith, Alice Foley *publisher, consultant*
Meredith, Ellis Edson *association and business executive*
Merilh, Marietta Paula *critical care nurse*
Merk, Elizabeth Thole *investment company executive*
Merlini, Sandra Ann *librarian, writer*
Merriam, Robert W. *engineering executive, educator*
Merrick, Dorothy Susan *interior designer*
Merrick, George Boesch *aerospace company executive*
Merrill, Abel Jay *lawyer*
†Merrill, Augustus Lee *poet, retired English educator*
Merrill, Frank Harrison *data processing executive, consultant*
Merrill, Jean Fairbanks *writer*
Merrill, Nathaniel *artistic director opera Colorado*
Merriman, Mary Ann *psychiatric nurse*
†Merritt, Eleanor Lynette *artist, educator*
Merritt, John Howard *secondary school educator*
Mesa, Jose Ramon *professional baseball player*
Meschke, Herbert Leonard *retired state supreme court justice*
†Mesenbrink, Shawna *library director*
Meserve, Walter Joseph *drama studies writer, publisher*
Meshel, Harry *state senator, political party official*
Messamore, Andrew Karl *anesthesiologist, pharmacist*
Messenkopf, Eugene John *real estate developer and hotel executive*
Metcalf, Pauline Cabot *architectural historian*
Metcalfe, Robert Davis, III *lawyer*
Metz, Frank Andrew, Jr. *data processing executive*
Metz, Steven William *small business owner*
Metz, T(heodore) John *librarian, consultant*
Metzner, Charles Miller *federal judge*
†Meunier, Robert Raymond *research electrical engineer, optical engineer*
Meyer, Andrew W. *publishing executive*
Meyer, Daniel Kramer *real estate executive*
Meyer, Frances Margaret Anthony *elementary and secondary school educator, health education specialist*
Meyer, George Wilbur *internist, health facility administrator*
Meyer, Greg Charles *psychiatrist*
Meyer, Harry Martin, Jr. *retired health science facility administrator*
Meyer, Kathleen Marie *English educator, editor, writer*
Meyer, Lasker Marcel *retail executive*
Meyer, Louis B. *judge, retired state supreme court justice*
Meyer, Mary-Louise *art gallery executive*
Meyer, Max Earl *lawyer*
Meyer, Robert Lee *secondary education educator*
Meyer, Roberta *mediator, communication consultant*
†Meyer, Sandra Palmer *financial executive*
Meyerink, Victoria Paige *film producer, actress*
Meyers, Jan *former congresswoman*
Meyers, Richard James *landscape architect*
Meyerson, Stanley Phillip *lawyer*
Mezzatesta, Michael Philip *art museum director*
Miah, Abdul Malek *electrical engineer, educator*
Mich, Connie Rita *mental health nurse, educator*
Michael, Donald Nelson *social scientist, educator*
Michael, Harold Kaye (Bud Michael) *sales and marketing executive*
Michels, Stanley E. *city official*
Michelsen, W(olfgang) Jost *neurosurgeon, educator, retired*
Michelson, Harold *production designer*
†Micucci, Dana Ann *writer*
†Middaugh, Gabrielle leSage *television news producer, entrepreneur*
Middaugh, Robert Burton *artist*
Middleton, Ellen Long *family nurse practitioner, educator*
Miele, Anthony William *retired librarian*
Might, Thomas Owen *newspaper company executive*
Mikel, Thomas Kelly, Jr. *laboratory administrator*
Mikhail, Mary Attalla *computer systems development executive*
Mikiewicz, Anna Daniella *marketing and sales representative*
Mikitka, Gerald Peter *investment banker, financial consultant*
Miknis, Lisa L. *neuroscience intensive care nurse*
Mikulski, Barbara Ann *senator*
Milano, Alyssa *actress*
Miles, Elsie E. *counselor, educator*
†Miles, Janet Ward *principal*
Miles, Jeanne Patterson *artist*
Miles, John Frederick *retired manufacturing company executive*
Miles, Kimberly Joy *critical care nurse*
Milhouse, Paul William *bishop*
Millard, Charles Phillip *manufacturing company executive*
Millard, Charles Warren, III *museum director, writer*
Miller, Alan Jay *financial consultant, author*
Miller, Allen Richard *mathematician*
Miller, Arjay *retired university dean*
Miller, Arthur *playwright, author*
Miller, Charles Edmond *library administrator*
Miller, Diane Doris *executive search consultant*
Miller, Dolores (Dee Miller) *intensive care nurse*
Miller, Donald LeSessne *publishing executive*
Miller, Ellen S. *marketing communications executive*
†Miller, Eric John *artist, muralist, ornament designer*
Miller, Esther Scobie Powers *real estate appraiser, professional watercolorist*
Miller, Frank William *legal educator*
Miller, Harold Edward *retired manufacturing conglomerate executive, consultant*
Miller, Jack Conway *landscape artist, art gallery director, owner*
Miller, Jacqueline Winslow *library director*
Miller, Jane Andrews *accountant*
Miller, Janet Dawn Hoover *nursing educator*
Miller, Jeffrey Veach *biochemist, researcher*
†Miller, Jennifer Ann *cleaning service owner*
Miller, Jerry Huber *retired university chancellor*
Miller, JP (James Pinckney Miller) *screenwriter, novelist, playwright*
Miller, Kenneth Roye, Jr. *state government administrator*
Miller, Lenore Wolf Daniels *speech-language pathologist*
Miller, Lillie M. *nursing educator*
Miller, Marilyn Lea *library science educator*
Miller, Nate *professional boxer*
Miller, Norman Charles, Jr. *journalism educator*
Miller, Pamela Joan *special events marketing executive*
Miller, Penelope Ann *actress*
Miller, Philip Gray *artist*
Miller, Reed *lawyer*
Miller, Reginald Wayne *professional basketball player*
Miller, Richard Franklin *educational consultant, researcher*
Miller, Robert Branson, Jr. *retired newspaper publisher*
Miller, Roberta Ann *gastroenterology nurse*
Miller, Ross Hays *retired neurosurgeon*
Miller, Ross M. *financial services company executive*
Miller, Shannon *Olympic athlete*
†Miller, Stuart Henry *radiologist, inventor*
Miller, Terry W. *academic adminstrator, legal consultant*
Miller, Thormund Aubrey *lawyer*
Miller, Vel *artist*
Miller, Vernon Dallace *retired minister*
Millett, Ralph Linwood, Jr. *retired newspaper editor*
Millhauser, Steven *writer*
Millican, Kirk *architect*
Milligan, Arthur Achille *retired banker*
Milligan, Reneé Ann *nursing educator, researcher*
Millikan, Clark Harold *physician*
Millimet, Erwin *lawyer*
Mills, Eugene Sumner *college president*
Mills, Kevin Lee *government executive*
Mills, Robert Harry *retired clergyman and church administrator*
Mills, Robert Lee *president emeritus*
Millsaps, Fred Ray *investor*
Milner, Irvin Myron *lawyer*
Mil'shtein, Samson *semiconductor physicist*
Miltner, Rebecca Suzanne *women's health nurse, pediatrics nurse*
Minami, Robert Yoshio *artist, graphic designer*
Mincy, Lisa Jo *nurse*
†Minczeski, John *poet*
Mindlin, Paula Rosalie *retired reading educator*
Miner, A. Bradford *journalist*
Miner-Farra, Tess Antoinette *English language educator, dean*
Minges, John Franklin, III *non-profit management consultant*
Mingle, James John *lawyer*
Minners, Howard Alyn *physician, research administrator*
Minnix, Bruce Milton *television and theatre director*
Minton, Jeffrey S. *writer*
Mintz, M. J. *lawyer*
Mintz, Morton Abner *author, former newspaper reporter*
Mintz, Patricia Pomboy *secondary education educator*
†Mirabelli, Eugene *English educator*
Miracle, Robert Warren *retired banker*
Mirisch, Walter Mortimer *motion picture producer*
Miscella, Maria Diana *humanities educator*
Mischke, Carl Herbert *religious association executive, retired*
Miselson, Alex J. (Jacob) *portfolio manager, securities analyst, investment theorist*
Miskowski, Lee R. *retired automobile executive*
Mislow, Kurt Martin *chemist, educator*
Misner, Lorraine *laboratory technologist*
Misrach, Richard Laurence *photographer*
Missan, Richard Sherman *lawyer*
Mitcham, Julius Jerome *accountant*
Mitchell, Adele Dickinson *health facility administrator*
Mitchell, Briane Nelson *lawyer*
Mitchell, Claybourne, Jr. *retired utilities executive*
Mitchell, Donald J. *former congressman*
Mitchell, Rick *journalist, writer*
Mitchem, Mary Teresa *publishing executive*
Mitelman, Bonnie Cossman *editor, writer, lecturer*
Mitrany, Devora *marketing consultant, writer*
Mitts, Marybeth Frazier *real estate company executive, consultant*
Mitzelfeld, Lisa Grayson *public relations executive*
Mitzner, Kenneth Martin *electrical engineering consultant*
Moak, Elizabeth *critical care and operating room nurse, legal nurse consultant*
Mobley, Patricia Ann (Trish Mobley) *lay church worker, church secretary*
Modigliani, Franco *economics and finance educator*
Modine, Matthew Avery *actor*
Moeckel, Bill Reid *retired university dean*
Moeller, Robert John *management consultant*
Moens, David Brian *manufacturing company executive*
Moffatt, Hugh McCulloch, Jr. *hospital administrator, physical therapist*
Moffatt, Katy (Katherine Louella Moffatt) *musician, vocalist, songwriter*
Moffatt, Laura L. *critical care nurse*
Moffatt, Mindy Ann *middle school educator, educational training specialist*
†Moffet, Penelope Jeanne *freelance writer, legal secretary*
Moffett, Samuel Hugh *retired educator, minister*
Moffitt, Susan Raye *critical care nurse*
Mogel, Leonard Henry *author*
Mohamed, Joseph *real estate broker*
Mohler, Brian Jeffery *diplomat*
Mojica, Aurora *training director*
Moliere, Jeffrey Michael *cardiopulmonary administrator*
†Molin, Paulette Fairbanks *university official, writer*
†Molinari, Ana Maria *salon owner*
Molitoris, Sallyann *eye care nurse*
Moll, David Carter *civil engineer*
Moller, Mary Denise *psychiatric nurse practitioner*
Molloy, Angela Margaret *advertising executive*
Molloy, Sylvia *Latin American literature educator, writer*
Moloff, Alan Lawrence *army officer, physician*
Molson, Robert Henry *obstetrician, gynecologist*
Moltzau, Hughitt Gregory *retired management training specialist*
Monacelli, Gianfranco *publishing executive*
Monaghan, Thomas Stephen *retired restaurant chain executive*
Monahan, Edward Charles *academic administrator, marine science educator*
Monck, Harry Nelson, IV *lawyer*
Monda, Marilyn *quality improvement consultant*
Mondale, Walter Frederick *former Vice President of United States, diplomat, lawyer*
Monninger, Robert Harold George *ophthalmologist, educator*
Monroe, Murray Shipley *lawyer*
Monsma, Robbie Elizabeth *lawyer, mediator, arbitrator, real estate executive*
Monson, David Carl *school superintendent, farmer, state legislator*
Montero, Fernan Gonzalo *retired advertising executive*
Montgomery, David Paul *professional baseball team executive*
Montgomery, James Morton *public relations, marketing executive, association executive*
Montgomery, Michael *secondary science educator*
Montgomery, Parker Gilbert *investment banker*
Montgomery, Roy Delbert *retired gas utility company executive*
Montgomery, Seth David *retired state supreme court chief justice*
†Montoya, Michael Evaristo *small busniess owner*
Montrose, Donald W. *retired bishop*
Monty, Charles Embert *utility company executive*
Moody, Graham Blair *lawyer*
Moody, Roland Herbert *retired librarian*
Moon, Katie Parmley *critical care nurse, home health care nurse*
Moore, Emily Allyn *pharmacologist*
†Moore, George William, III *sportswriter, editor*
Moore, John Cordell *retired lawyer*
Moore, John Plunkett Dennis *publisher*
Moore, John Ronald *manufacturing executive*
Moore, Linda Picarelli *insurance executive*
Moore, Lloyd Evans *retired lawyer*
Moore, Malcolm Frederick *manufacturing executive*
Moore, Powell Allen *government official*
Moore, Richard Alan *landscape architect*
Moore, Richard Earl *communications creative director*
Moore, Robert Henry *insurance company executive*
Moore, Robert William *professional organization executive*
Moore, Ruth Lambert Bromberg *retired clinical psychologist*
Moore, Thomas David *academic administrator*
Moore, Thomas Paul *retired broadcast executive*
Moore, Vernon Lee *agricultural consultant, retired food products company executive*
Moore, William Leroy, Jr. *career officer, physician*
Moorhead, Patrick Henry *secondary school administrator*
Moos, Daniel James *retired surgeon, educator*
Moosbruker, Jane Barbara *organization development consultant*
Moossy, John *neuropathologist, neurologist, consultant*
Moradi, Ahmad F. *software company executive, consultant*
Morahan, Stephanie *nursing administrator*
†Morales, Mario Roberto *adult education educator*
Moran, Ann *education educator*
Moran, Charles A. *securities executive*
Moran, John Arthur *oil company executive*
Moran, Nancy A. *ecology educator*
Morandi, John Arthur, Jr. *nursing administrator, educator, nurse*
Morang, Diane Judy *writer, television producer, business entrepreneur*
Moranis, Rick *actor*
Mordecai, Benjamin *theatrical producer, drama educator*
Morehead, Annette Marie *disabled children's facility administrator, child advocate*
Morehouse, Kathleen Salisbury Moore *writer*
Moreland, Alvin Franklin *veterinarian*
Morelli, Laura Baedor *nursing administrator*
Morelli, Peter Richard *electronic executive*
Morello, Joseph Albert *musician, educator*
Moreno, Jeanne Simonne *telemetry nurse*
Moreno, Patricia Frazier *legal assistant*
Morey, Nancy H. *medical/surgical nurse*
Morgan, Ann Lee *art historian, writer*
Morgan, Edmund Sears *history educator*
Morgan, Elizabeth *plastic and reconstructive surgeon*
Morgan, Evelyn Buck *nursing educator*
Morgan, James John *environmental engineering educator*
Morgan, Jane Hale *retired library director*
†Morgan, Janet Carol *library director*

Morgan, Mary Lou retired education educator, civic worker
Morgan, Robert Arthur accountant
Morgan, Ruth Prouse academic administrator, educator
Morgan, Thomas Rowland retired marine corps officer
Morgenroth, Earl Eugene entrepreneur
Moriarty, Donald William, Jr. banker
Moriarty, Michael actor
†Morin, Matthew Adrien producer
Morin-Miller, Carmen Aline writer
Morita, (Noriyuki) Pat actor, comedian
Morning, John graphic designer
Morreale, Ben retired history educator, novelist
Morrell, Gene Paul liquid terminal company executive
†Morrell, Kim Irving sales and marketing professional
Morrill, Penny Chittim art historian
Morrill, Thomas Clyde insurance company executive
Morris, Albert Jerome medical company executive
Morris, Diana Lee foundation executive
Morris, Dorothy Kay credit executive
Morris, Edward J(ames), Jr. retired insurance agent, small business owner
Morris, Frank Eugene banker
Morris, Robert G(emmill) retired foreign service officer
Morris, Stanley E. retired federal official
Morris, Winifred Walker art educator
†Morrisard-Larkin, Mary Angela foreign language educator
Morrison, Barbara Haney educational administrator
Morrison, Ian A(lastair) foundation executive
Morrison, James R. retired banker
Morrison, Sarah Lyddon author
Morrison, Shelley actress
Morrissey, Charles Thomas historian, educator
Morrow, Barry Nelson screenwriter, producer
Morrow, George Lester retired oil and gas executive
Morrow, Ralph Ernest historian, educator
Morrow, Rob actor
Morse, Flo writer
Morse, Richard Alan accountant
Morse, Robert Harry lawyer
Morse, Susan Edwina film editor
Mortensen, Peter banker
Mortimer, David William communications engineer
Mortola, Edward Joseph academic administrator emeritus
Morton, George Thomas reporter
Morton, Richard Lew retired military officer
Mosca, August artist
Mosca, Virginia retired language educator
Moscona, Aron Arthur biology educator, scientist
Moseley-Braun, Carol senator
Moser, Gerald M. emeritus educator
Moses, Michael James insurance company executive
Mosher, D. Russell cancer therapist
Mosler, John retired financial planner
Mosqueira, Charlotte Marianne dietitian
Moszawir, Harve H., Jr. retired lawyer
Moszkowicz, Virginia Marie quality administrator
Mott, Mary Elizabeth retired educational administrator
Mott, Stewart Rawlings business executive, political activist
Motto, Jerome Arthur psychiatry educator
Mould, Joan Powell social worker
Mount, Thomas H(enderson) motion picture and stage producer
Mountain, Clifton Fletcher surgeon, educator
Mowatt-Larssen, Erling transportation consultant
†Mowry, Elizabeth artist
Moy, Audrey retired retail buyer
Moyer, Jerry Mills financial services company executive
Moyers, Ernest Everett S. retired missile research scientist
Moylan, James Joseph lawyer
Moylan, Jay Richard medical products executive
Moynahan, John Daniel, Jr. retired insurance executive
Muckerman, Norman James priest, writer
Mudd, Roger Harrison news broadcaster, educator
Mudd, Sidney Peter former beverage company executive
Mudloff, Barbara medical/surgical nurse
Muecke, Charles Andrew (Carl Muecke) federal judge
Mueller, Barbara Stewart (Bobbie Mueller) youth drug use prevention specialist, volunteer
Mueller, Robert Louis business executive
Muhammad, Farid Ilyas social science educator
Muico-Mercurio, Luisa critical care nurse
Mujica, Mauro E. architect
Mukamal, David Samier sign manufacturing company executive
Mulcahy, Robert Edward management consultant
Mulcahy, Russell film director
Mulder, Douglas Wayne secondary educator
Muldoon, Thomas Lyman writer
Mulgrew, Katherine Kiernan actress
Mull, Charles Leroy, II retired naval officer and travel agency executive
Mullan, Donald William archbishop
Mullen, William Joseph, III military analyst, retired army officer
Muller, Margie Hellman financial services consultant
Muller, Peter lawyer, entertainment company executive, retail company executive, consultant
Mullikin, Steven Milton critical care nurse
Mumma, Albert Girard, Jr. architect
Muncey, James Arthur, Jr. architect
Munger, Bryce Leon physician, educator
Munic, Rachelle Ethel health services administrator
Munier, William Boss medical service executive
Munies, Seth Alix accountant
Muñoz, Carlos Ramón bank executive
Munsey, Virdell Everard, Jr. retired utility executive
Munson, Virginia Aldrich interior designer, decorator
Murdock, Mary-Elizabeth history educator
Murdza, Deanna Carol database administrator
Muren, Dennis E. visual effects director
†Murff, Elizabeth Jane Tipton mathematician, statistician, educator
Murphy, Benjamin Edward actor
Murphy, Bette Jane M. retired geriatrics nurse, nursing administrator
Murphy, Cindy L. medical/surgical and pediatrics nurse
Murphy, Donna Mae small business owner, social worker, lawyer
Murphy, Elisabeth Maria physical design engineer, consultant
Murphy, Francis English language educator
Murphy, Lewis Curtis lawyer, former mayor
Murphy, Margaret A. nursing educator, adult nurse practitioner
Murphy, Mary Kathleen family nurse practitioner, nursing educator
Murphy, Mary Kathleen Connors college administrator, writer
†Murphy, M(ichael) John neurologist, educator
Murphy, Sandra Robison lawyer
Murphy, Sheryl Warren rehabilitation nurse, consultant
Murphy, Timothy Aaron journalist
Murray, Albert L. writer, educator
Murray, Archibald R. lawyer
Murray, David George architect
Murray, Dorothy Speicher educator
Murray, Ernest Don artist, educator
Murray, Florence Kerins retired state supreme court justice
Murray, James D. physician
Murray, Leonard Hugh railroad executive
Murray, Robert Gray sculptor
Murrill, Paul Whitfield former utility executive, former university administrator
Musante, Tony (Anthony Peter Musante, Jr.) actor
Muson, Howard Henry writer, editor
Mutch, James Donald health therapist
Mydland, Gordon James judge
Myerowitz, P. David cardiologist, cardiac surgeon
Myers, Harold Mathews academic administrator
Myers, Jack Edgar biologist, educator
Myers, Jesse Jerome lawyer
Myers, John Herman investment management executive
Myers, John Thomas retired congressman
Myers, Mike actor, writer
Myers, Miller Franklin finance company executive, retail executive
Myers, Phillip Samuel mechanical engineering educator
Myers, Shirley Diana art book editor
Myerson, Alan director, film and television writer
Mysel, Randy Howard publishing company executive
Nabers, Claude Lowrey retired periodontist, writer
Nabholz, Mary Vaughan rehabilitation nurse
Nabrit, Samuel Milton retired embryologist
Nadel, Kenneth Alan editorial art director
Nader, Suzanne Nora Beurer elementary education educator
Nader-Heikenfeld, Rita Maria culinary educator, food writer
†Nagel, Robert Franklin lawyer
Nagel, Thomas philosopher, educator
Nagler, Barry lawyer
Naglieri, Eileen Sheridan special education educator
Nahman, Norris Stanley electrical engineer
Nahumck, Nadia Chilkovsky performer, dance educator, choreographer, author
Nair, Raghavan D. accountant, educator
Nairn, Charles Edward librarian, pastor, religious educator
†Najera, Peter Francisco military officer
Nakagawa, Allen Donald radiologic technologist
Nakahata, Tadaka retired consulting engineer, land surveyor
Nakamoto, Carolyn Matsue principal
Nakamura, Kazuo artist
Nakayama, Wataru engineering educator, consultant
Nance, David W. minister
Nank, Lois Rae financial executive
Napoleon, Donald Paul grocery store executive
Narath, Albert retired laboratory administrator
Nardi, Thomas James psychologist
Nardi Riddle, Clarine association administrator, judge
Narita, Hiro cinematographer
Nasgaard, Roald museum curator
Nash, Janet Rae geriatrics nurse
Nash, Susan Smith geologist
Nason, Dolores Irene computer company executive, counselor, eucharistic minister
Natcher, Stephen Darlington lawyer, business executive
Natkin, Robert painter
Nattras, Ruth A(nn) school nurse
Naugle, Jean Marie legal nurse consultant
Nava, Yolanda Margot broadcast journalist, author
Navalkar, Ramchandra Govindrao microbiologist, immunologist
Navarro, Karen Ann women's health care nurse practitioner
Navickas, John fluid dynamics engineer, researcher, consultant
Navratilova, Martina former professional tennis player
Nawy, Edward George civil engineer, educator
Naylor, Thomas Herbert economist, educator, consultant
Neal, Margaret Sherrill writer, editor
Neame, Ronald director, producer
Nearine, Robert James educational psychologist
Neary, Patricia Elinor ballet director
Necula, Nicholas electrical engineering consultant
Nederlander, James Laurence theater owner, producer
Nederveld, Ruth Elizabeth retired real estate executive
Needleman, Philip cardiologist, pharmacologist
Neel, James Van Gundia geneticist, educator
Neel, Judy Murphy association executive
Neely, Mark Edward, Jr. writer
Neff, Donald Lloyd news correspondent, writer
Neff, Jack Kenneth apparel manufacturing company executive
Neff, Lester Leroy administrator, minister
Nehrt, Lee Charles management educator
Neilson, Benjamin Reath lawyer
Neish, Francis Edward advertising agency executive
Nelligan, Kate (Patricia Colleen Nelligan) actress
Nelson, Barbara Kay insurance agent
Nelson, Ben, Jr. retired air force officer
Nelson, Carl Roger retired lawyer
Nelson, Craig T. actor
Nelson, Cynthia J. city official
Nelson, Edwin Clarence academic administrator, emeritus
Nelson, Helen Martha retired library director
Nelson, Jodie Lynn charity administrator
Nelson, John Howard food company research executive
Nelson, Kaye Lynn healthcare consultant
Nelson, Martha Jane magazine editor
Nelson, Martin Walter academic administrator, writer
Nelson, Norman Daniel government official
Nelson, Ralph Stanley lawyer
Nelson, Robert Charles newspaper executive
Nelson, Wallace Warren retired superintendent experimental station, agronomy educator
Nelson, Walter Gerald retired insurance company executive
Nemec, Josef retired organic chemist, researcher
Nemiroff, Maxine Celia art educator, gallery owner, consultant
Nesbit, Phyllis Schneider judge
Nesheim, Robert Olaf food products executive
Neshyba, Victor Peter retired aerophysics engineer
†Nesoff, Sandra Roberta journalist, social services administrator
Neswald, Barbara Anne advertising executive, writer
Netter, Cornelia Ann real estate broker
Netterville, George Bronson minister
Neuhaus, Joan T. finance company executive, private investigator
Neuman, Robert Harold communication executive
Neumann, Forrest Karl retired hospital administrator
Neumark, Gertrude Fanny materials science educator
Neunzig, Carolyn Miller elementary, middle and high school educator
Neuwirth, Allan Charles designer, director, screenwriter
†Neuwirth, Matthew Anthony marketing executive
Neville, Phoebe choreographer, dancer, educator
Neville-Babst, Lisa Ann medical/surgical nurse
Nevins, Sara Ann retired counselor
Nevins, Sheila television programmer and producer
†New, Thomas L. government executive
Newbern, William David retired state supreme court justice
Newborn, Jud anthropologist, writer, lyricist
Newbrun, Ernest oral biology and periodontology educator
Newby, James Edward education educator
Newcomb, Robert Carl real estate broker
Newell, William Talman, Jr. hospital administrator
Newland, James LeRoy retired bank executive
Newland, Larry J. orchestra conductor
Newman, Carol L. lawyer
Newman, Constance Berry museum administrator
Newman, Denis fund executive
Newman, Muriel Kallis Steinberg art collector
Newman, Paul actor, professional race-car driver, food company executive
Newman, Steven Harvey insurance company executive
Newman, Theodore Roosevelt, Jr. judge
Newman, William Guy producer, director, consultant
Newton, Barbara Benedetti artist, educator
Nicholas, Lawrence Bruce import company executive
Nicholas, Lynn Holman writer
Nicholas, Peter medical educator
Nichols, C. Walter, III retired trust company executive
Nichols, Carl Michael Internet media executive
Nichols, Iris Jean illustrator
Nichols, James Robbs university dean
Nichols, John David entrepreneur freelance
†Nichols, Kelley Maureen entertainment executive
Nichols, Mike stage and film director
Nichols, Sandra Lee community health nurse
Nicholson, June C. Daniels speech pathologist
Nicholson, Leland Ross retired utilities company executive, energy consultant
Nicholson, Richard Joseph trust banking executive
Nicklaus, Jack William professional golfer
Niclas, Karl Bernhard electronics engineer
Nicolas, Kenneth Lee international financial business executive
Nicolette, Lillian H. nursing administrator, consultant, educator
Nicotera, Cathy secondary education educator
Niehaus, Deborah Ann post-anesthesia care nurse
Nielsen, Glade Benjamin former mayor, former state senator
Nielsen, Karen Kay secondary education educator
Nielsen, Linda M. city councilwoman
Niemann, Lewis Keith lamp manufacturing company executive
†Niffenegger, Audrey Anne artist
Nigro, Ann K. geriatrics nurse, educator
Nilsson, A. Kenneth investor
Nish, Albert Raymond, Jr. retired newspaper editor
Nishimura, Joseph Yo retired retail executive, accountant
†Nissen, Lowell Allen education educator
Nix, Nancy Jean librarian, designer
Nixon, David dancer
Nixon, Marni singer
Nobles, Laurence Hewit retired geology educator
Nochman, Lois Wood Kivi (Mrs. Marvin Nochman) educator
Nodelman, Nancy Ziegler sculptor, designer
Noëldechen, Joan Marguerite writer
Noeth, Louise Ann journalist
Noland, Kenneth Clifton artist
Nolde, Shari Ann pediatrics, critical care nurse
Nolen, William Giles lawyer, accountant
†Noll, Danielle Renee healthcare policy analyst
Nolte, Nick actor
Nondorf, Janice Kathryn special education educator
Noonan, Julie Anne Carroll management consultant
Nord, Eric Thomas retired manufacturing executive
Nordby, Gene Milo engineering educator
Nordel, Patricia A. Olmstead medical/surgical, critical care, and obstetrical nurse
Nordley, Gerald David writer, investor
Nordlund, Donald Elmer manufacturing company executive
Norkin, Cynthia Clair physical therapist
Norman, Albert George, Jr. lawyer
Norman, Arlene Phyllis principal
Norman, Dudley Kent hospital administrator, nurse
Norman, E. Gladys business computer educator, consultant
Norman, Matthew West psychiatrist
Norris, Alfred Lloyd bishop
Norris, Darell Forest insurance company executive
Norris, June Rudolph minister
Norris, Katharine Eileen communications professional, educator
Norsworthy, John Randolph economist, educator
North, Gerald David William lawyer
North, John Adna, Jr. accountant, real estate appraiser
Norton, Andre Alice author
Norton, Judy actress
Norton, Karen Ann accountant
Norton, Nathaniel Goodwin marketing executive
Norton, Robert Michael mathematician, educator, statistician
Nosseck, Noel director
Nostrand, Howard Lee humanities educator
Nostrant, Timothy Thomas internist, gastroenterologist
Nothwanger, Rosemary Wood artist, geological illustrator
Nottingham, William Jesse retired church mission executive, minister
Nouriel, Margaret Cowan occupational health nurse
Nova, Craig writer
Novack, Alvin John physician
Novak, Alan Lee retired pharmaceutical company executive
Novak, Barbara art history educator
Novak, John Alfred mechanical engineer
Novas, Joseph, Jr. advertising agency executive
Novick, Julius Lerner theater critic, educator
Novinc, Judith Kaye medical/surgical nurse, administrator
Novotny, Deborah Ann management consultant
Nowaczek, Frank Huxley venture capital executive
Noyes, H(enry) Pierre physicist
Nuckols, William Marshall electrical goods manufacturing executive
Nugent, Shane Vincent lawyer
Nunn, Charles Burgess religious organization executive
Nunn, Trevor Robert director
Nurenberg, David retired oil company executive
Nusbaum, Geoffrey Dean psychotherapist
†Nusbaum, Margaret R.H. physician
Nygren, Malcolm Ernest minister
Nyman, David Harold retired nuclear engineer
Nymoen, Kristine Staples magazine editor
Oakes, Ellen Ruth psychotherapist, health institute administrator
Oakley, Andrew Arthur journalist, educator
Oates, Carl Everette lawyer
Oates, Joyce Marie psychiatrist
Obligacion, Freddie Rabelas sociology educator, researcher
Obrecht, Kenneth William banker
O'Brian, Hugh actor
O'Brien, Betty Alice theological librarian, researcher
O'Brien, Charles H. lawyer, retired state supreme court chief justice
O'Brien, J. Willard lawyer, educator
O'Brien, John Wilfrid economist, emeritus university president, educator
O'Brien, Mary Blichfeldt nursing consultant
O'Brien, MaryAnn Antoinette nursing educator
O'Brien, Orin Ynez musician, educator
†O'Brien, Sara Talis educator
O'Brien, Stephen James geneticist
O'Brien, Thomas Keith artist
Obushenko, Ivan Makarovich chemist
Ochs, Carol Rebecca theologian, philosophy and religion educator
O'Connell, Brian James priest, former university president
O'Connell, Philip Raymond retired lawyer, paper company executive
O'Connell, William Raymond, Jr. educational consultant
O'Connor, Doris Julia non-profit fundraiser, consultant
O'Connor, John Joseph operations executive
†O'Connor, Mallory McCane curator, art historian
Odell, Frank Harold banker
O'Dell, Joan Elizabeth lawyer, mediator, business executive
Oden, Jean Phifer special education educator
Odermatt, Robert Allen architect
O'Donnell, Brother Frank Joseph principal
O'Donnell, Kathleen Mary social services administrator
O'Donnell, Kevin retired metal working company executive
†O'Donnell, Sara Altshul editor
O'Driscoll, Marilyn Lutz elementary school educator
Oelman, Robert Schantz retired manufacturing executive
Offen, Ronald Charles retired school librarian
Ogden, Ann writer
Ogden, David William lawyer
Ogden, Denise Theresa marketing professional, educator
Ogg, George Wesley retired foreign service officer
O'Grady, Gail actress
†Ogren, Thomas L. township government administrator
O'Hara, Catherine actress, comedienne
O'Hare, James Raymond energy company executive
O'Hollaren, Paul Joseph former international fraternity administrator
Okada, Takuya retail executive
†O'Kane, Karen Ann English educator
Okolski, Cynthia Antonia psychotherapist, social worker
Okoshi-Mukai, Sumiye artist
Oksas, Joan Kay economist, educator
Oldfield, A(rthur) Barney writer, radio commentator
Olds, Jacqueline psychiatrist, educator
Oldshue, Paul Frederick financial executive
O'Leary, Denis Joseph retired physician, insurance company executive
O'Leary, Dennis Sophian medical organization executive
O'Leary, Patsy Baker writer, educator
O'Leary, Timothy Michael real estate corporation officer
Oliansky, Joel author, director
Oliphant, Ernie L. safety educator, public relations executive, consultant
Olive, David Michael magazine writer, magazine editor
Oliver, Marian Marie nurse
Oliver, Steven Wiles investment banker
Olivet, Joseph Francis elementary school educator
Olkinetzky, Sam artist, retired museum director and educator
†Ologbenla, Adesoji Olaposi financial advisor
Olsen, Clifford Wayne retired physical chemist, consultant
Olsen, George Edward retired insurance executive
Olsen, Jack writer
Olson, Dale C. public relations executive
Olson, James Clifton historian, university president
Olson, Paul Richard Spanish literature educator, editor
Olson, Phillip Roger naval officer
Olson, William Clinton international affairs educator, author, lecturer
Olson-Hagan, Arlene parochial school administrator
O'Malley, Thomas Patrick academic administrator
Omholt, Bruce Donald product designer, mechanical engineer, consultant
O'Neal, Harriet Roberts psychologist, psycholegal consultant
O'Neal, Ryan (Patrick Ryan O'Neal) actor

†O'Neal, Vanessa *educational association administrator*
O'Neil, Cleora Tanner *personnel specialist*
†O'Neill, James Benjamin *economics educator*
Ong, Bernard Tiu *global bank officer*
Onslow Ford, Gordon Max *painter*
Oppenheim, David Jerome *musician, retired university dean*
†Opsahl-Ong, Beale Hibbs *physicist*
O'Quinn, Nancy Diane *nurse, educator*
Ord, Linda Banks *artist*
Ordal, Caspar Reuben *business executive*
Oreluk, Mary M. *critical care nurse*
Orem, Cassandra Elizabeth *health systems administrator, educator, author, holistic health practitioner, entrepreneur*
Orlebeke, William Ronald *retired lawyer, writer*
Orloff, Neil *lawyer*
Ormasa, John *retired utility executive, lawyer*
Ornston, Darius Gray, Jr. *psychiatrist*
Oropallo, Deborah *artist, educator*
O'Rourke, Joan B. Doty Werthman *educational administrator*
Orr, Bobby (Robert Gordon Orr) *former hockey player*
Orr, Carol Wallace *book publishing executive*
Orr, Kenneth Bradley *academic administrator*
Orrmont, Arthur *writer, editor*
Ortiz, Angel Vicente *church administrator*
Ortiz, Francis Vincent, Jr. *retired ambassador*
Ortolano, Ralph J. *engineering consultant*
Orton, Patricia Osborn *marina owner, real estate investor*
Orttung, William Herbert *chemistry educator*
Osa, Douglas Lee *artist, printmaker*
Osborn, Kenneth Louis *financial executive*
Osborn, Susan Titus *editor*
Osborn, Terry Wayne *biochemist, executive*
Osborn, William George *savings and loan executive*
Osborne, James Alfred *religious organization administrator*
†Osborne, Linda Barrett *writer, editor*
O'Shea, Catherine Large *marketing and public relations consultant*
Osler, Dorothy K. *state legislator*
Osment, Lamar Sutton *retired dermatologist, educator*
Osmycki, Daniel A. *commercial real estate broker, consultant*
Osrin, Raymond Harold *retired political cartoonist*
Ossana, Diana Lynn *author, screenwriter*
Ostaszewski, Alyce Vitella *religion educator*
Oster, Lewis Henry *manufacturing executive, engineering consultant*
Osterhoff, James Marvin *retired telecommunications company executive*
O'Sullivan, Paul Kevin *business executive, management and instructional systems consultant*
Oswald, Robert Bernard *science administrator, nuclear engineer*
Otis, Denise Marie *editor, writer*
Otis, Jack *social work educator*
Otis, Lee Liberman *lawyer, educator*
Ott, Joseph John *computer specialist, writer*
Otto, Ingolf Helgi Elfried *banking institute fellow*
Oustrich, Josephine *elementary education educator*
Outka, Gene Harold *philosophy and Christian ethics educator*
Outland, Max Lynn *retired school system administrator*
Overcash, Shelia Ann *nurse*
Oviedo, Tamara Lenore *management consultant, photojournalist*
Owano, Mary Beth *pediatrics intensive care unit nurse*
Owens, Betsy Kingsolver *writer*
Owens, Charles Vincent, Jr. *diagnostic company executive and consultant*
Owens, John Franklin *health care administrator, consultant, nurse*
Ownbey, Lenore F. Daly *real estate investment specialist*
Oxyer, Mina Jane Stevens *nurse*
Pace, Charles Robert *psychologist, educator*
†Pachman, Ilene Munetz *writer, educator*
Pack, Allen S. *retired coal company executive*
Pack, Richard Morris *broadcasting executive*
Pack, Susan Joan *art consultant*
Packard, John Mallory *physician*
Padberg, Frank Thomas, Jr. *surgeon, educator*
Padberg, Harriet Ann *mathematics educator*
†Padrón, Ricardo *foreign language educator*
Paganelli, Charles Victor *physiologist*
Page, Lewis Wendell, Jr. *lawyer*
Page, Nancy Ellen *pediatrics nurse, nursing consultant*
Page, Willis *conductor*
Pai, Suren *telecommunications company executive*
Paige, Anita Parker *retired English language educator*
†Paine, Herbert *ballet administrator*
Painter, Robert Lowell *surgeon, educator*
Painton, Russell Elliott *lawyer, mechanical engineer*
Pal, Pratapaditya *museum curator*
Palade, George Emil *biologist, educator*
Palance, Jack *actor*
Palausi, Nicole (Nicole Galinat) *artist*
Palisi, Anthony Thomas *psychologist, educator*
Palizzi, Anthony N. *lawyer, retail corporation executive*
Pall-Pallant, Teri *paleontologist, inventor, behavioral scientist, design engineer, advertising agency executive*
Palmer, Bradley Beran *sportscaster*
Palmer, Dave Richard *retired military officer, academic administrator*
Palmer, Gary Andrew *portfolio manager*
Palmer, Irene Sabelberg *university dean and educator emeritus, nurse, researcher, historian*
Palmer, Langdon *banker*
Palmer, Larry George *chemist*
Palmer, Raymond Alfred *administrator, librarian, consultant*
Palmer, Ricky Samuel *physicist*
Palms, Roger Curtis *educator, editor, clergyman*
Palter, Robert Monroe *philosophy and history educator*
Palumbo, Matthew Aloysius *marketing executive*
Palvino, Jack Anthony *broadcasting executive*
†Panagakos, Michael Joseph *sales executive*
Panas, Sonya Lee Sawaya *retired gerontology and pediatrics nurse*
Pandya, Deanna Mears *family counselor, addiction counselor*
Pankratz, Carol Joyce *medical/surgical clinical nurse specialist*
†Pantzer, John G. *retired physician*
Paolucci, Anne Attura *playwright, poet, English and comparative literature educator*
Papadakos, Nicholas Peter *retired state supreme court justice*
Pappachristou, Joyce Flores *dietitian, educator*
†Pappas, Christine Jean *psychologist*
Paquin, Paul Peter *corporate finance executive*
Pardue, A. Michael *retired plastic and reconstructive surgeon*
Paredes-ManFredi, Lynn *college director*
Parent, Rodolphe Jean *Canadian air force official, pilot*
Parenti, Kathy Ann *sales professional*
Paret, John J. *clergyman*
Parins, Robert James *professional football team executive, judge*
Paris, Steven Mark *software engineer*
Park, John Thornton *academic administrator*
Park, Jon Keith *dentist, educator*
Park, Patricia Weill *controller*
Parker, Brent Mershon *retired medical educator, internist, cardiologist*
Parker, George *retired pen manufacturing company executive*
Parker, George Anthony *computer leasing company executive*
Parker, Gerald William *physician, medical administrator, retired*
Parker, Harry John *retired psychologist, educator*
Parker, Lee Fischer *sales executive*
Parker, Mel *editor*
Parker, Robert Brown *novelist*
Parker, Scott Lane *management consultant*
Parkman, Cynthia Ann *medical/surgical nurse, nurse educator*
Parks, Grace Susan *bank official*
Parks, Jane deLoach *retired law librarian, legal assistant*
Parode, Ann *lawyer*
Parreira, Helio Correa *physical chemist*
Parris, Nina Gumpert *curator, writer, researcher, photographer*
Parrish, Alma Ellis *elementary school educator*
Parrish, Matthew Denwood *psychiatrist*
Parrish, T. Michael *historian*
Parrott, Wanda Sue *writer, journalist*
Parry, Atwell J., Jr. *state senator, retailer*
Parsa, Brian Bahram *surgeon, military officer*
Parsons, Elmer Earl *retired clergyman*
Parsons, Harry Glenwood *retired surgeon*
Partington, James Wood *naval officer*
Partlow, Marianne Fairbank *artist, consultant, curator*
Partridge, Connie R. *advertising executive*
Pascale, Daniel Richard *circuit judge*
Pascoe, Patricia Hill *state senator, writer*
Paskawicz, Jeanne Frances *pain specialist*
Passmore, Michael Forrest *environmental research administrator*
Pastorek, Norman Joseph *facial plastic surgeon*
Pate, Joseph Michael *family nurse practitioner*
†Pate, Virginia Frances *artist, educator*
Patel, Roshni *social studies educator*
Patent, Dorothy Hinshaw *author, photographer*
Paterson, Robert E. *trading stamp company executive*
Patmos, Adrian Edward *university dean emeritus*
Patrick, Brenda Jean *educational consultant*
Patrick, Deval Laurdine *lawyer*
Patterson, Dennis Joseph *management consultant*
Patterson, Donis Dean *bishop*
Patterson, F. Ellen *social worker*
Patterson, Mildred Lucas *teaching specialist*
Patterson, Myrna Nancy *secondary education educator*
Patterson, Richard North *novelist, writer, lawyer*
Patterson, Robert Hudson *retired university library director*
Pattison, Jon Allen *computer scientist, consultant*
Patton, David Wayne *health care executive*
Patton, James Richard, Jr. *lawyer*
Patton, John Joseph *retired literature educator*
Pauken, Thomas Weir *venture capital executive, lawyer, mediator*
Paul, Evelyn Rose *critical care nurse*
Paul, Frank *retired consulting company executive*
Paul, Frank Allen *physician*
Paul, Richard Wright *lawyer*
Paul, Ron *congressman*
Paul, Vera Maxine *mathematics educator*
Paulsen, Frank Robert *college dean emeritus*
Paulson, Kenneth Alan *journalist, lawyer, business executive*
Paulson-Schiefelbein, Cindy Patrice *occupational therapist*
Paulus, Norma Jean Petersen *lawyer, state school system administrator*
Pauly, John Edward *anatomist*
Paup, Martin Arnold *real estate and securities investor*
Pautler, Maria Christine Sadusky *environmental scientist*
Paxton, Juanita Willene *retired university official*
Paxton, Laura Belle-Kent *English language educator, management professional*
Paxton, Tom *songwriter, entertainer, author*
Payne, Douglas DeFrees *cardiothoracic surgeon, educator*
Payne, Kevin Joseph *professional sports team executive*
Payne, Ladell *retired college president*
Pazdera, John Paul *regulatory services executive*
Pazienza, Vinny *professional boxer*
Peacock, Mary Willa *magazine editor*
Pear, Charles E., Jr. *lawyer*
Pearce, Paul Francis *retired aerospace electronics company executive*
Pearl, B. Michael *business owner*
Pearlmutter, Florence Nichols *psychologist, therapist*
Pearlstein, Philip *artist*
Pearson, Ralph Gottfrid *chemistry educator*
Pearson, Susan Winifred *dean, consultant*
Pearson, Wayman J. *waste management executive*
Pease, Sara Gooding *lay worker*
Peat, Wanda Jean *critical care nurse*
Peccarelli, Anthony Marando *lawyer*
Peck, Daniel Farnum *chemical company executive*
Peck, (Eldred) Gregory *actor*
Peck, Robert David *educational foundation administrator*
Peckham, Donald Eugene *retired utilities company executive*
Peckham, Ellen Stoepel *artist, poet*
Pedersen, Knud George *economics educator, academic administrator*
Peel, Mary Ann *nursing educator*
Peel, Victoria *elementary educator*
Peeples, Rufus Roderick, Jr. (Roddy Peeples) *farm and ranch news radio broadcaster*
Peers, Michael Geoffrey *archbishop*
Peete, Russell Fitch, Jr. *aircraft appraiser*
Peete, William Pettway Jones *surgeon*
Pefley, Norman Gordon *financial analyst*
Peixoto, Jose Ulysses *internist, researcher*
Péladeau, Marius Beaudoin *art consultant, retired museum director*
Pelkey, Mildred Loraine *volunteer*
Pell, Claiborne *former senator*
Pelotte, Donald Edmond *bishop*
Peltier, Eugene Joseph *civil engineer, former naval officer, business executive*
Pelz, Herman H. *physician*
†Peña, Federico Fabian *retired federal official*
Pena, Manuel, Jr. *retired state senator*
Penachio, Anthony Joseph, Jr. *psychotherapist, hypnotherapist, behavioral therapist*
Pendexter, Hugh, III *adult education educator*
Pendleton, Barbara Jean *retired banker*
Pendleton, Joan Marie *microprocessor designer*
Penke, Cynthia Marie *critical care nurse*
Penn, William Robert *critical care nurse*
Pennacchio, Linda Marie *secondary school educator*
Pennardt, Andre M. *emergency physician*
Pennington, Richard Maier *lawyer, retired insurance company executive*
†Pennywitt, Neil C. *educational organization administrator, fundraiser*
Penzer, Mark *lawyer, editor, corporate trainer, former publisher*
Peoples, John Arthur, Jr. *former university president, consultant*
Pepper, Dorothy Mae *nurse*
Pepper, Jeffrey Mackenzie *publishing executive*
Peppler, William Norman *aviation association executive*
Percy, Lee Edward *motion picture film editor*
Perdigó, Luisa Marina *foreign language and literature educator*
Perelman, Leon Joseph *paper manufacturing executive, university president*
Perez, Luz Lillian *psychologist*
Perez-Borja, Carlos M. *neurologist, hospital executive*
Perez-Gimenez, Juan Manuel *federal judge*
Peri, Winnie Lee Branch *educational director*
Perigo, Michael Gregory *director of development*
Perinelli, Marguerite Rose *women's health nurse, educator*
Perkins, Charles Theodore *real estate developer, consultant*
Perkins, Courtland D(avis) *engineering educator*
Perkins, Monte Leonard *musician, educator*
Perkins, Thomas Keeble *oil company researcher*
Perko, Walter Kim *computer consultant, songwriter, poet*
Perle, George *composer*
Perlis, Michael Steven *magazine publisher*
Perlman, Morton Henry *retired surgeon and educator*
Perlman, Richard Brian *lawyer*
Perlov, Dadie *management consultant*
Perlstein, William James *lawyer*
Perraud, Pamela Brooks *human resources professional*
Perreault, Sister Jeanne *college president*
Perrin, Gail *editor*
Perrin, Lisa C. *fiber artist*
Perrin, Michael Warren *lawyer*
Perritti, Martha Lou *writer*
Perrot, Paul Norman *museum director*
†Perry, Chris Nicholas *advertising executive*
Perry, George Williamson *lawyer*
Perry, James DeWolf *management consultant*
Perry, James E. *not-for-profit development executive*
Perry, Josephine *screen writer, playwright, educator*
Perry, Kenneth Walter *retired integrated oil company executive*
Perry, Matthew *actor*
Perry, Ruth *writer*
Perry, William James *educator, former federal official*
Peruzzo, Albert Louis *actuary, accountant*
Pesci, Joe *actor*
Pesola, Gene Raymond *physician, educator*
Petacque, Arthur M. *journalist*
Peter, Richard Ector *zoology educator*
Peterman, Donna Cole *communications executive*
Peters, Bernadette (Bernadette Lazzara) *actress*
Peters, Douglas Alan *nurse, case manager*
Peters, Douglas Cameron *mining engineer, geologist*
Peters, Elizabeth *nursing manager*
Peters, Kurt James *retired obstetrician, gynecologist*
Peters, Patricia L. *elementary education educator*
Peters, Ralph Frew *investment banker*
Peters, Robert Allen *retired drug company executive*
Peters, Robert Woolsey *architect*
Peters, Shirley Ann *pediatrics nurse*
Peters, Virginia *actress*
Petersen, Arne Joaquin *chemist*
Petersen, James Randall *lay religious leader, writer, theater artist*
Peterson, Ann Sullivan *physician, health care consultant*
†Peterson, Barbara Ann Bennett *history educator, television personality*
Peterson, Clark C. *announcer, writer*
Peterson, Kevin Bruce *newspaper editor, publishing executive*
Peterson, Kristin *artist*
†Peterson, Patricia Will *legal secretary*
Peterson, Robert Austin *manufacturing company executive retired*
Peterson, Sharon L. *community health nurse*
Petok, Samuel *retired manufacturing company executive*
Petoskey, Thomas W. *secondary school educator*
Petree, Betty Chapman *anesthetist*
Petrequin, Harry Joseph, Jr. *foreign service officer*
Petrie, Daniel Mannix *film, theatre and television director*
Petrie, Hugh Gilbert *philosophy of education educator*
Petrikas, Regina Marija *acute care nurse practitioner*
Petrina, Anthony J. *retired mining executive*
†Petterson, Margo *artist*
Pettigrew, L. Eudora *retired academic administrator*
Pettigrew, Steven Lee *healthcare management consultant*
Pettis-Roberson, Shirley McCumber *former congresswoman*
Pettit, Ghery DeWitt *retired veterinary medicine educator*
Pettit, John W. *administrator*
Pettitt, Jay S. *architect, consultant*
Pettolina, Anthony Michael *radio producer, computer systems analyst*
Petty, Lori *actress*
Pevear, Roberta Charlotte *retired state legislator*
Peyser, Joseph Leonard *author, translator, historial researcher*
Pezeshki, Kambiz A. *metallurgical engineer*
Pflanze, Otto Paul *history educator*
Phelan, Ellen *artist*
Phelps, Deanne Elayne *educational counselor, consultant*
Phillips, Carla Rahn *history educator*
Phillips, Charles Alan *accounting firm executive*
Phillips, Darrell *retail executive*
Phillips, Dianne Mooney *elementary school educator*
Phillips, Glynda Ann *editor*
Phillips, James Dickson, Jr. *federal judge*
Phillips, Joy Eugenia *counselor, consultant*
Phillips, Juanita M. *maternal/women's health and neonatal nurse*
Phillips, Julia Mae *physicist*
Phillips, Martha Henderson *organization executive*
Phinney, Frederick Warren *priest*
Pi, Wen-Yi Shih *aircraft company engineer, researcher*
Pick, Anthony J. *physician, educator*
Pick, James Block *management and sociology educator*
Pick, Robert Yehuda *orthopedic surgeon, consultant*
Pickens, Samuel C. *family physician, educator*
Pickle, Linda Williams *biostatistician*
Pick Reed, Eija Anneli *fundraising executive*
Picower, Warren Michael *editor*
Piehl, Donald Herbert *chemist, consultant*
Pielou, Evelyn C. *biologist*
†Pierce, David Hyde *actor*
Pierce, Fredric Charles *retired probation officer*
Pierce, Jennifer Ember *songwriter, author*
Pierce, Jim *recording industry producer*
Pierce, John Thomas *industrial hygienist, clinical toxicologist*
Pierce, Ponchitta Ann *TV host, producer, journalist, writer, consultant*
Pierce, Robert Nash *writer*
Pierce, Samuel Riley, Jr. *government official, lawyer*
Pierce-Beall, Tamara Ann *counselor, career consultant*
Pietrzyk, Leslie *writer*
Pifer, Alan (Jay Parrish) *former foundation executive*
Piga, Stephen Mulry *lawyer*
Pignataro, Evelyn Dorothy *trauma clinician, operating room nurse*
Pilcher, Ellen Louise *rehabilitation counselor*
Pilgrim, Deborah Annice *psychotherapist*
Pilisuk, Marc *community psychology educator*
Pinataro, Jean Eleanor *artist*
Pincus-Witten, Robert A. *art history educator, art gallery director, critic*
Pinter, Gabriel George *physiolog educator*
Pionke, Harry Bernhard *research leader and soil scientist*
Piore, Nora Kahn *economist, health policy analyst*
Pipchick, Margaret Hopkins *clinical specialist psychiatric nursing, therapist, consultant*
Piper, Fredessa Mary *school system administrator*
Piperno, Sherry Lynn *psychotherapist*
Pippin, James Adrian, Jr. *middle school educator*
Pippin, James Rex *health care management consultant*
Pippin, Linda Sue *pediatrics nurse*
Pirro, Alfred Anthony, Jr. *physician*
Pisney, Raymond Frank *international consulting services executive*
Pitasi, Judy *nurse*
Pitcher, Griffith Fontaine *lawyer*
Pitcher, Virginia Griffith Stein *fashion designer, graphic designer, poet*
Pitman, LaVern Frank *retired librarian*
†Pitman, Lemoine *sheet metal worker, trade union director*
Pitman, Sharon Gail *middle school counselor*
Pitrella, Francis Donald *human factors professional*
Pittelko, Roger Dean *clergyman, religious educator*
Pitts, Carl Thomas *secondary education educator*
Pitts, Terence Randolph *curator and museum director*
Piven, Joshua L. *journalist*
Pizzuro, Salvatore Nicholas *special education educator*
Pizzuto, Debra Kay *mathematics educator*
Pizzuto, Emanuelina Maria *concert pianist, composer*
Plangere, Jules Leon, Jr. *retired media company executive*
Plank, (Ethel) Faye *editor, photographer, writer*
Platt, Lewis Emmett *electronics company executive*
Platti, Rita Jane *educator, draftsman, author, inventor*
Plaza, Eva M. *lawyer*
Pleming-Yocum, Laura Chalker *religion educator*
Pleshette, Suzanne *actress, writer*
Pletcher, Eldon *editorial cartoonist*
Plottel, Gloria Susanne Stone *marketing professional*
†Plumly, Stanley *English educator, poet*
Plummer, Amanda *actress*
Plummer, Daniel Clarence, III *retired insurance consultant*
Plummer, Leone Poindexter *marriage and family therapist, nursing educator, nurse practitioner*
Plutro, Michele Ann *education specialist*
Plymyer, John Robert *retired professional association administrator*
Pniakowski, Andrew Frank *structural engineer*
Poad, Flora Virginia *retired librarian and educator*
Pockell, Leslie Mark *publishing company executive*
Pocock, Frederick James *environmental scientist, engineer, consultant*
Podhoretz, Norman *magazine editor, writer*
Pogue, Richard Welch *lawyer*
Poitier, Sidney *actor, director*
Pokras, Sheila Frances *retired judge*
Polacek, Deborah Jean *nursing consultant*
Polanco, Rosana Lim *grant writer*
Polatty, David P., III *military officer, federal agency administrator*
Poledouris, Basil K. *composer*
Poliakoff, Gary A. *lawyer, educator*
Polich, John Elliott *global marketing executive*
Polichino, Joseph Anthony, Jr. *wholesale company executive*
Policinski, Eugene Francis *author, newspaper editor, foundation executive*
Poling, Jerome Paul *journalist*
Polisar, Joseph Michael *protective services official*
Poll, Heinz *choreographer, artistic director*
Poll, Martin Harvey *film producer*
Pollack, Gerald Alexander *economist, government official*

Pollack, Sylvia Byrne retired educator, researcher, counselor
Pollan-Cohen, Shirley poet, educator
Pollard, Henry lawyer, mediator, arbitrator
†Pollet, Elizabeth writer, educator
Pollock, Karen Anne computer analyst
Pollock, Roy Van Horn animal health researcher
Polucci, Ashley Victor emergency staff nurse
Pomeroy, Kent Lytle physical medicine and rehabilitation physician
Pond, Phyllis Joan Ruble state legislator
Pool, Philip Bemis, Jr. investment banker
Pooley, Beverley John law educator, librarian
Pooley-Richards, Robin Lee critical care nurse
Poor, Anne artist
Poplawski, Joseph Walter retired glass manufacturing company executive
Porges, Walter Rudolf television news executive
Porretta, Emanuele Peter retired bank executive, consultant
†Porro-Salinas, Patricia Maria clinical psychologist
Portal, Gilbert Marcel Adrien oil company executive
Porte, Patricia Francis Skypeck geriatrics nursing administrator
Porter, Charles Henry photographer
Porter, Daniel Reed, III museum director
Porter, Dixie Lee insurance executive, consultant
Porter, Hayden Samuel computer science educator
Porter, Herbert M. retired pediatrician
Porter, Marie Ann neonatal nurse, labor and delivery nurse
Porter, Michael Pell lawyer
Porter, Nora Roxanne freelance graphic designer
Porter, Philip Thomas retired electrical engineer
Portis, Alan Mark physicist, educator
Portnoy, Sara S. lawyer
Porto, Mark writer
Posha, D. Richard real estate developer, home builder, designer
Posner, Sidney advertising executive
Poss, Jeffery Scott architect, educator
Post, Richard Bennett retired human resources executive
Poster, Steven Barry cinematographer, photgrapher, publisher, digital imaging consultant
†Postma, Martin J. economic development administrator
Poston, Ann Genevieve psychotherapist, nurse
Poston, Iona nursing educator
Poston, Tom actor
Poteat, James Donald diaconal minister, retired military officer
†Potempa Niedosik, Kim Marie sales executive
Potok, Chaim author, artist, editor
Potter, James Earl retired international hotel management company executive
Potter, Tanya Jean lawyer
Potts, Douglas Gordon retired neuroradiologist
Potts, Gerald Neal manufacturing company executive
Potts, Nancy Dee Needham psychologist
Potts, Ronald Clyde computer programmer, analyst
Potvin, Alfred Raoul engineering executive
Poulsen, Fern Sue special events and public relations consultant
Poulton, Roberta Doris nurse, consultant
Pound, Robert Vivian physics educator
Povish, Kenneth Joseph retired bishop
Powell, Clinton Cobb radiologist, physician, former university administrator
Powell, Earl Alexander, III art museum director
Powell, Karen Jean college program administrator
Powell, Kathleen Lynch lawyer, real estate executive
Powell, Marlys Kaye artist
Powell, Peter Irwin Augustus film producer and director
Powell, Sara Jordan musician, religious worker
Powell, Thomas Edward, III biological supply company executive, physician
Powers, Eldon Nathaniel computer mapping executive
Powers, Elizabeth Whitmel lawyer
Powers, John Henry industry executive
†Powers, Richard Augustine, III judge
Powless, David Griffin accountant
Pozzatti, Rudy Otto artist
Prabhu, Catherine Dudley school system administrator
Prady, Norman journalist, writer, advertising executive, marketing consultant
Prager, David retired state supreme court chief justice
Prakapas, Eugene Joseph art gallery director
Prange, Hilmar Walter neurology educator
Pratt, Alice Reynolds retired educational administrator
Pratt, David Terry engineering consultant
Pratt, Robert Windsor lawyer
Pratt, Veronica Kane writer
Pratte, Lise lawyer, corporate secretary, consultant
Precopio, Frank Mario chemical company executive
Preddy, Raymond Randall retired newspaper publisher, educator
Prescott, John Hernage aquarium executive
Prescott, Richard Chambers writer
Prescott, Tamy A. nurse practitioner
Preston, Seymour Stotler, III manufacturing company executive
Preszler, Sharon Marie psychiatric home health nurse
Prettyman-Baker, Sheila pediatrics, neonatal nurse
Preusser, Joseph William academic administrator
Prevost, Edward James paint manufacturing executive
Price, Ann Laurie senior health program manager
Price, Clifford Warren retired metallurgist, researcher
Price, Fredric Victor physician
Price, James Edward industrial engineer
Price, Nick professional golfer
Price, Paul Buford physicist, educator
Price, Robert electronics consultant
Price, Robert Ira coast guard officer
Price, Sandra Hoffman secondary school educator
Price, Thomas Frederick theatre educator
Price, Tom journalist
Price, William James, IV investment banker
Pride, Benjamin David advertising executive
Pridmore, Roy Davis government official
Priester, Horace Richard, Jr. retired quality assurance professional
Prieto, Claudio R. academic administrator, lawyer
Primes, Robert cinematographer
Primosch, James Thomas music educator, composer, musician
Prince, Andrew Steven lawyer, former government official
†Prince, Richard artist
Principe, Helen Mary medical case manager
Pring, Janice medical/surgical nurse
Prins, Robert Jack academic administrator
Prisco, Frank J. psychotherapist
Pritchard, Claudius Hornby, Jr. retired university president
Pritchard, Kathleen Jo not-for-profit association administrator
Pritikin, David T. lawyer
Pritsker, A. Alan B. retired engineering executive, educator
Pritts, Kim Derek state conservation officer, writer
Probasco, Dale Richard management consultant
Probasco, Patricia Lou software quality consultant
Procter, John Ernest former publishing company executive
Proctor, Richard J. geologist, consultant
Prokasy, William Frederick academic administrator
Prokopis, Emmanuel Charles computer company executive
Prominski, Eileen Alice school nurse, educator
Propst, Harold Dean retired academic administrator
Prosky, Robert Joseph actor
Protigal, Stanley Nathan lawyer
Proulx, (Edna) Annie writer
Provensen, Alice Rose Twitchell artist, author
Provenzano, Dominic information specialist
†Provost, Scott Edward social worker
Proxmire, William former senator
Pruett, Jo Ann marketing professional, special events coordinator
Prugh, George Shipley lawyer
Pruis, John J. business executive
Prusiner, Stanley Ben neurology and biochemistry educator, researcher
Pryce, Deborah D. congresswoman
Pryor, David Hampton former senator
Pryor, Harold S. retired college president
Przybyla, Leon Hugh, Jr. university director
Przybylski, Sandra Marie speech pathologist
Psillos, Susan Rose artist, educator
Ptasinski, Carol Mary nurse, educator
Pubillones, Joseph architect, educator
Pucek, Anthony J. psychiatric nurse practitioner
Puderbaugh, Kathleen Annette maternal/women's health nurse practitioner
Pudlewski, Judy Marie adult educator, consultant
Pudney, Gary Laurence television executive
Puetz, Pamela Ann human resources executive
Pugliese, Karen Olsen freelance public relations counsel
Pullen, Penny Lynne non-profit administrator, former state legislator
Pullen, Richard Owen lawyer, communications company executive
Pulliam, Brenda Jane retired secondary school educator
Pulliam, Yvonne Antoinette gifted education educator
Purcell, George Richard artist, postal employee
†Purpura, Antoinette Maria-Carmela elementary education educator
Pursey, Derek Lindsay physics educator
Purtill, Richard Lawrence philosopher, writer
Purtle, John Ingram lawyer, former state supreme court justice
Puryear, Alvin Nelson management educator
Pusateri, Lawrence Xavier lawyer
Pustilnik, Naum Alejandro investment banker
Putnam, Linda Lee communication educator, researcher
Putnam, Robert Ervin chemist
Putterman, Florence Grace artist, printmaker
Pyle, Robert Michael naturalist, writer
Pyles, Carol DeLong dean, consultant, educator
Pyper, James William chemist
Quaid, Dennis actor
Quaid, Randy actor
Quarles, Peggy Delores secondary school educator
Quattrone-Carroll, Diane Rose clinical social worker
Quehl, Gary Howard association executive, consultant
Quetglas, Moll Juan plastic and maxillofacial surgeon
Quigley, Leonard Vincent lawyer
Quillen, Cecil Dyer, Jr. lawyer, consultant
Quillen, Lloyd Douglas oil and gas executive
Quillen, William Tatem judge, lawyer, educator
Quinlan, J(oseph) Michael lawyer
Quinlan, Kathleen actress
Quinn, Anthony Rudolph Oaxaca actor, writer, artist
Quinn, Charles Nicholas journalist
Quinn, Irene S. critical care nurse
Quirk, Kenneth Paul accountant
Quiroz, Carole Elizabeth critical care nurse
Qutub, Musa Yacub hydrogeologist, educator, consultant
Raab, Herbert Norman retail executive
Rabadi, Wissam engineering executive, engineering educator
Rabago, Karl Roger lawyer
†Rabey, Stephen Alan writer
†Rabideau, Marilyn Ann elementary education educator
Rabiola, Samuel Charles English educator
Rabó, Jule Anthony chemical researcher, consultant
Rabson, Robert plant physiologist, retired science administrator
Rachkova, Mariana Ilieva physician, researcher
†Rachlin, Ellen Joan retired securities company executive
Rada, Ruth Byers college dean, author
Radabaugh, Michele Jo sales executive
Radcliffe, Redonia (Donnie Radcliffe) journalist, author
Rader, Dotson Carlyle author, journalist
Rader, Patrick Neil accountant
Radkowsky, Karen research and marketing consultant
Radlauer, Steve freelance writer, journalist
Radycki, Diane Josephine art historian, writer
Rafelson, Bob film director
Raffalli, Henri Christian lawyer, educator, criminologist
Ragland, Kathryn Marie dancer, educator
Ragland, Terry Eugene emergency physician
Rago, Dorothy Ashton retired educator
Ragsdale, Carl Vandyke motion picture producer
Ragucci, John Albert family practice physician
Ragusea, Stephen Anthony psychologist, educator
Raible, Peter Spilman minister, religious organization executive
Raichle, Marcus Edward radiology, neurology educator
Rainer, Rex Kelly civil engineer, educator
Raines, Franklin Delano corporate executive
Rainey, Claude Gladwin retired health care executive
Rainier, Ellen F. nurse
Rains, Sally Tippett writer
Rairdin, Craig Allen software company executive, software developer
Rairdon, Julia Agee nursing administrator
Raitt, Bonnie Lynn blues singer, guitarist
Rajski, Peggy film director, film producer
Raker, Gilbert Dunkin manufacturing executive, financial investor
Ralston, Roy B. petroleum consultant
Ram, Chitta Venkata physician
Ramaswami, Devabhaktuni chemical engineer
Ramesh, Nagarajan computer scientist
Ramirez, Maria C(oncepción) educational administrator
Ramirez-Rivera, Jose physician
Ramis, Harold Allen film director, screenwriter, actor
Ramos, Eleanor Lacson transplant nephrologist
Ramsay, Karin Kinsey publisher, educator
Ramsden, Karen McCoin writer
Ramsey, Douglas Arthur foundation executive
Ramsey, Henry, Jr. university official, lawyer, retired judge
Ramsey, Lucie Avra small business owner
Ramsey, Lynn Allison trade association, public relations professional
Ramsey, Patricia Gale psychology and education educator
Ramsey, Sandra Lynn psychotherapist
Ramsey Lines, Sandra forensic document examiner
Randall, Frankie professional boxer
Randall, Richard Harding, Jr. art gallery director
Randall, Richard Rainier geographer
Randall, Tony (Leonard Rosenberg) actor
Rander, Donna public information officer, city official
Randinelli, Tracey Anne magazine editor
Randolph, Judson Graves pediatric surgeon
Randolph, Nancy Adele nutritionist, consultant
Ranieri, Joseph John English language educator
Rank, Larry Gene management consultant
Rankin, Scott David artist, educator
Ranks, Anne Elizabeth retired elementary and secondary education educator
Ransom, Nancy Alderman sociology and women's studies educator, university administrator
Ransom, Richard Edward state supreme court justice
Ransome, Ernest Leslie, III retail company executive
Rao, Rama Krishna R. pharmaceutical company executive
Rapaport, Michael actor
Raper, Julia Taylor pediatric and neonatal nurse
Rapoport, Ronald Jon journalist
Rappaport, Linda Ellen lawyer
†Rappaport, Susan Elizabeth English language educator
Rappaport, Theodore Scott electrical engineering educator
Rasic, Janko architect
Raskin, Michael A. retail company executive
Rasmusson, Gary Henry medicinal chemist
Rassman, Joel H. real estate company executive, accountant
Rastegar-Djavahery, Nader E. venture capitalist
Rataj, Elizabeth Ann artist
Ratcliff, James Lewis administrator
Ratliff, Lois L. secondary school educator
Rattley, Jessie Menifield former mayor, educator
Ratzenberger, John Deszo actor, writer, director
Rauch, Paul David television producer
Raucher, Herman novelist, screenwriter
†Raven, Sheila Sherece management consultant
Raven-Riemann, Carolyn Sue actress, model, small business owner
Ravetch, Irving screenwriter
Rawls, Frank Macklin lawyer
Rawls, Nancy Lee Stirk nursing educator
Ray, Gayle Elrod sheriff
Ray, Marilyn Anne nursing educator, nursing researcher
Ray, Paula Dickerson elementary education educator
Ray, Richard Stanley accountant
Ray, Shirley Dodson educational administrator, consultant
Ray, Timothy Lionel artist
Rayl, India marketing executive
Raymond, Lee R. oil company executive
Raymond, Lloyd W. machinery company executive
Raymond, Robert Earl retired minister
Raymond, Susan Grant sculptor
Rayner, William Alexander retired newspaper editor
Raynolds, Harold, Jr. retired state education commissioner
†Read, Richard Eaton newspaper reporter
Reade, Steven Gordon lawyer
Reath, George, Jr. lawyer
Reber, Cheryl Ann consultant, social worker, program developer
Rechy, John Francisco author
Redburn, Amber Lynne nurse
†Reddy, Kishore P. internet services company executive
Redfield, Alfred Guillou physics and biochemistry educator
Redgrave, Lynn actress
Redgrave, Vanessa actress
Redlich, Fredrick Carl (Fritz) psychiatrist, educator
Redmond, Lawrence Craig lawyer
Redmont, Bernard Sidney university dean, journalism educator
†Redwine, Tina M. television journalist
Reece, David Bryson information systems administrator
Reed, David Patrick infosystems specialist
Reed, Diane Marie psychologist
Reed, Nancy Binns composer, poet, artist
Reed, Thomas Lee, II minister, elementary education educator
Reeder, James Arthur lawyer
Reeder, Robert Harry retired lawyer
Reeder, Thomas Allen television writer
Rees, Morgan Rowlands engineer, educator
Reese, Edward James, Jr. computer scientist
Reetz, Harold Frank, Jr. industrial agronomist
Reeves, David Charles secondary educator, construction executive
Reeves, Nancy Alice critical care nurse
Regalado, Raul Leo airport and parking consultant
Regan, Paul Jerome, Jr. manufacturing company executive, consultant
Regenstreif, Herbert lawyer
Regn Fraher, Bonnie special education educator
Rehm, Leo Frank civil engineer
Rehmus, Charles Martin educator, arbitrator
Reich, Harvey S. critical care physician
Reich, Robert Bernard former federal official, political economics educator
Reiche, Frank Perley lawyer, former federal commissioner
Reichman, Fredrick Thomas artist
Reichmanis, Elsa chemist
Reid, David Earl dentist, military officer
Reid, George Harrison marine consultant, writer
Reid, Harry senator
Reid, Joseph Browning retired architect
Reid-Bills, Mae editor, historian
Reidenbaugh, Lowell Henry retired sports editor
Reifsnider, Kenneth Leonard metallurgist, educator
Reigelsberger, Paul A. consultant, design artist
Reilly, Edward Francis, Jr. former state senator, federal agency administrator
Reilly, Robert Joseph counselor
†Reinalda, David Anthony elementary education educator
Reinertsen, Gloria May elementary education educator
Reinfelds, Juris computer engineering educator
Reinhardt, John Edward former international affairs specialist
Reinhardt, Stephen Roy federal judge
Reinke, Ralph Louis retired academic administrator
Reiss, Gwen North writer, poet, lecture agent
Reiss, Timothy James comparative literature educator, writer
Reister, Ruth Alkema lawyer, business executive
Reitan, Daniel Kinseth electrical and computer engineering educator
Reiter, Glenn Mitchell lawyer
†Reiter, Victoria A. writer, translator
†Rembold, Kristen Staby writer
Remer, Donald Sherwood engineering economist, cost estimator, educator
Reminger, Richard Thomas lawyer
Remley, Audrey Wright retired educational administrator, psychologist
Ren, Chung-Li engineer
Renaud, Bernadette Marie Elise author
Renda, Dominic Phillip airline executive
Rendal, Camille Lynn artist
Renfro, William Leonard futurist, lawyer, inventor, entrepreneur
Renick, Carol Bishop insurance planning company executive, consultant
Rennekamp, Rose Greeley marketing professional
Renouf, Anne technology commercialization financier
Replogle, Renata Julia art therapy educator, artist
Reppen, Norbjorn Dag electrical engineer, consultant
Requénez, Eunice Loida medical/surgical and community health nurse
Resing, Maryloretto Rachel elementary education educator, pastoral counselor
Resnick, Myron J. retired insurance company executive, lawyer
Retsky, Sidney Gerald retired company executive
Retzer, Michael L. political association executive
Reuber, Grant Louis banking insurance company executive
Reuther, Ronald Theodore museum director
Revor, Barbara Kay secondary school educator
Reyes, Silvestre congressman
Reynolds, Betty Ann elementary education educator
Reynolds, Billie Iles financial representative and counselor, former national association executive director
Reynolds, Edward book publisher
Reynolds, Ellen Aaker pediatrics and trauma nurse
Reynolds, H. Gerald lawyer
Reynolds, Harrah (H.) Robert conductor, artistic director
Reynolds, Jack W. retired utility company executive
†Reynolds, Janna Sue journalist
Reynolds, John Francis insurance company executive
Reynolds, Pamela Preston physician, historian
Reynolds, William Bradford lawyer
Rhame, Thomas Gene retired army officer
Rhea, Jerry Dwaine director consumer lending
Rhee, Albert lawyer, author
Rhett, John Taylor, Jr. government official, civil engineer
Rhoads, James Berton archivist, former government official, consultant, educator
Rhodes, John Jacob retired lawyer, former congressman
Rhodes, Mary O'Neil elementary education educator
Rhodes, Peter Edward label company executive
Riasanovsky, Nicholas Valentine historian, educator
Ricards, June Elaine nursing consultant, administrator
Riccardi, Robert advertising executive
Ricci, Mary Jean community health nurse, educator
Rice, Gary Russell special education educator
Rice, Joseph Albert banker
Rice, Otis LaVerne nursing home builder and developer
Rice, Patricia Oppenheim Levin special education educator, consultant
Rice, Richard Lee retired architect
Rice, Stan, Jr. poet, painter, English language educator
Rice, Stuart Alan chemist, educator
Rice, Walter Herbert federal judge
Rice-Dietrich, Therese Ann elementary education educator
Rich, Cynthia Gay elementary education educator
Rich, David Barry financial executive, accountant, entertainer
Rich, John film and television producer, director
Richard, Edward H. manufacturing company executive, former municipal government official
Richard, Oliver, III (Rick Richard) energy company executive
Richard, Susan Mathis communications executive, screenwriter
Richards, Ann actress, poet
Richards, Carmeleete A. computer training executive, network administrator
Richards, Mark Andrew radar signal processing research engineer
Richards, Michael actor, comedian
Richards, Morris Dick social work administrator, educator
Richards, Paul Linford physics educator, researcher
Richards, Susan R. management consultant
Richards, Wesley Jon newscaster, writer, producer
Richardson, Charles Clifton biochemist, educator
Richardson, Elsie Helen retired elementary education educator
Richardson, Jasper Edgar nuclear physicist
Richardson, John Carroll lawyer, tax legislative consultant
Richardson, Natasha Jane actress
Richardson, Richard Thomas retired banker

Richardson, Robert Dale, Jr. English language educator
Richardson, Robert John producer, director animation
Richardson, Thomas Andrew business executive, educator
Richardson, Wanda Louise Gibson nurse
Richburg, Billy Keith financial consultant and entrepreneur
Richburg, Kathryn Schaller nurse, educator
Richburg, W. Edward nurse educator
Richenburg, Robert Bartlett artist, retired art educator
Richey, Thomas Adam advertising executive
Richgels, Glen William mathematics educator
Richman, Alan magazine editor
Richman, Paul semiconductor industry executive, educator
Richman, Peter electronics executive
Richmond, Julius Benjamin retired physician, health policy educator emeritus
Richter, Carol Dean sales representative
†Richter, Mary Persis (Polly Richter) broadcast assistant
Richter, Nancy Ellen Sowers artist, graphic designer
Richter, Susan Mary medical and surgical nurse
Richter, W. D. screenwriter, director, producer
†Rickard, Norman Edward office equipment company executive
Rickard, Ruth David retired history and political science educator
Rickerd, Donald Sheridan foundation executive
Rickert, Jonathan Bradley retired foreign service officer
Ricketts, Sondra Lou librarian
Rickey, George Warren artist, sculptor, educator
†Riddell, Richard Anderson retired naval officer
Ridder, Paul Anthony newspaper executive
Riddick, Floyd Millard retired United States Senate parliamentarian, consultant
Riddle, Donald Husted former university chancellor
Riddle, Judith Lee lawyer
Riddle, Michael Lee lawyer
Rideout, Patricia Irene operatic, oratorio and concert singer
Rider, Paul Edward physicist, educator
Rider, Robert Farrington agribusiness executive
†Rider, Susan Marie musician
†Ridgway, James Mastin government official
Ridgway, Rozanne LeJeanne former diplomat, executive
Ridley-Thomas, Mark city official
Ridloff, Richard real estate executive, lawyer, consultant
Riecken, Henry William psychologist, research director
Riegel, John Kent retired corporate lawyer
Riegert, Peter actor
Riehecky, Janet Ellen writer
Riehle, Robert Arthur, Jr. medical director, surgeon
Riehm, Sarah Lawrence writer, arts administrator
Ries, Barbara Ellen alcohol and drug abuse services professional
Rifkin, Ned museum director
Riggin, Lee Pepper retired fraternal organization administrator
Righter, Walter Cameron bishop
Riker, Walter F., Jr. pharmacologist, physician
Riker, William Kay pharmacologist, educator
Riklis, Meshulam manufacturing and retail executive
Riley, Michael Joseph manufacturing company executive
Riley, Robert Shean Colonel, United States Army, retired
Rimel, Rebecca Webster foundation executive
Rimpila, Charles Robert physician
Rinaldi, Renee Zaira physician
Rinaldi, Robert R., Jr. artist, photographer, publisher
Rinder, Herbert Roy retired electrical engineer
†Rinehart, Marybeth E. elementary education educator, artist
Ring, Nancy Gail writer, artist
Ringler, Lenore educational psychologist, educator
Rinzel, Daniel Francis lawyer
Ripley, Alexandra Braid author
Riser, Carol Ann secondary education educator
Risk, Laura Jenny musician, educator
Risse, Diana Marie medical/surgical nurse, educator
Ritchey, Paul Andrew accountant
Ritchie, Anne educational administrator
Ritchie, Steven John foundation administrator, fundraising consultant
Ritta, Kurt V. painter, fine artist, illustrator
Ritter, Russell Joseph mayor, college official
Rittgers, Nancy J. nurse
Rivera, Oscar R. lawyer, corporate executive
Rivero, Jorge actor
Rivers, Kenneth Jay retired judicial administrator, consultant
Rivkind, Perry Abbot federal railroad agency administrator
Rizzolo, Robert Steven small business owner, historian
Roaden, Arliss Lloyd retired higher education executive director, former university president
†Robb, Lynda Johnson writer
Robbins, Charles Dudley, III manufacturing executive
Robbins, Frederick Chapman retired physician, medical school dean emeritus
Robbins, Jennifer Kay journalist
Robbins, Jessie Earl metallurgist
Robbins, Michael Warren magazine editor
Roberson, James O. foundation executive
†Roberson, Linwood John minister
Roberson, Pamela Kay secondary education educator
Roberts, Alan Silverman orthopedic surgeon
Roberts, Albert Dee internist
Roberts, Alfred Wheeler, III law firm executive
Roberts, Delmar Lee editor
Roberts, Doris actress
Roberts, (Ruth) Eleanor Sterett osteopathic physician
Roberts, Eric actor
Roberts, James Gordon foundation executive
Roberts, John Glover, Jr. lawyer
Roberts, Julia Baldwin retired banker
Roberts, Karen L(ee) geriatrics nurse
Roberts, Kathleen Donohoe special education educator
Roberts, Patricia Lee education educator
Roberts, Russell freelance writer
†Roberts, Russell L. artist
Roberts, Suzanne Catherine freelance reporter
Roberts, Wess author
Robertson, A. Haeworth actuary, benefit consultant, foundation executive
Robertson, Cliff actor, writer, director
Robertson, Jerry Lewis chemical engineer
Robertson, John Archibald Law nuclear scientist
Robertson, Mark Wayne investment specialist
Robertson, Mary Virginia retired elementary education educator
Robertson, Melvina construction company executive
Robertson, Wyndham Gay university official
Robick, Candace M. Younginger geriatrics nurse, educator
Robinette, Betty Lou occupational health and infection control nurse
Robins, Natalie poet, writer
Robins, Norman Alan strategic planning consultant, former steel company executive
Robinson, Angela Tomei clinical laboratory technologist
Robinson, Annettmarie entrepreneur
Robinson, Bob Leo retired international investment service executive
Robinson, Bruce Butler physicist
Robinson, Carmen Delores educator
Robinson, Caroleigh Hoffmann artist, educator
Robinson, Charlotte Hill artist
Robinson, Clayton David minister, educator
Robinson, David Adair neurophysiologist
Robinson, David Bradford scientific writer, poet
Robinson, David Brooks retired naval officer
Robinson, Gail Patricia mental health counselor, retired
Robinson, Glenda Carole pharmacist
Robinson, Henry, III office manager, legal consultant
Robinson, James Arthur university president emeritus, political scientist
Robinson, John Peter film composer, keyboardist
Robinson, Karen Sue psychiatric nurse
Robinson, Kathy S. trauma/emergency nurse
Robinson, Linda Gosden communications executive
Robinson, Lisa Gale Langley community health nurse, educator
Robinson, Lynda Hickox artist
†Robinson, Mary Frances retired French language educator
Robinson, Verna Cotten retired librarian, property management owner
Robinson, William Andrew health service executive, physician
Robison, Patricia Sue secondary school educator
Robison, William Christopher financial analyst
Robold, Alice Ilene retired mathematician, educator
Robson, Martin Cecil surgery educator, plastic surgeon
Roby, Christina Yen data processing specialist, educator
Rochberg, George composer, educator
Roche, Erin Wirtz elementary educator
Roche de Coppens, Peter George sociologist, educator
Rochelle, Lugenia academic administrator
Rochette, Ann Robinson clinical manager
Rock, Barry David social work educator
Rock, Chris actor, comedian
Rock, Richard Rand lawyer, former state senator
Rockafellow, Deborah S. career planning administrator
Rockall, Arthur Allison automotive designer
Rockburne, Dorothea Grace artist
Rockefeller, Winthrop P. state official
Rockstein, Morris science writer, editor, consultant
Rodbell, Clyde Armand distribution executive
†Rodenas, Paula author, journalist
Rodenburg, Clifton Glenn lawyer
Rodgers, Lawrence Rodney physician, educator
Rodgers, Nancy Lucille corporate executive
Rodgers, Nancy Lucille corporate executive
Rodino, Vincent Louis insurance company executive
Rodriguez, Alexander Emmanuel professional baseball player
Rodriguez-Orellana, Manuel law educator
Roe, Thomas Coombe former utility company executive
Roe, Wanda Jeraldean artist, retired educator, lecturer
Roebuck, Joseph Chester leasing company executive
Roehm, MacDonell, Jr. retail executive
Roehrig, C(harles) Burns internist, health policy consultant, editor
†Roelofs, Marina Banchero university official, consultant
Roesler, Rose Pieper retired geriatrics nurse
Roesner, Peter Lowell manufacturing company executive
Roethel, David Albert Hill consultant
Roetman, Orvil M. retired airplane company executive
Rogers, Bernard William military officer
Rogers, David playwright, novelist, actor
Rogers, Eva artist, poet
Rogers, Jack David plant pathologist, educator
Rogers, Justin Towner, Jr. retired utility company executive
Rogers, Kate Ellen interior design educator
Rogers, Laura M. medical/surgical nurse
Rogers, Margaret Ellen Jonsson civic worker
Rogers, Mimi actress
Rogers, Nathaniel Sims banker
Rogers, Peggy state agency administrator
Rogers, Sharon J. education consultant
Rogo, Kathleen safety engineer
Rohde, Tamera Annette oncological nurse
Rohlfing, Linda Anne physical therapist
Rohm, Robert Hermann sculptor, educator
Rohner, Bonnie-Jean small business owner, computer consultant
Rohr, Davis Charles aerospace consultant, business executive, retired air force officer
Rohrbach, Peter Thomas writer
Roiz, Myriam foreign trade marketing executive
Roland, Catherine Dixon entrepreneur
Rolewicz, Robert John estimating engineer
†Rollings, Alane poet, educator
Rollins, Alfred Brooks, Jr. historian, educator
Rollins, Arlen Jeffery osteopathic physician
†Rollins, Lisa L. journalist
Rolof, Marcia Christine sales executive
Roman, Ernan marketing executive
†Romano, Ray actor, comedian
Romanos, Nabil Elias business development manager
Romans, Donald Bishop corporate executive
Romans, Elizabeth Anne writer, artist, multimedia professional
Romeo, James Joseph retired army nurse corps officer, nursing researcher
Romeo, Luigi linguist, educator
Rondepierre, Edmond Francois insurance executive
Rook, Judith Rawie television producer, writer
Rooke, David Lee retired chemical company executive
Rooks, Charles Shelby minister
†Roper, Fred W. dean
Roper, John Lonsdale, III shipyard executive
Roper, Sally Ann health facility coordinator
Ropes, David Gardner advertising executive
Rosa, Vicky Lynn health facility administrator
Rosado, Elizabeth Schaar educator
Rose, Andrea writer, inventor, fashion designer, artist
Rose, Frederick Phineas builder and real estate executive
Rose, Jacobus producer
Rose, James Turner aerospace consultant
Rose, Joan Marie medical-surgical nurse
Rose, Marian Henrietta physics researcher
Rose, Robert John bishop
Rose, Wil foundation executive
Roseanne actress, comedienne, producer, writer
Roseman, Jack computer services company executive
Rosemberg, Eugenia physician, educator, medical research administrator
Rosen, Ana Beatriz electronics executive
Rosen, Arthur Marvin advertising executive
Rosen, Lawrence anthropology educator
Rosen, Martin Jack lawyer
Rosen, Myor harpist, educator
Rosen, Paul Peter pathologist
Rosenbaum, Irving M. retail store executive
Rosenbaum, Jonathan theology educator, college administrator
Rosenberg, Alison P. public policy official
Rosenberg, Carole art dealer, real estate broker
Rosenberg, David Alan military historian, educator
Rosenberg, John K. retired lawyer
Rosenberg, Leon Emanuel medical educator, geneticist, university dean
Rosenberg, Raymond David secondary education educator, consultant
Rosenblatt, Joseph poet, editor
Rosenblatt, Roger writer
Rosenblum, Mindy Fleischer pediatrician
Rosenblum Grevéy, Estelle retired dean, nursing educator
Rosenburgh, Dwayne Maurice electronics engineer
Rosenfeld, Albert Hyman science and medical writer
Rosenfeld, Mark Kenneth real estate developer
Rosenfield, James Harold communications executive
Rosenhouse, Howard retired lawyer
Rosenkilde, Carl Edward physicist
Rosenkoetter, Gerald Edwin engineering and construction company executive
Rosenn, Harold lawyer
Rosenstein, Mary Elisabeth Mallory retired clinical social worker
†Rosenstock, Robert diplomat, lawyer
Rosenthal, Arnold H. film director, producer, writer, graphic designer, calligrapher
Rosenthal, Arthur Jesse publisher
Rosenthal, Carla medical/surgical nurse
Rosenthal, James D. retired federal official, former ambassador, government and foundation executive
Rosmus, Anna Elisabeth writer
Rosner, Seth lawyer, educator
†Ross, Alan management consultant
Ross, Alberta Barkley retired chemist
†Ross, Alvin Paul educator
Ross, Ann Dunbar secondary school educator
Ross, Charlotte Pack social services administrator
Ross, Donald Roe federal judge
Ross, Elinor soprano
Ross, Molly Owings gold and silversmith, jewelry designer, small business owner
Ross, Robert Joseph head professional football coach
Rossavik, Ivar Kristian obstetrician, gynecologist
Rossello, Pedro governor of Puerto Rico
Rosset, Lisa Krug editor
Rossi, Mary Ann research scholar
Rossi, Peter Henry sociology educator
Rossman, Peggy Eyre Elrod retired nursing administrator, gerontology nurse
Rossman, Ruth Scharff artist, educator
†Rossotti, Charles Ossola federal agency administrator
Rostker, Bernard federal official
Roszkowski, Stanley Julian retired federal judge
Roth, Evelyn Austin retired elementary school educator
Roth, Loretta Elizabeth retired educator
Roth, Michael lawyer
Roth, Suzanne Allen financial services agent
Roth, Toby former congressman, political consultant
Rothenberger, Dolores Jane association administrator, actress, singer
Rothing, Frank John government official
Rothman, Deanna electroplating company executive
†Rothman, Robert science educator
Rothschild, Jennifer Ann artist, educator
Roubik, Susanne Eileen architect
Rouman, John Christ classics educator
Rourke, Arlene Carol publisher
Rourke, Mickey (Philip Andre Rourke, Jr.) actor
Rouse, Elaine Burdett retired secondary school educator
Rouse, Roscoe, Jr. librarian, educator
Roveto, Connie Ida financial services executive
Rowe, Bobby Louise art educator
Rowe, Joseph Everett electrical engineering educator, administrator
Rowe, William Davis financial services company executive
Rowell, Barbara Caballero office manager
Rowell, Lester John, Jr. retired insurance company executive
Rowlands, Gena actress
†Rowlett, Kimberly Jayne artist
Royal, Alice Calbert school health nurse
Royal, Allen Lamar engineer
Royalty, Kenneth Marvin lawyer
Royse, Brooke Sarno editor, writer
Royse, Mary Kay judge
Royston, Lloyd Leonard educational marketing consultant
Rubell, Bonnie Levine occupational therapist
Rubello, David Jerome artist
Rubin, Charles Alexis writer
Rubin, Martin N. meeting planner, consultant
Rubin, Nancy Zimman (Nancy Rubin Stuart) journalist, author, screenwriter
Rubin, Sandra Mendelsohn artist
Rubin, Vera Cooper research astronomer
Rubin, Zick psychology educator, lawyer, writer
Rubinovitz, Samuel diversified manufacturing company executive
Rubinstein, Eva (Anna) photographer
Rubnitz, Myron Ethan pathologist, educator
Ruchelman, Leonard Isadore urban studies and public administration educator
Rudan, Vincent Thaddeus nursing educator, administrator
Rudd, D(ale) F(rederick) chemical engineering educator
Ruderman, Armand Peter health economics educator, consultant, volunteer
Rudin, Anne Noto former mayor, nurse
Rudner, Sara dancer, choreographer
Rudolph, Wallace Morton law educator
Rudy, Raymond Bruce, Jr. retired food company executive
Rudzki, Eugeniusz Maciej chemical engineer, consultant
Ruegg, Donald George retired railway company executive
†Ruff, William Gerald special education educator
Ruffo, Michael painter
Ruggiero, Matthew John bassoonist
Ruggles, Rudy Lamont, Jr. investment banker, consultant
Ruhm, Thomas Francis retired lawyer, investor
Rui, Hallgeir cancer researcher
Ruland, Midlred Ardelia retail executive, retail buyer
Runde, Kathryn Joy oncology nurse
Rundio, Joan Peters (Jo Rundio) public administrator
Rundquist, Howard Irving investment banker
Runge, Donald Edward food wholesale company executive
Runyon, Elizabeth Behr mental health nurse
Ruoff, A. LaVonne Brown English language educator
Ruoho, Arnold Eino pharmacology educator
Rusch, Kathy Lynn school psychologist, educational advisor
Rush, Norman author
Rush, Richard Henry financial executive, writer, lecturer
Rushing, Rayburn Lewis evangelist
Russell, Anita S. Garber maternal/women's health, medical/surgical nurse
Russell, Attie Yvonne academic administrator, dean, pediatrics educator
Russell, Helen Diane retired museum curator, educator
Russell, Patrick James priest
Russell, Theresa Lynn actress
†Russell-Porath, Julie Ann advocate
Russi, Raul protective services official
Russo, Donna Marie lawyer
Russo, Jose pathologist
Russo, Roy Lawrence electronic design automation engineer, retired
Russo, Vincent Barney music educator
Rust, Robert Francis retired publishing executive
Rutherford, John Sherman, III (Johnny Rutherford) professional race car driver
Rutherford, Reid finance company executive
Ruzicka, Francis F., Jr. radiologist
Ryan, Allan James publishing executive, editor
Ryan, Carl Ray electrical engineer
Ryan, Cathrine Smith publisher
Ryan, Daniel John university administrator
Ryan, George H. governor, pharmacist
Ryan, Ione Jean Alohilani retired educator, counselor
Ryan, James insurance company executive
Ryan, James Frederick retired lawyer, educator
Ryan, John Michael landscape architect
Ryan, John William association executive
Ryan, Joyce Ethel publishing executive
Ryan, Raymond D. retired steel company executive, insurance and marketing firm executive
Ryan, William Joseph communications company executive
Ryder, Winona (Winona Laura Horowitz) actress
Rydholm, Ralph Williams advertising agency executive
Rydz, John S. educator
Ryerson, Marjorie Gilmour journalist, educator, poet, photographer
Ryk, Mary A. retired chaplain
Rymar, Julian W. manufacturing company executive
Ryskamp, Charles Andrew museum executive, educator
Saad, Barbara T. occupational health nurse, administrator
Saar, Betye (Irene Saar) artist
Sabatini, Nelson John government official
Sabat-Rivers, Georgina Latin American literature educator
Sabinson, Harvey Barnett theatrical organiztion administrator
Sacaccio, Margaret Mary critical care, geriatrics nurse
Saccente, Cary T. nurse
†Sacco, Tracy Lynn journalist
Sacerdote, Alan Scott endocrinologist
Sacha, Robert Frank osteopathic physician
Sachitano, Sheila Marie secondary school educator, small business owner
Sachs, William film director, producer, screenwriter
Sackellares, James Chris neurology educator
Saddler, George Floyd government economic adviser
Sadler, Graham Hydrick library administrator
Sadler, Sallie Inglis psychotherapist
Saeks, Richard Ephraim engineering executive
Safrey-Hoyt, Jennifer Ann newspaper editor, writer
Sagan, Stanley Daniel career officer, retired
Sagansky, Jeff broadcast executive
†Saiffe, Fernando Gonzalez organization administrator, lawyer
Saint, Eva Marie actress
St. Cyr, John Albert, II cardiovascular and thoracic surgeon
†Saint-Girard, Christian theatre director, choreographer, actor, educator
St. Pierre, Cathy M. family nurse practitioner
†Saks, Eric Maurice film producer, film director
Salaam, Rashaan professional football player
Salagi, Doris educational administrator, retired
Salako, Beatrice Olukemi accountant
Salamon, Miklos Dezso Gyorgy mining engineer, educator
†Salant, Katherine Blair columnist
Salathe, John, Jr. manufacturing company executive
Salatino, David critical care nurse
Salatka, Charles Alexander archbishop
Salazar, Luis Adolfo architect
Salbaing, Pierre Alcee retired chemical company executive
Salerno, Sister Maria nursing educator, adult and gerontological nurse
Salinger, Pierre Emil George journalist
Saliola, Frances retired corporate administrator

Shinn, George Latimer investment banker, consultant, educator
Shire, Talia Rose actress
Shirley, David Arthur chemistry educator, science administrator
Shirley, George Milton, Jr. chemicals executive
Shirley, Wayne Douglas music librarian
Shirley-Quirk, John concert and opera singer
Shishido, Calvin M. state agency administrator, retired
Shober, Eva Lee H. educational administrator
Shockley, Edward Julian retired aerospace company executive
Shoemaker, Marjorie Patterson textbook editor, consultant
Shook, Ann Jones lawyer
Shoop, Glenn Powell investment consultant
Shore, Harvey Harris business educator
Shore, Herbert writer, poet, educator
Shore, Stephen photographer
Shortz, Wilma Wildes writer, Arabian horse breeder
Shotwell, Malcolm Green retired minister
Shoun, Ellen Llewellyn retired secondary school educator
Shreiner, Curt educational technologist, consultant
Shreve, Susan Richards author, English literature educator
Shubb, William Barnet judge
Shuler, Jon Emmett securities industry professional
Shull, Claire documentary film producer, casting director
Shultis, Robert Lynn finance educator, cost systems consultant, retired professional association executive
Shultz, Linda Joyce retired library director
Shultz, Retha Mills retired missionary
Shumacker, Harris B., Jr. surgeon, educator, author
Shuman, Samuel Irving lawyer, law educator
Shuman, Thomas Alan correctional operations executive, consultant
Shur, Michael electrical engineer, educator, consultant
Shure, Myrna Beth psychologist, educator
Shuster, Frederick retired internist
Shuster, Robert G. electronics company executive, consultant
Shute, Richard Emil government official, engineer
Shutler, Mary Elizabeth academic administrator
Sices, David language educator, translator
Sicuro, Natale Anthony academic and financial administrator, consultant
Sidebottom, David Kirk writer, former engineer
Sidebottom, William George communications executive
Sider, Harvey Ray retired minister
Siefer, Stuart B. architect
Siegel, Jack Morton retired biotechnology company executive
Siegel, Mary Ann Garvin recruiter
†Siegel, Tara journalist
Siegel, Wilma Bulkin oncologist, educator, artist
Siejka, George John artist
Siemer, Deanne Clemence lawyer
†Siemon, James English language educator
Sievers, Ann Elisabeth Furiel clinical nurse specialist in otolaryngology
Sifontes, Jose E. pediatrics educator
Silberberg, Inga dermatologist
Silberman, Laurence Hirsch federal judge
Silberstein, Alan Mark financial services executive
Siljak, Dragoslav D. engineering educator
Sills, Richard Reynolds scientist, educator
Silva, Omega Logan physician
Silver, Daniel B. lawyer
Silver, George metal trading and processing company executive
Silver, Malcolm David pathologist, educator
Silver, Nina Gail writer, psychotherapist, singer-songwriter
Silverberg, Mark Victor lawyer, educator
Silverman, Elaine Roslyn retired secondary education educator
Silverman, Ira Norton news producer
Silverstein, Barbara Ann conductor, artistic director
Silverstein, Martin Elliot surgeon, author, consultant
Silvestri, Alan Anthony film composer
Silvia, Raymond Alan librarian
Simeral, William Goodrich retired chemical company executive
†Simkins, Gregory Dale secondary education educator
Simmons, Geoffrey Stuart physician
Simmons, James Gregg statistician
Simmons, Marguerite Saffold pharmaceutical sales professional
Simmons, Raymond Hedelius lawyer
Simms, John William retired foreign service officer, consultant
Simon, Barry Philip lawyer, airline executive
Simon, Jolene Marie nurse, educator
Simon, Melvin real estate developer, professional basketball executive
Simon, Melvin I. molecular biologist, educator
Simon, Michael Paul general contractor, realtor
Simon, Peter E. publishing executive
Simonet, John Thomas banker
Simons, Lewis Martin journalist
Simonson, Steven Neil psychotherapist
Simpers, Mary Palmer state legislator
Simpson, Frederick James retired research administrator
Simpson, Jack Benjamin medical technologist, business executive
Simpson, John Noel healthcare administrator
†Simpson, Mona Elizabeth English educator, writer
Simpson, Murray engineer, consultant
Sims, Kent Otway economist
Sinbad actor, comedian
Sinclair, Carole publisher, editor, author
Sinclair, Virgil Lee, Jr. judge, writer
Sincoff, Michael Z. human resources and marketing professional
†Siner, Maggie artist, educator
Singer, David Michael marketing and public relations company executive
Singer, Donna Lea writer, editor, educator
Singer, Marilyn writer
Singer, Markus Morton retired trade association executive
Singhvi, Virendra Singh consumer products company executive
Singletary, Patricia Ann minister
Singleton, Robert Culton graduate school administrator, Bible educator
Sires, Jonathan Paul sculptor
Sisemore, Claudia educational films and videos producer, director
Sitnyakovsky, Roman Emmanuil scientist, writer, inventor, translator
Siwe, Thomas Valentine musician, music educator
Siyan, Karanjit Saint Germain Singh software engineer
Sizemore, Barbara Ann Black studies educator
†Sizemore, Tom actor
Sjostrand, Fritiof Stig biologist, educator
Skaff, Joseph John retired state agency administrator, army officer
Skaggs, Bebe Rebecca Patten college dean, clergywoman
Skaggs, Kathy Cheryl writer, consultant
Skeels, Stephen Glenn civil engineer
Skene, G(eorge) Neil publisher, lawyer
Skibell, Joseph Freer writer, educator
Skinner, James Stanford physiologist, educator
Skinner, Knute rumsey poet, English educator
Skinner, Patricia Morag state legislator
Skinner, Shari L. dermatologist
Skinner, Thomas broadcasting and film executive
Sklar, Steven J. lawyer, legal educator, accountant
Skolnick, Lawrence neonatologist, medical administrator
Skolovsky, Zadel concert pianist, educator
Skowronski, Vincent Paul concert violinist, recording artist, executive producer, producer classical recordings
Skromme, Lawrence H. consulting agricultural engineer
Skurnik, Joan Iris special education evaluator, educator, consultant
Skwarczynski, Henryk Adam (Henryk Skwar) writer
Slade, Larry W. small business owner
†Slaughter, Djuanique Naté healthcare analyst, consultant
Slaughter, Freeman Cluff retired dentist
Slavit, David Hal otolaryngologist
Slavitt, David Walton retired lawyer
Slaydon-Wolbert, Jeanne Miller secondary school educator
Slayton, William Larew planning consultant, former government official
Slewitzke, Connie Lee retired army officer
Sloane, Arlene Loupus rehabilitation nurse, specialist
Sloyan, Gerard Stephen religious studies educator, priest
†Smaardyk, Sarah Lynn management professional
Smally, Donald Jay consulting engineering executive
Smiley, Ronald Michael communications executive
Smith, Ann Hamill retired religion educator
Smith, Anne Day writer
Smith, Arthur, Jr. pharmacist, pharmacy company executive
Smith, Barbara Dail school nurse
Smith, Barbara Jeanne retired librarian
Smith, Brian development director
Smith, Carter Blakemore broadcaster
Smith, Charles Conard refractory company executive
Smith, Charles Haddon geoscientist, consultant
Smith, Charlotte Reed retired music educator
Smith, Chester broadcasting executive
Smith, Christie Lisa radio announcer
Smith, Claudette Helms municipal official
Smith, Cynthia S. writer
†Smith, Daniel Leroy computer company executive
Smith, Dawn Christiana accountant
Smith, Debra Ann elementary education educator
Smith, Deirdre O'Meara lawyer
Smith, Dentye M. library media specialist
Smith, Doris Victoria educational agency administrator
†Smith, Edith MacNamara artist
Smith, Edward K. economist, consultant
Smith, Edward Reaugh retired lawyer, cemetery and funeral home consultant
Smith, Elmer W. retired federal government administrator
Smith, Ethel Farrington retired social worker, editor
Smith, Fern M. judge
Smith, Floyd Leslie insurance company executive
Smith, Frederick Coe manufacturing executive
Smith, George Drury publisher, editor, collagist, writer
Smith, George Patrick, II lawyer, educator
Smith, Geraldine Field medical/surgical nurse
†Smith, Gerrit Bruce foreign language educator
Smith, Goff industrial equipment manufacturing executive
Smith, Hedrick Laurence journalist, television comentator, author, lecturer
Smith, Howard McQueen librarian
Smith, Jack C. food service executive
Smith, James A. lawyer
Smith, James Alexander metal processing executive
Smith, James Parker accountant
Smith, Jane Marilyn Davis (Jane Maxwell) writer
Smith, Jean Broxton retired elementary education educator
Smith, Jean Kennedy former ambassador
Smith, Joban Jonathan security consultant
Smith, John Joseph, Jr. financial management executive
Smith, John M. bishop
Smith, John Wallace surgeon, educator
Smith, Jonathan David medical educator
Smith, Kathryn Ann advertising executive
Smith, Kenneth Edward academic administrator
Smith, Laverne Byrd educational association administrator
Smith, Lee Arthur professional baseball player
Smith, Leonard, Jr. medical/surgical and oncology nurse
Smith, Leonore Rae artist
Smith, Linda Wasmer writer
Smith, Lois Arlene actress, writer
Smith, Loren Allan federal judge
Smith, Loretta Mae contracting officer
Smith, M. Tacy computer applications trainer, consultant
Smith, Margaret Taylor volunteer
Smith, Martha Virginia Barnes retired elementary school educator
Smith, Martin Bernhard journalist
Smith, Martin Cruz author
Smith, Martin Henry pediatrician
Smith, Martin Lane biomedical researcher
Smith, Marya Jean writer
Smith, Maurice R. food products executive
Smith, Melissa Christine-Mary mental health nurse
Smith, Michael Elwin film company executive, director, producer
Smith, Michele Kathleen marriage and family therapist
Smith, (Tubby) Orlando Henry college basketball coach
Smith, Paul Vergon, Jr. corporate executive, retired oil company executive
Smith, Paula Marion urology and medical/surgical nurse
Smith, Richard Anthony investment banker
Smith, Robert Hugh engineering construction company executive
Smith, Robert Powell former ambassador, former foundation executive
†Smith, Rodney K. principal
Smith, Ronald Edward ophthalmologist
Smith, Ronald Ehlbert lawyer, referral-based distributor, public speaker, writer and motivator, real estate developer
Smith, Ronald Lynn health system executive
Smith, Roy Allen United States marshal
Smith, Russell Francis transportation executive
Smith, Shelly Gerald, Jr. small business owner, author
Smith, Sheryl Velting organization administrator
Smith, Sinjin beach volleyball player
Smith, Susan Lee history educator
†Smith, Suzanne F. writer
Smith, Thomas Winston cotton marketing executive
Smith, V. Kerry economics educator
Smith, Vangy Edith accountant, consultant, writer, artist
Smith, Vestal Beecher, Sr. physician
Smith, Virgil Baker retired electrical engineer
Smith, Virginia critical care nurse
Smith, Wilburn Jackson, Jr. retired bank executive
Smith, William Bridges diversified company executive
Smith-Epstein, Mary Kathleen dancer
Smither, Howard Elbert musicologist
Smits, Kathleen Curran artist, educator
Smock, Raymond William historian
Smoke, Richard Edwin lawyer, investment adviser
Smoker, Roy Ellis military officer
Smouse, H(ervey) Russell lawyer
Smuk, Kathy Ann community health nurse, educator
Smyth, Cornelius Edmonston retired hotel executive
Smyth, Nicholas Patrick D. surgeon
Sneed, Alberta Neal retired elementary education educator
Snelling, Barbara W. state official
Snelling, Robert Orren, Sr. franchising and employment executive
Snelson, Kenneth Duane sculptor
Snider, L. Britt government executive
Snider, Patricia Faye retired theater educator, small business owner
Snortland, Howard Jerome educational financial consultant
Snow, Claude Henry, Jr. information services executive, consultant
Snow, John William railroad executive
Snowden, Lawrence Fontaine retired aircraft company executive, retired marine corps general officer
Snyder, Alan Carhart financial services executive
Snyder, Marvin neuropsychologist
Snyder, Stephen Edward lawyer, mediator
Snyder, Susan Brooke retired English literature educator
Snyder, William Burton insurance executive
Soderbergh, Steven Andrew filmmaker
Soderquist, Ronald Bruce minister, ministry consultant
Sodolski, John retired association administrator
Soebbing, Janice Bromert occupational health nurse
Sojka, Sandra Kay investor, livestock conservator
Sokal, Robert Reuven biology educator, author
Soles, Ada Leigh former state legislator, government advisor
Sollender, Joel David management consultant, financial executive
Sollid, Faye Eising civic worker
Solomon, Amelia Kroll artist
Solomon, Beth Carol writer
Solomon, Risa Greenberg clinical social worker, child-family therapist
Solomon, Robert Charles philosopher, educator
Solow, Martha S. nonprofit management consultant, state legislator
Soltero-Harrington, Luis Rubén surgeon, educator
Somasundaran, Ponisseril surface and colloid engineer, applied science educator
Somers, Louis Robert retired food company executive
Sommer, Howard Ellsworth textile executive
Sommers, Louise lawyer
Sommers, William Paul management consultant, research and development institute executive
Sonderegger, Theo Brown psychology educator
Sondheim, Stephen Joshua composer, lyricist
Sonkowsky, Robert Paul classicist, educator, actor
Sonnenschein, Hugo Freund academic administrator, economics educator
Sontag, David B. producer, writer, communications executive
Sontag, Susan writer
Sooter, Will James executive search consultant
Soper, James Herbert botanist, curator
Sorel, Edward artist
SoRelle, Ruth Doyle medical writer, journalist
Sorensen, Jean artist
Sorensen, Sheila state senator
Sorgi, Deborah Bernadette educational software company executive
Soroca, Barbara J. performing company executive
Sotirhos, Michael ambassador
Souder, Howard R., Jr. customer support representative
Souders, Jean Swedell artist, educator
Soukup, Jeanne D'Arcy public health nurse
Soule, Sallie Thompson retired state official
Sousa, Barbara Jane community and school health nurse
Souter, David Hackett United States supreme court justice
Southerland, S. Duane manufacturing company executive
Southward, Glen Morris statistician, educator
Southwick, Charles Henry zoologist, educator
Southworth, Jamie MacIntyre education educator
Souveroff, Vernon William, Jr. business executive
Souw, Bernard Eng-Kie physicist, consultant
Sowers, William Armand civil engineer
Soyke, Jennifer Mae emergency and family physician
Spackman, Thomas James radiologist
Spada, James author, photographer, publisher
Spagnolo, Lucy W. hospice nurse
Spangler, Scott Michael retired private investor
Spanninger, Beth Anne lawyer
Sparey, John William retired animator
Sparks, William Sheral retired librarian
Spaulding, Frank Henry librarian
Speaker, Susan Jane lawyer
Speakes, Larry Melvin public relations executive
Speers, Roland Root, II lawyer
Speier, John Leo, Jr. retired chemist
Speight, James Glassford research company executive
Spejewski, Eugene Henry physicist, educator
Spelios, Lisa Garone nurse, educator
Spellman, Douglas Toby advertising executive
Spelson, Nicholas James engineering executive, retired
Spence, Andrew artist, painter
Spence, Dianna Jeannene software engineer, educator
Spence, Glen Oscar clergyman
Spence, Marjorie A. medical/surgical nurse
Spencer, David Anthony geologist, researcher
Spencer, Helen Elaine editor
Spencer, Milton Harry economics and finance educator
Spencer, Peter LeValley, Jr. editor
Spencer, Richard Glenn Stevens physician, nuclear magnetic resonance spectroscopist
Spero, Maddalena Ann nurse
Spero, Nancy artist
Sperry, Len Thomas psychiatry and preventive medicine educator
Sperry, Martin Jay lawyer
Speth, James Gustave United Nations executive, lawyer
Spicuzza, Jeanne Marie actor, writer, artist, poet
Spiegelman, James Michael international affairs expert
Spiegle, Harold Mark accountant
Spies, Karen Bornemann writer, education consultant
Spillman, Marjorie Rose producer, dancer
Spindel, Mark school system administrator
Spinelli, Jerry writer
Spingarn, Joel William small business owner
†Spink, Walter Milton art historian, educator
Spinks, Michael retired professional boxer
Spinnanger, Ruthe Thoverud writer, retired secondary school educator
Spinrad, Robert Joseph computer scientist
Spinweber, Cheryl Lynn psychologist, sleep specialist
Spitze, Steven Clyde army officer
Splane, Richard Beverley social work educator
Spliethoff, William Ludwig chemical company executive
Splitstone, George Dale retired hospital administrator
Spoehel, Ronald Ross communications company executive
Spoor, James Edward human resources executive, entrepreneur
Spottiswoode, Roger film director
Sprague, Charles Cameron medical foundation president
Sprague, George Frederick geneticist
Sprenger, Curtis Donald choir conductor, educator
†Sprewell, Latrell Fontaine professional basketball player
Spring, Michael Gerard international relations specialist
Springer, Gerald William sales executive
Springer, Robert Dale retired air force officer, consultant, lecturer
Sprinthall, Norman Arthur psychology educator
Sprowl, Dale Rae English educator
Sprung, Arnold lawyer
Squibb, Samuel Dexter chemistry educator
Squier, Jack Leslie sculptor, educator
Squires, Katherine Landey lawyer
Srinivasan, Venkataraman marketing and management educator
Sroge, Maxwell Harold marketing consultant, publishing executive
Srygley, Paul Dean marketing manager
Stabile, Alfonso C. city councilman
Stabile, Benedict Louis retired academic administrator, retired coast guard officer
Stack, Beatriz de Greiff lawyer
†Stackhouse, Robert sculptor
Stacy, Cheryl Anne critical care nurse
Stacy, Kathleen Mary critical care nurse
†Stadler, Craig Robert professional golfer
†Stahl, David orchestra and opera conductor
Stahl, Madonna retired judge
Staker, Robert Jackson federal judge
Stallone, Thomas Michael clinical psychologist
Stalon, Charles Gary retired economics educator, institute administrator
Stamm, Geoffrey Eaton retired arts administrator
Stamos, John James judge
Stamp, Frederick Pfarr, Jr. federal judge
Stamper, Malcolm Theodore publishing company executive
Stanfill, Dennis Carothers business executive
Stanfill, Shelton G. performing arts administrator
Stanford, Kathleen Theresa secondary school educator
Stanley, Duffy B. architect
Stanley, Margaret King performing arts administrator
Stanley, Marlyse Reed horse breeder
Stanley, Melinda Louise mental health nurse
Stanley, Myrtle Brooks minister, educational and religious consultant
Stanley, Robert Michael professional baseball player
Stanley, Scott, Jr. editor
Stano, Mary Gerardine writer, tax accountant
Stansell, Ronald Bruce investment banker
Stansil, Sheryl medical-surgical nurse
Stanton, John Jeffrey editor, broadcast journalist, government programs director, analyst, professional society administrator
Stanton, Louis Lee federal judge
Starer, Robert composer
Staresnick, Julie Chih school psychologist
Stark, Debra Pogrund lawyer
Stark, Diana public relations and promotion executive
Stark, Evelyn Brill poet, musician
Stark, Helen Morton secondary education educator
Starkweather, Teresa Madery artist, educator
Starr, David newspaper editor, publisher
Starr, Joyce Ives special education educator
†Starr, Kenneth Winston lawyer
Starr, Leon retired chemical research company executive
Stasek, Lorraine Anne elementary school educator
Stash, Susan Michele medical/surgical nurse
†Stashower, Daniel Meyer writer
Statman, Jackie C. career consultant
Stauber, Brandon Frederick consultant information technology and communications
Stauber, Cynthia B. medical/surgical nurse
Stavroulakis, Anthea Merrie biology educator
Stearns, Robert Leland curator
Stebbins, George Ledyard research botanist, retired educator

Stedman, Richard Ralph retired lawyer
Steed, Kelly Renée freelance writer and researcher
Steel, Kuniko June retired artist
Steele, Antonio L. principal, educator
Steele, Clarence Hart retired otolaryngologist
Steele, Vickie M. mental health nurse, nursing researcher
Steelsmith, Mary Joanne playwright, actress
Steen, Carlton Duane private investor, former food company executive
Stefanelli, Lisa Eileen elementary education educator
Stefano, George B. neurobiologist, researcher
Steffens, Dorothy Ruth political economist
Steffian, Emily Enders artist
Stegner, Lynn Nadene treasurer
Steiger, Dale Arlen publishing executive
Stein, Bennett Mueller neurosurgeon
Stein, Dale Franklin retired university president
Stein, Ellyn Beth mental health services professional
Stein, Gordon Edward mental health and chemical dependency nurse
†Stein, Lenore Von artistic director
Stein, Paul Arthur financial services executive
Steinberg, David comedian, author, actor
Steinberg, Joan Emily retired middle school educator
Steinberg, Marshall retired toxicologist
Steiner, Amy Leigh photo director, photographer
Steiner, Michael Louis pediatrician
Steiner, Shari Yvonne publisher, editor, journalist
Steinert, Leon Albert mathematical physicist
Steinhauser, Sheldon Eli sociology and gerontology educator, consultant
Steinmetz, John Charles geologist, paleontologist
Steir, Pat Iris artist
Stemberg, Thomas George retail executive
Sten, Johannes Walter control systems engineer, consultant
Stendahl, Krister retired bishop
Stengel, Ronald Francis management consultant
Stennett, William Clinton (Clint Stennett) radio and television station executive, state senator
Stentz, Steven Thomas researcher, project consultant
Stepak, Asa Martin writer
Stepanski, Anthony Francis, Jr. computer company executive
Stephens, Donald R(ichards) investor
†Stephens, Dorothy Lawrence elementary education educator
Stephens, Edward Carl communications educator, writer
Stephens, Elton Bryson bank executive, service and manufacturing company executive
Stephenson, Barbera Wertz lawyer
Stephenson, Toni Edwards publisher, investment management executive, communications executive
†Steris, Charles William sales executive
Stern, Arthur Paul electronics company executive
Stern, Charles retired foreign trade company executive
Stern, Daniel author, executive, educator
Stern, John Jules lawyer
Stern, Marilyn picture editor, photographer, writer
Stern, Milton chemical company executive
Stern, Nancy Fortgang mathematics and computer science, educator
Stern, S(eesa) Beatrice executive secretary, registered nurse
†Sterne, Rosanne L.P. consultant to nonprofit organizations
Sternhagen, Frances actress
Stettler, Carla Rice marketing executive
Stevens, Berton Louis, Jr. data processing manager
Stevens, Connie actress, singer
Stevens, Elizabeth psychotherapist, consultant
Stevens, John Flournoy priest
Stevens, Kathleen M. nurse
Stevens, Kenneth Allen retired defense department worker
Stevens, May artist
Stevens, Rhea Christina lawyer
Stevens, Shane novelist
Stevens, Warren actor
Stevenson, Bryan Allen lawyer
Stevenson, Elizabeth author, educator
Stevenson, Paul Michael physics educator, researcher
Stewart, Albert Elisha safety engineer, industrial hygienist
Stewart, Arthur Irving, III (Art Stewart) marketing communications executive
Stewart, Bruce Edmund, Sr. retired mechanical designer, writer
Stewart, Carleton M. banker, corporate director
Stewart, Clinton Eugene retired adult education educator
Stewart, Daniel Robert retired glass company executive
Stewart, Dorothy K. educator, librarian
Stewart, Gordon Curran insurance information association executive
Stewart, John Murray banker
Stewart, Joseph Turner, Jr. retired pharmaceutical company executive
Stewart, Miriam utilization review professional
Stewart, Paul Anthony, II trade association executive, author
Stewart, (William) Payne professional golfer
Stewart, Peter Beaufort retired beverage company executive
Stewart, Richard Alfred business executive
Stewart, Robert Gordon former museum curator
Stewart, Thomas James, Jr. baritone
Stewart, Whitney children's book writer
Stickle, David Walter microbiologist
Stickler, Fred Charles manufacturing company executive
Stickler, Gunnar Brynolf pediatrician
Stickney, Jessica former state legislator
Stickney, John Moore lawyer
Stiff, Robert Martin newspaper editor
Stiffler, Jack Justin electrical engineer
Stiglich, Jacob John, Jr. engineering consultant
Stiller, Jerry actor
Stiner, Carl Wade army officer
Stines, Fred, Jr. publisher
Stinsmuehlen-Amend, Susan artist
Stinson, Thomas Franklin economist, educator
Stipe, Michael musician
Stivers, William Charles forest products company executive
Stoecklin, Sister Carol Ann education educator
Stoesz, David Paul social work educator
Stofferson, Terry Lee financial officer
Stohlman, Connie Suzanne obstetrical gynecological nurse
Stoken, Jacqueline Marie physician
Stoker, Howard W. former education educator, educational administrator, consultant
Stokstad, Marilyn Jane art history educator, curator
Stolarik, M. Mark history educator
Stoll, Kimberly Jean music educator
Stollerman, Gene Howard physician, educator
Stolley, Richard Brockway journalist
†Stolovitsky, Mark Ian school administrator
Stone, Annette Elizabeth Calkins medical/surgical and occupational health nurse
†Stone, Douglas Bryan financial economist
Stone, Edward Herman lawyer
Stone, John Floyd soil physics researcher and educator
Stone, Kathy Sue secondary education educator
Stone, Lloyd corporate executive, state political party official
Stone, Oliver screenwriter, director
Stonecypher, David Daniel writer, retired psychiatrist and ophthalmologist
Stoneham, Edward Bryant technical company executive
Stonnington, Henry Herbert physician, medical executive, educator
†Storfer, James R. financial executive
Stotter, Harry Shelton banker, lawyer
Stouffer, Nancy Kathleen publishing company executive
Stover, Laura Elkins artist
†Stow, Gerald Lynn human services executive, speaker
Stowell, Maureen Frances county official
Strain, James Ellsworth pediatrician, retired association administrator
Strait, George country music vocalist
Stralser, Steven Michael marketing educator, consultant
†Strand, Mark poet
Strandjord, Ronald Millard architect
Strasser, Gabor management consultant
Strathairn, David actor
Stratman, Joseph Lee petroleum refining company executive, consultant, chemical engineer
Stratton, Julius Augustus psychologist, consultant
Stratton, Mariann retired naval nursing administrator
Stratton-Whitcraft, Cathleen Sue critical care and pediatrics nurse
Straub, Linda Catherine administrative assistant
Straub, Peter Francis novelist
Straulman, Ann Therese retired English language educator
Straus, Jerry Alan management consultant
Strauss, Peter actor
Stream, Arnold Crager lawyer, writer
Street, John Charles linguistics educator
Street, John F. city official
Streeter, Tal sculptor
Streicker, James Richard lawyer
Strick, Joseph film director
†Strickland, Stephanie poet
Strider, Marjorie Virginia artist, educator
Striker, Cecil Leopold archaeologist, educator
†Stringer, C. Vivian women's college basketball coach
Stringer, Mary Evelyn art historian, educator
Stringfield, Sherry actress
Stringham, Renée physician
Stripling, Betty Keith artist, nurse
Strisik, Paul artist
Strohm, Raymond William laboratory equipment manufacturing company executive
Strong, John David insurance company executive
Strong, Susan Clancey writer, communication consultant, editor
Strongin, Jonathan David physician
Strother, Patrick Joseph public relations executive
Strothman, James Edward editor
Stroud, John Franklin engineering educator, scientist
Stroud, Richard Hamilton aquatic biologist, scientist, consultant
Stroudsburg, Ty painter
Strouth, Baron Howard Steven geologist, mining engineer
Strukoff, Rudolf Stephen retired music educator
Stuart, Joseph Martin art museum administrator
Stuart, Mary actress
†Stuart, Reginald A. journalist
Stuart, Sandra Joyce computer information scientist
Stuckwisch, Clarence George retired university administrator
Studebaker, Glenn Wayne steel company executive
Studer, Carol A. creative director, graphic designer, consultant
Studness, Charles Michael economist
Stufano, Thomas Joseph criminologist, author, inventor
Stults, Walter Black management consultant, former trade organization executive
Stump, John Edward veterinary anatomy educator, ethologist
Stumpe, Warren Robert scientific, engineering and technical services company executive
Sturgeon, Charles Edwin management consultant
Sturtevant, Julian Munson biophysical chemist, educator
Sturtevant, Richard Pearce insurance consultant
Stutzman, Sandra Louise advanced nurse practitioner
Styne, Marlys Marshall retired English educator
Styron, William writer
Su, Hui-I Chen occupational therapist
Suarez, Michael Anthony civil engineer, consultant
Suber, Robin Hall former medical and surgical nurse
Subotnick, Stuart food service executive
Substad Lokensgard-Schimmelpfennig, Kathryn Ann small business owner, career consultant
Sugarman, Samuel Louis retired oil transportation and trading company executive, horse breeder
Sugerman, Andrew film producer
Sugnet, Linda A'Brunzo elementary education educator
Suhr, Geraldine M. medical/surgical nurse
Suits, Bernard Herbert philosophy educator
Sulc, Jean Luena (Jean L. Mestres) lobbyist, consultant
Sullivan, Ben Frank, Jr. real estate broker
Sullivan, Charles university dean, educator, author
Sullivan, Colleen Anne physician, educator
Sullivan, Daniel Joseph theater critic
†Sullivan, Evelin Elisabeth writer, educator
Sullivan, George Edward author
Sullivan, James Lenox clergyman
†Sullivan, James W. lobbyist
Sullivan, Leon Howard clergyman
Sullivan, Mary Rose English language educator
Sullivan, Nell Inklebarger administrative official, counselor
Sullivan, Nicholas G. science educator, speleologist
Sullivan, Patrick Raney labor management consultant
Sullivan, Sarah Louise management and technology consultant
Sumichrast, Jozef illustrator, designer
Summerfield, John Robert textile curator
Summers, Amy Elder neonatal nurse
Summitt, Patricia Head college basketball coach
Sundaresan, Mosur Kalyanaraman physics educator
Sunderman, Duane Neuman chemist, research institute executive
Sundquist, Maria Alexandra diplomat
Sunell, Robert John retired army officer
Sung, James Pang-Chieh surgeon
Sununu, John E. congressman
Suppes, Patrick statistics, education, philosophy and psychology educator
Suput, Ray Radoslav librarian
Suraci, Patrick Joseph clinical psychologist
Surles, Richard Hurlbut, Jr. retired law librarian
†Susak, David Michael electrical engineer
Sussman, Barry author, public opinion analyst and pollster, journalist
Sutherland, Debbora gerontological nurse practitioner
Sutlin, Vivian advertising executive
Sutton, Dolores actress, writer
Sutton, Julia Sumberg musicologist, dance historian
Sutton, Willis Anderson, Jr. sociology educator
Svenson, Bo actor, writer, director
Svensson, Lars Georg cardiovascular and thoracic surgeon
Svikhart, Edwin Gladdin investment banker
Svoboda, Janice June nurse
Svrcek, Debbie M. English educator
Swaim, David Dee diversified company financial executive
Swalm, Thomas Sterling aerospace executive, retired military officer
Swan, Charles E. not for-profit organizations consultant
Swanberg, Edmund Raymond investment counselor
Swanger, Sterling Orville appliance manufacturing company executive
Swanson, Georgia May retired speech communication educator
Swanson, Jennie Elizabeth Williams healthcare association administrator, church mentor, antique dealer
Swanson, Paul Rubert minister
Swanson, Ralph William aerospace executive, consultant, engineer
Swanson, William Russell marketing professional
Swanstrom, Thomas Evan economist
Swaters, Cherie Lynn Butler retired nurse
Sweeney, Deidre Ann lawyer
Sweeny, Mary Ellen nursing administrator, educator
Sweet, Philip W. K., Jr. former banker
Sweet, Robert Workman federal judge
Swenson, Lucyann medical/surgical and community health nurse
Swiff, Kelly small business owner, civic volunteer, author
Swift, Harriet writer, editor
Swift, Jonathan educator, tenor
Swig, Roselyne Chroman community consultant
Swindler, Daris Ray physical anthropologist, forensic anthropologist
†Switzer, Daniel Lewis construction company administrator
Switzer, Maurice Harold journalist
Switzman, Jessica (Heimberg) maternal/women's health nurse, medical/surgical nurse
Swoap, David Bruce government affairs consultant
Swope, Donald Downey retired banker
Sykora, Barbara Zwach state legislator
Symchowicz, Samson biochemist
Symmes, Daniel Leslie three-dimensional technology executive, producer, director
†Szabo, Yurika Lin marketing executive, advertising executive
Szantai, Linda Marie speech and language therapist
Szelenyi, Ivan educator
Szporn, Renee Marla religious studies and special education educator
†Szydlowski, Mary Vigliante writer
†Szydlowski, Ralph die maker, formability consultant
Tabandera, Kathlynn Rosemary secondary education educator
Tachi, Douglas Paul architect, interior designer
Tachmindji, Alexander John systems engineering consultant
Tack, Theresa Rose women's health nurse
†Tadlock, Anita Conner volunteer
Tagiuri, Consuelo Keller child psychiatrist, educator
Talal, Marilynn Glick poet
Talbott, Mary Ann critical care nurse
Tallerico, Delma Dolores museum educator
Tallet, Jorge Antonio philosopher, writer
Talley, Jim Allen minister, counselor
Talley, Kevin David legislative staff official
Talley, Robert Morrell aerospace company executive
Tally, Ted screenwriter
Talmadge, Philip Albert state supreme court justice, former state senator
Tamaro, George John consulting engineer
Tamen, Harriet lawyer
Tamm, Mary Anne DeCamp social services administrator
Tan, Hui Qian computer science and civil engineering educator
Tan, Veronica Y. psychiatrist
Tandler, Bernard cell biology educator
Tanenbaum, Jay Harvey lawyer
Tanguay, Norbert Arthur retired municipal police training officer
Tannenberg, Dieter E. A. retired manufacturing company executive
Tanner, Anita Louise physician assistant
Tanner, Laurel Nan education educator
Tanquary, Oliver Leo minister
Tansor, Robert Henry investor
Taplett, Lloyd Melvin human resources management consultant
Tapley, James Leroy retired lawyer, railway corporation executive
Taplin, Frank E., Jr. trustee education and arts institutions and associations
Tarar, Afzal Muhammad management consultant
Tarbi, William Rheinlander secondary education educator, curriculum consultant, educational technology researcher
Tardos, Anne artist, composer, writer
Taren, James Arthur neurosurgeon, educator
Tarjan, Robert Wegg retired information services executive, part-time math teacher
Tarkowski, Larry Michael municipal official
Tarnow, Malva May Wescoe post-anesthesia care nurse
†Tarozzi-Goldsmith, Marcella I. philosopher, writer
Tarr, Curtis W. business executive
Tarrance, Vernon Lance, Jr. public opinion research executive
†Tartakoff, Laura Ymayo political science educator
Tash, Martin Elias publishing company executive
Tate, Fran M. small business owner
Tatgenhorst, (Charles) Robert lawyer
Tauber, Sonya Lynn nurse
Taubman, A. Alfred real estate developer
Taunton, Kathryn Jayne accountant
Tauscher, Ellen O. congresswoman
Tavrow, Richard Lawrence lawyer, corporate executive
Tayler, Irene English literature educator
Taylor, Barbara Jo Anne Harris government official, civic and political worker
†Taylor, Beth educator
Taylor, David George retired banker
Taylor, Deborah Ann retired paralegal
Taylor, Dennis J. retired steel company executive
Taylor, Edna Jane retired employment program counselor
†Taylor, Eleanor Ross writer
Taylor, Elizabeth Rosemond actress
Taylor, Guy Watson symphonic conductor
Taylor, Hugh Pettingill, Jr. geologist, educator
Taylor, John Jackson (Jay) writer, international consultant, retired foreign service officer
Taylor, June Ruth retired minister
Taylor, Kathryn Lee mortgage broker
†Taylor, Lawrence sports commentator, former professional football player
Taylor, Linda Rathbun financial planner
Taylor, Margaret Turner clothing designer, writer, space planner, architectural designer
Taylor, Nathalee Britton nutritionist
Taylor, Peggy Horne artist, educator
Taylor, Randall William quality assurance administrator
Taylor, Richard James lawyer
†Taylor, Velande Pingel author, publisher
Teal, Edwin Earl retired engineering physicist, consultant
Tedesco, Paul Herbert humanities educator
Tedoldi, Robert Louis, Jr. financial planner, consultant
Teeple, Fiona Diane librarian, lawyer
†Teison, Herbert J. editor, publisher
Tejada, Louis, Jr. emergency medicine nurse, paramedic
Tellington, Wentworth Jordan engineer
Temerlin, Liener advertising agency executive
Temple, Joseph George, Jr. retired pharmaceutical company executive
Templeton, Carson Howard engineering executive, policy analyst
Templeton, John Alexander, II coal company executive
Tenhoeve, Thomas academic administrator
Tenney, Frank Putnam marketing executive
Tenney, Stephen Marsh physiologist, educator
Tennyson, Andala Mae nurse
Ter Horst, Jerald Franklin public affairs counsel
Teronde, Jeffrey Glenn controller
Terrell, G. Irvin lawyer
Terrell, Melvin C. academic administrator
Terrill, W(allace) Andrew international security analyst, educator
Terris, Susan physician, cardiologist
Terry, Clifford Lewis journalist
Terry, John Hart lawyer, former utility company executive, former congressman
Terry, Kay Adell marketing executive
Terry, Reese engineering executive
Terry, Richard Frank data transcriber
Terry, Wayne Gilbert healthcare executive, hospital administrator, consultant and mediator in health services management
Tesarek, Dennis George retired business consultant, writer, educator
Tetelbaum, Solomon David research engineer
Tetelman, Alice Fran consultant
Tetley, Glen choreographer
Tew, E. James, Jr. electronics company executive
Tewkesbury, Joan F. film director, writer
Textor, Robert Bayard cultural anthropology writer, consultant, educator
Thacker, Victor Larry educator
Thackray, Arnold Wilfrid historian, foundation executive
Thal, Herbert Ludwig, Jr. electrical engineer, engineering consultant
Tharp, Twyla dancer, choreographer
Thayer, Martha Ann small business owner
†Theis, Stuart H. water transport executive
Theobald, H Rupert retired political scientist
Theroux, Paul Edward author
Therrien, Anita Aurore elementary school educator
Thewlis, David actor
Thiel, Philip design educator
Thiele, Howard Nellis, Jr. lawyer
†Thielen, Jean Rose artist
Thiessen, Gordon George banker
Thom, Lilian Elizabeth secondary school educator
Thomas, Dale producer
Thomas, Ella Cooper lawyer
Thomas, Franklin Augustine lawyer, consultant
Thomas, Hilary Bryn telecommunications executive, interactivist, writer, speaker
Thomas, Joe Carroll retired human resources director
Thomas, Katherine Jane newspaper business columnist
Thomas, Leo J. retired imaging company executive
Thomas, Marlo (Margaret Julia Thomas) actress
Thomas, Patricia Faye educational administrator
Thomas, Patricia Goodnow journalist
Thomas, Rhonda Robbins marketing educator, consultant
†Thomas, Shelley Lynn technical writer
Thomas, Teresa Ann microbiologist, educator
Thomas, Tom retired plastics company executive
Thomas, William Kernahan retired federal judge
†Thomason, Harry E. lawyer, mechanical engineer, career officer
†Thomason, Harry Jack Lee, Jr. mechanical engineer
Thomopoulos, Anthony D. retired motion picture company executive
Thompson, Ana Calzada secondary education educator, mathematician
Thompson, Craig Dean sports association executive
Thompson, Craig Snover corporate communications executive
Thompson, Eugene Mayne retired minister
Thompson, Hunter Stockton author, political analyst, journalist
Thompson, J. Andy bank executive

Thompson, Jack Edward *mining company executive*
Thompson, Joseph Warren *osteopathic physician*
Thompson, Joyce Lurine *retired information systems specialist*
Thompson, Lawrence D. *marketing and sales executive*
Thompson, Mark Lee *art educator, sculptor*
Thompson, Ralph Newell *former chemical corporation executive*
Thompson, Raymond Eugene, Jr. *education educator*
Thompson, Richard Stephen *management consultant*
Thomson, Alex *cinematographer*
†Thomson, Caroline Helen *artist*
Thomson, James Adolph *medical group practice administrator*
Thomson, Mabel Amelia *retired elementary school educator*
Thongsak, Vajeeprasee Thomas *business planning executive*
Thorn, Brian Earl *retail company executive*
Thorn, Rosemary Kost *former librarian*
Thornton, John W., Sr. *lawyer*
Thornton, Mary Elizabeth Wells *critical care nurse, educator*
Thorsen, Marie Kristin *radiologist, educator*
Thorstenberg, (John) Laurence *oboe and English horn player*
Thottupuram, Kurian Cherian *priest, college director, educator*
Thrasher, Rose Marie *critical care and community health nurse*
Threefoot, Sam Abraham *physician, educator*
Threet, Jack Curtis *oil company executive*
Threlkeld, Richard Davis *broadcast journalist*
Throndson, Edward Warner *residential association administrator*
Thuillier, Richard Howard *meteorologist*
Thune, John *congressman*
†Thurin, Susan Schoenbauer *English educator*
Thurman, Jimmy Cline *sales executive*
Thurmond, John Peter, II *bank executive, rancher, archaeologist*
Tichenor, A. Caylen *elementary school educator*
Tiedge-Lafranier, Jeanne Marie *editor*
Tielke, James Clemens *retail and manufacturing management consultant*
Tienken, Arthur T. *retired foreign service officer*
†Tietz, Dietmar Juergen *computer Web engineer, scientist*
Tigges, John Thomas *writer, musician, lecturer*
Timmons, Sharon L. *retired elementary education educator*
Timpte, Robert Nelson *secondary school educator*
Tingley, Jay Allen *graphic designer*
Tinker, Mark Christian *producer, director*
Tipping, William Malcolm *social services administrator*
Tipples, Keith Howard *retired research director*
Tise, Larry Edward *association executive, historian*
Titus, Christina Maria *lawyer*
Tobias, Andrew Previn *columnist, lecturer*
Tobias, Richard *artist*
Tobias, Sheila *writer, educator*
Tobin, Michael Edward *banker*
Todd, Deborah J. *public health advisor*
Toensing, Victoria *lawyer*
Toevs, Alden Louis *management consultant*
Togerson, John Dennis *computer software company executive, retired*
Toirac, S(eth) Thomas *engineering executive, consultant*
Tokerud, Robert Eugene *electrical engineer*
Tokofsky, Jerry Herbert *film producer*
Toledo, Victor *educational consultant*
Tolins, Roger Alan *lawyer*
Tomasi, Donald Charles *architect*
Tombros, Peter George *pharmaceutical company executive*
Tomkiel, Judith Irene *small business owner*
Tomkow, Gwen Adelle *artist*
Tomlin, Lily *actress*
Tomlinson, Keith *state claims examiner*
Tomsky, Judy *fundraiser and event planner, importer*
Tone, Philip Willis *retired lawyer, former federal judge*
Tonello-Stuart, Enrica Maria *political economist*
Tong, Rosemarie *medical humanities and philosophy educator, consultant and researcher*
Tongue, Paul Graham *financial executive*
Tonkyn, Richard George *retired oil and gas company executive, researcher, consultant*
Toole, Linda Jernigan *quality control technician, cosmetics company admininstrator*
Tooley, Charles Frederick *communications executive, consultant*
Toor, Herbert Lawrence *chemical engineering educator, researcher*
Topik, Steven Curtis *history educator*
Torak, Elizabeth Lichtenstein *artist*
Torgerson, Larry Keith *lawyer*
Torkelson, Rita Katherine *medical/surgical nurse*
Torkildson, Raymond Maynard *lawyer*
Torok, John Anthony, III *dentist, financial analyst, portfolio manager*
Torre, Carolyn Talley *pediatric nurse practitioner*
Torregrossa, Joseph Anthony *lawyer*
Torres, Edwin *state judge, writer*
Torres, Ophelia Alvina Powell *pediatric and medical/surgical nurse, educator*
Torresyap, Pearl Marie *surgical nurse*
Toshach, Clarice Oversby *real estate developer, former computer executive*
Tower, Kathleen Ruth *librarian, consultant*
Towers, Bernard Leonard *medical educator*
Townsend, Jerrie Lynne *librarian*
Townsend, Susan Elaine *social service institute administrator, hostage survival consultant*
Tracanna, Kim *elementary and secondary physical education educator*
Tracey, Jay Walter, Jr. *retired lawyer*
Tracy, James *history educator*
†Tracy, Sean Michael *pilot*
Traeger, Charles Henry, III *lawyer*
Trafton, E. Joan *nursing educator*
Traher, William George *automotive model maker, retired*
†Traina, Anastasia Rose *playwright, screenwriter*
Traister, Robert Edwin *naval officer, engineer*
Tran, Nang Tri *electrical engineer, physicist*
Tranquada, Robert Ernest *medical educator, physician*
Trask, John Maurice, Jr. *property owner*
†Trautvetter, Lois Calian *chemistry educator, consultant*
Travanti, Daniel John *actor*
Travers, Rose Elaine *nursing supervisor*
Travis, Randy Bruce *musician*
Travolta, John *actor*
Traxler, Eva Maria *marketing administrator*
Traylor, William Robert *publisher*
Treacy, Vincent Edward *lawyer*
†Tregarthen, Suzanne Jo *writer, dean*
Treinavicz, Kathryn Mary *software engineer*
Trelease, Allen William *historian, educator*
Tremblay, Richard Ernest *psychology educator*
Tremko Housel, Laurie Ann *critical care nurse*
Trenery, Mary Ellen *librarian*
Treppler, Irene Esther *retired state senator*
Treynor, Jack Lawrence *financial advisor, educator*
Trezza, Alphonse Fiore *librarian, educator*
Triana, Gladys *artist*
Trice, William Henry *paper company executive*
Triece, Anne Gallagher *magazine publisher*
Trigg, Paul Reginald, Jr. *lawyer*
Trilling, Helen Regina *lawyer*
Trimble, Bernard Henry *tour guide, former trade association executive*
Trimble, Paul Joseph *retired lawyer*
Triolo, Peter *advertising agency executive, marketing educator, consultant*
Trippet, Susan Elaine *nursing educator*
Tronolone, Tracey Ann *social worker*
Troost, Bradley Todd *neurologist, educator*
Tropez-Sims, Susanne *pediatrician, educator*
Trotsky, Judith *writer*
Troupe, Marilyn Kay *education educator*
Trout, David E. *city planner*
Trout, Linda Copple *state supreme court justice*
Trudeau, Garretson Beekman (Garry Trudeau) *cartoonist*
Trueman, William Peter Main *broadcaster, newspaper columnist*
Truesdale, John Cushman *government executive*
Truitt, Barbara Ann *nurse*
Truman, Gary Tucker *photojournalist*
Truman, Margaret *author*
Trump, Donald John *real estate developer*
Trutter, John Thomas *consulting company executive*
Tsai, Wen-Ying *sculptor, painter, engineer*
Tsay, Ching Sow *anesthesiologist*
Tubman, William Charles *lawyer*
Tucci, Janis A(nn) *health unit administrator*
Tuchscherer, Marsha Smith *university art director*
Tuck, Mary Beth *nutritionist, educator*
Tuck, Russell R., Jr. *former college president*
Tucker, Charles Ray *metalworking company executive, sales and service engineer*
Tucker, Constance A. *critical care nurse*
Tucker, H. Richard *oil company executive*
Tucker, Jack William Andrew *writer, film editor, producer*
Tucker, Pierce Edward *air force officer*
Tucker-Osborne, Annette La Verne *legal nurse consultant, nursing home administrator*
Tudor, Mary Louise Drummond *elementary school educator*
Tuft, Mary Ann *executive search firm executive*
Tulley, Monica Elaine *marketing professional*
Tullis, Paul Rowan *journalist*
Tung, Yeishin *research scientist*
Tuohy, William *correspondent*
Tupper, Kent Phillip *lawyer*
Turco, Richard Peter *atmospheric scientist*
Turen, Barbara Ellen *lawyer*
Turk, Richard Errington *retired psychiatrist*
†Turkkan-Wille, Fatma *art historian*
Turnbull, John Neil *retired chemical company executive*
†Turnbull, Rebecca Jane Hemphill *educational administrator*
Turnbull, Vernona Harmsen *retired residence counselor, education educator*
Turner, Bonese Collins *artist, educator*
Turner, H(arry) Spencer *preventive medicine physician, educator*
Turner, Henry Brown *finance executive*
Turner, John Freeland *non-profit administrator, former federal agency administrator, former state senator*
†Turner, Joyce May *librarian*
Turner, Lee S., Jr. *civil engineer, consultant, former utilities executive*
Turner, Megan Whalen *author*
Turner, Nancy Kay *nurse*
Turner, Thomas Marshall *telecommunications executive, consultant*
Turner, Tina (Anna Mae Bullock) *singer*
†Turner-St. Clair, Linda Elaine *educator*
Turnipseed, Joel Thomas *writer*
†Turnoff, William Charles *magistrate judge*
Turok, Paul Harris *composer, music reviewer*
Turrill, Fred Lovejoy *surgeon*
Tussing, Lewis Benton, III (Tony Tussing) *secondary education educator, coach*
Tuttle, Jerry Owen *retired naval officer, business executive*
Tuttle, Laura Shive *healthcare educator, administrator*
Tuttle, Tammy Lynn *medical/surgical and pediatrics nurse*
Tuttle, William Julian *makeup artist*
Tuul, Johannes *physics educator, researcher*
Twardy, Stanley Albert, Jr. *lawyer*
Twichell, Chase *poet*
Tyler, Carl Walter, Jr. *physician, health research administrator, retired*
Tyler, Richard James *personal and professional development educator*
Tyler, Steven *singer*
Tyner, McCoy *jazz pianist, composer*
Tynes, John Cowan *publisher, writer, editor, graphic designer*
†Tyrrell, Lilian *craftsperson, artist*
Tyson, Eric *personal finance writer, finance counselor*
Tyson, H. Michael *retired bank executive*
Tytla, Peter T. *artist*
Tytler, Linda Jean *communications and public affairs executive, retired state legislator*
Ubell, Earl *magazine health editor*
Uchitel, Neil *composer*
†Uehling, Barbara Staner *educational administrator*
Uffelman, Malcolm Rucj *electronics company executive, electrical engineer*
Uhde, Larry Jackson *joint apprentice administrator*
Uhrich, Richard Beckley *hospital executive, physician*
Uken, Marcile Rena *music educator*
Ullman, Edwin Fisher *research chemist*
Ulrich, Richard William *finance executive*
Ulrich-Weaver, Judith L. *medical/surgical nurse, educator*
Uman, Martin Allan *electrical engineering educator, researcher, consultant*
UmBayemake, Linda *librarian*
Umpleby, Hannah Barbara Bennett *family therapist*
Underwood, Ralph Edward *computer systems engineer*
Undlin, Charles Thomas *banker*
Unger, Albert Howard *allergist, immunologist*
Unger, Roger Harold *physician, scientist*
Unithan, Dolly *visual artist*
Unser, Al *professional auto racer*
Updike, John Hoyer *writer*
Urciuoli, J. Arthur *investment executive*
Urdang, Laurence *lexicographer, publisher*
Usinger, Martha Putnam *counselor, educator*
Ussery, Luanne *retired communications consultant*
Ustinov, Sir Peter Alexander *actor, director, writer*
Utlaut, William Frederick *electrical engineer*
Utter, Robert French *retired state supreme court justice*
Uvena, Frank John *retired printing company executive, lawyer*
Vaccaro, Brenda *actress*
Vacco, Dennis C. *lawyer*
Vachher, Prehlad Singh *psychiatrist*
Vachon, Louis-Albert Cardinal *archbishop*
Vachon, Serge Jean *bank executive*
†Vagram-Nishanian, Violet *music educator*
Vai, Steve *guitarist*
Vaida, Veronica Fodor *publishing marketing reference professional*
Valderrama, Carlos *professional soccer player*
Valentine, I. T., Jr. (Tim Valentine) *former congressman*
Valentine, William Newton *physician, educator*
Valeskie-Hamner, Gail Yvonne *information systems specialist*
Valfre, Michelle Williams *nursing educator, administrator, author*
Valine, Delmar Edmond, Sr. *corporate executive*
Vallerand, Philippe Georges *sales executive*
Vallone, John Charles *motion picture production designer*
Valois, Robert Arthur *lawyer*
Valtman, Edmund *editorial cartoonist*
Vanaltenburg, Betty Marie *lumber company executive*
Vanatta, Bob *athletic administrator*
Van Atta, Cheri Marie *equine instructor*
VanBriggle, Denise Marie *secondary school educator*
Van Brunt, Edmund Ewing *physician*
Vance, David Alvin *management educator*
Vandenbroucke, Russell James *theatre director*
Vandenburg, Kathy Helen *career counselor*
Vanderhoof, Irwin Thomas *life insurance company executive*
van der Meer, Simon *physicist*
Vanderwalker, Diane Mary *materials scientist*
Vanderwest, Donald *income tax administrator*
VanDevere, Christian *fashion model, writer*
†van de Zilver, Peter A.L. *economist, business executive*
Van Dine, Alan Charles *advertising agency executive, writer*
Van Dreser, Merton Lawrence *ceramic engineer*
Van Duyn, Mona Jane *poet*
van Dyck, Nicholas Booraem *minister, foundation official*
Van Dyke, Henry Lewis *retired educator, writer*
Van Engen, Thomas Lee *state legislator*
Van Every, Kathleen Mary *contracts manager*
van Gestel, Allan *judge*
Vangieri, Louis C. *counselor, educator*
van Hengel, Maarten R. *financial executive*
Van Houten, Elizabeth Ann *corporate communications executive*
Vanier, Jacques *physicist*
van Itallie, Jean-Claude *playwright*
Vann, Diane E. Swanson *nursing educator*
Van Ness, John Ralph *university administrator, educator*
Van Ness, Patricia Catheline *composer, violinist*
Vannozzi, Thomas *cameraman*
Van Orden, Phyllis Jeanne *librarian, educator*
Van Patten, Joyce Benignia *actress*
Van Peebles, Mario *actor, director*
van Schilfgaarde, Jan *retired agricultural engineer, government agricultural research service administrator*
Van Solkema-Waitz, Terese Ellen *special education educator, consultant*
Van Tassel, James Henry *retired electronics executive*
Van Vleet, William Benjamin *retired lawyer, life insurance company executive*
Van Wagoner, Ammon Kim *health facility administrator*
†Vargas, Margarita *modern languages educator*
Vargas, Pattie Lee *author, editor*
Varis, Jina Aleksandra *voice teacher*
Varley, Michael Chris *communications executive*
Varner, David Eugene *lawyer*
Varney, Suzanne Glaab *health facility administrator*
Varrenti, Adam, Jr. *financial executive*
Vasily, John Timothy *information systems executive, state government official*
Vassil, Pamela *graphic designer, writer, administrator*
Vaughan, John Charles, III *horticultural products executive*
Vaughan, Nadine *psychologist*
Vaughn, Gregory Lamont *professional baseball player*
Vaughn, Kenneth J. *civil engineer, consultant*
Vaught, Darrel Mandel *accountant*
Vecci, Raymond Joseph *airline industry consultant*
Vega, Alberto Leon *financial executive*
Vega, J. William *aerospace engineering executive, consultant*
Velzy, Charles O. *mechanical engineer*
Venezia, Michael *painter, educator*
Verderber, Joseph Anthony *capital equipment company executive*
VerDorn, Jerry *actor*
Vermeule, Emily Townsend (Mrs. Cornelius C. Vermeule, III) *classicist, educator*
Verney, Judith La Baie *retired health program administrator*
Vernon, Carl Atlee, Jr. *retired wholesale food distributor executive*
Vero, Radu *freelance medical and scientific illustrator, educator, writer, consultant*
Veronis, George *geophysicist, educator*
Verplanck, William Samuel *psychologist, educator*
Vessey, John William, Jr. *army officer*
Vestweber, Susan Diane *operating room nurse*
Veta, D. Jean *lawyer*
Vickery, Byrdean Eyvonne Hughes (Mrs. Charles Everett Vickery, Jr.) *retired library services administrator*
Vieira, Robert *musical dramatist*
Vierra, Deborah *critical care, community health nurse*
†Vigness, Bryan *career officer*
Vigoda, Abe *actor*
Vila, Adis Maria *corporate executive, former government official, lawyer*
Vilenchik, Michael Marc *biophysicist, physician, virologist, radiobiologist*
Villareal, Roland *nurse*
†Villaveces, Jeffrey Roberto *educational organization worker*
Villella, Edward Joseph *ballet dancer, educator, choreographer, artistic director*
Vinar, Benjamin *lawyer*
Vincent, Bruce Havird *investment banker, oil and gas company executive*
Vincent, Gary Lee *federal employee, musician*
Vincent, Hal Wellman *marine corps officer, investor*
Violenus, Agnes A. *retired school system administrator*
Violette, Diane Marie *small business owner, consultant, editor*
Viorst, Judith Stahl *author*
Viorst, Milton *writer*
Virkhaus, Taavo *symphony orchestra conductor*
Viscelli, Therese Rauth *materials management consultant*
Visci, Joseph Michael *newspaper editor*
†Viswanathan, Meera Sushila *comparative literature and East Asian studies educator*
Vitaliano, Charles J(oseph) *geologist, educator*
†Vitolo, Robert V. *plastic and reconstructive surgeon*
Vitt, David Aaron *medical manufacturing company executive*
Vittone, John Michael *federal judge*
†Vlazny, John George *bishop*
Voelker, Margaret Irene (Meg Voelker) *gerontology, medical, surgical nurse*
Vohs, James Arthur *health care program executive*
Voight, Elizabeth Anne *lawyer*
Voight, Jon *actor*
Voigt, Cynthia *author*
Voigt, Robert Gary *numerical analyst*
Voketaitis, Arnold Mathew *bass-baritone, educator*
Volans, Ronald Paul *marketing professional*
Volcker, Paul A. *economist*
Voldman, Steven Howard *electrical engineer*
Volk, Patricia Gay *fiction writer, essayist*
Volkhardt, John Malcolm *food company executive*
Vollmer, Richard Wade *federal judge*
Volpe, Edmond L(oris) *college president*
von Furstenberg, Betsy *actress, writer*
Von Furstenberg, Diane Simone Michelle *fashion designer, writer, entrepreneur*
von Hoffman, Alexander *historian*
von Hoffman, Nicholas *writer, former journalist*
von Linsowe, Marina Dorothy *information systems consultant*
von Sauers, Joseph F. *lawyer*
von Sydow, Max (Carl Adolf von Sydow) *actor*
Vook, Frederick Ludwig *physicist, consultant*
Voorhees, James Dayton, Jr. *lawyer*
Voorhees, John Lloyd *columnist*
Vore, Mary Edith *pharmacology educator, researcher*
Voss, Carolyn Jean *nursing educator, consultant*
Voss, Omer Gerald *truck company executive*
†Voss, Varnell Von *elementary education educator*
Votava, Thomas Anthony *real estate and insurance professional*
Vradenburg, George, III *lawyer*
†Vujacic, Veljko M. *adult education educator*
Vytal, James Alfred *printing company executive*
Wachbrit, Jill Barrett *accountant, tax specialist*
†Wachtel, Jeffrey M. *management educator, management consultant*
Waddle, John Frederick *former retail chain executive*
Wadley, M. Richard *consumer products executive*
Wadsworth, Beverly Jane *retired nursing administrator*
Wadsworth, Jacqueline Dorèt *private investor*
Waggener, Theryn Lee *law enforcement professional*
Wagman, Robert John *journalist, author*
Wagner, Diana Mae *English language educator*
Wagner, Ellyn S(anti) *mathematics educator*
Wagner, Julia A(nne) *retired editor*
Wagner, Marilyn Faith *elementary school educator*
Wagner, Michael Duane *lawyer*
Wagner, Richard *athletics consultant, former baseball team executive*
Wagner, Robert *actor*
Wagner, Sigurd *electrical engineering educator, researcher*
†Wagner, Tom Edward *artist, dancer*
Wahl, Floyd Michael *geologist*
Wain, Christopher Henry Fairfax Moresby *actuary, insurance and investment consultant*
†Waisman, Carlos H. *sociologist*
Wait, Carol Grace Cox *organization administrator*
Waite, Frances W. *librarian, professional genealogist*
Walasek, Otto Frank *chemical engineer, biochemist, photographer*
Walden, Joseph Lawrence *career officer*
Waldon, Alton Ronald, Jr. *state senator*
Waldon, Grace Roberta *environmental company executive*
Waldrop, Gideon William *composer, conductor, former president music school*
Walenga, Jeanine Marie *medical educator, researcher*
Walken, Christopher *actor*
Walker, A. Harris *lawyer, manufacturing executive, retired*
Walker, Bradford C. *architect*
†Walker, Courtney G. *magazine editor*
Walker, Craig Michael *lawyer*
Walker, Debra *artist*
Walker, Donald Robert, Jr. *minister*
Walker, Gordon Davies *former government official, writer, lecturer, consultant*
Walker, John Sumpter, Jr. *lawyer*
Walker, Loren Haines *electrical engineer*
Walker, Mark A. *lawyer*
Walker, Mary L. *lawyer*
†Walker, Pamela *college administrator*
Wall, M. Danny *financial services company executive*
Wallace, F. Blake *aerospace executive, mechanical engineer*
Wallace, Jane House *retired geologist*
Wallace, Kenny *professional race car driver*
Wallace, Michael Arthur *aerospace executive*
Wallace, Michele *writer, educator*
Wallace, Robert Earl *geologist*
Wallace, Thomas C(hristopher) *editor, literary agent*
Wallace, William Augustine *philosophy and history educator*
Wallach, Amei Marione *journalist, art critic*
Wallach, Eli *actor*
Wallack, Rina Evelyn *lawyer*

Waller, Gary Fredric *English language educator, administrator, poet*
Waller, Ray Albert *statistician*
Wallerstein, Judith Saretsky *marriage and divorce researcher*
Walling, Sally Ann *health system administrator*
†Wallman, Lester Julian *retired medical educator*
Walls, Carmage Lee, Jr. *newspaper executive, consultant*
Walner, Robert Joel *lawyer*
Walrath, Daniel Laurens *physician*
†Walser, Clarke L. *management consultant*
Walsh, Diane *pianist*
Walsh, Dolores (Lorry)Ann Gonczo *special education educator*
Walsh, Edward Patrick *federal agency administrator*
Walsh, M. Emmet *actor*
Walsh, Michael Joseph *special operations consulting company executive*
Walsh, William Albert *management consultant, former naval officer*
Walston, Lola Inge *dietitian*
Walston, Ray *actor*
Walter, Ann Lynn *special education educator*
Walter, J. Jackson *consultant*
Walters, David Wayne *history and government educator, tennis coach*
†Walters, Jacqueline Lynsherrlye *college administrator*
Walters, Jo Lynn Blackburn *nursing administrator, psychiatric nurse*
Walters-Lucy, Jean Marie *personal growth educator, consultant*
Walton, Harold Vincent *former agricultural engineering educator, academic administrator*
Waltrip, Darrell Lee *professional stock car driver*
Waltz, Alan Kent *clergyman, denominational executive*
Waltz, Kenneth Neal *political science educator*
Wambaugh, Joseph *author*
Warberg, Willetta *concert pianist, author, piano educator*
Ward, Anthony G. *stock, options and futures exchange consultant*
†Ward, Cam *legislative staff member*
Ward, Edward Wells *telecommunications executive*
Ward, John J. *bishop*
†Ward, Nari *sculptor*
Ward, Vicki Dawne *family nurse practitioner, rural health specialist*
Warden, Jack *actor*
Warder, Richard Currey, Jr. *dean, mechanical aerospace engineering educator*
Ware, James Latané *plastic surgeon*
Ware, John E. *psychiatry educator, medical laboratory executive*
Ware, Leigh Ann Carter *neonatal critical care nurse*
Warner, Walter Duke *corporate executive*
Warnstadt, Steven H. *state legislator*
Warren, Cindy Michelle *author*
Warren, Mark Edward *foundation executive, lawyer*
Warren, Richard Ernest *advertising executive*
†Warren, Shelly Dee *academic administrator*
†Warren, Winnifred Patricia *human resources manager*
Warshawsky, Isidore *physicist, consultant*
Wartluft, David Jonathan *librarian, clergyman*
Washburn, Caryl Anne *occupational therapist*
Washburn, Dorothy A. *entrepreneur*
Washington, Charles Henderson *laser systems designer, consultant*
Washington, Denzel *actor*
Washington, Grover, Jr. *musician, producer, composer, arranger*
Washington, Josephine Harriet *biologist, endocrinologist, educator*
†Washington, Lester R. *insurance agent, small business owner*
Washington, Valora *foundation administrator*
Washington, Walter *retired academic administrator*
Washow, Paula Burnette *security company and investigation agency executive*
Wasserman, Anthony Ira *software company executive, educator*
Wasserstein, Wendy *playwright*
†Wasson, Brian Charles *editor*
Wasson, James Walter *aircraft manufacturing company executive*
Waters, Donald Eugene *academic administrator*
Waters, Ed (Edward Sarsfield Waters) *screenwriter, television producer, writer*
Waters, T. Wayne *journalist*
Wathen, Daniel Everett *state supreme court chief justice*
Watkins, James David *government official, naval officer*
†Watkins, James David *food products executive*
Watkins, Lewis Boone *artist*
Watkins, William David *editor, writer, consultant, agent*
Watko, Julie Anne *astrophysicist, actor*
Watson, Deborah Lynn *women's health nurse*
Watson, Marilyn Kaye *elementary education educator*
Watson, Rosemarie Memie *emergency medical technician*
Watt, John H. *financial executive*
Wattenberg, Albert *physicist, educator*
Watts, Glenn Ellis *union official*
Watts, Jeri Hanel *elementary education educator, writer*
Watts, Julia Ellen *writer, English educator*
Watts, Mary Ann *retired elementary education educator*
Watts, Ronald Lester *retired military officer*
Wawrose, Frederick Eugene *psychiatrist*
Waxman, Ronald *computer engineer*
Wayans, Damon *actor*
Wayans, Keenen Ivory *actor, producer*
Waymouth, John Francis *physicist, consultant*
Wearn, Wilson Cannon *retired media executive*
Weaver, Charles Horace *educator*
Weaver, Esther Ruth *medical and surgical, geriatrics and oncology nurse*
Weaver, Helen Grace *retired elementary education educator*
Weaver, Howard C. *newspaper executive*
Weaver, Peggy (Marguerite McKinnie Weaver) *plantation owner*
Weaver, William Charles *retired industrial executive*
Webb, David Allen *writer*
Webb, John Gibbon, III *lawyer*
Webber, Andrew Lloyd *composer*
Weber, Arthur *magazine executive*
Weber, Fred J. *retired state supreme court justice*
Weber, Garry Allen *city councilman*
Weber, John Walter *insurance company executive*
Weber, Laurie Ann *artist*

Weber, Linda Diane *occupational health nurse*
Weber, Mary Ellen Healy *economist*
†Weber, Shelly Ann *elementary music educator*
†Weber, William L. *economics educator*
†Webster, Andrew John *art educator*
Webster, John Kingsley Ohl, II *health administrator, rehabilitation manager*
Webster, Nicholas *director*
Webster, Susan Jean *medical/surgical nurse*
Wechsler, Sergio *automotive executive, consultant*
Wechter, Vivienne Thaul *artist, poet, educator*
Weckesser, Ernest Prosper, Jr. *publisher, educator*
Wedeen, Marvin Meyer *hospital executive*
Weeden, Mary Ann *real estate investment company executive*
†Weekley, David *real estate developer*
†Weeks, Mary Kathryn *secondary education educator, artist*
†Wegener, Robert Paul *communications educator*
Wegert, Mary Magdalene Hardel *retired special education director, consultant*
Wegman, William George *artist*
Wei, Hua-Fang *electrical engineer*
Weichler, Nancy Karen *pediatric nurse*
Weidner, Roswell Theodore *artist*
†Weier, Anita Carol *journalist*
Weightman, Esther Lynn *emergency trauma nurse*
Weikart, David Powell *educational research foundation administrator*
Weil, Inga Frenkel *psychiatrist*
Weil, Peter Henry *lawyer*
Weil, Rolf Alfred *economist, university president emeritus*
Weiland, Charles Hankes *lawyer*
Weimer, Gary W. *university development executive, consultant*
Weinberg, Sidney R. *physician*
Weinberg, Steven *physics educator*
Weinberger, Arnold *retired electrical engineer*
Weiner, Cherry *literary agent*
Weiner, Gershon Ralph *physician*
Weiner, Harold M. *retired radiologist*
Weiner, Jonathan David *writer*
Weiner, N. Alfred *publishing executive*
Weiner, Susan Marks *perinatal clinical nurse specialist, educator*
Weiner-Heuschkel, Sydell *theater educator*
Weinhauer, William Gillette *retired bishop*
Weinmann, Richard Adrian *lawyer*
Weinschel, Bruno Oscar *engineering executive, physicist*
†Weintraub, William H. *pediatric surgeon, educator*
Weir, Kenneth Wynn *marine corps officer, experimental test pilot*
Weir, Thomas Charles *banker*
Weis, Margaret Edith *writer, editor*
Weisbuch, Robert Alan *English educator*
Weisburger, Elizabeth Kreiser *retired chemist, editor*
Weisinger, Ronald Jay *government executive search consultant*
Weiskopf, Kim Robert *television producer, writer*
Weisman, Lorenzo David *investment banker*
Weisman, Paul Howard *lawyer*
Weismantel, Gregory Nelson *management consultant and software executive*
Weiss, Alan *musician, educator*
Weiss, Joseph W. *management educator, management consultant*
Weiss, Kenneth Jay *education educator, reading specialist, administrator*
Weiss, Max Tibor *retired aerospace company executive*
Weiss, Michael James *chemistry educator*
Weiss, Rita Sandra *transportation executive*
Weiss, Robert M. *urologist, educator*
Weissman, Jack (George Anderson) *editor*
Weissman, Samuel Isaac *chemistry educator*
Weissmann, Heidi Seitelblum *radiologist, educator*
Weitzel, Harvey M. *minister, counselor*
Weitzel, Marilyn Lee *nursing educator*
Welch, Madeleine Lauretta *medical/surgical and occupational health nurse*
Welch, Robyn Perlman *pediatric critical care nurse*
Weld, Tuesday Ker (Susan Ker Weld) *actress*
Weldon, Jeffrey Alan *lawyer*
Weldon, William Forrest *electrical and mechanical engineer, educator*
Weller, Debra Anne *elementary educator*
Welles, John Galt *retired museum director*
Welles, Virginia Chrisman *land use planner*
Wellman, Anthony Donald Emerson *advertising executive*
†Wellman, Mac *writer, educator*
Wells, Janet Ohlemiller *fundraiser*
Wells, Robert Hartley *chemistry professional*
Wells, Toni Lynn *accountant*
Wells, Victor Hugh, Jr. *retired advertising agency executive*
Welly, Michael Anthony *elementary school educator*
†Welsh, Thomas J. *retired bishop*
Welsome, Eileen *journalist*
Wendland, Claire *nursing administrator, geriatrics nurse*
Wendorf, Virginia Lou *retired accountant*
Wendt, George Robert *actor*
Wendt, Marilynn Suzann *elementary school educator, principal*
Wenzel, Loren Alvin *accounting educator*
Wenzel, Richard Putnam *internist*
Werlein, Donna Dabeck *community health care administrator*
Werman, Thomas Ehrlich *record producer*
Werner-Jacobsen, Emmy Elisabeth *developmental psychologist*
Werth, Andrew M. *telecommunications executive*
Wescoe, W(illiam) Clarke *physician*
Wesely, Marissa Celeste *lawyer*
Wessel, Morris Arthur *retired pediatrics educator*
Wessel, Peter *lawyer*
Wessler, Richard Lee *psychology educator, psychotherapist*
West, Gregory Alan *physician*
West, Jerry Alan *professional basketball team executive*
West, Raymond L. *nurse*
West, Rexford Leon *banker*
West, Warren Henry *securities trader*
Westall, Thomas George *pastoral counselor*
†Westergard, Sue Benzel *elementary education educator*
Westmoreland, Barbara Fenn *neurologist, electroencephalographer, educator*
Weston, Josh S. *retired data processing company executive*
Westwick, Carmen Rose *retired nursing educator, consultant*
Wetherill, Eikins *lawyer, stock exchange executive*

Wetzel, Donald Truman *engineering company executive*
Whalen, Alberta Dean *retired community health nurse*
Whalen, Charles William, Jr. *author, business executive, educator*
Whalen, Jane Claire *nurse, clinical specialist*
Whalen, Loretta Theresa *religious educational administrator*
Whalen-Blaauwgeers, Herma-Jozé *financial analyst*
Whalley, Joanne *actress*
Wharton, Hugh Davis, III *lawyer, judge*
Wheaton, Alice Alshuler *administrative assistant*
Wheaton, Mary Edwina *health facility administrator, educator*
Wheeler, Albin Gray *United States Army career officer, educator, retail executive, law firm executive*
Wheeler, Barbara J. *management consultant*
†Wheeler, Brannon M. *adult education educator*
Wheeler, Burton M. *literature educator, higher education consultant, college dean*
Wheeler, David Laurie *university dean*
Wheeler, John Charles *telecommunications professional*
Wheeler, R(ichard) Kenneth *lawyer*
Whelchel, Sandra Jane *writer*
Whildin, Donna *medical/surgical nurse*
Whistler, Roy Lester *chemist, educator, industrialist*
Whitaker, Shirley Ann *telecommunications company marketing executive*
Whitchurch, Charles Augustus *art gallery owner, humanities educator*
White, Annette Jones *retired early childhood educator/administrator*
White, Anthony Roy, Jr. *composer, educator*
White, Augustus Aaron, III *orthopedic surgeon*
White, Bertram Milton *chemicals executive*
White, Bonnie Yvonne *management consultant, retired educator*
White, Bruce Emerson, Jr. *business chain executive*
White, Charles Olds *aeronautical engineer*
†White, Claire Nicolas *writer, translator*
White, Erskine Norman, Jr. *management company executive*
White, Eugene Vaden *retired pharmacist*
White, Florence May *learning disabilities specialist*
White, Gerald Andrew *retired chemical company executive*
†White, Helene Nita *federal judge*
†White, Howard O., Jr. *musician, producer*
White, John Joseph, III *lawyer*
White, John Kiernan *lighting company executive*
White, John Wesley, Jr. *retired university president*
White, Juanita M. *staff nurse*
White, Julie *former foundation executive*
White, Katharine Stone *museum trustee*
White, Kerr Lachlan *retired physician, foundation director*
White, Larry D. *political science educator*
White, Loray Betty *public relations executive, writer, actress, producer*
White, Michael Craig *writer, illustrator*
White, Nancy Carolyn *publishing executive*
†White, Orion Forrest, Jr. *education educator*
White, Renee Allyn *judge*
White, Richard Clarence *lawyer*
White, Richard Thomas *radiologist*
White, Sarah Jowilliard *counselor*
White, Thomas Edward *retired government park official*
White, Willis Sheridan, Jr. *retired utilities company executive*
Whitehead, John Jed *healthcare and biotech company executive*
Whitehouse, Alton Winslow, Jr. *retired oil company executive*
Whitehouse, Sheldon *attorney general, lawyer*
Whitehurst, Rose Mae *education specialist*
Whiteley, Benjamin Robert *retired insurance company executive*
Whitener, Lawrence Bruce *political consultant, consumer advocate, educator, paralegal*
Whitesell, John Edwin *motion picture company executive*
White-Vondran, Mary-Ellen *retired stockbroker*
Whitfield, Lynn *actress*
Whitlock, Bennett Clarke, Jr. *retired association executive*
Whitlock, William Abel *retired lawyer*
Whitmore, Menandra M. *librarian*
Whitney, Jane *foreign service officer*
Whitney, Ruth Reinke *magazine editor*
Whitson, Angie *artist*
Whittaker, Mary Frances *educational and industrial company official*
Whyte, Bruce Lincoln *management executive, marketing professional*
Wiatr, Christopher Louis *microbiologist*
Wiatt, James Anthony *theatrical agency executive*
Wicker, Thomas Grey *retired journalist*
Wickersham, Amanda Kaye *retired elementary education educator*
Wickes, R(ichard) Paul *lawyer*
†Wickliffe, Mary *art historian*
Wickner, William Tobey *biochemistry educator*
Widmark, Richard *actor*
Wiebe, Leonard Irving *radiopharmacist, educator*
Wiebelhaus, Pamela Sue *school administrator, educator*
Wiebenson, Dora Louise *architectural historian, educator, author*
Wieber, Patricia McNally *medical/surgical nurse, orthopaedics nurse*
Wiedenhoeft, Ann Marie *psychotherapist, consultant*
Wiegenstein, John Gerald *physician*
Wieland, William Dean *health care consulting executive*
Wien, Stuart Lewis *retired supermarket chain executive*
Wiersma, Peggy Ann *nurse*
Wies, Barbara *editor, publisher*
Wiesen, Donald Guy *retired diversified manufacturing company executive*
Wieser, Siegfried *planetarium executive director*
Wiesner, John Joseph *retail chain store executive*
Wiessler, David Albert *correspondent*
Wiest, Dianne *actress*
Wiggins, Charles Edward *judge*
Wikarski, Nancy Susan *information technology consultant*
Wilamowski, Doris *psychotherapist*
Wilde, John *artist, educator*
Wildhack, William August, Jr. *lawyer*
Wiley, Carl Ross *timber company executive*
Wiley, Richard Arthur *lawyer*
Wilhelm, Charles Elliott *military officer*
Wilhelm, Morton *retired surgery educator*

Wilhelms, Don Edward *geologist*
Wilhelmsen, Harold John *accountant, operations controller*
†Wilhide, Angela Gail *secondary education educator*
Wilkening, Laurel Lynn *academic administrator, planetary scientist*
†Wilkins, Dick J. *engineering educator*
Wilkinson, Claude Henry *writer, artist, English literature educator*
Wilkinson, Doris *medical sociology educator*
Wilkinson, Stanley Ralph *agronomist*
Wilkinson, Todd Thomas *project engineer*
Will, Joanne Marie *food and consumer services executive, communications consultant, writer*
Wille, Wayne Martin *retired editor*
Willenbecher, John *artist*
Willey, Gordon Randolph *retired anthropologist, archaeologist, educator*
William, Thomas W. *electrical engineer*
Williams, Alfred Blythe *business communication educator*
Williams, Billy Dee *actor*
Williams, Charles Wesley *technical executive, researcher*
Williams, Cheryl A. *secondary education educator*
Williams, Christie Lee *journalist*
Williams, Cindy Jane *actress*
Williams, David Keith *technical trainer*
Williams, David Vandergrift *organizational psychologist*
Williams, Dennis Thomas *civil engineer*
Williams, Donald Allen, Jr. *writer, independent television/video producer*
Williams, Earle Carter *retired professional services company executive*
Williams, Ernest Going *retired paper company executive*
Williams, Ervin Eugene *religious organization administrator*
Williams, George Doyne, Jr. *cardiovascular surgeon*
Williams, Gregory Carl, Sr. *city official*
Williams, Gurney, III *journalist, educator*
Williams, Harriette Flowers *retired school system administrator, educational consultant*
Williams, Harry Edward *management consultant*
Williams, Heather Pauline *secondary education educator*
Williams, Helen Margaret *retired accountant*
Williams, Howard Walter *aerospace engineer, executive*
†Williams, Jeffrey P. *investment banker*
Williams, John Howard *architect, retired*
Williams, Joseph Theodore *oil and gas company executive*
Williams, Leona Rae *lingerie shop owner, consultant*
Williams, Lewis T. (Rusty Williams) *education educator*
Williams, Linda Hunt *organization executive*
Williams, Lisa *actress*
Williams, Louis Clair, Jr. *public relations executive*
Williams, Patrice Dale *linguist, educator*
Williams, Richard Clarence *retired librarian*
Williams, Robert Leon *psychiatrist, neurologist, educator*
Williams, Roger Stewart *physician*
Williams, Ronald Lee *pharmacologist*
Williams, Ross Arnold *computer systems engineer*
Williams, Thomas Arthur *lawyer*
Williams, Thomas B. *secondary school educator*
Williams, Thomas Lloyd *psychiatrist*
Williams, Thomas W. *electrical engineer*
Williams, Treat (Richard Treat Williams) *actor*
Williams, William John, Jr. *lawyer*
Williams-Barnard, Carol Lou *mental health nurse*
Williams-Maddox, Janice Helen *nurse*
Williamson, Edwin Dargan *lawyer, former federal official*
Williamson, Fletcher Phillips *real estate executive*
Williamson, Jo Ann *psychologist*
Williamson, Laird *stage director, actor*
Williamson, Myrna Hennrich *retired army officer, lecturer, consultant*
Williamson, William Allen *retired optometrist*
Willig, Karl Victor *computer firm executive*
Willingham, Ozella M. *medical/surgical and cardiac nurse*
Willis, Bettina Bentley *oncology nurse*
Willoughby, Kenneth Dwight *accountant, banking executive*
Wills, Charles Francis *former church executive, retired career officer*
Wills, William Ridley, II *former insurance company executive, historian*
Wilmore, Douglas Wayne *surgeon, educator*
Wilmoth, Margaret Chamberlain *oncology nurse, researcher*
Wilner, Freeman Marvin *retired hematologist, oncologist*
Wilner, Judith *journalist*
Wilpon, Fred *professional baseball team executive, real estate developer*
Wilshire, Robert Vidal *priest, theology educator*
Wilson, Almon Chapman *surgeon, physician, retired naval officer*
Wilson, C. Daniel, Jr. *library director*
Wilson, Colin Henry *writer*
Wilson, Dwight Liston *former military officer, investment advisor*
Wilson, Gary Thomas *engineering executive*
Wilson, Hugh Steven *lawyer*
Wilson, Jane *artist*
Wilson, Karen Lee *museum director*
Wilson, Kenneth Geddes *physics research administrator, educator*
Wilson, Lanford *playwright*
Wilson, Linda Ann *renal dialysis nurse*
Wilson, Mary Elizabeth *geriatrics nurse*
Wilson, Melvin Edmond *civil engineer*
Wilson, Michael Dean *business executive*
Wilson, Paul W., Jr. *lawyer, entrepreneur*
Wilson, Ralph Cookerly, Jr. *professional football team executive*
Wilson, Rhys Thaddeus *lawyer*
Wilson, Robin Scott *university president, writer*
†Wilson, Sandra Thomason *utility company executive*
Wilson, Sloan *author, lecturer*
Wilson, Warren Samuel *clergyman, bishop*
Wilson, William Glenn, Jr. *graphic designer*
Wilwerding, Kati Anne *critical care nurse*
Winchell, William Olin *mechanical engineer, educator, lawyer*
Winder, Robert Owen *retired mathematician, computer engineer executive*
Windom, William *actor*
Winfield, Paul Edward *actor*
Wing, Lilly Kelly Raynor *health services administrator*

Wingate, Bettye Faye *librarian, educator*
Winkler, Margaret Ann *geriatrics nurse, nursing administrator*
Winokur, Neil *photographer*
Winsor, David John *cost consultant*
Winston, Michael G. *corporate executive*
Winter, Alan *retired publishing company executive*
Winter, Harland Steven *pediatric gastroenterologist*
Winter, Richard Samuel, Jr. *computer training company owner, writer*
Winters, Jonathan *actor*
Winters, Sheila *family nurse practitioner*
Winthrop-St.Gery, Rhett *computer specialist*
Wintle, Rosemarie *bio-medical electronics engineer*
Winton, Howard Phillip *retired optometrist*
Winwood, Stephen Lawrence *musician, composer*
†Wioch, Christina Helena *artist*
Wirth, Russell D. L., Jr. *investment and merchant banker*
Wise, Karsonya Eugenia *filmmaker, writer*
Wise, Patricia *lyric coloratura*
Wise, Susan Tamsberg *management and communications consultant, speaker*
Wisehart, Mary Ruth *retired religious organization executive*
Wiseman, Douglas Carl *education educator*
Wishnia, Kenneth J.A. *writer, translator, language educator*
Wisniewski, Thomas Joseph *music educator*
Witcher, Daniel Dougherty *retired pharmaceutical company executive*
Witkowski, Joseph Albin *dermatologist*
Witt, Hugh Ernest *technology consultant*
Witt, Nancy Camden *artist*
Witte, Arline (Lyn Witte) *author/poet*
Witte, Merlin Michael *oil company executive*
Wittebort, Robert John, Jr. *lawyer*
Witthuhn, Norman Edward *minister*
Wittich, John Jacob *retired college president, corporation consultant*
Wittig, Raymond Shaffer *lawyer, technology transfer advisor*
†Wittman, Randy *professional basketball coach*
Woerner, Robert Lester *landscape architect*
Wohlfeld, Valerie Robin *writer*
Wold, Margaret Barth *religion educator, author*
Wolf, Dale Edward *state official*
Wolf, Edith Maletz *retired educator*
Wolf, Hans Abraham *retired pharmaceutical company executive*
†Wolf, Melinda Susan *social worker, poet*
Wolf, Muriel Hebert *soprano, opera director, music educator*
Wolf, Rosalie Joyce *financial executive*
Wolfberg, Melvin Donald *optometrist, educational administrator, consultant*
Wolfe, Frances Diane *medical secretary, artist*
Wolfe, Gregory Baker *international relations educator*
Wolfe, Jonathan A. *food wholesaler, retailer*
Wolff, Brian Richard *metal manufacturing company executive*
Wolff, Cynthia Griffin *humanities educator, author*
Wolff, Manfred Ernst *medicinal chemist, pharmaceutical company executive*
Wolff, Peter Adalbert *physicist, educator*
Wolfgang, Gary L. *orthopaedic surgeon*
Wolfman, Ira Joel *editor, writer*
Wolken, George, Jr. *patent lawyer*
Wollert, Gerald Dale *retired food company executive, investor*
Wollman Rusoff, Jane Susan *journalist, writer*
Woloshen, Jeffrey Lawrence *automobile executive, consultant, accountant*
Wolosonovich, Stephen *violinist*
Wolotkiewicz, Marian M. *household products company official*
Wolters, Oliver William *history educator*
Wolverton, Terry L(ynn) *writer, consultant*
Womack, Idalah Demina *social services administrator*
Wonders, William Clare *geography educator*
Wong, David Yue *academic administrator, physics educator*
Wong, Gwendolyn Ngit How Jim *former bank executive*
Wong, Rebecca Kimmae *mathematics educator, consultant*
Wong-Diaz, Francisco Raimundo *lawyer, educator*
Wong-Yozviak, Lisa Christine *music educator*
Woo, Jonathan C. G. *chemist, management consultant*
Woo, Savio Lau Ching *molecular medical geneticist*
Wood, Allen John *electrical engineer, consultant*
Wood, Arthur MacDougall *retired retail executive*
Wood, Diane Pamela *judge*
Wood, Donald Neal *educator in media, author*
Wood, Marian Starr *publishing company executive*
Wood, Norma J. *nurse practitioner*
Wood, Robert Charles *financial consultant*
Wood, Robert Coldwell *political scientist*
Wood, William Preston *author, lawyer*
Wood, Willis Bowne, Jr. *retired utility holding company executive*
Woodall, Lee *professional football player*
Woodard, Alfre *actress*
Woodard, Nina Elizabeth *banker*
†Woodard, Pamela J. *child care center administrator*
Woodcock, Richard Wesley *educational psychologist*
Wooden, John Robert *former basketball coach*
Woodman, Jean Wilson *educator, consultant*
Woodruff, Virginia *broadcast journalist, writer*
Woodruff, Warren Lane *music educator*
Woodrum, Patricia Ann *librarian*
Woods, Geraldine Pittman *health education consultant, educational consultant*
Woods, Harriett Ruth *retired political organization president*
Woods, J. P. *minister*
Woods, Phyllis Michalik *retired elementary school educator*
Woods, Reginald Foster *management consulting executive*
Woodside, George Robert *computer software developer*
Woodsworth, Anne *university dean, librarian*
Woodward, Clinton Benjamin, Jr. *civil engineering educator*
Woodward, John Russell *motion picture production executive*
Woodward, Thomas Morgan *actor*
Woodward, William Lee *retired savings bank executive*
†Woodwork, Bruce E. *physician, urologist*
Woolworth, Susan Valk *primary school educator*
Woosnam, Ian Harold *professional golfer*
Wooten, Frank Thomas *retired research facility executive*
Worcester, Peggy Jean *medical/surgical nurse*
Work, William *retired association executive*
Wormwood, Richard Naughton *retired naturalist, writer*
Worrell, Cynthia Celeste *school nurse*
Worthen, John Edward *academic administrator*
†Worthley, John Abbott *adult education educator, consultant, author*
Wozniak, Joyce Marie *sales executive*
Wren, Stephen Corey *corporation administrator, technologist, actuary, mathematician*
Wrenn, Diane Marie *medical/surgical nurse*
Wright, Beth Segal *art historian, educator*
Wright, Cathleen R. *administrator*
Wright, Charles Spaulding, II *writer, communications consultant*
Wright, Connie Sue *special education educator*
Wright, Frederick Lewis, II *lawyer*
Wright, Hassell Bradley *journalist, editor*
Wright, James David *sociology educator, writer*
Wright, Jane Brooks *retired university foundation professional*
Wright, Judith Rae *retired accountant*
Wright, Mae A. *engineering/nuclear waste management specialist*
Wright, Sir (John) Oliver *retired diplomat*
Wright, Randolph Earle *retired petroleum company executive*
Wright, Robert Payton *lawyer*
†Wright, Vera *social worker*
Wriston, Kathryn Dineen *lawyer, business executive*
Wroblowa, Halina Stefania *electrochemist*
Wruck, Erich-Oskar *retired foreign language educator*
Wrucke-Nelson, Ann C. *elementary education educator*
Wuellner, Kathleen D. *English educator*
Wujciak, Sandra Criscuolo *personnel executive*
Wulf, Janie Scott McIlwaine *gifted and talented education educator*
Wurst, Michael H. *critical care nurse, administrator*
Wussler, Robert Joseph *broadcasting executive, media consultant*
Wyatt, Lenore *civic worker*
Wyatt, Marcia Jean *fine arts educator, administrative assistant*
Wyatt, Rose Marie *clinical social worker*
Wyche, Ruth Skyler *rehabilitation contractor, researcher*
Wyer, Peter Charles *emergency physician*
Wylan, Barbara *artist*
Wyle, Noah *actor*
Wylie, Laurie Jean *nursing administrator*
Wyman, Louis Crosby *judge, former senator, former congressman*
Wyman, Viola Bousquet *elementary educator*
Wyngaarden, James Barnes *physician*
Wynstra, Nancy Ann *lawyer*
Wyrtki, Klaus *oceanography educator*
Wyse, Roy *retired labor union administrator*
†Xiao, John Qiang *education educator*
Yack, Patrick Ashley *editor*
Yaeger, Therese Francis *management professional*
Yakich, David Eli *international sales executive*
Yamaguchi, Kristi Tsuya *ice skater*
Yamane, George Mitsuyoshi *oral medicine and radiology educator*
Yampolsky, Phyllis *artist*
Yancey, Katherine Bean *editor*
Yang, Xiangzhong *research scientist, administrator, educator*
Yarbro, Alan David *lawyer*
Yared, Gabriel *composer*
Yarington, Charles Thomas, Jr. *surgeon, administrator*
Yarris, Elizabeth Lester *critical care nurse*
Yates, Charles Richardson *former arts center executive*
Yates, David John C. *chemist, researcher*
†Yates, Gary Lee *artist*
Yates, Linda Fae *women's health nurse*
Yates, Maurice Marvin, III *architect*
Yeager, Anson Anders *writer, former columnist and newspaper editor*
Yeager, Mark L. *lawyer*
Yearian, Mason Russell *retired physicist*
Yearwood, Jimette Berry *critical care nurse*
Yee, Henry Chan Myint *cardiologist*
†Yellin, Deena *journalist*
Yen, Duen Hsi *corporate executive, physicist*
Yeo, Ronald Frederick *librarian*
Yetto, John Henry *company executive*
Yglesias, Rafael Jose *novelist*
Yielding, K. Lemone *physician*
Ying, John L. *manufacturing executive*
Yitts, Rose Marie *nursery school executive*
Yntema, Mary Katherine *retired mathematics educator*
Yocam, Delbert Wayne *software products company executive*
Yochelson, Bonnie Ellen *museum curator, art historian*
Yodaiken, Ralph E. *pathologist, occupational medicine physician*
Yoh, Harold Lionel, Jr. *retired engineering, construction and management company executive*
Yollick, Bernard Lawrence *otolaryngologic surgeon*
Yolton, John William *philosopher, educator*
Yong, Raymond Nen-Yiu *civil engineering educator*
†Yook, Chong Chul *engineering educator*
Yool, George Richard *consultant*
York, Charles Albert *architect*
York, Walter Allen *cinematographer*
Yoshimoto, Tetsuyuki *neurosurgeon*
†Yoshimura, Valerie Nao *cultural organization administrator*
Yost, Bernice *detective agency owner*
Yost, Paula Lynn *accountant*
Yost, William Albert *psychology educator, hearing researcher*
Yother, Anthony Wayne *critical care nurse*
Youmans, Julian Ray *neurosurgeon, educator*
Young, Anna Lucia *communications professional*
Young, Burt *actor*
Young, Edwin S. W. *federal agency official*
Young, Gary A. *rehabilitation counselor*
Young, John Alan *electronics company executive*
Young, Joyce Henry *adult education educator, consultant*
Young, Judith Anne *animal conservationist*
Young, Kim Ann *health facility administrator*
Young, Larry Joe *insurance agent*
Young, Leo *electrical engineer*
Young, Margaret Chong *elementary education educator*
†Young, Mary Eming *physician*
Young, Mary Sean *actress*
Young, Michael Kent *lawyer, educator*
Young, Patrick *writer, editor*
Young, Richard Alan *association executive*
Young, Sharon Laree *mathematics educator*
Young, Susan Babson *retired library director*
Young, Susan Eileen *elementary education educator*
Young, Teresa Gail Hilger *adult education educator*
Young, Virgil Monroe *education educator*
Younger, Betty Nichols *social worker*
Youngs, Diane Campfield *learning disabilities specialist, educator*
Yount, William McKinley *minister, librarian, educator*
Yousef, Mona Lee *psychotherapist*
Yovicich, George Steven Jones *civil engineer*
Yu, Jessica *director, producer, writer, editor*
Yue, Alfred Shui-choh *metallurgical engineer, educator*
Yun, James Kyoon *electrical engineer*
Yung, Yiu Fai *statistician, educator*
Yunis, Jorge Jose *anatomy, pathology, and microbiology educator*
Yuriko, (Yuriko Kikuchi) *dancer, choreographer*
Yurman, Maria Anne *critical care nurse*
†Zacarías, Fernando Raul Kahlil *physician*
Zacharias, Donald Wayne *academic administrator*
Zachary, Louis George *chemical company consultant*
Zacks, Sumner Irwin *pathologist*
Zaferson, William S. *philosophy educator, publisher*
Zaffaroni, Alejandro C. *biochemist, medical research company executive*
Zagaski, Chester Anthony, Jr. *author, researcher*
Zagorin, Janet Susan *legal firm administrator, marketing professional*
†Zahedi, Caveh *filmmaker, video artist*
Zahrt, Merton Stroebel *investor*
Zaillian, Steven *screenwriter, director*
Zajac, Jack *sculptor, painter*
Zajac, Joseph Walter *mechanical engineer*
Zajas, J. Jonathan R. *management consulting company executive, principal*
Zaleski, Jan Franciszek *biochemist*
Zaleski, Jean *artist*
Zamansky, Jeffrey Ira *small business owner*
Zambrano, Debra Kay *community health nurse*
Zanetti, Joseph Maurice, Jr. *corporate executive*
Zapf, Hermann *book and type designer*
Zappa, Gail *record producer*
Zarb, Frank Gustave *investment executive*
Zarro, Janice Anne *lawyer*
Zauner, Christian Walter *university dean, exercise physiologist, consultant*
Zavala, Albert *research psychologist*
†Zavala, Alberto *real estate investment company executive*
Zayek, Francis Mansour *retired bishop*
Zehnder, Frederick John *retired automotive executive*
Zehr, Norman Robert *association administrator*
Zehring, Karen *information executive*
†Zeidan, Hissam Issa A. *family physician, air force officer, researcher*
Zeigler, L(uther) Harmon *political science educator*
Zeitler, Bill Lorenz *aviation engineer*
Zekman, Terri Margaret *graphic designer*
Zelinsky, Paul O. *illustrator, painter, author*
Zeller, John Frederick *engineering executive*
Zeller, Joseph Paul *advertising executive*
Zellmer, Darwin Llewelyn *radiation biophysicist*
Zendle, Howard Mark *software development researcher*
Zentz, Patrick James *artist, rancher*
Zercher, David Lowell *artist*
†Zernike, Kate *reporter*
Zevola, Donna Ruth *critical care nurse, educator*
Zheutlin, Dale *sculptor, educator*
Zhiglevich, Eugenia *writer, actress*
Zhu, Yong *research scientist*
Ziaka-Vasileiadou, Zoe Dimitrios *chemical engineer*
Zick, John Walter *retired accounting company executive*
Ziegler, Earl Keller *minister*
Ziegler, Jack (Denmore) *cartoonist*
Ziegler, Richard Ferdinand *lawyer*
Ziegler, Ronald Louis *association executive, former government official*
Ziegler, William Alexander *lawyer*
Zierath, Marilyn Jean *adult medical, surgical and pediatrics nurse*
†Zigmond, Michael J. *artist*
Zilbert, Allen Bruce *education educator, computer consultant*
†Zillman, Donald Norman *law educator*
Zimm, Bruno Hasbrouck *physical chemistry educator*
Zimmerman, Harold Samuel *retired state senator, newspaper editor and publisher, state administrator*
Zimmerman, James Robert *radiologist, engineer*
Zimny, Max *labor union administrator, lawyer*
†Zinn, Ellen Sherman *artist*
Zinnen, Robert Oliver *general management executive*
Zinner-Kemp, Susan Elizabeth *medical educator*
Zipf, Mark Edward *electrical engineer*
Zischke, Douglas Arthur *foreign service officer*
Zisholtz-Herzog, Ellen Naomi *arts administrator, consultant, cultural planner*
†Zive, Gregg William *judge*
Zodl, Joseph Arthur *international trade executive, consultant*
Zoelle, Andrea Marie *reference librarian*
Zoellick, Robert Bruce *political science administrator, lawyer*
Zohn, Martin Steven *lawyer*
†Zoller, James Alexander *educator*
†Zolov, Eric S. *historian, educator*
Zomber, Beverly Louise *medical, surgical, geriatric and psychiatric nurse, educator*
Zoritch, George *dance educator, choreographer*
Zowader, Sherry Lee *volunteer, artist*
Zox, Larry *artist*
Zube-Miles, Barbara J. *rehabilitation nurse*
Zuck, Alfred Miller *public administration educator*
Zuckerman, Harriet *sociologist, educator*
Zuckerman, Martin Harvey *personnel director*
Zufryden, Fred S. *academic administrator, marketing educator, researcher*
Zuiches, James Joseph *academic administrator*
Zukin, Paul *retired health research educator*
Zupsic, Matthew Michael *insurance company executive*
Zusy, Catherine *curator*
Zwain, Ismail Hassan *molecular endocrinologist*
Zweck, Ruth Edna Feeney *human services administrator, psychiatric nurse*
Zwerin, Charlotte Mitchell *film producer*
Zwislocki, Jozef John *neuroscience educator, researcher*
Zysblat, William Larry *accountant*

Professional Index

†New name in *Who's Who in America*, 54th Edition

AGRICULTURE

UNITED STATES

ALABAMA

Montgomery
Frazer, Stuart Harrison, III *cotton merchant*

Tuskegee Institute
Hill, Walter A. *agricultural sciences educator, researcher*

ARKANSAS

Hot Springs National Park
Baer, Kenneth Peter *farmer cooperative executive*

CALIFORNIA

Berkeley
Perloff, Jeffrey Mark *agricultural and resource economics educator*

Caliente
Rankin, Helen Cross *cattle rancher, guest ranch executive*

Davis
Carter, Harold O. *agricultural economics educator*

Modesto
Crawford, Charles McNeil *winery science executive*
Gallo, Ernest *vintner*

Napa
Chiarella, Peter Ralph *vintner*

Ontario
Johnson, Maurice Verner, Jr. *agricultural research and development executive*

Pacific Palisades
Jennings, Marcella Grady *rancher, investor*

Rutherford
Eisele, Milton Douglas *viticulturist*

San Diego
Caughlin, Stephenie Jane *organic farmer*

San Francisco
Hills, Austin Edward *vineyard executive*

COLORADO

Denver
Decker, Peter Randolph *rancher, former state official*

Fort Collins
Heird, James C. *agricultural studies educator*

DELAWARE

Dover
Carey, V. George *farmer, state legislator*

DISTRICT OF COLUMBIA

Washington
Boyd, F. Allen, Jr. *farmer, congressman*
Schmidt, Berlie Louis *agricultural research administrator*

FLORIDA

Gainesville
Nair, Ramachandran P.K. *agroforestry educator, researcher*

GEORGIA

Atlanta
Brooks, David William *farmer cooperative executive*
Stimpert, Michael Alan *agricultural products company executive*
Wright, Daniel *wine specialist, consultant*

HAWAII

Waialua
Singlehurst, Dona Geisenheyner *horse farm owner*

Waimanalo
†Okimoto, Dean J. *farmer, marketing consultant*

IDAHO

Twin Falls
Jones, Douglas Raymond *farming executive, state legislator*

ILLINOIS

Auburn
Burtle, Paul Walter *farmer*

Bloomington
Webb, O. Glenn *farm supplies company executive*

Champaign
Bentley, Orville George *retired agricultural educator, dean emeritus*

Danville
Konsis, Kenneth Frank *forester, educator*

Harvel
Zimmerman, Donald Dean *farmer, farm manager*

Homewood
Reed, Michael A. *agricultural products supplier*

Kenilworth
Clary, Rosalie Brandon Stanton *timber farm executive, civic worker*

Libertyville
Hattis, Albert Daniel *business executive, retired educator, journalist*

Macomb
North, Teresa Lynn *agricultural educator*

Mendota
Stamberger, Edwin Henry *farmer, civic leader*

Moline
Malicki, Gregg Hillard *agricultural equipment manufacturing executive*

Northfield
Bruns, Nicolaus, Jr. *retired agricultural chemicals company executive, lawyer*

Pekin
Frison, Rick *agricultural company executive*

Quincy
Randall, Robert Quentin *retired nursery executive*

Urbana
Cheryan, Munir *agricultural studies educator, biochemical engineering educator*
Hill, Lowell Dean *agricultural marketing educator*

INDIANA

Connersville
Bischoff, Lawrence Joseph *farmer*

Hanover
Heck, Richard T. *tree farmer*

Indianapolis
Arburn, Jerry William *farmer, vice president Indiana Farm Bureau*
Hegel, Carolyn Marie *farmer, farm bureau executive*

West Lafayette
Lechtenberg, Victor L. *agricultural studies educator*

IOWA

Akron
Hultgren, Dennis Eugene *farmer, management consultant*

Ames
Jacobson, Norman L. *retired agricultural educator, researcher*
Mullen, Russell Edward *agricultural studies educator*
Pearce, Robert Brent *agricultural studies educator*
Topel, David Glen *agricultural studies educator*

Decorah
Everman, Nancy Lidtke *farmer, organization executive*

Hubbard
Cook, Lisle *farmer*

Indianola
Mapel, Patricia Jolene *farmer, consultant*

Mason City
Kuhlman, James Weldon *retired county extension education director*

Muscatine
Kautz, Richard Carl *chemical and feed company executive*

POSTVILLE

Postville
Kozelka, Edward William *seed and feed company executive*

Vinton
Jorgensen, Ann *farmer*

Wilton
Lenker, Floyd William *farmer*

KANSAS

Claflin
Burmeister, Paul Frederick *farmer*

Ellsworth
†Thaemert, John C. *farmer*

Garden City
Reeve, Lee M. *farmer*

Haven
Schlickau, George Hans *cattle breeder, professional association executive*

Lewis
†Cross, David R. *farmer, livestock raiser*

Manhattan
McKee, Richard Miles *animal studies educator*

Topeka
Gatlin, Fred *agricultural program administrator, former state legislator*

KENTUCKY

Murray
Driskill, Charles Dwayne *agriculture educator, researcher*

LOUISIANA

Lake Charles
Stacey, Norma Elaine *farmer, civic worker*

MARYLAND

College Park
Fretz, Thomas A. *agricultural studies educator*

Havre De Grace
†Jay, Peter Augustus *writer, farmer*

MICHIGAN

Ann Arbor
Heydon, Peter Northrup *farmer, educator, philanthropist*

Howell
Cotton, Larry *ranching executive*

Pigeon
Maust, Joseph J. *agricultural products supplier*

MINNESOTA

Finlayson
Luoma, Judy *ranching executive*

Minneapolis
Joseph, Burton M. *retired grain merchant*

Saint Paul
Zylstra, Stanley James *farmer, food company executive*

MISSISSIPPI

Clarksdale
Williams, Kenneth Ogden *farmer*

Starkville
Gregg, Billy Ray *seed industry executive, consultant*
†Little, Randall Dean *agricultural economics educator, consultant*

MISSOURI

Knob Noster
†Corbett, Violet Jane *farmer, contracter*

Springfield
Strickler, Ivan K. *dairy farmer*

Warrensburg
Allen, Densil E., Jr. *agricultural studies educator*

MONTANA

Miles City
Fraser, Mac Robert (Rob Fraser) *livestock auction owner, auctioneer*

Pony
Anderson, Richard Ernest *agribusiness development executive, rancher*

Savage
Thiessen, Dwight Everett *farmer*

Utica
Stevenson, Sarah Schoales *rancher, business owner*

NEBRASKA

Elkhorn
Welch, Vern A. *retired corn breeder*

Funk
Sjogren, Donald Ernest *farmer*

Lincoln
Sheffield, Leslie Floyd *retired agricultural educator*

Scottsbluff
Weichenthal, Burton A. *beef cattle specialist*

NEVADA

Yerington
Scatena, Lorraine Borba *rancher, women's rights advocate*

NEW MEXICO

Cebolla
Berryman, Donald Carroll *cattle rancher*

Silver City
White, Don William *rancher, minister*

NEW YORK

Canandaigua
Sands, Marvin *wine company executive*

Ithaca
Bail, Joe Paul *agricultural educator emeritus*

South Dayton
Jones, Richard Allen *horse breeder, educator*

NORTH CAROLINA

Asheville
Ray, Ruth Alice Yancey *retired rancher, real estate developer*

Raleigh
Peacock, Charles H. *agricultural studies educator*

NORTH DAKOTA

Amidon
Bergquist, Gene Alfred *farmer, rancher, county commissioner*

Bismarck
Carlisle, Ronald Dwight *nursery owner*

Gilby
McLean, Burton Neil *farmer, rancher*

Regent
Krauter, Aaron Joseph *farmer, state senator*

Turtle Lake
Lindteigen, Susanna *rancher, state official*

OHIO

Columbus
Ockerman, Herbert W. *agricultural studies educator*

OKLAHOMA

Vinita
Gray, Donald Lyman *orchard owner*

OREGON

Medford
Smith, Robert F. (Bob Smith) *rancher, congressman*

Pendleton
†Reeder, Clinton Bruce *farmer*

PENNSYLVANIA

Carlisle
Freund, Roland Paul *farm management extension agent*

Imler
†Snider, Obie *farmer*

University Park
Hood, Lamartine Frain *agriculture educator, former dean*

SOUTH CAROLINA

Clemson
Wehrenberg, William Busse *agricultural studies educator*

Dillon
Chandler-Walton, Marcia Shaw Barnard *farmer*

Greer
Gregg, Marie Byrd *retired farmer*

Isle Of Palms
McKinley, Debra Lynn McKinney *dog show judge*

Pawleys Island
Kay, Thomas Oliver *agricultural consultant*

SOUTH DAKOTA

Belle Fourche
†Crabill, Mark Clare *agricultural specialist*

Brookings
Moore, Raymond A. *consultant, retired agriculture educator*

Elk Point
Chicoine, Roland Alvin *farmer, state official*
Gille, John Paul *agricultural extension educator*

Saint Lawrence
Lockner, Vera Joanne *farmer, rancher, legislator*

TENNESSEE

Cordova
Echols, James *agricultural products supplier*

Memphis
Simpson, Art *agricultural products supplier*

TEXAS

Carrizo Springs
†Myers, Jay Scott *cattle rancher*

College Station
Christiansen, James Edward *agricultural educator*
Hiler, Edward Allan *agricultural and engineering educator*

Dallas
Hewlett, Gloria Louise *rancher, retired educator, civic volunteer*

Devers
Boyt, Patrick Elmer *farmer, real estate executive*

Houston
Lee, Robert Leyne *plantation company executive, consultant*

Industry
Huitt, Jimmie L. *rancher, oil, gas, real estate investor*

San Antonio
Davenport, Pamela Beaver *rancher, small business owner*
Petty, Scott, Jr. *rancher*

Valley View
Wallace, Donald John, III *rancher, former pest control company executive*

Vega
Cook, Clayton Henry *rancher*

VIRGINIA

Blacksburg
Cannell, Robert Quirk *agricultural sciences educator*
Swiger, L. A. *agricultural studies educator*

Mc Lean
McIlwain, Clara Evans *agricultural economist, consultant*

Montross
Fountain, Robert Roy, Jr. *farmer, industrial executive, naval officer*

Prince George
Farrar, Andrew Lockett *agricultural education educator*

Springfield
Dean, John Wilson, Jr. *business consultant, retired army officer*

Warrenton
Smith, William Raymond *farmer, thoroughbred owner, breeder and trainer, retired history educator, philosophy educator*

WASHINGTON

Kirkland
Holden, Fred Stephen *industrial tree farmer*

Seattle
†Martensen, Keith Charles *cattle company executive*

Toppenish
Hefflinger, LeRoy Arthur *agricultural manager*

WEST VIRGINIA

Charles Town
McDonald, Angus Wheeler *farmer*

Morgantown
Maxwell, Robert Haworth *agricultural consultant*

WYOMING

Aladdin
Brunson, Mabel (Dipper) *researcher*

Douglas
†Willox, James Hugh *rancher*

Hulett
†Nuckolls, J. W. *rancher*

Lander
†Thompson, Douglas Lynn *rancher*

Wheatland
Bunker, John Birkbeck *cattle rancher, retired sugar company executive*

CANADA

ONTARIO

Blenheim
Thompson, Wesley Duncan *grain merchant*

ADDRESS UNPUBLISHED

Barrett, Barbara McConnell *ranch owner, community leader, lawyer*
Bohoskey, Bernice Fleming *mineral-land owner, writer*
†Britt, Lois G. *farming executive*
Brooks, Kenneth N. *forestry educator*
Byford, Emma *rancher*
Erwin, Elmer Louis *vintager, cement consultant*
Inbody, Dale Dewayne *farmer*
†Jensen, Edward Charles *forestry educator*
Johnson, Cyrus Edwin *grain farmer, former food products executive*
Jones, Norman Thomas *retired agricultural products company executive*
Kontny, Vincent J. *rancher, engineering executive*
Stanley, Marlyse Reed *horse breeder*
Van Atta, Cheri Marie *equine instructor*
Weaver, Peggy (Marguerite McKinnie Weaver) *plantation owner*

ARCHITECTURE AND DESIGN

UNITED STATES

ALABAMA

Auburn
Lechner, Norbert Manfred *architect, educator*
Millman, Richard George *architect, educator*

Birmingham
Barrow, Richard Edward *architect*
Gilchrist, William Aaron *architect*
Hecker, William Fulham, Jr. *architect*

Mobile
Winter, Arch Reese *architect*

Prattville
Lambert, Meg Stringer *interior designer, architect*

Tuskegee Institute
Pryce, Edward Lyons *landscape architect*

ALASKA

Eagle River
Brooks, Stuart Dale *building consultant*

ARIZONA

Phoenix
DeBartolo, Jack, Jr. *architect*
De Valeria, David Alan *architect, sculptor*
Elmore, James Walter *architect, retired university dean*
Gwozdz, Kim Elizabeth *interior designer*
Hawkins, Jasper Stillwell, Jr. *architect*
Schiffner, Charles Robert *architect*

Scottsdale
Ball, Donald Edmon *architect*
Brown, Shirley Margaret Kern (Peggy Brown) *interior designer*
Hooker, Jo *interior designer*
Klien, Wolfgang Josef *architect*
Rutes, Walter Alan *architect*
Soleri, Paolo *architect, urban planner*

Sedona
Iverson, Wayne Dahl *landscape architect, consultant*

Sonoita
Cook, William Howard *architect*

Sun City West
Madson, John Andrew *architect*
Mc Cune, John Francis, III *retired architect*

Tempe
Kenyon, David Lloyd *architect, architectural firm executive*
Mc Sheffrey, Gerald Rainey *architect, educator, city planner*

Tucson
Breckenridge, Klindt Duncan *architect*
Dinsmore, Philip Wade *architect*
Gourley, Ronald Robert *architect, educator*
Hershberger, Robert Glen *architect, educator*
McConnell, Robert Eastwood *architect, educator*
Nelson, Edward Humphrey *architect*
Wallach, Leslie Rothaus *architect*
Zube, Ervin Herbert *landscape architect, geographer, educator*

ARKANSAS

Fayetteville
Burggraf, Frank Bernard, Jr. *landscape architect, retired educator*
Jones, Euine Fay *architect, educator*

Little Rock
Blass, Noland, Jr. *retired architect*
Burruss, Terry Gene *architect*
Chilcote, Lugean Lester *architect*
Cromwell, Edwin Boykin *architect*
Truemper, John James, Jr. *retired architect*

CALIFORNIA

Altadena
Ziegler, Raymond Stewart *retired architect*

Bakersfield
McAlister, Michael H. *architect*

Berkeley
Blake, Laura *architect*
Brocchini, Ronald Gene *architect*
Burger, Edmund Ganes *architect*
Cardwell, Kenneth Harvey *architect, educator*
Hester, Randolph Thompson, Jr. *landscape architect, educator*
Olsen, Donald Emmanuel *architect, educator*
Stoller, Claude *architect*

Beverly Hills
Dillard, Suzanne *interior designer*
Eisenshtat, Sidney Herbert *architect*

Bodega Bay
King, Leland W. *architect*

Burbank
Naidorf, Louis Murray *architect*

Burlingame
Sadilek, Vladimir *architect*
Tanzi, Carol Anne *interior designer*

Camarillo
Field, Jeffrey Frederic *designer*

Carmel
Merrill, William Dickey *architect*

Chula Vista
Quisenberry, Robert Max *architect, industrial designer*

Corona Del Mar
Muller, David Webster *architectural designer*
Yeo, Ron *architect*

Coronado
Wagener, Hobart D. *retired architect*
Weiss-Cornwell, Amy *interior designer*

Costa Mesa
Dougherty, Betsey Olenick *architect*
Renne, Janice Lynn *interior designer*

Culver City
Morgan, Paul Evan *architect*
Moss, Eric Owen *architect*

Davis
†Francis, Mark Owen *landscape architecture educator*

El Cerrito
Komatsu, S. Richard *architect*

Escondido
Devine, Walter Bernard *naval architect, marine engineer*

Fresno
Darden, Edwin Speight, Sr. *architect*
Munyon, William Harry, Jr. *architect*

Patnaude, William E. *architect*
Pings, Anthony Claude *architect*
Putman, Robert Dean *golf course architect*

Glen Ellen
Rockrise, George Thomas *architect*

Glendale
†Holstad, Scott Cameron *writer, network specialist*
Stanfill, Latayne Colvett *non-fiction writer*

Huntington Beach
Lans, Carl Gustav *architect, economist*

Irvine
Kraemer, Kenneth Leo *architect, urban planner, educator*

La Jolla
Baesel, Stuart Oliver *architect*

Laguna Niguel
Axon, Donald Carlton *architect*

Long Beach
Perkowitz, Simon *architect*
Ruth, Steven J. *architectural firm executive*

Los Angeles
Berry, Richard Douglas *architectural educator, urban planner and designer*
Bobrow, Michael Lawrence *architect*
Brotman, David Joel *architectural firm executive*
Dworsky, Daniel Leonard *architect*
Fickett, Edward Hale *architect, planner, arbitrator*
Holdsworth, Ray W. *architectural firm executive*
Kline, Lee B. *architect*
Krag, Olga *interior designer*
Li, Gerald *architect, film producer and director*
†Madden-Lunsford, Kerry Elizabeth *writer*
Martin, Albert Carey *architect*
Moe, Stanley Allen *architect, consultant*
Myers, Barton *architect*
Nelson, Mark Bruce *interior designer*
Neutra, Dion *architect*
Phelps, Barton Chase *architect, educator*
Thoman, John Everett *architect, mediator*

Los Osos
Polk, Benjamin Kauffman *retired architect, composer, educator*

Manhattan Beach
Blanton, John Arthur *architect*

Marshall
Evans, Robert James *architect*

Mill Valley
†Owings, Alison June *writer, journalist*

Montecito
Burgee, John Henry *architect*

Montrose
Greenlaw, Roger Lee *interior designer*

Morgan Hill
Halopoff, William Evon *industrial designer, consultant*

Mountain View
Kobza, Dennis Jerome *architect*
Perkins, Nancy Jane *industrial designer*

Napa
Ianziti, Adelbert John *industrial designer*

Newport Beach
Bissell, George Arthur *architect*
Jacobs, Donald Paul *architect*
Richardson, Walter John *architect*

Oakland
Eckbo, Garrett *landscape architect, urban designer*
Matsumoto, George *architect*
Nicol, Robert Duncan *architect*
Winslow, Thomas Scudder, III *naval architect, marine consultant*

Oxnard
O'Connell, Hugh Mellen, Jr. *retired architect*

Palm Desert
Chambers, Milton Warren *architect*

Pasadena
Thomas, Joseph Fleshman *architect*

Pleasant Hill
Hassid, Sami *architect, educator*

Pleasanton
Fehlberg, Robert Erick *architect*

Redondo Beach
Shellhorn, Ruth Patricia *landscape architect*

Redwood City
Morrison, Murdo Donald *architect*

Sacramento
Dahlin, Dennis John *landscape architect, environmental consultant*
Hallenbeck, Harry C. *architect*
Lionakis, George *architect*
Ross, Terence William *architect*
Wasserman, Barry L(ee) *architect*

San Diego
Delawie, Homer Torrence *architect*
Henderson, John Drews *architect*
Holl, Walter John *architect, interior designer*
Livingston, Stanley C. *architect*
Munroe, Ronald L. *architect*
Paderewski, Sir Clarence Joseph *architect*
Wilson, Richard Allan *landscape architect*

San Francisco
Bull, Henrik Helkand *architect*
Del Campo, Martin Bernardelli *architect*
Field, John Louis *architect*
Hardison, Donald Leigh *architect*
Horan, Joseph Patrick *interior designer*
Kriken, John Lund *architect*
Minar, Paul G. *design consultant*
Moris, Lamberto Giuliano *architect*
Raeber, John Arthur *architect, construction consultant*
Ream, James Terrill *architect, sculptor*
Thistlethwaite, David Richard *architect*
Valentine, William Edson *architect*
Werner, William Arno *architect*

San Jose
Kwock, Royal *architect*
Richards, Lisle Frederick *architect*
Tanaka, Richard Koichi, Jr. *architect, planner*

San Juan Capistrano
Olson, Cal Oliver *golf architect*
Paul, Courtland Price *landscape architect, planner*

San Luis Obispo
Deasy, Cornelius Michael *architect*
Hasslein, George Johann *architectural educator*

San Marcos
Harmon, Harry William *architect, former university administrator*

San Mateo
Castleberry, Arline Alrick *architect*

San Rafael
Badgley, John Roy *architect*
Clark, Charles Sutter *interior designer*
Thompson, Peter Layard Hailey, Sr. *golf course architect*

Santa Barbara
Frizzell, William Kenneth *architect*
Kruger, Kenneth Charles *architect*

Santa Monica
Eizenberg, Julie *architect*
Friedrichs, Edward C. *architect*
Gehry, Frank Owen *architect*
Koning, Hendrik *architect*

Santa Rosa
Gilger, Paul Douglass *architect*

Sausalito
Leefe, James Morrison *architect*

Seal Beach
Rossi, Mario Alexander *architect*

Sierra Madre
Lyle, John Tillman *architect, landscape architecture educator*

Somerset
Setzekorn, William David *retired architect, consultant, author*

Sonoma
Allen, Rex Whitaker *architect*
Broderick, Harold Christian *interior designer*
Woodbridge, John Marshall *architect, urban planner*

South Pasadena
Girvigian, Raymond *architect*
Man, Lawrence Kong *architect*

Sunnyvale
Linn, Gary Dean *golf course architect*

Ventura
Okuma, Albert Akira, Jr. *architect*
Ruebe, Bambi Lynn *interior, environmental designer*

Villa Park
Buffington, Linda Brice *interior designer*

Visalia
Heidbreder, Gail *architect, educator*

COLORADO

Aspen
Alstrom, Sven Erik *architect*
Caudill, Samuel Jefferson *architect*

Boulder
Carlson, Devon McElvin *architect, educator*
Cowley, Gerald Dean *architect*
Hoffman, Charles Fenno, III *architect*

Colorado Springs
Phibbs, Harry Albert *interior designer, professional speaker, lecturer*

Denver
Abo, Ronald Kent *architect*
Anderson, John David *architect*
Brownson, Jacques Calmon *architect*
Dominick, Peter Hoyt, Jr. *architect*
Falkenberg, William Stevens *architect, contractor*
Fuller, Kenneth Roller *architect*
Havekost, Daniel John *architect*
Hoover, George Schweke *architect*
Steenhagen, Robert Lewis *landscape architect, consultant*
Wilk, Diane Lillian *architect, educator*
Williams, John James, Jr. *architect*
Wirkler, Norman Edward *architectural, engineering, construction management firm executive*
†Worthington, Carl August *architect*

Englewood
Eccles, Matthew Alan *golf course and landscape architect*

Fort Collins
Grandin, Temple *livestock equipment designer, educator*

Fort Garland
Boyer, Lester Leroy, Jr. *architecture educator, consultant*

Littleton
Huffman, Donna Lou *interior designer*
Williams, Sally *landscape designer*

Vail
Spaeh, Saundra Lee (Smith)
Vosbeck, Robert Randall *architect*

CONNECTICUT

Centerbrook
Simon, Mark *architect*

Cheshire
Martin, Glen Matthew *architect, landscape*
Rowland, Ralph Thomas *retired architect*
Saad, Edward Theodore *architect*

Essex
Grover, William Herbert *architect*

Fairfield
Everett, Wendy Ann *toy designer*

Greenwich
Drummond, Gillian M. *home furnishing company executive*
Hershaft, Elinor *space planner, interior designer*
Marks, Charles *architect*
Mock, Robert Claude *architect*

Hamden
Roche, (Eamonn) Kevin *architect*

Hartford
Leibin, Harvey Bruce *architect*

Lyme
Hoyt, Charles King *architect, editor*

Madison
Ingis, Gail *interior designer, educator, writer, photographer, artist*

New Canaan
Dean, Robert Bruce *architect*
Risom, Jens *furniture designer, manufacturing executive*

New Haven
Chilton, William David *architect*
Clarke, Fred W., III *architect, architectural firm executive*
†Haverland, Michael Robert *architect*
Newick, Craig David *architect*
Paniccia, Mario Domenic *architect*
Pelli, Cesar *architect*
Platner, Warren *architect*
Roth, Harold *architect*

Niantic
†Danos, Harry John *architect, educator, artist*

North Branford
Gregan, Edmund Robert *landscape architect*

Norwalk
Crosbie, Michael James *architect, writer, educator*
Irving, Michael Henry *architect*

Norwich
Sharpe, Richard Samuel *architectural company executive*

Orange
Miller, Henry Forster *architect*

Ridgefield
Bye, Arthur Edwin, Jr. *landscape architect*
Dimos, Helen *landscape designer*

Salisbury
White, Norval Crawford *architect*

Stonington
Stoddard, Alexandra *designer, writer, lecturer*

Stratford
Cowperthwaite, John Milton, Jr. *architect, construction consultant*

Trumbull
Watson, Donald Ralph *architect, artist, educator, author*

Waterbury
Bellemare, David John *architectural designer*

Westport
Ferris, Roger Patrick *architect*
Wayne, Kurt Christopher *architect*

Woodbury
Moeckel, Henry Theodore *architect*

DISTRICT OF COLUMBIA

Washington
Barr-Kumar, Raj *architect*
Bowie, Calvert S. *architect*
Chen, John Shaoming *architecture educator*
Coffin, Laurence Edmondston, Jr. *landscape architect, urban planner*
Cox, Warren Jacob *architect*
Cude, Reginald Hodgin *architect*
Fry, Louis Edwin, Jr. *architect*

Gentner, Paul LeFoe *architect, consultant*
Gordon, Harry Thomas *architectural firm executive*
Greenberg, Daniel Jeremy *computer game producer*
Hartman, George Eitel *architect*
Hellmuth, George William *architect*
Holladay, Wilhelmina Cole *interior design and museum executive*
Jacobsen, Hugh Newell *architect*
Kailian, Aram Harry *architect*
Keune, Russell Victor *architect, architectural association executive*
Keyes, Arthur Hawkins, Jr. *architect*
Landsburg, Alexander Charles *naval architect, researcher*
Lewis, Anne McCutcheon *architect*
MacDonald, William Lloyd *architectural historian*
Miller, Iris Ann *landscape architect, urban designer, educator*
Minkoff, Alice Sydney *interior designer, showroom owner*
Murray, Christopher Charles, III *architect*
Oehme, Wolfgang Walter *landscape architect*
Poppeliers, John Charles *architectural historian*
Schlesinger, B. Frank *architect, educator*
Siegel, Lloyd Harvey *architect, real estate developer, consultant*
White, George Malcolm *architect*
Wubbena, Kurt Wilharm *interior designer*
Yerkes, David Norton *architect*

FLORIDA

Boca Raton
McLeod, John Wishart *architect*

Bonita Springs
Trudnak, Stephen Joseph *landscape architect*

Boynton Beach
Stubbins, Hugh A(sher), Jr. *architect*

Bradenton
Hall, Ralph C. *retired architect, mechanical engineer*
Keane, Gustave Robert *architect, consultant*

Clearwater
Bertram, Frederic Amos *architect*

Coral Gables
Warburton, Ralph Joseph *architect, engineer, planner, educator*

Coral Springs
Schultz, Joel Sidney *architect*

Daytona Beach
Amick, William Walker *golf course architect*

Delray Beach
†Klein, Marilyn (Lynn) *interior designer, volunteer*
Love, Marsha Lynn *interior decorator*
Rippeteau, Darrel Downing *architect*

Fernandina Beach
Burns, Stephen Redding *golf course architect*

Fort Lauderdale
Ambrose, Judith Ann *designer*
Stone, Edward Durell, Jr. *landscape architect and planner*

Fort Pierce
Steel, Philip S. *architect, artist*

Gulf Breeze
French, Jere Stuart *landscape architect*

Hollywood
Harringer, Olaf Carl *architect, museum consultant*

Jacksonville
Morgan, William Newton *architect, educator*
Rumpel, Peter Loyd *architect, educator, artist*
Smith, Ivan Huron *architect*

Jupiter
Fazio, Tom *design firm executive, golf course designer*
Ostrout, Howard Francis, Jr. *landscape architect*

Lakeland
Garrott, Frances Carolyn *architectural technician*

Marco Island
Thorson, Oswald Hagen *architect*

Miami
Arango, Jorge Sanin *architect*
Chisholm, Robert E. *architect*
Cruz, Javier F. *architect*
Farcus, Joseph Jay *architect, interior designer*
Feito, Jose *architect*
Fort-Brescia, Bernardo *architect*
Hampton, Mark Garrison *architect*
Lapidus, Morris *retired architect, interior designer*
Martinez, Walter Baldomero *architect*
Plater-Zyberk, Elizabeth Maria *architectural educator*
Spear, Laurinda Hope *architect*
Telesca, Francis Eugene *architect*
Venet, Claude Henry *architect, acoustic engineer*

Miami Beach
Marcus, Arthur Jay *architect*

Naples
Jones, Richard Wallace *interior designer*
Lewis, Gordon Gilmer *golf course architect*

Orlando
Arnett, Warren Grant *interior designer*
Ellis, James Jolly *landscape resort official*
Vining, F(rancis) Stuart *architect, consultant*

Ormond Beach
Truitt, Richard byron *landscape architect*

Palm Beach
Wirtz, Willem Kindler *garden and lighting designer, public relations consultant*

Palm Beach Gardens
Christian, Robert Henry *architect*

Pensacola
Bullock, Ellis Way, Jr. *architect*
Woolf, Kenneth Howard *architect*

Punta Gorda
Bowman, Willard Nelson, Jr. *architect*

Saint Augustine
Matzke, Frank J. *architect, consultant*

Saint Petersburg
Wedding, Charles Randolph *architect*

Sanibel
Sappenfield, Charles Madison *architect, educator*

Sarasota
Smith, Mark Hallard *architect*

Stuart
Ankrom, Charles Franklin *golf course architect, consultant*

Tampa
Abell, Jan Meisterheim *architect*
Holmes, Dwight Ellis *architect*
Howey, John Richard *architect*
Jennewein, James Joseph *architect*

Venice
Appel, Wallace Henry *retired industrial designer*

Vero Beach
Ahrens, William Henry *architect*
Gibson, James Elliott *architect*
McGee, Humphrey Glenn *architect*
Tullis, Chaillé Handy *interior designer, volunteer*

Winter Haven
Burns, Arthur Lee *architect*
Leedy, Gene Robert *architect*

GEORGIA

Athens
Morrison, Darrel Gene *landscape architecture educator*

Atlanta
Bainbridge, Frederick Freeman, III *architect*
Cooper, Jerome Maurice *architect*
Diedrich, Richard Joseph *architect*
Fash, William Leonard *retired architecture educator, college dean*
Guest, Rita Carson *interior designer*
Hudspeth, Gregg William *landscape architect*
Lewcock, Ronald Bentley *architect, educator*
Moulthrop, Edward Allen *architect, artist*
Moynihan, James J. *architectural firm executive*
Nimmons, M(ajor) Stuart, III *architect*
Pulgram, William Leopold *architect, space designer*
Robison, Richard Eugene *architect*
Smith, Joseph Newton, III *retired architect, educator*
Surber, Eugene Lynn *architect*
White, Ortrude B. *architect*
Wilkes, George Gardner, Jr. *landscape architect*

Augusta
Woodhurst, Robert Stanford, Jr. *architect*

Conyers
Mc Intosh, James Eugene, Jr. *interior designer*

Macon
Dunwody, Eugene Cox *architect*
Garrett, Katherine Ann *interior designer*

Marietta
Rabon, William James, Jr. *architect*

Rome
Janowski, Thaddeus Marian *architect*

Saint Simons
Webb, Lamar Thaxter *architect*

Smyrna
Passantino, Richard J. *architect*

HAWAII

Haiku
Riecke, Hans Heinrich *architect*

Hanalei
Schaller, Matthew Fite *architect*

Honolulu
Botsai, Elmer Eugene *architect, educator, former university dean*
Cain, Raymond Frederick *landscape architect, planning company executive*
Hale, Nathan Robert *architect*
Hamada, Duane Takumi *architect*
Lau, Charles Kwok-Chiu *architect, architectural firm executive*
Sutton, Charles Richard *architect, designer*
Vidal, Alejandro Legaspi *architect*
Yeh, Raymond Wei-Hwa *architect, educator*

Kaneohe
Fisette, Scott Michael *golf course designer*

IDAHO

Boise
Hunsucker, (Carl) Wayne *architectural firm executive, educator*

ILLINOIS

Bloomington
Carlson, David Noel *landscape architect, sculptor*
Switzer, Jon Rex *architect*

Bolingbrook
Caddy, Edmund H.H., Jr. *architect*

Champaign
Baker, Jack Sherman *architect, designer, educator*
Hopkins, Lewis Dean *planner, educator*
Riley, Robert Bartlett *landscape architect*

Chicago
Allen, Janice M. *interior designer, nurse, office manager, actress, model*
Alschuler, John Haas *architect*
Amstadter, Laurence *retired architect*
Barney, Carol Ross *architect*
Beeby, Thomas H. *architect*
Belluschi, Anthony C. *architect*
Blankenship, Edward G. *architect*
Blutter, Joan Wernick *interior designer*
Brubaker, Charles William *architect*
Cook, Richard Borreson *architect*
Epstein, Sidney *architect and engineer*
Fowler, George Selton, Jr. *architect*
Gardunio, Joseph *landscaping company executive*
Gin, Jackson *architect*
Gold, Allan Harold *architect, structural engineer, educator*
Grunsfeld, Ernest Alton, III *architect*
Hackl, Donald John *architect*
Hayes, Richard Donald *architect*
Holabird, John Augur, Jr. *retired architect*
Jahn, Helmut *architect*
Kerbis, Gertrude Lempp *architect*
Mack, Alan Wayne *interior designer*
Macsai, John *architect*
Manny, Carter Hugh, Jr. *architect, foundation administrator*
Matthei, Edward Hodge *architect*
McCullagh, Grant Gibson *architect*
McCurry, Margaret Irene *architect, interior and furniture designer, educator*
Meyers, Lynn Betty *architect*
Osmond, Lynn *architecture executive*
Phillips, Frederick Falley *architect*
Pigozzi, Raymond Anthony *architect*
Quebe, Jerry Lee *architect*
†Robertson, Donna V. *architect, educator, dean*
Roupp, Albert Allen *architect*
Rugo, Steven Alfred *architect*
Schirn, Janet Sugerman *interior designer*
Schlossman, John Isaac *architect*
Schroeder, Douglas Fredrick *architect*
Schumann, Adolph Alfred, Jr. *architect*
Simovic, Laszlo *architect*
Smith, Adrian Devaun *architect*
Smith, Craig Malcolm *architect, consultant*
†Solwitz, Sharon *writer, educator*
Tigerman, Stanley *architect, educator*
Tobin, Calvin Jay *architect*
Tobin, Michael Alan *architect, real estate developer*
Torgersen, Torwald Harold *architect, designer*
Vagnieres, Robert Charles, Jr. *architect*
Valaskovic, David William *architect, designer*
Valerio, Joseph M. *architectural firm executive, educator*
VanderDeke, Patricia K. *architect*
Vinci, John Nicholas *architect, educator*
Weber, Hanno *architect*
Weese, Benjamin Horace *architect*

Collinsville
Morris, Calvin Curtis *architect*

Downers Grove
Kirkegaard, R. Lawrence *architectural acoustician*

Evanston
Friedman, Hans Adolf *architect*
Salzman, Arthur George *architect*
Zolomij, Robert William *landscape architect, consultant*

Glenview
Bradtke, Philip Joseph *architect*
Taylor, D(arl) Coder *architect, engineer*

Highland Park
Dubin, Arthur Detmers *architect*

Hinsdale
Akins, Marilyn Parker *interior designer*
Anderson, Harry Frederick, Jr. *architect*
Unikel, Eva Taylor *interior designer*

Lake Forest
Moylan, Stephen Craig *architect*

Lake Zurich
Krolopp, Rudolph William *retired industrial designer, consultant*

Lincolnshire
Dobrin, Sheldon L. *architect*

Lisle
Mehaffey, Scott Alan *landscape architect*

Mount Prospect
Thulin, Adelaide Ann *design company executive, interior designer*

Naperville
Balasi, Mark Geoffrey *architect*
Ramirez, Martin Ruben *architect, engineer, educator, cognitive scientist, consultant*

Northfield
Glass, Henry Peter *industrial designer, interior architect, educator*
Schneider-Criezis, Susan Marie *architect*

Oak Park
Kosanavich, Lisa A. *interior designer, industrial designer*
Worley, Marvin George, Jr. *architect*

Park Ridge
Sersen, Howard Harry *interior designer, cabinetry consultant*

Peoria
Corso, Frank, Jr. *architect, educator*
Kenyon, Leslie Harrison *architect*

Plainfield
Hofer, Thomas W. *landscape company executive*

Rockford
Seehausen, Richard Ferdinand *architect*

Schaumburg
Otis, James, Jr. *architect*

Skokie
Siegal, Burton Lee *product designer, consultant, inventor*

Urbana
Replinger, John Gordon *architect, retired educator*

Waukegan
Bleck, Thomas Frank *architect*

Wheeling
Klumpp, Stephen Paul *architect*

Winnetka
Piper, Robert Johnston *architect, urban planner*

INDIANA

Carmel
Eden, Barbara Janiece *commercial and residential interior designer*
Mc Laughlin, Harry Roll *architect*

Fort Wayne
Cole, Kenneth Duane *architect*

Indianapolis
Florestano, Dana Joseph *architect*
Moore, Brent Dale *landscape architect, horticulturist*
†Neville, Susan S. *writer, English educator*
Westcott, April Sue Cook *landscape architect*
Woollen, Evans *architectural firm executive*

Michigan City
Brockway, Lee J. *architect*

Mishawaka
Ponko, William Reuben *architect*
Troyer, LeRoy Seth *architect*

Muncie
Ernstberger, Eric *architectural company executive*

Nashville
Walsh, Alan John *architect*

South Bend
Bellalta, Esmée Cromie *landscape architect, retired educator*
Horsbrugh, Patrick *architect, educator, environologist*

West Lafayette
Molnar, Donald Joseph *landscape architecture educator*

IOWA

Ames
Kainlauri, Eino Olavi *architect*
Palermo, Gregory Sebastian *architect*

Cedar Rapids
Healey, Edward Hopkins *architect*
Stone, Herbert Marshall *architect*

Clear Lake
Broshar, Robert Clare *architect*

Davenport
Monty, Mitchell *landscape company executive*

Des Moines
Gardner, Richard Eugene *landscape architect*
Lewis, Calvin Fred *architect, educator*
Vande Krol, Jerry Lee *architect*

Iowa City
Anderson, Eugene Harold *retired architect, sculptor*
Neumann, Roy Covert *architect*

KANSAS

Lawrence
Grabow, Stephen Harris *architecture educator*

Manhattan
Foerster, Bernd *architecture educator*
Kremer, Eugene R. *architecture educator*

Pittsburg
Fish, David Carlton *architect*

Prairie Village
†Trussell, Donna Laura *writer*

Shawnee Mission
Colgrove, Thomas Michael *landscape architect*

Topeka
Karst, Gary Gene *architect*
Slemmons, Robert Sheldon *architect*

Wichita
Ellington, Howard Wesley *architect*
Kruse, Wilbur Ferdinand *architect*

KENTUCKY

Lexington
Halley, Samuel Hampton, III *architect*
Loghry, Richard M. *architecture and engineering services executive*
Romanowitz, Byron Foster *architect, engineer*

Liberty
Wright, Rodney H. *architect*

Louisville
Weyland, C. William *architect*

Salvisa
Lancaster, Clay *architecture/design educator, writer*

LOUISIANA

Baton Rouge
Baird, David Bryan *architect*
Desmond, John Jacob *architect*
Lee, Betty Redding *architect*
Markovich, Nicholas Charles *architect, designer, educator*
Reich, Robert Sigmund *landscape architect*
Scimeca, Raymond C. *architect*

New Orleans
Blitch, Ronald Buchanan *architect*
Favrot, Henri Mortimer, Jr. *architect, real estate developer*
Filson, Ronald Coulter *architect, educator, college dean*
Frantz, Phares Albert *architect*
Klingman, John Philip *architect, educator*
Mathes, Edward Conrad *architect*
Steinmetz, Robert Charles *architect*

Shreveport
Forte, Stephen Forrest *interior designer*
Haas, Lester Carl *retired architect*

MAINE

Edgecomb
Carlson, Suzanne Olive *architect*

New Harbor
Fradley, Frederick Macdonell *architect*

York
Lyman, William Welles, Jr. *retired architect*

MARYLAND

Annapolis
Lee, T. Girard *architect*
Miller, Richards Thorn *naval architect, engineer*
Wilkes, Joseph Allen *architect*

Baltimore
Adams, Harold Lynn *architect*
Brodie, M. J. (Jay Brodie) *architect, city planner, government executive*
Coulston, Stephen Brett *architect*
Donkervoet, Richard Cornelius *architect*
Ford, John Gilmore *interior designer*
Snead, James Arrington *architect*
Toomey, Sister Stephana *designer liturgical architectural space, nun*

Beltsville
Little, R. Donald *architect, administrator*

Bethesda
Hoenack, August Frederick *architect*

Bowie
Stone, Edward Harris, II *landscape architect*

Chevy Chase
Auerbach, Seymour *architect*
Oudens, Gerald Francis *architect, architectural firm executive*

College Park
Lewis, Roger Kutnow *architect, educator, author*

Columbia
Askew, Laurin Barker, Jr. *architect*
Slater, John Blackwell *landscape architect*

Damascus
Ventola, Dean Samuel *architect, architectural company executive*

Fort Washington
Miller, John Richard *interior designer*

La Plata
Firehock, Barbara A. *interior designer*

Olney
Delmar, Eugene Anthony *architect*

Port Republic
Miller, Ewing Harry *architect*

Rockville
Elliott, Benjamin Paul *architect*
Horowitz, Harold *architect*
Mount, G. Alan *architect*

Severna Park
Allison, John Langsdale *naval architect, marine engineer*

Silver Spring
†Spelman, Jon W. *writer, performer*
Ware, Thomas Earle *building consultant*

West Bethesda
Morgan, William Bruce *naval architect*
Spurling, Everett Gordon, Jr. *architect, construction specifications consultant*

MASSACHUSETTS

Amherst
Cornish, Geoffrey St. John *golf course architect*
†Grant, Daniel Howard *author*
Rupp, William John *architect*

Ashfield
Cudnohufsky, Walter Lee *landscape architect*

Bernardston
Harvey, Arthur John *landscape architect, golf course architect*

Boston
Alexander, James Garth *architect*
Anthony, Ethan *architect*
Beha, Ann Macy *architect*
Costa, Daniel Lawrence *architect*
Elkus, Howard Felix *architect*
Finegold, Maurice Nathan *architect*
Flansburgh, Earl Robert *architect*
Forbes, Peter *architect*
Glassman, Herbert Haskel *architect*
Goody, Joan Edelman *architect*
Harkness, John Cheesman *architect*
Joseph, J. Jonathan *interior designer*
Manfredi, David Peter *architect*
McKinnell, Noel Michael *architect, educator*
Rawn, William Leete, III *architect*
Sand, Michael *industrial designer*
Steffian, John Ames, Jr. *architect*
Tappé, Albert Anthony *architect*
Wolf, Gary Herbert *architect*
Wood, Henry Austin *architect*

Boxboro
Berry, Robert John *architect*

Brookline
†Walter, Eugene Victor *writer*

Cambridge
Anderson, Stanford Owen *architect, architectural historian, educator*
Bruck, Phoebe Ann Mason *landscape architect*
Burns, Carol J. *architect, educator*
Campbell, Robert *architect, writer*
Dewart, Christopher *architectural educator, furniture maker*
Downes, Gregory *architectural organization executive*
Green, Richard John *architect*
Hamner, W. Easley *architect*
Hass, Michael Shepherdson *architect*
Kobus, Richard Lawrence *architect, designer, executive*
Krieger, Alex *architecture and design educator*
Kruger, Kenneth *architect*
Moneo, José Rafael *architecture educator*
Newman, John Nicholas *naval architect educator*
Pollock, Wilson F. *architectural firm executive*
Porter, William Lyman *architect, educator*
Rosenfeld, Walter David, Jr. *architect, writer*
Rowe, Peter Grimmond *architecture educator, researcher*
Sekler, Eduard Franz *architect, educator*
†Silvetti, Jorge *architecture educator*
Szabo, Albert *architect, educator*
Tsoi, Edward Tze Ming *architect, interior designer, urban planner*

Concord
Alden, Peter Charles *author, naturalist*
Cutting, Heyward *designer, planner*

Holyoke
Baker, David S. *architect*

Hyde Park
†Clutz, Charles Nesbitt *architect*

Lexington
Frey, John Ward *landscape architect*

Lincoln
Merrill, Vincent Nichols *landscape architect*
Payne, Harry Morse, Jr. *architect*

Manchester
Shepley, Hugh *architect*

Nantucket
Lethbridge, Francis Donald *architect*

Newton
Korobkin, Barry Jay *architect*
Lam, Thomas Manpan *architect*
†Lewis-Kausel, Cecilia *interior design educator*
Oles, Paul Stevenson (Steve Oles) *architect, perspectivist, educator*

North Andover
Goldstein, Charles Henry *architect, consultant*

Shirley
Field, Hermann Haviland *architect, educator, author*

Somerville
Safdie, Moshe *architect*

South Yarmouth
Spilman, Raymond *industrial designer*

Stoughton
Ross, Edward Joseph *architect*

Waltham
Brooker, Richard I. *architect*
Notkin, Leonard Sheldon *architect*

Watertown
Dawson, Stuart Owen *landscape architect, urban designer*

Wayland
Huygens, Remmert William *architect*

Wellesley
Merguerian, Arshag *architect*

West Newton
Morris, Glenn Louis *architect*

West Springfield
Engebretson, Douglas Kenneth *architect, interior designer*

Weston
Fleming, Nancy McAdam *landscape designer*
Sturgis, Robert Shaw *architect*
Wood, Jeremy Scott *architect, urban designer*

Winchester
Jabre, Eddy-Marco *architect*

Winthrop
Costantino, Frank Mathew *architectural illustrator*

MICHIGAN

Ann Arbor
Beckley, Robert Mark *architect, educator*
Benford, Harry Bell *naval architect*
Flowers, Damon Bryant *architect, facility planner*
Fry, Richard E. *architectural firm executive*
Malkawi, Ali Mahmoud *architecture educator, researcher*
Marans, Robert Warren *architect, planner*
Metcalf, Robert Clarence *architect, educator*
Vakalo, Emmanuel-George *architecture and planning educator, researcher*

Birmingham
Van Dine, Harold Forster, Jr. *architect*

Bloomfield Hills
Allen, Maurice Bartelle, Jr. *architect*
Birkerts, Gunnar *architect*
Brown, Jack Wyman *architect*

Chelsea
Paulsen, Serenus Glen *architect, educator*

Detroit
Francis, Edward D. *architect*
Kessler, William Henry *architect*
†Monts, Rodd LyDell *writer, journalist*
Roehling, Carl David *architect*

Farmington
Reddig, Walter Eduard *architect, master cabinet maker*

Flint
Tolbert-Bey, Gregory Lee *landscape architect and planner*
Tomblinson, James Edmond *architect*

Grand Rapids
West, Terence Douglas *furniture company design executive*
Wold, Robert Lee *architect, engineer*

Gregory
Frank, Richard Calhoun *architect*

Jackson
Kendall, Kay Lynn *interior designer, consultant*

Kalamazoo
Carver, Norman Francis, Jr. *architect, photographer*

Macomb
Schmeiser, Jerome Richard *landscape architect, city planner*

Rockford
Boese, Ted C. *furniture designer*

Saint Joseph
Keech, Elowyn Ann *interior designer*

Saline
Babcock, Leo Aloysius *architect, scenic designer*

Southfield
Redstone, Daniel Aaron *architect*
Redstone, Louis Gordon *architect*

Traverse City
Brown, Paul Bradley *architect*

MINNESOTA

Duluth
Salmela, David Daniel *architect*
Whiteman, Richard Frank *architect*

Minneapolis
Clemence, Roger Davidson *landscape architect, educator*
Degenhardt, Robert Allan *architectural and engineering firm executive*
Faricy, Richard Thomas *architect*
Jacob, Bernard Michel *architect*
Martin, Roger Bond *landscape architect, educator*
Meese, Robert Allen *architect*
Parker, Leonard S. *architect, educator*
Rand, Peter Anders *architect*
†Satkowski, Leon George *architecture educator*
Susanka, Sarah Hills *architect*
Van Housen, Thomas Corwin, III *architect, designer, builder*
Weinzetl, Lawrence Martin *architect*

Northfield
Sovik, Edward Anders *architect, consultant*

Saint Paul
Close, Elizabeth Scheu *architect*

MISSISSIPPI

Biloxi
Zocchi, Louis Joseph *product designer, game company executive*

Columbus
Kaye, Samuel Harvey *architect, educator*

Greenwood
Evans, Randall Dean, Jr. *interior designer*

Mississippi State
Martin, Edward Curtis, Jr. *landscape architect, educator*

Starkville
Ford, Robert MacDonald, III *architect, educator*

Vicksburg
Richardson, Jeffrey Gunn *landscape architect*

MISSOURI

Clayton
Christner, Theodore Carroll *architect*

Columbia
Brent, Ruth Stumpe *design educator, researcher, educator*

Kansas City
Baker, Robert Thomas *interior designer*
Conrad, William Merrill *architect*
Seligson, Theodore H. *architect, interior designer, art consultant*
Shoemaker, Robert Shern *architect*

Saint Charles
Evans, James Bruce *urban planner*

Saint Louis
Becker, Rex Louis *architect*
Beuc, Rudolph, Jr. *architect, real estate broker*
Bextermiller, Theresa Marie Louise *architect, computer graphics*
Chivetta, Anthony Joseph *architect*
Cotton, W(illiam) Philip, Jr. *architect*
Ginsberg, Marvin A. *architect*
Hellmuth, George Francis *architect*
Ittner, H. Curtis *architect*
Krebs, Carol Marie *architect, psychiatric therapist*
Lickhalter, Merlin Eugene *architect*
Lovelace, Eldridge Hirst *retired landscape architect, city planner*
Michaelides, Constantine Evangelos *architect, educator*
Self, Larry Douglas *architectural firm executive*
Sincoff, Jerome J. *architect*
Thalden, Barry R. *architect*
Weese, Cynthia Rogers *architect, educator*

Springfield
Ownby, Jerry Steve *landscape architect, educator*

Turners
Hone, Randolph Cooper *architect*

Webster Groves
Kramer, Gerhardt Theodore *architect*

MONTANA

Bozeman
DeHaas, John Neff, Jr. *retired architecture educator*

Great Falls
Davidson, David Scott *architect*

NEBRASKA

Lincoln
Morrow, Andrew Nesbit *interior designer, business owner*
Mutunayagam, N. Brito *architecture and planning educator, associate dean*
Stange, James Henry *architect*
Steward, Weldon Cecil *architecture educator, architect, consultant*

Omaha
Bowen, Gary Roger *architect*
Polsky, Donald Perry *architect*
Ryan, Mark Anthony *architect*

NEW HAMPSHIRE

Fremont
Richardson, Artemas P(artridge) *landscape architect*

Goffstown
Gillmore, Robert *landscape designer, author, editor, publisher*

Hanover
Brooks, H. Allen *architectural educator, author, lecturer*

Holderness
Cutler, Laurence Stephan *architect, urban designer, advertising executive, educator*

New London
Sheerr, Deirdre McCrystal *architectural firm executive*

Peterborough
Alderman, Bissell *architect*

NEW JERSEY

Bernardsville
Lazor, Patricia Ann *interior designer*

Chatham
Johnston, Dennis Roy *computer systems integrator*

Clifton
Held, George Anthony *architect*

East Orange
Fielo, Muriel Bryant *space engineer, interior designer*

Englewood
Schmidt, Ronald Hans *architect*

Freehold
Pofsky, Norma Louise *interior designer, behavioral consultant*

Hackettstown
Kays, Elena J. *interior design educator*

Iselin
Kalafsky, Kurt M. *architect*

Jamesburg
Zeigen, Spencer Steven *architect*

Jersey City
Ortenzi, Regina (Gina Rae Ortenzi) *home fashion products designer, educator*

Lindenwold
†Farwati, Abdul Jalil *architect, civil engineer*

Medford
Dunn, Roy J. *landscape architect*

Montclair
Jones, Rees Lee *golf course architect*

Morristown
Cowles, Walter Curtis *naval architect*
Nadaskay, Raymond *architect*

Paramus
DiGeronimo, Suzanne Kay *architect*

Parsippany
†Mistry, Yogesh Balubhai *architect*

Pittstown
Bell, Frank Joseph, III *architect*

Princeton
Cooke, R(ichard) Caswell, Jr. *architect*
Etz, Lois Kapelsohn *architectural company principal*
Ford, Jeremiah, III *architect*
Graves, Michael *architect, educator*
Hillier, J(ames) Robert *architect*
Holt, Philetus Havens, III *architect*
Kehrt, Allan William *architectural firm executive*
Lerner, Ralph *architect, university dean*
Mills, Michael James *architect*

Ridgefield
Aybar, Romeo *architect*

Ridgewood
Celentano, Linda Nancy *industrial designer*
Ziv, Pat Valentine *interior designer*

Saddle River
Cappitella, Mauro John *architect*

Somerville
Shive, Richard Byron *architect*

South Orange
DeVaris, Panayotis Eric *architect*
Robinson, James LeRoy *architect, educator, developer*

Summit
Bottelli, Richard *retired architect*

Upper Montclair
Zivari, Bashir *architect, industrial designer*

NEW MEXICO

Albuquerque
Campbell, C(harles) Robert *architect*
Hakim, Besim Selim *architecture and urban design educator, researcher*
Hooker, Van Dorn *architect, artist*

Pirkl, James Joseph *industrial designer, educator, writer*
Sabatini, William Quinn *architect*

Questa
Sharkey, Richard David *architectural artisan, inventor, musician*

Santa Fe
Leon, Bruno *architect, educator*

NEW YORK

Auburn
Long, Michael Howard *landscape architect*

Bedford
Benedek, Armand *landscape architect*
Damora, Robert Matthew *architect*

Berlin
Stephens, Donald Joseph *retired architect*

Binghamton
Bearsch, Lee Palmer *architect, city planner*

Bronx
Blake, Peter Jost *architect*

Bronxville
Frost, A. Corwin *architect, consultant*

Brooklyn
Engersgard, Jorgen *architect*
†Hirsch, Charles Flynn *writer, editor*
Mui, Jimmy Kun *architect, network marketing executive*
Vasisko, Gerard F. *architect*
Weston, I. Donald *architect*
Woolley, Margaret Anne (Margot Woolley) *architect*

Buffalo
Coles, Robert Traynham *architect*

Carmel
Carruth, David Barrow *landscape architect*

Cold Spring
Brill, Ralph David *architect, real estate developer, venture capitalist*

Corona
Little, Frederick Anton *landscape architect, municipal administrator*

Cranberry Lake
Glavin, James Edward *landscape architect*

Dobbs Ferry
Guggenheimer, Tobias Immanuel Simon *architect*

East Hampton
Damaz, Paul F. *architect*

Elizaville
Koeppel, Harry Saul *interior designer, educator*

Flushing
Shirvani, Hamid *architect, educator, author, administrator*

Great Neck
Turofsky, Charles Sheldon *landscape architect*

Greenlawn
Stevens, John Richard *architectural historian*

Hastings On Hudson
Weinstein, Edward Michael *architect, consultant*

Ithaca
Becherer, Richard John *architecture educator*
Sims, William Riley *design and facility management educator, consultant*

Katonah
Baker, John Milnes *architect*
Kravitt, Martin Kenneth *architect*

Locust Valley
Bentel, Frederick Richard *architect, educator*
Bentel, Maria-Luise Ramona Azzarone (Mrs. Frederick R. Bentel) *architect, educator*
Webel, Richard Karl *landscape architect*

Long Island City
Sadao, Shoji *architect*

Manhasset
Corva, Angelo Francis *architect*
Grossi, Olindo *architect, educator*
Schiller, Arthur A. *architect, educator*

New Hyde Park
Hoffman, Maliza Mildred *interior designer*

New Lebanon
Baker, James Barnes *architect*

New Rochelle
Menzies, Henry Hardinge *architect*

New York
Ayotte, Richard L. *architect*
Barnes, Edward Larrabee *architect*
Beckhard, Herbert *architect*
Beckmann, John *architect, designer, writer*
Berman, Siegrid Visconti *interior designer*
Bland, Frederick Aves *architect*
Blinder, Richard Lewis *architect*
Bookhardt, Fred Barringer, Jr. *architect*
Borrelli, John Francis *architect*
Breger, William N. *architect, educator*
Breines, Simon *architect*
Brennan, Henry Higginson *architect*

Broches, Paul Elias *architect*
Brooks, Steven R. *architect*
Buatta, Mario *interior designer*
Butler, Jonathan Putnam *architect*
Cavaglieri, Giorgio *architect*
Chan, Lo-Yi Cheung Yuen *architect*
Clarke, Jerrold *architect*
Cobb, Henry Nichols *architect*
Czajka, James Vincent *architect*
Dattner, Richard *architect, educator*
David, Theoharis Lambros *architect, educator*
Davis, Jerry Albert *architect*
de Bethmann, Heidi Elizabeth *architect*
Decker, Dennis Dale *industrial designer*
De Vido, Alfredo Eduardo *architect*
Edelman, Judith H. *architect*
Eisenman, Peter David *architect, educator*
Fitch, James Marston *architectural preservationist, architectural historian, critic*
Fitzsimmons, Sophie Sonia *interior designer*
Fleischer, Joseph Linden *architect*
Franzen, Ulrich J. *architect*
Fratianne, David Michael *architect*
Freidin, Jack *architect*
Friedberg, Marvin Paul *landscape architect*
Fuston, Andrew D. *interior designer, educator, speaker, writer, environmentalist*
Gatje, Robert Frederick *architect*
Genaro, Donald Michael *industrial designer*
Georgis, William Theodore *architect*
†Geraci, Damiano *architect*
Gibbs, Jamie *landscape architect, interior designer*
Gifford, Steven *architect*
Ginsberg, David Lawrence *architect*
Glaser, Milton *graphic designer and illustrator*
Guise, David Earl *architect, educator*
Gwathmey, Charles *architect*
Halpin, Anna Marie *architect*
Halsband, Frances *architect*
Hardy, Hugh *architect*
Hariri, Gisue *architect, educator*
Hinz, Theodore Vincent *architect*
Holub, Martin *architect*
Holzman, Malcolm *architect*
Hoog, Marjorie *architect*
Ivy, Robert Adams, Jr. *architect, editor-in-chief*
Johansen, John MacLane *architect*
Kasakove, Susan *interior designer*
Kinnear, John Kenyon, Jr. *architect*
Kliment, Robert Michael *architect*
Kliment, Stephen Alexander *architect, editor, journalist*
Knowles, Edward F(rank) *architect*
Kohn, A. Eugene *architect*
Kondylis, Costas Andrew *architect*
Kuhl, William Bernard *landscape architect*
La Vita, Roberto *architect, art director, designer*
Lefferts, Gillet, Jr. *architect*
Leigh, Stephen *industrial designer*
Liebman, Theodore *architect*
Mandl, David *architect*
Masey, Jack *exhibition designer*
Meier, Richard Alan *architect*
Mellins, Thomas Harrison *architectural historian*
†Mondello, Robert Charles *architect, writer*
Palermo, Robert James *architect, consultant, inventor*
Parnes, Robert Mark *architect*
Pasanella, Giovanni *architect, architectural educator*
Pedersen, William *architect*
Pei, Chien Chung *architect*
Pei, Ieoh Ming *architect*
Peretz, Eileen *interior designer*
Perkins, Lawrence Bradford, Jr. *architect*
Pomeroy, Lee Harris *architect*
Pool, Mary Jane *design consultant, writer*
Quennell, Nicholas *landscape architect, educator*
Ranalli, George Joseph *architect, educator*
Rice, Richard Lee, Jr. *architect*
Rosenblatt, Arthur Isaac *architect, former museum director*
Rosenblatt, Lester *naval architect*
Rosenfeld, Norman *architect*
Rossant, James Stephane *architect, artist*
Sattan, William Daniel *interior designer*
Schwarz, Ekkehart Richard Johannes *architect, urban designer*
Slomanson, Lloyd Howard *architect, musician*
Smith, Ken *landscape architect*
Smotrich, David Isadore *architect*
Snibbe, Richard W. *architect*
Specter, David Kenneth *architect, interior designer*
Stern, Robert Arthur Morton *architect, educator, writer*
Tabler, William Benjamin *architect*
Tafel, Edgar *architect*
Tayar, Memduh Ali *architect*
Tozer, Elizabeth Farran *interior and floral designer, philanthropist*
Varney, Carleton Bates, Jr. *interior designer, columnist, educator*
Voorsanger, Bartholomew *architect*
†Wexler, Allan *architect, art educator*
Willis, Beverly Ann *architect*
Work, William H(enry) *architect, consultant*

Nyack
Degenshein, Jan *architect, planner*
Gaudy, Edward *landscape architect, consultant*

Oneida
Pittner, Andrew Peter *landscape architect*

Pleasantville
Annese, Domenico *landscape architect*

Pound Ridge
Abramovitz, Max *architect*

Purchase
Alfredo, Joseph Albert *landscape architect*

Rensselaerville
Dudley, George Austin *architect, planning consultant, educator*

Rye
Anderson, Allan *architectural firm executive*

Sands Point
Zalben, Steven *architect*

Syracuse
Skoler, Louis *architect, educator*

Tarrytown
Kenney, John Michel *architect*

Troy
Haviland, David Sands *architectural educator, researcher, administrator*

Wappingers Falls
Johnson, Jeh Vincent *architect*

Warwick
Mack, Daniel Richard *furniture designer*

Water Mill
D'Urso, Joseph Paul *interior designer*

Weedsport
Cichello, Samuel Joseph *architect*

White Plains
Papp, Laszlo George *architect*

NORTH CAROLINA

Asheville
King, Joseph Bertram *architect*

Boone
Oelberg, Robert Nathan *landscape architect*

Burlington
Stafford, Kenneth Dean *architect*

Cashiers
Runions, Sherman Curtis *landscape architect*

Chapel Hill
Dixon, Frederick Dail *architect*
Godschalk, David Robinson *architect, urban development planner, educator*

Charlotte
Estes, Christopher J. *landscape architect*
Ferebee, Stephen Scott, Jr. *architect*
Huberman, Jeffrey Allen *architect*
Melaragno, Michele *architecture educator*
Montague, Edgar Burwell, III (Monty Montague) *industrial designer*
Shive, Philip Augustus *architect*

Durham
Ramsay, Kerr Craige *architect*

Greensboro
Murrelle, Ronald Kemp *architectural designer*
†Wood, Ellen Dianne *drafting technician, artist*

High Point
Culler, Robert Ransom *furniture designing and product development company executive*

Kinston
Baker-Gardner, Jewelle *interior designer*

Pisgah Forest
Albyn, Richard Keith *retired architect*

Raleigh
Burns, Robert Paschal *architect, educator*
Clarke, Lewis James *landscape architect*
Flournoy, William Louis, Jr. *landscape architect*
Godwin, James Beckham *retired landscape architect*
Johnson, Marvin Richard Alois *architect*
Malecha, Marvin John *architect, academic administrator*

Robbinsville
Ginn, Ronn *architect, urban planner, general contractor*

Southern Shores
Vander Myde, Philip Louis *architectural design firm executive*

Winston Salem
Butner, Fred Washington, Jr. *architect*

NORTH DAKOTA

Fargo
Nelson, James Warren *architect, educator*

OHIO

Celina
Fanning, Ronald Heath *architect, engineer*

Chagrin Falls
Cordes, Loverne Christian *interior designer*

Cincinnati
Fitzgerald, James T. *architect*
Glendening, Everett Austin *architect*
Goetzman, Bruce Edgar *architecture educator*
Levinson, Charles Bernard *architect*
Luckner, Herman Richard, III *interior designer*
Meisner, Gary Wayne *landscape architect*
Nielsen, George Lee *architect*
Novak, Robert G. *architect*
Preiser, Wolfgang Friedrich Ernst *architect, educator, consultant, researcher*
Roche, Kevin R. *architect, retail design, retail strategist*
Roomann, Hugo *architect*
Senhauser, John Crater *architect*

Cleveland
Behnke, William Alfred *landscape architect, planner*
Bowen, Richard Lee *architect*
Eberhard, William Thomas *architect*
Gibans, James David *architect*
Hunter, Sally Irene *interior designer*
Kelly, John Terence *architect*

Little, Robert Andrews *architect, designer, painter*
Madison, Robert Prince *architect*
Melsop, James William *architect*
Sande, Theodore Anton *architect, educator, foundation executive*
Zung, Thomas Tse-Kwai *architect*

Columbiana
Richman, John Emmett *architect*

Columbus
Bohm, Friedrich (Friedl) K.M. *architectural firm executive*
Carpenter, Jot David *landscape architect, educator*
Kirk, Ballard Harry Thurston *architect*
Weinhold, Virginia Beamer *interior designer*

Cuyahoga Falls
Haag, Everett Keith *architect*

Dayton
Betz, Eugene William *architect*

Dublin
Cornwell, Paul M., Jr. *architect*

Kent
Centuori, Jeanine Gail *architecture educator*
Sommers, David Lynn *architect*

Shaker Heights
Gellert, Edward Bradford, III *architect, consultant*

Toledo
Hills, Arthur W. *architectural firm executive*
Martin, Robert Edward *architect*

Wauseon
Boyers, Janeth Mauree *interior designer*

Youngstown
Murcko, Donald Leroy *architect*

OKLAHOMA

Norman
Henderson, Arnold Glenn *architect, educator*
Henkle, James L. *industrial designer*
Sorey, Thomas Lester, Jr. *architect, educator*
Tuttle, Arthur Norman, Jr. *architect, university administrator, educational facilities planner*

Stillwater
Leider, Charles L. *landscape architect*

Tulsa
Ball, Rex Martin *urban designer, architect*
Jones, Robert Lawton *architect, planner, educator*
Kennedy, Nancy Louise *retired draftsman*

OREGON

Ashland
Mularz, Theodore Leonard *architect*

Beaverton
Ivester, (Richard) Gavin *industrial designer*

Clackamas
Merrill, William Dean *retired architect, medical facility planning consultant*

Eugene
†Mohr, Debbie (Doris Elaine) *author*

Medford
Skelton, Douglas H. *architect*
Straus, David A. *architectural firm executive*

Milwaukie
Michael, Gary Linn *architect, artist*

Otter Rock
Eaton, Leonard Kimball *retired architecture educator*

Portland
Bruechert, Beverly Ann *interior design consultant, recording artist, pianist*
Frasca, Robert John *architect*
Gunsul, Brooks R. W. *architect*
Hacker, Thomas Owen *architect*
Kilbourn, Lee Ferris *architect, specifications writer*
Ritz, Richard Ellison *architect, architectural historian, writer*

Springfield
Lutes, Donald Henry *architect*

Tualatin
Broome, John William *retired architect*

PENNSYLVANIA

Ambler
Brandow, Theo *architect*
Swansen, Donna Maloney *landscape designer, consultant*

Ardmore
Mirick, Henry Dustin *architect*

Bala Cynwyd
Bentivegna, Peter Ignatius *architectural company executive*

Bethlehem
Spillman, Robert Arnold *architect*

Butler
Kosar, John E. *architectural firm executive*

Cape May Point
Jordan, Joe J. *architect*

Cheltenham
Skaler, Robert Morris *architect, forensic architect*

Fort Washington
Lewis, Richard Arnold *architect*

Jenkintown
Clemmer, Leon *architect, planner*

Matamoras
Linden, Harold Arthur *interior designer, consultant*

New Cumberland
Peters, Ralph Edgar *architectural and engineering executive*

Philadelphia
Barnett, Jonathan *architect, city planner*
Brott, M. Paul *architectural firm executive*
Brown, Denise Scott *architect, urban planner*
†Carpenter, Amy Tacy *architect*
Dagit, Charles Edward, Jr. *architect, educator*
†DeLong, David G. *architect, urgan planner, educator*
Eiswerth, Barry Neil *architect, educator*
French, Jeffrey Stuart *architect*
Hamme, David Codrington *architect*
Hayes, John Freeman *architect*
Izenour, Steven *architect*
Jarvis, J. Andrew *architectural firm executive*
Kise, James Nelson *architect, urban planner*
Lavecchia, Benjamin L. *architectural firm executive*
Lawson, John Quinn *architect*
Magaziner, Henry Jonas *architect, writer*
Maxman, Susan Abel *architect*
McHarg, Ian Lennox *landscape architect, regional planner, educator*
Mitchell, Ehrman Burkman, Jr. *architect*
Patel, Pradeep R. *architectural firm executive*
Perkins, George Holmes *architectural educator, architect*
Rauch, John Keiser, Jr. *architect*
Rybczynski, Witold Marian *architect, educator, writer*
Rykwert, Joseph *architecture and art history educator*
Santos, Adele Naude *architect, educator*
Saylor, Peter M. *architect*
Sotnick, M.J. *architectural firm executive*
Stick, Thomas Howard Fitchett *corporate architect, construction litigation consultant*
Tremonte Spigonardo, Ada Mary *interior architect*
Tyng, Anne Griswold *architect*
Venturi, Robert *architect*
Vinh, Binh *architect*

Pittsburgh
Carter, Donald K. *architectural firm executive*
Damianos, Sylvester *architect, sculptor*
Gindroz, Raymond L. *architect*
Horowitz, Carole Spiegel *interior designer*
Horowitz, Don Roy *landscape company executive*
Levenson, Nathan Samuel *architect*
Loftness, Vivian Ellen *architecture educator*
Rosenblatt, Paul Mark *architect, educator*
Simonds, John Ormsbee *landscape architect*
Swain, William Grant *landscape architect*
Vater, David Joseph *architect*

Red Lion
Keener, Wayne B. *interior designer*

State College
Haas, John C. *architect*

University Park
Leslie, Donald Wilmot *landscape architecture educator*
Porterfield, Neil Harry *landscape architect, educator*
Wheeler, C. Herbert *architect, consultant, educator*

Wayne
Wheatley, William Arthur *architect, musician*

Willow Grove
Suer, Marvin David *architecture, consultant*

Wyomissing
Kessler, Leona Hanover *interior designer*

RHODE ISLAND

Jamestown
Todd, Thomas Abbott *architect, urban designer*

Newport
Burgin, William Lyle *architect*
Scoll, Eulalie Elizabeth *writer, researcher*
Tarpgaard, Peter Thorvald *naval architect*
Wurman, Richard Saul *architect*

Providence
Barnum, William Milo *architect*

SOUTH CAROLINA

Anderson
Pflieger, Kenneth John *architect*

Charleston
Goff, R. Garey *architect*
Lucas, Frank Edward *architect*

Clemson
Halfacre, Robert Gordon *landscape architect, horticulturist, educator*
Kishimoto, Yuji *architect, educator*
Young, Joseph Laurie *architecture educator*

Columbia
Hultstrand, Charles John *architect*
Turk, John Cobb *architect, educator*

Liskamm, William Hugo *architect, urban planner, educator*
Mazzarelli, Marc F. *landscape architect*
Mc Pheeters, Edwin Keith *architect, educator*
Meier, Henry George *architect*
Merrick, Dorothy Susan *interior designer*
Meyers, Richard James *landscape architect*
Miller, Jack Conway *landscape artist, art gallery director, owner*
Millican, Kirk *architect*
Moore, Richard Alan *landscape architect*
Mujica, Mauro E. *architect*
Mumma, Albert Girard, Jr. *architect*
Muncey, James Arthur, Jr. *architect*
Munson, Virginia Aldrich *interior designer, decorator*
Murray, David George *architect*
Odermatt, Robert Allen *architect*
Omholt, Bruce Donald *product designer, mechanical engineer, consultant*
Peters, Robert Woolsey *architect*
Pettitt, Jay S. *architect, consultant*
Poss, Jeffery Scott *architect, educator*
Pubillones, Joseph *architect, educator*
Rasic, Janko *architect*
Reid, Joseph Browning *retired architect*
Rice, Richard Lee *retired architect*
Rogers, Kate Ellen *interior design educator*
Roubik, Susanne Eileen *architect*
Ryan, John Michael *landscape architect*
Salazar, Luis Adolfo *architect*
Sande, Barbara *interior decorating consultant*
Schuth, Mary McDougle *interior designer, educator*
Siefer, Stuart B. *architect*
Stanley, Duffy B. *architect*
Stewart, Bruce Edmund, Sr. *retired mechanical designer, writer*
Strandjord, Ronald Millard *architect*
Tachi, Douglas Paul *architect, interior designer*
†Taylor, Velande Pingel *author, publisher*
Tomasi, Donald Charles *architect*
Walker, Bradford C. *architect*
Wiebenson, Dora Louise *architectural historian, educator, author*
Williams, John Howard *architect, retired*
Wilson, William Glenn, Jr. *graphic designer*
Woerner, Robert Lester *landscape architect*
Yates, Maurice Marvin, III *architect*
York, Charles Albert *architect*

ARTS: LITERARY. *See also* COMMUNICATIONS MEDIA.

UNITED STATES

ALABAMA

Auburn
Gilbert, Armida Jennings *American literature educator*

Birmingham
Lide, Neoma Jewell Lawhon (Mrs. Martin James Lide, Jr.) *poet*
Stallworth, Anne Nall *writer, writing educator*

Elmore
Williams, Glenda Carlene *writer*

Huntsville
Daly, Cecily A. *author, educator*

Tuscaloosa
†Martone, Michael *writer*

Tuskegee Institute
Roy, Rashmi *poet, adult education educator*

ALASKA

Anchorage
Molinari, Carol V. *writer, investment company executive, educator*
Strohmeyer, John *writer, former editor*
Thomas, Lowell, Jr. *author, lecturer, former lieutenant governor, former state senator*

Arctic Village
Tritt, Lincoln C. *writer, educator, musician*

Juneau
†Dauenhauer, Richard Leonard *writer*

ARIZONA

Bowie
Burke, Ruth *writer*

Flagstaff
Cline, Platt Herrick *author*

Mesa
Lengeman, William Irving, III *writer*

Paradise Valley
Cussler, Clive Eric *author*

Phoenix
Duyck, Kathleen Marie *poet, musician, retired social worker*
Ellison, Cyril Lee *literary agent, retired publisher*

Scottsdale
Carpenter, Betty O. *writer*

Sedona
Prather, Richard Scott *author*
Thorne, Kate Ruland *writer, publisher, editor*

Snowflake
Freyermuth, Gundolf S. *writer*

Sun City West
Bowkett, Gerald Edson *editorial consultant, writer*
†Manville, Greta C. *writer*

Tempe
Cortright, Barbara Jean *writer*
Raby, William Louis *author*

Tucson
Butcher, Russell Devereux *author, photographer*
†Inman, Billie Jo (Andrew) *writer, retired English educator*
Kingsolver, Barbara Ellen *writer*
†Lowe, Jonathan F. *writer*
Mason, Judith Ann *freelance writer*
Russ, Joanna *author*
Vicker, Ray *writer*
Warren, Bacil Benjamin *writer, publisher*
Young, Donald Allen *writer, consultant*

Yuma
Desmond, Leif *writer*
†Nelson, Rodney *writer, editor*

ARKANSAS

Eureka Springs
Dragonwagon, Crescent (Ellen Zolotow) *writer*

Fayetteville
Shafer, Carol Larsen *retired book reviewer*
Williams, Miller *poet, translator*

Hot Springs National Park
Stuber, Irene Zelinsky *writer, researcher*

Jonesboro
†Guffey, Marsha Kidd *grant writer, consultant*

Little Rock
Brown, Dee Alexander *author*

CALIFORNIA

Alameda
Grzanka, Leonard Gerald *writer, consultant*

Albany
†Cartier, Xam Ciaran *writer*

Albion
†Weiss, Ruth *poet*

Aliso Viejo
McCall, Elizabeth Kaye *columnist, consultant*

Altadena
Burden, Jean (Prussing) *poet, writer, editor*
†Davis, Christopher *writer, retired writing educator*

Antioch
Chu, Valentin Yuan-ling *author*

Apple Valley
Nolan, Ruth Marie *technical writer*

Aptos
†Wolff, Jean Walton *writer, artist*

Arcadia
Kenvin, Roger Lee *writer, retired English educator*
Sloane, Beverly LeBov *writer, consultant*

Belmont
Morris, Bruce Dorian *technical writer, literary historian, educator*

Berkeley
Burch, Claire Rita *writer*
Callenbach, Ernest *writer, editor*
†Chetin, Helen Campbell *writer*
Diamond, Sara Rose *writer, sociologist, lecturer*
Dundes, Alan *writer, folklorist, educator*
†Ellis, Ella Thorp *writer, retired educator*
Guest, Barbara *author, poet*
Katzen, Mollie *writer, artist*
Kingston, Maxine Hong *author*
Masson, Jeffrey Moussaieff *writer*
Meltzer, David *author, musician*
Milosz, Czeslaw *poet, author, educator*
Moon, Susan *writer, editor*
†Nunes, Susan Miho *writer*
Olsen, Tillie *author*
Temko, Allan Bernard *writer*
Wehner, Kay Y. *poet*
White, Richard Weddington, Jr. *writer, editor*

Beverly Hills
Basichis, Gordon Allen *author, screenwriter*
†Bass, Ronald *screenwriter*
Belknap, Maria Ann *writer*
Black, David *writer, educator, producer*
Bochco, Steven *screenwriter, television producer*
†Darabont, Frank *screenwriter, director*
Davenport, Robert Ralsey *writer*
†Farrelly, Bobby *writer, producer, director*
Flakes, Susan *playwright, screenwriter, director*
Gelbart, Larry *writer, producer*
Goldman, William *writer*
Manus, Willard *writer, journalist, critic*
Mazursky, Paul *screenwriter, theatrical director and producer*
Proft, Pat *screenwriter, film producer*
Rabe, David William *playwright*
Reiner, Annie *writer, psychotherapist*
Roth, Eric *screenwriter*
Schulian, John (Nielsen Schulian) *screenwriter, author*
Schulman, Tom *screenwriter*
Shepard, Sam (Samuel Shepard Rogers) *playwright, actor*
Towne, Robert *screenwriter*
Ward, David Schad *screenwriter, film director*

Bishop
Kelley, William *author, screenwriter*

Burbank
Goldstein, Kenneth F. *entertainment executive, software executive*

Camarillo
Alexander, John Charles *editor, writer*

Cameron Park
Frazer, Lance William *writer*

Canoga Park
McAuley, Milton Kenneth *author, book publisher*

Carmel
Shapiro, Stephen George *screenwriter, photographer*
Wolf, Dorothy Joan *poet*

Carmichael
Goodin, Evelyn Marie *writer*

Chico
Dorman, N.B. *writer*
Livingston, Myran Jay *author, film writer, director and producer*

Chula Vista
†Kowit, Steve Mark *poet, educator*
Trujillo, Teófilo-Carlos *writer, publisher, history educator*

Citrus Heights
Stadley, Pat Anna May Gough (Mrs. James M. Stadley) *author*

Claremont
Mezey, Robert *poet, educator*
Tilden, Wesley Roderick *author, retired computer programmer*

Clovis
Shields, Allan Edwin *writer, photographer, retired educator*

Colton
Witman-Glenn, Laura Kathleen *writer, security guard, silent alarm monitor*

Compton
Shiloh, Allen *writer, postal employee*

Concord
Albrecht, Donna G. *author*

Coronado
Stockdale, James Bond *writer, research scholar, retired naval officer*

Covina
More, Blake *writer, poet*

Crescent City
Ruffer, Joyce Sellars *poet, artist*

Cromberg
Kolb, Ken Lloyd *writer*

Culver City
Binder, Bettye B. *author, lecturer*
Crowe, Cameron *screenwriter, film director*
McNeill, Daniel Richard *writer*

Cypress
Edmonds, Ivy Gordon *writer*

Dana Point
Bullock, Harvey Reade *screenwriter*

Davis
Beagle, Peter Soyer *writer*
†Bunch, Richard Alan *writer, educator*
Major, Clarence Lee *novelist, poet, educator*

Del Mar
Smith, Robert Hamil *author, fund raiser*

El Segundo
Halloran, James Vincent, III *technical writer*
†Wilkinson, Sylvia Jean *writer, educator*

Encinitas
†Farrell, Warren Thomas *author*

Fallbrook
Johnston, Betty *writer*

Fresno
Garrison-Finderup, Ivadelle Dalton *writer*
Levine, Philip *poet, retired educator*
†Mullins, Cathy Layne *poet, bartender, manager*
Petrochilos, Elizabeth A. *writer, publisher*

Garden Valley
Price, Lew Paxton *writer, engineer, scientist*

Georgetown
Lengyel, Cornel Adam (Cornel Adam) *author*

Glendale
Darnell, Roger Kent *writer/producer*

Glendora
Phillips, Jill Meta *novelist, critic, astrologer*

Healdsburg
Erdman, Paul Emil *author*
Myers, Robert Eugene *writer, educator*

Hesperia
Du Lac, Lois Arline *writer*

Hollywood
Kurlander, Carl Litman *screenwriter*
Melchior, Ib Jorgen *author, television and motion picture writer, director*
Shurtleff, C. Michael *writer*
†Smith, Pamela Jaye *writer, producer, consultant*

Idyllwild
Schneider, Paul *writer*

Irvine
Brueske, Charlotte *poet, composer*
†Doan, Patrick Toai Van *writer, foundation administrator*
Shusterman, Neal Douglas *author, screenwriter*
Wolff, Geoffrey Ansell *novelist, critic, educator*

Kensington
Littlejohn, David *writer*

La Jolla
Antin, David *poet, critic*
Havis, Allan Stuart *playwright, theatre educator*
†Howe, Fanny Quincy *poet*

Lafayette
James, Muriel Marshall *author, psychotherapist*

Laguna Beach
Ghiselin, Brewster *author, English language educator emeritus*
Taylor, Theodore Langhans *author*

Laguna Niguel
Malott, John Raymond *writer, consultant*

Landers
Landers, Vernette Trosper *writer, educator, association executive*

Lodi
Schulz, Laura Janet *writer, retired secretary*

Long Beach
Dawson, Frances Emily *poet, nurse*

Los Alamitos
†Burke, Jan Helene *author*

Los Altos Hills
Cameron, Eleanor Cranston Fowle *author*

Los Angeles
Basil, Douglas Constantine *author, educator*
Bayless, Raymond Gordon *writer, artist, parapsychologist*
†Callaghan, Sheila *playwright, graphic designer*
Carlip, Hillary *author, screenwriter*
Carothers, A. J. *scriptwriter*
Cecchetti, Giovanni *poet, educator, literary critic*
Cohen, Leonard (Norman Cohen) *poet, novelist, musician, songwriter*
†Espey, John Jenkins *writer, English educator*
Fraser, Brad *playwright, theatrical director, screenwriter*
Good-Black, Edith Elissa (Pearl Williams) *writer*
†Gray, Ryan Christopher *writer, editor, graphic artist*
Highwater, Jamake *author, lecturer*
Hotz, Robert Lee *science writer, editor*
Jones, Janet Dulin *writer, film producer*
Kaplan, Nadia *writer*
Lettich, Sheldon Bernard *director, screenwriter*
Maker, Janet Anne *author, lecturer*
Mooser, Stephen *author*
Myers, Katherine Donna *writer, publisher*
Noguchi, Thomas Tsunetomi *author, forensic pathologist*
Raphael, Frederic Michael *author*
Rector, Margaret Hayden *writer*
Robert, Patrick *playwright*
Rubin, Bruce Joel *screenwriter, director, producer*
Russell, Pamela Redford *writer, film documentarian*
Schulberg, Budd *author*
Shapiro, Mel *playwright, director, drama educator*
Silverman, Treva *writer, producer, consultant*
Steel, Ronald Lewis *author, historian, educator*
Steinbrecher, Edwin Charles *writer, association director, film producer, astrologer*
†Vangelisti, Paul Louis *poet*
Weiser, Stanley *screenwriter*
Westheimer, David Kaplan *novelist*
†Williamson, Kevin *writer, producer, director*
Yoshiki-Kovinick, Marian Tsugie *author*

Los Gatos
Dahlberg, Thomas Robert *author, attorney, educator, software company executive*

Malibu
†Collings, Michael Robert *poet, educator*

Menlo Park
Dorset, Phyllis Flanders *technical writer, editor*

Monterey
von Drachenfels, Suzanne Hamilton *writer*

Moraga
Sestanovich, Molly Brown *writer*

Moreno Valley
†Brown, Frederick Courtney *writer*
Wilson, Robert Michael Alan *writer*

Napa
†Dow, Philip Donovan *poet, educator*
Wycoff, Charles Coleman *writer, retired anesthesiologist*

Newport Beach
Dovring, Karin Elsa Ingeborg *author, poet, playwright, communication analyst*
Wentworth, Diana von Welanetz *author*

Oakland
Bowman, Alison Frances *writer*
Cushman, Karen Lipski *writer*
Foley, Jack (John Wayne Harold Foley) *poet, writer, editor*
Narell, Irena *freelance writer, history educator*
Schacht, Henry Mevis *writer, consultant*
Silverberg, Robert *author*
Solomon, Norman *author, columnist*

Oceanside
Humphrey, Phyllis A. *writer*

PROFESSIONAL INDEX 5799 ARTS: LITERARY

Ojai
Weyl, Nathaniel *writer*

Orange
Lindskoog, Kathryn Ann *writer, educator*

Orinda
Berens, E. Ann *writer, mental health and youth advocate*

Pacific Grove
Fleischman, Paul *children's author*

Pacific Palisades
†Kirkgaard, Valerie Anne *writer, producer, consultant*
McGinn, James Thomas *writer, producer*

Palm Desert
Ryan, Allyn Cauagas *author, educator*

Palm Springs
Jamison, Warren *writer, lecturer, publisher*
Minahan, John English *author*

Palmdale
Hummer-Sharpe, Elizabeth Anastasia *genealogist, writer*

Palo Alto
†Briskin, Mae *writer*

Palomar Mountain
Day, Richard Somers *author, editorial consultant*

Palos Verdes Estates
Friesz, Mary Lee *poet, self-employed*

Pasadena
Arrieta, Marcia *poet, editor, publishing executive, educator*
Butler, Octavia Estelle *free-lance writer*
Holbrook, Sally Davis *author*

Penngrove
Chadwick, Cydney Marie *writer, art projects executive*

Petaluma
†Hass, Robert L. *writer, educator*
Hill, Debora Elizabeth *author, journalist, screenwriter*
†Knight, Kit Marie *poet, writer, movie critic*
Pronzini, Bill John (William Pronzini) *author*

Rancho Mirage
Olderman, Murray *columnist, cartoonist*

Rancho Santa Fe
Simon, William Leonard *film and television writer and producer, author*
Sommer-Bodenburg, Angela *author, artist*

Redondo Beach
Battles, Roxy Edith *novelist, consultant, educator*
Moretti, Constance Walton *author, genealogist*

Redwood City
Shoemaker, Dorothy Hays *technical writer*

Reedley
Carey, Ernestine Gilbreth (Mrs. Charles E. Carey) *writer, lecturer*

Rohnert Park
Haslam, Gerald William *writer, educator*

Roseville
Witt, Denise Marcia *writer, public relations specialist*

Sacramento
†Stenzel, Larry Gene *writer*
Tranum, Jean Lorraine *freelance writer*

San Anselmo
Torbet, Laura *author, artist, photographer, graphic designer*

San Carlos
Morrison, Ellen M. *writer, researcher*
†Torregian, Sotère *poet*

San Diego
Crumpler, Hugh Allan *author*
Koski, Donna Faith *poet*
Krull, Kathleen *juvenile fiction and nonfiction writer*
Lederer, Richard Henry *writer, educator, columnist*
†Lindbergh, Anne Spencer Morrow (Mrs. Charles Augustus Lindbergh) *author*
Linn, Edward Allen *writer*
March, Marion D. *writer, astrologer, consultant*
†Martén, Roger Evan *screenwriter*
Prescott, Lawrence Malcolm *medical and health science writer*
Sauer, David Andrew *writer, computer consultant*
Skwara, Erich Wolfgang *novelist, poet, educator, literary critic*
Smith, Stuart Craig *television and corporate writer and producer*
Stein, Eleanor Benson (Ellie Stein) *playwright*
Stewart-Pérez, Renice Ann *writer*
Yarber, Robert Earl *writer, retired educator*

San Francisco
Allen, Bruce John *writer, activist*
†Barayon, Ramon Sender *writer*
†Carlisle, Henry C. *author*
Chadwick, Whitney *writer, art historian, educator*
Corkery, Paul Jerome *author, editor*
Cousineau, Philip Robert *writer, filmmaker*
†Dillon, Millicent Gerson *writer*
Ferlinghetti, Lawrence *poet*
Graham, Toni *writer*
Gunn, Thom(son) (William) *poet*
†Hiemstra, Marvin Roy *poet, humorist, literary consultant*
†Kazalia, Marie Ann *writer*
Lai, Him Mark *writer*
Lau, Elizabeth Kwok-Wah *writer*
Lippitt, Elizabeth Charlotte *writer*
Lustgarten, Celia Sophie *freelance consultant, writer*
Montney, Marvin Richard *writer, poet, playwright*
O'Connor, Sheila Anne *freelance writer*
Pantaleo, Jack *writer, composer, social worker, harpist*
Paul, Don *writer, musician*
Quick, William Thomas *author, screenwriter*
Sachs, Marilyn Stickle *author, lecturer, editor*
†Taylor, (Paul) Kent *poet, medical researcher*
Taylor, Sabrena Ann *author, visual artist*
Whalen, Philip Glenn *poet, novelist*
†Winans, Allan Davis *poet, private investigator*

San Jose
Loventhal, Milton *writer, playwright, lyricist*

San Juan Capistrano
Kleiner, Richard Arthur *writer, editor*

San Luis Obispo
Bunge, Russell Kenneth *writer, poet, editor*
Sachs, Robert Michael *author*

San Luis Rey
Williams, Elizabeth Yahn *author, lecturer, lawyer*

San Rafael
Henry, Marie Elaine *poet*

Santa Barbara
Bock, Russell Samuel *author*
Cunningham, Julia Woolfolk *author*
Davidson, Eugene Arthur *author*
†Mitchell, Shawne Maureen *author*
Smith, Michael Townsend *author, editor, stage director*

Santa Clara
Simmons, Janet Bryant *writer, publisher*

Santa Cruz
†Houston, James D. *writer*
Sherman, Frieda Frances *writer*
†Yamashita, Karen Tei *writer*

Santa Monica
Courtney, Mary E. *writer, editor*
Launer, Dale Mark *screenwriter*
Mora, Philippe *screenwriter, producer, director, painter*

Santa Rosa
†Coleman, Wanda *poet, writer*
Gioia, (Michael) Dana *poet, literary critic*

Sausalito
†Hyde, Catherine Ryan *novelist, short story writer*

Sebastopol
Arnold, Marsha Diane *writer*
Kherdian, David *author*

Sherman Oaks
Ellison, Harlan Jay *author, screenwriter*
MacMullen, Douglas Burgoyne *writer, editor, retired army officer, publisher*
†Sonders, Scott Aleksander *writer, educator*

Sonoma
Jayme, William North *writer*
Kizer, Carolyn Ashley *poet, educator*

Soquel
Murray, Barbara Olivia *writer, retired psychologist*

South Pasadena
White, W. Robin *author*

Stanford
Berger, Joseph *author, educator, counselor*
Conquest, (George) Robert (Acworth) *writer, historian, poet, critic, journalist*
Gardner, John William *writer, educator*
Girard, René Noel *author, educator*
Steele, Shelby *writer, educator*
Wolff, Tobias (Jonathan Ansell Wolff) *author*

Studio City
Nelson, Anna Masterton *writer, digital effects artist*
Parish, James Robert *author, cinema historian*
Shavelson, Melville *writer, theatrical producer and director*
Whitney, Steven *writer, producer*

Sun Valley
Casey, Paul Arnold *writer, composer, photographer*

Templeton
Shahan, Sherry Jean *author, educator*

Venice
Eliot, Alexander *author, mythologist*
Padilla, Mario René *literature educator, writer, actor*
Seger, Linda Sue *script consultant, lecturer, writer*

West Hollywood
Grasshoff, Alex *writer, producer, director*
Thaw, Mort *writer*

Whittier
Caro, Evelyn Inga Rouse *writer*

Windsor
†Drake, Glendon Frank *writer*

COLORADO

Boulder
Boggs, Marcus Livingstone, Jr. *publisher, novelist, editor*
†Hurd, Jerrie *writer*
Martinez, Jose Rafael *writer, educator, poet*
Moore, George Barnard *poet, educator*
Waldman, Anne Lesley *poet, performer, editor, publisher, educational administrator*
†Wilmarth, Richard *poet*

Colorado Springs
Ball, Jennifer Leigh *writer, editor*
Dassanowsky, Robert von *writer, editor, educator, producer*
Leasure, Robert Ellis *writer, photographer*
Rhodes, Daisy Chun *writer, researcher, oral historian*
Whalin, W. Terry *author, editor*
Yaffe, James *author*

Commerce City
Hanson, Edward Alvin *technical writer*

Conifer
Kalla, Alec Karl *writer, rancher*

Denver
Carlson, Robert Ernest *freelance writer, architect, lecturer*
Ducker, Bruce *novelist, lawyer*
Grossman, Arnold Joseph *writer, producer*
MacGregor, George Lescher, Jr. *freelance writer*
Nemiro, Beverly Mirium Anderson *author, educator*
Osborn, Susan Chaney *educator, writer*
Sheldon Epstein, Vivian *author, publisher*

Durango
Korns, Leota Elsie *writer, mountain land developer, insurance broker*

Englewood
†Irwin, Mark *writer, educator*

Golden
†Dubois, Jean Hall *writer*
Eber, Kevin *science writer*

Grand Junction
Armstrong, Linda Jean (Gene) *writer, artist*

Greeley
Willis, Connie (Constance E. Willis) *author*

Littleton
Norman, Marcia Macy *writer, realtor*

Lyons
†Spring, Kathleen *writer*

Twin Lakes
†Zadeh, Firooz E. *author, real estate developer*

Vail
Knight, Constance Bracken *writer, realtor, corporate executive*

CONNECTICUT

Bethany
†Weber, Katharine *writer*

Darien
Hailey, Arthur *author*
Look, Alice *writer, producer, journalist*

East Hampton
Tucceri, Clive Knowles *science writer and educator, consultant*

Easton
Maloney, John Joseph *writer*

Fairfield
Barone, Rose Marie Pace *writer, retired educator, entertainer*

Greens Farms
St. Marie, Satenig *writer*

Greenwich
Ewald, William Bragg, Jr. *author, consultant*
Hoberman, Mary Ann *author*
Wallach, Magdalena Falkenberg (Carla Wallach) *writer*

Guilford
Peters, William *author, producer, director*

Hanover
Cheney, Glenn Alan *writer, educator*

Hartford
Hedrick, Joan Doran *writer*
†Schweitzer, N. Tina *fiction writer, photojournalist, television producer, director, international consultant public relations, media relations, government relations*

Madison
Carlson, Dale Bick *writer*

New Canaan
Prescott, Peter Sherwin *writer*

New Haven
Gallup, Donald Clifford *bibliographer, educator*
Hayden, Dolores *author, architect, educator*
†Johnson, Brian Curtis *poet, educator*
†Laughlin, Charles Andrew *literature educator*
†Reed, Janine Regale *freelance writer, English composition and language educator*
Scarf, Margaret (Maggie Scarf) *author*

Niantic
†Mountzoures, Harry Louis *writer*

Old Lyme
St. George, Judith Alexander *author*

Preston
Gibson, Margaret Ferguson *poet, educator*

Roxbury
Gurney, Albert Ramsdell *playwright, novelist, educator*

Stamford
†Herlands, E. Ward *poet, printmaker*

Storrs Mansfield
Rimland, Lisa Phillip *writer, composer, lyricist, artist*

Stratford
Walker, Gladys Lorraine *author*

Suffield
Tobin, Joan Adele *writer, scholar*

Waterbury
†Adamski, Richard Franklyn *writer, mental health consultant, technical theatre assistant*

Waterford
Commire, Anne *playwright, writer, editor*

West Cornwall
Klaw, Spencer *writer, editor, educator*

Weston
Diforio, Robert George *literary agent*
Kilty, Jerome Timothy *playwright, stage director, actor*

Westport
Hotchner, Aaron Edward *author*
†Klein, Woody *writer, editor, educator*
Martin, Ralph Guy *writer*

Wilton
Van Riper, Robert Austin *writer, retired public relations executive*

DELAWARE

Bridgeville
Burns, Vicki Lynn *writer, poet*

Frederica
Schulz, David A. *author*

Wilmington
Michel, Sandra Seaton *writer*
Ziolkowska-Boehm, Aleksandra *writer*

DISTRICT OF COLUMBIA

Washington
Alperovitz, Gar *author, educator*
Arndt, Richard Tallmadge *writer, consultant*
Atlas, Liane Wiener *writer*
Barnet, Richard Jackson *author, educator*
Birnbaum, Norman *author, humanities educator*
Burnham, David Bright *writer, educator*
Burns, David Mitchell *writer, musician, former diplomat*
Carter, Yvonne Johnson *writer, editor, English educator*
Childs, Timothy Winston *writer*
Cox, Eric Frederick *writer, book reviewer*
Friedan, Betty *author, feminist leader*
Furgurson, Ernest Baker, Jr. (Pat Furgurson) *writer*
Goldberg, Kirsten Boyd *science journalist*
Gorlin, Rena Ann *writer*
Hecht, Anthony Evan *poet*
Lilienthal, Alfred M(orton) *author, historian, editor*
†Long, Nancy *writer, lawyer*
MacLeish, Roderick *novelist, screenwriter, television producer*
May, Stephen *writer, former government official*
McCarthy, Abigail Quigley *writer, columnist, educator*
Ramsay, William Charles *writer*
Sattler, Stephen Charles *writer, editor, communications consultant*
Shaw, Russell Burnham *author, journalist*
Smith, Stuart Seaborne *writer, government official, union official*
Tannen, Deborah Frances *writer, linguist*
Taquey, Charles Henri *writer, consultant*
†Veronese, David *author*
Violante, Patricia *translator, speechwriter, interpreter*
†Wilkinson, Quintin Stanley *poet, speaker*
†Williams, Leaford Clemetson *writer, political scientist*
Wouk, Herman *writer*
Zelnick, Carl Robert *writer, educator*
Zietz, Karyl Lynn Kopelman *writer, opera critic, television correspondent, producer, documentary filmmaker*

FLORIDA

Babson Park
Morrison, Kenneth Douglas *author, columnist*

Belleair
Imparato, Edward Thomas *writer*

Big Pine Key
Cooper, John Charles *writer, educator*

Boca Raton
Doyle-Kimball, Mary *freelance writer, editor*
Keyes, Daniel *author*

Bokeelia
†Hausman, Gerald Andrews *writer*

Boynton Beach
Heckelmann, Charles Newman (Charles Lawton) *author, publishing consultant*

Cape Canaveral
†Albright, Judith Anne *writer*

Carrabelle
Campbell, Thomas Emory *author, researcher*

Citrus Springs
Tillery, Billy Carey writer, poet

Clearwater
Flagg, Helen Clawson writer

Coral Gables
†Balaban, John poet, educator in English, translator

Daytona Beach
Chesnut, Nondis Lorine screenwriter, consultant, reading and language arts educator
Mc Collister, John Charles writer, clergyman, educator, executive producer

Deland
Becker, Herbert Lawrence writer, accountant

Delray Beach
Burbank, Kershaw writer
Robinson, Richard Francis writer, author

Eustis
Chorosinski, Eugene Conrad writer, poet, author

Fort Lauderdale
Groshart, Caroline King technical writer, editor
Nash, James Lee poet, security official

Fort Myers
Hartman, Earl Kenneth writer
Powell, Richard Pitts writer

Gainesville
Smith, Jo Anne writer, retired educator

Hallandale
Geller, Bunny Zelda poet, writer, publisher, sculptor, artist

Highland Beach
†Tolf, Robert Walter writer

Hilliard
Nelson, Tommy Leon poet

Homosassa Springs
Burch, Annetta Jane writer

Indialantic
Lewis, Richard Stanley author, former editor

Islamorada
†Whyatt, Frances (Shylah Boyd) poet, novelist

Jacksonville
Moses, Daniel writer, singer

Lake Worth
Phipard, Nancy Midwood retired educator, writer

Lakeland
Niswonger, Jeanne Du Chateau author, biologist

Longboat Key
Hazan, Marcella Maddalena author, educator, consultant

Lynn Haven
Leonard, Venelda Hall writer

Maitland
Waltley, Douglas Dale writer

Melbourne
Lederer, William Julius author
†Schaaf, Martha Eckert author, poet, library director, musician, composer, educator, lecturer
Stone, Elaine Murray author, composer, television producer

Miami
Camner, Howard author, poet
McLaughlin, Margaret Brown educator, writer
Morgan, Marabel author
†Whitehead, John poet

Miami Beach
Gottlieb, Karla Lewis writer, college official

Mount Dora
Hart, Valerie Gail writer

Naples
Alpert, Hollis writer
Capelle-Frank, Jacqueline Aimee writer
Card, Orson Scott (Byron Walley) writer
Thompson, Didi Castle (Mary Bennett) writer, editor

New Smyrna Beach
Hauser, Sara Nooney writer, educator

Nokomis
Wendt, Lloyd writer

Oldsmar
Craft Davis, Audrey Ellen writer, educator

Orange Park
Goss, William Allan author, speaker

Orlando
Blum, Richard Arthur writer, media educator
Comfort, Iris Tracy writer
†Hubbard, Susan Mary writer, English educator
Raffa, Jean Benedict author, educator

Palm Beach
DiMartino, Christina writer

Palm Beach Gardens
Klein, Gail Beth Marantz freelance writer, dog breeder

Pensacola
Klepper, Robert Kenneth writer, silent film historian, journalist
Sargent, James O'Connor freelance writer

Port Saint Lucie
Jackson, George Mark writer, photographer

Punta Gorda
Wolff, Diane Patricia author, journalist, producer

Saint Augustine
Nolan, David Joseph author, historian

Saint Petersburg
Edwards, Fred L., Jr. writer, consultant
Oman, Robert Milton writer, consultant, educator
Wright, Fred W., Jr. writer

Sanibel
Walton, Chelle Koster travel writer

Sarasota
Jones, Sally Daviess Pickrell writer
Weeks, Albert Loren author, educator, journalist
Westcott, Joan Clark poet

South Bay
Oeffner, Barbara Dunning biographer, educator, screenwriter

Tallahassee
McCrimmon, Barbara Smith writer, librarian
Scott, Brenda D. writer
Sittig, Dennis Wayne poet, paper hanger
Tourtet, Christiane Andrée writer, artistic photographer, poetess

Tampa
Able, James Augustus, Jr. writer
Battle, Jean Allen writer, educator
Hanford, Grail Stevenson writer
†Thompson, Sandra Jean writer, editor

Tequesta
†Ragno, Nancy Nickell educational writer

Venice
Shaw, Bryce Robert author
Thomas, Terence Patrick writer, researcher, electronics design engineer

West Palm Beach
†Susman, Edward S. freelance writer

Winter Haven
†Bybee, Charles Forrest writer, poet

Winter Park
Hill, Elizabeth Starr writer

GEORGIA

Atlanta
Austin, Judy Essary scriptwriter
Calabria, Deb Flanagan playwright, director
Chapman, Paul H. author
Dunn, John Clinton writer, editor, organization executive
†Fehsenfeld, Martha Dow writer, editor
†Gates, Jeff writer
Knight, Deidre Elise Mosteller literary agent
Moore, Philip Nicholas author
Schwarz, Patrick Joseph screenwriter

Augusta
†Flythe, Starkey Sharp writer

Ellenwood
Walker, F. Darlene writer, researcher

Lizella
†Jones, Seaborn Gustavus poet

Savannah
Coffey, Thomas Francis, Jr. writer
Thomas, Dwight Rembert writer

Statesboro
Ragans, Rosalind Dorothy textbook author, retired art educator

Sugar Hill
Draughon, Deborah writer

Thomson
Wilson, Donna Owen author, artist

HAWAII

Honolulu
Arbeit, Wendy Sue researcher, writer
Halloran, Richard Colby writer, former research executive, former news correspondent
Statler, Oliver Hadley writer

Lanai City
Black, Anderson Duane writer, business consultant

Lihue
Stephens, Jack writer, photographer

IDAHO

Sun Valley
Briley, John Richard writer

Twin Falls
Fanselow, Julie Ruth writer

Wilder
Olsen, Helen May author

ILLINOIS

Abbott Park
Geist, Jill Marie medical writer

Arlington Heights
Griffin, Jean Latz writer, political strategist, small business owner

Buffalo Grove
Serbus, Pearl Sarah Dieck former freelance writer, former editor

Burbank
Juodvalkis, Egle writer

Carbondale
Williams, George Harvey author

Carlyle
Kottmeyer, Martin S. farmer, writer

Chicago
Brooks, Gwendolyn writer, poet
†Bruce, Debra M. poet, English language educator
Buehler, Evelyn Judy poet
†Calcagno, Anne writer, educator
Carpenter, Allan author, editor, publisher
†Crane, R.H. poet, editor
Ferguson, Margaret Geneva author, publisher, real estate broker
Fremon, David Kent writer, consultant
Hoover, Paul poet
Lach, Alma Elizabeth food and cooking writer, consultant
Littman, Margaret Rachel writer, magazine
Litweiler, John Berkey writer, editor
Madsen, Dorothy Louise (Meg Madsen) writer
Manelli, Donald Dean screenwriter, film producer
†Markus, Vasyl author, editor
†McManus, James Laughlin writer, educator
Muller, Leon writer
Nims, John Frederick writer, educator
†Perlberg, Mark poet, educator
†Schultz, John L. writer, educator
Stern, Richard Gustave author, educator
†Terkel, Studs (Louis Terkel) author, interviewer
Vita, Steven Edward poet
Vladem, Steven Allen author, motivational speaker
Wallingford, Anne writer, editor, project developer
Wisenberg, Sandra Leah writer

Crete
Scott, Whitney writer

Crystal Lake
Fleming, Marjorie Foster freelance writer, artist

Dekalb
†Stryk, Lucien Henry writer

Elmwood Park
Fiore, Mercia V. author

Evanston
Gibbons, William Reginald, Jr. poet, novelist, translator, editor

Fox River Grove
Kenzle, Linda Fry writer, artist

Galesburg
Litvin, Martin Jay author, lecturer

Glencoe
Glink, Ilyce Renée writer, publishing executive

Highland Park
Greenblatt, Miriam author, editor, educator

Homewood
†Heron, Frances Dunlap author, educator

Lake Forest
Swanton, Virginia Lee author, publisher, bookseller

Mchenry
Kenyon, Patricia Mae poet

Murphysboro
Millar, Barbara Lee technical writer, school administrator

Naperville
Schanstra, Carla Ross technical writer

North Riverside
Sedlak, S(hirley) A(gnes) freelance writer

Oak Brook
Kostrubala, Mark Anthony writer

Palatine
Crawford, Annmarie writer, model, actress, photographer
Pohl, Frederik writer

Paris
Sisson, Marilyn Sue writer

Peru
Kurtz, James Eugene freelance writer, minister

Rockford
Kelleghan, Kevin Michael writer, trainer

Round Lake
Anderson, Ruth Nathan syndicated columnist, TV news host, writer, recording artist, lyricist

Saint Charles
Dowd, James Patrick bookseller, writer

Savoy
Nelson, Clarence R. writer

Skokie
Gershon, William I. copywriter, voiceover actor, communications executive

South Barrington
Kissane, Sharon Florence writer, consultant, educator

Springfield
Jackson, Jacqueline Dougan educator, author

Stockton
†Anderson, Leone Marie Castell children's book author

Stoy
Rhoten, Kenneth D. writer

Urbana
Hale, Allean Lemmon writer, educator
Lieberman, Laurence poet, educator
Malone, Paul Scott writer, artist

Wheaton
Williams, Susan DeVore writer

Willowbrook
†McCormack, Emily Anna writer

Wilmette
Brill, Marlene Targ writer

INDIANA

Bloomington
Kibbey, Hal Stephen science writer
†Miller, Alyce fiction writer, educator
Mitchell, Bert Breon literary translator
Pfingston, Roger Carl writer photographer, retired educator
†Volkova, Bronislava poet, scholar

Chesterton
†Calengas, Leonardo writer
Petrakis, Harry Mark author

Crown Point
Palmeri, Sharon Elizabeth freelance writer, community educator

Fort Wayne
†Frost, Helen Marie writer
Gaff, Alan Dale writer
Lair, Helen May poet

Frankfort
Borland, Kathryn Kilby author

Howe
Bowerman, Ann Louise author, genealogist, educator

Indianapolis
Altman, Joseph author, neuroscientist
Budniakiewicz, Therese author
Carter, Jared poet
Friman, Alice Ruth poet, English educator
Hoppe, David Rutledge writer
Horvath, Terri Lynn writer, publishing company executive
†Quinn, Fran poet
Wilson, Margaret L. author, speaker
Wise, Rita J. writer, poet

Merrillville
†Birch-Vujovic, Judith Lee writer, lecturer, educator

Monticello
†Berry, Michael John author, medical and dental management consultant

Muncie
Eddy, Darlene Mathis poet, educator

Notre Dame
Goulet, Denis André development ethicist, writer

South Bend
Kline, Syril Levin writer, columnist, reporter, educational consultant, commentator, theatre critic

West Lafayette
†Smith, Robert Edward, Jr. communication educator, writer

IOWA

Ames
King, Michael Pearson writer, English educator
Smiley, Jane Graves author, educator

Cedar Falls
Clift, G.W. critic

Cedar Rapids
†McElmeel, Sharron Leila Hanson author, editor
Struthers, Eleanor Ann writer, educator

Charles City
†Krieger, Theodore Kent poet

Clinton
Warner, Jean Lollich poet

Dubuque
Gifford, Thomas Eugene writer

Fort Dodge
Wolf, Robert Charles writer, news correspondent

Iowa City
Bell, Marvin Hartley poet, English language educator
Graham, Jorie author
Johnson, Nicholas writer, lawyer, lecturer

Justice, Donald Rodney *poet, educator*
Stein, Robert A. *writer, educator*
Stern, Gerald Daniel *poet*

Muscatine
Collins, Max Allan *writer*

Waverly
Kampfe, Doris Elaine *storyteller, folk artist, poet*

West Des Moines
Hallagin, Janet Elaine *consultant, writer, editor*

KANSAS

Cherryvale
Wood, Ruby Fern *writer, retired elementary educator*

Galena
Heistand, Anita May *writer*

Kansas City
Sharpe, Bobbie Mahon *author*

Manhattan
Davis, Kenneth Sidney *writer*

Olathe
Kamberg, Mary-Lane *writer, journalist*

Pittsburg
Beer, Pamela Jill Porr *writer, retired vocational school educator*
Washburn, Laura Lee *poet, English literature and writing educator*

Shawnee Mission
Leifer, Loring *writer, information designer*
†Townley, Roderick Carl *writer*
Warren, Andrea Jean *writer*

Stilwell
Ledgin, Norman Michael *writer*

Wichita
†Dings, Fred *poet*

Winfield
Hartzell, John Mason *poet, service technician*

KENTUCKY

Campbellsburg
Mitchell, Mary Ann Carrico *poet*

Cumberland
†Collins, Jenny Galloway *poet, disc jockey, radio talk show host*

Frankfort
†Ellis, Normandi *writer*

Greenup
†Stuart, Jessica Jane *writer, poet*

Highland Heights
Maines, Leah *writer, business school director*

Lancaster
Hatton, Brenda Shirley (Linda Wellington) *writer, poet, songwriter*
Sea, Sherry Lynn *poet*

Lexington
Breckinridge, Scott Dudley, Jr. *author, government executive*
Johnson, Jane Penelope *freelance writer*
†Johnson, Paul Brett *writer, illustrator*

Louisville
Davenport, Gwen (Mrs. John Davenport) *author*
Morton, R. Meir *writer, editor*

Madisonville
May, Richard Warren *writer, consultant, inventor*

Middletown
†O'Dell, Mary Ernestine *poet, editor*

Morehead
†Bailey, Rebecca L. *writer*

Paducah
Milford, Judy Gill *author, poet*

LOUISIANA

Baton Rouge
Lee, Jean Clarisse *writer*
Madden, David *author*

Benton
†Charity, Nadine Ament *educator, poet*

Independence
Camp, Cynthia M. *writer, consultant*

Lake Charles
Butler, Robert Olen *writer, educator*

Metairie
Reinike, Irma *writer, artist, poet*

New Orleans
Friedmann, Patricia Ann *writer*
Grau, Shirley Ann (Mrs. James Kern Feibleman) *writer*
†McFerren, Martha Dean *writer, librarian*
Sexton, James Richard *author, photographer*

Shreveport
Williams, Patsy Ruth *poet*

MAINE

Bangor
Goss, Georgia Bulman *translator*
King, Stephen Edwin *novelist, screenwriter, director*

Belfast
Aaron, Hugh *writer*

Blue Hill
Taylor, Samuel A. *playwright*

Brooklin
Yglesias, Helen Bassine *author, educator*

Cushing
Taylor, Roger Conant *writer*

Farmington
Mueller, Lisel *writer, poet*

Hollowell
†Wormser, Baron Chesley *writer, educator*

Milbridge
Enslin, Theodore Vernon *poet*

Orono
Wilson, Dorothy Clarke *author*

Portland
Morgan, Robin Evonne *poet, author, journalist, activist, editor*
†Sholl, Betsy *poet, English educator*
Weir, Anne *writer*

Scarborough
†Begert, Jerome Francis *writer*

South Berwick
Carroll, Gladys Hasty *author*

Union
†Perrin, Arnold Strong *writer, editor*

MARYLAND

Aberdeen Proving Ground
Gibson, Annemarie *writer, editor*

Abingdon
Hosmer, Philip *writer, communications professional*

Adelphi
Mitchum, Cassandra *poet, writer*

Annapolis
Timperlake, Edward Thomas *writer*

Baltimore
Barth, John Simmons *writer, educator*
Brace, Margaret Denise *writer*
Eisenberg, Gerson G. *author, historian*
Epstein, Daniel Mark *poet, dramatist*
Fisher, Alan Hall *guidebook writer*
†Hayes, John M. *writer, sculptor, photographer*
Livingstone, Harrison Edward *writer, publisher*
†McGuiness, Ilona Maria *writing educator*
Purpura, Lia Rachel *poet, educator*
Tyler, Anne (Mrs. Taghi M. Modarressi) *author*

Bethesda
Dyer, Frederick Charles *writer, consultant*
Hartmann, Robert Trowbridge *author, consultant*
†Jennings, Lane Eaton *futurist writer, editor, translator*
Naylor, Phyllis Reynolds *author*
Simonds, Peggy Muñoz *writer, lecturer, retired literature educator*
Wimmel, Kenneth Carl *writer*

Burtonsville
Peck, Carol Faulkner *poet, writer, publisher, educator*

Chevy Chase
Bacon, Donald Conrad *author, editor*
Cron, Theodore Oscar *writer, editor, educator*
Krist, Gary Michael *writer*
Rosenbaum, Alvin Robert *writer, regional planner*

College Park
†Berlinski, Edward Gerard *writing educator, writer*
George, Gerald William *author, administrator*
Whittemore, Edward Reed, II *poet, retired educator*
Winton, Calhoun *literature educator*

Columbia
†Arnold, Karen L. *writer, consultant*

Dowell
Reeves, Connie Lynn *writer, retired army officer*

Fort Washington
Cameron, Rita Giovannetti *writer, publisher*

Garrett Park
Kornberg, Warren Stanley *science journalist*

Germantown
†Taylor, Douglas Howard *translator*
Weiner, Claire Muriel *freelance writer*

Mitchellville
Spieth, Martha Maxwell *writer*

Pasadena
Yelton, Robert Foster *playwright, poet*

Port Deposit
McMullen, Stanley Levon *author, composer*

Potomac
†Derricotte, Toi *poet, educator*
Kessler, Ronald Borek *author*
Pastan, Linda Olenik *poet*
Sowalsky, Patti Lurie *author*
Wartofsky, William Victor *writer*

Rockville
Madle, Robert Albert *writer*
McQuain, Jeffrey Hunter *writer, researcher*
Taube, Herman *author, educator*

Salisbury
Booker, Betty Mae *poet*

Severna Park
Davis, Clayton *writer, pilot*

Silver Spring
Ognibene, Peter John *writer*
Whitten, Leslie Hunter, Jr. *author, newspaper reporter, poet*

Williamsport
Hessler, Douglas Scott *screenwriter*

MASSACHUSETTS

Amherst
Bagg, Robert Ely *poet*
Jenkins, Paul Randall *poet, editor*
Lester, Julius B. *author*
Sandweiss, Martha A. *author, American studies and history educator*
Tate, James Vincent *poet, English educator*
Watson, Ellen Doré *poet, translator*

Andover
†Harrison, Jeffrey Woods *poet, educator*

Arlington
†Carver, Jeffrey A. *writer*

Barre
†Sullivan, James Edward *poet*

Bedford
Wind, Herbert Warren *writer*

Belmont
Cavarnos, Constantine Peter *writer, philosopher*
†Moore, Richard Thomas *writer, poet*

Boston
Andre, Rae *writer, organizational behavior educator*
Angelou, Maya *author*
Carroll, James *author*
Davis, William Arthur *writer, editor*
Greenwald, Sheila Ellen *writer, illustrator*
†Leonard, James Patrick *writer, editor, communications consultant*
Lowry, Lois (Hammersberg) *author*
Melnyczuk, Askold *writer*
Pinsky, Robert Neal *poet, educator*
Pynchon, Thomas Ruggles, Jr. *author*
Say, Allen *children's writer, illustrator*
Sklar, Holly L. *nonfiction writer*
Terrill, Ross Gladwin *author, educator*
Van Allsburg, Chris *author, artist*
Warren, Rosanna *poet*
Wiesel, Elie *writer, educator*

Braintree
Piraino, Thomas *writer, retired electrical engineer*

Burlington
†Vlock, Deborah Michele *writer, public relations company executive*

Byfield
Kozol, Jonathan *writer*

Cambridge
Buderi, Robert Bryan Hassan *author, journalist*
Desai, Anita *writer*
Heaney, Seamus Justin *poet, educator*
Kaplan, Justin *author*
MacDonald, Sandy *writer*
†Moore, Christine Palamidessi *writer*
Roazen, Paul *writer*
†Sylvester, Janet *poet, educator*
†Tyler, Elizabeth Cowley *writer*
Yergin, Daniel Howard *writer, consultant*

Centerville
Whouley, Kate *book industry consultant, writer*

Chestnut Hill
Valette, Jean Paul *writer*

Concord
Moore, Robert Lowell, Jr. (Robin Moore) *author*

Cummington
Smith, William Jay *author*
Wilbur, Richard Purdy *writer, educator*

Dover
Smith, William Henry Preston *writer, editor, former corporate executive*

East Dennis
†Ely, David (David E. Lilienthal, Jr.) *writer*

Easthampton
†Aalfs, Janet Elizabeth *poet, writer, martial arts educator*

Everett
Wright, Franz Paul *poet, writer, translator*

Great Barrington
Drew, Bernard Alger *writer*

Hatfield
Yolen, Jane *author*

Ipswich
Hamilton, Donald Bengtsson *author*

Jamaica Plain
Lowenthal, Michael Francis *writer, editor*

Leominster
Cormier, Robert Edmund *writer*

Leverett
†Pearson, Gayle Marlene *writer, editor*

Lexington
Kennedy, X. J. (Joseph Kennedy) *writer*
Topalian, Naomi Getsoyan *writer*

Lincoln
Donald, David Herbert *author, history educator*
Langton, Jane Gillson *writer, illustrator*
Mitchell, John Hanson *writer, editor*

Medford
DiPietro, Francis *writer*

Melrose
†Bond, Harold H. *poet*

Natick
Sutcliffe, Marion Shea *writer*

Needham
Walworth, Arthur *author*

Newton
Tuscher, Vincent James *author*
Zohn, Harry *author, educator*

Newton Hlds
Porter, Jack Nusan *writer, sociologist, educator, political activist*

North Dartmouth
†Hoagland, Everett H. *poet, English educator*

Northampton
Blumenfeld, Warren Jay *writer, educator*
Bowman, John Stewart *writer, editor*
Kaplan, James Lamport *writer, editor, publisher*
†Newman, Lesléa *writer*

Orleans
Hughes, Libby *author*

Provincetown
Oliver, Mary *poet*

Revere
†Recupero-Faiella, Anna Antonietta *poet*

Shirley
Shull, Ira David *writer*

Somerville
†Auspitz, Josiah Lee *writer, foundation administrator*

South Hadley
†Leithauser, Brad Edward *writer*
Viereck, Peter *poet, historian, educator*

Swampscott
Must, Dennis Patrick *writer, editor*

Truro
†Burr, Gray *poet, educator*
Woolley, Catherine (Jane Thayer) *writer*

Waltham
Ellenbogen, George *poet, educator*

Watertown
†Brownsberger, Susan Campbell *translator*
Spivack, Kathleen Romola Drucker *writer, educator*

Wellesley
Jacobs, Ruth Harriet *poet, playwright, sociologist, gerontologist*

Wellfleet
Piercy, Marge *poet, novelist, essayist*
†Wood, Ira *novelist*

West Newbury
Dooley, Ann Elizabeth *freelance writers cooperative executive, editor*

Westford
Olsen, David Leslie *author, consultant*

Williamsburg
Cahillane, James Francis *writer*

Williamstown
Burns, Joan Simpson *writer, editor*
Scull, Christina *writer*

Worcester
†Merrill, Christopher Lyall *writer*
Unger, Donald Nathan Stone *writer, editor*
Vick, Susan *playwright, educator, director, actress*

Yarmouth Port
Gorey, Edward St. John *author, artist*

MICHIGAN

Adrian
Fields, Harriet Leona *writer*

Ann Arbor
†Balducci, Carolyn Feleppa *writer*

†Dunning, Stephen (Arthur S. Dunning, Jr.) *writer, consultant, retired English educator*
Fraser, Russell Alfred *author, educator*
Henkin, Joshua Herbert *novelist, educator*

Battle Creek
Cline, Charles William *poet, pianist, rhetoric and literature educator*
Myer, Donna Gail *writer, health researcher*

Climax
Soule, Maris Anne *writer*

Detroit
Madgett, Naomi Long *poet, editor, educator*
McWilliams, Michael G. *writer, television critic*
Simmons, John Franklin *writer*

East Lansing
Perrin, Robert *editorial consultant, writer*
Wakoski, Diane *poet, educator*

Farmington Hills
†Wiloch, Thomas *writer, editor*

Grand Rapids
Foster, Linda Nemec *poet, educator*
VanderVorst, Mitchell S. *writer*

Holland
Nieuwsma, Milton John *writer, journalist*

Idlewild
Wooley, Geraldine Hamilton *writer, poet*

Ironwood
Vanooyen, Amy Joy *writer*

Kalamazoo
Arnold Hubert, Nancy Kay *writer*
Light, Christopher Upjohn *writer, computer musician, photographer*

Lansing
Klunzinger, Thomas Edward *writer, actor, director, township treasurer*

Plymouth
Wroble, Lisa Ann *writer, educator*

Rochester
Kienzle, William Xavier *author*

Shepherd
Herman, Mark Norman *translator*

Sterling Heights
Wilson-Pleiness, Christine Joyce *writer, poet, columnist*

Traverse City
Abeel, Samantha Lynn *juvenile fiction author*

Troy
McElmeel, Christopher John *writer*

Union Pier
Howland, Bette *writer*

Ypsilanti
Staicar, Thomas Edward *writer*

MINNESOTA

Appleton
Wilson, Orpha Hildred *writer*

Austin
Mauch, Matthew Douglas *poet, educator*

Eden Prairie
†Reed, Cheryl Lynn *writer, journalist*

Edina
Schwarzrock, Shirley Pratt *author, lecturer, educator*

Minneapolis
Baker, John Stevenson (Michael Dyregrov) *writer*
Bly, Robert *poet*
Christensen, Nadia Margaret *writer, translator, editor, educator*
Dommel, Darlene Hurst *writer*
Kennedy, Adrienne Lita *playwright*
Korotkin, Fred *writer, philatelist*
Lange, Katherine J. *writer*
St. Germaine-Lattig, Charles Edwin *political writer*
Verby, Jane Crawford *writer*

Richfield
Thompson, Steve Allan *writer*

Rochester
Mosher, Anthony Eugene *poet*

Saint Louis Park
Ramsey, Robert D. *writer*

Saint Paul
†Galt, Margot Fortunato *writer*
Keillor, Garrison Edward *writer, radio host*
Lambert, LeClair Grier *writer, lecturer, consultant, state government public information administrator*

MISSISSIPPI

Greenville
Keating, Bern *writer, journalist*

Gulfport
†Williams, Benjamin John *poet, playwright*

Jackson
Welty, Eudora *author*

Mathiston
Maddox, Marilyn Coleman *literature and composition educator*

Oxford
†Fox, Elizabeth Talbert *writer, artist*

Taylorsville
Windham, Velma Lee Ainsworth *writer, poet*

MISSOURI

Alton
Roe, Fredrick Evan *writer, farmer*

Ballwin
Haller, Karen Sue *writer*

Bloomfield
Ferrell, Paul Cleveland *author*

Carthage
Blackwood, Gary Lyle *author*

Columbia
†Bumas, E. Shaskan *writer, educator*

Fulton
†Mosley, Mary Ann Krehbiel *freelance writer/editor, lobbyist*

Hollister
McCall, Edith Sansom *writer*

Joplin
West, Diana D. *freelance writer, social worker*

Kansas City
Martin-Bowen, Lindsey *freelance writer*
Otteson, Holly Carol Harvick-Ward *poet*
Roth, Lawrence Frederick, Jr. (Larry Roth) *writer*

Maplewood
Schmidt, Skip Francis *writer*

Maryville
†Trowbridge, William Leigh *writer*

Pierce City
†Hays, Otis Earl, Jr. *writer*

Saint Charles
Castro, Jan Garden *author, arts consultant, educator*

Saint Louis
Baker, Martha Kaye *writer, editor*
Broeg, Bob (Robert William Broeg) *writer*
†Burgin, Richard Weston *writer, educator, editor*
Corbett, Suzanne Elaine *food writer, marketing executive, food historian*
Early, Gerald *writer*
Finkel, Donald *poet*
Gass, William H. *author, educator*
Lutz, John Thomas *author*
Sage, Linda Catherine *science writer, public relations professional*
Schlafly, Phyllis Stewart *author*
†Wayne, Jane Oxenhandler (Jane O. Wayne) *poet, writing educator*

Springfield
Asher, Sandra Fenichel *author, playwright*

Sweet Springs
Long, Helen Halter *author, educator*

Viburnum
West, Roberta Bertha *writer*

MONTANA

Bozeman
Aig, Dennis Ira *writer, film producer*

Helena
Haines, John Meade *poet, translator, writer*

Livingston
Clarke, Urana *writer, musician, educator*

Mc Leod
Hjortsberg, William Reinhold *author*

NEBRASKA

Lincoln
Blankenau, Gail Shaffer *writer*
†King, Robert Wandell *writer*
Magorian, James *author, poet*

Murdock
Klemme, Minnie Dorothy *writer*

Omaha
Brown, Marion Marsh *author, educator*
Ress, Patricia Colleen *author, travel and transportation industry writer*

Superior
Christensen, Donna Martin *writer*

NEVADA

Deeth
Jordan, Teresa Marie *writer*

Las Vegas
Eikenberry, Arthur Raymond *writer, service executive, researcher*
Latimer, Heather *writer*

Miller, Bobby W. *author*
Palmer, Lynne *writer, astrologer*

Reno
Grady, Sean Michael *writer*
Scrimgeour, Gary James *writer, educator*
Stratton, Bruce Cornwall *writer, landscape photographer, publisher*

NEW HAMPSHIRE

Bradford
Hersh, Burton David *author*

Concord
Yates, Elizabeth (Mrs. William McGreal) *author, editor*

Durham
Ford, Daniel (Francis) *writer*

Jefferson
Leiper, Esther Mather *writer*

Meriden
Demarest, Chris Lynn *writer, illustrator*

Peterborough
Thomas, Elizabeth Marshall *writer*

Suncook
Weiss, Joanne Marion *writer*

Walpole
Gooding, Judson *writer*

NEW JERSEY

Andover
Gioseffi, (Dorothy) Daniela *poet, performer, author, educator, jazz singer*

Basking Ridge
Allen, Katherine Spicer *writer, former chemist*

Bergenfield
Knowles, John *author*

Cape May Court House
Cohen, Daniel Edward *writer*
Cohen, Susan Lois *author*

Cherry Hill
Ballas, Nadia S. *writer, poet*
Chambers, Michele Denise *technical writer*
Gardner, Joel Robert *writer, historian*

East Hanover
†Mogendovich-Lubin, Eugene Michael *scholar, writer*

Edison
Duffy, James Patrick *writer*
Neves, Paula *writer, editor*
Wexler, Annette Frances *writer*

Egg Harbor Township
Reed, Frances Boogher *writer, actress*

Elizabeth
Aronowitz, Alfred Gilbert *writer*
Willis, Ben *writer, artist*

Fair Haven
Derchin, Dary Bret Ingham *writer*

Florham Park
Gibson, William Ford *author*

Gillette
Nathanson, Linda Sue *publisher, author, technical writer*

Glen Ridge
Drexel, John Frederick *poet, writer, editor*

Hoboken
Paradise, Paul Richard *writer, editor*

Hopewell
Halpern, Daniel *poet, editor, educator*
Wesselmann, Debbie Lee *novelist, short story writer*

Howell
Lance, Steven *author*

Island Heights
Noble, William Parker *writer, educator*

Lake Hopatcong
Tomlinson, Gerald Arthur *writer, publisher, editor*

Lebanon
Barto, Susan Carol *writer*

Lincroft
†Cody, James Patrick *writing educator*

Madison
Perriman, Wendy Karen *poet, educator*

Manahawkin
†Aurner, Robert Ray *author, corporate executive*

New Brunswick
†Blumenthal, Eileen Flinder *writer, theater educator*
Cheiten, Marvin Harold *writer, hardware manufacturing company executive*
Ostriker, Alicia Suskin *poet*

Newark
Dickson, Jim *writer, producer*

Oakland
Smith, Miranda Constance *writer, educator*

Paramus
Fader, Shirley Sloan *writer*

Pennington
Kluger, Richard *author, editor*

Princeton
Komunyakaa, Yusef (James Willie Brown, Jr.) *poet*
Morrison, Toni (Chloe Anthony Morrison) *novelist*
Muldoon, Paul *creative writing educator, poet*
Vincent, Emily (Jean Mulvey Friedmann) *book reviewer*
Weiss, Theodore Russell *poet, editor*

Princeton Junction
Pollard-Gott, Lucy *writer*

Ringwood
Murphy, Gloria Walter *novelist, screenwriter*

Robbinsville
Norback, Craig Thomas *writer*

Sayreville
†Rapp, Lea Bayers *author, journalist, show business consultant*

Ship Bottom
Turkot, Dorothy Regester Felton *writer, illustrator*

Short Hills
Middleton, Timothy George *writer*

South Orange
Willis, Meredith Sue *writer, educator*

Stewartsville
Elman, Robert *writer, editor*

Teaneck
Rizio, Ronald Robert *writer, information specialist*

Union
Irwin, James Richard, Jr. *writer, editor*

Upper Montclair
Delgado, Ramon Louis *educator, author, director, playwright, lyricist*

West Orange
Kushen, Betty Sandra *writer, educator*
Rayfield, Gordon Elliott *playwright, political risk consultant*

Westfield
Devlin, Wende Dorothy *writer, artist*

NEW MEXICO

Albuquerque
Barnes, Donald Ray *writer, genealogical researcher*
†Colbert, James E. *writer, educator*
†Currey, Richard *writer*
Durant, Penny Lynne Raife *author, educator*
Gregory, George Ann *writer, Native American educator*
†Malone, Henry Charles *writer, rare book dealer*
Miller, Michael *literary arts researcher, writer*
Moore, Todd Allen *poet*

Corrales
Page, Jake (James K. Page, Jr.) *writer, editor*

Galisteo
Lippard, Lucy Rowland *writer, lecturer*

La Plata
Kent, Mollie *writer, publishing executive, editor*

Las Cruces
Medoff, Mark Howard *playwright, screenwriter, novelist*
†Nelson-Humphries, Tessa *writer, educator*

Placitas
Dunmire, William Werden *author, photographer*

Portales
Williamson, Jack (John Stewart) *writer*

Rio Rancho
†Belovarski, Borislav V. *scriptwriter, writer*

Roswell
Rosemire, Adeline Louise *writer, publisher*

Santa Fe
Bergé, Carol *author*
Berne, Stanley *author*
†Candelaria, Nash *writer*
Gallenkamp, Charles *writer*
Gildzen, Alex *writer*
Hanson, Cappy Love *writer, musician, singer, composer*
Lamb, Elizabeth Searle *freelance writer, poet*
†Noyes, Stanley Tinning *writer, educator, arts administrator*
Tarn, Nathaniel *poet, translator, educator*
Wood, Nancy C. *author*

Taos
Lackey, Marcia Ann *writer*

Tesuque
Gose, Celeste Marlene *writer*

Tijeras
Berry, Dawn Bradley *writer, lawyer*

NEW YORK

Accord
Rivera, Beatriz writer, educator

Acra
Gaffney, Kathleen Mary writer, videographer

Albany
Black, Robert Charles author, lawyer
First, Tina Lincer writer
Hill, Mars Andrew writer, retired civil engineer
Kennedy, William Joseph novelist, educator

Amherst
Kurtz, Paul publisher, philosopher, educator

Annandale On Hudson
Achebe, Chinua writer, humanities educator
Manea, Norman writer, educator

Ballston Spa
Barba, Harry author, educator, publisher

Barrytown
Higgins, Dick (Richard Carter Higgins) writer, publisher, composer, artist

Bedford Hills
Ludlum, Robert author

Bethpage
Evers, Gene writer

Briarcliff Manor
Hopkins, Lee Bennett writer, educator

Bronx
Bingham, June author, playwright
Fast, Julius author, editor
Porter, Spence playwright
Shapiro, David Joel poet, art critic, educator

Bronxville
†Solomon, Barbara Probst writer

Brooklyn
†Bordao, Rafael educator, writer, poet
Chernow, Ron writer, columnist
Courtice, Katie freelance writer and editor, office consultant
Cullen-DuPont, Kathryn writer
Harmon, Mary Carol writer
†Lerner, Linda poet, English educator
Levi, Louise Landes poet, translator, musician
Lewin, Ted Bert writer, illustrator
Marcus, Leonard S. writer, book critic
†Morris, Traci D. poet, writer, educator
Mulvihill, Maureen Esther writer, educator, scholar
Nemser, Cindy writer
Pashman, Susan Ellen writer
Purdy, James writer
Sainer, Arthur writer, theater educator
†Whiting, Nathan poet, dancer
†Williams, Edward Frank poet, entertainment company executive

Buffalo
Creeley, Robert White author, English educator
Federman, Raymond novelist, English and comparative literature educator
Feldman, Irving poet

Carmel
Kinney, Harrison Burton writer

Chappaqua
George, Jean Craighead author, illustrator

Cherry Valley
†Plymell, Charley Douglass writer, educator

Clifton Park
de Colombí-Monguió, Alicia poet, foreign language educator

Corona
Levy, Barry Alan technical writer, songwriter

Dobbs Ferry
Mooney, Vicki playwright

Eastchester
†Weinberg, Dale G. technical writer, consultant

Esopus
Tetlow, Edwin author

Fairport
Germano, Mary Catherine writer

Flushing
†Dorn, Alfred poet, retired English educator
Givens, Janet Eaton writer
Goldsmith, Howard writer, consultant
†Sirowitz, Hal poet, special education educator
†Taylor, Conciere Marlana writer

Forest Hills
†Dybman, Nick Nison poet

Freeport
Terris, Virginia R. writer

Fulton
Long, Robert Emmet author

Garrison
Barnhart, Robert Knox writer, editor

Germantown
Linney, Romulus author, educator

Glen Cove
†Mulvihill, William Patrick writer

Goshen
Hawkins, Barry Tyler author, mental health services professional

Great Neck
†Burghardt, Linda F. writer
†Goldberger, Avriel Horwitz literary translator, retired French educator
Hurwitz, Johanna (Frank) author, librarian
Simon, Seymour writer, photographer
†Zeiger, David poet, retired English educator
†Zeiger, Lila L. creative writing educator

Greenfield Center
Fonseca, John dos Reis writer, former law educator

Greenlawn
†Roberts, Gloria Jean writer

Hamilton
Berlind, Bruce Peter poet, educator
Busch, Frederick Matthew writer, literature educator

Hastings On Hudson
Cooney, Patrick Louis writer

Hudson Falls
Bronk, William writer, retail businessman

Hyde Park
Eastwood, D(ana) Alan author, publisher, consultant

Interlaken
Bleiler, Everett Franklin writer, publishing company executive

Irvington
Massie, Robert Kinloch author

Ithaca
Ammons, Archie Randolph poet, English educator
Lurie, Alison author
†Shepherd, Reginald writer, educator

Jefferson Valley
Huyghe, Patrick Antoine science writer

Katonah
Crichton, (John) Michael author, film director

Keene Valley
†Neville, Emily Tam Lin writer, educator

Lockport
Cull, John Joseph novelist, playwright

Locust Valley
McGee, Dorothy Horton writer, historian

Mamaroneck
Randolph, Elizabeth writer

Millerton
Paretsky, Sara N. writer

Montauk
Lavenas, Suzanne writer, editor, consultant

Mount Kisco
Godilo-Godlevsky, Eugene Alexandrovich poet

Munnsville
Carruth, Hayden poet

New Rochelle
Branch, William Blackwell playwright, producer
Saperstein, David novelist, screenwriter, film director

New York
Adams, Alice writer
Albee, Edward Franklin author, playwright
Aliki, (Aliki Liacouras Brandenberg) author, illustrator children's books
Allen, Jay Presson writer, producer
Allen, Roberta fiction and nonfiction writer, conceptual artist
†Alvarez-Babin, Carmen Maria writer, retired educator
Andersen, Kurt Byars writer
Anderson, Poul William author
Anderson, Robert Woodruff playwright, novelist, screenwriter
Angell, Roger writer, magazine editor
Aronin, Marc Jacob playwright, artistic director, director
Ashdown, Marie Matranga (Mrs. Cecil Spanton Ashdown, Jr.) writer, lecturer
Ashton, Dore author, educator
Auchincloss, Louis Stanton writer
Auel, Jean Marie author
Auster, Paul writer
Balliett, Whitney writer, critic
Barrios, Richard (John) writer, film historian
Bauer, Marion Dane writer
Beattie, Ann author
Beim, Norman playwright, actor, director
Bel Geddes, Joan writer
Benchley, Peter Bradford author
Benedikt, Michael poet, educator, author, editor, free-lance consultant
†Benjamin, Ruth writer
Benjamin, Saragail Katzman writer, performer, composer
Berenbeim, Ronald Everett business writer, educator
Berendt, John Lawrence writer, editor
Berg, David author, artist
Berger, Thomas Louis author
†Bernikow, Louise writer
†Berry, Eliot Ward writer, appraiser
Birstein, Ann writer, educator
Bisson, Terry Ballantine author, editor
Bliven, Bruce, Jr. writer
Block, Francesca Lia writer
Blume, Judy Sussman author
Bolt, Thomas writer, artist
Borowik, Ann writer
Bouloukos, Theodore, II writer, editor
Bourjaily, Vance novelist
Bradbury, Ray Douglas author
Bradford, Barbara Taylor writer, journalist, novelist
Bradford, Richard Roark writer
Branch, Taylor writer
Braudy, Susan Orr author
Brenner, Erma author
†Brian, Laura Anna freelance writer
Brown, Rita Mae author
Bujold, Lois McMaster science fiction writer
Burnshaw, Stanley writer
Cabalquinto, Luis Carrazcal free-lance writer
Calisher, Hortense (Mrs. Curtis Harnack) writer
Caputo, Philip Joseph author, journalist, screenwriter
Carlson, P(atricia) M(cElroy) writer
Caro, Robert Allan author
Chapman, James Albion novelist, publisher
Christopher, Nicholas poet, novelist
Cisneros, Sandra poet, short story writer, essayist
Clancy, Thomas L., Jr. novelist
Clark, Matt science writer
Cleary, Beverly Atlee (Mrs. Clarence T. Cleary) author
Collier, Zena author
Connell, Evan Shelby, Jr. author
Conniff, Richard writer
Conroy, Pat (Donald Patrick Conroy) writer
Cook, Ferris writer, illustrator
Cook, Robin author
Cooper, Paulette Marcia writer
Corn, Alfred DeWitt poet, fiction writer, critic, educator
Cornwell, Patricia Daniels author
Creech, Sharon children's author
Crews, Harry Eugene author
Cryer, Gretchen playwright, lyricist, actress
Cummings, Josephine Anna writer
†Cunningham, Michael author, educator
Curie, Eve writer, lecturer
Curry, Jane Louise writer
Dailey, Janet novelist
Danto, Arthur Coleman author, philosopher, art critic
Danziger, Paula author
Davis, Lorraine Jensen writer, editor
de Hartog, Jan writer
†Denham, Alice writer
Denker, Henry playwright, author, director
Diamonstein-Spielvogel, Barbaralee writer, television interviewer/ producer
†Dickinson, Nathan Kilmer writer
Didion, Joan author
Dikeman, May writer
Dillard, Annie author
Doctorow, Edgar Lawrence novelist, English educator
Donaldson, Stephen Reeder author
Duffy, James Henry writer, former lawyer
†Duncan, Pearl Rose writer, poet
Dunne, John Gregory author
†Ellroy, James writer
Erdrich, (Karen) Louise fiction writer, poet
Espinoza, Galina magazine writer
Espy, Willard Richardson author
Fallaci, Oriana writer, journalist
Fast, Howard Melvin author
Fenichell, Stephen Clark writer
Fennell Robbins, Sally writer
Fierstein, Harvey Forbes playwright, actor
†Finch, Sheila writer, author science fiction
Fisher, Nancy writer, producer, director
Fleischman, Albert Sidney (Sid Fleischman) writer
Fleming, Thomas James writer
Fletcher, Colin author
Flexner, James Thomas author
Flint, Jerry writer
Fox, Paula (Mrs. Martin Greenberg) author
Francis, Dick (Richard Stanley Francis) novelist
Fratti, Mario playwright, educator
Friedman, B(ernard) H(arper) writer
Friedman, Philip novelist, screenwriter, producer
Frumkes, Lewis Burke writer, educator
Fulghum, Robert L. author, lecturer
Furnas, Joseph Chamberlain writer
Georgakas, Dan writer, educator
Gersoni-Edelman, Diane Claire author, editor
Giblin, James Cross author, editor
Giorno, John poet
Goldman, James playwright, screenwriter, novelist
†Goldsmith, Barbara author, social historian, journalist
Goldstein, Lisa Joy writer
†Gooch, Brad writer
Goodman, George Jerome Waldo (Adam Smith) author, television journalist, editor
Gordon, David playwright, director, choreographer
Gordon, Mary Catherine author
Goulden, Joseph Chesley author
Grafton, Sue novelist
Grant, Cynthia D. writer
Gray, Deborah Dolia business writing consultant
Grisham, John writer
Gross, Michael Robert writer, editor
Grumbach, Doris novelist, editor, critic, educator, bookseller
Guare, John playwright
†Gurganus, Allan writer, educator
Hadley, Leila Eliott-Burton (Mrs. Henry Luce, III) author
Hague, William Edward editor, author
Hamburger, Philip (Paul) writer
Hannibal, Edward Leo copywriter
Hardwick, Elizabeth author
Harris, E. Lynn writer
Haskell, Molly author
Hauptman, William playwright
†Haynes, Todd film writer, producer, director
Hazzard, Shirley author
†Heinemann, Larry C. writer
Heller, Joseph writer
Henley, Arthur author, editor, television consultant
Hentoff, Nathan Irving writer
Hernández, Roger Emilio newspaper columnist
Hesse, Karen (Sue) writer, educator
Hewitt, John Hamilton, Jr. editor, writer
Hillman, Howard Budrow author, editor, publisher, consultant
Hines, Anna Grossnickle author, illustrator
Hinton, S(usan) E(loise) author
Hinz, Dorothy Elizabeth writer, editor, international corporate communications and public affairs specialist
Hoffman, William M(oses) playwright, editor
Holland, Isabelle Christian writer
†Holman, Bob poet
Holroyd, Michael author
Horovitz, Israel Arthur playwright
Howie, Elizabeth Jane (Betsy Howie) writer, actress
Hull, David Stewart literary agency executive
Hussung, Alleen Mosette literary agent
Hwang, David Henry playwright, screenwriter
Irving, John Winslow writer
Isay, David Avram writer, radio producer
Jacker, Corinne Litvin playwright
†Jacoby, Coleman scriptwriter
Jakes, John author
Janeway, Elizabeth Hall author
Jhabvala, Ruth Prawer author
†Johnson, Angela children's book author
Jones, Diana Wynne writer
†Jones, Lawrence Worth poet, editor, performance art producer, songwriter
Jong, Erica Mann writer, poet
Kafka, Barbara Poses author
Kauffmann, Stanley Jules author
Kaufman, Bel author, educator
Keene, Donald writer, translator, language educator
Kehret, Peg writer
Kinnell, Galway poet, translator
Kisner, Jacob poet, editor, publisher
Klein, T(heodore) E(ibon) D(onald) writer
Kobler, John writer
Koch, Kenneth poet, playwright
Koke, Richard Joseph author, exhibit designer, museum curator
Koning, Hans (Hans Koningsberger) author
Koontz, Dean Ray writer
Kostelanetz, Richard writer, media and visual artist
Kotlowitz, Robert writer, editor
Kumin, Maxine Winokur poet, author
Kunitz, Stanley Jasspon poet, editor, educator
Lader, Lawrence writer
Lapierre, Dominique writer, historian, philanthropist
Lapine, James Elliot playwright, director
Lauber, Patricia Grace writer
Laurents, Arthur playwright
Leavitt, David Adam writer
Lelchuk, Alan author, educator
L'Engle, Madeleine (Mrs. Hugh Franklin) author
Leonard, Elmore John novelist, screenwriter
Levin, Ira author, playwright
Levitt, Sidney Mark author, illustrator, artist
Levoy, Myron author
†Levy, Owen writer
†Livingston, Bernard author
Lord, M. G. writer
Lunardini, Christine Anne writer, historian, consultant
Maas, Peter writer
Macer-Story, Eugenia Ann writer, artist
Mailer, Norman author
†Markson, David Merrill writer, educator
†Martin, Jacqueline Briggs author juvenile prose
Mason, Bobbie Ann novelist, short story writer
Matzner, Chester Michael writer
Maupin, Armistead Jones, Jr. writer
Mayer, Martin Prager writer
†McCourt, Frank writer
McCullough, Colleen author
McCullough, David author, educator
McDonald, Gregory Christopher author
McGarvey, Mary Hewitt writer
McGuane, Thomas Francis, III author, screenwriter
McMurtry, Larry Jeff author
†McNally, Terrence playwright
McPherson, James Lowell writer
McQuown, Judith Hershkowitz author, financial advisor
Meade, Marion author
Meltzer, Milton author
Minarik, Else Holmelund (Bigart Minarik) author
Mitgang, Herbert author, journalist
Mooney, Richard Emerson writer
Morgan, (George) Frederick poet, editor
Morgan, Thomas Bruce author, editor, public affairs executive
†Morris, Mary writer, educator
†Morris, Wright novelist, critic
Morrison, Patricia Kennealy author
Morton, Frederic author
†Mosley, Walter writer
†Munro, Alice author
Nash, N. Richard writer
†Neier, Aryeh author, human rights organization administrator
Nixon, Agnes Eckhardt television writer, producer
†Noonan, Tom playwright, actor, director
North, Charles Laurence poet, educator
Oates, Joyce Carol author
O'Brien, Tim writer
O'Doherty, Brian writer, filmmaker
Offit, Sidney writer, educator
†Oltion, Jerry author science fiction
Oppenheimer, Paul English comparative literature educator, poet, author
Osborne, Mary Pope writer
Ozick, Cynthia author
Pall, Ellen Jane writer
Paolucci, Robert D. translator
†Papell, Gertrude Helen poet, retired librarian
Passoff, Michelle writer
Paterson, Katherine Womeldorf writer
Peacock, Molly poet
Peck, Richard Wayne novelist
†Pendragon, Michael Malefica writer, poet
Pérez-Rivera, Francisco writer
†Peyton, Elizabeth Joy writer
Pirsig, Robert Maynard author
Plain, Belva writer
Plimpton, George Ames writer, editor, television host
Pogrebin, Letty Cottin writer, lecturer
Polacco, Patricia children's author, illustrator
†Pollack, Barbara Grace writer
Pollitt, Katha writer, poet, educator
Pomerantz, Charlotte writer
Poole, William Daniel writer, editor
Posner, Gerald author, lawyer
Price, Reynolds novelist, poet, playwright, essayist, educator
Rabinowitz, Anna poet
†Raphael, Phyllis writer
Ratcliff, Carter Goodrich writer, art critic, poet
Rathmann, Peggy author, illustrator
Reed, Ishmael Scott (Emmett Coleman) writer
Reig, June Wilson writer, director, producer
Reiss, Alvin writer
†Reza, Yasmina author, playwright
Rhodes, Richard Lee writer
Rice, Anne author
Rich, Adrienne writer
†Robinson, Kim Stanley science fiction author
†Rogers, Bruce Holland writer, author science fiction
Rogers, Michael Alan writer
Rollin, Betty author, television journalist
Rooney, Andrew Aitken writer, columnist
Root, William Pitt poet, educator
Rothenberg, Jerome author, visual arts and literary educator

†Rothenberg, Joyce Andrea (Joyce Joyce Andrea) *composer, poet, writer*
†Rothstein, Edward Benjamin *writer, critic*
Rudman, Mark *poet, educator*
Rylant, Cynthia *author*
†Sachar, Louis *writer prose*
Salant, Ari *medical advertising writer*
Sale, (John) Kirkpatrick *writer*
Salinger, Jerome David *author*
Salter, Mary Jo *poet*
†Sargent, Herb *writer, television producer*
Sargent, Pamela *writer*
Saul, John Woodruff, III *writer*
†Savage, Tom *poet, video librarian*
Schaffner, Cynthia Van Allen *writer, curator, lecturer*
†Schimel, Lawrence David *writer*
Schisgal, Murray Joseph *playwright*
Schlein, Miriam *author*
Schlesinger, Arthur (Meier), Jr. *writer, retired educator*
Schwed, Peter *author, retired editor and publisher*
Seaman, Barbara (Ann Rosner) *author*
Segal, Lore *writer*
†Seidman, Hugh *poet, technical writer*
Sendak, Maurice Bernard *writer, illustrator*
Shaffer, Peter Levin *playwright*
Shapiro, Harvey *poet*
Shapiro, Mary J. *writer, researcher, speech writer*
Sheehan, Susan *author*
Sheehy, Gail Henion *author*
Sheldon, Sidney *author, producer*
Sherrill, Stephen R. *writer*
Sherwood, James Webster, III *author, limousine company owner*
Shulevitz, Uri *author, illustrator*
Simon, Neil *playwright, television writer*
Slade, Bernard *playwright*
Smith, Betty *writer, nonprofit foundation executive*
Solomon, Andrew Wallace *author*
Sonnenberg, Ben *playwright, poet, editor, producer*
Sourian, Peter *writer, educator*
Southall, Ivan Francis *author*
Spiegelman, Art *author, cartoonist*
Spillane, Mickey (Frank Morrison Spillane) *author*
Steel, Danielle Fernande *author*
Stein, Joseph *playwright*
Steinem, Gloria *writer, editor, lecturer*
Stevenson, William Henri *author*
Stewart, Mary Florence Elinor *author*
Stone, Peter *playwright, scenarist*
Stone, Robert Anthony *author*
Stowers, Carlton Eugene *writer*
Swann, Brian *writer, humanities educator*
Talese, Gay *writer*
Tan, Amy Ruth *writer*
Taylor, Clyde Calvin, Jr. *literary agent*
Teachout, Terry *writer, critic*
Tomkins, Calvin *writer*
Toobin, Jeffrey Ross *writer, legal analyst*
Trillin, Calvin *writer, columnist*
Uhry, Alfred Fox *playwright*
Uris, Leon Marcus *author*
†Virga, Vincent Philip *writer, picture editor, researcher, designer*
†Volchok, Susan *writer*
Vonnegut, Kurt, Jr. *writer*
Wager, Walter Herman *author, communications director*
Wakefield, Dan *author, screenwriter*
Walker, Alice Malsenior *author*
Waller, Robert James *writer*
Ward, Geoffrey Champion *author, editor*
Wasserman, Albert *film producer, writer, director*
Watt, Douglas (Benjamin Watt) *writer, critic*
Weisberg, Barbara *writer, editor*
Wender, Phyllis Bellows *literary agent*
West, Paul Noden *author*
Weston, Carol *writer*
Whitney, Phyllis Ayame *author*
Wiener, Solomon *writer, consultant, former city official*
Wilds, Bonnie *author, community volunteer*
Wilson, August *playwright*
Wilson, F(rancis) Paul *novelist, screenwriter*
Windsor, Patricia (Katonah Summertree) *author, educator, lecturer*
Wise, David *author, journalist*
†Wisniewski, David *author juvenile prose*
Wolfe, Thomas Kennerly, Jr. *writer, journalist*
Wolff, Virginia Euwer *writer*
Yorinks, Arthur *children's author, writer, director*
York, Alexandra *writer, lecturer*
Zahn, Timothy *writer*
Zara, Louis *author, editor*
Zarka, Albert Abraham *author*
Zolotow, Charlotte Shapiro *author, editor*

Newburgh
Severo, Richard *writer*

Niagara Falls
Gromosiak, Paul *historian, consultant, science and math educator*
Powers, Bruce Raymond *author, English language educator, consultant*

North Boston
Herbert, James Alan *writer*

Nyack
Hendin, David Bruce *literary agent, author, consultant, numismatist*

Oceanside
Mills, James Spencer *author*

Olivebridge
Osborne, Seward Russell *writer*

Palisades
Davis, Dorothy Salisbury *author*

Pittsford
Green, Martin Lincoln *author, educator, publisher, consultant*

Plattsburgh
†Carrino, Michael *writing educator*

Pleasantville
Nelson, K. Bonita *literary agent*

Pomona
Brooks, Iris *writer, editor, musician*

Potsdam
DeGhett, Stephanie Coyne *writer, educator*

Poughkeepsie
Willard, Nancy Margaret *writer, educator*

Pound Ridge
Abramovitz, Anita Zeltner Brooks (Mrs. Max Abramovitz) *writer*

Rego Park
Brown, Kevin *writer*

Rochester
Hoch, Edward Dentinger *author*
†Nixon, David Michael *poet*
Rothberg, Abraham *author, educator, editor*
Scott, Joanna Jeanne *writer, English language educator*

Roslyn Heights
†Bruder, Judith *writer*

Rye
Hurwitz, Sol *writer, consultant*

Sagaponack
Appleman, Marjorie (M. H. Appleman) *playwright, educator, poet*
Appleman, Philip *poet, writer, educator*
Hagen-Stubbing, Yvonne Forrest *writer*

Saranac Lake
†Kenny, Maurice Francis *writer*

Saratoga Springs
Rogoff, Jay *poet, educator*

Scarsdale
Hershenson, Roberta Mantell *writer, photographer*

Schenectady
†Foley, Jeff *freelance writer*
Yamin-Garone, Mary Sultany *writer, graphic designer*

Searington
†Byalick, Marcia *author, columnist, reporter, educator*

Somers
†Newlin, George Christian *writer*

South Nyack
†Rumaker, Michael *writer, English educator*

Southampton
†Jones, Kaylie Ann *writing educator, writer*

Spencerport
Humphrey, Paul *commercial writer*

Staten Island
†Herman, Robert John *artist manager, author, music industry advisor*
Popp, Lilian Mustaki *writer, educator*
Porter, Darwin Fred *writer*

Sunnyside
Wallmann, Jeffrey Miner *author*

Syracuse
Ikins, Rachael Zacov *writer, illustrator, photographer*
Lloyd, David Thomas *writer, English educator*

Valley Stream
Rachlin, Harvey Brant *author*

Wainscott
Herzog, Arthur, III *author*

Warwick
Sierra, Victor, Jr. *poet*

Waverly
Forest, Bob *author, poet*

Webster
Shirkey, William Dan *writer*

West Nyack
Pringle, Laurence Patrick *writer*

White Plains
Benjamin, Barbara Bloch *writer, editor*
Cobb, Vicki *writer*
†Gordon, Susan J. *writer*

Woodstock
Godwin, Gail Kathleen *author*

Yonkers
†Baumel, Joan Patricia French *educator, writer, lecturer*
Lamagna, Joseph *author*
†Maritime, George *writer, photographer*

NORTH CAROLINA

Brevard
Jones, Sandy (Sandra F.) *writer, speaker, parenting expert*

Bryson City
Marr, Margaret Ann Lackey *writer*

Chapel Hill
Betts, Doris June Waugh *author, English language educator*
Little, Loyd Harry, Jr. *author*

Spencer, Elizabeth *author*

Charlotte
Finley, Glenna *author*
†Mager, Donald Northrop *poet, educator*
Schenck, Sydney Neel *writer*

Columbus
Blate, Michael *author, lecturer*
†Sauvé, Carolyn Opal *writer, journalist, poet*

Durham
Dunbar, Leslie Wallace *writer, consultant*
Ogede, Ode *literature educator*

Garner
†Monahan, Sherry Ann *writer*

Greensboro
†Gilbert, Marie Rogers *poet*
Sewell, Elizabeth *author, English educator*
Watson, Robert Winthrop *poet, English language educator*

Greenville
†Fay, Julie *writer*
†Twardy, Charles A., Jr. *writer*

Hillsborough
Williams, Virginia Parrott *writer, company executive*

Mount Olive
†Rigsbee, David E. *poet, educator*

Murfreesboro
Burke, Marguerite Jodi Larcombe *writer, computer consultant*

Pinehurst
Hopkins, Marjorie Johnson *writer*

Southern Pines
Yarborough, William Pelham *writer, lecturer, retired army officer, consultant*

Winston Salem
Ehle, John Marsden, Jr. *writer*
Gallimore, Margaret Martin *poet*
†Spach, John Thom *writer, educator*

NORTH DAKOTA

Fargo
†Ekberg, Susan Jane *writer, publisher*

Grand Forks
†Meek, Jay *educator, poet*

West Fargo
Parsley, Jamie Allen *writer*

OHIO

Akron
Moriarty, John Timothy *writer, transportation consultant*

Ashley
Thomas, Annabel Crawford *writer*

Athens
†Thorndike, John *writer*

Bellbrook
McClelland, Herbert Lee *retired publisher, author*

Berea
Bonds, Georgia Anna *writer, lecturer*

Blue Creek
†Novakovich, Josip A. *writer, English educator*

Chillicothe
Dickey, Phillip Nelson Theophilus (Philo Dickey) *poet, playwright*

Cincinnati
Barr, Kevin Curtis *poet*
Birmingham, Stephen *writer*
Braman, Heather Ruth *technical writer, editor, consultant, antiques dealer*
Hornbaker, Alice Joy *author*
Marks, Jeffrey Alan *writer*
Mulholland-Spaulding, Catherine A. *writer*
Oden, Fay Giles *author, educator*
Steinberg, Janet Eckstein *journalist*
†Zabel, Rick *writer*

Circleville
Strous, Allen *poet*

Cleveland
Coon, Sharon Ann *writer, public relations executive, educator*
Finn, Robert *writer, lecturer, broadcaster*
Gleisser, Marcus David *author, lawyer, journalist*
†Khabeer, Beryl M.A. *poet, playwright, educator*
Kovel, Ralph M. *author, antiques expert*
Kovel, Terry Horvitz (Mrs. Ralph Kovel) *author, antiques authority*
Pavlovich, Donald *educator, support person*
Sandburg, Helga *author*
Wood, Kathleen Oliver *writer, editor*
Woodson, Kevin *writer*

Columbus
Hilliker, Grant Gilbert *writer, former diplomat and educator*
Shook, Robert Louis *business writer*
†Young, Thomas Beetham *writer*

Dayton
Hayes, Stephen Kurtz *author*
Heath, Mariwyn Dwyer *writer, legislative issues consultant*

†Jelus, Susan Crum *writer, editor*
Thomas, Marianna *volunteer community activist, writer, speaker*

Granville
†Townsend, Ann C. *poet, English educator*

Kent
Hilliard, Bonnie Jean *writer, editor*

Marietta
†Dixon, Carol Ann *writer, educator*

Medina
†Foster, David Ben *creative writing educator, freelance writer*

Middletown
McClain, Michael H. *writer*

Niles
Markovich-Lytle, Darlene A. *author*

Oxford
†Finch, Annie R(idley) C(rane) *poet*
Goodman, Eric Keith *writer, educator*
†Reiss, James *poet, English educator, editor*

Perrysburg
Weaver, Richard L., II *writer, speaker, educator*

Sandusky
Behrens, Ellen Elizabeth Cox *writer, counselor, educator*

Springfield
Dobson, Janet Louise *writer*
Moon, Farzana *author*

Yellow Springs
Hamilton, Virginia (Mrs. Arnold Adoff) *author*
Keyes, Ralph Jeffrey *writer*

OKLAHOMA

Edmond
McCoy, William Ulysses *journalist*

Lawton
Spencer, Mark Morris *creative writing educator*
Stanley, George Edward *writer*

Norman
Owens, Rochelle *poet, playwright*
Scaperlanda, Maria d *writer, journalist, author*

Oklahoma City
Mather, Ruth Elsie *writer*
Mosby, Lee Emerson *writer*

Shawnee
†Windel, Frank E., Jr. *writer*

Stillwater
Shirley, Glenn Dean *writer*

Tulsa
Ezcchukwu, Bonnie Ok. *author, educator, counselor, poet, storyteller, multiculturalist, anti-drug and violence speaker*
Mojtabai, Ann Grace *author, educator*
Price, Alice Lindsay *writer, artist*

OREGON

Amity
†Skloot, Floyd *writer*

Applegate
Pursglove, Laurence Albert *technical writer, computer quality tester*

Ashland
Jackson, Elizabeth Riddle *writer, translator, educator*

Boring
Robinson, Jeanne Louise *lecturer, writer*

Culver
Siebert, Diane Dolores *author, poet*

Eugene
Wilhelm, Kate (Katy Gertrude) *author*

Grants Pass
Stafford, Patrick Purcell *poet, writer, management consultant*

Medford
Kent, Roberta B. *literary consultant*

Newport
Kennedy, Richard Jerome *writer*

Otis
King, Frank William *writer*

Pleasant Hill
Kesey, Ken *writer*

Portland
†Carlile, Henry David *poet, writer, educator*
Larson, Wanda Z(ackovich) *writer, poet*
Porter, Elsa Allgood *writer, lecturer*
Rutsala, Vern A. *poet, English language educator, writer*
Tuska, Jon *author, publisher*
Westin, Helen Tilda *writer, songwriter*

Salem
Ackerson, Duane Wright, Jr. *author*

Benson, Steven Donald *sheet metal research and marketing executive, sheet metal mechanic, programmer, author*
Yunker, Todd Elliott *writer*

Springfield
Kelso, Mary Jean *author*

PENNSYLVANIA

Altoona
†Moore, Dinty William *writer, educator*

Ambridge
Feinstein, Tikvah *writer, editor, publisher*

Ardmore
Kline, George Louis *author, translator, retired philosophy and literature educator*

Avondale
Foster, Paul *playwright*

Bridgeport
Kevis, David Ernest *author*

Broomall
Saunders, Sally Love *poet, educator*

Bushkill
Ellwood, Edith Muesing *free-lance writer*
Muesing Ellwood, Edith Elizabeth *writer, researcher, publisher, editor*

California
Langham, Norma *playwright, educator, poet, composer, inventor*

Clearfield
Grippo, James Joseph *writer, educator*

Cresco
Reinhardt, Susan Joan *writer*

Downingtown
Kovach, George Daniel *writer*

Doylestown
Cooke, Chantelle Anne *writer*

Drexel Hill
Alexander, Lloyd Chudley *author*

Glenside
Mazzucelli, Colette Grace Celia *author, university adminstrator, educator*

Greensburg
†Dorsey, John Victor *poet, screenwriter, editor*

Harrisburg
Kirkpatrick, David Warren *educational researcher, writer*

Hazleton
Reed, Cheryl *composition and writing educator*

Holtwood
Stein, Gloria *writer*

Howard
Carusone, Albert Robert *writer*

Indiana
Ferguson, Ronald Thomas *writer*
Mikkelsen, Nina Elizabeth Markowitz *writer, researcher*

Kennett Square
Martin, George (Whitney) *writer*

Lancaster
Baker, Mark Allen *author, historian, consultant*

Malvern
Figaniak, Laura Mary Ann *poet, executive assistant*

Merion Station
Jacobs, Suzanne *author*

Milford
Eckert, Allan Wesley *writer*
Le Guin, Ursula Kroeber *author*

Monroeville
Moenich, David Richard (D.R.M. Johnston) *writer*

Narvon
High, Linda Oatman *author*

Newtown
Pfeiffer, John Edward *author*

Philadelphia
Cooper, Jane Todd (J. C. Todd) *poet, writer, educator*
Fussell, Paul *author, English literature educator*
Klein, Esther Moyerman (Mrs. Philip Klein) *author*
Langston, Stephen Lewis *poet, carpenter*
Mangione, Jerre Gerlando *author, educator*
Paglia, Camille *writer, humanities educator*
Slavitt, David Rytman *writer*
†Thomson, Sharon Anne *writer, performer, director*

Phoenixville
Bretz, Connie *poet, storyteller*

Pittsburgh
Bleier, Carol Stein *writer, researcher*
Hodges, Margaret Moore *author, educator*
McHoes, Ann McIver *technical writer, computer systems consultant*
†Simms, Michael Arlin *poet, publishing executive*
Verlich, Jean Elaine *writer, public relations consultant*

Pottstown
Hylton, Thomas James *author*

Saint Davids
Shurkin, Lorna Greene *writer, publicist, fund raiser*

Sharon
Edwards, Patricia Ann *poet*

Shippensburg
Blair, Margaret Whitman *writer, researcher*

Southampton
Bendiner, Robert *writer, editor*
†Levin, Lynn Ellen *poet*

State College
Asbell, Bernard *author, English language educator*

Valley Forge
Miller, Betty Brown *freelance writer*

Villanova
Gould, Lilian *writer*
Nolan, Patrick Joseph *screenwriter, playwright, educator*

Wayne
Mackey, Betty Barr *writer*

West Mifflin
Carneal, Pamela Lynn *technical recruiter, technical, freelance writer*

Wyncote
Webb, Frances Moore *writer, educator*

Wynnewood
Meyers, Mary Ann *writer, consultant*

RHODE ISLAND

Barrington
Deakin, James *writer, former newspaperman*

Cranston
Feinstein, Alan Shawn *writer, financial adviser*

Pawtucket
Hoffman, Andrew Jay *writer*

Providence
Cassill, Ronald Verlin *author*
Coover, Robert *writer, scriptwriter, educator*
†Mandel, Peter Bevan *writer, columnist*
Schevill, James Erwin *poet, playwright*
†Vogel, Paula Anne *playwright*

Prudence Island
†McEntee, Grace Hall *writer, writing and education consultant*

Woonsocket
Gauvey, Ralph Edward, Jr. *writer, poet*

SOUTH CAROLINA

Aiken
Smith, Gregory White *writer*

Clemson
Byars, Betsy (Cromer) *author*

Folly Beach
Shutrump, Mary Jill *writer, editor, photographer, educator*

Georgetown
Isbell, Robert *writer*

Greenville
Weimer, Tonja Evetts *author, recording artist, consultant*

Hilton Head Island
Cross, Wilbur Lucius *writer, editorial consultant*

Little River
Ehrlich, John Gunther *writer*

Murrells Inlet
Lillemoen, Henry Daniel *retired writer*

Myrtle Beach
Uzenda, Jara Carlow *technical writer, residential contractor*

Rock Hill
Bristow, Robert O'Neil *writer, educator*

Seneca
Curry, Mary Earle Lowry *poet*

Spartanburg
Deku, Afrikadzata *Afrikan-scholar, researcher, writer, educator*

Sullivans Island
Humphreys, Josephine *novelist*

Summerville
Reisman, Rosemary Moody Canfield *writer, humanities educator*

Sumter
Justus, Adalu *writer, designer*

SOUTH DAKOTA

Brookings
Williams, Elizabeth Evenson *writer*

Kyle
Davies Silcott, Loma Geyer *freelance writer, English educator*

Mission Hill
Karolevitz, Robert Francis *writer*

TENNESSEE

Chattanooga
Callahan, North *author, educator*

Cleveland
Breuer, William Bentley *writer*

Cookeville
Underwood, Lucinda Jean *poet, playwright, small business owner, researcher*

Franklin
Bransford, Helen M. *writer, jewelry designer*

Gallatin
†Flynn, John David *writer, educator*

Knoxville
†Velazquez, Sheila Synnott *writer, newspaper columnist*

Madison
Simmons, Gary M. *writer, small business owner*
Williams, Edward Macon *poet*

Memphis
Casey, Paula F. *writer, speaker*
Foote, Shelby *author*
Gawehn-Frisby, Dorothy Jeanne *retired freelance technical writer*
†Parish, Barbara Shirk *writer, educator*
Sharpe, Robert F., Sr. *writer, lecturer, educator, consultant, publisher*

Nashville
Petty, Paula Gail *freelance writer, volunteer*
Winstead, Elisabeth Weaver *poet, writer, English language educator*

Newport
Dykeman, Wilma *writer, lecturer*

Whiteville
Traylor, Sharon Elain *writer, school food service staff member*

TEXAS

Abilene
Zachry, Juanita Daniel *writer, bookkeeper*

Arlington
Savage, Ruth Hudson *poet, writer, speaker*

Austin
Bishop, Amelia Morton *freelance writer*
†Blumenthal, Michael Charles *writer, educator*
†Favor, Lesli Joanna *writer, researcher*
Gustafsson, Lars Erik Einar *writer, educator*
White, Tom Martin *playwright, music publisher*

Bertram
Albert, Susan Wittig *writer, English educator*

Boerne
Price, John Randolph *writer*

Brookshire
Utley, Jane B. *poet*

China Spring
Weaver, Donna Kay *writer, genealogist*

College Station
Mason, Stephanie Jo *writer*

Conroe
Parle, Bertha Ibarra *writer short stories, poetry*

Corpus Christi
†Murray, E'Lane Carlisle *freelance writer*

Crystal Beach
Dunn, Glennis Mae *retired writer, lyricist*

Dallas
Ardoin, John Louis *author*
Davis, Elise Miller (Mrs. Leo M. Davis) *writer*
Harris, Leon A., Jr. *writer*
Hunter, Kermit *writer, former university dean*
†Monk, Cody James *writer*
Murray, John William, Jr. *writer, legal investigator*
Phillips, Betty Lou (Elizabeth Louise Phillips) *author, interior designer*
Sealander, John Arthur *writer, educator*
Sherwood, Rhonda Griffin *playwright, writer, designer*
Sundgaard, Arnold Olaf *playwright*
†Walker, Robert Martin *writer, minister*
Weeks, Jerome Christopher *writer, drama, book critic*

Double Oak
Watson, Beverly Hale *writer*

El Paso
†Cummings, Patricia Ann (Felicia Margarita Cruz) *writer, journalist, poet*
McCarthy, Cormac *writer*
Wilson, Leigh Ann *writer*

Fort Worth
Bean, Jack Vaughan *author, publisher*
Dover, Benjamin Franklin *writer, correspondent*
Laughlin, Christel Renate *translator, consultant*
Simmons, Naomi Charlotte *poet*

Galveston
Harrison, Dony *poet, writer, journalist, lecturer*

Hewitt
Watson, Jessica Lewis *writer*

Hico
Rice, James W. *author, illustrator*

Houston
Hirsch, Edward Mark *poet, English language educator*
Plunkett, Jack William *writer, publisher*
Schier, Mary Jane *science writer*
†Storey, Gail Donohue *writer, editor*
Summers, Joseph Frank *author, publisher*
†Thomas, Larry Dee *poet*

Hurst
Dooley, Lena Rose (Nelson) *writer, editor*

Katy
Harbour, Patricia Ann Monroe *poet*

Knippa
†Gracia, Brenda Lee *poet*

Liberty Hill
West, Felton *retired newspaper writer*

Lubbock
Bronwell, Nancy Brooker *writer*

Lufkin
Billingsley, Shirley Ann *writer, poet*

Mansfield
Parnell, Charles L. *speechwriter*

Murchison
Amos-Ganther, Linda *poet*

Port Arthur
Valsin, Bessie *poet*

Pottsboro
Jackson, Nona Armour *writer, illustrator*

Richardson
Bonura, Larry Samuel *writer*
†Wiesepape, Betty Holland *writing educator*

Saint Jo
Ashley, Raymond Weldon *writer*

Salado
Greene, A(lvin) C(arl) *author*

San Antonio
Ammann, Lillian Ann Nicholson *writer, health products distributor*
Fehrenbach, T(heodore) R(eed) *author, businessman*
Flynn, Robert Lopez *writer*
Glueck, Sylvia Blumenfeld *writer*
Knue, Joseph *writer, historian*
Laurence, Dan H. *author, literary and dramatic specialist*
Rogers, Frances Evelyn *author, retired educator and librarian*
Swiggett, Harold E. (Hal Swiggett) *writer, photographer*

Spring
Kerr, Alva Rae *writer, editor, association executive, playwright*

Springtown
Marrs, James F., Jr. (Jim Marrs) *author, journalist, educator*

UTAH

Park City
Solomon, Dorothy Jeanne Allred *writer, communications executive*

Salt Lake City
Black, Rosa Vida *writer, educator*
Skurzynski, Gloria Joan *writer*

Tooele
Rice, Stuart Evan *researcher, author*

VERMONT

Alburg
DiSipio, Rocco Thomas *writer*

Bennington
Glazier, Lyle *writer, educator*

Burlington
Hearon, Shelby *writer, lecturer, educator*

Castleton
†Lavin, Stuart Roy *writer, adult education educator*

Charlotte
Harris, Kathleen McKinley *writer*

Chester
Parsons, Cynthia *writer, educational consultant*

Dorset
†Pember, John Scott *poet*

Marlboro
†Dudley, Ellen Revie *writer, editor, publisher*

Middlebury
Blair, Patricia Wohlgemuth *economics writer*
Wright, Nancy Means *author, educator*

Middletown Springs
Asch, Frank *writer children's books, illustrator*

North Bennington
Belitt, Ben *poet, educator*

Norwich
Stetson, Eugene William, III *film producer*

South Royalton
Powers, Thomas Moore *author*

Thetford
Paley, Grace *author, educator*

VIRGINIA

Aldie
Weaver, Kitty Dunlap *author*

Alexandria
David, Joseph Raymond, Jr. *writer, periodical editor*
Tatham, Julie Campbell *writer*
Wallace, Barbara Brooks *writer*
Wells, Fay Gillis *writer, lecturer, broadcaster, aviation historian*

Annandale
Nowak, Jan Zdzislaw *writer, consultant*

Arlington
Bird, Caroline *author*
†Garfinkel, Patricia Gail *speech writer, policy analyst, poet*
Hittle, James Donald *writer, business consultant*
Page, Carolyn Ann *writer*

Ashburn
Boyne, Walter James *writer, former museum director*

Blacksburg
†Falco, Edward *writer, English educator*
†Poirier-Bures, Simone Thérèse *composition and creative writing educator, writer*

Burke
White, Terry Joe *writer, editor*

Chantilly
Priem, Richard Gregory *writer, information systems executive, entertainment company executive*

Charlotte Court House
Hoffman, William *author*

Charlottesville
Casey, John Dudley *writer, English language educator*
Dove, Rita Frances *poet, English language educator*
Viebahn, Fred *writer, journalist*

Fairfax
Bausch, Richard Carl *writer, educator*
Parrish-St. John, Florence Tucker *writer, retired government official*

Falls Church
Leighton, Frances Spatz *writer, journalist*
Morrison, H. Robert *writer, editor, politician*
Orben, Robert *editor, writer*
Whitehead, Kenneth Dean *author, translator, retired federal government official*

Fort Belvoir
Smith, Margherita *writer, editor*

Fredericksburg
Westebbe, Barbara Liebst *writer, sculptor*

Harrisonburg
Davis, Melodie Miller *writer, editor*

Hillsboro
Farwell, Byron Edgar *writer*

Lake Ridge
Englert, Helen Wiggs *writer*

Lexington
†Lyle, Katie Letcher *writer, educator*
†Solod, Lisa *writer*
Stuart, Dabney, III *poet, author, English language educator*

Lynchburg
Fulcher, Hugh Drummond *author*

Newport News
Buranelli, Vincent John *writer*

Norfolk
Berent, Irwin Mark *writer, software executive*
†Ruckdeschel, Susan *writing educator*

Petersburg
†Davis, Louise Minnie *writer*

Portsmouth
Mapp, Alf Johnson, Jr. *writer, historian*

Reston
Smith, Ralph Lee *author, musician*

Roanoke
Ayyildiz, Judy Light *writer, poet, educator*
Reiley, John Echols *writer*

Springfield
Hyland, Patricia Ann (Pat Hyland) *writer*

Vienna
Olshaker, Mark Bruce *author, film-maker*

Virginia Beach
Gunn, S. Jeanne *writer, artist, Reiki educator*
Seward, William W(ard), Jr. *author, educator*

Warrenton
Estaver, Paul Edward *writer, poet*

Woodville
Mc Carthy, Eugene Joseph *writer, former senator*

WASHINGTON

Bainbridge Island
†Snydal, James Matthew *poet*

Bellevue
Dickerson, Eugenie Ann *writer, journalist*

Bremerton
Hanf, James Alphonso *poet, government official*

Ellensburg
Paul, Virginia Otto *writer, administrator*

Gig Harbor
†Nelson, Jo Ann *writer, educator*

Issaquah
Trask, Robert Chauncey Riley *author, lecturer, foundation executive*

Kirkland
Szablya, Helen Mary *author, language professional, lecturer*

La Conner
Robbins, Thomas Eugene *author*

Lynnwood
Bear, Gregory Dale *writer, illustrator*
Moore, Susan Lynn *writer, television producer*

Manson
Hackenmiller, Thomas Raymond *writer, publisher*

Medina
Wong, Janet Siu *writer*

Mercer Island
Porad, Francine Joy *poet, painter*

Olympia
†Power, Marjorie *poet*

Port Angeles
Muller, Willard C(hester) *writer*

Redmond
†Enbysk, H. Monte *writer*
Vosevich, Kathi Ann *writer, editor, scholar*

Seattle
†Balk, Christianne Eve *writer*
Gross, Catherine Mary (Kate Gross) *writer, educator*
Kenney, Richard Laurence *poet, English language educator*
Kunkel, Georgie Bright *writer, retired school counselor*
McHugh, Heather *poet*
†Mc Intyre, Vonda Neel *author*
O'Mahony, Timothy Kieran *writer*
Pearce, Jeannie *writer, real estate agent*
Rimel, Linda June *writer*
Robb, Candace *novelist*
Singer, Sarah Beth *poet*
Sonnenfeld, Sandi *writer*
Sprague, Dale Joseph *writer*
Wagoner, David Russell *author, educator*

Spokane
†Brock, Randall J. *poet*
Kremers, Carolyn Sue *writer, musician, educator*
†Woodbury, Sara Jean *poet*

Tacoma
Douglas, Robert Owen *writer*
Maynard, Steven Harry *writer*

Vancouver
Hamby, Barbara Jean *writer, poet*

Walla Walla
Zipf, Teri M. *poet, writer*

Yakima
Jensen, Cherryl Kay *writer, public relations consultant*

WEST VIRGINIA

Huntington
Baber, Ralph King *writer, publisher*

Morgantown
Gagliano, Frank Joseph *playwright*

Newell
Spayth, Ann Schuyler *poet*

WISCONSIN

Appleton
†Dintenfass, Mark *writer, English educator*
Houk, Margaret *writer*
Rice, Ferill Jeane *writer, civic worker*

Argyle
Daley, Ron (Ronald Eugene Daley) *playwright, poet, director, producer*

Barneveld
†Welsh, Randy N. *writer*

De Pere
†Mori, Kyoko *writer, educator*

Elkhorn
Dunn, Walter Scott, Jr. *writer, former museum director, consultant*

Greenfield
Helland, Sherman M. *author*

Kenosha
†Tobin, Daniel Eugene *poet, English language educator*

Madison
Stone, John Timothy, Jr. *writer*
Wilson, Jacquelyn *writer*

Marshfield
†Carter, Alden Richardson *writer*

Menasha
Mills, Laurel *poet*

Milwaukee
Connelly, Mark *writer, educator*
†McIntyre, Virginia Ann *poet*
Reid, Margaret Kathleen *literature educator*

New Glarus
Marsh, Robert Charles *writer, music critic*

Racine
Wright, Betty Ren *children's book writer*

Shorewood
Cataldi, Phyllis Jean *writer, publisher of genealogies*

South Milwaukee
Thibaudeau, May Murphy *writer*

Wausau
Krause, Steven Albert *writer*

WYOMING

Jackson
†Sandlin, Tim Bernard *author, screenwriter*

Laramie
Boresi, Arthur Peter *author, educator*

Moose
Schreier, Carl Alan *writer, publisher*

Pinedale
Barlow, John Perry *writer*

CANADA

ALBERTA

Edmonton
Hughes, Monica *author*

BRITISH COLUMBIA

Chilliwack
Kinsella, William Patrick *author, educator*

North Vancouver
Harris, Christie Lucy *author*

Saanichton
Crozier, Lorna *poet, educator*

Vancouver
Bowering, George Harry *writer, English literature educator*

MANITOBA

Winnipeg
Oberman, Sheldon Arnold *writer, educator*

ONTARIO

Don Mills
Atwood, Margaret Eleanor *author*

London
Reaney, James Crerar *dramatist, poet, educator*

Ottawa
Lunn, Janet Louise Swoboda *writer*

Owen Sound
Bradford, Karleen *writer*

Port Hope
Mowat, Farley McGill *writer*

Scarborough
Hunter, Bernice Thurman *writer*

Sudbury
Havel, Jean Eugène Martial *author, educator*

Toronto
Bodsworth, Fred *author, naturalist*
Colombo, John Robert *poet, editor, writer*
Moore, Christopher Hugh *writer*
Parr, James Gordon *writer*
Shields, Carol Ann *writer, educator*

QUEBEC

Montreal
Bruemmer, Fred *writer, photographer*
Richler, Mordecai *writer*

MEXICO

San Luis Soyatlan
Sizemore, Deborah Lightfoot *writer, editor*

AUSTRALIA

Avalon
West, Morris Langlo *novelist*

ENGLAND

Cambridge
Steiner, George (Francis Steiner) *author, educator*

Hingham
Pollini, Francis *author*

London
Adams, Douglas Noel *writer*
Bawden, Nina (Mary) *writer*
Clarke, Sir Arthur Charles *author*
Cleese, John Marwood *writer, businessman, comedian*
Cope, Wendy *poet*
Cowles, Fleur (Mrs. Tom M. Meyer) *author, artist*
Deighton, Len *author*
Drabble, Margaret *writer*
Fine, Anne *author*
Follett, Kenneth Martin *author*
Fowles, John *author*
Galloway, Janice *writer, editor*
Hare, David *playwright*
Hughes, Winifred Shirley *writer, illustrator*
Hunter Blair, Pauline Clarke *author*
James, P(hyllis) D(orothy) (Baroness James of Holland Park of Southwold in County of Suffolk) *author*
le Carré, John (David John Moore Cornwell) *author*
Lessing, Doris (May) *writer*
Paton Walsh, Jill *author*
Pinter, Harold *playwright*
Read, Piers Paul *author*
Spark, Muriel Sarah *writer*
Stoppard, Tom (Tomas Straussler) *playwright*

Oxford
Aldiss, Brian (Wilson) *writer*
Pullman, Philip Nicholas *author*

Rottingdean
Matthews, John Floyd *writer, educator*

West Sussex
Aiken, Joan (Delano) *author*

Whitechurch
Adams, Richard George *writer*

FRANCE

Paris
Gallant, Mavis *author*
Williams, C(harles) K(enneth) *poet, literature and writing educator*

Ramatuelle
Collins, Larry *author, journalist*

IRELAND

Donegal
Friel, Brian (Bernard Patrick Friel) *author*

Mullingar
Donleavy, James Patrick *writer, artist*

Wicklow
McCaffrey, Anne Inez *author*

ITALY

Ravello
Vidal, Gore *writer*

Venice
Pasinetti, Pier Maria *author*

RUSSIA

Moscow
Solzhenitsyn, Aleksandr Isayevich *author*

TRINIDAD AND TOBAGO

Diego Martin
Walcott, Derek Alton *poet, playwright*

ADDRESS UNPUBLISHED

Allen, Danny Eugene *writer, naturalist, activitist*
Allen, Ralph Gilmore *dramatist, producer, drama educator*
Allen, Thomas B. *writer*
Aloff, Mindy *writer*
Anderson-Spivy, Alexandra *writer, editor*
†Angeline, Mary *poet*
Anton, Barbara *writer*
Ark, Laurine *writer*
Arlen, Michael J. *writer*
Askew, Dennis Lee *poet*
Bach, Mária-Cathérine *writer, researcher, translator*
Bacon-Smith, Camille *educator, writer*
†Bahr, Jane Marie *writer, retired English educator*
Bailey, William Waddell *writer, communications executive*
Baird, Alan C. *screenwriter*
Baldrige, Letitia *writer, management training consultant*
†Bang, Mary Jo *poet*
†Bapst, Donald Joseph, Jr. *writer*
Barker, Clive *artist, screenwriter, director, producer, writer*
Barkey, Brenda *technical writer, publications manager*
Barnes, Joanna *author, actress*
†Barnes, Kate *poet*
†Barrett, Katherine *writer, multimedia producer*
Barzun, Jacques *author, literary consultant*
Bassett, Elizabeth Ewing (Libby Bassett) *writer, editor*
Bauer, Caroline Feller *author*
Beach, Edward Latimer *writer, retired naval officer*
Beatts, Anne Patricia *writer, producer*
Bellow, Saul C. *writer*
Bender, Hy *writer*
†Bender, Sheila Sue *essayist, poet, author*
†Benson, Stephen Edward *writer*
†Berg, A(ndrew) Scott *author, biographer*
Berger, Linda Fay *writer*
Berndt, Jane Ann *writer, researcher, educator*
Bernstein, Jane *writer*
Berry, Richard Lewis *author, magazine editor, lecturer, programmer*
Billman, Larry Edward *writer, director*
Blair, Sandra Jean *author, publisher*
Block, Lawrence *author*
Block, Paul Alan *novelist, editor*
†Bogner, Norman *novelist, screenwriter, playwright*
†Bornstein, David Neil *writer*
Bourrie, Sally Ruth *writer*
Bova, Benjamin William *author, editor, educator*
Bracken, Peg *author*
Brandt, Ronald Stirling *writer*
†Branyan, W. David *novelist*
†Bronstein, Lynne *writer*
Brookman, Carol Joyce *writer*
Brookner, Anita *writer, educator*
Brown, Marcia Joan *author, artist, photographer*
Brumberg, G. David *history bibliographer*
Bryant, John *author, publisher*
Buckstein, Caryl Sue *writer*
Bulla, Clyde Robert *writer*
Bullins, Ed *author*
Burger, Robert Eugene *author, chess expert*
Burke, Doug *author, director, producer, inventor*
Burns, Kitty *playwright*
Campbell, Addison James, Jr. *writer*
Campbell, Will Davis *writer*
Caras, Roger Andrew *author, motion picture company executive, television correspondent, radio commentator*
Carner, Charles Robert, Jr. *screenwriter, director*
Carpenter, Edward Kearney *writer, editor*
Carpenter, Patricia Lynn *author*
Cartland, Barbara *author*
Castle, Sandie *writer, playwright, artist*
Cherryh, C. J. *writer*
Chesney, Susan Talmadge *writer, developer*
Chmielarz, Sharon Lee *writer, educator*
Choukas-Bradley, Melanie *writer, photographer*
Christina, Greta *book and film critic, writer, editor*
Claes, Gayla Christine *writer, editorial consultant*
Clark, Mary Higgins *author, business executive*
†Clifton, Lucille Thelma *author*
Coburn, D(onald) L(ee) *playwright*
Cogan, Karen Elizabeth *author, educator*
Cohen, Sherry Suib *writer*
†Conover, Jill M. *freelance writer*
Cook, Gloria Jean *writer*
Coonts, Stephen Paul *novelist*
Cory, Angelica Jo *author, spiritual consultant*
Couto, Nancy Vieira *poet, literary consultant*
Cowan, Andrew Glenn *television writer, producer, performer*
Crews, Mara Lynne *writer*
Crisman Carlson, Ruth Marie *writer*
†Cullen, Paula Bramsen *author*
Dageforde, Mary L. *technical writer, software designer*
†D'Ambrosio, Vinni Marie *writer*
†Darton, Eric *writer*
†Davies, Peter Ho *writer, educator*
†Davis, Don D., III *author, lawyer*
Davis, Luther *writer, producer*
Davis, Susanne Marie *writer, educator*
†De Mille, Barbara Munn *writer, former English literature educator*
Disch, Thomas M(ichael) *author*
Dolan, Edward Francis *writer*
Dolnick, Irene *financial services company official*
Dooling, Richard Patrick *writer, lawyer*
†Drake, Barbara Ruth *writer*
Drucker, Peter Ferdinand *writer, consultant, educator*
†Dubroff, Susanne *poet, former social worker*
Dunton-Downer, Leslie Linam *writer*
Eastup, Lavonda Jo *writer, poet, songwriter*
†Edelmann, Carolyn Foote *author, poet, editor*
Eglee, Charles Hamilton *television and movie writer, producer*
Elbin-Schell, Carol Gertrude *television promotion manager*
Ephron, Nora *writer, director*
Erickson, Donna Joy *writer, educator*
Erwin, Judith Ann (Judith Ann Peacock) *writer, photographer, lawyer*
†Espaillat, Rhina Polonia *poet*
Esty, John Cushing, Jr. *writer, teacher, advisor to non-profit boards*
Evangelista, Anita Loretta *freelance writer, emergency medical technician, nurse*
Ewart, Claire Lynn *author, illustrator*
Fadiman, Louise *writer, consultant*
Fammerée, Richard Arthur *poet, composer, performing artist*
†Farnsworth, John Seibert *writer*
†Farnsworth, Robert Lambton *poet, English educator*
†Farrelly, Peter John *screenwriter*
Fearrington, Ann Peyton *writer, illustrator, newspaper reporter, portraitist*
Feitlowitz, Marguerite *writer, literary translator*
Fell, Jennifer Anne *writer*
Fetler, Andrew *author, educator*
Fitzpatrick, Nancy Hecht *magazine editor*
Foote, Horton *playwright, scriptwriter*
Ford, Victoria *author, educator*
Fraser, Kathleen Joy *poet, creative writing educator*
Freed, Melvyn Norris *writer, retired higher education educator*
Freedman, Russell Bruce *author*
French, Marilyn *author, critic*
Fritz, Ethel Mae Hendrickson *writer*
†Fromm, Peter Francis *author*
Fryer, Thomas Waitt, Jr. *writer and editor*
Fuentes, Carlos *writer, former ambassador*
Fuller, Charles H, Jr *playwright*
Fuller, Elizabeth L. *writer, playwright*
Gardner, Nancy Bruff *writer*
†George, Linda Shumaker *writer, educator*
Gericke, Shane William *writer*
Gifford, Heidi *editor, writer*
Gilchrist, Ellen Louise *writer*
Gilroy, Frank Daniel *playwright*
Glick, Ruth Burtnick *author, lecturer*
Glück, Louise Elisabeth *poet*
Goble, Paul *author, illustrator, artist*
†Goldberg, Gerald Jay *writer, educator*
Gordimer, Nadine *author*
†Gordon, Fran diLustro *writer*
Gorham, George H. *playwright, lyricist*
Goss, Joel Francis *writer*
Gottlieb, Sherry Gershon *author, editor*
Grady, James Thomas *novelist*
†Grant, D(oris) Jean *writer*
Gray, Francine du Plessix *author*
†Graybill, Guy Oldt *writer*
Greenburg, Dan *author*
Greer, Germaine *author*
†Griffith, Patricia Browning *writer, educator*
†Grobel, Michael Lawrence *writer, editor*
Groening, Matthew *writer, cartoonist*
Gurvis, Sandra Jane *writer*
Guy, Eleanor Bryenton *writer*
Haas, Charlie *screenwriter*
Hahn, Mary Downing *author*
Haldeman, Joe William *novelist*
Hamit, Francis Granger *freelance writer*
Harden, Patrick Alan *journalist*
Hardy, Bridget McColl *screenwriter*
Harlow, Joan Beverley *writer*
Harrigan, Anthony Hart *author*
†Harris, Jana *writer, educator*
Harris, Jeanette Marianne *writer*
†Harshman, Marc *writer, poet, consultant*
Harvey, Willard Albertson, Jr. *writer, distribution company executive*
Haskell, Margaret Howard *writer, psychotherapist*
†Hawke, Simon Nicholas *writer, educator*
Hawkins, John *writer*
Helprin, Mark *author*
Henigson, Ann Pearl *freelance writer, songwriter, lyricist*
Henry, Joanne Landers *writer*
Herbert, Mary Katherine Atwell *freelance writer*
Herman, George Adam *writer*
Herman, Hank *writer*
Herstein, Howard Joseph *author*
Heymann, C(lemens) David *author*
Hiebel, William Raymond *writer, artist, composer, retired English educator*
Hijuelos, Oscar *novelist*
†Hill, Carol DeChellis *writer, novelist*
Hillerman, Tony *writer, former journalism educator*
Hirschberg, Vera Hilda *writer*
Hoban, Lillian *author, illustrator*
Hoffman, N.M. *poet*
Hollander, Anne *writer*
Holmes, Doloris Grant (Doloris Schwerner) *writer, social worker, theater director*
Holmes, Marjorie Rose *author*
†Hooper, Patricia *writer*
Houghtaling, Pamela Ann *technology writer, consultant*
Howell, Christopher Allen *technical writer*
Howes, Sophia DuBose *writer*
Hoyt, Mary Finch *author, editor, media consultant, former government official*
†Huffington, Arianna *writer*
†Hussman, Lawrence Eugene *writer, retired educator*
Huston, Nancy Louise *writer, educator*
†Imhof, Susan Anne *Poet*
†Isaacs, Anne Elizabeth *writer*
Isaacs, Susan *novelist, screenwriter*
Isbell, Harold M(ax) *writer, investor*
Jabs, Carolyn R. *writer*
Jackson, Charles Ian *writer, consultant*
†Jaffee, Annette Williams *novelist*
James, Tracey Faye *screenwriter*
†Janzen, Jean Wiebe *poet, educator*
Jenks, Tom *writer*
Jerace, Charlotte Louise *writer, consultant*
Johnson, Eydith G. Ivory *poet*
Jordan, Carrie Grayson *writer, poet, drama designer*
Jorden, William John *writer, retired diplomat*
Just, Ward Swift *author*
Kachuba, John Barrie *writer, editor*
Kanin, Fay *screenwriter*
†Kanter, Lynn *writer*
†Kantrowitz, Melanie Kaye *writer*
Kass, Jerome Allan *writer*
Katz, William Loren *author*
Katzenbach, John Strong Miner *author*
Kauffman, Dagmar Elisabeth *writer, researcher*
Keith, Carol Jean *writer, regional historian*
Kellerman, Faye Marder *novelist, dentist*
†Kemmett, William Joseph *poet, educator*
Kepes, Gyorgy *author, painter, photographer, educator*
Kessler, Stephen James *writer, editor*
Ketch, Tina *writer*
Khalid, Samy *writer*
Kidder, (John) Tracy *writer*
Kincaid, Jamaica *writer*
King, Joy Rainey *poet, retired medical secretary*
King, Larry L. *playwright, actor*
Klein, Roberta Phyllis *writer, editor, consultant, architect and designer*
Knowles, Jocelyn Wagner *health writer, women's health specialist*
†Koch, Margaret R. *writer, artist, historian*
Kocher, Margaret *technical writer*
Koepp, David *screenwriter*
†Kohn, Rita *author, playwright, journalist, educator*
Konigsburg, Elaine Lobl *author*
Koral, Marian *writer*
Kotlowitz, Alex *writer, journalist*
Krantz, Judith Tarcher *novelist*
†Kress, Nancy *writer*
Kristofferson, Karl Eric *writer*
†Krob, Melanie Gordon *writer*
Kuper, Daniela F. *writer, speaker*
Kushner, Tony *playwright*
Laboda, Amy Sue *writer*
Lally, Michael David *writer, actor*
Lambert, William Jesse, III *writer*
Lardner, Ring Wilmer, Jr. *author*
Larkin, Joan *poet, English educator*
Lashner, William Mark *writer*
Lawrence, Jerome *playwright, director, educator*
Lenard, Lisa H. *writer, educator*
Lenhart, Gary Alan *poet*
Levine, Israel E. *writer*
Lewis, Dennis Carroll *writer, publisher, educator*
Lindenberger, Herbert Samuel *writer, literature educator*
Line, Diane Jer'i *writer*
Lingle, Marilyn Felkel *freelance writer, columnist*
Link, William Theodore *television writer, producer*
Livo, Norma Joan *writer*
Lloyd, David Nigel *song writer, poet, performer*
Lober, Lionel M. *screenwriter, producer*
Long, (Lotus) Elaine *writer, editor*
Longstreet, Stephen (Chauncey Longstreet) *author, painter*
Lopez, Barry Holstun *writer*
Lord, Walter *author*
Lubell, Ellen *writer*
Luhn, Robert Kent *writer, magazine editor*
LyListon, William Phillip *writer, poet*
Macaulay, David (Alexander) *author, illustrator*
MacLachlan, Patricia *author*
Macleod, Normajean *writer*
Madrick, Jeffrey G. *writer, economic consultant*
Mamet, David Alan *playwright, director, essayist*
Manchester, William *writer*
Mann, Emily Betsy *writer, artistic director, theater director*
Mano, D. Keith *novelist*
Mansell Mayo, Catherine *writer, editor, economist*
Martin, Paul Raymond *writer*
Martindale, Nancy Elaine *writer, publisher, editor*
Marx, Anne (Mrs. Frederick E. Marx) *poet*
Mason, Connie Jeanne *writer*
Mathews, Harry Burchell *poet, novelist, educator*
Mathis, Sharon Bell *author, retired elementary educator and librarian*
McFall, Catherine Gardner *poet, critic, educator*
†McLaughlin, Patricia Ann *writer*
†McMillan, Gloria L. *writing educator*
McMillan, Terry L. *writer, educator*
†McNamee, Gregory Lewis *writer, editor*
Mc Phee, John Angus *writer*
McPherson, James Alan *writer, educator*
Mead, Loren Benjamin *writer, consultant*
Meaker, Marijane Agnes *author*
Meidav, Edie Emanuela *writer, educator*
Mele, Jim *writer*
Mendoza, George *poet, author*
†Merrill, Augustus Lee *poet, retired English educator*
Merrill, Jean Fairbanks *writer*
†Micucci, Dana Ann *writer*
Miller, Arthur *playwright, author*
Miller, JP (James Pinckney Miller) *screenwriter, novelist, playwright*
Millhauser, Steven *writer*
†Minczeski, John *poet*
Minton, Jeffrey S. *writer*
Mintz, Morton Abner *author, former newspaper reporter*
†Moffet, Penelope Jeanne *freelance writer, legal secretary*
Mogel, Leonard Henry *author*
Morang, Diane Judy *writer, television producer, business entrepreneur*
Morehouse, Kathleen Salisbury Moore *writer*
Morin-Miller, Carmen Aline *writer*
Morrison, Sarah Lyddon *author*
Morrow, Barry Nelson *screenwriter, producer*
Morse, Flo *writer*
Muldoon, Thomas Lyman *writer*
Murray, Albert L. *writer, educator*
Muson, Howard Henry *writer, editor*
Neal, Margaret Sherrill *writer, editor*
Neely, Mark Edward, Jr. *writer*
Nicholas, Lynn Holman *writer*
Noëldechen, Joan Marguerite *writer*
Nordley, Gerald David *writer, investor*
Norton, Andre Alice *author*
Nova, Craig *writer*
Ogden, Ann *writer*
Oldfield, A(rthur) Barney *writer, radio commentator*
O'Leary, Patsy Baker *writer, educator*
Oliansky, Joel *author, director*
Olsen, Jack *writer*
Orrmont, Arthur *writer, editor*
†Osborne, Linda Barrett *writer, editor*
Ossana, Diana Lynn *author, screenwriter*
Owens, Betsy Kingsolver *writer*
Paolucci, Anne Attura *playwright, poet, English and comparative literature educator*
Parker, Robert Brown *novelist*
Parrott, Wanda Sue *writer, journalist*
Patent, Dorothy Hinshaw *author, photographer*
Patterson, Richard North *novelist, writer, lawyer*
Perritti, Martha Lou *writer*
Perry, Josephine *screen writer, playwright, educator*
Perry, Ruth *writer*
Pierce, Robert Nash *writer*
Pietrzyk, Leslie *writer*
Polanco, Rosana Lim *grant writer*
Pollan-Cohen, Shirley *poet, educator*
†Pollet, Elizabeth *writer, educator*
Porto, Mark *writer*
Potok, Chaim *author, artist, editor*
Pratt, Veronica Kane *writer*
Prescott, Richard Chambers *writer*
Proulx, (Edna) Annie *writer*
†Rabey, Stephen Alan *writer*
Rader, Dotson Carlyle *author, journalist*
Rains, Sally Tippett *writer*
Ramsden, Karen McCoin *writer*
Raucher, Herman *novelist, screenwriter*
Ravetch, Irving *screenwriter*
Rechy, John Francisco *author*
Reeder, Thomas Allen *television writer*
Reiss, Gwen North *writer, poet, lecture agent*
†Reiter, Victoria A. *writer, translator*
†Rembold, Kristen Staby *writer*
Renaud, Bernadette Marie Elise *author*
Rice, Stan, Jr. *poet, painter, English language educator*
Richter, W. D. *screenwriter, director, producer*
Riehecky, Janet Ellen *writer*
Riehm, Sarah Lawrence *writer, arts administrator*
Ring, Nancy Gail *writer, artist*
Ripley, Alexandra Braid *author*
†Robb, Lynda Johnson *writer*
Roberts, Russell *freelance writer*
Roberts, Wess *author*
Robins, Natalie *poet, writer*
Robinson, David Bradford *scientific writer, poet*
Rockstein, Morris *science writer, editor, consultant*
†Rodenas, Paula *author, journalist*
Rogers, David *playwright, novelist, actor*
Rohrbach, Peter Thomas *writer*
†Rollings, Alane *poet, educator*
Romans, Elizabeth Anne *writer, artist, multimedia professional*
Rosenblatt, Joseph *poet, editor*
Rosenblatt, Roger *writer*
Rosenfeld, Albert Hyman *science and medical writer*
Rosmus, Anna Elisabeth *writer*
Royse, Brooke Sarno *editor, writer*
Rubin, Charles Alexis *writer*
Rush, Norman *author*
Sallis, James *writer*
†Sánchez-Llama, Inigo *Spanish literature educator*
Sanders, Theresa Lynn *writer, systems analyst, consultant*
Schaefer, Christina Kassabian *writer, genealogist*
Schatz, Lillian Lee *playwright, molecular biologist, educator*
Schenkkan, Robert Frederic *writer, actor*
Schickel, Richard *writer, film critic, producer*
Schneider, Phyllis Leah *writer, editor*
Schueler, Gerald Joseph *technical writer, service counselor*
Seamans, William *writer, commentator, former television and radio journalist*
Sears, Steven Lee *screenwriter, consultant*
Seidel, Frederick Lewis *poet*
Selby, Hubert, Jr. *writer*
Selz, Thalia Cheronis *writer, educator*
Shagan, Steve *screenwriter, novelist, film producer*
Shapiro, Karl Jay *poet, former educator*
†Shapiro, Molly Ann *writer*
Shattuck, Roger Whitney *author, educator*
Shauers, Margaret Ann *author*
Shep, Robert Lee *editor, publisher, textile book researcher*
Sherman, Susan Jean *writer, editor, educator*
Shindler, Merrill Karsh *writer, radio personality*
Shore, Herbert *writer, poet, educator*
Shortz, Wilma Wildes *writer, Arabian horse breeder*
Shreve, Susan Richards *author, English literature educator*
Sidebottom, David Kirk *writer, former engineer*
Silver, Nina Gail *writer, psychotherapist, singer-songwriter*
Singer, Donna Lea *writer, editor, educator*
Singer, Marilyn *writer*
Skibell, Joseph Freer *writer, educator*
Skinner, Knute rumsey *poet, English educator*
Skwarczynski, Henryk Adam (Henryk Skwar) *writer*
Smith, Anne Day *writer*
Smith, Cynthia S. *writer*
Smith, Jane Marilyn Davis (Jane Maxwell) *writer*
Smith, Martin Cruz *author*
Smith, Marya Jean *writer*
†Smith, Suzanne F. *writer*
Solomon, Beth Carol *writer*
Sontag, Susan *writer*
SoRelle, Ruth Doyle *medical writer, journalist*
Spada, James *author, photographer, publisher*
Spies, Karen Bornemann *writer, education consultant*
Spinelli, Jerry *writer*
Spinnanger, Ruthe Thoverud *writer, retired secondary school educator*
Stano, Mary Gerardine *writer, tax accountant*
Stark, Evelyn Brill *poet, musician*
†Stashower, Daniel Meyer *writer*
Steed, Kelly Renée *freelance writer and researcher*
Steelsmith, Mary Joanne *playwright, actress*
Stepak, Asa Martin *writer*
Stern, Daniel *author, executive, educator*
Stevens, Shane *novelist*
Stevenson, Elizabeth *author, educator*
Stewart, Whitney *children's book writer*
Stone, Oliver *screenwriter, director*
Stonecypher, David Daniel *writer, retired psychiatrist and ophthalmologist*
†Strand, Mark *poet*
Straub, Peter Francis *novelist*
†Strickland, Stephanie *poet*
Strong, Susan Clancey *writer, communication consultant, editor*
Styron, William *writer*
†Sullivan, Evelin Elisabeth *writer, educator*
Sullivan, George Edward *author*
Sussman, Barry *author, public opinion analyst and pollster, journalist*
Swift, Harriet *writer, editor*
†Szydlowski, Mary Vigliante *writer*
Talal, Marilynn Glick *poet*
Tally, Ted *screenwriter*
†Taylor, Eleanor Ross *writer*
Taylor, John Jackson (Jay) *writer, international consultant, retired foreign service officer*
Theroux, Paul Edward *author*
†Thomas, Shelley Lynn *technical writer*
Thompson, Hunter Stockton *author, political analyst, journalist*
Tigges, John Thomas *writer, musician, lecturer*
Tobias, Sheila *writer, educator*
†Traina, Anastasia Rose *playwright, screenwriter*
†Tregarthen, Suzanne Jo *writer, dean*
Trotsky, Judith *writer*
Truman, Margaret *author*
Tucker, Jack William Andrew *writer, film editor, producer*
Turner, Megan Whalen *author*
Turnipseed, Joel Thomas *writer*
Twichell, Chase *poet*
Updike, John Hoyer *writer*
Van Duyn, Mona Jane *poet*
Van Dyke, Henry Lewis *retired educator, writer*
van Itallie, Jean-Claude *playwright*
Viorst, Judith Stahl *author*
Viorst, Milton *writer*
Voigt, Cynthia *author*
Volk, Patricia Gay *fiction writer, essayist*
von Hoffman, Nicholas *writer, former journalist*
Wallace, Michele *writer, educator*
Wambaugh, Joseph *author*
Warren, Cindy Michelle *author*
Wasserstein, Wendy *playwright*

Watts, Julia Ellen *writer, English educator*
Webb, David Allen *writer*
Weiner, Cherry *literary agent*
Weiner, Jonathan David *writer*
Weis, Margaret Edith *writer, editor*
†Wellman, Mac *writer, educator*
Whalen, Charles William, Jr. *author, business executive, educator*
Whelchel, Sandra Jane *writer*
†White, Claire Nicolas *writer, translator*
White, Michael Craig *writer, illustrator*
Wilkinson, Claude Henry *writer, artist, English literature educator*
Williams, Donald Allen, Jr. *writer, independent television/video producer*
Wilson, Colin Henry *writer*
Wilson, Lanford *playwright*
Wilson, Sloan *author, lecturer*
Witte, Arline (Lyn Witte) *author/poet*
Wohlfeld, Valerie Robin *writer*
Wolverton, Terry L(ynn) *writer, consultant*
Wood, William Preston *author, lawyer*
Wright, Charles Spaulding, II *writer, communications consultant*
Yeager, Anson Anders *writer, former columnist and newspaper editor*
Yglesias, Rafael Jose *novelist*
Zagaski, Chester Anthony, Jr. *author, researcher*
Zaillian, Steven *screenwriter, director*
Zhiglevich, Eugenia *writer, actress*

ARTS: PERFORMING

UNITED STATES

ALABAMA

Birmingham
Dougherty, Dana Dean Lesley *television producer, educator*
Gilmore, Catherine Rye *arts administrator*
Hill, Stan Wayne *video producer*
Powell, Curtis Everett *music educator, college official*
†Westerfield, Richard *music director*

Huntsville
Mohan, Tungesh Nath *television and film producer, film educator*

Jacksonville
Fairleigh, James Parkinson *music educator*

Midfield
Bush, Dennis *radio personality*

Montgomery
Copeland, Jacqueline Turner *music educator*

Point Clear
Englund, Gage Bush *dancer, educator*

ALASKA

Indian
Wright, Gordon Brooks *musician, conductor, educator*

ARIZONA

Flagstaff
Aurand, Charles Henry, Jr. *music educator*

Fountain Hills
Tyl, Noel Jan *baritone, astrologer, writer*

Glendale
Zinn, Dennis Bradley *magician, actor, corporate skills trainer*

Mesa
Mason, Marshall W. *theater director, educator*

Phoenix
Aschaffenburg, Walter Eugene *composer, music educator*
DeMichele, Mark Anthony *stage director, educator, actor*
†Michael, Hermann *music director*
†Montague, Gray *performing company executive*
Nijinsky, Tamara *actress, puppeteer, author, librarian, educator*
Sibbio, Michael Gregory *promoter, concept developer, audio technical consultant*
Uthoff, Michael *dancer, choreographer, artistic director*

Scottsdale
Fosgate Heggli, Julie Denise *producer*
Peterson, John Willard *composer, music publisher*
Smith, Leonard Bingley *musician*

Sedona
Gregory, James *retired actor*
Griffin, (Alva) Jean *entertainer*
Rhines, Marie Louise *composer, violinist*

Teec Nos Pos
Smith, Mark Edward *music educator*

Tempe
Lombardi, Eugene Patsy *orchestra conductor, violinist, educator, recording artist*
Nagrin, Daniel *dancer, educator, choreographer, lecturer, writer*

Tucson
Armstrong, R(obert) Dean *entertainer*
Feliciano, José *entertainer*
Hanson, George *music director, conductor*
Malmgren, René Louise *educational theater administrator*
Puente, Tito Anthony *orchestra leader, composer, arranger*
Rich, Bobby *broadcast personality, radio programmer*
Seaman, Arlene Anna *musician, educator*

ARKANSAS

Clarksville
Pennington, Donald Harris *musician, retired physician*

Fort Smith
Husarik, Stephen *music educator*

Little Rock
†Itkin, David *music director, conductor*
Raney, Miriam Day *actress*

Paragould
Stallings, Phyllis Ann *music educator*

CALIFORNIA

Agoura Hills
Andrews, Ralph Herrick *television producer*
Healy, Kieran John Patrick *lighting designer, consultant*
Homer, Raymond Rodney *film producer, director*

Albany
Boris, Ruthanna *dancer, choreographer, dance therapist, educator*

Antioch
Adams, Liliana Osses *music performer, harpist*

Apple Valley
Beller, Gerald Stephen *professional magician, former insurance company executive*

Aptos
Penny, Steve *media producer, speaker*
Swenson, Kathleen Susan *music and art educator*

Arcadia
Zimmerman, Amy J. *producer, director*

Bakersfield
Owens, Buck (Alvis Edgar, Jr.) *singer, musician, songwriter, broadcast executive*

Benicia
Cummings, Barton *musician*

Berkeley
Dresher, Paul Joseph *composer, music educator, performer*
Imbrie, Andrew Welsh *composer, educator*
Kleiman, Vivian Abbe *filmmaker*
Ridgway, David Wenzel *educational film producer, director*
Thow, John H. *music educator, composer*

Beverly Hills
Ackerman, Andy *television director*
Affleck, Ben *actor*
Aiello, Danny *actor*
Alexander, Jason (Jay Scott Greenspan) *actor*
Allen, Debbie *actress, dancer, director, choreographer*
Allen, Joan *actress*
Amis, Suzy *actress*
Anders, Allison *film director, screenwriter*
Anderson, Louie *comedian*
Anderson, Richard Dean *actor*
Aniston, Jennifer *actress*
Ann-Margret, (Ann-Margret Olsson) *actress, performer*
Anspaugh, David *director, producer*
Anwar, Gabrielle *actress*
†Arau, Alfonso *film producer and director, writer*
Armstrong, Bess *actress*
†Armstrong, Gillian May *film director*
Arnold, Tom *actor, comedian, producer*
Arquette, Patricia *actress*
†August, Bille *film director*
Avildsen, John Guilbert *film director*
Aykroyd, Daniel Edward *actor, writer*
†Azaria, Hank *actor*
Bacon, Kevin *actor*
Bailey, John *cinematographer*
†Baird, Stuart *film editor, director*
Baker, Kathy Whitton *actress*
Baldwin, Daniel *actor*
Baldwin, William *actor*
Banderas, Antonio *actor*
†Barkin, Ellen *actress*
Bassett, Angela *actress*
Bates, Kathy *actress*
Bauer, Marty *talent agency execuive*
Baxter, Meredith *actress*
†Bay, Michael Benjamin *film director*
Beatty, (Henry) Warren *actor, producer, director*
Becks, Ronald Arthur *film producer*
Bedelia, Bonnie *actress*
Bellisario, Donald P. *TV writer, director, producer*
Belushi, James A. *actor*
Bening, Annette *actress*
Benson, Robby *actor, director, writer, producer*
†Berenger, Tom (Thomas Michael Moore) *actor*
Bergman, Andrew *motion picture director*
Berkeley, Elizabeth *actress*
†Berkus, James *talent agent*
Bernsen, Corbin *actor*
Bertinelli, Valerie *actress*
†Bevan, Tim *film producer*
Bigelow, Kathryn *film director*
Bisset, Jacqueline *actress*
Blake, Robert (Michael Gubitosi) *actor*
†Blethyn, Brenda Anne *actress*
†Bogdanovich, Peter *film director, writer, producer, actor*
Bonham-Carter, Helena *actress*
Bostwick, Barry *actor*
Branagh, Kenneth *actor, director*
Braun, Zev *motion picture and television producer*
Bridges, Beau (Lloyd Vernet Bridges, III) *actor*
Bridges, Jeff *actor*
Broderick, Matthew *actor*
Brokaw, Norman Robert *talent agency executive*
Bronson, Charles (Charles Buchinsky) *actor*
Brown, Clancy *actor, publishing executive*
Bullock, Sandra *actress*
Burke, Delta *actress*
Burnett, Carol *actress, comedienne, singer*
Burnett, Charles *film director*
†Burnham, John Ludwig *agent*
†Burns, Edward J., Jr. *actor, director*
Burstyn, Ellen (Edna Rae Gillooly) *actress*
Buscemi, Steve *actor*
†Busey, Gary *actor, musician*
Busfield, Timothy *actor*
Caan, James *actor, director*
†Campbell, Neve *actress*
Capshaw, Kate (Kathy Sue Nail) *actress*
†Carpenter, John Howard *director, screenwriter*
Carrere, Tia (Althea Janairo) *actress*
Carrey, Jim *actor*
Carroll, Diahann *actress, singer*
Carter, Chris *producer, director*
†Carter, Helena Bonham *actress*
Carter, Nell *actress, singer*
Caruso, David *actor*
Caton-Jones, Michael *film director*
Channing, Carol *actress*
Chaplin, Geraldine *actress*
Chritton, George A. *film producer*
Clayburgh, Jill *actress*
Clooney, George *actor*
Close, Glenn *actress*
†Coen, Joel *film director, writer*
Columbus, Chris Joseph *film director, screenwriter*
Connery, Sean (Thomas Connery) *actor*
Coolidge, Martha *film director*
Corbin, Barry *actor, writer*
Corman, Eugene Harold *motion picture producer*
Cox, Courteney *actress*
Coyote, Peter (Peter Cohon) *actor*
†Crawford, Cindy *model, actress*
Cronenberg, David *film director*
Crowe, Russell *actor*
†Crystal, Billy *comedian, actor*
Culp, Robert *actor, writer, director*
Curry, Tim *actor*
Curtis, Jamie Lee *actress*
Cusack, Joan *actress*
Cusack, John *actor*
D'Abo, Olivia *actress*
Dalton, Timothy *actor*
†Daly, Timothy *actor*
Damon, Matthew Paige *actor*
Danes, Claire *actress*
†Dante, Joe *film director*
Davidovich, Lolita *actress*
Davis, Andrew *film director, screenwriter*
Davis, Geena (Virginia Davis) *actress*
Dawber, Pam *actress*
Day-Lewis, Daniel (Daniel Michael Blake Day-Lewis) *actor*
Delaney, Kim *actress*
Delany, Dana *actress*
Demme, Jonathan *director, producer, writer*
De Niro, Robert *actor*
Dennehy, Brian *actor*
†Dern, Laura *actress*
DeVito, Danny Michael *actor, director, producer*
DiCaprio, Leonardo *actor*
†Doherty, Shannon *actress*
Donaldson, Roger *film director*
D'Onofrio, Vincent Philip *actor*
Donovan, Tate *actor*
Dotrice, Roy Louis *actor*
†Douglas, Kirk (Issur Danielovitch Demsky) *actor, motion picture producer*
Douglas, Michael Kirk *actor, film producer, director*
†Downey, Robert, Jr. *actor*
†Dreyfuss, Richard Stephan *actor*
Driver, Minnie *actress*
Duke, Patty (Anna Marie Duke) *actress*
Dunaway, (Dorothy) Faye *actress*
Dunne, Griffin *actor, producer*
†Dunst, Kirsten *actress*
Duvall, Robert *actor*
†Dye, John *actor*
Eden, Barbara Jean *actress*
Elwes, Cary *actor*
†Emmerich, Roland *director, producer, writer*
Everett, Rupert *actor*
Farentino, James *actor*
†Fellner, Eric *film producer*
Flaum, Marshall Allen *television producer, writer, director*
Foch, Nina *actress, creative consultant, educator, director*
†Foley, James *film director*
Fonda, Jane *actress*
†Forn, Rick *talent agent*
Foster, Lawrence *concert and opera conductor*
Fox, Michael J. *actor*
Fradis, Anatoly Adolf *film producer*
Franklin, Carl *director*
Fraser, Brendan *actor*
Frears, Stephen *film director*
Freeman, Morgan *actor*
†Friedkin, William *film director*
Friendly, Ed *television producer*
Gabler, Lee *talent agency executive*
†Garber, Victor *stage and film actor*
Garr, Teri (Ann) *actress*
George, Lynda Day *actress*
Gibson, Brian *film director*
Gillard, Stuart Thomas *film and television director, writer*
Gish, Annabeth *actress*
Glenn, (Theodore) Scott *actor*
Gless, Sharon *actress*
Glover, Danny *actor*
Glover, John *actor*
Goldblum, Jeff *actor*
Goodman, John *actor*
Grant, Hugh *actor*
Graves, Peter *actor*
Grey, Brad *producer, agent*
Griffith, Andy (Andrew Samuel Griffith) *actor*
Guest, Christopher *actor, director, screenwriter*
Hackford, Taylor *film director, producer*
Hagman, Larry *actor*
Hallstrom, Lasse *director*
Hamlin, Harry Robinson *actor*
Hanks, Tom *actor*
Hanson, Curtis *director, writer*
†Harlin, Renny (Renny Lauri Mauritz Harjola) *film director*
Harvey, Simon *actor, writer*
Haskell, Peter Abraham *actor*
Hawke, Ethan *actor*
Hawn, Goldie *actress*
Headly, Glenne Aimée *actress*
†Heaton, Patricia *actress*
Henderson, Florence (Florence Henderson Bernstein) *actress, singer*
Henry, Buck *actor, writer*
Heston, Charlton (John Charlton Carter) *actor*
†Hewitt, Jennifer Love *actress, singer*
Hill, Michael J. *film editor*
Hill, Walter *film director, writer, producer*
†Holland, Agnieszka *film director, screenwriter*
Hopkins, Sir Anthony (Philip) *actor*
†Hopper, Dennis *actor, writer, photographer, film director*
Howard, Ron *director, actor*
Hoy, William *film editor*
Hughes, John W. *film producer, screenwriter, film director*
Hulce, Tom *actor*
†Hunane, Kevin *talent agent*
Hunt, Linda *actress*
Hurd, Gale Anne *film producer*
†Hurt, William *actor*
Huston, Anjelica *actress*
Hutton, Timothy *actor*
Idle, Eric *actor, screenwriter, producer, songwriter*
Ingels, Marty *theatrical agent, television and motion picture production executive*
Jagger, Mick (Michael Philip Jagger) *singer, musician*
Joffe, Roland *film director*
Jones, Terry *film director, author*
Jordan, Glenn *director*
Kahn, Madeline Gail *actress*
Kane, Carol *actress*
†Kasdan, Lawrence Edward *film director, screenwriter*
Kaufman, Philip *film director*
Keaton, Diane *actress*
Keitel, Harvey *actor*
Keith, David Lemuel *actor*
Kellman, Barnet Kramer *film, stage and television director*
Kemper, Victor J. *cinematographer*
Khaiat, Laurent E. *producer, films*
Kilmer, Val *actor*
Kingsley, Ben *actor*
†Kingston, Alex(andra) *actress*
Kinski, Nastassja (Nastassja Nakszynski) *actress*
†Konchalovsky, Andrei *film director*
Kozak, Harley Jane *actress*
†Kravitz, Lenny *singer, guitarist*
Lahti, Christine *actress*
†Landis, John David *film director, writer*
Lane, Nathan (Joseph Lane) *actor*
Lange, Jessica *actress*
Langella, Frank *actor*
LaPaglia, Anthony *actor*
Lavin, Linda *actress*
Leary, Denis *comedian*
†Leder, Mimi *television director*
†Lee, Ang *filmmaker*
Lee, Jason Scott *actor*
†Lehmann, Michael Stephen *film director*
Leigh, Jennifer Jason (Jennifer Leigh Morrow) *actress*
Lemmon, Jack (John Uhler Lemmon, III) *actor*
Levant, Brian *film director*
Levy, Peter *cinematographer*
Lewis, Juliette *actress*
Limato, Edward Frank *talent agent*
Lindo, Delroy *actor*
Linkletter, Arthur Gordon *radio and television broadcaster*
†Linney, Laura *actress*
Liotta, Ray *actor*
Lloyd, Emily (Emily Lloyd Pack) *actress*
Loggia, Robert *actor*
Long, Shelley *actress*
Lopez, Jennifer *actress, dancer, singer*
Louis-Dreyfus, Julia *actress*
†Lourd, Bryan *talent agent*
Lovett, Richard *talent agency executive*
Lowell, Carey *actress*
Lowry, Dick M. *director*
Lumet, Sidney *film director*
Lynch, David K. *film director, writer*
Lyne, Adrian *film director*
Lynn, Jonathan Adam *film director, writer, actor*
Mac Dowell, Andie (Rose Anderson Mac Dowell) *actress*
MacLachlan, Kyle *actor*
MacMillan, Kenneth *cinematographer*
Madsen, Michael *actor*
Malkovich, John *actor*
†Manheim, Camryn *television and film actress*
†Mann, Michael K. *producer, director, writer*
Manulis, Martin *film producer*
Margulies, Julianna *actress*
†Martin, Kellie (Noelle) *actress*
Martin, Steve *comedian, actor*
Masterson, Mary Stuart *actress*
Mastrantonio, Mary Elizabeth *actress*
Masur, Richard *actor*
Matheson, Tim *actor*
Mathis, Samantha *actress*
Matlin, Marlee *actress*
Matovich, Mitchel Joseph, Jr. *motion picture producer, executive*
McAlpine, Andrew *production designer*
†McDaniel, James *actor*
McDermott, Dylan *actor*
†Mc Tiernan, John *film director*
Metcalf, Laurie *actress*
Milius, John Frederick *film writer, director*
Miner, Steve *film director*
†Minghella, Anthony *film director*
Moffat, Donald *actor*
Montalban, Ricardo *actor*
Moore, Demi (Demi Guynes) *actress*
Moore, Dudley Stuart John *actor, musician*
Moore, Julianne *actress*
Moore, Mary Tyler *actress*
Moore, Michael *film director*
Moriarty, Cathy *actress*
Morissette, Alanis *musician*
Mulroney, Dermot *actor*
Murphy, Eddie *comedian, actor*
Murray, Bill *actor, writer*
Najimy, Kathy *actress*
Nava, Gregory *film director*
Neeson, Liam *actor*
Neill, Sam *actor*
Nelson, Judd *actor*
Nicita, Rick *agent*
Nimoy, Leonard *actor, director*
Norris, Chuck (Carlos Ray) *actor*
Novak, Kim (Marilyn Novak) *actress*

Fuller, Larry *choreographer, director*
Furth, George *actor, playwright*
Garcia, Andy *actor*
Garofalo, Janeane *actress, comedienne*
†Garrett, Brad *actor, comedian*
Gavin, Delane Michael *television writer, producer, director*
Getty, Estelle *actress*
Gibbs, Marla (Margaret Gibbs) *actress*
Goldsmith, Jerry *composer*
Gooding, Cuba, Jr. *actor*
Goodman, David Bryan *musician, educator*
†Gordon, Mark, II *film producer*
Gould, Elliott *actor*
Grammer, Kelsey *actor*
Greenberg, Barry Michael *talent executive*
Grey, Joel *actor*
Griffithe, Todd Allen *television associate director*
†Griffiths, Rachel *actress*
†Gross, Matt G. *executive*
Guy, Jasmine *actress*
Hackman, Gene (Eugene Alden) *actor*
Haines, Randa *film director*
†Hancock, Herbert Jeffrey (Herbie Hancock) *composer, pianist, publisher*
Harris, Richard A. *film editor*
Hartke, Stephen Paul *composer, educator*
Harvey, Jackson *film producer*
Helgeland, Brian *film director, writer, producer*
Hemmings, Peter William *orchestra and opera administrator*
†Herek, Stephen *film director, producer*
Hiller, Arthur *motion picture director*
Hirsch, Judd *actor*
†Hoblit, Gregory *film director, television executive*
†Hopkins, Stephen *film director, producer*
Horovitz, Adam *recording artist*
Howe, John Thomas *film director, educator*
Hunt, Peter Roger *film director, writer, editor*
†Hyams, Peter *film director, producer, cinematographer*
Ireland, Kathy *actress*
Ivey, Judith *actress*
†Jackson, Janet Damita *singer, dancer*
†Jackson, Michael (Joseph) *singer*
†Jackson, Mick *film director, producer*
Jacobs, Stephen Jay *musician, composer, writer*
†Jennings, Willbur *musician, popular*
†Jeunet, Jean-Pierre *film director*
Johnson, Charles Floyd *television executive, producer*
Jones, Doug *travelog producer*
Kahan, Sheldon Jeremiah (Christopher Reed) *musician, singer*
Kahane, Jeffrey *music director*
Kaplan, Jonathan Stewart *film director, writer*
Keach, James P. *actor*
Kellerman, Sally Claire *actress*
Kelley, David E. *producer, writer*
Kelly, Maureen H. *actress*
Kennedy, George *actor*
†Kershner, Irvin *film director*
Kidman, Nicole *actress*
Klauss, Kenneth Karl *composer, educator*
Knotts, Don *actor*
Kovacs, Laszlo *cinematographer*
Kurtz, Swoosie *actress*
Lansing, Sherry Lee *motion picture production executive*
†Laudicina, Salvatore Anthony *film industry executive*
Leach, Britt *actor*
Lear, Norman Milton *producer, writer, director*
Leigh, Janet (Jeanette Helen Morrison) *actress*
Leighton, Robert *film editor*
Leo, Malcolm *producer, director, writer*
†Levinsohn, Gary *producer*
†Lloyd, Jake *actor*
London, Andrew Barry *film editor*
†Lunden, Joan *television personality*
MacGraw, Ali *actress*
Maher, Bill *talk show host, comedian, producer*
Main, Laurie (Laurence George Main) *actor*
Malden, Karl (Malden Sekulovich) *actor*
†Malick, Terrence (David Whitney, II) *film director*
†Malik, Terrence (David Whitney, II) *director, writer, producer*
Malone, Nancy *actor, director, producer*
Mann, Delbert *film, theater, television director and producer*
†Margosis, Daniel I. *television writer, producer*
Matthau, Walter *actor*
Mc Guire, Dorothy Hackett *actress*
†McKellen, Ian *actor*
McQueen, Justus Ellis (L. Q. Jones) *actor, director*
Merlis, George *television producer*
Metheny, Pat *jazz musician*
Meyer, Russ *film producer, director*
Milchan, Arnon *film producer*
Milsome, Douglas *cinematographer*
Mirisch, Lawrence Alan *motion picture agent*
Mirren, Helen *actress*
Moore, Ronald Bruce *visual effects producer*
†Moorhouse, Jocelyn Denise *film director*
Moreno, Rita *actress*
Morton, Joe *actor*
Mossman, Thomas Mellish, Jr. *television manager*
Mueller, Carl Richard *theater arts educator, author*
Muldaur, Diana Charlton *actress*
Mulligan, Richard M. *actor, writer*
†Mulligan, Robert Patrick *film director, producer*
Nettleton, Lois *actress*
Newhart, Bob *entertainer*
Newmar, Julie Chalane *actress, dancer, real estate businesswoman*
Nicholson, Jack *actor, director, producer*
Noble, James Wilkes *actor*
†Norman, Marc *screenwriter, producer*
†Norton, Edward *actor*
†Norwood, Brandy *singer, actress*
†Nunez, Victor *film director, producer, writer*
†O'Connor, Pat *film director*
O'Day, Anita Belle Colton *entertainer, singer*
Oldman, Gary *actor*
Olmsted, Sallie Lockwood *executive*
O'Neal, Tatum *actress*
Orbach, Jerry *actor, singer*
Paxton, Bill *actor, writer, director*
Peña, Elizabeth *actress*
Penn, Christopher *actor*
Penn, Sean *actor*
Peters, Brock *actor, singer, producer*
†Pettibon, Raymond *video artist*
Phillips, Lou Diamond *actor, director*
Pollack, Daniel *concert pianist*
Ponty, Jean-Luc *violinist, composer, producer*
Reynolds, Burt *actor, director*
†Reynolds, Gene *television producer, director*
†Reynolds, Kevin *film director, writer*
Rhys-Davies, John *actor*
Riche, Wendy *television producer*
Rickles, Donald Jay *comedian, actor*
Ritter, John(athan) (Southworth) *actor*
Rosenberger, Carol *concert pianist*
Ross, Herbert David *film director*
Ross, Marion *actress*
Rosten, Irwin *writer, producer, director*
Roth, Tim *actor*
Rothman, Claire Lynda *entertainment executive*
Rubin, Stanley Creamer *producer*
Rudolph, Alan *film director*
Ruskin, Joseph Richard *actor, director*
Saltzman, Barry *actor*
San Giacomo, Laura *actress*
Sargent, Joseph Daniel *motion picture and television director*
Sayles, John Thomas *film director, writer, actor*
Schwarzenegger, Arnold Alois *actor, author*
Schwimmer, David *actor*
Scott, Tony *film director*
Selleck, Tom *actor*
Seymour, Michael *production designer*
Shatner, William *actor*
Shea, Jack *television and film director, producer, writer*
Sherman, Eric *director, writer, educator*
Shire, David Lee *composer*
Silver, Ron *actor, director*
Silverstone, Alicia *actress*
Simmons, Jean *actress*
Smight, Alec Dow *film editor, consultant*
Smits, Jimmy *actor*
†Sommers, Stephen *film director*
Spelling, Aaron *film and television producer, writer, actor*
Spinotti, Dante *cinematographer*
Stapleton, Jean (Jeanne Murray) *actress*
Stern, Sandor *film writer, director*
Stevens, George, Jr. *film and television producer, writer, director*
Stevenson, Robert Murrell *music educator*
Strock, Herbert Leonard *motion picture producer, director, editor, writer*
Swit, Loretta *actress*
Tarantino, Quentin *film director, screenwriter*
Thomas, Betty *director, actress*
†Thompson, Andrea *actress*
Thompson, Sada Carolyn *actress*
Townsend, Barbara *actress*
Townsend, Robert *film director*
Tugend, Jennie Lew *film producer*
Tyson, Cicely *actress*
Ullman, Tracey *actress, singer*
Urioste, Frank J. *film editor*
†Van Der Beek, James *actor*
Verdon, Gwen (Gwyneth Evelyn) *actress, dancer, choreographer*
Villard, Dimitri Serrano *film producer, investment company executive*
†Wachowski, Andy *film director*
†Wachowski, Larry *film director*
Waite, Ralph *actor*
Waits, Thomas Alan *composer, actor, singer*
Waterston, Samuel Atkinson *actor*
†Watson, Emily *actress*
Webber, Peggy *actress, producer, director, writer*
Welch, Raquel *actress*
Welsh, John *actor*
Whitaker, Forest *actor, director, producer*
Winters, Barbara Jo *musician*
†Witherspoon, (Laura Jean) Reese *actress*
Yates, Peter *director, producer*
Young, Sean *actress*
Zemeckis, Robert L. *film director*
Ziskin, Laura *film producer*

Malibu
Almond, Paul *film director, producer, writer*
Harris, Ed(ward Allen) *actor*
Stöckwell, Dean *actor*
Vereen, Ben *actor, singer, dancer*

Martinez
DeWolfe, Martha Rose *singer, songwriter, publisher*

Mendocino
Woelfel, Robert William *broadcast executive, mayor*

Menlo Park
Baez, Joan Chandos *folk singer*

Mill Valley
Padula, Fred David *filmmaker*

Millbrae
Honor, Nicholas Kelly *disc jockey, accountant*

Mission Hills
Krieg, Dorothy Linden *soprano, performing artist, educator*

Monterey
Allen, Karen Jane *actress*

Montrose
Twitchell, Theodore Grant *music educator and composer*

Moorpark
Brunner, Robert Francis *composer, conductor*

Newport Beach
Morisseau, Nan Kruger *television personality*

North Hollywood
Baker, Rick *make-up artist*
Balmuth, Bernard Allen *retired film editor*
Diller, Phyllis *actress, author*
Kuter, Kay E. *writer, actor*
McMartin, John *actor*
Neill, Ve *make-up artist*
Null, Thomas Blanton *recording producer*
Powell, Stephanie *visual effects director, supervisor*
Reynolds, Debbie (Mary Frances Reynolds) *actress*
Smothers, Dick *actor, singer*
Smothers, Tom *actor, singer*
Walker, Mallory Elton *tenor*
†Warzel, Peter *international entertainment company consultant*
Woyt, James Charles (Jim Woyt) *actor*

Northridge
†Bregen, Louis *music professional*
Matsumoto, Shigemi *opera soprano, voice educator*

Oakland
Crocker, Joy Laksmi *concert pianist and organist, composer*
DeFazio, Lynette Stevens *dancer, choreographer, educator, chiropractor, author, actress, musician*
Elliott, Jack *folk musician*
Gordon, David Jamieson *tenor*
Perlmutter, Martin Lee *interactive media producer, recruiter, consultant, writer*
Randle, Ellen Eugenia Foster *opera and classical singer, educator*

Oceanside
Swoger, James Wesley *magician*

Ojai
Paxton, Glenn Gilbert *composer*

Oxnard
Gay, Marilyn Fanelli Martin *television producer, talk show hostess*

Pacific Palisades
Albert, Eddie (Edward Albert Heimberger) *actor*
Fabray, Nanette *actress*
Fisher, Frances *actress*
Holman, Bill *composer*

Palmdale
Luther, Amanda Lisa *producer*

Palo Alto
Lo, Yee On *composer*

Palos Verdes Estates
Benson, Francis M. *production engineer, radio producer*

Palos Verdes Peninsula
Giles, Allen *pianist, composer, music educator*
Lima, Luis Eduardo *tenor*

Panorama City
Loudon, Craig Michael *video specialist*

Pasadena
Adams, Elaine *art agent, publicist, writer*
Jones, Jennifer *actress*
Li Vigni, Shana Margaret Veronica Reichl *disc jockey*
Wilcox, Roberta Moat *music educator*

Pebble Beach
Klevan, Robert Bruce *music educator*

Petaluma
Daniel, Gary Wayne *motivation and performance consultant*

Pine Mountain
Edwards, Sarah Anne *radio, cable TV personality, clinical social worker*

Playa Del Rey
Berry, Jeffrey Alan *film director*

Pleasanton
Goddard, John Wesley *cable television company executive*

Poway
Burnworth, Randy James *video company executive*

Quartz Hill
McKain, Mary Margaret *musician*

Rancho Cucamonga
Robertson, Carey Jane *musician, educator*

Redondo Beach
Reed, John E. *producer, consultant*

Reseda
Alenikov, Vladimir *motion picture director and writer*

Richmond
†Lasseter, John P. *film director, computer animator*

Sacramento
†Gawthrop, Daphne Wood *performing company executive*
Nice, Carter *conductor, music director*

San Diego
Angelo, Sandra McFall *television and video producer, writer*
Burge, David Russell *concert pianist, composer, piano educator*
Campbell, Ian David *opera company director*
Flettner, Marianne *opera administrator*
Hooper, Robert Alexander *television producer, international educator*
Johnson, LaMont *composer, musician, producer, consultant*
McManus, Paul Robert *audio recording engineer*
Noehren, Robert *organist, organ builder*
Overton, Marcus Lee *performing arts administrator, actor, writer*
Ward-Steinman, David *composer, music educator, pianist*

San Dimas
Peters, Joseph Donald *filmmaker*

San Francisco
Balin, Marty (Martyn Jerel Buchwald) *musician*
Bennett, William *oboist*
Breeden, David *clarinetist*
Caniparoli, Val William *choreographer, dancer*
Chen, Joan (Chen Chong) *actress*
Crosby, Kathryn Grandstaff (Grant Crosby) *actress*
Dupont, Colyer Lee *television and film producer, video and film distributing company executive*
Etheridge, Melissa Lou *singer, songwriter*
Festinger, Richard *music educator, composer*
†Finley, Karen *actress*
George, Vance *conductor*
†Hardiman, David Alexander *music educator*
Hastings, Edward Walton *theater director*
Jacobus, Arthur *dance company administrator*
†King, Alonzo *artistic director, choreographer*
LeBlanc, Tina *dancer*
Maffre, Muriel *ballet dancer*
†McGegan, Nicholas *music director*
†Pastreich, Peter *orchestra executive director*
Peterson, Wayne Turner *composer, pianist*
Pitts, Orion Clark *theatre educator*
Runnicles, Donald *conductor*
Sheinfeld, David *composer*
Smuin, Michael *choreographer, director, dancer*
Stowell, Christopher R. *dancer*
Talbot, Stephen H. *television producer, writer*
Tiano, Anthony Steven *television producer, book publishing executive*
Tomasson, Helgi *dancer, choreographer, dance company executive*
Van Dyck, Wendy *dancer*
Wang, Wayne *film director*

San Jose
Dalis, Irene *mezzo-soprano, opera company administrator, music educator*
Grin, Leonid *conductor*
Hills, Alan R. *artistic director*
†Nahat, Dennis F. *artistic director, choreographer*
†Shuster, Diana *artistic director*
Shuster, Dianna *musical theatre company executive, choreographer*
†Toepfer, Karl Eric *theatre arts educator*

San Luis Obispo
†Davidson, Frances *film and video producer*

San Marino
Darian, Craig Charles *executive film producer*

San Pedro
Fritzsche, Kathleen (Dragonfire Fritzsche) *performing arts educator*

San Rafael
Hart, Mickey *rock musician*
Lucas, George W., Jr. *film director, producer, screenwriter*
Murphy, George *special effects expert*
Santana, Carlos *guitarist*
Squires, Scott William *special effects expert, executive*

Santa Ana
St. Clair, Carl *conductor, music director*
Sudbeck, Robert Francis *music educator, philosophy educator*

Santa Barbara
Ben-Dor, Gisèle *conductor, musician*
Brant, Henry *composer*
Brodhead, James E(aston) *actor, writer*
Howorth, David *producer, director*
Lange, Hope *actress*
Snyder, Allegra Fuller *dance educator*
Wayland, Newton Hart *conductor*

Santa Clarita
Bruno, Frank Eugene *television producer, videotape editor, telecine colorist*

Santa Cruz
Winston, George *pianist, guitarist, harmonica player*

Santa Monica
†Abrahams, Jim *film director*
Angel, Steven *musician*
Angier, Joseph *television producer, writer*
Black, Noel Anthony *television and film director*
†Brock, Phillip Leslie *talent agent*
Bruckheimer, Jerry *producer*
Cameron, James *film director, screenwriter, producer*
Chartoff, Robert Irwin *film producer*
†Cher, (Cherilyn Sarkisian) *singer, actress*
Cooper, Jackie *actor, director, producer*
Griffin, Merv Edward *former entertainer, television producer, entrepreneur*
Jewison, Norman Frederick *film producer, director*
†Kaminski, Janusz Zygmunt *cinematographer*
Kaplan, Mike *film and video producer, director, and distributor, marketing executive*
Leaf, Paul *producer, director, writer*
Marshall, Frank W. *film producer, director*
Nathanson, Michael *film company executive*
Norris, David Randolph *recording artist, philanthropist*
Pisano, A. Robert *entertainment company executive, lawyer*
Redford, Robert (Charles Robert Redford) *actor, director*
Rose, Michael Leonard *film, television and video producer*
†Rydell, Mark *film director, producer, actor*
Schroeder, William Robert *actor, graphic designer, linguist*
Smith, Anna Deavere *actor, educator, playwright*
Stack, Robert Langford *actor*
Summer, Donna (La Donna Adrian Gaines) *singer, actress, songwriter*
Suschitzky, Peter *cinematagrapher*
Taylor, James Vernon *musician*
Vacano, Jost *cinematographer*
Wexler, Haskell *film producer, cameraman*

Sherman Oaks
Bakula, Scott *actor*
Beals, Jennifer *actress*
Bergman, Alan *lyricist, writer*
Bergman, Marilyn Keith *lyricist, writer*
Blair, Linda Denise *actress*
Brennan, Eileen Regina *actress*
Clark, Susan (Nora Goulding) *actress*
Conrad, Robert (Conrad Robert Falk) *actor, singer, producer, director*
Gibbs, Antony (Tony) *film editor*
Hanna, William Denby *motion picture and television producer, cartoonist*
†Horner, James *composer*
Howard, Joseph B. (Joe Howard) *actor*
Karras, Alex *actor, former professional football player*

Lo Bianco, Tony actor
Majors, Lee actor
Peterson, Lowell cinematographer
Schlessinger, Laura radio talk show host
†Schroder, Rick actor
Sheen, Charlie (Carlos Irwin Estevez) actor
Shore, Howard Leslie composer
Sting, (Gordon Matthew Sumner) musician, songwriter, actor
Tesh, John television talk show host, musician
Williams, John Towner composer, conductor

Sonoma
Pollack, Phyllis Addison ballerina

Stanford
Cohen, Albert musician, educator
Lyons, Charles R. drama educator and critic

Stockton
Tregle, Linda Marie dance educator

Studio City
Carsey, Marcia Lee Peterson television producer
Devane, William actor
Duffield, Thomas Andrew art director, production designer
Gautier, Dick actor, writer
Hasselhoff, David actor
Jacobs, Ronald Nicholas television and motion picture producer/director
Kenney, H(arry) Wesley, Jr. producer, director
Lamothe, Irene Elise television producer, distributor
†Mandabach, Caryn television producer
Pressman, Michael film director
Richman, Peter Mark actor, painter, writer
Sertner, Robert Mark producer
Spencer, James H. art director, production designer
Sylbert, Paul production designer, art director
Sylbert, Richard production designer, art director
Taylor, Jack G., Jr. art director
Thomas, Wynn P. art director, production designer
Tomkins, Alan art director, production designer
Werner, Tom television producer, professional baseball team executive

Sunset Beach
Bettis, John Gregory songwriter

Sylmar
Foster, Dudley Edwards, Jr. musician, educator

Tarzana
Brook, Winston Rollins retired audio-video design consultant
Easton, Sheena rock vocalist

Temple City
Robbins, William Curtis, Jr. television and motion picture producer, director, writer, news reporter, cameraman
Weidaw, Kenneth Roe musician, educator, consultant

Thousand Oaks
Glieberman, Cary Hirsch film producer, director, writer
Rooney, Mickey (Joe Yule, Jr.) actor

Toluca Lake
Rustam, Mardi Ahmed film and television producer, publisher

Torrance
Harness, William Edward tenor

Universal City
†Bratt, Benjamin actor
Devin, Richard film industry executive
†Harmon, Angie actress
†Hill, Steven actor
Horak, Jan-Christopher film studies educator, curator
†LaBelle, Patti singer
Lansbury, Angela Brigid actress
Lovett, Lyle musician
†Merkerson, S. Epatha actress
Meyer, Ron agent
Midler, Bette singer, entertainer, actress
Reitman, Ivan film director, producer
†Simonds, Robert producer

Upper Lake
Scobey, Jan (Jeannette Marie Scobey) jazz musician, store owner, author

Vacaville
Russell, Rhonda Cheryl piano educator

Valencia
Simmons, Ann Lorraine actor

Valley Village
Toussaint, Christopher Andre video producer, director, writer

Van Nuys
Allen, Stephen Valentine Patrick William television comedian, author, pianist, songwriter

Venice
Bill, Tony producer, director

Walnut Creek
Stapp, Olivia Brewer opera singer

West Hollywood
Annakin, Kenneth Cooper film director, writer
Bloom, Claire actress
Blumofe, Robert Fulton motion picture producer, association executive
Cage, Nicolas (Nicolas Coppola) actor
†De Palma, Brian Russell film director, writer
Harper, Robert actor
Henley, Don singer, drummer, songwriter
Hill, Jack motion picture director, writer, educator
Jaglom, Henry David actor, director, writer
Krabbe, Jeroen Aart actor
Madonna, (Madonna Louise Veronica Ciccone) singer, actress
Males, William James film producer, make-up artist
McLaughlin, Stephen sound recording engineer
Shaye, Robert Kenneth cinema company executive
Sherman, Robert B(ernard) composer, lyricist, screenwriter
Verhoeven, Paul film director

Whittier
Korf, Leonard Lee theater arts educator

Woodland Hills
Baker, Joe Don actor
Evigan, Greg actor, musician
Gonzalez, Michael Joe multimedia producer
Horne, Lena singer
Klugman, Jack actor
Levy, Norman motion picture company executive
Small, Michael composer
Taylor, Rowan Shaw music educator, composer, conductor
Wester, Keith Albert film and television recording engineer, television executive

Yountville
Damé-Shepp, Diane art management administrator

Yreka
Beary, Shirley Lorraine retired music educator

COLORADO

Aspen
Ewing, Wayne Hilley film producer, director, writer
Harth, Robert James music festival executive
†Young, Henry executive director
Zinman, David Joel conductor

Boulder
Brakhage, James Stanley filmmaker, educator
Duckworth, Guy musician, pianist, educator
Fink, Robert Russell music theorist, former university dean
Kuchar, Theodore conductor, academic administrator, musician
†Lightfoot, William Carl performing arts association executive, symphony musician
Sarson, John Christopher television producer, director, writer
Symons, James Martin theater and dance educator

Colorado Springs
Bergman, Yaacov performing company executive
Wilkins, Christopher Putnam conductor

Denver
Bearden, Thomas Howard news program producer, correspondent
Burshtan, John Willis television producer
Ceci, Jesse Arthur violinist
Fredmann, Martin ballet artistic director, educator, choreographer
Keats, Donald Howard composer, educator
Moulton-Gertig, Suzanne Carey LeRoy musician, educator
Ozaki, Nancy Junko performance artist, educator
Robinson, Cleo Parker artistic director
Schwartz, Cherie Anne Karo storyteller, writer

Durango
Carey, Harry, Jr. actor
Hillers, Ellen Marsh film-television production coordinator

Estes Park
Bridges, Douglas M. musician, small business owner

Evergreen
White, John David composer, theorist, cellist

Glenwood Springs
Callier, Maria Cecile writer, actress

Grand Junction
Gustafson, Kirk performing company executive

Loveland
Balsiger, David Wayne television-video director, researcher, producer, writer

Niwot
Garvan, Stephen Bond artist manager

Ridgway
Weaver, Dennis actor

CONNECTICUT

Branford
Smith, Richard Emerson (Dick Smith) make-up artist

Bristol
Miller, Jon sports commentator
Nessler, Brad R. sports commentator

Chester
Hays, David Arthur theater producer, stage designer

Danbury
Jennings, Alfred Higson, Jr. music educator, actor, singer

East Haddam
Borton, John Carter, Jr. (Terry Borton) theatrical producer

Fairfield
Fash, Michael William cinematographer, director

Greenwich
Fates, Joseph Gilbert television producer
Rutgers, Katharine Phillips (Mrs. Frederik Lodewijk Rutgers) dancer
Tiegs, Cheryl model, designer

Hartford
Lankester, Michael performing company executive
Lyman, Peggy artistic director, dancer, choreographer, educator
†Lynn, Enid artistic director
Mc Lean, Jackie jazz saxophonist, educator, composer, community activist
Osborne, George Delano performing arts company director

Middle Haddam
Beaulieu, Dennis E. videographer

New Canaan
Richardson, Dana Roland video producer

New Haven
Baker, Robert Stevens organist, educator
Bly, Mark John dramaturg, playwriting educator
French, Richard Frederic retired music educator
Garvey, Sheila Hickey theater educator
Jordan, Paul music director
†Jung Ho, Pak artistic director
Piehler, Wendell Howard organist, choir director, fund-raiser
Tirro, Frank Pascale music educator, author, composer

New Preston
Grizzard, George actor

Newtown
Carroll, Thomas Lawrence, Jr. film and video producer
Mark, Marsha Yvonne Ismailoff artistic director

Norwalk
Eagan, Sherman G. producer, communications executive

Old Lyme
Hinman, Rosalind Virginia storyteller, drama educator

Ridgefield
Wyton, Alec composer, organist

Simsbury
Adams, (Lewis) Dean theater director

Southport
Walker, Charles Dodsley conductor, organist

Stamford
Karp, Steve producing director
Nierenberg, Roger symphony conductor
†Raphael, Brett artistic director, choreographer

Storrs Mansfield
Birdman, Jerome Moseley drama educator, consultant
†Crow, Laura Jean design educator, costume designer

Stratford
Rock, William Booth producer, announcer

Vernon Rockville
Williams, Julius Penson composer, conductor

Washington Depot
Mandler, Susan Ruth dance company administrator
Pendleton, Moses Robert Andrew dancer, choreographer
Tracy, Michael Cameron choreographer, performer, educator

Waterford
White, George Cooke theater director, foundation executive

West Hartford
Gryc, Stephen Michael composer, music educator
†Yueh, Chai-Lun voice educator, opera singer

Weston
Bellin, Harvey Forrest television producer, director
Fredrik, Burry theatrical producer, director
Kimmelman, Gregory M. television producer and director

Westport
Rose, Reginald television writer, producer
Solum, John Henry flutist, educator, author

Woodbridge
Nolan, Victoria theater director

DELAWARE

Newark
Cason, June Macnabb musician, educator, arts administrator

Wilmington
Brown Leatherberry, Thomas Henry gospel music company executive, clergy member
Copper, William P. composer, computer consultant
Gunzenhauser, Stephen Charles conductor
Wesler, Ken theater company manager

DISTRICT OF COLUMBIA

Washington
Ames, Frank Anthony percussionist, film producer
Ballou, Jeffrey Pierre producer
Brennan, Robin Lynn producer
Byers, Paul Heed television news producer, consultant
Collie, Kelsey Eugene producer, educator, director, playwright
Crowther, G(eorge) Rodney, III television production company executive, writer, photographer
†Day, Doris (Doris von Kappelhoff) singer, actress
Day, Mary artistic director, ballet company executive
Dryden, John Clifford radio syndicator
Forrest, Sidney clarinetist, music educator
Fricke, Heinz conductor
Green, Ricki Kutcher producer
Guggenheim, Charles E. motion picture and television producer
Harpham, Virginia Ruth violinist
Hay, George Austin actor, producer, director, musician, artist
Hewitt, Frankie Lea theater producer
Kahn, Michael stage director
Kendall, Peter Landis television news executive
Konstantinov, Tzvetan Krumov musician, concert pianist, educator
Kramer, Constance Ann songwriter
Laczko, Brian John theater director
Makris, Andreas composer
Moore, Elvi performing company executive
Mossel, Patricia L. opera executive
Parris, Robert composer
Ratner, Ellen Faith radio talk show host, writer
Royle, David Brian Layton television producer, journalist
Russell, Mark comedian
Sankaran, Shubha Silver musician, information management consultant
Schaefer, James Lee television news producer
Slatkin, Leonard Edward conductor, music director, pianist
†Sonneborn, Daniel Atesh composer, ethnomusicologist, producer, author
Spillane, Mary Catherine television producer
Stevens, Milton Lewis, Jr. trombonist
Sweet, Sam theater director
Thayer, Edwin Cabot musician
Thulean, Donald Myron symphony conductor
Webre, Septime ballet company artistic director, choreographer
†Wholey, Dennis Matthew television talk show host

FLORIDA

Boca Raton
Beck, Crafton music director
Fengler, John Peter television producer, director, advertising executive
Gold, Catherine Anne Dower music history educator

Bradenton
Lister, Thomas Mosie composer, lyricist, publishing company executive, minister

Coral Springs
Bachove, Jason Frost musician

Deland
Sorensen, Jacki Faye choreographer, aerobic dance company executive

Destin
Najarian, Betty Jo music educator

Dunedin
Flemm, Eugene William concert pianist, educator, conductor, chamber musician

Englewood
Brainard, Paul Henry musicologist, retired music educator

Eustis
Alfrey, Lydia Jean musician educator

Fort Lauderdale
Judd, James performing company executive
LeRoy, Miss Joy model, designer
†Nero, Peter pianist, conductor, composer, arranger
Randi, James (Randall James Hamilton Zwinge) magician, writer, educator

Fort Myers
Diers, Hank H. drama educator, playwright, director
Gorelik, Alla piano educator

Fort Pierce
Norton, Robert Howard entertainer, musical arranger, author

Gainesville
Paul, Ouida Fay music educator

Hallandale
Price, Ruthe Geier actress, writer, educator

Highland Beach
Settler, Eugene Brian record company executive

Inverness
Cook, George songwriter

Jacksonville
Stanley, Helen Camille composer, musician

Key West
Mitchell, John Dietrich theatre arts institute executive

Lake Buena Vista
Morgan, Linda Gail producer

Lake Helen
Finn, Stephen Martin producer

Lighthouse Point
Farr, Carole Anne Kleinrichert retired model, investor

Lutz
Hawkins, Lorraine C. symphony musician

Madison
Shaw, Kathleen Bentley violist

Melbourne
Slusher, Michael Dennis trombonist, arranger, producer

Miami
Allen, Charles Norman *television, film and video producer*
Catanzaro, Tony *dancer*
Davidson, Joy Elaine *mezzo-soprano*
Gibb, Robin *vocalist, songwriter*
Heuer, Robert Maynard, II *opera company executive*
Kwiat, David Mark *educator, actor*
Lawson, Eve Kennedy *ballet mistress*
Miller, Pamela Gardiner *performing arts company executive*
Nathanson, Andrew E(ric) *film location coordinator*
Reed, Alfred *composer, conductor*
Stephan, Egon, Sr. *cinematographer, film equipment company executive*

Miami Beach
Hecht, Donn *songwriter, screenwriter, agent*
Webb, Roy *television producer, writer*

Miami Lakes
Fletcher, Carlos Alfredo Torres *video and film production company executive*

Naples
Seaman, Christopher *perfoming arts company executive*
White, Roy Bernard *theater executive*

North Miami
Stills, Stephen *musician, vocalist, composer*

North Palm Beach
Hayman, Richard Warren Joseph *conductor*

Ocala
Robinson, Susan *conductor, musician*

Odessa
Cobb, Terri Reamer (Ceci Cobb) *film and video producer*

Orlando
†Ferrara, Katherine June *executive television producer*
Swedberg, Robert Mitchell *opera company director*
Walsh, James Anthony (Tony Walsh) *theater and film educator*

Ormond Beach
Hodkinson, Sydney Phillip *composer, educator*

Palm Beach
Cohen, Aaron Mitchell *producer, publisher, writer*
†Lappin, Bob *music director, conductor*

Pensacola
Rubardt, Peter Craig *conductor, educator*

Pompano Beach
MacLaren, Neil Moorley, Jr. *musician, music educator*
Waldman, Alan I. (Alawana) *songwriter, composer, lyricist, computer programmer, emergency medicine provider*
Walsh, Thomas Francis, Jr. *producer, writer, director*

Port Charlotte
Clark, Keith Collar *musician, educator*
Labousier, Susan Evelyn *choreographer, dancer*
Spatz, Hugo David *film producer*

Punta Gorda
Kavanaugh, Frank James *film producer, educator*

Royal Palm Beach
Curphey, Geraldine Casterline *church musician, retired*

Saint Petersburg
Carroll, Charles Michael *music educator*
MacMillan, Duncan Jay *music educator, pianist*

Sarasota
†Bjaland, Leif *artistic director, conductor*
McCollum, John Morris *tenor*

Spring Hill
Burnim, Kalman Aaron *theatre educator emeritus*

Tallahassee
†Bridger, Carolyn Ann *pianist, music educator*
Harsanyi, Janice *soprano, educator*
McConnell, Michael *opera company director*

Tampa
†Barrett, Stephen Michael *editor*
Edberg, Judith Florence *music educator*
Hankenson, E(dward) Craig, Jr. *performing arts executive*

Treasure Island
Dunn, Craig Andrew *entertainer, conductor, composer, educator*

Vero Beach
Schmidt, Ted *talent agent, entertainment producer*

West Palm Beach
†Hale, Marie Stoner *artistic director*
Robinson, Raymond Edwin *musician, music educator, writer*

Winter Park
Arman Gelenbe, Deniz *concert pianist*

GEORGIA

Athens
Staub, August William *drama educator, theatrical producer, director*

Atlanta
Bell, Jack Atkins *percussionist, educator*
Bridgewater, Herbert Jeremiah, Jr. *radio host*
†Chumbley, Robert Edward *artistic director*
†Domingo, Esther *music educator*
Hearn-Youngblood, Peggy Elaine *organist*
Kamm, Laurence Richard *television producer, director*
Kingsbury, Michael Bryant *organist, retired elementary and secondary education educator*
Knox, Charles Courtenaye *composer*
†McFall, John *artistic director*
Milhous, David Matthew *television network editor*
Reid, Antonio (L. A. Reid) *musician, songwriter*
Rex, Christopher Davis *classical musician*
Robinson, Florence Claire Crim *composer, conductor, educator*
Ski, Frank *radio disc jockey*
Taylor, Mary Rose *television anchor, journalist*

Augusta
Bradberry, Edward *opera company executive*
Cremer, Thomas Gerhard *music educator*

Columbus
Patrick, Carl Lloyd *theatre executive*

Decatur
Downs, Jon Franklin *drama educator, director*
Hamilton, Frank Strawn *jazz musician, folksinger, composer and arranger, educator*

Dunwoody
Clark, Faye Louise *drama and speech educator*

Kennesaw
Billingsley, Charles Clyde *musician, composer*

Mableton
Rowe, Bonnie Gordon *music company executive*

Macon
Johnson, Bonnie Sue *piano educator*

Marietta
Hlavaty, Patrick Dennis *educator, musician*
Wells, Palmer Donald *performing arts executive*

Rex
†Hodge, Douglas *entertainment executive*

Roswell
Siepi, Cesare *opera singer*

Saint Simons
Cedel, Melinda Irene *music educator, violinist*

Savannah
Greenberg, Philip B. *symphony orchestra conductor and music director*
Potts, Glenda Rue *music educator*

Toccoa
Thomas, Maurice W(illiam), Jr. *composer, lyricist*

HAWAII

Captain Cook
Link, Matthew Richard *video producer*

Ewa Beach
Kea, Jonathan Guy *instrumental music educator*

Honolulu
Furst, Dan (Daniel Christopher Furst, III) *producer, writer, actor*
Greenberg, Marvin *retired music educator*
Langhans, Edward Allen *drama and theater educator*
Smith, Barbara Barnard *music educator*
Williams, Mark Riley *video producer, director*

IDAHO

Boise
†Pimble, Toni *artistic director, choreographer, educator*

Idaho Falls
LoPiccolo, John *conductor, music director*

Pocatello
Stanek, Alan Edward *music educator, performer, music administrator*

Twin Falls
Halsell, George Kay *music educator*
Yost, Kelly Lou *pianist*

ILLINOIS

Alton
Schnabel, John Henry *retired music educator*

Aurora
Halfvarson, Lucille Robertson *music educator*

Bloomington
Brown, Jared *theater director, educator, writer*
Vayo, David Joseph *composer, music educator*

Brookfield
Pick, Richard Samuel Burns *educator, composer*

Champaign
Fredrickson, L(awrence) Thomas *composer*
Garvey, John Charles *violist, conductor, retired music educator*

Chicago
Aitay, Victor *concert violinist, music educator*
Akos, Francis *violinist*
Arpino, Gerald Peter *performing company executive*
Basden, Cameron *ballet mistress, dancer*
Boncher, Mary *talent agent*
Booth, Thomas Collins *musician*
Combs, Ronald T. *music educator*
†Conte, Lou *artistic director, choreographer*
Dabrowski, Edward John *television technical director*
DeMiles, Edward *agent*
Duell, Daniel Paul *artistic director, choreographer, lecturer*
Eaton, John C. *composer, educator*
†Falls, Robert Arthur *artistic director*
Farina, Dennis *actor*
Fogel, Henry *orchestra administrator*
†Freeman, Paul Douglas *symphony conductor*
Freidheim, Ladonna *dance company director*
Guastafeste, Roberta Harrison *cellist*
Hamarstrom, Patricia Ann *director, animation/multimedia specialist*
Herseth, Adolph Sylvester (Bud Herseth) *classical musician*
Jares, Terryl Lynn *musician*
Jean, Kenneth *conductor*
Kerros, Edward Paul *stage director, playwright*
Knapp, Donald Roy *musician, educator*
Lazar, Ludmila *concert pianist, pedagogue*
Lewis, Ramsey Emanuel, Jr. *pianist, composer*
Maggio, Michael John *artistic director*
Miles, Roberta *jazz singer, artist*
Moffatt, Joyce Anne *performing arts executive*
Padberg, Helen Swan *violinist*
Peters, Gordon Benes *musician*
Pokorni, Orysia *musician*
Ponné, Nanci Teresa *entertainment promoter, writer*
Prendergast, Carole Lisak *musician, educator*
Price, Henry Escoe *broadcast executive*
Ran, Shulamit *composer*
Ratner, Carl Joseph *theater director*
†Sandroff, Howard *composer, sound artist*
Schulfer, Roche Edward *theater executive director*
Scott, Stephen Brinsley *theater producer*
Sedelmaier, John Josef *film director, cinematographer*
Shapey, Ralph *composer, conductor, educator*
†Springer, Jerry *television talk show host*
Stifler, Venetia Chakos *dancer, choreographer, dance educator*
Tallchief, Maria *ballerina*
Wagner, Mark Anthony *videotape editor*
Wang, Albert James *violinist, educator*
Warfield, William Caesar *singer, actor, educator*
Wikman, Thomas S. *music director*
Winfrey, Oprah *television talk show host, actress, producer*
Wyszynski, Richard Chester *musician, conductor, educator*
Zajicek, Jeronym *music educator*
Zlatoff-Mirsky, Everett Igor *violinist*

Cicero
Levin, Michael David *musician*

Coal City
Major, Mary Jo *dance school artistic director*

Danville
Ball, James S. *orchestra conductor, educator, musician*

Downers Grove
Holt, William Harold, Jr. *film producer, consultant*
Shen, Sin-Yan *physicist, conductor, acoustics specialist, music director*

Elgin
Dodohara, Jean Noton *music educator*

Elmhurst
Daugherty, Richard Allen *musician, retired educator*
†Young, Wendy Unrath *musician*

Eureka
West, Nancy Lee *music educator, performance artist, entertainer*

Evanston
Beck, Eva-Carol *musician*
Eberley, Helen-Kay *opera singer, classical record company executive, poet*
Fitzgerald, Mary Joan *music educator*
Hemke, Frederick L. *music educator, university administrator*
Karlins, M(artin) William *composer, educator*
Kujala, Walfrid Eugene *musician, educator*
McDonough, Bridget Ann *music theatre company director*
Reimer, Bennett *music educator, writer*
Yoder, John Clifford *producer, consultant*

Grand Chain
†Ulrich, Eugene J. *music educator, composer*

Harvey
†Saldana, John Wesley, Jr. *songwriter, publisher*

Havana
Holmes, Lois Rehder *composer, piano and voice educator*

Highland Park
Mehta, Zarin *music festival administrator*
Scheuzger, Thomas Peter *audio engineer*

Joliet
Bartz, William Walter *musician*

Melrose Park
†Hillert, Richard Walter *composer, educator, author*

Naperville
†Schaeffer, Joan L. *theater company executive*

Normal
Pritner, Calvin Lee *actor, educator*

Northbrook
Magad, Samuel *orchestra concertmaster, conductor*
Slattery, James Joseph (Joe Slattery) *actor*

Olympia Fields
Villari, Jack C. *performing arts executive, arts entrepreneur*

Pana
Waddington, Irma Joann *music teacher*

Park Forest
Billig, Etel Jewel *theater director, actress*

Peoria
Price Boday, Mary Kathryn *choreographer, small business owner, educator*

Princeton
Tillman, June Torrison *musician*

Rockford
Larsen, Steven *orchestra conductor*
Masters, Arlene Elizabeth *singer*
Robinson, Donald Peter *musician, retired electrical engineer*

Round Lake
†Fejer, T. William *pianist, composer, architect, furniture designer*

Schaumburg
Kleppe, Joan Marie *entertainment executive*

Shorewood
Lombardo, David Albert *actor, writer, speaker, aviation educator*

Springfield
Ellis, Michael Eugene *documentary film producer, writer, director, marketing executive*
Nanavati, Grace Luttrell *dancer, choreographer, instructor*
Rogers, James Allan *music director, hymnoloigst, author, editor*

Urbana
Boardman, Eunice *retired music educator*
Burton, Herbert *composer*
†Haken, Rudolf *music educator*
Hedlund, Barbara Smith *musician, educator, music publisher*
Hedlund, Ronald *baritone*
Hobgood, Burnet McLean *theater educator*
Melby, John B. *composer, educator*

Wasco
Bach, Jan Morris *composer, educator*

Westchester
James, Joni *singer*

Wheaton
†Arasimowicz, George Zbigniew *composer, university dean*

Wilmette
Merrier, Helen *actress, writer*
Miller, Frederick Staten *retired music educator, academic administrator*

Winnetka
Hausfeld, James Frank *executive director*

INDIANA

Bloomington
Brown, Keith *musician, educator*
Klotman, Robert Howard *music educator*
Mac Watters, Virginia Elizabeth *singer, music educator, actress*
Pagels, Jürgen Heinrich *balletmaster, dance educator, dancer, choreographer, author*
Phillips, Harvey *musician, soloist, music educator, arts consultant*
Rousseau, Eugene Ellsworth *musician, music educator, consultant*
Strickholm, Peter William *composer, environmentalist*
Svetlova, Marina *ballerina, choreographer, educator*
Williams, Camilla *soprano, voice educator*
Wittlich, Gary Eugene *music theory educator*

Crawfordsville
Everett, Cheryl Ann *music educator, pianist*

Evansville
Savia, Alfred *conductor*

Fort Wayne
Franklin, Al *artistic director*
Tchivzhel, Edvard *music director*

Greencastle
Irwin, Stanley Roy *music educator, singer, conductor*

Indianapolis
Aliev, Eldar *artistic director, choreographer, educator*
Alvarez, Thomas *film/video producer, director, theater director, arts consultant*
Bolin, Daniel Paul *music educator*
Hammack, Julia Dixon *music educator*
Jarrett, Leslie Joe *video producer*
Leppard, Raymond John *conductor, harpsichordist*
†Nottingham, Theodore J. *video producer, writer*
Pugh, Daniel Wilbert *theatre educator*
Salewsky, Douglas Michael *video producer*
Suzuki, Hidetaro *violinist*
Thomas, John David *musician, composer, arranger, photographer, recording engineer, producer*

Knox
Weiss, Randall A. *television producer, supermarket executive*

Kokomo
Highlen, Larry Wade *music educator, piano rebuilder, tuner*

Muncie
Ghiglia, Oscar Alberto *classical guitarist*
McConnell, Sarah Stacey *film producer, French language educator*
†Whitaker, Sandra Sue *soprano, educator*

New Albany
Estep, Lawrence Robert *videographer, video producer*

Notre Dame
Pilkinton, Mark C. *theater educator*

Rolling Prairie
Eggleston, Alan Edward *musician, opera singer, Boy Scout executive*

Vincennes
Spurrier, James Joseph *theater educator*

Wabash
Zimmerman, Philip L. *performing arts and foundation executive*

West Lafayette
Wright, Alfred George James *band symphony orchestra conductor, educator*

IOWA

Anita
Everhart, Robert Phillip (Bobby Williams) *entertainer, songwriter, recording artist*

Cedar Falls
Fanelli, Michael Paul *music educator*
Gordon, Debra Gwen *music educator*

Cedar Rapids
†Tiemeyer, Christian *conductor*

Clinton
Unger, Gary Allen *recording industry executive, singer, lyricist*

Davenport
Dcamp, Charles Barton *educator, musician*

Des Moines
Blank, Myron Nathan *theater executive*
†Giunta, Joseph *conductor, music director*
Wannamaker, Mary Ruth *music educator*

Dubuque
Hemmer, Paul Edward *musician, composer, broadcasting executive*

Indianola
Larsen, Robert LeRoy *artistic director*
Mace, Jerilee Marie *opera company executive*
Snyder, Arlen Dean *actor*

Iowa City
Kottick, Edward Leon *music educator, harpsichord maker*
Mather, Roger Frederick *music educator, writer*
Taylor, Rachel Lee *pianist, educator*

Mount Etna
Sparks, (Theo) Merrill *entertainer, songwriter, translator, poet*

Sioux Center
Ringerwole, Joan Mae *music educator, recitalist*

Tipton
Farwell, Walter Maurice *vocalist, educator*

KANSAS

Hutchinson
Wendelburg, Norma Ruth *composer, pianist, educator*

Kansas City
Horseman, Barbara Ann *church musician, voice educator*

Lawrence
Duerksen, George Louis *music educator, music therapist*
Hilding, Jerel Lee *music and dance educator, former dancer*
Pozdro, John Walter *music educator, composer*

Manhattan
†Fedder, Norman J. *theatre educator, playwright*

Olathe
Smith, Katheryn Jeanette *music educator*

Overland Park
†Werner, Betty Jean *music educator*

Shawnee Mission
Julien, Gail Leslie *model, public relations professional*

Topeka
Pettijohn, Norma Agnes *organist, educator*
Rivers, Julie Elaine *concert pianist, composer, recording industry executive*

Wichita
Chen, Zuohuang *conductor*
Janzen, Janet Lindeblad *composer*
Johnson, Guy Charles *music educator, musician*

KENTUCKY

Frankfort
Fletcher, Winona Lee *theater educator*

Lexington
Monsen, Ronald Peter *musician, music educator, artist*

Louisville
Doyle, Billy Herman *film specialist, writer*
†Friedlander, Mitzi B. *artist*
Hardy, Michael C. *performing arts administrator*
Luvisi, Lee *concert pianist*
Miller, Marilee Hebert Slater *theatre administrator, producer, director, consultant*
Murrell, Deborah Anne *music educator, speaker, writer*
Schuster-Craig, John *music educator*

Richmond
Beranek, Carla Tipton *music educator*

LOUISIANA

Baton Rouge
Constantinides, Dinos Demetrios (Constantine Constantinides) *music educator, composer, conductor*
Norem, Richard Frederick, Sr. *musician, music educator*
Willett, Anna Hart *composer*

Hammond
Hemberger, Glen James *university band director, music educator*

Lafayette
Davis, Ruth Louise-Weingartner *video company administrator, former military officer*

New Iberia
Gonsoulin Ghattas, Wendy Ann *choreographer, dancer*

New Orleans
Baranovich, Diana Lea *music educator*
Cosenza, Arthur George *opera director*
Lyall, Robert H. *opera company executive*
†Seibel, Klauspeter *conductor*

Shreveport
Simons, Dennis *performing company executive*

Thibodaux
Klaus, Kenneth Sheldon *choral conductor, vocalist, music educator*

Zachary
Rogillio, Kathy June *musician, piano rebuilder, educator*

MAINE

Bangor
Moreau, James William *stuntman*

Biddeford
Konstantinovskaia, Valeria *puppeteer, puppet maker, sculptor, educator*

Blue Hill Falls
Stookey, Noel Paul *folksinger, composer*

Boothbay Harbor
Eriksen, Dan Oluf *film director*
Lenthall, Franklyn *theatre historian*

Brunswick
Schwartz, Elliott Shelling *composer, author, music educator*

Castine
Davis, Peter Frank *filmmaker, author*

Damariscotta
Waterman, Charles Albert *actor, director, retired sales executive*

Gorham
Stump, Walter Ray *drama educator*

Kittery
†Diggins, Dean Richard *dancer, artist*

Lewiston
Williams, Linda F. *music educator, jazz musician, ethnomusicologist*

Monhegan
Boehmer, Raquel Davenport *television producer, newsletter editor*

Portland
Shimada, Toshiyuki *orchestra conductor, music director*

Saint Albans
†Clark, Raymond Leroy *singer*

Surry
Sopkin, George *cellist, music educator*

Waldoboro
Fassett, Frances Nicholas (Kitty Fassett) *pianist, record producer*

West Baldwin
Simmonds, Rae Nichols *musician, composer, educator*

MARYLAND

Annapolis
Smith Tarchalski, Helen Marie *piano educator*

Baltimore
Allen, Rodney Desvigne *music educator*
Beer, Alice Stewart (Mrs. Jack Engeman) *retired musician, educator*
Benjamin, Thomas Edward *music educator, composer, conductor*

Harrison, Michael *opera company executive*
Hopps, Raymond, Jr. *film producer, lawyer*
Markey, Paul Victor *videographer, videotape editor*
Rauschenberg, Dale Eugene *music educator*
Robinson, Alice Jean McDonnell *drama and speech educator*
Southern, Hugh *retired performing arts manager*
†Temirkanov, Yuri *music director*

Bethesda
†Burkhalter, Susan Shively *music educator, organist*
Gray, James Gordon, Jr. *speech educator*
Hallsted, Nancy Ruth Everett *pianist, music educator*
Mastny-Fox, Catherine Louise *administrator, consultant*
†Proctor, Sondra Goldsmith *musician*

Bladensburg
†Gordon, Pamela Ann Wence *piano teacher*

Bryans Road
Boyer, Stephanie Ann *music educator*

Chestertown
Clarke, Garry Evans *composer, educator, musician, administrator*

College Park
Moss, Lawrence Kenneth *composer, educator*

Columbia
†Spicknall, Joan *music educator*

Davidsonville
Mahaffey, Redge Allan *movie producer, director, writer, actor, scientist*

Finksburg
†Giuffre, Anthony T. *television producer, lighting director*

Fort Washington
Hankerson, Charlie Edward, Jr. *music educator*

Germantown
Chambers, Helen McGraw *pianist*
Harris, William Norman *music educator*

Glen Burnie
Ruth, Shiela Grant *music educator*

Highland
Varga, Deborah Trigg *music educator, entertainment company owner*

Hyattsville
Dukes, Rebecca Weathers (Becky Dukes) *musician, singer, songwriter*

Potomac
Feinstein, Martin *performing arts consultant, art director*
Mapother, Margaret Loudermill *piano educator*
Wang, An-Ming *composer*

Reisterstown
Clews, William Vincent *producer, writer*

Rockville
Cain, Karen Mirinda *musician, educator*

Salisbury
Weber, Michael James *conductor*

Silver Spring
Crawford-Mason, Clare Wootten *television producer, journalist*
Eaton, James Coleman *music educator, therapist*
†Foucheux, Richard *actor, artist*
Neumann, Alfred John *music director*
Secular, Sidney *actor, model, mailorder marketing consultant*
†Smith, A(rletta) Renee *agent*

Westminster
Boudreaux, Margaret A. *music educator*

MASSACHUSETTS

Allston
†Burton, Gary *musician*

Amherst
Brandon, Liane *filmmaker, educator*
May, Ernest Dewey *music executive, organist, choirmaster*

Auburn
McDonald, Sean *video professional*

Barnstable
†Vila, Robert Joseph *television host, designer, real estate developer*

Belmont
Scanlan, Robert *theater director, writer*

Boston
†Brown, D. David *performing company executive*
Charnas, Fran Elka *theatre director, educator, author*
Del Sesto, Janice Mancini *opera company executive*
†Holmes, Anna-Marie *ballerina, ballet mistress*
Hoyt, Herbert Austin Aikins *television producer*
Jochum, Veronica *pianist*
Lesser, Laurence *musician, educator*
†Lockhart, Keith Alan *conductor, musician, teacher*
Maso, Michael Harvey *theatre administrator*
McPhee, Jonathan *music director, conductor, composer, arranger*
Miller, J. Philip *television producer, director, educator*
Moriarty, John *opera administrator, artistic director*
Rotenberg, Sheldon *violinist*
Schifrin, Lalo *composer*
Sharp, William Leslie *performing arts educator*

Totenberg, Roman *violinist, music educator*
Wahlberg, Mark *actor*
†Wardwell, Gerry E. *television producer, journalist*
Webber, Stephen William *music educator, composer*
Wheeler, W(illiam) Scott *composer, conductor, music educator*
Young, Laura *dance educator, choreographer*

Bridgewater
Kreiling, Jean Louise *music educator*
Moses, Nancy Lee Heise *dance educator*
Nicholeris, Carol Angela *music educator, composer, conductor*

Brookline
Epstein, Alvin *actor, director, singer, mime*

Cambridge
Cleary, David Michael *composer, library assistant*
de Varon, Lorna Cooke *choral conductor*
Epstein, David Mayer *composer, conductor, music theorist, educator*
Erdely, Stephen Lajos *music educator*
†Everett, Thomas Gregory *musician, music educator*
Layton, Billy Jim *composer*
Martino, Donald James *composer, educator*
Morris, Errol M. *filmmaker*
Orchard, Robert John *theater producer, educator*
Pinkham, Daniel *composer*
Russell, George Allen *composer, theoritician, author, conductor*
Shelemay, Kay Kaufman *music educator*
Sims, Ezra *composer*
†Somerville, Murray Forbes *organist, choral director*
Thomas, Edward LaBelle *technical director*
†Verba, Cynthia *music history educator*
Wiseman, Frederick *filmmaker*
Wunderlich, Renner *film producer, director, editor*

Dedham
Firth, Everett Joseph *timpanist*

Dennis Port
Marcus, Marie Eleanor *pianist*

Eastham
Lynne-O'Brien, Vincent *director, actor*

Fall River
Lynds, Lucinda *music educator*

Framingham
Bogard, Carole Christine *lyric soprano*

Gloucester
Zawinul, Josef *bandleader, composer, keyboardist, synthesist*

Great Barrington
Curtin, Phyllis *music educator, former dean, operatic singer*

Jamaica Plain
Florio, Christopher John *multimedia producer*

Lenox
Curtis, William Edgar *conductor, composer*

Littleton
Crandall Hollick, Julian Bernard Hugh *radio producer*

Marblehead
Kennedy, Elizabeth Mae *musician*

Medford
Anderson, Thomas Jefferson, Jr. *composer, educator*
DeVoto, Mark Bernard *music educator*

Nantucket
Rorem, Ned *composer, author*

Needham
Di Domenica, Robert Anthony *musician, composer*
Donahue, Arthur Thomas *television producer*

Newton
Brilliant, Barbara *television host, producer, columnist, journalist, communications and media consultant*
Sutherland, David Russell *filmmaker*

Newton Center
Schuller, Gunther Alexander *composer*

Newtonville
Gomberg, Sydelle *dancer educator*
Zimmardi, James Anthony *musician, music educator*

North Dartmouth
Dace, Tish *drama educator*

Northampton
Naegele, Philipp Otto *violinist, violist, music educator*

Plymouth
Gregory, Dick *comedian, civil rights activist*

Roxbury
Coleman, David Dennis, II *theater educator*
Weeks, Clifford Myers *musician, educational administrator*

South Lancaster
†Wada, Toshimasa Francis *conductor, educator*

Springfield
Smith, Mark Russell *symphony director*

Stockbridge
MacDonald, Sharon Ethel *dancer, choreographer, administrator*

Sudbury
Given, Ellen Marie *flutist*

Truro
Falk, Lee Harrison *performing arts executive, cartoonist*

Tyngsboro
Wetterwald, Audrey Lynn *dance educator*

Waltham
Boykan, Martin *composer, music educator*
Hill, John-Edward *theater executive*
Titcomb, Caldwell *music and theatre historian*
Wyner, Yehudi *composer, pianist, conductor, educator*

Watertown
Langstaff, John Meredith *musician*

Williamstown
Shainman, Irwin *music educator, musician*

Woburn
Reagan, Stevan Ray *cable company executive*

MICHIGAN

Alma
Scripps, Douglas Jerry *music educator, conductor, director*

Ann Arbor
Bassett, Leslie Raymond *composer, educator*
Bolcom, William Elden *musician, composer, educator, pianist*
Rosseels, Gustave Alois *music educator*
Scharp-Radovic, Carol Ann *choreographer, classical ballet educator, artistic director*
Sparling, Peter David *dancer, dance educator*

Benton Harbor
Wurz, Kevin Ross *theater educator, director*

Beverly Hills
Tolias, Linda Puroff *music educator*

Bloomfield Hills
Haidostian, Alice Berberian *concert pianist, civic volunteer and fundraiser*

Cadillac
Whitmer, Walter Glenn *band director*

Dearborn
Dzuiblinski, Gerard Arthur *theatre educator, artistic director*

Detroit
Alpert, Daniel *television executive*
Calarco, N. Joseph *theater executive*
Di Chiera, David *performing arts impresario*
Gulley, James Clarence, Jr. *television producer, marketing specialist, internet consultant*
Jarvi, Neeme *conductor*
Quayle, John Clare *video producer*

East Lansing
Kirk, Edgar Lee *musician, educator*
Whiting, Lisa Lorraine Dobson *video production educator, producer, director*

Grand Rapids
Spence, Brandon *music director*

Interlochen
Hanson, Byron Winslade *music educator*

Kalamazoo
Schrier, Steven Robert *television producer, director*
†Takeda, Yoshimi *music director*
Zupko, Ramon *composer, music professor emeritus*

Lansing
Blanchard, William Graham *film educator*

Midland
Buechner, Margaret *composer, music educator*

Oak Park
Martin, Vivian *soprano*

Redford
Goslin, Gerald Hugh *concert pianist, educator*

Rochester
Bajor, James Henry *musician, jazz pianist*

Southfield
McAuley, Philip Christopher *audio engineer*
Plummer, Glenn Rodney *radio and television producer*

Waterford
Blanchard, Danielle René *music educator*

MINNESOTA

Arnoka
Luther, Robert Alan *organist, educator*

Bemidji
Logan, P. Bradley *music educator, church musician*

Bloomington
Smith, Henry Charles, III *symphony orchestra conductor*

Eden Prairie
Nortwen, Patricia Harman *music educator*

Mankato
Hustoles, Paul John *theater educator*

Minneapolis
Doepke, Katherine Louise Guldberg *choral director, former music educator*
Fetler, Paul *composer*
Fleezanis, Jorja Kay *violinist, educator*
Larsen, Elizabeth B. (Libby Larsen) *composer*
Miller, John William, Jr. *bassoonist*
Oue, Eiji *performing company executive*
Severinsen, Doc (Carl H. Severinsen) *conductor, musician*
Skrowaczewski, Stanislaw *conductor, composer*
Smith, Kevin H. *performing company executive*
Strand, Dean Paul *disc jockey, audio engineer*
Thompson, Richard Nelson Christoph *producer, director*
Ware, D. Clifton *singer, educator*
Webb, Martha Jeanne *author, speaker, film producer*
Wollan, Curtis Noel *theatrical producer and director*

Moorhead
Rothlisberger, Rodney John *music educator*

Northfield
†McCleary, Harriet Caldwell *voice teacher, singer*

Saint Paul
Anderson, Clyde Bailey *musician, educator*
Biery, Marilyn Ruth *organist, conductor, educator, composer*
Nice, Pamela Michele *theatre director*
Tecco, Romuald Gilbert Louis Joseph *violinist, concertmaster*
Wolff, Hugh MacPherson *music director, conductor*

White Bear Lake
Gutché, Gene *composer*

MISSISSIPPI

Clinton
Eaves, Dorothy Ann Greene *music educator*

Grenada
Thomas, Ouida Power *music educator*

Jackson
Bobo, Len Davis *musician*
Pearce, Colman Cormac *conductor, pianist, composer*

MISSOURI

Arrow Rock
Bollinger, Michael *artistic director*

Branson
Bradley, Leon Charles *musician, educator, consultant*
Tillis, Mel(vin) *musician, songwriter*

Columbia
Archer, Stephen Murphy *retired theater educator*

Jefferson City
Greene, Thomasina Talley *concert pianist, educator*

Kansas City
Bolender, Todd *choreographer*
Bugg, Leon Hayes *music educator, performer, composer*
Costin, James D. *performing arts company executive*
Louis, William Joseph *theater educator, actor, director, artist, poet*
Whitener, William Garnett *dancer, choreographer*

Lees Summit
Bond-Brown, Barbara Ann *musician, educator*

Liberty
Harriman, Richard Lee *performing arts administrator, educator*

Maryville
Schultz, Patricia Bowers *vocal music educator*

Saint Joseph
Tritten, Donald Michael *music educator*

Saint Louis
Boddie, Don O'Mar *recording company executive, producer, recording artist*
Briccetti, Joan Therese *theater manager, arts management consultant*
Ehrlich, Ava *television executive*
Eichhorn, Arthur David *music director*
†Hylton, John Baker *music educator, university administrator*
Jackson, Paul Howard *multimedia producer, educator*
Radentz, Michael Grey *recording engineer, producer, composer, musician*
Schindler, Laura Ann *piano teacher, accompanist*
Stewart, John Harger *music educator*
Stumpf, Earlwayne Schwarze *actor, advertising executive*
Vonk, Hans *conductor*

Salem
†Jessen, Chris Michael *music educator*

Springfield
Moulder, T. Earline *musician*
Spicer, Holt Vandercook *speech and theater educator*

Warrensburg
Stagg, David Lee *music educator*

MONTANA

Billings
Barnea, Uri N. *music director, conductor, composer, violinist*

Bozeman
Savery, Matthew *music conductor, director, educator*

Great Falls
Johnson, Gordon James *artistic director, conductor*

Missoula
Knowles, William Leroy (Bill Knowles) *television news producer, journalism educator*
Listerud, (Lowell) Brian *choir director, music educator*

NEBRASKA

Chadron
Winkle, William Allan *music educator*

Hastings
Freed, Donald Callen *vocal and choral musician, educator*

Kearney
†Nabb, David Bruce *music educator*

Lincoln
Dixon, Wheeler Winston *film and video studies educator, writer*

Omaha
Bounds, Nancy *modeling and talent company executive*
Johnson, James David *concert pianist, organist, educator*
Yampelsky, Victor *music director*

Schuyler
Johnson, Dolores DeBower *consultant*

NEVADA

Carson City
Bugli, David *conductor, arranger, composer*

Henderson
Riske, William Kenneth *producer, cultural services consultant*

Las Vegas
Capelle, Madelene Carole *opera singer, educator, music therapist*
Castro, Joseph Armand *music director, pianist, composer, orchestrator*
Fuller, Dolores Agnes *songwriter, actress*
Gold, Hyman *cellist*
Healy, Mary (Mrs. Peter Lind Hayes) *singer, actress*
Kalb, Benjamin Stuart *television producer, director*
Knight, Gladys (Maria) *singer*
Leibovit, Arnold L. *film producer, director*
Lewis, Jerry (Joseph Levitch) *comedian*
Mitchell, Guy *singer, entertainer, actor*
†Vazquez, Jayme Jack *musician, songwriter, producer, technician*
Wiemer, Robert Ernest *film and television producer, writer, director*

Reno
Daniels, Ronald Dale *conductor*

NEW HAMPSHIRE

Bradford
Lettvin, Theodore *concert pianist*

Concord
Church, Gail Graham *former television producer, consultant*
Hodes, Paul William *record company executive, lawyer*
Lundahl, Steven Mark *musician, consultant*

East Alstead
Holloway, Robert Charles *orchestrator, arranger, composer*

Hanover
Ehrlich, David Gordon *film director, educator*

Lyme
Darion, Joe *librettist, lyricist*

Manchester
Carkin, Gary Bryden *performing arts educator*
Proulx, William John *producer*

Orford
Karol, John J., Jr. *producer, filmmaker*

Plymouth
Swift, Robert Frederic *music educator*

Walpole
Burns, Kenneth Lauren *filmmaker, historian*

Woodsville
†Page, Patti (Clara Ann Fowler) *vocalist*

NEW JERSEY

Allendale
Ruth, Rodney *musician, music consultant, contractor, educator*

Allenhurst
Tognoli, Era M. *performing company executive, artistic director*

Atlantic City
Chambers, Robert Arthur *entertainment director*

Basking Ridge
Estes, Simon Lamont *opera singer, bass-baritone*

Bayonne
†Goldman, Edward Merrill *musician*

†Lyndeck, Edmund *actor*

Belle Mead
Carroll, David Joseph *actor*

Cherry Hill
Clauser, Donald Roberdeau *musician*

Clayton
Bertenshaw, William Howard, III *radio and television producer*

Cliffside Park
Perhacs, Marylouise Helen *musician, educator*

Clifton
Herman, Josh Seth *actor, clown, magician*

East Brunswick
Hurst, Gregory Squire *artistic director, director, producer*
Kupchynsky, Jerry Markian *orchestra conductor, educator*
Mooney, William Piatt *actor*
Yttrehus, Rolv Berger *composer, educator*

East Hanover
†Ori, Nancy Jean *video producer and director, photographer*

East Orange
Oderman, Stuart Douglas *pianist, composer, playwright*

Englewood
Zwilich, Ellen Taaffe *composer*

Flemington
Castellanos, Diego Antonio *television personality, writer, educator*

Florham Park
Atkins, Richard Bart *film, television producer*

Fort Lee
Houston, Whitney *vocalist, recording artist*

Glassboro
†DiBlasio, Denis *musician, educator*
Robinette, Joseph Allen *theater educator, playwright*

Glen Ridge
Bracken, Eddie (Edward Vincent) *actor, director, writer, singer, artist*

Hackensack
Angelakis, Manos G(eorge) *filmmaker, communications executive*

Hoboken
†Einreinhofer, William Michael, Jr. *television producer and director, educator*

Iselin
Bragg, William David *film producer, screenwriter*
Rosenthal, David Michael *musician, songwriter, composer, producer, synthesizer programmer*

Jersey City
Owens, Dana (Queen Latifah) *recording artist, actress*
Rázim, William Wendell *former radio broadcasting producer*

Lawrenceville
†Tipton, June Frank *music educator*

Leonia
Deutsch, Nina *pianist*

Livingston
Bertenshaw, Bobbi Cherrelle *producer*

Madison
Monte, Bonnie J. *performing company executive, director, educator*

Metuchen
Roma-Scott, Mary Lou *music educator*

Montclair
†Cioffi, Patrizia *soprano, voice educator, arts consultant*
†Nirenberg, Nelson Marcio *conductor, educator*
Sierra, Roberto *composer, music educator*
Walker, George Theophilus, Jr. *composer, pianist, music educator*

Mount Laurel
Torres, Robert Alvin *dancer, singer, actor, sign language interpreter*

Newark
Macal, Zdenek *conductor*
Monty, Gloria *former television producer, film executive*
Silipigni, Alfredo *opera conductor*
Storrer, William Allin *consultant*
†Tamburri, Lawrence J. *artistic director*

Paramus
Dirr, John Charles (Jack Dirr) *television producer and director*

Parlin
Chernow, Jay Howard *music industry executive*
†Griffin, Martin Edward *music educator*

Peapack
Gustafson, Robert Eric *artistic director*

Perth Amboy
Richardson-Melech, Joyce Suzanne *music educator, singer*

Pitman
Carpenter, Hoyle Dameron *music educator emeritus*

Princeton
Estey, Audree Phipps artistic director
Levy, Kenneth music educator
Orphanides, Nora Charlotte ballet educator
Rosen, Marvin Abraham music educator
Vizzini, Carol Redfield symphony musician, music educator
Westergaard, Peter Talbot composer, music educator

Red Bank
Hughes, Barnard actor

Ridgefield
Shapira, Benjamin cellist

River Vale
Moderacki, Edmund Anthony music educator, conductor

Rockaway
Laine, Cleo (Clementina Dinah Dankworth) singer

Rumson
Topham, Sally Jane ballet educator

Somerville
Dixon, Joanne Elaine music educator

Teaneck
Bullough, John Frank organist, music educator
Reid, Rufus Lamar jazz bassist, educator

Totowa
Wesp, Wendy Louise vocalist, songwriter

Trenton
†Fields, L. Marc producer, director, writer, educator

Vineland
†Warren, Corky radio personality

Warren
Maull, George Marriner music director, conductor

West Paterson
King, Deborah Simpkin music, voice educator

Woodcliff Lake
Morath, Max Edward entertainer, composer, writer

NEW MEXICO

Albuquerque
Evans, Bill (James William Evans) dancer, choreographer, educator, arts administrator
Lockington, David conductor
Rice, Linda Angel music educator
Smyer, Myrna Ruth drama educator

Edgewood
Hamilton, Jerald musician

Las Cruces
Pinnow, Timothy Dayne theater educator, fight choreographer

Santa Fe
Ballard, Louis Wayne composer
Crosby, John O'Hea conductor, opera manager
Gaddes, Richard performing arts administrator
Miller, Dwight Richard cosmetologist, corporate executive, hair designer
Peterson, Harry Austin, Sr. television producer, writer
Rubenstein, Bernard orchestra conductor
Wilson, Bart Allen media director, marketing consultant, educator

NEW YORK

Amherst
Braun, Kazimierz Pawel theatrical director, writer, educator
Coover, James Burrell music educator

Astoria
Morrow, Scott Douglas choreographer, educator

Baldwinsville
†Niemiec, Paul Wallace, Jr. artist, pharmacist

Bayside
Zinn, William violinist, composer, business executive

Bedford
Chase, Chevy (Cornelius Crane Chase) comedian, actor, author

Bethpage
Sapan, Joshua Ward cable TV executive

Binghamton
Mac Lennan, Susan Mary performing company executive

Briarcliff Manor
Del Colle, Paul Lawrence communications administrator, educator
Kennell, Richard Wayne recording artist, business manager
Ostrofsky, Anna music educator, violinist

Bronx
Sherman, Judith Dorothy producer, recording company owner, recording engineer
Somary, Johannes Felix conductor
Sprecher, Baron William Gunther pianist, composer, conductor, diplomat

Bronxville
Biscardi, Chester composer, educator
Farber, Viola Anna dancer, choreographer, educator

Brooklyn
Anderson, James Noel (Jim Anderson) recording engineer, producer
Barnes, John Wadsworth director, writer
Bergen, Christopher Brooke opera company administrator, translator, editor
†Creshevsky, Noah Ephriam music educator, composer
†Doss, Amanda D. producer
Ham, Karen music educator
Hopkins, Karen Brooks performing arts executive
Jarman, Joseph jazz musician
Jenkins, Leroy violinist, composer
Kazan, Basil Gibran religious music composer
Koppel, Audrey Feiler electrologist, educator
†Lee, Spike (Shelton Jackson Lee) filmmaker
Lichtenstein, Harvey performing arts executive
Rucker, Bronwyn actress, writer, social worker
Salzman, Eric composer, writer
Spano, Robert performing company executive, conductor
Zawadi, Kiane musician

Buffalo
Manes, Stephen Gabriel concert pianist, educator

Cortland
Hischak, Thomas Stephen theater educator, writer

Crugers
Norman, Jessye soprano

Deer Park
D'Amore, Victor director, choreographer, dance educator

Dobbs Ferry
Kapp, Richard P. conductor, arts administrator
Litwin, Burton Lawrence entertainment industry executive, theatrical producer, lawyer

East Hampton
Dello Joio, Norman composer

Elmira
Amchin, Robert A. music educator

Flushing
†Saylor, Bruce Stuart composer, educator
Silver, Sheila Jane composer, music educator
Smaldone, Edward Michael composer
†Yeo, Kim Eng artist

Forest Hills
†Gorbaty, Jan pianist, music educator
Polakoff, Abe baritone
Prager, Alice Heinecke music company executive

Germantown
Rollins, (Theodore) Sonny composer, musician

Gilbertsville
Roos, Casper actor

Glen Head
Sutherland, Denise Jackson (Denise Suzanne Jackson) ballerina

Greenfield Center
Conant, Robert Scott harpsichordist, music educator

Harrison
†Wedge, Chris animation director

Hastings On Hudson
D'Antoni, Philip producer
Fischler, Steven Alan film producer
Parrott, Billy James film director, communications executive
Wolfe, Stanley composer, educator

Hempstead
Chapman, Ronald Thomas musician, educator
Graffeo, Mary Thérèse music educator, performer

Hewlett
Wolff, Eleanor Blunk actress

Hicksville
Estrin, Morton pianist, music educator

Hillsdale
Dufault, Peter Kane writer, musician

Hurley
Bedford, Brian actor

Islip
†Lombardi, Carlo pianist, educator

Ithaca
Hester, Karlton Edward composer, performer, music educator
Husa, Karel Jaroslav composer, conductor, educator

Jamaica
Desser, Maxwell Milton artist, art director, filmstrip producer
Rose, Jodi opera company founder and artistic director

Lindenhurst
Farrell-Logan, Vivian actress

Long Eddy
Hoiby, Lee composer, concert pianist

Manhasset
Brand, Oscar folksinger, author, educator

Margaretville
Brockway-Henson, Amie producing artistic director

Massapequa Park
Klein, Kenneth orchestra conductor, educator

Millbrook
Nowak, Grzegorz music educator

Millerton
Hastings, Donald Francis actor, writer

New Rochelle
Cleary, James C. audio-visual producer
Gay, Elisabeth Feitler actress
Merrill, Robert baritone

New York
Adams, Joey comedian, author
Adler, Richard composer, lyricist
†Ahrens, Lynn lyricist
Ailes, Roger Eugene television producer, consultant
Alcantara, Theo conductor
Alenikoff, Frances choreographer, performer, writer, dancer, artist
Allen, Betty (Mrs. Ritten Edward Lee, III) mezzo-soprano
Allen, Nancy musician, educator
Allen, Woody (Allen Stewart Konigsberg) actor, filmmaker, author
†Alterman, Barry performing company executive
†Altman, Robert B. film director, writer, producer
Amara, Lucine opera and concert singer
Anagnost, Dino artistic director
Araiza, Francisco (José Francisco Araiza Andrade) opera singer
Asakawa, Takako dancer, dance teacher, director, choreographer
Ashley, Elizabeth actress
Asner, Edward actor
Aurilia, Christine Marie administrative assistant
†Avgerakis, George Harris video producer
Ax, Emanuel pianist
Azzoli, Val music company executive
Babyface, (Kenny Edmonds) popular musician
Bacall, Lauren actress
Baker-Riker, Margery television executive
Baldwin, Stephen actor
Banks, Helen Augusta singer, actress
Barber, Russell Brooks Butler television producer
Bardos, Karoly television and film educator, writer, director
Barker, Charles conductor
Barker, Edwin Bogue musician
Barrie, Barbara actress
Barsalona, Frank Samuel theatrical agent
†Bart, Roger actor
Bartoli, Cecilia coloratura soprano, mezzo soprano
Becofsky, Arthur Luke arts administrator, writer
Beeson, Jack Hamilton composer, educator, writer
Behrens, Hildegard soprano
Belkin, Boris David violinist
Bennett, Tony (Anthony Dominick Benedetto) entertainer
Benton, Nicholas theater producer
Bergen, Polly actress
Berger, Miriam Roskin creative arts therapy director, educator, therapist
Bernardi, Mario conductor
Bernstein, Elliot Louis television executive
Berry, Halle actress
†Besterman, Douglas composer, orchestrator
Bikel, Theodore actor, singer
Birkenhead, Thomas Bruce theatrical producer and manager, educator
Bishop, André artistic director, producer
Boelzner, Gordon orchestral conductor
Bohrman, David Ellis television news producer
Bolotowsky, Andrew Ilyitch flutist, composer
Bonazzi, Elaine Claire mezzo-soprano
Bonynge, Richard opera conductor
Borge, Victor entertainer, comedian, pianist
Bosco, Philip Michael actor
Bowden, Sally Ann choreographer, teacher, dancer
Braden, Martha Brooke concert pianist, educator
Braxton, Toni popular musician
Brechner, Stanley artistic director
Brecker, Michael saxophonist
Bregman, Martin film producer
Brendel, Alfred concert pianist
Brewster, Robert Gene concert singer, educator
Brinkley, Christie model, spokesperson, designer
†Brohn, William David conductor, orchestrator
Brothers, Joyce Diane television personality, psychologist
Brown, Carolyn Rice dancer, choreographer
Brown, David motion picture producer, writer
Brown, Trisha dancer
Browning, John pianist
†Buckley, Betty Lynn actress
Bumbry, Grace soprano
†Burns, Ralph conductor, orchestrator
Burrell, Orville Richard popular musician
Button, Richard Totten television and stage producer, former figure skating champion
Byer, Diana performing arts company executive
Calabrese, Rosalie Sue arts management consultant, writer
Cannon, John actor, performing arts association executive
Cantrell, Lana actress, singer, lawyer
Capalbo, Carmen Charles director, producer
Caples, Richard James dance company executive, lawyer
Carlson, Marvin Albert theater educator
Carney, Michael orchestra leader
Carpenter, Patricia music educator
Carter, Elliott Cook, Jr. composer
Carthay, R. Jon hand model, actor
Caruso, Rocco Andrew television producer
Castel, Nico tenor, educator
Cazeaux, Isabelle Anne Marie retired musicology educator
Chambless, Anne Devon wig and make-up artist
Champion, Marge (Marjorie Celeste Champion) actress, dancer, choreographer
Chang, Marian S. filmmaker, composer
Channer, Harold Hudson television producer, interviewer
Channing, Stockard (Susan Stockard) actress
Charnin, Martin theatrical director, lyricist, producer
†Chenoweth, Kristin actress
Christensen, Dieter ethnomusicologist
Clapton, Eric musician
Cohen, Selma Jeanne dance historian
Colbath, Brian (Brian Colbath Watson) actor, script and live performance writer
Cole, Vinson tenor
Coleman, Cy pianist, composer, producer
Coleman, George Edward tenor, alto and soprano saxophonist
Colvin, Shawn recording artist, songwriter
Comfort, Jane choreographer, director
Conlon, James Joseph conductor
Conway, Kevin actor, director
Coolio popular musician
Cooperman, Alvin television and theatrical producer
Corigliano, John Paul composer
Corsaro, Frank Andrew theater, musical and opera director
Cory, Jeffrey television, film, stage, event and creative director
Craven, Wes film director
†Crosby, David musician
†Cullman, Joan theatrical producer
†Cumming, Alan actor
Cunningham, Merce dancer
Curtin, Jane Therese actress, writer
Curtis, Paul James mime
Curtis, Tony (Bernard Schwartz) actor
Dakin, Christine Whitney dancer, educator
Dale, Jim actor
d'Amboise, Jacques Joseph dancer, choreographer
Darvarova, Elmira violinist, concertmaster
David, Hal lyricist
Davies, Dennis Russell conductor, music director, pianist
Davis, Leonard violist
Davis, Luane Ruth theatrical director, performer
Davis, Rece anchor, reporter
Davison, Bruce actor
de Lappe, Gemze dancer, educator, choreographer
DeLay, Dorothy (Mrs. Edward Newhouse) violinist, educator
Dendy, Mark choreographer
†Diawara, Manthia film and literature educator, writer, filmmaker
Diaz, Justino bass-baritone
Dichter, Misha concert pianist
Diggins, Peter Sheehan arts administrator
†Dillon, Matt actor
†Dion, Celine musician
Dissette, Alyce Marie television newsmedia and theatrical producer, non-profit foundation executive
Dlugoszewski, Lucia artistic director
Dodson, Daryl Theodore ballet administrator, arts consultant
†Domingo, Placido tenor
Donelian, Armen pianist, composer, author
Doty, Shayne Taylor organist
Downs, Hugh Malcolm radio and television broadcaster
Drake, Laura director, performer
Duchin, Peter Oelrichs musician
Dufour, Val (Albert Valery Dufour) actor
Dulaine, Pierre ballroom dancer
Dunn, Mignon mezzo-soprano
Duquesnay, Ann actress, singer
†Dutoit, Charles conductor
Dylan, Bob (Robert Allen Zimmerman) singer, composer
Eger, Joseph conductor, music director
Elias, Rosalind mezzo-soprano
Ellis, Scott theatrical director
Englander, Roger Leslie television producer, director
Entremont, Philippe conductor, pianist
†Eschenbach, Christoph conductor, pianist
Everly, Jack conductor
Ewing, Maria Louise soprano
Fairbanks, Douglas Elton, Jr. actor, producer, writer, corporation director
Falletta, Jo Ann musician
Farberman, Harold conductor, composer
Farley, Carole soprano
Faulkner, Julia Ellen opera singer
Feist, Gene theater director
Feld, Eliot dancer, choreographer
Ferber, Laurence Robert television producer
Feuer, Cy motion picture and theatrical producer, director
Fisher, Jules Edward producer, lighting designer, theatre consultant
†Flaherty, Stephen composer, orchestrator
Flanagan, Tommy (Lee) jazz pianist
Fleming, Renée L. opera singer
Fontana, Thomas Michael producer, scriptwriter
Ford, Eileen Otte (Mrs. Gerard W. Ford) modeling agency executive
Foreman, Laura dancer, choreographer, conceptual artist, writer, educator
Foreman, Richard theater director, playwright
Formento, Daniel radio company executive, writer
Forst, Judith Doris mezzo-soprano
Frankel, Gene theater director, author, producer, educator
Franklin, Aretha singer
Freizer, Louis A. radio news producer
Freni, Mirella soprano
Frisell-Schröder, Sonja Bettie opera producer, stage director
Frith, Michael Kingsbury artistic director, illustrator, performing company executive
Fryer, Robert Sherwood theatrical producer
†Gagne, David Ward music educator
Galway, James flutist
Gazzara, Ben actor
Geffen, Betty Ada theatrical personal manager
Gibb, Barry vocalist, songwriter
Gillies, Trent Donald television producer
†Glass, Philip composer, musician
Glover, Savion actor, dancer
Goldsmith, Merwin actor, theater director
Goodman, Roger Mark television director
Gordon, Mark actor, theater director, theater educator
Gottlieb, Morton Edgar theatrical and film producer
†Greco, Jose choreographer
Grier, David Alan actor
Grodnick, Scott Randall internet executive, music company executive
Guettel, Henry Arthur retired arts executive
Hackett, Buddy actor
Haden, Charles jazz bassist, composer
Hagen, Uta Thyra actress
†Haimes, Todd artistic director
Halmi, Robert film producer
Hance, Wiley Francis executive producer
Hancock, Gerre Edward musician
Hardy, Gordon Alfred music educator, music school president
Harkarvy, Benjamin artistic director
Harmon, Jane theatrical producer
Harnick, Sheldon Mayer lyricist
Harrell, Lynn Morris cellist
Harrow, Nancy (Mrs. Jan Krukowski) jazz singer, songwriter, editor
Harth, Sidney musician, educator
†Hartley, Hal film director
Hastings, Deborah bass guitarist
Hearn, George actor

Hebert, Bliss Edmund *opera director*
Henderson, Skitch (Lyle Russell Cedric) *pianist, conductor*
Henrickson, Richard Ralph *composer, lyricist, musician, record producer*
Hepburn, Katharine Houghton *actress*
Herrera, Paloma *dancer*
Herstand, Theodore *theatre artist, educator*
Hewitt, Don S. *television news producer*
Heyward, Andrew John *television producer*
Hill, George Roy *film director*
†Hill, Lauryn *vocalist*
Hoffman, Dustin Lee *actor*
Hoffman, Esther *pianist, educator*
Holbrook, Anna *actress*
Holder, Geoffrey Lamont *dancer, actor, choreographer, director*
Holey, Brett Allen *television director, producer*
Holland, Beth *actress*
Holliday, Polly Dean *actress*
†Horn, Shirley *vocalist, pianist*
Houghton, Charles Norris *stage director, author, educator*
Hull, Charles *performing company executive*
Hupp, Robert Martin *artistic director, educator*
†Ibi, Keiko *film director*
Ienner, Don *music company executive*
Imus, Don *radio host*
Ivory, James Francis *film director*
Jackson, Anne (Anne Jackson Wallach) *actress*
Jackson, Isaiah *conductor*
Jacobs, Jim *playwright, composer, lyricist, actor*
†Jacobs-Furey, Marilyn Sandra *television director*
Jacobson, Lawrence Seymour *television executive producer*
Jaffe, Susan *ballerina*
James-Dunston, Janet Renée *orchestral music teacher, composer, flutist*
Jamison, Judith *dancer*
Jeffers, Kevin Allen *vocalist*
Jenkin, James Thomas *videotape editor*
Johnson, James M. *orchestra executive*
Johnsson, Hillary Crute *soloist, opera singer*
Jones, Bill T. *dancer, choreographer*
Jung, Doris *dramatic soprano*
Kalmanoff, Martin *composer*
Kamlot, Robert *performing arts executive*
Karchin, Louis Samuel *composer, educator*
Kassel, Virginia Weltmer *television producer, writer*
Kaufman, Lloyd *film director, producer*
Kellogg, Cal Stewart, II *conductor, composer*
Kent, Julie *ballet dancer, actress, model*
Kent, Linda Gail *dancer*
†Kernis, Aaron Jay *composer*
Kessler, Fredric Lee *video producer, computer animation artist*
Khanzadian, Vahan *tenor*
Khasday, Alyce Field *literary and film agent, psychic consultant, business owner*
Kinberg, Judy *television producer, director*
King, B. B. (Riley B. King) *singer, guitarist*
Klein, Dyann Leslie *theater properties company executive*
Klein, Joseph Michelman *musical director*
Klein, Peter *theatrical producer*
Kline, Kevin Delaney *actor*
†Krakauer, David *musician, educator*
Krauss, Alison *country musician*
†Krizer, Jodi *performing arts executive*
Krosnick, Joel *cellist*
Krupska, Danya (Mrs. Ted Thurston) *theater director, choreographer*
Kulin, Keith David *cinematographer*
Kusmin, Ellyn Sue *music administrator*
Kusturica, Emir *film director*
Laderman, Michael Aaron *flutist, music educator*
Lampert, Zohra *actress*
Lane, Kenneth Robert *producer, distributor*
Lane, Louis *musician, conductor*
Lang, Pearl *dancer, choreographer*
Langsam, Ida S. *press agent, consultant*
Lansbury, Edgar George *theatrical producer*
Larmore, Jennifer *mezzo-soprano*
Last, Ruth Edith *actress*
Laufer, Beatrice *composer*
Leach, Robin *producer, writer, television host*
Leavitt, Michael P(aul) *arts manager, concert producer, music industry record distributor*
LeCompte, Elizabeth *theater director*
Lee, Dai-Keong *composer*
†Lee, Iara *filmmaker*
Legrand, Michel Jean *composer*
Lemon, Ralph *choreographer*
Leritz, Lawrence R. *choreographer, dancer, actor, producer, director, songwriter*
Letterman, David *television personality, comedian, writer*
Levine, James *conductor, pianist, artistic director*
Libin, Paul *theatre executive, producer*
LiBretto, John Charles *television director*
Liebermann, Lowell *composer, pianist, conductor*
†Limbaugh, Rush Hudson *radio and talk show host*
Loney, Glenn Meredith *drama educator*
Loudon, Dorothy *actress*
†Louis, Murray *dancer, choreographer, dance teacher*
Lubovitch, Lar *dancer, choreographer*
Lucas, James E(vans) *operatic director*
Lucci, Susan *actress*
Ludgin, Chester Hall *baritone, actor*
Lunn, Kitty Elizabeth *actress*
LuPone, Patti *actress*
Luther, Bruce Charles *sound technician*
Macurdy, John Edward *basso*
Mainieri, Mike *vibraphonist, producer, arranger, composer*
Malkin, Barry *film editor, consultant*
Maltby, Richard Eldridge, Jr. *theater director, lyricist*
Mamlok, Ursula *composer, educator*
†Manahan, Anna *actress*
Mansouri, Lotfollah (Lotfi Mansouri) *opera stage director, administrator*
Mantegna, Joe Anthony *actor, playwright*
Maraynes, Allan Lawrence *filmmaker, television producer*
Marder, Samuel *violinist*
†Marion, Cynthia Anne *stage director*
Marsalis, Branford *musician*
Marsh, Jean Lyndsey Torren *actress, writer*
Martin, Elliot Edwards *theatrical producer*
†Martin, Ricky *vocalist*
Martinelli, Johnnie *agent*
Martini, Richard K. *theatrical producer*
Martins, Peter *ballet master, choreographer, dancer*
Masur, Kurt *conductor*
Maxwell, Carla Lena *dancer, choreographer, educator*
May, Elaine *actress, theatre and film director*
Maysles, Albert H. *filmmaker*
Mazzola, John William *former performing arts center executive, consultant*
†McDonald, Audra Ann *actress*
McDormand, Frances *actress*
McKenzie, Kevin Patrick *artistic director*
McLachlan, Sarah *composer, musician*
McTeer, Janet *actress*
Meadow, Lynne (Carolyn Meadow) *theatrical producer and director*
Menken, Alan *composer*
Merchant, Ismail Noormohamed *film producer and director*
Merritt, Michael Monroe *musician*
Michaels, Lorne *television writer, producer*
†Michel, Prakazrel (Pras) *musician, singer*
Milnes, Sherrill E. *baritone*
Minnelli, Liza *singer, actress*
Mintz, Shlomo *conductor, violist, violinist*
Mitchell, Arthur *dancer, choreographer, educator*
Mollica, Santo *percussionist, songwriter, performer*
Monk, Debra *actress*
Monk, Meredith Jane *artistic director, composer, choreographer, film maker, director*
Moore, Michael Watson *musician, string bass, educator*
Morris, James Peppler *bass*
Morris, John *composer, conductor, arranger*
Morris, Mark William *choreographer*
Moseley, Carlos DuPre *former music executive, musician*
Moskovitz, Jim *radio, television and film producer, writer*
†Mullen, Marie *actress*
Muller, Jennifer *choreographer, dancer*
Munzer, Cynthia Brown *mezzo-soprano*
Murphy, Donna *actress*
Murphy, Rosemary *actress*
Murphy, Russell Stephen *dance company executive*
†Murphy, Tom *actor*
†Nash, Graham William *singer, composer*
Neal, Patricia *actress*
Nebgen, Stephen Wade *stage producer*
Nederlander, James Morton *theater executive*
Nelson, Barry *actor*
Nelson, Edwin Stafford *actor*
Niesen, James Louis *theater director*
Nugent, Nelle *theater, film and television producer*
Nussbaum, Jeffrey Joseph *musician*
†O'Brien, Conan *writer, performer, talk show host*
O'Donnell, Rosie *television personality, comedienne, actress*
Ohira, Kazuto *theatre company executive, writer*
O'Horgan, Thomas Foster *composer, director*
†O'Leary, Mary Louise *television producer, educator*
O'Neal, Hank *entertainment producer, business owner*
†Oz, Frank (Frank Richard Oznowicz) *puppeteer, film director*
†Ozawa, Seiji *conductor, music director*
†Page, James Patrick (Jimmy Page) *musician*
Palmer, Wayne Lewis *television director and producer*
Parker, Alice *composer, conductor*
Parks, Gordon Roger Alexander *film director, author, photographer, composer*
Parseghian, Gene *talent agent*
Parsons, Estelle *actress*
Paul, Les *entertainer, inventor*
Pavarotti, Luciano *lyric tenor*
Payton-Wright, Pamela *actress*
Pennebaker, Donn Alan *film director, lecturer*
Perahia, Murray *pianist*
Peress, Maurice *symphony conductor, musicologist*
Perkins, Leeman Lloyd *music educator, musicologist*
Perlman, Itzhak *violinist*
Perlmutter, Alvin Howard *television and film producer*
Perry, Douglas *opera singer*
Peters, Roberta *soprano*
†Plant, Robert Anthony *singer, composer*
Poor, Peter Varnum *producer, director*
Porizkova, Paulina *model, actress*
Porter, Karl Hampton *orchestra musical director, conductor*
Porter, Stephen Winthrop *stage director*
Posin, Kathryn Olive *choreographer*
Powers, Scott *producer, actor*
Previn, Andre *composer, conductor*
Price, Leontyne *concert and opera singer, soprano*
Prince, Harold *theatrical producer*
Protas, Ron *dance company executive*
Pryce, Jonathan *actor*
Queler, Eve *conductor*
Ramirez, Tina *artistic director*
Ramsay, Gustavus Remak *actor*
Ramsier, Paul *composer, psychotherapist*
Rand, Calvin Gordon *arts and education producer and consultant*
Randolph, David *conductor*
Raphael, Sally Jessy *talk-show host*
Reed, Lou *musician*
Reich, Steve *composer*
Reilly, Charles Nelson *actor, director*
Reinking, Ann H. *actress, dancer*
Renick, Kyle *artistic director*
Rhodes, Samuel *violist, educator*
Rice, Barbara Lynn *stage manager*
†Richard, Ellen *theater executive*
Richards, Keith *musician*
Richards, Lloyd George *theatrical director, university administrator*
†Rifkin, Ron *actor*
Rigg, Dame Diana *actress*
Rivera, Chita (Conchita del Rivero) *actress, singer, dancer*
Rivera, Geraldo *television personality, journalist*
Robards, Jason Nelson, Jr. *actor*
Rosen, Nathaniel Kent *cellist*
Rosenblum, M. Edgar *theater producer*
Ross, Audrey *theatrical publicist*
Rostropovich, Mstislav Leopoldovich *musician*
Rothschild, Amalie Randolph *filmmaker, producer, director, digital artist, photographer*
Rudel, Julius *conductor*
Rudin, Scott *film and theatre producer*
Saddler, Donald Edward *choreographer, dancer*
Salerno-Sonnenberg, Nadja *violinist*
Salonen, Esa-Pekka *conductor*
Salonga, Lea *actress, singer*
Sandler, Adam *actor*
Santiago-Hudson, Ruben *actor*
Saunders, Arlene *opera singer*
Schafer, Milton *composer, pianist*
Schechner, Richard *theater director, author, educator*
Scheeder, Louis *theater producer, director, educator*
Schickele, Peter *composer*
Schlang, Joseph *performing company executive*
Schoonmaker Powell, Thelma *film editor*
Schorer, Suki *ballet teacher*
Schrade, Rolande Maxwell Young *composer, pianist, educator*
Schroeder, Aaron Harold *songwriter*
Schuhart, Anne Dashley (Susan Schuhart Zito) *actress*
Schwartz, Stephen Lawrence *composer, lyricist*
Scorsese, Martin *film director, writer*
†Scott, Willard Herman *radio and television performer*
Scotto, Renata *soprano*
Seal *popular musician*
Seary, Lawrence Anthony *cinematographer, news assignment editor*
Sedaka, Neil *singer, songwriter*
†Seeger, Pete *folk singer, songwriter*
Segal, George *actor*
Seldes, Marian *actress*
Seltzer, Leo *documentary filmmaker, educator, lecturer*
Serebrier, José *musician, conductor, composer*
Severs, William Floyd *actor*
Shane, Rita *opera singer, educator*
Shelley, Carole *actress*
Sherman, Arthur *theater educator, writer, actor, composer*
†Shircore, Jenny *make-up artist*
Shostakovich, Maxim Dmitriyevich *symphonic conductor*
Shull, Richard Bruce *actor*
Shuman, Earl Stanley *songwriter, music publisher*
Siegel, Marc Monroe *television and film producer, writer, director*
Silver, Joan Micklin *film director, screenwriter*
Silvers, Sally *choreographer, performing company executive*
Simon, Carly *singer, composer, author*
Smith, Malcolm Sommerville *bass*
Soll, Joseph M. *psychotherapist*
Solomon, Maynard Elliott *music historian, former recording company executive*
Solomons, Gus, Jr. (Gustave Martinez) *choreographer, dancer, writer*
Solov, Zachary *choreographer, ballet artist*
Sorel, Claudette Marguerite *pianist*
Soto, Jock *dancer*
Soyer, David *cellist, music educator*
Spacey, Kevin *actor*
Speller, Robert Ernest Blakefield, Jr. *choreographer*
Spinella, Stephen *actor*
Springer, Ashton, Jr. *theatrical producer*
Springsteen, Bruce *singer, songwriter, guitarist*
Stattel, Robert *actor*
Steinberg, Roy Bennett *television producer, director, educator*
Stern, Howard Allan *radio personality, television show host*
Stern, Isaac *violinist*
Stiefel, Ethan *dancer*
Stilwell, Richard Dale *baritone*
Stocker, Jeffrey David *film acting coach*
Stoltzman, Richard Leslie *clarinetist*
Storch, Arthur *theater director*
Strasfogel, Ian *stage director*
†Streb, Elizabeth A. *choreographer*
Stroman, Susan *choreographer*
Stutzmann, Nathalie *classical vocalist*
Sult, Jeffery Scot *performing company executive, playwright, director, actor*
Sutherland, Dame Joan *retired soprano*
Talmi, Yoav *conductor, composer*
Taylor, Paul *choreographer*
†Taymor, Julie *theater, film and opera director and designer*
Thigpen, Lynne *actress*
Thorne, Francis *composer*
Tilson Thomas, Michael *symphony conductor*
†Tobon, Maria-Elena *conductor, flutist*
Torn, Rip (Elmore Rual Torn, Jr.) *actor, director*
Townshend, Peter *musician, composer, singer*
Tracey, Margaret *dancer*
Tree, Michael *violinist, violist, educator*
Tregellas, Patricia *musical director, composer*
Tuckwell, Barry Emmanuel *musician, music educator*
Tune, Tommy (Thomas James Tune) *musical theater director, dancer, choreographer, actor*
Turturro, John *actor*
Uggams, Leslie *entertainer*
Ulrich, Lars *drummer*
Upbin, Shari *theatrical producer, director, agent, educator*
Uppman, Theodor *concert and opera singer, voice educator*
Upshaw, Dawn *soprano*
Vandross, Luther *singer*
Van Halen, Eddie *guitarist, rock musician*
†Varone, Douglas Joseph *choreographer*
Vedder, Eddie *singer*
Viertel, Jack *theatrical producer, writer*
Volpe, Joseph *opera company administrator*
Von Brandenstein, Patrizia *production designer*
Wagner, Alan Cyril *television and film producer*
Wallace, Stewart F. *composer*
†Warbeck, Stephen *composer*
Warfield, Gerald Alexander *composer, writer*
†Waters, John *film director, writer, actor*
Wedgeworth, Ann *actress*
Weldon, Charles Jauverni *actor*
Westwood, Donald C. *opera executive*
Wexler, Peter John *producer, director, designer*
Whitehead, Robert *theatrical producer*
†Wilcox, T.J. *filmmaker*
†Williams, James Edward *musician, composer, author, producer, lecturer*
Wilson, Robert M. *theatre artist*
Winslet, Kate *actress*
Wittstein, Edwin Frank *stage and film production designer*
Wolfe, George C. *theater director, producer, playwright*
Wong, B.D. *actor*
†Wood, Frank *actor*
Wood, Ronald *musician*
Woodward, Joanne Gignilliat *actress*
Worth, Irene *actress*
Wuorinen, Charles Peter *composer*
†Wyclef, Jean *singer, record producer*
Yellin, Victor Fell *composer, music educator*
†Young, Neil *musician, songwriter*
Zaks, Jerry *theatrical director, actor*
Zhu, Ai-Lan *opera singer*
†Zipay, Joanne Margaret *theatre educator, director, dramaturge*
Zosike, Joanie Fritz *theater director, actor*
Zucker, Stefan *tenor, writer, editor, radio broadcaster*

Nyack
Borst, John Noble *television director, producer*

Orangeburg
†Seymour, James Craig *theater educator, actor, director*

Orchard Park
Geiger, Loren Dennis *classical musician*

Oswego
Lisk, Edward Stanley *musician, educator, conductor*
Nesbitt, Rosemary Sinnett *theatre educator*

Palisades
Krainin, Julian Arthur *film director, producer, writer, cinematographer*

Pawling
Jones, James Earl *actor*

Pelham
Weiss, Stuart Lloyd *television and radio producer, tax attorney*

Pittsford
Benson, Warren Frank *composer, educator*

Port Washington
Tarleton, Robert Stephen *producer and distributor fine arts videos*

Poughkeepsie
Wilson, Richard Edward *composer, pianist, music educator*

Purchase
Kornfeld, Lawrence *theatre director, educator*
Magaziner, Elliot Albert *musician, conductor, educator*

Putnam Valley
Amram, David Werner *composer, conductor, musician*

Quogue
Macero, Teo *composer, conductor*

Red Hook
Boretz, Benjamin Aaron *composer, music educator*

Rego Park
Cronyn, Hume *actor, writer, director*

Rhinebeck
Flexner, Josephine Moncure *musician, educator*

Rochester
Cherchi Usai, Paolo *film curator, film historian*
Diamond, David Leo *composer*
†Fagan, Garth *choreographer, artistic director, educator*
Harrison, Daniel Gordon *music educator, musician*
Kowalke, Kim H. *music educator, musicologist, conductor, foundation executive*
Marcellus, John Robert, III *trombonist, educator*
†Reynolds, Verne *musician, retired music educator*
Rouse, Christopher Chapman, III *composer*
Schwantner, Joseph *composer, educator*
†Shahin, Raymond J. *music educator, composer*
Weiss, Howard A. *violinist, concertmaster, conductor, music educator*

Roscoe
DeFilippo, Dominic Joseph *special effects inventor*

Roslyn Heights
Bauer, William Henry *musician*
Senft, Mason George *musician*

Saratoga Springs
Dasgupta, Gautam *theater educator, journal editor and publisher*
De Vizzio, Nicholas Joseph *violinist, educator, conductor*
†Myers, Philip Henry *artist*
Porter, David Hugh *pianist, classicist, academic administrator, liberal arts educator*

Scarsdale
Brooks, Lorraine Elizabeth *music educator*

Sea Cliff
Popova, Nina *dancer, choreographer, director*

Southampton
Joel, Billy (William Martin Joel) *musician*

Sparkill
Dahl, Arlene *actress, author, designer, cosmetic executive*

Sparrow Bush
Murray, William Bruce *opera singer*

Spencer
†Grunberg, Slawomir *film and television producer and director, director of photography*

Staten Island
Cross, Ronald *musicologist, educator*
Hardee, Lewis Jefferson, Jr. *educator*
Mastroianni, Armand *director*
Miller, Wayne *actor, designer, impresario*
Robison, Paula Judith *flutist*
Tessa, Marian Lorraine *talk show host, writer, producer, educator*
†Thomas, Charles Columbus *educator, artist*

Sunnyside
Giaimo, Kathryn Ann *performing arts company executive*

Syracuse
Elms, Ben *actor, director*
Wolff, Catherine Elizabeth *opera company executive*

PROFESSIONAL INDEX 5817 ARTS: PERFORMING

Tarrytown
†Frisch, Albert T. *composer*
Kroll, Nathan *film producer, director*

Tivoli
Cary, Gregory J. *dance center executive, dancer, choreographer, artist*

Troy
Snyder, Patricia Di Benedetto *theater director and administrator*

West Hurley
Martucci, Vincent James *composer, pianist*

West Islip
Keller, Joyce *television and radio host, counselor, writer,*

White Plains
Daraio, Robert Reid *technical/video engineer*
Sedelmaier, J. J. *filmmaker*

Willow
Bley, Carla Borg *jazz composer*

Yonkers
Baumel, Herbert *violinist, conductor*
Saslow, Steve *television director, editor*

NORTH CAROLINA

Asheville
Neese, Heidi Sue *television news assignment editor*
Weed, Maurice James *composer, retired music educator*

Boiling Springs
Vaughan, Ted Wayne *music and communications educator, musician*

Boone
Falvo, Robert J. *music educator*

Brevard
†Effron, David Louis *conductor, music director*

Cary
Bates, Roger Alan *entertainer*

Chapel Hill
†Adamson, Judy *theater educator*
Hammond, David Alan *stage director, educator*
Newman, William Stein *music educator, author, pianist, composer*
Parker, Scott Jackson *theatre manager*
Powell, Carolyn Wilkerson *music educator*

Creedmoor
Cross, June Crews *retired music educator*

Durham
Caesar, Shirley *gospel singer, evangelist*
Nakarai, Charles Frederick Toyozo *music educator, adjudicator*
Ward, Robert *composer, conductor, educator*
Watts, Toni Eileen *actress*
Zaranka, Albert J. *musical director, pianist, educator*

Fayetteville
†Curtis, Marvin Vernell *music educator*

Greensboro
Green, Jill I. *dance educator, researcher*
Middleton, Herman David, Sr. *theater educator*
Russell, Peggy Taylor *soprano, educator*
Styles, Teresa Jo *producer, educator*

Greenville
Alexander, Samuel Rudolph *retired concert manager, educational administrator*
Chauncey, Beatrice Arlene *music educator*

Hendersonville
Hathorne, Gayle Gene *musician, genealogical educator, writer*

Hudson
Kincaid, Tina *entertainer, producer*

Kernersville
Bruno, Frank A. *film producer*

Lincolnton
Hallman, Patricia Ann *music educator*

Misenheimer
Smith, Thomas Harold, III *instrumental music educator, musician*

New Bern
Smith, Jean Lenora *music educator*

Raleigh
Garriss, Phyllis Weyer *music educator, performer*
Harper, Dixon Ladd *broadcast director*
†Muddell, Jeffrey Allan *television news producer*
Waschka, Rodney Anthony, II *composer, educator*
†Zimmerman, Gerhardt *music director*

Rougemont
Nilsson, Mary Ann *music educator*

Statesville
Stewart, Patricia Canup *vocal music educator*

Tuckasegee
Lominac, Harry Gene *retired theater educator, designer*

Wilmington
Cameron, Kay *conductor, music director, arranger*

Winston Salem
Carney, Karen Rose *music educator, jazz, popular, classical pianist*
†Perret, Peter James *symphony conductor*
Trautwein, George William *conductor*

NORTH DAKOTA

Zeeland
Wolf, Trudy J. Fraase *music educator, librarian*

OHIO

Akron
Kazle, Elynmarie *producer, performing arts executive*
Schubert, Barbara Schuele *performing company executive*

Bowling Green
Burnett, Frances *concert painist, teacher of piano*
Duling, Edward Burger *music education educator*

Canton
†Moorhouse, Linda Virginia *symphony orchestra administrator*

Cincinnati
Beggs, Patricia K. *performing company executive*
Belew, Adrian *guitarist, singer, songwriter, producer*
Benner, Charles Henry *retired music educator*
Galloway, Lillian Carroll *modeling agency executive, consultant*
Herman, Donald Aloys *radio station personality and official*
Hoffman, Joel Harvey *composer*
Kunzel, Erich, Jr. *conductor, arranger, educator*
Lopez-Cobos, Jesus *conductor*
†Monder, Steven I. *orchestra executive*
†Morgan, Victoria *artistic director*
†Pendle, Karin *music educator*
Tocco, James *pianist*
Ward, Sherman Carl, III (Buzz Ward) *theater manager*

Cleveland
Adams, Leslie *composer*
Bamberger, David *opera company executive*
DesRosiers, Anne Booke *performing arts administrator, consultant*
Dohnanyi, Christoph von *musician, conductor*
Erb, Donald *composer*
Giannetti, Louis Daniel *film educator, film critic*
Gladden, Dean Robert *arts administrator, educator, consultant*
Mc Farlane, Karen Elizabeth *concert artists manager*
Morris, Thomas William *symphony orchestra administrator*
Najar, Leo Michael *conductor, arranger, educator*
Perry, Frederick John *theater educator*
Topilow, Carl S. *symphony conductor*
†von Dahnányi, Christoph *music director*

Columbus
Dederer, William Bowne *music educator, administrator*
Drvota, Mojmir *cinema educator, author*
†Franano, Susan Margaret Ketteman *orchestra administrator, soprano*
†Hagerman, James Brien *speech and drama educator*
Harris, Donald *composer*
Lowe, Clayton Kent *photography, cinema, and video educator*
Rosenstock, Susan Lynn *orchestra manager*
†Russell, William Fletcher, III *opera company director*
†Siciliani, Alessandro Domenico *conductor*
Wagner, Robert Walter *photography, cinema and communications educator, media producer, consultant*

Dayton
Clamme, Marvin Leslie *recording engineer, electronic engineer*
Gittleman, Neal *orchestra conductor*
Walters, Jefferson Brooks *musician, retired real estate broker*

Delaware
Jamison, Roger W. *pianist, piano educator*

Delta
Monahan, Leonard Francis *musician, singer, composer, publisher*

East Cleveland
Soule, Lucile Snyder *pianist, music educator*

Findlay
Musser, Saundra Jeanne (Berry) *music educator, composer*

Hudson
Shaw, Doris Beaumar *film and video producer, executive recruiter*

Kent
Nguyen, Phong Thuyet *ethnomusicologist, musician, educator*
†Prioleau, Darwin E. *dance educator, choreographer*

Lakewood
Brodhead, Thomas McCourtney *music engraver, computer programmer*

Lynx
Watters, Cora Tula *musician*

Middletown
†Combopiano, Charles Angelo *opera company executive*

New Concord
Brown, Karen Rima *orchestra manager, Spanish language educator*

Oberlin
Boe, David Stephen *musician, educator, college dean*
Polivnick, Paul *conductor, music director*

South Euclid
Janson, Patrick *singer, actor, conductor, educator*

Strongsville
Oltman, C. Dwight *conductor, educator*

Tiffin
Galipeau, Peter Armand *video producer, advertising account executive*
Talbot-Koehl, Linda Ann *dancer, ballet studio owner*

Toledo
†Heritage, Lee Morgan *music educator, composer*
Knorr, John Christian *entertainment executive, bandleader, producer*
Massey, Andrew John *conductor, composer*

Willoughby
Baker, Charles Stephen *music educator*

OKLAHOMA

Altus
Muse, John Scott *video and animation producer*

Anadarko
†Kidd, Lovetta Monza *music educator*

Clinton
Askew, Penny Sue *choreographer, artistic director, ballet instructor*

Mounds
Fellows, Esther Elizabeth *musician, music educator*
Halsey, James Albert *international entertainment impressario, theatrical producer, talent manager*

Norman
Budai, William H. *music educator*
Carey, Thomas Devore *baritone, educator*
Ross, Allan Anderson *music educator, university official*

Oklahoma City
Bell, Tony Cliffton *radio show host, producer*
Levine, Joel *music director, conductor*
Mardis, Richard Lyle *television producer and director, production manager*
McCoy, Wesley Lawrence *musician, conductor, educator*
Moore, Billy Don *video scriptwriter, producer*
Payne, Gareld Gene *vocal music educator, medical transcriptionist*
Thomas, Gary Wayne *actor*
Twyman, Nita (Venita) *music educator*

Stillwater
Smeyak, Gerald Paul *telecommunication educator*

Stonewall
McDonald, Mary Elizabeth *singer, songwriter*

Tulsa
†Crawford, Carol I. *opera company artistic director*
Moore, David Arthur *composer, music educator*
Owens, Jana Jae *entertainer*
Saied, James Guy *conductor, consultant*

OREGON

Ashland
Shaw, Arthur E. *conductor*

Eugene
Bailey, Exine Margaret Anderson *soprano, educator*
Bergquist, Ed Peter, Jr. *music educator emeritus*
Harth-Bedoya, Miguel *conductor*

Medford
Tevis, Barry Lee *television producer, marketing executive*

Portland
Bailey, Robert C. *opera company executive*
Berentsen, Kurtis George *music educator, choral conductor*
Blumberg, Naomi *symphony musician, educator*
Boston, Gretha *mezzo-soprano, actress*
Brown, Deborah Elizabeth *television producer*
†DePreist, James Anderson *conductor*
Huggett, Monica *performing company executive*
Jensen, Marion Pauline *singer*
Leyden, Norman *conductor*
Prlain, Pete *producer, writer, actor*

PENNSYLVANIA

Allentown
Beltzner, Gail Ann *music educator*
Fox, Jean *piano educator*

Annville
Condran, Cynthia Marie *gospel musician*

Avoca
†Keelan, Hugh *music director*

Beaver Falls
Copeland, Robert Marshall *music educator*

Berwick
Michael, Phyllis Callender *composer*

Bethlehem
Allen, Beatrice *music educator, pianist*
†Zerkle, Paula Ring *music educator*

Bloomsburg
Stropnicky, Gerard Patrick *theater director, consultant*

Bristol
Atkinson, Susan D. *producing artistic director, theatrical consultant*

Bryn Mawr
Goutman, Lois Clair *retired drama educator*
Stucky, Steven (Edward) *composer*

Chadds Ford
Swensson, Evelyn Dickenson *conductor, composer, librettist*

Cheyney
Bagley, Edythe Scott *theater educator*

Delaware Water Gap
Woods, Philip Wells (Phil Woods) *jazz musician composer*

Drexel Hill
Martino, Michael Charles *entertainer, musician, actor*

Edinboro
Weinkauf, David *film, animation, and photography educator*

Gouldsboro
Duricko, Erma O. *stage director, educator*

Hatboro
Carroll, Lucy Ellen *choral director, music coordinator, educator*

Hershey
Fowler, Susan Robinson *theatre executive*

Huntingdon Valley
Goldstein, Neil Warren *filmmaker*

Indiana
Perlongo, Daniel James *composer*

Irwin
Runser, Dianne Strong *music educator, music director*

Jenkintown
Driehuys, Leonardus Bastiaan *conductor*

Kingston
Weisberger, Barbara *artistic director, educator, choreographer*

Lancaster
†Barnett, Elizabeth Lucinda (Lucy) *television news producer*
Buchanan, Lovell *entertainer*
†Grochowski, Jelsia *music educator*
Simmons, Deidre Warner *performing company executive*

Lenhartsville
Adams, Faye Ann *musician, educator*

Mc Kean
Chitester, Robert John *television producer*

McKees Rocks
Butala, Anthony Francis *vocalist, entertainer, small business owner*

Mechanicsburg
†Boughter, Ronald Edward *video specialist*
Clousher, Fred Eugene (Freddie Cee Clousher) *entertainment producer, booking agent, musician*

Media
Leonard, Vincent Albert *music composer*

New Hope
Stahl, Stephen Lee *theater director, writer, producer*

New Wilmington
Pitman, Grover Allen *music educator*

Philadelphia
†Anzalone, Frank Michael *stage manager*
Blavat, Jerry (Gerald Joseph Blavat) *radio and television personality, actor*
Bookspan, Michael Lloyd *musician*
Borovik, Alexei Peter *ballet dancer, educator*
Coppock, Ada Gregory *theatre executive*
Cornelius, Jeffrey Michael *music educator*
Crumb, George Henry *composer, educator*
Garonzik, Sara Ellen *stage director*
Glazer, Tom (Thomas Zacariah Glazer) *folksinger, writer, composer*
Graffman, Gary *pianist, music educator*
Havard, Bernard *theater producer*
Hsu, Samuel *music history educator, concert pianist*
Kaiser, Roy *artistic director*
King, Darryl Eric *filmmaker, director*
LaMay, Roger C. *television news director*
Meyer, Leonard B. *musician, educator*
Mostovoy, Marc Sanders *conductor, music director*
Remick, Lloyd Zane *sports, communications and entertainment lawyer*
Sawallisch, Wolfgang *conductor*
Smith, Lloyd *musician*
†Tomlinson, Gary Alfred *music educator*
Wernick, Richard Frank *composer, conductor*

Pittsburgh
Balada, Leonardo *composer, educator*
Bardyguine, Patricia Wilde *ballerina, ballet theatre executive*
Capobianco, Tito *opera director*
Cardenes, Andres Jorge *violinist, music educator*
†Colwell, Denis *music director*
†Gounaridou, Kiki *theater educator*
Hollingsworth, Samuel Hawkins, Jr. *bassist*
LeBaron, Alice Anne *musician*
Libman, Steven Bradley *performing arts administrator*
Marshall, Cak (Catherine Elaine Marshall) *music educator, composer*
Miller, Mildred *opera singer, recitalist*
†Neft Byers, Suzi Terry *television producer*

†Orr, Terrence S. *dancer, ballet master, artistic director*
Petrov, Nicolas *dance educator, choreographer*
Rogers, Fred McFeely *television producer and host*
Sciannameo, Franco Ludovico Orlando *music educator*
Taylor, Mark Chandlee *choreographer*
Toeplitz, Gideon *symphony society executive*
†Weinstein, Mark Jay *opera general director*
Wilde, Patricia *retired artistic director*
Wilson, Wanda Lee Davis *entertainment promotions professional, casting director*

Scranton
†Whitman, Roy Eric *television specialist*

Swarthmore
Devin, (Philip) Lee *dramaturg, theater educator*

University Park
Baisley, Robert William *music educator*

Villanova
Steele, Robert Dennis *radio producer, announcer*

Warminster
Koch, Nancy Joy *music educator, choral director, vocal coach*

West Chester
Burton, John Bryan *music educator*
Pettigrew, Claire Rudolph *music educator*
Villella, John William *music education educator*

West Grove
Allman, William Berthold *musician, engineer, consultant*

RHODE ISLAND

Cumberland
Rossi, Joseph Anthony *film and television make-up artist, educator*

Harrisville
Jubinska, Patricia Ann *ballet instructor, choreographer*

Newport
Malkovich, Mark Paul, III *musician, artistic director, scientist, sports agent*

Providence
Barnhill, James Orris *theater educator*
Berenson, Stephen *actor, educator*
Dempsey, Raymond Leo, Jr. *radio and television producer, moderator, writer*
Hutchinson, Park William, Jr. *theatre educator*
McEleney, Brian *actor*
Nelson, Ron *composer, conductor, educator*
Rachleff, Larry *performing company executive*

SOUTH CAROLINA

Charleston
Redden, Nigel A. *performing company executive*

Columbia
Cleveland, Elbin L. *theatre design and technology educator*
Gasque, (Allard) Harrison *disc jockey, volunteer*
†Starrett, William *dancer, artistic director*

Edisto Island
Van Metre, Margaret Cheryl *artistic director, dance educator*

Florence
†Fisher, Christine S. *music educator*

Greenville
Kline, David Jonathan *video producer*
Robinson, Benjamin Pierce *theater director, coach, actor*
Selvy, Barbara *dance instructor*

Spartanburg
Feinstein, Marion Finke *artistic director, dance instructor*
White, Robert Bruce *keyboard instruments company acoustical consultant*

SOUTH DAKOTA

Rapid City
Lee, Jamie Lee *video specialist*

TENNESSEE

Antioch
Ely, Joe *singer and songwriter*

Brentwood
Tucker, Tanya Denise *singer*

Franklin
Bull, Sandy (Alexander Benjamin Bull) *musician, composer*
Stafford, Clay *film producer, director, writer, actor, educator, public speaker*

Germantown
Lensch, Kristin Marie *organist, recitalist*

Hendersonville
Cash, June Carter *singer*

Hermitage
Axton, Hoyt Wayne *singer, composer*

Johnson City
Jenrette, Thomas Shepard, Jr. *music educator, choral director*

Kingsport
Davis, Tammie Lynette *music educator, director*

Knoxville
Trevor, Kirk David Niell *orchestra conductor, cellist*

La Vergne
†Ingram, David *entertainment company executive*

Madison
Prince, Anna Lou *composer, music publisher, construction company executive*

Memphis
Ching, James Michael *artistic director opera company*
Hathcock, John Edward *vocalist*
Head, Willis Stanford *music educator, performer*
†Maxwell, Martha Ellen *performing company executive*
McRee, Celia *composer*
Piazza, Marguerite *opera singer, actress, entertainer*
Pugh, Dorothy Gunther *artistic director ballet company*
Williams, David Russell *retired music educator*

Murfreesboro
†Gilbert, Linda Arms *music educator*

Nashville
Carpenter, Mary Chapin *singer, songwriter*
Dalzell, Jeffrey Alexander *agent, musician*
Fleck, Bela *country musician*
†Foxworthy, Jeff *comedian, actor, writer*
Gill, Vince *country musician, singer*
Houk, Benjamin Noah *artistic director, choreographer*
Hutchison, Barbara Bailey *singer, songwriter*
James, Hugh Neal *video, record, movie producer, director*
Judd, Wynonna *vocalist, musician*
Kurek, Michael Henry *music educator*
Lange, Robert John (Mutt Lange) *producer*
Lee, Douglas A. *music educator*
Montgomery, Dillard Brewster *musician, educator*
Penterman, Carol A. *opera company executive*
Reeves, Robert Grant *artist manager*
Schermerhorn, Kenneth *music director*
†Skaggs, Ricky *country musician*
Smith, Michael W. *popular musician*
Stuart, Marty *country music singer, musician, songwriter*
Sumner, Rachel Diane *vocalist, educator*
Tillis, Pam *country singer, songwriter*
Tippin, Aaron *country music singer, songwriter*
Twain, Shania *country musician*
Valentine, Alan Darrell *symphony orchestra executive*
Whitten-Frickey, Wendy Elise *entertainer*
Yearwood, Trisha *country music singer, songwriter*

TEXAS

Arlington
Witt, Anne Cleino *musician, education educator*

Aubrey
Pizzamiglio, Nancy Alice *performing company executive*

Austin
Adair, Dwight Rial *film director, educator*
Antokoletz, Elliott Maxim *music educator*
†Bay, Peter *orchestra conductor*
Brockett, Oscar Gross *theatre educator*
Gimble, Johnny *country musician*
Holtzman, Joan King *musician, composer*
Jennings, Coleman Alonzo *theatre educator*
Kennan, Kent Wheeler *composer, educator*
†King, Carole *songwriter, singer*
Lary, Banning Kent *video producer, publisher*
Sharir, Yacov *artistic director, choreographer*

Borger
Allen, Bessie Malvina *music educator, church organist*

Cedar Hill
Kilgore, Janice Kay *musician, educator*

Cleburne
Palmer, Lynn Landry *conductor, musician*

Cleveland
White, Cecile Renee Kingsbury *dance educator*

College Station
†Schultz, Roger Herman *theater educator*

Corpus Christi
Allison, Joan Kelly *music educator, pianist*
Brown, Marguerite Johnson *music educator*

Dallas
Anderson, Robert Theodore *music educator, organist*
Atkinson, Bill *artistic director*
†Brinson, Barbara Ann *music educator*
Eagar, Stephen Wade *television news anchor, reporter*
Elder, Sheri Lynne *symphony orchestra official*
Etgen, Ann *ballet educator*
Fogelman, Evan Marr *literary agent, entertainment consultant, lawyer*
Foutch, Michael James *actor, dancer, lighting designer, producer*
Freiberger, Katherine Guion *composer, retired piano educator*
Galt, John William *actor, writer*
Karayanis, Plato Steven *opera company executive*
Kline, George William, II *television producer*
Litton, Andrew *musical director*
Palmer, Christine (Clelia Rose Venditti) *operatic singer, performer, pianist, vocal instructor, lecturer, entertainer*
Pell, Jonathan Laurence *artistic administrator*
Perry, Edward Gordon, III *record production executive*
Pride, Charley *singer*
Thomas, Paul Lindsley *composer, organist, music director*
Young, Kay Lynn *dance educator, small business owner*

De Soto
Tyrer-Ferraro, Polly Ann *music instructor, software developer*

Denton
†Cohen, Nicki Sandra *music educator, music therapist*
Latham, William Peters *composer, former educator*
Paul, Pamela Mia *concert pianist*

Farmers Branch
Walsh, Elizabeth Jameson *musician*

Fort Hood
Booker, Shirley Ruth *entertainment specialist*

Fort Worth
Cliburn, Van (Harvey Lavan Cliburn, Jr.) *concert pianist*
Ely, Glen Sample *television and video producer*
Giordano, John Read *conductor*
Lipkin, Seymour *pianist, conductor, educator*
†Mejia, Paul Roman *choreographer, dancer*
Whillock, David Everett *film and television educator, consultant*

Hallsville
Hutcherson, Donna Dean *retired music educator*

Harlingen
Godfrey, Aline Lucille *music specialist, church organist*

Houston
Adams, Daniel Clifford *music educator*
Berger, Sidney L. *theater educator, director*
†Brosh, Rita *performing company executive*
Brown, Glenda Ann Walters *ballet director*
Buyse, Leone Karena *orchestral musician, educator*
Cesario, Robert James *music educator, performer*
Clark, Ron D(ean) *cosmetologist*
Crain, Richard Charles *school district music director*
Douglas, P C *producer, director, reporter, editor*
Englesmith, Tejas *actor, producer, curator*
Girouard, Peggy Jo Fulcher *ballet educator*
Gockley, (Richard) David *opera director*
Guilliouma, Larry Jay, Jr. *performing arts administrator, music educator*
Hammond, Michael Peter *music educator, dean*
Jones, Florence M. *music educator*
Maness, Darrell Ray *television producer, editor*
Marion, Suzanne Margaret *music educator*
Ostrow, Stuart *theatrical producer, educator*
Rigsby, Carolyn Erwin *music educator*
Stevenson, Ben *artistic director*

Huntsville
†Gratz, Cindy Carpenter *dance educator, choreographer*
Russell, George Haw *video production company executive*

Irving
Milgrim, Samuel G. *television producer*
Wahlstrom, Paul Burr *television producer*

Lackland AFB
Lydic, Garry Keith *producer*

Lubbock
Aykal, Gürer *conductor*
King, Linda Carol *music educator*
Lucas, Don John *music educator*
van Appledorn, Mary Jeanne *composer, music educator, pianist*

Mcallen
Mohner, Carl Martin Rudolf *movie actor, artist*

Mesquite
Montgomery, Marvin *musical producer*

Midland
Powers, Patricia Kennett *piano and organ educator*

Pasadena
Gilley, Mickey Leroy *musician*

Richardson
Valenti, Frederick Alan *actor, screenwriter*

Rockwall
Wallace, Mary Elaine *opera director, author*

San Antonio
Burns, Leslie Kaye *documentary video producer and director*
Corrales, Frank Campa *composer, writer, guitarist*
Greenberg, Nat *orchestra administrator*
Jiménez, Leonardo *popular accordionist*

Spring
Mackay, Cynthia Jean *music educator*

Stephenville
Levisay, Leesa Dawn *music educator, composer*

Temple
Chamlee, Ann Combest *music educator*

Tyler
Hatfield, James Allen *theater arts educator*
Rogers, Cheryl Lynn *music and dance educator*

Vernon
Cook, Marcella Kay *drama educator*

Waco
Colvin, (Otis) Herbert, Jr. *musician, educator*

Whitehouse
Baker, Rebecca Louise *musician, music educator, consultant*

Wichita Falls
†Schaffer, Candler Gareld *conductor, hornist, educator*

UTAH

Provo
†Jaccard, Jerry-Louis *music educator, translator*
Pratt, Rosalie Rebollo *harpist, educator*

Salem
Hahn, Joan Christensen *retired drama educator, travel agent*

Salt Lake City
†Ewers, Anne *opera company director*
Grant, Raymond Thomas *arts administrator*
Hamill, Mark Richard *actor*
Hill, Kenneth O. *performing company executive*
†Jacobs, Johann *performing arts company executive*
Johnson, Mary Perrine *musician, educator*
†Kåge, Jonas *ballet company artistic director*
Kelm, Linda *opera singer*
Morey, Charles Leonard, III *theatrical director*
Ottley, Jerold Don *choral conductor, educator*
Silverstein, Joseph Harry *conductor, musician*
Van Wagenen, Sterling *film producer, director*
†Verdoia, Kenneth Louis *documentary producer*

VERMONT

Brattleboro
Brofsky, Howard *musician, music educator*

Burlington
Varricchio, Louis *radio producer, science writer, personality, public relations executive*

Johnson
Whitehill, Angela Elizabeth *artistic director*

Tunbridge
Stewart, Donald George *musician, music industry executive, composer*

Weston
Stettler, Stephen F. *performing company executive*

VIRGINIA

Alexandria
Erion, Carol Elizabeth *music educator*

Arlington
Kelley, Virginia (Judy) Wiard *dance educator*

Burke
Holmes, Stephanie Eleanor *music educator, violinist*

Charlottesville
Chapel, Robert Clyde *stage director, theater educator*
Ross, Walter Beghtol *music educator, composer*
Stanley, Ralph *bluegrass musician*

Chester
Gray, Frederick Thomas, Jr. ('Rick Gray) *actor, educator*

Clifton Forge
Stump, Pamela Ferris *music educator*

Fairfax
Hilbrink, William John *violinist*
Ziff, Irwin (Irv Ziff) *actor*

Falls Church
Ezard, Gary Carl *video editor*

Lynchburg
Luck, Ray Egan *pianist, music educator*

Manassas
Bahner, Sue (Florence Suzanna Bahner) *radio broadcasting executive*

Mc Lean
Domeyko, Cecilia *television producer*
†Skantze, Pat *model, consultant*
Vazsonyi, Balint *concert pianist, television producer*
Youngs, William Ellis *motion picture engineer, projectionist*

Moneta
Pfeuffer, Robert John *musician*

Mount Crawford
German, Lynne Cummings *music educator*

Newport News
Edmonds, Michael Darnell *music educator*

Norfolk
Hailstork, Adolphus Cunningham *composer*
Mark, Peter *director, conductor*
Musgrave, Thea *composer, conductor*
Rohrer, Susan Earley *film producer, writer, director*
†Scott, Karen Cain *vice educator, soprano*

Radford
†Camphouse, Mark David *music educator, dean, composer, conductor*
James, Clarity (Carolyne Faye James) *mezzo-soprano*

Richmond
Campbell, Neal Franklin *musician, educator*
Winslett, Stoner *artistic director*

Roanoke
†Wiley, David *music director*

Smithfield
Wynne, John Boyce *performing company executive*

Springfield
Eastman, Donna Kelly *composer, music educator*

Staunton
Balsley, Philip Elwood *entertainer*

Sterling
Jefferson, Sandra Traylor *choreographer, ballet coach*

Vienna
†Feld, Kenneth *performing company executive*
Kinsolving, Sylvia Crockett *musician, educator*
Witman, Kim Pensinger *opera company executive*

Virginia Beach
Freyss, David *producer, director*
Gibbs, Jordan Smith *music educator, artist*

Williamsburg
Hornsby, Bruce Randall *composer, musician*

WASHINGTON

Bainbridge Island
Moyemont, Terry Walter *video producer, videographer*

Bellingham
Larner, Daniel M. *theater educator, playwright, author*

Bremerton
Rickerson, Jean Marie *video producer, journalist, photographer*

Coupeville
Lotzenhiser, George William *music educator, university administrator, composer*

Everett
Waldron, Richard Frederick *musician, educator*

Friday Harbor
Waite, Ric *cinematographer*

Issaquah
Hunt, Robert William *theatrical producer, data processing consultant*

Kent
Pettigrew, Dana Mary *musician, insurance agent*

Longview
Williamson, Debra Faye *performing arts educator*

Mercer Island
Francis, Carolyn Rae *music educator, musician, author, publisher*

Seattle
Collier, Tom Ward *musician, educator*
Denke, Conrad William *motion picture producer*
Elyn, Mark *retired opera singer, educator*
Forbes, David Craig *musician*
Jenkins, Speight *opera company executive, writer*
Jones, Samuel *conductor*
Moore, Benjamin *theatrical producer*
Nishitani, Martha *dancer*
Russell, Francia *ballet director, educator*
Ryder, Hal *theater educator, director*
Samuel, Gerhard *orchestra conductor, composer*
Sateren, Terry *theater technical production*
Smith, Jeffrey L. (The Frugal Gourmet) *cooking expert, television personality, author*
Staryk, Steven Sam *violinist, concertmaster, educator*
Stowell, Kent *ballet director*
Talvi, Ilkka Ilari *violinist*
Thomas, Karen P. *composer, conductor*
Tsutakawa, Deems Akihiko *musician, composer, record producer*

Snohomish
Philpott, Larry La Fayette *horn player*

Spokane
Bray, R(obert) Bruce *music educator*
Durham, Warren John *television and radio producer*
Mechetti, Fabio *orchestra conductor*
†Phillips, John (Jack) Grant *theatre director*
Rimbach, Evangeline Lois *retired music educator*

Woodinville
Sanders, Richard Kinard *actor*

WEST VIRGINIA

Charleston
Conlin, Thomas (Byrd) *conductor*
Ilar, Craig Scott *audio engineer*

Fairmont
O'Connor, John Edward *theater educator, director*

Inwood
Rizzetta, Carolyn Teresa *musical instrument, sound recording entrepreneur*

Mannington
Schumacher, Theresa Rose (Terry Schumacher) *singer, musician, legal assistant*

Morgantown
Wiedebusch, Mary Kathryne *dance educator*

Salem
Raad, Virginia *pianist, lecturer*

Spencer
Kosowicz, Francis John *concert organist*

Westover
Trythall, Harry Gilbert *music educator, composer*

Wheeling
Worby, Rachael Beth *conductor*

WISCONSIN

Appleton
†Biringer, Gene Douglas *music educator, theorist*
†Damp, George Edward *music educator*
†Schaphorst, Kenneth W. *music educator, composer*

Cadott
Blair, David Chalmers Leslie *composer, writer*

De Pere
†Tepe, Judith Mildred *vocal music teacher, choral director*

Delavan
Lepke, Charma Davies *musician, educator*

Dodgeville
Dentinger, Ronald Lee *comedian, speaker, freelance writer*

Eau Claire
Cunningham, Michael Gerald *composer, music educator*
Patterson, Donald Lee *music educator*

Greenfield
McKillip, Patricia Claire *operatic soloist*

Madison
Burns, Elizabeth Murphy *media executive*
Davis, Richard *musician, music educator*
Dembski, Stephen Michael *composer, university music composition professor*
Latimer, James Harold *percussionist, conductor, composer, educator*
Rosser, Annetta Hamilton *composer*

Menomonee Falls
Chicorel, Ralph *composer, lyricist, playwright*

Milwaukee
†Boese, Lillian R. *performing company executive*
Delfs, Andreas *performing company executive*
Downey, John Wilham *composer, pianist, conductor, educator*
Hansen-Rachor, Sharon Ann *conductor, choral music educator*
Hanthorn, Dennis Wayne *performing arts association administrator*
Ovitsky, Steven Alan *musician, symphony orchestra executive*
Rosenblatt, Suzanne Maris *performance artist, poet, visual artist*
†Thompson, Basil F. *ballet master*
Uecker, Bob *actor, radio announcer, former baseball player, TV personality*

Oak Creek
Semmes, Sally Peterson *dance educator, performer, speech educator, choreographer*

Oshkosh
McWilliams, Robert Lindsay *music educator, musician, conductor*

Racine
McPheron, JoAnn Marie B. *music educator, poet*
Schoening, Ruth Irene *music educator, retired, musician*

Washington Island
Schweikert, Norman Carl *musician*

Waupaca
Moerschel, Blanche Lenore *pianist, composer, educator*

TERRITORIES OF THE UNITED STATES

PUERTO RICO

Bayamon
Ortiz, William *composer, music educator*

CANADA

ALBERTA

Alberta
Nissinen, Mikko Pekka *dancer*

Calgary
†Epton, Gregg *performing company executive*
Graf, Hans *conductor*
Monk, Allan James *baritone*

BRITISH COLUMBIA

North Vancouver
Anderson, Gillian *actress*
Duchovny, David *actor*

Qualicum Beach
Little, Carl Maurice *performing arts administrator*

Vancouver
Comissiona, Sergiu *conductor*

Murray, Anne *singer*
Wright, James W. *entertainment company executive*

Victoria
Horn, Paul Joseph *musician*
McCoppin, Peter *symphony orchestra conductor*

MANITOBA

Winnipeg
Lewis, Andre Leon *artistic director*
Spohr, Arnold Theodore *artistic director, choreographer*
Tovey, Bramwell *conductor, composer*
Turner, Robert Comrie *composer*
†Wilhelm-Boyles, Andrew *performing company executive*

NOVA SCOTIA

Halifax
†Dunnel, Leslie B. *conductor*

ONTARIO

Cambridge
Eldred, Gerald Marcus *retired performing arts association executive*

Don Mills
Applebaum, Louis *composer, conductor*

Dundas
Shaw, John Firth *orchestra administrator*

Hamilton
Lipton, Daniel Bernard *conductor*

Kitchener
Coles, Graham *conductor, composer*

London
†Brian, Jackson *artistic director*
Stafford, Earl *conductor*
William, David *director, actor*

Mississauga
Peterson, Oscar Emmanuel *pianist*

Ottawa
†Decker, Franz Paul *symphony conductor, educator*
Franca, Celia *ballet director, choreographer, dancer, narrator*
Gillingham, Bryan Reginald *music educator*

Thornhill
Nimmons, Phillip Rista *composer, conductor, clarinetist, educator*

Toronto
Beckwith, John *musician, composer, educator*
Boswell, Philip John *opera administrator*
Bradshaw, Richard James *conductor*
Cahill, Catherine M. *orchestra executive*
Chan Hon Goh *ballerina*
Colgrass, Michael Charles *composer*
Drabinsky, Garth Howard *entertainment company executive*
Egoyan, Atom *film director*
Eklof, Svea Christine *ballet dancer*
Freedman, Harry *composer*
Girard, Francois *film director*
Glasco, Kimberly *ballet dancer*
Israelievitch, Jacques H. *violinist, conductor*
Kudelka, James *choreographer, artistic director*
Kuerti, Anton Emil *pianist, composer*
†Lamon, Jeanne *music director, concertmaster, educator*
Oliphant, Betty *ballet school director*
Ottmann, Peter *choreologist, ballet master*
Pedersen, Paul Richard *composer, educator*
Rasky, Harry *producer, director, writer*
Schramek, Tomas *ballet dancer, educator*
Shearing, George Albert *pianist, composer*
Staines, Mavis Avril *artistic director, ballet principal*
Stefanschi, Sergiu *dancer*
Wilder, Valerie *ballet company administrator*
Wilkins, Ormsby *music director, conductor, pianist*

Windsor
†Haig, Susan *conductor*

QUEBEC

Montreal
†Dancyger, Alain *performing company executive*
Gulkin, Harry *arts administrator, film producer*
Rhodes, Lawrence *artistic director*
Trogani, Monica *ballet mistress*
†Turovsky, Yuli *conductor*
Uzan, Bernard *general and artistic director*
Woszczyk, Wieslaw Richard *audio engineering educator, researcher*

Sainte Foy
Pasquier, Joël *music educator*

AUSTRALIA

Kings Cross
Davis, Judy *actress*

Mona Vale
Seale, John Clement *director, cinematographer*

Surry Hills
†Blanchett, Cate *actress*

Sydney
†Miller, George *film director*

CAYMAN ISLANDS

Grand Cayman
Crockett, James Grover, III *musician, former music publisher*

CHINA

Kowloon
†Woo, John *film director*

COSTA RICA

San José
Hoffman, Irwin *orchestra conductor*

ENGLAND

Askett Bucks
Irons, Jeremy John *actor*

Balcombe
Scofield, Paul *actor*

Brighton
Watkin, David *film director, cinematographer*

Cambridge
Bream, Julian *classical guitarist and lutanist*
Hogwood, Christopher Jarvis Haley *music director, educator*

Isle of Wight
Stigwood, Robert Colin *theater, movie, television and record producer*

London
Ashkenazy, Vladimir Davidovich *concert pianist, conductor*
Barshai, Rudolf Borisovich *conductor*
Bertolucci, Bernardo *film director*
†Bourne, Matthew *performing company executive, artistic director*
Cellan-Jones, James Gwynne *television producer, director*
Christie, Julie *actress*
Codron, Michael Victor *theatrical producer*
Conti, Tom *actor, writer, director*
Dowell, Anthony James, Sr. *ballet dancer*
Dudley, Anne *composer*
Gielgud, Sir (Arthur) John *actor, director*
Hawthorne, Nigel Barnard *actor*
Holm, Sir Ian *actor*
Hoskins, Bob (Robert William Hoskins) *actor*
John, Elton Hercules (Reginald Kenneth Dwight) *musician*
Jordan, Neil Patrick *film director*
Leigh, Mike *film director*
Levi, Yoel *orchestra conductor*
Le Vien, John Douglas (Jack Le Vien) *motion picture and television producer, director*
Lloyd-Webber, Lord Baron, of Syomonton *composer*
Mackerras, Sir (Alan) Charles (Maclaurin) *conductor*
Mackintosh, Cameron *musical theater producer*
McCowen, Alec *actor*
†McGregor, Ewan Gordon *actor*
McIntyre, Donald Conroy *opera singer, baritone*
Miller, Jonathan Wolfe *theater and film director, physician*
Minton, Yvonne Fay *mezzo-soprano*
Nelson, John Wilton *symphonic conductor*
Nucci, Leo *baritone*
Palin, Michael Edward *actor, screenwriter, author*
Phillips, Sian *actress*
Plowright, Joan Anne *actress*
Radford, Michael *director*
Rattle, Simon *conductor*
Rea, Stephen *actor*
Ricci, Ruggiero *violinist, educator*
Richardson, Miranda *actress*
Schaufuss, Peter *dancer, producer, choreographer, ballet director*
Smith, Dame Maggie *actress*
Starr, Ringo (Richard Starkey) *musician, actor*
Wallis, Diana Lynn *artistic director*
Winner, Michael Robert *film director, writer, producer*
York, Susannah *actress*

Manchester
Wilson, Keith Dudley *media and music educator*

North Wales
Hands, Terence David (Terry Hands) *theater and opera director*

Oxford
Tureck, Rosalyn *concert performer, author, editor, educator*

Richmond
Attenborough, Baron Richard Samuel *actor, producer, director, goodwill ambassador*
Te Kanawa, Kiri *opera and concert singer*

FINLAND

Helsinki
†Saraste, Jukka-Pekka *conductor*

FRANCE

Ferney-Voltaire
Morgenstern, Sheldon Jon *symphony orchestra conductor*

Paris
Annaud, Jean-Jacques *film director, screenwriter*
Boulez, Pierre *composer, conductor*
de Havilland, Olivia Mary *actress*
Deneuve, Catherine (Catherine Dorleac) *actress*
Jolas, Betsy *composer, educator*
Kurtz, Eugene Allen *composer, educator, consultant*

Marceau, Marcel pantomimist, actor, director, painter, poet
Raimondi, Ruggero opera singer

GERMANY

Berlin
Abbado, Claudio conductor
Goodman, Alfred composer, musicologist

Dresden
Schreier, Peter tenor

Forst
DeVol, Luana dramatic soprano, consultant, arts administrator

Hamburg
Neumeier, John choreographer, ballet company director

Munich
Schell, Maximilian actor, director

Stuttgart
Anderson, Reid Bryce ballet company artistic director

IRELAND

Dublin
Sheridan, Jim director, screenwriter

Galway
†Hynes, Garry theatre director

ISRAEL

Tel Aviv
Mehta, Zubin conductor, musician

ITALY

Rome
†Benigni, Roberto actor, writer, director, producer
Loren, Sophia actress
†Piovani, Nicola composer

MONACO

Monte Carlo
†Marton, Eva opera singer

NEW ZEALAND

Wellington
Paquin, Anna actress

NORWAY

Oslo
†Jansons, Mariss orchestra conductor

PERU

Lima
Castro-Pozo, Talía dancer, educator

THE PHILIPPINES

Makati City
Aramian, Marc composer, music producer

SCOTLAND

Edinburgh
McMaster, Brian John artistic director

SPAIN

Barcelona
de Larrocha, Alicia concert pianist

Madrid
Frühbeck de Burgos, Rafael conductor

SWEDEN

Stockholm
Soederstrom, Elisabeth Anna opera singer

SWITZERLAND

Geneva
Barenboim, Daniel conductor, pianist

Staad
Moore, Roger George actor

Zurich
Jones, Gwyneth soprano

ADDRESS UNPUBLISHED

Aaron, Roy Henry entertainment company executive
Aasen-Hull, Audrey Avis music educator
Adams, Bryan vocalist, composer
†Adams, Hilary Shiels theater director
†Adams, Marilyn Kay music educator
Adaskin, Murray composer
Adato, Perry Miller documentary producer, director, writer
Adler, Samuel Hans retired conductor, composer
Alberghetti, Anna Maria singer, actress
Alberts, David artistic director, mime
Alda, Alan actor, writer, director
Allen, Marilyn Myers Pool theater director, video producer
Alley, Kirstie actress
Alonso, Maria Conchita actress, singer
Andrews, Julie actress, singer
Applegate, Christina actress
Apted, Michael David film director
Aquino-Kaufman, Florence (Florence Anglin) actress, playwright
Arenal, Julie (Mrs. Barry Primus) choreographer
Arnold, Robert Jeffrey musician
Aronson, Luann Marie actress
Arthur, Beatrice actress
Assante, Armand actor
Atherton, William actor
Auberjonois, René Murat actor
Avian, Bob choreographer, producer
†Bach, Jean Enzinger filmmaker
†Bacharach, Burt composer, conductor
Badalamenti, Angelo composer, conductor
Badham, John MacDonald motion picture director
Baker, Susan Marie Victoria, Rev. writer, artist
Balaban, Bob actor, director
Baldwin, Alec (Alexander Rae Baldwin, III) actor
Balser, Robert Edward animation film producer, director
Balter, Alan conductor, music director
Bank, Marji D. actress
Baranski, Christine actress
†Barkai, Ornit television producer, broadcast journalist
Barselou, Paul Edgar actor, writer
Bauer, Elaine Louise ballet dancer
Beebe, Hank composer
Begley, Ed, Jr. actor
Behlmer, Rudy H., Jr. director, writer, film educator
Belafonte, Harry singer, concert artist, actor
Bencini, Sara Haltiwanger concert pianist
Bennett, Sharon Kay music educator
Benowitz, Roy composer, orchestrator, copyist, organist, pianist
Benton, Robert film director, screenwriter
†Beresford, Bruce film director
Berezin, Tanya acting coach, actress
Berg, Peter actor
Bergen, Candice actress, writer, photojournalist
Bergeron, Earleen Fournet actress
Berkofsky, Martin concert pianist
Berle, Milton (Milton Berlinger) actor
Berlind, Roger Stuart stage and film producer
Berlinger, Warren actor
†Berloff, Andrea performing arts company official
Berman, Sanford Solomon motion picture sound designer, composer, arranger, artist
Bierley, Paul Edmund musician, author, publisher
Bill, Karen S. actress
Binoche, Juliette actress
Birch, Patricia choreographer, director
Biziou, Peter cinematographer
Bjerknes, Michael Leif dancer
Black, Karen actress
Black, Rilla Alma violinist, library assistant, poet
Blake, Ran jazz pianist, composer
Blattner, Florence Anne music educator
Bloomquist, Kenneth Gene music educator, university bands director
Blossom, Beverly choreographer, dance educator
Bluestein, Steve Franklin comedian, writer
Bobbie, Walter theatrical director
Bochner, Hart actor
Bock, Jerry (Jerrold Lewis) composer
Bogart, Rebecca A. musician, educator
Bogosian, Eric actor, writer
Bond, Victoria Ellen conductor, composer
Bonerz, Peter actor, director
Bonnard, Raymond theater director
Borchardt, Donald Arthur visual and performing arts educator
Borgnine, Ernest actor
Boyd, Julianne Mamana theater director
Boyd, Liona Maria musician
Boyle, Peter actor
Bracco, Lorraine actress
Brandauer, Klaus Maria actor
Brando, Marlon, Jr. actor
Braugher, Andre actor
Brecker, Randal Edward musician, arranger
†Briggle, Gary Lee singer, actor, director
Brimley, Wilford actor
Brock, John Morgan, Jr. composer, synthesist
Brooks, Albert (Albert Einstein) actor, writer, director
Brooks, Garth (Troyal Garth Brooks) country music singer
Brosnan, Peter Lawrence documentary filmmaker
Brosnan, Pierce actor
Brown, Jim (James Nathaniel Brown) film actor, former professional football player
Buck, William Joseph theatrical designer, educator
Bunim, Mary-Ellis television producer
Burton, Al producer, director, writer
Byrne, David musician, composer, artist, director
Caesar, Sid actor, comedian
Caldwell, Sarah opera producer, conductor, stage director and administrator
Calegari, Maria ballerina
Cameron, JoAnna actress, director
†Campion, Jane director, screenwriter
Cannon, Dyan actress
Capice, Philip Charles television production executive
Carney, Arthur William Matthew actor
Carr, Paul Wallace actor
Carradine, Keith Ian actor, singer, composer
Carvey, Dana actor, stand up comedian
Casei, Nedda mezzo-soprano
Cash, Johnny entertainer
Cassel, Seymour actor
Cates, Phoebe actress
Cavender, Michael Charles broadcast news executive
Ceraso, Chris dramatist, actor
Chang, Helen Chung-Hung piano pedagogy specialist
Chapman, William baritone
Charles, Walter actor
Charry, Michael R(onald) musician, conductor
Child, Julia McWilliams (Mrs. Paul Child) cooking expert, television personality, author
Christopher, Russell Lewis baritone
Cimino, Michael film director, writer
Clark, Candy actress
Clark, Steven Marston film producer, real estate licensee
Claver, Robert Earl television director, producer
Cleveland, Ashley musician
Cloonan, Patrick Michael radio news producer, writer
Coburn, James actor
Cohen, Alexander H. theatrical and television producer
Cohen, Larry film director, producer, screenwriter
Coleman, Dabney W. actor
Coleman, Malcolm James, Jr. band director, music educator, flute educator
Collins, Joan Henrietta actress
Collins, Kathleen Anne artistic director
Cone, Edward Toner composer, emeritus music educator
Conrad, Richard A. opera singer, educator
Consoli, Marc-Antonio composer
Constantine, Michael actor
Cook, Fielder producer, director
Cooper, Hal television director
Cooper-Avrick, Anita Beverly television stage manager
†Copperfield, David (David Kotkin) illusionist, director, producer, writer
Coppola, Francis Ford film director, producer, writer
Corey, Jeff actor, director, educator
†Corto, Diana Maria lyric-coloratura, producer, educator
Corvino, Ernesta ballet dancer
Cosby, Bill actor, entertainer
†Cosmatos, George Pan film director
Cossa, Dominic Frank baritone
Costa-Gavras, (Konstaninos Gavras) director, writer
Cotrubas, Ileana opera singer, lyric soprano, retired
Coukis, Peter George musician, composer
†Crenshaw, Barclay MacBride film producer, writer
Crosby, Julie Lynne theater industry executive, educator
Crosby, Norman Lawrence comedian
Crouse, Lindsay actress
Cruise, Tom (Tom Cruise Mapother, IV) actor
Cruz-Romo, Gilda soprano
Culkin, Macaulay actor
Cummings, Constance actress
†Cunningham, Ron choreographer, artistic director
Currie, Fergus Gardner performing arts educator
Currier, Ruth dancer, choreographer and educator
Curson, Theodore musician
Dabbs, Henry Erven television and film producer, educator
Dafoe, Willem actor
Dailey, Irene actress, educator
Daly, Tyne actress
D'Angelo, Beverly actress
Daniels, Jeff actor
Daniels, Ronald George theater director
†Danza, Tony actor
D'Arbanville-Quinn, Patti actress
Darling, Robert Edward designer, stage director
Davidovsky, Mario composer
Davis, Anthony composer, pianist, educator
Davis, Danny (George Joseph Nowlan) musician
Davis, Debra Greer music educator, pianist
†Davis, Nathan actor
Dean, Dearest (Lorene Glosup) songwriter
Dean, Leesa Jane musician
de Blasis, James Michael artistic director, producer, stage director
Debus, Eleanor Viola retired business management company executive
De Felitta, Frank Paul producer, writer, director
†Demissie, Yemane I. filmmaker
†De Mornay, Rebecca actress
†Dench, Judith Olivia actress
Deutsch, Herbert Arnold music educator
Devlin, Michael Coles bass-baritone
Dewey, Donna director, actress
Diaz, Cameron actress
Dick, James Cordell concert pianist
Dickinson, Peter composer
Diemer, Emma Lou composer, music educator
DiGirolamo, Glen Francis actor
Dishy, Bob actor
Dixon, William Robert musician, composer, educator
Dolin, Samuel Joseph composer, educator
Dorn, Dolores actress
†Dorsky, Nathaniel filmmaker
Downey, Michael Peter public television executive
Downey, Roma actress
Doyle, Gillian actress
Drake, Ervin Maurice composer, author
Druzinsky, Edward musician
Duigan, John film director
Duke, Bill film director, actor
Dunlap, Richard Donovan artistic director
Durning, Charles actor
†Dusan, Makavejev film director, film producer
Dyer, L. Keith entertainment company producer
Dysart, Richard A. actor
Eagle, Jack commercial actor, comedian
Easterly, Susan music and humanities educator
Eastwood, Clint actor, director, former mayor
Ebb, Fred lyricist, librettist
Edwards, Anthony actor
Edwards, Ryan Hayes baritone
Ehrling, Sixten orchestra conductor
†Eisenberg, Daniel filmmaker
Elgart, Larry Joseph orchestra leader
Elikann, Lawrence S. (Larry Elikann) television and film director
Elizondo, Hector actor
Elliot, Willard Somers retired musician, composer
Erbe, Yvonne Mary music educator, marketing specialist
Everett, Tom actor
Everhart, Rex actor, director, photographer
†Fahey, Jeff actor
Falk, Peter actor
Farrell, Mike actor
Felton, Norman Francis motion picture producer
Fenn, Sherilyn actress
Ferrara, Abel film director
†Field, Sally actress
Fields, Freddie producer, agent
Fiennes, Ralph Nathaniel actor
Figgis, Mike film director
Filerman, Michael Herman television producer
Fincher, David film director
Fine, Deborah Jane researcher, author
Fiorentino, Linda actress
First, Craig Patrick composer, educator
Firstenberg, Samuel film director
Fischer, Clare composer
Fisher, Carrie Frances actress, writer
Fitzgerald, Geraldine actress
Fletcher, Louise actress
Foldi, Andrew Harry retired singer, educator
Fonda, Bridget actress
Fonda, Peter actor, director, producer
†Forbes, Michelle television and film actress
†Ford, Faith actress
Ford, Harrison actor
Ford, Nancy Louise composer, scriptwriter
Forest, Eva Brown songwriter, producer
†Forster, Robert actor, speaker
Forsythe, Henderson actor
Foss, Lukas composer, conductor, pianist
Franciosa, Anthony (Anthony Papaleo) actor
Franken, Al humorist, actor, writer
†Frankenheimer, John Michael film and stage director
Freston, Thomas E. cable television programming executive
Frey, Glenn songwriter, vocalist, guitarist
Fuerstner, Fiona Margaret Anne ballet company executive, ballet educator
Gagnon, Edith Morrison ballerina, singer, actress
Gallagher, Peter actor
Garner, James (James Scott Bumgarner) actor
Garniss, Joan Brewster musician, educator
Gehm, Denise Charlene ballerina, arts administrator
Geller, Norman Harvey music arranger, conductor
Gelman, Larry actor, director
Gelotte, Bob Gunnar musician
Gere, Richard actor
Gill, Richard Thomas opera singer, economic analyst
Gilliam, Terry Vance film director, actor, illustrator, writer
Gilman, Richard drama educator, author
Glover, Crispin Hellion actor
Glynn, Carlin (Carlin Masterson) actress
Goddard, James Russell producer, writer, actor
Goen, Bob television show host
Goldberg, Whoopi (Caryn Johnson) actress
Goldin, Marion Freedman television news producer, reporter
Goldman, Barbara Deren film and theatrical producer
Goldman, Mia film editor
Goldstone, James film, television and stage director
Goodman, Erika dancer, actress
Gordon, Marjorie lyric coloratura soprano, opera producer, teacher
Gorman, Cliff actor
Gossett, Louis, Jr. actor
Gould, Harold actor
Goz, Harry G. actor, singer
Graff, Randy actress
†Graham, Heather actress
Grant, Alexander Marshall ballet director
Grant, Lee (Lyova Haskell Rosenthal) actress, director
Grant, Merrill Theodore producer
Graves, Denyce Antoinette mezzo-soprano
Graves, Lorraine Elizabeth dancer, educator, coach
Gray, Diane dancer, choreographer
Gray, Vicki Lou Pharr music educator
Greenberg, Bonnie Lynn music industry executive
Grey, Jennifer actress
Grier, Pamela actress, writer, singer
Griffith, Melanie actress
Grimm, Roberta Pauline Johnson performing arts company director
Grody, Donald actor, judge, lawyer, arbitrator
Groskopf, Aubrey Bud motion picture television executive
Gross, Gil radio talk show host, columnist
Gross, Terry R. radio producer, host
Guinness, Sir Alec actor
Gutierrez, Gerald Andrew theatrical director
Guttenberg, Steve actor
†Guttman, Irving Allen opera stage director
Hall, Arsenio actor, comedian
Hall, Conrad L. cinematographer
Hall, James Stanley jazz guitarist, composer
Hall, Monty television producer, actor
Hamlisch, Marvin composer, conductor, pianist, entertainer
Hanman, Ted E. music educator, choral conductor
Harper, Richard Henry film producer, director
Harris, Harry H. television director
Harris, Margaret pianist, conductor, composer
Harris, Theodore Clifford songwriter, music publisher
Harrison, Gregory actor
Hart, Dorothy actress, international affairs speaker
Harwood, Vanessa Clare ballet dancer
Hawkins, Roberta Rosenthal theater educator
†Hayek, Salma actress
Hays, Robert actor
Healey, Myron Daniel actor
Heard, Ronald Roy motion picture producer
†Heche, Anne actress
Heckart, Eileen actress
†Heckerling, Amy film director
Hedahl, Gorden Orlin theatre educator, university dean
Henderson, Scott jazz guitarist
Hendl, Walter conductor, pianist, composer
Henes, Donna celebration artist, ritualist, writer
Henner, Marilu actress
Herbig, Günther conductor
Herson, Arlene Rita producer, journalist, television program host
Hines, Gregory Oliver actor, dancer
Hingle, Pat actor
Hite, Catharine Leavey orchestra manager
Hodges, Ann actress, singer, dancer
Hoggard, Lara Guldmar conductor, educator
Holbrook, Hal (Harold Rowe Holbrook, Jr.) actor
Holly, Lauren actress
Hooper, Josh screen actor, director, producer, writer
Hopkins, Robert Elliott music educator
Horisberger, Don Hans conductor, musician
Houghton, Katharine actress
Houser, Thomas Henri voice educator
Howard, David ballet school administrator
Hubbard, Elizabeth actress
Hudson, Ernie actor
Hughes, Michaela Kelly actress, dancer
Huning, Devon Gray actress, dancer, audiologist, photographer, video producer and editor
Hunt, Helen actress
Hunter, Kim (Janet Cole) actress
Ichino, Yoko ballet dancer
Irey, Charlotte York dance educator
Irving, George Steven actor
Jackson, Nagle stage director, playwright
Jackson, Samuel L. actor

ARTS: VISUAL

UNITED STATES

ALABAMA

Andalusia
†Rich, Lonnie Keven art educator, artist

Birmingham
Carmichael, Mary Alice artist, genealogist
Fleming, Frank sculptor
Keller, Armor artist, arts advocate
Price, Rosalie Pettus artist

Decatur
Bennett, Rebecca Eaton *artist*

Mobile
Clausell, Deborah Deloris *artist, songwriter*
Goff, William M., Jr. *art director, graphic designer*

Montgomery
Jensen, Suzanne E. *artist, art educator*

Normal
Dawkins, Jimmie Angela *art educator*

ALASKA

Anchorage
Shadrach, (Martha) Jean Hawkins *artist*

Juneau
DeRoux, Daniel Grady *artist*

Ketchikan
McDermott, David (John) *artist, writer, photographer*

Nome
Sloan, Patrice S. *artist*

ARIZONA

Apache Junction
Coe, Anne Elizabeth *artist*

Bisbee
Stiles, Knute *artist*

Chandler
Matus, Nancy Louise *artist*

Douglas
Dusard, Jay *photographer*

Eagar
McCain, Buck *artist*

Fountain Hills
York, Tina *painter*

Green Valley
Nasvik-Dennison, Anna *artist*
Page, John Henry, Jr. *artist, educator*

Lake Montezuma
Burkee, Irvin *artist*

Mesa
Kaida, Tamarra *art and photography educator*

Oracle
Rush, Andrew Wilson *artist*

Oro Valley
Loeh, Corinne Rachow *artist*

Paradise Valley
Heller, Jules *artist, writer, educator*

Peoria
Willard, Garcia Lou *artist*

Phoenix
Bluth, Don *animator, director, screenwriter*
Dignac, Geny (Eugenia M. Bermudez) *sculptor*
Drakulich, Martha *arts educator*
Herranen, Kathy *artist, graphic designer*
Schaumburg, Donald Roland *art educator, ceramic artist*
Williams, Joyce Marilyn *artist, business owner*

Prescott
Stasack, Edward Armen *artist*
Willoughby, James Russell *artist, author*

Scottsdale
Blanchet, Jeanne Ellene Maxant *artist, educator, performer*
Chase, James Keller *retired artist, museum director, educator*
Fratt, Dorothy *artist*
Kleppe, Shirley R. Klein *artist*
Lang, Margo Terzian *artist*
†Lloyd, Sally-Heath Fahnestock *artist*
Pitcher, Helen Ione *advertising director*
Rosenthal, Charles Louis *artist, educator*
Scholder, Fritz *artist*
Simmons, Julie Lutz *artist*
Van Dusen, Peter *artist*

Sedona
Ware, Peggy Jenkins *photographer, writer, artist, dancer*

Tempe
Kinney, Raleigh Earl *artist*
Turk, Rudy Henry *artist, retired museum director*

Tucson
†Bannard, Ann *sculptor*
†Bautzmann, Nancy Annette *artist*
Conant, Howard Somers *artist, educator*
Hamilton, Ruth Hellmann *design company owner*
Root, Nile *photographer, educator*
Schaffer, Richard E(nos) *artist, registrar*
Solomon, Vita Petrosky *artist*

ARKANSAS

Arkadelphia
†Fendley-Herbert, Debi Lynn *artist, art educator*

Berryville
Brown, Frances Louise (Grandma Fran Brown) *artist, art gallery owner*

Conway
Maakestad, Erik Paul *artist, educator*
†Ruehle, Jon *sculptor*

Fayetteville
Wilson, Charles Banks *artist*

Huntsville
Musick, Pat *artist, sculptor, art educator*

Jonesboro
Christiano, Melissa *artist, educator*

Little Rock
Fowler, Jennefer Rae *sculptor*
Tara-Casciano, Gertrude Ann *artist*

Russellville
Sullivan, John M. *graphic designer*

State University
Lindquist, Evan *artist, educator*

CALIFORNIA

Acampo
Eger, Marilyn Rae *artist*

Alameda
Biscevic, Nancy Lunsford *photographer*

Albion
†Darcy, John Arthur *artist*

Altadena
Bockus, Herman William, Jr. *artist, educator, writer*

Anaheim
Bennett, Genevieve *artist*
Nelipovich, Sandra Grassi *artist*

Aptos
Howe, Susan Leone *artist, printmaker, design consultant*
Schy, Gay *artist, investor*

Arcadia
Danziger, Louis *graphic designer, educator*

Arcata
Anderson, William Thomas *art educator, artist*

Aromas
Nutzle, Futzie (Bruce John Kleinsmith) *artist, author, cartoonist*

Bakersfield
Reep, Edward Arnold *artist*

Benicia
Shannonhouse, Sandra Lynne Riddell *sculptor*

Berkeley
Brixey, Shawn Alan *digital media artist, media educator, director*
Cantor, Rusty Sumner *artist*
Genn, Nancy *artist*
Hack, Elizabeth *artist*
Hartman, Robert Leroy *artist, educator*
Kasten, Karl Albert *painter, printmaker, educator*
McNamara, John Stephen *artist, educator*
Miyasaki, George Joji *artist*
Moore, Frank James *artist, educator*
Rapoport, Sonya *artist*
Simpson, David William *artist, educator*
Sussman, Wendy Rodriguez *artist, educator*
†Tanahashi, Kazuaki *artist, writer*
Theiss, Vernon G. *designer, educator, artist*
Washburn, Stan *artist*

Beverly Hills
Scott, Deborah L. *costume designer*

Bodega
Hedrick, Wally Bill *artist*

Bolinas
Harris, Paul *sculptor*
Okamura, Arthur Shinji *artist, educator, writer*

Boonville
Hanes, John Ward *sculptor, civil engineer consultant*

Burbank
†Holder, Donald *lighting designer*
Wu, Shu-Lin Sharon *animation educator*

Burlingame
Voelker, Elizabeth Anne *artist*

Cambria
Harden, Marvin *artist, educator*

Canoga Park
Rosenfeld, Sarena Margaret *artist*
†Song, Yanming *artist*

Cardiff By The Sea
Sargent, J(ean) McNeil *artist, art educator*

Carlsbad
Diaz, David *illustrator*

Carmel
Andreason, Sharon Lee *sculptor*
Kenna, Michael *photographer*

Carmichael
Sahs, Marjorie Jane *art educator*

Carpinteria
Hansen, Robert William *artist, educator*

Carson
Hirsch, Gilah Yelin *artist, writer*

Castro Valley
Erwin, Frances Suzanne *artist*
Knight, Andrew Kong *visual artist, educator*

Chatsworth
Wells, Annie *photographer*

Chico
†Williams, Mark Grayson *artist*

Claremont
Benjamin, Karl Stanley *art educator*
Blizzard, Alan *artist*
Casanova, Aldo John *sculptor*
†Dunye, Cheryl *artist, film maker*
Reiss, Roland Martin *artist, educator*
Zornes, Milford *artist*

Corona Del Mar
Brandt, Rexford Elson *artist*
Delap, Tony *artist*

Coronado
Hubbard, Donald *marine artist, writer*

Costa Mesa
Muller, Jerome Kenneth *photographer, art director, editor*

Culver City
†Grant, Joan Julien *artist, poet*
Pittard, William Blackburn (Billy Pittard) *television graphic designer*

Cupertino
Quirke, Lillian Mary *retired art educator*

Cypress
Bloom, Julian *artist, editor*
George, Patricia Byrne *artist*

Daggett
Bailey, Katherine Christine *artist, writer*

Danville
Handa, Eugenie Quan *graphic designer*

Davis
Petersen, Roland *artist, printmaker*

Desert Hot Springs
Hall, Anthony R. *photographer*

Diamond Springs
Tarbet, Urania Christy *artist, writer*

El Cajon
Harvey, Elaine Louise *artist, educator*

Encinitas
Breslaw, Cathy Lee *artist, educator*
Perine, Robert Heath *artist, writer*

Encino
Badham, Julia Aileen *artist*
Jones, John Harding *photographer*

Escondido
Sternberg, Harry *artist*

Eureka
Marak, Louis Bernard, Jr. *artist, educator*

Fairfax
Toney, Anthony *artist*

Fallbrook
Ragland, Jack Whitney *artist*

Ferndale
†Silver, Emily Ann *artist, educator*

Flintridge
†Johnston, Oliver Martin, Jr. *animator*
†Thomas, Franklin Rosborough *retired animator*

Folsom
Campbell, Ann Marie *artist*

Forest Ranch
Morrison, Martha Kaye *photolithography engineer, executive*

Fullerton
Curran, Darryl Joseph *photographer, educator*
Macaray, Lawrence Richard *art educator*
Woodhull, Patricia Ann *artist*

Galt
†Nunes, Judy Omai *artist*

Garden Grove
Bell, Melodie Elizabeth *artist, massage therapist*

Glendale
Spatny, Mark Scott *production designer, production manager*

Greenbrae
Blatt, Morton Bernard *medical illustrator*

Hayward
Jordahl, Kathleen Patricia (Kate Jordahl) *photographer, educator*

Highland
†Vanderveer, David Bryan *artist*

Hollywood
†Huang, Wen-xiang *artist, educator*

Huntington Beach
Berry, Kim Lauren *artist*
†Hazelton, Astor Miller *artist*

Inglewood
Vario, Joyce *graphic designer*

Inverness
Welpott, Jack Warren *photographer, educator*

Irvine
Berryhill, Georgia Gene *graphic designer, educator*
Giannulli, Mossimo *designer, apparel business executive*

Kensington
Loran, Erle *artist*

Kingsburg
Olson, Maxine Louise *artist, lecturer*

La Jolla
Inverarity, Robert Bruce *artist*
Low, Mary Louise (Molly Low) *documentary photographer*
Merrim, Louise Meyerowitz *artist, actress*
Silva, Ernest R. *visual arts educator, artist*
Whitaker, Eileen Monaghan (Eileen Monaghan) *artist*

La Mirada
Feldman, Roger Lawrence *artist, educator*

La Quinta
Barr, Roger Terry *sculptor*

Lafayette
Monheit, Molly Jane *artist, writer*
Shurtleff, Akiko Aoyagi *artist, consultant*

Laguna Beach
Blacketer, James Richard *artist*
DiGenova, Silvano Antonio *rare coin and fine art dealer*
Powers, Runa Skötte *artist*

Laguna Hills
Walker, Virginia L. *art educator*

Laguna Niguel
Apt, Charles *artist*

Laguna Woods
Saudek, Martha Folsom *artist, educator*

Lagunitas
Holman, Arthur Stearns *artist*

Lakewood
Barton, Billie Jo *artist, educator*

Lancaster
Swart, Bonnie Blount *artist*

Larkspur
Napoles, Veronica Kleeman *graphic designer, consultant*

Long Beach
Nielsen, Pamela Jeanne *artist, writer*
Viola, Bill *artist, writer*

Los Angeles
Amdur, Judith Devorah *artist, cook*
Apple, Jacqueline B (Jacqueline B. Apple) *artist, writer, educator*
Bangs, Cate (Cathryn Margaret Bangs) *film production designer, interior designer*
Barth, Uta *artist, educator*
Block, Amanda Roth *artist*
Bothwell, Dorr *artist*
Boyett, Joan Reynolds *arts administrator*
Caroompas, Carole Jean *artist, educator*
Di XX Miglia, Gabriella *artist, conservationist*
Ewing, Edgar Louis *artist, educator*
Frame, John Fayette *sculptor*
Galanos, James *fashion designer*
†Gray, Bruce Gordon *sculptor*
Hamilton, Patricia Rose *artist's agent*
Hess, Frederick Scott *artist*
Hockney, David *artist*
Janowski, Karyn Ann *artist*
†Johnson, Betsey Lee *fashion designer*
Johnston, Ynez *artist*
Judge, Mike *animator*
†Kersels, Martin *artist*
Ketchum, Robert Glenn *photographer, print maker*
Kory, Michael A. *graphics computer animator*
Layton, Harry Christopher *artist, lecturer, consultant*
Lem, Richard Douglas *painter*
Manolakas, Stanton Peter *watercolor artist*
McGraw, Deloss Holland *illustrator, painter*
†Pastor, Jennifer *sculptor*
Pederson, Con *animator*
†Pujol, Ernesto *artist*
Rankaitis, Susan *artist*
Saar, Alison *sculptor*
†Sobieszek, Robert A. *photographer, educator*
Stone, George *artist, art educator*
Tyler, Richard *fashion designer*
Welles, Melinda Fassett *artist, educational psychologist*
Williamson, Edwin Lee *wardrobe and costume consultant*
Woelffer, Emerson Seville *artist*
Wright, Bernard *artist*

Los Banos
Peterson, Stanley Lee *artist*

Lucerne Valley
Johnson, Jane Oliver *artist*

Malibu
Bowman, Bruce *art educator, writer, artist*

Manhattan Beach
Lee, Gloria Deane *artist, educator*
Posner, Judith Lois *art dealer*

Marina Del Rey
Lange, Gerald William *book artist, typographer*

Mckinleyville
Berry, Glenn *educator, artist*

Mendocino
†Sharkey, Virginia Grace *artist*

Mill Valley
Jones, Pirkle *photographer, educator*

Mission Viejo
Samuelson, Norma Graciela *architectural illustrator, artist*

Modesto
Bucknam, Mary Olivia Caswell *artist*

Montecito
Levinson, Betty Zitman *artist*

Monterey
Gilpin, Henry Edmund, III *photographer, educator*
Karsh, Yousuf *photographer*

Morgan Hill
Freimark, Robert (Bob Freimark) *artist*

Mountain View
Clark, Jonathan L. *photographer, printer, publisher*

Napa
Garnett, William *photographer*
Norman, Sheri Hanna *artist, educator, cartographer*

Newport Beach
Spitz, Barbara Salomon *artist*

North Hollywood
Knoll, William Lee *animation director*

Northridge
Bassler, Robert Covey *artist, educator*
Weatherup, Wendy Gaines *graphic designer, writer*

Oakhurst
Cantwell, Christopher William *artist*

Oakland
Alba, Benny *artist*
Beasley, Bruce Miller *sculptor*
Brewster, Andrea B. *artist*
Frey, Viola *sculptor, educator*
Gonzalez, Arthur Padilla *artist, educator*
Harper, Rob March *artist, educator*
Levine, Marilyn Anne *artist*
Melchert, James Frederick *artist*
Rath, Alan T. *sculptor*
†Sheridan, John Lucas *artist, art consultant*

Oceanside
Sarkisian, Pamela Outlaw *artist*

Orinda
Epperson, Stella Marie *artist*

Oxnard
Sweet, Harvey *theatrical, scenic and lighting designer*

Pacific Palisades
Chesney, Lee Roy, Jr. *artist*
†Sasaki, John Eric *art company executive*
Zivelonghi, Kurt Daniel *computer graphics artist, art director, designer*

Palm Desert
Kaufman, Charlotte King *artist, retired educational administrator*
Moroles, Jesus Bautista *sculptor*

Palm Springs
Maree, Wendy *painter, sculptor*

Palo Alto
Eisenstat, Benjamin *artist*
Kiser, Stephen *artist, educator*
McCluskey, Lois Thornhill *photographer*
Rich, Lesley Mosher *artist*
Weakland, Anna Wu *artist, art educator*

Pasadena
Gill, Gene *artist*
Howe, Graham Lloyd *photographer, curator*
†Iturbide, Graciela *photographer*
Marrow, Marva Jan *photographer, writer, video and multimedia producer, web designer, publisher*
Pashgian, Margaret Helen *artist*
Sakoguchi, Ben *artist, art educator*
Savedra, Jeannine Evangeline *art educator, artist*
Zammitt, Norman *artist*

Pebble Beach
Mortensen, Gordon Louis *artist, printmaker*

Petaluma
Fuller-McChesney, Mary Ellen *sculptor, writer, publisher*
McChesney, Robert Pearson *artist*
Reichek, Jesse *artist*
Skalagard, Hans Martin *artist*

Phelan
Erwin, Joan Lenore *artist, educator*

Piedmont
Wood, Wayne Barry *photojournalist*

Pinole
Gerbracht, Robert Thomas (Bob Gerbracht) *painter, educator*

Placentia
Nettleship, William Allan *sculptor*

Porterville
†Golightly, Douglas Raymond *artist*

Prunedale
Garman, Dale S., Jr. *sculptor*

Rancho Santa Fe
Dieffenbach, AliceJean *artist*

Redondo Beach
Lytal, Patricia Lou *art educator*

Richmond
Huckeby, Karen Marie *graphic arts executive*
Wessel, Henry *photographer*

Riverside
Medel, Rebecca Rosalie *artist*

Sacramento
Allan, William George *painter, educator*
Cosgrove, James *artist, industrial designer*
Dalkey, Fredric Dynan *artist*
Drachnik, Catherine Meldyn *art therapist, artist, counselor*
Nye, Gene Warren *retired art educator*

Salinas
Puckett, Richard Edward *artist, consultant, retired recreation executive*

San Carlos
Oliver, Nancy Lebkicher *artist, retired elementary education educator*
Sullivan, Shirley Ross (Shirley Ross Davis) *art collector*

San Diego
Barone, Angela Maria *artist, researcher*
Beaumont, Mona *artist*
Farmer, Janene Elizabeth *artist, educator*
†Howard, Mildred *sculptor*
Linton, Roy Nathan *graphic arts company executive*
Nyiri, Joseph Anton *sculptor, art educator*
†Siegal, Barbara Leatrice *visual artist*
Sorby, J(oseph) Richard *artist, educator*

San Francisco
Autio, Rudy *artist educator*
Babcock, Jo *artist, educator*
Beall, Dennis Ray *artist, educator*
†Blood, Brian Ellis *artist*
Brooke, Pegan Struthers *artist, art educator*
Chartrand, April Martin *designer*
Chin, Sue Soone Marian (Suchin Chin) *conceptual artist, portraitist, photographer, community affairs activist*
DeSoto, Lewis Damien *art educator*
Dickinson, Eleanor Creekmore *artist, educator*
Dreibelbis, Ellen Roberts *artist*
Hahner, Linda R. R. *artist, creative director*
Hershman, Lynn Lester *artist*
Hobbs, C. Fredric *artist, filmmaker, author*
Howard, David E. *artist*
Huntting, Cynthia Cox *artist*
Kehlmann, Robert *artist, critic*
Komater, Christopher John *artist*
†LeGrady, George *photographer, educator*
Lobdell, Frank *artist*
Martin, Fred *artist, college administrator*
Maxim, David Nicholas *artist*
Mayeri, Beverly *artist, ceramic sculptor, educator*
McClintock, Jessica *fashion designer*
Muranaka, Hideo *artist, educator*
Phillips, Thomas Embert *artist*
Piccolo, Richard Andrew *artist, educator*
Raciti, Cherie *artist*
Rascón, Armando *artist*
Roloff, John Scott *artist, art educator*
Sassone, Marco Massimo *artist*
Van Hoesen, Beth Marie *artist, printmaker*
Villa, Carlos Pedro *artist, activist, educator*
Wall, Brian Arthur *sculptor*
†West, Alice Clare *artist*
Wilson, Allan Byron *graphics company executive*

San Jose
Ellner, Michael William *art educator*
Estabrook, Reed *artist, educator*
Gunther, Barbara *artist, educator*
Lopez, Angelo Cayas *freelance illustrator*
Nguyen, Long Duc *artist*

San Juan Capistrano
Burns, Toni Anthony *artist*

San Leandro
Chilcoat, Dale Allen *artist, visual and performing arts educator*

San Luis Obispo
Dickerson, Colleen Bernice Patton *artist, educator*
Ruggles, Joanne Beaule *artist, educator*

San Marino
Medearis, Roger Norman *artist*

San Mateo
Chester, Sharon Rose *photographer, natural history educator, writer, illustrator*
Huxley, Mary Atsuko *artist*

San Pedro
Crutchfield, William Richard *artist, educator*
Strasen, Barbara Elaine *artist, educator*

Santa Barbara
Cavat, Irma *artist, educator*
Eguchi, Yasu *artist*
Wallin, Lawrence Bier *artist*

Santa Clara
Lane, Holly Diana *artist*

Santa Cruz
Bartlett Abood, Kathleen Gene *artist, educator*
Leites, Barbara Lee (Ara Leites) *artist*

Massaro, Karen Thuesen *artist*
Summers, Carol *artist*

Santa Monica
Fellows, Alice Combs *artist*
Fukuhara, Henry *artist, educator*
Jenkins, George *stage designer, film art director*
†Kay, Jeremy H. *cartoonist*
Mitchell, Kathleen Ann *illustrator, graphic designer*

Santa Rosa
Mancusi, Timothy John *artist, illustrator*
Monk, Diana Charla *artist, stable owner*
Rider, Jane Louise *artist, educator*
Thistlethwaite, Aline McQuiston *artist*

Saratoga
Sherwood, Patricia Waring *artist, educator*

Sausalito
Holmes, Robert Edward *photographer*
Kuhlman, Walter Egel *artist, educator*

Sherman Oaks
†Hoover, Richard *set designer*
Platus, Libby *artist, sculptor*
†Powell, Sandy *costume designer*
Weiss, Julie *costume designer*

Sierra Madre
Converse, Elizabeth Sheets *artist, writer*

Simi Valley
Shawn, Eric *software and consumer products company executive*

Solana Beach
Beck-von-Peccoz, Stephen George Wolfgang *artist*

Somis
Kehoe, Vincent Jeffré-Roux *photographer, author, cosmetic company executive*

Sonoma
Anderson, Gunnar Donald *artist*

Sonora
Sharboneau, Lorna Rosina *artist, educator, author, poet, illustrator*

South Lake Tahoe
Darvas, Endre Peter *artist*

South Pasadena
Askin, Walter Miller *artist, educator*

Studio City
Wissner, Gary Charles *motion picture art director, production designer*

Summerland
Calamar, Gloria *artist*

Sylmar
Scheib, Gerald Paul *fine art educator, jeweler, metalsmith*

Tehachapi
†Dewar, Robert Earl *artist*

Thousand Oaks
Heyer, Carol Ann *illustrator*
Relkin, Michele Weston *artist*

Torrance
Everts, Connor *artist*

Upper Lake
Twitchell, Kent *mural artist*

Vacaville
Ford, John T., Jr. *art, film and video educator*

Van Nuys
Graham, Roger John *photography and journalism educator*
Sandel, Randye Noreen *artist*

Venice
Bengston, Billy Al *artist*
Eversley, Frederick John *sculptor, engineer*
Garabedian, Charles *artist*
Hartley, Corinne *painter, sculptor, educator*
Shelton, Peter T. *artist*

Watsonville
†Hannula, Tarmo *photographer*
Hansen, Elizabeth Jean *appraiser, author*

West Covina
Shiershke, Nancy Fay *artist, educator, property manager*

West Hollywood
†Chillida, Eduardo *sculptor*

Woodland Hills
Bonassi, Jodi *artist, marketing consultant*

COLORADO

Arvada
Halley, Diane Esther *artist*

Aspen
Berkó, Ferenc *photographer*
Soldner, Paul Edmund *artist, ceramist, educator*

Boulder
Bierman, Sandra Lee *artist*
Bolomey, Roger Henry *sculptor*
Chong, Albert Valentine *artist, educator*
Friedman, Pamela Ruth Lessing *art consultant, financial consultant*
Iris (Silverstein), Bonnie *artist, writer, educator*

Matthews, Eugene Edward *artist*
†Rosato, Antonette *visual artist*

Colorado Springs
Fox, Gwen *artist, educator*
Goehring, Kenneth *artist*

Cortez
Winterer-Schulz, Barbara Jean *art designer, author*

Crestone
†Manno, Angela Linda *artist*

Denver
Alcott Tempest Temple, Leslie *artist*
Graham, Pamela Smith *artist, distributing company executive*
Hakeem, Muhammad Abdul *artist, educator*
McElhinney, James Lancel *artist, educator*
Ragland, Bob *artist, educator*
Shwayder, Elizabeth Yanish *sculptor*

Durango
Reber, Mick *artist, educator*

Estes Park
†Berkeley, Seamus Osborne *artist, consultant*

Fort Collins
†Simons, Stephen Richard *artist*
Weimer, Dawn *sculptor*

Greeley
Ursyn, Anna *computer graphics artist, educator*

La Veta
Zehring, Peggy Johnson *artist*

Loma
†Young, David Bennion *artist*

Longmont
King, Jane Louise *artist*

Louisville
Day, Robert Edgar *retired artist, educator*

Loveland
Weresh, Thelma Faye *sculptor, artist*

Nederland
†Border, William Lawson *artist*

Salida
Miller, Marian Lofton *artist, musician*

San Luis
Wardlaw, Diane *graphic designer*

Snowmass Village
Beeman, Malinda Mary *artist, program administrator*

Telluride
Hadley, Paul Burrest, Jr. (Tabbit Hadley) *domestic engineer, photographer*
Smith, Samuel David *artist, educator*

Westcliffe
Merfeld, Gerald Lydon *artist*

Woodland Park
Cockrille, Stephen *art director, business owner*

Yellow Springs
†Sholtis, Michelle Lea *potter, educator*

CONNECTICUT

Ashford
McCaughtry, Charles H. *artist, painter*
Spencer, Editha Mary (Hayes) *artist*
Spencer, Harold Edwin *retired art educator, art historian, painter*

Bethel
Ajay, Abe *artist*

Bloomfield
Hammer, Alfred Emil *artist, educator*

Branford
LeVasseur, Lee Allan *fine artist*
Milgram, Judith Lee *art educator, administrator, artist*

Bridgeport
Mahmud, Shireen Dianne *photographer*

Colebrook
Ash, Hiram Newton *graphic designer*

Cornwall Bridge
Pfeiffer, Werner Bernhard *artist, educator*

Cos Cob
Kane, Margaret Brassler *sculptor*

Danbury
Saghir, Adel Jamil *artist, painter, sculptor*

Enfield
Loomis, Janice Kaszczuk *artist*

Fairfield
Bullard, Roger Perrin *artist*
Trager, Philip *photographer, lawyer*

Falls Village
Cronin, Robert Lawrence *sculptor, painter*

Farmington
Smith, Cary Christopher *artist*

Georgetown
Roberts, Priscilla Warren *artist*

Greenwich
Adrian, George Panaitisor *graphic designer*
Baer, Adam Scott *artist*
†Moonie, Liana M. *artist*
Pope, Ingrid Bloomquist *sculptor, lecturer, poet*
Sandbank, Henry *photographer, film director*

Groton
Franciosi, Barbara Lee *designer, fiber artist*

Hampton
Jones, William Anthony *artist, educator, illustrator*

Hartford
Fitzgerald, Michael Cowan *art historian*
Menses, Jan *artist, draftsman, etcher, lithographer, muralist*
Uccello, Vincenza Agatha *artist, director, educator emerita*

Madison
Cappetta, Anna Maria *art educator*
Clendenen, Corinna Pakenham *art critic, writer, auctioneer*
Kronauer, Lisa Elliott *art director*

Meriden
Bertolli, Eugene Emil *sculptor, goldsmith, designer, consultant*

Milford
Curt, Denise Morris *artist, limner, photographer*
Dodd, Alan Charles *art educator*

Monroe
Wheatley, Sharman B. *art educator, artist*

Naugatuck
Mannweiler, Mary-Elizabeth *painter*

New Britain
Deckert, Clinton Allen *artist*
Kot, Marta Violette *artist, art educator*

New Canaan
Antupit, Samuel Nathaniel *art director*
Caesar, Henry A., II *sculptor*
†Ervin, Wilma Jean *painter, photographer*
Kovatch, Jak Gene *artist*
Rendl-Marcus, Mildred *artist, economist*
Richards, Walter DuBois *artist, illustrator*
Sweeny, Kenneth S. *graphic design consultant*

New Haven
Bailey, William Harrison *artist, educator*
†Feinstein, Rochelle *artist, educator*
Gralla, Howard Irwin *graphic designer*
Grausman, Philip *sculptor*
Jacobson, Susana Viola (Susan Jacobson) *artist*
Johnson, Lester Fredrick *artist*
Lindroth, Linda (Linda Hammer) *artist, curator, writer*
Papageorge, Tod *photographer, educator*
Pease, David Gordon *artist, educator*

Newtown
†Christensen, Betty *artist*

Noank
Bates, Gladys Edgerly *sculptor*

Norwalk
Perry, Charles Owen *sculptor*

Norwich
Montford, James Giordani, Jr. *artist*

Old Lyme
Chandler, Elisabeth Gordon (Mrs. Laci De Gerenday) *sculptor, harpist*
de Gerenday, Laci Anthony *sculptor, educator*
Rooney, Maria Dewing *photographer*

Redding
Isley, Alexander Max *graphic designer, lecturer*

Ridgefield
Kromer, Ann Marie *artist*
†Pitman, Ann Bridgman *artist*

Shelton
Lewis, Peter David *artist, educator*

Stamford
Koch, Robert *art educator*
Rudman, Joan Eleanor *artist, educator*
Strosahl, William Austin *artist, art director*

Storrs Mansfield
Jones, Clyde Adam *art educator, artist*

Torrington
†McKenzie, Kathleen Julianna *artist*

Wallingford
Lauttenbach, Carol *artist*

Warren
Abrams, Herbert E. *artist*

Waterford
Patnode, Mark W. *artist, graphic designer*

West Cornwall
Prentice, Tim *sculptor, architect*

West Hartford
White, Joan Michelson *artist*

Weston
Bleifeld, Stanley *sculptor*
Cadmus, Paul *artist, etcher*

Westport
Chernow, Ann Levy *artist, art educator*
Fisher, Leonard Everett *artist, writer, educator*
Reilly, Anne Caulfield (Nancy Reilly) *painter*
†Siff, Marlene Ida *artist, designer*

Wilton
Maruyama, Karl Satoru *graphic designer*

Winchester
Firimita, Florin Ion *artist, educator, curator*

Woodbridge
†Roche, Raymond Laird *artist*

DELAWARE

Greenville
Reynolds, Nancy Bradford duPont (Mrs. William Glasgow Reynolds) *sculptor*

Hockessin
Sawin, Nancy Churchman *educator, artist, historian*

New Castle
Almquist, Don *illustrator, artist*

Newark
Brown, Hilton *visual arts educator, artist*
Hunsperger, Elizabeth Jane *art and design consultant, educator*
Rowe, Charles Alfred *artist, designer, educator*

Rockland
Harvey, Andre *sculptor*

Wilmington
Bounds-Seemans, Pamella J. *artist*
Lewis, Mary Therese *artist*
Rothrock, Richard Edward *sculptor, stone specialist*

DISTRICT OF COLUMBIA

Washington
Auld, Albert Michael *sculptor*
Basch, Richard Vennard *photographer, producer, writer, director*
Biddle, Catharina Baart *artist*
Blair, James Pease *photographer*
Bowman, Dorothy Louise *artist*
Brown, John Carter *art and education consultant, federal agency administrator*
Brown, Pamela Wedd *artist*
†Buster, Kendall *art educator*
Cleary, Manon Catherine *artist, educator*
Coppola, John Francis *exhibits director*
Costigan, Constance Frances *artist, educator*
Dana, Richard L. *painter, arts administrator*
DiPerna, Frank Paul *photographer, educator*
Forrester, Patricia Tobacco *artist*
Giles, Patricia Cecelia Parker *retired art educator, graphic designer*
Gonzalez-Ceron, Oscar *visual artist*
†Goslee, Patricia Claire *artist, graphic designer*
Gossage, John Ralph *photographer*
Gumpert, Gunther *artist*
†Ihrie, John Richard, III *art educator*
†Kim, Sook Cha *artist*
Koller, Shirley Leavitt *sculptor*
Krebs, Rockne *artist*
Millon, Henry Armand *fine arts educator, architectural historian*
Muhn, B.G. *artist, educator*
Permutter, Jack *artist, lithographer*
Polan, Annette Lewis *artist, educator*
Rankine, V.V. *sculptor/painter*
Rode, Meredith Eagon *art educator, artist*
†Schaap, Aletta Johanna *artist*
Shinolt, Eileen Thelma *artist*
Shrader, Carl Michael *photography and pre-press production executive*
†Simes, Anastasia Ryurikov *artist*
Skolnick, Judith A. Colton *artist*
Smith, Donald Eugene *executive*
Steadham, Richard Lynn *magazine art director*
Sthreshley, Charles Archie *sculptor*
Summerford, Ben Long *retired artist, educator*
Tacha, Athena *sculptor, educator*
Truitt, Anne Dean *artist*
Ulvestad, Anne Elizabeth *art director*

FLORIDA

Alachua
†Tilton, John Ellsworth *ceramic artist*

Aventura
Cerri, Robert Noel *photographer*

Bay Harbor Islands
†Kitner, Harold *artist, educator*

Boca Raton
McFarren, Naza *artist*
Ortlip, Mary Krueger *artist*
Ortlip, Paul Daniel *artist*
Pelish, Susan Marion *sculptor, painter*
Pepper, Beverly *artist, sculptor*
Wertheimer, Esther *sculptor*

Boynton Beach
Birkenstock, Joyce Ann *artist*
Harwood, Bernice Baumel *artist, community volunteer*

Bradenton
Garrison, Richard Neil *artist*
†McClish, Jerry F. *artist*
Voorhees, Stephanie Robin Nee Faught *retired art educator*

Clearwater
†Walker, William Russell *artist*

Clermont
Cox, Margaret Stewart *photographer*

Cocoa Beach
Blum, June *artist, curator*
Herbstman, Loretta *sculptor*

Coral Gables
Bannard, Walter Darby *artist, art critic*

Dania
†Satin, Claire Jeanne *sculptor, illustrator*

Daytona Beach
Alvarez, Marianne *artist, photographer, educator*

Deland
Hupalo, Meredith Topliff *artist, illustrator*

Delray Beach
Lerner, Norman *photographer, educator*
Mills, Agnes Eunice Karlin *artist, printmaker, sculptor*
Ross, Beatrice Brook *artist*

Dunedin
Allison, Brooke Hastings *artist*

Englewood
Sisson, Robert F. *photographer, writer, lecturer, educator*
Tracy, Lois Bartlett *painter*

Fernandina Beach
DelPesco Thornton, Nancy Rose *artist, educator*

Fort Lauderdale
Gianguzzi, Joseph Custode *sculptor*

Fort Myers
Dean, Jean Beverly *artist*
Frank, Elizabeth Ahls *art educator, artist*
Schwartz, Carl Edward *artist, printmaker*

Fort Pierce
Peterson, Barbara Owecke *artist, nurse, realtor*
†Walker, Dennis *artist*

Gainesville
Grant, Elizabeth Jane Thurmond *graphic design educator, consultant*
Kerslake, Kenneth Alvin *artist, printmaker, art educator*
Morgan, Anne Barclay *artist, author*
†Murray, Kate Shakeshaft *artist*
Williams, Hiram Draper *artist, educator*

Gulf Breeze
McDonald, Marianne M. *artist*

Gulfport
Marshall, Nathalie *artist, writer, educator*

Hollywood
Sadowski, Carol Johnson *artist*

Indialantic
Pavlakos, Ellen Tsatiri *sculptor*

Indian Harbor Beach
Osmundsen, Barbara Ann *sculptor*
Traylor, Angelika *stained glass artist*

Jacksonville
Eden, F(lorence) Brown *artist*
Loomis, Jacqueline Chalmers *photographer*

Jupiter
†Sadow, Harvey Seynour, Jr. *artist*

Key Biscayne
Napp, Gudrun F. *artist*

Lake Helen
Dillashaw, Eula Catherine *artist, graphic artist*

Lake Mary
Bachmann, Bill *photographer*

Lake Park
Heaton, Janet Nichols *artist, art gallery director*

Lake Worth
Greer, Brian R. *commercial photographer, futurist*
Hein, Laurie Snow *artist, educator*

Lakeland
Stark, Bruce Gunsten *artist*

Maitland
Schubert, Jeanne *artist*

Marathon
Giffen, Lois Key *artist, psychosynthesis counselor*

Marco Island
Kingsley, Judith *artist*

Melbourne
Conneen, Mari M. *artist*
Failla, Sophia Lynn *artist, educator*

Melrose
Harley, Ruth *artist, educator*

Miami
Alexenberg, Mel *artist, art educator*
Balás, Irene Barbara *artist*
Brito, Maria Cristina *sculptor, educator*
†DeCristofaro, John George *artist, designer*
DePasquale, Laura *artist, art education administrator*
Hanna, Ronald Everette *art educator, consultant*
Kislak, Jean Hart *art director*
Maddern, David *artist*
Marks, Shirley I. *artist*
Strickland, Thomas Joseph *artist*
Tschumy, Freda Coffing *artist, educator*

Miami Beach
McManus, Michael Edward *artist, educator*

Mulberry
Oettinger, Kathleen Linda *artist, writer*

Naples
Eldridge, David Carlton *art appraiser*
†Poehlmann, Christopher Eric *artist, designer*

New Smyrna Beach
Ledbetter, Benton L. *sculptor*
Leeper, Doris Marie *sculptor, painter*

Ocala
†Knief, Helen Janett *artist*

Okeechobee
Chilcutt, Dorthe Margaret *art educator, artist*

Orange Park
Kennedy, James Frederick *artist*

Orlando
Haxton, David *computer graphics educator, computer animator, photographer*
Renee, Lisabeth Mary *art educator, artist, galley director*
Robertson, Lorna Dooling *artist, real estate developer*
†Softic, Tanja *artist*
Warren, Dean Stuart *artist*

Ormond Beach
†Frank, Robert E. *artist*

Osprey
Robinson, Sally Winston *artist*

Palm Bay
Galitello-Wolfe, Jane Maryann *artist, writer*

Palm Beach
Krois, Audrey *artist*
Myers, Eugene Ekander *art consultant*
Wenzel, Joan Ellen *artist*

Palm City
Sloan, Richard *artist*

Palm Harbor
Giavis, Theodore Demetrios *commercial illustrator, artist*
Katzen-Guthrie, Joy *performance artist, engineering services executive*

Parkland
Janice, Barbara *illustrator*

Pembroke Pines
Abbott, Linda Joy *stained glass artisan, educator*

Pensacola
Burke-Fanning, Madeleine *artist*
Cooper, Elva June *artist, writer*

Plant City
Knoderer, David Letterfly *artist, educator*

Plantation
Ballantyne, Maree Anne Canine *artist*

Pompano Beach
Roberts, Karen Barbara *art educator*
Saleeby, Cherie Lee *sculptor*

Port Charlotte
Leslie, John *artist, designer, photographer, sculptor*

Safety Harbor
Banks, Allan Richard *artist, art historian, researcher*
Banks, Holly Hope *artist*

Saint Augustine
Gillilland, Thomas *art gallery director*
†Hall, Robert *art educator, artist*

Saint Petersburg
Bryant, Laura Militzer *artist*
Peterson, Eric Lang *art appraiser, art consultant, gallery owner*
Ransom, Brian Charles *artist, educator, musician, composer*

Sanibel
Keogh, Mary Cudahy *artist*

Sarasota
Altabe, Joan Augusta Berg *artist, writer, art and architecture critic*
Burkett, Helen *artist*
Cashin, Patricia Jeanne (Pat Cashin) *artist, educator*
Harmon, (Loren) Foster *art consultant*
Krate, Nat *artist*
Makau, John *artist*
Winterhalter, Dolores August (Dee Winterhalter) *art educator*

Sebastian
Pieper, Patricia Rita *artist, photographer*

Tallahassee
Hicken, Russell Bradford *art dealer, appraiser*
Kessler, Mitzi Lyons *artist*
Pond-Koenig, donalee *artist*

Tampa
Costin, John Edward *graphic artist*

Temple Terrace
Kashdin, Gladys Shafran *painter, educator*

Vero Beach
†Scott, Charlotte Patricia *artist*

West Palm Beach
Gronlund, Robert B. *art collector, fund raising consultant*

Winter Haven
Clement, Elizabeth Stewart *artist*

Winter Springs
San Miguel, Manuel *painter, historian, composer, poet*

GEORGIA

Alpharetta
Needle, Charles Richard *photographer*
Wu, Wayne Wen-Yau *artist*

Aragon
Hardin, Sherrie Ann Asfoury *commercial photographer*

Athens
Clements, Robert Donald *sculptor*
DeZurko, Edward Robert *retired art educator*
Edison, Diane *artist, educator, administrator*
Herbert, James Arthur *artist, filmmaker*
Kaufman, Glen Frank *art educator, artist*
Kent, Robert B. *artist, educator*
Olsen, Richard James *artist, art educator*
Paul, William Dewitt, Jr. *artist, educator, photographer, museum director*

Atlanta
Brown, Sarah M. *artist, gallery owner, educator, publisher*
Callahan, Harry Morey *photographer*
Deremer, Susan René *artist*
†Gibson, Michael *artist*
Grumet, Priscilla Hecht *fashion specialist, consultant, writer*
Guberman, Sidney Thomas *painter, writer*
Holden, Laurence Preston *artist*
Lide, Janet Elizabeth *graphic designer, artist*
Lucero, Michael *sculptor*
Malone, James Hiram *graphic artist, painter, writer*
McLean, James Albert *artist, educator*
†Rodriguez, Rocío *artist*
Schneeberger, Helen Haynes *artist*

Augusta
Rosen, James Mahlon *artist, art historian, educator*

Avondale Estates
Carroll, Jane Hammond *artist, author, poet*

Bainbridge
Kwilecki, Paul *photographer*

Duluth
†Garner, Karen Burnette *artist, administrative assistant*

Gainesville
Taylor, Mary Jane *art educator, artist*

Jasper
Sutter, Jean *sculptor*

Macon
Weaver, Jacquelyn Kunkel Ivey *artist, educator*

Marietta
Daresta, Pamela Beagle *artist*
Lahtinen, Silja Liisa *artist*
Wegodsky, Gail Eleanor *artist*

Mount Berry
Mew, Thomas Joseph, III (Tommy Mew) *artist, educator*

Peachtree City
Robben, Mary Margaret *portrait artist, painter*

Powder Springs
Collins Burns, Lisa Diane *art educator*

Roswell
†Christopher, Lin *artist*

Savannah
†Andrews, Christine Marie *graphic designer*
Aquadro, Jeana Lauren *graphic designer, educator*
Foley, Marilyn Lorna *artist*
Gabeler-Brooks, Jo *artist*
†Neely, C. Michael *graphic designer, illustrator*
Oelschig, Augusta Denk *retired artist, art educator*
Shang, Xuhong *art educator, artist*
†Spradley, Dorothy Radford *art educator, sculptor*

HAWAII

Hanalei
Helder, David Ernest *artist, educator*

Honolulu
Amor, Simeon, Jr. *photographer*
Belknap, Jodi Parry *graphic designer, writer, business owner*
Betts, Barbara Stoke *artist, educator*
Chang, Rodney Eiu Joon *artist, dentist*
Pickens, Frances Jenkins *jewelry/metal artist, art educator*
Uhl, Philip Edward *marine artist*

Kapaa
Kahn, Martin Jerome *art gallery owner*

Kapaau
Jankowski, Theodore Andrew *artist*

Kihei
†Yamada, Shige *artist*

Lahaina
Sato, Tadashi *artist*

Lihue
Lai, Waihang *art educator*

IDAHO

Harrison
Carlson, George Arthur *artist*

Lewiston
Scott, Linda Byrne *artist*

Nampa
Shaffer, Mary Louise *art educator*

ILLINOIS

Addison
†Leiber, Annete Perone *artist, art association administrator*

Barrington
Nadolski, Stephanie Lucille *artist, designer*

Beardstown
Gross, Shirley Marie *artist, farm manager*

Bloomington
Casey-Beich, Micheal Louanna *artist*

Carbondale
Benjamin-Kruge, Siona *artist, educator*

Champaign
Jackson, Billy Morrow *artist, retired art educator*
Kotoske, Roger Allen *artist, educator*

Charleston
Boshart, Jeffrey Glenn *sculptor, educator*

Chicago
Altman, Edith G. *sculptor*
Bender, Janet Pines *artist*
Bent, Geoffrey Steven *artist, librarian*
Boggess, Thomas Phillip, III *graphic arts company executive*
Bowman, Leah *fashion designer, consultant, photographer, educator*
†Campos-Pons, Maria Magdalena *artist*
Castillo, Mario Enrique *artist, educator*
Chambers, Richard Leon *retired Turkish language and civilization educator*
Crane, Barbara Bachmann *photographer, educator*
Dompke, Norbert Frank *retired photography studio executive*
Feeley, Henry Joseph, Jr. (Hank Feeley) *artist, former advertising agency executive*
Gaines, Anne Farley *artist, art educator*
Garner, Ted *artist*
Gray, Richard *art dealer, consultant, holding company executive*
†Gunning, Tom *art educator*
†Hards, Richard Charles *artist*
Heinecken, Robert Friedli *art educator, artist*
Henriquez-Freeman, Hilda Josefina *fashion design executive*
Hill, Gary *video artist*
Himmelfarb, John David *artist*
Ida, Shoichi *artist*
Jachna, Joseph David *photographer, educator*
Kearney, John Walter *sculptor, painter*
Kearney, Lynn Marilyn Haigh *arts administrator, curator*
King, Andre Richardson *architectural graphic designer*
Klopack, Kenneth Barthon *art educator, artist*
Koga, Mary *artist, photographer, social worker*
Look, Dona Jean *artist*
McGrail, Jeane Kathryn *artist, educator, poet, curator*
Mitchell, Dennis L. *artist, educator*
Novak, Marlena *artist, educator, writer, curator*
Olson, Patricia Joanne *artist, educator*
Pantuso, Michael Vincent *graphic design company executive*
Paul, Arthur *artist, graphic designer, illustrator, art and design consultant*
Phelan, Mary Helen *artist, educator*
Pilarski, Jeffrey H. *graphic designer, consultant*
†Pukelis, Larry S. *art educator*
Regensteiner, Else Friedsam (Mrs. Bertold Regensteiner) *textile designer, educator*
†Samuels, Fern Jacqueline *artist, educator*
Sigler, Hollis *artist, educator, author*
Skrebneski, Victor *photographer*
Tessing, Louise Scire *graphic designer*
†Thall, Robert *photographer, educator*
Thompson, George Everet *graphic designer, educator*
Wilson, Anne Gawthrop *artist, educator*
Wolin, Jeffrey Alan *artist*
Workman, Robert Peter *artist, cartoonist*
Yamada, Takeshi *artist, language and cultural consultant, educator*

Cicero
Welborn, Sarah *photographer, writer, poet*

Dekalb
Dorn, Gordon Joseph *artist, art educator*
Merritt, Helen Henry *retired art educator, ceramic sculptor, art historian*

Des Plaines
Banach, Art John *graphic artist*

Edwardsville
†Hampton, Phillip Jewel *artist, educator*
Malone, Robert Roy *artist, art educator*

Elmhurst
†Hookham, Eleanor King *painter*
King Hookham, Eleanor *artist*

Evanston
Conger, William Frame *artist, educator*
Nakoneczny, Michael Martin *artist*
Rasco, Kay Frances *antique dealer*
Vanderstappen, Harrie Albert *Far Eastern art educator*

Geneva
Mishina, Mizuho *artist*

Glencoe
Morrissey, Terri Jo *artist*

Grayslake
Nicholas, Willadene Louise *artist*

Highland Park
Slavick, Ann Lillian *art educator, arts*

Hudson
Mills, Frederick VanFleet *art educator, watercolorist*

Lombard
Ahlstrom, Ronald Gustin *artist*
Hudson, Samuel Campbell, Jr. *art educator, artist, sculptor*

Palatine
Fortunato, Nancy *artist*
Miletto, David Gregory *artist*

Park Forest
Cribbs, Maureen Ann *artist, educator*

Park Ridge
Charewicz, David Michael *photographer*
Lesiak, Lucille Ann *graphic designer*
Orlow, Daniel John *photographer, artist*

Pekin
Hupke, David R. *photographer*

Quincy
†Mejer, Robert Lee *art educator, curator*

Rantoul
†Rosakopf, Arthur W. *artist*

River Forest
Sloan, Jeanette Pasin *artist*
White, Philip Butler *artist*

Rockford
Apgar, Jean E. *artist, consultant*

Rolling Meadows
Rebbeck, Lester James, Jr. *artist*

Scales Mound
Lieberman, Archie *photographer, writer*

Skokie
Goldsmith, Barbara Cecile *sculptor, curator*

Sleepy Hollow
†Galitz, Robert Walter *art broker, dealer*

South Holland
Fota, Frank George *artist*

Table Grove
†Thomson, Helen Louise *artist*

Waukegan
Bleck, Virginia Eleanore *illustrator*

Wheaton
Lowrie, Pamela Burt *educator, artist*

Winnetka
Plowden, David *photographer*

Zion
Hettich, Paul Joseph *theatre designer, technician, military officer*

INDIANA

Albany
Patrick, Alan K. *artist*

Anderson
Case, Hank *wine importer, retired art educator, photographer*
Olson, Carol Lea *lithographer, educator, photographer*

Bloomington
Bardzell, Jeffrey Scott *graphics designer*
Datcu, Ioana *visual artist*
Lowe, Marvin *artist*
O'Hearn, Robert Raymond *stage designer*
Stirratt, Betsy *artist, gallery director*

Crown Point
Scheub, Richard Herman *photographer*

Evansville
Brown, William Fredrick *art educator*
Roth, Carolyn Louise *art educator*

Fort Wayne
Bock-Tobolski, Marilyn Rose *artist, art educator*

Gary
Rosen, Kay *painter*

Goshen
Mishler, John Joseph *sculptor, art educator*
Neterer, Christopher Dean *mural painter, manufacturing company official*

Indianapolis
Jacobson, Marc Peter *art educator*
Schaad, Dee Edwin *art educator*
†Van Lone Trieschman, Janet Anne *graphic arts educator*
Willoughby, David Charles *photographer, forensics illustrator*

Milltown
Chapman, Sue Turner *artist*

Morgantown
Boyce, Gerald G. *artist, educator*

Nashville
Brown, Peggy Ann *artist*
Gurnack, Dean Hilton *artist*
Kriner, Sally Gladys Pearl *artist*

Purdue University
Bannatyne, Mark William McKenzie *technical graphics educator*

Richmond
Kennedy, Barbara Ellen Perry *art therapist*

Terre Haute
†Hay, Dick *artist, educator*
Lamis, Leroy *artist, retired educator*
Tió, Adrian Ricardo *artist, art educator*

Valparaiso
Olson, Lynn *sculptor, painter, writer*

West Lafayette
Ichiyama, Dennis Yoshihide *design educator, consultant, administrator*

Winamac
Ligocki, Gordon Michael *artist, educator*

IOWA

Ames
Zimmerman, William *artist*

Bettendorf
Herdman, Susan *art educator, artist*

Britt
†Castillo, Leanne Marlow *artist, nurse*

Burlington
Trickler, Sally Jo *technical illustrator*

Cedar Rapids
†Zmolek, Gloria Jean *artist*

Davenport
Jecklin, Lois Underwood *art corporation executive, consultant*

Decorah
Maurland, Anne Elisabeth *potter*

Des Moines
Reece, Maynard Fred *artist, author*
†Truck, Frederick John *artist*

Dubuque
Gibbs, Robert T. (Tom) *sculptor, consultant*

Iowa City
Merkel-Hess, Mary Lynne *artist*
Morice, David Jennings *illustrator, writer*
Schmidt, Julius *sculptor*

Mallard
Grethen, Cheryl Ann *artist*

Marion
Prall, Barbara Jones *artist*

Mason City
Dotson, John Ray *oil painter*

Mount Pleasant
Scarff, Hope Dyall *photographer*

KANSAS

Augusta
†Bolick, Jan Marie *art educator*

Great Bend
Nuss, Joanne Ruth *sculptor, artist*

Hays
†Oiler, Dorilou Wemlinger *artist*

Hutchinson
Girst, Jack Alan *computer graphic artist, writer, illustrator*

Lawrence
Dooley, Patrick John *graphic designer, design educator*
Hermes, Marjory Ruth *machine embroidery and arts educator*
†McCrea, Judith *artist, educator*
Pilkington, Jeremy James *graphic designer*
Vaccaro, Nick Dante *painter, educator*

Leawood
Kordash, Dorothy Mae *artist*

Lenexa
Barkley-Lueders, Elaine Kay *production art manager*

Ottawa
Howe, William Hugh *artist*

Overland Park
Hurcomb, Laura Grace *visual artist*

Topeka
Navone, Edward William *artist, educator*
†Taylor, Glend Marie *art educator*

KENTUCKY

Adairville
Lyne, Alison Davis *illustrator*

Bowling Green
†Smith, Malcolm Mobutu *art educator*

Frankfort
†Lanham, Sallie Clay *artist, educator*

Lexington
Gohde, Kurt R.D. *artist*
Sandoval, Arturo Alonzo *art educator, artist*

Louisville
†Fitzpatrick, Joseph Lloveras *artist, art educator*
Leightty, Sharon Howerton *artist, fine arts educator*
Marsh, Virginia Jean *art educator*
Wilson, Melissa Elizabeth *artist, educator*

Paducah
Farr, Warren Earl *artist*

LOUISIANA

Baton Rouge
†Barkemeyer, Marsha D. *artist, educator*

Cecilia
†Girouard, Tina *artist, curator*

Dubach
Guin, Jeffery Keith *graphic designer*

Metairie
Ales, Beverly Gloria Rushing *artist*
Killeen, Edward Joseph *actor, designer*

New Orleans
Bailey, Barry Stone *sculptor, educator*
Best, Susan Marie *artist, educator*
†Gertjejansen, Doyle *artist, educator*
Harshfield, Neil Alan *sculptor, educator*
†Liljeberg, Genevieve Brocato *artist*
Scott, John Tarrell *art educator, sculptor*
Simons, Dona *artist*
Thornell, Jack Randolph *photographer*
Wegmann, Mary Katherine *art director*
Weiss, Susette Marie *technical and photographic consultant, mass communications/media specialist*

Shreveport
Hughes, Mary Sorrows *artist*
Ragland, Preston Lamar *designer, small business owner*
Wray, Geraldine Smitherman (Jerry Wray) *artist*

Thibodaux
Howes, Michael *sculptor, educator*

MAINE

Auburn
Webb, Todd (Charles Clayton Webb) *photographer, writer*

Bar Mills
Buchanan, Bruce *metal artist, photographer*

Blue Hill
Wenglowski, Joyce *painter*

Boothbay Harbor
Cavanaugh, Tom Richard *artist, antiques dealer, retired art educator*
Eames, John Heagan *etcher*

Caribou
Hutcheon, Wilda Vilene Burtchell *artist*

Castine
Mancuso, Leni *artist, poet, educator*

China
†Dwelley, Marilyn Joan *artist*

Cushing
Magee, A. Alan *artist*

Damariscotta
Robinson, Walter George *arts management and funding consultant*

East Boothbay
Peters, Andrea Jean *artist*

Fairfield
†Carpenter, David Ronnie *artist*

Gorham
Bearce, Jeana Dale *artist, educator*

Guilford
Staley, Thomas Eugene *artist*

Jefferson
Fiore, Joseph Albert *artist*

Kennebunk
Betts, Edward *artist*

New Harbor
Lyford, Cabot *sculptor*

Ogunquit
†Nudelman, Stuart *artist, educator*

Port Clyde
Thon, William *artist*

Portland
Ventimiglia, John Thomas *artist, art educator*

Saint George
Bailey, Jonathan E. *photographer*

Sanford
†Trask, James Stephen *artist, forester*

Scarborough
Warg, Pauline *artist, educator*

South Portland
Huntoon, Abby Elizabeth *artist, teacher*
Townshend, Sharon *artist*

Tenants Harbor
Quint-Rose, Marilyn Iris *artist*

Trevett
Mathias, Cordula *art dealer*

Vinalhaven
†Morton, Barbara Murphy *artist*

Wells
Hero, Barbara Ferrell *visual and sound artist, writer*

Wiscasset
Leslie, Seaver *artist*

Yarmouth
†Clark, Gail Theroux *artist*

York
Hallam, Beverly (Beverly Linney) *artist*

MARYLAND

Abingdon
Moore, Brad Elliot *art educator, artist, printmaker*

Annapolis
Alderdice, Cynthia Lou *artist*
Gurlik, Philip John *artist*
Markman, Ronald *artist, educator*

Arnold
†Kolb, Joyce Diana *artist, educator*

Baltimore
Carroll, Karen *art educator*
Fisher, Phoebe Gerber *painter, antique dealer*
Hartigan, Grace *artist*
Kramer, Norma Domenica Andrea *artist*
Miller, Melvin Orville, Jr. *artist*
Norris, Rebecca *design firm executive*
Parsons, Ivy *artist, sculptor, educator*
Rothschild, Amalie Rosenfeld *artist*
Tatum, Arthur, III *educator, lexicographer, pianist*
Zaruba, Allen Scott Harmon *sculptor*

Bethesda
Day, Marylouise Muldoon (Mrs. Richard Dayton Day) *appraiser*
Dox, Ida *artist, medical illustrator*
Elliott, George Armstrong, III *artist, journalist*
†Hughes, Gary L. *artist, sculptor*
Koenig, Elizabeth Barbara *sculptor*
Safer, John *artist, lecturer, banker, real estate developer*
Tanenbaum, Jill Nancy *graphic designer*

California
Dobry, Aliki Calirroe *artist*

Centreville
Amos, James Lysle *photographer*

Chevy Chase
Duvall, Bernice Bettum *artist, exhibit coordinator, jewelry designer*
Kainen, Jacob *artist, former museum curator*
Kranking, Margaret Graham *artist*

Clinton
†Hamilton, Jaqueline Buckner *artist, landscaper*

College Park
DeMonte, Claudia Ann *artist, educator*
Lapinski, Tadeusz Andrew *artist, educator*

Crisfield
†Ryan, Jerome Francis *artist*

Crofton
Andrysiak, Frank Louis *videographer*

Cumberland
†Decosta, Frank *artist*

Denton
Doster, Rose Eleanor Wilhelm *artist*

Glen Echo
Stevenson, A. Brockie *retired artist*

Hagerstown
Paxton, Alice Adams *artist, architect and interior designer*

Kensington
†Banner, Marilyn Ruth *artist, educator*

North East
Marie, Linda *artist, photographer*

Owings Mills
Kissel, William Thorn, Jr. *sculptor*

Oxford
Zachai, Dohrn Dorian *artist*

Perryville
Ciampaglio, Jeff William *sculptor*

Potomac
Keil, Marilyn Martin *artist*

Quantico
Scott, David Winfield *artist, consultant*

Silver Spring
Barkin, Robert Allan *graphic designer, newspaper executive, consultant*
†Golembe, Carla Dru *artist*
Neuhäuser, Mary Helen *artist, writer, playwright*
Peiperl, Adam *kinetic sculptor, photographer*

Towson
Ruppert, John Hutchins *sculptor*

Upper Fairmount
Dougherty, Barbara Lee *artist, writer*

Woodbine
Nuss, Barbara Gough *artist*

MASSACHUSETTS

Allston
†D'Angora, Kendra Marie *artist, preschool educator*

Amherst
Dabrowski, Thaddeus E. *educator, painter*
Hendricks, James Powell *artist*
Lasch, Pat *artist, educator*
Liebling, Jerome *photographer, educator*
Yarde, Richard Foster *art educator*

Belmont
†Pappas, Marilyn R. *art educator*

Beverly
Manheim, Michael Philip *photographer*
Roy, Robert William *artist, educator*

Boston
Ablow, Joseph *artist, educator*
Avison, David *photographer*
Fink, Aaron *artist*
†Gallagher, Ellen *artist*
Gibran, Kahlil *sculptor*
Gold, Gretchen *painter, educator, jeweler*
McDaniel, Joyce L. *artist, educator*
Parker, Olivia *photographer*

Braintree
Conlon, Eugene *artist, administrator*

Brookfield
Couture, Ronald David *art administrator, design consultant*

Brookline
Barron, Ros *artist*
Reingardt, Ragnhild Sigrid Augusta *sculptor, artist*
Rubin-Katz, Barbara *sculptor, human services administrator*
Schiller, Sophie *artist, graphic designer*
Wilson, John *artist*

Burlington
DeCrosta, Susan Elyse *graphic designer*

Cambridge
Ackerman, James Sloss *fine arts educator*
Alcalay, Albert S. *artist, design educator*
Bakanowsky, Louis Joseph *visual arts educator, architect, artist*
Chandler, Fay Martin *artist*
Feininger, Theodore Lux *artist*
Handford, Martin John *illustrator, author*
Hilt, Mary Louise *artist*
Kulikovskaya, Svetlana Romanovna *artist, costume designer, self-employed*
Mazur, Michael *artist*
Mc Kie, Todd Stoddard *artist*
Slosburg-Ackerman, Jill Rose *artist, educator*
†Wodiczko, Krzysztof *artist, architect, educator*

Chilmark
Geyer, Harold Carl *artist, writer*
Low, Joseph *artist*

Concord
Ihara, Michio *sculptor*

East Bridgewater
Heywood, Anne *artist, educator*

East Orleans
Burkert, Robert Randall *artist*

Fall River
†Andrade, Manuela Pestana *art educator*

Framingham
†Aronson, Benjamin *artist*
†Casselman, Frederick Lee *computer artist*

Gloucester
Donnelly, Barbara *artist, educator*

Greenfield
†Young, Thomas Steven *artist, educator*

Harwich
Geberth, Frances White *painter*
†Steward, Aleta Joanna *artist*

Hingham
†Kilroy, John Michael *artist, educator*
Reardon, Mary Agnes *painter, muralist, design consultant*

Hull
Burgess, David Lowry *artist*

Indian Orchard
Warren, Alice Louise *artist*

Leeds
Baskin, Leonard *sculptor, graphic artist*

Lexington
Burwen, Barbara R. *painter*

Littleton
Harland, William Robert, Sr. *painter*

Lynn
Denzler, Nancy J. *artist*
Farris, Robert Harold, Jr. *artist, educator*

Manchester
†St. Clair, Lynn Owen *artist, illustrator*

Marblehead
Heins, Esther *botanical artist, painter*

Marshfield
Arapoff, John Richard *artist*

Marshfield Hills
Krause, Dorothy Simpson *fine artist, educator*

Millers Falls
Ryan, Richard E. *painter*

Nantucket
Devaney, John Goodwin *painter, muralist*
†Sherry, William Joseph, III *sculptor, gallery owner*

Natick
Geller, Esther (Bailey Geller) *artist*
Gregory, John C. *artist, sculptor*
Morgan, Betty Mitchell *artist, educator*

Needham
Carr, Iris Constantine *artist, writer*

Newburyport
Vernon, Alexandra Reiss *artist*

Newton
†Avishai, Susan E. *artist, illustrator*
Masi, Robin *artist, writer, educator*

Newtonville
Polonsky, Arthur *artist, educator*

North Brookfield
Neal, Avon *artist, author*
Parker, Ann (Ann Parker Neal) *photographer, graphic artist, writer*

North Eastham
DeMuth, Vivienne Blake McCandless *artist, illustrator*

North Grafton
†Stokowski, Leonard James *artist*

North Hatfield
†Moser, Arthur Barry *designer, illustrator, educator*

Northampton
Rupp, Sheron Adeline *photographer, educator*

Norwell
Brett, Jan Churchill *illustrator, author*
Wentworth, Murray Jackson *artist, educator*

Oak Bluffs
Hardman, Della Brown Taylor *art educator, retired*

Peabody
Dee, Pauline Marie *artist*

Pittsfield
Adams, Shelby Lee *photographer*

Provincetown
†Black, Constance Jane *artist*
Hutchinson, Peter Arthur *artist*

Rockland
†Crimi, Paul *artist*

Rockport
Calabro, Joanna Joan Sondra *artist*
Mosher, Donald Allen *artist*

Seekonk
Backes, Joan *artist*

Sherborn
Pickhardt, Carl Emile, Jr. *artist*

Somerville
Cooper, Mark Fredrick *artist, sculptor, art educator*
Halevi, Marcus *photographer*
†Taft, Nellie Leaman *artist*
†Valincius, Irene *artist*

Southampton
†Slater, Jess Everett *artist*

Southborough
Gohlke, Frank William *photographer*

Springfield
Frey, Mary Elizabeth *artist*

Stockbridge
†Kalischer, Clemens *photographer*

Sudbury
Aronson, David *artist, retired art educator*

Swansea
Caswell, Sally Ellen *artist, art educator*

Townsend
†Thorpe, Samuel Stanley, Jr. *artist*

Vineyard Haven
McIntosh, Jon Charles *illustrator*

Waltham
†Alexandrov, Simona *artist, art educator, administrator*

Watertown
Kupferman, David Cobb *painter*

Wayland
Dergalis, George *artist, educator*

Wellesley
Fontaine, Eudore Joseph, Jr. *artist, art historian*
McGibbon, Phyllis Isabel *artist, educator*

Wellfleet
Coughlin, Jack *printmaker, sculptor, art educator*
Coughlin, Joan Hopkins *artist, educator*

West Barnstable
Kennedy, Michele Lyn *artist*

West Brookfield
Higgins, Brian Alton *art gallery executive*

West Springfield
Barrientos, Jane Ellen *art educator*

West Stockbridge
Yanoff, Arthur Samuel *artist, art therapist*

Westwood
Philbrick, Margaret Elder *artist*

Williamstown
Hedreen, Guy Michael *art educator*

Winchester
Neuman, Robert Sterling *art educator, artist*

Worcester
Clifford, Jay *artist*

MICHIGAN

Ann Arbor
Cassara, Frank *artist, printmaker*
Cox, Dennis E. *photographer*
Kamrowski, Gerome *artist*
†Keller, Martha Rock *artist, educator*
Mártonyi, Csaba Lászlo *ophthalmic photographer/imager*

Auburn Hills
Mandiberg, David Michael *sculptor*

Beverly Hills
Grey, Joseph Edward, II *artist*

Big Rapids
Barnum, Robert Lyle *artist, art educator*

Birmingham
Ashleigh, Caroline *art and antiques appraiser*
Ortman, George Earl *artist*

Blissfield
†Thompson, Kenneth M. *sculptor, educator*

Bloomfield Hills
Burnett, Patricia Hill *artist, author, sculptor, lecturer*

Bruce Crossing
Waara, Maria Esther *artist*

Caledonia
Duren, Stephen D. *artist*

Capac
Wagner, Dorothy Marie *retired senior creative designer, artist*

Carleton
Falls, Kathleene Joyce *photographer*

Coldwater
Fisher, Estelle Maude *artist*

Dearborn
Cape, James Odies E. *fashion designer*

Deckerville
Jarmolowicz, C. Renee *artist, art educator*

Detroit
Bulka, Douglas Glenn *artist*
Day, Burnis C. *artist, educator*
Kachadoorian, Zubel *artist, educator*
Merriweather, Robert Everett *illustrator*
Mitchell, Peyton Leslie *photographer*
Moldenhauer, Judith A. *graphic design educator*
Schwing, Mark David *artist*

East Lansing
Leepa, Allen *artist, educator*

Farmington Hills
Donald, Edward Milton, Jr. *marketing company executive*

Fort Gratiot
Rowark, Maureen *fine arts photographer*

Grand Rapids
Jackoboice, Sandra Kay *artist*
Kemper, Donna Mae *fine art and layout artist*

Grosse Ile
Stump, M. Pamela *sculptor*

Hillsdale
†Frudakis, Anthony Parker *sculptor, educator*

Holly
Stolpin, William Roger *artist, printmaker, retired engineer*

Houghton
Ex, Tom *sculptor, gallery owner*

Howell
Watkins, Curtis Winthrop *artist*

Jackson
Abbott, Mary Elaine *photographer, lecturer, researcher*

Kalamazoo
Solomon, Paul Robert *artist, educator*
Taylor, Joy Holloway *artist*

Lawton
†Bowman, Jerry Wayne *artist, research scientist*

Mount Pleasant
Traines, Rose Wunderbaum *sculptor, educator*

Oak Park
Smith, Nelson David *artist educator*

Olivet
Stevens, Charlotte Whitney *artist, retired art educator*

Orchard Lake
Maniscalco, Joseph *artist, educator*

Petoskey
Switzer, Carolyn Joan *artist, educator*

Plainwell
Flower, Jean Frances *art educator*

Plymouth
Heitman, Susan Marie *artist*

Pontiac
†Brychtova, Jaroslava *sculptor*

Riverdale
Kirby, Kent Bruce *artist, educator*

Roseville
Geck, Francis Joseph *furniture designer, educator, author*

Sparta
Stevens, Richard *visual artist*

Warren
Barr, David John *artist, educator*

Wyandotte
†Croci, Mary Ellen *artist, mental health specialist*
Dunn, Gloria Jean *artist*

MINNESOTA

Arden Hills
Alexander, Marjorie Anne *artist, hand papermaker, art consultant*

Clarkfield
Richter, Franz Allbert *artist, historian*

Duluth
Chee, Cheng-Khee *artist*
Ojard, Bruce Allen *photographer, educator*

Excelsior
†Oas, Joan Margaret *artist*

Frazee
Ulmer, James Howard *potter*

Glenwood
Olson, Nancy Ann *artist, educator*

Harmony
Webster, Jeffrey Leon *graphic designer*

International Falls
Westphal, Rolf Werner *sculptor, educator*

Inver Grove Heights
†Blaisdell, Elena Marie Marmo *artist, printer*

Minneapolis
Bleeker, Bernard Martin *designer, graphic*
†Bougie, Peter John *artist, educator*
Hallman, Gary L. *photographer, educator*
Innmon, (Tara) Arlene Katherine *artist, dancer, writer, storyteller, healer*
Jirka, Brad Paul *sculptor, art educator*
†Jonsson, Egil Sigurd *artist*
Larkin, Eugene David *artist, educator*
Myers, Malcolm Haynie *artist, art educator*
Pollock, Tony Joe *graphic designer, writer*
Preuss, Roger E(mil) *artist*
Rich, David *visual artist*
Rose, Thomas Albert *artist, art educator*
†Sagar, Michal *art educator, artist*
Weinberger, Adrienne *artist, appraiser*

Minnetonka
La Liberte, Ann Gillis *graphic artist, consultant, designer, educator*

Monticello
Ingeman, Jerry Andrew *artist*

Northfield
Lloyd, Timothy Lee *art educator*

Saint Joseph
Gordin, Misha *photographer*

Saint Paul
Anderson, Kurt Lewis *artist*
Matteson, Clarice Chris *artist, educator*
Tylevich, Alexander V. *sculptor, architect, educator*

MISSISSIPPI

Belzoni
Halbrook, Rita Robertshaw *artist, sculptor*

Jackson
Wolfe, Mildred Nungester *artist*

Pascagoula
Smith, Donald Vaughan *artist, educator*

University
Shelnutt, Gregory William *sculptor, educator*

MISSOURI

Blue Springs
†Rice, Durwin Dan *artist, art dealer*

Bourbon
Heitsch, Leona Mason *artist, writer*

Chesterfield
Morse, Stacey Ann *art studio owner*

Columbia
Larson, Sidney *art educator, artist, writer, painting conservator*
Robins, Betty Dashew *antiques and arts dealer*
Stack, Frank Huntington *painter, educator*
Zemke, Deborah Esther *illustrator*

Des Peres
Mason, Jane Musselman *artist*

Hermann
Mahoney, Catherine Ann *artist, educator*

Jefferson City
Craver, Charles Henry *illustrator*

Kansas City
Arnold, Kathryn *artist, educator*
Boyer, Helen King *artist*
Lee, Margaret Norma *artist*
Mast, Kande White *artist*
Schnell, Shirley Luke *art educator*
Verbeek-Cowart, Pauline M. *textile designer, educator*

Kirksville
Adkins, Dean Phillip *painter*

Lewistown
Terpening, Virginia Ann *artist*

Liberty
†Bortko, Daniel John *photographer, educator*

Licking
White, Charles McBride *sculptor*

Nevada
Brown, Fermon *photographer, advertising professional*

Osage Beach
Orr, Rita Hope *artist*

Parkville
Pettes, Robert Carlton *artist*

Saint Charles
Eckert, William Dean *retired educator, artist*

Saint Louis
Burkett, Randy James *lighting designer*
Carter, Carol *artist, educator*
Duhme, H(erman) Richard, Jr. *sculptor, educator*
Dunivent, John Thomas *artist, educator*
†Flavin, D. Aeschliman *artist, lecturer, educator*
Fondaw, Ronald Edward *artist, educator*
†Hansman, Robert G. *art educator, artist*
Kodner, Martin *art dealer, consultant*
Kunc, Karen *artist, educator*
Levi, Hans Leopold *artist, educator*
Lipan, Petruta E. *artist, curator, semiotician*
Ott, Sabina *art educator*
Sago, Janis Lynn *photography educator*
Stanton, Frank Lawrence, Jr. *graphic designer, illustrator, educator*
†Ward-Brown, Denise *sculptor, educator*

Sikeston
†Schuchart, Ann Murphy *artist, educator*

Springfield
†Lin, Zhi *art educator*
Thompson, Wade S. *artist, art and design educator*

Webster Groves
Osver, Arthur *artist*

MONTANA

Bozeman
Buck, John E. *sculptor, print maker, educator*
Selyem, Bruce Jade *photographer*

Hot Springs
Erickson, James Gardner *retired artist, cartoonist*

Kalispell
von Krenner, Walther G. *artist, writer, art consultant and appraiser*

Miles City
†Larson, Gene L. *illustrator*

Missoula
Morin, Paula Marie Yvette (Maryan Morin) *photographer, artist, photo researcher*
Rippon, Thomas Michael *art educator, artist*

Whitefish
†Fielder, Maryann *artist, consultant*

NEBRASKA

Chadron
Hazen, Vincent Allan *painter, printmaker*

Crete
†Martin, Gary John *art educator, artist*

Lincoln
Brownson, Elwyn James *artist, educator, art therapist*
Neal, Mo (P. Maureen Neal) *sculptor*
Rogge, Kathleen Ruth *domestic engineer, art educator*
Rowan, C. Patrick *art educator*

Mc Cook
Dernovich, Donald Frederick *artist, educator*

Omaha
Burkholder, Roger Glenn *artist, author*
Golden, Dona Lee *artist*
Seng, Jeffrey Frazier *artist, poet*

Plattsmouth
Ellington, Carol J. *artist, printmaker*

NEVADA

Henderson
Hara-Isa, Nancy Jeanne *graphic designer, county official*

Las Vegas
Gideon-Hawke, Pamela Lawrence *fine arts small business owner*
Goldblatt, Hal Michael *photographer, accountant*

Reno
Albrecht, Carol Heath *artist, educator*
Goin, Peter Jackson *art educator*
Hilts, Ruth *artist*
Newberg, Dorothy Beck (Mrs. William C. Newberg) *portrait artist*
Waddell, Theodore *painter*

NEW HAMPSHIRE

Bennington
Willis, Barbara Florence *artist*
Willis, Sidney Frank *artist, educator*

Concord
†Raskin, Joy Lynn *art educator, silversmith*

Dover
Casey, Kimberlyn Lorettre *artist, painter, educator*
Mitchell, William Clark *printmaker, graphic artist*

Exeter
Dailey, Daniel Owen *artist, educator, designer*

Gorham
Robitaille, Paul Réne *photographer*

Hampstead
Bolton, (Margaret) Elizabeth *artist, poet*

Hancock
Pollaro, Paul Philip *artist*

Hanover
Boghosian, Varujan Yegan *sculptor*
Moss, Ben Frank, III *art educator, painter*

New London
Bott, John Crist *artist, educator*

Plaistow
Collins, James Francis *wildlife artist*

Winchester
Tandy, Jean Conkey *art educator*

Wolfeboro
Bonin, Suzanne Jean *artist*

NEW JERSEY

Absecon
†Sweeten, E. Marshall *lighting designer*

Asbury
Konrad, Adolf Ferdinand *artist*

Avenel
†Appezzato, Marc Robert *graphic artist*

Barnegat Light
Smith, Gail Hunter *artist*

Bayonne
Gorman, William David *artist, graphic artist*
McMahon, Eileen Marie *artist's agent*
Searle, Ronald *artist*

Bernardsville
Spofford, Sally (Hyslop) *artist*

Blairstown
Bean, Bennett *artist*

Browns Mills
DeWitt, Edward Frances *artist*

Califon
Rosen, Carol Mendes *artist*

Cliffside Park
†Hayes, Michael *artist, editor*

Colonia
Wiesenfeld, Bess Gazevitz *interior designer, real estate developer*

Cranford
†Casale, Paul Joseph *illustrator*

Cresskill
Smyth, Craig Hugh *fine arts educator*

Edison
†Arakawa, Peter Stanhope *artist, educator*
Behr, Marion Ray *artist, author, business executive*
Wendel, Christopher Mark *exhibition designer*

Englewood
Anuszkiewicz, Richard Joseph *artist*

Ewing
Sanders, Philip F., Jr. *artist, computer art educator*

Fair Lawn
Parker, Adrienne Natalie *art educator, art historian*

Fairfield
de Smet, Lorraine May *artist*

Franklin Lakes
Baker, Cornelia Draves *artist*

Freehold
Flynn, Pamela *artist, educator*

Hammonton
Grefe, Bruce Paul *art educator, artist*

Hazlet
Wunsch, Anna Catherine Mary O'Brien Horton *artist, consultant*

Hightstown
Howard, Barbara Sue Mesner *artist*

Hoboken
Forman, Robert *painter*

Iselin
Tice, George A(ndrew) *photographer*

Jersey City
Carmi, Giora *illustrator*
Gurevich, Grigory *visual artist, educator*

Keasbey
Hari, Kenneth Stephen *painter, sculptor, writer*

Lebanon
Svoboda, Joanne Dzitko *artist, educator*

Long Branch
Stamaty, Clara Gee Kastner *artist*

Mahwah
Patten, Eileen Dunlevy *fine art consultant, public relations consultant*

Mendham
Smith, Elizabeth *artist*

Mercerville
Reiley, Matthew Canney *sculptor*

Middletown
Craney, Rose Stigliano *artist, sculptor*

Milford
Carter, Clarence Holbrook *artist*

Montclair
Beerman, Miriam *artist, educator*

Morristown
Prince, Leah Fanchon *art educator and research institute administrator*

New Brunswick
Goffen, Rona *art educator*
Ortiz, Raphael Montañez *performance artist, educator*
Spencer, J. Ken *artist*

Newark
D'Astolfo, Frank Joseph *graphic designer*

Newton
Dagley, Mark *artist*

Oakland
†Dressel, Margaret Jane *artist, art educator*

Orange
†Juliano, Kathryn Marie *artist*
Lewis, Peter Wayne *art educator, painter*

Park Ridge
De Pol, John *artist*

Pemberton
Witkin, Isaac *sculptor*

Piscataway
Rosalsky, Barbara Ellen *artist, home health aide*

Princeton
†Benarde, Anita E. *artist*
Bunnell, Peter Curtis *photography and art educator, museum curator*
†Diller, Elizabeth E. *artist, educator*
George, Thomas *artist*
Grabar, Oleg *art educator*
Seawright, James L., Jr. *sculptor, educator*
†Treves, George David *graphic artist*
Wilmerding, John *art history educator, museum curator*

River Vale
Peleg, Ephraim *sculptor*
Sommerhoff, Herrat H. *painter, educator*

Rockleigh
Heslin, Cathleen Jane *artist, designer, entrepreneur*

Roosevelt
Landau, Jacob *artist*

Rutherford
Petrie, Ferdinand Ralph *illustrator, artist*

Somerset
†Tarantino, Vera Dean *art educator*
Young, James Earl *ceramics educator, educational administrator*

South Bound Brook
Weir, Sonja Ann *artist*

Springfield
DeVone, Denise *artist, educator*
Marino, Natalie Marie *artist*

Stillwater
Finkelstein, Louis *retired art educator*

Stockton
Mahon, Robert *photographer*
Schoenherr, John (Carl) *artist, illustrator*
Taylor, Rosemary *artist*

Summit
Rousseau, Irene Victoria *artist, sculptor*

Teaneck
Indick, Janet *sculptor, educational administrator*

Tenafly
Koons, Irvin Louis *design and marketing executive, graphic artist, consultant*

Toms River
Cattani, Dante Thomas *artist, art teacher, writer*

Trenton
Sakson, Robert George *artist*
Weld, Alison Gordon *artist, contemporary art curator*

Union
Korn, Neal Mark *painter, art educator*

Ventnor City
Robbins, Hulda Dornblatt *artist, printmaker*

Verona
Ayaso, Manuel *artist*

Wayne
Cetrulo, Jerry *sculptor*
Katz, Leandro *artist, filmmaker*

West Caldwell
Trozzi, Patricia Lynn *graphic artist*

West Orange
Schreiber, Eileen Sher *artist*

West Paterson
St. John, Catherine *painter*
Seiffer, Neil Mark *photographer*

Whippany
Petitto, Barbara Buschell *artist*

Whitehouse Station
Harvey Gibbs, Jane *graphic designer*

Woodbridge
†Nagy-Hartnack, Lois Ann *art educator*
†Scolamiero, Peter *retired artist*

NEW MEXICO

Albuquerque
Adams, Clinton *artist, historian*
Antreasian, Garo Zareh *artist, lithographer, art educator*
Aubin, Barbara Jean *artist*
Barrow, Thomas Francis *artist, educator*
Barry, Steve *sculptor, educator*
Cia, Manuel Lopez *artist*
Coleman, Barbara McReynolds *artist*
Culpepper, Mabel Claire *artist*
Dunn, Dennis Steven *artist, illustrator*
Easley, Loyce Anna *painter*
Green, Mae Maera *artist*
Hovel, Esther Harrison *art educator*
Humphries, Sandra Lee Forger *artist, teacher*
Keating, David *photographer*
Lee-Smith, Hughie *artist, educator*
Multhaup, Merrel Keyes *artist*
Nagatani, Patrick Allan Ryoichi *artist, art educator*
†Nevin, Jean Shaw *artist*
Pritchard, Betty Jean *art educator*
Townsend, Alvin Neal *artist*
Weems, Mary Ann *art gallery owner*
Witkin, Joel-Peter *photographer*

Alto
Zeitelhack, Gloria Jeanne *artist*

Arroyo Hondo
Davis, Ronald *artist, printmaker*

Gallup
Cattaneo, Jacquelyn Annette Kammerer *artist, educator*

Hobbs
Garey, Patricia Martin *artist*

Jemez Springs
Bennett, Noël *artist, author*

Las Cruces
Perroni, Carol *artist, painter*
Ritter, Sallie *painter, sculptor*

Los Alamos
Sarracino, Margaret C. *artist*

Navajo
†Boomer, John D. *artist, sculptor*

Nogal
Moeller, Susan Elaine *artist*

Ranchos De Taos
Marx, Nicki Diane *sculptor, painter*

Rio Rancho
Duitman, Lois Robinson *artist, writer*
Warder, William *artist*

Rociada
Reed, Carol Louise *designer*

Roswell
Wiggins, Kim Douglas *artist, art dealer*

Santa Fe
Adams, Phoebe *sculptor*
Allen, Page Randolph *artist*
Allen, Terry *artist*
Bauer, Betsy (Elizabeth Bauer) *artist*
Clift, William Brooks, III *photographer*
Dechert, Peter *photographer, writer, foundation administrator*
†Jackson, Polly *artist*
LeRose, Thomas M. *photographer*
Lindsay, Richard Paul *artist, jewelry designer*
Longley, Bernique *artist, painter, sculptor*
†Racuya-Robbins, Ann Elizabeth *artist*
Randolph, Somers *sculptor*
Shubart, Dorothy Louise Tepfer *artist, educator*
Stedman, Myrtle Lillian *artist*

Taos
Bell, Larry Stuart *artist*
†Grunthal, Donna Marie *art gallery executive, artist*
Manzo, Anthony Joseph *painter*
Martin, Agnes *artist*
Scott, Doug *sculptor*

Tesuque
Novak, Joe *artist*

NEW YORK

Accord
Ryan, Michael Paul *artist*

Afton
Schwartz, Aubrey Earl *artist*

Albany
Herrick, Kristine Ford *graphic design educator*
Lawton, Nancy *artist*
Shankman, Gary Charles *art educator*

Albion
†Bannister, Richard D *sculptor*

Alfred
Billeci, Andre George *art educator, sculptor*
Higby, (Donald) Wayne *artist, educator*

Ancramdale
Weinstein, Joyce *artist*

Ardsley
†Fasanella, Ralph P. *artist*
Sokolow, Isobel Folb *sculptor*

Armonk
Elson, Charles *stage designer, educator*

Babylon
Haley, Priscilla Jane *artist, printmaker*

Bayside
Adoquei, Sam *art educator, artist*
Lee, Long Looi *artist*

Bearsville
Sands, Martha Mercer (Nichole René) *artist, musician, performing artist, poet*
Szyszka, Roswita Evelyn *artist*

Bedford Hills
Jensen-Carter, Philip Scott *advertising and architectural photographer, medical photographer*

Bellport
†Trahan, Janet Marie *artist, gallery owner*

Bloomington
Ruffing, Anne Elizabeth *artist*

Bridgehampton
Jackson, Lee *artist*

Bronx
Adams, Alice *sculptor*
Behnken, William Joseph *art educator, artist*
†Brickner, Alice *painter, illustrator*

Gerardi, Joan Lois *art educator*
Gonzalez, Rose A-Navarro *artist*
Kassoy, Hortense (Honey Kassoy) *artist, sculptor, painter, printmaker*
Kitt, Olga *artist*
Schwam, Marvin Albert *graphic design company executive*

Brooklyn
Allman, Avis Asiye *artist, poet, Turkish and Islamic culture educator*
Amendola, Sal John *artist, educator, writer*
Amy, Michaël Jacques *art historian, educator, art critic*
Azank, Roberto *artist*
Carlile, Janet Louise *artist, educator*
Daley, Sandra *retired artist, filmmaker, photographer*
Del Rosario, Mariano Boras, Jr. *artist*
Del Valle, Cezar Jose *artist, writer, theatre historian*
Diamond, Jessica *artist*
Dinnerstein, Harvey *artist*
Dinnerstein, Simon Abraham *artist, educator*
Evans, Garth *artist, educator*
Fisher, Joel Anthony *sculptor*
Gabris, George Steven *sculptor, welder*
†Giusti, Karin F. *artist, educator*
Grado, Angelo John *artist*
Haum, Barbara Rose *artist, researcher*
Hazlitt, Donald Robert *artist*
Hoepfner, Karla Jean *designer, artist*
Jones, Susan Emily *fashion educator, administrator, educator*
Kemp, James William *graphic artist*
Kjok, Solveig *artist, art historian, linguist*
Lederman, Stephanie Brody *artist*
Marcano, Soraya *visual artist*
Mehlman, Ronald Walter *sculptor, educator*
†Neal, Florence Arthur *artist*
†Neill, Margaret Ann *artist, writer*
†Otterness, Tom *artist*
Pearlstein, Seymour *artist*
Peker, Elya Abel *artist*
Pitynski, Andrzej Piotr *sculptor*
Plaut, Jane Margaret *art educator*
Rocco, Ron *artist*
Schaefer, Marilyn Louise *artist, writer, educator*
Shechter, Ben-Zion *artist, illustrator*
Shechter, Laura Judith *artist*
Silverstein, Louis *art director, designer, editor*
Sonenberg, Jack *artist*
von Rydingsvard, Ursula Karoliszyn *sculptor*
Zakanitch, Robert Rahway *artist*
Zhang, Berni *painter*
†Zweig, Janet *artist, sculptor*

Buffalo
Berlyn, Sheldon *art educator*
Henrich, Jean MacKay *painter, sculptor, educator*
Kazmierczak, Elzbieta Teresa *graphic designer, illustrator, educator, semiotician*
Rogovin, Milton *documentary photographer, retired optometrist*

Buskirk
Johanson, Patricia Maureen *artist, architect, park designer*

Campbell Hall
Greenly, Colin *artist*

Canaan
†Knebel, Constance *potter, ceramicist*
Walker, William Bond *painter, retired librarian*

Catskill
Howie, Philip Wesley *sculptor*

Central Square
BuMann, Sharon Ann *sculptor*

Clarence
Hubler, Julius *artist*

Climax
Adler, Lee *artist, educator, marketing executive*

Corning
Buechner, Thomas Scharman *artist, retired glass manufacturing company executive, museum director*

Cornwall On Hudson
Abrams-Collens, Vivien *artist*

Cortlandt Manor
Rosenberg, Marilyn Rosenthal *artist, visual poet*

Cross River
Kelsey, Sterett-Gittings *sculptor*

Croton On Hudson
Rubinfien, Leo H. *photographer, filmmaker*

Cutchogue
Strimban, Robert *graphic designer*

Denver
Koutroulis, Aris George *artist, educator*

Dix Hills
Pugliese, Paul Jones *cartographer*

East Hampton
Jaudon, Valerie *artist*
Petersen, Ellen Anne *artist*
Scott, Rosa Mae *artist, educator*
Stein, Ronald Jay *artist, airline transport pilot*

East Herkimer
Kroft, Glenn Vincent *painter*

East Islip
Rogers, Jeanne Valerie *art educator, artist*

East Northport
†Meares, Elsi Junas *artist*

East Setauket
Badalamenti, Fred Leopoldo *artist, educator*

Notarbartolo, Albert *artist*
Ohlson, Douglas Dean *artist*
Okuhara, Tetsu *artist, photographer*
Oldenburg, Claes Thure *artist*
Oldham, Todd *fashion designer*
Olitski, Jules *artist*
Olivere, Raymond Louis *illustrator, artist, portrait painter*
Ono, Yoko *conceptual artist, singer, recording artist*
†Opie, Catherine *photographer*
†Orozco, Gabriel *artist*
†Osorio, Pepon *artist*
Pace, Stephen Shell *artist, educator*
Park, Chung *painter, educator, computer software developer*
Parker, Nancy Winslow *artist, writer*
Pavone, Joseph Anthony *designer, display*
†Pearson, Bruce *artist*
Pearson, Henry Charles *artist*
Peckolick, Alan *graphic designer*
†Perlman, Cara Janet *artist*
Pier, Gwen Marie *art gallery director*
Plavinskaya, Anna Dmitrievna *artist*
Poons, Larry *artist*
Porter, Liliana Alicia *artist, photographer, painter, print and filmaker*
†Prieto, Monique N. *artist*
Quackenbush, Robert Mead *artist, author, psychoanalyst*
Rabinowitch, David George *sculptor*
Rada, George Andrew *painter*
Radunsky, Alexander *designer, lighting*
Rankin-Smith, Pamela *photographer*
Rauschenberg, Robert *artist*
Reddy, Krishna Narayana *artist, educator*
Reiback, Earl Martin *artist*
Reininghaus, Ruth *artist*
Remington, Deborah Williams *artist*
Resika, Paul *artist*
Richter, Gerhard *artist*
Ringgold, Faith *artist*
Rivelli, William Raymond Allan *photographer*
Rivers, Larry *artist*
Robb, Carole *artist*
Rodriguez, Geno (Eugene Rodriguez) *artist, arts administrator*
†Romberg, Osvaldo *artist*
†Rose, Aaron *artist*
Rose, Leatrice *artist, educator*
†Rosenberg, Alex Jacob *art dealer, curator, fine arts appraiser, educator*
Rosenhouse, Irwin J. *artist, designer*
Rosenthal, Tony (Bernard) *sculptor*
Ross, Charles *artist*
Ross, John T. *artist, educator*
Ruscha, Edward *artist*
Rushefsky, Steven *graphic artist*
Ryman, Robert Tracy *artist*
St. Clair, Michael *art dealer*
Santlofer, Jonathan *artist, educator*
Sassoon, Countess Ingrid Anny von Siemering Shuenemann de Gehrs *writer, illustrator, graphic artist, educator*
Schapiro, Miriam *artist*
Schneider, JoAnne *artist*
Schneider, Martin Aaron *photojournalist, filmmaker, public advocate*
Schwartz, Daniel Bennett *artist*
Seborovski, Carole *artist*
Segal, George *sculptor*
Seidler, Sheldon *graphic designer, art director, inventor, educator, painter, sculptor*
Seldin, Penny G. *creative director, artist*
Seliger, Mark Alan *photographer*
Seltzer, Joanne Lynn *artist*
Serrano, Andres *artist*
†Shambroom, Paul *artist, photographer*
Shapiro, Ellen M. *graphic designer, writer, inventor*
Shapiro, Joel Elias *artist*
Sharp, Anne Catherine *artist, educator*
Shaw, (George) Kendall *artist, educator*
Sherin, Robin *artist*
Sherman, Cindy *artist*
Shulman, Mildred *artist, inventor*
Sigal-Ibsen, Rose *artist*
†Sikander, Shahzia *artist*
Silverman, Burton Philip *artist*
Simonds, Charles Frederick *artist*
Singer, Barbara Helen *photographer*
Sis, Peter *illustrator, children's book author, artist, filmmaker*
Sisson, H. Michael *graphic designer, marketing professional*
Skupinski, Bogdan Kazimierz *artist*
Slavin, Arlene *artist*
Slavin, Neal *photographer*
Sleigh, Sylvia *artist, educator*
Slone, Sandi *artist*
Slothower, Dena Natalie *art educator*
†Smith, Kiki *artist*
†Smith, Phil Denise *artist, writer, art dealer*
Smith, Shirley *artist*
Smith, Vincent DaCosta *artist*
Snider, Stephen William *art director, graphic designer*
†Soldwedel, Kipp *fine arts painter, founder, president*
Solman, Joseph *artist*
Sonneman, Eve *artist*
Sopanen, Jeri Rainer *photography director*
Southworth, Linda Jean *artist, critic, educator, poet*
Sperakis, Nicholas George *artist*
Starr, Steven Dawson *photographer*
Sterling, David Mark *graphic designer*
Sterrett, Jane Evelyne *illustrator, artist*
†Stewart, Allison Dean *artist, editor*
Stiebel, Gerald Gustave *art dealer*
Stine, Catherine Morris *artist*
Storrs, Immi Casagrande *sculptor*
Strang, John *association executive*
†Sui, Anna *fashion designer*
Sullivan, Jim *artist*
†Sundukov, Alexei *artist*
Surrey, Milt *artist*
Swain, Robert *artist*
Tàpies, Antoni *painter, sculptor*
†Thomasos, Denyse *artist*
Thrall, Donald Stuart *artist*
†Tiravanija, Rirkrit *sculptor*
Tisma, Marija Stevan *artist*
Tooker, George *artist*
Torreano, John Francis *painter, sculptor*
Trakas, George *sculptor*
Trigere, Pauline *fashion designer*
Tscherny, George *graphic designer*
Uehling, Judith Olson *artist, painter, printmaker, sculptor*
Upright, Diane Warner *art dealer*
Vass, Joan *fashion designer*
Vicente, Esteban *artist*
†Villarreal, Raul *artist, graphic designer*
Vitorovic, Nadezda *artist, poet*
Viviano, Sam Joseph *illustrator*
Von Ringelheim, Paul Helmut *sculptor*
Wald, Sylvia *artist*
†Walker, Kara *artist*
Walton, Anthony John (Tony Walton) *theater and film designer, book illustrator*
Wechsler, Gil *lighting designer*
Weems, Carrie Mae *photographer*
Weiner, Lawrence Charles *artist*
Weitz, John *designer, writer*
†Wels, D. (Deborah Wels) *artist, educator*
Wenegrat, Saul S. *arts administrator, art educator, consultant*
Weschler, Anita *sculptor, painter*
Wesley, John Mercer *artist*
White, Alexander William *graphic designer, educator*
†Williams, Sue *artist*
†Williamson, Philemona *artist*
Willis, Thornton Wilson *painter*
†Winters, Terry *artist*
Wolins, Joseph *artist*
Wright, Faith-dorian *artist*
Wunderman, Jan Darcourt *artist*
Wurmfeld, Sanford *artist, educator*
Wyeth, James Browning *artist*
York, Richard Travis *art dealer*
Youngerman, Jack *artist, sculptor*
Zimmerman, Kathleen Marie *artist*
Zlowe, Florence Markowitz *artist*
Zuniga, Francisco *sculptor, graphic artist*

Newark
Hughes, Owen Willard *artist*

Newburgh
†Ochs, Richard Wayne *artist, gallery owner*

North Tonawanda
Rusin, Len M. *painter, educator*

Northport
Hohenberger, Patricia Julie *fine arts and antique appraiser, consultant*

Nyack
Vaugel, Martine Olga *sculptor, educator*

Old Chatham
Teng, Juliet *artist*

Oneonta
†Michaelsen, Niels Henrik *painter, illustrator*

Orangeburg
Adams, Barbara *artist, designer*

Orchard Park
Fortunato, Pat Deakin *fine artist*

Oswego
Baitsell, Wilma Williamson *artist, educator, lecturer*
Fox, Michael David *art educator, visual imagist artist*

Owego
McCann, Jean Friedrichs *artist, educator*

Palisades
Knowlton, Grace Farrar *sculptor, photographer, painter*

Peekskill
Shea-Bergeron, Kevin Michael *artist, art therapist*
†Umland, James Frederick *painter*

Piermont
Berkon, Martin *artist*

Pittsford
Majchrzak, David Joseph *artist, printer*

Plainview
Fein, Leona Moss *artist*

Port Jefferson Station
†Pepi, Vincent *artist*

Port Washington
Kossin, Sanford Marshall *illustrator*

Poughkeepsie
Davis, Harvey *commercial photographer, videographer*
†Gesek, Thaddeus *artist*

Pound Ridge
Ferro, Walter *artist*
Schwebel, Renata Manasse *sculptor*

Purchase
Rainer, Renata Urbach *artist, photographer, educator*

Rensselaer
Nack, Claire Durani *artist, author*

Rhinebeck
Rabinovich, Raquel *painter, sculptor*

Riverdale
Greenberg, Arline Francine *artist, photographer*

Rochester
†Dill-Kocher, Laurie *textile artist*
Feuerherm, Kurt Karl *artist, educator*
Lotta, (Anthony) Tom *artist*
Margolis, Richard Martin *photographer, educator*
Merritt, Howard Sutermeister *retired art educator*
Saisselin, Remy Gilbert *fine arts educator*
Yager, William Stewart *sculptor*

Roslyn
Finke, Leonda Froehlich *sculptor*

Roslyn Heights
Newmark, Marilyn *sculptor*

Rye
Lehman, Myra Harriet *sculptor, dental hygienist*
Troller, Fred *graphic designer, painter, visual consultant, educator*

Sagaponack
Butchkes, Sydney *artist*

Saratoga Springs
Upton, Richard Thomas *artist*

Scarsdale
Newman, Stacey Clarfield *artist, curator*
Ries, Martin *artist, educator*

Schenectady
†Blood, Robert Alvin *sculptor*

Shady
Ruellan, Andree *artist*

Shelter Island
Culbertson, Janet Lynn *artist*
Gurevitz, Bernard Herman *painter*

Shelter Island Heights
Slade, Roy *artist, college president, museum director*

Shoreham
Spier, Peter Edward *artist, author*

Slingerlands
Carroll, Corlis Faith *artist*

Snyder
Breverman, Harvey *artist*

Southampton
Kanovitz, Howard *artist*

Sparkill
Myers, Adele Anna *artist, educator, nun*

Staten Island
Hermus, Lance Jay *art appraiser*
Locke Monda, Robin *graphic designer, artist*
Nelson, Carey Boone *sculptor*

Sterling
Seawell, Thomas Robert *artist, retired educator*

Stony Brook
Pekarsky, Melvin Hirsch *artist*
Pindell, Howardena Doreen *artist*

Sugar Loaf
Endico, Mary Antoinette *artist*

Syracuse
McCoubrey, Sarah *artist and art educator*
Thomas, Sidney *fine arts educator, researcher*

Tappan
Dell, Robert Christopher *geothermal sculptor, scenic artist*
Nickford, Juan *sculptor, educator*

Tivoli
Schade, Arthur George *sculptor, educator*

Troy
Hampshire, John Carr, III *artist, educator*

Tuxedo Park
Domjan, Joseph (Spiri Domjan) *artist*

Utica
Gape, Serafina Vetrano *decorative artist and designer*
Labuz, Ronald Matthew *design educator*
Pribble, Easton *artist*

Valley Cottage
Greene, Stephen *painter*
Shaderowfsky, Eva Maria *photographer, writer, computer specialist*

Wading River
Marlow, Audrey Swanson *artist, designer*

Wainscott
Russo, Alexander Peter *artist, educator*

Walden
Hraniotis, Judith Beringer *artist*

Wallkill
Koch, Edwin Ernest *artist, interior decorator*

Wantagh
Glaser, David *painter, sculptor*
Urbaitis, Elena *artist*

Warwick
Franck, Frederick Sigfred *artist, author, dental surgeon*

Westbury
Barboza, Anthony *photographer, artist*
Sherbell, Rhoda *artist, sculptor*

White Plains
Erla, Karen *artist, painter, collagist, printmaker*

Williamsville
Whitcomb, James Stuart *videographer, photographer, production company executive*

Woodhaven
Zizi *artist*

Woodstock
Banks, Rela *sculptor*
Currie, Bruce *artist*
†Hahne Hofsted, Janet Lorraine *artist*
†Hamel, Manette C. *artist, writer*

Yonkers
O'Donnell, Robert George *fine artist*

Yorktown Heights
Jones, Lauretta Marie *artist, graphic designer, computer interface designer*

NORTH CAROLINA

Asheville
Allen, Heather Lindsey *textile artist, art educator, writer*
†Chapman, Gary H. *artist, educator*
Jones, J. Kenneth *art dealer, former museum administrator*
Levin, Robert Alan *glass artist*

Brevard
Murray, Douglas Timothy *sculptor, art educator*

Burnsville
Bernstein, William Joseph *glass artist, educator*
Doyle, John Lawrence *artist*

Carrboro
Anderson, Arthur Lee *sculptor, writer*

Chapel Hill
Brown, Mark Walden *artist*
Hirschfield, Jim *artist, educator*
McKay, Renee *artist*
Murphy, Dan *sculptor*
Stipe, Robert Edwin *design educator*

Charlotte
Chaikin, Alyce *artist*
Reed, Rita *artist*
†Strawn, Martha Ann *art educator, photographer*
Triplette, Laurance Daltroff *art advisor and appraiser*

Clarkton
Wuebbels, Theresa Elizabeth *visual art educator*

Davidson
Jackson, Herb *artist, educator*

Durham
Cooley, Jacob Alan *painter*

Franklin
Judernatz, Mary Seegers *artist*

Greensboro
Ananian, Michael Fred *artist*
Barker, Walter William, Jr. *artist, educator*
†Gaucher, Kim Elizabeth *artist, art director*

Greenville
Wallin, Leland Dean *artist, educator*

Hillsborough
†Fantazos, Henryk Michael *painter, graphic artist*

Kings Mountain
†Snow, Alice M. *artist*

Landis
Lynch, Samuel Curlee, Jr. (Sir Sami Lynch) *painter, sculptor, writer*

Leasburg
Treacy, Sandra Joanne Pratt *art educator, artist*

Lenoir
Michaux, Henry Gaston *art educator*

Lewisville
Desley, John Whitney *medical illustrator*

Newport
Burge, Larry Brady *artist*

Penland
†Schulman, Norman *artist*

Raleigh
†Gomez, Andrea Hope *artist*

Sanford
Higgins, George Edward *sculptor*

Tyner
Sams, Robin Dahl *artist*

Valdese
Atkin, Andrew Scott *artist*

Waynesville
Nickerson, John Henry *artist, sculptor, designer*

Weaverville
Kledis, Jarel Emanuel *sculptor*

Whitsett
Fennell, Richard Arthur *artist*

Winston Salem
Faccinto, Victor Paul *artist, gallery administrator*
†Lubin, David Martin *art and American studies educator*

NORTH DAKOTA

Grand Forks
Owens, Morgan Kasian *painter*

Jamestown
†Cox, Sharon G. *art educator*

Mandan
Hodge, Ann Linton *artist*

Richardton
Miller, Jean Patricia Salmon *art educator*

OHIO

Akron
†Borowiec, Andrew *art educator, photographer*
Keener, Polly Leonard *illustrator*

Athens
Boothe, Power *visual artist, filmmaker, set designer*
†Parkinson, Sharran Fell *design educator*

Aurora
Lawton, Florian Kenneth *artist, educator*

Beavercreek
†McCullough, Margie Lu *artist*

Bowling Green
Ocvirk, Otto George *artist*

Canton
Strauss, John Leonard *artist*

Chesterland
†Wood, Kenneth Anderson *artist, designer, consultant*

Cincinnati
Brod, Stanford *graphic designer, educator*
Daniels, Astar *artist*
Knipschild, Robert *artist, educator*
Rexroth, Nancy Louise *photographer*
Smittle, Nelson Dean *artist*
Sullivan, Connie Castleberry *artist, photographer*
Weston, Phyllis Jean *art gallery director*
Wygant, Foster Laurance *art educator*

Cleveland
†Beckwith, Karen Danette *artist, printer*
Cassill, Herbert Carroll *artist*
Deming, David Lawson *art educator*
Zurawski, Dale L. *art director, graphic designer, illustrator*

Columbus
Black, David Evans *sculptor, painter*
†Gall, Linda Lee *artist, administrator*
Gilliom, Bonnie Lee *arts educator, consultant*
Goff, Wilmer Scott *photographer*
Jung, Diana Lynn *graphic designer*
†Lewis, Sharon Kay *artist, craftsman*
McGuire, Mark Joseph *graphic designer, art educator*
Roth, Susan King *design educator*
Simson, Bevlyn *artist*
Sunami, John Soichi *designer*
Ultes, Elizabeth Cummings Bruce *artist, retired art historian and librarian*
†Wong, Albert Y. *artist*

Coshocton
Parkhill, Harold Loyal *artist*

Cuyahoga Falls
Ohm, Joseph Ronald *industrial designer*

Dayton
Laird, John *photographer*
Wilkins, John *graphic designer*
Zahner, Mary Anne *art educator*

Hamilton
†Jones, Rick H. *arts administrator*

Hilliard
Cupp, David Foster *photographer, journalist*

Kent
Kwong, Eva *artist, educator*

Kimbolton
†Thomas, Richard Duane *artist*

LaGrange
Kaatz, Lynn Robert *artist, graphic designer*

Lakewood
Smith, Marvin D. *artist*

Loveland
Newton, Baldwin Charles *artist, educator*

Massillon
Lawrence, Alice Lauffer *artist, educator*

Masury
Wagner, Julie Ann *newspaper designer*

Miamisburg
Michaelis, Betty Jane *sculptor, retired small business owner*

New Carlisle
Bowlin, Gloria Jean *artist*

New Richmond
Scott, Michael Lester *artist, educator*

North Canton
Rodriguez, Irene Tobias *artist, art educator*

Oberlin
Reinoehl, Richard Louis *artist, scholar, martial artist*

Okeana
Bloch, Rosemarie *artist, musician*

Oxford
†Ewing, Susan R. *artist, educator*

Pepper Pike
Fallon, Pat *artist, art educator*
Rule-Hoffman, Richard Carl *art therapist, educator, counselor*

Perrysburg
Autry, Carolyn *artist, art history educator*

Reynoldsburg
Boiman, Donna Rae *artist, art academy executive*

Salem
†Babb, Elizabeth *artist, graphic artist*

Sandusky
†Rothermel, Joan Ashley *artist*

Seven Hills
Stanczak, Julian *artist, educator*

Shaker Heights
Held, Lila M. *art appraiser*

Springfield
Patterson, Martha Ellen *artist, art educator*

Toledo
Brower, James Calvin *graphic artist, painter*
Cousino, Joe Ann *sculptor*
Khan, Munawwar Jehan (Meena) *librarian, investor*
McGlauchlin, Tom *artist*
Nordin, Phyllis Eck *sculptor, painter, consultant*

Twinsburg
†Spagg, Jim *artist*

Urbana
Bronkar, Eunice Dunalee *artist, art educator*

Wadsworth
Neumann, Jeffrey Jay *photographer, minister*

Wakeman
Krupp, Barbara D. *artist*

West Alexandria
†Sappington, Lynda Louisa Burton *artist*

Yellow Springs
Hudson, Jon Barlow *sculptor*

Youngstown
Zordich, Steve *retired art educator, artist*

Zanesville
Westgerdes, Gerald Lee *sculptor, art educator*

OKLAHOMA

Broken Arrow
†Byarse, Anthony *artist*

Chickasha
Brown, Steven L. *art educator*
Good, Leonard Phelps *artist*

Midwest City
Gonzalez, Richard Theodore *photographer*

Norman
Day, Adrienne Carol *artist, art educator*

Oklahoma City
Alaupovic, Alexandra Vrbanic *artist, educator*
Boston, Billie *costume designer, costume history educator*
Whitener, Carolyn Raye *commercial artist*

Shawnee
Hicks, Steve L. *artist, art educator*

Tulsa
†Irvin, Mary Eleanor Yturria *artist*
†Neal, E(verett) G(ilbert) *sculptor, clown, small business owner*
Spencer, Laurie Lee *sculptor, art educator*
Spencer, Winifred May *art educator*
Vaughn, Rosalind Nzinga *artist*

Vinita
Castor, Carol Jean *artist, teacher*

OREGON

Applegate
Boyle, (Charles) Keith *artist, educator*

Bandon
Lindquist, Louis William *artist, writer*

Bend
Acosta, Cristina Pilar *artist*

Cannon Beach
Greaver, Harry *artist*

Dayton
Gilhooly, David James, III *artist*

Eugene
Hoy, Harold Henry *artist*

Grants Pass
Marchini, Claudia Cilloniz *artist*
Remington, Mary *artist, author*

Medford
Johnson, Morgan Burton *artist, writer*

Newberg
Keith, Pauline Mary *artist, illustrator, writer*

Pendleton
Harper, Gloria Janet *artist, educator*

Portland
Ace, Katherine *artist*
Canfield, James *art director*
†Hall, Mike Burt (Marshall B.) *artist, educator*
†Lorenz, Nancy *artist*
Ramsby, Mark Delivan *lighting designer and consultant*
Savinar, Tad Lee *artist*
Thompson, Terrie Lee *graphic designer*

Salem
Forgue, Kerry Jo *artist, educator*

PENNSYLVANIA

Allentown
Moller, Hans *artist*

Ardmore
Noone, Kathleen Mary *art educator*

Bala Cynwyd
Blumberg, June Beth *artist*

Boyertown
Slider, Dorla Dean (Freeman) *artist*

Breinigsville
Brady, Jeffrey Kevin *photographer*

Bryn Mawr
Beck, Christine Safford *photographer, publisher, volunteer*
Kline, John Charles *painter, educator*

Buffalo Mills
Housel, Donna Jane *artist*

Butler
Bashline, Aryl Ann *photographer, fiber artist*

Camp Hill
Rowe, Michael Duane *artist*

Carlisle
Davenny, Ward Leslie *artist, educator*

Chambersburg
Boretz, Naomi Messinger *artist, educator*

Cochranville
Sazegar, Morteza *artist*

Coraopolis
Bacher, Lutz *film, video and photography educator*

East Stroudsburg
†Lane, Miharu Qualkinbush *artist, educator*

Edinboro
Kemenyffy, Steven *artist, art educator*

Elkins Park
Erlebacher, Martha Mayer *artist, educator*
Schatz, Charlotte Asness *artist, educator*

Emmaus
Greenslade, Kathryn Elizabeth *art director*

Eranheim
Murphy, Mary Marguerite *artist*

Erie
†Dempsey, Jennifer Camille *art educator, artist*

Fairless Hills
Marable, Simeon-David *artist*

Fairview
Krider, Margaret Young *art educator*

Fleetwood
†Zucco, Doug *artist*

Glen Mills
Turner, Janet Sullivan *painter*

Glenmoore
DeGuatemala, Joyce *sculptor*

Glenside
Bardliving, Clifford Lee, Jr. *graphic designer*
Frudakis, Zenos Antonios *sculptor, artist*
Taylor, Judith Ann *art educator, artist*

Havertown
Craley, Carol Ruth *art educator, academic administrator*

Huntingdon Valley
Edelman, Janice *artist, educator*
Stephenson, Helene Ruth *painter, consultant*

Indiana
†LaRoche, Lynda *artist, educator*

Jessup
Karluk, Lori Jean *craft designer, copy editor*

Kimberton
Williams, Lawrence Soper *photographer*

Lederach
Hallman, H(enry) Theodore, Jr. *artist, textile designer*

Lehigh Valley
Kocsis, James Paul *artist*

Lumberville
Katsiff, Bruce *artist*

Mechanicsville
Bye, Ranulph DeBayeux *artist, author*

Narberth
Grenald, Raymond *architectural lighting designer*

New Castle
Blair, Phyllis E. *artist, sculptor, illustrator*

New Holland
Kermes, Constantine John *artist, industrial designer*

New Hope
Patterson, Donald William *painter*

Newtown
Smith, Karen Ann *visual artist*

Norristown
Gerdes, Michelle Ann *designer*

North Wales
Rayevsky, Robert *illustrator*

Oxford
Palser, Beth Anne *painter*

Philadelphia
†Brady, Thomas Geoffrey *artist*
Camp, Donald Eugene *experimental photographer, educator*
Cramer, Richard Charles *artist, educator*
Druckrey, Inge Heide *graphic designer, educator*
Faraghan, George Telford *photographer*
Franklin, Harold Leroy *graphic artist, filmmaker*
Gerber, Jack *artist*
Hyder, Frank J. *artist, educator*
†Kirsch, Marilyn *artist*
†Lavins, Marilyn Edith *artist*
Le Clair, Charles George *artist, retired university dean*
Levy, Rochelle Feldman *artist*
Maitin, Sam(uel Calman) (Sam Maitin) *artist*
McCormick, Rod *sculptor, art educator*
Osborne, Judith Barbour *artist, art educator*
Paone, Peter *artist*
Remenick, Seymour *artist, educator*
Saul, April *photographer*
Schaff, Barbara Walley *artist*
Spandorfer, Merle Sue *artist, educator, author*
Willet, E(verett) Crosby *artist*
Williams, James Boughton *artist, art educator*
Zuchman, Philip Abrim *artist, educator*

Phildelphia
Wiesner, David *illustrator, children's writer*

Phoenixville
Allen, Carol Linnea Ostrom *art educator*

Pittsburgh
Bickel, Minnette Duffy *artist*
Kamienska-Carter, Eva Hanna *designer, artist*
Kelly, Richard Dale *photographer, multimedia producer, filmmaker*
†Nelson, James Potter *artist*
†Quinn, Elizabeth Anna *artist, art educator*
Rogers, Bryan Leigh *artist, art educator*
Schwalb, Harry *artist*
Spalding, Rita Lee *artist*
Vrscak, William Martin *artist, art educator*
Wilkins, David George *fine arts educator*
Williams, John Wesley *fine arts educator*

Reading
†Miller, Regina Dancull Gouger *artist, designer, educator*

Richboro
Burtt, Larice A.R. *artist*

Roscoe
O'Hara, Paul Anthony, Jr. *retired art educator, artist*

Rydal
Roediger, Janice Anne *artist, educator*

Scenery Hill
Schaltenbrand, Philip Edward *art educator*

Scranton
†Alexander, Steven *artist, educator*

Selinsgrove
Connolly, Elma Troutman *artist, contractor, designer*

Shickshinny
Luksha, Rosemary Dorothy *art educator*

Shippensburg
Sturtz-Davis, Shirley Zampelli *retired arts administrator/educator, fashion archivist*

Silverdale
Grande, Alexander, IV *artist*

Solebury
Anthonisen, George Rioch *sculptor, artist*

Spring Grove
Helberg, Shirley Adelaide Holden *artist, educator*

Tyrone
Shaw, Marilyn Margaret Mitchell *artist, photographer*

Upper Darby
Gasparro, Frank *sculptor*

Wellsboro
Driskell, Lucile G. *artist*

West Grove
Allman, Margo Hutz *sculptor, painter*

Wexford
Osby, Larissa Geiss *artist*

Wilkes Barre
Joyce, Ann Iannuzzo *art educator*

Williamsport
Waggaman, John Floyd, II *photographer*

Wrightsville
†Burkhart, Dennis Lloyd *artist, illustrator*

Yardley
Ahrens, Henry William *art educator, consultant, puppeteer*

York
Springer, Joel Henry *artist, educator*

RHODE ISLAND

Hope Valley
Devin, Carl Eric *artist*

Jamestown
Prip, Janet *metalsmith*
Worden, Katharine Cole *sculptor*

Narragansett
Bentley-Scheck, Grace Mary *artist*
Sullivan, Paul Joseph *artist*

Newport
†Rogers, Rita *artist, conservator*

North Kingstown
Kilguss, Elsie Schaich *artist, gallery owner*

Providence
Dewing, Linda Thimann *sculptor*
Feldman, Walter Sidney *artist, educator*
Geisser, Peter James *artist, educator for hearing impaired*
Grimaldi, Vince *artist*
Heyman, Lawrence Murray *printmaker, painter*
Howes, Lorraine de Wet *fashion designer, educator*
Leviten, Riva Shamray *artist*
Ockerse, Thomas *graphic design educator*
Wunderlich, Alfred Leon *artist, art educator*

Wakefield
Leete, William White *artist*

Westerly
Hence, Jane Knight *designer*

SOUTH CAROLINA

Aiken
Ristow, Gail Ross *art educator, paralegal, children's rights advocate*

Bethune
Ogburn, Thomas Willis *artist*

Central
Smith-Cox, Elizabeth Shelton *art educator*

Chapin
†McNinch, Michel Cottingham *artist, educator*

Charleston
McCallum, Corrie *painter, printmaker*

Columbia
Elkins, Toni Marcus *artist, art association administrator*
Floyd, Timothy Sherwood *graphic designer*
Hansen, Harold John (Harry) *artist, educator*

Greenville
Alberga, Alta Wheat *artist*
Earle, Patricia Nelson *artist*

Hilton Head Island
†Shepard, Steven Louis *graphic artist, painter*

Mount Pleasant
Ayres, Paul Erdman *artist*

Orangeburg
Hampton, Raymond *painter*

Summerville
Vorwerk, E. Charlsie *artist*

SOUTH DAKOTA

Huron
Bryant, James Arthur *painter*

Rapid City
Mabon, William Clarence *photographer, sales executive*

Sioux Falls
Aldern, Robert Judson *architectural, liturgical and landscape artist*
Grupp, Carl Alf *art educator, artist*
†Kolb, John Joseph *art educator*
Peters, John Henry *artist*

Spearfish
Termes, A. Dick *artist*

Vermillion
Freeman, Jeffrey Vaughn (Jeff Freeman) *art educator, artist*

TENNESSEE

Bristol
Mueller, Roy Clement *graphic arts company executive*

Chattanooga
Martin, Chester Y. *sculptor, painter*
Mills, Olan, II *photography company executive*
†Trew, Reba C. *artist*

Dandridge
Weatherly-McWaters, Barbara Cannon *artist*

East Brainerd
Swanger, Daniel A.I. *artist*

Germantown
Stevens, Colleen Newport *artist*

Greenback
†Rollins, Freddie Wayne *artist, graphic design*

Hendersonville
†Morgan, Gerald Lee *artist*

Humboldt
Lynch, Elizabeth Humphreys *artist, educator*

Jackson
Benson, Aaron Lee *art educator*

Kingsport
Hyder, Betty Jean *art educator*

Kingston
Worden, Marny *artist, musician*

Knoxville
Drinnon, Janis Bolton *artist, poet, author, volunteer*
Sublett, Carl Cecil *artist*
Turner, Peggy Ann *graphic designer, visual artist, educator*

Lookout Mountain
Aplin, James Granger *artist*
Wyeth, Andrew *artist*

Memphis
De Mere-Dwyer, Leona *medical artist*
†McCarthy, David Patterson *art educator*
McPherson, Larry E(ugene) *photographer, educator*
Riss, Murray *photographer, educator*
†Smith, Kimberly Ann *art educator*

Nashville
Oates, Sherry Charlene *portraitist*
Pennington, Harold Thomas *graphic designer*

Oak Ridge
Runtsch, Clarence Frederick *artist, sculptor*
†Yzadi, Kay Tisko *artist*

TEXAS

Amarillo
McDuff, Lightnin *sculptor*

Arlington
Munoz, Celia Alvarez *artist*

Austin
Fearing, William Kelly *art educator, artist*
Goldstein, Peggy R. *sculptor*
Guerin, John William *artist*
Hatgil, Paul Peter *artist, sculptor, educator*
High, Timothy Griffin *artist, educator, writer*
Long, Bert Louis, Jr. *artist*
Mayer, Susan Martin *art educator*
McCoy, John Denny *artist*
†Robinson, Priscilla *artist*
Sawyer, Margo Lucy *artist, educator*
†Smith, Jeffrey Chipps *art educator*
Weismann, Donald Leroy *art educator, artist, filmmaker, writer*

Bedford
Lentz, Luther Eugene *graphic arts technical specialist*

Blanco
Evett, Philip John *sculptor, educator*

Cleveland
Surls, James *sculptor*

College Station
†Stone, Mary Elizabeth *artist*

Corpus Christi
Kemmerer, Dennis Allen *artist, educator*
Ullberg, Kent Jean *sculptor*
Worden, Elizabeth Ann *artist, comedy writer, singer, playwright*

Dallas
Blessen, Karen Alyce *free lance illustrator, designer*
Emerson, Walter Caruth *artist, educator*
†Haydel, Raymond *computer animation artist*
†Henderson, Michael Howard *artist, educator*
Hudgins, Louise Nan *art educator*
†Lawrence, Annette *artist*
Richards, Jeanne Herron *artist*
Roman, Patricia Ann *sculptor*
Rushton, Lynn Noelle *artist*
Smither, Edward Murray *art consultant, appraiser*
Whitehead, Michael Richard *painter*

Denton
Cox, Barbara Claire *costume designer, educator*
Washmon, Gary Brent *artist, educator*

Dripping Springs
Pellicone, William *artist, sculptor, writer, architect*

Duncanville
Terry, Martin Michael *visual artist, art therapist*

El Paso
Cox, Helen Adelaide (Holly Cox) *artist, writer*
Drake, James *sculptor*
Weitz, Jeanne Stewart *artist, educator*

Euless
Leding, Anne Dixon *artist, educator*

Flower Mound
Rohm, Robert Roy *artist*

Fort Worth
†Allen, William Marion, III *retired graphic designer, artist*
Durham, Jo Ann Fanning *artist*
Phillips, Mary Ann *artist, writer, retired legal secretary*
Schoolar, Steve Sherman *sculptor, theatrical technician*

Gainesville
Killian, Lawrence Harding (Larry H.), II (Larry H. Killian) *sculptor*

Granbury
†Jones, Collette Ann *artist*

Haltom City
Rickett, Carolyn Kaye Master *artist, criminologist*

Houston
Camfield, William Arnett *art educator*
Christie, Richard Joel *studio executive*
†Davenport, Bill *sculptor*
Gorski, Daniel Alexander *art educator*
Hamilton, Jacqueline *art consultant*
Honeycutt, George Leonard *photographer, retired*
Hulce, Durward Philip *theatrical lighting designer*
Jackson, Susanne Leora *creative placement firm executive*
King, Kay Wander *design educator, fashion designer, consultant*
Larrey, Inge Harriette *jazz and blues freelance photographer*
Loro, Antonio *artist*
O'Neil, John *artist*
Orr, Carole *artist*
Shelley, Clyde Burton *artist*
Solomon, Marsha Harris *draftsman, artist*
Ward, Bethea *artist, small business owner*

Huntsville
Lea, Stanley E. *artist, educator*

Katy
Huffaker, E. Wayne *artist*

Kerrville
Frudakis, Evangelos William *sculptor*

Laredo
Knapp, Thomas Edwin *sculptor, painter*
Watson, Helen Richter *educator, ceramic artist*

League City
Williams, Richard Robert *artist, educator*

Longview
Cromer-Campbell, Tammy *commercial and fine art photographer*
Hearne, Carolyn Fox *art, history educator, artist, art museum director*

Lubbock
†Kennedy, Linda Carol *art and art educator*

Marfa
Meyer, Ellen Adams *arts consultant*

Mcallen
Troester, Waltraud *artist, graphic designer, consultant*

Mission
McClendon, Maxine *artist*

Odessa
Phillips, Barry *artist, educator*

Pasadena
†Ballard, Carrie *artist*

Plano
†Cotter-Smith, Cathleen Marie *art educator, artist*

Pleasanton
†Wilson, Karen Ford *artist*

Richardson
Bellamy, Jennifer Rachelle *artist*

San Antonio
Broderick, James Allen *art educator*
Field, Charles Twist *artist, art educator*
†Puckett, Terry Gay *art educator, artist*
Rowe, Reginald *artist*
Summers, Barbara June *artist*
Von Honts, Jacqueline Jay *artist*

Sonora
Earwood, Barbara Tirrell *artist*

Spicewood
Carrell, Hammel Lee *jewelry designer*

Waco
Kagle, Joseph Louis, Jr. *artist, arts administrator*

UTAH

American Fork
Reinhold, Allen Kurt *graphic design educator*

Bountiful
Powell, Ted Ferrell *micrographics specialist*

Monroe
Kirby, Orville Edward *potter, painter, sculptor*

Salt Lake City
Hartley, Elise Moore *theatrical milliner, costume designer*
Pierce, Diane Jean *artist*
Wyness, Steven Charles *illustrator*
†Zemmels, David Russell *theatre educator, lighting designer*

Smithfield
Rasmuson, Brent (Jacobsen) *photographer, graphic artist, lithographer*

Spring City
Bennion, Joseph Wood *potter*

VERMONT

Bennington
Adams, Pat *artist, educator*

Bridgewater
Bramhall, Peter *artist, sculptor, designer, craftsman*

Cavendish
Shapiro, David *artist, art historian*

East Calais
Gahagan, James Edward, Jr. *artist*
Gahagan, Patricia de Gogorza *sculptor*

Enosburg Falls
Svendsen, Alf *artist, art educator*

Hardwick
Holtz, Laurence *artisan, photographer*

Manchester Center
Dunning, Steven *painter*

Marlboro
Poster, Lauren Olitski *art administrator, artist*

Middletown Springs
Lloyd, Robert Andrew *art educator*

Newark
Van Vliet, Claire *artist*

Newbury
McGarrell, James *artist, educator*

Putney
†Hunt, Bill *artist, educator*

Saxtons River
Aho, Eric *artist*

South Royalton
Jones, Timothy Mark *graphic designer, painter*

Springfield
Thayer, Rosealyce Cullen *artist*

Weston
Kasnowski, Chester Nelson *artist, educator*

VIRGINIA

Alexandria
Harwood, Matthew David *artist*
†Sogoian, Mikael F. *artist*
†Tesler, Diane Elaine *artist*
Triefeldt, Rein *sculptor, educator*
Wasko-Flood, Sandra Jean *artist, educator*

Arlington
Kotler, Wendy Illene *art educator, social studies educator, grants coordinator*
Reed, Paul Allen *artist*

Blacksburg
Calvera, Jorge *artist*
Crawford, Peggy Smith *design educator*
Davis, Carole Carrera *watercolor artist*
Gablik, Suzi *art educator, writer*

Charlottesville
Priest, Hartwell Wyse *artist*

Chesapeake
Katz, MaryAnne *artist, educator*

Chincoteague
Payne, Nancy Sloan *retired visual arts educator*

Clifton
Hennesy, Gerald Craft *artist*

Colonial Heights
Grizzard-Barham, Barbara Lee *artist*

Draper
Whitehurst, Mary Tarr *artist, poet, writer*

Fairfax
Krupinski, Christine Margaret *artist*

Falls Church
†Thompson, Carol S. *artist*

Farmville
Whaley, Michael David *graphic designer*

Fredericksburg
Detwiler, Joseph Alden *artist*
Herndon, Cathy Campbell *artist, art educator*

Schmutzhart, Berthold Josef *sculptor, educator, art and education consultant*

Glen Allen
†Vaughn, Ann Marie *art educator, artist*

Hot Springs
Trotter, Susan Collins *artist*

Independence
Craig, James Hicklin *fine arts consultant*

Lanexa
Green, Richard Bertram *sculptor*

Linden
Cole, Crystal Lynn *artist*

Louisa
Black, James David *woodcarver, English educator, editor, poet*

Lynchburg
Hudson, Walter Tiree *artist*

Marshall
Han, Nong *artist, sculptor, painter*

Mc Lean
Harrison, Carol Love *fine art photographer*
Johnson, Mary Zelinda *artist*
Rugala, Karen Francis (Karen Francis) *artist, television producer*

McLean
†Somogyi, Maria M. *artist*

Middleburg
†Luco, Wende *artist*
Robinson, Michael Francis *private art dealer and appraiser*

Newport News
Abbott, Beverly Stubblefield *artist*

Norfolk
Frieden, Jane Heller *art educator*
Jones, Leon Herbert, Jr. (Herb Jones) *artist*

Oak Hill
†Adler, Dale Ann *artist*

Radford
Shell, Robert Edward Lee *photographer, writer*

Reston
Heginbotham, Jan Sturza *sculptor*
Ovissi, Nasser *artist*

Richmond
Freed, David Clark *artist*
Kevorkian, Richard *artist*
Levit, Heloise B. (Ginger Levit) *art dealer, art consultant*
Martin, Bernard Murray *painter, educator*
Rowley, Frank Selby, Jr. *artist*
Savedge, Anne Creery *artist, photographer*

Staunton
†Fultz, Sara Spitler *art educator*

Swoope
Avery, Robert Newell *sculptor*

Virginia Beach
Ruben, Leonard *retired art educator*
Stevens, Suzanne Duckworth *artist, educator*

Wachapreague
Wilkins, (Ira) Guy *painter, art teacher*

Waynesboro
Prye, Ellen Ross *graphic designer*

Williamsburg
Coleman, Henry Edwin *art educator, artist*
Lorenz, Hans Ernest *photographer*
Robinson, Jay (Thurston) *artist*
Roseberg, Carl Andersson *sculptor, educator*
Stanley, Shirley Davis *artist*

WASHINGTON

Anacortes
Mc Cracken, Philip Trafton *sculptor*

Bainbridge Island
Carlson, Robert Michael *artist*

Battle Ground
Hansen, James Lee *sculptor*

Bellevue
Warsinke, Norman George *interior designer, sculptor*

Coupeville
Canfield, Stella Stojanka *artist, art gallery owner*

Edmonds
Deering, Anne-Lise *artist, real estate salesperson*
Johnson, d'Elaine Ann Herard *artist*

Ellensburg
Housner, Jeanette Ann *artist, jeweler*
Parker-Fairbanks, Dixie *artist*

Everett
Krahn, Thomas Frank *photographer*

Goldendale
Musgrave, Lee *artist, museum administrator*

Kent
†Klennert, Daniel Charles *artist*

Pierce, Danny Parcel *artist, educator*

La Conner
†Mack, James Willard *artist, educator*

Lilliwaup
McGrady, Corinne Young *design company executive*

Mercer Island
Berman, Gizel *sculptor*
Langhout-Nix, Nelleke *artist*
Steinhardt, Henry *photographer*

Monroe
Nguyen-Ely, Darlene *sculptor*

North Bend
Kaplan, Donna Elaine *artist, educator*

Olympia
Fitzgerald, Betty Jo *artist, educator, juror, curator*
Haseltine, James Lewis *artist, consultant*
Randlett, Mary Willis *photographer*

Palouse
Duffy, Irene Karen *artist*

Puyallup
Chalk, Earl Milton *retired art director*

Redmond
†McIntosh, Molly Jean *interior designer*

Seattle
Berger, Paul Eric *artist, photographer*
Blomdahl, Sonja *artist*
Bruch, Barbara Rae *artist, educator*
†Calderon, Mark A. *artist, sculptor*
Dailey, Michael Dennis *painter, educator*
De Alessi, Ross Alan *lighting designer*
†Farbanish, Thomas *sculptor*
Gardiner, T(homas) Michael *artist*
Garvens, Ellen Jo *art educator, artist*
Govedare, Philip Bainbridge *artist, educator*
Guzak, Karen Jean Wahlstrom *artist*
Hirondelle, Anne Elizabeth *ceramic artist*
Huchthausen, David Richard *sculptor, real estate developer*
Lawrence, Jacob *artist, educator*
Pawula, Kenneth John *artist, educator*
Royal, Richard *artist*
Skoor, John Brian *art educator, art consultant*
Spafford, Michael Charles *artist*
Tift, Mary Louise *artist*
Trimpin *artist*
Washington, James Winston, Jr. *artist, sculptor*
Weiss, Dick Joseph *artist*
Wenick, Dean *photographer*

Spokane
Bonuccelli, Dominic Arizona *photographer*

Tenino
Orsini, Myrna J. *sculptor, educator*

Vancouver
Hulburt, Lucille Hall *artist, educator*

WEST VIRGINIA

Morgantown
Pearce, Meredith *graphic designer*

Parkersburg
Gilbert, Kenneth G. *art educator*

Philippi
Lambert, Olivia Sue *commercial artist, writer*

Sutton
Hopen, William Douglas (Bill Hopen) *sculptor*

Wheeling
Phillis, Marilyn Hughey *artist*

WISCONSIN

Appleton
Amm, Sophia Jadwiga *artist, educator*

Beloit
Simon, Michael Alexander *photographer, educator*

Berlin
Martin, Rebecca Ann *artist, graphic designer*

Eau Claire
Lawler, John Griffin *graphic designer, educator*

Germantown
Hargan, Charles James *lithographer, village official*

Green Bay
†Style, Christine L. *art educator, curator*

Hartland
Stamsta, Jean F. *artist*

Hollandale
Colescott, Warrington Wickham *artist, printmaker, educator*
Myers, Frances *artist*

Iola
Rosenberger, Carolyn Ann *art educator*

Lake Mills
Quest, Kristina Kay *art educator*

Madison
Becker, David *artist, educator*
Greenwald, Caroline Meyer *artist*
†Lakes, Diana Mary *artist*
Launder, Yolanda Marie *graphic design director*

Link, O(gle) Winston *photographer*
†Racette, Elizabeth Anne *artist*
Rogers, Katherine Kuelbs *artist, writer*

Marshfield
Gardner, Ella Haines *artist*

McNaughton
Bradshaw, Glenn Raymond *art educator*

Mequon
Smith, Leila Hentzen *artist*

Milwaukee
Gjerdset, Kristin Anne *art educator, artist*
Heiloms, May (Mrs. Samuel Heiloms) *artist*
Helbert, Clifford L. *graphic designer, journalism educator*
Herr, Richard Joseph *sculptor, educator*
Michaels-Paque, Joan M. *artist, educator*
Thrall, Arthur Alvin *artist*

Monona
Fritz, Bruce Morrell *photographer*

New Richmond
Schwan, LeRoy Bernard *artist, retired educator*

Oconomowoc
Vespa, Ned Angelo *photographer*

Oshkosh
Deniston-Trochta, Grace Marie *educator, artist*
Hu, Li *art educator*

South Milwaukee
Knoll, Gregg A. *artist, printmaker, educator*

Stoughton
†McEvoy, James H. *artist*

Viroqua
†Possehl, Robert *visual artist*

Wausau
Fleming, Thomas Michael *artist, educator*

Whitewater
Gauger, Michele Roberta *photographer, studio administrator, corporate executive*

WYOMING

Centennial
Russin, Robert Isaiah *sculptor, educator*

Cheyenne
Moore, Mary French (Muffy Moore) *potter, community activist*

Laramie
Reif, (Frank) David *artist, educator*

Saratoga
†Palen, Jerry *artist*

CANADA

ALBERTA

Edmonton
Jungkind, Walter *design educator, writer, consultant*

BRITISH COLUMBIA

Duncan
Hughes, Edward John *artist*

Salt Spring Island
Raginsky, Nina *artist*

Victoria
Harvey, Donald *artist, educator*

MANITOBA

Winnipeg
Eyre, Ivan *artist*

NOVA SCOTIA

Toronto
Tolmie, Kenneth Donald *artist, author*

Wolfville
Colville, David Alexander *artist*

ONTARIO

London
Livick, Stephen *fine art photographer*

Niagara-on-the-Lake
Scott, Campbell *artist*

Toronto
Astman, Barbara Ann *artist, educator*
Braswell, Paula Ann *artist*
Kramer, Burton *graphic designer, educator*
Semak, Michael William *photographer, educator*
Winter, Frederick Elliot *fine arts educator*

Waterloo
Urquhart, Tony *artist, educator*

QUEBEC

Beaconsfield
Harder, Rolf Peter *graphic designer, painter*

Montreal
Charney, Melvin *artist, architect, educator*
McEwen, Jean *painter*

Saint Lambert
Archambault, Louis *sculptor*

SASKATCHEWAN

Saskatoon
Bornstein, Eli *artist, sculptor*

MEXICO

Mexico City
†Friedeberg, Pedro *painter, sculptor, designer*

Morelos
Cauduro, Rafael *painter, muralist*

AUSTRALIA

Ringwood
Base, Graeme Rowland *illustrator, author*

BRITISH WEST INDIES

Grand Cayman Island
Ronald, Pauline Carol *retired art educator*

ENGLAND

London
†Brotherston, Lez *set designer, costumer*
†Hiller, Susan *artist*

FRANCE

Arles
Clergue, Lucien Georges *photographer*

Malakoff
Boltanski, Christian *painter, photographer*

Paris
Lacroix, Christian Marie Marc *fashion designer*
Renouf, Edda *artist*
Ungaro, Emanuel Matteotti *fashion designer*

GERMANY

Frankfurt
Ammann, Jean-Christophe *art director*

ITALY

Florence
Cecil, Charles Harkless *artist, educator*

JAPAN

Kanagawa
Swarz, Sahl *sculptor*

Tokyo
Kusama, Yayoi *sculptor, painter*

THE NETHERLANDS

Amsterdam
Baer, Jo *painter*

PAKISTAN

Lahore
Geoffrey, Iqbal (Mohammed Jawaid Iqbal Jafree) *artist, lawyer*

PORTUGAL

Lisbon
†Berger, Jason *artist, printmaker*

SPAIN

Seville
Sanchez, Leonedes Monarrize Worthington (His Royal Highness Duke de Leonedes of Spain Sicily Greece) *fashion designer*

SWEDEN

Bralanda
Emilson, Henry Bertil *artist*

ADDRESS UNPUBLISHED

Abadi, Fritzie *artist, educator*

Abbe, Elfriede Martha sculptor, graphic artist
Abeles, Kim Victoria artist
Abramowicz, Janet painter, print-maker
Adkins, Terry R. artist
Aldredge, Theoni Vachliotis costume designer
Alexander, Peter Houston artist
Allen, Jane Ingram artist, educator
Anastasi, William Joseph artist
Ancona, George E. photographer, film producer, author
Andrade, Edna artist, art educator
Andrews, Jean artist, writer
Annus, John Augustus artist
†Argraves, Hugh Oliver poet, artist, playwright
†Arnold, Gloria Malcolm artist, educator
Aronson, Marc artist
Arrott, Patricia Graham artist, art instructor
Astaire, Carol Anne Taylor artist, educator
August, Louise artist, illustrator, educator
August, Robert William designer, educator
Austin, Janet Hays artist
Bacon, Benjamin B. title designer
Bader, Lorraine Greenberg textile stylist, designer, consultant
Barlow, Jean art educator, artist
Barth, Frances Dorothy artist
Bateman, Robert McLellan artist
Baughman, J. Ross photographer, writer, educator
Becker, Jon Andrew arts and education consultant
†Beloff, Zoe artist, educator
Benton, Fletcher sculptor
Benzel, Ilona Fran artist
Benzle, Curtis Munhall artist, art educator
Bergmann, Meredith Gang sculptor
Berman, Aaron art appraiser, director, consultant
Berman, Eleanore artist
†Berridge, Mary photographer
Bethlen, Ilona R. designer, educator
†Biedermann, Paul Frederick graphic designer
Bigbee, Ivy Cave photographer, author
Binch, Caroline Lesley illustrator, photographer
Bissell, James Dougal, III motion picture production designer
Blair, Robert Noel artist
Blinder, Janet art dealer
Blitt, Rita Lea artist
Blumenfeld, Rochelle S. Reznik artist
Bolles, Susan production designer
Bowen-Forbes, Jorge Courtney artist, author, poet
†Bower, Marilyn Kay landscape artist
Boxer, Stanley Robert artist, sculptor
Bradley, Marilynne Gail advertising executive, advertising educator
Bradshaw, Dove artist
†Bridge, Andrew theatrical lighting designer
Brigeois, Evelyne Brigitte artist, publisher
Broadbent, Amalia Sayo Castillo graphic arts designer
Brown, Alice Elste artist
Brown, Carol (Rose) artist
Browne, Diana Gayle artist, social services
Brugioni, David Michael graphic designer, illustrator, artist
Bryan, Sukey artist
Bryant, Daryl Leslie painter, educator
†Buell, Dexter artist, sculpture
Bundi, Renee art director, graphic designer
†Burger, Werner Carl retired art educator
Burke, Bill art educator
Burlingame, Lloyd Lamson retired design instructor
†Burns, Ellen Jean arts educator
Burrows, E. Michael art educator, artist
Butterfield, Deborah Kay sculptor
†Calabrese, Karen Ann artist, educator
Campanelli, Pauline Eble artist
Campbell, Demarest Lindsay artist, designer, writer
Campbell, Patton stage designer, educator
†Canavan, Patrick Joseph artist
Cantliffe, Jeri Miller artist, art educator
Caporaso, Pat Marie art dealer
Caro, Anthony (Alfred Caro) sculptor
Carroll, Marie-Jean Greve educator, artist
Carter, Nanette Carolyn artist
Casey, Thomas Warren graphic design company executive, architect
Causey-Jeffery, Tracy Ann art dealer, art historian
Celentano, Francis Michael artist, art educator
†Centofanti, Joyce Michelina artist, educator
Chapin, Deborah artist
†Child, Abigail artist, educator
Child, Judith artist
Chinni, Peter Anthony artist
†Claiborne, Liz (Elisabeth Claiborne Ortenberg) fashion designer
Clark, Larry photographer
Clarke, John Clem artist
Clauser, Kenneth Alton professional photographer, banjo player
Clement, Alain Gérard photographer
Cobb, Ruth artist
Cobb, Virginia Horton artist, educator
Cogan, John Dennis artist
Colker, Edward artist, educator
Conrader, Constance Ruth artist, writer, librarian
Conroy, Tamara Boks artist, special education educator, former nurse
†Cook, James Anthony artist, educator
Coover, Doris Dimock artist
Coplans, John Rivers artist
Cornell, Thomas Browne artist, educator
Cox, Pat artist
Craw, Freeman (Jerry Craw) graphic artist
Crilley, Joseph James artist
Crispo, Richard Charles artist, ethnologist, minister
†Crowley-Kiggins, Margaret Louise artist
Cumming, Robert Hugh artist, photographer
Cummings, David William artist, educator
Currie, Steven Ray artist
Dallmann, Daniel F. artist, educator
†Darlow, Andrew J. photographer
Davis, Christina artist
Davis, Mary Christine artist, art educator
Debevoise, A. Clay artist
De Blasi, Tony (Anthony Armando De Blasi) artist
Dechar, Peter Henry artist
DeGeest, Elaine Beck artist
De Looper, Willem Johan artist, museum curator
DeLoyht-Arendt, Mary I. artist
†DeLuca, Kristin Leigh graphic designer
Deutsch, David Allan artist
Dill, Laddie John artist
DiPasquale, Paul Albert sculptor
Dixon, Michael Wayne designer, writer, researcher
Dogançay, Burhan C. artist, photographer, sculptor
Dolbin, Steven Michael sculptor, educator
Dominguez, Eddie artist
Donath, Therese artist, author
Downes, Rackstraw artist
Doyle, Tom sculptor, retired educator
Drasler, Gregory John artist
Drooyan, John Neal visual artist, photographer, fine artist
Du Boise, Kim Rees artist, photographer, art educator
Duguid, Dorothy Ann Ramseyer artist
Dunbar, Bruce Stephen photographer, gallery administrator
†Duval-Carrié, Edouard artist
Dyer, Geraldine A. (Geri A. Dyer) artist, poet
†Easterson, Sam artist
†Eckert, Tom W. artist, educator
Eddy, Don artist
Elcik, Elizabeth Mabie fashion illustrator
Emmons, Beverly lighting designer
†Eveleth, Emily artist
Fahey-Cameron, Robin artist, photographer
Farah, Cynthia Weber photographer, publisher
Farrar, Elaine Willardson artist
Faxon, Alicia Craig art educator
Ferreira, Armando Thomas sculptor, educator
Fetter, William Allan computer graphics executive
Finn, Mary Ralphe artist
Firestein, Cecily Barth artist
Firestone, Evan Richard art educator, art historian
Fish, Janet Isobel artist
Fisher, Vernon artist, educator
Forester, Russell artist
†Forsman, Catherine Anne poet, webmaster
Frailey, Stephen A. photographer
Frank, Leona Veda artist
†Fratkin, Leslie photographer
†Frederick, Craig Matthew sculptor
Freilicher, Jane artist
Friday, Katherine Orwoll artist
Fritz, Charles John artist
Fulco, Paula artist
†Furth, Karen J. artist, art educator
Gallagher, Cynthia artist, educator
Gard, Judy Richardson artist, educator
Gause, Charles Marvin artist
†Gay, Tito (Virginia Lewis Gray Findlay) artist, educator
Gechtoff, Sonia artist
†George, Anna book designer, artist
†Georgiades, Aristotle artist, educator
†Gervits, Leonid art educator, artist
Gimbolo, Aleksei Frank Charles (Cimbolo) artist, philosopher, author
†Gipson, Shelley R. artist, educator
Giusti, Robert George artist, educator
Gleason, John James theatrical lighting designer
†Gloman, David J. artist
†Godbee, Gary Russell artist
Goldberg, Bradley Jay artist
Goldberger, Blanche Rubin sculptor, jeweler
Golden, Judith Greene artist, educator
Goolsby, Charles William artist, educator
Graham, Kathleen Margaret (K. M. Graham) artist
†Grant, Gretchen Gullicksen artist
Greeff, Adele Montgomery Burcher artist
Greenberg, Albert art director
Groban, Lee David artist
Grunbaum, Marianne Hettner artist
Gumen, Murad artist, writer, film director and producer
Gurwitz-Hall, Barbara Ann artist
Guthrie, Timothy Sean art educator, artist
Haberl, Judy Ann artist, educator
Hale, Christy illustrator, designer, art educator
Hall, Susan Laurel artist, educator, writer
Halsey, Gary illustrator
Hanan, Laura Molen artist
Hankin, Charles Edward sculptor
Hanson, Janice Crawford artist, financial analyst
Hanson, Jo artist
Harari, Hananiah artist
Harper, James Robert graphic designer
Hasson, Raymond Edward, III artist, writer
Havens, Keith Cornell artist
Hawkes, Kevin Cliff illustrator, author
Hayes, David Vincent sculptor
Helander, Bruce Paul artist
Heller, Dorothy artist
Henry, John Raymond sculptor
Herman, David Henry artist, violin restorer and dealer
Herzberg, Thomas artist, illustrator
†Hickman, Patricia artist, craftswoman
†Higgins, Margaret Christie photographer
Hodges, Judith Anne artist, art educator
Holden, Rebecca Lynn artist
Holler, Rita Atwell photojournalist
†Holton, William artist
Holzer, Jenny artist
†Holzman, Sandra artist, educator
Horton, Patricia Mathews artist, violist and violinist
Huber, Colleen Adlene artist
Hudson, Jacqueline artist
†Huffington, Anita sculptor
Hull, Margaret Ruth artist, educator, consultant
†Jackson, Michelle A. artist
Jacob, Ted Manas biomedical and forensic photographer
Jacobs, Ferne Kent artist
Janko, May graphic artist
Jansen, Angela Bing artist, educator
Jay, Norma Joyce artist
†Jenkins, Marie P. art educator
Jimenez, Luis Alfonso, Jr. sculptor
Johnston, William Medford artist, retired educator
Jones, Claire Burtchaell artist, teacher, writer
Jones, Cynthia Rector artist
†Jones, Taylor Burnett cartoonist
Josephson, Kenneth Bradley artist, retired educator
Kahl, David Burr artist
Kahn, Susan Beth artist
Kalin, D(orothy) Jean artist, educator
Kalina, Richard artist
Kannenstine, Margaret Lampe artist
Karawina, Erica artist, stained glass designer
Karnofsky, Mollyne artist, poet, art educator
Katayama, Toshihiro artist, educator
Kauffman, Kaethe Coventon art educator, artist, author
Kearns, James Joseph artist
Keiser, Carol Jane artist
Kelly, Ellsworth painter, sculptor
Kipniss, Robert artist
Kiskadden, Robert Morgan artist, educator
Kleiman, Alan Boyd artist
Klein, Lynn Ellen artist
Klement, Vera artist
Knapp, Candace Louise sculptor
Knapp, Stephen Albert artist
Kohn, Karen Josephine graphic and exhibition designer
Kolean, Bonita LaMae artist, educator
Kotler, Martin Joseph painter
Krulik, Barbara S. director, curator
Kunin, Jacqueline Barlow art educator
Kyle, Gene Magerl merchandise presentation artist
Laemmle, Cheryl Marie Vicario artist
Lafleur, Laurette Carignan artist
†LaMantia, Paul Christopher (W. Zombek) artist
†Landa, Robin Lois design educator, writer
La Rocca, Isabella artist, educator
Lassiter, Kenneth T. photography educator, consultant
Laufer, William Hervey artist, printmaker
†Lazzara, Joyce Evelyn artist
†LÊ, An-My photographer, educator
Leak, Nancy Marie artist
Lee, Andrea K. artist
Leeds, Nancy Brecker sculptor, lyricist
†Legere, Kathy Ann artist
Lehman, Todd Wilson artist
Leiber, Judith Maria designer, manufacturer
†Leiva, Nicolas artist
Lekan, Briana Marker photographer
Lembark, Connie Wertheimer art consultant
†Lerner, Ilya artist
LeRoy, G. Palmer art dealer
Levi, Josef Alan artist
Levin, Morton D(avid) artist, printmaker, educator
Levine, Jack artist
Leys, Sue Ellen Rohrer designer, costume
†Libensky, Stanislav art educator
Lieberman, Louis (Karl Lieberman) artist
Liljegren, Frank Sigfrid artist, art association official
Liman, Ellen painter, writer, arts advocate
Linhares, Judith Yvonne artist, educator
Lipman, Carol Koch designer
Littleton, Harvey Kline artist
Livingston-MacIrelan, Joan Persilla artist
Lockart, Barbetta fabric designer, artist, jeweler, art educator
Lowenthal, Susan artist, designer, retired finance executive
Ludwig, Allan Ira photographer, artist, author
Lund, David Nathan artist
Lynch, Peter George artist
Lyshak-Stelzer, Frances artist
Machado, Paulo Almeida art educator
Maginnis, Tara Michele costume designer, educator
Maher, Jan Colleen artist, educator
Mahfouz, Ilham Badreddine artist
Mangold, Sylvia Plimack artist
†Marchman, Frederick Alan artist
Marion, John Louis fine arts auctioneer and appraiser
Mark, Mary Ellen photographer
Marlowe, Willie fine arts educator, artist
Marsh, Merrilyn Delano sculptor, painter
†Marti, Virgil artist
Martin, Noel graphic design consultant, educator
Martyl, (Mrs. Alexander Langsdorf, Jr.) artist
Mason, J. Day painter, poet, actress, educator
Massey, Stephen Charles auctioneer
Matlow, Linda Monique photographic agency executive, publishing executive
Mauney, Thomas Lee theater designer
Maxwell, Ruth Elaine artist, interior designer, decorative painter
†McClean, Karen Leslie photographer
McCully, Emily Arnold illustrator, writer
McCurdy, Michael Charles illustrator, author
†McGee, Carrie L. artist
McKnight, Thomas Frederick artist
McLaughlin, Jean Wallace art director, artist
McMillan, Stephen Walker artist
McMillen, Elizabeth Cashin artist
McPeters, Sharon Jenise artist, writer
McVicker, Jesse Jay artist, educator
Medinger, C. Wynn design and branding consultant
Meil, Kate sculptor
Melamid, Alexander artist
Meneeley, Edward Sterling artist
†Merritt, Eleanor Lynette artist, educator
Middaugh, Robert Burton artist
Miles, Jeanne Patterson artist
†Miller, Eric John artist, muralist, ornament designer
Miller, Philip Gray artist
Miller, Vel artist
Minami, Robert Yoshio artist, graphic designer
Misrach, Richard Laurence photographer
Morning, John graphic designer
Morris, Winifred Walker art educator
Mosca, August artist
†Mowry, Elizabeth artist
Murray, Ernest Don artist, educator
Murray, Robert Gray sculptor
Nadel, Kenneth Alan editorial art director
Nakamura, Kazuo artist
Natkin, Robert painter
Nemiroff, Maxine Celia art educator, gallery owner, consultant
Neuwirth, Allan Charles designer, director, screenwriter
Newman, Muriel Kallis Steinberg art collector
Newton, Barbara Benedetti artist, educator
Nichols, Iris Jean illustrator
†Niffenegger, Audrey Anne artist
Nodelman, Nancy Ziegler sculptor, designer
Noland, Kenneth Clifton artist
Nothwanger, Rosemary Wood artist, geological illustrator
O'Brien, Thomas Keith artist
Okoshi-Mukai, Sumiye artist
Olkinetzky, Sam artist, retired museum director and educator
Onslow Ford, Gordon Max painter
Ord, Linda Banks artist
Oropallo, Deborah artist, educator
Osa, Douglas Lee artist, printmaker
Pack, Susan Joan art consultant
Palausi, Nicole (Nicole Galinat) artist
Partlow, Marianne Fairbank artist, consultant, curator
†Pate, Virginia Frances artist, educator
Pearlstein, Philip artist
Peckham, Ellen Stoepel artist, poet
Péladeau, Marius Beaudoin art consultant, retired museum director
Perrin, Lisa C. fiber artist
Peterson, Kristin artist
†Petterson, Margo artist
Phelan, Ellen artist
Pinataro, Jean Eleanor artist
Pitcher, Virginia Griffith Stein fashion designer, graphic designer, poet
Poor, Anne artist
Porter, Charles Henry photographer
Porter, Nora Roxanne freelance graphic designer
Powell, Marlys Kaye artist
Pozzatti, Rudy Otto artist
†Prince, Richard artist
Provensen, Alice Rose Twitchell artist, author
Psillos, Susan Rose artist, educator
Purcell, George Richard artist, postal employee
Putterman, Florence Grace artist, printmaker
Rankin, Scott David artist, educator
Rataj, Elizabeth Ann artist
Ray, Timothy Lionel artist
Raymond, Susan Grant sculptor
Reichman, Fredrick Thomas artist
Rendal, Camille Lynn artist
Replogle, Renata Julia art therapy educator, artist
Richardson, Robert John producer, director animation
Richenburg, Robert Bartlett artist, retired art educator
Richter, Nancy Ellen Sowers artist, graphic designer
Rickey, George Warren artist, sculptor, educator
Rinaldi, Robert R., Jr. artist, photographer, publisher
Ritta, Kurt V. painter, fine artist, illustrator
†Roberts, Russell L. artist
Robinson, Caroleigh Hoffmann artist, educator
Robinson, Charlotte Hill artist
Robinson, Lynda Hickox artist
Rockall, Arthur Allison automotive designer
Rockburne, Dorothea Grace artist
Roe, Wanda Jeraldean artist, retired educator, lecturer
Rogers, Eva artist, poet
Rohm, Robert Hermann sculptor, educator
Rose, Andrea writer, inventor, fashion designer, artist
Rosenberg, Carole art dealer, real estate broker
Ross, Molly Owings gold and silversmith, jewelry designer, small business owner
Rossman, Ruth Scharff artist, educator
Rothschild, Jennifer Ann artist, educator
Rowe, Bobby Louise art educator
†Rowlett, Kimberly Jayne artist
Rubello, David Jerome artist
Rubin, Sandra Mendelsohn artist
Rubinstein, Eva (Anna) photographer
Ruffo, Michael painter
Saar, Betye (Irene Saar) artist
Samuels, Hanna artist
†Santini, Debrah Ann artist, educator
Scharf, William artist
Schiff, Jeffrey Allen art educator
Schmalz, Carl Nelson, Jr. artist, educator, printmaker
†Schmitz, Barbara art preservationist
Schultz, Eileen Hedy graphic designer
Schultz, Gerald A. (Jerry Schultz) graphic designer
Schwartz, Lillian Feldman artist, filmaker, art analyst, writer, nurse
Schwegman, Monica Joan artist
†Scofidio, Ricardo artist
Seddon, Priscilla Tingey painter
Servello, Joseph Domenick artist, illustrator
†Shafran, Faith artist
Shapiro, Peter Efimovich sculptor
Shaughnessy, Marie Kaneko artist, business executive
Sheaff, Richard Dana graphic designer
Sheridan, Laurie artist
Sheridan, Sonia Landy artist, retired art educator
Sherman, Ruth Tenzer artist, fixtures company executive
Shore, Stephen photographer
Siejka, George John artist
†Siner, Maggie artist, educator
Sires, Jonathan Paul sculptor
†Smith, Edith MacNamara artist
Smith, Leonore Rae artist
Smits, Kathleen Curran artist, educator
Snelson, Kenneth Duane sculptor
Solomon, Amelia Kroll artist
Sorel, Edward artist
Sorensen, Jean artist
Souders, Jean Swedell artist, educator
Spence, Andrew artist, painter
Spero, Nancy artist
Squier, Jack Leslie sculptor, educator
†Stackhouse, Robert sculptor
Stamm, Geoffrey Eaton retired arts administrator
Starkweather, Teresa Madery artist, educator
Steel, Kuniko June retired artist
Steffian, Emily Enders artist
Steir, Pat Iris artist
Stevens, May artist
Stinsmuehlen-Amend, Susan artist
Stover, Laura Elkins artist
Streeter, Tal sculptor
Strider, Marjorie Virginia artist, educator
Stripling, Betty Keith artist, nurse
Strisik, Paul artist
Stroudsburg, Ty painter
Studer, Carol A. creative director, graphic designer, consultant
Sumichrast, Jozef illustrator, designer
Tardos, Anne artist, composer, writer
Taylor, Margaret Turner clothing designer, writer, space planner, architectural designer
Taylor, Peggy Horne artist, educator
Thiel, Philip design educator
†Thielen, Jean Rose artist
Thompson, Mark Lee art educator, sculptor
†Thomson, Caroline Helen artist
Tingley, Jay Allen graphic designer
Tobias, Richard artist
Tomkow, Gwen Adelle artist
Torak, Elizabeth Lichtenstein artist
Triana, Gladys artist
Turner, Bonese Collins artist, educator
†Tyrrell, Lilian craftsperson, artist
Tytla, Peter T. artist
Unithan, Dolly visual artist
Vassil, Pamela graphic designer, writer, administrator
Venezia, Michael painter, educator
Vero, Radu freelance medical and scientific illustrator, educator, writer, consultant
Von Furstenberg, Diane Simone Michelle fashion designer, writer, entrepreneur
†Wagner, Tom Edward artist, dancer
Walker, Debra artist
†Ward, Nari sculptor
Watkins, Lewis Boone artist
Weber, Laurie Ann artist
†Webster, Andrew John art educator
Wechter, Vivienne Thaul artist, poet, educator
Wegman, William George artist
Weidner, Roswell Theodore artist
Whitson, Angie artist
Wilde, John artist, educator

Willenbecher, John *artist*
Wilson, Jane *artist*
Winokur, Neil *photographer*
†Wioch, Christina Helena *artist*
Witt, Nancy Camden *artist*
Wylan, Barbara *artist*
Yampolsky, Phyllis *artist*
†Yates, Gary Lee *artist*
York, Walter Allen *cinematographer*
Zajac, Jack *sculptor, painter*
Zaleski, Jean *artist*
Zapf, Hermann *book and type designer*
Zekman, Terri Margaret *graphic designer*
Zelinsky, Paul O. *illustrator, painter, author*
Zentz, Patrick James *artist, rancher*
Zercher, David Lowell *artist*
Zheutlin, Dale *sculptor, educator*
†Zigmond, Michael J. *artist*
†Zinn, Ellen Sherman *artist*
Zox, Larry *artist*

ASSOCIATIONS AND ORGANIZATIONS. *See also* specific fields.

UNITED STATES

ALABAMA

Athens
Hawley, Harold Patrick *educational consultant*

Birmingham
Carter, Frances Tunnell (Fran Carter) *fraternal organization administrator*
Gross, Iris Lee *association executive*
Kirkley, D. Christine *non-profit organization administrator*
Moran, William Madison *fundraising executive*
Newton, Don Allen *chamber of commerce executive*
Parker, Israel Frank *national association consultant*
Rynearson, W. John *foundation administrator*

Epes
Zippert, John *association administrator, editor, publisher*

Huntsville
Motz, Kenneth Lee *former farm organization official*

Mobile
Lindsey, Bebe Gustin *fundraiser*
McCann, Clarence David, Jr. *special events coordinator, museum curator and director, artist*

Montgomery
Jones, Charles William *association executive*

Vestavia Hills
Diasio, Ilse Wolfartsberger *volunteer*

ALASKA

Anchorage
Jones, Mark Logan *educational association executive, educator*
Marcey, Jean LaVerne *educational association administrator*
O'Regan, Deborah *association executive, lawyer*
Thrasher-Livingston, Kara Scott *program director*

Fairbanks
Wilkniss, Peter E. *foundation administrator, researcher*

Nome
McCoy, Douglas Michael *social services administrator, clergyman*

ARIZONA

Dewey
Burch, Mary Lou *organization consultant, housing advocate*

Dragoon
Woosley, Anne I. *cultural organization administrator*

Phoenix
Daniels, Barbara Ann *non-profit organization executive*
Dorland, Byrl Brown *retired civic worker*
Hassett, Brian Thomas *administrator local chapter of United Way*
Hays, E. Earl *youth organization administrator*
Murphy, John W. *foundation executive*
Smith, Stuart Robert *foundation executive*

Scottsdale
Ferree, John Newton, Jr. *fundraising specialist, consultant*
Jacobson, Frank Joel *cultural organization administrator*
Muller, H(enry) Nicholas, III *foundation executive*

Sedona
Stoufer, Ruth Hendrix *community volunteer*

Sierra Vista
Morrow, Bruce William *educational administrator, business executive, consultant, author*

Tempe
Sullivan-Boyle, Kathleen Marie *association executive*

Tucson
Johnson, Robert Bruce *company director*
Jones, John Stanley *director special projects, Tucson*
Langum, W. Sue *civic worker*
Powers, Stephen *educational researcher, consultant*
Riggs, Frank Lewis *foundation executive*
Ross, Robert *health agency administrator*
Sickel, Joan Sottilare *foundation administrator*
Tirrell, John Albert *organization executive, consultant*

Wickenburg
Baker, Carolyn *musician*

ARKANSAS

Morrilton
†Tugwell, Franklin *think-tank executive*

North Little Rock
Doyle, William Lynn *fundraising consultant*

CALIFORNIA

Alamo
Hardy, Lois Lynn *educational training company executive*

Aliso Viejo
Reading, Phyllis Ann *professional association executive, nurse*

Altadena
Griswold, Martha Kerfoot *social worker*

Arroyo Grande
†Battles, Lara *counselor, psychotherapist*

Atherton
King, Jane Cudlip Coblentz *volunteer educator*

Berkeley
Myers, Miles Alvin *educator, educational association administrator*

Beverly Hills
Davis, Bruce *cultural organization administrator*
O'Keefe, John Francis *fundraiser*
Pavlik, John Michael *performing arts association executive*

Burbank
†Rawlinson, Joseph *foundation executive*

Burlingame
Mahoney, Ann Dickinson *fundraiser*

Canoga Park
Lederer, Marion Irvine *cultural administrator*

Carlsbad
Liddicoat, Richard Thomas, Jr. *professional society administrator*

Carmel
Morain, Mary Stone Dewing *volunteer association executive*

Chico
Burks, Rocky Alan *independent living center executive, consultant*

Citrus Heights
Leisey, Donald Eugene *educational materials company executive, educator*

Claremont
Warder, Michael Young *think tank executive*

Culver City
Netzel, Paul Arthur *fundraising management executive, consultant*

Daly City
Civitello-Joy, Linda Joan *association executive*

Dana Point
Reed, David Andrew *foundation executive*

Davis
Hays, Myrna Mantel *educational association administrator, fashion consultant*
Wydick, Judith Brandli James *volunteer*

El Monte
Last, Marian Helen *social services administrator*

Elk Grove
McIntyre-Ragusa, Mary Maureen *social services consultant*

Encino
Baker, William Morris *cultural organization administrator*

Foster City
Carter, William Gerald *non-profit corporation executive*

Glendora
Day-Gowder, Patricia Joan *retired association executive, consultant*

Hawthorne
Gruenwald, James Howard *association executive, consultant*

Hollywood
Blakeney, Karen Elizabeth *social work administrator, consultant*

Irvine
Fouste, Donna H. *association executive*

Keene
Rodriguez, Arturo Salvador *labor union official*

Kentfield
Blum, Joan Kurley *fundraising executive*

La Canada Flintridge
Racklin, Barbara Cohen *fundraising consultant*

La Jolla
Knox, Elizabeth Louise *community volunteer, travel consultant*

Lee Vining
McQuilkin, Geoffrey James *enviromental association administrator*

Lodi
Nusz, Phyllis Jane *retired fundraising consultant, meeting planner*

Long Beach
Muchmore, Don Moncrief *museum, foundation, educational, financial fund raising and public opinion consulting firm administrator, banker*
Patino, Douglas Xavier *foundation, government agency, and university administrator*

Los Altos
Farber, Geraldine Ossman *civic worker*
Orr, Susan Packard *business owner*
Wilbur, Colburn Sloan *foundation administrator, chief executive officer*

Los Angeles
Banks, Melissa Richardson *fund raising professional*
Berenbaum, Michael Gary *foundation admnistrator, theology educator*
Chassman, Leonard Fredric *labor union administrator*
Christopher, James Roy *executive director*
Ellsworth, Frank L. *non-profit executive*
Hubbs, Donald Harvey *foundation executive*
Lindley, F(rancis) Haynes, Jr. *foundation president emeritus, lawyer*
Mack, J. Curtis, II *civic organization administrator*
Marrow, Deborah *foundation executive, art historian*
Marshall, Mary Jones *civic worker*
Munitz, Barry *foundation administrator*
O'Daniel, Damon Mark *development assistant*
Orsatti, Alfred Kendall *organization executive*
†Poole, Robert William, Jr. *foundation executive*
Pope, Alexander H. *non-profit administrator, former lawyer*
Rice, Susan F. *fundraising counsel executive*
Schine, Wendy Wachtell *foundation administrator*
†Shakely, John Bower (Jack Shakely) *foundation executive*
Smith, Jean Webb (Mrs. William French Smith) *civic worker*
Walton, Brian *labor union executive*
Wendlandt, Wendy Ann *political organizer*
Wilson, Gayle Ann *civic worker*
Wlaschin, Ken *cultural organization administrator, writer*

Manhattan Beach
Devitt-Grasso, Pauline Virginia *civic volunteer, nurse*

Marina Del Rey
Stebbins, Gregory Kellogg *foundation executive*

Menlo Park
†Altman, Drew E. *foundation executive*
Fairbank, Jane Davenport *editor, civic worker*
†Johansen, Bob *think-tank executive*
Nichols, William Ford, Jr. *foundation executive, business executive*
Pallotti, Marianne Marguerite *foundation administrator*
†Shulman, Lee S. *foundation executive*

Modesto
Whiteside, Carol Gordon *foundation executive*

Monterey
Krasno, Richard Michael *educational organization executive, educator*

Morongo Valley
Lindley, Judith Morland *cat registry administrator*

Mountain View
Bills, Robert Howard *political party executive*
Karp, Nathan *political activist*
Serra, Patricia Janet *social services administrator*

Napa
Loar, Peggy Ann *foundation administrator*

Newbury Park
McCune, Sara Miller *foundation executive, publisher*

Newport Beach
Greenfield, James M. *fund raiser*
Kallman, Burton Jay *foods association director*
Poole, Thomas Richard *endowment capital campaign director, fund raising counsel*

North Hollywood
Grasso, Mary Ann *theater association executive*

Northridge
Syms, Helen Maksym *educational administrator*

Oakland
†Hawkins, Robert B. *think tank executive*
Macmeeken, John Peebles *foundation executive, educator*

Oceanside
Roberts, James McGregor *retired professional association executive*

Orinda
Fisher, Robert Morton *foundation administrator, university administrator*

Palm Springs
Hearst, Rosalie *philanthropist, foundation executive*

Pasadena
Staehle, Robert L. *foundation executive*

Pleasanton
Whisnand, Rex James *association executive*

Pomona
Lyon, Carolyn Bartel *civic worker*

Porterville
Mullen, Rod *nonprofit organization executive*

Redwood City
Spangler, Nita Reifschneider *volunteer*

Riverside
Hodgen, Maurice Denzil *foundation executive*

Sacramento
Dunlap, John Daniel, III *association administrator*
Hayward, Fredric Mark *social reformer*
Larsen, Kenneth Marshall *art and human services advocate, consultant*
Meyer, Rachel Abijah *foundation director, artist, theorist, poet*

Salinas
Chester, Lynne *foundation executive, artist*

San Andreas
Breed, Allen Forbes *correctional administrator*

San Bernardino
Traynor, Gary Edward *association administrator*

San Diego
Beattie, Geraldine Alice (Geri Beattie) *advocate*
Carleton, Mary Ruth *foundation administrator, consultant*
Dolan, James Michael, Jr. *zoological society executive*
Grosser, T.J. *administrator, developer, fundraiser*
Krejci, Robert Harry *non-profit organizations development consultant*
Lane, Gloria Julian *foundation administrator*
Lovelace, Susan Ellen *professional society administrator*

San Francisco
Canales, James Earl, Jr. *foundation administrator*
†Collins, Dennis Arthur *foundation executive*
Du Bain, Myron *foundation administrator*
Eastham, Thomas *foundation administrator*
Fuller, William P. *president Asia Foundation*
Giovinco, Joseph *nonprofit administrator, writer*
†Goldman, Richard N. *foundation administrator*
Grose, Andrew Peter *foundation executive*
Hayes, Randall L. *environmental organizer, lecturer*
Hickman, Maxine Viola *social services administrator*
Jacobs, John Howard *professional society administrator*
Madson, David John *fundraising executive*
†Mimi, Haas *volunteer*
Murdoch, Colin *cultural organization administrator*
Nee, D. Y. Bob *think tank executive, engineering consultant*
Newirth, Richard Scott *cultural organization administrator*
†Pipes, Sally C. *think-tank executive*
Pope, Carl *professional society administrator*
Tobin, Gary Allan *cultural and community organization educator*
Wolfe, Burton H. *non-profit organization executive*

San Jose
†Nguyen, Lan Ba *cultural center administrator, educator*
Westendorf, Elaine Susan *social worker*

San Luis Obispo
Jamieson, James Bradshaw *foundation administrator*

San Marino
Hull, Suzanne White *retired administrator, author*

San Mateo
Diehr, David Bruce *social service administrator*
†Speirn, Sterling K. *foundation administrator*

San Pedro
Gammell, Gloria Ruffner *professional association administrator*

Santa Barbara
Looper, Kevin Charles *non-profit executive*
Mc Coy, Lois Clark *emergency services professional, retired county official, magazine editor*
Redick, Kevin James *cultural organization administrator*
Shreeve, Susanna Seelye *educational planning facilitator*

Santa Cruz
McLean, Hulda Hoover *volunteer, conservationist, naturalist, artist*

Santa Monica
Abarbanel, Gail *social service administrator, educator*
Foley, Jane Deborah *foundation executive*
Greene, C. Michael *art association administrator*
Rich, Michael David *research corporation executive, lawyer*
Thomson, James Alan *research company executive*
Van Dyk, Frederick Theodore *foundation executive*

Santa Rosa
Bowen, Robin Janine *non-profit agency executive*

Sherman Oaks
Marckwardt, Harold Thomas *association executive*

Sonoma
Stadtman, Verne August *former foundation executive, editor*

South Lake Tahoe
Nason, Rochelle *conservation organization administrator*
Prescott, Barbara Lodwich *educational administrator*

Stanford
Lyman, Richard Wall *foundation and university executive, historian*

Stockton
Blodgett, Elsie Grace *association executive*

Studio City
Frumkin, Simon *political activist and columnist*

Sylmar
Froelich, Beverly Lorraine *foundation director*

Tiburon
Cook, Lyle Edwards *retired fund raising executive, consultant*

Trinidad
Marshall, William Edward *historical association executive*

Truckee
Johnston, Bernard Fox *author, foundation executive*

Universal City
Gumpel, Glenn J. *association executive*

Visalia
Keenan, Robert Joseph *trade association executive*
Taylor, Helen Shields *civic worker*

Walnut
Chaney, Gene Paul Russ *trade association administrator*

Walnut Creek
Duke, Ellen Kay *community activist, playground professional*

West Hollywood
Hoffenblum, Allan Ernest *political consultant*

Whittier
Harvey, Patricia Jean *educator, administrator, retired*
Meardy, William Herman *association executive*

COLORADO

Boulder
Heath, Josephine Ward *foundation administrator*
Jonsen, Richard Wiliam *educational administrator*

Colorado Springs
Hawley, Nanci Elizabeth *social services administrator*
Killian, George Ernest *educational association administrator*
MacLeod, Richard Patrick *foundation administrator*
Miller, Zoya Dickins (Mrs. Hilliard Eve Miller, Jr.) *civic worker*
Rochette, Edward Charles *retired association executive*

Denver
Blish, Eugene Sylvester *trade association administrator*
Bryan, A(lonzo) J(ay) *service club official*
Campagna, Timothy Nicholas *institute executive*
Faatz, Jeanne Ryan *educational association director*
Fujioka, Jo Ann Ota *educational administrator, consultant*
Gloss, Lawrence Robert *fundraising executive*
Groff, JoAnn *organization administrator*
Hirschfeld, Arlene F. *civic worker, homemaker*
Hixon, Janet Kay Erickson *education specialist*
Hogan, Curtis Jule *union executive, industrial relations consultant*
Jones, Jean Correy *organization administrator*
Loeup, Kong *cultural organization administrator*
Low, Merry Cook *civic worker*
Nelson, Bernard William *foundation executive, educator, physician*
Osborn, Bonita Genevieve *school board association administrator*
Read, Patricia Ellen *administrator non-profit organization, editor*
Ward, Lester Lowe, Jr. *arts executive, lawyer*
Weelans, Andrea J. *professional association executive*

Englewood
Chesser, Al H. *union official*
†Lessey, Samuel Kenric, Jr. *foundation administrator*
Reese, Monte Nelson *agricultural association executive*

Golden
Dickinson, Carol Rittgers *arts administrator, writer, executive director*

Grand Junction
McCarthy, Mary Frances *hospital foundation administrator*

Greeley
Schrenk, Gary Dale *foundation executive*

Greenwood Village
Walker, Eljana M. du Vall *civic worker*

Guffey
Ward, Larry Thomas *social program administrator*

Highlands Ranch
Massey, Leon R. (R.L. Massey) *professional association administrator*

Indian Hills
Johnston, Laurance Scott *foundation director*

Littleton
Doty, Della Corrine *organization administrator*
Keogh, Heidi Helen Dake *advocate*

U S A F Academy
Coppock, Richard Miles *nonprofit association administrator*

CONNECTICUT

Branford
Resnick, Idrian Navarre *foundation administrator*

Bridgeport
Hendricks, Edward David *speaker, educator, consultant*
Ward, Thomas Joseph *association executive, lecturer, researcher, writer*

Darien
Marshall, Susan Lockwood *civic worker*

Fairfield
Ford, Maureen Morrissey *civic worker*

Falls Village
Toomey, Jeanne Elizabeth *animal activist*

Farmington
†Ort, Eric D. *fundraising executive*

Greenwich
Baptist, Thomas R. *association administrator*
Bjornson, Edith Cameron *foundation executive, communications consultant*

Guilford
Macy, Terrence William *social services administrator*

Hartford
Behuniak, Peter, Jr. *educational administrator, consultant*
Decko, Kenneth Owen *trade association administrator*
Gibbons, Mary Peyser *civic volunteer*

Madison
Houghton, Alan Nourse *association executive, educator, consultant*

Middletown
Carrington, Virginia Gail (Vee Carrington) *professional society administrator, librarian*

Milford
Myers, David Richard *youth organization financial executive*
Wall, Robert Emmet *educational administrator, novelist*

Mystic
Connell, Hugh P. *foundation executive*
Smith, Norman Clark *fund raising and non-profit management consultant*

New Canaan
Noxon, Margaret Walters *community volunteer*
Thomsen, Donald Laurence, Jr. *institute executive, mathematician*

New Fairfield
Meyers, Abbey S. *foundation administrator*

New Haven
Dechant, Virgil C. *fraternal organization administrator*
Hadley, Nancy Lynne *community foundation executive*

New London
Renaud, Robert (Edwin) *college administrator*

New Milford
Sallani, Marion Davis (Mrs. Werner Sallani) *social work administrator, therapist*

Newington
Sumner, David George *association executive*

North Branford
Logan, John Arthur, Jr. *retired foundation executive*

Norwalk
Fulweiler, Patricia Platt *civic worker*
Hyatt, Dorothy Ann *volunteer*

Old Lyme
Bond, Niles Woodbridge *cultural institute executive, former foreign service officer*

Old Saybrook
Spencer, William Courtney *foundation executive, international business executive*

Riverside
Coulson, Robert *retired association executive, arbitrator, author*

Rocky Hill
Dubin, Joseph William *union representative*

Roxbury
Styron, Rose Burgunder *human rights activist, poet, journalist*

Simsbury
Calvert, Lois Wilson *civic worker*

Stamford
Brakeley, George Archibald, Jr. *fundraising consultant*
Chisolm, Barbara Wille *world affairs organization executive*
McNamara, Francis Joseph, Jr. *foundation executive, lawyer*
Rilla, Donald Robert *social services administrator*
Stillings, Irene Ella Grace Cordiner *organization executive*
Wunsch, Bonnie Rubenstein *fraternal organization executive*

Waterbury
†Jorge, Juan B. *cultural organization administrator, writer*

Weston
Alcosser, Lois Harmon *cultural organization administrator*

Westport
Milton, Catherine Higgs *public service entrepreneur*
†Strmecki, Marin J. *foundation executive*

Wilton
Forger, Robert Durkin *retired professional association administrator*
†Hughes, Joan Mottola *education association representative*

DELAWARE

Bethany Beach
Gale, Robert L. *educational association administrator, consultant*

Dover
Ornauer, Richard Lewis *retired educational association administrator*

Montchanin
Hall, Robert Paul *social services administrator*

Newark
Curtis, James C. *cultural organization administrator/ history educator*
Gronka, M(artin) Steven *educational association executive, film and television producer*
Mitchell, Peter Kenneth, Jr. *educational consultant, association administrator*
Townsend, Brenda S. *educational association administrator*

Newport
†Bayard, Richard H. *political party official*

Rehoboth Beach
Warden, Richard Dana *government labor union official*

Wilmington
Battaglia, Basil Richard *political party official, company executive*
Emmert, Richard Eugene *retired professional association executive*
†Hall, Gene M. *consumer protection agency administrator*
†Milbury-Steen, Sally (Sarah) Louise *administrator not-for-profit association, advocate*
Peterson, Russell Wilbur *former association executive, former state governor*
†Simon, Elisabeth Page *nonprofit organization administrator*
Wheeler, M. Catherine *organization executive*

DISTRICT OF COLUMBIA

Washington
Abbott, Corinne *fundraiser*
Able, Edward H. *association executive*
Abrams, Elliott *think-tank executive, writer, foreign affairs analyst*
Ahmann, Mathew Hall *social action organization administrator, consultant*
Allen, Edward Lawrence, Jr. *government relations executive, lobbyist*
Ambach, Gordon Mac Kay *educational association executive*
Anderson, Dean William *educational administrator*
Andrews, Laureen E. *foundation administrator*
Andrews, Lewis Davis, Jr. *trade association executive*
Appleberry, James Bruce *higher education association executive*
Arlook, Ira Arthur *non-profit association executive*
Armacost, Michael Hayden *research institution executive, ambassador*
Arnold, William Edwin *foundation administrator, consultant*
Atherton, Alfred Leroy, Jr. *former foreign service officer*
Auerbach, Stuart Charles *development loan fund administrator, journalist*
Avery, Byllye Yvonne *health association administrator*
Babby, Ellen Reisman *education administrator*
Bagge, Carl Elmer *association executive, lawyer, consultant*
Bahr, Morton *trade union executive*
Barrow, Robert Earl *retired agricultural organization administrator*
Barry, John J. *labor union leader*
Bartlett, Charles Leffingwell *foundation executive, former newspaperman*
Barto, Cheryl *educational association administrator, researcher*
†Becker, Jerome David *writer*
Bednash, Geraldine Polly *association executive*
Bender, David Ray *library association executive*
Berner, Keith *foundation administrator executive*
Berry, Morrell John *cultural organization administrator*
Biller, Morris (Moe Biller) *union executive*
Binkley, Marilyn Rothman *educational research administrator*
Birdsall, Nancy *professional association administrator*
Blair, Louis Helion *foundation executive*
Blitzer, Charles *educational administrator*
Boaz, David Douglas *foundation executive*
Bode, Barbara *foundation executive, Internet consultant, entrepreneur*
Bond, Julian *civil rights leader*
Bonosaro, Carol Alessandra *professional association executive, former government official*
Book, Edward R. *consultant, retired association executive*
Bookbinder, Hyman H(arry) *public affairs counselor*
Borut, Donald J. *professional society administrator*
Boyle, John Edward Whiteford *cultural organization administrator*
Brightup, Craig Steven *lobbyist*
Brintnall, Michael Arthur *association executive, political scientist*
Brobeck, Stephen James *consumer advocate*
Brosnan, Carol Raphael Sarah *retired arts administrator, musician*
Brown, Norman Allen *consultant, educator*
Cagney, Michael Joseph *foundation adminstrator*
Calhoun, John Alfred *social services administrator*
Calingaert, Michael *nonprofit organization executive*
Cameron, Don R. *educational association administrator*
Campiglia, Michael Edward *association executive*
Canes, Michael Edwin *trade association administrator, economist*
Chan, Wing-Chi *cultural organization administrator, musicologist*
Chavez-Thompson, Linda *labor union administrator*
Chilcote, Samuel Day, Jr. *trade association administrator*
Cochran, John Thomas *professional association executive*
Coia, Arthur A. *labor union executive*
Colbert, Robert Ivan *education association administrator*
Coleman, Stephen William *community development executive, consultant*
Collie, H. Cris, III *trade association executive*
Cope, James Dudley *trade association executive*
Crane, Edward Harrison, III *institute executive*
Crerar, Ken A. *association executive*
Croser, Mary Doreen *educational association executive*
Cross, Christopher T. *association executive*
Crouch, Toni L. *association executive, educator*
Dallara, Charles H. *think tank executive, financial analyst*
Damgard, John Michael *trade association executive*
Davis, Christopher Lyth *professional association executive*
Deegan, Michael Warren *volunteer overseas organization administrator*
Deets, Horace *association executive*
Dettke, Dieter M. *foundation executive*
DiConti, Michael Andrew *trade organization executive*
†Dinges, Charles V. *professional association executive*
Ditlow, Clarence M. *think-tank executive*
Dobriansky, Paula Jon *business executive*
Dole, Elizabeth Hanford *former charitable organization administrator, former secretary of labor, former secretary of transportation*
Dolibois, Robert Joseph *trade association administrator*
Donahue, Thomas Reilly *trade union official*
Dooley, Betty Parsons *educational association administrator*
Dority, Douglas H. *association executive*
Dorn, Jennifer Lynn *charitable organization administrator*
Eisenberg, Pablo Samuel *non-profit organization executive*
Elliott, Thomas Michael *executive, educator, consultant*
Elsey, George McKee *foundation administrator*
Engel, Ralph *manufacturers association executive*
Feldman, Sandra *labor union administration*
Fink, Matthew Pollack *trade association executive, lawyer*
Finkle, Jeffrey Alan *professional association executive*
Finley, Julie Hamm *political party official*
Fisher, William P. *association executive*
Foard, Douglas W. *educational association administrator*
Foreman, Carol Lee Tucker *consumer advocate*
†Foster, Serrin Marie *non-profit organization executive*
Fowler, Raymond Dalton *professional association executive, psychologist*
Francois, Francis Bernard *association executive, lawyer*
†Franz, Marian C. *association administrator*
Franz, Wanda *association administrator*
Frederick, Robert Melvin *farm organization executive*
Fried, Bruce Merlin *health services director*
Friedman, Miles *trade association executive, financial services company executive, university lecturer*
Fritz, Thomas Vincent *association and business executive*
Fujito, Wayne Takeshi *international business company executive*
Fulbright, Harriet Mayor *foundation administrator*
Fuller, Kathryn Scott *environmental association executive, lawyer*
Fulton, Kenneth Ray *professional association administrator*
†Furchgott, David Max *cultural programs executive*
Gans, Curtis B. *think tank administrator*
Georgine, Robert Anthony *union executive*
Gershman, Carl Samuel *foundation administrator*
Gilliam, Arleen Fain *labor union administrator, finance executive*
Gobeli, Virginia C. *national program leader*
Goldman, Aaron *foundation executive, writer*
Goldstein, Laurence Alan *trade association executive*
Golodner, Jack *labor association official*
Gore, Tipper (Mary Elizabeth Gore) *wife of the vice president of the United States*
Gorham, William *organization executive*
Greenstein, Robert M. *non-profit organization director*
Griffenhagen, George Bernard *trade association executive*
Hamilton, Lee Herbert *educational organization administrator, former congressman*
Hanley, Frank *labor union official*
Harrison, Monika Edwards *business development executive*
Hawkinson, Brian Patrick *professional association executive*
Hays, Cindy Shelton *fundraising company executive*
Healey, John G. *human services organization executive*
Heinz, Teresa F. *foundation administrator*
†Henick, Henry Christopher *lobbyist*
Hills, John Merrill *educational administrator, consultant, former public policy research center executive*
Hoffman, Ann Fleisher *labor union official, lawyer*
Holloway, James Lemuel, III *foundation executive, retired naval officer*
Holmer, Alan Freeman *trade association executive, lawyer*
Houghton, Arthur A. *professional society administrator*
Howard, Glen Scott *foundation executive, lawyer*
Hoyt, John Arthur *humane society executive*
Huband, Frank Louis *educational association executive*
Hudnut, William Herbert, III *senior resident fellow, political scientist*

Hughes, Thomas Lowe *foundation executive*
Ingram, Richard Thomas *educational association executive*
Ireland, Patricia *association executive*
Isaacs, Amy Fay *political organization executive*
Ivey, William James *foundation executive, writer, producer*
Jackson, Patricia Pike *association executive*
Jacobson, Michael Faraday *consumer advocate, writer*
Jensen, James E. *director congressional and government affairs*
Joe, Thomas *think-tank*
†Johnson, Victor Charles *association executive*
Jones, George Fleming *foundation executive*
Kamber, Victor Samuel *political consultant*
Karpinski, Gene Brien *non-profit group administrator, think tank executive*
Kavanaugh, Everett Edward, Jr. *trade association executive*
Kearns, Kevin Lawrence *political association executive, lawyer*
Keeny, Spurgeon Milton, Jr. *association executive*
Keltz, Amy Lynn *political science organization administrator*
Kemp, John D. *professional society administrator*
Kempner, Jonathan L. *professional society administrator*
Kennan, Stephanie Ann *advisor*
†Kennedy, Craig *foundation administrator*
†Knapp, Andrew C. *political association administrator*
Knapp, Richard Maitland *association executive*
Knippers, Diane LeMasters *association president*
Kolb, Charles Chester *humanities administrator*
Kossak, Shelley *think-tank executive*
Kratovil, Jane Lindley *think tank associate, developer/fundraiser*
Kreig, Andrew Thomas *trade association executive*
Krepinevich, Andrew F. *organization administrator*
Kressley, Larry *foundation administrator*
Ku, Charlotte *professional association administrator*
Kullberg, John Francis *foundation administrator*
LaHaye, Beverly *cultural organization administrator*
Lampl, Peggy Ann *social services administrator*
LaPidus, Jules Benjamin *educational association administrator*
Larson, Charles Fred *trade association executive*
La Sala, James *labor union administrator*
Lawson, Richard Laverne *trade association executive, retired military officer*
LeBlanc, James Leo *business executive, consultant*
Lewis, Henry Donald *fundraising consultant*
Liederman, David Samuel *child welfare administrator*
Limon, Lavinia *social services administrator*
†Liu, Xiaozhu Drew *institute administrator, editor*
Longin, Thomas Charles *education association administrator*
Low, Stephen *foundation executive, educator, former diplomat*
Lucas, C. Payne *development organization executive*
Luciano, Peter Joseph *professional society administrator*
Lynch, Robert L. *art association administrator*
†MacLeod, Laurel A. *lobbyist, researcher*
Magrath, C. Peter *educational association executive*
Marshall, Brian Laurence *trade association executive*
Marshall, William, III *think tank executive*
Martin, Jerry Lee *organization executive, educator*
Masters, Edward E. *association executive, former foreign service officer*
†Maury, Samuel L. *association executive*
Maynes, Charles William *foundation administrator*
McEntee, Gerald W. *labor union official*
Mc Kay, Emily Gantz *civil rights professional*
McNulty, Robert Holmes *non-profit executive*
McSteen, Martha Abernathy *organization executive*
Melendez, Sara E. *non-profit organization executive*
Messner, Howard Myron *professional association executive*
Michelman, Kate *advocate*
Miller, John Francis *association executive, social scientist*
Miller, Margaret Alison *education association administrator*
Moore, Jacquelyn Cornelia *labor union official, editor*
Mtewa, Mekki *foundation administrator*
Mueller, Sharon Lee (Sherry Mueller) *educational organization executive*
Muir, Patricia Allen *professional association administrator*
Munson, Richard Jay *congressional policy analyst*
Murray, James Joseph, III *association executive*
Musil, Robert Kirkland *professional society administrator*
Nader, Ralph *consumer advocate, lawyer, author*
Narasaki, Karen Keiko *civil rights organization executive, lawyer*
Nicholson, Jim *political organization administrator*
Nicholson, Richard Selindh *educational association administrator*
†Nickens, Paula *political organization administrator*
Nikkel, Ronald Wilbert *social services administrator*
Norton, James J. *union official*
†Obrecht, Margaret M. H. *cultural organization administrator*
O'Day, Paul Thomas *trade association executive*
Ogilvie, Donald Gordon *bankers association executive*
Ottley, William Henry *professional association director, consultant*
Paal, Douglas H. *educational association administrator*
Paulson, Stanley Fay *educational association administrator*
Pearson, Roger *organization executive*
Pelavin, Sol Herbert *research company executive*
Pierce, David R. *educational administrator*
Pinstrup-Andersen, Per *educational administrator*
Platts, Howard Gregory *scientific, educational organization executive*
Pleasure, Robert Jonathan *association director, lawyer*
Pollack, Ronald F(rank) *foundation executive, lawyer*
Portney, Paul Rogers *research and educational organization executive*
Puryear, Jeffrey Merrill *cultural association administrator*
Radin, Alex *former association executive, consultant*
Raizen, Senta Amon *educational administrator, researcher*
Rayburn, Wendell Gilbert *educational association executive*
Reger, Lawrence Lee *trade association administrator*
Reich, Alan Anderson *executive*
Reumann-Moore, Andrew Owens *nonprofit executive*
†Rhame, Jean Graham *professional society administrator*
Rice, David Eugene, Jr. *trade association administrator, lawyer, consultant*
Rich, Dorothy Kovitz *educational administrator, author*
Richardson, Ann Bishop *foundation executive, lawyer*
Riehle, B. Hudson *trade association executive*
Roberts, Cecil Edward, Jr. *labor union administrator*
Robey, Kathleen Moran (Mrs. Ralph West Robey) *civic worker*
Robinson, Kenneth Leonard, Jr. *trade association executive*
Robinson, Leonard Harrison, Jr. *international government consultant, business executive*
Rodgers, Kirk Procter *international organization executive, environmentalist*
Rodman, Peter Warren *foreign policy specialist*
Rudder, Catherine Estelle *political science association administrator*
Russell, William Joseph *educational association administrator*
†Saffuri, Khaled Ahmad *cultural organization executive*
Salisbury, Dallas L. *research institute executive*
Samuel, Howard David *union official*
†Satloff, Robert B. *think-tank executive*
Scanlon, Terrence Maurice *public policy foundation administrator*
Schatz, Thomas Andrew *nonprofit organization executive, lawyer*
Schlickeisen, Rodger Oscar *non-profit environmental organization executive*
Schubert, Richard Francis *consultant*
Seldman, Neil Norman *cultural organization administrator*
Sewell, John Williamson *research association executive*
Shlaes, John B. *consultant*
Siciliano, Rocco Carmine *institute executive*
Sieverts, Frank Arne *association executive*
Sims, Robert Bell *professional society administrator, public affairs official, newspaper publisher*
Skaggs, David E. *association administrator, lawyer, educator*
Slade, John Danton *lobbyist*
†Slakey, Francis *association administrator, physics educator*
Smith, Daniel Martin *nonprofit research organization administrator*
Snyder, John Michael *lobbyist, public relations director*
Solinger, Janet Weiland *cultural association director*
Soller, R. William *association executive, pharmacologist*
Sombrotto, Vincent R. *postal union executive*
†Sparks, Kenneth R. *association executive*
Spence, Sandra *professional administrator*
Splete, Allen Peterjohn *association executive, educator*
Staats, Elmer Boyd *foundation executive, former government official*
†Stein, John Hollister *non-profit organization executive*
Stephens, John Frank *association executive, researcher*
Stern, Andrew L. *labor union administrator*
Stern, Paula *international trade advisor*
Stone, Jeremy Judah *professional society administrator*
†Stover, Mark R. *lobbyist*
Strachan, David E. *trade association executive*
Strong, Henry *foundation executive*
Sutherland, Alan Roy *foundation administrator*
Sweeney, John Joseph *labor union administrator*
Szaz, Zoltan Michael *association executive*
Tarr-Whelan, Linda *policy center executive*
Theodore, Eustace D. *educational association executive, consultant*
Tipton, E. Linwood *trade association executive*
Tobias, Robert Max *labor leader, lawyer*
Tonkin, Leo Sampson *educational foundation administrator*
Tracy, Alan Thomas *trade association administrator*
Trumka, Richard Louis *labor leader, lawyer*
Unsell, Lloyd Neal *energy organization executive, former journalist*
Vander Horst, Kathleen Purcell *nonprofit association administrator*
Vanderryn, Jack *philanthropic foundation administrator*
Van Lare, Barry Lee *social welfare executive*
Veatch, Elizabeth Wilson *educational administrator*
Veliotes, Nicholas Alexander *professional association executive, former ambassador and assistant secretary of state*
Viola, Herman Joseph *curator*
von Kann, Clifton Ferdinand *aviation and space executive, software executive*
Walker, John Denley *foundation director, former government official*
†Wallace Douglas, Jean *foundation founder, conservationist*
Ward, Michael Delavan *international agency administrator*
Warren, David Liles *educational association executive*
Weinstein, Allen *educator, historian, non-profit administrator*
Wertheimer, Fredric Michael *public policy advocate*
West, Jake *labor union administrator*
Weyrich, Paul Michael *political organizations executive*
Whitehead, Alfred K. *labor union administrator*
Williams, Eddie Nathan *research institution executive*
Williams, Lawrence Floyd *conservation organization official*
Williams, Maurice Jacoutot *development organization executive*
Williams, Ronald L. *pharmaceutical association executive*
Wilson, Glen Parten *professional society administrator*
Wise, William Harvey, IV *human service executive*
Wiseman, Laurence Donald *foundation executive*
Wolfe, Leslie R. *think-tank executive*
Woolley, John Edward *trade association executive*
Work, Jane Magruder *professional society administrator*
Yost, Paul Alexander, Jr. *foundation executive, retired coast guard officer*
Yzaguirre, Raul Humberto *civil rights leader*
Zielinski, Paul Bernard *grant program administrator, civil engineer*

FLORIDA

Bal Harbour
Ash, Dorothy Matthews *civic worker*

Boca Raton
Jessup, Jan Amis *arts volunteer, writer*
Kirkbride, Patricia Capell *educational aministrator*

Boynton Beach
Blodee, Merle Huie *civic worker*
Rogers, John S. *retired union official*

Coral Gables
†Jones, Susan Tamny *fundraising executive*

Coral Springs
Burg, Ralph *art association executive*

Delray Beach
Stewart, Patricia Carry *foundation administrator*

Destin
De Revere, David Wilsen *professional society administrator*

Englewood
Schultz, Arthur Joseph, Jr. *retired trade association executive*

Estero
Brown, William Robert *association executive, consultant*

Fort Lauderdale
Calhoun, Peggy Joan *fundraising executive*
McAusland, Randolph M. N. *arts administrator*
Miller, Jerome M. *civic worker*
Washington, Alice Hester *human services professional*

Fort Pierce
Stock, Grace Emma *civic volunteer*

Haines City
Ware, Clarkie May Flake *civic worker*

Hallandale
Contney, John Joseph *trade association administrator*

Heathrow
Darbelnet, Robert Louis *automobile association executive*

Hialeah
Phelps, Dorothy Frink *civic worker*

Jacksonville
†Beitz, William Charles *religious charity executive*
Bennett, Michael Wayne *social services administrator, consultant*
Glover, Richard Bernard *foundation administrator*
Johnson, Leland "Lee" Harry *social services administrator*
†Magill, Sherry *foundation administrator*
Morris, Max King *foundation executive, former naval officer*

Lake Worth
Goldstein, Jerome Charles *professional association executive, surgeon, otolaryngologist*

Lakeland
Santangelo, Daniel L. *association administrator*
Spencer, Mary Miller *civic worker*

Lauderdale By The Sea
Wynne, Brian James *former association executive, consultant*

Longboat Key
Dorsey, Eugene Carroll *former foundation and communications executive*

Longwood
Dunne, Nancy Anne *retired social services administrator*

Maitland
Lovelace, Dorothy Louise *volunteer*

Melbourne
Dale, Cynthia Lynn Arpke *educational administrator, retired*

Miami
Beckley, Donald K. *fundraiser*
Bennett, Olga Salowich *civic worker, graphic arts researcher, consultant*
Blanco, Josefa Joan-Juana (Jossie Blanco) *social services administrator*
Brinkman, Paul Del(bert) *foundation executive*
Cullom, William Otis *trade association executive*
Dickason, John Hamilton *retired foundation executive*
Heiens, Richard Allen *education foundation executive*
Hills, Lee *foundation administrator, newspaper executive, consultant*
†Montes-Bradley, Saul Mariano *foundation administrator*
VanBrode, Derrick Brent, IV *trade association administrator*

Miami Beach
†Hair, Gilbert Martin *foundation administrator*

Miccosukee Cpo
Humphrey, Louise Ireland *civic worker, equestrienne*

Naples
Rowe, Herbert Joseph *retired trade association executive*

Nocatee
Turnbull, David John (Chief Piercing Eyes-Penn) *cultural association executive*

Nokomis
Holec, Anita Kathryn Van Tassel *civic worker*

North Palm Beach
Crawford, Roberta *association administrator*
Woodard, Wallace William, III *quality advocate*

Okeechobee
Bishop, Sid Glenwood *union official*

Ormond Beach
Lively, Carol A. *professional society administrator*

Osprey
Harrington, Nancy Regina O'Connor *volunteer*

Palm Beach
Chittick, Elizabeth Lancaster *association executive, women's rights activist*
Elson, Suzanne Goodman *community activist*
Hope, Margaret Lauten *civic worker*
Mandel, Carola Panerai (Mrs. Leon Mandel) *foundation trustee*
Moloney, Thomas Walter *consulting firm executive*
Rinker, Ruby Stewart *foundation administrator*

Palm Beach Gardens
Falk, Bernard Henry *trade association executive*

Panama City Beach
Schafer, John Stephen *foundation administrator*

Pensacola
Furlong, George Morgan, Jr. *health care foundation executive, retired naval officer*
Walker, Peggy Jean *social work agency administrator*

Pinellas Park
West, Wallace Marion *cultural organization administrator*

Ponte Vedra
Watson, John Lawrence, III *former trade association executive*

Ponte Vedra Beach
Van Nelson, Nicholas Lloyd *business council executive*

Punta Gorda
Clinton, Mariann Hancock *educational association administrator*

Saint Augustine
Fevurly, Keith Robert *educational administrator*
Marsolais, Harold Raymond *trade association administrator*
Rountree, John Griffin Richardson *association and retail executive*

Saint Petersburg
Allshouse, Merle Frederick *educational organization administrator*

Sanibel
Ball, Armand Baer *former association executive, consultant*

Sarasota
Bausch, James John *foundation executive*
Spencer, Lonabelle (Kappie Spencer) *political agency administrator, lobbyist*
Tamberrino, Frank Michael *professional association executive*

Stuart
Hutchinson, Janet Lois *historical society administrator*

Tallahassee
Hammer, Marion Price *association executive*
Harbin, Merline Johnson *social service agency administrator*
Ryll, Frank Maynard, Jr. *professional society administrator*
Turnbull, Marjorie Reitz *foundation executive, state legislator*
Valencic, Cynthia *foundation administrator*

Tampa
Callan, Joseph Patrick *social service administrator*
Catoe, Paul *cultural organization administrator*
Ingalls, Rick Lee *fundraising consulting executive*
Lowe, Peter Stephen *non-profit company executive*
Tapp, Mamie Pearl *educational association administration*

Wesley Chapel
Holloway, Marvin Lawrence *retired automobile club executive, rancher, vintager*

West Palm Beach
Atkinson, Regina Elizabeth *medical social worker*
DeMoss, Nancy *foundation administrator*
Engh, Fredric Charles *educational association administrator*

Winter Haven
Gobie, Henry Macaulay *philatelic researcher, retired postal executive*

Winter Park
Myers, Norman Lewis *fund development consultant*
Olsson, Nils William *former association executive*

Zephyrhills
Powell, David Thomas, Jr. *retired association administrator*

GEORGIA

Americus
Fuller, Millard Dean *charitable organization executive, lawyer*

Atlanta
Axon, Michael *education association field representative*
Barnes, Harry G., Jr. *human rights activist, conflict resolution specialist, retired ambassador*
Birdsong, Alta Marie *volunteer*
Brandt, Gene Stuart *fundraising consultant*
DeConcini, Barbara *association executive, religious studies educator*
Harrison, John Raymond *foundation executive, retired newspaper executive*
Jones, Joseph W. *foundation administrator*
Kelly, William Watkins *educational association executive*
King, Coretta Scott (Mrs. Martin Luther King, Jr.) *educational association administrator, lecturer, writer, concert singer*
King, Philip Jerome *internet retailer, music business consultant*
Lehfeldt, Martin Christopher *nonprofit association executive*
McTier, Charles Harvey *foundation administrator*
Petty, E. James *community service director*
Philipp, Alicia *community foundation executive*
†Riordan, Bridget Guernsey *educational administrator*
Robertson, Kimberly Harden *social welfare administrator*
Scarpucci, Penelope Alderman *fundraising executive*
Scott, William Fred *cultural organization administrator*
Spillett, Roxanne *social services administrator*
Starr, Charles Christopher *foundation executive, priest*
Thumann, Albert *association executive, engineer*
Walker, Jennie Louise *research director*
White, Ann Wells *community activist*

Augusta
Davison, Frederick Corbet *foundation executive*

College Park
Mays, Jill Duncan *social services administrator, counselor*

Decatur
Garrett, Gloria Susan *social services professional*

Duluth
Reed, Ralph Eugene, Jr. *association executive, writer*

Lagrange
Gresham, James Thomas *foundation executive*

Macon
Mills, Cynthia Spraker *association executive*

Norcross
Hill, I. Kathryn *medical certification agency executive*
LaFramboise, Patrick Joseph *trade association administrator*

Peachtree City
Pulin, Carol *fine arts organization administrator*

Riverdale
Rhoden, Mary Norris *educational center director*

Roswell
Glassick, Charles Etzweiler *academic foundation administrator*
Thibaudeau, Mary Frances *cultural organization administrator*

Sautee Nacoochee
Hill, Ronald Guy *non profit organization consultant*

Savannah
Hill, Dorothy Bennett *community activist*

Summerville
Spivey, Suzan Brooks Nisbet *association administrator, medical technologist*

Tucker
McNair, Nimrod, Jr. *foundation executive, consultant*

Winterville
Shockley, W. Ray *travel trade association executive*

HAWAII

Hawaii National Park
Nicholson, Marilyn Lee *arts administrator*

Honolulu
Bornhorst, Marilyn *Democrat party chariwoman*
Furuyama, Renee Harue *association executive*
Jordan, Amos Azariah, Jr. *foreign affairs educator, retired army officer*
Kahikina, Michael Puamamo *social services administrator, state legislator*
†Morrison, Charles *think-tank executive*
Robinson, Robert Blacque *foundation administrator*
Schoenke, Marilyn Leilani *foundation administrator*
White, Emmet, Jr. *retirement community administrator*
Witeck, John Joseph *labor union representative, educator*

Lihue
Lenthall, Judith Faith *non-profit corporation administrator*
Pironti, Lavonne De Laere *developer, fundraiser*

IDAHO

Boise
Craig, Kara Lynn *chief executive officer*

Coeur D Alene
Sanderson, Holladay Worth *domestic violence advocate*

Homedale
Patterson, Beverly Ann Gross *fund raising consultant, grant writer, federal grants administrator, social services administrator, poet*

Salmon
†Nisbet, Marian Frances *community and political activist*

ILLINOIS

Arlington Heights
Nerlinger, John William *trade association administrator*

Barrington
Dykla, K.H.S. Edward George *retired social services administrator*

Belleville
Brian, Patricia Ann *social services administrator*

Belvidere
Luhman, William Simon *community development administrator*

Carlinville
Bellm, Joan *civic worker*
Goudy, Josephine Gray *social services administrator*

Champaign
Clark, Roger Gordon *educational administrator*

Chicago
Barker, Emmett Wilson, Jr. *trade association executive*
Benson, Sally Jean *development manager*
Bloch, Ralph Jay *professional association executive*
Bourdon, Cathleen Jane *executive director*
Bushman, Mary Laura Jones *developer, fundraiser*
Clevenger, Penelope *international business consultant*
Connelly, John Dooley *social service organization executive*
Creighton, Neal *foundation administrator, retired army officer*
Daffron, Sandra Ratcliff *professional society administrator*
Dolan, Thomas Christopher *professional society administrator*
Donnell, Harold Eugene, Jr. *professional society administrator*
English, Henry L. *not-for-profit association executive*
Feldstein, Charles Robert *fund raising consultant*
Frazin, Rhona Sondra *non-profit executive*
Hayes, Richard Johnson *association executive, lawyer*
Herbert, Victor James *foundation administrator*
Jackson, Jesse Louis *civic and political leader, clergyman*
Jonas, Harry S. *professional society administrator*
Kelly, Jerry Bob *social services administrator*
Kinnamon, Ron *administrator*
Kleiman, Kelly (Ruth B.) *non-profit organization consultant, lawyer*
Koenig, Bonnie *international non-profit organization consultant*
Kudo, Irma Setsuko *not-for-profit executive director*
Leff, Deborah *non-profit executive*
Lerner, Alexander Robert *association executive*
†López, Cecilia Luisa *educational association administrator*
MacDougal, Gary Edward *corporate director, foundation trustee*
Mathieu-Harris, Michele Suzanne *association executive*
Mercer, David Robinson *cultural organization administrator*
Miller, Jay Alan *civil rights association executive*
Minow, Josephine Baskin *civic worker*
Murphy, Ellis *association management executive*
Nebenzahl, Paul *fundraising executive, museum executive*
Newman, Wade Davis *trade association executive*
Olsen, Rex Norman *trade association executive*
Ree, Donna *social services administrator, educator*
†Regenstein, Joseph, Jr. *foundation executive*
Rehage, Kenneth J. *educational association administrator*
Richman, Harold Alan *social welfare policy educator*
Rielly, John Edward *educational association administrator*
Rodgers, James Foster *association executive, economist*
Saliga, Pauline Andrea *administrator*
Scalish, Frank Anthony *labor union administrator*
Schaefer, Helene G(eraldine) *social services professional*
Schimberg, Barbara Hodes *organizational development consultant*
Skolnick, Sherman Herbert *media host/producer, researcher, court reformer*
So, Frank S. *educational association administrator*
†Socolow, Daniel James *foundation administrator*
Vogelzang, Jeanne Marie *professional association executive, attorney*
Wallerstein, Mitchel Bruce *foundation executive*
Weber, Daniel E. *association executive*
Weigand, Russell Glen *fundraising consulting firm executive*
Wilhelm, David C. *political organization administrator*
Wright, Helen Kennedy *professional association administrator, publisher, editor, librarian*

Crystal Lake
Chamberlain, Charles James *railroad labor union executive*
Linklater, Isabelle Stanislawa Yarosh-Galazka (Lee Linklater) *foundation administrator*

Deerfield
Stavropoulos, Rose Mary Grant *community activist, volunteer*

Des Plaines
Quellmalz, Frederick *foundation executive, editor*

East Hazel Crest
Ruyle-Hullinger, Elizabeth Smith (Beth Ruyle) *association executive*

Elgin
Kelly, Matthew Edward *association executive, retired*

Elmhurst
Hildreth, R(oland) James *foundation executive, economist*
Noffs, David Sharrard *foundation administrator*

Evanston
Abnee, A. Victor *trade association executive*
Gordon, Julie Peyton *foundation administrator*
Raymond, Frank Joseph *association executive*
Thrash, Patricia Ann *educational association administrator*
Yoder, Frederick Floyd *fraternity executive*

Galena
Hermann, Paul David *retired association executive*

Glen Ellyn
Jens, Elizabeth Lee Shafer (Mrs. Arthur M. Jens, Jr.) *civic worker*

Harvey
Dunn, Eraina Burke *non-profit organization administrator, city official*

Hoffman Estates
Roach, William Russell *training and education executive*

Joliet
Holzrichter, Fred William *foundation executive*

Kankakee
Gurney, Pamela Kay *social services official*

La Grange Park
Brown, Helen Sauer *fund raising executive*

Lake Bluff
Schreiber, George Richard *association executive, writer*

Lake Forest
Fetridge, Bonnie-Jean Clark (Mrs. William Harrison Fetridge) *civic volunteer*
Taylor, Barbara Ann Olin *educational consultant*

Long Grove
Connor, James Richard *foundation administrator*

Mooseheart
Ross, Donald Hugh *fraternal organization executive*

Naperville
L'Allier, James Joseph *educational multimedia company executive, instructional designer*

Oak Brook
John, Richard C. *enterprise development organization executive*

Orion
Magee, Elizabeth Sherrard *civic organization volunteer*

Ottawa
Thornton, Edmund B. *philanthropist*

Palatine
Brod, Catherine Marie *foundation administrator*
Walker, Sally Y. *educational association administrator*

Park Ridge
Bailey, Marianne Therese *social service administrator*
Ewald, Robert Frederick *insurance association executive*
Kleckner, Dean Ralph *trade association executive*

Peoria
Bussone, Frank Joseph *foundation executive, television broadcaster*
Kroehler, Ralph S. *association executive*
Laible-White, Sherry Lynne *welfare reform administrator*
Quanstrom, Roy Fred *non-profit organization executive*

Percy
Rice, Charles Dale *labor relations specialist, writer*

Riverside
Dengler, Robert Anthony *professional association executive*

Rock Falls
Julifs, Sandra Jean *community action agency executive*

Rockford
Falzone, John F. *association executive*
Heinke, Warren E. *social services administrator*

Rosemont
Good, William Allen *professional society executive*

Schaumburg
Little, Bruce Washington *professional society administrator*
Tompson, Marian Leonard *professional society administrator*

Skokie
Gleason, John Patrick, Jr. *trade association executive*

Springfield
Puckett, Carlissa Roseann *non-profit association executive*

Tiskilwa
McCauley, Helen Nora *civic worker*

Urbana
Sturtevant, William T. *fundraising executive, consultant*

Vernon Hills
Michalik, John James *legal educational association executive*

Waukegan
Drapalik, Betty Ruth *civic worker, artist*

West Peoria
McBride, Sharon Louise *counselor, technical communication educator*

Wilmette
Brink, Marion Francis *trade association administrator*
Hansen, Andrew Marius *retired library association executive*

Winfield
McNutt, Kristen Wallwork *consumer affairs executive*

Winnetka
Andersen, Kenneth Benjamin *retired association executive*
Owens, Luvie Moore *association consultant*

INDIANA

Batesville
St. Pierre, William Edward *regional director*

Bloomington
Wilson, Kathy Kay *foundation executive*

Cedar Lake
Loudermilk, Mary Ruth *local government volunteer*

Elkhart
Shackle, Karen Ann *non-profit association executive*

Evansville
Early, Judith K. *social services director*
Halterman, Martha Lee *social services administrator, counselor*
Tilley, Sheryl J. (Sherry Tilley) *nonprofit organization executive*

Fishers
Gatto, Louis Constantine *educational authority executive*

Fort Wayne
Archer-Sorg, Karen S. *association coordinator*
Chapman, Paula Anne *cultural organization administrator*
Clay, Juanita Loundmon *mental health consultant*

Friendship
Miller, John *foundation administrator*

Hanna
Stephenson, Dorothy Maxine *volunteer*

Indianapolis
Barcus, Robert Gene *educational association administrator*
Beazley, Hamilton Scott *volunteer health organization executive*
Blaydes, June Louise *volunteer*
Clark, Charles M., Jr. *research institution adminstrator*
Dortch, Carl Raymond *former association executive*
Finley, Katherine Mandusic *professional society administrator*
Maxwell, Florence Hinshaw *civic worker*
Recker, Thomas Edward *fraternal organization executive*
Robbins, N. Clay *foundation administrator*
Shaffer, Alfred Garfield (Terry) *service organization executive*
Skvarenina, Joseph Lee *development/public relations professional, editor*
Sweezy, John William *political party official*
Vereen, Robert Charles *retired trade association executive*

Michigan City
Blake, George Alan, Jr. *non-profit association executive, consultant*

North Manchester
Horn, Carol Garver *foundation administrator*
Myers, Anne M. *development director*

North Vernon
Williams, John Albert *developmental disabilities agency director*

Santa Claus
Platthy, Jeno *cultural association executive*

Shelby
Kurzeja, Richard Eugene *professional society administrator*

South Bend
Hunt, Mary Reilly *organization executive*

Terre Haute
Aldridge, Sandra *civic volunteer*

West Lafayette
Watlington, Sarah Jane *community volunteer, retired military officer*

IOWA

Carroll
De Moss, Lloyd G. *community service executive*

Cedar Rapids
Berry, Roberta Mildred *civic worker*
Whipple, William Perry *foundation administrator*

Decorah
Barnes-Guzman, Beth Yvette *grants administrator*

Des Moines
Nelson, Charlotte Bowers *public administrator*
Peterson, Michael K. *Democrat party chairman*
Powell, Sharon Lee *social welfare organization administrator*
Womack, Doug C. *labor union representative*

Iowa City
Bailey, Regenia Dee *non-profit executive*
Blake, Darlene Evelyn *political worker, consultant, educator, author*
Ferguson, Richard L. *educational administrator*

Larchwood
Zangger, Russell George *organization executive, flying school executive*

Mason City
Moneir, Tarek *community development administrator*

Muscatine
Steinmaus, Mary Carol *foundation administrator*

Sioux City
Waller, Ephraim Everett *retired professional association executive*

West Branch
Forsythe, Patricia Hays *development professional*

KANSAS

Fort Riley
Spurrier-Bright, Patricia Ann *executive director*

Kansas City
Campbell, Joseph Leonard *trade association executive*

Lawrence
Bowman, Laird Price *retired foundation administrator*
Mona, Stephen Francis *golf association executive*

Manhattan
Flaherty, Roberta D. *educational association administrator*

Overland Park
Benjamin, Janice Yukon *foundation development executive*

Shawnee Mission
Green, John Lafayette, Jr. *education executive*
Slater, William Adcock *retired social services organization executive*

Topeka
Beachy, William R. *non-profit executive*
Menninger, Roy Wright *medical foundation executive, psychiatrist*
Powers, Ramon Sidney *historical society administrator, historian*

Weskan
Okeson, Dorothy Jeanne *educational association administrator*

Wichita
Lowrey, Annie Tsunee *retired cultural organization administrator*

Winfield
Gray, Ina Turner *fraternal organization administrator*

KENTUCKY

Berea
Stephenson, Jane Ellen *educational association administrator*

Bowling Green
Pannell, Patricia Gay *independent living specialist, state official*

Corbin
Barton-Collings, Nelda Ann *political activist, newspaper, bank and nursing home executive*

Frankfort
Cody, Wilmer St. Clair *educational administrator*
Dringenburg, Duane Clinton *social services executive*
†McCloud, Ronald B. *political organization executive*

La Grange
Livers, Thomas Henry *fundraiser for nonprofit organizations*

Lexington
Lewis, Robert Kay, Jr. *fundraising executive*
†Scudder, Brooks Alfred *public administrator*

Louisville
Bentley, James Robert *association curator, historian, genealogist*
Early, Jack Jones *foundation executive*
Fleming, Laura Elizabeth *non-profit executive*
Watts, Beverly L. *civil rights executive*

Morehead
†Barker, Garry Gene *art center administrator*

LOUISIANA

Baton Rouge
Conerly, Evelyn Nettles *educational consultant*
Francis, Michael G. *political party official*
Jeffers, Ben *political organization executive*
Moore, Robert Wesley *foundation administrator*
†Odom, Bob *state agricultural and forestry commissioner*
Warren, John William *professional society administrator*

Metairie
Kramer, Helene G. *political and civic association executive*

New Orleans
Benjamin, Adelaide Wisdom *community volunteer and activist*
†Cohen, Rosalie *civic worker*
Rathke, Dale Lawrence *community organizer and financial analyst*
Sullivan, Daniel Edmond *fundraising executive*
Weeks, Lana Carol *clinical social worker*

Ruston
Sabin, Paul Edgar *developer*

Shreveport
Goodman, Sylvia Klumok *volunteer*
Magness, Nan Jean *social services administrator*

MAINE

Augusta
Gervais, Paul Nelson *foundation administrator, psychotherapist, public relations executive*
†Hall, Christopher *political party official*
Trites, Donald George *human service consultant*

Camden
†Keogh, Kevin *political party official*

Caribou
Bosse, Denise Frances *educational administrator, education educator*

Friendship
Merrill, Mary Lee *professional society administrator*

Georgetown
Chapin, Maryan Fox *civic worker*

Kittery Point
Howells, Muriel Gurdon Seabury (Mrs. William White Howells) *volunteer*

Old Town
Pajama, Helen *advocate*

Orrs Island
Porter, Maxiene Helen Greve *civic worker*

Pemaquid
Howell, Jeanette Helen *retired cultural organization administrator*

Portland
Konkel, Harry Wagner *civic volunteer, retired career officer*
Scott, Aurélia Carmelita *non-profit organization executive, writer*

S Portland
Harris, Penny Smith *fundraising consultant*

Spruce Head
Bird, Mary Alice *fund raising consultant*

West Baldwin
Pierce, Elizabeth Gay *civic worker*

Windham
Mulvey, Mary Crowley *retired adult education director, gerontologist, senior citizen association administrator*

York
Smart, Mary-Leigh Call (Mrs. J. Scott Smart) *civic worker*

MARYLAND

Aberdeen Proving Ground
Tobin, Aileen Webb *educational administrator*

Annapolis
Brady, Frank Benton *retired technical society executive*
Iannoli, Joseph John, Jr. *university development executive*
Stahl, David Edward *trade association administrator, retired*

Baltimore
Alpern, Linda Lee Wevodau *health agency administrator*
Backas, James Jacob *foundation administrator*
Chang, Debbie I-Ju *health services director*
Deffenbaugh, Ralston H., Jr. *immigration agency executive, lawyer*
DeKuyper, Mary Hundley *non-profit consultant*
Dickinson, Jane W. *social services administrator*
Douglass, Robert Lee *electronics association executive, city councilman*
†Embry, Robert C. *foundation administrator*
Ephross, Paul Hullman *social work educator*
Freeze, James Donald *administrator, clergyman*
Fuentealba, Victor William *professional society administrator*
Kemp, Suzanne Leppart *educator, clubwoman*
Pinkard, Anne Merrick *foundation administrator*
Safran, Linda Jacqueline *fundraising consultant*
Weber, Nancy Walker *charitable trust administrator*

Bethesda
Beall, Robert Joseph *foundation executive*
Buhler, Leslie Lynn *institute administrator*
Cleary, Timothy Finbar *professional society administrator*
Day, Robert Dwain, Jr. *foundation executive, lawyer*
Grady, Patricia A. *health institute director, researcher*
Grandy, Fred *foundation administrator, former congressman, former actor*
Grau, John Michael *trade association executive*
Hartnett, Elizabeth A. *trade association executive*
Hershaft, Alex *organization executive*
Hodes, Richard J. *think tank executive, immunologist, researcher*
Hyman, Steven Edward *federal agency administrator, psychiatrist, educator*
Leshner, Alan Irvin *science foundation administrator*
Nelligan, William David *professional association executive*
Oddis, Joseph Anthony *associations executive*
Salisbury, Tamara Paula *foundation executive*
Saunders, Charles Baskerville, Jr. *retired association executive*
Sprott, Richard Lawrence *foundation administrator, researcher*
Tape, Gerald Frederick *former association executive*
Thursz, Daniel *retired service organization executive, consultant*
Wright, Helen Patton *professional society administrator*

Bowie
Stultz, Katherine Diane *genealogical society administrator*

Chevy Chase
Allison, Adrienne Amelia *voluntary organization administrator*
Dulin, Maurine Stuart *volunteer*
Hunt, Frederick Talley Drum, Jr. *association executive*
Pogue, Mary Ellen E. (Mrs. L(loyd) Welch Pogue) *youth and community worker*
Sauer, Richard John *non-profit executive*

College Park
Stover, Carl Frederick *foundation executive*

Columbia
Bailey, John Martin *retired transportation planner, educator*
Gray, Kirk Lamond *social investment firm executive, anthropologist*
Kasprick, Lyle Clinton *volunteer, financial executive*
Willging, Paul Raymond *trade association executive*

Crofton
Ross, E(dwin) Clarke *association executive, educator*

Elkton
Scherf, Christopher N. *trade association administrator*

Ellicott City
Benton, Bill Browning *human services consultant*

Forestville
†Thompson, Elwood Ray *union executive, career consultant*

Fort Washington
Coffey, Matthew B. *trade association executive*

Gaithersburg
Hansen, Paul Walden *conservation organization executive*

Germantown
Searles, Thomas Daniel *society administrator*

Hagerstown
Peters, Marjorie Spanninger *historical society executive*

Kensington
Hurt, Frank *labor union administrator*

Lanham Seabrook
Littlefield, Roy Everett, III *association executive, legal educator*

Lexington Park
Sprague, Edward Auchincloss *retired association executive, economist*

Linthicum Heights
Lavin, Charles Blaise, Jr. *association executive*

Montgomery Village
Avedisian, Archie Harry *community organization executive*

North Bethesda
Sherman, Deane Murray *culture organization administrator*
Stearman, William Lloyd *military association executive, author*

Owings Mills
Siegel, Bernard *foundation administrator*

Potomac
Noonan, Patrick Francis *conservation executive*
Rosenberg, Sarah Zacher *institute arts administration executive, humanities administration consultant*

Randallstown
Ross, Norman Everett *cultural organization administrator*

Rockville
Anderson, Walter Dixon *trade association management consultant*
Kline, Raymond Adam *professional organization executive*
Maxwell, Robert James *trade association administrator*
Murphy, Gerard Norris *trade association executive*
Pillote, Barbara Wiegand *volunteer*
Scardelletti, Robert A. *labor union administrator*
Spahr, Frederick Thomas *association executive*
Standing, Kimberly Anna *educational researcher*
Sumberg, Alfred Donald *professional association executive*

Saint Leonard
Sugarman, Jule M. *children's services consultant, former public administrator*

Salisbury
Leonard, Joseph Howard *association organization executive*
†Thursfield, Fred F. *foundation administrator*

Severna Park
Hall, Marcia Joy *non-profit organization administrator*

Silver Spring
Camphor, James Winky, Jr. *educational administrator*
Davis, Regina Catherine (Gina Davis) *advocate*
Fanelli, Joseph James *retired public affairs executive, consultant*
Fockler, Herbert Hill *foundation executive*
Havis, Lee *executive director educational association*
Hayman, Harry *association executive, electrical engineer*
Hermanson Ogilvie, Judith *foundation executive*
†Hoehn, Richard Albert *association executive, clergyman*
Hunt, Mary Elizabeth *association executive*
Jaffeson, Richard Charles *association executive administrator*
Kirkland, (Joseph) Lane *labor union official*
Rasi, Humberto Mario *educational administrator, editor, minister*
Smedley, Lawrence Thomas *retired organization executive*
Wallace, C. Elizabeth McFarland *retired association director*
Winston, Michael Russell *foundation executive, historian*

Takoma Park
Lancaster, Alden *educational and management consultant*

Towson
Scott, Elizabeth *social service administrator*

MASSACHUSETTS

Amherst
Holmes, Helen Bequaert *project director*

Attleboro
†Tuniewicz, Mark Anthony *political organization administrator*

Boston
Brown, Lloyd David *association executive, management educator*
Burkhardt, Charles Henry *professional society executive, author, lecturer, consultant*
Cabot, Louis Wellington *foundation trustee*
Deissler, Mary Alice *foundation executive*
Fuerst, Rita Antoinette *management and fundraising consultant*
Garcia, Frieda *community foundation executive*
Glass, Renée *educational health foundation executive*
†Gratz, Donald Burr *educational administrator, writer, consultant*
Guild, Richard Samuel *trade association management company executive*
†Inman, Jean A. *political party official*
Knight, Norman *philanthropist, former broadcast executive*
Kohring, Dagmar Luzia *fundraiser, consultant*
†Malloy, William Francis, Jr. *lobbyist, navy officer*
Mayer, Henri André Van Huysen *association executive*
†O'Byck, Robert William, Jr. *association administrator*
Sullivan, James Leo *organization executive*
Tarlov, Alvin Richard *former philanthropic foundation administrator, physician, educator, researcher*
Tucker, Louis Leonard *retired historical society administrator*

Braintree
Wilson, Blenda Jacqueline *foundation administrator*

Brookline
Wax, Bernard *research and development consultant, lecturer*
Zoll, Miriam Hannah *activist, writer, communication specialist*

Cambridge
Berlowitz, Leslie *cultural organization administrator*
†Bloomfield, Steven B. *think-tank executive*
de Marneffe, Barbara Rowe *volunteer*
Harris, William Wolpert *treasurer political action committee*
Kovach, Bill *educational foundation administrator*
†Mason, Linda A. *social services administrator*
Truesdell, Stephanie *development officer*
Wenger, Luke Huber *educational association executive, editor*

Charlton
Williams, Russell Eugene *administrator, educator, economist*

Chelmsford
Elwell, Barbara Lois Dow *community organizer*

Devens
Anthony, Sylvia *social welfare organization executive*

Dorchester
Daly, Charles Ulick *foundation executive*

Essex
Broome, Roger Greville Brooke, IV *fundraiser*

Fitchburg
Niemi, Beatrice Neal *social services professional*

Framingham
Harrington, Joseph Francis *educational company executive, history educator*
Welte, A. Theodore *chamber of commerce executive*

Great Barrington
Gilmour, Robert Arthur *foundation executive, educator*

Groton
Searle, Andrew Barton *fund raising consultant*

Haverhill
Walker, Robert Ross *social worker*

Ipswich
†Moules, Deborah Ann *non-profit organization administrator*
Munro, Donald William, Jr. *non-profit organization executive*
Wilson, Doris H. *volunteer*

Lowell
Mazur, Stella Mary *former organization administrator*

Medford
O'Connell, Brian *community organizer, public administrator, writer, educator*

Milton
Corcoran, Robert Joseph *fund raising executive*

Nantucket
Pollard, Margaret Louise *association administrator*

Northampton
Rice, Elisabeth Jane *volunteer*

Plymouth
Baker, Peggy MacLachlan *cultural organization administrator*

Quincy
Chin, Jean Lau *health and mental health executive*

Wayland
Humphrey, Diana Young *fund raiser, travel consultant*

Wellesley
Henderson, Mary Louise *civic worker*

Westford
Geary, Marie Josephine *art association administrator*

Weston
†Wesley, Judith Ann *educational administrator*

MICHIGAN

Ann Arbor
Diana, Joseph A. *retired foundation executive*
Kennedy, David Boyd *foundation executive, lawyer*
Porter, John Wilson *education executive*
Ware, Richard Anderson *foundation executive*

Auburn
Gregory, Richard Joseph *youth services professional*

Battle Creek
Davis, Laura Arlene *retired foundation administrator*
DeVries, Robert Allen *foundation administrator*
Mawby, Russell George *retired foundation executive*
Richardson, William Chase *foundation executive*
Wendt, Linda M. *educational association administrator*

Bloomfield Hills
Waller, Irene Bazan *social services agency administrator*

Brighton
Darlington, Judith Mabel *clinical social worker, Christian counselor*

Dearborn Heights
Donoian, George *association executive*

Detroit
Andrews-Worthy, Rosalind *foundation consultant*
Davis, Kathryn Ward *fundraising consultant*
Montgomery, Michael John *fundraiser, consultant and administrator*
Noland, Mariam Charl *foundation executive*
Schuster, Elaine *civil rights professional, state official*
Vaitkevicius, Vainutis Kazys *foundation administrator, medical educator*
Yokich, Stephen P. *labor union administrator*

Dowagiac
Ott, C(larence) H(enry) *citizen ambassador, accounting educator*

East Lansing
Mitstifer, Dorothy Irwin *honor society administrator*
Munger, Benson Scott *professional society administrator*

Flint
Belcher, Max *social services administrator, college dean*
White, William Samuel *foundation executive*

Grand Rapids
Mauren, Kris Alan *non-profit organization executive*

Grosse Pointe Shores
Smith, Frank Earl *retired association executive*

Harbor Springs
†Bailey, Thomas C. *conservancy executive*

Holland
Foster, Glenn Kevin *former christian relief agency executive, social service agency executive*

Howell
Heinel, Robert Steven *social services administrator*

Lansing
Croxford, Lynne Louise *social services administrator*
†Pruss, Stanley F. *consumer protection administrator*

Madison Heights
O'Hara, Thomas Edwin *professional administrator executive*

Manistee
Behring, Daniel William *educational and business professional, consultant*

Oak Park
Piper, Annette Cleone *social services administrator, researcher*

Plymouth
Porter, Karen Collins *non-profit administrator, counselor*

Pontiac
Chamberlain, Jean Nash *county government department director*
Weeks, Timotheus *educational administrator*

Redford
Krec, George Frank, Jr. *fundraiser*

Southfield
Fleming, Mac Arthur *labor union administrator*
†Liebold, William Henry *fundraiser*
McDonald, Patricia Anne *professional society executive*

Southgate
Jacob, Robert Edward *small business and non-profit tax consultant*

Traverse City
Keilitz, Gene Martin *retired association administrator*

Troy
Hunia, Edward Mark *foundation executive*
Marshall, John Elbert, III *foundation executive*

MINNESOTA

Clear Lake
Casey, Daniel L. *school counselor*

Minneapolis
Fawcett, Marie Ann Formanek (Mrs. Roscoe Kent Fawcett) *civic leader*
†Gilson, Gary *professional society administrator, journalist*
Johnson, John Warren *retired association executive*
King, Reatha Clark *community foundation executive*
King, Robert Cotton *professional society consultant*
Skillingstad, Constance Yvonne *social services administrator, educator*
Speer, Nancy Girouard *educational administrator*
Terry, Paul Edward *health foundation administrator*

Minnetonka
Choate, Bradford Eugene *foundation executive*
Fogelberg, Paul Alan *continuing education company executive*

Moorhead
Pierce, John Stuart *fund raiser*

Owatonna
Groff, Stanley Allen *human services administration executive, educator*

Rochester
Shulman, Carole Karen *professional society administrator*
Wojcik, Martin Henry *foundation development official*

Roseville
Hughes, Jerome Michael *education foundation executive*

Saint Paul
Anderson, Gordon Louis *foundation administrator*
Archabal, Nina M(archetti) *historical society director*
Bruener, James William *fundraiser*
Calvin, Rochelle Ann *development association administrator*
Doermann, Humphrey *economics educator*
Fesler, David Richard *foundation director*
Goff, Lila Johnson *historical society administrator*
Kielsmeier, James Calvin *nonprofit corporation executive*
Kolehmainen, Jan Waldroy *professional association administrator*
Parsons, Mark Frederick *college development officer*
Pruzan, Irene *arts administrator, music educator, flutist, marketing and public relations specialist*
Senese, Dick *Democrat party chairman*

Saint Peter
Nelsen, William Cameron *foundation executive, former college president*

Wayzata
Shannon, James Patrick *foundation consultant, retired food company executive*

MISSISSIPPI

Bay Saint Louis
†Fabian, Lori Foltz *grant consultant, singer, actress, producer*

Fayette
La Salle, Arthur Edward *historic foundation executive*

Jackson
Risley, Rod Alan *education association executive*
Sullivan, John Magruder, II *government affairs administrator*
Thrash, Edsel E. *educational administrator*

Long Beach
Kanagy, Steven Albert *foundation administrator*

Madison
Hays, Mary Katherine Jackson *civic worker*

Pontotoc
Roberts, Rose Harrison *social services administrator, consultant*

MISSOURI

Bridgeton
Kenison, Raymond Robert *fraternal organization administrator, director*

Columbia
Palo, Nicholas Edwin *professional society administrator*

Earth City
Anderhalter, Oliver Frank *educational organization executive*

Independence
Potts, Barbara Joyce *retired historical society executive*

Ironton
Douma, Harry Hein *social service agency administrator*

Jefferson City
McDaniel, Sue Powell *cultural organization administrator*

Kansas City
Bugher, Robert Dean *professional society administrator*
Hanson, Phillip John *united way executive*
Haw, Bill *association executive*
Levi, Peter Steven *chamber of commerce executive, lawyer*
Sparks, Donald Eugene *interscholastic activities association executive*
Wilson, Eugene Rolland *foundation executive*
Wingfield, Laura Allison Ross *fraternal organization executive*

Kirksville
French, Michael Francis *non-profit education agency administrator*

Lees Summit
St. John, Shay *fundraising executive*

O'Fallon
Lottes, Patricia Joette Hicks *foundation administrator, retired nurse*

Saint Louis
†Anderson, Bruce John *foundation administrator*
Bascom, C. Perry *foundation administrator*
Duhme, Carol McCarthy *civic worker*
Hall, Mary Taussig *volunteer*
†Hickman, Charles Wallace *educational association administrator*
Hunter, Earle Leslie, III *professional association executive*
Maxwell, Dorothea Bost Andrews *civic worker*
Melman, Joy *civic volunteer*
Pope, Robert E(ugene) *fraternal organization administrator*
Robins, Marjorie McCarthy (Mrs. George Kenneth Robins) *civic worker*
Sutter, Elizabeth Henby (Mrs. Richard A. Sutter) *civic leader, management company executive*
Winter, Mildred M. *educational administrator*

Springfield
Morris, Ann Haseltine Jones *social welfare administrator*

MONTANA

Billings
Peterson, Arthur Laverne *foundation administrator*
Sample, Joseph Scanlon *foundation executive*

Bozeman
Sanddal, Nels Dodge *foundation executive, consultant*

Harrison
Jackson, Peter Vorious, III *retired association executive*

Helena
Aleksich-Akey, Sue *Republican party chairman*

Missoula
Kemmis, Daniel Orra *cultural organization administrator, author*
Wolfe, Gary John *foundation administrator, wildlife biologist*

Park City
Abrams, Ossie Ekman *fundraiser*

NEBRASKA

Grand Island
Abernethy, Irene Margaret *civic worker, retired county official*

Harrison
Coffee, Virginia Claire *civic worker, former mayor*

Lincoln
Gray, Joni Nadine *state agency administrator*
Hunhoff, Sister Phyllis *foundation administrator*
Rosenow, John Edward *foundation executive*
Swartz, Jack *chamber of commerce executive*

North Platte
Davis, Moraine Taylor *non-profit organization administrator*

Ogallala
†Bourque, Richard Michael *foundation administrator*

Omaha
Bell, C(lyde) R(oberts) (Bob Bell) *foundation administrator*
Fettig, John Michael *fund raising executive*
Flickinger, Thomas Leslie *hospital alliance executive*
†Foreman, Julie Lynn *volunteer coordinator*
Monasee, Charles Arthur *retired healthcare foundation executive*

Seward
Vrana, Verlon Kenneth *retired professional society administrator, conservationist*

South Sioux City
†Poland, Amy Lynn *social services administrator*

NEVADA

Carson City
Ayres, Janice Ruth *social service executive*

Henderson
Freyd, William Pattinson *fund raising executive, consultant*

Las Vegas
Martin, Myron Gregory *foundation administrator*
Pray, Donald Eugene *foundation administrator, lawyer*
Segerblom, Sharon B. *social services administrator*
Wunstell, Erik James *non-profit organization administrator, communications consultant*

Pahrump
Nowell, Linda Gail *organization executive*

Reno
Leipper, Diane Louise *association administrator*
Winzeler, Judith Kay *foundation administrator*

NEW HAMPSHIRE

Concord
†Busselle, James A. *educational administrator*
Crosier, John David *trade association administrator*
†Woodburn, Jeff *political party official*

Londonderry
Michaud, Norman Paul *association administrator, logistics consultant*

Marlborough
Walton, Russell Sparey *foundation administrator*

Peterborough
Eppes, William David *civic worker, writer*

Randolph
Bradley, William Lee *retired foundation executive, educator*

Tilton
Stanley, George Joel *social services administrator*

NEW JERSEY

Atlantic City
Jamieson, John Edward, Jr. *social services administrator, minister, bioethicist*

Basking Ridge
Probert, Edward Whitford *foundation executive, volunteer*

Bernardsville
Cooperman, Saul *foundation administrator*

East Brunswick
†Gawlikowski, Vladimir C. *organization executive*

East Rutherford
Kempner, Michael W. *public relations executive*

Elizabeth
Layden, Thomas John *social services supervisor*

Englewood
Orlando, George (Joseph) *union executive*

Fort Dix
Stankiewicz, John Jay *staff administrator*

Glen Ridge
Pendley, Donald Lee *association executive*

Harrington Park
Covello, John Anthony *water utility lobbyist*

Highland Park
†Kolodzei, Natalia A. *art foundation administrator, art historian*

Hightstown
Smith, Datus Clifford, Jr. *former foundation executive, publisher*

PROFESSIONAL INDEX 5841 ASSOCIATIONS AND ORGANIZATIONS

Jersey City
Degatano, Anthony Thomas *educational association administrator*
Goria, Ellen Theresa *professional society administrator*
Kahrmann, Robert George *educational administrator*
Niemiec, Edward Walter *professional association executive*

Kendall Park
Goldberg, Bertram J. *social agency administrator*

Lambertville
Mackey, Philip English *non-profit organization consultant*

Lebanon
O'Neill, Elizabeth Sterling *trade association administrator*

Lyndhurst
Ridenour, James Franklin *fund raising consultant*

Montclair
Campbell, Stewart Fred *foundation executive*
Mason, Lucile Gertrude *fundraiser, consultant*
Steiner, Roberta Dance *not-for-profit organization executive*
Tennen, Jane Savitt *consultant to non-profit organizations, writer*

Morristown
Murray, Charles Robert. *charitable fundraiser, educator*
Spence, Janet Blake Conley (Mrs. Alexander Pyott Spence) *civic worker*

Mount Laurel
Ciociola, Cecilia Mary *science education specialist*
Moyer, Cheryl Lynn *non-profit administrator*

New Providence
Westerland, Maureen A. *fundraiser*
Wilderotter, Peter Thomas *non-profit executive*

New Vernon
Dugan, John Leslie, Jr. *foundation executive*

Newark
Morris-Yamba, Trish *educational and social service association director*

Paterson
Chiles, Lawton, III *non-profit organization executive*

Pennington
Calvo, Roque John *professional society administrator*
Mitchell, Janet Aldrich *fund raising executive, reference materials publisher*

Plainfield
Limpert, John H., Jr. *fund raising executive*

Port Murray
Stokes, Eileen Margaret *historic society administrator*

Princeton
Altman, Robert Allen *educational assessment executive*
Balch, Stephen Howard *professional society administrator*
De Lung, Jane Solberger *independent sector executive*
†Doyle, Michael W. *think-tank executive*
Hearn, Ruby Puryear *foundation executive*
Jellinek, Paul S. *foundation executive, health economist*
Kassof, Allen H. *foundation administrator*
Kenyon, Regan Clair *educational research executive*
Plaks, Livia Basch *foundation executive*
Stern, Gail Frieda *historical association director*

Ridgewood
Herink, Richie *education company executive*
Kahlenberg, Jeannette Dawson *retired civic organization executive*

Roseland
Hochberg, Mark Stefan *foundation president, cardiac surgeon*

Rumson
Brenner, Theodore Engelbert *retired trade association executive*
Freeman, David Forgan *retired foundation executive*

Scotch Plains
Ungar, Manya Shayon *volunteer, education consultant*

Somerville
Brown, Susie Warrington *foundation executive*

Springfield
Stoller, Mitchell Robert *non-profit organization administrator*

Trenton
Binder, Elaine Kotell *consultant to associations*
†Giblin, Thomas Patrick *labor union administrator*
†Jones, Arburta Elizabeth *development specialist*

Union Beach
Gilmartin, Clara T. *volunteer*

Upper Montclair
†Courson, William A. *association administrator*

Verona
McGinley, Daniel Joseph *association executive*

Voorhees
Layton, Amanda Emigh *non-profit organization fundraiser*

Woodcliff Lake
Watson, Christopher D. *fundraising and communications consultant*

NEW MEXICO

Albuquerque
Cole, Terri Lynn *organization administrator*
Roberts, Dennis William *association executive*

Farmington
Mathers, Margaret *charitable agency consultant, copy editor*

Las Cruces
Eriksson, Anne-Marie *social services executive, educator*

Playas
Clifton, Judy Raelene *association administrator*

Santa Fe
Charles, Cheryl *non-profit and business executive*
Lukac, George Joseph *fundraising executive*

NEW YORK

Albany
Axelrod, Susan L. *fundraiser*
Hobart, Thomas Yale, Jr. *union president*

Amherst
Clark, Donald Malin *professional association executive*

Armonk
Bergson, Henry Paul *professional association administrator*

Astoria
Davidson, Rex L. *association executive*

Bedford Hills
Waller, Wilhelmine Kirby (Mrs. Thomas Mercer Waller) *civic worker, organization official*

Binghamton
Kingsley, Robert Thomas *developer*

Breesport
Peckham, Joyce Weitz *foundation administrator, former secondary education educator*

Briarcliff Manor
Luck, Edward Carmichael *professional society administrator*

Bronx
†Fox, Geoffrey E. *educational administrator*

Brooklyn
Crawford, Patricia Alexis Ann *social justice and healthcare advocate, writer*
Herman, Allen Ian *foundation administrator*
Isaacson, Arline Levine *association administrator*
Sage, Robert Ephram *social service agency administrator*

Buffalo
Clarkson, Elisabeth Ann Hudnut *civic worker*
Sanders, Wendy Lee *development professional*

Canaan
†Van Schaick, Laura *non-profit social service administrator*

Caroga Lake
Nilsen, Richard H. *foundation administrator, consultant*

Chappaqua
de Janosi, Peter Engel *research manager*

Clinton
Couper, Richard Watrous *foundation executive, educator*

Congers
Commanday, Peter Martin *educator*

Corona
Afulezi, Uju N. *economic association administrator, professor, librarian, author, consultant*

Dobbs Ferry
Miss, Robert Edward *fundraiser*

East Quogue
Weiss, Elaine Landsberg *community development management official*

Elizabethtown
Lawrence, Richard Wesley, Jr. *foundation executive*

Elmhurst
Matsa, Loula Zacharoula *social services administrator*

Endicott
Englehart, Joan Anne *trade association executive*

Flushing
Fichtel, Rudolph Robert *retired association executive*
Madden, Joseph Daniel *trade association executive*
Wells, David I. *retired labor union administrator*

Garrison
Pierpont, Robert *fund raising executive, consultant*

Germantown
Callanan, Laura Patrice *foundation manager*

Glens Falls
Depan, Mary Elizabeth *civic volunteer, nurse*

Glenville
Pontius, James Wilson *foundation administrator*

Harrison
Wadsworth, Frank Whittemore *foundation executive, literature educator*

Hudson
Miner, Jacqueline *political consultant*

Huntington
Schulz, William Frederick *human rights association executive*

Ithaca
Grainger, Mary Maxon *civic volunteer*
Stein, Irene Wald *social services administrator*

Jamaica
Keys, Martha McDougle *educational administrator*

Jamestown
†Thompson, Birgit Dolores *civic worker, writer*

Lake Grove
Brayson, Albert Aloysius, II *educational association administrator*

Larchmont
Hinerfeld, Ruth G. *civic organization executive*

Long Island City
Hoffman, Merle Holly *political activist, social psychologist, author*

Merrick
Doyle, James Aloysius *retired association executive*

Montauk
Butler, Thomas William *retired health and social services administrator*

New Rochelle
Black, Page Morton *civic worker*

New York
Allmendinger, Paul Florin *retired engineering association executive*
Amitin, Mark Hall *cultural organization administrator, educator, writer*
Andrulis, Dennis P. *health policy analyst executive, researcher*
Appel, Marsha Ceil *association executive*
Auld, Larry Elwood *foundation executive*
Ball, Susan *arts association administrator, art historian*
Beardsley, Theodore S(terling), Jr. *professional society administrator*
Belden, David Leigh *professional association executive, engineering educator*
Bellamy, Carol *international organization executive*
Bergman, Charles Cabe *foundation executive*
Berkman, Lillian *foundation executive, corporation executive, art collector*
†Berley, Marc S. *foundation administrator, English educator*
Berry, Nancy Michaels *philanthropy consultant*
Bird, Mary Lynne Miller *professional society administrator*
Bobbitt, Juanita Marilyn Crawford *international organization executive*
Brainerd, Michael Charles *international exchange organization executive*
Braverman, Robert Jay *international consultant, public policy educator*
Brown, Terrence Charles *art association executive, researcher, lecturer*
Buckman, Thomas Richard *foundation executive, educator*
Campbell, Colin Goetze *foundation president*
Canada, Geoffrey *social welfare administrator*
†Cannon, Steve *non-profit organization administrator*
Cassella, William Nathan, Jr. *organization executive*
Catley-Carlson, Margaret *professional organization administrator*
Cavanagh, Carroll John *business advisor, lawyer, principal art services company*
Chapin, Schuyler Garrison *cultural affairs executive, university dean*
Chatfield-Taylor, Adele *arts administrator, historic preservationist*
Christopher, Maurine Brooks *foundation administrator, writer, editor*
Cicerchi, Eleanor Ann Tomb *fundraising executive*
Clarke, Garvey Elliott *educational association administrator, lawyer*
Codding, Mitchell A. *cultural organization administrator*
†Cohen, Cynthia Price *institute administrator*
Cole, Elma Phillipson (Mrs. John Strickler Cole) *social welfare executive*
Coly, Lisette *foundation executive*
Conarroe, Joel Osborne *foundation administrator, educator, editor*
Cook, John Wesley *foundation administrator*
Cornell, Thomas Charles *peace activist, writer*
David, Miles *association and marketing executive*
Davis, Karen *fund executive*
Davis, Kathryn Wasserman *foundation executive, writer, lecturer*
Dean, Diane D. *youth service agency executive, fund development consultant*
Dennis, Everette Eugene, Jr. *foundation executive, journalism educator, writer*
DeVita, M. Christine *foundation administrator*
Diamond, Irene *foundation administrator*
Dirks, Nicholas B. *cultural research organization administrator/history educator*
Drake, Owen Burtch Winters *association administrator*
Dressner, Howard Roy *foundation executive, lawyer*
Easum, Donald Boyd *consultant, educator, former institute executive, diplomat*
Eisenberg, Alan *professional society administrator*
Ekman, Richard *foundation executive, educator*
Elliott, Dolores *disabilities advocate, film producer*
Engelhardt, Sara Lawrence *organization executive*
†Evans, Eli Nachamson *foundation administrator*
Fehr, Donald M. *baseball union executive*
Feldt, Gloria A. *social service administrator*
Feuerstein, Paul Bruck *social services agency executive*
Feurey, Claudia Packer *not-for-profit executive*
Finberg, Barbara Denning *nonprofit executive*
Flicker, John *foundation executive*
Foerst, John George, Jr. *fundraising executive*
Fox, Daniel Michael *foundation administrator, author*
Foxman, Abraham H. *advocacy organization administrator*
Franklin, Phyllis *professional association administrator*
Furlong, James Christopher *art program administrator, stage director*
†Gallagher, Edward Peter *foundation administrator*
Garrison, John Raymond *organization executive*
Gaudieri, Millicent Hall *association executive*
Goldblatt, Eileen Witzman *foundation executive*
Gotbaum, Betsy *historical society director*
Granik, Russell T. *sports association executive*
Grimaldi, Nicholas Lawrence *social services administrator*
Guenther, Paul Bernard *volunteer*
Handberg, Irene Deak *educational organization executive*
Hanley, William H. *association executive*
Hansen, Peter *international organization executive*
Hanvik, Jan Michael *arts promoter, writer*
Harris, David Alan *not-for-profit organization executive*
Hart, Kitty Carlisle *arts administrator*
Helton, Arthur Cleveland *advocate, lawyer*
Hesselbein, Frances Richards *foundation executive, consultant, editor*
Hester, James McNaughton *foundation administrator*
Hester, Melvyn Francis *labor union executive*
Hoffman, Linda R. *social services administrator*
Holtzman, Ellen A. *foundation executive*
Hope, Judith H. *Democrat party chairman*
Ilchman, Alice Stone *foundation administrator, former college president, former government official*
Innis, Roy Emile Alfredo *organization executive*
Jacobsen, Theodore H. (Ted H. Jacobsen) *labor union official, educator*
Jacobson, Gaynor I. *retired association executive*
Jacobson, Gilbert H. *association executive, lawyer*
Jaffe, Andrew Mark *organization executive, editor, publisher, lecturer*
Jerome, Fred Louis *science organization executive*
Jones, David R(ussell) *not-for-profit executive*
Jones, Elaine R. *civil rights advocate*
Kaggen, Lois Sheila *non-profit organization executive*
Kahan, Marlene *professional association executive*
Kahn, Alfred Joseph *social worker and policy scholar, educator*
†Kaiser, Michael *performing company, foundation administrator*
Kaplan, Jay *cultural organization administrator, editor*
Kardon, Peter Franklin *foundation administrator*
Karr, Norman *trade association executive*
Kaskell, Peter Howard *association executive, lawyer*
Kramberg, Ross *arts administrator*
Kuh, Joyce Dattel *education administrator*
Kuyper, Joan Carolyn *foundation administrator*
Labunski, Stephen Bronislaw *professional society administrator*
LaMotta, Connie Frances *association executive*
Landy, Joanne Veit *foreign policy analyst*
Lawson-Johnston, Peter Orman *foundation executive*
Lee, Clement William Khan *trade association administrator*
Lewis, Sylvia Davidson *association executive*
Luce, Henry, III *foundation executive*
Luckman, Sharon Gersten *arts administrator*
Luks, Allan Barry *executive director*
Mahoney, Margaret Ellerbe *foundation executive*
Mangan, Mona *association executive, lawyer*
Marincola, John *association administrator*
Marks, Edward B. *international relief administrator*
Maynard, Virginia Madden *charitable organization executive*
Mazur, Jay J. *trade union official*
McCormack, Elizabeth J. *foundation administrator*
McCrary, Eugenia Lester (Mrs. Dennis Daughtry McCrary) *civic worker, writer*
McLean, Mora *institute administrator*
McNamara, Mary E. *nonprofit executive, asset manager, minister*
Metcalf, Karen *foundation executive*
Milbank, Jeremiah *foundation executive*
Millett, Kate (Katherine Murray Millett) *political activist, sculptor, artist, writer*
Moran, Martin Joseph *fundraising company executive*
Morehouse, Ward *human rights organization executive, publisher*
Odenweller, Robert Paul *philatelist, association executive, airline pilot*
Olyphant, David *cultural, educational association executive*
O'Neil Bidwell, Katharine Thomas *fine arts association executive, performing arts executive*
Oppenheimer-Nicolau, Siobhan *think tank executive*
Osborn, Frederick Henry, III *foundation executive*
Ovadiah, Janice *cultural institute executive*
Peters, Robert Wayne *organization executive, lawyer*
Phillips, Russell Alexander, Jr. *retired foundation executive*
Preston, Frances Williams *performing rights organization executive*
Price, Hugh B. *foundation executive, lawyer*
Rattazzi, Serena *art museum and association administrator*
Riordan, John Thomas *trade association executive*
Robinson, David Zav *non-profit agency consultant*
Robinson, Nan Senior *not-for-profit organization consultant*
†Rogers, Raymond Franklin, Jr. *labor union professional*
Rose, Joanna Semel *cultural activist*
†Rosenthal, Joel Howard *think-tank executive*
Rosoff, Jeannie I. *nonprofit organization administrator*
Scaffidi, Judith Ann *school volunteer program administrator*
Schlittler, Gilberto Bueno *former UN official, political science educator*
Schor, Laura Strumingher *executive director, historian*
Schubart, Mark Allen *arts and education executive*
Seuk, Kook Jing (Joon Ho) *foundation administrator*
Sharp, Daniel Asher *foundation executive*
Shelp, Ronald Kent *non-profit business and trade association executive, author, lecturer, consultant*

Sherman, Fred Sweney *marine transport executive, foundation executive*
Sherrod, Lonnie Ray *foundation administrator, researcher, psychologist*
†Short, Thomas C. *theatre union executive*
Sills, Beverly (Mrs. Peter B. Greenough) *performing arts organization executive, coloratura soprano*
Simpson, David Livingstone, Jr. *fraternal organization executive, fundraiser*
Singer, Arthur Louis, Jr. *foundation executive*
Singh, Jyoti Shankar *international organization executive*
Slater, Joseph Elliott *educational institute administrator*
Slutsky, Lorie Ann *foundation executive*
Sokol, Marc Jeffrey *arts administrator*
Solender, Stephen David *philanthropic organization executive*
Spero, Joan Edelman *foundation president*
Spira, Patricia Goodsitt *association executive*
Spurgin, Nora Martin *social welfare organization executive*
Steedman, Doria Lynne Silberberg *organization executive*
Straus, Oscar S., II *foundation executive*
Sultanik, Kalman *professional society administrator*
Sussman, Leonard Richard *foundation executive*
Touborg, Margaret Earley Bowers *non-profit executive*
Tudryn, Joyce Marie *professional society administrator*
†Turnbaugh, Douglas Blair *arts administration executive, author*
Wallach, John Paul *foundation administrator, author*
†Walton, Kara Ann *research and educational administrator*
Wattleton, (Alyce) Faye *educational association administrator*
Weeks, David Frank *foundation administrator*
Weintraub, Daniel Ralph *social welfare administrator*
Weisl, Edwin Louis, Jr. *foundation executive, lawyer*
Weissman, Susan *social services professional*
Wellington, Sheila Wacks *foundation administrator, psychiatry educator*
Whiteside, Duncan *disability and child welfare foundation executive*
Wiener, Malcolm Hewitt *foundation executive*
Wright, Hugh Elliott, Jr. *association executive, writer*
Young, Jordan Marten *cultural organization administrator, educator*
Young, Steve G. *labor union administrator*
†Zelin, Madeleine *think-tank executive*
Zollar, Jawole Willa Jo *art association administrator*

Niagara Falls
Laubaugh, Frederick *association executive, consultant*

Nyack
Paru, Marden David *fundraising executive*

Oyster Bay
Russell, Mary Wendell Vander Poel *non-profit organization executive, interior*

Palisades
Miller, Roberta Balstad *science administrator*

Potsdam
Stevens, Sheila Maureen *teachers union administrator*

Purchase
Staley, Harry Lee *fund raising executive*

Rochester
DeMarco, Roland R. *foundation executive*
†Haschmann, Thomas Edwin *social services agency administrator*
Lebman, Robert Richard *social services administrator*
Pacala, Leon *retired association executive*
Strand, Marion Delores *social service administrator*

Saranac
Smith, J. Kellum, Jr. *foundation executive, lawyer*

Scarborough
Beglarian, Grant *foundation executive, composer, consultant*

Scarsdale
Bruck Lieb Port, Lilly *retired consumer advisor, broadcaster, columnist*
Hemley, Eugene Adams *trade association executive*
†Johnson, Katharyn Price (Mrs. Edward F. Johnson) *civic worker*
Paulin, Amy Ruth *civic activist, consultant*
Rosow, Jerome Morris *institute executive*
Wile, Julius *former corporate executive, educator*

Schenectady
Chestnut, Harold *foundation administrator, engineering executive*

Staten Island
Meeker, Susan Stewart *economic development organization administrator*

Stony Brook
Brandwein, Ruth Ann *social welfare educator*

Syracuse
Rountree, Patricia Ann *youth organization administrator*

Tarrytown
Dobkin, John Howard *art administrator*

Tonawanda
Browning, James Franklin *professional society executive*

Troy
Carovano, John Martin *not-for-profit adminstrator, conservationist*

Valley Stream
Haies, Evelyn S(olomon) *fundraiser, educator, writer*

Watertown
Henderson, Gladys Edith *retired social welfare examiner*

Webster
Theis, Nancy Nichols *community activist, mental retardation specialist*

Westbury
†Mondello, Joseph N. *political party chairman*

White Plains
†Berliner, David C. *foundation administrator*
Stalerman, Ruth *civic volunteer, poet*

Yonkers
Karpatkin, Rhoda Hendrick *consumer information organization executive, lawyer*
Neal, Leora Louise Haskett *social services administrator*

NORTH CAROLINA

Asheville
Murdock, William Joseph *foundation adminstrator, educator*
Summers, Ruth T. *cultural organization executive*

Black Mountain
Hibbard, Carl Roger *social services administrator*

Brevard
Bertrand, Annabel Hodges *civic worker, artist, calligrapher*

Cary
Martin, William Royall, Jr. *retired association executive*

Chapel Hill
Dickman, Catherine Crowe *retired human services administrator*
Kenan, Thomas Stephen, III *philanthropist*
MacGillivray, Lois Ann *organization executive*
Slack, Lewis *organization administrator*
Wicker, Marie Peachee *civic worker*

Charlotte
Griep, Ann Marie *education association education coordinator*
Locke, Elizabeth Hughes *foundation administrator*
McCall, Billy Gene *charitable trust executive*
Pyle, Gerald Fredric *medical geographer, educator*

Durham
Bevan, William *retired foundation executive*
Lozoff, Bo *nonprofit organization administrator*
Semans, Mary Duke Biddle Trent *foundation administrator*

Greensboro
Kornegay, Horace Robinson *trade association executive, former congressman, lawyer*

Raleigh
Bull, Leonard S. *educational association administrator*
Davis, Robin Reed *lobbyist, feminist advocate*
Graham, Kent Hill *philanthropist, museum guide*
Harvey, Glenn F. *association executive*
McDowell, Timothy Hill *lobbyist*

Research Triangle Park
Miller, Robert Reese *trade association executive*

Smithfield
Taylor, Ellen Borden Broadhurst *civic worker*

Wingate
Dodd, John Robert *non-profit organization administrator*

Winston Salem
Carter, Henry Moore, Jr. *retired foundation executive*

NORTH DAKOTA

Minot
Moe, Vida Delores *civic worker*

OHIO

Akron
Collier, Alice Elizabeth *retired community organization executive*
Fordyce, James Stuart *non-profit organization executive*
Frank, John V. *foundation executive*
Martino, Frank Dominic *union executive*

Berea
Brannen, Daniel Jude *children's services administrator*

Canal Winchester
Bacus, Terrence Lee *labor relations consultant*

Canton
Mason, Judith Snyder *fund development consultant*

Chagrin Falls
Ostendorf, Joan Donahue *fund raiser, volunteer*
Sivak, Madeline Ann *nonprofit organization executive, nurse*
Vail, Iris Jennings *civic worker*

Chardon
Langer, Edward L. *trade association administrator*
Reinhard, Sister Mary Marthe *educational organization administrator*

Cincinnati
Adlard, Carole Rechtsteiner *adoption educational agency executive*
Conley, Robert T. *educational administrator*
Fontana, Michael *educational foundation administrator, writer, poet*
Hiatt, Marjorie McCullough *service organization executive*
Sowder, Fred Allen *foundation administrator, alphabet specialist*
Wilson, Arthur Henry *charitable institution executive*
Zola, Gary Phillip *religious educational administrator, rabbi,*

Cleveland
†Begala, John Adelbert *human service administrator*
Bender, Peggy Wallace *fundraising consultant*
Bergholz, David *foundation administrator*
Buescher, Thomas Paul *labor market analyst*
Calabrese, Leonard M. *social services administrator*
Calkins, Hugh *foundation executive*
Cleary, Michael J. *educational administrator*
Cooper, James Clinton *social services administrator, consultant*
Faller, Dorothy Anderson *international agency administrator*
Garrison, William Lloyd *cemetery executive*
Hartley, Duncan *fundraising executive*
Lord, James Gregory *organizational and philanthropic counsel to consultants*

Cleveland Heights
Shorey, Amy Guy *fundraiser*

College Corner
Gilmore, Robert Witter *foundation administrator*

Columbus
Chu, Roderick Gong-Wah *educational administrator*
Colburn, Julia Katherine Lee *volunteer, educator*
Hamilton, Harold Philip *fund raising executive*
Luck, James I. *foundation executive*
Newman, Diana S. *development consultant*
†Olesen, Doug *think tank executive*
Selby, Diane Ray Miller *fraternal organization administrator*
†Webb, Kevin Roger *executive*

Dayton
Daley, Robert Emmett *foundation executive, retired*
Mathews, David *foundation executive*
Schwartzhoff, James Paul *foundation executive*
Yeager, Tamara Layne *educational association executive*

Dublin
Needham, George Michael *association executive*

Independence
Jenson, Jon Eberdt *association executive*

Materials Park
Putnam, Allan Ray *association executive*

Mentor
Andrassy, Timothy Francis *trade association executive*

Middletown
Kohler, Edith A. *senior citizen's organization executive*

New Philadelphia
Robinson, Scott Alan *social services administrator*

Oberlin
Cartier, Brian Evans *association executive*
Cooke, Lloyd Miller *former organization executive*
Taylor, Gail Richardson *civic worker, lawyer, former university official*

Oxford
Becker, Stephen Bradbury *fraternal organization administrator*
Miller, Robert James *educational association administrator*

Shaker Heights
Provan, Carol McLaughlin *fundraising executive*

Waverly
Carlson, Carolin McCormick Furst *civic worker*

Westlake
Distelhorst, Garis Fred *trade association executive*

Worthington
Newkirk, Peggy Rose Wills *civic volunteer*

Yellow Springs
Graham, Jewel Freeman *social worker, lawyer, educator*

Youngstown
Westenbarger, Don Edward *retired association executive*

Zoar
Fernandez, Kathleen M. *cultural organization administrator*

OKLAHOMA

Big Cabin
Stinson, Marion Dennis *regional association administrator*

Durant
Gumm, Jay Paul *association executive*

Lawton
Brooks, (Leslie) Gene *cultural association administrator*

Norman
Hammon, Norman Harold *fundraising counsel and development consultant*
Morgan, Elizabeth Anne *foundation consultant, writer*

Oklahoma City
Gumerson, Jean Gilderhus *health foundation executive*
McLaughlin, Lisa Marie *educational administrator*
Van Rysselberge, Charles H. *organization administrator*
Woods, Pendleton *retired college official, author*

Tulsa
Wagner, Clarence H., Jr. *charitable organization administrator*
Wesenberg, John Herman *professional society administrator*

OREGON

Bandon
Millard, Esther Lound *foundation administrator, educator*

Beaverton
Bruce, John Allen *foundation executive, educator*

Bend
Evers-Williams, Myrlie *cultural organization administrator*
Goodman, Susan Kathleen *charitable organization administrator, educator*

Corvallis
Wilkins, Caroline Hanke *consumer agency administrator, political worker*

Eugene
†Gersten, Russell Monroe *educational foundation administrator*
Hale, Dean Edward *social services administrator*

Gold Beach
Dillon, Robert Morton *retired association executive, architectural consultant*

Grants Pass
Boling, Judy Atwood *civic worker*

Gresham
Nicholson, R. Stephen *organization administrator*

Junction City
Humphry, Derek *association executive, writer*

Medford
Sours, James Kingsley *association executive, former college president*

Portland
Collins, Maribeth Wilson *foundation president*
Henderson, George Miller *foundation executive, former banker*
Hudson, Jerry E. *foundation administrator*
McClave, Donald Silsbee *professional society administrator*
Orloff, Chet *cultural organization administrator*
Pine, William Charles *foundation executive*
Rooks, Charles S. *foundation administrator*

Salem
Atkinson, Perry *political organization administrator*
†Barnett, Kerry Evan *state business administrator*

Summerville
Hopkins, Gerald Frank *trade association administrator*

PENNSYLVANIA

Allentown
Farr, Lona Mae *non-profit executive, business owner*

Allison Park
Wood, Edward Manning *fund raising counsel*

Ardmore
Ginsburgh, Brook *association executive*

Aston
Gambescia, Stephen Francis *higher education administrator*

Beaver
James, Robert Brandon *social service agency administrator*

Berwyn
Reed, Clarence Raymond *retired association executive*

Bethlehem
Dorward, Judith A. *association executive*

Blue Bell
Bell, Michael G. *trade association administrator*

Bryn Mawr
Cooney, Patricia Ruth *civic worker*
Moll, Robin Bitterlich *fundraising executive, consultant*
Richards, Rhoda Root Wagner *civic worker*

Chadds Ford
King, M. Jean *association executive*

Chambersburg
Lesher, Richard Lee *association executive, retired*

Dillsburg
Bowers, Glenn Lee *retired professional society administrator*

PROFESSIONAL INDEX 5843 ASSOCIATIONS AND ORGANIZATIONS

Drexel Hill
Schiazza, Guido Domenic (Guy Schiazza) *educational association administrator*

Easton
Danjczek, Michael Harvey *social service administrator*
Yost, Robert R. *social services agency administrator*

Elizabethtown
Madeira, Robert Lehman *professional society administrator*

Erie
Egan, Corrine Halperin *trade association administrator*

Exton
Newhall, John Harrison *non profit company executive*
Penrose, Charles, Jr. *professional society administrator*

Gettysburg
Nelson-Small, Kathy Ann *foundation administrator*

Gibsonia
Haas, Eileen Marie *homecare advocate*

Glenside
Carter, Ruth B. (Mrs. Joseph C. Carter) *foundation administrator*

Harrisburg
Breslin, Michael Joseph, III *social services administrator, educator*
†Novak, Alan P. *political party official*
Ross, Sheila Moore *philanthropic executive*
Staub, Shalom David *cultural organization administrator*
Stone, Thomas Richardson *cultural center president*
Wissler-Thomas, Carrie *professional society administrator, artist*

Kempton
Lenhart, Cynthia Rae *conservation organization executive*

King Of Prussia
Carter, S. Daniel *corporate administrator, computer consultant, political consultant*

Kingston
Friedman, Pauline Poplin *civic worker, consultant*

Latrobe
Hager, Edward Paul *development executive*

Laverock
Block, Isaac Edward *professional society administrator*

Lititz
Lord, Kathleen Virginia Anderson *fundraising executive, educator*

McConnellsburg
Taylor, Margaret Uhrich *professional society administrator*

Millerton
Lyon, Berenice Iola Clark *civic worker*

Newtown
Keenan, Terrance *foundation executive*

Philadelphia
Bodine, James Forney *retired civic leader*
Foti, Margaret Ann *association executive, publisher, editor*
Friedman, Murray *civil rights official, historian*
Klein, Arthur *foundation executive*
McKenna, Thomas Morrison, Jr. *social services organization executive*
Pak, Hyung Woong *foundation executive*
Pizzi, Charles Peter *association president*
Ray, Evelyn Lucille *arts association administrator, meeting planner*
Stevenson, Josiah, IV *cultural arts administrator*
Tucker, Cynthia Delores Nottage (Mrs. William M. Tucker) *political party official, former state official*
†Turchi, Ralph P. Ray, Jr. *retired labor union administrator*
Watson, Bernard Charles *foundation administrator*

Pittsburgh
Cheever, Meg *non-profit organization administrator*
Dybeck, Alfred Charles *labor arbitrator*
Grinberg, Meyer Stewart *educational institute executive*
Horan, Justin Thomas *retired association executive*
Ketchum, David Storey *retired fundraising executive*
Mellon, Richard Prosser *charitable foundation executive*
Pasnick, Raymond Wallace *labor union official, editor*
Petersen, Jean Snyder *association executive*
Thorner, John *professional society administrator*
Wishart, Alfred Wilbur, Jr. *foundation administrator*

Radnor
†Harper, Charles Little, Jr. *foundation administrator, planetary scientist*

Reading
Mattern, Donald Eugene *retired association executive*
Morrill, Michael William *consumer activist*
Murphy, Kevin Keith *foundation executive*

Red Lion
Hartman, Charles Henry *nonprofit management consultant*

Saint Davids
Denenberg, Herbert Sidney *journalist, lawyer, former state official*

Saxonburg
†Howell, Cherie Ann *volunteer recruitment coordinator, educator*

Sewickley
Ryan, George H. *foundation administrator*

State College
DeVoss, James Thomas *community foundation administrator, retired*
Phillips, Janet Colleen *educational association executive, editor*
Santavicca, Pamela Ferguson *social welfare administrator*

Stroudsburg
Batistoni, Ronald *educational association administrator*

University Park
Feller, Irwin *think-tank executive, economics educator*

Valley Forge
Kunin, Richard H. *educational association administrator, artist*

Villanova
Friend, Theodore Wood, III *foundation executive, historian*
Smith, Standish Harshaw *non-profit company executive*

Warrendale
Rumbaugh, Max Elden, Jr. *professional society administrator*
Scott, Alexander Robinson *engineering association executive*

Wayne
Annenberg, Leonore A. *foundation administrator*
Etris, Samuel Franklin *trade association administrator*

West Newton
Sever, Tom *labor union administrator*

Wilkes Barre
Dewey, George Willis, III *non-profit corporation executive*

Williamsport
Pittman-Schulz, Kimberley C. *foundation executive*

Wynnewood
Freeman, Morton S. *former bar association executive, retired lawyer*

York
Binder, Mildred Katherine *retired public welfare agency executive*
Russell, Stephen Speh *lawyer*

RHODE ISLAND

Kingston
Schmidt, Charles T., Jr. *labor and industrial relations educator*

North Providence
Maciel, Patricia Ann *development professional*

Providence
Klyberg, Albert Thomas *historical society administrator*

Warwick
Worthington, Samuel Andrew *social welfare administrator*

West Warwick
†Lancellotta, John Jerry-Louis *public service administrator*

Woonsocket
Dubuc, Mary Ellen *educational administrator*

SOUTH CAROLINA

Aiken
Ely, Duncan Cairnes *non profit/human services executive, civic leader*

Charleston
Hughes, Blake *retired architectural institute administrator, publisher*
Mesic, Harriet Lee Bey *medical support group administrator*

Columbia
†Barton, Rayburn *educational administrator*
Bell, Ronald Mack *university foundation administrator*
Bjontegard, Arthur Martin, Jr. *foundation executive*
McGill, Jennifer Houser *non-profit association administrator*
Resch, Mary Louise *social services administrator*
Shabazz, Aiysha Muslimah *social work administrator*

Edgefield
Allen, Jerry Wayne *organization executive*

Green Pond
Ittleson, H(enry) Anthony *foundation executive*

Greenville
Hendrix, Susan Clelia Derrick *civic worker*

Hilton Head Island
Tucker, Frances Laughridge *civic worker*

Lancaster
Bundy, Charles Alan *foundation executive*

Murrells Inlet
†Flannery, Joseph Edward *retired education association executive*

Rock Hill
Viault, Sarah Underhill *civic volunteer*

Spartanburg
Richards, Marty Grover *university foundation director*

Winnsboro
McMaster, Mary Rice *civic worker*

Woodruff
Childers, Bob Eugene *educational association executive*

SOUTH DAKOTA

Aberdeen
Eldredge, Robert John *social services administrator, psychologist*

Rapid City
Erickson, John Duff *retired educational association administrator*

Sioux Falls
Brown, Sue *foundation executive*
Layton, Jean C. *non-profit association administrator*

Watertown
Schumacher, Ervin *retired social services administrator*

Yankton
Piper, Kathleen *Democrat party chairwoman*

TENNESSEE

Chattanooga
Sargeant, Jonathan Douglas *professional organization administrator*

Cleveland
Lockhart, Madge Clements *educational organization executive*

Knoxville
Froula, James DeWayne *national honor society director, engineer*

Lebanon
Howard, Lounita Cook *nonprofit executive director*

Memphis
Glasgow, Agnes Jackie *social welfare administrator, therapist*
Kaplan, (Claudia) Claudette S. *volunteer, professional leader, philanthropist*
Tibbs, Martha Jane Pullen *civic worker*
Whitesell, Dale Edward *retired association executive, natural resources consultant*

Nashville
Benson, Edwin Welburn, Jr. *trade association executive*
Davis, Terry L. *historical association executive*
Henderson, Milton Arnold *professional society administrator*
Johnson, Hollis Eugene, III *foundation executive*
Lodowski, Charles Alan *business association executive*
Purcell, William Paxson, III *university policy center administrator*
†Richard G., Rhoda *educational administrator*
†Saltsman, John B. *political party executive*
Siegfried, John *association officer*
Turk, Thomas Liebig *cultural organization administrator*

Newport
Kridler, Jamie Branam *children's advocate, social psychologist*

TEXAS

Abilene
Kyker, Christine White (Chris Kyker) *human services consultant*

Addison
Waldrep, Alvis Kent, Jr. *non-profit foundation administrator*

Amarillo
Utterback, Will Hay, Jr. *labor union administrator*

Angleton
Handy, Robert Truman *association administrator*

Austin
Banks, Virginia Anne (Ginger Banks) *association administrator*
Barnes, Thomas Joseph *migration program administrator*
Bonjean, Charles Michael *foundation executive, sociologist, educator*
Green, Shirley Moore *public affairs and communications executive*
Hinkley Thompson, Carol Joyce *philanthropy consultant, motivational speaker, writer*
Malcolm, Mollybeth *political party official, counselor*
Mc Kinney, Michael Whitney *trade association executive*
Stoner, James Lloyd *retired foundation executive, clergyman*
West, Glenn Edward *business organization executive*

College Station
Vandiver, Frank Everson *institute administrator, former university president, author, educator*

Colleyville
Love, Ben Howard *retired organization executive*

Dallas
Evans, Linda Perryman *foundation adminstrator*
†Frano, Ronald A. *non-profit executive*
Hay, Betty Jo *civic worker*
Juergens, Bonnie Kay *not-for-profit company executive*

El Paso
Deckert, Myrna Jean *youth organization executive*
Goodman, Gertrude Amelia *civic worker*
Peak, James Matthew *fundraising executive*

Fort Worth
Miller, Travis Milton *association executive, accountant*
Wilkie, Valleau, Jr. *foundation executive*

Galveston
Baker, Robert Ernest, Jr. *retired foundation executive*
Newman, Frances Moody *foundation executive*
Valentine, John Henry, Jr. *foundation president, secondary education educator*

Georgetown
Busfield, Roger Melvil, Jr. *retired trade association executive, educator*

Houston
Crispin, Andre Arthur *international trading company executive*
Grace, Priscilla Anne *labor union executive*
†Hearne, Barbra M. *foundation administrator*
Knotts, Glenn R(ichard) *foundation administrator*
McCleary, Beryl Nowlin *civic worker, travel agency executive*
Shankel, Gerald Marvin *professional society administrator*
Strong, George Walter *political consultant*
Zorn Pickens, Caroline Mae *social services administrator*

Irving
Gorman, MaureenU. *foundation administrator*
Olson, Herbert Theodore *trade association executive*
Stern, Ilene *executive fund raiser*

Jonesville
Vaughan, Martha Louise *agency administrator*

Lubbock
Gibbons, Connie Sue *art association administrator*
Johnson, Ronda Janice *professional not-for-profit fundraiser*

Odessa
Boyd, Claude Collins *educational specialist, consultant*

Richardson
Adamson, Dan Klinglesmith *science association executive*
Bray, Carolyn Scott *educational administrator*

San Antonio
Jacobson, Helen Gugenheim (Mrs. David Jacobson) *civic worker*
Krier, Joseph Roland *chamber of commerce executive, lawyer*
Leal, Barbara Jean Peters *fundraising executive*
Montecel, Maria Robledo (Cuca Robledo Montecel) *educational association administrator*
Spears, Diane Shields *art academy administrator*
White, Mary Ruth Wathen *social services administrator*

Sugar Land
Hosley, Marguerite Cyril *volunteer*

Texarkana
Hines, Betty Taylor *women's center administrator*

Waco
Russell, Inez Snyder *non-profit organization executive*

Waxahachie
Cockerham, Sidney Joe *professional society administrator*

Weatherford
Bergman, Anne Newberry *civic activist*

Webster
Shaffer, Anita Mohrland *counselor, educator*

UTAH

Provo
Lee, Blaine Nelson *executive consultant, educator, author*

Saint George
Martin, George Wilbur *trade association administrator*

Salt Lake City
Bishop, Rob *political party executive*
Clark, Deanna Dee *civic leader and volunteer*
Cofield, Philip Thomas *educational association administrator*
Evans, Max Jay *historical society administrator*
Holbrook, Meghan Zanolli *fundraiser, public relations specialist, state pol*
Melich, Doris S. *public service worker*

Sandy
Littleton, Gaye Darlene *nonprofit executive director*

Woods Cross
Ingles, Joseph Legrand *social services administrator, political science educator*

VERMONT

Bennington
Perin, Donald Wise, Jr. *former association executive*

Bradford
Mallary, Gertrude Robinson *civic worker*

Brattleboro
Akins, Zane Vernon *association executive*
Cramer, Walter Elwood, II *educational administrator*

Burlington
Neale, Gail Lovejoy *non-profit organization management consultant*
Richardson, Gail Marguerite *community services agency executive*

Montpelier
Barbieri, Christopher George *professional society administrator*

Poultney
Edwards, Charles Arthur *college administrator*

Shelburne
Ryerson, William Newton *non profit organization executive*

Weybridge
Berens, Betty Kathryn McAdam *community program administrator*

VIRGINIA

Abingdon
Jones, Mary Trent *endowment fund trustee*

Alexandria
Bachus, Walter Otis *retired army general, former association executive*
Ball, Robert M(yers) *social security, welfare and health policy specialist, writer, lecturer*
Baroody, Michael Elias *trade association executive*
Bezold, Clement *think tank executive*
Bolger, Robert Joseph *retired trade association executive*
Brown, Quincalee *professional society administrator*
Byrd, Barbara A. *professional society administrator*
Byrnside, Oscar Jehu, Jr. *professional society administrator*
Carter, Gene R. *professional society administrator*
Clower, William Dewey *trade association executive*
Cooney, David Martin *organization administrator, retired naval officer*
Cooper, David E.K. *foundation executive*
Crane, Stephen Charles *professional society administrator*
Culkin, Charles Walker, Jr. *trade association administrator*
De Barbieri, Mary Ann *nonprofit management consultant*
Dietrich, Laura Jordan *international policy advisor*
Farrell, William Christopher *lobbyist*
Gould, Phillip *defense planner, engineer*
Greenstein, Ruth Louise *research institute executive, lawyer*
Henton, Melissa Kaye *strategic technology and arms control analyst*
Kolar, Mary Jane *trade and professional association executive*
Leach, Debra Ann *alcohol beverage association executive*
Lenz, Edward Arnold *trade association executive, lawyer*
Losey, Michael Robert *professional society administrator*
Lovejoy, Bret D. *vocational association administrator*
Magazine, Alan Harrison *association executive, consultant*
McCulloch, William Leonard *trade association administrator*
Merrick, Roswell Davenport *educational association administrator*
Murray, Robert John *think-tank executive*
Murtagh, William John *preservationist, educator*
Noland, Royce Paul *association executive, physical therapist*
Paul, Andrew Robert *trade association executive*
Rasmus, John Charles *trade association executive, lawyer*
Rector, John Michael *association executive, lawyer*
Reed, Leon Samuel *policy analyst, writer, photographer*
Scheibel, James Allen *volunteer service executive*
Schwartz, Richard *consumer association executive*
Sciulla, Michael Garri *association executive*
Southworth, R. Morrison *fundraising counsel*
Spadin, Gaile Luanne *association administrator*
Turner, Mary Jane *educational administrator*
Williams, Jody *political organization administrator*
Wurzel, Mary V. *past association executive*

Annandale
Herbst, Robert LeRoy *organization executive*

Arlington
Bast, James Louis *trade association executive*
Bertenthal, Bennett Ira *foundation administrator*
Bossman, David A. *trade association administrator*
Del Duca, Betty Spahr *association executive*
Fabian, John McCreary *non-profit company executive, former astronaut, former air force officer*
Gauvin, Charles F. *professional society administrator*
Gibbons, Miles J., Jr. *foundation administrator*
Hendrickson, Jerome Orland *trade association executive, lawyer*
Hickman, Elizabeth Podesta *retired counselor, educator*
Hunter, J(ohn) Robert *insurance consumer advocate*
Jankowski, John Edward, Jr. *government administrator*
Kirtley, Jane Elizabeth *professional society administrator, lawyer*
Lampe, Margaret Sanger *community activist*
Langworthy, Everett Walter *association executive, natural gas exploration company executive*
Makonnen, Sophia Mehret *international development/Africa specialist*
Marcuccio, Phyllis Rose *association executive, editor*
McMasters, Paul Kenneth *foundation executive*
McShane, Michael John *lobbyist*
McWethy, Patricia Joan *educational association administrator*
Paynter, Harry Alvin *retired trade association executive*
Rees, Clifford Harcourt, Jr. (Ted Rees) *association executive, retired air force officer*
Richtol, Herbert Harold *science foundation program director*
Roach, Arthur Hudgins *fund raising consultant*
Roberts, James Milnor, Jr. *professional society administrator*
Rosenker, Mark Victor *trade association executive*
Shannon, Thomas Alfred *retired educational association administrator emeritus*
Smith, Elise Fiber *international non-profit development agency administrator*
Stackpole, Kerry Clifford *association executive*
Stolgitis, William Charles *professional society executive*
Taylor, Robert William *professional society administrator*
Teem, John McCorkle *retired association executive*
Vaught, Wilma L. *foundation executive, retired air force officer*
Watson, Alexander Fletcher *organization executive, former ambassador*
Wells, Christine *foundation executive*
Wilson, Minter Lowther, Jr. *retired officers association executive*

Brookneal
Elson, James Martin *historic foundation director, college music educator, fine arts administrator*

Burke
†Zelasko, Nancy Faber *education association manager*

Chantilly
†Matthews, Stephen Philip *association executive*
Sroka, John Walter *trade association executive*

Charlottesville
Jordan, Daniel Porter, Jr. *foundation administrator, history educator*
Mallory, Michael Anthony *foundation executive*
Wilson, Mitchell B. *fraternal organization administrator*

Chesapeake
Tate, Randall J. (Randy Tate) *former congressman*

Fairfax
Cullison, Alexander C. (Doc Cullison) *mediator, arbitrator*
Emely, Charles Harry *trade association executive, consultant*
Emely, Mary Ann *association executive*
Gray, William H., III *association executive, former congressman*
Grunder, Fred Irwin *program administrator, industrial hygienist*
Hollans, Irby Noah, Jr. *retired association executive*
Molino, Michael Anthony *trade association executive*
Mund, Richard Gordon *foundation executive*
Smith, J. Daniel *maritime association administrator*
Wood, C(harles) Norman *association executive*
Woodruff, C(harles) Roy *professional association executive*

Falls Church
Tamondong, Susan Daet *international social scientist*
Thomsen, Samuel Borron *non-profit executive, consultant*

Flint Hill
Dietel, William Moore *former foundation executive*

Franklin
Feldt, Glenda Diane *educational administrator*

Front Royal
Greco, Barbara Ruth Gomez *literacy organization administrator*
Marx, Paul Benno *author, social service administrator, missionary*

Great Falls
DiBona, Charles Joseph *retired trade association executive*
Schwartz, Robert Terry *professional association executive*
Whipple, David Doty *retired professional society administrator*

Harrisonburg
Helmuth, Les N. *fund raising executive, non-profit consultant*

Keswick
Nosanow, Barbara Shissler *art association administrator*

Louisa
Small, William Edwin, Jr. *association and recreation executive*

Lynchburg
Johnson, Robert Bruce *historic preservationist*

Manassas
Cypess, Raymond Harold *bioscience organization executive*
Jakub, Paula Sue *association administrator*
Slayton, Gus *foundation administrator*

Mc Lean
Mars, Virginia Cretella *civic worker*
McInerney, James Eugene, Jr. *trade association executive*
Rogers, Thomas Francis *foundation administrator*
Schweiker, Richard Schultz *trade association executive, former senator, former cabinet secretary*

Newport News
Hawkins, J. Michael *housing development administrator*
Mazur, Rhoda Himmel *community volunteer*

Norfolk
Filer, Emily Symington Harkins *social services administrator*
Wilson, Lloyd Lee *organization administrator*

Reston
Brennan, Norma Jean *professional society publications director*
Chattman, Raymond Christopher *foundation executive*
Curry, John Joseph *professional organization executive*
Davis, James E. *professional association executive*
Gates, James David *retired association executive, consultant*
Hope, Samuel Howard *accreditation organization executive*
Madry-Taylor, Jacquelyn Yvonne *educational administrator*
Mahlmann, John James *music education association administrator*
Minton, Joseph Paul *retired safety organization executive*
Mogge, Harriet Morgan *educational association executive*

Richmond
Combs, Sandra Lynn *state parole board official*
DeWitt, Brydon Merrill *development consultant*
Grover, Peter Dun *cultural organization administrator*
Horwitz, Marcia J. *fundraiser, writer*
Kline, Robert H. *foundation administrator*
Linkonis, Suzanne Newbold *community corrections case manager, counselor*
†Plum, Kenneth *political organization administrator*
Rada, Heath Kenneth *social service organization executive*
Spitzer, William John *healthcare social work administrator*
Wood, Jeanne Clarke *charitable organization executive*

Roanoke
Schlegel, Beverly Faye *private club administrator*

Spotsylvania
Hardy, Dorcas Ruth *business and government relations executive*

Springfield
Bartlow, Gene Steven *association executive, retired air force officer*
Larson, Reed Eugene *foundation administrator*

Stafford
Sedlak, James William *organization administrator*

Sterling
Munger, Paul David *educational administrator*

Upperville
Smart, Edith Merrill *civic worker*

Vienna
Spiro, Robert Harry, Jr. *foundation and business executive, educator*
West, Richard Luther *defense consultant, retired army officer*

Virginia Beach
Bryant, Jacqueline Eola *educational consultant, urban specialist*

Warrenton
Fox, Raymond Graham *educational technologist*
Sass, Arthur Harold *educational executive*

Williamsburg
Longsworth, Charles R. *foundation administrator*
Wilburn, Robert Charles *institute executive*

Woodstock
Hull, Linda Weaver *outreach coordinator*

WASHINGTON

Battle Ground
Fineran, Diana Lou *association administrator*

Bellevue
Arnold, Ronald Henri *nonprofit organization executive, consultant*
Kiest, Alan Scott *social services administrator*

Blaine
James, Herb Mark (Jay James) *foundation and insurance executive, free trade consultant*

Bothell
Hoffman, Marianne Macina *corporate relations administrator*

Edmonds
Monroe, James Walter *retired organization executive*

La Center
Holley, Lawrence Alvin *retired labor union official*

Mill Creek
Corbally, John Edward *foundation director*

Olympia
†Bland, Marybeth *volunteer, artist*
Olson, Steven Stanley *social service executive*
Stohl, Esther A. *senior citizen advocate*

Port Townsend
Woolf, William Blauvelt *retired association executive*

Seattle
Arthur, William Lynn *environmental foundation administrator*
Baker, Roland Jerald *trade association administrator*
Brooke, Francis John, III *foundation administrator*
Mathis, Teresa Gale *association executive*
Moore, Judith Ann *educational administrator*
Ray, Marianne Yurasko *social services administrator*

Shelton
Mullen, Cathryne Anne *civic worker*

Spokane
Coker, Charlotte Noel *political activist*
Falkner, James George *foundation executive*
Murphy, Mary Ann *human services administrator*
Twohig, Kevin *foundation administrator*

Tacoma
Garner, Carlene Ann *fundraising consultant*
Graybill, David Wesley *chamber of commerce executive*
Rieke, William Oliver *foundation director, medical educator, former university president*

Vancouver
Ferguson, Larry Emmett *educational administrator*
Smith, Sam Corry *retired foundation executive, consultant*

Woodinville
Manevich, Leonard A. *cultural organization administrator, composer*

Yakima
Nelson, Bryan H(erbert) *non-profit agency administrator*

WEST VIRGINIA

Charleston
Chapman, John Andrew *association executive*
Tyson, David Richard *lawyer, political party official*

Hillsboro
Pierce, William Luther *association executive, writer*

Oak Hill
Janney, Sally Baggs *civic worker*

Parkersburg
Burdette, Jane Elizabeth *nonprofit association executive, consultant*

WISCONSIN

Altoona
James, Henry Thomas *former foundation executive, educator*

Eau Claire
†Hart, Holly Joy *educational administrator*

Elm Grove
Halvorsen, Morrie Edward *trade association administrator*

Fond Du Lac
†Ward, JoAnn Boettner *convention and tourist bureau administrator*

Greenfield
Havey, Francis Powers *fund raising executive, lawyer*

Kenosha
Adler, Seymour Jack *social services administrator*

La Crosse
Schumacher, Philip Gerard *fundraising executive*

Madison
Higby, Gregory James *historical association administrator, historian*
Jacobs, Eleanor R. *retired volunteer*
Porter, Andrew Calvin *educational administrator, psychology educator*
Schmidt, Martha Bubeck *educator, counselor*
†Spring, Terri *political organization executive*

Milwaukee
Ballweg, Mary Lou *nonprofit association administrator and founder, writer, consultant*
Blankenship, Jay Randall *social services executive*
Brever, Michael Stephen *non-profit executive director, alderman*
Joyce, Michael Stewart *foundation executive, political science educator*
Rader, I. A. *electronic components manufacturing company executive*
Ritz, Esther Leah *civic worker, volunteer, investor*
Taylor, Allen M. *community foundation executive*
Zeidler, Frank P. *former association administrator, mayor, arbitrator, mediator, fact-finder*

Mineral Point
Olson, John W. *advocate*

Onalaska
†Pertzsch, Evelyn Maria *civic worker*

Racine
†Bray, Charles William, III *foundation executive*
Rosser, Richard Franklin *higher education consultant*

Shawano
Lyon, Thomas L. *agricultural organization administrator*

St Francis
Schaubel, Harry Albert *volunteer*

Wausau
Connor, Mary Roddis *foundation administrator*

Whitewater
Kolda, Thomas Joseph *non-profit organization executive*

PROFESSIONAL INDEX 5845 ASSOCIATIONS AND ORGANIZATIONS

WYOMING

Cheyenne
Noe, Guy *retired social services administrator*

Laramie
Darnall, Roberta Morrow *association executive*
Hanson, Mary Louise *retired social services administrator*

CANADA

ALBERTA

Calgary
Raeburn, Andrew Harvey *performing arts association executive, record producer*
Roberts, John Peter Lee *cultural advisor, administrator, educator, writer*

Edmonton
Christian, Ralph Gordon *agricultural research administrator*

BRITISH COLUMBIA

Vancouver
Saywell, William George Gabriel *foundation administrator*

NEW BRUNSWICK

Fredericton
Lewell, Peter A. *international technology executive, researcher*

NOVA SCOTIA

Halifax
Sparling, Mary Christine *foundation executive*

Wolfville
Elliott, Robbins Leonard *consultant*

ONTARIO

Mississauga
Burrell, Carol Ann *trade association executive*

Ottawa
Davies, Gareth John *lawyer, trade executive*
Ecroyd, Lawrence Gerald *trade association administrator*

Toronto
Goodenow, Robert W. *labor union administrator*
Kossuth, Selwyn Barnett *trade association consultant*
Montgomery, Donald Russell *labor consulting firm executive*
Troubetzkoy, Alexis Serge *foundation administrator, educator*
Wildman, Charles Jackson *political organization official*
Wilson, Ian Edwin *cultural organization administrator, archivist*

Willowdale
Bulloch, John Frederick Devon *foundation administrator*

QUEBEC

Montreal
Alain, Robert *foundation administrator*

Outremont
Letourneau, Jean-Paul *business association executive and consultant*

Rosemere
Hopper, Carol *meeting and trade show administrator*

MEXICO

Mexico City
Bruton, John Macaulay *trade association executive*

ENGLAND

Brighton
Bezanson, Keith Arthur *administrative educational executive*

London
†McNulty, Sally *political association executive*

FRANCE

Nanterre
Mestrallet, Gérard *professional society administrator*

ITALY

Rome
Wilson, George Peter *international organization executive*

JAPAN

Minato-ku Tokyo
Scullion, Tsugiko Yamagami *non-profit organization executive*

SWITZERLAND

Bern
Leavey, Thomas Edward *international organization administrator*

Geneva
Purcell, James Nelson, Jr. *international organization administrator*
Schweitzer, Theodore Gottlieb, III *United Nations administrator*
Weber, George *international social welfare administrator*

ADDRESS UNPUBLISHED

Allerton, John Stephen *association executive*
Allison, Andrew Marvin *church executive*
Amstutz, Daniel Gordon *international trade association administrator, former grain dealer, government and intergovernment official*
Andringa, Patricia Perkins *fundraiser, consultant*
Anguiano, Lupe *business executive*
Annenberg, Walter H. *philanthropist, diplomat, editor, publisher, broadcaster*
Armour, David Edward Ponton *trade association administrator*
Aron, Peter Arthur *charitable foundation executive, private investor*
Arthur, Rochelle Linda *creative director*
Ashman, Alicia Koninska *civic activist*
Atchison, Richard Calvin *trade association director*
Babb, Roberta Joan *educational administrator*
Bagley, Steven Robert *food bank organization executive, consultant*
Balter, Frances Sunstein *civic worker*
Barker, Judy *foundation executive*
Barone, Janine Mason *foundation administrator*
Bashore, Irene Saras *research institute administrator*
Beitz, Alexandra Grigg *political activist*
Benton, Robert Dean *educational organization executive*
Berresford, Susan Vail *philanthropic foundation executive*
†Biddle, Albert G. W. *trade association executive*
Biggers, Joan Nevill *social services organization administrator*
Blair, Fred Edward *social services administrator*
Bloch, Julia Chang *foundation administrator, former bank executive, educator*
†Blumstein, Susan Bender *fundraiser*
Boal, Dean *retired arts center administrator, educator*
Boeker, Paul Harold *non-profit organization official, diplomat*
Branch, Anne Heather *fund raiser*
Brawer, Catherine Coleman *foundation executive, curator*
Bricker, William Rudolph *organization executive*
Brim, Orville Gilbert, Jr. *former foundation administrator, author*
Brooks Shoemaker, Virginia Lee *volunteer, librarian*
Brown, Anne Rhoda Wiesen *civic worker*
†Brown, David R. *think-tank executive*
Brune, Eva *fundraiser*
Buck, Linda Dee *civic worker*
Burki, Fred Albert *labor union official*
Bush, Barbara Pierce *volunteer, wife of former President of the United States*
Campbell, Edwin Denton *consultant*
Carey, Ronald *former labor union leader*
Carroll, Brenda Sandidge *retired civic worker*
Carter, (William) Hodding, III *foundation executive, former journalist, public official and educator*
Casey, Robert J. *international trade association executive*
Cesnik, James Michael *union official, newspaperman, printer, consultant*
Chernish, Lelia Margaret *fundraiser*
Clark, Margaret Pruitt *education and advocacy executive administrator*
†Cohen, Mark D. *social service admnistrator*
Collyer, Robert B. *trade association administrator*
Cooper, Bobbie (Minna Louise Morgan Cooper) *volunteer*
Cooper, Charles Donald *association executive, editor, retired career officer*
†Corn, Lovick P. *retired foundation executive*
Coughlan, William David *professional society administrator*
Covell, Christopher Greene *management executive*
Cowles, Elizabeth Hall *program consultant*
Crane, Stacey Lynn *association executive*
Day, Neil McPherson *trade association executive*
De Moss, Robert George *religious foundation executive*
Dennis, Kimberly Ohnemus *philanthropy consultant*
Desmarais, Maurice *trade association administrator*
DeVos, Elisabeth *political association executive*
Dorman, Richard Frederick, Jr. *association executive, consultant*
Eastman, Francesca Marlene *volunteer, art historian*
Easton, Michelle *foundation executive*
Ellis, Anne Elizabeth *fundraiser*
Epperson, Margaret Farrar *civic worker*
Estep, Sarah Virginia *association executive*
Evans, Rosemary Hall *civic worker*
Fabry, Paul Andrew *international association executive*
Fahlbeck, Douglas Alan *corporate development executive*
Farinella, Paul James *retired arts institution executive*
Farris, Robert Earl *transportation consultant, corporate executive*
Ferris, Katherine Ann *civic worker*
Fluth, John Adam *educational administrator*
Flynn, Paul Bartholomew *foundation executive*
Forbes, Marjorie Webster *counselor*
Foster, Charles Henry Wheelwright *former foundation officer, consultant,author*
Friedman, Frances Wolf *political fund raiser*
†Fuller, Norine L. *lobbyist, educational administrator*
Gabria, Joanne Bakaitis *health and education volunteer, former information processing systems equipment company executive*
Gallagher, John Paul *association administrator*
Gammon, Samuel Rhea, III *association executive, former ambassador*
Gasper, Jo Ann *consulting firm executive*
Gertenbach, Robert Frederick *medical research organization executive, accountant, lawyer*
Gilchrest, Thornton Charles *retired association executive*
Goldberg, Norma Lorraine *retired public welfare administrator*
Goldman, Rachel Bok *civic volunteer*
Goodwin, Felix Lee *retired educational administrator, retired army officer*
Grace, Helen Kennedy *retired foundation administrator*
Griggs, Bobbie June *civic worker*
Gunderson, Judith Keefer *golf association executive*
Guthman, Sandra Polk *foundation executive*
Hadas, Julia Ann *social services administrator*
Hanford, George Hyde *retired educational administrator*
Heap, Sylvia Stuber *civic worker*
Helm, DeWitt Frederick, Jr. *consultant, professional association administrator*
Henricks, Roger Lee *retired social services administrator*
Hicks, Dolores Kathleen (De De Hicks) *association executive*
Hines, JoAnn R. *professional association executive and consultant*
Hobday, John Charles *foundation administrator*
Hoffheimer, Minette Goldsmith *community service volunteer*
Hoopes, Townsend Walter *business consultant, former government official*
Horsch, Kathleen Joanne *social services administrator, educator, consultant*
Houchin, Susan Kay *social services administrator*
Huggins, Robert Brian *nonprofit organization official*
Hyatt-Smith, Ann Rose *non-profit organization executive, consultant*
Ikeda, Tsuguo (Ike Ikeda) *social services center administrator, consultant*
Isaacson, Edith L. *civic leader*
Johnson, Marlene M. *nonprofit executive*
Johnson, Mary Murphy *social services administrator, writer*
Jones, Dorothy Joanne *social services professional*
Kabat, Linda Georgette *civic leader*
Kahn, Pauline Gitman *volunteer*
Kane, Ryan Thomas *corporate executive*
Kaskowitz, Edwin *social services executive*
Keil, M. David *retired international association executive*
Kelly, Nancy Folden *arts administrator*
Kezlarian, Nancy Kay *social services administrator, family counselor*
King, Rosalyn Mercita *social science researcher*
Kinslow, Margie Ann *volunteer worker*
Klopfleisch, Stephanie Squance *social services agency administrator*
Knauer, Virginia Harrington (Mrs. Wilhelm F. Knauer) *consumer consultant, former government official*
Koller, Karen Kathryn *social services administrator*
Kunstadter, Geraldine Sapolsky *foundation executive*
Kurtz, Dolores May *civic worker*
Kussrow, Nancy Esther *educational association administrator*
Lancaster, Sally Rhodus *non-profit consultant*
†Lash, Donna Rose *non-profit administrator, lobbyist, writer*
Ledwig, Donald Eugene *association executive, former broadcasting executive, former naval officer*
Leggett, Roberta Jean (Bobbi Leggett) *social services administrator*
Leland, David J. *political association executive*
Lester, Virginia Laudano *education administrator*
†Levin, Judith Maria *consultant to non-profit organizations*
Liddell, Jane Hawley Hawkes *civic worker*
Livingston, Margaret Gresham *civic leader*
Lubic, Ruth Watson *association executive, nurse midwife*
Luckey, Doris Waring *civic volunteer*
MacCarthy, Talbot Leland *civic volunteer*
Malek, Marlene Anne *cultural organization, foundation executive*
Marquardt, Sandra Mary *activist, lobbyist, researcher*
Marsh, Michael L.H. *trade association administrator*
Mason, John E. *political association executive*
Massaro, Linda P. *science foundation executive*
McCloskey, J(ohn) Michael *retired association administrator*
McCone, Michael F. *retired cultural organization administrator*
McDaniel, Mike *political association executive*
McFate, Patricia Ann *foundation executive, scientist, educator*
McIntyre, Carol Chrisman *social services administrator*
McKinney, Louise Chestnut *volunteer*
McMurray, Ron *political association executive*
McMurtry, Florence Jean *educational administrator*
Mende, Robert Graham *retired engineering association executive*
Mercuri, Joan B. *foundation executive*
Meredith, Ellis Edson *association and business executive*
Miller, Pamela Joan *special events marketing executive*
Mojica, Aurora *training director*
Moore, Robert William *professional organization executive*
Morris, Diana Lee *foundation executive*
Morrison, Barbara Haney *educational administrator*
Morrison, Ian A(lastair) *foundation executive*
Nardi Riddle, Clarine *association administrator, judge*
Neel, Judy Murphy *association executive*
Nelson, Jodie Lynn *charity administrator*
O'Connor, Doris Julia *non-profit fundraiser, consultant*
O'Donnell, Kathleen Mary *social services administrator*
O'Hollaren, Paul Joseph *former international fraternity administrator*
†O'Neal, Vanessa *educational association administrator*
O'Rourke, Joan B. Doty Werthman *educational administrator*
Peck, Robert David *educational foundation administrator*
Pelkey, Mildred Loraine *volunteer*
†Pennywitt, Neil C. *educational organization administrator, fundraiser*
Peppler, William Norman *aviation association executive*
Peri, Winnie Lee Branch *educational director*
Perigo, Michael Gregory *director of development*
Perry, James E. *not-for-profit development executive*
Phillips, Martha Henderson *organization executive*
Pick Reed, Eija Anneli *fundraising executive*
Pifer, Alan (Jay Parrish) *former foundation executive*
Plymyer, John Robert *retired professional association administrator*
Powers, John Henry *industry executive*
Pratt, Alice Reynolds *retired educational administrator*
Pritchard, Kathleen Jo *not-for-profit association administrator*
Pullen, Penny Lynne *non-profit administrator, former state legislator*
Quehl, Gary Howard *association executive, consultant*
Ramsey, Douglas Arthur *foundation executive*
Ramsey, Lynn Allison *trade association, public relations professional*
Retzer, Michael L. *political association executive*
Richards, Morris Dick *social work administrator, educator*
Rickerd, Donald Sheridan *foundation executive*
Riggin, Lee Pepper *retired fraternal organization administrator*
Rimel, Rebecca Webster *foundation executive*
Ritchie, Steven John *foundation administrator, fundraising consultant*
Roberson, James O. *foundation executive*
Roberts, James Gordon *foundation executive*
Roethel, David Albert Hill *consultant*
Rogers, Margaret Ellen Jonsson *civic worker*
Rose, Wil *foundation executive*
Rosenberg, Alison P. *public policy official*
Ross, Charlotte Pack *social services administrator*
Rothenberger, Dolores Jane *association administrator, actress, singer*
Rowell, Barbara Caballero *office manager*
†Russell-Porath, Julie Ann *advocate*
Ryan, John William *association executive*
Sabinson, Harvey Barnett *theatrical organiztion administrator*
†Saiffe, Fernando Gonzalez *organization administrator, lawyer*
Sampson, Robert Neil *natural resources consultant*
Sanford, Sarah J. *healthcare executive*
Schiaffino, S(ilvio) Stephen *retired medical society executive, consultant*
Scott, August Jeryl *public speaker*
Sebela, Vicki D. *association executive, freelance writer*
Seggerman, Anne Crellin *foundation executive*
Semler, Margot Strong *association administrator*
Siegel, Mary Ann Garvin *recruiter*
Singer, Markus Morton *retired trade association executive*
Smith, Brian *development director*
Smith, Laverne Byrd *educational association administrator*
Smith, Margaret Taylor *volunteer*
Smith, Sheryl Velting *organization administrator*
Sodolski, John *retired association administrator*
Sollid, Faye Eising *civic worker*
Stewart, Paul Anthony, II *trade association executive, author*
Sulc, Jean Luena (Jean L. Mestres) *lobbyist, consultant*
†Sullivan, James W. *lobbyist*
†Tadlock, Anita Conner *volunteer*
Tamm, Mary Anne DeCamp *social services administrator*
Taplin, Frank E., Jr. *trustee education and arts institutions and associations*
Thomas, Patricia Faye *educational administrator*
Throndson, Edward Warner *residential association administrator*
Tipping, William Malcolm *social services administrator*
Tise, Larry Edward *association executive, historian*
Tomsky, Judy *fundraiser and event planner, importer*
Townsend, Susan Elaine *social service institute administrator, hostage survival consultant*
Trimble, Bernard Henry *tour guide, former trade association executive*
Turner, John Freeland *non-profit administrator, former federal agency administrator, former state senator*
†Uehling, Barbara Staner *educational administrator*
Uhde, Larry Jackson *joint apprentice administrator*
Van Ness, John Ralph *university administrator, educator*
†Villaveces, Jeffrey Roberto *educational organization worker*
Wait, Carol Grace Cox *organization administrator*
Walter, J. Jackson *consultant*
Warren, Mark Edward *foundation executive, lawyer*
Washington, Valora *foundation administrator*
Watts, Glenn Ellis *union official*
Weikart, David Powell *educational research foundation administrator*
Wells, Janet Ohlemiller *fundraiser*
Whalen, Loretta Theresa *religious educational administrator*
White, Julie *former foundation executive*
Whitlock, Bennett Clarke, Jr. *retired association executive*
Williams, Linda Hunt *organization executive*
Womack, Idalah Demina *social services administrator*
Woods, Harriett Ruth *retired political organization president*
Work, William *retired association executive*
Wright, Jane Brooks *retired university foundation professional*
Wyatt, Lenore *civic worker*
Wyse, Roy *retired labor union administrator*
†Yoshimura, Valerie Nao *cultural organization administrator*
Zehr, Norman Robert *association administrator*
Ziegler, Ronald Louis *association executive, former government official*
Zimny, Max *labor union administrator, lawyer*
Zisholtz-Herzog, Ellen Naomi *arts administrator, consultant, cultural planner*
Zoellick, Robert Bruce *political science administrator, lawyer*
Zowader, Sherry Lee *volunteer, artist*
Zuck, Alfred Miller *public administration educator*

ATHLETICS

UNITED STATES

ALABAMA

Auburn
†Ellis, Cliff *college basketball coach*
Housel, David *athletic director*
Marsh, David *university swimming coach*
Reeve, Thomas Gilmour *physical education educator*
Shore, Eric *coach*

Hueytown
Allison, Robert Arthur *race car owner, retired professional stock car driver*

Montgomery
Olson, Michele Scharff *kinesiology/physical education educator*

Normal
Parham, Press *university women's basketball coach*

Phenix City
Merritt, Martin David *tennis professional, educator, musician*

Tuscaloosa
Crompton-Moorer, Cassandra *basketball player*
Moody, Rick Michael *collegiate basketball coach*

ARIZONA

Flagstaff
Sanders, Meg *women's basketball coach*

Phoenix
Ainge, Danny Ray *professional basketball coach*
Bell, Jay Stuart *baseball player*
Benes, Andrew Charles *professional baseball player*
Bidwill, William V. *professional football executive*
Colangelo, Bryan *professional sports team executive*
Colangelo, Jerry John *professional basketball team executive*
Fitzsimmons, (Lowell) Cotton *professional basketball executive, broadcaster, former coach*
†Garagiola, Joe, Jr. *baseball team executive*
†Gillom, Jennifer *professional basketball player*
Hemond, Roland A. *professional baseball team executive*
Johnson, Kevin Maurice *professional basketball player*
Johnson, Randall David (Randy Johnson) *professional baseball player*
Kidd, Jason *professional basketball player*
Manning, Daniel Ricardo *professional basketball player*
†Miller, Cheryl DeAnn *professional basketball coach, broadcaster*
†Murrell, Adrian Bryan *professional football player*
Pettis, Bridget *basketball player*
†Plummer, Jason Steven (Jake) *professional football player*
†Roenick, Jeremy *professional hockey player*
Showalter, Buck (William Nathaniel Showalter, III) *major league baseball team manager*
Swann, Eric Jerrod *professional football player*
Timms, Michele *professional basketball player*
Tkachuk, Keith *professional hockey player*
Tobin, Vincent Michael *professional football coach, former sports team executive*
Van Arsdale, Dick *professional basketball team executive*
Williams, Aeneas Demetrius *professional football player*
Williams, Matt (Matthew Derrick Williams) *professional baseball player*

Tempe
Hoke, Judy Ann *physical education educator*
Lein, Randy *coach*
Moore, Rob *professional football player*
Snyder, Bruce Fletcher *coach*
Snyder, Lester M. *sports association executive*
Thorne, Charlie Turner *women's collegiate basketball coach*
White, Kevin M. *athletic director*

Tucson
Bonvincini, Joan M. *university women's basketball coach*
Case, Richard W. *sports association executive*
Kearney, Joseph Laurence *retired athletic conference administrator*
Olson, Lute *university athletic coach*

ARKANSAS

Conway
Titlow, Larry Wayne *physical education and kinesiology educator*

Fayetteville
Blair, Gary *women's collegiate basketball coach*
McDonnell, John *coach*
†Richardson, Nolan *university athletic coach*

Russellville
Jackson, Shelia Lucyle *physical education educator, consultant*

State University
Dowd, Barry *athletic director*
Hollis, Joe *coach*
Mittie, Jeff *university women's basketball coach*

CALIFORNIA

Alameda
Davis, Allen *professional football team executive*
Gordon, Darrien X. Jamal *professional football player*
Gruden, Jon *professional football coach*
Herrera, John *professional football team executive*
Howard, Desmond Kevin *professional football player*
Wisniewski, Stephen Adam *professional football player*

Anaheim
Bavasi, William Joseph *professional sports team executive*
Collins, Terry *professional baseball manager*
DiSarcina, Gary Thomas *baseball player*
Edmonds, James Patrick (Jim Edmonds) *baseball player*
Fielder, Cecil Grant *professional baseball player*
Finley, Chuck (Charles Edward Finley) *baseball player*
Kariya, Paul *professional hockey player*
McDowell, Jack Burns *professional baseball player*
Salmon, Timothy James *professional baseball player*
Selanne, Teemu *hockey player*
Stark, Milton Dale *sports association executive*
Tavares, Tony *professional hockey and baseball leagues executive*
Vaughn, Maurice Samuel (Mo Vaughn) *professional baseball player*

Berkeley
Braun, Benjamin *basketball coach*
Kasser, John *athletic director*
Milano, Robert *baseball coach*
Thornton, Nort *swimming coach*
Weiner, Barry Frederick *gymnastics coach*

Beverly Hills
Lott, Ronnie (Ronald Mandel Lott) *retired professional football player, T.V. broadcaster*
Shoemaker, Bill (William Lee Shoemaker) *retired jockey, horse trainer*

Clovis
Mort, Gary Steven *physical education educator*

Coronado
Axelson, Joseph Allen *professional athletics executive, publisher*

Culver City
Johnson, Earvin (Magic Johnson) *professional sports team executive, former professional basketball coach*

Cypress
Dorn, Marian Margaret *educator, sports management administrator*

Danville
Behring, Kenneth E. *professional sports team owner*

El Segundo
Rock, Angela *volleyball player*

Fountain Valley
Treadway-Dillmon, Linda Lee *athletic trainer, actress, stuntwoman*

Fresno
Bohl, Allen *coach*
Hill, Pat *coach*

Fullerton
Curry, Denise *university women's basketball coach*

Inglewood
Bryant, Kobe *basketball player*
Dixon, Tamecka *professional basketball player*
Ferraro, Ray *hockey player*
†Harper, Derek *professional basketball player*
Harris, Del William *professional basketball coach*
Jackson, Philip Douglas *professional basketball coach*
Kupchak, Mitchell *professional sports team executive*
Leslie, Lisa *professional basketball player*
Mabika, Mwadi *basketball player*
McGee, Pamela *basketball player*
O'Neal, Shaquille Rashaun *professional basketball player*
Rice, Glen Anthony *professional basketball player*
Robinson, Larry Clark *professional hockey coach*
Rodman, Dennis Keith *basketball player*
Roski, Edward P. *professional sports team executive*
Sharman, William *professional basketball team executive*
Toler, Penny *professional basketball player*
†Woolridge, Orlando *professional basketball coach*

Irvine
Adams, Mark *coach*

Lake Arrowhead
Barnett, Michael *sports agent, business manager*

Long Beach
Boychuk, Dallas *university head women's basketball coach*
Gimmillaro, Brian *university head women's volleyball coach*

Los Angeles
Abdul-Jabbar, Kareem (Lewis Ferdinand Alcindor) *retired professional basketball player, sports commentator*
Baker, Guy *coach*
Barretta-Keyser, Jolie *professional athletics coach, author, film and TV casting director*
Baylor, Elgin Gay *professional basketball team executive*
Brown, James Kevin *professional baseball player*
Ford, Chris *professional basketball coach*
Gillespie, Mike J. *university baseball coach*
Grudzielanek, Mark James *professional baseball player*
Hundley, Todd Randolph *professional baseball player*
†Johnson, Davey (David Allen Johnson) *baseball team manager*
Karros, Eric Peter *baseball player*
Lasorda, Thomas Charles (Tommy Lasorda) *professional baseball team manager*
Lavin, Stephen Michael *basketball coach*
Mondesi, Raul *baseball player*
†Olivier, Kathy *college basketball coach*
†Olowokandi, Michael *professional basketball player*
†Park, Chan Ho *professional baseball player*
†Robitaille, Luc *professional hockey player*
†Russell, Bill *coach*
Scates, Allen Edward *coach*
Schubert, Mark *university swimming coach*
Sheffield, Gary Antonian *professional baseball player*
Sherfy, Bradley L. *golf coach*
†Stacy, Hollis *professional golfer*
Sterling, Donald T. *professional basketball team executive*
Wilhoit, Julie *women's collegiate basketball coach*
Williams, John *coach*

Malibu
Trakh, Mark *university head women's basketball coach*

Marina Del Rey
Banks, Ernest (Ernie Banks) *retired professional baseball player*
Kiraly, Karch (Charles Kiraly) *professional volleyball player*
Steffes, Kent *volleyball player*

Oakland
Bogues, Tyrone Curtis (Muggsy Bogues) *professional basketball player*
Carlesimo, P. J. (Peter J. Carlesimo) *professional basketball coach*
Cohan, Christopher *professional sports team executive*
†Hofman, Ken *professional sports team executive*
Howe, Art (Arthur Henry Howe, Jr.) *professional baseball manager*
†Phillips, Keith Anthony (Tony) *professional baseball player*
Raines, Timothy *professional baseball player*
St. Jean, Garry *professional basketball coach*
†Schott, Stephen C. *professional sports team executive*
†Starks, John Levell *professional basketball player*

Palm Springs
Jumonville, Felix Joseph, Jr. *physical education educator, realtor*

Palo Alto
Van Derveer, Tara *university athletic coach*

Pasadena
†Cienfuegos, Mauricio *professional soccer player*
†Del Prado, Sergio *professional soccer team executive*
†Schmid, Sigi *professional soccer coach*

Rancho Santa Margarita
Montana, Joseph C., Jr. *former professional football player*
†Pruett, Scott *race car driver*

Sacramento
†Adelman, Rick *professional basketball coach*
†Allen, Sonny *professional basketball coach*
Bolton-Holifield, Ruthie *basketball player*
Burgess, Linda *basketball player*
Byears, Latasha *professional basketball player*
Fox, Ned *professional sports team owner*
Hardmon, Lady *professional athlete*
Petrie, Geoff *professional basketball team executive*
†Reynolds, Jerry Owen *sports team executive*
Thomas, Jim *professional basketball team executive*
†Webber, Chris, III (Mayce Edward Christopher Webber) *professional basketball player*

San Diego
Addis, Thomas Homer, III *professional golfer*
Beathard, Bobby *professional football team executive*
Bochy, Bruce *professional sports team manager, coach*
Carney, John Michael *professional football player*
Gwynn, Anthony Keith (Tony Gwynn) *professional baseball player*
Harbaugh, James Joseph *professional football player*
Hoffman, Trevor William *professional baseball player*
Lucchino, Lawrence *sports team executive, lawyer*
†Magadan, David Joseph *professional baseball player*
†McKeon, John Aloysius (Jack) (Jack McKeon) *professional baseball team executive*
Means, Natrone Jermaine *professional football player*
Metcalf, Eric Quinn *professional football player*
Moores, John *professional sports team executive*
Myers, Randall Kirk (Randy Myers) *professional baseball player*
†Riley, Michael (Mike Riley) *professional football coach*
Sanders, Reginald Laverne (Reggie Sanders) *professional baseball player*
Seau, Junior (Tiana Seau, Jr.) *professional football player*
†Spanos, Alexander Gus *professional football team executive*
†Towers, Kevin *baseball team executive*

San Francisco
Baker, Dusty (Johnnie B. Baker, Jr.) *professional baseball team manager*
Bonds, Barry Lamar *professional baseball player*
†Cepeda, Orlando *retired professional baseball player*
Kent, Jeffrey Franklin *baseball player*
Magowan, Peter Alden *professional baseball team executive, grocery chain executive*
Nen, Robert Allen (Robb Nen) *professional baseball player*
†Sabean, Brian R. *professional baseball team executive*

San Jose
†Cerritos, Ronald *professional soccer player*
Damphousse, Vincent *professional hockey player*
McEnery, Tom *professional sports team executive*
Nicholls, Bernard Irvine *hockey player*
Nolan, Owen *professional hockey player*
Payne, Gregory *physical education educator*
†Quinn, Brian *professional soccer coach*
Vernon, Mike *professional hockey player*
Wughalter, Emily Hope *physical education educator*
†Wynalda, Eric *professional soccer player*

Santa Barbara
French, Mark *women's basketball coach university level*

Santa Clara
†Chastain, Brandi Denise *professional soccer player*
Hanks, Merton Edward *professional football player*
†Hearst, (Gerald) Garrison *professional football player*
Mariucci, Steve *coach professional and college football*
McDonald, Tim *professional football player*
Norton, Kenneth Howard *professional football player*
Rice, Jerry Lee *professional football player*
Walsh, William *former football coach*
Young, Bryant Colby *football player*
Young, Steven *professional football player*

Sausalito
Casals, Rosemary *professional tennis player*

Sherman Oaks
Hamilton, Scott Scovell *professional figure skater, former Olympic athlete*

Stanford
†Montgomery, Mike *university basketball coach*

Stockton
Dunning, John *university volleyball coach*

Valley Village
Bench, Johnny Lee *retired professional baseball player*

Walnut Creek
Hallock, C. Wiles, Jr. *athletic official*

COLORADO

Alamosa
Layton, Terry Wayne *college basketball coach*

Boulder
Neinas, Charles Merrill *athletic association executive*
Tharp, Richard *athletic director*

Colorado Springs
Armstrong, Lance *professional cyclist*
Badger, Sandra Rae *health and physical education educator*
Barrowman, Mike *Olympic athlete, swimmer*
Barton, Gregory Mark *Olympic athlete, kayak racer*
Beard, Amanda *swimmer, Olympic athlete*
†Bennett, Brooke *Olympic athlete*
Berkoff, David *Olympic athlete, swimmer*
Biondi, Matt *Olympic athlete, swimmer*
Botsford, Beth *swimmer, Olympic athlete*
Burgess, Greg *Olympic athlete, swimming*
Byrd, Chris *amateur boxer*
Carlton, Steven Norman *retired professional baseball player*
Dello Joio, Norman *olympic athlete, equestrian*
Diebel, Nelson *Olympic athlete, swimmer*
†Dolan, Tom *Olympic athlete*
Donovan, Anne *coach*
Evans, Janet *Olympic swimmer*
Foth, Bob *Olympic athlete, riflery*
Granato, Catherine (Cammi Granato) *hockey player*
†Haislett, Nicole *Olympic athlete*
†Kwan, Michelle *figure skater*
Lewis, Steve *Olympic athlete, track and field*
Lipinski, Tara Kristen *figure skater*
Morales, Pablo *Olympic athlete, swimmer*
Morris, Jason *Olympic athlete*
Murray, Ty (King of the Cowboys) *professional rodeo cowboy*
Rhode, Kim *Olympic athlete*
Rouse, Jeff *Olympic athlete, swimmer*
Sanders, Summer *former olympic athlete, television correspondent*
Scherr, James E. *sports association executive*
Schultz, Richard Dale *national athletic organizations executive*
†Stewart, Melvin *Olympic athlete, swimmer*
Thomas, Debi (Debra J. Thomas) *ice skater*
Tueting, Sarah *hockey player*
Van Dyken, Amy *swimmer, Olympic athlete*

Denver
Balboa, Marcelo *soccer player*
Bichette, Alphonse Dante *professional baseball player*
†Bravo, Paul *professional soccer player*
Castilla, Vinivio Soria *professional baseball player*
†D'Antoni, Mike *professional basketball coach*
Forsberg, Peter *professional hockey player*
Gebhard, Bob *professional baseball team executive*
†Hartley, Bob *hockey coach*
Kile, Darryl Andrew *baseball player*
Lemieux, Claude *professional hockey player*
Leyland, James Richard *professional baseball team manager*
Lyons, Charles *professional sports team executive*
†McDyess, Antonio *professional basketball player*
†Myernick, Glenn *professional soccer coach*
Reid, David *Olympic athlete*
Roy, Patrick *professional hockey player*
Sakic, Joseph Steve *professional hockey player*
Van Exel, Nickey Maxwell *professional basketball player*
Volk, Jan *professional sports team executive*
Walker, Larry Kenneth Robert *professional baseball player*

Englewood
Beake, John *professional football team executive*
Bowlen, Patrick Dennis *holding company executive, lawyer, professional sports team executive*
Carter, Dale Lavelle *professional football player*
Craw, Nicholas Wesson *motor sports association executive*
†Davis, Terrell *football player*
Elway, John Albert *professional football player*
Shanahan, Mike *professional football coach*
†Sharpe, Shannon *professional football player*
†Smith, Neil *professional football player*

Fallbrook
Spahn, Warren *retired baseball player*

Fort Collins
Collen, Tom *coach*

U S A F Academy
†DeBerry, Fisher *college football coach*

CONNECTICUT

Bristol
Corso, Lee *former football coach, football analyst*
Reynolds, Harold Craig *professional baseball player*

Fairfield
Doris, Eugene Patrick *athletics director*

Hamden
Barberi, Matthew *physical education and health educator*

Hartford
Jones, K. C. *professional basketball coach*

New London
Pinhey, Frances Louise *physical education educator*

Stamford
McGuire, Bartlett *sports association executive*
Taylor, Stephen Hosmer *sports entertainment executive, photographer*

Storrs
Stevens, Nancy *coach*

Storrs Mansfield
Auriemma, Geno *university athletic coach*
Calhoun, Jim *college basketball coach*

West Hartford
Jones, Allison *basketball coach*

DELAWARE

Bear
Cairns, Sara Albertson *physical education educator*

Dover
DeVane, Jackie *head coach women's basketball*

Newark
Baiul, Oksana *figure skater*
Martin, Tina *basketball coach*

DISTRICT OF COLUMBIA

Washington
Burge, Heidi *basketball player*
Casserly, Charley *professional football team executive*
Chin, Allen E., Sr. *athletic administrator, educator*
†Darsch, Nancy *professional basketball coach*
Green, Darrell *professional football player*
Harvey, Kenneth Ray *professional football player*
Hathaway, Carmrid Glaston *sports association executive, real estate investor*
Howard, Juwan *professional basketball player*
Jenkins, Robert Emerson *coach*
Knapp, Patrick *women's basketball coach*
Kohl, Herbert *professional sports team executive, former senator*
McEnroe, John Patrick, Jr. *professional tennis player, commentator*
McKeown, Joe *women's basketball coach*
Mitchell, Brian Keith *professional football player*
O'Malley, Susan *professional basketball team executive*
Patrick, Richard M. *professional hockey team executive*
Pollin, Abe *professional basketball team executive, builder*
†Richmond, Mitchell James *professional basketball player*
Ritzenberg, Albert (Allie Ritzenberg) *tennis professional*
†Snyder, Daniel *professional sports team executive, communications executive*
Thatcher, Jeff *women's collegiate basketball coach*
Thompson, John *retired college basketball coach*
Tyler, Sanya *coach*
Upshaw, Gene *sports association executive*
Wilson, Ronald Lawrence *professional hockey coach*

FLORIDA

Coral Gables
†Hamilton, J. Leonard *college basketball coach*
Labati, Ferne *women's basketball coach*

Davie
Johnson, Jimmy *professional football coach*
Jones, Eddie J. *professional football team executive*
Marino, Daniel Constantine, Jr. *professional football player*
†McDuffie, Otis James (O.J.) *professional football player*
Wannstedt, David Raymond *professional football team coach*
Webb, Richmond Jewel *professional football player*

Daytona Beach
Alcott, Amy Strum *professional golfer*
†Ammaccapane, Danielle *professional golfer*
Andrews Reeves, Donna *golfer*
Bodine, Brett *professional race car driver*
Burton, Brandie *professional golfer*
Craven, Ricky *professional race car driver*
†Davies, Laura *golfer*
†DeLuca, Annette *professional golfer*
†Dunn, Moira C. *golf professional*
Earnhardt, (Ralph) Dale *professional race car driver*
†Figg-Currier, Cindy *professional golfer*
Gordon, Jeff *race car driver*
Inkster, Juli *professional golfer*
King, Betsy *professional golfer*
Klein, Emilee *professional golfer*
Mallon, Meg *professional golfer*
McGann, Michelle *professional golfer*
Neumann, Liselotte *professional golfer*
Pepper, Dottie *professional golfer*
†Robbins, Kelly *professional golfer*
†Rudd, Ricky *professional race car driver*
Schrader, Ken *professional race car driver*
Sheehan, Patty *professional golfer*
Sorenstam, Annika *professional golfer*
Speed, Lake *professional race car driver*
Spencer, Jimmy *professional race car driver*
†Steinhauer, Sherri *professional golfer*
Stephenson, Jan Lynn *professional golfer*
†Tschetter, Kris *professional golfer*
†Votaw, Ty M. *golf association commissioner*
Wallace, Rusty *race car driver*
Webb, Karrie *professional golfer*
Whitworth, Kathrynne Ann *professional golfer*
Yarborough, William Caleb *former professional stock car race driver*

Deerfield Beach
King, Don *boxing promoter*
Tyson, Mike G. *professional boxer*

Deland
†Wilkes, Glenn Newton *athletics educator, consultant*

Fort Lauderdale
Ciccarelli, Dino *professional hockey player*
Clark, Mary Ellen *Olympic athlete*
Ford, Edward Charles (Whitey Ford) *retired baseball player*
†Welton *professional soccer player*
†Wortmann, Ivo *professional soccer coach*

Gainesville
Alexander, Stewart Murray (Buddy Alexander) *golf coach*
Brandi, Andy *tennis coach*
†Donovan, Billy *university basketball boach*
Duvenhage, Ian *head tennis coach*
Jones, Tom *track and field coach*
Ross, Julia Carol *basektball coach*
Singer, Robert Norman *motor behavior educator*
†Spurrier, Steve *university athletic coach, former professional football player*
Varnes, Jill Tutton *university official, health educator*

Indian Creek
Shula, Don Francis *former professional football coach, team executive*

Jacksonville
†Brunell, Mark Allen *football player*
Capers, Dominic *professional football coach*
Coughlin, Tom *professional football coach*
Lake, Carnell Augustino *professional football player*
†Taylor, Fred *professional football player*
Weaver, Wayne *professional sports team executive*

Lady Lake
Hartzler, Genevieve Lucille *physical education educator*

Miami
†Boles, John *professional baseball coach, manager*
Dombrowski, David *baseball team executive*
Farmer, Hiram Leander *physical education educator*
Hardaway, Timothy Duane *basketball player*
†Henry, John W. *professional sports team executive*
†Kotsay, Mark Steven *baseball player*
Mourning, Alonzo *professional basketball player*
†Pfund, Randy (Randell Pfund) *sports team executive, former professional basketball coach*
Porter, Terry *professional basketball player*
Riley, Patrick James *professional basketball coach*

Micco
Cognata, Joseph Anthony *retired football commissioner*

Orlando
De Vos, Daniel G. *sports team executive, marketing professional*
Ford, Kisha *basketball player*
Gabriel, John *sports team executive*
Hardaway, Anfernee Deon (Penny Hardaway) *professional basketball player*
†Janzen, Lee *professional golfer*
Kruczek, Mike *coach*
Moore, Yolanda *basketball player*
†Peck, Carolyn *professional basketball coach*
†Rivers, Glenn Anton (Doc) *professional basketball coach, former basketball player*
Sharkey, Colleen Mary *sports association administrator*
Sloan, Steve *athletic director*
Vander Weide, Bob *professional sports team executive*
Vander Weide, Cheri DeVos *sports team executive, marketing professional*
Wilkins, (Jacques) Dominique *professional basketball player*
Williams, Pat *professional basketball team executive*

Ormond Beach
Wendelstedt, Harry Hunter, Jr. *umpire*

Palm Beach
Floyd, Raymond Loran *professional golfer*

Palm Beach Gardens
†Andrade, William Thomas *professional golfer*
Awtrey, Jim L. *sports association executive*
Couples, Frederick Steven *professional golfer*
Daly, John *professional golfer*
Duval, David Robert *golfer*
Furyk, James Michael *professional golfer*
Haas, Jay *professional golfer*
Henninger, Brian *professional golfer*
Huston, John *professional golfer*
Jacobsen, Peter Erling *professional golfer*
Langer, Bernhard *professional golfer*
†Leonard, Justin *professional golfer*
†Lickliter, Frank Ray, II *professional golfer*
†Love, Davis Milton, III *professional golfer*
†Maggert, Jeffrey Allan *professional golfer*
†Mickelson, Phil *professional golfer*
Miller, John Laurence *professional golfer*
Montgomerie, Colin *professional golfer*
Olazabal, Jose Maria *professional golfer*
†O'Meara, Mark *professional golfer*
†Ozaki, Jumbo *professional golfer*
Parnevik, Jesper Bo *golfer*
Perry, James Kenneth *professional golfer*
†Roberts, Loren Lloyd *professional golfer*
Stankowski, Paul Francis *golfer*
Strange, Curtis Northrop *professional golfer*
†Verplank, Scott Rachal *professional golfer*
†Westwood, Lee *professional golfer*
Woods, Tiger (Eldrick Woods) *professional golfer*

Palm City
Mc Hale, John Joseph *baseball club executive*

Pompano Beach
Elder, Robert Lee *professional golfer*

Ponte Vedra Beach
Azinger, Paul *professional golfer*
Cook, John *professional golfer*
Elkington, Steve *professional golfer*
Forsman, Dan Bruce *professional golfer*
Frost, David *professional golfer*
Pavin, Corey Allen *professional golfer*
Rodriguez, Chi Chi (Juan Rodriguez) *professional golfer*
†Sluman, Jeff *professional golfer*
Wadkins, Lanny *professional golfer*
Washington, MaliVai *professional tennis player*

Saint Petersburg
Boggs, Wade Anthony *professional baseball player*
Canseco, Jose *professional baseball player*
Lauber, Christopher Joseph *sports event promoter*
McGriff, Fred (Frederick Stanley McGriff) *baseball player*
†Rothschild, Larry *professional baseball executive*

Sunrise
Bure, Pavel *professional hockey player*
McLean, Kirk *professional hockey player*
Murray, Bryan Clarence *professional sports team executive*
Torrey, William Arthur *professional hockey team executive*

Tallahassee
Bowden, Bobby *university athletic coach*
Farmer, Claudette *collegiate basketball coach*
Owens, Steven Mark *health education educator*
Semrau, Sue *university head women's basketball coach*

Tampa
†Alstott, Michael Joseph (Mike Alstott) *professional football player*
†Dilfer, Trent *professional football player*
Dungy, Tony *professional sports team executive*
Glazer, Malcolm *professional sports team executive*
Hankinson, Tim *soccer coach*
Nickerson, Hardy Otto *football player*
Sakiewicz, Nick *professional sports team executive*

West Palm Beach
Player, Gary Jim *professional golfer, businessman, golf course designer*

GEORGIA

Athens
Diaz, Manuel *university tennis coach*
Landers, Andy *head coach women's basketball*
Wallace, Jeff *tennis coach*

Atlanta
Aaron, Henry L. (Hank Aaron) *professional baseball team executive*
Arani, Ardy A. *professional sports marketing executive, lawyer*
Babcock, Peter Heartz *professional sports executive*
Baylor, Don Edward *professional baseball manager*
Bellamy, Walter Jones *retired basketball player*
Berenato, Agnus McGlade *women's basketball coach*
†Blaylock, Mookie (Daron Oshay Blaylock) *professional basketball player*
Boone, Bret Robert *professional baseball player*
Cox, Bobby (Robert Joe Cox) *professional baseball manager*
Cremins, Bobby *college basketball coach*
Douglas, (Charles) Lee *executive vice president basketball team*
Galarraga, Andres Jose *professional baseball player*
Gearon, John Michael *professional basketball team executive*
Gibson, Althea *retired professional tennis player, golfer, state official*
Glavine, Tom (Thomas Michael Glavine) *professional baseball player*
†Jones, Larry Wayne "Chipper" *baseball player*
Kasten, Stanley Harvey *sports association executive*
King, Marian Emma *health and physical education educator*
Maddux, Greg(ory Alan) *professional baseball player*
Moses, Edwin *former track and field athlete*
Mutombo, DiKembe (Dikembe Mutombo Mpolondo Mukamba Jean Jacque Wamutombo) *professional basketball player*
Schuerholz, John Boland, Jr. *professional baseball executive*
Smith, Steven Delano *professional basketball player*
Smoltz, John Andrew *professional baseball player*
Wilkens, Leonard Randolph, Jr. (Lenny Wilkens) *professional basketball coach*
Yoculan, Suzanne *gymnastics coach*

Columbus
Mize, Larry Hogan *professional golfer*

Kennesaw
Waples, David Lloyd *athletic director*

Marietta
Devigne, Karen Cooke *retired amateur athletics executive*

Statesboro
Cram, Rusty *basketball coach*

Suwanee
†Anderson, Jamal Sharif *professional football player*
†Chandler, Christopher Mark (Chris) *professional football player*
†Dickerson, Eric Demetric *former professional football player*
Mathis, Terance *professional football player*
Reeves, Daniel Edward *professional football coach*
Smith, Taylor *professional football team executive*
Tuggle, Jessie Lloyd *professional football player*

HAWAII

Honolulu
Goo, Vince *women's collegiate basketball coach*
Shoji, Dave *women's collegiate volleyball coach*

IDAHO

Twin Falls
†Studebaker, William Vern *sports and literature educator, writer*

ILLINOIS

Belleville
Connors, Jimmy (James Scott Connors) *professional tennis player*

Bourbonnais
Peters, Betty A. *physical education educator*

Carbondale
Hart, James Warren *university athletic director, restaurant owner, former professional football player*

Champaign
Birmingham, Carolyn *recreation educator*
Hayasaki, Yoshi *coach*
Turner, Ron *coach*

Charleston
Ankenbrand, Larry Joseph *physical education educator*

Chicago
†Agoos, Jeff *professional soccer player*
Akers, Michelle Anne *soccer player*
Amonte, Anthony Lewis *professional hockey player*
Arena, Bruce *professional soccer coach*
†Baumgardt, Justi Michelle *soccer player*
Beck, Rodney Roy *baseball player*
Blauser, Jeffrey Michael *professional baseball player*
†Bradley, Bob *professional soccer coach*
Cannon, Bennie Marvin *physical education educator*
†Cromwell, Amanda Caryl *soccer player, coach*
Daze, Eric *professional hockey player*
Diaz-Arce, Raul *soccer player*
DiCicco, Tony *soccer coach*
†Ducar, Tracy *soccer player*
†Fawcett, Joy Lynn *soccer player*
Fitzpatrick, Mark *professional hockey player*
Floyd, Tim *professional basketball coach, former collegiate basketball coach*
†Fotopoulos, Danielle *soccer player*
†Foudy, Julia Maurine *soccer player*
†Gabarra, Carin Leslie *professional soccer player*
†Gaetti, Gary *baseball player*
Gilmour, Doug *professional hockey player*
Grace, Mark Eugene *baseball player*
Gregg, Lauren *women's soccer coach*
Hamm, Mariel Margaret *soccer player*
†Jones, Cobi *professional soccer player*
†Keller, Deborah Kim *soccer player*
King, Billie Jean Moffitt *former professional tennis player*
Krause, Jerry (Jerome Richard Krause) *professional basketball team executive*
†Kreis, Jason *professional soccer player*
†Kukoc, Toni *professional basketball player*
Lee, Marva Jean *counselor, physical education educator, consultant*
Lilly, Kristine Marie *soccer player*
Lynch, Edward Francis *professional sports team executive*
†MacMillan, Shannon Ann *soccer player*
†MacPhail, Andrew B. *professional sports team executive*
†Manuel, Jerry *manager professional athletics*
†Milbrett, Tiffeny Carleen *professional soccer player*
Morardini, Michael Robert *baseball player*
†Overbeck, Carla Werden *soccer player, coach*
†Parlow, Cynthia Marie *soccer player*
Pizer, Howard Charles *sports and entertainment executive*
†Razov, Ante *professional soccer player*
Reinsdorf, Jerry Michael *professional sports teams executive, real estate executive, lawyer, accountant*
Riggleman, James David *professional baseball team manager*
†Roberts, Tiffany Marie *soccer player*
Sandberg, Ryne *former professional baseball player*
Santiago, Benito Rivera *professional baseball player*
Savard, Denis Joseph *former professional hockey player, coach*
Schwartz, Alan Gifford *sport company executive*
†Schwoy, Laurie Annette *soccer player*
Scurry, Briana Collette *soccer player*
†Sobrero, Kathryn Michele *soccer player*
Sosa, Samuel (Sammy Sosa) *professional baseball player*
†Staples, Thori Yvette *soccer player*
†Streiffer, Jen *soccer player*
Thomas, Frank Edward *professional baseball player*
†Venturini, Tisha Lea *professional soccer player*
†Whalen, Sarah Eve *soccer player*

Elk Grove Village
Meyer, Raymond Joseph *former college basketball coach*

Evanton
Olkowski, June *women's collegiate basketball coach*

Glendale Heights
Spearing, Karen Marie *physical education educator, coach*

Lake Forest
Jaeger, Jeff Todd *professional football player*
McCaskey, Edward W. *professional football team executive*
McCaskey, Michael B. *professional football team executive*

Lincolnshire
Schauble, John Eugene *physical education educator*

Moline
Carls, Judith Marie *physical education educator, golf coach*

Peoria
Freitag, Donna *head women's basketball coach*

Rock Island
Correll, Dan Eugene *physical education educator*

Rockford
Keating, Patricia Ann Stacy *retired physical education educator*

Roscoe
Young, Larry Eugene *baseball umpire*

Urbana
Thompson, Margaret M. *physical education educator*

Wheaton
Breckenfelder, Lynn E. *health and physical education educator*

INDIANA

Bloomington
Counsilman, James Edward *physical education educator*
Knight, Bob *college basketball coach*

Evansville
Bennett, Kathi *women's basketball coach*
Wilson, Gregory Scott *kinesiology educator, coach*

Indianapolis
Adkins, Derrick Ralph *Olympic athlete*
Ashford, Evelyn *former track and field athlete*
Austin, Charles *Olympic athlete*
Barnes, Eric Randolph *Olympic athlete*
Bates, Michael *Olympic athlete, track and field*
Batten, Jane Kimberly *olympic athlete*
Bennett, Cornelius *professional football player*
Bird, Larry Joe *professional basketball coach, former professional basketball player*
Borden, Amanda *gymnast, Olympic athlete*
Buford-Bailey, Tonja Yevette *track and field Olympic athlete*
Burrell, Leroy Russel *track and field athlete*
Chow, Amy *gymnast, Olympic athlete*
Conley, Michael Alexander *track and field athlete*
Conway, Hollis *track and field athletie, Olympic athlete*
†Dawes, Dominique *gymnast, Olympic athlete*
Decker Slaney, Mary Teresa *Olympic athlete*
Dimas, Trent *Olympic athlete, gymnast*
Favor-Hamilton, Suzanne Marie *track and field athlete, Olympian*
†Ganassi, Chip *professional race car executive, owner*
Gray, Johnny *track and field athlete, Olympic athlete*
Greene, Joe *Olympic athlete, track and field*
†Harrison, Kenny *Olympic athlete*
Irsay, James Steven *professional football team owner*
Johnson, Allen *Olympic athlete*
Johnson, Dave *Olympic athlete, track and field*
Johnson, Michael *track and field Olympic athlete*
†Kingdom, Roger *olympic athlete*
Lenzi, Mark *Olympic athlete, springboard diver*
†Manning, Peyton *professional football player*
Marsh, Michael Lawrence *track and field athlete*
Mitchell, Dennis A. *Olympic athlete, track and field*
Mora, James Ernest *professional football coach, professional sports team executive*
Mullin, Chris(topher) Paul *professional basketball player*
O'Brien, Daniel Dion *track and field athlete, Olympic athlete*
Phelps, Jaycie *gymnast, Olympic athlete*
Pierce, Jack *Olympic athlete, track and field*
Powell, Mike *olympic athlete, track and field*
Rose, Jalen *professional basketball player*
Simon, Herbert *professional basketball team executive*
Smits, Rik *professional basketball player*
Torrence, Gwen *Olympic athlete*
†Tracy, Paul Anthony *race car driver*
†Vasser, Jimmy *professional race car driver*
Walsh, Donnie *sports club executive*
Watts, Quincy Dushawn *track and field athlete*
Young, Kevin *track and field athlete*

Notre Dame
Auriol, Yves *university women's head fencing coach*
McGraw, Muffet *women's basketball coach*
Petrucelli, Chris *soccer coach*
Poulin, David James *hockey coach*

Oakland City
Schafer, Patricia Day *physical education educator*

Rochester
Neff, Kathy S. *swimming and water safety educator*

Terre Haute
Campbell, Judith May *physical education educator*
Reeve, Cheryl Ann *basketball coach*

West Lafayette
†Sims-Curry, Kristy *women's college basketball coach*

IOWA

Ames
Bourke, Kevin *coach*
Fennelly, William *basketball coach*
McCarney, Dan *coach*
Smith, Eugene D. *coach*

Cedar Falls
DiCecco, Tony *university head women's basketball coach*

Des Moines
Bluder, Lisa *women's collegiate basketball coach*

Iowa City
†Alford, Steve *college basketball coach*
Bowden, Terry Wilson *coach*
Bowlsby, Bob *athletic director*

KANSAS

Lawrence
†Osness, Wayne H. *physical education educator*
Washington, Marian *women's basketball coach*
Williams, Roy *university athletic coach*

Leawood
Byers, Walter *athletic association executive*

Manhattan
Patterson, Deb *university women's head basketball coach*
Urick, Max *athletic director*

Overland Park
Dempsey, Cedric W. *sports association administrator*

Shawnee Mission
Watson, Thomas Sturges *professional golfer*

KENTUCKY

Lexington
Boucher, Larry Gene *sports association commissioner*
Krone, Julie *jockey*
Mattox, Bernadette *university head women's basketball coach*
Mumme, Hal *coach*
Stevens, Gary *professional jockey*

Louisville
Clapp, Martin *university co-head women's basketball coach*
Crum, Denny (Denzel Edwin Crum) *collegiate basketball coach*
White, Sara *university co-head women's basketball coach*

Madisonville
Ramsey, Frank *retired basketball player*

Morehead
Litter, Laura *women's basketball coach*

Murray
Fields, Eddie *women's collegiate basketball coach*

Richmond
Inman, Larry Joe *coach*

LOUISIANA

Baton Rouge
Dinardo, Gerry *coach*
Gunter, Sue *women's basketball coach*

Grambling
Robinson, Eddie Gay *college football coach*

Metairie
Ambrose, Ashley Avery *football player*
Benson, Tom *professional football executive*
Ditka, Michael Keller *professional football coach*
Martin, Shirley A. *physical education educator*

Natchitoches
Wilkes, Charles Newton *sports administration and health and physical education educator*

New Orleans
Martin, Gerald Wayne *professional football player*
Roaf, William Layton *professional football player*
†Scelfo, Chris *university football coach*

Ruston
Barmore, Leon *head basketball coach*
Jordan, Carl David *physical education educator*

Shreveport
†Sutton, Hal Evan *professional golfer*

Thibodaux
Bonin, Do *basketball coach*

MARYLAND

Baltimore
†Anderson, Brady Kevin *professional baseball player*
Angelos, Peter G. *professional sports team executive, lawyer*
Baines, Harold Douglass *professional baseball player*
Belle, Albert Jojuan *professional baseball player*
Bordick, Michael Todd *professional baseball player*
Clark, Will (William Nuschler Clark, Jr.) *professional baseball player*
Conine, Jeffrey Guy *professional baseball player*
Hoch, David Allen *physical education educator, athletic director*
†Miller, Ray *professional baseball team manager*
Mussina, Michael Cole *baseball player*
†Newsome, Ozzie *manager professional athletics*
Ripken, Calvin Edwin, Jr. (Cal Ripken) *professional baseball player*
†Wren, Frank *professional baseball team executive*

Bethesda
Leonard, Sugar Ray (Ray Charles Leonard) *retired professional boxer*
Palmer, James Alvin *baseball commentator*

College Park
Williams, Gary *collegiate basketball team coach*

Columbia
Maier, William Otto *martial arts school administrator, educator, consultant*

Landover
†Strickland, Rodney *professional basketball player*
†Unseld, Westley Sissel *professional sports team executive, former professional basketball coach, former professional basketball player*

Owings Mills
†Billick, Brian *professional football coach*
Burnett, Robert Barry *professional football player*
Modell, Arthur B. *professional football team executive*
Turner, Eric Ray *professional football player*
Woodson, Roderick Kevin *professional football player*

Silver Spring
Schuster, Claire Rachel *health educator*

Towson
Seaman, Tony *university athletic coach*

West Case
Murray, Eddie Clarence *baseball player*

MASSACHUSETTS

Arlington
Samuelson, Joan Benoit *professional runner*

Boston
†Allison, Jason *professional hockey player*
Aparicio, Luis Ernesto *retired baseball player*
Auerbach, Arnold (Red Auerbach) *professional basketball team executive*
Bourque, Ray *professional hockey player*
Burns, Pat *professional hockey coach*
Carr, Michael Leon *professional sports team executive, former professional basketball player*
Duquette, Daniel F. *professional baseball team executive*
†Garciaparra, Nomar (Anthony Nomar Garciaparra) *professional baseball player*
Gaston, Paul E. *professional basketball team executive*
Harrington, John Leo *baseball company executive*
†Khristich, Dimitri *professional hockey player*
Kleinfelder, Carole *lacrosse head coach*
†Martinez, Pedro Jaime *professional baseball player*
Martinez, Ramon Jaime *professional baseball player*
Neely, Cameron Michael *former professional hockey player*
Offerman, Jose Antonio Dono *professional baseball player*
†Paxson, James Joseph, Jr. *sports team executive, former professional basketball player*
Pitino, Richard *professional basketball coach, former collegiate basketball coach*
Saberhagen, Bret William *professional baseball player*
Schram, Stephen C. *professional basketball team executive*
Sinden, Harry *professional hockey team executive*
Skinner, Al *college basketball coach*
Smith, Kathy Delaney *basketball coach*
Strickler, Gary *university athletic director*
Thomas, Lee *professional sports team executive*
Valentin, John William *professional baseball player*
†Walker, Antoine Devon *professional basketball player*
†Williams, Jimy *baseball team manager*
Wolf, Dennis *university basketball coach*
Yastrzemski, Carl Michael *former baseball player, public relations executive*

Cambridge
Parker, Harry Lambert *university rowing coach*

Chestnut Hill
Inglese, Cathy *university head women's basketball coach*

Foxboro
Armstrong, Bruce Charles *professional football player*
Bledsoe, Drew *professional football player*
Carroll, Pete *professional football coach*
Coates, Ben Terrence *professional football player*
†Edwards, Robert *professional football player*
Kraft, Robert K. *professional sports team executive*
Savarese, Giovanni *professional soccer player*
†Zenga, Walter *professional soccer player*

Lawrence
Brophy, Susan Dorothy *adapted physical education educator*

Lynnfield
Kerrigan, Nancy *professional figure skater, former Olympic athlete*

Springfield
Archibald, Nathaniel *retired basketball player*
Goodrich, Gail Charles, Jr. *retired basketball player*
Greer, Harold Everett *retired basketball player*
Hagan, Clifford O. *retired basketball player*
Harris-Stewart, Lusia *retired basketball player*
Havlicek, John J. (Hondo Havlicek) *former professional basketball player*
Hawkins, Cornelius L. (Connie) *retired basketball player*
Hayes, Elvin Ernest *retired basketball player*
Lovellette, Clyde *retired basketball player*
McGuire, Richard Joseph *retired basketball player*
Miller, Ralph *coach, retired*
Newell, Peter *retired basketball coach*
Wanzer, Robert *retired basketball player*

Wilmington
Hayes, Carol Jeanne *physical education educator*

Worcester
Gibbons, William Patrick *coach*

MICHIGAN

Auburn Hills
Abraham, Tajama *basketball player*
†Brondello, Sandy *professional basketball player*
Dumars, Joe, III *retired professional basketball player*
†Gentry, Alvin *professional basketball coach*
Hill, Grant *professional basketball player*
†Hlede, Korie *professional basketball player*
Laettner, Christian Donald *professional basketball player*
Lieberman-Cline, Nancy *professional basketball coach, former player*
Montross, Eric Scott *professional basketball player*
Wilson, Thomas S. *professional basketball team administrator*

Berrien Springs
Ali, Muhammad (Cassius Marcellus Clay) *retired professional boxer*

Detroit
Bowman, William Scott "Scotty" *professional hockey coach*
Chelios, Christos K *professional hockey player*
Clark, Wendel *hockey player*
Devellano, James Charles *professional hockey manager*
Fedorov, Sergei *hockey player*
†Holland, Ken *sports team executive*
Ilitch, Marian *professional hockey team executive, food service executive*
Ilitch, Michael *professional hockey team executive*
†Larionov, Igor *professional hockey plaery*
†McHale, John, Jr. *professional sports team executive*
Osgood, Chris *professional hockey player*
†Parrish, Larry *manager professional athletics*
Shanahan, Brendan Frederick *professional hockey player*
Yzerman, Steve *professional hockey player*

East Lansing
†Izzo, Thomas *college basketball coach*
Langeland, Karen *basketball coach*

Mount Pleasant
Flynn, Dick *coach*
Voll, Fran *women's basketball coach university level*

Pontiac
Moore, Herman Joseph *professional football player*
Sanders, Barry *retired football player*
Schmidt, Chuck *professional football team executive*

Traverse City
Howe, Gordon *former professional hockey player, sports association executive*

MINNESOTA

Eden Prairie
Anderson, Gary Allan *professional football player*
Carter, Cris *professional football player*
Cunningham, Randall *professional football player*
Green, Dennis *professional football coach*
Hoard, Leroy *professional football player*
†McCombs, Billy Joe (Red McCombs) *professional football team executive*
McDaniel, Randall Cornell *professional football player*
†Moss, Randy *professional football player*
†Woods, Gary *professional football team executive, former professional basketball team executive*

Mankato
Taylor, Glen *professional sports team executive, printing and graphics company executive*

Minneapolis
†Agler, Brian *professional basketball coach*
Aguilera, Richard Warren (Rick Aguilera) *baseball player*
Cordova, Martin Keevin (Marty Cordova) *baseball player*
Kelly, Tom (Jay Thomas Kelly) *major league baseball club manager*
†Lehman, Tom *professional golfer*
Littlejohn, Cherly *university head women's basketball coach*
Lucia, Donald J. *head coach men's ice hockey*
McHale, Kevin Edward *former professional basketball player, sports team executive*
Moor, Rob *professional basketball team executive*
Nanne, Louis Vincent *professional hockey team executive*
Pohlad, Carl R. *professional baseball team executive, bottling company executive*
Puckett, Kirby *professional baseball team executive, former player*
Ryan, Terry *professional sports team executive*
Saunders, Philip D. *professional basketball coach*
Steinbach, Terry Lee *professional baseball player*

Saint Paul
Swanson-Schones, Kris Margit *developmental adapted physical education educator*

MISSISSIPPI

Hattiesburg
Giles, Michael Comer *physical education educator, aquatics consultant*

Itta Bena
Ware, William Levi *physical education educator, researcher*

Jackson
Pennington, Andrew *women's basketball coach*

†Raymond, Lisa *tennis player*
Reneberg, Richard (Richey Reneberg) *professional tennis player*
Rubin, Chanda *professional tennis player*
†Schnyder, Patty *professional tennis player*
Wheaton, David *professional tennis player*
†Williams, Serena *professional tennis player*
†Williams, Venus *tennis player*

Yonkers
Williams, Ted Vaughnell *physical education educator*

NORTH CAROLINA

Asheville
Quinn, Barbara Ann *athletics administrator, educator*
Weber, Kathleen *basketball coach*

Chapel Hill
†Guthridge, Bill *university basketball coach*
Shelton-Scroggs, Karen *hockey coach*
Smith, Dean Edwards *university basketball coach*

Charlotte
Baldwin, Ed *coach*
Bodine, Geoff *professional race car driver*
Bullett, Vicky *professional basketball player*
Coleman, Derrick D. *professional basketball player*
Davis, Eric Wayne *professional football player*
Gibbs, Joe Jackson *former professional football coach, broadcaster, professional sports team executive*
Greene, Kevin Darwin *professional football player*
Irvan, Ernie (Swervin' Irvan) *professional race car driver*
Manning, Sharon *professional athlete*
Mapp, Rhonda *professional basketball player*
Mason, Anthony George Douglas *professional basketball player*
†Meadors, Marynell *professional basketball coach*
†Reid, Tracy *professional basketball player*
Rypien, Mark Robert *professional football player*
Shinn, George *professional sports team executive*
†Silas, Paul *professional basketball coach*
Stinson, Andrea *professional basketball player*
Thompson, David O'Neal *retired basketball player*
Walls, Charles Wesley *football player*

Conover
Jarrett, Dale *professional race car driver*

Cooperstown
Perry, Gaylord Jackson *former professional baseball player*

Durham
Goestenkors, Gail *head basketball coach*
Krzyzewski, Mike *university athletic coach*

Greensboro
Agee, Lynne *university head basketball coach*

Greenville
Hamrick, Mike Alan *athletic director*
Workman, Lee DeWayne *collegiate athletics administrator*

Harrisburg
Bell, Walter Clayton *drag car racer, small business owner*
Labonte, Terry *professional race car driver*
†Waltrip, Michael *professional race car driver*

High Point
†Burton, Ward *professional race car driver*

Huntersville
†Stewart, Tony *professional race car driver*

Mooresville
Benson, Johnny *professional race car driver*
†Cope, Derrike *professional race car driver*
†Earnhardt, Dale, Jr. *professional stock race car driver*
†Little, Charles Glen, Jr. (Chad) *professional race car driver*
Marlin, Sterling *professional race car driver*
Martin, Mark *professional race car driver*
Mayfield, Jeremy *professional race car driver*

Morrisville
Francis, Ron *professional hockey player*
Karmanos, Peter, Jr. *professional sports team executive*
†Maurice, Paul *pro hockey coach*
†Peca, Michael *professional hockey player*
Rutherford, Jim *professional sports team executive*

Randleman
Andretti, John *professional race car driver*
†Petty, Kyle *professional stock car driver*
Petty, Richard *retired professional race car driver*

Trinity
Labonte, Bobby *professional race car driver*

Welcome
†Skinner, Mike *professional race car driver*

NORTH DAKOTA

Minot
Cederstrom, Gary Lynn *professional baseball umpire*

OHIO

Akron
Murphy, Bob *professional golfer*
Owens, Lee *coach*
Zoeller, Fuzzy *professional golfer*

Berea
Brown, Lomas, Jr. *professional football player*

Bowling Green
Blackney, Gary *university football coach*
Clark, Jaci *women's collegiate basketball coach*

Cadiz
Hoffman, Barbara Jo *health and physical education educator, athletic director*

Canton
Elliott, Peter R. *athletic organization executive, retired*
Grant, Bud (Harry Peter Grant) *retired professional football coach*
Greene, Joe (Charles Edward Greene) *former professional football player, professional football coach*
†Mack, Tom *retired professional football player*
Selmon, Lee Roy *retired football player*
†Shaw, Billy *retired professional football player*
Smith, Jackie *former professional football player*

Cincinnati
Avery, Steven Thomas *professional baseball player*
Blake, Jeff *professional football player*
Bowden, Jim *professional sports team executive*
Brown, Mike *professional sports team executive*
Coslet, Bruce N. *professional football coach*
Huggins, Bob *college basketball coach*
Knowlton, Austin E. (Dutch Knowlton) *professional football team executive*
Larkin, Barry Louis *professional baseball player*
Minter, Richard (Rick) *football coach*
Neagle, Dennis Edward (Denny Neagle) *professional baseball player*
Pirtle, Laurie Lee *women's basketball coach, university level*
Sawyer, John *professional football team executive*
Schott, Marge *professional baseball team executive*

Cleveland
Agassi, Andre Kirk *tennis player*
Alomar, Roberto Velazquez *professional baseball player*
Alomar, Sandy, Jr. (Santos Velazquez Alomar) *professional baseball player*
Brown, Rushia *basketball player*
Burns, Duffy *women's basketball coach university level*
†Calcavecchia, Mark *professional golfer*
Clark, Dwight Edward *sports team executive, former professional football player*
Cordero, Wilfredo Nieva *professional baseball player*
Courier, Jim (James Spencer Courier, Jr.) *tennis player*
Edwards, Michelle Denise *professional basketball player*
Faldo, Nick *professional golfer*
Fijalkowski, Isabelle *professional basketball player*
Gardocki, Christopher *football player*
†Gooden, Dwight Eugene *professional baseball player*
Hargrove, Mike (Dudley Michael Hargrove) *professional baseball team manager*
Hart, John *professional sports team executive*
†Hill-McDonald, Linda *professional basketball coach*
Jackson, Michael Ray *baseball player*
Jones, Merlakia *basketball player*
Justice, David Christopher *baseball player*
Kemp, Shawn T. *professional basketball player*
Langston, Mark Edward *professional baseball player*
Lopez, Nancy *professional golfer*
Nemcova, Eva *professional basketball player*
†Palmer, Chris *professional football coach*
Pierce, Mary *professional tennis player*
Policy, Carmen A. *professional sports team executive*
Ramirez, Manuel Aristides (Manny Ramirez) *professional baseball player*
Rothstein, Ronald *professional basketball coach*
Seles, Monica *tennis player*
†Singh, Vijay *professional golfer*
Vizquel, Omar Enrique *professional baseball player*

Columbus
Burns, Beth *women's collegiate basketball coach*
†Cooper, John *university football coach*
†Fitzgerald, Tom *professional soccer coach*
McBride, Brian *soccer player*
Noe, Fred J. *sports association administrator*
†O'Brien, Jim *university basketball coach*

Fairfield
Robertson, Oscar Palmer (Big O Robertson) *chemical company executive, former professional basketball player*

Gahanna
†Douglas, James (Buster) *boxer*

Hilliard
†Herta, Bryan *race car driver*

Kent
Lindsay, Bob *basketball coach*
Pees, Russell Dean *coach*

Owensville
Davis, Valerie Jeanne *physical education educator*

Oxford
Pont, John *football coach, educator*

Parma Heights
†Konchan, Kenneth Joseph *humanities educator*

Westlake
Peterson, Amy *Olympic athlete*

Youngstown
DeBartolo, Edward John, Jr. *professional football team owner, real estate developer*
†Wathen, Norman Daniel *athletic trainer*

OKLAHOMA

Norman
Coale, Sherri *university women's basketball coach*

Oklahoma City
Fernandez, Lisa *softball player*
Porter, Don E. *sports administrator*
Richardson, Dot *softball player*
Smith, Michele *softball player*

Stillwater
Holder, Mike *coach*

Tulsa
Huber, Fritz Godfrey *physical education educator, excercise physiologist*

OREGON

Eugene
Runge, Jody *coach*

Portland
†Dunleavy, Michael Joseph *professional basketball coach*
Glickman, Harry *professional basketball team executive*
Grant, Brian Wade (General Grant) *professional basketball player*
Kolde, Bert *professional basketball team executive*
Weinberg, Lawrence *professional basketball team owner*
Whitsitt, Bob *sports team executive*
Whitsitt, Robert James *professional basketball team executive*

PENNSYLVANIA

Bethel Park
Bohn, James Francis *physical education educator*

Bethlehem
Troyan, Sue *university head coach women's basketball*

Bradford
Ross, Jean Louise *physical education educator*

Easton
Holmes, Larry, Jr. *retired professional boxer*

Harrisburg
Farrell, Kelly Jean *health and physical education educator*

Hazleton
Roslevich, James Andrew *athletic trainer*

Lewisburg
Fedorjaka, Kathy *university basketball coach*

Long Pond
Mattioli, Joseph Reginald, Jr. *raceway executive, former dentist*

Meadville
Irwin, Melinda Kay *physical education educator*

Millersville
Kabacinski, Stanley Joseph *health and physical education educator, consultant, speaker*

Philadelphia
Brantley, Jeffrey Hoke *professional baseball player*
Brind'Amour, Rod Jean *professional hockey player*
Brown, Lawrence Harvey (Larry Brown) *basketball coach*
Clarke, Robert Earle (Bobby Clarke) *hockey executive*
†Croce, Pat *sports team executive*
Fish, Elizabeth Ann *physical education educator*
†Francona, Terry Jon *manager professional athletics*
Gant, Ron (Ronald Edwin Gant) *professional baseball player*
Garcia, Richard Raul *major league umpire*
Green, Tyler Scott *professional baseball player*
Hextall, Ron *professional hockey player*
Hill, Tyrone *professional basketball player*
Holmgren, Paul *professional hockey coach*
Iverson, Allen *basketball player*
†King, Billy *sports team executive*
Landeta, Sean *professional football player*
Lindros, Eric Bryan *professional hockey player*
Lurie, Jeffrey *professional sports team executive*
McRae, Hal (Harold Abraham McRae) *major league baseball team manager*
Miller, John *basketball coach*
Murphy, Kevin *women's collegiate basketball coach*
†Neilson, Roger *professional hockey coach*
Roe, John Andrew (Rocky) *major league baseball umpire, consultant*
†Rolen, Scott Bruce *professional baseball player*
†Schilling, Curtis Montague *professional baseball player*
Scott, Joseph C. *professional hockey team executive*
Snider, Edward Malcolm *professional hockey club executive*
Thomas, William Harrison *professional football player*
Vanbiesbrouck, John *professional hockey player*

Pittsburgh
Bettis, Jerome Abram *professional football player*
Cowher, Bill *professional football coach*
Dawson, Dermontti Farra *professional football player*
Jagr, Jaromir *professional hockey player*
Kendall, Jason Daniel *professional baseball player*
Kirkland, Lorenzo Levon *football player*
Lamont, Gene *professional baseball team manager*
Lemieux, Mario *retired professional hockey player*
†McClatchy, Kevin *professional sports team executive*
Noll, Charles Henry *former professional football coach*
Patrick, Craig *professional hockey team executive*
Rooney, Daniel M. *professional football team executive*
Stargell, Willie (Wilver Dornel Stargell) *professional sports team coach, former baseball player*
†Stewart, Kordell *professional football player*
†Straka, Martin *professional hockey player*

Reading
Unser, Alfred, Jr. *professional race car driver*

University Park
Kaidanov, Emmanuil Gregory *coach*
Portland, Rene *university athletic coach*
Williams, Julie *coach*

Youngstown
Palmer, Arnold Daniel *professional golfer*

RHODE ISLAND

Providence
Burr, Jean Marie *university women's basketball coach*
†Faxon, Brad *professional golfer*

SOUTH CAROLINA

Charleston
Conrad, Thomas *basketball coach*
Kreese, John L. *basketball coach*

Charlotte
†Seifert, George *professional football coach*

Clemson
Adair, Trevor *soccer coach*
†Davis, Jim *university basketball coach*
Kriese, Charles (Chuck) *tennis coach*

Conway
LeForce, Alan *women's basketball coach*

Florence
Hardouin, Bernard Michael, III *fitness specialist*

Greenville
Carter, Sherry *women's basketball coach*
Hortis, Athena Maria *physical education educator*

Mount Pleasant
Bennett, Janet Sandhoff *physical education educator*

TENNESSEE

Chattanooga
Miles, Bradley James *athletic trainer*

Clarksville
Gardner, Susanne *women's basketball coach*

Copperhill
Jacobi, Joe *Olympic athlete, canoeist*

Gray
Bailey, Donovan *Olympic athlete*

Johnson City
Kemp, Karen *women's basketball coach*

Memphis
Drinkard, D(onald) Dwight, Sr. *sports event director*

Nashville
Diller, John C. *professional athletics executive*
Fisher, Jeff *professional football coach*
†George, Eddie *professional football player*
Griffith, Jerry Lynn *physical education educator*
Holovak, Mike *sports association executive*
†McNair, Steve *professional football player*

TEXAS

Arlington
Alicea, Luis Rene *professional baseball player*
Burkett, John David *professional baseball player*
Gonzalez, Juan (Alberto Vazquez) *professional baseball player*
†Kelly, Roberto Conrado (Bobby Kelly) *professional baseball player*
Melvin, Robert Douglas *professional sports team executive*
Oates, Johnny Lane *professional baseball team manager*
Palmeiro, Rafael Corrales *professional baseball player*
Rodriguez, Ivan Torres *professional baseball player*
†Ryan, Nolan *former professional baseball player*
†Schieffer, J. Thomas *professional baseball team executive*
Wetteland, John Karl *professional baseball player*
†Zeile, Todd Edward *baseball player*

Austin
Crenshaw, Ben *professional golfer*
Garrido, Augie *university athletic coach*

Brownfield
Swoopes, Sheryl *professional basketball player*

Carrollton
†Strockbine, Richard Lewis *athletics administrator*

College Station
Galloway-McQuitter, Liz *university head basketball coach*
Slocum, Richard Copeland (R.C.) *university athletic coach*

Coppell
Foster, William Edwin (Bill Foster) *nonprofessional basketball coach*

Dallas
†Dir, Dave *professional soccer coach*
†Jordan, Matt *professional soccer player*
Landry, Tom (Thomas Wade Landry) *former professional football coach*
Millican, Chestella Alvis Hudel *athletics educator*
Nelson, Donald Arvid (Nellie Nelson) *professional basketball coach*
†Sheffield, Cinnamon *coach, dance educator, choreographer*

Trevino, Lee Buck *professional golfer*
Ussery, Terdema L. *professional sports team executive*

Houston

Alexander, Leslie Lee *professional sports team executive*
†Alou, Moises *professional baseball player*
Arcain, Janeth *professional athlete*
Bagwell, Jeff (Jeffrey Robert Bagwell) *professional baseball player*
Barkley, Charles Wade *professional basketball player*
†Bell, Derek *baseball player*
Biggio, Craig *professional baseball player*
Burden, Rhea Ann *athletic trainer*
†Chancellor, Van *professional basketball coach*
Cooper, Cynthia *professional basketball player*
Dierker, Larry *professional baseball team manager*
Dirks, Mike *golf coach*
Donie, Scott *Olympic athlete, platform diver*
Eusibio, Raul Antonio *baseball player*
Foreman, George *boxer, minister, boxing broadcaster*
Foyt, A(nthony) J(oseph), Jr. *auto racing crew chief, former professional auto racer*
Helton, Kim *coach*
Hunsicker, Gerry *professional sports executive*
Jackson, Tammy *basketball player*
Kim, Pyung-Soo *martial arts educator*
Lewis, Carl (Frederick Carlton Lewis) *Olympic track and field athlete*
McLane, Drayton, Jr. *professional baseball team executive*
Murphy, Calvin Jerome *professional sports team executive*
Olajuwon, Hakeem Abdul *professional basketball player*
Patterson, Steve *professional football team executive*
Perrot, Kim *basketball player*
Pippen, Scottie *professional basketball player*
Smith, Tal *sports association administrator*
Thompson, Tina *professional basketball player*
Tomjanovich, Rudolph *professional athletic coach*

Irving

Aikman, Troy *professional football player*
Allen, Larry Christopher *football player*
†Belfour, Ed *professional hockey player*
†Gailey, Thomas Chandler *professional football coach*
†Hitchcock, Ken *professional hockey coach*
Hull, Brett A. *professional hockey player*
Irvin, Michael Jerome *professional football player*
Ismail, Raghib (Rocket Ismail) *professional football player*
Jones, Jerry (Jerral Wayne Jones) *professional football team executive*
Lett, Leon *professional football player*
Lites, James R. *professional hockey team executive*
†Modano, Michael *professional hockey player*
Sanders, Deion Luwynn *football player*
Smith, Emmitt J., III *professional football player*
Stepnoski, Mark Matthew *professional football player*
Warren, Christopher Collins *professional football player*
Williams, Erik George *professional football player*
Woodson, Darren Ray *professional football player*

Leander

Erickson, Ralph D. *retired physical education educator, small business owner, consultant*

Lubbock

Sharp, Marsha *basketball coach*
Wilson, Margaret Eileen *retired physical education educator*

Odessa

Norvell, Nancy Lynn *health/physical education educator*

San Angelo

†Keith, Susan *kinesiology educator*

San Antonio

†Duncan, Tim *professional basketball player*
Elliot, Sean Michael *professional basketball player*
†Holt, Peter M. *sports team executive*
†Popovich, Gregg *professional basketball coach*
Robinson, David Maurice *professional basketball player*

Spring

Moceanu, Dominique *gymnast, Olympic athlete*

Waco

†Fulmer, Phillip *university football coach*
Hogg, Sonja *university athletics coach*
†Tomey, Dick *university football coach*

UTAH

Cedar City

Morrison, Craig Somerville *physical education educator*

Ogden

†Fullerton, Douglas B. *sports association adminstrator*

Park City

†Bergoust, Eric *olympic athlete*
†Dunn, Shannon *olympic athlete*
McIntyre, Elizabeth Geary *United States downhill skier*
Moe, Tommy (Thomas Sven Moe) *skier, former Olympic athlete*
†Moseley, Jonny *olympic athlete, free style skier*
†Powers, Ross *olympic athlete*
Roffe-Steinrotter, Diann *Olympic athlete*
†Stone, Nikki *retired olympic athlete*
Street, Picabo *Olympic athlete*

Provo

Shippen, Trent *university head women's basketball coach*

Salt Lake City

Baranova, Elena *basketball player*
†Dydek, Malgorzata *professional basketball player*

Hornacek, Jeffrey John *professional basketball player*
Howells, R. Tim *professional sports team executive*
Layden, Francis Patrick (Frank Layden) *professional basketball team executive, former coach*
Majerus, Rick *collegiate basketball team coach*
Malone, Karl *professional basketball player*
Miller, Larry H. *professional sports team executive, automobile dealer*
Palmer, Wendy *professional basketball player*
Sloan, Jerry (Gerald Eugene Sloan) *professional basketball coach*
Stockton, John Houston *professional basketball player*
Tremitiere, Chantel *basketball player*

VIRGINIA

Abingdon

†Hamilton, Bobby *professional race car driver*

Ashburn

Cooke, John Kent *professional sports management executive*
Turk, Matt *football player*
Turner, Norv *professional football coach*

Blacksburg

†Henrickson, Bonnie *college basketball coach*

Charlottesville

Ryan, Debbie *university athletic coach*

Fairfax

Cicala, Jac *soccer coach*

Falls Church

Theismann, Joseph Robert *former professional football player, announcer*

Ferrum

Sandidge, June Carol *physical education educator*

Hampton

Cage-Bibbs, Patricia *coach*

Harrisonburg

Childers, Bud *university head basketball coach*
Morgan, Christy *university head field hockey coach*

Herndon

†Etcheverry, Marco *professional soccer player*
†Harkes, John *professional soccer player*
Lassiter, Roy *soccer player*
†Moreno, Jaime *professional soccer player*
Payne, Kevin *professional soccer organization executive*
†Rongen, Thomas *professional soccer coach*

Mc Lean

†Blair, Bonnie *former professional speedskater, former Olympic athlete*
Chang, Michael *tennis player*
Martin, Todd *professional tennis player*

Norfolk

Larry, Wendy *head coach women's basketball*

Reston

†DeFrantz, Anita *physical education educator*

Richmond

Daniel, Beth *professional golfer*

Suffolk

Gray, Marcia Lanette *health, physical education and recreation educator*

WASHINGTON

Cheney

Pfeifer, Jocelyn *women's collegiate basketball coach*

Kirkland

Brown, Chadwick Everett *football player*
Collins, Mark *professional football player*
Glover, Kevin *football player*
Holmgren, Mike *professional football coach*
Kennedy, Cortez *professional football player*
Watters, Richard James *professional football player*

Olympia

†Thiel, Joseph William *golf professional*

Pullman

†Sampson, Kelvin Dale *college basketball coach*

Seattle

Ackerley, Barry *professional basketball team executive, communications company executive*
Armstrong, Charles G. *professional baseball executive, lawyer*
Baker, Vincent Lamont *basketball player*
Buhner, Jay Campbell *baseball player*
Ellis, John W. *professional baseball team executive, utility company executive*
Griffey, Ken, Jr. (George Kenneth Griffey, Jr.) *professional baseball player*
Martinez, Edgar *professional baseball player*
Payton, Gary Dwayne *professional basketball player*
Piniella, Louis Victor *professional baseball team manager*
Slocumb, Heathcliff *professional baseball player*
Swift, William Charles *professional baseball player, Olympic athlete*
Walker, Walter Frederick *professional basketball team executive*
†Westphal, Paul *professional basketball coach*

Spokane

Barney, Kellee *university athletics coach*
†Monson, Dan *college basketball coach*

WEST VIRGINIA

Harpers Ferry

Startzell, David N. *sports association executive*

Huntington

Simpson, Juliene *university head women's basketball coach*

WISCONSIN

Green Bay

Favre, Brett Lorenzo *professional football player*
†Freeman, Antonio Michael *professional football player*
Harlan, Robert Ernest *professional football team executive*
†Levens, (Herbert) Dorsey *professional football player*
Rhodes, Raymond Earl *professional sports team executive*
White, Reggie (Reginald Howard White) *retired professional football player*

Greendale

Kuhn, Roseann *sports association administrator*

Kenosha

†Lindgren, Scott Arthur *athletic educator*

Madison

Mtalika Banda, Kelekeni *university soccer coach*
Richter, Pat *university athletic director*
Sauer, Jeff *university hockey coach*

Milwaukee

†Garner, Phil *professional baseball manager*
†Grissom, Marquis Dean *professional baseball player*
†Jansen, Daniel Ervin *professional speedskater, marketing professional, former Olympic athlete*
Lanier, Bob *former professional sports team executive, former basketball player*
Nomo, Hideo *professional baseball player*
Selig, Allan H. (Bud Selig) *professional baseball team executive*
†Selig-Prieb, Wendy *sports team executive*
Steinmiller, John F. *professional basketball team executive*
Weinhauer, Bob *professional sports team executive*
†Witty, Christine (Chris Witty) *speed skater*

CANADA

ALBERTA

Calgary

Bartlett, Grant A. *professional sports team executive*
Edwards, N. Murray *professional sports team owner*
Hotchkiss, Harley N. *professional hockey team owner*
Libin, Alvin G. *business executive*

Edmonton

Low, Ron Albert *professional hockey coach*
Sather, Glen Cameron *professional hockey team executive, coach*
Weight, Doug *professional hockey player*

BRITISH COLUMBIA

Richmond

Zeigler, Earle Frederick *physical education-kinesiology educator*

Vancouver

†Abdul-Rahim, Shareef *professional basketball player*
Chapple, John H. *professional sports team executive*
Hill, Brian *professional basketball team coach*
Jackson, Stu *professional sports team executive, former university basketball coach*
McCaw, John E., Jr. *professional sports team executive*
Messier, Mark Douglas *professional hockey player*
Mogilny, Alexander *professional hockey player*

ONTARIO

Kanata

Dudley, Rick *professional hockey coach*
†Rhodes, Damian *professional hockey player*
†Yashin, Alexei *hockey player*

Mississauga

Gaston, Cito *former professional baseball manager*

Toronto

Ash, Gordon Ian *professional sports team executive*
†Berezin, Sergei *professional hockey player*
Browning, Kurt *figure skating champion*
†Carter, Butch *professional basketball coach, former sports team executive*
†Carter, Vince *professional basketball player*
Chamberlain, Wilton Norman *retired professional basketball player*
†Dryden, Ken *sports team executive*
Fernandez, Tony (Octavio Antonio Castro Fernandez) *baseball player*
Fletcher, Darrin Glen *baseball player*
Fregosi, James Louis *professional baseball team manager*
Hentgen, Patrick George *baseball player*
Hollins, David Michael *professional baseball player*
Joseph, Curtis Shayne *professional hockey player*
Kelly, Patrick Franklin *baseball player*
King, Kris *professional hockey player*

---

†Quinn, Pat (John Brian Patrick Quinn) *professional sports team manager*
Stavro, Steve A. *professional hockey team executive*
†Sundin, Mats Johan *professional hockey player*
†Thomas, Steve *professional hockey player*
Wells, David Lee *professional baseball player*
Willis, Kevin Alvin *professional basketball player*

QUEBEC

Montreal

Alou, Felipe Rojas *professional baseball manager*
Beattie, James Louis *professional sports team executive*
Brochu, Claude Renaud *professional baseball team executive*
Corson, Shayne *professional hockey player*
†Guerrero, Vladimir *professional baseball player*
Lemaire, Jacques *professional hockey coach*
Menard, Louis Jacques *professional sports team executive*
Stoneman, William Hambly, III *professional baseball team executive*
†Widger, Chris *professional baseball player*

Saint Lazare

Fanning, William James *professional baseball team executive, radio and television broadcaster*

MEXICO

La Noria

Campos, Jorge *professional soccer player*

Mexico City

Chavez, Julio Cesar *professional boxer*
Joppy, William *professional boxer*

AUSTRALIA

Sydney

Norman, Gregory John *professional golfer*

DOMINICAN REPUBLIC

Santo Domingo

Marichal Sanchez, Juan Antonio *retired baseball player, agency administrator*

ENGLAND

Leicester

Keller, Kasey *professional soccer player*

GERMANY

Cologne

Sabatini, Gabriela *retired tennis player*

LEVERKUSEN

Tannenberg

Reyna, Claudio *soccer player*

NIGERIA

Abuja

†Milutinovic, Bora *soccer coach*

SOUTH AFRICA

Klippoortjie

Els, Theodore Ernest *professional golfer*

SPAIN

Santander

Ballesteros, Severiano *professional golfer*

VENEZUELA

Turmero

†Botha, Francois (Frans) *professional boxer*

ADDRESS UNPUBLISHED

Allen, Eric Andre *professional football player*
Alvarez, Barry *university football coach*
Anderson, Sparky (George Lee Anderson) *broadcast analyst, former baseball team manager*
Andretti, Mario *race car driver*
Andretti, Michael Mario *professional race car driver*
†Barrett, Tina *professional golfer*
Bertman, Skip *baseball coach*
Bishop, Blaine Elwood *football player*
Blanchard, Cary *football player*
Boling, Robert Bruce *physical education educator*
Bonifay, Cam *professional sports team executive*
†Bowe, Riddick Lamont *professional boxer*
Bradley, Patricia Ellen *professional golfer*
Bridgewater, Brad *Olympic athlete*
†Burton, Jeff *professional race car driver*
Byrne, Catherine *swimmer*
Camacho, Hector *boxer*
Caminiti, Kenneth Gene *professional baseball player*
Carbajal, Michael *boxer*
Carew, Rodney Cline *batting coach, former professional baseball player*
Crawford, Marc *professional hockey coach*
Crawford, Margaret Jean Barnes *physical education educator, consultant*

Curry, Hugh Robert *tennis player*
†Dallenbach, Wally *professional race car driver*
Davidson, Bonnie Jean *gymnastics educator, sports management consultant*
Davila, Rebecca Tober *health and physical education educator*
Desjardins, Eric *professional hockey player*
Drabek, Doug (Douglas Dean Drabek) *baseball player*
†Drexler, Clyde *retired professional basketball player*
Duva, Lou *boxing promoter, manager*
†Elliott, Bill *professional rac car driver*
†Embry, Wayne Richard *former basketball executive*
Evert, Christine Marie (Chris Evert) *retired professional tennis player*
Fernandez, Mary Joe *professional tennis player*
Fingers, Roland Glen *retired baseball player*
Gainey, Robert Michael *professional hockey coach, former player*
Gamble, Harry T. *professional football team executive*
Geddes, Jane *professional golfer*
†Girton, Marcy *athletic director*
Graf, Steffi *professional tennis player*
Guthrie, Janet *professional race car driver*
Haberl, Valerie Elizabeth *physical education educator, company executive*
Hall, J. Tillman *physical education educator, administrator, writer*
Hamill, Dorothy Stuart *professional ice skater*
Hanson, Erik Brian *professional baseball player*
Hatchell, Sylvia *basketball coach*
Hill, Virgil *professional boxer*
†Hoch, Scott Mabon *professional golfer*
Hollandsworth, Todd Mathew *baseball player*
Holmes, Keith *professional boxer*
Hopkins, Bernard (The Executioner Hopkins) *professional boxer*
Hurtado, Eduardo *soccer player*
†Irwin, Kenny *professional race car driver*
†Issel, Daniel Paul *sports team executive, former professional basketball coach*
Johnson, Kenneth Lance *baseball player*
Jones, Roy *professional boxer*
Jordan, Michael Jeffrey *retired professional basketball player, retired baseball player*
†Karl, George *professional basketball coach*
Kavalek, Lubomir *chess expert*
Kent, Betty Dickinson *horsemanship educator*
Kitchen, Paul Howard *hockey historian*
Kite, Thomas O., Jr. *professional golfer*
Kluka, Darlene Ann *human performance educator, researcher*
Koufax, Sandy *retired baseball player*
Kundla, John Albert *coach, retired*
Lacko, J. Michelle *physical education, health and science educator*
Lacroix, Pierre *professional sports team professional*
LeClair, John Clark *professional hockey player*
†Levering, Judy A. *sports association executive*
Liles, Frank *professional boxer*
Littler, Gene Alec *professional golfer*
Lofton, Kenneth *professional baseball player*
Lopez, Ricardo *professional boxer*
Lynch, Jair *Olympic athlete*
†Malone, Kevin *sports team executive*
Manahan, Joan Elsie *health and physical education educator*
Martin, Christy *professional boxer*
Mason, Linda *physical education educator, softball and basketball coach*
McCarthy, Jean Jerome *retired physical education educator*
Mellanby, Scott Edgar *professional hockey player*
Mesa, Jose Ramon *professional baseball player*
Miller, Nate *professional boxer*
Miller, Reginald Wayne *professional basketball player*
Miller, Shannon *Olympic athlete*
Montgomery, David Paul *professional baseball team executive*
Navratilova, Martina *former professional tennis player*
Nicklaus, Jack William *professional golfer*
Orr, Bobby (Robert Gordon Orr) *former hockey player*
Parins, Robert James *professional football team executive, judge*
Payne, Kevin Joseph *professional sports team executive*
Pazienza, Vinny *professional boxer*
Price, Nick *professional golfer*
Randall, Frankie *professional boxer*
Rodriguez, Alexander Emmanuel *professional baseball player*
Ross, Robert Joseph *head professional football coach*
Rutherford, John Sherman, III (Johnny Rutherford) *professional race car driver*
Salaam, Rashaan *professional football player*
†Sanderson, Geoff *hockey player*
†Savon, Felix *Olympic athlete*
Schottenheimer, Martin Edward *professional football coach*
Schrempf, Detlef *professional basketball player*
Seldin, David *professional sports team executive*
Sharpe, Sterling *former professional football player, sports commentator*
Smith, Lee Arthur *professional baseball player*
Smith, (Tubby) Orlando Henry *college basketball coach*
Smith, Sinjin *beach volleyball player*
Spinks, Michael *retired professional boxer*
†Sprewell, Latrell Fontaine *professional basketball player*
†Stadler, Craig Robert *professional golfer*
Stanley, Robert Michael *professional baseball player*
Stewart, (William) Payne *professional golfer*
†Stringer, C. Vivian *women's college basketball coach*
Summitt, Patricia Head *college basketball coach*
Thompson, Craig Dean *sports association executive*
Unser, Al *professional auto racer*
Valderrama, Carlos *professional soccer player*
Vanatta, Bob *athletic administrator*
Vaughn, Gregory Lamont *professional baseball player*
Wagner, Richard *athletics consultant, former baseball team executive*
Wallace, Kenny *professional race car driver*
Waltrip, Darrell Lee *professional stock car driver*
West, Jerry Alan *professional basketball team executive*
Wilpon, Fred *professional baseball team executive, real estate developer*
Wilson, Ralph Cookerly, Jr. *professional football team executive*
†Wittman, Randy *professional basketball coach*

Woodall, Lee *professional football player*
Wooden, John Robert *former basketball coach*
Woosnam, Ian Harold *professional golfer*
Yamaguchi, Kristi Tsuya *ice skater*

BUSINESS. *See* **FINANCE; INDUSTRY.**

COMMUNICATIONS. *See* **COMMUNICATIONS MEDIA; INDUSTRY: SERVICE.**

COMMUNICATIONS MEDIA. *See also* **ARTS: LITERARY.**

UNITED STATES

ALABAMA

Anniston
Ayers, Harry Brandt *editor, publisher, columnist*

Auburn
Harvey, James Mathews, Jr. *instructional media producer, columnist*

Birmingham
Allen, Christopher C. *publishing executive*
Barrett, Ellen Colby *magazine editor*
Carlton, Michael *magazine editor*
Casey, Ronald Bruce *journalist*
Crichton, Douglas Bentley *editor, writer*
Francavilla, Donna T. *news reporter*
Griffin, Eleanor *magazine editor*
Hanson, Victor Henry, II *newspaper publisher*
Hickson, Marcus Lafayette, III *communication educator, consultant*
Kennedy, Joe David, Jr. (Joey Kennedy) *editor*
Lynch, Kevin *publishing executive*
Nunnelley, Carol Fishburne *editor newspaper*
Scarritt, Thomas Varnon *newspaper editor*
Seitz, Karl Raymond *editor*
Sheppard, Scott *magazine publisher*
Stephens, James T. *publishing executive*

Fairhope
†Propp, Sheila Margaret *newspaper editor*

Jacksonville
Merrill, Martha *instructional media educator*

Mobile
†Clark, Veronica Ann Wilds (Ronni Patriquin Clark) *journalist*
Hearin, William Jefferson *newspaper publishing company executive*

Montgomery
Brooks, Michael *broadcast executive*
Bullock, Mark William *broadcast journalist*
Hayes, John Edward *broadcasting executive*
Hertenstein, Myrna Lynn *publishing executive*
Johnson, Mary Elizabeth *editor, author*
Oppmann, Andrew James *newspaper editor*
Sottile, Kathy Watson *publisher, writer*
Woods, David *television executive*

Tuscaloosa
Nelson, Debra Jean *sales manager, journalist, public relations executive, consultant*
Reinhart, Kellee Connely *journalist*
Thomson, H. Bailey *editor, educator*

ALASKA

Anchorage
Cowell, Fuller A. *publisher*
Crawford, Sarah Carter (Sally Carter Crawford) *broadcast executive*
Hill, Erik Bryan *newspaper photographer*
Pearson, Larry Lester *journalism educator, internet presence provider*

Fairbanks
Berry, Kathryn Allen *editor in chief science publication*
Mitchell, Susan E. *editor, desktop publisher*

Glennallen
Smelcer, John E. *publishing company executive*

Homer
Beach, Geo *journalist, poet*

North Pole
Chamberland, Anna Margaret Pickett *communitcations professional, small business owner*

ARIZONA

Bisbee
Eppele, David Louis *columnist, author*

Flagstaff
Hammond, Howard David *retired botanist and editor*
Helford, Paul Quinn *communications educator, academic administrator*
Siegmund, Mark Alan *editor, publisher, business consultant, design scientist*

Gilbert
Kenney, Thomas Frederick *broadcasting executive*

Glendale
Joseph, Gregory Nelson *media critic, writer*

Phoenix
Edens, Gary Denton *broadcasting executive*
Genrich, Mark L. *newspaper editorial writer, columnist*
Godwin, Mary Jo *editor, librarian consultant*
Grafe, Warren Blair *cable television executive*
Gunty, Christopher James *newspaper editor*
Hardin, Terrence Armstrong *radio broadcasting manager*
Harnett, Lila *retired publisher*
Johnson, Pam *newspaper editor*
Kaiser, Robert Blair *journalist*
Kelley, Patricia Austin *publishing executive*
Kolbe, John William *newspaper columnist*
Leach, John F. *newspaper editor, journalism educator*
Miller, William *broadcast executive*
Moyer, Alan Dean *retired newspaper editor*
North, Patrick *broadcasting executive*
Oppedahl, John Fredrick *publisher*
Reyes, Anna Maria *broadcast executive*
Schatt, Paul *newspaper editor*
Steckler, Phyllis Betty *publishing company executive*
Weber, Fredric G. *broadcast executive*
Weil, Louis Arthur, III *newspaper publishing executive*

Prescott
Anderson, Parker Lynn *editorial columnist, playwright*

Scottsdale
Allison, Stephen Galender *broadcast executive*
Everingham, Harry Towner *editor, publisher*
Frischknecht, Lee Conrad *retired broadcasting executive*
Johnson, Micah William *television newscaster, director*
Mc Knight, William Warren, Jr. *publisher*

Sedona
Chicorel, Marietta Eva *publisher*

Tempe
Allen, Charles Raymond *television station executive*
Douglas, Michael *publishing executive*
Owens, Michael L. *radio station executive*
Rankin, William Parkman *educator, former publishing company executive*
Richards, Gale Lee *communication educator*
Sabine, Gordon Arthur *educator, writer*

Tucson
Coffman, Roy Walter, III *publishing company executive*
Cox, Stephen F. *retired publishing company executive*
Foran, Kevin Richard *television station executive*
Grimes, James Cahill *retired publishing executive, advertising executive*
Hale, William Bryan, Jr. *newspaper editor*
Hutchinson, Charles Smith, Jr. *book publisher*
Jackel, Lawrence *publishing company executive*
Martin, June Johnson Caldwell *journalist*
Roos, Nestor Robert *consultant*
Stein, Mary Katherine *writer, editor, photographer, communications executive*
Villa, Jacqueline Irene *newspaper editor*
Weber, Samuel *editor, retired*
White, Jane *See journalist*

ARKANSAS

Brookland
†Angleman-Noble, Sharon Ann *journalist*

Cedarville
Whitaker, Ruth Reed *retired newspaper editor*

Conway
Plotkin, Helen Ann *writer, editor*

Fayetteville
Masterson, Michael Rue *journalist, educator, editor*

Hot Springs National Park
Lauber, Joseph Lincoln *publisher's representative*

Little Rock
†Barham, Steven Gary *public radio station executive*
Greenberg, Paul *newspaperman*
Hobbs, Ray David *editor*
Portis, Charles McColl *reporter, writer*
Smith, Griffin, Jr. *editor*
Starr, John Robert *retired newspaper editor, political columnist*
†White, Ray D. *newspaper designer*

Magnolia
Reppert, James Eugene *mass communications educator*

Mountain Home
Anderson, Kenneth Norman *retired magazine editor, author*

Springdale
Martin, Becca Bacon *editor, journalist*

CALIFORNIA

Agoura Hills
Chagall, David *journalist, author*
Teresi, Joseph *publishing executive*

Alamo
Reed, John Theodore *publisher, writer*

Alhambra
Duke, Donald Norman *publisher*

Alpine
Greenberg, Byron Stanley *newspaper and business executive, consultant*

Aptos
†Winters, Paul Andrew *editor*

Arcata
Swanson, Carolyn Rae *news reporter, counselor*

Avila Beach
Kamm, Herbert *journalist*

Belmont
Carlson, Gary R. *publishing executive*

Belvedere
Benet, Carol Ann *journalist, career counselor, teacher*

Belvedere Tiburon
Kramer, Lawrence Stephen *journalist*

Berkeley
Bagdikian, Ben Haig *journalist, emeritus university educator*
Browne, G.M. Walter Shawn Browne *journalist, chess player*
Fulton, Katherine Nelson *journalist, consultant*
Helson, Henry Berge *publisher, retired mathematics educator*
Lesser, Wendy *literary magazine editor, writer, consultant*
Matthews, Mildred Shapley *scientific editor, freelance writer*

Beverly Hills
Beck, Marilyn Mohr *columnist*
†Bollenbach, Stephen Frasier *entertainment executive*
Bradshaw, Terry *sports announcer, former professional football player*
Chernin, Peter *motion picture company executive*
Corwin, Stanley Joel *book publisher*
Farhat, Carol Sue *motion picture company executive*
Fernandez, Giselle *newscaster, journalist*
Filosa, Gary Fairmont Randolph V., II *multimedia executive, financier, writer*
Gerber, William Norman *motion picture executive*
Grazer, Brian *film company executive*
Grushow, Sandy *broadcast executive*
Harris, Fran *sportscaster, former basketball player*
Hefner, Hugh Marston *editor-in-chief*
Heller, Paul Michael *film company executive, producer*
Hill, David *broadcast executive*
Kuhn, Michael *motion picture company executive*
Lond, Harley Weldon *editor, publisher*
Mechanic, William M. *television and motion picture industry executive*
Rifkin, Arnold *film company executive*
Rosenzweig, Richard Stuart *publishing company executive*
†Rothman, Thomas Edgar *production executive*
Rush, Herman E. *television executive*
Schneider, Charles I. *newspaper executive*
Stambler, Irwin *publishing executive*
Yomtov, Michelle Rene *journalist*
Zanuck, Richard Darryl *motion picture company executive*

Brisbane
England, Cheryl *publisher, editorial director*

Burbank
Ancier, Garth Richard *television broadcast executive*
Arkoff, Samuel Z. *motion picture executive, producer*
†Black, Carole *broadcast executive*
Brogliatti, Barbara Spencer *television and motion picture executive*
Daly, Robert Anthony *former film executive*
DiBonaventure, Lorenzo *film company executive*
Disney, Roy Edward *broadcasting company executive*
Eisner, Michael Dammann *entertainment company executive*
Hashe, Janis Helene *editor*
Jonas, Tony *television executive*
Kellner, Jamie *broadcasting executive*
Lieberfarb, Warren N. *broadcast executive*
†Liss, Walter C. *television station executive*
Liss, Walter C., Jr. *television station executive*
Mestres, Ricardo A., III *motion picture company executive*
Robertson, Richard Trafton *entertainment company executive*
Roth, Joe *motion picture company executive*
Roth, Peter *broadcast executive*
Schneider, Peter *film company executive*
Schumacher, Thomas *film company executive*
Semel, Terry *former entertainment company executive*
Shriver, Maria Owings *news correspondent*
Sweeney, Anne M. *cable television company executive*
Thyret, Russ *recording industry executive*
Wolper, David Lloyd *motion picture and television executive*

Burlingame
Mendelson, Lee M. *film company executive, writer, producer, director*

Byron
Alexander, Frank *publisher, editor*

Calabasas
†Dunphy, Jerry Raymond *television news anchor, lyric writer*

Camarillo
DePatie, David Hudson *motion picture company executive*
Doebler, Paul Dickerson *publishing management executive*

Cambria
Blundell, William Edward *journalist, consultant*

Canoga Park
Destler, Dave M. *publisher, editor, journalist*

Cardiff By The Sea
Sheldon, Deena Lynn *television camera operator*

Carlsbad
Brown, Jack *magazine editor*

Carmel
Bohannon-Kaplan, Margaret Anne *publisher, lawyer*
Koeppel, Gary Merle *publisher, art gallery owner, writer*
Mollman, John Peter *book publisher, consultant electronic publishing*

Century City
†Fili-Krushel, Patricia *broadcast executive*

Chino Hills
Hemenway, Stephen James *record producer, author*

Chula Vista
Blankfort, Lowell Arnold *newspaper publisher*

Concord
MacDonald, Angus *writer, editor*

Corona Del Mar
Crump, Spencer *publisher, business executive*

Costa Mesa
Dinkel, John George *magazine editor*
Jabbari, Ahmad *publishing executive*

Culver City
Buyse, Emile Jules *film company executive*
Calley, John *motion picture company executive, film producer*
Feingold, Benjamin S. *broadcast executive*
Feltheimer, Jon *entertainment company executive*
Fisher, Lucy J. *motion picture company executive*
Hu, Lincoln *media technology executive, computer scientist*
†Kaplan, Andy *broadcast executive*
Littlefield, Warren *television executive*
Pascal, Amy *film company executive*
†Tannenbaum, Eric *broadcast executive*
Wigan, Gareth *film company executive*

Davis
Motley, Michael Tilden *communication educator*

Del Mar
Faludi, Susan C. *journalist, scholarly writer*
Kaye, Peter Frederic *television editor*

El Dorado Hills
Schlachter, Gail Ann *publishing company executive*

El Segundo
Conrad, Paul Francis *editorial cartoonist*
McKee, John Morrison *broadcast executive*

Emeryville
Fenwick, James H(enry) *editor*

Encino
Holman, Harland Eugene *retired motion picture company executive*
Lowy, Jay Stanton *music industry executive*
Rawitch, Robert Joe *journalist, educator*
Rose, Doyle *broadcast executive*

Eureka
Lollich, Leslie Norlene *journalist, educator*

Fair Oaks
Davidson, (Marie) Diane *publisher*

Fairfax
Codoni, Frederick Peter *editor*

Fall River Mills
Caldwell, Walter Edward *editor, small business owner*

Flintridge
Fry, Donald Owen *broadcasting company executive*

Foster City
Ball, John Paul *publishing company executive*

Frazier Park
Nelson, Harry *journalist, medical writer*

Fresno
Hart, Russ Allen *telecommunications educator*
Mettee, Stephen Blake *publishing executive*
Moyer, J. Keith *newspaper editor*
†Waters, Charles R. *executive editor*
Wilson, James Ross *communications educator, broadcasting executive*

Fullerton
Lewandoski, Robert Henry *editor, publisher*

Hanford
†Harris, Mildred Staeger *retired broadcast executive*

Hayward
Funston, Gary Stephen *publishing and advertising executive*

Hollywood
Adjenian, Robert *publisher*
†Drudge, Matt *journalist*
Sarley, John G. *broadcast executive, writer*

Huntington Beach
De Massa, Jessie G. *media specialist*
Frye, Judith Eleen Minor *editor*

Indio
Ellis, Lee *publisher, editor*

Inyokern
Stallknecht-Roberts, Clois Freda *publisher, publicist*

Irvine
Bartkus, Richard Anthony *magazine publisher*
Hardie, Robert C. *newspaper publishing executive*
Lesonsky, Rieva *editor*
Power, Francis William *newspaper publisher*
Rosse, James N. *newspaper publishing executive*

La Canada
Paniccia, Patricia Lynn *journalist, writer, lawyer, educator*

La Habra
Oliver, Joyce Anne *journalist, editorial consultant, columnist*

La Jolla
Copley, David C. *newspaper publishing company executive*
Copley, Helen Kinney *newspaper publisher*
Hallin, Daniel Clark *communications educator*
Harris, T. George *magazine editor*
Schudson, Michael Steven *communications educator*

Lafayette
Alexander, Kenneth Lewis *editorial cartoonist*
Stewart, Leslie Mueller *editor, writer*

Laguna Hills
James, Sidney Lorraine *television executive*

Lake Forest
Wetenkamp, Herbert Delos, Jr. *publisher*

Linden
Smith, Donald Richard *editor, publisher*

Loma Linda
Bell, Denise Louise *newspaper reporter, photographer, librarian*

Long Beach
Adler, Jeffrey D. *political consultant, public affairs consultant, crisis management expert*
Bond, Frances Curtis *retired editor*
Byles, Torrey Koppe *communications technolgy specialist*
Ellis, Harriette Rothstein *editor, writer*
†Kelly, Wayne Fred *journalism educator*
Ruszkiewicz, Carolyn Mae *newspaper editor*

Los Altos
Miller, Ronald Grant *author, critic*

Los Angeles
Archerd, Army (Armand Archerd) *columnist, television commentator*
Beard, John Jackson, III *journalist*
Belnap, David F. *journalist*
Benty, Cameron Todd *magazine editor*
Bernstein, William *film company executive*
Berry, Stephen Joseph *reporter*
Bloomberg, Stu *broadcast executive*
Boyarsky, Benjamin William *journalist*
Boyle, Barbara Dorman *motion picture company executive*
Byrne, Gerard Anthony *publishing company executive, marketing consultant*
Camron, Roxanne *editor*
Carey, Chase *broadcast executive*
Clarke, Peter *communications and health educator*
Cordova, Jeanne Robert *publisher, journalist, activist*
Crippens, David Lee *broadcast executive*
Darling, Juanita Marie *correspondent*
Del Olmo, Frank *newspaper editor*
†DeLuca, Michael *film company executive*
Delugach, Albert Lawrence *journalist*
Drewry, Elizabeth *newspaper publishing executive*
Duffy, Patrick *broadcast executive*
Dwyre, William Patrick *journalist, public speaker*
Fein, Irving Ashley *television and motion picture executive*
Field, Ted (Frederick Field) *film and record industry executive*
Firstenberg, Jean Picker *film institute executive*
Flanigan, James J(oseph) *journalist*
Foster, Mary Christine *motion picture and television executive*
Friedman, Robert Lee *film company executive*
Furlong, Thomas Castle *newspaper editor*
Garry, William James *magazine editor*
Garza, Oscar *newspaper editor*
Gauff, Lisa *broadcast journalist*
Getlin, Josh *reporter*
Gilmore, Mikal George *critic, journalist, author*
Glass, Herbert *music critic, lecturer, editor*
Groves, Martha *newspaper writer*
Gudea, Darlene *publishing company executive*
Hammond, Teena Gay *editor*
Hart, John Lewis (Johnny Hart) *cartoonist*
†Hiltzik, Michael *journalist*
Hines, William Everett *publisher, producer, cinematographer, writer*
Horowitz, David Charles *consumer commentator, newspaper columnist*
Hudson, Christopher John *publisher*
Iafrate, Gerald Carl *motion picture company executive, lawyer*
Iovine, Jimmy *recording industry executive*
Israel, David *journalist, screenwriter, producer*
Jacobson, Sidney *editor*
Jarmon, Lawrence *developmental communications educator*
Katleman, Harris L. *television executive*
Kaye, Jhani *radio station manager, owner production company*
King, Michael *syndicated programs distributing company executive*
Kraft, Scott Corey *correspondent*
Kristof, Kathy M. *journalist*
Laventhol, David Abram *newspaper editor*
Lazarus, Mell *cartoonist*
Lee, Stan (Stanley Martin Lieber) *cartoon publisher, writer*
†Lehmkuhl, Lynn *publishing executive*
Levine, Jesse E. *publishing executive*
Li, Lilia Huiying *journalist*
Loehwing, Rudi Charles, Jr. *publicist, radio broadcasting executive, journalist*
Maltin, Leonard *television commentator, writer*
Mann, Wesley F. *newspaper editor*
Margulies, Lee *newspaper editor*
Masters, Lee *broadcast executive*
McCluggage, Kerry *television executive*
Michaud, Michael Gregg *publishing executive, writer*
Michel, Donald Charles *editor*
Miles, Jack (John Russiano) *journalist, educator*
†Miller, Percy *record company executive*
Moonves, Leslie *television company executive*
Morgan, Dirck *broadcast journalist*
Mottek, Frank *broadcaster, journalist*
Murphy, Philip Edward *broadcast executive*
Murray, James Patrick *newspaper columnist*
Neal, Howard *broadcasting executive*
Nelson, Bryce Eames *journalist, educator*
Neufeld, Mace *film company executive*
†O'Neil, W. Scott *publishing executive*
O'Reilly, Richard Brooks *journalist*
Parks, Michael Christopher *journalist*
†Perez, Denise Therese *editor*
Perlmutter, Donna *music and dance critic*
Petersen, Robert E. *publisher*
†Philips, Chuck *journalist*
Phillips, Geneva Ficker *editor*
Plate, Thomas Gordon *newspaper columnist, educator*
Radloff, William Hamilton *editor, writer*
Reardon, John E. *broadcast executive*
Reich, Kenneth Irvin *journalist*
Rense, Paige *editor, publishing company executive*
Rich, Alan *music critic, editor, author*
Richmond, Ray S(am) *journalist*
Romo, Cheryl Annette *writer, editor*
Rosenberg, Howard Anthony *journalist*
Rotello, Gabriel *journalist*
Russell, James Brian *broadcast executive, media consultant*
Saltzman, Joseph *journalist, producer, educator*
Sarnoff, Thomas Warren *television executive*
Saylor, Mark Julian *editor*
Scott, Kelly *newspaper editor*
Scully, Vincent Edward *sports broadcaster*
Shapazian, Robert Michael *publishing executive*
Shaw, David Lyle *journalist, author*
†Shea, Fran *broadcast executive*
Shuster, Alvin *journalist, newspaper editor*
Sigband, Norman Bruce *management communication educator*
Simpson, O. J. (Orenthal James Simpson) *former professional football player, actor, sports commentator*
Sinay, Hershel David *publisher*
Smith, Lane Jeffrey *automotive journalist, technical consultant*
Sonnberg, Mark *television executive*
Sperling-Orseck, Irene *publishing company executive*
Steele, Bruce Carl *editor*
Stern, Leonard Bernard *television and motion picture production company executive*
Stern, Mitchell *broadcast executive*
Tarses, Jamie *television network executive*
Trembly, Cristy *television executive*
Tulsky, Fredric Neal *journalist*
Turner, Craig *journalist*
Unterman, Thomas *newspaper publishing company executive, lawyer*
Valentine, Dean *broadcast executive*
Vargas, Diana L *television station executive*
Ward, Leslie Allyson *journalist, editor*
†Wardlow, Bill *record industry consultant, entertainer*
Warner, James *broadcast executive*
Wilbraham, Craig *broadcast executive*
Willes, Mark Hinckley *media industry executive*
Wilson, Charles Zachary, Jr. *newspaper publisher*
Wolinsky, Leo C. *newspaper editor*
Wright, Donald Franklin *retired newspaper executive*
Youpa, Donald G. *broadcast executive*

Los Gatos
Meyers, Ann Elizabeth *sports broadcaster*

Malibu
MacLeod, Robert Fredric *editor, publisher*

Marina
Grenfell, Gloria Ross *freelance journalist*

Marina Del Rey
Engel, Geoffrey Byron *editor*
Evans, Thomas R. *magazine publisher*
Rojany, Lisa Adrienne *publishing company executive*

Menlo Park
Bull, James Robert *publishing executive*
Nichols, Alan *newspaper publishing executive*
Wright, Rosalie Muller *magazine and newspaper editor*

Merced
Boese, Sandra Jean *publishing executive*

Mill Valley
Leslie, Jacques Robert, Jr. *journalist*
McNamara, Stephen *newspaper executive*

Monterey
Gotshall, Cordia Ann *publishing company executive, distributing executive*

Monterey Park
Stapleton, Jean *journalism educator*

Newport Beach
Dean, Paul John *magazine editor*
McMahon, Brian *publishing executive*
Van Mols, Brian *publishing executive*
Weber, Mark Edward *editor, historian*

North Hollywood
Feola, Louis *broadcast executive*
Horowitz, Zachary I. *entertainment company executive*
Koran, Dennis Howard *publisher*
Lindheim, Richard David *television company executive*
Powers, Melvin *publishing executive*

Novato
Pfeiffer, Phyllis Kramer *publishing executive*

Oakhurst
Carlin, Sidney Alan *music publisher, arranger*

Oakland
†Brevetti, Francine Clelia *journalist*
Burt, Christopher Clinton *publisher*
Christopher, L. Carol *communication researcher, freelance writer*
Conway, Nancy Ann *editor*
Dailey, Garrett Clark *publisher, lawyer*
Erlich, Reese William *journalist*
Haiman, Franklyn Saul *author, communications educator*
Kelso, David William *fine arts publishing executive, artist*
McKinney, Judson Thad *broadcast executive*
Schrag, Peter *editor, writer*
Wood, Larry (Mary Laird) *journalist, author, university educator, public relations executive, environmental consultant*

Oceanside
Delienne, Jacquelyn E. *e-commerce developer and publisher, management consultant, electronic comme*
Howard, Robert Staples *newspaper publisher*

Ontario
†Evans, Daniel Joseph *journalist*
†McAfee, I. Paul, III *editor*
Wagner, Rob Leicester *newspaper editor, writer*

Orange
Fletcher, James Allen *video company executive*
Zweifel, Donald Edwin *editor, civic affairs volunteer, consultant*

Pacific Grove
Davis, Robert Edward *retired communication educator*

Pacific Palisades
Hadges, Thomas Richard *media consultant*
Pitkin, Roy Macbeth *editor*
Price, Frank *motion picture and television company executive*
Purcell, Patrick B. *consultant*

Palm Desert
Ayling, Henry Faithful *writer, editor, consultant*
Crider, Jeffrey John *public relations executive*
Godfrey, Alden Newell *communications educator*

Palm Springs
Browning, Norma Lee (Mrs. Russell Joyner Ogg) *journalist*
Jones, Milton Wakefield *publisher*
Mann, Zane Boyd *editor, publisher*

Palo Alto
Hamilton, David Mike *publishing company executive*
Hellyer, Constance Anne (Connie Anne Conway) *writer, musician*
Perlman, Steve *multimedia broadcast executive*

Palos Verdes Peninsula
King, Nancy *communications educator*

Paradise
Fulton, Len *publisher*

Pasadena
Bergholz, Richard Cady *political writer*
Carey, Keith Grant *editor, publishing executive*
Diehl, Digby Robert *journalist*
Hopkins, Philip Joseph *journalist, editor*
Roth, Irma Doris Brubaker *editor*
Spector, Phil *record company executive*

Paso Robles
Brown, Benjamin Andrew *journalist*

Pebble Beach
Ketcham, Henry King *cartoonist*

Portola Valley
Garsh, Thomas Burton *publisher*

Rancho Palos Verdes
Hillinger, Charles *journalist, writer*

Rancho Santa Fe
McNally, Connie Benson *editor, publisher, antiques dealer*

Rancho Santa Margarita
Miller, Elliot Ivan *editor*

Richmond
Doyle, William Thomas *retired newspaper editor*

Ridgecrest
Roberts, Jerry Bill *publishing company executive*

Riverside
Foreman, Thomas Elton *drama critic*
Mc Laughlin, Leighton Bates, II *journalism educator, former newspaperman*
McQuern, Marcia Alice *newspaper publishing executive*
Opotowsky, Maurice Leon *newspaper editor*
Robbins, Karen Diane *editor*
†Rodrigue, George P. *editor*
Sokolsky, Robert Lawrence *journalist, entertainment writer*
Zappe, John Paul *city editor, educator, newspaper executive*

Rolling Hills Estates
Bradford, Susan Anne *political consultant, writer*

Sacramento
Baltake, Joe *film critic*
Block, Alvin Gilbert *journal executive editor*
Bottel, Helen Alfea *columnist, writer*
Endicott, William F. *journalist*
†Favre, Gregory *publishing executive*
Glackin, William Charles *arts critic, editor*
Grossman, Marc Richard *media consultant*
†Heaphy, Janis D. *newspaper executive*
Knudson, Thomas Jeffery *journalist*
LaMont, Sanders Hickey *journalist*
Lundstrom, Marjie *newspaper editor*
McClatchy, James B. *editor, newspaper publisher*
†Potts, Erwin Rea *newspaper executive*
Pruitt, Gary B. *newspaper executive*

Shaw, Eleanor Jane *newspaper editor*
Walsh, Denny Jay *reporter*
Walters, Daniel Raymond *political columnist*

Saint Helena
Allegra, Antonia *editor, writer*

San Carlos
Jones, Georgia Ann *publisher*

San Clemente
Singer, Kurt Deutsch *news commentator, author, publisher*

San Diego
Beauchamp, Miles Philip *newspaper editor-columnist, education consultant*
Bell, Gene *newspaper publishing executive*
Bennett, Ronald Thomas *photojournalist*
Borden, Diane Lynn *communications educator*
Brown, Darrell *broadcast executive*
Da Rosa, Alison *travel editor*
Donahoe, Jim *broadcast executive*
Fike, Edward Lake *newspaper editor*
Freedman, Jonathan Borwick *journalist, author, lecturer*
Glickenhaus, Mike *radio station executive*
Kaufman, Julian Mortimer *broadcasting company executive, consultant*
Klein, Herbert George *newspaper editor*
Krulak, Victor Harold *newspaper executive*
Langer, Eva Marie *audio video systems manager*
McCarthy, Kevin *broadcast executive*
Morgan, Neil *author, newspaper editor, lecturer, columnist*
Myrland, Doug *broadcast executive*
O'Laughlin, Joanie *broadcast executive*
Owen, Charles Theodore *journalist, publisher*
Pfeffer, Rubin Harry *publishing executive*
Pincus, Robert Lawrence *art critic, cultural historian*
Quinn, Edward J. *broadcasting company executive*
Ristine, Jeffrey Alan *reporter*
Rowe, Peter A. *newspaper columnist*
Slater, Leonard *writer, editor*
Stafford, Mike *broadcast executive*
Steen, Paul Joseph *retired broadcasting executive*
†Toth, Simone Lee *reporter*
†Trageser, James Michael *editor*
Walton, Bill (William Theodore Walton, III) *sportscaster, former professional basketball player*
Winner, Karin *newspaper editor*

San Francisco
†Ahern, Joseph A. *television station executive*
Anders, George Charles *journalist, author*
Baker, Kenneth *art critic, writer*
Barnum, Alexander Stone *journalist*
Batlin, Robert Alfred *editor*
Bauer, Michael *newspaper editor*
Bitterman, Mary Gayle Foley *broadcasting executive*
†Bronstein, Phil *executive editor*
Chapin, Dwight Allan *columnist, writer*
Chase, Marilyn *journalist*
Close, Sandy *journalist*
Curley, John Peter *sports editor*
Dickey, Glenn Ernest, Jr. *sports columnist*
Donnally, Patricia Broderick *newspaper editor*
Duscha, Julius Carl *journalist*
Eastwood, Susan *medical scientific editor*
Eaton, Jerry *television executive*
Falk, Steven B. *newspaper publishing executive*
Finefrock, James Alan *editor*
Freeman, Marshall *publishing executive*
Garchik, Leah Lieberman *journalist*
George, Donald Warner *online columnist and editor, freelance writer*
German, William *newspaper editor*
Graysmith, Robert *political cartoonist, author*
Heuring, Wayne Robert *newspaper journalist*
Hill, Greg *newspaper bureau chief*
Hochschild, Adam *writer, commentator, journalist*
Hoppe, Arthur Watterson *columnist*
Jenkins, Bruce *sportswriter*
Johns, Roy (Bud Johns) *publisher, author*
Junker, Howard Henry *periodical editor*
†Kelleher, Kevin Paul *journalist*
Kelly, Kevin *editor*
Klein, Jeffrey *editor-in-chief*
Klein, Marc S. *newspaper editor and publisher*
Lara, Adair *columnist, writer*
Lewis, Andrea Elen *editor*
Louie, David A. *television journalist*
Luckoff, Michael *broadcast executive*
Marino, Richard J. *publishing executive*
†Marshall, Carolyn D. *journalist, author*
Meyer, Thomas James *editorial cartoonist*
Minton, Torri *journalist*
Morgan, Michael Brewster *publishing company executive*
Nachman, Gerald Weil *columnist, critic, author*
Osterhaus, William Eric *television executive*
Oxarart, Frank *broadcast executive*
Pazour, Don *publishing executive*
Perlman, David *science editor, journalist*
Pimentel, Benjamin Impelido *journalist*
Reed, Robert Daniel *publisher*
Rice, Jonathan C. *retired educational television executive*
†Roberts, Jerry *newspaper editor*
Rogoff, Alice Elizabeth *writer, editor*
Rosenheim, Daniel Edward *journalist, television news director*
Rossetto, Louis *editor, publisher*
Rubenstein, Steven Paul *newspaper columnist*
Rusher, William Allen *writer, commentator*
Salvadore, Tony *broadcast executive*
Saunders, Debra J. *columnist*
Schrier, Eric *publisher*
Schwarz, Glenn Vernon *editor*
Shulgasser, Barbara *writer*
Sias, John B. *multi-media company executive, newspaper publisher, publishing executive*
Steinberg, Michael *music critic, educator*
Strupp, Joseph Paul *reporter*
Susskind, Teresa Gabriel *publisher*
Taylor, Belinda Carey *magazine editor, writer*
†Taylor, Wendy *editor*
Tobin, Shannon R. *media trade show producer*
Wade, Booker *television executive*
Watkins, Rufus Nathaniel *newspaper professional*
Wilner, Paul Andrew *journalist*
Wilson, Matthew Frederick *newspaper editor*
Winn, Steven Jay *critic*
Wolaner, Robin Peggy *internet and magazine publisher*
Yamamoto, Michael Toru *journalist*

San Jose
Brown, Barbara Mahone *communications educator, poet, consultant*
Carey, Peter Kevin *reporter*
†Ceppos, Jerome Merle *newspaper editor*
Doctor, Kenneth Jay *editor*
Elder, Robert Laurie *newspaper editor*
†Harris, Jay Terrence *newspaper editor*
Ingle, Robert D. *newspaper editor, newspaper executive*
Love, Amy Dundon *business executive, marketing and sales executive*
Migielicz, Geralyn *photojournalist*
Rubinfien, Elisabeth Sepora *journalist*

San Luis Obispo
Busselen, Steven Carroll *journalist, editor*
Campbell, Renoda Gisele *human resources administrator*

San Marcos
Branch, Robert Hardin *radio and television educator, broadcast executive*
Carroll, William *publisher*

San Mateo
Landry, Richard *publishing executive*
Motoyama, Catherine Tomoko *communications educator*

San Pablo
†Thompson, Sandra Leniese *publishing company executive, consultant*

San Rafael
Roffman, Howard *motion picture company executive*
Sansweet, Stephen Jay *journalist, author, marketing executive*

Santa Ana
Cheverton, Richard E. *newspaper editor*
Katz, Tonnie *newspaper editor*
Lawrence, David Norman *broadcasting executive, consultant*
Treshie, R. David *newspaper publishing executive*

Santa Barbara
Ackerman, Marshall *publishing company executive*
Brantingham, Barney *journalist, writer*
Brown, J'Amy Maroney *journalist, media relations consultant, investor*
Campbell, William Steen *publishing executive, writer, speaker*
Duntley, Linda Kathleen Day *network executive, artist, educator, author, educator, researcher*
Gibney, Frank Bray *publisher, editor, writer, foundation executive*
Segal, Helene Rose *editor*
Smith, Robert Nathaniel *broadcasting executive, lawyer*
Tapper, Joan Judith *magazine editor*

Santa Clarita
Adams, Jack *film company executive, screenwriter, producer, educator*

Santa Cruz
†Young, Gary Eugene *editor, poet*

Santa Monica
Baer, Walter S. *research executive*
†Derevlany, John *television writer/producer*
Halperin, Stuart *entertainment company executive*
Kirschenman, Karl Aaron *editor*
Mancuso, Frank G. *entertainment company executive*
Palmatier, Malcolm Arthur *editor, consultant*
Renetzky, Alvin *publisher*
Rozenfeld, Kim David *television company executive and producer*

Santa Rosa
Callum, Myles *magazine editor, writer*
Locher, Richard Earl *editorial cartoonist*
Person, Evert Bertil *newspaper and radio executive*
Schulz, Charles Monroe *cartoonist*
Swofford, Robert Lee *newspaper editor, journalist*

Sausalito
Brand, Stewart *editor, writer*
†Hansen, Charles Morton *genealogy editor, retired military officer*

Scotts Valley
Esposito, Joseph John *publishing company executive*

Seal Beach
Caesar, Vance Roy *newspaper executive*

Sebastopol
Barnes, Grant Alan *book publisher*

Sherman Oaks
Davidson, Bill (William John Davidson) *entertainment journalist, author*
Firestone, Roy *sportscaster*
Perth, Rod *network entertainment executive*
Wilcox, Robert Kalleen *journalist*
Yasnyi, Allan David *communications company executive*

Sierra Madre
Dewey, Donald William *magazine publisher, editor, writer*

Simi Valley
Killion, Jack Charles *newspaper columnist*

Solana Beach
Parker, John Brian *broadcast executive*

Sonoma
Beckmann, Jon Michael *publisher*
Hass, Robert Michael *editor*

South Pasadena
Mantell, Suzanne Ruth *editor*

Stanford
Andreopoulos, Spyros George *writer*
Baker, Patricia Ann *publishing executive*
Breitrose, Henry S. *communications educator*
Chaffee, Steven Henry *communication educator*
†Glasser, Theodore L. *journalism educator*
Maharidge, Dale Dimitro *journalist, educator*
Pope, Norris *publishing executive*
Risser, James Vaulx, Jr. *journalist, educator*
Roberts, Donald Frank, Jr. *communications educator*
Salisbury, David Francis *science and technology writer*

Stockton
Lovell, Emily Kalled *journalist*

Summerland
Cannon, Louis Simeon *journalist, author*
Hall, Lee Boaz *publishing company consultant, author*
Mitchell, Maurice B. *publishing executive, educator*

Tehachapi
Mitchell, Betty Jo *writer, publisher*

Toluca Lake
Ragan, Ann Talmadge *media and production consultant, actor*

Torrance
Adelsman, (Harriette) Jean *newspaper editor*

Tulare
Baradat, Raymond Alphonse *recording industry executive*

Ukiah
Toms, Michael Anthony *broadcast journalist, editor, writer, producer*

Universal City
Geffen, David *recording company executive, producer*
Katzenberg, Jeffrey *motion picture studio executive*
Paul, Charles S. *motion picture and television company executive*
Wasserman, Lew R. *film, recording and publishing company executive*

Van Nuys
Sludikoff, Stanley Robert *publisher, writer*

Ventura
Kirman, Charles Gary *photojournalist*
Moran, Rita Jane *music, drama, restaurant critic, travel writer*

Vista
Klungness, Elizabeth Jane *publisher, writer, retired accountant*

Walnut Creek
Borenstein, Daniel Asa *newspaper political editor*
Satz, Louis K. *publishing executive*
Trousdale, Stephen Richard *newspaper editor*

Watsonville
Condon, Thomas Joseph *editor, writer*

Westminster
Milligan, Ronald Edgar *journalist*

Wilton
Harrison, George Harry, III (Hank Harrison) *publishing executive, author*

Woodland Hills
Beasley, Larry *newspaper publishing executive*
DeWitt, Barbara Jane *journalist*
Kinkade, Kate *magazine editor, insurance executive*
Lund, Robert W. *newspaper editor*
Shuster, Fred Todd *journalist, commentator*

Yreka
Smith, Vin *sports editor, business owner, novelist*

COLORADO

Aspen
Hayes, Mary Eshbaugh *newspaper editor*

Aurora
Savage, Eric Wayne *multimedia developer*

Boulder
Birkenkamp, Dean Frederick *editor, publishing executive*
Bowers, John Waite *communication educator*
Gaines, James Russell *magazine editor, author*
Horii, Naomi *editor*
Rienner, Lynne Carol *publisher*

Cherry Hills Village
Stapleton, Katharine Hall (Katie Stapleton) *food broadcaster, author*

Colorado Springs
Barbre, Erwin S. *publishing company executive*
Mehlis, David Lee *publishing executive*
Nolan, Barry Hance *publishing company executive*
Ogrean, David William *sports executive*
†Smith, Steven Alan *newspaper editor*
Zapel, Arthur Lewis *book publishing executive*

Denver
Bates, James Robert *newspaper editor*
Bradley, Jeff(rey Mark) *arts critic*
Britton, Dennis A. *newspaper editor, newspaper executive*
†Brooke, James Bettner *news correspondent*
Burdick, Robert W. *newspaper editor*
Cubbison, Christopher Allen *editor*
Dallas, Sandra *correspondent, writer*
Dance, Francis Esburn Xavier *communication educator*
Drake, Sylvie (Jurras Drake) *theater critic*
Dubroff, Henry Allen *newspaper editor*
Engdahl, Todd Philip *newspaper editor*
Geiser, Elizabeth Able *publishing company executive*
Giffin, Glenn Orlando, II *music critic, writer, newspaper editor*
Hamblin, Kenneth Lorenzo *radio talk show host, columnist*
Haselbush, Ruth Beeler *retired newspaper editor*
†Mattiace, Peter *journalist*
McKibben, Ryan Timothy *newspaper executive*
Morgese, James N. *broadcast executive*
Odgen, Roger *television station executive*
Otto, Jean Hammond *journalist*
Rockford, Marv *television executive*
Rothman, Paul Alan *publisher*
Saltz, Howard Joel *newspaper editor*
Sardella, Edward Joseph *television news anchor*
Scudder, Richard B. *newspaper executive*
Simone, Robert M. *broadcast executive*
†Strutton, Larry D. *newspaper executive*
†Taylor, Scott David *broadcast executive*
Ulevich, Neal Hirsh *photojournalist*
Weinberg, Hedy Leah *journalist*
Zimmer, Larry William, Jr. *sports announcer*

Dillon
Follett, Robert John Richard *publisher*

Durango
Ballantine, Morley Cowles (Mrs. Arthur Atwood Ballantine) *newspaper editor*

Eastlake
Roberts, David Lowell *journalist*

Englewood
†Harbaugh, Teresa Gabriel *publisher, artist*
O'Brien, James B. *broadcast executive*

Evergreen
Dobbs, Gregory Allan *journalist*

Flagler
†Bredehoft, Thomas Evan *newspaper publisher*

Fort Collins
Christiansen, Norman Juhl *retired newspaper publisher*
Sons, Raymond William *journalist*

Georgetown
Stern, Mort(imer) P(hillip) *journalism and communications educator, academic administrator, consultant*

Granby
Johnson, William Potter *newspaper publisher*

Greeley
Camp, Ronald Stephen *educational technologist, television producer, educator*

Gunnison
Venturo, Frank Angelo *communications educator, college offical*

Idaho Springs
Kelley, Louanna Elaine *newspaper columnist, researcher*

Littleton
Udevitz, Norman *publishing executive*

Longmont
Davis, Donald Alan *author, news correspondent, lecturer*
Thompson, Michael James *news editor*

Morrison
Myers, Harry J., Jr. *retired publisher*

Niwot
Rinehart, Frederick Roberts *publisher*

Pueblo
Rawlings, Robert Hoag *newspaper publisher*

Silverton
Denious, Sharon Marie *publisher*

Sterling
Widhalm, Michele Ann *reporter, writer*

Strasburg
†Nesland, Matt J. *journalist, photojournalist*

Westminster
Wirkkala, John Lester *cable company executive*

CONNECTICUT

Bridgeport
Henderson, Albert Kossack *publishing company executive, dairy executive, consultant*
Walsh, Charles Hagen *columnist, writer*

Bristol
Adamle, Mike *sports commentator*
Aldridge, David *sports announcer*
Beil, Larry *sports announcer*
Berman, Chris *sports anchor*
Bernstein, Al *sports commentator*
Bernstein, Bonnie *reporter*
Cyphers, Steve *reporter*
Eisen, Rich *reporter*
Gammons, Peter *columnist*
Kernan, John William *auto racing reporter*
Kiper, Mel *sports commentator*
Kremer, Andrea *sports correspondent*
Malone, Mark *sports reporter*
Melrose, Barry James *sportscaster, former professional hockey team coach*
Morganti, Al *reporter*
Parsons, Benny *auto racing commentator*
Patrick, Bill *sports network host*
Patrick, Dan *sportscaster*
Patrick, Mike *sports commentator*
Pidto, Bill *sports network anchorman*
Punch, Jerry *sports reporter*
Raftery, Bill *basketball analyst*
Ravech, Karl *sports anchor, reporter*

McBride, Martha Gene Shultz editor, actress
McCormally, Kevin Jay editor
McDowell, Charles R. columnist, news analyst, lecturer
McElveen, Joseph James, Jr. author, journalist, public broadcasting executive
Mc Grory, Mary columnist
McLellan, Joseph Duncan critic, journalist
Means, Marianne political columnist
Mears, Walter Robert journalist
Melendy, David Russell broadcast journalist
Melton, Carol A(nne) media executive
Merry, Robert William publishing executive
Meszar, Frank publishing executive, former army officer
Meyer, Cord columnist
Meyer, Lawrence Robert journalist
Meyerson, Adam foundation executive
Miklaszewski, James Alan television news correspondent
Miller, Loye Wheat, Jr. journalist, corporate communications specialist
Miller, Mark Karl journalist
Millie, Harold Raymond editor
Mitchell, Andrea journalist
Moore, Miles David journalist
Morris, Daniel Kearns journalist
Moser, Donald Bruce magazine editor
Moss, Madison Scott editor
Murray, Alan Stewart publishing executive
Myers, Elissa Matulis publisher, association executive
Naylor, Brian news correspondent
Neal, Charlie sports broadcaster
Nelson, John Howard (Jack Howard Nelson) journalist
Nelson, Lars-Erik newspaperman
†Nesmith, Jeff journalist
Novak, Robert David Sanders newspaper columnist, television commentator
O'Brien, Timothy Andrew writer, journalist, lawyer
Ochs, Charlie broadcast executive
Orr, J. Scott newspaper correspondent
Ottaway, David Blackburne journalist
Padden, Preston broadcast executive
Page, Clarence E. newspaper columnist
Page, Tim music critic
Palmer, Stacy Ella periodical editor
Pancake, John newspaper editor
Paxson, Richard newspaper editor
Peirce, Neal R. journalist
Perkins, Lucian photographer
Peters, Charles Given, Jr. editor
Phlegar, Benjamin Focht retired magazine editor
Pincus, Walter Haskell editor
Plante, William Madden news correspondent
Porter, Barbara anchorwoman, writer, educator
Potter, Blair Burns editor
Potter, Deborah Ann news correspondent, educator
Prah, Pamela Marie journalist
Prina, L(ouis) Edgar journalist
Pruden, James Wesley newspaper editor, columnist
Putzel, Michael journalist, consultant, educator
Randall, Gene news correspondent, anchor
Rankin, Robert Arthur journalist
Raspberry, William James journalist
Richard, Paul art critic
Richburg, Keith Bernard journalist, foreign correspondent
Richman, Phyllis Chasanow newspaper critic
Ridgeway, James Fowler journalist
Roberts, Corinne Boggs "Cokie" (Cokie Roberts) correspondent, news analyst
Rogers, Warren Joseph, Jr. journalist
Rosen, Gerald Robert editor
Rosen, James Martin journalist
Rosenbloom, Morris Victor author, publisher, public relations executive, government official
Rosenfeld, Stephen Samuel newspaper editor
Ross, Robinette Davis publisher
Ross, Wendy Clucas newspaper editor, journalist
Rowan, Carl Thomas columnist
Rowson, Richard Cavanagh publisher
Rushnell, Squire Derrick television executive
Russert, Timothy John broadcast journalist, executive
Safire, William journalist, author
Salhani, Claude photojournalist
Sawyer, Forrest newscaster
Scheibel, Kenneth Maynard journalist
Schieffer, Bob broadcast journalist
Schiff, Margaret Scott newspaper publishing executive
Schram, Martin Jay journalist
Seidman, L(ewis) William television commentator, publisher
Senior, William Curtis editor
Serafin, Barry D. television news correspondent
Shales, Thomas William television and film critic, writer, journalist
Shanks, Hershel editor, writer
Shanks, Judith Weil editor
Shannon, Donald Hawkins retired newspaperman
Shapiro, Walter Elliot political columnist
Sharpe, Rochelle Phyllis journalist
Shaw, Bernard television journalist
Shaw, Gaylord newspaper executive
Shearer, Alan newspaper editor
Sheehan, Neil reporter, scholarly writer
Shenon, Philip journalist
Sherman, Charles Edwin broadcasting executive, educator
Shogan, Robert news correspondent
Shosky, John Edwin communications consultant, speechwriter
Shribman, David Marks editor
Sibolski, John Alfred, Jr. educational association executive
Sidey, Hugh Swanson correspondent
Siegel, Robert Charles broadcast journalist
Silver, Brian Quayle broadcast journalist, musician, educator
†Simons, Carol Lenore magazine editor
Slenker, Richard Dreyer, Jr. broadcast executive
Sloyan, Patrick Joseph journalist
Smith, D(aisy) Mullett publisher
Smith, Dean communications advisor, arbitrator
Smith, Mignon C. publishing executive
Smith, Stephen Grant journalist
Snow, Robert Anthony journalist
Snyder, James P. audio and digital television technician, videographer engineer, editor
Solomon, George M. newspaper editor
Sperling, Godfrey, Jr. journalist
Spoon, Alan Gary communications and publishing executive
Stamberg, Susan Levitt radio broadcaster
Stepp, Laura Sessions journalist
Stern, Carl Leonard former news correspondent, federal official
Sullivan, John Fox publisher
Suskind, Ronald Steven journalist
Sweet, Lynn D. journalist
Szulc, Tad journalist, commentator
Talbott, Strobe journalist
Terzian, Philip Henry journalist
Theis, Paul Anthony publishing executive
Thomas, Helen A. (Mrs. Douglas B. Cornell) newspaper bureau executive
Tiede, Tom Robert journalist
Tillery, Richard Lee television executive
Toedtman, James Smith newspaper editor, journalist
Tolchin, Martin newspaper reporter, author
Toledano, Ralph de columnist, author, poet
Tolson, John J. writer, editor
Totenberg, Nina journalist
Trafford, Abigail editor, writer, columnist
Turner, Douglas Laird writer, editor, columnist
Utley, Jon Basil entrepreneur, journalist
Valenti, Jack Joseph motion picture executive
†Van Susteren, Greta Conway news anchor, lawyer
Von Drehle, David James journalist
Walker, Ronald C. magazine publisher
Wallace, Christopher broadcast television correspondent
Walsh, Kenneth T. journalist
Walsh, Kenneth Thomas journalist
Warren, Albert publishing executive
Warren, Clay communication educator
Warren, Daniel Yeomans publishing executive
Warren, Paul Lansing publishing company executive
Watson, George Henry, Jr. journalist, broadcaster
†Weglarczyk, Bartosz journalist
Weinberger, Caspar Willard publishing executive, former secretary of defense
Weiner, Timothy Emlyn newspaper journalist
Weissman, Cheryl Ann editor
White, Robert M., II newspaper executive, editor, columnist
Wiessler, Judy Burton news editor
Wilkins, Amy P. publishing executive
Will, George Frederick editor, political columnist, news commentator
Williams, Earl Patrick, Jr. editor, freelance writer
Williams, James R., III broadcast executive
Williamson, Michael Stanley photojournalist, writer
Winter, Thomas Swanson editor, newspaper executive
Witcover, Jules Joseph newspaper columnist, author
Woodruff, Judy Carline broadcast journalist
Woodward, Robert Upshur newspaper reporter, writer
†Wright, Lisa Lyons media specialist
Yardley, Jonathan journalist, columnist
Young, Thomas Wade journalist
Zwadiuk, Oleh radio executive

FLORIDA

Apalachicola
Cronkite, Mary Sue Riddle journalist, fiction writer

Aventura
Babson, Irving K. publishing company executive
Cohen, Alex retired publisher

Boca Grande
Heffernan, John William retired journalist

Boca Raton
Frank, Stanley Donald publishing company executive
Johnson, Martin Allen publisher
Levine, Irving Raskin news commentator, university dean, author, lecturer
McQueen, Scott Robert broadcasting company executive

Boynton Beach
Klein, Bernard publishing company executive

Bradenton
McFarland, Richard Macklin retired journalist
White, Dale Andrew journalist

Clearwater
Kumar, Anita reporter
VanMeer, Mary Ann publisher, writer, researcher

Coconut Grove
Sweeny, Donna Bozzella writer, editor

Coral Gables
Stano, Carl Randolph (Randy Stano) newspaper editor, art director, educator

Daytona Beach
Davidson, Herbert M. (Tippen), Jr. newspaper owner
O'Reilly, Don reporter, writer, photographer
†Wanjohi, Elsie Wairimu communications educator

Delray Beach
Robinson, Brenda Kay editor, public relations professional
Salsberg, Arthur Philip publishing company executive
Walker, Fred Elmer broadcasting executive

Dover
Pearson, Walter Donald editor, columnist

Fort Lauderdale
Eisner, Will publishing company executive
Greenberger, Sheldon Lee newspaper advertising executive
Halpern, Steven Jay editor, newspaper columnist, freelance writer
Hartz, Deborah Sophia editor, critic
Maucker, Earl Robert newspaper editor, newspaper executive
Pettijohn, Fred Phillips retired newspaper executive, consultant
Reisinger, Sandra Sue columnist
Schulte, Frederick James newpaper editor
Soeteber, Ellen journalist, newspaper editor
Williamson, William Paul, Jr. journalist

Fort Myers
Barbour, William Rinehart, Jr. retired book publisher
Gustafson, Jim broadcast executive
Jacobi, Fredrick Thomas newspaper publisher

Fort Pierce
Gawel, Maureen Saltzer newspaper executive

Gainesville
Barber, Charles Edward newspaper executive, journalist
Bedell, George Chester retired publisher, educator, priest
Danforth, Glenn R. magazine publisher
Henson, (Betty) Ann media specialist, educator
Hollien, Harry Francis speech and communications scientist, educator
Kaplan, John photojournalist, consultant, educator
Maple, Marilyn Jean educational media coordinator

Hialeah
Hernandez, Roland broadcast executive

Hollywood
Anger, Paul newspaper editor
Fell, Frederick Victor publisher
Korngold, Alvin Leonard broadcasting company executive
Ohms, Cosmo recording and production company executive

Homestead
Crouse, John Oliver, II journalist, publisher

Indian Harbor Beach
Covault, Craig editor

Indian Rocks Beach
†Kephart, Robert Dennis publisher

Jacksonville
Brown, Lloyd Harcourt, Jr. newspaper editor
†Cannon, Carl N. publisher
Hartmann, Frederick William newspaper editor
Loomis, Henry former broadcasting company executive, former government official
Vincent, Norman Fuller broadcasting executive
Walters, John Sherwood retired newspaperman

Jupiter
Anderson, Thomas Jefferson publisher, rancher, public speaker, syndicated columnist
Barhyte, Donald James retired newspaper executive

Key Biscayne
Smith, Harrison Harvey journalism consultant

Kissimmee
†Cody, Aldus Morrill journalist, retired editor, typographer

Lake Mary
Strang, Stephen Edward magazine editor, publisher

Lake Worth
Pecker, David J. magazine publishing company executive

Lakeland
Perez, Louis Michael newspaper editor

Lantana
Coz, Steve editor-in-chief, publishing executive

Longboat Key
Estrin, Richard William retired newspaper editor, real estate broker

Longwood
Argirion, Michael editor
Chernak, Jerald Lee television executive

Lutz
Kolb, Richard Maurice sports writer, sportscaster

Maitland
Heller, Ira Louis research executive
Prizer, Edward Levis retired magazine publisher

Marco Island
Figge, Frederick Henry, Jr. retired publishing executive
Wheeler, Warren G(age), Jr. retired publishing executive

Melbourne
Krieger, Robert Edward publisher

Melrose
Burt, Alvin Victor, Jr. journalist

Miami
Balmaseda, Liz columnist
Barry, Dave columnist, author
Black, Creed Carter newspaper executive
Chapman, Alvah Herman, Jr. newspaper executive
Clarke, Jay Marion editor, author
Dickey, Arden newspaper publishing executive
Fichtner, Margaria journalist
Foster, Kathryn Warner newspaper editor
Goldberg, Bernard R. news correspondent
Hampton, John Lewis retired newspaper editor
Harris, Douglas Clay newspaper executive
Huber, Michael Frederick journalist, educator
Ibarguen, Alberto newspaper executive
Lawrence, David, Jr. journalist, early childhood development advocate
Lewis, John Milton cable television company executive
Miller, Gene Edward newspaper reporter and editor
Morin, James Corcoran editorial cartoonist
Muir, Helen journalist, author
Natoli, Joe newspaper publishing executive
Pope, John Edwin, III newspaper sports editor
Rodriguez, Ray broadcast executive
Russell, James Webster, Jr. newspaper editor, columnist
Sanchez, Robert Francis journalist
Savage, James Francis editor
Smiley, Logan Henry journalist, public concern consultant
Steinback, Robert Lamont newspaper columnist
Terilli, Samuel A., Jr. newspaper publishing executive
Wax, William Edward photojournalist
Wickstrom, Karl Youngert publishing company executive

Miami Beach
Blakley, John Clyde telecommunications consultant
Perkel, Robert Simon photojournalist, educator

Mount Dora
Trussell, Charles Tait columnist

Mulberry
Mueller, Michael Lee editor

Naples
†Breitenstein, David E. newswriter
Clapp, Roger Howland retired newspaper executive
Clarke, John Patrick retired newspaper publisher
Cobb, Brian Eric broadcasting executive
Hedberg, Paul Clifford broadcasting executive
Norins, Leslie Carl publisher
Taishoff, Lawrence Bruce publishing company executive
Wodlinger, Mark Louis broadcast executive
Wyant, Corbin A. newspaper publisher

North Miami
Kopenhaver, Lillian Lodge journalism educator

North Palm Beach
Edwards, William James broadcasting executive
Lavine, Alan columnist, writer

Ocala
Stock, Stephen Michael broadcast journalist

Opa Locka
Rushin, Jerry broadcast executive

Orlando
Boyar, Jay Mitchell film critic
Dunn, William Bruna, III journalist
Golinkin, Webster Fowler media executive
Grant, Joanne Cummings film company executive
Guest, Larry Samuel newspaper columnist
Healy, Jane Elizabeth newspaper editor
Maupin, Elizabeth Thatcher theater critic
O'Keefe, Maurice Timothy editor, photographer
Puerner, John newspaper publishing executive
Quinn, Jane journalist
Reese, Charles Edgar columnist
Wall, Arthur Edward Patrick editor

Osprey
Allen, George Howard publishing management consultant

Palm Beach
Lickle, William Cauffiel publisher
Monath, Norman publishing company executive
Pryor, Hubert editor, writer
Roberts, Margaret Harold editor, publisher
Rukeyser, M.S., Jr. television consultant, writer

Palm City
Wirsig, Woodrow magazine editor, trade organization executive, business executive

Penney Farms
Meyer, Marion M. editorial consultant

Pensacola
Bowden, Jesse Earle newspaper editor, author, cartoonist, journalism educator
Cox, Amie C. publisher

Pompano Beach
Legler, Bob publishing company executive
Noland, Josh recording company executive
Roen, Sheldon R. publisher, psychologist
Thaung journalist

Port Saint Lucie
Sommers, Robert Thomas editor, publisher, author

Saint Augustine
†Baker, Harold Wayne retired news editor, anchor
Nolan, Joseph Thomas journalism educator, communications consultant
Robbins, Rima journalist, public relations consultant

Saint Petersburg
Barnes, Andrew Earl newspaper editor
Belich, John Patrick, Sr. journalist
Benbow, Charles Clarence retired writer, critic
Buchan, Russell Paul publisher, gas company executive, entrepreneur
Corty, Andrew P. publishing executive
Foley, Michael Francis newspaper executive
†French, Thomas journalist
Haiman, Robert James newspaper editor, journalism educator, media consultant
Hooker, Robert Wright journalist
Jenkins, Robert Norman newswriter, editor
Johnson, Edna Ruth editor
Liebert, Larry Steven journalist
Martin, Susan Taylor newspaper editor
Naughton, James Martin journalist
Patterson, Eugene Corbett retired editor, publisher
Pittman, Robert Turner retired newspaper editor
Roales, Judith newspaper publisher
Squires, Patricia Eileen Coleman freelance journalist, writer
Tash, Paul Clifford newspaper editor

Santa Rosa Beach
Gilmore, Beverly J retired journalist, gallery owner

Sarasota
Hackl, Alphons J. publisher
†Jackson, Jody journalist
Loomis, Wesley Horace, III former publishing company executive
Marino, Eugene Louis publishing company executive
Matthews, Lynn O. publisher

Matz, Kenneth H., Jr. *retired newscaster*
†McFarlin, Diane Hooten *newspaper editor*
North, Marjorie Mary *columnist*
Proffitt, Waldo, Jr. *newspaper editor*
Wetstone, Janet Meyerson *designer, journalist*
Wilson, Kenneth Jay *writer*

Steinhatchee
Grubbs, Elven Judson *retired newspaper publisher*

Stuart
Erlick, Everett Howard *broadcasting company executive*

Sun City Center
Fleischman, Sol Joseph, Sr. *retired television broadcasting executive*

Tallahassee
Dadisman, Joseph Carrol *newspaper executive*
Holcomb, Terri Lynn *computer graphic consultant*
McBride, Donna Jannean *publisher*
Morgan, Lucy Ware *journalist*
Raymond, Leland Francis *editor, desktop publisher*
Roberts, Michael Joseph *journalist*

Tampa
Ashe, Reid *publishing executive*
Benjamin, Robert Spiers *foreign correspondent, writer, publicist*
Friedlander, Edward Jay *journalism educator*
Gossett, Forrest Scott *publishing executive*
Locker, Raymond Duncan *editor*
Major, Jim *broadcasting executive*
Manion, Beatrice (B.C. Manion) *journalist*
†Miller, Randy E. *journalism educator, writer*
Roberts, Edwin Albert, Jr. *newspaper editor, journalist*
Ruth, Daniel John *journalist*
Shevy, Allen Earl, Jr. *publishing executive*
Smith, W. Gordon *magazine editor*
Snyder, James Robert *professional sports executive*
Thelen, Gil *newspaper editor*
Tully, Darrow *newspaper publisher*
White, Nancy G. *journalism educator*
Witwer, Bruce *newspaper editor*

Tarpon Springs
Parks, Karl Eaton, Jr. *publisher*

Venice
Corrigan, William Thomas *retired broadcast news executive*

Vero Beach
Parkyn, John William *editor, writer*

Wellington
Kravetz, Cheryl DuPree *reporter*

West Palm Beach
Fairbanks, Richard Monroe *broadcasting company executive*
O'Hara, Thomas Patrick *managing editor*
Passy, Charles *arts critic*
Sears, Edward Milner, Jr. *newspaper editor*
Wright, Donald Conway *editorial cartoonist*

Weston
Randolph, Jennings, Jr. (Jay Randolph) *sportscaster*

GEORGIA

Alpharetta
Dovey, Laurie Lee *magazine editor, writer, photographer*

Athens
Agee, Warren Kendall *journalism educator*
Corey, Stephen Dale *magazine editor, poet, educator*
Feldman, Edmund Burke *art critic*
Fink, Conrad Charles *journalism educator, communications consultant*
Hester, Albert Lee *retired journalism educator*
Holder, Howard Randolph, Sr. *broadcasting company executive*
Hynds, Ernest *journalism educator*

Atlanta
†Allen, Natalie *cable news anchor*
Bisher, James Furman *journalist, author*
Boyd, Kenneth Wade *publishing company executive, consultant*
Brady, Kimberly Ann *editorial director*
Burgess, Chester Francis, III *journalist, television producer*
Burke, William A. *broadcast executive*
Campbell, Colin McLeod *journalist*
Chambers, Anne Cox *newspaper executive, former diplomat*
†Chen, Joie *cable news anchor*
Collier, Diana Gordon *publishing executive*
Connelly, Terrence John, Sr. *television station executive*
†Cossack, Roger *newscaster*
Davis, Sterling Evan *television executive*
Dobson, Bridget McColl Hursley *television executive and writer*
Dotson, Robert Charles *news correspondent*
Easterly, David Eugene *communications executive*
Ellis, Elmo Israel *broadcast executive, consultant, columnist*
†Fortin, Judy *cable news anchor*
Furnad, V. R. (Bob Furnad) *television news executive*
Gilmer, Harry Wesley *publishing executive, educator*
Grogan, Paula Cataldi *newspaper editor*
†Grubic, Adrianne *journalist*
†Hall, Rebekah A. *journalist, editor*
Harris, Henry Wood *cable television executive*
Henderson, Charles William *health and medical publishing executive*
Hulbert, Daniel Joyce *theater critic, entertainment writer*
Johnson, Tom *broadcasting executive*
Johnson, W. Thomas, Jr. *media executive*
Johnson, Wyatt Thomas, Jr. (Tom Johnson) *cable news executive*
Jones, J. Kenley *journalist*
Kanov, Mark *radio station executive*
†Kaplan, Richard N. *broadcast executive, cable*
Kennedy, James C. *publishing and media executive*
†Kintzel, Roger *publisher*
Kloer, Philip Baldwin *television critic*
Landess, Mike (Malcolm Lee Landess, III) *television news anchorman*
Martin, Ron *newspaper editor-in-chief*
McHugh, Gene *television executive*
Mequirk, Terry *broadcast executive*
Merdek, Andrew Austin *publishing/media executive, lawyer*
Neil, Robert F. *broadcast executive*
Nelson, Brian James *broadcast journalist*
Ottley, John K. *publisher*
Phillips, John David *media company executive*
Polk, James Ray *journalist*
Puckett, Susan *newspaper editor*
†Roberts, Chuck *cable news anchor*
Rosenfeld, Arnold Solomon *newspaper editor*
Roth, Teresa Ann *broadcast executive*
Sansone, Victor *broadcast executive*
†Savidge, Martin *cable news anchor*
Schwartz, William A(llen) *broadcasting and cable executive*
Sibley, Celestine (Mrs. John C. Strong) *columnist, reporter*
Sink, John Davis *leadership consultant, scientist*
Smith, Jay *publishing executive*
Stewart, Michael McFadden *professional speaker*
Tarver, Jackson Williams *newspaper executive*
Teepen, Thomas Henry *newspaper editor, journalist*
Tharpe, Frazier Eugene *journalist*
Thomas, Barbara Ann *record company executive*
Toner, Michael F. *journalist*
Tucker, Cynthia Anne *journalist*
Tullis, Bill *broadcasting company executive, sound engineer, music producer*
Turner, Ted (Robert Edward Turner) *television executive*
Walden, Philip Michael *recording company executive, publishing company executive*
Walker, Robert *broadcast executive*
Walker, John *newspaper editor*
Walton, Jim *sports news network executive*
Ward, Janet Lynn *magazine editor, sports wire reporter*
†Waters, Lou *anchorman, correspondent*
†White, Jacinta Victoria *book distribution company owner*
Whitt, Richard Ernest *reporter*

Augusta
†Morris, William Shivers, III *newspaper executive*

Blackshear
Vaughan, Mittie Kathleen *journalist*

Buford
Garwood, Robert Ashley, Jr. *network communications analyst*

Clarkesville
Dowden, Thomas Clark *telecommunication executive*

Clarkston
Love, Nancy Lorene *communication and political strategist, educator*
Wieck, Stewart Douglas *publisher, writer*

Dahlonega
Meyer, Sylvan Hugh *editor, magazine executive, author*

Decatur
Knight, Walker Leigh *editor, publisher, clergyman*
Shaw, Jeanne Osborne *editor, poet*
†Veach, Daniel Lee *editor*

Fayetteville
Turnipseed, Barnwell Rhett, III *journalist, public relations consultant*

Jekyll Island
McKinley, Douglas Webster (Webb McKinley) *consultant*

Macon
Savage, Randall Ernest *journalist*

Marietta
Dunwoody, Kenneth Reed *magazine and book editor*
Hays, Robert William *communications consultant, educator, writer*
Michel, Elizabeth Cheney *communications strategist, educator, consultant*

Newnan
Skinner, Walter Winston *journalist, minister*

Norcross
Lyne, James Coleman, Jr. *magazine editor, magazine writer*

Oxford
Sitton, Claude Fox *newspaper editor*

Peachtree City
Yother, Michele *publisher*

Savannah
†Edeawo, Gale Paula *publishing company executive, writer*

Stone Mountain
Speed, Billie Cheney (Mrs. Thomas S. Speed) *retired editor, journalist*

HAWAII

Aiea
Walker, Welmon, Jr. (Rusty Walker) *publisher, consultant*

Ewa Beach
Lewis, Mary Jane *communication specialist, video producer, writer*

Haleiwa
Austen, Shelli Oetter *radio news anchor, consultant*

Honolulu
Baker, Kent Alfred *broadcasting company executive*
Flanagan, John Michael *editor, publisher*
†Gatti, Jim *editor*
Jellinek, Roger *editor*
Kamemoto, Garett Hiroshi *reporter*
Kim, Joung-Im *communication educator, consultant*
Krauss, Bob *newspaper columnist, author*
Rexner, Romulus *publishing executive*
Simonds, John Edward *newspaper editor*
Smyser, Adam Albert *newspaper editor*
Sparks, Robert William *retired publishing executive*
Tehranian, Majid *political economy and communications educator*
Twigg-Smith, Thurston *newspaper publisher*
Varner, Helen *communication educator*

Kailua
Bone, Robert William *writer, photojournalist*

Kailua Kona
Wageman, Virginia Farley *editor, writer*

Kaneohe
McGlaughlin, Thomas Howard *publisher, retired naval officer*

Pahoa
Lewis, Jack (Cecil Paul Lewis) *publishing executive, editor*

Wailuku
Isbell, Alan Gregory *editor, writer, publisher*

IDAHO

Boise
†Boren, Robert Reed *communication educator*

Coeur D Alene
†Rosdahl, Nils *educator*

Idaho Falls
Harris, Darryl Wayne *publishing executive*

Moscow
Anderson, Clifton Einar *writer, communications consultant*

ILLINOIS

Arlington Heights
Baumann, Daniel E. *newspaper executive*
Catrambone, Kathy *journalist*
Lampinen, John A. *newspaper editor*
Paddock, Robert Young *retired publisher*
Ray, Douglas Kent *newspaper executive*
Shuman, Nicholas Roman *journalist, educator*

Barrington
Bash, Philip Edwin *publishing executive*

Belleville
Berkley, Gary Lee *newspaper publisher*

Bloomingdale
Richard, David Dean *publishing executive*

Bloomington
Merwin, Davis Underwood *newspaper executive*

Brookfield
Hansen, Donald Marty *journalist, accountant*

Buffalo Grove
Dimond, Robert Edward *publisher*

Burr Ridge
Finnegan, James John, Jr. *editor, publisher*
Sund, Jeffrey Owen *publishing company executive*

Byron
Oneil, Susan Jean *media specialist*

Carbondale
Jaehnig, Walter Bruno, Jr. *communications educator*

Carol Stream
Gaukel, Erich John *magazine editor*
Myra, Harold Lawrence *publisher*
Shorney, George Herbert *publishing executive*
Taylor, Kenneth Nathaniel *publishing executive, author*

Champaign
Christians, Clifford Glenn *communications educator*
Hays, Robert Glenn *journalism educator*
†Kroner, Fred L. *journalist*
McCulloh, Judith Marie *editor*
Meyer, August Christopher, Jr. *broadcasting company executive, lawyer*
Watts, Robert Allan *publisher, lawyer*
Wentworth, Richard Leigh *editor*

Charleston
Kaufman, Susan Jane *journalist, educator*

Chicago
Agema, Gerald Walton *broadcasting company executive*
Ahern, Joseph A. *television station executive*
Allen, Richard Blose *legal editor, lawyer*
Anderson, Jon Stephen *newswriter*
Artner, Alan Gustav *art critic, journalist*
Baltic, Scott Michael *magazine editor*
Barr, Emily *television station executive*
Bell, Clark Wayne *business editor, educator*
Bennett, Lerone, Jr. *magazine editor, author*
Boers, Terry John *sportswriter, radio and television personality*
Bratcher, Juanita *journalist*
Brewster, Gregory Bush *telecommunications educator*
Brotman, Barbara Louise *columnist, writer*
Brumback, Charles Tiedtke *retired newspaper executive*
Brummel, Mark Joseph *magazine editor*
Cahill, Kathleen *broadcast executive*
Callaway, Karen A(lice) *journalist*
Camper, John Jacob *press secretary*
Cappo, Joseph C. *publisher*
Christiansen, Richard Dean *newspaper editor*
Cohodes, Eli Aaron *publisher*
Connors, Dorsey *television and radio commentator, newspaper columnist*
Cooper, Ilene Linda *magazine editor, author*
Cross, Robert Clark *journalist*
Curwen, Randall William *journalist, editor*
Darby, Edwin Wheeler *retired newspaper financial columnist*
Davis, Jack Wayne, Jr. *internet publisher*
DeBat, Donald Joseph *media consultant, columnist*
Dold, Robert Bruce *journalist*
Donovan, Dianne Francys *journalist*
Dyson, Mary *broadcast executive*
Ebert, Roger Joseph *film critic*
Epstein, David M. *publishing executive*
Essex, Joseph Michael *visual communication planner*
Evans, Mariwyn *periodical editor*
Everhart, Bruce *radio station executive*
Fair, Hudson Randolph *recording company executive*
Feder, Robert *television and radio columnist*
Fetridge, Clark Worthington *publisher*
Field, Marshall *business executive*
Flock, Jeffrey Charles *news bureau chief*
Fornek, Scott Patrick *journalist*
Frankson-Kendrick, Sarah Jane *publisher*
Fuller, Jack William *writer, publishing executive*
Gaines, William Chester *journalist*
Gilbert, Vincent Newton *publisher*
Goldsborough, Robert Gerald *publishing executive, author*
Grant, Dennis *newspaper publishing executive*
Greene, Robert Bernard, Jr. (Bob Greene) *broadcast television correspondent, columnist, author*
Gruber, William Paul *journalist*
Haddix, Carol Ann Mighton *journalist*
Hallinan, Joseph Thomas *journalist, correspondent*
Harvey, Paul *news commentator, author, columnist*
Hefner, Christie Ann *publishing and marketing executive*
Hengstler, Gary Ardell *publisher, editor, lawyer*
Higgins, Jack *editorial cartoonist*
Huntley, Robert Stephen *newspaper editor*
Husar, John Paul *newspaper columnist, television panelist, broadcaster*
Jones, Linda *communications educator*
Judge, Bernard Martin *editor, publisher*
Kaiserlian, Penelope Jane *publishing company executive*
†Kelly, Curtis Hartt *publishing executive*
Kisor, Henry Du Bois *newspaper editor, critic, columnist*
Klaviter, Helen Lothrop *magazine editor*
Koester, Robert Gregg *record company executive*
Koppes, Steven Nelson *science writer, editor*
Kotulak, Ronald *newspaper science writer*
Kramer, Weezie Crawford *broadcast executive*
Krueger, Bonnie Lee *editor, writer*
Kupcinet, Irv *columnist*
Kyle, Robert Campbell, II *publishing executive*
Landers, Ann (Mrs. Esther P. Lederer) *columnist*
Lazarus, George Milton *newspaper columnist*
†Leckey, Andrew A. *financial columnist*
Leff, Donna Rosene *journalism educator*
Lewis, Sylvia Gail *journalist*
Lindberg, Richard Carl *editor, author, historian*
Lipinski, Ann Marie *newspaper editor*
Loesch, Katharine Taylor (Mrs. John George Loesch) *communication and theatre educator*
Longworth, Richard Cole *journalist*
Lundberg, George David, II *medical editor in chief, pathologist*
Lyon, Jeffrey *journalist, author*
Lythcott, Marcia A. *newspaper editor*
Madigan, John William *publishing executive*
Margolis, Rob *publisher*
McCarron, John Francis *columnist*
McDaniel, Charles-Gene *journalism educator, writer*
McDougal, Alfred Leroy *publishing executive*
McNally, Andrew, IV *publishing executive*
Meade, Robin Michele *news anchor, reporter*
Migala, Lucyna Jozefa *broadcast journalist, arts administrator, radio station executive*
Mironovich, Alex *publisher*
Nault, William Henry *publishing executive*
Neal, Steven George *journalist*
Needleman, Barbara *newspaper executive*
Neubauer, Charles Frederick *investigative reporter*
O'Dell, James E. *newspaper publishing executive*
O'Loughlin, Donna *editor periodical*
Pallasch, Abdon Maxim, III *journalist*
Parisi, Joseph (Anthony) *magazine editor, writer-consultant, educator*
Peerman, Dean Gordon *magazine editor*
Peres, Judith May *journalist*
Phelps, Richard William *journal editor, consultant*
Philipson, Morris *university press director*
Pierson, Don *sports columnist*
Pilchen, Ira A. *editor*
Pitt, Judson Hamilton *publisher, author*
Plotnick, Harvey Barry *publishing executive*
Plotnik, Arthur *author, editorial consultant*
Pope, Kerig Rodgers *magazine executive*
Primm, Earl Russell, III *publishing executive*
Pruter, Robert Douglas *editor*
Quaal, Ward Louis *broadcast executive*
Quade, Victoria Catherine *editor, writer, playwright, producer*
Radler, Franklin David *publishing holding company executive*
Reedy, Jerry Edward *editor, writer*
Rice, Linda Johnson *publishing executive*
Rice, William Edward *newspaper columnist*
Richardson, Julieanna Lynn *cable television executive*
Roeper, Richard *columnist*
Rosenbaum, Jonathan Daniel *film critic*
Rosenberg, Sheli *broadcast executive*
Rosenbloom, Steve *sportswriter*
Ross, Michael *publishing executive*
Ross, Michael Neil *publishing executive*
†Roth, Robert A. *newspaper executive*
Rynkiewicz, Stephen Michael *journalist*
Sabin, Neal *broadcast executive*
Scanlan, Thomas Cleary *publishing executive, editor*
Schmeltzer, John Charles *financial writer*
Schultz, Paul Neal *electronic publishing executive*
Shere, Dennis *publishing executive*
Sherman, Joseph J. *newspaper publishing executive*
Smith, Sam Pritzker *columnist, author*
Sneed, Michael (Michele) *columnist*
Stark, Henry *technology educator*

Stone, Steven Michael *sports announcer, former baseball player*
Tyner, Howard A. *publishing executive, newspaper editor, journalist*
Varro, Barbara Joan *editor*
von Rhein, John Richard *music critic, editor*
Vukas, Ronald *publishing executive*
Wade, Nigel *editor in chief*
Wasiolek, Edward *literary critic, language and literature educator*
Weinberg, Lila Shaffer *writer, editor*
Weintraub, Joseph Barton *publishing executive*
Wells, Joel Freeman *editor, author*
Wier, Patricia Ann *publishing executive, consultant*
Wolfe, Sheila A. *journalist*
Wycliff, Noel Don *journalist, newspaper editor*
Youngman, Owen Ralph *newspaper executive*
Zaslow, Jeffrey Lloyd *syndicated columnist*
Zekman, Pamela Lois (Mrs. Fredric Soll) *reporter*
Zorn, Eric John *newspaper columnist*

Crystal Lake
Keller, William Francis *publishing consultant*

Dekalb
Vance Siebrasse, Kathy Ann *newspaper publishing executive*

Des Plaines
Clapper, Marie Anne *magazine publisher*
Decker, William Alexander *editor*
Grahn, Barbara Ascher *publisher*
Hlavacek, Roy George *publishing executive, magazine editor*

Dixon
Shaw, Thomas Douglas *newspaper executive*

Edwardsville
Gauen, Patrick Emil *newspaper correspondent*

Elmhurst
Pruter, Margaret Franson *editor*

Evanston
Borcover, Alfred Seymour *journalist*
Downing, Joan Forman *editor*
Felknor, Bruce Lester *editorial consultant, writer*
Galvin, Kathleen Malone *communications educator*
Hannan, Bradley *educational publishing consultant and executive*
Jacobs, Norman Joseph *publishing company executive*
Jones, Robert Russell *magazine editor*
Kuenster, John Joseph *magazine editor*
Larson, Roy *journalist, publisher*
McCleary, Elliott Harold *magazine editor*
Otwell, Ralph Maurice *retired newspaper editor*
Peck, Abraham *editor, writer, educator, magazine consultant*
Protess, David Lewis *journalism educator*
Schwarzlose, Richard Allen *journalism educator*
Wagner, Durrett Former publisher, *picture service executive*
Wefler, Wilson Daniel *publisher, editor, management consultant*
Whitaker, Charles F. *journalism educator*
White, Willmon Lee *magazine editor*
†Wilhelm, Frank Leo *publisher, writer*
Wills, Garry *journalist, educator*
Ziomek, Jonathan S. *journalist, educator*

Genoa
Brown, Katherine Jane *editor, retired, chamber of commerce executive*

Glen Ellyn
Kirkpatrick, Clayton *former newspaper executive*
Murphy, Jerome Eugene *communications consultant*

Glenview
Biedron, Theodore John *newspaper advertising executive*
Mabley, Jack *newspaper columnist, communications consultant*
Witting, Christian James, Jr. (Chris Witting) *broadcast executive*

Greenville
Flowers, Creole Duane *publishing executive*

Highland Park
Johnson, Curtis Lee *publisher, editor, writer*
Pattis, S. William *publisher*
Rutenberg-Rosenberg, Sharon Leslie *retired journalist*

Hinsdale
Dussman, Judith Ann *publishing executive*

Hoffman Estates
†Geller, Bruce *music publisher, composer*

Jerseyville
Graham, Lester Lynn *radio journalist*

Kenilworth
Cook, Stanton R. *media company executive*

La Grange
Mermigas, Diane Cynthia Stefanos *business journalist*

Lake Forest
Barnes, Sandra Henley *publishing company executive*
Schulze, Franz, Jr. *art critic, educator*

Libertyville
True, Raymond Stephen *writer, editor, analyst, consultant*

Lincolnwood
Krejcsi, Cynthia Ann *textbook editor*
Pattis, Mark R. *publishing company executive*

Macomb
McLean, Deckle *journalism educator*

Mount Vernon
Withers, W. Russell, Jr. *broadcast executive*

Mount Zion
Burns, B. Thomas *broadcasting executive*

Mundelein
Terris, William *publishing executive*

Naperville
†Moore, Brian Michael *newspaper copy editor, journalist*
Raccah, Dominique Marcelle *publisher*
Spiotta, Raymond Herman *editor*

Normal
Gottschalk, Keith Edward *journalist*

Northbrook
Elleman, Barbara *editor*
Klemens, Thomas Lloyd *editor*
Pesmen, Sandra (Mrs. Harold William Pesmen) *editor*
Snader, Jack Ross *publishing company executive*

Oak Brook
Lane, James Frederick, IV *publishing executive*

Oak Park
Forst, Edmund Charles, Jr. *communications educator, consultant*

Park Ridge
Johnson, Kenneth Stuart *publisher, printer*

Pekin
Dancey, Charles Lohman *newspaper executive*

Peoria
Colvin, Connie Lou *administrative specialist, author*
McConnell, John Thomas *newspaper executive, publisher*
Murphy, Sharon Margaret *educator*

Peru
Carus, Andre Wolfgang *educational publishing firm executive*
Carus, Milton Blouke *publisher children's periodicals*

Plainfield
Cook, Bruce Lawrence *research analyst, educator*
Diercks, Eileen Kay *educational media coordinator, elementary school educator*

Prospect Heights
Robinson, Martin (Marty) *television and radio broadcaster, media consultant*

Quincy
Moritz, Betty Ann *retired editor*

River Forest
†Zimbrakos, Paul William *editor*

Riverside
Gwinn, Robert P. *publishing executive*

Riverwoods
Smith, Carole Dianne *editor, writer, product developer*

Rockford
Fleming, Thomas J. *editor, publishing executive*
Green, Lisa R. *journalist*

Rolling Meadows
Miles, Frank Charles *retired newspaper executive*

Saint Charles
Vance, Leslie Edwin *multimedia technologist*

Schaumburg
Edmunds, Jane Clara *communications consultant*
Schlossberg, Howard Barry *editor, freelance writer*

Skokie
Manos, John *editor-in-chief*
Wasik, John Francis *editor, writer, publisher*

Springfield
Harper, William Wayne *broadcast executive*
Pistorius, Alvin William, Jr. (Bill Miller) *communications educator*

Sullivan
Hagen, Daniel Urban *editor, writer*

Tinley Park
Flanagan, John F. *publishing executive*

Urbana
Dash, Leon DeCosta, Jr. *journalist*

West Chicago
Franzen, Janice Marguerite Gosnell *magazine editor*

Wheaton
Hollingsworth, Pierce *publishing executive*
Taylor, Mark Douglas *publishing executive*

Wheeling
Kuennen, Thomas Gerard *journalist*

Wilmette
Klein, Robert Edward *publishing company executive, educator*
Markus, Robert Michael *journalist, retired*

INDIANA

Anderson
Nuwer, Henry Joseph (Hank Nuwer) *journalist, educator*

Angola
Bevington, Cindy *reporter*

Bloomington
Gough, Pauline Bjerke *magazine editor*
Jacobi, Peter Paul *journalism educator, author*
Schroeder, Judith Lois *editor, communications executive*
Schurz, Scott Clark *journalist, publisher*
Weaver, David Hugh *journalism educator, communications researcher*
Wilhoit, G. Cleveland *journalism educator*

Cambridge City
Slonaker, Mary Joanna King *columnist*

Elkhart
Schreiber, David Raymond *reporter*

Evansville
Mathews, Walter Garret *columnist*
Ryder, Thomas Michael *newspaper editor*

Fort Wayne
†Inskeep, Richard Glenn *publishing executive*
Jarosh, Andrew T. *journalist*
Klugman, Stephan Craig *newspaper editor*
Lockwood, Robert Philip *publishing executive*
Pellegrene, Thomas James, Jr. *editor, researcher*
Sandeson, William Seymour *cartoonist*
†Skufca, Sherry Lee *newspaper editor*

Greenwood
Jacobs, Harvey Collins *newspaper editor, writer*

Indianapolis
Birky, Nathan Dale *publishing company executive*
Borman, Laurie D. *magazine editor-in-chief*
†Brown, Daniel Stewart, Jr. *communications educator, university official*
Caldwell, Howard Clay *retired broadcast journalist, writer*
Caperton, Albert Franklin *newspaper editor*
Chase, Alyssa Ann *editor*
Coffey, Charles Moore *communication research professional, writer*
Cohen, Gabriel Murrel *editor, publisher*
Comiskey, Nancy *newspaper editor*
†Duncan, Dale A. *publishing executive*
Fleming, Marcella *journalist*
Forliti, Amy Marie *reporter*
Garmel, Marion Bess Simon *journalist*
Gaus, David Sheerin *publisher*
Greenberg, Stephen S. *publishing executive*
Griggs, Ruth Marie *retired journalism educator, writer, publications consultant*
Lyst, John Henry *newspaper editor*
McKeand, Patrick Joseph *newspaper publisher, educator*
Nancrede, Sarah Elizabeth (Sally Nancrede) *reporter*
Natz, Jacques *news director*
†Pearce, Jason Alexander *communications administrator, editor*
Pratt, Arthur D. *printing company executive*
Price, (John) Nelson author, *journalist*
Pulliam, Eugene Smith *newspaper publisher*
†Robertson, Jean Ellis *art critic, art history educator*
Russell, Frank Eli *retired newspaper publishing executive*
Schilling, Emily Born *editor, association executive*
SerVaas, Beurt Richard *corporate executive*
Staff, Charles Bancroft, Jr. *music and theater critic*
Wheeler, Daniel Scott *management executive, editor*
Whitchurch, Gail G. *communication educator*
Wright, David Burton *retired newspaper publishing company executive*
Yates, Robin Corriene *journalism instructor, freelance writer*

Lafayette
Finch, Robert Jonathan *communications engineering consultant*

Ligonier
Sharp, Susan Gene *media educator*

Martinsville
Kendall, Robert Stanton *newspaper editor, journalist*

Monroe City
Teverbaugh, Kerry Dean *television meteorologist, promotional consultant*

Muncie
Bell, Stephen Scott (Steve Bell) *journalist, educator*
Ingelhart, Louis Edward *journalism educator, retired*
†Massé, Mark Henry *journalism educator*

Munster
Colander, Patricia Marie *newspaper publisher*
Moore, Carolyn Lannin *video specialist*

Noblesville
Feigenbaum, Edward D. *legal editor, publisher, consultant*

Notre Dame
Langford, James Rouleau *university press administrator*
Rice, (Ethel) Ann *publishing executive, editor*

Plymouth
Nixon, William Rusty *sportswriter*

Poseyville
Joos, Steven Lee *sports editor*

Rushville
Moore, Helen Elizabeth *reporter*

Saint Meinrad
Cody, Aelred Joseph *editor, priest*

South Bend
Lampkin, Ralph, Jr. *vocalist, nightclub consultant, producer, writer, coach*
Schurz, Franklin Dunn, Jr. *media executive*
Smith, E. Berry *television and radio executive*
Wensits, James Emrich *newspaper editor*

IOWA

Ames
Gartner, Michael Gay *editor, television executive*
Smith, Kim Anthony *journalist, educator*

Cedar Rapids
Keller, Eliot Aaron *broadcasting executive*
Quarton, William Barlow *broadcasting company executive*

Council Bluffs
Kelly, Patricia Ann *communication arts educator*

Davenport
Brocka, Bruce *editor, educator, software engineer*
Brown, Colleen *broadcast executice*
Gottlieb, Richard Douglas *media executive*

Des Moines
Boyle, Bruce James *publisher*
Byal, Nancy Louise *food editor*
DeAngelo, Anthony James *media specialist, architect, writer, communication specialist*
Graham, Diane E. *newspaper editor*
Henry, Barbara A. *publishing executive*
Kerr, William T. *publishing and broadcasting executive*
Kruidenier, David *newspaper executive*
Lawless, James L. *editor, columnist*
Leach, Dave Francis *editor, musician*
Lemmon, Jean Marie *editor-in-chief*
Myers, Mary Kathleen *publishing executive*
†O'Donnell, Thomas Richard *reporter*
Peterson, David Charles *photojournalist*
Rhein, Dave *newspaper editor*
Rood, Lee *newspaper editor*
†Ryerson, Dennis *editor*
†Shao Collins, Jeannine *magazine publisher*
Van Zante, Shirley M(ae) *magazine editor*
Witke, David Rodney *newspaper editor*

Dubuque
Kolz, Beverly Anne *publishing executive*
Leblond, Jack James *multimedia executive*

Iowa City
Bloom, Stephen G *journalist, educator*
Campion, Daniel Ray *editor*
Duck, Steve Weatherill *communications educator*
Soloski, John *journalism and communications educator*

Marshalltown
Roe, Sue Lynn *journalist, free lance writer*

Mason City
Collison, Jim *business executive*

Sioux City
†Schoenherr, Julie Ann *newspaper reporter*

Spirit Lake
van der Linden, John Edward *newspaper broker, consultant*

Urbandale
Alumbaugh, JoAnn McCalla *magazine editor*

West Des Moines
Burnett, Robert A. *retired publisher*
Dooley, Donald John *retired publishing executive*

Westside
Stiles, Virginia Lee *newspaper editor, clergy*

KANSAS

Fort Scott
Emery, Frank Eugene *publishing executive*

Hugoton
Goering, Sherrill Anita *newspaper editor*

Hutchinson
Baumer, Beverly Belle *journalist*
Buzbee, Richard Edgar *newspaper editor*

Iola
Lynn, Emerson Elwood, Jr. *newspaper editor/publisher*

Lawrence
Dickinson, William Boyd, Jr. *editorial consultant*
Ginn, John Charles *journalism educator, former newspaper publisher*
Orel, Harold *literary critic, educator*
Pickett, Calder Marcus *retired journalism educator*
Secor, James L. *editor*
Simons, Dolph Collins, Jr. *newspaper publisher*

Lindsborg
†Barbo, Beverly Ann *printing and publishing company executive*

Manhattan
Seaton, Edward Lee *newspaper editor and publisher*
Watt, Willis Martin *academic administrator, communications and leadership educator*

Newton
Houser, Gordon Sinclair *editor*
†Newton, Jennifer Christine *newspaper reporter*

North Newton
Snider, Marie Anna *syndicated columnist*

Russell
Manion, Kay Daureen *newspaper executive*

Saint Marys
Latham, Dudley Eugene, III (Del Latham) *printing and paper converting executive*

Salina
Entriken, Robert Kersey, Jr. *motorsport writer, retired newspaper editor*

Hansen, Donna Lauree *court reporting educator*
Parker, Maryland (Mike Parker) *reporter, photographer*

Shawnee Mission
†Hayes, Colleen Ballard *writer, photographer*
Martin, Donna Lee *publishing company executive, retired*

Topeka
Black, Kirk J. *television executive*
Cornish, Kent M. *television executive*
Crahan, Ann Teresa *magazine editor*
Ferguson, Lewis LeRoy *senior correspondent*
Powers, Harris Pat *retired broadcasting executive*
Sipes, Karen Kay *newspaper editor*
Stauffer, Stanley Howard *retired newspaper and broadcasting executive*

Valley Falls
†Wilson, Robert Eugene *publisher*

Wichita
Curtright, Robert Eugene *newspaper critic and columnist*
Dill, Sheri *publishing executive*
Getz, Robert Lee *newspaper columnist*
Hatteberg, Larry Merle *photojournalist*

KENTUCKY

Bowling Green
†Bauer, David Christopher L. *newspaper editor*
Quinn, Paula Miner *publisher, healer, musician, educator*

Calvert City
Stice, Dwayne Lee *broadcasting company executive*

Carlisle
Wolf, John Howell *retired publisher*

Covington
Michaels, Randy *broadcast executive*
Trimble, Vance Henry *retired newspaper editor*

Crescent Springs
†Ott, James Daniel *journalist, educator*

Danville
†Frank, John *editor*

Fort Knox
Barnes, Larry Glen *journalist, editor, educator*

Frankfort
Cross, Alvin Miller (Al Cross) *political columnist, writer*
Smith, Sherri Long *journalist, secondary education educator*

Glasgow
†Knicely, Carroll Franklin *publishing executive*

Goshen
Strode, William Hall, III *photojournalist, publisher*

Lexington
Allison, James Claybrooke, II *broadcasting executive*
†Dooley, Karla Jeanette *reporter*
Keeling, Larry Dale *journalist*
Kelly, Timothy Michael *newspaper publisher*
Kissling, Fred Ralph, Jr. *publishing executive, insurance agency executive*

London
Giles, William Elmer *newspaper editor*

Louisville
Atcher, Randy *musician, narrator, entertainer, retired realtor*
Brones, Lisa Ann Mari *news anchorperson, reporter*
Bullard, Claude Earl *newspaper, commercial printing and radio and television executive*
Collyer, George Stanley, Jr. *magazine editor*
Hawpe, David Vaughn *newspaper editor, journalist*
Ivory, Bennie *editor*
Landau, Herman *newspaperman retired*
Manassah, Edward E. *publisher*
Melnykovych, Andrew O. *journalist*
Scheu, Lynn McLaughlin *scientific publication editor*
Schulman, Robert *journalist*
Tinsley, Tuck, III *book publishing executive*
Towles, Donald Blackburn *retired newspaper publishing executive*

Pewee Valley
Gill, George Norman *newspaper publishing company executive*

Propect
Shipley, Alden Peverly *broadcaster, broadcasting executive*

LOUISIANA

Alexandria
Smith, Joe Dorsey, Jr. *retired newspaper executive*

Baton Rouge
Calato, Damian *television executive*
†Gay, Pamela Diane *dance critic, historian*
Gilmore, Clarence Percy *writer, magazine editor*
Jenkins, Louis (Woody) *television executive, state legislator*
LeBlanc, Hanson Paul, III *communications educator, researcher*
Manship, Douglas *broadcast and newspaper executive*
Pastorek, John *news director*
Phillabaum, Leslie Ervin *publisher*
Windhauser, John William *journalism educator*

Covington
Stroup, Sheila Tierney *columnist*

Gonzales
Young, David Nelson *media and communications consultant*

Gretna
Calhoun, Milburn *publishing executive, rare book dealer, physician*

Iowa
†Guilbeau, Brian Gerald *sportswriter*

Lake Charles
Beam, James C. (Jim Beam) *editor, newspaper*

Natchitoches
Masson, Stephanie Reese *journalist*

New Orleans
Amoss, Walter James, III *editor*
Ball, Millie (Mildred Porteous Ball) *editor, journalist*
Barker, Larry Lee *communications educator*
Crumley, David Oliver *publisher, author, foundation executive*
Curry, Dale Blair *journalist*
Dennery, Linda *newspaper publishing executive*
Ferguson, Charles Austin *retired newspaper editor*
Gebauer, August William *editor*
Handelsman, Walt *cartoonist*
Phelps, Ashton, Jr. *newspaper publisher*
Plymale, Ida Ruth Duffey *journalist, educator*
Pope, John M. *journalist*
Schleifstein, Mark Edwin *newspaper reporter*
†Wilkie, Curtis Carter, Jr. *journalist*

Shreveport
Beaird, Charles T. *publishing executive*
Lazarus, Allan Matthew *retired newspaper editor*
†Robinson, Edna Earle *publishing company executive*
Robinson, Garry Lewin *television news executive*

Thibodaux
Delahaye, Alfred Newton *retired journalism educator*

MAINE

Bangor
Warren, Richard Jordan *newspaper publisher*
Warren, Richard Kearney *newspaper publisher*

Berwick
Bufithis, Cynthia Billings *media specialist*

Bristol
Sabin, William Albert *editor*

Camden
Anderson, George Harding *broadcasting company executive*

Castine
Hall, David *sound archivist, writer*

Chebeague Island
Traina, Albert Salvatore *publishing executive*

Damariscotta
Blake, Bud (Julian Watson) *cartoonist*

Eliot
†Delgen, Amy Lynn *copywriter*

Ellsworth
Dudman, Richard Beebe *communications company executive, journalist*
Wiggins, James Russell *newspaper editor*

Falmouth
Sawyer, Wellington Oliver *radio announcer*

Lincoln
Kneeland, Douglas Eugene *retired newspaper editor*

Lyman
Reeves, Thomas William, Jr. *record label owner*

Orono
Bennett, Carolyn L. *journalist, writer*

Orrs Island
Lowndes, Janine Marie Herbert *journalist*

Portland
Neavoll, George Franklin *newspaper editor*

Sebago Lake
Murray, Wallace Shordon *publisher, educator*

Sedgwick
Schroth, Thomas Nolan *editor*

Waldoboro
Hewett, David Edgar *journalist*

York
†Perry, Herbert Peter *newswriter*

MARYLAND

Annapolis
Casey, Edward Dennis *newspaper editor*
Chambers, Ronald D. *book publishing executive*
Miller, John Grider *magazine editor*
Rubin, Samuel Bruce *speech communication educator*

Baltimore
Alexander, Marcellus W., Jr. *television station executive*
Beckenstein, Myron *journalist*
Bor, Jonathan Steven *journalist*
Broening, Walter Stephens, Jr. *journalist, history educator*
Brunson, Dorothy Edwards *broadcasting executive*
Carroll, John Sawyer *newspaper editor*
Cohn, Gary Dennis *journalist*
Dolan, Jim *broadcast executive*
Dorsey, John Russell *journalist*
Giuliano, Michael Philip *arts journalist, educator*
Glasgow, Jesse Edward *newspaper editor*
Jackson, Harold *journalist*
Junck, Mary *newspaper publishing executive*
Lee, Denise Elizabeth *editor*
Marimow, William Kalmon *journalist*
Montgomery, Paula Kay *publisher*
Pollak, Lisa *columnist*
Price, Debbie Mitchell *journalist*
Rodricks, Daniel John *columnist, television commentator*
Rousuck, J. Wynn *theater critic*
Steinbach, Alice *journalist*
Sterne, Joseph Robert Livingston *newspaper editor, educator*
Stevens, Elisabeth Goss (Mrs. Robert Schleussner, Jr.) *writer, journalist, graphic artist*
Sullam, Brian Eliot *journalist*
Tepper, Michael Howard *publishing company executive*
Thomas, Jacqueline Marie *journalist, editor*

Bethesda
Boshart, Edgar David *editor, journalist, photographer*
Capaldini, Mark Laurence *online information service executive*
Chronister, Gregory Michael *newspaper editor*
Cornish, Edward Seymour *magazine editor*
Dudley, Don *broadcast journalist, communications consultant*
Frank, Richard Sanford *retired magazine editor*
Harney, Kenneth Robert *editor, columnist*
Hendricks, John S. *broadcast executive*
Herman, Edith Carol *journalist*
Hoover, Roland Armitage *publisher, printer*
Jeppson, Lawrence Smith *publisher fine arts, consultant*
Johnson, Richard Kent *publishing executive*
Larrabee, Donald Richard *publishing company executive*
Nessen, Ronald Harold *broadcast executive*
Pickerell, James Howard *photojournalist*
Pratt, Dana Joseph *publishing consultant*
Rooney, William Richard *magazine editor*
Rubin, William *editor*
Smirnow, Virgil *publisher, consultant*
Wagner, Cynthia Gail *editor, writer*

Bowie
Towle, Laird Charles *book publisher*

Chevy Chase
Adler, James Barron *publisher*
Bruno, Harold Robinson, Jr. *retired journalist, educator, writer*
Chaseman, Joel *media executive*
Felton, Gordon H. *retired publishing executive*
Kingsley, Nathan *journalist, consultant, educator*
Kriegsman, Alan M. *retired critic*
Shipler, David Karr *journalist, correspondent, author*
Toth, Robert Charles *retired polling consultant, journalist*

College Park
Beasley, Maurine Hoffman *journalism educator, historian*
Gomery, Douglas *communications educator, writer*
Grunig, James Elmer *communications educator, researcher, public relations consultant*
Hiebert, Ray Eldon *educator, author, consultant*
Johnson, Haynes Bonner *author, journalist, television commentator*
Winik, Jay B. *writer, political scientist, consultant*

Columbia
Barrow, Lionel Ceon, Jr. *communications and marketing consultant*
Drummond, LaCreda Renee *journalist*
Hall, Wiley A. *columnist, journalist*

Easton
†Wilson, Laura Ann *newspaper editor*

Ellicott City
Harding, John Walter *art critic*

Frederick
Archibald, Fred John *newspaper executive*
Delaplaine, George Birely, Jr. *newspaper editor, cable television executive*

Gaithersburg
Wicklein, John Frederick *journalist, educator*

Greenbelt
Hill, Ben *broadcast executive*

Hagerstown
Fisher, Charles Worley *editor*
Warner, Harry Backer, Jr. *retired journalist, freelance writer*

Havre De Grace
Wetter, Edward *broadcasting executive*

Hollywood
Powledge, Fred Arlius *freelance writer*

Lanham
Hencke, Paul Gerard *editor, writer, broadcaster*

Lanham Seabrook
Lyons, James Edward *publishing executive*

Lexington Park
Lineback, Harvey Lee *media specialist*

Lutherville Timonium
Cedrone, Louis Robert, Jr. *critic*

North Potomac
Lide, David Reynolds *handbook and database editor*
Willis, Norman Hunt *new media writer, director, producer*

Owings Mills
Hirsh, Allan Thurman, Jr. *publishing executive*
Holdridge, Barbara *book publisher*

Potomac
Christian, John Kenton *organization executive, publisher, writer, marketing consultant*
Crowley, Mary Elizabeth (Mary Elizabeth Crowley-Farrell) *journalist, editor*
Dykewicz, Paul Gregory *journalist*
Fox, Arthur Joseph, Jr. *editor*
Karnow, Stanley *journalist, writer*
Mason, Dan *broadcast executive*

Princess Anne
Franklin, Robert Allen *broadcast executive, radio producer*

Rockville
†Hoover, Carol Faith *publisher*
Kohlmeier, Louis Martin, Jr. *newspaper reporter*
Langley, Roger Richard *editor*
Macafee, Susan Diane *reporter*
Regeimbal, Neil Robert, Sr. *retired journalist*
Yamazaki, Kazutami *journalist*

Severna Park
Moore, John Leo, Jr. *journalist, writer, editor*
Pumphrey, Janet Kay *editor, publisher*

Silver Spring
Bennett, Carol(ine) Elise *reporter, actress*
Carson, Steven Lee *newspaper publisher*
Eiserer, Leonard Albert Carl *publishing executive*
Hoar, William Patrick *editor, author*
Howze, Karen Aileen *newspaper editor, lawyer, multi-cultural communications consultant*
Lee, Sheng Yen *editor*
Mooney, James Hugh *newspaper editor*
Vernon, Weston, III (Wes Vernon) *broadcaster, writer, actor*
Wooster, Martin Morse *author, editor*
†Zubkoff, Harry M. *news analyst*

Street
Spangler, Ronald Leroy *retired television executive, aircraft executive, automobile collector*

Towson
Williams, Harold Anthony *retired newspaper editor*

MASSACHUSETTS

Acton
Haver, Thomas M. *publishing company executive*
Kittross, John Michael *retired communications educator*

Allston
Becton, Henry Prentiss, Jr. *broadcasting company executive*

Amherst
Wilcox, Bruce Gordon *publisher*

Andover
Lerch, Robert Bond *cable television executive*

Bedford
Goodman, William Beehler *editor, literary agent*

Boston
Adams, Phoebe-Lou *journalist*
Atwan, Helene *publishing executive*
Baughman, James Carroll *information and communication educator*
Berube, Margery Stanwood *publishing executive*
Bourne, Katherine Day *journalist, educator*
Burack, Sylvia Kamerman *editor, publisher*
Bursma, Albert, Jr. *publishing company executive*
Caldwell, Gail *book critic*
Carr, Jay Phillip *critic*
Carroll, Matthew Shaun *reporter*
Cohen, Rachelle Sharon *journalist*
Collins, Monica Ann *journalist*
Cook, David *editor*
Costello, Andrew F. *newspaper editor*
Daly, Christopher Burke *journalist, educator*
Daniloff, Nicholas *journalist, educator*
Darehshori, Nader Farhang *publishing sales executive*
†Darst, Guy B., Jr. *journalist*
Davison, Peter Hubert *editor, poet*
Daya, Jackie *publishing company executive*
DeFleur, Margaret H. *communications educator*
Dodge, Steven B. *broadcast executive*
Donovan, Helen W. *newspaper editor*
Eder, Richard Gray *newspaper critic*
Fanning, Katherine Woodruff *editor, journalism educator*
Feder, Donald Albert *syndicated columnist*
Feeney, Mark *newspaper editor*
Flanders, Jefferson *publishing executive*
Gendron, George *magazine editor*
Gibson, Barry Joseph *magazine editor*
Goldman, Ed *broadcast executive*
Grimes, Heilan Yvette *publishing executive*
Grossfeld, Stan *newspaper photography executive, author*
Harris, Roy Jay, Jr. *editor, business journalist*
Hatfield, Julie Stockwell *journalist, newspaper editor*
Hillery, Thomas Hungiville *journalist, financial consultant*
Hilts, Philip James *correspondent*
Hoffman, Stanley Marc *editor*
Hostetter, Amos Barr, Jr. *cable television executive*
Huff, William Braid *publication company executive*
Katz, Larry *writer, columnist*
Kauffman, Godfrey *newspaper publishing executive*
†Ketter, William B. *journalist, educator*
Kimball, George Edward, III *sports columnist*
King, Nick *magazine editor*
Klarfeld, Jonathan Michael *journalism educator*
Knox, Richard Albert *journalist*
Krakoff, Robert Leonard *publishing executive*
Larkin, Alfred Sinnott, Jr. *newspaper editor*
Larkin, Michael John *newspaper editor, journalist*
Lawrence, Merloyd Ludington *editor*
Lee, Donald Young (Don Lee) *publishing executive, editor, writer*
Leland, Timothy *newspaper executive*

Lewis, Anthony *newspaper columnist*
Loew, Brenda *publisher*
Lyman, Henry *retired publisher, marine fisheries consultant*
Manning, Robert Joseph *editor*
Manning, William Frederick *wire service photographer*
Mason, Charles Ellis, III *magazine editor*
Menzies, Ian Stuart *newspaper editor*
†Moore, Gregory L. *editor*
Morris, Gerald Douglas *newspaper editor*
Moyes, Norman Barr *journalism educator, writer, photographer*
Newman, Richard Alan *publisher, editor and consultant*
Norment, Eric Stuart *newspaper editor*
Purcell, Patrick Joseph *newspaper publisher*
Raeder, William Munro *publishing executive*
Rhoads, Linda Smith *editor*
Santos, Gilbert Antonio (Gil Santos) *radio and television sportscaster*
Schulz, John Joseph *communications educator*
Schwartz, Lloyd *music critic, poet*
Sigman, Stuart J. *communications educator*
Silvey, Anita Lynne *editor*
Smyth, Peter Hayes *radio executive*
Stevens, Marilyn Ruth *editor*
Storin, Matthew Victor *newspaper editor*
Strothman, Wendy Jo *book publisher*
Szep, Paul Michael *editorial cartoonist*
Taylor, Benjamin B. *newspaper publishing executive*
Taylor, Stephen Emlyn *publishing executive*
Taylor, William Osgood *newspaper executive*
†Thys, Frederic Georges Rene *journalist*
Turek, Sonia Fay *journalist*
Utiger, Robert David *medical editor*
Warsh, David Lewis *economic journalist*
Whitworth, William A. *magazine editor*
Wilson, David Bruce *journalist*

Brewster
O'Brien, Gregory Francis *book publisher, writer, producer*

Bridgewater
Al-Obaidi, Jabbar A. *communication educator, film producer*

Brookline
Caso, Adolph *publishing company executive*

Cambridge
Aronson, Michael Andrew *editor*
†Ascher, Maria Louise *translator, editor*
Bane, Bernard Maurice *publishing company executive*
†Berners-Lee, Tim *World Wide Web executive*
Bouvier, Linda Fritts *publishing executive*
Eldridge, Larry (William Lawrence Eldridge) *journalist*
†Fiore, Lois Frances *editor, artist*
Koyanis, Melinda T. *publishing executive, lawyer*
Kuttner, Robert Louis *editor, columnist*
Nordell, Hans Roderick *journalist, retired editor*
†Picardi, Gerard A. *publisher*
Sisler, William Philip *publishing executive*
Squire, James Robert *retired publisher, consultant*
Urbanowski, Frank *publishing company executive*
Wilcox, Maud *editor*

Canton
Roman, John Joseph *cartoonist, illustrator*

Chestnut Hill
Knez, Brian *publishing executive*
Smith, Richard Alan *publishing and specialty retailing executive*

Cohasset
Replogle, David Robert *publishing company executive*

Danvers
†Ronan, John J. *communications educator*

Dedham
Janson, Barbara Jean *publisher*

Dorchester
Brelis, Matthew Dean Burns *journalist*
Bruzelius, Nils Johan Axel *journalist*
Goodman, Ellen Holtz *journalist*
Greenway, Hugh Davids Scott *journalist*

Dover
Salhany, Lucille S. *broadcast executive*

Duxbury
Habgood, Robert P. *publishing executive*

Easton
†Chichetto, James William *editor, educator*

Fall River
†Dion, Marc Munroe *newspaper columnist*

Fitchburg
Wieland, Paul Richard *broadcast executive*

Framingham
Crohan, Margaret Elizabeth *communications educator, consultant*
Levy, Joseph Louis *publishing company executive*

Gloucester
Baird, Gordon Prentiss *publisher*

Great Barrington
Lewis, Karen Marie *writer, editor*

Hanover
†Driscoll, Kathleen J *writer, research analyst*

Holyoke
Dwight, William, Jr. *former newspaper executive, restaurateur*

Hyannis
Makkay, Albert *broadcast executive*
Makkay, Maureen Ann *broadcast executive*

Miller, Timothy Alan *newspaper entertainment editor, film critic*

Lee
Rich, Philip Dewey *publishing executive*

Lenox
Meyer, Peter Barrett *journalist*

Lincoln
Nenneman, Richard Arthur *retired publishing executive*

Lowell
†Peters, Janice C. *cable company executive*

Marblehead
Quigley, Stephen Howard *executive editor*

Medford
Siegal, Kenneth Harvey *editor*

Middleton
Stover, Matthew Joseph *communications executive*

Millis
Masterson, Patricia O'Malley *publications editor, writer*

Needham
La Camera, Paul A. *television station executive*
Meisner, Mary Jo *editor*

Newburyport
Berggren, Dick *editor*

Newton
Barnet, Bruce *publishing executive*
Kardon, Brian *publishing company executive*
Knupp, Ralph *publishing company executive*
Neth, Jerry *publishing company executive*
Norton, (William) Elliot *retired drama critic*

Newton Center
Sandman, Peter M. *communication educator, consultant*

North Adams
Thurston, Donald Allen *broadcasting executive*

North Chatham
Rowlands, Marvin Lloyd, Jr. *publishing and communications consultant*

North Chelmsford
Osenton, Thomas George *publisher*

Northampton
Gardner, Thomas Neville *communications educator*
†Kitchen, Denis Lee *publisher, artist*

Norwell
Rolnik, Zachary Jacob *publishing company executive*

Orleans
Dessauer, John Phillip *publisher, financial management company executive*

Quincy
Dunning, Thomas E. *newspaper editor*
Lippincott, Joseph P. *photojournalist, educator*

Rockland
Bowes, Frederick, III *publishing executive*
Pallai, David Francis *publishing executive*

Rockport
Bissell, Phil (Charles P. Bissell) *cartoonist*
Fillmore, Laura *publisher*

Sandwich
Porter, John Stephen *retired television executive*

Scituate
Ryan, George Edward *journalist*

South Harwich
Micciche, Salvatore Joseph *retired journalist, lawyer*

Springfield
Garvey, Richard Conrad *journalist*
Gordon, Ronni Anne *journalist*
Haggerty, Thomas Francis *newspaper editor*
McDermott, Larry Arnold *newspaper publisher, newspaper editor*
Mish, Frederick Crittenden *editor*
Morse, John M. *book publishing executive*

Waltham
Fleming, Samuel Crozier, Jr. *health care publishing and consulting firm executive*
Mills, Matt *broadcast executive*

Wellesley
Gladstone, Richard Bennett *retired publishing company executive*
Myers, Arthur B. *journalist, author*
Tarr, Robert Joseph, Jr. *publishing executive, retail executive*

Wellfleet
Limpitlaw, John Donald *retired publishing executive, clergyman*

West Tisbury
Méras, Phyllis Leslie *journalist*

Weston
Oelgeschlager, Guenther Karl *publisher*
Sanzone, Donna S. *publishing executive*

Williamsburg
Mazor, David S. *film distribution company executive*

Winchester
Ewing, David Walkley *magazine editor*

Ockerbloom, Richard C. *newspaper executive*

Winthrop
Lutze, Ruth Louise *retired textbook editor, public relations executive*
Vettel, Niki Marcia (Monica Marcia Scher) *broadcasting executive*

Woburn
Speerstra, Karen M. *publishing executive*

MICHIGAN

Ann Arbor
Beaver, Frank Eugene *communication educator, film critic and historian*
Bedard, Patrick Joseph *editor, writer, consultant*
Bradsher, Keith Vinson *journalist*
Csere, Csaba *magazine editor*
Day, Colin Leslie *publisher*
Eisendrath, Charles Rice *journalism educator, manufacturer, farmer, consultant*
Fitzsimmons, Joseph John *publishing executive*
Mangouni, Norman *publisher*
Martin, Bruce James *newspaper editor*

Bad Axe
Riegle, Karen Dewald *communications educator*

Bay City
†Hiner, John Patrick *newspaper editor*

Birmingham
McIntyre, Bruce Herbert *media and marketing consultant*

Bloomfield Hills
Brown, Lynette Ralya *journalist, publicist*
James, William Ramsay *cable television executive*

Clinton
Anderson, Denice Anna *editor*

Davison
Schelske, Donald Melvin *newspaper editor*

Dearborn
Hogan, Brian Joseph *editor*

Detroit
Albom, Mitch David *sports columnist*
Anstett, Pat *newspaper editor*
Antoniotti, Steve *broadcast executive*
Ashenfelter, David Louis *reporter, former newspaper editor*
Behrmann, Joan Gail *newspaper editor*
Berman, Laura *journalist*
Blomquist, David Wels *journalist*
Bullard, George *newspaper editor*
Burzynski, Susan Marie *newspaper editor*
Cantor, George Nathan *journalist*
Colby, Joy Hakanson *art critic*
Dickerson, Brian *columnist*
Diebolt, Judith *newspaper editor*
Falls, Joseph Francis *sportswriter, editor*
Fezzey, Mike *radio station executive*
Frank, Alan W. *television station executive*
Green, Verna S. *broadcast executive*
†Henderson, Angelo B. *journalist*
James, Sheryl Teresa *journalist*
Kelleher, Timothy John *publishing company executive*
Kiska, Timothy Olin *newspaper columnist*
Kramer, Mary Louise *journalist*
Laughlin, Nancy *newspaper editor*
McGruder, Robert *newspaper publishing executive*
Meriwether, Heath J. *newspaper publisher*
Parry, Dale D. *newspaper editor*
Penberthy, Stanley Josiah, Jr. *publisher*
Pepper, Jonathon L. *newspaper columnist*
Ruffner, Frederick G., Jr. *book publisher*
†Silverman, Mark *publisher*
†Smith, Jennette Helen *journalist*
Smyntek, John Eugene, Jr. *newspaper editor*
Stark, Susan R. *film critic*
Stroud, Joe Hinton *newspaper editor*
Talbert, Bob *newspaper columnist*
Teagan, John Gerard *newspaper executive*
Vega, Frank J. *newspaper publishing executive*
Vincent, Charles Eagar, Jr. *sports columnist*
Waldmeir, Peter Nielsen *journalist*
White, Joseph B. *reporter*

Durand
Cook, Bernadine Fern *book publisher, writer*

East Lansing
Freedman, Eric *journalist, educator, writer*
Gardner, Mary Adelaide *retired journalism educator*
Greenberg, Bradley Sander *communications educator*
Levy, Mark Robert *communication educator*
Morton, Jerry Lee *journalist*
Soffin, Stan *journalism educator*

Farmington Hills
Bryfonski, Dedria Anne *publishing company executive*
Harwell, William Earnest (Ernie Harwell) *broadcaster*

Ferndale
Baker, Elaine R. *radio station executive*

Flint
Samuel, Roger D. *newspaper publishing executive*

Grand Rapids
†Crawford, Joseph Patrick *editor*
Kaczmarczyk, Jeffrey Allen *journalist, classical music critic*
Kregel, James R. *publishing executive*
Lloyd, Michael Stuart *newspaper editor*
Mayo, David Wayne *sportswriter*
Petersen, Jonathan William *publishing executive, media consultant*
Ryskamp, Bruce E. *publishing executive*

Grosse Pointe
Christian, Edward Kieren *broadcasting station executive*

DeVine, (Joseph) Lawrence *drama critic*
Elsila, David August *editor*
Hill, Draper *editorial cartoonist*
Holsapple, Linda Harris *retired editor*
McWhirter, Glenna Suzanne (Nickie McWhirter) *retired newspaper columnist*
Whittaker, Jeanne Evans *former newspaper columnist*

Jackson
Weaver, Franklin Thomas *newspaper executive*

Kalamazoo
Carver, Joan Willson *publishing executive, artist*
Gilmore, James Stanley, Jr. *broadcast executive*
Jamison, Frank Raymond *communications educator*

Lansing
Brown, Nancy Field *editor*
McCoy, Bernard Rogers *television anchor*

Marquette
Manning, Robert Hendrick *media consultant*

Mears
Binder, L(eonard) James *magazine editor, retired*

Midland
Messing, Carol Sue *communications educator*

Mount Pleasant
Petrick, Michael Joseph *journalism educator*
Tait, Alice Ann *journalism educator*

Novi
Opre, Thomas Edward *magazine editor, film company executive, corporate travel company executive*

Petoskey
Vernon, Doris Schaller *retired writer*

Saginaw
Chaffee, Paul Charles *newspaper editor*

Saint Clair Shores
Shine, Neal James *journalism educator, former newspaper editor, publisher*

Sandusky
Johnson, John Douglas *newspaper publisher*

Southfield
Clayton, James A. *broadcast executive*
Dunlop, Michael *broadcast executive*
Gilchrist, Grace *television station executive*
Makupson, Amyre Porter *television station executive*

Sterling Heights
Dipboye, Marilyn Joyce *publisher, editor, writer*

Sturgis
Hair, Robert Eugene *editor, writer, historian*

Troy
Lorencz, Mary *media relations administrator*
Moore, Oliver Semon, III *publishing executive, consultant*

Ypsilanti
Evans, Gary Lee *communications educator and consultant*

MINNESOTA

Annandale
Johnson, Jon E. *magazine editor and publisher*

Birchwood Village
Oliver, Marlys Mae *retired editor, writer*

Bloomington
Johnson, Leslie Carole *editor, publisher*

Castle Rock
Ericson, Harold Louis *communications executive*

Center City
Hammond, Bill *publishing executive*

Chisholm
†Anderson, Brian Keith *editor*

Duluth
Latto, Lewis M. *broadcasting company executive*

Eagan
Collier, Ken O. *editor*
Miller, Alan M. *editor, educator, writer*

Eden Prairie
Degnan, Amy Marie *journalist*

Edina
Trouten, Douglas James *journalist*

Ely
Swenson, L. Anne *publisher*

Fergus Falls
Rinden, David Lee *editor*

Minneapolis
Armitage, Shannon Lyn *editor-in-chief newspaper*
Bisping, Bruce Henry *photojournalist*
Boyd, Belvel James *newspaper editor*
Buoen, Roger *newspaper editor*
Carter, Roy Ernest, Jr. *journalist, educator*
Cope, Lewis *journalist*
Cowles, John, Jr. *publisher, women's sports promoter*
Crosby, Jacqueline Garton *newspaper editor, journalist*
†Fine, Pam *newspaper editor*
Flanagan, Barbara *journalist*

PROFESSIONAL INDEX 5861 COMMUNICATIONS MEDIA

Franklin, Robert Brewer *journalist*
Ison, Christopher John *investigative reporter*
Johnson, Cheryl (CJ) *newspaper columnist*
Johnson, Gary LeRoy *publisher*
Jones, Will(iam) (Arnold) *writer, former newspaper columnist*
Kalman, Marc *radio station executive*
Kinderwater, Joseph C. (Jack Kinderwater) *publishing company executive*
Kramer, Joel Roy *journalist, newspaper executive*
Laing, Karel Ann *magazine publishing executive*
Lerner, Harry Jonas *publishing company executive*
Marshall, Sherrie *newspaper editor*
McDaniel, Jan *television station executive*
McEnroe, Paul *reporter*
†McGuire, Tim *editor*
Meador, Ron *newspaper editor, writer*
Mohr, L. Thomas *newspaper executive*
Moraczewski, Robert Leo *publisher*
Murphy, Joseph Edward, Jr. *broadcast executive*
Opperman, Dwight Darwin *publishing company executive*
Roberts, Katherine Erin *journalist*
Roloff, Marvin L. *publishing executive*
Salyer, Stephen Lee *broadcast executive*
Scallen, Thomas Kaine *broadcasting executive*
Spendlove, Steve Dale *vice president and general manager*
Steinmetz, Mark S. *broadcast executive*
Strickler, Jeff *newspaper movie critic*
Swartz, Donald Everett *television executive*
Watson, Catherine Elaine *journalist*
†Werner, Lawrence H. *editor*
White, Robert James *newspaper columnist*
Whittemore, Brian *broadcast executive*
Wright, Frank Gardner *retired newspaper editor*
Youngblood, Richard Neil *columnist*
Ziebarth, E. William *news analyst, educator*

Rochester
Swanson, David Elmer *journalist*

Rushford
†Schober, Myron Jerome *newspaper editor and publisher*

Saint Cloud
†Allenspach, Kevin Ray *sportswriter*
Porter, Laurinda Wright *communication educator*

Saint Joseph
Rowland, Howard Ray *mass communications educator*

Saint Paul
Aggergaard, Steven Paul *journalist, musician*
Blanchard, J. A. *publishing executive*
Bree, Marlin Duane *publisher, author*
Burkart, Jeffrey Edward *communications educator*
Clark, Ronald Dean *newspaper editor*
Hubbard, Stanley Stub *broadcast executive*
Huntzicker, William Edward *journalism educator*
Kling, William Hugh *broadcasting executive*
Lundy, Walker *newspaper editor*
Sadowski, Richard J. *publishing executive*
†Sadowski, Rick *publisher*
Wehrwein, Austin Carl *newspaper reporter, editor, writer*
Weschcke, Carl Llewellyn *publishing executive*

Sartell
Dominik, John Julius *retired advertising company executive*

Two Harbors
McMillion, John Macon *retired newspaper publisher*

West Saint Paul
Cento, William Francis *retired newspaper editor*

MISSISSIPPI

Biloxi
Weeks, Roland, Jr. *newspaper publisher*

Brandon
Buckley, Frank Wilson *newspaper executive*

Calhoun City
†Spencer, Thomas M. *journalist*

Clinton
McWilliams, Anne Washburn *retired journalist, writer*

Gulfport
Branan, Bradley Thomas *journalist*
Hash, John Frank *broadcasting executive*

Itta Bena
Harbor, Kingsley Okoro *communications and journalism educator, researcher*

Jackson
Petty, David *newspaper editor*
Whitsett, Paul Timothy, Jr. (Tim Whitsett) *executive*

Kosciusko
Shoemaker, William C. *journalist*

Mississippi State
Hutenstine, Marian Louise *journalism educator*

Tupelo
Armistead, John Grayson *journalist*

University
Bass, Jack *journalism educator*

Vicksburg
Briuer, Elke Moersch *editor*

Yazoo City
Brown, Marion Lipscomb, Jr. *publisher, retired chemical company executive*

MISSOURI

Ashland
Flink, Jane Duncan *publisher*

Chesterfield
Higgins, Edward Aloysius *retired newspaper editor*

Clayton
Marcus, Larry David *broadcasting executive*

Columbia
Brenner, Donald John *journalism educator*
†Lambert, Edward Charles *journalism educator, broadcaster*
Loory, Stuart Hugh *journalist*
Sanders, Keith Page *journalism educator*
Woelfel, Stacey William *news director*

Fayette
Davis, H(umphrey) Denny *publisher*

Higginsville
Rhodes, Robert Charles *cable company executive, consultant*

Joplin
Massa, Richard Wayne *communications educator*

Kansas City
†Allan, Clayton Paul *publishing executive*
Anderson, James Keith *retired magazine editor*
Andrews, Kathleen W. *book publishing executive*
†Audy, Lynn *editor*
Batiuk, Thomas Martin *cartoonist*
Brisbane, Arthur Seward *newspaper publisher*
Busby, Marjorie Jean (Marjean Busby) *journalist*
Cantrell, (Thomas) Scott *newspaper music critic*
Crumpley, Charles Robert Thomas *journalist*
Davis, James Robert *cartoonist*
Gusewelle, Charles Wesley *journalist*
†Hickok, Gloria Vando *publisher, editor, poet*
Larson, Gary *cartoonist*
McDermott, Alan *newspaper editor*
Mc Meel, John Paul *newspaper syndicate and publishing executive*
McSweeney, William Lincoln, Jr. *retired publishing executive*
Oliphant, Patrick *cartoonist*
Palmer, Cruise *newspaper editor*
Petosa, Jason Joseph *publisher*
Roush, Sue *newspaper editor*
†Ryan, William James *communication educator*
Salem, Lee *editor*
Tammeus, William David *journalist, columnist*
Thornton, Thomas Noel *publishing executive*
Townsend, Harold Guyon, Jr. *publishing company executive*
Van Buren, Abigail (Pauline Friedman Phillips) *columnist, author, writer, lecturer*
Zieman, Mark *newspaper editor*

Kirksville
†Tatro, Norbert *journalist, educator*

Saint Louis
Barnes, Harper Henderson *movie critic, editor*
Bauman, George Duncan *former newspaper publisher*
Buck, Jack *sportscaster, broadcast executive*
Campbell, Cole C. *journalist, educator*
Dill, John Francis *retired publishing company executive*
Domjan, Laszlo Karoly *newspaper editor*
Elkins, Ken Joe *broadcasting executive*
Engelhardt, Thomas Alexander *editorial cartoonist*
Ferguson, Gary Warren *retired public relations executive*
Green, Joyce *book publishing company executive*
Hays, Howard H. (Tim Hays) *editor, publisher*
Kanne, Marvin George *newspaper publishing executive*
Killenberg, George Andrew *newspaper consultant, former newspaper editor*
Kirby, Dianna Lea *broadcast executive*
Korando, Donna Kay *journalist*
Linder, Aaron Mark *telelearning specialist, legal video specialist*
Norman, Charles Henry *broadcasting executive*
Olshwanger, Ron *photojournalist*
Olson, Clarence Elmer, Jr. *newspaper editor*
Pennick, Paul Patrick *newspaper editor*
Penniman, Nicholas Griffith, IV *newspaper publisher*
Pollack, Joe *retired newspaper critic and columnist, writer*
Pulitzer, Michael Edgar *publishing executive*
Regnell, Barbara Caramella *retired media educator*
Waters, Richard *retired publishing company executive*
Wiley, Gregory Robert *publisher*

Springfield
Champion, Norma Jean *communications educator, state legislator*
Glazier, Robert Carl *publishing executive*
Harris, Ralph William *religious journalist*
Horn, Kenneth Leroy *editor*
Sylvester, Ronald Charles *newspaper writer*

University City
Benson, Joseph Fred *journalist, legal historian*

Verona
Jay, Jerry Leon, Sr. *retired publishing executive, industrial engineer*

Warrensburg
Adams, Wilburn Clifton *communication educator*
Carr, Richard Raymond *editor, public relations administrator*

MONTANA

Butte
van der Veur, Paul Roscoe *communication educator, researcher*

Havre
Gallus, Charles Joseph *journalist*

Helena
Malcolm, Andrew Hogarth *journalist, writer*

Kalispell
Ruder, Melvin Harvey *retired newspaper editor*

Missoula
†Riggs, Thomas Jeffries, IV *editor*

Whitefish
James, Marion Ray *magazine founder, editor*

NEBRASKA

Cozad
Peterson, Marilyn Ann Whitney *journalism educator*

Friend
De Bevoise, Lee Raymond *editor, nurse, writer, photographer, webmaster*

Kearney
Wice, Paul Clinton *news director, educator*

Lincoln
Davis, Fred *journalist, educator*
Dyer, William Earl, Jr. *retired newspaper editor*
†Lewis, Michael Ray *book editor*
Raz, Hilda *editor-in-chief periodical, English educator*
Ross, Daniel J.J. *publishing executive*
†Vetscher, Timothy John *reporter, anchor on TV news show*

Omaha
Andersen, Harold Wayne *contributing editor, newspaper executive*
Batchelder, Anne Stuart *former publisher, political party official*
Donaldson, William L. *retired newspaper publishing company executive*
†Finney, Michael J. *publishing executive*
Lipschultz, Jeremy Harris *communication educator*
Sands, Deanna *editor*
†Woldt, Harold Frederick, Jr. *newspaper publishing executive*

York
Givens, Randal Jack *communications educator*

NEVADA

Boulder City
Kidd, Hillery Gene *educational publisher*

Fernley
Weniger-Phelps, Nancy Ann *media specialist, photographer*

Henderson
Martin, Donald Walter *author, publisher*
Wills, Robert Hamilton *retired newspaper executive*

Incline Village
Diederich, J(ohn) William *internet publisher*

Las Vegas
†Frederick, Sherman *publishing executive*
Jaffe, Herb *retired newspaper editor, columnist*
Kelley, Michael John *newspaper editor*
Magliocco, Peter Anthony *editor, writer*
Norman, Jean Reid *journalist*

Reno
†Carrigan, Michael Andrew *journalism educator, journalist, writer*
Clark-Johnson, Susan *publishing executive*
Miller, Newton Edd, Jr. *communications educator*
Ogle, James Richard, Jr. *news executive*

NEW HAMPSHIRE

Concord
Brown, Tom Christian *newspaper publisher*
Fahey, Patricia Anne *editor*

Dover
†Handy, Carolyn *newspaper editor*
Wentworth, William Edgar *journalist*

Dublin
Hale, Judson Drake, Sr. *editor*

Hanover
Gardner, Peter Jaglom *publisher*
Olcott, William Alfred *magazine editor*

Jackson
Johnson, Ned (Edward Christopher Johnson) *publishing company executive*

Jaffrey
Schulte, Henry Frank *journalism educator*

Lyme
Dwight, Donald Rathbun *newspaper publisher, corporate communications executive*

Manchester
McQuaid, Joseph Woodbury *newspaper executive*
Perkins, Charles, III *newspaper editor*

Merrimack
Kotelly, George Vincent *editor, writer, electrical engineer*

Peterborough
Dawes, Lyell Clark *publishing company executive*

Portsmouth
Hopkins, Jeannette Ethel *book publisher, editor*
Silverman, George Alan *broadcasting executive*
Thornhill, Arthur Horace, Jr. *retired book publisher*

Salem
Smith, Laurence Roger *journal editor*

NEW JERSEY

Allenwood
†Kerber, Beth-Ann *editor, reporter*

Bergenfield
Clark, Fred *legal writer, editor*

Bernardsville
Parker, Nancy Knowles (Mrs. Cortlandt Parker) *publishing executive*

Blackwood
Cloyd, Thomas Earl *broadcast designer, consultant*

Bridgewater
Freeman, Henry McCall *newspaper publisher*

Caldwell
Mann, Robert Christopher *communications educator, television host, producer*

Cape May
Fox, Matthew Ignatius *publishing company executive*

Chatham
Gormley, Robert John *book publisher*

Cherry Hill
Baxter, Robert Theodore Stewart *arts critic*
Callaway, Ben Anderson *journalist*
Del Colliano, Gerard Anthony *publisher*
Rudman, Solomon Kal *magazine publisher*

Concordia
Reichek, Morton Arthur *retired magazine editor, writer*

Cranbury
Miller, Isadore *television executive, consultant*
Yoseloff, Julien David *publishing company executive*
Yoseloff, Thomas *publisher*

Deal
Becker, Richard Stanley *music publisher*

Dover
Kassell, Paula Sally *editor, publisher*

Dumont
Sadock, Karen *editor, writer*

East Brunswick
Kabela, Frank, Jr. *broadcast executive*

East Rutherford
Krockman, Arnold Francis *publisher, advertising executive*

Edison
Comstock, Robert Ray *journalism educator, newspaper editor*
Hunter, Michael *publishing executive*

Englewood
Friedman, Emanuel *publishing company executive*
Griffin, Robert Douglas *publishing executive, genealogist*

Englewood Cliffs
Haltiwanger, Robert Sidney, Jr. *book publishing executive*
Perry, Douglas Matthew *publishing executive, editor*
Saible, Stephanie Irene *magazine editor*
Vane, Dena *magazine editor-in-chief*

Fair Lawn
Mazel, Joseph Lucas *publications consultant*

Fanwood
Whitaker, Joel *publisher*

Fords
Blond, Stuart Richard *newsletter editor*

Fort Lee
Bolster, William Lawrence *broadcast executive*
†Cohn, Scott *television news correspondent*
Fischel, Daniel Norman *publishing consultant*
†Jamison, George Hill III *broadcast company executive, writer*
Levy, Valery *publisher*
†Nadeine, Vladimir *journalist, editor*

Garwood
Smith, Joan Lowell *syndicated columnist, feature writer*

Glen Rock
Krebs, Gary Michael *editor, author*
Winstead, Clint *financial publisher*

Hackensack
Ahearn, James *newspaper columnist*
†Comandini, Michele Louise *newspaper reporter*
Margulies, James Howard *editorial cartoonist*
Waixel, Vivian *journalist*

Hackettstown
Scalza, Margaret T. *publishing executive*

Haddonfield
Cheney, Daniel Lavern *retired magazine publisher*

Highland Lakes
Ludwig, Gregory Brian *editor, writer*

Hightstown
Wham, George Sims *retired publishing executive*

Hillsborough
Yuster-Freeman, Leigh Carol *publishing company executive*

Hillsdale
DiBlasi, Dianne Clark *editor*

Hoboken
Regazzi, John James, III *publishing executive*
Shafran, Michael Wayne *editor*
†Stohr, Katherine A. *journalist*

Hopatcong
Bowen, Robert William *publishing executive*

Jersey City
Ingrassia, Paul Joseph *publishing executive*
Katz, Colleen *publisher*
Kollar, Mark Patrick *newsletter editor*
Larkins, Robert Joseph *journal editor*
Levine, Richard James *publishing executive*
Wagner, Douglas Walker Ellyson *journal editor*

Lawrenceville
Onyshkevych, Larissa M. L. Zaleska *educator, editor*
†Wang, Minmin *communications educator*

Lebanon
Goulazian, Peter Robert *retired broadcasting executive*

Linwood
McCormick, Robert Matthew, III *newspaper executive*

Little Falls
Glasser, Lynn Schreiber *publisher*
Glasser, Stephen Andrew *publishing executive, lawyer*

Livingston
Cone, Edward Christopher *newspaper publisher*
Kurtz, Ellen R. *journalist*

Long Branch
Lagowski, Barbara Jean *writer, book editor*

Mahwah
Lynch, Kevin A. *book publishing executive*

Manahawkin
†Harlan, Heather Gordon *reporter*

Marlton
Forbes, Gordon Maxwell *sports journalist, commentator*

Medford
Henderson, Rita Elizabeth *literary agent, journalist*
Hogan, Thomas Harlan *publisher*

Metuchen
Smyth, David *editor, author*

Middletown
Wyndrum, Ralph William, Jr. *communications company executive*

Montclair
Gogick, Kathleen Christine *magazine editor, publisher*

Montvale
Politi, Beth Kukkonen *publishing services company executive*
Sifton, David Whittier *magazine editor*

Montville
Coleman, Earl Maxwell *publishing company executive*
Teubner, Ferdinand Cary, Jr. *retired publishing company executive*

Moorestown
†Dudley, Edward James *retired news manager*

Morris Plains
O'Neill, Robert Edward *business journal editor*

Morristown
Ahl, David Howard *writer, editor*
Geyer, Thomas Powick *newspaper publisher*
Tullen, Colton (Skipp Tullen) *recording engineer*

Mount Holly
Brown, Hershel M. *retired newspaper publisher*

Mountain Lakes
LaForce, William Leonard, Jr. *photojournalist, columnist*

Neptune
†Breen, Stephen P. *editorial cartoonist*
Clurfeld, Andrea *editor, food critic*
†Collins, Robert T. *publisher*
Ollwerther, William Raymond *newspaper editor*
Plangere, Jules L., III *newspaper company executive*
†Siegel, Harris G. *managing editor*

Neptune City
Axelrod, Glen Scott *publishing company executive*

New Brunswick
Horowitz, Irving Louis *publisher, educator*
Taliaferro, James Hubert, Jr. *communications educator*
Wilson, Donald Malcolm *publishing executive*

New Providence
Cooper, Carol Diane *publishing company executive*
†Esser, Joseph Allen *editor*
Hollister, Dean *publishing company executive*
Roycroft, Edward J. *publishing company executive*

Newark
Aregood, Richard Lloyd *editor*
Bartner, Martin *newspaper executive*
Everett, Richard G. *newspaper editor*
Kanzler, George *journalist, critic*
Lenehan, Art *newspaper editor*
Newhouse, Donald E. *newspaper publishing executive*
Newhouse, Mark William *publishing executive*
Willse, James Patrick *newspaper editor*

Newton
†Mielo, Gary John *journalism educator*

North Caldwell
Siegel, Ira T. *publishing executive*

Northfield
Pollock, Michael Jeffrey *periodical editor*

Northvale
Aronson, Jason *publisher*
Kurzweil, Arthur *publisher, writer, educator*

Oldwick
Snyder, Arthur *publishing company executive*

Oradell
Nesoff, Robert *newspaper publisher*

Paramus
Brissie, Eugene Field, Jr. *publisher*

Parsippany
Smay, Connie R. *educational media specialist, educator*

Pennington
Harris, Frederick George *publishing company executive*

Pennsauken
Helmetag, Steven Charles *recording industry executive*

Piscataway
Fogiel, Max *publishing executive*
Hernandez, Prospero Medalla *book publisher, consultant*
Wasserman, Marlie P(arker) *publisher*

Pleasantville
Bennett, Eileen Patricia *copy editor, reporter*
Briant, Maryjane *newspaper editor*
†Peele, Thomas *journalist, writer*

Pompton Plains
Costello, Gerald Michael *editor*

Princeton
Buttenheim, Edgar Marion *publishing executive*
Grossman, Allen Neil *publishing executive*
Harayda, Janice *newspaper book editor, author*
Lippincott, Walter Heulings, Jr. *publishing executive*
Nied, Thomas H. *media company executive*
O'Donnell, Laurence Gerard *editorial consultant*
Palsho, Dorothea Coccoli *information services executive*
Steele, Marta F. Nussbaum *writer, editor, book*
Weiss, Renée Karol *editor, writer, musician*

Ramsey
Underwood, Steven Clark *publishing executive*

Ridgefield Park
D'Avella, Bernard Johnson, Jr. *publishing company executive, lawyer*

Ridgewood
Haveliwala, Hozefa Y.A. *journalist, writer*
Kiernan, Richard Francis *publisher*
Mitgang, Lee David *journalist, author, lecturer*

Rumson
Macdonald, Donald Arthur *publishing executive*

Rutherford
Davis, Joe David *broadcast executive*
Mongelli, Thomas Guy *broadcast executive, radio personality*

Saddle River
Dowden, Carroll Vincent *publishing company executive*
Noyes, Robert Edwin *publisher, writer*

Secaucus
Bailey, Steven Frederick *publishing executive*
Bender, Bruce F. *book publishing executive*
Black, Hillel Moses *publisher*
Fredericks, Alan *editor-in-chief*
†Gibson, John *news anchor, correspondent*
Lane, David Paul *publishing executive*
†O'Brien, Soledad *newscaster*
Povich, Lynn *journalist, magazine editor*
Verdi, David Joseph *broadcast news executive*
†Williams, Brian *news anchor, correspondent*

Short Hills
Soderlind, Sterling Eugene *newspaper industry consultant*
Winter, Ruth Grosman (Mrs. Arthur Winter) *journalist*

South Orange
Roseman, Martin Richard *publisher*

South River
Rachel, Eric Mark *recording industry executive*

Sparta
Spence, Robert Leroy *publishing executive*

Stockholm
dePaolo, Ronald Francis *editor, writer*

Summit
Scudder, Edward Wallace, Jr. *newspaper and broadcasting executive*

Teaneck
Ehrenfeld, Phyllis Rhoda *editor, playwright, book reviewer*

Toms River
Leone, Judith Gibson *educational media specialist, video production company executive*
Wagner, Edward Kurt *publishing company executive*

Trenton
Christopherson, Elizabeth Good *broadcast executive*
Joseph, Edith Hoffman *retired editor*

Upper Saddle River
Dojny, Richard Francis *publishing company executive*

Verona
Meyer, Helen (Mrs. Abraham J. Meyer) *retired editorial consultant*

Vineland
DeVivo, Sal J. *newspaper executive*

West Caldwell
Reboli, John Anthony *publishing executive*

Woodcliff Lake
Jacobs, Charles Nathan *editor, writer*

Wyckoff
Butterfield, Bruce Scott *publishing, communications and education executive, consultant*
Eiger, Richard William *retired publisher*

NEW MEXICO

Albuquerque
Danziger, Jerry *broadcasting executive*
Davidson, Juli *creativity consultant*
Hadas, Elizabeth Chamberlayne *publisher*
Lang, Thompson Hughes *publishing company executive*
McNeil, Mark Frasher *broadcast executive*
Tackman, Arthur Lester *newspaper publisher, management consultant*

Las Cruces
Pennington, Robert Michael *communications educator, consultant*

Los Alamos
Mendius, Patricia Dodd Winter *editor, educator, writer*

Santa Fe
Calloway, Larry *columnist*
Dirks, Lee Edward *newspaper executive*
Forsdale, (Chalmers) Louis *education and communication educator*
Groseclose, Everett Harrison *retired editor*
Hice, Michael *editor, marketing professional*
†Kaiser, Don *media trainer*
Lichtenberg, Margaret Klee *publishing company executive*
Mc Kinney, Robert Moody *newspaper editor and publisher*
Stieber, Tamar *journalist*

Silver City
†Hall, Edward Payson, Jr. *communication educator*
Hall, Jean Quintero *communication educator*

Taos
Bacon, Wallace Alger *speech communications educator, author*

NEW YORK

Albany
Cornell, Ralph Lawrence, Jr. *publishing executive*
Jakes, Lara Christine *newspaper reporter*
Mueller, I. Lynn *strategic planning and communications consultant*
Olmsted, Ruth Martin *editor*
Ortloff, George Christian, Sr. (Chris Ortloff) *journalist, state legislator*
Rosenfeld, Harry Morris *editor*
Smith, Rex William *journalist*
Tyksinski, Eugene Kory *broadcast executive*

Albertson
Ferber, Samuel *publishing executive*

Armonk
Korn, Steven Eric *medical publisher*
Sharpe, Myron Emanuel *publisher, editor, writer*

Astoria
Salzberg, Russ *sportscaster*
Somers, Steve *sportscaster*

Bainbridge
Goerlich, Shirley Alice Boyce *publisher, educator, consultant*

Baldwin Place
Kurian, George Thomas *publisher*

Ballston Lake
Silverman, Gerald Bernard *journalist*

Bayport
Poli, Kenneth Joseph *editor, writer, photographer*

Beacon
Mc Keown, William Taylor *magazine editor, author*

Bedford
Bowman, James Kinsey *publishing company executive, rare book specialist*

Bellport
Roland, David Leonard *broadcast production educator*
Townsend, Terry *publishing executive*

Bethpage
Dolan, Charles Francis *media, entertainment company executive*
Sweeney, Daniel Thomas *cable television company executive*

Binghamton
Cohen, William Mark *publisher*
Marella, Philip Daniel *broadcasting company executive*
Steffens, Martha Moutoux *newspaper editor, civic journalism consultant*

Bohemia
Maccarone, Frances Mary *publishing executive*

Brewster
Shepard, Jean Heck *publishing company consultant, author, agent*
Simon, Andrew L. *educational publishing executive*

Briarcliff Manor
Rinaldo, Peter Merritt *publishing executive*

Bridgehampton
Phillips, Warren Henry *publisher*

Bronx
†DeVivo, Darren Douglas *broadcast executive, announcer*
Moritz, Charles Fredric *book editor*
†Obioha, McLord Chinedum *magazine editor*
Regan, Harold James *publishing executive*
†Stein, Bernard L. *publishing executive*
Zalaznick, Sheldon *editor, journalist*

Bronxville
Greenwald, Martin *publishing company executive*
Keller, LeRoy *journalist, consultant*
Lombardo, Philip Joseph *broadcasting company executive*
Shuker, Gregory Brown *publishing and production company executive*

Brooklyn
Bianco, Anthony Joseph, III *newswriter*
Burlacu, Constantin *journalist, educator*
Cardoza, Avery *writer, publisher*
Daly, Joe Ann Godown *publishing company executive*
Newbauer, John Arthur *editor*
Ortner, Everett Howard *magazine editor, writer*
Ressner, Philip *editor*
Reynolds, Nancy Remick *editor, writer*
Sanford, David Boyer *writer, editor*
Walsh, George William *publishing company executive, editor*
Walz, Steven K. *newspaper editor*
Wiener, Hesh (Harold Frederic Wiener) *publisher, editor, consultant*

Buffalo
Brady-Borland, Karen *reporter*
Collins, J. Michael *public broadcasting executive*
Goldhaber, Gerald Martin *communication educator, author, consultant*
Halpert, Leonard Walter *retired editor*
Lee, Genevieve Bruggeman *publishing company executive*
Light, Murray Benjamin *newspaper editor*
Robinson, David Clinton *reporter*
†Sullivan, Margaret M. *managing editor*
Toles, Thomas Gregory *editorial cartoonist*
Trotter, Herman Eager, Jr. (Herman Trotter) *music critic*
Urban, Henry Zeller *newspaperman*
Vogel, Michael N. *journalist, writer, historian*
Woelfel, Joseph Donald *communications educator*

Campbell Hall
Ottaway, James Haller, Jr. *newspaper publisher*

Centerport
McQueeney, Henry Martin, Sr. *publisher*
Tunick, Laraine Donisi *publishing executive*

Chappaqua
Gstalder, Herbert William *publisher*
Ujifusa, Grant Masashi *editor*

Cherry Valley
Sapinsky, Joseph Charles *magazine executive, photographer*

Croton On Hudson
Shatzkin, Leonard *publishing consultant*
Straka, Laszlo Richard *publishing consultant*
Turner, David Reuben *publisher, author*

Dobbs Ferry
Downey, John Harold *publishing executive*
Holtz, Sidney *publishing company executive*
Simon, Lothar *publishing company executive*

East Hampton
De Bruhl, Marshall *writer, editor, publishing consultant*
Harmon, Marian Sanders *writer, sculptor*
Keagy, Dorothy (Dotti Keagy) *copywriter*

Elba
Kauffman, William Joseph *editor, writer*

Elmsford
Miranda, Robert Nicholas *publishing company executive*

Farmingdale
Steckler, Larry *publisher, editor, author*

Flushing
Cathcart, Robert Stephen *mass media consultant*
Chook, Paul Howard *publishing executive*
Kiner, Ralph McPherran *sports commentator, former baseball player*
Lopez-Pumarejo, Tomas Alberto *communications educator, marketing consultant*

Gardner, Janet Paxton journalist, video producer
Gardner, Joseph Lawrence editor, writer
Gardner, Roberta Joan library director
Garrett, Jane Nuckols editor, priest
Gebauer, Rüdiger publishing company executive
Gehringer, Richard George publishing executive
Gelb, Arthur newspaper editor
Gelb, Leslie Howard organization president, lecturer
Germano, William Paul publisher
Gershon, Bernard broadcast executive
Gerson, Robert Elisha periodical editor-in-chief
Gewirtz-Friedman, Gerry editor
Gharib, Susie television newscaster
†Gibaldi, Joseph publishing executive
Gibson, Charles DeWolf broadcast journalist
Gibson, Chip publishing executive
Giddins, Gary Mitchell music critic, columnist
Gilbert, Hamlin Miller, Jr. publishing executive
Giles, Robert Hartmann journalist, educator
Gilman, Richard H. newspaper publishing executive
Giniger, Kenneth Seeman publisher
Giraldi, Robert Nicholas film director
Giroux, Robert editor, book publisher, author
Gissler, Sigvard Gunnar, Jr. journalism educator, former newspaper editor
Godoff, Ann book editor
Goldberg, Sidney editor
Goldberger, Paul Jesse architecture critic, writer, educator, editor
Golden, Soma newspaper editor
Goldsmith, Robert Lewis youth association magazine executive
Goldstein, Norm editor, writer
Gollin, Albert Edwin media research executive, sociologist
Gollob, Herman Cohen retired publishing company, editor
Golson, George Barry editor
Goodstein, Les newspaper publishing executive
Gordevitch, Igor publishing company executive
Gottlieb, Paul publishing company executive
Gottlieb, Robert Adams publisher
Gould, Eleanor Lois (Eleanor Gould Packard) editor, grammarian
Grader, Patricia Alison Lande editor
Gralla, Lawrence publishing company executive
Grann, Phyllis publisher, editor
Graves, Earl Gilbert publisher
Greco, Albert Nicholas communications educator
Green, Dan publishing company executive
Green, George Joseph publishing executive
Greene, Richard H. journalist
Greenfield, (Henry) Jeff news analyst
Grenquist, Peter Carl consultant
Grigonis, Richard William technical editor
Grigsby, Henry Jefferson, Jr. editor
Gropp, Louis Oliver editor in chief
Grose, William Rush publishing executive
Grossman, Janice magazine publishing company executive
Grune, George Vincent publishing company executive
Guccione, Robert Charles Joseph Edward Sabatini publisher
Guiher, James Morford, Jr. publisher, writer
Gumbel, Greg sportscaster
Gwertzman, Bernard newspaper editor
Hager, Larry Stanley book editor, publishing executive
Haire, Jack magazine publisher
Halasz, Robert Joseph editor
Hall, Abram publishing production manager
Hall, Nancy Christensen publishing company executive, author, editor
Hallett, E. Bruce, III publishing executive
†Hansen, Nanette Elizabeth anchorwoman, correspondent
Harden, Blaine Charles journalist
Hartford, William Henry magazine editor, writer, lecturer
Hauck, Marguerite Hall broadcasting executive
Hauser, Gustave M. cable television and electronic communications company executive
Hearst, Randolph Apperson publishing executive
Heins, John publishing executive
Heller, Jamie Gale editor, lawyer
Heloise columnist, lecturer, broadcaster, author
Henriques, Diana Blackmon journalist
†Herald, George William foreign correspondent
Herder, Gwendolin Elisabeth Maria publishing executive
Herman, R(obert) Thomas journalist
Herman, Scott Hunt radio station executive
Hertz, Leon publishing executive
Hicks, Tyler Gregory publishing company executive, writer
Hill, Wallace Harry sports television consultant
Hills, Frederic Wheeler editor, publishing company executive
Hinckley, David Malcolm journalist, editor, critic
Hinojosa, Maria L. news correspondent
Hippeau, Eric book publishing executive
Hirsch, George Aaron publisher
Hirsch, Roseann Conte publisher
Hiss, Tony writer
Hoffman, Michael Eugene editor, publisher, museum curator
Holch, Gregory John children's book editor, author
Holland, Bernard Peabody music critic
Holmes, Miriam H. publisher
Holt, Donald Dale magazine editor
Holt, Sidney Clark journalist
Honan, William Holmes journalist, writer
Hopkins, Jan journalist, news anchor
House, Karen Elliott company executive, former editor, reporter
Howat, Kevin John publishing executive
Hoyt, Anthony S. publishing executive
Hudson, Richard McLain, Jr. journalist, researcher
Hughes, Allen music critic
Hunter-Bone, Maureen Claire magazine editor
Hurewitz, Miriam F. copyeditor
Hurley, Cheryl Joyce book publishing executive
Huxtable, Ada Louise architecture critic
Iger, Robert A. broadcast executive
Innesa, Levkova-Lamm art critic, writer, curator
Isaacson, Walter Seff editor
Isenberg, Steven Lawrence publishing executive, retired
†Jackson, Ann Williams publisher
Jameson, Richard magazine editor, film critic
Jamison, Jayne magazine publisher
Janssen, Peter Anton magazine editor and publisher
Jaroff, Leon Morton magazine editor
†Jay-Z (Jigga), (Sean Carter) music company executive
†Jeanson, Cedric film company executive
Jefferson, Margo L. journalist
Jellinek, George broadcast executive, writer, music educator
Jenkins, Anthony Charles correspondent
Jennings, Peter Charles television anchorman
Jensen, Michael Charles journalist, lecturer, author
Jewler, Sarah magazine editor
Johnson, John broadcast journalist
Johnson, John H. publisher, consumer products executive
Johnston, Catherine V. magazine publisher
Jones, Alex S. journalist, writer, broadcaster
Jones, David Rhodes retired newspaper editor, consultant
Jones, Laurie Lynn magazine editor
Juran, Sylvia Louise editor
Kael, Pauline film critic, author
Kahn, Jim magazine publisher
Kahn, Nancy Valerie publishing and entertainment executive, consultant
†Kakutani, Michiko critic
Kalajian-Lagani, Donna publishing executive
†Kalech, Marc newspaper editor
Kamhi, Michelle Marder editor, writer
Kann, Peter Robert journalist, newspaper publishing executive
Kaplan, Jerry magazine publisher
Karmazin, Mel broadcast executive
Karpel, Craig S. journalist, editor
Kaufman, Victor A. broadcast executive, former film company executive
Keane, Bil cartoonist
†Keller, Bill journalist
Kellogg, David publisher
Kennedy, Marla Hamburg publisher, gallery director
Kenney, Thomas Michael publisher
Keppler, Herbert publishing company executive
Kesting, Theodore magazine editor
Kiechel, Walter, III editor
Kiely, Garrett Paul publishing executive
King, Roger M. syndicated programs distributing company executive
Kirchner, Jake publishing executive
Kirk, Susanne Smith editor
Kirshbaum, Laurence J. book publishing executive
Kirshenbaum, Jerry editor, journalist
Kislik, Richard William publishing executive
Kismaric, Carole Lee editor, writer, book packaging company executive
Kissel, Howard William drama critic
Kjellberg, Ann C. editor
Kleinwald, Martin (Martin Littlefield) book publishing executive
Klingensmith, Mike publishing executive
Klinghoffer, David journalist
Knowlton, Leslie Brooks journalist
Kolatch, Myron magazine editor
Korman, Lewis J. entertainment/media company executive, lawyer
Koslow, Sally editor-in-chief
Kosner, Edward A(lan) magazine editor and publisher
Koster, Elaine Landis publishing executive
Koteff, Ellen periodical editor
Kozodoy, Neal magazine editor
†Krajick, Kevin Rudolph journalist
Krebsbach, Karen Anton journalist
Kreda, Allan Jay journalist
Krenek, Debby newspaper editor
Krents, Milton Ellis broadcast executive
Kristof, Nicholas Donabet journalist
Kroft, Steve news correspondent, editor
†Kuchment, Anna M. journalist
Kummerfeld, Donald David publisher
Lack, Andrew broadcast executive
Lamirande, Arthur Gordon editor, author, musician, actor
Lamm, Donald Stephen publishing company executive
Lamont, Lansing journalist, public affairs executive, author
Landau, Sidney I. publishing executive
Landy, Rona broadcast executive
Lane, Nancy editor
†Lang, Christof television journalist
Lang, Vera J. publishing company executive
Lapham, Lewis Henry editor, author, television host
Lauer, Matt broadcast journalist
Laurence, Leslie journalist
†Laybourne, Geraldine broadcasting executive
Leahey, Lynn editor-in-chief
Leahy, Michael Joseph newspaper editor
LeDoux, Harold Anthony cartoonist, painter
Lee, Frances Helen editor
Lee, Sally A. editor-in-chief
Lees, Alfred William writer, former magazine editor
Lehmann-Haupt, Christopher Charles Herbert book reviewer
Lelyveld, Joseph Salem newspaper editor, correspondent
Leonard, Rachel Rauh editor
Levin, Alan M. television journalist
Levin, Gerald M. media and entertainment company executive
Levin, Martin P. publishing executive, lawyer
Levine, Charles Michael publishing company executive, consultant
Levine, Ellen R. magazine editor
Levinson, Warren Mitchell broadcast journalist
Levitas, Mitchel Ramsey editor
Levitz, Paul Elliot publishing executive
Levy, Alan Joseph editor, journalist, writer
†Levy, George Harold publishing company executive
†Lewis, Edward T. publisher
Lewis, Russell T. newspaper publishing executive
Lingeman, Richard Roberts editor, writer
Littleford, William Donaldson retired publishing executive
Loeb, Marshall Robert journalist
Logan, Don publishing executive
Long, David L. magazine publisher
Long, Elizabeth Valk magazine publisher
Long, Lisa Valk communications company executive
Longley, Marjorie Watters newspaper executive
Loomis, Carol J. journalist
Loomis, Robert Duane publishing company executive, author
Lord, Robert Wilder retired editor and writer
Losee, Thomas Penny, Jr. publisher
Low, Richard H. broadcasting executive, producer
Lurie, Ranan Raymond political cartoonist, political analyst, artist, lecturer
Lynne, Michael film company executive
Lynton, Michael publishing executive
†Mabrey, Vicki news correspondent, anchor
MacGowan, Sandra Firelli publishing executive, publishing educator
Machlin, Milton Robert magazine editor, writer
Macri, Theodore William book publisher
Madden, John television sports commentator, former professional football coach
Malamed, Seymour H. motion picture company executive
Maleska, Martin Edmund publishing executive
Maletta, Lou broadcast executive
Mapes, Glynn Dempsey newspaper editor
Mardin, Arif music industry executive, musician
Marlette, Douglas Nigel editorial cartoonist, comic strip creator
Martin, Judith Sylvia journalist, author
Martin, Paul Ross editor
Martz, Lawrence Stannard periodical editor
†Maslin, Janet film critic
Mathews, Jack Wayne journalist, film critic
Maurer, Gilbert Charles media company executive
Mazzola, Anthony Thomas editor, art consultant, designer, writer
McAniff, Nora P. publishing executive
McCarrick, Edward R. magazine publisher
McCarthy, Patrick magazine publishing executive
†McCarty, V.K. publisher
McCormack, Thomas Joseph retired publishing company executive
McCrie, Robert Delbert editor, publisher, educator
McCurdy, Charles Gribbel publishing company executive
McDonell, Robert Terry magazine editor, novelist
McDowell, Edwin S. journalist, novelist
McEwen, James publishing executive
†McEwen, Mark anchor
McFadden, Robert Dennis reporter
McFeely, William Drake publishing company executive
McGee, Henry broadcast executive
McGill, Frank media consulting firm specialist
McGill, Jay magazine publisher
McGinnis, Arthur Joseph publisher
McGrath, Charles Arthur editor, writer
McGrath, Eleanor Burns editor, writer
McGrath, Judith broadcast executive
McGraw, Harold Whittlesey, Jr. publisher
Mc Kay, Jim television sports commentator
McKenna, Kevin Patrick newspaper editor
†McLaughlin, David broadcast executive
McMorrow, Eileen editor periodical
Mc Pherson, Paul Francis publishing and investment banking executive
Meagher, James Proctor editor
Means Coleman, Robin Renee' communication educator
Medenica, Gordon publisher
Mehta, A. Sonny publishing company executive
Mehta, Julie Mahendra editor, writer
Meigs, James B. editor-in-chief
Melloan, George Richard editor, columnist, writer
Melvin, Russell Johnston magazine publishing consultant
Mencher, Melvin journalist, retired educator
†Mendini, Douglas A. publishing company executive, writer
Meserve, Mollie Ann publisher
Metz, Robert Roy publisher, editor
Meyer, Karl Ernest journalist
Meyer, Pucci newspaper editor
Meyers, John Allen magazine publisher
Michaels, Alan Richard sports commentator
Michaels, James Walker magazine editor
Michaud, Christopher journalist
Mikita, Joseph Karl broadcasting executive
Miller, Caroline editor-in-chief
Miller, Darcy M. publishing executive
Miller, Michael Jeffrey editor, columnist
Minard, Everett Lawrence, III journalist, magazine editor
Mirenburg, Barry Leonard publisher, company executive, educator
Mohler, Mary Gail magazine editor
Molho, Emanuel publisher
Montorio, John Angelo magazine editor
Moore, Ann S. magazine executive
†Morgan, Jeffrey D. publisher
†Morillo, Mariano journalist
Morris, Douglas Peter recording company executive
Morton, Brian writer, editor, educator
Moskin, John Robert editor, writer
Mottola, Thomas entertainment company executive
Moyers, Bill D. journalist
Moyers, Judith Davidson television producer
†Muldow, Susan publishing executive
Muller, Henry James journalist, magazine editor
Murdoch, (Keith) Rupert publisher
Murphy, Ann Pleshette magazine editor-in-chief
Murphy, Helen recording industry executive
Muth, John Francis newspaper editor, columnist
Nagourney, Herbert publishing company executive
Naiburg, Irving B., Jr. publisher
Nathan, Paul S. editor, writer
Navasky, Victor Saul magazine editor, publisher
Negroponte, John Dimitri publishing company official, former diplomat
Newcomb, Jonathan publishing executive
Newhouse, Nancy Riley newspaper editor
Newman, David Robert magazine editor
Newman, Nancy publishing executive
Newman, Rachel magazine editor
Nibley, Andrew Mathews editorial executive
Nielsen, Nancy publishing executive
Nielsen Hayden, Patrick editor
Norris, Floyd Hamilton financial journalist
Norville, Deborah news correspondent
Novitz, Charles Richard television executive
Novogrod, Nancy Ellen editor
Nyren, Neil Sebastian publisher, editor
Oakes, John Bertram writer, editor
O'Brien, Geoffrey Paul editor, writer
Ochs, Michael editor, librarian, music educator
O'Connell, Margaret Ellen editor, writer
O'Dair, Barbara editor
Okrent, Daniel magazine editor, writer
Oldham, Joe editor
†Olson, Peter publishing executive
O'Neil, James Peter financial printing company executive
Orwoll, Mark Peter magazine editor
†Osgood, Charles news broadcaster, journalist
Osnos, Peter Lionel Winston publishing executive
Ostling, Richard Neil journalist, author, broadcaster
O'Sullivan, John editor
Pace, Eric Dwight journalist
Packard, George Randolph journalist, educator
Paneth, Donald Joseph editor, writer
Paradise, Robert Richard publishing executive
Paro, Jeff publisher
Patterson, Perry William publishing company executive
Pauley, Jane television journalist
†Pearce, Carol Ann editor, writer
Pearlstine, Norman editor
Peck, Thomas newspaper publishing executive
Penn, Stanley William journalist
Peper, George Frederick editor
Perney, Linda newspaper editor
Pesin, Ella Michele journalist, public relations professional
Petersen, Barry Rex news correspondent
Petzal, David Elias editor, writer
Pfeiffer, Jane Cahill former broadcasting company executive, consultant
Pfund, Niko publishing executive
Phillips, Reneé magazine editor, author, public speaker
Phillips, Stone newscaster
Piel, Gerard science editor, publisher
Podd, Ann newspaper editor
Polito, Robert writer
†Pope, Leavitt Joseph broadcast company executive
Pope, Liston, Jr. writer, journalist
Portale, Carl publishing executive
Porterfield, Christopher magazine editor, writer
Post, David Alan internet technology executive
Povich, (Maurice) Maury Richard broadcast journalist, talk show host, television producer
Press, Michelle editor
Prestbo, John Andrew newspaper editor, journalist, author
Pursley, Joan Muyskens editor
Quindlen, Anna journalist, author
Quinn, Jane Bryant journalist, writer
Quinn, Sally journalist
Quinson, Bruno Andre publishing executive
Raab, Selwyn journalist
Ragan, David publishing company executive
Raines, Howell Hiram newspaper editor, journalist
Ramirez, Carlos David publisher
Rashad, Ahmad sports broadcaster, former professional football player
Rather, Dan broadcast journalist
Rauch, Rudolph Stewart, III periodical editor, arts education executive
Rawson, Eleanor S. publishing company executive
Rawson, Hugh Robert book publishing executive, writer
Ray, C. Claiborne editor, columnist
Ray, William Melvin newsletter publishing consultant
Reed, James Donald journalist, author
Regan, Judith Theresa publishing executive
Reichl, Ruth Molly editor
Reidy, Carolyn Kroll publisher
Reilly, William Francis media company executive
Remelius, Roger Martin broadcasting and licensing executive
Remnick, David J. journalist, editor
Rescigno, Richard Joseph editor
Reuther, David Louis children's book publisher, writer
Reyburn, Pamela Sue journalist
Reynolds, Mary Robbin publishing company executive
Reynolds, Warren Jay retired publisher
Rhoads, Geraldine Emeline editor
Rhone, Sylvia recording industry executive
Rich, Frank Hart critic
†Richardson, Elaina magazine editor
Richardson, Ralph Ernest publisher
Rigby, Paul Crispin artist, cartoonist
Riggio, Leonard book publishing executive
Riggs, Michael David magazine editor, writer
Rigney, Jane copy editor, writer
Ripp, Joseph Allen publishing executive
†Robelot, Jane anchor
Roberts, Elizabeth McCreery magazine editor
†Roberts, John news anchor
Roberts, Madelyn Alpert publishing executive
†Robinson, Janet publishing executive
Robinson, Maurice Richard, Jr. publishing executive
Rogin, Gilbert Leslie editor, author
Roland, John newscaster
Rollins, Sherrie Sandy television executive
Romain, Pierre R. commercial and television production executive, producer
Ronson, Raoul R. publishing executive
Rooney, Michael Francis publisher
Rose, Charles television journalist
Rosen, Carole cable television executive
Rosensweig, Dan publishing executive
Rosenthal, Abraham Michael journalist
Rosenthal, Andrew newspaper editor
Rosenthal, Jacob (Jack Rosenthal) newspaper editor
Rosenthal, Lucy Gabrielle writer, educator, editor
Ross, Norman Alan publisher
Rosset, Barnet Lee, Jr. publisher
Rothberg, Gerald editor, publisher
Rubin, Harry Meyer entertainment industry executive
Rubin, Stephen Edward editor, journalist
Rudin, Max Allen publishing executive
Ryan, Michael E. newspaper publishing executive
Ryan, Regina Claire (Mrs. Paul Deutschman) editor, book packager, literary agent
Sabat, Robert Hartman magazine editor
Sabino, Catherine Ann magazine editor
Sabosik, Patricia Elizabeth publisher, editor
Safer, Morley journalist
Salembier, Valerie Birnbaum publishing executive
Saltz, Carole Pogrebin publisher
Samelson, Judy editor
Sanders, Richard Louis executive editor
†Sandum, Howard E. literary agent
Sawyer, (L.) Diane television journalist
Saxon, Wolfgang Erik Georg journalist
Scannell, Herb broadcast executive
Scarborough, Charles Bishop, III broadcast journalist, writer
Schaap, Richard Jay journalist
Schein, Gerald D. publishing executive
Schiffrin, Andre publisher
Schillinger, Liesl Katharine journalist
Schlosser, Herbert S. broadcasting company executive
Schmemann, Serge journalist
Schmertz, Mildred Floyd editor, writer
Schmidt, Stanley Albert editor, writer
Schoell, William Robert editor, author
Schonberg, Harold Charles music critic, columnist
Schrader, Michael Eugene columnist, editor
Schulz, Ralph Richard publishing consultant
Schuman, Patricia Glass publishing company executive, educator
Scribner, Charles, III publisher, art historian, lecturer
Seave, Ava publishing executive
Segal, Jonathan Bruce editor
Seligman, Daniel editor

Semple, Robert Baylor, Jr. newspaper editor, journalist
Servodidio, Pat Anthony broadcast executive
Settipani, Frank G. news correspondent
Seymore, James W., Jr. magazine editor
Seymour, Lesley Jane magazine editor-in-chief
Shaine, Frederick Mordecai newspaper executive, consultant
Shanks, David publishing executive
Sheinman, Morton Maxwell editor, consultant, writer, photographer
Shepard, Stephen Benjamin journalist, magazine editor
Shepard, Thomas Rockwell, III advertising sales executive
Shepherd, Kathleen Shearer Maynard television executive
Sherman, Robert broadcaster
Shestack, Melvin Bernard editor, author, filmmaker, television producer
Sheward, David John newspaper editor and critic
Shewchuk, Robert John television executive
Shier, Shelley M. production company executive
Shnayerson, Robert Beahan editor
Shortz, Will puzzle editor
Siegal, Allan Marshall newspaper editor
Siegel, Joel Steven television news correspondent
Siegel, Marvin newspaper editor
Siek, Rainer broadcast executive
Sifton, Elisabeth book publisher
Sikorsky, Robert Bellarmine syndicated columnist
Silberman, James Henry editor, publisher
Silver, Shelly Andrea media artist
Silverman, Stephen Meredith journalist, screenwriter, producer
Silvers, Robert Benjamin editor
Simmons, Russell recording industry executive
†Simon, Bob news correspondent, anchor
Simonson, Lee Stuart broadcast company executive
Singer, Niki publishing executive, public relations executive
Singerman, Martin newspaper publishing executive
Singleton, Donald Edward journalist
Skillin, Edward Simeon magazine publisher
†Skinner, Peter Graeme publishing executive, lawyer
Sleed, Joel columnist
Sloan, Allan Herbert journalist
Smith, Charles Carter, Jr. publishing executive
Smith, Corlies Morgan publishing executive
Smith, Joseph Phelan film company executive
Smith, Leigh Randall newspaper reporter
Smith, Liz (Mary Elizabeth Smith) newspaper columnist, broadcast journalist
Smith, Patrick John editor, writer
Smith, Richard Mills editor in chief, magazine executive
†Smith, Todd magazine editor-in-chief
Smith, Warren Allen editor
Snyder, Richard Elliot publishing company executive
Solvano, Steve media specialist
Sonenberg, David Alan personal manager
Soren, Tabitha L. television newscaster, writer
Speller, Robert Ernest Blakefield publishing executive
Spence, James Robert, Jr. television sports executive
Spengler, Cindy J. publisher
Spring, Michael editor, writer
†Squires, John publishing executive
Stahl, Lesley R. journalist
Stamaty, Mark Alan cartoonist, author, artist
Stanger, Ila writer, editor
Steiger, Paul Ernest newspaper editor, journalist
Steinfeld, Thomas Albert publisher
Stephenson, Michele editor
Stern, Robert D. publishing executive
Stern, Roslyne Paige magazine publisher
†Sterritt, David John film critic, educator
†Stone, Laurie journalist, writer
Stossel, John news analyst
Straus, Roger W., Jr. publishing company executive
Stringer, Howard television executive
Stuart, Carole publishing executive
Stuart, Jane Elizabeth film and video executive
Stuart, Lyle publishing company executive
Studin, Jan publishing executive
Sturtevant, Peter Mann, Jr. television news executive
Sugihara, Kenzi publishing executive
Sugiyama, Kazunori music producer
Sullivan, Timothy J. journalist
Sulzberger, Arthur Ochs newspaper executive
Sulzberger, Arthur Ochs, Jr. newspaper publisher
Summer, Sharon publisher
Summerall, Pat (George Allan Summerall) sportscaster
Sussman, Gerald publishing company executive
Sustendal, Diane consultant
Sutton-Straus, Joan M. journalist
Sweed, Phyllis publishing executive
Sweezy, Paul Marlor editor, publisher
Swenson, Steven M. broadcast executive
Sykes, Jolene publishing executive
Szenasy, Susan Selma magazine editor
Talese, Nan Ahearn publishing company executive
Talley, Truman Macdonald publisher
Tatum, Wilbert Arnold editor, publisher
Taylor, Sherril Wightman broadcasting company executive
Taylor, Susan L. editor, magazine
Taylor, Terry R. editor, educator
Temple, Wick journalist
Thomas, Brooks publishing company executive
Thompson, Martin Christian news service executive
Tober, Barbara D. (Mrs. Donald Gibbs Tober) editor
Toff, Nancy Ellen book editor
Tomlinson, James Francis retired news agency executive
Tong, Kaity anchor
Torres, Louis editor, writer
Toussaint, Allen Richard recording studio executive, composer, pianist
Townsend, Alair Ane publisher, municipal official
Townsend, Charles H. publishing executive
Tuchman, Gary Robert television news correspondent
Tuchman, Phyllis critic
Tucker, Alan David publisher
Ubell, Robert Neil editor, publisher, consultant
Uchitelle, Louis journalist
Udell Turshen, Rochelle Marcia publishing executive
Ungaro, Susan Kelliher magazine editor
Urdang, Alexandra book publishing executive
Valand, Theodore Lloyd media company executive
Valenti, Carl M. retired newspaper publisher
Van Sant, Peter Richard news correspondent
Vaughan, Linda publishing executive
Vaughan, Samuel Snell editor, author, publisher
Vecsey, George Spencer sports columnist
Vega, Marylois Purdy journalist
Vitale, Alberto Aldo publishing company executive
Vitale, Dick commentator, sports writer
Vittorini, Carlo publishing company executive
Voorhees, David William editor, historian
Wald, Richard Charles broadcasting executive
Walker, Mort cartoonist
†Wall, Carolyn Raimondi communications executive
Wallace, G. David magazine editor
Wallace, Ken magazine publisher
Wallace, Mike television interviewer and reporter
Wallace, Patrick T. broadcast executive
Wallace, Thomas J. magazine editor-in-chief
Walters, Barbara television journalist
Walters, Raymond, Jr. newspaper editor, author
Wang, Arthur Woods retired publisher
Warner, Peter David publishing executive
Waxenberg, Alan M. publisher
Weber, Robert Maxwell cartoonist
Wechsler, Bradley J. film company executive
Weinstein, Harvey film company executive
Weinstein, Robert film company executive
Weintz, Walter Louis book publishing company executive
Welling, Kathryn Marie editor
Wells, Linda Ann editor-in-chief
Welsh, Donald Emory publisher
Wenner, Jann Simon editor, publisher
Westin, David broadcast executive
Wetschler, Ed editor
Wheeler, Michael broadcast executive
Whitaker, Mark Theis magazine editor
White, Kate editor-in-chief
White, Russell publishing executive
White, Timothy Thomas Anthony writer, editor, broadcaster
Whiteman, Douglas E. publisher
Whittell, Polly (Mary) Kaye editor, journalist
Wiggers, Charlotte Suzanne Ward magazine editor
Wiley, Bradford publishing executive
Wilford, John Noble, Jr. news correspondent
Williams, Alun Gwyn publishing company executive
Willis, John Alvin editor
Winfrey, Carey Wells journalist, magazine editor
Winship, Frederick Moery journalist
Wintour, Anna editor
Wittenberg, Kate editor
Wittman, Allan Henry publishing executive
Wogan, Robert broadcasting company executive
Wolmer, Bruce Richard magazine editor
Woodcock, Les editorial director
Woodruff, Mark Reed magazine editor
Wössner, Mark Matthias publishing company executive
Wright, Bob broadcasting executive
Wright, Robert broadcast executive
Yablon, Leonard Harold publishing company executive
Young, Ethan editor
Young, Genevieve Leman publishing executive, editor
Yunich, Peter B. publishing executive
Yurkiw, Mark Leo executive
Zackheim, Adrian Walter editor
Zahn, Paula newscaster
Zanetti, Richard Joseph publisher
Zeldin, Richard Packer publisher
Zerman, Melvyn Bernard publishing company executive, author
Zevon, Susan Jane editor
Zimbalist, Efrem, III publishing company executive
Zimmerman, William Edwin newspaper editor, publisher, writer
Zuckerman, Mortimer Benjamin publisher, editor, real estate developer

North Salem
Burlingame, Edward Livermore book publisher
Larsen, Jonathan Zerbe journalist

Nyack
Flood, (Hulda) Gay editor, consultant
Oursler, Fulton, Jr. editor, writer

Old Brookville
Fairman, Joel Martin broadcasting executive

Old Westbury
O'Brien, Adrienne Gratia communications educator

Ossining
Carter, Richard publisher, writer
Stein, Sol publisher, writer, editor in chief

Oswego
Loveridge-Sanbonmatsu, Joan Meredith communication studies educator

Palisades
Polk, Milbry Catherine media specialist

Pelham
Minick, Michael publishing executive

Plainview
Newman, Edwin Harold news commentator

Pleasantville
Krefting, Robert J(ohn) publishing company executive
Willcox, Christopher Patrick magazine editor

Port Washington
Candido, Arthur Aldo publishing and distribution company executive
Jay, Frank Peter writer, educator

Poughkeepsie
Kim, David Sang Chul publisher, evangelist, retired seminary president
VanBuren, Denise Doring media relations executive

Purchase
Sandler, Irving Harry art critic, art historian

Remsenburg
Billman, Irwin Edward publishing company executive

Rhinecliff
Dierdorff, John Ainsworth retired editor

Riverdale
Chimsky, Mark Evan publishing consultant
Ellentuck, Elmer journal editor

Rochester
Fallesen, Gary David journalist
Lank, Edith Handleman columnist, educator
Moore, Matthew Scott publisher, deaf advocate, author
Pitoniak, Scott Michael sports columnist
Prosser, Michael Hubert communications educator
Rosenhouse, Michael Allan lawyer, editor, publishing executive
†Young, Cynthia Nason magazine editor, artist

Rockville Centre
McFaul, Patricia Louise editor

Rome
Waters, George Bausch newspaper publisher

Ronkonkoma
Pati, Christopher Martin musician, record company executive

Roslyn
Risom, Ole Christian publishing company executive

Rye
Goodenough, Andrew Lewis publishing executive
Stoller, Ezra photojournalist

Scarborough
†Byrne, Robert Eugene chess columnist

Scarsdale
Arond, Miriam magazine editor, writer
Frackman, Noel art critic
Frankel, Stanley Arthur columnist, educator, business executive
†Gertler, Stephanie Jocelyn journalist
Heese, William John music publishing company executive
O'Neill, Michael James editor, author
Topping, Audrey Ronning photojournalist, author
Topping, Seymour publishing executive, educator

Setauket
Robinson, Richard M. technical communication specialist

Somers
Boudreaux, John public relations/internet specialist
Cohn, Howard retired magazine editor

South Nyack
Leiser, Ernest Stern journalist

South Salem
Moore, Raymond Lionel recording engineer, record producer

Southampton
Graham, Howard Barrett publishing company executive
Smith, Dennis (Edward) author, publisher

Spencertown
Lieber, Charles Donald publisher

Staten Island
Diamond, Richard Edward publisher
Newhouse, Samuel I., Jr. publishing executive
†Silverstein, Arthur publishing executive

Stony Brook
Booth, George cartoonist
Harvey, Christine Lynn publishing executive
Manvich, Donna multimedia copyright researcher, consultant, permissions specialist

Sugar Loaf
Rogers, James Tracy editor, author

Syosset
Rudman, Michael P. publishing executive

Syracuse
Bunn, Timothy David newspaper editor
Kennedy, Samuel Van Dyke, III journalism educator
LaRue, William David television critic
Mesrobian, Arpena Sachaklian publisher, editor, consultant
Rogers, Stephen newspaper publisher

Tarrytown
Ashburn, Anderson magazine editor
LeGrice, Stephen magazine editor
Neill, Richard Robert retired publishing company executive
Whipple, Judith Roy book editor
Wood, Roger publishing executive

Troy
Friedman, Sue Tyler technical publications executive
Goode, Jean publishing company executive
Rubens, Philip communications educator, technical writer

Utica
Donovan, Donna Mae newspaper publisher

Valley Cottage
Stolldorf, Genevieve Schwager media specialist

Valley Stream
Lehrer, Stanley magazine publisher, editorial director, corporate executive

Wading River
Budd, Bernadette Smith newspaper executive, public relations consultant

Wainscott
Henderson, William Charles editor

Warwick
Simon, Dolores Daly copy editor

Watertown
Brett, James Clarence retired journalism educator
Johnson, John Brayton editor, publisher

White Plains
Goodman, Walter author, editor
Minsker, Eliot A. publishing executive
Patman, Jean Elizabeth journalist
†Ritter, Robert W. editor
Scott-Williams, Wendy Lee information technology specialist
Silverman, Al editor
Vick, James Albert publishing executive, consultant

Woodbury
Bell, William Joseph cable television company executive
McEnroe, Kate broadcast executive

Woodhaven
†Liu, Weihong art critic

Yonkers
Denver, Eileen Ann magazine editor
Eimicke, Victor W(illiam) publishing company executive
Leo, Jacqueline M. television executive, editor

Yorktown Heights
Wade, James O'Shea publisher

NORTH CAROLINA

Asheville
Damtoft, Walter Atkinson editor, publisher

Boone
Aluri, Rao book publisher

Brevard
Phillips, Euan Hywel publishing executive

Burlington
Buckley, J. Stephen newspaper publisher

Carrboro
Boggs, Robert Newell editor

Cary
McCarty, Thomas Joseph publishing company executive

Chapel Hill
Lauder, Valarie Anne editor, educator

Charlotte
Barrows, Frank Clemence newspaper editor
Buckner, Jennie newspaper editor
Curtis, Mary C. journalist
Haines, Kenneth H. television broadcasting executive
Horner, Bob broadcast executive
Neill, Rolfe retired newspaper executive
†Powell, Dannye Romine news columnist
†Ridder, Peter B. publishing executive
Sharits, Dean Paul motion picture company executive
Swicegood, Steven Lloyd reporter
Williams, Edwin Neel newspaper editor

Dunn
Adams, Hoover newspaper founder

Durham
Cooper, Charles Howard photojournalist, newspaper publishing company executive
Fiske, Edward Bogardus editor, journalist, educational consultant
Harrell, (Benjamin) Carlton columnist, retired editor
Hawkins, William E. N. newspaper editor
Rollins, Edward Tyler, Jr. newspaper executive
Rossiter, Alexander, Jr. news service executive, editor

Edenton
Walklet, John James, Jr. publishing executive

Fayetteville
†Swain, Mary Margaret editor, marketing consultant

Goldsboro
Price, Eugene newspaper editor

Greensboro
Blackwell, William Ernest broadcast industry executive
Gill, Evalyn Pierpoint writer, editor, publisher
Herman, Roger Eliot professional speaker, consultant, futurist, writer
Jellicorse, John Lee communications and theatre educator
McKissick-Melton, S. Charmaine mass communications educator

Greenville
†Eribo, Festus mass communication educator, journalist

Hampstead
Unger, Stephen Allen publishing executive, editor

Harrisburg
Economaki, Chris Constantine (Christopher Economaki) publisher, editor
Ethridge, Mark Foster, III writer, publisher, media consultant

Highlands
Tietze, Phyllis Somerville retired media specialist

Hillsborough
Bolduc, Jean Plumley journalist, education activist

Jefferson
Franklin, Robert McFarland book publisher

Laurel Springs
Gilbert-Strawbridge, Anne Wieland journalist

Lenoir
†Hicks, Cecilia Perkins *editor*

Lillington
Harrington, Anthony Ross *radio announcer, educator*

Morganton
†Jones, Geraldine Mary Florence *journalist*

Newton
Harris, Gerald Wayne *retired radio advertising sales executive*

Pittsboro
Bailey, Herbert Smith, Jr. *retired publisher*
Hauser, Charles Newland McCorkle *newspaper consultant*
Shurick, Edward Palmes *television executive, rancher*

Raleigh
Cohen, David Michael *newspaper editor, journalist*
Crisp, Fred *publishing executive*
Daniels, Frank Arthur, Jr. *newspaper publisher*
Daniels, Frank Arthur, III *publishing executive*
Effron, Seth Alan *editor, journalist*
Entman, Robert Mathew *communications educator, consultant*
Hendricks, Chris *publisher*
Kauffman, Terry *broadcast and creative arts communication educator, artist*
Paschal, Beth Cummings *journalist, editor*
Powell, Drexel Dwane, Jr. *editorial cartoonist*
Reeves, Ralph B., III *publisher, editor*
Scogin, Troy Pope *publishing company executive, accounts executive*

Salisbury
Post, Rose Zimmerman *newspaper columnist*

Saluda
Mc Cutcheon, John Tinney, Jr. *journalist*

Smyrna
†Doble, Richard deGaris *editor, publisher, photographer*

Spindale
Trautmann, Patricia Ann *communications educator, storyteller*

Waxhaw
Lamparter, William C. *printing and publishing consultant, digital printing and information systems specialist*

Winston Salem
†Dykers, Carol Reese *communications educator*
Graybeal, Barbara *editor, writer*
King, Wayne Edgar *educator, journalist*
†Poston, William Roger, II *biomedical communications educator*
Tursi, Frank Vincent *journalist*

Wrightsville Beach
Mc Ilwain, William Franklin *newspaper editor, writer*

NORTH DAKOTA

Bismarck
Thomas, John *communications technologist*

Fargo
Hipschman, David *editor*
Littlefield, Robert Stephen *communication educator, training consultant*
Paulson, John Doran *newspaper editor, retired*

Finley
Devlin, William Russell *newspaper owner*

Garrison
Gackle, Donald Christoph *publisher*

OHIO

Akron
Dotson, John Louis, Jr. *newspaper publisher*
Fuentez, Tania Michele *copy editor, writer*
Leach, Janet C. *publishing executive*

Athens
Metters, Thomas Waddell *sports writer*
Sanders, David *university press administrator*
Scott, Charles Lewis *photojournalist*
Stempel, Guido Hermann, III *journalism educator*

Berea
Harf, Patricia Jean Kole *syndicated columnist, educational consultant, lecturer, clinical psychologist, family therapist*

Bowling Green
Cadegan, Jaime B. *educational administrator*
†Cassara, Catherine *journalism educator*
Clark, Robert King *communications educator emeritus, lecturer, consultant, actor, model*
†Norton, Wayne Anderson *journalism educator, public relations specialist*
Thomas, Marie Elena *newspaper editor*

Canton
Maxwell, John Alexander, Jr. *retired newspaper editor, consultant*

Chagrin Falls
Lange, David Charles *journalist*

Cincinnati
Beckwith, Barbara Jean *journalist*
Borgman, James Mark *editorial cartoonist*
Burleigh, William Robert *newspaper executive*
Constant, Anita Aurelia *publisher*
Dooley, Jo Ann Catherine *retired publishing company executive*
Fryxell, David Allen *publishing executive*
Gelfand, Janelle Ann *music critic*
Harmon, Patrick *newspaperman*
Irwin, Miriam Dianne Owen *book publisher, writer*
King, Margaret Ann *communications educator*
Klaserner, James *publishing executive*
Knue, Paul Frederick *newspaper editor*
McMullin, Ruth Roney *publishing executive, trustee, management fellow*
Mechem, Charles Stanley, Jr. *former broadcasting executive, former golf association executive*
Petty, Priscilla Hayes *writer, columnist, producer*
Scripps, Robert P. *publishing executive*
Silvers, Gerald Thomas *publishing executive*
Smith, C. LeMoyne *publishing company executive*
Whipple, Harry M. *newspaper publishing executive*
Winternitz, Felix Thomas *editor, educator, writer*

Cleveland
Brandt, John Reynold *editor, journalist*
†Clark, Gary R. *newspaper editor*
Clifton, Douglas C. *newspaper editor*
Conrad, Robert David *broadcast executive, educator*
Davis, David Aaron *journalist*
Fabris, James A. *journalist*
Greer, Thomas H. *newspaper executive*
Hamilton, Thomas Woolman *publishing company executive*
Jensen, Kathryn Patricia (Kit) *public radio station executive*
Jindra, Christine *editor*
Kanzeg, David George *radio programming director*
Klein, George Robert *periodical distribution company executive*
Kovacs, Rosemary *newpaper editor*
Lebovitz, Harold Paul (Hal Lebovitz) *journalist*
†Lee, Jae-won *journalism educator, political campaign consultant*
Long, Robert M. *newspaper publishing executive*
Lowry, Joan Marie Dondrea *broadcaster*
Machaskee, Alex *newspaper publishing company executive*
McKenna, Joseph Francis *journalist, communications consultant*
Miller, Arnold *retired newspaper editor*
Miyares, Benjamin David *editor, publisher, consultant*
Modic, Stanley John *business editor, publisher*
Molyneaux, David Glenn *newspaper travel editor*
Pascarella, Perry James *author, editor, speaker*
Shaw, Scott Alan *photojournalist*
Strang, James Dennis *editor*
Thompson, Stephen Arthur *publishing executive*
Wareham, Jerry *broadcast executive*
Zubal, John Thomas *book exchange executive, publisher, bibliographer*

Cleveland Heights
Drane, Walter Harding *publishing executive, business consultant*

Columbus
Barry, James P(otvin) *writer, editor*
Campbell, Richard Rice *retired newspaper editor*
Charles, Bertram *radio broadcasting executive*
†Cole Wardell, Kirstin *television news anchor*
Collins, Michael Edward *religious newspaper editor*
Cox, Mitchel Neal *editor*
Curtin, Michael Francis *editor*
Dawson, Virginia Sue *newspaper editor*
Dervin, Brenda Louise *communications educator*
DeVassie, Terry Lee *newspaper executive*
Flanagan, Harry Paul *publishing executive*
Fornshell, Dave Lee *educational broadcasting executive*
Grossberg, Michael Lee *theater critic, writer*
Hanrahan, Barbara *university press executive*
Johnston, Jeffery W. *publishing executive*
Kefauver, Weldon Addison *publisher*
Kiefer, Gary *newspaper editor*
Lucier, P. Jeffrey *publishing executive*
Massie, Robert Joseph *publishing company executive*
Mitchell, Carol Elaine *publishing executive, writer, educator*
Murphy, Andrew J. *managing news editor*
Sherrill, Thomas Boykin, III *retired newspaper publishing executive*
Stallworth, Sam *television executive*
Stephenson, David D. *journalist*
Strode, George K. *sports editor*
Tabor, Mary Leeba *literary magazine editor, author*
Weaver, Leah Ann *journalist, speech writer*
Weisgerber, David Wendelin *editor, chemist*

Crestline
Brouwer, Mark Nicholas *publisher, newspaper, retired*

Cuyahoga Falls
Hamilton, Donald Dow Webb *publisher, freelance writer*

Dayton
†Carollo, Russell *journalist*
Cawood, Albert McLaurin (Hap Cawood) *newspaper editor*
Duncan, Richard Leo *communications educator*
Hamlin, Tom *radio and television sportcaster, realtor*
Matheny, Ruth Ann *editor*
Peterson, Skip (Orley R. Peterson, III) *newspaper photographer*
Tillson, John Bradford, Jr. *newspaper publisher*

Fairview Park
Condon, George Edward *journalist*

Hamilton
James, Ronald Bruce *journalist*

Kirtland
Ryan, William Joseph *multimedia and distance education designer*

Lakewood
Chabek, Daniel James *journalist, writer, public relations professional*

Lima
†Lucente, Thomas John, Jr. *editor*

Lyndhurst
Kastner, Christine Kriha *newspaper correspondent*

Mason
Nichols, Dennis Arnold *newspaper editor*

Miamisburg
†Brown, Paul William *publishing executive*
Gieskes, Hans *information services and publishing executive*

Mount Gilead
Gress, Allen E. *newspaper editor*

Newark
Hopson, James Warren *publishing executive*

Oxford
Sanders, Gerald Hollie *communications educator*

Parma
Wells Bradley, Charlena Renee *editor, writer*
Yanda, Timothy George *cable television engineer*

Pataskala
†Caw, Thomas William *retired publisher and editor*

Pepper Pike
O'Neill, Katherine Templeton *journalist, museum administrator, former nursing educator*

Portsmouth
Deaterla, Michael Franklin *journalist, publicity specialist*

Shaker Heights
†Mendel, Roberta *editor, publisher, writer*

Sidney
Laurence, Michael Marshall *magazine publisher, writer*
Lawrence, Wayne Allen *publisher*
Stevens, Robert Jay *magazine editor*

Springfield
Maddex, Myron Brown (Mike Maddex) *broadcasting executive*
Mauriello, Tracie Lynn *journalist*

Toledo
Block, John Robinson *newspaper publisher*
Block, William K., Jr. *newspaper executive*
Rosenbaum, Kenneth E. *journalist, editor*
Royhab, Ronald *journalist, newspaper editor*
Stankey, Suzanne M. *editor*
Willey, John Douglas *retired newspaper executive*
Yonke, David Arthur *music critic, journalist, writer*

Warren
Rush, William John *newspaper executive*

Westerville
Ellis, E. Addison, III *publishing executive*

Willoughby
Campbell, Talmage Alexander *newspaper editor*
Corrigan, Faith *journalist, educator*
O'Toole, Thomas J. *journalist, photographer*

Wooster
August, Robert Olin *journalist*

Youngstown
†Flick, James Dennis *journalist, free lance writer*
Przelomski, Anastasia Nemenyi *retired newspaper editor*
†Villani, Jim Nicholas *publisher, English educator*

OKLAHOMA

Ada
Reese, Patricia Ann *retired editor, columnist*

Broken Arrow
Hale, Richard Lee *magazine editor*

Duncan
Adams, Brenda Kay *publications administrator, consultant*

Edmond
Pydynkowsky, Joan Anne *journalist*

Norman
Dary, David Archie *journalism educator, author*
Drayton, John N. *publishing executive*
Kaid, Lynda Lee *communications educator*
Morton, Linda P. *journalism educator*

Oklahoma City
Gaylord, Edward Lewis *publishing company executive*
Gourley, James Leland *editor, publishing executive*
Hight, Joe Irvin *editor*
Mitrovgenis, James William, Jr. *journalist*
Triplett, E. Eugene *editor*

Ponca City
Collins, Walter Lloyd George *editor*

Sallisaw
Mayo, James Watie (Jim Mayo) *publishing executive*

Tulsa
Bender, John Henry, Jr. (Jack Bender) *editor, cartoonist*
Bishop, Mary Fern *editor*
Haring, Robert Westing *newspaper editor*
Jones, Jenk, Jr. *editor, educator*
Jones, Jenkin Lloyd *retired newspaper publisher*
Lafitte, Bobby Gene *radio announcer*
Major, John Keene *radio broadcasting executive*
Reddicliffe, Steven *periodical editor-in-chief*
Scott, John Prosser *television program producer, management consultant*
†Smith, Edwin Bernard *journalism and advertising educator*
Upton, Howard B., Jr. *management writer, lawyer*
Worley, Joe *editor*

OREGON

Albany
Wood, Kenneth Arthur *retired newspaper editor, writer*

Beaverton
Sanford, David Roy *journalist, educator*

Coquille
Taylor, George Frederick *newspaper publisher, editor*

Corvallis
Coffin, Chris *managing editor*
Hall, Don Alan *editor, writer*

Eugene
Ambrose, Daniel Michael *publishing executive*
Baker, Alton Fletcher, III *newspaper editor, publishing executive*
Baker, Bridget Downey *newspaper executive*
Baker, Edwin Moody *retired newspaper publisher*
Calvert, Leonard James *editor, writer*
Hess, Suzanne Harriet *newspaper administrator, photographer*
Hildenbrand, Donald Gerald *editor*
Sherriffs, Ronald Everett *communication and film educator*
Tykeson, Donald Erwin *broadcasting executive*

Florence
Serra, Robert Emmett *newspaper editor*

Medford
†Ryder, Stephen Willis *newspaper publisher*
Shinn, Duane K. *music publisher*

Portland
Bhatia, Peter K. *editor, journalist*
Crabbs, Roger Alan *publisher, consultant, small business owner, educator*
†Hart, Jack Robert *newspaper editor*
Johnston, Virginia Evelyn *editor*
Loewenthal, Nessa Parker *communications educator*
Mapes, Jeffrey Robert *journalist*
Murphy, Francis Seward *journalist*
Rowe, Sandra Mims *newspaper editor*
Sterling, Donald Justus, Jr. *retired newspaper editor*
Stickel, Frederick A. *publisher*
†Stickel, Patrick Francis *publishing executive, newspaper*
Stilson, Christie Carol *publications executive, business owner*
Treleaven, Phillips Albert *retired publishing company executive*
Woodward, Stephen Richard *newspaper reporter*

Salem
Frank, Gerald Wendel *civic leader, journalist*
Martin, Jim *copy editor, writer*
Wallace, Julia Diane *newspaper editor*

Tigard
Nokes, John Richard *retired newspaper editor, author*

Wallowa
Wizard, Brian *publisher, author*

PENNSYLVANIA

Albrightsville
Wilson, George Wharton *newspaper editor*

Allentown
Hovey, Graham Billings *public affairs journalist*
Shorts, Gary K. *newspaper publisher*

Ardmore
Gerbner, George *communications educator, university dean emeritus*

Bala Cynwyd
Begley, Dennis *radio station executive*
Field, Joseph Myron *broadcast executive*
Hosey, Sheryl Lynn Miller *editor*
Kates, Gerald Saul *printing executive*
Lee, Jerry *broadcast executive*

Bensalem
Kang, Benjamin Toyeong *writer, clergyman*

Bethlehem
Friedman, Sharon Mae *science journalism educator*

Bloomsburg
Ulloth, Dana Royal *communications educator*

Broomall
Cohen, Philip D. *book publishing executive*

Bryn Mawr
Broido, Arnold Peace *music publishing company executive*
Mc Lean, William L., III *publisher*

Camp Hill
Holliday, Albert Edwards *publisher*

Carlisle
Fish, Chester Boardman, Jr. *retired publishing consultant, writer*
Talley, Carol Lee *newspaper editor*

Clarion
Siddiqui, Dilnawaz Ahmed *communications educator, international communication planning advisor, consultant*

Clarksville
Ankrom, Barbara Burke *journalist*

Clearfield
Ulerich, William Keener *publishing company executive*

PROFESSIONAL INDEX 5867 COMMUNICATIONS MEDIA

Collegeville
Mellanby, Ian John *publisher*

Coudersport
Rigas, John *broadcast executive*

Danielsville
Billings, Johanna Schmidt *journalist, antiques consultant*

Doylestown
Morgnanesi, Lanny M. *journalist*
Smith, Charles Paul *newspaper publisher*

East Stroudsburg
Rosenblum, Stewart Irwin *recording industry executive*

Easton
†Engler, Brian Keith *radio broadcast personality*
Stitt, Dorothy Jewett *journalist*

Emmaus
Beldon, Sanford T. *publisher*
Bricklin, Mark Harris *magazine editor, publisher*
Daniels, Jonathan Paul *web developer*
Lafavore, Michael J. *magazine editor*
Rodale, Ardath *publishing executive*

Flourtown
Lee, Adrian Iselin, Jr. *journalist*

Forest City
Kameen, John Paul *newspaper publisher*

Gettysburg
Gritsch, Ruth Christine Lisa *editor*

Gibsonia
Pochapin, Jay Frank *marketing executive*

Gladwyne
Murray, William D.G. *publishing executive*

Gwynedd Valley
†Strasburg, William Edward *retired newspaper publisher*

Harrisburg
DeKok, David *writer, reporter*
Drachler, Stephen Edward *press secretary*
Gover, Raymond Lewis *newspaper executive*
Huntington, Thomas Mansfield *editor*

Hellertown
McCullagh, James Charles *publishing company executive*

Hermitage
†Woge, Mairy Jayn *reporter*

Hollidaysburg
McPhee, Norma Howatt *publishing executive, author*

Honesdale
Brown, Kent Louis, Jr. *magazine editor*
Clark, Christine May *editor, author*

Horsham
Dariano, Joseph *publishing company executive*
Fisher, Darryl *information services company executive*

Kennett Square
Landstrom, Elsie Hayes *editor*

King Of Prussia
Enge, Vernon Reier *editor health care publications*

Lancaster
Shaw, Charles Raymond *journalist*
Shenk, Willis Weidman *newspaper executive*

Levittown
Halberstein, Joseph Leonard *retired associate editor*
Oppenheimer, Sanford (Sandy Oppenheimer) *newspaper editor*

Mechanicsburg
†Davis, Frank Daniel *retired journalist*

Millville
Shoup, Michael C. *newspaper reporter, editor*

Montoursville
Woolever, Naomi Louise *retired editor*

New Kensington
Demmler, Albert William, Jr. *retired editor, metallurgical engineer*

North Wales
Szabo, Joseph George *publisher, journalist, cartoonist, editor*

Oakmont
Ockershausen, Jane Elizabeth *journalist*

Oaks
Lenfest, Harold Fitz Gerald *cable television executive, lawyer*

Paoli
Gallagher, Terrence Vincent *editor*

Philadelphia
†Alexander, Marcellus W. *television station executive*
Backman, Robert Marc *television and radio station executive*
Biddle, Daniel R. *editor, reporter*
Binzen, Peter Husted *columnist*
Boasberg, Leonard W. *reporter*
Boldt, David Rhys *journalist*
Bradley, Kevin J. *publishing company executive*
Brodsky, Julian A. *broadcasting services, telecommunications company executive*
Bykofsky, Stuart Debs *newspaper columnist*
Carey, Arthur Bernard, Jr. *editor, writer, columnist*
Cooper, Richard Lee *newspaper editor, journalist*
Cortes, Ron *reporter*
Drake, Donald Charles *journalist*
Ferrick, Thomas Jerome, Jr. *journalist*
Foster, David John *journalist*
Gordon, Anne Kathleen *editor*
Gross, Larry Paul *communications educator*
Gruliow, Rebecca Agnes Lindsay *editor, translator, artist*
Hall, Robert J. *newspaper executive*
Halpern, Eric Franklin *university publishing director*
Haynes, Gary Allen *photographer, journalist, newspaper editor*
Hillgren, Sonja Dorothy *journalist*
Klein, Julia Meredith *newspaper reporter*
Leary, Michael Warren *journalist*
Leebron, Elizabeth Joanne *broadcast educator, video producer*
Leiter, Robert Allen *journalist, magazine editor*
Lent, John Anthony *journalist, educator*
Lyon, William Carl *sports columnist*
Moore, Acel *journalist*
Morgan, Arlene Notoro *newspaper editor, reporter, recruiter*
Nalle, Peter Devereux *publishing company executive*
Nussbaum, Paul Eugene *journalist*
Othmer, David Artman *television and radio station executive*
Parry, Lance Aaron *newspaper executive*
Patel, Ronald Anthony *newspaper editor*
Perkins, Russell Alexander *publisher, consultant*
Pollock, Lawrence J. *television broadcast company executive*
Prendergast, John Thomas *editor, writer*
Randall, Roger David *publishing executive*
Rogers, Mary Martin *publishing company executive*
Rorer, John Whiteley *publisher, consultant*
Rosenthal, Robert Jon *newspaper editor, journalist*
Saline, Carol Sue *journalist*
Searcy, Jarrell D. (Jay Searcy) *sportswriter*
Shapiro, Howard *newspaper editor*
Stalberg, Zachary *newspaper editor*
Taylor, Robin Lynn *anchorperson, reporter*
Teacher, Stuart *book publishing company executive*
Vitez, Michael *reporter*
Wilkinson, Signe *cartoonist*
Winfrey, Marion Lee *television critic*
Woestendiek, (William) John, Jr. *columnist*

Pittsburgh
Apone, Carl Anthony *journalist*
Croan, Robert James *music critic, singer*
Graham, Laurie *editor, writer*
Harrell, Edward Harding *newspaper executive*
Heindl, Mary Lynn *magazine editor*
Howell, John A. *television station executive*
King, Maxwell E. P. *newspaper editor*
Leo, Peter Andrew *newspaper columnist, writing educator*
Lopes, Jerry *broadcast executive*
Miller, Cynthia Ann *publisher*
†Rial, Martha *photographer*
Roof, Robert L. *broadcast executive, sales executive*
Ross, Madelyn Ann *newspaper editor*
Swann, Lynn Curtis *sportscaster, former professional football player*

Pottstown
Kelly, Thomas Joseph, III *photojournalist*

Quakertown
†Hauff, Sara Jeannette *newspaper editor*

Radnor
Baxter, John Michael *editor*
Zucker, Herbert *publishing executive*

Scottdale
Miller, Levi *publishing administrator*

Scranton
Lynett, George Vincent *newspaper publisher*
Lynett, William Ruddy *publishing, broadcasting company executive*
Rogers, Edwin Earl *newspaper editor*
Singleton, David Earl *newspaper reporter*

Sharon
Chaudhri, Amin Qamar *film company executive*

Solebury
Hulko, Robert Lee *recording studio executive*

State College
Heldman, Louis Marc *newspaper publisher and executive*
Kowalczyk, Kim Jan *editor, writer*

Trevose
Gerace, Diane *journalist*

Uniontown
Curry, Kimberly M. *communications consultant*

University Park
Benson, Thomas Walter *rhetoric educator, writer*
Mansfield-Richardson, Virginia Dell *communications educator, researcher*
Thatcher, Sanford Gray *publishing executive*

Valley Forge
Polli, G. Patrick *publishing executive*

Warrendale
Snyder, Linda Ann *book editor*

Warrington
Ward, Hiley Henry *journalist, educator*

Wayne
Youman, Roger Jacob *editor, writer*

West Chester
Begley, Kathleen A. *communications trainer and writer*
Mahoney, William Francis *editor/author*
Schickling, Barry *editor, newspaper*
Segel, Joseph M. *broadcasting executive*

Williamsport
Rosebrough, Carol Belville *cable television company executive*

Worcester
Curtis, Alton Kenneth *film company executive, clergyman*

Wynnewood
Singer, Samuel L(oewenberg) *journalist*

Yardley
Zulker, Charles Bates *broadcasting company executive*

York
†Liberante, Carrie A. *reporter*

RHODE ISLAND

Charlestown
Ungaro, Joseph Michael *newspaper publishing executive, consultant*

Cranston
Parravano, Amelia Elizabeth (Amy Beth Parravano) *recording industry executive*

Johnston
MacDonald, Cindy Marie *publisher, consultant*

Newport
Holloway, Jerome Knight *publisher, former military strategy educator, retired foreign service officer*

Portsmouth
Needham, Richard Lee *magazine editor*

Providence
Dujardin, Richard Charles *journalist*
Farmer, Susan Lawson *broadcasting executive, former secretary of state*
†Iven, Chris *journalist*
Olmsted, Audrey June *communications educator*
Rosenberg, Alan Gene *newspaper editor*
Smith, Robert Leslie *journalist*
†Sutton, Howard G. *publishing executive*
Watkins, John Chester Anderson *newspaper publisher*
Whitcomb, Robert Bassett *journalist, editor*

Wakefield
Wyman, James Vernon *newspaper executive*

Warwick
Halperson, Michael Allen *publishing company executive*

West Kingston
Haring, Howard Jack *newsletter editor*

Westerly
Algier, Angela Jane *newspaper editor*
Day, Chon *cartoonist*

SOUTH CAROLINA

Anderson
Urakami, Akio *manufacturing company executive*

Bennettsville
Kinney, William Light, Jr. *newspaper editor, publisher*

Cayce
McElveen, William Lindsay *broadcasting executive, lecturer*

Charleston
Abbott-Lyon, Frances Dowdle *journalist, civic worker*
Anderson, Ivan Verner, Jr. *newspaper publisher*
Brown, Linda Meggett *reporter*
Chaplin, George *newspaper editor*
French, Kenneth Wayne *radio station executive, consultant*
Gilbreth, Frank Bunker, Jr. *retired communications executive, writer*
Langley, Lynne Spencer *newspaper editor, columnist*
Manigault, Peter *media executive*
†Parker, James H. *business reporter*
Reed, Stanley Foster *editor, author, publisher, lecturer*
Schreadley, Richard Lee *writer, retired newspaper editor*
Tarleton, Larry Wilson *newspaper editor*
Thompson, William Birdsall *journalist*

Clinton
Franklin, Larry Brock *publishing executive*

Columbia
†Breedin, Berryman Brent *journalist, public relations, historian, consultan*
Fry, Catherine Howard *publishing executive*

Easley
Failing, George Edgar *editor, clergyman, educator*

Greenville
Eskew, Rhea Taliaferro *newspaper publisher*
Lloyd, Wanda Smalls *newspaper editor*

Hilton Head Island
Baumgardner, Barbara Borke *publishing consultant*
McKinney, Donald Lee *magazine editor*

Landrum
Wyche, Samuel David *sportscaster*

Orangeburg
Sims, Edward Howell *editor, publisher*

Piedmont
Davis, Robert Barry *technician, religious studies educator*

Rock Hill
†Milstead, John David *newspaper editor*

Simpsonville
Gilstrap, Leah Ann *media specialist*

Winnsboro
King, Robert Thomas *editor, free-lance writer*

SOUTH DAKOTA

Bison
Wishard, Della Mae *newspaper editor*

Philip
†Cook, Andrea Jenelle *newspaper editor, rancher*

Rapid City
Wells-Johnson, Vesta Lynn *audio/video production company executive*

Sioux Falls
Ellis, Peter *editor*
Garson, Arnold Hugh *newspaper publisher*

Vermillion
†Sanford, Geraldine Agnes *editor, retired English educator*

TENNESSEE

Brentwood
Flanagan, Van Kent *journalist*

Chattanooga
Anderson, Lee Stratton *newspaper publisher, editor*
Holmberg, Albert William, Jr. *publishing company executive*
Holmberg, Ruth Sulzberger *publishing company executive*
Lutgen, Robert Raymond *newspaper editor*
MacManus, Yvonne Cristina *editor, videoscripter, writer, consultant*

Crossville
Moser, Michael R. *newspaper editor*

Gatlinburg
Hooper, William Edward *broadcast journalist*

Johnson City
†Wozniak, James Lawrence *reporter*

Knoxville
Hohenberg, John *journalist, educator*
Penland, Barbara Hubbard *multi media publishing company executive*
Pulliam, Walter Tillman *newspaper publisher*
Rukeyser, William Simon *journalist*
Siler, Jennifer *university press administrator*
†Sitton, Ronald William *editor*
Teeter, Dwight Leland, Jr. *journalism educator*
Woodard, H. Tom *entertainment company executive*

Lookout Mountain
Cavett, Van Andrew *retired journalist*

Mc Minnville
Martin, Ron *editor, superintendent of schools, consultant, minister*

Memphis
Brooks, Kathleen *journalist*
Emery, Sue McHam *bulletin editor, owner bridge studio*
Kushma, David William *journalist*
McEachran, Angus *newspaper editor*
Smith, Whitney Bousman *music and drama critic*
Stokes, Henry Arthur *journalist*
Turner, Bernice Hilburn *recording industry executive*
Yawn, David McDonald *journalist*

Nashville
Battle, William Robert (Bob Battle) *retired newspaper executive*
Boyd, Theophilus Bartholomew, III *publishing company executive*
Dohrmann, Richard Martin *computer software publishing executive*
Du Bois, Tim *recording industry executive*
Frey, Herman S. *publishing company executive*
Green, Lisa Cannon *business editor*
†Hargrave, James Lee *editor, consultant*
Hauk, Gary H. *associate director, discipleship and family group*
Lowe, Harold Gladstone, Jr. *photojournalist, small business owner, farmer*
Mayhew, Aubrey *music industry executive*
Rayburn, Ted Rye *newspaper editor*
Roberts, Sandra *editor*
Rogers, Barbara Jean (B.J. Rogers) *writer, editor*
Russell, Fred McFerrin *journalist, author, lawyer*
Seigenthaler, John Lawrence *retired newpaper executive*
Shaw, Carole *editor, publisher*
Shaw-Cohen, Lori Eve *magazine editor*
Sherborne, Robert *editor*
Stone, Lawrence Mynatt *publishing executive*
Sutherland, Frank *publishing executive, editor*
Sweeney, Mark Owen *publisher*
†Taylor, Richard Kevin *magazine editor*

Sevierville
Stone, Mary Overstreet *newspaper editor*

TEXAS

Abilene
Boyll, David Lloyd *broadcasting company executive*
Marler, Charles Herbert *journalism educator, historian, consultant*

Amarillo
Spies, Dennis J. *editor*

Arlington
Fields, Valerie Daralice *journalist*
Otto, Ludwig *director, publisher, educator*

Austin
Carpenter, Elizabeth Sutherland *journalist, author, equal rights leader, lecturer*
Casabonne, Richard J. *publishing company executive*
Conine, Ernest *newspaper commentator, writer*
†Crowley, Robert Kenan *radio station executive*
Danielson, Wayne Allen *journalism and computer science educator*
Hitchcock, Joanna *publisher*
†Hughes, Cynthia L. *festival director, writer, editor*
Ivins, Molly *columnist, writer*
†Knowles, Harry *communications executive*
Laine, Katie Myers *communications consultant*
Mayes, Wendell Wise, Jr. *broadcasting company executive*
Oppel, Richard Alfred *newspaper executive*
Ricks, Patricia Wynn *author, publisher*
Stout, Patricia A. *communications educator*
Teague, Hyman Faris *former publishing company executive*
Tinsley, Anna Melissa *reporter*

Beaumont
Roth, Lane *communications educator*

Bedford
Lieber, David Leslie *journalist*

Bellaire
Ballanfant, Kathleen Gamber *newspaper executive, public relations company executive*

Big Spring
†Walker, John Hester *newspaper editor, author*

Bryan
†Borden, Robert Christian *editor*

Canyon Lake
Phelan, Charlotte Robertson *journalist, book critic*

Cedar Park
Dorsch, Jeffrey Peter *journalist*

Chandler
Jacobsen, Shirley Marie *editor, songwriter, artist*

College Station
Meier, Kenneth John *political science journal editor*
Rotell, Thomas M. *publishing executive*

Dallas
Adriance, Brenda *broadcast executive*
Bailon, Gilbert *newspaper editor*
Bersano, Bob *newspaper editor*
Blackistone, Kevin *sports columnist*
Blow, Steve *newspaper columnist*
Blumenthal, Karen *newspaper executive*
Brown, Stephen Bryan *real estate editor*
Burns, Scott *columnist*
Cox, James William *newspaper executive*
Creany, Cathleen Annette *television station executive*
Cummins, James Duane *correspondent, media executive*
Davis, Gregory T. *radio station executive*
Decherd, Robert William *newspaper and broadcasting executive*
DeOre, Bill *editorial cartoonist*
Dillon, David Anthony *journalist, lecturer*
Dufner, Edward Joseph *business newswriter*
Finn, Peter Michael *television production executive*
Flournoy, John Craig *newspaper reporter*
Galloway, Randy *newspaper sports columnist*
Glines, Carroll Vane, Jr. *magazine editor*
Griffith, Dotty (Dorothy Griffith Stephenson) *journalist, speaker*
Hall, Cheryl *newspaper editor*
Hare, John *radio station executive*
Holmes, Bert Otis E., Jr. *retired newspaperman*
Huey, Ward L(igon), Jr. *media executive*
Johnson, Kevin Orlin *publisher, writer*
Jordan, Karen Leigh *newspaper travel editor*
Klehfoth, Jay Gordon *publisher, writer, consultant*
Kutner, Janet *art critic, book reviewer*
Lane, Shawn Lanard *journalist, motivational speaker*
Langer, Ralph Ernest *journalist, newspaper executive and editor*
Long, Joann Morey *publishing company executive, editor*
Maddoux, Marlin *broadcast executive, journalist, author*
Maza, Michael William *newspaper editor, columnist*
Osborne, Burl *newspaper publisher, editor*
Patterson, Ronald Paul *publishing company executive, clergyman*
Pederson, Rena *newspaper editor*
Powell, Larry Randall *columnist*
Ryan, Timothy Christopher *anchor, reporter*
Schwartz, Marilyn *columnist*
Siegfried, Tom *newspaper editor*
Smith, David Lee *newspaper editor*
Smith, Sue Frances *newspaper editor*
Stepherson, Karen Evette *administrative assistant*
Weinkauf, William Carl *instructional media company executive*
Wuntch, Philip Samuels *journalist, film critic*

Denton
Flansburg, James McCauley *editor*
Jeffrey, Shirley Ruthann *publisher*
Levin, Carolyn Melinda *media educator, documentary filmmaker*
Shelton, James Keith *journalism educator*

Duncanville
Pierce, Robert Ray *secondary education educator*

El Paso
Treadwell, Hugh Wilson *publishing executive*

Fort Worth
Eliasoph, Jeffrey Paul *television news anchor*
Everitt, Julie Joy *newspaper reporter*
Jones, Brian *television station executive*
Malone, Dan F. *journalist*
Peipert, James Raymond *journalist*
Price, Michael Howard *journalist, critic, composer, cartoonist*
Record, Phillip Julius *newspaper executive*
Tinsley, Jackson Bennett *newspaper editor*
Turner, Wesley R. *publishing executive*

Hochheim
Redman, Violet Jane *printer, writer, genealogist*

Houston
Aguilar, Melissa Ward *newspaper editor*
Barlow, Jim B. *newspaper columnist*
Bischoff, Susan Ann *newspaper editor*
Boudreaux, Bob *broadcast journalist*
Bunch, Fred *newspaper picture editor*
Clark, Judith Redmond *editor, writer*
Clark, Scott *newspaper editor*
Clarke, Jeff *television station executive*
Crist, Lynda Lasswell *editor, historian*
Criswell, Ann *newspaper editor*
de Castro, Jimmy *radio station executive*
Downing, Margaret Mary *newspaper editor*
Frieden, Kit *newspaper editor*
Ganter, Garland *radio station executive*
George, Deveral D. *editor, journalist, advertising consultant*
Gerraughty, David R. *newspaper editor*
Gray, Robert Steele *publishing executive, editor*
Griffin, Oscar O'Neal, Jr. *writer, former oil company executive*
Hale, Leon *newspaper columnist*
Hammond, Ken *newspaper magazine editor*
†Hawes, William Kenneth *communication educator*
Heinsen, Lindsay *newspaper editor*
Hobby, William Pettus *broadcast executive, retired*
Holmes, Ann Hitchcock *journalist*
Holmes, Cecile Searson *religion editor*
Jackson, Ernest, Jr. *broadcasting executive*
Jetton, Steve *newspaper editor*
Johnson, Richard James Vaughan *newspaper executive*
Johnston, Marguerite *journalist, author*
Kientz, Renee *newspaper editor*
Loftis, Jack D. *newspaper editor, newspaper executive*
Lynch, Bob (Robert Wayne Lynch, Jr.) *newspaper editor, educator*
Marshall, Jane Pretzer *newspaper editor*
Marshall, Thom *columnist*
McDavid, George Eugene (Gene Mc David) *retired newspaper executive*
Millar, Jeffery Lynn *columnist*
Miller, John Pendleton (Jack) *publishing company executive*
Morris, David Hargett *broadcast executive, rancher*
Oren, Bruce Clifford *newspaper editor, artist*
Osgood, Christopher Mykel *radio account executive*
Osterberg, Susan Snider *communications educator, farmer*
Pederson, Tony Weldon *newspaper editor*
Powers, Hugh William *newspaper executive*
Read, Michael Oscar *editor, consultant*
†Shook, Barbara Rhines *journalist, consultant*
Thomas, Edred *broadcast executive*
Tice, Pamela Paradis *scientific editor, writer*
Walbridge, Willard Eugene *broadcasting executive*
Walls, Martha Ann Williams (Mrs. B. Carmage Walls) *newspaper executive*
Ward, David Henry (Dave Ward) *television news reporter, anchorman*
Wasserman, Steve *broadcast executive*
Weber, Owen *broadcast executive*

Irving
Halter, Jon Charles *magazine editor, writer*
†Owen, Joe David *editor*
Young, J. Warren *magazine publisher*

Jefferson
Lawrence, Sharon Orleans *publishing executive, writer*

Kelly A F B
Stringer, Jerry Ray *magazine editor*

Kerrville
Williams, William Henry, II *publisher*

Lewisville
Vacca, John Joseph, Jr. *television executive*

Livingston
Perkins, Sue Dene *editor*

Midlothian
†Davis, Brenda D. *journalist*

Mount Pleasant
Palmer, Robert Blunden *newspaper, printing executive*

New Braunfels
Bryant, Dennis Michael *publisher, educator*

Overton
Warren, Sandra Kay (Sandy Warren) *journalist, photographer*

Plano
Senderling, Jon Townsend *journalist, public affairs specialist*

Port Aransas
Noble, James Kendrick, Jr. *media industry consultant*

Richardson
Patrick, James Nicholas, Sr. *radio, television, newspaper commentator, consultant*

San Angelo
†Henry, Holly Ann *journalist*

San Antonio
Alexander, F. Wiley *columnist*
Clark, Robert Phillips *newspaper editor, consultant*
Davis, Jolene Bryant *magazine publishing executive consultant*
†Dunkelberg, Lee *journalist*
Emerson, Arthur Rojas *broadcast executive*
Giust, Steve *television station executive*
Gwathmey, Joe Neil, Jr. *broadcasting executive*
Johnson, Sammye LaRue *communications educator*
Jones, Jay, II *radio station executive*
Joslyn, James *television station executive*
Lenke, Joanne Marie *publishing executive*
Marbut, Robert Gordon *communications and broadcast executive, investor*
Marrou, Chris René *television newscaster*
Mays, L. Lowry *radio station executive*
Michaels, Willard A. (Bill Michaels) *retired broadcasting executive*
Rivard, Robert *editor*
†Wilkinson, Kenton Todd *communications educator*
Winik, Joanne *broadcast executive*
Yerkes, Susan Gamble *newspaper columnist*

Spring
Mohalley, Patricia JoAnn *library media specialist*

The Woodlands
Logan, Mathew Kuykendall *journalist*

Tiki Island
Kahn, Kathleen Pica *photojournalist, journalist, mediator, arbitrator*

Tyler
Berry, David Val *newspaper editor*
Brock, Dee Sala *television executive, educator, writer, consultant*

Wharton
Jackson, Larry C. *publishing executive*

UTAH

Midway
Zenger, John Hancock *training company executive*

Ogden
Trundle, W(infield) Scott *publishing executive newspaper*

Provo
Bennett, Bill *publishing company executive*
Hatch, Steven Graham *publishing company executive*
Tata, Giovanni *publishing executive*

Salt Lake City
Chase, Randal Stuart *communication educator, consultant*
Evensen, Jay Douglas *newspaper editor*
Fehr, J. Will *newspaper editor*
Gallivan, John William *publisher*
Harrie, Daniel Andrew *newspaper reporter*
Hatch, George Clinton *television executive*
Hatch, Wilda Gene *broadcast company executive*
Lustica, Katherine Grace *marketing executive, artist, consultant*
Moore, Carrie A. *journalist*
Mortimer, William James *newspaper publisher*
Newell, Clayton Coke *media professional, writer*
Robison, Barbara Ann *retired newspaper editor*
Shelledy, James Edwin, III *editor*
Smith, Donald E. *broadcast engineer, manager*
Todd, Jay Marlyn *editor*
Welch, Dominic *publishing executive*

Sandy
Fullmer, Timothy Shawn *printing company executive*

West Jordan
Carter, Paul Edward *publishing company executive*

VERMONT

Bennington
†Burkhardt, Frederick Henry *editor*

Burlington
Liley, Elizabeth Ellen *journalist, educator*

Charlotte
Monsarrat, Nicholas *newspaper editor, writer, educator*

Chester
Coleman, John Royston *newspaper publisher*

Dorset
Ketchum, Richard Malcolm *editor, writer*

Fair Haven
Barnouw, Erik *broadcasting educator, writer*

Hartland Four Corners
Brady, Upton Birnie *editor, literary agent*

Lincoln
Kompass, Edward John *consulting editor*

Lyndonville
James, Bruce Allan *radio station owner, general manager*

Montpelier
Good, Jeffrey *journalist*

North Pomfret
Crowl, John Allen *retired publishing company executive*

Norwich
Lamperti, Claudia Jane McKay *editor*

Perkinsville
Harris, Christopher *publisher, designer, editor*

Rochester
Schenkman, Joseph *publishing executive*

White River Junction
Rutter, Frances Tompson *publisher*

VIRGINIA

Alexandria
Barbato, Joseph Allen *writer*
Brownfeld, Allan Charles *columnist*
Comeau, Kathy Darr *publishing executive*
Dillman, Grant *journalist*
DuVall, Jack *television executive, fund raiser, speechwriter*
Fichenberg, Robert Gordon *newspaper editor, consultant*
Fleming, Douglas Riley *journalist, publisher, public affairs consultant*
Foster, Robert Francis *communications executive*
Foxwell, Elizabeth Marie *editor, writer*
Francis, Samuel Todd *columnist*
Hewitt, Charles C. *broadcast executive*
Hobbs, Michael Edwin *broadcasting company executive*
Jolly, Bruce Overstreet *retired newspaper executive*
Kotok, Alan *publishing association executive*
Morrison, Tiffany L. *cable television executive*
Morse, Burnham Spottswood *broadcast executive*
Radewagen, Fred *publisher, organization executive*
Weiser, John Conrad *photography administrator*
Wright, Mary James *managing editor*
Yoder, Edwin Milton, Jr. *columnist, educator, editor, writer*

Arlington
Adams, John Hanly *retired magazine editor, writer, consultant*
Bodley, Harley Ryan, Jr. *editor, writer, broadcaster*
Bullard, Marcia *publishing executive*
†Bussman, Charles Haines *publisher*
Bussmann, Charles Haines *publisher*
Clayton, James Edwin *journalist*
Cole, Benjamin Richason *newspaper executive*
Curley, John J. *diversified media company executive*
Curley, Thomas *newspaper executive*
Dentzer, Susan *journalist*
Feller, Mimi *newspaper publishing executive*
Ferguson Kennedy, Barbara Brownell *journalist*
Fleishman, Phil *radio news executive*
Gniewek, Raymond Louis *newspaper editor*
Goodman, Mark *journalist, educator*
Jurgensen, Karen *newspaper editor*
Lester, Barnett Benjamin *editor, foreign affairs officer*
Lorell, Monte *newspaper editor*
Lynch, Patricia Gates *broadcasting organization executive consultant, former ambassador*
MacDougall, William Lowell *magazine editor*
MacNeil, Robert Breckenridge Ware *retired broadcast journalist, writer*
Mathews, Linda McVeigh *newspaper editor*
Mazzarella, David *newspaper editor*
McKinley, Sarah Elizabeth *journalist*
McNamara, Tom *newspaper editor*
McWethy, John Fleetwood *journalist*
Mirrielees, James Fay, III *publishing executive*
Neikirk, William Robert *journalist*
Neuharth, Allen Harold *newspaper publisher*
Obermayer, Herman Joseph *newspaper publisher*
Perry, Bill *photojournalist*
Quinn, John Collins *publishing executive, newspaper editor*
Reiss, Susan Marie *editor, writer*
Ritter, Hal *newspaper editor*
Rockefeller, Sharon Percy *broadcast executive*
Samsot, Robert Louis *newspaper editor, consultant*
Schreurs, Brian Frederick *editor, publisher*
Simonson, David C. *retired newspaper association executive*
Simpson, John Mathes *newspaper editor*
Smith, Ellen Elisabeth *publisher, journalist*
Tanzer, Lester *editor*
Terzian, Grace Paine *publisher*
Tyrrell, Robert Emmett, Jr. *periodical editor, writer*
Vesper, Carolyn F. *newspaper publishing executive*
Walker, Cecil L. *broadcast executive*
Weiss, Susan *newspaper editor*
White, Dale Timothy (Tim White) *television journalist, producer*

Blacksburg
Warren, William Kermit *media company executive*

Bridgewater
Bittel, Muriel Helene *managing editor*

Bristol
Macione, Joe *television station executive*

Chantilly
†Chrzanowski, Leye Jeanette *publisher*

Charlottesville
Brownrigg, Walter Grant *cartoonist, corporate executive*
Daniel, Leon *journalist, newspaper columnist, editor*
Foard, Susan Lee *editor*
Loo, Beverly Jane *publishing company executive*
Parrish, David Walker, Jr. *legal publishing company executive*
Worrell, Anne Everette Rowell *newspaper publisher*

Chesapeake
Collins, Carolyn Herman *school media specialist, legislative aide*
Green, Barbara-Marie *publisher, journalist, poet*

Covington
Rohr, Dwight Mason *news director, radio marketing consultant*

Crozet
Crosby, James Earl *newspaper publisher*

Danville
†Wenger, Lisa Marie *reporter*

Fairfax
Jackman, Thomas M. *newspaper reporter, columnist*

Fairfax Station
Abuzaakouk, Aly Ramadan *publishing executive*

Falls Church
Benton, Nicholas Frederick *publisher*
Conde, Carlos Danache *journalist*
Cromley, Allan Wray *journalist*
Kaplow, Herbert Elias *journalist*

PROFESSIONAL INDEX 5869 COMMUNICATIONS MEDIA

Stone, Marvin Lawrence *journalist, government official*

Fredericksburg
†Strahan, Bradley Russel *publisher, poet, educator*

Great Falls
Garrett, Wilbur (Bill) *magazine editor*

Hampton
Barnes, Myrtle Sue Snyder *editor*
Brauer, Harrol Andrew, Jr. *broadcasting executive*

Harrisonburg
Rollman, Steven Allan *communication educator*

Luray
Burzynski, Norman Stephen *editor*

Manassas
Houston, Caroline Margaret *editor*
Wilson, Robert Spencer *magazine editor*

Marion
Elledge, Glenna Ellen Tuell *journalist*

Mason Neck
Mc Curdy, Patrick Pierre *editor, consultant*

Mc Lean
†Early, Gregg Steven *executive editor*
Fromm, Joseph *retired magazine editor, foreign affairs consultant*
Parshall, Gerald *journalist*
Roellig, Paul David *publishing executive*
Salzinger, Mark Alan *editor, violinist*
Wong, Andrew *telecommunications company executive*

Middleburg
Evans, John Derby *telecommunications company executive*

Midlothian
Chapman, Gilbert Whipple, Jr. *publishing company executive*
Pearson, Gregory David *publisher, media specialist*

Mineral
Speer, Jack Atkeson *publisher*

Mount Vernon
Brownson, Anna Louise Harshman *publishing executive, editor*

Newport News
Evans, Robert August, Jr. *newspaper reporter, editor*
Perry, Donald A. *cable television consultant*

Norfolk
Addis, Kay Tucker *newspaper editor*
Barry, Richard Francis, III *publishing executive*
Batten, Frank *newspaper publisher, cable broadcaster*
Bonko, Larry Walter *columnist, writer, radio personality*
Fitzpatrick, William Henry *retired journalist*
Ritter, Alfred Francis, Jr. *communications executive*
Sizemore, William Howard, Jr. *newspaper editor*

Orange
†Burke, Robert Lawrence *consultant*

Petersburg
Isom, Rebecca Jayne *newspaper editor, newspaper columnist*

Radford
Thomas, Robert Wilburn *media and advertising executive*
Wille, Lois Jean *retired newspaper editor*

Reston
Clapp, Stephen Caswell *journalist*
Mallette, Malcolm Francis *newspaper editor, educator*
Miller, Donald Lane *publishing executive*
Powell, Anne Elizabeth *editor*
Pyle, Thomas Alton *instructional television and motion picture executive*

Richmond
†August, Albert T., III *publishing executive*
Baker, Donald Parks *journalist, educator*
Bryan, John Stewart, III *newspaper publisher*
Bustard, Clarke *music critic, newswriter, radio producer*
Estes, Gerald Walter *newspaper executive*
Goodykoontz, Charles Alfred *newspaper editor, retired*
Mackenzie, Ross *newspaper editor*
Neman, Daniel Louis *movie critic*
Owen, Howard Wayne *journalist, writer*
Robertson, William Franklin *publishing executive*
Saunders, Dero Ames *writer, editor*
Seals, Margaret Louise *newspaper editor*
Smith, Ted Jay, III *mass communications educator*
Sydnor, Charles Wright *broadcast executive, historian*

Roanoke
Beagle, Benjamin Stuart, Jr. *columnist*
Easterling, Eddie Jean *publisher*
Rugaber, Walter Feucht, Jr. *newspaper executive*
Zomparelli, Wendy *newspaper executive*

Saint Paul
Gregory, Ann Young *editor, publisher*

Springfield
Finnegan, Philip *journalist*
Hastings, Melanie (Melanie Jean Wotring) *television news anchor*
Hillis, John David *television news executive, producer, writer*

Stanardsville
Anns, Arlene Eiserman *publishing company executive*

Sterling
Pittman, Robert Warren *entertainment executive*
Sanfelici, Arthur H(ugo) *editor, writer*

Tazewell
Garner, June Brown *journalist*

Vienna
Browning, Charles *publishing executive*
Mc Arthur, George *journalist*
Miller, Claire Ellen *periodical editor*

Virginia Beach
Christy, Larry Todd *publisher*
Quicke, Andrew Charles *cinema-television educator, consultant, writer*
Robertson, Pat (Marion Gordon Robertson) *religious broadcasting executive*
Smith, A. Robert *editor, author*
Wicker, Richard Fenton, Jr. *editor*

Williamsburg
Winstead, Joy *journalist, consultant*

Winchester
Byrd, Harry Flood, Jr. *newspaper executive, former senator*

WASHINGTON

Bellevue
Berkley, James Donald *clergyman*
Smith, Lester Martin *broadcasting executive*
Speer, Paul Alan *record producer, recording artist*

Bellingham
Doerper, John Erwin *publisher, editor*

Edmonds
Decker, Sharyn Lynn *newspaper reporter*
Owen, John *retired newspaper editor*

Ferndale
Jordan, Marvin Evans, Jr. *record company executive*

Longview
Natt, Theodore McClelland *newspaper editor, publisher*

Lynnwood
Krause, Thomas Evans *record promotion and radio consultant*

Olympia
McClelland, Kamilla Kuroda *news reporter, proofreader, book agent*

Port Angeles
Brewer, John Charles *journalist*

Port Orchard
Bonsell, Thomas Allen *journalist, publisher*

Port Townsend
†MacLean, Barbara Hotmacher *journalist*

Pullman
†Green, Paul John *independent critic*

Puyallup
Mowery, Gerald Eugene *publisher, writer*

Redmond
†Kinsley, Michael E. *magazine editor*

Seabrook
Pitman, Randy Ernest *publisher, editor*

Seattle
Alexander, Jasper D. *publishing executive*
Anderson, Ross *columnist*
Blethen, Frank A. *newspaper publisher*
Boardman, David *newspaper editor*
Buckner, Philip Franklin *newspaper publisher*
Bunting, Kenneth Freeman *newspaper editor*
Crumb, Robert *cartoonist*
Culp, Mildred Louise *corporate executive*
Ellegood, Donald Russell *publishing executive*
Fancher, Michael Reilly *newspaper editor, newspaper publishing executive*
Godden, Jean W. *columnist*
Gouldthorpe, Kenneth Alfred Percival *publisher, state official*
Grimley, Janet Elizabeth *newspaper editor*
Gwinn, Mary Ann *newspaper reporter*
Hartl, John George *film critic*
Hills, Regina J. *journalist*
†Horsey, David *editorial cartoonist*
Johnson, Wayne Eaton *writer, editor, former drama critic*
Lacitis, Erik *journalist*
Medved, Michael *film critic, author, talk show host*
Nalder, Eric Christopher *investigative reporter*
Nash, Cynthia Jeanne *journalist*
†Parks, Michael James *publisher, editor*
Payne, Ancil Horace *retired broadcasting executive*
Rinearson, Peter Mark *journalist, author, software developer*
†Ross, David Lawrence *broadcaster*
Scott, Patrick *broadcast executive*
Shipman, Keith Bryan *sportscaster*
Sizemore, Herman Mason, Jr. *newspaper executive*
Soden, John P. *publishing executive*
Stanton, Michael John *newspaper editor*
Steele, Cynthia *literary critic, translator, educator*
Szeto, Hung *publisher*
Thiel, Arthur Warren *journalist*
Turner, Wallace L. *reporter*

Spokane
Blewett, Stephen Douglas *journalism educator, public relations consultant*
Cowles, William Stacey *publisher*
Gray, Alfred Orren *retired journalism educator, communications specialist*
Kafentzis, John Charles *journalist, educator*
Kunkel, Richard Lester *public radio executive*
Peck, Christopher *editor*
Steele, Karen Dorn *journalist*

Tacoma
Gilbert, Ben William *retired newspaper editor*
†Mladenich, Ronald E. *publishing executive*
Warren, Dale Andrew *publishing company executive*

Tukwila
Lamb, Ronald Alfred *editor*

Vancouver
Power, Margaret Rae (Margo Power) *publisher*

Vashon
Mann, Claud Prentiss, Jr. *retired television journalist, real estate agent*

WEST VIRGINIA

Berkeley Springs
†Thorman, Richard Kahn *editor, writer*

Bluefield
Haag, Mark Waldo, II *director network operations*

Buckhannon
Ifert, Danette Eileen *communication educator*

Charleston
Chilton, Elizabeth Easley Early *newspaper executive*
Grimes, Richard Stuart *editor, writer*
Haught, James Albert, Jr. *journalist, newspaper editor, author*

Clarksburg
Highland, Cecil Blaine, Jr. *newspaper publisher, lawyer, banker*

Greenville
Warner, Kenneth Wilson, Jr. *editor, association and publications executive*

Huntington
Miller, Jerry Brian *radio broadcaster*
Reynolds, Marshall Truman *printing company executive*
Ritchie, Garry Harlan *television broadcast executive*

Nitro
Atkinson, Tommy Ray *sportscaster, sportswriter*

Shepherdstown
Snyder, Joseph John *editor, historian, author, lecturer, consultant*
Wilson, Miriam Janet Williams *publishing executive*

Summit Point
Woods, David Lyndon *publishing and broadcast executive, former federal agency executive*

Weston
†Billeter, Robert James *newspaper publisher*

WISCONSIN

Black River Falls
Michaels, Marion Cecelia *writer, editor, news syndicate executive*

Brookfield
Lessiter, Frank Donald *magazine editor*

Cedar Grove
Feider, Gary Joseph *newspaper editor*

Delafield
Behrendt, David Frogner *journalist*

Edgerton
Everson, Diane Louise *publishing executive*

Fitchburg
Hill, Michael John *newspaper editor*

Fort Atkinson
†Knox, Brian Victor *newspaper publisher and editor*
Knox, William David *publishing company executive*
Meyer, Eugene Carlton *retired editor*
Sager, Donald Jack *publisher, former librarian*

Green Bay
Daley, Arthur James *retired magazine publisher*

Greendale
†Kaiser, Ann Christine *magazine editor*

Iola
Krause, Chester Lee *publishing company executive*
Mishler, Clifford Leslie *publisher*
Van Ryzin, Robert Richard *magazine editor*

Janesville
Fitzgerald, James Francis *cable television executive*

Kenosha
Brown, Howard Jordan *newspaper publisher*

Madison
Brann, Edward R(ommel) *editor*
Burgess, James Edward *newspaper publisher, executive*
Denton, Frank M. *newspaper editor*
Drechsel, Robert Edward *journalism educator*
Fitchen, Allen Nelson *publisher*
Govier, Gordon Oliver *radio news broadcaster, consultant*
Hachten, William Andrews *journalism educator, author*
Haslanger, Philip Charles *journalist*
Hoyt, James Lawrence *journalism educator, athletic administrator*
Kleinmaier, Judith Marie Raddant *journalist*
McNelly, John Taylor *journalist, educator*
Miller, Frederick William *publisher, lawyer*
Wineke, William Robert *reporter, clergyman*
Wolman, J. Martin *retired newspaper publisher*
Zweifel, David Alan *newspaper editor*

Menomonie
Cutnaw, Mary-Frances *emeritus communications educator*
Hecker, Margo Joan *editor, writer*

Milwaukee
Armstrong, Douglas Dean *journalist*
Auer, James Matthew *art critic, journalist*
Berkman, Dave *mass communications educator*
Farris, Trueman Earl, Jr. *retired newspaper editor*
Foster, Richard *journalist*
Garbaciak-Bobber, Joyce Katherine *news anchor*
Henry, Rick *broadcast executive*
Hinkley, Gerry *newspaper editor*
Hinshaw, Edward Banks *broadcasting company executive*
Hoffmann, Gregg J. *journalist, author*
Huston, Margo *journalist*
Jaques, Damien Paul *theater critic*
Kaiser, Martin *newspaper editor*
Kritzer, Paul Eric *media executive, communications lawyer*
Leonard, Richard Hart *journalist*
†Lickel, Robin L. *editor*
McCann, Dennis John *columnist*
†McNally, Joel Douglas *newspaper editor, columnist*
Sandler, Lawrence *newspaper reporter*
Schaleben, Arville *newspaper editor, writer, educator*
Spore, Keith Kent *newspaper executive*
Stratton, Bradley Jon *magazine editor*
Sullivan, Edward *periodical editor*

Montello
Burns, Robert Edward *editor, publisher*

Neshkoro
Eiche, Candace Rose *journalist*

Pelican Lake
Martin, Mary Wolf *newspaper editor*

Pewaukee
Lee, Jack (Jim Sanders Beasley) *broadcast executive*

Phillips
Peterson, Catherine Lois *newspaper reporter*

Racine
Doll, David Michael *journalist*
Miller, Yolanda *publisher, writer*

Schofield
Gettelman, Robin Claire *media specialist*

Sheboygan
Hanson, Paul Anthony *publisher*

Soldiers Grove
Zimmer, Paul Jerome *publisher, editor, poet, retired*

Stoughton
Brenz, Gary Jay *publishing executive*

Superior
Billig, Thomas Clifford *publishing and marketing executive*

Verona
Schroeder, Henry William *publisher*

Waukesha
Dreyfus, Lee Sherman *international speaker*
Gruber, John Edward *editor, railroad historian, photographer*
Larson, Russell George *magazine publisher*

Wauwatosa
Fibich, Howard Raymond *retired newspaper editor*

West Bend
Fraedrich, Royal Louis *magazine editor, publisher*

WYOMING

Cheyenne
Schliske, Rosalind Routt *journalism educator, journalist*

Laramie
Gowdy, Curtis *sportscaster*

Riverton
Peck, Robert A. *newspaper publisher*

TERRITORIES OF THE UNITED STATES

PUERTO RICO

Bayamon
Berio, Blanca *editor*

VIRGIN ISLANDS

Saint John
Walker, Ronald R. *writer, newspaper editor, educator*

CANADA

ALBERTA

Calgary
Shaw, Jim, Jr. *broadcast executive*

Edmonton
Hughes, Linda J. *newspaper publisher*

BRITISH COLUMBIA

Vancouver
Yaffe, Barbara Marlene *journalist*

Victoria
Poole, Robert Anthony *journalist*
Tighe, James C. *publisher*

MANITOBA

Winnipeg
Buchko, Garth *broadcasting executive*
Chalmers, Jane *broadcast executive*
Wreford, David Mathews *magazine editor*

ONTARIO

Brockville
McLeod, Philip Robert *publishing executive*

Don Mills
French, William Harold *retired newspaper editor*

Kanata
†Martin, Jacques *professional hockey coach*

Kitchener
MacDonald, Wayne Douglas *publisher*

London
Cornies, Larry Alan *journalist, educator*

North York
Hanna, William Brooks *book publisher*

Ottawa
Beatty, Perrin *broadcasting company executive*
Clever, W(arren) Glenn *editor, publishing executive, poet, writer, educator*
Davey, Clark William *newspaper publisher*
Macklem, Michael Kirkpatrick *publisher*
Mills, Russell Andrew *newspaper publisher*
Saucier, Guylaine *broadcast executive*

Pickering
Irwin, John Wesley *publisher*

Richmond Hill
Carson, Edward John *book publisher*

Scarborough
Besse, Ronald Duncan *publishing company executive*
Knycha, Josef *journalist*
Mitchell, Arthur Harris *newspaper columnist*

Toronto
Alvarez, Frank *radio station executive*
Berton, Pierre *journalist, author*
Black, Conrad Moffat *publishing corporate executive*
Boultbee, John Arthur *publishing executive*
Bregg, Peter *photojournalist*
Clancy, Louis John *newspaper editor, journalist*
Downing, John Henry *columnist, journalist*
Egan, Vincent Joseph *journalist, newspaper columnist*
Galloway, David Alexander *publishing company executive*
Godfrey, Paul *publisher*
Harris, Nicholas George *publisher*
Honderich, John Allen *newspaper publisher*
Karp, Allen *motion picture company executive*
King, John Charles Peter *newspaper editor*
Landsberg, Michele *journalist*
Lasker, David Raymond *newspaper editor, musician*
Lewis, Robert *periodical editor, journalist*
Lombardi, John Barba-Linardo *broadcasting executive*
Rauhala, Ann Elaine *reporter*
Roberts, William D. *broadcasting executive*
Slaight, Gary *broadcasting executive*
Thall, Burnett Murray *newspaper executive*
Tory, John A. *newspaper publishing executive*

Willowdale
Dean, Geoffrey *book publisher*
Kerner, Fred *book publisher, writer*

QUEBEC

Dollard
Des Roches, Antoine *retired newspaper executive*

Montreal
Beaubien, Philippe de Gaspe, II *communications executive*
Braide, Robert David *broadcast executive*
Juneau, Pierre *broadcasting company executive*
Landry, Roger D. *publishing company executive*
Pépin, Marcel *broadcast executive*
Romanelli, G. Jack *journalist*
Webster, Norman Eric *journalist, charitable foundation administrator*

SASKATCHEWAN

Regina
Hughes, Robert Lachlan *newspaper executive*

AUSTRALIA

Sydney
Guerin, Didier *magazine executive*

BELGIUM

Brussels
Kempe, Frederick Schumann *newspaper editor, author*

CHINA

Hong Kong
Laurie, James Andrew *journalist, broadcaster*
Lehner, Urban Charles *journalist*

ENGLAND

Buckinghamshire
Elegant, Robert Sampson *journalist, author*

Cambridge
Kermode, (John) Frank *literary critic, educator*

London
Green, Richard Lancelyn (Gordon) *editor, writer*
Hoge, Warren M. *newspaper and magazine correspondent, editor*
Kramer, Sidney B. *publisher, lawyer, literary agent*
Oliver, Diane Frances *publisher, writer*
Scardino, Albert James *journalist*
Scardino, Marjorie Morris *publishing company executive*
Stapleton, Nigel John *multinational information publishing executive*

Surrey
Babb, Michael Paul *engineering magazine editor*

FIJI

Suva
Usher, Sir Leonard Gray *retired news association executive*

FRANCE

Neuilly Cedex
Goldmark, Peter Carl, Jr. *publishing executive*

Nice
Spivak, Jonathan M. *journalist*

Paris
Dahlburg, John-Thor Theodore *newspaper correspondent*
Dubs, Patrick Christian *publisher*
Lewis, Flora *journalist*

GERMANY

Gütersloh
†Middelhoff, Thomas *publishing executive*

Munich
Saur, Klaus G. *publisher*

HONG KONG

Causeway Bay
Ignatius, Alan (Adi) *magazine editor*

ISRAEL

Savyon
Bushinsky, Jay (Joseph Mason) *journalist, radio/TV correspondent, columnist*

ITALY

Rome
Wynn, Coy Wilton *journalist*

JAPAN

Tokyo
Akutsu, Yoshihiro *communications educator*
Krisher, Bernard *foreign correspondent*
Nagata, Akira *publishing executive*
WuDunn, Sheryl *journalist, correspondent*
Yates, Ronald Eugene *newspaper editor, journalist*

THE NETHERLANDS

Aerdenhout
Vinken, Pierre Jacques *publishing executive, neurosurgeon*

Amsterdam
Bruggink, Herman *publishing executive*

PORTUGAL

Oeiras
Howe, Marvine Henrietta *newspaper reporter*

SOUTH AFRICA

Johannesburg
Berk, Philip Woolf *journalist*

SWITZERLAND

Geneva
Rohrer, Maurice Pierre *journalist*

ADDRESS UNPUBLISHED

Abercrombie, Stanley *magazine editor*
Achorn, Robert Comey *retired newspaper publisher*
†Ackerman, Robert Keith *journalist*
Ackermann, Karen *publishing executive*
Adams, Christopher Paul *journalist*
Adelson, Merv Lee *entertainment and communication industry executive*
Agarwal, Suman Kumar *editor*
Ainsworth, Harriet Crawford *journalist, public relations consultant*
Akiyama, Carol Lynn *motion picture industry executive*
Aldrich, Patricia Anne Richardson *retired magazine editor*
Allen, Donald Merriam *editor, publisher*
Andrisani, John Anthony *editor, author, golf consultant*
Angulo, Gerard Antonio *publisher, investor*
†Archambault, George Francis *editor, pharmaceutical consultant*
Arden, Sherry W. *publishing company executive*
†Armstrong, Terry Lee *publishing executive, carpenter*
Arnold, Henri *cartoonist*
Aronson, Norman Leonard *publishing executive, consultant*
Ashton, Betsy Finley *broadcast journalist, author, lecturer*
Audet, Paul Andre *retired newspaper executive*
Avnet, Jonathan Michael *motion picture company executive, film director*
†Azhar, Rubaina Shameem *journalist*
Baggett, Donnis Gene *journalist, editor*
Bahbah, Bishara Assad *editor*
Baltz, Antone Edward, III *journalist, writer, academic administrator*
Barhydt, Sally J. *publishing company executive*
Bartlett, David *journalist*
†Batsell, Jacob Paul *journalist*
Baumann, Michelle Renae *editor, writer*
Beamish, Mary Kathryn *copy editor*
Benn, Julie Eve Arend *writer, communications specialist*
Bennack, Frank Anthony, Jr. *publishing company executive*
Berkowitz, Steve *publishing company executive*
Berman, William H. *publishing company executive*
Bernheimer, Martin *music critic*
Bernstein, Peter Walter *publisher*
Bernstein, Richard Allen *company executive*
Bieber-Roberts, Peggy Eilene *communications educator, editor, journalist, researcher*
Bishop, Gordon Bruce *journalist*
Bisnette, Dena Lynn *journalist*
Black, Barbara Ann *publisher*
Blanco, Laura *film producer*
Block, William *newspaper publisher*
Bluhm, Gene Elwood *trade journal editor and publisher*
Bohle, Robert Henry *journalism educator*
Bordy, Bill (William James Bordy) *publisher*
Borger, Gloria *journalist, editor*
Borysewicz, Mary Louise *editor*
Braden, Thomas Wardell *news commentator*
Bram, Leon Leonard *publishing company executive*
Bratzler, Mary Kathryn *desktop publisher*
Breathed, Berkeley *cartoonist*
Brekke, Gail Louise *broadcasting administrator*
Bremer, Victor John *broadcasting executive*
Brinberg, Herbert Raphael *information management, publishing company executive*
Broadwater, James E. *publisher*
Brockway, Laurie Sue *editor, journalist, author, minister*
Brooks, Babert Vincent *publisher*
Broude, Ronald *music publisher*
Broussard, Carol Madeline *writer, literary consulting agent, photographer*
Brown, Britt *retired publishing company executive*
Brown, Richard Carlos *journalism educator, editor*
Brown, Tina *magazine editor*
Buchanan, Patrick Joseph *journalist*
Buckley, William Elmhirst *publishing consultant*
Buffkins, Archie Lee *public television executive*
Burns, Bebe Lyn *journalist*
†Burrows, Edwin Gladding *retired broadcaster, writer, poet*
Bush, Larry *sportswriter*
Butler, George Frank *editor, literary historian*
Byrne-Dempsey, Cecelia (Cecelia Dempsey) *journalist*
Caffee, Marcus Pat *publishing company executive*
Cairns, Diane Patricia *motion picture executive*
Calder, Iain Wilson *publishing company executive*
Callander, Bruce Douglas *journalist, free-lance writer*
Calvano-Smith, Rita *journalist, small business owner*
Camp, Clifton Durrett, Jr. *newspaper consultant, rancher*
Campbell, Byron Chesser *publishing company executive*
Caputo, Salvatore *critic*
Cardone, Bonnie Jean *photojournalist*
Cardwell, Nancy Lee *editor, writer*
Carillo, Mary *broadcaster, tennis analyst*
†Carlson, Donald Otto *magazine publisher, editor*
Carlson, Natalie Traylor *publisher*
Carmichael, Judy Lea *record industry executive, concert jazz pianist*
Carper, James David *magazine editor*
Cassin, James Richard *broadcast educator*
Cavill, Karen A. *writer, editor*
Chang, T. Susan *book editor*
Charnin, Jade Hobson *magazine executive*
Chercover, Murray *television executive*
Ciccone, F. Richard *retired newspaper editor*
Clapper, Lyle Nielsen *magazine publisher*
†Clark, Don Alan *journalist, reporter*
Clark, James Covington *journalist, historian*
Clark, Peter Bruce *newspaper executive*
Cloud, Stanley Wills *journalist, editor, writer*
Cohen, Allan Richard *broadcasting executive*
Cohen, Mark Herbert *broadcasting company executive*
Collier, Robert Steven *broadcast technician*
†Constable, Burt Wilson *newspaper columnist*
Conyers, Claude Brunson *retired publishing executive*
Cornett, Gregg *newspaper publisher, newspaper editor, computer company executive*
Costa, Michael F. *multimedia communications executive*
Costas, Bob (Robert Quinlan Costas) *sportscaster*
Crawford, Harold Bernard *publisher*
Crecente, Brian David *writer, journalist*
Crowther, James Earl *radio and television executive, lawyer*
Cullen, Robert John *publishing executive, financial consultant*
Curtis, Mary Ellen (Mary Curtis Horowitz) *publishing company executive*
Dahlgren, Carl Herman Per *educator, arts administrator*
D'Alessio, David Wesley *communications educator*
Daly, Chuck (Charles Jerome Daly) *sports commentator, professional basketball coach*
D'Amato, Anthony Roger *recording company executive*
Daniel, Elbert Clifton *journalist*
Davatzes, Nickolas *broadcast executive*
Daves, Donald Rae *entertainment industry executive*
Davis, Kristin W. *periodical editor*
Day, Anthony *newspaper writer*
Dean, Walter Jeryl Jerry *newswriter*
DeCamp, Graydon *journalist*
Dedman, Bill *journalist*
Deitz, Susan Rose *newspaper advice columnist*
de Leon, Lidia Maria *magazine editor*
Desbarats, Peter Hullett *journalist, academic administrator*
Dickman, James Bruce *photojournalist*
Dietrich, William Alan *author, journalist*
Dills, James Arlof *retired publishing company executive*
Dittmer, Linda Jean *retired photojournalist, photographer, computer artist*
Dolgen, Jonathan L. *motion picture company executive*
Doolittle, James H. *retired cable television systems company executive*
Dosti, Rose *newspaper columnist, author*
Downing, Kathryn M. *publishing executive, lawyer*
Draznin, Jules Nathan *journalism and public relations educator, consultant*
Drew, Elizabeth Heineman *publishing executive*
Dreyfuss, Joel Philippe *magazine editor*
Duerr, Herman George *retired publishing executive*
Duncan, James Richard *systems administrator*
Dunham, Benjamin Starr *editor, arts administrator*
Dunkelberger, Steve Walter *journalist*
Eaker, Ira *publishing executive*
Edgren, Gretchen Grondahl *magazine editor*
Edwards, Geoffrey Hartley *newspaper publisher*
Ehrlich, Amy *editor, writer*
Enger, Edward Henry, Jr. *editor, writer*
Erlicht, Lewis Howard *broadcasting company executive*
Esterline, Shirley Jeanne *lithograph company executive*
Evans, Gene M. *publishing executive*
Ewell, Miranda Juan *journalist*
†Fadda Eastman, Julie Suzanne *editor*
Farnsworth, Elizabeth *broadcast journalist*
Federici, William Vito *newspaper reporter*
Feiffer, Jules *cartoonist, writer, playwright*
Felton, Guy Page, III *website publisher, consultant*
Fernald, Harold Allen *publishing executive*
Ferre, Antonio Luis *newspaper publisher*
Fiddick, Paul William *broadcasting company executive*
Fink, John Francis *retired newspaper editor, columnist, writer*
Finnegan, Sara Anne (Sara Lycett) *publisher*
†Fiore, Michele Mercia *reporter*
Fisher, Robert Charles Haru *publishing company executive, editor*
Flood, James Tyrrell *broadcasting executive, public relations consultant*
Fodiman, Aaron Rosen *publishing executive*
Forcinio, Hallie Eunice *editor*
†Fossum, Judy Kaye *radio news reporter*
Francke, Linda Bird *journalist*
Frankel, Glenn *journalist*
Franklin, Jon Daniel *writer, journalist, educator*
Friedman, Richard Burtram *journalist*
Fritz, Mark Francis *journalist*
Fuchs, Joseph Louis *retired magazine publisher*
Fuchs, Michael Joseph *television executive*
Gannon, James Patrick *newspaper editor*
Garfield, Robert Edward *newspaper columnist*
Gartenberg, Seymour Lee *retired recording company executive*
Gates, Laura Jean Cummings *journalist*
Gates, Susan Inez *magazine publisher*
Gay, Susan Matthews *publishing professional*
Geis, Bernard *book publisher*
Geller, Lisa Michele *copy editor*
Gerber, Seymour *retired publishing company executive*
Gifford, Frank Newton *sportscaster, commentator, former professional football player*
Gill, Henry Herr *photojournalist*
Giuffrida, Tom A. *publisher*
Glover, William Harper *theater critic*
Godwin, Naomi Nadine *editor*
Goellner, Jack Gordon *publishing executive*
†Gold, Matea Jenny *journalist, educator*
Gold, Sylviane *entertainment editor, writer, critic*
Goldsmith, Arthur Austin *magazine editor*
Goldwater, John Leonard *publisher, writer*
Goode, Stephen Hogue *publishing company executive*
Goodkin, Michael Jon *publishing company executive*
†Gordon, Kenneth Antony *publisher*
†Gowen, Kay S. *communications educator*
Gralla, Milton *publisher*
Gray, Gordon L. *communications educator*
Gray, Thomas Stephen *newspaper editor*
†Grayson, Richard Steven (Lord of Mursley) *foreign correspondent, international legal and political management consultant, educator*
†Greenhouse, Carol Joan *editor, writer, educator*
Greenwald, John Edward *newspaper and magazine executive*
Gretser, George Westfall *publisher*
Guittar, Lee John *retired newspaper executive*
†Gumbel, Bryant Charles *broadcaster*
Hagel, Raymond Charles *publishing company executive, educator*
Hahn, Helene B. *motion picture company executive*
Halfen, David *publishing executive*
Hall, David *newspaper editor*
Hamill, (William) Pete *newspaper columnist, author, editor*
Harding, John T. *journalist*
Harkness, Peter Anthony *editor, publisher*
Harmon, Debra Mae *journalist*
Harris, Louis *public opinion analyst, columnist*

Hast, Adele editor, historian
†Hearst, George Randolph, Jr. publishing executive, diversified ranching and real estate executive
Hechler, David Samuel journalist
Hedler, Kenneth Bruce journalist
Heiman, Grover George, Jr. magazine editor, author
Heldrich, Eleanor Maar publisher
Heller, Richard H. writer, editor, book critic, publisher
Hemperly, Rebecca Sue publishing manager
Henig, Robin Marantz journalist
Henry, Frances Ann journalist, educator
Herdeck, Donald Elmer publishing executive, retired humanities educator
Herguth, Robert John columnist
Hering, Doris Minnie dance critic
Hess, David Willard journalist
Hieb, Mario Kirk broadcast engineer, inventor, writer, consultant
Hilker, Helen-Anne journalist
Hill, Steven John journalist, political reformer
Himmelfarb, Milton editor, educator
Hobbs, Avaneda Dorenza publishing company executive, minister, singer
Holland, David Thurston former editor
Holton, Robert Page publishing executive
Holzman, D. Keith record company executive, producer, arts consultant
House, Kay Seymour editor
Hubley, Reginald Allen publisher
†Huckman, Michael Andrew reporter
Hudson, Jerry Charles communications educator
Hudson, Julie Danielle newspaper editor
Hurd, Byron Thomas newspaper executive, retired
Hurst, Kenneth Thurston publisher
Huttner, Richard M. publishing executive
Idaszak, Jerome Joseph economic journalist
Innerst, Carol Jean journalist
Ismach, Arnold Harvey retired journalism educator
Jenkins, Billie Beasley film company executive
Jensen, Jack Michael publishing executive
Jiler, William Laurence publisher
Jinks, Robert Larry retired newspaper publisher
John, Mertis, Jr. record company executive
Johnson, Malcolm Clinton, Jr. publishing consultant
Johnson, Patricia Mary publisher
Jones, Leonade Diane media publishing company executive
Jordan, Fred publishing company executive
Kagan, Julia Lee magazine editor
†Kahlenberg, Susan Gale communications educator
†Kamin, Blair Douglass newspaper critic
†Kamuf, Rachael L. reporter
Karol, Michael Alan editor
Kash, Wyatt Keith publishing executive
Kassulke, Natasha Marie reporter
Kayfetz, Victor Joel writer, editor, translator
Keena, J. Bradley political commentator
Kelly, Michael Joseph, Jr. publishing executive
Kennedy, Harvey Edward science information publishing executive
Kennedy, Orin film company executive
Kenny, Patrick Edward publishing executive
Kesend, Michael publishing executive
Key, Ted cartoonist
Keyes, Saundra Elise newspaper editor
†Khinoy, Andrew journalist
Killgore, Le journalist, political columnist
Kilpatrick, James Jackson, Jr. columnist, author
Kimes, Beverly Rae editor, writer
King, (Lenard) Glen broadcasting educator, composer
Klein, Chuck private investigator
Klein, Edward Joel editor, author, lecturer
Kleinberg, Howard J. newspaper columnist
Knell, Gary Evan media executive, lawyer
Koehler, George Applegate broadcasting company executive
Koltun, Frances Lang editor, publisher, broadcaster
Koppett, Leonard columnist, journalist, author
Koren, Edward Benjamin cartoonist, educator
Kramer, Donovan Mershon, Sr. newspaper publisher
Kraslow, David retired newspaper publishing executive, reporter, author, consultant
Krauss, Mitchell E. journalist
Krauthammer, Charles columnist, editor
Kuehn, James Marshall newspaper editor
†Lader, Phyllis S. journalist
Laidlaw, Robert Richard publishing company executive
Laitin, Joseph journalist, former government spokesman and public relations consultant
Lalli, Cele Goldsmith retired editor
Lalli, Frank magazine editor
Lander, Howard entertainment newspaper publisher
Landis, James David publishing company executive, retired, author
Lape, Robert Cable broadcast journalist
Leason, Jody Jacobs newspaper columnist
Leavitt, William Douglas editor
†Lee, Daniel Sewhin radio language specialist, announcer, producer
Lee, Marianna retired editor
Lehrman, Nat magazine editor
Lehtinen, Merja Helen Kokkonen journalist, researcher, publisher
Leirer, Jennifer Lea journalist, beauty consultant
Lepkowski, Wil (Wilbert Charles Lepkowski) journalist
†Lessy, Harriet Gail columnist
†Levin, Robert Barry motion picture company executive
Levine, David M. newspaper editor
Lewin, K(atherine) Tamar reporter
Lewis, L(inda) Maureen publishing executive
Liberman, Gail Jeanne editor
Lipman, David multimedia consultant
Littlewood, Thomas Benjamin retired journalism educator
Lloyd, Michael Jeffrey recording producer
Loper, James Leaders broadcasting executive
Lord, Roy Alvin retired publisher
Lorente, Rafael journalist
Love, Laurie Miller science editor
Lucentini, Mauro journalist
Lugenbeel, Edward Elmer publisher
Lumpkin, Anne Craig retired television and radio company executive
†Lyons, Michelle Cherie journalist
MacDonald, Robert Taylor newspaper executive
MacFarlane, Andrew Walker media specialist, educator
†MacFarquhar, Larissa journalist
Main, Robert Gail communications educator, training consultant, television and film producer, former army officer
Mallo-Garrido, Josephine Ann advertising agency owner
Malloy, Michael Terrence journalist, newspaper editor
Malott, Adele Renee editor
Manley, Joan A(dele) Daniels retired publisher
Manning, Richard Dale writer
Marcus, Greil Gerstley critic
Marino, Joseph Anthony retired publishing executive
Marmer, Nancy editor
Martarella, Franc David television executive
Masket, Edward Seymour television executive
Mason, John Oliver free-lance journalist
Maxwell, Linda Jeanne newspaper reporter, photographer
Mayer, Allan media consultant, writer
McCallister, Duane newspaper executive
McCoy, Georgia Sideris magazine editor, writing consultant
McDarrah, Gloria Schoffel editor, author
†McDonald, Peter Jeffrey journalist
McGarry, Kevin Vincent retired newspaper executive
McGuirk, Terrence former broadcasting company executive
McHenry, Robert (Dale) editor
McIntyre, Douglas Alexander magazine publisher
McManus, Jason Donald editor, retired
†Mear, Annie M. communications educator
Medavoy, Mike motion picture company executive
Medina, Kathryn Bach book editor
Mellema, Donald Eugene retired radio news reporter and anchor
Melody, Michael Edward publishing company executive
Meredith, Alice Foley publisher, consultant
Meyer, Andrew W. publishing executive
†Middaugh, Gabrielle leSage television news producer, entrepreneur
Might, Thomas Owen newspaper company executive
Miller, Donald LeSessne publishing executive
Miller, Norman Charles, Jr. journalism educator
Miller, Robert Branson, Jr. retired newspaper publisher
Millett, Ralph Linwood, Jr. retired newspaper editor
Miner, A. Bradford journalist
Mitchell, Rick journalist, writer
Mitchem, Mary Teresa publishing executive
Monacelli, Gianfranco publishing executive
†Moore, George William, III sportswriter, editor
Moore, John Plunkett Dennis publisher
Moore, Thomas Paul retired broadcast executive
Morton, George Thomas reporter
Mudd, Roger Harrison news broadcaster, educator
Murphy, Timothy Aaron journalist
Myers, Shirley Diana art book editor
Mysel, Randy Howard publishing company executive
Nava, Yolanda Margot broadcast journalist, author
Neff, Donald Lloyd news correspondent, writer
Nelson, Martha Jane magazine editor
Nelson, Robert Charles newspaper executive
†Nesoff, Sandra Roberta journalist, social services administrator
Nichols, Carl Michael Internet media executive
Nish, Albert Raymond, Jr. retired newspaper editor
Noeth, Louise Ann journalist
Novick, Julius Lerner theater critic, educator
Nymoen, Kristine Staples magazine editor
Oakley, Andrew Arthur journalist, educator
†O'Donnell, Sara Altshul editor
Olive, David Michael magazine writer, magazine editor
Orr, Carol Wallace book publishing executive
Osborn, Susan Titus editor
Osrin, Raymond Harold retired political cartoonist
Otis, Denise Marie editor, writer
†Pachman, Ilene Munetz writer, educator
Pack, Richard Morris broadcasting executive
Palmer, Bradley Beran sportscaster
Palvino, Jack Anthony broadcasting executive
Parker, Mel editor
Paulson, Kenneth Alan journalist, lawyer, business executive
Peacock, Mary Willa magazine editor
Peeples, Rufus Roderick, Jr. (Roddy Peeples) farm and ranch news radio broadcaster
Pepper, Jeffrey Mackenzie publishing executive
Perlis, Michael Steven magazine publisher
Perrin, Gail editor
Petacque, Arthur M. journalist
Peterson, Kevin Bruce newspaper editor, publishing executive
Phillips, Glynda Ann editor
Picower, Warren Michael editor
Pierce, Jim recording industry producer
Piven, Joshua L. journalist
Plangere, Jules Leon, Jr. retired media company executive
Plank, (Ethel) Faye editor, photographer, writer
Pletcher, Eldon editorial cartoonist
Pockell, Leslie Mark publishing company executive
Podhoretz, Norman magazine editor, writer
Policinski, Eugene Francis author, newspaper editor, foundation executive
Poling, Jerome Paul journalist
Porges, Walter Rudolf television news executive
Prady, Norman journalist, writer, advertising executive, marketing consultant
Preddy, Raymond Randall retired newspaper publisher, educator
Price, Tom journalist
Pudney, Gary Laurence television executive
Putnam, Linda Lee communication educator, researcher
Quinn, Charles Nicholas journalist
Radcliffe, Redonia (Donnie Radcliffe) journalist, author
Radlauer, Steve freelance writer, journalist
Ramsay, Karin Kinsey publisher, educator
Randinelli, Tracey Anne magazine editor
Rapoport, Ronald Jon journalist
Rayner, William Alexander retired newspaper editor
†Read, Richard Eaton newspaper reporter
†Redwine, Tina M. television journalist
Reid-Bills, Mae editor, historian
Reidenbaugh, Lowell Henry retired sports editor
Reynolds, Edward book publisher
†Reynolds, Janna Sue journalist
Richards, Wesley Jon newscaster, writer, producer
Richman, Alan magazine editor
Ridder, Paul Anthony newspaper executive
Robbins, Jennifer Kay journalist
Robbins, Michael Warren magazine editor
Roberts, Delmar Lee editor
Roberts, Suzanne Catherine freelance reporter
†Rollins, Lisa L. journalist
Rosenthal, Arthur Jesse publisher
Rosset, Lisa Krug editor
Rourke, Arlene Carol publisher
Rubin, Nancy Zimman (Nancy Rubin Stuart) journalist, author, screenwriter
Rust, Robert Francis retired publishing executive
Ryan, Allan James publishing executive, editor
Ryan, Cathrine Smith publisher
Ryan, Joyce Ethel publishing executive
Ryerson, Marjorie Gilmour journalist, educator, poet, photographer
†Sacco, Tracy Lynn journalist
Safrey-Hoyt, Jennifer Ann newspaper editor, writer
Sagansky, Jeff broadcast executive
†Salant, Katherine Blair columnist
Salinger, Pierre Emil George journalist
†Salvatore, Diane J. editor
Samway, Patrick H. journal editor
Sanders, Marlene anchor, journalism educator
Sapsowitz, Sidney H. entertainment and media company executive
Sarris, Andrew George film critic
Schleuning, Jay James reporter
†Schmaler, Tracy Alice newspaper journalist, writer
†Schmedel, Scott Rollings journalist
Schooley, Jennifer Lynn broadcasting executive
Schorr, Daniel Louis broadcast journalist, author, lecturer
Schragis, Steven M. publisher, lawyer
Schwartz, Lloyd Marvin newspaper and magazine correspondent, broadcaster
Schweickart, Russell Louis communications executive, astronaut
Scruggs, Charles G. editor
†Sedlacek, Michal journalist
Serwatka, Walter Dennis publishing executive
Sewell, Leslie television producer, journalist
Shelton, Stephani broadcast journalist, consultant
Shoemaker, Marjorie Patterson textbook editor, consultant
Shreiner, Curt educational technologist, consultant
†Siegel, Tara journalist
Simon, Peter E. publishing executive
Simons, Lewis Martin journalist
Sinclair, Carole publisher, editor, author
Skene, G(eorge) Neil publisher, lawyer
Skinner, Thomas broadcasting and film executive
Smith, Carter Blakemore broadcaster
Smith, Chester broadcasting executive
Smith, George Drury publisher, editor, collagist, writer
Smith, Hedrick Laurence journalist, television comentator, author, lecturer
Smith, Linda Wasmer writer
Smith, Martin Bernhard journalist
Spencer, Helen Elaine editor
Spencer, Peter LeValley, Jr. editor
Stamper, Malcolm Theodore publishing company executive
Stanley, Scott, Jr. editor
Stanton, John Jeffrey editor, broadcast journalist, government programs director, analyst, professional society administrator
Starr, David newspaper editor, publisher
Steiger, Dale Arlen publishing executive
Steiner, Amy Leigh photo director, photographer
Steiner, Shari Yvonne publisher, editor, journalist
Stennett, William Clinton (Clint Stennett) radio and television station executive, state senator
Stephens, Edward Carl communications educator, writer
Stern, Marilyn picture editor, photographer, writer
Stiff, Robert Martin newspaper editor
Stines, Fred, Jr. publisher
Stolley, Richard Brockway journalist
Stouffer, Nancy Kathleen publishing company executive
Strothman, James Edward editor
†Stuart, Reginald A. journalist
Sullivan, Daniel Joseph theater critic
Switzer, Maurice Harold journalist
Tash, Martin Elias publishing company executive
†Taylor, Lawrence sports commentator, former professional football player
†Teison, Herbert J. editor, publisher
Terry, Clifford Lewis journalist
Thomas, Katherine Jane newspaper business columnist
Thomas, Patricia Goodnow journalist
Thomopoulos, Anthony D. retired motion picture company executive
Threlkeld, Richard Davis broadcast journalist
Tiedge-Lafranier, Jeanne Marie editor
Tobias, Andrew Previn columnist, lecturer
Traylor, William Robert publisher
Triece, Anne Gallagher magazine publisher
Trudeau, Garretson Beekman (Garry Trudeau) cartoonist
Trueman, William Peter Main broadcaster, newspaper columnist
Truman, Gary Tucker photojournalist
Tullis, Paul Rowan journalist
Tuohy, William correspondent
Tynes, John Cowan publisher, writer, editor, graphic designer
Ubell, Earl magazine health editor
Urdang, Laurence lexicographer, publisher
Vaida, Veronica Fodor publishing marketing reference professional
Valtman, Edmund editorial cartoonist
Vargas, Pattie Lee author, editor
Visci, Joseph Michael newspaper editor
Voorhees, John Lloyd columnist
Wagman, Robert John journalist, author
Wagner, Julia A(nne) retired editor
†Walker, Courtney G. magazine editor
Wallace, Thomas C(hristopher) editor, literary agent
Wallach, Amei Marione journalist, art critic
Walls, Carmage Lee, Jr. newspaper executive, consultant
†Wasson, Brian Charles editor
Waters, T. Wayne journalist
Watkins, William David editor, writer, consultant, agent
Wearn, Wilson Cannon retired media executive
Weaver, Howard C. newspaper executive
Weber, Arthur magazine executive
Weckesser, Ernest Prosper, Jr. publisher, educator
†Wegener, Robert Paul communications educator
†Weier, Anita Carol journalist
Weiner, N. Alfred publishing executive
Weissman, Jack (George Anderson) editor
Welsome, Eileen journalist
Werman, Thomas Ehrlich record producer
White, Nancy Carolyn publishing executive
Whitesell, John Edwin motion picture company executive
Whitney, Ruth Reinke magazine editor
Wicker, Thomas Grey retired journalist
Wies, Barbara editor, publisher
Wiessler, David Albert correspondent
Wille, Wayne Martin retired editor
Williams, Christie Lee journalist
Williams, Gurney, III journalist, educator
Wilner, Judith journalist
Winter, Alan retired publishing company executive
Wolfman, Ira Joel editor, writer
Wollman Rusoff, Jane Susan journalist, writer
Wood, Donald Neal educator in media, author
Wood, Marian Starr publishing company executive
Woodruff, Virginia broadcast journalist, writer
Woodward, John Russell motion picture production executive
Wright, Hassell Bradley journalist, editor
Wussler, Robert Joseph broadcasting executive, media consultant
Yack, Patrick Ashley editor
Yancey, Katherine Bean editor
†Yellin, Deena journalist
Young, Patrick writer, editor
Young, Richard Alan association executive
†Zernike, Kate reporter
Ziegler, Jack (Denmore) cartoonist

EDUCATION. For postsecondary education, *See also* specific fields.

UNITED STATES

ALABAMA

Albertville
Sheets, Dorothy Jane retired school librarian and educator

Andalusia
Windham, Susan Kay Harper early childhood educator

Anniston
Smith, Judith Day early childhood educator

Auburn
Alderman, Charles Wayne university dean
Galbraith, Ruth Legg retired university dean, home economist
Kribel, Robert Edward academic administrator, consultant physicist
Lishak, Lisa Anne secondary education educator
Miller, Wilbur Randolph university educator and administrator
Muse, William Van academic administrator
Owens, John Murry dean
Philpott, Harry Melvin former university president
Voitle, Robert Allen college dean, physiologist

Bessemer
Stephens, Betsy Bain retired elementary school educator

Birmingham
Berte, Neal Richard college president
Branham, Grady Eugene principal
†Bridges, James Edward, Jr. dean
Carter, John Thomas retired educational administrator, writer
Clarke, Juanita M. Waiters education educator
Corts, Thomas Edward university president
Edwards, Margaret McRae college administrator, lawyer
Goldman, Jay industrial engineer, educator, former dean
Hames, Carl Martin educational administrator, art dealer, consultant
Hendley, Dan Lunsford retired university official
†Hill, David Geoffrey college administrator
Mc Callum, Charles Alexander university official
†O'Neil, Peter V. provost
Reynolds, W(ynetka) Ann academic administrator, educator
Wood, Clinton Wayne middle school educator

Centre
Clark, Kathleen Vernon special education educator

Clanton
Davenport, Betty special education educator

Crossville
Blessing, Maxine Lindsey secondary education educator

Daphne
†Henson, Pamela Taylor secondary education educator, biology

Dothan
Garner, Alto Luther retired education educator

Enterprise
Rikard, Yvonne H. elementary educator

Florence
Potts, Robert Leslie academic administrator
Zarate, Ann Gairing academic administrator, lawyer

Foley
Wood, Linda Sherrill secondary education educator

Fort Payne
Harris, Melba Iris secondary school educator, state agency administrator

Guntersville
Patterson, Harold Dean retired superintendent of schools
Sparkman, Brandon Buster educator, writer, consultant

Hartselle
Smith, Pamela Rodgers elementary education educator

Homewood
Hart, Virginia Wade elementary education educator

Hoover
Wyers, Mary Shuttlesworth *secondary school educator, coach*

Huntsville
Black, Daniel Hugh *retired secondary school educator*
Franz, Frank Andrew *university president, physics educator*
†Hall, Elizabeth Murchie *retired special education educator, consultant*
Hession, Alice Irene *principal*
Hoppe, Lea Ann *elementary education educator*
Krueger, Kathleen Susan *special education administrator*
Leslie, Lottie Lyle *retired secondary education educator*
Lundquist, Charles Arthur *university official*
Morgan, Beverly Hammersley *middle school educator, artist*
Quick, Jerry Ray *academic administrator*

Irondale
Karr, Beverly Ann *counselor*

Jacksonville
Austin, Dan *retired dean*
Boswell, Rupert Dean, Jr. *retired academic administrator, math educator*
Hale, Judy Ann *education educator*
McGee, Harold Johnston *academic administrator*

Livingston
DeMay, Patricia Ann *elementary educator, education educator*
Green, Asa Norman *university president*

Maxwell AFB
Kline, John Alvin *academic administrator*

Mobile
Byrd, Mary Jane *education educator*
Copeland, Lewis *principal*
Dansak, Daniel Albert *medical educator, consultant*
Floyd, Cinthia Ann *secondary school educator, coach*
McElhaney, Lynne Meyer *chemistry and biology educator*
Vacik, James Paul *university administrator*
Whiddon, Frederick Palmer *academic administrator*
†White, Mary Gormandy *college executive*
Zawistowski, Lori Anne *academic administrator*

Montgomery
Bigham, Wanda Ruth *college president*
Brannan, Eulie Ross *education consultant*
Harris, William Hamilton *academic administrator*
May, Cecil Richard, Jr. *academic administrator*
Ritvo, Roger Alan *vice chancellor, health management-policy educator*

Mountain Brook
Dixon, Michel L. *educational administrator*

Muscle Shoals
Smith, Harry Delano *educational administrator*

Normal
†Jarrett, Alfred A. *social administration educator, consultant*

Opp
Patterson, Polly Jones *academic director*

Ozark
Dobson, Rebecca Elizabeth *secondary education educator, retired*

Perdido
Curry, Debbie Hartley *secondary education educator*

Pinson
Turberville, Dee Johnson *secondary school media specialist*

Prattville
Burrows, Henry Peter, III *secondary education educator*

Scottsboro
McGill, Judy Annell McGee *early childhood and elementary educator*

Southside
Hill, Anita Griffith *retired principal*

Sylacauga
McDonough, Sandra Morris *secondary school educator*

Talladega
Paris, Virginia Hall (Ginger Paris) *elementary school educator*

Theodore
Weeks, Charlotte Lynne *elementary education educator*

Troy
Hawkins, Jack, Jr. *academic administrator*
Long, John Maloy *university dean*

Tuscaloosa
Barrett, Nancy Smith *university administrator*
Gunther, William David *university administrator, economics educator*
Jackson, Cynthia Williford *special education educator*
Meredith, Thomas C. *academic administrator*
Mitchell, Herbert Hall *former university dean, educational consultant*
Searcy, Jane Berry *educational administrator*
Smith, Lois Colston *secondary school educator*
Sorensen, Andrew Aaron *academic administrator*
Southern, James Terry *secondary education educator*
Thomas, Joab Langston *retired university president, biology educator*

Tuscumbia
Hutchens, Eugene Garlington *college administrator*

Tuskegee
Green, Elbert P. *retired university official*
Payton, Benjamin Franklin *college president*

Wetumpka
Tracy, Patricia Ann Koop *secondary school educator*
†Welch, Judy Faulkner *primary education educator*

ALASKA

Anchorage
Anthony, Susan *secondary education educator*
Behrend, Donald Fraser *educator, university administrator*
Bowie, Phyllis *secondary education educator*
Byrd, Milton Bruce *college president, former business executive*
Gillam, David Allen *elementary school educator*
Gorsuch, Edward Lee *chancellor*
Hale, Mary Helen Parker *university administrator*
†Johnson, Daniel M. *provost*
Matsui, Dorothy Nobuko *elementary education educator*
Wedel, Millie Redmond *secondary school educator*

Chiniak
Griffin, Elaine B. *educator*

Fairbanks
Alexander, Vera *dean, marine science educator*
Burch, Barbara Jean *special education educator, administrator*
Doran, Timothy Patrick *educational administrator*
Lind, Marshall L. *academic administrator*
Reichardt, Paul Bernard *provost, chemistry educator*
Wood, William Ransom *retired university president, city official, corporate executive*

Juneau
Cary, Suzanne *elementary education educator*
Romesburg, Kerry D. *state education administrator*

Nome
Dunaway, Samantha Jo *secondary school educator*

Sitka
Ross, Dona Ruth *education program director, retired*

Tuntutuliak
Daniel, Barbara Ann *elementary and secondary education educator*

Wasilla
Moore, Toni Floss *elementary education educator*

ARIZONA

Arizona City
Donovan, Willard Patrick *retired elementary education educator*

Avondale
Huffman, Thomas Patrick *secondary education educator*
Thompson, Bonnie Ransa *secondary educator, chemistry educator*

Buckeye
Burton, Edward Lewis *retired industrial procedures and training consultant, educator*

Cave Creek
†Kastelic, Robert L. *education educator*
†Valentine, Margo *secondary education educator*

Chandler
Barnard, Annette Williamson *elementary school principal*
Rowe, Ernest Ras *education educator, academic administrator*
Stewart, Nancy Sue Spurlock *educator*

Flagstaff
†Connell, Charles W. *provost*
Hooper, Henry Olcott *academic administrator, physicist*
Lovett, Clara Maria *university administrator, historian*
Ratzlaff, Vernon Paul *elementary education educator, consultant*
Reyhner, Jon Allan *education educator*

Fort Huachuca
Adams, Frank *education specialist*

Fountain Hills
Humes, Charles Warren *counselor, educator*

Glendale
Altersitz, Janet Kinahan *principal*
Bret, Donna Lee *elementary education educator*
Edwards, Vicki Ann *elementary school assistant principal*
Louk, Donna Pat *elementary education educator, music educator*
Throp, George Lawrence *secondary education educator, mathematics educator*

Goodyear
Asadi, Robert Samir *high school principal*

Green Valley
Barich, Dewey Frederick *emeritus educational administrator*
Smith, Raymond Lloyd *former university president, consultant*

Holbrook
Palmer, Arthur Arvin *dean, rancher*
†Passer, Gary Louis *college president*

Many Farms
Hamilton, Jimmy Ray *secondary education educator*

Mesa
Carter, Sally Packlett *elementary education educator*
†Christiansen, Larry K. *college president*
Colbert, George Clifford *college official*
†Darling, Sandra Kay *educational consultant, school administrator*
Garwood, John Delvert *former college administrator*
Mead, Linda McCullough *secondary education educator, adult educator*
Philbrick, Douglas Robert *principal, librarian, educator, mental health professional*
Ramirez, Janice L. *assistant school superintendent*

Miami
†Ladendorff, Linda Hardin-Reed *early childhood education educator*

Page
Hart, Marian Griffith *retired reading educator*

Phoenix
Barela, Bertha Cicci *elementary education educator, artist*
Cain, Robert Joseph *elementary school educator*
Camous, Louise Michelle *secondary education educator, sister*
Culnon, Sharon Darlene *reading specialist, special education educator*
Donnelly, Charles Robert *retired college president*
Fitzgerald, Joan *principal*
Hughes, Robert Edward *elementary education educator*
Hutchinson, Ann *development director*
Linderman, William Earl *elementary school educator, writer*
Melinosky, Karen Elizabeth *special education educator*
Minor, Willie *college department chair*
†Schilling, John Michael *education director*
Smith-Hart, Ann Aurelia *instructional services administrator*
Wendel, O. Theodore, Jr. *university associate provost*
†Whitlow, Donna Mae *daycare and primary school administrator*
Wood, Barbara Butler *secondary language arts and television production educator*

Pine
Gurney, Evalyn Hartung *retired secondary school educator*

Prescott
Beaumont, Roderick Fraser *education consultant*
Rheinish, Robert Kent *university administrator*

Prescott Valley
Peoples, Esther Lorraine *elementary education educator*

Roll
Jorajuria, Elsie Jean *elementary education educator*

Safford
Riddlesworth, Judith Himes *elementary and secondary education educator*

San Manuel
Hawk, Dawn Davah *secondary education educator*
Hawk, Floyd Russell *secondary school educator*
Lemley, Diane Claire Beers *principal*

Scottsdale
Esquer, Deborah Anne *elementary education educator*
Hill, Louis Allen, Jr. *former university dean, consultant*
Mayer, Robert Anthony *retired college president*
Wright, C. T. Enus *former academic administrator*

Sedona
Goldberg, Melvyn *retired educator*

Sierra Vista
Michelich, Joanna Kurdeka *academic administrator*

Sun City West
Cohen, Abraham J. (Al Cohen) *educational administrator*

Sun Lakes
Smith, Eleanor Jane *university chancellor, retired, consultant*
Thompson, Loring Moore *retired college administrator, writer*

Tempe
†Codell, Julie Francia *university administrator*
Coor, Lattie Finch *university president*
Forsyth, Ben Ralph *academic administrator, medical educator*
Guzzetti, Barbara Jean *education educator*
Lunsford, Jack William *community colleges official*
Overman, Glenn Delbert *college dean emeritus*
Pijawka, David *environmental educator, researcher*
Saunders, Karen Estelle *secondary school educator*
Scott, Judith Myers *elementary education educator*
Simmons, Howard Lee *education educator*
Wallen, Carl J. *education educator*
†Warner, Michael Dennis *educator*
Wills, J. Robert *academic administrator, drama educator, writer*

Tucson
Cate, Rodney Michael *academic administrator*
Chidester, Otis Holden *retired secondary education educator*
Cutrone, Lawrence Gary *school system administrator, consultant, writer*
Dyer-Raffler, Joy Ann *special education diagnostician, educator*
Eribes, Richard *dean*
Evans, Arthur Haines, Jr. *educational consultant, researcher*
Garner, Girolama Thomasina *retired educational administrator, educator*
Giorgi, Peter Bonnard *educator*
Heins, Marilyn *college dean, pediatrics educator, author*
Hurt, Charlie Deuel, III *dean, educator*
Johnson, Christopher Gardner *technology educator*
Johnson, John Gray *retired university chancellor*
Kaltenbach, C(arl) Colin *dean, educator*
Larson, L. Jean *educational administrator*
Leavitt, Jerome Edward *childhood educator*
Likins, Peter William *university administrator*
Madden, James A. *gifted and talented educator*
Maker, Carol June *gifted and talented educator*
Reid, Charles Phillip Patrick *academic administrator, researcher, educator*
Sander, Eugene George *vice provost, dean*
Stoffle, Carla Joy *university library dean*
Tomoeda, Cheryl Kuniko *academic researcher*
Weaver, Albert Bruce *university administrator*

Yuma
Rivera, Jaime Arturo *secondary education educator, principal*

ARKANSAS

Alma
†Dyer, V. Jeffrey *principal*

Arkadelphia
Butler, Dartha Jean *middle school educator*
Dunn, Charles DeWitt *academic administrator*
Elrod, Ben Moody *academic administrator*
Grant, Daniel Ross *retired university president*
Mueller, Gene Albert *dean, social sciences educator*
Thomas, Herman L. *school system administrator*

Camden
Bradshaw, Otabel *retired primary school educator*
Owen, Larry Gene *academic administrator, educator, electronic and computer integrated manufacturing consultant*

Conway
Die, Ann Marie Hayes *college president, psychology educator*
Horton, Joseph Julian, Jr. *academic dean, educator*
Thompson, Winfred Lee *university president, lawyer*

Crossett
†Smith, Connie Simpson *secondary school educator*

Dermott
Bynum, Judith Lane *special education educator*

Des Arc
Branham, Elizabeth Mullen *educational administrator*

Fayetteville
Ferritor, Daniel E. *educator*
Naseem, Hameed Ahmad *educator*
Schoppmeyer, Martin William *education educator*
Van Patten, James Jeffers *education educator*
Williams, Doyle Z. *university dean, educator*

Fort Smith
Gooden, Benny L. *school system administrator*
Montgomery, M. Darlene *secondary education educator, English educator*
Paxton, Jackie Lee *education educator, writer, consultant*

Glenwood
Klopfenstein, Philip Arthur *high school educator*

Greenbrier
†Burgin, Karen Jean *special education educator*

Hartford
Roller Hall, Gayle Aline *gifted and talented education educator*

Hindsville
Peirce, Carole *secondary school educator*

Hot Springs
Brinson, Harold Thomas *retired university president emeritus*

Hot Springs National Park
Farris, Jefferson Davis *university administrator*

Jonesboro
†Lavers, Norman *adult education educator*
Nelsen, Evelyn Rigsbee Seaton *retired educator*
Smith, Eugene Wilson *retired university president and educator*

Little Rock
Anderson, Joel E., Jr. *university administrator*
Berry, Evalena Hollowell *retired secondary educator, writer*
Chesser, Thelma Jo Sykes *early childhood educator, administrator*
Fribourgh, James Henry *university administrator*
Hathaway, Charles E. *academic administrator*
Keaton, William Thomas *academic administrator, pastor*
Nelson, Susan Branon *coordinator comprehensive system personnel development*
O'Neal, Nell Self *retired principal*
Truex, Dorothy Adine *retired university administrator*
Wilson, I. Dodd *dean*
Wohlleb, James Carl *academic director*

Lowell
†Hill, Roger L. *principal*

Magnolia
Gamble, Steven G. *academic administrator*

Newark
†Webb, Mary Ann *principal*

North Little Rock
Johnson, Mark D. *college administrator*
Sawyer, Anita Dawn *special education educator*

Pine Bluff
Davis, Lawrence A. *academic administrator*

PROFESSIONAL INDEX 5873 EDUCATION

Scott, Vicki Sue *school system administrator*

Rogers
Spainhower, James Ivan *retired college president*

Russellville
Morris, Lois Lawson *education educator*

Searcy
Burks, David Basil *academic administrator, educator*
†Morgan, Jan Chesshir *academic administrator*

Springdale
Cordell, Beulah Faye *special education educator*
Hill, Peggy Sue *principal*
Rollins, Jimmy Don *school system administrator*

Stamps
Moore-Berry, Norma Jean *secondary school educator*

State University
Rampp, Lary Charles *educational consultant*
Wyatt, Leslie *academic administrator*

CALIFORNIA

Alameda
Carter, Roberta Eccleston *therapist, counselor*
Hooke, Michael Peter *secondary education educator*

Albany
Chook, Edward Kongyen *university administrator, disaster medicine educator*

Alta Loma
Haskvitz, Alan Paul *educational consultant, school educator*
Lucas, Elizabeth Marie Coughlin *educator*
†Young, Jerry Wayne *college president*

Altadena
Montanez, Mary Ann Chavez *vocational rehabilitation counselor, writer, producer*

Anaheim
Guajardo, Elisa *counselor, educator*
Jackson, David Robert *school system administrator*

Angwin
Maxwell, Donald Malcolm *college president, minister*

Antioch
Bedell, Jay Dee *educator, writer*

Apple Valley
Tishner, Keri Lynn *secondary education educator*

Aptos
Bohn, Ralph Carl *educational consultant, retired educator*

Arcadia
Baltz, Patricia Ann (Pann Baltz) *elementary education educator*

Arcata
Bowker, Lee Harrington *academic administrator*
McCrone, Alistair William *university president*

Atherton
Lane, Joan Fletcher *educational administrator*

Avenal
Barr, Maurice Alan *elementary education educator*

Azusa
Felix, Richard E. *academic administrator*

Bakersfield
Arciniega, Tomas Abel *university president*
Hefner, John *principal*
Hodash, Bob (Robert A. Hodash) *principal*
Ice, Marie *education educator*
Litherland, Donna Joyce *counselor*
Powell, Patricia Ann *secondary school educator*
Thomas, Tom Eldon *corrections educator*

Banning
Finley, Margaret Mavis *retired elementary school educator*

Bayside
Bank, Ron *principal*

Beaumont
†Mayer, Harvey Ethan *educator*

Bellflower
Cook, Karla Joan *elementary education educator*

Benicia
Garrop, Barbara Ann *elementary education educator*

Berkeley
Bender, Richard *university dean, architect, educator*
Berdahl, Robert Max *academic administrator, historian, educator*
†Black, Richard W. *director, financial aid*
Bowker, Albert Hosmer *retired university chancellor*
Cieslak, William *academic administrator*
Cross, Kathryn Patricia *education educator*
Freedman, Sarah Warshauer *education educator*
Glenny, Lyman Albert *retired education educator*
Johnson, Mary Katherine *elementary education educator*
Kay, Herma Hill *dean*
Kerr, Clark *academic administrator emeritus*
Leonard, Thomas Dean *dean, educator*
Maslach, George James *former university official*
Merrill, Richard James *educational director*
Miles, Raymond Edward *former university dean, organizational behavior and industrial relations educator*
Montgomery, Roger *dean*
Ralston, Lenore Dale *academic policy and program analyst*
Rice, Robert Arnot *school administrator*
Rohwer, William D., Jr. *university dean*
Schell, Orville *dean*
Shoemaker, Cameron David James *dean, educator*
Tien, Chang-Lin *engineer, educator*
†Tyson, Laura D'Andrea *dean, economist, educator*

Beverly Hills
Grant, Michael Ernest *educational administrator, institutional management educator*
Van de Kamp, Andrea Louise *academic administrator*

Bloomington
Llanusa, Steven Michael *elementary education educator*

Blythe
Thomas, Marcella Elaine *elementary education educator*

Bonita
Barnard, Arlene *retired secondary education educator*

Boulder Creek
Billings, Judith Diane *elementary education educator*

Buena Park
Papin, Nancy Sue *educational computer coordinator*
Turkus-Workman, Carol Ann *educator*

Burbank
Godwin, Annabelle Palkes *retired early childhood education educator*
Kelly, Michael Joseph *academic administrator, consultant*
Walters, Kenneth C. *retired educator*

Burlingame
Raffo, Susan Henney *elementary education educator*

Camarillo
Evans, James Handel *university administrator, architect, educator*

Campo
Beierle, Herbert Leonard *dean*

Canyon Lake
Knight, Vick, Jr. *author, educator, counselor*

Carlsbad
Gardner, David Chambers *education educator, psychologist, business executive, author*

Carmel
Faul, George Johnson *former college president*
Faul, June Patricia *education specialist*

Carson
Quijada, Angélica Maria *elementary education educator*

Chatsworth
Miller, Robert Steven *secondary school educator*

Chico
Esteban, Manuel Antonio *university administrator, educator*
Robinson, Beulah Lobdell *retired educator*

Chino
†Forsyth, Barbara Jean *elementary reading specialist, writer, poet*

Chula Vista
Hanson, Eileen *principal*
Livziey, James Gerald *secondary school educator*
Maggi, Gayle J.B. *secondary school educator*
Wyatt, Edith Elizabeth *elementary education educator*

Claremont
Alexander, John David, Jr. *college administrator*
Bekavac, Nancy Yavor *academic administrator, lawyer*
Douglass, Enid Hart *educational program director*
Faranda, John Paul *college administrator*
Fucaloro, Anthony Frank *dean*
Gann, Pamela Brooks *academic administrator*
Liggett, Thomas Jackson *retired seminary president*
Maguire, John David *academic administrator, educator, writer*
Platt, Joseph Beaven *former college president*
Riggs, Henry Earle *academic administrator, engineering management educator*
Stanley, Peter William *academic administrator*
Stark, Jack Lee *academic administrator*
Strauss, Jon Calvert *academic administrator*
Wettack, F. Sheldon *academic administrator*

Clayton
Bower, Fay Louise *retired academic administrator, nursing educator*

Colton
Dybowski, Douglas Eugene *education educator, economist*
Slider, Margaret Elizabeth *elementary education educator*

Compton
Williams, Vivian Lewie *college counselor*

Corona
Steiner, Barbara Anne *secondary school educator*

Costa Mesa
†Austin, David John *curriculum developer, writer*

Cotati
Hill, Ray Allen *educator*

Crockett
†Adams, Carol Jean *educator*

Cypress
Hall, Georgianna Lee *special education educator*

Danville
Sekera, Cynthia Dawn *secondary education educator*

Davis
Ginosar, D. Elaine *elementary education educator*
Green, Bonnie Jean *early childhood administrator*
Grey, Robert Dean *academic administrator, biology educator*
Hawke, Deborah Sue *academic counselor*
Pritchard, William Roy *former university system administrator*
Smiley, Robert Herschel *university dean*
Vanderhoef, Larry Neil *academic administrator*

Del Mar
†Walshok, Mary Lindenstein *academic administrator, sociology educator*

Delano
Lucas, Stephanie Heune *elementary education educator*

Desert Hot Springs
†Price, Cynthia Rose *elementary educator, entrepreneur*

Diamond Bar
Domeño, Eugene Timothy *elementary education educator, principal*

Dinuba
McKittrick, Joseph Terrence *school administrator, educator*

Downey
Brooks, Lillian Drilling Ashton *adult education educator*
Carrico, Deborah Jean *special education teacher*
Gogolin, Marilyn Tompkins *educational administrator, language pathologist*
Ruecker, Martha Engels *retired special education educator*

Duarte
Tse, Man-Chun Marina *special education educator*

Dunlap
Gair, Kevin Lindsey *learning director, educator*

El Cajon
Palafox, Mari Lee *private school educator*
Thomas, Esther Merlene *elementary education educator*

El Centro
Patterson, Melissa *elementary education educator*

El Monte
Deaver, Sharon Mae *special education educator*

Elk Grove
Landon, JoJene Babbitt *special education educator*
Sparks, Jack Norman *college dean*

Encinitas
Galiley, C. Jerome *secondary education educator*

Encino
Bach, Cynthia *educational program director, writer*

Escondido
†Friedman, Alan Howard *education educator, writer*
Moore, Marc Anthony *university administrator, writer, retired military officer*

Fair Oaks
Lemke, Herman Ernest Frederick, Jr. *retired elementary education educator, consultant*
†Staley, James Kelly *secondary school educator*

Fairfield
Kirkorian, Donald George *college official, management consultant*

Fallbrook
Evans, Anthony Howard *university president*

Forestville
Kielsmeier, Catherine Jane *school system administrator*

Fortuna
Fisher, Bruce David *elementary school educator*

Foster City
Berman, Daniel K(atzel) *educational consultant, university official*
Evans, Darrell J. *higher education educator*

Fountain Valley
†Purdy, Leslie *community college president*

Fresno
Coleman, Donald Gene *education educator*
Dandoy, Maxima Antonio *education educator emeritus*
Haak, Harold Howard *university president*
Howard, Katsuyo Kunugi *counselor, educator, consultant*
Keen, Derl Walter *child development educator*
Klassen, Peter James *academic administrator, history educator*
†Ortiz, John Michael *provost*
Welty, John Donald *academic administrator*

Fullerton
Barchi, Barbara Ann *education and training services consultant*
Donoghue, Mildred Ransdorf *education educator*
Gordon, Milton Andrew *academic administrator*
Hopping, Richard Lee *college president emeritus*
†Martinez, Vera *academic administrator*
O'Donnell, Edith J. *educational and information technology consultant, author, musician*
Pullen, Rick Darwin *dean*
Smith, Ephraim Philip *academic administrator, former university dean, educator*
Snider, Jane Ann *elementary school educator*

Glendale
Empey, Donald Warne *educational administrator*
Odier, Pierre Andre *educator, writer, photographer, artist*
Whalen, Lucille *academic administrator*

Glendora
Acevedo, Elizabeth Morrison *special education educator*
Schiele, Paul Ellsworth, Jr. *educational business owner, writer*

Hayward
Dance, Maurice Eugene *college administrator*
Gin, Hal Gabriel *university administrator*
Harris, Penelope Claire *children's center administrator, consultant*
Laycock, Mary Chappell *gifted and talented education educator, consultant*
McCune, Ellis E. *retired university system chief administrator, higher education consultant*
Rees, Norma S. *academic administrator*

Highland
†Odell, Brenda W. *principal*

Hillsborough
Hower, Donna Wilson *elementary education educator*

Hollister
Turpin, Calvin Coolidge *retired university administrator, educator*

Huntington Beach
Davidson-Shepard, Gay *secondary education educator*
Shishkoff, Muriel Mendelsohn *educational writer*
†Yglesias, Kenneth Dale *college president*

Huntington Park
Veis, Fred Alan *special education educator*

Indian Wells
Trotter, F(rederick) Thomas *retired academic administrator*

Indio
Houghton, Robert Charles *secondary education educator*

Irvine
Beach, Christopher John *American literary arts educator*
Block, Sandra Linda *special education educator*
Fleischer, Everly Borah *academic administrator*
†Hartmann, Dale Walter *librarian*
Kleeman, Nancy Gray Ervin *special education educator*
Moghadam, Amir *consultant, educational administrator*
Peltason, Jack Walter *foundation executive, educator*

Kelsey
Rankin, Graham M. *educator, consultant*

Kenwood
Richardson, Mary Weld *education administrator, development consultant*

La Habra
Ahn, Peter Pyung-choo *dean*

La Jolla
Alksne, John F. *dean*
†Ande, Jan Lee *educator, poet*
Cavenee, Webster K. *director*
Dreilinger, Charles Lewis (Chips Dreilinger) *dean*
†Dynes, Robert C. *academic administrator*
Frieman, Edward Allan *academic administrator, educator*
Lee, Jerry Carlton *university administrator*
Masys, Daniel Richard *medical school director*
Mitry, Darryl Joseph *educator, writer, strategic advisor*

La Mesa
Black, Eileen Mary *elementary school educator*
Tarson, Herbert Harvey *university administrator emeritus*

La Palma
Akubuilo, Francis Ekenechukwu *secondary school educator*

La Verne
Coray, Jeffrey Warren *assistant principal, instructor*
Fleck, Raymond Anthony, Jr. *retired university administrator*
Morgan, Stephen Charles *academic administrator*

Lafayette
†Thomas, Ramsay Berry *secondary educator*

Laguna Beach
Mirone-Bartz, Dawn *secondary school and community college educator*
Ryder, Virginia Pinkus *retired school system administrator*

Laguna Woods
Epley, Thelma Mae Childers *retired gifted and talented education educator*

Lake Arrowhead
Hubbard, Jeffrey Charles *educational administrator*

Lake Sherwood
Steadman, Lydia Duff *elementary school educator, symphony violinist*

Lakeport
Jones, Brenda Gail *school district administrator*

Lancaster
Bohannon, Linda Sue *special education educator*

Lemon Grove
Mott, June Marjorie *school system administrator*

Lemoore
Krend, William John *secondary education educator*

Livermore
Roshong, Dee Ann Daniels *dean, educator*

Lodi
Bishop-Graham, Barbara *secondary school educator, journalist*

Loma Linda
Joyce, Vicki Marie *special education educator*
Klooster, Judson *academic administrator, dentistry educator*

Long Beach
Anatol, Karl W. E. *provost*
Armstrong, Joanna *education educator*
Beljan, John Richard *university administrator, medical educator*
Best, Gary Allen *special education educator*
Blazey, Michael Alan *educator*
Dublin, Stephen Louis *secondary school educator, singer, musician*
Duke, Phyllis Louise Kellogg Henry *school administrator, management consultant*
Feldman, Stephen *academic administrator*
Fleming, Jane Williams *retired educator, author*
Hext, Kathleen Florence *internal audit college administrator*
Hobgood, E(arl) Wade *college dean*
Lathrop, Irvin Tunis *retired academic dean, educator*
Lauda, Donald Paul *university dean*
Maxson, Robert C. *university president*
McDonough, Patrick Dennis *academic administrator*
Porter, Priscilla *elementary education educator*
Reed, Charles Bass *chief academic administrator*

Los Altos
Gonzales, Richard Robert *academic administrator*
Keller, James Warren *college administrator*

Los Altos Hills
Johnson, Penelope Anne *university dean*

Los Angeles
Allums, Henriene *elementary education educator*
Ansley, Julia Ette *educator, poet, writer, consultant*
Armstrong, Lloyd, Jr. *university official, physics educator*
Burman, Sheila Flexer Zola *special education educator*
Campo, Todd Russell *principal, law enforcement educator*
Carnesale, Albert *university chancellor*
Cohen, Arthur M. *education educator*
Dalis, Peter T. *athletic director*
Dewey, Donald Odell *university dean*
Ecklund, Judith Louise *academic administrator*
Edwards, Kathryn Inez *instructional media consultant*
Feldman, Frances Lomas *educator, consultant*
Girvin, Shirley Eppinette *elementary education educator, journalist*
Gosfield, Margaret *educator, educational administrator, consultant, editor*
Gothold, Stuart Eugene *school system administrator, educator*
Grose, Elinor Ruth *retired elementary education educator*
†Haley, Roslyn Trezevant *educational program director*
Harris, F. Chandler *retired university administrator*
Harvey, James Gerald *educational counselor, consultant, researcher*
Hayes, Robert Mayo *university dean, library and information science educator*
Hoffman, Neil James *academic administrator*
Hubbard, John Randolph *university president emeritus, history educator, diplomat*
Jackson, Kingsbury Temple *educational contract consultant*
Kaback, Elaine *career counselor, consultant*
Kennelly, Sister Karen Margaret *college president*
Kleingartner, Archie *founding dean, educator*
Lieber, David Leo *university president*
Lim, Larry Kay *university official*
Lucente, Rosemary Dolores *educational administrator*
Lynch, Beverly Pfeifer *education and information studies educator*
†Mamer, John William *adult education educator*
Mandel, Joseph David *academic administrator, lawyer*
Marlin, Robert Matthew *secondary school educator*
†Martin, Shane Patrick *education educator, consultant*
McCabe, Edward R. B. *academic administrator, educator, physician*
Merrifield, Donald Paul *university chancellor*
Mitchell, Theodore R. *academic administrator*
Moore, Donald Walter *academic administrator, school librarian*
Moran, Thomas Harry *university administrator*
Mori, Allen Anthony *university dean, consultant, researcher*
Parks, Debora Ann *private school director*
Pierskalla, William Peter *university dean, management-engineering educator*
Polon, Linda Beth *elementary school educator, writer, illustrator*
Prejean, Kattie Calvin *educational administrator*
Rosser, James Milton *academic administrator*
Sample, Steven Browning *university executive*
Shearer, Derek Norcross *international studies educator, diplomat, administrator*
Silverman, Leonard M. *university dean, electrical engineering educator*
Slaughter, John Brooks *university administrator*
Sloane, Robert Malcolm *university administrator*
†Spangler, Mary *college president*
Steinberg, Warren Linnington *school principal*
Taylor, Leigh Herbert *college dean*
Toledo, Robert *football coach*
Wagner, William Gerard *university dean, physicist, consultant, information scientist, investment manager*
Wazzan, A(hmed) R(assem) Frank *engineering educator, dean*
Wexler, Robert *university administrator*
†Williams, William J. *educator, consultant, writer*
Young, Charles Edward *university chancellor emeritus*

Los Gatos
Dunham, Anne *educational institute director*

Malibu
Davenport, David *university president, lawyer*
Phillips, Ronald Frank *academic administrator*

Menifee
Kandus, Richard Jay *adult education educator*

Milpitas
Leonardi, Rosarius Roy *special education educator*

Mineral
Hoofard, Jane Mahan Decker *elementary education educator*

Mission Viejo
McGinnis, Joán Adell *retired secondary school educator*
Sabaroff, Rose Epstein *retired education educator*

Modesto
Bairey, Marie *principal*
Harrison-Scott, Sharlene Marie *elementary education educator*
Naeve, Catherine Ann *secondary education educator*
Sibitz, Michael William *school superintendent*
Tidball, Lee Falk *elementary education educator*

Mojave
Shelby, Tim Otto *secondary education educator*

Montebello
Cabrera, Carmen *secondary education educator*
Kolbeck, Sister Ann Lawrence *school principal*

Monterey
Di Girolamo, Rosina E. *education educator*
†Morgan, Edwin Philip *academic administrator*
Oder, Broeck Newton *school emergency management consultant*

Monterey Park
Meysenburg, Mary Ann *principal*
†Moreno, Ernest H. *college president*

Moreno Valley
Mullen, Terri Ann *special education educator*
Twedell, Lester Ralph, Jr. *secondary school educator*

Mountain View
Craig, Joan Carmen *secondary school educator, drama teacher*

Napa
Ervin, Margaret Howie *elementary education educator, special education educator*
Moore, William Joseph *retired educator*
Rada, Alexander *university official*
Renfrow, Patricia Anne *secondary education educator*

Newport Beach
Wyatt, Brett Michael *secondary school educator*

North Hollywood
Chang, Wung *researcher, lecturer, business advisor*

Northridge
Curzon, Susan Carol *university administrator*
Falk, Heinrich Richard *theater and humanities educator*
†Shaw, Victor N. *educator*
Tanis, Norman Earl *retired university dean, library expert*

Novato
†Morrissey, Michael Patrick *educational research consultant, educator*
Patterson, W. Morgan *college president*
†White, Linda Lee Locy *secondary educator*

Oakland
Anderson, Brother Mel *academic administrator*
Atkinson, Richard Chatham *university president*
Diaz, Sharon *education administrator*
DuMont, Virginia Peterson *educator, writer*
Fries, Lita Linda *school system administrator*
Goldstine, Stephen Joseph *college administrator*
Gomes, Wayne Reginald *academic administrator*
Griego, Elizabeth Brownlee *college dean*
Griffin, Betty Jo *elementary school educator*
Heydman, Abby Maria *dean*
†McCloskey, Mark *educator*
Stewart, John Lincoln *university administrator*
Tomlinson-Keasey, Carol Ann *university administrator*

Oceanside
Pena, Maria Geges *academic services administrator*

Ontario
Kennedy, Mark Alan *middle and secondary school educator*
Peters, Jacqueline Mary *secondary education educator*

Orange
Doti, James L. *academic administrator*
Hamilton, Harry Lemuel, Jr. *academic administrator*

Orinda
Glasser, Charles Edward *university president*

Oroville
Tamori, David Isamu *secondary education educator*

Oxnard
Hamm, George Ardeil *retired secondary education educator, hypnotherapist, consultant*
Herrera, Sandra Johnson *school system administrator*

Pacific Grove
Eadie, Margaret L. *educational and career consultant*
Wangberg, Elaine Gregory *university administrator*

Pacific Palisades
†Grimstad, Kirsten Julia *educator*

Palm Desert
Hester, Gerald LeRoy *retired school system administrator*
Hoffmann, Joan Carol *retired academic dean*
Sexson, Stephen Bruce *educational writer, educator*

Palm Springs
Gill, Jo Anne Martha *middle school educator*
Hartman, Rosemary Jane *special education educator*
Owings, Thalia Kelley *elementary school educator*
Satcher, Clement Michael *Art education educator*

Palo Alto
Bohrnstedt, George William *educational researcher*
Bolitho, Louise Greer *educational administrator, consultant*
Case, Robbie *education educator, author*
Loveless, Edward Eugene *education educator, musician*
Parker, Thomas G. *educator*

Palos Verdes Estates
Fischer, Robert Blanchard *university administrator, researcher*
Hara, Tadao *educational administrator*
Lazzaro, Anthony Derek *university administrator*

Palos Verdes Peninsula
Baxter, Betty Carpenter *educational administrator*
Copeland, Phillips Jerome *former academic administrator, former air force officer*
Gaines, Jerry Lee *secondary education educator*

Pasadena
Albert, Sidney Paul *philosophy and drama educator*
Baltimore, David *academic administrator, microbiologist, educator*
Brooks, Edward Howard *college administrator*
Brown, David R. *academic administrator*
Cepielik, Elizabeth Lindberg *educator*
Everhart, Thomas Eugene *retired university president, engineering educator*
Freise, Earl Jerome *univeristy administrator, materials engineering educator*
Gilman, Richard Carleton *retired college president*
Levy, David Steven *college administrator*
Lingenfelter, Sherwood Galen *university provost, anthropology educator*
Meye, Robert Paul *retired seminary administrator, writer*
Peter, Kenneth Shannon *elementary school educator*
Pings, Cornelius John *educational consultant, director*
Siemon-Burgeson, Marilyn M. *education administrator*
Stolper, Edward Manin *secondary education educator*

Paso Robles
Gruner, George Richard *retired secondary education educator*

Pinole
Grogan, Stanley Joseph *educational and security consultant*

Playa Del Rey
†Reed, Timothy Max *secondary education educator*

Pleasant Hill
†Edelstein, Mark Gerson *college president*
Lundgren, Susan Elaine *counselor, educator*

Pleasanton
Aladeen, Lary Joe *secondary school educator*

Pomona
Ambrose, William Wright, Jr. *college dean, accounting educator, tax researcher*
Demery, Dorothy Jean *secondary school educator*
†Dishman, Rose Marie Rice *academic administrator, researcher*
Fine, Aubrey Howard *educator*
Suzuki, Bob H. *university president*

Porterville
Hayes, Shirley Ann *special education educator*

Portola Valley
Dixon, Andrew Derart *retired academic administrator*
Oscarson, Kathleen Dale *writing assessment coordinator, educator*

Poway
Shippey, Lyn *reading center director*
Vitti, Anthony Mark *secondary education educator*

Quartz Hill
Nettelhorst, Robin Paul *academic administrator, writer*

Rancho Cordova
Hendrickson, Elizabeth Ann *retired secondary education educator*

Rancho Palos Verdes
Schach, Barbara Jean *elementary education educator*

Rancho Santa Margarita
Munsell, Joni Anne *middle school educator*

Red Bluff
Kennedy, James William, Jr. (Sarge Kennedy) *special education administrator, consultant*

Redding
†Grant, James Martin *academic administrator*

Redlands
Appleton, James Robert *university president, educator*
†Burgess, Charlotte Gaylord *dean*
Healy, Daniel Thomas *secondary education educator*
Jennings, Irmengard Katharina *academic administrator*

Redondo Beach
Marsee, Stuart (Earl) *educational consultant, retired*

Redway
Branzei-Velasquez, Sylvia Carol *secondary education educator*

Reseda
Anstad, Neil *director*
Moss, Debra Lee *special education educator*

Rialto
Bauza, Christine Diane *special education educator*
Straight, James Wesley *secondary education educator*

Ridgecrest
Matulef, Gizelle Terese *secondary education educator*

Riverside
Allen, William Merle *university administrator, museum director*
Balow, Irving Henry *retired education educator*
†Bulloch, Kathleen Louise *educational professional*
Diamond, Richard *secondary education educator*
Finan, Ellen Cranston *secondary education educator, consultant*
Geraty, Lawrence Thomas *academic administrator, archaeologist*
Hendrick, Irving Guilford *dean, education educator*
Lacy, Carolyn Jean *elementary education educator, secondary education educator*
Naugle, Charlotte June *principal, educator*
†Pianca, Marina *educator, researcher, writer*
Williams, Pamela R. *elementary school administrator*
Yacoub, Ignatius I. *university dean*

Rohnert Park
Arminana, Ruben *academic administrator, educator*
Babula, William *university dean*

Sacramento
Gerth, Donald Rogers *university president*
†Harris, Robert M. *college president*
†Howes, Edward Herbert *college educator*
Kellough, Richard Dean *educator*
Lasley, Mona Carol *elementary education educator, consultant*
Law, Nancy Enell *school system administrator*
McKim, Harriet Megchelsen *education educator*
O'Leary, Marion Hugh *university dean, chemist*
Reed-Graham, Lois L. *administrator, secondary education educator*
†Smith, Marie B. *college president*
Steinhaus, Patricia *university administrator*
Stuart, David R. *academic administrator*
Zaidi, Emily Louise *retired elementary school educator*
†Zito, Michael Steven *educational administrator*

San Andreas
Millsaps, Rita Rae *elementary school educator*

San Bernardino
Crowell, Samuel Marvin, Jr. *education educator*
Norton, Ruth Ann *education educator*
Pendleton, Ronald Kenneth *education educator*

San Carlos
Mark, Lillian Gee *educational administrator*

San Diego
Ashton, Tamarah M. *special education educator*
Brose, Cathy *principal*
Castruita, Rudy *school system administrator*
Charles, Carol Morgan *education educator*
Clement, Betty Waidlich *literacy educator, consultant*
Clifton, Mark Stephen *administrator*
Donley, Dennis Lee *school librarian*
Fay, Helyn *college counselor*
Feinberg, Lawrence Bernard *university dean, psychologist*
Golding, Brage *former university president*
Hayes, Alice Bourke *university official, biology educator*
Hays, Garry D. *academic administrator*
Heath, Berthann Jones *education administrator*
Henig, Suzanne *retired educator, writer, editor*
Hoye, Walter Brisco *retired college administrator*
Kuc, Joseph A. *education educator, consultant*
Le Blanc, Deborah Sims *public administration educator*
Lomeli, Marta *elementary education educator*
Mir, Marilyn *retired educator*
Morris, Henry Madison, Jr. *education educator*
Prodor, Leah Marie *secondary education educator*
Reynolds, Hallie Bellah *elementary education educator*
Schade, Charlene Joanne *adult and early childhood education educator*
Schwartz, Alfred *university dean*
Walker, Donald Ezzell *retired academic administrator*
Weber, Stephen Lewis *university president*
Woodford, Mary Imogene Steele *secondary school educator*

San Dimas
Cameron, Judith Lynne *secondary education educator, hypnotherapist*
Lindly, Douglas Dean *elementary school educator, administrator*

San Francisco
Albino, Judith Elaine Newsom *university president*
Buidang, George (Hada Buidang) *educator, administrator, consultant, writer*
Cain, Leo Francis *retired special education educator*
Corrigan, Robert Anthony *academic administrator*
Davis, James Wesley *university program administrator, artist, writer, composer*
Dullea, Charles W. *university chancellor emeritus, priest*
Egan, Patricia Jane *former university development director, writer*

PROFESSIONAL INDEX 5875 EDUCATION

Fleishhacker, David school administrator
Fromm, Hanna educational administrator
Hall, Zach Winter academic administrator
†Jay, Cheryl Ann neurology educator
†Julius, Daniel J. university administrator, educator
Kleinberg, David Lewis education administrator
Kozloff, Lloyd M. university dean, educator, scientist
Krevans, Julius Richard university administrator, physician
LaBelle, Thomas Jeffrey academic administrator
Lo, Bernard education educator
Lo Schiavo, John Joseph university executive
Manson, Malcolm Hood educational administrator
Metz, Mary Seawell retired university dean, retired college president
Naegele, Carl Joseph university academic administrator, educator
O'Neill, Michael academic administrator
Rippel, Clarence W. academic administrator
Schlegel, John Peter academic administrator
†Schroffel, Bruce university executive
Stauffer, Thomas Michael university president
Stephens, Elisa art college president, lawyer
Torrey, Ella King academic administrator
Ury, Claude Max educational consultant, book reviewer
Zhu, Bo-qing cardiovascular research specialist

San Jose
Arvizu, Charlene Sutter elementary education educator
†Bain, Linda L. academic administrator
Caret, Robert Laurent university president
Collett, Jennie principal
Cruz, B. Robert academic administrator
Cryer, Rodger Earl educational administrator
Duncan, Gloria Celestine elementary educator
Elsorady, Alexa Marie secondary education educator
Holyer, Erna Maria adult education educator, writer, artist
Jordan, Bernice Bell elementary education educator
Martin, Bernard Lee former college dean
Merriam, Janet Pamela special education educator
Okerlund, Arlene Naylor university official
Pflughaupt, Jane Ramsey secondary school educator
Silver, Roberta Frances (Bobbi Silver) educator, writer
Waterer, Bonnie Clausing high school educator
Whitney, Natalie White primary school educator
Wise, Joseph Stephen secondary education educator, artist

San Leandro
Nehls, Robert Louis, Jr. school system administrator

San Lorenzo
†Clum, Gerard W. academic administrator
Glenn, Jerome T. secondary school principal
Schultz, Frederik Emil academic administrator

San Luis Obispo
Bailey, Philip Sigmon, Jr. university official, chemistry educator
Baker, Warren J(oseph) university president
Dalton, Linda Catherine university administrator
Ericson, Jon Meyer academic administrator, rhetoric theory educator
Haile, Allen Cleveland educator and administrator
Waller, Julia Reva financial aide counselor

San Marcos
†Boggs, George Robert academic administrator
Lilly, Martin Stephen university dean

San Marino
Footman, Gordon Elliott educational administrator
Mothershead, J. Leland, III dean

San Mateo
Bonnell, William Charles secondary education educator
Danker, Mervyn Kenneth director of education
Patnode, Darwin Nicholas academic administrator, professional parliamentarian

San Pablo
Colfack, Andrea Heckelman elementary education educator

San Rafael
Fink, Joseph Richard college president
Thomas, Mary Ann McCrary counselor, school system administrator

Santa Ana
†Eddy, Charles Christopher educator
Kato, Terri Emi elementary school and gifted and talented educator
Verhaegen, Terri Lynn Foy middle school educator
Watts, Judith-Ann White academic administrator

Santa Barbara
Allaway, William Harris retired university official
Boyan, Norman J. retired education educator
Cirone, William Joseph educational administrator
Korenic, Lynette Marie librarian
Kuehn, David Laurance music academy administrator
Mac Intyre, Donald John college president
O'Dowd, Donald Davy retired university president
Sinsheimer, Robert Louis retired university chancellor and educator
Sprecher, David A. university administrator, mathematician
Yang, Henry T. university chancellor, educator

Santa Clara
Locatelli, Paul Leo academic administrator
Nordmeyer, Mary Betsy retired vocational educator

Santa Clarita
Lavine, Steven David academic administrator

Santa Cruz
Brothers, Cheryl Marianne Morris school superintendent
Greenwood, M. R. C. college dean, biologist, nutrition educator
†Laue, John Otto Everett educator

Santa Maria
Dunn, Judith Louise secondary school educator

Johnsen, Peggy Winchell education administrator

Santa Monica
†Robertson, Piedad F. academic administrator

Santa Rosa
Christiansen, Peggy principal
Foster, Lucille Caster school system administrator, retired
Moore, Arlene Joy elementary school educator
Webb, Charles Richard retired university president

Santee
Deckard, Steve Wayne science educator, academic administrator

Saratoga
Houston, Elizabeth Reece Manasco correctional education consultant
Whalen, Margaret Cavanagh retired secondary school educator

Seal Beach
†Egertson, Thilda Amanda retired librarian and elementary educator
Melton, Cheryl Ann educator, small business owner

Seaside
Eke, Kenoye Kelvin academic administrator

Sherman Oaks
Fortuna, Anthony Frank retired educator, consultant
Horner, Sandra Marie Groce (Sandy Heart) educator, poet, songwriter, lyricist

Signal Hill
Vandament, William Eugene retired academic administrator

Silverado
Mamer, James Michael secondary education educator

Simi Valley
Bullock, Donald Wayne elementary education educator, educational computing consultant
Jackson, Thirston Henry, Jr. retired adult education educator

Solana Beach
DeMarco-Dennis, Eleanor (Poppy DeMarco-Dennis) elementary education educator, community activist

Sonoma
Hobart, Billie education educator, consultant

South San Francisco
Shelton, Leslie Habecker adult literacy program director

Springville
Meredith, Marilyn writer, writing educator

Stanford
Baron, James Neal organizational behavior and human resources educator, researcher
Gross, Richard Edmund education educator
Harrison, Wendy Jane Merrill university official
Henriksen, Thomas Hollinger university official
Kays, William Morrow university administrator, mechanical engineer
Kirst, Michael Weile education educator, researcher
Metzenberg, Robert L. education educator
Naimark, Norman M. academic administrator
Palm, Charles Gilman university official
Raisian, John academic administrator, economist
Spence, Andrew Michael dean, finance educator
Stone, William Edward unversity adminstrator
Strober, Myra Hoffenberg education educator, consultant
Veinott, Arthur Fales, Jr. universtiy research administrator

Stockton
Addie, Harvey Woodward retired secondary education educator, music director
DeRicco, Lawrence Albert college president emeritus
Jantzen, J(ohn) Marc retired education educator
Sorby, Donald Lloyd university dean

Sun Valley
Mayhue, Richard Lee dean, pastor, writer

Sylmar
Lisalda, Sylvia Ann primary education educator

Tarzana
Yablun, Ronn secondary education educator, small business owner

Temecula
Randall, John Albert, III elementary and secondary education educator

Temple City
Matsuda, Stanley Kazuhiro secondary education educator
Provenzano, Maureen Lynn secondary school educator

Thousand Oaks
Cipriano, Patricia Ann secondary education educator, consultant
†Powe, Larry Kenneth clinical researcher
†Tierney, Nathan Llywellyn educator

Torrance
Culton, Paul Melvin retired counselor, educator, interpreter
Dickerson, Joe Bernard principal, educator
McNamara, Brenda Norma secondary education educator

Tujunga
Mayer, George Roy educator

Turlock
Amrhein, John Kilian retired dean
Hughes, Marvalene academic administrator

Twaddell, Karen Grace elementary education educator
Volk, Gregory Thomas secondary education educator

Tustin
Greene, Wendy Segal special education educator

Twentynine Palms
Clemente, Patrocinio Ablola psychology educator

Union City
Lockhart, Patsy Marie secondary education educator
Nacario, Robert John educational administrator

Valencia
Volpe, Eileen Rae special education educator

Venice
Dixon, Neil Edward elementary school educator, paleoanthropologist

Ventura
Renger, Marilyn Hanson elementary education educator

Victorville
Peterson, Leroy retired secondary education educator

Visalia
Goulart, Janell Ann elementary education educator

Vista
Tiedeman, David Valentine education educator

Walnut
Spencer, Constance Marilyn secondary education educator

Walnut Creek
Carver, Dorothy Lee Eskew (Mrs. John James Carver) retired secondary education educator
Mackay, Patricia McIntosh counselor
Wolf, Harry retired dean and educator

Weimar
Kerschner, Lee R(onald) academic administrator, political science educator

Westlake Village
†Woodard, Matthew Jay martial arts instructor

Whittier
Ash, James Lee, Jr. academic administrator
De Lorca, Luis E. educational administrator, educator, speaker
†Long, Peggy Jo principal
Shackelford, Anastasia Marie secondary school educator
Tunison, Elizabeth Lamb education educator
Zanetta, Joseph Michael university administrator, lawyer

Woodland Hills
†Inocencio, E. Bing college president
Zeitlin, Herbert Zakary retired college president, real estate company excutive

Woodside
Lee, Hamilton H. education educator

Yorba Linda
Lunde, Dolores Benitez retired secondary education educator

Yuba City
Dalpino, Ida Jane secondary education educator
Perry, Phillip Edmund middle school educator

COLORADO

Alamosa
Rickey, June Evelyn Million retired educator

Arvada
Bert, Carol Lois educational assistant
Hammond-Blessing, DiAnn A. elementary education educator
Young, Bonnie Darline primary school educator
Zetterman, Polly Davis retired secondary school educator

Aurora
Fedak, Barbara Kingry technical center administrator
†Gieskieng, Janice Carol assistant principal
Jarvis, Mary G. principal
Young, Gordon elementary education educator
Zuschlag, Nancy Hansen environmental science/ nature resources educator

Boulder
Anderson, Ronald Delaine education educator
Buechner, John C. academic administrator
Dilley, Barbara Jean college administrator, choreographer, educator
Enarson, Harold L. university presidentemeritus
Hawkins, Brian L. academic administrator, educator
Healy, James Bruce cooking school administrator, writer
†Knierim, Willis M. educator
Marshall, James Kenneth academic administrator
†Mavrogianes, Mark educator
Sirotkin, Phillip Leonard educational administrator
Williams, James Franklin, II university dean, librarian
Wilson, Kenneth Allen educator

Broomfield
Ekey, Carrie Rae elementary education educator
Little, Mark Douglas secondary school educator

Calhan
Fuller, Janice Marie secondary school educator
Henderson, Freda LaVerne elementary education educator

Canon City
Baumann, Ernst Frederick college president
Perrin, Cynthia Suzanne secondary education educator

Cheyenne Wells
Palmer, Rayetta J. technology coordinator, educator

Colorado Springs
Adams, Bernard Schroder retired college president
Burnley, Kenneth Stephen school system administrator
Guy, Mildred Dorothy retired secondary school educator
Hinkle, Betty Ruth educational administator
†Jones, Vernon Dale educator
Mohrman, Kathryn academic administrator
Rothenberg, Harvey David educational administrator
Ruch, Marcella Joyce retired educator, biographer
Shade, Linda Bunnell university chancellor
Wilcox, Rhoda Davis elementary education educator
†Wilson, Todd Andrew college administrator in public relations

Deer Trail
Malson, Verna Lee special education educator

Denver
Antonoff, Steven Ross educational consultant, author
Bautista, Michael Phillip school system administrator
Beckman, L. David university chancellor
Billig, Shelley Hirschl educational research and training consultant
Bowden, Randall Glen academic adminstrator
Cannon, Elizabeth Anne special education educator
Craine, Thomas Knowlton non-profit administrator
DePew, Marie Kathryn retired secondary school educator
Drake, Lucius Charles, Jr. school administrator, university consultant, educator
Driggs, Margaret educator
Ellis, Sylvia D. Hall development and library education consultant
Fielden, C. Franklin, III early childhood education consultant
Fulginiti, Vincent university dean
Fulkerson, William Measey, Jr. college president
Greenspahn, Barbara university administrator, law educator, librarian
†Groth, Mark Adam audio visual specialist, photographer
Grounds, Vernon Carl seminary administrator
Hafenstein, Norma Lu educator, administrator
Halgren, Lee A. academic administrator
Hill, Kathleen Lois performing art school executive
Jacobson, Eugene Donald educator, administrator, researcher
Kaplan, Sheila academic administrator
Lane, Peggy Lee educator
Linenbrink, Cecilia educator
Mc Clenney, Byron Nelson community college administrator
Messer, Donald Edward theological school president
Miller, Clara Burr education educator
Palmreuter, Kenneth Richard Louis principal
Parsell, Roger Edmund retired educator, civic worker
Ritchie, Daniel Lee academic administrator
Vogel, Robert Lee college administrator, clergyman
Weber-Shadrick, Dorothy Jo management consultant
Wright, Carole Dean reading specialist
Zaranka, William F. academic administrator, author

Durango
Jones, Joel Mackey academic administrator

Englewood
Dawson, Eugene Ellsworth university president emeritus
Nelson, Barbara Louise secondary education educator
†Schmahl, John Howard counseling
Shields, Marlene Sue elementary school educator
Whiteaker, Ruth Catherine retired secondary education educator, counselor
Zernial, Susan Carol educator, consultant, acquisitions editor

Estes Park
Guest, Linda Sand education educator
Johnson, Carol Lynn secondary school counselor
Stanton, Lea Kaye elementary school educator, counselor

Evergreen
Berger, Sue Anne secondary education educator, chemist
†Grunska, Gerald P(aul) former secondary educator, sports official

Fort Collins
Cook, Dierdre Ruth Goorman school administrator, secondary education educator
Crabtree, Loren William provost, academic administrator, history educator
Fotsch, Dan Robert elementary education educator
Harper, Judson Morse university administrator, consultant, educator
Jaros, Dean university official
Weiser, Timothy L. athletic director
Yates, Albert Carl academic administrator, chemistry educator

Golden
Bickart, Theodore Albert university president
Lyons, Cherie Ann educational administrator, author
Mueller, William Martin former academic administrator, metallurgical engineering educator
†Stevenson, Cynthia Mary school system administrator
Truly, Richard H. academic administrator, former federal agency administrator, former astronaut

Grand Junction
Bergen, Virginia Louise principal, language arts educator
Moberly, Linden Emery educational administrator

Greeley
Duff, William Leroy, Jr. university dean emeritus, business educator

Green, Vickie Lee *gifted and talented educator, music educator*
Griffin, Peggy *university administrator*
Mason, Carolyn Sue *career coordinator*
Smythe, Valerie Ann *special education educator*
†Thompson, Paul N. *college president*

Highlands Ranch
Jeffryes, Mark Allen *elementary school educator, administrator*

Idaho Springs
Block, Kerry Reagan *special education educator*

Idalia
†Rossbach, Lucille K. *secondary education educator, reading specialist*

Lakewood
Forrest, Kenton Harvey *science educator, historian*
Mc Bride, Guy Thornton, Jr. *college president emeritus*
West, Marjorie Edith *elementary education educator*

Littleton
Bush, Stanley Giltner *secondary school educator*
†Butler, Dena Louise *mathematics educator*
Feist, Edward Joseph *secondary education educator*
Greenberg, Elinor Miller *college official, consultant*
Lening, Janice Allen *physical education educator*
†Lesh-Laurie, Georgia Elizabeth *university administrator, biology educator, researcher*
Wallisch, Carolyn E. *principal*
Whalen, Cathryn Ann *reading specialist*

Pueblo
Lightell, Kenneth Ray *education educator*
Poole, Rita Ann *secondary education educator*
Sisson, Ray L. *retired dean*
†Swanson, Bret Robert *elementary education educator*
†Wong, Leslie Eric *academic administrator*

Sterling
Hunter, Frank A. *secondary education educator*

Westminster
Eaves, Stephen Douglas *educator, vocational administrator*

CONNECTICUT

Bloomfield
Foster, Benjamin, Jr. *educational administrator*
Hilsenrath, Baruch M. *principal*

Bridgeport
Dworkin, Irma-Theresa *school system administrator, researcher, educator*

Bristol
†Furniss, Keith Richard *educational administrator*

Cheshire
Maddaloni, Betty *elementary education educator*

Columbia
Malchiodi, Joanne Marie *elementary education educator, reading consultant*

Cos Cob
Sorese, Denise Powers *reading consultant, educator*

Coventry
Foster, Lloyd Arthur *principal*

Danbury
Arbitelle, Ronald Alan *elementary school educator*
Hawkes, Carol Ann *university dean*
Heller, Maryellen *special education educator*
Roach, James R. *university president*

Enfield
Reuter, Joan Copson *program director*

Fairfield
Boskello, Dennis Jon *elementary education educator*
Boskello, Margo Lynn *elementary education educator*
Cernera, Anthony Joseph *academic administrator*
Hauck, Madeline (Agnes) *special and adult basic education educator*
Kelley, Aloysius Paul *university administrator, priest*
Michael, Mary Amelia Furtado *retired educator, freelance writer*
Miles, Leland Weber *university president*
†Paolini, Claire Jacqueline *dean, educator*

Falls Village
Gaschel-Clark, Rebecca Mona *special education educator*
Purcell, Dale *college president, consultant*

Farmington
Deckers, Peter John *dean*
Jestin, Heimwarth B. *retired university administrator*
Kedderis, Pamela Jean *academic administrator*

Glastonbury
†Cavanaugh, Marianne *secondary educator*
Hatch, D. Patricia P. *principal*

Greenwich
Halley, Janet Carnahan *secondary education educator*

Groton
English, James Fairfield, Jr. *former college president*
Oberg, Judith Ovrebo *retired physical education educator*

Hamden
Brown, Jay Marshall *retired secondary education educator*

Hartford
†Barber, Joseph Clifford *college administrator*
†Cibes, William Joseph, Jr. *chancellor, educator*
Dobelle, Evan Samuel *college administrator*
Frost, James Arthur *former university president*
Malone, Thomas Francis *academic administrator, meteorologist*
Morris, Richard Knowles *retired education and anthropology educator*
Reynolds, Scott Walton *academic administrator*
Salafia, Rose Marie Brocka *educator*
Schulz, Brigitte Helene *educator, researcher*
Skerker, Arthur J. *secondary education educator*
Stoker, Warren Cady *university president*
Tonkin, Humphrey Richard *academic administrator*

Meriden
†Johnson, James *principal*

Middletown
Bennet, Douglas Joseph, Jr. *university president*
Kerr, C(larence) William *retired university administrator*
†McCormick, Elizabeth Johnston *college official*

Milford
Cox, Robert Claude *retird educator and school system administrator*

Monroe
Kranyik, Elizabeth Ann *secondary education educator*

Naugatuck
Stauffer, Elizabeth Clare *elementary education educator, music choral director, consultant*

New Britain
Hampton, John James *university dean, consulting company executive*
Judd, Richard Louis *academic administrator*
Rosa, Peter Manuel *university administrator, researcher*

New Canaan
Norman, Christina Reimarsdotter *secondary education language educator*

New Haven
Adanti, Michael J. *academic administrator*
Anderson, Carl Albert *academic administrator, lawyer*
†Benjamin, Donna Miller *university official, elementary education educator*
†Golan, Romy *educator*
Kessler, David A. *dean, medical educator*
Lamar, Howard Roberts *educational administrator, historian*
Lorimer, Linda Koch *university educator*
Passarelli, Giulio Domenic (G. Dom Passarelli) *educational administrator*
Waxman, Merle *dean*
Yandle, Stephen Thomas *dean*
Yeager, Louise Barbara Lehr *secondary education educator*

New Milford
†Shusdock, Alice Cecilia *elementary education educator*

Newington
D'Annolfo, Suzanne Cordier *educational administrator, educator*

Niantic
Ashley, Eleanor Tidaback *retired elementary educator*

North Haven
Bennett, Harry Louis *college educator*
Fuggi, Gretchen Miller *education educator*
McCauley, Lisa Francine *secondary education educator*

North Stonington
Keane, John Patrick *retired secondary education educator*

Norwalk
Bray, William Scott *retired school system administrator*

Old Lyme
Nidzgorski, Barbara Helen *gifted and talented education educator, puppeteer*

Prospect
Thornley, Wendy Ann *educator, sculptor*

Ridgefield
Brewster, Carroll Worcester *former academic administrator*
Leonard, Sister Anne C. *superintendent, education director*
Wallace, Ralph *superintendent*

Stamford
†Fredo, Bart *educator*
Megrue, Suzanne Jacobsen *primary education educator*
†Peters, Clifford Simpson *secondary school educator*

Storrs
Nieforth, Karl Allen *university dean, educator*

Storrs Mansfield
Austin, Philip Edward *university president*
Cohen, Marcia Alice *special education administrator*
Gutteridge, Thomas G. *academic administrator, consultant and labor arbitrator*
Kerr, Kirklyn M. *university administrator, veterinary pathologist, researcher*
Lee, Tsoung-Chao *education educator*
Smith, Robert Victor *university administrator*

Stratford
Conti-O'Brien, Yvonne *elementary education educator*
Hageman, Richard Philip, Jr. *educational administrator*
Hall, Shelley Stevenson *special education educator*

Suffield
D'Aleo, Penny Frew *special education educator, consultant*
Friedman, Dian Debra *elementary education educator*

Trumbull
Lang, James Richard *education consultant*
Nevins, Lyn (Carolyn A. Nevins) *educational supervisor, trainer, consultant*
Norcel, Jacqueline Joyce Casale *educational administrator*
Smith, Gail Marie *special education educator, educational consultant*
Weiner, Mary Lou *elementary education educator*

Wallingford
Hay, Leroy E. *school system administrator*

Waterbury
†Arias, Bridget Carser *elementary educator*
Brown, Lillian Hill *retired educator*
†Richard, Peter Wayne *educator*

West Hartford
Dunn, Robert Elbert *education consultant, principal*
Echols, Ivor Tatum *retired educator, assistant dean*

West Haven
Allen, Jerry L. *university dean, communication educator*
DeNardis, Lawrence J. *academic administrator*
Farquharson, Patrice Ellen *primary school educator*
Kern, Bernadette *rehabilitation services educator, consultant*
Simone, Angela Paolino *elementary education educator*
†Solano, Mona *elementary education educator*

West Redding
†Holder, Barbara June *educator in English and literature*

Weston
Boesch, Diane Harriet *elementary education educator*

Westport
†Battenfeld, John Leonard *educator, journalist*

Wethersfield
Edwards, Kenneth S. *principal*

Willimantic
Carter, David George, Sr. *university administrator*
Enggas, Grace Falcetta *university administrator*
Peagler, Owen F. *college administrator*
Stoloff, David L. *education educator*

Wilton
Greene, Howard Roger *educational consultant*
Grunewald, Donald *former college president, educator*

Wolcott
Gerace, Robert F. *secondary school principal*

DELAWARE

Bear
Hersi, Dorothy Talbert *education educator*
Stewart, Shirley Anne *assistant principal*

Dover
Braverman, Ray Howard *secondary school educator*
Delauder, William B. *academic administrator*
Gorum, Jacquelyne W. *dean, social work educator*
Smith, Charles Nathaniel *academic administrator*
Wagner, Nancy Hughes *secondary school educator, state legislator*
Wilson, Clealyn Bullock *elementary education educator*

Laurel
Kile, Kenda Jones *educational consultant*

Lewes
Smith, George H.P. *retired elementary educator*

Milford
Ferrari, Mercedes V *secondary education educator*
Walls-Culotta, Sandra L. *educational administrator*

Millsboro
Derrickson, Shirley Jean Baldwin *elementary school educator*

New Castle
†Doberstein, Audrey K. *college president*

Newark
Carter, Mae Riedy *retired academic official, consultant*
†Lemay, J.A. Leo *American literature educator*
Lewis, Horacio Delano *consultant, educator*
Lynch, Thomas Gregory *educational program administrator*
McLain, William Tome *principal*
†Nahera, Kristina Luckanish *educator*
Poplos, Charles Mitchell, III *social science educator, educational technologist*
Schiavelli, Melvyn David *academic administrator, chemistry educator, researcher*

Seaford
Petrea, Patricia Beth *special education educator*

Wilmington
Graves, Thomas Ashley, Jr. *educational administrator*
†Hockersmith, Charles Edwin *information technology educator*
Olson, Leroy Calvin *retired educational administration educator*
†Tankersley, Julianne Grandell *elementary and secondary education educator*

DISTRICT OF COLUMBIA

Washington
Alatis, James Efstathios *university dean emeritus*
Alton, Bruce Taylor *educational consultant*
Anderson, Beverly Jacques *academic administrator*
Arnez, Nancy Levi *educational leadership educator*
Audrey-Taylor, Davida *secondary education educator*
Bader, Rochelle Linda (Shelley Bader) *educational administrator*
Bailey, Nancy Joyce *educator*
Barrett, Richard David *university director, consultant, bank executive*
Battle, Lucius Durham *retired educational institution administrator, former diplomat*
Beckham, Edgar Frederick *educational consultant*
Bennett, Carl Roosevelt *secondary education teacher*
†Biggs, Jeffrey Robert *educator*
Bolling, Landrum Rymer *retired academic administrator, writer, consultant*
Bulger, Roger James *academic health center executive*
Burgin, Walter Hotchkiss, Jr. *educational administrator*
Burris, James Frederick *federal research administrator, educator*
Cebe, Juanita *academic administrator*
Chandler, John Wesley *educational consultant*
Christian, Mary Jo Dinan *educator, real estate professional*
Cornett, Richard Orin *research educator, consultant*
Cronin, Richard James *university official, educator*
†Crowley, John Charles *academic director*
Dougherty, Jude Patrick *dean*
Duffey, Joseph Daniel *educational administrator*
Elliott, Emerson John *education consultant, policy analyst*
†Felbinger, Claire Louise *adult education educator, administrator*
Ferrara, Steven *educational researcher, test developer*
Ferris, William Reynolds *folklore educator*
Fisher, Miles Mark, IV *education and religion educator, minister*
Flaherty, Sister Mary Jean *dean, nursing educator*
Fosler, R. Scott *academic administrator*
Gaff, Jerry Gene *academic administrator*
†Goodman, Alan Paul *academic administrator, business educator*
Goodman, Steven Roy *educational consultant, lawyer*
Graves, Ruth Parker *educational executive, educator*
Hagan, Philip Edward, Jr. *academic administrator*
Halperin, Samuel *education and training policy analyst*
Herbert, James Charles *education executive*
Herbster, William Gibson *university administrator, consultant*
Hernandez, Christine *educational consultant*
Hoi, Samuel Chuen-Tsung *art school dean*
Horan, Harold Eugene *university administrator, former diplomat*
†Ibish, Yusuf Hussein *retired educator*
Ikenberry, Stanley Oliver *education educator, former university president*
Ingold, Catherine White *academic administrator*
Jenkins, John Smith *academic dean, lawyer*
Jones-Wilson, Faustine Clarisse *education educator emeritus*
Jordan, Irving King *university president*
Keeley, Robert Vossler *retired academic administrator, retired ambassador*
†Kerwin, Cornelius Martin *dean, public affairs educator*
Kirkien-Rzeszotarski, Alicja Maria *academic administrator, researcher, educator*
†Klaits, Joseph A. *education program director, historian*
Kramer, Robert *dean*
Kyhos, M. Gaither Galleher *private school educator*
†Ladner, Benjamin *university president*
Leon, Donald Francis *university dean, medical educator*
Livingston, Robert Gerald *university official, political scientist*
MacDonald, John Thomas *educational administrator*
Malveaux, Floyd Joseph *academic dean*
Martin, David Standish *education educator*
Mattar, Philip *institute director, editor*
Maxted, William C. *dean*
Maxwell, David E. *academic executive, educator*
Moore, Marsha Lynn *elementary education educator*
Moskowitz, Faye Stollman *educator*
Myers, Marjorie Lora *elementary school principal*
Nelson, Jacqueline Dunham *elementary education educator*
Nwagbaraocha, Joel Onukwugha *academic administrator, educator*
O'Connor, John Dennis *academic administrator*
O'Donovan, Leo Jeremiah *university president, theologian, priest*
Osten, Janice Anne *education chief nurse*
Peck, Malcolm Cameron *educational exchange specialist*
Perley, James E. *education association professional*
Porter, John Weston *guidance counsellor*
Preer, Jean Lyon *information science educator, dean*
Pruitt, Anne Loring *academic administrator, education educator*
Ranck, Edna Runnels *academic administrator, researcher*
Rogers, Ailene Kane *secondary school educator*
Salamon, Linda Bradley *English literature educator*
Sibolski, Elizabeth Hawley *academic administrator*
Smuckler, Ralph Herbert *university dean, political science educator*
Solomon, Henry *university dean*
Steigman, Andrew L. *academic dean*
Stone, Elizabeth Wenger *retired dean*
†Stopford, Michael John *university administrator*
Thompson, Bernida Lamerle *principal, consultant, educator*
Timpane, Philip Michael *education educator, policy analyst*
Trachtenberg, Stephen Joel *university president*
Treibley, Pete Vance *principal*
Turaj, Frank *university dean, literature and film educator*
Williams, Frances Elizabeth *secondary education educator*

FLORIDA

Alachua
Marston, Robert Quarles *university president*

Altamonte Springs
Huyett, Debra Kathleen *elementary education educator*
Poland, Phyllis Elaine *secondary school educator, consultant*

Apalachicola
Galloway, Brenda Mabrey *school system administrator*

Apopka
Calhoun, Emily Mitchell *elementary education educator*

Atlantic Beach
Herge, Henry Curtis, Sr. *education educator, dean emeritus*

Auburndale
Wean, Karla Denise *middle school educator, secondary education educator*

Babson Park
Hodapp, Shirley Jeaniene *curriculum administrator*

Boca Raton
Arden, Eugene *retired university provost*
Caputi, Marie Antoinette *university official*
Catanese, Anthony James *academic administrator*
Connor, Frances Partridge *retired education educator*
Connor, Leo Edward *special education administrator*
Guglielmino, Lucy Margaret Madsen *education educator, researcher, consultant*
Leary, William James *educational administrator*
Miller, Eugene *university official, business executive*
Rebel, Amy Louise *elementary education educator*
Ross, Donald Edward *university administrator*
Tennies, Robert Hunter *headmaster*

Bonita Springs
†DiSerafino, Reneé Marie *elementary education educator*
Finger, Iris Dale Abrams *elementary school educator*
Johnson, Franklyn Arthur *academic administrator*

Boynton Beach
Costa, Terry Ann *educational administrator*
Cotton, John Pierce *principal*

Bradenton
Pedersen, Norman Arno, Jr. *retired headmaster, literary club director*

Brandon
Straub, Susan Monica *special education educator*

Brooksville
Capps, David Edward, Jr. *assistant dean*
Harvey, Joseph Howard *mathematics educator, musician*
Schutte, Carla Daniels *elementary education educator*

Cape Coral
Lane, William C., Jr. *principal*
Vilardi, Charles Ronald *elementary education educator*

Clearwater
Mattice, Howard LeRoy *education educator*
Stilwell, Charlotte Finn *vocational counselor*

Cocoa
Drake, James Alfred *higher education administrator*
Gamble, Thomas Ellsworth *academic administrator*
†King, Maxwell Clark *academic administrator*

Coral Gables
†Bourgoignie, Marie Helene *educator*
Carney, Martin Joseph, Jr. *university administrator*
Lewis, Elisah Blessing *university official*
†Lopez, Ruben *engineer, educational administrator*
Moss, Ambler Holmes, Jr. *academic administrator, educator, lawyer, former ambassador*
†Trowbridge, Mark Alan *educational consultant*
Yarger, Sam Jacob *dean, educator*

Coral Springs
Colton, Susan Adams *educational administrator*
Heydet, Nathalie Durbin *gifted and talented education educator*
Murray, John Ralph *former college president*

Crawfordville
Black, B. R. *retired educational administrator, consultant*

Daytona Beach
Ebbs, George Heberling, Jr. *university executive*
†Hartsell, Horace Ed *college president*
Lampe, Harriett Richmond *retired educator, artist*

Deerfield Beach
Davis, Ronald P. *secondary school educator*

Deland
Brakeman, Louis Freeman *retired university administrator*
Dascher, Paul Edward *university dean, accounting educator*
Duncan, Pope Alexander *college administrator*
Gill, Donald George *education educator*
Langston, Paul T. *music educator, university dean, composer*
Lee, Howard Douglas *academic administrator*
Morland, Richard Boyd *retired educator*

Deltona
Bondinell, Stephanie *counselor, former educational administrator*
Neal, Dennis Melton *middle school administrator*

Destin
Asher, Betty Turner *academic administrator*

Englewood
Lantz, Joanne Baldwin *academic administrator emeritus*

Estero
Brush, George W. *college president*

Fernandina Beach
Fishbaugh, Carole Sue *secondary school educator*

Flagler Beach
Wadsworth, Frances Faulkner *retired educator*

Fort Lauderdale
Carton, Cristina Silva-Bento *elementary educator*
†Edmund, Norman W. *educational researcher*
Feldman, Myrna Lee *elementary education educator*
Fischler, Abraham Saul *education educator, retired university president*
Hanbury, George Lafayette, II *academic administrator*
†Klein, Stacy Lynn *educator*
Lewis, Ovid C. *dean, law educator, lawyer*
McCan, James Lawton *education educator*
Miller, Stephen Warren *dean*
Ornstein, Libbie Allene *primary school educator*
Pallowick, Nancy Ann *special education educator*
Spungin, Charlotte Isabelle *retired secondary education educator, writer*
†Young Olson, Brenda *elementary education educator*

Fort Myers
Canham, Pruella Cromartie Niver *retired educator*
†Chambers, Jim Arthur *educator*
Kish, Elissa Anne *educational administrator, consultant*
Mac Master, Harriett Schuyler *retired elementary education educator*
†Sneddon, Robert J. *educator elementary schools*
Warner, Elizabeth Jane Scott *exceptional education educator*
Whittaker, Douglas Kirkland *school system adminstrator*

Fort Pierce
†Massey, Edwin R. *college president*

Fort Walton Beach
Sanders, Jimmy Devon *public administration and health services educator*
Stevenson, Mary Eva Blue *retired elementary education educator*

Gainesville
App, James Leonard *assistant dean*
Bartlett, Rodney J. *chemistry and physics educator*
†Brodeur, Michael Stephen *dean*
Bryan, Robert Armistead *university administrator, educator*
†Butler, Henry James *academic administrator, consultant*
Candelas, Teresa Bush *special education educator*
Chait, Andrea Melinda *special education educator*
Challoner, David Reynolds *university official, physician*
Cheek, Jimmy Geary *university administrator, agricultural education and communications educator*
Gets, Lispbeth Ella *educational administrator*
Humphrey, Stephen *college dean*
Lombardi, John V. *university administrator, historian*
Lowenstein, Ralph Lynn *university dean emeritus*
Meyer, Harvey Kessler, II *retired academic administrator*
Neims, Allen Howard *univeristy dean, medical scientist*
Oppenheim, Paul *vocational educator*
Price, Donald Ray *university official, agricultural engineer*
Reeves, Tracey Elizabeth *director*
Schneider, Richard Harold *university dean, educator*
Thornton, J. Ronald *technology center director*
Viessman, Warren, Jr. *academic dean, civil engineering educator, researcher*
York, E. Travis *academic administrator, former university chancellor, consultant*

Goulds
Cooper, Kenneth Stanley *educational administrator*

Graceville
Collier, Evelyn Myrtle *elementary school educator*
Kinchen, Thomas Alexander *college president*

Green Cove Springs
Yelton, Eleanor O'Dell *retired reading specialist*

Gulfport
Athanson, Mary Catheryne *school system administrator*

Hialeah
Legg, Morris Burke *secondary school educator*

Hollywood
Bivens, Constance Ann *retired elementary education educator*
Goldberg, Icchok Ignacy *retired special education educator*

Holmes Beach
Dunne, James Robert *academic administrator, management consultant, business educator*

Homestead
Bachmeyer, Steven Allan *secondary education educator*

Indian Harbor Beach
Haggis, Lewanna Strom *educator, author, consultant*

Indian Rocks Beach
Rocheleau, James Romig *retired university president*

Jacksonville
Carver, Joan Sacknitz *university dean*
Cloud, Linda Beal *retired secondary school educator*
†Johnson, Crystal Maria *primary school educator*
Kinne, Frances Bartlett *chancellor emeritus*
Main, Edna (June) Dewey *education educator*
Osborn, Marvin Griffing, Jr. *educational consultant*
Piotrowski, Sandra A. *elementary education educator*
Sandercox, Robert Allen *college official, clergyman*
Simms, Jacqueline Kamp *secondary education educator*
†Wallace, Steven R. *college president*
Wiles, Jon W(hitney) *education educator, consultant*

Jacksonville Beach
Pugh-Marzi, Sherrie *daycare center administrator*

Jupiter
Loper, Lucia Ann *retired elementary school educator*
Sproull, Robert Lamb *retired university president, physicist*

Kissimmee
Avery, Kay Beth *secondary school educator*
Boswell, Tommie C. *middle school educator*
Evans-O'Connor, Norma Lee *secondary school educator, consultant*
Jablon, Elaine *education consultant*
Kintner, Treva Carpenter *retired education educator*
†Rattie, Margaret Elizabeth (Beth Rattie) *educator*
Toothe, Karen Lee *elementary and secondary school educator*

Lady Lake
Head-Hammond, Anna Lucille *retired secondary education educator*
Staub, Martha Lou *retired elementary education educator*

Lake Mary
Brown, Barbara Jean *special and secondary education educator*

Lake Worth
†Gallon, Dennis P. *college president*
Taylor, Clifford Otis *retired principal*

Lakeland
Wade, Ben Frank *college administrator*
Wetzel-Tomalka, Mary Margerithe *retired secondary educator*

Land O'Lakes
Branham, Pamela Helen *special education educator*

Largo
Gall, Keith M. *director*
Hinesley, J. Howard *superintendent*

Lecanto
Mathia, Mary Loyola *parochial school educator, nun*
Walker, Mary Diane *secondary school educator*

Longboat Key
Kaye Johnson, Susan *educational consultant*

Lutz
Pfeuffer, Dale Robert *secondary school social studies educator*

Marianna
Connor, Catherine Brooks *educational media specialist*
Flowers, Virginia Anne *academic administrator emerita*

Melbourne
Addicott, Beverly Jeanne *elementary school educator*
Cahill, Gerard Albin *university educator*
Hollingsworth, Abner Thomas *university dean*
Weaver, Lynn Edward *academic administrator, consultant, editor*

Merritt Island
McClanahan, Leland *academic administrator*
Thompson, Hugh Lee *academic administrator*
Walter, George Anthony *elementary education educator*

Miami
Banas, Suzanne *middle school educator*
†Berkman, Ronald M. *dean, educator*
Bitter, John *university dean emeritus, musician, businessman, diplomat*
Clarkson, John G. *academic administrator, ophthalmologist*
Cohen, Eugene Erwin *university health institute administrator, accounting educator emeritus*
Dottin, Erskine S. *education educator*
Foote, Edward Thaddeus, II *university president, lawyer*
Geis, Tarja Pelto *educational coordinator, consultant, counselor, teacher, professor*
Henderson, William Eugene *education educator*
Krissel, Susan Hinkle *university official*
Lee, J. Patrick *academic administrator*
†Lewis, Clifton *principal*
Love, Mildred Allison *retired secondary school educator, historian, writer, volunteer*
Maidique, Modesto Alex *academic administrator*
McCabe, Robert Howard *college president*
O'Laughlin, Sister Jeanne *university administrator*
Price, Barbara Gillette *college administrator, artist*
Richards, Bobbie Jo *secondary education educator*
Riecken, Ellnora Alma *retired music educator*
Stern, Joanne Thrasher *elementary school educator*
Stiehm, Judith Hicks *university official, political science educator*
Thornton, Sandi Tokoa *elementary education educator*
Warren, Emily P. *retired secondary school educator*
†Wright, Pamela Jean *administrator*

Miami Beach
Danzis, Rose Marie *emeritus college president*
Gitlow, Abraham Leo *retired university dean*
LaVorgna, Judith Phelps *educational administrator*
Rube, Miriam Shoshana *principal, educator*

Milton
Moorer, Lela Irene *elementary education educator*
Seaton, Carolle Carter *educator, writer*

Miramar
†Lee-Murphy, Karen Simone *education specialist*

Monticello
Hooks, Mary Linda *adult education educator*

Mount Dora
Scharfenberg, Margaret Ellan *retired elementary educator*

Mulberry
Bowman, Hazel Lois *retired English language educator*

Naples
Abbott, John Sheldon *law school dean and chancellor emeritus*
Loft, Bernard Irwin *education educator, consultant*
Marcy, Jeannine Koonce *retired educational administrator*
†Nelson, John Charles *retired educator*
Sigman, Susan Bell *educator, writer*

New Smyrna Beach
Jesup, Cynthia Smith (Cindy Jesup) *elementary education educator*
Shaffer, Joye Coy *reading specialist*

Nokomis
Lockledge, Jack E. *principal, retired*

North Miami
†Klinger, Donald E. *educator*
Vogel, Barry Robert *university official*

North Miami Beach
Sorosky, Jeri Ruth *academic administrator*

North Palm Beach
Portera, Alan August *elementary education educator*

North Port
†Coleman-Triana, Karen L. *media specialist*

Oakland Park
Adams, Nancy Ann *school system administrator*
Krauser, Janice *special education educator*

Ocala
DeLong, Mary Ann *educational administrator*

Opa Locka
Hopton, Janice *elementary school principal*

Orange Park
Myers, Bertina Satterfield *secondary education business educator, administrator*
Ratzlaff, Judith L. *secondary school educator*
†Roman, Theresa Kay *educational administrator*

Orlando
Baggott, Brenda Jane Lamb *elementary educator*
Bias, Kimberly Vance *special education educator*
Brookes, Carolyn Jessen *early childhood education educator*
Clinton, Stephen Michael *academic administrator*
Colbourn, Trevor *retired university president, historian*
Crane, Glenda Paulette *private school educator*
Crawford, Patricia Ann *education educator*
†Gianini, Paul C., Jr. *college university*
Hardesty, Stephen Don *secondary education educator*
Hitt, John Charles *academic administrator*
Hollis, Judy Wilson *curriculum resource educator*
Levreault, Kathryn Sue *school system official, information specialist*
Qadri, Yasmeen *educational administrator, consultant*
Reagan, Larry Gay *college vice president*
Spears, Robert Edward *instructional technologist*
Watson, Jimmy Lee *academic administrator*
Witengier, Mary Joan MacGilvray *retired special education educator, physical therapist*
Wunder, James George, III *educator*

Ormond Beach
Boyle, Susan Jean Higle *elementary school educator*

Oviedo
MacKenzie, Charles Sherrard *academic administrator*

Palm Bay
Boley, Andrea Gail *secondary school educator*

Palm Beach
Steere, Anne Bullivant *retired student advisor*

Palm Beach Gardens
Orr, Joseph Alexander *educational administrator*

Palm City
Ammarell, John Samuel *retired college president, former security services executive*

Palm Coast
Dickson, David Watson Daly *retired college president*
DiUlus, Frederick Alfonso-Edward *business educator*

Palm Harbor
Fanning, Wanda Gail *retired elementary school educator*
Fernandez, Joseph Anthony *educational administrator*

Panama City
Mulligan, Barbara Laird Welch *school system administrator*
Smith, Jani Marie *special education educator*

Pensacola
Abercrombie, Charlotte Manning *reading specialist, supervisor*
†Bare, Charles Lambert *education director*
Franklin, Godfrey *adult education educator*
Galloway, Sharon Lynne *special education educator*
Marx, Morris Leon *academic administrator*
McLeod, Stephen Glenn *education educator, language educator*
Olsen, John Richard *education consultant*
Sisk, Rebecca Benefield *educator, business owner*

Pompano Beach
Bookbinder, Robert Max *superintendent of schools*

Johnson, Dorothy Curfman elementary education educator

Ponte Vedra Beach
†Patterson, Oscar, III university program administrator

Port Orange
Hiatt, Charles F., II secondary education educator

Punta Gorda
Goodman, Donald C. university administrator
Hill, Richard Earl academic administrator

Rockledge
Sutton, Betty Sheriff elementary education educator

Royal Palm Beach
†Robinson, Dolores Olivia educational consultant, grantwriter

Saint Augustine
†Naughton, René Patricia primary school educator
Proctor, William Lee college president
Sappington, Sharon Anne retired school librarian

Saint Cloud
Kandrac, Jo Ann Marie school administrator

Saint Leo
Hale, Charles Dennis education educator

Saint Petersburg
Armacost, Peter Hayden academic administrator
Griffin, Dennis Joseph middle school principal
†Griggs, Catherine M. educator
†Kuttler, Carl Martin, Jr. academic administrator
Meisels, Gerhard George academic administrator, chemist, educator
Meyer, Robert Allen human resource management educator
Nussbaum, Leo Lester retired college president, consultant
†Peterson, Sheryl Swan academic administrator, psychologist
Smith, Betty Robinson elementary education educator
Southworth, William Dixon retired education educator
Westall, Sandra Thornton special education educator

San Mateo
Wood, Shelton Eugene college educator, consultant, minister

Sarasota
Atwell, Robert Herron higher education executive
Bassis, Michael Steven academic administrator
Biegel, Alice Marie secondary school educator
Christ-Janer, Arland Frederick college president
Highland, Marilyn M. principal
Kelly, Debra Ann adult education educator
Lee, Ann McKeighan secondary school educator
Thompson, Annie Figueroa academic director, educator
Williams, Julia Rebecca Keys secondary school educator
Wilson, Marsha L. consultant
Wilson, Ned Bruce university academic administrator

Sebastian
Mauke, Otto Russell retired college president

Seffner
†Allen, Claudette A. educational administrator

Spring Hill
Weber, Mary Linda preschool educator

Stuart
Maktouf, Samir education company executive

Sun City Center
Gummere, Walter Cooper educator, consultant

Tallahassee
Adams, Perry Ronald former college administrator
Barker, Jeanne Wilson principal, computer educational consultant
Baum, Werner A. former academic administrator, meteorologist
Bert, Clara Virginia home economics educator, administrator
†Bower, Beverly Lynne education educator
Burkman, Ernest, Jr. education educator
Burnette, Ada M. Puryear educational administrator
Bye, Raymond Erwin, Jr. academic administrator
Crider, Irene Perritt education educator, small business owner, consultant
D'Alemberte, Talbot (Sandy D'Alemberte) academic administrator, lawyer
Daniels, Irish C. principal
Deutsch, Alleen Dimitroff university administrator
Foss, Donald John university dean, research psychologist
†Grant, Sydney Robert educator
†Harding, James Raymond, II special education educator
Hayward, Patricia Carroll university administrator
Herbert, Adam William, Jr. chancellor
Humphries, Frederick S. university president
Ladd, Kristi Lynn special education educator
†Leon, Karen Renée elementary education educator
Lick, Dale Wesley adult education educator
Mayo, John dean
Mills, Belen Collantes early childhood education educator
Morgan, Robert Marion educational research educator
Riley, Kenneth Jerome athletic director
Smith, Clayton Alexander college administrator
†Wetherell, Thomas Kent college president

Tampa
Anderson, Robert Henry educator
Barksdale-Ladd, Mary Alice education educator
Bondi, Joseph Charles, Jr. education educator, consultant
Bradley, Charles Ernest educational leadership consultant, music educator
Cannella, Deborah Fabbri elementary school educator
†Dunne, Peter Benjamin university administrator
Givens, Paul Ronald former university chancellor
Heck, James Baker university official
Hegarty, Thomas Joseph academic administrator, history educator
Hoover, Betty-Bruce Howard private school educator
Luddington, Betty Walles library media specialist
Mc Alister, Linda Lopez educator, philosopher
McCook, Kathleen de la Peña university educator
McIntosh, Martha Ann retired teacher, director of religious education
Nevsimal, Ervin L. elementary education educator
Reese-Brown, Brenda primary education educator, mathematics specialist
Sanchez, Mary Anne retired secondary school educator
Streeter, Richard Barry academic official

Tarpon Springs
Byrne, Richard Hill counselor, educator

Tierra Verde
Schmitz, Dolores Jean primary education educator

Titusville
Bush, Patricia Eileen education educator
Furci, Joan Gelormino early childhood education educator
Linscott, Jacqueline C. education consultant, retired educator

Valrico
Benjamin, Sheila Pauletta secondary education educator

Venice
Jamrich, John Xavier retired university administrator
Myers, Virginia Lou education educator
Thomas, David Ansell retired university dean

Wellington
McGee, Lynne Kalavsky principal

West Melbourne
Robsman, Mary Louise education educator

West Palm Beach
Abdo, Deborah J. school administrator
Clark, Claudia Pia preschool administrator
Corts, Paul Richard college president
Cox-Gerlock, Barbara academic administrator, consultant
Turner, Arthur Edward college administrator

Winter Haven
Mc Anulty, Mary Catherine Cramer retired principal, educator
Peck, Maryly VanLeer college president, headmaster, chemical engineer

Winter Park
Bornstein, Rita academic administrator
Markland, Barbara Carolyn administrative assistant
McDowell, Annie R. retired counselor

GEORGIA

Adel
Darby, Marianne Talley elementary school educator

Albany
Carter-Wommack, Barbara retired educator
Keith, Carolyn Austin secondary school counselor
Paschal, James Alphonso counselor, educator secondary school

Americus
Capitan, William Harry university president emeritus
McGrady, Clyde A. secondary school principal
Nichols, Harold James university dean
Stanford, Henry King college president

Athens
Adams, Michael Fred university president, political communications specialist
Andrews, Grover Jene adult education educator, administrator
Coley, Linda Marie secondary school educator
Crowley, John Francis, III university dean
Crowther, Ann Rollins dean, political science educator
Douglas, Dwight Oliver university administrator
†Dowling, John Clarkson educator
Fincher, Cameron Lane education educator
†Jones, Betty Kay academic administrator
Marable, Robert Blane secondary education agriculture educator
Pettis, Victoria Elaine secondary school educator
Reid, Leonard N. academic administrator
Russell, J. Thomas dean
Smagorinsky, Peter education educator
Speering, Robin educator, computer specialist
West, Marsha elementary school educator
Younts, Sanford Eugene university administrator

Atlanta
Aaberg, Thomas Marshall, Sr. academic administrator, ophthalmology educator
Aczel, Mollie Goodman educational administrator
Affonso, Dyanne D. dean, nursing educator
Alexander, Cecil Abraham college official, architect, consultant
Bailey, Joy Hafner counselor, educator
Bickerton, Jane Elizabeth university research coordinator
Bright, David Forbes academic administrator, classics and comparative literature educator
†Chace, William M. university executive
Chace, William Murdough university administrator
†Chopp, Rebecca S. provost
Clough, Gerald Wayne academic administrator
Cole, Johnnetta Betsch university president emeritus, educator
Cole, Thomas Winston, Jr. chancellor, college president, chemist
Curry, Toni Griffin counseling center executive, consultant
D'Andrea, Frances Mary special education educator
Delaney-Lawrence, Ava Patrice secondary school educator
†Dorsey, David Frederick dean, humanities educator
Ferris, James Leonard academic administrator
Frye, Billy Eugene university administrator, biologist
Galloway, Thomas D. dean
Henry, Ronald James Whyte university official
Higgins, Richard J. educational administrator
Hogan, John Donald college dean, finance educator
Hough, Leslie Seldon educational administrator
†Hugee, Elton Bernard university official, retired military enlisted man
Ignatonis, Sandra Carole Autry special education educator
Keiller, James Bruce college dean, clergyman
Lockett, Jennifer Elisabeth middle school educator
Manley, Audrey Forbes college president, physician
McPherson, Judy Beth education educator
McQueen, Sandra Marilyn educator, consultant
Meyer, Ellen L. academic administrator
Moon, Anne Trippe secondary school educator
Norris, Mary Penn elementary education educator
Parko, Edith Margaret special education educator
Parko, Joseph Edward, Jr. emeritus educator
Pattillo, Manning Mason, Jr. academic administrator
Patton, Carl Vernon academic administrator, educator
Rogers, Brenda Gayle educational administrator, educator, consultant
Schuppert, Roger Allen university official
Shannon, David Thomas, Sr. reitred academic administrator
Thompson, Wallace Reeves, III physical education educator
Tummala, Rao Ramamohana engineering educator
Yancey, Carolyn Dunbar educational policy maker

Augusta
Bloodworth, William Andrew, Jr. academic administrator
Kirch, Darrell Gene dean
Lambert, Vickie Ann dean
Lee, Emma McCain counselor
Martin, Willie Pauline elementary school educator, illustrator
Moore, Nancy Fischer elementary school educator
Tedesco, Francis Joseph university administrator

Avondale Estates
Fowler, Andrea teachers academy administrator

Barnesville
Hatcher, Wayne academic administrator

Bonaire
Griffin, Barbara Conley kindergarten and adult educator, antique store owner, retailer

Bremen
McBrayer, Laura Jean H. school media specialist

Brunswick
†Brinson, Cora Katherine principal
Harper, Janet Sutherlin Lane educational administrator, writer
Lyons, Kathleen Marie elementary school educator
Talbott, Mary Ann Britt secondary education educator

Buford
Carswell, Virginia Colby primary school educator, special education educator

Carrollton
Harden, Gail Brooks elementary school educator
Kielborn, Terrie Leigh secondary education educator
Sethna, Beheruz Nariman university president, marketing, management educator

Cartersville
Barnett, Harold Thomas school system superintendent

Chamblee
Lass, Teresa Lee secondary school and special education educator

Chatsworth
Beasley, Troy Daniel secondary education educator

Cochran
Halaska, Thomas Edward academic administrator, director, engineer

Columbus
Averill, Ellen Corbett secondary education science educator, administrator
Brown, Frank Douglas academic administrator
Duncan, Frances Murphy retired special education educator
Dunson, Diane Elaine elementary education educator, computer specialist
Edwards, Joan Annette elementary art educator
Jinright, Noah Franklin vocational school educator
Montgomery, Anna Frances elementary school educator
Newton, Gwendolyn Stewart elementary school educator
Sims, Guy Willis superintendent schools

Conyers
DeVane, Patricia Ann Doss educational administrator
Pearce, Sara Margaret Culbreth middle school educator

Crawford
Bower, Douglas William pastoral counselor, psychotherapist, clergyman

Cumming
Enterline, Susan Carole elementary educator, writer
†Fuqua, Jane Boyd principal

Cuthbert
Treible, Kirk college president

Dalton
Frerichs, Joy Roberta elementary education educator

Danielsville
Bond, Joan elementary school educator

Decatur
Baker, Stephen Monroe school system administrator
Jones, Sherman J. academic administrator, management educator, investment executive
Keaton, Mollie M. elementary school educator
Losh, Charles Lawrence vocational education administrator
Myers, Orie Eugene, Jr. university official

Douglasville
Landy, Lois Clouse principal, counselor
Vance, Sandra Johnson secondary school educator

Duluth
Neuman, Ted R. principal

East Point
Gloster, Hugh Morris retired college president, college association consultant

Fairburn
†Brooks, Janice Willena educator

Fayetteville
Fleckenstein, James William elementary school educator
Phillips, Gary Lee principal

Fitzgerald
Lewis, Charles Wesley secondary education educator, English educator

Franklin
Lipham, William Patrick principal, educator

Gainesville
Burd, John Stephen academic administrator, music educator

Hawkinsville
Mixon, Julia Jean Sanders primary school educator
Sheffield, Gloria Carol elementary education educator

Hogansville
Spradlin, Charles Leonard secondary school educator

Jonesboro
Smith, Robyn Doyal elementary and middle school educator
Ziegler, Robert Oliver retired special education educator

Kennesaw
Ouyang, Ronghua adult education educator
Siegel, Betty Lentz university president

La Fayette
Hendrix, Bonnie Elizabeth Luellen elementary school educator

Lagrange
Ault, Ethyl Lorita special education educator, consultant

LaGrange
Shelton, Natalie Heard college administrator

Lithonia
Magill, Dodie Burns early childhood education educator

Locust Grove
Crawford, Sue Ellen elementary education educator

Lookout Mountain
Haddad, Daphne Wharton education educator

Macon
Bayliss, Sister Mary Rosina principal
Dantzler, Deryl Daugherty dean, law educator
Dessem, R. Lawrence dean, law educator
Godsey, R(aleigh) Kirby university president
Innes, David Lyn university official, educator
Popper, Virginia Sowell education educator
Sims, David Suthern university facilities official
Steeples, Douglas Wayne university dean, consultant, researcher
Warren, Russell Glen academic administrator

Madison
Jones, Henry Wayne secondary education educator

Marietta
Cheshier, Stephen Robert former university president, electrical engineer
Douglas, Darcy special education educator
Houston, Dorothy Middleton elementary education educator
Laframboise, Joan Carol middle school educator
†Lawson, James Gregory university administrator
Matias, Patricia Trejo secondary education educator
Oliver, Ann Breeding secondary education educator
Ramsey, Virginia Carol Marshall middle school educator
Rivers, Alma Faye secondary education educator
Rossbacher, Lisa Ann university president, geology educator, writer

Maysville
Herriman, Jean Ann elementary education educator

Midway
Smith, Hazel Gwynn elementary school educator

Milledgeville
Deal, Therry Nash college dean
Hill, Helen Marguerite Thacker academic administrator

Millwood
King, Mary Ann secondary education educator

Morrow
Smith-Jones, Mary Emily *elementary school physical education educator*

Mount Berry
†Colley, John Scott *college president, English literature educator*
Mathis, Luster Doyle *college administrator, political scientist*
Shatto, Gloria McDermith *academic administrator*

Mount Vernon
†Julian, Larry G. *education educator*
Williamson, C. Dean *university official*

Nahunta
Thrift, Sharron Woodard *secondary education program director*

Newnan
Ferzacca, William *education educator, consultant*
Royal, Nancy B. *primary school educator*

Norcross
Burnett, Cassie Wagnon *middle school educator*
†Miller, Norma Jean *principal*

Peachtree City
Wilde, Mary *secondary education educator*

Riverdale
Sprayberry, Roslyn Raye *secondary school educator*

Robins AFB
Hunnicutt, Victoria Anne Wilson *retired school system administrator, educator*

Roopville
Butler, Jody Talley *gifted education educator*

Roswell
Lackey, Deborah K. *art educator*

Saint Simons
Tomberlin, William G. *principal*

Savannah
Burnett, Robert Adair *university administrator, history educator*
Coberly, Patricia Gail *elementary education educator, adult education educator*
Leighton, Richard Frederick *retired dean*
Rowan, Richard G. *academic administrator*
Shealy, Catherine Clarke *elementary school educator*
Strauser, Beverly Ann *education educator*
Thompson, Larry James *gifted educatin educator*

Snellville
Gerson, Martin Lyons *secondary school educator*

Statesboro
Beasley, John Julius *child and family development educator*
Green, Edward Thomas, Jr. *education educator*
Henry, Nicholas Llewellyn *college president, political science educator*

Stone Mountain
Dees, Julian Worth *retired academic/research administrator*

Swainsboro
Malone, Frankie Wheeler *primary school educator*

Thomaston
McPhail, Charles L., Jr. *school system support personnel*

Thomson
Smith, Robert L. *principal*

Tiger
DuBois, Karen York *secondary school educator*

Toccoa Falls
Alford, Paul Legare *college and religious foundation administrator*
Diehl, Donna Rae *education educator*
Reese, David George *adult education educator*

Tunnel Hill
Martin, Teresa Ann Hilbert *special education educator*

Union City
†Arnold, Dorothy Harrison *assistant principal*

Valdosta
Bailey, Hugh Coleman *university president*
Bridges, James A. *vocational school educator*
†Capps, Susan Marie *elementary school educator*

Willacoochee
Gillis, Judy Wingate *elementary educator*

Winder
Hutchins, Cynthia Barnes *special education educator*

Winterville
Anderson, David Prewitt *retired university dean*

Woodstock
Everiss, Dana Ford *middle school educator*
†Tull, Trent Ashley *director activities*

Young Harris
Putnam, Joanne White *college financial aid administrator, bookkeeper*

HAWAII

Eleele
Takanishi, Lillian K. *elementary school educator*

Hilo
Best, Mary Lani *university program coordinator*

Honolulu
Bogart, Louise Berry *education educator*
Bopp, Thomas Theodore *university administrator, chemistry educator*
Gee, Chuck Yim *dean*
Inaba, Lawrence Akio *educational director*
Keith, Kent Marsteller *academic administrator, corporate executive, government official, lawyer*
King, Arthur R., Jr. *education educator, researcher*
Kunishige, Lynn Leiko Kimura *secondary education educator*
Masters, Elaine *educator, writer*
Mortimer, Kenneth P. *academic administrator*
Nelson, Jeanne Francess *secondary education educator*
Pacific, Joseph Nicholas, Jr. *educator*
Perkins, Frank Overton *university official, marine scientist*
Souza, Joan of Arc *educational administrator*
Timbers, Judith Ann *academic administrator, writer*
Tito, Maureen Louise *educational administrator*
Wright, Chatt Grandison *academic administrator*

Kailua
Tokumaru, Roberta *principal*

Kailua Kona
Clewett, Kenneth Vaughn *college official*
Diama, Benjamin *retired educator, artist, composer, writer*
Feaver, Douglas David *retired university dean, classics educator*
Spitze, Glenys Smith *retired educator*

Kapaa
Outcalt, David Lewis *academic administrator, mathematician, educator, consultant*

Keaau
Kawachika, Jean Keiko *middle school educator*

Lihue
†Cabanting, Judy Bayuca *elementary educator*
Shigemoto, April Fumie *English educator secondary school*

Paia
†Loomis, James Cook *educator*

Pearl City
Lee, Kenneth *secondary education educator*
Rhinelander, Esther Richard *secondary school educator*
Tokuno, Kenneth Alan *college dean, poet*

Waipahu
Casey, James Leroy *curriculum director*

IDAHO

Bancroft
Larsen, Aileen *principal*
Pristupa, David William *secondary education educator*

Boise
Andrus, Cecil Dale *academic administrator*
Baird, Donald Robert *secondary school educator*
Ellis-Vant, Karen McGee *elementary and special education educator, consultant*
Maloof, Giles Wilson *academic administrator, educator, author*
Ruch, Charles P. *academic administrator*
†Starry, Pamela Faye *elementary educator*
Wentz, Catherine Jane *elementary education educator*
Yang, Baiyin *adult education educator*

Caldwell
Hendren, Robert Lee, Jr. *academic administrator*

Coeur D Alene
Dunnigan, Mary Ann *former educational administrator*
Medved, Sandra Louise *elementary education educator*

Kellogg
Haller, Ann Cordwell *secondary school educator*

Menan
Webb, Marilyn McCoy *middle school educator*

Middleton
Brown, Ilene De Lois *special education educator*

Moscow
Hatch, Charles R. *university dean*
Hendee, John Clare *university research educator*
Hoover, Robert Allan *university president*
Jankowska, Maria Anna *librarian, educator*

Mountain Home
Graves, Karen Lee *high school counselor*
Krueger, Candice Jae *assistant principal*

Mountain Home A F B
Borchert, Warren Frank *elementary education educator*

Nampa
Hopkins, Martha Jane *education educator*

New Plymouth
Matthews-Burwell, Vicki *elementary education educator*

Pocatello
Bowen, Richard Lee *academic administrator, political science educator*
†DeTienne, Darcy A. *university administrator*
Eichman, Charles Melvin *career assessment educator, school counselor*
†Larsen, Stephen Allan *endowment administrator, financial planner*

Pemberton, Cynthia Lee A. *physical education educator*
Sagness, Richard Lee *education educator, former academic dean*

Post Falls
Mikles, Chris *secondary school educator*

Saint Anthony
Blower, John Gregory *special education educator*

Shelley
Thompson, Sandra Jane *secondary school educator*

Twin Falls
Anderson, Marilyn Nelle *elementary education educator, librarian, counselor*

ILLINOIS

Anna
Wolfe, Martha *elementary education educator*

Antioch
Zeman, Don *secondary education educator, coach*

Arlington Heights
Di Prima, Stephanie Marie *educational administrator*
Placek-Zimmerman, Ellyn Clare *school system administrator, educator, consultant*

Aurora
Easley, Pauline Marie *retired elementary school educator*
Settles, William Frederick *secondary and university educator, administrator*
Sloan, Michael Lee *secondary education educator*
†Stallons, James C. *secondary education educator*
†Thompson, John Tyrus *secondary education educator, consultant*
Zarle, Thomas Herbert *academic administrator*

Barrington
Hicks, Jim *secondary education educator*
Riendeau, Diane *secondary school educator*

Beecher
Termuende, Edwin Arthur *retired chemistry educator*

Belleville
Tinoco, Patricia Ann *elementary education educator*

Benton
Glasco, Sue Alice *retired educator*

Bethalto
Gallinot, Ruth Maxine *educational consultant*
Wilson, Sandra Jean *principal*

Bethany
Syfert, Samuel Ray *retired librarian*

Bloomington
Key, Otta Bischof *retired educator*
Myers, Minor, Jr. *academic administrator, political science educator*
Simpson, J. Christopher *academic administrator*
Watkins, Lloyd Irion *university president*

Bradley
Anderson, Janice Lee Ator *secondary education mathematics educator*

Bridgeport
McMillen, Julie Lynn *educator*

Cahokia
Wade, Susan Kaye *elementary education educator*

Calumet City
Jandes, Kenneth Michael *superintendent of schools*
Palagi, Robert Gene *college administrator*

Carbondale
Cordoni, Barbara Keene *special education educator*
Dixon, Billy Gene *academic administrator*
†Gilbert, Sharon L. *education educator*
Helstern, Linda Lizut *university administrator, poet*
Mead, John Stanley *university administrator*
Sanders, John Theodore *academic administrator*
Snyder, Carolyn Ann *university dean, librarian*

Carlinville
Koplinski, Sarah E. Pruitt *college development director*
Pride, Miriam R. *college president*

Carol Stream
Choice, Priscilla Kathryn Means (Penny Choice) *gifted education educator, international consultant*

Carterville
Dews, Henry *environmental educator, minister, recycler*

Champaign
Aiken, Michael Thomas *academic administrator*
Cammack, Trank Emerson *retired university dean*
Crum, Becky Sue *supervisor, educator*
Dulany, Elizabeth Gjelsness *university press administrator*
Espeseth, Robert D. *park and recreation planning educator*
Hellmer, Lynne Beberman *education educator*
Mann, Lawrence Robert *university administrator*
Schowalter, William Raymond *college dean, educator*
Spodek, Bernard *early childhood educator*
Ward, James Gordon *education administration educator*

Charleston
Jorns, David Lee *university president*
Moler, Donald Lewis *educational psychology educator*
Rich, Steven Wayne *director alumni affairs*

Rives, Stanley Gene *university president emeritus*
Surles, Carol D. *academic administrator*

Chatham
Hoots, Charles Wayne *principal*

Chicago
Adelson, Duffie Ann *music school administrator*
†Allen, Julie Michelle *secondary education educator*
Anderson, Lorraine *secondary education educator*
Andreoli, Kathleen Gainor *dean, nurse*
Ayman, Iraj *international education consultant*
Baird, Douglas Gordon *law educator*
Baker, Robert J. *medical academic dean, surgeon*
Baworowsky, John Michael *academic administrator*
Beane, Marjorie Noterman *academic administrator*
Beck, Irene Clare *educational consultant, writer*
Birnbaum, Barry William *special education educator*
Bloom, Benjamin S. *education educator*
Blumenthal, Carlene Margaret *vocational-technical school educator*
Bornholdt, Laura Anna *university administrator*
Bowman, Barbara Taylor *institute president*
†Broski, David C. *chancellor*
†Brown, Delores *academic administrator*
Brusky, Linda L. *middle school mathematics and science educator*
Buckley, Janice Marie *school administrator*
Buniak, Raymond *educational professional*
Champagne, Ronald Oscar *academic administrator, mathematics educator*
Coe, Donald Kirk *university official*
†Cole, Dana T. *adult educator, researcher*
Coleman, Roy Everett *secondary education educator, computer programmer*
Collens, Lewis Morton *university president, legal educator*
Cooper, Wylola *retired special education educator*
Coy, Patricia Ann *special education director, consultant*
Culp, Kristine Ann *dean, theology educator*
Cummings, Maxine Gibson *elementary school educator*
†deRoulet, Daniel N. *college dean*
DeWyn, Kenneth Lee *development executive, arts administrator, actor*
Dobrov, Gregory W. *adult education educator, researcher*
Drechney, Michaelene *secondary education educator*
Einoder, Camille Elizabeth *secondary education educator*
Ellison, Jeffrey Alan *educator*
Elwin, James William, Jr. *dean, lawyer*
Felton, Cynthia *educational administrator*
Fish, Stanley Eugene *university dean, English educator*
Furlong, Patrick David *educator, researcher*
Graham, Patricia Albjerg *education educator, foundation executive*
Gross, Theodore Lawrence *university administrator, author*
Hamada, Robert S(eiji) *economist, educator*
Hawkins, Loretta Ann *secondary school educator, playwright*
Henikoff, Leo M., Jr. *academic administrator, medical educator*
Heuer, Michael Alexander *dean, endodontist educator*
Hirsch, James Alan *executive director*
Jegen, Sister Carol Frances *religion educator*
Johnson, Barbara Elaine Spears *education educator*
Johnson, Mary Ann *computer training vocational school owner*
Jones, Trina Wood *special education educator*
Kelly, Michael Thomas *educator*
Kim, Mi Ja *dean*
Kubistal, Patricia Bernice *educational consultant*
Kurty, John Thomas *secondary school administrator*
Lach, Michael C. *educator*
Larson, Mark Allen *educator*
Lewis, Philip *educational and technical consultant*
Looney, Claudia Arlene *academic administrator*
Lynn, Laurence Edwin, Jr. *university administrator, educator*
†Lysakowski, Richard Stanley *secondary education educator, economic analyst*
Macklin, Jeanette *secondary education educator*
†Mason, Sandra Renee *dean*
Matasar, Ann B. *former dean, business and political science educator*
McCray, Curtis Lee *university president*
McDowell, Orlando *educator*
Merwin, Peter Matthew *teacher, writer*
Meyer, Michael Jon *education educator, writer*
Minogue, John P. *academic administrator, priest, educator*
Mirza, Leona Lousin *educator*
Mlotek, Herman Victor *former religious education educator*
Mora, Carol Ann *early childhood educator, lecturer*
Moss, Gerald S. *dean, medical educator*
Mulligan, Robert William *university official, clergyman*
O'Reilly, Charles Terrance *university dean*
Perlman, Carole Lachman *education professional*
Petitan, Debra Ann Burke *educator, education counselor, design engineer, writer, author*
†Petty, Linda C. *academic administrator, educator*
Piderit, John J. *university educator*
Reinke, John Henry *educational administrator, clergyman*
Reynolds, Ruth Carmen *school administrator, secondary school educator*
Richardson, John Thomas *academic administrator, clergyman*
Rosenbluth, Marion Helen *educator, consultant, psychotherapist*
Rury, John Leslie *education educator*
Schieser, Hans Alois *education educator*
Schommer, Carol Marie *principal*
Schubert, William Henry *curriculum studies educator*
Scribner, Margaret Ellen *school evaluator, senior consultant*
Scrimshaw, Susan Crosby *dean*
Snodgrass, Klyne Ryland *seminary educator*
Spearman, David Leroy *elementary education educator, administrator*
†Steinberg, Salme Elizabeth Harju *university president, historian*
Steven, Donald Anstey *educator, composer*
Stowell, Joseph, III *academic administrator*
Strong, Dorothy Swearengen *educational administrator*
Sulkin, Howard Allen *college president*
Swanson, Don Richard *university dean*
Swanson, Patricia K. *university official*
†Taylor, Bernice *academic administrator*

Tuckson, Reed V. *academic administrator*
Walker-Ricks, Gloria Deloise *secondary education educator*
Wall, Michael Joseph *academic administrator*
Wasan, Darsh Tilakchand *university official, chemical engineer educator*
Weiman, Heidi *early childhood education educator*
Wooten-Bryant, Helen Catherine *principal*
Young, Lauren Sue Jones *education educator*
Zonka, Constance Z. *educational organization administrator*

Country Club Hills
Scherer, George Robert *secondary education educator*

Crystal Lake
†Davidson, Shirley Jean *elementary and secondary educator*

Danville
†Steward, Irene A. *academic administrator*

Dekalb
Coakley, Michael James *university administrator*
Healey, Robert William *school system administrator*
James, Marilyn Shaw *secondary education educator, social service worker*
King, Kenneth Paul *secondary education educator*
Kuropas, Myron Bohdon *elementary education educator*
La Tourette, John Ernest *academic administrator*
Marcano, Rosita Lopez *education educator*
Monat, William Robert *university official*
†Moody, Jesse Carroll *educational administrator*
Morrison, Harriet Barbara *retired education educator*
Niemi, John Arvo *adult education educator*
Williams, Hope Denise *administrator, business consultant*

Des Plaines
Appelson, Marilyn Irene *director of college development*
Coburn, James LeRoy *educational administrator*
Jakubek, Helen Majerczyk *retired secondary school educator*

Dolton
Whitehurst, Steven Laroy *telecommunications administrator*

Downers Grove
†Kunnemann, Nancy Bush *special education educator*
LaRocca, Patricia Darlene McAleer *middle school mathematics educator*
Punt, Leonard Cornelis *educational services company executive*

East Moline
Polios, Nancy Louise *secondary school educator*

East Saint Louis
†Finch, Janet Mitchell *academic administrator*
Wright, Katie Harper *educational administrator, journalist*

Edinburg
†Jones, Kenneth D. *secondary education educator, coach*

Edwardsville
Lazerson, Earl Edwin *academic administrator emeritus*
May, Mary Louise *elementary education educator*
Riley, Dawn C. *educational philosopher, researcher*

Effingham
Pickett, Steven Harold *elementary education educator*

Elgin
Hopkins, John Kendall *college administrator, architect*
Machowicz, Michele A. *secondary education educator, consultant*
Mason, Stephen Olin *nonprofit association administrator*
Matthaeus, Renate G. *high school principal*
Schmalholz, Deborah Lynn *education educator*

Elmhurst
†Babyar, Margaret *school counselor*
Begando, Joseph Sheridan *retired university chancellor, educator*
Cureton, Bryant Lewis *college president, educator*

Eureka
Hearne, George Archer *academic administrator*

Evanston
Boye, Roger Carl *academic administrator, journalism educator, writer*
Christian, Richard Carlton *university dean, former advertising agency executive*
†Cubbage, Alan Kennett *academic administrator*
Herron, Orley R. *college president*
†Jacobs, Donald P. *dean, banking and finance educator*
Lafont, Cristina *educator*
Lewis, Dan Albert *education educator*
McCoy, Marilyn *university official*
Miller, Thomas Williams *former university dean*
Musa, Samuel Albert *university executive*
Weber, Arnold R. *academic administrator*
Williams-Monegain, Louise Joel *retired science educator, ethnographer*
Zarefsky, David Harris *academic administrator, communication studies educator*

Evergreen Park
†Daw, Maureen Bridgette *special education educator, administrator*

Flossmoor
Ferreira, Daniel Alves *secondary education Spanish language educator*
Schillings, Denny Lynn *history educator*

Fox Lake
Vida, Diane *high school administrator*

Frankfort
Hattendorf, Diane Lynn *principal*

Franklin Park
Currie, Leah Rae *special education educator*

Galesburg
Haywood, Bruce *retired college president*
Sunderland, Jacklyn Giles *former alumni affairs director*

Gardner
Coulter, Julienne Ellen *secondary education educator, consultant*

Geneva
Irwin, John Thomas *retired counselor*
Weigand, Jan Christine *elementary education educator, computer specialist*

Gillespie
†Alepra, Sherry Jo *elementary school educator*

Glen Ellyn
†Nilsson, Ronald Allan *academic administrator*
Patten, Ronald James *retired university dean*

Glenview
Corley, Jenny Lynd Wertheim *elementary education educator*
Livingston, Richard Alan *retired secondary education educator*
Traudt, Mary B. *elementary education educator*

Godfrey
†Woods, Karen Dies *educator*

Granite City
Eftimoff, Anita Kendall *educational consultant*
Humphrey, Owen Everett *retired education administrator*

Grayslake
Taylor, Sharen Rae (McCall) *special education educator*

Hanover Park
Winterstein, James Fredrick *academic administrator*

Hazel Crest
Chapman, Delores *elementary education educator*
Potts, Clifford Albert *retired educator, church musician*

Highland
Franklin, Patricia Lynn *special education educator*

Highland Park
Gordon, Paul *metallurgical educator*
Hoffman, Sharon Lynn *adult education educator*

Hillsboro
McCafferty, Marlyn Jeanette *elementary education educator*

Hinsdale
Burrows, Donald Albert *college dean, artist, painter,*
Taylor, T(homas) Roger *educational consultant, educator*

Homer
Gilliaus, Barbara Jean *secondary education home economics educator*

Huntley
Van Horn, John Henry *secondary school educator*

Ina
Weston, Kevin David *adult education educator*

Indianhead Park
Lundin, Shirley Matcouff *early childhood and adult educator, consultant*

Ingleside
Krentz, Eugene Leo *university president, educator, minister*

Jacksonville
Hansmeier, Barbara Jo *elementary education educator*
Johns, Beverley Anne Holden *special education administrator*
Moe-Fishback, Barbara Ann *counseling administrator*
Pfau, Richard Anthony *college president*
Welch, Rhea Jo *special education educator*

Joliet
Bartow, Barbara Jené *university program administrator*
Caamano, Kathleen Ann Folz *gifted education professional*
Scott, Linda Ann *assistant principal, elementary education educator*

Kankakee
Bowling, John C. *academic administrator*
Wintrode, Kelly Rose *elementary education educator*

La Grange
Jaffe-Notier, Peter Andrew *secondary education educator*

Lake Bluff
Van Clay, Mark *schools superintendant*

Lake Forest
Adelman, Pamela Bernice Kozoll *education educator*
Bransfield, Joan *principal*
Crowley, Anna Avra *secondary education educator, historian*
Hotchkiss, Eugene, III *retired academic administrator*
†Yanella, Donald *educator*

Lansing
Guzak, Debra Ann *special education educator*
Olson, Jaynie L. *secondary school counselor*

Libertyville
†Belluomini, Ronald Joseph *secondary education educator, poet*
Bermingham, John Scott *associate dean*
Kremkau, Paul *principal*

Lincolnshire
Martin, John Driscoll *school administrator*

Lincolnwood
Greenblatt, Deana Charlene *elementary education educator*

Lisle
Simpson, Jayne Lou *academic administrator*

Macomb
†Adams, John Quincy *educator, consultant*
Goehner, Donna Marie *retired university dean*
Hayes, Paul Robert *special education educator*
†Kyllonen Rose, Julie Frances *college program administrator*
Witthuhn, Burton Orrin *university official*

Madison
Pope, Sarah Ann *elementary education educator*

Mapleton
Wendelin, Barbara Lynn *elementary school educator*

Marion
Howell, Catherine Jeanine *retired secondary education educator*

Markham
Peacock, Marilyn Claire *primary education educator*

Mason City
Breedlove, Jimmie Dale, Jr. *elementary education educator*

Matteson
Pedziwater, Kaye Lynn *elementary education educator*

Mc Leansboro
Brinkley, William John *secondary education educator*

Mchenry
Dodds, David William *superintendent*
†Shelton, Kevin Patrick *secondary education educator*

Minooka
Nellett, Gaile H. *university level educator*

Moline
†Healy, Donald Eugene, Jr. *special education educator, consultant*
Luebbers, Rita Mary *religious education director*
†Washington, Helene Maria *eduator*

Morton
Corey, Judith Ann *educator*

Mount Olive
Rogers, Ke'an Seth *elementary school educator*

Murphysboro
Gersbacher, Eva Elizabeth *special education administrator*
Hall, James Robert *secondary education educator*
Merz, Kathy Maureen *elementary education educator*

Naperville
Burton, Kay Fox *retired secondary education educator, guidance counselor*
Florence, Ernest Estell, Jr. *special education educator*
†Huffman, Louise Tolle *elementary education educator*
Martin, Joan Ellen *secondary education educator*
PoPolizio, Vincent *retired secondary education educator*
Rosenthal, Edward Leonard *secondary school educator*
Wilde, Harold Richard *college president*

Niles
Gillet, Pamela Kipping *special education educator*

Normal
Ball, Linda Ann *secondary education educator*
Matsler, Franklin Giles *retired education educator*
Parry, Sally Ellen *academic administrator, english educator*
†Vogt, W. Paul *dean*

North Chicago
Booden, Theodore *dean*
Kovacek, Duane Michael *secondary school educator*

Northbrook
Hestad, Marsha Anne *educational administrator*

O'Fallon
Herrington, James Patrick *secondary education educator*

Oak Forest
Hull, Charles William *special education educator*

Oak Lawn
†Leon, Jay *educator*

Oak Park
Adelman, William John *university labor and industrial relations educator*
Kahn, Peter R. *secondary school educator*

Oakbrook Terrace
Cason, Marilynn Jean *technological institute official, lawyer*

Oglesby
Zeller, Francis Joseph *dean*

Orion
Nicholson, Tom Cotton *school district administrator*

Orland Park
Anderson, Arthur Rodney *secondary education educator*
Price, Nancy Molander *educational administrator, school psychologist*

Palatine
Stephens, LaVerne C. *middle school educator*

Palos Hills
Crawley, Vernon Obadiah *academic adminstrator*

Palos Park
Nicholls, Richard Allen *middle school social studies educator*

Park Forest
Moore, D(eane) Stanley *educator*

Pekin
Schurter, Richard Allen *secondary school history educator*

Peoria
Kelly, Grace Dentino *secondary education educator*
McMullen, David Wayne *education educator*
Miller, Wilma Hildruth *education educator*
Nielsen, Eloise Wilma *elementary education educator*

Peoria Heights
Bergia, Roger Merle *educational administrator*

Peru
Benning, Joseph Raymond *principal*

Petersburg
Smith, Catherine Ann *principal*

Quincy
Morrison, John Alexander *retired educator, foreign policy analyst*

Richton Park
Burt, Gwen Behrens *elementary school administrator*
Piucci, Virginio Louis *academic administrator*

River Forest
Lund, Sister Candida *college chancellor*

River Grove
Stein, Thomas Henry *social science educator*

Robbins
Fulson, Lula M. *educator*

Rock Falls
Johnson, Virginia Gayle *secondary education educator*

Rock Island
Horstmann, James Douglas *college official*
Tredway, Thomas *college president*

Rockford
Bates, David Vliet *religious school administrator, minister*
Holder, Judith Anne *guidance counselor*
Howard, John Addison *former college president, institute executive*
Johnson, Elizabeth Ericson *retired educator*
†KC, Lisa Louise *school system administrator, jeweler*
Marelli, Sister Sister Mary Anthony *secondary school principal*
Martas, Julia Ann *special education administrator*
Rauch, Janet Melodie *elementary school educator*
Steele, Carl Lavern *academic administrator*
Wilke, Duane Andrew *educator*

Rolling Meadows
Peekel, Arthur K. *secondary school educator*

Schaumburg
†Cicarelli, James S. *college dean*
Hedke, Richard Alvin *gifted education educator*
Hlousek, Joyce B(ernadette) *school system administrator*
Silver, Bella Wolfson *daycare center executive, educator*
†Williams, Kay Janene *elementary education educator*

Shabbona
†Prestegaard, Kathy Anne *secondary education educator*

Shelbyville
Storm, Sandy Lamm *secondary education educator*

Skokie
Arandia, Carmelita S. *school administrator*
Sloan, Judi C. *physical education educator*

Springfield
Cipfl, Joseph John, Jr. *university administrator*
Cowles, Ernest Lee *academic administrator, educator, consultant, researcher*
Craig, John Charles *educational researcher, consultant*
Lynn, Naomi B. *academic administrator*
Moy, Richard Henry *academic dean, educator*
Penning, Patricia Jean *elementary education educator*
Poorman, Robert Lewis *education consultant, former college president*
Shahidian, Hammed *adult education educator*
†Skelton, Luther William, III *educator, consultant*
†Stephens, Norman L. *academic administrator*

PROFESSIONAL INDEX 5881 EDUCATION

Sterling
Albrecht, Beverly Jean *special education educator*
Donahue, Shirley Ohnstad *elementary education educator*

Streamwood
Polkowski, Delphine Theresa *elementary education educator, speech therapist*

Sycamore
Johnson, Yvonne Amalia *elementary education educator, science consultant*

Tinley Park
Kostka, Elmer Bohumil *secondary school educator*

University Park
Peterson, Kenneth Allen, Sr. *retired superintendent of schools*

Urbana
Bloomfield, Daniel Kermit *college dean, physician*
Glick, Karen Lynne *college administrator*
Goodman, David Gordon *Japanese, comparative literature educator, writer*
Holt, Donald A. *university administrator, agronomist, consultant, researcher*
Horsfall, William Robert *educator*
McConkie, George Wilson *educational psychology educator*
†Michelson, Bruce Frederic *academic administrator, educator*
Stukel, James Joseph *academic administrator, mechanical engineering educator*
Wedgeworth, Robert *dean, university librarian, former association executive*
Weir, Morton Webster *retired academic administrator, educator*

Villa Park
Peterson, Elaine Grace *technology director*
Smith, Barbara Ann *gifted education coordinator*
Taylor, Ronald Lee *school administrator*

Virden
McGartland, Steven Ross *secondary education music educator*

Waverly
†Stahr, Ellen Marie *secondary school educator*

Westchester
Kinney, Thomas J. *adult education educator*

Wheaton
†Abbott, Lenice C. *education educator, administrator*
Algeo, John Thomas *retired educator, association executive*

Wheeling
†Johnson, Jeffrey Carl *elementary education educator*
Tash, Suzan Sclove *child care center executive*

Wilmette
Rhoad, Richard Arthur *secondary school educator, writer*
Smutny, Joan Franklin *academic director, educator*

Winnetka
†Baule, Steven Michael *secondary education educator, author*
Bundy, Blakely Fetridge *early childhood educator, advocate*
Fink, Eloise Bradley *educator, writer, editor*
Huggins, Charlotte Susan Harrison *secondary school educator, author, travel speciali*
McCrea, Philip James *secondary school and college science educator*
Schwartz, Daniel Joel *educational administrator*

Woodridge
Huffman, Sarilee Shesol *elementary school educator*

Woodstock
Totz, Sue Rosene *secondary school educator*

INDIANA

Anderson
Leak, Arthur James *registrar*
Neidert, David Lynn *administrator*
Nicholson, Robert Arthur *college president*
Shank, Cheryl Lynn *university administrator*

Angola
Reynolds, R. John *acadmemic administrator*

Auburn
Workman, Kenneth D. *school system administrator*

Batesville
Volk, Cecilia Ann *elementary education educator*

Bloomington
Aman, Alfred Charles, Jr. *dean*
Arnove, Robert Frederick *education educator*
Barnes, A. James *academic dean*
Boyd, Rozelle *university administrator, educator*
Brand, Myles *academic administrator*
Brown, Trevor *dean*
Collins, Dorothy Craig *retired educational administrator*
Crowe, James Wilson *university administrator, educator*
†Dalton, Dan R. *college dean*
Glenn, G(eorge) Dale *principal*
Gros Louis, Kenneth Richard Russell *university chancellor*
Hopkins, Jack Walker *former university administrator, environmental educator*
Johnson, Owen Verne *program director*
Mehlinger, Howard Dean *education educator*
Mobley, Tony Allen *university dean, recreation educator*
Nelms, Charlie *academic administrator*
Otteson, Schuyler Franklin *former university dean, educator*
Palmer, Judith Grace *university administrator*
Ryan, John William *academic administrator*
Sanders, Steve *university official, political science educator*
Smith, Carl Bernard *education educator*
Vontz, Thomas Scott *education educator*
Webb, Charles Haizlip, Jr. *retired university dean*
Williams, Edgar Gene *university administrator*

Brooklyn
Roach, Eleanor Marie *elementary education educator*

Charlestown
†Bowen, Donna Darlyn *educator*
Fellows, Marilyn Kinder *elementary education educator*

Chesterton
Nelson, Paul James *educator*

Connersville
Herald, Sandra Jean *elementary education educator*

Crawfordsville
Ford, Andrew Thomas *academic administrator*
Pribbenow, Paul P. *higher education administrator, consultant*
Servies, Richard L. *secondary education educator*
Spurgeon, Nannette SuAnn (Susie Spurgeon) *special education educator*

Crown Point
Jones, Walter Dean *community program director*

Culver
Manuel, Ralph Nixon *private school executive*

East Chicago
Platis, James George *secondary school educator*
Platis, Mary Lou *media specialist*

Evansville
Huff, Sheila Lindsey *secondary education educator, coach*
Jerrel, Bettye Lou *science educator*
†Schultz, John Edward *principal*
Vinson, James Spangler *academic administrator*

Fort Wayne
Aikman, Carol Chidester *education educator*
Andorfer, Donald Joseph *university president*
Auburn, Mark Stuart *educator, administrator*
Balthaser, Linda Irene *academic administrator*
†Beckner, Walton Thomas (Tom) *adult education educator, academic administrator*
Carter, George Edward *education educator*
Cutshall-Hayes, Diane Marion *elementary education educator*
Hamrick, Linda L. *educator*
Hickey, Dixie Marie *school system administrator*
†Jordan, Pamela Lee *educator*
Lewark, Carol Ann *special education educator*
Pease, Ella Louise *elementary education educator*
Stebbins, Vrina Grimes *retired elementary school educator, counselor*
†Wartell, Michael A. *academic administrator*
Weicker, Jack Edward *educational administrator*

Fortville
Demegret, A. Jean Hughes *secondary education educator, artist*

Franklin
Bender, Larry Wayne *vocational educator*
Martin, William Bryan *chancellor, lawyer, minister*

Fremont
Elliott, Carl Hartley *former university president*

Garrett
Baker, Suzon Lynne *secondary education mathematics educator*

Gary
Davis, Venita Paula *elementary school educator*
Hall, James Rayford, III *adult educator*
Kang, Young Woo *special education educator*
Smith, Vernon G. *education educator, state representative*

Georgetown
Dailey, Donald Harry *adult education educator, volunteer*

Goshen
Meyer, Albert James *educational researcher*
Stoltzfus, Victor Ezra *retired university president, academic consultant*
†Weaver, Henry David *retired educational administrator, consultant*

Greencastle
Bottoms, Robert Garvin *academic administrator*
†Martin, Marilyn Mann *librarian*
Rosenberger, James Robert *counselor*

Greenfield
Saunders, James Kevin *principal*

Griffith
†Wean, Charles Raymond, Jr. *retired secondary education educator*

Hagerstown
†Jones, Sarah Louise *principal*

Hammond
Delph, Donna Jean (Maroc) *education educator, consultant, university administrator*
DeVaney, Cynthia Ann *elementary education educator, real estate broker*
Kadow, Cathi *academic counselor*
Yovich, Daniel John *educator*

Hobart
†Brandenburg, Jamie Enrico *elementary education educator*

Huntington
Dowden, G. Blair *academic administrator*
Lahr, Beth M. *college administrator*

Indianapolis
Bannister, Geoffrey *university president, geographer*
Bepko, Gerald Lewis *university administrator, law educator, lecturer, consultant, lawyer*
Brown, Freezell, Jr. *private school educator*
Dickeson, Robert Celmer *retired university president, foundation executive, political science educator*
Dykstra, Clifford Elliot *chemistry educator, researcher*
†Edwards, Terri Michele *special education educator*
Evans, Daniel Fraley *college administrator, banker, retail executive*
Evenbeck, Scott Edward *university official, psychologist*
Fadely, James Philip *admission and financial aid director, educator*
Felicetti, Daniel A. *academic administrator, educator*
Gooldy, Patricia Alice *retired elementary education educator*
Hamilton, Cheryl Louise *elementary education educator*
Hill, Patricia Jo *special education educator*
Huffman-Hine, Ruth Carson *adult education administrator, educator*
Metzner, Barbara Stone *university counselor*
Miner, Susan K. *special education administrator*
Motsinger, Linda Sue *university official*
Ney, Michael Vincent *university administrator*
†Reed, Suellen K. *superintendent public instruction*
†Rosentraub, Mark S. *educator*
Schafer, Matthew T. *English language educator, coach*
Solomon, Marilyn Kay *educator, consultant*
Speth, Gerald Lennus *education and business consultant*
Sullender, Joy Sharon *elementary school educator*
Watkins, Sherry Lynne *elementary school educator*

Jamestown
Waymire, John Thomas *principal*

Kokomo
Hill, Emita Brady *academic administrator*
Lopes, Dominic M. McIver *educator*

Kouts
Miller, Sarabeth *secondary education educator*

Lafayette
Troutner, Joanne Johnson *school technology administrator, educator, administrator, consultant*

Lagrange
Young, Rebecca Lee *special education educator*

Leesburg
Pryor, Dixie Darlene *elementary education educator*

Lincoln City
Blessinger, Timothy Louis *secondary school educator*

Marion
Barnes, James Byron *university president*
Philbert, Robert Earl *secondary school educator*

Merrillville
Kamanaroff, Charlene *elementary education educator*

Mishawaka
†Wilson, Rebecca Jo *dean, education educator*

Monroeville
Sorgen, Elizabeth Ann *retired educator*

Morocco
Fernandez, Martin Andrew *secondary school educator*

Muncie
Adams, Thomas Wayne *chemistry educator*
Alford, Jeffrey Whitwam *university administrator*
Amman, E(lizabeth) Jean *university official*
Holt, Gerald Wayne *retired counseling administrator*
Linson, Robert Edward *university administrator emeritus*
†McAllister, Peter A. *music education educator*
Swetnam, Ruth E. Danglade *curriculum director*
Wiedmer, Terry Lynn *educational administration educator, consultant*

Munster
Fies, James David *elementary education educator*
Platis, Chris Steven *educator*

New Albany
Kaiser, Michael Bruce *elementary education educator*
Riehl, Jane Ellen *education educator*

New Castle
†Ratcliff, Richard Pickering *secondary education educator*

New Harmony
Koch, Jane Ellen *secondary school educator*

Noblesville
Thacker, Jerry Lynn *school administrator*

North Manchester
Sponseller, Kay Lynn *secondary school educator, college educator*
Williams, Leonard A., Jr. *educator*

Notre Dame
Castellino, Francis Joseph *university dean*
Crosson, Frederick James *former university dean, humanities educator*
Hatch, Nathan Orr *university administrator*
Johnstone, Joyce Visintine *education educator*
O'Meara, Onorato Timothy *academic administrator, mathematician*

Pendleton
Phenis, Nancy Sue *educational administrator*

Pittsboro
Hassfurder, Leslie Jean *principal*

Plainfield
Lucas, Georgetta Marie Snell *retired educator, artist*

Plymouth
Cardinal-Cox, Shirley Mae *education educator*
Jurkiewicz, Margaret Joy Gommel *secondary education educator*

Portage
Zuick, Diane Martina *elementary education educator*

Portland
†Bisel, Marsha McCune *elementary education educator*

Purdue University
Beering, Steven Claus *academic administrator, medical educator*

Richmond
Bennett, Douglas Carleton *academic administrator*
Robinson, Dixie Faye *school system administrator*

Schererville
Griffin, Anita Jane *elementary education educator*

South Bend
Charles, Isabel *university administrator*
†Owens, Ora Lee *elementary education educator*
Perrin, Kenneth Lynn *university chancellor*
Rodgers, Grace Anne *university official*
Shirley, Randall Delron *university dean*

Terre Haute
Hulbert, Samuel Foster *college president*
Hunt, Effie Neva *former college dean, former English educator*
Landini, Richard George *university president, emeritus English educator*
Leach, Ronald George *educational administration educator*
Moore, John William *university president*
†Myers, Andrea Lee *university administrator*
†Summers, Jerry Andy *education educator*
Van Til, William *education educator, writer*

Union Mills
Johnson, Bruce Ross *elementary education educator*

Upland
Harbin, Michael Allen *religion educator, writer*
Kesler, Jay Lewis *academic administrator*
Kitterman, Joan Frances *education educator*

Valparaiso
Harre, Alan Frederick *university president*
Miller, John Albert *university educator, consultant*
Mundinger, Donald Charles *college president retired*
Schnabel, Robert Victor *retired academic administrator*
Serpe-Schroeder, Patricia L. *elementary education educator*

Vincennes
Nead, Karen L. *university professor*

Wabash
Whitehead, Wendy Lee *special education educator*

Warren
Pattison, Deloris Jean *retired counselor, university official*

Warsaw
Stump, Christine Jo *daycare provider*

West Lafayette
Baumgardt, Billy Ray *university official, agriculturist*
Cox, Beverly E. *educational researcher, educator*
Gappa, Judith M. *university administrator*
Gennett, Timothy *academic administrator*
Gentry, Don Kenneth *academic dean*
Hill, Rebecca Sue Helm *educator*
Moskowitz, Herbert *management educator*
Ringel, Robert Lewis *university administrator*
Shertzer, Bruce Eldon *education educator*
Stone, Beverley *former university dean, former dean of students*
Tacker, Willis Arnold, Jr. *medical educator, researcher*
Tilton, Mark Campbell *educator*
Weidenaar, Dennis Jay *college dean*

Westville
Alspaugh, Dale William *university administrator, aeronautics and astronautics educator*

Whiting
Fies, Ruth Elaine *media specialist*

Winona Lake
†Plaster, David Roy *college executive*

Yorktown
Downing, Barbara Kay *principal*
Stephenson, Julie *secondary school educator*

Zionsville
Hansen, Arthur Gene *former academic administrator, consultant*

IOWA

Albia
Putnam, Bonnie Colleen *elementary education educator*

Ames
Crabtree, Beverly June *retired college dean*
Dyrenfurth, Michael John *vocational technical and industrial technology educator, consultant*
Ebbers, Larry Harold *education educator*
Jischke, Martin C. *academic administrator*
Manatt, Richard *education educator*

Rabideau, Peter Wayne *university dean, chemistry educator*
Schuh, John Howard *adult education educator, academic administrator*
†Whitaker, Faye P. *education educator*

Ankeny
Gilbert, Fred D., Jr. *college official*

Bettendorf
†Sandvick, Doris S. *elementary educator*

Boone
†Taylor, Sheila Marie *principal*

Burlington
Brocket, Judith Ann *elementary education mathematics educator*
Lundy, Sherman Perry *secondary school educator*

Cedar Falls
†Edginton, Christopher R. *educator, academic administrator*
Ishler, Margaret Fisher *education educator*

Cedar Rapids
Feld, Thomas Robert *academic administrator*
Haines, Cathy Jean *elementary education educator*
Holder, Kathleen *elementary education educator*
Hutton, Mary J. *guidance counselor*
Plagman, Ralph *principal*
Rosberg, Merilee Ann *education educator*
Smith, Cindy Thompson *special education educator*
Stirler, Karen Sue *special education educator, adult education educator*
Williams, Colin Dale *school system administrator*

Clear Lake
Schultz, Patricia Ann *secondary education educator*

Clinton
Winkler, Joann Mary *secondary school educator*

Council Bluffs
Roberts, Antonette *special education educator*

Davenport
Dcamp, Richard Manley *secondary education educator*
Hudson, Celeste Nutting *education educator, reading clinic administrator, consultant*
Rogalski, Edward J. *university administrator*
†Stephans, Patrice Ann *dean*

Des Moines
Beisser, Sally Rapp *educator*
†Gaines, Ruth Ann *educator*
Jeschke, Thomas *gifted education educator*
Mattern, David Bruce *elementary education educator*
Schmidt, Barbara J. *educational consultant*
Webb, Mary Christine *special education educator*
Wessendorf Knau, Suana Le *special education educator*

Dubuque
Dunn, M. Catherine *college administrator, educator*
Peterson, Walter Fritiof *academic administrator*
Phillips, Betty Joan *retired educator in student services*
Toale, Thomas Edward *school system administrator, priest*

Elliott
Hunt, Colleen A. *educational consultant*

Emmetsburg
Wells, Martha Johanna *elementary education educator*

Essex
Raynor, Patricia Ann Herbert *special education educator*

Fairfield
†Joshi, Prabhakar G. *educator*

Fort Madison
Wallerich, Omer Kay *secondary education educator*

Garner
Mestad, Gary Allen *education educator*

George
†Martens-Rosenboom, Marcia Ann *secondary education educator*

Grinnell
Osgood, Russell King *dean*

Honey Creek
Hansen, Cherry A. Fisher *special education educator*

Hopkinton
Pounds, Buzz R. *educator*

Iowa City
Boyd, Willard Lee *academic administrator, museum administrator, lawyer*
Brennan, Robert Lawrence *educational director, psychometrician*
†Coleman, Mary Sue *academic administrator*
Davis, Julia McBroom *college dean, speech pathology and audiology educator*
Duffy, William Edward, Jr. *retired education educator*
Feldt, Leonard Samuel *university educator and administrator*
Hines, N. William *dean, law educator, administrator*
Kennedy, Jack *secondary education journalism educator*
†McCarville, Sheila Ann *special education educator, elementary educator*
†Newman, Robert Preston *educator*
Porter, Nancy Lefgren *reading recovery educator*
Roe, Gerald Bruce *director*
Skorton, David Jan *university official, physician, educator, researcher*
Vaughan, Emmett John *academic dean, insurance educator*
Venzke, Kristina Lea *academic administrator*
Whitmore, Jon Scott *university official, play director*

Iowa Falls
Sessler, Donna Jean Hotz *secondary education educator*

Mason City
Olson, Paul Buxton *retired social studies, marketing, and business educator*

Mount Vernon
Will, Frederic *university president, writer*

Newton
Ponder, Marian Ruth *retired mathematics educator*

Oakdale
Spriestersbach, Duane Caryl *university administrator, speech pathology educator*

Orange City
†Druliner, Marcia Marie *education educator*

Osceola
Vanderflught, Jack Ray *secondary educator, marketing professional*

Oskaloosa
Burrow, Paul Irving *educator*

Ottumwa
†Dinsmore, Susan Marie *secondary education educator*

Sergeant Bluff
†Moore, Daniel Alan *secondary school principal*

Sioux City
Dillman, Kristin Wicker *middle school educator, musician*
Marker, David George *university president*
Mounts, Nancy *secondary education educator*
†Orwig, Timothy Thomas *academic administrator, writer*
Wick, Sister Margaret *college administrator*
Wilson, Kim Robin *reading educator*

Spencer
Martindale, Donald Patrick *elementary education educator*

Storm Lake
†McDaniel, Timothy Elton *educator*

University Park
Rickman, W. Edward *college president*

Walnut
Myers, Gloria Jean *elementary education educator*

Waverly
Fredrick, David Walter *university administrator*

West Des Moines
Holderness, Susan Rutherford *at-risk educator*

KANSAS

Andover
†Cost, Stephen James *principal*

Anthony
Carr, Cynda Annette *elementary education educator*

Arkansas City
Kroeker, Lisa Dawn *secondary education educator*

Ashland
Lehman, Julie Aimée *secondary education educator*

Atchison
Seago, Diana Marie *college administrator*
†Still, Vickye Sue *elementary educator*

Baldwin City
Lambert, Daniel Michael *academic administrator*

Baxter Springs
O'Neal, Vicki Lynn *elementary education educator*

Concordia
†Raines, Louis Edward *school administrator*

Council Grove
Grimsley, Bessie Belle Gates *special education educator*

Derby
Delamarter, Thelda Jean Harvey *secondary education educator*

Dodge City
Sapp, Nancy L. *educational administrator*

Downs
La Barge, William Joseph *tutor, researcher*

Effingham
Figgs, Linda Sue *educational administrator*

El Dorado
Cahalen, Shirley Leanore *retired secondary education educator*
Fangmann, Heather Ann *secondary educator, English*

Emporia
†Mallein, Darla J. *educator*
Schallenkamp, Kay *academic administrator*

Fort Leavenworth
†Willbanks, James Hal *educator, retired military officer*

Hays
Boldra, Sue Ellen *social studies educator, business owner*
Hammond, Edward H. *university president*
Harbin, Calvin Edward *retired educator*
Harman, Nancy June *elementary education educator, principal*

Hiawatha
Pennel, Marie Lucille Hunziger *retired elementary education educator*

Hoyt
Lierz-Ziegler, Stacey Elizabeth *educational consultant*

Hutchinson
Green, Thereasa Ellen *elementary education educator*
Stevens, Leota Mae *retired elementary education educator*

Kansas City
Clifton, Thomas E. *seminary president, minister*
Hagen, Donald Floyd *university administrator, former military officer*
Whelan, Richard J. *director special education and pediatrics programs, academic administrator*

Lawrence
Frederickson, Horace George *former college president, public administration educator*
Greenberg, Marc L. *education educator*
Hemenway, Robert E. *academic administrator, language educator*
Locke, Carl Edwin, Jr. *academic administrator, engineering educator*
Peterson, Nancy *special education educator*
Pinet, Frank Samuel *former university dean*
Schiefelbusch, Richard Louis *retired language educator, research administrator*
Schnose, Linda Mae *special education educator*
Turnbull, Ann Patterson *special education educator, consultant*

Leavenworth
Pedigo, Sheila Denise *dean*
Zaretski, Ann Pikaart *special education educator*

Liberal
Rodenberg, Anita Jo *academic administrator*

Lindsborg
Humphrey, Karen A. *college director*
Michael, Ronald Roy *registrar, librarian*

Louisburg
†Best, Pamela LaFeuer *secondary school educator*

Macksville
Rohr, Brenda Ann *band and vocal director*

Manhattan
Coffman, James Richard *academic administrator, veterinarian*
Richter, William Louis *university administrator*
†Wefald, Jon *university president*

Meade
Brannan, Cleo Estella *retired elementary education educator*

Mulvane
George, Donald Richard *retired principal*

Newton
Hymer, Martha Nell *elementary education educator*

Oakley
Wolfe, Mindy René *early childhood education educator*

Olathe
Goodwin, Becky K. *secondary education educator*
Martin, Daniel James *university official, lawyer*
Shelton, Jody *school system administrator*
Stevens, Diana Lynn *elementary education educator*

Overland Park
Lamb, Bill Henry *college administrator, educator*

Pittsburg
Darling, John Rothburn, Jr. *university president, business educator*

Pomona
Gentry, Alberta Elizabeth *elementary education educator*

Prairie Village
Breidenbach, Monica Eileen *educator, career counselor*

Pratt
DePew, Monette Evelyn *educator*

Saint John
Wibright, Eddy Ann *secondary education educator*

Salina
†Delap, Joe Gene *educator*
Dubuc, Deborah Jo *special education educator*
Miller, Jeffery Dean *university admissions director, consultant*

Shawnee
Bunch, Jolene Regina *educator*

Shawnee Mission
†Crossen, Shani Kathryn *secondary school educator, tax preparer*
Kaplan, Marjorie Ann Pashkow *school district administrator*
Laing, Linda Jeanne *school counselor*
Stilwell, Connie Kay *secondary school educator*

Stilwell
Snodgrass, Connie Sue *secondary education educator*

Sublette
Swinney, Carol Joyce *secondary education educator*

Topeka
Lukert-Devoe, Linda Pauline *special education educator*
†Smith, Loran Bradford *educator*

Ulysses
Nordyke, Robyn Lee *primary school educator*

Uniontown
Conard, Norman Dale *secondary education educator*

Wichita
†Beggs, Donald Lee *university chancellor*

Winfield
Willoughby, John Wallace *former college dean, provost*

KENTUCKY

Arjay
Hoskins, Barbara R(uth) Williams *elementary educator, elementary principal*

Bowling Green
Carlock, Janet Lynne *middle school educator*

Bronston
Mitchell, Steve Harold *child development specialist*

Campbellsville
Skaggs, Karen Gayle *elementary school educator*

Cynthiana
Glascock, Robin *secondary school educator*

Danville
Breeze, William Hancock *college administrator*
Rowland, Robert E. *secondary school principal*
Ward, John Chapman *academic affairs dean*

Elizabethtown
Lee, William Christopher *vocational school educator*

Erlanger
Cheser, Karen Denise *school system administrator, writer*

Falmouth
Mudd, Sheryl Kay *secondary school educator, guidance counselor*

Florence
Adams, Sandra Lynn *principal*

Fort Thomas
Gaston, Paul Lee *academic administrator, English educator*

Frankfort
McDaniel, Karen Jean *university library administrator, educator*

Harlan
Greene, James S., III *school administrator*

Harrodsburg
Lunger, Irvin Eugene *university president emeritus, clergyman*
Redwine, Donna J. *middle school education educator*

Henderson
Wayne, Bill Tom *secondary school educator, coach*

Highland Heights
Boothe, Leon Estel *university president emeritus, consultant*
Brennan, Ronald Wesley *retired secondary school educator*
†Mauldin, Rosetta Johnson *dean, social work educator*

Hindman
Still, James *adult education educator, writer*

Lexington
Bosomworth, Peter Palliser *university medical administrator*
Cole, Henry Philip *educational psychology educator*
Fleming, Juanita W. *academic administrator*
Kewin, Cynthia McLendon *secondary education educator*
Lawson, Frances Gordon *child guidance specialist*
Matheny, Samuel Coleman *academic administrator*
Pruitt, Beth Anne *special education educator*
Singletary, Otis Arnold, Jr. *university president emeritus*
Thelin, John Robert *academic administrator, education educator, historian*
Wethington, Charles T., Jr. *academic administrator*
Zinser, Elisabeth Ann *academic administrator*

Louisville
Bash, Lee *educational administrator*
Bradford, Gail Idona *minister*
Bratton, Ida Frank *secondary school educator*
†Cabal, Theodore James *dean, religious studies educator*
Cecil, Bonnie Susan *elementary education educator*
Egginton, Everett *educational administrator*
Garfinkel, Herbert *university official*
Highland, Martha (Martie) *retired education educator, consultant*
Kmetz, Donald R. *retired academic administrator*
Martin, Janice Lynn *special education educator*
Mohler, Richard Albert, Jr. *academic administrator, theologian*
†Newby, Elizabeth Ann *elementary education educator*
Nystrand, Raphael Owens *university dean, educator*
Oates, Thomas R. *university executive*
Schneider, Jayne B. *school librarian*
Shumaker, John William *academic administrator*

Smith, Mary Elinor *retired dean, mathematics educator, counselor*
†Stone, Nancy Jon *special education educator*
Swain, Donald Christie *retired university president, history educator*
Taylor, Robert Lewis *academic administrator*
†Truitt, Benjamin *elementary education educator*
Wilson, Denise Watts *secondary school educator*

Madisonville
Aubrey, Sherilyn Sue *elementary school educator*

Maysville
Hunter, Nancy Donehoo *education educator*

Middlesboro
Potter, Karen Ann *secondary school educator*

Morehead
†Newby, Earl Fernando *educator*

Murray
Bumgardner, Cloyd Jeffrey *school principal*

Nancy
Watts, Brenda Sue *elementary education educator, retired*

Newport
Clinkenbeard, James Howard *principal*

Nicholasville
Crouch, Dianne Kay *secondary school guidance counselor*

Paintsville
Wells, Zella Faye *assistant school superintendent, consultant*

Pikeville
Smith, Harold Hasken

Pineville
Miracle, Donald Eugene *elementary school educator*

Princeton
Holt, Linda Fitzgerald *elementary education educator*

Russell
†Heck, Charles Ralph *university dean*

Somerset
Caron, Anita Jo *secondary education educator*

Union
Cook, Janice Eleanor Nolan *retired elementary school educator*
Wiener, Kathleen Marie *elementary education educator*

Vine Grove
Gray, Paul Clell *secondary school educator*

Winchester
Farmer, Rebecca Anne *educator*

LOUISIANA

Alexandria
Maples, Mary Lou *elementary education educator*

Arabi
Stierwald, Marlene Lydia *elementary school educator*

Baton Rouge
Boyce, Bert Roy *university dean, library and information science educator*
Brun, Judith *principal*
Caffey, H(orace) Rouse *university official, agricultural consultant*
Costonis, John J. *law educator, lawyer*
Doty, Gresdna Ann *education educator*
Hamilton, John Maxwell *university dean, writer*
Harrelson, Clyde Lee *secondary school educator*
Kelly, Mary Joan *librarian*
Mc Cameron, Fritz Allen *retired university administrator*
Prestage, James Jordan *university chancellor*
†Saccopoulos, Christos-Anastasios Argyriou *university dean, architect*
†Yates, Marvin L. *retired academic administrator*

Bossier City
Darling, Shannon Ferguson *special education educator*

Boutte
Breaux, Marion Mary *secondary education educator*

Chalmette
Crouchet, Kathleen Hunt *elementary educator, reading educator*

Church Point
Romine, Donna Mae *middle school educator*

Denham Springs
Perkins, Arthur Lee, Sr. *retired principal, real estate broker, insurance agent*

Destrehan
Greene, Glen Lee *secondary school educator*

Franklin
Fairchild, Phyllis Elaine *school counselor*

Golden Meadow
Strickland, Tara Lynn *elementary education educator*

Gramercy
Deroche, Kathleen Samrow *elementary educator, mathematics consultant*

Grant
†Hahler, Gary Edwards *secondary school educator, coach*

Hammond
Bender, Victor M. *educational administrator*
Parker, Clea Edward *retired university president*

Houma
Bordelon, Dena Cox Yarbrough *retired special education educator*
Lemoine, Pamela Allyson *principal*

Iowa
Leonard, Linda Faye *secondary education educator*

Kenner
Cook, Willie Chunn *retired elementary school educator*
Regan, Siri Lisa Lambourne *gifted education educator*

Lafayette
†Akin, Jonathan Andrew *educator*
Cosper, Sammie Wayne *educational consultant*
Moody, Janet Lynne *elementary education educator*
Redding, Evelyn A. *dean, nursing educator*

Lake Charles
Bradley, Judy Faye *elementary school educator*
Dronet, Virgie Mae *educational technology educator*
Earhart, Lucie Bethea *volunteer, former secondary school educator*
Fields, Anita *dean*
Hebert, Robert D. *academic administrator*
Leder, Sandra Juanita *elementary school educator*

Leesville
Farley, Michelle Renae *secondary school educator*

Mandeville
†Miller, Joseph Claude *principal*

Many
†Rains, Laura Jean Ponselle *special education educator, farmer*

Metairie
Caruso, Kay Ann Pete *elementary education educator*
Johnson, Beth Michael *school administrator*

Monroe
Vankeerbergen, Bernadette Chantal *college educator*
†Zander, Arlen Ray *academic director*

Natchitoches
Wolfe, George Cropper *retired private school educator, artist, author*

New Orleans
†Aymond, Gregory M. *academic administrator*
†Baudoin, Larry Anthony *academic administrator*
Carter, James Clarence *university administrator*
Chambers, Thomas Edward *college president, psychologist*
†Cowen, Scott S. *university president*
Danahar, David C. *academic administrator, history educator*
Gordon, Joseph Elwell *university official, educator*
Hamlin, James Turner, III *university dean, physician*
Hassenboehler, Donalyn *principal*
Johnson, Clifford Vincent *college administrator*
Jones, John Anderson, Jr. *school system administrator*
Kelly, Eamon Michael *university president emeritus*
Mackin, Cooper Richerson *university chancellor*
McCall, John Patrick *college president, educator*
McFarland, James W. *academic administrator*
McMahon, Maeve *middle school administrator*
O'Brien, Gregory Michael St. Lawrence *university official*
Pedersen, Lynn Colton *primary school educator*
Ross, Kathleen *elementary and secondary school educator, author*
Simoneaux, Catherine M. *academic administrator*
Vanselow, Neal Arthur *university administrator, physician*
Washington, Robert Orlanda *social policy educator, former university official*

New Roads
Christophe, Josita Lejuan *special education educator*

Pride
Jones, LaCinda *assistant principal*

Ruston
Maxfield, John Edward *retired university dean*
Reneau, Daniel D. *academic administrator*
Taylor, Foster Jay *retired university president*

Saint Gabriel
Knight, Diane *special education educator*

Shreveport
Joshua, Percy *English educator*
Smith, Harriet Gwendolyn Gurley *secondary school educator, writer*
Thomas, Bessie *primary education educator*

Sicily Island
Dale, Sam E., Jr. *retired educational administrator*

Slidell
Dabdoub, Paul Oscar *academic administrator*
Faust, Marilyn B. *middle school principal*
Schexnayder, Manfred Jean *secondary education educator*
Schofield, Barbara Curtright *school administrator*

Sorrento
Welch, Joe Ben *academic administrator*

West Monroe
Reighney, Mary Kathryn *secondary education educator*

Westwego
Brehm, Loretta Persohn *secondary art educator, librarian, consultant*

MAINE

Arrowsic
Stone, Albert Edward *educator*

Ashland
Morrow, David Andrew *secondary education educator*

Augusta
Asmussen, J. Donna *educational administrator, consultant*
Sanders, Estelle Watson *school system adminstrator*

Bangor
McKinnon, Carolyn Ann *child care center director*

Bar Harbor
Carman, John Herbert *elementary education educator*
†Little, Carl von Kienbusch *academic director, writer*
Swazey, Judith Pound *institute president, sociomedical science educator*

Bar Mills
Burns, Maryann Margaret *elementary education educator*

Biddeford
Featherman, Sandra *university president, political science educator*
Ford, Charles Willard *university administrator, educator*

Boothbay Harbor
Davison, Ruth Hilton *elementary education educator*

Brunswick
Edwards, Robert Hazard *college president*
Greason, Arthur LeRoy, Jr. *university administrator*

Bucksport
Williams, Christine Hewes *elementary education educator*

Cumb Foreside
Dill, William Rankin *college president*

Damariscotta
Johnson, Arthur Menzies *retired college president, historian, educator*

Ellsworth
Remick, Oscar Eugene *academic administrator*

Farmington
Kalikow, Theodora June *university president*

Fort Kent
Taggette, Deborah Jean *special education educator*

Lewiston
Harward, Donald *academic official*
†Roy, Jean Ann *eduator*
Umpierre, Luz Maria *women studies educator, foreign language educator*

Lubec
Hudson, Miles *special education educator*

Machias
Rosen, David Matthew *education educator*

North Yarmouth
Fecteau, Rosemary Louise *educational administrator, educator, consultant*

Old Orchard Beach
Bartner, Jay B. *school system administrator*

Old Town
†Alex, Joanne DeFilipp *educator Montesorri school*

Orono
Butterfield, Stephen Alan *education educator*
Radke, Margaret Hoffman *retired secondary school educator*
Rauch, Charles Frederick, Jr. *retired academic official*
Wiersma, G. Bruce *dean, forest resources educator*

Portland
Gilmore, Roger *college president*
Pattenaude, Richard Louis *university executive*

Presque Isle
Huffman, Durward Roy *academic administrator, electrical engineer*

Rumford
Kent, Richard B. *secondary education educator*

Saco
Queally, Christopher *secondary education educator, theatre director*

South Paris
Martin, Charles Seymour *middle school educator*

Topsham
Nulle, Christopher Reynolds *secondary education educator*

Waterville
†Barnard, Bruce K. *academic administrator*
Cook, Susan Farwell *alumni relations director*
Cotter, William Reckling *college president*
Nelson, Robert E. *geology professor*

West Boothbay Harbor
Ryan, Marylou *education consultant*

Yarmouth
Bischoff, David Canby *retired university dean*
Bissonnette, Jean Marie *elementary school educator, polarity therapist*
Hart, Loring Edward *academic administrator*

MARYLAND

Adelphi
Langenberg, Donald Newton *academic administrator, physicist*

Annapolis
Cordts, Thomas James *elementary education educator*
Parham, Carol Sheffey *school system administrator*
Rosenthal, Michael Ross *academic administrator, dean*

Baltimore
Ajmani, Ranjeet Singh *educator*
Boughman, Joann Ashley *dean*
Bradshaw, Cynthia Helene *educational administrator*
Brewer, Nevada Nancy *elementary education educator*
Brewster, Gerry Leiper *educator, lawyer*
Bryan, Thelma Jane *university administrator, English educator*
Buser, Carolyn Elizabeth *correctional education administrator*
Donaldson, Sue Karen *dean, nursing educator*
Donovan, Sharon Ann *educator*
Ellis, Brother Patrick (H. J. Ellis) *academic administrator*
Fitzgerald, Thomas Rollins *university administrator*
Fletcher, Sherryl Ann *higher education administrator*
Gifford, Donald George *academic dean*
Grasmick, Nancy S. *superintendent of schools*
Hinson, Karen Elizabeth *secondary education educator*
Howland, Kristine Kay *college administrator*
Hrabowski, Freeman Alphonsa, III *university president*
Jackson, Stanley Edward *retired special education educator*
Keller, George Charles *higher education consultant, writer*
Kessler, Wallace Frank *school director, tour developer*
Klitzke, Theodore Elmer *former college dean, arts consultant*
Kroto, Joseph John *secondary educator*
Lazarus, Fred, IV *college president*
McPartland, James Michael *university official*
Mohraz, Judy Jolley *college president*
Norris, Douglas Martin *principal*
Palmucci Jr., John A. *college administration executive*
Poehler, Theodore Otto *university provost, engineer, researcher*
Ranney, Richard Raymond *dental educator, researcher*
Reinhart, Walter Josef *educator*
Ross, Richard Starr *medical school dean emeritus, cardiologist*
Schnell, Eugene Richard, IV *education director*
Smith, Hoke LaFollette *university president*
Tiefenwerth, William Philip *university program director*
Wallis, Sandra Rhodes *educator*

Bel Air
Miller, Dorothy Eloise *education educator*
Phillips, Bernice Cecile Golden *retired vocational education educator*

Beltsville
Lewis, Bette Louise *school principal*

Berlin
Crawford, Norman Crane, Jr. *academic administrator, consultant*

Bethesda
August, Diane L. *independent education consultant, policy researchr*
Buccino, Alphonse *university dean emeritus, consultant*
Corn, Milton *academic dean, physician*
Dykstra, Vergil Homer *retired academic administrator*
Gleazer, Edmund John, Jr. *retired education educator*
Hemming, Val G. *university dean*
Jameson, Sanford Chandler *education educator*
Leibowitz, Deborah Golub *early childhood, gifted and parent education consultant*
Manasse, Henri Richard, Jr. *academic administrator, pharmacy administration educator*

Capitol Heights
McKinney-Ludd, Sarah Lydelle *middle school education, librarian*
Pressley, Denise M. *special education educator*

Catonsville
Woolley, Alma Schelle *nursing educator*

Centreville
†Cupani, Jean Evelyn Morgan *elementary education educator*

Chevy Chase
Brenner, Marcella Siegel *retired education educator*
Ferguson, James Joseph, Jr. *physician, academic administrator, researcher*
Holloway, William Jimmerson *retired educator*
Ostar, Allan William *academic administrator, higher education consultant*
†Shosteck, Ruth Dub (Ruth Shosteck) *clinical social worker, educator*

Clinton
†Sauls, Carlton Rathele *academic administrator*

Cobb Island
Rudy, Linda Mae *secondary school educator*

Cockeysville
Cuninggim, Whitty Daniel *educator*

College Park
Anroman, Gilda Marie *assistant director, lecturer, educator*
Briggs, Sue *academic administrator*
†Bushrui, Suheil Badi *educator*
Dieter, George Elwood, Jr. *university official*
Dorsey, John Wesley, Jr. *university administrator, economist*
Finkelstein, Barbara *education educator*
†Frank, Howard *college dean*
Gass, Saul Irving *educator*
Geoffroy, Gregory L. *academic administrator*
†Kaplan, Barbara Beigun *university official, educator*
†Kasser, Joseph E. *educational administrator*
Massey, Thomas Benjamin *educator*
Polakoff, Murray Emanuel *university dean, economics and finance educator*
Prentice, Ann Ethelynd *university dean*
Satin, Karen W. *university publications director*
Schwab, Susan Carroll *university dean*
†Southerland, Wallace, III *academic administrator, consultant*
Stewart, Teresa Elizabeth *elementary school educator*
Toll, John Sampson *university president, physics educator*

Columbia
Bruley, Duane Frederick *academic administrator, consultant, engineer*
Davis, Janet Marie Gorden *secondary education educator*
Folkenberg, Lois Waxter *principal, educator, psychologist*
Whiting, Albert Nathaniel *former university chancellor*

Cumberland
Jancuk, Kathleen Frances *educational administrator*
Johnson, Rex Ray *automotive education educator*
Shelton, Bessie Elizabeth *school system administrator*

Delmar
Ennis, Sharon Lynn *elementary education educator*

Elkton
Howe, Patricia Moore *adult education educator*

Ellicott City
Leonard, Florence Jones *retired university graduate program director*
Powell, Lillian Marie *retired music educator*
Zimmer, Janie Louise *school system administrator*

Emmitsburg
Houston, George R. *college president*

Frederick
Church, Martha Eleanor *retired academic administrator, scholar*
Cuffie, Kevin Lamont *academic administrator, educational consultant*
Hindman, Margaret Horton *college administrator*
Klein, Elaine Charlotte *educational administrator*

Frostburg
Gira, Catherine Russell *university president*

Gaithersburg
Horman, Karen Loeb *elementary education educator*
†Keifer, Amy Jo *educator*
Rowe, Joseph Charles *elementary education educator, administrator*

Gambrills
Trimnal, Wanda Lee *secondary school educator*

Germantown
Stroud, Nancy Iredell *retired secondary school educator, freelance writer, editor*

Glen Burnie
†Gaither, Nina Denise *special education educator*

Glenwood
Rossetti, Linda Elaine *special education educator*

Greenbelt
Boarman, Gerald L. *principal*
Green, Patricia Pataky *school system administrator, consultant*
Kalnay, Eugenia *university administrator, meteorologist*

Hagerstown
†Foor, Jane A. *school counselor*
McCoy, Mildred Brookman *elementary eduation educator, retired*

Hurlock
Bowens, Emma Marie *elementary education educator*

Hyattsville
Moylan, John L. *secondary school principal*
Rodgers, Mary Columbro *academic administrator, English educator, author*

Joppa
Bates, Charles Benjamin *elementary school administrator*
Rehrig, William Harold *band and orchestra director*

Kensington
Hudson, Yvonne Morton *elementary education educator*

Largo
Wright, R. Russell *educator, musician*

Laurel
Barcome, Marigail *special education educator*
Lang, Colleen Anne *secondary education educator*
Wales, Patrice *school system administrator*

Lusby
Ladd, Culver Sprogle *secondary education educator*

Owings Mills
Berg, Barbara Kirsner *health education specialist*

Oxon Hill
†Shoap, Carla Shipman *community instructional educator*

Phoenix
Hairston, Walter Albert *school system administrator*

Port Republic
Karol, Eugene Michael *school system administrator*

Potomac
Jung, Richard Kieth *headmaster*
Karch, Karen Brooke *principal*
Stupak, Ronald Joseph *dean, management educator, researcher, consultant*

Prince Frederick
Karol, Victoria Diane *educational administrator*

Princess Anne
McKinney, Frances Hathaway *university program administrator*

Queenstown
Bowie, Norman Ernest *university official, educator*
Ryans, Reginald Vernon *music education educator, special education educator*

Randallstown
Myers, Debra Taylor *elementary school educator, writer*

Rockville
Levine, Barbara Gershkoff *early childhood education educator, consultant*
Rosenberg, Judith Lynne *middle school educator*
Sparks, David Stanley *university administrator*
Stansfield, Charles W. *educational administrator*
Stenger, Judith Antoinette *middle school educator*

Salisbury
Merritt, Carole Anne *secondary school educator*
Woolford, Dornell Larmont *academic administrator*

Sandy Spring
Cope, Harold Cary *former university president, higher education association executive*

Severna Park
Picken, Edith Daryl *school principal*

Silver Spring
Bonner, Bester Davis *school system administrator*
Coles, Anna Louise Bailey *retired university official, nurse*
Jackson, Mary Jane McHale Flickinger *principal*
Moseley, Theresa *guidance counselor, actress*
Poinsett-White, Sadie Ruth *elementary education educator*
Rankin, Rachel Ann *retired media specialist*
Schick, Irvin Henry *academic administrator, educator*
Shira, Robert Bruce *university administrator, oral surgery educator*
Whalen, John Philip *retired educational administrator, clergyman, lawy*
Williams, Barbara Ivory *educational researcher*

Sparks
Smith, Frances Rider *academic administrator*

Stevenson
Hyman, Mary Bloom *science education programs coordinator*

Stevensville
Agreen, Linda Kerr *secondary eduacation educator*

Suitland
Speier, Peter Michael *mathematics educator*

Sykesville
†Foor-Hogue, Robert L. *secondary educator*

Towson
Chappell, Annette M. *university dean*

Upper Marlboro
Elwood, Patricia Cowan *education specialist, political consultant*
Street, Patricia Lynn *secondary education educator*

Waldorf
Hastings, Lee L. *secondary education educator*
Robey, Sherie Gay Southall Gordon *secondary education educator, consultant*
Walker, Diane Marie *special education educator*

Westminster
Chambers, Robert Hunter, III *college president, American studies educator*
Jenne, Arthur Kirk *secondary school educator*

Westover
†Scott, Christy Wright *elementary education educator*

Whaleyville
Truitt, Shirley Ann Bowdle *middle school educator*

MASSACHUSETTS

Acton
Tamaren, Michele Carol *special education educator*

Amherst
Adrion, William Richards *academic administrator, computer and information sciences educator, author*
Bliss, Katherine Elaine *Latin American history educator*
Costa, Kevin *post secondary education educator*
Gerety, Tom *college administrator, educator*
Prince, Gregory Smith, Jr. *academic administrator*
Rohan, Virginia Bartholome *college development director*
†Zuniga, Ximena U. *education educator, researcher*

Andover
Wise, Kelly *private school educator, photographer, critic*

Arlington
Blinn, Cynthia Lees *middle school educator*
Fulmer, Vincent Anthony *retired college president*

Auburn
Donnelly, Carol Burns *education educator*

Babson Park
Higdon, Leo I., Jr. *dean, finance educator*

Bedford
Schafer, Eva Cady *elementary school teacher, musician*

Belmont
†Dober, Richard Patrick *campus and facility planner, writer*
Harvey, Kenneth Richard *middle education educator, writer*

Beverly
Smith, Merelyn Elizabeth *elementary and middle school educator*

Boston
Argyris, Chris *organizational behavior educator*
Baker, Brent *dean*
Banks, Henry H. *academic dean, physician*
Berk, Lee Eliot *college president*
Caldwell, Ann Wickins *academic administrator*
Cass, Ronald Andrew *dean*
Chobanian, Aram Van *medical school dean, cardiologist*
Davies, Don *education educator*
DePaola, Dominick Philip *academic administrator*
Dluhy, Deborah Haigh *college dean*
Dujon, Diane Marie *director, activist*
Eisner, Sister Janet Margaret *college president*
Greene, Robert Allan *former university administrator*
†Harden, Patricia Keegan *financial aid officer*
Hedlund, Ronald David *academic administrator, researcher, educator*
Henry, Joseph Louis *university dean*
Hyatt, Raymond Russell, Jr. *educator*
Kaplan, Robert Samuel *educator*
Kerwin, Mark Broderick *chief financial officer, accountant*
Kirkpatrick, Edward Thomson *college administrator, mechanical engineer*
Klafter, Craig Evan *university administrator, legal historian*
†Knowles, Em Claire *dean*
†Kohn, Livia *educator*
Melton, David Van *dean, minister*
Morris, Robert *educator*
†Nelson, Steven Ryerson *finance educator*
Norris, Lonnie Harold *dean*
†Paine, Lisa Lynn *university administrator*
Palter, Elizabeth Ann Schneck *dean*
Penney, Sherry Hood *university president, educator*
Roemer, Linda *educator, academic administrator*
Ronayne, Michael Richard, Jr. *academic dean*
Rush, Sean Charles *higher education consultant*
†Sacchetti, Dominic Vincent *school system administrator*
Sargent, David Jasper *university official*
Shirley, Dennis Lynn *education educator*
†Shore, Eleanor Gossard *university dean*
Silber, John Robert *university chancellor, philosophy and law educator*
†Tilchin, William Neal *educator*
Van Domelen, John Francis *academic administrator*
Vernon, Heidi *international business educator*
Westling, Jon *university administrator*

Braintree
Gittleman, Sol *university official, humanities educator*

Bridgewater
Casabian, Edward K., Jr. *secondary education educator*
Nelson, Marian Emma *education educator*
Tinsley, Adrian *college president*

Brookline
†Cofield, Sherdena Dorsey *education director*
Ruthchild, Rochelle Goldberg *education educator*

Burlington
Dubois, Cindy A. *guidance counselor*

Cambridge
Baldine, Joanne *academic administrator, researcher*
Bruce, James Donald *academic administrator*
Daukantas, George Vytautas *counseling practitioner, educator*
Eurich, Nell P. *educator, author*
Fineberg, Harvey Vernon *university official, physician, educator*
Fischer, Kurt Walter *education educator*
Fox, Ellen *academic administrator*
Fox, John Bayley, Jr. *university dean*
Gray, Paul Edward *academic official*
Greyser, Linda Lorraine *education educator*
Howitt, Arnold Martin *university researcher, administrator, educator*
Johnson, Howard Wesley *former university president, business executive*
Kassman, Deborah Newman *university administrator, writer, editor*
McKenna, Margaret Anne *college president*
McKenna, Martha Barry *college dean*
Miller, Chandra Marie *educator*
Mitchell, William J. *dean, architecture educator*
†Page, Daniel Bennett *dean, musician*
Rowe, Mary P. *academic administrator, management educator*
Rudenstine, Neil Leon *academic administrator, educator*
†Schmalensee, Richard Lee *dean, economist, former government official, educator*
Sharp, Phillip Allen *academic administrator, biologist, educator*
Stacey, Roger Foy *educator*
Thiemann, Ronald Frank *dean, religion educator*
Tucker, John Avery *academic administrator, electrical engineer*
Vest, Charles Marstiller *academic administrator*
Whitcavitch-DeVoy, Julia Elizabeth *educational consultant*
Whitlock, Charles Preston *former university dean*
Wilson, Linda Smith *academic administrator*

Carlisle
†Helenius-LaPorte, Susan Ann *elementary education educator*

Casa Blanca
Ortiz, Diana M. *curriculum coordinator, tribal services executive*

Centerville
Kiernan, Owen Burns *educational consultant*

Charlestown
Mc Menimen, Kathleen Brennan *secondary education educator*

Charlton
†Denault, Linda Ellen Stone *educational administrator, educator*

Chestnut Hill
Altbach, Philip *higher education director, educator*
Herbeck, Dale Alan *educator*
Leahy, William P. *academic administrator, educator*
Monan, James Donald *university administrator*

Chicopee
Czerwiec, Irene Theresa *gifted education educator*

Concord
Brown, Linda Weaver *academic administrator*

Danvers
Traicoff, George *college president*

Dedham
Nichols, Nancy Ruth *elementary educator*

Duxbury
†Meier, Carl William *retired educator*

East Longmeadow
Wald, Gloria Sue *educational consultant*

Easthampton
†Melnick, Ralph *library director, secondary school educator,*

Fairhaven
Goes, Kathleen Ann *secondary education educator, choral director*

Fall River
Horvitz, Susan Smith *educator*
Ingles, James H. *community college dean*

Fitchburg
Mara, Vincent Joseph *college president*
Riccards, Michael Patrick *academic administrator*

Framingham
LeDuc, Karen Lorain Leacu *elementary and middle school education educator*

Gardner
Cosentino, Patricia Byrne *English educator, poet*
Coulter, Sherry Parks *secondary education educator*
Marceau, Judith Marie *elementary education educator*

Grafton
Tite, John Gregory *secondary school educator*

Great Barrington
Rodgers, Bernard F., Jr. *academic administrator, dean*

Greenfield
†Hassett, sulvia Ann *educator*

Hanover
Mickunas, Nancy Ann *special education educator*

Haverhill
Dimitry, John Randolph *academic administrator*
†Hosman-Nelson, Jill Marie *special education educator*

Holland
McGrory, Mary Kathleen *retired college president*

Holliston
O'Connor, Jude *special education educator, consultant*

Holyoke
†O'Connor, Mary Ellen *principal*

Housatonic
Charpentier, Gail Wigutow *private school executive director*

Hudson
†Mixter, Jean E. *educational administrator*

Hyde Park
Harris, Emily Louise *special education educator*

Indian Orchard
†Daley, Veta Adassa *educational administrator*

Ipswich
Kennan, Elizabeth Topham *former university president and history educator*
Sturwold, Sister Rita Mary *educational administrator*

Jamaica Plain
Nance, Marjorie Greenfield *educator*

Kingston
Squarcia, Paul Andrew *school superintendent*

Lawrence
Stanley, Malchan Craig *school system administrator, psychologist*

Lenox
Vincent, Shirley Jones *secondary education educator*

Lexington
Levy, Steven Z. *elementary education educator*

Lincoln
Muirhead, Kevin James *middle school administrator*

Longmeadow
Leary, Carol Ann *academic administrator*
Wallace, Ruth Helpern *special education educator*

Lowell
Hayes, Donald Paul, Jr. *elementary and secondary education educator*

Lynn
Astuccio, Sheila Margaret *educational administrator*
Ryder, Edward Francis *secondary education educator*

Malden
Feeney, Lynda Jean *secondary education educator*

Marblehead
†Orlen, Gerald Lawrence *secondary education educator*

Marlborough
†Moorman, Janet Elizabeth *secondary education educator*

Mattapoisett
Andersen, Laird Bryce *retired university administrator*

Maynard
Holway, Ellen Twombly Hay *primary education educator*

Medford
DiBiaggio, John A. *university president*
Mumford, George Saltonstall, Jr. *former university dean, astronomy educator*
†Wachman, Alan Michael *educator*

Methuen
Heron, Virginia Grace *secondary education educator*

Millers Falls
Hutcheson, Thomas Worthington *educational administrator*

Milton
Warren, John Coolidge *private school dean, history educator*
Wengler, Marguerite Marie *educational therapist*

Monson
St. Louis, Paul Michael *foreign language educator*

Needham
Zambone, Alana Maria *special education educator*

New Bedford
Bullard, John Kilburn *university administrator*

Newbury
Hamond, Karen Marie Koch *secondary education educator*

North Adams
Conklin, Jack Lariviere *education educator*

North Andover
†Wojtas, Susan A. *college administrator*

North Chelmsford
†Trivers, Dianne H. *elementary educator*

North Dartmouth
Cressy, Peter Hollon *university chancellor, retired naval officer*
Waxler, Robert Phillip *university educator, consultant*

North Easton
Ratcliffe, Barbara Jean *special education educator*

Northampton
Lightburn, Anita Louise *dean, social work educator*
Nickles, Herbert Leslie *college administrator*
†Sherr, Richard J. *educator*
Simmons, Ruth J. *academic administrator*

Norton
Marshall, Dale Rogers *college president, political scientist, educator*

Oakham
Poirier, Helen Virginia Leonard *elementary education educator*

Oxford
Stevens, D(onna) Lyn *preschool provider*

Palmer
Roy, Alicia M. *secondary education educator*

Paxton
†Locke, John R. *principal*

Plymouth
Freyermuth, Virginia Karen *secondary art educator*
Goggin, Joan Marie *school system specialist*

Quincy
Adams, Ronald G. *middle school educator*
Cawthorne, Alfred Benjamin *education educator*
Hill, Kent Richmond *college president*

Revere
Ferrante, Olivia Ann *retired educator, consultant*

Rockland
Gauquier, Anthony Victor *special education counselor*

Rockport
Bakrow, William John *college president emeritus*

Salem
Harrington, Nancy D. *college president*

Saugus
Austill, Allen *dean emeritus*

Scituate
†Spangler, Stanley Eugene *international relations educator*

Sharon
Douglas, Joanne M. Kaerwer *elementary education educator*

Somerset
Camara, Pauline Francoeur *secondary school educator*

South Attleboro
Hanson, Barbara Jean *education educator*

South Dartmouth
Ward, Richard Joseph *university dean, educator, author*

South Deerfield
Fritz, Nancy H. *educational researcher, administrator*

South Hadley
Creighton, Joanne Vanish *academic administrator*

Springfield
Caprio, Anthony S. *university president*
Cleland, Thomas Edward, Jr. *secondary school educator*
Courniotes, Harry James *academic administrator*
Vella, Sandra Rachael *principal*

Sudbury
Campbell, Elaine Josephine *educational director, writer, critic, educator*

Taunton
Buote, Rosemarie Boschen *special education educator*
Croteau, Gerald A., Jr. *school system administrator*

Tewksbury
DeAngelis, Michele F. *school system administrator*
Talford, Ginamarie *secondary education educator*

Tyngsboro
Lee, Joan Roberta *elementary education educator*

Waltham
Adamian, Gregory Harry *academic administrator*
Parrella, Susan Irene *special education administrator*
Reinharz, Jehuda *academic administrator, history educator*
†Reis, Arthur Henry, Jr. *academic administrator*

Wareham
Gustafson, Deborah Lee *educational administrator, educator*

Wellesley
Auerbach, Jerold S. *university educator*
Baum, Laura *educator*
Heartt, Charlotte Beebe *university official*
Ragone, David Vincent *former university president*
Walsh, Diana Chapman *academic administrator, social and behavioral sciences educator*
Wong, Bella Toy Funnd *secondary school educator, lawyer*

Wenham
Baker, Ruth Holmes *retired secondary education educator*
†Sciola, Charlotte Ann *school system administrator*

West Springfield
Dunphy, Maureen Ann *educator*

Westford
Brady, Shelagh Ann *elementary education educator*

Weymouth
†Scott, Susan Shattuck *secondary education educator*

Whitman
Anderson, Beth Ellen *English literature and composition educator*
Delaney, Matthew Michael *school administrator, fine arts educator*
Thompson, Andrew Ernest *secondary school educator*

Williamstown
†Beilin, Katarzyna Olga *educator*
Birrell, Stephen Reynolds *college administrator*

Winchendon
†Blair, C. Jackson *school administrator*

Winchester
Harris, Carole Ruth *educational consultant, researcher*
Meesa, Janet Jean *elementary educator*

Woburn
Tramonte, Michael Robert *education educator*

Worcester
Bowen, Alice Frances *school system administrator*
Brooks, John Edward *college president emeritus*
†DeHoratius, Edmund Francis *secondary education educator*
Grogan, William Robert *university dean*
Johnson, Nancy Ann *education educator*
Loew, Franklin Martin *educational administrator, biologist, consultant*
O'Neil, William Francis *academic administrator*
Onorato, Nicholas Louis *program director, economist*
Palmer, John Anthony, III *secondary educatin educatorr*
Traina, Richard Paul *academic administrator*
†Ulbrich, Mary Parsons *educator, administrator*

Yarmouth Port
Hall, James Frederick *retired college president*

MICHIGAN

Adrian
Caine, Stanley Paul *college administrator*

Allendale
Lubbers, Arend Donselaar *academic administrator*
Niemeyer, Glenn Alan *academic administrator, history educator*
Philbin, John Harper *educator*
†Stark, Gary Duane *dean*

Alma
Stone, Alan Jay *college administrator*
Swanson, Robert Draper *college president*

Alpera
Lancour, Karen Louise *secondary education educator*

Ann Arbor
Anderson, Austin Gothard *university administrator, lawyer*
Bonner, Michael David *adult education educator, researcher*
†Cho, Eun-su *adult education educator*
Cole, David Edward *university administrator*
Copeland, Carolyn Abigail *retired university dean*
Curtis, Christopher Bryan *secondary education educator*
Davis, Wayne Kay *university dean, educator*
Duderstadt, James Johnson *academic administrator, engineering educator*
Dumas, Rhetaugh Etheldra Graves *university official*
†Farghaly, Ali S. *educator*
Fleming, Robben Wright *retired educator*
Fleming, Suzanne Marie *university official, chemistry educator*
†Gonzalez, John M. *educator*
Judge, Charles Arthur *academic administrator*
Omenn, Gilbert Stanley *academic administrator, physician*
Paul, Ara Garo *university dean*
Porretta, Louis Paul *education educator*
Reinarz, Alice G. *academic administrator*
Robbins, Jerry Hal *educational administration educator*
Stark, Joan Scism *education educator*
Sussman, Alfred Sheppard *university educator*
Tice, Carol Hoff *middle school educator, consultant*
Van Houweling, Douglas Edward *university administrator, educator*
Warner, Robert Mark *university dean, archivist, historian*
Watkins, Paul B. *academic research center administrator, medical educator*
†White, B. Joseph *university dean*
Xie, Yu *adult education educator*

Armada
Kummerow, Arnold A. *superintendent of schools*

Auburn Hills
Etefia, Florence Victoria *academic and behavior specialist*

Battle Creek
Bishop, Joyce Ann *special programs counselor*
McPhee, Paula Ann *elementary education educator*

Bay City
Rakowski, Barbara Ann *principal*

Berrien Springs
Lesher, William Richard *retired academic administrator*

Bingham Farms
Harvey, Judith Gootkin *elementary education educator, real estate agent*
†Mills, Helene Audrey *education educator*

Birmingham
Van der Tuin, Mary Bramson *headmistress*

Bloomfield Hills
Doyle, Jill J. *elementary school principal*
Gavin, Robert Michael, Jr. *college president*
Piliawsky, Monte Eddy *college program director*
†Thompson, Richard Thomas *academic administrator*
Wermuth, Mary Louella *secondary education educator*

Brighton
Jensen, Baiba *principal*

Buchanan
Falkenstein, Karin Edith *elementary school principal*
†Wade, Melvin Pitt *principal*

Centerline
†Sexton, Catherine M. *health occupations educator, nurse*

Chesterfield
Broad, Cynthia Ann Morgan *special education educator, consultant*
Suchecki, Lucy Anne *elementary education educator*

Clarkston
Mousseau, Doris Naomi Barton *retired elementary school principal*

Clinton Township
Zanni, Christina Marie *art educator*

Clio
McCabe, Donald James *educational research director*

Coloma
Groff, Charlotte Virginia *elementary education educator*

Commerce Township
Boynton, Irvin Parker *retired educational administrator*

De Tour Village
Kemp, Patricia Ann *principal*

Dearborn
Dziuba, Henry Frank *university official*
Fair, Jean Everhard *education educator*
Orlowska-Warren, Lenore Alexandria *art educator, fiber artist*
Romatowski, Jane A. *education educator, associate dean*

Dearborn Heights
Johns, Diana *secondary education educator*

Detroit
Alford, Sandra Elaine *university official*
†Brooks, Charlotte Marie *educator, counselor*
Brynski, Christina Halina *school system administrator, consultant, educator*
Edelstein, Tilden Gerald *academic administrator, history educator*
Fay, Sister Maureen A. *university president*
Hagman, Harlan Lawrence *education educator*
Jackson, Claudreen *special education educator*
†Jackson, Murray Earl *academic administrator, educator*
†Johnson, Cathy Adams *educational administrator*
Johnson, Sylvia S. *retired secondary school educator*
†Miller, Annetta *university administrator*
Pietrofesa, John Joseph *education educator*
Reid, Irvin D. *academic official*
Rogers, Richard Lee *educator*
Semanik, Anthony James *instructional technology coordinator*
†Shannon, Timothy T. *educational adminstrator*
Shorter, Michelle Anne *secondary educator*
Skoney, Sophie Essa *educational administrator*
Smith, Gary Richard *technology educator*
†Tan, Chin An *educator*

Dowagiac
Gourley, Everett Haynie *educator*
Mulder, Patricia Marie *education educator*

East Lansing
Abbett, William S. *dean*
Brophy, Jere Edward *education educator, researcher*
Byerrum, Richard Uglow *college dean*
†Fernandez, Ramona Esther *adult education educator*
Harrison, Jeremy Thomas *dean*
Honhart, Frederick Lewis, III *academic director*
†Labaree, David Fleming *eduator*
Mackey, Maurice Cecil *university president, economist, lawyer*
McPherson, Melville Peter *academic administrator, former government official*
Pierre, Percy Anthony *university president*
Simon, Lou Anna Kimsey *academic administrator*
Snoddy, James Ernest *education educator*
Wronski, Stanley Paul *education educator*

Farmington Hills
Faxon, Jack *headmaster*
Hartman-Abramson, Ilene *adult education educator*
Hechler, Ellen Elissa *elementary education educator*

Flint
Dismuke, Leroy *special education educator, coordinator*
Duckett, Bernadine Johnal *retired elementary principal*
Hayes, Joyce Merriweather *secondary education educator*
Lorenz, John Douglas *college official*

Flushing
Barnes, Robert Vincent *elementary and secondary school art educator*

Fort Gratiot
Mueller, Don Sheridan *retired school administrator*

Frankfort
Acker, Nathaniel Hull *retired educational administrator*
†Bell, Sheila Sue *primary school educator*

Franklin
†Reinhart, Anne Christine *special education educator, consultant*

Fruitport
Collier, Beverly Joanne *elementary education educator*

Gaylord
Magsig, Judith Anne *early childhood education educator, retired*

Grand Rapids
†Calkins, Richard W. *college president*
Cline, Sister Barbara Jean *educational administrator*
Diekema, Anthony J. *college president emeritus, educational consultant*
Lyons, David Eugene *secondary education educator*
VanHarn, Gordon Lee *college administrator and provost*
VanScoy, Holly Carole *educational researcher*

Grosse Pointe
Collinson, Vivienne Ruth *education educator, researcher, consultant*

Robie, Joan *elementary school principal*

Hancock
Puotinen, Arthur Edwin *college president, clergyman*

Hillsdale
Kline, Faith Elizabeth *college official*
Roche, George Charles, III *college administrator*

Holland
Hill, JoAnne Francis *retired elementary education educator*
Jacobson, John Howard, Jr. *college president*
Nyenhuis, Jacob Eugene *college official*
Van Wylen, Gordon John *former college president*
Witkowski, Kristen Ann *academic administrator*

Houghton
Tompkins, Curtis Johnston *university president*

Hudson
Wollett, Eleanor Leigh *general education curriculum coordinator*

Ionia
Kunze, Linda Joye *educator*

Jackson
Haglund, Bernice Marion *elementary school educator*
Straayer, Carole Kathleen *retired elementary education educator*
Trap, Jennifer Josephine *special education administrator*

Jenison
Headley, Kathryn Wilma *secondary education educator*

Kalamazoo
Badra, Robert George *philosophy, religion and humanities educator*
Cody, Frank Joseph *secondary school administrator, education educator*
Donoghue, George Edward *retired secondary educator*
†Gómez Lance, Betty Rita *sciences and foreign language educator, writer*
Gordon, Alice Jeannette Irwin *secondary and elementary education educator*
Haenicke, Diether Hans *university president emeritus, educator*
Jones, James Fleming, Jr. *college president, Roman language and literature educator*
†Kobrak, Peter Max *educator*
LoVerme, Charles *intermedia educator*
†Mingus, Matthew Scott *educator*
Muncey, Barbara Deane *university associate consultant*
Ransford, Sherry *secondary education educator*
Strong, Russell Arthur *university administrator*
Stufflebeam, Daniel LeRoy *education educator*

Kincheloe
Light, Kenneth Freeman *college administrator*

Lake Orion
Brewer, Judith Anne *special education educator*

Lansing
Brennan, Thomas Emmett *law school president*
Butcher, Amanda Kay *retired university administrator*
†Drake, Douglas Craig *university official*
†Miller, Christine Ann *academic administrator*
Piveronus, Peter John, Jr. *education educator*
Warrington, Willard Glade *former university official*

Lapeer
Spray, Pauline Etha Mellish *retired elementary educator, writer*

Lawrence
Fudge, Mary Ann *vocational school educator*

Livonia
Babineau, Margaret Louise *music educator*
Van de Vyver, Sister Mary Francilene *academic administrator*

Long Beach
Woodrome, Harvey Niles *education educator*

Ludington
Puffer, Richard Judson *retired college chancellor*

Macomb
Farmakis, George Leonard *education educator*

Maple City
Morris, Donald Arthur Adams *college president*

Marquette
†Bailey, Judith Irene *university official, consultant*
Roy, Michael Joseph *higher education administrator*
Suomi, Paul Neil *alumni association director*

Midland
Barker, Nancy Lepard *university official*
†Grzesiak, Katherine Ann *primary educator*

Milford
Black, Denise Louise *secondary school educator*

Mount Pleasant
†Davenport, Richard W. *academic administrator*
Deromedi, Herb *athletic director*
Justice-Malloy, Rhona Jean *educator, theatrical artist*
†Martin, Sue Ann *dean*
Plachta, Leonard E. *academic administrator*

Muskegon
†Opel, Patricia *counselor, artist*

Niles
Metty, Michael Pierre *college dean*

Okemos
Velicer, Janet Schafbuch *elementary school educator*

Olivet
†Halseth, James A. *academic administrator*

Ontonagon
Clark, Raymond John *Academic Administrator*

Petoskey
†Baird, Greg Ross *university program director, theater educator*
Meyer, Catherine Lynn *elementary school educator*

Plymouth
Belobraidich, Sharon Lynn Goul *elementary education educator*

Pontiac
Decker, Peter William *academic administrator*

Portland
Adams, Bill *principal*
Rainey, Derek Rexton *educator, sculptor*

Rochester
†Connellan, William Wesley *higher education administrator*
Packard, Sandra Podolin *education educator, consultant*
Polis, Michael Philip *university dean*
Russi, Gary D. *academic administrator*

Rockford
Pappas, William John *principal, educator*

Royal Oak
†Beyerlein, Susan Carol *educational administrator*

Saginaw
Blue, Robert Lee *secondary education educator*
Sudhoff, Virginia Rae *retired elementary education educator*

Saint Clair Shores
Doutt, Geraldine Moffatt *retired educational administrator*

Saint Joseph
Skale, Linda Dianne *elementary education educator*

Sidney
Tammone, William Whitmore *academic administrator, science educator*

Southfield
Chambers, Charles MacKay *university president*
Leavell, Debbie Susann *secondary education educator*
Lorenz, Sarah Lynne *secondary education educator*
Olsen, Douglas H. *superintendent*
Swain, Melinda Susan *elementary education educator*

Stanton
Winchell, George William *curriculum and technology educator*

Sterling Heights
Cutter, Jeffrey S. *secondary education educator, music educator*
Pierson, Kathleen Mary *child care center administrator, consultant*

Tawas City
Jacob, Elizabeth Ann *elementary education educator*

Taylor
Beebe, Grace Ann *special education educator*

Temperance
Jan, Colleen Rose *secondary school educator*
Kinney, Mark Baldwin *fellowship executive, educator*

Traverse City
Petersen, Evelyn Ann *education consultant*
Stepnitz, Susan Stephanie *special education educator*
Zimmerman, Paul Albert *retired college president, minister*

Troy
Maierle, Bette Jean *director nursery school*

University Center
†Boyse, Peter Dent *academic administrator*
Gilbertson, Eric Raymond *academic administrator, lawyer*
†Hill, Paul Christian *dean*

Utica
Olman, Gloria *secondary education educator*

Vicksburg
Garrett, Christopher Arthur *secondary education educator*

Walled Lake
Peal, Christopher John *educational administrator*

Warren
Lorenzo, Albert L. *academic administrator*
Quay, Gregory Harrison *secondary school educator*

Waterford
†Anderson, Francile Mary *secondary education educator*
Fontanive, Lynn Marie *special education educator*

Wayne
Carpenter, Arthur Lloyd *education educator*

West Bloomfield
Sandler, Kevin Scott *education educator, film studies educator*

Westland
Mullinix, Barbara Jean *special services director*

Williamston
Johnson, Tom Milroy *academic dean, medical educator, physician*

Wolverine Lake
†Arraf, Shreen *school system administrator*

Yale
Vuylsteke, Thomas A. *secondary education educator*

Ypsilanti
Boone, Morell Douglas *academic administrator, information and instructional technology educator*
Fleming, Thomas A. *academic affairs assistant director, former special education educator*
Gerber, Lucille D. *elementary education educator*
†Griffin, Carolyn Leigh *English educator, genealogist*
Lewis-White, Linda Beth *elementary school educator*
Shelton, William Everett *university president*
Tobias, Tom, Jr. *elementary school educator*

MINNESOTA

Ada
†Sillerud, Arlen Roger *retired educator*

Albert Lea
Rechtzigel, Sue Marie (Suzanne Rechtzigel) *child care center executive*

Bertha
Peterson, Myra M. *special education educator*

Bloomington
Allen, Mary Louise Hook *secondary education educator*
Larson, Beverly Rolandson *elementary education educator*
Powell, Christa Ruth *educational training executive*

Buffalo
Swanson, Fern Rose *retired elementary education educator*

Burnsville
Freeburg, Richard L. *elementary education educator*

Cannon Falls
Bonde, Linda Merilyn *elementary school educator*

Champlin
Hersch, Russell LeRoy *secondary education educator*

Cloquet
Ellison, David Charles *special education educator*

Collegeville
Reinhart, Dietrich Thomas *university president, history educator*

Cushing
Perfetti, Robert Nickolas *educational consultant*

Dassel
Kay, Craig *principal*

Detroit Lakes
†Sycks, Elaine Marie *deaconess*

Duluth
Stauber-Johnson, Elizabeth Jane *retired elementary mathematics education educator*

Edina
Meyer, Warren George *vocational educator*

Elysian
Nickerson, James Findley *retired educator*

Gary
Anderson, Alden Alvin *music educator*

Hackensack
Mentzer, Merleen Mae *retired adult education educator*

Hopkins
Zins, Martha Lee *elementary education educator, media specialist*

Kelliher
Hughes, Patricia E. *secondary education educator*

Lakeland
Helstedt, Gladys Mardell *vocational education educator*

Long Lake
Lowthian, Petrena *college president*

Mankato
Hustoles, Mary Jo *elementary education educator*
Rush, Richard R. *academic administrator*

Minneapolis
Avella, Joseph Ralph *university executive*
†Barceló, Nancy Virginia (Rusty Barceló) *academic administrator*
Buggey, Lesley JoAnne *education educator, consultant*
Cerra, Frank Bernard *dean*
DiGangi, Frank Edward *academic administrator*
Dooley, David J. *elementary school principal*
Eckberg, E. Daniel *secondary education educator*
Gardebring, Sandra S. *academic administrator*
Gardner, William Earl *university dean*
Jernberg, Sandra Kay *elementary education educator*
Johnson, Carol R. *school system administrator*
Jorgensen, Daniel Fred *academic executive*
Kirschner, Ruth Brin *elementary education educator*
Knoell, Nancy Jeanne *kindergarten educator*
Kvavik, Robert Berthel *university administrator*
Lindell, Edward Albert *former college president, religious organization administrator*
Matson, Wesley Jennings *educational administrator*
†Morrison, James Kent *higher education administrator*
Nolting, Earl *academic administrator*
†Phillips, Carl Vincent *educator*
Ramberg, Patricia Lynn *college president*
Rand, Sidney Anders *retired college administrator*
Redmon, Rose Marie *secondary school educator*
†Rojas, Guillermo *educator*
Schuh, G(eorge) Edward *university dean, agricultural economist*
Slorp, John S. *academic administrator*
Southall, Francis Geneva *retired education educator music*
Wehrwein-Hunt, Jeri Lynn *elementary education educator*

Minnetonka
Wigfield, Rita L. *elementary education educator*

Moorhead
Dille, Roland Paul *college president*
Emmel, Bruce Henry *secondary education mathematics educator*
Treumann, William Borgen *university dean*

Morris
†Hall, Rickey Lee *academic administrator*

Mounds View
Calvin, Stafford Richard *academic administrator*

North Mankato
Coomes, Sally Payne *secondary educator*

Northfield
Edwards, Mark U., Jr. *college president, history educator, author*
Kowalewski, Michael John *educator*
McKinsey, Elizabeth *college dean*

Osseo
Long, June *school system consultant*

Plymouth
Fish, James Stuart *college dean, advertising consultant*

Preston
Hokenson, David Leonard *secondary school educator*

Remer
McNulty-Majors, Susan Rose *special education administrator*

Richfield
Devlin, Barbara Jo *school district administrator*

Rochester
Loutzenhiser, Carolyn Ann *elementary education educator*
Sherman, Thomas Francis *education educator*

Rosemount
Trygestad, JoAnn Carol *secondary education educator*

Saint Cloud
Berling, John George *academic dean*
†Grube, Bruce F. *academic official*
†McKay, Joane Williams *college dean*
†Sahlstrom, Stanley D. *retired college president and regent*
Wertz, John Alan *secondary school educator*

Saint James
Jones, Patricia Louise *elementary counselor*

Saint Joseph
†Hendley, W. Clark *academic provost*

Saint Louis Park
Svendsbye, Lloyd August *college president, clergyman, educator*

Saint Paul
Anderson, Charles S. *college president, clergyman*
Brushaber, George Karl *college-theological seminary president, minister*
Dykstra, Robert *retired education educator*
Graham, Charles John *university educator, former university president*
†Hartford, Douglas Bennett *university administrator*
Holt, Nancy Irene *elementary education educator*
Huber, Sister Alberta *college president*
Kerr, Sylvia Joann *educator*
Kirchhoff, Frederick Thomas *academic administrator, dean*
†Kuzer, Mindy Susan *educator*
McPherson, Michael Steven *academic administrator, economics educator*
Osnes, Larry G. *academic administrator*
Pampusch, Anita Marie *foundation administrator*
Rathburn, Robert Charles *retired educator*
Rogers, Karen Beckstead *gifted studies educator, researcher, consultant*
Stroud, Rhoda M. *elementary education educator*
Sullivan, Alfred Dewitt *academic administrator*

Shoreview
O'Brien, Thomas E. *educator, priest*

Ulen
Harmon, Kay Yvonne *elementary education educator*

Upsala
Piasecki, David Alan *social studies educator*

Waseca
Frederick, Edward Charles *university official*

Wayzata
Jamrogiewicz, Debra Lynn *educational consultant*

Winona
Beyer, Mary Edel *primary education educator*
Boseker, Barbara Jean *education educator*
DeThomasis, Brother Louis *college president*

Haugh, Joyce Eileen Gallagher education educator
Krueger, Darrell William university president
Nasstrom, Roy Richard education educator, consultant
White, Marjorie Mary elementary school educator

MISSISSIPPI

Alcorn State
Mitchell, Jackie Williams university administrator, consultant

Batesville
Neal, Joseph Lee vocational school educator

Biloxi
Brown, Sheba Ann elementary education educator
Cadney, Carolyn secondary education educator
Manners, Pamela Jeanne middle school educator

Brandon
Okojie, Felix A. research administrator

Brookhaven
†Wells, Peggy Lynn educator

Cleveland
Baker-Branton, Camille counselor, educator
Wyatt, Forest Kent university president

Clinton
Whitlock, Betty secondary education educator

Columbus
Rent, Clyda Stokes academic administrator

Hattiesburg
Culberson, James O. retired rehabilitation educator
Lucas, Aubrey Keith retired academic administrator
Noonkester, James Ralph retired college president
Saucier Lundy, Karen college dean, educator

Hazlehurst
Nelson, Alberta Catchings secondary education educator

Holly Springs
Beckley, David Lenard academic administrator

Itta Bena
†Baral, Ram Chandra educator, special education

Jackson
Broome, Kathryn secondary education educator
Chambers-Mangum, Fransenna Ethel special education educator
Conerly, Albert Wallace academic administrator, dean
Creel, Sue Cloer secondary education educator
Harmon, George Marion college president
†Layzell, Thomas D. academic administrator
†Lindsay, Susan Ruchti school principal
Rogers, Oscar Allan, Jr. college president
Sardin, James Earl school system administrator

Long Beach
Burnham, Tom state school system administrator
White, Edith Roberta Shoemake elementary school educator
Williams, James Orrin university administrator, educator

Lorman
Bristow, Clinton, Jr. academic administrator

Louisville
Hill, Wayne Thomas school administrator, minister

Mathiston
Hutchins, J. Mark university administrator

Meridian
Hoskins, Mable Rose secondary education educator, English language educator
Phillips, Patricia Jeanne retired school administrator, consultant

Mississippi State
Gunter, John Edward dean
Hawkins, Merrill Morris, Sr. college administrator
Hughes, Patricia Newman academic administrator
Mabry, Donald Joseph university administrator, history educator
McGilberry, Joe Herman, Sr. university administrator
Nelson, Rachael Aine mechanical engineering
†Nybakken, Elizabeth educator
Watson, James Ray, Jr. education educator
†Wilkinson, Dehlia Rae educator

Nettleton
Hairald, Mary Payne vocational education educator, coordinator

Noxapater
Sumner, Margaret Elizabeth elementary school educator

Oxford
Moorhead, Sylvester Andrew education educator retired
Walton, Gerald Wayne retired university official

Pascagoula
McKee, Ronald Gene vocational education educator

Perkinston
†Mellinger, Barry Lee community college president, vocational educator

Starkville
Knight, Aubrey Kevin vocational education educator
Martin, Theodore Krinn former university administrator (deceased)
Roberts, Willard John secondary school educator
Townsend, John M. education educator

Taylorsville
Dilmore, Cindy Corley special education educator

Thaxton
†Dean, Michael P. dean

University
Khayat, Robert Conrad chancellor
Lindgren, Carl Edwin educational consultant, antiquarian, photographer, priest
Martin, Jeanette St. Clair adult education educator
Meador, John Milward, Jr. university dean
Smith, Allie Maitland university dean

Whitfield
Whitehead, Zelma Kay special education educator

MISSOURI

Ballwin
†Harris, Terry Allen associate principal

Blue Springs
†Brock, Linda M. educator
Wood, Cynthia L. secondary education educator

Boonville
Schuster, Joyce Anne curriculum director

Camdenton
Hosman, Sharon elementary education educator

Cape Girardeau
Haugland, Susan Warrell education educator
Keys, Paul Ross university dean
McMahan, Gale Ann Scivally education educator
†Reinmann, Carol Sue elementary educator

Centralia
†Adams, Barbara Karen special education teacher, real estate agent

Chula
Murphy, Jenny Lewis special education educator

Columbia
Adams, Algalee Pool college dean, art educator
Brouder, Gerald T. academic administrator
Fluharty, Charles William policy research institute director, consultant, researcher
George, Melvin Douglas retired university president
Gysbers, Norman Charles education educator
Keith, Everett Earnest educator, education administrator
Kierscht, Marcia Selland academic administrator, psychologist
Miller, Paul Ausborn adult education educator
Nolan, Michael Francis college program director
Pacheco, Manuel Trinidad academic administrator
Payne, Thomas L. university official
Petersen, George James educational administration educator
Staley, Marsha Lynn elementary school educator, principal

Conception
†Neenan, Benedict Thomas academic administrator, rector

Drexel
Williams, Shirley J. daycare provider, educator, writer

Eagleville
Hendren, Linda Sue secondary education educator

Eureka
Warren, Kathryn Beckcom elementary school educator

Farmington
†Massie, Maureen Teresa elementary school educator
†Waters, David Lloyd principal, educator

Fayette
†Chaney, Sara Jo college official, clergywoman
Inman, Marianne Elizabeth college administrator

Florissant
Barnes, Rebecca Marie assistant principal
Bartlett, Robert James principal
Carman, Robert Eugene elementary school educator
James, Dorothy Louise King special education educator
Payuk, Edward William elementary education educator
Ulrich, Janet M. retired elementary school educator

Fulton
Swiney, Doyle James principal

Gallatin
Smith, Joann Jewell retired educator
Wilsted, Joy elementary education educator, reading specialist, parenting consultant

Grandview
Daugherty, Tonda Lou special education educator

Hannibal
Carty, Raymond Wesley academic administrator

Hillsboro
Adkins, Gregory D. higher education administrator
†Russell, Brenda Carol technical educator

Hollister
Head, Mary Mae elementary education educator

Houston
Ruckert, Rita E. retired elementary education educator

Imperial
Usher, Mary Margaret special education educator

Independence
Camper, Deniece Ann special education educator
Henley, Robert Lee school system administrator
Marlow, Lydia Lou elementary education educator

Jefferson City
Gonder, Sharon special education educator

Jennings
Robards, Bourne Rogers elementary education educator

Joplin
Allman, Margaret Ann Lowrance counselor

Kansas City
Brown, Zania Faye elementary education educator
Buford, Ronetta Marie music educator
†Cundiff, Jerry H. secondary music educator, church choir director
Doyle, Wendell E. retired band director, educator
Durig, James Robert college dean
Eubanks, Eugene Emerson education educator, consultant
Martin, Deanna Coleman university director
McCollum, Clifford Glenn college dean emeritus
Roos, Kathleen Marie special education educator
Sherwood, Joan Karolyn Sargent career counselor
Simmonds, Corwin (Corey) Shawn dean
Ward, Todd Pope educational resources executive
Washington, Patricia Lane retired school counselor
Wilkins, Arthur Norman retired college administrator

Kirksville
TenBrink, Terry Dean academic administrator

Kirkwood
†Black, Richard A. community college president
Warner, Alvina (Vinnie Warner) principal
Wiecher, Delilah Lee secondary school educator

Lees Summit
Boehm, Toni Georgene seminary dean, nurse
Griffith-Thompson, Sara Lynn resource reading educator
†Halsey, Joyce Leslie secondary education educator
Reynolds, Tommy secondary school educator

Liberty
†Sizemore, William Christian academic administrator
Tanner, Jimmie Eugene college dean

Marceline
†Engelhard, Barbara Jo education educator

Marionville
Estep, Mark Randall secondary education educator

Marshall
Huff, Jane Van Dyke secondary education educator

Maryville
Hubbard, Dean Leon university president

Moberly
Staley, Richard Lynn school system administrator

Mount Vernon
Pulliam, Frederick Cameron educational administrator

Plato
Wood, Joetta Kay special education educator

Point Lookout
Anderson, Ruth G. education educator, consultant

Raytown
Blaine, Robert Virgil principal

Rogersville
Hetherington, John Scott principal

Rolla
Warner, Don Lee dean emeritus

Saint Charles
Biggerstaff, Randy Lee academic administrator, sports medicine rehabilitation consultant
Cox, Glenda Jewell elementary school educator
Frey, Laura Marie special education administrator
Huckshold, Wayne William elementary education educator
Mager, Margaret Julia Eckstein special education educator

Saint Joseph
Murphy, Janet Gorman college president

Saint Louis
Allen, Renee principal
Baker, Shirley Kistler university administrator
Biondi, Lawrence university administrator, priest
Borst, William Adam educator, radio personality, writer
Briggs, Cynthia Anne educational administrator, clinical psychologist
Bubash, Patricia Jane special education educator
Byrnes, Christopher Ian academic dean, researcher
Cain, James Nelson arts school and concert administrator
Chism, Michelle secondary education educator
†Combs, W. William college administrator
Danforth, William Henry retired academic administrator, physician
Deal, Joseph Maurice university dean, art educator, photographer
Dodge, Paul Cecil academic administrator
Donohue, Patricia Carol academic administrator
Dunn, Jane Grace retired educator
Ellis, Dorsey Daniel, Jr. dean, lawyer
Flanagan, Joan Wheat (Maggie Flanagan) educational therapist
Fowler, Marti secondary education educator
Gerdine, Leigh retired academic administrator
Gilligan, Sandra Kaye private school director
Greenbaum, Stuart I. economist, educator
Hall, Homer L. journalism educator
†Harris, Edwin B. educator, administrator
Hendricks, Flora Ann former case manager, former special education educator
Kelly, Ann Terese elementary education educator
Khinduka, Shanti Kumar university administrator, educator
Koff, Robert Hess foundation administrator
Lackey, Kayle Diann elementary education educator
Lovin, Keith Harold university administrator, philosophy educator
†Luebbert, Karen M. academic administrator
Mahan, David James university official
Marsh, James C., Jr. secondary school principal
Martens, Patricia Frances adult education educator
Maupin, Stephanie Zeller educator, consultant
McGannon, John Barry university chancellor
Miller, Jo Ann education educator, college official
Monteleone, Patricia academic dean
O'Neill, Sheila principal
Pfefferkorn, Michael Gene, Sr. secondary school educator, writer
Pfefferkorn, Sandra Jo secondary school educator
Reid, Lorene Frances middle school educator
Reinert, Paul Clare university chancellor emeritus
Robinson, John Philip secondary educator
Rodriguez, Katie Claire advocate disability awareness
†Schoeffel, Georgia B. secondary education educator
Seligman, Joel dean
Stephenson, Gwendolyn W. academic administrator
Stodghill, Ronald school system administrator
Sutter, Jane Elizabeth educator, writer
Thomas, Pamela Adrienne special education educator
Touhill, Blanche Marie university chancellor, history-education educator
†Triplett, Charles Lawrence secondary education educator
Turner, Harold Edward education educator
Watkins, Hortense Catherine middle school educator
Weiss, Robert Francis former academic administrator, religious organization administrator, consultant
Weldon, Virginia V. university administrator

Salem
Dent, Catherine Gale secondary education educator

Savannah
Walker, Frances Morine retired special education educator

Sedalia
Hazen, Elizabeth Frances retired special education educator

Springfield
Allcorn, Terry Alan principal, educator
Groves, Sharon Sue elementary education educator
†Keiser, John Howard university president
Moore, John Edwin, Jr. college president
Quiroga, Ninoska university official
Slye, Gail Lynn educator
Smith, Donald L. social sciences educator
Smith, Judith Ann academic administrator
Stovall, Richard L. academic administrator
†Wilson, Judith Ann educator

Troy
Simmons, Karen Elaine secondary education educator

Verona
Youngberg, Charlotte Anne education specialist

Warrensburg
Elliott, Eddie Mayes academic administrator
Limback, E(dna) Rebecca vocational education educator

Washington
Chambers, Jerry Ray school system administrator

Webster Groves
Schenkenberg, Mary Martin principal

Windyville
Clark, Laurel Jan adult education educator, author, editor, minister
Condron, Daniel Ralph academic administrator, metaphysics educator

MONTANA

Antelope
Olson, Betty-Jean retired elementary education educator

Belt
Anderson, Harold Sterling retired adult education educator

Billings
DeRosier, Arthur Henry, Jr. college president
May, Michael Wayne technical school executive
McDaniel, Susan Roberta academic administrator

Bozeman
Goering, Kenneth Justin college administrator
Monaco, Paul academic administrator, educator, artist, writer

Butte
Sherrill, Barbara Ann Buker elementary school educator

Crow Agency
Pease-Pretty On Top, Janine B. community college administrator

Dayton
Catalfomo, Philip retired university dean

Great Falls
†Smith, Clayton Nowlin academic administrator

Helena
Crofts, Richard A. academic administrator
Dorrance, Debra Ann secondary school educator
†Guiliani, Marilyn Kay educator

Scott, Joyce Alaine *university official*

Kalispell
Ormiston, Patricia Jane *elementary education educator*

Lewistown
Edwards, Linda L. *elementary education educator*

Miles City
Emilsson, Elizabeth Maykuth *special education educator*
†Oberlander, Dale Eugene *college administrator*

Missoula
Barnett, Mary Louise *elementary education educator*
Brown, Perry Joe *university dean*
Dennison, George Marshel *academic administrator*
Kindrick, Robert LeRoy *academic administrator, dean, English educator*

Superior
Tull, Steven Gerald *secondary education educator*

NEBRASKA

Atkinson
Martens, Helen Eileen *elementary school educator*

Bellevue
Hightower, Pauline Patricia *elementary education educator*
James, Geneva Behrens *secondary school educator*
Muller, John Bartlett *university president*

Blair
Christopherson, Myrvin Frederick *college president*

Chadron
Ayres, Elizabeth *educator*

Columbus
Rieck, Janet Rae *special education educator*

Grand Island
†Giddings, William Glenn *community college president*
Zichek, Shannon Elaine *secondary school educator*

Gretna
Riley, Kevin M. *principal*

Hastings
Kort, Betty *secondary education educator*

Hayes Center
Fornoff, Ann Lynette *secondary school educator*

Inman
Keil, Holly Mae *elementary education educator*

Kearney
Middleton, James G. *education educator, counselor*
Ramage, Jean Carol *former univesity dean, psychology educator*

Lincoln
Ballinger, Royce Eugene *academic administrator, educator*
Bradley, Richard Edwin *retired college president*
Byrne, C. William, Jr. *athletics program director*
†Cavett, Dorcas C. *elementary educator*
Grew, Priscilla Croswell *university official, geology educator*
Hendrickson, Kent Herman *university administrator*
Hermance, Lyle Herbert *college official*
Janzow, Walter Theophilus *retired college administrator*
Laursen, Paul Herbert *retired university educator*
Lingle, Muriel Ellen *retired elementary education educator*
†Moeser, James Charles *university chancellor, musician*
Nelson, Darrell Wayne *university administrator, scientist*
†Ollerenshaw, JoAnne *elementary education educator*
Omtvedt, Irvin Thomas *academic administrator, educator*
Powers, David Richard *educational administrator*
Robak, Kim M. *academic administrator*
Smith, Lewis Dennis *academic administrator*
Tonack, DeLoris *elementary school educator*

Mc Cook
Creasman, Virena Welborn (Rene Creasman) *retired elementary and secondary school educator, genealogist, researcher*

Norfolk
Mortensen-Say, Marlys (Mrs. John Theodore Say) *school system administrator*
Timmer, Margaret Louise (Peg Timmer) *educator*

North Platte
Boerner, Sheila Gertrude *secondary education educator*

Omaha
Baer, Richard Myron *retired college administrator*
Bauer, Otto Frank *university official, communication educator*
Dixon, Terry Phillip *academic administrator, educational consultant*
Dougherty, Charles John *university administrator, philosophy and medical ethics educator*
Fjell, Mick *principal*
Francis, Connie L. *retired secondary education educator*
Haselwood, Eldon LaVerne *education educator*
Hill, John Wallace *special education educator*
Ho, David Kim Hong *educator*
Kosalka, Teresa Marie *elementary education educator*
McEniry, Robert Francis *education educator*
Morrison, Michael Gordon *university president, clergyman, history educator*
Mueller, Suzanne *secondary school educator*
Newton, John Milton *acadmeic administrator, psychology educator*
O'Brien, Richard L(ee) *academic administrator, physician, cell biologist*
Rosse, Therese Marie *reading and special education educator, curriculum, school improvement and instruction specialist*
Schlessinger, Bernard S. *retired university dean*
Tucker, Michael *elementary school principal*

Plainview
Mauch, Jeannine Ann *elementary education educator*

Rochester Hills
Westerfield, Michael Wayne *college administrator*

South Sioux City
Wilson, Esther Elinore *technical college educator*

Stuart
Larabee, Brenda J. *secondary education educator*

Verdigre
†Schweers, Margie Lou *elementary education educator*

Waverly
Trout, Shirley Kay *parent educator, writer, speaker*

Wayne
Sweeney, Karen J. *educator*

NEVADA

Boulder City
Holmes, BarbaraAnn Krajkoski *secondary education educator*

Carson City
Hull, Dennis Jacques *counselor*
Wadman, William Wood, III *educational director, technical research executive, consulting company executive*

Elko
Lovell, Walter Benjamin *secondary education educator*

Fallon
Dwyer, Doris Dawn *adult education educator*
Plants, Walter Dale *elementary education educator, minister*

Gardnerville
Pyle, David *elementary education educator*

Hawthorne
Graham, Lois Charlotte *retired educator*

Henderson
Benson, James DeWayne *university administrator*

Las Vegas
Brown, Lori Lipman *secondary school educator*
Carroll, Rossye O'Neal *college administrator*
Chance, Patti Lynn *adult education educator*
Cinque, Thomas Joseph *dean*
Cloud, Barbara Lee *adult education educator*
Cram, Brian Manning *school system administrator*
Cwerenz-Maxime, Virginia Margaret *primary educator, secondary education educator*
Gaspar, Anna Louise *retired elementary school teacher, consultant*
Gelfer, Jeffrey Ian *early childhood education educator*
Hair, Kittie Ellen *secondary educator*
Harter, Carol Clancey *university president, English language educator*
Kassouf, Esther Kay *middle school education educator*
McDonald, Malcolm Gideon *education educator*
Phillips, Karen *secondary education educator*
Ring, David C. *school administrator*
Shuman, R(obert) Baird *academic program director, writer, English language educator, educational consultant*
Skoll, Pearl A. *retired mathematics and special education educator*
Vaccaro, Louis Charles *college president*
Zehm, Stanley James *education educator*

Minden
Tyndall, Gaye Lynn *secondary education educator*
Zabelsky, William John *choral and band director*

North Las Vegas
Jacks, Roger Larry *secondary education educator*
Moore, Richard *academic administrator*
Sullivan, Debra Kae *elementary education educator*

Reno
Crowley, Joseph Neil *university president, political science educator*
Daugherty, Robert Melvin, Jr. *university dean, medical educator*
Humphrey, Neil Darwin *university president, retired*
Jarvis, Richard S. *academic administrator*
Kaylor, Andrea Lynn *secondary school counselor*
King, Charles Thomas *retired school superintendent, educator*
Lord, Jacklynn Jean *student services representative*
McKay, Alice Vitalich *academic administrator*
†Poore, Coral Deane *educator*
Salls, Jennifer Jo *secondary school educator*
Walen, Joanne Michele *secondary education educator, consultant*
Westfall, David Patrick *academic administrator, educator*

Summerlin
Johnson, Mary Elizabeth *retired elementary education educator*

NEW HAMPSHIRE

Amherst
Collins, Paul Daniel *principal*
Willis, John Osgood *educational evaluator, educator*

Bedford
Seidman, Alan *educational administrator*

Belmont
†Donovan, Vicki A. *elementary school teacher*

Claremont
Marashio, Paul William *educational administrator, educator*
Rich, Betty An *early childhood educator*

Concord
Porter, G. William *education administrator*

Dover
Pelletier, Marsha Lynn *secondary school educator, state legislator*

Durham
DeMitchell, Todd Allan *education educator*
Eggers, Walter Frederick *academic administrator*
Farrell, William Joseph *university chancellor*
Leitzel, Joan Ruth *university president*
Mazzari, Louis W. *program director*
Perry, Bradford Kent *academic administrator*

Epping
Boynton, James Robert *educational institute professional*

Farmington
Meyers, James B. *secondary education educator*

Hampton
Prentiss, Barbara Ann *principal*

Hanover
†Bharucha, Jamshed *dean*
Carfora, John Michael *economics and political science educator*
Danos, Paul *dean, finance educator*
Freedman, James Oliver *university president, lawyer*
Hennessey, John William, Jr. *academic administrator*
Howe, Harold, II *academic administrator, former foundation executive, educator*
Wright, James Edward *college president, history educator*

Haverhill
†Brickner, Roger Kenneth *secondary school educator*

Henniker
Cummiskey, J. Kenneth *former college president*

Hooksett
Gustafson, Richard Alrick *college president*

Keene
Hickey, Delina Rose *education educator*

Lebanon
Nagy, Laura Lee *educator, writer, editor*
Tinker, Averill Faith *special education educator*

Londonderry
Kennedy, Ellen Woodman *elementary and home economics educator*

Manchester
Auclair, Louise A. *education educator*
Descoteaux, Carol J. *academic administrator*
Horton, Joseph Matthew *college dean, humanities educator*
Jenkins, Margaret Constance *elementary education educator*

Nashua
Hansen, Michele Simone *secondary education educator*
Johnson, Arthur V., II *secondary education educator*
Mitsakos, Charles Leonidas *education educator, consultant*
Purington, David W. *elementary education educator*

New London
Mc Laughlin, David Thomas *academic administrator, business executive*
Vulgamore, Melvin L. *retired college president*

North Haverhill
Charpentier, Keith Lionel *school system administrator*

Pelham
Holmes, Richard Dale *secondary education educator, historical consultant*

Raymond
Reynolds, Debbie *educational administrator*

Rindge
†Forest, James Jared-Franzen *educator, reseacher*
Killion, Richard Joseph *college official, political science educator*

Somersworth
Tully, Hugh Michael *music educator*

Tilton
Schultz, Judith *educational administrator, consultant*

Wilton
Potter, Robert Wallace, Jr. *educator*

Wolfeboro
Pierce, Edward Franklin *retired academic administrator*

NEW JERSEY

Absecon
†Hiltner, Dawn Marie *elementary education educator*

Atlantic Highlands
Crowley, Cynthia Johnson *secondary school educator*

Basking Ridge
Giglio, William Vito *secondary education educator*
O'Neill, Adrienne *academic administrator*

Bayonne
Martinez, Lisa Lynn *elementary education educator*
Wanko, Michael Andrew *school system administrator*
Zuckerman, Nancy Carol *learning disabilities specialist, consultant*

Beach Haven
†Houlihan, Gail Lanier *child advocate, educator*

Bergenfield
Alfieri, John Charles, Jr. *educational administrator*

Berkeley Heights
Shaffer, Gail Dorothy *secondary education educator*

Bernardsville
Robinson, Maureen Loretta *retired secondary school educator*

Bloomfield
†Hemeleski, John Peter *retired academic administrator*

Bloomsbury
Clymer, Jerry Alan *educational administrator*

Bogota
Oldenhage, Irene Dorothy *elementary education educator*

Brick
Godbold, Barbara Louise *secondary education educator*

Bridgewater
Mack, Robert William *secondary school educator*

Brigantine
Kickish, Margaret Elizabeth *elementary education educator*

Browns Mills
Di Nunzio, Dominick *educational administrator*

Caldwell
Werner, Patrice (Patricia Ann Werner) *college president*

Camden
†Cummings, Melvin O'Neal *educator elementary school, administrator*
Gordon, Walter Kelly *retired provost, English language educator*
†Miller, Audrey G. *vice principal elementary school*

Cape May
Margolis, Jeffrey Allen *guidance counselor*

Cherry Hill
Brenner, Lynnette Mary *reading specialist, educator*
Bryan, Henry Collier *retired secondary school educator, clergyman*
Gutin, Myra Gail *communications educator*

Chester
Fluker, Jay Edward *middle school art educator*

Cliffside Park
Colagreco, James Patrick *school superintendent*

Clifton
Laskey, Frances M. *secondary school educator*
McCoy, Linda Korteweg *media specialist*
Meyer, John Anthony *vice principal*
Rodgers, John Joseph, III *educational administration consultant*

Colts Neck
Gall, Michael Louis *educator*

Delmont
†Troyanovich, Stephen John *educational program director, poet*

Denville
Gangloff, Linda Lee *secondary education educator, underwater photographer, writer*

Dover
Byrnes, Robert William *secondary school educator*

East Brunswick
Haupin, Elizabeth Carol *retired secondary school educator*

East Hanover
Tamburro, Peter James, Jr. *social studies secondary school educator*

East Orange
†Eldridge-Howard, Joyce *principal*
Jones Gregory, Patricia *secondary art educator*

Edison
Hynes-Lasek, Nancy Ellen *secondary education educator*
Maeroff, Gene I. *academic administrator, journalist*
McKiernan, Robert E. *career management consultant*
Robinson, Donald Warren *educator, artist*

Elizabeth
Morgan, Sister Ruth Zelena *educator*

Elmer
Slavoff, Harriet Emonds *learning disabilities teacher, consultant*

Emerson
Finch, Carol Anne *former secondary education educator*

Englewood
Hornblass, Bernice Miriam *educational evaluator, reading and learning disabilities specialist*

Englewood Cliffs
†Kim, Jae Taik *educator*

Fair Lawn
Wallace, Mary Monahan *elementary and secondary schools educator*

Flemington
Schneider, Kimberly Jane *special education educator*

Fort Lee
Sugarman, Alan William *educational administrator*

Franklinville
DiGregory, Nicholas A. *secondary educator, coach*

Freehold
Avella, John Thomas *principal, school administrator*

Garfield
Kobylarz, Joseph Douglas *secondary education educator*

Glassboro
Holdcraft, Janet R. *academic administrator*
James, Herman Delano *college administrator*
†Libro, Antoinette C. *university dean*

Hackensack
Cicchelli, Joseph Vincent *secondary education educator*
†Jones, Charles T. *principal*
Parisi, Cheryl Lynn *elementary school educator*

Hackettstown
†Sheninger, Arthur Wayne *principal*

Haddon Heights
Gwiazda, Stanley John *university dean*

Haddonfield
Kinee-Krohn, Patricia *special education educator*

Harrington Park
Grantuskas, Patricia Mary *elementary education educator*

Hillside
†Jean-Mary, Joseph Belladere *educator*

Hoboken
Woodward, Holly Lowell *former educator, writer*

Irvington
Steele-Hunter, Teresa Ann *elementary education educator*

Jackson
Vacchiano, Julie Catherine *special education educator*

Jersey City
Barrett, Kathleen Anne *assistant principal*
Johanson, Martha Cecilia *elementary educator*
Miller, Adele Engelbrecht *educational administrator*
Pesce, Phyllis Anne *elementary education educator*
Stencer, Mark Joseph *academic administrator, consultant*

Johnsonburg
Cioffi, Eugene Edward, III *educational administrator*

Lake Hopatcong
Ollo, Michael Anthony *educational coordinator, educator*

Lakewood
Rodgers, Dianna Sue *private school educator*
Williams, Barbara Anne *college president*

Lawrenceville
Leonard, Patricia Louise *education educator, consultant*
Luedeke, J. Barton *academic administrator*
Tharney, Leonard John *education educator, consultant*

Linden
Bedrick, Bernice *retired science educator, consultant*
Malec, Ruth Ellen *special services director*

Little Falls
Blanton, Lawton Walter *retired dean*

Livingston
Bottone, Frank Michael *secondary education educator*
DiGiovachino, John *special education educator*

Lodi
Rozman, Francene Catherine *science educator*

Long Branch
Youssef, Nadine S. *secondary school educator*

Madison
Somers, Sarah Pruyn *elementary school educator*

Magnolia
Warden, Karen Barbara *special education educator*

Mahwah
Hunt, Diana Dilger *university administrator, educator*
Scott, Robert Allyn *college president*

Manahawkin
Zalinsky, Sandra H. Orlofsky *school counselor*

Manalapan
Barratt, Donna Lee *elementary school educator*

Marlton
†Arzt, Noam H. *academic administrator, consultant*
Benjamin, Leni Bernice *elementary education educator*
Haines, Lisa Ann *secondary education educator*

Mays Landing
†May, John T. *college president*

Medford
Galbraith, Frances Lynn *educational administrator*
McGettigan, Katheryn Jones *curriculum and instruction coordinator*

Metuchen
†D'Augustine, Robert *university administrator, lawyer*
Massey, Eleanor Nelson *school librarian, media specialist*

Middlesex
McGuire, Catherine Frances *elementary education educator*

Middletown
Shields, Patricia Lynn *educational broker, consultant*

Midland Park
Dunn, Patricia Ann *school system administrator, English language educator*

Monmouth Junction
Lawton, Deborah Simmons *educational media specialist*

Montclair
Coffin, Charlsa Lee *Montessori school educator, writer, artist*

Moorestown
Weeks, Maurice Richard, Jr. *educational consultant, academic administrator*

Morris Plains
Fielding, Maralyn Joy *principal, consultant*

Morristown
†Felsenstein, Frank Arjeh *educator*
Venezia, William Thomas *school system administrator, counseling consultant*

Mountain Lakes
King, Georgeann Camarda *elementary education educator*

Neptune
Baccarella, Theresa Ann *primary school educator*

New Brunswick
Chasek, Arlene Shatsky *academic director*
Dill, Ellis Harold *university dean*
Durnin, Richard Gerry *education educator*
†Foley, Richard *academic administrator*
Garner, Charles William *educational administration educator, consultant*
Kansfield, Norman J. *seminary president*
Lawrence, Francis Leo *university president, language educator*
Nelson, Jack Lee *education educator*
†Sapirman, Nadine Kadell *university official*
Somville, Marilyn F. *dean*
Strickland, Dorothy *education educator*
Tanner, Daniel *curriculum theory educator*

New Providence
Boise, Audrey Lorraine *education educator*
Miskiewicz, Susanne Piatek *elementary education educator*

Newark
Bergen, Stanley Silvers, Jr. *retired university president, physician*
Flagg, E(loise) Alma Williams *educational administrator*
Healy, Phyllis M. Cordasco *school social worker*
Hollander, Toby Edward *education educator*
Jackson, Nancy Lee *geography educator*
†Liman, Joan Pamela *university dean*
Pfeffer, Edward Israel *educational administrator*
Thomas, Gary L. *academic administrator*

Newton
Cutshall, Janet Marie *educator*
Koerber, Joan C. *retired educator*
MacMurren, Margaret Patricia *secondary education educator, consultant*

North Bergen
Zondler, Joyce Evelyn *kindergarten educator*

North Branch
Gartlan, Philip M. *secondary school director*

North Brunswick
Kahrmann, Linda Irene *child care supervisor*

North Haledon
Onove, Daniel James *elementary educator*

Oakland
Butterfield, Charles Edward, Jr. *educational consultant*

Ocean
†Marley, Melissa *educator*

Ocean City
Gross, Kathleen Frances *parochial school mathematics educator*

Oceanport
Meibauer, Amery Filippone *special education educator*

Old Bridge
Swett, Stephen Frederick, Jr. *principal, educator*

Old Tappan
Gaffin, Joan Valerie *secondary school educator*

Orange
Monacelli, Jeffrey Paul *elementary education educator*

Parsippany
Ceurvels, Warren Steven *school system administrator*

Paterson
Sico, John Joseph *secondary education educator*

Patterson
Murez, John *music education director, educator*

Penns Grove
Graham, Albert Darlington, Jr. *educational administrator*

Pennsauken
†Robinson, Mae F. *secondary education educator*

Perth Amboy
Santiago, Theresa Marie *special education educator*

Piscataway
Colaizzi, John Louis *college dean*
Coppola, Sarah Jane *special education educator*
French, Kathleen Patricia *educational administrator*
Lee, Barbara Anne *educator, lawyer*
†Wernoski, Richard Scott *academic department administrator*
You, Aleta *education educator*

Pleasantville
London, Charlotte Isabella *secondary education educator, reading specialist*
Mento, Joseph Natale *guidance counselor*

Pomona
Colijn, Geert Jan *academic administrator, political scientist*
Comfort, Priscilla Maria *college official, human resources professional*
Farris, Vera King *college president*
†Henderson, Dee Wursten *dean*
Krogh-Jespersen, Mary-Beth *academic administrator*

Princeton
Cole, Nancy Stooksberry *educational research executive*
Fenske, Edward Charles *special education educator, consultant*
George, Robert Peter *educator, lawyer*
Gillespie, Thomas William *theological seminary administrator, religion educator*
Hitz, Frederick Porter *educator, lawyer*
Howarth, William (Louis) *education educator, writer*
Labalme, Patricia Hochschild *educational administrator*
†Leaver, Robin A. *educator*
Malkiel, Nancy Weiss *college dean, history educator*
Rosenblatt, Louise Michel *emerita educator*
Shapiro, Harold Tafler *academic administrator, economist*
Trussell, James *dean*

Randolph
Capsouras, Barbara Ellen *college official*
†Zulauf, Sander William *educator*

Red Bank
Post, Barbara Joan *elementary education educator*

Ridgewood
Riccio-Sauer, Joyce *art educator*

Robbinsville
†Buono, Frederick Joseph *secondary school educator*

Rockaway
Allen, Dorothea *secondary education educator*

Roseland
Ventola, Elizabeth Eve *educational administrator*

Roselle
Bizub, Barbara L. *elementary school educator*
Di Marco, Barbaranne Yanus *multiple handicapped special education educator*

Roselle Park
Scarpelli, Vito *adult education educator, administrator*

Saddle River
Farmer, Martha Louise *retired college administrator*

Scotch Plains
†Rebimbas, Lisa Vale *secondary foreign language educator*

Short Hills
Robbins-Wilf, Marcia *educational consultant*

Sicklerville
Vivarelli, Daniel George, Sr. *special education and learning disabilities educator, consultant*

Skillman
Rhett, Haskell Emery Smith *educator*

South Amboy
Kosmoski, Mary Lou Teresa *special education educator*
Moskal, Anthony John *former dean, professor, management and education consultant*

South Orange
†Ahr, Peter *academic administrator*
Blackburn, Terence Lee *dean*
Gruenwald, Renee *special education educator*
Peterson, Thomas R. *academic administrator*
†Sheeran, Robert T. *academic administrator*

South Plainfield
Munger, Janet Anne *education administrator*

Stone Harbor
Macconi, Mary Davis *secondary education educator*

Succasunna
Davies, Mary Elizabeth *principal*
Freimauer, Jacqueline Linda *secondary educator*
Wilkens, Christopher William *educator*

Summit
Rossey, Paul William *school superintendent, university president*
Starks, Florence Elizabeth *retired special education educator*
†Tehie, Janice Beveridge *education educator*

Swedesboro
†Vaughan, Celeste Marie-Therese *school psychologist*

Teaneck
†Hernandez, Amie Susan *academic director*
Mahoney, Maureen E. *retired secondary education educator*
Mertz, Francis James *university president*
Pischl, Adolph John *school administrator*
Smith, Susan Elizabeth *guidance director*
Walker, Lucy Doris *secondary school educator, writer*

Tenafly
Sanchez, Evelyn-Clare *secondary education educator*

Toms River
Adickes, Louis Wyckoff *educator*

Trenton
Carbone, David A. *academic administrator*
†Conrad, Andrew William *dean, writer*
Donahue, Donald Francis *secondary education educator*
Lacy, John Russell *state government administrator*
Nini, Rose Cornelia *dean*
Pruitt, George Albert *academic administrator*
Scheiring, Michael James *college official*
Smallwood, Robert Albian, Jr. *secondary education educator*

Union
Applbaum, Ronald Lee *academic administrator*
Hennings, Dorothy Grant (Mrs. George Hennings) *education educator*
Lederman, Susan Sturc *public administration educator*
Weiger, Myra Barbara *educational administrator*

Union City
Bull, Inez Stewart *special education and gifted music educator, coloratura soprano, pianist, editor, author*
Kaden, Lori Jill *school counselor*
Ortizio, Debra Louise *elementary education educator*
Sheehy, Janice Ann *elementary education educator, technology facilitator*

Upper Montclair
†Lynde, Richard A. *academic administrator*
†Narrett, Carla Marie *university administrator*

Vernon
Megna, Steve Allan *elementary education educator*
Roche, Susan Lynn *elementary education educator*

Voorhees
†Bailey, Linda A. *educator*

Washington
De Sanctis, Vincent *college president*

Wayne
†Ansari, Maboud *education educator*
Garcia, Ofelia *dean*
Goldstein, Marjorie Tunick *special education educator*
Hochman, Naomi Lipson *special education educator, consultant*
Laruccia, Stephen Dominic *university official*
Speert, Arnold *academic administrator, chemistry educator*
†Strasser, Janis Koeppel *education educator*
Younie, William John *special education educator, researcher*

West Long Branch
Lutz, Francis Charles *university dean, civil engineering educator*
Stafford, Rebecca *academic administrator, sociologist*

West New York
Shapiro, Sandra Libby Rosenberg *dean, business education educator*

West Orange
Bearg, Esther Marilyn *school counselor*

West Paterson
†DeLouise, Tia Caputi *university executive*
Marren, Maryann Fahy *primary school educator*

Westfield
Besch, Lorraine W. *special education educator*
Cummin, Sylvia Esther *secondary education educator*

Westwood
Wright, Norman Albert, Jr. *middle school educator*

Willingboro
Chagnon, Lucille Tessier *literacy and developmental learning specialist*
Jackson, Wayne Samuel *university administrator, communications educator*

Woodbridge
Chesky, Pamela Bosze *school system administrator*

Woodbury
Banks, Theresa Ann *retired elementary education educator*

Duffield-Myers, Arlene Anna *elementary education educator*
Lamey, Mary Cocove *elementary guidance counselor*

Woodstown
Tatnall, Ann Weslager *reading educator*

Yardville
Telencio, Gloria Jean *elementary education educator*

NEW MEXICO

Alamogordo
Lee, Joli Fay Eaton *elementary education educator*

Albuquerque
Anaya, Rudolfo *educator, writer*
Benson, Sharon Stovall *primary school educator*
Caplan, Edwin Harvey *university dean, accounting educator*
Cass, Barbara Fay *elementary school educator*
Donovan, Leslie Ann *honors division educator, consultant*
Drummond, Harold Dean *education educator*
Fleury, Paul Aimé *university dean, physicist*
Garcia, F. Chris *academic administrator, political science educator, public opinion researcher*
†Gordon, William C. *college administrator*
Graff, Pat Stuever *secondary education educator*
Hadley, William Melvin *college dean*
Howard, Jane Osburn *educator*
Hull, McAllister Hobart, Jr. *retired university administrator*
Jorgensen, Gary C. *elementary and secondary education educator*
Lattman, Laurence Harold *retired academic administrator*
May, Gerald William *university administrator, educator, civil engineering consultant*
Miller, Mickey Lester *retired school administrator*
Peck, Richard Earl *academic administrator, playwright, novelist*
†Stitelman, Leonard *educator*
Stuart, Cynthia Morgan *university administrator*
White, Jennifer Phelps *counselor*
Zink, Lee Berkey *academic administrator, economist, educator*

Artesia
Horner, Elaine Evelyn *secondary education educator*
Sarwar, Barbara Duce *educational consultant*

Bluewater
Marquez, Martina Zenaida *retired elementary education educator*

Carlsbad
D'Antonio, Kay Bishop *special education educator*
Gossett, Janine Lee *middle school educator*

Crownpoint
Tolino, Arlene Becenti *elementary education educator*

Farmington
Luttrell, Mary Lou *elementary educator*

Gallup
Miller, Elizabeth Heidbreder *dean instruction*

Las Cruces
Bird, Mary Francis *secondary education educator*
Boykin, William Edward *principal*
†Conroy, William B. *university administrator*
Easterling, Kathy *school system administrator*
Gale, Thomas Martin *university dean*
Sharp, George Lawrence *counselor*
Thayer, Michael J. *secondary education educator*

Lordsburg
Renteria, Donna Jo Gonzales *elementary education educator*

Los Alamos
Nekimken, Judy Marie *secondary school educator*
Ramirez, Carlos Brazil *college administrator*
Seidel, Tammy Sue *secondary education educator*

Montezuma
Geier, Philip Otto, III *college president*

Portales
†Dixon, Steven Michael *university administrator*

Rio Rancho
Meyerson, Barbara Tobias *elementary school educator*

Ruidoso
Heger, Herbert Krueger *education educator*
Stover, Carolyn Nadine *middle school educator*

Santa Fe
Agresto, John *college president*
Ferguson, Glenn Walker *consultant, writer, lecturer*
Harcourt, Robert Neff *educational administrator, journalist, genealogist*
†Morris, Sidney Helen *educational administrator*
Torres, Gilbert Vincent *elementary education educator*
Wise, Janet Ann *college official*

Shiprock
Hill, Melodie Anne *special education educator*

Silver City
French, Laurence Armand *social science educator, psychology educator*
Snedeker, John Haggner *university president*

Smith Lake
Hansen, Harold B., Jr. *principal*

Taos
Martin, Kena Sue *educator*

Vaughn
Maes, Pat Julian *secondary education educator*

NEW YORK

Afton
Rafter, Sandra Joy *special education educator*

Albany
†Baaklini, Abdo Iskandar *educator*
Branigan, Helen Marie *educational administrator*
†Clifford, George W. *college administrator*
Edmonds, Richard H. *dean*
Enemark, Richard Demeritt *educational administrator*
Fadeley, Eleanor Adeline *secondary education educator*
Faul, Karene Tarquin *art department administrator*
†Forsberg, Caroline Bernice *acadamic administrator*
Garner, Doris Traganza *educator*
Kadamus, James Alexander *educational administrator*
Long, David Russell *academic program director*
†Peinovich, Paula E. *academic administrator*
†Perone, Filomena Maria *university administrator*
Quackenbush, Roger E. *retired secondary school educator*
Robbins, Cornelius (Van Vorse) *education administration educator*
†Sánchez-Murray, Rita Zunilda *secondary Spanish language and culture educator*
Shadrick, Betty Patterson *university administrator, consultant*
Stevens, Gregory Irving *university administrator, educator*
Thornton, Maurice *retired academic administrator*
Williams, C(harles) Wayne *education educator*

Alfred
Coll, Edward Girard, Jr. *university president*
Ott, Walter Richard *academic administrator*

Alfred Station
Love, Robert Lyman *educational consulting company executive*

Amherst
Anisman, Martin Jay *academic administrator*
Hartwick, Patrick James *special education educator*
†Schultz, Susan M. *school principal*
Wiesenberg, Jacqueline Leonardi *lecturer*

Amityville
Gicola, Paul *middle school science educator, administrator*

Andover
Witherow, Catherine Saslawsky *secondary school educator*

Annandale On Hudson
Botstein, Leon *college president, music historian, conductor*

Attica
Taylor, Karen Marie *education educator*

Auburn
†Bragger, Stacey Eileen *elementary education educator*
Eldred, Thomas Gilbert *secondary education educator, historian*
†Ohl, Thomas Anthony *school counselor*

Aurora
Leybold-Taylor, Karla Jolene *college official*

Averill Park
Costello, Amelia Fusco *educator*

Baldwinsville
Kline, Carole June *special education educator*

Barrytown
Shimmyo, Theodore Tadaaki *seminary president*

Batavia
Steiner, Stuart *college president*

Bay Shore
Pinsker, Tillene Giller *special education administrator*

Bayside
Yin, Henry Chih-Peng *educator*

Beacon
Stokes, Catherine Ann *elementary education educator*

Bedford
Kluge, Steve *secondary education educator*

Bellmore
Harris, Ira Stephen *secondary education educator, administrator*

Bellport
†Baxter, Louise T. *educational administrator*

Binghamton
Beach, Beth *elementary educator*
Coffey, Margaret Tobin *education educator, county official*
Dantini, Julie Ann *educational administrator, director, counselor*
DeFleur, Lois B. *university president, sociology educator*
Feisel, Lyle Dean *university dean, electrical engineering educator*
†Swain, Mary Ann Price *university official*

Blasdell
Hope, Christopher Lawrence *middle school educator*

Bohemia
Ortiz, Germaine Laura De Feo *secondary education educator, counselor*

Brentwood
Manning, Randolph H. *academic administrator*

Brewster
Vichiola, Christopher Michael *educator, writer*

Briarwood
Takacs, Michael Joseph *educator*

Bridgehampton
Edwards, John W. *school superintendent*
McMenamin, Joan Stitt *headmistress*

Bridgeport
Sheldon, Thomas Donald *educational organization administrator*

Brockport
Campbell, Jill Frost *university official*
Gemmett, Robert James *university dean, English language educator*
Ludwig, Kurt James *residence director*

Bronx
Damico, Debra Lynn *college official, English and French educator*
Fernandez, Ricardo R. *university administrator*
George, Deinabo Dabibi *writer, computer specialist, educator*
Hadaller, David Lawrence *dean*
Hilliard, John Mauk *university official*
Kravath, Alan Wolfe *education evaluator*
Mooney, Mary Ann *early childhood educator*
†Mottus, Jane E. *college administrator, historian*
Nathanson, Melvyn Bernard *university provost, mathematician*
Payson, Martin Saul *secondary school educator, mathematician*
Posner, Bruce Frederick *independent school administrator, consultant*
Reichert, Marlene Joy *secondary school educator, writer*
Riba, Netta Eileen *secondary school educator*
Scanlan, Thomas Joseph *college president, educator*
†Schroth, Raymond Augustine *university official, journalism educator, priest*
Wille, Rosanne Louise *higher education administrator*

Bronxville
Mau, Dwayne Holger *minister*
Myers, Michele Tolela *college president*

Brooklyn
Alfano, Edward Charles, Jr. *elementary education educator*
Arcuri, Leonard Philip *elementary education educator*
Bakakos, Diana *middle school educator*
Birenbaum, William M. *former university president*
†Bofay, Fred *university administrator*
Bugliarello, George *university chancellor*
†Chowdhury, Mohammed Shamsul *educator*
Cohen, Harris Saul *dean*
Curry, David *guidance staff developer*
†Flateau, John *academic administrator*
Goldstein, Brenda Iris *retired elementary school educator*
Gura, Timothy James *speech educator*
Harris, James Arthur, Sr. *school system administrator, economist, consultant*
Hill, Elizabeth Anne *academic administrator, lawyer*
Kurz, Irwin *principal*
Largo, Gerald Andrew *academic adminstrator*
Lattin, Vernon Eugene *academic administrator*
O'Connor, Sister George Aquin (Margaret M. O'Connor) *college president, sociology educator*
†Palm, Marion *educator*
Parker, Barbara L. *educator*
Poloyger, Iran *retired principal*
†Rosario-Olmedo, Carmen Gloria *principal*
Soldo, John J. *educator*
Thompson, William C., Jr. *school system administrator*
Wapner, Myrna *retired principal*
Williams, Emma Louise *elementary education educator*
Williams, Vida Veronica *guidance counselor*
Williams, William Magavern *headmaster*
Wolfe, Ethyle Renee (Mrs. Coleman Hamilton Benedict) *college administrator*
†Zibrin, Michael *academic administrator*

Buffalo
Alderdice, Douglas Alan *secondary education educator*
Anderson, Wayne Keith *dean*
Ansar, Ahmad *career counselor*
Biggs, Edmund Logan *college administrator*
†Choi, Namkee Gang *educator*
Dewey, Henry S., Jr. *elementary education educator*
Greiner, William Robert *university administrator, educator, lawyer*
Herdlein, Richard Joseph, III *college official and dean, educator*
Hrycik, Pauline Emily *educator*
Krucenski, Leonard Joseph *secondary education educator*
Monaco-Hannon, Kelli Ann *secondary school educator*
†Moore, Muriel A. *college president*
†Muir, Geraldine Marie *student affairs administrator*
Novak, Mary Theresa *parochial school educator*
Oak, H(elen) Lorraine *academic administrator, geography educator*
Schmidli, Keith William *vocational education administrator, educator, researcher*
Shaner, Bronwyn Marian *elementary education educator*
Shick, Richard Arlon *academic dean*
Thorpe, John Alden *academic administrator, mathematician*
Triggle, David John *university dean, consultant*
Vitagliano, Kathleen Alyce Fuller *secondary education educator*
Wilbur, Barbara Marie *elementary education educator*

Camillus
Davis, Lynn Harry *secondary education educator*

Canandaigua
Malinowski, Patricia A. *community college educator*
Williams, Carolyn Woodworth *retired elementary education educator, consultant*

Canastota
Lawson, Eric Wilfred, Sr. *educator*

Carthage
Rishel, Kenn Charles *school superintendent*

Cassadaga
†Sack, Marianne Sorensen *career educator, counselor*

Castleton On Hudson
Lanford, Oscar Erasmus, Jr. *retired university vice chancellor*

Catskill
Tompkins, Sharon Lee *primary education educator*
Wolfe, Geraldine *administrator*

Cedarhurst
Seyfert, Wayne George *secondary education educator, anatomy educator*
Van Raalte, Polly Ann *reading and writing specialist, photojournalist*

Center Moriches
Cullen, Valerie Adelia *secondary education educator*

Centereach
Cutrone, Dee T. *retired elementary education educator*

Central Islip
Griffith, Philip Arthur *elementary school educator*

Cicero
Mirucki, Maureen Ann *academic administrator*

Circleville
Moore, Virginia Lee Smith *elementary education educator*

Clarence
Bish, L. Ann *retired secondary education educator*

Clifton Park
†Golden, David M. *educator*
Murphy, Mary Patricia *elementary education educator*

Clinton
Fuller, Ruthann *principal*
Rose, Alan Arthur *university administrator*
Tobin, Eugene Marc *academic administrator*

Cohoes
Tabner, Mary Frances *secondary school educator*

Combria Heights
Davis-Jerome, Eileen George *principal*

Commack
Gittman, Elizabeth *educator*

Congers
Nelson, Marguerite Hansen *special education educator*

Corinth
Winslow, Norma Mae *elementary education educator*

Cortland
†Alsen, Eberhard *educator*

Crown Point
Dajany, Innam *academic administrator*

Cutchogue
Aldcroft, George Edward *guidance counselor*

Davidson
†LeFauve, Linda Marie *college administrator*

Delmar
Quackenbush, Cathy Elizabeth *secondary school educator*

Dix Hills
Braun, Ludwig *educational technology consultant*

Douglaston
†Hornick, Susan Florence *secondary education educator, fine arts educator*

Durham
Dearing, David Richard *secondary education educator*

East Aurora
Birch, David William *college official*
Spahn, Mary Attea *retired educator*
Weidemann, Julia Clark *principal, educator*
Woodard, Carol Jane *educational consultant*

East Islip
Orsomarso, Don Frank *school system administrator*
Somerville, Daphine Holmes *elementary education educator*

East Meadow
Beyer, Norma Warren *secondary education educator*

East Setauket
Barcel, Ellen Nora *secondary school educator, free-lance writer, editor*

Elmhurst
†Gregg-Mullings, Linda *educator*
Lester, Lance Gary *education educator, researcher*
Maurer-Buterakos, Kathleen Ann *educational administrator, supervisor*

Elmira
Meier, Thomas Keith *college president, English educator*

Fairport
Holtzclaw, Diane Smith *elementary school educator*

PROFESSIONAL INDEX 5891 EDUCATION

Lavoie, Dennis James *secondary education educator*
Pearles, Linda Terry *secondary education educator*
Wiener, David L. *secondary education educator*

Far Rockaway
†Mithcell, Lillian Adassa *educator*

Farmingdale
Cipriani, Frank Anthony *college president*

Farmingville
Di Marco, Anthony Sabatino *retired educational administrator*

Fayetteville
Hiemstra, Roger *adult education educator, writer, networker*

Floral Park
Scricca, Diane Bernadette *principal*

Flushing
Buell, Frederick Henderson *educator*
Capra, Linda Ann *elementary education educator*
Erickson, Raymond *academic dean, music historian, musician*
Erwin, Elizabeth Joy *early childhood and special education specialist*
Kobliner, Richard *secondary school educator*
Ritchin, Barbara Sue *educational administrator, consultant*
Roberts, Kathleen Joy Doty *school administrator, educator*
Uter, Carmenlita *secondary school educator, genealogist*

Forest Hills
Kane, Sydell *elementary school principal*

Fort Edward
Horn, Thomas Joseph, Jr. *educator*

Frankfort
Conigilaro, Phyllis Ann *retired elementary education educator*

Fredonia
Collingwood, Tracy Lynn *academic advisor, career counselor*
Mac Vittie, Robert William *retired college administrator*
Sedota, Gladys Elizabeth *secondary education educator*

Freeport
Martorana, Barbara Joan *secondary education educator*

Gainesville
MacWilliams, Debra Lynne *primary reading specialist, consultant*

Garden City
†Anziano, Gale Mary *guidance counselor, social worker*
Atkins, William Allen *academic administrator*
†Fanelli, Sean A. *college president*
Okulski, John Allen *principal*
Webb, Igor Michael *academic administrator*

Gardiner
Schneider, Evelyn Jean *educational consultant, English educator*

Geneva
Hersh, Richard H. *academic administrator*
Woodard, Richard Charles *college administrator*

Glen Cove
Chun, Arlene Donnelly *special education educator*

Glen Head
Boyrer, Elaine M. *principal*
Swift, Ronni *special education educator*

Gloversville
†Casey, Kathleen Margaret *secondary education educator*

Grand Island
Beach, Sandra Marie Yudichak *secondary education educator*
Muck, Ruth Evelyn Slacer (Mrs. Gordon E. Muck) *education educator*

Granville
†Stoddard, Andrea Louise *special education educator, small business owner*

Great Neck
†Epstein, Marc A. *school system administrator*
Harris, Marilyn *retired academic administrator*
Hecht, Marie Bergenfeld *retired educator, author*

Greenvale
Cook, Edward Joseph *college president*
Steinberg, David Joel *academic administrator, historian, educator*
Westermann-Cicio, Mary Louise *academic administrator, library studies educator*

Greenville
Overbaugh, Maryanne W. *elementary educator*

Greenwich
†Targan, Barry *educator*

Greenwood
Rollins, June Elizabeth *elementary education educator*

Hamburg
Witt, Dennis Ruppert *secondary school mathematics educator*

Hamilton
Jones, Howard Langworthy *retired educational administrator, consultant*

†Wilhelm, Simi Ruth *college administrator*

Harrison
McElwaine, Theresa Weedy *academic administrator, artist*
Paulli, Carla Nadene *secondary education educator*

Hartsdale
Aker, Susan K. *elementary education educator*
Wallace, Arthur, Jr. *retired college dean*

Hempstead
Berliner, Herman Albert *university provost and dean, economics educator*
Bowe, Frank G. *educator*
†Carty, Heidi Marlene *educator, researcher*
Conway-Gervais, Kathleen Marie *reading specialist, educational consultant*
Haynes, Ulric St. Clair, Jr. *university dean*
Shuart, James Martin *academic administrator*
Yndigoyen, Eloy *guidance counselor*

Highland
Kurzdorfer, Peter John *chess educator, writer*

Highland Mills
Gazzaniga, Antonette J. *secondary school educator*

Hilton
Ratigan, Hugh Lewis *middle school and elementary school educator*

Holbrook
Senholzi, Gregory Bruce *secondary school educator*

Hopewell Junction
Cznarty, Donna Mae *secondary education educator*

Houghton
Chamberlain, Daniel Robert *college president*
Luckey, Robert Reuel Raphael *retired academic administrator*

Howard Beach
Iorio, John Emil *retired education educator*
Livingston, Barbara *special education educator*

Hudson
Vile, Sandra Jane *leadership training educator*

Huntington
D'Addario, Alice Marie *school administrator*
Levinthal, Beth Ellen (Kuby Levinthal) *educator*

Huntington Station
Boxwill, Helen Ann *primary and secondary education educator*

Hurley
Opdahl, Viola Elizabeth *secondary education educator*

Hyde Park
Baker, Jennifer L. *secondary education educator*
Nihoff, John J. *vocational educator, business owner*

Irvington
Harris, Maria Loscutoff *special education educator, consultant*

Ithaca
Ben Daniel, David Jacob *entrepreneurship educator, consultant*
Firebaugh, Francille Maloch *university official*
Halpern, Bruce Peter *academic administrator, researcher, educator*
Hopcroft, John Edward *dean, computer science educator*
†Johnson, Stephen Philip *educational administrator*
McCarroll, Earl *educator, director*
Nesheim, Malden C. *academic administrator, nutrition educator*
†Randel, Don M. *academic administrator*
Rawlings, Hunter Ripley, III *university president*
Rhodes, Frank Harold Trevor *university president emeritus, geologist*
Sass, Stephen Louis *education educator*
†Schettino, Leslie A. *program director*
Scott, Norman Roy *academic administrator, agricultural engineering educator*
Streett, William Bernard *retired university dean, engineering educator*
†Swieringa, Robert Jay *dean, accountant, educator*
Weinstein, Leonard Harlan *institute program director, educator*
Whalen, James Joseph *college president emeritus*

Jamaica
Bartilucci, Andrew Joseph *university administrator*
Ekbatani, Glayol *educator, program director, author*
Faust, Naomi Flowe *education educator, poet*
Harmon, W. David *academic administrator*
Harrington, Donald James *university president*
Mangru, Basdeo *secondary education educator*
Mullen, Frank Albert *former university official, clergyman*
Sciame, Joseph *university administrator*

Jamestown
Benke, Paul Arthur *college president*
Martin, Margaret Gately *elementary education educator*
Seguin, David Gerard *community college official*

Jericho
Mandery, Mathew M. *principal*

Johnstown
†Bell, Priscilla J. *academic administrator*

Katonah
†Ferrarone, Teresa Lane *educational consultant*

Kendall
Rak, Linda Marie *elementary education educator, consultant*

Kew Gardens
Marks, Lillian Shapiro *secretarial studies educator, author*

Kings Point
Mazek, Warren F(elix) *academic administrator, economics educator*

Kingston
Bruck, Arlene Lorraine *secondary education educator*
Stellar, Arthur Wayne *educational administrator*

Krumville
†Nagi, Catherine Raseh *retired educational administrator, financial planner*

Lake Placid
Reiss, Paul Jacob *college president*

Lake Ronkonkoma
Spahr, Clinton S., Jr. *elementary education educator*

Lancaster
Kappan, Sandra Jean *elementary education educator*

Latham
McGoldrick, William Patrick *educational consultant*

Le Roy
Ruekberg, David Remington *secondary English educator*

Levittown
Auteri, Rose Mary Patti *school system administrator*
Wieland, Thomas J. *headmaster*

Liberty
†Luckner-Smassanow, Lucille *school system administrator*

Lido Beach
†Hoyt, James John *educator*

Liverpool
Miller, Eileen Renee *counselor*
Munoz, Charlotte Marie *English educator*
Trombley, Edward Francis, III *educational administrator*
Williams, John Alan *secondary education educator, coach*

Lockport
Godshall, Barbara Marie *educational administrator*

Locust Valley
†Mathews, Walter Michael *university administrator*

Long Beach
Ostroy, Joseph *education educator*

Long Eddy
Van Swol, Noel Warren *secondary education educator and administrator*

Long Island City
Bowen, Raymond Cobb *academic administrator*
†Matsushita, Marimi *educator, mathematician*

Loudonville
†Mackin, Kevin Eugene *academic administrator, clergyman*
Toal, James Francis *academic administrator*

Lowville
Daley, Laurana Bush *elementary education educator*

Lyons
Olson, Daniel Anthony *secondary education educator*

Malone
Premo, Angela Mary *special education educator*

Manhasset
Sessler, Jane Virginia *secondary school educator*

Marcellus
DeForge, Katherine Ann *secondary education educator*

Marlboro
Pollak, Joel Michael *school superintendent*

Massena
Perez, Loretta Ann Bronchetti *secondary education educator, small business owner*
Vazquez, Sue Ellen *elementary education educator*

Mastic Beach
Casciano, Paul *school system administrator*
Pagano, Alicia I. *education educator*

Medford
Haig, Monica Elaine Nachajski *special education educator*

Merrick
Garfinkel, Lawrence Saul *academic administrator, educator, television producer*

Middle Village
Thoering, Robert Charles *elementary education educator*

Middleport
Massaro, Joseph James *secondary school educator*

Middletown
Teabo-Sandoe, Glenda Patterson *elementary education educator*

Montrose
Matthias, George Frank *educator*

Mount Sinai
†Bricka, Evelyn Chantel *educator*

Mount Vernon
Walters, Carolyn Maria *secondary school educator*

Nanuet
Magner, Martha Mary *education educator, consultant*
Miney, Maureen Elizabeth *middle school educator*
Rosenberg, Janice Carol Berman *principal, librarian, mentor*

Nesconset
Goldstein, Joyce *special education educator*

New City
Mellon, Joan Ann *educator*

New Paltz
Emanuel-Smith, Robin Lesley *special education educator*
Whittington-Couse, Maryellen Frances *education administrator*

New Rochelle
Capasso, Frank Louis *secondary school educator*
Donahue, Richard James *secondary school educator*
Gallagher, John Francis *education educator*
Kelly, Sister Dorothy Ann *college chancellor*
†Nodiff, David Marc *elementary education educator*
Shrage, Laurette *special education educator*
Wolotsky, Hyman *retired college dean*

New York
Alfano, Michael Charles *dental school dean*
Begley, Evelyn Maria *special education educator*
†Berkowitz, Alan Steven *educator, poet*
Borkon, Doris *educational administrator, entrepreneur*
Bouton, Marshall Melvin *academic administrator*
Brademas, John *retired university president, former congressman*
Brenner, Egon *university official, education consultant*
Budig, Gene Arthur *former chancellor, professional sports executive*
Burton, John Campbell *university dean, educator, consultant*
Campbell, Mary Schmidt *dean art school*
Caputo, David Armand *university president, political scientist educator*
Carey, James William *university dean, educator, researcher*
Cargill, Ursula Bardot *university official*
Charendoff, Mark Stuart *educator*
Chelstrom, Marilyn Ann *political education consultant*
Claster, Jill Nadell *university administrator, history educator*
Cochran, Raymond Martin *university financial administrator*
Cohen, Saul Bernard *former college president, geographer*
Consagra, Sophie Chandler *academy administrator*
Crocetti, Gino *elementary and secondary education educator*
†Crumpacker, Margery Ann *educator*
Daly, George Garman *college dean, educator*
Dimino, Sylvia Theresa *elementary and secondary educator*
Dobrinsky, Herbert Colman *university administrator*
Durkin, Dorothy Angela *university official*
Durst, Carol Goldsmith *educator*
Eckel, Thomas Warne *secondary education educator, musician*
†Elmarsafy, Ziad Magdy *educator*
Elster, Samuel Kase *college dean, medical educator, physician*
†Embree, Catherine M. *university official*
†Essandoh, Hilda Brathwaite *kindergarten educator*
Ewers, Patricia O'Donnell *university administrator*
Fabian, Larry Louis *university administrator*
Feldberg, Meyer *university dean*
†Fisher, Michael Charles *school administrator*
Gartner, Alan P. *university official, author*
Gatto, John Taylor *educational consultant, writer*
†Gibson, Arlene Joy *headmaster*
Gillespie, John Thomas *university administrator*
Goldsmith, Cathy Ellen *special education educator*
†Gotian, Ruth *educational program administrator*
Gourgey, Karen Luxton *special education educator*
Grabois, Neil Robert *association executive, former college president*
Gregorian, Vartan *academic administrator*
Haffner, Alden Norman *university official*
Hartstein, Sam *educational administrator*
†Haythe, Pamela Fleming *secondary education educator*
Hejduk, John Quentin *dean, architect*
†Hoehn, Natasha Diane *elementary education educator*
Hoffner, Marilyn *university administrator*
Horowitz, Frances Degen *academic administrator, psychology educator*
Hoxie, Ralph Gordon *educational administrator, author*
†Huppauf, Bernd R. *educator*
Ilchman, Warren Frederick *university administrator, political science educator*
Iselin, John Jay *university president*
Jelinek, Vera *university director*
Jennings, Charles Robert *educator*
Jeynes, Mary Kay *college dean*
Kimmich, Christoph Martin *academic administrator, educator*
Klopf, Gordon John *educational consultant, former college dean*
Konner, Joan Weiner *university administrator, educator, publisher, broadcasting executive, television producer*
Kopp, Wendy *teaching program administrator*
Koshi, Annie K. *education educator, researcher*
Lamm, Norman *academic administrator, rabbi*
Lange, Phil C. *retired education educator*
Lanquetot, Roxanne *special education educator, writer*
Leiman, Joan Maisel *university administrator*
Levine, Arthur Elliott *academic administrator, educator*
Levine, Naomi Bronheim *university administrator*
†Levitz, Paul H. *educator*
Lloyd, Jean *early childhood educator, television producer*

Lynch, Gerald Weldon *academic administrator, psychologist*
Macchiarola, Frank Joseph *academic administrator*
Marcuse, Adrian Gregory *academic administrator*
Marshall, Geoffrey *retired university official*
Maubert, Jacques Claude *headmaster*
McPherson, Mary Patterson *academic administrator*
Mesrop, Alida Yolande *academic administrator*
Mikhail, Mona N. *education educator*
Mitterand, Henri C. *education educator, writer*
†Moore, Frank Randolph *university official*
Moses, Yolanda T. *academic administrator*
Nelson, Iris Dorothy *retired guidance and rehabilitation counselor*
Nentwich, Michael Andreas Erhart *educator, consultant*
Noddings, Nel *education educator, writer*
†O'Connell, Jane B. *school administrator*
O'Hare, Joseph Aloysius *academic administrator, priest*
Oliva, Lawrence Jay *academic administrator, history educator*
Oreskes, Susan *private school educator*
Palmeri, Marlaina *principal*
Paquette, Brian Christopher *university administrator, dean*
Patriarca, Silvana *education educator*
Pigott, Irina Vsevolodovna *educational administrator*
Polisi, Joseph W(illiam) *academic administrator*
Pratt, Richardson, Jr. *retired college president*
Pulanco, Tonya Beth *special education educator*
Reutter, Eberhard Edmund, Jr. *education and law educator*
Rhodes, David J. *academic administrator*
Richardson, Richard Colby, Jr. *leadership and policy studies educator, researcher*
Robinson, Joyce McPeake *administrator*
Rosenthal, Albert Joseph *university dean, law educator, lawyer*
†Rossbach, Janet Bache *college administrator*
Rowe, John Wallis *university administrator, medical executive*
Rowland, Esther E(delman) *college dean, retired*
Rubenstein, Arthur Harold *medical school official and dean, physician*
Rubino, Victor Joseph *academic administrator, lawyer*
Rumschitzki, David Sheldon *chemical engineering educator*
Rupp, George Erik *academic administrator*
Schur, Joan Brodsky *secondary education educator, curriculum developer*
Seidenberg, Rita Nagler *education educator*
Seitz, Frederick *former university administrator*
Selby, Cecily Cannan *dean, educator, scientist*
Shea, Dion Warren Joseph *university official, fund raiser*
Silverman, Martin Morris Bernard *secondary education educator*
Snitow, Virginia Levitt *educator*
Soros, Susan Weber *educational administrator*
Sussman, George David *academic administrator*
Tapley, Donald Fraser *university official, physician, educator*
Townsend-Butterworth, Diana Barnard *educational consultant, author*
Tschumi, Bernard *dean*
Vernon, Arthur *educational administrator*
Walton, R. Keith *academic administrator, lawyer*
Walzer, Judith Borodovko *academic administrator, educator*
Waren, Stanley Arnold *university administrator, theatre and arts center administrator, director*
Weinstein, Sidney *university program director*
Wilbur, Melissa Ellen *educator*
Wilson, Basil *academic administrator*
†Witherspoon, Roger *academic administrator*
Wylie, James Malcolm *educator*
Yetman, Leith Eleanor *academic administrator*

Newburgh
Geiser, William Francis *education educator*
Joyce, Mary Ann *principal*
Saturnelli, Annette Miele *school system administrator*

Niagara University
O'Leary, Daniel Francis *university dean*

Nicksville
†Moshoyannis, Phillip Demetri Alexander *educator*

North Babylon
Löwenborg-Coyne, Kim *school administrator, musician*

Northport
Diamond, Stuart *educator, lawyer, business executive, consultant*

Norwich
†Nassar, Elizabeth Fox *secondary educator*

Nyack
†Johnson, Judith Misner *educator*
Sandmeier, Harriet Virginia Heit *educational administrator*

Oakdale
Meskill, Victor P. *college president, educator*

Old Westbury
Schure, Matthew *college president*
van Wie, Paul David *secondary school educator, historian, educator*

Oneida
Moller, Jacqueline Louise *elementary education educator*

Oneonta
Detweiler, Richard Allen *college president, psychology educator*
Donovan, Alan Barton *college president*
Gotsch, Susan D. *academic administrator, dean*
Matthews, Harry Bradshaw *dean*

Orangeburg
Hennessy, James Ernest *academic administrator, telecommunications executive, retired*

Orchard Park
Holmes, Kathleen Marie *secondary education educator*

Ossining
†Monroe, Stephen A. *educational administrator, financial consultant*
†Perlman, John Niels *educator, poet*
Pungello, Johanna Margaret *elementary education educator*
Rothman, Barbara Schaeffer *speciali education educator*

Oswego
Moody, Florence Elizabeth *education educator, retired college dean*
Presley, John Woodrow *academic administrator*

Oyster Bay
†Gambone, Kenneth F. *secondary education educator, English educator*

Patchogue
Fogarty, James Vincent, Jr. *special education administrator, educator*
Orlowski, Karel Ann *elementary school educator*
Watkins, Linda Theresa *educational researcher*

Pawling
†Barbaro, Salvatore *educator*
†Thomas, Cheryl Ann *educational administrator*

Penfield
†O'Kane, John Joseph *special education educator, administrator*

Penn Yan
Williams, Renee Arlene *secondary education educator*

Piermont
Dusanenko, Theodore Robert *retired educator, county official*

Pine Plains
†Finley, Madison K. *dean*

Pittsford
Cupini, Mariellen Louise *school district administrator*

Plattsburgh
Worthington, Janet Evans *academic director, English language educator*

Pleasantville
Antonecchia, Donald A. *principal*

Port Chester
Penney, Linda Helen *music educator*

Port Jefferson
Lipitz, Elaine Kappel *secondary education fine arts educator*

Port Washington
Futter, Joan Babette *former school librarian*
Williams, George Leo *retired secondary education educator*

Potsdam
Ha, Andrew Kwangho *education educator*
†Henry, Richard Michael *educator*
Rudiger, Lance Wade *secondary school educator*
Sarnoff, Joseph C. *academic administrator*
Stoltie, James Merle *academic administrator*
Stone, Irving Thomas *educator*

Poughkeepsie
Brakas, Nora Jachym *education educator*
†Currie, Stephen *educator, writer*
Davis, Mary Lou *secondary education educator*
Fergusson, Frances Daly *college president, educator*
Filor, Anna May *secondary education educator*
†Joyce, Michael *educator*
†Lewis, Richard Laurence *academic administrator, digital artist*
Opdycke, Leonard Emerson *retired secondary education educator, publisher*

Purchase
Lacy, Bill *college president, architect*

Ransomville
Mayer, George Merton *retired elementary education educator*

Rensselaer
Kennedy, Linda Louise *secondary education educator*

Rexford
Schmitt, Roland Walter *retired academic administrator*

Richmond Hill
†Sharif, Choudhry M. *secondary education educator*

Riverdale
Hauser, Bernice Worman *inter-campus director*
Lerner, Laurence M. *college administrator*
†Llena, Rey Lapiceros *secondary education educator, consultant*

Rochester
Balch, Glenn McClain, Jr. *academic administrator, minister, author*
Bernstein, Paul *retired academic dean*
Campbell, Alma Jacqueline Porter *elementary education educator*
Cantore Green, Jean *secondary education educator*
Cohen, Jules *physician, educator, former academic dean*
†Costanza, Marie *secondary education educator*
Ernsthausen, Carol Knasel *educator*
†Farley, Susan Strack *elementary educator*
†Hacker, Robert Gordon *educator, consultant*
Hurt, Davina Theresa *educator*
Jackson, Thomas Humphrey *university president*

Joynt, Robert James *academic administrator*
Kirschenbaum, Howard *educator*
†Mattice, David Shane *student affairs administrator*
†McKenzie, Stanley Don *academic administrator, English educator*
Metzler, Ruth Horton *genealogical educator*
Munson, Harold Lewis *education educator*
Plosser, Charles Irving *university dean, economics educator*
Serrano, Rose Arlene *vice principal*
†Shuffelton, Frank C. *educator*
Simone, Albert Joseph *academic administrator*
Stone, Gail Ann *elementary and secondary education educator*
Thompson, Brian John *university administrator, optics educator*
Yarnall, Susanne Lusink *elementary school educator*

Rockville Centre
Becker, Nettie *preschool administrator*

Ronkonkoma
Heiserer, Albert, Jr. *automotive educator, small business owner*

Roslyn
Kutscher, Eugene Bernard *educational administrator*
Stracher, Dorothy Altman *education educator, consultant*

Roslyn Heights
Jordan, Patricia James *secondary education educator*

Saint Bonaventure
Doyle, Mathias Francis *university president, political scientist, educator*

Sanborn
Schmidt-Bova, Carolyn Marie *vocational school administrator, consultant*
†Stoll, Marsal P. *academic administrator*

Sands Point
Cullinan, Bernice E(llinger) *education educator*

Saranac Lake
Jakobe, Virginia Ellis *retired educator*
Szwed, Beryl J. *school system administrator, mathematics educator*

Saratoga Springs
Ratzer, Mary Boyd *secondary education educator, librarian*

Scarsdale
Collins, Ann N. *secondary school educator*
Del Duca, Rita *educator*
Griffiths, Daniel Edward *dean emeritus*
Naughton, Ann Elsie *educator*

Schenectady
Bond, Michele Denise *early childhood educator*
Helmar-Salasoo, Ester Anette *literacy educator, researcher*
Hull, Roger Harold *college president*
Wallner, Ludwig John *principal*

Schoharie
Stiver, Patricia Abare *elementary education educator*

Seaford
Moore, Sister Mary Francis *parochial school educator*

Sidney
Haller, Irma Tognola *secondary education educator*

Southampton
Ferrara-Sherry, Donna Layne *education educator*

Springville
Loockerman, William Delmer *educational administrator*

Staten Island
†Affron, Mirella Jona *academic administrator*
Berman, Barbara *educational consultant*
Brady, Christine Ellen *education coordinator*
Reing, Alvin Barry *special education educator, psychologist*
Smith, Norman Raymond *college president*
Springer, Marlene *university administrator, educator*

Stony Brook
Cochran, James Kirk *dean, oceanographer, geochemist, educator*
Geyer, Dennis Lynn *university administrator and registrar*
Kenny, Shirley Strum *university administrator*
†Richmond, Rollin C. *academic administrator*
Shamash, Yacov *dean, electrical engineering educator*

Suffern
Harvuot, Cathleen Mary *elementary education educator, principal*

Syosset
†Collins, James Michael *principal*
Nydick, David *school superintendent*

Syracuse
Charters, Alexander Nathaniel *retired adult education educator*
Geisinger, Kurt Francis *university administrator, psychometrician*
Hollis, Susan Tower *college dean*
Krathwohl, David Reading *education educator emeritus*
†Manke, Jeffrey Gerard *college administrator*
Rubin, David M. *dean, educator*
Shaw, Kenneth Alan *university president*
Waite, Peter Arthur *literacy educator, educational consultant*
Ware, Bennie *university administrator*
Weiss, Volker *university administrator, educator*
Whaley, Ross Samuel *academic administrator*

Thendara
Voce, Joan A. Cifonelli *retired elementary school educator*

Troy
Kahl, William Frederick *retired college president*
McAllister, Edward William Charles *educator*
Romond, James *principal*
Wait, Samuel Charles, Jr. *academic administrator, educator*
Wilson, Jack Martin *dean, scientific association executive, physics educator*

Tuxedo Park
Groskin, Sheila Marie Lessen *primary school educator*

Utica
Boyle, William Leo, Jr. *educational consultant, retired college president*

Valhalla
†Hankin, Joseph Nathan *college president*

Victor
†Schmidt, Douglas Karl *elementary education educator*

Waccabuc
Reid, Mary Louise *educational consultant*

Walden
Konior, Jeannette Mary *elementary school educator*

Wallkill
Leopold, Richard William *middle school educator*

Wantagh
Marcatante, John Joseph *educational administrator*

Wappingers Falls
Wolfson, Ann Helene *secondary school educator*

Watertown
Smith, Marcia Jeanne *secondary school educator*

Webster
Herman, Richard Charles *educator*

Wellsville
Tezak, Edward George *dean*

West Leyden
Kornatowski, Susan Carol *elementary education educator*

West Sand Lake
Rogers, James Edwin *secondary school educator, retired*

White Plains
Barrow, Marie Antonette *elementary school educator*
Boeringer, Greta *librarian*
†Greenup, Marion Teresa *not-for-profit health organization administrator*
Mattison, Donald Roger *dean, physician, educator, military officer*
Peck, Alexander Norman *elementary education educator*
Ryan, Joseph F. *educator*
Szolnoki, John Frank *special education educator, administrator*
Taub, Larry Steven *education administrator*

Whitesboro
†Blake, Edward Stephens *secondary education educator*

Whitestone
Dressler, Brenda Joyce *health educator, consultant, book and film reviewer*
Lodico, Cheryl Madeline *secondary education educator*

Williamson
Ross, Kathleen Marie Amato *secondary school educator*

Windsor
Decker, Susan Carol *elementary education educator*

Yonkers
Liggio, Jean Vincenza *adult education educator, artist*
Weston, Francine Evans *secondary education educator*

Yorktown Heights
Bennett, Charles H. *director programs*
†Delmoro, Ronald Anthony *elementary school principal*

NORTH CAROLINA

Asheboro
Talley, Doris Lanier *instructional technology specialist*

Asheville
Boyce, Emily Stewart *retired library and information science educator*
Carver, M. Kyle *secondary education educator*
Pickard, Carolyn Rogers *secondary school educator*
Reed, Patsy Bostick *academic administrator*
†Ulrey, Lee Williams *educator*

Balsam
†Merritt, Mark Francis *educator*

Banner Elk
Thomas, John Edwin *retired academic administrator*

Battleboro
Hardy, Linda Lea Sterlock *media specialist*

Boiling Springs
White, Martin Christopher *academic administrator*

Bolivia
Johnson, Melba Edwards *secondary education educator*

Boone
Borkowski, Francis Thomas *university administrator*
Duke, Charles Richard *academic dean*
Durham, Harvey Ralph *academic administrator*
Greene, Melanie Anita Ward *education educator*
Land, Ming Huey *college dean*
Pollard, William Barlow, III *university educator*
Robinson, Linda *college program administrator*
Woollcombe, Graham Douglas *dean*

Buies Creek
Wiggins, Norman Adrian *university administrator, legal educator*

Cary
Bat-haee, Mohammad Ali *educational administrator, consultant*
Summers, Suzanne Frances Hememway *elementary education educator*

Chapel Hill
Biles, Cindy Clemente *academic administrator*
Broad, Margaret (Molly) Corbett *university executive*
Campbell, B(obby) Jack *university official*
Carboni, Lisa Wilson *education educator*
Carroll, Roy *academic administrator*
Cole, Richard Ray *university dean*
Cunningham, James William *literacy education educator, researcher*
Edwards, Richard LeRoy *academic dean, social work educator, non-profit management consultant*
Fordham, Christopher Columbus, III *university dean and chancellor, medical educator*
Freund, Cynthia M. *dean, nursing educator*
Friday, William Clyde *university president emeritus*
Ganley, Oswald Harold *university official*
Hill, Deborah Ann *special education educator*
Hooker, Michael Kenneth *university chancellor*
†Howes, Jonathan B. *planning and public policy educator*
Melchert, Harold Craig *adult education educator*
Murphy, James Lee *college dean, economics educator*
Parker, John Albert *adult education educator*
Plow, Jean Osmann *special education educator*
†Poock, Michael C. *educator*
Reid, Jeffrey Paul *higher education administrator, consultant*
Simmons, Michael Anthony *dean*
Ware, William Brettel *education educator*
Whybark, David Clay *educational educator, researcher*

Charlotte
Burke, Mary Thomas *university administrator, educator*
Clark, Ann Blakeney *educational administrator*
Colvard, Dean Wallace *emeritus university chancellor*
†DeForrest, Matthew McCoy *educator, freelance writer*
Ellis, Carolyn McClain *educator*
Eppley, Frances Fielden *retired secondary education educator, author*
Fretwell, Elbert Kirtley, Jr. *retired university chancellor, consultant*
Greene, William Henry L'Vel *academic administrator*
Hardin, Elizabeth Ann *academic administrator*
Schaffer, Eugene Carl *education educator*
Smylie, John Edwin *education executive*
Spear, Andrea Ashford *principal, educator*
Witzel, Barbara Binion *elementary education educator*
Woodward, James Hoyt *academic administrator, engineer*

Chocowinity
Castle, William Eugene *retired academic administrator*

Clayton
Jenkins, Elaine Parker *secondary school educator*

Clinton
Friedman, Deborah Leslie White *educational administrator*

Cullowhee
Bardo, John William *university administrator*
Coulter, Myron Lee *retired academic administrator*
DuVall, Rick *education educator*
Gurevich, Robert *international development administrator*
Reed, Alfred Douglas *university administrator*

Davidson
Kuykendall, John Wells *academic administrator, educator*
Spencer, Samuel Reid, Jr. *educational consultant, former university president*

Dudley
Kelly, Edward John, V *counselor*

Dunn
Spence, Othniel Talmadge *education minister, broadcast executive*

Durham
†Adams, Rex *dean*
Beckum, Leonard Charles *academic administrator*
Brown, Patricia Anita *university official*
Chambers, Julius LeVonne *academic administrator, lawyer*
†Delucca, Robert Kenneth *adult education educator, writer, translator*
Dowell, Earl Hugh *university dean, aerospace and mechanical engineering educator*
Hall, Conrad Alden *history educator*
†Harrington-Austin, Eleanor Joyce *educator*
Huestis, Charles Benjamin *former academic administrator*
Keohane, Nannerl Overholser *university president, political scientist*
Kuniholm, Bruce Robellet *university administrator*
Lindsey, Lydia *education educator, researcher*
Richardson, Vanessa *education educator*
Schmalbeck, Richard Louis *university dean, lawyer*
Stanley, Carol Jones *academic administrator, educator*
†Wallace, Maurice Orlando *educator, pastor*

Elon College
Tolley, Jerry Russell *university administrator*

Fairmont
Kemp, Charles E. *secondary education educator, history*

Fayetteville
Dowd, John P., III *academic administrator*
Lydon, Kerry Raines *school director*
Smith, Karla Salge Jordan *early childhood education educator*

Fremont
Whaley, Connie G. *middle school educator*

Gibsonville
Crawford, Kathrine Nelson *special education educator*

Graham
Corbett, Lenora Meade *community college educator*

Greensboro
†Agesa, Richard Ugunzi *economics educator*
Barnett, Dorothy Prince *retired university dean*
Canipe, Stephen Lee *educational administrator*
Hazelton, Catherine Lynette *elementary school educator*
Hoffman, Lynn Renee *elementary education educator*
Hosier, Linda G. *educator*
McNemar, Donald William *academic administrator*
Miller, Robert Louis *university dean, chemistry educator*
Prodan, James Christian *university administrator*
Rogers, William Raymond *college president emeritus, psychology educator*
Sullivan, Patricia A. *academic administrator*
Wright, John Spencer *school system administrator*

Greenville
Bearden, James Hudson *university official*
Eakin, Richard Ronald *academic administrator, mathematics educator*
Foley, Charles Bradford *university dean, music educator*
Howell, John McDade *retired university chancellor, political science educator*
Leggett, Donald Yates *academic administrator*
Leggett, Nancy Porter *university administrator*

Hampstead
McManus, Hugh F. *principal*

Hendersonville
Payne, Gerald Oliver *retired elementary education educator*

High Point
Martinson, Jacob Christian, Jr. *academic administrator*

Hillsborough
Dula, Rosa Lucile Noell *retired secondary education educator*

Huntersville
Brownlee, Sarah Hale *elementary special education educator*

Kinston
Matthis, Eva Mildred Boney *college official*
Petteway, Samuel Bruce *college president*

Lake Junaluska
Stanton, Donald Sheldon *academic administrator*

Lewisville
Gould, Anne Austin *special education educator*

Lillington
Overton, Elizabeth Nicole *elementary school educator, aerobics instructor*

Lumberton
Harding, Barry *school system administrator, educational consultant*

Mooresville
Neill, Rita Jarrett *elementary school educator*

Mount Airy
Short, Linda Matthews *elementary education educator*

Mount Olive
Raper, William Burkette *retired college president*

Mount Ulla
Kluttz, Henry G. *principal*

Murfreesboro
Brett, Mauvice Winslow *retired educational administrator, consultant*
Lott, Stanley G. *college president*
Whitaker, Bruce Ezell *college president*

New Bern
Hemphill, Jean Hargett *college dean*

Pembroke
Meadors, Allen Coats *health administrator, educator*

Pittsboro
Magill, Samuel Hays *retired academic administrator, higher education consultant*

Polkton
Heilman, Thomas Lewis *educational administrator*

Pope AFB
Vaughan, Clyde Vernelson *program director*

Princeton
Harrell, Michelle *special education educator*

Raleigh
Buchanan, David Royal *associate dean*
Burris, Craven Allen *retired education administrator, educator*
Dolce, Carl John *education administration educator*
Drew, Nancy McLaurin Shannon *counselor, consultant*
Fletcher, Oscar Jasper, Jr. *college dean*
Gulledge, Karen Stone *educational administrator*
Howell, Bruce Inman *academic administrator*
Jarrett, Polly Hawkins *secondary education educator, retired*
Jenkins, Clauston Levi, Jr. *college president*
Maidon, Carolyn Howser *teacher education director*
Mann, Thurston Jeffrey *academic administrator*
Monteith, Larry King *chancellor emeritus*
Page, Anne Ruth *gifted education educator, education specialist*
Poulton, Bruce Robert *former university chancellor*
Robinson, Prezell Russell *academic administrator*
Russell, Thomas Lee *academic administrator*
Sardi, Elaine Marie *special education educator*
Shaw, Talbert O. *university president*
†Singh, Munindar P. *adult education educator*
Stewart, Debra Wehrle *university dean and official, educator*
Thompson, Cleon F., Jr. *university administrator*
Winstead, Nash Nicks *university administrator, phytopathologist*
Wynne, Johnny Calvin *university dean, plant breeding researcher*

Rockingham
Robertson, Ralph S. *secondary school principal*

Rocky Mount
Jackson, Reed McSwain *educational administrator*
Sulfaro, Joyce A. *school program director*
†Watson, Elizabeth Anne *elementary education educator*

Ronda
Dobbins, Brenda Lorraine Adams *secondary school educator*

Roxboro
Daniel, Lori Edwards *assistant principal*
†Woodall, Carolyn Glascoe *school counselor*

Rutherfordton
Conley, Katherine Logan *religious studies educator*
Metcalf, Ethel Edgerton *retired elementary school educator*

Sanford
York, Carolyn Pleasants Stearns *English educator*

Smithfield
Wiggs, Shirley JoAnn *retired secondary school educator*

Southern Pines
Kaufmann, Rachel Norsworthy *educator*

Wake Forest
Buchanan, Edward A. *education educator*

Warrenton
Spence, Faye Yvonne *elementary school educator*

Washington
†Alligood, Lola Lurvey *educator*

Whiteville
Scott, Stephen Carlos *academic administrator*

Williamston
Hoggard, Minnie Coltrain *gifted education educator, consultant*

Wilmington
Cahill, Charles L. *university administrator, chemistry educator*
Dewey, Ralph Jay *headmaster*
Funk, Frank E. *retired university dean*
Hucks, Cynthia Stokes *university finance officer, accountant*
Leutze, James Richard *academic administrator, television producer and host*
Rorison, Margaret Lippitt *reading consultant*

Wilson
Bailey, Grace Daniel *retired secondary school educator*

Winston Salem
†Brown, David G. *academic administrator*
Crowder, Lena Belle *retired special education educator*
Ewing, Alexander Cochran *chancellor*
Hearn, Thomas K., Jr. *academic administrator*
Janeway, Richard *university official*
Jarrell, Iris Bonds *elementary school educator, business executive*
Roth, Marjory Joan Jarboe *special education educator*
†Runde, Craig Eric *academic director*
Suttles, Donald Roland *retired academic administrator, business educator*
Thrift, Julianne Still *academic administrator*
Volz, Annabelle Wekar *learning disabilities educator, consultant*

NORTH DAKOTA

Bismarck
Evanson, Barbara Jean *middle school education educator*
Keeley, Ethel S. *secondary education program director*

Devils Lake
Fixen, Randall Robert *academic director*
Tande, Teresa Lyn *secondary educator*

Dickinson
Brauhn, Richard Daniel *university administrator*

Ellendale
Larson, Lavonne Fay *educator*

Fargo
†Lipp, William Victor *secondary education educator*
Stone, Robert Rueben, Jr. *educational administrator*

Glenfield
Spickler, JoAnn Dorothy *secondary education educator*

Grand Forks
Ashe, Kathy Rae *special education educator*
Baker, Kendall L. *academic administrator*
Davis, W. Jeremy *dean, law educator, lawyer*
Jacobs, Christopher Paul *adult education educator, writer*
Page, Sally Jacquelyn *university official*
Wilson, H. David *dean*

Jamestown
Walker, James Silas *academic administrator*

Mandan
Novak, Laura J. *secondary school educator*

Minot
Jermiason, John Lynn *elementary school educator, farmer, rancher*
Shaar, H. Erik *academic administrator*

Northwood
Braaten, Linda Marie Skurdell *secondary education educator*

West Fargo
†Boutiette, Vickie Lynn *educator*
Cwikla, Rich I. *secondary education educator*

OHIO

Ada
Freed, DeBow *college president*

Akron
Auburn, Norman Paul *university president*
Barker, Harold Kenneth *former university dean*
Childs, Sally Johnston *elementary and secondary education administrator*
Kelley, Frank Nicholas *dean*
Phillips, Dorothy Ormes *elementary education educator*
†Price, Susan Stem *primary education educator, antique dealer*
†Ruebel, Marion A. *university president*

Alliance
Brown, Elizabeth Anne *elementary educator*
Dunagan, Gwendolyn Ann *special education educator*
Fugelberg, Nancy Jean *elementary music specialist, educator*
†Henning, John Edward *secondary school educator in English, researcher*
Sheetz, Ernest Austin *academic administrator, educator*

Archbold
McDougle, Larry George *academic administrator*

Ashland
Kerr, Margaret Ann *elementary education educator*

Ashville
Brown, Edith Toliver *retired educator*

Athens
Bruning, James Leon *university official, educator*
Bugeja, Michael Joseph *educator, writer*
†Flaherty, Stephen Matthew *academic administrator*
Glidden, Robert Burr *university president, musician, educator*
Krendl, Kathy *dean*
Moreno, Rosa-Maria *academic program coordinator*
Parmer, Jess Norman *university official, educator*

Avon Lake
Gwiazda, Caroline Louise *school system administrator*

Barberton
Samples, Iris Lynette *elementary school educator*

Batavia
†Tissandier, Holly Jo *teacher of developmentally handicapped*

Bath
Bowman-Dalton, Burdene Kathryn *education testing coordinator, computer consultant*

Bay Village
Barney, Susan Leslie *academic administrator*

Beachwood
Sneiderman, Marilyn Singer *secondary and elementary school educator*

Beavercreek
Busch, Sharon Lynne *elementary and secondary education educator*

Bedford
Hodakievic, James Joseph *secondary education educator*

Berea
Malicky, Neal *college president*

Bergholz
McElwain, Edwina Jay *elementary education educator*

Bowerston
McBride, Mildred Maylea *retired elementary school educator*

Bowling Green
†Blinn, John Robert *secondary school educator*
Gehring, Donald D. *education educator*
Knight, William Edward *university administrator, educator*
†Ribeau, Sidney A. *academic administrator*
Zwierlein, Ronald Edward *athletics director*

Brooklyn
Burns, Brenda Carolyn *retired special education administrator*

Bryan
Mabus, Barbara Jean *secondary science educator*
Stevens, Muriel Kay *elementary educator*

Bucyrus
Frey, Judith Lynn *elementary education educator*

Cambridge
Dray, Dwight Leroy *retired school system administrator*

Canton
Cummings, Carole Edwards *special education educator*
Thomas, Suzanne Ward *public relations director, communications educator*

Celina
Grapner-Mitchell, Pamela Kay *primary education educator*
Wolfe, John Raymond *education educator*

Chagrin Falls
Brown, Jeanette Grasselli *university official*

Chesapeake
Harris, Bob L(ee) *retired educational administrator*

Chillicothe
Basil, Brad L. *technology education educator*
†Jayne, Cristina Marsh *retired elementary education educator*
Leedy, Emily L. Foster (Mrs. William N. Leedy) *retired education educator, consultant*

Cincinnati
†Apanites, Jennifer Moore *elementary educator*
Backherms, Kathryn Anne *parochial school educator*
Berwanger, Kathleen A. *secondary school educator*
Briggs, Henry Payson, Jr. *headmaster*
Emmich, Linda L. *secondary education educator, guidance counselor*
Fischer, Patricia Ann *middle school educator*
Goin, Robert G. *athletic director*
Gottschalk, Alfred *college chancellor*
Greengus, Samuel *academic administrator, religion educator*
Harrison, Donald Carey *university official, cardiology educator*
Hess, Marcia Wanda *retired educator*
Hoff, James Edwin *university president*
Hoffman, Donna Coy *learning disabilities educator*
Hoke, Eugena Louise *special education educator*
Iachetti, Rose Maria Anne *retired elementary education educator*
Johnson, Betty Lou *secondary education educator*
Kamp, Cynthia Lea *elementary education educator*
Kohl, David *dean, librarian*
Lambert, Rebecca Jean *secondary educator*
†Livingston, Mitchel Dean *academic administrator, education educator*
Margello, Frank Michael *vocational educator*
Nester, William Raymond, Jr. *retired academic administrator and educator*
O'Connor, Patricia Walker *education educator*
O'Reilly, Rosann Tagliaferro *computer educator*
Patterson, Claire Ann *vocational educator*
Sanford, Wilbur Lee *retired elementary education educator*
Skilbeck, Carol Lynn Marie *elementary educator and small business owner*
Smith, Gregory Allgire *college administrator*
Steger, Joseph A. *university president*
Wagner, Thomas Edward *academic administrator, educator*
Werner, Robert Joseph *college dean, music educator*
Wilson, Frederick Robert *counselor educator*
Winkler, Henry Ralph *retired academic administrator, historian*
Zimmerman, Sheldon *college president, rabbi*

Circleville
Carpenter, Amy Lynn *elementary education educator*

Cleveland
Ainsworth, Joan Horsburgh *university development director*
†Auston, David Henry *university administrator, educator*
Bassett, John E. *dean, English educator*
Brooten, Dorothy *dean, nursing educator*
Cerone, David *academic administrator*
Conrad, Loretta Jane *educational administrator*
Cox, Clifford Ernest *business executive former school administration*
Cullis, Christopher Ashley *dean, biology educator*
Goll, Paulette Susan *secondary education educator*
Hardman, Corlista Helena *school system administrator*
Jirkans, Maribeth Joie *school counselor*
Jones, Rosemary *college official*
Kennedy, Frederick Morgan *retired secondary education educator*
McArdle, Richard Joseph *academic administrator*
McCullough, Joseph *college president emeritus*
Neal, Bennie F. *school administrator, educator*
Nickerson, Gary Lee *secondary education educator*
Parker, Robert Frederic *university dean emeritus*
Prater-Fipps, Eunice Kay *educational administrator*
Pytte, Agnar *academic administrator*
Queen, Joyce Ellen *elementary school educator*
Quigney, Theresa Ann *special education educator*
Sabik, Joseph Andrew *psycho-educational assessment specialist*
Samson, Gordon Edgar *educator, consultant*
Thomas, Faye Evelyn J. *elementary and secondary school educator*
†Thornton, Jerry Sue *community college president*
Van Ummersen, Claire A(nn) *academic administrator, biologist, educator*
Weidenthal, Maurice David (Bud Weidenthal) *educational administrator, journalist*
Zdanis, Richard Albert *academic administrator*

Cleveland Heights
Bruhn, Paul Robert *principal*
King, George *academic administrator*
Travis, Frederick Francis *academic administrator, historian*

Columbus
Beller, Stephen Mark *university administrator*
Blankenship, Dolores Moorefield *principal, music educator, retired*
Cole, Clarence Russell *college dean*
Cottrell, David Alton *school system administrator*
Culbertson, Jack Arthur *education educator*
de la Chapelle, Albert *education educator*
Dietrich, Carol Elizabeth *educator, former dean*
Francis, John Wayne *educator*
Hart, Mildred *counselor*
Heinlen, Daniel Lee *alumni organization administrator*
Koenigsknecht, Roy A. *education administrator*
Kucinich-Horn, Sandra Lee McCarthy *secondary education educator*
Lindsay, Dianna Marie *educational administrator*
Magliocca, Larry Anthony *education educator*
Mathis, Lois Reno *retired elementary education educator*
Meuser, Fredrick William *retired seminary president, church historian*
Miller, Wayne Clayton *student services director*
Moore, Margaret Docherty *educator*
Otte, Paul John *academic administrator, consultant, trainer*
Oxley, Margaret Carolyn Stewart *elementary education educator*
Pritchard, Kristiane *history educator*
Reilly, Joy Harriman *theatre educator, playwright, actress, director*
Smith, Linda Sue *special education educator*
Speck, Samuel Wallace, Jr. *academic administrator*
Stephens, Thomas M(aron) *education educator*
Stewart, Mac A. *educator*
Willke, Thomas Aloys *university official, statistics educator*

Cortland
Lane, Sarah Marie Clark *elementary education educator*

Coshocton
Havelka, Thomas Edward *secondary education educator*

Crestline
Maddy, Janet Marie *retired educator, dean of students*

Dayton
Allen, Rose Letitia *special education educator*
Bowman, Ed *school administrator*
Coil, Carolyn Chandler *educational consultant*
Crowe, Shelby *educational specialist, consultant*
Fitz, Brother Raymond L. *university president*
†Flack, Harley E. *university president*
Goldenberg, Kim *university president, internist*
Kankey, Roland Doyle *academic administrator*
Lasley, Thomas J., II *education educator*
Martin, James Gilbert *university provost emeritus*
McIntosh, Linda Clair *special education program specialist*
†Mullins, Robert P. *educator*
Ponitz, David H. *academic administrator*
†Pringle, Mary Beth *educator, writer*
†Sifferlen, Ned *university president*
Taylor, Elisabeth Coler *secondary school educator*
Twale, Darla Jean *education educator*
Uphoff, James Kent *education educator*
Williams, Charles Vernon, III *education administrator*

Defiance
Harris, James Thomas, III *college administrator, educator*
Slocum, Lori Sue *secondary school educator*

Delaware
Courtice, Thomas Barr *academic administrator*
Pettigrew, Carolyn Landers *theological school official, minister*

Delta
Miller, Beverly White *past college president, education consultation*

Dublin
Bordelon, Carolyn Thew *elementary school educator*
Conrad, Marian Sue (Susan Conrad) *special education educator*
Hagar, Jack *mathematics and science educator*

East Liverpool
Ash, Thomas Phillip *superintendent of schools*

East Palestine
Patterson, Paula Jeanne *secondary education educator*

Eastlake
Kerata, Joseph J. *secondary education educator*

Elyria
Hughes, Kenneth G. *elementary school educator*
Wood, Jacalyn Kay *education educator, educational consultant*

Findlay
Sipes, Theodore Lee *educator*

Franklin
Foley, Harriet Elizabeth Fealy *retired school librarian*

Fremont
Johnson, Laurence F. *college executive*
Sattler, Nancy Joan *educational administrator*

Gambier
†Daugherty, Craig A. *college financial aid director*
†Oden, Robert A., Jr. *college president*
†Will, Katherine H. *university administrator*

Garfield Heights
Chamberlin, Joan Mary *assistant principal, academic services director*

Gates Mills
Altman, Leslie Joan *secondary school educator*
†Lazos, Stergios John *secondary education educator*
O'Malley, Mary Kay *elementary education educator*

Groveport
Keck, Vicki Lynn *special education educator*

Hamilton
Royer, Diana Amelia *educator*
†Zahner, Anne Colette *preschool educator*

Harrison
†Cron, Marc C. *secondary education educator*
Stoll, Robert W. *principal*

Highland Hills
Zahs, David Karl *secondary school educator, educational administrator*

Hiram
Jagow, Elmer *retired college president*
Oliver, G(eorge) Benjamin *educational administrator, philosophy educator*
Rose, Jane Preston *dean*

Hubbard
Vukovich, Ruth Ann *secondary educator*

Hudson
Ellis, Christine Jo *middle school educator*

Ironton
Murnahan, Vera Mae *elementary school educator*
Nourse, Michael Duane *special education educator*

Kent
Buttlar, Rudolph Otto *retired college dean*
Cartwright, Carol Ann *university president*
Schwartz, Michael *university president, sociology educator*

Kettering
Denlinger, Vicki Lee *secondary school physical education educator*

Kingston
Mathew, Martha Sue Cryder *retired education educator*

Lancaster
Young, Nancy Henrietta Moe *retired elementary education educator*

Lewis Center
Strip, Carol Ann *gifted education specialist, educator*

Liberty Center
Jones, Marlene Ann *family and consumer sciences educator*

Lodi
Cox, Hillery Lee *primary school educator*

Magnolia
Zimmerman, Judith Rose *elementary art educator*

Mansfield
Gregory, Deirdre Dianne *secondary educator*
Hartman, Ruth Ann *educator*
Reynolds Westerfelt, Debra Kay *education educator, consultant*
Riedl, John Orth *university dean*
†Wheeler, Joyce Nadine *child care company professional*

Marietta
Wilson, Lauren Ross *academic administrator*

Marion
Badertscher, Doris Rae *elementary education educator*

Massillon
Walker, James William *secondary education educator, freelance writer*

Mechanicsburg
Maynard, Joan *education educator*

Medina
Meacher, Earl Robert *vocational educator*

Mentor
Towns, Gregory Wayne *elementary educator*

Miller City
Raudabaugh, James Eugene *secondary education educator*

Millersport
Thogmartin, Mark Bruce *elementary education educator, writer*

Mogadore
Kelly, Janice Helen *elementary school educator*

Moreland Hills
Hardie, James Carl *college administrator*

Mount Vernon
†Bennett, Marguerite M. *college administrator, mathematics educator*
Nease, Stephen Wesley *college president*
Shriver, William Russell *secondary education educator*

New Bremen
Wierwille, Marsha Louise *elementary education educator*

New Concord
Van Tassel, Daniel Ellsworth *academic administrator, consultant, educator*

New Middletown
Ade, Barbara Jean *secondary education educator*

New Philadelphia
Goforth, Mary Elaine Davey *secondary education educator*

New Vienna
Howell, Michelle Elane Davis *educator*

Newark
Fortaleza, Judith Ann *school system administrator*
Paul, Rochelle Carole *special education educator*
Van Dervort, Sharyn L. *secondary education educator*

North Canton
Foster, James Caldwell *academic dean, historian*

North Olmsted
Middleton, Mary *secondary education educator*
Smolen, Cheryl Hosaka *special education educator*

Northfield
Buzzelli, Charlotte Grace *educator*

Norton
Kun, Joyce Anne *secondary education educator, small business owner*

Norwood
Tubbs, Robin Lee *secondary education educator*

Oberlin
Brown, John Lott *educator*
Dye, Nancy Schrom *academic administrator, history educator*
MacKay, Alfred F. *dean, philosophy educator*
MacKay, Gladys Godfrey *adult education educator*

Oregon
Crain, John Kip *school system administrator*

Orrville
Warner, Patricia Ann *secondary school educator*

Oxford
†Garland, James C. *college president*
Pearson, Paul Guy *academic administrator emeritus*
†Powell, Myrtis H. *university administrator*
Shriver, Phillip Raymond *academic administrator*

Painesville
Davis, Barbara Snell *college educator*

Parma
McFadden, Nadine Lynn *secondary education Spanish educator*
Pisarchick, Sally *special education educator*
Shirey, Connie Mae *secondary school educator*
Tener, Carol Joan *retired secondary education educator*

Peninsula
Brobeck, David George *middle school administrator*

Perrysburg
Carpenter, J. Scott *vocational school educator*
Zuchowski, Beverly Jean *chemistry educator*

Pettisville
Switzer, Stephen Stuart *school superintendent*

Pickerington
Rana-Collins, Arlene *secondary education educator*
Young, Glenna Asche *elementary education educator*

Plain City
Brown, D. Robin *elementary school educator*

Polk
Welch, Karen Joan *secondary education educator*

Port Clinton
Ewersen, Mary Virginia *retired educator*

Portsmouth
Billiter, Freda Delorous *elementary education educator, retired*
Chapman, James Paul *university official*

Richfield
Feola, David Craig *secondary school administrator*

Richmond
Martin, Clara Rita *elementary education educator*

Rio Grande
Shibley, Ralph Edwin, Jr. *special education, vocational education educator*

Rootstown
†Boex, James Richard *academic administrator, medical researcher*

Shaker Heights
Lichtman, Lillian Margaret Yaeger *special education educator*

Sidney
Seitz, James Eugene *retired college president, freelance writer*

Springboro
Ramey, Rebecca Ann *elementary education educator*

Springfield
Dominick, Charles Alva *college official*

Kinnison, William Andrew *retired university president*

Steubenville
Cummiskey, Raymond Vincent *academic administrator*

Streetsboro
Drugan, Cornelius Bernard *school administrator, psychologist, musician*

Strongsville
Shambaugh, Catherine Anne *elementary education educator*

Sylvania
Rabideau, Margaret Catherine *media center director*

Tallmadge
Starcher-Dell'Aquila, Judy Lynn *special education educator*

Toledo
Billups, Norman Fredrick *college dean, pharmacist*
Braithwaite, Margaret Christine *elementary education educator*
Flaskamp, Ruth Ehmen Staack *retired elementary education educator*
Horton, Frank Elba *university official, geography educator*
Kozbial, Richard James *elementary education educator*
Moon, Henry *academic administrator*
†Puligandla, Ramakrishna *educator*
Romanoff, Marjorie Reinwald *education educator*

Upper Arlington
†Evans, David Charles *elementary education educator*

Valley View
Miller, Susan Ann *school system administrator*

Vandalia
†Schear, Peggy Simmons *educator*

Vermilion
Bersche, James H. *secondary education educator*

Vincent
Meek, Barbara Susan *elementary education educator*

Wadsworth
Rastok, Stacie Lynn *elementary school principal*

Westerville
Anderson, Jane Ellsworth *secondary school educator*
DeVore, Carl Brent *college president, educator*
Diersing, Carolyn Virginia *educational administrator*
Husarik, Ernest Alfred *educational administrator*
Kerr, Thomas Jefferson, IV *academic official*
Lattimore, Joy Powell *preschool administrator*
Min, Linda Lou *elementary education educator*
VanSant, Joanne Frances *academic administrator*

Westfield Center
Spinelli, Anne Catherine *elementary education educator*

Westlake
Loehr, Marla *spiritual care coordinator*

Willoughby
Grossman, Mary Margaret *elementary education educator*
Lillich, Alice Louise *retired secondary education educator*

Wooster
Shepherd, Mary Anne *elementary education educator*

Xenia
Richey, William Keith *secondary education educator*
Zellner, Sharon Michelle *special education educator*

Youngstown
Cochran, Leslie Herschel *university administrator*
Coleman, Esther Mae Glover *educator*
Loch, John Robert *educational administrator*
Zitto, Richard Joseph *physics educator*
Zorn, Robert Lynn *education educator*

Zanesville
Jones, Marlene Wiseman *elementary education educator, reading specialist*
Koncar, George Alan *secondary education educator*

OKLAHOMA

Ada
Dennison, Ramona Pollan *special education educator*

Ardmore
Thompson, John E. *principal*

Bartlesville
Risner, Anita Jane *career planning administrator*

Broken Arrow
Roberson, Deborah Kay *secondary school educator*

Checotah
Mann, Patsy Sue *secondary education educator*

Cushing
†Evans, Cheryl Lynn *elementary school principal*
Olesen, Sylvia Lawrence *educator, administrator*

Disney
Hamilton, Carl Hulet *retired academic administrator*

Drummond
Harris, Joyce Faye *elementary education educator*

Durant
Christy, David Hardacker *secondary school educator, music educator*

Edmond
Bailey, Elizabeth Anne *middle school education educator*
Harryman, Rhonda L. *education educator*

Enid
Dyche, Kathie Louise *secondary school educator*
Mabry, Betsy *elementary education educator*
Taylor, Donna Lynne *adult training coordinator*

Erick
Chittum, Jamey Eve *principal*

Goodwell
Goldsmith, Dale Campbell *university official*

Guthrie
Dowdy, Fredella Mae *secondary school educator*
Scott-Christian, Tres Mali *employment counselor, consultant*

Hinton
Pasby, Garry Edward *assistant principal*

Keota
Davis, Thomas Pinkney *secondary school educator*

Lawton
Calaway, James *elementary education educator*
Cates, Dennis Lynn *education educator*
Davis, Don Clarence *university president*
Gardner, Carol Elaine *elementary school educator*

Miami
Vanpool, Cynthia Paula *special education educator, special services consultant*

Newkirk
Mullin, Melissa Yvonne *secondary English educator*

Norman
Boren, David Lyle *academic administrator*
Dalton, Deborah Whitmore *dean*
†Dyer, Suzette Morales *higher education administrator*
Haring, Kathryn Ann *special education educator, research scientist*
Hodgell, Murlin Ray *university dean*
†Olasiji, Thompson Dele *educator*
Pappas, James Pete *university administrator*
Schindler, Barbara Francois *education educator*
Sharp, Paul Frederick *former university president, educational consultant*
Stover, Curtis Sylvester *retired vocational school educator*
†Stroud, Clarke *university official*
Van Horn, Richard Linley *academic administrator*
Zapffe, Nina Byrom *retired elementary education educator*

Oklahoma City
Bogle, Ronald E. *academic administrator*
Brown-Kuykendall, Donita *early childhood educator*
Forni, Patricia Rose *dean, nursing educator*
Garrett, Sandy Langley *school system administrator*
Holder, Lee *educator and university dean emeritus*
Holloway, Othelle June *elementary school educator*
Jennings, Stephen Grant *academic administrator*
Johnson, James Terence *college chancellor*
Kraker, Deborah Schovanec *special education educator*
Mason, Betty G(wendolyn) Hopkins *school system administrator*
Murphy, Deborah Hill *education cosultant, psychotherapist*
Noakes, Betty LaVonne *retired elementary school educator*
†Quaid, Gloria J. *school administrator*
Shirey, Margaret (Peggy Shirey) *elementary school educator*
Waldo, Catherine Ruth *private school educator*
Wheat, Willis James *retired university dean, management educator*

Okmulgee
Turner, Michael Dan *university administrator*

Paden
Adams, Darlene Agnes *secondary education educator*

Pauls Valley
Pesterfield, Linda Carol *school administrator, educator*

Ponca City
Surber, Joe Robert *assistant superintendent of schools*
Tatum, Betty Joyce *secondary school educator*

Prague
Stefansen, Peggy Ann *special education educator*

Pryor
Burdick, Larry G. *school system administrator*

Shawnee
Hill, Bryce Dale *school administrator*
Wilks, Jacquelin Holsomback *educational counselor*
Zuhdi, Omar *secondary education educator*

Stillwater
Boger, Lawrence Leroy *university president emeritus*
Browning, Charles Benton *retired university dean, agricultural educator*
Curl, Samuel Everett *university dean, agricultural scientist*
Halligan, James Edmund *university administrator, chemical engineer*
Hayes, Kevin Gregory *university administrator*
Mc Collom, Kenneth Allen *retired university dean*
Sandmeyer, Robert Lee *university dean, economist*

Tahlequah
†Clark, Mark William *dean, educator*

Howard, James Kenton *university administrator, journalist*
Williams, Larry Bill *academic administrator*

Tinker AFB
Scott, Carol Lee *child care educator*

Tulsa
Buthod, Mary Clare *school administrator*
Knaust, Clara Doss *retired elementary school educator*
Kukura, Rita Anne *elementary school educator*
Lawless, Robert William *academic administrator*
Undernehr, Laura Lee *elementary education educator*
Wood, Emily Churchill *educator, educational consultant*

Warr Acres
Weir, Richard Dale *elementary education educator*

Woodward
Fisher, Deena Kaye *social studies education, administrator*
Selman, Minnie Corene Phelps *elementary school educator*

OREGON

Ashland
Kreisman, Arthur *higher education consultant, humanities educator emeritus*
Smith, G(odfrey) T(aylor) *academic administrator*

Astoria
Bainer, Philip La Vern *retired college president*
†Lee, Kristen Kae *education professional*

Beavercreek
Lawler, Alice Bonzi (Mrs. Oscar T. Lawler) *retired college administrator, civic worker*

Coos Bay
†Wright, Deborah George *dean, author*

Corvallis
†Arnold, Roy *provost, university administrator*
Byrne, John Vincent *higher education consultant*
Davis, John Rowland *university administrator*
Healey, Deborah Lynn *education administrator*
Johnson, Duane P. *academic administrator*
Lumpkin, Margaret Catherine *retired education educator*
Parker, Donald Fred *college dean, human resources management educator*
Risser, Paul Gillan *academic administrator, botanist*
†Stephens, Kay Kuipers *education educator*
Young, Roy Alton *university administrator, educator*

Cottage Grove
Miller, Joanne Louise *middle school educator*

Creswell
Briggs, Bonnie Jean *secondary school educator*

Dayton
Purcell, Kevin Brown *director of special services*

Eugene
Bassett, Carol Ann *journalism educator, writer*
Cox, Joseph William *academic administrator*
†Frank, David Anthony *educator*
Frohnmayer, David Braden *university president*
Gall, Meredith Damien (Meredith Mark Damien Gall) *education educator, author*
Grossen, Bonnie Joy *education research scientist*
Moseley, John Travis *university administrator, research physicist*
Wood, Daniel Brian *educational consultant*

Forest Grove
Moeller, Bonnie Jean *elementary school educator*
Singleton, Francis Seth *dean*

Gresham
Light, Betty Jensen Pritchett *former college dean*
†Vela, Joel E. *college president*
Webb, Donna Louise *academic director, educator*

Hillsboro
Cleveland, Charles Sidney *secondary education educator*

Jacksonville
Lowe, Barbara Annette *retired elementary education educator*

Joseph
Gilbert, David Erwin *retired academic administrator, physicist*

Lake Oswego
Le Shana, David Charles *retired academic administrator*
Meltebeke, Renette *career counselor*

Madras
Hillis, Stephen Kendall *secondary education educator*

Mcminnville
Walker, Charles Urmston *retired university president*

Merrill
Porter, Roberta Ann *counselor, educator, school system administrator*

Myrtle Creek
Hull, Tom Allan *mechanics educator*

North Bend
de Sá e Silva, Elizabeth Anne *secondary school educator*

Oceanside
Wadlow, Joan Krueger *academic administrator*

Portland
Bennett, Charles Leon *vocational and graphic arts educator*
Blumel, Joseph Carlton *university president*
Cantelon, John Edward *academic administrator*
Henry, Samuel Dudley *educator*
Johnson, Thomas Floyd *former college president, educator*
Koblik, Stevens S. *academic administrator*
Lawrence, Sally Clark *academic administrator*
Lynch, Nita Marie Smith *vocational curriculum developer, ballroom dancer*
Martin, Ernest Lee *academic administrator, historian, theologian, writer*
Mooney, Michael Joseph *college president*
Perry, Judith Ann *educator*
Reardon, Michael F. *university provost*
Sedgwick, Levonne *retired school program administrator*
Seliner, Barbara Ann *elementary education educator*
Shaff, Beverly Gerard *educational administrator*
Sherrer, Charles David *college dean, clergyman*
Tufts, Robert B. *academic administrator*
Walker, James Bradley *academic institution administrator*
Whitefoot, Tabitha Bernier *alternative education educator*
Wiest, William Marvin *education educator, psychologist*

Roseburg
Johnson, Doris Ann *educational administrator*
Tilson, Daniel *elementary education educator*

Salem
Janota, Debilyn Marie *school principal*

Sandy
Thies, Lynn Wapinski *elementary education educator*

Shady Cove
†Torres-Staicoff, Sue Anne *secondary education educator, artist*

Toledo
MacKenroth, Joyce Ellen *secondary school educator*

White City
Acord-Skelton, Barbara Burrows *counselor, educator, artist*

PENNSYLVANIA

Abington
Magison, Deborah Helen *elementary education educator*
Scheuer, Donald William, Jr. *educational administrator*

Albion
†Olson, David R. *elementary school principal*

Aliquippa
Drobac, Nikola (Nick Drobac) *educator*

Allentown
†Bruckner, Michael Stewart *college official*
Buenaflor, Judith Luray *secondary education educator*
Taylor, Arthur Robert *college president, business executive*
Yoder, Myron Eugene *secondary school educator*

Allison Park
Korchnak, Lawrence Charles *educational administrator, consultant, writer*

Altoona
Larsen, Carlton Keith *academic administrator*
Vreeland-Flynn, Tracy Lynn *elementary education educator*

Annville
Grieve-Carlson, Gary Robert *secondary education educator*

Ashland
Lucas, Harry David *secondary education educator*

Bala Cynwyd
Chiu, Helen Lienhard *educator*
Furey, Susan Mary *elementary education educator*
Oswald, James Marlin *education educator*
†Robinson, James Alfred *retired educator*
Sutnick, Alton Ivan *dean, educator, researcher, physician*

Bally
Kelsch, Joan Mary *elementary education educator*

Barto
Isett, Deborah Michele Gunther *elementary education educator*

Beaver
Sefton, Mildred McDonald *retired educator*

Beaver Falls
Mulhollen, Phyllis Marie *special education educator, instructional support coordinator*

Belle Vernon
Kline, Bonita Ann *middle school guidance counselor, educator*

Bensalem
Klingerman, Karen Nina *elementary school educator, teacher consultant, course coordinator*

Bethel Park
Douds, Virginia Lee *elementary education educator*

Bethlehem
Bergethon, Kaare Roald *retired college president*
†Farrington, Gregory C. *university administrator*
†Markley, Nelson G. *academic administrator*
†Spengler, Mark Glenn *educator*

Blue Bell
Brendlinger, LeRoy R. *college president*

Brookhaven
DiRosa, Steven Joseph *primary and secondary school educator*

Brownsville
†Martin, Richard H. *principal*

Bryn Mawr
Salisbury, Helen Holland *education educator*
Smith, Nona Coates *academic administrator*
†Vickers, Nancy J. *academic administrator*
Worrall, Charles Harrison *elementary education educator*
Wright, James Clinton *dean, archaeology educator*

Butler
Rettig, Carolyn Faith *educator*

Cambridge Springs
Learn, Richard Leland *corrections school principal*
Youngblood, Constance Mae *elementary school principal*

Canonsburg
Mascetta, Joseph Anthony *principal*

Carlisle
Blackledge, David William *academic administrator*
Mentzer, Marsha Lee *secondary school educator*

Carnegie
†Whitfield, Tammy J. *educator*

Catasauqua
Fogelson, Brian David *educational administrator*

Chadds Ford
Witcher, Phyllis Herrmann *secondary education educator*

Chalfont
Hauber, Patricia Anne *educator*

Charleroi
Kravec, Frances Mary *elementary education educator*

Chester
Bruce, Robert James *university president*
Buck, Lawrence Paul *academic administrator*
Jackson, Cynthia Marie *elementary school educator*
Moll, Clarence Russel *retired university president, consultant*
Wepner, Shelley Beth *education educator, software developer*

Chester Springs
Simms, Amy Lang *writer, educator*

Claridge
Perich, Terry Miller *secondary school educator*

Clearfield
Reighard, Edward Buzard *retired education executive director*

Coatesville
Fitzgerald, Susan Helena *elementary educator*
Smith, Patricia Anne *special education educator*

Collegeville
Richter, Richard Paul *academic administrator*
Strassburger, John Robert *academic administrator*

Columbia
McTaggart, Timothy Thomas *secondary education educator*

Conestoga
Fritz, Eugene Earl *university administrator*

Cooperstown
Hogg, James Henry, Jr. *retired education educator*

Cornwall
McGill, William James, Jr. *academic administrator, writer*

Cranberry Township
Conti, Carolyn Ann *elementary school educator*

Cresson
†Strange, Russell Littlejohn *school system administrator*

Dallas
Johnson MacDowell, Tina *elementary education educator*

Danville
Wert, Barbara J. Yingling *special education consultant*

Dayton
Patterson, Madge Lenore *elementary education educator*

Devon
Garbarino, Robert Paul *retired administrative dean, lawyer*

Doylestown
Murray, Karen Lee *special education educator*

Drums
†Frask, Robin Ann Kostanesky *secondary school educator*

Du Bois
Kearney, Linda Lee *secondary education educator*
Nye, George N *secondary school educator*

Eagles Mere
Sample, Frederick Palmer *former college president*

East Petersburg
Stuempfle, Catherine Diane *secondary education educator*

East Stroudsburg
Brackbill, Nancy Lafferty *elementary education educator*
Dillman, Robert John *academic administrator*

Easton
†Bartolocci, Paulette E Marie *elementary school educator, aerobic instructor*
Kaye, Daniel Barnett *secondary education educator, consultant*
Rothkopf, Arthur J. *college president*
Snyder, Charles Terry *director*

Edinboro
†Brown, Lisa Rochell *academic administrator*
Cox, Clifford Laird *university administrator, musician*
Curry-Carlburg, Joanne Jeanne *elementary education educator*

Elizabethtown
Ritsch, Frederick Field *academic administrator, historian*

Erie
Barber, Michele A. *title one educator*
Chrisman, Marlene Santia *special education educator*
Drexler, Nora Lee *retired educator, writer, illustrator*
Eberlin, Richard D. *education educator*
Faulkner, Bonita Louise *enrichment education educator*
Lilley, John Mark *academic administrator, dean*
McDyer, Susan Spear *academic administrator*

Exeter
Stocker, Joyce Arlene *retired secondary school educator*

Exton
Shollenberger, Sharon Ann *secondary school educator*

Fairview
Graziani, Linda Ann *secondary education educator*

Flourtown
Lambert, Joan Dorety *elementary education educator*
Moore, Sandra Kay *counselor, administrator*

Folsom
White, Barbara Cloud *principal, educator*

Franklin
Lytle, Elizabeth Ann *secondary education educator, writer*
Moore, Mary Julia *educator*

Frederick
†Sekellick, Ronald E. *special education educator*

Freeland
Rudawski, Joseph George *educational administrator*

Gibsonia
Szymanski, George Joseph *school administrator*

Glen Rock
Hortman, David Jones *secondary education educator*

Glenside
Mee, Carolyn Jean *education educator*
†Sacks, Robert D. *educational administrator, fund raiser*

Grantham
Kraybill, Donald Brubaker *college provost*

Greensburg
†Cassell, Frank Alan *university president, history educator*

Greenville
Lillie, Marshall Sherwood *college safety and security director, educator*
Rugen, Richard Hall *college administrator*

Gwynedd Valley
Feenane, Sister Mary Alice *principal*

Hamburg
Weiss, Gerald Francis, Jr. *secondary education educator, coach*

Hanover
Barnhart, Nikki Lynn Clark *elementary school educator*
Clark, Sandra Marie *school administrator*
Hazel, Marianne Elizabeth *educational administrator*
Toft, Thelma Marilyn *secondary school educator*

Harleysville
†Johnson, Andrew W. *secondary education educator*

Harrisburg
†Baehre, Edna Victoria *college president*
Baird, Irene Cebula *educational administrator*
Brown, John Walter *vocational education supervisor*
Burns, Rebecca Ann *educator, librarian*
McCormick, James Harold *academic administrator*
Partin, Daniel Ray *secondary school educator*
Popnik, Marlene Alita *school librarian*
Woods, Willie G. *dean, English language and education educator*

Harrison City
McWilliams, Samuel Robert *secondary education educator*

Harrisville
Amon, Cheryl Ann Attridge *elementary education educator*

Haverford
Brownlow, Donald Grey *private school educator*
Gollub, Jerry *academic administrator*
†Hansen, Elaine T. *academic administrator*
Tritton, Thomas Richard *academic administrator, biology educator*

Havertown
Beck, Elaine Kushner *elementary and secondary school educator*

Hollidaysburg
Robinson, Gary David *principal*

Hollsopple
†Spory, Catherine Jane *primary school educator, education educator*

Homestead
Dithrich, Marie *elementary education educator*

Honesdale
Barbe, Walter Burke *education educator*
Campbell, Linda Sue *guidance counselor*
Stanton, Sara Baumgardner *retired secondary school educator*

Horsham
Strock, Gerald E. *school system administrator*

Hunlock Creek
Zimmerman, Anita Eloise *elementary education educator*

Huntingdon
Kepple, Thomas Ray, Jr. *college administrator*

Huntingdon Valley
Danielewski, Donna Krystyna *secondary school educator*
†Silverman, Ray *educator*

Immaculata
Manning, Kevin James *academic administrator*
McKee, Sister Kathleen Helen *nun, educator, college administrator*

Indiana
Baker, Janice Marie *special education educator, researcher*
Kulis, Ellen Mae *elementary education educator*
Pettit, Lawrence Kay *university president*
Princes, Carolyn Diane Wilbon *educational director*

Jenkintown
Baldwin, David Rawson *retired university administrator*
DiSandro, Linda Anita *counselor*

Jermyn
Crotti, Rose Marie *special education educator*

Johnstown
Bowser, Edwin Leonard *academic counselor*
Boyle, Robert James *special education school director*
Grove, Nancy Carol *academic administrator*
Jones, Thomas William *secondary education educator, consultant*
Lindberg, Stephen *secondary education educator*
McKnight, Joyce Sheldon *adult educator, community organizer, mediator*
†Morrison, Sharon Renee *elementary education educator*
Wemple, Arthur Gerard *English educator*

Kennett Square
Martin, Helen Elizabeth *secondary education educator*
†Vosburgh, Bruce Howard *educational administrator*

King Of Prussia
Gallis, Carole Campbell *secondary education educator*
Hawes, Nancy Elizabeth *mathematics educator*

Kingston
Godlewski, James Bernard *elementary school educator, principal, consultant*

Knox
Rupert, Elizabeth Anastasia *retired university dean*
†Schwab, Joyce Lynn *educator*

Kutztown
Laub, Mary Lou *elementary education educator*
McFarland, David E. *university official*
Spencer, JoAnn Nora *education educator*
Watrous, Robert Thomas *academic director*

La Plume
Boehm, Edward Gordon, Jr. *university administrator, educator*

Lafayette Hill
†King, Diane Averbach *education educator*
Slagle, Robert Lee, II *elementary and secondary education educator*

Lake Ariel
Casper, Marie Lenore *middle school educator*

Lancaster
Byler, Vickie Lynne Jennifer *educator, athletic director*
Drum, Alice *college administrator*
Ebersole, Mark Chester *emeritus college president*
Kneedler, Alvin Richard *college president*
Linton, Joy Smith *primary school educator*

Langhorne
Babb, Wylie Sherrill *college president*

Lansdale
Cusimano, Adeline Mary Miletti *educational administrator*
Rosen, Bonnie *elementary school principal, consultant*

Lebanon
Synodinos, John Anthony *academic administrator*

Lehman
Williams, Thomas Alan *secondary education educator, coach*

Levittown
McAllister, Sally L. *learning center administrator*
Wolverton, Carolyn Patricia *English language educator*

Lewisburg
Adams, William D. *university president*
Hetherington, Bonita Elizabeth *elementary education educator*

Lincoln University
Jackson, Katherine Church *former elementary school educator, reading educator*

Lock Haven
Almes, June *retired education educator, librarian*
Willis, Craig Dean *academic administrator*

Loretto
Wilson, David Patrick *academic administrator*

Lower Burrell
Rose, Robert Henry *arts education administrator*

Macungie
Rubin, Arthur Herman *university administrator, consultant*

Malvern
Swymer, Stephen *principal*

Manheim
Geib, Violet M. *elementary education educator*

Marietta
†Lawrence, James David *principal*

Mc Donald
Craig, Trisha Ann Varish *secondary school teacher*
Maurer, Karen Ann *special education educator*

Meadville
Dixon, Armendia Pierce *school program administrator*

Mechanicsburg
Rudolph, Robert Norman *secondary school educator, adult education educator*

Media
Comeforo, Jean Elizabeth *hearing-impaired educator*
Coyle, Edward J. *physical education coordinator*
Dunlap, Richard Frank *school system administrator*

Mercersburg
Fegan, Martina Kriner *secondary education educator*

Merion Station
Kulp, Jonathan B. *elementary school educator*
Pearcy, Lee Theron *secondary education educator, writer*

Meyersdale
Cober, Kay Ann *secondary school educator*

Middletown
Jordan, Lois Wenger *university official*
South, James Dawson, II *university administrator*

Milford
Reynolds, Edwin Wilfred, Jr. *retired secondary education educator*

Millersville
Caputo, Joseph Anthony *university president*
Suskie, Linda Anne *academic administrator*

Monroeville
Sehring, Hope Hutchison *library science educator*

Mont Alto
Caldwell, Corrinne Alexis *academic administrator*

Moon Township
†Kiliany, Mary Catherine *program director, communications educator*

Moosic
Owens, Evelyn *elementary education educator*

Mount Pleasant
Dangelo, Eugene Michael *elementary education educator*

Myerstown
Heiser, Janet Dorothy *physical education educator*

Natrona Heights
Baldassare, Louis J. *school superintendent*

Nazareth
†Ferraro, Margaret Louise (Peg Ferraro) *educator*

New Castle
Denniston, Marjorie McGeorge *retired elementary education educator*
Halm, Nancye Studd *private school administrator*
Roux, Mildred Anna *retired secondary school educator*

New Holland
Cox, James Michael *school district administrator, psychologist*

New Hope
Knight, Douglas Maitland *educational administrator, optical executive*

New Wilmington
Deegan, John, Jr. *academic administrator, researcher*

Newtown
†Bursk, Christopher I. *educator*
Duncan, Stephen Robert *elementary education educator*

Newville
Rand, Sharon Kay *elementary education educator*

Norristown
Del Collo, Mary Anne Demetris *school administrator*
Nelson, Dawn Marie *middle school science and math educator*
†Woolf, Steven *principal*

Northampton
Greenleaf, Janet Elizabeth *principal*

Oakdale
Gilden, Robin Elissa *elementary education educator*

Old Forge
Rakauskas, Matthew *vice-principal*

Ottsville
Hughes, Charles Martin *retired educator*

Palmyra
Miller, John Patrick *secondary education educator*

Penn Valley
Berman, Phillip Lee *religious institute administrator, author*

Perkasie
Ferry, Joan Evans *school counselor*

Philadelphia
Armstrong, Clay *physiology educator*
Bates, James Earl *academic administrator*
Blumberg, Baruch Samuel *academic research scientist*
Brucker, Paul C. *academic administrator, physician*
Cohen, David Walter *academic administrator, periodontist, educator*
Cooperman, Barry S. *educational administrator, educator, scientist*
Delacato, Carl Henry *education educator*
Eddy, Julia Veronica *educator*
Erichsen, Peter Christian *university official, lawyer*
Gerbino, Philip Paul *university president, consultant*
Gerrity, Thomas P. *dean*
Giegengack, Robert *university administrator*
Goldman, Richard Paul *educational administrator*
Gusoff, Patricia Kearney *elementary education educator*
Gustafson, Sandra Lynne *secondary education educator*
†Guyer, Hedy-Ann Klein *special education educator*
Hack, Gary Arthur *dean*
Hackney, Francis Sheldon *university president*
†Ingram, George Herschel *university administrator, writer*
Jacoby, Thomas S. *school system administrator*
Jamieson, Kathleen Hall *dean, communications educator*
Krewer, Julie-Ann *scholar*
Lancaster, Burnella W. *special education educator*
Lang, Norma M. *dean, nursing educator*
Meyerson, Martin *university executive, professor, urban and regional planner*
Monahan, Diane Maire *university educator*
Osborne, Frederick Spring, Jr. *academic administrator, artist*
Padulo, Louis *university administrator*
Papadakis, Constantine N. *university executive*
Peirce, Donald Oluf *elementary education educator*
Presseisen, Barbara Zemboch *educational director, researcher*
†Richardson, Joanne *elementary education educator, counselor*
Rodin, Judith Seitz *academic administrator, psychology educator*
Rovner, Leonard Irving *physical education educator*
Rudczynski, Andrew B. *academic administrator, medical researcher*
Sheehan, Donald Thomas *academic administrator*
Smith, Robert Rutherford *university dean, communication educator*
Solmssen, Peter *academic administrator*
Sutman, Francis Xavier *university dean*
Swan, Ralph Edward *higher education educator*
Tawyea, Edward Wayne *university administrator, librarian*
Taylor, Jeffrey Matthew *principal*
Vargus, Ione Dugger *university administrator*
Veon, Dorothy Helene *educational consultant*
Wachman, Marvin *university chancellor*
Wagner, Daniel A. *human developement educator, academic administrator*
Walker, Valaida Smith *university administrator*
Walters, Donald Lee *education educator*

Philipsburg
†Genesi, Susan Petrovich *educator*

Pittsburgh
†Barazzone, Esther Lynn *academic administrator, educator*
Boyce, Doreen Elizabeth *lecturer, civic development foundation executive*
Christiano, Paul P. *academic administrator, civil engineering educator*
†Cohon, Jared L. *university administrator*
Curry, Nancy Ellen *educator, psychoanalyst, psychologist*
Dempsey, Jacqueline Lee *special education director*
Dobos, Sister Marion *parochial school educator*
Dunn, Douglas Murray *university dean*
Epperson, David Ernest *dean, educator*
†Hanchett-Serbin, Karen Lynn *community college administrator*
†Harvey, John Hertford *academic and athletics administrator, consultant*
†Hayden, Gary Thomas *contract management director*

Johnson, Douglas Wayne *secondary education educator*
Kimm, Sue Young Sook *academic administrator, researcher*
Landon, Marie Catherine *school system administrator, educator*
Laughlin, Patricia *university dean*
Lorensen, Frederick Hamilton *educational administrator, consultant*
McDuffie, Keith A. *literature educator, magazine director*
McNulty, Cindy *educator*
Michalopoulos, George Konstantine *academic administrator*
†Miller, Debra Lee *special education educator, supervisor*
Posvar, Wesley Wentz *university president, educator, consultant*
Rago, Ann D'Amico *university official, public relations professional*
Smartschan, Glenn Fred *school system administrator*
Stella, Janet Louise *special education educator*
Sullivan, Loretta Roseann *elementary education educator*
Suzuki, Jon Byron *dean, periodontist, educator*
Van Dusen, Albert Clarence *university official*
†Vincent, Timothy C. *secondary school educator*
Wallace, Richard Christopher, Jr. *school system administrator, educator*
Weidman, John Carl, II *education educator, consultant*
Wilson, George David *school administrator*

Plymouth Meeting
Delacato, Janice Elaine *learning consultant, educator*

Pottstown
White, Thomas David, II *academic administrator*

Punxsutawney
Graffius, Richard Stewart, II *middle school educator*

Quarryville
Schreiner, Helen Ann *special education educator*

Reading
Bowles, Patricia Mary *secondary education educator*
Buckendorff, Rosemary Hauseman *secondary education educator*

Red Lion
Van Kouwenberg, Martha Nester *secondary education educator*

Ridley Park
Brittell-Whitehead, Diane Peeples *secondary education educator, addiction counselor*

Roaring Spring
Dell, Linda Treese *gifted and talented education educator*

Robesonia
Evaul, Charleen McClain *education educator*
†Fuhrman, Gwendolyn Sue *secondary school educator*

Russell
†Thomas, Bryan Valentine *secondary school educator, artist*

Russellton
Curtis, Paula Annette *elementary and secondary education educator*

Saint Davids
Baird, John Absalom, Jr. *college official*

Saltsburg
Pidgeon, John Anderson *headmaster*

Saxton
†Curfman, Walter L. *school system administrator*

Schnecksville
Kiechel, Barbara Bernadette *vocational school educator*

Scottdale
Lee, John Lawrence, Jr. *educational administrator*

Scranton
McShane, Joseph Michael *priest, academic administrator, theology educator*
Nee, Sister Mary Coleman *college president emeritus*
Passon, Richard Henry *academic administrator*
Reap, Sister Mary Margaret *college administrator*
†Zaboski, Gerald Christopher *academic administrator*

Selinsgrove
Cunningham, Joel Luther *university president*

Sewickley
Newell, Byron Bruce, Jr. *Episcopalian pastor, director pastoral services*

Shippensburg
Ceddia, Anthony Francis *university administrator*
Gay, Mathew Frank *secondary education educator*
Kujawa, Lorraine Frances *elementary educator*

Slippery Rock
Bickel, Nora Kathryn *elementary education educator*
Gordon, Tom Lee *education educator*
Smith, Grant Warren, II *university administrator, physical sciences educator*

Solebury
Sellers, Susan Taylor *principal*

Springfield
Carter, Frances Moore *educator, writer*

State College
†Cabrera, Alberto F. *education educator*
Hoffa, Harlan Edward *retired university dean, art educator*
Max, Elizabeth *educator*

Mills, Rilla Dean *university administrator, consultant*
Remick, Forrest Jerome, Jr. *former university official*
Spencer, Priscilla James *physical education educator*
Toombs, William Edgar *professor*

Summerdale
Young, James Alan *academic administrator*

Swarthmore
Berger, Dianne Gwynne *educator*
Bloom, Alfred Howard *college president*

Sweet Valley
Aldrow-Liput, Priscilla R. *elementary education educator*

Titusville
Campasino, Ellen Marie *elementary education educator*

Topton
Allison, Robert Harry *school counselor*
Bloom, Ruth Elsa *educator, administrator*

University Park
Askov, Eunice May *adult education educator*
†Brighton, John *academic administrator*
Dupuis, Victor Lionel *retired curriculum and instruction educator*
Erickson, Rodney Allen *dean, educator*
Hammond, J. D. *university dean, insurance executive*
Herr, Edwin Leon *educator, academic administrator*
Jordan, Bryce *retired university president*
Koopmann, Gary Hugo *educational center administrator, mechanical engineering educator*
Larson, Russell Edward *university provost emeritus, consultant agriculture research and development*
Levin, James *education educator*
MacCarthy, Stephen Justin *university amdinistrator, consultant*
Martorana, Sebastian Vincent *educator, educational consultant*
Neff, Robert Wilbur *academic administrator, educator*
Nicely, Robert Francis, Jr. *education educator, administrator*
Spanier, Graham Basil *academic administrator, family sociologist, demographer, marriage and family therapist*
Whitko, Jean Phillips *academic administrator*
Yoder, Edgar Paul *education educator*

Upper Darby
Hudiak, David Michael *academic administrator, lawyer*
Leiby, Bruce Richard *secondary education educator, writer*

Upper Saint Clair
Dunkis, Patricia B. *school system administrator*

Vandergrift
Quader, Patricia Ann *elementary education educator*

Villanova
Clement, Barbara Koltes Sadtler *academic administrator*
Dobbin, Edmund J. *university administrator*
Fitzpatrick, M. Louise *dean, nursing educator*
Ricks, Thomas Miller *university administrator, historian*

Wallingford
Cruz-Sáenz, Michèle Frances Schiavone de *educator, researcher*
Maull, Ethel Mills *retired special education educator*

Washington
Burnett, Howard Jerome *college president*
†Longo, James McMurtry *college administrator*

Wayne
Cavitt, Lorraine DiMino *reading specialist, elementary educator*
McArdle, Joan Terruso *parochial school mathematics and science educator*
†Smedley, David Robert *college official, educator*

Wernersville
Panuska, Joseph Allan *academic administrator*

West Aliquippa
Peya, Prudence Malava *retired gifted and talented education educator*

West Chester
Adler, Madeleine Wing *academic administrator*
Bove, Patrice Magee *elementary education educator*
Hickman, Janet Susan *college administrator, educator*
Lamm, Sharon Lea *corporate educator, consultant*
Morgan, John David *middle school educator*
†Van Liew, Maria Christina *adult education educator*

West Mifflin
DiCioccio, Gary Francis *secondary education educator*

West Nanticoke
†Gardner, Judith Ann *secondary school and university educator*

Wexford
Hutchinson, Barbara Winter *middle school educator*
Myers, Renée Leslie *school system administrator, educator*

Williamsport
Douthat, James Evans *college administrator*
Meyers, Judith Ann *education educator*

Windber
Baltzer, Patricia Germaine *elementary school educator*

Wrightsville
Sonneborn, Sylvia Lou Hott *secondary school educator*

Wyncote
Ciao, Frederick J. *educational administrator, educator*

Wyomissing
Cellucci, Peter T. *principal*
Moran, William Edward *academic administrator*

Yardley
Breitenfeld, Frederick, Jr. *educational consultant, former public broadcasting executive*
Elliott, Frank Nelson *retired college president*
Metzger, Mary Catherine *special education educator*

York
Aarestad, James Harrison *retired educational administrator, army officer*
Barton, Dawn Kanani *elementary school educator*
†Kroh, Mark Sinclair *educational administrator*
Link, Rebecca Clagett *registrar*
Madama, Patrick Stephen *academic official*
Owens, Marilyn Mae *elementary school educator, secondary school educator*
Paraskevakos, Kelly Diane *secondary education educator*

Zelienople
Moyer, Christina Beth *elementary education educator, reading specialist*

RHODE ISLAND

Barrington
Graser, Bernice Erckert *elementary school principal*

Bristol
†Boulé, Denise Marguerite *educational administrator*
Schipper, Michael *university official*

Central Falls
Leclerc, Leo George *guidance counselor*

Cumberland
LaFlamme-Zurowski, Virginia M. *secondary school special education educator*

East Providence
†Spaught, Maureen Whalen *primary educator*

Kingston
Carothers, Robert Lee *academic administrator*
Gaulin, Lynn *experiential education educator*
McKinney, William Lynn *education educator*
†Schroeder, Jonathan Edward *business administration educator*
Sullivan, Richard Ernest *educator*
Youngken, Heber Wilkinson, Jr. *former university administrator, pharmacy educator*

Lincoln
Brites, José Baptista *secondary education educator, writer, artist*

Middletown
Jackson, John Edward *educator, logistician, retired naval officer*
Ponte, Stephen Carl *school system administrator*

Narragansett
Pierson, Douglas H. *special education educator*

Newport
Flowers, Sandra Joan *elementary education educator*
Wood, Berenice Howland *educator*

North Kingstown
Resch, Cynthia Fortes *secondary education educator*

Portsmouth
Mello, Michael William *educational administrator*

Providence
†Carey, Russell Christopher *university administrator, lawyer*
Cooper, Caroline Ann *hospitality faculty dean*
†Farmer, Richard Edward *college dean*
Filomeno, Linda Jean Harvey *elementary education educator*
Gee, Elwood Gordon *university administrator*
Greer, David S. *university dean, physician, educator*
Mandle, Earl Roger *design school president, former museum executive*
Marsh, Donald Jay *medical school dean, medical educator*
McMahon, Eleanor Marie *education educator*
Nazarian, John *academic administrator, mathematics educator*
Shapiro, Raquel *school psychologist, counselor*
Sweeney, Judith Kiernan *secondary education educator*

Saunderstown
Donovan, Gerald Alton *retired academic administrator, former university dean*

South Kingstown
Zarrella, Arthur M. *superintendent schools*

Warwick
Izzi, John *educator, author*

West Kingston
†Sullivan, Nancy *retired educator, poet*

Wood River Junction
Carlson-Pickering, Jane *gifted education educator*

SOUTH CAROLINA

Aiken
Alexander, Robert Earl *university chancellor, educator*
Salter, David Wyatt *secondary school educator*
Tully, Susan Sturgis *adult education educator*

Anderson
Norris, Joan Clafette Hagood *educational administrator*

Barnwell
Miller, Elizabeth Jane *secondary education educator*

Batesburg
Covington, Tammie Warren *elementary education educator*

Beaufort
Plyler, Chris Parnell *dean*
Sheldon, Jeffrey Andrew *college official*

Bennettsville
Best, Carolyn Anne Hill *middle school education educator*

Cayce
McGill, Cathy Broome *gifted and talented education educator*

Charleston
Coleman, Dorothy Zipper *retired educational administrator*
Edwards, James Burrows *university president, oral surgeon*
Greenberg, Raymond Seth *academic administrator, educator*
Gunn, Morey Walker, Jr. *secondary school educator, choir director, organist*
Hinman, Eve Caison *academic administrator*
Hunter, Jairy C., Jr. *academic administrator*
Karesh, Janice Lehrer *special education consultant*
†Kuzenski, John C. *educator*
†Parson, Jack *academic administrator, political science educator*
President, Toni Elizabeth *guidance counselor, former elementary educator*
Sanders, Tence Lee Walker *elementary education educator*
Sarasohn, Evelyn Lois Lipman *principal*
Siewicki, Jean Ann *middle school educator*
Simms, Lois Averetta *retired secondary education educator, musician*
Sutusky, John Charles *higher education educator*
Whelan, Wayne Louis *higher education administrator*

Clemson
Cheatham, Harold Ernest *university dean, counselor, educator*
Curris, Constantine William *university president*
Kelly, John William, Jr. *university administrator*
Nilson, Linda Burzotta *director center for teaching*
Underwood, Sandra Jane *planning and management director*
Vogel, Henry Elliott *retired university dean and physics educator*

Clinton
†Cox, Kevin Monterey *school administrator*
Griffith, John Vincent *academic official*

Clio
McLeod, Marilynn Hayes *educational administrator, farmer*

Columbia
Aelion, C. Marjorie *adult education educator*
†Akhavi, Shahrough *educator*
Blachman, Morris J. *dean, management consultant*
Broome, Michael Cortes *college administrator*
Cilella, Mary Winifred *director*
†Cobbs, Charlene Rene' *parent educator*
†Davis, Bertha L. *dean women, Bible educator*
Friedman, Myles Ivan *education educator*
King, John Ethelbert, Jr. *education educator, former academic administrator*
LeClair, Betty Jo Cogdill *special education and early childhood educator*
Luna, Gene Irving *academic administrator, education educator*
McCulloch, Anne Merline Jacobs *college dean*
Miller, Johnny Vincent *academic administrator*
†Mitchell, J. Joseph, Jr. *educator, administrator, consultant*
Mohr, Laura Lee *school system administrator*
Muzekari, Thomasine Dabbs *adult education educator*
Palms, John Michael *academic administrator, physicist*
Petty, Donna Matthews *middle school educator*
Reisz, Howard Frederick, Jr. *seminary president, theology educator*
†Schramm, Susan Lynn *education educator*
Smith, Debra Marie *special education educator*
Waites, Candy Yaghjian *former state official*

Conway
Sarvis, Elaine Magann *assistant principal*
Squatriglia, Robert William *university dean, educator*
Wiseman, Dennis Gene *university dean*

Due West
Koonts, Jones Calvin *retired education educator*

Easley
Cole, Lois Lorraine *retired elementary school educator*
Henderson, Stephen Keith *academic administrator*

Elgin
Peake, Frank *middle school educator*

Florence
Rutherford, Vicky Lynn *special education educator*
Smith, Walter Douglas *retired college president*

Fort Mill
Honeycutt, Brenda *secondary education educator*

Gaffney
Davis, Lynn Hambright *culinary arts educator*
Griffin, Walter Roland *college president, educator, historian*
Suttle, Helen Jayson *retired education educator*

Greenville
Alford, Robert Wilfrid, Jr. *elementary school educator*
Hardin, Frankie Creamer *elementary education educator*
Hill, Grace Lucile Garrison *education educator, consultant*
Payne, George Frederick *educational administrator*
Smith, Philip Daniel *academic administrator, education educator*
†Turner, Barbara F. *elementary educator*
Whitmire, John Lee *daycare provider*

Greenwood
Jackson, Larry Artope *retired college president*
Mecca, Thomas Vincent *college administrator*
Morgan, John Augustine *university executive, consultant*

Greer
Poore, Timothy Shawn *elementary educator*

Hartsville
Daniels, James Douglas *academic administrator*

Hilton Head Island
Exley, Winston Wallace *middle school educator*
Fleischman, Kathryn Agnes *secondary education educator*
Mirse, Ralph Thomas *former college president*
Pustilnik, Jean Todd *elementary education educator*

Holly Hill
Niemeyer, Sandra Kay *secondary education educator*

Kershaw
Lucas, Dean Hadden *retired educator*

Kiawah Island
Bernard, Lowell Francis *academic administrator, educator, consultant*

Ladson
Cannon, Major Tom *special education educator*
Diamond, Michael Shawn *science and math educator, computer consultant*

Lake City
Hawkins, Linda Parrott *school system administrator*

Laurens
Dixon, Albert King, II *retired university administrator*

Lexington
Gatch, Charles Edward, Jr. *academic administrator*

Mount Pleasant
Gilbert, James Eastham *academic administrator*

North Charleston
Reilly, David Henry *university dean*

Orangeburg
Briggman, Jessie B. *secondary education educator*
Creekmore, Verity Veirs *media specialist*

Pawleys Island
Proefrock, Carl Kenneth *academic medical administrator*

Pendleton
†Owens, Gwendolyn Billups *education educator*

Pickens
†Shields, William George *elementary education educator*

Prosperity
Hause, Edith Collins *college administrator*

Rock Hill
Di Giorgio, Anthony J. *college president*
Wilson, Melford Alonzo, Jr. *secondary education educator*

Saluda
Nussbaumer, Melany Hamilton *program director*

Society Hill
King, Amanda Arnette *elementary school educator*

Spartanburg
Agnew, Janet Burnett *secondary education educator*
Gray, Nancy Ann Oliver *college administrator*
Gregg, Paula Ann *middle school educator*
Lesesne, Joab Mauldin, Jr. *college president*
Mahaffey, James Perry *education educator, consultant*
McGehee, Larry Thomas *university administrator*
Moore, Charles Gerald *educational administrator*
Stephens, Barbara Jane *academic administrator*
Stephens, Bobby Gene *college administrator, consultant*

Sumter
Abbott, Vicky Lynn *educational administrator*

Union
Lorenz, Latisha Jay *elementary education educator*

York
Huffman, Mervin Nicky *educator*

SOUTH DAKOTA

Aberdeen
†Akkerman, Charlotte Ann *principal*
Tebben, Sharon Lee *education educator*

Brookings
Elliott, Peggy Gordon *university president*

Kadoka
Stout, Maye Alma *educator*

Madison
Tunheim, Jerald Arden *academic administrator, physics educator*

Mitchell
Schilling, Katherine Lee Tracy *retired principal*
Swigart Johnson, Mary Colleen *special education educator*

Parkston
Coleman, Gary William *elementary school educator*

Pierre
Benson, Bernice LaVina *elementary education educator*
Perry, Robert Tad *educational official*

Rapid City
Han, Kenneth *dean*
Hughes, William Lewis *former university official, electrical engineer*
†Ochse, Ann *special education educator, consultant*
Schleusener, Richard August *college president*

Selby
Akre, Donald J. *school system administrator*

Sioux Falls
Ashworth, Julie *elementary education educator*
Balcer, Charles Louis *college president emeritus, educator*
Talley, Robert Cochran *medical school dean and administrator, cardiologist*
Tucker, William Vincent *vocational evaluator, former college president*
Wagoner, Ralph Howard *academic administrator, educator*

Spearfish
Thie, Genevieve Ann *retired secondary school educator*

Sturgis
†Musilek, Betty Marie *elementary education educator*

Vermillion
Dahlin, Donald C(lifford) *academic administrator*

Yankton
Crandall, Terrence Lee *counselor*

TENNESSEE

Ashland City
†Hall, Steve Harris *educator*

Athens
†Pfeifer, Diane M. *dean*
Stevenson, Jean Myers *education educator*

Bolivar
Buchanan, Bennie Lee Gregory *special education educator*

Bristol
Anderson, Jack Oland *retired college official*

Buchanan
Frensley, Joe Thomas *elementary education educator*

Chapel Hill
Christman, Luther Parmalee *retired university dean, consultant*

Chattanooga
Obear, Frederick Woods *academic administrator*
Stacy, Bill Wayne *academic administrator*
Tucker, Stanley R. *headmaster*
Young, Michael J. *secondary education educator, pastor*

Chuckey
Casteel, DiAnn Brown *principal*

Clarksville
Eaves, Arthur Joseph *English literature educator*
Manson, Tony James *education educator*

Cleveland
Lawson, Billie Katherine *elementary school educator*
Owens, Kelly Ann *elementary education educator*
Suttles, David Clyde *educator*

Collierville
Schmidt, Ronald R. *academic administrator*

Columbia
Cantrell, Sharron Caulk *secondary school educator*
Loper, Linda Sue *learning resources center director*

Cookeville
Alfred, Suellen *English education educator*
Elkins, Donald Marcum *dean, agronomy educator*
Peters, Ralph Martin *education educator*
Volpe, Angelo Anthony *university administrator, chemistry educator*

Dickson
Thomas, Janey Sue *elementary school principal*

Franklin
Awalt, Marilene Kay *principal*
Daniel, Cathy Brooks *tutor, educational consultant*
Guthrie, Glenda Evans *educational company executive*

Gallatin
Whiteside, Ann Birdsong *university public relations director*

Germantown
Allison, Beverly Gray *seminary president, evangelism educator*

Goodlettsville
Vatandoost, Nossi Malek *art school administrator*

Greeneville
†Carter, William Randall *educator, administrator*

Henderson
England, Richard C., Jr. *special education educator*

Hermitage
Quaintance, Alice Lynn *elementary school media specialist*

Huntsville
Ellis, Lonnie Calvert *educator*

Jackson
Agee, Bob R. *university president, educator, minister*
Bailey, James Andrew *middle school educator*
Barefoot, Hyran Euvene *academic administrator, educator, minister*

Jefferson City
Krug, John Carleton (Tony Krug) *college administrator, library consultant*
Maddox, Jesse Cordell *academic administrator*
Milligan, Karen Little *education educator*

Johnson City
Alfonso, Robert John *university administrator*
Franks, Ronald Dwyer *university dean, psychiatrist, educator*

Knoxville
Armistead, Willis William *university administrator, veterinarian*
Bales, William Joseph *academic administrator*
Beam, Richard Kenneth *college administrator*
Bodenheimer, Sally Nelson *reading educator*
Boling, Edward Joseph *university president emeritus, educator*
Brown, Billy Charlie *secondary school educator*
Griffin, Mary Jane Ragsdale *educational consultant, writer, small business owner*
Grubb, Rick *secondary education educator*
Harris, Roland Arsville, Jr. *college official*
Mankel, Francis Xavier *former principal, priest*
†Mooney, Wanda *school administrator*
Moran, James D., III *child development educator, university administrator*
Ratliff, Eva Rachel *elementary education educator*
Reynolds, Marjorie Lavers *nutrition educator*
Schumann, Jane Anne *education educator*
†Snyder, William T. *university chancellor*
South, Stephen A. *academic administrator*
†Thomas, Laurel Lynn *educational administrator, consultant*
Walsh, Joanne Elizabeth *retired educator, librarian*

Louisville
Wheeler, George William *university provost, physicist, educator*

Lynchburg
Logan, Debora Joyce *elementary and special education educator*

Manchester
Woodworth, Gene Boswell *educational writer, educator*

Mascot
Roberts, Sharon *gifted and talented education educator*

Mc Minnville
Henry, Mary Lou Smelser *elementary education educator*

Memphis
Barnes, Janice Bryant *elementary educator*
Brownell, Blaine Allison *university administrator, history educator*
†Call, M. Douglas *university administrator*
Carter, Michael Allen *college dean, nursing educator*
Coker, Georgina Harris *elementary education educator*
Dreyfus, Susan Kahn *elementary education educator*
Dunathan, Harmon Craig *college dean*
Ford, Kimball Sudderth *middle school educator*
Gagne, Ann Marie *special education educator*
Gaskins, Linda Carol *educator*
Gourley, Dick R. *college dean*
Hunt, James Calvin *academic administrator, physician*
Jones, Teresa A. *college official*
Legg, J. Ivan *academic administrator*
Nesin, Jeffrey D. *academic administrator*
Ranta, Richard Robert *university dean*
Rawlins, V. Lane *university president*
Tuggle, Gloria Harris *school system administrator*
Watson, Ada *secondary education educator*
Wheeler, Orville Eugene *university dean, civil and mechanical engineering educator*

Morristown
Hopper, Peggy F. *education educator*

Murfreesboro
Doyle, Delores Marie *elementary education educator*
Hayes, Janice Cecile *education educator*
Leaming, Deryl Ray *dean*
Walker, James E. *academic administrator, educator*

Nashville
Armstrong, Jeanette *education director*
†Baggett, Janet Rosalind *secondary education educator*
†Beasley, John Snodgrass, II *university administrator*
†Bourne, John R. *educator*
Chambers, Carol Tobey *elementary school educator*
Chaney, Sharon Henderson *secondary education educator, consultant*
Chapman, John Edmon *university dean, pharmacologist, physician*
Clinton, Barbara Marie *university health services director, social worker*
Clouse, R. Wilburn *education educator*
Conway-Welch, Colleen *dean, nurse midwife*
†Daniel, George Emmett *academic administrator*
Emans, Robert LeRoy *academic administrator, education educator*

Freudenthal, Ernest Guenter *technology and business educator*
Geisel, Martin Simon *college dean, educator*
Greene, Lydia Abbi Jwuan *elementary education educator*
Hamilton, Russell George, Jr. *academic dean, Spanish and Portuguese language educator*
Heard, (George) Alexander *retired educator and chancellor*
Hefner, James A. *academic administrator*
McMurry, Idanelle Sam *educational consultant*
†Murrell, Henry James *principal*
Pellegrino, James William *college dean, psychology educator*
Ridley, Carolyn Fludd *social studies educator*
Sharp, Bert Lavon *retired education educator, retired university dean*
Whitaker, Evans Parker *academic administrator*
Williams, Mary Helen *elementary education educator*
Wise, Bill *school system administrator*
Wyatt, Joe Billy *academic administrator*

Newport
Ball, Travis, Jr. *educational consultant, editor*
Runnion, Cindie J. *elementary school educator*

Oak Ridge
†Cragle, Donna Lynne *university administrator, researcher*

Ooltewah
Ratz, Kathy Ann Farmer *secondary education educator*

Pulaski
Croft, Janet Brennan *library director, fiber artist, costume designer*

Rogersville
Fairchild, Dorcas Sexton *English educator*

Sewanee
Croom, Frederick Hailey *college administrator, mathematics educator*
Lorenz, Anne Partee *special education educator, consultant*
Patterson, William Brown *university dean, history educator*

Somerville
†Cross, Rose Marie *school administrator*

Tazewell
Herrell, Virgil Lee *secondary education educator, English educator*

Tullahoma
Collins, S(arah) Ruth Knight *education educator*
McCay, Thurman Dwayne *university official*

Unicoi
Hatcher, James Mitchell *principal*

White House
Boyd, Becky M. *secondary school educator*

TEXAS

Abilene
Crymes, Mary Cooper *secondary school educator*
Hobbs, Karen French *development officer*
McCaleb, Gary Day *university official*
Shimp, Robert Everett, Jr. *academic administrator, historian*

Aledo
Lindsay, John, IV *principal*

Alpine
Morgan, Raymond Victor, Jr. *university administrator, mathematics educator*
Ortego y Gasca, Felipe de *education educator*

Amarillo
Sutterfield, Deborah Kay *special education educator*

Andrews
Scarbrough, Glenda Judith *elementary education educator*

Aransas Pass
Hamilton, Kathleen Allen *secondary education educator*

Arlington
Hawkins, Robert A. *college administrator*
Pickard, Myrna Rae *dean*
Sobol, Harold *retired dean, manufacturing executive, consultant*
Sorensen, Jeff Merwyn *university director*

Athens
Hawkins, Audrey Denise *academic administrator, educator*
Malcom, Carl Ray *secondary education educator*

Austin
Auvenshine, Anna Lee Banks *school system administrator*
Ayres, Robert Moss, Jr. *retired university president*
†Boehm, P. Diann *elementary education educator*
Brewer, Thomas Bowman *retired university president*
Campbell, Grover Stollenwerck *university official*
Cannon, William Bernard *retired university educator*
Cardozier, Virgus Ray *higher education educator*
Cleaves, Peter Shurtleff *university and foundation official*
Cunningham, William Hughes *academic administrator, marketing educator*
Dalton, Don *principal*
Flawn, Peter Tyrrell *businessman, retired university president, educator*
†Fonté, Richard W. *university administrator*
Franklin, Billy Joe *international higher education specialist*
Franklin, G(eorge) Charles *academic administrator*
Gardner, David Walton *educational administration educator*
Gill, Clark Cyrus *retired education educator*
Guzma'n, Ana Margarita *university administrator*
Haneke, Dianne Myers *education educator*
Harris, Ben M. *education educator*
Hetzler, Susan Elizabeth Savage *educational administrator*
Hunter, Brother Eagan *education educator*
Jeffrey, Robert Campbell *university dean*
Johnson, Sandra Lynn *education consultant*
Kennamer, Lorrin Garfield, Jr. *retired university dean*
Lehmann-Carssow, Nancy Beth *secondary school educator, coach*
Lewis, Nancy Louine Lambert *school counselor*
Livingston, William Samuel *university administrator, political scientist*
†Lund, Jeffrey Nelson *university official, human resources consultant*
Martin, Earin Miller *program director, educator, trainer*
Mathews, Steven Conrad *educational company executive*
†Matwiczak, Kenneth Matthew *university educator, consultant*
McCarty, Sally F. *educational consultant, entrepreneur*
†Parker, Randall Martin *educator*
Passons, Donna Janelle *academic administrator*
Quinn, Mike *dean*
Rogers, Lorene Lane *university president emeritus*
Roueche, John Edward, II *education educator, leadership program director*
Royal, Darrell K. *university official, former football coach*
†Sullivan, Charlotte Ann *educator*
Vliet, Donna Love *educator*
†Ziegler, Sharon Northrud *educational administrator*

Baytown
Black, Sarah Joanna Bryan *secondary school educator*
Culp, Barbara June *secondary school educator*

Beaumont
Brentlinger, William Brock *college dean*
Gagne, Mary *secondary school principal*

Beeville
Myers, Patricia Louise *college administrator*

Belton
Andreason, George Edward *university administrator*
Parker, Bobby Eugene, Sr. *college president*

Big Lake
†McCarson, Roberta Joan *educator in English, art, theatre*

Big Spring
Simmons, Lorna Womack *elementary school educator*

Boerne
Daugherty, Linda Hagaman *private school executive*

Bonham
Youree, Cheryl Ann *secondary education educator*

Borger
Brown, Roger Dale *college dean*

Brownfield
Cameron, Glenda Faye *secondary education educator*

Brownsville
Boze, Betsy Vogel *university dean, marketing educator*
Caballero, Bertha Lucio *gifted and talented education educator*

Brownwood
Tumlinson, Michael Ray *educational administrator*

Bryan
Bear, Robert Emerson *secondary education art educator*
Hill, Henry Carl *college administrator*
Hubert, Frank William Rene *retired university system chancellor*

Candelaria
Chambers, Johnnie Lois (Tucker) *retired elementary school educator, rancher*

Canyon
Long, Russell Charles *academic administrator*

Carrollton
Maher, Sheila *secondary school principal*

Channelview
Wallace, Betty Jean *elementary school educator, lay minister*

College Station
Adkisson, Perry Lee *university system chancellor*
†Balfour, Stephen Paul *educational analyst*
Calhoun, John C., Jr. *academic administrator*
†Cantrell, Carol Whitaker *educational administrator*
Carpenter, Delbert Stanley *educational administration educator*
Cocanougher, Arthur Benton *university dean, former business administration educator*
Erlandson, David Alan *education administration educator*
Haden, Clovis Roland *university administrator, engineering educator*
Kennedy, Robert Alan *educational administrator*
Monroe, Haskell Moorman, Jr. *university educator*
Perrone, Ruth Ellyn *university administrator*
Slater, Robert Owen *education educator*

Colleyville
†Berges, Juneria Parr *middle school principal*
Jones, Pamela Susan *middle school educator*

Comanche
Droke, Edna Faye *elementary school educator, retired*

Commerce
Schmidt, L. Lee, Jr. *university official*

Conroe
Marsh, Sue Ann *special education educator*

Converse
Hulsey, Rachel Martinez *secondary education educator*
Vontur, Ruth Poth *elementary school educator*

Coppell
Smothermon, Peggi Sterling *middle school educator*

Copperas Cove
Wright, David Ray *secondary school educator*

Corinth
Church, Jo Hall *educator*

Corpus Christi
Abdelsamad, Moustafa Hassan *dean*
Azopardi, Korita Marie *secondary school educator*
Chodosh, Robert Ivan *retired middle school educator, coach*
Early, William James *education educator*
Furgason, Robert Roy *university president, engineering educator*
Hamrick, Bill Allen *principal, retired*
Harper, Sandra Stecher *university administrator*
Stone-Magner, Rose Marie *vocational educator*

Corrigan
Murphy, Linda Marie *school district administrator*

Corsicana
Orsak, Charlie George *community college administrator*

Crockett
LaClair, Patricia Marie *physical education director, medical technician*

Cypress
Hamilton, Phyllis *principal*
Sorrell, Adrian Lloyd *education educator*

Dallas
Beidel, John Michael *headmaster, pastor*
Berkeley, Marvin H. *management educator, former university dean*
Bonelli, Anthony Eugene *former university dean*
Cook, Gary Raymond *university president, clergyman*
Davis, Patricia M. *literacy educator*
Gajewski, Ronald S. *consulting and training company executive*
Haayen, Richard Jan *university official, insurance company executive*
Harbaugh, Lois Jensen *secondary education educator*
Harrison, Frank *former university president*
†Helfman, Carolyn Rae *middle school educator*
Jaffe-Blackney, Sandra Michelle *special education educator*
†Mittlestet, Stephen *academic administrator*
Morse-McNeely, Patricia *poet, writer, middle school educator*
Novack, Lynne Dominick *academic and international programs administrator*
Poindexter, Barbara Glennon *secondary school educator*
Qualls, June Carol *elementary education educator*
Robbins, Jane Lewis *elementary school educator*
Smith, Valerie Gay *school counselor*
Taylor, Martha Ellen *private school educator*
Thomas, Sarah Elaine *elementary music educator*
Turner, Robert Gerald *university president*
Weaver, Betsy Dianne *elementary school educator*
Wenrich, John William *college president*
Williams, Bryan *university dean, medical educator*
†Wise, Kurt Alan *educator*

Decatur
Jordan, Linda Susan Darnell *elementary school educator*

Denton
Carlson, William Dwight *college president emeritus*
Cobb, Jeanne Beck *education educator, researcher, consultant*
Hurley, Alfred Francis *academic administrator, historian, retired military officer*
Palermo, Judy Hancock *elementary school educator*
Pettigrew, Johnnie Delonia *educational diagnostician*
Smith, Howard Wellington *education educator, dean emeritus*
Swigger, Keith *dean*
Thompson, Leslie Melvin *college dean, educator*
Turner, Philip Michael *university official and dean, author*

Edinburg
Nevarez, Miguel A. *university president*

El Paso
Beckley, Michele Anise Bennett *elementary education educator*
Erskine, William Crawford *academic administrator, accountant, health facility administrator*
Hernandez, Roberto Reyes *secondary school educator*
Jaraba, Martha E. (Betty Jaraba) *secondary school educator*
Jesinsky, Susan Gail *special education educator*
Natalicio, Diana Siedhoff *academic administrator*
Riter, Stephen *university administrator, electrical engineer*
Schecter, Erline Dian *educational administrator*
Tess, Alice Charlene *secondary school educator*
von Tungeln, George Robert *retired university administrator, economics consultant*

Fort Worth
Alland, Lawrence Martin *pastoral counselor, marriage and family therapist*
Bickerstaff, Mina March Clark *university administrator*
Collins Block, Cathy *education educator, writer, educational consultant*
Coonrod, Delberta Hollaway (Debbie Coonrod) *elementary education educator, consultant, freelance writer*
†De La Garza, Leonardo *university administrator*
Ferrari, Michael Richard, Jr. *university administrator*
Helton, Lucille Henry Hanrattie *academic administrator*
Hernandez, Daniel Arthur *elementary school educator*
Miller, Paula Colker *education consultant, staff developer*
Rainwater, Joyce Kelley *special education educator, consultant*
Saenz, Michael *college president*
Schrum, Jake Bennett *university administrator*
Tucker, William Edward *academic administrator, minister*
Von Rosenberg, Gary Marcus, Jr. *parochial school educator*
Walwer, Frank Kurt *dean, legal educator*
White, Warren Travis *educational consultant firm executive*
Wilson-Webb, Nancy Lou *adult education administrator*

Freeport
Baskin, William Gresham *counselor, music educator, vocalist*

Friendswood
Kennedy, Priscilla Ann *elementary school educator*

Gainesville
Dietz, David W. *elementary education educator*

Galveston
Banet, Charles Henry *academic administrator, clergyman*
Carrier, Warren Pendleton *retired university chancellor, writer*
Clayton, William Howard *retired university president*
Darst, Mary Lou *elementary education educator*
Goodwin, Sharon Ann *academic administrator*
Heins, Sister Mary Frances *educational administrator, nun*

Garland
Foster, Rebecca Anne Hodges *secondary school educator*
Goheen, Debra Elaine *secondary education educator*
Tabor, Beverly Ann *retired elementary school educator*

Georgetown
Shilling, Roy Bryant, Jr. *academic administrator*

Granbury
McWilliams, Chris Pater Elissa *elementary school educator*

Grapevine
Carter, Terri Gay Manns *Latin language educator*
Hirsh, Cristy J. *school counselor*
Kraft, Karen Ann *secondary school educator*

Greenville
Rice, Melva Gene *retired education educator*

Hallsville
†Dunlap, James Elvie *school superintendent, educator*

Harlingen
Zaslavsky, Robert *secondary school educator*

Hillsboro
Auvenshine, William Robert *academic administrator*

Houston
Adams, Elaine Parker *college administrator*
Adamson, Janice Lynne *fundraiser, grant writer, event coordinator*
†Ballard, Linda C. *director financial aid*
Banks, Evelyn Yvonne *middle school educator*
Berti, Margaret Ann *early childhood education educator*
Bowden, Nancy Butler *school administrator*
†Burgos-Sasscer, Ruth *chancellor*
Butler, William Thomas *college chancellor, physician, educator*
Camerino, Pat W. *medical college official*
Caram, Dorothy Farrington *educational consultant*
Carpenter, Dana Lynn *elementary educator*
Carroll, Michael M. *academic dean, mechanical engineering educator*
Darby, Anita Loyce *secondary school educator*
Davis, Bruce Gordon *retired principal*
Dent, Leanna Gail *secondary education educator*
†Djerejian, Edward Peter *institute administrator, former diplomat*
Douglas, James M. *universtiy president*
Doyle, Joseph Francis, III *art educator*
Ehlinger, Janet Ann Dowling *elementary school educator*
Feigin, Ralph David *medical school president, pediatrician, educator*
Fisher, Janet Warner *secondary school educator*
Gause, Val Hollis *middle school educator*
Georgiades, William Den Hartog *educational administrator*
Gillis, (Stephen) Malcolm *academic administrator, economics educator*
Hamilton, Lorraine Rebekah *adult education consultant*
Hitchman, Cal McDonald, Sr. *secondary education educator*
Ho, Yhi-Min *university dean, economics educator*
Hodo, Edward Douglas *university president*
Hoffman, Philip Guthrie *former university president*
Jimmar, D'Ann *elementary education educator, fashion merchandiser*
Johnson, Judy Dianne *elementary education educator*
†Johnson, Sandra Ann *elementary educator educator*
Kellar, William Henry *university official, history educator*
Kendall, Kay L. Orth *university official*
Kendrick, Robert Warren *county administrator, superindendent*
Kinnaird, Susan Marie *special education educator*
Mansell, Joyce Marilyn *special education educator*
McIntire, Mary Beth *university dean and official*
Meyer, Dianne Scott Wilson *secondary school educator, librarian*
Miller, Harry Freeman *university administrator*
Paul, Alida Ruth *secondary school educator*

Pendergraft, Roy Daniel *medical educator, physician*
Pickering, James Henry, III *academic administrator, educator*
Poats, Lillian Brown *education educator*
Polhemus, Mary Ann *elementary school principal, educator*
Rice, Emily Joy *retired secondary school and adult educator*
Roos, Sybil Friedenthal *retired elementary school educator*
Sayer, Coletta Keenan *gifted education educator*
Sharp, Douglas Andrew *secondary school educator*
Sheehan, Linda Suzanne *educational administrator*
Smith, Arthur Kittredge, Jr. *academic administrator, political science educator*
†Smith, Roland Blair *university administrator*
Smythe, Cheves McCord *dean, medical educator*
Stryker, Daniel Ray *adult education educator*
van Cleave, Kirstin Dean (Kit van Cleave) *martial arts educator, writer, educator, publishing executive*
†Wade, Freddie, III *program director*
Webb, Marty Fox *principal*
Weber, Wilford Alexander *education educator*
Wesse, David Joseph *higher education consultant*
Whitaker, Gilbert Riley, Jr. *academic administrator, business economist*
Williames, Lee John *university official, history educator*

Howe
Jarma, Donna Marie *secondary education educator*

Humble
St. Pé, Carolyn Ann *elmentary education educator*

Huntsville
Bowers, Elliott Toulmin *university president*
LeBlanc, Jacob D. *vice principal*
Marks, Bobby Kees *academic administrator, educator*
Payne, David Emer *university administrator*
Ward, Richard Hurley *university administrator, writer*
Warner, Laverne *education educator*

Hurst
Bennett, Lori Jayne *elementary school educator*

Irving
Bielss, Otto William, Jr. *secondary school educator*
Cannon, Francis V., Jr. *academic administrator, electrical engineer, economist*
Chase, Pearline *adult education educator*
Martin, Thomas Lyle, Jr. *university president*
McVay, Barbara Chaves *secondary education mathematics educator*
Messina, Paul Francis *education consultant*
Sasseen, Robert Francis *university educator*

Karnes City
Davis, Troy Arnol *reflexologist, hypnotherapist*

Katy
Gibert, Charlene West *gifted education educator*
Hughes, Sandra Michelle *education administrator, educator*

Kempner
Parker, Catharine Janet *education administrator, consultant, entrepreneur*

Kilgore
†Holda, William Michael *academic administrator*

Killeen
†Anderson, James Raymond *academic administrator*
Book, Barbara Nell *elementary school educator*
Montgomery, Marietta H. (Bunnie Montgomery) *secondary education educator*
Reid, Sharon Lea *educational facilitator*
Reid, Thomas Michael *middle school educator*

Kingsville
†Cortazar, Alejandro *educator*
Ibanez, Manuel Luis *university official, biological sciences educator*
Robins, Gerald Burns *education educator*
Wiley, Millicent Yoder *retired secondary school educator, realtor*

Klein
Esmond, Cheri Sue *secondary school educator*

Lake Creek
Smith, Shirley Ann Nabors *secondary school educator*

LaPorte
†Defee, Vicki Jean *elementary education educator*

Laredo
Black, Clifford Merwyn *academic administrator, sociologist, educator*
Fierros, Ruth Victoria *retired secondary school educator*
Reuthinger, Georgeanne *special education educator*

Leander
Reed, Carol Brady Summerlin *secondary education educator*

Levelland
†Taylor, James Lynn *college administrator*

Lewisville
Myers, Madeleine Becan *secondary school educator*

Livingston
Horner, Jennie Linn *retired educational administrator, nurse*
Oliver, Debbie Edge *elementary education educator*

Longview
Fouse, Anna Beth *education educator*
LeTourneau, Richard Howard *retired college president*
Martin, John Foster *university official*
Pursley-Davis, Alice Janet *elementary school educator*

Lubbock
Askins, Billy Earl *education educator, consultant*
†Burns, John Mitchell *academic administrator*
Haragan, Donald Robert *university administrator, geosciences educator*
Hisey, Lydia Vee *educational administrator*
Huggins, Cannie Mae Cox Hunter *retired elementary school educator*
Nelson, Toza *elementary school educator*
Nugent, Connie *elementary education educator*
Pike, Douglas Eugene *educator*
Schmidly, David J. *academic administrator, dean, biology educator*

Lufkin
†Shaw, Dianne Elizabeth *school administrator*
Strohschein, Helen Frances *educational administrator*

Mcallen
Gonzalez, Rolando Noel *secondary school educator, religion educator, photographer*
Ramirez, Leo Armando *secondary school educator*
Sands, Norman Earl *elementary school educator, composer*

Mercedes
Alaniz, Theodora Villarreal *elementary education educator*

Midland
Lankford, Jill *elementary school principal*
McAfee, John Wilson, Sr. *retired principal*

Mount Pleasant
Caskey, Judith Ann *educational director*

Nacogdoches
Ball, Margie Barber *elementary school educator*

New Braunfels
Oestreich, Charles Henry *retired university president*

North Richland Hills
Urquhart, Chris Holowiak *school administrator, educator*

Odessa
Folsom, Hyta Prine *educational grant writer, consultant*
Sorber, Charles Arthur *academic administrator*
Watson, Kay *school system administrator, retired*

Pampa
Anderson, Donna Elaine *elementary and secondary school educator*
Kibbe, Kay Lynn *secondary education educator, counselor*

Pasadena
†Blue, Monte Lynn *college president*
Reyna, Wanda Wong *early childhood education educator*

Pecos
Busby, Shannon Nixon *special education educator*

Perryton
Doerrie, Bobette *secondary education educator*

Pflugerville
†Null, James Wesley *educator*

Plainview
Norris, Kathy Horan *school counselor*

Plano
Anderson, Robin Marie *secondary education educator*
†Anthony, John H. *college administrator*
Burns, Kristi J. *school counselor*
France-Deal, Judith Jean *English as a Second Language educator*
Reidling, Valerie Ann *secondary school educator*

Pyote
Thomas, Beverly Irene *special education educator*

Redwater
Edwards, Maya Michelle *secondary education educator*

Rhome
Brammer, Barbara Rhudene *retired secondary education educator*

Richardson
Dunn, David E. *university dean*
Keenan, Deborah Duane LeFevre *special education educator, student assistance specialist*
Kelly, Rita Mae *academic administrator, researcher*
Turner, Frederick *interdisciplinary educator*
Weaver, Jo Nell *retired elementary school educator*
Wildenthal, Bryan Hobson *university administrator*

Rockdale
Estell, Dora Lucile *retired educational administrator*

San Angelo
Maedgen, Cynthia Ann *secondary school educator*

San Antonio
†Bostick, Betty Jane *retired elementary education educator*
Boyers, John Martin *principal*
Brazil, John Russell *academic administrator*
†Chidgey, Terri J. *educator, principal*
Cummings Persellin, Diane Y. *music education educator*
Dudley, Brooke Fitzhugh *educational consultant*
†Elaydi, Saber Nasr *educator*
Frith, Lynda Kathryn *principal*
Gibbons, Robert Ebbert *university official*
Goelz, Paul Cornelius *university dean*
†Groff, James Edward *education educator, academic administrator*
Henderson, Dwight Franklin *dean, educator*
Kalkwarf, Kenneth Lee *academic dean*
Koym, Zala Cox *elementary education educator*
Leal, J. Terri *academic facility administrator*
LeCoeur, Jo *adult education educator*
Ledvorowski, Thomas Edmund *secondary education educator*
Lloyd, Susan Elaine *middle school educator*
Madrid, Olga Hilda Gonzalez *retired elementary education educator, association executive*
Marshall, Joyce Ramsey *elementary education educator*
Mayo, Sandra Marie *college dean*
†McBee, Lucy A. *elementary education educator, administrator*
McDonald, Mary Helen *special education educator*
Moder, John Joseph *academic administrator, priest*
Moss, Betty Harris *secondary education educator*
†Oliver, Beverly *secondary school principal, administrator*
Owens, Amelia Anne *elementary education educator*
Paloczy, Susan Therese *elementary school principal*
Potts, Martha Lou *elementary education educator*
Ramsey, Sara Annette *elementary education educator*
Silva, Aurelia Davila *education educator*
Terry, James Crockett *school system administrator, mediator*
Tomkewitz, Marie Adele *elementary school educator*
†White, Charles B. *academic administrator*
Wimpee, Mary Elizabeth *elementary school educator*
Windham, Janice Gay *principal*
Young, James Julius *university administrator, retired army officer*

San Diego
Pena, Modesta Celedonia *retired principal*

San Juan
Shelby, Nina Claire *special education educator*

San Marcos
Barragán, Celia Silguero *elementary education educator*
Fite, Kathleen Elizabeth *education educator*
Miloy, Leatha Faye *university program director*
Schiflett, Peggy L. Kucera *secondary school educator, consultant*
Supple, Jerome H. *academic administrator*

Seabrook
†Niksich, Peggy Linda *elementary education educator*

Sherman
Jordan, David William *college administrator, faculty dean*
Page, Oscar Cletice *academic administrator*
†Williams, Ruby Jo *retired principal*

Skidmore
Barnes, Patricia Ann *art teacher*

Southlake
Allen, Eleanor Kathleen (Missy Allen) *elementary education educator*

Stafford
Herrera, Mary Cardenas *education educator, music minister*

Stephenville
Sims, Larry Kyle *secondary school educator*

Sugar Land
Duvall, Cathleen Elaine *elementary school educator, consultant*

Sulphur Springs
Gibson, Jannette Poe *educator, consultant*

Temple
Van Ness, James Samuel *academic administrator, historian*

Terrell
†Perry, Lanny Joseph *secondary education educator, clergyman*

The Woodlands
Sharman, Diane Lee *secondary school educator*

Tyler
Baker, Deborah Kay *secondary education educator*
Davidson, Jack Leroy *academic administrator*
†Lewis, Linda Katherine *elementary education educator*
Waller, Wilma Ruth *retired secondary school educator and librarian*

Universal City
McElveen-Combs, Gail Marie *middle school educator*

Uvalde
Wilson, Benjamin Franklin, Jr. *education educator*

Victoria
Haynes, Karen Sue *university president, social work educator*

Vidor
Stokely, Joan Barbara *elementary school educator*

Waco
Belew, John Seymour *academic administrator, chemist*
Brooks, Roger Leon *university president*
Hollingsworth, Martha Lynette *secondary school educator*
Lindsey, Jonathan Asmel *development executive, educator*
Moseley, Mary Prudence *education educator*
Moshinskie, James Francis *educational technology educator*
Reynolds, Herbert Hal *academic administrator*
†Sloan, Robert B. *university president*

Waxahachie
Hastings, Ronnie Jack *secondary school educator*

Weatherford
Estes, Carolyn Ann Hull *retired elementary school educator*

Weslaco
Jordan, Timothy Edward *secondary education educator*

Wharton
Gonzalez, Antonio *academic administrator, mortgage company executive*

Whitehouse
Stansell, Aiszeleen *secondary school educator*

Whitewright
Watkins, Regina Gail *elementary education educator*

Wichita Falls
Cates, Sue Sadler *educational diagnostician*
Harvill, Melba Sherwood *university librarian*
Pemberton, Merri Beth Morris *educator*
Rodriguez, Louis Joseph *university president, educator*

Willis
McCrary, Linda Hulon *elementary school educator*

Woodway
Mulholland, Barbara Ann *school director*

UTAH

Bountiful
Rawlins, Jan *principal*

Cedar City
Stauffer, Gregory L(ynn) *program director*
†Templin, Carl Ross *college dean, educator*

Clearfield
Daniels, Robert Paul *special education administrator*

Clinton
Johnson, Charles N. *elementary education educator*

Logan
†Ahlstrom, Callis Blythe *university official*
Hunsaker, Scott Leslie *gifted and talented education educator*
McKell, Cyrus M. *retired college dean, plant physiologist*
Shaver, James Porter *education educator, university dean*

Magna
McDonough, Karel Joy Doop *secondary education educator, musician*

Mount Pleasant
Schade, Wilbert Curtis *educational administrator*

Ogden
Eisler, David Lee *provost*
Graff, Darrell Jay *physiology educator*
Mecham, Steven Ray *school system administrator*
Smith, Robert Bruce *college administrator*
Thompson, Paul Harold *university president*

Orem
Green, John Alden *university director study abroad program*

Price
†Donaldson, Rebecca S. *elementary education educator, reading specialist*

Provo
Bangerter, Vern *secondary education educator*
Bateman, Merrill Joseph *university president*
Christensen, Bruce LeRoy *academic administrator, former public broadcasting executive*
Densley, Colleen T. *elementary education educator, curriculum facilitator*
Fleming, Joseph Clifton, Jr. *dean, law educator*
Hansen, H. Reese *dean, educator*
Huber, Clayton Shirl *university dean*
Keele, Alan Frank *adult education educator*
Stahmann, Robert F. *education educator*
Todd, Sally McClay *teacher gifted and talented, psychologist*
Whatcott, Marsha Rasmussen *elementary education educator*

Riverton
Rockwood, Linn Roy *retired recreation executive, educator*

Salt Lake City
Cannell, Cyndy Michelle *elementary school principal*
Chivers, Laurie Alice *state educational administrator*
Drew, Clifford James *university administrator, special education and educational psychology educator*
Fink, Kristin Danielson *secondary education educator*
Gough, Eugene V. *vocational education educator*
Magleby, Florence Deming *special education educator*
Matsen, John Martin *academic administrator, pathologist*
Matthews, Patricia Deneise *special education educator*
McCleary, Lloyd E(verald) *education educator*
McIntyre, Jerilyn Sue *academic administrator*
Miller, William Charles *college dean, architect*
Morris, Sylvia Marie *university official*
Peterson, Chase N. *university president*
Pickering, AvaJane *specialized education facility executive*
†Purdie, Tonya Marie Thomas *college academic counselor*
Simmons, Lynda Merrill Mills *educational administrator*
Smith, J(ames) Scott *elementary education educator*
†Sorensen, Parry Daniel *educator*
Stock, Peggy A(nn) *college president, educator*
Thatcher, Blythe Darlyn *assistant principal*

Sandy
Liddle, Jacqueline S. *secondary education educator*
Pierce, Ilona Lambson *educational administrator*

PROFESSIONAL INDEX 5901 EDUCATION

Sabey, J(ohn) Wayne *academic administrator, consultant*
Volpe, Ellen Marie *middle school educator*

Tooele
Lawrence, Stephen Lee *elementary school principal, mechanic*

Wendover
Arnoldson, Earl Randon *educator*

West Jordan
Shepherd, Paul H. *elementary school educator*

VERMONT

Arlington
Pentkowski, Raymond J. *superintendent*

Bennington
Coleman, Elizabeth *college president*
Cooper, Charleen Frances *special and elementary education educator*
†DeBey, Mary *educator*

Burlington
Allard, Judith Louise *secondary education educator*
Brandenburg, Richard George *university dean, management educator*
Della Santa, Laura *principal*
Ferrari, Dennis M. *secondary education educator*
Frymayer, John W. *dean*
LaRue, S. Renee *middle level educator*
Miller, Jane Cutting *elementary education educator*
Ramaley, Judith Aitken *university president, endocrinologist*

Castleton
†Miller, Judith *adult education educator*

Colchester
Fellows, Diana Potenzano *educational administrator*
Thompson, Ellen Ann *elementary education educator*

East Burke
Burnham, Robert Alan *educator, academic administrator*

Hinesburg
Forauer, Robert Richard *elementary education educator*

Ludlow
Davis, Vera *elementary school educator*

Middlebury
McCardell, John Malcolm, Jr. *college administrator*
†Napolitano, Peter Joseph *academic administrator*
O'Brien, George Dennis *retired university president*
Rader, Rhoda Caswell *academic program director*

North Troy
Weingart, Carol Jayne *university administrator, educator, psychotherapist*

Plymouth
Crandell, Sarah Allen *dean*

Saint Johnsbury
Mayo, Bernier L. *secondary school principal*

South Hero
Bisson, Roger *middle school educator*

South Royalton
Doria, Anthony Notarnicola *college dean, educator*
Foose, Robert A. *higher education administrator*

Waterbury
Bunting, Charles I. *academic administrator*

Woodstock
Chiefsky, Susan Justine *secondary education educator*

VIRGINIA

Abingdon
Mashburn, Donald Eugene *educator*

Alexandria
Fairey, Chad Christopher *secondary education educator*
Jarrard, James Paul *school program administrator*
Johnson, William David *retired university administrator*
LaMarca, Mary Margaret *elementary education educator*
†Lane, Debra Elizabeth *principal*
Latson, Richard Charles *audio visual manager*
Pastin, Mark Joseph *association executive*
†Schmidt, Elaine Melotti *assistant principal*
Stout, Mary Webb *supervisory educational services specialist, educator*

Amherst
Campbell, Catherine Lynn *elementary and middle school educator*
Herbert, Amanda Kathryn *special education educator*

Annandale
†Ernst, Richard James *academic administrator*

Arlington
Bartlett, Elizabeth Susan *audio-visual specialist*
Berg, Sister Marie Majella *university chancellor*
Hill, Donald Wain *education accreditation commission executive*
Houston, Paul David *school association administrator*
Leibensperger, Philip Wetzel *secondary education educator*
McCaskill, James H. *secondary education educator, consultant*
Peterson, Paul Quayle *retired university dean, physician*
Smerdon, Ernest Thomas *academic administrator*
Violand-Sanchez, Emma Natividad *school administrator, educator*
Welsford, James Joseph *secondary school educator*

Ashland
Chandler, Kimberley Lynn *gifted education resource specialist*
Henshaw, William Raleigh *middle school educator*
Martin, Roger Harry *college president*

Baskerville
Simmons, Barry William *university official, consultant*

Bedford
Henry, Nancy Sinclair *middle school educator*

Blacksburg
†Archer, Vanessa *education program director*
Brown, Gregory Neil *university administrator, forest physiology educator*
Campbell, Joan Virginia Loweke *secondary school educator, language educator*
Carlisle, Ervin Frederick *university provost, educator*
Edwards, Patricia K. *dean*
†Goodsell, Charles T. *educator*
Harris, Sally Lee *public relations coordinator*
†Hirt, Joan B. *education educator*
Lynch, Sherry Kay *counselor*
†Meszaros, Peggy *academic administrator*
†Muffo, John Anthony *administrator*
Poole, Calvert King *elementary school educator*
Smith, Robert McNeil *university dean*
Steger, Charles William *university administrator*
Tillar, Thomas Cato, Jr. *university alumni relations administrator, consultant*
Torgersen, Paul Ernest *academic administrator, educator*

Boyd Tavern
Darden, Donna Bernice *special education educator*

Bridgewater
Geisert, Wayne Frederick *educational consultant, retired administrator*

Charlottesville
†Adams, Lawrence Earl *educator*
Brandt, Richard Martin *education educator*
Breneman, David Worthy *dean, educator*
Bunker, Linda Kay *dean, physical education educator*
Carey, Robert Munson *university dean, physician*
Casteen, John Thomas, III *university president*
Cooper, James Michael *education educator*
Corse, John Doggett *university official, lawyer*
Fornadel, William Mark *university dean*
Keats, Patricia Hart *counselor, educator*
Keene, Rhonda Leigh *secondary education educator*
Lancaster, (Barbara) Jeanette *dean, nursing educator*
Matson, Robert Edward *public management educator, leadership consultant*
McDonough, William Andrew *dean*
O'Neil, Robert Marchant *university administrator, law educator*
Reynolds, Robert Edgar *academic administrator, physician*
Smith, Clyde Ray *dean*
†Snyder, Edward Adams *dean, economics educator*
Thompson, Kenneth W(infred) *educational director, author, editor, administrator, social science educator*
Verstegen, Deborah A. *education educator*

Chesapeake
Harris, Brenda Lee *college administrator*
Lewter, Helen Clark *elementary education educator, retired*
Nicely, Denise Ellen *elementary education educator*
†Niemeyer, Antonio Bilisoly, Jr. *school system administrator*
Pearce, Patsy Beasley *elementary education educator*
Spady, Benedict Quintin *secondary education educator*

Chester
Spindler, Judith Tarleton *elementary school educator*

Clifton
Latt, Pamela Yvonne *school system administrator*

Clifton Forge
Allen, M(ilford) Ray *secondary education educator*

Clintwood
†Baker, George Brian *principal*

Courtland
†Smith, Cynthia Lynne *educator*

Covington
†Worley, Wesley F. *secondary education educator*

Culpeper
Furgiuele, Margery Wood *vocational school educator*

Dahlgren
Bales, Ruby Jones *retired elementary school educator and principal*

Delaplane
Harris, Charles Upchurch *seminary president, clergyman*

Emporia
Bottoms, Brenda Pinchbeck *elementary education educator*

Fairfax
Carr, Patricia Warren *adult education educator*
Havlicek, Sarah Marie *educator, artist, small business owner*
Johnson, George William *retired academic administrator*
Merten, Alan Gilbert *academic administrator*
Miller, Linda Karen *educator*
†Potter, David L. *academic administrator*
Powell, Karan Hinman *university program administrator, consultant*
Vance, Mary Lee *academic administrator*

Falls Church
Cleland, Sherrill *college president*
Rice, Sue Ann *dean, industrial and organizational psychologist*
†Willison, Kimberly Schumaker *gifted education educator*

Fort Defiance
Livick, Malcolm Harris *school administrator*

Fredericksburg
Craig, N(orville) Wayne *secondary education educator*
Jenks-Davies, Kathryn Ryburn *retired daycare provider and owner, civic worker*
Jones, Julia Pearl *elementary school educator*

Glen Allen
Alves, Constance Dillenger *special education educator*

Great Falls
Benen, Elaine Carol *educational administrator*

Hampden Sydney
Wilson, Samuel V. *college president*

Hampton
Fox, Margaret Louise *retired secondary education educator*
Steele, James Eugene *school system administrator, educator*

Harrisonburg
Aley, Shelley B. *composition and rhetoric educator*
Carrier, Ronald Edwin *university administrator*
Hedrick, Joyce Ann Coryell *educational support services professional*

Haysi
Deel, George Moses *elementary school educator*

Herndon
†Ross, Barbara Ann *gifted/talented education educator*

Keswick
Ackell, Edmund Ferris *university president*
Fletcher, John Caldwell *bioethicist, educator*

Keysville
Carwile, Nancy Ramsey *educational administrator*

Lake Ridge
Hinnant, Hilari Anne *educator, educational consultant*

Leesburg
Rader, Toni Christine *secondary education educator*

Lexington
Elrod, John William *university president, philosophy and religion educator*
Knapp, John Williams *retired college president*
McCloud, Anece Faison *academic administrator*
†Pierpaoli, Paul George *educator*
Young, Kenneth Evans *educational consultant*

Lynchburg
†Cushman, Valerie Jean *athletic director*
Simms, Alice Jane *secondary school educator*
Sullivan, Gregory Paul *secondary education educator*
Swain, Diane Scott *principal*

Machipongo
Bonniwell, Ann Glenn *educational administrator*

Manassas
Archer, Chalmers, Jr. *education educator*
†Beirne-Patey, Marian Josephine *secondary educator*
Edwards, Peter *educator, writer*

Mc Lean
Michalowicz, Karen Dee *secondary education educator*

Middleburg
Coven, Robert Michael *secondary school educator, researcher, writer*
Larmore, Catherine Christine *university official*

Midlothian
Alligood, Mary Sale *special education educator*

Monroe
Sandidge, Oneal Cleaven *academic administrator, educator*

Monterey
Kirby, Mary Weeks *elementary education educator, reading specialist*

Newport News
Hightower, John Brantley *arts administrator*
Powell, Jouett Lynn *college dean, philosophy and religious studies educator*
Tracy, Tracy Faircloth *special education educator*
Wiatt, Carol Stultz *elementary education educator*

Norfolk
Curry, Robert Furman, Jr. *educator, academic advisor*
†Gora, JoAnn M. *academic administrator*
Jones, Franklin Ross *education educator*
†Kimbrough, Walter Mark *university activities director*
Koch, James Verch *academic administrator, economist*
Myers, Donald Allen *university dean*
Perkins, Annie Suite *adult education educator*
Ritz, John Michael *education educator*
†Tonelson, Stephen W. *special education educator*
Wheeler, Jock Rogers *dean, medical educator*

Oakton
Hough, Edythe S. Ellison *dean*
Hu, Sue King *elementary and middle school educator*

Ophelia
Simonsen, August Henry *education director*

Portsmouth
Agricola, Dianne G. *secondary education educator, tutor*
Dudley, Delores Ingram *secondary education educator, poet, writer*

Pulaski
Cox, David Alan *superintendent of schools*

Reston
Keefe, James Washburn *educational writer, researcher, consultant*

Richmond
Blank, Florence Weiss *literacy educator, editor*
Cooper, William Edwin *university president, educator*
Ellis, Anthony John *education educator*
Hamel, Dana Bertrand *academic administrator*
Heilman, E. Bruce *academic administrator*
James, Allix Bledsoe *retired university president*
Jones, Jeanne Pitts *director early childhood school*
Kontos, Hermes Apostolou *dean*
Leary, David Edward *university dean*
McGee, Henry Alexander, Jr. *university official*
McLees, Ainslie Armstrong *secondary education educator*
Minor, Marian Thomas *elementary and secondary school educational consultant*
Morrill, Richard Leslie *university administrator*
Reveley, Walter Taylor, III *dean*
Rosenblum, John William *dean*
Sasser, Ellis A. *gifted and talented education educator*
Simmons, S. Dallas *former university president*
Torrence, Rosetta Lena *educational consultant*
Trani, Eugene Paul *academic administrator, educator*
Waite-Franzen, Ellen Jane *academic administrator*
†White, Shelley Reaves *educator, counselor*
Williams, Deborah Yvonne *secondary education educator*

Roanoke
Coleman, Sallye Terrell *retired social studies educator*
†Harrison, John Todd *social studies teacher*
Nickens, Harry Carl *academic administrator*

Salem
Gring, David M. *academic administrator*

Spotsylvania
Westwood, Geraldine E. *elementary school educator*

Springfield
Jones, Bonnie Damschroder *special education specialist*
Leavitt, Mary Janice Deimel *special education educator, civic worker*
Minetree, James Lawrence, III *military officer, educator*
Ray, Carol Lynn *special education educator*

Staunton
Tyson, Cynthia Haldenby *academic administrator*

Suffolk
Matson, Virginia Mae Freeberg (Mrs. Edward J. Matson) *retired special education educator, author*

Sugar Grove
Greer, Carole Kilby *reading specialist*

Urbanna
Salley, John Jones *university administrator, oral pathologist*

Vienna
†Colosi, Thomas R. *educator*
Cramer, Roxanne Herrick *gifted and talented education educator*
Tordiff, Hazel Midgley *education director*

Virginia Beach
Barriskill, Maudanne Kidd *primary school educator*
Budd, Richard Wade *university official, communications scientist*
Corbat, Patricia Leslie *special education educator*
Jones, Robert Clair *middle school educator*
Kawczynski, Diane Marie *elementary and middle school educator, composer*
†MacDonald, Douglas Alexander *educator*
Morgan, Raymond Franklin *education educator*
Phillips, Joey Heyward *special education educator*
Richardson, Daniel Putnam *director*
Selig, William George *university official*
Von Mosch, Wanda Gail *middle school educator*
Wiggins, Samuel Paul *education educator*

Warrenton
Norskog, Eugenia Folk *elementary education educator*

Waynesboro
Clark, Olive Iola *retired secondary and elementary education educator*

Williamsburg
Birney, Robert Charles *retired academic administrator, psychologist*
Humphreys, Homer Alexander *former principal*
Jones, David Proctor *academic administrator*
McBeth, Elaine Susan *university administrator*
Mc Kean, John Rosseel Overton *university dean*
†Mills, Joan Elizabeth *educator*
Pipes, Robert Byron *retired academic administrator, mechanical engineer*
Scholnick, Robert J. *college dean, English language educator*
Smith, James Brown, Jr. *secondary school educator*
Van Tassel-Baska, Joyce Lenore *education educator*

Winchester
Braswell, Gary Joseph *secondary school educator, military officer*
Pleacher, David Henry *secondary school educator*
Smith, Lanna Cheryl *secondary school educator*
Tisinger, Catherine Anne *college dean*

Wise
Lemons, L. Jay *academic administrator*
Smiddy, Joseph Charles *retired college chancellor*

Woodbridge
Derrickson, Denise Ann *secondary school educator*
Packard, Mildred Ruth *middle school educator*

Yorktown
Forrest, Kay V. *educator, editor, writer*
Rogers, Sheila Wood *elementary and secondary school educator*

WASHINGTON

Auburn
Eaton, Edgar Eugene *retird educator, writer*

Bainbridge Island
Milander, Henry Martin *educational consultant*

Bellevue
Bergstrom, Marianne Elisabeth *program coordinator, special education educator*
†Pastore, Michael Anthony *college administrator*

Bellingham
Becker, Michael Kelleher *university administrator, consultant*
Little, Marie Ann *ESL educator, program facilitator*
Morse, Karen Williams *academic administrator*

Bothell
Banks, Cherry Ann McGee *education educator*
Icenhower, Rosalie B. *retired elementary school principal*

Bremerton
Garrison, Eva Heim *school counselor*

Centralia
Kirk, Henry Port *academic administrator*

Cheney
†Jordan, Stephen M. *university president*

Chimacum
Hollenbeck, Dorothy Rose *special education educator*

Colton
†Straughan, Gene Thomas *educator*

Deer Park
Griffin, Leslie Dee *educational administrator*

Edmonds
Bell, Nancy Lee Hoyt *real estate investor, middle school educator, volunteer*
†Bell, Ralph Rogers *retired superintendent schools, genealogist*
DeForeest, Joanne Marie *educator*

Ellensburg
†Janke, John Eric *secondary educator*
Nelson, Ivory Vance *academic administrator*

Everett
Hundley, Ronnie *academic administrator*

Federal Way
Duggan, Edward Martin *secondary education educator*

Gig Harbor
Bratrud, Linda Kay *secondary education educator*

Goldendale
Nygaard, Mary Payne *primary school educator*

Issaquah
Newbill, Karen Margaret *elementary school educator, education educator*

Kennewick
Knight, Janet Ann *elementary education educator*

Kent
Hickey, Shirley Louise Cowin *elementary education educator*
Irwin, Deborah Jo *secondary education educator, flutist*
Johnson, Dennis D. *elementary school principal*

Kirkland
Rich, Clayton *retired university official and educator*
Tyllia, Frank Michael *university official, educator*

Lacey
Kuniyasu, Keith Kazumi *secondary education educator*
†Reilich, Eileen *education educator*
Spangler, David Robert *college administrator, engineer*

Lakewood
Oakes, DuWayne Earl *retired principal*

Leavenworth
Wadlington, William Jewell *principal, secondary education educator*

Longview
Campbell, Kristine Koetting *academic administrator*

Lynnwood
†Oharah, Jack *academic administrator*

Mill Creek
Larson, Mary Bea *elementary education educator*

Mount Vernon
Bogensberger, Joan Helen Hess *school administrator, consultant*
Cline, Pauline M. *educational administrator*

Nine Mile Falls
Payne, Arlie Jean *parent education administrator*

Odessa
Pitts, Michael Duane *secondary education educator*

Olympia
Averill, Ronald Henry *political science educator, retired military officer*
†Bergeson, Teresa *state system administrator*
Hogan, Nancy Kay *elementary education educator*
Jervis, Jane Lise *college official, science historian*
Lambert, Kathy L. *elementary educator, legislator*

Port Angeles
Chase, John David *university dean, physician*

Poulsbo
Pack, Nancy J. *special education educator, speech therapist*

Pullman
Bataille, Gretchen *academic administrator*
Hatch, Lynda Sylvia *education educator*
Hatley-Brickey, Lael Ann *university administrator*
Lewis, Norman G. *academic administrator, researcher, consultant*
Nelson, Douglas Michael *school system administrator, educator*
Rennebohm Franz, Kristi *primary education educator*

Renton
Frank, Ronald Ray *elementary school educator*
Lockridge, Alice Ann *secondary education educator*
Schoenrock, Cheri Michelle *elementary education educator*

Richland
Miller, James Vince *university president*
Piippo, Steve *educator*

Seattle
Abbott, Robert Dean *education scientist*
Banks, James Albert *educational research director, educator*
Beaumonte, Phyllis Ilene *secondary school educator*
Brown, Kristi *principal*
Carlson, Dale Arvid *university dean*
Coulter, John Arthur *academic administrator*
Cox, Frederick Moreland *retired university dean, social worker*
Debro, Julius *university dean, sociology educator*
Denny, Brewster Castberg *retired university dean*
Drew, Jody Lynne *secondary education educator*
Fischer, Mary E. *special education educator*
Gardiner, John Jacob *leadership studies educator, author, philosopher*
Gerberding, William Passavant *retired university president*
Gibaldi, Milo *dean*
Goodlad, John Inkster *education educator, author*
Guskin, Alan E. *university president*
Hampton, Shelley Lynn *hearing impaired educator*
Hegyvary, Sue Thomas *nursing school dean*
†Huntsman, Lee *university provost, academic administrator*
Jennerich, Edward John *university official and dean*
Koerber, Linda René Givens *educator, counselor*
Korn, Jessica Susan *education educator, researcher, ambassador*
McCormick, Richard Levis *academic administrator*
McMahon, John Joseph *college official*
†Murakami, Christine Sybil *university official, educational technologist*
Ostrom, Katherine Elma *retired educator*
†Palais, James B. *educator*
Ray, Charles Kendall *retired university dean*
Siegel, Shepherd *education administrator*
Silver, Michael *school superintendent*
Stringer, William Jeremy *university official*
Terrell, W(illiam) Glenn *university president emeritus*
Thompson, Dwight Alan *vocational rehabilitation expert*
Tschernisch, Sergei P. *academic administrator*
†Warlum, Michael Frank *rraining, consulting and writing company executive*
Woods, Nancy Fugate *dean, women's health nurse*

Sequim
Barton, Jay *university administrator, biologist*

Shelton
St. George, Laura Mae *retired middle school educator*

Spanaway
Paris, Kathleen *secondary school educator*
Roberts-Dempsey, Patricia E. *secondary school educator*

Spokane
Barnes, Steve James *elementary education educator*
Coughlin, Bernard John *university chancellor*
Matters, Clyde Burns *former college president*
McManus, Patrick Francis *educator, writer*
Nyman, Carl John, Jr. *university dean and official*
Robinson, William P. *academic administrator, consultant, speaker*

Tacoma
Baldassin, Michael Robert *secondary school educator*
Davis, Albert Raymond *secondary education educator*
Ingram, Artonyon S. *psychology educator*
King, Gundar Julian *retired university dean*
Lewis, Jan Patricia *education educator*
Maloney, Patsy Loretta *university official, nursing educator*

Toppenish
Ross, Kathleen Anne *college president*

Vancouver
Ovens, Mari Camille *school system administrator, dietitian*
Tehrani, Diane Hawke *English as a second language educator*

Vaughn
Schottland, Robert Milton *secondary school educator*

Wenatchee
Krebs, Sherry Lynn *elementary education educator*

Yakima
Dorsett, Judith A. *elementary education educator*
Eng, Joan Louise *retired special education educator*

WEST VIRGINIA

Arthurdale
Hall, Marilee Alice *elementary education educator*

Athens
Beasley, Jerry Lynn *academic administrator*
Marsh, Joseph Franklin, Jr. *emeritus college president, educational consultant*

Barboursville
Lucas, Carol McCann *vocational education educator*

Bethany
Cummins, Delmer Duane *academic administrator, historian*

Bluefield
Auville, Frances Carter *educational administrator*
Blevins, Thomas E. *college administrator, educator*
Hager, Donald Wayne *secondary education educator*
Patsel, E. Ralph, Jr. *registrar*

Caldwell
Diem, Debra R. *elementary school educator*

Charleston
Arrington, Carolyn Ruth *education consultant*
Brown, Kathryn Elizabeth *development director*
Davis, Billie Johnston *school counselor*
Minear, Alana Wilfong *development director*
Simmons, Virginia Gill *educational administrator*
Welch, Edwin Hugh *academic administrator*

Clay
Gillespie, Larry *secondary school principal*

Crab Orchard
Janney, Patra Ellen *principal*

Dailey
Kolsun, Bruce Alan *special education educator*

Dunbar
Russell, James Alvin, Jr. *college administrator*

Fairmont
Hardway, Wendell Gary *former college president*
Saunders-Starn, Rose *elementary education educator*

Farmington
Lambert, Delores Elaine *secondary education educator*

Glen Jean
Beverly, Laura Elizabeth *special education educator*

Huntington
Gilley, James Wade *university president*
Gould, Alan Brant *academic administrator*
Hayes, Robert Bruce *former college president, educator*
Hooper, James William *educator*
Kent, Calvin Albert *university administrator*
McKown, Charles H. *dean*
Morgan, Linda Rice *secondary education educator*

Lahmansville
Harman, Jo Ann Snyder *secondary school educator*

Man
Saunders, Brenda Rhea *secondary education educator*

Martinsburg
Hoffmaster, Beverly Ann *elementary education educator*

Morgantown
Allamong, Betty D. *academic administrator*
Bajura, Richard Albert *university administrator, engineering educator*
Biddington, William Robert *university administrator, dental educator*
Brooks, Dana D. *dean*
Bucklew, Neil S. *educator, past university president*
D'Alessandri, Robert M. *dean*
Haggett, Rosemary Romanowski *dean*
Hardesty, David Carter, Jr. *university president*
Stewart, Guy Harry *university dean emeritus, journalism educator*

Nitro
Lucas, Panola *elementary education educator*

Parkersburg
Robinson, Robert Joseph *elementary school educator, art educator*

Petersburg
Garber, Harold David *school system superintendent, columnist*

Ridgeley
Unger, Roberta Marie *special education educator*

Saint Albans
Smith, Robert Carlisle *department administrator, welding educator*

Salem
Ohl, Ronald Edward *academic administrator*

Shady Spring
Reed, Cathy Lorraine *elementary education educator*

South Charleston
Drummond, Patrica Ferguson *secondary education educator*
Garnett, Susan Ellen *special education educator*

Spencer
Chapman, William Ervin *elementary education educator*
Parker, Theresa Ann Boggs *special education educator*

Vienna
Acree, Wilma Katheryn *retired secondary school educator*

Wheeling
Campbell, Clyde Del *academic administrator*

WISCONSIN

Amherst
Reed, Penny Rue *special education educator, administrator*

Appleton
Tincher, Barbara Jean *university official*
Warch, Richard *academic administrator*

Bayfield
Wilhelm, Sister Phyllis *principal*

Beloit
Ferrall, Victor Eugene, Jr. *college administrator, lawyer*
Melvin, Charles Alfred, III *superintendent of schools*

Brodhead
O'Neil, J(ames) Peter *computer software designer, educator*

Brookfield
Gradeless, Donald Eugene *secondary education educator*
Zimmerman, Jay *secondary education educator*

Cambria
Bronson, Martha Ann *secondary education educator*

Cedarburg
Cass, Richard Eugene *English language educator*

Columbus
Schellin, Patricia Marie Biddle *educator*

De Pere
†Frechette, Bonnie L. *secondary education educator*
Manion, Thomas A. *college president*

Deerfield
†Banaszynski, Carol Jean *educator*

Delafield
Kurth, Ronald James *university president, retired naval officer*

Denmark
Martens, Lyle Charles *state education administrator*

Dunbar
†Horn, Samuel Edgar *academic administrator*

Eagle River
Nieuwendorp, Judy Lynell *special education educator*

Eau Claire
Brill, Donald Maxim *educator, writer, researcher*
Mash, Donald J. *college president*
Richards, Jerry Lee *academic administrator, religious educator*

Elkhorn
Reinke, Doris Marie *retired elementary education educator*

Elm Grove
Barth, Karl Luther *retired seminary president*

Fish Creek
Abegg, Martin Gerald *retired university president*

Fond Du Lac
Mailer, Kathleen *academic administrator*

Fox Point
Stahl, Mary Gail *elementary educator*

Freedom
Moscinski, David Joseph *educational administrator, school psychologist*

Glendale
Moeser, Elliott *principal*
Schenker, Eric *university dean, economist*

Green Bay
Weidner, Edward William *university chancellor, political scientist*

Hales Corners
Michalski, (Żurowski) Wacław *adult education educator*

Holmen
Meyer, Karl William *retired university president*

Hudson
Benson, Sandra Jean *media specialist*

Dahle, Johannes Upton *academic administrator*

Janesville
Taylor, Timothy Leon *college dean*
Thomas, Margaret Ann *educational administrator, art educator*

Kenosha
Akalin, Roberta Ann *education counselor*
Campbell, F(enton) Gregory *college administrator, historian*
Levis, Richard George *secondary school educator*

Kimberly
Van Boxtel, Randall Anthony *secondary education educator*

La Crosse
Medland, William James *college president*
Novotney, Donald Francis *superintendent of schools*

Lake Geneva
†Nelson, Dawn Lynelle *secondary education educator*
Williams, Joanne Molitor *elementary education educator, retired*

Laona
†Sturzl, Alice A. *school district administrator*

Madison
†Aberle, Elton David *dean*
†Beissinger, Margaret Hiebert *educator*
Busby, Edward Oliver *retired dean*
Ebben, James Adrian *college president*
Kreuter, Gretchen V. *academic administrator*
Lemberger, August Paul *university dean, pharmacy educator*
Lyall, Katharine C(ulbert) *academic administrator, economics educator*
Mertens, Diane K. *secondary education educator*
Mitby, Norman Peter *college president*
Odden, Allan Robert *education educator*
Olien, David William *academic administrator*
Policano, Andrew J. *university dean*
Ward, David *academic administrator, educator*
Wermers, Donald Joseph *registrar*
Yuill, Thomas MacKay *academic administrator, microbiology educator*

Manitowoc
Butler, Robin Erwin *retired vocational technical educator, consultant*
Schuh, Martha Schuhmann *mathematics educator*

Menomonee Falls
Hinnrichs-Dahms, Holly Beth *middle school educator*

Mequon
Dohmen, Mary Holgate *retired primary school educator*
Ellis, William Grenville *academic administrator, management consultant*
Watson-Boone, Rebecca A. *library & information studies educator, researcher*

Merrill
Gravelle, John David *secondary education educator*

Milton
Hosler, Russell John *retired education educator*

Milwaukee
Aman, Mohammed Mohammed *university dean, library and information science educator*
†Blumberg, Sherry Helene *Jewish education educator*
Bovée, Warren Gilles *retired journalism educator*
Coffman, Terrence J. *academic administrator*
Dunn, Michael J. *dean*
Dupuis, Kateri Theresa *elementary education educator*
Fuller, Howard *education educator, academic administrator*
Geyer, Sidna Priest *business education educator*
Hansen, John Herbert *university administrator, accountant*
Hatton, Janie R. Hill *principal*
†Hill, James Warren *college dean*
Lesniewski, Christine Veronica *special education educator, consultant*
Lietz, Jeremy Jon *educational administrator, writer*
Masland, Susan Wistar *retired education educator*
†McGinnity, Thomas G. *university administrator*
Read, Sister Joel *academic administrator*
Reed, John Kennedy Emanuel *elementary school teacher*
Rheams, Annie Elizabeth *education educator*
Rhoten, Juliana Theresa *retired school principal*
Sankovitz, James Leo *retired development director, lobbyist*
Schroeder, John H. *university chancellor*
Smith, John Allen *English educator*
Spann, Wilma Nadene *educational administrator*
Szmanda, Lucille Marie *retired vocational school educator*
Viets, Hermann *college president, consultant*
Waller, Mary Bellis *psychotherapist, education educator, consultant*
†Wild, Robert Anthony *university president*

New Glarus
Etter, Peter Erich *school district administrator*

New London
Fitzgerald, Laurine Elisabeth *university dean, educator*

Oak Creek
Thomae, Mary Joan Pangborn *special education educator*

Oconto Falls
Schlieve, Hy C. J. *principal*

Osceola
Finster, James Robert *library media specialist*

Oshkosh
Herzog, Barbara Jean *secondary school educator, administrator*

Kerrigan, John E. *academic administrator*
Mocker, Donald W. *dean*

Palmyra
Hammiller, Ruth Ellen *school psychologist*

Pleasant Prairie
Knudtson, Diane Marie *elementary education educator*

Racine
Petrie, Marie Rose *educational specialist*

Rhinelander
Cohen, Nancy L. *high school teacher*

River Falls
Thibodeau, Gary A. *academic administrator*

Saint Croix Falls
Finster, Diane L. Stelten *secondary educator, media specialist, home economics educator*

Sheboygan
†Dussault, Nicholas F. *educator*
Fritz, Kristine Rae *secondary education educator*

Sun Prairie
†Ford, Dorothy Mary *principal*

Superior
Peterson, Charlene Marie *educational administrator*

Thiensville
Hobbs, Walter Clarence *retired educator*

Waukesha
Falcone, Frank S. *academic administrator*
Garrot, Patricia Mary *secondary education educator*

West Bend
Fabian, Thomas Robert *superintendent of schools*
Rodney, Joel Morris *dean, campus executive officer*

Whitefish Bay
McInerny, Paul Michael *educational administrator*

Whitewater
Greenhill, H. Gaylon *academic administrator*
Ulbricht, Walter Louis *university public affairs administrator*

Wisconsin Rapids
Weiland, Teri Ann *principal*

WYOMING

Afton
Hoopes, Farrel G. *secondary education educator*

Buffalo
Urruty, Katherine Jean *secondary school educator*

Casper
Wilkes, Shar (Joan Charlene Wilkes) *elementary education educator*

Cheyenne
Richardson, Earl Wilson *elementary education educator, retired*

Cody
Fees, Nancy Fardelius *special education educator*

Gillette
Brown, Toni Cyd *elementary, middle, and secondary school educator*

Jackson
Massy, William Francis *education educator, consultant*

Laramie
Forster, Bruce Alexander *dean*
McBride, Judith *elementary education educator*
Schmitt, Diana Mae *elementary education educator*

Newcastle
Sample, Bette Jeane *elementary educator*

Rock Springs
Kathka, David Arlin *director educational services*
Magnuson, Dennis Duane *secondary education educator*

Sheridan
Schatz, Wayne Ardale *district technology coordinator, computer educator*

Thermopolis
†Krisko, Mary Ellen *primary school educator*

Wheatland
Morrison, Samuel Ferris *secondary school educator*

Worland
Wise, Kathryn Ann *middle school educator*

TERRITORIES OF THE UNITED STATES

GUAM

Hagatna
Alano, Ernesto Olarte *secondary education educator*

Mangilao
Lee, Chin-Tian *academic administrator, agricultural studies educator*

Talofofo
Taylor, James John *academic administrator*

PUERTO RICO

Aguadilla
Jaramillo, Juana Segarra *dean*

Bayamon
Bonilla, Daisy Rose *parochial school English language educator*

Ceiba
DeMaio, Dorothy Walters *tutorial school administrator, consultant*

Guayama
Febres-Santiago, Samuel F. *university chancellor*

Humacao
Castrodad, Felix A. *university administrator*
Delgado-Rodriguez, Manuel *secondary school educator*

Rio Piedras
López de Mendez, Annette Giselda *education educator*

Sabana Seca
Sierra Millán, Daniel *school administrator*

San German
Mojica, Agnes *academic administrator*

San Juan
Basols, Jose Andres *school director, priest*
Carreras, Francisco José *retired university president, foundation executive*
Cortes, Ivette *elementary education educator*
del Toro, Ilia *retired education educator*
Maldonado, Norman I. *academic administrator, physician educator*
Matheu, Federico Manuel *university chancellor*

MILITARY ADDRESSES OF THE UNITED STATES

EUROPE

APO
Johnson, Melissa Ann *early childhood educator*
Niles, Thomas Michael Tolliver *university administrator*

CANADA

ALBERTA

Calgary
Neale, E(rnest) R(ichard) Ward *retired university official, consultant*
Rasporich, Anthony Walter *university dean*
Watanabe, Mamoru *former university dean, physician, researcher*
White, Terrence Harold *academic administrator, sociologist*

Edmonton
Adams, Peter Frederick *university president, civil engineer*
Tyrell, Lorne S. *university dean*

BRITISH COLUMBIA

Cobble Hill
Cox, Albert Reginald *academic administrator, physician, retired*

Kelowna
Muggeridge, Derek Brian *dean, engineering consultant*

Vancouver
Andrews, John Hobart McLean *education educator*
Finnegan, Cyril Vincent *retired university dean, zoology educator*
Haycock, Kenneth Roy *educator, consultant, administrator*
Lusztig, Peter Alfred *university dean, educator*
McNeill, John Hugh *pharmaceutical sciences educator*
Webber, William Alexander *university administrator, physician*

Victoria
Strong, David F. *university administrator*
Welch, S(tephen) Anthony *university dean, Islamic studies and arts educator*

MANITOBA

Winnipeg
Poettcker, Henry *retired seminary president*

NEW BRUNSWICK

Fredericton
McGreal, Rory Patrick *educational administrator*
Parr-Johnston, Elizabeth *academic administrator*

NEWFOUNDLAND

Saint John's
May, Arthur W. *university president*

NOVA SCOTIA

Halifax
Murray, Thomas John (Jock Murray) *medical humanities educator, medical researcher, neurologist*
Ozmon, Kenneth Lawrence *university president, educator*

Timberlea
Verma, Surjit K. *retired school system administrator*

Truro
Mac Rae, Herbert Farquhar *retired college president*

Wolfville
Ogilvie, Kelvin Kenneth *university president, chemistry educator*

ONTARIO

Hamilton
Shaw, Denis Martin *university dean, former geology educator*

London
Davenport, Paul *university administrator, economics educator*
McMurtry, Robert Y. *academic dean*

Ottawa
Kroeger, Arthur *university chancellor, former government official*
Labarge, Margaret Wade *medieval history educator*
Malouin, Jean-Louis *university dean, educator*
Philogene, Bernard J. R. *academic administrator, science educator*
Seely, John F. *dean*

Peterborough
Theall, Donald Francis *retired university president*

Thunder Bay
Locker, J. Gary *university official, civil engineering educator*

Toronto
Aberman, Arnold *dean*
Armstrong, Robin Louis *university official, physicist*
Evans, John Robert *former university president, physician*
†Gasque, Laurel *educator*
Hayhurst, James Frederick Palmer *career and business consultant, inspirational speaker, writer*
Korey-Krzecowski, George J. M. Kniaz *university administrator, management consultant*
Kushner, Eva *academic administrator, educator, author*
Macdonald, Hugh Ian *university president emeritus, economist, educator*
Ostry, Sylvia *academic administrator, economist*
Prichard, John Robert Stobo *academic administrator, law educator*
Runte, Roseann *academic administrator*

Waterloo
Berczi, Andrew Stephen *academic administrator, educator*
Kay-Guelke, Jeanne *dean, educator*
Rosehart, Robert George *university president, chemical engineer*
Smith, Rowland James *educational administrator*
Wright, Douglas Tyndall *business executive, university executive emeritus*

QUEBEC

Montreal
Cloutier, Gilles Georges *academic administrator, research executive*
Freedman, Samuel Orkin *university official*
French, Stanley George *university dean, philosophy educator*
Granger, Luc Andre *university dean, psychologist*
Johnston, David Lloyd *academic administrator, lawyer*
Lajeunesse, Marcel *university administrator, educator*
Lowy, Frederick Hans *university president, psychiatrist*
Vinay, Patrick *university dean*

Quebec
Gervais, Michel *academic administrator*

Sainte Anne de Bellevue
Buckland, Roger Basil *university dean, educator, vice principal*

SASKATCHEWAN

Regina Beach
Barber, Lloyd Ingram *retired university president*

Saskatoon
Knott, Douglas Ronald *college dean, agricultural sciences educator, researcher*
Popkin, David Richard *academic dean, obstetrician, gynocologist*
Stewart, John Wray Black *college dean*

AUSTRALIA

Melbourne
†Stark, Janice Ann *elementary education educator*

Sydney
Albinski, Henry Stephen *academic research center director, writer*

CAPE VERDE

Santa Catarina
Kern, Jean Glotzbach *elementary education educator, gifted education educator*

CHILE

Concepcion
Trzebiatowski, Gregory L. *education educator*

CHINA

Guangzhou
Mundorf, Nancy Knox *early childhood educator*

EGYPT

Cairo
Miller, Harry George *education educator*

ENGLAND

London
Peckham, Michael John *academic administrator*

Manchester
McGuigan, Patrick *college official, operatic baritone*

Milton Keynes
Daniel, Sir John Sagar *academic administrator, metallurgist*

Surrey
Petrek, William Joseph *college president emeritus*

FRANCE

Paris
Simpson, Michael Kevin *university president, political science educator*

HONG KONG

Pokfulam
†Wang, Aihe *educator*

IRELAND

Ballyvaughan
Wicks, Eugene Claude *college president, art educator*

SCOTLAND

Aberdeen
Rice, Charles Duncan *university official*

SOUTH AFRICA

Auckland Park
Koekemoer, Carl Lodewicus *university official, business consultant*

SWITZERLAND

Geneva
Kessinger, Tom G. *academic administrator*

TAIWAN

Chungli
†Chen, Hsin-Hwa *education educator, researcher*

UNITED ARAB EMIRATES

Abu Dhabi
Preska, Margaret Louise Robinson *education educator, administrator*

Al Ain
Voth, Douglas W. *academic dean*

ADDRESS UNPUBLISHED

†Aaron, Melissa D. *education educator*
Aaslestad, Halvor Gunerius *college dean, retired*
Adams, Alfred Hugh *college president*
Adams, Renee Bledsoe *elementary school educator*
Agar, John Russell, Jr. *school district administrator*
Albers, Edward James, Sr. *retired secondary school educator*
Alford, Joyce Wray *educational administrator*
Allen, Charles Eugene *college administrator, agriculturist*
Alligood, Elizabeth Ann Hiers *retired special education educator*
Alstat, George Roger *special education educator*
Ammeraal, Brenda Ferne *secondary school educator*
Anderson, Charles Lee Royal *retired academic administrator*
Anderson, Iris Anita *retired secondary education educator*
Anderson, Susan Elaine Mosshamer *education and organizational consultant*
Andrews, Carol *primary education educator*
†Anspacher, Stephen J. *university official*
†Archer, Mary Kathryn *elementary education educator*
Archuleta, Walter R. *educational consultant, language educator*
Areen, Judith Carol *dean*
Aretz, Barbara Jane *reading specialist, educator*
Armacost, Mary-Linda Sorber Merriam *former college president, educational consultant*
Armstrong-Law, Margaret *school administrator*
Arnold, Leslie Ann *special education educator*
Arnold, P. A. *special education educator*
Arnold, Ruth Ann *elementary education educator*
Ataie, Judith Garrett *middle school educator*
Ausburn, Lynna Joyce *vocational and technical curriculum developer, consultant*
†Azrael, Judith Anne *educator*
Babbitt, Samuel Fisher *retired university official*
Bachtel, Ann Elizabeth *educational consultant, researcher, educator*
Bade, Carl August *retired secondary education educator*
Bailar, Benjamin Franklin *academic administrator, administration educator*
Baiocco, Sharon A. *college administrator*
Baker, C. B. *retired day care director, organizer, communicator*
Baker, Carol Ann *elementary school educator*
Ball, Howard Guy *education specialist educator*
Barber, Kimberly Lisanby *elementary education educator*
Barnett, Linda Kay Smith *vocational guidance counselor*
Barone, John Anthony *university provost emeritus*
Barone, Stephanie Lynn *academic administrator, psychology researcher*
Barrett, Evelyn Carol *retired secondary education educator*
Barrett, Janet Tidd *academic administrator*
Bartel, Arthur Gabriel *educational administrator, city official*
Barville, Rebecca Penelope *elementary school educator*
Bassist, Donald Herbert *retired academic administrator*
Baxter, Cecil William, Jr. *retired college president*
Beck, Karen Portsche *elementary education educator*
Becker, Richard Charles *retired college president*
Becker, Walter Heinrich *vocational educator, planner*
Beckwith, Sidney Johnson *director special programs, curriculum administrator*
Belanger, Cherry Churchill *elementary school educator*
†Bell, Gary M. *college dean*
Beresford, Wilma *elementary and gifted education educator*
Bergman, Hermas John (Jack Bergman) *retired college administrator*
Berman, Harry J. *educator, college administrator*
Bernath, Mary Therese *special education educator*
Bernhardt, Jean Louise *special education educator*
Bernstein, I(rving) Melvin *university official and dean, materials scientist*
Beston, Rose Marie *retired college president*
Birkmayer, Donald Tefft *college official*
Birman, Linda Lee *elementary education educator*
Bishop, Charles Edwin *university president emeritus, economist*
Bishop, June A. *secondary education educator*
Bishop, (Ina) Sue Marquis *dean, psychiatric and mental health nurse educator, researcher*
Bivans, Maurita W. *school administrator*
Bivens, Lynette Kupka *elementary education educator*
Black, Georgia Ann *educational administrator*
Black, Rhonda Stout *special education educator*
Blair, Charlie Lewis *elementary school educator*
Blazey, Judith Leiston *school district administrator*
Blecke, Arthur Edward *principal*
Bloodworth, Gladys Leon *educator*
Blummer, Kathleen Ann *counselor*
Borntrager, John Sherwood *principal*
Borst, Phillip West *academic administrator*
Bost, Raymond Morris *retired college president*
Boyenga, Cindy A. *secondary education educator*
Brackenhoff, Lonnie Sue *principal*
Bragdon, Paul Errol *educator*
†Braid, Bernice *program director, dean*
Brain, George Bernard *university dean*
Branyan, Robert Lester *retired university administrator*
Brawner, Sharon Lee *bilingual education educator, researcher*
Brewer, Carey *retired academic administrator*
Brock, Russell Ernest *educational administrator*
Brooks, Dennis Mark *secondary education educator*
†Brower, Sara E. Maskell *elementary education educator*
Brown, David Grant *university president*
Brownlee, Paula Pimlott *educational consultant, former academic administrator*
Brunnett, Kathleen Shannon *secondary educator*
Bryan, Lawrence Dow *college president*
Buckler, Marilyn Lebow *school psychologist, educational consultant*
Bulcken, Carolyn Anne Brooks *retired special education educator*
Bullock, Molly *retired elementary education educator*
Bunker, Debra J. *elementary education educator*
Burbridge, Ann Arnold *elementary school educator, music educator*
Burke, Joseph C. *former university official*
Burns, James Milton *retired educator*
Burns, Marie T. *retired secondary education educator*
Caldwell, William Edward *educational administration educator, arbitrator*
Cameron, J. Elliot *retired parochial educational system administrator*
Cameron, Lucille Wilson *retired dean of libraries*
Camp, Kristin Mary *primary school educator*
Campbell, Clarence Bowen *retired educator, real estate developer, columnist*
Campbell, Susan Carrigg *secondary education educator*
†Campbell-ray, Kecia Lynn *elementary school teacher*
Carey, John Jesse *academic administrator, religion educator*
Carlin, Betty *educator*
Carlson, Freda Ellen *educator, consultant*
Carr, Bessie *retired middle school educator*
Carroll, Joanne Zlate *elementary education educator*
Carter, Herbert Edmund *former university official*
Casoni, Richard Albert *marine technologist, educator*
Casper, Gerhard *academic administrator, law educator*
Cassell, William Comyn *retired college president*
Castor, Betty *academic administrator*
†Cavalcante-Fleming, Maria A. *preschool educator, language educator, translator*
†Cavender, Patricia Patten *director program*
†Celentino, Victor Gerard *special education educator*
Cercelle, Audrey Lynn *school psychologist*
Cerveny, Kathryn M. *educational administrator*
Chaim, Robert Alex *dean, educator*
Chandler, Alice *higher education consultant, university president*
Charlton, Shirley Marie *educational consultant*
Chase, Edith Newlin *preschool educator, poet*
Chase, James Richard *retired college president*
Chater, Shirley Sears *health educator*
Cheeger, Jeff *education educator*
Chemla, Daniels S. *director, adult education educator*
Christensen, Caroline *vocational educator*
Cimino, Ann M. *education educator*
Clark, James Milford *college president, retired*
Clark, Sharon Jackson *private school administrator*
Clarke, Lambuth McGeehee *retired college president*
Clawson, Roxann Eloise *college administrator, computer company executive*
Cleary, Sue Ellen *secondary school educator*
Clifford, Brother Peter *academic administrator, religious educator*
Clough, Lauren C. *retired special education educator*
Clum, Debra Sue *elementary education educator*
Cluxton, Joanne Genevieve *elementary school educator*
Cochrane, Walter E. *education administrator, writer*
Coffee, Joseph Denis, Jr. *retired college chancellor*
Cohen, Shirley Mason *educator, writer, civic worker*
Coleman, Robert Elliott *retired secondary education educator*
Colgate-Lindberg, Catharine Pamella *educator*
Collier, Herman Edward, Jr. *retired college president*
Coluccio, Josephine Catherine *primary and elementary school educator*
Compton, Norma Haynes *retired university dean, artist*
†Conklin, Sarah C. *health education educator*
Connell, George Edward *former university president, scientist*
Connes, Alain *education educator*
Conole, Clement Vincent *business administrator*
Conover, Mona Lee *retired adult education educator*
Cooke, Thomas Paul *education educator*
Copeland, Henry Jefferson, Jr. *former college president*
†Corbin, Tracy Dianne *researcher*
Corley, Charles J. *middle school educator*
†Cornwell, Marguerite Kelsey *college administrator*
Cortlund, Joan Marie *educator*
Cosnotti, Richard Louis *development director*
Costantini, Mary Ann C. *writer, editor, retired elementary educator*
Craiglow, James Hawkins *graduate school official*
Cramer, Robert Vern *retired college administrator, consultant*
Crawford, Kenneth Charles *educational institute executive, retired government official*
Craymer, Helen Stoughton *educator*
Cromwell, Ronald R. *educator*
Crosby, (Claire) Marena Lienhard *retired college administrator*
Cross, Dolores Evelyn *university administrator, educator*
Crouse, Carol K. Mavromatis *elementary education educator*
Dahse, Kenneth William *educator, photojournalist*
Davenport, Lawrence Franklin *school system administrator*
Davidson, James Melvin *academic administrator, researcher, educator*
Davies-McNair, Jane *retired educational consultant*
Davion, Ethel Johnson *school system administrator, curriculum specialist*
Davis, Anna Jane Ripley *elementary education educator*
Davis, Joseph Lloyd *educational administrator, consultant*
Day, Charlotte Ellen *education administrator*
Debs, Barbara Knowles *former college president, consultant*
†Deconinck, Isabelle F. *marketing and promotion specialist, writer*
De Jong, Arthur Jay *education consultant, former university president*
Delahanty, Rebecca Ann *school system administrator*
DeLong, Janice Ayers *education educator*
De Long, Katharine *retired secondary education educator*
Denham, Caroline Virginia *retired college official*
Denton, David Edward *retired education educator*
Denton, Joan Cameron *reading consultant, former educator*
†de Russy, Candace Uter *education reformer*
Dey, Carol Ruth *secondary education educator*
Dickinson, Gail Krepps *educational administrator, educator*
Dickson, Max Charles *retired career counselor, coordinator*
DiSalle, Michael Danny *secondary education educator*
Dobler, Donald William *retired college dean, consultant, corporate executive*
Donaldson, Wilma Crankshaw *elementary education educator*
Dorsey, Rhoda Mary *retired academic administrator*
Dowling, Paul Dennis *bilingual special education educator*
Drake, George Albert *college president, historian*
Dresbach, Mary Louise *state educational administrator*
Dubois, Nancy Q. *elementary school educator*
Dudycha, Anne Elizabeth *retired special education educator*
Duff, John Bernard *college president, former city official*
Duffy, John Joseph *retired academic administrator, history educator*
Dunham, Rebecca Betty Beres *school administrator*
Dunn, Deborah Dechellis *special education educator*
Dunworth, John *retired college president*
Dutson, Thayne R. *university dean*
DuVall, Patricia Arlene *secondary education educator*
Dwinell, Ann Jones *special education educator*
Eacho, Esther MacLively *special education educator*
Ebbert, Arthur, Jr. *retired university dean*
Edens, Betty Joyce *reading recovery educator*
Edington, Robert Van *university official*
Edwards, Ardis Lavonne Quam *retired elementary education educator*
Eliot, Charles William John *former university president*
Ellingson, Irmgard Hein *secondary education educator*
Ellner, Carolyn Lipton *university dean, business executive*
Emekli, Mahi Suzanne *counselor, researcher*
Endicott, Jennifer Jane *education educator*
Ertl, Rita Mae *elementary education educator*
Essig, Kathleen Susan *university official, education consultant*
†Evans, Fred Lynn *principal*
Evans, Geraldine Ann *academic administrator*
Fadum, Ralph Eigil *university dean*
Fair, Marcia Jeanne Hixson *retired educational administrator*
Falk, Marshall Allen *retired university dean, physician*
Farquhar, Robin Hugh *former university president*
Farrar, Richard Bartlett, Jr. *secondary education educator*
Feerick, John David *dean, lawyer*
Feldstein, Joshua *educational administrator*
Fenton, Marjorie *university official, consultant*
Fernández-V., Juan Ramon *university chancellor*
Fessler, Patricia Lou *retired library and media coordinator*
Fetters, Doris Ann *retired secondary education educator*
Fife, Jonathan Donald *higher education educator*
Firestone, Sheila Meyerowitz *retired gifted and talented education educator*
Fitzpatrick, Ruth Ann *education educator*
Fitzwater, Ivan W. *retired superintendant*
Fleetwood, Mary Annis *education association executive*
Fleming, Barbara Joan *retired university administrator*
Fleming, Sylvia Shackelford *secondary school educator, writer*
Foltiny, Stephen Vincent *special education educator*
Folz, Kathleen Louise *elementary education educator*
†Ford, S. Theodore, Jr. *academic administrator*
Forney, Ronald Dean *elementary school educator, consultant, educational therapist*
Forney, Virginia Sue *educational counselor*
Foronda, Elena Isabel *secondary school educator*
Foster, Martha Tyahla *educational administrator*
†Foster, Michele *educator*
Fountain, Andre Ferchaud *academic program director*
Fox, Warren Halsey *academic administrator, consultant*
Freeman, Meredith Norwin *former college president, education educator*
Freeman, Peter A. *computer science educator, dean*
Frey, Katie Manciet *educational administrator*
Frick, Ivan Eugene *college president emeritus, education consultant*
Frison, George C. *education educator*
Fritschler, A. Lee *retired college president, public policy educator*
Frost, Everett Lloyd *academic administrator*
Fuenning, Esther Renate *adult education educator*
Fuller, Maxine Compton *retired secondary school educator*
Fullerton, Gail Jackson *university president emeritus*
Gabel, Katherine *academic administrator*
Galdi-Weissman, Natalie Ann *secondary education educator*
Gamsky, Neal Richard *university administrator, psychology educator*
†Garcia-Guzman, Barbara Mari *secondary education educator*
Garcia-Mely, Rafael *retired education educator*
Garrett, Cheryl Gay *secondary education educator, writer*
Gates, Donna Marie *special education educator*
Genovese, Lawrence Matthew *secondary education educator*
Gentilcore, John C. *school principal*
Gibbons, Erin *secondary education educator*
Giblett, Phylis Lee Walz *middle school educator*
†Giddings, Paula Jane *author, educator*
Gilberg, Margot D. *secondary school Spanish educator*
Gillin, Carol Ann *middle school educator*
Gischlar, Karen Lynn *elementary education educator*
Giusti, Joseph Paul *retired*
Gladstone, Carol Lynn *assistant principal*
Glaze, Lynn Ferguson *development consultant*
Glenn, Richard Alan *adult education educator*
Glennen, Robert Eugene, Jr. *retired university president*
†Glenz, Nancy L. *educator*
Gleue, Lorine Anna *elementary education educator*
Glower, Donald Duane *university executive, mechanical engineer*
†Glynn, Edward *college dean*
Godfrey, Margaret Ann *educator*
Goerke, Glenn Allen *university administrator*
Goewey, Gordon Ira *university administrator*
Goff, Jane E. *secondary school educator*
Golden, Beth *Special Olympics administrator*
Goldinger, Shirley Anne *elementary education educator*
Good, Linda Lou *elementary education educator*
Goodrich, Kenneth Paul *retired college dean*
Goodrich, Robert Lawrence, Jr. *educator, accountant*
Gordis, David Moses *academic administrator, rabbi*
Gordon-Spearman, Florida Lee *nursing educator*
Graupner, Sheryll Ann *elementary education educator*
Graves, Wallace Billingsley *retired university executive*
Grebstein, Sheldon Norman *university administrator*
Green, Nancy Loughridge *academic administrator*
Greenberg, Ina Florence *retired elementary education educator*
†Greer, Kathleen E. *college registrar*
Gregory, Mary Sharon *educator*
Grier, Dorothy Ann Pridgen *secondary education specialist*
Griffie, Gayle G. *retired principal*
Grine, Florence May *secondary education educator*
Groat, Pamela Ferne *school media specialist*
†Gross, Steven Jay *education educator*
Grove, Myrna Jean *elementary education educator*
Groves, Bernice Ann *educator*
Gudnitz, Ora M. Cofey *secondary education educator*
Gustafson, Denise Krupka *special education educator*
Guyon, John Carl *retired university administrator*
Habkirk, Sue Ann *education educator*
Haeberle, Rosamond Pauline *retired educator*
Hagan, Joseph Henry *university administrator*
Hammond, Vernon Francis *school administrator*
Hamrock, Margaret Mary *retired educator, writer*

Hanna, Noreen Anelda retired adult education administrator, consultant
Hannewald, Norman Eugene secondary school educator
Hansen, Enid Eileen secondary education educator
†Haque, Akhlaque Ul educator, researcher
Hardin, Clifford Morris retired university chancellor, cabinet member
Hardison, Diane Sorrell Parker special education educator
Hardy De Jesus, Georgette Marilyn university administrator
Harmston, Robert Albert secondary education educator
Harrigan, Rosanne Carol dean, nursing educator
Harrington, Jean Patrice college president
Harris, Annie Rene elementary school teacher
Harris, Delmarie Jones elementary education educator
Harris, Merle Wiener college administrator, educator
Harrison, Earl Grant, Jr. educational administrator
†Harrod, Lois Marie secondary school educator, poet
Harsha, Amy Beth elementary education educator
Hart, Sharown educator
Hartley, Craig Sheridan mechanical and materials engineering educator
Hartman, Elizabeth Diane retired elementary education educator
Harville Smith, Martha Louise special education educator
Hasselmo, Nils university official, linguistics educator
Haug, Marilyn Ann reading and mathematics educator
†Heath, Jerome Bruce information systems educator
Heaton-Marticorena, Jean early childhood educator
Hebert, Christine Anne educator
Heestand, Diane Elissa educational technology educator, medical educator
Hegarty, George John university president, English educator
Heidt-Dunwell, Debra Sue vocational education educator
Helman, Alfred Blair retired college president, education consultant
Henkel, Cynthia Leigh elementary education educator
†Herman, Deborah Ann secondary education educator
†Hetzmark, Abby M. secondary education educator
Hickey, Sharon Marie middle school educator
Higgins, Dorothy Marie academic dean
Hines, Voncile special education educator
Hinson, Claudia Burns elementary school educator
Hitchcock, Walter Anson educational consultant, retired educational administrator
Hlywa, Jennifer Lyn secondary educator
Hoffman, Judy Greenblatt preschool director
Hoft, Lynne Ann educator, remedial specialist, educational consultant
Holmes, Erline Morrison retired educational administrator, consultant
Holtkamp, Susan Charlotte elementary education educator
Hood, Luann Sandra special education educator
Hoover, Davonna Maria primary education educator
Horan, Mary Jo adult education educator, consultant
Horner, Matina Souretis retired college president, corporate executive
Hosman, Sharon Lee music educator
Howard, Clarice Hardee special education educator
Huff, Janet House special education educator
Huffman, Carol Koster retired middle school educator
Hull, Louise Knox retired elementary educator, administrator
Humphrey, Arthur Earl university administrator, retired
Hunt-Clerici, Carol Elizabeth academic administrator
Huntington, Irene Elizabeth special education educator
Huse, Johna Kathleen secondary school educator
Huttenback, Robert Arthur academic administrator, educator
Iadipaolo, Donna Marie educator, writer, director, artist, performer
Iceman, Sharon Lorraine elementary education educator
Ierardi, Eric Joseph school system administrator
Inglett, Betty Lee retired media services administrator
†Ita, John Bradley history educator
Jackson, Bart educator, game developer
Jackson, Lambert Blunt academic administrator
Jackson, Miles Merrill retired university dean
Jacobs, Delores Hamm secondary education educator
Jacobs, Linda Rotroff elementary school educator
Jakubauskas, Edward Benedict college president
Jenkins, Brenda Gwenetta early childhood/special education specialist
†Jennings, La Vinia Delois educator
Jerrytone, Samuel Joseph trade school executive
†Jett, Terri Renee educator
Jimmink, Glenda Lee retired elementary school educator
John, Ralph Candler retired college president, educator
Johnson, Kirsten Denise elementary education educator
Johnson, LaVerne St. Clair retired elementary school educator
Johnson, Olin Chester education educator
Johnson, Sylvia Sue university administrator, educator
Johnston, F. Bruce, Jr. educator
†Jones, Catherine Elaine educational administrator
Jones, Lawrence Neale university dean, minister
Jones, Ted C(ooke) distance learning educator
Jones, Therese M. special education educator
Jordan, Joseph Louis education educator, government official
Jurasek, Randall John educational consultant
Kachur, Betty Rae elementary education educator
Kampe, Carolyn Jean elementary art and special education educator
Kamstra, Bettye Maurice secondary education educator
Kappner, Augusta Souza academic administrator
Karben, Shelley Valerie elementary and special education school educator
Karber, Johnnie Faye elementary education educator
Kasberger-Mahoney, Elvera A. educational administrator
Kaschak, Virginia Ruth elementary education educator
†Kasper, Victor, Jr. economics educator
Kaspin, Susan Jane child care specialist
Kazmarek, Linda Adams secondary education educator
Keller, Jami Ann special education educator
Kelley, Patricia Colleen educator, researcher
Kelts, David William elementary education educator
Kempner, Maximilian Walter law school dean, lawyer
Kerins, Francis Joseph college president
Kern, Charles William retired university official, chemistry educator
Kersting, Edwin Joseph retired university dean
Ketron, Carrie Sue secondary school educator
Keyes, Joan Ross Rafter education educator, author
†Kidd, Feda Sutton elementary education educator
Kiehlbauch, Sheryl Lynn elementary education educator
Kimbrough, Lorelei elementary education educator
King-Garner, Miria elementary education educator
†Kirk, Rea Helene (Rea Helene Glazer) special education educator
Kissling, Helen Grey elementary education educator
Kittrell, Marie Beckner retired educator
Kliebhan, Sister M(ary) Camille academic administrator
†Klucking, Gail Marie educator
Knapp, Lonnie Troy elementary education educator
Knight, Rebecca Jean secondary education educator
†Knoll, M.J. college administrator
†Knowles, Eddie Ade dean
Koch, Joanne Ellen guidance counselor
†Koehler, Marilyn Joiner principal, educator
Koenig, Allen Edward higher education consultant
Kolb, Dorothy Gong elementary education educator
Koleilat, Betty Kummer middle school educator, mathematician
Koleson, Donald Ralph retired college dean, educator
Komisar, David Daniel retired university provost
Kormondy, Edward John university official, biology educator
Koveleski, Kathryn Delane retired special education educator
Kozma, Helene Joyce Marie adult educator
†Kraemer, Alfred Robert school librarian
Kraft, Arthur academic dean
Kravetz, Nathan educator, author
Kristensen, Marlene early childhood education educator
Krueger, Christine Marie assistant principal
Krueger, Eugene Rex academic program consultant
Kryzak, Linda Ann educational administrator
Kubiak, John Michael academic administrator
Kuttner, Donna Holberg health education specialist
Lackenmier, James Richard college president, priest
Laible, Jon Morse retired mathematics educator, dean
Lambrix, Winifred Marie McFarlane elementary education educator
†Langley, Carolyn Chesson kindergarten teacher
Langley, Joellen S. music educator
†Langley, Lester Danny educator
Langworthy, William Clayton college official
Lawrence, Betty Jean elementary education educator
Leahey, Margaret Joan academic administrator
Leal, Herbert Allan Borden former university chancellor, former government official
Leavitt, Maura Lynn elementary education educator
Ledbury, Diana Gretchen adult education educator
†Ledet, Phyllis L. educational administrator
Lee, Corinne Adams retired educator
Lee, William Franklin, III association administrator, musician, composer
Legington, Gloria R. middle school educator
Leistner, Mary Edna retired secondary education educator
LeMense, Fay Ann special education educator
Lennon, Joseph Luke college official, priest
Lester, Robin Dale educator, author, former headmaster
Levin, Richard Charles academic administrator, economist
†Lichterman, Paul R. educator
Lindegren, Jack Kenneth elementary and secondary education educator
Lindenmeyer, Mary Kathryn secondary education educator
Lipschutz, Marian Shaw secondary education educator, writer
Lipscomb-Brown, Edra Evadean retired childhood educator
Lockwood, Theodore Davidge former academic administrator
Long, Jennifer L. elementary educator
Looser, Donald William academic administrator
Loring, Mildred Rogers elementary educator, reading specialist
Loser, Joseph Carlton, Jr. dean, retired judge
Love, Sara Elizabeth retired educator
Lovell, Mary Ann secondary education educator
Lovinger, Warren Conrad emeritus university president
Low, Robert Teh-Pin educator
Lueke, Donna Mae yoga instructor, reiki practitioner
†Luft, Gary Alan secondary education educator
Lundgren, Leonard, III retired secondary education educator
Lynch, John Daniel secondary education educator, state legislator
Lynch, Laura Ellen elementary education educator
Lyne, Dorothy-Arden educator
Machen, Ethel Louise Lynch retired academic administrator
†Macinskas, Wendy Lasser secondary education educator
Mack, Rebecca Ann primary education educator
MacLeod, Donald William secondary school educator
Macmillan, William Hooper university dean, educator
MacPhee, Donald Albert academic administrator
Major, Patrick Webb, III principal
†Maldonado-Mendez, Nilsa B. language educator
Mallory, Arthur Lee university dean, retired state official
Malti-Douglas, Fedwa educator
Mañas, Rita educational administrator
Mans, Thomas Charles dean
Marlatt, Dorothy Barbara university dean
Marshak, Robert Reuben former university dean, medical educator, veterinarian
Martin, John Swanson retired educator
Martin, Marta learning disability specialist, educator
Martin, Mary secondary education educator
†Mason, Gloria secondary education educator
Mason, Johanna Hendrika Anneke retired secondary education educator
Mason, Martha elementary education consultant, former educator
Matera, Frances Lorine elementary educator
Maurer, Beverly Bennett school administrator
†Maxwell, Mark S. secondary education educator, novelist
Maybury, Greg J academic administrator
Mayfield, Robert Charles university official, geography educator
Mazur, Deborah Joan counselor
Mazzatenta, Rosemary Dorothy retired school administrator
McCall, Patricia Alene secondary music education educator
McCarthy, Joanne Mary reading specialist
†McCaslin, Robert Brian educator
McConnell, Albert Lynn educational official
McCoy, David Brion middle school educator
Mc Isaac, George Scott business policy educator, government official, former management consultant
†McKelton, Drue-Marie academic director
McKnight, Patricia Marie elementary education educator
McLaughlin, Michael Rob secondary school educator, coach
McLean, Amy C. secondary school educator
†Mc Mahon, Barbara A. teacher
Mc Mahon, George Joseph academic administrator
McMorrow, Margaret Mary (Peg McMorrow) retired educator
McPeak, Allan career services director, educator, lawyer, consultant
Mc Pherson, Peter university president
Medley, Donald Matthias education educator, consultant
Mehne, Paul Randolph associate dean, medical educator
Meier, Enge preschool educator
Meinert, Bobbi Irene college program administrator
Melady, Thomas Patrick academic administrator, ambassador, author, public policy expert, educator
Melman, Cynthia Sue special education educator
Merritt, John Howard secondary school educator
Meyer, Frances Margaret Anthony elementary and secondary school educator, health education specialist
Meyer, Robert Lee secondary education educator
Miles, Elsie E. counselor, educator
†Miles, Janet Ward principal
Miller, Arjay retired university dean
Miller, Jerry Huber retired university chancellor
Miller, Richard Franklin educational consultant, researcher
Mills, Eugene Sumner college president
Mills, Robert Lee president emeritus
Mindlin, Paula Rosalie retired reading educator
Mintz, Patricia Pomboy secondary education educator
Moeckel, Bill Reid retired university dean
Moffatt, Mindy Ann middle school educator, educational training specialist
†Molin, Paulette Fairbanks university official, writer
Monahan, Edward Charles academic administrator, marine science educator
Monson, David Carl school superintendent, farmer, state legislator
Montgomery, Michael secondary science educator
Moore, Thomas David academic administrator
Moorhead, Patrick Henry secondary school administrator
†Morales, Mario Roberto adult education educator
Moran, Ann education educator
Morgan, Mary Lou retired education educator, civic worker
Morgan, Ruth Prouse academic administrator, educator
Mortola, Edward Joseph academic administrator emeritus
Mott, Mary Elizabeth retired educational administrator
Mulder, Douglas Wayne secondary educator
Murphy, Mary Kathleen Connors college administrator, writer
Murray, Dorothy Speicher educator
Myers, Harold Mathews academic administrator
Nader, Suzanne Nora Beurer elementary education educator
Nader-Heikenfeld, Rita Maria culinary educator, food writer
Naglieri, Eileen Sheridan special education educator
Nakamoto, Carolyn Matsue principal
Neff, Lester Leroy administrator, minister
Nelson, Edwin Clarence academic administrator, emeritus
Nelson, Martin Walter academic administrator, writer
Neunzig, Carolyn Miller elementary, middle and high school educator
Newby, James Edward education educator
Nichols, James Robbs university dean
Nicotera, Cathy secondary education educator
Nielsen, Karen Kay secondary education educator
†Nissen, Lowell Allen education educator
Nondorf, Janice Kathryn special education educator
Norman, Arlene Phyllis principal
Norris, Alfred Lloyd bishop
†O'Brien, Sara Talis educator
O'Connell, William Raymond, Jr. educational consultant
Oden, Jean Phifer special education educator
O'Donnell, Brother Frank Joseph principal
O'Driscoll, Marilyn Lutz elementary school educator
Offen, Ronald Charles retired school librarian
Olivet, Joseph Francis elementary school educator
Olson-Hagan, Arlene parochial school administrator
O'Malley, Thomas Patrick academic administrator
Orr, Kenneth Bradley academic administrator
Oustrich, Josephine elementary education educator
Outland, Max Lynn retired school system administrator
Palmer, Irene Sabelberg university dean and educator emeritus, nurse, researcher, historian
Paredes-ManFredi, Lynn college director
Park, John Thornton academic administrator
Parrish, Alma Ellis elementary school educator
Patmos, Adrian Edward university dean emeritus
Patterson, Mildred Lucas teaching specialist
Patterson, Myrna Nancy secondary education educator
Paulsen, Frank Robert college dean emeritus
Paxton, Juanita Willene retired university official
Payne, Ladell retired college president
Pearson, Susan Winifred dean, consultant
Peel, Victoria elementary educator
Pendexter, Hugh, III adult education educator
Pennacchio, Linda Marie secondary school educator
Peoples, John Arthur, Jr. former university president, consultant
Perreault, Sister Jeanne college president
Perry, William James educator, former federal official
Peters, Patricia L. elementary education educator
Petoskey, Thomas W. secondary school educator
Petrie, Hugh Gilbert philosophy of education educator
Pettigrew, L. Eudora retired academic administrator
Phelps, Deanne Elayne educational counselor, consultant
Phillips, Dianne Mooney elementary school educator
Phillips, Joy Eugenia counselor, consultant
Pierce-Beall, Tamara Ann counselor, career consultant
Piper, Fredessa Mary school system administrator
Pippin, James Adrian, Jr. middle school educator
Pitman, Sharon Gail middle school counselor
Pitts, Carl Thomas secondary education educator
Pizzuro, Salvatore Nicholas special education educator
Platti, Rita Jane educator, draftsman, author, inventor
Plutro, Michele Ann education specialist
Powell, Karen Jean college program administrator
Prabhu, Catherine Dudley school system administrator
Preusser, Joseph William academic administrator
Price, Sandra Hoffman secondary school educator
Prieto, Claudio R. academic administrator, lawyer
Prins, Robert Jack academic administrator
Pritchard, Claudius Hornby, Jr. retired university president
Prokasy, William Frederick academic administrator
Propst, Harold Dean retired academic administrator
Pryor, Harold S. retired college president
Przybyla, Leon Hugh, Jr. university director
Pudlewski, Judy Marie adult educator, consultant
Pulliam, Brenda Jane retired secondary school educator
Pulliam, Yvonne Antoinette gifted education educator
†Purpura, Antoinette Maria-Carmela elementary education educator
Pyles, Carol DeLong dean, consultant, educator
Quarles, Peggy Delores secondary school educator
†Rabideau, Marilyn Ann elementary education educator
Rada, Ruth Byers college dean, author
Rago, Dorothy Ashton retired educator
Ramirez, Maria C(oncepción) educational administrator
Ramsey, Henry, Jr. university official, lawyer, retired judge
Ranks, Anne Elizabeth retired elementary and secondary education educator
Ratcliff, James Lewis administrator
Ratliff, Lois L. secondary school educator
Ray, Paula Dickerson elementary education educator
Ray, Shirley Dodson educational administrator, consultant
Redmont, Bernard Sidney university dean, journalism educator
Reeves, David Charles secondary educator, construction executive
Regn Fraher, Bonnie special education educator
†Reinalda, David Anthony elementary education educator
Reinertsen, Gloria May elementary education educator
Reinke, Ralph Louis retired academic administrator
Remley, Audrey Wright retired educational administrator, psychologist
Resing, Maryloretto Rachel elementary education educator, pastoral counselor
Revor, Barbara Kay secondary school educator
Reynolds, Betty Ann elementary education educator
Rhodes, Mary O'Neil elementary education educator
Rice, Gary Russell special education educator
Rice, Patricia Oppenheim Levin special education educator, consultant
Rice-Dietrich, Therese Ann elementary education educator
Rich, Cynthia Gay elementary education educator
Richardson, Elsie Helen retired elementary education educator
Riddle, Donald Husted former university chancellor
†Rinehart, Marybeth E. elementary education educator, artist
Riser, Carol Ann secondary education educator
Ritchie, Anne educational administrator
Roaden, Arliss Lloyd retired higher education executive director, former university president
Roberson, Pamela Kay secondary education educator
Roberts, Kathleen Donohoe special education educator
Roberts, Patricia Lee education educator
Robertson, Mary Virginia retired elementary education educator
Robertson, Wyndham Gay university official
Robinson, James Arthur university president emeritus, political scientist
Robison, Patricia Sue secondary school educator
Roche, Erin Wirtz elementary educator
Rochelle, Lugenia academic administrator
Rockafellow, Deborah S. career planning administrator
†Roelofs, Marina Banchero university official, consultant
Rogers, Sharon J. education consultant
†Roper, Fred W. dean
Rosado, Elizabeth Schaar educator
Rosenberg, Raymond David secondary education educator, consultant
Rosenblum Grevéy, Estelle retired dean, nursing educator
†Ross, Alvin Paul educator
Ross, Ann Dunbar secondary school educator
Roth, Evelyn Austin retired elementary school educator
Roth, Loretta Elizabeth retired educator
Rouse, Elaine Burdett retired secondary school educator
†Ruff, William Gerald special education educator
Russell, Attie Yvonne academic administrator, dean, pediatrics educator
Ryan, Daniel John university administrator
Ryan, Ione Jean Alohilani retired educator, counselor
Rydz, John S. educator
Sachitano, Sheila Marie secondary school educator, small business owner
Salagi, Doris educational administrator, retired
†Sanders, Janis Serpas elementary education educator
Sandford, Virginia Adele vocational school educator

†Sarrel, Robert school system administrator
Sartorius, Gregg Steven educational administrator
Sauer, Henry Jack elementary school educator, small business owner
Sawyer, Felicia Ivez elementary school educator
Scaffidi-Wilhelm, Gloria Angelamarie elementary education educator
Schmidt, Ruth Ann college president emerita
Schmoldt, Peggy Sue cosmetology educator
Schneider, Carolyn Alice Brauch elementary education educator
Schneider, Mary Louise retired elementary education educator
Schrage, Rose educational administrator
Schuckman, Nancy Lee retired principal
Schumacher, Vernon A. education educator
Schure, Alexander university chancellor
Schuster, Nancy Jones reading specialist
Sciaroni, Linda Gillingham high school educator
Scott, Loretta Claire elementary education educator
Scudero, Leslie Jeannine preschool teacher
Seeligson, Molly Fulton professsional life coach, educational consultant
Sellers, William Hugh academic administrator
Sessoms, Allen Lee academic administrator, former diplomat, physicist
Sestini, Virgil Andrew retired biology educator
Shagam, Marvin Hückel-Berri private school educator
Shannon, Isabelle Louise education director
Sharples, D. Kent college administrator
Sharwell, William Gay retired university president and company executive
Shaw, David Robert secondary school educator, theater director
Shearer, Charles Livingston academic administrator
Shields, Cynthia Rose college administrator
Shober, Eva Lee H. educational administrator
Shoun, Ellen Llewellyn retired secondary school educator
Shutler, Mary Elizabeth academic administrator
Sicuro, Natale Anthony academic and financial administrator, consultant
Silverman, Elaine Roslyn retired secondary education educator
†Simkins, Gregory Dale secondary education educator
Singleton, Robert Culton graduate school administrator, Bible educator
Sizemore, Barbara Ann Black studies educator
Skaggs, Bebe Rebecca Patten college dean, clergywoman
Skurnik, Joan Iris special education evaluator, educator, consultant
Slaydon-Wolbert, Jeanne Miller secondary school educator
Smith, Debra Ann elementary education educator
Smith, Jean Broxton retired elementary education educator
Smith, Kenneth Edward academic administrator
Smith, Martha Virginia Barnes retired elementary school educator
†Smith, Rodney K. principal
Sneed, Alberta Neal retired elementary education educator
Snortland, Howard Jerome educational financial consultant
Sonnenschein, Hugo Freund academic administrator, economics educator
Southworth, Jamie MacIntyre education educator
Spindel, Mark school system administrator
Stabile, Benedict Louis retired academic administrator, retired coast guard officer
Stanford, Kathleen Theresa secondary school educator
Staresnick, Julie Chih school psychologist
Stark, Helen Morton secondary education educator
Starr, Joyce Ives special education educator
Stasek, Lorraine Anne elementary school educator
Statman, Jackie C. career consultant
Steele, Antonio L. principal, educator
Stefanelli, Lisa Eileen elementary education educator
Stein, Dale Franklin retired university president
Steinberg, Joan Emily retired middle school educator
†Stephens, Dorothy Lawrence elementary education educator
Stewart, Clinton Eugene retired adult education educator
Stewart, Dorothy K. educator, librarian
Stoecklin, Sister Carol Ann education educator
Stoker, Howard W. former education educator, educational administrator, consultant
†Stolovitsky, Mark Ian school administrator
Stone, Kathy Sue secondary education educator
Stuckwisch, Clarence George retired university administrator
Sugnet, Linda A'Brunzo elementary education educator
Sullivan, Charles university dean, educator, author
Szelenyi, Ivan educator
Szporn, Renee Marla religious studies and special education educator
Tabandera, Kathlynn Rosemary secondary education educator
Tanner, Laurel Nan education educator
Tarbi, William Rheinlander secondary education educator, curriculum consultant, educational technology researcher
†Taylor, Beth educator
Tenhoeve, Thomas academic administrator
Terrell, Melvin C. academic administrator
Therrien, Anita Aurore elementary school educator
Thom, Lilian Elizabeth secondary school educator
Thompson, Ana Calzada secondary education educator, mathematician
Thompson, Raymond Eugene, Jr. education educator
Thomson, Mabel Amelia retired elementary school educator
Tichenor, A. Caylen elementary school educator
Timmons, Sharon L. retired elementary education educator
Timpte, Robert Nelson secondary school educator
Toledo, Victor educational consultant
Tracanna, Kim elementary and secondary physical education educator
Troupe, Marilyn Kay education educator
Tuchscherer, Marsha Smith university art director
Tuck, Russell R., Jr. former college president
Tudor, Mary Louise Drummond elementary school educator
†Turnbull, Rebecca Jane Hemphill educational administrator
Turnbull, Vernona Harmsen retired residence counselor, education educator
†Turner-St. Clair, Linda Elaine educator
Tussing, Lewis Benton, III (Tony Tussing) secondary education educator, coach
VanBriggle, Denise Marie secondary school educator
Vandenburg, Kathy Helen career counselor
Van Solkema-Waitz, Terese Ellen special education educator, consultant
Varis, Jina Aleksandra voice teacher
Violenus, Agnes A. retired school system administrator
Volpe, Edmond L(oris) college president
†Voss, Varnell Von elementary education educator
†Vujacic, Veljko M. adult education educator
Wagner, Marilyn Faith elementary school educator
†Walker, Pamela college administrator
Walsh, Dolores (Lorry)Ann Gonczo special education educator
Walter, Ann Lynn special education educator
†Walters, Jacqueline Lynsherrlye college administrator
Walters-Lucy, Jean Marie personal growth educator, consultant
Warder, Richard Currey, Jr. dean, mechanical aerospace engineering educator
†Warren, Shelly Dee academic administrator
Washington, Walter retired academic administrator
Waters, Donald Eugene academic administrator
Watson, Marilyn Kaye elementary education educator
Watts, Jeri Hanel elementary education educator, writer
Watts, Mary Ann retired elementary education educator
Weaver, Charles Horace educator
Weaver, Helen Grace retired elementary education educator
†Weber, Shelly Ann elementary music educator
†Weeks, Mary Kathryn secondary education educator, artist
Wegert, Mary Magdalene Hardel retired special education director, consultant
Weiss, Kenneth Jay education educator, reading specialist, administrator
Weller, Debra Anne elementary educator
Welly, Michael Anthony elementary school educator
Wendt, Marilynn Suzann elementary school educator, principal
†Westergard, Sue Benzel elementary education educator
†Wheeler, Brannon M. adult education educator
Wheeler, David Laurie university dean
White, Annette Jones retired early childhood educator/administrator
White, Florence May learning disabilities specialist
White, John Wesley, Jr. retired university president
†White, Orion Forrest, Jr. education educator
Whitehurst, Rose Mae education specialist
Wickersham, Amanda Kaye retired elementary education educator
Wiebelhaus, Pamela Sue school administrator, educator
†Wilhide, Angela Gail secondary education educator
Wilkening, Laurel Lynn academic administrator, planetary scientist
Williams, Cheryl A. secondary education educator
Williams, Harriette Flowers retired school system administrator, educational consultant
Williams, Heather Pauline secondary education educator
Williams, Lewis T. (Rusty Williams) education educator
Williams, Thomas B. secondary school educator
Wilson, Robin Scott university president, writer
Wiseman, Douglas Carl education educator
Wittich, John Jacob retired college president, corporation consultant
Wolf, Edith Maletz retired educator
Wong, David Yue academic administrator, physics educator
†Woodard, Pamela J. child care center administrator
Woods, Phyllis Michalik retired elementary school educator
Woodsworth, Anne university dean, librarian
Woolworth, Susan Valk primary school educator
Worthen, John Edward academic administrator
†Worthley, John Abbott adult education educator, consultant, author
Wright, Connie Sue special education educator
Wrucke-Nelson, Ann C. elementary education educator
Wulf, Janie Scott McIlwaine gifted and talented education educator
Wyman, Viola Bousquet elementary educator
†Xiao, John Qiang education educator
Yitts, Rose Marie nursery school executive
Young, Joyce Henry adult education educator, consultant
Young, Margaret Chong elementary education educator
Young, Susan Eileen elementary education educator
Young, Teresa Gail Hilger adult education educator
Young, Virgil Monroe education educator
Youngs, Diane Campfield learning disabilities specialist, educator
Zacharias, Donald Wayne academic administrator
Zauner, Christian Walter university dean, exercise physiologist, consultant
Zilbert, Allen Bruce education educator, computer consultant
†Zoller, James Alexander educator
Zufryden, Fred S. academic administrator, marketing educator, researcher
Zuiches, James Joseph academic administrator

ENGINEERING

UNITED STATES

ALABAMA

Auburn
Aldridge, Melvin Dayne electrical engineering educator
Cochran, John Euell, Jr. aerospace engineer, educator, lawyer
Irwin, John David electrical engineering educator
Jaeger, Richard Charles electrical engineer, educator, science center director
Turnquist, Paul Kenneth agricultural engineer, educator
Walsh, William Kershaw textile engineering educator

Birmingham
Adams, Alfred Bernard, Jr. environmental engineer
Appleton, Joseph Hayne civil engineer, educator
Bunt, Randolph Cedric mechanical engineer
Edmonds, William Fleming retired engineering and construction company executive
Hidy, George Martel chemical engineer, executive
Makarov, Yuri Viktorovich electrical engineering educator, researcher
Scott, Owen Myers, Jr. nuclear engineer
Szygenda, Stephen A. electrical and computer engineering educator, researcher

Decatur
Taylor, Paul retired engineer

Dozier
Grantham, Charles Edward broadcast engineer

Elberta
Brennan, Lawrence Edward electronics engineer

Hoover
Hemmings, Robert Leslie chemical engineer

Huntsville
Bramon, Christopher John aerospace engineer
Bridwell, G. Porter retired aerospace engineer
Chassay, Roger Paul, Jr. engineering executive, project manager
Componation, Paul Joseph industrial and systems engineer, educator
Emerson, William Kary engineering company executive
Hunter, Herbert Erwin aerospace engineer
Kim, Young Kil aerospace engineer
Mc Donough, George Francis, Jr. retired aerospace engineer, consultant
Moore, Fletcher Brooks engineering company executive
Reece, Wanda G. space station training engineer, writer
Schonberg, William Peter aerospace, mechanical, civil engineering educator
Schroer, Bernard Jon industrial engineering educator
Theisen, Russell Eugene electrical engineer
Vaughan, Otha H., Jr. retired aerospace engineer, research scientist
Vinz, Frank Louis electrical engineer
Watson, Raymond Coke, Jr. engineering executive, academic administrator
Wu, Ying Chu Lin Susan engineering company executive, engineer
Yang, Hong-Qing mechanical engineer

Loachapoka
Schafer, Robert Louis agricultural engineer, researcher

Madison
Adams, Gary Lee systems engineer
Barbour, Blair Allen electro-optical engineer, researcher
Dannenberg, Konrad K. aeronautical engineer
Evensen, Alf John engineer, researcher, sales executive
Hawk, Clark Williams mechanical and aerospace engineering educator
Reddy, Thikkavarapu Ramachandra electrical engineer

Mobile
Hamid, Michael electrical engineering educator, consultant

Montgomery
Paddock, Austin Joseph engineering executive

Muscle Shoals
Barrier, John Wayne engineer, management consultant

Redstone Arsenal
Clark, Mark Anthony electrical engineer
Hollowell, Monte J. engineer, operations research analyst
Smith, Troy Alvin aerospace research engineer

Thomasville
Davis, Gene civil engineer

Tucson
Murray, Dale Norris engineering scientist, researcher

Tuscaloosa
Barfield, Robert F. retired mechanical engineer, educator, dean
Bryan, Colgan Hobson aerospace engineering educator
Doughty, Julian Orus mechanical engineer, educator
Griffin, Marvin Anthony industrial engineer, educator
Morley, Lloyd Albert electrical engineering educator
Moynihan, Gary Peter industrial engineering educator
Warren, Garry Wilbur engineering educator

ALASKA

Anchorage
Baker, Grant Cody civil engineering educator
Leman, Loren Dwight civil engineer
†McKay, Thomas W. petroleum engineer
Pressley, James Ray electrical engineer
Watts, Michael Arthur materials engineer

Fairbanks
Tilsworth, Timothy retired environmental/civil engineering educator

ARIZONA

Chandler
Fordemwalt, James Newton microelectronics engineering educator, consultant
Myers, Gregory Edwin aerospace engineer

Flagstaff
Somerville, Mason Harold mechanical engineering educator, university dean

Glendale
Harris, Warren Lynn development engineer
Landrum, Larry James computer engineer

Goodyear
Bailey, Thomas Everett engineering company executive

Hereford
Hirth, John Price metallurgical engineering educator

Mesa
Rummel, Robert Wiland aeronautical engineer, author

Paradise Valley
Ratkowski, Donald J. mechanical engineer, consultant
Russell, Paul Edgar electrical engineering educator

Phoenix
Amavisca, Edward Dean electrical engineer
Bachus, Benson Floyd mechanical engineer, consultant
Banerjee, Ajoy Kumar engineer, constructor, consultant
Burchard, John Kenneth chemical engineer
Chisholm, Tom Shepherd environmental engineer
Ehst, Eric Richard aerospace engineer
Faul, Gary Lyle electrical engineering supervisor
Freyermuth, Clifford L. structural engineering consultant
Fullmer, Steven Mark systems engineer
Goldman, Charles electromechanical engineer
Hamilton, Darden Cole flight test engineer
Jorgensen, Gordon David engineering company executive
Kaliszek, Andrew Wojciech mechanical engineer
Leeland, Steven Brian electronics engineer
McGuire, Gerard Joseph engineering executive
Miller, Michael Jon survey engineer, local government manager
Nishioka, Teruo (Ted Nishioka) electrical engineer

Prescott
Bieniawski, Zdzislaw Tadeusz Richard engineering educator emeritus, writer, consultant
Chesson, Eugene, Jr. civil engineering educator, consultant
Hasbrook, A. Howard aviation safety engineer, consultant
Kahne, Stephen James systems engineer, educator, academic administrator, engineering executive

Prescott Valley
Wynn, Robert Raymond retired engineer, consultant

Rio Verde
Jordan, Richard Charles engineering executive

Scottsdale
Eckelman, Richard Joel engineering specialist
Fisher, John Richard engineering consultant, former naval officer
Gilson, Arnold Leslie retired engineering executive
Gookin, Thomas Allen Jaudon civil engineer
Kiehn, Mogens Hans aviation engineer, consultant
Lee, Dennis Turner civil engineer, construction executive
Newman, Marc Alan electrical engineer
Ragland, Samuel Connelly industrial engineer, management consultant
Roberts, Peter Christopher Tudor engineering executive

Sierra Vista
Plum, Richard Eugene retired flight engineer
Ricco, Raymond Joseph, Jr. computer systems engineer

Sun City
Vander Molen, Jack Jacobus engineering executive, consultant

Sun City West
Coté, Ralph Warren, Jr. mining engineer, nuclear engineer
Woodruff, Neil Parker agricultural engineer

Sun Lakes
Richardson, Robert Carleton engineering consultant

Tempe
Balanis, Constantine Apostle electrical engineering educator
Berman, Neil Sheldon chemical engineering educator
Ferry, David Keane electrical engineering educator
Hempfling, Gregory Jay mechanical engineer
Karady, George Gyorgy electrical engineering educator, consultant
Kaufman, Irving retired engineering educator
Mense, Allan Tate research and development engineering executive
Robertson, Samuel Harry, III transportation safety research engineer, educator
Schroder, Dieter Karl electrical engineering educator
Shaw, Milton Clayton mechanical engineering educator
Si, Jennie engineering educator
Stephenson, Frank Alex engineer, consultant

Tonopah
Brittingham, James Calvin nuclear engineer

Tucson
Arnell, Walter James William mechanical engineering educator, consultant
Brooks, Donald Lee civil engineering and scientific consulting firm executive
Brunton, Daniel William mechanical engineer
Coates, Wayne Evan agricultural engineer
Cook, Paul Christopher engineering psychologist
Cuello, Joel L. biosystems engineer, educator
Fasel, Hermann F. aerospace and mechanical engineering educator
Harrington, Roger Fuller electrical engineering educator, consultant
Hiskey, J. Brent metallurgical engineer, educator
Hunt, Bobby Ray electrical engineering educator, consultant
Kerwin, William James electrical engineering educator, consultant

Kinney, Robert Bruce *mechanical engineering educator*
Mitchell, Robert Campbell *nuclear consultant*
Ogilvie, T(homas) Francis *engineer, educator*
Prince, John Luther, III *engineering educator*
Renard, Kenneth George *civil engineer*
Rubendall, Richard Arthur *civil engineer*
Sells, Kevin Dwayne *marine engineer*
Winarski, Daniel James *mechanical engineer, educator*

Vail
Hunnicutt, Robert William *engineer*

Youngtown
Gross, Al *electrical engineer, consultant*

ARKANSAS

Fayetteville
Andrews, John Frank *civil and environmental engineering educator*
Gaddy, James Leoma *chemical engineer, educator*
Thornton, Mitchell Aaron *engineering educator, consultant*
White, John Austin, Jr. *engineering educator, chancellor*

Hot Springs National Park
Wennerstrom, Arthur John *aeronautical engineer*

Little Rock
Hocott, Joe Bill *chemical engineer*

CALIFORNIA

Agoura Hills
Chang, Chong Eun *chemical engineer*
Hokana, Gregory Howard *engineering executive*

Alamo
More, Vishwas *engineering laboratory administrator*

Alpine
Roberts, Dwight Loren *engineering consultant, novelist*

Alta Loma
Bordner, Gregory Wilson *chemical engineer*

Altadena
Coles, Donald Earl *retired aeronautics educator*

Anaheim
Franklin, Cheryl Jean *engineer, author*
Kimme, Ernest Godfrey *communications engineer*
Watson, Oliver Lee, III *aerospace engineering manager*

Arcadia
Broderick, Donald Leland *electronics engineer*
Massier, Paul Ferdinand *mechanical engineer*

Atherton
Rosen, Charles Abraham *electrical engineer, consultant*

Auburn
Sun, Haiyin *optical engineer, educator*

Azusa
Forbes, Judie *program manager*
Works, Madden Travis, Jr. (Pat Works) *operations executive, author, skydiving instructor, skydiving publications executive*

Belvedere Tiburon
Cooke, James Barry *civil engineer, consultant*

Benicia
Lipsky, Ian David *mechanical engineering executive*

Berkeley
Bea, Robert G. *civil engineering educator*
Bell, Alexis T. *chemical engineer*
Berger, Stanley Allan *mechanical engineering educator*
Birdsall, Charles Kennedy *electrical engineer*
Bogy, David B(euregard) *mechanical engineering educator*
Brodersen, Robert W. *engineering educator*
Cairns, Elton James *chemical engineering educator*
Chang-Hasnain, Constance Jui-Hua *educator*
Chopra, Anil Kumar *civil engineering educator*
Denn, Morton Mace *chemical engineering educator*
Dornfeld, David Alan *engineering educator*
Finnie, Iain *mechanical engineer, educator*
Frisch, Joseph *mechanical engineer, educator, consultant*
Fuerstenau, Douglas Winston *mineral engineering educator*
Garrison, William Louis *civil engineering educator*
Goldsmith, Werner *mechanical engineering educator*
Gray, Paul Russell *electrical engineering educator*
Grossman, Lawrence Morton *nuclear engineering educator*
Harris, Guy Hendrickson *chemical research engineer*
Hodges, David Albert *electrical engineering educator*
Hsu, Chieh Su *applied mechanics engineering educator, researcher*
Hu, Chenming *electrical engineering educator*
Kastenberg, William Edward *engineering and applied science educator*
Katz, Randy H. *electrical engineering, computer sciences educator*
Kuh, Ernest Shiu-Jen *electrical engineering educator*
Leitmann, George *mechanical engineering educator*
Lewis, Edwin Reynolds *biomedical engineering educator*
Lieberman, Michael A. *electrical engineer, educator*
Maron, Melvin Earl *engineer, philosopher, educator*
May, Adolf Darlington *civil engineering educator*
Monismith, Carl Leroy *civil engineering educator*
Muller, Richard Stephen *electrical engineer, educator*
Neureuther, Andrew R. *engineering educator*
Newman, John Scott *chemical engineer, educator*
Oldham, William George *electrical engineering and computer science educator*
Ott, David Michael *engineering company executive*
Pagni, Patrick John *mechanical and fire safety engineering science educator*
Pask, Joseph Adam *ceramic engineering educator*
Penzien, Joseph *structural engineering educator*
Pigford, Thomas Harrington *nuclear engineering educator*
Polak, Elijah *engineering educator, computer scientist*
Popov, Egor Paul *engineering educator*
Schwarz, Steven Emanuel *electrical engineering educator, administrator*
Scordelis, Alexander Costicas *civil engineering educator*
Stonebraker, Michael R. *electrical engineering & computer science educator*
Susskind, Charles *engineering educator, author, publishing executive*
Tomizuka, Masayoshi *mechanical engineering educator, researcher*
Van Duzer, Theodore *electrical engineer*
Whinnery, John Roy *electrical engineering educator*
White, Richard Manning *electrical engineering educator*
Wiegel, Robert Louis *consulting engineering executive*
Zadeh, Lotfi Asker *engineering educator*

Berry Creek
Miller, Joseph Arthur *retired manufacturing engineer, educator, consultant*

Buena Park
Wiersema, Harold LeRoy *aerospace engineer*

Burlingame
Chen, Basilio *engineering executive*

Calistoga
Moorhouse, Douglas C. *retired engineering executive*

Camarillo
Lam, Cheung-Wei *electrical engineer*
MacDonald, Norval (Woodrow) *safety engineer*
Parker, Theodore Clifford *electronics engineer*

Cambria
DuFresne, Armand Frederick *management and engineering consultant*

Campbell
Ross, Hugh Courtney *electrical engineer*

Canoga Park
Kivenson, Gilbert *engineering consultant, patent agent*

Capitola
Barna, Arpad Alex *electrical engineering consultant*

Carmel
Alsberg, Dietrich Anselm *electrical engineer*

Cayucos
Theurer, Byron W. *aerospace engineer, business owner*

Cerritos
Subramanya, Shiva *aerospace systems engineer*

Chatsworth
Lu, Guiyang *electrical engineer*

Chico
Allen, Charles William *mechanical engineering educator*

Claremont
Dym, Clive Lionel *engineering educator*
Molinder, John Irving *engineering educator, consultant*
Monson, James Edward *electrical engineer, educator*
Tanenbaum, Basil Samuel *engineering educator*
Yurist, Svetlan Joseph *mechanical engineer*

Compton
Wang, Charles Ping *scientist*

Concord
Cassidy, John Joseph *hydraulic and hydrologic engineer*
Lee, Low Kee *electronics engineer, consultant*

Corona Del Mar
Richmond, Ronald LeRoy *aerospace engineer*

Coronado
Crilly, Eugene Richard *engineering consultant*

Corralitos
Short, Harold Ashby *imaging engineer*

Costa Mesa
Buchtel, Michael Eugene *optical mechanical engineer*
Carpenter, Frank Charles, Jr. *retired electronics engineer*

Crockett
Leporiere, Ralph Dennis *quality engineer*

Culver City
Kumar, Anil *nuclear engineer*
Sensiper, Samuel *consulting electrical engineer*
Wood, Paul Nigel *film and television engineer*

Cupertino
Fenn, Raymond Wolcott, Jr. *retired metallurgical engineer*

Cypress
Magdosku, Christopher Lee *civil engineer*

Dana Point
Furst, Raymond Bruce *engineer, consultant*

Davis
Akesson, Norman Berndt *agricultural engineer, emeritus educator*
Beadle, Charles Wilson *retired mechanical engineering educator*
Brandt, Harry *mechanical engineering educator*
Chancellor, William Joseph *agricultural engineering educator*
Cheney, James Addison *civil engineering educator*
Dorf, Richard Carl *electrical engineering and management educator*
Fridley, Robert Bruce *agricultural engineering educator*
Gates, Bruce Clark *chemical engineer, educator*
Ghausi, Mohammed Shuaib *electrical engineering educator, university dean*
Hakimi, S. Louis *electrical and computer engineering educator*
Krener, Arthur J. *systems engineering educator*
Krone, Ray Beyers *civil and environmental engineering educator, consultant*
Larock, Bruce Edward *civil engineering educator*
Levy, Bernard C. *electrical engineer, educator*
Orlob, Gerald Thorvald *civil engineer, engineering educator, reseacher*
Wang, Shih-Ho *electrical engineer, educator*

Del Mar
Wilkinson, Eugene Parks *nuclear engineer*

Desert Hot Springs
Halasz, Stephen Joseph *retired electro-optical systems engineer*

Diamond Bar
Mirisola, Lisa Heinemann *air quality engineer*

Dinuba
Leps, Thomas MacMaster *civil engineer, consultant*

Downey
Baumann, Theodore Robert *aerospace engineer, consultant, army officer*
Demarchi, Ernest Nicholas *aerospace engineering administrator*
Grooms, Henry Randall *civil engineer*
Nash, Richard Eugene *aerospace engineer*
Nichols, Mark Edward *engineer*

Edwards
Garcia, Andrew B. *chemical engineer*
Hamlin, Edmund Martin, Jr. *engineering manager*

El Cajon
Summers, Stanley Eugene *mechanical engineer*

El Segundo
Banuk, Ronald Edward (Ron) *mechanical engineer*
Bauer, Jerome Leo, Jr. *chemical engineer*
Begert, Matthew *engineering company official*
Lantz, Norman Foster *electrical engineer*
Mathur, Ashok *telecommunications engineer, educator, researcher*
Maxwell, Floyd Dawson *research engineer, consultant*
Mirza, Zakir Hussain *aerospace company consultant*
Pugay, Jeffrey Ibanez *mechanical engineer*
Tamrat, Befecadu *aeronautical engineer*

Emeryville
Bresler, Boris *consulting engineer*
Zwoyer, Eugene Milton *consulting engineering executive*

Encinitas
Frank, Michael Victor *risk assessment engineer*
Morrow, Charles Tabor *aerospace consulting engineer*

Encino
Acheson, Louis Kruzan, Jr. *aerospace engineer and systems analyst*
Friedman, George Jerry *aerospace company executive, engineer*
Knuth, Eldon Luverne *engineering educator*

Escondido
Ghandhi, Sorab Khushro *electrical engineering educator*

Fair Oaks
Smiley, Robert William *industrial engineer*

Folsom
Ettlich, William F. *electrical engineer*

Foster City
Ham, Lee Edward *civil engineer*

Fountain Valley
Khalessi, Mohammad R. *structural engineer, researcher*
Tu, John *engineering executive*

Fremont
Engelbart, Doug *engineering executive*
Le, Thuy Trong *research scientist, educator*
Wu, James Chen-Yuan *aerospace engineering educator*

Fresno
Huffman, David George *electrical engineer*

Fullerton
Gunness, Robert Charles *chemical engineer*

Glendale
Stemmer, Jay John *safety engineer, consultant*
Vilnrotter, Victor Alpár *research engineer*

Glendora
Haile, Benjamin Carroll, Jr. *retired chemical and mechanical engineer*

Goleta
Tulin, Marshall P(eter) *engineering educator*

Granite Bay
Borum, William Donald *engineer*

Greenbrae
Elder, Rex Alfred *civil engineer*

Hacienda Heights
Love, Daniel Joseph *consulting engineer*

Hanford
Zack, Teresa Ison *civil engineer*

Hawthorne
Burns, Brent Emil *electrical engineer*

Hayward
Hunnicutt, Richard Pearce *metallurgical engineer*

Hermosa Beach
McDowell, Edward R. H. *chemical engineer*

Hillsborough
Blume, John August *consulting civil engineer*

Huntington Beach
Leveton, Ian Sinclair *civil engineer*
Stillman, Alfred William, Jr. *design and support engineer*

Irvine
Bershad, Neil Jeremy *electrical engineering educator*
Currivan, Bruce Joseph *electronics engineer*
Guymon, Gary LeRoy *civil engineering educator, consultant*
Jacobsen, Eric Kasner *consulting engineer*
Kinsman, Robert Preston *biomedical plastics engineer*
†Nicholas, Henry Thompson, III *engineering executive*
Orme, Melissa Emily *mechanical engineering educator*
Samueli, Henry *electrical engineering educator, entrepreneur*
Sirignano, William Alfonso *aerospace and mechanical engineer, educator*
Sklansky, Jack *electrical and computer engineering educator, researcher*
Stubberud, Allen Roger *electrical engineering educator*
Ting, Albert Chia *bioengineering researcher*

Kensington
Oppenheim, Antoni Kazimierz *mechanical engineer*

La Canada Flintridge
Price, Humphrey Wallace *aerospace engineer*

La Jolla
Chang, William Shen Chie *electrical engineering educator*
Chien, Shu *physiology and bioengineering educator*
Coler, Myron A(braham) *chemical engineer, educator*
Conn, Robert William *engineering science educator*
Counts, Stanley Thomas *aerospace consultant, retired naval officer, retired electronics company executive*
Fung, Yuan-Cheng Bertram *bioengineering educator, author*
Hall, Harold Robert *retired computer engineer*
Helstrom, Carl Wilhelm *electrical engineering educator*
Levy, Ralph *engineering executive, consultant*
Milstein, Laurence Bennett *electrical engineering educator, researcher*
Penner, Stanford Solomon *engineering educator*
Rudee, Mervyn Lea *engineering educator, researcher*
Rudolph, Walter Paul *engineering research company executive*
Schmid-Schoenbein, Geert Wilfried *biomedical engineer, educator*
Simnad, Massoud T. *engineering educator*
Sung, Kuo-Li Paul *bioengineering educator*
Sung, Lanping Amy *biomedical engineer*
Williams, Forman Arthur *engineering science educator, combustion theorist*
Wolf, Jack Keil *electrical engineer, educator*

Lafayette
Krueger, Robert Edward *manufacturing executive, mechanical engineer*

Laguna Beach
Bushman, Edwin Francis Arthur *engineer, plastics consultant, rancher*
Larson, Harry Thomas *electronics engineer, executive, consultant*

Laguna Hills
Green, Leon, Jr. *mechanical engineer*
Hammond, R. Philip *chemical engineer*
Lederer, Jerome *aerospace safety consultant, engineer*

Laguna Niguel
Shifrin, Bruce Carl *electrical engineer*

Lake Forest
Sheehy, Jerome Joseph *electrical engineer*

Lancaster
Cooper, James Ralph *engineering executive*
Hodges, Vernon Wray *mechanical engineer*

Livermore
Carley, James French *chemical and plastics engineer*
Cassens, Nicholas, Jr. *ceramics engineer*
Christensen, Richard Monson *mechanical engineer, materials engineer*
Edmondo, Douglas Brian *marine engineer*
Hill, John Earl *mechanical engineer*
Johnson, Roy Ragnar *electrical engineer*
King, Ray John *electrical engineer*
Sheem, Sang Keun *fiber optics engineering professional*

Lomita
Balcom, Orville *engineer*

Long Beach
Cummings, Darold Bernard *aircraft engineer*
Dillon, Michael Earl *engineering executive, mechanical engineer, educator*
Donald, Eric Paul *aeronautical engineer, inventor*
Elliott, John Gregory *aerospace design engineer*
Jager, Merle LeRoy *aerospace engineer*
Kumar, Rajendra *electrical engineering educator*
Robinson, Michael R. *aeronautical engineer*

Los Altos
Bell, Chester Gordon *computer engineering company executive*
Bergrun, Norman Riley *aerospace executive*
Kazan, Benjamin *research engineer*
Moll, John Lewis *electronics engineer, retired*
Peterson, Victor Lowell *aerospace engineer, management consultant*
Sharpe, Roland Leonard *engineering company executive, earthquake and structural engineering consultant*
Zebroski, Edwin Leopold *consulting engineer*

Los Altos Hills
Fondahl, John Walker *civil engineering educator*

Los Angeles
Abdou, Mohamed A. *mechanical, aerospace, and nuclear engineering educator*
Alwan, Abeer *electrical engineering educator*
Atluri, Satya N(adham) *aerospace engineering educator*
Breuer, Melvin Allen *electrical engineering educator*
Bucy, Richard Snowden *aerospace engineering and mathematics educator, consultant*
Charwat, Andrew Franciszek *engineering educator*
Cheng, Hsien Kei *aeronautics educator*
Cheng, Tsen-Chung *electrical engineering educator*
Crombie, Douglass Darnill *aerospace communications system engineer*
Dhir, Vijay K. *mechanical engineering educator*
Dorman, Albert A. *consulting engineer executive, architect*
Elliott, Robert S(tratman) *electrical engineer, educator*
Friedlander, Sheldon Kay *chemical engineering educator*
Handy, Lyman Lee *petroleum engineer, chemist, educator*
Hovanessian, Shahen Alexander *electrical engineer, educator*
Huang, Sung-cheng *electrical engineering educator*
Incaudo, Joseph August *engineering company executive*
Itoh, Tatsuo *engineering educator*
James, William Langford *aerospace engineer*
Johnston, Roy G. *consulting structural engineer*
Karplus, Walter J. *engineering educator*
†Kiang, Ching-Hwa *chemical engineering educator*
Klinger, Allen *engineering and applied science educator*
Kuehl, Hans Henry *electrical engineering educator*
Leal, George D. *engineering company executive*
Lin, Tung Hua *civil engineering educator*
Lindsey, William C. *engineering educator*
Lynn, Katherine Lyn *quality engineer, chemist*
MacKenzie, John Douglas *engineering educator*
Marmarelis, Vasilis Zissis *engineering educator, author, consultant*
Martin, J(ohn) Edward *architectural engineer*
McKellop, Harry Alden *biomechanical engineering educator*
Meecham, William Coryell *engineering educator*
Mendel, Jerry Marc *electrical engineering educator*
Mortensen, Richard Edgar *engineering educator*
Muntz, Eric Phillip *aerospace engineering and radiology educator, consultant*
Nadler, Gerald *engineering educator, management consultant*
Nobe, Ken *chemical engineering educator*
Okrent, David *engineering educator*
O'Neill, Russell Richard *engineering educator*
Orchard, Henry John *electrical engineer*
Perrine, Richard Leroy *environmental engineering educator*
Perry, Robert Michael *international engineering company executive*
Portenier, Walter James *aerospace engineer*
Ramo, Simon *engineering executive*
Rauch, Lawrence Lee *aerospace and electrical engineer, educator*
Rubinstein, Moshe Fajwel *engineering educator*
Safonov, Michael George *electrical engineering educator, consultant*
Scholtz, Robert Arno *electrical engineering educator*
Sheppard, William Vernon *engineering and construction executive*
Shinozuka, Masanobu *civil engineer, educator*
Udwadia, Firdaus Erach *engineering educator, consultant*
Urena-Alexiades, Jose Luis *electrical engineer*
Wagner, Christian Nikolaus Johann *materials engineering educator*
Weber, Charles L. *electrical engineering educator*
Welch, Lloyd Richard *electrical engineering educator, communications consultant*
Willner, Alan Eli *electrical engineer, educator*
Yang, Bingen *mechanical engineering educator*
Yeh, William Wen-Gong *civil engineering educator*
Yen, Teh Fu *civil and environmental engineering educator*

Los Gatos
Naymark, Sherman *consulting nuclear engineer*
Rosenheim, Donald Edwin *electrical engineer*

Malibu
Bedrosian, Edward *electrical engineer*
Clewett, Raymond Winfred *mechanical design engineer*
Hooper, Catherine Evelyn *senior development engineer*
Vickers, Deborah Janice *electrical engineer, researcher*

Manhattan Beach
Bradburn, David Denison *engineer, retired air force officer*
Ricardi, Leon Joseph *electrical engineer*

Mcclellan AFB
Herrlinger, Stephen Paul *flight test engineer, air force officer, educator*

Menlo Park
†Cardozo, Oscar F. *engineering executive*
Edson, William Alden *electrical engineer*
Honey, Richard Churchill *retired electrical engineer*
Kohne, Richard Edward *retired engineering executive*
Levenson, Milton *chemical engineer, consultant*
McCarthy, Roger Lee *mechanical engineer*
Shah, Haresh Chandulal *civil engineering educator*

Milpitas
McDonald, Mark Douglas *electrical engineer*
Mian, Guo *electrical engineer*
Parruck, Bidyut *electrical engineer*
Wang, Huai-Liang William *mechanical engineer*
Wolters, Christian Heinrich *systems engineer*

Mission Hills
Cramer, Frank Brown *engineering executive, combustion engineer, systems consultant*

Mission Viejo
Ljubicic Drozdowski, Miladin Peter *consulting engineer*
Subramanian, Sundaram *electronics engineer*

Moffett Field
Dacles-Mariani, Jennifer Samson *engineering educator*
Erzberger, Heinz *aeronautical engineer*
Kerr, Andrew W. *aerodynamics researcher*
McCroskey, William James *aeronautical engineer*
Statler, Irving Carl *aerospace engineer*

Monarch Beach
Dougherty, Elmer Lloyd, Jr. *retired chemical engineering educator, consultant*

Monrovia
Mac Cready, Paul Beattie *aeronautical engineer*
Pray, Ralph Emerson *metallurgical engineer*

Monterey
Butler, Jon Terry *computer engineering educator, researcher*
Marto, Paul James *retired mechanical engineering educator, consultant, researcher*
Newberry, Conrad Floyde *aerospace engineering educator*

Monterey Park
Waiter, Serge-Albert *retired civil engineer*

Moorpark
Bahn, Gilbert Schuyler *retired mechanical engineer, researcher*

Morro Bay
Wagner, Peter Ewing *physics and electrical engineering educator*

Mountain View
Heffelfinger, David Mark *optical engineer*
Johnson, Conor Deane *mechanical engineer*
Savage, Thomas Warren *engineering director*
Subramanian, Ravi *electrical engineer*

Murphys
Moody, Frederick Jerome *mechanical engineer, consultant thermal hydraulics*

Newport Beach
†Cheng, Yuhua *electrical engineer*
Kraus, John Walter *former aerospace engineering company executive*
Sharbaugh, W(illiam) James *plastics engineer, consultant*

Northridge
Bradshaw, Richard Rotherwood *engineering executive*
Kiddoo, Robert James *engineering service company executive*
Stout, Thomas Melville *control systems engineer*
Torgow, Eugene N. *electrical engineer*

Oakland
Brown, Stephen Lawrence *environmental consultant*
De Ford, Douglas Atmetlla *biochemical, biomechanical and industrial engineer*
King, Cary Judson, III *chemical engineer, educator, university official*
Kint, Arne Tonis *industrial engineer, mechanical engineer*
Madabhushi, Govindachari Venkata *retired civil engineer*
Musihin, Konstantin K. *electrical engineer*
Pister, Karl Stark *engineering educator*
Tsztoo, David Fong *civil engineer*
Vallerga, Bernard A. *engineering administrator*

Occidental
Rumsey, Victor Henry *electrical engineering educator emeritus*

Oceanside
Clark, Arthur Bryan *engineer*

Orange
Fisk, Edward Ray *retired civil engineer, author, educator*
Monsees, James Eugene *engineering executive, consultant*
Vice, Charles Loren *electromechanical engineer*

Orinda
Gilbert, Jerome B. *consulting environmental engineer*

Oxnard
Harrower, Thomas Murray *electro-mechanical design engineer*

Pacific Palisades
Abzug, Malcolm *flight mechanics engineer*
Herman, Elvin E. *retired consulting electronic engineer*

Palm Desert
Morrison, Robert Thomas *aerospace engineering and marketing consultant*
Osborne, Bartley Porter, Jr. *aeronautical engineer*

Palmdale
Moule, William Nelson *electrical engineer*

Palo Alto
Brown, David Randolph *electrical engineer*
†Daniels, Keith Allen *materials engineering manager*
Diffie, Whitfield *computer and communications engineer*
Fujitani, Martin Tomio *software quality engineer*
Hodge, Philip Gibson, Jr. *mechanical and aerospace engineering educator*
Kelley, Robert Suma *systems engineer*
Lender, Adam *electrical engineer*
London, A(lexander) L(ouis) *retired mechanical engineering educator*
Pierce, John Robinson *electrical engineer, educator*
Quate, Calvin Forrest *engineering educator*
Shelton, Robert Charles *electrical engineer*
Szczerba, Victor Bogdan *electrical engineer, sales engineer*
Taylor, John Joseph *nuclear engineer*
Youngdahl, Paul Frederick *mechanical engineer*

Palos Verdes Peninsula
Denke, Paul Herman *aircraft engineer*
Frassinelli, Guido Joseph *retired aerospace engineer*
Lowi, Alvin, Jr. *mechanical engineer, consultant*
Mirels, Harold *aerospace engineer*
Rechtin, Eberhardt *retired aerospace executive, retired educator*
Seide, Paul *civil engineering educator*
Spinks, John Lee *retired engineering executive*
Wang, Tony Kar-Hung *automotive and aerospace company executive*
Weiss, Herbert Klemm *retired aeronautical engineer*

Paradise
Learned, Vincent Roy *electrical engineer , educator*

Pasadena
Barrett, Robert Mitchell *electrical engineer*
Boulos, Paul Fares *civil and environmental engineer*
Breckinridge, James Bernard *optical science engineer, program manager*
Bridges, William Bruce *electrical engineer, researcher, educator*
Carroll, William Jerome *civil engineer*
Cass, Glen Rowan *environmental engineer*
Dallas, Saterios (Sam) *aerospace engineer, researcher, consultant*
Davis, Mark E. *chemical engineering educator*
Elachi, Charles *aerospace engineer*
Farr, Donald Eugene *engineering scientist*
Gavalas, George R. *chemical engineering educator*
Gould, Roy Walter *engineering educator*
Hatheway, Alson Earle *mechanical engineer*
Heer, Ewald *engineer*
Hemann, Raymond Glenn *research company executive*
Hilbert, Robert S(aul) *optical engineer*
Housner, George William *retired civil engineering educator, consultant*
Jacobs, Joseph John *engineering company executive*
Jennings, Paul Christian *civil engineering educator, academic administrator*
Knauss, Wolfgang Gustav *engineering educator*
Knowles, James Kenyon *applied mechanics educator*
List, Ericson John *environmental engineering science educator, engineering consultant*
Marble, Frank E(arl) *engineering educator*
Martin, Craig Lee *engineering company executive*
Otoshi, Tom Yasuo *electrical engineer, consultant*
Perez, Reinaldo Joseph *electrical engineer*
Presecan, Nicholas Lee *environmental and civil engineer, consultant*
Raichlen, Fredric *civil engineering educator, consultant*
Roshko, Anatol *aeronautic engineer*
Sabersky, Rolf Heinrich *mechanical engineer*
Schlinger, Warren Gleason *retired chemical engineer*
Seinfeld, John Hersh *chemical engineering educator*
Simon, Marvin Kenneth *electrical engineer, consultant*
Smith, Michael Robert *electro-optical engineer, physicist*
Stewart, Homer Joseph *engineering educator*
†Tolaney, Murli *environmental engineering executive*
Trussell, R(obert) Rhodes *environmental engineer*
Weisbin, Charles Richard *nuclear engineer*
Wood, Lincoln Jackson *aerospace engineer*
Wu, Theodore Yao-Tsu *engineer*
Yamarone, Charles Anthony, Jr. *aerospace engineer, consultant*
Yao, Xiaotian Steve *electrical engineer, optical scientist*
Yariv, Amnon *electrical engineering educator, scientist*
Yeh, Paul Pao *electrical and electronics engineer, educator*

Penn Valley
Morgenthaler, John Herbert *chemical engineer*
Throner, Guy Charles, Jr. *engineering executive, scientist, engineer, inventor, consultant*

Penryn
Bryson, Vern Elrick *nuclear engineer*

Petaluma
†Ghane, Kamran *computer engineer*

Pismo Beach
Saveker, David Richard *naval and marine architectural engineering executive*

Playa Del Rey
Tai, Frank *aerospace engineering consultant*

Pleasant Hill
Hopkins, Robert Arthur *retired industrial engineer*

Pleasanton
Jarnagan, Harry William, Jr. *project control manager*
Novak-Lyssand, Randi Ruth *engineer, computer scientist*

Pomona
Kauser, Fazal Bakhsh *aerospace engineer, educator*
Teague, Lavette Cox, Jr. *systems educator, consultant*

Poway
Dean, Richard Anthony *mechanical engineer, engineering executive*

Rancho Mirage
Bennett, Grover Bryce *engineering consultant*
Kramer, Gordon *mechanical engineer*

Rancho Palos Verdes
Raue, Jorg Emil *electrical engineer*

Redondo Beach
Brodsky, Robert Fox *aerospace engineer*
Buchta, Edmund *engineering executive*
Cohen, Clarence Budd *aerospace engineer*
Sackheim, Robert Lewis *aerospace engineer, educator*

Redwood City
Herrin, Stephanie Ann *retired aerospace engineer*

Ridgecrest
Pearson, John *mechanical engineer*

Riverside
Beni, Gerardo *electrical and computer engineering educator, robotics scientist*

Rocklin
Tovar, Nicholas Mario *mechanical engineer*

Rodeo
Emmanuel, Jorge Agustin *chemical engineer, environmental consultant*

Rohnert Park
Lord, Harold Wilbur *electrical engineer, electronics consultant*
†Tortorici, Peter Christopher *metallurgical engineer*

Rolling Hills Estates
Diaz-Zubieta, Agustin *nuclear engineer, executive*
Wong, Sun Yet *engineering consultant*

Sacramento
Bezzone, Albert Paul *structural engineer*
Carleone, Joseph *aerospace executive*
Cavigli, Henry James *petroleum engineer*
Collins, William Leroy *telecommunications engineer*
Crimmins, Philip Patrick *metallurgical engineer, lawyer*
Forsyth, Raymond Arthur *civil engineer*
Ishmael, William Earl *land use planner, civil engineer*
Lathi, Bhagawandas Pannalal *electrical engineering educator*
Roberts, James E. *civil engineer*
Simeroth, Dean Conrad *chemical engineer*
Soriano, Bernard C. *engineering executive*

San Bernardino
French, Kirby Allan *transportation engineer, computer programmer*
Holtz, Tobenette *aerospace engineer*

San Carlos
Symons, Robert Spencer *electronic engineer*

San Clemente
Cramer, Eugene Norman *nuclear power engineer, computer educator*
White, Stanley Archibald *research electrical engineer*

San Diego
Anderson, Karl Richard *aerospace engineer, consultant*
Anderson, Paul Maurice *electrical engineering educator, researcher, consultant*
Beyster, John Robert *engineering company executive*
Brown, Alan J. *electrical engineer*
Burke, Arthur Thomas *engineering consultant*
Butler, Geoffrey Scott *systems engineer, educator, consultant*
Chen, Carlson S. *mechanical engineer*
Chen, Kao *consulting electrical engineer*
Conly, John Franklin *engineering educator, researcher*
Crocker, Valerie Marian *mechanical engineer*
Crook, Sean Paul *aerospace systems program director*
Evans, Ersel Arthur *consulting engineer executive*
Frederick, Norman L., Jr. *electrical engineer*
Geffe, Philip Reinhold *electrical engineer, consultant*
Gray, Gavin Campbell, II *computer information engineer, computer consultant*
Gross, Jeffrey *software engineer*
Hills, Linda Launey *advisory systems engineer*
Hobbs, Marvin *engineering executive*
Hoffman, Robert James *retired electronics engineer*
Huang, Chien Chang *electrical engineer*
Kropotoff, George Alex *civil engineer*
Marple, Stanley Lawrence, Jr. *electrical engineer, signal processing researcher*
†Martin, Bruce Daniel *engineering executive*
McLeod, John Hugh, Jr. *mechanical and electrical engineer*
Powell, Robert Francis *manufacturing engineer*
St. Clair, Hal Kay *electrical engineer*
Sell, Robert Emerson *electrical engineer*
Sesonske, Alexander *nuclear and chemical engineer*
Sheaffer, Richard Allen *electrical engineer*
Slate, John Butler *biomedical engineer*
Tom, Lawrence *engineering executive*
Tricoles, Gus Peter *electromagnetic engineer, physicist, consultant*
Viterbi, Andrew James *electrical engineering and computer science educator, business executive*
Ward, Charles Raymond *systems engineer*
Youngs, Jack Marvin *cost engineer*

San Dimas
Zhang, Guotai *process engineer, researcher, ethylene furnace specialist*

San Fernando
Bridges, Robert McSteen *mechanical engineer*

San Francisco
Angell, James Browne *electrical engineering educator*
Bechtel, Riley Peart *engineering company executive*
Bechtel, Stephen Davison, Jr. *engineering company executive*
Brooks, William George *aeronautical engineer*
†Chan, Daisy S. W. *manufacturing engineer*
Cheng, Kwong Man *structural engineer*
Cheng, Wan-Lee *mechanical engineer, industrial technology educator*
Danziger, Bruce Edward *structural engineer*
Dolby, Ray Milton *engineering company executive, electrical engineer*

Engelmann, Rudolph Herman *electronics consultant*
Gerwick, Ben Clifford, Jr. *construction engineer, educator*
Hamburger, Ronald Owen *structural engineering executive*
Keller, Edward Lowell *electrical engineer, educator*
Koffel, Martin M. *engineering company executive*
Lin, Tung Yen *civil engineer, educator*
Marshall, John Paul *broadcast technologist*
Mattern, Douglas James *electronics reliability engineer*
Shor, Samuel Wendell Williston *naval engineer*
Shushkewich, Kenneth Wayne *structural engineer*
Tank, Man-Chung *civil engineer*
Vreeland, Robert Wilder *electronics engineer*
Wrona, Peter Alexander *structural engineer*
Wyllie, Loring A., Jr. *structural engineer*
Yuan, Shao Wen *aerospace engineer, educator*

San Jose
Cao, Jie-Yuan *electronics engineer, researcher*
Chamberlin, Donald Dean *computer engineer*
Chandramouli, Ramamurti *electrical engineer*
Contos, Paul Anthony *engineer, investment consultant*
Dennison, Ronald Walton *engineer*
Gallar, John Joseph *mechanical engineer, educator*
Gill, Hardayal Singh *electrical engineer*
Haque, Mohammed Shahidul *electrical engineer*
Hoang, Loc Bao *electrical engineer*
Hodgson, Gregory Bernard *software systems architect*
†Hoff, Marcian Edward, Jr. *electronics engineer*
Huang, Francis Fu-Tse *mechanical engineering educator*
Israel, Paul Neal *computer design engineer, author*
Jacobson, Albert Herman, Jr. *industrial and systems engineer, educator*
Kirk, Donald Evan *electrical engineering educator, dean*
Levy, Salomon *mechanical engineer*
Morimoto, Carl Noboru *computer system engineer, crystallographer*
Shaw, Charles Alden *engineering executive*
Tran, Jack Nhuan Ngoc *gas and oil reservoir engineer*
Valentine, Ralph Schuyler *chemical engineer, research director*
Wu, Dongping (Don Wu) *optical and electrical engineer*
Zhang, Jianping *electrical engineer*

San Juan Capistrano
Korb, Robert William *former materials and processes engineer*

San Luis Obispo
Anderson, Warren Ronald *electrical engineering educator*

San Luis Rey
Melbourne, Robert Ernest *civil engineer*

San Marcos
Jeffredo, John Victor *aerospace engineer, manufacturing company executive, inventor*
Purdy, Alan Harris *biomedical engineer*

San Pedro
Ellis, George Edwin, Jr. *chemical engineer*
McCarty, Frederick Briggs *electrical engineer*

San Rafael
Wright, Frederick Herman Greene, II *computer systems engineer*

Santa Ana
Amoroso, Frank *retired communication system engineer, consultant*
Bauer, Bruce F. *aerospace engineer*
Bentley, William Arthur *electro-optical consultant, engineer*
†Cagle, Thomas M. *electronics engineer*
Kelly, James Patrick, Jr. *retired engineering and construction executive*
Waaland, Irving Theodore *retired aerospace design executive*

Santa Barbara
Chmelka, Bradley Floyd *chemical engineering educator*
Coldren, Larry Allen *engineering educator, consultant*
Crispin, James Hewes *engineering and construction company executive*
Fredrickson, Glenn Harold *chemical engineering and materials educator*
Hedgepeth, John M(ills) *aerospace engineer, mathematician, engineering executive*
Iselin, Donald Grote *civil engineering and management consultant*
Israelachvili, Jacob Nissim *chemical engineer*
Kokotovic, Petar V. *electrical and computer engineer, educator*
Kramer, Edward John *materials science and engineering educator*
Kroemer, Herbert *electrical engineering educator*
Lawrance, Charles Holway *civil and sanitary engineer*
Meriam, James Lathrop *mechanical engineering educator*
Mitra, Sanjit Kumar *electrical and computer engineering educator*
Russell, Charles Roberts *chemical engineer*
Swalley, Robert Farrell *structural engineer, consultant*
Tirrell, Matthew *chemical engineering, materials science educator*
Wade, Glen *electrical engineer, educator*
Wooldridge, Dean Everett *engineering executive, scientist*

Santa Clara
Aguinsky, Richard Daniel *software and electronics engineer*
Carlsen, John Richard *engineer*
Chan, Shu-Park *electrical engineering educator*
Falgiano, Victor Joseph *electrical engineer, consultant*
Gupta, Rajesh *industrial engineer, quality engineer*
Hoagland, Albert Smiley *electrical engineer*
Jung, Henry Hung *mechanical engineer*
Kaneda, David Ken *electrical engineering company executive*
Kershaw, David Joseph *process engineer*
Olvera, Carlos Nelson *mechanical engineer, executive*
Parden, Robert James *engineering educator, management consultant*
Philipossian, Ara *engineer, semiconductor process technologist*
Vu, Quat Thuong *electrical engineer*
Weinberg, William Henry *chemical engineer, chemical physicist, educator*
Yan, Pei-Yang *electrical engineer*
Zhang, Xiao-Feng *power system engineer, researcher*

Santa Clarita
Abbott, John Rodger *electrical engineer*
Granlund, Thomas Arthur *engineering executive, consultant*

Santa Cruz
Langdon, Glen George, Jr. *electrical engineer*

Santa Monica
Gritton, Eugene Charles *nuclear engineer*
Kayton, Myron *engineering company executive*
Kummer, Wolfgang H. *electrical engineer*
McGuire, Michael John *environmental engineer*
Roney, Robert Kenneth *retired aerospace company executive*
Sherman, Zachary *civil and aerospace engineer, consultant*

Santa Rosa
Apfel, Joseph H. *optical engineer, research scientist*

Saratoga
Brown, Paul Fremont *aerospace engineer, educator*
Dix, Gary Errol *engineering executive*
Johnson, Noel Lars *biomedical engineer*
Rawson, Eric Gordon *optical engineer*
Reilly, Patrick John *engineering, construction company executive*
Syvertson, Clarence Alfred *engineering and research management consultant*

Seal Beach
Wiberg, Donald Martin *electrical engineering educator, consultant*

Sebastopol
Norman, Arnold McCallum, Jr. *engineer*

Simi Valley
Ahsan, Omar Faruk *computer engineer, manager, consultant*

Sonoma
Muchmore, Robert Boyer *engineering consultant executive*
Scott, John Walter *chemical engineer, research management executive*

South Pasadena
Kopp, Eugene Howard *electrical engineer*

Stanford
Aziz, Khalid *petroleum engineering educator*
Boudart, Michel *chemical engineer, chemist, educator*
Bracewell, Ronald Newbold *electrical engineering educator*
Bradshaw, Peter *engineering educator*
Bryson, Arthur Earl, Jr. *retired aerospace engineering educator*
Cannon, Robert Hamilton, Jr. *aerospace engineering educator*
Carlson, Robert Codner *industrial engineering educator*
Cox, Donald Clyde *electrical engineering educator*
Dutton, Robert W. *electrical engineer*
Eshleman, Von Russel *electrical engineering educator*
Eustis, Robert Henry *mechanical engineer*
Franklin, Gene Farthing *engineering educator, consultant*
Gere, James Monroe *civil engineering educator*
Gibbons, James Franklin *electrical engineering educator*
Goodman, Joseph Wilfred *electrical engineering educator*
Gray, Robert M(olten) *electrical engineering educator*
Harris, Stephen Ernest *electrical engineering and applied physics educator*
Herrmann, George *mechanical engineering educator*
Hesselink, Lambertus *electrical engineering and physics educator*
Hewett, Thomas Avery *petroleum engineer, educator*
Jameson, Antony *aerospace engineering educator*
Kailath, Thomas *electrical engineer, educator*
Kane, Thomas Reif *engineering educator*
Kino, Gordon Stanley *electrical engineering educator*
Kruger, Charles Herman, Jr. *mechanical engineering educator*
Levitt, Raymond Elliot *civil engineering educator*
Linvill, John Grimes *engineering educator*
Macovski, Albert *electrical engineering educator*
Madix, Robert James *chemical engineer, educator*
McCarty, Perry Lee *civil and environmental engineering educator*
McCluskey, Edward Joseph *engineering educator*
Miller, Daniel James *systems engineer*
Moin, Parviz *mechanical engineering educator*
Orr, Franklin Mattes, Jr. *petroleum engineering educator*
Ortolano, Leonard *civil engineering educator, water resources planner*
Parkinson, Bradford Wells *astronautical engineer, educator*
Pease, Roger Fabian Wedgwood *electrical engineering educator*
Reynolds, William Craig *mechanical engineer, educator*
Roberts, Paul V. *civil and environmental engineering educator*
Siegman, Anthony Edward *electrical engineer, educator*
Spreiter, John Robert *engineering researcher, educator, space physics scientist*
Springer, George Stephen *mechanical engineering educator*
Steele, Charles Richard *biomedical and mechanical engineering educator*
Street, Robert Lynnwood *civil, mechanical and environmental engineer*
Tsai, Stephen Wei-Lun *aeronautical educator*
Van Dyke, Milton Denman *aeronautical engineering educator*
Vincenti, Walter Guido *aeronautical engineer, emeritus educator*
White, Robert Lee *electrical engineer, educator*

Sunnyvale
Can, Sumer *research electrical engineer*
Devgan, Onkar Dave N. *technologist, consultant*
Kim, Wan Hee *electrical engineering educator, business executive*
†Lin, Chong Ming *engineer*
†Lopatin, Sergey Dmitrievich *microelectronic scientist, electrochemist*
Peline, Val P. *engineering executive*
Robbins, James Edward *electrical engineer*
Yin, Gerald Zheyao *technology and business executive*

Sylmar
Madni, Asad Mohamed *engineering executive*

Tarzana
Hansen, Robert Clinton *electrical engineering consultant*
Macmillan, Robert Smith *electronics engineer*

Temecula
Minogue, Robert Brophy *retired nuclear engineer*
Petersen, Vernon Leroy *communications and engineering corporations executive*

Thousand Oaks
Deisenroth, Clinton Wilbur *electrical engineer*
Krumm, Charles Ferdinand *electrical engineer*

Torrance
Kucij, Timothy Michael *engineer, musician, minister*
Mazzolini, James William *engineering administrator*
Mende, Howard Shigeharu *mechanical engineer*
Sorstokke, Susan Eileen *systems engineer*
Wylie, Richard Thornton *aerospace engineer*

Tracy
Nelson, Kenneth Arthur *electrical engineer*

Truckee
Forsen, Harold Kay *retired engineering executive*

Tustin
†De Veirman, Geert Adolf *engineer*

Vallejo
Hudak, Paul Alexander *retired engineer*

Van Nuys
Lagasse, Bruce Kenneth *structural engineer*

Ventura
Gaynor, Joseph *chemical engineer, technical-management consultant*

Victorville
Lagomarsini, George Caesar *engineering and mathematics educator, consultant*
Sedeño, Eugene Raymond *electronics engineer, consultant*

Walnut
Caudron, John Armand *accident reconstructionist, forensic investigator*

Walnut Creek
Burgarino, Anthony Emanuel *environmental engineer, consultant*
Crandall, Ira Carlton *consulting electrical engineer*
Lagarias, John Samuel *engineering executive*
Lee, William Chien-Yeh *electrical engineer*
†Yake, Daniel Glen *civil engineer*

Watsonville
Brown, Alan Charlton *retired aeronautical engineer*

Weed
Kyle, Chester Richard *mechanical engineer*

Westlake Village
Caligiuri, Joseph Frank *retired engineering executive*

Westminster
Armstrong, Gene Lee *systems engineering consultant, retired aerospace company executive*

Westport
Anderson, Terry Marlene *civil engineer*

Whittier
Lillevang, Omar Johansen *civil engineer*

Woodland Hills
Brozowski, Laura Adrienne *mechanical engineer*
Meeks, Crawford Russell, Jr. *mechanical engineer*
Yackle, Albert Reustle *aeronautical engineer*

Woodside
Frank, Victor Robert *electrical engineer*

Yorba Linda
Kennedy, Robert P. *civil engineer*
Porcello, Leonard Joseph *engineering research and development executive*

COLORADO

Arvada
Loomis, Christopher Knapp *metallurgical engineer*

Aurora
Osterberg, Jorj O. *retired civil engineer*
Schwartz, Lawrence *aeronautical engineer*

Boulder
Barnes, Frank Stephenson *electrical engineer, educator*
Breddan, Joe *systems engineering consultant*
Cathey, Wade Thomas *electrical engineering educator*
Corotis, Ross Barry *civil engineering educator, academic administrator*
†Evans, Hugh Williams *retired mining engineer, consultant*
Gupta, Kuldip Chand *electrical and computer engineering educator, researcher*
Hanna, William Johnson *electrical engineering educator*
Hauser, Ray Louis *research engineer, entrepreneur*
Hill, David Allan *electrical engineer*
Joy, Edward Bennett *electrical engineer, educator*
Kompala, Dhinakar Sathyanathan *chemical engineering educator, biochemical engineering researcher*
Lemp, John, Jr. *telecommunications engineer*
Peters, Max Stone *chemical engineer, educator*
Reitsema, Harold James *aerospace engineer*
Rodriguez, Juan Alfonso *technology corporation executive*
Sani, Robert LeRoy *chemical engineering educator*
Seebass, Alfred Richard, III *aerospace engineer, educator, university dean*
Shanahan, Eugene Miles *flow measurement instrumentation company executive*
Skaar, Daniel (Leif) *engineering executive*
Smith, Ernest Ketcham *electrical engineer*
Sodal, Ingvar Edmund *electrical engineer, scientist*
Strauch, Richard G. *electrical engineering educator*
Tary, John Joseph *engineer, consultant*
Timmerhaus, Klaus Dieter *chemical engineering educator*
Uberoi, Mahinder Singh *aerospace engineering educator*

Canon City
McBride, John Alexander *retired chemical engineer*

Colorado Springs
Adnet, Jacques Jim Pierre *astronautical and electrical engineer, consultant*
James, Wayne Edward *electrical engineer*
Watts, Oliver Edward *engineering consultancy company executive*
Witte, Robert Alan *electrical engineer*
Ziemer, Rodger Edmund *electrical engineering educator, consultant*

Craig
Violette, Glenn Phillip *transportation engineer*

Denver
Chamberlain, Adrian Ramond *transportation engineer*
Colvis, John Paris *aerospace engineer, mathematician, scientist*
Devitt, John Lawrence *consulting engineer*
East, Donald Robert *civil engineer*
Fay, Richard James *mechanical engineer, executive, educator*
Flanders, George James *mechanical engineer, engineering development manager*
Frevert, Donald Kent *hydraulic engineer*
†Hamilton, Barry Alan *aerospace engineer, software engrineer*
Long, Francis Mark *retired electrical engineer, educator*
McCandless, Bruce, II *aerospace engineer, former astronaut*
Mehring, Clinton Warren *engineering executive*
Perez, Jean-Yves *engineering company executive*
Poirot, James Wesley *engineering company executive*
Smith, William French *environmental safety adminstrator*
Stephens, Larry Dean *engineer*
Young, Lester Rex *engineering and construction company executive*
Ziernicki, Richard Mieczyslaw *engineering firm executive*

Durango
Langoni, Richard Allen *civil engineer*

Englewood
Aguirre, Vukoslav Eneas *environmental engineer*
Bingham, Paris Edward, Jr. *electrical engineer, computer consultant*

Estes Park
Blumrich, Josef Franz *aerospace engineer*
Ojalvo, Morris *civil engineer, educator*
Webb, Richard C. *engineering company executive*

Evergreen
Jesser, Roger Franklyn *former brewing company engineering executive, consultant*
Newkirk, John Burt *metallurgical engineer, administrator*

Fort Collins
Cermak, Jack Edward *engineer, educator*
Emslie, William Arthur *electrical engineer*
Grigg, Neil S. *civil engineering educator*
Heermann, Dale Frank *agricultural engineer*
Kaufman, Harold Richard *mechanical engineer and physics educator*
Mesloh, Warren Henry *civil and environmental engineer*
Morgan, David Allen *electronic engineer*
Richardson, Everett Vern *hydraulic engineer, educator, administrator, consultant*
Woolhiser, David Arthur *hydrologist*

Golden
Clausen, Bret Mark *industrial hygienist, safety professional*
Ervin, Patrick Franklin *nuclear engineer*
Gentry, Donald William *mine engineering executive*
Hager, John Patrick *metallurgy engineering educator*
Sloan, Earle Dendy, Jr. *chemical engineering educator*
Yarar, Baki *metallurgical engineering educator*

Grand Junction
Rybak, James Patrick *engineering educator*

Greenwood Village
Peterson, Ralph R. *engineering executive*

Lafayette
Middlebrooks, Eddie Joe *environmental engineer*

Lakewood
Danzberger, Alexander Harris *chemical engineer, consultant*
Elkins, Lincoln Feltch *petroleum engineering consultant*
Johnstone, James George *engineering educator*

Littleton
Brychel, Rudolph Myron *engineer, consultant*
Harney, Patricia Rae *nuclear analyst*
Kazemi, Hossein *petroleum engineer*
Kullas, Albert John *management and systems engineering consultant*
Ulrich, John Ross Gerald *aerospace engineer*
Whitehouse, Charles Barton *avionics educator*

Longmont
†Keene, Samuel James, Jr. *reliability engineer researcher, educator*
Muench, Lothar Wilhelm *electrical engineer, consultant*

Loveland
Taylor, Marian Alecia *manufacturing development engineer*

Olathe
Shriver, Allen Keith *electrical engineer, contractor, executive*

Pueblo
Giffin, Walter Charles *retired industrial engineer, educator, consultant*

Telluride
Kuehler, Jack Dwyer *engineering consultant*

Westminster
Dalesio, Wesley Charles *former aerospace educator*

Wheat Ridge
Barrett, Michael Henry *civil engineer*
Scherich, Erwin Thomas *civil engineer, consultant*

CONNECTICUT

Avon
McIlveen, Walter *mechanical engineer*

Bethel
DeLugo, Ernest Mario, Jr. *electrical engineer*

Bloomfield
De Maria, Anthony John *electrical engineer*
Kissa, Karl Martin *electrical engineer*
Leonberger, Frederick John *electrical engineer, photonics manager*
Nye, Edwin Packard *mechanical engineering educator*

Bolton
Banas, Conrad Martin *mechanical engineer, chief scientist*

Branford
Cohen, Myron Leslie *business executive, mechanical engineer*
Wegener, Peter Paul *engineering educator, author*

Bridgeport
Brunale, Vito John *aerospace engineer*
Gagnon, Robert James, Jr. *manufacturing engineer*
Hmurcik, Lawrence Vincent *electrical engineering educator*

Cheshire
†Cassagneres, Everett *engineer, consultant, pilot*
Eppler, Richard Andrew *chemical engineer, educator, consultant*

Cos Cob
Snowdon, Jane Louise *industrial engineer*
Zang, Joseph Albert, Jr. *chemical engineer, consultant*

Darien
Bays, John Theophanis *consulting engineering*
Forman, J(oseph) Charles *chemical engineer, consultant, writer*
Glenn, Roland Douglas *chemical engineer*

East Hartford
Cassidy, John Francis, Jr. *industrial technology executive*
Day, William Hudson *mechanical engineer, turbomachinery company executive*
Foyt, Arthur George *electronics research administrator*
LeJambre, Charles R. *aeronautical engineer*
Pfeifer, Howard Melford *mechanical engineer*
Rhie, Chae Myung *mechanical engineer, aeronautical engineer, aerospace engineer*
Zacharias, Robert M. *mechanical engineer, aeronautical engineer, aerospace engineer*

Ellington
Setzer, Herbert John *chemical engineer*

Farmington
†Minges, James Seth *consultaing engineer, planner*

Greenwich
Nadel, Norman Allen *civil engineer*

Groton
Benn, Raymond Christopher *materials engineer*
Sheets, Herman Ernest *marine engineer*

Hamden
Walker, Charles Allen *chemical engineer, educator*

Hartford
Bronzino, Joseph Daniel *electrical engineer*
Cornell, Robert Witherspoon *engineering consultant*
Gieras, Jacek Franciszek *electrical engineering educator, scientist*
Link, Henry Joseph *environmental engineer*

Manchester
Brazeal, Earl Henry, Jr. *electrical engineer*

Mansfield Center
Aldrich, Robert Adams *agricultural engineer*

Mystic
Thompson, Robert Allan *aerospace engineer*

New Britain
Czajkowski, Eva Anna *aerospace engineer, educator*
Sarisley, Edward F. *engineering technology educator, consultant*

New Canaan
Halverstadt, Robert Dale *mechanical engineer, metals manufacturing company*

New Fairfield
Daukshus, A. Joseph *systems engineer*

New Haven
Apfel, Robert Edmund *mechanical engineering educator, applied physicist, research scientist*
Cunningham, Walter Jack *electrical engineering educator*
Horváth, Csaba *chemical engineering educator, researcher*
Ricard, Thomas Armand *electrical engineer*

North Branford
Crossley, Francis Rendel Erskine *engineering educator*

North Stonington
Helm, John Leslie *mechanical engineer, company executive*

Old Lyme
Doersam, Charles Henry, Jr. *engineer*

Orange
Lobay, Ivan *mechanical engineering educator*

Ridgefield
McConnell, John Edward *electrical engineer, company executive*
Tomanic, Joseph P(aul) *retired research scientist*

Rocky Hill
Chuang, Frank Shiunn-Jea *engineering executive, consultant*
McCullough, Jefferson Walker *industrial engineering consultant*

South Windsor
Hobbs, David Ellis *mechanical engineer*

Southbury
Rubin, Jacob Carl *mechanical research engineer*

Stamford
Sahota, Gurcharn Singh *mechanical engineer*
Wheeler, Wesley Dreer *marine engineer, naval architect, consultant*

Storrs Mansfield
DiBenedetto, Anthony Thomas *engineering educator*
Long, Richard Paul *civil engineering educator, geotechnical engineering consultant*
Pitkin, Edward Thaddeus *aerospace engineer, consultant*

Stratford
Douglas, Karin Nadja *engineer*
Kassapoglou, Christos *aeronautical engineer*
†Sipprell, George Sidney *engineering professional*

Tariffville
Johnson, Loering M. *design engineer, historian, consultant*

Tolland
Wilde, Daniel Underwood *computer engineering educator*

Trumbull
Garelick, Melvin Stewart *engineering educator, aerospace engineer*
Gladki, Hanna Zofia *civil engineer, hydraulic mixer specialist*

Waterbury
Colbenson, Mary Elizabeth Dreisbach *materials engineer*

Waterford
Hinkle, Muriel Ruth Nelson *naval warfare analysis company executive*

Watertown
Wuthrich, Paul *electrical engineer, researcher, consultant*

Weston
Offenhartz, Edward *aerospace executive*

Wilton
Juran, Joseph Moses *engineer*
Martimucci, Richard Anthony *engineering company executive*

DELAWARE

Dover
Jones, Jay Paul *environmental engineer*

Newark
Allen, Herbert Ellis *environmental chemistry educator*
Bareford, William John *chemical engineer*
Barteau, Mark Alan *chemical engineering and chemistry educator*
Cheng, Alexander Hung-Darh *engineering educator, consultant*
Christy, Charles Wesley, III *industrial engineering educator*
Grayson, Richard Andrew *aerospace engineer*
Lomax, Kenneth Mitchell *agricultural engineering educator*
Nye, John Calvin *agricultural engineer, educator*
Sandler, Stanley Irving *chemical engineering educator*
Szeri, Andras Z. *engineering educator*

Smyrna
Hutchison, James Arthur, Jr. *architectural and engineering company executive*

Wilmington
Busche, Robert Marion *chemical engineer, consultant*
Igwe, Godwin Joseph *chemical engineer*
†Ji, Zhenghua *computer engineer*
Kutemeyer, Peter Martin *industrial engineering executive*
Liew, Fah Pow *mechanical engineer*
Murphy, Arthur Thomas *systems engineer*
Nwankwo, Emeka Obioma *chemical engineer, educator, entrepreneur*
Perez, Eduardo Hector *mechanical engineering consultant*
Salzstein, Richard Alan *biomedical engineer, bioprocessing engineer*
Thurman, Herman Robert, Jr. *structural engineer*
Trainham, James A., III *chemical engineer*

DISTRICT OF COLUMBIA

Washington
Arkilic, Galip Mehmet *mechanical engineer, educator*
Bainum, Peter Montgomery *aerospace engineer, consultant*
†Baronas, Jean Marie *computer systems engineer, educator*
Blanchard, Bruce *environmental engineer, government official*
Brahms, Thomas Walter *engineering institute executive*
Buckelew, Robin Browne *aerospace engineer*
Burton, William Joseph *engineering executive*
Canter, Howard Raphael *nuclear engineer*
Carioti, Bruno M. *civil engineer*
Chiang, George Djia-Chee *engineer, educator*
Deason, Jonathan Pierce *environmental engineer, federal agency administrator*
DeLuca, Mary *telecommunications engineer*
Diaz, Nils Juan *nuclear engineer, federal commissioner, regulator*
Diehl, William Henry S. *civil engineer*
Dinneen, Gerald Paul *electrical engineer, former government official*
Divone, Louis Vincent *aerospace engineer, educator, author, government official*
Eisner, Howard *engineering educator, engineering executive*
Freund, Deborah Miriam *transportation engineer*
Friedman, Arthur Daniel *electrical engineering and computer science educator, investment management company executive*
Fuhrman, Ralph Edward *civil and environmental engineer*
Giallorenzi, Thomas Gaetano *optical engineer*
Hershey, Robert Lewis *mechanical engineer, management consultant*
Hodder, James Edward *industrial engineer*
Jones, Howard St. Claire, Jr. *electronics engineering executive*
Kahn, Walter Kurt *engineering and applied science educator*
Kappaz, Michael H. *engineering company executive*
Khozeimeh, Issa *electrical engineer*
Kim, John Chan Kyu *electrical engineer*
Klein, Perry Ian *electronics engineer*
Lebow, Irwin Leon *communications engineering consultant*
Lee, Charlyn Yvonne *chemical engineer*
MacDonald, Bruce Walter *aerospace engineer, government official*
Menendez, Adolfo *engineering company executive*
Monroe, Robert Rawson *engineering construction executive*
Page, Robert Wesley *engineering and construction company executive, federal official*
Pickholtz, Raymond Lee *electrical engineering educator, consultant*
Quinn, Pat Maloy *engineering company executive*
Reis, Victor H. *mechanical engineer, government official*
Replogle, Michael A. *civil engineer, urban planner*
Rust, William David, Jr. *retired structural engineer*
Salmon, William Cooper *mechanical engineer, engineering academy executive*
Sanchez, Rafael Antonio *chemical engineer*
Shalowitz, Erwin Emmanuel *civil engineer*
Shon, Frederick John *nuclear engineer*
Skinner, Robert Earle, Jr. *civil engineer, engineering executive*
Skolnik, Merrill I. *electrical engineer*
Stanwick, Tad *retired systems engineer*
Stuart, Charles Edward *electrical engineer, oceanographer*
Thigpen, Lewis *engineering educator*
Townsend, Marjorie Rhodes *aerospace engineer, business executive*
Van Dusen, Carl James *broadcast engineer*
Wang, John Cheng Hwai *communications engineer*
Warnick, Walter Lee *mechanical engineer*
White, Robert Roy *retired chemical engineer*
White, Roy Martin *engineering manager*
Whitworth, Horace Algernon *mechanical engineer*
Wilhelm, Peter G. *aeronautical and astronautical engineer*
Wu, Carl Cherng-Miin *ceramic engineer*

FLORIDA

Amelia Island
Jesser, Benn Wainwright *chemical engineering and construction company executive*

Boca Raton
Han, Chingping Jim *industrial engineer, educator*
Johnson, James Robert *ceramic engineer, educator*
Lin, Y. K. *engineer, educator*
Reynolds, George Anthony, Jr. *engineering executive*
Su, Tsung-Chow Joe *engineering educator*

Bonita Springs
Katzen, Raphael *consulting chemical engineer*

Boynton Beach
Vesely, Alexander *civil engineer*

Bradenton
Baker, Walter Louis *retired engineering company executive*
Friedrich, Robert Edmund *retired electrical engineer, corporate consultant*
Patterson, Homer Stephen *electronics maintenance supervisor*

Brooksville
Miller, Kenneth Edward *mechanical engineer, consultant*

Cape Coral
Dietrich, Jonathan Austin *chemical process engineer*
Longo, Paul Albert *retired industrial engineer, consultant*
Smith, Bruce William *safety engineer*

Clearwater
Cowles, Sandra Lynne *metallurgical engineer*
Tanner, Craig Richard *fire and explosion engineer*

Cocoa
Luecke, Conrad John *aerospace educator*

Coral Gables
Kline, Jacob *biomedical engineering educator*
Saffir, Herbert Seymour *structural engineer, consultant*
Young, Tzay Y. *electrical and computer engineering educator*

Coral Springs
Dzieduszko, Janusz Wladyslaw *electrical engineer*
Valasquez, Joseph Louis *industrial engineer*

Dania
Weissman-Berman, Deborah *sandwich composites engineer, researcher*

Daytona Beach
Jacobson, Ira David *aerospace engineer, educator, researcher*
Millar, Gordon Halstead *mechanical engineer, agricultural machinery manufacturing executive*
†Sloane, James Robert *chemical engineer*

Delray Beach
Smith, Charles Oliver *engineer*

Deltona
Tiblier, Fernand Joseph, Jr. *municipal engineering administrator*

Dundee
Johnson, Gordon Selby *consulting electrical engineer*

Eglin AFB
Franzen, Larry William *aerospace electronics engineer*
Snyder, Donald Robert, III *electronic imaging engineer*

Fernandina Beach
Lilly, Wesley Cooper *marine engineer, ship surveyor*

Fort Lauderdale
Cassidy, Terrence Patrick, Jr. *engineering consultant*
Fishe, Gerald Raymond Aylmer *engineering executive*
Schear, Betty Z. *engineering executive, consultant*

Fort Myers
Disney, Ralph L(ynde) *retired industrial engineering educator*
Mergler, Harry Winston *engineering educator*
Moeschl, Stanley Francis *electrical engineer, management consultant*
Scott, Kenneth Elsner *mechanical engineering educator*
Sechrist, Chalmers Franklin, Jr. *electrical engineering educator*

Fort Walton Beach
Bergschneider, John *city engineer*

Gainesville
Abbaschian, Reza *materials science and engineering educator*
Anderson, Timothy J. *chemical engineering educator*
Balabanian, Norman *electrical engineering educator*
Capehart, Barney Lee *industrial and systems engineer*
Cristescu, Nicolaie Dan *engineering educator*
Delfino, Joseph John *environmental engineering sciences educator*
Drucker, Daniel Charles *engineer, educator*
†Farber, Erich A. *mechanical engineer*
Fossum, Jerry George *electrical engineering educator*
Isaacs, Gerald William *retired agricultural engineering educator, consultant*
Kurzweg, Ulrich Hermann *engineering science educator*
Law, Mark Edward *electrical engineer, educator*
Lindholm, Fredrik Arthur *electrical engineering educator*
Malvern, Lawrence Earl *engineering educator, researcher*
Neugroschel, Arnost *electrical engineering educator*
Ohanian, Mihran Jacob *nuclear engineering educator, research dean*
Pearce, Joseph Huske *industrial engineer*
Peebles, Peyton Zimmerman, Jr. *electrical engineer, educator*
Phillips, Winfred Marshall *dean, mechanical engineer, academic administrator*
Polasek, Edward John *electrical engineer, consultant*
Sah, Chih-Tang *electrical and computer engineering educator*
Schmertmann, John Henry *civil engineer, educator, consultant*
Sheng, Yea-Yi Peter *oceanographic engineer, educator, researcher*
Sherif, S. A. *mechanical engineering educator*

Harvego, Edwin Allan *mechanical engineer*
Jacobsen, Richard T *mechanical engineering educator*
Miller, Gregory Kent *structural engineer*
Paik, Seungho *mechanical engineer*
Riemke, Richard Allan *mechanical engineer*

Inkom
Ambrose, Tommy W. *chemical engineer, executive*

Moscow
DeShazer, James Arthur *biological engineer, educator, administrator*
Jackson, Melbourne Leslie *chemical engineering educator and administrator, consultant*
Johnson, Brian Keith *electrical engineering educator*
Woodall, David Monroe *research engineer, dean*

Nampa
Franklin, Leonard G. *engineer*

ILLINOIS

Argonne
Chang, Yoon Il *nuclear engineer*
Haupt, H. James *mechanical design engineer*
Kumar, Romesh *chemical engineer*
Miller, Shelby Alexander *chemical engineer, educator*
Panchal, Chandrakant B. *chemical engineer, researcher*
Till, Charles Edgar *nuclear engineer*

Ashland
Benz, Donald Ray *nuclear safety engineer, researcher*

Bloomingdale
Wolfe, Carl Dean *electrical engineer*

Bolingbrook
Relwani, Nirmal Murlidhar (Nick Relwani) *mechanical engineer*

Broadview
Cousins, William Thomas *industrial engineer, educator*

Carol Stream
Darling, Lawrence Dean *engineering computing executive*

Carthage
Erbes, John Robert *engineering executive*

Champaign
Korst, Helmut Hans *mechanical engineer, educator*

Chicago
Acs, Joseph Steven *transportation engineering consultant*
Agarwal, Gyan Chand *engineering educator*
Aggarwal, Suresh Kumar *mechanical and aerospace engineering educator*
Babcock, Lyndon Ross, Jr. *environmental engineer, educator*
Banerjee, Prashant *industrial engineering educator*
Breyer, Norman Nathan *metallurgical engineering educator, consultant*
Brouse, John Ammon, Jr. *fiber optics engineer*
Cha, Soyoung Stephen *mechanical engineer, educator*
Chen, Wai-Kai *electrical engineering and computer science educator, consultant*
Chung, Paul Myungha *mechanical engineer, educator*
Cooper, Stuart Leonard *chemical engineering educator, researcher, consultant*
Datta, Rathin *chemical engineer*
Davis, DeForest P. *architectural engineer*
Dix, Rollin C(umming) *mechanical engineering educator, consultant*
Epstein, Raymond *engineering and architectural executive*
Fabisch, Gale Warren *civil engineer*
Fahnestock, Jean Howe *retired civil engineer*
Gerstner, Robert William *structural engineering educator, consultant*
Graupe, Daniel *electrical and computer engineering educator, systems and biomedical engineer*
Gupta, Krishna Chandra *mechanical engineering educator*
Guralnick, Sidney Aaron *civil engineering educator*
Hanson, Martin Philip *mechanical engineer, farmer*
Hartnett, James Patrick *engineering educator*
Jaramillo, Carlos Alberto *civil engineer*
†Jones, R(oger) Kent *civil engineer, educator*
Kennedy, Lawrence Allan *mechanical engineering educator*
Lin, James Chih-I *biomedical and electrical engineer, educator*
Linden, Henry Robert *chemical engineering research executive*
Martin, Wesley George *electrical engineer*
Minkowycz, W. J. *mechanical engineering educator*
Minneste, Viktor, Jr. *retired electrical company executive*
Munoz, Mario Alejandro *civil engineer, retired consultant*
Murata, Tadao *engineering and computer science educator*
Oskouie, Ali Kiani *chemical and environmental engineer*
Pandit, Bansi *nuclear engineer*
Riches, Kenneth William *nuclear regulatory engineer*
Rikoski, Richard Anthony *engineering executive, electrical engineer*
Rozenblat, Anatoly Isaacovich *scientist, inventor*
Russo, Gilberto *engineering educator*
Shieh, Ching-Long *structural engineering executive*
Sresty, Guggilam Chalamaiah *environmental engineer*
Stecich, John Patrick *structural engineer*
Wadden, Richard Albert *environmental engineer, educator, consultant, research director*

Clarendon Hills
Moritz, Donald Brooks *mechanical engineer, consultant*

Crystal Lake
Dabkowski, John *electrical engineering executive*

Decatur
Koucky, John Richard *metallurgical engineer, manufacturing executive*

Dekalb
Lorence, William George *county engineer, consultant*

Des Plaines
Winfield, Michael D. *engineering company executive*

Downers Grove
Hsiao, Ming-Yuan *nuclear engineer, researcher*

Dunlap
Reinsma, Harold Lawrence *design consultant, engineer*

East Moline
Taylor, Byron Keith *industrial engineer*

Elgin
Koepke, Donald Herbert *retired mechanical engineer and real estate professional*

Elmhurst
Burton, Darrell Irvin *engineering executive*

Evanston
Achenbach, Jan Drewes *engineering educator, scientist*
Bankoff, Seymour George *chemical engineer, educator*
Bazant, Zdenek Pavel *structural engineering educator, scientist, consultant*
Belytschko, Ted Bohdan *civil and mechanical engineering educator*
Bobco, William David, Jr. *consulting engineering company executive*
Brazelton, William Thomas *chemical engineering educator*
Butt, John Baecher *chemical engineering educator*
Carr, Stephen Howard *materials engineer, educator*
Cheng, Herbert Su-Yuen *mechanical engineering educator*
Daskin, Mark Stephen *civil engineering educator*
Fessler, Raymond R. *metallurgical engineering consultant*
Fine, Morris Eugene *materials engineer, educator*
Fourer, Robert Harold *industrial engineering educator, consultant*
Frey, Donald Nelson *industrial engineer, educator, manufacturing company executive*
Goldstick, Thomas Karl *biomedical engineering educator*
Haddad, Abraham Herzl *electrical engineering educator, researcher*
Keer, Leon Morris *engineering educator*
Kliphardt, Raymond A. *engineering educator*
Krizek, Raymond John *civil engineering educator, consultant*
Kung, Harold Hing-Chuen *engineering educator*
Lee, Der-Tsai *electrical engineering and computer science educator, researcher, consultant*
Liu, Shu Qian *biomedical engineer, researcher, educator*
Liu, Wing Kam *mechanical and civil engineering educator*
Marhic, Michel Edmond *engineering educator, entrepreneur, consultant*
Murphy, Gordon John *electrical engineer*
Ottino, Julio Mario *chemical engineering educator, scientist*
Rubenstein, Albert Harold *industrial engineering and management sciences educator*
Shah, Surendra Poonamchand *engineering educator, researcher*
Smith, Spencer Bailey *engineering and business educator*
Sobel, Alan *electrical engineer, physicist*
Taflove, Allen *electrical engineer, educator, researcher, consultant*
Van Ness, James Edward *electrical engineering educator*

Fairfield
Arakkal, Antony Lona *engineering executive, researcher*

Gilman
Ireland, Herbert Orin *engineering educator*

Glenview
Hutter, Gary Michael *environmental engineer*
Logani, Kulbhushan Lal *civil and structural engineer*
Panarese, William C. *civil engineer*
Parker, James John *engineering and marketing manager*
Russell, Henry George *structural engineer*
Van Zelst, Theodore William *civil engineer, natural resource exploration company executive*

Grayslake
Schmoll, George Frederick, III *research engineer*

Gurnee
Sommerlad, Robert Edward *environmental research engineer*
Theis, Peter Frank *engineering executive, inventor*

Hinsdale
Copley, Stephen Michael *materials science and technology engineer, consultant*

Joliet
Ellebracht, Harold Mark *marine engineer*

Kankakee
Dodson, Carl Edward *nuclear engineer, real estate agent, executive, minister, assistant superintendent*

La Grange
Mehlenbacher, Dohn Harlow *civil engineer*

Lake Bluff
Fortuna, William Frank *architectural engineer, architect*

Lake Forest
Bell, Charles Eugene, Jr. *industrial engineer*
Lambert, John Boyd *chemical engineer, consultant*
Smith, Sidney Talbert *biomedical engineer*

Lemont
Chen, Shoei-Sheng *mechanical engineer*

Lisle
McCaul, Joseph Patrick *chemical engineer*
Vora, Manu Kishandas *chemical engineer, quality consultant*

Lombard
Swanson, Bernet Steven *consulting engineer, former educator*

Marshall
Cork, Donald Burl *electrical engineer*

Moline
Harrington, Roy Edwards *agricultural engineer, author*
Skromme, Arnold Burton *educational writer, engineering consultant*
Smith, David William

Morton Grove
Blanchard, James Arthur *engineer, computer systems specialist, financial planner*

Mount Prospect
Avila, Arthur Julian *metallurgical engineer*
Scott, Norman Laurence *engineering consultant*

Naperville
Coplien, James O. *engineering researcher*
Craigo, Gordon Earl *quality systems consultant*
Crawford, Raymond Maxwell, Jr. *nuclear engineer*
Garg, Vijay Kumar *telecommunications engineer*
Kimmel, Frank Edward *engineer*
Koeppe, Eugene Charles, Jr. *electrical engineer*
Krishnamachari, Sadagopa Iyengar *mechanical engineer, consultant*
Peters, Boyd Leon *agricultural engineer*

Niles
Obermann, George *engineering executive*

North Riverside
Mockus, Joseph Frank *electrical engineer*

Northbrook
Adler, Robert *electronics engineer*
Polsky, Michael Peter *mechanical engineer*

Oak Brook
Degerstrom, James Marvin *retired engineering executive*
Xu, Tao *mechanical engineer*
Young, Steven Scott *managing director*

Oak Forest
Kogut, Kenneth Joseph *consulting engineer*

Oak Park
Clark, John Peter, III *engineering consultant*
Morkovin, Mark Vladimir *aerospace and mechanical engineer*

Olympia Fields
Menees, John Robert *mechanical engineer*

Orland Park
Knop, Charles Milton *electrical engineer*

Palatine
Nixon, Wayne Robert *engineering manager*

Park Forest
Williams, Jack Raymond *civil engineer*

Park Ridge
Bridges, Jack Edgar *electronics engineer*
McIntosh, Don Leslie *electrical engineer*

Peoria
Kroll, Dennis Edwards *industrial engineering educator*
Polanin, W. Richard *engineering educator*

Plainfield
Chakrabarti, Subrata Kumar *marine research engineer*

Prophetstown
Sanders, Gary Glenn *electronics engineer, consultant*

Rantoul
Valencia, Rogelio Pasco *electronics engineer*

Rock Island
Osborn, David Lee *engineer*

Rockford
Casagranda, Robert Charles *industrial engineer*
Eliason, Jon Tate *electrical engineer*
Hornby, Robert Ray *mechanical engineer*
Shepler, John Edward *engineering executive*

Romeoville
Cizek, David John *sales engineer, small business owner*

Roscoe
Jacobs, Richard Dearborn *consulting engineering company executive*

Sauget
Baltz, Richard Arthur *chemical engineer*

Schaumburg
Dahn, Carl James *aerospace engineer*
Zhao, Jinsong Jason *engineer, researcher, administrator*

Skokie
Corley, William Gene *engineering research executive*
Siegal, Rita Goran *engineering company executive*

Springfield
Ballenger, Hurley René *electrical engineer*
Chen, Eden Hsien-chang *engineering consultant*
Fleck, Gabriel Alton *electrical engineer*
Hahin, Christopher *metallurgical engineer, corrosion engineer*
Lyons, J. Rolland *civil engineer*
Porter, William L. *electrical engineer*
Reed, John Charles *chemical engineer*

Urbana
Addy, Alva Leroy *mechanical engineer*
†Ahmad, Irfan Saleem *agricultural engineer, researcher*
Axford, Roy Arthur *nuclear engineering educator*
Basar, Tamer *electrical engineering educator*
Bergeron, Clifton George *ceramic engineer, educator*
Blahut, Richard Edward *electrical and computer engineering educator*
Chao, Bei Tse *mechanical engineering educator*
Chato, John Clark *mechanical and bioengineering educator*
Clausing, Arthur Marvin *mechanical engineering educator*
Coleman, Paul Dare *electrical engineering educator*
Conry, Thomas Francis *mechanical engineering educator, consultant*
Cook, Harry Edgar *engineering educator*
Cusano, Cristino *mechanical engineer, educator*
Dobrovolny, Jerry Stanley *engineering educator*
Eden, James Gary *electrical engineering and physics educator, researcher*
Gaddy, Oscar Lee *electrical engineering educator*
Goering, Carroll E. *agricultural engineering educator*
Hall, William Joel *civil engineer, educator*
Hannon, Bruce Michael *engineer, educator*
Hanratty, Thomas Joseph *chemical engineer, educator*
Herrin, Moreland *civil engineering educator, consultant*
Hess, Karl *electrical and computer engineering educator*
Holonyak, Nick, Jr. *electrical engineering educator*
Huang, Thomas Shi-Tao *electrical engineering educator, researcher*
Jones, Benjamin Angus, Jr. *retired agricultural engineering educator, administrator*
Kang, Sung-Mo (Steve Kang) *electrical engineering educator*
Kumar, Panganamala Ramana *electrical and computer engineering educator*
May, Walter Grant *chemical engineer*
Mayes, Paul Eugene *engineering educator, technical consultant*
Miley, George Hunter *nuclear engineering educator*
Miller, Robert Earl *engineer, educator*
Pai, Anantha Mangalore *electrical engineering educator, consultant*
Rao, Nannapaneni Narayana *electrical engineer*
Siess, Chester Paul *civil engineering educator*
Stallmeyer, James Edward *engineer, educator*
Swenson, George Warner, Jr. *electronics engineer, radio astronomer, educator*
Trick, Timothy Noel *electrical and computer engineering educator, researcher*
Trigger, Kenneth James *mechanical and industrial engineering educator*
Wang, Shicai *research engineer*
Wert, Charles Allen *metallurgical and mining engineering educator*
Westwater, James William *chemical engineering educator*
Yen, Ben Chie *water resources engineering educator*
Yoerger, Roger Raymond *agricultural engineer, educator*

Vernon Hills
Gnaedinger, John Phillip *structural engineer, consultant*

Warrenville
Symuleski, Richard Aloysius *chemical engineer*

Washington
Hallinan, John Cornelius *mechanical engineering consultant*

West Chicago
Kieft, Gerald Nelson *mechanical engineer*

Westchester
Tutins, Antons *electrical and audio engineer*

Wheeling
Ebeling, Arthur William *mechanical engineer*

Wilmette
Barnett, Ralph Lipsey *engineering educator*
McCabe, Thomas James *civil engineer*
Muhlenbruch, Carl W. *civil engineer*

Winnetka
Fraenkel, Stephen Joseph *engineering and research executive*
Nell, Janine Marie *metallurgical and materials engineer*

Wood River
Stevens, Robert Edward *engineering company executive*

INDIANA

Avon
Shartle, Stanley Musgrave *consulting engineer, land surveyor*

Bloomington
Dawson, James Richard *fire and safety engineer*
Harder, John E. *electrical engineer*

Carmel
Kalwara, Joseph John *engineer*
Ong, James Shaujen *mechanical engineer*

Chesterfield
Fry, Meredith Warren *civil engineer, consultant*

Columbus
Fadarishan, Stephen Robert *systems engineer*
Flynn, Patrick Francis *engineering executive*

Connersville
Stanton, William Taylor *manufacturing engineer*

Corydon
Speth, Camille *engineer*

Crane
Waggoner, Susan Marie *electronics engineer*

Evansville
Bennett, Paul Edmond *engineering educator*
Blandford, Dick *electrical engineering and communications educator*
Gerhart, Philip Mark *engineering educator*

Fort Wayne
Joffe, Benjamin *mechanical engineer*
Lyons, Jerry Lee *mechanical engineer*

Goshen
Heap, James Clarence *retired mechanical engineer*

Hammond
Pierson, Edward Samuel *engineering educator, consultant*

Indianapolis
Battle, Joe David *engineer*
Brannon-Peppas, Lisa *chemical engineer, researcher*
Collins, James Duffield *marine engineer, editor*
Dillon, Howard Burton *civil engineer*
Evans, Richard James *mechanical engineer*
Gable, Robert William, Jr. *aerospace engineer*
Mundell, John Anthony *environmental engineer, consultant*
Vlach, Jeffrey Allen *environmental specialist*

Kokomo
Miller, Robert Frank *retired electronics engineer, educator*
Nierste, Joseph Paul *software engineer*

Lafayette
Bement, Arden Lee, Jr. *engineering educator*
Etzel, James Edward *environmental engineering educator*
Fox, Robert William *mechanical engineering educator*
Geddes, Leslie Alexander *bioengineer, physiologist, educator*
Gustafson, Winthrop Adolph *aeronautical and astronautical engineering educator*
Lindenlaub, J. C. *electrical engineer, educator*
Ott, Karl Otto *nuclear engineering educator, consultant*

Middlebury
Siegel, Harvey Robert *engineering and product development executive*

Muncie
Bennon, Saul *electrical engineer, transformer consultant*
Seymour, Richard Deming *technology educator*

Newburgh
Feldbusch, Michael F. *engineering company executive*

Noblesville
Monical, Robert Duane *consulting structural engineer*

Notre Dame
Gray, William Guerin *civil engineering educator*
Incropera, Frank Paul *mechanical engineering educator*
Jerger, Edward William *mechanical engineer, university dean*
Kohn, James Paul *engineering educator*
Michel, Anthony Nikolaus *electrical engineering educator, researcher*
Sain, Michael Kent *electrical engineering educator*
Schmitz, Roger Anthony *chemical engineering educator, academic administrator*
Szewczyk, Albin Anthony *engineering educator*
Varma, Arvind *chemical engineering educator, researcher*

Peru
McMinn, William Lowell, Jr. *engineer*

Purdue University
Bernhard, Robert James *mechanical engineer, educator*
Liley, Peter Edward *mechanical engineering educator*

South Bend
Jorgensen, Robert William *product engineer*
Littrell, Carl Paul *civil engineer*

Terre Haute
Malooley, David Joseph *electronics and computer technology educator*

West Lafayette
Albright, Lyle Frederick *chemical engineering educator*
Altschaeffl, Adolph George *civil engineering educator*
Andres, Ronald Paul *chemical engineer, educator*
Barany, James Walter *industrial engineering educator*
Bogdanoff, John Lee *aeronautical engineering educator*
Chao, Kwang-Chu *chemical engineer, educator*
Chen, Wai-Fah *civil engineering educator*
Cohen, Raymond *mechanical engineer, educator*
Cooper, James Albert, Jr. *electrical engineering educator*
Delleur, Jacques William *civil engineering educator*
Drnevich, Vincent Paul *civil engineering educator*
Eckert, Roger E(arl) *chemical engineering educator*
Friedlaender, Fritz Josef *electrical engineering educator*
Greenkorn, Robert Albert *chemical engineering educator*
Hinkle, Charles Nelson *retired agricultural engineering educator*
Koivo, Antti Jaakko *electrical engineering educator, researcher*
Landgrebe, David Allen *electrical engineer*
Leimkuhler, Ferdinand Francis *industrial engineering educator*
Lin, Pen-Min *electrical engineer, educator*
†Lyrintis, Anastasios Sotirios *engineering educator*
Lyrintzis, Anastasios Sotirios *aerospace engineering professor*
Marshall, Francis Joseph *aerospace engineer*
Mc Gillem, Clare Duane *electrical engineering educator*
Mc Laughlin, John Francis *civil engineer, educator*
Michael, Harold Louis *civil engineering educator*
Neudeck, Gerold Walter *electrical engineering educator*
Ong, Chee-Mun *engineering educator*
Peppas, Nikolaos Athanassiou *chemical engineering educator, consultant*
Ramadhyani, Satish *mechanical engineering educator*
Richey, Clarence Bentley *agricultural engineering educator*
Salvendy, Gavriel *industrial engineer*
Schwartz, Richard John *electrical engineering educator, researcher*
Sozen, Mete Avni *civil engineering educator*
Stevenson, Warren Howard *mechanical engineering educator*
Taber, Margaret Ruth *electrical engineering technology educator, electrical engineer*
Tomovic, Mileta Milos *mechanical engineer, educator*
Viskanta, Raymond *mechanical engineering educator*
Wankat, Phillip Charles *chemical engineering educator*
Williams, Theodore Joseph *engineering educator*
Wright, Jeff Regan *civil engineering educator*

IOWA

Ames
Anderson, Robert Morris, Jr. *electrical engineer*
Basart, John Philip *electrical engineering and radio astronomy researcher, educator*
Baumann, Edward Robert *environmental engineering educator*
Black, James Robert *industrial engineer*
Brown, Robert Grover *engineering educator*
Buchele, Wesley Fisher *retired agricultural engineering educator*
Bullen, Daniel Bernard *mechanical engineering educator*
Cleasby, John LeRoy *civil engineer, educator*
Colvin, Thomas Stuart *agricultural engineer, farmer*
Hobson, Keith Lee *civil engineer, consultant*
Inger, George Roe *aerospace engineering educator*
Johnson, Howard Paul *agricultural engineering educator*
Jones, Edwin Channing, Jr. *electrical engineering educator*
Larsen, William Lawrence *materials science and engineering educator*
Mischke, Charles Russell *mechanical engineering educator*
Okiishi, Theodore Hisao *mechanical engineering educator*
Riley, William Franklin *mechanical engineering educator*
Sanders, Wallace Wolfred, Jr. *civil engineer*
Skarshaug, David Paul *industrial engineer*
Tenek, Lazarus *mechanical engineer*
Venkata, Subrahmanyam Saraswati *electrical engineering educator, electric energy and power researcher*
Wilder, David Randolph *materials engineer, consultant*
Young, Donald Fredrick *engineering educator*

Belmond
Johnson, Roger Christie *environmental engineer*

Bettendorf
Heyderman, Arthur Jerome *engineer, civilian military employee*

Cedar Falls
Hall, Teresa Joanne Keys *manufacturing engineer, educator*
Johnson, Curtis Scott *engineer*

Davenport
Bartlett, Peter Greenough *engineering company executive*
Pedersen, Karen Sue *electrical engineer*

Decorah
Erdman, Lowell Paul *civil engineer, land surveyor*

Des Moines
Israni, Kim *civil engineer*

Iowa City
Arora, Jasbir Singh *engineering educator*
Eyman, Earl Duane *electrical science educator, consultant*
Haug, Edward Joseph, Jr. *mechanical engineering educator, simulation research engineer*
Kusiak, Andrew *manufacturing engineer, educator*
Lonngren, Karl Erik *electrical and computer engineering educator*
Marshall, Jeffrey Scott *mechanical engineer, educator*
Patel, Virendra Chaturbhai *mechanical engineering educator*
Rim, Kwan *biomedical engineering educator*

Madrid
Handy, Richard Lincoln *civil engineer, educator*

Muscatine
Stanley, Richard Holt *consulting engineer*
Thomopulos, Gregs G. *consulting engineering company executive*

Pocahontas
Camp, Steven John *civil engineer*

KANSAS

Andover
Whiteside, Glenn G. *aircraft design engineer*

Caney
Barbi, Josef Walter *engineering, manufacturing and export companies executive*

Emporia
Woods, Warren Chip *civil engineer*

Fort Leavenworth
Brown, Richard Francis *command and control systems engineer, military off*

Hutchinson
Dukelow, Samuel Griffith *engineering consultant*
Jaisinghani, Manish Kumar *manufacturing engineer*
Munger, Harold Hawley, II *city engineer*

Lawrence
Benjamin, Bezaleel Solomon *architecture and architectural engineering educator*
Darwin, David *civil engineering educator, researcher, consultant*
Green, Don Wesley *chemical and petroleum engineering educator*
Lucas, William Max, Jr. *structural engineer, university dean*
McCabe, John Lee *engineer, educator*
McCabe, Steven Lee *structural engineer*
Moore, Richard Kerr *electrical engineering educator*
Muirhead, Vincent Uriel *aerospace engineer*
Roskam, Jan *aerospace engineer*
Rowland, James Richard *electrical engineering educator*
Vossoughi, Shapour *chemical and petroleum engineering educator*

Leavenworth
Camery, John William *computer engineer*
Hamilton, Mark Alan *electrical engineer*
Meister, Kimberly Lenore Baltzer *civil engineer, consultant*

Leawood
Karmeier, Delbert Fred *consulting engineer, realtor*

Manhattan
Johnson, William Howard *agricultural engineer, educator*
†King, Terry Scot *engineering educator*
Lee, E(ugene) Stanley *engineer, mathematician, educator*
Simons, Gale Gene *nuclear and electrical engineer, educator*

Mcpherson
Grauer, Douglas Dale *civil engineer*

Olathe
Bertrand, Robert Simeon *manufacturing engineer*

Overland Park
Callahan, Harry Leslie *civil engineer*
Dunn, Robert Sigler *engineering executive*
Smith, Sidney Ted *environmental engineer, consultant*

Salina
Crawford, Lewis Cleaver *engineering executive*
Robb, David Dow *electrical engineer, consultant*
Selm, Robert Prickett *engineer, consultant*

Shawnee Mission
Bartlett, Roger Danforth *engineering executive*

Topeka
Metzler, Dwight Fox *civil engineer, retired state official*

Wichita
Alvarez, Pablo *aeronautical and aerospace engineer*
Hansen, Ole Viggo *chemical engineer*
Holland, Phillip Kent *aerospace engineer*
Kice, John Edward *engineering executive*
Wentz, William Henry, Jr. *aerospace engineer, educator*
Wilhelm, William Jean *civil engineering educator*

KENTUCKY

Bellevue
†Lemlich, Robert *educator*

Bowling Green
Russell, Josette Renee *industrial engineer*

Catlettsburg
Fischer, Robert Lee *engineering executive, educator*

Elizabethtown
Guthrie, Michael Steele *magnetic circuit design engineer*

Lexington
Baker, Merl *engineering educator*
Caroland, William Bourne *structural engineer*
Cremers, Clifford John *mechanical engineering educator*
Drake, David Lee *electronics engineer*
Drake, Vaughn Paris, Jr. *electrical engineer, retired telephone company executive*
Foree, Edward Golden *environmental engineer, consultant*
Grimes, Craig Alan *electrical engineering educator*
Grimes, Dale Mills *physics and electrical engineering educator*
Hanson, Mark Tod *engineering mechanics educator*
Male, Alan Thomas *engineering educator, association executive*
Nasar, Syed Abu *electrical engineering educator*
Steele, Earl Larsen *electrical engineering educator*
Tauchert, Theodore Richmond *mechanical engineer, educator*

Louisville
Clark, John Hallett, III *consulting engineering executive*
Garcia, Rafael Jorge *retired chemical engineer*
Hanley, Thomas Richard *engineering educator*
Moll, Joseph Eugene *chemical engineer, chemical company executive*
†Moore, Charles Damon, Jr. *technology educator*
Reinbold, Darrel William *energy engineering specialist*
Siewert, Robin Noelle *chemical engineer*
Smith, Robert F., Jr. *civil engineer*
Tran, Long Trieu *industrial engineer*

Union
Hochstrasser, John Michael *environmental engineer, industrial hygienist*

Wickliffe
Gray, Carol Hickson *chemical engineer*

LOUISIANA

Baton Rouge
Anderson, George Hugo *chemical engineer*
Arman, Ara *civil engineering educator*
Chen, Peter Pin-Shan *electrical engineering and computer science educator, data processing executive*
Constant, William David *chemical engineer, educator*
Corripio, Armando Benito *chemical engineering educator*
Gammon, Malcolm Ernest, Sr. *surveying and engineering executive*
Khonsari, Michael M. *mechanical engineering educator*
Marshak, Alan Howard *electrical engineer, educator*
Pike, Ralph Webster *chemical engineer, educator, university administrator*
Reible, Danny David *environmental chemical engineer, educator*
Sajo, Erno *nuclear engineer, physicist, consultant, educator*
Stopher, Peter Robert *civil and transportation engineering educator, consultant*
Tipton, Kenneth Warren *agricultural administrator, researcher*
Triantaphyllou, Evangelos *industrial engineering educator*
Tumay, Mehmet Taner *geotechnical consultant, educator, academic administrator*
Valsaraj, Kalliat Thazhathuveetil *chemical engineering educator*

Bossier City
Guenther, Gordon P. *mechanical engineer*

Columbia
Davis, (Shelton) Delane *petroleum engineer*

Dubach
Straughan, William Thomas *engineering educator*

Kenner
Siebel, Mathias Paul *mechanical engineer*

Lafayette
Domingue, Emery *consulting engineering company executive, retired*
Fang, Cheng-Shen *chemical engineering educator*
Hepguler, Gregory Gokhan *petroleum engineer*
Luppens, John Christian *petroleum engineer*
Rieke, Herman Henry, III *petroleum engineering educator, consultant*

Lake Charles
Levingston, Ernest Lee *engineering company executive*

Mandeville
Hruska, Francis John *marine surveyor and consultant*

Maurice
Larsen, Henrik Aslak *mechanical engineer*

Metairie
Nicoladis, Michael F. *engineering company executive*
N'Vietson, Tung Thanh *civil engineer*

New Orleans
†Boh, Robert Henry *civil engineer, construction company executive*
Lannes, William Joseph, III *electrical engineer*
Lee, Griff Calicutt *civil engineer*
Nelson, Waldemar Stanley *civil engineer, consultant*
O'Connor, Kim Claire *chemical engineering and biotechnology educator*
Quirk, Peter Richard *engineering company executive*
Solomonow, Moshe *biomedical engineer, scientist, educator*

Ruston
Barron, Randall Franklin *mechanical engineer, educator, consultant*
Hale, Paul Nolen, Jr. *engineering administrator, educator*
Painter, Jack Timberlake *civil engineer*

Slidell
Grantham, Donald James *engineer, educator, author*
Tewell, Joseph Robert, Jr. *electrical engineer*

Vivian
Collier, Samuel Melvin *aerospace engineer*

MAINE

Bangor
Hsu, Yu Kao *aerospace scientist, mathematician, educator*

Brunswick
Watts, Helen Caswell *civil engineer*

East Boothbay
Smith, Merlin Gale *engineering executive, researcher*

Eastport
Kennedy, Robert Spayde *electrical engineering educator*

Falmouth
Rohsenow, Warren Max *retired mechanical engineer, educator*

Gray
Durgin, Scott Benjamin *radio frequency engineer, physics educator*

Orono
Ruthven, Douglas Morris *chemical engineering educator*

Portland
Raisbeck, Gordon *systems engineer*

MARYLAND

Aberdeen Proving Ground
Cozby, Richard Scott *electronics engineer, reserve army officer*

Annapolis
Caldwell, Curtis Irvin *acoustical engineer*
DiAiso, Robert Joseph *civil engineer*
Granger, Robert Alan *mechanical and aerospace engineering educator*
Heller, Austin Norman *chemical and environmental engineer*
Johnson, Bruce *engineering educator*
Rapkin, Jerome *defense industry executive*
Schoenfeld, William Patton *aerospace mechanical engineer*
Tuttle, Kenneth Lewis *engineering educator, consultant*

Baltimore
Anandarajah, Annalingam *civil engineer, educator*
Broadbent, J. Street *engineering executive*
Corn, Morton *environmental engineer, educator*
Degenford, James Edward *electrical engineer, educator*
Ellingwood, Bruce Russell *structural engineering researcher, educator*
Emerick, Norman Cooper *consulting engineer*
Fisher, Jack Carrington *environmental engineering executive*
Girovich, Mark Jacob *mechanical engineer*
Jelinek, Frederick *electrical engineer, educator*
Katz, Joseph Louis *chemical engineer, educator*
Kelman, Gary F. *environmental engineer*
Knoedler, Elmer L. *retired chemical engineer*
Lemer, Andrew Charles *engineer, economist*
Mc Cord, Kenneth Armstrong *consulting engineer*
Norris, Joseph, III *computer engineer*
O'Melia, Charles Richard *environmental engineering educator*
Popel, Aleksander S. *engineering educator*
Prince, Jerry Ladd *engineering educator*
Scanlan, Robert Harris *civil engineer, educator*
Sharpe, William Norman, Jr. *mechanical engineer, educator*
Stolberg, Ernest Milton *retired environmental engineer, consultant*

Bethesda
Ballhaus, William Francis, Jr. *aerospace industry executive, research scientist*
Briskman, Robert David *engineering executive*
Burdeshaw, William Brooksbank *engineering executive*
Freedman, Joseph *sanitary and public health engineering consultant*
Kemelhor, Robert E(lias) *mechanical engineer*
Koltnow, Peter Gregory *engineering consultant*
Nimeroff, Phyllis Ruth *electronic engineer, visual artist*
Pritchard, Wilbur *telecommunications engineering executive*
Saville, Thorndike, Jr. *coastal engineer, consultant*

Brooklandville
Azola, Martin Peter *civil engineer, construction manager*

California
Jessup, Edwin Harley, III *aerospace engineering executive*

Chevy Chase
Edelson, Burton Irving *electrical engineer*
Rockwell, Theodore *nuclear engineer*
Short, Steve Eugene *engineer*

Clarksville
Brancato, Emanuel Leonard *electrical engineering consultant*

Cockeysville Hunt Valley
Barr, Irwin Robert *retired aeronautical engineer*

College Park
Anderson, John David, Jr. *aerospace engineer*
Ayyub, Bilal M. *civil engineering educator, researcher, executive*
Barbe, David Franklin *electrical engineer, educator*
Cunniff, Patrick Francis *mechanical engineer*
Ephremides, Anthony *electrical engineering educator*
Gentry, James Walter *chemical engineer, educator*
Gessow, Alfred *aerospace engineer, educator*
Granatstein, Victor Lawrence *electrical engineer, educator*
Gupta, Ashwani Kumar *mechanical engineering educator*
Kirk, James Allen *mechanical engineering educator*
Lee, Chi Hsiang *electrical engineer, educator*
Levine, William Silver *electrical engineering educator*
Lin, Hung C. *electrical engineer educator*
Marcus, Steven Irl *electrical engineering educator*
Mote, Clayton Daniel, Jr. *mechanical engineer, educator, administrator*
Newcomb, Robert Wayne *electrical engineer educator*
Taylor, Leonard Stuart *engineering educator, consultant*

Columbia
Franks, David A. *computer engineer*
Vu, Cung *chemical engineer*

Crofton
Laurenson, Robert Mark *mechanical engineer*

Easton
Buescher, Adolph Ernst (Dolph Buescher) *aerospace company executive*

Ellicott City
Gagnon, Robert Michael *engineering executive, educator*

Finksburg
Konigsberg, Robert Lee *electrical engineer*

Fort Washington
Caveny, Leonard Hugh *mechanical engineer, aerospace scientist, consultant*

Frederick
Nayyar, Mohinder Lal *mechanical engineer*
Wolf, Donald Joseph *industrial engineer*

Gaithersburg
Cookson, Alan Howard *electrical engineer, researcher*
Fong, Jeffrey Tse-Wei *mechanical engineer*
Gravatt, Claude Carrington, Jr. *research and development executive*
Jahanmir, Said *materials scientist, mechanical engineer*
Levine, Robert Sidney *chemical engineer, consultant*
Nickle, Dennis Edwin *electronics engineer, church deacon*
Rabinow, Jacob *electrical engineer, consultant*
Stever, Horton Guyford *aerospace scientist and engineer, educator, consultant*
Tesk, John Aloysius *materials scientist*
†Wang, Francis Wei-Yu *biomedical materials scientist, researcher*
Wiederhorn, Sheldon Martin *materials scientist engineer*
Wisniewski, John William *mining engineer, bank engineering executive*
Wright, Richard Newport, III *civil engineer, retired government official*
Yang, Xiang Yang *engineer, entrepreneur*

Germantown
Lee, Lin-Nan *communications engineer, engineering executive*
Peratt, Anthony Lee *electrical engineer, physicist*
Singh, Braj Kumar *mechanical engineer*

Glen Arm
Harris, Benjamin Louis *chemical engineer, consultant*

Glen Burnie
Smalts, David H. *civil engineer*

Greenbelt
Cooper, Robert Shanklin *engineering executive, former government official*
Ku, Jentung *mechanical and aerospace engineer*
Levitt, Gerald Steven *engineering services executive*
Steiner, Mark David *engineering executive*

Havre De Grace
Huang, Yung-Hui *chemical engineer*

Hunt Valley
Kinstlinger, Jack *engineering executive, consultant*
Krotiuk, William John *mechanical engineer*

Hyattsville
Sindoris, Arthur Richard *electronics engineer, government official*

Kingsville
Pullen, Keats A., Jr. *electronics engineer*

Lanham
Criscimagna, Ned Henry *mechanical engineer*

Lanham Seabrook
Yen, Wen Liang *aerospace engineer*

Largo
Freeman, Ernest Robert *engineering executive*

Laurel
Eaton, Alvin Ralph *aeronautical and systems engineer, research and development administrator*

Linthicum
O'Brien, Sean Delaney *acoustical engineer*

Linthicum Heights
Skillman, William Alfred *consulting engineering executive*

New Market
Billig, Frederick Stucky *mechanical engineer*

North Potomac
Dorsey, William Walter *aerospace engineer, engineering executive*

Patuxent River
Adams, Richard Eugene *aerospace engineer, project manager*

Phoenix
Lade, Poul Vestergaard *civil engineering educator, researcher, consultant*

Potomac
Williams, Peter Maclellan *nuclear engineer*

Queenstown
Kearns, Robert William *manufacturing inventor*

Rockville
Burdick, William MacDonald *biomedical engineer*
Hutchin, Nancy Lee *process engineering and change management consultant*
McDonald, Capers Walter *biomedical engineer, corporate executive*
Seagle, Edgar Franklin *environmental engineer, consultant*
Ulbrecht, Jaromir Josef *chemical engineer*

Saint Inigoes
Masters, George Windsor *electrical engineer, educator*
Scruitsky, Robert Lee *senior project engineer*

Severna Park
Davis, John Adams, Jr. *electrical engineer, roboticist, corporate research executive*
Retterer, Bernard Lee *electronic engineering consultant*

Silver Spring
Chang, Cheng-Shien *reliability engineering executive, consultant*
Eades, James Beverly, Jr. *aeronautical engineer*
Foresti, Roy, Jr. *chemical engineer*
Hermach, Francis Lewis *consulting engineer*
Mikata, Yozo *mechanical engineer, software engineer*
Mok, Carson Kwok-Chi *structural engineer*
Shames, Irving Herman *engineering educator*

Stevensville
Trescott, Sara Lou *water resources engineer*

Sykesville
Whittle, Joseph F., Jr. *engineering executive, consultant*

Timonium
Mitchell, Keith Phillip *electrical engineer*

West Bethesda
Sevik, Maurice *acoustical engineer, researcher*

MASSACHUSETTS

Acton
Clayton, John *retired engineering executive and consultant*
Hicks, Walter Joseph *electrical engineer*

Amherst
Abbott, Douglas Eugene *engineering educator*
Franks, Lewis E. *electrical and computer engineering educator, researcher*
Haensel, Vladimir *chemical engineering educator*
Koren, Israel *electrical and computer engineering educator*
Laurence, Robert Lionel *chemical engineering educator*
Nash, William Arthur *civil engineer, educator*
Swift, Calvin Thomas *electrical and computer engineering educator*
Targonski, Stephen Donald *electrical engineering researcher*
Vogl, Otto *polymer science and engineering educator*

Andover
Chung, Tchang-Il *engineer*
Jakes, William Chester *electrical engineer*
Marsh, Robert Buford *chemical engineer, consultant*

Arlington
Gumpertz, Werner Herbert *structural engineering company executive*

Bedford
Cronson, Harry Marvin *electronics engineer*
Fante, Ronald Louis *engineering scientist*
Lackoff, Martin Robert *engineer, physical scientist, researcher*

Belmont
Bowen, H. Kent *engineering educator*
Durgin, Frank Herman, II *aeronautical engineer*
Haralampu, George Stelios *electric power engineer, former engineering executive electric utility company*
Merrill, Edward Wilson *chemical engineering educator*

Boston
Cassandras, Christos George *engineering educator, consultant*
De Luca, Carlo John *biomedical engineer*
Fine, Samuel *biomedical engineering educator, consultant*
Gilbert, Arthur Charles *aerospace engineer, consulting engineer*
Harrington, Joseph John *environmental engineering educator*
Hines, Marion Ernest *electronic engineering consultant*
Langer, Robert Martin *retired chemical engineering company executive, consultant*
Levitin, Lev Berovich *engineering educator*
Moore, Richard Lawrence *structural engineer, consultant*
Pierce, Allan Dale *engineering educator, researcher*
Raemer, Harold Roy *electrical engineering educator*
Saleh, Bahaa E. A. *electrical engineering educator*
Teich, Malvin Carl *electrical engineering educator*
†Weng, Zhiping *biomedical engineering educator*
Zaldastani, Othar *structural engineer*

Boxboro
Lee, Shih-Ying *mechanical engineering educator*

Boxford
Laderoute, Charles David *engineer, economist, consultant*

Brockton
Jellows, Tracy Patrick *software engineer*
Park, Byiung Jun *textile engineer*
Wiegner, Allen Walter *biomedical engineering educator, researcher*

Brookline
Eden, Murray *electrical engineer, emeritus educator*
Felsen, Leopold B. *engineering educator*
Keil, Alfred Adolf Heinrich *marine engineering educator*

Burlington
Weatherby, David John *engineering company executive*

Cambridge
Abelson, Harold *electrical engineer, educator*
Abernathy, Frederick Henry *mechanical engineering educator*
Argon, Ali Suphi *mechanical engineering educator*
Baggeroer, Arthur Bernard *electrical engineering educator*
Baron, Judson Richard *aerospace educator*
Baron, Sheldon *research and development company executive*
Battin, Richard Horace *astronautical engineer*
Beér, János Miklós *engineering educator*
Ben-Akiva, Moshe Emanuel *civil engineering educator*
Beranek, Leo Leroy *acoustical consultant*
Bras, Rafael Luis *engineering educator*
Brenner, Howard *chemical engineering educator*
Brockett, Roger Ware *engineering and computer science educator*
Brown, Robert Arthur *chemical engineering educator*
Carmichael, Alexander Douglas *engineering educator*
Chen, Sow-Hsin *nuclear engineering educator, researcher*
Cohen, Robert Edward *chemical engineering educator, consultant*
Colton, Clark Kenneth *chemical engineering educator*
Corbato, Fernando Jose *electrical engineer and computer science educator*
Crandall, Stephen Harry *engineering educator*
Cummings-Saxton, James *chemical engineer, consultant, educator*
de Neufville, Richard Lawrence *engineering educator*
Dewey, Clarence Forbes, Jr. *engineering educator*
Drake, Elisabeth Mertz *chemical engineer*
Dubowsky, Steven *mechanical engineering educator*
Duffy, Robert Aloysius *aeronautical engineer*
Dugundji, John *aeronautical engineer*
Elias, Peter *electrical engineering educator*
Fay, James Alan *mechanical engineering educator*
Flowers, Woodie Claude *mechanical engineering educator and researcher, engineering director*
Fujimoto, James G. *electrical engineering educator*
Furman, Thomas D., Jr. *engineering company executive*
Gallager, Robert Gray *electrical engineering educator*
Gatos, Harry Constantine *engineering educator*
Glaser, Peter Edward *mechanical engineer, consultant*
Golay, Michael Warren *nuclear engineering educator*
Greitzer, Edward Marc *aeronautical engineering educator, consultant*
Guerra, John Michael *optical engineer*
Hansen, Kent Forrest *nuclear engineering educator*
Harleman, Donald Robert Fergusson *environmental engineering educator*
Harris, Wesley L. *aeronautics engineering educator*
Haus, Hermann Anton *electrical engineering educator*
Heney, Joseph Edward *environmental engineer*
Heywood, John Benjamin *mechanical engineering educator*
Howard, Jack Benny *chemical engineer, educator, researcher*
Ippen, Erich Peter *electrical engineering educator*
Jensen, Klavs Flemming *chemical engineering educator*
Kamm, Roger Dale *biomedical engineer, educator*
Kassakian, John Gabriel *research electrical engineer, engineering director*
Kazimi, Mujid Suliman *nuclear engineer, educator*
Kerrebrock, Jack Leo *aeronautics and astronautics engineering educator*
Kyhl, Robert Louis *retired electrical engineering educator*
Ladd, Charles Cushing, III *civil engineering educator*
Laibinis, Paul Edward *chemical engineering educator*
Lala, Jaynarayan Hotchand *computer engineer*
Latanision, Ronald Michael *materials science and engineering educator, consultant*
Leehey, Patrick *mechanical and ocean engineering educator*
LeMessurier, William James *structural engineer*
Lim, Jae Soo *engineering educator, information systems*
Longwell, John Ploeger *chemical engineering educator*
Makhoul, John Ibrahim *electrical engineer, researcher*
Mann, Robert Wellesley *biomedical engineer, educator*
Marini, Robert Charles *environmental engineering executive*
Markey, Winston Roscoe *aeronautical engineering educator*
Masubuchi, Koichi *marine engineer, educator*
McClintock, Frank Ambrose *mechanical engineer*
McGarry, Frederick Jerome *civil engineering educator*
Mei, Chiang Chung *civil engineer, educator*
Meyer, John Edward *nuclear engineering educator*
Milgram, Jerome H. *marine and ocean engineer, educator*
Miller, Rene Harcourt *aerospace engineer, educator*
Parker, Ronald R. *electrical engineer*
Parthum, Charles Albert *civil engineer*
Penfield, Paul Livingstone, Jr. *electrical engineering educator*
Pian, Theodore Hsueh-Huang *engineering educator, consultant*
Probstein, Ronald Filmore *mechanical engineering educator*
Reid, Robert Clark *chemical engineering educator*
Rivest, Ronald L. *engineer*
Rogers, Peter Phillips *environmental engineering educator, city planner*
Roos, Daniel *engineering educator*
Ruina, Jack Philip *electrical engineer, educator*
Russell, Kenneth Calvin *metallurgical engineer, educator*
Saltzer, Jerome Howard *computer science educator*
Satterfield, Charles Nelson *chemical engineer, educator*
Sheridan, Thomas Brown *mechanical engineering and applied psychology educator, researcher, consultant*
Siebert, William McConway *electrical engineering educator*
Slaughter, E. Sarah *civil engineering educator*
Smith, Henry Ignatius *engineering educator*
Smith, Kenneth Alan *chemical engineer, educator*
Sonin, Ain A. *mechanical engineering educator, consultant*
Staelin, David Hudson *electrical engineering educator, consultant*
Stephanopoulos, Gregory *chemical engineering educator, consultant, researcher*

Stevens, Kenneth Noble *electrical engineering educator*
Suh, Nam Pyo *mechanical engineering educator*
Thomas, Harold Allen, Jr. *civil engineer, educator*
Todreas, Neil Emmanuel *nuclear engineering educator*
Triantafyllou, Michael Stefanos *ocean engineering educator*
Trilling, Leon *aeronautical engineering educator*
Troxel, Donald Eugene *electrical engineering educator*
Tuller, Harry Louis *materials science and engineering educator*
Ungar, Eric Edward *mechanical engineer*
Vander Velde, Wallace Earl *aeronautical and astronautical educator*
Vér, István László *noise control consultant*
Vunjak-Novakovic, Gordana *chemical engineer, educator*
Wang, Daniel I-Chyau *biochemical engineering educator*
Wechsler, Alfred Elliot *engineering executive, consultant, chemical engineer*
White, David Calvin *electrical engineer, energy educator, consultant*
Whitman, Robert Van Duyne *civil engineer, educator*
Williams, James Henry, Jr. *mechanical engineer, educator, consultant*
Wuensch, Bernhardt John *ceramic engineering educator*
Yannas, Ioannis Vassilios *polymer science and engineering educator*

Canton
Costa, Pat Vincent *automation sciences executive*

Concord
Aldrich, Harl Preslar, Jr. *retired civil engineer, consultant*
Drew, Philip Garfield *consultant engineering company executive*
Osepchuk, John Moses *engineering physicist, consultant*
Villers, Philippe *mechanical engineer*
Woll, Harry J. *electrical engineer*

Dover
Kovaly, John Joseph *consulting engineering executive, educator*

Dracut
†Pieslak, Richard Alphonse *civil engineer*

East Longmeadow
Green, Frank Walter *industrial engineer*

Foxboro
Pierce, Francis Casimir *civil engineer*
Ryskamp, Carroll Joseph *chemical engineer*

Framingham
Bose, Amar Gopal *electrical engineering educator*
Crossley, Frank Alphonso *former metallurgical engineer*
Lindsay, Leslie *packaging engineer*

Franklin
Shastry, Shambhu Kadhambiny *scientist, engineering executive, consultant*

Hanscom AFB
Schmitt, Stephen Richard *electronics engineer*

Harwich
Bush, Richard James *engineering executive, lay worker*

Holden
Cole, Theron Metcalf *engineer*

Jamaica Plain
Shapiro, Ascher Herman *mechanical engineer, educator, consultant*

Lancaster
Richter, Henry Andrew *electrical engineer*

Leicester
Rogers, Randall Lloyd *mechanical engineer*

Lenox
Coffin, Louis Fussell, Jr. *mechanical engineer*

Lexington
Aronin, Lewis Richard *metallurgical engineer*
Bailey, Fred Coolidge *retired engineering consulting company executive*
Brookner, Eli *electrical engineer*
Cooper, William Eugene *consulting engineer*
Davidson, Frank Paul *retired macroengineer, lawyer*
Fortmann, Thomas Edward *research and development company executive*
Freed, Charles *engineering consultant, researcher*
Keicher, William Eugene *electrical engineer*
Kerr, Thomas Henderson, III *electrical engineer, researcher*
Kingston, Robert Hildreth *engineering educator*
Morrow, Walter Edwin, Jr. *electrical engineer, university laboratory administrator*
Stiglitz, Martin Richard *electrical engineer*
Sussman, Martin Victor *chemical engineering educator, inventor, consultant*

Longmeadow
Ferris, Theodore Vincent *chemical engineer, consulting technologist*
Hopfe, Harold Herbert *retired chemical engineer*

Lowell
Paikowsky, Samuel G. *civil engineering educator*

Lynn
D'Entremont, Edward Joseph *infosystems engineer, educator*
Kercher, David Max *mechanical engineer*

Malden
Miller, Kenneth William, II *research, development, engineering executive*

Manchester
Arntsen, Arnt Peter *engineer, consultant*

Marblehead
Ehrich, Fredric F. *aeronautical engineer*
Hoffman, Thomas Edgar *mechanical engineer*

Marlborough
Bennett, C. Leonard *consulting engineer*

Medford
Astill, Kenneth Norman *mechanical engineering educator*
Brosnan, David Patrick *structural engineer*
Greif, Robert *mechanical engineering educator*
Nelson, Frederick Carl *mechanical engineering educator*
Uhlir, Arthur, Jr. *electrical engineer, university administrator*

Medway
Hoag, David Garratt *aerospace engineer*

Milford
Carson, Charles Henry *microwave engineer*
Gliksberg, Alexander David *engineering executive*

Millbury
Pan, Coda H. T. *mechanical engineering educator, consultant, researcher*

Natick
DeCosta, Peter F. *chemical engineer*

Needham
Pucel, Robert Albin *electronics research engineer*

New Bedford
Soares, Carl Lionel *quality control engineer, metrologist*

Newton
Saffran, Kalman *engineering consulting company executive, entrepreneur*

Newton Center
Mark, Melvin *consulting mechanical engineer, educator*

North Attleboro
Inskeep, James R. *process control engineer*

North Dartmouth
Law, Frederick Masom *engineering educator, structural engineering firm executive*

Norwood
Fuller, Samuel Henry, III *computer engineer*
Mc Feeley, John Jay *chemical engineer*
Sheingold, Daniel H. *electrical engineer*

Peabody
Goldberg, Harold Seymour *electrical engineer, educator*
Peters, Leo Francis *environmental engineer*

Pittsfield
Feigenbaum, Armand Vallin *systems engineer, systems equipment executive*

Quincy
Colgan, Sumner *manufacturing engineer, chemical engineer*
Kelley, James Francis *civil engineer*

Reading
Melconian, Jerry Ohanes *engineering executive*

Sharon
Wisotsky, Serge Sidorovich *engineering executive*

South Hadley
Todorovic, John *chemical engineer*

South Hamilton
Spears, Howard Calvin Knox *power plant design engineer*

South Wellfleet
Bargellini, Pier Luigi *electrical engineer*

Sudbury
Fowler, Charles Albert *electronics engineer*

Swampscott
Kaufman, William Morris *engineer consultant*

Taunton
Lambert, Eugene Louis *engineer, manufacturing executive*

Tewksbury
Speltz, Michael John *program manager*
Wilson, Daniel Donald *engineering executive*

Vineyard Haven
Porter, James H. *chemical engineering executive*

Waltham
Hatsopoulos, George Nicholas *mechanical engineer, thermodynamicist, educator*

Watertown
Katz, William Emanuel *chemical engineer*
True, Edward Keene *architectural engineer*

Wayland
Stekly, Z.J. John *mechanical engineer*

Wellesley
Tierney, Thomas J. *business management consultant*
Weil, Thomas Alexander *electronics engineer, retired*

Westborough
Berthiaume, Wayne Henry *electrical engineer*

Gionfriddo, Maurice Paul *aeronautical engineer, research and development manager*

Weston
Kendall, Julius *consulting engineer*
Landis, John William *engineering and construction executive, government advisor*
Resden, Ronald Everett *medical devices product development engineer*

Westwood
Foster, Arthur Rowe *mechanical engineering educator*
Old, Bruce Scott *chemical and metallurgical engineer*

Weymouth
Crandlemere, Robert Wayne *engineering executive*
Imbault, James Joseph *manufacturing company executive*

Wilmington
Faccini, Ernest Carlo *mechanical engineer*

Winchester
Hirschfeld, Ronald Colman *retired consulting engineering executive*

Woburn
By, Andre Bernard *engineering executive, research scientist*

Worcester
Clarke, Edward Nielsen *engineering science educator*
DeFalco, Frank Damian *civil engineering educator*
Katz, Robert Nathan *ceramic engineer*
Norton, Robert Leo, Sr. *mechanical engineering educator, researcher*
Parrish, Edward Alton, Jr. *electrical and computer engineering educator, academic administrator*
Peura, Robert Allan *electrical and biomedical engineering educator*
Weiss, Alvin Harvey *chemical engineering educator, catalysis researcher and consultant*
Wilbur, Leslie Clifford *mechanical engineering educator*
Zwiep, Donald Nelson *mechanical engineering educator, administrator*

Yarmouth Port
Stott, Thomas Edward, Jr. *engineering executive*

MICHIGAN

Allen Park
Kulkarni, Kumar Balakrishna *automotive engineer*

Ann Arbor
Adamson, Thomas Charles, Jr. *aerospace engineering educator, consultant*
†Ambaruch, Arthur H. *engineer*
Assanis, Dennis N. (Dionissios Assanis) *mechanical engineering educator*
†Barber, James Richard *mechanical engineering educator*
Becher, William Don *electrical engineering educator, engineering consultant*
Bilello, John Charles *materials science and engineering educator*
Bitondo, Domenic *engineering executive*
Calahan, Donald Albert *electrical engineering educator*
Carnahan, Brice *chemical engineer, educator*
Chaffin, Don Brian *industrial engineering educator, research director*
Director, Stephen William *electrical and computer engineering educator, academic administrator*
England, Anthony Wayne *electrical engineering and computer science educator, astronaut, geophysicist*
Faeth, Gerard Michael *aerospace and mechanical engineering educator, researcher*
Friedmann, Peretz Peter *aerospace engineer, educator*
Gibala, Ronald *metallurgical engineering educator*
Gilbert, Elmer Grant *aerospace engineering educator, control theorist*
Haddad, George Ilyas *engineering educator, research scientist*
Hanson, Robert Duane *civil engineering educator*
Hayes, John Patrick *electrical engineering and computer science educator, consultant*
†Kannatey-Asibu, Elijah *engineering educator*
Kozma, Adam *electrical engineer*
Leith, Emmett Norman *electrical engineer, educator*
Macnee, Alan Breck *electrical engineer, educator*
Martin, William Russell *nuclear engineering educator*
McClamroch, N. Harris *aerospace engineering educator, consultant, researcher*
Meitzler, Allen Henry *electrical engineering educator, automotive scientist*
†Ni, Jun *mechanical engineering educator, researcher*
Pehlke, Robert Donald *materials and metallurgical engineering educator*
Petrick, Ernest Nicholas *mechanical engineer*
Pollock, Stephen Michael *industrial engineering educator, consultant*
Root, William Lucas *electrical engineering educator*
Rumman, Wadi (Saliba Rumman) *civil engineer*
Schwank, Johannes Walter *chemical engineering educator*
Scott, Norman Ross *electrical engineering educator*
Senior, Thomas Bryan A. *electrical engineering educator, researcher, consultant*
Solomon, David Eugene *engineering company executive*
Tai, Chen-To *electrical engineering educator*
Ulaby, Fawwaz Tayssir *electrical engineering and computer science educator, research center administrator*
Upatnieks, Juris *optical engineer, researcher, educator*
Willmarth, William Walter *aerospace engineering educator*
Wilson, Richard Christian *engineering firm executive*
Wylie, Evan Benjamin *civil engineering educator, consultant, researcher*
Young, Edwin Harold *chemical and metallurgical engineering educator*

Auburn Hills
Brady, Michael John *chemical engineer, automotive engineer*

Augusta
Barr, William Robert *industrial engineer, consultant*

Bay City
Morrill, Geary Steven *entrepreneur*

Big Rapids
Thapa, Khagendra *survey engineering educator*

Bingham Farms
Gratch, Serge *mechanical engineering educator*
McKeen, Alexander C. *engineering consulting company owner*

Birmingham
Park, Richard John *value engineer*

Bloomfield Hills
Cuffe, Stafford Sigesmund *automotive engineer, consultant*
Jeffe, Sidney David *automotive engineer*
Roy, Ranjit Kumar *mechanical engineer*
Stivender, Donald Lewis *mechanical engineering consultant*

Canton
Kendall, Laurel Ann *geotechnical engineer*

Carleton
Rancourt, James Daniel *optical engineer*

Clarkston
Colucci, Joseph Michael *mechanical engineering consultant*
Erkfritz, Donald Spencer *mechanical engineer*

Dearborn
Cairns, James Robert *mechanical engineering educator*
Gjostein, Norman Arthur *materials engineer, consultant, educator*
Libertiny, Susan Fryc *mechanical engineer*
Linnansalo, Vera *engineer*
Little, Robert Eugene *mechanical engineering educator, materials behavior researcher, consultant*
Lou, Zheng (David) *mechanical engineer, biomedical engineer*
Luettgen, Michael John *engineer*
Olson, Richard Gottlieb *nuclear engineer*
Orthwein, William Coe *mechanical engineer*
Wagner, Harvey Arthur *nuclear engineer*

Detroit
Batcha, George *mechanical and nuclear engineer*
Brammer, Forest Evert *electrical engineering educator*
Helmle, Ralph Peter *computer systems developer, manager*
Holness, Gordon Victor Rix *engineering executive, mechanical engineer*
Kline, Kenneth Alan *mechanical engineering educator*
Kummler, Ralph H. *chemical engineering educator*
Pulkkinen, Jyrki Tuomo Juhani *structural engineer*
Putchakayala, Hari Babu *engineering company executive*
Schmidt, Robert *mechanics and civil engineering educator*
Sengupta, Dipak Lal *electrical engineering and physics educator, researcher*
Stynes, Stanley Kenneth *retired chemical engineer, educator*
Trim, Donald Roy *consulting engineer*
Uicker, Joseph Bernard *engineering company executive*

East Lansing
Andersland, Orlando Baldwin *civil engineering educator*
Anderson, Donald Keith *chemical engineering educator*
Chen, Kun-Mu *electrical engineering educator*
Cutts, Charles Eugene *civil engineering educator*
Foss, John Frank *mechanical engineering educator*
Goodman, Erik David *engineering educator*
Lloyd, John Raymond *mechanical engineering educator*
Mukherjee, Kalinath *materials science and engineering educator, researcher*
Snell, John Raymond *civil engineer*
Soutas-Little, Robert William *mechanical engineer, educator*
von Bernuth, Robert Dean *agricultural engineering educator, consultant*
Von Tersch, Lawrence Wayne *electrical engineering educator, university dean*

Eastport
Tomlinson, James Lawrence *mechanical engineer*

Farmington
Chou, Clifford Chi Fong *research engineering executive*
Neyer, Jerome Charles *consulting civil engineer*

Farmington Hills
Ellis, Robert William *engineering educator*

Flint
Novak, Jo-Ann Stout *chemical engineer*

Grand Blanc
Bell, Donald Lloyd *retired engineer*
Riley, Ronald Jim *inventor, consultant*

Grand Rapids
Garver, Frederick Merrill *industrial engineering executive*

Greenbush
Paulson, James Marvin *engineering educator*

Grosse Pointe
Beltz, Charles Robert *engineering executive*
Cross, Ralph Emerson *mechanical engineer*
Maleitzke, Kenneth Eugene *automotive engineer, retired*

Houghton
Goel, Ashok Kumar *electrical engineering educator*

Heckel, Richard Wayne *metallurgical engineering educator*
Huang, Eugene Yuching *civil engineer, educator*

Kalamazoo
Engelmann, Paul Victor *plastics engineering educator*
Van Vlack, Lawrence Hall *engineering educator*

Lansing
Shirtum, Earl Edward *retired civil engineer*

Laurium
Pippenger, John Junior *fluid power engineer*

Livonia
Duffy, James Joseph *engineer*

Mason
Toekes, Barna *chemical engineer, polymer consultant*

Midland
Carson, Gordon Bloom *engineering executive*
Leng, Douglas Ellis *chemical engineer, scientist*
Meister, Bernard John *chemical engineer*
Seiler, Wallace Urban *chemical engineer*

North Branch
Stevenson, James Laraway *communications engineer, consulting*

Okemos
Giacoletto, Lawrence Joseph *electronics engineering educator, researcher, consultant*

Plymouth
Champa, John Joseph *telecommunications engineer, consultant*
Clark, Kenneth William *mechanical engineer*
Hsi, Morris Yu *mechanical engineer, applied researcher*

Pontiac
Danielewicz, Claudia Anne *quality assurance engineer*
Meldrum, Richard James *electrical engineer*

Port Huron
Maraldo, Angela Marie *civil engineer*

Redford
†Ravi Shankar, Suggan V. *software development engineer*

Rochester Hills
Hicks, George William *automotive and mechanical engineer*

Rockford
Westveld, Belinda Joyce *reliability and quality engineer, educator*

Romulus
Archer, Hugh Morris *consulting engineer, manufacturing professional*

Royal Oak
Smith, John William Hugh *civil engineer*

Saline
Bender, Robert John *ceramic engineer*

Shelby Township
Babar, Raza Ali *industrial engineer, utility consultant, futurist, management educator, marketing strategist, author, publisher*
Kortsha, Gene Xhevat *industrial hygienist*

Southfield
Hanisko, John-Cyril Patrick *electronics engineer, physicist*
†Liu, Huimin *engineering executive, consultant*
Washington, Anthony Nathaniel *mechanical engineer*

Sterling Heights
Smith, Gregory Robert *engineer, educator, marketing consultant*

Three Rivers
Mackay, Edward *engineer*

Traverse City
†Sidor, Stanley *engineer*

Troy
Bautz, Jeffrey Emerson *mechanical engineer, educator, researcher*
Hart, James Francis *civil engineer*
Johnston, Timothy Sidney *computer engineer*

Walled Lake
Williams, Sam B. *engineering executive*

Warren
Gallopoulos, Nicholas Efstratios *chemical engineer*
Jacovides, Linos Jacovou *electrical engineering research manager*
Krygier, Michael Robert *mechanical engineer*
Lett, Philip Wood, Jr. *defense consultant*
Nagy, Louis Leonard *engineering executive, researcher*

Waterford
Hampton, Phillip Michael *consulting engineering company executive*

Wyandotte
Beaudette, Robert Lee *transportation and logistics consultant*

MINNESOTA

Bloomington
Beckwith, Larry Edward *mechanical engineer*
Norris, William C. *engineering executive*

Burnsville
Lai, Juey Hong *chemical engineer*

Chanhassen
Thorson, John Martin, Jr. *electrical engineer, consultant*

Eden Prairie
Higgins, Robert Arthur *electrical engineer, educator, consultant*
Svärd, N. Trygve *electrical engineer*

Golden Valley
Ng, Christine S. *chemical engineer*

Hopkins
Karls, Nicholas James *engineering executive*

Lutsen
Napadensky, Hyla Sarane *engineering consultant*

Madison
Husby, Donald Evans *engineering company executive*

Maple Grove
Setterholm, Jeffrey Miles *systems engineer*

Minneapolis
Anderson, John Edward *mechanical engineering educator*
Bakken, Earl Elmer *electrical engineer, bioengineering company executive*
Cohen, Arnold A. *electrical engineer*
Davis, Howard Ted *engineering educator*
Fairhurst, Charles *civil and mining engineering educator*
Fletcher, Edward Abraham *engineering educator*
Galambos, Theodore Victor *civil engineer, educator*
Gerberich, William Warren *engineering educator*
Goldstein, Richard Jay *mechanical engineer, educator*
Hawkinson, Thomas Edwin *environmental and occupational health engineer*
Hawley, Sandra Sue *electrical engineer*
Hillstrom, Thomas Peter *engineering executive*
Johnson, Walter Kline *civil engineer*
Joseph, Daniel Donald *aeronautical engineer, educator*
Kain, Richard Yerkes *electrical engineer, researcher, educator*
Keller, Kenneth Harrison *engineering educator, science policy analyst*
Kvalseth, Tarald Oddvar *mechanical engineer, educator*
Lambert, Robert Frank *electrical engineer, consultant*
Lemberg, Steven Floyd *electrical engineer*
Liu, Benjamin Young-hwai *engineering educator*
Ogata, Katsuhiko *engineering educator*
Oriani, Richard Anthony *metallurgical engineering educator*
Persson, Erland Karl *electrical engineer*
Pfender, Emil *mechanical engineering educator*
Scriven, L. E(dward) *chemical engineering educator, scientist*
Sheikh, Suneel Ismail *aerospace engineer, researcher*
Shulman, Yechiel *engineering educator*
†Stelson, Kim Adair *mechanical engineering educator*
Tennyson, Joseph Alan *engineering executive*

Minnetonka
Johnson, Lennart Ingemar *materials engineering consultant*

New Brighton
Norling, Irwin Denison *retired measurement specialist, photographer*

North Oaks
Staehle, Roger Washburn *metallurgical engineer*

Park Rapids
Olsonawski, David Allen *civil engineer*

Plymouth
Ripp, Bryan Jerome *geological engineer*

Rochester
†Baxter, Duane Willard *electrical engineer, consultant*
Huffine, Coy Lee *retired chemical engineer, consultant*
Krivoshik, Andrew Peter *engineer*
Melby, Paul Elliott *electrical engineer*
O'Hare, Daniel John *electrical engineer*
Rentschler, Alvin Eugene *mechanical engineer*

Saint Paul
Goodell, John Dewitte *electromechanical engineer*
Goodman, Lawrence Eugene *structural analyst, educator*
Lampert, Leonard Franklin *mechanical engineer*
Myren, David James *aeronautical engineer*

Woodbury
Benforado, David M. *environmental engineer*

MISSISSIPPI

Hamilton
Ward, Robert Earl, Jr. *chemical engineer, chemical company administrator*

Hattiesburg
Fournier, Donald Joseph, Jr. *mechanical engineer, consultant, educator*

Jackson
†Balentine, William (Ray) *civil engineer*
Pearce, David Harry *biomedical engineer*

Mississippi State
Bumgardner, Joel David *biomedical engineer, educator*
Cliett, Charles Buren *aeronautical engineer, educator, academic administrator*
Taylor, Clayborne Dudley *engineering educator*
Thompson, Joe Floyd *aerospace engineer, educator*

Nettleton
Newell, Harold Joe *quality assurance engineer*

Pascagoula
Chapel, Theron Theodore *quality assurance engineer*

Starkville
Carley, Charles Team, Jr. *mechanical engineer*
Jacob, Paul Bernard, Jr. *electrical engineering educator*

Stennis Space Center
Corbin, James H. *executive engineer, meteorologist, oceanographer*

University
Chen, Wei-Yin *chemical engineering educator, researcher*
Horton, Thomas Edward, Jr. *mechanical engineering educator*
Uddin, Waheed *civil engineer, educator*

Vicksburg
McRae, John Leonidas *civil engineer*
Stafford, James Polk, Jr. *civil engineer*

MISSOURI

Ava
Murray, Delbert Milton *manufacturing engineer*

Ballwin
Cornell, William Daniel *mechanical engineer*

Centralia
Harmon, Robert Wayne *electrical engineering executive*

Chesterfield
Yardley, John Finley *aerospace engineer*

Columbia
Frisby, James Curtis *agricultural engineering educator*
O'Connor, John Thomas *civil engineering educator*
Pringle, Oran Allan *mechanical and aerospace engineering educator*
Viswanath, Dabir Srikantiah *chemical engineer*
Yasuda, Hirotsugu Koge *chemical engineering professor*

Florissant
Tomazi, George Donald *retired electrical engineer*
Ziemer, John Robert *software engineer*

Fortuna
Ramer, James LeRoy *civil engineer*

Hazelwood
Bruns, Billy Lee *electrical engineer, consultant*

Joplin
†Shaheen, Esber Ibrahim *engineering consultant, writer*

Kansas City
Acheson, Allen Morrow *retired engineering executive*
Adam, Paul James *engineering company executive, mechanical engineer*
Rodman, Len C. *civil and communication engineering executive*
Wade, Robert Glenn *engineering executive*

Kirkwood
Holsen, James Noble, Jr. *retired chemical engineer*

Lake Lotawana
Heineman, Paul Lowe *consulting civil engineer*

Lampe
Linden, Paul Allen *optical engineer*

Maryland Heights
Beumer, Richard Eugene *engineer, architect, construction firm executive*
Goldfarb, Marvin Al *retired civil engineer*

Rolla
Adams, Craig David *environmental engineering educator*
Barr, David John *civil, geological engineering educator*
Crosbie, Alfred Linden *mechanical engineering educator*
Dagli, Cihan Hayreddin *engineering educator*
Finaish, Fathi Ali *aeronautical engineering educator*
Munger, Paul R. *civil engineering educator*
Numbere, Daopu Thompson *petroleum engineer, educator*
Saperstein, Lee Waldo *mining engineering educator*
Sarchet, Bernard Reginald *retired chemical engineering educator*
Sauer, Harry John, Jr. *mechanical engineering educator, university administrator*
Tsoulfanidis, Nicholas *nuclear engineering educator, university official*

Saint Charles
Izuchukwu, John Ifeanyichukwu *industrial and mechanical engineer*

Saint Louis
Amini, Amir Arsham *biomedical engineering researcher, educator*
Antonacci, Anthony Eugene *controls engineer*
Birman, Victor Mark *mechanical and aerospace engineering educator*
Brasunas, Anton de Sales *metallurgical engineering educator*
Breihan, Erwin Robert *civil engineer, consultant*
Briggs, William Benajah *aeronautical engineer*
Cairns, Donald Fredrick *engineering educator, management consultant*
Cox, Jerome Rockhold, Jr. *electrical engineer*
Dudukovic, Milorad P. *chemical engineering educator, consultant*
Erickson, Robert Anders *optical engineer, physicist*
Ghosh, Soumitra Kumar *electrical engineer*
Gould, Phillip Louis *civil engineering educator, consultant*
Howard, Walter Burke *chemical engineer*
Hundelt, Craig Thomas *engineering executive, realtor*
McKelvey, James Morgan *chemical engineering educator*
Muller, Marcel W(ettstein) *electrical engineering educator*
Peters, David Allen *mechanical engineering educator, consultant*
Richardson, Thomas Hampton *design consulting engineer*
Rogers, John Russell *manufacturing company executive, engineer*
Ross, Monte *electrical engineer*
Shrauner, Barbara Wayne Abraham *electrical engineering educator*
Sutera, Salvatore Philip *mechanical engineering educator*
Szabo, Barna Aladar *mechanical engineering educator, mining engineer*
Trout, Keith William *electrical engineer*
Winter, David Ferdinand *electrical engineering educator, consultant*
Wolfe, Charles Morgan *electrical engineering educator*
Zaborszky, John *electrical engineer, educator*
Zurheide, Charles Henry *consulting electrical engineer*

Springfield
Hansen, John Paul *metallurgical engineer*
Rogers, Roddy Jack *civil, geotechnical and water engineer*

Webb City
Nichols, Robert Leighton *civil engineer*

MONTANA

Bozeman
Berg, Lloyd *chemical engineering educator*
Billau, Robin Louise *engineering and consulting executive*
Cokelet, Giles Roy *biomedical engineering educator*
Sanks, Robert Leland *environmental engineer, emeritus educator*
Stanislao, Joseph *consulting engineer, educator*

Great Falls
Walker, Leland Jasper *civil engineer*

Helena
Johnson, David Sellie *civil engineer*
†Watson, Thomas M. *civil engineer*

Missoula
Rice, Steven Dale *electronics educator*

Philipsburg
Bauer, Robert Forest *petroleum engineer*

NEBRASKA

Beatrice
Coker, William B. *electrical engineer*

Clay Center
Hahn, George LeRoy *agricultural engineer, biometeorologist*

Lincoln
Allington, Robert William *instrument company executive*
Bahar, Ezekiel *electrical engineering educator*
Edison, Allen Ray *electrical engineer, educator*
Edwards, Donald Mervin *biological systems engineering educator, university dean*
Elias, Samy E. G. *engineering executive*
Hoffman, Glenn Jerrald *agricultural engineering educator, consultant*
Splinter, William Eldon *agricultural engineering educator*
Ullman, Frank Gordon *electrical engineering educator*
Woollam, John Arthur *electrical engineering educator*

Omaha
Ben-Yaacov, Gideon *computer system designer*
Coy, William Raymond *civil engineer*
Hultquist, Paul Fredrick *electrical engineer, educator*
Kelpe, Paul Robert *engineer, consultant*
Matthies, Frederick John *architectural engineer*
Zerbs, Stephen Taylor *telecommunications development engineer*

NEVADA

Boulder City
Wyman, Richard Vaughn *engineering educator, exploration company executive*

Carson City
Hughes, Robert Merrill *control system engineer*

Incline Village
Thompson, David Alfred *industrial engineer*

Las Vegas
Boehm, Robert Foty *mechanical engineer, educator, researcher*
Broca, Laurent Antoine *aerospace scientist*
Culp, Gordon Louis *consulting engineer*
Haas, Robert John *aerospace engineer*
Herzlich, Harold J. *chemical engineer*
Messenger, George Clement *engineering executive, consultant*
Mulvihill, Peter James *fire protection engineer*

Minden
Bently, Donald Emery *electrical engineer*
Muszynska, Agnieszka (Agnes Muszynska) *mechanical engineering research scientist*

PROFESSIONAL INDEX 5917 ENGINEERING

Reno
Danko, George *engineering educator*
Lee, David DeWitt *industrial hygienist*
Reddy, Rajasekara L. *mechanical engineer*
Weinbrenner, George Ryan *aeronautical engineer*

Silver City
Bloyd, Stephen Roy *environmental manager, educator, consultant*

Sparks
Kleppe, John Arthur *electrical engineering educator, business executive*

NEW HAMPSHIRE

Center Sandwich
Simmons, Alan Jay *electrical engineer, consultant*

Concord
Caswell, William Stephen, Jr. *civil engineer*
Smart, Melissa Bedor *environmental consulting company executive*

Hanover
Dean, Robert Charles, Jr. *mechanical engineer, entrepreneur, innovator*
Garmire, Elsa Meints *electrical engineering educator, consultant*
Hutchinson, Charles Edgar *engineering educator*
Long, Carl Ferdinand *engineering educator*
Queneau, Paul Etienne *metallurgical engineer, educator*
Wallis, Graham Blair *engineer, educator*

Jaffrey
Foster, Walter Herbert, III *mechanical and manufacturing engineer, executive*

Marlow
Lindholm, Ulric Svante *engineering research institute executive, retired*

Merrimack
Uy, Philip M. *aeronautical engineer*

Nashua
Fallet, George *civil engineer*
Woodruff, Thomas Ellis *electronics consulting executive*

New Castle
Klotz, Louis Herman *structural engineer, educator, consultant*

Peterborough
Farnham, Sherman Brett *retired electrical engineer*

Portsmouth
Baumann, Hans D. *engineering executive*

Salem
Bonacorsi, Gregory James *mechanical engineer*

Seabrook
McLean, James Nelson *structural engineer*

West Lebanon
MacAdam, Walter Kavanagh *consulting engineering executive*

NEW JERSEY

Atco
Conrad, George John *retired design engineer, planner*

Barnegat
Hawk, Frank Carkhuff, Sr. *industrial engineer*

Basking Ridge
Drewry, Don Neal *fire protection engineer*

Bedminster
David, Edward Emil, Jr. *electrical engineer, business executive*

Berkeley Heights
Rabiner, Lawrence Richard *electrical engineer*

Bloomfield
Dohr, Donald R. *metallurgical engineer, researcher*

Bridgewater
Newman, Stephen Alexander *chemical engineer, thermodynamicist*

Burlington
Kennedy, Christopher Robin *ceramist*

Cherry Hill
Alexander, Eugene Morton *electronics engineer*
Fuentevilla, Manuel Edward *chemical engineer*
Melick, George Fleury *mechanical engineer, educator*

Clark
Walsh, Daniel Stephen *systems engineering consultant*

Clinton
Swift, Richard J. *engineering company executive*

Columbus
Litman, Bernard *electrical engineer, consultant*

Cranbury
Hochreiter, Joseph Christian, Jr. *engineering company executive*

Cranford
Schink, Frank Edward *electrical engineer*

Denville
Price, Robert Edmunds *civil engineer*

Edison
Olszewski, Jerzy Adam *electrical engineer*
Pruden, Ann Lorette *chemical engineer, researcher*

Elmwood Park
Semeraro, Michael Archangel, Jr. *civil engineer*

Englewood
Deresiewicz, Herbert *mechanical engineering educator*

Fairfield
Johnson, David Blackwell *safety engineer*

Florham Park
Bhagat, Phiroz Maneck *mechanical engineer*
Kenney, William F. *process engineer, safety engineer, sports official*

Fort Lee
Screpetis, Dennis *nuclear engineer, consultant*

Fort Monmouth
Perlman, Barry Stuart *electrical engineering executive, researcher*

Freehold
Christ, Duane Marland *computer systems engineer*
Schwartz, Perry Lester *information systems engineer, consultant*
Stirrat, William Albert *electronics engineer*

Green Village
Castenschiold, René *engineering company executive, author, consultant*

Hackensack
Mavrovic, Ivo *chemical engineer*
Yagoda, Harry Nathan *system engineering executive*
Zimmerman, Marlin U., Jr. *chemical engineer*

Haddonfield
Chu, Horn Dean *chemical engineer*
Siskin, Edward Joseph *engineering and construction company executive*

Hewitt
Selwyn, Donald *engineering administrator, researcher, inventor, educator*

Highland Park
Spencer, Herbert Harry *structural engineering researcher, computer analyst*

Hightstown
Johnson, Walter Curtis *electrical engineering educator*

Hoboken
Abel, Kate *researcher*
Boesch, Francis Theodore *electrical engineer, educator*
Bruno, Michael Stephen *ocean engineering educator, researcher*
Griskey, Richard George *chemical engineering educator*
Savitsky, Daniel *engineer, educator*
Sisto, Fernando *mechanical engineering educator*

Holmdel
Boyd, Gary Delane *electro-optical engineer, researcher*
Erfani, Shervin *electrical engineer, educator, scientist, writer*
Lang, Howard Lawrence *electrical engineer*
Meadors, Howard Clarence, Jr. *electrical engineer*
Opie, William Robert *retired metallurgical engineer*
Ross, Ian Munro *electrical engineer*

Jersey City
Adlershteyn, Leon *naval architect, engineer, educator, researcher*

Kinnelon
Haller, Charles Edward *engineering consultant*

Lawrenceville
Enegess, David Norman *chemical engineer*
Kihn, Harry *electronics engineer, manufacturing company executive*

Lincroft
Heirman, Donald Nestor *training engineering company executive, consultant*

Livingston
Daman, Ernest Ludwig *mechanical engineer*

Lodi
Melignano, Carmine (Emanuel Melignano) *video engineer*

Long Branch
Nahavandi, Amir Nezameddin *retired engineering firm executive*

Maplewood
Moore, Robert Condit *civil engineer*

Marlton
Singh, Krishna Pal *mechanical engineer*
Woods, Howard James, Jr. *civil engineer*

Middletown
Linker, Kerrie Lynn *systems engineer*
O'Neill, Eugene Francis *communications engineer*

Monmouth Junction
Carneiro, Mervyn Joseph *mechanical engineer*

Montclair
Clech, Jean Paul Marie *mechanical engineer*
Eager, George Sidney, Jr. *electrical engineer, business executive*
Hutchins, Carleen Maley *acoustical engineer, violin maker, consultant*

Morristown
Heilmeier, George Harry *electrical engineer, researcher*
Kagan, Val Alexander *engineer, researcher, educator*
Lieberman, Lester Zane *engineering company executive*
Personick, Stewart David *electrical engineer*

Mount Arlington
Jacobs, Richard Moss *consulting engineer*

Mount Laurel
Stallings, Viola Patricia Elizabeth *certified project manager, systems engineer, educational systems specialist*
Vidas, Vincent George *engineering executive*

Mountainside
Luckenbach, Edward Cooper *chemical engineer*

Murray Hill
Potamianos, Alexandros *electrical engineer, researcher*

Neptune
Amedu, Davis Jimoh *industrial engineer*
Zurick, Jack *electrical engineer*

New Brunswick
Awan, Ahmad Noor *civil engineer*
Jaluria, Yogesh *mechanical engineering educator*
Karol, Reuben Hirsh *civil engineer, sculptor*
Katz, Carlos *electrical engineer*
Smith, Fredric Charles *electronic technician, consultant*
Wolfe, Robert Richard *bioresource engineer, educator*

New Providence
Cho, Alfred Yi *electrical engineer*
Dodabalapur, Ananth *electrical engineer*

Newark
Bar-Ness, Yeheskel *electrical engineer, educator*
Dubrovsky, Roman *engineering educator*
Friedland, Bernard *engineer, educator*
Hanesian, Deran *chemical engineer, chemistry and environmental science educator, consultant*
Hrycak, Peter *mechanical engineer, educator*
Hsu, Cheng-Tzu Thomas *civil engineering educator*
Khera, Raj Pal *civil and environmental engineering educator*
Leu, Ming Chuan *engineering educator*
Pfeffer, Robert *chemical engineer, academic administrator, educator*
Pignataro, Louis James *engineering educator*
Rosato, Anthony Dominick *mechanical engineer, educator*
Siginer, Dennis A(ydeniz) *mechanical engineering educator, researcher*
Spillers, William Russell *civil engineering educator*
Yu, Yi-Yuan *mechanical engineering educator*

North Caldwell
Stevens, William Dollard *consulting mechanical engineer*

Ocean
Reich, Bernard *retired telecommunications engineer*

Ocean City
Reiter, William Martin *chemical engineer*
Speitel, Gerald Eugene *consulting environmental engineer*

Parsippany
Marscher, William Donnelly *engineering company executive*

Passaic
Lindholm, Clifford Falstrom, II *engineering executive, mayor*

Phillipsburg
Cooper, Paul *mechanical engineer, research director*

Picatinny Arsenal
Janow, Chris *mechanical engineer*

Pilesgrove Township
Robinson, John Abbott *mechanical engineer*

Piscataway
Flanagan, James Loton *electrical engineer, educator*
Freeman, Herbert *computer engineering educator*
Frenkiel, Richard Henry *systems engineer, consultant*
Guo, Qizhong *engineering educator, researcher*
Mammone, Richard James *engineering educator*
Salkind, Alvin J. *electrochemical engineer, educator, dean*
Sannuti, Peddapullaiah *electrical engineering educator*
Strachan, William John *optical engineer*
Welkowitz, Walter *biomedical engineer, educator*
Williams, James Richard *human factors engineering psychologist*
Zhao, Jian Hui *electrical and computer engineering educator*

Plainfield
Granstrom, Marvin Leroy *civil and sanitary engineering educator*
Reilly, Michael Thomas *chemical engineer*

Plainsboro
Sorensen, Henrik Vittrup *electrical engineering educator*

Pomona
Sharobeam, Monir Hanna *engineering educator*

Princeton
Anderson, Bruce James *electrical engineer, consultant*
Bartolini, Robert Alfred *electrical engineer, researcher*
Billington, David Perkins *civil engineering educator*
Blair, David William *mechanical engineer*
Cakmak, Ahmet Sefik *civil engineering educator*
Curtiss, Howard Crosby, Jr. *mechanical engineer, educator*
Debenedetti, Pablo Gaston *chemical engineering educator*
Denlinger, Edgar Jacob *electronics engineering research executive*
Dickinson, Bradley William *electrical engineering educator*
Durbin, Enoch Job *aeronautical engineering educator*
Fusillo, Thomas Victor *environmental engineer*
Gibson, James John *electronics engineer, consultant*
Gillham, John Kinsey *chemical engineering educator*
Glassman, Irvin *mechanical and aeronautical engineering educator, consultant*
Hough, Robert Alan *civil engineer*
Jackson, Roy *chemical engineering educator*
Johnson, Ernest Frederick *chemical engineer, educator*
Lechner, Bernard Joseph *consulting electrical engineer*
Linke, Richard A. *systems engineer, researcher*
Lo, Arthur Wu-nien *electrical engineering educator*
Miles, Richard Bryant *mechanical and aerospace engineering educator*
Nikain, Reza *civil engineer*
Platt, Judith Roberta *electrical engineer*
Poor, Harold Vincent *electrical engineering educator*
Prud'homme, Robert Krafft *chemical engineering educator*
Russel, William Bailey *engineering educator*
Saville, Dudley Albert *chemical engineering educator*
Schroeder, Alfred Christian *electronics research engineer*
Socolow, Robert Harry *engineering educator, scientist*
Stengel, Robert Frank *mechanical and aerospace engineering educator*
Torquato, Salvatore *civil engineering educator*
†Tsui, Daniel C. *electrical engineering educator*
Vahaviolos, Sotirios John *electrical engineer, scientist, corporate executive*
VanMarcke, Erik Hector *civil engineering educator*
Walton, Clifford Wayne *chemical engineer, researcher*
Wei, James *chemical engineering educator, academic dean*
Weimer, Paul K(essler) *electrical engineer, consultant*
Weinstein, Norman Jacob *chemical engineer, consultant*
Wolf, Wayne Hendrix *electrical engineering educator*
Zatz, Irving J. *structural engineer*

Princeton Junction
Bair, William Alois *engineer*
Lull, William Paul *engineering consultant*

Rahway
Buckland, Barry C. *chemical engineer*
Drew, Stephen Walker *chemical engineer*

Red Bank
Lucky, Robert Wendell *electrical engineer*
Schneider, Sol *electronic engineer, consultant, researcher*

Ridgewood
Abplanalp, Glen Harold *civil engineer*

Robbinsville
Goldstein, Norman Robert *safety engineer*

Rumson
Rowe, Harrison Edward *electrical engineer*

Salem
Crymble, John Frederick *chemical engineer, consultant*

Scotch Plains
Domeshek, Sol *aeronautical engineer*

Short Hills
Wharton, Lennard *engineering company executive*

Shrewsbury
De Chino, Karen Linnia *engineering business analyst*

Skillman
Brill, Yvonne Claeys *engineer, consultant*
Shah, Hash N. *plastics technologist, researcher*

Somerset
Murthy, Srinivasa K. *engineering corporation executive*

South Plainfield
Kennedy, John William *engineering company executive*

Sparta
Truran, William Richard *electrical engineer*

Springfield
Goldstein, Irving Robert *mechanical and industrial engineer, educator, consultant*
Perilstein, Fred Michael *electrical engineer, consultant*

Summit
Fukui, Hatsuaki *electrical engineer, art historian*

Teaneck
Ehrlich, Ira Robert *mechanical engineering consultant*

Towaco
Pasquale, Frank Anthony *engineering executive*

Upper Saddle River
Wallace, William, III *engineering executive*

Warren
Biswas, Dhrubes *electrical engineer*
Ellerbusch, Fred *environmental engineer*
Salem, Eli *chemical engineer*

Watchung
Michaelis, Paul Charles *engineering physicist executive*
Tornqvist, Erik Gustav Markus *chemical engineer, research scientist*

Wayne
Arturi, Anthony Joseph *engineering executive, consultant*
Cheng, David Hong *mechanical engineering educator*

West Caldwell
Wray, Gilbert Andrew *mechanical and civil engineer*

West New York
Gruenberg, Elliot Lewis *electronics engineer and company executive*

Wyckoff
Mirza, Muhammad Zubair *product development company executive, researcher, engineering consultant, inventor*

NEW MEXICO

Albuquerque
Anderson, Lawrence Keith *electrical engineer*
Austin, Edward Marvin *retired mechanical engineer, researcher*
Baum, Carl Edward *electromagnetic theorist*
Brown, James Randall *mechanical engineer*
Byrne, Raymond Harry *electrical engineer*
Dorato, Peter *electrical and computer engineering educator*
Emlen, Warren Metz *computer-related services company owner*
Fuchs, Beth Ann *research engineer*
Gross, William Allen *mechanical engineer*
Gruchalla, Michael Emeric *electronics engineer*
Haertling, Gene Henry *ceramic engineering educator*
Hall, Jerome William *research engineering educator*
Hausner, Jerry *electronics engineer, consultant*
Karni, Shlomo *engineering and religious studies educator*
Lederer, John Martin *retired aeronautical engineer*
Molzen, Dayton Frank *consulting engineering executive*
Orman, John Leo *software engineer, writer*
Peck, Ralph Brazelton *civil engineering educator, consultant*
Prindle, Robert William *geotechnical engineer*
Samara, George Albert *engineer*
Studer, James Edward *geological engineer*
Vizcaino, Henry P. *mining engineer, consultant*
Wood, Gerald Wayne *electrical engineer*

Belen
Toliver, Lee *mechanical engineer*

Embudo
Rogers, Benjamin Talbot *consulting engineer, solar energy consultant*

Farmington
Finch, Thomas Wesley *corrosion engineer*
Garretson, Owen Loren *mechanical and chemical engineer*

Kirtland AFB
Voelz, David George *electrical engineer*

Las Cruces
Colbaugh, Richard Donald *mechanical engineer, educator, researcher*
Ford, Clarence Quentin *mechanical engineer, educator*
Matthews, Larryl Kent *mechanical engineering educator*
Morgan, John Derald *electrical engineer*

Los Alamos
Jackson, James F. *nuclear engineer*
McDonald, Thomas Edwin, Jr. *electrical engineer*
†Pond, Daniel James *ergonomist*
Stoddard, Stephen Davidson *ceramic engineer, former state senator*
Van Tuyle, Gregory Jay *nuclear engineer*
†Weaver, Michael James *mechanical engineer*

Santa Fe
Baerwald, John Edward *traffic and transportation engineer, educator*
Miller, Edmund Kenneth *retired electrical engineer, educator*
Tenison, John Hughes *civil engineer, retired military officer*
Turney, Thomas Charles *civil engineer*

White Sands
Kestner, Robert Richard, II *engineering psychologist*

White Sands Missile Range
Arthur, Paul Keith *electronic engineer*

NEW YORK

Afton
Church, Richard Dwight *electrical engineer, scientist*

Akron
Greatbatch, Wilson *biomedical engineer*

Albany
Brunner, Robert Vincent, Jr. *civil engineer*
Fanuele, Frank John *engineering executive*
Happ, Harvey Heinz *electrical engineer, educator*
McKay, Donald Arthur *mechanical engineer*
Roy, Rob J. *biomedical engineer, anesthesiologist*
Ting, Joseph K. *mechanical engineer*

Alfred
Spriggs, Richard Moore *ceramic engineer, research center administrator*

Amherst
Chang, Ching Ming (Carl Chang) *business executive, mechanical engineer, educator*

Armonk
Donofrio, Nicholas M. *computer engineer*

Ballston Lake
Fiedler, Harold Joseph *electrical engineer, consultant*

Bath
†Wu, Shiming *materials scientist, researcher*

Big Flats
Orsillo, James Edward *computer systems engineer, company executive*

Binghamton
Cornacchio, Joseph Vincent *engineering educator, computer researcher, consultant*

Briarcliff Manor
Cugnini, Aldo Godfrey *electrical engineer*

Brooklyn
Armenakas, Anthony Emmanuel *aerospace educator*
Beaufait, Frederick W(illiam) *civil engineering educator*
Bertoni, Henry Louis *electrical engineering educator*
Goodman, Alvin S. *engineering educator, consultant*
Helly, Walter Sigmund *engineering educator*
Kempner, Joseph *aerospace engineering educator*
McLean, William Ronald *electrical engineer, consultant*
Mernyk, Ross Lou *electronics engineer*
Ortiz, Mary Theresa *biomedical engineer, educator*
Pan, Huo-Hsi *mechanical engineer, educator*
Rice, John Thomas *architecture educator*
Roess, Roger Peter *engineering educator*
Shaw, Leonard Glazer *electrical engineering educator, consultant*

Buffalo
Anderson, Wayne Arthur *electrical engineering educator*
Benenson, David Maurice *engineering educator*
Drury, Colin Gordon *engineering consultant, educator*
Hida, George T. *chemical and ceramic engineer*
Karwan, Mark Henry *engineering educator, dean*
Kinzly, Robert Edward *engineering company executive*
Kreuz, Daniel Edward *city engineer*
Landi, Dale Michael *industrial engineer, academic administrator*
Lee, George C. *civil engineer, university administrator*
Meredith, Dale Dean *civil engineering educator*
Metzger, Ernest Hugh *aerospace engineer, scientist*
Reismann, Herbert *engineer, educator*
Ruckenstein, Eli *chemical engineering educator*
Sarjeant, Walter James *electrical and computer engineering educator*
Shaw, David Tai-Ko *electrical and computer engineering educator, university administrator*
Weber, Thomas William *chemical engineering educator*
Weller, Sol William *chemical engineering educator*
Wozniak, Richard Anthony *computer engineer*

Canandaigua
Innes, David George *environmental and safety engineer*

Carmel
Bardell, Paul Harold, Jr. *electrical engineer*

Chappaqua
O'Neill, Robert Charles *inventor, consultant*
Pomerene, James Herbert *retired computer engineer*

Clifton Park
Panek, Jan *electrical power engineer, consultant*

Clinton
Pagani, Albert Louis *aerospace system engineer*

Cold Spring
Pugh, Emerson William *electrical engineer*

Corning
Ackerman, Roger G. *ceramic engineer*
Havewala, Noshir Behram *chemical engineer*

Corona
Miele, Joel Arthur, Sr. *civil engineer*

Cortland
†Hurwitz, Mark Francis *filtration company executive, research engineer*

Deer Park
Taub, Jesse J. *electrical engineering researcher*

Delmar
†Campas, Anna Penelope *civil engineer, architect*
Shen, Thomas To *environmental engineer*

East Amherst
Soong, Tsu-Teh *engineering science educator*

East Norwich
Rosen, Meyer Robert *chemical engineer*

East Syracuse
Wiley, Richard Gordon *electrical engineer*

Endicott
Schwartz, Richard Frederick *electrical engineering educator*

Fairport
Oldshue, James Y. *chemical engineering consultant*

Farmingdale
Bolle, Donald Martin *retired engineering educator*
Bongiorno, Joseph John, Jr. *electrical engineering educator*
Klosner, Jerome Martin *mechanical engineer, educator*
LaTourrette, James Thomas *retired electrical engineering and computer science educator*
Youla, Dante C. *electric engineer*

Fayetteville
Dosanjh, Darshan S(ingh) *aeronautical engineer, educator*

Flushing
Milone, James Michael *occupational health-safety forensic engineering technology executive, evironmental engineer*
Stahl, Frank Ludwig *civil engineer*

Garden City
Fleisig, Ross *aeronautical engineer, engineering manager*

Glen Cove
Conti, James Joseph *chemical engineer, educator*
Makris, Constantine John *infosystems engineer*

Glenham
Douglas, Fred Robert *cost engineering consultant*

Glens Falls
Fawcett, Christopher Babcock *civil engineer, construction and water resources company executive*

Glenville
Anderson, Roy Everett *electrical engineering consultant*

Great Neck
Shaffer, Bernard William *mechanical and aerospace engineering educator*

Greenlawn
Bachman, Henry Lee *electrical engineer, engineering executive*
Newman, Edward Morris *engineering executive*

Harrison
Schulz, Helmut Wilhelm *chemical engineer, environmental executive*

Hauppauge
de Lanerolle, Nimal Gerard *process engineer*

Hawthorne
Bisdikian, Chatschik *electrical engineer*
Colmenares, Narses Jose *electrical engineer*

Hempstead
Goldstein, Stanley Philip *engineering educator*
Maier, Henry B. *environmental engineer*

Holbrook
Jugueta, Eduardo Malubay *mechanical engineer*

Holtsville
Musteric, Peter *engineering director*

Huntington
Christiansen, Donald David *electrical engineer, editor, publishing consultant*

Huntington Station
Agosta, Vito *mechanical and aerospace engineering educator*
Lanzano, Ralph Eugene *civil engineer*
Richardson, Charles Marsh *electrical engineer, educator*

Ithaca
Berger, Toby *electrical engineer*
Boedo, Stephen *mechanical engineer, consultant*
Carlin, Herbert J. *electrical engineering educator, researcher*
Dalman, Gisli Conrad *electrical engineering educator*
De Boer, Pieter Cornelis Tobias *mechanical and aerospace engineering educator*
Dick, Richard Irwin *environmental engineer, educator*
Eastman, Lester Fuess *electrical engineer, educator*
Greenberg, Donald P. *engineering educator*
Leibovich, Sidney *engineering educator*
Loucks, Daniel Peter *environmental systems engineer*
Lynn, Walter Royal *civil engineering educator, university administrator*
Maxwell, William Laughlin *retired industrial engineering educator*
McGuire, William *civil engineer, educator*
McIsaac, Paul Rowley *electrical engineer, educator*
Meyburg, Arnim Hans *transportation engineer, educator, consultant*
Moon, Francis C. *mechanical engineer*
Moore, Franklin Kingston *mechanical engineer, educator*
Nation, John Arthur *electrical engineering educator, researcher*
O'Rourke, Thomas Denis *civil engineer, educator*
Phelan, Richard Magruder *mechanical engineer*
Rodriguez, Ferdinand *chemical engineer, educator*
Shuler, Michael Louis *biochemical engineering educator, consultant*
Sudan, Ravindra Nath *electrical engineer, physicist, educator*
Tang, Chung Liang *engineering educator*
Wang, Kuo-King *manufacturing engineer, educator*

Jamestown
Leising, David Michael *industrial engineer*

Jericho
Casem, Conrado Sibayan *civil, structural engineer*
Shinners, Stanley Marvin *electrical engineer*

Katonah
Bashkow, Theodore Robert *electrical engineering consultant, former educator*

Latham
Lvovsky, Yuri *physicist, applied superconductivity engineer*

Little Falls
Bunk, George Mark *civil engineer, consultant*

Lockport
Shah, Ramesh Keshavlal *researcher, engineering educator*

Locust Valley
Schaffner, Charles Etzel *consulting engineering executive*

Long Island City
Theodoru, Stefan Gheorghe *civil engineer, writer*

Manlius
Jefferies, Michael John *retired electrical engineer*

Massapequa Park
Plotkin, Martin *retired electrical engineer*

Melville
Bilenas, Jonas *mechanical engineer, educator*
Chan, Jack-Kang *undersea warfare engineer, mathematician*

Middle Island
Crowder, Lillie Mae Brown *retired architectural engineer*

Mineola
Lizardos, Evans John *mechanical engineer*
Newman, Malcolm *mechanical and civil engineering consultant*

Montrose
Reber, Raymond Andrew *retired chemical engineer*

New Hartford
Gupta, Subhash Chandra *metallurgical engineer*

New Hyde Park
Hyman, Abraham *electrical engineer*

New York
Acrivos, Andreas *chemical engineering educator*
Aghassi, William J. *mechanical engineer, consultant*
Ahmad, Jameel *civil engineer, researcher, educator*
Baum, Richard Theodore *engineering executive*
Binger, Wilson Valentine *civil engineer*
Boley, Bruno Adrian *engineering educator*
Bove, John Louis *chemistry and environmental engineering educator, researcher*
Brazinsky, Irv(ing) *chemical engineering educator*
Cantilli, Edmund Joseph *safety engineering educator, writer*
Chang, Jenghwa *biomedical and electrical engineer, medical physicist*
Cheh, Huk Yuk *engineering educator, electrochemist*
Chen, Tak-Ming *civil engineer*
Cowin, Stephen Corteen *biomedical engineering educator, consultant*
Daniel, Charles Timothy *transportation engineer, consultant*
Darsin, Jose A. *transportation engineer*
DiMaggio, Frank Louis *civil engineering educator*
†Fields, Lennon *engineer*
Fogel, Irving Martin *consulting engineer*
†Footen, John Anthony *video engineer*
Frost, Daniel Allen *financial engineer*
Glover, Norman James *engineering executive*
Gordon, Frederick *marine engineer*
Greenfield, Seymour Stephen *mechanical engineer*
Happel, John *chemical engineer, researcher*
Haratunian, Michael *engineering company executive*
Harris, Colin Cyril *mineral engineer, educator*
Hennessy, John Francis, III *engineering executive, mechanical engineer*
Jaffe, William J(ulian) *industrial engineer, educator*
Kim, Se Jung *civil engineer*
Klein, Morton *industrial engineer, educator*
Knobler, Alfred Everett *ceramic engineer, manufacturing company executive, publisher*
Lai, W(ai) Michael *mechanical engineer, educator*
Landau, Ralph *chemical engineer*
Lee, Sidney Phillip *chemical engineer, state senator*
Lenton, Roberto Leonardo *research facility and environmental administrator*
Manassah, Jamal Tewfek *electrical engineering and physics educator, management consultant*
Michel, Henry Ludwig *civil engineer*
Morfopoulos, V. *metallurgical engineer, materials engineer*
Mow, Van C. *engineering educator, researcher*
Paaswell, Robert Emil *civil engineer, educator*
Robertson, Leslie Earl *structural engineer*
Ross, Donald Edward *engineering company executive*
Sadegh, Ali M. *mechanical engineering educator, researcher, consultant*
Schoenfeld, Robert Louis *biomedical engineer*
Schwartz, Mischa *electrical engineering educator*
Schwarz, Ralph Jacques *engineering educator*
See, Saw-Teen *structural engineer*
†Siah, Armajani *civil engineer*
Simkhovich, Semen Lasarevich *cryogenic engineer, researcher, educator*
Smith, Gordon H. *civil engineer*
Sobel, Kenneth Mark *electrical engineer, educator*
Soejima, Daisuke *international trade engineer, economist*
Subak-Sharpe, Gerald Emil *electrical engineer, educator*
Themelis, Nickolas John *metallurgical and chemical engineering educator*
Thornton, Charles H. *engineering executive*
Tsividis, Yannis P. *electrical engineering educator*
Vergilis, Joseph Semyon *mechanical engineering educator*
Vogelman, Joseph Herbert *scientific engineering company executive*
†Wakeman, Thomas Herbert, III *civil engineer, regional administrator*
Watkins, Charles Booker, Jr. *mechanical engineering educator*
Weinbaum, Sheldon *biomedical engineer*
Weinstein, Herbert *chemical engineer, educator*
Wetterau, James Bernard *electrical engineer*
Yao, David Da-Wei *engineering educator*
Yegulalp, Tuncel M. *mining engineer, educator*
Zakkay, Victor *aeronautical engineering educator, scientist*
Zuck, Alfred Christian *consulting mechanical engineer*

Niagara Falls
Dojka, Edwin Sigmund *civil engineer*

Niskayuna
Huening, Walter Carl, Jr. *retired consulting application engineer*

Johnson, Ingolf Birger *retired electrical engineer*
Omidvar, Bijan *structural engineer, researcher*

North Babylon
Tipirneni, Tirumala Rao *metallurgical engineer*

Northport
Litchford, George B. *aeronautical engineer*
Weber, Ray Everett *engineering executive, consultant*

Old Westbury
Nelson, Edward Alan *electrical engineering educator*

Orangeburg
Ye, Biqing *biomedical engineer, researcher*

Owego
Smoral, Vincent J. *electrical engineer*

Pittsford
Marshall, Joseph Frank *electronic engineer*

Plainview
Rothenberg, Richard Lee *audio engineering executive*

Plattsburgh
Treacy, William Joseph *electrical and environmental engineer*

Pleasantville
Urban, Joseph Jaroslav *engineer, consultant*

Port Washington
Gaddis, M. Francis *mechanical and marine engineer, environmental scientist*

Potsdam
Busnaina, Ahmed Ali *mechanical engineering educator*
Chin, Der-Tau *chemical engineer, educator*
Mochel, Myron George *mechanical engineer, educator*
Pillay, Pragasen *engineering educator*
Sathyamoorthy, Muthukrishnan *engineering researcher, educator*

Poughkeepsie
Chu, Richard Chao-Fan *mechanical engineer*
De Cusatis, Casimer Maurice *fiber optics engineer*
Logue, Joseph Carl *electronics engineer, consultant*

Rochester
Bouyoucos, John Vinton *research and development company executive*
Carstensen, Edwin Lorenz *biomedical engineer, biophysicist*
Gans, Roger Frederick *mechanical engineering educator*
Holzbach, James Francis *civil engineer*
Joos, Felipe Miguel *mechanical engineer*
Kinnen, Edwin *electrical engineer, educator*
Lessen, Martin *engineering educator, consulting engineer*
Loewen, Erwin G. *precision engineer, educator, consultant*
Palmer, Harvey John *chemical engineering educator, consultant*
Parker, Kevin James *electrical engineer educator*
Sackett, David Harrison *electrical engineer*
Schmidhammer, Robert Howard *environmental executive, engineering consultant*

Rockville Centre
†Cronacher, Warren William *consulting engineer*

Rome
Coppola, Anthony *electrical engineer*

Rye
Lehman, Lawrence Herbert *consulting engineering executive*

Rye Brook
Landegger, George F. *engineering executive*

Scarsdale
Borg, Robert Frederic *civil engineer*
Florman, Samuel Charles *civil engineer*

Schenectady
Barthold, Lionel Olav *engineering executive*
Bucinell, Ronald Blaise *mechanical engineer, educator*
De Mello, F. Paul *electrical engineer*
Kliman, Gerald Burt *electrical engineer*
Matta, Ram Kumar *aeronautical engineer*
Ringlee, Robert James *consulting engineering executive*
Walsh, George William *engineering executive*
Wolfe, Frederick Andrew *engineering educator*

Setauket
Irving, A. Marshall *marine engineer*
Levine, Sumner Norton *industrial engineer, educator, editor, author, financial consultant*

Slingerlands
Wilcock, Donald Frederick *mechanical engineer*

Staten Island
Garzi, John Joseph *maintenance engineer*
Johansen, Robert John *electrical engineer*
Singer, Edward Nathan *radio engineer, consultant*

Stony Brook
Cope, Randolph Howard, Jr. *electronic research and development executive, educator*
Zemanian, Armen Humpartsoum *electrical engineer, mathematician*

Syracuse
Cheng, David Keun *engineering educator*
Drucker, Alan Steven *mechanical engineer*
Hamlett, James Gordon *electronics engineer, management consultant, educator*
Konski, James Louis *civil engineer*
Sargent, Robert George *engineering educator*

Tarrytown
Anderson, John Erling *chemical engineer*
Bacaloglu, Radu *chemical engineer*
Farrell, Gregory Alan *biomedical engineer*

Tonawanda
Drozdziel, Marion John *aeronautical engineer*

Troy
Abetti, Pier Antonio *consulting electrical engineer, technology management and entrepreneurship educator*
Belfort, Georges *chemical engineering educator, consultant*
Bergles, Arthur Edward *mechanical engineering educator*
Block, Robert Charles *nuclear engineering and engineering physics educator*
Brunelle, Eugene John, Jr. *mechanical engineering educator*
Desrochers, Alan Alfred *electrical engineer*
Duquette, David Joseph *materials science and engineering educator*
Dvorak, George J. *mechanics and materials engineering educator*
Fish, Jacob *civil engineer, educator*
Gerhardt, Lester A. *engineering educator, dean*
Gill, William Nelson *chemical engineering educator*
Glicksman, Martin Eden *materials engineering educator*
Gutmann, Ronald J. *electrical engineering educator*
Hirsa, Amir H. *aerospace engineer, educator*
Hsu, Cheng *decision sciences and engineering systems educator*
Jordan, Mark Henry *consulting civil engineer*
Krempl, Erhard *mechanics educator, consultant*
Lahey, Richard Thomas, Jr. *nuclear engineer, fluid mechanics engineer*
Lemnios, Andrew Zachery *aerospace engineer, educator, researcher*
Littman, Howard *chemical engineer, educator*
McDonald, John Francis Patrick *electrical engineering educator*
Nelson, John Keith *electrical engineer*
Oppenheim, Sheldon Frederick *chemical engineer*
Sanderson, Arthur Clark *engineering educator*
Saridis, George Nicholas *electrical, computers and system engineering educator, robotics and automation researcher*
Shuey, Richard Lyman *engineering educator, consultant*
Stoloff, Norman Stanley *materials engineering educator, researcher*
Woods, John William *electrical, computer and systems engineering educator, consultant*
Zimmie, Thomas Frank *civil engineer, educator*

Upton
Fthenakis, Vasilis *chemical engineer, consultant, educator*
Qian, Shinan *optical engineer, researcher, educator*
Radeka, Veljko *electronics engineer*
Steinberg, Meyer *chemical engineer*
Susskind, Herbert *biomedical engineer, educator*

Valhalla
Paik, John Kee *structural engineer*

Washingtonville
Guarino, Louis Joseph *mechanical engineer, consultant*

West Kill
Dwon, Larry *retired electrical engineer, educator, consultant*

West Nyack
Hornik, Joseph William *civil engineer*

West Point
Shoop, Barry LeRoy *electrical engineer, educator*

White Plains
Busch, Paul L. *engineering executive*
Foster, John Horace *consulting environmental engineer*
Mitchell, Robert Dale *consulting engineer*
Westerhoff, Garret Peter *environmental engineer, executive*

Woodstock
Smith, Albert Aloysius, Jr. *electrical engineer, consultant*

Yorktown Heights
Dennard, Robert Heath *engineering executive, scientist*
Dill, Frederick Hayes *electrical engineer*
Hong, Se June *computer engineer*
Lavenberg, Stephen S. *electrical engineer, researcher*
Romankiw, Lubomyr Taras *materials engineer*
Terman, Lewis Madison *electrical engineer, researcher*
Troutman, Ronald R. *electrical engineer*
Wajda, Tadeusz *engineer*

NORTH CAROLINA

Asheville
Born, Robert Heywood *consulting civil engineer*
Lowery, Douglas Lane *retired environmental engineer*

Bunn
Boblett, Mark Anthony *civil engineering technician*

Burlington
Patterson, Robert Campbell, Jr. *civil engineer*

Canton
Hooper, Carl Glenn *civil engineer, software author, contractor*

Cary
Conrad, Hans *materials engineering educator*
Khan, Masrur Ali *nuclear and chemical engineer, physicist*
Miranda, Constancio Fernandes *civil engineering educator*
Vick, Columbus Edwin, Jr. *civil engineering design firm executive*

Chapel Hill
Coulter, Norman Arthur, Jr. *biomedical engineering educator emeritus*
Huang, Herman Fu *transportation researcher*
Kuhn, Matthew *engineering company executive*
Lucas, Carol Lee *biomedical engineer*
Okun, Daniel Alexander *environmental engineering educator*
Singer, Philip Charles *environmental engineer, educator*
Stidham, Shaler, Jr. *operations research educator*

Charlotte
Keanini, Russell Guy *mechanical engineering educator, researcher*
King, L. Ellis *civil engineer, educator, consultant*
Phibbs, Garnett Ersiel *engineer, educator, minister, religious organization administrator*
Toth, James Joseph *power systems engineer*

Conover
Kundu, Debabrata *mechanical engineer*

Durham
Bejan, Adrian *mechanical engineering educator*
Casey, H(orace) Craig, Jr. *electrical engineering educator*
Fisher, Charles Page, Jr. *consulting geotechnical engineer*
Garg, Devendra Prakash *mechanical engineer, educator*
Harman, Charles Morgan *mechanical engineer*
Hochmuth, Robert Milo *mechanical and biomedical engineer, educator*
McKinney, Ross Erwin *civil engineering educator*
Petroski, Henry *engineer educator*
Plonsey, Robert *electrical and biomedical engineer*
Strohbehn, John Walter *engineering science educator*
Utku, Senol *civil engineer, computer science educator*
Vatavuk, William Michael *chemical engineer, author*
†Wilson, Blake Shaw *electrical engineer, researcher*

Granite Falls
Humphreys, Kenneth King *engineer, educator, association executive*

Greensboro
Adewuyi, Yusuf Gbadebo *chemical engineering educator, researcher, consult*
Bailey, William Nathan *systems engineer*
Elliott, Benny Lee, Jr. *mechanical engineer*
Shivakumar, Kunigal Nanjundaiah *aerospace engineer*

Hendersonville
Schooley, Charles Earl *electrical engineer, consultant*

High Point
Huston, Fred John *retired automotive engineer*

Huntersville
†Church, John W. *quality engineer*

Morrisville
Cofer, John Isaac, IV *mechanical engineer*

Mount Airy
Ratliff, Robert Barns, Jr. *mechanical engineer*

Murphy
Kerr, Walter Belnap *retired missile instrumentation engineer, English language researcher, consultant*

New Bern
Baughman, Fred Hubbard *aeronautical engineer, former naval officer*
Love, Darryl Lewis *quality engineer*
Moeller, Dade William *environmental engineer, educator*
Whitehurst, Brooks Morris *chemical engineer*

Newport
Williams, Winton Hugh *civil engineer*

Raleigh
Baliga, Bantval Jayant *electrical engineering educator, research administrator*
Beatty, Kenneth Orion, Jr. *chemical engineer*
Bitzer, Donald Lester *electrical engineering educator, retired research laboratory administrator*
Church, Kern Everidge *engineer, consultant*
DeJarnette, Fred Roark *aerospace engineer*
Dudziak, Donald John *nuclear engineer, educator*
Foley, Gary J. *research chemical engineer, computer scientist, federal agency administrator*
Gardner, Robin Pierce *engineering educator*
Hanson, John M. *civil engineering and construction educator*
Hauser, John Reid *electrical engineering educator*
Havner, Kerry Shuford *civil engineering and solid mechanics educator*
Hinton, David Owen *retired electrical engineer*
Holton, William Coffeen *electrical engineering executive*
Keshk, Mamdouh M. (Mike Keshk) *design engineer*
Kriz, George James *agricultural research administrator, educator*
Meier, Wilbur Leroy, Jr. *industrial engineer, educator, former university chancellor*
Skaggs, Richard Wayne *agricultural engineering educator*
Sneed, Ronald Ernest *engineering educator emeritus*
Stannett, Vivian Thomas *chemical engineering educator*
Taylor, Kaaryn Wilaine *civil engineer*
Turinsky, Paul Josef *nuclear engineer, educator*
Williams, Hugh Alexander, Jr. *retired mechanical engineer, consultant*

Swannanoa
Stuck, Roger Dean *electrical engineering educator*

Washington
Hackney, James Acra, III *industrial engineer, consultant, retired manufacturing company executive*

Winston Salem
Henderson, Richard Martin *retired chemical engineer*

NORTH DAKOTA

Bismarck
Carmichael, Virgil Wesly *mining, civil and geological engineer, former coal company executive*

Fargo
Li, Kam Wu *mechanical engineer, educator*
Rogers, David Anthony *electrical engineer, educator, researcher*
Varma, Amiy *civil engineer, educator*

Grand Forks
Schmitz, Daniel Dean *mechanical engineer*

OHIO

Akron
Brown, David Rupert *engineering executive*
Isayev, Avraam Isayevich *polymer engineer, educator*
Mettler, Gerald Phillip *reliability engineer*
Miller, Irving Franklin *chemical engineering educator, biomedical engineering educator, academic administrator*
Salkind, Michael Jay *technology administrator*
Sancaktar, Erol *engineering educator*
Symens, Ronald Edwin *electrical engineer, consultant*

Athens
Dinos, Nicholas *engineering educator, administrator*
Robe, Thurlow Richard *engineering educator, university dean*

Aurora
Kirchner, James William *retired electrical engineer*
Rocco, James Robert *civil engineer*

Barberton
Kitto, John Buck, Jr. *mechanical engineer*
Zbacnik, Raymond Eric *process engineer*

Batavia
Bower, Kenneth Francis *electrical engineer*
McDonough, James Francis *civil engineer, educator*

Brookpark
Wilson, Jack *aeronautical engineer*

Brunswick
Rohlik, Harold Edward *engineer*

Canton
Ceroke, Clarence John *engineer, consultant*
Hoecker, David *engineering executive*
Pedoto, Gerald Joseph *supplier quality analyst*

Chandlersville
Herron, Janet Irene *industrial manufacturing engineer*

Cincinnati
Adams, Donald Scott *engineer, pharmacist*
Agrawal, Dharma Prakash *engineering educator*
Bahr, Donald Walter *chemical engineer*
Bahrani, Al Sattar *mechanical engineer*
Bostian, Harry Edward *chemical engineer*
Gardner, Leonard Burton, II *retired industrial automation engineer*
†Garg, Prem K. *civil engineer*
Greenberg, David Bernard *chemical engineering educator*
Hodge, Bobby Lynn *mechanical engineer, manufacturing executive*
Johnson, K(enneth) O(dell) *aerospace engineer*
Kowel, Stephen Thomas *electrical engineer, educator*
Martin, John Bruce *chemical engineer*
Mital, Anil *engineering educator*
Pancheri, Eugene Joseph *chemical engineer*
Ratliff, Thomas Asbury, Jr. *retired engineer*
Rubin, Stanley Gerald *aerospace engineering educator*
Schrantz, Donald Lee *mechanical engineer*
Simitses, George John *engineering educator, consultant*
Smith, Leroy Harrington, Jr. *mechanical engineer, aerodynamics consultant*
Toftner, Richard Orville *engineering executive*
Weisman, Joel *nuclear engineering educator, engineering consultant*

Cleveland
Angus, John Cotton *chemical engineering educator*
Baer, Eric *engineering and science educator*
Bahniuk, Eugene *mechanical engineering educator*
Bluford, Guion Stewart, Jr. *engineering company executive*
Brosilow, Coleman Bernard *chemical engineering educator*
Burghart, James Henry *electrical engineer, educator*
Coulman, George Albert *chemical engineer, educator*
DellaCorte, Christopher *engineer, tribologist*
Fernandez, René *aerospace engineer*
Fritz, Dwain Eldon *engineer*
Goldstein, Marvin Emanuel *aerospace scientist, research center administrator*
Harkins, Richard Wesley *marine engineer, naval architect*
Heuer, Arthur Harold *ceramics engineer, educator*
Ko, Wen-Hsiung *electrical engineering educator*
Lee, Jinho *research engineer, consultant*
†Lee, Kenneth Young *application engineer*
Liu, Chung-Chiun *chemical engineering educator*
Madden, James Desmond *forensic engineer*
McWhorter, John Francis *manufacturing engineer*
Mofflin, Lionel Hugh (Harry Mofflin) *biomedical engineer, physician*
Nguyen, Pram *engineer, consultant*
Reshotko, Eli *aerospace engineer, educator*
Rudy, Yoram *biomedical engineer, biophysicist, educator*
Saada, Adel Selim *civil engineer, educator*
Savinell, Robert Francis *engineering educator*
Siegel, Robert *heat transfer engineer*
Wagner, James Warren *engineering educator*
Wessel, Dennis James *mechanical engineering administrator*

Columbus
Alexander, Carl Albert *ceramic engineer, educator*

Altan, Taylan *engineering educator, mechanical engineer, consultant*
Arps, David Foster *electronics engineer*
Bailey, Cecil Dewitt *aerospace engineer, educator*
Bechtel, Stephen E. *mechanical engineer, educator*
Bedford, Keith Wilson *civil engineer, atmospheric science educator*
Bhushan, Bharat *mechanical engineer*
Boulger, Francis William *metallurgical engineer*
Brodkey, Robert Stanley *chemical engineering educator*
Chovan, John David *biomedical engineer*
Cruz, Jose Bejar, Jr. *engineering educator*
Duckworth, Winston Howard *retired ceramic engineer*
Ensminger, Dale *mechanical engineer, electrical engineer*
Fenton, Robert Earl *electrical engineering educator*
Grant, Michael Peter *electrical engineer*
Hadipriono, Fabian Christy *engineering educator, researcher*
Harris, Ronald David *chemical engineer*
Horowitz, Stanley H. *electrical engineer*
Houser, Donald Russell *mechanical engineering educator, consultant*
Jacox, John William *mechanical engineer and consulting company executive*
Kouyoumjian, Robert G. *electrical engineering educator*
Ksienski, Aharon Arthur *electrical engineer*
Leissa, Arthur William *mechanical engineering educator*
Liu, Ming-Tsan *computer engineering educator*
Miller, Don Wilson *nuclear engineering educator*
Moulton, Edward Quentin *civil engineer, educator*
Ozkan, Umit Sivrioglu *chemical engineering educator*
†Patel, Vipinchandra Natwarlal *computer engineer*
Peters, Leon, Jr. *electrical engineering educator, research administrator*
Rapp, Robert Anthony *metallurgical engineering educator, consultant*
Redmond, Robert Francis *nuclear engineering educator*
Rubin, Alan J. *environmental engineer, chemist*
Sahai, Yogeshwar *engineering educator*
St. Pierre, George Roland, Jr. *materials science and engineering administrator, educator*
Singh, Rajendra *mechanical engineering educator*
Smith, George Leonard *industrial engineering educator*
Smith, Marion Leroy *college dean emeritus, mechanical engineer*
Smith, Philip John *industrial and systems engineering educator*
Taiganides, E. Paul *agricultural and environmental engineer, consultant*
Turchi, Peter John *aerospace and electrical engineer, educator*
Uotila, Urho Antti Kalevi *geodesist, educator*
Wagoner, Robert Hall *engineering educator, researcher*
Waldron, Kenneth John *mechanical engineering educator, researcher*
Ware, Brendan John *retired electrical engineer and utility executive*
Whitlatch, Elbert Earl, Jr. *engineering educator*
Zakin, Jacques Louis *chemical engineering educator*
Zande, Richard Dominic *civil engineering firm executive*

Continental
Dranchak, Lawrence John *retired mechanical engineer*

Dayton
Cowden, Roger Hugh, II *systems engineer*
Houpis, Constantine Harry *electrical engineering educator*
†Koubek, Richard John *engineering educator*
Lamont, Gary Byron *electrical engineer*
Pajak, Michael E. *mechanical engineer*
Phillips, Chandler Allen *biomedical engineer*
Repperger, Daniel William *electrical engineer*
Schmitt, George Frederick, Jr. *materials engineer*
Shaw, George Bernard *consulting engineer, educator*

Delaware
Kraus, John D. *electrical engineer, educator*

Delphos
Staup, John Gary *safety engineer*

Dublin
Major, Coleman Joseph *chemical engineer*

Eastlake
Spohn, Wayne Robert *mechanical engineer*

Elyria
Dunaevsky, Valery *mechanical engineer, researcher*

Fairborn
Conklin, Robert Eugene *electronics engineer*

Gates Mills
Enyedy, Gustav, Jr. *chemical engineer*
Pace, Stanley Carter *retired aeronautical engineer*

Logan
Carmean, Jerry Richard *broadcast engineer*

Lyndhurst
Sevin, Eugene *engineer, consultant, educator*

Maineville
Laybourne, George Thomas *scientist, quality control engineer, consultant*

Mansfield
Stander, Richard Ramsay, Sr. *retired civil engineer and construction engineer*

Marblehead
Haering, Edwin Raymond *chemical engineering educator, consultant*

Marion
Tozzer, Jack Carl *civil engineer, surveyor*

Marysville
Baik-Kromalic, Sue S. *metallurgical engineer*

Miamisburg
Peterson, George P. *mechanical engineer, research and development firm executive*

Middletown
Gilby, Steve *metallurgical engineering researcher*
Newby, John Robert *metallurgical engineer*

Newark
Green, John David *engineering executive*

North Olmsted
Lundin, Bruce Theodore *engineering and management consultant*

Oxford
Ward, Roscoe Fredrick *engineering educator*

Painesville
Jayne, Theodore Douglas *technical research and development company executive*

Perrysburg
Khan, Amir U. *agricultural engineering consultant*
Lieder, W. Donald *chemical engineer*

Powell
Schwab, Glenn Orville *retired agricultural engineering educator, consultant*

Rocky River
Masters, Albert Townsend *mechanical engineer*
Schoun, Mila *mechanical engineer*

Rossford
Salmon, Stuart Clive *manufacturing engineer*

Shauck
Garvick, Kenneth Ryan *broadcast engineer, announcer, educator*

Shelby
Moore, Florian Howard *electronics engineer*

South Lebanon
Campbell, David Rogers *engineer*

Springboro
Saxer, Richard Karl *metallurgical engineer, retired air force officer*

Toledo
Benham, Linda Sue *civil engineer*
Brown, James Edward *safety engineer*
Dukkipati, Rao Venkateswara *engineering educator, researcher, scientist*
Nycz, Joseph Donald *engineer*
Oh, Keytack Henry *industrial engineering educator*
Wolfe, Robert Kenneth *engineering educator*
Wolff, Edwin Ray *retired construction engineer, consultant*

Trotwood
Caldwell, Ronald DeWitt, Sr. *industrial engineer, consultant*

Wadsworth
Brumbaugh, John A., Jr. *electrical engineer*

Westlake
Huff, Ronald Garland *mechanical engineer*

Wickliffe
Anthony, Donald Barrett *engineering executive*

Willoughby
Hassell, Peter Albert *electrical and metallurgical engineer*

Worthington
Compton, Ralph Theodore, Jr. *electrical engineering educator*
Giannamore, David Michael *electronics engineer*

Wright Patterson AFB
Agnes, Gregory Stephen *engineering educator, military officer*
D'Azzo, John Joachim *electrical engineer, educator*
Haritos, George Konstantinos *engineer, educator, military officer*
Mitchell, Philip Michael *aerospace engineer, consultant, educator*

Yellow Springs
Trolander, Hardy Wilcox *engineering executive, consultant*

Youngstown
Fok, Thomas Dso Yun *civil engineer*
Lacivita, Michael John *safety engineer*
Mossman, Robert Gillis, IV *civil and environmental engineer*
Stahl, Joel Sol *plastic and chemical engineer*

OKLAHOMA

Bartlesville
Johnson, Marvin Merrill *chemical engineer, chemist*
Lai, Young-Jou *industrial engineer*
Mihm, John Clifford *chemical engineer*

Collinsville
Councilman, Richard Robert *product development engineer*

Cushing
Kyker, James Charles *engineering executive, computer programmer*

Midwest City
Smith, Wayne Calvin *chemical engineer*

Norman
Bert, Charles Wesley *mechanical and aerospace engineer, educator*
Campbell, John Morgan *retired chemical engineer*

Crane, Robert Kendall *engineering educator, researcher, consultant*
Denison, Gilbert Walter *chemical engineer, administrator*
Mallinson, Richard Gregory *chemical engineering educator*
Muraleetharan, Kanthasamy Kadirgamar *civil engineering educator*
O'Rear, Edgar Allen, III *chemical engineering educator*
Zaman, Musharraf *civil engineering educator*
Zelby, Leon Wolf *electrical engineering educator, consulting engineer*

Oklahoma City
Hofener, Steven David *civil engineer*
Lovelace, George David, Jr. *quality engineer*
Mikkelson, Dean Harold *geological engineer*
Miller, Herbert Dell *petroleum engineer*
Paden, Larry J. *electronics engineer, lawyer*
Thompson, Guy Thomas *safety engineer*
Wickens, Donald Lee *engineer executive, consultant, rancher*

Stillwater
Barfield, Billy Joe *agricultural engineer, educator*
Brusewitz, Gerald Henry *agricultural engineering educator, researcher*
Case, Kenneth Eugene *industrial engineering educator*
Hoberock, Lawrence Linden *mechanical engineer, educator*
Hughes, Michael *civil engineer*
Mize, Joe Henry *industrial engineer, educator*
Noyes, Ronald Tacie *agricultural engineering educator*
Thompson, David Russell *engineering educator, academic dean*

Tulsa
Blanton, Roger Edmund *mechanical engineer*
Blenkarn, Kenneth Ardley *mechanical engineer, consultant*
Brill, James P. *petroleum engineer, educator*
Cobbs, James Harold *engineer, consultant*
Earlougher, Robert Charles, Sr. *petroleum engineer*
Parker, Robert Lee, Sr. *petroleum engineer, drilling company executive*
Prayson, Alex Stephen *drafting and mechanical design educator*
Williams, David Rogerson, Jr. *engineer, business executive*
Williams, John Horter *civil engineer, oil, gas, telecommunications and allied products distribution company executive*

Weatherford
Schwartz, John Charles *chemical engineer*

Yale
Berger, Billie David *corrosion engineer*

Yukon
Morgan, Robert Steve *mechanical engineer*

OREGON

Ashland
Berkman, James L. *bicycle builder, publisher*

Beaverton
Chartier, Vernon Lee *electrical engineer*

Brookings
Nolan, Benjamin Burke *retired civil engineer*

Corvallis
Engelbrecht, Rudolf *electrical engineering educator*
Hansen, Hugh Justin *agricultural engineer*
Knudsen, James George *chemical engineer, educator*
Miner, John Ronald *bioresource engineer*
Mohler, Ronald Rutt *electrical engineering educator*
Rapier, Pascal Moran *chemical engineer, physicist*
Temes, Gabor Charles *electrical engineering educator*

Eugene
Martin, John Stewart *software engineer*
Richards, James William *electromechanical engineer*

Florence
Ericksen, Jerald Laverne *educator, engineering scientist*

Hillsboro
Rotithor, Hemant Govind *electrical engineer*

Junction City
Sharples, Thomas Davy *retired mechanical engineer*

Klamath Falls
Hunsucker, Robert Dudley *physicist, electrical engineer, educator, researcher*

Lake Oswego
Kovtynovich, Dan *civil engineer*

Lincoln City
Gehrig, Edward Harry *electrical engineer, consultant*

Medford
Davenport, Wilbur Bayley, Jr. *electrical engineering educator*
Horton, Lawrence Stanley *electrical engineer, apartment developer*

Myrtle Point
Walsh, Don *marine consultant, executive*

Portland
Becker, Bruce Douglas *mechanical engineer*
Cassidy, Richard Arthur *environmental engineer, governmental water resources specialist*
Daly, Donald F. *engineering company executive*
Dryden, Robert D. *engineering educator*
Forsberg, Charles Alton *computer, information systems engineer*
Grappe, Harold Hugo *civil engineer*
Kennedy, R. Evan *engineering executive, consultant, retired structural engineer*

Khalil, Mohammad Aslam Khan *environmental science and engineering educator, physics educator*
McCoy, Eugene Lynn *civil engineer*
Pham, Kinh Dinh *electrical engineer, educator, administrator*
Yamayee, Zia Ahmad *engineering educator, dean*

Salem
Butts, Edward Perry *civil engineer, environmental consultant*

Sunriver
Clough, Ray William, Jr. *civil engineering educator*

Tigard
Nice, James William *digital field service technician, educator*

Tualatin
Webster, Merlyn Hugh, Jr. *manufacturing engineer, information systems consultant*

Wilsonville
Isberg, Reuben Albert *radio communications engineer*

PENNSYLVANIA

Acme
Randza, Jason Michael *engineer*

Allentown
Dwyer, John James *mechanical engineer*
Gewartowski, James Walter *electrical engineer*
Lesak, David Michael *safety engineer, educator, consultant*
Singhal, Kishore *engineering administrator*

Apollo
Musselman, Larry L. *chemical engineer*

Bethel Park
Korchynsky, Michael *metallurgical engineer*
O'Donnell, William James *engineering executive*

Bethlehem
Anderson, David Martin *environmental health engineer*
Beedle, Lynn Simpson *civil engineering educator*
Chen, John C. *chemical engineering educator*
Durkee, Jackson Leland *civil engineer*
Erdogan, Fazil *mechanical engineer*
Fisher, John William *civil engineering educator*
Georgakis, Christos *chemical engineer educator, consultant, researcher*
Karakash, John J. *engineering educator*
Levy, Edward Kenneth *mechanical engineering educator*
Pense, Alan Wiggins *metallurgical engineer, academic administrator*
Tuzla, Kemal *mechanical engineer, scientist*
Wenzel, Leonard Andrew *engineering educator*

Birdsboro
Mengle, Tobi Dara *mechanical engineer, consultant*

Blue Bell
Cartlidge, Edward Sutterley *mechanical engineer*

Boalsburg
Gettig, Martin Winthrop *retired mechanical engineer*

Bridgeville
Andersen, Theodore Selmer *engineering manager*

Broomall
Emplit, Raymond Henry *electrical engineer*

Bryn Mawr
Mani, Korah Thattunkal *engineer, consultant*

Butler
Kay, George Paul *environmental engineer*
†Simms, Donald Ray *engineer*

Chadds Ford
Isakoff, Sheldon Erwin *chemical engineer*

Cheltenham
Weinstock, Walter Wolfe *systems engineer*

Chester
Kornfield, Nathaniel Richard *computer engineer educator*

Conshohocken
Rippel, Harry Conrad *mechanical engineer, consultant*

Coopersburg
Peserik, James E. *electrical, controls and computer engineer, consultant, forensics and safety engineer, fire cause and origin investigator*
Siess, Alfred Albert, Jr. *engineering executive, management consultant*
Winters, Arthur Ralph, Jr. *chemical and cryogenic engineer, consultant*

Coraopolis
Al-Qudsi, Hassan Shaban *engineer, project manager*
Moretti, Edward Charles *environmental engineer, consultant*

Ebensburg
Ramsdell, Richard Adoniram *marine engineer*

Elizabethtown
Woodward, Vern Harvey *retired engineering sales executive*

Erie
Crankshaw, John Hamilton *mechanical engineer*
Gray, Robert Beckwith *electrical engineer, consultant*

Evans City
Zellers, Robert Charles *materials engineer, consultant, speaker*

Export
Colborn, Harry Walter *electrical engineering consultant*
Hampton, Edward John *engineering company executive*
Wagner, Charles Leonard *electrical engineer, consultant*

Flourtown
Di Maria, Charles Walter *mechanical and automation engineer, consultant*

Fort Washington
Pillai, Raviraj Sukumar *chemical engineer, researcher*
Visek, Albert James *retired computer engineer*

Gibsonia
Shoub, Earle Phelps *engineer, industrial hygienist, educator*

Glen Mills
Churchill, Stuart Winston *chemical engineering educator*

Glenside
Hargens, Charles William, III *electrical engineer, consultant*

Greensburg
Guyker, William Charles, Jr. *electrical engineer, researcher*

Harrisburg
Cate, Donald James *mechanical engineer, consultant*
Dietz, John Raphael *consulting engineer executive*

Havertown
Sheppard, Walter Lee, Jr. *chemical engineer, consultant*

Hellertown
Viest, Ivan M(iroslav) *consulting structural engineer*

Hideout Lake Ariel
Tague, Charles Francis *retired engineering, construction and real estate development company executive*

Horsham
Goff, Kenneth Wade *electrical engineer*

Huntingdon Valley
Bloor, W(illiam) Spencer *electrical engineer, consultant*
West, A(rnold) Sumner *chemical engineer*

Indiana
Soule, Robert D. *safety and health educator, administrator*

Jenkintown
Haythornthwaite, Robert Morphet *civil engineer, educator*
Mifsud, Lewis *electrical engineer, fire origin investigator, physicist*

Johnstown
Kuhn, Howard Arthur *engineering executive, educator*

Kulpsville
Pavlov, Gregory Charles *engineer*

Lancaster
Ebersole, J. Glenn, Jr. *engineering, marketing, management and public relations executive*

Langhorne
Touhill, C. Joseph *environmental engineer*

Lansdowne
Popovics, Sandor *civil engineer, educator, researcher*

Lewisburg
Kim, Jai Bin *civil engineering educator*
Lowe, John Raymond, Jr. *mechanical engineer*
Orbison, James Graham *civil engineer, educator*

Ligonier
Mattern, Gerry A. *engineering consultant*

Madison
Nair, Bala Radhakrishnan *engineer*

Monroeville
Campbell, Donald Acheson *nuclear engineer, consultant*
Jacobi, William Mallett *nuclear engineer, consultant*

Moon Township
Rabosky, Joseph George *engineering consulting company executive*

Murrysville
McWhirter, James Herman *consulting engineering business executive, financial planner*
Schlabach, Leland A. *electrical engineer*

New Alexandria
Ackerman, Robert Lloyd *chemical engineer, environmental tree farmer*

New Brighton
Baldwin, Clarence Jones, Jr. *electrical engineer, manufacturing company executive*

New Cumberland
Scheiner, James Ira *engineering company executive*

New Hope
Bertele, William *environmental engineer*

New Kensington
Jarrett, Noel *chemical engineer*
Pien, Shyh-Jye John *mechanical engineer*

Newtown
Luo, Nianzhu *mechanical engineer*

Newtown Square
Perrone, Nicholas *mechanical engineer, business executive*
Yeh, George Chiayou *engineering company executive*

Philadelphia
Batterman, Steven Charles *engineering mechanics and bioengineering educator, forensic engineering and biomechanics consultant*
Beard, Richard Burnham *engineering educator emeritus, researcher*
Bischoff, Kenneth Bruce *chemical engineer, educator*
†Brader, William R. *engineer, architectural firm executive*
Byer, Harold George *environmental engineer*
Chance, Henry Martyn, II *engineering executive*
Cho, Young Il *mechanical engineering educator*
Cohen, Ira Myron *aeronautical and mechanical engineering educator*
Eisenstein, Bruce Allan *electrical engineering educator*
El-Sherif, Mahmoud A. *electrical engineering educator*
Engheta, Nader *electrical engineering educator, researcher*
Falkie, Thomas Victor *mining engineer, natural resources company executive*
Fegley, Kenneth Allen *systems engineering educator*
Gaither, William Samuel *civil engineering executive, consultant*
Graham, Walter S. *environmental engineer*
Jaron, Dov *biomedical engineer, educator*
Joner, Bruno *aeronautical engineer*
Kritikos, Haralambos N. *electrical engineering educator*
Kuruvilla, Kollanparampil *electrical engineer*
Lawley, Alan *materials engineering educator*
Lewin, Peter Andrew *electrical engineer, educator*
Litt, Mitchell *chemical engineer, educator, bioengineer*
Morlok, Edward Karl *engineering educator, consultant*
Mortimer, Richard Walter *mechanical engineering educator*
Quinn, John Albert *chemical engineering educator*
Rumpf, John Louis *civil engineer, consultant*
Schwan, Herman Paul *electrical engineering and physical science educator, research scientist*
Showers, Ralph Morris *electrical engineer educator*
Siderer, Jack Philip *engineering executive*
Stabenau, Walter Frank *systems engineer*
Sun, Hun H. *electrical engineering and biomedical engineering educator*
Terzian, Karnig Yervant *civil engineer*
Tomiyasu, Kiyo *consulting engineer*
Van der Spiegel, Jan *engineering educator*

Pittsburgh
Anderson, John Leonard *chemical engineering educator*
Archer, David Horace *process engineer, consultant*
Badics, Zsolt *electrical engineer, researcher*
Bergmann, Carl Adolf *chemical engineer, researcher*
Birks, Neil *metallurgical engineering educator, consultant*
Boczkaj, Bohdan Karol *structural engineer*
Casasent, David Paul *electrical engineering educator, data processing executive*
Charap, Stanley Harvey *electrical engineering educator*
Chigier, Norman *mechanical engineering educator*
Conti, Ronald Samuel *electronics engineer, fire prevention engineer*
D'Appolonia, Elio *civil engineer, educator*
Freudenrich, David Robert *civil engineer, traffic engineer*
Gottfried, Byron Stuart *engineering educator*
Griffin, Donald Spray *mechanical engineer, consultant*
Grossmann, Ignacio Emilio *chemical engineering educator*
Harder, Edwin L. *electrical engineer*
Hendrickson, Chris Thompson *civil and environmental engineering educator, researcher*
Hoburg, James Frederick *electrical engineering educator*
Hung, Tin-Kan *engineering educator, researcher*
Jordan, Angel Goni *electrical and computer engineering educator*
Li, Ching-Chung *electrical engineering and computer science educator*
Luthy, Richard Godfrey *environmental engineering educator*
Maly, Wojciech P. *engineering educator, researcher*
McAvoy, Bruce Ronald *engineer, consultant*
Meiksin, Zvi H. *electrical engineering educator*
Milnes, Arthur George *electrical engineer, educator*
Morgan, Daniel Carl *civil engineer*
Murphy, Thomas Michael *civil engineer*
Nathanson, Harvey Charles *electrical engineer*
Neuman, Charles P. *electrical and computer engineering educator*
Peterson, Robert Scott *electrical engineer*
Pettit, Frederick Sidney *metallurgical engineering educator, researcher*
Pohland, Frederick George *environmental engineering educator, researcher*
Raimondi, Albert Anthony *mechanical engineer*
Rohrer, Ronald Alan *electrical and computer engineering educator, consultant*
Russell, Alan James *chemical engineering and biotechnology educator*
Schultz, Jerome Samson *biochemical engineer, educator*
Simaan, Marwan *electrical engineering educator*
Sinclair, Glenn Bruce *mechanical engineering educator, researcher*
Spanovich, Milan *retired civil engineer*
Stahl, Laddie L. *electrical engineer, manufacturing company executive*
Tierney, John William *chemical engineering educator*
Vogeley, Clyde Eicher, Jr. *engineering educator, artist, consultant*
Westerberg, Arthur William *chemical engineering educator*
Woo, Savio Lau-Yuen *bioengineering educator*
Yang, Wen-Ching *chemical engineer*

Reading
Hollander, Herbert I. *consulting engineer*
Moriarty, John Klinge *electronics engineer, consultant*

Somerset
†Minarik, John Paul *engineer, writer*

Springfield
Gordon, Robert Bruce *mechanical engineer*

State College
Barnoff, Robert Mark *civil engineering educator*
Foderaro, Anthony Harolde *nuclear engineering educator*
Maneval, David Richard *mineral engineering consultant*
Olson, Donald Richard *mechanical engineering educator*
Wysk, Richard A. *engineering educator, researcher*

Swarthmore
Krendel, Ezra Simon *systems and human factors engineering consultant*

Tobyhanna
Weinstein, William Steven *technical engineer*

University Park
Aplan, Frank Fulton *metallurgical engineering educator*
Bose, Nirmal Kumar *electrical engineering, mathematics educator*
Brown, John Lawrence, Jr. *electrical engineering educator*
Cross, Leslie Eric *electrical engineering educator*
Davids, Norman *engineering science and mechanics educator, researcher*
Duda, John Larry *chemical engineering educator*
Elliott, Herschel *agricultural engineer, educator*
Feng, Tse-yun *computer engineer, educator*
Geselowitz, David Beryl *bioengineering educator*
Ham, Inyong *industrial engineering educator*
Holl, John William *engineering educator*
Kabel, Robert Lynn *chemical engineering educator*
Knott, Kenneth *engineering educator, consultant*
Kulakowski, Bohdan Tadeusz *mechanical engineering educator*
Lakshminarayana, Budugur *aerospace engineering educator*
Mathews, John David *electrical engineering educator, research director, consultant*
Matthews, Berry *ceramic engineer*
McCormick, Barnes Warnock *aerospace engineering educator*
McDonnell, Archie Joseph *environmental engineer*
McWhirter, John Ruben *chemical engineering educator*
Mentzer, John Raymond *electrical engineer, educator*
Nisbet, John Stirling *electrical engineering educator*
Ramani, Raja Venkat *mining engineering educator*
Ruud, Clayton Olaf *engineering educator*
Scanlon, Andrew *structural engineering educator*
Tavossi, Hasson M. *process engineering educator, consultant*
Thompson, William, Jr. *engineering educator*
Tittmann, Bernhard Rainer *engineering science and mechanics educator*
Vannice, M. Albert *chemical engineering educator, researcher*
Webb, Ralph Lee *mechanical engineering educator*
Witzig, Warren Frank *nuclear engineer, educator*

Villanova
Tomlinson, J. Richard *engineering services company executive*

Wallingford
Parker, Jennifer Ware *chemical engineer, researcher*

Warminster
†Bodkin, Thomas William *architectural engineer*
Tatnall, George Jacob *aeronautical engineer*

Warrington
Moneghan, John Edward *aerospace engineer*

Washington
†Gleason, James Edward, Jr. *mining engineer*

Wayne
Grigg, William Clyde *electrical engineer*

West Chester
Murphy, Stephan David *electrical engineer*
Weston, Roy Francis *environmental consultant*

West Conshohocken
Ceccola, Russ *electrical engineer, writer*
Ivanov, Vladimir Gennadievich *biomedical engineer*

West Mifflin
Ardash, Garin *mechanical engineer*

Wexford
DoVale, Fern Louise *civil engineer*

Wynnewood
Schmaus, Siegfried H. A. *engineering executive, consultant*

York
Horn, Russell Eugene *engineering executive, consultant*
Miller, Donald Kenneth *engineering consultant*
Moore, Walter Calvin *retired chemical engineer*

RHODE ISLAND

Cranston
Fang, Pen Jeng *engineering executive and consultant*
Thielsch, Helmut John *engineering company executive*

East Greenwich
Juechter, John William *retired mechanical engineer, consultant*

Kingston
Polk, Charles *electrical engineer, educator, biophysicist*
Tufts, Donald Winston *electrical engineering educator*

Portsmouth
Becken, Bradford Albert *engineering executive*

Providence
Clifton, Rodney James *engineering educator, civil engineer, consultant*
Freund, Lambert Ben *engineering educator, researcher, consultant*
Glicksman, Maurice *engineering educator, former dean and provost*
Gurland, Joseph *engineering educator*
Hazeltine, Barrett *electrical engineer, educator*
Hurt, Robert Howard *chemical engineering educator*
Needleman, Alan *mechanical engineering educator*
Preparata, Franco Paolo *computer science and engineering educator*
Richman, Marc Herbert *forensic engineer, educator*
Suuberg, Eric Michael *chemical engineering educator*
Symonds, Paul Southworth *mechanical engineering educator, researcher*
Weiner, Jerome Harris *mechanical engineering educator*

Rumford
Findley, William Nichols *mechanical engineering educator*

Wakefield
Boothroyd, Geoffrey *industrial and manufacturing engineering educator*

Warwick
Baffoni, Frank Anthony *biomedical engineer, consultant*

SOUTH CAROLINA

Aiken
Groce, William Henry, III *environmental engineer, consultant*
Hootman, Harry Edward *retired nuclear engineer, consultant*
Johnston, Carolyn Judith *construction engineer*
Murphy, Edward Thomas *engineering executive*
Williamson, Thomas Garnett *nuclear engineering and engineering physics educator*

Beaufort
Pinkerton, Robert Bruce *mechanical engineer*

Charleston
Baron, Seymour *engineering and research executive*

Clemson
Bunn, Joe Millard *retired agricultural engineering educator*
Golan, Lawrence Peter *mechanical engineering educator, energy researcher*
Han, Young Jo *agricultural engineer, educator*
Leonard, Michael Steven *industrial engineering educator*
Pursley, Michael Bader *electrical engineering educator, communications systems research and consulting*
Williamson, Robert Elmore *agricultural engineering educator*
Zumbrunnen, David Arnold *mechanical engineering educator, consultant*

Columbia
Baskin, C(harles) R(ichard) *retired civil engineer, physical scientist*
Ernst, Edward Willis *electrical engineering educator*
Ma, Fashang *mechanical engineering educator*

Florence
†Jiang, Longzhi *mechanical engineer*

Greenville
Fernandez, Miguel Angel *process safety, design engineer, energy consultant*
Schneider, George William *retired aircraft design engineer*

Hampton
Platts, Francis Holbrook *plastics engineering manager*

Hartsville
Menius, Espie Flynn, Jr. *electrical engineer*
Stallings, Frank, Jr. *industrial engineer*

Hilton Head Island
Huckins, Harold Aaron *chemical engineer*
Windman, Arnold Lewis *retired mechanical engineer*

Jenkinsville
Loignon, Gerald Arthur, Jr. *nuclear engineer*

Laurens
Bost, John Rowan *retired manufacturing executive, engineer*

North Charleston
Fei, James Robert *engineer*

Orangeburg
Graule, Raymond (Siegfried) *metallurgical engineer*
Isa, Saliman Alhaji *electrical engineering educator*
†Sandrapaty, Ramanchandra Rao *engineering educator*

Pawleys Island
Alexander, William D., III *civil engineer, consultant, former army air force officer*

Pineland
Centgraf, Damian Louis *broadcast engineer*

Rock Hill
Hardin, William Beamon, Jr. *electrical engineer*

Salem
Jones, Charles Edward *mechanical engineer*

Spartanburg
Schultz, Warren Robert *manufacturing administrator*

West Union
Klutz, Anthony Aloysius, Jr. *health, safety and environmental manager*

SOUTH DAKOTA

Brookings
Hamidzadeh, Hamid Reza *mechanical engineer, educator, consultant*
Nass, James Charles *utilities engineering manager*

Dakota Dunes
Healy, William Charles *electrical engineer*

Pierre
Templeton, Barbara Ann *civil engineering technologist*

Rapid City
Gowen, Richard Joseph *electrical engineering educator, academic administrator*
Klock, Steven Wayne *engineering executive*
Lefevre, Donald Keith *electrical engineer*
Riemenschneider, Albert Louis *retired engineering educator*
Scofield, Gordon Lloyd *mechanical engineer, educator*

TENNESSEE

Arnold AFB
Davis, John William *government science and engineering executive*

Brownsville
Stevenson, William Edward *chemical engineer*

Chattanooga
Cox, Ronald Baker *engineering and management consultant, university dean*
Manaker, Arnold Martin *mechanical engineer, consultant*
Williams, Robert Carlton *electrical engineer*

Cleveland
Knight, Sandra Norton *civil engineer*

Cookeville
Chowdhuri, Pritindra *electrical engineer, educator*
Sissom, Leighton Esten *engineering educator, dean, consultant*
Ting, Kwun-Lon *engineer, educator, consultant*

Crossville
Hovmand, Svend *chemical engineer, engineering executive*
Pitt, Woodrow Wilson, Jr. *engineering educator*

Dandridge
†Menzel, William Clarence, Jr. *nuclear engineer*

Elizabethton
Claussen, Lisa Renee *engineering executive*

Greenbrier
Newell, Paul Haynes, Jr. *engineering educator, former college president*

Johnson City
†Lucas, R. Robert *finance engineer, corporate tax planner*

Kingsport
Gibson, David Allen *civil engineer*
Reasor, Roderick Jackson *industrial engineer*
Siirola, Jeffrey John *chemical engineer*

Knoxville
Bose, Bimal Kumar *electrical engineering educator*
Bressler, Marcus N. *consulting engineer*
Campbell, William Buford, Jr. *materials engineer, chemist, forensic consultant*
Cliff, Steven Burris *engineering executive*
Garrison, Arlene Allen *engineering executive, engineering educator*
Gonzalez, Rafael Ceferino *electrical engineering educator*
Hung, James Chen *engineer, educator, consultant*
LeVert, Francis Edward *nuclear engineer*
Mc Dow, John Jett *agricultural engineering educator*
Mise, Jesse Sherden *structural engineer, consultant*
Pearce, James Walker *electronics engineer*
Richards, Stephen Harold *engineering educator*
Richardson, Don Orland *agricultural educator*
Roth, J(ohn) Reece *electrical engineer, educator, researcher-inventor*
Schuler, Theodore Anthony *retired civil engineer, retired city official*
Uhrig, Robert Eugene *nuclear engineer, educator*

Lenoir City
Brown, Donald Vaughn *technical educator, engineering consultant*

Maryville
Oakes, Lester Cornelius *retired electrical engineer, consultant*

Memphis
Fountain, Robert Allen *organizational management executive*
Kellogg, Frederic Hartwell *civil engineer, educator*
Maksi, Gregory Earl *engineering educator*
McIntosh, John Osborn *engineering consultant*
Williams, Edward F(oster), III *environmental engineer*

Nashville
Brodersen, Arthur James *electrical engineer*
Cadzow, James Archie *engineering educator, researcher*
Collins, Jerry Clayton *biomedical engineering educator*
Cook, George Edward *electrical engineering educator, consultant*
Galloway, Kenneth Franklin *engineering educator*
Hahn, George Thomas *materials engineering educator, researcher*
Harrawood, Paul *civil engineering educator*
Harris, Thomas Raymond *biomedical engineer, educator*
House, Robert William *technology management educator*
Potter, John Leith *mechanical and aerospace engineer, educator, consultant*
Schnelle, Karl Benjamin, Jr. *chemical engineering educator, consultant, researcher*
Speece, Richard Eugene *civil engineer, educator*
Thackston, Edward Lee *engineer, educator*

Oak Ridge
Brown, Robert Frederick *industrial systems engineer, technology applications, industrial systems and management systems consultant*
Fontana, Mario H. *nuclear engineer*
Hurt, Nathan Hampton, Jr. *mechanical engineer*
Kasten, Paul Rudolph *nuclear engineer, educator*
Rosenthal, Murray Wilford *chemical engineer, science administrator*
Trauger, Donald Byron *nuclear engineering laboratory administrator*

South Pittsburg
Cordell, Francis Merritt *instrument engineer, consultant*

Summertown
Emanuel, William Gilbert *electrical engineer*

Tullahoma
Baucum, William Emmett, Jr. *electrical research engineer*
Butler, R. W. *engineering company executive*
Garrison, George Walker, Jr. *mechanical and industrial engineering educator*
Hill, Susan Sloan *safety engineer*

Vonore
Lownsdale, Gary Richard *mechanical engineer*

TEXAS

Amarillo
Elkins, Lloyd Edwin, Sr. *petroleum engineer, energy consultant*
Keaton, Lawrence Cluer *safety engineer, consultant*

Anahuac
Fontenot, Jackie Darrel *safety and health consultant*

Arlington
Anderson, Dale Arden *aerospace engineer, educator*
Chen, Mo-Shing *electrical engineering educator*
Clark, Dayle Meritt *civil engineer*
Deaver, Pete Eugene *civil and aeronautical engineer*
Fung, Adrian Kin-Chiu *electrical engineering educator, researcher*
Lewis, Frank Leroy *electrical engineer, educator, researcher*
Mc Elroy, John Harley *electrical and industrial engineering educator*
Ptaszkowski, Stanley Edward, Jr. *civil engineer, structural engineer*
Qasim, Syed Reazul *civil and environmental engineering educator, researcher*
Rollins, Albert Williamson *civil engineer, consultant*
Stevens, Gladstone Taylor, Jr. *industrial engineer*

Austin
Adcock, Willis Alfred *electrical engineer, educator*
Armstrong, Neal Earl *civil engineering educator*
Baker, Lee Edward *biomedical engineering educator*
Beard, Leo Roy *civil engineer*
Breen, John Edward *civil engineer, educator*
Brock, James Rush *chemical engineering educator*
Bronaugh, Edwin Lee *electromagnetic compatibility engineer, consultant*
Brown, Stephen Neal *computer engineer*
Burns, Ned Hamilton *civil engineering educator*
Carey, Graham Francis *engineering educator*
Carlton, Donald Morrill *research, development and engineering executive*
Carrasquillo, Ramon Luis *civil engineering educator, consultant*
Castaldi, Frank James *environmental engineer, consultant*
Caudle, Ben Hall *petroleum engineering educator*
Cragon, Harvey George *computer engineer*
Cywar, Adam Walter *management engineer*
Dougal, Arwin Adelbert *electrical engineer, educator*
Dupuis, Russell Dean *electrical engineer, research scientist*
Fair, James Rutherford, Jr. *chemical engineering educator, consultant*
Feiner, Robert Franklin *petroleum and mechanical engineer*
Ford, Davis L. *sanitary & environmental engineer*
Fowler, David Wayne *architectural engineering educator*
Fults, Kenneth Wyatt *civil engineer, surveyor*
Gloyna, Earnest Frederick *environmental engineer, educator*
Goodenough, John Bannister *engineering educator, research physicist*
Grifel, Stuart Samuel *management engineer, consultant*
Harris, Richard Lee *engineering executive, retired army officer*
Himmelblau, David Mautner *chemical engineer*
Hixson, Elmer L. *engineering educator*
Howell, John Reid *mechanical engineering educator*
Hull, David George *aerospace engineering educator, researcher*
Jirsa, James Otis *civil engineering educator*
Koen, Billy Vaughn *mechanical engineering educator*
Koros, William John *chemical engineering educator*
Lake, Larry Wayne *petroleum engineering educator, researcher*
Lamb, Jamie Parker, Jr. *mechanical engineer, educator*
Ling, Frederick Fongsun *mechanical engineering educator*
Loehr, Raymond Charles *engineering educator*
Luedecke, William Henry *mechanical engineer*
Mc Ketta, John J., Jr. *chemical engineering educator*
Nicastro, David Harlan *forensic engineer, consultant, author*
Nichols, Steven Parks *mechanical engineer, university official*
Oden, John Tinsley *mathematician, theoretical mechanics consultant*
O'Geary, Dennis Traylor *contracting and engineering company executive*
Paul, Donald Ross *chemical engineer, educator*
Perkins, Richard Burle Jamail, II *chemical engineer, international consultant*
Raina, Rajesh *computer engineer*
Reese, Lymon Clifton *civil engineering educator*
Richards-Kortum, Rebecca Rae *biomedical engineering educator*
Rylander, Henry Grady, Jr. *mechanical engineering educator*
Sandberg, Irwin Walter *electrical and computer engineering educator*
Saunders, Jimmy Dale *aerospace engineer, physicist, naval officer*
Schapery, Richard Allan *engineering educator*
Schechter, Robert Samuel *chemical engineer, educator*
Schmidt, Philip S. *mechanical engineering educator*
Sciance, Carroll Thomas *chemical engineer*
Sohie, Guy Rose Louis *electrical engineer, researcher*
Steinfink, Hugo *chemical engineering educator*
Stokoe, Kenneth H., II *civil engineer, educator*
Straiton, Archie Waugh *electrical engineering educator*
Streetman, Ben Garland *electrical engineering educator*
Su, Jie *researcher, engineer*
Swartzlander, Earl Eugene, Jr. *engineering educator, former electronics company executive*
Tesar, Delbert *machine systems and robotics educator, researcher, manufacturing consultant*
Thurston, George Butte *mechanical and biomedical engineering educator*
Tucker, Richard Lee *civil engineer, educator*
Umeadi, Albert Nkuni *civil engineer, consultant*
Vliet, Gary Clark *mechanical engineering educator*
Walton, Charles Michael *civil engineering educator*
Wehring, Bernard William *nuclear engineering educator*
Welch, Ashley James *engineering educator*
Woodson, Herbert Horace *retired electrical engineering educator*
Wright, Stephen Gailord *civil engineering educator, consultant*

Baird
Rodenberger, Charles Alvard *aerospace engineer, consultant*

Beaumont
Mueller, Lisa Maria *process engineer*

Bellaire
Moore, Pat Howard *engineering and construction company executive*
Wisch, David John *structural engineer*

Big Spring
Fryrear, Donald William *agricultural engineer*

Boerne
Mitchelhill, James Moffat *civil engineer*

Brownsville
Marz, Loren Carl *environmental engineer, chemist, meteorologist*

Bryan
Samson, Charles Harold, Jr. (Car Samson) *retired engineering educator, consultant*

Bushland
Howell, Terry Allen *agricultural engineer*

Carrollton
Schulz, Richard Burkart *electrical engineer, consultant*

Cedar Creek
Akins, Vaughn Edward *retired engineering company executive*

College Station
Baskharone, Erian Aziz *mechanical and aerospace engineering educator*
Bhattacharyya, Shankar Prashad *electrical engineer, educator*
Buth, Carl Eugene *civil engineer*
Cochran, Robert Glenn *nuclear engineering educator*
Cohen, Aaron *aerospace engineer*
Ehsani, Mehrdad (Mark Ehsani) *electrical engineering educator, consultant*
Fletcher, Leroy Stevenson *mechanical engineer, educator*
Godbey, Luther David *architectural and engineering executive*
Hall, Kenneth Richard *chemical engineering educator, consultant*
Isdale, Charles Edwin *chemical engineer*
Junkins, John Lee *aerospace engineering educator*
Kunze, Otto Robert *retired agricultural engineering educator*
Kuo, Way *industrial engineer, researcher*
Lee, William John *petroleum engineering educator, consultant*
Lowery, Lee Leon, Jr. *civil engineer*
Mathewson, Christopher Colville *engineering geologist, educator*
Page, Robert Henry *engineer, educator, researcher*
Painter, John Hoyt *electrical engineer*
Parlos, Alexander George *systems and control engineering educator*
Patton, Alton DeWitt *electrical engineering educator, consultant, research administrator*
Reinschmidt, Kenneth Frank *engineering and construction executive*
Richardson, Herbert Heath *mechanical engineer, educator, institute director*
Roesset, Jose M. *civil engineering educator*
Urbanik, Thomas, II *research civil engineer*
Wagner, John Philip *safety engineering educator, science researcher*
Weese, John Augustus *mechanical engineer, educator*
Yao, James Tsu-Ping *civil engineer*

Corpus Christi
Umfleet, Lloyd Truman *electrical engineering technology educator*

Dallas
Brown, Phillip James *systems engineer*
Bruene, Warren Benz *electronic engineer*
Chadbourne, John Frederick, Jr. *engineering executive*
Chatterjee, Pal *electrical engineer, manufacturing executive*
Cruikshank, Thomas Henry *energy services and engineering executive*
Durkee, Joe Worthington, Jr. *nuclear engineer*
Fix, Douglas Martin *electrical engineer*
Fontana, Robert Edward *electrical engineering educator, retired air force officer*
Hammerlindl, Donald James *petroleum consultant*
Hart, David Royce *structural engineer*
Honkanen, Jari Olavi *electrical engineer*
Kilby, Jack St. Clair *electrical engineer*
Knight, Gary Charles *mechanical engineer*
Schulze, Richard Hans *engineering executive, environmental engineer*
Williams, Charles Edward *engineer*
Zimmerman, S(amuel) Morton (Mort Zimmerman) *electrical and electronics engineering executive*

Deer Park
Sandstrum, Steve D. *engineering executive*

El Paso
Diong, Billy Ming *control engineering researcher*
Friedkin, Joseph Frank *consulting engineering executive*
Grieves, Robert Belanger *engineering educator*
Heide, John Wesley *engineering executive*
Shadaram, Mehdi *electrical engineering educator*
Sheng, Zhuping *geological engineer, hydrogeologist*

Fair Oaks Ranch
Dixon, Robert James *aerospace consultant, former air force officer, former aerospace company executive*

Fort Hood
Porter, Bruce Jackman *military engineer, computer software engineer*

Fort Worth
Buckner, John Kendrick *aerospace engineer*
Cunningham, Atlee Marion, Jr. *aeronautical engineer*
Kenderdine, John Marshall *petroleum engineer, retired army officer*
Nichols, James Richard *civil engineer, consultant*
Pray, Donald George *retired aerospace engineer*
Romine, Thomas Beeson, Jr. *consulting engineering executive*

Freeport
Tsai, Tom Chunghu *chemical engineer*

Friendswood
Wood, Loren Edwin *aerospace engineering administrator, consultant*

Galveston
†Frederickson, Christopher John *neuroscientist*
Otis, John James *civil engineer*
Sheppard, Louis Clarke *biomedical engineer, educator*

Garland
Bohli, Harry John, Jr. *structural engineer, consultant*
Christensen, Allan Robert *electrical engineer, enrolled agent*

Grapevine
Killebrew, James Robert *architectural engineering firm executive*

Greenville
Johnston, John Thomas *engineering executive*

Hollywood Park
Smith, Richard Thomas *electrical engineer*

Houston
Antalffy, Leslie Peter *mechanical engineer*
Bomba, John Gilbert *civil engineer, consultant*
Bovay, Harry Elmo, Jr. *retired engineering company executive*
Bozeman, Ross Elliot *engineering executive*
Cheatham, John Bane, Jr. *retired mechanical engineering educator*
Chiquelin, David Bryan *mechanical engineer*
Cizek, John Gary *safety and fire engineer*
Claridge, Elmond Lowell *retired engineering educator, consultant*
Clark, John William, Jr. *electrical engineer, educator*
Colaco, Joseph P. *civil engineer*
Collipp, Bruce Garfield *ocean engineer, consultant*
Davis, Michael Jordan *civil engineer, natural gas company executive*
Duerr, David *civil engineer*
Duke, Michael B. *aerospace scientist*
Edwards, Victor Henry *chemical engineer*
Eichberger, LeRoy Carl *mechanical engineer, consultant, stress analyst*
Elliot, Douglas Gene *chemical engineer, engineering company executive, consultant*
Epright, Charles John *aerospace engineer*
Focht, John Arnold, Jr. *geotechnical engineer*
Frankhouser, Homer Sheldon, Jr. *engineering and construction company executive*
Geer, Ronald Lamar *mechanical engineering consultant, retired oil company executive*
Gernon, George Owen, Jr. *civil engineer*
Gidley, John Lynn *engineering executive*
Goins, William C., Jr. *engineering executive*
Halyard, Raymond James *aerospace engineer, mathematics educator*
Heilman, Robert Edward *mechanical engineer*
Hellums, Jesse David *chemical engineering educator and researcher*
†Henley, Ernest Justus *chemical engineering educator, consultant*
Hightower, Joe Walter *chemical engineering educator, consultant*
Hirasaki, George Jiro *chemical engineer, educator*
Hsu, Thomas Tseng-Chuang *civil engineer, educator*
Ivins, Marsha S. *aerospace engineer, astronaut*
Kirby, Sarah Ann Van Deventer *aerospace engineer*

Kobayashi, Riki *chemical engineer, educator*
Krause, William Austin *engineering executive*
Larks, Jack *forensic engineer, consultant*
Lechner-Fish, Teresa Jean *chemical engineer, analytical chemist*
Levy, Robert Edward *management consultant*
Lienhard, John Henry, IV *mechanical engineering educator*
Luss, Dan *chemical engineering educator*
Maligas, Manuel Nick *metallurgical engineer*
Matney, William Brooks, VII *electrical engineer, marine engineer*
Matthews, Charles Sedwick *petroleum engineering consultant, research advisor*
McIntire, Larry Vern *chemical engineering educator*
Meinke, Roy Walter *electrical engineer, consultant*
Miele, Angelo *engineering educator, researcher, consultant, author*
Miller, Charles Rickie *thermal and fluid systems analyst, engineering manager*
Miller, Mike *mechanical engineer*
Morris, Owen Glenn *engineering corporation executive*
Nordgren, Ronald Paul *engineering educator, researcher*
Pearson, James Boyd, Jr. *electrical engineering educator*
Peng, Liang-Chuan *mechanical engineer*
Pham, Cuong Huy *chemical engineer*
Pomeroy, Carl Fredrick *petroleum engineer*
Powell, Alan *engineer-scientist*
Prats, Michael *petroleum engineer, educator*
Rhodes, Allen Franklin *engineering executive*
†Rodgers, James Turner *petroleum engineer, oil industry executive*
Rypien, David Vincent *engineering executive*
Shen, Liang Chi *electrical engineer, educator, researcher*
Skov, Arlie Mason *petroleum engineer, consultant*
Sloan, Harold David *chemical engineering consultant*
Smalley, Arthur Louis, Jr. *engineering and construction company executive*
Souza, Marco Antonio *civil engineer, educator*
Spanos, Pol Dimitrios *engineering educator*
Sun, Wei-Joe *aerospace engineer, consultant*
Sweet, Christopher William *computer company executive*
Tiras, Herbert Gerald *engineering executive*
Tucker, Randolph Wadsworth *engineering executive*
Van Doesburg, Hans *chemical engineer, management consultant*
Veletsos, A(nestis) *civil engineer, educator*
Warren, J(oseph) E(mmet) *petroleum engineer*
Woodward, Clifford Edward *chemical engineer*
Wren, Robert James *aerospace engineering manager*
Yu, Aiting Tobey *engineering executive*

Irving
Longwell, H.J. *petroleum engineer, executive*
†McCormack, Grace Lynette *civil engineering technician*
Potter, Robert Joseph *technical and business executive*
Rainwater, R. Steven *systems engineer*

Keller
White, Lee Alvin *mechanical engineer, engineering executive*

Kerrville
Matlock, (Lee) Hudson *civil engineer, educator*

Kilgore
Carter, Michael Wayne *electrical engineer*

Kingwood
Bowman, Stephen Wayne *quality assurance engineer, consultant*

League City
Senyard, Corley Price, Jr. *engineering executive, consultant*

Lindale
Bockhop, Clarence William *retired agricultural engineer*

Lubbock
Archer, James Elson *engineering educator*
Dudek, Richard Albert *engineering educator*
Giesselmann, Michael Guenter *electrical engineer, educator, researcher*
Ishihara, Osamu *electrical engineer, physicist, educator*
Kristiansen, Magne *electrical engineer, educator*
Portnoy, William Manos *electrical engineering educator*
Zhang, Hong-Chao *manufacturing engineer, educator*

Midland
Helms, Micky *engineering executive*

Parker
Dawes, Robert Leo *research company executive*

Pearland
Allman, Mark C. *engineer, physicist*

Perryton
Edens, Fred Joe *petroleum engineer*

Port Aransas
Lehmann, William Leonardo *electrical engineer, educator*

Port Neches
Langford, Roland Everett *environmental safety scientist, author*

Prairie View
Akujuobi, Cajetan Maduabuchukwu *systems engineer, electrical engineering educator, researcher*

Randolph A F B
Lahser, Carl William, Jr. *environmental engineer*

Richardson
Biard, James Robert *electrical engineer*
Lutz, Raymond Price *industrial engineer, educator*
Witherspoon, W(illiam) Tom *engineering consultant*

Rockport
Minor, Joseph Edward *civil engineer, educator*

Rockwall
Griffith, James William *engineer, consultant*

Rosenberg
Tourtellotte, Mills Charlton *mechanical and electrical engineer*

Round Rock
Kopp, Debra Lynn *manufacturing engineer, consultant*

Salado
Carroll, Irwin Dixon *engineer*

San Antonio
Abramson, Hyman Norman *engineering and science research executive*
Buster, Alan Adair *control engineer*
Cutshall, Jon Tyler *aerospace engineer, researcher*
Gomes, Norman Vincent *retired industrial engineer*
Hubbard, Walter Bryan *engineer, consultant*
Migachyov, Valery *mechanical engineer*
Sarangapani, Jagannathan *intelligent systems and controls engineer, educator*
Singer, Merton *engineer*
Singh, Yesh Pal *mechanical engineering educator, consultant*

San Marcos
Nguyen, Philong *electrical engineer*

Sanger
Head, Gregory Alan *mechanical engineer, consultant*

Southlake
Roth, Robert William *technical consultant*

Spring
Ho, Hwa-Shan *engineering executive, civil engineer, consultant, drilling engineer*

Sugar Land
†Lin, Norman C.C. *project controls manager*
Romero, Mario H. *engineering executive*
Weispfennig, Klaus *chemical engineer, educator*
Westphal, Douglas Herbert *engineering company executive*

Temple
Patureau, Arthur Mitchell *chemical engineer, consultant*

The Woodlands
Lewis, Daniel Edward *systems engineer, computer company executive*
Norton, David Jerry *mechanical research engineer*

Tyler
Morgan, Freeman Louis, Jr. *engineer, consultant*

Universal City
Atchley, Curtis Leon *mechanical engineer*

Waco
Dow, William Gould *electrical engineer, educator*
Farison, James Blair *electrical biomedical engineer, educator*

Waxahachie
McLane, William Delano *mechanical engineer*
†Speed, Randall Sherman *engineering consultant*

Webster
Kobayashi, Herbert Shin *electrical engineer*

Wharton
Schulze, Arthur Edward *biomedical engineer, researcher*

Wichita Falls
Peterson, Holger Martin *electrical engineer*

UTAH

Brigham City
Krejci, Robert Henry *aerospace engineer*

Farmington
Gutzman, Philip Charles *aerospace executive, logistician*

Fort Duchesne
Cameron, Charles Henry *petroleum engineer*

Logan
Hargreaves, George Henry *civil and agricultural engineer, researcher*
Keller, Jack *agricultural engineering educator, consultant*

Ogden
Davidson, Thomas Ferguson *chemical engineer*
Ritchey, Harold W. *retired chemical engineer*

Orem
Harris, Michael James *software engineer*
Nordgren, William Bennett *engineering executive*

Provo
Jonsson, Jens Johannes *electrical engineering educator*
Merritt, LaVere Barrus *engineering educator, civil engineer*

Salt Lake City
Barney, Kline Porter, Jr. *retired engineering company executive, consultant*
Crawford, Kevan Charles *nuclear engineer, educator*
Dahlstrom, Donald Albert *former chemical-metallurgical engineering educator*
De Vries, Kenneth Lawrence *mechanical engineer, educator*
Epperson, Vaughn Elmo *civil engineer*
Gandhi, Om Parkash *electrical engineer*
Hereth, Lyle George *electrical engineering technologist*
Jacobsen, Stephen C. *biomedical engineer*
Judd, Thomas Eli *electrical engineer*
Lazzi, Gianluca *electronics engineer, researcher*
Pershing, David Walter *chemical engineering educator, researcher*
Seader, Junior DeVere (Bob) *chemical engineering educator*
Silver, Barnard Joseph Stewart *mechanical and chemical engineer, consultant, inventor*
Sohn, Hong Yong *chemical and metallurgical engineering educator*
Stringfellow, Gerald B. *engineering educator*

Sandy
Jorgensen, Leland Howard *aerospace research engineer*

VERMONT

Burlington
Anderson, Richard Louis *electrical engineer*
Critchlow, Dale *electrical engineer*
Pinder, George Francis *engineering educator, scientist*

Charlotte
Pricer, Wilbur David *electrical engineer*

Colchester
Hazelett, S(amuel) Richard *mechanical engineer*

Essex Junction
†Ishaq, Mousa Hanna *materials engineer*
Lee, Mankoo *device engineer/scientist, design engineer*

Montpelier
Ross, Frederick W., III *transportation engineer*

White River Junction
Linnell, Robert Hartley *environment, safety consultant*

VIRGINIA

Alexandria
Cook, Charles William *aerospace consultant, educator*
Darling, Thomas, Jr. *retired rural electrification specialist*
Heacock, Phillip Kaga *aerospace executive*
Jokl, Alois Louis *electrical engineer*
MacLaren, William George, Jr. *engineering executive*
Mandil, I. Harry *nuclear engineer*
Marschall, Albert Rhoades *engineer*
Murray, Russell, II *aeronautical engineer, defense analyst, consultant*
Scurlock, Arch Chilton *chemical engineer*
Searle, Willard F., Jr. *marine and salvage engineer*
Studebaker, John Milton *utilities engineer, consultant, educator*
Taylor, William Brockenbrough *engineer, consultant, management consultant*
Thompson, LeRoy, Jr. *radio engineer, military reserve officer*
Weiner, Robert Michael *engineering design company executive, retired consulting engineer*
Weisberg, Leonard R. *retired research and engineering executive*

Arlington
Bordogna, Joseph *engineer, educator*
Brown, Gardner Russell *engineering executive*
Coleman, Howard S. *engineer, physicist*
Fernandez, Fernando Lawrence *aeronautical engineer, research company executive*
Gooding, Robert C. *engineering administrator*
Hagn, George Hubert *electrical engineer, researcher*
Hall, Carl William *agricultural and mechanical engineer*
Heineken, Frederick George *biochemical engineer*
Henderson, Robert Earl *mechanical engineer, educator, consultant*
Katona, Peter Geza *biomedical engineer, educator*
Kostoff, Ronald Neil *aerospace scientist*
Larsen-Basse, Jorn *mechanical and materials engineering educator, researcher, consultant*
Lau, Clifford *electrical engineer, researcher*
Lazich, Daniel *aerospace engineer*
Meyers, Sheldon *engineering company executive*
Morgan, Robert Peter *engineering educator*
Poehlein, Gary Wayne *chemical engineering educator*
Reagan, Lawrence Paul, Jr. *systems engineer*
Reynik, Robert John *materials scientist, research and education administrator*
Sewell, William George, III *electronics engineer*
Stevens, Donald King *retired aeronautical engineer, consultant*
Sutton, George Walter *research laboratory executive, mechanical engineer, physicist*
Webb, David Owen *petroleum engineer, association executive*

Blacksburg
Batra, Romesh Chander *engineering mechanics educator, researcher*
Blackwell, William Allen *electrical engineering educator*
Boardman, Gregory Dale *environmental engineer, educator*
Brown, Gary Sandy *electrical engineering educator*
Byers, Albert Samuel *aerospace education specialist*
de Wolf, David Alter *electrical engineer, educator*
Fabrycky, Wolter Joseph *engineering educator, author, industrial and systems engineer*
Glasser, Wolfgang Gerhard *wood science and chemical engineering researcher, educator*
Gray, Festus Gail *electrical engineer, educator, researcher*
Haugh, Clarence Gene *agricultural engineering educator*
Hibbard, Walter Rollo, Jr. *retired engineering educator*
Lee, Fred C. *electrical engineering educator*
Mitchell, James Kenneth *civil engineer, educator*
Murray, Thomas Michael *civil engineering educator, consultant*
Perumpral, John Verghese *agricultural engineer, administrator, educator*
Phadke, Arun G. *electrical engineering educator*
Price, Dennis Lee *industrial engineer, educator*
Randall, Clifford Wendell *civil engineer*
Squires, Arthur Morton *chemical engineer, educator*
Stutzman, Warren Lee *electrical engineer, educator*

Blue Ridge
Elmore, Walter A. *electrical engineer, consultant*

Burke
Lynch, Charles Theodore, Sr. *materials science engineering researcher, consultant, educator*

Charlottesville
Bly, Charles Albert *nuclear engineer, research scientist*
Dorning, John Joseph *nuclear engineering, engineering physics and applied mathematics educator*
Edlich, Richard French *biomedical engineering educator*
Flack, Ronald Dumont *mechanical engineering educator*
Gaden, Elmer Lewis, Jr. *chemical engineering educator*
Gilruth, Robert Rowe *aerospace consultant*
Haimes, Yacov Yosseph *systems and civil engineering educator, consultant*
Herakovich, Carl Thomas *civil engineering, applied mechanics educator*
Hoel, Lester A. *civil engineering educator*
Hudson, John Lester *chemical engineering educator*
Inigo, Rafael Madrigal *retired electrical engineering educator*
Johnson, W(alker) Reed *nuclear engineering educator*
Krzysztofowicz, Roman *systems engineering and statistical science educator, consultant*
McGinnis, Charles Irving *civil engineer*
Morton, Jeffrey Bruce *aerospace engineering educator*
Reynolds, Albert Barnett *nuclear engineer, educator*
Theodoridis, George Constantin *biomedical engineering educator, researcher*
Thompson, Anthony Richard *electrical engineer, astronomer*
Townsend, Miles Averill *aerospace and mechanical engineering educator*

Chesapeake
Donohue, David Patrick *engineering executive, retired navy rear admiral*
Farmer, Dwight L. *transportation engineer, educator*
Sorey, Cecil Earl, Jr. *civil engineer*

Dahlgren
Evans, Alan George *electrical engineer*

Edinburg
Trindal, Wesley Steele *mechanical engineer*

Elkton
Buot, Francisco Jose *industrial engineer*

Fairfax
Beale, Guy Otis *engineering educator, consultant*
Cook, Gerald *electrical engineering educator*
Coulter, David Creswell *research engineer*
Gollobin, Leonard Paul *chemical engineer*
Hatch, Ross Riepert *weapon system engineering executive*
Jamieson, John Anthony *engineering consulting company executive*
Langley, Rolland Ament, Jr. *retired engineering technology company executive*
Larsen, Phillip Nelson *electrical engineer*
Levis, Alexander Henry *systems engineer, educator, consultant*
Lott, Wayne Thomas *systems engineer*
Warfield, John Nelson *engineering educator, consultant*

Fairfax Station
Coaker, James Whitfield *mechanical engineer*

Falls Church
Jones, Russel Cameron *civil engineer*
Lorenzo, Michael *engineer, government official, real estate broker*
May, Carol Lee *mechanical engineer*
Sowell, Dale Anthony *civil engineer*
Villarreal, Carlos Castaneda *engineering executive*

Fort Belvoir
Barnholdt, Terry Joseph *chemical, industrial, and general engineer*
Clarke, Frederick James *civil engineer*

Fredericksburg
Medding, Walter Sherman *environmental engineer*

Great Falls
Skeen, David Ray *systems engineer, consultant*

Hampton
Adeyiga, Adeyinka A. *engineering educator*
Bartels, Robert Edwin *aerospace engineer*
Duberg, John Edward *retired aeronautical engineer, educator*
Dwoyer, Douglas Leon *engineering executive*
Farrukh, Usamah Omar *electrical engineering educator, researcher*
Joshi, Suresh Meghashyam *research engineer*
Kelly, Jeffrey Jennings *mechanical engineer*
Krueger, Ronald *aerospace engineer*
Mehrotra, Sudhir C. *engineering company executive*
Meyers, James Frank *electronics engineer*
Phillips, William H. *aeronautical engineer*
Singleterry, Robert Clay, Jr. *aerospace technologist, material research engineer*
Sobieski, Jaroslaw *aerospace engineer*
Tessler, Alexander *aerospace engineer*
Whitesides, John Lindsey, Jr. *aerospace engineering educator, researcher*

Hartfield
Lovell, Robert R(oland) *engineering executive*

Herndon
Dodd, Steven Louis *systems engineer*

Snyder, Franklin Farison *hydrologic engineering consultant*

Huddleston
Kopp, Richard Edgar *electrical engineer*

King George
Hoglund, Richard Frank *research and technical executive*

Lynchburg
Barkley, Henry Brock, Jr. *research and development executive*
Latimer, Paul Jerry *non-destructive testing engineer*

Madison
Brewer, Philip Warren *civil engineer*
McGhee, Kenneth Hamilton *civil engineer, consultant*

Marion
Pratt, Mark Ernest *mechanical engineer*

Mc Lean
Bivins, Susan Steinbach *systems engineer*
Carnicero, Jorge Emilio *aeronautical engineer, business executive*
Dobson, Donald Alfred *retired electrical engineer*
Klopfenstein, Rex Carter *electrical engineer*
Larson, Arvid Gunnar *electrical engineer*
Loven, Andrew Witherspoon *environmental engineering company executive*
Rosenbaum, David Mark *engineering executive, consultant, educator*
Schmeidler, Neal Francis *engineering executive*
Sonnemann, Harry *electrical engineer, consultant*
Stasior, William F. *engineering company executive*
Tomeh, Osama Adnan *civil engineer*
Walsh, John Breffni *aerospace consultant*

McLean
†Metters, Samuel *engineering executive*
Singley, George T., III *mechanical engineer, federal agency administrator*

Mechanicsville
Jones, Stuart Cromer *mechanical engineer*

Newport News
Beach, Harry Lee, Jr. *mechanical engineer, aerospace engineer*
Corlett, William Albert *retired aerospace engineer*
Donaldson, Coleman duPont *aerodynamics and aerospace consulting engineer*
Gies, Robert Jay *mechanical engineer*
Hubbard, Harvey Hart *aeroacoustician, noise control engineer, consultant*
Laroussi, Mounir *electrical engineer*
Noblitt, Nancy Anne *aerospace engineer*

Norfolk
Denyes, James Richard *industrial engineer*
Mc Gaughy, John Bell *civil engineer*
Wiltse, James Clark *civil engineer*

Oak Hill
Hubbard, Carl Aubrey *aerospace engineer, management consultant*

Oakton
Curry, Thomas Fortson *electronics engineer, defense industry executive*

Palmyra
Leslie, William Cairns *metallurgical engineering educator*
Ramsey, Forrest Gladstone, Jr. *retired engineering company executive*

Radford
Phelps, George Graham *computer systems engineer, consultant*

Reston
Choi, Michael Kamwah *aerospace engineer, mechanical engineer, thermal engineer, researcher*
Duscha, Lloyd Arthur *engineering executive*
Harvey, Aubrey Eaton, III *industrial engineer*
Mumzhiu, Alexander *optical and imaging processing engineer, researcher*

Richmond
Compton, Olin Randall *consulting electrical engineer, researcher*
Mattauch, Robert Joseph *electrical engineering educator*
Palik, Robert Richard *mechanical engineer*
Sprinkle, William Melvin *engineering administrator, audio-acoustical engineer*
Washington, James MacKnight *former chemical engineer*
Wist, Abund Ottokar *biomedical engineer, radiation physicist, educator*

Roanoke
Coar, Richard John *mechanical engineer, aerospace consultant*
Jackson, Daniel Wyer *electrical engineer*
Jiang, John Jianzhong *materials engineer*
†Journiette, Melvin Diago *civil engineer*
Shaffner, Patrick Noel *retired architectural engineering executive*
Stadler, Donald Arthur *management engineer*

Spotsylvania
Kozloski, Lillian Terese D. *history of aerospace technology educator*

Springfield
Broome, Paul Wallace *engineering research and development executive*
Casazza, John Andrew *electrical engineer, business executive, educator*
Duff, William Grierson *electrical engineer*
Meikle, Philip G. *engineer, retired government agency executive*
Schlegelmilch, Reuben Orville *electrical engineer, consultant*

Stafford
Tallent, Robert Glenn *chemical and environmental engineer, entrepreneur*

Sterling
Bockwoldt, Todd Shane *nuclear engineer*
Paraskevopoulos, George *aerospace engineer*

Vienna
Keiser, Bernhard Edward *engineering company executive, consulting telecommunications engineer*
Salah, Sagid *retired nuclear engineer*
Woodward, Kenneth Emerson *retired mechanical engineer*
Zeitlin, Gerald Mark *electrical engineer*

Virginia Beach
Glenn, Joe Davis, Jr. *retired civil engineer, consultant*

Waynesboro
McNair, John William, Jr. *civil engineer*

Williamsburg
Dunn, Ronald Holland *civil engineer, management executive, consultant*
Hughes, George Farant, Jr. *retired safety engineer*
Lambert, Stephen Robert *electrical engineer, consultant*
Lynn, Larry (Verne Lauriston Lynn) *engineering executive*
Spitzer, Cary Redford *avionics consultant, electrical engineer*

WASHINGTON

Auburn
Duhnke, Robert Emmet, Jr. *retired aerospace engineer*
Westbo, Leonard Archibald, Jr. *electronics engineer*

Bainbridge Island
Eber, Lorenz *aeronautical engineer, civil engineer, inventor*
Glosten, Lawrence Robert *engineering executive*

Bellevue
Dow, Daniel Gould *electrical engineering educator*
Edde, Howard Jasper *retired engineering executive*
Erickson, Virginia Bemmels *chemical engineer*
Hibbard, Richard Paul *industrial ventilation consultant, lecturer*
Parks, Donald Lee *mechanical engineer, human factors engineer*
†Passage, James Thompson *engineering executive*
Schairer, George Swift *aeronautical engineer*
Williams, Jerald Arthur *mechanical engineer*
Wright, Theodore Otis *forensic engineer*

Bellingham
Albrecht, Albert Pearson *electronics engineer, consultant*
Jansen, Robert Bruce *consulting civil engineer*
Johnstone, Kenneth Ernest *electronics and business consultant*

Black Diamond
Morris, David John *mining engineer, consultant, mining executive*

Bothell
Cao, Thai-Hai *industrial engineer*
Jacobs, Harold Robert *mechanical engineering educator, practitioner*

Bremerton
Joseph, James Edward *mechanical engineering technician*
†Shephard, Deane Anthony *mechanical and design engineer*

Dupont
Pettit, Ghery St. John *electronics engineer*

Edmonds
Peckol, James Kenneth *consulting engineer*
Schmit, Lucien André, Jr. *structural engineer*
Terrel, Ronald Lee *civil engineer, business executive, educator*

Federal Way
Mast, Robert F. *structural engineer*
Studebaker, Irving Glen *mining engineering consultant*

Issaquah
Reid, John Mitchell (Jack Reid) *biomedical engineer, researcher*

Kenmore
Guy, Arthur William *electrical engineering educator, researcher*

Kent
Bangsund, Edward Lee *former aerospace company executive, consultant*
Williams, Max Lea, Jr. *engineer, educator*

Kirkland
Boxleitner, Warren James *electrical engineer, researcher*
Szablya, John Francis *electrical engineer, consultant*
Wenk, Edward, Jr. *civil engineer, policy analyst, educator, writer*

Lummi Island
Ewing, Benjamin Baugh *environmental engineering educator, consultant*

Marysville
McClure, Allan Howard *materials engineer, space contamination specialist, space materials consultant*

Mill Creek
Bacon, Vinton Walker *civil engineer*

Mukilteo
Bohn, Dennis Allen *electrical engineer, executive*

Olympia
Loftness, Marvin O. *electrical engineer*

Pullman
Funk, William Henry *environmental engineering educator*
Guzman, Armando *electrical research engineer*
Scheer, Gary Werner *electrical engineer*
Stock, David Earl *mechanical engineering educator*
Torruellas, William Eugene *electrical engineer, educator*

Redmond
Lane, James F. *software engineer*
Willard, H(arrison) Robert *electrical engineer*

Renton
Trenkler, Tina Louise *nuclear engineer*

Richland
Khaleel, Raziuddin *groundwater hydrologist*
Lutter, Delores Kay *environmental engineer*
Piper, Lloyd Llewellyn, II *engineer, government and service industry executive*
†Trent, Donald Stephen *thermo fluids engineer*

Seattle
Babb, Albert Leslie *biomedical engineer, educator*
Bowen, Jewell Ray *chemical engineering educator*
Calkins, Robert Bruce *aerospace engineer*
Christiansen, Walter Henry *aeronautics educator*
Clark, Robert Newhall *electrical and aeronautical engineering educator*
Davis, Earl James *chemical engineering educator*
Fadden, Delmar McLean *electrical engineer*
Fay, Christopher Wayne *mechanical engineer, consultant*
Finlayson, Bruce Alan *chemical engineering educator*
Gartz, Paul Ebner *systems engineer*
Gilbert, Paul H. *engineering executive, consultant*
Haralick, Robert Martin *electrical engineering educator*
Hertzberg, Abraham *aeronautical engineering educator, university research scientist*
Hoffman, Allan Sachs *chemical engineer, educator*
Hom, Richard Yee *research engineer*
Ii, Jack Morito *aerospace engineer*
Ishimaru, Akira *electrical engineering educator*
Joppa, Robert Glenn *aeronautics educator*
Kapur, Kailash Chander *industrial engineering educator*
Kippenhan, Charles Jacob *mechanical engineer, retired educator*
Kobayashi, Albert Satoshi *mechanical engineering educator*
Laing, Thomas Dallas, Jr. *marine surveyor, salvage consultant*
Lauritzen, Peter Owen *electrical engineering educator*
Martin, George Coleman *aeronautical engineer*
Mc Feron, Dean Earl *mechanical engineer*
Meditch, James Stephen *electrical engineering educator*
Oliver, Donny Glen *electronics engineer*
Oman, Henry *retired electrical engineer, engineering executive*
Peden, Irene Carswell *electrical engineer, educator*
Raisbeck, James David *engineering company executive*
Rudolph, Thomas Keith *aerospace engineer*
Skilling, John Bower *structural and civil engineer*
Sleicher, Charles Albert *chemical engineer*
Spindel, Robert Charles *electrical engineering educator*
Vesper, Karl Hampton *business and mechanical engineering educator*
Weissman, Eugene Yehuda *chemical engineer*
Wood, Stuart Kee *retired engineering manager*
Woodruff, Gene Lowry *nuclear engineer, university dean*

Snohomish
Meister, John Edward, Jr. *consultant, technical educator, systems analyst*

South Bend
Heinz, Roney Allen *civil engineering consultant*

Spokane
Ladd, Dean *mechanical engineer*
Maus, John Andrew *computer systems engineer*

Sumner
Olson, Ronald Charles *aerospace executive*

Sunnyside
Capener, Regner Alvin *electronics engineer, minister, author, inventor*

Tacoma
Gates, Thomas Edward *civil engineer, waste management administrator*
Holman, Kermit Layton *chemical engineer*

Vancouver
Taylor, Carson William *electrical engineer*

Woodinville
McGavin, Jock Campbell *airframe design engineer*

Woodland
Mairose, Paul Timothy *mechanical engineer, consultant*

WEST VIRGINIA

Charleston
Koleske, Joseph Victor *chemical engineer, consultant*
Whittington, Bernard Wiley *electrical engineer, consultant*

Montgomery
Gourley, Frank A., Jr. *engineering educator*

Morgantown
Guthrie, Hugh Delmar *chemical engineer*
Kent, James A. *consulting chemical engineer, author, consultant*
Schroder, John L., Jr. *retired mining engineer*

Ravenswood
Hamrick, Leslie Wilford, Jr. *metallurgy supervisor*

South Charleston
Nielsen, Kenneth Andrew *chemical engineer*

WISCONSIN

Brookfield
Krueger, John Anthony *biomedical engineer, musician*
Robles, Ted Canillas *electrical engineering educator*
Thomas, John *mechanical engineer, research and development*

Frederic
Rudell, Milton Wesley *aerospace engineer*

Madison
Abubakr, Said Mohammed *chemical engineering educator*
Beachley, Norman Henry *mechanical engineer, educator*
Behrend, William Louis *electrical engineer*
Berthouex, Paul Mac *civil and environmental engineer, educator*
Bird, Robert Byron *chemical engineering educator, author*
Bohnhoff, David Roy *agricultural engineer, educator*
Boyle, William Charles *civil engineering educator*
Bubenzer, Gary Dean *agricultural engineering educator, researcher*
Callen, James Donald *nuclear engineer, plasma physicist, educator*
Carbon, Max William *nuclear engineering educator*
Chang, Y. Austin *materials engineer, educator*
Converse, James Clarence *agricultural engineering educator*
Dietmeyer, Donald Leo *retired electrical engineer, educator*
Duffie, John Atwater *chemical engineer, educator*
Emmert, Gilbert Arthur *engineer, educator*
Hill, Charles Graham, Jr. *chemical engineering educator*
Kulcinski, Gerald LaVerne *nuclear engineer, educator*
Lasseter, Robert Haygood *electrical engineering educator, consultant*
Lightfoot, Edwin Niblock, Jr. *chemical engineering educator*
Lipo, Thomas A. *electrical engineer, educator*
Long, Willis Franklin *electrical engineering educator, researcher*
Loper, Carl Richard, Jr. *metallurgical engineer, educator*
Lovell, Edward George *mechanical engineering educator*
Malkus, David Starr *mechanics educator, applied mathematician*
Novotny, Donald Wayne *electrical engineering educator*
Ray, Willis Harmon *chemical engineer*
Seireg, Ali A(bdel Hay) *mechanical engineer*
Skiles, James Jean *electrical and computer engineering educator*
Stewart, Warren Earl *chemical engineer, educator*
Thesen, Arne *industrial engineering educator*
Uyehara, Otto Arthur *mechanical engineering educator emeritus, consultant*
Webster, John Goodwin *biomedical engineering educator, researcher*

Menomonie
†Asthana, Rajiv *engineering educator, researcher*

Milwaukee
Bartel, Fred Frank *consulting engineer executive*
Battocletti, Joseph Henry *electrical engineer, biomedical engineer, educator*
Boettcher, Harold Paul *engineer, educator*
Chan, Shih Hung *mechanical engineering educator, consultant*
Demerdash, Nabeel Aly Omar *electrical engineer*
Fournelle, Raymond Albert *engineering educator*
Gaggioli, Richard Arnold *mechanical engineering educator*
Heinen, James Albin *electrical engineering educator*
James, Charles Franklin, Jr. *engineering educator*
Landis, Fred *mechanical engineering educator*
Reid, Robert Lelon *mechanical engineering educator*
Widera, Georg Ernst Otto *mechanical engineering educator, consultant*
Wilsdon, Thomas Arthur *product development engineer, administrator*
Zelazo, Nathaniel K. *engineering executive*

Neenah
Tsai, Fu-Jya *polymer scientist and engineer*

Pewaukee
Dupies, Donald Albert *retired civil engineer*
Schaefer, Mark Donald *mechanical engineer*

Racine
Hodges, Lawrence H. *agricultural engineer*

Spooner
Frey, Paul Howard *chemical engineer, engineering consultants company executive*

Sussex
Dantzman, Gregory Peter *design engineer*

Watertown
Cech, Joseph Harold *chemical engineer*

Waukesha
Mielke, William John *civil engineer*

Wauwatosa
Bub, Alexander David *acoustical engineer*

WYOMING

Casper
Hinchey, Bruce Alan *environmental engineering company executive*

Gillette
Sharp, Pamela Ann *quality assurance engineer*

Laramie
Bellamy, John Cary *civil engineer, meteorologist*
Mingle, John Orville *engineer, educator, lawyer, consultant*
†Pell, Kynric Martin *engineering educator*
Rechard, Paul Albert *civil engineering consulting company executive*
Stewart, Larry Ray *engineer, financial director, quality consultant*

Riverton
Pursel, Harold Max, Sr. *mining engineer, civil engineer, architectural engineer*

Wilson
Lawroski, Harry *nuclear engineer*

TERRITORIES OF THE UNITED STATES

PUERTO RICO

Dorado
Ortiz-Quiñones, Carlos Ruben *electronics engineer, educator*

MILITARY ADDRESSES OF THE UNITED STATES

PACIFIC

APO
Turner, David Lowery *system safety engineer*

CANADA

ALBERTA

Calgary
Glockner, Peter G. *civil and mechanical engineering educator*
Heidemann, Robert Albert *chemical engineering educator, researcher*
Malik, Om Parkash *electrical engineering educator, researcher*
McDaniel, Roderick Rogers *petroleum engineer*

Edmonton
Koval, Don O. *electrical engineering educator*
Lock, Gerald Seymour Hunter *retired mechanical engineering educator*
McDougall, John Roland *civil engineer*
Morgenstern, Norbert Rubin *civil engineering educator*
Offenberger, Allan Anthony *electrical engineering educator*
Otto, Fred Douglas *chemical engineering educator*
Rajotte, Ray V. *biomedical engineer, researcher*

BRITISH COLUMBIA

Vancouver
Crawford, Carl Benson *retired civil engineer, government research administrator*
Grace, John Ross *chemical engineering educator*
Jull, Edward V. *electrical engineer, radio scientist, educator*
Klohn, Earle Jardine *engineering company executive, consultant*
Meisen, Axel *chemical engineering educator, university dean*
Peters, Ernest *metallurgy educator, consultant*
Salcudean, Martha Eva *mechanical engineer, educator*
Young, Lawrence *electrical engineering educator*

Victoria
Antoniou, Andreas *electrical engineering educator*
Lind, Niels Christian *civil engineering educator*

Westbank
Wedepohl, Leonhard Martin *electrical engineering educator*

MANITOBA

Winnipeg
Kuffel, Edmund *electrical engineering educator*
Morrish, Allan Henry *electrical engineering educator*

NEW BRUNSWICK

Fredericton
Faig, Wolfgang *survey engineer, engineering educator*

NEWFOUNDLAND

Saint John's
Clark, Jack I. *civil engineer, researcher*

NOVA SCOTIA

Hammonds Plains
Wilson, Frank Henry *retired electrical engineer*

Kentville
Baker, George Chisholm *engineering executive, consultant*

ONTARIO

Burlington
Harris, Philip John *engineering educator*

Hamilton
Bandler, John William *electrical engineering educator, consultant*
Campbell, Colin Kydd *electrical and computer engineering educator, researcher*
Crowe, Cameron Macmillan *chemical engineering educator*
Parnas, David Lorge *engineering educator, computer scientist*

Kingston
Bacon, David Walter *chemical engineering educator*
Batchelor, Barrington de Vere *civil engineer, educator*

London
Davenport, Alan Garnett *civil engineer, educator*
Inculet, Ion I. *electrical engineering educator, research director, consultant*
Wilson, Gerald Einar *mechanical and industrial engineer, business executive*

North York
Buzacott, John Alan *engineering educator*

Ottawa
Cockshutt, E(ric) Philip *engineering executive, research scientist, energy consultant*
Georganas, Nicolas D. *electrical engineering educator*
Gussow, William Carruthers *petroleum engineer, geologist*
Moore, William John Myles *electrical engineer, researcher*
Morand, Peter *investment company executive*

Saint Catharines
Picken, Harry Belfrage *aerospace engineer*

Toronto
Balmain, Keith George *electrical engineering educator, researcher*
Davison, Edward Joseph *electrical engineering educator*
Endrenyi, Janos *research engineer, educator*
Foster, John Stanton *nuclear engineer*
Ganczarczyk, Jerzy Jozef *civil engineering educator, wastewater treatment consultant*
Goring, David Arthur Ingham *chemical engineering educator, scientist*
Janischewskyj, Wasyl *electrical engineering educator*
Kunov, Hans *biomedical and electrical engineering educator*
Mackiw, Vladimir Nicholaus *metallurgical consultant*
Meagher, George Vincent *mechanical engineer*
Rimrott, Friedrich Paul Johannes *engineer, educator*
Runnalls, (Oliver) John (Clyve) *nuclear engineering educator*
Salama, C. Andre Tewfik *electrical engineering educator*
Sedra, Adel Shafeek *electrical engineering educator, academic administrator*
Semlyen, Adam *electrical engineering educator*
Slemon, Gordon Richard *electrical engineering educator*
Smith, Peter William Ebblewhite *electrical engineering educator, scientist*
Venetsanopoulos, Anastasios Nicolaos *electrical engineer, educator*
Wonham, Walter Murray *electrical engineer, educator*

Waterloo
Penlidis, Alexander *chemical engineering educator*
Rempel, Garry Llewellyn *chemical engineering educator, consultant*
Sherbourne, Archibald Norbert *civil engineering educator*
Vlach, Jiri *electrical engineering educator, researcher*

Windsor
Hackam, Reuben *electrical engineering educator*

QUEBEC

Montreal
Alepian, Taro *engineering and construction executive*
Cameron, Alastair Duncan *engineering consultant*
Carreau, Pierre *chemical engineering educator*
Corinthios, Michael Jean George *electrical engineering educator*
Dealy, John Michael *chemical engineer, educator*
Haccoun, David *electrical engineering educator*
Kearney, Robert Edward *biomedical engineering educator*
Ladanyi, Branko *civil engineer*
Lamarre, Bernard *engineering, contracting and manufacturing advisor*
Martel, Jacques G. *engineer, adminstrator*
Paidoussis, Michael Pandeli *mechanical engineering educator*
Ramachandran, Venkatanarayana Deekshit *electrical engineering educator*
Saint-Pierre, Guy *engineering executive*
Selvadurai, Antony Patrick Sinnappa *civil engineering educator, applied mathematician, consultant*

Quebec
Lecours, Michel *electrical engineering educator*
Tavenas, François *civil engineer, educator*

Saint Lambert
Terreault, Charles *engineer, management educator, researcher*

Sainte Anne de Bellevue
Broughton, Robert Stephen *irrigation and drainage engineering educator, consultant*

Sillery
La Rochelle, Pierre-Louis *civil engineering educator*

Trois Rivieres
Lavallee, H.-Claude *chemical engineer, researcher*

Varennes
Bartnikas, Raymond *electrical engineer, educator*

SASKATCHEWAN

Regina
Mollard, John Douglas *engineering and geology executive*

Saskatoon
Billinton, Roy *engineering educator*
Kumar, Surinder *electrical engineering educator, consultant*
Sachdev, Mohindar Singh *engineering educator*

AUSTRALIA

Brisbane Queensland
Chang, Weilin Parrish *construction and engineering educator, administrator, researcher*

CHINA

Beijing
Shu, Wenlong *environmental engineer, educator*
Xue, Lan *engineering educator*

Chengdu
Zeng, Xuegang *telecommunications engineer, engineering educator*

Hong Kong
Chang, H. K. *biomedical engineer, educator*
Li, Victor On-Kwok *electrical engineering educator*
Liou, Ming-Lei *electrical engineer*
Wang, Jun *engineering educator*

Jiangsu
Xia, Jiding *chemical engineering educator*

Taipei
Lin, Yeou-Lin *engineer, consultant*

ENGLAND

Cambridge
Broers, Sir Alec Nigel *engineering educator*
Ffowcs Williams, John Eirwyn *acoustical engineer*
Hawthorne, Sir William (Rede) *aerospace and mechanical engineer, educator*

London
Baxendell, Sir Peter (Brian) *petroleum engineer*

GERMANY

Aachen
Pischinger, Franz Felix *engineer, researcher*

Bonn
Wohlleben, Rudolf *microwave and antenna researcher*

Dortmund
Freund, Eckhard *electrical engineering educator*

Erlangen
Lips, H. Peter *systems engineer director*

Munich
Hein, Fritz Eugen *engineer, consultant, architect*

GREECE

Athens
Arnis, Efstathios Constantinos *space naval designer*
Hatzakis, Michael *retired electrical engineer, research executive*
Ligomenides, Panos Aristides *electrical and computer engineering educator, consultant*

Thessaloniki
Angelides, Demosthenes Constantinos *civil engineer*

GUATEMALA

Guatemala
Loesener, Otto Robert *aerospace engineer*

HONG KONG

Clear Water Bay
Tang, Wilson Hon-chung *engineering educator*

Wan Chai
Kao, Charles Kuen *electrical engineer, educator*

JAPAN

Aichi
Abe, Yoshihiro *ceramic engineering educator, materials scientist*

Kanagawa
Shimazaki, Yoji *civil engineering educator*

Kitakyushu
Mine, Katsutoshi *instrumentation educator*

Nagoya
Sendo, Takeshi *mechanical engineering educator, researcher, author*
Tasaka, Shuji *engineering educator*

Oita
Ishibashi, Eiichi *engineering researcher and educator*

Shimizu
Anma, So *engineering consultant*

Tokyo
Aoyama, Hiroyuki *structural engineering educator*
Kaneko, Hisashi *engineering executive*
Saito, Shuzo *electrical engineering educator*
Sakuta, Masaaki *engineering educator, consultant*
Yasufuku, Sachio *electrical engineer, educator*

THE NETHERLANDS

Roosendaal
van Deventer, Arie Pieter *agricultural engineer*

THE PHILIPPINES

Manila
Stepanich, Fred Charles *civil and water resources engineer*

REPUBLIC OF KOREA

Pusan
Ha, Chang Sik *polymer science educator*

SAUDI ARABIA

Riyadh
Uygur, Mustafa Eti *materials and mechanical engineering educator*

SWITZERLAND

Zurich
Bailey, James Edwin *chemical engineer*
Morari, Manfred *chemical engineer, educator*

TAIWAN

Tainan
Huang, Ting-Chia *chemical engineering educator, researcher*
Shih, Tso Min *mining engineering educator*

Taipei
Pao, Yih-Hsing *engineer, educator*
Young, Der-Liang Frank *civil engineering educator, researcher*

WALES

Gwynedd
Owen, Walter Shepherd *materials science and engineering educator*

ADDRESS UNPUBLISHED

Alexander, Melvin Taylor *quality assurance engineer, statistician*
Allison, John McComb *retired aeronautical engineer*
Al-Qadi, Imad Lutfi *civil engineering educator, researcher*
Amann, Charles Albert *mechanical engineer*
†Anderson, Eric David *electrical engineer*
Anderson, John Gaston *electrical engineer*
Anderson, Thomas Patrick *mechanical engineer, educator*
Arden, Bruce Wesley *computer science and electrical engineering educator*
Baddour, Raymond Frederick *chemical engineer, educator, entrepreneur*
Bakht, Baidar *civil engineer, researcher, educator*
Baltazzi, Evan Serge *engineering research consulting company executive*
Bamberger, Joseph Alexander *mechanical engineer, educator*
Bar-Cohen, Avram *mechanical engineering educator*
Bardin, Rollin Edmond *electrical engineering executive*
Barker, Lisa Ann *aerospace engineer*
Bartlett, Desmond William *engineering company executive*
Bartoo, Richard Kieth *chemical engineer, consultant*
Bascom, Willard Newell *engineer, scientist, underwater archaeologist*
Bauer, Richard Carlton *nuclear engineer*
Beckjord, Eric Stephen *nuclear engineer, energy researcher*
Bellow, Donald Grant *mechanical engineering educator*
Berger, Frederick Jerome *electrical engineer, educator*
Bergey, John M. *retired technology executive*
Berkholtz, Nicholas Evald *engineering manager, consultant*

Bers, Abraham electrical engineering and physics educator
Bertin, John Joseph aeronautical engineer, educator, researcher
Bigham, James George structural engineer
Bissell, Allen Morris engineer, consultant
Bjorndahl, David Lee electrical engineer
Bloch, Erich retired electrical engineer, former science foundation administrator
Bolie, Victor Wayne engineering educator emeritus
Bollinger, Kenneth John aerospace engineer, computer and space scientist
Bornhorst, Kenneth Frank electromagnetics and systems engineer
Bose, Anjan electrical engineering educator, academic administrator
Brickell, Charles Hennessey, Jr. marine engineer, retired military officer
Bridger, Baldwin, Jr. electrical engineer
Briggs, James Henry, II engineering administrator
†Bronsdon, Robert Lawrence acoustical engineer, artist
Brooks, Mark Hunter systems engineering manager, consultant
Brown, Ronald Malcolm engineering corporation executive
Bunch, Jennings Bryan, Jr. electrical engineer
†Burlingame, Anson Hollyday retired engineer
Burns, Richard Francis mechanical engineer
Bussgang, Julian Jakob electronics engineer
Byrd, Lloyd Garland civil engineer
Carreker, John Russell retired agricultural engineer
Carrera, Rodolfo nuclear engineer, physicist
Carroll, Philip Joseph engineering company executive
Carta, Franklin Oliver retired aeronautical engineer
Carter, Thomas Allen retired engineering executive, consultant
Cassidy, Kevin Andrew retired engineering company executive
Cerny, Louis Thomas civil engineer, association executive
Chance, Kenneth Donald engineer
Chandra, Abhijit engineering educator
Chapanis, Alphonse human factors engineer, ergonomist
Chastain-Knight, Denise Jean process engineer
Cheston, Theodore C. electrical engineer
Childress, Dudley Stephen biomedical engineer, educator
Chin, Robert Allen engineering graphics educator
†Chizeck, Howard Jay engineering educator
Cloonan, Clifford B. electrical engineer, educator
Coble, Hugh Kenneth engineering and construction company executive
Conway, Richard Ashley environmental engineer
Cooper, Austin Morris chemist, chemical engineer, consultant, researcher
Cormia, Frank Howard industrial engineering administrator
Crowley, Joseph Michael electrical engineer, educator
Cullingford, Hatice Sadan chemical engineer
Dally, James William mechanical engineering educator, consultant
Dargan, Pamela Ann systems and software engineer
Davis, Keigh Leigh aerospace engineer
Dawson, Gerald Lee engineering company executive
Deere, Don U. civil engineer
Diamond, Fred I. electronic engineer
Dietz, Patricia Ann engineering administrator
Dietz, William retired aeronautics engineer, consultant
Divine, Theodore Emry electrical engineer
Dodd, Joe David safety engineer, consultant, administrator
Dong, Zhaoqin materials and testing engineer, researcher
Donohue, Marc David chemical engineering educator
Dougherty, Floyd Wallace design engineer
Dull, William Martin engineering executive
Durrani, Sajjad Haidar retired space communications engineer
Dyer, Ira ocean engineering educator, consultant
Eaglet, Robert Danton electrical engineer, aerospace consultant, retired military officer
Eberstein, Arthur former biomedical engineering educator, researcher
Edgar, Thomas Flynn chemical engineering educator
Edmundson, Charles Wayne mechanical engineer, communications executive
Eissmann, Robert Fred manufacturing engineer
Ellis, Michael David aerospace engineer
Engleman, Dennis Eugene electrical engineer
Ettinger, Harry Joseph industrial hygiene engineer, project manager
Ferderber-Hersonski, Boris Constantin process engineer
Fero, Lester K. aerospace engineer, consultant
Fetrow, George Lawrence retired roadway engineering executive
Finger, Harold B. energy, space, nuclear energy, urban affairs and government management consultant
Fingerson, Leroy Malvin engineering executive, mechanical engineer
Fish, Andrew Joseph, Jr. electrical engineering educator, researcher
Fishman, Bernard mechanical engineer
Fleischer, Gerald Albert industrial engineer, educator
Flick, Carl electrical engineer, consultant
Ford, Oral Ivan (Van Ford) retired engineer
Fraser, Donald C. engineering executive, educator
Fritcher, Earl Edwin civil engineer, consultant
Garriott, Owen Kay astronaut, scientist
Gassert, Richard Adam engineering company executive
Genovese, Philip William civil engineer
Gens, Ralph Samuel electrical engineering consultant
Gerhardt, Heinz Adolf August aircraft design engineer
Gerhardt, Jon Stuart mechanical engineer, engineering educator
Germany, Daniel Monroe aerospace engineer
Godo, Einar computer engineer
Goetzel, Claus Guenter metallurgical engineer
Gorenberg, Norman Bernard aeronautical engineer, consultant, retired
Gouse, S. William, Jr. engineering executive, scientist
Graessley, William Walter retired chemical engineering educator
Gray, Harry Joshua electrical engineer, educator
Griffith, Dewey Maurice mechanical engineer, investor
Griswold, Gary Norris engineering company executive
Guerber, Howard P. retired electrical engineer
Gupta, Ramesh Chandra geotechnical engineer, consultant
Haberman, Charles Morris mechanical engineer, educator
Hallett, William Jared nuclear engineer
Halpin, Daniel William civil engineering educator, consultant
Halushynsky, George Dobroslav systems engineer
Hamilton, William Eugene, Jr. electrical engineer
Hammam, M. Shawky electrical engineer, educator
Hanneman, Rodney Elton metallurgical engineer
Hanson, Wendy Karen chemical engineer
Harris, Patricia Lee engineering executive
Harris, Roy Hartley electrical engineer
Hearn, Charles Lee petroleum reservoir engineer
Hecker, Michael Hanns Louis retired electrical engineer, speech scientist
Hellman, Martin Edward retired electrical engineering educator
Henderson, Charles Brooke research company executive
Herbel, LeRoy Alec, Jr. telecommunications engineer
Herman, William Arthur engineering and physics laboratory administrator
Higby, Edward Julian safety engineer
Hoffer, Roy Daniel forensic electrical engineer
Hoffman, John D. engineering educator
Hogan, Neville John mechanical engineering educator, consultant
Hornby-Anderson, Sara Ann metallurgical engineer, marketing professional
Howard, Dean Denton electrical engineer, researcher, consultant
Hunsberger, Robert Earl mechanical engineer, manufacturing executive
Hunt, Donald Edward planning and engineering executive
Hunt, Donnell Ray retired agricultural engineering educator
Hutchinson, John Woodside applied mechanics educator, consultant
Iaquinto, Joseph Francis electrical engineer
Imtiaz, Kauser Syed aerospace engineer
Jensen, Marvin Eli retired agricultural engineer
Johnson, Arnold Ivan civil engineer
†Johnson, Leonard R. industrial engineer, educator
Johnson, Mary Elizabeth Susan consulting engineer
†Johnson, Paul Eugene telecommunications engineer, consultant
Johnson, Robert Walter marine engineer, priest
Johnson, Stewart Willard civil engineer
Jordan, Howard Emerson retired engineering executive, consultant
Kaplan, Ozer Benjamin environmental health specialist, consultant
Kemper, John Dustin mechanical engineering educator
Kimbriel-Eguia, Susan engineering planner
Kinzie, Daniel Joseph biomedical engineer
Kisak, Paul Francis engineering company executive
Klein, Martin ocean engineering consultant
Klink, Robert Michael consulting engineer, management consultant, financial consultant, property developer
Kodali, Hari Prasad electrical engineer
Korab, Arnold Alva engineering executive
Kretschmer, Frank Frederick, Jr. electrical engineer, researcher, consultant
Kubo, Isoroku mechanical engineer
Kuesel, Thomas Robert civil engineer
Kurfess, Thomas Roland mechanical engineering educator
Landgren, George Lawrence electrical engineer, consultant
Landis, William J. mechanical engineer
Legal, Kenneth Joseph control systems engineer
Levinson, Herbert Sherman civil and transportation engineer
Levinson, Stephen Eliot engineering educator, electrical engineer
Li, Tingye electrical engineer
Libertiny, Thomas Gabor mechanical engineer, administrator
Lie, Yu-Chun Donald electrical engineer
Lin, Ping mechanical engineer
Lipsky, Stephen Edward engineering executive, electronic warfare engineer
Liu, Alan Fong-Ching mechanical engineer
Liu, Young King biomedical engineering educator
Lodge, Arthur Scott mechanical engineering educator
Longobardo, Anna Kazanjian engineering executive
Lowe, John, III consulting civil engineer
Luger, Donald R. engineering company executive
Magnabosco, Louis Mario chemical engineer, researcher, consultant
Mahle, Christoph Erhard electrical engineer
Mai, Chao Chen engineer
Mak, Ben Bohdan engineer
Marietta, Elizabeth Ann industrial engineer
Maropis, Nicholas engineering executive
Marshall, Gerald Francis optical engineer, consultant, physicist
Martin, Lee mechanical engineer
Mason, John Latimer engineering executive
Mason, Robert Lester engineer, small business computer consultant
Mates, Robert Edward mechanical engineering educator
McClellan, Robert Edward civil engineer
McCorkle, Michael electrical engineer
McDermott, Kevin J. engineering educator, consultant
McFadden, Peter William retired mechanical engineering educator
McGaughy, Richard Wayne nuclear consultant
McGonigle, John Leo, Jr. civil engineer
McLaughlin, William Irving space technical manager
McLellon, Richard Steven aerospace engineer, consultant
Merriam, Robert W. engineering executive, educator
†Meunier, Robert Raymond research electrical engineer, optical engineer
Miah, Abdul Malek electrical engineer, educator
Mitzner, Kenneth Martin electrical engineering consultant
Moll, David Carter civil engineer
Morgan, James John environmental engineering educator
Mortimer, David William communications engineer
Moyers, Ernest Everett S. retired missile research scientist
Murphy, Elisabeth Maria physical design engineer, consultant
Myers, Phillip Samuel mechanical engineering educator
Nahman, Norris Stanley electrical engineer
Nakayama, Wataru engineering educator, consultant
Navickas, John fluid dynamics engineer, researcher, consultant
Nawy, Edward George civil engineer, educator
Necula, Nicholas electrical engineering consultant
Neshyba, Victor Peter retired aerophysics engineer
Niclas, Karl Bernhard electronics engineer
Nordby, Gene Milo engineering educator
Novak, John Alfred mechanical engineer
Nyman, David Harold retired nuclear engineer
Oliphant, Ernie L. safety educator, public relations executive, consultant
Ortolano, Ralph J. engineering consultant
Peltier, Eugene Joseph civil engineer, former naval officer, business executive
Perkins, Courtland D(avis) engineering educator
Peters, Douglas Cameron mining engineer, geologist
Pezeshki, Kambiz A. metallurgical engineer
Pi, Wen-Yi Shih aircraft company engineer, researcher
Pniakowski, Andrew Frank structural engineer
Porter, Philip Thomas retired electrical engineer
Potvin, Alfred Raoul engineering executive
Pratt, David Terry engineering consultant
Price, James Edward industrial engineer
Pritsker, A. Alan B. retired engineering executive, educator
Rabadi, Wissam engineering executive, engineering educator
Rainer, Rex Kelly civil engineer, educator
Ramaswami, Devabhaktuni chemical engineer
Rappaport, Theodore Scott electrical engineering educator
Rees, Morgan Rowlands engineer, educator
Rehm, Leo Frank civil engineer
Reifsnider, Kenneth Leonard metallurgist, educator
Reinfelds, Juris computer engineering educator
Reitan, Daniel Kinseth electrical and computer engineering educator
Remer, Donald Sherwood engineering economist, cost estimator, educator
Ren, Chung-Li engineer
Reppen, Norbjorn Dag electrical engineer, consultant
Richards, Mark Andrew radar signal processing research engineer
Rinder, Herbert Roy retired electrical engineer
Robertson, Jerry Lewis chemical engineer
Roetman, Orvil M. retired airplane company executive
Rogo, Kathleen safety engineer
Rohr, Davis Charles aerospace consultant, business executive, retired air force officer
Rolewicz, Robert John estimating engineer
Rosenburgh, Dwayne Maurice electronics engineer
Rosenkoetter, Gerald Edwin engineering and construction company executive
Rowe, Joseph Everett electrical engineering educator, administrator
Royal, Allen Lamar engineer
Rudd, D(ale) F(rederick) chemical engineering educator
Rudzki, Eugeniusz Maciej chemical engineer, consultant
Russo, Roy Lawrence electronic design automation engineer, retired
Ryan, Carl Ray electrical engineer
Saeks, Richard Ephraim engineering executive
Salamon, Miklos Dezso Gyorgy mining engineer, educator
Salvatorelli, Joseph J. engineer, consultant
Samorek, Alexander Henry electrical engineer, mathematics and technology educator
Sandry, Karla Kay Foreman industrial engineering educator
Savrun, Ender engineering executive, researcher, engineer
Schachter, Max retired engineering services company executive
Schell, Allan Carter retired electrical engineer
Scherer, A. Edward nuclear engineering executive
Schey, John Anthony metallurgical engineering educator
Schnapf, Abraham aerospace engineer, consultant
Schoeffmann, Rudolf consulting engineer
Schoen, Allen Harry retired aerospace engineering executive
Schultz, Albert Barry engineering educator
Schurmeier, Harris McIntosh aeronautical engineer
Schwinn, Donald Edwin environmental engineer
Scott, Charles David chemical engineer, consultant
Seamans, Robert Channing, Jr. astronautical engineering educator
Seymour, Frederick Prescott, Jr. industrial engineer, consultant
Shank, Maurice Edwin aerospace engineering executive, consultant
Sherman, Frank William engineer
Shur, Michael electrical engineer, educator, consultant
Siljak, Dragoslav D. engineering educator
Simpson, Murray engineer, consultant
Sitnyakovsky, Roman Emmanuil scientist, writer, inventor, translator
Siyan, Karanjit Saint Germain Singh software engineer
Skeels, Stephen Glenn civil engineer
Skromme, Lawrence H. consulting agricultural engineer
Smally, Donald Jay consulting engineering executive
Smith, Virgil Baker retired electrical engineer
Somasundaran, Ponisseril surface and colloid engineer, applied science educator
Sowers, William Armand civil engineer
Spelson, Nicholas James engineering executive, retired
Sten, Johannes Walter control systems engineer, consultant
Stewart, Albert Elisha safety engineer, industrial hygienist
Stiffler, Jack Justin electrical engineer
Stiglich, Jacob John, Jr. engineering consultant
Stroud, John Franklin engineering educator, scientist
Stumpe, Warren Robert scientific, engineering and technical services company executive
Suarez, Michael Anthony civil engineer, consultant
†Susak, David Michael electrical engineer
Swalm, Thomas Sterling aerospace executive, retired military officer
Tachmindji, Alexander John systems engineering consultant
Tamaro, George John consulting engineer
Tellington, Wentworth Jordan engineer
Templeton, Carson Howard engineering executive, policy analyst
Terry, Reese engineering executive
Tetelbaum, Solomon David research engineer
Thal, Herbert Ludwig, Jr. electrical engineer, engineering consultant
†Thomason, Harry Jack Lee, Jr. mechanical engineer
Tokerud, Robert Eugene electrical engineer
Toor, Herbert Lawrence chemical engineering educator, researcher
Tran, Nang Tri electrical engineer, physicist
Treinavicz, Kathryn Mary software engineer
Tsai, Wen-Ying sculptor, painter, engineer
Turner, Lee S., Jr. civil engineer, consultant, former utilities executive
Uman, Martin Allan electrical engineering educator, researcher, consultant
Utlaut, William Frederick electrical engineer
Van Dreser, Merton Lawrence ceramic engineer
Vaughn, Kenneth J. civil engineer, consultant
Vega, J. William aerospace engineering executive, consultant
Velzy, Charles O. mechanical engineer
Voldman, Steven Howard electrical engineer
Wagner, Sigurd electrical engineering educator, researcher
Walasek, Otto Frank chemical engineer, biochemist, photographer
Walker, Loren Haines electrical engineer
Walton, Harold Vincent former agricultural engineering educator, academic administrator
Washington, Charles Henderson laser systems designer, consultant
Waxman, Ronald computer engineer
Wei, Hua-Fang electrical engineer
Weinberger, Arnold retired electrical engineer
Weinschel, Bruno Oscar engineering executive, physicist
Weldon, William Forrest electrical and mechanical engineer, educator
Wetzel, Donald Truman engineering company executive
White, Charles Olds aeronautical engineer
†Wilkins, Dick J. engineering educator
Wilkinson, Todd Thomas project engineer
William, Thomas W. electrical engineer
Williams, Charles Wesley technical executive, researcher
Williams, Dennis Thomas civil engineer
Williams, Howard Walter aerospace engineer, executive
Williams, Thomas W. electrical engineer
Wilson, Gary Thomas engineering executive
Wilson, Melvin Edmond civil engineer
Winchell, William Olin mechanical engineer, educator, lawyer
Wintle, Rosemarie bio-medical electronics engineer
Wood, Allen John electrical engineer, consultant
Woodward, Clinton Benjamin, Jr. civil engineering educator
Yong, Raymond Nen-Yiu civil engineering educator
†Yook, Chong Chul engineering educator
Young, Leo electrical engineer
Yovicich, George Steven Jones civil engineer
Yue, Alfred Shui-choh metallurgical engineer, educator
Yun, James Kyoon electrical engineer
Zajac, Joseph Walter mechanical engineer
Zeitler, Bill Lorenz aviation engineer
Zeller, John Frederick engineering executive
Ziaka-Vasileiadou, Zoe Dimitrios chemical engineer
Zipf, Mark Edward electrical engineer

FINANCE: BANKING SERVICES. *See also* FINANCE: INVESTMENT SERVICES.

UNITED STATES

ALABAMA

Birmingham
Horsley, Richard David banker
Jones, D. Paul, Jr. banker, lawyer
Morgan, Hugh Jackson, Jr. bank executive
Nash, Warren Leslie banker
Northen, Charles Swift, III banker
Powell, William Arnold, Jr. retired banker
Sellers, Fred Wilson accountant
Stone, Edmund Crispen, III banker
Weatherly, Robert Stone, Jr. banker

Guin
†Lolley, Steven V. banker

Huntsville
Boykin, Betty Ruth Carroll mortgage loan officer, bank executive

Mobile
Coker, Donald William economic, management, banking, evaluation & healthcare consultant

Montgomery
Hoffman, Richard William banker

ALASKA

Anchorage
Cuddy, Daniel Hon bank executive
Harris, Roger J. mortgage company executive, entrepreneur
Rasmuson, Elmer Edwin banker, former mayor

ARIZONA

Gilbert
Duran, Michael Carl bank executive

Green Valley
Miner, Earl Howard retired trust banker

Phoenix
Bradley, Gilbert Francis retired banker

Prescott
Moore, Elizabeth Jane banker

Scottsdale
Gray, Walter Franklin retired banker

Tubac
Miller, Frederick Robeson *banker*

Tucson
Ross, Mark L. *mortgage broker*

ARKANSAS

Conway
Daugherty, Billy Joe *banker*

Forrest City
Stipe, John Ryburn *bank executive*

Little Rock
Bowen, William Harvey *banker, lawyer*
Butler, Richard Colburn *banker, lawyer*
Gulley, Wilbur Paul, Jr. *former savings and loan executive*
McAdams, Herbert Hall, II *banker*

CALIFORNIA

Aptos
Dobey, James Kenneth *banker*

Arcadia
Baillie, Charles Douglas *banker*

Beverly Hills
Goldsmith, Bram *banker*
Spivak, Jacque R. *bank executive*

Burbank
DeMieri, Joseph L. *bank executive*
Miller, Clifford Albert *merchant banker, business consultant*

Burlingame
Costa, John Anthony *loan assistant*

Calistoga
Dillon, James McNulty *retired banker*

Crestline
Douglas, Cindy Holloway *mortgage company executive*

Danville
Puffer, Sharon Kaye *residential loan officer*

Davis
Morgan, Charles Edward Phillip *bank executive*

Escondido
Newman, Barry Ingalls *retired banker, lawyer*

Fallbrook
David, Ward Stanton *bank officer, retired federal agency executive*

Fresno
Huizenga, Edward Richard *mortgage banker*
Smith, Richard Howard *banker*

Glendale
Cross, Richard John *banker*

Glendora
†Thomas, Andree K *assistant vice president*

Huntington Beach
MacCauley, Hugh Bournonville *banker*

La Mesa
Schmidt, James Craig *retired bank executive, bankruptcy examiner*

Lafayette
Dethero, J. Hambright *banker*

Laguna Hills
Pelton, Harold Marcel *mortgage broker*

Long Beach
Hancock, John Walker, III *banker*
Keller, J(ames) Wesley *credit union executive*

Los Angeles
Badie, Ronald Peter *banker*
Buchman, Mark Edward *banker*
Lenard, Michael Barry *merchant banker, lawyer*
Magner, Rachel Harris *banker*
McLarnan, Donald Edward *banker, corporation executive*
Wu, Li-Pei *banker*

Menlo Park
Schmidt, Chauncey Everett *banker*

Monterey Park
Crawford, Philip Stanley *bank executive*

Newport Beach
Frederick, Dolliver H. *merchant banker*
Harley, Halvor Larson *banker, lawyer*

Orange
Starr, Richard William *retired banker*

Palo Alto
Cotsakos, Christos Michael *internet financial services company executive*

Pasadena
Patton, Richard Weston *retired mortgage company executive*
Ulrich, Peter Henry *banker*
Vaughn, John Vernon *banker, industrialist*

Pebble Beach
Burkett, William Andrew *banker*

Piedmont
Hoover, Robert Cleary *retired bank executive*

Playa Del Rey
Blomquist, Carl Arthur *medical and trust company executive, insurance executive*

Pomona
McDonough, Julie Marie *mortgage company executive, consultant*

Rancho Cucamonga
Horton, Michael L. *mortgage company executive, publishing executive*

Rolling Hills Estates
Chuang, Harold Hwa-Ming *banker*

Roseville
Hennessey, David Patrick *banker*

Sacramento
Waller, Larry Gene *mortgage banking executive*

San Diego
Blakemore, Claude Coulehan *banker*
Kendrick, Ronald H. *banker*
Lindh, Patricia Sullivan *banker, former government official*
Reinhard, Christopher John *merchant banking, venture capital executive*
Wiesler, James Ballard *retired banker*

San Francisco
Aldinger, William F., III *banker*
August-deWilde, Katherine *banker*
Baumhefner, Clarence Herman *banker*
Bee, Robert Norman *banker*
Demarest, David Franklin, Jr. *banker, former government official*
Dorfman, Paul Michael *bank executive*
Eckersley, Norman Chadwick *bank executive*
Gillette, Frankie Jacobs *retired savings and loan executive, social worker, government administrator*
Hazen, Paul Mandeville *banker*
Jacobs, Rodney L. *bank executive*
Lee, Pamela Anne *bank executive, accountant, business analyst*
Luikart, John Ford *investment banker*
Miller, John Nelson *banker*
Olds, John Theodore *banker*
Oliver, John Edward *bank strategic management and training consultant*
Peters, Raymond Robert *bank executive*
Peterson, Rudolph A. *banker*
Rosenberg, Richard Morris *banker*
Trowbridge, Thomas, Jr. *mortgage banking company executive*
Tyran, Garry Keith *banker*
Vogt, Evon Zartman, III (Terry Vogt) *merchant banker*
Warner, Harold Clay, Jr. *banker, investment management executive*

San Luis Obispo
Carr, Roxanne Marie *mortgage company executive*

Santa Barbara
Anderson, Donald Meredith *bank executive*
Tilton, David Lloyd *savings and loan association executive*

Santa Monica
Morgan, Monroe *retired savings and loan executive*
Weil, Leonard *banker*

Simi Valley
Harris, Richard Anthony Sidney *trust company executive*
Shirilla, Robert M. *bank executive*

Turlock
Wallström, Wesley Donald *bank executive*

Vacaville
Sawyer, Nelson Baldwin, Jr. *credit union executive*

Walnut Creek
McGrath, Don John *banker*
Rhody, Ronald Edward *banker, communications executive*

Woodland Hills
Floyd, Brett Alden *mortgage banker*

COLORADO

Boulder
Martin, Phillip Dwight *bank consulting company executive, mayor*

Colorado Springs
Olin, Kent Oliver *banker*

Denver
Fugate, Ivan Dee *banker, lawyer*
Grant, William West, III *banker*
Levinson, Shauna T. *financial services executive*
Malone, Robert Joseph *bank executive*
Nicholson, Will Faust, Jr. *bank holding company executive*
Rockwell, Bruce McKee *retired banker and foundation executive*

Englewood
Corboy, James McNally *investment banker*
Rosser, Edwin Michael *mortgage company executive*
Sims, Douglas D. *bank executive*

Fort Collins
Koessel, Donald Ray *retired banker*

Georgetown
Hildebrandt-Willard, Claudia Joan *banker*

Greeley
Smith, Jack Lee *bank executive*

Greenwood Village
Davidson, John Robert (Jay) *banking executive*

Lakewood
Orullian, B. LaRae *bank executive*

Pueblo
Meek, Charles Ronald

CONNECTICUT

Avon
†Dodd, David K. *banker*

Bloomfield
†Klinger, Douglas Evan *money management executive*

Bridgeport
Freeman, Richard Francis *banker*

Cobalt
Stevens, Robert Edwin *bank executive, former insurance company executive*

Cos Cob
Kane, Jay Brassler *banker*

Darien
Mapel, William Marlen Raines *retired banking executive*

Essex
Miller, Elliott Cairns *retired bank executive, lawyer*

Fairfield
Brett, Arthur Cushman, Jr. *banker*
DeCarlo, Deena M. *mortgage company executive*

Greenwich
Bachenheimer, Ralph James *merchant banker*
Birle, James Robb *investment banker*
de Visscher, Francois Maria *investment banker*
Egbert, Richard Cook *retired banker*
Shanks, Eugene Baylis, Jr. *banker*
Weppler, Jay Robert *merchant banking executive*
Weyher, Harry Frederick, III *merchant banker*

Hamden
Williams, Edward Gilman *retired banker*

Hartford
Kraus, Eileen S. *bank executive*
Newell, Robert Lincoln *retired banker*

New Canaan
MacEwan, Nigel Savage *merchant banker*

Ridgefield
Bernstein, William Robert *banker*
Mesznik, Joel R. *investment banker*

Stamford
Baylis, Robert Montague *investment banker*
Philipps, Edward William *banker, real estate appraiser*

Westport
Rastegar, Farzad Ali *investment banker*

Whitneyville
Miller, Walter Richard, Jr. *banker*

DELAWARE

Montchanin
Freytag, Richard Arthur *banker*

Newark
Cawley, Charles M. *banker*

Wilmington
Porter, John Francis, III *banker*
St. Clair, Jesse Walton, Jr. *retired savings and loan executive*
Wright, Vernon Hugh Carroll *bank executive*

DISTRICT OF COLUMBIA

Washington
Aguirre-Sacasa, Francisco Xavier *international banker, diplomat*
Baxter, Nevins Dennis *bank consultant*
†Brown, Mark Malloch *bank executive*
†Burki, Shahid Javed *bank executive*
D'Aniello, Daniel *merchant banker*
†Dervis, Kemal *bank executive*
DuCran, Claudette Deloris *bank officer*
Fitz-Hugh, Glassell Slaughter, Jr. *bank executive*
Flack, Ronald David *diplomat, public service educator, banker*
Graham, William Pierson *investment banker, entrepreneur*
Greenspan, Alan *central banker, economist*
Guenther, Jack Donald *banker*
Higgins, Mark C. *development banker*
†Linn, Johannes *bank executive*
†Logan, Ann D. *financial company executive*
Mathias, Edward Joseph *merchant banker*
McNamara, Robert Strange *former banking executive, cabinet member*
Miller, G(eorge) William *merchant banker, business executive*
Murphy, Shaun Edward *bank executive*
Palmer, R(obie Marcus Hooker) Mark *banker*
Robinson, Daniel Baruch *banker*
Rotberg, Eugene Harvey *investment banker, lawyer*
Shihata, Ibrahim Fahmy Ibrahim *bank executive, lawyer*
Tanous, Peter Joseph *banker*
†Wolfensohn, James David *international public officer*

FLORIDA

Boca Raton
Barnes, Donald Winfree *financial services executive*
Cannon, Herbert Seth *investment banker*
†Hoppenstein, Abraham Solomon *investment and merchant banker, consultant*

Boynton Beach
Jacobs, C. Bernard *banker*

Clearwater
†Johnson, Randall C. *mortgage banker*

Coral Gables
Weiner, Morton David *banker, insurance agent*

Dunedin
Rosa, Raymond Ulric *retired banker*

Gulfport
Kruse, James Joseph *merchant banker*

Jacksonville
Lane, Edward Wood, Jr. *retired banker*
Rice, Charles Edward *bank executive*
Swartz, Stephen Arthur *banker, lawyer*

Jupiter
Cotter, Joseph Francis *retired hotel and bank executive*

Lantana
Shanahan, Robert B. *banker*

Manalapan
Brennan, Donald P. *merchant banker*

Marco Island
Cooper, Thomas Astley *banking executive*

Miami
Brownell, Edwin Rowland *banker, civil engineer, land surveyor*
Giller, Norman Myer *banker, architect, author*

Naples
Craighead, Rodkey *banker*
Hampton, Philip McCune *banker*
Hooper, John Allen *retired banker*
Kley, John Arthur *banker*
Martinuzzi, Leo Sergio, Jr. *banker*

North Palm Beach
†Connor, John Thomas *retired bank and corporate executive, lawyer*
Lynch, William Walker *banker*
Shaw, Stephen Ragsdale *trust investment executive*

Orlando
Shirek, John Richard *retired savings and loan executive*

Palm Beach
Callaway, Trowbridge *banker*
Curry, Bernard Francis *former banker, consultant*

Palm Harbor
Dunbar, David Wesley *bank executive*

Pompano Beach
Kester, Stewart Randolph *banker*

Ponte Vedra Beach
de Selding, Edward Bertrand *retired banker*
O'Brien, Raymond Vincent, Jr. *banker*

Punta Gorda
Haswell, Carleton Radley *banker*

Santa Rosa Beach
Wright, John Peale *retired banker*

Temple Terrace
Rink, Wesley Winfred *banker*

Tequesta
Turrell, Richard Horton, Sr. *retired banker*

Venice
O'Keefe, Robert James *retired banker*

Vero Beach
Sheehan, Charles Vincent *investment banker*

GEORGIA

Atlanta
Barron, Patrick Kenneth *bank executive*
Carlisle, Patricia Kinley *mortgage company executive, paralegal*
Chapman, Hugh McMaster *banker*
†Estes, Joseph O'Bryant, II *mortgage corporation executive*
Forrestal, Robert Patrick *banker, lawyer*
Halwig, Nancy Diane *banker*
Hollis, Timothy Martin *bank executive*
Ivey, Michael Wayne *mortgage broker*
Snelling, George Arthur *banker*
Spiegel, John William *banker*
Watts, Anthony Lee *bank executive*
Williams, James Bryan *banker*

Flowery Branch
Monroe, Melrose *retired banker*

Marietta
Schuelke, Constance Patricia *mortgage company executive*

Savannah
Giblin, Patrick David *retired banker*
Howard, Constance Adair *bank officer*

Sea Island
LaWare, John Patrick *retired banker, federal official*

HAWAII

Honolulu
Dods, Walter Arthur, Jr. *bank executive*
Hoag, John Arthur *retired bank executive*
Johnson, Lawrence M. *banker*
Keir, Gerald Janes *banker*
Midkiff, Robert Richards *financial and trust company executive, consultant*
Stephenson, Herman Howard *retired banker*
Wolff, Herbert Eric *banker, former army officer*

IDAHO

Eagle
Tschacher, Darell Ray *mortgage banking executive*

ILLINOIS

Batavia
Schilling, Arlo Leonard *bank executive*

Belleville
Bailey, Susan Carol *commercial banking executive*

Blue Island
Yager, Vincent Cook *banker*

Champaign
Selby, Barbara Kenaga *bank executive*

Chicago
Bakwin, Edward Morris *banker*
Barrow, Charles Herbert *investment banker*
Bartter, Brit Jeffrey *investment banker*
Bobins, Norman R. *banker*
Bolger, David P. *bank executive*
Cole, Stephen Salisbury *bank executive*
Dancewicz, John Edward *investment banker*
Darr, Milton Freeman, Jr. *banker*
De Leonardis, Nicholas John *bank executive, financial lecturer, educator*
Eddy, David Latimer *banker*
Finley, Harold Marshall *investment banker*
Franke, Richard James *retired investment banker*
Goldberg, Sherman I. *banking company executive, lawyer*
Griffiths, Robert Pennell *banker*
Hart, Pamela Heim *banker*
Heagy, Thomas Charles *banker*
Hollis, Donald Roger *banking consultant*
Istock, Verne George *banker*
Keating, Terry Michael *commercial banker*
Kinzie, Raymond Wyant *banker, lawyer*
Klapperich, Frank Lawrence, Jr. *investment banker*
Klebba, Raymond Allen *property manager*
Kramer, Ferdinand *mortgage banker*
McCoy, John Bonnet *banker*
McKay, Neil *banker*
Montgomery, Charles Howard *retired bank executive*
Paulus, Michael John *bank executive, economist*
Pollock, Alexander John *banker*
Rizzi, Joseph Vito *banker*
Roberts, Theodore Harris *banker*
Schroeder, Charles Edgar *banker, investment management executive*
Socolofsky, Jon Edward *banker*
Stevens, Mark *banker*
Stewart, Patricia Ann *banker*
Stirling, James Paulman *investment banker*
Theobald, Thomas Charles *banker*
Thomas, Richard Lee *banker*
Vander Wilt, Carl Eugene *banker*
Vitale, David J. *banker*
Williams, Edward Joseph *banker*

Deerfield
Bagley, Thomas Steven *private equity investor*

Dundee
Weck, Kristin Willa *bank executive*

Edelstein
†Hickey, Bernard J. *bank executive*

Fox River Grove
Abboud, Alfred Robert *banker, consultant, investor*

Godfrey
Miller, Donald Edward *banking executive*

Golf
Fellingham, Warren Luther, Jr. *retired banker*

Havana
Sinnock, Elizabeth Anne *bank officer*

Highwood
Brown, Lawrence Haas *banker*

Hinsdale
Kinney, Kenneth Parrish *retired banker*

Hoffman Estates
Weston, Roger Lance *banker*

Hopedale
Birky, John Edward *banker, consultant, financial advisor*

Kenilworth
Corrigan, John Edward, Jr. *banker, lawyer*

Lake Bluff
Anderson, Roger E. *bank executive*

Lake Forest
Ross, Robert Evan *bank executive*

Moline
Parise, Marc Robert *banker*

Northbrook
Gratalo, John, Jr. *mortgage banker, business owner*
Keehn, Silas *retired bank executive*
Lezak, Jeffrey Mayer *mortgage broker*

Palatine
†Chalupa, Vlastislav John *retired bank executive*
Fitzgerald, Gerald Francis *retired banker*

Springfield
Ferguson, Mark Harmon *banker, lawyer*
Lohman, Walter Rearick *banker*

Washington
Blumenshine, Mahlon *banker*

INDIANA

Columbus
Abts, Henry William *banker*
Nash, John Arthur *bank executive*

Evansville
McCutchan, William Mark *banker*

Fort Wayne
Kirkwood, Maurice Richard *banker*
Shaffer, Paul E. *retired banker*

Granger
Skodras, Vicki Herring *banker*

Indianapolis
Dietz, William Ronald *financial services executive*
Meyer, William Michael *mortgage banking executive*

Monticello
Howarth, David H. *retired bank executive*

Muncie
Anderson, Stefan Stolen *bank executive*

Portage
Gasser, Wilbert (Warner), Jr. *retired banker*

Tell City
Smith, Mary Katherine *banker*

Terre Haute
Smith, Donald E. *banker*

IOWA

Baxter
Edge, John Forrest *banker*

Cedar Rapids
Nebergall, Donald Charles *rural consultant*

Des Moines
Bucksbaum, Matthew *real estate investment trust company executive*

Dubuque
Dunn, Frank M. (Francis Michael Dunn) *banker*

Maquoketa
Tubbs, Edward Lane *banker*

Traer
Hulme, Darlys Mae *banker*

KANSAS

Coldwater
Adams, Elizabeth Herrington *banker*

Leawood
Ballard, John William, Jr. *banker*
Linn, James Herbert *retired banker*

Manhattan
Stolzer, Leo William *bank executive*

Pratt
Loomis, Howard Krey *banker*

Roeland Park
Morgan, Bruce Blake *banker*

Shawnee Mission
Gregory, Lewis Dean *trust company executive*
McEachen, Richard Edward *banker, lawyer*
Schwartz, Lawrence Michael, Jr. *retired investment banker*

Tonganoxie
Torneden, Connie Jean *bank officer*

Topeka
Aleshire, Richard Joe *banker*
Dicus, John Carmack *thrift savings bank executive*
Johnson, Arnold William *mortgage company executive*
Rolley, Alan W. *banker*

KENTUCKY

Inez
Duncan, Robert Michael *banker, lawyer, Republican national committeeman*

Lexington
Savage, William Earl *bank executive, religious educator*

Louisa
Burton, John Lee, Sr. *banker*

Louisville
Guillaume, Raymond Kendrick *banker*
Hower, Frank Beard, Jr. *retired banker*
Showalter, Robert Earl *banker*
Tyrrell, Gerald Gettys *banker*

Shepherdsville
†Pike, Burlyn *bank director, lawyer*

LOUISIANA

Alexandria
Bolton, Robert Harvey *banker*

Baton Rouge
Moyse, Hermann, III *banker*

Covington
Blossman, Alfred Rhody, Jr. *banker*

Lafayette
Stuart, Walter Bynum, III *banker*

New Orleans
Creamer, German Gonzalo *bank executive, educator*
Wakefield, Benton McMillin, Jr. *banker*

Ruston
Marbury, William Ardis *banker*

Shreveport
Nelson, George Dalman, Jr. *banker*

MAINE

Andover
Ellis, George Hathaway *retired banker and utility company executive*

Bangor
Bullock, William Clapp, Jr. *banker*

Bristol
Schmidt, Thomas Carson *international development banker*

Portland
Saufley, William Edward *banker, lawyer*

MARYLAND

Annapolis
McGuirk, Ronald Charles *banker*
Schleicher, Nora Elizabeth *banker, treasurer, accountant*

Baltimore
Baldwin, Henry Furlong *banker*
Couper, William *banker*
Liberto, Joseph Salvatore *retired banker*
Morrel, William Griffin, Jr. *banker*
Murray, Joseph William *banker*
Schaefer, Robert Wayne *banker*
Shattuck, Mayo Adams, III *investment bank executive*
Stainrook, Harry Richard *banker*

Bethesda
Comings, William Daniel, Jr. *mortgage banker, housing development executive*
Petty, John Robert *financier*
Rosenbaum, Greg Alan *merchant banker, consultant*
Veniard, Jose M. *bank officer*

Chestertown
Williams, Henry Thomas *retired banker, real estate agent*

Chevy Chase
Broumas, John George *retired banker, retired theatre owner*
Saul, B. Francis, II *bank executive*

College Park
†Bento, Antonio Miguel R. *banking consultant*

Crownsville
Wright, Harry Forrest, Jr. *retired banker*

Elkton
Harrington, Benjamin Franklin, III *retired business consultant*

Ellicott City
Faulstich, Albert Joseph *banking consultant*

Frederick
Hoff, Charles Worthington, III *banker*

Hagerstown
†Kelly, Philip A. *bank executive*

Montgomery Village
Byrne, James Edward *international banking expert*

Potomac
Bibby, Douglas Martin *mortgage association executive*
Schonholtz, Joan Sondra Hirsch *banker, civic worker*

Rockville
Meyer, F. Weller *bank executive*

Saint Michaels
Shipley, L. Parks, Jr. *banker*

Sparks Glencoe
Swackhamer, Gene L. *bank executive*

MASSACHUSETTS

Boston
Alden, Vernon Roger *corporate director, trustee*
Berg, Gordon Hercher *banker*
Brown, William L. *banker*
Carter, Marshall Nichols *banker*
Comeau, Susan *bank executive*
Fallon, John Golden *banker*
Finnegan, Neal Frances *banker*
Gifford, Charles Kilvert *banker*
Hamill, John P. *bank executive*
Hill, Richard Devereux *retired banker*
Little, Arthur Dehon *investment banker*
Murray, Terrence *banker*
Phillips, Daniel Anthony *trust company executive*
Ray, William F. *banker*
Safe, Kenneth Shaw, Jr. *fiduciary firm executive*
Sheehan, Monica Mary *banker*
Simard, Patricia Gannon *economic development finance administrator*
Stepanian, Ira *banking executive*
Vermilye, Peter Hoagland *banker*
†Weisberg, Bruce Steven *bank executive*
Williams, Charles Marvin *commercial banking educator*

Cambridge
Edgerly, William Skelton *banker*

Dedham
Bachman, Carol Christine *trust company executive*

Dover
Aldrich, Frank Nathan *banker*
Crittenden, Gazaway Lamar *retired banker*
Stockwell, Ernest Farnham, Jr. *banker*

Longmeadow
Lo Bello, Joseph David *bank executive*

Medford
Sloane, Marshall M. *banker*

Newburyport
MacWilliams, Kenneth Edward *investment banker*

Salem
McLaughlin, Michael Angelo *mortgage consultant, author*

Wellesley
Small, Parker Adams, III *investment banker*

West Bridgewater
Worrell, Cynthia Lee *bank executive*

Weston
Aquilino, Daniel *banker*

Westover AFB
Martin, Glenn Michael *mortgage banker*

Westwood
Riley, Henry Charles *banker*

Winchester
Brennan, Francis Patrick *banker*

Woburn
Curry, John Michael *investment banker*

Worcester
Hunt, John David *retired banker*
Spencer, Harry Irving, Jr. *retired banker*

MICHIGAN

Bay City
Van Dyke, Clifford Craig *retired banker*

Bloomfield Hills
Colladay, Robert S. *trust company executive, consultant*
Houston, E. James, Jr. *bank officer*
Rusin, Edward A. *banker*

Detroit
Babb, Ralph W., Jr. *banker*
Greenwood, Harriet Lois *environmental banker, researcher*
Jeffs, Thomas Hamilton, II *banker*
Miller, Eugene Albert *banker*

Farmington Hills
Ebert, Douglas Edmund *banker*
Heiss, Richard Walter *former bank executive, consultant, lawyer*

Flint
Piper, Mark Harry *retired banker*
Taeckens, Pamela Webb *banker*

Frankfort
Foster, Robert Carmichael *banker*

Gaylord
Weiss, Debra S. *bank commission official*

Grand Rapids
Canepa, John Charles *banking consultant*

Grosse Pointe
Richardson, Dean Eugene *retired banker*
Surdam, Robert McClellan *retired banker*
Thurber, Cleveland, Jr. *trust banker*

Kalamazoo
Holland, Harold Herbert *banker*

Linden
†Piper, William Howard *banker*

Saginaw
Evans, Harold Edward *banker*

Wirz, Pascal Francois *trust company executive*
Wolff, William F., III *investment banker*
Wriston, Walter Bigelow *retired banker*
Wu, Sarah Zheng *investment banker*
Young, Robert Craig *banker*
Zwerling, Gary Leslie *investment bank executive*

Niskayuna
Whittingham, Harry Edward, Jr. *retired banker*

Oyster Bay
Schwab, Hermann Caspar *banker*

Plandome
Williams, Morgan Lloyd *retired investment banker*

Pomona
Kapnick, Stewart *investment banker*

Queensbury
Mead, John Milton *banker*

Ridgewood
Jones, Harold Antony *banker*

Rochester
Lohouse, Dennis Elmer *banker, investment manager*
Simon, Leonard Samuel *banker*

Rye
Lerner, Frederic Howard *financial executive, educator*

Saratoga Springs
Wait, Charles Valentine *banker*

Scarsdale
Hines, William Eugene *banker*

Stamford
Bergleitner, George Charles, Jr. *investment banker*

Staten Island
Chapin, Elliott Lowell *retired bank executive*

Syracuse
Gray, Charles Augustus *banker*

Tonawanda
Haller, Calvin John *banker*

Utica
Schrauth, William Lawrence *banker, lawyer*

West Harrison
Verano, Anthony Frank *retired banker*

Westbury
Tulchin, Stanley *banker, lecturer, author, business reorganization consultant*

White Plains
Bober, Lawrence Harold *retired banker*

Whitesboro
Raymonda, James Earl *retired banker*

NORTH CAROLINA

Charlotte
Browning, Roy Wilson, III *mortgage banking executive*
Crutchfield, Edward Elliott, Jr. *banking executive*
Georgius, John R. *bank executive*
Hance, James Henry, Jr. *bank executive*
†Lewis, Kenneth D. *banker*
McColl, Hugh Leon, Jr. *bank executive*
Wilson, Milner Bradley, III *retired banker*

Fairmont
Byrne, James Frederick *banker*

Gastonia
Teem, Paul Lloyd, Jr. *bank executive*

Highlands
Bell, William Henry, Jr. *banker*

Pinehurst
Schneider, Donald Frederic *banker*

Raleigh
Hardin, Eugene Brooks, Jr. *retired banker*
Holding, Lewis R. *banker*
Stevenson, Denise L. *business executive, banking consultant*

Rocky Mount
Wilkerson, William Holton *banker*

Wilmington
Fulrath, Andrew Wesley *bank executive*

Wilson
Stewart, Burton Gloyden, Jr. *retired banker*

Winston Salem
Austell, Edward Callaway *banker*
Baker, Leslie Mayo, Jr. *banker*
Cramer, John Scott *retired banker*
McNair, John Franklin, III *banker*
Medlin, John Grimes, Jr. *banker*
Runnion, Howard J., Jr. *banker*
Wanders, Hans Walter *banker*

OHIO

Akron
Blackstone, Patricia Clark *banker, psychotherapist*

Beachwood
Brandon, Edward Bermetz *retired banking executive*

Canton
Carpenter, Noble Olds *banker*

Chagrin Falls
Obert, Charles Frank *banker*

Cincinnati
Brumm, Paul Michael *banker*
Schaefer, George A., Jr. *bank executive*
Thiemann, Charles Lee *banker*

Cleveland
Daberko, David A. *banker*
Gillespie, Robert Wayne *banker*
Glickman, Carl David *banker*
Koch, Charles Joseph *banker*
Powers, Richard Daniel *banker*
Redus, Darrin Miguel *banker*
Rupert, John Edward *retired savings and loan executive, business and civic affairs consultant*
†Schmid, William Gregory *bank executive*
Schutter, David John *banker*
Siefers, Robert George *banker*

Columbus
Glaser, Gary A. *bank executive*
Leiter, William C. *banking executive*
McNennamin, Michael J. *bank executive*
O'Donnell, F. Scott *banker*
Page, Linda Kay *banking executive*

Dublin
†Mullen, Thomas J. *mortgage company executive*

Hamilton
Pontius, Stanley N. *bank holding company executive*

Miamisburg
Tozer, Theodore William *mortgage company executive*

Newark
Manning, Ronald Lee *banker*
McConnell, William Thompson *commercial banker*

Pepper Pike
Mc Call, Julien Lachicotte *banker*

Perrysburg
Yager, John Warren *retired banker, lawyer*

Sylvania
Bergsmark, Edwin Martin *mortgage bank executive*

Toledo
Carson, Samuel Goodman *retired banker, company director*
Koppus, Betty Jane *retired savings and loan association executive*
Kunze, Ralph Carl *retired savings and loan executive*
Nitschke, Shaun Michael *bank officer*

Willoughby
Abelt, Ralph William *bank executive*

OKLAHOMA

Bartlesville
Doty, Donald D. *retired banker*

Konawa
Rains, Mary Jo *banker*

Oklahoma City
Brown, Kenneth Ray *banker*
Browne, John Robinson *banker*
Trost, Louis Frederick, Jr. *banker, financial planner*
Williams, William Ralston *retired bank and trust company executive*

Tulsa
Hawkins, Francis Glenn *banker, lawyer*

OREGON

Eugene
Drennan, Michael Eldon *banker*
Winnowski, Thaddeus Richard (Ted Winnowski) *bank executive*

Gold Beach
Gores, Gary Gene *credit union sales manager*

Medford
Lantis, Donna Lea *retired banker, art educator, artist*

Milwaukie
Staver, Leroy Baldwin *banker*

Portland
Jensen, Edmund Paul *retired bank holding company executive*
McKay, Laura L. *banker, consultant*

PENNSYLVANIA

Bala Cynwyd
Bausher, Verne C(harles) *banker*

Erie
Bracken, Charles Herbert *banker*

Gettysburg
Ozag, David *human resources executive*

Gratz
Herb, Jane Elizabeth *banker*

Hanover
Stevenson, Paul J. *bank executive, bank officer*

Harleysville
Daller, Walter E., Jr. *banking executive*

Harrisburg
Campbell, Carl Lester *banker*
Rishel, Richard Clinton *banker*

Kennett Square
Jewitt, David Willard Pennock *retired banker*

Lancaster
Ashby, Richard James, Jr. *bank executive, lawyer*
Fritsch, Richard Elvin *trust company executive*

Lansdale
Fawley, John Jones *retired banker*

Lebanon
Parrott, Charles Norman *bank executive*

Leola
McElhinny, Wilson Dunbar *banker*

Lititz
Bolinger, Robert Stevens *banker*

Malvern
Bedrosian, Gregory Ronald *investment banker*

Media
Cooke, M(erritt) Todd *banker*

Philadelphia
Boehne, Edward George *banker*
†Cohen, Betsy Z. *bank executive*
Foulke, William Green *retired banker*
Kardon, Robert *mortgage company executive*
Larsen, Terrance A. *bank holding company executive*
Murdoch, Lawrence Corlies, Jr. *retired banker, economist*
Potamkin, Meyer P. *mortgage banker*
Reintzel, Warren Andrew *trust company executive*
Spolan, Harmon Samuel *banker*
Walker, Douglas C. *banker*

Pittsburgh
Alexander, Andrew James *commercial lender*
Cahouet, Frank Vondell *banking executive*
Clyde, Larry Forbes *banker*
Hansen, Stephen Christian *banker*
Lahey, Regis Henry *bank executive*
McGuinn, Martin Gregory *banker, lawyer*
Milsom, Robert Cortlandt *banker*
Morby, Jeffrey Lewis *banker, investment banker*
O'Brien, Thomas Henry *bank holding company executive*
O'Hanlon, Charles Francis, III *bank executive*
Pearson, Nathan Williams *investment management executive*

Plymouth Meeting
†Silver, Louis Edward *investment banker, management consultant*

Radnor
Eagleson, William Boal, Jr. *banker*

Reading
Erdman, Carl L. N. *retired banker*
Roesch, Clarence Henry *banker*

Saint Davids
Pollard, Edward Ellsberg *banker*
Sheftel, Roger Terry *merchant bank executive*

Scranton
Janoski, Henry Valentine *banker, former investment counselor, realtor*

Sewickley
Ostern, Wilhelm Curt *retired holding company executive*

Shippensburg
Grim, Patricia Ann *banker*

Souderton
Hoeflich, Charles Hitschler *banker*

Telford
Hagey, Walter Rex *retired banker*

Washington
†Starek, John T. *banker*

West Chester
Swope, Charles Evans *bank president, lawyer*
Taylor, Bernard J., II *banker*

West Conshohocken
Boenning, Henry Dorr, Jr. *investment banker*

Wyomissing
Moll, Lloyd Henry *banker*

RHODE ISLAND

Providence
Burns, Robert E. *bank executive*
Gardner, Thomas Earle *investment banker, managment/financial consultant*

Westerly
Devault, David V. *bank executive*

SOUTH CAROLINA

Columbia
Boggs, Jack Aaron *banker, municipal government official*

SOUTH DAKOTA

Centerville
Thomson, John Wanamaker *bank executive*

Sioux Falls
Allmendinger, Betty Lou *retired bank employee*
Engen, Lee Emerson *savings and loan executive*

TENNESSEE

Brentwood
Wood, Stephen Fletcher *mortgage banker, software executive*

Cleveland
Johnson, Beverly Phillips *chairman, bank officer*

Clinton
Birdwell, James Edwin, Jr. *retired banker*

Harrogate
Robertson, Edwin Oscar *banker*

Johnson City
Surface, James Louis, Sr. *trust officer, lawyer*

Maryville
Lawson, Fred Raulston *banker*

Memphis
Booth, Robert Lee, Jr. *banker*
Horn, Ralph *bank executive*

Murfreesboro
Ford, William F. *banker*

Nashville
Bottorff, Dennis C. *banker*
Cook, Charles Wilkerson, Jr. *banker, former county official*
Daane, James Dewey *banker*
Fleming, Samuel M. *banker*
Harrison, Clifford Joy, Jr. *banker*
Maihafer, Harry James *retired banker, former army officer, writer*

TEXAS

Abilene
Bentley, Clarence Edward *savings and loan executive*

Alamo
Fellenstein, Cora Ellen Mullikin *retired credit union executive*

Amarillo
Burgess, C(harles) Coney *bank executive*
Williams, Jerry Don *bank executive*

Austin
Bunten, William Daniel *retired banker*
Deal, Ernest Linwood, Jr. *banker*
Howard, John Loring *retired trust banker*
Stone, Leon *banker*

Dallas
Brown, Gloria Vasquez *banker*
Cochran, George Calloway, III *retired bank executive, lawyer*
Hughes, Keith William *banking and finance company executive*
Mason, Barry Jean *retired banker*
McTeer, Robert D., Jr. *banker*
Pistor, Charles Herman, Jr. *former banker, academic administrator*
Reid, Langhorne, III *merchant banker*

Hearne
Moore, Loretta Westbrook *retired banker*

Houston
Bass, Daniel Thomas *banker*
Elkins, James Anderson, Jr. *banker*
Elkins, James Anderson, III *investment banker*
Geis, Duane Virgil *retired investment banker*
Gibbs, Mary Bramlett *banker*
Knapp, David Hebard *banker*
Petit, Brenda Joyce *credit bureau sales executive*

Pasadena
Moon, John Henry, Sr. *banker*

Plano
†Brown, Richard Harris *information technology executive*

San Antonio
Keyser-Fanick, Christine Lynn *banking executive, marketing and strategic planning professional*
Pina, Alberto Buffington *trust company official*
Post, Gerald Joseph *retired banker, retired air force officer*

Tyler
Bell, Henry Marsh, Jr. *banking executive*

Victoria
Stubblefield, Page Kindred *banker*

UTAH

Ogden
Browning, Roderick Hanson *banker*
Draper, Richard Nelson *banker*
Manning, Donna *banker*

Park City
Montgomery, James Fischer *savings and loan association executive*

Saint George
Beesley, H(orace) Brent *savings and loan executive*

Salt Lake City
Eccles, Spencer Fox *banker*
Hemingway, W(illiam) David *banker*
Lamborn, W. John *bank executive*
Simmons, Roy William *banker*

VERMONT

Manchester
Carey, James Henry *banker*

VIRGINIA

Alexandria
Birely, William Cramer *investment banker*
Woelflein, Kevin Gerard *banker*

Arlington
Leland, Marc Ernest *trust advisor, lawyer*
Rogers, James Frederick *banker, management consultant*

Ashburn
Pavsek, Daniel Allan *banker, educator*

Bluefield
Spracher, John C. *banking executive*

Charlottesville
Bull, George Albert *retired banker*

Falls Church
Geithner, Paul Herman, Jr. *banker*

Lynchburg
Quillian, William Fletcher, Jr. *retired banker, former college president*

Mc Lean
Brendsel, Leland C. *federal mortgage company executive*
Glenn, David Wright *mortgage company executive*
Kimberly, William Essick *investment banker*
Ramsey, Lloyd Brinkley *retired savings and loan executive, retired army officer*
Schools, Charles Hughlette *banker, lawyer*

Norfolk
Cutchins, Clifford Armstrong, III *banker*
Williamson, Jean Elizabeth *office manager*

Phenix
Davis, Peggy Hamlette *banking executive*

Purcellville
Kok, Frans Johan *investment banker*

Richmond
Black, Robert Perry *retired banker, executive*
Broaddus, John Alfred, Jr. *bank executive, economist*
Henley, Vernard William *banker*
Jones, Catesby Brooke *retired banker*
Moore, Andrew Taylor, Jr. *banker*
Talley, Charles Richmond *commercial banking executive*
Tilghman, Richard Granville *banker*

Virginia Beach
Harrison, William Wright *retired banker*
Mann, Harvey Blount *retired banker*

Williamsburg
Bernhardt, John Bowman *banker*

WASHINGTON

Bellevue
Davidson, Robert William *merchant banker*

Friday Harbor
Buck, Robert Follette *retired banker, lawyer*

Kirkland
Melby, Orville Erling *retired banker*

Mercer Island
Spitzer, Jack J. *banker*

Oak Harbor
Piercy, Gordon Clayton *bank executive*

Olympia
Alfers, Gerald Junior *retired banker*

Seattle
Andrew, Lucius Archibald David, III *bank executive*
Arnold, Robert Morris *banker*
Campbell, Robert Hedgcock *investment banker, lawyer*
Cockburn, John F. *retired banker*
Cullen, James Douglas *banker, finance company executive*
Faulstich, James R. *retired bank executive*
Green, Joshua, III *banker*
Greenwood, W. R., III *investment banker*
Killinger, Kerry Kent *bank executive*
Porter, Walter Thomas, Jr. *bank executive*
Rice, Norman B. *bank executive, former mayor*

Sequim
Laube, Roger Gustav *retired trust officer, financial consultant*

Spokane
Lindsay, Donald Parker *former savings bank executive*
McWilliams, Edwin Joseph *banker*

Tacoma
Fetters, Norman Craig, II *banker*
Odlin, Richard Bingham *retired banker*
Owen, Thomas Walker *banker, broker*

WEST VIRGINIA

Charleston
Martin, Jerry Harold *bank examiner*

WISCONSIN

Brookfield
Bauer, Chris Michael *banker*

Kenosha
Seitz, Florian Charles *retired banker*

Marinette
Staudenmaier, Mary Louise *banker, lawyer*

Menomonee Falls
Walters, Ronald Ogden *mortgage banker*

Milwaukee
Fitzsimonds, Roger Leon *bank holding company executive*
Long, Robert Eugene *banker*
Samson, Allen Lawrence *bank executive*
†Schmidt, Christian E. *bank executive*
†Weening, Richard William, Jr. *banker, finance and communications executive, venture capitalist*

WYOMING

Cheyenne
Knight, Robert Edward *banker*

CANADA

BRITISH COLUMBIA

Vancouver
Gardiner, William Douglas Haig *bank executive*

ONTARIO

Hamilton
Johnston, Malcolm Carlyle *bank executive*

Ottawa
Freedman, Charles *bank executive*

Toronto
Augustine, Jerome Samuel *merchant banker*
Baillie, Alexander Charles, Jr. *banker*
Barrett, Matthew W. *banker*
Bickford, James Gordon *banker*
Brooks, Robert Leslie *bank executive*
Cleghorn, John Edward *bank executive*
Flood, A. L. (Al Flood) *retired bank executive*
Fullerton, R. Donald *banker*
†Godsoe, Peter Cowperthwaite *banker*
Greenwood, Lawrence George *banker*
Hayes, Derek Cumberland *banking executive, lawyer*
Kluge, Holger *retired bank executive*
Lawson, Jane Elizabeth *bank executive*
MacDougall, Hartland Molson *corporate director, retired bank executive*
Styles, Richard Geoffrey Pentland *retired banker*
Taylor, Allan Richard *retired banker*
Thomson, Richard Murray *retired banker*
Webb, Anthony Allan *banker*

QUEBEC

Laval
Pichette, Claude *former banking executive, university rector, research executive*

Montreal
Beaudoin, François *financial institution president, chief executive officer*
Berard, André *bank executive*
Turmel, Jean Bernard *banker*

ARGENTINA

Buenos Aires
Sacerdote, Manuel Ricardo *banker*

AUSTRALIA

Sydney
Olsen, Robert John *savings and loan association executive*

ENGLAND

London
Barren, Bruce Willard *merchant banker*
Binney, Robert Harry *bank executive*
Catto of Cairncatto, Baron Stephen Gordon *banker*
Collins, Paul John *banker*
Pennant-Rea, Rupert Lascelles *banker, economist*

Ross on Wye
Barlow, Matthew Blaise Joseph *merchant banker*

FRANCE

La Couture Boussey
Karnath, Lorie Mary Lorraine *bank officer, consultant*

INDIA

New Delhi
Mehta, Ravi Ravinder Singh *banking trainer and researcher, trade specialist*

ITALY

Milan
Bruno, E. *bank company executive*

SINGAPORE

Singapore
†Doctoroff, Mark Gunther *bank officer*

SWITZERLAND

Zurich
Gut, Rainer E. *banker*
Papadakis, Panagiotis Agamemnon *banker, international business executive*

TAIWAN

Taipei
Yeh, Kuo Hsing *bank executive*

ADDRESS UNPUBLISHED

Ackerman, Jack Rossin *investment banker*
Alvord, Joel Barnes *retired bank executive*
Baker, Henry S., Jr. *retired banker*
Ballantine, John Wallis *retired banker*
Barrett, William Joel *investment banker*
Biklen, Stephen Clinton *retired student loan company executive*
Bird, Phillip Craig *mortgage company executive*
Bitner, John William *banker*
Bowen, James Ronald *banker*
Boykin, Robert Heath *banker*
Boyle, Richard James *banker*
Boyles, James Kenneth *retired banker*
Britt, John Roy *banker*
Browning, Colin Arrott *retired banker*
Buckels, Marvin Wayne *savings and loan executive*
Burden, Ordway Partridge *investment banker*
Busch, Noel Henry *banker*
Busse, Leonard Wayne *banker, financial consultant*
Christenson, Gregg Andrew *bank executive*
Clark, Raymond Oakes *banker*
Clifton, Russell B. *banking and mortgage lending consultant, retired mortgage company executive*
Coleman, Lewis Waldo *bank executive*
Cooney, John Thomas *retired banker*
Costello, Daniel Walter *retired bank executive*
Crozier, William Marshall, Jr. *bank holding company executive*
†Diaz, Javier Vicente *bank executive*
Dittenhafer, Brian Douglas *banker, economist*
†Dobson, James Lane *bank executive*
Dodson, Samuel Robinette, III *investment banker*
Eaton, Curtis Howarth *banker, state agency administrator*
Fahey, Joseph Francis, Jr. *banker, financial consultant*
Fahringer, Catherine Hewson *retired savings and loan association executive*
Figlar, Anita Wise *banker*
Fitzmaurice, Laurence Dorset *bank executive*
Fix, John Neilson *banker*
Ford, William Francis *retired bank holding company executive*
Foster, Stephen Kent *banker*
Franchini, Roxanne *banker*
Frankel, Charles James, III *banker*
Gaffney, Thomas *banker*
Gainor, Thomas Edward *banker*
Gallagher, Lindy Allyn *banker, financial consultant*
Germanotta, Jeffrey Steven *investment banker*
Gilchrist, James Beardslee *banker*
Graham, Cynthia Armstrong *banker*
Grant, James Colin *banker*
Greer, K. Gordon *banker*
Gros, Francisco Roberto André *banker*
Grosland, Emery Layton *banker*
Groves, Michael *banker*
†Harenza, Brian James *international banker*
Harrison, William Burwell, Jr. *banker*
Hayes, Mary Phyllis *savings and loan association executive*
Higginson, Jerry Alden, Jr. *bank executive*
Hogan, Robert Henry *trust company executive, investment strategist*
Howard, Donald Searcy *banker*
Ingersoll, Paul Mills *banker*
James, William W. *banker*
Jennings, Joseph Ashby *banker*
Jones, Richard Melvin *bank executive, former retail executive*
Keehner, Michael Arthur Miller *investment bank executive*
Klein, Robert Majer *retired bank executive*
Klett, Gordon A. *retired savings and loan association executive*
Kooken, John Frederick *retired bank holding company executive*
Korpal, Eugene Stanley *banker, former army officer*
Lafley, Alan Frederick *retired banker*
Lankford, Duane Gail *investment banker, mountaineer*
Larr, Peter *banker*
Levine, Gerald Richard *investment stockbroker, mortgage banker*
Liu, Ernest K. H. *international banking executive, international financial consultant*
Lumpkin, John Henderson *retired banker*
†Lyttle, Kim Eugene *bank officer*
Mayo, Robert Porter *banker*
McAlmond, Russell Wayne *bank executive*
Milligan, Arthur Achille *retired banker*
Miracle, Robert Warren *retired banker*
Montgomery, Parker Gilbert *investment banker*
Moriarty, Donald William, Jr. *banker*
Morris, Frank Eugene *banker*
Morrison, James R. *retired banker*
Mortensen, Peter *banker*

Muñoz, Carlos Ramón *bank executive*
Newland, James LeRoy *retired bank executive*
Newman, Denis *fund executive*
Nichols, C. Walter, III *retired trust company executive*
Nicholson, Richard Joseph *trust banking executive*
Obrecht, Kenneth William *banker*
Odell, Frank Harold *banker*
Oliver, Steven Wiles *investment banker*
Ong, Bernard Tiu *global bank officer*
Osborn, William George *savings and loan executive*
Otto, Ingolf Helgi Elfried *banking institute fellow*
Palmer, Langdon *banker*
Paquin, Paul Peter *corporate finance executive*
Parks, Grace Susan *bank official*
Pendleton, Barbara Jean *retired banker*
Porretta, Emanuele Peter *retired bank executive, consultant*
Pustilnik, Naum Alejandro *investment banker*
Raines, Franklin Delano *corporate executive*
Reuber, Grant Louis *banking insurance company executive*
Rice, Joseph Albert *banker*
Richardson, Richard Thomas *retired banker*
Roberts, Julia Baldwin *retired banker*
Rogers, Nathaniel Sims *banker*
Rundquist, Howard Irving *investment banker*
Schaut, Joseph William *retired banker*
Searle, Philip Ford *banker*
Shah, Bipin Chandra *banker*
Silberstein, Alan Mark *financial services executive*
Simonet, John Thomas *banker*
Smith, Richard Anthony *investment banker*
Smith, Wilburn Jackson, Jr. *retired bank executive*
Stephens, Donald R(ichards) *investor*
Stephens, Elton Bryson *bank executive, service and manufacturing company executive*
Stewart, Carleton M. *banker, corporate director*
Stewart, John Murray *banker*
†Storfer, James R. *financial executive*
Stotter, Harry Shelton *banker, lawyer*
Sweet, Philip W. K., Jr. *former banker*
Swope, Donald Downey *retired banker*
Taylor, David George *retired banker*
Thiessen, Gordon George *banker*
Thompson, J. Andy *bank executive*
Thurmond, John Peter, II *bank executive, rancher, archaeologist*
Tobin, Michael Edward *banker*
Tyson, H. Michael *retired bank executive*
Undlin, Charles Thomas *banker*
Vachon, Serge Jean *bank executive*
Vega, Alberto Leon *financial executive*
Weir, Thomas Charles *banker*
West, Rexford Leon *banker*
Wong, Gwendolyn Ngit How Jim *former bank executive*
Woodard, Nina Elizabeth *banker*
Woodward, William Lee *retired savings bank executive*

FINANCE: FINANCIAL SERVICES

UNITED STATES

ALABAMA

Birmingham
Chin, Kai Chi *financial analyst*
Espey, Linda Ann Glidewell *accountant*
Hall, Robert Alan *financial company executive*
Hardman, Daniel Clarke *accountant*
Powers, Edward Latell *accountant*
Raabe, William Alan *tax author and educator*

Bremen
Weathersby, Cecil Jerry *accounting and finance manager*

Chapman
Miller, James Rumrill, III *finance educator*

Decatur
Michelini, Sylvia Hamilton *auditor*
Talley, Richard Woodrow *accountant*

Dothan
Cross, Steven Jasper *finance educator*

Florence
Richardson, Ruth Delene *business educator*

Huntsville
Graves, Benjamin Barnes *business administration educator*
Morgan, Ethel Branman *accountant, retired electronics engineer*

Mobile
Booker, Larry Frank *accountant*

Montgomery
†Childree, Robert L. *comptroller*
Frazer, Nimrod Thompson *financial services company executive*
Smith, Larry Steven *financial analyst, farmer, accountant*

Pelham
Reed, Terry Allen *accountant*

Point Clear
Hart, Eric Mullins *finance company executive*

Russellville
Malone, Susie Hovater *business educator*

Silas
Jenkins, Randall David *accountant*

Tuscaloosa
Gup, Benton Eugene *banking educator*
Lee, Thomas Alexander *accountant, educator*
Mayer, Morris Lehman *marketing educator*

ALASKA

Anchorage
Price, Margaret Ruth *financial services company executive*
Rylander, Robert Allan *financial service executive*

Barrow
Parkin, Sharon Kaye *bookkeeper*

North Pole
†Prax, Glenn Michael *financial consultant*

ARIZONA

Avondale
Rosztoczy, Ferenc Erno *business executive*

Carefree
Galda, Dwight William *financial company executive*

Eagar
Saunders, James Harwood *accountant*

Flagstaff
Lockwood, Chris A. *business educator, consultant*

Fort Huachuca
Kelly, Maureen Ann *management accountant*

Gilbert
Larson, Dorothy Ann *business educator*

Glendale
Ricks, David Artel *business educator, editor*

Mesa
Tennison, William Ray, Jr. *financial planner, stockbroker, resort owner*

Paradise Valley
Duff, James George *retired financial services executive*

Phoenix
Barnes, Stephen Paul *financial planner*
Burg, Jerome Stuart *financial planning consultant*
Daniel, James Richard *accountant, computer company financial executive*
Fulk, Roscoe Neal *retired accountant*
Gibbs, William Harold *finance company executive*
Holloway, Edgar Austin *retired diversified business executive*
Jungbluth, Connie Carlson *accountant, tax professional*
Krueger, John Charles *financial planner, investment advisor*
Linxwiler, Louis Major, Jr. *retired finance company executive*
Mullen, Daniel Robert *finance executive*
Schabow, John William *accountant*
Stern, Richard David *investment company executive*
Upson, Donald V. *financial executive, retired*
Veit, William Arthur *financial planner*

Scottsdale
Dalton, Howard Edward *retired accounting executive*
Hansen, Donald W. *insurance and financial services executive*

Sun City
Roberts, Anna Ruth *financial consultant*

Sun City West
Person, Robert John *financial management consultant*
Schrag, Adele Frisbie *business education educator*

Tempe
Ger, Shaw-Shyong *accountant*
Kaufman, Herbert Mark *finance educator*
Oakes, Thomas Chapas *financal analyst*
Pany, Kurt Joseph *accounting educator, consultant*
Poe, Jerry B. *financial educator*
Roy, Asim *business educator*

Tucson
Braswel, Kerry *tax accountant, horsewoman*
Schulman, Elizabeth Weiner *financial consultant*
Seay, Suzanne *financial planner, educator*
Taveggia, Thomas Charles *management consultant*

ARKANSAS

Arkadelphia
Webster, Robert Lee *accounting educator, researcher*

Conway
Horton, Finis Gene *financial services company executive*
Moore, Herff Leo, Jr. *management educator*

Fayetteville
Cook, Doris Marie *accountant, educator*
Hay, Robert Dean *retired management educator*
Orr, Betsy *business education educator*
Rosenberg, Leon Joseph *marketing educator*

Fort Smith
Craig, David Clarke *finanacial advisor, instructor*

Hot Springs National Park
Wallace, William Hall *economic and financial consultant*

Little Rock
Conger, Cynthia Lynne *financial planner*
Goodner, Norman Wesley *governmental relations specialist*
Paul, Richard (Aaron) *financial planner, consultant*
Scivally, Bart Murnane *accountant, auditor*

Maumelle
Lewis, Barbara Grimes *financial administrator*

North Little Rock
George, James Edward *accountant*

Pine Bluff
†Sellers, Jennifer Lynn *accountant*

State University
Ruby, Ralph, Jr. *vocational business educator*

CALIFORNIA

Aliso Viejo
Hamilton, Allen Philip *financial advisor*

Anaheim
Lano, Charles Jack *retired financial executive*

Atherton
Barker, Robert Jeffery *financial executive*
Chetkovich, Michael N. *accountant*

Bakersfield
Bacon, Leonard Anthony *accounting educator*

Bell Canyon
Labbett, John Edgar *senior financial executive*

Belvedere Tiburon
Cook, Robert Donald *financial service executive*

Berkeley
Bucklin, Louis Pierre *business educator, consultant*
McKeever, Mike Pierce *economics and business educator*
Staubus, George Joseph *accounting educator*

Beverly Hills
Matzdorff, James Arthur *investment banker, financier*
McGagh, William Gilbert *financial consultant*
Taggart, Sondra *financial planner, investment advisor*
Widaman, Gregory Alan *financial executive, accountant*

Brea
Greytak, Lee Joseph *financial services and real estate development company executive*

Burbank
Gold, Stanley P. *diversified investments executive*
Marinace, Kenneth Anthony *financial advisor*
Petersen, Gladys *accounting clerk, writer*

Calabasas
Goldfield, Emily Dawson *finance company executive, artist*

Carlsbad
Billingsley, William Scott *accountant, controller*
Buckley, Greta Paula *auditor*
Peasland, Bruce Randall *financial executive*

Carmel
Bonfield, Andrew Joseph *tax practitioner*
Steele, Charles Glen *retired accountant*

Carmichael
Areen, Gordon E. *finance company executive*

Cathedral City
Konwin, Thor Warner *financial executive*

Cerritos
Ayloush, Cynthia Marie *financial executive*

Chico
Olsen, Robert Arthur *finance educator*
Van Auken, Stuart *marketing educator*

Chiriaco Summit
Myers, William Elliott *financial consultant*

Chula Vista
Scozzari, Albert *portfolio manager*

Corona Del Mar
Helphand, Ben J. *actuary*

Coronado
Allen, Charles Richard *retired financial executive*

Costa Mesa
Kolanoski, Thomas Edwin *financial company executive*

Covina
Cottrell, Janet Ann *controller*

Culver City
Abarbanell, Gayola Havens *financial planner*
Eckel, James Robert, Jr. *financial planner*

Cupertino
Davis, Barbara Joyce Wiener *accountant, investment manager, financial consultant, educator*
Hill, Claudia Adams *tax consultant*
Supan, Richard Matthew *finance company executive*

Daly City
Dee, Jon Facundo *financial services executive*

Dana Point
Kesselhaut, Arthur Melvyn *financial consultant*
Montanus, Mary Rosamond *accountant*

Davis
Tsai, Chih-Ling *management educator*

Dublin
Murdock, Steven Kent *business consultant, educator*

El Segundo
Pettersen, Thomas Morgan *accountant, finance executive*

Encino
Dor, Yoram *accountant, firm executive*
Fuld, Steven Alan *financial advisor, insurance specialist*

Fallbrook
Freeman, Harry Lynwood *accountant*

Fremont
Jensen, Paul Edward Tyson *business educator, consultant*
Yee, Keith Philip *accountant*

Fresno
Emrick, Terry Lamar *financial business consultant*
Pinkerton, Richard LaDoyt *management educator*
Tellier, Richard Davis *management educator*

Fullerton
Oh, Tai Keun *business educator*
Peralta, Joseph Soriano *financial planner*

Glendale
Tripoli, Masumi Hiroyasu *financial consultant and diplomat*

Granada Hills
Lehtihalme, Larry (Lauri) K. *financial planner*

Hemet
Rowe, Mary Sue *accounting executive*

Hollister
Grace, Bette Frances *certified public accountant*

Huntington Beach
Boysen, Lars *financial consultant*
Strutzel, J(od) C(hristopher) *escrow company executive*

Irvine
Feldstein, Paul Joseph *management educator*

La Canada
Tookey, Robert Clarence *consulting actuary*

La Crescenta
Fisk, Irwin Wesley *financial investigator*

La Habra
Schoppa, Elroy *accountant, financial planner*

La Jolla
Dorsey, Dolores Florence *corporate treasurer, business executive*
Jeub, Michael Leonard *financial executive*
Purdy, Kevin M. *estate planner*

La Mesa
Bailey, Brenda Marie *accountant*

Laguna Hills
†Ortiz, Alfred T. *financial executive*

Lodi
†Miller, Barry Lee *strategic planner*

Long Beach
Morrow, Sharon R. *financial advisor*
Walker, Linda Ann *financial planner*

Los Altos
Halverson, George Clarence *business administration educator*
Sanchez, Marla Rena *controller*

Los Angeles
Allison, Laird Burl *business educator*
Anderson, Kenneth Jeffery *family financial planner, accountant, lawyer*
Bennis, Warren Gameliel *business administration educator, author, consultant*
Borsting, Jack Raymond *business administration educator*
Broad, Eli *financial services executive*
Chan, David Ronald *tax specialist, lawyer*
Cohen, William Alan *marketing educator, author, consultant*
Drummond, Marshall Edward *business educator, university administrator*
Garrison, P. Gregory *diversified financial services company executive*
Gillis, Nelson Scott *financial executive*
Goldberg, Harvey *financial executive*
Goldwyn, Ralph Norman *financial company executive*
Hein, Leonard William *accounting educator*
Knapp, Cleon Talboys *business executive*
Larson, Karin Louise *financial analyst*
Lee, Shi-Chieh (Suchi Lee) *international tax specialist*
Lin, Thomas Wen-shyoung *accounting educator, researcher, consultant*
Meloan, Taylor Wells *marketing educator*
Mock, Theodore Jaye *accounting educator*
Moffatt, Robert Henry *accountant, publisher, writer, consultant*
Morrison, Donald Graham *business educator, consultant*
Morrow, Winston Vaughan *financial executive*
Mosich, Anelis Nick *accountant, author, educator, consultant*
O'Toole, James Joseph *business educator*
Roussey, Robert Stanley *accountant, educator*
Siegel, David Aaron *accountant*
Stancill, James McNeill *finance educator, consultant*
Tuttle, Rick *city controller*
Weston, John Frederick *business educator, consultant*
Williams, Julie Ford *mutual fund officer*

Madera
Kellam, Becky *business educator, consultant*

Malibu
Baskin, Otis Wayne *business educator*

Marina Del Rey
Allmon, Michael Bryan *financial consultant*

Menlo Park
McDonald, Warren George *accountant, former savings and loan executive*
Schleh, Edward Carl *business analyst*
Wolfson, Mark Alan *investor, business educator*

Midway City
McCawley, William Dale, II *accountant, writer, ethnohistorian*

Mill Valley
Ware, David Joseph *financial consultant*

Monterey Park
Lin, Lawrence Shuh Liang *accountant*
Tseng, Felix Hing-Fai *accountant*

Moraga
Coleman, Henry James, Jr. *management educator, consultant*

Napa
Hennings, Dorothy Ann *financial adviser*

Newbury Park
Kocen, Lorraine Ayral *accountant*

Newport Beach
Anyomi, Samuel Mawuena Kweku *business educator*
Indiek, Victor Henry *finance corporation executive*
†Johnson, William S. *financial planning company executive, educator*
Randolph, Steven *insurance and estate planner*
Wood, George H. *investment executive*

North Hollywood
Boulanger, Donald Richard *financial services executive*

Northridge
Ruley, Stanley Eugene *cost analyst*

Oakland
Barlow, William Pusey, Jr. *accountant*
Helvey, Julius Louis, II *finance company executive*
Randisi, Elaine Marie *accountant, educator, writer*
Tran, Nguyet T. *accountant*
Tyndall, David Gordon *business educator*

Oceanside
Garfin, Louis *actuary*
Taverna, Rodney Elward *financial services company executive*

Ontario
Coney, Carole Anne *accountant*

Orange
Kathol, Anthony Louis *finance executive*
Smith, Jack Daryl *accountant, stockbroker*

Palo Alto
Breyer, James William *venture capitalist*
Herrick, Tracy Grant *fiduciary*
Kohler, Fred Christopher *tax specialist*

Palos Verdes Estates
Hughs, Mary Geraldine *accountant, social service specialist*
Manning, Christopher Ashley *finance educator, consultant*

Palos Verdes Peninsula
Barab, Marvin *financial consultant*

Pasadena
Axelson, Charles Frederic *retired accounting educator*
Gillis, Christine Diest-Lorgion *financial planner, stockbroker*
O'Connor, William Charles *automobile agency finance executive*
Walendowski, George Jerry *accounting and business educator*

Petaluma
Cuggino, Michael Joseph *financial executive*

Piedmont
Cole, Peter William *financial executive*

Pleasanton
Majure, Allison Scott *product marketing professional*

Pollock Pines
Johnson, Stanford Leland *marketing educator*

Pomona
Patten, Thomas Henry, Jr. *management, human resources educator*

Poway
Tello, Donna *tax strategist*

Redlands
Barnes, A. Keith *management educator*

Reseda
Chavez, Albert Blas *financial executive*

Riverside
Carpenter, Susan Ann *financial planner*
Harrison, Ethel Mae *financial executive*
Mc Cormac, Weston Arthur *retired educator, retired career officer*
Sheppard, Howard Reece *accountant*

Rocklin
Dwyer, Darrell James *financial executive*

Sacramento
†Fansler, Brian Caldwell *budget analyst*
Herman, Irving Leonard *business administration educator*
Putney, Mary Engler *federal auditor*

Salinas
Stevens, Wilbur Hunt *accountant*

San Clemente
Petruzzi, Christopher Robert *business educator, consultant*

San Diego
Branson, Harley Kenneth *finance executive*
Brimble, Alan *business executive*
Bruggeman, Terrance John *financial corporate executive*
Disney, Michael George *financial services executive*
Gengor, Virginia Anderson *financial planning executive, educator*
Markowitz, Harry M. *finance and economics educator*
Masotti, Louis Henry *management educator, consultant*
Pierson, Albert Chadwick *business management educator*
Riedy, Mark Joseph *finance educator*
Robins, Mitchell James *accountant, management consultant*
Sabin, Gary Byron *financial company executive, investment advisor*
Spanos, Dean A. *business executive*

San Francisco
Buckner, John Knowles *pension administrator*
Entriken, Robert Kersey *retired management educator*
Fuller, James William *financial director*
Gruber, George Michael *accountant, financial systems consultant*
Hallstrom, Robert Chris *government actuary*
Herringer, Frank Casper *diversified financial services company executive*
Jimenez, Josephine Santos *portfolio manager*
Kahn, Linda McClure *actuary, consultant*
Kuhns, Craig Shaffer *business educator*
Larson, Mark Allan *financial executive*
MacNaughton, Angus Athole *finance company executive*
Mayer, Patricia Jayne *financial officer, management accountant*
Mumford, Christopher Greene *corporate financial executive*
Nord, Paul Elliott *accountant*
Olshen, Abraham Charles *actuarial consultant*
Palmer, William Joseph *accountant*
Paterson, Richard Denis *financial executive*
Ramos, Charles Joseph (Joe Ramos) *wealth management consultant*
Savage, Thomas Joseph *executive development company executive, priest*
Tyau, Gaylore Choy Yen *business educator*
Uri, George Wolfsohn *accountant*
Weihrich, Heinz *management educator*
Witter, Wendell Winship *financial executive, retired*
Zobel, Jan A. *tax consultant*

San Gabriel
Bilecki, Ronald Allan *financial planner*

San Jose
Ackerman, Arlene Alice *accountant, business consultant, artist, writer*
Ball, James William *check cashing company executive*
Delucchi, George Paul *accountant*
Kertz, Marsha Helene *accountant, educator*
Morrison, William Fosdick *business educator, retired electrical company executive*
Simons, Roger Mayfield *tax specialist*

San Luis Obispo
Blakeslee, Diane Pusey *financial planner*

San Mateo
Johnson, Charles Bartlett *mutual fund executive*
Johnson, Rupert Harris, Jr. *finance company executive*
Lamson, Kristin Anne *finance company executive*

San Rafael
Heller, H(einz) Robert *financial executive*

Santa Ana
Schulte Shields, Mary Ann *finance executive*

Santa Barbara
Mehra, Rajnish *finance educator*

Santa Monica
Markoff, Steven C. *finance company executive*
Taylor, Nigel Brian *financial planner*

Santa Rosa
Harris, David Joel *financial planner*
Root, Charles Joseph, Jr. *finance executive, consultant*

Sherman Oaks
Hein, Todd Jonathan *accountant*
Rich, Gareth Edward *financial planner*
Tsiros, John Andreas *accountant*

Simi Valley
McBride, Joyce Browning *accountant*
Rehart, Margaret Lee *controller*

Sonora
Wheeler, Elton Samuel *financial executive*

Stanford
†Beaty, Shannon Michelle *financial consultant*
Beaver, William Henry *accounting educator*
Holloway, Charles Arthur *public and private management educator*
Leavitt, Harold Jack *management educator*
McDonald, John Gregory *financial investment educator*
Montgomery, David Bruce *marketing educator*
Pfeffer, Jeffrey *business educator*
Porterfield, James Temple Starke *business administration educator*
Saloner, Garth *management educator*

Stockton
Goldstrand, Dennis Joseph *business and estate planning executive*
Taylor, Francis Michael *auditor, municipal official*
Vargo, Richard Joseph *accounting educator, writer*

Temecula
Locklin, William Ray *financial planner*

Thousand Oaks
Allen, David Harlow *business educator, logistician, consultant*

Toluca Lake
Morris, Janet Eloise *webdesigner, poet*

Universal City
Baker, Richard Eugene *corporate executive*

Upland
Jones, Nancy Langdon *financial planning practitioner*

Vacaville
†Yerkes, Jay Alan *financial planner*

Vallejo
Feil, Linda Mae *tax preparer*

Visalia
Neeley, James K. *credit agency executive*

Vista
Ferguson, Margaret Ann *tax consultant*
Helmuth, Philip Alan *tax consultant*

Walnut
Craig, Karen Lynn *accountant, controller*

Walnut Creek
Boland, Margaret Camille *financial services administrator, consultant*
Coit, R. Ken *financial planner*
Dasovich, E. Martin *accountant*
Fridley, Saundra Lynn *internal audit executive*
McCauley, Bruce Gordon *financial consultant*

Westlake Village
Cammalleri, Joseph Anthony *financial planner, retired air force officer*
Cucina, Vincent Robert *retired financial executive*
Detterman, Robert Linwood *financial planner*

Westminster
Smith, William Hugh, Sr. *retired audit manager, consultant*

Whittier
Maxwell, Raymond Roger *accountant*

Willits
Akins, George Charles *accountant*

Woodland Hills
Anaya, Richard Alfred, Jr. *accountant, investment banker*
Babayans, Emil *financial planner*
Harmon, David *finance company executive*
Taubitz, Fredricka *financial executive*

COLORADO

Arvada
Laidig, Eldon Lindley *financial planner*
Wambolt, Thomas Eugene *financial consultant*

Aurora
Bauman, Earl William *accountant, government official*

Boulder
Bangs, F(rank) Kendrick *former business educator*
Baugh, L. Darrell *financial executive*
Baughn, William Hubert *former business educator and academic administrator*
Goldstein, Michael Aaron *finance educator*
Melicher, Ronald William *finance educator*
Schlander, Mark D. *financial consultant*
Stanton, William John, Jr. *marketing educator, author*
Thomas, Daniel Foley *financial services company executive*

Broomfield
Affleck, Julie Karleen *accountant*

Castle Rock
Eppler, Jerome Cannon *private financial advisor*

Colorado Springs
Bressan, Robert Ralph *accountant*
Gagne, Margaret Lee *accounting educator*
Homan, Ralph William *finance company executive*
Wheeler, Larry Richard *accountant*

Columbine Valley
Wittbrodt, Edwin Stanley *consultant, former bank executive, former air force officer*

Denver
Barber, Larry Eugene *financial planner*
Bell, Steven H. *financial company executive*
Brown, Mark Ransom *financial advisor*
Cook, Albert Thomas Thornton, Jr. *financial advisor*
Gampel, Elaine Susan *investment management analyst and consultant*
Hall, Richard Murray, Jr. *finance executive, consultant*
Herz, Leonard *financial consultant*
Knights, Ronald Michael *business educator*
Leraaen, Allen Keith *financial executive*
Lincoln, Alexander, III *financier, lawyer, private investor*
Sandler, Thomas R. *accountant*
Woodward, Albert Bruce, Jr. *investment advisor, radio broadcaster, arbitrator, expert witness*

Engelwood
Townsend, James Douglas *accountant*

Englewood
Anderson, Peggy Rees *accountant*
Bondi, Bert Roger *accountant, financial planner*
Schwartz, Michael Lee *financial planner, consultant*
Shannon, Richard Stoll, III *financial executive*
Sprincz, Keith Steven *financial services company professional*

Erie
Alpers, John Hardesty, Jr. *financial planning executive, retired military officer*

Fort Collins
Ewing, Jack Robert *accountant*
Kinnison, Robert Wheelock *retired accountant*
Switzer, Ralph V., Jr. *accounting and taxation educator*
Thomas, Jeanette Mae *public accountant*

Greenwood Village
Barnard, Rollin Dwight *retired financial executive*

Lakewood
Keller, Shirley Inez *accountant*

Littleton
Bass, Charles Morris *financial and systems consultant*
Hadley, Marlin LeRoy *direct sales financial consultant*
Newell, Michael Stephen *finance company executive, international finance, protective services consultant*
Ryan, Evonne Ianacone *capital management company executive*

Wheat Ridge
Gerlick, Helen J. *tax practitioner, accountant*
Leino, Deanna Rose *business educator*
Nichols, Vicki Anne *financial consultant, librarian*

CONNECTICUT

Bridgeport
Watson, David Scott *financial services executive*

Brookfield
Foncello, Martin John, Jr. *business and intelligence analyst, consultant*

Danbury
Gezurian, Dorothy Ellen *accounting executive*
Proctor, Richard Jerome, Jr. *business educator, accountant, expert witness*

Darien
Schell, James Munson *financial executive*

East Hampton
†Jamsheed, Jacqueline Tahminey *financial manager*

East Hartford
Barredo, Rita M. *auditor*
Conwell, Theresa Gallo *financial services representative*

Fairfield
Detmar-Pines, Gina Louise *business strategy and policy educator*
Gad, Lance Stewart *investment advisor, lawyer, private investor*
McCain, Arthur Williamson, Jr. *retired pension investment consultant*

Greenwich
Allen, Paul Howard *financial institutions investor*
Fleisher, Jerrilyn *financial planner*
Glick, Steven Lawrence *financial consultant*
Higgins, Jay Francis *financial executive*
Horton, Jared Churchill *retired corporation executive*
Larkin, James Thomas *financial services company executive*
Lockhart, James Bicknell, III *risk management software and services executive*
Miles, Jesse Mc Lane *retired accounting company executive*
Moonie, Clyde Wickliffe *financial consultant*
Moskowitz, Stanley Alan *financial executive*
Seznec, Jean-Francois *international trade and investment manager*
Smith, Rodger Field *financial executive*
von Braun, Peter Carl Moore Stewart *company executive*

Hamden
Tomasko, Edward A. *financial planner*

Hartford
†Bobrow, Marc Adam *auditor, accountant*
Campbell, Timothy Reid *financial services company executive*
Centofanti, Joseph *accountant*
Generas, George Paul, Jr. *finance educator, lawyer*
Mitchell, William Patrick *auditor*
Rabushka Lysik, Michèle *financial advisor*
Trail, Margaret Ann *employee benefits company executive*

Litchfield
Kenagy, Robert Coffman *planning consulting company executive*
Shrady, Alexander James S. *accountant*

New Haven
Abdelsayed, Wafeek Hakim *accounting educator*
Buck, Donald Tirrell *finance educator*
Buckley, Richard Bennett *asset management company executive*
Fried, Charles A. *accountant, financial executive*
Malkin, Moses Montefiore *employee benefits administration company executive*
Williams, Willie, Jr. *credit consultant, writer*

Newington
Foley, Patricia Jean *accountant*

North Haven
Fein, Russ Stuart *financial executive*

North Stonington
Nolf, David M. *financial executive*

North Stormington
Mills, Joshua Redmond *financial executive*

Norwalk
Foster, John McNeely *accounting standards executive*
Freedman, Howard Martin *financial planner*
Mueller, Gerhard G(ottlob) *financial accounting standard setter*
Schmalzried, Marvin Eugene *financial consultant*

Old Greenwich
Fignar, Eugene Michael *financial company executive, lawyer*

Old Lyme
Fairfield-Sonn, James Willed *management educator and consultant*

Portland
Chapman, Allen Floyd *management educator, college dean*

Prospect
Powell, Raymond William *financial planner, school administrator*

Rocky Hill
Roy, Thomas David *accountant*

Stamford
Chamberlain, Jill Frances *financial service executive*
Christophe, Cleveland Aleridge *investment company executive*
Godfrey, Robert R. *financial services executive*
Harris, Wiley Lee *financial services executive*
James, John Whitaker, Sr. *financial services executive*
Jason, J. Julie *money manager, author, lawyer*
Loh, Arthur Tsung Yuan *finance company executive*
Lupia, David Thomas *corporate financial advisor, management consultant*
Marsden, Charles Joseph *financial executive*
McNear, Barbara Baxter *retired financial communications executive, consultant*
Pansini, Michael Samuel *tax and financial consultant*
Popelyukhin, Aleksey *actuary, researcher*
Tully, Daniel Patrick *financial services executive*
Vivian, Jay (R.L. Vivian, Jr.) *retirement funds manager*

Stonington
Rees, Charles H. G. *retired financial officer, investor, consultant*

Thompson
Fisher, William Thomas *business administration educator*

Torrington
Adorno, Monica S. *taxpayer representative*

West Cornwall
Jones, Mark Richard *financial advisor*

Westport
Hayden, Vern Clarence *financial planner*
McElroy, Abby Lucille Wolman *financial consultant*
Ready, Robert James *financial company executive*
Rodiger, W. Gregory, III *financial executive*

Wilton
Campbell, Robert Ayerst *accounting company executive*
Cook, Jay Michael *accounting company executive*
Copeland, James E., Jr. *financial service executive*
Hersh, Ira Paul *tax and financial planning consultant*
Kangas, Edward A. *accounting firm executive*

DELAWARE

Claymont
Doto, Paul Jerome *accountant*

Newark
Bolton, Carile Orville Bogy *auditor, accountant*
Stiner, Frederic Matthew, Jr. *accounting educator, consultant, writer*

Wilmington
†Baker, Pamela W. *accountant*
Griffin, Jo Ann Thomas *retired financial planner, tax specialist*
Porter, Kenneth Wayne *actuary*
Rogoski, Patricia Diana *financial executive*

DISTRICT OF COLUMBIA

Washington
Allbritton, Joe Lewis *diversified holding company executive*
†Antonelli, Angela Maria *policy analyst*
†Armstrong, Alexandra *financial advisor*
Arnold, G. Dewey, Jr. *accountant*
Arundel, John Howard *financial consultant*
Blair, Thomas Delano *inspector general Smithsonian Institution*
†Brown, Stuart L. *tax specialist*
Buzzell, Robert Dow *management educator*
Byron, William James *management educator, former university president*
†Castro, Laura Ellen *accountant*
Edwards, Bert Tvedt *accountant*
Esposito, Mark Alan *stock market executive*
Fischetti, Michael Joseph *accounting educator*
Flood, Mark Damien *finance educator*
†Funches, Jesse L. *financial administrator*
†Gould, W. Scott *financial administrator*

Helfer, Ricki Tigert banking and finance consultant
Hough, Lawrence A. former financial organization executive
†Izard, C. Douglass tax specialist
Johnson, James A. financial organization executive
Kanter, Arnold Lee international businesss consultant, policy analyst
Larsen, Richard Gary accounting firm executive
Le Goc, Michel Jean-Louis business educator
Leonard, H. Jeffrey finance executive
Levy, Michael B. business educator
Lindquist, Robert John accountant, financial investigator
Litke, Arthur Ludwig business executive
MacIntyre, John Alexander financial planner
MacLaury, Bruce King research institution executive
Malek, Frederic Vincent finance company executive
McAllister, Jennifer Rae financial controller
Miller, Carl Frank financial executive, vending controller
Morriss, Nicholas Anson financial consultant
Mosso, Lyle David accountant
Murphy, Lezell Wanda stock market analyst
†Musick, Anthony financial executive
Nordlinger, Gerson, Jr. investor
Page, Harry Robert business administration educator
Penn, Damon Ernest financial company executive, small business owner
†Picciotto, Robert bank executive
Poole, Darryl Vernon financial and executive management consultant
†Seed, Charles J. accountant
Silver, David financial executive, lawyer
Small, Lawrence M. financial organization executive
†Sutcliffe, Ronald Eugene business educator, university dean
Taylor, David Kerr international business educator, consultant
†Thomas, Christopher Paul financial executive
Tuggle, Francis Douglas management educator, consultant, corporate director
Walker, David A(lan) finance educator
Walker, David Michael comptroller
White, Margit Triska financial advisor
Young, Loretta Ann auditor
†Zenker, Wendy financial executive

FLORIDA

Aventura
Kliger, Milton Richard financial services executive

Belleview
Bellis, Arthur Albert financial executive, government official

Boca Raton
Bartunek, Kenneth Steven finance educator
Ferris-Waks, Arlene Susan financial analyst
Jaffe, Leonard Sigmund financial executive
Jessup, Joe Lee business educator, management consultant
Karmelin, Michael Allen financial executive
Kelley, Eugene John business educator
Sigel, Marshall Elliot financial consultant

Boynton Beach
Bartholomew, Arthur Peck, Jr. accountant

Clearwater
Campolettano, Thomas Alfred contract manager
Clingerman, Edgar Allen, Sr. financial services executive
Loos, Randolph Meade financial planner
Sassouni, Chris Garo financial consultant
Teets, Charles Edward international business consultant, lawyer

Cocoa Beach
Wirtschafter, Irene Nerove tax consultant

Coral Gables
Lampert, Wayne Morris corporate financier

Coral Springs
Sommerer, John accountant

Crestview
Scott, George Gallmann accountant

Crystal River
Schlumberger, Robert Ernest accountant

Deerfield Beach
Nolan, Lone Kirsten financial advisor

Deland
Horton, Thomas Roscoe business advisor

Delray Beach
Gatewood, Robert Payne financial planning executive

Fort Lauderdale
Abraham, Rebecca Jacob finance educator
Cobb, David Keith business executive
Kennedy, Beverly (Kleban) Burris financial consultant, tv and radio talk show host
Pohlman, Randolph A. business administration educator, dean
Shoemaker, William Edward financial executive

Fort Myers
Adams, Todd Porter financial and investment advisor

Fort Pierce
Lucy, Donald Michael business and accounting educator, accountant

Gainesville
Davis, John Allen, Jr. (Jeff Davis) financial planner

Gulfport
Keistler, Betty Lou accountant, tax consultant

Hialeah
Shaw, Steven John retired marketing educator, academic administrator

Hobe Sound
DeHority, Edward Havens, Jr. retired accountant, lawyer
Vanderbilt, Oliver Degray financier

Jacksonville
Allen, Ronald Wesley financial executive
Edwards, Marvin Raymond investment counselor, economic consultant
Lindner, Carl Henry, Jr. financial holding company executive
Tomlinson, William Holmes management educator, retired army officer

Jacksonville Beach
Forrest, Allen Wright tax and financial services firm executive, accountant, financial planner

Jupiter
Guilarte, Pedro Manuel holding company executive

Lake Wales
Luing, Gary Alan financial management educator

Largo
Shillinglaw, Gordon accounting educator, consultant

Lauderhill
Sokolowski, Theodor Matwig retired accountant

Lighthouse Point
Shein, Jay Lesing financial planner

Longwood
†Seem, Robert Paul financial planner

Melbourne
Roub, Bryan R(oger) financial executive

Miami
Camacho, Alfredo accountant
Capraro, Franz accountant
Day, Kathleen Patricia financial planner
Dessler, Gary S. business educator, author, consultant, administrator
Duncanson, Harry Richard accountant, financial executive
Ehrlich, Morton international finance executive
Esteves, Vernon Xavier financial consultant, investment advisor
Fishel, Peter Livingston accounting business executive
Flinn, David Lynnfield financial consultant
Guerra, Charles Albert financial consultant and executive
Hallbauer, Rosalie Carlotta business educator
Hendrickson, Harvey Sigbert retired accounting educator
Hodgetts, Richard Michael business management educator
Kregg, Judith Lynne accountant
Lavin, David accountant, educator
Maynard, Cecil Darwin, III auditor, accountant
Nunez-Lawton, Miguel G. international finance specialist
Pomeranz, Felix accounting educator
Ramirez de la Piscina, Julian diversified financial services company executive
Satuloff, Barth accounting executive, dispute resolution professional
Torres, Hugo R. financial analyst, international credit analyst, telecommunications analyst

Naples
Berry, Donald Lee accountant
de Saint Phalle, Thibaut investment banker, educator, lawyer, financial consultant
Handy, Charles Brooks accountant, educator
Ordway, John Danton retired pension administrator, lawyer, accountant
Thomas, Gary Lynn financial executive
Weeks, Richard Ralph marketing educator

Nokomis
Meyerhoff, Jack Fulton financial executive

North Palm Beach
Frevert, James Wilmot financial planner, investment advisor

Ocklawaha
Silagi, Barbara Weibler corporate administrator

Ocoee
Davis, Elena Denise accountant

Orange Park
Glenn, Steven Claude financial executive

Orlando
Armacost, Robert Leo management educator, former coast guard officer
Gray, Anthony Rollin capital management company executive

Palm Beach
Bishop, Warner Bader finance company executive
Cook, Edward Willingham diversified industry executive
Fitilis, Theodore Nicholas portfolio manager

Palm Beach Gardens
Herrick, John Dennis financial consultant, former law firm executive, retired food products executive
Howard, Melvin financial executive

Palmetto
Patton, Ray Baker financial consultant, real estate broker

Pensacola
Carper, William Barclay management educator
Commins, Ernest Altman (Ernie Commins) certified financial planner

Plantation
Garrett, Linda Silverstein financial planner

Pompano Beach
Mulvey, John Thomas, Jr. financial consultant

Ponte Vedra Beach
Brink, John William financial corporation executive
Roland, Melissa Montgomery accountant

Punta Gorda
Bulzacchelli, John G. financial executive

Saint Petersburg
Blumenthal, Herman Bertram accountant
Freeman, Corinne financial services, former mayor
Maier, Karl George estate and financial planner
Putnam, J. Stephen financial executive
Raissi, Joseph financial planner
Wasserman, Susan Valesky accountant

Sarasota
Arreola, John Bradley diversified financial service company executive, financial planner
Bailey, Robert Elliott financial executive
Bewley, David Charles financial planner
Cummings, Erika Helga business consultant
Dryce, H. David accountant, consultant
Lambert, John Phillip financial executive, consultant
Miles, Arthur J. financial planner, consultant
Roberts, Don E. accountant

Spring Hill
Aldrich, David Alan accountant

Stuart
O'Connor, Francis X. financial executive
White, Donald Francis financial planner, insurance agent

Tampa
Alexander, William Olin finance company executive
Becatti, Lance Norman finance company executive
Bradish, Warren Allen internal auditor, operations analyst, management consultant
Carter, James A. finance executive
Hanford, Agnes Rutledge financial adviser
Harriman, Malcolm Bruce investment advisor
Henard, Elizabeth Ann controller
Hernandez, Gilberto Juan accountant, auditor, management consultant
Holder, Anna Maria holding company executive
Nord, Walter Robert business administration educator, researcher, consultant
Schine, Jerome Adrian retired accountant

Venice
Buckley, John William financial company executive

Vero Beach
Danforth, Arthur Edwards finance executive
Fetter, Robert Barclay retired administrative sciences educator
Koontz, Alfred Joseph, Jr. financial and operating management executive, consultant
Riefler, Donald Brown financial consultant

Wesley Chapel
Mendelsohn, Louis Benjamin financial analyst

West Palm Beach
Eppley, Roland Raymond, Jr. retired financial services executive
Livingstone, John Leslie accountant, management consultant, business economist, educator
Robertson, Sara Stewart portfolio manager

Weston
Holtzman, Gary Yale administrative and financial executive

Winter Park
Bevc, Carol-Lynn Anne financial officer
Coulter, Fredrik Vladimir accountant, consultant
Plane, Donald Ray management science educator
Starr, Martin Kenneth management educator
Therrien, Francois Xavier, Jr. business and tax consultant

GEORGIA

Alpharetta
Edmondson, Damon Wayne financial analyst, consultant
Kurtz, Robert Arthur finance company executive
Zimmermann, John financial consultant

Athens
Bamber, Linda Smith accounting educator
Miller, Herbert Elmer accountant
Zinkhan, George Martin, III marketing educator

Atlanta
Averitt, Richard Garland, III financial services company executive
Benston, George James accountant, economist
Brooks, James Joe, III accountant
Chambers, Robert William financial company executive
Dykes, John Henry, Jr. retired finance executive
†Flynn, Marty J. investment company administrator
†Fox, Jack financial service executive
Gross, Stephen Randolph accountant
Hanna, Frank Joseph credit company executive
Hawkins, Robert Garvin management educator, consultant
Hays, William Grady, Jr. corporate financial and bank consultant
Henry, William Ray business administration educator
Hiller, George Mew financial advisor, investment manager, lawyer
Lobb, William Atkinson financial services executive
Martinez, Tino Max financial services company executive
Nelson, Robert Earl, Jr. financial services company executive
O'Haren, Thomas Joseph financial services executive
Parsons, Leonard Jon marketing educator, consultant
Plummer, Michael Kenneth financial consultant
Reid, Joseph William consultant
Sheth, Jagdish Nanchand business administration educator
†Sinclair, Robert P., Jr. accountant
Stubbs, Thomas Hubert company executive
Whitmer, William Eward retired accountant

Augusta
Powell, James Kevin financial planner

Columbus
Huff, Lula Eleanor controller, accounting educator
Segrest, Roger W. auditor, municipal official

Conyers
Spearman, Maxie Ann financial analyst, administrator

Dalton
Winter, Larry Eugene accountant

Decatur
Anderson, Jonpatrick Schuyler financial consultant, therapist, archivist
Frank, Ronald Edward marketing educator
Manners, George Emanuel business educator, emeritus dean
Myers, Clark Everett retired business administration educator
Rodgers, Richard Malcolm management accountant

Duluth
Rogers, William Brookins financial consultant, business appraiser

East Point
McMullan, James Franklin financial planner

Fayetteville
Brown, L(arry) Eddie tax practitioner, real estate broker, financial planner

Hinesville
†Wise, Carl Stamps accounting educator

Kennesaw
Aronoff, Craig Ellis management educator, consultant

Lagrange
Turner, Fred Lamar accountant, lawyer

Macon
Owens, Garland Chester accounting educator

Marietta
Carlin, Stewart Henry accounting executive
Edwards, Charles Mundy, III financial consultant
Panter, Terry Eve accountant

Milledgeville
Engerrand, Doris Dieskow business educator

Norcross
Massey, Lewis finance company executive

Oakwood
Martin, Johnny Benjamin accountant

Peachtree City
Moulder, Wilton Arlyn financial management consultant

Statesboro
Murkison, Eugene Cox business educator

Thomasville
Stepanek, David Leslie financial services company executive

Washington
Mansfield, Norman Connie bookkeeper

Woodstock
Aromin, Mercedes Fung portfolio manager, investment advisor, consultant
Austin, John David retired financial executive

HAWAII

Honolulu
Betts, James William, Jr. financial analyst, consultant
Fukushima, Barbara Naomi financial consultant
Haig, David M. property and investment manager
Hook, Ralph Clifford, Jr. business educator
Ng, Wing Chiu accountant, computer software consultant, educator, activist
Palia, Aspy Phiroze marketing educator, researcher, consultant
Pilar, L. Prudencio R. financial services executive
Solidum, James finance and insurance executive
†Yim, Mario K.M. financial planner

IDAHO

Boise
Gray, Lonna Irene indemnity fund executive
Mock, Stanley Clyde certified financial planner, investment advisor
Pomeroy, Horace Burton, III accountant, corporate executive
Porter, Barbara Reidhaar accounting executive
Randall, Sherri Lee accountant

Hayden
Morris, Mary Ann bookkeeper

Idaho Falls
Call, Joseph Rudd accountant
Riddoch, Hilda Johnson accountant

PROFESSIONAL INDEX 5935 FINANCE: FINANCIAL SERVICES

ILLINOIS

Addison
Baillie-David, Sonja Kirsteen *controller*

Aurora
Halloran, Kathleen L. *financial executive, accountant*

Belleville
Fietsam, Robert Charles *accountant*

Bloomington
Friedman, Joan M. *accounting educator*
Hinojosa, David *fraud examiner*

Bolingbrook
Katsianis, John Nick *financial executive*

Buffalo Grove
Johnson, Craig Theodore *portfolio manager*
Leonetti, Michael Edward *financial planner*

Cahokia
Healy, Steven Michael *accountant, city official*

Carol Stream
Gale, Neil Jan *internet consultant, computer consultant*

Champaign
Bailey, Andrew Dewey, Jr. *accounting educator*
Brighton, Gerald David *accounting educator*
†Ganguly, Ananda Roop *business management educator*
Perry, Kenneth Wilbur *accounting educator*
Schoenfeld, Hanns-Martin Walter *accounting educator*

Charleston
Cooper, George Kile *business educator*

Chicago
Almeida, Richard Joseph *finance company administrator*
Alonzi, Loreto Peter *finance executive*
Baniak, Sheila Mary *accountant*
Bocci, Raymond Perry *auditor*
Bott, Harold Sheldon *accountant, management consultant*
Bryan, William Royal *finance educator*
Calvanico, Joseph James *financial company executive*
Carlson, Richard Gregory *accountant*
Chapman, Alger Baldwin *finance executive, lawyer*
Chookaszian, Dennis Haig *financial executive*
Deli, Anne Tynion *financial services executive*
Eppen, Gary Dean *business educator*
Epstein, Stephen Roger *financial executive*
Falkowski, Patricia Ann *investment consultant, financial analyst*
Fensin, Daniel *diversified financial service company executive*
Fitzgerald, Robert Maurice *financial executive*
Fleming, Richard H. *finance executive*
Forbes, John Edward *financial consultant*
Friend, Robert Nathan *financial counselor, economist, market technician*
Garrigan, Richard Thomas *finance educator, consultant, editor*
Hansen, Claire V. *financial executive*
Haydock, Walter James *banker*
Hicks, Cadmus Metcalf, Jr. *financial analyst*
Hogarth, Robin Miles *business educator, university official*
Howard, Christy J. *actuary*
Kamin, Kay Hodes *financial planner, lawyer, entrepreneur, educator*
†Kleckner, Robert A. *accounting firm executive*
Knowles, Thomas William *business educator, consultant*
Kudish, David J. *financial executive*
Kullberg, Duane Reuben *accounting firm executive*
Lindskog, Norbert F. *business and health administration educator, consultant*
Longman, Gary Lee *accountant*
Lorie, James Hirsch *business administration educator*
Lyman, Arthur Joseph *financial executive*
Mallory, Robert Mark *controller, finance executive*
Mayer, Raymond Richard *business administration educator*
McCormack, Robert Cornelius *investment banker*
Miller, Merton Howard *finance educator*
Moor, Roy Edward *finance educator*
Nelson, Thomas George *consulting actuary*
Parcells, Margaret Ross *deputy auditor general*
Perlmutter, Norman *finance company executive*
Pump, Bernard John *finance company executive*
Rachwalski, Frank Joseph, Jr. *financial executive*
Rauschenberg, Mary Edna *accountant*
†Ropp, Daniel Nels *actuary*
Rosenbaum, Michael A. *investor relations consultant*
Ryan, Leo Vincent *business educator*
Sandor, Richard Laurence *financial company executive*
Schornack, John James *accountant*
Schueppert, George Louis *financial executive*
Seitzinger, Sean Christopher *strategic consultant*
Silva, Cheryl Lynn *financial economist*
Sorgel, Sylvia *financial services executive*
Sullivan, Bernard James *accountant*
Velisaris, Chris Nicholas *financial analyst*
Verschoor, Curtis Carl *business educator, consultant*
Vitale, Gerald Lee *financial services executive*
Weil, Roman Lee *accounting educator*
Wishner, Maynard Ira *finance company executive, lawyer*
Wittenberg, Jon Albert *accountant*
Yacktman, Donald Arthur *financial executive, investment counselor*
Zimmerman, Martin E. *financial executive*

Cicero
†Kreuz, Jeanette C. *accountant, school official*

Crestwood
Cowie, Norman Edwin *credit manager*

De Kalb
Hanna, Nessim *marketing educator*

Decatur
Decker, Charles Richard *investment executive*

Deerfield
Boyd, Joseph Don *financial services executive*
Chromizky, William Rudolph *accountant*
Lifschultz, Phillip *financial and tax consultant, accountant, lawyer*
Russell, William Steven *finance executive*
Serwy, Robert Anthony *accountant*

Des Plaines
Rosenson, Irwin Dale *accountant*

Downers Grove
Morefield, Michael Thomas *financial executive*

Elgin
O'Connor, Peggy Lee *communications manager*

Elk Grove Village
Bandel, David Brian *accountant*

Evanston
Cassell, Frank Hyde *business educator*
Catlett, George Roudebush *accountant*
Corey, Gordon Richard *financial advisor, former utilities executive*
Duncan, Robert Bannerman *strategy and organizations educator*
Lavengood, Lawrence Gene *management educator, historian*
Prince, Thomas Richard *accountant, educator*
Scott, Walter Dill *management educator*
Stern, Louis William *marketing educator, consultant*

Gays
Finley, Gary Roger *financial company executive*

Geneseo
Allen, Leonard Brown *retired tax manager*

Geneva
Young, Jack Allison *financial executive*

Glen Ellyn
Drafke, Michael Walter *business educator, consultant*
Grundy, Roy Rawsthorne *marketing educator*

Glencoe
Silver, Ralph David *financial consultant and arbitrator*

Glenview
Faig, Kenneth Walter *actuary, publisher*
Levin, Donald Robert *business and finance executive, motion picture producer, professional sports team owner*
Mack, Stephen W. *financial planner*

Hanover Park
Schoeld, Constance Jerrine *financial planner*

Jacksonville
Kirchhoff, Michael Kent *economic development executive*

Joliet
Chalmers, Diana Jean *office administrator*
Colonna, William Mark *accountant*

Lake Forest
Reichert, Norman Vernon *financial services consultant*

Libertyville
Feit, Michael *controller*
Harding, James Warren *finance company executive*

Lincolnshire
Kramer, Alexander Gottlieb *financial director*
Mathieson, Michael Raymond *controller*
Pappano, Robert Daniel *financial company executive*

Macomb
Bauerly, Ronald John *marketing educator*

Matteson
Keenan, Robert Arthur *financial executive*

Mchenry
Koehl, Camille Joan *accountant*

Melrose Park
Quirk, Donna Hawkins *financial analyst*

Naperville
Tan, Li-Su Lin *accountant, insurance executive, investment consultant*

Northbrook
Afterman, Allan B. *accountant, educator, researcher, consultant*
Feibel, Frederick Arthur *finanical consultant*
Fischer, Aaron Jack *accountant*
Hill, Thomas Clarke, IX *accountant, systems specialist, entrepreneur*
Mandel, Karyl Lynn *accountant*
Newman, Lawrence William *financial executive*
Roehl, Kathleen Ann *financial executive*
Stearns, Neele Edward, Jr. *diversified holding company executive*

Northfield
Seaman, Jerome Francis *actuary*

Oak Brook
Miller, Robert Stevens, Jr. *finance professional*

Oakbrook Terrace
Catalano, Gerald *accountant, oil company executive*
Ciccarone, Richard Anthony *financial executive*
Keller, Dennis James *management educator*

Oregon
Cain, Vernon *information services executive*

Palatine
Butler, John Musgrave *business financial consultant*
Spinner, Lee Louis *accountant*

Quincy
Mallory, Troy L. *accountant*

Riverdale
Hoekwater, James Warren *treasurer*

Riverside
Perkins, William H., Jr. *finance company executive*

Riverwoods
Yarrington, Hugh *corporate lawyer, communications company executive*

Rockford
Albert, Janyce Louise *business educator, banker*
Davit, Frank Torino *accountant*

Rolling Meadows
O'Connell, Edward Joseph, III *financial executive, accountant*

Roselle
Waite, Darvin Danny *accountant*

Rosemont
Aitken, Rosemary Theresa *financial planner, consultant*

Springfield
Kuhn, Kathleen Jo *accountant*

Sterling
Attebury, Janice Marie *accountant*

Urbana
Bedford, Norton Moore *accounting educator*
Williamson, John Maurice *accountant*

Wheaton
Holman, James Lewis *financial and management consultant*

Wilmette
Hufnagel, Henry Bernhardt *financial advisor*

INDIANA

Beech Grove
Clapper, George Raymond *retired accountant, computer consultant*

Bloomington
Belth, Joseph Morton *retired business educator*
DeHayes, Daniel Wesley *management executive, educator*
Gordon, Paul John *management educator*
Hustad, Thomas Pegg *marketing educator*
Wentworth, Jack Roberts *business educator, consultant*

Columbus
Berman, Lewis Paul *financial executive*

Evansville
Luckett, John Mills, III *construction company financial executive*
McGuire, Brian Lyle *educator, health science facility consultant*

Fishers
Boegel, Nick Norbert *accountant, lawyer*

Fort Wayne
Graf, Robert Arlan *retired financial services executive*
Gretencord, David C. *tax consultant*
Gutreuter, Jill Stallings *financial consultant, financial planner*
Sipe, Roger Wayne *accountant, consultant*

Franklin
Link, E.G. (Jay Link) *corporate executive, family wealth counselor*

Goshen
Lehman, Karl Franklyn *accountant*

Granger
Engel, Brenda Bolton *controller*

Indianapolis
Beuter, Richard William *accountant*
Boggs, Christopher B. *accountant, auditor*
Braham, Delphine Doris *government accountant*
Carlock, Mahlon Waldo *financial consultant, former high school administrator*
†Fiers, John Robert *business executive, police chaplain*
Fisher, Gene Lawrence *financial executive*
Furlow, Mack Vernon, Jr. *retired financial executive, treasurer*
Goodwin, William Maxwell *financial executive*
Gutermuth, Scott Alan *accountant, pharmaceutical company executive*
Israelov, Rhoda *financial planner, writer, entrepreneur*
Kellison, Donna Louise George *accountant, educator*
Kressley, George John, Jr. *financial analyst*
Long, Clarence William *accountant*
Mathioudakis, Michael Robert *life insurance and estate planning executive*
Sales, Angel Rodolfo *financial executive*
Stutz, Jay Francis *controller*
Vietor, John J. *audit manager*
Warstler, David John *auditor*
Williams, Gregory Keith *accountant*
Winemiller, James D. *accountant*

Jasper
Kane, James Robert *financial executive*

Lafayette
Helmuth, Ned D *financial planner*

Muncie
Ball, Virginia Beall *investor*

Notre Dame
Reilly, Frank Kelly *business educator*
Shannon, William Norman, III *marketing and international business educator, food service executive*
Vecchio, Robert Peter *business management educator*

Portage
Cunningham, R. John *retired financial consultant*
Sullivan, Donna Dianne *accountant*

Rensselaer
Slaby, Frank *financial executive*

South Bend
Agbetsiafa, Douglas Kofi *financial and management consultant*
Cohen, Ronald S. *accountant*
Harriman, Gerald Eugene *retired business administrator, economics educator*
Murphy, Christopher Joseph, III *financial executive*
Wrenn, Walter Bruce *marketing educator, consultant*

West Lafayette
Cooper, Arnold Cook *management educator, researcher*
Cosier, Richard A. *business educator, consultant*
Lewellen, Wilbur Garrett *management educator, consultant*

IOWA

Ankeny
Boelens, Patricia Ann *accountant, nurse*

Cedar Falls
Greer, Willis Roswell, Jr. *accounting educator*

Cedar Rapids
Knapp, Barbara Allison *financial services, oncological nurse consultant*
Meyer, Curtis Ray *accountant*
Speicher, Gary Dean *financial planner*

Dallas Center
Snyder, Dana Renee Nelson *business executive*

Davenport
Asadi, Anita Murlene *business educator*
Brocka, M. Suzanne *controller*
Kruse, Rosalee Evelyn *accountant, auditor*

Des Moines
Hyon, Won Sop *certified public accountant, auditor*
Shepherd, Tom Richard *financial executive*
Yetmar, Scott Andrew *accountant, educator*

Fonda
Tamm, Eleanor Ruth *retired accountant*

Iowa City
Collins, Daniel W. *accountant, educator*
Riesz, Peter Charles *marketing educator, consultant*

Muscatine
McMains, Melvin L(ee) *controller*

New Hampton
Babcock, Judy Ann *auditor*

Pacific Junction
Krogstad, Jack Lynn *accounting educator*

Pella
Rudd, Orville Lee, II *finance company executive*
Shimp, Karen Ann *accountant, municipal financial executive*

Sioux City
Knowler, Robert Gene *county treasurer*
Silverberg, David Stanley *financial consultant*

KANSAS

Emporia
Hashmi, Sajjad Ahmad *business educator, university dean*

Hutchinson
Harris, Bill Dean *card services manager*

Kansas City
Globoke, Joseph Raymond *accountant*

Lawrence
Beedles, William LeRoy *finance educator, financial consultant*

Leawood
Byrum, Judith Miriam *accountant*

Lecompton
Conard, John Joseph *financial official*

Mcpherson
Hull, Robert Glenn *retired financial administrator*

Overland Park
Buchanan, William Murray *consulting actuary*
Johnson, Sharon Denise *executive*

Pratt
Jones, Debra K. *accountant*

Shawnee Mission
Hoffman, Alfred John *retired mutual fund executive*
Lucas, James Raymond *author, business executive, management consultant*

Topeka
Reser, Elizabeth (Betty) May *bookkeeper*

Westwood
Ketter, James Patrick *accountant*

KENTUCKY

Bowling Green
Rahim, M. Afzalur *management educator, editor*

Fort Thomas
Hill, Esther Dianne *business education educator*

Frankfort
Chadwell, James Russell, Jr. *controller*
Hatchett, Edward Bryan, Jr. *state auditor, lawyer*

Goshen
McClinton, Donald George *diversified holding company executive*

Louisville
Besser, Lawrence Wayne *corporate accountant*
Carr, Larry Dean *financial services executive*
Dalton, Jennifer Faye *accountant*
Min, Hokey *business educator*

Murray
Boston, Betty Lee *financial consultant, financial planner*

Richmond
Kensicki, Peter Robert *insurance, finance educator*

Scottsville
Porter, Charles Michael *retail company executive*

Versailles
Humes, David Walker *accountant*

LOUISIANA

Baton Rouge
Bedeian, Arthur George *business educator*
†Breaux, Cindy Addison *accountant*
Brown, Raymond Jessie *financial and insurance company executive*
Crumbley, Donald Larry *accounting educator, writer, consultant*
†Czerwinski, Sally Huffman *information systems manager*
DeVille, Donald Charles *accountant*
D'Souza, Alan S. *tax consultant, real estate agent, pianist, writer*
McGarr, Charles Taylor *accountant*

Covington
Files, Mark Willard *business and financial consultant*
Foil, Donald Carl *accountant*

Crowley
Martin, Edythe Louviere *business educator*

Gonzales
Leake, Anita Robin *accountant, financial analyst*

Kenner
Scherich, Edward Baptiste *retired diversified company executive*

Leesville
Wimberly, Beadie Reneau (Leigh Wimberly) *financial services executive*

Metairie
Boazman, Franklin Meador *financial consultant*
Doody, Louis Clarence, Jr. *accountant*
McShan, Clyde Griffin, II *financial executive*
Whitehorn, W. Elizabeth Randazzo *accountant*

Monroe
Wolfe, Michael David *management educator*

New Orleans
Dunbar, Prescott Nelson *investment company executive*
Hansel, Stephen Arthur *holding company executive*
Ingraham, Joseph Edwin *financial officer*
Ledbetter, Linda Carol *pension fund executive, professional organization executive*
Suber, Margaret Adele *controller*
Vella, Joseph Bayer *portfolio manager*
Wild, Dirk Jonathan *accountant*

Ruston
Marbury, Virginia Lomax *insurance and investment executive*
Pullis, Joe Milton *business administration educator, writer*

Shreveport
†Jacobs, Catherine Heriot *financial advisor*
Lenard, Lloyd Edgar *financial consultant*

Thibodaux
Delozier, Maynard Wayne *marketing educator*
Fairchild, Joseph Virgil, Jr. *accounting educator*

MAINE

Augusta
†Whitney, Carol F. *controller*

Bangor
Albrecht, Ronald Lewis *financial services executive*
Albrecht, Rondi Kim *financial services executive*

Friendship
MacIlvaine, Chalmers Acheson *retired financial executive, former association executive*

Hampden
Stratton, Frances Ruth *retired bookkeeper*

South Portland
Martin, Joseph Robert *financial executive*

Topsham
Palesky, Carol East *tax accountant*

MARYLAND

Aberdeen Proving Ground
Leonard, Virginia Kathryn *public financial manager*

Annapolis
Smith, Robert Myron *investment company executive*

Baltimore
Ambler, Bruce Melville *energy company executive*
Buggs, Elaine S. *financial analyst*
Duke, George Wesley *financial executive*
†Hilgenberg, John Christian *financial executive, corporate director, consultant*
Jacobs, Richard James *banker, educator*
Killebrew, Robert Sterling, Jr. *investment manager*
Ourednik, Patricia Ann *accountant*
Pratt, Joan M. *comptroller*
Siegel, Melvyn Harry *financial consultant, securities company executive*
Tringali, Joseph *financial planner, accountant*
Wist, Paul Gabriel *accountant*

Bethesda
Burt, Marvin Roger *financial advisor, investment manager*
Castelli, Alexander Gerard *accountant*
Cornelius, Maria G. *financial advisor*
Nason, Charles Tuckey *financial services executive*
Rankin, James Patrick *financial services company executive*
Soffer, Lowell Charles *financial executive*

Bozman
Wyatt, Wilson Watkins, Jr. *communications and public affairs executive*

Brandywine
Jacob, Sharon Rose *accountant, consultant*

Cambridge
Higgins, Michael Edward *finance executive*

Chevy Chase
Smith, Peter Leonard *diversified financial services company executive*

College Park
Gordon, Lawrence Allan *accounting educator*
Gupta, Anil Kumar *management educator*
Kolodny, Richard *finance educator*
Lamone, Rudolph Philip *business educator*
Sims, Henry P., Jr. *management educator*
Stehman, Betty Kohls *financial and management consultant*

Easton
Crowder, Jo Anne Corkran *certified public accountant*

Elkridge
Calton, Sandra Jeane *accountant*

Ellicott City
Clive, Craig N. *compensation executive*

Gaithersburg
Johnson, George H. *financial services company executive*
Ruth, James Perry *financial planning executive*

Hagerstown
Bever, Melanie Sue *credit company manager*

Hanover
Schmidt, Sandra Jean *financial analyst*

Joppa
Kott, Beverly Parat *financial counselor*

Laurel
Kuska, John Joseph, Jr. *accountant*

Lusby
Hutchins, Edith Elizabeth *payroll administrator*

Mitchellville
Hagans, Robert Reginald, Jr. *financial executive*

Montgomery Village
Malhotra, Deepak *accountant*

Owings Mills
Hoffman, Craig Allan *finance executive*

Potomac
Gowda, Narasimhan Ramaiah *financial consultant*

Rockville
Gillick, Betsy Brinkley *financial analyst*
Jacques, Joseph William *investment advisor*
Milan, Thomas Lawrence *accountant*
Sherman, Howard D. *financial consultant*
Smith, Raymond Douglas *management educator*

Salisbury
Ezell-Grim, Annette Schram *business management educator, academic administrator*
Hoffman, Richard Curzon, IV *business administration educator*

Silver Spring
Grubbs, Donald Shaw, Jr. *retired actuary*
Schwarz, Louis Jay *financial advisor*
Simon, Donald John *employee benefits administrator, insurance and investment broker*
Yasher, Michael *accountant*

Stevenson
Hyman, Sigmund M. *benefits consultant*

Sykesville
Vreeland, Russell Glenn *accountant, consultant*

Waldorf
Gregan, John Patrick *finance executive, small business owner*

Woodstock
Price, John Roy, Jr. *financial executive*

Wye Mills
Schnaitman, William Kenneth *finance company executive*

MASSACHUSETTS

Acton
Coughlin, Cornelius Edward *accounting company executive*

Allston
Mills, Daniel Quinn *business educator, consultant, author*

Amherst
Levine, Michael Lawrence *financial planner*
Manz, Charles C. *management educator*

Arlington
Corrigan, Terence Martin *tax specialist, accountant*

Babson Park
Stephenson, Craig Allen *financial educator*

Bedford
Kouyoumjian, Charles H. *diversified financial services company executive*
Peiser, Robert Alan *financial executive*

Belmont
Rich, Sharon Lee *financial planner*

Boston
Aber, John William *finance educator*
Akin, Steven Paul *financial company executive*
Baker, Charles Duane *business administration educator, former management executive*
Barbee, George E. L. *financial services and business executive*
Bower, Joseph Lyon *business administration educator*
Boyd, David Preston *business educator*
Bruns, William John, Jr. *business administration educator*
Christensen, Carl Roland *business administration educator*
Christenson, Charles John *retired business educator*
Colburn, Kenneth Hersey *financial executive*
Crook, Robert Wayne *mutual funds executive*
D'Alessandro, David Francis *financial services company executive*
Dupill, Michael Joseph *tax accountant*
Eastman, Thomas George *investment management executive*
Ebsworth, William Robert *investment company executive*
Elfner, Albert Henry, III *mutual fund management company executive*
Farb, Thomas Forest *financial executive*
Fletcher, Cathy Ann *auditor*
Gifford, Nelson Sage *financial company executive*
Gould, James Spencer *financial consultant*
Gulman, Richard Bruce *tax accountant*
Hayes, Robert Herrick *technology management educator*
Hayes, Samuel Linton, III *business educator*
Johnson, Edward Crosby, III *financial company executive*
Kanter, Rosabeth Moss *management educator, consultant, writer*
Karafotias, Nicholas Charles *finance professional*
Karelitz, Richard Alan *financial executive, lawyer*
Kingman, William Lockwood *financial consultant*
Lawrence, Paul Roger *retired organizational behavior educator*
Lee, Jonathan Owen *financial services company executive, lawyer*
Lodge, George C(abot) *business administration educator*
Lovett, Miller Currier *management educator, clergyman*
MacArthur, Sandra Lea *financial services executive*
Marshall, Martin Vivan *business administration educator, business consultant*
Maxwell, J. B. *financial and marketing consultant*
McArthur, John Hector *business educator*
McCraw, Thomas Kincaid *business history educator, editor, author*
McFarlan, Franklin Warren *business administration educator*
Park, William H(erron) *financial executive*
Pitts, James Atwater *financial executive*
Reiling, Henry Bernard *business educator*
Schnitzer, Iris Taymore *financial management executive, lawyer*
Schwister, Jay Edward *portfolio manager*
Shames, Jeffrey *financial services company executive*
Skinner, Wickham *business administration educator*
Sloane, Carl Stuart *business educator, management consultant*
Stevenson, Howard Higginbotham *business educator*
Stobaugh, Robert Blair *business educator, business executive*
Temkin, Robert Harvey *accountant*
Tucker, Richard Lee *financial executive*
Vatter, Paul August *business administration educator, dean*
Weiss, James Michael *financial analyst, portfolio manager*
Wheatland, Richard, II *fiduciary services executive, museum executive*
†Widmann, John Andrew *account administrator, musician*

Brewster
Hickok, Richard Sanford *retired accountant*

Brockton
Clark, Carleton Earl *tax consultant*

Brookline
Olenick, Arnold Jerome *accountant, financial management consultant*
Reedy, Harry Lee *financial services executive*

Burlington
Pettinella, Nicholas Anthony *financial executive*

Cambridge
Deshpandé, Rohit *marketing educator*
French, Kenneth Ronald *finance educator*
Hauser, John Richard *marketing and management science educator*
Hax, Arnoldo Cubillos *management educator, industrial engineer*
Kelley, Albert Joseph *global management strategy consultant*
Leonard, Herman Beukema (Dutch Leonard) *public finance and management educator*
Little, John Dutton Conant *management scientist, educator*
Magnanti, Thomas L. *management and engineering educator*
Pounds, William Frank *management educator*
Safran, Edward Myron *financial service company executive*
Urban, Glen L. *management educator*

Canton
Kurzman, Stephen Alan *accountant*
Tockman, Ronald Chester *accountant*
†Walsh, Donna Lee *treasurer*

Chestnut Hill
Fouraker, Lawrence Edward *retired business administration educator*

Concord
Smith, Peter Walker *finance executive*

Eastham
Souther, Jean Lorraine *accounting and management educator, accountant*

Everett
Jenkins, Alexander, III *business executive*

Foxboro
Bush, Raymond T. *accountant, corporate professional*

Framingham
Jones, Clark Powell, Jr. *financial services executive*
Rosenberg, Victor Laurence *management educator, entrepreneur*

Gloucester
Means, Elizabeth Rose Thayer *financial consultant, lawyer*

Hingham
Hart, Richard Nevel, Jr. *financial exective, consultant*

Hopkinton
McGuire, Frank Joseph *accountant*

Leominster
Ford, John Stephen *treasurer*

Lexington
Muldowney, Michael Patrick *finance executive*
Wyss, David Alen *financial service executive*

Longmeadow
Constance, Barbara Ann *financial planner, small business owner, consultant*
Skelton, Don Richard *consulting actuary, retired insurance company executive*

Lowell
Teague, Bernice Rita *accountant*

Milford
Samojla, Scott Anthony *accountant*

Millbury
Noonan, Stephen Joseph *accounting firm executive*

Nantucket
Louderback, Peter Darragh *accountant, consultant*

Newton
Churchill, Daniel Wayne *management and marketing educator*

North Dartmouth
†Ainscough, Thomas Lee, Jr. *business educator, internet marketing consultant*

Osterville
Silk, Alvin John *business educator*

Pepperell
Osten, Patricia Ann *tax specialist*

Pittsfield
Gregware, James Murray *financial planner*

Quincy
Werner, Joanne Loucille *financial executive*

Randolph
Cammarata, Richard John *financial advisor*

Salem
Gruhl, Suzanne Swiderski *accountant*
†Popkin, Nancy Popkin *financial planner*

Sherborn
Kaplan, Harley Lance *financial planner*

Stoneham
Astill, Robert Michael *credit manager*

Stoughton
Bestgen, William Henry, Jr. *financial planner*

Sudbury
Meltzer, Donald Richard treasurer

Swampscott
Wolff, Richard Carl financial planner, insurance agency and pension planning company executive

Swansea
Hjerpe, Edward Alfred, III finance and banking executive

Waban
Tofias, Allan accountant

Wakefield
Coffman, Dallas Whitney financial consultant

Waltham
Klein, Lawrence Allen accounting educator

Weston
Ives, J. Atwood financial executive
Rockwell, George Barcus financial consultant
Valente, Louis Patrick (Dan) business and financial executive

Wilmington
Bartlett, John Bruen financial executive

Worcester
Banks, McRae Cave, II management educator, consultant
Greenberg, Nathan accountant

MICHIGAN

Ada
Van Andel, Steve Alan business executive

Allendale
Veazey, Richard Edward accounting educator

Ann Arbor
Cornelius, Kenneth Cremer, Jr. finance executive
Elger, William Robert, Jr. accountant
Foster, Alan Herbert financial consultant, educator
Huntington, Curtis Edward actuary
Kim, E. Han finance and business administration educator

Arcadia
Ogilvie, Bruce Campbell financial consultant

Auburn Hills
Drexler, Mary Sanford financial executive
Kulesza, Chester Stephen (Bud Kulesza) finance executive
Trebing, David Martin financial executive

Battle Creek
Jagner, Ronald Paul financial administrator, consultant

Birmingham
Buczak, Douglas Chester financial advisor, lawyer
McDonald, Alonzo Lowry, Jr. business and financial executive

Bloomfield Hills
Gulati, Vipin accountant
Marks, Craig management educator, consultant, engineer
Poth, Stefan Michael retired sales financing company executive

Clarkston
Forrester, Alan McKay capital company executive

Conway
Sedgwick-Hirsch, Carol Elizabeth financial executive

Dearborn
Lee, Hei Wai finance educator, researcher

Dearborn Heights
Bajaria, Bharat Jamnadas accountant

Detroit
Adams, William Johnston financial and tax consultant
Carlson, John Dennis, Jr. accountant
Cavanagh, Gerald Francis business educator
DeChellis, Giacomo John controller, accountant
Guilfoyle, James Joseph financial executive, accountant
Kahalas, Harvey business educator

East Lansing
Arens, Alvin Armond accountant, educator
Hollander, Stanley Charles marketing educator

Farmington Hills
Helppie, Charles Everett, III financial consultant
Michlin, Arnold Sidney finance executive

Flint
Rappleye, Richard Kent financial executive, consultant, educator

Grand Rapids
Parrish, Kenneth Dale treasurer, accountant
Thauer, Edwin William, Jr. financial services executive
†Vander Steen, Dirk Willem financial executive
Welton, Michael Lee financial advisor

Grosse Pointe
Weingart, Robert Paul financial consultant

Holland
Zick, Leonard Otto accountant, manufacturing executive, consultant

Ishpeming
Cope, Robert Gary management educator, author, consultant

Jackson
Collins, Dana Jon financial executive
Hildreth, Patricia Yvonne accounting executive

Lansing
Feight, Theodore J. financial planner

Livonia
Valerio, Michael Anthony financial executive

Midland
Weisenberger, Elaine Sue tax specialist, accountant

Monroe
Mlocek, Sister Frances Angeline financial executive

Muskegon
Butler, Mark Sherman controller
Delong, Donald R. accountant

Niles
Truesdell, Timothy Lee financial consultant, real estate investor

Oak Park
Walker, Audrey Hope business and finance executive

Plymouth
Garpow, James Edward financial executive

Port Huron
Ragle, George Ann accountant

Portland
Rich, Joseph John accountant

Rochester
Giordano, Joseph, Jr. financial planner, investment consulting firm executive
Horwitz, Ronald M. business administration educator

Saint Joseph
Eversole, Gregory Charles accountant

Southfield
Boyce, Daniel Hobbs financial planning company executive
Cantwell, Dennis Michael finance company executive
Drebus, John Richard financial consultant
Gargaro, John Timothy financial executive
McCuen, John Joachim building company and financial company executive
Neiheisel, Stephen Walter controller

Stanwood
Cawthorne, Kenneth Clifford retired financial planner

Traverse City
Taylor, Donald Arthur marketing educator
Williams, Madonna Jo accountant

MINNESOTA

Bloomington
Chadwick, John Edwin financial counselor and planner
Wicker, Franklin Michael financial consultant

Crookston
Shol, Kim Durand accountant, computer program

Duluth
Feroz, Ehsan Habib accounting educator, researcher, writer
Fryberger, Elizabeth Ann financial consultant
Nelson, Dennis Lee finance educator

Excelsior
Hugh, Gregory Joseph finance company executive

Mankato
Janavaras, Basil John university business educator, consultant

Minneapolis
Berry, David J. financial services company executive
Berryman, Robert Glen accounting educator, consultant
Bromelkamp, David John investment officer
Fitch, Mary Killeen salary design and human resources specialist
†Fritts, William D., Jr. financial executive
Goldberg, Luella Gross corporation executive
Hoffmann, Thomas Russell business management educator
Kinney, Earl Robert mutual funds company executive
Montgomery, Andrew Stuart financial advisor
Montgomery, Henry Irving financial planner
Petersen, Douglas Arndt financial development consultant
Pillsbury, George Sturgis investment adviser
Rudelius, William marketing educator
Schwartz, Howard Wyn business/marketing educator, consultant

Minnetonka
Jacobson, Anna Sue finance company executive
Sorteberg, Kenneth Warren executive accountant

Mound
Sidders, Patrick Michael financial executive

Nevis
Stibbe, Austin Jule accountant

Nisswa
Marmas, James Gust retired businees educator, retired college dean

Ottertail
Hanson, Al financial newsletter editor and publisher

Plymouth
Hauser, Elloyd finance company executive

Saint Louis Park
Wesselink, David Duwayne finance company executive

Saint Paul
Bry, Jeffrey Allen auditor
Connors, William Edward lawyer
Palmer, Roger Raymond accounting educator

Wayzata
†Tripp, Thomas William monetary specialist

White Bear Lake
Goldin, Martin Bruce financial executive, consultant

Woodbury
Vaughn, John Rolland auditor

MISSISSIPPI

Clarksdale
Walters, William Lee accountant

Hattiesburg
†Duhon, David Lester business educator, management consultant

Indianola
†Horton, W. Mike financial company executive

Jackson
Elliott, Mitchell Lee financial analyst

Meridian
Thomas, Kenneth Eugene auditor

Mississippi State
Nash, Henry Warren marketing educator

Robinsonville
Askins, Arthur James accountant, finance management and auditing executive

Starkville
George, Ernest Thornton, III financial consultant
Rigsby, John Thomas, Jr. accounting educator
Thomas, Garnett Jett accountant

MISSOURI

Arnold
†McGraw, Bryan Kelly financial company executive

Blue Springs
Accurso, Catherine Josephine asset manager
Foudree, Charles M. financial executive

Cape Girardeau
Farrington, Thomas Richard financial executive, investment advisor

Chesterfield
Armstrong, Theodore Morelock financial executive
Henry, Roy Monroe financial planner
Liggett, Hiram Shaw, Jr. retired diversified industry financial executive

Clayton
Nagelvoort, Charles Wendell financial advisor

Columbia
DeJarnette, Shirley Shea treasurer
Nikolai, Loren Alfred accounting educator, author
Stockglausner, William George accountant
Wagner, William Burdette business educator

Farmington
Lees, William Glenwood finance executive, retail executive

Fulton
Geiger, Mark Watson management educator

Kansas City
Baker, Roy E. accountant, retired educator
Bloch, Henry Wollman tax preparation company executive
Boysen, Melicent Pearl finance company executive
Cruess, Leigh Saunders financial executive
Funkouser, Mark auditor, municipal official
Garrison, Larry Richard accounting educator
Hansen, Eric Lloyd accountant
Lock, Robert Joseph accountant
Mustard, Mary Carolyn financial executive
Rozell, Joseph Gerard accountant
Shaw, Richard David marketing and management educator
Stevens, James Hervey, Jr. retired financial advisor

Kearney
Shrimpton, James Robert controller

Marshall
Cox, Sandra Annette economic developer

Moberly
Ornburn, Kristee Jean accountant

Neosho
Weber, Margaret Laura Jane retired accountant

Parkville
Mitchell, Robert Lee, III auditor

Raytown
Johnson, Sondra Lea accountant

Saint Charles
Spencer, Richard Andrew financial planner, investment advisor, artist

Saint Louis
Arthur, Charles Gemmell, IV accountant
Badalamenti, Anthony financial planner
Bloemer, Rosemary Celeste bookkeeper
Brown, Melvin F. corporate executive
Burch, Stephen Kenneth financial services company executive, real estate investor
Carlson, Arthur Eugene accounting educator
Cohen, Edwin Robert financial executive
Crider, Robert Agustine international financier, law enforcement official
Dill, Virginia S. accountant
Driscoll, Charles Francis financial services company executive, investment adviser
Green, Darlene comptroller, municipal official
Horwitz, William J. treasurer
Kniffen, Jan Rogers finance executive
Maschmann, Michael Wayne controller
O'Donnell, Mark Joseph accountant
Osborn, John David credit union executive
Roberts, Hugh Evan business investment services company executive
Sandbach, Charlie Bernard accountant
Schmidt, Clarence Anton financial consultant
Schmidt, Robert Charles, Jr. finance executive
Shepperd, Thomas Eugene accountant
Spindler, Michelle Lee accountant
Walsh, John E., Jr. business educator, consultant
Wiggins, Dewayne Lee financial executive
Winter, Richard Lawrence financial and health care consulting company executive

Saint Paul
Unterreiner, C. Martin financial advisor

Springfield
Buschert, Jason Lee accountant
Shealy, Michael Ivan financial consultant, geologist

Unionville
Sparks, (Lloyd) Melvin appraiser

Wildwood
†Braun, David Joseph financial executive

MONTANA

Bozeman
Davis, Nicholas Homans Clark finance company executive

Cut Bank
McCormick, Betty Leonora accountant

Stevensville
Laing-Malcolmson, Sally Anne enrolled tax agent, tax consultant

Troy
Sherman, Signe Lidfeldt portfolio manager, former research chemist

NEBRASKA

Dickens
Rausch, Paul Matthew financial executive

Dodge
Inman, Mitchell Lee, Jr. accountant

Fremont
Dunklau, Rupert Louis personal investments consultant

Lincoln
Digman, Lester Aloysius management educator
Foy, Edward Donald financial planner
Johnson, Margaret Kathleen business educator
Lienemann, Delmar Arthur, Sr. accountant, real estate developer
†North, Christopher William portfolio manager, securities analyst

Norfolk
Wehrer, Charles Siecke business and education educator

Omaha
Christensen, Jon finance company executive, former congressman
Drummer, Donald Raymond financial services executive
Erickson, James Paul retired financial service company executive
Nigh, Jay Jackson Casey investment analyst
Pitts, Robert Eugene, Jr. marketing educator, consultant

Papillion
Miller, Drew financial management company executive

NEVADA

Incline Village
Henderson, Paul Bargas, Jr. economic development consultant, educator

Las Vegas
Hobbs, Guy Stephen financial executive
Nold, Aurora R. business educator
Rodgers, Steven Edward tax practitioner, educator
Rogers, David Hughes finance executive
Wendt, Steven William business educator

North Las Vegas
Williams, Mary Irene business education educator

Reno
Garcia, Katherine Lee comptroller, accountant

NEW HAMPSHIRE

Gilmanton
Osler, Howard Lloyd *controller*

Goffstown
Martel, Eva Leona *accountant*

Hanover
Anthony, Robert Newton *management educator emeritus*

Lincoln
Hogan, Lori Ann *finance director, accountant*

Nashua
Hemming, Walter William *business financial consultant*
Perkins, George William, II *financial services executive, film producer*

NEW JERSEY

Annandale
Appelbaum, Michael Arthur *finance company executive*

Avon By The Sea
Bruno, Grace Angelia *accountant, retired educator*

Belmar
Branco, James Joseph *estate planner*

Bloomfield
Conta, Richard Vincent *actuary*

Bloomingdale
Wanamaker, Ellen Ponce *tax specialist*

Brielle
Christofi, Andreas *finance educator*

Budd Lake
Bauer, Jean Marie *accountant*

Camden
Homan, Kenneth Lewis *auditor*
Jones, Larry Darnell *tax specialist*
Law, Robert *finance director*

Carlstadt
Bonis, Joseph John *financial executive*

Cherry Hill
Newell, Eric James *financial planner, tax consultant, former insurance executive*

Convent Station
Healy, Gwendoline Frances *controller*

Cranbury
Kemmerer, Peter Ream *financial executive*

Edison
Hecht, William David *accountant*
†Visco, Nicholas *controller*

Elmwood Park
Nadzick, Judith Ann *accountant*

Fair Haven
Aumack, Shirley Jean *financial planner, tax preparer*

Fairfield
Byer, Theodore Scott *accountant*

Florham Park
Henning, Neil Scott *financial consultant*

Fort Lee
Yoo, Choon Wang *financial consultant*

Gladstone
Caspersen, Finn Michael Westby *diversified financial services company executive*

Hackensack
Mehta, Jay *financial executive*

Hasbrouck Heights
†Granoff, Michael *investment agency manager*

Haworth
Posner, Roy Edward *finance executive, retired*

Hightstown
Moustafa, Fikry Sayed *accountant*

Ho Ho Kus
Munschauer, Robert Lloyd *accountant*

Hoboken
Jurkat, Martin Peter *management educator*

Holmdel
Ayub, Yacub *financial consultant*

Iselin
Accardi, Joseph Ronald *accountant*
De Rose, Louis John *financial services executive*
Sangiuliano, Barbara Ann *tax consultant*

Jackson
Hagberg, Carl Thomas *financial executive*

Lawrenceville
Farrar, Donald Keith *retired financial executive*

Lincroft
Keenan, Robert Anthony *financial services company executive, educator, consultant*

Little Falls
Armellino, Michael Ralph *retired asset management executive*
Birnberg, Jack *financial executive*

Marlton
Gorenberg, Charles Lloyd *financial services executive*

Matawan
Wubbenhorst, Clifford C. *financial analyst*

Mendham
Hesselink, Ann Patrice *financial executive, lawyer*

Milltown
Holland, Joseph John *financial manager*

Monmouth Beach
Herbert, LeRoy James *retired accounting firm executive*

Montvale
Brecht, Warren Frederick *business executive*
Showalter, David Scott *accounting executive*

Montville
Klapper, Byron D. *financial company executive*

Morristown
Cregan, Frank Robert *financial executive, consultant*
Ross, Thomas J., Jr. *personal financial adviser*

Mount Laurel
Shoe, Margaret Ellen *accountant*

Mountainside
Newler, Jerome Marc *accountant*

Mullica Hill
Sparks, Barbara L. *financial planner*

New Brunswick
Mills, George Marshall *insurance consultant*

Newark
Arabie, Phipps *marketing educator, researcher*
Clymer, Brian William *insurance company executive, former state official*
Contractor, Farok *business and management educator*
Darr, Walter Robert *financial analyst*
Hadley, John Bart *financial analyst*
Norwood, Carolyn Virginia *business educator*
Rosenberg, Jerry Martin *business administration educator*

Oakhurst
Fasthuber-Grande, Traudy *financial services company executive*

Oldwick
Kellogg, C. Burton, II *financial analyst*

Paramus
Balter, Leslie Marvin *business communications educator*
Weinstock, George David *financial services company executive*

Parsippany
Wechter, Ira Martin *tax specialist, financial planner*

Plainsboro
Holmes, Suzon Tropez *financial analyst*

Princeton
Cleary, Lynda Woods *financial advisor, consultant*
Cohen, Isaac Louis (Ike Cohen) *financial consultant*
Cox, Douglas Lynn *financial corporation executive*
Goldfarb, Irene Dale *financial planner*
Harvey, Norman Ronald *finance company executive*
Henbest, Jon Charles *accountant, consultant*
Henkel, William *financial services executive*
Kerney, Thomas Lincoln, II *investments and real estate professional*
Loss, Stuart Harold *financial executive*
Neff, Robert Arthur *business and financial executive*
Osei, Edward Kofi *financial analyst, educator, strategic planner*
Pimley, Kim Jensen *financial training consultant*

Princeton Junction
Cohen, Florence Emery *financial services executive*

Raritan
Licetti, Mary Elizabeth *business analysis director*

Red Bank
McCann, John Francis *retired financial services company executive*
Oberst, Robert John *financial analyst*

Ridgewood
McBride, William Bernard *treasurer*

River Edge
Gass, Manus M. *accountant, business executive*

River Vale
Becker, Murray Leonard *corporate financial consultant, consulting actuary*

Rockaway
Reeves, Marylou *financial planner*

Rutherford
Liptak, Irene Frances *retired business executive*

Saddle Brook
Donahoe, Maureen Alice *accounting consultant*

Secaucus
Rothman, Martin *finance company executive, accountant*

Short Hills
Gibson, William Lee *financial consultant*

Mebane, William Black *controller, financial consultant*
Price, Michael F. *money management executive*
Pyle, Robert Milner, Jr. *financial services company consultant*
Winters, David John *securities analyst*

Skillman
Wheelock, Keith Ward *retired consulting company executive, educator*

Somerset
Gruchacz, Craig M. *financial executive*

Somerville
Cohen, Walter Stanley *accountant, financial consultant*

Southampton
Knortz, Walter Robert *accountant, former insurance company executive*

Spring Lake
Wrege, Charles Deck *management educator*

Summit
Cragoe, John Henry *investment company executive*
Vogel, Julius *consulting actuary, former insurance company executive*

Teaneck
Naadimuthu, Govindasami *business educator, university official*

Toms River
Boisseau, Jerry Philip *financial services company executive*

Trenton
Kaschak, David James *accountant*

Waldwick
Surdoval, Donald James *accounting and management consulting company executive*

Warren
Hartman, David Gardiner *actuary*
Mahecha, Juan Carlos, Jr. *financial services administrator*

West Long Branch
Boronico, Jess Stephen *management science educator, academic dean*
Holland, John Joseph, Jr. *economics educator*

West Orange
Weiner, Mervyn *retired mergers and acquisitions executive*

Westfield
Frungillo, Nicholas Anthony, Jr. *accountant*

Whitehouse Station
Atieh, Michael Gerard *accountant*

NEW MEXICO

Albuquerque
D'Anza, Lawrence Martin *marketing educator*
Kroll, Paul Benedict *auditor*
Lowranee, Muriel Edwards *program specialist*
Mitchell, Lindell Marvin *financial planner*
Royle, Anthony William *accountant*

Las Cruces
Bell, M. Joy Miller *financial planner, real estate broker*
Constantini, Louis Orlando *financial consultant, stockbroker*
Peterson, Robin Tucker *marketing educator*

Placitas
Bencke, Ronald Lee *financial executive*

Portales
Morris, Donald *tax specialist*
†Poynor, Clifford Franklin *credit corporation owner, rancher*

Santa Fe
Brown, Alan Whittaker *accountant*
Watkins, Stephen Edward *accountant, newspaper executive*

Silver City
Hamlin, Don Auer *financial executive*

NEW YORK

Albany
Alexander, Ellin Dribben *financial marketing company executive*
Blount, Stanley Freeman *marketing educator*
†Corcoran, Colleen Marie *grant and contract administrator*
Farley, Eugene Joseph *accountant*
Hancox, David Robert *audit administrator, educator*
†Hancox, Steven J. *auditor, state official*
Holstein, William Kurt *business administration educator*
Philip, George Michael *pension fund administrator*

Amherst
Jen, Frank Chifeng *finance and management educator*

Bedford
†Krensky, Harry F. *fund manager, educator*

Binghamton
Murry, William Douglas *human resource management educator, consultant*
Shillestad, John Gardner *financial services company executive*

Bohemia
Rogé, Ronald William *financial planner, investment management executive*

Brewster
Neugroschl, Jill Paulette *financial planning company executive*

Bridgehampton
Needham, James Joseph *retired financial services executive*

Bronx
Sedacca, Angelo Anthony *police officer, scholar, philanthropist*
Stuhr, David Paul *business educator, consultant*

Bronxville
Auriemmo, Frank Joseph, Jr. *financial holding company executive*
Connola, Donald Pascal, Jr. *management consultant, educator*
Martin, R. Keith *business and information systems educator, consultant*
Sharp, Donald Eugene *bank consultant*

Brooklyn
Banjoko, Alimi Ajimon *financial planner*
DeLustro, Frank Joseph *financial executive, consultant*
Hechtman, Howard *financial analyst*
Levine, Nathan *business educator*
Morgan, Mary Louise Fitzsimmons *fund raising executive, lobbyist*
Pino, Richard Edmund *financial analyst, financial planner*
Sweet, Marc Steven *financial executive*

Buffalo
Draper, Verden Rolland *accountant*
Gruen, David Henry *financial executive, consultant*
Jacobs, Jeremy M. *diversified holding company executive, hockey team owner*
Koontz, Eldon Ray *management and financial consultant*
Layton, Rodney Eugene *controller, newspaper executive*
Oliver, Dominick Michael *business educator*
Southwick, Lawrence, Jr. *management educator*

Canandaigua
Read, Eleanor May *financial analyst*

Canton
Pollard, Fred Don *finance company executive*

Cedarhurst
Cohen, Philip Herman *accountant*

Chittenango
Cassell, William Walter *retired accounting operations consultant*

Dobbs Ferry
Weisman, Benjamin Brucker *finance educator, consultant*

East Garden City
Baker, J. A., II *management consultant, monetary architect, financial engineer*

East Greenbush
Mucci, Patrick John *financial consultant, realtor, commercial loan broker*

East Meadow
Mondello, John Paul *financial consultant*

East Rochester
Murray, James Doyle *accountant*

Endicott
Heide, Hans Dieter, Jr. *accountant*

Fairport
Garg, Devendra *financial executive*
Reidy, Thomas Michael *financial executive*
Talty, Lorraine Caguioa *accountant*

Far Rockaway
Epstein, Samuel Abraham *stock and bond broker, petroleum consultant*

Flushing
Overton, Rosilyn Gay Hoffman *financial services executive*

Garden City
Kurlander, Neale *accounting and law educator, lawyer*
Smith, Paul Thomas *financial services company executive*

Glen Falls
†Hall, Michael L. *business educator*

Hamburg
Keenan, John Paul *management educator, consultant, psychologist*

Hampton Bays
Yavitz, Boris *business educator, corporate director*

Hauppauge
Amore, Michael Joseph *financial and administrative executive*
Heller, Stanley Martin *accountant*

Hawthorne
Kiamie, Don Albert Najeeb *accountant*

Hempstead
Comer, Debra Ruth *management educator*
Lee, Keun Sok *business educator, consultant*
Montana, Patrick Joseph *management educator*

Hicksville
Stein, Melvin A. *accountant*

Holtsville
Martin, Christopher Edward *accountant, personal finance consultant*

Hoosick Falls
Canedy, Nancy Gay *comptroller, accountant, educator*

Horseheads
Huffman, Patricia Joan *retired accounting coordinator*

Huntington
Slutsky, Leonard Alan *finance executive, consultant*

Ithaca
Dyckman, Thomas Richard *accounting educator*
Elliott, John *accountant, educator, dean*
Lesser, William Henri *marketing educator*
Van Houtte, Raymond A. *financial executive*

Kew Gardens
Schnakenberg, Donald G. *financial administrator*

Le Roy
Smukall, Carl Franklin *accountant*

Lewiston
LoTempio, Julia Matild *accountant*

Lynbrook
O'Malley, Edward Joseph, Jr. *financial services administrator*

Manhasset
Lotruglio, Anthony F. *financial consultant*

Massapequa
Arbiter, Andrew Richard *accountant*
Odol, Marilyn Elaine *accountant*

Medford
Barna, Douglas Peter *collection agency executive*
Snyder, Mark Jeffrey *financial consultant, actuary*

Merrick
Kaplan, Steven Mark *accountant*

Mineola
Parola, Frederick Edson, Jr. *county comptroller*

Mount Kisco
Keesee, Thomas Woodfin, Jr. *financial consultant*

New Hyde Park
Grassi, Louis C. *accountant*

New York
Adams, Carl Fillmore, Jr. *finance company executive*
Adams, Robert B. *financial services company executive*
Alexander, Barbara Toll *investment banker*
Altfest, Lewis Jay *financial and investment advisor*
Assael, Henry *marketing educator*
Atwater, Verne Stafford *finance educator*
Bains, Harrison MacKellar, Jr. *financial executive*
Banks, Russell *financial planner, consultant*
Barnett, Bernard *accountant*
Barrett, Martin Jay *financial executive*
Batchvarov, Alexander Ivanov *financial analyst*
Becker-Roukas, Helane Renée *securities analyst, financial executive*
†Benfield, James Haines *treasurer*
Bland, Teresa P. *financial analyst, consultant*
Bloomberg, Michael Rubens *finance and information services company executive*
Bradford, Phillip Gnassi *financial analytics developer*
Brittain, Willard W., Jr. (Woody Brittain) *diversified financial services company executive*
Brooke, Paul Alan *finance company executive*
Brown, James Nelson, Jr. *accountant*
Brustein, Lawrence *financial executive*
Butler, Stephen Gregory *accountant*
Camps, Jeffrey Lowell *financial services company general agent*
Canes, Brian Dennis *professional services company official*
Chadick, Susan Linda *executive search consulting executive*
Chenault, Kenneth Irvine *financial services company executive*
Chester, John E., III *financial services company executive*
Clark, Charles Alan *financial analyst*
Clark, Howard Longstreth, Jr. *finance company executive*
Cohen-Sabban, Nessim *auditor, accountant*
Colby, Marvelle Seitman *business management educator, administrator*
Connor, Joseph E. *accountant*
Cosenza, Vincent John *accountant*
Cronson, Caroline Mary *financial executive*
Daidone, Lewis Eugene *financial services company executive*
Darcy, Keith Thomas *finance company executive, educator*
Dawson, Thomas Cleland, II *financial executive*
Delgado, George Ernest *financial consultant*
Deupree, Marvin Mattox *accountant, business consultant*
DeWitt, Eula *accountant*
Dimon, James *financial services executive*
Donaldson, William Henry *financial executive*
Edwards, James D. *accounting company executive*
Efrat, Isaac *financial analyst, mathematician*
Eig, Norman *investment company executive*
Eisner, Richard Alan *accountant*
Ellegard, Roy Whitney *appraiser*
Emmerman, Michael N *financial analyst*
Eveillard, Jean-Marie *financial company executive*
Ezrati, Milton Joseph *investment manager, economist*
Fahey, James Edward *financial executive*
Felix, Ted Mark *accountant*
Ferguson, Robert *financial services executive, educator, writer*
Fontana, John Arthur *employee benefits specialist*
†Foster, Mary Frances *accounting firm executive, accountant*
Freiberg, Lowell Carl *financial executive*
Frye, Clayton Wesley, Jr. *financial executive*
Garba, Edward Aloysius *financial executive*
Garrett, Robert *financial advisory executive*
Gaughan, Eugene Francis *accountant*
Gill, Ardian C. *actuary, photographer*
Gladstone, William Louis *accountant*
Goldberg, Edward L. *financial services executive*
Golden, William Theodore *trustee, corporate director*
Goldschmidt, Robert Alphonse *financial executive*
Golub, Gerald Leonard *accounting company executive*
Golub, Harvey *financial services company executive*
Gorewitz, Rubin Leon *accountant, financial consultant*
Gorman, Lawrence James *banker*
Gowens, Walter, II *financial and business services executive*
Graf, Peter Gustav *accountant, lawyer*
Grafton, W. Robert *professional services company executive*
Green, David O. *accounting educator, educational administrator*
Gross, Robert Emanuel *collateral loan broker*
Groves, Ray John *accountant*
Hajim, Edmund A. *financial services executive*
Halloran, Leo Augustine *retired financial executive*
Harrison, John Alexander *financial executive*
Harrison, Warren *finance company executive*
Hazen, William Harris *finance executive*
Heintz, Joseph E. *financial services company executive*
Henning, Michael Anthony *diversified financial company executive*
Hewitt, Dennis Edwin *financial executive*
Hibel, Bernard *financial consultant, former apparel company executive*
Hickman, J. Kenneth *accounting company executive*
Hornstein, Mark *financial executive*
Jacobs, Mark Neil *financial services corporation executive, lawyer*
Johnson, Clarke Courtney *financial consultant, educator*
Johnson, Freda S. *public finance consultant*
Johnson, J. Chester *financial executive, poet*
Joseph, Michael Sarkies *accountant*
Kamarck, Martin Alexander *financial services executive*
Kaye, Walter *financial executive*
Kearns, Richard P. *diversified financial services company executive*
Kennedy, John Joseph *bank financial officer*
Kimsey, William L. *diversified financial services company executive*
Kirk, Donald James *accounting educator, consultant*
Kirsch, Donald *financial consultant, author*
Kirsh, Michael Alan *financial estate planner*
Koeppel, Noel Immanuel *financial planner, securities and real estate broker*
Kolesar, Peter John *business and engineering educator*
Komansky, David H. *financial services executive*
Kopelman, Richard Eric *management educator*
Kra, Ethan Emanuel *actuary*
Ladjevardi, Hamid *fund manager*
Lambert, Abbott Lawrence *retired accountant*
Lamensdorf, Sam Fielding, Jr. *financial services company executive*
Lammie, James L. *financial planner, consultant*
Langbert, Mitchell Berke *business educator*
Langford, Laura Sue *ratings analyst*
Laskawy, Philip A. *accounting and management consulting firm executive*
Lebouitz, Martin Frederick *financial services industry executive, consultant*
Lessing, Brian Reid *actuary*
Lewins, Steven *security analyst, investment advisor, corporate executive, diplomatic advisor*
Libby, John Kelway *financial services company executive*
Lindquist, Richard James *portfolio manager*
Lipson, Charles Barry *finance company executive*
Loeb, Peter Kenneth *money manager*
Lowell, Stanley Edgar *accountant*
Lubow, Nathan Myron *accountant*
Lust, Herbert Cohnfeldt, II *finance executive*
Madden, Michael Daniel *finance company executive*
Madonna, Jon C. *accounting firm executive*
Mandelbaum, Harold Neil *accountant*
Martin, Glenn *financial manager, consultant*
Mathisen, Harold Clifford *portfolio management executive*
Maurer, Jeffrey Stuart *finance executive*
McCutchen, William Walter, Jr. *management educator*
McDonald, Thomas Paul *controller*
McGraw, Harold Whittlesey, III (Terry McGraw) *information company executive*
Midanek, Deborah Hicks *portfolio manager, director*
†Miller, Heidi G. *diversified financial company executive*
Miller, John R. *accountant*
Miller, Neil Stuart *financial officer, advertising executive*
Misthal, Howard Joseph *accountant, lawyer*
Moore, Nicholas G. *finance company executive*
Moyles, Philip Vincent, Jr. *financial services company executive*
†Nelson, Roger R. *financial company executive*
Ng, Helen M. *financier, civil engineer*
Nichols, Edie Diane *executive recruiter*
Norman, Stephen Peckham *financial services company executive*
†Noveck, Madeline I. *financial company executive*
Paddock, Anthony Conaway *financial consultant*
Palion, Peter Thaddeus *financial planner*
Palitz, Bernard G. *finance company executive*
Pappas, Michael *financial services company executive*
Peppet, Russell Frederick *accountant*
Peritz, Abraham Daniel *business executive*
Pinna, Michael Anthony *financial consultant*
Prehle, Tricia Anne *accountant*
Presby, J. Thomas *financial advisor*
Purcell, Philip James *financial services company executive*
Raad, Elias Antoine *finance educator, consultant, researcher*
Rabinovitz, Brian Keith *accountant*
Raffelson, Michael *financial executive*
Ramin, Kurt *accounting executive*
Reich-Berman, Eunice Thelma *fixed income analyst*
Rein, Catherine Amelia *financial services executive, lawyer*
Reiss, Dale Anne *accounting executive, investment company executive*
Riegelhaupt, Edward Irwin *financial consultant*
Rinaldini, Luis Emilio *investment banker*
Ritch, Kathleen *diversified company executive*
†Roberts, John J. *accounting firm executive*
Robinson, James D., III *corporate executive, investor*
Rockefeller, Laurance S. *philanthropist*
Roethenmund, Otto Emil *financial and banking executive*
Rogers, Pier Camille *management educator*
Rose, June H. *healthcare financial executive*
Rosenthal, Charles Michael *financial executive*
Ross, Coleman DeVane *accountant, insurance company consultant*
Saint-Donat, Bernard Jacques *finance company executive*
Salom, Roberto *financial executive*
Sappin, Edward Jonathan *financial advisor*
Schlesinger, David Adam *newspaper editor*
Segal, Martin Eli *retired actuarial and consulting company executive*
†Setia, Rajiv Kumar *research analyst*
Shapoff, Stephen H. *financial executive*
Sharp, J(ames) Franklin *finance educator, investment portfolio manager*
Shaw, Alan Roger *financial executive, educator*
Siegel, Arthur Herbert *executive*
Siguler, George William *financial services executive*
Silverman, Herbert R. *corporate financial executive*
Simmons, John Derek *financial consultant*
Simons, Eric Ward *financial executive*
Skomorowsky, Peter P. *retired accounting company executive, lawyer*
Slifka, Alan Bruce *investment manager*
Smith, Harold Charles *private pension fund executive*
Smith, Raymond W. *finance company executive*
Smith, Rona *finance company executive*
Soros, George *fund management executive*
Sorter, George Hans *accounting and law educator, consultant*
Speziale, Richard Salvatore *financial executive*
Stockman, David Allen *former federal official, congressman, financier*
Stovall, Robert H(enry) *money management company executive*
†Styblo Beder, Tanya *financial engineer, educator*
Tarantino, Dominic A. *retired professional services firm executive*
Tavel, Mark Kivey *money management company executive, economist*
Tisch, Preston Robert *finance executive*
Tognino, John Nicholas *financial services executive*
Toohey, Edward Joseph *financial services company executive*
Updike, Helen Hill *investment manager, financial adviser*
Visconti, John C. *financial consultant*
Vitale, Paul *accountant*
Volk, Norman Hans *financial executive*
†Walsh, James Francis, Jr. *financial services executive*
Walsh, Thomas Gerard *actuary*
Weaver, Richard Lindsay Newton *financial services executive*
Weingrow, Howard L. *financial executive, investor*
Weiss, Myrna Grace *business consultant*
Wells, Patricia Trent *auditor*
Wilson, Christian Gideon *portfolio manager*
Wright, Richard John *business executive*
Young, George Haywood, III *investment banker*
Yuen, Janet *financial analyst*
Zand, Dale Ezra *business management educator*

Newburgh
Copans, Kenneth Gary *accountant*

Niagara Falls
Shaghoian, Cynthia Lynne *accountant*

Northport
Krahel, Thomas Stephen *account executive*

Norwich
†Broten, James M. *accountant*

Nyack
Bryant, Karen Worstell *financial advisor, investment company executive*

Oceanside
Reed, James William, Jr. *financial services, not for profit and injury prevention consultant*

Old Westbury
Barbera, Anthony Thomas *accountant, educator*

Orchard Park
Thomas, Jimmy Lynn *financial executive*

Oyster Bay
Amato, Camille Jean *manufacturing executive*

Pittsford
Gallea, Anthony Michael *portfolio manager*
Herge, Henry Curtis, Jr. *consulting firm executive*

Plainview
Feller, Benjamin E. *actuary*

Plattsburgh
Dossin, Ernest Joseph, III *credit consulting company executive*

Pleasant Valley
Odescalchi, Edmond Péry *international financial consultant, author*

Pleasantville
Reps, David Nathan *finance educator*

Port Washington
Phelan, Arthur Joseph *financial executive*

Poughkeepsie
Handel, Bernard *accountant, actuarial and insurance consultant, lawyer*
Hansen, Karen Thornley *accountant*
McFadden, John Thomas *financial planner, insurance agent, investor*

Pound Ridge
Webb, Richard Gilbert *financial executive*

Purchase
Muschio, Edward Charles *accountant*
Noonan, Frank Russell *business executive*
Papaleo, Louis Anthony *accountant*
Sacco, John Michael *accountant*

Queens Village
Cook, Michael Anthony *financial services executive*

Queensbury
Bitner, William Lawrence, III *retired banker, educator*

Rhinebeck
Longden, Claire Suzanne *financial planner, investment advisor*

Riverdale
†Lee, Dong Hwan *business adminstration educator*

Rochester
Golisano, B. Thomas *finance company director, human resources director*
Goyer, Virginia L. *accountant*
Kessler, Roslyn Marie *financial analyst*
Laschenski, John Patrick *accountant*
Marriott, Marcia Ann *business educator, consultant*
Schwert, G(eorge) William, III *finance educator*
Watts, Ross Leslie *accounting educator, consultant*

Rye
Beldock, Donald Travis *financial executive*
Finnerty, John Dudley *investment banker, financial educator*

Saint Bonaventure
Parikh, Rajeev Natvarlal *educator, university administrator, accountant*

Saratoga Springs
Dickinson, Richard Henry *accountant*

Scarsdale
Breslow, Marilyn Ganon *portfolio manager*
Eforo, John Francis *financial officer*
Gollin, Stuart Allen *accountant*

Schenectady
Barber, Nicholas Carl *tax specialist, real estate executive*

Sleepy Hollow
Ferguson, Douglas Edward *financial executive*

Somers
Gulick, Donna Marie *accountant*

Staten Island
Gelbein, Jay Joel *accountant*
Storberg, Eric Philip *financial planner*

Suffern
Orazio, Paul Vincent *financial planner*

Sunnyside
Turek, Charles Saul *bookkeeper*

Syracuse
Butler, Richard John *business educator*
Marcoccia, Louis Gary *accountant, university administrator*
†O'Keefe, Sean Charles *public adminstration educator*
Ortiz, Fernando, Jr. *economic small business development consultant*

Tarrytown
Ferrari, Robert Joseph *business educator, former banker*

Troy
St. John, William Charles, Jr. *business educator, administrator*

Valley Stream
Ellis, Bernice *financial planning company executive, investment advisor*
Rosenberg, Lee Evan *financial planner*

Vestal
Piaker, Philip Martin *accountant, educator*

Wappingers Falls
Kells, Albert John *financial consultant*

Water Mill
Kreimer, Michael Walter *financial planner, investment company official*

Webster
McCormack, Stanley Eugene *financial consultant*
Nicholson, Douglas Robert *accountant*
Southard, Paul Raymond *financial executive*

White Plains
Gillingham, Stephen Thomas *financial planner*
Keegan, Warren Joseph *business educator, consultant*
Lipsky, Leonard *merger, management and acquisition specialist, financial and marketing consultant*
Ryan, Theresa Ann Julia *accountant*

Williamsville
Mack, Gregory John *financial executive and consultant*

Yonkers
Alessi, George Anthony *financial advisor, consultant*
Johansen, Robert Joseph *consulting actuary*

York
Coleman, David Cecil *financial executive*

Yorktown Heights
Donovan, Andrew Joseph *financial consultant*

NORTH CAROLINA

Advance
Herpel, George Lloyd *marketing educator*

Beaufort
Pagano, Filippo Frank *financial broker, commercial loan consultant*

Boone
Dean, James M. *investment adviser*

Cary
Hagan, John Aubrey *financial executive*

Chapel Hill
Langenderfer, Harold Quentin *accountant, educator*
Morgan, Frank T. *business educator, consultant*
Perreault, William Daniel, Jr. *business administration educator*
Rondinelli, Dennis A(ugust) *business administration educator, research center director*
Rosen, Benson *business administration educator*
Roth, Aleda Vender *business educator*

Charlotte
Almond, Giles Kevin *accountant, financial planner*
Anderson, Gerald Leslie *financial executive*
Evans, David Shawn *financial executive*
Halas, Paul Anthony, Jr. *business appraisal and valuation specialist, consultant*
Knox, Havolyn Crocker *financial consultant*
Labardi, Jillian Gay *financial planner, insurance agent*
†Patrick, Timothy K. *securities analyst*
Rajani, Prem Rajaram *transportation company financial executive*
Schulz, Walter Kurt *accountant, information technology consultant*
Wheeler, Norman K. *consultant*

Dunn
Robison, Frederick Mason *financial executive*

Durham
Bettman, James Ross *management educator*
Staelin, Richard *business administration educator*

Fayetteville
†Ayadi, Olusegun Felix *finance educator*

Greensboro
Mecimore, Charles Douglas *retired accounting educator*
Starling, Larry Eugene *auditor*

Greenville
Schellenberger, Robert Earl *management educator and department chairman*

Havelock
Lindelof, William Christian, Jr. *financial company executive*

Hendersonville
Goehring, Maude Cope *retired business educator*

High Point
Smith, Michael Sterling *insurance and financial services executive*

Jacksonville
Hutto, James Calhoun *retired financial executive*

Kernersville
Metcalf, Corwin Moore (Mickey) *business educator, businessman, consultant*

Mount Airy
Rotenizer, R. Eugene *financial planner*

Oak Ridge
Johnson, Mark Cyrus *financial planner, tax preparer*

Pembroke
Bukowy, Stephen Joseph *accounting educator*

Raleigh
Aldridge, Adrienne Yingling *accountant, business analyst*
†Gerlach, Daniel J. *budget and tax policy analyst*
Hill, Hulene Dian *accountant*
Jessen, David Wayne *accountant*
Nation, Philip David *financial planner*
Renfrow, Edward *state auditor*

Southern Pines
Matney, Edward Eli *financial advisor*

Tryon
Flynn, Kirtland, Jr. *accountant*

West End
Harman, Henry M., Jr. *accountant, educator*

Wilkesboro
Thomas, David Lloyd *accountant, consultant*
Waller, Jim D. *holding company executive*

Wilson
†Lenard, Mary Jane *accounting and information systems educator*

Winston Salem
Gallo, Vincent John *financial planner*
Hardwick, James Carlton, Jr. *business and financial planner*
Middaugh, Jack Kendall, II *management educator*
Smunt, Marsha Lynn Haeflinger *financial executive*

NORTH DAKOTA

Fargo
Ness, Gary Gene *accountant*
Risher, Stephan Olaf *investment officer*

Grand Forks
Berge, Scott Jerry *accountant*
Wambsganss, Jacob Roy *accounting educator, small business consultant*

Minot
McQuarrie, Michelle Lee *accountant*

OHIO

Ada
Cooper, Ken Errol *management educator*

Akron
Moore, Walter Emil, Jr. *financial planner*

Amelia
Hayden, Joseph Page, Jr. *company executive*

Andover
Mole, Richard Jay *accounting company executive*

Athens
Rakes, Ganas Kaye *finance and banking educator*

Aurora
Nelson, Hedwig Potok *financial executive*

Austintown
Gorcheff, Nick A. *controller*

Bowling Green
Lunde, Harold Irving *management educator*

Brunswick
Reed, Jane Garson *accounting educator, consultant*

Chagrin Falls
Poza, Ernesto Juan *business consultant, educator*

Cincinnati
Biery, Charles John, Sr. *accountant*
Conaton, Michael Joseph *financial service executive*
Dougherty, Charlotte Anne *financial planner, insurance and securities representative*
Evans, Barry Craig *financial services company exexutive*
Huenefeld, Thomas Ernst *financial consultant, retired banker*
Johnson, Norma Louise *accountant*
Lawson, Randall Clayton, II *financial executive*
Lindner, Robert David *finance company executive*
Lintz, Robert Carroll *financial holding company executive*
Mantel, Samuel Joseph, Jr. *management educator, consultant*
Nelson, Mary Ellen Dickson *actuary*
Rand, Carolyn *financial executive*
Rebel, Jerome Ivo *financial planner*
Shoemaker, Hal Alan *accountant*
Siekmann, Donald Charles *accountant*
Williamson, Vikki Lyn *financial executive*
Wulker, Laurence Joseph *portfolio manager, educator, financial planner*

Cleveland
Chester, Russell Gilbert, Jr. *accountant, auditor*
Dossey, Richard Lee *accountant*
Fitzmaurice, Catherine Theresa *auditor*
Harrington, Nancy Lynn *tax accountant*
Hawkinson, Gary Michael *financial services company executive*
Krulitz, Leo Morrion *financial executive*
Manley, David Thomas *employment benefit plan administration company executive*
Mayne, Lucille Stringer *finance educator*
Myeroff, Kevin Howard *financial planner*
Noetzel, Arthur Jerome *business administration educator, management consultant*
Petina, David Anthony *private company analyst*
Pierson, Marilyn Ehle *financial planner*
Roberts, James Owen *financial planning executive, consultant*
Seaton, Robert Finlayson *retired planned giving consultant*
Skolnik, David Erwin *financial analyst*
Stratton-Crooke, Thomas Edward *financial consultant*
Thomas, Richard Stephen *financial executive*

Columbus
Amatos, Barbara Hansen *accounting executive*
Ballou, Charles Herbert *financial executive*
Berry, William Lee *business administration educator*
Chesser, Kerry Royce *financial director*
Fidler, Carol Ann *accountant*
Kasper, Larry John *accountant, litigation support consultant*
Knisely, Douglas Charles *accountant*
Koehn, Susan Michele *accountant*
Kreager, Eileen Davis *administrative consultant*
LaLonde, Bernard Joseph *educator*
Leong, G. Keong *operations management educator*
Milligan, Glenn Wesley *business educator*
Nikias, Anthony Douglas *accountant, educator*
Ruhlin, Peggy Miller *investment adviser, financial planner*

Cuyahoga Falls
Hessler, William Gerhard *tax consultant*
Moses, Abe Joseph *international financial consultant*

Dayton
McCutcheon, Holly Marie *accountant*
Singhvi, Surendra Singh *finance and strategy consultant*
Wilson, Robert M. *financial executive*

Dublin
Heneman, Robert Lloyd *management educator*
Madigan, Joseph Edward *financial executive, consultant, director*

East Liverpool
Feldman, Marvin Herschel *financial consultant*

Fairfield
Royer, Thomas Jerry *financial planner*

Fremont
Recktenwald, Fred William *financial executive*

Gallipolis
†Mingus, Deborah Lynn *treasurer*

Greenville
Franz, Daniel Thomas *financial planner*

Harrison
Kocher, Juanita Fay *retired auditor*
Wuest, Larry Carl *tax examiner*

Hudson
Ashcroft, Richard Carter *controller*

Lancaster
Voss, Jack Donald *international business consultant, lawyer*

Liberty Township
Bartlett, Shirley Anne *accountant*

Mansfield
Haldar, Frances Louise *business educator, accountant, treasurer*
Shah, James M. *actuarial consultant*

Mason
Drees, Stephen Daniel *financial services executive, strategy, marketing and product development executive*
Roemer, John Alan *financial executive*

Maumee
Tigges, Kenneth Edwin *retired financial executive*

North Canton
Lynham, C(harles) Richard *foundry company executive*

North Olmsted
Brady, Michael Cameron *investment consultant*

Oxford
Snavely, William Brant *management educator and consultant*
Wilson, James Ray *international business educator*

Parma
Krise, Jack Cloyde, Jr. *treasurer*

Pepper Pike
Fredrickson, Sharon Wong *accountant*

Reynoldsburg
Gunnels, Lee O. *retired finance and management educator, manufacturing company executive*

Rocky River
Grmek, Dorothy Antonia *accountant*

Shaker Heights
Donnem, Sarah Lund *financial analyst, non-profit and political organization consultant*

Springboro
Mishler, Mark David *financial executive, educator*

Steubenville
White, Vicki Lee *bank service representative*

Sylvania
Sampson, Wesley Claude *auditor, software inventor*

Toledo
Eberly, William Somers *financial consultant*
Shoffer, Jeffrey David *financial planner*

Twinsburg
Rose, Brendan J. *accountant*

Warren
Platthy, Terrance Lee *accountant*
Robbins, Robert Marvin *accountant*

Westerville
Hoyt, Rosemary Ellen *tax accountant*

Willoughby
Trennel, Lawrence William *accountant*

Wilmington
Hodapp, Larry Frank *accountant*
Mongold, Sandra K. *corporate executive*

OKLAHOMA

Bethany
†Powell, Cynthia Diane *finance educator*

Durant
England, Dan Benjamin *accountant*

Edmond
Tucker, Leslie Ray *accountant, historian*

Moore
Harrington, Gary Burnes *retired controller*

Norman
Lis, Anthony Stanley *retired business administration educator*

Oklahoma City
Acers, Patsy Pierce *financial seminars company executive*
Cassel, John Elden *accountant*
Tolbert, James R., III *financial executive*
Trent, Richard O(wen) *financial executive*
Woody, Mark Edward *financial planner*

Stillwater
†Mowen, John C. *business educator*
Trennepohl, Gary Lee *finance educator*

Tahlequah
Carment, Thomas Maxwell *accounting educator, consultant, researcher*

Tulsa
Berlin, Steven Ritt *business educator*
Candreia, Peggy Jo *financial analyst*
Duncan, Maurice Greer *accountant, consultant*
Hoe, Richard March *insurance and securities consultant, writer*
Imhoff, Pamela M. *marketing educator*
Jones, Michael Lynn *financial consultant, operations manager*
Williams, Patricia *financial analyst*

OREGON

Ashland
Chatfield, Michael *accounting educator*
Farrimond, George Francis, Jr. *management educator*

Eugene
Hamren, Nancy Van Brasch *bookkeeper*
Lindholm, Richard Theodore *economics and finance educator*

Grants Pass
Smith, Barnard Elliot *management educator*

Lake Oswego
Cooper, Rachel Bremer *accountant*
Mylnechuk, Larry Herbert *financial executive*

Madras
Brooks, Marian *retired comptroller and credit manager*

Newberg
McMahon, Paul Francis *finance company executive*

Portland
Dow, Mary Alexis *auditor*
Epperson, Eric Robert *financial executive, film producer*
Finley, Lewis Merren *financial consultant*
Hill, Mary Lou *accountant, business consultant*
Hinckley, Gregory Keith *financial executive*
Stewart, Marlene Metzger *financial planning practitioner, insurance agent*
Watne, Donald Arthur *accountant, educator*
White, Roberta Lee *comptroller*

PENNSYLVANIA

Allentown
Balog, Ibolya *accountant*
Bleiler, Catherine Ann *financial executive*
Fortune, Robert Russell *financial consultant*
Heitmann, George Joseph *business educator, consultant*

Allison Park
LaDow, C. Stuart *consultant financial services*

Ambler
Wald, Mary S. *risk management and personal finance educator*

Baden
Hodge, Daniel Ray *auditor*

Bala Cynwyd
Isdaner, Lawrence Arthur *accountant*
McGill, Dan Mays *insurance business educator*
Miller, L. Martin *accountant, financial planning specialist*

Bath
Smith, Cathy Dawn *administrator*

Bedford
Koontz, Brad Matthew *accountant*

Bethlehem
Barsness, Richard Webster *management educator, administrator*
Hobbs, James Beverly *business administration educator, writer*

Blue Bell
Scheuring, David Keith, Sr. *financial services company executive*
Villwock, Kenneth James *procurement executive*
Weinbach, Lawrence Allen *business executive*

Braddock
Slack, Edward Dorsey, III *financial systems professional, consultant*

Bryn Mawr
Moyer, F. Stanton *financial executive, advisor*

Butler
Coleman, Arthur Robert *retired accountant*
Kendall, George Jason *accountant, financial planner, computer consultant*

Chester
DiAngelo, Joseph Anthony, Jr. *management educator, academic dean*

Collegeville
Maco, Teri Regan *accountant, engineer*

Coraopolis
Giliberti, Michael Richard *financial planner*

Cresson
Griffith, Madlynne Veil *controller*

Danville
Coffman, David Ervin *accountant, valuation analyst*

Doylestown
Kohlhepp, Edward John *financial planner*

Dunmore
Pencek, Carolyn Carlson *treasurer, educator*

Easton
Burkhart, Glenn Randall *corporate internal auditor*
Moore, Joyce Kristina *financial planner*

Erie
Monahan, Thomas Andrew, Jr. *accountant*

Exton
Bush, Joanne Tadeo *financial consultant, corporate executive*

Fairview
Wondra, Norbert Francis *accountant, controller*

Flourtown
Christy, John Gilray *financial company executive*

Greensburg
Foreman, John Daniel *financial executive*

Harrisburg
Dean, Eric Arthur *auditor, accountant*
Lincoln, Carl Clifford, Jr. *auditor*
Willow, Judith Ann Loye *tax preparer*

Haverford
Bell, Philip Wilkes *accounting and economics educator*
Merrill, Arthur Alexander *financial analyst*

Havertown
Brinker, Thomas Michael *finance executive*

Horsham
†Van Buren, John Martin *actuary*

Indiana
†Pressly, Thomas Richard *accounting educator*

Kutztown
Coyle, Charles A. *marketing educator*
Ogden, James Russell *marketing educator, consultant, lecturer, trainer*

Lafayette Hill
King, Leon *financial services executive*

Lancaster
Freeman, Clarence Calvin *financial executive*
Spatcher, Dianne Marie *finance executive*
Taylor, Ann *business consultant, human resource educator*

Lima
Newett, Edward J., Jr. *accountant*

Malvern
Hendrix, Stephen C. *financial executive*

Mc Donald
Tannehill, Norman Bruce, Jr. *consultant, educator*

Meadowbrook
Baeckstrom, Marianne *actuary*

Media
Baitzel, Gregory Wilson *accounting executive*
Hemphill, James S. *investment management executive, financial advisor*

Monaca
Nutter, James Randall *management educator*

Nanticoke
McHale, Maureen Bernadette Kenny *controller*

Nazareth
Rayner, Robert Martin *financial executive*

New Castle
Moore, Janet Marie *accountant, state official*

Newtown
Fiore, James Louis, Jr. *public accountant, educator, professional speaker, trainer consultant*
Wurster, Julie Anne *financial executive*

Newtown Square
Graf, Arnold Harold *employee benefits executive, financial planner*
Steinman, Robert Cleeton *accountant*

Philadelphia
Alexander, William Herbert *business educator, former construction executive*
Anderson, Jerry Allen *financial analyst*
Anderson, Rolph Ely *marketing educator*
Andrisani, Paul *business educator, management consultant*
Babbel, David Frederick *finance and insurance educator*
Blume, Marshall Edward *finance educator*
Booth, Anna Belle *accountant*
Daly, Donald Francis *investment counsel*
de Vassal, Vladimir *investment management executive*
Fisher, Marshall Lee *operations management educator*
Flores, J. Terry *accountant*
Francescone, John Bernard *accountant*
Friedman, Sidney A. *financial services executive*
Gilmour, D(avid) James *strategic planner, systems analyst*
Glusman, David Howard *accountant*
Goodman, Charles Schaffner *marketing educator*
Harvey, Rebecca Suzanne *accountant, management consultant*
Joglekar, Prafulla Narayan *information systems management educator, consultant*
Kandel, Donald Harry *financial analyst*
Keim, Donald Bruce *finance educator*
Kelley, William Thomas *marketing educator*

Kelly, Joseph J. *accountant*
Kimberly, John Robert *management educator, consultant*
Kozlowski, Bette Marie *accountant*
Ksansnak, James E. *service management company executive*
Mazzarella, James Kevin *business administration educator*
Micko, Alexander S. *financial executive*
Mihaly, George Harry, Jr. *accountant*
Moore, Brian Clive *actuary*
Nadley, Harris Jerome *accountant, educator, author*
odish, Leonard Melvin *marketing educator, entrepreneur*
Ralston, Steven Philip *portfolio manager, financial analyst*
Robinson, Robert L. *financial service company executive, lawyer*
Rose, Robert Lawrence *financial services company executive*
Rosenbloom, Bert *marketing educator, consultant, writer*
Rowan, Richard Lamar *business management educator*
Saidel, Jonathan A. *city controller*
Saks, Stephen Howard *accountant*
Santomero, Anthony M. *business educator*
Sanyour, Michael Louis, Jr. *financial services company executive*
Saul, Ralph Southey *financial service executive*
Selles, Robert Hendrikus *actuary, consultant*
†Shils, Edward B. *management educator, lawyer*
Smith, Frederick Samuel, Jr. *accountant*
Staloff, Arnold Fred *financial executive*
Taylor, Wilson H. *diversified financial company executive*
Webber, Ross Arkell *management educator*
Ziegler, Donald Robert *accountant*
Zucker, William *retired business educator*

Pittsburgh
Bernt, Benno Anthony *financial executive, entrepreneur and investor*
Bly, James Charles, Jr. *financial services executive*
Broker, Jeffrey John *accountant*
Czuszak, Janis Marie *former credit company official, researcher*
Franklin, Kenneth Ronald *franchise company executive, consultant*
Haggerty, Gretchen R. *accounting and finance executive*
Haley, Roy W. *financial services executive*
Ijiri, Yuji *accounting and economics educator*
Kahn, Herman L. (Bud Kahn) *financial advisor*
Kilmann, Ralph Herman *business educator*
King, William Richard *business educator, consultant*
Kraus, John Delbert *investment advisor*
Kriebel, Charles Hosey *management sciences educator*
Sees, Kay Anne *accountant, healthcare consultant*
Smrekar, Karl George, Jr. *financial planner*
Stevens, William Talbert *financial services executive*
Thorne, John Reinecke *business educator, venture capitalist*

Plymouth Meeting
Litman, Raymond Stephen *financial services consultant*

Radnor
Stearns, Milton Sprague, Jr. *financial executive*

Reading
Gebbia, Robert James *tax executive*

Richboro
Higginbotham, Kenneth James *financial services executive*

Saint Davids
Bertsch, Frederick Charles, III *business executive*
Rogers, James Gardiner *accountant, educator*

Scranton
Eckersley, Richard Laurence *accountant*
Ostrowski, Thomas John *accountant*
Volk, Thomas *accountant*

Sewickley
Jehle, Michael Edward *financial executive*

Springfield
Berenato, Anthony Francis *financial executive*
Blazek, Wayne Joseph *auditor*

Towanda
Hulslander, Marjorie Diane *auditor*

University Park
Jaffe, Austin Jay *business administration educator*
Junker, Edward P., III *retired diversified financial services company executive*
McKeown, James Charles *accounting educator, consultant*

Wayne
Mestre, Oscar Luis *financial consultant*
Sims, Robert John *financial planner*

West Chester
Blasiotti, Robert Vincent *accountant, consultant*
Handzel, Steven Jeffrey *accountant*
McMeen, Albert Ralph, Jr. *investment advisor*

West Conshohocken
Richard, Scott F. *portfolio manager*

White Haven
Phillips, David George *financial planner*

Williamsport
Bellmore, Lawrence Robert, Jr. *financial planner*

Wyomissing
Stephen, Dennis John *financial planner*

York
Day, Ronald Richard *financial executive*
Fontanazza, Franklin Joseph *accountant*

RHODE ISLAND

Cranston
Ahlgren, Charles Stephen *business and public policy consultant*

East Providence
Horton, Debbi-Jo *accountant*
Tripp, Michael Windsor *accountant*

Johnston
†Castellone, Natalie Lynné *accountant*

Kingston
Mazze, Edward Mark *marketing educator, consultant*
Stark, Dennis Edwin *finance executive*

Lincoln
Carter, Wilfred Wilson *financial executive, controller*

Pawtucket
Davison, Charles Hamilton *financial executive*

Providence
Harris, Richard John *diversified holding company executive*
Marot, Lola *accountant*
McNeil, Paul Joseph, Jr. *employment security interviewer*
Satterthwaite, Franklin Bache, Jr. *management educator, executive coach*

Smithfield
Ready, Christopher James *accountant*

SOUTH CAROLINA

Charleston
Prewitt, William Chandler *financial executive*
Stewart, Brent Allen *business educator*

Clemson
Mabry, Rodney Hugh *economics and finance educator*
Sheriff, Jimmy Don *accounting educator, academic dean*

Columbia
Davis, Barbara Langford *financial advisor*
Edwards, James Benjamin *accountant, educator*
Flynn, Cheryl Dixon *accountant*
Hollis, Charles Eugene, Jr. *savings and loan association executive*
Luoma, Gary A. *accounting educator*
Monahan, Thomas Paul *accountant*
Powell, J(ohn) Key *estate planner, consultant*

Georgetown
Bowen, William Augustus *financial consultant*
McGrath, James Charles, III *financial services company executive, lawyer, consultant*

Greenville
Rogers, Jon Martin *financial consultant, financial company executive*

Johns Island
Rhea, Marcia Chandler *accountant*

Summerville
Sexton, Donald Lee *retired business administration educator*

Sumter
Van Bulck, Hendrikus Eugenius *accountant*

Williamston
Alewine, James William *financial executive*

SOUTH DAKOTA

Burbank
Simmons, Joseph Thomas *accountant, educator*

Platte
Pennington, Beverly Melcher *financial services company executive*

Sioux Falls
Brandt, David Dean *accountant, financial planner, valuation analyst*

Spearfish
Anderson, Thomas Caryl *financial and administrative systems professional*

Vermillion
Korte, Leon Lee *accountant, educator*

TENNESSEE

Alamo
Finch, Evelyn Vorise *financial planner*

Blountville
Grau, Garry Lee *business educator*

Brentwood
McClary, Jim Marston *accounting executive, consultant*
McNamara, Kevin Michael *accountant*

Bristol
Sessoms, Stephanie Thompson *accountant*

Chattanooga
Matherley, Steve Allen *cost accountant*
Randall, Kay Temple *accountant, real estate agent, retired*
Russe, Conrad Thomas Campbell *accountant*

Cleveland
Callais, Elaine Denise Rogers *accountant*

Cookeville
Gentry, Ricky Glyn *accountant*

Crossville
Lansford, Edwin Gaines *accountant*

Elizabethton
Taylor, Wesley Alan *accountant, consultant*

Goodlettsville
Stickel, Lisa Mays *accountant*
Tongate, Darrel Edwin *accountant*

Jackson
Garner, Jeffrey L. *accountant*
Holt, Michael Kenneth *management and finance educator, consultant*

Johnson City
†Spritzer, Allan D. *business educator*

Knoxville
Carcello, Joseph Vincent *accounting educator*

Memphis
Agrawal, Surendra P. *accountant, educator*
Blake, Norman Perkins, Jr. *finance company executive*
Brandon, Elvis Denby, III *financial planner*
Forell, David Charles *financial executive*
Hale, Danny Lyman *financial executive*
Iles, Roger Dean *accountant*
Lang, Lillian Owen *accountant*
†Pruitt, Stephen Wallace *finance educator*

Murfreesboro
Lee, John Thomas *finance educator, financial planner*

Nashville
Brophy, Jeremiah Joseph *financial company official, former army officer*
Brown, Norman James *financial manager*
Dykes, Archie Reece *financial services executive*
Gibbs, Brian J. *behavioral scientist, business educator*
Holsen, Robert Charles *accountant*
†Phillips, Clyde M. *accounting executive*
Richmond, Samuel Bernard *management educator*
Saunders, Ted Elliott *accountant*
Sircy, Bob C., Jr. *accountant, financial executive*
Ullestad, Merwin Allan *tax services executive*
Van, George Paul *international money management consultant*
Weingartner, H(ans) Martin *finance educator*

Soddy Daisy
Swafford, Douglas Richard *corporate credit executive*

TEXAS

Addison
Tull, C. Thomas *investment advisor*

Amarillo
Martin, Luan *accountant, payroll and timekeeping supervisor*
Sowers, Thomas Edwin *accountant, auditor*
Streu, Raymond Oliver *financial planner, securities executive*

Argyle
Pettit, John Douglas, Jr. *management educator*

Arlington
Dickinson, Roger Allyn *business administration educator*
Quant, Harold Edward *financial services company executive, rancher*
Reilly, Michael Atlee *financial company executive, venture capital investor*
Sambaluk, Nicholas Wayne *auditor*
Swanson, Peggy Eubanks *finance educator*
Witt, Robert E. *marketing educator*

Austin
Alpert, Mark Ira *marketing educator*
Anderson, Urton Liggett *accounting educator*
Crum, Lawrence Lee *banking educator*
Cundiff, Edward William *marketing educator*
Doenges, Rudolph Conrad *finance educator*
Drew, Aubrey Jay *accountant*
Fehle, Frank Rudolf *finance educator*
Granof, Michael H. *accounting educator*
Graydon, Frank Drake *retired accounting educator, university administrator*
Kimberlin, Sam Owen, Jr. *financial institutions consultant*
Larson, Kermit Dean *accounting educator*
Lemens, William Vernon, Jr. *banker, finance company executive, lawyer*
McElroy, Maurine Davenport *financier, educator*
Peterson, Robert Allen *marketing educator*
Robertson, Jack Clark *accounting educator*
†Taylor, Joseph Arthur *internation communication educator*
Wolf, Harold Arthur *finance educator*

Bellaire
Richardson, William Wightman, III *personnel and employee benefits consultant*

Brenham
Rothermel, James Douglas *retired finance educator*

Brownsville
Cohen, Barry Mendel *financial executive, educator*

Brownwood
Bell, Mary E. Beniteau *accountant*

Burleson
Manning, Walter Scott *accountant, former educator, consultant*

Cedar Hill
Shower, Robert Wesley *financial executive*

Cedar Park
†Vela, Wesley James *finance director*

College Station
Evans, Carol Ann Butler *consultant, lecturer*
Plum, Charles Walden *retired business executive and educator*
Wichern, Dean William *business educator*

Commerce
Avard, Stephen Lewis *finance educator*

Corpus Christi
Vaughan, Alice Felicie *accountant, real estate executive, tax consultant*

Dallas
Bateman, Giles Hirst Litton *finance executive*
Caldwell, Thomas Howell, Jr. *accountant, financial management consultant*
Cameron, Glenn Nilsson *loan executive*
Coldwell, Philip Edward *financial consultant*
Coy, Christopher Hartmann *finance executive*
Dugger, Joe E. *accountant*
Garner, Paul Trantham *data services administrator*
Grant, Joseph Moorman *finance executive*
Graves, Deidra Nicole *international tax consultant*
Harris, Lucy Brown *accountant, consultant*
Hay, Jess Thomas *retired finance company executive*
Jennings, Dennis Raymond *accountant*
Jobe, Larry Alton *financial company executive*
Lam, Chun Hung *finance educator, consultant*
Lebos, Richard Jesse *lawyer*
Mackey, Stacy Leigh *accounting assistant*
Mahadeva, Manoranjan *financial executive, accountant*
Mahr, George Joseph *financial service executive, real estate developer*
McElvain, David Plowman *retired manufacturing company financial executive*
McElyea, Jacquelyn Suzanne *accountant, real estate consultant*
Moore, Thomas Joseph *financial company executive*
Murrell, William Ivan *accountant*
Pruitt, Brad Alexander *business executive*
Reinganum, Marc Richard *finance educator*
Shimer, Daniel Lewis *corporate executive*
Smiles, Ronald *management educator*
Solender, Robert Lawrence *financial executive*
Tannebaum, Samuel Hugo *accountant*

Denton
Brock, Horace Rhea *accounting educator*
Prybutok, Victor Ronald *business educator*
Taylor, Sherrill Ruth *management educator*

Duncanville
Trotter, Ide Peebles *financial planner, investment manager*

El Paso
DeGroat, James Stephen *financial services executive*
Hoagland, Jennifer Hope *accountant*
Kelley, Sylvia Johnson *financial services firm executive*
Preston, Letricia Elayne *financial planner*

Fort Worth
Clark, Emory Eugene *financial planning executive*
Dominiak, Geraldine Florence *accounting educator*
Pappas-Speairs, Nina *financial planner, educator*
Warren, Peter Gigstad *financial consultant, investment advisor*

Frisco
Bloskas, John D. *financial executive*

Galveston
Selig, Oury Levy *financial consultant*
Short, James Ferebee *portfolio manager*
Welch, Ronald J. *actuary*

Garland
Hughes, Arthur Hyde *accountant, consultant*
Lord, Jacqueline Ward *accountant, photographer, artist*
McGill, Maurice Leon *financial executive*

Houston
Arnold, Daniel Calmes *finance company executive*
Braden, John Alan *accountant*
Coffey, Clarence W. *treasurer*
D'Agostino, James Samuel, Jr. *financial executive*
Daily, James L., Jr. *retired financial executive*
Dunn, James Randolph *corporate executive*
Gauer, William Keith *accountant*
Getz, Lowell Vernon *financial advisor*
Goldberg, William Jeffrey *accountant*
Griffith Fries, Martha *controller*
Hargrove, James Ward *financial consultant*
Hlozek, Carole Diane Quast *financial services company officer*
Horvitz, Paul Michael *finance educator*
Jordan, David Thomas *financial analyst, consultant*
Kelly, Margaret Elizabeth *financial analyst, planner*
Knauss, Robert Lynn *international business educator, corporate executive*
Malone, Lisa R. *accountant, scheduler*
McComas, Marcella Laigne *marketing educator*
Metyko, Michael Joseph *owner, manager development company*
Nollen, Margaret Roach *financial administrator*
†Pace, Allan Jay *financial advisor*
†Priwin, Daniel *finance company executive*
Rasbury, Julian George *financial services company executive*
Rawson, Jim Charles *accountant, executive*
Rockwell, Elizabeth Dennis *retirement specialist, financial planner*
Sims, Rebecca Gibbs *accountant, certified fraud examiner, journalist, editor*
Starkey, Elizabeth LaRuffa *accountant*
Thacker, Shannon Stephen *financial advisor*
Van Caspel, Venita Walker *retired financial planner*
Van Dusen, Glenn T. *controller, secretary, treasurer*
Wells, Damon, Jr. *investment company executive*
Wilcox, Barbara Montgomery *accountant*
Wilkinson, Harry Edward *management educator and consultant*
Williams, James Lee *financial industries executive*
Young, Jeanette Cochran *corporate planner, reporter, analyst*
Zeff, Stephen Addam *accounting educator*

Irving
Clinton, Tracy Peter, Sr. *financial executive, systems analyst*
Forson, Norman Ray *controller*
Geisinger, Janice Allain *accountant*
Martin, Stacey *accountant*
Meredith, Karen Ann *accountant, financial executive*
Mobley, William Hodges *management educator, researcher*
Norris, Richard Anthony *accountant*
†Roig, Daniel G. *finance company executive*
Sensabaugh, Mary Elizabeth *financial consultant*
Stevens, Dennis Max *audit director*
Whitaker, Heidi Sue *accountant, systems developer, project manager*

Katy
†Coleman, Curtis H. *financial executive*

Kingsville
Stanford, Jane Herring *business administration educator*

Lubbock
Chavarria, Dolores Esparza *financial service executive*
Stem, Carl Herbert *business educator*
Wolfe, Verda Nell *pension consultant, financial planner*

Mc Kinney
Brewer, Ricky Lee *investment broker, estate planner*
Goldstein, Lionel Alvin *personal financial and investment advisor*
Kessler, John Paul, Jr. *financial planner*

Midland
Groce, James Freelan *financial consultant*
Tom, James Robert *accountant*

Navasota
Smith, Jo Ann Costa *comptroller*

Odessa
Casparis, Alexander Lamar *accountant*

Pasadena
Scott, William Floyd *accountant*

Pearland
Thomas, James Raymond *accountant*

Plano
Bode, Richard Albert *retired financial executive*
Carter, Rodney *corporate finance executive*
Muir, Duncan *financial public relations executive*
Wayne, Jeanette Marie *auditor*

Port Aransas
Beimers, George Jacob *financial executive*

Richardson
Thomas, Robert Lee *financial services company executive, consultant*

Round Rock
Puri, Rajendra Kumar *business and tax specialist, consultant*

San Antonio
Atnip, Betty Louise *accountant*
Carroll, William Marion *financial services executive*
Fawcett, Leslie Clarence, Jr. *accountant*
Griffin-Thompson, Melanie *accounting firm executive*
Hannah, John Robert, Sr. *accountant*
Jensen-White, Teresa Elaine *financial planner*
Jones, James Richard *business administration educator*
Roth-Roffy, Paul William *accountant*
Terracina, Roy David *private investor*

Sugar Land
Keefe, Carolyn Joan *tax accountant*

Tyler
Moore, David L. *financial consultant*

Universal City
Smith, James Earlie, Jr. *financial services auditor*

Victoria
Satava, David Richard *accountant, educator*

Waco
Collins, Robert Craig *business educator*
Rose, John Thomas *finance educator*

Wichita Falls
Silverman, Gary William *financial planner*

Wimberley
Skaggs, Wayne Gerard *financial services company executive, retired*

UTAH

Provo
Hunt, H(arold) Keith *business management educator, marketing consultant*

Saint George
Day, Steven M. *accounting educator, accountant*

Salt Lake City
Burdette, Robert Soelberg *accountant*
Cousins, Richard Francis *diversified financial services company executive*
Joseph, Kevin Mark *financial services executive*
Nelson, Roger Hugh *management educator, business executive*
Nicolatus, Stephen Jon *financial consultant*
Sullivan, Claire Ferguson *retired marketing educator*
Young, Scott Thomas *business management educator*

Sandy
†Jayne, Fred Eugene *financial planner*

VERMONT

Burlington
Thimm, Alfred Louis *management educator*

East Fairfield
Long, Joan Hazel *accountant*

Perkinsville
Freeburg, Richard Gorman *financial derivatives company executive*

Rutland
Haley, John Charles *financial executive*
Wright, William Bigelow *retired financial executive*

Vergennes
Sinkewicz, Robert William *financial analyst, accountant*

Windsor
Hydrisko, Stanley Joseph *financial company executive*

VIRGINIA

Abingdon
Graham, Howard Lee, Sr. *corporate executive*

Alexandria
Brickhill, William Lee *international finance consultant*
Coryell, Glynn Heath *financial service executive*
†Hammad, Alam E. *international business consultant, educator*
†Huh, Jae Young *finance company executive*
Le, Thuy Xuan *financial control systems developer, consultant, metaphysics scientist*
Smith, Robert Luther *management educator*

Annandale
Connair, Stephen Michael *financial analyst*
Jones, David Charles *international financial and management consultant*

Arlington
Allard, Scott Morgan *cost, benefit analyst, information professional*
†Amlin, Gary W. *finance administrator*
Bianchi, Charles Paul *technical and business executive, money manager, financial consultant*
Bruck, William *business executive*
Davis, Maynard Kirk *accountant*
Lewis, Hunter *financial advisor, publisher*
McClure, William Earl *financial advisor*
Merrifield, Dudley Bruce *business educator, former government official*
Vernon, Anthony Cliffe *financial systems support specialist*
Wesberry, James Pickett, Jr. *financial management consultant, auditor, international organization executive*

Blacksburg
Brozovsky, John A. *accounting educator*
Moore, Laurence John *business educator*
Patterson, Douglas MacLennan *finance educator*

Bridgewater
Armstrong, Martha Susan *accountant, educator*

Bristol
Creger, David Lee *financial planner, insurance executive*

Broad Run
Kube, Harold Deming *retired financial executive*

Charlottesville
Broome, Oscar Whitfield, Jr. *accounting educator, administrator*
Davis, Edward Wilson *business administration educator*
Dunn, Wendell Earl, III *business educator*
Ellett, John Spears, II *retired taxation educator, accountant, lawyer*
Gwin, John Michael *marketing educator, consultant*
Kehoe, William Joseph *business educator, researcher, consultant*
Mc Kinney, George Wesley, Jr. *banking educator*
Minehart, Jean Besse *tax accountant*
Scott, Charlotte H. *business educator*
Shenkir, William Gary *business educator*
Sihler, William Wooding *finance educator*
Thompson, David William *business educator*
Trent, Robert Harold *business educator*
Wheeler, David Wayne *accountant*

Chesapeake
Shirley, Charles William *insurance and investment advisor, farm owner*

Chester
Roane, David James, Jr. *information technology auditor*

Duffield
Reynolds, James Allen, Jr. *financial analyst, marketing professional*

Fairfax
Bowden, Howard Kent *accountant*
†Johnson, Kelly Hal *performance analyst*
Kautt, Glenn Gregory *financial planner*
Khoury, Riad Philip *corporation executive, financial consultant*
Maul, Kevin Jay *financial consultant*
McCrohan, Kevin Francis *business educator*
Spage, Catherine Marie *budget analyst*
Tompros, Andrew Elias *financial analyst*

Falls Church
Drake, Diana Ashley *financial planner*
Hahn, Thomas Joonghi *accountant*
Kaplan, Jocelyn Rae *financial planning firm executive*
Purvis, Ronald Scott *financial counselor, real estate executive*
Rosenberg, Theodore Roy *financial executive*

Glen Allen
Fairbank, Richard *diversified financial services company executive*

Haymarket
Phillips, Robert Benbow *financial planner*

Herndon
Polemitou, Olga Andrea *accountant*

Keswick
Pochick, Francis Edward *financial consultant*

Leesburg
Davidson, Noreen Hanna *financial services company executive*

Lexington
DeVogt, John Frederick *management science and business ethics educator, consultant*

Lynchburg
Gilmore, Philip Nathanael *finance educator, accountant*

Mc Lean
Baldassari, Robert Gene *accountant*
Drew, K *financial advisor, management consultant*
Halaby, Najeeb E. *financier, lawyer*
Landfield, James Seymour *financial manager*

Mechanicsville
Mann, Stephen Ashby *financial counselor*

Mount Vernon
Saadian, Javid *accountant, consultant*

Newport News
Le Mons, Kathleen Ann *portfolio manager, investment officer*

Norfolk
Bullington, James Richard *business educator, former ambassador*
McKee, Timothy Carlton *taxation educator*
Powell, Stephen Kenneth *financial planner*
West, Roger Seiker, III *finance executive*

Palmyra
Sahr, Morris Gallup *financial planner*

Petersburg
†Challa, Chandrashekar Dutt *business educator*

Reston
Fox, Edward A. *business executive*

Richmond
Capps, Thos E. *diversified financial services company executive*
Gottwald, Bruce Cobb, Jr. *treasurer analyst*
Hull, Rita Prizler *accounting educator*
King, Robert Leroy *business administration educator*
†Landsidle, William Edward *comptroller*
Scott, George Cole, III *investment advisor*
Scott, Sidney Buford *financial services company executive*
Thompson, Francis Neal *financial services consultant*
Trumble, Robert Roy *business educator*
Upton, David Edward *finance educator*

Roanoke
Hudick, Andrew Michael, II *finance executive*
Mitchell, Sharon Stanley *supply analyst, accountant*

Upperville
Smart, Stephen Bruce, Jr. *business and government executive*

Urbanna
Hudson, Jesse Tucker, Jr. *financial executive*

Vienna
Urbanas, Alban William *estate planner*
Zoeller, Jack Carl *financial executive*

Virginia Beach
Burke, Thomas Joseph *accountant*
DiCarlo, Susanne Helen *financial analyst*
O'Brien, Robert James *financial consultant, business owner*
Price, Alan Thomas *business and estate planner*

Waterford
Harper, James Weldon, III *finance consultant*

Williamsburg
Fulmer, Robert M. *business educator, management consultant*
Kottas, John Frederick *business administration educator*
Messmer, Donald Joseph *business management educator, marketing consultant*
O'Connell, William Edward, Jr. *finance educator*
Pearson, Roy Laing *business administration educator*
Regan, Donald Thomas *financier, artist, lecturer*
Strong, John Scott *finance educator*
Warren, William Herbert *business administration educator*

Winchester
Proe, John David *business educator, consultant, administrator*
†Sample, Travis Lamar *business educator*

Woodbridge
Dillaber, Philip Arthur *budget and resource analyst, economist, consultant*
Rose, Marianne Hunt *business educator*

Wytheville
Wright, Donald Gene *accountant*

WASHINGTON

Bellevue
Graham, John Robert, Jr. *financial executive*

Gig Harbor
Cuzzetto, Charles Edward *accountant, financial analyst, educator*

Medical Lake
Grub, Phillip Donald *business educator*

Mount Vernon
Gaston, Margaret Anne *retired business educator*

Mountlake Terrace
Rapp, Nina Beatrice *financial company executive*

Olympia
Christensen, Robert Wayne, Jr. *financial and leasing company executive*
Myers, Sharon Diane *auditor*
†Thompson, Richard *financial executive*

Richland
Craven, William Donald *internal auditor, consultant*

Seattle
Bunting, Robert Louis *accounting firm executive, management consultant*
Collett, Robert Lee *financial company executive*
Dively, Dwight Douglas *finance director*
Etcheson, Warren Wade *business administration educator*
Evans, Richard Lloyd *financial services company executive*
Feiss, George James, III *financial services company executive*
Gaskill, Herbert Leo *accountant, engineer*
Harder, Virgil Eugene *business administration educator*
Kasama, Hideto Peter *accountant, business advisor, real estate consultant*
MacLachlan, Douglas Lee *marketing educator*
Patterson, Beverley Pamela Grace *accountant*
Sandstrom, Alice Wilhelmina *accountant*
Saxberg, Borje Osvald *management educator*
Tollett, Glenna Belle *accountant, mobile home park operator*

Sequim
Walker, Raymond Francis *business and financial consulting company executive*

Shoreline
Hanson, Kermit Osmond *business administration educator, university dean emeritus*

Spokane
Burton, Robert Lyle *accounting firm executive*
Hoyt, Bradley James *financial advisor*
Teets, Walter Ralph *accounting educator*

WEST VIRGINIA

Charleston
Morton, Mark Edward *accountant, clothing store executive*

Inwood
Cloyd, Helen Mary *accountant, educator*

Weirton
Robinson, Charles Warren *controller*

WISCONSIN

Baraboo
Smith, Walter DeLos *accountant, professional speaker*

Belgium
Slater, John Greenleaf *financial consultant*

Beloit
Rodeman, Frederick Ernest *accountant*

Brookfield
Breu, George *accountant*
Hundt, Paul Anthony *financial planner*
Roder, Ronald Ernest *accountant*

De Pere
Rueden, Henry Anthony *accountant*

Eau Claire
Weil, D(onald) Wallace *business administration educator*

Germantown
Fischer, Roberta Jane *accountant*

Green Bay
Fisher, Robert Warren *accountant*

Greenfield
Neal, Jon C(harles) *accountant, consultant*

Kenosha
Wright, David Jonathan *finance educator*

La Crosse
Kastantin, Joseph Thomas *accounting educator*

Madison
Aldag, Ramon John *management and organization educator*
Baron, Alma Fay S. *management educator*
Bielinski, Daniel Walter *management consultant*
Brachman, Richard John, II *financial services consultant, banking educator*
Eisler, Millard Marcus *financial executive*
Googins, Louise Paulson *financial planner*
Hansen, James John *accountant*
Nevin, John Robert *business educator, consultant*
Prieve, E. Arthur *arts administration educator*
Wade, Royce Allen *financial services representative*

Mequon
Berry, William Martin *financial consultant*

Middleton
Foss, Karl Robert *auditor*

Milwaukee
Einhorn, Stephen Edward *mergers and acquisitions executive, consultant, investment banker*
Ertel, Gary Arthur *accountant*
Huf, Carol Elinor *tax service company executive*
Kendall, Leon Thomas *finance and real estate educator, retired insurance company executive*

Minocqua
Pickert, Robert Walter *accountant*

Muskego
Stefaniak, Norbert John *business administration educator*

Oconto Falls
Leifker, Dale Alan *accountant*

Pleasant Prairie
Schutte, Richard David *financial officer*

Solon Springs
Robek, Mary Frances *business education educator*

Superior
Jordan, Robert Earl *business educator*

Waupun
Wendt, Thomas Gene *controller*

Whitewater
Thatcher, Janet Solverson *finance educator*

Wisconsin Rapids
Kenney, Richard John *paper company finance executive*

WYOMING

Afton
Hunsaker, Floyd B. *accountant*

Cheyenne
Ferrari, David Guy *auditor*
Price, Keith Glenn *accountant*

Cody
Riley, Victor J., Jr. *financial services company executive*

Green River
Thoman, Mary E. *business and marketing educator, rancher*

Riverton
Clark, Stanford E. *accountant*

Rock Springs
Schumacher, Jon Walter *accountant, educator*

Sheridan
Ryan, Michael Louis *controller*

Wheatland
Whitney, Ralph Royal, Jr. *financial executive*

TERRITORIES OF THE UNITED STATES

PUERTO RICO

Hato Rey
Vilches-O'Bourke, Octavio Augusto *accounting company executive*

CANADA

ALBERTA

Calgary
Maher, Peter Michael *management educator*

BRITISH COLUMBIA

Vancouver
Mahler, Richard Terence *finance executive*
Mattessich, Richard Victor (Alvarus) *business administration educator*

NEW BRUNSWICK

Saint Andrews
Anderson, John Murray *operations executive, former university president*

ONTARIO

Islington
White, Adrian Michael Stephen *financial executive*

London
Osbaldeston, Gordon Francis *business educator, former government official*

Mississauga
Turnbull, Adam Michael Gordon *financial executive, accountant*

Toronto
Cockwell, Jack Lynn *financial executive*
Cunningham, Gordon Ross *financial executive*
Greig, Thomas Currie *retired financial executive*
Hirst, Peter Christopher *consulting actuary*
Lowe, Robert Edward *financial company executive*
Mann, George Stanley *real estate and financial services corporation executive*
Payton, Thomas William *corporate finance consultant executive*
†Pollock, Samuel *diversified financial services company executive*
Poprawa, Andrew *financial services executive, accountant*
†Schwartz, Gerald Wilfred *financial executive*
Silk, Frederick C.Z. *financial consultant*
Skinner, Alastair *accountant*
Sloan, David Edward *retired corporate executive*
†Steinberg, Gregg Martin *financial and management consultant, investment banker*
Weldon, David Black *company director*

QUEBEC

Montreal
Black, William Gordon *pension consultant*
Crowston, Wallace Bruce Stewart *management educator*
Daly, Gerald *accountant*
Desmarais, Paul *holding company executive*
†Gratton, Robert *diversified financial services company executive*
Laurin, Pierre *finance company executive*
Mintzberg, Henry *management educator, researcher, writer*
Olivella, Barry James *financial executive*
Picard, Laurent A(ugustin) *management educator, administrator, consultant*
Saumier, Andre *finance executive*
Speirs, Derek James *diversified corporation financial executive*
Thompson, John Douglas *financier*
Weir, Stephen James *financial executive*

Quebec
Saint-Pierre, Michel R. *financial services executive*

Verdun
Lessard, Michel M. *finance company executive*

SASKATCHEWAN

Saskatoon
Irvine, Vernon Bruce *accounting educator, administrator*

MEXICO

Veracruz
Janssens, Joe Lee *controller*

BELGIUM

Brussels
†Moschetta, Philippe *financial executive*

CHINA

Hong Kong
Gundersen, Mary Lisa Kranitzky *finance company executive*

ENGLAND

London
Berger, Thomas Jan *financial company executive*
†Ellis, Claud M. Buddy *diversified financial services company executive*
Frank, Charles Raphael, Jr. *financial executive*
Gyllenhammar, Pehr Gustaf *finance company executive, retired automobile company executive, writer*
Pacter, Paul Allan *accounting standards researcher*

FRANCE

Clermont Ferrand
Bourdais de Charbonniére, Eric *financial executive*

ISRAEL

Jerusalem
Masri, Jane Martyn *finance and operations administrator*

JAPAN

Irumagun
Kobayashi, Noritake *business educator*

Kyoto
Shima, Hiromu *management educator*

Suita
Ohashi, Shoichi *business administration educator*

THE NETHERLANDS

Noordwijk
†van der Lugt, Robert Jan *development consultant*

SAUDI ARABIA

Riyadh
Olayan, Suliman Saleh *finance company executive*

SWITZERLAND

Geneva
Farman-Farmaian, Ghaffar *investment company executive*

ADDRESS UNPUBLISHED

Abbott, Edward Leroy *finance executive*
Abels, Robert Frederick *tax consultant*
Abromson, Irving Joel *financial services professional*
Adam, Orval Michael *retired financial executive, lawyer*
Adams, Sharon Farrell *financial analyst*
Alberternst, Judith Ann *pension administrator*
Allen, Anna Marie *financial executive*
Aloisio, Maria Theresa *tax accountant*
Alper, Merlin Lionel *financial executive*
Amdahl, Byrdelle John *business consulting executive*
Ames, Steven Reede *financial planner*
Anderson, Karl Peter *controller*
Arenberg, Julius Theodore, Jr. *retired accounting company executive*
Assunto, Richard Anthony *payroll executive*
Atcheson, Sue Hart *business educator*
Balderston, William, III *retired banker*
Barney, Austin Dunham, II *estate planner*
Beck, Andrew Robert *accountant*
Beebe, John Eldridge *financial service executive*
Beller, Luanne Evelyn *accountant*
Belluomini, Frank Stephen *accountant*
Benenson, Claire Berger *investment and financial planning educator*
Bennett, Peter Dunne *retired marketing educator*
Berger, Stephen *financial services company executive*
Bertucelli, Robert Edward *accountant, educator*
Blasco, Alfred Joseph *business and financial consultant*
Bliss, William Stanley, Jr. *corporate financial and marketing consultant*
Blum-Veglia, Cheryl Ann *accountant*
Booth, George Geoffrey *finance educator*
Borum, Rodney Lee *financial business executive*
Bowne, Shirlee Pearson *finance and housing consultant*
Boyd, Danny Douglass *financial counselor, marriage and family counselor*
Boyd, Edward Lee *financial executive*
Boyd, Francis Virgil *retired accounting educator*
Braisted, Madeline Charlotte *financial planner*
Brigham, John Allen, Jr. *financial executive, environmentalist, polition*
Brown, Henry Bedinger Rust *financial management company executive*
Brown, Michael Robert *finance specialist*
Brune, David Hamilton *financial corporation executive, lawyer*
†Butrimovitz, Gerald Paul *financial planner, securities analyst, investment advisor*
Cain, Patricia Jean *accountant*
Carter, Richard Duane *business educator*
Caso, Philip Michael *financial services company executive, educator*
Charlton, Jesse Melvin, Jr. *management educator, lawyer*
Chattin, Gilbert Marshall *financial analyst*
Chelberg, Bruce Stanley *holding company executive*
Chin, Cindy Lai *accountant*
Christen, Paul Richert *financial company executive*
Clapp, Beverly Booker *accountant*
Clayton, Richard Reese *retired holding company executive*
Collette, Frances Madelyn *retired tax consultant, lawyer*
Contillo, Lawrence Joseph *financial and computer company executive*
Crisler, Paul Richard *retired auditor*
Dallwein, Edward K. *controller*
Davis, Deborah Cecilia *auditor*
Davis, Robert H. *financial executive, arbitrator, mediator, educator*
Deli, Steven Frank *financial services executive*
Derchin, Michael Wayne *financial analyst*
†DeRosa, David Francis *finance educator, trading company executive*
Dickman, Bernard Harold *statistics educator*
Dickson, Eva Mae *credit manager*
Doherty, Thomas Joseph *financial services industry consultant*
†Dolan, Peter J. *corporate financial consultant*
Doty, Philip Edward *accountant*
Downing, M. Scott *budget systems analyst*
Dunbar, Patricia Lynn *new product development consultant*
Dunlap, James Riley, Sr. *former financial executive, credit manager*
Durst, Roberta J. *accountant, healthcare consultant*
Ernstthal, Henry L. *management educator*
Estrin, Herbert Alvin *financial consultant, entertainment company executive*
Farrall, Harold John *retired accountant*
Fenster, Craig Michael *actuary*
Fitzgerald, Susan Inge *credit analyst*
Folz, Carol Ann *financial analyst*
Forest, Philip Earle *housing finance consultant*
Forsgren, John H., Jr. *financial executive*
Fox, Kelly Diane *financial advisor*
France, Richard William *finance executive*
Frank, Edgar Gerald *retired financial executive*
Franklin, William Emery *international business educator*
Fravel, Elizabeth Whitmore *accountant*
Fuller, Stephen Herbert *business administration educator*
†Furst, E. Kenneth *accountant*
Gabriel, Rennie *financial planner*
Gaiber, Lawrence Jay *financial company executive*
Garbacz, Stephen Lawrence *financial director*
Geer, James Hamilton, Jr. *counselor, consultant*
Giles, James Francis *financial executive*
Gleijeses, Mario *holding company executive*
Goodson, Raymond Eugene *business educator, former automotive executive*
Gregg, Walter Emmor, Jr. *financial corporation executive, accountant, lawyer*
Griffin, Carleton Hadlock *accountant, educator*
Griggs, John Robert *financial and consumer credit services executive*

Gruber, Fredric Francis *financial planning and investment research executive*
Guimond, John Patrick *retired financial consultant*
Haddock, Harold, Jr. *retired accounting firm executive*
Handy, Edward Otis, Jr. *financial services executive*
†Hannah, Gregg S. *business educator*
Hanson, Carl Malmrose *financial company executive*
Harlow, Charles Vendale, Jr. *finance educator, consultant*
Harper, W(alter) Joseph *financial consultant*
Harris, Gretchen Elizabeth *treasury analyst, consultant*
†Harrison, Jonathan Edward *accountant, law enforcement consultant*
Henne, Andrea Rudnitsky *business educator*
Hershberger, Steven Kaye *controller*
Heyward, Harold *financial consultant*
Hintz, Charles Bradley *diversified financial executive*
Hodges, Kenneth Stuart *controlller*
Holder, Trudy H. *accounting director*
Holloran, Thomas Edward *business educator*
Holtmeier, Robert J. *accountant*
Holton, Grace Holland *accountant*
Hoy, Harold Joseph *marketing educator, retail executive, management consultant, author, military officer*
Hubbe, Henry Ernest *financial forecaster, funds manager*
Hudak, Thomas F(rancis) *finance company executive*
Hunter, Rebecca Kathleen *accountant, personnel administrator*
Impellizeri, Monica *pension fund administrator, consultant*
Jacques, Andre Charles *financial consultant*
Jamison, John Callison *business educator, investment banker*
Johnson, Bruce Alan *financial company executive*
Johnson, Philip *investment banking executive*
Jones, Kacy Douglas *accountant*
†Jones, Robert A. *equity finance company exeucutive*
Kaplan, Leonard Eugene *accountant*
Kaufman, Charles David *controller*
Keegan, Kenneth Donald *financial consultant, retired oil company executive*
Kennedy, Thomas Patrick *financial executive*
Kidd, Robert [illegible]ugh *financial executive, accountant*
King, Algin Braddy *marketing educator*
Kingsbery, Walton Waits, Jr. *retired accounting firm executive*
Kreitzer, Lois Helen *personal investor*
Krug, Karen-Ann *healthcare financial executive, accountant*
La Blanc, Robert Edmund *consulting company executive*
Lally, William Joseph *financial planner*
Lamont, Alice *accountant, consultant*
Larizadeh, M(ohammed) R(eza) *business educator*
Larson, Gerald Lee *auditor*
Lawrence, Robert MacLaren *retired marketing educator, consultant*
Lesher, John Lee, Jr. *consulting services company executive*
Leventhal, Ellen Iris *portfolio manager, financial services executive*
Levy, Louis Edward *retired accounting firm executive*
Lewis, Gordon Carter *auditor*
Lieberman, Anne Marie *financial executive, retired*
Lindberg, Francis Laurence, Jr. *management consultant*
Lombard, Marjorie Ann *financial officer*
Loren, Mary Rooney *controller*
Magnano, Salvatore Paul *retired financial executive, treasurer*
Malhotra, Pulin *financial infrastructure consultant*
Mand, Martin G. *financial executive*
Mandel, Jack Kent *marketing and advertising educator, publishing consultant*
†Marcille, Lorraine May *finance company executive, accountant*
Mauldin, Jean Ann *controller*
†Maymind, Ilana *accountant*
Mayoras, Donald Eugene *corporate executive, writer, consultant, educator*
McBride, Jack J. *financial services executive*
McLennan, Robert Gordon *asset management company executive*
McNamara, David Joseph *financial and tax planning executive*
Mednick, Robert *accountant*
†Meyer, Sandra Palmer *financial executive*
Miller, Jane Andrews *accountant*
Miselson, Alex J. (Jacob) *portfolio manager, securities analyst, investment theorist*
Mitcham, Julius Jerome *accountant*
Morgan, Robert Arthur *accountant*
Morse, Richard Alan *accountant*
Mosler, John *retired financial planner*
Moyer, Jerry Mills *financial services company executive*
Muller, Margie Hellman *financial services consultant*
Munies, Seth Alix *accountant*
Myers, Miller Franklin *finance company executive, retail executive*
Nair, Raghavan D. *accountant, educator*
Nank, Lois Rae *financial executive*
Nehrt, Lee Charles *management educator*
Neuhaus, Joan T. *finance company executive, private investigator*
Nichols, John David *entrepreneur freelance*
North, John Adna, Jr. *accountant, real estate appraiser*
Norton, Karen Ann *accountant*
Oldshue, Paul Frederick *financial executive*
†Ologbenla, Adesoji Olaposi *financial advisor*
Osborn, Kenneth Louis *financial executive*
Palmer, Gary Andrew *portfolio manager*
Park, Patricia Weill *controller*
Pefley, Norman Gordon *financial analyst*
Peruzzo, Albert Louis *actuary, accountant*
Phillips, Charles Alan *accounting firm executive*
Pick, James Block *management and sociology educator*
Powless, David Griffin *accountant*
Puryear, Alvin Nelson *management educator*
Quirk, Kenneth Paul *accountant*
Rader, Patrick Neil *accountant*
Rastegar-Djavahery, Nader E. *venture capitalist*
Ray, Richard Stanley *accountant*
Reigelsberger, Paul A. *consultant, design artist*
Reynolds, Billie Iles *financial representative and counselor, former national association executive director*
Rhea, Jerry Dwaine *director consumer lending*
Rich, David Barry *financial executive, accountant, entertainer*
Richburg, Billy Keith *financial consultant and entrepreneur*
Ritchey, Paul Andrew *accountant*
Robertson, A. Haeworth *actuary, benefit consultant, foundation executive*
Robison, William Christopher *financial analyst*
Roth, Suzanne Allen *financial services agent*
Roveto, Connie Ida *financial services executive*
Rowe, William Davis *financial services company executive*
Ruggles, Rudy Lamont, Jr. *investment banker, consultant*
Rush, Richard Henry *financial executive, writer, lecturer*
Rutherford, Reid *finance company executive*
Salako, Beatrice Olukemi *accountant*
Sardou, Brian D. *controller, consultant*
Sarther, Lynette Kay *accountant*
Sayles, Leonard Robert *management educator, consultant*
Scanlon, Peter Redmond *accountant*
Scheel, Nels Earl *financial executive, accountant*
Schoen, William Jack *financier*
Sellers, Dawn Kathleen *accountant, auditor*
Sheridan, Patrick Michael *finance company executive, retired*
Shields, H. Richard *tax consultant,business executive*
Shoop, Glenn Powell *investment consultant*
Shore, Harvey Harris *business educator*
Shultis, Robert Lynn *finance educator, cost systems consultant, retired professional association executive*
Smith, Dawn Christiana *accountant*
Smith, James Parker *accountant*
Smith, John Joseph, Jr. *financial management executive*
Smith, Vangy Edith *accountant, consultant, writer, artist*
Snelling, Robert Orren, Sr. *franchising and employment executive*
Snyder, Alan Carhart *financial services executive*
Spiegle, Harold Mark *accountant*
Srinivasan, Venkataraman *marketing and management educator*
Stegner, Lynn Nadene *treasurer*
Stein, Paul Arthur *financial services executive*
Stofferson, Terry Lee *financial officer*
Stralser, Steven Michael *marketing educator, consultant*
Taunton, Kathryn Jayne *accountant*
Taylor, Kathryn Lee *mortgage broker*
Taylor, Linda Rathbun *financial planner*
Tedoldi, Robert Louis, Jr. *financial planner, consultant*
Teronde, Jeffrey Glenn *controller*
Thacker, Victor Larry *educator*
Tongue, Paul Graham *financial executive*
Treynor, Jack Lawrence *financial advisor, educator*
Turner, Henry Brown *finance executive*
Tyler, Richard James *personal and professional development educator*
Tyson, Eric *personal finance writer, finance counselor*
Ulrich, Richard William *finance executive*
Vance, David Alvin *management educator*
van Hengel, Maarten R. *financial executive*
Varrenti, Adam, Jr. *financial executive*
Vaught, Darrel Mandel *accountant*
Wachbrit, Jill Barrett *accountant, tax specialist*
Wain, Christopher Henry Fairfax Moresby *actuary, insurance and investment consultant*
Wall, M. Danny *financial services company executive*
Watt, John H. *financial executive*
Weiss, Joseph W. *management educator, management consultant*
Wells, Toni Lynn *accountant*
Wendorf, Virginia Lou *retired accountant*
Wenzel, Loren Alvin *accounting educator*
Whalen-Blaauwgeers, Herma-Jozé *financial analyst*
Wilhelmsen, Harold John *accountant, operations controller*
Williams, Helen Margaret *retired accountant*
Willoughby, Kenneth Dwight *accountant, banking executive*
Wolf, Rosalie Joyce *financial executive*
Wood, Robert Charles *financial consultant*
Wren, Stephen Corey *corporation administrator, technologist, actuary, mathematician*
Wright, Judith Rae *retired accountant*
Yost, Paula Lynn *accountant*
Zick, John Walter *retired accounting company executive*
Zysblat, William Larry *accountant*

FINANCE: INSURANCE

UNITED STATES

ALABAMA

Birmingham
Currie, Larry Lamar *insurance company executive*
Johnson, Creighton Ernest *insurance company executive, retired*
Rushton, William James, III *insurance company executive*

Foley
Russell, Ralph Timothy *insurance company executive, mayor*

Mobile
Adams, Jeffrey Paul *insurance agent, insurance company executive*

Montgomery
Robinson, Kenneth Larry *insurance company executive*

ALASKA

Anchorage
Gill, William Haywood *insurance broker, consultant*
Trevithick, Ronald James *underwriter*

ARIZONA

Carefree
Wise, Paul Schuyler *insurance company executive*

Flagstaff
Mullens, William Reese *retired insurance company executive*

Green Valley
Brissman, Bernard Gustave *insurance company executive*

Lake Havasu City
Shervheim, Lloyd Oliver *insurance company executive, lawyer*

Paradise Valley
Day, Richard Putnam *marketing, strategic planning and employee benefits consultant, arbitrator*

Phoenix
Fugiel, Frank Paul *insurance company executive*
Healy, Barbara Anne *insurance company executive, financial planner*
Melner, Sinclair Lewis *insurance company executive, retired*

Prescott
Osborn, DeVerle Ross *insurance company executive*

Scottsdale
Burr, Edward Benjamin *life insurance company executive, financial executive*
Tyner, Neal Edward *retired insurance company executive*
Vairo, Robert John *insurance company executive*

Tubac
Fey, John Theodore *retired insurance company executive*

Tucson
Gerhart, Dorothy Evelyn *insurance executive, real estate professional*
Martin, Paul Edward *retired insurance company executive*

ARKANSAS

Fayetteville
Dulan, Harold Andrew *former insurance company executive, educator*

Jonesboro
Calaway, Dennis Louis *insurance company executive, real estate broker, financial executice*

Pine Bluff
Bradford, Jay Turner *insurance executive, state legislator*

CALIFORNIA

Agoura Hills
Cannon, Nancy Gladstein *insurance agent*

Alpine
Keller, Susan Agnes *insurance executive*

Auburn
Jeske, Howard Leigh *retired life insurance company executive, lawyer*

Bradbury
Christensen, Donn Wayne *insurance executive*

Brea
Spiegel, Ronald Stuart *insurance company executive*

Camarillo
Halperin, Kristine Briggs *insurance sales and marketing professional*

Carlsbad
Haney, Robert Locke *retired insurance company executive*

Dana Point
Lang, George Frank *insurance executive, consultant, lawyer*

Encino
Webster, David Arthur *life insurance company executive*

Garden Grove
Williams, J(ohn) Tilman *insurance executive, real estate broker, city official*

Gold River
Gray, Myles McClure *retired insurance company executive*

La Mesa
Schlador, Paul Raymond, Jr. *insurance agent*

Los Angeles
Boynton, Donald Arthur *title insurance company executive*
Erickson, Richard Beau *insurance and financial company executive*
Faulwell, Gerald Edward *insurance company executive*
Gurash, John Thomas *insurance company executive*
Holden, William Willard *insurance executive*
Houston, Ivan James *insurance company executive*
Inman, James Russell *claims consultant*
Johnson, E. Eric *insurance executive*
Milgrim, Darrow A. *insurance broker, recreation consultant*
Rinsch, Charles Emil *insurance company executive*
Stewart, James M. *insurance and securities broker*
Winthrop, Kenneth Ray *insurance executive*

Mill Valley
Clark, Edgar Sanderford *insurance broker, consultant*

Newman
Carlsen, Janet Haws *retired insurance company owner, mayor*

Newport Beach
Cosgrove, Cameron *technology executive*
Gerken, Walter Bland *insurance company executive*
Marcoux, Carl Henry *former insurance executive, writer, historian*
Sutton, Thomas C. *insurance company executive*

Novato
Leaton, Marcella Kay *insurance representative, business owner*

Oakland
Ching, Eric San Hing *health care and insurance administrator*

Orange
Godeke, Raymond Dwight *insurance company executive, accountant*

Petaluma
Skup, David Alan *insurance company executive*

Pismo Beach
Brisbin, Robert Edward *insurance agency executive*

Rancho Cordova
Alenius, John Todd *insurance executive*

Sacramento
Basconcillo, Lindy *insurance and financial services company executive*

San Diego
Baxter, Robert Hampton, III *insurance executive*
Hayes, Robert Emmet *retired insurance company executive*
Jeffers, Donald E. *retired insurance executive, consultant*
Johnson, Vicki R. *insurance company executive*
Purcifull, Robert Otis *insurance company executive*
Ross, Vonia Pearl *insurance agent, small business owner*

San Francisco
Broome, Burton Edward *insurance company executive*
Drexler, Fred *insurance executive*
Enfield, D(onald) Michael *insurance executive*
Grager, Steven Paul *life insurance and trust consultant*
Grove, Douglas David *insurance company executive*
Lamberson, John Roger *insurance company executive*
Levine, Norman Gene *insurance company executive*

San Jose
Jackson, Patrick Joseph *insurance executive*

San Rafael
Djordjevich, Michael *insurance company executive*
Keegan, Jane Ann *insurance executive, consultant*

Sonoma
Bow, Stephen Tyler, Jr. *insurance and computer industry consultant*

Thousand Oaks
Gregory, Calvin *insurance service executive*

Vista
Fuhlrodt, Norman Theodore *retired insurance executive*

Woodland Hills
Berry, Carol Ann *insurance executive*

Woodside
Freitas, Antoinette Juni *insurance company executive*

COLORADO

Aurora
Volpe, Richard Gerard *insurance accounts executive, consultant*

Colorado Springs
Michels, Patricia A. *insurance agent*

Denver
Axley, Hartman *underwriter*
Conroy, Thomas Francis *insurance company executive*

Englewood
Hardy, Wayne Russell *insurance and investment broker*

Fort Collins
Schendel, Winfried George *insurance company executive*
Stephens, Taylor Lane *insurance company executive*

Kremmling
Lewis, Charles D. *rancher, consultant*

Longmont
Simpson, Velma Southall *insurance agent*

Parker
Nelson, Marvin Ray *retired life insurance company executive*

Pueblo
Kelly, William Bret *insurance executive*

CONNECTICUT

Avon
Hickey, Kevin Francis *healthcare executive*
Mazur, Edward John, Jr. *insurance agent*
Stowe, Joyce Lundy *life insurance company official, educator*

Collinsville
Ford, Dexter *retired insurance company executive*

Danbury
Gogliettino, John Carmine *insurance broker*

Glastonbury
Budd, Edward Hey *retired insurance company executive*

Goshen
†Morris, John M. *insurance agency administrator*

Greenwich
Berkley, William Robert *insurance holding company executive*
Clements, Robert *insurance executive*
Flanagan, Robert Daniel *life insurance agent*
Fuller, Theodore *retired insurance executive*
Heer, Edwin LeRoy *insurance executive*
Schiff, Jayne Nemerow *underwriter*

Hartford
Abbot, Quincy Sewall *retired insurance executive*
Ayer, Ramani *insurance company executive*
†Donahue, John F. *insurance executive*
Fiondella, Robert William *insurance company executive*
Huber, Richard Leslie *insurance company executive*
Mullane, Denis Francis *insurance executive*
Sargent, Joseph Denny *insurance executive*
Scully, John Carroll *life insurance marketing research company executive*
Wenner, Gary Michael *information technology company executive*
Westervelt, James Joseph *insurance company executive*
Wilde, Wilson *insurance company executive*
Wilder, Michael Stephen *insurance company executive*
Wise, Richard Evans *corporate executive*

Ledyard
White, Harold R. *insurance and health care inforamtion company executive*

New Canaan
Cohen, Richard Norman *insurance executive*
Ylvisaker, James William *insurance executive*

Stamford
Block, Ruth *retired insurance company executive*
Chickering, Howard Allen *insurance company executive, lawyer*
Ferguson, Ronald Eugene *reinsurance company executive*
Hudson, Harold Jordon, Jr. *retired insurance executive*
Kellogg, Tommy Nason *reinsurance corporation executive*
McWilliams, Thomas Henry *life reinsurance underwriter professional*

Tolland
Simons, Barry *underwriter, insurance consultant*

Vernon Rockville
Wolff, Gregory Steven *insurance company executive*

West Hartford
DeLibero, Mary Smellie *insurance company professional, pianist, soprano*
Gingold, George Norman *insurance company executive, lawyer*

Weston
Thompson, N(orman) David *insurance company executive*

Westport
Frankel, Paul Warren *insurance executive, physician*

Windsor
Koussa, Harold Alan *insurance account executive*

DELAWARE

Greenville
Dombeck, Harold Arthur *insurance company executive*

Wilmington
Pollock, Paul Edward *insurance executive*

DISTRICT OF COLUMBIA

Washington
Conrad, Donald Glover *insurance executive*
Freeman, Robert Turner, Jr. *insurance executive*
†Geer, Dennis F. *insurance executive*
Howes, Theodore Clark *claims examiner*
†Lynn, James Thomas *investment banker, insurance company executive, government executive, lawyer*
†Martin, Julie A. *insurance executive*
Nicely, Olza M. (Tony) *insurance company executive*
Oakley, Diane *insurance executive, benefit consultant*
Parde, Duane Arthur *association executive*
Simpson, Louis A. *insurance company executive*
Turner, Marvin Wentz *insurance company executive*

FLORIDA

Altamonte Springs
Hull, John Doster *retired insurance company executive*

Boca Raton
Knudsen, Rudolph Edgar, Jr. *insurance company executive*
Lynn, Eugene Matthew *insurance company executive*
Richardson, R(oss) Fred(erick) *insurance executive*
Sena, John Michael *insurance agent*

Boynton Beach
Bryant, Donald Loyd *insurance company executive*
Caras, Joseph Sheldon *life insurance company executive*

Bradenton
Phelan, John Densmore *insurance executive, consultant*

Brooksville
Linn, James Eldon, II *insurance company executive*

Clearwater
Caronis, George John *insurance executive*
Fraser, John Wayne *insurance executive, consultant, underwriter*

Coral Gables
†Evarist, Milian, Jr. *insurance company executive*
Landon, Robert Kirkwood *philanthropist, retired insurance company executive*
Rodriguez, Nestor Joaquin *insurance broker*

Coral Springs
†Miller, Karl Frederick *insurance manager*
Tharp, Karen Ann *insurance agent*

Daytona Beach
Adams, John Carter, Jr. *insurance executive*

Fort Lauderdale
Lilley, Mili Della *insurance company executive, entertainment management consultant*
Zumbano, Anthony Ralph *risk, claims management executive*

Fort Myers
Pearson, Paul Holding *insurance company executive*

Gainesville
Niblack, Nancy Lee Parham *insurance agent, financial consultant*
Robertson, James Cole *consultant*

Gulf Breeze
DeBardeleben, John Thomas, Jr. *retired insurance company executive*

Islamorada
Boruszak, James Martin *insurance company executive*

Jacksonville
Kitchens, Frederick Lynton, Jr. *insurance company executive*
Lyon, Wilford Charles, Jr. *insurance executive*
Morehead, Charles Richard *insurance company executive*
Ohnsman, David Robert *insurance consultant*

Key Largo
Daenzer, Bernard John *insurance company executive, legal consultant*

Largo
Guthrie, John Craver *insurance agency owner*

Longwood
Brown, Donald James, Jr. *insurance company executive*

Melbourne
Love, Charles Anthony *insurance inspector, evangelist*

Miami
Denison, Floyd Gene *insurance executive*
Frost, Philip *insurance company executive*
Gabor, Frank *insurance company executive*
George, Stephen Carl *reinsurance executive, educator, consultant*
Gindy, Benjamin Lee *insurance company executive*
Heggen, Arthur William *insurance company executive*
Rivero, Andres *insurance executive*
Shusterman, Nathan *life underwriter, financial consultant*
Toro, Carlos Hans *insurance/financial products marketing executive*
Van Wyck, George Richard *insurance company executive*

Naples
Barnhill, Howard Eugene *insurance company executive*
Kennedy, Donald Davidson, Jr. *retired insurance company executive*
Mc Queen, Robert Charles *retired insurance executive*
Parish, John Cook *insurance executive*

New Port Richey
Hanahan, James Lake *insurance executive*

Orange Park
Hudson, William Mark *insurance company executive, owner*

Ormond Beach
Burt, Wallace Joseph, Jr. *insurance company executive*

Oviedo
Brethauer, William Russell, Jr. *claim investigator*

Saint Petersburg
Hoche, Philip Anthony *life insurance company executive*

Sarasota
Bushey, Alan Scott *retired insurance holding company executive*

Tallahassee
Gabor, Jeffrey Alan *insurance and financial services executive*
Gunter, William Dawson, Jr. (Bill Gunter) *insurance company executive*
Hunt, John Edwin *insurance company executive, consultant*

Tampa
Ayers, Charles Allen *insurance risk management executive*
Flagg, Barry David *insurance, corporate benefits, estate planning consultant*
Hanisee, Mark Steven *employee benefits professional*
Poe, William Frederick *insurance agency executive, former mayor*
Vanderburg, Paul Stacey *insurance executive, consultant*

Tequesta
Holmes, Melvin Almont *insurance company executive*

Titusville
Hardister, Darrell Edward *insurance executive*

Vero Beach
Burton, Arthur Henry, Jr. *insurance company executive*

Village Of Golf
Bates, Edward Brill *retired insurance company executive*

Wellington
Beshears, Charles Daniel *insurance executive, retired*

Winter Haven
Rossbacher, John Robert *retired insurance broker, musician, writer*

Winter Park
Conrad, Judy L. *insurance company executive*
Kraft, Kenneth Houston, Jr. *insurance agency executive*

GEORGIA

Alpharetta
Clary, Ronald Gordon *insurance agency executive*
Fowler, Vivian Delores *insurance company executive*

Atlanta
Atkinson, A. Kelley *insurance company executive*
Black, Kenneth, Jr. *retired insurance executive and educator, author*
Buck, Lee Albert *retired insurance company executive, evangelist*
Fox, Lloyd Allan *insurance company executive*
Garner, Thomas Emory, Jr. *health insurance executive*
Gregory, Mel Hyatt, Jr. *retired insurance company executive*
Peacock, George Rowatt *retired life insurance company executive*
Witty, Robert Wilkes *insurance services company executive*

Chamblee
Fried, Lawrence Philip *insurance company executive*

Columbus
Amos, Daniel Paul *insurance executive*
Amos, Paul Shelby *insurance company executive*
Cloninger, Kriss, III *insurance company executive*
†Loudermilk, Joey M. *insurance corporation executive, corporate lawyer*

Duluth
Burns, Carroll Dean *insurance company executive*

Lagrange
Hudson, Charles Daugherty *insurance executive*

Lithonia
Shakespeare, Easton Geoffrey *insurance broker, consultant*

Norcross
Yancey, Wallace Glenn *retired insurance company executive*

Savannah
Dodge, William Douglas *insurance company consultant*
Standbridge, Peter Thomas *retired insurance company executive*

Statesboro
Parrish, Benjamin Emmitt, II *insurance executive*

Stone Mountain
Denney, Laura Falin *insurance company executive*

HAWAII

Honolulu
Hu, Joseph Kai Ming *insurance company executive*
Lee, Marcia Ellen *insurance agent*
Lindsay, Karen Leslie *insurance company executive*
Matthews, Norman Sherwood, Jr. *insurance company executive*
Okada, Ronald Masaki *insurance agent*

IDAHO

Idaho Falls
Parkinson, Howard Evans *insurance company executive*

Nampa
Heidt, Raymond Joseph *insurance company executive*

ILLINOIS

Bloomington
Axley, Dixie L. *insurance company executive*
Callis, Bruce *insurance company executive*
Curry, Alan Chester *insurance company executive*
Engelkes, Donald John *insurance company executive*
Johnson, Earle Bertrand *insurance executive*
Joslin, Roger Scott *insurance company executive*
Rodman, Raymond G. *insurance company executive*
Rust, Edward Barry, Jr. *insurance company executive, lawyer*
Shelley, Edward Herman, Jr. *retired insurance company executive*
Ward, Jon David *insurance company executive*

Burr Ridge
Greulich, Robert Charles *insurance company marketing executive*

Calumet City
Strubbe, Thomas R. *insurance industry executive*

Champaign
Peterson, Roger Lyman *insurance company executive*
Wills, Bart Francis *insurance company executive*

Chicago
Bartholomay, William C. *insurance brokerage company executive, professional baseball team executive*
Chang, Yi-Cheng *insurance agent*
Cizza, John Anthony *insurance executive*
DeMoss, Jon W. *insurance company executive, lawyer*
Dudash, Linda Christine *insurance executive*
Engel, Philip L. *insurance company executive*
Hinkelman, Ruth Amidon *insurance company executive*
Ingram, Donald *insurance company executive*
Janecek, Lenore Elaine *insurance specialist, consultant*
Jerome, Jerrold V. *insurance company executive*
Johnson, Caroline Janice *insurance company executive*
Lishka, Edward Joseph *insurance underwriter*
Lorenz, Hugo Albert *retired insurance executive, consultant*
Parcells, Frederick R. *product management*
Parks, Corrine Frances *insurance agency owner*
Preble, Robert Curtis, Jr. *insurance executive*
Ryan, Patrick G. *insurance company executive*
Tocklin, Adrian Martha *insurance company executive, lawyer*
Tyree, James C. *insurance company executive*
Zucaro, Aldo Charles *insurance company executive*

Decatur
Braun, William Joseph *life insurance underwriter*

Deerfield
Cruikshank, John W., III *life insurance underwriter*

Des Plaines
Pannke, Peggy M. *long term care insurance agency executive*

Evanston
Peponis, Harold Arthur *insurance agent, broker*

Fairfield
Smith, Terry G. *insurance sales professional*

Freeport
Pascoe, E(dward) Rudy *insurance sales executive*

Galena
Crandall, John Lynn *insurance consultant, retired insurance company executive*

Geneva
Goulet, Charles Ryan *retired insurance company executive*

Glencoe
Webb, James Okrum, Jr. *insurance company executive*

Highland Park
Nathan, Robert Burton *life insurance agent*

Hinsdale
Denton, Ray Douglas *insurance company executive*

Lake Forest
Brown, Cameron *insurance company consultant*
Eckert, Ralph John *insurance company executive*
Peterson, Donald Matthew *insurance company executive*

Moline
Middleton, Marc Stephen *corporate insurance risk manager*

Naperville
Desch, Theodore Edward *retired health insurance company executive, lawyer*

Northbrook
Liddy, Edward M. *insurance company executive*
Saunders, Kenneth D. *insurance company executive, consultant, arbitrator*
Shape, Steven Michael *insurance executive, lawyer*

Oak Brook
Muschler, Audrey Lorraine *insurance broker*

Oakbrook Terrace
Anderson, Stephen Francis *insurance company executive*
Shalek, James Arthur, Jr. *insurance agent, financial consultant*

Orland Park
Schultz, Barbara Marie *insurance company executive*

Peoria
Michael, Jonathan Edward *insurance company executive*

Prospect Heights
Clark, Donald Robert *retired insurance company executive*

Rock Island
Cheney, Thomas Ward *insurance company executive*
Lardner, Henry Petersen (Peter Lardner) *insurance company executive*

Skokie
Hedien, Wayne Evans *retired insurance company executive*

Springfield
Dodge, Edward John *retired insurance executive*

Wheaton
Hamilton, Robert Appleby, Jr. *insurance company executive*

INDIANA

Bloomington
Long, John D. *retired insurance educator*

Carmel
Hilbert, Stephen C. *insurance company executive*

Fort Wayne
Clarke, Kenneth Stevens *insurance company executive*
Dunsire, P(eter) Kenneth *insurance company executive*
Robertson, Richard Stuart *insurance holding company executive*
Rolland, Ian McKenzie *insurance executive, retired*
Steiner, Paul Andrew *retired insurance executive*
Vachon, Marilyn Ann *retired insurance company executive*
West, Thomas Meade *insurance company executive*

Greenwood
Calvano, Linda Sue Ley *insurance company executive*
Daniel, Michael Edwin *insurance agency executive*

Indianapolis
Christenson, Le Roy Howard *insurance company officer*
Cramer, Betty F. *life insurance company executive*
Funk, James William, Jr. *insurance agency administrator, business owner*
Gagel, Barbara Jean *health insurance administrator*
Gaunce, Michael Paul *insurance company executive*
Henderson, Bruce Wingrove *insurance executive*
Husman, Catherine Bigot *insurance company executive, actuary*
Lytle, L(arry) Ben *insurance company executive, lawyer*
McCarthy, Harold Charles *retired insurance company executive*
McKinney, E. Kirk, Jr. *retired insurance company executive*
Norman, LaLander Stadig *insurance company executive*
Robinson, Larry Robert *insurance company executive*
Wolsiffer, Patricia Rae *insurance company executive*

Lafayette
Whitsel, Robert Malcolm *retired insurance company executive*

Merrillville
Collie, John, Jr. *insurance agent*

Pendleton
Kischuk, Richard Karl *insurance company executive*

IOWA

Cedar Rapids
Fick, E(arl) Dean *insurance executive*

Council Bluffs
Johnson, Michael Randy *insurance company executive*
Nelson, H. H. Red *insurance company executive*

Des Moines
Brooks, Roger Kay *insurance company executive*
Drury, David J. *insurance company executive*
Ellis, Mary Louise Helgeson *insurance company executive*
Kalainov, Sam Charles *insurance company executive*
Kelley, Bruce Gunn *insurance company executive, lawyer*
Richards, Riley Harry *insurance company executive*
Schneider, William George *former life insurance company executive*
Speas, Raymond Aaron *retired insurance company executive*
Williams, Carl Chanson *insurance company executive*

West Des Moines
Bobenhouse, Nellie Yates *insurance company executive*

KANSAS

Manhattan
Ball, Louis Alvin *insurance company executive*

Newton
Morford, Marie Arlene *insurance company executive*

Overland Park
Golec, Jennifer Jane *insurance underwriter*
Jones, Charles Calhoun *estate and business planning consultant*

Shawnee Mission
Hays, Paul Lee, Jr. *insurance company executive*
Holliday, John Moffitt *insurance company executive*

Landau, Mason Stephen *business broker, insurance professional*
Miller, Stanford *reinsurance exeuctive, lawyer*

Topeka
Morris, Michael Allen *insurance executive*

Wichita
Henry, Cecil James, Jr. *insurance sales broker*
Van Milligen, James M. *health care administrator*

KENTUCKY

Fountain Run
Shanks, Gerald Robert *retired insurance company executive*

Lexington
Johnston, Patrick Richard *risk management specialist, county official*

Louisville
Baxter, James William, III *investment executive*
Haddaway, James David *retired insurance company official*
Rosky, Theodore Samuel *insurance company executive*

Owensboro
Ford, Steven Milton *insurance agent*

LOUISIANA

Baton Rouge
Greer, Robert Stephenson *insurance company executive*
Mathews, John William (Bill Mathews) *insurance executive*

Kenner
Kuebler, David Wayne *insurance company executive*

Metairie
Milam, June Matthews *life insurance agent*

New Orleans
Grau, Jean Elizabeth *retired insurance agent*
Hardy, Thomas Cresson *insurance company executive*
Purvis, George Frank, Jr. *life insurance company executive*

Shreveport
Harbuck, Edwin Charles *insurance agent*

MAINE

Cape Eliz
Dalbeck, Richard Bruce *insurance executive*

Lewiston
Buckley, Paul Richard *insurance executive*

Portland
Candage, Howard Everett *insurance management consultant, agent, broker*
Freilinger, James Edward *insurance and investments company executive*
Orr, James T., III *insurance company executive*
Reid, Rosemary Anne *insurance agent*

MARYLAND

Baltimore
Dishon, Cramer Steven *sales executive*
Goodman, William Richard *insurance adjusting company executive*
Hecht, Alan Dannenberg *insurance executive*
Morris, David Michael *insurance executive, lawyer*

Brandywine
Jaffe, Morris Edward *insurance executive*

Chester
Dabich, Eli, Jr. *insurance company executive*

Cockeysville Hunt Valley
Spinella, J(oseph) John *insurance company executive*

Columbia
Hayes, Charles Lawton *insurance company executive, holding company executive*

Easton
Howard, Ann Hubbard *insurance agency executive*

Frederick
†Offutt, Thomas Francis *insurance company executive*

Gaithersburg
Boddiger, George Cyrus *insurance corporate executive, consultant*

Lutherville Timonium
Kolker, Roger Russell *insurance executive*

Mount Airy
Collins, Henry James, III *insurance company executive*

Owings Mills
Disharoon, Leslie Benjamin *retired insurance executive*
Walsh, Semmes Guest *retired insurance company executive*

Oxford
Radcliffe, George Grove *retired life insurance company executive*

Parkton
Cummins, Paul Zach, II *insurance company executive*

Severna Park
Ebersberger, Arthur Darryl *insurance company executive, consultant*

Silver Spring
Jaskot, John Joseph *insurance company executive*

Timonium
Brustein, Abram Isaac *insurance company executive*

MASSACHUSETTS

Acton
Hartz, Luetta Bertha *account executive*

Boston
Aborn, Foster Litchfield *insurance company executive*
Brown, Michael *information technology executive*
Brown, Stephen Lee *insurance company executive*
Chilvers, Derek *insurance company executive*
Conners, John Brendan *insurance company executive*
Countryman, Gary Lee *insurance company executive*
Farnam, Walter Edward *insurance company executive*
Kamer, Joel Victor *insurance company executive, actuary*
Kelley, Kevin H. *insurance company executive*
King, Robert David *insurance company executive*
Mansfield, Christopher Charles *insurance company legal executive*
Morton, Edward James *insurance company executive*
Scipione, Richard Stephen *insurance company executive, lawyer*
Shafto, Robert Austin *retired insurance company executive*
Shemin, Barry L. *insurance company executive*
Taylor, Edward Michael *insurance and risk management consultant*

Brockton
Conboy, Martin Daniel *insurance broker, historian*

Brookline
Shaw, Samuel Ervine, II *retired insurance company executive, consultant*

Duxbury
Wangler, William Clarence *retired insurance company executive*

East Longmeadow
Miller, Nancy Janet *insurance agent*

Eastham
McLaughlin, Richard Warren *retired insurance company executive*

Framingham
Oleskiewicz, Francis Stanley *retired insurance executive*

Great Barrington
Schenck, Benjamin Robinson *insurance consultant*

Haverhill
Morris, Robert *reinsurance analyst*

Holyoke
Bluh, Cynthia Hubbard *insurance company executive*

Lynnfield
Gianino, John Joseph *retired insurance executive*

Newton
Rodman, Sumner *insurance executive*

North Chatham
O'Brien, Robert Emmet *insurance company executive*

North Dighton
Silvia, David Alan *insurance broker*

Pittsfield
Cornelio, Albert Carmen *insurance executive*

South Orleans
Hale, Margaret Smith *insurance company executive, educator*

Springfield
Clark, William James *retired insurance company executive*
Johnson, Robert Allison *life insurance company executive*
Wheeler, Thomas Beardsley *insurance company executive*

Upton
Monahan, John Harry *insurance company business analyst*

Waltham
O'Connell, Jeanne *financial planner, insurance broker*

Westborough
Russell, John William *insurance executive*

Weston
Boothroyd, Herbert J. *insurance company executive*
Fish, David Earl *insurance company executive*

Winchester
Cowgill, F(rank) Brooks *retired insurance company executive*

Worcester
Davidson, Lee David *insurance executive*
O'Brien, John F. *insurance company executive*
Olson, Robert Leonard *retired insurance company executive*

MICHIGAN

Grand Rapids
Kuiper, Douglas Scott *insurance executive*
Sommers, Dana Eugene *insurance agency executive*

Kalamazoo
Curry, John Patrick *insurance company executive, management consultant*

Lansing
Billard, William Thomas *insurance company executive*

Naubinway
Smith, Richard Ernest *retired insurance company executive*

Olivet
Hubbel, Michael Robert *insurance company executive, educator*

Royal Oak
Andrzejak, Michael Richard *insurance agent*

Traverse City
Chang, Ching-I Eugene *insurance executive*

Unionville
Othersen-Khalifa, Cheryl Lee *insurance broker, realtor*

MINNESOTA

Arden Hills
Van Houten, James Forester *insurance company executive*

Bemidji
Bridston, Paul Joseph *strategic consultant*

Edina
Boyle, Barbara Jane *insurance company executive*

Ivanhoe
Hoversten, Ellsworth Gary *insurance executive, producer*

Mankato
Denn, Cyril Joseph *insurance agent*

Minneapolis
Anton, Frank Leland *insurance company executive*
Blomquist, Robert Oscar *insurance company executive*
Eitingon, Daniel Benjamin *insurance consultant*
Gandrud, Robert P. *fraternal insurance executive*
Keets, John David, Jr. *insurance company executive*
Konieczny, Sharon Louise *insurance company executive*
McErlane, Joseph James *insurance company executive*
Mitchell, James Austin *insurance company executive*
Stiles, Donald Alan *insurance company executive*

Minnetonka
Robbins, Orem Olford *insurance company executive*

Saint Paul
Anderson, Gregory Shane *insurance executive*
Boudreau, James Lawton *insurance company executive*
Johnson, James Erling *insurance executive*
Kane, Stanley Phillip *insurance company executive*
Leatherdale, Douglas West *insurance company executive*
Martin, Steven S. *healthcare executive*
Sinklar, Robert *insurance company executive*

Woodbury
Darr, John *insurance company executive*

MISSISSIPPI

Brandon
Nash, Jimmy Ray *life insurance sales executive*

Clinton
Montgomery, Keith Norris, Sr. *insurance executive, state legislator*

Diamondhead
Jones, Lawrence David *insurance and medical consultant*

Gulfport
Hewes, William Gardner, III *insurance executive, real estate agent, legislator*

Jackson
Stovall, Jerry (Coleman Stovall) *insurance company executive*

Madison
Dean, Jack Pearce *retired insurance company executive*

MISSOURI

Camdenton
Decker, Malcolm Doyle *insurance agent*

Columbia
Knies, Paul Henry *former life insurance company executive*

Fordland
Frazier, James Martell, Jr. *retired insurance company official*

Kahoka
Huffman, Robert Merle *insurance company executive*

PROFESSIONAL INDEX 5947 FINANCE: INSURANCE

Kansas City
Bixby, Walter E. *insurance company executive*
Malacarne, C. John *insurance company executive, lawyer*
Mc Gee, Joseph John, Jr. *former insurance company executive*
Reaves, Charles William *insurance company executive, writer, educator, investment advisor*

Saint Louis
Cramer, Michael William *insurance executive*
Haberstroh, Richard David *insurance agent*
Hogan, Michael Ray *diversified company executive*
LeBlanc, Michael Stephen *insurance and risk executive*
Liddy, Richard A. *insurance company executive*
Powers, Pierce William, Jr. *insurance specialist*
Werner, Burton Kready *insurance company executive*
Winer, Warren James *insurance executive*

Springfield
Ostergren, Gregory Victor *insurance company executive*

Wildwood
Crist, Lewis Roger *insurance company executive*

MONTANA

Kalispell
Lopp, Susan Jane *insurance underwriter*

Whitefish
Hemp, Ralph Clyde *retired reinsurance company executive, consultant, arbitrator, umpire*

NEBRASKA

Holdrege
Hendrickson, Bruce Carl *life insurance company executive*

Lincoln
Angle, John Charles *retired life insurance company executive*
Arth, Lawrence Joseph *insurance executive*
Campbell, John Dee *retired insurance executive*

North Platte
Carlson, Randy Eugene *insurance executive*

Omaha
Ames, George Ronald *insurance executive*
Barrett, Frank Joseph *insurance company executive*
Bookout, John G. *insurance company executive*
Conley, Eugene Allen *retired insurance company executive*
Jay, Burton Dean *insurance actuary*
Jetter, Arthur Carl, Jr. *insurance company executive*
Sigerson, Charles Willard, Jr. *insurance company executive*
Skutt, Thomas James *insurance company executive*
Strevey, Guy Donald *insurance company executive*
Weekly, John William *insurance company executive*

NEVADA

Henderson
Johnson, Joan Bray *insurance company consultant*

Reno
Delaney, William Francis, Jr. *reinsurance broker*

NEW HAMPSHIRE

Grantham
Smith, Dudley Renwick *retired insurance company executive*

Hanover
Kemp, Karl Thomas *insurance company executive*

Rochester
Dworkin, Gary Steven *insurance company executive*

NEW JERSEY

Berkeley Heights
Gottheimer, George Malcolm, Jr. *insurance executive, educator*

Bloomfield
Feldman, Max *insurance executive*

Cherry Hill
Vaughan, Lynn Katherine *insurance agent*

Cranford
Crow, Lynne Campbell Smith *insurance company representative*

East Brunswick
Todd, Edward Francis, Jr. *risk management consultant, insurance broker*

Florham Park
Bossen, Wendell John *insurance company executive*

Freehold
Prideaux, John Raymond, Jr. *insurance company executive*

Glen Rock
Mc Elrath, Richard Elsworth *retired insurance company executive*

Holmdel
Meyer, Robert Alan *reinsurance company executive*

Lambertville
Batshaw, Marilyn Seidner *insurance professional*

Lawrence Harbor
DeMatteo, Gloria Jean *insurance saleswoman*

Madison
Calligan, William Dennis *retired life insurance company executive*
Leak, Margaret Elizabeth *insurance company executive*
Parker, Henry Griffith, III *insurance executive*

Morristown
Munson, William Leslie *insurance company executive*
Newhouse, Robert J., Jr. *insurance executive*

Mountain Lakes
Cook, Charles Francis *insurance executive*

Newark
Nelson, Douglas Lee *insurance company executive*
Ryan, Arthur Frederick *insurance company executive*

Parsippany
McGirr, David William John *insurance executive*
Weiner, Marian Murphy *insurance executive, consultant*

Princeton
Christie, David George *insurance company executive*
†Wentz, Sidney Frederick *insurance company executive, foundation executive*

Rumson
Creamer, William Henry, III *insurance company executive*

Short Hills
MacKinnon, Malcolm D(avid) *retired insurance company executive*

Somerset
Brophy, Joseph Thomas *information company executive*

Spring Lake
Bonhag, Thomas Edward *insurance company executive, financial consultant, financial planner*

Summit
Gerathy, E. Carroll *former insurance executive, real estate developer*
Keith, Garnett Lee, Jr. *investment executive*

Warren
Chubb, Percy, III *insurance company executive*
O'Hare, Dean Raymond *insurance company executive*

Westfield
Dzury, Stephen Daniel *insurance company official*

Wyckoff
Lane, Nathan *insurance agency executive*
Miller, Walter Neal *insurance company consultant*

NEW MEXICO

Albuquerque
Liss, Norman Richard *insurance executive*
Parsley, Steven Dwayne *title company executive*
Wainio, Mark Ernest *insurance company consultant*

Las Cruces
Cochrun, John Wesley *financial consultant*

Tucumcari
Woodard, Dorothy Marie *insurance broker*

NEW YORK

Albany
Cole, John Adam *insurance executive*

Armonk
†Dunton, Gary C. *insurance company executive*
Elliott, David H. *insurance company executive*

Binghamton
Best, Robert Mulvane *insurance company executive*

Bronx
Miller, Barry H. *insurance company executive*

Bronxville
Knapp, George Griff Prather *insurance consultant, arbitrator*

Brooklyn
Faison, Seth Shepard *retired insurance broker*
Satterfield-Harris, Rita *workers compensation representative*

Buffalo
Deasy, Jacqueline Hildegard *insurance consultant*
Roehner, Linda Gail *claims consultant*

Cobleskill
Wilson, Lewis Lansing *insurance executive*

Cohocton
Sarfaty, Wayne Allen *insurance agent, financial planner*

Dryden
Baxter, Robert Banning *insurance company executive*

Fayetteville
Sager, Roderick Cooper *retired life insurance company executive*

Flushing
Sanborn, Anna Lucille *pension and insurance consultant*

Garrison
Impellizzeri, Anne Elmendorf *insurance company executive, non-profit executive*

Glens Falls
Trombley, Joseph Edward *insurance company executive, underwriter, financial planner*

Hicksville
Rough, Herbert Louis *insurance company executive*

Kingston
Reis, Frank Henry *insurance agency executive*

Lindenhurst
Hungerford, Gary A. *insurance executive, columnist, author, editor*

Malverne
Knight, John Francis *insurance company executive*

Merrick
Cherry, Harold *insurance company executive*
O'Brien, Kenneth Robert *life insurance company executive*

Mineola
Miller, Loring Erik *insurance agent, broker*

New York
Agnew, William Harold *insurance company executive*
†Alviggi, Christopher *insurance broker*
†Benmosche, Robert H. *insurance company executive*
Berdick, Leonard Stanley *insurance broker*
Biggs, John Herron *insurance company executive*
†Borelli, Francis J(oseph) (Frank Borelli) *insurance brokerage and consulting firm financial executive*
Borut, Josephine *insurance executive*
Briggs, Philip *insurance company executive*
Burns, John Joseph, Jr. *financial and insurance holding company executive*
Caouette, John Bernard *insurance company executive*
Corry, James Michael *insurance executive, educator*
Coyne, Frank J. *insurance industry executive*
Crystal, James William *insurance company executive*
Darer, John David *insurance company executive*
Dolan, Raymond Bernard *insurance executive*
Earls, Kevin Gerard *insurance company executive*
Emek, Sharon Helene *risk management consultant*
Gammill, Lee Morgan, Jr. *insurance company executive*
Goodstone, Edward Harold *retired insurance company executive*
Greenberg, Maurice Raymond *insurance company executive*
Hansen, Richard Arthur *insurance company executive, psychologist*
Harris, David Henry *retired life insurance company executive*
Henry, Catherine Theresa *insurance company executive*
Hohn, Harry George *retired insurance company executive, lawyer*
Hollis, Louicle *risk control administrator, educator*
Hutchings, Peter Lounsbery *insurance company executive*
†Jacobson, Sibyl *insurance company executive*
Kaplan, Keith Eugene *insurance company executive, lawyer*
Kaplan, Theodore Norman *insurance company executive*
Klinck, James William *insurance company executive*
Leaf, Robert Jay *dental insurance consultant*
†Lee, Alvin Yin-Hang *financial risk management specialist*
MacDonald, Ronald Francis *financial services company executive*
†Manton, Edwin Alfred Grenville *insurance company executive*
Markowitz, Robert *insurance executive*
McCormack, John Joseph, Jr. *insurance executive*
McLaughlin, Michael John *insurance company executive*
Melone, Joseph James *insurance company executive*
Milton, Christian Michel *insurance executive*
Murray, Richard Maximilian *insurance executive*
Nagler, Stewart Gordon *insurance company executive*
Nail, John Joseph *insurance company executive*
Olsen, David Alexander *insurance executive*
Papa, Vincent T. *insurance company executive*
Ross, Donald Keith *retired insurance company executive*
Sandler, Robert Michael *insurance company executive, actuary*
Sargent, Joseph Dudley *insurance executive*
Schwartz, Robert George *retired insurance company executive*
Slavutin, Lee Jacob *estate planning insurance executive*
Smiley, Irwin *insurance agency executive*
Smith, Alexander John Court *insurance executive*
Smith, John Matthew *insurance company executive*
Smith, Michael Alan *insurance industry analyst*
Somers, John Arthur *insurance company executive*
Sternberg, Seymour *insurance company executive*
Underhill, Jacob Berry, III *retired insurance company executive*
†Vant, Elizabeth D. *health insurance company official*
Vidal, David Jonathan *insurance company executive, journalist*
Washington, Clarence Edward, Jr. *insurance company executive*
Waters, Michael Robert *insurance management executive*
Wisner, Frank George *insurance company executive, former ambassador*
Wolf, James Anthony *insurance company executive*
Worthington, Lorne Raymond *insurance executive*
Yalen, Gary N. *insurance company executive*
Zucchi, Donna Marie *insurance company executive*

Oceanside
Rubin, Hanan *retired insurance company executive*

Penfield
Klose, Charlotte Ann *insurance agency owner*

Point Lookout
Stack, Maurice Daniel *retired insurance company executive*

Pound Ridge
Bennett, Edward Henry *reinsurance executive*

Rock Hill
Lombardi, Kent Bailey *insurance company administrator*

Rockville Centre
Burton, Daniel G. *insurance executive*

Scarsdale
Decaminada, Joseph Pio *insurance company executive, educator*

Schenectady
Murray, Edward Rock *insurance broker*

Southampton
Dublis, Raymond Anthony *insurance executive*

Staten Island
Gavrity, John Decker *insurance company executive*

Syosset
Barry, Richard Francis *retired life insurance company executive*
Kniffin, Paula Sichel *insurance sales executive*

Utica
Austin, Michael Charles *insurance company executive*
Cuccaro, Ronald Anthony *insurance adjusting company executive*
Ehre, Victor Tyndall *insurance company executive*

Watertown
Rankin, Bonnie Lee *insurance executive*

Yonkers
Wolfson, Irwin M. *insurance company executive*

NORTH CAROLINA

Camden
Hammond, Roy Joseph *reinsurance company executive*

Chapel Hill
Fine, J(ames) Allen *insurance company executive*
Karlin, Gary Lee *insurance executive*
Kittredge, John Kendall *retired insurance company executive*
Stewart, Richard Edwin *insurance consulting company executive*

Charlotte
Maday, Clifford Ronald *insurance professional*
Mendelsohn, Robert Victor *insurance company executive*

Durham
Clark, Arthur Watts *insurance company executive*
Collins, Bert *insurance executive*

Greensboro
Hall, William Edward, Jr. *insurance agency executive*
Soles, William Roger *insurance company executive*
Tugman, Stuart Grady, Jr. *insurance executive*

Hendersonville
Stokes, William Finley, Jr. *insurance executive*

Nashville
Coggin, Michael Wright *insurance marketing and training executive*

Pinehurst
O'Loughlin, John Kirby *retired insurance executive*

Raleigh
Whitehead, Ian *insurance company executive*

Roxboro
†Phillips, Mark T. *insurance agent*

Winston Salem
Buselmeier, Bernard Joseph *insurance company executive*

NORTH DAKOTA

Fargo
Kane, David Sheridan *insurance company executive*
Rice, Jon Richard *managed care administrator, physician*

Grand Forks
Wogaman, George Elsworth *insurance executive, financial consultant*

OHIO

Akron
†Craig, Marci Lynne *insurance claims administrator*
†Lalli, Anthony *insurance agent*

Blacklick
Doyle, Patrick Lee *retired insurance company executive*

Canton
Caswell, Linda Kay *insurance agency executive*
Schauer, Thomas Alfred *insurance company executive*

Chillicothe
Copley, Cynthia Sue Love *insurance adjuster*

Cincinnati
Aniskovich, Paul Peter, Jr. *insurance company executive*
Byers, Kenneth Vernon *insurance company executive*
Clark, James Norman *insurance executive*
Horrell, Karen Holley *insurance company executive, lawyer*
Klein, Jerry Emanuel *insurance and financial planning executive*
Klinedinst, Thomas John, Jr. *insurance agency executive*
Krohn, Claus Dankertsen *insurance company executive*
Puthoff, Francis Urban *insurance salesman*
Scheineson, Irwin Bruce *insurance and investment company executive*

Cleveland
Lewis, Peter Benjamin *insurance company executive*

Columbus
Carlson, Larry Vernon *insurance company executive*
Castlen, Peggy Lou *insurance company executive*
Cook, John Roscoe, Jr. *insurance executive*
Duryee, Harold Taylor *insurance executive*
Emanuelson, James Robert *retired insurance company executive*
Fullerton, Charles William *retired insurance company executive*
McCutchan, Gordon Eugene *lawyer, insurance company executive*
McFerson, Diamond Richard *insurance company executive*

Dayton
Kinsey, Douglas Paul *insurance agent, financial planner*

Delta
Rees, Erica Sue *insurance company executive*

Geneva
Foote, David Ward, Jr. *insurance agency executive*

Grove City
Purdy, Dennis Gene *insurance company executive, education consultant*

Hamilton
Marcum, Joseph LaRue *insurance company executive*

Maumee
Oakes, Frank Leslie, Jr. *retired insurance agency executive*
Seymour, Dale Joseph *insurance company executive*

North Canton
Malcolm, Douglas Raymond *insurance agent, business consultant*

Rocky River
Riedthaler, William Allen *risk management professional*

Springfield
Rowland-Raybold, Roberta Rae *insurance agent, music educator*

Uniontown
Allison, Dianne J. Hall *insurance company official*

Westfield Center
Blair, Robert Cary *insurance company executive*

Youngstown
Tierno, Edward Gregory *insurance company executive*

OKLAHOMA

Oklahoma City
Hamilton, Thomas Allen *independent insurance agent*
Ille, Bernard Glenn *insurance company executive*
Lee, Ellen Faith *insurance company associate*

Perry
Doughty, Michael Dean *insurance agent*

Tulsa
Abbott, William Thomas *claim specialist*

OREGON

Hillsboro
Yates, Keith Lamar *retired insurance company executive*

Portland
Galbraith, John Robert *insurance company exeuctive*
Hill, James Edward *insurance company executive*
Lang, Philip David *former state legislator, insurance company executive*

Salem
Rasmussen, Neil Woodland *insurance agent*

Tualatin
Chambers, Lois Irene *insurance automation consultant*

Waldport
Ginter, Carol(yn) Augusta Romtvedt *retired bond underwriter*

West Linn
Dunstan, Larry Kenneth *insurance company executive*

PENNSYLVANIA

Abington
Biddle, Richard B. *retired life insurance executive*

Ardmore
Beebe, Leo Clair *industrial equipment executive, former educator*

Bala Cynwyd
Shepard, Geoffrey Carroll *insurance executive*

Berwyn
McIntyre, James Owen *insurance executive*

Bethlehem
Schumacher, Susan Louise *underwriter*

Bloomsburg
Miller, David Jergen *insurance executive*

Camp Hill
Gunn, G. Greg *insurance executive*
Mead, James Matthew *insurance company executive*

Cheltenham
Hart, William C. *insurance underwriter, educator, writer*

Downingtown
Glitz, Donald Robert *insurance underwriting executive*

Erie
Hagen, Thomas Bailey *business owner, former state official, former insurance company executive*

Fort Washington
Ross, Roderic Henry *insurance company executive*

Greentown
Schumaker, William Thomas *insurance company executive*

Harrisburg
Dunn, Kenneth Ralph *insurance company executive*
Patterson, Robert Eugene *government official*

Hatboro
Quigley, Robert Charles *insurance industry consultant*

Haverford
Zalinski, Edmund Louis Gray *insurance executive, mutual funds and real estate executive, investor*

Hazleton
Nenstiel, Susan Kisthart *fundraising professional*

Hershey
Moffitt, Charles William *insurance sales executive*

Jenkintown
Silver, Leonard J. *insurance and risk management company executive*

King Of Prussia
Katz, Arnold Martin *insurance brokerage firm executive*
Volpe, Ralph Pasquale *insurance company executive*

Newtown
Scull, Charles D. *insurance company executive*

Newtown Square
Staats, Dean Roy *retired reinsurance executive*

Norristown
Clemens, Alvin Honey *insurance company executive*

Olyphant
Paoloni, Virginia Ann *insurance company executive*

Philadelphia
Fleetwood, Rex Allen *insurance company executive*
Frohlich, Kenneth R. *insurance executive*

Pittsburgh
Duval, Robert *leasing company executive*
McDaniel, Norwood Allan *insurance broker*

Ridgway
Aiello, Gennaro C. *insurance company executive*

Spring House
van Steenwyk, John Joseph *health care plan consultant, educator*

Wayne
†DiPietro, Michele A. *insurance underwriter*
Yoskin, Jon William, II *insurance company executive*

RHODE ISLAND

Foster
Sawyer, Mildred Clementina *real estate agent*

Little Compton
MacKowski, John Joseph *retired insurance company executive*

Warwick
Sloan, Robert Hood, Jr. *insurance agent*

SOUTH CAROLINA

Columbia
Averyt, Gayle Owen *insurance executive*

Greenville
Clark, Elizabeth Annette *retired insurance company administrator*
Hipp, William Hayne *insurance and broadcasting executive*

Spartanburg
Stewart, James Charles, II *insurance agent*

SOUTH DAKOTA

Aberdeen
Stoia, Viorel G. *life underwriter*

Mitchell
Widman, Paul Joseph *insurance agent*

TENNESSEE

Chattanooga
Chandler, J. Harold *insurance company executive*

Memphis
Lowery, F(loyd) Lynn, Jr. *insurance company executive*

Nashville
†Carson, Paul Eugene *insurance examiner*
Davis, James Verlin *insurance brokerage executive*
Elberry, Zainab Abdelhaliem *insurance company executive*
Gaultney, John Orton *life insurance agent, consultant*
Howell, John Floyd *insurance company executive*

Seymour
Steele, Ernest Clyde *retired insurance company executive*

TEXAS

Austin
Caldwell, William McNeilly *insurance agent*
Ellis, Glen Edward, Jr. *insurance agent, financial planner*
Golden, Edwin Harold *insurance company executive*
Mullen, Ron *insurance company executive*
Nolen, William Lawrence, Jr. *insurance agency owner, real estate investor*
Payne, Eugene Edgar *insurance company executive*
Payne, Tyson Elliott, Jr. *retired insurance executive*
Spielman, David Vernon *retired insurance, finance and publications consultant*

Corpus Christi
Vargas, Joe Flores *insurance claims executive*

Crockett
Jones, Don Carlton *insurance agent*

Dallas
Beck, Luke Ferrell Wilson *insurance specialist*
Cline, Bobby James *insurance company executive*
Forêt, Randy Blaise *insurance executive*
Guthrie, M. Philip *insurance company executive*
Hogan, Thomas Victor *insurance company executive*
Rinne, Austin Dean *insurance company executive*
Weakley, Clare George, Jr. *insurance executive, theologian, entrepreneur*
White, Irene *insurance professional*

Fort Worth
Blackburn, Wyatt Douglas *insurance executive*
Brannon, Treva Lee (Wood) *insurance company executive*
Kern, Edna Ruth *insurance executive*

Galveston
Monts, Elizabeth Rose *insurance company executive*

Houston
Alexander, Harold Campbell *insurance consultant*
Bickel, Stephen Douglas *insurance company executive*
Couch, Jesse Wadsworth *retired insurance company executive*
Davis, Rex Lloyd *insurance company executive*
Dean, Robert Franklin *insurance company executive*
Devlin, Robert Manning *financial services company executive*
Harris, Richard Foster, Jr. *insurance company executive*
Hook, Harold Swanson *management consulting executive*
Kellison, Stephen George *insurance executive*
Lindsey, John Horace *insurance agency executive*
Lyons, Phillip Michael, Sr. *insurance accounting and real estate executive*
Martin, Kenneth Frank *insurance company executive*
Poulos, Michael James *insurance company executive*
Skalla, John Lionell *insurance agent*
Thomas, Marilyn Jane *insurance agent, agency owner*
Tidwell, Mary Ellen *loss control coordinator*
Woodson, Benjamin Nelson, III *insurance executive*

Irving
Cooper, Alcie Lee, Jr. *insurance executive*

Lake Jackson
Elbert, James Peak *independent insurance agent, minister*

Mcallen
Whisenant, B(ert) R(oy), Jr. *insurance company executive*

Palestine
Douthitt, Shirley Ann *insurance agent*

Plano
Hardy, Tom Charles, Jr. *medical equipment company*

Richardson
Slaight, Mark Franklin *insurance claims adjuster*

San Antonio
Colyer, Kirk Klein *insurance executive, real estate investment executive*
Herres, Robert Tralles *financial services executive*
Wellberg, Edward Louis, Jr. *insurance company executive*

Spring
Templeton, Randall Keith *insurance company executive*

Stafford
Friedberg, Thomas Harold *insurance company executive*

Waco
Rapoport, Bernard *life insurance company executive*

UTAH

Ogden
Buckner, Elmer La Mar *insurance executive*

Salt Lake City
Allen, Roy Verl *life insurance company executive*
Engar, Richard Charles *insurance executive, dentist, educator*

Sandy
Macumber, John Paul *insurance company executive*

VERMONT

East Calais
Harding, John Hibbard *insurance company executive*

Quechee
Baney, John Edward *insurance company executive*

Woodstock
Blackwell, David Jefferson *retired insurance company executive*

VIRGINIA

Alexandria
Casey, Michael Kirkland *business executive, lawyer*

Arlington
Clarke, Frederic B., III *risk analysis consultant*

Charlottesville
Long, Charles Farrell *insurance company executive*

Eastville
†Cowling, Colin Douglas, Jr. *insurance executive*

Fairfax
Tringale, Anthony Rosario *insurance executive*

Herndon
Mandine, Salvador G. *insurance executive*

Linden
Poulin, Claude R. *actuarial consultant*

Lynchburg
McRorie, William Edward *life insurance company executive*
Stewart, George Taylor *insurance executive*

Mc Lean
Connelly, Mary Creedon *insurance company executive*

Midlothian
Coleman, Ronald Lee *insurance claims executive*

Newport News
Miller, W. Marshall, II *insurance consultant*

Norfolk
Dungan, William Joseph, Jr. *insurance broker, economics educator*

Richmond
Payne, William Sanford *insurance company executive*

Roanoke
Berry, John Coltrin *insurance executive*
†Miles, Sherry Celestine *disabilty determinatin analyst*

Virginia Beach
Ellis, John Carroll, Jr. *life insurance sales executive*

Williamsburg
Herrmann, Benjamin Edward *former insurance executive*
Sisk, Albert Fletcher, Jr. *retired insurance agent*
Webster, Robert Louis *insurance company executive*

Woodstock
Walker, Charles Norman *retired insurance company executive*

WASHINGTON

Auburn
Colburn, Gene Lewis *insurance and industrial consultant*

Bellevue
Clay, Orson C. *insurance company executive*

Kennewick
Stevens, Henry August *insurance agent, educator*

Kirkland
McDonald, Joseph Lee *insurance broker*

Mountlake Terrace
English, Donald Marvin *loss control representative*

Olympia
†Senn, Deborah *insurance commissioner*

Seattle
Dubes, Michael John *insurance company executive*
Duckworth, Tara Ann *insurance company executive*

Dyer, Philip E. *insurance company executive*
Eigsti, Roger Harry *insurance company executive*
Kibble, Edward Bruce *insurance-investment advisory company executive*
LaPoe, Wayne Gilpin *retired business executive*
Robb, Bruce *former insurance company executive*

Spokane
Garrett, Paul Edgar *insurance executive, writer, poet*

Walla Walla
Perry, Louis Barnes *retired insurance company executive*

WEST VIRGINIA

Grafton
Knotts, Robert Lee *insurance executive*

WISCONSIN

Brookfield
Trytek, David Douglas *insurance company executive*

Delafield
Roberts, Thomas Blair *retired insurance broker*

Madison
DuRose, Stanley Charles, Jr. *insurance executive*
Larson, John David *life insurance company executive, lawyer*
Mathwich, Dale F. *insurance company executive*
Sims, Terre Lynn *insurance company executive*
†Spencer, C. Stanley *insurance executive*
Waldo, Robert Leland *retired insurance company executive*

Merrill
Whitburn, Gerald *insurance company executive*

Milwaukee
Kelley, Lyle Ardell *insurance company executive*
Manko, Wesley Daniel *insurance advisor*
Zore, Edward John *insurance company executive*

Nashotah
Vincent, Norman L. *retired insurance company executive*

Sun Prairie
Rollette, Harold Henry *insurance company executive*

Wausau
Huebner, Suzanne Marie *insurance company executive*

WYOMING

Glenrock
Bennington, Leslie Orville, Jr. *insurance agent*

CANADA

MANITOBA

Winnipeg
†McFeetors, Raymond L. *insurance company executive*

ONTARIO

Etobicoke
Howe, James Tarsicius *retired insurance company executive*

London
Allan, Ralph Thomas Mackinnon *insurance company executive*

Toronto
†D'Alessandro, Dominic *financial executive*
Nesbitt, Mark *management consultant*

AUSTRALIA

Sydney
Melkonian, Harry G. *insurance executive, rancher*

BERMUDA

Hamilton
Kramer, Donald *insurance executive*

Pembroke
Stempel, Ernest Edward *insurance executive*

CHINA

Hong Kong
Tse, Edmund Sze-Wing *insurance company executive*

FRANCE

Paris
Blondeau, Jacques Patrick Adrien *reinsurance company executive*
Peugeot, Patrick *insurance executive*

SWITZERLAND

Zurich
Fitzpatrick, John Henry *insurance company executive*

ADDRESS UNPUBLISHED

Adam, John, Jr. *insurance company executive emeritus*
Alpert, Ann Sharon *insurance claims examiner*
Anker, Robert Alvin *retired insurance company executive*
Armocida, Patricia Anne *managed health care official*
Armstrong, F(redric) Michael *retired insurance company executive, consultant*
Balkcom, Carol Ann *insurance agent*
Bare, Bruce *retired life insurance company executive*
Beattie, Nora Maureen *insurance company executive, actuary*
Bellamy, James Carl *insurance company executive*
Bertrand, Frederic Howard *retired insurance company executive*
Brouillette, Yves *insurance company executive*
†Brown, Joseph W., Jr. (Jay Brown) *insurance company executive*
Buck, Earl Wayne *insurance investigator, private detective*
Carver, Kendall Lynn *insurance company executive*
Childress, Walter Dabney, III *insurance executive, financial planner*
Cooper, Charles Gordon *insurance consultant, former executive*
Dackow, Orest Taras *insurance company executive*
Dannenberg, Martin Ernest *retired insurance company executive*
Deering, Fred Arthur *retired insurance company executive*
DiPiazza, Michael Charles *insurance company executive*
Dodds, Linda Carol *insurance company executive*
Ellis, John Munn, III *insurance company financial executive*
Fibiger, John Andrew *life insurance company executive*
Gummere, John *insurance company executive*
Hanks-DeCrescenzo, Jame Melisse *insurance company executive*
Hartsell, Samuel David *insurance agent*
Hauenstein, George Carey *life insurance executive*
Hawk, Carole Lynn *insurance company executive, research analyst*
Hensley, Stephen Allan *insurance executive*
Hibner, Rae A. *insurance company official, nurse*
Hinds, Edward Dee *insurance and investment professional, financial planner*
Hirst, Heston Stillings *former insurance company executive*
†Hohl, Craig Stephen *risk management executive*
†Hunter, Tanya Antoinette *insurance biller*
Jacobson, James Bassett *insurance executive*
Johnson, Glendon E. *retired insurance company executive*
Johnson, William Ray *insurance company executive*
Juredine, David Graydon *insurance company executive*
Kanter, Jerome Jacob *insurance company executive*
Knizeski, Justine Estelle *insurance company executive*
Kolde, Richard Arthur *insurance company executive, consultant*
Lacey, Cloyd Eugene *retired insurance company executive*
Ladd, Joseph Carroll *retired insurance company executive*
Lamel, Linda Helen *professional society executive, former insurance company executive*
Lee, J. Daniel, Jr. *retired insurance company executive*
Levine, Michael Joseph *economic development executive*
Lipsey, John C. (Jack Lipsey) *insurance company executive*
Maatman, Gerald Leonard *insurance company executive*
Maloney, Therese Adele *insurance company executive*
McKenna, Terence Patrick *insurance company executive*
Mehdizadeh, Parviz *insurance company executive*
Minges, John Franklin, III *non-profit management consultant*
Moore, Linda Picarelli *insurance executive*
Moore, Robert Henry *insurance company executive*
Morrill, Thomas Clyde *insurance company executive*
Morris, Edward J(ames), Jr. *retired insurance agent, small business owner*
Moses, Michael James *insurance company executive*
Moynahan, John Daniel, Jr. *retired insurance executive*
Nelson, Barbara Kay *insurance agent*
Nelson, Walter Gerald *retired insurance company executive*
Newman, Steven Harvey *insurance company executive*
Norris, Darell Forest *insurance company executive*
Olsen, George Edward *retired insurance executive*
Plummer, Daniel Clarence, III *retired insurance consultant*
Porter, Dixie Lee *insurance executive, consultant*
Renick, Carol Bishop *insurance planning company executive, consultant*
Resnick, Myron J. *retired insurance company executive, lawyer*
Reynolds, John Francis *insurance company executive*
Rodino, Vincent Louis *insurance company executive*
Rondepierre, Edmond Francois *insurance executive*
Rowell, Lester John, Jr. *retired insurance company executive*
Ryan, James *insurance company executive*
Sanders, Franklin D. *insurance and reinsurance consultant*
Schoonover, Hugh James *insurance agent*
Scott, John Burt *life insurance executive*
Sharick, Merle Dayton, Jr. *mortgage insurance company executive*
Smith, Floyd Leslie *insurance company executive*
Snyder, William Burton *insurance executive*
Stewart, Gordon Curran *insurance information association executive*
Strong, John David *insurance company executive*
Sturtevant, Richard Pearce *insurance consultant*
Vanderhoof, Irwin Thomas *life insurance company executive*

†Washington, Lester R. *insurance agent, small business owner*
Weber, John Walter *insurance company executive*
Whiteley, Benjamin Robert *retired insurance company executive*
Wills, William Ridley, II *former insurance company executive, historian*
Young, Larry Joe *insurance agent*
Zupsic, Matthew Michael *insurance company executive*

FINANCE: INVESTMENT SERVICES

UNITED STATES

ALABAMA

Birmingham
Comer, Donald, III *investment company executive*
Culp, Charles Allen *financial executive*
Haworth, Michael Elliott, Jr. *investor, former aerospace company executive*
Marks, Charles Caldwell *retired investment banker, retired industrial distribution company executive*
Massey, Richard Walter, Jr. *investment counselor*
Tucker, Thomas James *investment manager*

Montgomery
Blount, Winton Malcolm, III *investment executive*
Taylor, Watson Robbins, Jr. *investment banker*

Sylacauga
Comer, Braxton Bragg, II *entrepreneur*

ALASKA

Anchorage
Hickel, Walter Joseph *investment firm executive, forum administrator*
Jay, Christopher Edward *stockbroker*
Rose, David Allan *investment manager*

Juneau
Bushre, Peter Alvin *investment company executive*

ARIZONA

Paradise Valley
Doede, John Henry *investment company executive*

Phoenix
Currie, Constance Mershon *investment services professional*
Scarbrough, Ernest Earl *stockbroker, financial planner*

Scottsdale
Budge, Hamer Harold *mutual fund company executive*
Cormie, Donald Mercer *investment company executive*
Luke, David Kevin *investment company executive*
Myers, Clay *retired investment management company executive*

Tucson
Grubb, L(ewis) Craig *investment company executive, consultant*
Lomicka, William Henry *investor*
Schannep, John Dwight *brokerage firm executive*

Yuma
Stuart, Gerard William, Jr. *investment company executive, city official*
Talbot, Devon Vvictor *precious metals dealer, writer*

ARKANSAS

Fort Smith
Hembree, Hugh Lawson, III *diversified holding company executive*

Little Rock
Good, Mary Lowe (Mrs. Billy Jewel Good) *investment company executive, educator*
Light, Jo Knight *stockbroker*
Reeves, Rosser Scott, III *retired investment company executive*

CALIFORNIA

Arcadia
Kalm, Arne *investment banker*

Bakersfield
Zeviar-Geese, Gabriole *stock market investor*

Benicia
Szabo, Peter John *investment company executive, financial planner, mining engineer, lawyer*

Beverly Hills
Evans, Louise *investor, clinical psychologist, philanthropist*
Gambrell, Thomas Ross *investor, retired physician, surgeon*
Israel, Richard Stanley *investment banker*
Seidel, Joan Broude *stockbroker, investment advisor*
Walker, William Tidd, Jr. *investment banker*

Burlingame
Heath, Richard Raymond *investment executive*
Most, Nathan *mutual fund executive*

Carmel
Jordan, Edward George *business investor, former college president, former railroad executive*

Century City
Feiman, Thomas E. *investment manager*

Chico
Houx, Mary Anne *investments executive*

Covina
Colley, Janet Scritsmier *investment consultant*

Cupertino
Horn, Christian Friedrich *venture capital company executive*

Cypress
Grant, Alan J. *business executive, educator*

Dixon
Molina Villacorta, Rafael Antonio *technology management investment company executive*

Encinitas
Smith, Benjamin Eric *venture capitalist, executive*

Escondido
Allen, Donald Vail *investment executive, writer, concert pianist*

Fresno
Buzick, William Alonson, Jr. *investor, lawyer, educator*
Dauer, Donald Dean *investment executive*

Hollywood
Marshall, Conrad Joseph *entrepreneur*

La Jolla
Stone, Donald D. *investment and sales executive*

Lake Arrowhead
Fitzgerald, John Charles, Jr. *investment banker*

Larkspur
Kirk, Gary Vincent *investment advisor*

Long Beach
Schinnerer, Alan John *entrepreneur*

Los Altos
Carsten, Jack Craig *venture capitalist*

Los Angeles
Angeloff, Dann Valentino *investment banking executive*
Bradshaw, Carl John *investor, lawyer, consultant*
DeBard, Roger *investment executive*
Drew, Paul *entrepreneur*
Emmeluth, Bruce Palmer *investment company executive, venture capitalist*
Gebhart, Carl Grant *security broker*
Gordy, Berry *entrepreneur, record company executive, motion picture executive*
Hamilton, Beverly Lannquist *investment management professional*
Horning, Robert Alan *securities broker*
Hurt, William Holman *investment management company executive*
Hurwitz, Lawrence Neal *investment banking company executive*
Kaye, Barry *investment company executive*
Koffler, Stephen Alexander *investment banker*
Latzer, Richard Neal *investment company executive*
Mann, Nancy Louise (Nancy Louise Robbins) *entrepreneur*
Ogle, Edward Proctor, Jr. *investment counseling executive*
Reed, George Ford, Jr. *investment executive*
Riordan, George Nickerson *investment banker*
Tennenbaum, Michael Ernest *private investor*
Trumbull, Stephen Michael *entrepreneur*
Winkler, Howard Leslie *investment banker, business and financial consultant*

Malibu
Ortiz, Geoffrey *stock broker, retirement planning specialist*

Menlo Park
Fenton, Noel John *venture capitalist*
Hoagland, Laurance Redington, Jr. *investment executive*
Lucas, Donald Leo *private investor*
†McCown, George E. *venture banking company executive*
Walsh, William Desmond *investor*

Moraga
Ittner, Helen Louise *entrepreneur*

Mountain View
Crowley, Jerome Joseph, Jr. *investment company executive*

Napa
Strock, David Randolph *brokerage house executive*

Newport Beach
Giannini, Valerio Louis *investment banker*
Harris, Brent Richard *investment company executive*
Hinshaw, Ernest Theodore, Jr. *private investor, former Olympics executive, former financial executive*
Thorp, Edward Oakley *investment management company executive*

Oakland
Alford, Joan Franz *entrepreneur*

Oceanside
Rosier, David Lewis *investment banker*

Orinda
Bach, Martin Wayne *stockbroker, owner antique clock stores*
Rosenberg, Barr Marvin *investment advisor, economist*

Oxnard
Woodworth, Stephen Davis *investment banker*

Pacific Palisades
Hagenbuch, Rodney Dale *stock brokerage house executive*

Palm Desert
Krallinger, Joseph Charles *entrepreneur, business advisor, author*

Palm Springs
Lougheed, Arthur Lawrence *investment advisor, tax and pension consultant*

Palo Alto
Berg, Olena *investment company executive, former federal official*
Markkula, A. C., Jr. *entrepreneur, computer company executive*

Palos Verdes Estates
Mennis, Edmund Addi *investment management consultant*

Pasadena
Arnott, Robert Douglas *investment company executive*
Baum, Dwight Crouse *investment banking executive*
Liebau, Frederic Jack, Jr. *investment manager*

Rancho Santa Fe
Polster, Leonard H. *investment company executive*

Ross
Rosenbaum, Michael Francis *securities dealer*

Sacramento
†Rualo, Hector Ramos *investment management executive*

San Diego
Dunn, David Joseph *financial executive*
Koehler, John Edget *entrepreneur*
Martinez, John Stanley *entrepreneur*

San Francisco
Apatoff, Michael John *finance executive*
Colwell, Kent Leigh *venture capitalist*
Dachs, Alan Mark *investment company executive*
Dellas, Robert Dennis *investment banker*
De Lutis, Donald Conse *investment manager, consultant*
Dunn, Richard Joseph *retired investment counselor*
Gale, Michael Jonathan *entrepreneur*
Gardner, James Harkins *venture capitalist*
Greber, Robert Martin *financial investments executive*
Gund, George, III *financier, professional sports team executive*
Hagenbuch, John Jacob *investment banker*
Halliday, John Meech *investment company executive*
Hellman, F(rederick) Warren *investment advisor*
Hsieh, Michael Thomas *venture capitalist*
Mahoney, Michael James *investment executive*
Matthews, Gilbert Elliott *investment banker*
McGettigan, Charles Carroll, Jr. *investment banker*
Morgan, Christina *venture capital firm executive*
Pfau, George Harold, Jr. *stockbroker*
Redo, David Lucien *investment company executive*
Rock, Arthur *venture capitalist*
Rosenberg, Claude Newman, Jr. *investment adviser*
Rosner, Robert Mendel *securities analyst*
Smelick, Robert Malcolm *investment bank executive*
Strock, James Martin *entrepreneur, writer*
Timmins, James Donald *venture capitalist*
Turner, Marshall Chittenden, Jr. *venture capitalist, consultant*
Turner, Ross James *investment corporation executive*
Vallee, Jacques Fabrice *venture capitalist*
Veitch, Stephen William *investment counselor*
Welsh, Stacey Lau *investment banker*
Wiley, Thomas Glen *retired investment company executive*
Winblad, Ann *investment company executive*

San Jose
Hall, Robert Emmett, Jr. *investment banker, realtor*

San Juan Capistrano
Robinson, Daniel Thomas *brokerage company executive*

San Leandro
Pansky, Emil John *entrepreneur*

San Rafael
Bertelsen, Thomas Elwood, Jr. *investment banker*

Santa Barbara
Bartlett, James Lowell, III *investment company executive*
Egan, Susan Chan *security analyst*
Hansen, Robert Gunnard *philatelist, entrepreneur*

Santa Clara
Lynch, Charles Allen *investment executive, corporate director*

Santa Monica
D'Angelo, Victoria Scott *entrepreneur, writer*

Sherman Oaks
Koonce, John Peter *investment company executive*

South Pasadena
Zimmerman, William Robert *entrepreneur, engineering based manufacturing company executive*

Templeton
Guenther, Robert Stanley, II *investment and property executive*

Thousand Oaks
Horton, Kenneth *investor*

Torrance
Enright, Stephanie Veselich *investment company executive*

Walnut Creek
Cervantez, Gil Lawrence *venture capital company executive*

Westlake Village
Fredericks, Ward Arthur *venture capitalist, food industry consultant*
Valentine, Gene C. *securities dealer*

Woodside
Isaacson, Robert Louis *investment company executive*

COLORADO

Boulder
Kimmel, Mark *writer, retired venture capital company executive*
Mehalchin, John Joseph *entrepreneur, finance executive*

Colorado Springs
Bennett, Brian Richard *investment broker*
Silliman, Brian Allen *numismatist, authenticator*

Denver
Berger, William Merriam Bart *investment management company executive*
Imhoff, Walter Francis *investment banker*
Stephenson, Arthur Emmet, Jr. *corporate and investment company executive*
Sutton, Robert Edward *investment company executive*
Wagner, Judith Buck *investment firm executive*
Welch, J(oan) Kathleen *entrepreneur*

Englewood
Van Loucks, Mark Louis *venture capitalist, business advisor*

Grand Junction
Skogen, Haven Sherman *investment company executive*

Kersey
Guttersen, Michael *ranching and investments professional*

Placerville
Monferrato, Angela Maria *entrepreneur, investor, writer, designer*

Snowmass Village
Bancroft, Paul, III *investment company executive*
Le Buhn, Robert *investment executive*

CONNECTICUT

Bristol
Morgan, Joe Leonard *investment company executive, former professional baseball player*

Darien
Koontz, Carl Lennis, II *investment counselor*
Moltz, James Edward *brokerage company executive*
Morse, Edmond Northrop *investment management executive*

Farmington
Bigler, Harold Edwin, Jr. *investment company executive*
Flynn, Daniel Francis *investment company executive*

Greenwich
Cervoni, Robert Angelo *financial executive, consultant*
Lewis, Perry Joshua *investment banker*
Nevin, Crocker *investment banker*
Rider, Gregory Ashford *investment company executive*
Schneider, John Arnold *business investor*
Tournillon, Nicholas Brady *trade finance, international investments company executive*

Hartford
Fiszel, Geoffrey Lynn *investment banker, investment advisor*

Litchfield
Booth, John Thomas *investment banker*

New Canaan
Gilbert, Steven Jeffrey *venture capitalist, screenwriter, lawyer*
Grace, Julianne Alice *investor relations firm executive*
Mountcastle, Kenneth Franklin, Jr. *retired stockbroker*
Penny, Susan Caroline Voelker *investment manager*
Pike, William Edward *business executive*
Snyder, Nathan *entrepreneur*

North Haven
†Bowles, Richard Robert *retired investor, art appraiser*

Norwalk
Alderman, Rhenus Hoffard, III *investment company executive*
†Danvers, David Bell *equity broker*
Hathaway, Carl Emil *investment management company executive*

Southport
Sheppard, William Stevens *investment banker*
Wilbur, E. Packer *investment company executive*

Stamford
Beyman, Jonathan Eric *information officer*
Hawley, Frank Jordan, Jr. *venture capital executive*

Washington
Darlow, George Anthony Gratton *investor*

Weston
Zimmerman, Bernard *investment banker*

Westport
Frey, Dale Franklin *financial investment company executive, manufacturing company executive*
Kelly, Paul Knox *investment banker*
O'Keefe, John David *investment specialist*
Walton, Alan George *venture capitalist*
Wayne, Neil Russell *investment management company executive*

Wilton
Scheinman, Stanley Bruce *international financial executive, lawyer*

DELAWARE

Greenville
DeWees, Donald Charles *securities company executive*

Wilmington
Kalil, James, Sr. *investment executive*
Laird, Walter Jones, Jr. *investment professional*

DISTRICT OF COLUMBIA

Washington
Ansary, Cyrus A. *investment company executive, lawyer*
Bonde, Count Peder Carlsson *investment company executive*
Brody, Kenneth David *investment banker*
Caldwell, John L. *international company executive*
Darman, Richard G. *investor, educator, former government official, former investment banker*
Dickson, Mark Allan *investment company executive*
Douglas, Leslie *investment banker*
Ferris, George Mallette, Jr. *investment banker*
Fisher, Robert Dale *stockbroker, retired naval officer*
Fitts, C. Austin *investment adviser*
Gibson, Paul Raymond *international trade and investment development executive*
†Halpin, Peter G. *investment company executive*
Hartwell, Stephen *investment company executive*
Lister, Harry Joseph *financial company executive, consultant*
Macomber, John D. *industrialist*
McIlwain, John Knox *real estate investment administrator*
Middendorf, J. William, II *investment banker*
Overman, Eric Mario *international trade and finance consultant*
Selin, Ivan *entrepreneur*
Sethness, Charles Olin *international financial official*
Shrier, Adam Louis *investment firm executive, consultant*
Silver, Jonathan Moses *investment management executive*
Simpich, George Cary *investment banker*
Spears, David D. *trading commission executive*
Stearns, James Gerry *retired securities company executive*
Tener, George E. *investor*
Tomlinson, Alexander Cooper *investment banker, consultant*
Tucker, Howard McKeldin *investment banker, consultant*
Wortley, George Cornelius *government affairs consultant, investor*

FLORIDA

Boca Raton
Barbarosh, Milton Harvey *merchant banking executive*
†Chestnov, Richard Franklin *private investor*
Cohen, Melvyn Douglas *securities company executive*
Landry, Michael Gerard *investment company executive*
Schmoke, L(eroy) Joseph, III *entrepreneur*
Skurnick, Sam *stockbroker, investment manager*

Boynton Beach
Allison, Dwight Leonard, Jr. *investor*

Bradenton
Nelson, Ralph Erwin *investment company executive, coin dealer*
Seim, Andrew *investment company executive, venture capitalist*

Cantonment
Crook, Penny Loraine *investment broker*

Clearwater
Grala, Jane M. *securities firm executive*

Coral Gables
Nunez-Portuondo, Ricardo *investment company executive*
Steinberg, Alan Wolfe *investment company executive*

Coral Springs
Levitz, John Blase *investment management consultant*

Destin
Horne, Thomas Lee, III *entrepreneur*

Englewood
Simis, Theodore Luckey *investment banker, information technology executive*

Fort Lauderdale
Donoho, Tim Mark *entrepreneur*
Huizenga, Harry Wayne *entrepreneur, entertainment corporation executive, professional sports team executive*
Niehaus, Robert James *investment banking executive*
Thayer, Charles J. *investment banker*
Vladem, Paul Jay *investment advisor, broker*

Hobe Sound
Hotchkiss, Winchester Fitch *retired investment banker*
Parker, H. Lawrence *investor, rancher, retired investment banker*

Hollywood
Nicolas, Carl-Richard *commodities trading company executive, translator*

Homosassa
Nagy, Albert N. *entrepreneur, consultant*

Jacksonville
Monsky, John Bertrand *investment banking executive*
Schultz, Frederick Henry *investor, former government official*

Jupiter
Kulok, William Allan *entrepreneur, venture capitalist*
Malm, Rita H. *securities executive*

Longboat Key
Dale, Martin Albert *investment banking executive, retired*
Levitt, Irving Francis *investment company executive*
Phillips, Howard William *investment banker*

Madeira Beach
Ashton, Thomas Walsh *investment banker*

Marco Island
Blackwell, John Wesley *securities industry executive, consultant*
Pettersen, Kjell Will *stockbroker, consultant*

Miami
Batcheller, Joseph Ann *entrepreneur*
Bishopric, Karl *investment banker, real estate executive, advertising executive*
†DeMueller, Lucia *investment consultant*
Dorion, Robert Charles *entrepreneur, investor*
Gonzalez, Manuel John *investment broker, international trade executive*
Kuczynski, Pedro-Pablo *investor*
Rubens, Jeffrey David *investment executive*

Miami Lakes
Zwigard, Bruce Albert *brokerage house executive*

Naples
Elliott, Edward *investment executive, financial planner*
Finley, Jack Dwight *investments and consultation executive*
Oliver, Robert Bruce *retired investment company executive*
Osias, Richard Allen *international financier, investor, real estate investment executive, corporate investor*

New Smyrna Beach
Grummer, Eugene Merrill *commodity futures market development executive*

Nokomis
Hawley, Phillip Eugene *investment banker*

North Miami Beach
Capdevielle, Xavier O. *builder, constructor*

Orlando
Jasica, Andrea Lynn *investor, former mortgage banking executive*
Managhan, James L., Jr. *entrepreneur, entertainer*

Palm Beach
Andrews, Holdt *investment banker*
Bagby, Joseph Rigsby *financial investor*
Gundlach, Heinz Ludwig *investment banker, lawyer*
Johnson, Theodore Mebane *investment executive*

Palm Beach Gardens
Hannon, John Robert *investment company executive*

Palm City
Spears, Doris Ann Hachmuth *entrepreneur, writer, publisher, real estate and management consultant*

Pensacola
†Lovoy, Joseph T. *investment advisor*

Pompano Beach
Rifenburgh, Richard Philip *investment company executive*

Port Saint Lucie
Olson, Edward Charles *entrepreneur, conservationist, writer, environmental consultant, banker, business consultant, foundation administrator*

Saint Petersburg
Emerson, William Allen *retired investment company executive*
Franke, Thomas *investment company executive*
Galbraith, John William *securities company executive*
Godbold, Francis Stanley *investment banker, real estate executive*
James, Thomas A. *investment company executive*
Julien, Jeffrey P. *investment company executive*
Scott, Lee Hansen *retired holding company executive*

Sarasota
Balliett, John William *entrepreneur, real estate executive*
Prade, Jean Noël Cresta *entrepreneur*

Tamarac
Brown, Ted Leon, Jr. *investment company executive*

Tampa
Ault, Jeffrey Michael *investment banker*
Holder, Harold Douglas, Sr. *investor, industrialist*
Lykes, Joseph T., III *investments manager*
Michaels, John Patrick, Jr. *investment banker, media broker*
Sigety, Charles Birge *investment company executive*

Tierra Verde
Gaffney, Thomas Francis *investment company executive*

Venice
Hackett, Edward Vincent *investment research company executive*
Xanthopoulos, Philip, Sr. *brokerage house executive*

Vero Beach
Clawson, John Addison *financier, investor*
Glassmeyer, Edward *investment banker*
Thompson, William David *investment banking executive*
Wilson, Robert James Montgomery *investment company executive*

West Palm Beach
Jenkins, Stanley Michael *stockbroker*
Zisson, James Stern *investment management consultant*

GEORGIA

Atlanta
Blackwell, Michael Sidney *broker, financial services executive*
†Bledsoe, Susan McCallum *operations manager, stockbroker*
Dietz, Arthur Townsend *investment counseling company executive*
Green, Holcombe Tucker, Jr. *investment executive*
Jackson, Geraldine *entrepreneur*
Keough, Donald Raymond *investment company executive*
McMahon, Donald Aylward *investor, corporate director*
McNabb, Dianne Leigh *investment banker, accountant*
Moss, Dan, Jr. *stockbroker*
Nash, Charles D. *investment banker*
Sands, Jerome D. *investment company executive*
Thomas, James Edward, Jr. *brokerage house executive*
Thompson, Nils Roy, III *investment company executive*
Uys, Jurgen Peter Brinker *securities analyst*
Williams, Ralph Watson, Jr. *retired securities company executive*

Columbus
Diaz-Verson, Salvador, Jr. *investment advisor*

Duluth
Street, David Hargett *investment company executive*

Lawrenceville
Greene, William Joshua, III *investment executive and consultant*

Sea Island
Brown, Ann Catherine *investment company executive*

HAWAII

Honolulu
Haight, Warren Gazzam *investor*
Ho, Stuart Tse Kong *investment company executive*
Mau, William Koon-Hee *financier*

Kailua
Amos, Wally *entrepreneur*

Kaneohe
Fukumoto, Geal S. *investment representative*

IDAHO

Boise
Hendren, Merlyn Churchill *investment company executive*

ILLINOIS

Barrington
Leon, Edward *investor*
Porter, Stuart Williams *investment company executive*

Champaign
Spice, Dennis Dean *venture capitalist*

Chicago
Atristain-Carrion, Ramiro Javier *investment company executive*
Bergonia, Raymond David *venture capitalist*
Blair, Edward McCormick *investment banker*
Block, Philip Dee, III *investment counselor*
Boris, James R. *investment company executive*
Brodsky, William J. *options exchange executive*
Buckle, Frederick Tarifero *international holding company executive, political and business intelligence analyst*
Case, Donni Marie *investment company executive*
Chaleff, Carl Thomas *brokerage house executive*
Clarke, Philip Ream, Jr. *investment banker*
Cloonan, James Brian *investment executive*
Crown, James Schine *investment executive*
Fahn, Jay *commercial bank executive, consultant, art dealer*
Fenton, Clifton Lucien *investment banker*
Foster, James Reuben *investment company executive*
Freehling, Stanley Maxwell *investment banker*
Gilbert, Debbie Rose *entrepreneur*
Gorter, James Polk *investment banker*
Greenberg, Steve *brokerage house executive*
Harris, Ronald William *commodities trader*
Hickey, Jerome Edward *investment company executive*
Kelly, Arthur Lloyd *management and investment company executive*
Kirsch, Jeffrey Scott *securities executive*
Knox, Lance Lethbridge *venture capital executive*
Kuhn, Ryan Anthony *information industry investment banker*
Lewis, Charles A. *investment company executive*
Logan, David Samuel *investment banker*
Luthringshausen, Wayne *brokerage house executive*
McCausland, Thomas James, Jr. *brokerage house executive*
McConahey, Stephen George *securities company executive*
Melamed, Leo *investment company executive*
Miner, Thomas Hawley *international entrepreneur*
Mulvihill, Terence Joseph *investment banking executive*
Nash, Donald Gene *commodities specialist*
O'Brien, Brien Michael *investment firm executive*
Oliver, Harry Maynard, Jr. *retired brokerage house executive*
Osborn, William A. *investment company executive*
Rasin, Rudolph Stephen *corporate executive*
Reece, Beth Pauley *commodities broker*
Ross, Darius Alexander *merger and acquisition specialist*
Schulte, David Michael *investment banker*
Slansky, Jerry William *investment company executive*
Spears, Jackson E., Jr. *investment banker*
Stanton, Benjamin R. *investment company executive*
Stead, James Joseph, Jr. *securities company executive*
Stevens, Paul G., Jr. *brokerage house executive*
Swift, Edward Foster, III *investment banker*
Towson, Thomas D. *securities trader*
Underwood, Robert Leigh *venture capitalist*
Varwig, David Lee *investment banker*
Waite, Dennis Vernon *investor relations consultant*
Weitzman, Robert Harold *investment company executive*
Wilmouth, Robert K. *commodities executive*
Woods, Robert Archer *investment counsel*
Young, Ronald Faris *commodity trader*
Zeid, Paula Klein *metals broker*

Deerfield
Howell, George Bedell *equity investing and managing executive*

Elgin
Freeman, Corwin Stuart, Jr. *investment adviser*

Glenview
Gillis, Marvin Bob *investor, consultant*
Mukoyama, James Hidefumi, Jr. *securities executive*

Highland Park
Uhlmann, Frederick Godfrey *commodity and securities broker*

Lake Forest
Beitler, Stephen Seth *private equity and venture capital executive*

Lincolnshire
Caballero, Mario Gustavo *investment company executive, gaming executive*
†Sheble, Ronald Walter *financial manager*

Lombard
Cihak, Erwin Frank *retired securities trader, real estate developer*

Naperville
Penisten, Gary Dean *entrepreneur*
Vanagas, Rimantas Andrius (Ray Vanagas) *entrepreneur*

Oak Brook
Kelly, Donald Philip *entrepreneur*

Oak Forest
Jashel, Larry Steven (L. Steven Rose) *entrepreneur, media consultant*

Palos Hills
Johnson, Audrey Ann *options trader, stockbroker*

Peoria
Vaughan, David John *distribution company executive*

River Forest
Wirsching, Charles Philipp, Jr. *retired brokerage house executive, private investor*

Schaumburg
Balasa, Mark Edward *investment consultant*
Patzke, Frank Thomas *investment advisor*

Villa Park
Tang, George Chickchee *investment company executive*

Wheaton
Back, Robert Wyatt *investment executive, pharmaceutical company executive consultant*

Wilmette
Albright, Townsend Shaul *investment banker, government benefits consultant*
Ryan, Mike *investment management consultant*

Winnetka
Martin, Patrick Albert *investment adviser*
Mathers, Thomas Nesbit *financial consultant*
Sick, William Norman, Jr. *investment company executive*

INDIANA

Anderson
Cox, Archibald, Jr. *investment banker*

Columbus
Hollansky, Bert Voyta *stock brokerage executive*

Evansville
Brill, Alan Richard *entrepreneur*

Fort Wayne
Detwiler, Susan Margaret *information brokerage executive*

Indianapolis
Fritz, Cecil Morgan *investment company executive*
King, Kay Sue *investment company executive*
Price, Thomas Allan *entrepreneur*
Stayton, Michael Bruce *financial entrepreneur, corporate professional*

Merrillville
Reitmeister, Noel William *financial planner, investment and insurance executive, author, consultant, columnist, television host and producer, educator*

Munster
Shields, Robert Francis *stockbroker*

IOWA

Bettendorf
Rathje, James Lee *broker*

Cedar Falls
Oster, Merrill James *entrepreneur, publisher, author, lecturer*

Des Moines
†Blazek, Steven Joseph *investment company executive, sales executive*

Spencer
Franker, Stephen Grant *investment executive*

West Des Moines
Reilly, Michael J. *stockbroker*
Shoafstall, Earl Fred *entrepreneur, consultant*

KANSAS

De Soto
Wilson, Darrell Glenn *investment banker, software developer*

Olathe
Fraser, David Charles *investment banker*

Shawnee Mission
Tucker, Keith A. *investment company executive*
Van Tuyl, Cecil L. *investment company executive*

Topeka
Hedrick, Lois Jean *retired investment company executive, state official*

Wichita
Barry, Donald Lee *investment broker*

KENTUCKY

Harrods Creek
Chandler, James Williams *retired securities company executive*

Lexington
Wagner, Alan Burton *entrepreneur*

Louisville
Porter, Henry Homes, Jr. *investor*

Whitesburg
Smith, Roger Keith *investment executive*

LOUISIANA

New Orleans
Dahlberg, Carl Fredrick, Jr. *entrepreneur*
Flower, Walter Chew, III *investment counselor*

MAINE

Augusta
Moody, Stanley Alton *entrepreneur, financial consultant*

Bryant Pond
Conary, David Arlan *investment company executive*

Cumberland Center
Thomas, Charles Carroll *investment management executive*

Norway
Skolnik, Barnet David *entrepreneur*

Portland
Anderson, Stephen Mills *investment broker*
Harte, Christopher McCutcheon *investment manager*

Rockport
Rohrbach, Lewis Bunker *investment company executive*

MARYLAND

Baltimore
Bacigalupo, Charles Anthony *brokerage company executive*
Brinkley, James Wellons *investment company executive*
Cashman, Edmund Joseph, Jr. *investment banker*
Curley, John Francis, Jr. *mutual fund executive*
Ellsworth, Robert Fred *investment executive, former government official*
Hardiman, Joseph Raymond *securities industry executive*
Harvey, Curran Whitthorne, Jr. *investment management executive*
Himelfarb, Richard Jay *securities firm executive*
Hopkins, Samuel *retired investment banker*
Kent, Edgar Robert, Jr. *investment banker*
McManus, Walter Leonard *investment executive*
Preston, Mark I. *investment company executive*
Semans, Truman Thomas *investment company executive*
Shaeffer, Charles Wayne *investment counselor*

Bethesda
Drazin, Lisa *real estate and corporate investment banker, financial consultant*
Meakem, Carolyn Soliday *investment executive, financial planner, money manager, consultant*

Chesapeake City
Albert, Harry Francis *investments executive*

Chestertown
Sener, Joseph Ward, Jr. *securities company executive*

Chevy Chase
Freeman, Harry Louis *investment executive*

Hagerstown
Baer, John Metz *entrepreneur*

Lutherville Timonium
Cappiello, Frank Anthony, Jr. *investment advisor*

Rockville
Freedman, Marc Allan *investment company executive*
Proffitt, John Richard *business executive, educator*

Towson
Young, William Sherban *investment broker*

Westminster
Yingling, Jacob Matthias *independent investor*

MASSACHUSETTS

Boston
Aikman, William Francis *venture capitalist*
Bailey, Richard Briggs *investment company executive*
Bennett, George Frederick *investment manager*
Benson, James M. *investment company executive*
Calderwood, Stanford Matson *investment management executive*
Cantella, Vincent Michele *stockbroker*
Carey, John Andrew *investment company executive*
Cox, Howard Ellis, Jr. *venture capitalist*
de Burlo, Comegys Russell, Jr. *investment advisor, educator*
Driscoll, James S. *entrepreneurial strategist*
Ederle, Douglas Richard *investment manager*
Elfers, William *retired investment company director*
Estin, Hans Howard *investment executive*
Fitzgerald, Daniel Louis *securities dealer*
Gozonsky, Edwin O. O. *investment broker*
Hagler, Jon Lewis *investment executive*
Hale, Martin de Mora *investor*
Hart, Douglas Edward *investment company executive*
†Johnson, Abigail *investment company executive*
Langermann, John W. R. *institutional equity salesperson*
Lasser, Lawrence J. *investment company executive*
Lieberman, Gail Forman *investment company executive*
Lovell, Francis Joseph *investment company executive*
Markoff, Gary David *investment executive*
†Mc Carthy, Denis Michael *investment executive*
McCullen, Joseph T., Jr. *venture capitalist*
Morby, Jacqueline *venture capitalist*
Morrison, Gordon Mackay, Jr. *investment company executive*
Morton, William Gilbert, Jr. *stock exchange executive*
Oates, William Armstrong, Jr. *investment company executive*
Philbin, Ann Margaret *brokerage house executive*
Shaw, William Frederick *investment company executive*
Sobin, Julian Melvin *international consultant*
Tempel, Jean Curtin *venture capitalist*
Thorndike, John Lowell *investment executive*
Towles, Stokley Porter *commercial and investment banking executive*
†Treacy, Michael Edmund Francis *venture capitalist*

Brookline
Strassler, Robert B. *investment professional*

Cambridge
Bedrosian, Edward Robert *investment management company executive*
Davis, Paul Robert *investment manager, portfolio manager*
Lloyd, Boardman *investment executive*
Metcalfe, Murray Robert *venture capitalist*
Pardee, Scott Edward *securities dealer*
Rowe, Stephen Cooper *venture capitalist, entrepreneur*

Carlisle
Fohl, Timothy *consulting and investment company executive*

Concord
Schiller, Pieter Jon *venture capital executive*
Wickfield, Eric Nelson *investment company executive*

Great Barrington
Wampler, Barbara Bedford *entrepreneur*

Lincoln
Holberton, Philip Vaughan *entrepreneur, educator, professional speaker*

Lynn
Zykofsky, Stephen Mark *investment counselor*

Marion
Stone, David Barnes *investment advisor*

Marlborough
Moran, James J., Jr. *insurance executive*

Newton
Svrluga, Richard Charles *entrepreneur*

Quincy
Markham, Charles Rinklin *financial executive, tax accountant*

Reading
Burbank, Nelson Stone *investment banker*

Scituate
Keating, Margaret Mary *entrepreneur, business consultant*

South Deerfield
Paladino, Albert Edward *venture capitalist*

Stoneham
Mc Donald, Andrew Jewett *securities firm executive*

Taunton
Ricciardi, Louis Michael *brokerage house executive*

Waban
Henderson, Kenneth Atwood *investment counseling executive*

Wakefield
Spaulding, William Rowe *investment consultant*

Wellesley
Chandra, Rob S. *venture capitalist*

Weston
Alcock, George Lewis, Jr. (Peter Alcock) *investor, business strategist*

Westwood
Gillette, Hyde *retired investment banker*

Wilbraham
Gaudreau, Jules Oscar, Jr. *insurance and financial services company executive*

Woburn
Eddison, Elizabeth Bole *entrepreneur, information specialist*
McCulloch, James Callahan *corporate executive*

MICHIGAN

Beulah
Auch, Walter Edward *securities company executive*

Birmingham
Sallen, Marvin Seymour *investment company executive*

Bloomfield Hills
†Beachum, James Curtis *stockbroker*

Farmington Hills
Ellmann, Sheila Frenkel *investment company executive*

Flint
Elieff, Lewis Steven *stockbroker*

Grosse Pointe
Lane, James McConkey *investment executive*
Mengden, Joseph Michael *retired investment banker*
Simonds, Richard Kimball *investment executive*

Madison Heights
Janke, Kenneth *investment consultant*

Oak Park
Novick, Marvin *investment company executive, former automotive supplier executive, accountant*

West Bloomfield
Mamut, Mary Catherine *retired entrepreneur*

MINNESOTA

Anoka
Ward, Bart James *investment executive*

Edina
Burbank, John Thorn *entrepreneur*

Excelsior
Fazio, Anthony Lee *investment company executive*

Minneapolis
Appel, John C. *investment company executive*
Dale, John Sorensen *investment company executive, portfolio manager*
Fauth, John J. *venture capitalist*
Gallagher, Gerald Raphael *venture capitalist*
Lindau, James H. *grain exchange executive*
Lindau, Philip *commodities trader*
Piper, Addison Lewis *securities executive*
Schreck, Robert *commodities trader*
Sit, Eugene C. *investment executive*

Savage
Bean, Glen Atherton *entrepreneur*

Stillwater
Horsch, Lawrence Leonard *venture capitalist, corporate revitalization executive*

Wayzata
Wyard, Vicki Shaw *investment and insurance company executive*

MISSOURI

Hannibal
Galloway, Daniel Lee *investment executive*

Jefferson City
Beatty, Grover Douglas *stockbroker*

Kansas City
Braude, Michael *commodity exchange executive*
De Vries, Robert John *investment banker*
Latshaw, John *entrepreneur*
Rowland, Landon Hill *diversified holding company executive*

Lees Summit
Korschot, Benjamin Calvin *investment executive*

Saint Louis
Aldridge, Charles Ray *brokerage house executive, trade director*
Bachmann, John William *securities firm executive*
Bernstein, Donald Chester *brokerage company executive, lawyer*
Bickel, Floyd Gilbert, III *investment counselor*
Costigan, Edward John *investment banker*
Edwards, Benjamin Franklin, III *investment banker*
Jackson, Gayle Pendleton White *venture capitalist, international energy specialist*
†Langenberg, Oliver M. *securities dealer, analyst*
Maguire, John Patrick *investment company executive*
Moore, Patricia Kay *investor, public relations director*
O'Neill, Eugene Milton *mergers and acquisitions consultant*

NEBRASKA

Dalton
Swanson, Lauren A. *entrepreneur, educator, researcher*

Lincoln
†Bennie, Bob *investment company executive*

Omaha
Buffett, Warren Edward *entrepreneur*
Cross, W. Thomas *investment company executive*
Johnson, Richard Walter *entrepreneur*
Sokolof, Phil *industrialist, consumer advocate*
Soshnik, Joseph *investment banking consultant*
Velde, John Ernest, Jr. *investment company executive*
Wild, Stephen Kent *securities broker, dealer*

NEVADA

Glenbrook
Jabara, Michael Dean *investment banker, entrepreneur*

Incline Village
Johnson, James Arnold *business consultant, venture capitalist*
Kleinman, George *commodities executive*

Las Vegas
Di Palma, Joseph Alphonse *investment company executive, lawyer*
Fernandez, Linda Flawn *entrepreneur, social worker*
Holland, Robert Debnam, Sr. *investment company executive*
Stock, Lincoln Frederick *stockbroker, retired*

Logandale
Smiley, Robert William, Jr. *investment banker*

Reno
Newberg, William Charles *stock broker, real estate broker, automotive engineer*

Smith
Weaver, William Merritt, Jr. *investment banker*

NEW HAMPSHIRE

Dover
Parks, Joe Benjamin *entrepreneur, former state legislator*

Exeter
Verzone, Ronald D. *insurance brokerage executive, investment advisor*

Manchester
Levins, John Raymond *investment advisor, management consultant, educator*

Portsmouth
Balding, Bruce Edward *investment executive*

NEW JERSEY

Avenel
Berg, Louis Leslie *investment executive*

Cliffside Park
Goldstein, Howard Bernard *investment banker, advertising and marketing executive*

Cranford
Bardwil, Joseph Anthony *investments consultant*

Dover
Hurwitz, David *entrepreneur, consultant*

Edison
†Critchley, John J., Jr. *stock options trader*
Provitera, Michael J. *investment company executive*

Florham Park
Clayton, William L. *investment banking executive*
Lovell, Robert Marlow, Jr. *retired investment company executive*

Fort Lee
Lippman, William Jennings *investment company executive*

Franklin Lakes
†Baker, Philip Douglas *consultant, retired investment banker*

Hackensack
Heilborn, George Heinz *investments professional*

Haddonfield
Carter, Joan Pauline *investment company executive*

Hampton
Lovejoy, Lee Harold *investment company executive*

Jersey City
Kaplan, Ben Augustus *financial services executive*
Lang, Everett Francis, Jr. *brokerage house executive*
Smith, James Frederick *securities executive*

Little Silver
Turbidy, John Berry *investor, management consultant*

Livingston
Levine, Harry Bruce *stockbroker*

Marlboro
Friedman, Howard Martin *financial executive*

Mendham
Kirby, Allan Price, Jr. *investment company executive*
Skidmore, Francis Joseph, Jr. *securities company executive*

Montclair
Kidde, John Lyon *investment manager*

Morganville
Sternfeld, Marc Howard *investment banker*

Morristown
Kearns, William Michael, Jr. *investment banker*

Mount Holly
†Moffitt, Ronald James *entrepreneur*

New Brunswick
Mills, Dorothy Allen *investor*

Newark
Cortez, Ricardo Lee *investment management executive*
O'Leary, Paul Gerard *investment executive*
Scott, James Hunter, Jr. *investment executive*

Nutley
Olmsted, David John *capital management company executive*

Parsippany
Winograd, Bernard *real estate and financial adviser*

Plainsboro
Schreyer, William Allen *retired investment firm executive*

Point Pleasant
Caponegro, Ernest Mark *stockbroker, financial planner*

Princeton
Chamberlin, John Stephen *investor, former cosmetics company executive*
Ehrenberg, Edward *executive, consultant*
Johnston, Robert Fowler *venture capitalist*
Lobo, Jennifer Helena *investment banker, venture capitalist*
Schafer, Carl Walter *investment executive*
Treu, Jesse Isaiah *venture capitalist*

Red Bank
Hertz, Daniel Leroy, Jr. *entrepreneur*
Weiant, William Morrow *investment banking executive*

Ridgewood
Ege, Hans Alsnes *securities company executive*
Tuthill, Jay Dean, II *investment executive*

Rockleigh
Heslin, John Thomas *entrepreneur, historic preservationist*

Roseland
Golden, Robert Charles *financial services executive*

Rumson
Strong, George Hotham *private investor, consultant*

Saddle River
Giovannoli, Joseph Louis *entrepreneur, lawyer*

Scotch Plains
Bishop, Robert Milton *former stock exchange official*

Short Hills
†Bartels, Stanley Leonard *investment banker*

Skillman
Burns, Patrick Owen *venture capital company executive*

Summit
Malin, Robert Abernethy *investment management executive*

Sussex
†Davis, Thomas Philip *investment banker*

Teaneck
Lehmann, Esther Strauss *investment company executive*

Toms River
Boyd, Roger Allen *investment consultant*
Cone, Michael McKay *venture capitalist*

Tuckerton
Dinges, Richard Allen *entrepreneur*

Weehawken
Hess, Dennis John *investment banker*

Westfield
Simon, Martin Stanley *commodity marketing company executive, economist*

Wyckoff
Bucko, John Joseph *investment corporation executive*

NEW MEXICO

Albuquerque
†Fermin, John Enriquez *investor*

Corrales
Eisenstadt, Pauline Doreen Bauman *investment company executive*

Santa Fe
Davis, Shelby Moore Cullom *investment executive, consultant*
Dreisbach, John Gustave *investment banker*
Nurock, Robert Jay *investment analysis company executive*

Taos
Holte, Debra Leah *investment executive, financial analyst*
Lipscomb, Anna Rose Feeny *entrepreneur, arts organizer, fundraiser*

NEW YORK

Albany
Leichman, Kenneth William *investment executive*

Armonk
Gerstner, Louis Vincent, Jr. *diversified company executive*

Bay Shore
Williams, Tonda *entrepreneur, consultant*

Binghamton
Kunjukunju, Pappy *insurance company financial executive*

Brooklyn
Leyh, Richard Edmund, Sr. *retired investment executive*
Strohbehn, Edward Allen *investment company executive*

Buffalo
Irwin, Robert James Armstrong *investment company executive*
Littlewood, Douglas Burden *business brokerage executive*

Croton On Hudson
Rath, Bernard Emil *entrepreneur*

Dobbs Ferry
Grunebaum, Ernest Michael *investment banker*

Garden City
Gordon, Barry Joel *investment advisor*
Hinds, Glester Samuel *financier, program specialist, tax consultant*

Glen Head
Sutherland, Donald James *investment company executive*

Glens Falls
Pearsall, Glenn Lincoln *brokerage house executive*

Great Neck
Appel, Gerald *investment advisor*
Hampton, Benjamin Bertram *brokerage house executive*
Lyons, Laurence *securities executive, retired*

Hartsdale
Katz, John *investment banker*

Huntington
Pettersen, Kevin Will *investment company executive*

Irvington
Peyser, Peter A. *former congressman, investment management company executive*

Ithaca
Cornish, Elizabeth Turverey *stockbroker*

Jamestown
Bargar, Robert Sellstrom *investor*

Jericho
Fialkov, Herman *investment banker*

Lake Grove
Braff, Howard *brokerage house executive, financial analyst*

Latham
Mitchell, Mark-Allen Bryant *state government administrator*

Locust Valley
Benson, Robert Elliott *investment banker, consultant*

Mamaroneck
Topol, Robert Martin *retired financial services executive*

Manhasset
Brackett, Ronald E. *investment company executive, lawyer*

Massapequa
Molitor, Michael A. *entrepreneur, consultant*

Melville
Clinard, Joseph Hiram, Jr. *securities company executive*

Merrick
Poppel, Seth Raphael *entrepreneur*

New Hyde Park
Richards, Bernard *investment company executive*

New York
Acampora, Ralph Joseph *brokerage firm executive*
Albers, Charles Edgar *investment manager*
Ames, George Joseph *investment banker*
Andersen, K(ent) Tucker *investment executive*
†Anderson, Timothy R. *investment banker*
Aronson, Edgar David *venture capitalist*
Atwa, Salem Aldasouki *entrepreneur*
Ball, Damon Howard *investment management executive*
Ballard, Charles Alan *investment banker*
Barr, Michael Charles *securities trader*
Barry, Thomas Corcoran *investment counsellor*
Bartges, Hans *investment company executive*
Bartlett, Peter B. *investment company executive*
Bedrij, Orest *investment banker, scientist*
Beinecke, Frederick William *investment company executive*
Bell, Martin Allen *investment company executive*
Bellas, Albert Constantine *investment banker, advisor*
Bergreen, Bernard D. *investment company executive*
Beringer, Stuart Marshall *investment banker*
Berlin, Howard Richard *investment advisory company executive*
Berlin, Jordan Stuart *investment company executive*
Berris, Brian A. *investment company executive*
Bewkes, Eugene Garrett, Jr. *investment company executive, consultant*
Bickford, Jewelle Wooten *investment banker*
Biderman, Mark Charles *investment banker*
Biggs, Barton Michael *investment company executive*
Birkelund, John Peter *investment banking executive*
Blalock, Sherrill *investment advisor*
Boissevain, Benjamin Mathew *investment banker*
Brittenham, Raymond Lee *investment company executive*
Britz Lotti, Diane Edward *investment company executive*
Brody, Alan Jeffrey *investment company executive*
Brody, Eugene David *investment company executive*
Brown, Fred Elmore *investment executive*
Brown, Walter H. *investment company executive*
Brunie, Charles Henry *investment manager*
Buck, James E. *financial exchange executive*
Buckles, Robert Howard *retired investment company executive*
Bulow, George Mitchell *entrepreneur*
Burke, James Joseph, Jr. *investment banker*
Cannaliato, Vincent, Jr. *investment banker, mathematician*
Carey, William Polk *investment banker*
Carpenter, Michael Alan *financial services executive*
Casey, Thomas Jefferson *investment banker, venture capitalist*
Cecil, Donald *investment company executive*
Chalsty, John Steele *investment banker*
Chapman, Max C. *investment company executive*
Chapman, Peter Herbert *investment company executive*
Chavers, Kevin G. *investment company executive*
Clarens, John Gaston *investment executive*
Cogan, Marshall S. *entrepreneur*
Cohen, Abby Joseph *investment strategist*
Cohen, Claire Gorham *investors service company executive*
Cohen, Jonathan Little *investment banker*
Cohen, Joseph M. *investment company executive*
Cohn, Bertram Josiah *investment banker*
Cole, Carolyn Jo *brokerage company executive*
Collins, Timothy Clark *holding company executive*
Condron, Christopher M. Kip *investment company executive*
Conway, Richard Francis *investment company executive*
Culp, Michael Bronston *securities company executive, research director*
†Curry, Ravenel Boykin *investment manager*
Cushing, Harry Cooke, IV *investment banker*
Dallen, Russell Morris, Jr. *investment company executive, lawyer*
Daly, John Neal *investment company executive*
D'Angelo, Ernest Eustachio *brokerage house executive*
Davis, Martin S. *investment company executive*
DeBusschere, David Albert *brokerage executive, retired professional basketball player and team executive*
DeNunzio, Ralph Dwight *investment banker*
Dillon, Clarence Douglas *retired investment company executive*
Dimond, Thomas *investment advisory company executive*
Doyle, William Stowell *venture capitalist*
Dugan, Edward Francis *investment banker*
Ealy, Carleton Cato *investment banker*
Edlow, Kenneth Lewis *securities brokerage official*
Einiger, Carol Blum *investment executive*
Ercklentz, Alexander Tonio *investment executive*
Evnin, Anthony Basil *venture capital investor*
Fan, Linda C. *investment company executive*
Fein, Bernard *investments executive*
Feskoe, Gaffney Jon *investment banker, management consultant*
Fetscher, Paul George William *brokerage house executive*
Filatov, Victor Simeonovich *investment professional*
Filimonov, Mikhail Anatolyevitch *investment company executive*
Fisher, Richard B. *investment banker*
Fiumefreddo, Charles A. *investment management company executive*
Fort, Randall Martin *investment banking executive*
Fowler, Henry Hamill *investment banker*
Frackman, Richard Benoit *investment banker*
France, Joseph David *securities analyst*
Frank, Frederick *investment banker*
Franklin, Edward Ward *international investment consultant, lawyer, actor*
Frantzen, Henry Arthur *investment company executive*
Fried, Albert, Jr. *investment banker*
Friedenberg, Daniel Meyer *financial investor, writer*
Friedman, Alvin Edward *investment executive*
Furman, Roy L. *investment banker, theatrical executive*
Galbraith, Evan Griffith *investment banker*
Gant, Donald Ross *investment banker*
Garner, Albert Headden *investment banker*
Garon, Ross Anden *investment banker*
Geller, Jeffrey Lawrence *financier*
Gellert, Michael Erwin *investment banker*
Gero, Anthony George *securities and commodities trader*
Goelet, Robert G. *investment executive*
Gold, Jeffrey Mark *investment banker, financial adviser*
Goldberg, David Alan *investment banker, lawyer*
Goldsmith, John H. *investment company executive*
Gonzalez, Eugene Robert *investment banker*
Gottesman, David Sanford *investment executive*
Grasso, Richard A. *stock exchange executive*
Grau, Marcy Beinish *real estate broker, former investment banker*
Gray, Arthur, Jr. *investment counselor*
Green, Adam Mitchell *investment banker*
Greenberg, Alan Courtney (Ace Greenberg) *stockbroker*
Grijns, Laine *investment company executive*
Grusky, Robert R. *investor*
Haas, Eleanor A. (Mrs. Peter Ralph Haas) *investment banker*
Hallingby, Paul, Jr. *investment banker*
Halpern, Merril Mark *investment banker*
Hanau, Kenneth John, III *venture capitalist*
Hansmann, Ralph Emil *investment executive*
Hanson, John C. *investment company executive*
Harris, D. George *entrepreneur*
Hart, Gurnee Fellows *investment counselor*
Hashimoto, Kyosuke *investment company executive*
Haskell, John Henry Farrell, Jr. *investment banking company executive*
Head, Glenn Oakes *investment company executive*
Hedley, David Van Houten *investment banker*
Heimann, John Gaines *investment banker*
Hennessy, John M. *brokerage house executive*
Hensel, Katherine Ruth *investment strategist, securities analyst*
Herbst, Edward Ian *brokerage firm executive*
Herkness, Lindsay Coates, III *securities broker*
Herrmann, Lacy Bunnell *investment company executive, financial entrepreneur, venture capitalist*
Hertog, Roger *investment company executive*
Herzog, John E. *securities dealer*
Heyman, William Herbert *financial services executive*
Hieber, William George, Jr. *stockbroker*
Hill, J(ames) Tomilson *investment banker*
Hillman, Rita *investor*
Hilton, Andrew Carson *investor, management consultant, former manufacturing company executive*
Hoffman, Robert Howard *investment banker*
†Holden, James Daniel *investment company executive*
Holland, Michael Francis *investment company executive*
Horowitz, Gedale Bob *investment banker*
Howard, Nathan Southard *investment banker, lawyer*
Huntington, Lawrence Smith *investment banker*
Hurst, Robert Jay *securities company executive*
Hussein, Ahmed Dia *investment banker*
Hyman, John Allen *securities executive*
Hyman, Seymour *capital and product development company executive*
Isnard, Arnaud *venture capitalist*
Jacoby, A. James *securities brokerage firm executive*
Janiak, Anthony Richard, Jr. *investment banker*
Janney, Stuart Symington, III *investment company executive*
Jepson, Hans Godfrey *investment company executive*
Johnson, Johnnie Dean *investor relations consultant*
Jones, Abbott C. *investment banking executive*
Jones, Barclay Gibbs, III *investment banker*
Jordan, John W., II *holding company executive*
Kaiser, Suzanne Billo *investment banker*
Kautz, James Charles *investment banker*
Kellogg, Peter R. *securities dealer*
Kelly, Brian *commodities trader*
Kelly, William Michael *investment executive*
Kinsman, Sarah Markham *investment company executive*
Kirsch, Arthur William *investment consultant*
Klamm de Betas, Ullrich *investor*
Klingenstein, Frederick Adler *investment banking executive*
Kressel, Henry *venture capitalist*
Kretschmer, Keith Hughes *investor*
Krimendahl, Herbert Frederick, II *investment banker*
Lamle, Hugh Roy *investment advisor, consultant*
Lasser, Joseph Robert *investment company executive*
Lauder, Ronald Stephen *investor*
Laverge, Albert Johannes *investment banker*
Lavine, Lawrence Neal *investment banker*
Lawrence, Bryan Hunt *investment banking executive*
Lazaroff, Shneur Zalmen *stockbroker*
Lebec, Alain *investment banker*
Lee, Victor J. *venture capitalist*
Leighton, Lawrence Ward *investment banker*
Levy, Leon *investment company executive*
Levy, Matthew Degen *investment company executive, consumer products executive, management consultant*
Lewis, Sherman Richard, Jr. *investment banker*
Liddell, Donald Macy, Jr. *retired investment counsellor*
Lipper, Kenneth *investment banker, author, producer*
Loeb, John Langeloth, Jr. *investment counselor*
Logue-Kinder, Joan *investment brokerage firm executive*
Long, Thomas Michael *investment banker, private equity fund manager*
Lyall, Michael Rodney *investment banker*
MacDermott, Thomas Jerome *investment banking executive*
†Mack, John J. *investment company executive*
Mager, Ezra Pascal *investment management company executive*
Mahoney, Thomas Henry, IV *investment banker*
Main, Patricia Englander *investor*
Marks, Edwin S. *investment company executive*
Marlas, James Constantine *holding company executive*
Marron, Donald Baird *investment banker*
Masinter, Edgar Martin *investment banker*
Maughan, Deryck C. *investment banker*
Maxwell, Anders John *investment banker*
Mayer, William Emilio *investor*
Mazzilli, Paul John *investment banker*
McBride, Rodney Lester *investment counselor*
McCarter, Thomas N., III *investment counseling company executive*
McCleary, Benjamin Ward *investment banker*
†McGlynn, William Charles *brokerage house executive*
Mc Lendon, Heath Brian *securities investment company executive*
McMullan, William Patrick, III *investment banker*
Menschel, Richard Lee *investment banker*
Metz, Emmanuel Michael *investment company executive, lawyer*
Michele, Robert Charles *investment management, portfolio manager*
Miller, B. Jack *investment company executive*
Miller, Douglas L. *stockbroker, money manager*
Mintz, Walter *investment company executive*
†Mlynarczyk, Francis Alexander, Jr. *securities broker, investment manager*
Morris, William Charles *investor*
Morrissey, Dolores Josephine *investment executive*
Murphy, John Joseph, Jr. *investment company executive*
Nabi, Stanley Andrew *investment executive*
Nadel, Elliott *investment firm executive*
Nadelberg, Eric Paul *brokerage house executive*
Nazem, Fereydoun F. *venture capitalist, financier*
Necarsulmer, Henry *investment banker*
Needham, George Austin *investment banker*
Neuberger, Roy R. *investment counselor*
Niemiec, David Wallace *investment managment*
Obernauer, Marne, Jr. *business executive*
Obolensky, Ivan *investment banker, foundation consultant, writer, publisher*
O'Connell, Daniel S. *private investments professional*
Offit, Morris Wolf *investment management executive*
O'Grady, Beverly Troxler *investment executive, counselor*
Okun, Melanie Anne *venture capitalist*
Olinger, Chauncey Greene, Jr. *investment executive, editorial consultant*
O'Neill, George Dorr *business executive*
O'Neill, Joseph J. *futures market executive*
Openshaw, Helena Marie *investment company executive, portfolio manager*
Orben, Jack Richard *investment company executive*
Osborne, Stanley de Jongh *investment banker*
Ostrander, Thomas William *investment banker*
Page, Jonathan Roy *investment analyst*
Palitz, Clarence Yale, Jr. *commercial finance executive*
Paton, Leland B. *investment banker*
Paul, Andrew Mitchell *venture capitalist*
†Paulson, Henry Merritt, Jr. *venture capitalist, investment banker*
Perlmutter, Louis *investment banker, lawyer*
Perrette, Jean Rene *investment banker*
Peterson, Peter G. *investment company executive*
Pettit, William Dutton, Sr. *investment executive, consultant*
Piper, Thomas Laurence, III *investment banker*
Pollack, Stephen J. *stockbroker*
Pope, Albert Augustus *financier*
Potter, William James *investment banker*
†Potts, Christopher Franklyn *financial derivatives controller*
Pouschine, John Laurence *private equity investment executive*
Prountzos, Tina *investment banker*
Pulling, Thomas Leffingwell *investment advisor*
Quick, Peter *brokerage firm executive*
Quick, Thomas Clarkson *brokerage house executive*
Quirk, John James *investment company executive*
Rahl, Leslie *risk advisor, entrepreneur*
Rand, Lawrence Anthony *investor and financial relations executive*
Read, Russell *investment company executive*
Reis, Judson Patterson *investment manager*
Rickert, Edwin Weimer *investment consultant*
†Roby, Joe Lindell *investment banker*
Rogers, Theodore Courtney *investment company executive*
Roosevelt, Theodore, IV *investment banker*
†Rosa, John Vincent *investment company executive*
Rose, Robert Neal *brokerage house executive*
Rosenbloom, Daniel *investment banker, lawyer*
Rosenthal, Daniel *investment company executive*
Rothfeld, Michael B. *theatrical productions executive, investor*
Rothstein, Gerald Alan *investment company executive*
Rouhana, William Joseph, Jr. *business executive*
Rubin, Robert Samuel *investment banker*
Sabet, Hormoz *entrepreneur*
Sacerdote, Peter M. *investment banker*
Santoro, Charles William *investment banker*
Scaturro, Philip David *investment banker*
Schick, Harry Leon *investment company executive*
Schiff, David Tevele *investment banker*
Schiff, Marlene Sandler *entrepreneur*
Schiro, James J. *brokerage house executive*
Schless, Phyllis Ross *investment banker*
Schoen, Rem *investment executive*
Seff, Leslie S. *securities trader*
Seidman, Samuel Nathan *investment banker, economist*
Selby, Frederick Peter *investment banker*
Shallcross, Deanne *investment company executive*
Shapiro, Robert Frank *investment banking company executive*
Sherrill, H. Virgil *securities company executive*
Sherva, Dennis G. *investment company executive*
Siebert, Muriel *brokerage house executive, former state banking official*
Simon, Jonathan Paul *equity derivatives trader*
Slotkin, Todd J. *holding company executive, venture capitalist*
Smith, Malcolm Bernard *investment company executive*
Sorte, John Follett *investment firm executive*
Speciale, Richard *investment advisor*
Spielvogel, Sidney Meyer *investment banker*
Spira, Robert Alan *securities company executive*
Steffens, John Laundon *brokerage house executive*
Stein, Bernard *stockbroker*
Stein, David Fred *investment executive*
Steinberg, Saul Phillip *holding company executive*
Stern, James Andrew *investment banker*
Stern, Walter Phillips *investment executive*
Stewart, E(dward) Nicholson *investment management executive*
Stiles, Thomas Beveridge, II *investment banking executive*
Stoddard, George Earl *investment company financial executive*
Straton, John Charles, Jr. *investment banker*
Sulimirski, Witold Stanislaw *banker*
Suskind, Dennis A. *investment banker*
Svenson, Charles Oscar *investment banker*
Swarz, Jeffrey Robert *securities analyst, neuroscientist*
Swensen, J. Scott *investment manager*
Tanner, Harold *investment banker*
Taylor, Richard William *investment banker, securities broker*
Tempelman, Jerry Henry *investment funds trader*
Tenenbaum, Bernard Hirsh *entrepreneur, educator*
Thaler, Richard Winston, Jr. *investment banker*
Tierney, Paul E., Jr. *investment company executive*
Tizzio, Thomas Ralph *brokerage executive*
Towbin, A(braham) Robert *investment banker*
Tozer, W. James, Jr. *investment company executive*
Train, John *investment counselor, writer, government official*
Trapp, Peter Jarl Rudolf *investment banker, farmer*
Treitel, David Henry *financial consultant*
Ule, Guy Maxwell, Jr. *stockbroker*
Van Dine, Vance *investment banker*
Wages, Robert Coleman *equity investor*
Wagner, Donald Arthur *securities group executive*
Walters, Milton James *investment banker*
Wareham, Raymond Noble *investment banker*
Warner, Miner Hill *investment banker*
†Wayner, Richard A. *investment banker, novelist*
Weathersby, George Byron *association management executive*
Webster, John Kimball *investment executive*
Weinberg, John Livingston *investment banker*
Weintz, Jacob Frederick, Jr. *retired investment banker*
Wellin, Keith Sears *investment banker*
Whiting, Gordon James *investment banker*
Whitman, Martin J. *investment banker*
Whitney, Edward Bonner *investment banker*
Wigmore, Barrie Atherton *investment banker*
Williams, Dave Harrell *investment executive*
Wit, Harold Maurice *investment banker, lawyer, investor*
Wizen, Sarabeth Margolis *compliance operations principal*
Wolff, Alexander Nikolaus *writer*
Wolitzer, Steven Barry *investment banker*
Woods, Ward Wilson, Jr. *investment company executive*
Wruble, Brian Frederick *private investor*
Yancey, Richard Charles *investment banker*
Yeager, George Michael *investment counsel executive*
Zeuschner, Erwin Arnold *investment advisory company executive*
Zoullas, Deborah Anne *auction company executive*

Pelham
Niehoff, Karl Richard Besuden *financial executive*

Plainview
McCaffrey, John Anthony *brokerage house executive*

Pleasantville
†Bruckenstein, Joel P. *investment company executive, financial planner*

Rochester
Rulison, Joseph Richard *investment advisor*
Spurrier, Mary Eileen *investment advisor, financial planner*
Whitney, William Gordon *investment management company executive*

Rockville Centre
Rogers, Eugene Charles *retired investment firm executive*

Roslyn Heights
Jaffe, Melvin *securities company executive*

Rye
Gambee, Robert Rankin *investment banker*

Rye Brook
Smethurst, E(dward) William, Jr. *brokerage house executive*

Scarsdale
Abbe, Colman *investment banker*
Stamas, Stephen *investment executive*

Southampton
Atkins, Victor Kennicott, Jr. *investment banker*
Brokaw, Clifford Vail, III *investment banker, business executive*

Syosset
Schiff, Peter Grenville *venture capitalist*

Wainscott
Dubow, Arthur Myron *investor, lawyer*

Wantagh
Zinder, Newton Donald *stock market analyst, consultant*

Warwick
Greenwood, John Edward Douglas *investment banker, lawyer*

Westbury
Fogg, Joseph Graham, III *investment banking executive*

Williamsville
McDuffie, Michael Anthony *investment company executive*

Woodstock
Ober, Stuart Alan *investment consultant, book publisher*

Yonkers
Smith, Aldo Ralston, Jr. *brokerage house executive*

NORTH CAROLINA

Boone
Mackorell, James Theodore, Jr. *entrepreneur, small business owner*

Charlotte
Gay, David Braxton *stockbroker*
Grimaldi, James Thomas *investment fund executive*
Hardin, Thomas Jefferson, II *investment counsel*
May, Benjamin Tallman *securities specialist, administrator*
Prud'homme, Albert Fredric *securities company executive, financial planner*
Ragan, Robert Allison *private investment executive, financial consultant*
Ruff, Edward Carr *investment company executive*

Durham
Scott, Lee Allen, Sr. *securities company executive*

Greensboro
Johnson, Marshall Hardy *investment company executive*

High Point
Phillips, Earl Norfleet, Jr. *financial services executive*

North Wilkesboro
Pardue, Dwight Edward *venture capitalist*

Raleigh
McKinney, Charles Cecil *investment company executive*

Winston Salem
Strickland, Robert Louis *corporations director*

NORTH DAKOTA

Fargo
Tallman, Robert Hall *investment company executive*

OHIO

Alpha
James, Francis Edward, Jr. *investment counselor*

Beachwood
Charnas, Michael (Mannie Charnas) *investment company executive*

Bryan
Oberlin, Earl Clifford, III *securities brokerage company executive*

Cincinnati
Lucke, Robert Vito *merger and acquisition executive*

Cleveland
Brentlinger, Paul Smith *venture capital executive*
Hook, John Burney *investment company executive*
Shepard, Ivan Albert *securities and insurance broker*
Summers, William B. *brokerage house executive*
Swetland, David Wightman *investment company executive*
Warren, Russell James *investment banking executive, consultant*

Columbus
Barthelmas, Ned Kelton *investment and commercial real estate banker*
Hewitt, William Harley *investment and marketing executive*
Pointer, Peter Leon *investment executive*
Roberts, William Eric *investment company executive*

Delaware
Hamre, Gary Leslie William *entrepreneur*

Franklin
Wilkey, Mary Huff *investor, writer, publisher*

Galion
Cobey, Ralph *industrialist*

Hudson
Kempe, Robert Aron *venture management executive*

Kent
Kline, Vicki Ann *investment consultant*

Lancaster
Hurley, Samuel Clay, III *investment management company executive*

Pomeroy
Edwards, John David *investment executive*

Richmond Heights
Acheampong, Robert Kwabena *investment consultant*

Rocky River
O'Brien, John Feighan *investment banker*

Tipp City
†Hogan, John Terry *investment company executive*

Toledo
Geisler, Nathan David *financial consultant*

Westerville
Barr, John Michael *investor, training and management consultant*

OKLAHOMA

Oklahoma City
Munhollon, Samuel Clifford *investment brokerage house executive*

Tulsa
Healey, David Lee *investment company executive*
Neas, John Theodore *investment company executive*
Sanditen, Edgar Richard *investment company executive*

OREGON

Bend
Fain, Jay Lindsey *brokerage house executive, consultant*

Depoe Bay
Fish, Barbara Joan *investor, small business owner*

Lake Oswego
Stewart, Thomas Clifford *trading and investment company executive*

Medford
Hennion, Carolyn Laird (Lyn Hennion) *investment executive*

Portland
Rutherford, William Drake *investment executive, lawyer*

PENNSYLVANIA

Bensalem
Graf, William J. *entrepreneur*

Bethlehem
Stella, John Anthony *investment company executive*

Blue Bell
Giordano, Nicholas Anthony *stock exchange executive*
Gleklen, Donald Morse *investment company executive*

Boothwyn
Bagley, Mark Joseph *investment analyst*

Bryn Mawr
Cannon, John *investment consultant*
Lewis, James Earl *financier*

Camp Hill
Custer, John Charles *investment broker*

Canonsburg
Prado, Gerald M. *investment banker*

Conshohocken
Cheung, Peter Pak Lun *investment company executive, chemistry educator*

Easton
Lear, Floyd Raymond, III *entrepreneur*

Ephrata
Sager, Gilbert Landis *investment company executive*

Erie
Ryan, Gerald Anthony *financial advisor, venture capitalist*

Gladwyne
Geisel, Cameron Meade, Jr. *investment professional*

Havertown
Godwin, Pamela June *financial services executive*

King Of Prussia
Cannon, Lynne Marple *investment management company executive*

Ligonier
Mellon, Seward Prosser *investment executive*

Newtown Square
Turner, George Pearce *consulting company executive*

Paoli
Denny, William Murdoch, Jr. *investment management executive*

Philadelphia
Borer, Edward Turner *investment banker*
Johnson, Craig Norman *investment banker*
Palmer, Russell Eugene *investment executive*
Savitz, Samuel J. *actuarial consulting firm executive*
Simpson, Carol Louise *investment company executive*
Wilde, Norman Taylor, Jr. *investment banking company executive*
Wolitarsky, James William *securities industry executive*
Woosnam, Richard Edward *venture capitalist, lawyer*

Pittsburgh
Casturo, Don James *venture capitalist*
Donahue, John Francis *investment company executive*
Feldman, Robert Elliot *investment company executive*
Fisher, Henry *investment banker*
Hillman, Henry L. *investment company executive*
Hunter, David Wittmer *security brokerage executive*
Hyman, Lewis Neil *investment company executive, investment advisor*
Knapp, George Robert *investment executive, business advisor, lawyer*
Mathieson, Andrew Wray *investment management executive*
Maurer, Richard Michael *investment company executive*
Walton, James M. *investment company executive*
Walton, Joseph Carroll *investor*

Radnor
Buck, James Mahlon, Jr. *venture capital executive*
Humes, Graham *investment banker*

Reading
White, Timothy Paul *brokerage house executive*

Sewickley
Chaplin, James Crossan, IV *securities firm executive*

Valley Forge
Bogle, John Clifton *investment company executive*

Villanova
Lewis, Wayne H. *investment company executive*

West Conshohocken
Miller, Paul Fetterolf, Jr. *retired investment company executive*

Wilkes Barre
Yarmey, Richard Andrew *portfolio manager*

Williamsport
McDonald, Peyton Dean *brokerage house executive*

York
Thornton, George Whiteley *investment company executive*

RHODE ISLAND

Cranston
Langlois, Michael A(rthur) *brokerage house executive*

East Greenwich
Hunter, Garrett Bell *investment banker*

Newport
Stone, Edward Luke *private equity investor, realtor*

Providence
Bogan, Mary Flair *stockbroker*
Joukowsky, Artemis A. W. *private investor*
Manchester, Robert D. *venture capitalist*

SOUTH CAROLINA

Aiken
Hanna, Carey McConnell *securities and investments executive*

Columbia
Gore, David Curtiss *investment banker, consultant*

Greenville
Oxner, Glenn Ruckman *financial executive*

Johns Island
Cameron, Thomas William Lane *investment company executive*

Pawleys Island
Hudson-Young, Jane Smither *investor*

Sullivans Island
Romaine, Henry Simmons *investment consultant*

Taylors
†Frederes, Marshall *stockbroker*

TENNESSEE

Johnson City
Wilkes, Clem Cabell, Jr. *stockbroker*

Knoxville
Barker, Keith Rene *investment banker*
Penn, Dawn Tamara *entrepreneur*

Nashville
Bradford, James C., Jr. *brokerage house executive*
Burch, John Christopher, Jr. *investment banker*
Byrd, Andrew Wayne *investment company executive*
Hanselman, Richard Wilson *entrepreneur*
Kuhn, Paul Hubert, Jr. *investment counsel*
Nelson, Edward Gage *merchant banking investment company executive*
Roberts, Kenneth Lewis *investor, lawyer, foundation administrator*
Sullivan, Allen Trousdale *securities company executive*

Parsons
Franks, Hollis B. *retired investment executive*

TEXAS

Abilene
Owen, Dian Grave *investment corporation executive*

Addison
Smith, Cece *venture capitalist*

Austin
Baumgartner, Robert *consultant*
Inman, Bobby Ray *investor, former electronics executive*

Cibolo
Smith, Harry Leroy *securities firm executive*

Corsicana
Dyer, James Mason, Jr. *investment company executive*

Dallas
Bond, Myron Humphrey *investment executive*
Buchholz, Donald Alden *stock brokerage company executive*
Collins, Michael James *investment company executive*
Crockett, Dodee Frost *brokerage firm executive*

Glatstein, David *investment company executive*
†Hicks, Thomas O. *buyout firm executive, professional baseball team executive*
London, W(illiam) Boyd, Jr. *investment company executive*
Lutes, Benjamin Franklin, Jr. *investor*
McClure, Frederick Donald *investment banker, lawyer*
Parent, David Hill *investment company executive*
Philipson, Herman Louis, Jr. *investment banker*
Whitson, James Norfleet, Jr. *retired diversified company executive*

De Soto
Harrington, Betty Byrd *entrepreneur*

El Paso
Wootten, John Robert *investor*

Fort Worth
Asher, Garland Parker *investment holding company executive*

Garland
McGrath, James Thomas *real estate investment company executive*

Horseshoe Bay
Anderson, Kenneth Ward *investor, consultant*

Houston
Anderson, William (Albion), Jr. *investment banker*
Barrere, Clem Adolph *business brokerage company executive*
Bollich, Elridge Nicholas *investment executive*
Cunningham, R. Walter *venture capitalist*
Currie, John Thornton (Jack Currie) *retired investment banker*
Duncan, Charles William, Jr. *investor, former government official*
Glassell, Alfred Curry, Jr. *investor*
Metzger, Lewis Albert *brokerage house executive, financial consultant*
Neuhaus, Philip Ross *investment banker*
O'Connor, Ralph Sturges *investment company executive*
Page, Ann *stock brokerage executive*
Parsons, Edmund Morris *investment company executive*
Richards, Leonard Martin *investment executive, consultant*
Riesser, Gregor Hans *arbitrage investment advisor*
Williams, Edward Earl, Jr. *entrepreneur, educator*

Lakeway
Boswell, Gary Taggart *investor, former electronics company executive*

Rockport
Morel, Eugene Allen *entrepreneur*

San Antonio
Arnold, Stephen Paul *investment professional*
Duncan, A. Baker *investment banker*
McClane, Robert Sanford *former bank holding company executive, entrepreneur*

Stafford
Franks, Charles Leslie *investments executive*

Texas City
Legan, Robert William *securities analyst*

Waco
†Veselka, Nancy C. *entrepreneur*

UTAH

Provo
Anderson, Mark T. *business developer, entrepreneur, financier*

Riverton
Gaustad, Richard Dale *financier*

Salt Lake City
Ballard, Melvin Russell, Jr. *investment executive, church official*
Brady, Rodney Howard *holding company executive, broadcast company executive, former college president, former government official*
Meldrum, Peter Durkee *venture capital/biotechnology company executive*
Wallace, Matthew Walker *retired entrepreneur*

VERMONT

Quechee
DeRouchey, Beverly Jean *investment company executive*

VIRGINIA

Alexandria
Furash, Edward E. *investment company executive, writer, lecturer*
Hirsch, Robert Louis *energy research-development-management consultant*
Pabarcius, Algis *investment executive*
Rainwater, Joan Lucille Morse *investment company executive*
Richards, Darrie Hewitt *investment company executive*

Arlington
Gregg, David, III *investment banker*
Lampe, Henry Oscar *stockbroker*
Sands, Frank Melville *investment manager*

Charlottesville
Gunter, Bradley Hunt *capital management executive*
Monroe, Brooks *investment banker*
Newman, James Wilson *business executive*

Falls Church
Han, Syung D. *international trade consultant, financier*
Isaac, William Michael *investment firm executive, former government official*

Mc Lean
Searles, Dewitt Richard *retired investment firm executive, retired air force officer*
Smith, Thomas Eugene *investment company executive, financial consultant*

Middleburg
Heckler, John Maguire *stockbroker, investment company executive*
Parkinson, James Thomas, III *investment consultant*

Preston
Biddle, A. G. W., III (Jack Biddle) *venture capitalist*

Reston
†Backus, John Carlton, Jr. *venture capitalist*

Richmond
Binns, Walter Gordon, Jr. *investment management executive*
Gorr, Louis Frederick *investment consultant*
Hong, James Ming *industrialist, venture capitalist*
Phillips, Thomas Edworth, Jr. *financial advisor, senior consultant*
Powell, Kenneth Edward *investment banker*
Rowe, Mae Irene *investment company executive*
Washburn, John Rosser *entrepreneur*

Stanardsville
Anns, Philip Harold *international trading executive, former pharmaceutical company executive*

Williamsburg
Gordon, Baron Jack *stockbroker*
Montgomery, Joseph William *finance company executive*
Roberson, Robert S. *investment company executive*

WASHINGTON

Bellevue
Arnold, Robert Lloyd *investment broker, financial advisor*
Jones, John Wesley *entrepreneur*
Wells-Henderson, Ronald John *investment counselor*

Kirkland
Ryles, Gerald Fay *private investor, business executive*

Redmond
Pacholski, Richard Francis *retired securities company executive, financial advisor, consultant*

Seattle
Alberg, Tom Austin *investment company executive, lawyer*
Bayley, Christopher T. *public affairs consultant*
McAleer, William Harrison *software venture capitalist*
Nelson, Allen F. *investor relations company executive*

Spokane
Fowler, Walton Berry *franchise developer, educator*

Tacoma
Habedank, Gary L. *brokerage house executive*

WISCONSIN

Madison
Chu, Hsien Ming *investment company executive*

Milwaukee
Kasten, G. Frederick, Jr. *investment company executive*
Lubar, Sheldon Bernard *venture capitalist*
Samson, Richard Max *investments and real estate executive*
Schnoll, Howard Manuel *investment banking and managed asset consultant*

Wauwatosa
Ladd, Louise Elizabeth *investments company executive*

West Allis
Mayer, Anthony John *investment company executive*

Zenda
Sills, William Henry, III *investment banker*

WYOMING

Cheyenne
Myers, Rolland Graham *investment counselor*

Wilson
Chrystie, Thomas Ludlow *investor*
Sage, Andrew Gregg Curtin, II *corporate investor, manager*

TERRITORIES OF THE UNITED STATES

PUERTO RICO

Hato Rey
Ferrer, Miguel Antonio *brokerage firm and investment bank executive*

San Juan
Uribe, Javier Miguel *investment executive*

CANADA

ALBERTA

Calgary
Cumming, Thomas Alexander *stock exchange executive*
Seaman, Donald Roy *investment company executive*

BRITISH COLUMBIA

Vancouver
Belzberg, Samuel *investment professional*
Budzinsky, Armin Alexander *investment banker*
Harwood, Brian Dennis *securities industry executive*
Saunders, Peter Paul *investor*

MANITOBA

Winnipeg
Alexander, Norman James *investment consultant*
Watchorn, William Ernest *venture capitalist*

NOVA SCOTIA

Bedford
Hennigar, David John *investment broker*

ONTARIO

Chatham
McKeough, William Darcy *investment company executive*

Oakville
Holmes, James *investment company executive*

Toronto
Bloomberg, Lawrence S. *securities executive, art collector*
†Bloomberg, Lawrence S. *securities executive, art collector*
Hore, John Edward *commodity futures educator*
Lindsay, Roger Alexander *investment executive*
Petrillo, Leonard Philip *corporate securities executive, lawyer*
Weston, Sr., W. Galen *diversified holdings executive*

QUEBEC

Montreal
Cedraschi, Tullio *investment management company executive*
Elie, Jean André *investment banker*
Schwartz, Roy Richard *holding company executive*
Torrey, David Leonard *investment banker*

MEXICO

Cabo San Lucas
Morrow, James Thomas *investment banker, financial executive*

BAHAMAS

Nassau
Templeton, John Marks *investment counsel, financial analyst*

BERMUDA

Tuckers Town
Heizer, Edgar Francis, Jr. *venture capitalist*

BRAZIL

Sao Paulo
Leighton, Robert Bruce *investment company executive*

CHINA

Beijing
Melville, Richard Allen *investment company executive*

Hong Kong
Chun, Wendy Sau Wan *investment company executive*

ENGLAND

London
Hale, Charles Martin *stockbroker*
Hayden, Richard Michael *investment banker*
Jourdren, Marc Henri *investment banking company executive*
Keevil, Philip Clement *investment banker*
Mulford, David Campbell *finance company executive*
Solberg, Ronald Louis *investment banker, fixed-income strategist*

GERMANY

Moglingen
Meyberg, Bernhard Ulrich *entrepreneur*

IRELAND

Dublin
Montle, Paul Joseph *entrepreneur*

MONGOLIA

Ulaanbaatar
Mandel, Leslie Ann *investment advisor, business owner, author*

NIGERIA

Lagos
†Omole, Gabriel Gbolabo *international venture capitalist*

SOUTH AFRICA

Marshalltown
Chen, Philip Minkang *investment banker, corporate executive, lawyer, engineer*

SWITZERLAND

Geneva
Berger, Andrew L. *investment banker, lawyer*

Lausanne
Bloemsma, Marco Paul *investor*

ADDRESS UNPUBLISHED

Ackerman, Melvin *investment company executive*
Aljian, James Donovan *investment company executive*
†Allen, Herbert *investment banker*
Anderson, Mary Theresa *investment manager*
Apel-Brueggeman, Myrna L. *entrepreneur*
Armstrong, Michael David *investment banker*
Arp Lotter, Donna *investor, venture capitalist*
Auerbach, Jonathan Louis *securities trader*
Aurin, Robert James *entrepreneur*
Bacharach, Melvin Lewis *retired venture capitalist*
Bailey, Rita Maria *investment advisor, psychologist*
Bansak, Stephen A., Jr. *investment banker, financial consultant*
Bantry, Bryan *entrepreneur, producer, director*
Birnbaum, Stevan Allen *investment company executive*
Black, Richard Bruce *business executive, consultant*
Blum, Barbara Davis *investor*
Bondarenko, Hesperia Aura Louis *entrepreneur*
Bowles, Barbara Landers *investment company executive*
Bratt, Nicholas *investment management and research company executive*
Brosda, Alexander Christian *investment banker*
Brown, Samuel *retired corporate executive*
†Burkett, Robert L. *investment company executive*
Burks, Jack D. *investment executive*
Burns, Donald Snow *registered investment advisor, financial and business consultant*
Callard, David Jacobus *private equity investor*
Campbell, William Yates *investment banker*
Carr, Harold Noflet *investment corporation executive*
†Chin, Tanya Jade *policy analyst*
Cockrum, William Monroe, III *investment banker, consultant, educator*
Coleman, Leon Horn *real estate investor*
†Coolidge, Anne R. *investment company executive*
Cooper, James Hayes Shofner (Jim Cooper) *investment company executive, former congressman, lawyer*
Czarnecki, Gerald Milton *investment banking and venture capital*
Davies, Michael S. *security analyst*
Doherty, Charles Vincent *investment counsel executive*
Dorland, Dodge Oatwell *investment advisor*
Drake, Rodman Leland *investment company executive, consultant*
Dunn, John Raymond, Jr. *stockbroker*
Duval, Michael Raoul *investment banker*
Dwyer, Charles Breen *arbitrage and Eurobond specialist*
Emmett, Rita *professional speaker*
Falker, John Richard *investment advisor*
FitzAlan-Howard, Bennett-Thomas Henry Robert *consultant, public administration and policy analyst, political theorist*
Frank, Judith Ann (Jann Frank) *retired entrepreneur, small business owner*
Frankenberger, Bertram, Jr. *investor, consultant*
Friedlander, Charles Douglas *space consultant*
Froehlke, Robert Frederick *financial services executive*
Fuld, Richard Severin, Jr. *investment banker*
Geissinger, Frederick Wallace *investment banking executive*
Glasberg, Laurence Brian *private investor, business executive*
Goldman, Alan Ira *investment banking executive*
Good, Walter Raymond *investment executive*
Goyan, Michael Donovan *stockbroker, investment executive*
Graffis, Julie Anne *entrepreneur, retail consultant, interior designer*
Greene, Frank Sullivan, Jr. *investment management executive*
Groezinger, Leland Becker, Jr. *investment professional*
Haber, Warren H. *investment company executive*
Hambrecht, William R. *retired venture capitalist*
Hansen, Hal T. *investment company executive*
Hapner, Mary Lou *securities trader and dealer*
Hays, Thomas Chandler *holding company executive*
Heine, Leonard M., Jr. *investment executive*
Hentic, Yves Frank Mao *investment banker, industrial engineer*
Hickey, Joseph Michael *investment banker*
Hochheimer, Frank Leo *brokerage executive*
Howard, James Webb *investment banker, lawyer, engineer*
Hudson, Donald J. *retired stock exchange executive*

Ihlanfeldt, William *investment company executive, consultant*
Jaenike, William F. *retired investment company executive*
Jepson, Robert Scott, Jr. *international investment banking specialist*
Johnson, Michael Warren *international relations specialist*
Kahn, Herta Hess (Mrs. Howard Kahn) *retired stockbroker*
Kain, Rikki Floyd *investment company executive*
Kapor, Mitchell David *venture capitalist*
Kawano, James Conrad *investment analyst*
Kotler, Steven *investment banker*
Lafair, Theodore *investment company executive, financial consultant*
Landis, Robert Kumler, III *investment banker, lawyer*
Landsman, Richard *investment company executive, finance educator*
Lee, David Stoddart *retired investment counselor*
Lohrer, Richard Baker *investment consultant*
Loucks, Ralph Bruce, Jr. *investment company executive*
Luke, Douglas Sigler *business executive*
Lynch, Thomas Peter *securities executive*
Marks, Leonard, Jr. *retired corporate executive*
Marler, Larry John *private investor, leadership consultant*
Mascheroni, Eleanor Earle *investment company executive*
Mc Gill, Archie Joseph *venture capitalist*
McNeill, Robert Patrick *investment counselor*
McRae, Thomas Kenneth *retired investment company executive*
Mendez, Albert Orlando *industrialist, financier*
Merk, Elizabeth Thole *investment company executive*
Mikitka, Gerald Peter *investment banker, financial consultant*
Miller, Alan Jay *financial consultant, author*
Miller, Ross M. *financial services company executive*
Millsaps, Fred Ray *investor*
Moran, Charles A. *securities executive*
Morgenroth, Earl Eugene *entrepreneur*
Myers, John Herman *investment management executive*
Nilsson, A. Kenneth *investor*
Nowaczek, Frank Huxley *venture capital executive*
Pauken, Thomas Weir *venture capital executive, lawyer, mediator*
Paup, Martin Arnold *real estate and securities investor*
Peters, Ralph Frew *investment banker*
Pool, Philip Bemis, Jr. *investment banker*
Price, William James, IV *investment banker*
†Rachlin, Ellen Joan *retired securities company executive*
Renouf, Anne *technology commercialization financier*
Robertson, Mark Wayne *investment specialist*
Robinson, Annettmarie *entrepreneur*
Robinson, Bob Leo *retired international investment service executive*
Roehm, MacDonell, Jr. *retail executive*
Roland, Catherine Dixon *entrepreneur*
Scharff, Monroe Bernard *investor relations consultant*
Sells, Boake Anthony *private investor*
Shinn, George Latimer *investment banker, consultant, educator*
Shuler, Jon Emmett *securities industry professional*
Sojka, Sandra Kay *investor, livestock conservator*
Spangler, Scott Michael *retired private investor*
Stanfill, Dennis Carothers *business executive*
Stansell, Ronald Bruce *investment banker*
Steen, Carlton Duane *private investor, former food company executive*
Svikhart, Edwin Gladdin *investment banker*
Swanberg, Edmund Raymond *investment counselor*
Tansor, Robert Henry *investor*
Urciuoli, J. Arthur *investment executive*
Vincent, Bruce Havird *investment banker, oil and gas company executive*
Ward, Anthony G. *stock, options and futures exchange consultant*
Washburn, Dorothy A. *entrepreneur*
Weisman, Lorenzo David *investment banker*
West, Warren Henry *securities trader*
White-Vondran, Mary-Ellen *retired stockbroker*
†Williams, Jeffrey P. *investment banker*
Wirth, Russell D. L., Jr. *investment and merchant banker*
Zahrt, Merton Stroebel *investor*
Zarb, Frank Gustave *investment executive*

FINANCE: REAL ESTATE

UNITED STATES

ALABAMA

Albertville
†Patterson, Jeffery Allen *realtor*

Anniston
Landholm, Dawn Renae *land use planner*

Arab
Hammond, Ralph Charles *real estate executive*

Birmingham
Copeland, Hunter Armstrong *real estate executive*
Ingram, Margi *real estate broker*

Mobile
Perkins, Marie McConnell *real estate executive*

Montgomery
Cassels, Martha Beasley *realtor, developer*

Pelham
Liu, Sarah Jo *urban planner*

Saraland
Smith, Paul Lowell *realtor, minister*

ALASKA

Anchorage
Faulkner, Sewell Ford *real estate executive*
Kelly, Maxine Ann *retired property developer*

Girdwood
†Trauter, John James *real estate executive*

ARIZONA

Cottonwood
Izzo, Mary Alice *real estate broker*

Mesa
McCollum, Alvin August *real estate company executive*

Peoria
Morrison, Manley Glenn *real estate investor, former army officer*

Phoenix
Clements, John Robert *real estate professional*
†Gronseth, Daniel Edward *park ranger*
Lewis, Orme, Jr. *investment company executive, land use advisor*
Montague, Sidney James *real estate developer*
Rau, David Edward *real estate company executive*
Snare, Carl Lawrence, Jr. *business executive*
Woods, Donald Peter *real estate executive, marketing professional*

Prescott
†Anderson, Walter Lee *environmental educator, artist, photographer*
Martinez, Anthony Joseph *real estate appraiser*

Scottsdale
Garling, Carol Elizabeth *real estate executive and developer*
†Grogan, James J. *real estate company executive*

Sun City
Lutin, David Louis *real estate development and finance consultant*

Tucson
Best, Gary Thorman *commercial real estate broker*
Bodinson, Holt *conservationist*
Irvin, Mark Christopher *real estate consultant, broker and developer*
Lehrling, Terry James *real estate broker*
Longan, George Baker, III *real estate executive*

West Sedona
Lane, Margaret Anna Smith *property manager developer*

ARKANSAS

Bella Vista
Cooper, John Alfred, Jr. *community development company executive*

Fayetteville
Jackson, Robert Lee *real estate agent*

Fort Smith
Taylor, James Lynn (Jimmie Taylor) *real estate executive*

Hot Springs National Park
Craft, Kay Stark *real estate broker*

Jonesboro
Peters, Mary Helen *real estate agent*

Little Rock
McConnell, John Wesley *real estate-resort developer, corporate executive*

CALIFORNIA

Apple Valley
Ledford, Gary Alan *real estate developer*

Arcadia
Freedman, Gregg *real estate appraisal company executive*

Belmont
†Keller, Eric Trent *real estate manager*

Belvedere Tiburon
Caselli, Virgil P. *real estate executive*

Berkeley
Grimes, Ruth Elaine *city planner*
Wachs, Martin *urban planning educator, author, consultant*
Worrell, Ernst *energy and environmental analyst, researcher*

Beverly Hills
†Glazer, Guilford *real estate developer*
Seeger, Melinda Wayne *realtor*
Shapell, Nathan *financial and real estate executive*
Tamkin, Curtis Sloane *real estate development company executive*
Victor, Robert Eugene *real estate corporation executive, lawyer*

Brentwood
Albers, Lucia Berta *land developer*

Burbank
Garcia, Daniel P. *real estate manager*

Campbell
Nicholson, Joseph Bruce *real estate developer*

Cypress
Osgood, Frank William *urban and economic planner, writer*

Diamond Bar
Gong, Carolyn Lei Chu *real estate agent*

El Macero
Wheeler, Douglas Paul *conservationist, government official, lawyer*

Fair Oaks
Yarrigle, Charlene Sandra Shuey *realtor, investment counselor*

Fountain Valley
Smith, Marie Edmonds *real estate agent, property manager*

Fresno
Donaldson, George Burney *environmental consultant*

Glendale
Bitterman, Melvin Lee *real estate developer*

Goleta
Koart, Nellie Hart *real estate investor and executive*

Grass Valley
Ozanich, Charles George *real estate broker*

Hemet
Coad, Dennis Lawrence *real estate broker*

Huntington Beach
Jackle, Karen Dee *real estate executive*

Irvine
Chronley, James Andrew *real estate executive*
Stack, Geoffrey Lawrence *real estate developer*
Tully, John Peter *land use planner*
Wiley, Matthew Forrest *real estate broker*

Jackson
Steele, John Roy *real estate broker*

La Habra
Lundberg, Lois Ann *political consultant, property manager executive*

La Jolla
Anthony, Harry Antoniades *city planner, architect, educator*
Foley, L(ewis) Michael *real estate executive*
Ripley, Stuart McKinnon *real estate consultant*

La Mesa
Ligon, Patti-Lou E. *real estate investor, educator*

Lafayette
Peters, Ray John *surveyor*

Laguna Beach
Hanauer, Joe Franklin *real estate executive*

Laguna Niguel
York, James Orison *real estate executive*

Lancaster
Roths, Beverly Owen *organization executive*

Long Beach
MeGann, John Milton *real estate executive*
Rosenberg, Jill *realtor, civic leader*

Los Angeles
Abernethy, Robert John *real estate developer*
Bergman, Nancy Palm *real estate investment company executive*
Best, Roger Norman *inventor, real estate manager, consultant*
Furlotti, Alexander Amato *real estate development company executive*
†Green, Richard E. *real estate company executive*
Linsk, Michael Stephen *real estate executive*
Nelson, James Augustus, II *real estate executive, architect, banker*
Schnebelen, Pierre *resort planner and developer, consultant*
Swartz, Roslyn Holt *real estate investment executive*
West, Robert Johnson *appraisal company executive*

Manhattan Beach
Schoenfeld, Lawrence Jon *real estate developer, asset lender*

Menlo Park
Fischer, Michael Ludwig *environmental executive*
Goodman, Beatrice May *real estate professional*

Mission Viejo
Harris, Ruby Lee *realtor*

Moorpark
Bush, June Lee *real estate executive*

National City
Potter, J(effrey) Stewart *property manager*

Newbury Park
Fredericks, Patricia Ann *real estate executive*

Newport Beach
Bren, Donald L. *real estate company executive*
Fawcett, John Scott *real estate developer*
Kenney, William John, Jr. *real estate development executive*
McClune, Michael Marlyn *real estate executive*
Mink, Maxine Mock *real estate executive*
Tow, Marc Raymond *lawyer, real estate investor*

North Hollywood
Schultz, Phyllis May *financial property manager*

Oakland
Anthony, Elaine Margaret *real estate executive, interior designer*

Ontario
Ariss, David William, Sr. *real estate developer, consultant*

Palm Desert
Wiedle, Gary Eugene *real estate management company executive*

Palmdale
Anderson, R(obert) Gregg *real estate company executive*

Palo Alto
Wong, Y(ing) Wood *real estate investment company executive, venture capital investment company executive*

Pasadena
Crowley, John Crane *real estate developer*
Van Karnes, Kathleen Walker *realtor*

Placerville
Burnett, Eric Stephen *environmental consultant*
Craib, Kenneth Bryden *resource development executive, physicist, economist*

Rancho Santa Fe
Kessler, A. D. *business, financial, investment and real estate advisor, consultant, lecturer, author, broadcaster, producer*

Rolling Hills Estates
Allbee, Sandra Moll *real estate broker*

Rough And Ready
Nix, Barbara Lois *real estate broker*

Sacramento
Lukenbill, Gregg *real estate developer, sports promoter*
Oliva, Stephen Edward *resource conservationist, lawyer*

San Bernardino
Willis, Harold Wendt, Sr. *real estate developer*

San Diego
Davis, James McCoy *real estate executive*
†Herzog, Lawrence Arthur *city planning educator*
Mc Comic, Robert Barry *real estate development company executive, lawyer*

San Fernando
Aguilar, Julia Elizabeth *real estate associate, writer*

San Francisco
Bracken, Thomas Robert James *real estate investment executive*
Brower, David Ross *conservationist*
Freund, Fredric S. *real estate broker, property manager*
Shorenstein, Walter Herbert *commercial real estate development company executive*

San Jose
Rothblatt, Donald Noah *urban and regional planner, educator*

San Juan Capistrano
Hough, J. Marie *real estate company official*

San Luis Obispo
Hempenius, Gerald Edward *real estate broker*

San Marino
Grantham, Richard Robert *real estate company consultant*

San Rafael
Roulac, Stephen E. *real estate consultant*

Santa Ana
Danoff-Kraus, Pamela Sue *shopping center development executive*

Santa Barbara
Arnold, Michael Neal *real property appraiser, consultant*

Santa Cruz
Dilbeck, Charles Stevens, Jr. *real estate company executive*
Hersley, Dennis Charles *environmentalist, software systems consultant*

Sausalito
Klingensmith, Arthur Paul *business and personal development consultant*
Klotsche, Charles Martin *real estate development company executive, writer*

Tracy
Dittman, Deborah Ruth *real estate broker*

Tustin
Pauley, Richard Heim *real estate counselor*
Prizio, Betty J. *property manager, civic worker*

Twain Harte
Kinsinger, Robert Earl *property company executive, educational consultant*

Upland
Lewis, Goldy Sarah *real estate developer, corporation executive*

Venice
†Mikesekk, Richard Hugh *real estate*

Vista
Cavanaugh, Kenneth Clinton *retired housing consultant*

Watsonville
†Eadie, Charles D. *city planner, consultant, writer*

West Hills
Struhl, Stanley Frederick *real estate developer*

Westminster
†Reasonover, Robert Pretceille (Huy-manh Nguyen) *real estate broker, educator*

Yorba Linda
Vilardi, Agnes Francine *real estate broker*

COLORADO

Aurora
Lochmiller, Kurtis L. *real estate entrepreneur*

Boulder
Clifford, Lawrence M. *real estate company executive*
Hammell, Grandin Gaunt *real estate consultant*
Morris, John Theodore *planning official*
Stepanek, Joseph Edward *industrial development consultant*

Breckenridge
O'Reilly, Thomas Mark *real estate executive*

Colorado Springs
Bowers, Zella Zane *real estate broker*
Bruce, Douglas E. *real estate investor*
Christensen, C(harles) Lewis *real estate developer*

Denver
Mugler, Larry George *regional planner*
Norman, John Edward *petroleum landman*

Englewood
Ellsworth, Joseph Cordon *real estate executive, lawyer*
Smyth, David Shannon *real estate investor, commercial and retail builder and developer*

Fort Collins
Driscoll, Richard Stark *land use planner*
Frink, Eugene Hudson, Jr. *business and real estate consultant*

Golden
Sacks, Arthur Bruce *environmental and liberal arts educator*

Grand Junction
Nelsor, Paul William *real estate broker*

Lakewood
Keatinge, Cornelia Wyma *architectural preservationist consultant, lawyer*

Pueblo
Heizer, Ida Ann *retired real estate broker*

Snowmass
Lovins, L. Hunter *public policy institute executive*

CONNECTICUT

Berlin
Carroll, Adorna Occhialini *real estate executive*

Bethel
Kurfehs, Harold Charles *real estate executive*

Bridgeport
Ciszak, Lynn Marie *city planner*
Despres, Robert Leon *urban planner*
Schwartz, James Peter *real estate broker*

Danbury
Anderson, Alan Reinold *real estate executive, communications consultant*

East Hartford
Bonin, Paul Joseph *real estate and banking executive*

Fairfield
Beers, Anne Cole *real estate broker*

Greenwich
Gottlieb, Lester M. *entrepreneur*
Lee, Lloyd Eng-Meng *real estate private equity investment*
Urstadt, Charles J. *real estate executive*

Ledyard
Haase, William R., IV *urban planner*

New Haven
Alexander, Bruce Donald *real estate executive, educator*
Harrison, Henry Starin *real estate educator, entrepreneur*

New London
Langfield, Raymond Lee *real estate developer*

Newtown
Pilchard, Melissa Meyer *realtor, appraiser*

North Haven
Pearce, Herbert Henry *real estate company executive*

Norwalk
†Brooks, Torrey D. *real estate executive*

Plymouth
Hall, William Smith, Jr. *land surveyor*

Stamford
Koproski, Alexander Robert *real estate executive*

Stratford
Chase, J. Vincent *shopping center executive, justice of the peace*

Trumbull
Renz, William Franklin *real estate investor*

Waterbury
†Ogrodnik, Lana Kathleen *real estate broker*

DELAWARE

Dover
Taylor, Suzonne Berry Stewart *real estate broker*

Newark
Byrne, John Michael *energy and environmental policy educator, researcher*
†Wilder, Margaret G. *urban policy educator*

Rehoboth Beach
Truitt, Suzanne *real estate broker*

Wilmington
Lerner, Alfred *real estate and financial executive*
Maley, Patricia Ann *preservation planner*
†Thomes, Harry Scott *real estate consultant*

DISTRICT OF COLUMBIA

Washington
†Bennett, Douglas Philip *real estate executive, lawyer*
Blackwelder, Brent Francis *environmentalist*
Blair, William Draper, Jr. *conservationist*
McMahon, Neil Michael *real estate executive*
Meyer, Alden Merrill *environmental association executive*
Oge, Margo Tsirigotis *environmentalist*
Osgood, Barbara Travis *conservationist, sociologist*
Reardon, Pearl Rance *real estate executive, writer*
†Rymland, Richard Sylvan *real estate developer*
Soule, Jeffrey Lyn *urban planner, consultant*
Stegman, Michael Allen *city and regional planning educator*
Stollman, Israel *city planner*
Stone, Roger David *environmentalist*
Wehe, David Carl *real estate developer*

FLORIDA

Arcadia
Schmidt, Harold Eugene *real estate company executive*

Boca Raton
Borg, Dean Jeremy *real estate developer*
Carr-Allen, Elizabeth *real estate and mortgage broker, metaphysician*
†Goray, Gerald Allen *investor, business executive, lawyer*
Hersh, Sid *real estate developer*
Innes-Brown, Georgette Meyer *real estate and insurance broker*
Konrad, Agnes Crossman *retired real estate agent, retired educator*
Lagin, Neil *landscape designer, consultant*
Siegel, Ned Lawrence *real estate developer*

Bradenton
Prettyman, Jon Allison *urban planner*

Cedar Key
Starnes, Earl Maxwell *urban and regional planner, architect*

Clearwater
Wyllie, Alfred Linn *real estate broker, mortgage broker*

Cocoa
Papa, Michael Joseph *real estate broker*

Coral Gables
Blumberg, Philip Flayderman *real estate developer*
Stover, James Howard *real estate executive*

Dade City
Currier, Douglas Gilfillan, II *urban planner*

Daytona Beach
Hastings, Mary Lynn *real estate broker*
Perschmann, Lutz Ingo *property manager, real estate consultant*

Deland
Caccamise, Alfred Edward *real estate executive*
Tedros, Theodore Zaki *educator, real estate broker, appraiser*

Dunnellon
Sawick, Karen Ann *real estate salesperson*

Fort Lauderdale
Bird, Linda W. *realtor*
Cummings, Virginia (Jeanne) *retired real estate company executive*
Moraitis, Karen Karl *real estate broker*
Wietor, Michael George *real estate executive, commodity trading advisor, export purchasing agent*

Fort Myers
Heath, Glenn Edward *planner*
†Wassersug, Stephen Robert *environmental consultant*

Fort Walton Beach
Cooke, Fred Charles *real estate broker*

Gainesville
Nozzi, Dom *urban planner*
Stein, Jay M. *planning and design educator, consultant*
York, Vermelle Cardwell *real estate broker and developer*

Gulf Breeze
Jenkins, Robert Berryman *real estate developer*

Jacksonville
Parker, David Forster *real estate development consultant*
Pearce, Jennifer Sue *real estate appraiser*
Sibley, Richard Carl *real estate executive*

Jupiter
Mutters, David Ray *real estate broker*

Key West
Green, Sandra Staap *mortgage broker, real estate appraiser*

Lakeland
Smith, Levie David, Jr. *real estate appraiser, consultant*

Lantana
Weeks, Charles, Jr. *real estate executive, retired publishing company executive*

Longboat Key
Black, Martin Patrick *urban planner*

Longwood
Gasperoni, Emil, Sr. *realtor, developer*

Maitland
Vallee, Judith Delaney *environmentalist, writer, fundraiser*

Marathon
Davidson, Ed *tour operator*

Marco Island
Genrich, Judith Ann *real estate executive*
Llewellyn, Leonard Frank *real estate broker*

Melbourne
Evans, Arthur Forte *real estate developer*
Glindeman, Henry Peter, Jr. *real estate developer*

Miami
Glogower, Michael Howard *public housing senior functional specialist*
Guerra, Roland *regional property manager*
Lopez-Munoz, Maria Rosa P. *land development company executive*
Nestor Castellano, Brenda Diana *real estate executive*
Norton, Susan Marlene *real estate agent*
Raffel, Leroy B. *real estate development company executive*
Salvaneschi, Luigi *real estate and development executive, business educator*
Taylor, Adam David *real estate executive*

Naples
Corkran, Virginia B. *realtor*
Evans, Elizabeth Ann West *retired realtor*

Niceville
Rasmussen, Robert Dee *real estate appraiser*

North Miami
Markson, Daniel Ben *real estate developer, consultant, syndicator*

Ocala
Booth, Jane Schuele *real estate broker, executive*

Orlando
†Bailey, William Ray *transportation planner*
Watson, Barry Lee *real estate and mortgage broker, investor, contractor, builder, developer*

Palm Beach
Bagby, Martha L. Green *real estate holding company, novelist, publisher*
Shepherd, Charles Clinton *real estate executive*

Palmetto
Rains, Gloria Cann *environmentalist company executive*

Plantation
Lehman, Joan Alice *real estate executive*

Ponte Vedra
Davis, Kim McAlister *real estate sales executive, real estate broker*
Moore, Philip Walsh *appraisal company executive*

Port Charlotte
Wall, Edward Millard *environmental consulting executive*

Punta Gorda
Beever, Lisa Britt-Dodd *transportation and environmental planner, researcher*
Graham, William Aubrey, Jr. *real estate broker*

Saint Pete Beach
Hurley, Frank Thomas, Jr. *realtor*

Saint Petersburg
Baiman, Gail *real estate broker*
Layton, William George *management consultant, human resources executive, export-import executive*
Rummel, Harold Edwin *real estate development executive*
Smyth, Walter G. *real estate broker*
VanButsel, Michael R. *real estate broker and developer*

Sanibel
Courtney, James Edmond *real estate developer*

Sarasota
Bennett, Lois *real estate broker*
Byron, E. Lee *real estate broker*
Scheitlin, Constance Joy *real estate broker*
Tate, Manley Sidney *real estate broker*

Sebastian
Muller, Henry John *real estate developer*

Sebring
Sherrick, Daniel Noah *real estate broker*

Starke
†Solze, Richard C. *real estate appraiser*

Sunrise
Cronin, Mary Haag *real estate referral agent*

Tallahassee
Doan, Petra Leisenring *urban planner, educator*
Johnson, Benjamin F., VI *real estate developer, consulting economist*
Lisenby, Dorrece Edenfield *realtor*
Morgan, Constance Louise *real estate executive*
Tookes, James Nelson *real estate investment company executive*

Tampa
Corbitt, Doris Orene *real estate agent, dietitian*
Purcell, Henry, III *real estate developer*

Titusville
Shafer, Lorene Leggitt *real esate agent*

Valrico
Parrado, Peter Joseph *real estate executive*

Weston
Austin, Grant William *real estate appraiser*

Winter Park
Strawn, Frances Freeland *real estate executive*

GEORGIA

Atlanta
†Adams, Corey Emile *planner, analyst*
Adams, David Porterfield, III *business appraiser*
Bragdon, Katherine McCoy *urban planner, civilian military employee*
Comstock, Robert Donald, Jr. *real estate executive*
Cupp, Robert Erhard *golf course architect, land use planner*
Curtis, Philip Kerry *real estate developer*
Glover, John Trapnell *real estate executive*
Raines, Tim D. *real estate corporation executive*
Regenstein, Lewis Graham *conservationist, author, lecturer, speech writer*
Simpson, Allan Boyd *real estate company executive*
Winchester, Jesse Gregory *commercial real estate company executive*
Wolbrink, James Francis *real estate investor*

Augusta
Mayberry, Julius Eugene *realty company owner, investor*

Bainbridge
†Provence, Daniel Joseph *realtor, farmer*

Carrollton
Dunnavant, Tracy Lynn *planning administrator*

College Park
Charania, Barkat *real estate consultant*

Folkston
Crumbley, Esther Helen Kendrick *realtor, retired secondary education educator*

Gainesville
Gravitt, Nancy Canup *realtor*

Indian Springs
Lamb, Deryle Jean *preservationist*

Marietta
Cline, Robert Thomas *retired land developer*

Savannah
Cadle, Farris William *land title abstractor*

Scottdale
Borochoff, Ida Sloan *real estate executive, artist*

Suwanee
Colgan, George Phillips *real estate developer, real estate analyst*

Toccoa
Maypole, John Floyd *real estate holding company executive*

HAWAII

Honolulu
Baker, Helen Doyle Peil *realtor*
Gillmar, Jack Notley Scudder *real estate company executive*
Luke, Lance Lawton *real estate and construction consultant*
Olsen, Harris Leland *real estate and international business executive, educator, diplomat*

Koloa
Cobb, Rowena Noelani Blake *real estate broker*

IDAHO

Boise
Jones, Donna Marilyn *real estate broker, legislator*

Idaho Falls
Thorsen, Nancy Dain *real estate broker*
Williams, Phyllis Cutforth *retired realtor*

Stanley
Kimpton, David Raymond *natural resource consultant, writer*

Troy
Hepler, Merlin Judson, Jr. *real estate broker*

ILLINOIS

Aurora
Stephens, Steve Arnold *real estate broker*

Barrington
Fowler, Susan Michele *real estate broker, entrepreneur*

Buffalo Grove
Shields, Patrick Thomas, Jr. *retired property manager*

Champaign
Guttenberg, Albert Ziskind *planning educator*

Chicago
Amato, Isabella Antonia *real estate executive*
Beban, Gary Joseph *real estate corporation officer*
Benson, Sara Elizabeth *real estate broker, real estate appraiser*
Bohn, Charlotte Galitz *retired real estate executive*
Bynoe, Peter Charles Bernard *real estate developer, lawyer*
Campbell, Gavin Elliott *real estate investor and developer*
Daley, Vincent Raymond, Jr. *real estate executive, consultant*
Daly, Patrick F. *real estate executive, architect*
Field, Karen Ann (Karen Ann Schaffner) *real estate broker*
Galowich, Ronald Howard *real estate investment executive, venture capitalist*
Geoga, Douglas Gerard *real estate development company executive, lawyer*
Gerbie, S. Ralph *real estate executive, property investor*
Good, Sheldon Fred *realtor*
Hayes, Jacqueline Crement *real estate broker and developer*
Kelly, Robert Francis *real estate consultant*
Kramer, Anthony Ferdinand *real estate company executive*
Lapidus, Dennis *real estate developer*
Matanky, James E. *real estate developer*
†Michaels, Robert A. *real estate development company executive*
Morrill, R. Layne *real estate broker, executive, professional association administrator*
Pappas, Philip James *real estate company executive*
Reschke, Michael W. *real estate executive*
Rowe, Randall Keith *real estate executive*
Rubenstein, Eric Davis *real estate executive*
Schwab, James Charles *urban planner*
†Skoien, Gary *real estate company executive*
†Spoerri, Robert C. *real estate company executive*
Strobeck, Charles LeRoy *real estate executive*
Totlis, Gust John *retired title insurance company executive*
Travis, Dempsey Jerome *real estate executive, mortgage banker*
Wirtz, William Wadsworth *real estate and sports executive*
Wood Prince, William Norman *investments and real estate professional*

Deerfield
Barker, Barbara *real estate professional*

Dundee
Ulakovich, Ronald Stephen *real estate developer*

Hinsdale
Nibeck, Susan Nelson *real estate sales agent*
Stastny, John Anton *real estate executive*

Lake Zurich
Schultz, Carl Herbert *real estate management and development company executive*

Libertyville
O'Leary, Timothy Francis *real estate developer*

Long Grove
Van Der Bosch, Susan Hartnett *real estate broker*

Macomb
Maguire, Dave *real estate owner, manager*

Normal
Bender, Paul E. *title insurance executive*

Northbrook
†D'Arcy, Thomas P. *real estate company executive*
Levy, Arnold S(tuart) *real estate company executive*
Michna, Andrea Stephanie *real estate consultant and developer*

Northfield
Kleinman, Burton Howard *real estate investor*
Stein, Paula Jean Anne Barton *hotel real estate consultant*

O'Fallon
Cecil, Dorcas Ann *property management executive*
Ottwein, Merrill William George *real estate company executive, veterinarian*

Oak Brook
Goodwin, Daniel L. *real estate company executive*
Wheeler, Paul James *real estate executive*

Ottawa
Breipohl, Walter Eugene *real estate broker*

Peoria
Rushford, Eloise Johnson *land manager*

Plainfield
Fichter, David Harry *conservationist, environmentalist*

Rockford
Hart, Jay Albert Charles *retired real estate broker*

Rosemont
Jenkins, Walter Donald *real estate executive*

Saint Charles
Urhausen, James Nicholas *real estate developer, construction executive*

Schaumburg
Barrett, Jeffrey Scott *real estate company executive*

Spring Valley
Crowley, Michael Ryan *real estate appraiser/analyst, educator*

Springfield
†Golemo, Timothy Franklin *urban planner*

Wilmette
Eigel, Christopher John *real estate executive*

INDIANA

Bloomington
Blankenfeld, Beverly (B. J. Blankenfeld) *real estate professional*

Carmel
McCool, Richard Bunch *real estate developer*

Evansville
Matthews, C(harles) David *real estate appraiser, consultant*

Fort Wayne
Hirschy, Gordon Harold *real estate agent, auctioneer*

Indianapolis
Borns, Robert Aaron *real estate developer*
Frisch, Fred I. *real estate executive*
Jewett, John Rhodes *real estate executive*
Knapp, Madonna Faye *property manager, administrator*
Mullen, Thomas Edgar *real estate consultant*
Simon, David *real estate company officer*
Sokolov, Richard Saul *real estate company executive*

Jeffersonville
Reisert, Charles Edward, Jr. *real estate executive*

Lafayette
Shook, James Creighton *real estate executive*

Newburgh
Tierney, Gordon Paul *real estate broker, genealogist*

Terre Haute
Perry, Eston Lee *real estate and equipment leasing company executive*

IOWA

Ankeny
Nash, John J(oseph) *real estate manager, computer programmer*

Cedar Rapids
Baermann, Donna Lee Roth *property executive, retired insurance analyst*
Knepper, Eugene Arthur *realtor*
†Ripma, Barbara Jean *realtor*
Rohlena, Robert Charles *retired real estate manager*

Des Moines
Leonard, George Edmund *real estate, bank, and consulting executive*

Dubuque
Felderman, Robert John *real estate appraiser, realtor*

Iowa City
Milkman, Marianne Friedenthal *retired city planner*

Spencer
Lemke, Alan James *environmental specialist*

KANSAS

Lawrence
Strauss, Eric James *urban planning educator, lawyer, consultant*

Overland Park
McChesney, Samuel Parker, III *real estate executive*

Prairie Village
Taylor, Ralph Orien, Jr. *real estate developer, investor*

Wichita
Lusk, William Edward *real estate and oil company executive*

KENTUCKY

Bowling Green
Stewart, Harold Sanford *real estate investment and supply executive*

Lexington
Gable, Robert Elledy *real estate investment company executive*

London
Gregory, Jerry *real estate agent*

Louisville
Gott, Marjorie Eda Crosby *conservationist, former educator*

LOUISIANA

Baton Rouge
Marvin, Wilbur *real estate executive*
Mohr, Jeffrey Michael *real estate and insurance executive*

Harvey
Chee, Shirley *real estate broker*

Metairie
Myers, Iona Raymer *real estate and property manager*
Perrin, Roy Albert, Jr. *real estate developer, investor*

New Orleans
Jones, Glenn Earle *property management executive*
Lupo, Robert Edward Smith *real estate developer and investor*

Shreveport
Brock, Eric John *urban planner, historian, consultant*

MAINE

Bangor
Foster, Walter Herbert, Jr. *real estate company executive*

Gray
Cahill, Richard Frederic *city planner*

Lincolnville
Williams, Robert Luther *city planning consultant*

MARYLAND

Aberdeen Proving Ground
Docken, Edsel Ardean, Sr. (Dean Docken) *urban planner*

Baltimore
DeVito, Mathias Joseph *retired real estate executive*
Mierzwicki, Anthony Joseph *real estate executive*
Millspaugh, Martin Laurence *real estate developer, urban development consultant*
Shrestha, Shiva Kumar *urban planner*

Bel Air
Baumgardner, Renee Elaine *urban planner*

Bethesda
Clark, A. James *real estate company executive*
Gilreath, Jerry Hollandsworth *community planner*
†Halpert, Stuart D. *real estate company executive*
John, Frank Herbert, Jr. *real estate appraiser, real estate investor*
Kibbe, James William *real estate broker*
Sams, James Farid *real estate development company executive*
Walker, Mallory *real estate executive*

Burtonsville
Kammeyer, Sonia Margaretha *real estate agent*

Chevy Chase
Lee, Edward Brooke, Jr. *real estate executive, fund raiser*

Clinton
Ives, Adriene Diane *real estate executive*

Cockeysville
Bart, Polly Turner *real estate developer*

Columbia
Cook, Stephen Bernard *homebuilding company executive*
Hilderbrandt, Donald Franklin, II *urban designer, landscape architect, artist*
McCuan, William Patrick *real estate company executive*

Dunkirk
Vining, Pierre Herbert *real estate consultant*

Port Republic
Hanke, Byron Reidt *residential land planning and community associations consultant*

Rockville
†Guttman, Steven J. *real estate company executive*
Kusterer, Thomas *environmental planner*

Takoma Park
Urciolo, John Raphael, II *real estate developer, real estate and finance educator*

MASSACHUSETTS

Amherst
Bentley, Richard Norcross *regional planner, writer, educator*
Larson, Joseph Stanley *environmentalist, educator, researcher*

Arlington
†Van Orman, Jeanne *planning consultant*

Auburndale
Nahigian, Robert John *real estate development broker*

Boston
Beal, Robert Lawrence *real estate executive*
Constable, William Gordon *real estate development executive, lawyer*
Dacey, Brian Francis *real estate executive*
Gerrity, Daniel Wallace *real estate developer*
Holland, James R. *real estate corporation executive*
Lovejoy, George Montgomery, Jr. *real estate executive*

Radloff, Robert Albert *real estate executive*
Thibedeau, Richard Herbert *environmental planner, administrator*

Bourne
Fantozzi-Pacheco, Peggy Ryone *environmental planner*

Cambridge
Fleming, Ronald Lee *urban designer, administrator, preservation planner, environmental educator*
Spunt, Shepard Armin *real estate executive, management and financial consultant*
Susskind, Lawrence Elliott *urban and environmental planner, educator, mediator*
Vigier, François Claude Denis *city planning educator*

East Bridgewater
Farrell, Sharon Elaine *real estate broker*

Fairhaven
Hotchkiss, Henry Washington *real estate broker and financial consultant*

Gloucester
Johnson, Janet Lou *real estate executive*

Milton
Comeau, Lorene Anita Emerson *real estate developer*

Newton
Havens, Candace Jean *planning consultant*

North Andover
Michaels, Patricia Palen *urban planner*

Northampton
Russell, Joel Samuel *land use consultant*

Pepperell
Holmes, Jean Louise *real estate investor, Holocaust scholar, educator*

Sudbury
Watson, Dorothy Colette *real estate broker*

Topsfield
Arnold, Alice Marie *real estate management executive*

Waltham
Fagans, Karl Preston *real estate facilities administration executive*
Nelson, Arthur Hunt *real estate management development company executive*

West Tisbury
Logue, Edward Joseph *development company executive*

Weymouth
Coughlin, H. Richard *real estate broker*

Winchester
Blackham, Ann Rosemary (Mrs. J. W. Blackham) *realtor*

MICHIGAN

Ada
Van Dellen, Chester, Jr. *environmental consultant, real estate appraiser*

Ann Arbor
Gooch, Nancy Jane *realtor, mortgage executive*
†Rabe, Barry George *natural resources and environment educator*
Rycus, Mitchell Julian *urban planning educator, urban security and energy planning consultant*
Sosnowski, David Joseph *environmental protection specialist*
Surovell, Edward David *real estate company executive*

Bloomfield Hills
Halso, Robert *real estate company executive*

Clarkston
Ylvisaker, John Richard *real estate developer, consultant*

Dearborn
Werling, Donn Paul *environmental educator*

East Lansing
Palinski, Kay Marie *real estate broker*

Fenton
Manuel, Dennis Lee *real estate broker*

Grosse Ile
Smith, Veronica Latta *real estate corporation officer*

Grosse Pointe
Dunlap, Connie Sue Zimmerman *real estate professional*

Indian River
Heidemann, Mary Ann *community planner*

Lansing
†Huard, Jeffrey Scott *community planner*
Tipton, James Alva *real estate agent, farmer*

Livonia
Borin, Jeffrey Nathan *real estate developer*
Borin, Ralph *real estate developer*

Marquette
Coleman, Patrick J. *urban planner*

Reed City
†Freeman, George Stanley *city manager, city and regional planner*

Saginaw
Cline, Thomas William *real estate leasing company executive, management consultant*

Saint Clair Shores
Field, Thomas Lee *business executive, politician*

Southfield
Arroyo, Rodney Lee *city planning and transportation executive*

Traverse City
McCafferty, John Martin *real estate executive, commodities trader*

White Lake
Clyburn, Luther Linn *real estate broker, appraiser, ship captain*

MINNESOTA

Aitkin
Morton, Craig Richard *real estate investor*

Bloomington
Dahlberg, Burton Francis *real estate corporation executive*

Coon Rapids
Elvig, Merrywayne *real estate manager*

Detroit Lakes
Remmen, Lawrence P. *city planner*

Duluth
Bowman, Roger Manwaring *real estate executive*

Minneapolis
Fine, William Irwin *real estate developer*
Gilbertson, Steven E(dward) Satyaki *real estate broker, guidance counselor*
Gladhill, Bethany *community advocate, historic preservation consultant*
Kreiser, Frank David *real estate executive*
Linoff, Alan Lee *real estate development company executive*
O'Keefe, Nancy Jean *real estate company executive*
Stuebner, James Cloyd *real estate developer, contractor*
Vergin, Timothy Lynn *commercial real estate appraiser and broker*

Saint Louis Park
†Nickerson, Ronald George *park planner*

Saint Paul
McDonald, Malcolm Willis *real estate company executive*

Saint Peter
Turnbull, Charles Vincent *retired real estate broker*

MISSISSIPPI

Clarksdale
Magdovitz, Lawrence Maynard *real estate executive, lawyer*

Hattiesburg
Johnson, Ellen Randel *real estate broker*

Meridian
Church, George Millord *real estate executive*

MISSOURI

Ash Grove
Johnson, Iver Christian *valuation company executive*

Chesterfield
Schierholz, William Francis, Jr. *real estate developer*

Columbia
Northway, Wanda I. *realty company executive*

Holden
Martin, Laura Belle *real estate and farm land owner and manager*

Independence
Francis, Mary Frances Van Dyke *real estate executive, editor*

Kansas City
Buckner, William Claiborne *real estate broker*
Dumovich, Loretta *real estate and transportation company executive*
Mazzetti, Timothy Alan *commercial real estate executive*
Shutz, Byron Christopher *real estate executive*

Marshfield
Herren, Cline Champion *real estate agent*

Raymore
DeLuca, John Richard, II *city planning administrator, geography educator*

Saint Joseph
Miller, Lloyd Daniel *real estate agent*
Rachow, Sharon Dianne *realtor*

Saint Louis
†Keller, Theodore G., Jr. *real estate manager*
Koehler, Harry George *real estate executive*
Marking, T(heodore) Joseph, Jr. *transportation and urban planner*
Meissner, Edwin Benjamin, Jr. *retired real estate broker*
Morley, Harry Thomas, Jr. *real estate executive*
Ruwitch, Ann Rubenstein *urban planner executive*
†Wielansky, Lee S. *real estate company executive*

Springfield
Ash, Sharon Kaye *real estate company executive*
Condellone, Trent Peter *real estate developer*

Stockton
Jackson, Betty L. Deason *real estate developer*

MONTANA

Great Falls
Coffman, Barbara LeAnn *environmentalist, state official*
Stevens, George Alexander *realtor*

Sidney
Beagle, John Gordon *real estate broker*

NEBRASKA

Madison
Wozniak, Richard Michael, Sr. *retired city and regional planner*

Omaha
Gallagher, Paula Marie *real estate appraiser*
Neal, Bonnie Jean *real estate professional*

Wausa
Pfeil, Don Curtis *retired real estate executive*

NEVADA

Carson City
Empey, Gene F. *real estate executive*
McLain, John Lowell *resource specialist, consultant*

Las Vegas
Maravich, Mary Louise *realtor*
Pulliam, Francine Sarno *real estate broker and developer*
Tate, Evelyn Ruth *real estate broker*

North Las Vegas
Fiori, Frank Anthony *land use planner, historic preservation consultant*

Reno
Davenport, Janet Lee *real estate saleswomen, small business owner*
Jennison, Brian L. *environmental specialist*

West Wendover
Psenka, Robert Edward *real estate developer, behavioral scientist*

Winnemucca
Clemons, Lynn Allan *land use planner*

NEW HAMPSHIRE

Hanover
Meadows, Donella *environmentalist*

Lebanon
Umling, David Arthur *urban planner*

Newfields
Wilson, Donald Alfred *land boundary consultant, surveyor*

NEW JERSEY

Bridgeport
Walters, Charles Joseph *real estate developer*

Butler
Wingert, Hannelore Christiane *real estate sales executive, chemical company executive*

Camden
Roberts, Thomas Andrew, II *urban development executive*

Chatham
Lax, Philip *land developer, space planner*

Cherry Hill
Burke, Linda Judith *real estate broker*

Clifton
Svendsen, Joyce R. *real estate company executive*

Colts Neck
Rode, Leif *retired real estate personal computer consultant*

East Orange
Anderson, Zina-Diane *real estate executive*

Flemington
Salamon, Renay *real estate broker*

Florham Park
Katona, Bruce Richard *real estate company executive*

Green Brook
Elias, Donald Francis *environmental consultant*

Hackensack
Gingras, Paul Joseph *real estate management company executive*

Hanover
†Von Moltke, Konrad *environmental policy educator*

Haworth
Stokvis, Jack Raphael *urban planner, entrepreneur computer consultnt and developer, government agency administrator*

Hazlet
Fisher, David Bruce *land development executive*

Hopewell
Pariso, Jean Brunner *real estate professional*

Millburn
Tanguay, Anita Walburga *real estate broker*

Old Tappan
Terranova, Carl *real estate broker*

Plainfield
Nierstedt, William James *planner*

Princeton
Broad, Barbara Prentice *real estate agent*

Randolph
Femminella, Charles Joseph, Jr. *real estate appraiser, tax assessor, broker*

Sea Isle City
Boeshe, Barbara Louise *real estate executive*

Somerset
DiMeglio, Nicolas Joseph *real estate broker, small business owner*

Union
†David, Ivo A. *real estate broker, artist*

Upper Saddle River
Marron, Darlene Lorraine *real estate development executive, financial and marketing consultant*

NEW MEXICO

Alamogordo
Black, Maureen *realty company executive*

Albuquerque
Godfrey, Richard George *real estate appraiser*
Navarro, Janyte Janine *environmental educator*
Stahl, Jack Leland *real estate company executive*
Tinnin, Thomas Peck *real estate professional*

Mora
Hanks, Eugene Ralph *land developer, cattle rancher, forester, retired naval officer*

Santa Fe
Montgomery, Michael Davis *real estate investor*
Pearson, Margit Linnea *development company executive*
Perkins, Linda Gillespie *real estate executive*

NEW YORK

Albany
Matuszek, John Michael, Jr. *environmental scientist, educator, consultant*

Annandale On Hudson
Mayo-Winham, Carolyn Ann *development executive*

Baldwinsville
†Hansen, Beverly Anne *environmental policy educator*

Brewster
Killackey, Dorothy Helen *real estate professional, former educator*

Briarcliff Manor
Pasquarelli, Joseph J. *real estate, engineering and construction executive*

Bronx
Morrow, Phillip Henry *real estate development company executive*
Robinson, John Gwilym *conservationist*

Brooklyn
Balbi, Kenneth Emilio *environmental lead specialist, researcher*
Blackman, Robert Irwin *real estate developer and investor, lawyer, accountant*
Hill, Isabel Thigpen *urban planner*
Markgraf, Rosemarie *real estate broker*

Canaan
Belknap, Michael H. P. *real estate developer*

Central Islip
McGowan, Harold *real estate developer, investor, scientist, author, philanthropist*

Clifton Park
Miller, Robert Carl *real estate developer*

Cold Spring
Miller, Timothy Earl *planning company executive*

Cooperstown
Huntington, Robert Graham *environmental business consultant*

Elmsford
Raymond, George Marc *city planner, educator*

Goshen
Ward, William Francis, Jr. *real estate investment banker*

Great Neck
Zirinsky, Daniel *real estate investor and photographer*

Hicksville
Urschel, Effie Caroline Krogmann *real estate broker, appraiser, poet, author*

Irvington
Trent, Bertram James *real estate executive*

Ithaca
Goldsmith, William Woodbridge *city and regional planning educator*

Jamestown
†Bargar, Nancy Gay *real estate company executive*

Jericho
Axinn, Donald Everett *real estate investor, developer*

Larchmont
Levi, James Harry *real estate executive, investment banker*

Melville
Florea, Robert William *real estate investment executive*
Niebuhr, Fred J(ohn) *real estate consultant*

Mill Neck
von Briesen, Edward Fuller *builder, real estate developer*

New Hyde Park
Cooper, Milton *real estate investment trust executive*

New York
Anderson, Richard Theodore *urban planner, association executive*
Benenson, Edward Hartley *realty company executive*
Bolt, Dawn Maria *real estate agent, financial adviser*
Borecki, Kenneth Michael *real estate investment consultant*
Cannon, John J(oseph) *real estate sales and marketing executive*
Clancy, John Patrick *real estate company executive*
Coudert, Dale Hokin *real estate executive, marketing consultant*
Cuneo, Jack Alfred *real estate investment executive*
†Fascitelli, Michael D. *real estate executive*
Fiedler, Lawrence Elliot *real estate investment company executive*
Fox-Freund, Barbara Susan *real estate executive*
Garfield, Leslie Jerome *real estate executive*
Gochberg, Thomas *real estate investor, financial executive*
Goddess, Lynn Barbara *commercial real estate broker*
Godwin, Ralph Lee, Jr. *real estate executive*
Goldenberg, Charles Lawrence *real estate company executive*
Hernstadt, Judith Filenbaum *city planner, real estate executive, broadcasting executive*
Howell, William Page *real estate executive*
Hutton, Ernest Watson, Jr. *urban designer, city planner*
Kalikow, Peter Stephen *real estate developer, former newspaper owner, publisher*
Keith, John Pirie *urban planner*
Lachman, Marguerite Leanne *real estate investment advisor*
Marder, John G. *real estate investor, marketing consultant, corporate director*
Marshall, Alton Garwood *real estate counselor*
Mirante, Arthur J., II *real estate company executive*
Mueller, Shirley Anne *lawyer, real estate broker*
†Newman, William *real estate executive*
Nichols, Carol D. *real estate professional, association executive*
Nimetz, Gloria Lorch *real estate broker, photographer*
Perry-Widney, Marilyn (Marilyn Perry) *international finance and real estate executive, television producer*
Petz, Edwin V. *real estate executive, lawyer*
Purse, Charles Roe *real estate investment company executive*
Rose, Daniel *real estate company executive, consultant*
Rose, Elihu *real estate executive*
Roskind, E. Robert *real estate company executive*
Schlang, David *real estate executive, lawyer*
Scott, Stanley DeForest *real estate executive, former lithography company executive*
Scurry, Richardson Gano, Jr. *investment management company financial executive*
Sinclair, David Macowan *marine surveyor*
Stein, Ellen Gail *executive manager*
Strum, Brian J. *real estate executive*
Thomas, Violeta de los Angeles *real estate broker*
Tishman, John L. *realty and construction company executive*
Toote, Gloria E. A. *developer, lawyer, columnist*
Urstadt, Charles Deane *real estate executive*
Warsawer, Harold Newton *real estate appraiser and consultant*
Wolf, Peter Michael *investment management and land planning consultant, educator, author*
Zacharias, Thomas Elling *real estate executive*

Newburgh
Koskella, Lucretia C. *real estate broker, appraiser*

Oakdale
Bragdon, Clifford Richardson *city planner, educator*

Palisades
Anderson, Margaret Tayler *real estate broker, career consultant*

Pawling
Wood, Christopher L. J. *consumer goods company executive*

Pelham
Pough, Richard Hooper *conservationist*

Rochester
Nutter, David George *urban planner*

Rye
Feinberg, Norman Maurice *real estate executive*
Mintz, Stephen Allan *real estate company executive, lawyer*

Saratoga Springs
Smith, Vincent De Paul *realtor, real estate company executive*

Scarsdale
Goldberg, Harriet David *urban planner*

Schenectady
Corcoran, Kevin James *town planner*
Demar-Salad, Geraldine *real estate sales and development executive, management consultant*

Stanfordville
Zeyher, Mark Lewis *real estate investor*

Stony Brook
Koppelman, Lee Edward *regional planner, educator*

Syracuse
De Long, Jacob Edward *real estate broker*

White Plains
McCarthy, John Robert *real estate firm officer*

Wyandanch
Barnett, Peter John *property development executive, educator*

NORTH CAROLINA

Asheville
Cragnolin, Karen Zambella *real estate developer, lawyer*
West, Michael J. *real estate developer, business owner*

Boone
†McCoy, Todd Edward *real estate appraiser*

Chapel Hill
Rohe, William Michael *urban planning educator*
Waldon, Roger Stephen *urban planner*
Weiss, Shirley F. *urban and regional planner, economist, educator*

Charlotte
Cox, Linda Smoak *real estate broker*
Diemer, Arthur William *real estate executive*
Fortenberry, Carol Lomax *real estate appraiser*
Wiggins, Nancy Bowen *real estate broker, market research consultant*

Fayetteville
Kendrick, Mark Cleveland *real estate executive*

Greensboro
Conrad, David Paul *business broker, retired restaurant chain executive*

Murphy
Pezzella, Jerry James, Jr. *investment and real estate executive*

Raleigh
Redman, William Walter, Jr. *realtor*
Willer, Edward Herman *real estate broker*

Sanford
Hopkins, Cassandre' F. *land use planner*

Winston Salem
Doggett, Aubrey Clayton, Jr. *real estate executive, consultant*

NORTH DAKOTA

Bismarck
Christianson, James Duane *real estate developer*
Clairmont, William Edward *developer*

OHIO

Cincinnati
Chatterjee, Jayanta *educator, urban designer*
Dunigan, Dennis Wayne *real estate executive*
Randman, Barry I. *real estate developer*
Schuler, Robert Leo *appraiser, consultant*
Shenk, Richard Lawrence *real estate developer, photographer, artist*
Weiskittel, Ralph Joseph *real estate executive*

Cleveland
Adler, Thomas William *real estate executive*
†Cleary, Martin Joseph *real estate company executive*
Gould, Bonnie Marincic *realtor*
Jacobs, Richard E. *real estate executive, sports team owner*

Columbus
†Glimcher, David J. *real estate executive*
†Glimcher, Herbert *real estate company executive*
McCurdy, Kurt Basquin *real estate corporation officer*
Voss, Jerrold Richard *city planner, educator, university official*

Concord
Conway, Neil James, III *title company executive, lawyer, writer*

Dayton
Frydman, Paul *real estate broker and developer*
Miles, Alfred Lee *real estate broker, educator*
Stout, Donald Everett *real estate developer, environmental preservationist*
Wertz, Kenneth Dean *real estate executive*

Elyria
Stefanik, Janet Ruth *realtor*

Hebron
Slater, Wanda Marie Worth *rental property manager*

Hudson
Stec, John Zygmunt *real estate executive*

Jefferson
Gibbs, Arland LaVerne *retired real estate agent*

Lodi
Berry, Beverly A. *real estate investment executive*

Mount Vernon
Meharry, Ronald Lee *real estate investor, inn keeper*

New Albany
Kessler, John Whitaker *real estate developer*

North Canton
Jackson, David Lee *real estate executive*

Parma
Verba, Betty Lou *real estate executive, investor*

Salem
Barcey, Harold Edward Dean (Hal Barcey) *real estate counselor*

Shaker Heights
Solganik, Marvin *real estate executive*
Winter, John Alexander *realtor, real estate appraiser*

Toledo
Batt, Nick *property and investment executive*

Worthington
Winston, Janet Margaret *real estate professional, civic volunteer*

Youngstown
Camacci, Michael A. *commercial real estate broker, development consultant*

OKLAHOMA

Ada
Davison, Victoria Dillon *real estate executive*

Norman
Zelby, Rachel *realtor*

Oklahoma City
Bradford, Dennis Doyle *real estate broker, developer*
Randall, Mike *urban planner, municipal official*

Tahlequah
Campbell, Jane Turner *former educator and realtor*

Tulsa
Henderson, James Ronald *industrial real estate developer*
Hill, Josephine Carmela *realtor*
Mahoney, Jack *real estate broker, software developer*
Matthews, Dane Dikeman *urban planner*
Murphy, Patrick Gregory *real estate company executive*
Roberson, Jerry Donn *urban planner*
Vincent, Carl G., Jr. *real estate portfolio manager*

OREGON

Beaverton
Parrish, Stanley Glenister *real estate broker*

Grants Pass
Comeaux, Katharine Jeanne *realtor*

Lake Oswego
Morse, Lowell Wesley *banking and real estate executive*

Portland
Dickinson, Janet Mae Webster *relocation consulting executive*
Lilly, Elizabeth Giles *mobile park executive*
Standring, James Douglas *real estate developer*

Springfield
Davis, George Donald *executive land use policy consultant*

PENNSYLVANIA

Acme
Weeks, Julia E. *real estate broker*

Allentown
Saab, Deanne Keltum *real estate appraiser, broker*

Allison Park
†Evans, David Richard *land use administrator*

Ardmore
Winsor, Eleanor Webster *dispute resolution company executive*

Bryn Mawr
Segal, Donald Henry Gilbert *real estate developer*

Cleona
Carpenter, Roxanne Sue *realtor*

Doylestown
Carson, John Thompson, Jr. *environmental consultant*

Elkins Park
Havir, Bryan Thomas *urban planner*

Erie
Gottschalk, Frank Klaus *real estate company executive*

Johnstown
†Pasquerilla, Frank J. *real estate executive*
†Pasquerilla, Mark E. *real estate company executive*
†Zamias, Damian George *real estate executive*

King Of Prussia
†Gantman, Lewis I. *real estate company executive*
†Snyder, Wayne L. *real estate company executive*

Lester
DiGiamarino, Marian Eleanor *realty administrator*

Meadville
Cable, Mabel Elizabeth *urban planner, artist*

Mohnton
Hart, LeRoy Banks *financial software executive, real estate developer*

Newtown Square
Klein, Mark Paul *real estate developer*

Norristown
Heyser, William H. *landscape contractor*

Philadelphia
Bacon, Edmund Norwood *city planner*
Bonett, Edward Joseph, Jr. *law clerk, public housing manager*
†Glickman, Edward A. *real estate investment executive*
Henry, Rene Arthur, Jr. *environmental agency administrator*
Mellman, Leonard *real estate investor and advisor*
Peck, Robert McCracken *naturalist, science historian, writer*
Pew, Robert Anderson *retired real estate corporation officer*
†Rubin, Ronald *real estate executive*
Strong, Ann Louise *planning educator*
Zalecky, Donna Michelle *land use planner, landscape architect*

Pittsburgh
Brown, Kevin James *real estate broker, consultant*
†Drovdlic, Fred G. *community planner*
Leney, George Willard *consulting engineer*
McGinn, Mary Lyn *real estate company executive*
Robert, Maria Cecilia *urban and regional planner, consultant*
Sarraf, Roberta Jean *planning consultant*
Stephenson, Robert Clay *real estate company executive*

Plymouth Meeting
Levinson, Gary Howard *real estate investor*

Somerset
Barkman, Annette Shaulis *real estate management executive*

Southeastern
Zlotolow-Stambler, Ernest *real estate executive, architectural executive*

Springfield
Reeves, Thomas A. *naturalist*

State College
†Watson, Jennifer Annette *urban planner, landscape architect*

University Park
Golany, Gideon Salomon *urban designer*

Willow Grove
Moore, Norma Jean *real estate associate broker*

RHODE ISLAND

Wakefield
Morrison, Fred Beverly *real estate consultant*

Warwick
Lachapelle, Cleo Edward *real estate broker*

SOUTH CAROLINA

Beaufort
Chambers, Henry Carroll *realty broker*

Columbia
†DePass, William Brunson, Jr. *commercial and industrial real estate broker*

Easley
Spearman, Patsy Cordle *real estate broker*

Florence
Dupre, Judith Ann Neil *real estate agent, interior decorator*

Greenville
Crawford, William David *real estate broker, consultant*
Simmons, David Jeffrey *real estate executive*

Hilton Head Island
Cramer, Laura Schwarz *realtor*
Gruchacz, Robert S. *real estate executive*
Kemp, Mae Wunder *real estate broker, consultant*

Port Royal
Wilson, Thomas David, Jr. *urban planner*

Salem
Harbeck, William James *real estate executive, lawyer, international consultant*

Spartanburg
Gray, Gwen Cash *real estate broker*

Summerville
†Christie, Joseph Francis *city planner*

Taylors
Dean, Cheryl Ann *urban planner*

Union
Berry, Peter DuPre *real estate executive*

SOUTH DAKOTA

Sioux Falls
Kilian, Thomas Randolph *rural economic developer, consultant*

TENNESSEE

Alamo
Raines, Irene Freeze *real estate broker*

Brentwood
†Banks, Halbert Jay *real estate executive*
Raskin, Edwin Berner *real estate executive*

Chattanooga
Elder, Thomas Woodrow *real estate consultant*
Porter, Dudley, Jr. *environmentalist, foundation executive, lawyer*

Hampton
McClendon, Fred Vernon *real estate professional, business consultant, equine and realty appraiser, financial consultant*

Knoxville
Cossé, R. Paul *realty company executive*

Memphis
Connolly, Matthew B., Jr. *conservationist*
Cooper, Irby *real estate development company executive*
Haizlip, Henry Hardin, Jr. *real estate consultant, former banker*

Nashville
Beck, Robert Beryl *real estate executive*
Driscoll, Joseph Francis *real estate executive*
Estes, Moreau Pinckney, IV *real estate executive, lawyer*
Greer, Herschel Lynn, Jr. *real estate broker*

TEXAS

Austin
†Edgecomb, Virginia *real estate broker*
Mathias, Reuben Victor (Vic Mathias) *real estate executive, investor*
Toubin, Charles Irving *commercial real estate executive, writer*

Bay City
Aylin, Elizabeth Twist Pabst *real estate broker, developer*

Bayou Vista
Schlotfeldt, William (Bill) West *real estate investor*

Bullard
Buckner, John Hugh *retired real estate broker, retired construction company executive, retired air force officer*

Calvert
Alemán, Marthanne Payne *environmental planner, consultant*

College Station
Goode-Haddock, Celia Ross *title company executive*

Conroe
Judge, Dolores Barbara *real estate broker*

Corpus Christi
Norman, Wyatt Thomas, III *landman, consultant*

Cypress
Peck, Edwin Russell *real estate management executive*

Dallas
Cansler, Denise Ann *real estate executive*
Curran, David Bernard, Jr. *real estate executive*
Doran, Mark Richard *real estate financial executive*
Garison, Lynn Lassiter *real estate executive*
Gidel, Robert Hugh *real estate investor*
Hamilton, David Lee *retired environmental company executive*
Moss, Robert Williams *real estate developer*
†Perkins, John W. *real estate company executive*
Perot, H. Ross, Jr. *real estate developer, sports team executive*
Rutherford, Paris *planning and urban development executive*
Santamaria, Rose Faye *real estate agent*
Yeslow, Rosemarie *real estate professional*

El Paso
Karch, Robert E. *real estate company executive*
Lyle, James Arthur *real estate broker*

Elgin
Osborne, Michael James *real estate executive, energy executive, author*

Fort Worth
Coslik, Stephen *real estate executive*
Davis, Carol Lyn *research consultant*
†Reed, Linda Ann *real estate company property manager*
Regan, Charlotte Marie *real estate broker, cosmetics consultant*
Underwood, Harvey Cockrell *real estate executive*

Granbury
Almy, Earle Vaughn, Jr. (Buddy Almy) *real estate executive*

Hitchcock
Teague, Mary Kay *realtor*

Houston
Barrere, Jamie Newton *real estate executive*
Goldsmith, Billy Joe *real estate broker*
Harris, Lyttleton Tazwell, IV *property management-investment company executive*
Henry, Randolph Marshall *company executive, real estate broker*
Holcomb, William A. *retired oil and gas exploration, pipeline executive, retired real estate broker, consultant*
Kollaer, Jim C. *real estate executive, architect*
Lanier, Robert C. (Bob Lanier) *real estate owner, developer, former mayor*
Lassiter, James Morris, Jr. *real estate investment executive*
Lehrer, Kenneth Eugene *real estate advisor, economic consultant*
Lestin, Eric Hugh *real estate investment banking executive*
Ling, Lily Hsu-Chiang *real estate executive, accountant*
†McDonald, Scott *real estate company executive*
Raia, Carl Bernard *commercial real estate executive and developer*

Irving
Basinger, Lawrence Edwin *real estate executive*

Laredo
Nixon-Mendez, Nina Louise *urban planner*

Longview
Harper, Verne Jay *petroleum landman*

Lubbock
Wall, Betty Jane *real estate consultant*

Mico
Shockey, Thomas Edward *real estate executive, engineer*

Midland
Wade, Margaret Gaston *real estate property manager, educator*

Salado
Mackie, Donald John, Jr. *real estate developer*

San Antonio
Bryan, Richard Ray *real estate development executive, construction executive*
Cottingham, Stephen Kent *real estate development executive, researcher*
Emick, William John *real estate investor, retired federal executive*
Joiner, Lorell Howard *real estate development and investment executive*
Maring, Michael William *property management company executive*

Sanger
Foote, Ruth Annette *business executive, land developer*

Spring
Coy, Elba Boone *retired real estate developer*

Temple
Aldrich, C. Elbert *real estate broker*
Moore, Joanna Elizabeth *real estate professional*

The Woodlands
Wortham, James Mason *gas supply representative*

Waco
Rusling, Barbara N(eubert) *real estate executive, state commisioner*

UTAH

Draper
Mecham, Lee *real estate director*

Midvale
Teerlink, J(oseph) Leland *real estate developer*

Ogden
Southwick, James Albert *realtor*

Provo
Diepholz, Daniel R. *real estate consultant, accountant*

VERMONT

Shelburne
Carpenter, Donald Blodgett *real estate appraiser*

VIRGINIA

Accomac
Manter, Sandra *county planner*

Alexandria
Gilchrist, Richard Irwin *real estate developer*
Holland, Dianna Gwin *real estate broker*

Annandale
Hollis, Linda Eardley *urban planning consultant*

Arlington
Guruswamy, Dharmithran *urban planner*
Koury, Agnes Lillian *real estate owner and manager*
Sawhill, John Crittenden *conservationist, economist, university president, government official*
†Siegel, Laurence C. *real estate investment executive*

Charlottesville
Greenwood, Virginia Maxine McLeod *real estate executive, broker*

Fairfax
Boerner-Nilsen, Jo M. *real estate trainer*

Falls Church
Frazier, Walter Ronald *real estate investment company executive*

Gwynn
Pickle Beattie, Katherine Hamner *real estate agent*

Haymarket
Crafton-Masterson, Adrienne *real estate executive, writer, poet*

Mc Lean
Alberts, Henry Celler *real estate company executive*
McLean, Robert, III *real estate company executive*

Newport News
Goldberg, Ivan Baer *real estate executive*
Goldberg, Stanley Irwin *real estate executive*

Reston
Miller, Lynne Marie *environmental company executive*

Richmond
DeWitt, Michele Mixner *community planner*
Dickinson, Alfred James *realtor*
Tuck, Grayson Edwin *real estate agent, former natural gas transmission executive*
Wender, Herbert *title company executive*

Springfield
Borum, Olin Henry *realtor, former government official*

Vienna
Van Putten, Mark *environmentalist*

Virginia Beach
Gallagher, Vicki Smith *real estate agent*
Pefley, Charles Saunders *real estate broker*
†White, Stephen James *city planner, educator*

Williamsburg
Holt, Paul deCourcy, III *city planner*

WASHINGTON

Bellevue
Edwards, Kirk Lewis *real estate company executive*

Everett
Adams, Victoria Eleanor *retired realty company executive*

Renton
Kredlo, Thomas Andrew *real estate appraiser*

Rollingbay
Morris, Donald Charles *commercial real estate mergers and acquisitions*

Seattle
Dillard, Marilyn Dianne *property manager*
Gerrodette, Charles Everett *real estate company executive, consultant*
McKinnon, James Buckner *real estate sales executive, writer, researcher*
Sander, Susan Berry *environmental planning engineering corporation executive*
Sasaki, Tsutomu (Tom Sasaki) *real estate company executive, international trading company executive, consultant*
Wesley, Virginia Anne *real estate property manager*

Spokane
Kirschbaum, James Louis *real estate company administrator*

Tacoma
Wolf, Frederick George *environmentalist*

WEST VIRGINIA

Fairmont
York, Linda Kay *real estate appraiser, executive*

Huntington
Davis, Donald Eugene *real estate management executive*

WISCONSIN

Appleton
Brehm, William Allen, Jr. *urban planner*

Beaver Dam
Butterbrodt, John Ervin *real estate executive*
Manthe, Cora De Munck *real estate and investment company executive*

Cambridge
Stevens, Chester Wayne *real estate executive*

Lake Mills
Lazaris, Pamela Adriane *community planning and development consultant*

Madison
Evans, Donald LeRoy *real estate company executive*
Mullins, Jerome Joseph *real estate developer, consulting engineer*
Ring, Gerald J. *real estate developer, insurance executive*
Vandell, Kerry Dean *real estate and urban economics educator*

Mequon
Ryan, Mary Nell H. *training consultant*

Milwaukee
Glazer, Gerald Sherwin *real estate broker*

Minocqua
Utt, Glenn S., Jr. *motel investments and biotech industry company executive*

Pewaukee
Jasiorkowski, Robert Lee *real estate broker, computer consultant*

Woodruff
DeBauche, Jacqueline Jean *wildlife rehabilitator*

TERRITORIES OF THE UNITED STATES

PUERTO RICO

San Juan
Ocasio Belén, Félix E. *real estate development company executive*

VIRGIN ISLANDS

Saint Thomas
Duarte, Patricia M. *real estate and insurance broker*

CANADA

ALBERTA

Calgary
McEwen, Alexander Campbell *cadastral studies educator, former Canadian government official, surveying consultant*
Milavsky, Harold Phillip *real estate executive*

BRITISH COLUMBIA

Vancouver
Goldberg, Michael Arthur *land policy and planning educator*

NOVA SCOTIA

Stellarton
Sobey, Donald Creighton Rae *real estate developer*

ONTARIO

London
Pearson, Norman *urban and regional planner, administrator, academic and planning consultant, writer*

Newmarket
Wood, Neil Roderick *real estate development company executive*

North York
Carrothers, Gerald Arthur Patrick *environmental and city planning educator*

Ottawa
MacNeill, James William *international environment consultant*

Toronto
†Braithwaite, J(oseph) Lorne *real estate executive*
Cullingworth, Larry Ross *residential and real estate development company executive*
Dimma, William Andrew *real estate executive*
Grier, Ruth *environmentalist*

Weston
McIntyre, John George Wallace *real estate development and management consultant*

QUEBEC

Montreal
Gabbour, Iskandar *city and regional planning educator*

Rimouski
Larivée, Jacques *conservationist*

ENGLAND

London
Hall, Sir Peter Geoffrey *urban and regional planning educator*
†Scott, Stuart L. *real estate company executive*

JAPAN

Tokyo
Sakai, Akiyoshi *urban redevelopment consultant*

ADDRESS UNPUBLISHED

Ahlgren, Gibson-Taylor *real estate broker*
Aulbach, George Louis *property investment company executive*
Barrett, Linda L. *real estate executive*
Beal, Merrill David *conservationist, museum director*
Bond, Audrey Mae *real estate broker*
Brady, George Moore *real estate executive, mortgage banker*
Brooks, Michael Paul *urban planning educator*
Brown, Ann Lenora *community economic development professional*
Burgess, Diane Glenn *real estate broker, paralegal*
Carlucci, Gino Dominic, Jr. *urban planner, policy analyst*
Chesler, Doris Adelle *real estate professional*
Coffey, Nancy Ann *commercial real estate broker*
Corey, Kenneth Edward *geography and urban planning educator, researcher*
Cranford, James Blease *retired real estate executive*
Davis, Mary Byrd *conservationist, researcher*
DeBock, Ronald Gene *real estate company executive*
Dendrinos, Dimitrios Spyros *urban planning educator*
Desloge, Christopher Davis, Sr. *real estate and merchant banking executive*
DeWitt, Sallie Lee *realtor*
Dickey, Robert Marvin (Rick Dickey) *property manager*
Doyle, Judith Stovall *real estate executive, retired*
Economou-Pease, Bessie Carasoulas *city planner, consultant*
Ellett, Alan Sidney *real estate development company executive*
Ellis, William Ben *environmental educator, retired utility executive*
Epstein, Jaye Mark *city planner*
Fetterly, Lynn Lawrence *real estate broker, developer*
Fino, Marie Georgette Keck *retired real estate broker*
Fischer, Zoe Ann *real estate and property marketing company executive, consultant*
Friedman, Howard W. *retired real estate company executive*
Frost, Anne *real estate broker, author, publisher*
Gasper, Ruth Eileen *real estate executive*
Gayle, Margot *preservationist, writer*
Gellman, Isaiah *environmental consultant*
Gilbert, Frederick E. *development planner, Africanist, consultant*
Gilmour, David Patton *economic and community planner*
Goldspiel, Arnold Nelson *real estate executive*
Gutstein, Carol Feinhandler *realtor*
Hakala, Karen Louise *retired real estate adminstrator*
Hodson, Nancy Perry *real estate agent*
Holway, James Michael *regional planner, state agency administrator*
Hufschmidt, Maynard Michael *resources planning educator*
Irwin, Lamour Mitch *real estate developer*
Johnson, Kay Durbahn *real estate manager, consultant*
Jungbluth, Kirk E. *real estate appraiser, mortgage banking executive*
Karakey, Sherry JoAnne *financial and real estate investment company executive, interior designer*
Kiefer, Robert Harry *real estate broker*
Kirtley, Hattie Mae *retired real estate broker*
Kohn, Robert Samuel, Jr. *real estate investment consultant*
Kopis, F. Jan *real estate broker*
Kremer, Honor Frances (Noreen Kremer) *real estate broker, small business owner*
Lamy, M(ary) Rebecca *land developer, former government official*
Ledford, Janet Marie Smalley *real estate appraiser, consultant*
Lynch, Florence Jones *real estate counselor, property manager*
Maguire, Robert Francis, III *real estate investor*
Maier, Robert Henry *real estate executive*
Mann, Clarence Charles *real estate company official*
McDonald, Barbara Jean *real estate broker*
McManus, Joseph Warn *urban planner, architect*
McNeil, Edward Warren *real estate executive*
Mercurio, Renard Michael *real estate corporation executive*
Messenkopf, Eugene John *real estate developer and hotel executive*
Meyer, Daniel Kramer *real estate executive*
Miller, Esther Scobie Powers *real estate appraiser, professional watercolorist*
Mitts, Marybeth Frazier *real estate company executive, consultant*
Mohamed, Joseph *real estate broker*
Nakahata, Tadaka *retired consulting engineer, land surveyor*
Nederveld, Ruth Elizabeth *retired real estate executive*
Netter, Cornelia Ann *real estate broker*
Newcomb, Robert Carl *real estate broker*
O'Leary, Timothy Michael *real estate corporation officer*
Osmycki, Daniel A. *commercial real estate broker, consultant*
Ownbey, Lenore F. Daly *real estate investment specialist*
Perkins, Charles Theodore *real estate developer, consultant*
Posha, D. Richard *real estate developer, home builder, designer*
Powell, Kathleen Lynch *lawyer, real estate executive*
Rassman, Joel H. *real estate company executive, accountant*
Ridloff, Richard *real estate executive, lawyer, consultant*
Rose, Frederick Phineas *builder and real estate executive*
Rosenfeld, Mark Kenneth *real estate developer*
Saunders, Alexander Hall *real estate executive*
Schwerin, Warren Lyons *real estate developer*
Senerchia, Dorothy Sylvia *urban planner, author*
Sherf, Sandee Croft *real estate corporation executive*
Simon, Melvin *real estate developer, professional basketball executive*
Slayton, William Larew *planning consultant, former government official*
Sullivan, Ben Frank, Jr. *real estate broker*
Taubman, A. Alfred *real estate developer*
Toshach, Clarice Oversby *real estate developer, former computer executive*
Trask, John Maurice, Jr. *property owner*
Trout, David E. *city planner*
Trump, Donald John *real estate developer*
Votava, Thomas Anthony *real estate and insurance professional*
Wadsworth, Jacqueline Dorèt *private investor*
Waldon, Grace Roberta *environmental company executive*
Weeden, Mary Ann *real estate investment company executive*
†Weekley, David *real estate developer*
Weisinger, Ronald Jay *government executive search consultant*
Welles, Virginia Chrisman *land use planner*
Williamson, Fletcher Phillips *real estate executive*
Young, Judith Anne *animal conservationist*
†Zavala, Alberto *real estate investment company executive*

GOVERNMENT: AGENCY ADMINISTRATION

UNITED STATES

ALABAMA

Athens
Wilson, Lucy Lynn Willmarth *postal service administrator*

Cullman
Munger, James Guy *protective services executive*

Huntsville
†Wolfe, Jackie Lee, Jr. *protective services professional*

Mobile
Cashdollar, Dick *protective services official*
Cochran, Samuel M. *protective services official*
Moore, Robert J. *United States marshal*

Montgomery
Harris, Joseph Lamar *state official*
†Hector, Henry Joseph *state commission administrator*
McKee, John William, Jr. *protective services official*
†Richardson, Edward R. *state agency administrator*

Redstone Arsenal
Schumann, J. Paul *federal agency administrator*

Springville
Dover, Derek Jason *corrections officer*

ALASKA

Anchorage
†Udland, Duane S. *protective services official*
Udland, Dwane *protective services official*

Fairbanks
Davis, Charles Lee *fire marshal*

Juneau
†Burke, Marianne King *state agency administrator, financial executive*
†Holloway, Shirley J. *state agency administrator*
†Kirkpatrick, Willis F. *state banking and securities administrator*
†Martin, Robert, Jr. *state agency administrator*
†Perdue, Karen *state agency administrator*

ARIZONA

Grand Canyon
Arnberger, Robert *federal administrator*

Phoenix
Bishop, C. Diane *state agency administrator, educator*
Boozer, James L. *federal agency administrator*
Brunacini, Alan Vincent *fire chief*
†Houseworth, Richard Court *state agency administrator*
†Keegan, Lisa Graham *state education agency adminstrator*
Meridith, Denise Patricia *government official*
Nielson, Theo Gilbert *law enforcement official, university official*
North, Warren James *government official*
Wilson, Stephen Rip *public policy consultant*

Scottsdale
Hill, Robert Martin *police detective, forensic document examiner, consultant, lecturer*

Tucson
Casper, Wayne Arthur *state government official, educator*
Done, Robert Stacy *consultant*
Smith, David Mitchell *fire and explosion consultant*
Walker, Franklin Curtis *national park administrator*

ARKANSAS

Jonesboro
Humway, Ronald Jimmie *state agency administrator*

Little Rock
†Simon, Raymond *state education administrator*

CALIFORNIA

Anaheim
Bowman, Jeffrey R. *protective services official*
Gaston, Randall Wallace *police chief*
Jung, Charlene *city treasurer*

Auburn
Warren, Marshall Thomas *protective service official*

Bakersfield
Brummer, Steven E. *police chief*

Benicia
von Studnitz, Gilbert Alfred *state official*

Burbank
Chaffee, James Albert *protective services official*

Capo Beach
Ely-Chaitlin, Marc Eric *government official*

Castro Valley
Palmer, James Daniel *inspector*

Cupertino
Compton, Dale Leonard *retired space agency executive, consultant*

El Centro
Steensgaard, Anthony Harvey *federal agent*

Fremont
†Eastin, Delaine Andree *state agency administrator*
Steckler, Craig Theodore *law enforcement official*

Fresno
Rank, Everett George *government official*
Winchester, Ed *protective services official*

Garden Grove
Sherrard, Raymond Henry *retired government official*

La Jolla
Knauss, John Atkinson *former federal agency administrator, oceanographer, educator, former university dean*

Lagunitas
Mann, Karen *consultant, educator*

Long Beach
Jeffery, James Nels *protective services official*
Luman, Robert M. *protective services official*

Los Angeles
Bangs, John Wesley, III *law enforcement administrator*
Fisher, Barry Alan Joel *protective services official*

Malibu
Kmiec, Douglas William *government official, law educator, columnist*

Oakland
Samuels, Joseph, Jr. *police chief*

Ontario
Bernard, Alexander *airport police official*

Palos Verdes Estates
Basnight, Arvin Odell *public administrator, aviation consultant*

Pasadena
Parker, Robert Allan Ridley *government administrator, astronaut*

Placerville
Palmieri, Rodney August *state agency administrator, pharmacist*

Redwood City
†O'Keefe, Donald Martin *county protective services officer*

Roseville
†Spampinato, Francis Cesidio, Jr. *federal administrator*

Sacramento
Callahan, Ronald *federal investigator, historian*
Costamagna, Gary *fire chief City of Sacramento*
Drown, Eugene Ardent *federal agency administrator*
Dunaway, Margaret Ann (Maggie Dunaway) *state agency consultant*
Enomoto, Jerry Jiro *protective services official*
Helmick, D.O. *protective services official*
Lopes, Brenda M. *state agency administrator*
McLennan, Geoffrey Thomas *state agency real estate executive*
Muehleisen, Gene Sylvester *retired law enforcement officer, state official*
Neville, Monica Mary *state assembly program executive*
Stoker, Mike Brian *state agency executive*
Venegas, Arturo, Jr. *chief police*

San Bernardino
Birge, Anne Constantin *protective services official*
Dean, Lee *protective services executive*
Farmer, Wesley Steven *police officer*

San Bruno
Kell-Smith, Carla Sue *federal agency administrator*

San Diego
Osby, Robert Edward *protective services official*
Sanders, Jerry *protective services official*

San Francisco
Axtell, Keith Elton *federal agency administrator*
Coye, Molly Joel *state agency administrator*
Lau, Fred H. *protective services official*
Tarnoff, Peter *business consultant*
Yin, Dominic David *police officer, educator, lawyer*

San Jose
†Monica, Martin J. *law enforcement officer, educator*

Santa Ana
†Walters, Paul *protective services official*

Santa Monica
Winchell, Robert Allen *government agency administrator, auditor*

Shingle Springs
Guay, Gordon Hay *postal service executive, marketing educator, consultant*

Sonora
Efford, Michael Robert *police administrator, educator*

South Pasadena
†Remy, Ray *state government official*

Stockton
Chavez, Edward *police chief*
Ratto, Douglas C. *protective services official*

Visalia
Rodriguez, Carlos *fire chief*

Yuba City
Doscher, Richard John *protective services official*

COLORADO

Aurora
Barnes, Raymond Edward *fire department official*
Moser, Jeffery Richard *economic director, public affairs and public management executive, artist, writer, former state official*
Vincent, Verne Saint *protective services official*

Colorado Springs
Kramer, Lorne C. *protective services official*
Navarro, Manuel *protective services official*

Denver
†Cooke, Paul Lewis *state fire marshall*
†Gonzales, Richard L. *fire department chief*
Logan, James Scott, Sr. *federal agency administrator*
McGraw, Jack Wilson *government official*
Simons, Lynn Osborn *federal education official*
Woerner, Robert Eugene *federal agency administrator, editor*
Woodward, Dean Allen *state agency administrator*

Englewood
†Vallin, Travis L. *state government administator*

Golden
Olson, Marian Katherine *emergency management executive, consultant, publisher*
Stewart, Frank Maurice, Jr. *federal agency administrator*

Lakewood
†Kourlis, Thomas A. *state commissioner*

Littleton
Hayes, Roger Matthew *deputy sheriff*

Longmont
Kaminsky, Glenn Francis *deputy chief of police retired, business owner, teacher*

Monument
Miele, Alfonse Ralph *former government official*

Vail
McGee, Michael Jay *fire marshal, educator*

CONNECTICUT

Cheshire
McKee, Margaret Jean *federal agency executive*

East Hartford
Franklin, Robert Richard *retired federal agency administrator, farmer*

Hartford
Berube, Jeanne Ann *state government policy director*
†Burke, John P. *state agency administrator*
Krpata, Richard Martin *state agency administrator*
†Nappier, Denise L. *state agency administrator*
Piotrowski, Richard Francis *state agency administrator, council chairman*
†Sergi, Theodore S. *state agency administrator*

New Haven
O'Connor, John R. *protective services official*

Newtown
Furhman, Herbert Gary *police officer*

Waterbury
†Epstein, Carl Plakcy *public information officer*
Plummer, John Mitchell *postal clerk*

Wethersfield
†Armstrong, John J. *state agency administrator*

DELAWARE

Dover
Britt, Maisha Dorrah *protective services official*
Ellingsworth, Alan D. *police superintendent*
Lowell, Howard Parsons *government records administrator*
†Tarburton, John F. *state agency administrator*
†Taylor, Stan *corrections department commissioner*
Williams, Donna Lee H. *state agency adminstrator*

Georgetown
Pippin, Kathryn Ann *state agency administrator*

Newark
Keene, William Blair *state education official*

Wilmington
Benson, Barbara Ellen *state agency administrator*
Caruso, Nicholas Dominic *protective services official*
Eichler, Thomas P. *state agency administrator*
†Mullaney, Timothy P. *United States marshall*
Vattilana, Joseph William *retired chief state safety inspector*

DISTRICT OF COLUMBIA

Washington
Ackerman, Kenneth David *federal agency administrator*
Adamsons, Uldis *government official*
Alberts, Bruce Michael *federal agency administrator, foundation administrator, biochemist*
Allen, Frederick Warner *federal agency executive*
†Allen, Melissa J. *federal agency administrator*
†Altenhofen, Jane Ellen *federal agency administrator, auditor*
Alvarez, Aida *federal agency administrator*
Anderson, David Turpeau *government official, judge*
Anfinson, Thomas Elmer *government financial administrator*
Armstrong, David Andrew *federal agency official, retired army officer*
†Armstrong, Michael J. *federal agency administrator*
†Armstrong, Robert *retired federal agency administrator*
Ashe, Lincoln Emil *police officer*
Attaway, David Henry *retired federal research administrator, oceanographer*
Atwood, John Brian *federal agency administrator*
†Ayres, David T. *senatorial administrator*
Bacon, Elinor R. *goverment agency administrator*
†Bacon, Kenneth H. *federal agency administrator, editor, journalist*
†Bahret, Mary Ellen *press secretary*
Bailey, Betty L. *federal agency administrator*
Baker, James Robert *federal agency administrator*
Balutis, Alan *federal agency administrator*
Baquet, Charles R., III *federal agency administrator*
†Barlow, Larry S. *federal agency administrator*
†Barr, Mari R. *federal agency administrator*
Barram, David J. *federal agency administrator*
Barry, Donald J. *government official*
Barry, Donald James *government official*
Barton, William Russell *government official*
Bateman, Paul William *government official, business executive*
†Beecher, Donna D. *human resources administrator*
Beecher, William Manuel *government official*
†Beers, Rand *narcotics and law enforcement administrator*
Bell, Hubert Thomas *government official*
Beller, Melanie *federal agency administrator*
Beneke, Patricia Jane *federal agency administrator*
†Benton, Marjorie Craig *federal agency administrator*
Berry, Mary Frances *federal agency administrator, history and law educator*
Berube, Raymond P. *federal agency administrator*
Biddle, Livingston Ludlow, Jr. *former government official, author, consultant*
Biechman, John Charles *federal agency official*
Bigelow, Donald Nevius *educational administrator, historian, consultant*
Biter, Richard M. *federal official*
Blum, Margaret D. *federal agency administrator*
†Boesel, Charles Mather *communications professional*
Born, Brooksley Elizabeth *lawyer*
Bragg, Lynn Munroe *federal agency administrator*
Brenner, Robert David *federal agency administrator*
Bresee, James Collins *federal agency scientist*
Brickhouse, Eugene A. *federal agency administrator*
†Briggs, Ethel D. *federal agency administrator*
Broun, Richard Hadas *government administrator*
†Brown, Alvin *housing and urban development administrator*
Brown, Bradford Clement *government relations public affairs executive*
Brown, Dale Susan *government administrator, educational program director, writer*
Brown, Harold *former secretary of defense, corporate director*
†Brown, Terrence J. *federal agency administrator*
Browner, Carol *federal agency administrator*
Brush, Peter Norman *retired federal agency administrator, lawyer*
†Bucella, Donna A. *federal official*
†Burbano, Fernando *federal agency administrator*
Byrne, Leslie Larkin *former federal agency administrator, former congresswoman*
†Callear, Mildred O. *federal agency administrator*
†Campbell, Arthur C. *federal agency adminstrator*
Caponiti, James *federal government official*
Carey, E. Fenton *federal agency associate administrator*
Chamberlin, John Charlton *federal agency administrator*
†Chesser, Judy Lee *federal agency administrator, lawyer*
Childress, Kerri J. *federal agency administrator*
†Clampitt, Susan *federal agency administrator*
†Clark, Jamie Rappaport *fish and wildlife service administrator*
Coleman, John V. *government official*
Congel, Frank Joseph *federal agency administrator, physicist*
†Conrad, Roan *federal agency administrator*
Conway, John Thomas *government official, lawyer, engineer*
†Conway, Sean *press secretary*
†Coonrod, Robert T. *federal agency administrator*
†Cooper, Cardell *housing and urban development administrator*
†Cordes, John F., Jr. *federal agency administrator*
Corlett, Cleve Edward *government administrator*
Coro, Alicia Camacho *federal executive*
Cotruvo, Joseph Alfred *federal agency administrator*
Cousar, Gloria *government official*
Coyle, Philip E. *federal agency administrator, engineer*
†Coyner, Kelley S. *federal agency administrator*
†Crapa, Joseph R. *federal agency administrator*
Craun, James *federal agency administrator*
Crawford, Carol Tallman *government executive*
Crawford, Jackie R. *federal agency administrator*
Creel, Harold Jennings, Jr. *federal commission administrator, lawyer*
Cunningham, George Woody *federal official, metallurgical engineer*
Cunninghame, Donna Holt *former government official*
Cuomo, Andrew *federal agency administrator*
†Cushing, Michael *federal agency administrator*
Dalrymple, John *federal agency administrator*
†Daniels, Legree S. *federal agency administrator*
Daniels, Stephen M. *government official*
†David, James *information officer*
Davis, Nathan Chilton *federal agency administrator*
†Davis, Thurman M. *federal agency administrator*
Dawson, Robert Kent *government relations expert*
†Day, Elizabeth A. *press secretary*
DeCell, Hal C. *federal agency administrator*
†De Leon, Rudy *government official*
delJunco, Tirso *federal agency administrator*
Denniston, Scott F. *federal agency administrator*
Derby, Adele *government agency administrator*
†De Santi, Susan S. *federal agency administrator*
Diehl, Philip N. *federal government official*
DiMario, Michael Francis *federal agency official, lawyer*
†Duffy, Dennis M. *federal agency administrator*
†Edward, Thomas L. *federal agency administrator*
Eggenberger, Andrew Jon *federal agency administrator*
Elkinton, Steven *government agency administrator*
Erdreich, Ben Leader *federal agency executive*
Falkner, Juliette *federal agency administrator*
Farmer, Greg *former federal agency administrator*
Ferguson, Thomas *federal agency administrator*
Fingerhut, Marilyn Ann *federal agency administrator*
Finkel, Adam *government agency administrator*
Fitz-Pegado, Lauri J. *telecommunications executive*
Flynn, Cathal *federal agency amdinistrator*
Flynn, Nancy Marie *government executive*
Ford, William R. *federal agency administrator*
Fosdick, Cora Prifold (Cora Prifold Beebe) *government official*
Fowler, William E., Jr. *government official*
Fox, Lynn Smith *federal government official*
Freeh, Louis Joseph *federal agency administrator*
Freeman, Chas. W., Jr. *government official, ambassador, author*
†French, Richard Vaughn *federal agency administrator*
Friday, Elbert Walter, Jr. *federal agency administrator, meteorologist*
Fried, Edward R. *government official*
Friedlander, Bernice *federal program administrator*
†Fulton, Scott C. *federal agency administrator*
Gainer, Terrance W. *police official*
Gall, Mary Sheila *federal agency administrator*
Gallegos, Lou *federal agency administrator*
Gardiner, David *federal agency administrator*
Garvey, Jane *federal aviation administrator*
Gearan, Mark D. *federal agency administrator*
†Gensler, Gary *federal agency administrator*
†Gianni, Gaston L., Jr. *federal agency administrator*
Gibson, Thomas Fenner, III *public affairs strategist, political cartoonist*
Gillingham, Robert Fenton *federal agency administrator, economist*
Gilliom, Judith Carr *government official*
Gleiman, Edward Jay *federal agency administrator*
Gober, Hershel W. *government official*
Godwin, Kimberly Ann *federal agency administrator, lawyer*
Goldin, Daniel S. *federal agency administrator*
†Good, David P. *federal agency administrator*
Goodman, Margaret Gertrude *government administrator*
†Goss, Kay Collett *government official*
Gottemoeller, Rose E. *federal agency administrator*
Gottlieb, James Rubel *federal agency administrator, lawyer*
Greaux, Cheryl Prejean *federal agency administrator*
†Greeson, Jennifer *press secretary*
Gretch, Paul *federal agency administrator*
†Griffin, Richard J. *federal agency administrator*
†Griffith, Reginald W. *federal agency administrator*
Haass, Richard Nathan *federal agency administrator, educator*
Hale, Robert Fargo *government official*
Hall, James Evan *federal agency administrator, lawyer*
Hall, Michael Lee *federal government agency grants administrator*
Haltzel, Michael Harris *federal agency administrator*
Hammond, Jerome Jerald *government program administrator, agricultural economist*
†Hanley, Edward J. *federal agency administrator*
Hanley, Edward John *federal government executive*
†Hanson, John *federal agency administrator*
†Harder, Cherie S. *public information officer*
†Harrison, Gregory *public information officer*
†Hart, Clyde J., Jr. *federal agency administrator*
Hayes, Paula Freda *governmental official*
Hempel, Fred *federal government administrator*
Henderson, Peter Harry *non-profit organization administrator*
Henderson, William J. *postmaster general*
Henry, Sherrye *federal agency administrator*
†Hensley, Sue L. *communications director*
†Herr, Phillip Ray *federal agency administrator*
Heumann, Judith *federal agency administrator*
Higgins, Kathryn O'Leary *government official*
Hill, Jefferson Borden *regulatory oversight officer, lawyer*
Hill, Jimmie Dale *retired government official*
Hollis, Walter Winslow *government official*
Holum, John D. *federal agency administrator*
†Holz, Arnold G. *federal agency administrator*
†Horn, Floyd P. *federal agency administrator*
Horner, Constance Joan *federal agency administrator*
†Hotmire, Erik Joseph *press secretary*
Hove, Andrew Christian *federal agency administrator*
Hsu, Ming Chen *federal agency administrator*
†Hubbard, Daniel T., Jr. *public information officer*
Igasaki, Paul M. *federal agency administrator*
Jackson, Shirley Ann *federal agency administrator, physicist*
Jacobs, David E. *federal agency administrator*
Jeffress, Charles N. *government agency administrator*
Jenson, William G. *federal agency administrator*
Johnson, Arlene Lytle *government agency official*
†Johnson, Jacqueline *Native American program administrator*
Josephson, Diana Hayward *government agency official*
Kamensky, John Michael *federal agency administrator*
Kammerer, Joseph T. *government official*
†Kane, Allen *postal service executive*
Karnas, Fred G., Jr. *government agency administrator*
Karpan, Kathleen Marie *former state official, lawyer, journalist*
Kearney, Stephen Michael *corporate treasurer*
†Keilty, Bryan T. *government agency administrator*
Kelley, Edward Watson, Jr. *federal agency administrator*
†Kelly, Raymond W. *federal agency administrator*
†Kemble, Penn *government official*
Kennard, William Earl *federal agency administrator, lawyer*
†Kenney, Dennis Jay *criminal justice researcher, educator*
†Kerr, T. Michael *federal official*

Kilgore, Edwin Carroll *retired government official, consultant*
†Killefer, Nancy *federal agency administrator*
Kinsey, Mark A. *government official*
Kitzmiller, William Michael *government official*
†Knisely, Robert A. *federal agency administrator*
†Koehnke, Donna R. *federal agency administrator*
Kutscher, Ronald Earl *retired federal government executive*
†Lachance, Janice Rachel *federal agency administrator, lawyer*
†Lago, Marisa *federal agency administrator*
†Lane, Maury *communications director*
Lane, Neal Francis *federal administrator, physics researcher, former university provost*
†Larkin, Barbara Mills *federal agency administrator*
Lash, Terry R. *federal agency administrator*
†Lathen, Deborah A. *federal agency administrator*
†Layden, John F. *federal agency chairman*
†Lemmon, David *press secretary*
Lentini, Joseph Charles *government agency management analyst*
Levitt, Arthur, Jr. *federal agency administrator, securities and publishing executive*
†Lewis, John Van Dusen *federal agency administrator, anthropologist*
Lieberman, James *federal agency administrator*
Lindsey, Alfred Walter *federal agency official, environmental engineer*
†Linton, Gordon J. *federal agency administrator*
Lissakers, Karin Margareta *federal agency administrator*
Loach, Robert Edward *federal agency administrator*
Lobron, Neil Richard *federal civil servant*
†Lockwood, Maggie L. *press secretary*
Loy, Frank Ernest *government official*
Luck, Andrew Peter *federal agency administrator*
†Ludecke, Kristen M. *press secretary*
†Lundsager, Meg *federal agency administrator*
Lynn, William James, III *federal agency administrator*
†Maco, Paul S. *securities and exchange administrator*
Mader, David *federal agency administrator*
†Madison, Christopher King *communications director*
Maillett, Louise Elizabeth *government official*
Mann, John L. *federal agency administrator*
Martinez, Eluid *government official*
†Martinez, Ricardo *federal agency administrator*
†Masten, Charles C. *federal agency administrator*
Maxwell, David Ogden *former government official and financial executive*
Mc Afee, William *government official*
McAteer, J. Davitt *federal agency administrator*
†McCam, Shelia *federal agency administrator*
McCreight, Robert Edwin *federal agency administrator, educator*
†McKelvie, Darina C. *federal agency administrator*
McLucas, William Robert *federal agency director*
McQueen, James T. *federal agency administrator*
†McTaggart, Timothy Robert *state agency administrator, lawyer*
†Mead, Kenneth Minor *federal agency administrator*
Medish, Mark *federal government official*
Mehle, Roger W. *federal agency administrator*
Menczer, William B. *government agency executive*
Mlay, Marian *retireed government official*
†Molitoris, Jolene M. *federal agency administrator*
Moniz, Ernest Jeffrey *government official, former physics educator*
Moreno, G(ilberto) Mario *federal agency administrator*
Morgan, Linda Joan *federal agency administrator*
†Morris, Joann Sebastion *federal agency admnistrator*
†Morse, Jerome Samuel *government administrator, trade specialist*
†Mosley, Raymond A. *federal agency administrator*
†Munoz, George *federal agency administrator*
Murr, James Coleman *retired federal government official*
†Naher, Raymond *federal agency administrator*
Neal, Darwina Lee *government official*
Nethery, John Jay *government official*
†Okin, Carol J. *federal agency administrator*
Oliver, LeAnn Michelle *government official*
O'Neill, Richard Paul *federal agency administrator*
Opfer, George J. *federal agency executive*
Owendoff, James M. *federal agency administrator*
†Palast, Geri Deborah *federal agency administrator, Lawyer*
Pari, Brigitta Gulya *federal government official*
Patron, June Eileen *former government official*
Patterson, Sally Jane *government affairs consultant*
Pepper, Robert *federal agency administrator*
Perciasepe, Robert *federal agency administrator*
Phillips, Pamela Kelly *public affairs specialist*
†Pincus, Aileen *press secretary*
Pincus, Ann Terry *federal agency administrator, editor, writer*
†Porras, M. Richard *postal services executive*
Posey, Ada Louise *federal agency administrator*
†Potok, Nancy Ann *federal agency administrator*
†Pressley, Donald L. *federal agency administrator*
Quello, James Henry *government official*
Rao, Potarazu Krishna *government executive*
Reed, Anne F. Thomson *government official*
Reilly, Patrick William *government official*
Reinsch, William Alan *government executive, educator*
†Riccobono, Richard M. *federal agency administrator*
Richardson, Margaret Milner *accounting firm executive, lawyer*
Richlen, Scott Lane *federal government program administrator*
Riggs, John Alan *institute administrator*
Riley, John Patrick *legislative advisor*
Risbrudt, Christopher Dave *federal agency administrator, economist*
Rivera, Fanny *government agency administrator*
Rivlin, Alice Mitchell *federal agency administrator, economist*
Roberts, Alan L. *federal agency administrator*
†Robertson, Linda L. *federal agency administrator*
Rogers, Raymond Jesse *federal railroad associate administrator*
†Romero, Henry *federal associate director*
Rominger, Richard *federal agency administrator*
†Rood, Sally A. *federal agency administrator*
Rosendhal, Jeffrey David *federal science agency administrator, astronomer*
Rosenstock, Linda *federal agency administrator, medical educator*
†Ross, David Gray *child support administrator*
†Roth, Stanley Owen *federal agency administrator*
Rothenberg, Joseph Howard *federal agency administrator*
Rottman, Ellis *public information officer*
Rubinoff, Roberta Wolff *government administrator*
Rushton, Emory Wayne *government official*
Ryan, John E. *federal agency administrator*
†Sanders, David G. *federal agency administrator*
Savage, Phillip Hezekiah *federal agency administrator*
Schapiro, Mary *federal agency administrator, lawyer*
Schloss, Howard Monroe *federal agency administrator*
Schneider, Mark Lewis *government official*
Schoenberg, Mark George *government agency administrator*
Schuerch, William *federal agency official*
Searing, Marjory Ellen *government official, economist*
Shapiro, Michael Henry *government executive*
Shearer, Paul Scott *government relations professional*
†Sheehy, Daniel Edward *arts administrator, musician*
†Shelton, Henry H. *federal agency administrator*
†Shelton-Colby, Sally *federal agency administrator*
Singerman, Phillip A. *federal agency administrator*
†Slocombe, Walter Becker *government official, lawyer*
†Smith, Nancy M. *federal agency administrator*
Smith, Wendy Haimes *federal agency administrator*
Smith, William Lee *federal administrator, educator*
Solecki, Ray *government agency administrator*
†Sonderquist, Randy *public information officer*
Spector, Eleanor Ruth *government executive*
Springer, Fred Everett *federal agency administrator*
Springer, Michael Louis *federal agency administrator*
†Standefer, Richard B. *federal agency administrator*
Stanley, Elaine Gerber *government official*
Starek, Roscoe, III *federal agency official*
†Stark, Janice Roberta *operations administrator*
Stayman, Allen Paul *federal agency administrator*
Steele, Ana Mercedes *former government official*
Stevenson, Katherine Holler *federal agency administrator*
Stillman, Robert Donald *government official*
Stonehill, Robert Michael *federal agency administrator*
Stoner, John Richard *federal government executive*
Straub, Chester John, Jr. *government official*
Summers, Lawrence *government official*
†Sutton, Jeffrey E. *associate administrator management*
†Swedin, Kris *federal agency administrator*
Sweedler, Barry Martin *federal agency administrator*
Swoope, Anthony *government agency administrator*
†Taft, Julia V. *population, refugees and migration administrator*
Takamura, Jeanette Chiyoko *federal government official*
Tanoue, Donna A. *federal agency administrator*
Tarrants, William Eugene *government official*
†Tates-Macias, Cheryl *federal agency administrator*
Tenet, George John *government agency official*
Thompson, Lawrence Hyde *federal agency official*
Tichenor, Charles Beckham, III *federal agency management and program analyst*
†Tinsley, Nikki Lee *federal agency administrator*
Tomb, Rex Skelton *federal agency administrator*
Toner, John *federal agency administrator*
Towey, Carroll Francis *senior education specialist*
Tuck, John Chatfield *former federal agency administrator, public policy advisor*
Tull, John E., Jr. *federal agency commissioner*
†Ucelli, Loretta M. *federal agency administrator*
Vanderveen, John E. *federal agency administrator, emeritus scientist*
†Van de Water, Mark E. *federal agency administrator*
Verstandig, Toni Grant *federal agency administrator*
Vest, Gary D. *federal agency administrator*
Wagner, G. Martin *federal agency administrator*
†Warner, Edward L., III *federal agency administrator*
Washburn, Abbott McConnell *government official*
Washburn, Kathryn Hazel *government agency executive*
†Washington, Bonnie *healthcare administrator*
†Watkins, Dayton J. *federal agency administrator*
Watson, Harlan L(eroy) *federal official, physicist, economist*
Weinstein, Kenneth N. *federal government administrator*
Weirich, Richard Denis *government official*
Weisberg, Stuart Elliot *federal official, lawyer*
Wells, Linton, II *government official*
†Wenzel, Bob *federal agency administrator*
White, George *government official, physical scientist*
White, John *federal agency administrator*
Williamson, Richard Hall *federal association executive*
Williamson, Rushton Marot, Jr. *information technology project manager*
†Wilson, Ross *political advisor*
Winkler, Vera Cortada (Nina Winkler) *government executive*
†Winokur, Robert S. *federal agency administrator*
†Winter, Michael Alex *federal agency administrator*
Winter, Roger Paul *government official*
Winters, Sam *federal agency administrator, lawyer*
Withrow, Mary Ellen *federal agency administrator*
Witt, James Lee *federal agency administrator, director*
Wolanin, Thomas Richard *educator, researcher*
†Worden, Robert Leo *government agency administrator, researcher*
†Wright, Christopher J. *federal agency administrator*
Wrigley, William David *protection services official*
Wytkind, Edward *federal agency administrator*
†Yeager, Brooks *policy and international affairs administrator*
Zaffos, Gerald *federal agency executive*
Zenowitz, Allan Ralph *government official*
Zok, James J. *federal agency administrator*

FLORIDA

Boca Raton
Boggess, Jerry Reid *protective services official*

Bradenton
McGarry, Marcia *community service coordinator*
Thompson, Barbara Storck *state official*

Cocoa Beach
Choromokos, James, Jr. *former government official, consultant*

Coconut Creek
Limmer, Ezekiel *retired federal agency administrator, economist*

Debary
†Tauber, James G. *fire chief*

Delray Beach
Liguori, Joseph John, Jr. *fire fighter, paramedic consultant*

Fort Lauderdale
Etling, Terry Douglas *state agency administrator*

Fort Walton Beach
Culver, Dan Louis *federal agency administrator*

Gulf Breeze
Larson, Kurt Paul *fire chief*

Gulf Stream
Nalen, Craig Anthony *government official*

Havana
Macmillan, Tyler Lash *state agency administrator*

Hialeah
Bolanos, Rolando D. *protective services officer*
Horsley, Ernest *city administrator*

Homestead
Ring, Richard G. *national park service administrator*

Jacksonville
Glover, Nathaniel, Jr. *sheriff*
Mishael, Rochelle Jaaziel *retired correctional officer*
Potter, William *city executive*

Kennedy Space Center
Bridges, Roy Dubard, Jr. *federal agency administrator*

Miami
Fern, Emma Elsie *state agency administrator*

Saint Petersburg
Barca, James Joseph *fire department administrative services executive*
Callahan, James K. *fire chief*
Stephens, Darrel W. *protective services official*

Stuart
Laska, Paul Robert *protective services official, writer, educator*

Tallahassee
Ashler, Philip Frederic *international trade and development advisor*
Braswell, Jackie Boyd *state agency administrator*
Coe, Thomas R. *police chief*
Drayton, Carey M. *police administrator*
Ehlen, Martin Richard *state agency administrator, management analyst*
Milligan, Robert Frank *state agency administrator*
Thomas, James Bert, Jr. *government official*
Varn, Herbert Fred *state agency administrator*

Tampa
Holder, Ben R. *protective services official*
†Liedke, Guy Arthur *public administrator*
Moreland, Don *protective services official*
Nesmith, William Leonard *protective services official*

GEORGIA

Atlanta
†Chapman, William S. *state agency administrator*
†Ford-Roegner, Patricia A. *health services professional*
Garner, Edwin Bruce *government official*
†Garner, J. Wayne *state agency administrator*
†Gayle, Helene D. *federal agency administrator, pediatrician*
Harvard, Beverly Joyce Bailey *protective service official*
McMichael, Robert Henry *protective services official*
†Miles, Sid R. *state agency administrator*
Millar, John Donald *occupational and environmental health consultant, educator*
Minor, Winston L. *city fire chief*
Rucker, Kenneth Lamar *law enforcement officer, educator*
†Toomey, Kathleen E. *state agency administrator*
Wilson, Norman Eugene *adminstrator department Georgia penal institution*

Columbus
Collins, Wayne Winford *protective services official*
Johnson, Herman James *correctional facility administrator*
Miller, Luther C. *protective services official*

Conyers
†Vaighn, Arthur Augustus *state agency administrator*

Douglasville
Paterson, Paul Charles *private investigator, security consultant*

Glynco
†Basham, W. Ralph *federal agency administrator*

Hapeville
Bugg, Owen Bruce *state agency administrator*

Robins AFB
Lewis, Clinton *federal agency administrator*

Savannah
Caldwell, John Walter *United States marshal*

HAWAII

Honolulu
Devaney, Donald Everett *law enforcement official*
Kudo, Emiko Iwashita *former state official*
Roseberry, Edwin Southall *state agency administrator*
Saiki, Patricia (Mrs. Stanley Mitsuo Saiki) *former federal agency administrator, former congresswoman*
Seely, Marilyn Ruth *state agency administrator*

Kaneohe
Ikeda, Moss Marcus Masanobu *retired state education official, lecturer, consultant*

IDAHO

Boise
†Alcorn, James M. *state insurance administrator*
Heitman, Gregory Erwin *state official*
Peterson, Eileen M. *state agency director, administrator*
†Takasugi, Patrick A. *state agency administrator*

Moscow
Butterfield, Samuel Hale *former government official and educator*

ILLINOIS

Carol Stream
LaPorte, Stephen Walter *police officer*

Chicago
Jibben, Laura Ann *state agency administrator*
Koppe, William Paul *deputy sheriff*
Kuczwara, Thomas Paul *postal inspector, lawyer*
Rumsfeld, Donald Henry *former government official, corporate executive*
Spagnolo, Joseph A., Jr. *state agency administrator*
Van Pelt, Robert Irving *firefighter*
Wayman, David Anthony *state agency administrator*
Wilson, Richard Harold *government official*

Chicago Heights
Bohlen, Jeffrey Brian *protective services official*

Decatur
Erlanson, Deborah McFarlin *state program administrator*

Downers Grove
Hasen-Sinz, Susan Katherine *state agency administrator, actress*
Ruffolo, Paul Gregory *police officer, educator*

Godfrey
Ford, Terry Lynn *fire department executive*

La Grange Park
Calhamer, Allan Brian *retired postal worker*

Maywood
Farley, Robert Hugh *police detective, child abuse consultant*

Northlake
Haack, Richard Wilson *retired police officer*

Palatine
Hellyer, Timothy Michael *protective services officer*

Romeoville
Nagel, Kurt E. *police officer*

Savanna
Kuk, Michael Louis *protective services official*

Springfield
†Doyle, Rebecca Carlisle *state agency administrator*
Mogerman, Susan *state agency administrator*
Moore, Robert *protective services official*
Schroeder, Joyce Katherine *state agency administrator, research analyst*
Shim, Sang Koo *state mental health official*
†Washington, Odie *state agency administrator*

Tinley Park
Freitag, Carol Wilma *state official*

INDIANA

Indianapolis
†Carraway, Melvin J. *protective services official*
†Feldman, Richard David *health commissioner*
Gerdes, Ralph Donald *fire safety consultant*
†Jones, Stanley *state agency administrator*
†Nass, Connie Kay *state auditor*
Smith, Keith *protective services official*

La Porte
Hiler, John Patrick *former government official, former congressman, business executive*

Logansport
†Mayfield, Kristina Sue *protective services administrator*

Lowell
Reed, Gerald Wilfred *protective services official*

Mishawaka
Brogan-Werntz, Bonnie Bailey *retired police officer, photographer*

Schererville
Opacich, Milan *protective services official, musician*

IOWA

Cedar Rapids
Blome, Dennis H. *United States marshal*

Davenport
Wilson, Frances Edna *protective services official*

Des Moines
†Atchison, Christopher George *public health director*
Brickman, Kenneth Alan *state lottery executive*
Cherry, Linda Lea *federal agency official*
†Cochran, Dale M. *state agency administrator*
Henry, Phylliss Jeanette *United States Marshal*
Moulder, William H. *chief of police*
Porter, Russell Mark *law enforcement executive, educator, trainer*
†Stilwill, Ted *state agency administrator*
†Vaughan, Therese Michele *insurance commissioner*

Mc Callsburg
Lounsberry, Robert Horace *former state government administrator*

Treynor
†Guttau, Michael K. *state agency administrator, banker*

Waterloo
Newcomer, James Henry *government executive*

KANSAS

Colby
Finley, Philip Bruce *retired state adjutant general*

Lawrence
Gerry, Martin Hughes, IV *federal agency administrator, lawyer*

Olathe
Strieby, Douglas Hunter *law enforcement officer*

Pittsburg
†Emerson, Anne *state director*

Topeka
†Carlson, Scott Brandon *state agency administrator*
†Matson, Michael J. *press secretary*
McClinton, James Alexander *stage agency administrator, councilman*
Webb, Marvin Russell *former state agency director*

Wichita
Watson, William M. *chief of police*

KENTUCKY

Bowling Green
Wells, Jerry Wayne *police official*

Frankfort
†Herberg, Paul Thomas *state agency administrator*
†Rose, Gary *protective services official*
†Smith, Billy Ray *state commissioner*
Whaley, Charles E. *state agency administrator*

Irvine
†Carter, Jeffrey Scott *correctional officer*

Lexington
Calvert, C(lyde) Emmett *state agency administrator, retired*

Louisville
Adams, Robert Waugh *state agency administrator, economics educator*
†Potter, Eugenia Kelly *state agency administrator, publisher*
Sanders, Russell Edward *protective services official*

Madisonville
Veazey, Doris Anne *state agency administrator, retired*

Owensboro
†Miller, Scott Bryan *public administration specialist*

Warsaw
†LeGrand, William R. *retired postmaster, insurance agent*

LOUISIANA

Baton Rouge
†E. Joseph, Savioe *state education agency administrator*
†Golsby, Marsanne *press secretary*
Granger, Frank, III *assessor*
†Mann, Robert Townley *press secretary*
Parks, James William, II *public facilities executive, lawyer*
Phares, Greg *protective services officer*
†Picard, Cecil *state education agency administrator*
Stalder, Richard L. *corrections official*
†Whittington, William R. *protective services official*

Bogalusa
Henke, Shauna Nicole *police dispatcher, small business owner*

New Orleans
McDaniels, Warren *fire official*
Pennington, Richard J. *protective service official*

MAINE

Portland
†Gilbert, Laurent F., Sr. *state agency administrator*

MARYLAND

Annapolis
Taussig, Joseph Knefler, Jr. *retired government official, lawyer*
†Virts, Henry A. *veterinarian, state agency administrator*

Baltimore
Anderson, John William *protective services official*
†Apfel, Kenneth S. *federal government official*
†Colvan, Carolyn W. *federal agency administrator*
Frazier, Thomas C. *protective services official*
Gallups, Vivian Lylay Bess *federal contracting officer*
Hart, Robert Gordon *federal agency administrator*
†Huber, Jay D. *state agency administrator*
†Huse, James G. *federal agency administrator*
Johnson, Elaine McDowell *retired federal government executive, educator*
McKinney, George K. *protective services official*
†Richardson, Sally Keadle *state health care administrator*
Uhl, Scott Mark *state agency administrator*
Wainwright, Joan *federal agency administrator*
Wheeler, Peter Martin *federal agency administrator*
Williams, Herman, Jr. *protective services offical*

Beltsville
Tso, Tien Chioh *federal agency official, plant physiologist*

Bethesda
†Battey, James F. *federal agency administrator*
Brown, Ann *federal agency administrator*
Fefferman, Hilbert *lawyer, government official*
†Ficca, Stephen A. *federal agency administrator*
†Frye, Robert Edward *federal agency administrator*
Funk, Sherman Maxwell *former government official, writer, consultant*
†Gilbert, Pamela *federal agency administrator*
†Gorden, Phillip *federal agency administrator*
Hundt, Reed Eric *federal agency administrator, lawyer*
Joyce, Bernita Anne *federal government agency administrator*
Klausner, Richard D. *federal agency administrator, cell biologist*
Larrabee, Barbara Princelau *retired intelligence officer*
Lee, Young Jack *federal agency administrator*
†Murr, Thomas W., Jr. *federal agency administrator*
O'Callaghan, Jerry Alexander *government official*
Richardson, John *retired international relations executive*
Schambra, Philip Ellis *federal agency administrator, radiobiologist*
Skirboll, Lana R. *federal health policy director*
Twiss, John Russell, Jr. *federal government agency executive*
Varmus, Harold Eliot *government health institutes administrator, educator*
Vigil, Eugene Leon *federal agency administrator, cell biologist*
Wente, Van Arthur *consultant, retired government official*
Whaley, Storm Hammond *retired government official, consultant*
Young, Frank Edward *former federal agency administrator, religious organization administrator*

Chester
Svahn, John Alfred *government official*

Chevy Chase
†Gaines, Michael Johnston *parole commissioner*
Hudson, Anthony Webster *retired federal agency administrator, minister*
Pitofsky, Robert *federal agency administrator, law educator*
Quinn, Eugene Frederick *government official, clergyman*
Weiss, Ernest *federal agency administrator*

Clinton
Kennedy, G. Alfred *retired federal agency administrator*

Crofton
Harding-Clark, Jessica Rose *public affairs specialist, journalist*

Fort Washington
Stiver, William Earl *retired government administrator*
Weaver, Frank Cornell *government agency administrator*

Frederick
†Pearson, Jennie Sue *retired government administrator*

Gaithersburg
Hertz, Harry Steven *government official*
Johnson, Frederick Carroll *federal government executive*
Kammer, Raymond Gerard, Jr. *government official*
Snell, Jack Eastlake *federal agency administrator*

Glen Burnie
Zabetakis, Thomas John *federal agency administrator*

Hyattsville
Bell, Harriette Elizabeth *stock agency administrator*

Ijamsville
Chen, Philip S., Jr. *government official*

Kensington
Glower, Raphael *personnel management administrator, program analyst*
Suraci, Charles Xavier, Jr. *retired federal agency administrator, aerospace education consultant*

Laurel
Chrismer, Ronald Michael *federal agency administrator*

Madison
Hoffman, Alicia Coro *retired federal executive*

Millersville
Vlavianos, John G. *retired federal agency administrator*

North Bethesda
White, Bonnie Havana *retired federal agency official*

Ocean City
Skidmore, Linda Carol *science and engineering consultant*

Potomac
Frey, James McKnight *government official*
Rotberg, Iris Comens *social scientist*

Rockville
Aamodt, Roger Louis *federal agency administrator*
Chavez, Nelba *federal agency administrator*
†Couig, Mary Patricia *federal agency administrator*
Fouchard, Joseph James *retired government agency administrator*
Fox, Claude Earl *federal health official*
Friedman, Michael A. *food and drug agency commissioner*
Galaty, Carol Popper *health policy administrator*
Kelsey, Frances Oldham (Mrs. Fremont Ellis Kelsey) *government official*
McGaffigan, Edward, Jr. *federal agency administrator*
Rheinstein, Peter Howard *government official, physician, lawyer*
Simpson, Lisa Ann *government agency administrator, physician*
†Stoiber, Carlton Ray *government agency official*
†Zoon, Kathryn Christine *biologics research administrator*

Silver Spring
†Hall, J. Michael *federal agency administrator, oceanographer*
Kline, Jerry Robert *government official, ecologist*
Maas, Joe (Melvin Joseph Maas) *retired federal agency administrator*
Manheimer, Bernard Henry *federal agency administrator, consultant*
Telesetsky, Walter *government official*
Weisman, Herman Muni *retired emergency research administrator*
Williams, Paul *retired federal agency administrator*

Waldorf
Gray, Tammi Terrell *federal agency analyst, writer*

MASSACHUSETTS

Beverly
McMahon, Joyce Arlene *public information director*

Boston
Evans, Paul F. *protective services official*
McLeod, Andrew Harvey *conservationalist*
Pierce, Martin E., Jr. *fire commissioner*
Sullivan, Dorothy Rona *state official*
Woerner, Fred Frank *federal agency*

Cambridge
Deutch, John Mark *federal agency administrator, chemist, academic administrator*
Donahue, John David *public official, educator*

Dorchester
Garrison, Althea *government official*

Everett
Shedden, Kenneth Charles *fire department official, business owner*

Framingham
†Hillman, Reed V. *protective services official*

Hingham
Zieper, Matthew Howard *policy analyst*

Medfield
Heffernan, Peter John *state official*

New Bedford
Benoit, Richard Armand *retired police chief, lawyer*

Plymouth
Forman, Peter *sheriff, former state legislator*

Westborough
Horwitz, Eleanor Catherine *information and education official*

MICHIGAN

Ann Arbor
Schmitt, Mary Elizabeth *postal supervisor*

Atlanta
†Francisco, Wayne H. *criminalist, educator*

Bloomfield Hills
Jones, John Paul *probation officer, psychologist*

Detroit
Budny, James Charles *federal agency administrator*
Forbes-Richardson, Helen Hilda *state agency administrator*

Flint
Becker, Michael Edward *police and emergency medical services executive*

Idlewild
Bullett, Audrey Kathryn *retired public administrator*

Lanse
Butler, Patricia *protective services official*

Lansing
Beardmore, Dorothy *state education official*
Brook, Susan G. *state agency administrator, horse farmer*
Mee, Richard James *state agency administrator*

New Haven
Shaw, Charles Rusanda *government investigator*

Okemos
Montgomery, James Huey *state government administrator, consultant*

MINNESOTA

Excelsior
Brekke, Judy Lynn *state agency administrator*

Fort Snelling
†Morris, Raymond Walter *state agency administrator*

Minneapolis
Olson, Robert K. *police chief*
Stark, Matthew *higher education and civil rights administrator*

Robbinsdale
Manning, Edward Peter *protective services official*

Saint Paul
Davis, Richard Carlton *state agency administrator*
Finney, William K. *police chief*
Hall, Beverly Joy *police officer*
Stanek, Richard Walter *police captain, Minneapolis*
†Wedl, Robert J. *state agency commissioner*

Stillwater
Carlson, Norman A. *government official*

MISSISSIPPI

Jackson
†Anderson, James V. *state agency administrator*
Bennett, Marshall Goodloe, Jr. *state official, lawyer*
Durr, Eisenhower *protective services official*
†Garriga, Mark *state government administrator*
†Ingram, James *state agency administrator*
Laster, Rhonda Renée *juvenile probation/parole officer*
Ranck, Edward L. *state agency administrator*
†Spell, Lester James *state agency administrator*

Oxford
Crews, David *protective services official*
Johnson, Joyce Thedford *state agency administrator*

Stennis Space Center
Estess, Roy S. *federal agency administrator*

MISSOURI

Blue Springs
†Snyder, James Robert *protective services official, educator*

Cape Girardeau
†Schulte, Tom *public information officer*

Creve Coeur
Luzio, Timothy Joseph *protective services official*

Gladstone
†Hasty, Michael Joe *protective services official*

Jefferson City
Bartman, Robert E. *state education official*
Forbis, Bryan Lester *state agency administrator*
Karll, Jo Ann *state agency administrator, lawyer*
Mahfood, Stephen Michael *governmental agency executive*
Peeno, Larry Noyle *state agency administrator, consultant*
†Saunders, John L. *state agency administrator*
†Vincent, Trish *state agency administrator*
†Wilnoit, W. L. *protective services official*

Kansas City
English, R(obert) Bradford *marshal*
Fairchild, Sharon Elaine *corrections administrator*
McLendon, Jesse Lawrence *protective services official*
Parker, Dennis Gene *former sheriff, karate instructor*

Lambert Airport
Griggs, Leonard LeRoy, Jr. *federal agency administrator*

Saint Louis
Domahidy, Mary Rodgers *public policy educator*
Henderson, Ronald *police chief*
Scheffing, Donald George *county government administrator*

Springfield
Green, David Ferrell *law enforcement official*
Gruhn, Robert Stephen *parole officer*
Luttrull, Shirley JoAnn *protective services official*

Wheeling
†Roe, Mary Ann *postmaster*

MONTANA

Helena
†Lewis, Dave *state agency administrator*
†Peck, Ralph *state agency administrator*
†Reap, Craig T. *protective services officer*

NEBRASKA

Arlington
Boerrigter, Glenn Charles *educational administrator*

PROFESSIONAL INDEX 5965 GOVERNMENT: AGENCY ADMINISTRATION

Lincoln
†Christensen, Douglas *state agency administrator*
†Kilgarin, Karen *state official, public relations consultant*

Norfolk
Heineman, Gregory Lyle *government agency administrator*

O'Neill
Hedren, Paul Leslie *national park administrator, historian*

Omaha
†Hansen, James Allen *state agency administrator*
Thorogood, John Harry *protective service official*

NEVADA

Carson City
†Finn, Jack *press secretary*
†Peterson, Mary L. *state agency official*
Rankin, Teresa P. Froncek *state agency administrator, insurance educator*

Henderson
Perkins, Richard Dale *police official, state legislator*

Las Vegas
Klein, Freda *retired state agency administrator*
Lally, Norma Ross *federal agency administrator, retired*
Martin, Michael Albert *surveillance agent*
Spencer, Carol Brown *association executive*
Trevino, Mario H. *protective services official*
†Troncoso, Jose Gerardo *United States marshall*
Wieting, Gary Lee *federal agency executive*
Wood, Benjamin Carroll, Jr. *safety professional*

North Las Vegas
Marchand, Russell David, II *fire chief*

Reno
†Iverson, Paul *government agency administrator*

NEW HAMPSHIRE

Concord
Brunelle, Robert L. *retired state education director*
Day, Russell Clover *state agency administrator*
Mevers, Frank Clement *state archivist, historian*
Risley, Henry Brainard *protective service official*
†Taylor, Stephen H. *state commissioner*

Derry
MacDonald, Wayne Douglas *fraud investigator*

Exeter
DeLucia, Gene Anthony *government administrator, computer company executive*

NEW JERSEY

Absecon
Byrne, Shaun Patrick *law enforcement officer*

Adelphia
Carter, Harry Robert *fire chief*

Irvington
Huber, Donald Mark *protective services official*

Jamesburg
Wolfe, Deborah Cannon Partridge *government education consultant*

Lakeland
Connor, Wilda *government health agency administrator*

Lawrenceville
Hunt, Wayne Robert, Sr. *state government official*
Stockton, John Potter, III *retired state agency administrator*

Madison
Kluck, Edward Paul *chief of police*

Maplewood
Rabadeau, Mary Frances *protective services official*

Mount Holly
†Holba, Annette M. *county detective, educator*

Mountainside
Weigele, Richard Sayre *police officer*

New Brunswick
Stewart, Ruth Ann *public policy analyst, professor*

Newark
Cunningham, Glenn Dale *protective services official*
†Santiago, Joseph J. *protective services official*
Young, Darlene *post office executive*

Toms River
Rupert, Wayne Richard *protective services official*

Trenton
†Brown, Arthur R. *state agency administrator*
Salgado, Luis José *state agency official*
Traier, John *state agency administrator*
†Yull, Peter Martin *state agency administrator*

Weehawken
Murphy, Barbara Ann *protective services official*

Willingboro
Greene, Natalie Constance *protective services official*

NEW MEXICO

Albuquerque
Gordon, Larry Jean *public health administrator and educator*
Huling, Morris *fire chief*
Jaramillo, Mari-Luci *federal agency administrator*
Maestas, Alex Walter *state agency clerk*
Manz, Bruno Julius *retired government agency executive*
Marsh, William David *government operations executive*

Santa Fe
Knapp, Edward Alan *retired government administrator, scientist*
Mitio, John, III *state agency administrator*
Rogers, Jerry L. *federal agency administrator*
Saurman, Andrew (Skip Saurman) *state agency executive*
†Verant, William J. *state agency administrator*
Wentz, Christopher James *state agency administrator*
†White, Darren *state agency administrator*

NEW YORK

Albany
Borys, Theodor James *state agency data center administrator*
Bradley, Edward James *state official, computer programmer and analyst*
Cross, Robert Francis *city official*
Granderath, Walter Joseph *tax administrator*
Horn, Martin F. *state agency administrator*
†Mills, Richard P. *state agency administrator*
†Patton, Gerald Wilson *state agency administrator*
†Polan, David Ray *public administrator*
Shields, Robert Michael *state agency administrator*

Brooklyn
Bigger, Philip Joseph *judicial branch official*
Von Essen, Thomas *protective services official*

Buffalo
Keane, Cornelius John *fire commissioner*

Deer Park
Maher, James Richard *protective services offical*

Flushing
Viegas, Louis Paul *postmaster*

Fredonia
Mallory, George Wolcott *retired federal agency officer*
Strauser, Jeffrey Arthur *public safety official*

Great Neck
Blumberg, Barbara Salmanson (Mrs. Arnold G. Blumberg) *retired state housing official, housing consultant*

Guilderland
†Reiff, Robert L. *federal agency specialist*

Hartsdale
Jones, Donald Kelly *state agency executive*

Ithaca
Murphy, Eugene Francis *retired government official, consultant*

Kingston
Salzmann, Richard Thomas *protective services official*

Lackawanna
Smith, Michael Joseph *protective services official*

Latham
Standfast, Susan J(ane) *state official, researcher, consultant, educator*

New York
Alexander, Jane *federal agency administrator, actress, producer*
Beausoleil, Doris Mae *federal agency administrator, housing specialist*
†Burke, Martin J. *United States marshall*
Cremer, Leon Earl *federal agent, lawyer*
FitzGerald, Gerald P. *state agency executive*
Gelb, Bruce Stuart *city commissioner, consultant*
Holzer, Harold *public information officer, historian, writer*
Korb, Lawrence Joseph *government official*
Lord, Barbara Joanni *public official, lawyer*
Mahon, John Joseph *federal agency adminstrator*
†Noman, Omar *program manager, writer*
Safir, Howard *police commissioner*
Sorensen, Gillian Martin *United Nations official*
Steinlight, Stephen Mark *public policy director*
Talbot, Phillips *Asian affairs specialist*

Rochester
†Duffy, Robert John *police chief*
Jones-Atkins, DeBorah Kaye *state official*
McCaffrey, John P. *protective services official*
Meloni, Andrew P. *protective services official*

Schenevus
Fielder, Dorothy Scott *postmaster*

South Nyack
†Colsey, Alan Blair *public safety executive*

Syracuse
Naum, Christopher John *fire protection management and training consultant, educator*

Valhalla
Czarnecki, Anthony J. *correction administrator, educator*

Yonkers
Pasquale, Terry *police department administrator*

NORTH CAROLINA

Asheville
Edminster, Walter B. *protective services official*
Roberts, Bill Glen *retired fire chief, investor, consultant*

Burlington
Kee, Walter Andrew *former government official*

Corolla
Schrote, John Ellis *retired government executive*

Durham
†Aldridge, Geoffrey *security consultant*

Elizabeth City
Lewis, Tola Ethridge, Jr. *retired state agency administrator, martial arts instructor*

Greensboro
Lindemeyer, Nancy Jo *public information officer*
Reed, William Edward *government official, educator*
Wallace, Becky Whitley *protective services official*

Raleigh
Maness, Edwin Clinton, III *highway patrol officer, video coordinator*

NORTH DAKOTA

Bismarck
Clark, Tony *state agency administrator*
Isaak, Larry A. *state agency administrator*
Sanstead, Wayne Godfrey *state superintendent, former lieutenant governor*

OHIO

Akron
†Irvine, Edward D. *police chief*

Burton
Snyder, Timothy H. *police officer, lawyer*

Centerville
Baver, Roy Lane *retired protection services official, consultant*

Cleveland
Grabow, Raymond John *mayor, lawyer*
Harris, Clayton *police chief*
Jettke, Harry Jerome *retired government official*
Jones, Thomas F. *protective services official*
Troutman, David W. *protective services official*

Columbus
Bianco, Don Christopher *civil servant, retired*
Dresser, Karen Kerns *state agency administrator*
Gillmor, Karen Lako *state agency administrator, strategic planner*
†Goff, John *state agency administrator*
Jackson, G. James *protective services official*
McInturff, Floyd M. *retired state agency administrator*
Metzler, Eric Harold *retired state agency administrator, researcher*
Ray, Frank David *government agency official*
Thompson, James W., Jr. *state official*

Dayton
Hines, Jeff G. *environmental protection administrator*
†Lowe, Ronald, Sr. *chief of police*
Sweeney, James Lee *retired government official*

Montpelier
Deckrosh, Hazen Douglas *retired state agency educator and administrator*

Munroe Falls
Stahl, Steve Allen *protective services official*

Olmsted Falls
Kiessling, Ronald Frederick *retired federal government executive*

Pomeroy
Brockert, Joseph Paul *government executive, writer, editor, designer*

Reynoldsburg
†Daily, Fred L.

Toledo
Smith, Robert Nelson *former government official, anesthesiologist*

Upper Arlington
Holcomb, Dwight A. *city chief of police*

Zanesville
O'Sullivan, Christine *executive director social service agency*

OKLAHOMA

Chickasha
Beets, Freeman Haley *retired government official*

Oklahoma City
†Buchanan, Rick *press secretary*
Collins, William Edward *aeromedical administrator, researcher*
Daxon, Tom *state agency administrator*
Gonzales, Sam C. *protective service official*
Harbour, Robert Randall *state agency administrator*
†Wheeler, Jane Frances *protective services official*

Tulsa
Blackstock, Virginia Lee Lowman (Mrs. LeRoy Blackstock) *civic worker*
Deihl, Michael Allen *federal agency administrator*
Palmer, Ronald *police chief*

Wanette
Thompson, Joyce Elizabeth *retired state education official*

OREGON

Medford
Cole, Richard George *public administrator*

Portland
†Brockley, John P. *state agency executive, airport executive*
Erickson, Pamela Sue *state agency administrator*
†Thorne, Mike *state agency administrator*
Wall, Robert *fire chief*

Salem
DeLuca, Peter *state agency administrator, lawyer*
Howland, L.R. *protective services official*

PENNSYLVANIA

Allentown
McElroy, Janice Helen *government agency executive*

Butler
Rickard, Dennis Clark *sheriff, educator*

Castle Shannon
Selkowitz, Lucy Ann *security officer*

Franklin
Miller, John Karl *protective services official*

Gettysburg
Roach, James Clark *government official*

Harrisburg
†Evanko, Paul J. *commissioner, colonel Pennsylvania state police*
†Hayes, Samuel E., Jr. *state agency administrator*
†Hickok, Eugene W. *state agency administrator*
†Mazia, Theodore L. *state agency administrator*
Salomone, Anthony William, Jr. *state agency administrator*

Hawley
Hudak, Joseph David *state police investigator, educator, forensic engineer*

Mont Alto
Sourbier, James Henry, IV *police chief*

New Hope
Connolly, Janet Elizabeth *retired sociologist and criminal justice educator*

Philadelphia
Brown, Betty Marie *government agency administrator*
Hackney, Sheldon *federal agency administrator, academic administrator*
Hairston, Harold B. *protective services official*

Pittsburgh
Fullerton, Ernest Leroy *special agent, investigator, educator*

Scranton
Sokolowski, Walter D. *protective services official*

University Park
Lee, Robert Dorwin *public affairs educator*

Wallingford
Cook, Harvey Carlisle *law enforcement official*

Washington Crossing
Castle, Eric F. *administrator historic site*

RHODE ISLAND

Newport
Tuchman, Adam Michael *federal contract negotiator*

Providence
†Hulbert, Stephen *state agency administrator*
Leyden, John James *protective services official*
†McWalters, Peter *state agency administrator*
†Volpe, Stephen *agency administrator*

Warwick
Florio, David Peter *probation and parole counselor*

SOUTH CAROLINA

Charleston
Gaillard, John Palmer, Jr. *former government official, former mayor*
†Nielsen, Barbara Stock *state educational administrator*
†Rennhack, Joan Lee *safety enforcement official*

Columbia
Brooks, Israel, Jr. *protective services official*
Duffie, Virgil Whatley, Jr. *state agency administrator*
Inkley, Scott Russell, Jr. *state agency administrator*
Jennings, William R. *state agency administrator*

Georgetown
†Walters, Alan Wayne *police officer*

Hilton Head Island
Ink, Dwight A. *government agency administrator*

North
Moran, John Bernard *government official*

TENNESSEE

Brighton
King, James Andrew *protective services educator and administrator*

Dresden
McWherter, Ned Ray *government administrator, farmer, investor*

Gatlinburg
Wade, Karen *national parks administrator*

Knoxville
Crowell, Craven H., Jr. *federal agency administrator*
Fowler, Joseph Clyde, Jr. *protective services official*

Memphis
Knight, H. Stuart *law enforcement official, consultant*

Nashville
Guy, Sharon Kaye *state agency executive*
†Mathews, Robert C.H. *state agency executive*
Smith, Charles Edward *state agency administrator*
†Walters, Jane *state agency administrator*

Pickwick Dam
Casey, Beverly Ann *postmaster*

TEXAS

Amarillo
Bull, Walter Stephen *police officer*

Arlington
†Kunkle, David M. *police chief*

Austin
†Combs, Susan *commissioner of agriculture*
†Knee, Stanley La Moyne *protective services official*
†Molina, Eduardo *state agency administrator*
Paulsgrove, Robin *fire chief*
Richardson, Freda Leah *state agency executive*

Baytown
Leiper, Robert Duncan *local government official*

Bryan
Owens, Harold B. *former state agency consultant*

Corpus Christi
Alvarez, Peter, Jr. *police chief*

Dallas
Click, Bennie R. *protective services official*
Hill, Jesse Hoyt *training specialist, economics & business educator*
Miller, Dodd *protective services official*
Robb, Aaron David *child protective services investigator*
Thomas, Chester Wiley *special agent*

El Paso
†Grijalva, J. R. *police chief*

Fort Worth
Windham, Thomas *protective services official*

Galena Park
Price, Joe Sealy *law enforcement officer*

Houston
Bradford, C.O. *protective services officer*
Corral, Edward Anthony *fire marshal*
Kaup, David Earle *law enforcement officer*
Russell, Anna *city administrator*

Randolph AFB
Newton, Lloyd Warren *federal agency administrator, career officer*

Richardson
Cox, Sue *non-profit agency administrator*

San Antonio
Dean, Jack *protective services official*
Philippus, Al A. *protective services official*
Sessions, William Steele *lawyer, former government official*

Selma
†Lee, Allen Scott *protective services official*

Stonewall
Betzer, Roy James *retired national park service ranger*

UTAH

Brigham City
McCullough, Edward Eugene *patent agent, inventor*

Murray
†Haun, Henry Lamar *corrections department executive*

Salt Lake City
Gold, Rick L. *federal government executive*
†Leary, G. Edward *state finance commisioner*
Porter, Bruce Douglas *federal agency administrator, educator, writer*
Terry, David Thames *government administrator*

VERMONT

Springfield
Putnam, Paul Adin *retired government agency official*

Waterbury
Recchia, Christopher *state agency environmental administrator*

VIRGINIA

Alexandria
Christie, Thomas Philip *federal agency administrator, research manager*
Connally, Ernest Allen *retired federal agency administrator*
Connell, John Gibbs, Jr. *former government official*
Danaher, James William *retired federal government executive*
Duggan, Ervin S. *federal agency administrator*
Hughes, Grace-Flores *former federal agency administrator, consultant*
Leestma, Robert *federal agency administrator, educator*
†Patrick, Erline M. *federal agency administrator*
Senese, Donald Joseph *former government official, research administrator*
Williams, Justin W. *government official*

Annandale
Hedrick, Floyd Dudley *retired government official, author*

Arlington
Alford, Paula N. *federal agency administrator*
†Baum, Robert L. *federal agency executive*
Boyle, Robert Patrick *retired government agency consultant, lawyer*
Brandt, Werner William *federal agency official*
Clutter, Mary Elizabeth *federal official*
Ehrman, Madeline Elizabeth *federal agency administrator*
†Fredericks, Michael Edwin *criminal investigator*
Gonzalez, Eduardo *federal agency administrator*
Harrison-Jones, Virginia M. *federal government agency employee*
Hunkele, Lester Martin, III *retired federal agency administrator*
Knowlton, William Allen *political and military consultant, educator*
†Lasowski, Anne-Marie F. *federal agency administrator*
Lieberman, Robert J. *federal agency administrator*
Marzetti, Loretta A. *government agency executive, policy analyst*
Norris, James Arnold *federal agency administrator*
Patrick, Michele Mary *government official*
†Pugliese, Frank P., Jr. *federal agency administrator*
Reeder, Franklin S. *retired federal agency administrator*
†Tarbell, David S. *federal agency administrator*
Verburg, Edwin Arnold *federal agency administrator*

Burgess
Towle, Leland Hill *retired government official*

Burke
Daski, Robert Steven *federal civil servant*

Chesapeake
†Best, R. Stephen, Sr. *fire chief*
†Carrmun, L. Conklin *police chief*

Fairfax
Fisher, Mary Maurine *federal agency official, retired*
Hill, Christopher Thomas *administrator, educator*
Stone, Gregory Michael *law enforcement and public safety consultant*

Fairfax Station
Kaminski, Paul Garrett *federal agency administrator, investment banker*
Taylor, Eldon Donivan *government official*

Falls Church
Fischer, Dennis James *government official*
Padden, Anthony Aloysius, Jr. *federal government official*
†Spencer, Ralph Edwin *federal government official*

Fort Belvoir
Molholm, Kurt Nelson *federal agency administrator*
†Reed, William H. *federal agency administrator*

Fredericksburg
Dyal, William M., Jr. *federal agency administrator*

Hampton
Daniels, Cindy Lou *space agency executive*

Lorton
Francis, Richard Haudiomont *government administrator*

Manassas
Webb, Dennis Wayne *protective services official*

Mc Lean
Calio, Anthony John *scientist, business executive*
Duncan, Robert Clifton *retired government official*
Hathaway, William Dodd *federal agency administrator*
Mahan, Clarence *retired govenment official, writer*
Martin, Marsha Pyle *federal agency administrator*
Reswick, James Bigelow *former government official, rehabilitation engineer, educator*
Spaulding, Wallace Holmes *retired federal agency professional*
Turner, Stansfield *former government official, lecturer, writer, teacher*
Verhalen, Robert Donald *consultant*
Yancik, Joseph John *government official*

Mineral
Donald, James Robert *federal agency official, economist, outdoors writer*

Newport News
Ray, Randy *state agency administrator*

Norfolk
High, Melvin C. *protective services official*
McCarthy, Dennis M. *deputy director*
Wakeham, Ronald T. *protective services official*

Oakton
Entzminger, John Nelson, Jr. *federal agency administrator, electronic engineer, researcher*
Mosemann, Lloyd Kenneth, II *business executive*

Portsmouth
DaMoude, Denise Ann *postal worker*

Quantico
LeDoux, John Clarence *law enforcement official*
Mangan, Terence Joseph *retired police chief*

Reston
Sherwin, Michael Dennis *government official*

Richmond
Effinger, Steven Craig *state agency administrator*
†Huggins, M. Wayne *protective services agency administrator*
Macleod, Cynthia Ann *national park service official, historian*
Pollard, Overton Price *state agency executive, lawyer*

Roseland
Arey, William Griffin, Jr. *former government official*

Ruther Glen
Bush, Mitchell Lester, Jr. *retired federal agency administrator*

Springfield
Edwards, Renee Camille *logistics engineer, public relations professional*

Sterling
Port, Arthur Tyler *retired government administrator, lawyer*

Vienna
†Baity, William F. *federal agency administrator*

Virginia Beach
Carter, James Walton *fire chief*

Williamsburg
Drum, Joan Marie McFarland *federal agency administrator*
Gentry, James William *retired state official*

WASHINGTON

Lakewood
Buchanan, Enid Jane *healthcare professional, housing administrator*

Olympia
†Lehman, Joseph D. *state agency administrator*
†Long, Marsha Tadano *state official*
Robertson, Eric Eugene *state trooper*

Redmond
Simpson, Linda Anne *retired police detective, municipal official*

Richland
Dunigan, Paul Francis Xavier, Jr. *federal agency administrator*

Seattle
†Melendez, Rosa Maria *United States marshall*
Peddy, Julie Ann *admininstrative officer*
Stamper, Norman H. *police chief*

Sequim
Meacham, Charles Harding *government official*

Spokane
Dashiell, G. Ronald *marshal*
Williams, Robert Stone *protective services official*

WEST VIRGINIA

Charleston
†Adkins, Charles M., Jr. *United States marshall*
Douglass, Gus Ruben *state agency administrator*
†Marockie, Henry R. *state school system administrator*
†Rader, John B. *state agency administrator*

Clarksburg
†Trupo, Leonard Joseph *United States marshall*

WISCONSIN

Belleville
†Tomlin, Nicholas John *chief of police*

Beloit
Tubbs, Charles Allan *protective services official*

Green Bay
Day, Douglas Eugene *public information officer*

Madison
†Benson, John T. *state agency administrator*
†Brancel, Ben *state agency administrator*
Cronin, Patti Adrienne Wright *state agency administrator*
†Litscher, Jon E. *protective services official*
Parrino, Cheryl Lynn *federal agency administrator*

Milwaukee
Trindal, Joseph William *federal law enforcement official*

Wisconsin Rapids
Gignac, James E. *municipal fire chief, consultant*

WYOMING

Casper
Reed, James Earl *fire department commander*

Cheyenne
†Catchpole, Judy *state agency administrator*
†Helart, August Marvin *state agency administrator*

Lander
†Price, Raymond E. *state agency administrator*

Yellowstone National Park
Finley, Michael *national park administrator*

TERRITORIES OF THE UNITED STATES

PUERTO RICO

Hato Rey
Wirshing, Herman *protective services official*

CANADA

BRITISH COLUMBIA

Victoria
MacPhail, Joy K. *provincial agency administrator*

NEW BRUNSWICK

Campbellton
Blanchard, Edmond P. *Canadian government official*

Moncton
McKenna, Frank Joseph *Canadian government official, lawyer*

NOVA SCOTIA

Lawrencetown
Pottie, Roswell Francis *Canadian federal science and technology consultant*

ONTARIO

Gloucester
MacFarlane, John Alexander *former federal housing agency administrator*

Ontario
McNally, Joseph Lawrence *retired space agency executive*

Ottawa
Gusella, Mary Margaret *commissioner*
Harvie, James Duncan *nuclear regulator*
Ingstrup, Ole Michaelsen *Canadian government agency official*
Lapointe, Lucie *government agency executive*
Murray, Joseph Philip Robert *Canadian protective services official*
Penner, Keith *Canadian government official*

Toronto
Fraser, William Neil *government official, retired*
Gillespie, Alastair William *former Canadian government official*
Hodgson, Chris *Canadian provincial official*
Saunderson, William *Canadian provincial official*
Tsubouchi, David H. *Canadian provincial official*

SASKATCHEWAN

Regina
Teichrob, Carol *Canadian provincial official*

ENGLAND

London
Adams, Gordon Merritt *federal agency administrator*
Russell, Thomas *British government official*

SWITZERLAND

Signy
Murphy, Edmund Michael *federal agency administrator, demographer*

ADDRESS UNPUBLISHED

Acker, Woodrow Louis (Lou Acker) *security and protection professional*
Adelman, Rodney Lee *federal agency administrator*
Anderson, Wayne Carl *public information officer, former corporate executive*
Arveson, Raymond Gerhard *retired state official*
Baigis, Wendy Sue *probation and parole officer*
Bayer, Robert Edward *retired defense department official, consultant*
†Behrouz, Elizabeth J. *service director*
Belton, Deborah Carolyn Knox *state information systems administrator*
Boozer, Howard Rai *retired state education official*
Boysen, Thomas Cyril *state school system administrator*
†Braunworth, Brent Taylor *firefighter, paramedic, police officer*
Brubaker, Crawford Francis, Jr. *government official, aerospace consultant*
Burgess, Marjorie Laura *protective services official*

Camdessus, Michel (Jean) *federal agency administrator, international organization executive*
Camp, Alethea Taylor *executive and organizational design consultant*
Campbell, Arthur Andrews *retired government official*
Campbell, Donald Alfred *retired government official*
†Carter, Paul Milton, Jr. *federal agency administrator*
Cassidy, Esther Christmas *retired government official*
Clark, Thomas Ryan *retired federal agency executive, business and technical consultant*
Claytor, Richard Anderson *retired federal agency executive, consultant*
Conway, James Valentine Patrick *forensic document examiner, former postal service executive*
Day, Rosalee P. *probation officer*
De Herrera, Juan Abran *United States marshal*
†Del Valle, Irma *protective services official, poet*
Didlo, Larry L. *security officer, educator*
†Drymon, David E. *investigative consultant, background investigator*
Dunn, Michael V. *federal agency administrator*
Edwards, William Henry Von, III *United States marshal*
Ehrman, John *federal agency official, historian*
Eisenberg, Albert Charles *federal agency administrator*
Flanders, Raymond Alan *dentist, governmental health agency administrator*
Flint, Lou Jean *retired state education official*
†Fox, Anne C. *state agency administrator*
Franklin, Bonnie Selinsky *federal agency administrator*
Frazier, Henry Bowen, III *retired judge, government official, lawyer*
Fulbright-Brock, Vivian *supervisory probation officer*
Gardner, Guy S. *government official*
Golding, Carolyn May *former government senior executive, consultant*
Goldoff, Anna Carlson *public administration educator*
Gordon, Peter Lowell *immigration and naturalization administrator*
Griffith, Carl Leslie *protective services official*
Griffith, David L. *protective services official*
Guild, Nelson Prescott *retired state education official*
Hale, Kenneth Byron *retired law enforcement officer, eudcator*
Harder, Robert Clarence *state official*
Harmon, James Allen *federal agency administrator*
Hedrick, Basil Calvin *state agency administrator, ethnohistorian, educator, museum and multicultural institutions consultant*
Helms, J. Lynn *former government agency administrator*
Henson, Ralph Eugene *sheriff, retired*
Hepburn, Valerie Ann *state agency administrator*
Heyman, Ira Michael *federal agency administrator, museum executive, law educator*
Hladky, William George *protective service official*
Hodsoll, Francis Samuel Monaise *government official*
Johnson, Ralph Raymond *ambassador, federal agency administrator*
Johnson, Rodney Dale *retired law enforcement officer, photographer*
Johnstone, Stowell *former state agency administrator*
†Joseph, Jofi John *policy analyst*
Kelso, John Hodgson *former government official*
Kezer, Pauline Ryder *state government executive*
†Klagholz, Leo F. *state agency administrator*
Kusserow, Richard Phillip *government official, business executive*
LaBarre, Carl Anthony *retired government official*
Landon, William J. *intelligence officer*
Le, Diana Lynn *county worker*
Lewis, Samuel Winfield *retired government official, former ambassador*
†Lisi, Anthony Salvatore *police officer*
Lovelace, Rose Marie Sniegon *federal space agency administrator*
Mancher, Rhoda Ross *federal agency administrator, strategic planner*
†Martin, Keith Mitchel *state ageny administrator*
McCoy, Mary Ann *state official*
Mc Coy, Tidal Windham *former government official*
Mc Fee, Thomas Stuart *retired government agency administrator*
McGee, Patrick Edgar *postal service clerk*
†Noll, Danielle Renee *healthcare policy analyst*
Passmore, Michael Forrest *environmental research administrator*
Pierce, Fredric Charles *retired probation officer*
Polisar, Joseph Michael *protective services official*
Raffalli, Henri Christian *lawyer, educator, criminologist*
Ramsey Lines, Sandra *forensic document examiner*
Rander, Donna *public information officer, city official*
Ray, Gayle Elrod *sheriff*
Reilly, Edward Francis, Jr. *former state senator, federal agency administrator*
Rhett, John Taylor, Jr. *government official, civil engineer*
Riddick, Floyd Millard *retired United States Senate parliamentarian, consultant*
Rivkind, Perry Abbot *federal railroad agency administrator*
Rogers, Peggy *state agency administrator*
†Rossotti, Charles Ossola *federal agency administrator*
Russi, Raul *protective services official*
Saddler, George Floyd *government economic adviser*
Schoenberger, James Edwin *federal agency adminstrator*
Schrenko, Linda C. *state agency administrator*
†Schumacher, David L. *state administrator*
Scott, William Herbert *state agency administrator*
Shanahan, Michael George *police officer*
Shasteen, Donald Eugene *government official*
Shishido, Calvin M. *state agency administrator, retired*
Shuman, Thomas Alan *correctional operations executive, consultant*
Shute, Richard Emil *government official, engineer*
Skaff, Joseph John *retired state agency administrator, army officer*
Smith, Doris Victoria *educational agency administrator*
Smith, Elmer W. *retired federal government administrator*
Smith, Roy Allen *United States marshal*
Swan, Charles E. *not for-profit organizations consultant*
Tanguay, Norbert Arthur *retired municipal police training officer*
Truesdale, John Cushman *government executive*
van Schilfgaarde, Jan *retired agricultural engineer, government agricultural research service administrator*
Waggener, Theryn Lee *law enforcement professional*
Walker, Gordon Davies *former government official, writer, lecturer, consultant*
Walsh, Edward Patrick *federal agency administrator*
White, Thomas Edward *retired government park official*
Williams, Gregory Carl, Sr. *city official*
Young, Edwin S. W. *federal agency official*

GOVERNMENT: EXECUTIVE ADMINISTRATION

UNITED STATES

ALABAMA

Bessemer
Bains, Lee Edmundson *state official*

Birmingham
Arrington, Richard, Jr. *mayor*
Boomershine, Donald Eugene *bureau executive, development official*

Huntsville
De Shields, Carla Veonecia *county official*

Mobile
Bell, John *state agency executive*
Bostwick, Robert O. *municipal staff member*
Delaney, Thomas Caldwell, Jr. *city official*
Scott, Brenda *muncipal or county official*

Montgomery
Austin, Hugh S., Jr. *city official*
Austin, Hugh Sam *municipal department administrator*
Bennett, James Ronald *secretary of state*
Blalock, Brenda Gale *city official*
James, Fob, Jr. (Forrest Hood James) *former governor*
Pryor, William Holcombe, Jr. *state attorney general*
Siegelman, Don Eugene *governor*
Wallace, Art *municipal government official*
Williamson, Donald Ellis *state official*
†Windom, Stephen Ralph *state official, lawyer*

ALASKA

Anchorage
Barbee, Robert D. *state official*
Brown, Dean Naomi *state official, geologist*
Selby, Jerome M. *mayor*

Juneau
Botelho, Bruce Manuel *state attorney general, mayor*
†Condon, Wilson Leslie *commissioner*
Knowles, Tony *governor*
Meacham, Charles P. *president, capital consulting*
Twomley, Bruce Clarke *commissioner, lawyer*
Ulmer, Frances Ann *state official*

Ninilchik
Oskolkoff, Grassim *Native American Indian tribal chief*

Sterling
Steckel, Barbara Jean *retired city financial officer*

ARIZONA

Green Valley
Egger, Roscoe Lynn, Jr. *consultant, former IRS commissioner*

Kingman
McAfee, Susan Jacqueline *county official*
†Wickstrom, Clifton Duane *county executive, educator*

Mesa
Brown, Wayne J. *mayor*
Wong, Willie *former mayor, automotive executive*

Phoenix
†Allen, Verna L. *state commissioner*
Bayless, Betsey *state official*
Christensen, Bradford William *state official*
Curcio, Christopher Frank *city official*
DiCiccio, Sal *city official*
Hull, Jane Dee *governor, former state legislator*
Lingner, Doug *city official*
Lyons, Lionel Dale *city equal opportunity director*
Meister, Frederick William *state official, lawyer*
Napolitano, Janet Ann *state attorney general*
†Noyes, Francie *state official*
Pettle, Cecile *city director*
Quayle, James Danforth (Dan) *former vice president United States, entrepreneur*
Rimsza, Skip *mayor*
West, Tony *state official*

Scottsdale
Dobronski, Mark William *judge, justice of the peace*
Warnas, Joseph John *municipal official*

Sun City
Farwell, Albert Edmond *retired government official, consultant*

Tempe
Smith, Carol Estes *city councilman*
Tambs, Lewis Arthur *diplomat, historian, educator*

Tucson
Crawford, Michael *city council*
Garza, Elizeo *director solid waste management, Tucson*
Ibarra, Jose *city council*
Leal, Steve *city council*
Marcus, Janet *city council*
Meyerson, Ronald L. *director of operations, Tucson*
Miller, George *mayor*
Paez, Antonio Contreras *director transportation Tucson*
Partridge, William Russell *retired federal executive*
Scott, Shirley *city council*

ARKANSAS

Bella Vista
Medin, Myron James, Jr. *city manager*

Conway
Polk, William Allen *city planner, architect*

Heber Springs
Rawlings, Paul C. *retired government official*

Little Rock
†Alexander, Don *state official*
†Barton, Kay G. *state official*
Cheek, James Richard *ambassador*
Fisher, Jimmie Lou *state official*
Goss, Kay Gentry Collett *federal official*
†Harris, Jim *state official*
Huckabee, Michael Dale *governor*
Priest, Sharon Devlin *state official*
†Pryor, Mark Lunsford *state attorney general*

Marshall
Johnston, James Joel *foreign service officer, publisher*

Warren
Reep, Robert Gregg *mayor*

CALIFORNIA

Anaheim
Daly, Tom *mayor*
Hill, David *city human resources director*
Sohl, Lee *municipal official*

Arcadia
†Boeskin, Bryan Edward *public administrator*

Bakersfield
†Krishnamurthy, Sriram *planner*
Price, Robert Otis *mayor*

Berkeley
Hamilton, Randy Haskell *city manager*
Rice, Edward Earl *former government official, author*

Beverly Hills
Covitz, Carl D. *state official, real estate and investment executive*

Big Bear Lake
†Carlsen, Russell Arhtur *city manager*

Century City
Wilson, Pete *former governor*

Chula Vista
Vignapiano, Louis John *municipal official*

Claremont
Pedersen, Richard Foote *diplomat and academic administrator*

Concord
Davis, Robert Leach *retired government official, consultant*

Coronado
Hostler, Charles Warren *international affairs consultant*

Costa Mesa
Hugo, Nancy *county official, alcohol and drug addiction professional*

Davis
Kaplan, Douglas Allen *county official*

Downey
Schoettger, Theodore Leo *city official*

El Cajon
Pollock, Richard Edwin *former county administrator*
Thigpen, Mary Cecelia *city official, consultant*

El Monte
Wallach, Patricia *mayor*

Felicity
Istel, Jacques Andre *mayor*

Fremont
Lydon, Daniel T. *city official*
Morrison, Gus (Angus Hugh Morrison) *mayor, engineer*
Perkins, Jan *municipal official*

Fresno
Patterson, James *mayor*

Fullerton
Sa, Julie *council woman*

La Jolla
Shakespeare, Frank *ambassador*

La Verne
Cozad, Lyman Howard *city manager*

Laguna Hills
Hussey, William Bertrand *retired foreign service officer*

Long Beach
Bontá, Diana M. *city manager*
Burroughs, Gary L. *city official*
O'Neill, Beverly Lewis *mayor, former college president*
Sato, Eunice Noda *former mayor, consultant*
Schick, Susan F. *municipal official, developer*

Los Angeles
Adelman, Andrew A. *city manager*
Antonovich, Michael D. *city manager*
Brown, Kathleen *state treasurer, lawyer*
Brownridge, J. Paul *city manager*
Christopher, Warren *lawyer, former government official*
Cisneros, Henry G. *former federal official, broadcast executive*
Comrie, Keith Brian *city administrative officer*
Driscoll, John J. *city manager*
†Fong, Matthew Kipling *state official*
Galanter, Ruth *city official*
Howe, Con Edward *city manager*
Hwang, John Dzen *municipal official*
Mattingly, Gary *city manager*
Morris, Sharon Hutson *city manager*
Nodal, Adolfo V. *city manager*
Reagan, Nancy Davis (Anne Francis Robbins) *volunteer, wife of former President of United States*
Reagan, Ronald Wilson *former President of United States*
Riordan, Richard J. *mayor*
Schnabel, Rockwell Anthony *ambassador*
Smith, Ann Delorise *municipal official*
Toman, Mary Ann *federal official*
Torres-Gil, Fernando M. *federal official, academic administrator*
Young, Caprice Yvonne *municipal official*

Martinez
Uilkema, Gayle Burns *county official, mayor, councilwoman, business educator*

Menlo Park
Lane, Laurence William, Jr. *retired ambassador, publisher*

Mill Valley
Davis, Linda Jacobs *municipal official*

Milpitas
†Larson, Greg Edward *city manager*

Mission Viejo
Wilson, Eleanor McElroy *county official*

Monterey
Barrett, Archie Don *consultant , former federal official*
Wright, Mary Rose *state park superintendent*

Monterey Park
Smith, Betty Denny *county official, administrator, fashion executive*

Moreno Valley
†McClellan, Barry Dean *city manager*

Mountain View
†Duggan, Kevin Charles *city manager*

Napa
Battisti, Paul Oreste *county supervisor*

Nevada City
†Cassella, Dennis Gene *county official*

Newport Beach
Toren, Mark *state official, econometrician*

Oakland
†Brown, Edmund Gerald, Jr. (Jerry Brown) *mayor, former governor*
Musgrove, George *city official*

Oceanside
Lyon, Richard *mayor, retired naval officer*

Ontario
Dastrup-Hamill, Faye Myers *city official*

Oxnard
Takasugi, Nao *state official, business developer*

Pasadena
Bean, Maurice Darrow *retired diplomat*

Placerville
McIntosh, Paul Eugene *county government official*

Rancho Mirage
Ford, Gerald Rudolph, Jr. *former President of United States*

Redlands
Hanson, Gerald Warner *retired county official*

Riverside
Loveridge, Ronald Oliver *mayor*
Nicol, Colleen *municipal official*
Whyld, Steve *municipal official*

Roseville
Gray, Robert Donald *retired mayor*
Lungren, Daniel Edward *former state attorney general*

Sacramento
Betts, Bert A. *former state treasurer, accountant*
Burns, John Francis *state official, educator*
†Bustamante, Cruz M. *state official*
Contreras, Dee (Dorthea Contreras) *municipal official, educator*
Davis, Gray *governor*
Dunnett, Dennis George *state official*
Friery, Thomas P. *city treasurer*
Hodgkins, Francis Irving (Butch Hodgkins) *county official*
Jones, Bill *state official, rancher*

Lake, Molly Anne state official
†Lockyer, Bill state attorney general
Peck, Ellie Enriquez retired state administrator
†Quackenbush, Chuck insurance commissioner
Serna, Joe, Jr. mayor
Terhune, C.A. state official
Trounstine, Philip John state official
Tubbs, William Reid, Jr. public service administrator
Walston, Roderick Eugene state government official

Salinas
Wong, Walter Foo county official

San Bernardino
†Larkin, Donald James, Jr. county government official

San Diego
Freeman, Myrna Faye county schools official
Golding, Susan mayor
Gwinn, Casey city attorney San Diego, California
Robinson, David Howard lawyer
Vargas, Juan city official

San Francisco
Achtenberg, Roberta former federal official
Brown, Willie Lewis, Jr. mayor, former state legislator, lawyer
Frank, Anthony Melchior federal official, former financial executive
†Hewitt, Conrad W. state superintendant of banks
Kaufman, Barbara municipal official
Leal, Susan city official
Taylor, John Lockhart city official
Ward, Doris M. recorder/ assessor, San Francisco
Yaki, Michael J. municipal official

San Jose
†Coons, Larry R. public parks administrator
Dando, Pat city official
Gallo, Joan Rosenberg city attorney
†Gonzales, Ron mayor, former county supervisor
Winslow, Frances Edwards city official

San Luis Obispo
Shlaudeman, Harry Walter retired ambassador

San Pedro
Keller, Larry A. city manager

Santa Ana
Williams, Cleveland muncipal or county official
Zepeda, Susan Ghozeil county official

Santa Monica
Rice, Donald Blessing business executive, former secretary of air force

Santa Rosa
Frowick, Robert Holmes retired diplomat

Solana Beach
Beard, Ann Southard government official, travel company executive
Ernst, Roger Charles former government official, natural resources consultant, association executive
Gildred, Theodore Edmonds ambassador

South Gate
Mosby, Dorothea Susan municipal official

South Lake Tahoe
†Miller, Kerry Lee city manager

Stanford
Shultz, George Pratt former government executive, economics educator

Stockton
Giottonini, James B. public works director Stockton, California
Meissner, Katherine Gong city clerk
Pinkerton, Steven James city director housing and redevelopment
Samsell, L. Patrick municipal official
Samsell, Lewis Patrick municipal finance executive

Sunnyvale
Crabill, Linda Jean municipal government official

Union City
Lewis, Mark Earldon city manager

Ventura
Smith, Bill city manager

Yuba City
Kemmerly, Jack Dale retired state official, aviation consultant

COLORADO

Aurora
Sheffield, Nancy city neighborhood services director
Tauer, Paul E. mayor, educator
Young, Donna L. city official

Bayfield
Giller, Edward Bonfoy retired government official, retired air force officer

Boulder
Bolen, David B. ambassador, former corporation executive
Callen, Lon Edward county official

Colorado Springs
Cousar, Ronny city official
Makepeace, Mary Lou mayor
Milton, Richard Henry retired diplomat, children's advocate
Mullen, James H. city manager
Zelenek, David S. city official

Denver
Brown, Keith Lapham retired ambassador
Cohen, Cheryl Denise municipal official
†Davidson, Donetta state government official
†Ehnes, Jack state insurance commissioner
Frontera, Michael P. municipal official
Gallagher, Dennis Joseph municipal official, state senator, educator
Mejia, James Edward city official
Minger, Terrell John public administration and natural resource institute executive
Moulton, Jennifer T. city and county official, architect
Muja, Kathleen Ann state official, consultant
Owens, Bill governor
Paramo, Patricia Ann city/county official
Rodriguez, Rosemary E. municipal official
†Rogers, Joe state official
Romer, Roy R. former governor
†Salazar, Kenneth L. state attorney general
Webb, Wellington E. mayor

Golden
Kopel, David Benjamin lawyer

Lakewood
Morton, Linda mayor

Morrison
Solin, David Michael state official

Pueblo
Occhiato, Michael Anthony city official

Sterling
Gustafson, Randall Lee city manager

CONNECTICUT

Easton
Meyer, Alice Virginia state official

Hamden
Westerfield, Carolyn Elizabeth Hess city planner

Hartford
Blumenthal, Richard state attorney general
Bysiewicz, Susan state official
†Coleman, Garey E. state legislative administrator
†De Rocco, Andrew Gabriel state commissioner, scientist, educator
†Harriman, Stephen A. state public health commissioner
Killian, Robert Kenneth former lieutenant governor
Noonan, John G(erard) state financial management specialist
Peters, Michael P. mayor
Rapoport, Miles S. state official
Rell, M. Jodi lieutenant governor
Rowland, John G. governor, former congressman
†Shiffrin, Mark A. commissioner, state

New Milford
Peitler, Arthur Joseph mayor, lawyer

Northford
James, William Hall former state official, educator

Stamford
Dennies, Sandra Lee city official
Malloy, Dannel Patrick mayor

Wethersfield
†Mann, Edward H. state official

DELAWARE

Dover
†Amato, Anthony J. director state aviation department
Bookhammer, Eugene Donald state government official
Carper, Thomas Richard governor
Freel, Edward J. state official
Minner, Ruth Ann state official
†Sylvester, Gregg C. state official, physician
Warner, Raymond Melvin county official
†Woodruff, Sheri L. state official

Newark
Woo, S. B. (Shien-Biau Woo) former lieutenant governor, physics educator

Wilmington
Brady, M. Jane state attorney general
†DeMatteis, Claire state director
Ianni, Francis Alphonse state official, former army officer
Morris, Ronald Anthony county official

DISTRICT OF COLUMBIA

Fort Mcnair
Swihart, James W., Jr. diplomat

Washington
Aaron, David L. diplomat
Abshire, David Manker diplomat, research executive
Acheson, Eleanor Dean federal government official
†Albicker, Robert federal official
Albright, Madeleine Korbel federal official, diplomat, political scientist
Alexander, Dawn Alicia public relations executive
Alvarez, Scott G. federal official
Andersen, Robert Allen retired government official
Anderson, Samuel David government affairs consultant
Angula, Helmut Kangulohi Namibian government official
Anschuetz, Norbert Lee retired diplomat, banker
Anthony, Sheila Foster government official
Atherton, Charles Henry federal commission administrator
Auten, John Harold government official
Ayres, Mary Ellen government official
Azcuenaga, Mary Laurie government official
Babbitt, Bruce Edward federal official
Bachula, Gary R. federal official
Baldyga, Leonard J. retired diplomat, international consultant
Barnes, Shirley Elizabeth foreign service officer
Barringer, Philip E. retired government official
Barshefsky, Charlene diplomat
Bassin, Jules foreign service officer
Bell, Robert G. federal agency official
Bellows, Michael Donald foreign service officer
Benedick, Richard Elliot diplomat
Benedict, Lawrence Neal foreign service officer
Berg, Stephen Warren government official
†Berger, Samuel R. federal official
Bernstein, Joan Z. government official
†Bosworth, Stephen Warren ambassador
Breul, Jonathan Dutro government official
Brewster, Robert Charles diplomat, consultant
Britton, Leann G. federal official
†Bromwich, Michael Ray federal official
Brotzman, Donald Glenn government official, lawyer
Brown, Elizabeth Ann foreign service officer
Brown, June Gibbs government official
Buck, Carolyn J. federal official
†Burns, R. Nicholas federal official
Burson, Charles W. federal official, former state attorney general
Busby, Morris D. ambassador
Caldera, Louis Edward federal official
Callahan, John J. federal official
†Cantú, Norma V. federal official
Casstevens, Kay L. federal official
Catlett, D. Mark federal official
†Celeste, Richard F. ambassador, former governor
Charles, Leslie Bermann government official
Chorba, Timothy A. former ambassador to Singapore
Chrétien, Raymond A. J. ambassador
†Clark, Donald Scott federal official
Cleland, Joseph Maxwell (Max Cleland) state official
Clinton, Hillary Rodham First Lady of United States, lawyer
Clinton, William Jefferson President of the United States
†Cohen, Bonnie R. government official
Cohen, William Sebastian federal official, former senator
Cole, Tom state official
†Collins, James Franklin ambassador
Collins, Keith federal executive
Connell, Marion Fitch government official
Cook, Michael Blanchard government executive
Cooke, David Ohlmer government official
Copps, Michael Joseph commerce administrator
Cotter, Michael William retired ambassador, business consultant
Courtney, William Harrison diplomat
Crawford, William Rex, Jr. former ambassador
Crocker, Chester Arthur diplomat, scholar, federal agency administrator
†Crocker, Ryan C. ambassador
Cropp, Linda W. city official
Crowe, William James, Jr. diplomat, think tank executive
†Culshaw, Robert Nicholas British diplomat
Cutler, Walter Leon diplomat, foundation executive
Daley, William M. federal government official
Danvers, William consultant
Danvers, William C. federal official
†Danzig, Richard Jeffrey government official, lawyer
Deal, Timothy government executive
Dean, Edwin Robinson government official, economist
DeSeve, G. Edward federal official
dev Frierson, Robert federal official
Dewhurst, Stephen B. government official, lawyer
Dobbins, James Francis, Jr. foreign service officer
Duemling, Robert Werner diplomat, museum director
Eastham, Alan Walter, Jr. foreign service officer, lawyer
Ebbitt, James Roger government official
Eddy, John Joseph diplomat
Eizenstat, Stuart E. ambassador, lawyer
Elliott, Lee Ann government official
Ely-Raphel, Nancy diplomat
†Farr, George F. federal official
Feierstein, Mark Barry diplomat
Ferrara, Peter Joseph federal official, lawyer, author, educator
Ferren, John Maxwell lawyer
Fishel, Andrew S. director, federal
FitzGerald, William Henry G. diplomat, corporation executive
Fleisher, Eric Wilfrid retired foreign service officer
Flyzik, James J. federal official
Foglietta, Thomas Michael diplomat, former congressman
†Foley, Thomas Stephen diplomat, former speaker House of Representatives
Franklin, Barbara Hackman business executive, former government official
Frawley Bagley, Elizabeth government advisor, ambassador
†Fried, Daniel ambassador
Gaffney, Susan federal official
Galloway, William Jefferson former foreign service officer
†Gansler, Jacques Singleton executive in acquisition and technology
Gantt, Harvey B. former mayor
Garaufis, Nicholas G. federal official
Garthoff, Raymond Leonard diplomat, diplomatic historian
Gati, Toby T. international advisor
Gatons, Anna-Marie Kilmade government official
Gaviria Trujillo, Cesar international organization administrator, former president of Colombia, economist
Geisel, Harold Walter diplomat
Gelbard, Robert Sidney ambassador
Gessaman, Donald Eugene consultant, former government executive
†Giffin, Gordon D. ambassador, lawyer
Ginsberg, Marc C. former diplomat, investment company executive
Glauthier, T. J. federal official
Glickman, Daniel Robert federal official
Gnehm, Edward W., Jr. ambassador
Goldberg, Joseph Philip government official
Gore, Albert, Jr. Vice President of the United States
Green, Arthur E. media strategist
Grove, Brandon Hambright, Jr. diplomat, public and international affairs consultant
†Hall, Kathryn Walt ambassador
Halsted, David Crane diplomat
Hamburg, Margaret Ann (Peggy Hamburg) city commissioner
Harrop, William Caldwell retired ambassador, foreign service officer
Hayes, Allene Valerie Farmer government administrator
†Hecklinger, Richard E. ambassador
Herman, Alexis M. federal official
Hernreich, Nancy federal official
†Holmes, Henry Allen government official
†Horslund, Jens-Otto diplomat
Hrinak, Donna Jean ambassador
Huddle, Franklin Pierce, Jr. diplomat
Hughes, Morris Nelson, Jr. foreign service officer
Hurley, John Arthur government official
Indyk, Martin S. diplomat
†Irving, Clarence L., Jr. (Larry Irving) federal official
Jordan, Mary Lucille commissioner
Joseph, James Alfred ambassador
Kaiser, Philip Mayer diplomat
Kauzlarich, Richard Dale ambassador, foreign service officer
Keating, Robert B. ambassador
Keevey, Richard Francis government official, educator
Kennedy, Patrick F. federal official
Kerber, Frank John diplomat
†Kim, Sung Yup diplomat
†Kiss, Tibor military attache
Klosson, Michael foreign service officer
Komer, Robert William government official, consultant
Koskinen, John Andrew federal government executive
Kovach, Eugene George government official, consultant
Kraemer, Sylvia Katharine government official, historian
†Kurtzer, Daniel ambassador
Laird, Melvin Robert former secretary of defense
Lanza, Kenneth Anthony foreign service officer
†La Rocque, Gene Robert retired naval officer, government official, author
†Larson, Alan Philip federal official
Lastowka, James Anthony former federal agency executive, lawyer
Levitt, Mark Howard government official
Lew, Jacob federal official
Lilly, William Eldridge government official
†Linehan, Lou Ann state official
Livingood, Wilson S. law enforcement official
Lovell, Malcolm Read, Jr. public policy institute executive, educator, former government official, former trade association executive
Lowe, Mary Frances federal government official
Lowenstein, James Gordon former diplomat, international consultant
Lucas, James Walter federal government official
†Luedtke, Thomas associate administrator procurement for NASA
†Lyles, Lester L. director
Lyons, James Robert federal official
MacKay, Kenneth Hood, Jr. (Buddy MacKay) federal official
†Magaw, John W. federal law enforcement official
Magee, Charles Thomas international consultant, retired diplomat
Marcotte, Michael Steven municipal administrator
Marquez, Awilda Rose federal official
Matheson, Michael J. federal official
Mathews, Jessica Tuchman policy researcher, columnist
McCaffrey, Barry Richard federal official, retired army officer
Mc Donald, John Warlick diplomat, global strategist
McGinty, Kathleen federal official
McGue, Christie federal official
McGuire, Roger Alan retired foreign service officer
McKee, Alan R. foreign service officer
McMichael, Guy H., III federal official
McNeil, Patricia Wentworth federal agency executive
McNicol, David Leon federal official
Messenger, Jon Carleton government project manager
Meyer, Armin Henry retired diplomat, author, educator
Meyer, Laurence Harvey federal official
Michaud, Michael Alan George diplomat, writer
Michel, James H. ambassador, lawyer
Miles, Richard diplomat
Miller, Marcia E. federal government official
Miller, William Green ambassador
Moore, George S., Jr. government, executive
Morningstar, Richard L. diplomat
†Muasher, Marwan J. Jordanian diplomat
Murphy, Gerald retired government official, consultant
†Myers, Margaret E. performance assessment director
†Neal, Robert L., Jr. director
Neas, Lindsey Rutledge legislative assistant
Nemfakos, Charles Panagiotis government official
Neumann, Ronald Eldredge diplomat
†Newsom, Eric D. federal official
Newton, David George diplomat
Norland, Donald Richard retired foreign service officer
Oakley, Phyllis Elliott diplomat
O'Bryon, James Fredrick defense executive
Ochmanek, David Alan defense analyst
O'Hara, Clifford Bradley commission administrator
†Olson, Lyndon Lowell, Jr. ambassador
Orr, Paul Welles government relations consultant
Owen, Henry former ambassador, consultant
Palmer, Steven O. federal official
†Parris, Mark Robert ambassador
Pashayev, Hafiz Mir Jalal diplomat, physics educator
Passage, David diplomat
Patterson, Kathy city official
Pearl, Laurence Dickson retired federal government executive
Pendleton, Miles Stevens, Jr. diplomat
Perle, Richard Norman government official
†Peters, F. Whitten federal official
Phillips, Christopher Hallowell diplomat
Phillips, James D. retired diplomat
Pickering, Thomas Reeve diplomat
Pierce, Margaret Hunter government official
Pines, Robert H. federal official
Placke, James A(nthony) foreign service officer, international affairs consultant
Quainton, Anthony Cecil Eden diplomat
Ransom, David Michael retired ambassador
†Ratchford, William federal official
†Rawls, William Lee state official
Reed, John Hathaway former ambassador
Reicher, Dan William federal agency executive
†Remez, Shereen G. chief information officer
Render, Arlene ambassador
Reno, Janet federal official, lawyer
†Retsinas, Nicolas P. federal official
†Reyes Heroles, Jesus Mexican government official
†Rice, Susan Elizabeth federal agency official

Richard, Mark M. *government official, lawyer*
Richardson, William Blaine *federal official*
Riley, Richard Wilson *federal official*
Roberts, Douglas B. *state official*
Robinson, James Kenneth *federal official*
Robinson, Laurie Overby *assistant attorney general*
†Roby, Cheryl J. *deputy assistant secretary*
Rogowsky, Robert Arthur *trade commission operations director, professor*
Romani, Paul Nicholas *government official*
†Romero, Edward L. *diplomat, environmental engineering executive*
†Rosenthal, Neal H. *federal commissioner*
Rosewater, Ann *federal official*
Ross, Christopher Wade Stelyan *diplomat*
†Rubin, Eric S. *foreign service officer*
Rubin, Robert E. *former secretary of treasury*
Rugh, William Arthur *diplomat*
Rupel, Dimitrij *diplomat*
Ruscio, Domenic *legislative consultant, public affairs specialist*
†Ryan, Mary A. *diplomat*
Sacksteder, Frederick Henry *former foreign service officer*
Samet, Andrew *government official*
Sasser, James Ralph (Jim Sasser) *ambassador, former senator*
Sayre, Robert Marion *ambassador*
Scarbrough, Frank Edward *government official*
†Schindler, Sol *foreign affairs analyst, writer*
†Schmitten, Rolland Arthur *government official*
†Schneider, Cynthia Perrin *ambassador, art history educator*
Schneiter, George Robert *government executive*
Scott-Finan, Nancy Isabella *government administrator*
Seck, Mamadou Mansour *ambassador, career officer*
Seidel, Samuel Learned Richard Carton *governmental researcher*
Sellin, Theodore *foreign service officer, consultant*
Shalala, Donna Edna *federal official, political scientist, educator, former university chancellor*
Shane, Jeffrey Neil *lawyer*
Sheehan, Michael Andrew *diplomat*
Shelly, Christine Deborah *foreign service officer*
Shelton, L. Robert *federal official*
†Shibley, Gail *public affairs director transportation department*
Shinn, David Hamilton *diplomat*
Shumate, John Page *diplomat*
Simmons, Anne L. *federal official*
Simon, Jeanne Hurley *federal commissioner*
Simpson, Daniel H. *ambassador*
Skelly, Thomas P. *federal agency executive*
Skodon, Emil Mark *diplomat*
†Skolfield, Melissa T. *government official*
Slater, Rodney E. *federal official*
Smith, Elaine Diana *foreign service officer*
Smith, Marshall Savidge *government official, academic dean, educator*
†Smittcamp, Lisa M. *state official*
Somerville, Walter Raleigh, Jr. *government official*
Sommerfelt, Soren Christian *foreign affairs, international trade consultant, former Norwegian diplomat, lawyer*
Sonnenfeldt, Helmut *former government official, educator, consultant, author*
†Spalter, Jonathan H. *government information officer*
Steinberg, Donald Kenneth *diplomat*
Stern, Todd D. *federal government official*
Storing, Paul Edward *foreign service officer*
†Strauss, David *federal official*
Stuart, Sandra Kaplan *federal official*
†Sullivan, Michael John *ambassador, former governor*
†Sullivan, Suzanne *administrator federal aviation administration*
Sutter, Eleanor Bly *diplomat*
†Swanick, Anthony Joseph *congressional communications director*
Swing, William Lacy *ambassador*
Thomas, Ralph Charles, III *federal official*
Thomas, Scott E. *federal government executive, lawyer*
Thompson, Joseph *federal official*
Thompson, Sally Engstrom *state official*
Torkelson, Jodie Rae *executive branch staff member*
†Touraine Moulin, Françoise *scientific attache*
†Toye, Nelson E. *financial officer*
Trezise, Philip Harold *government official*
†Truman, Edwin Malcolm *federal official*
Twining, Charles Haile *ambassador*
Underwood, Robert Anacletus *congressional delegate, university official*
†Viadero, Roger C. *government official*
Vogel, Frederick John *diplomat*
Wachtmeister, Count Wilhelm H. F. *diplomat*
Ware, Thaddeus Van *government official*
Watson, Arthur Dennis *government official*
Wayne, Stephen J. *government educator, academic director, writer*
Webster, Christopher White *foreign service officer*
Welch, Charles David *diplomat*
Wendt, E. Allan *ambassador*
West, Togo Dennis, Jr. *federal official, former aerospace executive*
Wexler, Anne *government relations and public affairs consultant*
Wiles, William Wharton *retired federal government official*
†Williams, Anthony A. *mayor*
Williams-Bridgers, Jacquelyn *federal government official*
Wilson, Joseph Charles, IV *ambassador*
Winograd, Morley Alec *government consultant, retired sales executive*
Winter, Harvey John *government official*
Wirth, Timothy Endicott *foundation official, former senator*
Witajewski, Robert M. *diplomat*
Won, Delmond J.H. *commissioner*
Woodward, Robert Forbes *retired government official, consultant*
Worthy, Patricia Morris *municipal official, lawyer*
†Yalowitz, Kenneth Spencer *ambassador*
Yates, John Melvin *ambassador*
Yellen, Janet Louise *government official, economics educator*
†Zaidman, Steven *associate official Federal Aviation Administration*
Ziglar, James W. *federal official, lawyer, investment banker*
Zwach, David Michael *foreign service officer*

FLORIDA

Bal Harbour
Horton, Jeanette *municipal government official*

Boynton Beach
Polinsky, Janet Naboicheck *state official, former state legislator*

Brooksville
Anderson, Richard Edmund *city manager, management consultant*

Coral Gables
Arcos, Cresencio S. *ambassador*

Coral Springs
Richardson, Peter Mark James *town official*
†Tomeo, Louis Anthony *county official*

Deerfield Beach
†Moore, Terrence Raenale *city administrator*

Fort Lauderdale
Garver, James Amos *municipal official*
Pallans, Mark David *city official, telecommuncations specialist*

Fort Pierce
Ginns, David Richard *county official*

Gainesville
Heflin, Martin Ganier *foreign service officer, international political economist*
Jones, Elizabeth Nordwall *county government official*

Hialeah
Deloach, Daniel *city clerk*
Farach, Ruben *city administrator*
†Martinez, Raul L. *mayor, publisher*

Hollywood
Giulianti, Mara Selena *mayor, civic worker*
†Mostel, Claire Roberta *county official*

Jacksonville
Delaney, John Adrian *mayor*
Francis, Miles N., Jr. *muncipal official*
Jones, Harold C. *director agriculture*
Mousa, Sam E. *municipal official*
Park, Christopher S. *chairman civil service board*
Roberts, Lynwood *county official*

Kennedy Space Center
Banks, Lisa Jean *government official*

Merritt Island
Thomas, James Arthur *retired government official, electrical engineer*

Miami
Carollo, Joe *mayor*
Cates, Nelia Barletta de *diplomat of Dominican Republic*
León, Eduardo A. *diplomat, business executive*
Lichacz, Sheila Enit *diplomat, artist*
Moorman, Rose Drunell *county administrator, systems analyst*
†Ojeda, Jose Antonio, Jr. *county official*
†Rivera, David M. *government official*
Spratt, Stephen Michael *county government official*

North Lauderdale
Stunson, John *city manager*

Ormond Beach
Burton, Alan Harvey *city official*

Palm City
Henry, David Howe, II *retired diplomat*

Panama City
Stark, S. Daniel, Jr. *convention and visitors bureau executive*

Plant City
McDaniel, James Roosevelt *municipal official*

Punta Gorda
Knoble, William Avery *government finance officer, accountant*
Piacitelli, John Joseph *county official, educator, pediatrician*
Smith, Marilyn Patricia *city government official, management consultant and facilitator*

Saint Petersburg
Fischer, David J. *mayor*
Mussett, Richard Earl *city official*
Turner, Robert H. *administrator*

Sanibel
Gibson, Roy L. *city planner*

Sarasota
Hennemeyer, Robert Thomas *diplomat*

Sebastian
White, Thomas Patrick *county official, small business owner*

Tallahassee
†Bush, John Ellis *governor*
Butterworth, Robert A. *state attorney general*
Crawford, Bob *state commissioner*
†Harris, Katherine *state official*
Mortham, Sandra Barringer *former state official*
†Nelson, Bill *state treasurer*
Ramsey, Sally Ann Seitz *retired state official*
Spooner, Donna *public administrator*

Tampa
Brookins, Wayne *municipal official*
Ferlita, Ross *municipal government official*
Freedman, Sandra Warshaw *former mayor*
Greco, Dick A. *mayor, hardware company executive*
McConnell, Joan Tronco *municipal government official*
Metcalf, Ralph *director sanitation department*
Noriega, Fernando, Jr. *municipal official*
Studer, William Allen *county official*

Treasure Island
Williams, Bonnie Lee *city official*

Venice
Williams, Justin *retired government official*

GEORGIA

Athens
Hillenbrand, Martin Joseph *diplomat, educator*

Atlanta
Archard, Douglas Bruce *foreign service officer*
Baker, Thurbert E. *state attorney general*
Bell, Griffin B. *lawyer, former attorney general*
Campbell, Bill *mayor*
Carter, Jimmy (James Earl Carter, Jr.) *former President of United States*
†Cox, Cathy *state official*
del Rosario, Remedios K. *commissioner water department Atlanta*
Dobbins, Michael A. *city planning and development commissioner*
Howard, Pierre *state official*
Hyde, Richard Lee *investigator*
Irvin, Thomas T. *state commissioner of agriculture*
Laney, James Thomas *former ambassador, educator*
Malone, Perrillah Atkinson (Pat Malone) *retired state official*
Maple, Terry L. *county official*
McCarty, Deborah Ownby *city commissioner, lawyer*
Middleton, Jarvis Darnell *city commissioner*
Miller, Zell Bryan *former governor*
Myrick, Bismarck *diplomat*
Orr, John Mark *senior planner Athens-Clarke County*
Schwartz, William B., Jr. *ambassador*
Streeb, Gordon Lee *diplomat, economist*
†Taylor, Mark *state official*

Bowdon
Henson, Diana Jean *county official*

Cartersville
Harris, Joe Frank *former governor*

Columbus
Ellis, Patrick R. *municipal official*
Land, Martin J. *city official*

Conyers
Kelly, John Hubert *diplomat, business executive*

Decatur
Gay, Robert Derril *public agency director*

Martinez
Cheng, Wu C. *patent examiner*

Rome
Williams, Blaine Henry *city government administrator*

Saint Simons
Douglas, William Ernest *retired government official*

Savannah
Rousakis, John Paul *former mayor*

Stone Mountain
Bowers, Michael Joseph *former state attorney general*

HAWAII

Camp H M Smith
Teare, Richard Wallace *ambassador*

Honolulu
Bronster, Margery S *state attorney general*
Cayetano, Benjamin Jerome *governor, former state senator and representative*
†Goto Sabas, Jennifer *state official*
Harris, Jeremy *mayor*
Hirono, Mazie Keiko *state official*
†Kitamura, Michael *state director*
†Obata, Randy *executive assistant to governor of Hawaii*
Okimoto, Glenn Michiaki *state official*
†Wakatsuki, Lynn Y. *commissioner*

IDAHO

Boise
Benham, James H. *state official*
Cenarrusa, Pete T. *secretary of state*
†Gee, Gavin M. *state government official*
Hawkins, James Victor *state official*
Kempthorne, Dirk Arthur *governor*
Lance, Alan George *state attorney general*
Otter, Clement Leroy *lieutenant governor*
†Spalding, James C. *state official*
Terteling, Carolyn Ann *city official*
†Williams, J. D. *state controller*
Wilson, Jack Fredrick *retired federal government official*

Donnelly
†Edwards, Lydia Justice *state official*

Moscow
Kennedy, Mary Virginia *diplomat*

Soda Springs
†Clark, Trent L. *federal affairs manager*

ILLINOIS

Beecher
Barber, Robert Owen *village administrator*

Bone Gap
Putt, Jerry Wayne *municipal official*

Bourbonnais
Koehler, Frank James *city manager*

Cahokia
†Hoffman, Marc Olin *state official*

Chicago
Bishop, Oliver Richard *state official*
Buchanan, John *city official*
Burnett, Walter, Jr. *city official*
Chandler, Michael D. *city official*
Cherry, Robert Steven, III *municipal agency administrator*
Daley, Richard Michael *mayor*
de Vos, Peter Jon *ambassador*
Dixon, Lorraine *city official*
†Emmanuel, Rahm *federal official*
Enenbach, Mark Henry *community action agency executive, educator*
Gabinski, Theri *city official*
Giles, Percy Z. *city official*
Johnson, Donald Harry, Jr. *government official, educator*
Keryczynskyj, Leo Ihor *lawyer, county official, educator*
Laski, James J. *city clerk*
Mell, Richard F. *city official*
Murphy, Hugh *city official*
Murphy, Thomas W. *city official*
Natarus, Burton F. *government executive*
O'Connor, Patrick J. *city official*
Olivo, Frank *city official*
Olk, Frederick James *county official, paralegal*
Olson, Roy Arthur *government official*
O'Shaw, Robert (Bob) *city official*
†Parks, Carolyn Lightford *public administrator*
Peterson, Terry *city official*
Rice, Judith C. *city commissioner*
Rothstein, Ruth M. *county health official*
Rugai, Virginia A. (Ginger) *city official*
Solis, Daniel S. *city official*
Stone, Bernard Leonard *vice mayor, alderman, lawyer*
Suarez, Ray *city official*
Thomas, Cherryl T. *city buildings commissioner*
Topinka, Judy Baar *state official*
Turner-Coleman, Shirley A. *city official*
Vroustouris, Alexander *inspector general*
Walker, Thomas Ray *city transportation commissioner*

Cicero
Kociolko, John Stephen *town official*

Decatur
Rockefeller, Margaretta Fitler Murphy (Happy Rockefeller) *widow of former vice president of United States*

Evanston
Ingersoll, Robert Stephen *former diplomat, federal agency administrator*

Glencoe
Morris, Robert Barrett *city manager*

Joliet
O'Connell, James Joseph *port official*

Lake Zurich
Dixon, John Fulton *village manager*

Morrison
Gallagher, John Robert, Jr. *county official*

Oak Brook
Veitch, Stephen Boies *city manager*

Rochester
†Shaw, Linda K. *municipal official, librarian*

Springfield
†Boozell, Mark Eldon *state official*
Edgar, Jim *former governor*
Gamble, Douglas Irvin *state official, educator*
Morford, Lynn Ellen *state official*
†Riedl, Stephen Thomas *state government official*
Ryan, James E. *state attorney general*
Schmidt, Mark James *state public health official*
†White, Jesse *state official*
†Wood, Corinne *state official*

Waukegan
†Flanyak, Chrisann Marie *county court manager*

Westchester
Crois, John Henry *local government official*

Wheaton
Gow, Olivia Greco *public official, former English language educator*

INDIANA

Columbus
Carter, Pamela Lynn *former state attorney general*

Crawfordsville
Boland, Joseph Anthony *state official*

Fort Wayne
Helmke, (Walter) Paul *mayor, lawyer*
Lee, Timothy Earl *international agency executive, paralegal*

Indianapolis
Bradford, James *city official*
Brents, Maggie M. *city official*
Cohen, Edward *state official*
Gilroy, Sue Anne *state official*

Goldsmith, Stephen *mayor*
Modisett, Jeffrey A. *state attorney general*
O'Bannon, Frank Lewis *governor, lawyer*
Usher, Phyllis Land *state official*

Notre Dame
Wadsworth, Michael A. *athletic director, former ambassador*

Spencer
Tucker, Mary Margaret *county government official*

Tell City
Gebhard, Diane Kay *county administrator, political advisor*

IOWA

Cedar Rapids
Novetzke, Sally Johnson *former ambassador*
Wright, Walter Edward *county official, retired army officer*

Des Moines
Anderson, Eric Anthony *city manager*
†Anderson, James Donald *state official*
Bergman, Bruce E. *municipal official*
Corning, Joy Cole *former state official*
†Culver, Chester J. *state official*
†Daniels, Preston A. *mayor*
†Eisenhower, Cynthia P. *state official*
Ferrell, Lynn DuWayne *county official*
Fitzgerald, Michael Lee *state official*
Jones, Floyd A. *municipal official*
Miller, Thomas J. *state attorney general*
Odell, Mary Jane *former state official*
†Pederson, Sally *state official*
Riper, Kevin *city official*
†Vilsack, Thomas *governor*

Harlan
Jacobsen, Linda Mary *county official*

Hiawatha
Merriam, Oliver Steven *city manager*
Pate, Paul Danny *secretary of state*

Laurens
Barrett, Patricia Ruth *government official*

Nevada
Bilyeu, Gary Edward *government official*
Jamison, David Dwight *county treasurer*

Steamboat Rock
Taylor, Ray *state senator*

Waterloo
Johannsen, Sonia Alicia *retired county official*
O'Rourke, Thomas Allan *county public health director*
Sass, Patricia Sharon *county official*

West Des Moines
Branstad, Terry Edward *former governor, lawyer*

KANSAS

El Dorado
Adkins, William Lloyd *state official*

Eudora
Miller, David Groff *political party executive*

Kinsley
Carlson, Mary Isabel (Maribel Carlson) *county treasurer*

Leavenworth
Kansteiner, Beau Kent *city official*

Leawood
McKay, Robert George *city official*

Manhattan
†Mattson, Gary A. *city planning educator*
†Tummala, Krishna Kumar *public administration educator*

Marion
Bateman, Jeannine Ann *county official*

Mcpherson
Steffes, Don Clarence *state senator*

Shawnee
Chaffee, Paul David *city official*

Shawnee Mission
Bortko, Edward Joseph *retired city official*

Topeka
Carlson, E. Dean *state official*
Freden, Sharon Elsie Christman *state education assistant commissioner*
†Glasscock, Joyce H. *public information officer*
Gordon, Thelma Hunter *state official*
Graves, William Preston *governor*
†Mitchell, Gary R. *state official*
†Murray, Robert A. *state official*
†Nichols, Rocky *state representative, non-profit administrator*
†Rarrick, C. Steven *state official*
Sebelius, Kathleen Gilligan *state commissioner*
Simmons, Charles E. *state official*
Stovall, Carla Jo *state attorney general*
Thornburgh, Ron E. *state official*

Wichita
Knight, Robert G. *mayor, investment banker*

KENTUCKY

Covington
Bates, Patti Jean *communications specialist in public safety*

Frankfort
†Armstrong, David Love *attorney general*
Brown, John Y., III *state official*
Chandler, Albert Benjamin III *attorney general*
Freeman, Arthur L. *state commissioner*
Hamilton, John Kennedy *state treasurer*
Henry, Stephen Lewis *state official, orthopedic surgeon, educator*
Palmore, Carol M. *state official*
Patton, Paul E. *governor*
†Sapp, Wayne Douglass *state official*
Strong, Marvin E., Jr. *state official*

Lexington
Cantrell, Donna Alexander *county commissioner finance*
Hughes, Carl Andrew *municipal construction executive*
Miller, Pamela Gundersen *mayor*
Ramsey, Robert *county official, retired career officer*
Yates, Isabel McCants *city council vice mayor*

London
Jensen, Tom *political party executive, lawyer*

Morganfield
†Edmondson, Austin Harold *city manager*

Paducah
†Earles, Pat *city administrator*

LOUISIANA

Baton Rouge
Bankston, Nathaniel D. *city registrar*
Blanco, Kathleen Babineaux *lieutenant governor*
Bohlinger, Lewis Hall *state government official*
Foster, M. J., Jr. (Mike Foster) *governor*
Ieyoub, Richard Phillip *state attorney general*
Marino, Anthony *airport commission*
McKeithen, Walter Fox *secretary of state*
†Nickel, James W. *state director*
Nijoka, Donald Wayne *metropolitan council administrator*
†Sheppard, John B., Jr. *state official*
Young, Eugene A. *county official*

Boyce
Chilton, Alice Pleasance Hunter (Mrs. St. John Poindexter Chilton) *former state official, vocational counselor*

Kenner
Levell, Edward, Jr. *city official*

Lake Charles
Mount, Willie Landry *mayor*

New Orleans
Hunter, Sue Persons *former state official*
Jeff, Morris F.X., Jr. *muncipal or county official*
Keller, Louis, Sr. *municipal official*
Morial, Marc Haydel *mayor*
Ortique, Revius Oliver, Jr. *city official*
Roesler, Robert Harry *city official*
Schaefer, Ralph *municipal government official*
Stansbury, Harry Case *state commissioner*
Sylvain, Vincent Todd Adams *muncipal or county official*

Slidell
Dearing, Reinhard Josef *city official*

MAINE

Auburn
Adams, Mark A. *city manager*

Augusta
†Bailey, Dennis *state official*
†Denaco, Parker Alden *state official*
Gwadosky, Dan A. *secretary of state*
Ketterer, Andrew *state attorney general*
King, Angus S., Jr. *governor of Maine*
Waldron, Janet E. *state commissioner*

Belfast
Worth, Mary Page *mayor*

Presque Isle
Brown, James Walker, Jr. *city government planning and development administrator*

Windham
Diamond, G. William *former secretary of state*
Walker, Steve Sweet *town official*

MARYLAND

Annapolis
Coulter, James Bennett *state official*
Florestano, Patricia Sherer *state official*
Glendening, Parris Nelson *governor, political science educator*
†Johnson, Dean LaLander *mayor*
Townsend, Kathleen Kennedy *state official*
Wasserman, Martin P. *former state official*
Willis, John T. *state official*

Baltimore
Balog, George G. *city director of public works*
Bell, Lawrence A. *city official*
Carmichael, Richard E. *government official, financial manager, educator*
Curran, J. Joseph, Jr. *state attorney general*
†Daniels, Susan M. *commissioner*
Glassman, Jon David *business executive*
Graves, Charles C., III *city planning director*
Henson, Daniel P., III *housing and community development commissioner*
Jones, Raymond Moylan *strategy and public policy educator*
Meima, Ralph Chester, Jr. *corporate executive, former foreign service officer*
Schmoke, Kurt L. *mayor*
Welch, Agnes *city councilwoman*

Bethesda
Bowsher, Charles Arthur *retired government official, business executive*
Fleming, Patricia Stubbs *federal official*
Gallagher, Hubert Randall *government consultant*
Green, Jerome George *federal government official*
Hempstone, Smith, Jr. *diplomat, journalist*
Ingraham, Edward Clarke, Jr. *foreign service officer*
Kidd, Charles Vincent *former civil servant, educator*
Kirby, Harmon E. *ambassador*
Laingen, Lowell Bruce *diplomat*
Lewis, James Histed *retired foreign service officer*
Morgan, John Davis *consultant*
Neill, Denis Michael *international consultant*
Neumann, Robert Gerhard *ambassador, consultant*
North, William Haven *foreign service officer*
Peck, Edward Lionel *retired foreign service officer, corporate executive*
Rowell, Edward Morgan *retired foreign service officer, lecturer*
Sober, Sidney *retired diplomat, education educator*
Vest, George Southall *diplomat*

Burkittsville
Aughenbaugh, Deborah Ann *mayor, retired educator*

Chevy Chase
Albright, Raymond Jacob *government official*
Bush, Frederick Morris *federal official*
Korth, Penne Percy *ambassador*
†Lewis, Jon Roderick *political advisor*
Lukens, Alan Wood *retired ambassador and foreign service officer*
Mansfield, Julian Peter *city manager*
†O'Leary, Hazel R. *former federal official, lawyer*
Prince, Julius S. (Bud Prince) *retired foreign service reserve officer*
Sampas, Dorothy Myers *government official*
†Sorenson, Roger A. *international relations consultant*

College Park
Broadnax, Walter D. *public policy educator*
Peterson, David Frederick *government agency executive*

Columbia
Cargo, William Ira *ambassador, retired*
Scates, Alice Yeomans *former government official, consultant*

Crownsville
Hanna, James Curtis *state official*

Ellicott City
Galinsky, Deborah Jean *county official*
Longuemare, R. Noel, Jr. *former federal official*

Emmitsburg
†Brown, Carrye Burley *federal agency administrator*

Fort Washington
Eddy, Elsbeth Marie *retired government official, statistician*
Smoot, Burgess Howard *federal official*

Frederick
Deale, Robert Elmer, Jr. *state official*
Shackelford, Dan Elbert *federal procurement analyst*

Gaithersburg
French, Judson Cull *government official*
Warshaw, Stanley Irving *government official*

Grasonville
Andrews, Archie Moulton *government official*

Kensington
Rosenthal, Alan Sayre *former government official*

La Plata
Fisher, Gail Feimster *government official*

Laurel
Sharpless, Joseph Benjamin *former county official*

Owings Mills
Nes, David Gulick *retired diplomat*

Potomac
Kernan, Barbara Desind *senior government executive*
Newhouse, Alan Russell *retired federal government executive*
Shepard, William Seth *government official, diplomat, writer*

Rockville
Chiogioji, Melvin Hiroaki *former government official, entrepreneur*
Corley, Rose Ann McAfee *government official*
Dicus, Greta Joy *federal commissioner*
Ewing, Blair Gordon *local government official*
†Holston, Sharon Smith *government official*
Hubbard, William Keith *government executive*
Krahnke, Betty Ann *county official*
Sacchet, Edward Michael *foreign service officer*
Szabo, Daniel *government official*
Weiss, Stuart *government official*
Woodcock, Janet *federal official*

Silver Spring
Ahmad, Mirza Muzaffar *economic advisor*
Bindenagel, James Dale *diplomat*
†Foster, Nancy Marie *environmental analyst, government official*
Goott, Daniel *government official, consultant*

Tall Timbers
Morgan, Dennis Alan *federal official*

Westminster
Cronin, Susan Gayle *county program coordinator*

MASSACHUSETTS

Boston
Allukian, Myron, Jr. *government administrator, public health educator, dental educator*
Cellucci, Argeo Paul *state official*
Collins, Edward J., Jr. *city financial officer*
Galvin, William Francis *secretary of state, lawyer*
Harshbarger, Scott *law educator, former state attorney general*
Markel, Robert Thomas *mayor*
Menino, Thomas M. *mayor*
Merrill, Stephen *former governor*
O'Brien, Shannon P. *state treasurer*
O'Brien, Thomas N. *city economic development officer*
Swift, Jane Maria *state official*
Wild, Victor Allyn *lawyer, educator*

Cambridge
Beasley, David Muldrow *former governor*
Busch, Marc Lawrence *government educator*
Hunt, Swanee G. *public policy educator, former ambassador*
Kelman, Steven Jay *management educator*
Porter, Roger Blaine *government official, educator*
Widnall, Sheila Evans *aeronautical educator, former secretary of the airforce, aeronautical educator, former university official*

Duxbury
McAuliffe, Eugene Vincent *retired diplomat and business executive*

Fall River
Connors, Robert Leo *city official*

Greenfield
Thidemann, Norman Ellis *town official*

Lowell
Natsios, Nicholas Andrew *retired foreign service officer*

Lynn
McManus, Patrick J. *mayor, lawyer, accountant*

Marlborough
Petrin, John Donald *town administrator*

Melrose
Maloney, Robert L. *municipal official*

Salem
Prokopy, John Alfred *government consultant*

Shelburne Falls
McClatchy, Kate *political candidate*

Sherborn
Levin, Burton *diplomat*

South Boston
Flynn, Raymond Leo *ambassador to the Vatican, former mayor*

South Dartmouth
†Theodore, Joseph, Jr. *city electrical inspector*

South Deerfield
Grist, John *retired government official, engineering consultant*

Southborough
Railsback, David Phillips *state official, laywer*

Springfield
Albano, Michael J. *mayor*
†Reilly, Thomas F. *state attorney general*

Taunton
Lopes, Maria Fernandina *commissioner*

Waltham
Fuchs, Lawrence Howard *government official, educator*

Wellesley
Parker, William H., III *federal official*

Wenham
Davis, Marjorie Alice *former city official*

West Hyannisport
Devine, Nancy *postmaster*

Westwood
†Jaillet, Michael André *town administrator*

Worcester
Gurwitz, Arnold *city official, pediatrician*

Yarmouth Port
Nichols, Robert Lyman *retired foreign service officer, lecturer*

MICHIGAN

Ann Arbor
Sheldon, Ingrid Kristina *mayor*

Bloomfield Hills
Fauver, John William *mayor, retired business executive*

Detroit
Archer, Dennis Wayne *mayor, lawyer*
Cleveland, Clyde *city official*
Currie, Jackie L. *city clerk*
†Doss, Rianne Simone *juvenile protection officer, business executive*

PROFESSIONAL INDEX 5971 GOVERNMENT: EXECUTIVE ADMINISTRATION

Martin, Fred *retired municipal official*
McNamara, Edward Howard *county official, former mayor*
Pavledes, E. Louis *city official*
Polakowski, William J. *municipal official*
Scott, Brenda M. *city official*
Worden, William Michael *city agency administrator, preservation consultant*

Flint
Stanley, Woodrow *mayor*

Grand Rapids
Hooker, William *administrative services officer*
Hoyt, William *city planner*
Logie, John Hoult *mayor, lawyer*

Hastings
†Rahn, L. Joseph *municipal official, business educator*

Lansing
Bell Wilson, Carlotta A. *state official, consultant*
Cannon, Patrick D. *federal offical, broadcaster*
†Granholm, Jennifer Mulhern *state attorney general*
†McGinnis, Kenneth L. *state official*
Miller, Candice S. *state official*
Muchmore, Dennis C. *governmental affairs consultant*
Posthumus, Richard Earl *state official, farmer*
Svec, Sandra Jean *state official*
†Truscott, John *state official*

Marquette
Wellington, Rosemary *economic development coordinator*

Mount Clemens
Kolakowski, Diana Jean *county commissioner*

Muskegon
Kuhn, Robert Herman *city and county official, engineer*
Roy, Paul Emile, Jr. *county official*

Negaunee
Friggens, Thomas George *state official, historian*

Saint Clair Shores
Weis, Lawrence Frederick *city official*

Tecumseh
Sackett, Dianne Marie *city treasurer, accountant*

Traverse City
Childs, K. Ross *county administrator, consultant*

Warren
Goldsmith, Aaron Clair *federal government executive*

MINNESOTA

Bloomington
Fellner, Michael Joseph *government execuive, educator*

Coon Rapids
Backes, Betty Lou *city clerk*

Hugo
Museus, Robert Allen *city manager*

Minneapolis
Carlson, Arne Helge *former governor*
Humphrey, Hubert Horatio, III *state attorney general*
Joseph, Geri Mack (Geraldine Joseph) *former ambassador, educator*
Mondale, Joan Adams *wife of former Vice President of United States*
O'Brien, Kathleen *muncipal or county official*
Quinlan, C. Patrick *retired diplomat, educator*
Sayles Belton, Sharon *mayor*

Northfield
Flaten, Robert Arnold *retired ambassador*

Saint Paul
Coleman, Norm *mayor*
†Hatch, Mike *state attorney general*
Kessler, Robert W. *director license, inspections, environmental rules*
†Kiffmeyer, Mary *state official*
O'Keefe, Thomas Michael *government official*
†Roberts, A(rthur) Wayne *organization administrator*
†Schunk, Mae *state official*
Shaffer, Thomas Frederic *state official*
†Ventura, Jesse *governor*

Saint Peter
Conlon, Kathryn Ann *county official*

MISSISSIPPI

Gulfport
Dickerson, Monar Steve *city official*
Easton, Jill Johanna *state official*
Mc Call, Jerry Chalmers *retired government official*

Jackson
Clark, Eric C. *state official*
Fordice, Kirk (Daniel Kirkwood Fordice, Jr.) *governor, construction company executive, engineer*
†Johnson, Harvey, Jr. *mayor*
Moore, Mike *state attorney general*
Musgrove, David Ronald *state official*
Musgrove, Ronnie *state official*
†Wilbur, Robert W. (Robbie) *state official*
Winter, William Forrest *former governor, lawyer*

Natchez
Harris, W. D. *city housing inspector, small business owner*

Pascagoula
†Touart, George F. *county official*

MISSOURI

Bolivar
Helton, Terry L. *city administrator*

Chaffee
Kitchen, Ellen Carleen *municipal official*

Columbia
Lubensky, Earl Henry *diplomat, anthropologist*

Jefferson City
Carnahan, Mel *governor, lawyer*
Cook, Rebecca McDowell *state official*
Hanson, Richard A. *state commissioner*
Holden, Bob *state official*
Madison, Eddie Lawrence, Jr. *public relations consultant, editor, writer*
Nixon, Jeremiah W. (Jay Nixon) *state attorney general*
Stroup, Kala Mays *state higher education commissioner*
Wilson, Roger Byron *lieutenant governor, school administrator*

Kansas City
Archer, J(ohn) Barry *municipal official*
†Arnold, Eric Daniell *budget analyst*
†Barnes, Kay *mayor of Kansas City, Missouri*
†Christensen, Courtney Waide *municipal administrator*
Danner, Kathleen Frances Steele *federal official*
Davis, Richard Francis *city government official*
Edwards, Horace Burton *former state official, former oil pipeline company executive, management consultant*
†Faulwell, Bond R. *government executive*
Price, Charles H., II *former ambassador*
Reed, Janice Moen *municipal employee*
Rocha, Catherine T. *municipal official*

Platte City
Knight, Betty Ann *county commissioner*

Rockville
McAvey, Maureen *municipal official*

Saint Charles
Lang, Danny Robert *municipal development official*

Saint Louis
Baker, Nannette A. *lawyer, city official*
Brendle, Steven Michael *municipal official, accountant*
Carpenter, Sharon Quigley *municipal official*
Geary, Daniel Patrick *postal service worker*
Harmon, Clarence *mayor*
Kuss, Joseph *municipal official*
Lester, Jacqueline *executive director city civil rights enforcement*
Pon-Salazar, Francisco Demetrio *diplomat, educator, deacon, counselor*
Russell-Davis, Valerie Sid *Saint Louis executive director employment and training*
Wiechart, Ralph *superintendent military memorial museum*

Saint Peters
†Brooks, Richard Eugene *cultural affairs administrator*

Springfield
Montgomery, Linda Stroupe *county official*

MONTANA

Billings
Larsen, Richard Lee *former mayor and city manager, business, municipal and labor relations consultant, arbitrator*

Fairfield
Graf, Ervin Donald *municipal administrator*

Havre
Mayer Lossing, Emily Ann *city official*

Helena
Cooney, Mike *state official*
Ekanger, Laurie *state official*
†Hutchinson, Donald Wilson *state commissioner of financial institutions*
Kolstad, Allen C. *state official*
Mazurek, Joseph P. *state attorney general, former state legislator*
†O'Keefe, Mark David *state official*
Racicot, Marc F. *governor*

Superior
Schneider, Brenda Laureen *town official*

NEBRASKA

Benkelman
Whiteley, Rose Marie *city clerk, treasurer*

Lincoln
Beermann, Allen J. *former state official*
Heineman, David *state official*
†Johanns, Michael O. *governor*
†Maurstad, David Ingolf *lieutenant governor, insurance agency executive*
Moore, Scott *state official*
Moul, Maxine Burnett *state official*
Stenberg, Donald B. *state attorney general*

North Bend
Johnson, Lowell C. *state commissioner*

North Platte
Hawks, James Wade *county highway superintendent, county surveyor*

Omaha
Daub, Hal *mayor of Omaha, former congressman*
†Janssen, Tom *state director*
Nelson, E. Benjamin *former governor, lawyer*
Peters, Robert *municipal official*

NEVADA

Carson City
†Augustine, Kathy *state official*
Del Papa, Frankie Sue *state attorney general*
†Guinn, Kenny C. *governor*
Heller, Dean *state official*
Hunt, Lorraine T. *state official*
†Molasky-Arman, Alice A. *state insurance commissioner*
†Walshaw, L. Scott *commissioner*

Henderson
McKinney, Sally Vitkus *state official*

Las Vegas
†Ciski, Leslie A. *government official*
Hammargren, Lonnie *former lieutenant governor*
Hudgens, Sandra Lawler *retired state official*
Jackson, Barbara Patricia *city manager*
Jones, Jan Laverty *mayor*
Miller, Robert Joseph *governor, lawyer*
Regan, John Bernard (Jack Regan) *community relations executive, senator*
Shackelford, Ralph *municipal official*
Vandever, Judith Ann *county official*
Walter, Randall H. *county official*

NEW HAMPSHIRE

Concord
Gardner, William Michael *state official*
Hill, Donald S. *commissioner, state*
†Maiola, Joel W. *state official*
McLaughlin, Philip T. *state attorney general*
Shaheen, C. Jeanne *governor*
Thomas, Georgie A. *state official*
†Twomey, Elizabeth Ann Molloy *education commissioner*

Grantham
Feldman, Roger Bruce *government official*

New Durham
Herman, William George *municipal government executive*

NEW JERSEY

Atlantic City
Mora, Kathleen Rita *state judicial administrator*

East Newark
Huhn, Darlene Marie *county official, poet*

Eatontown
Chomsky, Martin S. *county executive director*

Egg Harbor Township
Blee, Francis J. *municipal official*

Fort Monmouth
Washington, William Nicolai *government official*

Freehold
Nicholson, Henry Rexon *county transportation director*

Hoboken
Sasso, Frank Sergio *health officer*

Irvington
Paden, Harry *municipal official*

Jersey City
Gallagher, Thomas M. *city official Jersey City*
Schundler, Bret Davis *mayor*

Lakewood
Edwards, Francis Charles *municipal official*
†Valentino, Brian Joseph *public administrator*

Maplewood
Bigelow, Page Elizabeth *public policy professional*

Monmouth Junction
Olsen, Raymond T. *township official*

Moonachie
Malley, Raymond Charles *retired foreign service officer, industrial executive*

Morristown
MacKinnis, Ann Phelps *municipal government and land use management*

Newark
Harris, Carleina Hampton *muncipal or county official, educator*
James, Sharpe *mayor*
Martin, James Hanley *deputy state attorney general*
Scales, John Thomas *state official*
Stoute, Gayle Casandra Tisdale *postal service official*

Point Pleasant
Woolley-Dillon, Barbara Allen *city planner*

Princeton
Matlock, Jack Foust, Jr. *diplomat*

Sea Isle City
Tull, Theresa Anne *retired ambassador*

Seabrook
Joyce, Louis Cyril, IV *township administrator, planner*

Trenton
Di Eleuterio, James *state official*
Fishman, Len *state commissioner*
McElroy, George John *state government official*
†Soaries, DeForest B., Jr. *state official*
Verniero, Peter *state attorney general*
Whitman, Christine Todd *governor*

Union City
Dulack, David Donald *retired city inspector*

NEW MEXICO

Albuquerque
Baca, Jim *mayor*
Baca Archulata, Margie *city clerk*
Gonzales, Stephanie *state official*
Grossetete, Ginger Lee *retired gerontology administrator, consultant*
Harden, Clinton Dewey, Jr. *restaurant owner, state official*
Haulenbeek, Robert Bogle, Jr. *government official*
Kotchian, Sarah *municipal government official*
Lamberson, Anna Weinger *state legislative finance director, economist*
†McGuire, Susan G. *state director*
Ortiz y Pino, Gerald *municipal official*
Rael, Lawrence *city administrator*
†Rios, Phillip Peña *village administrator*
Sedillo, Orlando Delano *city solid waste management director*

Los Lunas
Behrend, Betty Ann *municipal official*

Santa Fe
Bradley, Walter D. *lieutenant governor, real estate broker*
Johnson, Gary Earl *governor*
Johnson, William Hugh, Jr. *state official, hospital administrator*
†Kinderwater, Diane *state official*
Lewis, James Beliven *state government official*
†Madrid, Patricia Ann *state attorney general, lawyer*
Montoya, Michael A. *state treasurer, accountant*
Vigil-Giron, Rebecca *state official*

NEW YORK

Albany
Berman, Carol *commissioner*
Chretien, Margaret Cecilia *public administrator*
Clarey, Donald Alexander *government affairs consultant*
†Croce, Alan J. *government agency executive*
†Donohue, Mary *state official*
Herman, Robert Samuel *former state official, economist, educator*
Murphy, Thomas Joseph *governmental official*
Murray, Kevin Francis *commissioner*
Pataki, George E. *governor*
Reynolds, Karl David *state official*
†Spitzer, Eliot *state attorney general*
Treadwell, Alexander F. *state official*

Ballston Lake
Cotter, William Donald *state commissioner, former newspaper editor*

Briarcliff Manor
Bates, Barbara J. Neuner *retired municipal official*

Brooklyn
Golden, Howard *muncipal or county official*
Rabiu, Badru I.D. *federal official*

Buffalo
DeLisle, Alan H. *city commissioner*
Durawa, Daniel T. *state commissioner*
Giambra, Joel Anthony *city comptroller*
Hassett, Eva M. *city commissioner*
Masiello, Anthony M. (Tony Masiello) *mayor*
Nowak, Carol Ann *city official*
Rochwarger, Leonard *former ambassador*

Chappaqua
Laun, Louis Frederick *government official*

Chatham
†DeGroodt, Jesse *municipal official, sports writer*

City Island
†George, James *retired diplomat, foundation executive*

Clinton
Burns, Bernard O. *county legislator*

East Elmhurst
Marshall, Helen M. *city official*

Floral Park
Corbett, William John *government and public relations consultant, lawyer*

Huntington
†Israel, Steve *town councilman*

Long Island City
Trent, James Alfred *city official*

Mineola
Salten, David George *county agency administrator, academic administrator*

Monticello
Sorensen, Alan John *county official*

New City
†Karben, Ryan Scott *county legislator*

New York
Andrews, Earl, Jr. *commissioner, state and local*
Annan, Kofi A. *diplomat*
Atsada, Chaiyanam *diplomat*
Baker, James Estes *foreign service officer*

Barbera, Jose Eduardo *international trade professional*
Blinken, Donald *ambassador, investment banker*
†Bowles, Erskine *White House staff member*
Brown, Carroll *diplomat, association executive*
Burleigh, A. Peter *ambassador*
Bystryn, Marcia Hammill *city program administrator*
Calovski, Naste *diplomat*
Carlson, Mitchell Lans *international technical advisor*
Chaves, Jose Maria *diplomat, foundation administrator, lawyer, educator*
Clark, William, Jr. *political advisor*
Cohn, David Herc *retired foreign service officer*
Curley, Walter Joseph Patrick *diplomat, investment banker*
Dangue Rewaka, Denis *diplomat*
†Dawson, Stephanie Elaine *city manager*
Dayson, Diane Harris *superintendent, park ranger*
DeCosta, Steven C. *municipal official*
Dejammet, Alain *diplomat*
†Doherty, Patrick William *city official*
Edighoffer-Murray, Anna Barbel *procurement officer, pharmacist, political scientist*
Eisenstadt, G. Michael *diplomat, author, lecturer, research scholar*
Eitel, Antonius *diplomat*
Elaraby, Nabil A. *Egyptian diplomat*
†Espinoza, Noemi Ruth *diplomat, researcher*
Fowler, Robert Ramsay *Canadian government official*
Fulci, Francesco Paolo *diplomat*
Gardner, Richard Newton *diplomat, lawyer, educator*
Giuliani, Rudolph W. *mayor, former lawyer*
Grunwald, Henry Anatole *ambassador, editor, writer*
Guillot, Cyril Etienne *international organization administrator*
Hevesi, Alan G. *muncipal or county official*
†Holbrooke, Richard Charles Albert *ambassador, government official*
Jargalsaikhany, Enkhsaikhan *diplomat*
Jones, James Robert *ambassador, former congressman, lawyer*
Katz, Abraham *retired foreign service officer*
Khan, Ahmed Kamal *ambassador*
Koch, Edward I. *former mayor, lawyer*
Lavrov, Sergei Viktorovich *ambassador*
Lehman, Orin *retired state official*
Levin, Herbert *diplomat, foundation executive*
McMullan, Alexander Joseph *municipal official*
†Mendez, Ruben Policarpio *diplomat*
Messinger, Ruth W. *borough president*
Miller, A. Gifford *city official*
Motyl, Alexander John *political science educator*
Murphy, Richard William *retired foreign service officer, Middle East specialist, consultant*
Ney, Edward N. *ambassador, advertising and public relations company executive*
Ober, Robert Fairchild, Jr. *college president, retired government official*
Okun, Herbert Stuart *diplomat, educator*
Petrella, Fernando Enrique *diplomat*
Platt, Nicholas *Asian affairs specialist, retired ambassador*
Polonetsky, Jules *city commissioner*
Qin Huasun *diplomat*
Ranald, Ralph Arthur *former government official, educator*
Rao, Sethuramiah Lakshminarayana *demographer, United Nations official*
†Roberts, Richard Todd *commissioner*
Rohatyn, Felix George *ambassador*
Rowan, John Patrick *city official*
Rzewnicki, Janet C. *state official*
Sobol, Thomas *state education commissioner*
Staehelin, Jenö Charles Albert *diplomat*
†Stephanopoulos, George Robert *federal official*
Stern, Henry Jordan *commissioner, state and local*
Stupp, Herbert William *municipal official*
Sucharipa, Ernst *diplomat*
Tello Macias, Manuel *diplomat*
Tharoor, Shashi *world organization official, writer*
Tomka, Peter *Slovakian diplomat*
†Vural, Volkan *Turkish representative to UN*
†Wibisono, Makarim *diplomat*
Wiener, Annabelle *United Nations official*
†Wyzner, Eugeniusz *diplomat*
Young, Paula Eva *city official, journalist, writer*
Zimiles, Eric Ian *government official*

Newtonville
†Conroy-LaCivita, Diane Catherine *city administrator*

Ogdensburg
Krol, John Casimir *city manager, municipal planner*

Ossining
Chervokas, John Vincent *town supervisor*

Oswego
†Wallace, Jason Joseph *city official*

Oyster Bay
Bell, James Thomas *town official*

Prt Jefferson
Strong, Robert Thomas *mayor, middle school educator*

Rochester
Burch, Bridgette *press secretary City of Rochester, New York*
Hannon, Richard W. *director budget bureau*
Johnson, William A., Jr. *mayor*
Kingsley, Linda S. *corporation counsel*

Romulus
Ostrander, Robert Edwin *retired United Nations interregional advisor, petroleum company executive*

Sprngfld Gdns
Bourne, John David *city finance executive*

Staten Island
Landau-Crawford, Dorothy Ruth *local social service executive*

Watertown
Coe, Benjamin Plaisted *retired state official*

West Seneca
Kelly, Anne Catherine *retired city official*

Yonkers
Alexander, Stanley F. *municipal agency administrator*
Celli, Joseph *municipal government official*
Farmer, Joe *municipal official*
Kaiser, Ann *municipal agency administrator*
LaPerche, James *municipal agency admiminstrator*
Liszewski, John *municipal official*
McGovern, Frank J. *municipal official*
Sialiano, Salvatore *municipal agency administrator*
Tutoni, Mitchell A. *municipal official*

NORTH CAROLINA

Apex
Ellington, John David *retired state official*

Cary
Saunders, Barry Wayne *state official*

Charlotte
McCarley, DeWitt *municipal official*
McCrory, Patrick *mayor*

Durham
Kerckhoff, Sylvia Stansbury *mayor*

Greensboro
Nussbaum, V. M., Jr. *former mayor*

High Point
Pate, William Patrick *city manager*

New Bern
Antry, Ronald Virgel *county official*

Raleigh
Boyles, Harlan Edward *state official*
Easley, Michael F. *state attorney general*
Graham, James A. *state commissioner*
Hunt, James Baxter, Jr. *governor, lawyer*
James, Perry Edwin, III *director Raleigh finance department*
Johnston, Linda Tidwell *municipal official*
Kirkpatrick, Jayne F. *director public affairs*
Marshall, Elaine Folk *state official*
Payne, Harry Eugene, Jr. *state labor commissioner*
†Sean, Walsh *press secretary*
Seiber, Frank *director information services*
Smith, Gail Grady *municipal official*
Stevens, Richard Yates *county official*
†Wheeler, Dan *state commissioner*
Wicker, Dennis A. *state official*

Southern Pines
Toon, Malcolm *former ambassador*

Wilson
Wyatt, Edward Avery, V *city manager*

NORTH DAKOTA

Bismarck
Gilmore, Kathi *state treasurer*
Heitkamp, Heidi *state attorney general*
Jaeger, Alvin A. (Al Jaeger) *secretary of state*
Myrdal, Rosemarie Caryle *state official, former state legislator*
Pomeroy, Glenn *state insurance commissioner*
Schafer, Edward T. *governor*

Grand Forks
Glassheim, Eliot Alan *program officer*

Mandan
Paul, Jack Davis *retired state official, addictions consultant*

Minot
Turner, Jane Ann *federal agent*

OHIO

Akron
Kidder, Joseph P. *city service director*
†Plusquellic, Donald L. *mayor*
Romanoski, George A. *municipal official*
Rothal, Max *director law department, lawyer*
Woolford, Warren L. *municipal official*

Celina
Giesige, Mark Richard *county official, auditor*

Cincinnati
Hardrick, Maria Darshell *government official, tax examiner*
†Holscher, Robert F. *county official*
†McInerney, Timothy P. *city manager*
Qualls, Roxanne *mayor*
Williams, Roy A. *municipal official*

Cleveland
Chema, Thomas V. *government official, lawyer*
Denihan, William M. *city official*
Everett, Ronald Emerson *government official*
Konicek, Michael *city official*
Robiner, Donald Maxwell *federal official, lawyer*
White, Michael Reed *mayor*

Columbus
Blackwell, J. Kenneth *state official*
†Burton, Barry Alan *county official*
Carter, Melinda *municipal official*
Draghi, Raymond Amadea *retired postal worker*
Filipic, Matthew Victor *state official*
Goldsmith, Jocelyn Stone *state employment professional*
Kingseed, Wyatt *city official*
Lashutka, Gregory S. *mayor, lawyer*
McGrath, Barbara Gates *city manager*
Montgomery, Betty Dee *state's attorney general, former state legislator*
Myers, William C. *city commissioner*
†O'Connor, Maureen *state official, lawyer*
Rice, Thomas W. *city public safety official*
Taft, Bob *governor*
Teater, Dorothy Seath *county official*
Ventresca, Joseph Anthony *energy coordinator*

Dayton
Hill, William E. *director technology services city government*
Lashley, William Bartholomew *county official*
Williams, Clarence E. *muncipal official*

Hamilton
Earley, Kathleen Sanders *municipal official*

Jacksontown
Schultz, Charles Edward *state official*

Mansfield
Prater, Willis Richard *county government agency official*

Maumee
Pauken, Stephen J. *mayor*

Mentor
Traub, Ronald Matthew *municipal administrator*

Navarre
Monroe, Kevin Anthony *municipal official*

Niles
Rizer, Janet Marlene *city tax administrator*

Toledo
Cardwell, Larry *executive director Toledo Youth Commission*
Finkbeiner, Carlton S. (Carty Finkbeiner) *mayor*
Kovacik, Thomas L. *chief operating officer and safety director Toledo*
Raczkowski, Dale Peter *city government administrator*
Reams, Anthony L. *director Toledo public service department*

University Heights
Rothschild, Beryl Elaine *mayor*

Wilmington
Hackney, Howard Smith *retired county official*

Wright Patterson AFB
Caudill, Tom Holden *governmental policy and analysis executive*

OKLAHOMA

Ada
Anoatubby, Bill *governor*

Lawton
Ellenbrook, Edward Charles *county official, small business owner*

Norman
Corr, Edwin Gharst *ambassador*
Perkins, Edward J. *diplomat*
Price, Linda Rice *community development administrator*

Oklahoma City
Butkin, Robert *state treasurer*
Clark, Gary Ray *licensing board executive*
Cooper, George *superintendent animal welfare Oklahoma City*
Craig, Jon Lee *state environmental program administrator*
Dungan, Paul Barnes *director city-county health department*
Edmondson, William Andrew *state attorney general*
Fallin, Mary Copeland *state official*
Hendrick, Howard H. *state government administrator*
Humphreys, Kirk *mayor*
†Hunter, Michael James *state government official, lawyer, educator*
Hurley, Thomas P. *city clerk*
Keating, Francis Anthony, II *governor, lawyer*
McKenzie, Clif Allen *Indian tribe official, accountant*
McNitt, Susan *municipal official*
Norick, Ronald J. *former mayor*
Ricks, Bob Alonzo *state official*
Rush, Richard P. *chamber of commerce executive*
Terrell, Danny *director general svcs*

Park Hill
Mankiller, Wilma Pearl *tribal leader, retired*

Poteau
†Kerr, Robert Samuel, III *state official*

Tulsa
Savage, Susan M. *mayor*

OREGON

Eugene
Bascom, Ruth F. *retired mayor*

Florence
Day, John Francis *city official, former savings and loan executive, former mayor*

Lake Oswego
Campbell, Colin Herald *former mayor*
Gawf, John Lee *foreign service officer*

Portland
Burton, Mike *regional government officer*
Kafoury, Marge *city official*
Katz, Vera *mayor, former college administrator, state legislator*
Kleim, E. Denise *city official*
Moose, Charles A. *state official*
Rosenberger, Michael F. *county official*

Salem
Hill, Jim *state official*
Keisling, Phillip Andrew *state official*
Kitzhaber, John Albert *governor, physician, former state senator*
Myers, Hardy *state attorney general, lawyer*

PENNSYLVANIA

Akron
Imhoff, Reed *retired city manager*

Allentown
Glaessmann, Doris Ann *former county official, consultant*
Smith, Robert Grant, Jr. *public official, retired hotel executive*

Bloomsburg
†Holdren, Murray F. *municipal official*

Carlisle
Russell, Theodore Emery *diplomat*

Chambersburg
Ross, Larry Michael *county economic development official*

Donora
Todd, Norma Jean Ross *retired government official*

Du Bois
Donahue, Ross Donald *state official*

Erie
Savocchio, Joyce A. *mayor*

Gettysburg
Schmoyer, Richard Harvey *county official*

Girardville
Dempsey, Thomas Joseph *postmaster*

Harrisburg
Banks, Albert Victor, Jr. *government administrator*
Bittenbender, Robert A. *state official*
Cauley, Alvin Paul *state government administrator*
Fisher, D. Michael *state attorney general*
Hafer, Barbara *state official*
†Koken, M. Diane *commissioner, state*
Lourie, Norman Victor *government official, social worker*
Nyce, Robert Eugene *state official*
†Pizzingrilli, Kim *state official*
†Reeves, Tim *state official*
Ridge, Thomas Joseph *governor, former congressman*
Schweiker, Mark S. *lieutenant governor*
Zogby, Charles Bernard *political office staff member*

Hollidaysburg
†Eichelberger, John H., Jr. *county commissioner*

Johnstown
Whittle, Randolph Gordon, Jr. *retired city manager*

King Of Prussia
†Wagenmann, Ronald George *township manager*

Lewisburg
Lenhart, Lorraine Margaret *county official*

Lititz
Koch, Bruce R. *diplomat*

Media
Dunion, Celeste Mogab *consultant, township official*

Mount Joy
D'Agostino, Raymond *city manager*

New Cumberland
Rose, Bonnie Lou *state official*

Newtown
Brennan, Thomas John *city and state official, consultant, educator*

Philadelphia
Basora, Adrian Anthony *ambassador*
Di Bernadinis, Michael *commissioner recreation Philadelphia*
DiCiccio, Frank J. *city official*
Fernandez, Happy Craven (Gladys Fernandez) *city council member*
Harris, Raymond Jesse *retired government official*
Hayllar, Ben *city finance director*
Knapton, David Robert *city planner*
Kromer, John *city official*
Longstreth, W. Thacher *city official*
Miller, Donna Reed *city official*
Mullin, Stephen Paul *municipal official*
Murray, Kathleen *municipal official*
Rendell, Edward Gene *mayor, lawyer*
Uhler, Walter Charles *government official, writer, reviewer*
Verna, Anna Cibotti *city council official*
Wolfe, J. Matthew *lawyer*

Pittsburgh
Charochak, Dale Michael *county official*
Cherna, Marc Kenneth *human services executive*
Costa, Guy *city official*
Donahoe, David Lawrence *state and city official*
Hennigan, Paul *municipal official*
Hirsch, Eloise *city administrator*
Kraus, Kathleen *acting director public safety, Pittsburgh*
Lowe, Stanley A. *housing authority executive*
Murphy, Thomas J., Jr. *mayor*

Pottstown
Prowant, Gregory E. *township manager*

PROFESSIONAL INDEX 5973 GOVERNMENT: EXECUTIVE ADMINISTRATION

Skippack
Stonehouse, Daniel *municipal officer*

Somerset
Thomas, Darlene Jean *state employee*

Spring House
†Canavan, Christophe R. *municipal manager*

State College
Lamb, Robert Edward *diplomat*

Waynesboro
Christopher, Michael Anthony *township manager*

West Chester
Dinniman, Andrew Eric *county commissioner, history educator, academic program director, international studies educator*

RHODE ISLAND

King Hou
Sundlun, Bruce *former governor*

Narragansett
Loontjens, Maurice John, Jr. *town manager*

Newport
Scott, Gerald Wesley *American diplomat*

North Providence
Mollis, A. Ralph *mayor*

Pawtucket
Metivier, Robert Emmett *retired mayor*

Providence
Almond, Lincoln *governor, lawyer*
Fogarty, Charles Joseph *state official*
Langevin, James R. *state official*
Pine, Jeffrey Barry *state attorney general*
Sanderson, Edward French *state official*
†Younkin, Richard Ambrose *state official, air quality specialist*

SOUTH CAROLINA

Anderson
Howard, Gerald Kelly *county official*

Chester
Driggers, Edward Rosemond *city administrator*

Clemson
Wiley, Byron Anthony *state official*

Columbia
Adams, Weston *diplomat, lawyer*
Condon, Charles Molony *state attorney general*
†Hodges, James H. *governor*
Miles, Jim *state official*
Patterson, Grady Leslie, Jr. *state treasurer*
Peeler, Bob *state official*
Walker, Richard Louis *former ambassador, educator, author*

Lexington
Morris, Earle Elias, Jr. *retired state official, business executive*

Patrick
Privette, Rosa Lee Millsaps *county official*

Sumter
Dawson-August, Annie Lee *state official*

SOUTH DAKOTA

Pierre
Barnett, Mark William *state attorney general*
Hazeltine, Joyce *state official*
Hillard, Carole *state official*
Janklow, William John *governor*

Redfield
†Morrison, Janet Kay *county treasurer*

Sioux Falls
†Erpenbach, Steve W. *state director*

Timber Lake
Flynn, Peggy Lou *county official*

TENNESSEE

Brentwood
Martin, William Edwin *government official*

Clarksville
Shelton, William Scott *former city official*

Cleveland
Wood, George Ambos *city manager*

Germantown
†Mills, William Barney *municipal official*

Madison
North, Jo Ann McLendon *county assessor*

Memphis
Herenton, Willie W. *mayor*

Nashville
Babbitt, Robert T. *municipal official*
Bredesen, Philip Norman *mayor*
Browning, T. Jeff *commissioner, state and local*
†Campbell, Donal *state official*
Cupit, Jim (Thomas) *county official*
Darnell, Riley Carlisle *state government executive, lawyer*
Fyke, James H. *city official*
Horton, Teresa Evetts *municipal official*
†Houston, Bill *state commissioner*
Hunt, Walter *county government official*
Levy, Bruce P. *muncipal or county official*
Murphy, James L., III *muncipal or county official*
Nolan, Eugene F. *muncipal or county official*
Palmer-Hass, Lisa Michelle *state official*
†Perrey, Ralph Martin *state government administrator*
†Sizemore, Douglas M. *state commerce and insurance commissioner*
Skoney, Bob *municipal official*
†Summers, Paul *state attorney general*
Sundquist, Don *governor, former congressman, sales corporation executive*
Swing, Marilyn S. *metropolitan clerk*
Wadley, Fredia Stovall *state commissioner*
Walkup, John Knox *state attorney general*
Wilder, John Shelton *state official, former state legislator*

Portland
†Ryan, Hans Thomas *government official, political consultant*

Sparta
Pearson, Margaret Donovan *former mayor*

Springfield
Nutting, Paul John *city manager*

TEXAS

Arlington
Odom, Elzie D. *mayor*

Austin
Ashworth, Kenneth Hayden *public affairs specialist, educator*
Barnes, James Randal *state official*
†Bomer, Elton *state official*
Bush, George W. *governor*
Cooke, Carlton Lee, Jr. *mayor*
Cornyn, John *state attorney general*
Gates, Charles W., Sr. *city official*
Johnson, Lady Bird (Mrs. Lyndon Baines Johnson) *widow of former President of United States*
McReynolds, Mary Maureen *municipal environmental administrator, consultant*
Morales, Dan *state attorney general*
†Moses, Mike *commissioner*
†Perry, Rick *state official*
Richards, Ann Willis *former governor*
Todd, Bruce M. *public affairs executive, former mayor*
Townsend, Richard Marvin *government insurance executive, city manager, consultant*
Watson, Kirk *mayor*
White, Alice Virginia *volunteer health corps administrator*

Beaumont
Lord, Evelyn Marlin *former mayor*

Breckenridge
†Rominger, James Corridon *political party administrator*

Brenham
Pipes, Paul Ray *county commissioner*

Brooks AFB
Monk, Richard Francis *air force officer, health care administrator*

Burleson
Godbey, Helen Kay *city official*

Clarendon
Chamberlain, William Rhode *county official*

Corpus Christi
Allin, Bonnie A. *city official*
Peterson, Harold R. *municipal official*

Dallas
†Caramia, Philip Dominick *government official*
Cheney, Dick (Richard Bruce Cheney) *former secretary of defense, former congressman*
Dyer, Paul D. *municipal official*
Johnson, Alonzo Bismark *city official, court administrator*
Kirk, Ron *mayor, lawyer*
†Kirk, Ronald *mayor*
Lake, Joseph Edward *ambassador*
Lee, Jimmy Che-Yung *city planner*
Melton, Robert W. *city auditor*
Poss, Mary *mayor*
Rubottom, Roy Richard, Jr. *retired diplomat and educator, consultant*

Denton
Hill, David Mark *city planning director*

El Paso
Ramirez, Carlos Moises *mayor*

Fort Worth
Barr, Kenneth L. *mayor*
McMillen, Howard Lawrence *municipal government official*

Garland
Baker, John *director engineering*
Bickerstaff, Jeffery Wayne *municipal official*
Kauffman, George *financial administrator*
Spence, Jim *mayor*

Harlingen
Matz, James Richard *county official*

Houston
Brown, Lee Patrick *federal official, law enforcement educator*
Bush, George Herbert Walker *former President of the United States*
DeLeön, John Joseph *city agency executive*
desVignes-Kendrick, Mary *municipal official*
Driscoll, Ray F. *city official*
Flack, Joe Fenley *county and municipal official, former insurance executive*
Fowler, Robert Asa *diplomat, consultant, business director*
†Lanier, Bob *mayor*
Lewis, Richard D. *municipal official*
Manero, Joseph Anthony *political consultant, lobbyist*
Schechter, Arthur Louis *lawyer*
Spellman, Oliver B., Jr. *city official*
Yarbrough, Michael *city councilman*

Irving
Sweat, Jason Ellis *government official, consultant*

Jacksboro
Webb, Michael Alan *city manager*

Kingwood
Romere, Mary Elaine *public health services manager*

La Feria
Philip, Sunny Koipurathu *municipal official*

Laredo
Colón, Phyllis Janet *city official*

Lubbock
Cooke, Alex "Ty", Jr. *mayor*
Sitton, Windy *mayor of Lubbock, Texas*

Muenster
Broyles, Stephen Douglas *public administrator*

New Braunfels
Krueger, Robert Charles *ambassador, former senator, former congressman*

Port Arthur
†Thigpen, Albert Thaeto *municipal administrator*

San Antonio
Brechtel, Terry M. *San Antonio budget and analysis director*
Catto, Henry Edward *former government official, former ambassador*
Flores, Roger *city official*
Henderson, Connie Chorlton *city planner, artist and writer*
Moore, Steve *executive director San Antonio convention bureau*
Peak, Howard W. *mayor*
Pena, Octavio *director city internal revenue department*

UTAH

Salt Lake City
†Allen, Joi Lin *government official*
Alter, Edward T. *state treasurer*
†Bowen, Melanie *state official*
Corradini, Deedee *mayor*
†Foxley, Cecelia Harrison *commissioner*
Graham, Jan *state attorney general*
Hilbert, Robert Backus *county water utility administrator*
Johnson, Frank *retired state official, educator*
Leavitt, Michael Okerlund *governor, insurance executive*
†Minson, Dixie L. *state director*
†Thorne, Kim S. *state official*
†Varela, Vicki *deputy chief of staff Governor of Utah*
Walker, Olene S. *lieutenant governor*

West Valley City
Wright, Gearld Lewis *mayor, retired educator*

VERMONT

Barre
Milne, James *former secretary of state*

Burlington
Glitman, Maynard Wayne *foreign service officer*

Middlebury
Kunin, Madeleine May *ambassador to Switzerland, former governor*

Montpelier
Costle, Elizabeth Rowe *commissioner*
Dean, Howard *governor*
†Markowitz, Deborah L. *state government official*
†Pelham, Tom *commissioner, state*
Racine, Doug *state official*
Sorrell, William H. *state attorney general*

Peacham
Engle, James Bruce *ambassador*

South Londonderry
Spiers, Ronald Ian *diplomat*

Washington
Brynn, Edward Paul *former ambassador*

VIRGINIA

Alexandria
Aller, John Cosmos *diplomat*
Costagliola, Francesco *former government official, macro operations analyst*
Ensslin, Robert Frank, Jr. *retired association executive and military officer*
Fisher, Joseph Allen *retired government official*
Fitton, Harvey Nelson, Jr. *former government official, publishing consultant*
Havens, Harry Stewart *former federal assistant comptroller general, government consultant*
Helman, Gerald Bernard *government official*
Hilton, Robert Parker, Sr. *national security affairs consultant, retired naval officer*
Price, James Edward *federal government executive*
Pringle, Robert Maxwell *diplomat*
†Schanzer, Steven T. *defense security director*
Skoug, Kenneth Nordly, Jr. *diplomat*
Watkins, Birge Swift *government contractor*

Amelia Court House
Wallace, John Robert *county administrator*

Annandale
Christianson, Geryld B. *government relations consultant*
Rogers, Stephen Hitchcock *former ambassador*
Tontz, Robert L. *government official*

Arlington
Aggrey, Orison Rudolph *former ambassador, university administrator*
Allen, David *government official*
Bolster, Archie Milburn *retired foreign service officer*
†Boster, Davis Eugene *retired ambassador*
Brazeal, Aurelia Erskine *former ambassador*
Bune, Karen Louise *criminal justice official*
Covington, James Edwin *government agency administrator, psychologist*
Davis, Ruth A. *ambassador*
Edmondson, William Brockway *retired foreign service officer*
Everett, Warren Sylvester *consultant, former government official*
Grandmaison, J. Joseph *federal agency executive*
Hamed, Martha Ellen *government administrator*
Itoh, William H. *former ambassador*
Keel, Alton Gold, Jr. *ambassador*
Krys, Sheldon Jack *retired foreign service officer, career minister*
Kull, Joseph *government administrator*
Smith, Myron George *former government official, consultant*
Taggart, G. Bruce *government program executive*
Umminger, Bruce Lynn *government official, scientist, educator*
Verville, Elizabeth Giavani *federal official*
Wilkie, Julia Bullard *government affairs representative*
Yount, George R. *admiral commander*

Burke
Pfister, Cloyd Harry *consultant, former career officer*

Charlottesville
Newsom, David Dunlop *foreign service officer, educator*

Chesapeake
Ward, William E. *mayor*

Chesterfield
†Stegmaier, James J.L. *county administrator*

Dumfries
Wolle, William Down *foreign service officer*

Fairfax
Beckler, David Zander *government official, science administrator*
Pyatt, Everett Arno *government official*

Falls Church
Beyer, Donald Sternoff, Jr. *state official*
Block, John Rusling *former secretary of agriculture*
Ward, George Frank, Jr. *ambassador*

Fort Belvoir
Daverede, Heidi Marianne *government official*
Diercks, Frederick Otto *government official*

Front Royal
Stanley, Douglas Parnell *county planner*

Great Falls
Savage, Michael Thomas *federal executive*
Zimmermann, Warren *former foreign service officer*

Hampton
Beauregard, Leslie Michelle *budget analyst, legislative liaison*

Haymarket
Doolittle, Warren T. *retired federal official*

King George
Newhall, David, III *former government official*

Lynchburg
Davenport, James Robert *retired city official, retired utility executive*
Stephens, Bart Nelson *former foreign service officer*

Mc Lean
Cahill, Harry Amory *diplomat, educator*
Cannon, Mark Wilcox *government official, business executive*
Healy, Theresa Ann *former ambassador*
McCormack, Richard Thomas Fox *government official, former ambassador*
Norris, Genie M. *senior government official*
Smith, Russell Jack *former intelligence official*

Newport News
Williamson, Jack *city official*

Norfolk
Andrews, Mason Cooke *mayor, obstetrician, gynecologist, educator*
Daughtrey, R. Breckenridge *city clerk*
Davies, George Patrick *city official*
Griffith, Charles Dee, Jr. *state official*
Keifer, John M. *director Norfolk public works department*
Washington, Ann S. *city official*

Richmond
Adiele, Nkwachukwu Moses *state official*
Earley, Mark Lawrence *state attorney general*
Gilmore, James Stuart, III *governor*
Hager, John Henry *state official*
Holcomb, Richard D. *state commissioner*

King, Ronald L. *state official, English educator*
Kinsey, David Jonathan *state official, meteorologist*
Kronzer, Lance *city auditor, Richmond, Virginia*
Lockhart, Mack L. *Richmond City Assessor*
†Marcus, M. Boyd, Jr. *state official*
†Miner, Mark Aaron *state official*
†Petera, Anne P. *state official*
Sgro, Beverly Huston *head of collegiate school, state official, educator*
Showalter, J. Kirk *general registrar, Richmond, Virginia*
†Tillet, Ronald *state official*
Wilder, Eunice *city official*

Springfield
Hunt, Robert Gayle *former government official*
Stottlemyer, David Lee *government official*

Suffolk
Hope, James Franklin *mayor, civil engineer, consultant*

Susan
Ambach, Dwight Russell *retired foreign service officer*

The Plains
Gibbons, John Howard (Jack Gibbons) *government official, physicist*

Vienna
DeWitt, Charles Barbour *federal government official*
Marinelli, Ada Santi *retired government official, real estate broker*
Palmer, Stephen Eugene, Jr. *government official*
Tucker, Alvin Leroy *retired government official*

Virginia Beach
Atkinson, John T. *treasurer City of Virginia Beach*
Cowart, Gwen *municipal official*
Friedman, Andrew *director housing and neighborhood preservation*
Grochmal, David *municipal government official*
†King, Stephen Miles *public administration educator*
Maxwell, Donald L. *municipal official*
Oberndorf, Meyera E. *mayor*
Ricketts, James *municipal official*
Smith, Ruth Hodges *city clerk*
Sullivan, David C. *municipal agency administrator*

Woodstock
Duceman, Mark Eugene *county zoning administrator, planner*

WASHINGTON

Bainbridge Island
Huntley, James Robert *government official, international affairs scholar and consultant*

Bellevue
†Burleson, Hugh Latimer, II *retired foreign service officer, translator*

Bothell
Cothern, Barbara Shick *county official*

Centralia
Brunswig, Jessie *executive assistant*

Dayton
McFarland, Jon Weldon *retired county commissioner*

Marysville
Bartholomew, Shirley Kathleen *municipal official*

Medina
Ward, Marilyn Beeman *commissioner*

Olympia
Godfrey, Patrick Lewis *state government official*
Locke, Gary *governor*
†Love, Keith Sinclair *communications director Governor of Washington*
Munro, Ralph Davies *state government official*
Murphy, Michael Joseph *state official*
O'Brien, Robert S. *state official*
Owen, Bradley Scott *lieutenant governor*

Pullman
Halvorson, Alfred Rubin *retired mayor, consultant, education educator*

Renton
Lowry, Mike *former governor, former congressman*

Seattle
Covington, Germaine Ward *municipal agency administrator*
Diers, James A. *director department of neighborhoods Seattle*
Knox, Venerria L. *municipal or county official*
Krochalis, Richard F. *municipal government official*
Schell, Paul E. S. *mayor*
Skidmore, Donald Earl, Jr. *government official*
Smith, Le Roi Matthew-Pierre, III *municipal administrator*
Voget, Jane J. *city official, lawyer*

Sequim
Huston, Harriette Irene Otwell (Ree Huston) *retired county official*
McMahon, Terrence John *retired foreign service officer*

Spokane
Adolfae, Michael H. *municipal government official*
Greenwood, Collette P. *municipal official, finance officer*
Harden, Harvey *director civil service department, Spokane*
Kobluk, Michael D. *municipal official*
Lengyel, Larry *director employment and training, Spokane*
Pfister, Terri *city clerk*
Sciuchetti, Dale *municipal government official*

Sumas
Hemry, Larry Harold *former federal agency official, writer*

Tacoma
†Ebersole, Brian *mayor*
Luttropp, Peter C. *director of finance, Tacoma*
Vlasak, Walter Raymond *state official, management development consultant*

Vancouver
Ogden, Daniel Miller, Jr. *government official, educator*

Wenatchee
Montague, Gary Leslie *county commissioner, retired newspaper advertising executive*

Yakima
Sveinsson, Johannes *former city and county government official*

WEST VIRGINIA

Charleston
†Clark, Hanley C. *state insurance commissioner*
Hechler, Ken *state official, former congressman, political science educator, author*
Mc Graw, Darrell Vivian, Jr. *state attorney general*
Melton, G. Kemp *former mayor*
†Miles, Jill Leone *state official*
Tomblin, Earl Ray *state official*
Underwood, Cecil H. *governor, company executive*

Harpers Ferry
Cooley, Hilary Elizabeth *county official*

WISCONSIN

Appleton
Lillge, Eugene Francis *county official*

Ashland
Smith, Jane Schneberger *retired city administrator*

Fox Point
†Robertson, Susan Elendra *municipal government administrator*

Juneau
Ebert, Dorothy Elizabeth *county clerk*

Madison
Doyle, James E(dward) *state attorney general*
Earl, Anthony Scully *former governor of Wisconsin, lawyer*
La Follette, Douglas J. *secretary of state*
Mack, Kirbie Lyn *municipal official*
McCallum, Scott *state official*
Saunders, Charles David *state official*
Thompson, Tommy George *governor*
Voight, Jack C. *state official*

Marinette
†Lawton, Robert Cushman *county official*

Milwaukee
Henry, Julietta *commissioner, state and local*
Norquist, John Olof *mayor*
Penman, Julie A. *commissioner, state and local*
Szallai, Kenneth J. *muncipal or county official*

Oshkosh
†Rojahn, Elizabeth J. *diplomat*

Pleasant Prairie
Pollocoff, Michael R. *village administrator*

Superior
Ciccone, Margaret *mayor*

WYOMING

Cheyenne
Geringer, James E. *governor*
†McBride, John P. *state insurance commissioner*
Ohman, Diana J. *state official, former school system administrator*
†Rodekohr, Diane E. *state official*
Smith, Stanford Sidney *state treasurer*
Thomson, Thyra Godfrey *former state official*
†Woodhouse, Gay Vanderpoel *state attorney general*

Laramie
Dickman, Francois Moussiegt *former foreign service officer, educator*
Meyer, Joseph B. *state official, former academic administrator*

TERRITORIES OF THE UNITED STATES

AMERICAN SAMOA

Pago Pago
†Mailo, Toetagata Albert *territory attorney general*
Sunia, Tauese *governor*
Tulafono, Togiola T.A. *state official*

GUAM

Agana
Bordallo, Madeleine Mary (Mrs. Ricardo Jerome Bordallo) *lieutenant governor*
Gutierrez, Carl T. C. *governor*

NORTHERN MARIANA ISLANDS

Saipan
†Tenorio, Pedro Pangelinan *government official*

PUERTO RICO

San Juan
Burgos, Norma *secretary of state*
†Velez Silva, Xenia *Puerto Rican government official*

REPUBLIC OF MARSHALL ISLAND

Majuro
Plaisted, Joan M. *diplomat*

VIRGIN ISLANDS

Charlotte Amalie
Aubain, Joseph F. *municipal official*
†James, Gerard Amwur, II *lieutenant governor*
Stapleton, Marylyn Alecia *diplomat*

Saint Thomas
Schneider, Roy *former US Virgin Islands government official*
†Simmonds, Ruby *government official*
†Turnbull, Charles W. *governor*

MILITARY ADDRESSES OF THE UNITED STATES

ATLANTIC

APO
Alexander, Leslie M. *ambassador*
Baltimore, Richard Lewis, III *foreign service officer*
Carner, George *foreign service executive, economic strategist*
Creagan, James Francis *diplomat*
Gutierrez, Lino *diplomat*
Jett, Dennis Coleman *foreign service officer*
Kamman, Curtis Warren *ambassador*
Maisto, John F. *ambassador*

EUROPE

APO
Cook, Frances D. *diplomat*
Fowler, Wyche, Jr. *ambassador*
Kornblum, John Christian *ambassador*
Lino, Marisa Rose *diplomat*
Milam, William Bryant *diplomat, economist*
Walker, Edward S., Jr. *diplomat*

London
Bartholomew, Reginald *diplomat*

PACIFIC

APO
Beeman, Josiah Horton *diplomat*
Holmes, Genta Hawkins *diplomat*

FPO
Boucher, Richard A. *ambassador*

CANADA

ALBERTA

Calgory
McCrank, Michael Neil *government official*

Edmonton
Day, Stockwell Burt *government official*

BRITISH COLUMBIA

Kaleden
Siddon, Thomas Edward *Canadian government official, environmental consultant*

Vancouver
Duncan, Mark *government official*
Harcourt, Michael Franklin *retired premier of Province of British Columbia, lawyer, educator*

Victoria
Gardom, Garde Basil *lieutenant governor of British Columbia*
Penikett, Antony David John *Canadian government official*

MANITOBA

Winnipeg
Curtis, Charles Edward *Canadian government official*
Downey, James Erwin *government official*
Filmon, Gary Albert *Canadian provincial premier, civil engineer*
†Liba, Peter Michael *Canadian government official, former communications executive*
Praznik, Darren Thomas *provincial legislator*

NEW BRUNSWICK

Fredericton
LeBreton, Paul M. *government official*

NEWFOUNDLAND

Saint Johns
Gibbons, Rex Vincent *geologist*

NOVA SCOTIA

Halifax
Cosman, Francene Jen *government official*
Kinley, John James *government official*

Waverley
Grady, Wayne J. *government official*

ONTARIO

London
Haskett, Dianne Louise *mayor, lawyer*

Manotick
Prince, Alan Theodore *former government official, engineering consultant*

Nepean
Stanford, Joseph Stephen *diplomat, lawyer, educator*

Nobleton
Embleton, Tony Frederick Wallace *retired Canadian government official*

Ottawa
Ablonczy, Diane *member Canadian parliament*
Anderson, David *Canadian government official*
Armstrong, Henry Conner *former Canadian government official, consultant*
Assadourian, Sarkis *member of parliament*
Augustine, Jean *member of parliament*
Axworthy, Lloyd *Canadian government official*
Barnes, Susan Carol *member of parliament*
Beaumier, Colleen *member Canadian Parliament*
Beehan, Cathy *government official, lawyer*
Bélair, Réginald *Canadian government official*
Bélisle, Paul C. *Canadian government official*
Bellemare, Eugene *member of parliament*
Bernier, Gilles *member of parliament*
Bigras, Bernard *Canadian government official*
Blaikie, William *government official*
Breitkreuz, Garry *member of parliament*
Brown, Bonnie *Canadian parliamentarian*
Buchanan, John MacLennan *Canadian provincial official*
Cameron, Christina Stuart *government official*
Catterall, Marlene *Canadian legislator*
Cauchon, Martin *Canadian government official*
Chan, Raymond *Canadian government minister*
Chatters, Dave *member of parliament*
Chrétien, (Joseph Jacques) Jean *prime minister of Canada, lawyer*
Collenette, David M. *Canadian government official*
Copps, Sheila *Canadian government official*
Dawson, Mary E. *government official*
DeVillers, Paul *member of parliament*
Dhaliwal, Herb *Canadian government official*
Dingwall, David C. *Canadian government official*
Dion, Stéphane *federal official*
Discepola, Nunzio (Nick) *Canadian government official*
Dromisky, Stan *Canadian government official*
Duhamel, Ronald J. *Canadian government official*
Duncan, John M. *Canadian government official*
Eggleton, Arthur C. *Canadian government official, member of Parliament*
Fairbairn, Joyce *Canadian government official*
Finestone, Sheila *Canadian government official*
Finlay, John Baird *government official*
Finn, Gerard *federal government official*
†Fry, Hedy *government minister*
Gagliano, Alfonso *Canadian government official*
Gilmour, William *government official*
Giroux, Robert-Jean-Yvon *retired Canadian government official*
Gold, Lorne W. *Canadian government official*
Goodale, Ralph E. *Canadian government minister*
Gouk, James William *government official*
†Graham, B. Alasdair *government official*
Gray, Herbert Eser *Canadian government official*
Grey, Deborah Cleland *Canadian government official*
Harb, Mac *Canadian government official*
Harder, V. Peter *government official*
Hill, Jay *member of parliament*
Jaffer, Rahim *parliamentarian*
Kerpan, Allan *government official*
Kingsley, Jean-Pierre *government official*
Kirkwood, David Herbert Waddington *Canadian government official*
Lalonde, Francine *member of parliament*
LaRocque, Judith Anne *federal official*
LeBlanc, Roméo *Canadian Governor General*
MacAulay, Lawrence A. *Canadian government official*
MacDonald, Flora Isabel *Canadian government official*
Manley, John *Canadian government official*
Marleau, Diane *Canadian government official*
Martin, Paul *Canadian government official*
Massé, Marcel *Canadian government minister*
McGuire, Joe *federal official*
McLellan, A. Anne *Canadian government official*
McLure, John Douglas *government relations*
McNally, Grant *member of parliament*
Mifflin, Fred John *Canadian government official*
Mills, Bob *member of parliament*
Minna, Maria *member of parliament*
Mitchell, Andy *Canadian federal official*
Morrison, Lee *member of parliament*
Murray, Ian *member of parliament*
†Normand, Gilbert *government official*
Nunziata, John *member of parliament*
O'Brien, Lawrence *member of parliament*
Paradis, Denis *member of parliament*
Perić, Janko *government official*
Peterson, Jim *member of parliament*
Picard, Pauline *Canadian government official*
Pickard, Jerry *member of parliament*
Pilliteri, Gary *member of parliament*
Poulin, Marie-Paule *Canadian government official*
Proud, George *member of parliament*
Ramsay, Jack *federal official*
Riis, Nelson *member of parliament*
Robertson, Robert Gordon *retired Canadian government official*

Robichaud, Fernand *Canadian government official*
Robillard, Lucienne *federal official*
Robinson, Svend J. *member of parliament*
Rock, Allan Michael *Canadian government official*
Roland, Anne *registrar Supreme Court of Canada*
Scott, Andy *government official*
Shepherd, Alex *member of parliament*
Silverman, Ozzie *consulting strategist*
Steckle, Paul *federal official*
Tait, John Charles *Canadian government official*
Vanclief, Lyle *federal official*
Withers, Ramsey Muir *government consultant, former government official*
Yalden, Maxwell Freeman *Canadian diplomat*
Yeomans, Donald Ralph *Canadian government official, consultant*

Rockcliffe
Marchi, Sergio Sisto *Canadian government official*

Toronto
Gotlieb, Allan E. *former ambassador*
Holyday, Douglas Charles *city councillor*
Lastman, Melvin D. *mayor*
Turner, John Napier *former prime minister of Canada, legislator*
Wilson, Jim *Canadian provincial official*

QUEBEC

Chelsea
Warren, Jack Hamilton *former diplomat and trade policy adviser*

Hull
Blondin-Andrew, Ethel *Canadian government official*
Stewart, Christine Susan *Canadian government official*
Stewart, Jane *Canadian federal official*

Montreal
Bourque, Pierre *mayor*
Mulroney, (Martin) Brian *former prime minister of Canada*
Pendleton, Mary Catherine *foreign service officer*

Nemaska
Coon Come, Matthew *Native American tribal chief*

Quebec
Bouchard, Lucien *Canadian government official*
Pronovost, Jean *government official*

Quebec City
Marchand, Jean-Paul *government official*

SASKATCHEWAN

Regina
Atkinson, Patricia *minister of health*
Romanow, Roy John *provincial government official, barrister, solicitor*
Shillington, Edward Blain *government official*
Wiebe, J. E. N. *province official*

Saskatoon
Blakeney, Allan Emrys *Canadian government official, lawyer*

MEXICO

Mexico City
Cervantes Aguirre, Enrique *Mexican government official*
†Davidow, Jeffrey *ambassador to Mexico*
de la Fuente Ramirez, Juan Ramon *Mexican government official*
de Maria y Campos, Mauricio *United Nations official*
Green Macias, Rosario *United Nations official*
Ruiz Sacristán, Carlos *Mexican government official*
Zedillo Ponce de León, Ernesto *president of Mexico*

BAHRAIN

Manaman
†Young, Johnny *foreign service officer*

BRAZIL

Brasilia
†Lopes Borio, Pedro Henrique *diplomat*

CAPE VERDE

Praia
McNamara, Francis T. *ambassador*

CHILE

Santiago
†O'Leary, John Joseph, Jr. *ambassador*
Wilkey, Malcolm Richard *retired ambassador, former federal judge*

CZECH REPUBLIC

Prague
Shattuck, John *diplomat, civil rights lawyer, university administrator*

ECUADOR

Quito
Sanbrailo, John A. *mission director*

EGYPT

Cairo
Boutros-Ghali, Boutros *former United Nations official*

ENGLAND

London
Elizabeth, Her Majesty II (Elizabeth Alexandra Mary) *Queen of United Kingdom of Great Britain and Northern Ireland, and her other Realms and Territories, head of the Commonwealth, Defender of the Faith*
Lader, Philip *government official, diplomat, business executive, university president*
MacLaren, Roy *Canadian government official, publisher*
Orr, Bobette Kay *diplomat*
Streator, Edward *diplomat*

FRANCE

Audierne
Smalley, Robert Manning *government official*

Beduer
Ezelle, Robert Eugene *diplomat*

Paris
Dean, John Gunther *diplomat*
Ferriter, John Pierce *diplomat*
Myerson, Jacob Myer *former foreign service officer*

Sannois
Cornell, Robert Arthur *retired international government official, consultant*

GERMANY

Berlin
Saloom, Joseph A., III *diplomat*

INDONESIA

Jakarta
Roy, J(ames) Stapleton *ambassador*

ITALY

Rome
Barbanti, Sergio *diplomat*
Bertini, Catherine Ann *United Nations official*
Cassiers, Juan *diplomat*

JAPAN

Minato-ku Tokyo
Manz, Johannes Jakob *Swiss diplomat*

Tokyo
Owada, Hisashi *diplomat*

RWANDA

Kigali
Gribbin, Robert E., III *former ambassador*

SLOVAKIA

Bratislava
Lankford, Richard Oliver *diplomat*

SOUTH AFRICA

Arcadia
Berry, Ann Roper *diplomat*

SRI LANKA

Colombo
Smyth, Richard Henry *foreign service officer*

SWITZERLAND

Geneva
Amorim, Celso Luiz Nunes *government official*
Brown, Kent Newville *ambassador*

TAIWAN

Taipei
Chang, Parris Hsu-cheng *law-maker, political science educator, writer*

TUNISIA

Tunis
Raphel, Robin *ambassador*

URUGUAY

Montevideo
†Dodd, Thomas J. *ambassador, educator*

VIETNAM

Hanoi
Peterson, Douglas Pete (Pete Peterson) *ambassador, former congressman*

Ho Chi Minh City
Ray, Charles Aaron *foreign service officer*

ADDRESS UNPUBLISHED

Abramowitz, Morton I. *former ambassador*
Adams, Edwin Melville *former foreign service officer, actor, author, lecturer*
Adams, James Blackburn *former state government official, former federal government official, lawyer*
Adams, Michael John *air force non-commissioned officer*
Albertson, Susan L. *retired federal government official*
Allen, Edgar Burns *records management professional*
Anderson, Nils, Jr. *former government official, retired business executive, industrial historian*
†Arias, Incencio F. *diplomat*
Armstrong, Anne Legendre (Mrs. Tobin Armstrong) *former ambassador, corporate director*
Bailey, Donnis Aaron David *county official*
Barkley, Richard Clark *ambassador*
Batt, Philip E. *former governor*
Benson, Joanne E. *former lieutenant governor*
†Bentsen, Lloyd *former government official, former senator*
Berlincourt, Marjorie Alkins *government official, retired*
Betti, John Anso *federal official, former automobile manufacturing company executive*
Beyer, Gordon Robert *foreign service officer*
Binsfeld, Connie Berube *former state official*
Blood, Archer Kent *retired foreign service officer*
Boyatt, Thomas David *former ambassador*
Brauchli, Marcus Walker *foreign correspondent*
Brenner, Jane Segrest *former city council member*
†Brogan, Frank T. *lieutenant governor*
†Brown, James H., Jr. *state insurance commissioner, lawyer*
Bryant, Winston *former state attorney general*
Burchman, Leonard *government official*
Burris, Frances White *retired state official*
Bush, Richard Clarence, III *federal government executive*
Bushnell, Prudence *former diplomat, management consultant, trainer*
Cannon, Isabella Walton *mayor*
†Carney, Timothy Michael *diplomat*
Carter, Rosalynn Smith *wife of former President of United States*
Cary, Anne O. *retired diplomat*
†Chen, Stephen S. F. *diplomat*
Christie, Walter Scott *retired state official*
Clarke, Henry Lee *foreign service officer, former ambassador*
Cleaver, Emanuel, II *former mayor, minister*
†Clifford, Edward R. *municipal official*
Cockrum, Bob *city official*
Cohen, Roberta Jane *government executive*
Condayan, John *retired foreign service officer, consultant*
Coop, Frederick Robert *retired city manager*
Coppie, Comer Swift *state official*
Corkery, James Caldwell *retired Canadian government executive, mechanical engineer*
Cornish, Richard Joseph *international affairs consultant, retired diplomat*
Cougill, Roscoe McDaniel *mayor, retired air force officer*
Dalton, John Howard *Former Secretary of the Navy, financial consultant*
Dawson, Horace Greeley, Jr. *former diplomat, government official*
†De Fronzo, Joseph Michael *village manager*
†Dickerson, Justin Brandt *financial and telecommunications policy analyst*
Dillon, Robert Sherwood *retired government official*
Drennen, William Miller, Jr. *cultural administrator, film executive, producer, director, mineral resource executive*
†Drennon-Gala, Donney Thomas *correctional treatment specialist, sociologist*
Dunford, David Joseph *foreign service officer, ambassador*
Dyrstad, Joanell M. *former lieutenant governor, consultant*
Egan, Wesley William, Jr. *ambassador*
Eisenhower, John Sheldon Doud *former ambassador, author*
Emmons, Robert Duncan *diplomat*
Engler, John *governor*
Essenfeld, Ann Paula *government official*
Eu, March Fong *ambassador, former state official*
Evans, Gregory Thomas *retired commissioner, retired justice*
Evatt, Parker *former state commissioner, former state legislator*
Ewing, Raymond Charles *retired ambassador*
Fisher, Allan Michael *government official, educator*
Ford, Ford Barney *retired government official*
Franke, Wayne Thomas *retired government affairs director, consultant*
Fraser, Donald MacKay *former mayor, former congressman, educator*
Fréchette, Louise *Canadian diplomat*
Frederick-Mairs, T(hyra) Julie *administrative health services official*
Gallucci, Robert Louis *diplomat, federal government official*
†Gorbell, Michael Randall *federal agency and business management executive*
Graeve, Peter John *county official*
Greenwood, Janet Kingham *sanitarian, county official*
Gregoire, Christine O. *state attorney general*
Grossman, Marc *diplomat*
Growe, Joan Anderson *former state official*
Gumppert, Karella Ann *federal government official*
Hall, Keith R. *federal official*
Hanmer, Stephen Read, Jr. *retired government executive*
Haydock, Michael Damean *building and code consultant, writer*
Hess, Jeanette Ruth *county official*
Hester, Nancy Elizabeth *county government official*
Hett, Joan Margaret *civic administrator*
Hilsman, Roger *government educator*
Hockeimer, Henry Eric *business executive*
Holiday, Edith Elizabeth *former presidential adviser, cabinet secretary*
Howard, Robert Elliott *former federal official, consultant, educator*
Huenemann, Rodney Karl *state administrator, executive*
Isom, Harriet Winsar *ambassador*
Jarvis, William Esmond *retired Canadian government official*
Johnson, Karla Ann *county official*
Joseph, Shirley Troyan *retired executive*
Keim, Betty Adele T. *mayor*
Kelley, Wayne Plumbley, Jr. *retired federal official*
Kendig, William Lamar *retired government official, accountant*
Kendrick, Joseph Trotwood *former foreign service officer, writer, consultant*
Kernan, Joseph E. *state official*
Kissinger, Henry Alfred *former secretary of state, international consulting company executive*
†Kniesler, Frederick Cornelius *retired municipal official*
†Kohl, Linda Weir *city official*
Korn, Peter A. *city manager*
Kulstad, Guy Charles *public works official*
†Lackey, Ken *goverment administrator*
Lalley, Frank Edward *federal government official*
Layton, John C. *goverment official, management consultant*
Ledogar, Stephen J. *diplomat, retired*
Lee, Chester Maurice *government official*
Lee, James Matthew *Canadian politician*
Lenahan, Walter Clair *retired foreign service officer*
Levitsky, Melvyn *ambassador*
Levy, Leah Garrigan *federal official*
Lindsay, John Vliet *former mayor, former congressman, author, lawyer*
Loiello, John Peter *diplomat*
Lorenzo Franco, José Ramón *Mexican government official*
MacLean, John Angus *former premier of Prince Edward Island*
Maestrone, Frank Eusebio *diplomat*
†Mameli, Peter Angelo *city official, public management educator*
Maradona, Remigio Martin *international delegate, poet*
Martin, James Kay *government official*
Martz, Judy Helen *state official*
Marvin, William Glenn, Jr. *former foreign service officer*
Mathews, Mary Kathryn *retired government official*
Mattingly, Mack Francis *former ambassador, former senator, entrepreneur*
Mazankowski, Donald Frank *Canadian government official*
McBee, Robert Levi *retired federal government official, writer, consultant*
†McBryde, Daphne Michelle *government official*
McClinton, James Leroy *city administrator*
McLaughlin, Audrey *Canadian government official*
McLean, Walter Franklin *international consultant, pastor, legislator*
Mendonsa, Arthur Adonel *retired city official*
Miller, Kenneth Roye, Jr. *state government administrator*
Mills, Kevin Lee *government executive*
Mohler, Brian Jeffery *diplomat*
Mondale, Walter Frederick *former Vice President of United States, diplomat, lawyer*
Moore, Powell Allen *government official*
Morris, Robert G(emmill) *retired foreign service officer*
Morris, Stanley E. *retired federal official*
Nelson, Cynthia J. *city official*
Nelson, Norman Daniel *government official*
†New, Thomas L. *government executive*
Nielsen, Glade Benjamin *former mayor, former state senator*
Ogg, George Wesley *retired foreign service officer*
†Ogren, Thomas L. *township government administrator*
Ortiz, Francis Vincent, Jr. *retired ambassador*
†Peña, Federico Fabian *retired federal official*
Petrequin, Harry Joseph, Jr. *foreign service officer*
Pierce, Samuel Riley, Jr. *government official, lawyer*
†Postma, Martin J. *economic development administrator*
Pridmore, Roy Davis *government official*
Pritts, Kim Derek *state conservation officer, writer*
Rattley, Jessie Menifield *former mayor, educator*
Raynolds, Harold, Jr. *retired state education commissioner*
Reich, Robert Bernard *former federal official, political economics educator*
Reinhardt, John Edward *former international affairs specialist*
Rickert, Jonathan Bradley *retired foreign service officer*
†Ridgway, James Mastin *government official*
Ridgway, Rozanne LeJeanne *former diplomat, executive*
Ritter, Russell Joseph *mayor, college official*
Rockefeller, Winthrop P. *state official*
†Rosenstock, Robert *diplomat, lawyer*
Rosenthal, James D. *retired federal official, former ambassador, government and foundation executive*
Rossello, Pedro *governor of Puerto Rico*
Rostker, Bernard *federal official*
Rothing, Frank John *government official*
Rudin, Anne Noto *former mayor, nurse*
Rundio, Joan Peters (Jo Rundio) *public administrator*
Ryan, George H. *governor, pharmacist*
Sabatini, Nelson John *government official*
Salmaggi, Guido Godfrey *former diplomat, opera impresario*
Scanlan, John Douglas *foreign service officer, former ambassador*
Schoettler, Gail Sinton *former state official*
Schwartz, Carol Levitt *government official*
Scott, Clarence, III *city official*
Sherrer, Gary *state lieutenant governor*
Simms, John William *retired foreign service officer, consultant*
Smith, Claudette Helms *municipal official*
Smith, Jean Kennedy *former ambassador*
Smith, Robert Powell *former ambassador, former foundation executive*
Snelling, Barbara W. *state official*
Snider, L. Britt *government executive*
Sotirhos, Michael *ambassador*
Soule, Sallie Thompson *retired state official*
Speth, James Gustave *United Nations executive, lawyer*
Spiegelman, James Michael *international affairs expert*

Stevens, Kenneth Allen retired defense department worker
Stowell, Maureen Frances county official
Sundquist, Maria Alexandra diplomat
Swoap, David Bruce government affairs consultant
Tarkowski, Larry Michael municipal official
Taylor, Barbara Jo Anne Harris government official, civic and political worker
Tienken, Arthur T. retired foreign service officer
Tomlinson, Keith state claims examiner
Vanderwest, Donald income tax administrator
Vincent, Gary Lee federal employee, musician
Watkins, James David government official, naval officer
Whitehouse, Sheldon attorney general, lawyer
Whitney, Jane foreign service officer
Wolf, Dale Edward state official
Wright, Sir (John) Oliver retired diplomat
Zischke, Douglas Arthur foreign service officer

GOVERNMENT: LEGISLATIVE ADMINISTRATION

UNITED STATES

ALABAMA

Birmingham
Allen, Maryon Pittman former senator, journalist, lecturer, interior and clothing designer

Guntersville
Hefner, W. G. (Bill Hefner) former congressman

Jacksonville
Browder, John Glen former congressman, educator

Jasper
Bevill, Tom retired congressman, lawyer

Mobile
Callahan, Sonny (H.L. Callahan) congressman
Edwards, Jack former congressman, lawyer

Montgomery
Dixon, Larry Dean state legislator
Langford, Charles Douglas state legislator, lawyer
†Lee, Charles McDowell legislative staff member

Tuscumbia
Heflin, Howell Thomas former senator, lawyer, former state supreme court chief justice

ALASKA

Anchorage
Rieger, Steven Arthur state legislator, business consultant

Eagle River
Cotten, Samuel Richard former state legislator, fisherman

Juneau
†King, Robert Wilson gubernatorial staff member
Kohring, Victor H. state legislator, construction executive

North Pole
James, Jeannette Adeline state legislator, accountant

ARIZONA

Phoenix
Burchfield, Don R. counselor, youth services administrator
Nelson, John councilman, engineering executive
Siebert, Dave councilman
Williams, A. Cody councilman
†Wold, Kimberly G. legislative staff member

Scottsdale
Rudd, Eldon retired congressman, political consultant

Tucson
Bartlett, David Carson state legislator

Waddell
Turner, Warren Austin state legislator

ARKANSAS

Fayetteville
Malone, David Roy state senator, university administrator

Fort Smith
Miles, Travis Anthony state senator
Pollan, Carolyn Joan state legislator, job research administrator

Greenwood
Walters, Bill state senator, lawyer

Little Rock
Sherman, William Farrar lawyer, state legislator

Searcy
Beebe, Mike state senator, lawyer

Sherwood
Wood, Marion Douglas state legislator, lawyer

CALIFORNIA

Alamo
Baker, William P. (Bill Baker) former congressman

Campbell
†Beyer, Casey K. legislative staff member

Garden Grove
Dornan, Robert Kenneth former congressman

Glendale
Moorhead, Carlos J. former congressman

Inglewood
Dymally, Mervyn Malcolm retired congressman, international business executive

Los Altos
Cranston, Alan former senator
Thurber, Emily Forrest political consultant

Los Angeles
Bernson, Hal city councilman
Chick, Laura councilwoman
Goldberg, Jackie councilwoman
Holden, Nate city councilman
Svorinich, Rudy, Jr. councilman
Wachs, Joel city councilman
Walters, Rita councilwoman

Newport Beach
Cox, (Charles) Christopher congressman

Sacramento
Alarcon, Richard state senator, former councilman
Alpert, Dede Whittleton (Dede Alpert) state legislator
Hammond, Lauren Rochelle senate consultant
Holmes, Robert Eugene state legislative consultant, journalist
Knight, William J. (Pete Knight) state senator, retired air force officer
Leslie, (Robert) Tim state legislator
Russell, Newton Requa retired state senator
Schmidt, Gregory Palmer secretary California senator, historian

San Diego
McCarty, Judy city councilwoman
Stallings, Valerie Aileen councilwoman
†Stein, Greg legislative staff member
Stevens, George L. city councilman
Warden, Barbara city councilwoman
Wear, Byron councilman

San Francisco
Ammiano, Tom county and municipal official

San Jose
Fiscalini, Frank city councilman

West Covina
Torres, Esteban Edward former congressman, business executive

COLORADO

Colorado Springs
Sinclair, William Donald church official, fundraising consultant, political activist

Denver
Bishop, Tilman Malcolm state senator, retired college administrator
†Dicks, Patricia K. state senate employee
Kurtz, Karl Theodore government executive
Meiklejohn, Alvin J., Jr. state senator, lawyer, accountant
†Palmer, Robert legislative administrator
Wham, Dorothy Stonecipher state legislator

Golden
Hopper, Sally state legislator

Greeley
Brown, Hank former senator, university administrator

CONNECTICUT

Hamden
Villano, Peter F. state legislator

Hartford
Caruso, Christopher L. state legislator
Cook, Cathy Welles state senator
Currey, Melody Alena state legislator
Daily, Eileen M. state legislator
DePino, Chris Anthoney state legislator
Dillon, Patricia Anne state legislator
Eberle, Mary U. state legislator
Fahrbach, Ruth C. state legislator
Flaherty, Patrick John state legislator, economist
Gerratana, Theresa B. state legislator
Gunther, George Lackman state senator, natureopathic physician, retired
Harp, Toni N. state legislator
Hess, Marilyn Ann state legislator
Kirkley-Bey, Marie Lopez state legislator
McGrattan, Mary K. state legislator
Orefice, Gary James state legislator
Peters, Melodie state legislator
Sawyer, Pamela Z. state legislator
Scalettar, Ellen state legislator
Simmons, Robert Ruhl state legislator, educator
Upson, Thomas Fisher state legislator, lawyer

Mansfield Center
Merrill, Denise state legislator

New Britain
Bozek, Thomas state legislator

New Haven
Dyson, William R. state legislator, educator

Riverside
Powers, Claudia McKenna state legislator

Tolland
†Wyman, Nancy S. state legislator

Vernon Rockville
Herbst, Marie Antoinette former state senator

DELAWARE

Bear
Davis, Richard Frank state legislator

Dover
Bair, Myrna Lynn state senator
Cook, Nancy W. state legislator
Henry, Margaret Rose state legislator
Maroney, Jane P. state legislator
Vaughn, James T. former state police officer, state senator

Harrington
Quillen, George R. state legislator

New Castle
Spence, Terry R. state legislator

Newark
Amick, Steven Hammond senator, lawyer
Neal, James Preston state senator, project engineer

Wilmington
†Ahn, James Jongho legislative aide
Blevins, Patricia M. state legislator
George, Orlando John, Jr. state representative, college administrator

DISTRICT OF COLUMBIA

Washington
Abercrombie, Neil congressman
Abraham, Spencer senator
Ackerman, Gary Leonard congressman
Aderholt, Robert B. congressman
Akaka, Daniel Kahikina senator
†Alexander, Brad L. legislative staff member
Allard, A. Wayne senator, veterinarian
Allen, Thomas H. congressman, lawyer
Andrews, Robert E. congressman
Archer, William Reynolds, Jr. (Bill Reynolds) congressman
Ashcroft, John David senator
Bachus, Spencer T., III congressman, lawyer
†Backlin, Jim legislative staff member
†Baird, Brian N. congressman
Baker, Richard Hugh congressman
Baldacci, John Elias congressman
Ballenger, Thomas Cass congressman
Barcia, James A. congressman
Barr, Robert Laurence, Jr. congressman, lawyer
Barrett, Thomas M. congressman
Barrett, William E. congressman
Bartlett, Roscoe G. congressman
Bass, Charles F. congressman
Bateman, Herbert Harvell congressman
Baucus, Max S. senator
Bayh, Evan senator, former governor
Becerra, Xavier congressman, lawyer
Bennett, Robert F. senator
Bentsen, Kenneth E., Jr. congressman
Bereuter, Douglas Kent congressman
†Berger, Jonathan M. legislative staff member
Berkley, Shelley congresswoman
Berman, Howard Lawrence congressman
Berry, Marion congressman
Biden, Joseph Robinette, Jr. senator
Biggert, Judith Borg congresswoman, lawyer
Bilbray, Brian P. congressman
Bilirakis, Michael congressman, lawyer, business executive
Bingaman, Jeff senator
Bishop, Sanford Dixon, Jr. congressman
Blagojevich, Rod R. congressman
Blumenauer, Earl congressman
Blunt, Roy D. congressman
†Blyth, Jonathan J. legislative staff member
Boehlert, Sherwood Louis congressman
Boehner, John A. congressman
†Bogdanovich, Michele L. legislative staff member
Bond, Christopher Samuel (Kit Bond) senator, lawyer
†Bonham, (Andrew) Kent legislative staff member
Bonilla, Henry congressman, broadcast executive
Bonior, David Edward congressman
Bono, Mary congresswoman
Borski, Robert Anthony congressman
Boswell, Leonard L. congressman
Boucher, Frederick C. congressman, lawyer
Boxer, Barbara senator
†Boyagian, Levon legislative administrator
Brady, Kevin congressman
†Brady, Robert A. congressman
Breaux, John B. senator, former congressman
Brown, Corrine congresswoman
Brown, Sherrod congressman, former state official
Brownback, Sam senator
Bryan, Richard H. senator
Bryant, Edward congressman
Bumpers, Dale L. former senator, former governor
Burns, Conrad Ray senator
†Burns, William Stuart legislative administrator
Burr, Richard M. congressman
Burton, Dan L. congressman
Buyer, Steve Earle congressman, lawyer
Byrd, Robert Carlyle senator
Calvert, Ken congressman
Camp, Dave congressman
Campbell, Ben Nighthorse senator
†Campbell, Douglas J. legislative staff member
Campbell, Thomas J. congressman
Canady, Charles Terrence congressman, lawyer
Cannon, Christopher B. congressman
Capps, Lois Ragnhild Grimsrud congresswoman, school nurse
†Capuano, Michael Everett congressman
Cardin, Benjamin Louis congressman
Carlisle, Margo Duer Black government official
Carr, Bob former congressman, lawyer
†Carr, Bobby G. legislative staff member
Carson, Julia M. congresswoman
Castle, Michael N. congressman, former governor, lawyer
Chabot, Steven J. congressman
Chafee, John Hubbard senator
Chambliss, Saxby congressman
Chapman, James L. (Jim Chapman) former congressman
Chenoweth, Helen P. congresswoman
Christensen, Donna Marie congresswoman
Clark, Dick former senator, ambassador, foreign affairs specialist
Clay, William Lacy congressman
Clayton, Eva M. congresswoman, former county commissioner
Cleland, Max senator
Clement, Bob congressman
Clyburn, James E. congressman
Coats, Daniel Ray former senator
Cobb, Jane Overton legislative staff member
Coburn, Tom A. congressman
Coelho, Tony former congressman
Coleman, E. Thomas congressman
Collins, Michael A. (Mac Collins) congressman
Collins, Susan M. senator
Combest, Larry Ed congressman
Condit, Gary Adrian congressman
Conrad, Kent senator
Conyers, John, Jr. congressman
Cook, Merrill A. congressman, explosives industry executive
†Cooper, Barbara federal agency administrator
Costello, Jerry F., Jr. congressman, former county official
Coverdell, Paul Douglas senator
Coyne, William Joseph congressman
Craig, Larry Edwin senator
Cramer, Robert E., Jr. (Bud Cramer) congressman
Crane, Philip Miller congressman
Crapo, Michael Dean senator, former congressman, lawyer
†Crowley, Joseph congressman
Cubin, Barbara Lynn congresswoman, former state legislator
Cummings, Elijah E. congressman
Cunningham, Randy congressman
†Dammann, Julie Ann legislative staff member
Danner, Patsy Ann (Mrs. C. M. Meyer) congresswoman
Daschle, Thomas Andrew senator
Davis, Jim congressman, lawyer
Davis, Thomas M., III congressman
†Day, Kristen Valade legislative staff member
Deal, Nathan J. congressman, lawyer
DeFazio, Peter A. congressman
Delahunt, William D. congressman
DeLauro, Rosa L. congresswoman
DeLay, Thomas D. (Tom DeLay) congressman
Dellums, Ronald V. former congressman, health facility administrator
Deutsch, Peter R. congressman, lawyer
DeWine, R. Michael senator, lawyer
Diaz-Balart, Lincoln congressman
Dickey, Jay W., Jr. congressman, lawyer
Dicks, Norman De Valois congressman
†Di Martino, David legislative staff member
Dingell, John David congressman
Dixon, Julian Carey congressman
Dodd, Christopher J. senator
Doggett, Lloyd congressman, former state supreme court justice
Domenici, Pete V. (Vichi Domenici) senator
Dooley, Calvin Millard congressman
Doolittle, John Taylor congressman
Dorgan, Byron Leslie senator
Doyle, Michael F. congressman
Dreier, David Timothy congressman
Duncan, John J., Jr. congressman
Dunn, Jennifer Blackburn congresswoman
Durbin, Richard Joseph senator
†Edgell, Bradley Gaskins legislative staff member
Edwards, Chet congressman
†Edwards, John R. senator, lawyer
Ehrlich, Robert L., Jr. congressman
Emerson, Jo Ann congresswoman
Engel, Eliot L. congressman
English, Philip Sheridan congressman
Enzi, Michael Bradley senator, accountant
Eshoo, Anna Georges congresswoman
Etheridge, Bob congressman
Evans, Lane congressman
Everett, Terry congressman
Ewing, Thomas William congressman, lawyer
Faleomavaega, Eni Fa'auaa Hunkin congressman
†Faletti, Tom legislative staff member
Farr, Sam congressman
Fattah, Chaka congressman, former state legislator
Feingold, Russell Dana United States senator, lawyer
Feinstein, Dianne senator
Filner, Bob congressman
†Fletcher, (Robert) Ernie congressman
Foley, Mark Adam congressman
Forbes, Michael P. congressman
Ford, Harold Eugene congressman
Fossella, Vito John congressman
†Foust, Robert Schmertz legislative director
Fowler, Tillie Kidd congresswoman
Fox, Jon D. congressman
Frank, Barney congressman
Frelinghuysen, Rodney P. congressman
Frist, William H. senator, surgeon
Frost, Jonas Martin, III congressman
Funderburk, David Britton consultant, former congressman and ambassador
Gallegly, Elton William congressman
Ganske, J. Greg congressman, plastic surgeon
†Gartzke, Dana G. legislative administrator
Gejdenson, Sam congressman
Gekas, George William congressman
Gephardt, Richard Andrew congressman
Gest, Kathryn Waters public affairs professional
Gibbons, James Arthur congressman
Gilchrest, Wayne Thomas congressman, former high school educator
†Gill, Shayne H. legislative staff member
Gillmor, Paul E. congressman, lawyer
Gilman, Benjamin Arthur congressman
†Glass, Wayne legislative staff member
†Glenn, Harry J. legislative administrator
†Gonzalez, Charles A. congressman
Goode, Virgil H., Jr. congressman
Goodlatte, Robert William (Bob Goodlatte) congressman, lawyer
Goodling, William F. congressman
Gordon, Barton Jennings (Bart Gordon) congressman, lawyer
Gorton, Slade senator

Graham, D. Robert (Bob Graham) senator, former governor
Graham, Lindsey O. congressman
Gramm, William Philip (Phil Gramm) senator, economist
Grams, Rodney D. senator, former congressman
Grassley, Charles Ernest senator
†Green, Mark Andrew congressman, lawyer
Greenwood, James Charles congressman
Gregg, Judd senator, former governor
†Griffin, Keith E. legislative administrator
Gutierrez, Luis V. congressman, elementary education educator
Gutknecht, Gilbert William, Jr. congressman, former state legislator, auctioneer
Hagel, Charles senator
Hall, Ralph Moody congressman
Hall, Tony P. congressman
†Hancock, John Alva legislative staff member
Hansen, James Vear congressman
Harkin, Thomas Richard senator
Harman, Jane congresswoman, lawyer
Hastert, (J.) Dennis congressman
Hastings, Alcee Lamar congressman, former federal judge
Hastings, Doc congressman
Hattan, Susan K. legislative staff member
†Hayes, Richard L. government executive
†Hayes, Robert (Robin Hayes) congressman
Hayworth, John David, Jr. congressman, sportscaster, commentator, broadcaster
Hefley, Joel M. congressman
Helms, Jesse senator
Herger, Wally W. congressman
†Hill, Baron P. congressman
Hill, Rick Allan congressman
Hilleary, Van congressman
Hilliard, Earl Frederick congressman, lawyer
Hinchey, Maurice D., Jr. congressman
Hinojosa, Ruben congressman
Hobson, David Lee congressman, lawyer
†Hoeffel, Joseph M. congressman, lawyer
Hoekstra, Peter congressman, manufacturing executive
†Hoffman, Robert Phillip legislative staff member
Holden, Tim congressman, protective official
Hollings, Ernest Frederick senator
†Holt, Rush Dew congressman, physics educator, researcher, consultant
Hooley, Darlene congresswoman, county commissioner
Horn, Stephen congressman, political science educator
Horton, Frank former congressman, lawyer
Hostettler, John N. congressman
Houghton, Amory, Jr. congressman
†Howard, Henry state legislator
Hoyer, Steny Hamilton congressman
Hulshof, Kenny congressman
Hutchinson, Asa congressman
Hutchinson, Tim senator
Hyde, Henry John congressman
Inhofe, James M. senator
Inouye, Daniel Ken senator
†Inslee, Jay R. congressman, lawyer
†Isakson, Johnny congressman
†Isom, Charles L. legislative staff member
Istook, Ernest James, Jr. (Jim Istook) congressman, lawyer
Jackson, Jesse, Jr. congressman
Jackson Lee, Sheila congresswoman
Jarvis, Charlene Drew council member
Jefferson, William L. (Jeff Jefferson) congressman
Jeffords, James Merrill senator
Jenkins, William L. (Bill Jenkins) congressman
John, Chris congressman
Johnson, Eddie Bernice congresswoman
†Johnson, Eric legislative administrator
Johnson, Jay Withington former congressman
Johnson, Nancy Lee congresswoman
Johnson, Samuel (Sam Johnson) congressman
Johnson, Timothy Peter senator
Johnston, John Bennett, Jr. former senator
†Jones, Stephanie Tubbs congresswoman, lawyer
Jones, Walter Beaman, Jr. congressman
†Jordan, Samantha legislative staff member
Kanjorski, Paul Edmund congressman, lawyer
Kaptur, Marcia Carolyn congresswoman
Kasich, John R. congressman
†Kassiday, Joel David legislative staff member
Kasten, Robert W., Jr. former senator
†Keenum, Mark E. legislative chief of staff
Kelly, Sue W. congresswoman
Kennedy, Edward Moore senator
Kennedy, Patrick J. congressman
Kennelly, Barbara B. former congresswoman, federal agency administrator
Kerrey, Bob (J. Robert Kerrey) senator
Kerry, John Forbes senator
Kildee, Dale Edward congressman
Kilpatrick, Carolyn Cheeks congresswoman
Kind, Ron congressman
King, Peter Thomas congressman, lawyer
Kingston, Jack congressman
Kleczka, Gerald D. congressman
†Klein, Bill legislative staff member
Klink, Ron congressman, reporter, newscaster
Knollenberg, Joseph (Joe Knollenberg) congressman
Kolbe, James Thomas congressman
Kucinich, Dennis J. congressman
Kundanis, George congressional aide
Kuykendall, Steven T. congressman
Kyl, Jon L. senator
La Falce, John Joseph congressman, lawyer
LaHood, Ray congressman
Lampson, Nick congressman
Landrieu, Mary L. senator
†Lankler, Gregory M. legislative administrator
Lantos, Thomas Peter congressman
Largent, Steve congressman, former professional football player
†Larson, John Barry congressman, insurance executive
Latham, Tom congressman
LaTourette, Steven C. congressman
Laughlin, Gregory H. (Greg Laughlin) former congressman
Lautenberg, Frank R. senator
Lazio, Rick A. congressman, lawyer
Leach, James Albert Smith congressman
Leahy, Patrick Joseph senator
Lee, Barbara congresswoman
Lent, Norman Frederick, Jr. former congressman
Levin, Carl senator
Levin, Sander M. congressman
Lewis, Charles Jeremy congressman
Lewis, John R. congressman
Lewis, Ron congressman
Lieberman, Joseph I. senator
Lincoln, Blanche Lambert senator
Linder, John E. congressman, dentist
Lipinski, William Oliver congressman
Livingston, Robert Linlithgow, Jr. (Bob Livingston, Jr.) former congressman
LoBiondo, Frank A. congressman
Lofgren, Zoe congresswoman
†Lofton, James H. legislative staff
Lott, Trent senator
Lowey, Nita M. congresswoman
Lucas, Frank D. congressman
†Lucas, Ken congressman
Lugar, Richard Green senator
Luther, William P. congressman
Mack, Connie, III (Cornelius Mack) senator
†Mahr, Thomas D. legislative staff member
Maloney, Carolyn Bosher congresswoman
Manzullo, Donald A congressman, lawyer
Markey, Edward John congressman
†Martinage, Ashley E. legislative staff member
Martinez, Matthew Gilbert congressman
Mascara, Frank congressman
Matsui, Robert Takeo congressman
McCain, John Sidney, III senator
McCarthy, Karen P. congresswoman, former state representative
Mc Collum, Ira William, Jr. (Bill Mc Collum) congressman
McConnell, Addison Mitchell, Jr. (Mitch McConnell, Jr.) senator, lawyer
McCrery, James (Jim McCrery) congressman
McDermott, James A. congressman, psychiatrist
†McDonald, Patricia Ann legislative administrator
†McGarey, Patrick O. legislative staff member
†McGill, Michael S. legislative staff member
McGovern, James P. congressman
McHugh, John Michael congressman, former state senator
McInnis, Scott Steve congressman, lawyer
McIntosh, David M. congressman
McIntyre, Mike congressman
McKeon, Howard P. (Buck McKeon) congressman, former mayor
McKinney, Cynthia Ann congresswoman
McNulty, Michael Robert congressman
Meehan, Martin Thomas congressman, lawyer
Meek, Carrie P. congresswoman
Meeks, Gregory Weldon congressman
†Mellow, Jane E. legislative administrator
Menendez, Robert congressman, lawyer
Metcalf, Jack congressman, retired state senator
Metz, Craig Huseman legislative administrator
Millender-McDonald, Juanita congresswoman, former school system administrator
Miller, Dan congressman
†Miller, Gary G. congressman
Miller, George congressman
Minge, David congressman, lawyer, law educator
Mink, Patsy Takemoto congresswoman
Moakley, John Joseph congressman
Mollohan, Alan B. congressman, lawyer
Monagan, John Stephen writer, lecturer, retired congressman and lawyer
†Moore, Dennis congressman
Moran, James Patrick, Jr. congressman, stockbroker
Moran, Jerry congressman
Morella, Constance Albanese congresswoman
Morrison, Bruce Andrew government executive, former congressman
Moynihan, Daniel Patrick senator, educator
Murkowski, Frank Hughes senator
†Murphy, Patrick M. legislative staff member
Murray, Patty senator
Murtha, John Patrick congressman
Myrick, Sue congresswoman, former mayor
Nadler, Jerrold Lewis congressman, lawyer
†Napolitano, Grace F. congresswoman
†Naylor, Mary A. legislative staff member
Neal, Richard Edmund congressman, former mayor
Nelson, Gaylord Anton former senator, association executive
Nethercutt, George Rector, Jr. congressman, lawyer
Ney, Robert W. congressman
†Nichols, Rob legislative staff member
Nickles, Donald (Don Nickles) senator
Northup, Anne Meagher congresswoman
Norton, Eleanor Holmes congresswoman, lawyer, educator
Norwood, Charles W., Jr. congressman
†Novak, Jana legislative staff member
Nussle, James Allen congressman
Oberstar, James L. congressman
Obey, David Ross congressman
Olver, John Walter congressman
Ortiz, Solomon P. congressman
Ose, Douglas congressman
Owens, Major Robert Odell congressman
Oxley, Michael Garver congressman
Packard, Ronald C. congressman
Pallone, Frank, Jr. congressman
Pascrell, William J., Jr. congressman
Pastor, Edward congressman
Paxon, L. William former congressman
Payne, Donald M. congressman
Pease, Edward congressman
Pelosi, Nancy congresswoman
Peterson, Collin C. congressman
Peterson, John E. congressman
Petri, Thomas Evert congressman
†Pfeiffer, Tom legislative staff member
†Phelps, David D. congressman
Pickering, Charles W., Jr. congressman
Pickett, Owen B. congressman
Pitts, Joseph R. congressman
Pombo, Richard congressman, rancher, farmer
Pomeroy, Earl R. congressman, former state insurance commissioner
Porter, John Edward congressman
Portman, Rob congressman
Pressler, Larry senator
†Pressler, Laurel A. legislative staff member
Quinn, Jack congressman, English language educator, sports coach
Radanovich, George P. congressman
Rahall, Nick Joe, II (Nick Rahall) congressman
Ramstad, Jim congressman, lawyer
Rangel, Charles Bernard congressman
Reed, John Francis (Jack Reed) senator
Regula, Ralph congressman, lawyer
†Reynolds, Thomas M. congressman
†Ribbentrop, Richard Lyn legislative staff member
Riley, Robert congressman, entrepreneur, cattleman
Rivers, Lynn N. congresswoman
Robb, Charles Spittal senator, lawyer
Roberge, M. Sheila state legislator
Roberts, Charles Patrick (Pat Roberts) senator
Rockefeller, John Davison, IV (Jay Rockefeller) senator, former governor
Rodriguez, Ciro D. congressman
Roemer, Timothy J. congressman
Rogan, James E. congressman
Rogers, Harold Dallas (Hal Rogers) congressman
Rohrabacher, Dana congressman
Romero-Barceló, Carlos Antonio congressman, former governor of Puerto Rico
Ros-Lehtinen, Ileana congresswoman
Roth, William V., Jr. senator
Rothman, Steven R. congressman
Roukema, Margaret Scafati congresswoman
Roybal-Allard, Lucille congresswoman
Royce, Edward R. (Ed Royce) congressman
†Rucker, Kelly legislative staff member
†Rudesill, Dakota Sundance legislative assistance
Rudman, Warren Bruce former senator, lawyer, think tank executive
Rush, Bobby L. congressman
†Ryan, Paul congressman
Ryun, Jim congressman
Sabo, Martin Olav congressman
Salmon, Matt congressman
Sanchez, Loretta congresswoman
Sanders, Bernard (Bernie Sanders) congressman
Sandlin, Max Allen, Jr. congressman
Sanford, Marshall (Mark Sanford) congressman
Santorum, Rick senator
Sarbanes, Paul Spyros senator
Sawyer, Thomas C. congressman
Saxton, H. James congressman
Scarborough, Joe congressman
Schaefer, Dan L. former congressman
Schaffer, Robert (Bob Schaffer) congressman
†Schakowsky, Janice congresswoman
†Schmidt, Derek Larkin legislative aide
Schroeder, Patricia Scott (Mrs. James White Schroeder) trade association administrator, former congresswoman
Schumer, Charles Ellis senator
Scott, Robert Cortez congressman, lawyer
Sensenbrenner, Frank James, Jr. congressman, lawyer
Serrano, Jose E. congressman
Sessions, Jefferson Beauregard, III senator
†Sewer, Loán C. legislative staff member
Shadegg, John B. congressman
†Shaffron, J. Janet legislative administrator
Shaw, E. Clay, Jr. (Clay Shaw) congressman
Shays, Christopher congressman
Shelby, Richard Craig senator, former congressman
Sherman, Bradley James congressman
†Sherwood, Donald Lewis congressman
Shimkus, John Mondy congressman
†Shows, Ronnie congressman
Shuster, Bud congressman
†Simpson, Michael K. congressman
Sisisky, Norman congressman, soft drink bottler
Skeen, Joseph Richard congressman
Skelton, Isaac Newton, IV (Ike Skelton) congressman
Slaughter, Louise McIntosh congresswoman
Smith, Adam congressman
Smith, Christopher Henry congressman
Smith, D. Adam congressman
Smith, Frank councilman
†Smith, Gene legislative staff member
Smith, Gordon Harold senator
Smith, Lamar Seeligson congressman
Smith, Nick congressman, farmer
Smith, Robert Clinton senator
Snowe, Olympia J. senator
Snyder, Vic congressman, physician
Solomon, Gerald Brooks Hunt former congressman
Souder, Mark Edward congressman
Specter, Arlen senator
Spence, Floyd Davidson congressman
Spratt, John McKee, Jr. congressman, lawyer
Stabenow, Deborah Ann congresswoman
Stark, Fortney Hillman (Pete Stark) congressman
Stearns, Clifford Bundy congressman, business executive
Stenholm, Charles W. congressman
Stevens, Theodore Fulton senator
Stokes, Louis former congressman, lawyer
Strickland, Ted congressman, clergyman, psychology educator, psychologist
Stump, Bob congressman
Stupak, Bart T. congressman, lawyer
†Sweeney, John E. congressman
†Szemraj, Roger R. legislative staff member
Talent, James M. congressman, lawyer
Tancredo, Thomas G. congressman
Tanner, John S. congressman, lawyer
Tauzin, W. J. Billy, II (Wilbert J. Tauzin) congressman
Taylor, Charles H. congressman
Taylor, Gene congressman
†Terry, Lee R. congressman, lawyer
†Thom, Gregory F. legislatvie staff member
Thomas, Craig senator
Thomas, William Marshall congressman
Thompson, Bennie G. congressman
Thompson, C. Michael congressman
Thompson, Fred senator
Thompson, Jill Lynette Long former congresswoman
Thornberry, Mac congressman
Thurman, Karen L. congresswoman
Thurmond, Strom senator
Tiahrt, W. Todd congressman, former state senator
Tierney, John F. congressman, lawyer
†Toomey, Patrick J. congressman
Torricelli, Robert G. senator
Towns, Edolphus congressman
Traficant, James A., Jr. congressman
†Turner, James congressman
Turner, Jim congressman
†Udall, Mark congressman
Udall, Thomas congressman
Upton, Frederick Stephen congressman
†Van Heuvelen, Robert legislative staff member
Vazirani-Fales, Heea legislative staff member, lawyer
Velazquez, Nydia M. congresswoman
Vento, Bruce Frank congressman
†Vermilye, Andrew R. legislative staff
Visclosky, Peter John congressman, lawyer
†Vitter, David congressman
Voinovich, George V. senator, former governor
†Walden, Greg congressman
†Waldman, Thomas L. legislative staff member
Walker, Robert Smith former congressman
Walsh, James Thomas congressman
Wamp, Zach congressman
Warner, John William senator
Waters, Maxine congresswoman
Watkins, Wesley Wade congressman
Watt, Melvin L. congressman, lawyer
Watts, J. C., Jr. congressman
Waxman, Henry Arnold congressman
Weiss, Gail Ellen legislative staff director
Weldon, David Joseph, Jr. congressman, physician
Weldon, W(ayne) Curtis congressman
Weller, Gerald C. congressman
Wellstone, Paul senator
Wexler, Robert congressman
Weygand, Bob A. congressman
†White, Stanley legislative administrator
Whitfield, Edward (Wayne Whitfield) congressman
Wicker, Roger F. congressman
†Williams, Tony J. legislative staff member
Wilson, Charles (Charlie Wilson) former congressman
Wilson, Heather Ann congresswoman
†Wilson, Kevin M. legislative staff member
†Wingate, Heather legislative staff member
Wise, Robert Ellsworth, Jr. (Bob Ellsworth) congressman
Wofford, Harris Llewellyn former senator, national service executive
Wolf, Frank R. congressman, lawyer
Woolsey, Lynn congresswoman
Wu, David congressman
Wyden, Ron senator
Wynn, Albert Russell congressman
†Yost, Paul A., III legislative staff
Young, C. W. (Bill Young) congressman
Young, Donald E. congressman

FLORIDA

Bradenton
Woodson-Howard, Marlene Erdley former state legislator

Jacksonville
Bennett, Charles Edward former congressman, educator
Hipps, Alberta city councilwoman
Holzendorf, King, Jr. city councilman
†Siegmund, Susan legislative staff member
Soud, Ginger city councilwoman
Williams, Lance Lamont legislative assistant

Miami
Cosgrove, John Francis lawyer, state legislator

Miami Beach
Gordon, Jack David senator, foundation executive

Pensacola
Hutto, Earl retired congressman

Saint Petersburg
Cretekos, George Nick district assistant

Tallahassee
†Blanton, Faye Wester legislative staff member
†Phelps, John B. legislative official

Tampa
Davis, Helen Gordon former state senator
Glickman, Ronnie Carl state official, lawyer

West Palm Beach
Johnston, Harry A., II former congressman

Winter Park
Mica, John L. congressman

GEORGIA

Americus
Hooks, George Bardin state senator, insurance and real estate company executive

Atlanta
Henson, Michele state legislator
Martin, James Francis state legislator, lawyer
Murphy, Thomas Bailey state legislator
Nunn, Samuel (Sam Nunn) former senator
Purcell, Ann Rushing state legislator, office manager medical business

Augusta
Barnard, Druie Douglas, Jr. former congressman, former bank executive

Jonesboro
King, Glynda Bowman state legislator

Lawrenceville
Wall, Clarence Vinson state legislator

Marietta
†Aiken, V. Fred legislative staff member

Smyrna
Atkins, William Austin, Sr. (Bill Atkins) former state legislator

HAWAII

Hilo
Ushijima, John Takeji state senator, lawyer

Honolulu
Cachola, Romy Munoz state representative
Chun Oakland, Suzanne Nyuk Jun state legislator
Fasi, Frank Francis state senator
Fong, Hiram Leong former senator
Takumi, Roy Mitsuo state representative

Kailua
Young, Jacqueline Eurn Hai state legislator, consultant

Wailuku
Baker, Rosalyn Hester economic development administrator

IDAHO

Boise
Black, Pete *retired state legislator, educator*

ILLINOIS

Aurora
Etheredge, Forest DeRoyce *former state senator, university administrator*

Belleville
Holbrook, Thomas Aldredge *state legislator*

Carbondale
Simon, Paul *former senator, educator, author*

Carterville
Poshard, Glenn W. *former congressman*

Chicago
Allen, Thomas *alderman*
Banks, William J. P. *alderman*
Beavers, William M. *alderman*
Berman, Arthur Leonard *state senator*
Bernardini, Charles *alderman*
Bugielski, Robert Joseph *state legislator*
Burke, Edward M. *alderman*
†Cohen, Ira *legislative staff member*
Colom, Vilma *alderman*
Davis, Danny K. *congressman*
Doherty, Brian Gerard *alderman*
Granato, Jesse D. *alderman*
Hansen, Bernard J. *alderman*
Laurino, Margaret *alderman*
Levar, Patrick *alderman*
Moore, Joseph Arthur *alderman, lawyer*
Munoz, Ricardo *alderman*
Ocasio, Billy *alderman*
Shiller, Helen *alderman, adult education educator*
Smith, Mary Ann *alderman*
Tillman, Dorothy Wright *alderman*
Troutman, Arenda *alderman*
†Whidmayer, Christopher A. *legislative staff member*
Yates, Sidney Richard *former congressman, lawyer*

Deerfield
†Kohn, David Lupo *legislative staff member*

Jacksonville
Findley, Paul *former congressman, author, educator*

Joliet
†Wilson, Reed J. *legislative staff member*

Lake Forest
Frederick, Virginia Fiester *state legislator*

Naperville
Cowlishaw, Mary Lou *state legislator*

Palatine
†Fitzgerald, Peter Gosselin *senator, lawyer*

Springfield
Carroll, Howard William *state senator, lawyer*
Currie, Barbara Flynn *state legislator*
Geo-Karis, Adeline Jay *state senator*
Madigan, Michael Joseph *state legislator*
Moore, Andrea S. *state legislator*
Philip, James (Pate Philip) *state senator*

Urbana
†Greene, Terry J. *legislative staff member*

Westmont
Bellock, Patricia Rigney *state legislator*

Wheaton
Fawell, Beverly Jean *state legislator*

INDIANA

Attica
Harrison, Joseph William *state senator*

Columbus
Garton, Robert Dean *state senator*

Fort Wayne
Goeglein, Gloria J. *state legislator*

Indianapolis
Black, Elwood C. *councilman*
Dowden, William *councilman*
Gilmer, Gordon *councilman*
Golc, Jeff *councilman*
Gray, Monroe, Jr. *councilman*
Jacobs, Andrew, Jr. *former congressman, educator*
Jones, Paul *councilman*
Klinker, Sheila Ann J. *state legislator, middle school educator*
McClamroch, William Tobin *councilman*
O'Dell, Cory *councilman*
Schneider, William *councilman*
Scholer, Sue Wyant *state legislator*
Short, Frank T. *councilman*
Tilford, Jody *councilwoman*
†Tinkle, Carolyn J. *legislative staff member*

IOWA

Des Moines
Deluhery, Patrick John *state senator*
Drake, Richard Francis *state senator*
Grundberg, Betty *state legislator, property manager*
Harper, Patricia M. *state legislator*
Rosenberg, Ralph *former state senator, lawyer, consultant, educator*
Szymoniak, Elaine Eisfelder *state senator*

Sioux City
Andersen, Leonard Christian *former state legislator, real estate investor*

West Des Moines
Churchill, Steven Wayne *former state legislator, marketing professional*

KANSAS

Clay Center
Braden, James Dale *former state legislator*

Coffeyville
Garner, Jim D. *state legislator, lawyer*

Hutchinson
Kerr, David Mills *state legislator*
O'Neal, Michael Ralph *state legislator, lawyer*

Lawrence
Ballard, Barbara W. *state legislator*
Winter, Winton Allen, Jr. *lawyer, state senator*

Olathe
O'Connor, Kay *state legislator*
Snowbarger, Vince *congressman*

Prairie Village
Langworthy, Audrey Hansen *state legislator*

Salina
Horst, Deena Louise *state legislator*

Shawnee Mission
Sader, Carol Hope *former state legislator*

Topeka
†Findley, Troy R. *state legislator, bank officer*
Frahm, Sheila *association executive, former government official, academic administrator*
Mays, M. Douglas *state legislator, financial consultant*
Salisbury, Alicia Laing *state senator*
†Saville, Pat *state senate official*

Wichita
Pottorff, Jo Ann *state legislator*

KENTUCKY

Crestview Hills
Harper, Kenneth Franklin *retired state legislator, real estate broker*

Frankfort
†Ferguson, Barbara *legislative staff member*
Richards, Jody *state legislator, journalism educator, small business owner*

Villa Hills
Celella, Jan Gerding *retired legislative staff member*

LOUISIANA

La Place
Landry, Ronald Jude *lawyer, state senator*

Marksville
Riddle, Charles Addison, III *state legislator, lawyer*

Monroe
Cooksey, John Charles *congressman, ophthalmic surgeon*

New Orleans
Boggs, Corinne Claiborne (Lindy Boggs) *former congresswoman*

MAINE

Augusta
Ahearne, Douglas *state legislator*
Amero, Jane Adams *state legislator*
Barth, Alvin Ludwig, Jr. *state legislator*
Daggett, Beverly Clark *state legislator*
Desmond, Mabel Jeannette *state legislator, educator*
Hatch, Pamela H. *state legislator*
Kilkelly, Marjorie Lee *state legislator, community development official*
Martin, John L. *state legislator*
Paradis, Judy *state legislator*
Saxl, Jane Wilhelm *state legislator*
Stevens, Kathleen *state legislator*
Townsend, Elizabeth *state legislator*

Bangor
Donnelly, James Owen *state legislator, bank executive*

Brunswick
Pfeiffer, Sophia Douglass *state legislator, lawyer*

Cape Eliz
Simonds, Stephen Paige *former state legislator*

Cumberland Center
Butland, Jeffrey H. *former state senator, retail company official*
Taylor, Joseph B. *former state legislator*

Dover Foxcroft
Cross, Ruel Parkman *state legislator*

Hampden
Plowman, Debra D. *state legislator*

Island Falls
Joy, Henry Lee *state legislator*

North Haven
Pingree, Rochelle M. *state legislator*

Portland
†Sullivan, Mark *legislative staff member*

MARYLAND

Annapolis
†Addison, William B.C., Jr. *state senate employee*
Astle, John Chandlee *state legislator*
Davis, Clarence *state legislator*
Dixon, Richard N. *state legislator*
Hixson, Sheila Ellis *state legislator*
Howard, Carolyn J. B. *state legislator*
Kelley, Delores Goodwin *state legislator*
Klima, Martha Scanlan *state legislator*
Love, Mary Ann E. *state legislator*
Madden, Martin Gerard *state legislator*
McCabe, Christopher J. *state legislator*
Menes, Pauline H. *state legislator*
Miller, Thomas V. Mike, Jr. *state legislator*
Roesser, Jean Wolberg *state legislator*
Ruben, Ida Gass *state senator*
Teitelbaum, Leonard H. *state legislator*

Baltimore
Branch, Paula Johnson *city councilwoman*
Cain, John L. *city councilman*
Clinger, William Floyd, Jr. *former congressman*
Curran, Robert *councilman*
D'Adamo, Nicholas C. *city councilman*
Dixon, Sheila *councilwoman*
Hoffman, Barbara A. *state legislator*
Hughes, Brenda Bethea *state legislator*
Malley, Martin *councilman, lawyer*
Marriott, Salima Siler *state legislator, social work educator*
Mfume, Kweisi *former congressman*
Rawlings, Stephanie *city councilwoman*
Spector, Rochelle *city councilwoman*
Stidman, Edith (Janet) Scales *parliamentarian*
Stone, Norman R., Jr. *state legislator*
Stukes, Melvin L. *councilman*

Bel Air
Riley, Catherine Irene *former state senator, legislative staff member*

Bethesda
Gude, Gilbert *former state and federal legislator, nurseryman, writer*
Metzenbaum, Howard Morton *former senator, consumer organization official*
Reed, Miriam Bell *legislative staff*

Chevy Chase
Beilenson, Anthony Charles *former congressman*
†Lubalin, Eve *legislative staff aide*

Columbia
†Quinter, Neil F. *legislative staff member*

Easton
Schisler, Kenneth David *state legislator*

Frederick
Byron, Beverly Butcher *congresswoman*

Rockville
Petzold, Carol Stoker *state legislator*

Silver Spring
Weiss, Leonard *senate staff director, mathematician, engineer*

MASSACHUSETTS

Boston
Amorello, Matthew John *state senator*
Bertonazzi, Louis Peter *federal agency administrator*
Canavan, Christine Estelle *state legislator*
Cleven, Carol Chapman *state legislator*
Cuomo, Donna Fournier *state legislator*
DiMasi, Salvatore Francis *state legislator*
Donovan, Carol Ann *state legislator*
Flavin, Nancy Ann *state legislator*
Hyland, Barbara Claire *state legislator*
Kennedy, Joseph Patrick, II *former congressman*
Larkin, Peter J. *state legislator*
†Menard, Joan M. *state legislator*
Moore, Richard Thomas *state legislator*
Murray, Therese *state legislator*
Paulsen, Anne M. *state legislator*
Rogeness, Mary Speer *state legislator*
†Scanlan, Patrick Francis *legislative staff member*
Simmons, Mary Jane *state legislator*
Sprague, Jo Ann *state legislator*
Story, Ellen *state legislator*
Studds, Gerry Eastman *former congressman*
Walrath, Patricia A. *state legislator*

Cambridge
Cronin, Bonnie Kathryn Lamb *legislative staff executive*
Simpson, Alan Kooi *former senator*

Fall River
Correia, Robert *state legislator*

Gardner
Hawke, Robert Douglas *retired state legislator*

Marblehead
Petersen, Douglas W. *state legislator*

New Bedford
Koczera, Robert Michael *state legislator*

Stoughton
†Robichaud, Holly *political strategist*

Taunton
Fagan, James H. *state legislator*

Worcester
Binienda, John J. *state legislator*

MICHIGAN

Brighton
Chrysler, Richard R. *former congressman*

Detroit
Cockrel, Sheila M. *councilwoman*
Everett, Kay *councilwoman*
Hood, Nicholas *councilman*
Mahaffey, Maryann *councilwoman*

Farmington Hills
Dolan, Jan Clark *former state legislator*

Grand Rapids
Ehlers, Vernon James *congressman*

Holland
†Jelgerhuis, Jane Marie *legislative staff member*

Kalamazoo
Welborn, John Alva *former state senator, small business owner*

Lansing
Bullard, Willis Clare, Jr. *state legislator*
Emmons, Joanne *state senator*
Geake, Raymond Robert *state senator*
Geiger, Terry *state legislator*
Jellema, Jon *state legislator*
Kaza, Greg John *state representative, economist*
LaForge, Edward *state legislator*
McManus, George Alvin, Jr. *state senator, cherry farmer*
Perricone, Charles *state legislator*
Schwarz, John J.H. *state senator, surgeon*
Sikkema, Kenneth R. *state legislator*

MINNESOTA

Austin
Leighton, Robert Joseph *state legislator*

Mankato
Hottinger, John Creighton *state legislator, lawyer*

Minneapolis
Oliver, Edward Carl *state senator, retired investment executive*
Reichgott Junge, Ember D. *state legislator, lawyer*

New Brighton
Pellow, Richard Maurice *former state legislator*

Ottertail
Anderson, Bob *state legislator, business executive*

Saint Paul
Carlson, Lyndon Richard Selvig *state legislator, educator*
Carruthers, Philip Charles *public official, lawyer*
Frederickson, Dennis Russel *senator, farmer*
Greenfield, Lee *state legislator*
†Hugoson, Gene *state legislator, farmer*
Kiscaden, Sheila M. *state legislator*
Knoblach, James Michael *state represenative*
Leppik, Margaret White *state legislator*
Luther, Darlene *state legislator*
McGuire, Mary Jo *state legislator*
Molnau, Carol *state legislator*
Seagren, Alice *state legislator*
Solberg, Loren Albin *state legislator, secondary education educator*
Spear, Allan Henry *state senator, historian, educator*
Vellenga, Kathleen Osborne *former state legislator*

MISSISSIPPI

Amory
Bryan, Wendell Hobdy, II (Hob Bryan) *senator*

Brookhaven
Parker, Michael (Mike Parker) *former congressman*

Columbia
Simmons, Miriam Quinn *state legislator*

Hattiesburg
Saucier, Gene Duane *state legislator*

Jackson
Tuck, Amy *state senator, lawyer*

Southaven
†Flowers, Merle G. *legislative staff member*

MISSOURI

Chesterfield
Hale, David Clovis *former state representative*

Harrisonville
Hartzler, Vicky J. *state legislator*

Jefferson City
Bray, Joan *state legislator*
Clay, William Lacy, Jr. *state legislator*
Farnen, Ted William *state legislator*
McClelland, Emma L. *state legislator*
Westfall, Morris *state legislator*

Saint Louis
Hoblitzelle, George Knapp *former state legislator*

MONTANA

Helena
†Cramer, Chuckie *state senate official*
Hargrove, Don *state senator*

Missoula
Williams, Pat *former congressman*

NEBRASKA

Lincoln
Curtis, Carl Thomas *former senator*
Engel, L. Patrick *state legislator*
Exon, J(ohn) James *former senator*
Landis, David Morrison *state legislator*
Marsh, Frank (Irving) *former state official*
Schimek, DiAnna Ruth Rebman *state legislator*
Stuhr, Elaine Ruth *state legislator*
Wesely, Donald Raymond *state senator*
Will, Eric John *state senator*

Omaha
Pirsch, Carol McBride *county official, former state senator, community relations manager*

NEVADA

Carson City
O'Connell, Mary Ann *state senator, business owner*

Las Vegas
Ensign, John E. *former congressman*
Vucanovich, Barbara Farrell *former congresswoman*

Rego Park
Manton, Thomas Joseph *former congressman*

Reno
Raggio, William John *state senator*

Yerington
Dini, Joseph Edward, Jr. *state legislator*

NEW HAMPSHIRE

Barrington
Lovejoy, George *former state senator*

Belmont
Bartlett, Gordon E. *state legislator*

Concord
Arnold, Thomas Ivan, Jr. *legislator*
Cote, David Edward *state legislator*
Dunlap, Patricia C. *state legislator*
Fields, Dennis H. *state legislator*
Franks, Suzan L. R. *state legislator*
Fraser, Marilyn Anne *state legislator*
Hager, Elizabeth Sears *state legislator, social services organization administrator*
Jacobson, Alf Edgar *state legislator*
Jean, Loren *state legislator*
Lovejoy, Marian E. *state legislator*
Lozeau, Donnalee M. *state legislator*
McNamara, Wanda G. *state legislator*
Merritt, Deborah Foote *state legislator, vocational coordinator*
Moore, Carol *state legislator*
Pignatelli, Debora Becker *state legislator*
Pratt, Irene Agnes *state legislator*
Richardson, Barbara Hull *state legislator, social worker*
Snyder, Clair A. *state legislator*
Spear, Barbara L. *state legislator*

Cornish
Allison, David C. *state legislator*

Derry
Colantuono, Thomas Paul *state legislator*
Dowd, Sandra K. *state legislator*
Katsakiores, George Nicholas *state legislator, retired restauranteur*

Dover
Pelletier, Arthur Joseph *state legislator, educator*

Durham
Wheeler, Katherine Wells *state legislator*

Etna
Copenhaver, Marion Lamson *state legislator*

Franklin
Feuerstein, Martin *state legislator*

Hanover
Crory, Elizabeth L. *former state legislator*
Guest, Robert Henry *state legislator, management educator*

Henniker
Currier, David P. *retired state legislator*

Hillsboro
Sargent, Maxwell D. *state legislator*

Jackson
Zeliff, William H., Jr. *former congressman*

Jaffrey
Royce, H. Charles *state legislator*

Kingston
Welch, David A. *state legislator*
Weyler, Kenneth L. *state legislator*

Laconia
Holbrook, Robert George *state legislator*
Turner, Robert H. *state legislator*

Lancaster
Pratt, Leighton Calvin *state legislator*

Lebanon
Below, Clifton C. *state legislator*

Littleton
Eaton, Stephanie *state legislator*

Manchester
Ahern, Richard Favor *state legislator*

Arnold, Barbara Eileen *state legislator*
McCarty, Winston H. *state legislator*
Nardi, Theodora P. *former state legislator*
Turgeon, Roland M. *state legislator*

Milton Mills
McKinley, Robert E. *state legislator, retired mechanical engineer*

Moultonborough
Foster, Robert W. *state legislator*

Nashua
Bergeron, Normand R. *retired state legislator*
Holley, Sylvia A. *state legislator*

New Castle
Cohen, Burton Joseph *state senator*

Newport
Stamatakis, Carol Marie *state legislator, lawyer*

Nottingham
Case, Margaret A. *state legislator*

Plaistow
Senter, Merilyn P(atricia) *former state legislator and freelance reporter*

Portsmouth
Crossman, Harold G., Jr. *former state legislator*

Randolph
Bradley, Paula E. *retired state legislator*

Rindge
White, Jean Tillinghast *former state legislator*

Rumney
King, Wayne Douglas *former state senator*

Somersworth
Vincent, Francis C. *state legislator*

Windham
Arndt, Janet S. *state legislator*

Wyndham
Delahunty, Joseph Lawrence *state senator, business investor*

NEW JERSEY

Asbury Park
Smith, Thomas S. *state legislator*

Atlantic Highlands
Corodemus, Steven James *state legislator, lawyer*

Bayonne
Doria, Joseph V., Jr. *state legislator*

Bordentown
Malone, Joseph R. *state legislator*

Camden
Bryant, Wayne Richard *state legislator*

Ewing
Turner, Shirley K. *state legislator*

Fair Lawn
Felice, Nicholas R. *state legislator*

Flemington
Lance, Leonard *state legislator*
Schluter, William E. *state legislator*

Freehold
Farragher, Clare M. *state legislator*

Hamilton
Inverso, Peter A. *state legislator*

Jamesburg
Wright, Barbara W. *state legislator, nurse*

Middletown
Kyrillos, Joseph M. *state legislator*

Morris Plains
DeCroce, Alex *state legislator*
Murphy, Carol J. *state legislator*

New Brunswick
Lynch, John A. *lawyer, state senator*

Newark
Bradley, Bill *former senator*
Martini, William J. *former congressman*

Ocean City
Hughes, William John *former congressman, diplomat*

Ocean View
Gibson, John C. *state legislator*

Plainfield
Green, Gerald B. *state legislator*

Princeton
Baker, Nancy Kassebaum (Nancy Kassebaum) *former senator, foundation official*

Red Bank
Arnone, Michael J. *state legislator, dentist*

Ridgewood
†Ciannella, Joeen Moore *legislative staff member, small business owner*

Short Hills
Ogden, Maureen Black *retired state legislator*

Somerville
Pappas, Michael *former congressman*

Teaneck
Weinberg, Loretta *state legislator*

Trenton
Ben-Asher, Daniel Lawrence *legislative researcher, writer*
DiFrancesco, Donald T. *state senator, lawyer*
Gill, Nia H. *state legislator*
Haytaian, Garabed (Chuck) *state legislator*

Turnersville
Matheussen, John J. *state legislator*

Union
Franks, Robert D. (Bob Franks) *congressman*

Woodbury
Stuhltrager, Gary W. *state legislator*
Zane, Raymond J. *state senator, lawyer*

NEW MEXICO

Albuquerque
Rutherford, Thomas Truxtun, II *former state senator, county commissioner*

Hobbs
Reagan, Gary Don *state legislator, lawyer*

Los Alamos
Redmond, Bill *former congressman, minister*
Wallace, Jeannette Owens *state legislator*

Roswell
Casey, Barbara A. Perea *state representative, school superintendent*

NEW YORK

Albany
Canestrari, Ronald *state legislator*
Destito, RoAnn M. *state legislator*
Farley, Hugh T. *state senator, law educator*
Ferrara, Donna *state legislator*
Glick, Deborah J. *state legislator*
Greene, Aurelia *state legislator*
Hannon, Kemp *state senator*
Harenberg, Paul E. *state legislator*
Hill, Earlene Hooper *state legislator*
Hochberg, Audrey G. *state legislator*
Jacobs, Rhoda S. *state legislator*
Kuhl, John R., Jr. *state legislator*
Lack, James J. *state senator, lawyer*
Leichter, Franz S. *state senator*
Matusow, Naomi C. *state legislator*
Mayersohn, Nettie *state legislator*
O'Neil, Chloe Ann *retired state legislator*
Paterson, David Alexander *state senator*
Proskin, Arnold W. *state assemblyman, lawyer*
Reynolds, William Peter *legislative aide*
Santiago, Nellie *state legislator*
Sullivan, Frances Taylor *state legislator*
Velella, Guy John *state legislator*
Vitaliano, Eric Nicholas *state legislator, lawyer*
Volker, Dale Martin *state senator, lawyer*

Bath
Davidsen, Donald R. *state legislator*

Binghamton
Libous, Thomas William *state senator*

Bronx
Cruz, Lucy *city councilwoman*
Eisland, June M. *councilwoman*
Foster, Wendell *councilman*
Rivera, Jose *city councilman*
Warden, Lawrence A. *councilman*

Brooklyn
Dibrienza, Stephen *city councilman*
Fisher, Kenneth K. *councilman*
Henry, Lloyd *councilman*
Malave-Dilan, Martin *councilman*
Robinson, Annette *councilwoman*
Robles, Victor L. *city councilman*
Weiner, Anthony D. *congressman*
Wooten, Priscilla A. *councilwoman*

Derby
Pordum, Francis J. *former state legislator, educator*

Flushing
Harrison, Julia *councilwoman*
Stavisky, Leonard Price *state legislator*

Forest Hills
Koslowitz, Karen *councilwoman*

Glendale
Maltese, Serphin Ralph *state senator, lawyer*

Great Neck
†Goldes, Jordan *legislative staff member*

Jackson Heights
Sabini, John D. *city councilman*

Jamaica
Flake, Floyd Harold *former congressman*
Spigner, Archie *councilman*
White, Thomas *city councilman*

Laurelton
Watkins, Juanita *city councilwoman*

Middle Village
Ognibene, Thomas V. *councilman*

Middletown
†Aumick, Amalia *legislative staff member*

Milford
Seward, James L. *state legislator*

New City
Gromack, Alexander Joseph *state legislator*

New York
Berman, Herbert E. *councilman*
Duane, Thomas K. *councilman*
Eldridge, Ronnie *councilwoman*
Eristoff, Andrew S. *councilman*
Farrell, Herman D., Jr. *state legislator*
Fields, C. Virginia *city councilwoman*
Forbes, John Francis *government official*
Freed, Kathryn E. *councilwoman, lawyer*
Goodman, Roy Matz *state senator, business executive*
Linares, Guiller *city councilman*

North Syracuse
Bragman, Michael J. *state legislator*

Oneida
Magee, William *state legislator*

Pearl River
Colman, Samuel *assemblyman*

Plainview
Sidikman, David S. *state legislator*

Port Chester
Oppenheimer, Suzi *state senator*

Rochester
John, Susan V. *state legislator*

Seneca Falls
Nozzolio, Michael F. *state legislator*

Smithtown
Wertz, Robert Charles *state legislator*

Staten Island
Connelly, Elizabeth Ann *state legislator*
Molinari, Guy Victor *municipal official*
O'Donovan, Jerome *councilman*
Straniere, Robert A. *state legislator*

Yonkers
Singer, Cecile Doris *state legislator*

NORTH CAROLINA

Advance
Cochrane, Betsy Lane *state senator*

Burlington
Holt, Bertha Merrill *state legislator*

Chapel Hill
Price, David Eugene *congressman, educator*

Clinton
Faircloth, Duncan McLauchlin (Lauch Faircloth) *former senator, businessman, farmer*

Fayetteville
Tyson-Autry, Carrie Eula *legislative consultant, researcher, small business owner*

Hickory
†Luckadoo, Thomas D. *legislative staff member*

New Bern
Perdue, Beverly E. *state legislator, geriatric consultant*

Raleigh
Lancaster, H(arold) Martin *former congressman, former advisor to the President, academic adminstrator*
†Pruitt, Janet *state senate official*
Sutton, Ronnie Neal *state legislator, lawyer*
Tally, Lura Self *state legislator*

Winston Salem
Ward, Marvin Martin *retired state senator*

NORTH DAKOTA

Ashley
Kretschmar, William Edward *state legislator, lawyer*

Dickinson
†Goetz, William G. *state legislator*

Edgeley
Schimke, Dennis J. *former state legislator*

Fargo
Mathern, Tim *state senator, social worker*

Fessenden
Streibel, Bryce *state senator*

Grand Forks
DeMers, Judy Lee *state legislator, university dean*
Stenehjem, Wayne Kevin *state senator, lawyer*

Minot
Mickelson, Stacey *state legislator*

Williston
Rennerfeldt, Earl Ronald *state legislator, farmer, rancher*
Yockim, James Craig *state senator*

OHIO

Akron
Seiberling, John Frederick *former congressman, law educator, lawyer*

Cleveland
Oakar, Mary Rose *former congresswoman*

Columbus
Furney, Linda Jeanne *state legislator*
Glenn, John Herschel, Jr. *former senator*
Hollister, Nancy *state legislator*
Hottinger, Jay *state legislator*
Kearns, Merle Grace *state legislator*
McLin, Rhine Lana *state senator, funeral service executive, educator*
Mead, Priscilla *state legislator*
Neely, Scott Hays *legislative liaison*

Dayton
Reid, Marilyn Joanne *state legislator, lawyer*

Gallipolis
Cremeans, Frank A. *former congressman*

Hillsboro
Snyder, Harry Cooper *retired state senator*

Kettering
Horn, Charles F. *state senator, lawyer, electrical engineer*

Lima
Cupp, Robert Richard *state senator, attorney*

OKLAHOMA

Oklahoma City
Ford, Charles Reed *state senator*
†Ward, Lance D. *state senate official*

OREGON

Beaverton
Strobeck, Ken Leslie *state legislator, healthcare organization executive*

Bend
Cooley, Wes *former congressman*

Portland
Furse, Elizabeth *former congresswoman, small business owner*
Hatfield, Mark Odom *former senator*

Salem
Brown, Kate *state legislator*
Taylor, Jacqueline Self *state legislator*

PENNSYLVANIA

Centre Hall
Rudy, Ruth Corman *former state legislator*

Cheswick
Dermody, Frank *state legislator, lawyer*

Elizabeth
Levdansky, David Keith *state legislator*

Erie
Boyes, Karl W. *state legislator*

Harrisburg
Armstrong, Gibson E. *state senator*
Armstrong, Thomas Errol *state legislator*
Barley, John E. *state legislator*
Bebko-Jones, Linda *state legislator*
Cohen, Lita Indzel *state legislator*
Forcier, Teresa Elaine *state legislator*
Fox, Miriam Annette *state legislative fiscal analyst*
Gruitza, Michael *state legislator, lawyer*
Hart, Melissa A. *state senator*
Helfrick, Edward W. *state legislator*
Herman, Lynn Briggs *state legislator*
Itkin, Ivan *state legislator*
Kukovich, Allen Gale *legislator, lawyer*
Lepore, Anthony W(illiam) *legislative staff member*
Loeper, F. Joseph *state senator*
Manderino, Kathy *state legislator*
Miller, Sheila M. *state legislator*
Mundy, Phyllis *state legislator*
Schwartz, Allyson Y. *state senator*
Steelman, Sara Gerling *state legislator*
Tangretti, Thomas Alan *state legislator*
†Tartaglione, Christine *state senator*
True, Katie *state legislator*
Vance, Patricia H. *state legislator*
Washington, LeAnna M. *state legislator*

Johnstown
Wozniak, John N. *senator*

Lampeter
Schuler, Jere W. *state legislator*

Lebanon
Brightbill, David John *state senator, lawyer*

Lewisberry
Smith, Bruce I. *state legislator*

Lock Haven
Hanna, Michael K. *state legislator*

Martinsburg
Stern, Jerry Allen *state legislator*

Peckville
Mellow, Robert James *state senator*

Penn Hills
†D'Alesandro, Paul J. *legislative staff member*

Philadelphia
Cohen, David *councilman*
Johns, Michael Douglas *government relations executive, policy analyst, health care consultant*
Krajewski, Joan L. *councilwoman*
Mariano, Richard *city councilman*
Nutter, Michael A. *councilman*
O'Neill, Brian J. *councilman*
Rizzo, Frank *city councilman*
Roebuck, James Randolph, Jr. *state legislator*
Tasco, Marian B. *councilwoman*

Reading
Rohrer, Samuel Edward *state legislator*

Red Lion
Saylor, Stanley E. *state legislator*

Upper Darby
†Fleitz, John *legislative administrator*

Wayne
Rubley, Carole A. *state legislator*

Waynesboro
Punt, Terry Lee *state legislator*

Wellsboro
Baker, Matthew Edward *state legislator*

Williamsport
Madigan, Roger Allen *state legislator*

York
Stetler, Stephen H. *state legislator*

RHODE ISLAND

Adamsville
Quick, Joan B. *state legislator*

Bristol
Parella, Mary A. *state legislator*

Central Falls
Lyle, John William, Jr. *former state senator, lawyer, social studies educator*

Cranston
Lanzi, Beatrice A. *state legislator*

Newport
Cicilline, J. Clement *state legislator*

Providence
Ajello, Edith H. *state legislator*
Algiere, Dennis Lee *state senator*
Cambio, Bambilyn Breece *state legislator*
Gibbs, June Nesbitt *state senator*
Goodwin, Maryellen *state legislator*
Henseler, Suzanne Marie *state legislator, social studies educator, majority whip*
†Hoyas, Raymond T. *state senate official*
Iannitelli, Susan B. *state legislator*
Lima, Charlene *state legislator*
Metts, Harold M. *state legislator*
Naughton, Eileen Slattery *state legislator*
Paiva Weed, M(arie) Teresa *state legislator*
Perry, Rhoda E. *state legislator*
Sasso, Eleanor Catherine *state senator*
Williams, Anastasia P. *state legislator*

Rumford
Irons, William V. *state legislator*

Saunderstown
Carter, Kenneth *state legislator, restauranteur*

Wakefield
Garvey, Eugene Francis *state legislator*

Warwick
Ginaitt, Peter Thaddeus *state legislator*
Revens, John Cosgrove, Jr. *state senator, lawyer*
†Russo, James Michael *legislative staff member*

SOUTH CAROLINA

Columbia
Courson, John Edward *state senator, insurance company executive*
Harvin, Charles Alexander, III *state legislator, lawyer*
†King, Sam B, III *legislative staff member*
Leatherman, Hugh Kenneth, Sr. *state senator, business executive*
†Nance, Robert M. *legislative staff member*

Greenville
Inglis, Robert D. (Bob Inglis) *former congressman, lawyer*
Manly, Sarah Letitia *state legislator, ophthalmic photographer, angiographer*
Mann, James Robert *congressman*

Mc Cormick
Clayton, Verna Lewis *retired state legislator*

Spartanburg
Patterson, Elizabeth Johnston *former congresswoman*

West Columbia
Wilson, Addison Graves (Joe Wilson) *state senator, lawyer*

SOUTH DAKOTA

Black Hawk
Maicki, G. Carol *former state senator, consultant*

Brookings
McClure-Bibby, Mary Anne *former state legislator*

Miller
Morford, JoAnn (JoAnn Morford-Burg) *state senator, investment company executive*

Pierre
†Adam, Patricia A. *state legislator*
†Hurd, Paula *state official*
Pederson, Gordon Roy *state legislator, retired military officer*

Sioux Falls
Paisley, Keith Watkins *state senator, small business owner, retired*

Sturgis
Ingalls, Marie Cecelie *former state legislator, retail executive*

TENNESSEE

Kingsport
Quillen, James Henry (Jimmy Quillen) *former congressman*

Nashville
Kisber, Matthew Harris *state legislator*
Person, Curtis S., Jr. *state senator, lawyer*

Union City
†Hill, Joe H. *legislative staff member*

TEXAS

Abilene
Hunter, Robert Dean (Bob Hunter) *state legislator, retired university official*

Arlington
†Samuels, Harold D. *legislative staff member*

Austin
Brown, J. E. (Buster Brown) *state senator, lawyer*
Bullock, Robert D. (Bob Bullock) *lawyer, lieutenant governor, state legislator*
Denny, Mary Craver *state legislator, rancher*
†King, Betty D. *state senate employee*
Sansom, Andrew *state agency administrator*
Turner, Sylvester *state legislator, lawyer*

Beaumont
Brooks, Jack Bascom *congressman*

Dallas
Blumer, Donna *councilwoman*
Bryant, John Wiley *former congressman*
Cain, David *state senator, lawyer*
Duncan, Larry Edward *councilman*
Hicks, Donald W., Sr. *councilman*
Leedom, John Nesbett *distribution company executive, state senator*
Mallory, Barbara Len *councilwoman*
Walne, Alan *councilman*

Fort Worth
Geren, Pete (Preston Geren) *former congressman*
Willis, Doyle Henry *state legislator, lawyer*

Garland
Driver, Joe L. *state legislator, insurance agent*

Houston
Bell, Chris *city councilman*
Boney, Jew Don *councilman*
Castillo, John E. *councilman*
Fraga, Felix *councilman*
Green, Gene *congressman*
Roach, Joe *councilman*
Sanchez, Orlando *city councilman*

Humble
Fields, Jack Milton, Jr. *former congressman*

Irving
Armey, Richard Keith (Dick Armey) *congressman*

Laredo
Zaffirini, Judith *state senator, small business owner*

Lubbock
Montford, John Thomas *state legislator, academic administrator, lawyer*

Midland
Craddick, Thomas Russell *state representative, investor*

Plainview
Kirchhoff, Mary Virginia *city council member*

San Antonio
Gonzalez, Henry Barbosa *former congressman*
Guerrero, Debra Ann *council woman*
Morales, Rolando *city official San Antonio*
†Ricks, Philip L., II *legislative director*

Stafford
†Lindsey, Dawn S. *legislative staff member*

UTAH

Alpine
Tanner, Jordan *state legislator*

Bountiful
Burningham, Kim Richard *former state legislator*

Cedar City
Hunter, R. Haze *former state legislator*

Corinne
Ferry, Miles Yeoman *state official*

Ogden
Montgomery, Robert F. *state legislator, retired surgeon, cattle rancher*

Orem
Peterson, Craig Anton *former state senator*

Provo
Valentine, John Lester *state legislator, lawyer*

Salt Lake City
Bennett, Janet Huff *legislative staff member*
Black, Wilford Rex, Jr. *state senator*
Carnahan, Orville Darrell *retired state legislator, retired college president*
Garn, Edwin Jacob (Jake Garn) *former senator*
Greene, Enid *former congresswoman*
†Martinez, Art L. *legislative staff member*
†Moore, Annette B. *state senate employee*
Orton, William H. (Bill Orton) *former congressman, lawyer*
Shepherd, Karen *former congresswoman*

Tremonton
Kerr, Kleon Harding *former state senator, educator*

VERMONT

Brattleboro
Milkey, Virginia A. *state legislator*

Essex Junction
Parizo, Mary Ann *state legislator*

Hartland
Dunne, Matthew Bailey *state legislator*

Montpelier
†LaClair, Jolinda *legislative staff member*
May, Edgar *former state legislator, nonprofit administrator*
Paquin, Edward H., Jr. *state legislator*
†Peterson, Julie *public information officer*
Ready, Elizabeth M. *state legislator*
Rivers, Cheryl P. *state legislator*
Steele, Karen Kiarsis *state legislator*
Valsangiacomo, Oreste Victor *state legislator*

Putney
Darrow, Steve *state legislator*

Saint Johnsbury
Crosby, George Miner *former state legislator*

South Londonderry
Coleman, Wendell Lawrence *former state legislator*

White River Junction
Bohi, Lynn *state legislator*

VIRGINIA

Alexandria
Collins, Cardiss *former congresswoman*
Molinari, Susan *former congresswoman*
Montgomery, Gillespie V (Sonny Montgomery) *former congressman*
Riggs, Frank *former congressman*
Sauer, H. Arthur *legislative staff member*
Ticer, Patricia *state senator*

Arlington
Fazio, Vic *former congressman*
Volkmer, Harold L. *former congressman*

Burke
Smeeton, Thomas Rooney *governmental affairs consultant*

Halifax
Anderson, Howard Palmer *former state senator*

Leesburg
Mims, William Cleveland *state legislator, lawyer*

Marshall
Rose, Charles Grandison, III (Charlie Rose) *former congressman*

Mc Lean
Burke, Sheila P. *legislative staff member*
Callahan, Vincent Francis, Jr. *state legislator, publisher*
St. Germain, Fernand Joseph *congressman*

Merrifield
Miller, Emilie F. *former state senator, consultant*
Scott, James Martin *state legislator, healthcare system executive*

Newport News
Keator, Margaret Whitley *legislative aide*
Trible, Paul Seward, Jr. *former United States senator*

Norfolk
Miller, Yvonne Bond *state senator, educator*

Norton
Kennedy, J. Jack, Jr. *court administrator, bank director, lawyer*

Richmond
Forbes, J. Randy *state senator*
Schaar, Susan Clarke *state legislative staff member*

Vienna
Higginbotham, Wendy Jacobson *political adviser, writer*
Kim, Jay *former congressman*

Woodbridge
Garon, Richard Joseph, Jr. *chief of staff, political worker*

WASHINGTON

Everett
Nelson, Gary *county councilman, engineer*

Gig Harbor
McMahan, Lois Grace *former state legislator*

Lake Stevens
Quigley, Kevin Walsh *state legislator, lawyer*

Olympia
Ballard, Clyde *state legislator*
†Cook, Tony Michael *legislative staff member*
Kessler, Lynn Elizabeth *state legislator*
Kohl-Welles, Jeanne Elizabeth *state senator, sociologist, educator*
Long, Jeanine Hundley *state legislator*
Neeld, Michael Earl *legislative staff administrator*
Spanel, Harriet Rosa Albertsen *state senator*

Ritzville
Schoesler, Mark Gerald *state legislator, farmer*

Seattle
Evans, Daniel Jackson *former senator*

Tacoma
†Beckett, Kurt A. *legislative staff member*

Vancouver
Smith, Linda A. *former congresswoman*

WEST VIRGINIA

Charleston
†Small-Plante, Susan *legislative administrator*

Elkins
Spears, Jae *state legislator*

Martinsburg
†Slaven, Chip *district director*

Parkersburg
Brum, Brenda *state legislator, librarian*

WISCONSIN

Janesville
Neumann, Mark W. *former congressman*
Wood, Wayne W. *state legislator*

Juneau
Fitzgerald, Scott *state legislator*

Madison
†Baldwin, Tammy *congresswoman*
Barish, Lawrence Stephen *nonpartisan legislative staff administrator*
Burke, Brian B. *state senator, lawyer*
Farrow, Margaret Ann *state legislator*
Hardie, Anthony D. *legislative staff member, social welfare administrator*
Klug, Scott Leo *former congressman*
Krusick, Margaret Ann *state legislator*
Moen, Rodney Charles *state senator, retired naval officer*
Porter, Cloyd Allen *state representative*
Roessler, Carol Ann *state senator*
Rude, Brian David *state legislator*
Swoboda, Lary Joseph *state legislator*
Turner, Robert Lloyd *state legislator*
Young, Rebecca Mary Conrad *state legislator*

Waterford
Gunderson, Scott Lee *state legislator*

WYOMING

Casper
Donley, Russell Lee, III *former state representative*
Meenan, Patrick Henry *state legislator*

Cody
Shreve, Peg *state legislator, retired elementary educator*

Jackson
LaLonde, Robert Frederick *state senator, retired*

Lander
Tipton, Harry Basil, Jr. *state legislator, physician*

Laramie
Hansen, Matilda *state legislator*
Maxfield, Peter C. *state legislator, law educator, lawyer*

Rock Springs
Blackwell, Samuel Eugene *state legislator*

TERRITORIES OF THE UNITED STATES

AMERICAN SAMOA

Pago Pago
Lutali, A. P. *senator*

GUAM

Agana
San Agustin, Joe Taitano *Guamanian senator, financial institution executive, management researcher*

PUERTO RICO

San Juan
Acevedo-Vila, Anibal *state legislator, lawyer*

CANADA

BRITISH COLUMBIA

Vancouver
McWhinney, Edward Watson *Canadian government legislator*

Victoria
Boone, Lois Ruth *legislator*
Weisgerber, John Sylvester *provincial legislator*

ONTARIO

Brampton
Malhi, Gurbax Singh *legislator*

Ottawa
Abbott, Jim *member of Canadian parliament*
Austin, Jacob (Jack Austin) *Canadian senator*
Bevilacqua, Maurizio *member of Canadian parliament*
Bonin, Raymond *member of Canadian parliament*
Borotsik, Rick *member of Canadian parliament*
Boudria, Don *Canadian government official*
Carroll, M(argaret) Aileen *member of Canadian parliament*
Casson, Rick *member of Canadian parliament*
Chamberlain, Brenda Kay *member of Canadian parliament*
Charbonneau, Yvon *member of parliament*
Clouthier, Hector *member of Canadian parliament*
Dalphond-Guiral, Madeleine *member of Canadian parliament*
Doyle, Norman E. *member of Canadian parliament*
Doyle, Richard James *retired Canadian senator, former editor*
Easter, Wayne Arnold *Parliament member*
Elley, Reed *member of parliament*
Forseth, Paul *member of parliament*
Grose, Ivan *member of parliament*
Hart, James *member of Canadian parliament*
Ianno, Tony *member of Canadian parliament*
Jackson, Ovid *member of parliament*
Johnston, Dale *member of parliament*
Kilgour, David *Canadian member of parliament*
Lee, Derek *member of parliament*
Lincoln, Clifford *member of parliament*
Lowther, Eric *member of parliament*
Lynch-Staunton, John *Canadian senator*
MacEachen, Allan Joseph *retired parliamentarian*
Maheu, Shirley *Canadian legislator*
Maloney, John *member of parliament*
Martin, Keith Philip *member of parliament, physician*
Mayfield, Philip *member of parliament*
McCormick, Larry *member of parliament*
Milliken, Peter Andrew Stewart *legislator*
Mills, Dennis J. *member of parliament*
Muise, Mark *member of parliament*
Murray, Lowell *Canadian senator*
Parent, Gilbert *member Canadian House of Commons*
Penson, Charlie *member of parliament*
Pettigrew, Pierre S. *politician, member of parliament*
Richardson, John *member of parliament*
Robichaud, Louis Joseph *Canadian senator*
St. Denis, Brent *member of parliament*
St-Hilaire, Caroline *member of parliament*
Schmidt, Werner *member of parliament*
Serré, Ben *member of parliament*
Soloman, John *member of parliament*
Telegdi, Andrew *member of parliament*
Torsney, Paddy Ann *member of parliament*
Ur, Rose-Marie *member of parliament*
Valeri, Tony *member of parliament*
Wappel, Tom *member of parliament*
Whelan, Susan *member of parliament*
White, Randy *member of parliament*
White, Ted *member of parliament*
Wood, Bob *member of parliament*

Toronto
Eyton, John Trevor *senator, business executive*

ADDRESS UNPUBLISHED

Baker, Howard Henry, Jr. *former senator, lawyer*
Barnhart, Jo Anne B. *government official*
Barton, Joe Linus *congressman*
†Batchelder, Jennifer Jo *legislative staff member*
Beals, Nancy Farwell *state legislator*
Bell, Clarence Deshong *state senator, lawyer*
Berman, Lori Beth *legislative staff member*
Bilbray, James Hubert *former congressman, lawyer, consultant*
Blaschke, Renee Dhossche *alderman*
Bliley, Thomas Jerome, Jr. *congressman*
Bonsack, Rose Mary Hatem *state legislator, physician*
Brown, Richard E. *state legislator*
Bunning, Jim *senator, former professional baseball player*
Burton, Joseph Alfred *state legislator*
Charlton, Betty Jo *retired state legislator*
Churchill, Robert Wilson *state legislator, lawyer*
Coble, Howard *congressman, lawyer*
Cochran, Thad *senator*
Collins, Barbara-Rose *former congresswoman*
Culp, Faye Berry *former state legislator*
Danforth, John Claggett *former senator, lawyer, clergyman*
Davis, Crystal Michelle *oil company administrator*
de la Garza, Kika (Eligio de la Garza) *former congressman*
†DeMint, James Warren *congressman, marketing executive*
Doderer, Minnette Frerichs *state legislator*
Drake, Robert Alan *state legislator, animal nutritionist, mayor*
Farmer, Elaine Frazier *retired state legislator*
†Federing, Eric K. *congressional communications director, motion picture preservationist, lecturer*
Fields, Cleo *state senator*
Ford, Wendell Hampton *former senator*
Franks, Gary Alvin *former congressman, real estate professional*
Gingrich, Newt(on Leroy) *former congressman*
Gordly, Avel Louise *senator, community activist*
Goss, Porter J. *congressman*
Granger, Kay *congresswoman*
Hammerschmidt, John Paul *retired congressman, lumber company executive*
Hatch, Orrin Grant *senator*
Hawkins, Mary Ellen Higgins (Mary Ellen Higgins) *former state legislator, public relations consultant*
Hearn, Joyce Camp *retired state legislator, educator, consultant*
Heath, Roger Charles *state senator, writer*
Hickey, Winifred E(spy) *former state senator, social worker*
Hill, Anita Carraway *retired state legislator*
Hoke, Martin Rossiter *former congressman*
Holliday, Robert Kelvin *retired state senator, former newspaper executive*
Hunter, Duncan Lee *congressman*
Hutchison, Kay Bailey *senator*
Kindness, Thomas Norman *former congressman, lawyer, consultant*
Kleven, Marguerite *state senator*
Knight, Alice Dorothy Tirrell *state legislator*
Konnyu, Ernest Leslie *former congressman*
†Maloney, James Henry *congressman*
McCarthy, Carolyn *congresswoman*
McDade, Joseph Michael *former congressman*
Mc Govern, George Stanley *former senator*
McHale, Paul *former congressman, lawyer*
Meshel, Harry *state senator, political party official*
Meyers, Jan *former congresswoman*
Mikulski, Barbara Ann *senator*
Mitchell, Donald J. *former congressman*
Moseley-Braun, Carol *senator*
Myers, John Thomas *retired congressman*
Nielsen, Linda M. *city councilwoman*
Osler, Dorothy K. *state legislator*
Parry, Atwell J., Jr. *state senator, retailer*
Pascoe, Patricia Hill *state senator, writer*
Paul, Ron *congressman*
Pell, Claiborne *former senator*
Pena, Manuel, Jr. *retired state senator*
Pettis-Roberson, Shirley McCumber *former congresswoman*
Pevear, Roberta Charlotte *retired state legislator*
Pond, Phyllis Joan Ruble *state legislator*
Proxmire, William *former senator*
Pryce, Deborah D. *congresswoman*
Pryor, David Hampton *former senator*
Reid, Harry *senator*
Reyes, Silvestre *congressman*
Roth, Toby *former congressman, political consultant*
Satterthwaite, Helen Foster *retired state legislator*
Searle, Rodney Newell *state legislator, farmer, insurance agent*
Seastrand, Andrea H. *former congresswoman*
Sessions, Pete *congressman*
Simpers, Mary Palmer *state legislator*
Skinner, Patricia Morag *state legislator*
Soles, Ada Leigh *former state legislator, government advisor*
Sorensen, Sheila *state senator*
Stabile, Alfonso C. *city councilman*
Stickney, Jessica *former state legislator*
Sununu, John E. *congressman*
Sykora, Barbara Zwach *state legislator*
Talley, Kevin David *legislative staff official*
Tauscher, Ellen O. *congresswoman*
Thune, John *congressman*
Treppler, Irene Esther *retired state senator*
Valentine, I. T., Jr. (Tim Valentine) *former congressman*
Van Engen, Thomas Lee *state legislator*
Waldon, Alton Ronald, Jr. *state senator*
†Ward, Cam *legislative staff member*
Warnstadt, Steven H. *state legislator*
Weber, Garry Allen *city councilman*
Zimmerman, Harold Samuel *retired state senator, newspaper editor and publisher, state administrator*

HEALTHCARE: DENTISTRY

UNITED STATES

ALABAMA

Birmingham
Fullmer, Harold Milton *dentist, educator*
King, Charles Mark *dentist, educator*
Manson-Hing, Lincoln Roy *dental educator*

ARIZONA

Oro Valley
Oro, Debra Ann *dentist*

Tucson
Davis, Richard Calhoun *dentist*
Geistfeld, Ronald Elwood *retired dental educator*
Hawke, Robert Francis *dentist*
Nadler, George L. *orthodontist*
†Oro, Robert John *dentist, consultant, writer*

ARKANSAS

Fayetteville
Grammer, Frank Clifton *oral surgeon, researcher*

CALIFORNIA

Arcadia
Gamboa, George Charles *oral surgeon, educator*

Arcata
Hise, Mark Allen *dentist*

Balboa Island
Petersen, Richard Craig *dentist*

Claremont
Valdez, Arnold *dentist, lawyer*

Eureka
Welling, Gene B. *dental association executive*

Loma Linda
Feller, Ralph Paul *dentist, educator*

Los Angeles
Dummett, Clifton Orrin *dentist, educator*

Northridge
Logan, Lee Robert *orthodontist*

Pacific Palisades
Hooley, James Robert *oral and maxillofacial surgeon, educator, dean*

Pasadena
Mc Carthy, Frank Martin *oral surgeon, surgical sciences educator*

Pebble Beach
Kim, Han Pyong *dentist, researcher*

San Francisco
Bensinger, David August *dentist, university dean*
Dugoni, Arthur A. *orthodontics educator, university dean*
Greene, John Clifford *dentist, former university dean*
Greenspan, Deborah *oral medicine educator*
Greenspan, John S. *dentistry educator, scientist, administrator*
Khosla, Ved Mitter *oral and maxillofacial surgeon, educator*
Mack, Ronald Brand *pediatric dentist, clinician, educator, writer, lecturer*
Rouda, Robert E. *dentist*
Wirthlin, Milton Robert, Jr. *periodontist*

San Jose
Yoshizumi, Donald Tetsuro *dentist*

San Rafael
Gryson, Joseph Anthony *orthodontist*

Vacaville
Dedeaux, Paul J. *orthodontist*

West Hollywood
Etessami, Rambod *endodontist*

Whittier
Lowe, Oariona *dentist*

COLORADO

Boulder
Colbert, Elbert Lynn *dentist, recording artist*
Schaffer, Joel Lance *dentist*

Denver
Berkey, Douglas Bryan *dental educator, researcher, gerontologist, clinician*
Doida, Stanley Y. *dentist*
Patterson, Daniel William *dentist*

Golden
Christensen, Robert Wayne *oral maxillofacial surgeon, minister*

Highlands Ranch
Boraz, Robert Alan *dentist, surgery and pediatrics educator*

CONNECTICUT

Avon
Boucher, Louis Jack *retired dentist, educator*
Weiss, Robert Michael *dentist*

Brookfield
Cohen, Mark Steven *dentist*

Middletown
Valentine, George Edward *dentist*

Norwich
†Young, Pamela Jean *dental hygienist*

Sharon
†Nweeia, Martin Thomas *dentist, musician, composer, anthropologist*

DELAWARE

Dover
Lorton, Lewis *researcher, computer executive, dentist*

Wilmington
Wachstein, Joan Martha *dental hygienist*

DISTRICT OF COLUMBIA

Washington
Calhoun, Noah Robert *oral maxillofacial surgeon, educator*

Sazima, Henry John *oral and maxillofacial surgery educator*
Sinkford, Jeanne Craig *dentist, retired dean, educator*
Stromfers, Eric Robert *dental assistant*

FLORIDA

Bay Harbor Islands
Rosenbluth, Morton *periodontist, educator*

Boca Raton
Lerner, Theodore Raphael *dentist*

Boynton Beach
Kronman, Joseph Henry *orthodontist*

Clearwater
Stewart, Michael Ian *orthodontist*

Fort Lauderdale
Dorn, Samuel O. *endodontist*
Oliet, Seymour *endodontics educator, dean, dentist*

Fort Myers
Laboda, Gerald *oral and maxillofacial surgeon*

Gainesville
Javid, Nikzad Sabet *dentist, prosthodontist educator*
Widmer, Charles Glenn *dentist, researcher*

Jupiter
Nessmith, H(erbert) Alva *dentist*

Melbourne
Elder, Stewart Taylor *dentist, retired naval officer*

Miami
Glenn, Frances Bonde *dentist*
Higley, Bruce Wadsworth *orthodontist*
Iver, Robert Drew *dentist*
Leeds, Robert *dentist*
Parnes, Edmund Ira *oral and maxillofacial surgeon*

Sarasota
Gugino, Carl Frank *orthodontist, educator*

Tampa
Pasetti, Louis Oscar *dentist*
Perret, Gerard Anthony, Jr. *orthodontist*

Winter Haven
Turnquist, Donald Keith *orthodontist*

Winter Park
Bush-Counts, Christine Gay *dental hygienist*
McKean, Thomas Wayne *dentist, retired naval officer*

GEORGIA

Atlanta
Freedman, Louis Martin *dentist*

Macon
Holliday, Peter Osborne, Jr. *dentist*
Walton, DeWitt Talmage, Jr. *dentist*

Marietta
Braswell, Laura Day *periodontist*

HAWAII

Honolulu
Nishimura, Pete Hideo *oral surgeon*
Scheerer, Ernest William *dentist*
Tamura, Neal Noboru *dentist, consultant*

Pearl City
Sue, Alan Kwai Keong *dentist*

ILLINOIS

Alton
Dickey, Keith Winfield *dentist, dental educator*

Batavia
Bicknell, Brian Keith *dentist*

Chicago
Abt, Sylvia Hedy *dentist*
Barr, Sanford Lee *dentist*
Diefenbach, Viron Leroy *dental, public health educator, university dean*
Eisenmann, Dale Richard *dental educator*
Glenner, Richard Allen *dentist, dental historian*
Goepp, Robert August *dental educator, oral pathologist*
Graber, Thomas M. *orthodontist*
Hardaway, Ernest, II *oral and maxillofacial surgeon, public health official*
Hirsch, Martin Alan *dentist*
Horowitz, Fred Lee *dentist, administrator, consultant*
Jackson, Gregory Wayne *orthodontist*
McNeely, Carol J. *dentist*
Santangelo, Mario Vincent *dentist*
Scott, Karen Ann *dentist*
Weclew, Victor T. *dentist*
Yale, Seymour Hershel *dental radiologist, educator, university dean, gerontologist*

Elburn
Willey, James Lee *dentist*

Geneva
Kallstrom, Charles Clark *dentist*
Lazzara, Dennis Joseph *orthodontist*

Godfrey
King, Ordie Herbert, Jr. *oral pathologist*

Jacksonville
Loughary, Thomas Michael *dentist*

Kenilworth
Edson, Wayne E. *retired dentist, consultant*

La Grange
Morelli, Anthony Frank *pediatric dentist*

Lake Forest
Jones, Gordon Kempton *dentist*
McClellan, Mart Gaynor *orthodontist*

Mount Vernon
Stephen, Richard Joseph *oral and maxillofacial surgeon*

Naperville
Grimley, Jeffrey Michael *dentist*

Park Ridge
Kenney, John Patrick *dentist*

Riverwoods
Douglas, Bruce Lee *oral and maxillofacial surgeon, medical director, educator, workplace health consultant, gerontology consultant*

Roselle
Kao, William Chishon *dentist*

Taylorville
Gardner, Jerry Dean *dentist, military officer*

INDIANA

Anderson
Stohler, Michael Joe *dentist*

Columbus
Arthur, Jewell Kathleen *dental hygienist*

Elkhart
Bryan, Norman E. *dentist*

Evansville
Fritz, Edward Lane *dentist*
Raibley, Parvin Rudolph *dentist*

Gary
Stephens, Paul Alfred *dentist*

Indianapolis
Behner, Elton Dale *dentist*
Christen, Arden Gale *dental educator, researcher, consultant*
Reese, Ted M. *dentist*
Sarbinoff, James Adair *periodontist, consultant*
Standish, Samuel Miles *oral pathologist, college dean*
Tolliver, Kevin Paul *dentist*

New Albany
Johnson, John Edwin *orthodontist*

Peru
Davidson, John Robert *dentist*

Terre Haute
Roshel, John Albert, Jr. *orthodontist*

IOWA

Iowa City
Bishara, Samir Edward *orthodontist*
Bjorndal, Arne Magne *endodontist*
Ogesen, Robert Bruce *dentist*
Olin, William Harold *orthodontist, educator*

KANSAS

Shawnee
Eshelman, Enos Grant, Jr. *prosthodontist*

Topeka
Fyler, Carl John *dentist*

Wellington
Willis, Robert Addison *dentist*

KENTUCKY

Lexington
Wesley, Robert Cook *dental educator*

Louisville
Crim, Gary Allen *dental educator*
Gist, William Claude, Jr. *dentist*
Parkins, Frederick Milton *dental educator, university dean*
Stewart, Arthur Van *dental educator, geriatric health administrator*

LOUISIANA

Shreveport
Lloyd, Cecil Rhodes *pediatric dentist*

MARYLAND

Baltimore
McCauley, H(enry) Berton *retired public health dentist*
Spitznagel, John Keith *periodontist, researcher*

Bethesda
Kruger, Gustav Otto, Jr. *oral surgeon, educator*

Columbia
Rovelstad, Gordon H. *dentist, researcher*

Gaithersburg
Frome, David Herman *dentist*

Potomac
Cotton, William Robert *retired dentist*

MASSACHUSETTS

Boston
Frankl, Spencer Nelson *dentist, university dean*
†Friedman, Paula K. *dentist, dental school administrator*
Goldhaber, Paul *dental educator*
Shklar, Gerald *oral pathologist, periodontist, educator*
White, George Edward *pedodontist, educator*

Bridgewater
Hodge-Spencer, Cheryl Ann *orthodontist*

Dorchester
Lee, June Warren *dentist*

Hanover
Lonborg, James Reynold *dentist, former professional baseball player*

Medfield
Hein, John William *dentist, educator*

North Quincy
Segelman, Allyn Evan *dentist, researcher, insurance executive*

MICHIGAN

Ann Arbor
Asgar, Kamal *dentistry educator, consultant*
Ash, Major McKinley, Jr. *dentist, educator*
Christiansen, Richard Louis *orthodontics educator, research director, former dean*
Craig, Robert George *dental science educator*
Reese, James W. *orthodontist*

Dearborn
Sarkisian, Edward Gregory *dentist*

Grand Rapids
Bander, Thomas Samuel *dentist*

Midland
Thompson, Seth Charles *retired oral and maxillofacial surgeon*

Warren
Woehrlen, Arthur Edward, Jr. *dentist*

MINNESOTA

Alexandria
Monahan, Edward Joseph, III *orthodontist*

Byron
Nolting, Frederick William *dentist*

Duluth
Kramer, Alex John *dentist*

Kenyon
Jacobson, Lloyd Eldred *retired dentist*

Mankato
Dumke, Melvin Philip *dentist*
Johnson, William W. *dental educator*

Minneapolis
Shapiro, Burton Leonard *oral pathologist, geneticist, educator*
Wolff, Larry F. *dental educator, researcher*

Saint Louis Park
Weisman, Herbert Neal *dentist, financial planner*

Saint Paul
Jensen, James Robert *dentist, educator*

MISSISSIPPI

Keesler AFB
Linehan, Allan Douglas *prosthodontist*

MISSOURI

Chesterfield
Biebel, Curt Fred, Jr. *dentist*
Selfridge, George Dever *retired dentist, retired naval officer*

Kansas City
†Johnson, Gregory Kent *dentist, educator*
Moore, Dorsey Jerome *dentistry educator, maxillofacial prosthetist*
Scott, Ruth Lois *dental hygiene educator*

Mexico
Rice, Marvin Elwood *dentist*

Saint Louis
Manne, Marshall Stanley *periodontist*
Osborn, Mark Eliot *dentist*
Schmidt, Gunter *dentist*

MONTANA

Hardin
MacClean, Walter Lee *dentist*

NEBRASKA

Fremont
Roesch, Robert Eugene *dentist*

Lincoln
Chisholm, George Nickolaus *dentist*

Omaha
Lynch, Benjamin Leo *oral surgeon educator*
Zaiman, K(oichi) Robert *dentist*

NEW JERSEY

Denville
†Chung, Robert *dentist, educator*

Edison
Wallerstein, Seth Michael *dentist*

Englewood
Schwartz, Howard Alan *periodontist*

Fort Lee
Kiriakopoulos, George Constantine *dentist*

Hackettstown
Brock, David Lawrence *periodontist*
Wiedemann, Charles Louis *dentist*

Hammonton
Stephanick, Carol Ann *dentist, consultant*

Ho Ho Kus
Van Slooten, Ronald Henry Joseph *dentist*

Kearny
Perricci, Jeffrey Michael *dentist*

Lakewood
Brod, Morton Shlevin *oral surgeon*

Leonia
Armstrong, Edward Bradford, Jr. *oral and maxillofacial surgeon, educator*

Marmora
Ingaglio, Diego Augustus *dentist*

Montclair
Bolden, Theodore Edward *denist, educator, dental research consultant*

Newark
Kantor, Mel Lewis *dental educator, researcher*

Ridgewood
Lucca, John James *retired dental educator*
Picozzi, Anthony *dentist*

Rochelle Park
Dadurian, Medina Diana *pediatric dentist, educator*

Sparta
Alberto, Pamela Louise *oral and maxillofacial surgeon, educator*

Westfield
Feret, Adam Edward, Jr. *dentist*

Woodbridge
Galkin, Samuel Bernard *orthodontist*

NEW MEXICO

Farmington
Graham, Warren Kirkland *dentist*

NEW YORK

Albany
Sbuttoni, Michael James *orthodontist, building contractor*

Beacon
†Rosenfeld, Stephen S. *dentist*

Bronx
Friedman, Joel Matthew *oral and maxillofacial surgeon, educator*

Brooklyn
Cranin, Abraham Norman *oral and maxillofacial surgeon, researcher, implantologist*

Buffalo
Ciancio, Sebastian Gene *periodontist, educator*
Drinnan, Alan John *oral pathologist*
Gogan, Catherine Mary *dental educator*

Camillus
Caryl, William R., Jr. *orthodontist*

Flushing
†Parise, Frank Benjamin *dentist*
Weiss, George Arthur *orthodontist*

Grand Island
Hennigar, William Grant, Jr. *dentist*

Locust Valley
Zambito, Raymond Francis *oral surgeon, educator*

Massena
Pellegrino, James Martin *dentist*

Nanuet
Andreen, Aviva Louise *dentist, researcher, academic administrator, educator*

New York
Arvystas, Michael Geciauskas *orthodontist, educator*
Ashkinazy, Larry Robert *dentist*
Brzustowicz, Stanislaw Henry *clinical dentistry educator*
Denmark, Stanley Jay *orthodontist*
Di Salvo, Nicholas Armand *dental educator, orthodontist*
Kaslick, Ralph Sidney *dentist, educator*
†Kimura, Hiroshi *periodontist*
Klatell, Jack *dentist*
Kulik, Lewis Tashrak *dentist*
Mandel, Irwin Daniel *dentist*
Marder, Michael Zachary *dentist, researcher, educator*
Mulvihill, James Edward *periodontist*
†Rapp, Henry Conrad, III *dentist*
Scarola, John Michael *dentist, educator*
Sendax, Victor Irven *dentist, educator, dental implant researcher*

Poughkeepsie
†Welker, William D. *dentist*

Rochester
Billings, Ronald J. *dental research administrator*
Bowen, William Henry *dental researcher, dental educator*

Rockville Centre
Epel, Lidia Marmurek *dentist*

Rye
Hopf, Frank Rudolph *dentist*

Shelter Island
†Moran, Daniel Thomas *dentist*

Sleepy Hollow
Zegarelli, Edward Victor *retired dental educator, researcher*

Smithtown
Goldstein, Leonard Barry *dentist, educator*

Stony Brook
Sreebny, Leo M. *oral biology and pathology educator*

Wantagh
Ross, Sheldon Jules *dentist*

Wappingers Falls
Engelman, Melvin Alkon *retired dentist, business executive, scientist*

West Hempstead
Tartell, Robert Morris *retired dentist*

Woodbury
Kitzis, Gary David *periodontist, educator*

Yonkers
Torrese, Dante Michael *prosthodontist, educator*

NORTH CAROLINA

Asheville
Scully, John Robert *oral and maxillofacial surgeon*

Chapel Hill
Arnold, Roland R. *dental educator and researcher*
Baker, Ronald Dale *dental educator, surgeon, university administrator*
Barker, Ben Dale *dentist, educator*
Bawden, James Wyatt *dental educator, dental scientist*
Hershey, H(oward) Garland, Jr. *university administrator, orthodontist*
Proffit, William Robert *orthodontics educator*
Stamm, John William Rudolph *dentist, educator, academic dean*
White, Raymond Petrie, Jr. *dentist, educator*

Charlotte
Misiek, Dale Joseph *oral and maxillofacial surgeon*
Owen, Kenneth Dale *orthodontist, real estate broker*
Twisdale, Harold Winfred *dentist*

NORTH DAKOTA

Williston
Bekkedahl, Brad Douglas *dentist*

OHIO

Cincinnati
MacKnight, David Laurence *dentist*
Steinbrunner, Sally Oyler *dental consultant, hygienist*

Cleveland
De Marco, Thomas Joseph *periodontist, educator*
Robertson, Edward Neil *dentist*

Columbus
Austin, David George *dentist*
Horton, John Edward *periodontist, educator*
Jolly, Daniel Ehs *dental educator*
Patrick, George Milton *dentist*
Stevenson, Robert Benjamin, III *prosthodontist, writer*
Vermilyea, Stanley George *prosthodontist, educator*

Cuyahoga Falls
Barsan, Robert Blake *dentist*

Fairfield
Cutter, John Michael *dentist*

Hilliard
Relle, Attila Tibor *dentist, geriodontist*

Lancaster
Burns, Glenn Richard *dentist*

Milford
Creath, Curtis Janssen *pediatric dentist*

North Royalton
Iacobelli, Mark Anthony *dentist*

Rocky River
Montgomery, Gary *dentist*

Solon
†Layman, Martin W. *dentist*

Toledo
Kastner, Michael James *dentist*

Uniontown
Naugle, Robert Paul *dentist*

Willoughby
Stern, Michael David *dentist*

OKLAHOMA

Durant
Craige, Danny Dwaine *dentist*

Edmond
Brown, William Ernest *dentist*

Oklahoma City
Shillingburg, Herbert Thompson, Jr. *dental educator*

OREGON

Portland
Clarke, J(oseph) Henry *dental educator, dentist*

PENNSYLVANIA

Clarion
Foreman, Thomas Alexander *dentist*

Danville
Kleponis, Jerome Albert *dentist*
Lessin, Michael Edward *oral-maxillofacial surgeon*

Harrisburg
Prioleau, Sara Nelliene *dentist*

Lansdale
Strohecker, Leon Harry, Jr. *orthodontist*

Mount Pleasant
Juriga, Raymond Michael *dentist*

New Holland
Amor, James Michael *dentist, actor*

Norristown
Steinberg, Arthur Irwin *periodontist, educator*

Philadelphia
Breitman, Joseph B. *prosthodonist, dental educator*
Fielding, Allen Fred *oral and maxillofacial surgeon, educator*
Fonseca, Raymond J. *dental medicine educator*
Listgarten, Max Albert *periodontics educator*
Winkler, Sheldon *dentist, educator*

Pittsburgh
Ismail, Yahia Hassan *dentist, educator*
Laurenzano, Robert Salvatore *dentist*
Miller, Charles Jay *dentist*
Stiff, Robert Henry *dentist, educator*

Radnor
Vanarsdall, Robert Lee, Jr. *orthodontist, educator*

Wayne
Guernsey, Louis Harold *retired oral and maxillofacial surgeon, educator*

SOUTH CAROLINA

Charleston
Johnson, Dewey E(dward), Jr. *dentist*
Salinas, Carlos Francisco *dentist, educator*

Columbia
Witherspoon, Walter Pennington, Jr. *orthodontist, philanthropist*

Greenville
Mitchell, William Avery, Jr. *orthodontist*

Lake City
TruLuck, James Paul, Jr. *dentist, vintner*

Manning
DuBose, James Daulton *dentist*

TENNESSEE

Knoxville
Gotcher, Jack Everett, Jr. *oral and maxillofacial surgeon*

Memphis
Butts, Herbert Clell *dentist, educator*
Harris, Edward Frederick *orthodontics educator*
Jurand, Jerry George *periodontology educator, researcher*
McCullar, Bruce Hayden *oral and maxillofacial surgeon*

Millington
Reed, Erbie Loyd *dentist*

Nashville
Medwedeff, Fred M(arshall) *dentist*

TEXAS

Dallas
Al-Hashimi, Ibtisam *oral scientist, educator*
DeSpain, Becky Ann *dental educator*

Flower Mound
Kolodny, Stanley Charles *oral surgeon, air force officer*

Houston
Allen, Don Lee *dentistry educator*
Burroughs, Jack Eugene *dentist, management consultant*
Heath, Frank Bradford *dentist*
Sweet, James Brooks *oral and maxillofacial surgeon*

Missouri City
Chang, Jeffrey Chai *dentist, educator, researcher*

Plainview
†Crawford, Felix Conkling *dentist*

Plano
Findley, John Sidney *dentist*
Taylor, Paul Peak *pediatric dentist, educator*

Salado
Willingham, Douglas Barton *dentist*

San Antonio
Palmer, Hubert Bernard *dentist, retired military officer*
Parker, Warren Andrew *public health dentist, consultant*
Pigno, Mark Anthony *prosthodontist, educator, researcher*

VERMONT

Essex Junction
Lampert, S. Henry *dentist*

Shelburne
Sawabini, Wadi Issa *retired dentist*

VIRGINIA

Pearisburg
Morse, F. D., Jr. *dentist*

Portsmouth
Cox, William Walter *dentist*

Richmond
Laskin, Daniel M. *oral and maxillofacial surgeon, educator*

Virginia Beach
Lowe, Cameron Anderson *dentist, endodontist, educator*
Zimmerman, Solomon *dentist, educator*

WASHINGTON

Everett
Oliver, William Donald *orthodontist*

Lynnwood
Woodruff, Scott William *cosmetic, reconstructive and maxillofacial surgeon*

Seattle
Dworkin, Samuel Franklin *dentist, psychologist*
Hall, Stanton Harris *dental educator, orthodontist*
Herring, Susan Weller *dental educator, oral anatomist*
Page, Roy Christopher *periodontist, scientist, educator*

Spokane
Foster, Ruth Mary *dental association administrator*
Steadman, Robert Kempton *oral and maxillofacial surgeon*

WISCONSIN

Beloit
Green, Harold Daniel *dentist*

Green Bay
Martens, Donald Mathias *orthodontist*
Swetlik, William Philip *orthodontist*

Madison
Wanek, Ronald Melvin *orthodontist*

Milwaukee
Bogdon, Glendon Joseph *orthodontist*

New Glarus
Sippy, David Dean *dentist*

Racine
Moles, Randall Carl *orthodontist*

Sikora, Suzanne Marie *dentist*

WYOMING

Casper
Keim, Michael Ray *dentist*

CANADA

BRITISH COLUMBIA

Vancouver
Beagrie, George Simpson *dentist, educator, dean emeritus*

ONTARIO

Markham
Ten Cate, Arnold Richard *dentistry educator*

QUEBEC

Montreal
Bentley, Kenneth Chessar *oral and maxillofacial surgeon, educator*

Sainte Foy
Maranda, Guy *oral maxillofacial surgeon, Canadian health facility executive, educator*

GERMANY

Witten
Gaengler, Peter Wolfgang *dentist, researcher*

NORWAY

Österås
Löe, Harald *retired dentist, educator, researcher*

SWEDEN

Göteborg
Bona, Christian M. *dentist, psychotherapist*

ADDRESS UNPUBLISHED

Bates, Richard Mather *dentist*
Brooke, Ralph Ian *dental educator*
Garnick, Jerry Jack *periodontist, educator*
Hammer, Wade Burke *retired oral and maxillofacial surgeon, educator*
Herman, David Jay *orthodontist*
Hoffman, Jerry Irwin *dental educator*
Jacobsen, Egill Lars *dentist, educator*
Jochum, Lester H. *dentist*
Kessler, Pete William *dentist*
Lambert, Joseph Parker *dentist*
Lippert, Christopher Nelson *dentist, consultant*
Makins, James Edward *retired dentist, dental educator, educational administrator*
McClelland, Richard Lee *dentist*
Mele, Joanne Theresa *dentist*
Nabers, Claude Lowrey *retired periodontist, writer*
Newbrun, Ernest *oral biology and periodontology educator*
Park, Jon Keith *dentist, educator*
Reid, David Earl *dentist, military officer*
Slade, Larry W. *small business owner*
Slaughter, Freeman Cluff *retired dentist*
Torok, John Anthony, III *dentist, financial analyst, portfolio manager*

HEALTHCARE: HEALTH SERVICES

UNITED STATES

ALABAMA

Auburn
Barker, Kenneth Neil *pharmacy administration educator*
†Tullier, Michael Joseph *nonprofit blood center administrator*

Birmingham
Bennett, James Patrick *healthcare executive*
Booth, Rachel Zonelle *nursing educator*
Booth, Wendy Christina *nursing educator*
Cooper, Karen René *health facility administration nurse*
Devane, Denis James *health care company executive*
Hammond, C(larke) Randolph *healthcare executive*
Holmes, Suzanne McRae *nursing supervisor*
Jones, Moniaree Parker *occupational health nurse*
Miller, Dennis Edward *health medical executive*
Perry, Helen *home care nurse, educator*
Quintana, José Booth *health care executive*
Richards, J. Scott *rehabilitation medicine professional*
Roth, William Stanley *hospital foundation executive*
Smith, Steve Allen *nursing administrator*
Stephens, Deborah Lynn *health facility executive*
Todsen, Dana Rognar *health care executive*
Weinsier, Roland Louis *nutrition educator and director*

Cusseta
Striblin, Lori Ann *critical care nurse, Medicare coordinator, nursing educator*

Daphne
Bennett, Anne Marie *nursing administrator*

Dauphin Island
Levenson, Maria Nijole *retired medical technologist*

Dothan
Jackson, Alisa Simmons *geriatrics nurse, administrator*

Evergreen
†Castleberry, Carolyn P. *mental health therapist and counselor*

Fairfield
Lloyd, Barbara Ann *nurse, educator*

Florence
Davis, Ernestine Bady *nurse educator, administrator*
Kyzar, Patricia Parks *maternity nurse*

Gadsden
Lefelhocz, Irene Hanzak *nurse, business owner*

Gallant
Lively, Brenda Mae R. *women's health nurse*

Huntsville
Loux, Jean McCluskey *housewife, registered nurse*
Noble, Ronald Mark *sports medicine facility administrator*

Mobile
Clark, Jack *retired hospital company executive, accountant*
Stevens, Gail Lavine *community health nurse, educator*

Montgomery
Farrell, Robert Joel, II *counselor, education therapist, educator, minister*
Myers, Ira Lee *physician*
Rowan, John Robert *retired medical center director*
Ternus, Mona Pearl *critical care nurse, flight nurse, educator*

New Brockton
Taylor, William Michael *medical/surgical and critical care nurse*

Ozark
DuBose, Elizabeth (Bettye DuBose) *community health nurse*

Pelham
Ferris, Michelle L. *women's health nurse*
Lee, James A. *health facility finance executive*

Sylacauga
Bledsoe, Mary Louise *medical, surgical nurse*
Dye, Elaine Gibson *home health nurse*

Theodore
Hollis, Julia Ann Roshto *critical care and medical/ surgical nurse*

Troy
Adcock, Anthony Green *health education educator*

Tuscaloosa
Neathery, Patricia Astleford *retired nutritionist, consultant*
Prigmore, Charles Samuel *social work educator*
Wyatt, Michael Thomas *healthcare quality analyst*

ALASKA

Anchorage
Devens, John Searle *natural resources administrator*
Gillette, Muriel Delphine *nurse*
Harris, Jan Caplan *health care administrator*
Madsen, Linda Ann *pediatrics nurse*
Meddleton, Daniel Joseph *health facility administrator*
Teague, Bruce Williams *chiropractor*

Bethel
Selby, Naomi Ardean *women's health nurse, medical/surgical nurse*

Fairbanks
Blake, Robert Philip *human services administrator, music therapist*
Brody, Bonnie *clinical social worker*

Homer
Scruggs, Mary Ann *women's health nurse*

Juneau
Johnson, Mark Steven *public health administrator*

Sitka
Carlson, Susan Spevack *medical director, family physician*

ARIZONA

Apache Junction
Winslow, Lillian Ruth *nurse*

Casa Grande
Hutchison, Pat *nurse, administrator*
McGillicuddy, Joan Marie *psychotherapist, consultant*

Chandler
Graham, Anita Louise *correctional and community health nurse*
Shousha, Annette Gentry *retired critical care nurse*

Cottonwood
Peck, Donald Harvey *chiropractor*

Flagstaff
Wetzel, Wendy Sue *women's health nurse practitioner, holistic health nurse*

Fredonia
Pickett-Trudell, Catherine *family therapist*

Gilbert
Bourne, Elfreda O. *community health nurse*
Conger-White, Christine Kathleen *utilization management coordinator*

Glendale
Cassidy, Barry Allen *physician assistant, clinical medical ethicist*

Green Valley
Johnson, Onalee H. *retired nursing educator*

Hereford
Schenk, Quentin Frederick *retired social work educator, mayor, psychologist*

Mesa
Boyd, Leona Potter *retired social worker*
Evans, Don A. *healthcare company executive*
†Fleisher, Mark *health care executive*
Klosowski-Gorombei, Deborah Ann *nursing administrator, flight nurse*

Morenci
Subia, Eva M. *medical/surgical and community health nurse*

Paradise Valley
McKinley, Joseph Warner *health science facility executive*

Payson
Lasys, Joan *medical nurse, writer, educator, publisher*

Phoenix
Chan, Michael Chiu-Hon *chiropractor*
Dillenberg, Jack *public health officer*
Fitzgerald-Verbonitz, Dianne Elizabeth *nursing educator*
Henely, Geraldine Josephine *medical/surgical nurse*
Lang, Patricia Ann *school nurse*
Manning-Weber, Claudia Joy *medical radiography administrator, consultant*
Mertes, Sharon Colleen *women's health nurse*
Mitchell, Wayne Lee *health care administrator*
Piatt, Malcolm Keith, Jr. *medical center administrator*
Seiler, Steven Lawrence *health facility administrator*
Sullivan, Mary Kathleen *nurse*
Van Kilsdonk, Cecelia Ann *retired nursing administrator, volunteer*
Welliver, Charles Harold *hospital administrator*
Williams, Arleen Rolling *pediatrics nurse*

Pima
Shafer, James Albert *health care administrator*

Prescott
Goodman, Gwendolyn Ann *nursing educator*
Mc Cormack, Fred Allen *state social services administrator*
Rindone, Joseph Patrick *clinical pharmacist, educator*

Rio Verde
Ramsey, David Selmer *retired hospital executive*

Scottsdale
Eide, Imogene Garnett *nursing consultant*
Kane-Villela, Grace McNelly *maternal, women's health and pediatrics nurse*
Meyers, Marlene O. *hospital administrator*
Troxell, Mary Theresa (Terry Troxell) *geriatrics services professional*

Sedona
Catterton, Marianne Rose *occupational therapist*

Sierra Vista
Cowger, Phyllis *nurse*

Sun City West
Mc Donald, Barbara Ann *psychotherapist*

Surprise
Shipley, Linda Diane Stuff *gerontology and medical/ surgical nurse*

Tempe
Lange, Lynette Patricia *nurse*
Mason, Terence K. *critical care nurse*
Missimer, Denise Louise *mental health nurse*
Wesbury, Stuart Arnold, Jr. *health administration and policy educator*

Thatcher
Heaton, Debbie Ann *mental health services worker*

Tucson
Andersen, Luba *electrologist, electropigmentologist*
Bennett, Pamela Yvonne *diabetes resource nurse, pediatrics nurse*
Brewer, Barbara Bagdasarian *nursing administrator*
Bryning, Susan Mary *critical care nurse, adult nurse practitioner*
Horan, Mary Ann Theresa *nurse*
Huggins, Delma Bustamante *community nurse, family nurse practitioner*
Kany, Judy C(asperson) *health policy analyst, former state senator*
Kerr, Frederick Hohmann *health care company executive*
Kmet, Rebecca Eugenia Patterson *pharmacist*
Lyman, Darlice Murphy *critical care nurse*
Magnotto, Rebecca Adiutori *community and mental health nurse*
McAllister, Patricia L. *nurse*
McCabe, Monica Jane *oncological nurse*
McCanless, Lauri Lynn *neonatal and pediatrics nurse*
Nation, James Edward *retired speech pathologist*
Rhoads, Preston Mark *pharmacist, consultant*

Shropshire, Donald Gray *hospital executive*
Tang, Esther Don *development consultant, retired social worker*
Vidal, Delia *medical/surgical and oncological nurse*
Weber, Charles Walter *nutrition educator*
Wilson, Teresa Ann *maternal/newborn nurse*

Winslow
Wolfe, Janice Kay *oncological nurse*

ARKANSAS

Enola
Brown, Lois Heffington *health facility administrator*

Forrest City
Creasey, Katherine Yvonne *family nurse practitioner*

Fort Smith
Banks, David Russell *health care executive*
Decker, Josephine I. *health clinic official*

Hot Springs National Park
Farley, Roy C. *rehabilitation researcher, educator*
McDaniel, Ola Jo Peterson *social worker, educator*

Little Rock
Hueter, Diana T. *health facility executive*
Mitchell, Jo Kathryn *hospital technical supervisor*
Nichols, Sandra B. *public health service officer*
Pierson, Richard Allen *hospital administrator*
Staggs, Michelle Denise *flight nurse*

Lonoke
Adams, Mary Raprich *retired nursing education administrator*

Magazine
Fleck, Mariann Bernice *health scientist*

Melbourne
Rosa, Idavonne Taylor *community health nurse*

Mt Ida
Harmon, Kay Madelon *occupational therapist*

North Little Rock
Funk, Dorothea *public health nurse*
Wilson, LaVerne *nurse, administrator*

Paris
Hawkins, Naomi Ruth *nurse*

Springdale
Phillips, Linda Lou *pharmacist*

State University
Rutherford, Mary Jean *laboratory administrator, science educator*

CALIFORNIA

Agoura Hills
Merchant, Roland Samuel, Sr. *hospital administrator, educator*

Alameda
Herrick, Sylvia Anne *health service administrator*

Alhambra
Obert, Jessie Craig *nutritionist, consultant*

Aliso Viejo
Boccia, Judy Elaine *home health agency executive, consultant*
Buncher, James Edward *healthcare management executive*

Altadena
Branin, Joan Julia *health services management educator*

Arcadia
Anderson, Holly Geis *women's health facility administrator, commentator, educator*
Razor, Beatrice Ramirez (Betty Razor) *enterostomal therapy nurse, educator, consultant*

Arcata
Janssen-Pellatz, Eunice Charlene *healthcare facility administrator*

Artesia
†Choo, Michael Owen *executive, consultant*

Atascadero
Lamore, Bette *rehabilitation counselor, motivational speaker*

Auburn
Leonard, Angeline Jane *psychotherapist*

Azusa
Smith, Beverly *nursing educator*

Bakersfield
Amerine, Wendy L. *community health and gerontology nurse*
McMillan, Leonard David *family life specialist, consultant, lecturer*
Murillo, Velda Jean *social worker, counselor*
Watkins, Judith Ann *nurse administrator*
Wong, Wayne D. *nutritionist*

Berkeley
Calloway, Doris Howes *nutrition educator*
Carpenter, Kenneth John *nutrition educator*
Cohn, Theodore Elliot *optometry educator, vision scientist*
Day, Lucille Lang *health facility administrator, educator, author*
Enoch, Jay Martin *vision scientist, educator*
Friedman, Mendel *hospital administration executive*
Gilbert, Neil Robin *social work educator, author, consultant*

Hafey, Joseph Michael *health association executive*
†Haggstrom, Jane *mental health nursing educator, administrator*
Harris, Michael Gene *optometrist, educator, lawyer*
Hill, Lorie Elizabeth *psychotherapist*
Lashof, Joyce Cohen *public health educator*
Margen, Sheldon *public health educator, nutritionist emeritus*
Westheimer, Gerald *optometrist, educator*

Beverly Hills
†Priselac, Thomas M. *health facility administrator*

Brea
Pierpoint, Karen Ann *marriage, family and child therapist*
Ramsey, Nancy Lockwood *nursing educator*
Schlose, William Timothy *health care executive*

Burbank
Hartshorn, Terry O. *health facility administrator*

Camarillo
Rieger, Elaine June *nursing administrator*

Camp Pendleton
Branson-Berry, Karen Marie *nurse*

Capitola
Sprenkel, Joanne Noce *employee health nurse*

Carlsbad
Hrenoff, Natalia Olympiada *nurse*

Carmel
Elmstrom, George P. *optometrist, writer*

Carson
Chan, Peter Wing Kwong *pharmacist*

Castro Valley
Bennett, Shoshana Stein *post partum counselor, consultant, lecturer*

Cedar Ridge
Bruno, Judyth Ann *chiropractor*

Chatsworth
Stephenson, Irene Hamlen *biorhythm analyst, consultant, editor, educator*

Chico
Etz, (Helen) Jane *hospital utilization*
Ward, Chester Lawrence *physician, retired county health official, retired military officer*

Citrus Heights
Barth, Sharon Lynn *nurse*

Claremont
Hartford, Margaret Elizabeth (Betty Hartford) *social work educator, gerontologist, writer*
Martin, Jay Herbert *psychoanalysis and English educator*

Cloverdale
Neuharth, Daniel J., II *psychotherapist*

Concord
Koffler, Herbert *health plan administrator, educator*

Costa Mesa
Klein, (Mary) Eleanor *retired clinical social worker*

Culver City
Davidson, Valerie LaVergne *institute administrator*
Stoughton, W. Vickery *healthcare executive*

Daly City
Reuss von Plauen, Prince-Archbishop Heinrich XXVI *Metropolitan, nursing, legal consultant, psychologist, educator*

Davis
Fowler, William Mayo, Jr. *rehabilitation medicine physician*
King, Janet Carlson *nutrition educator, researcher*
Lewis, Jonathan *health care association administrator*
Schneeman, Barbara Olds *nutritionist*
Stern, Judith S. *nutritional researcher, educator*
Turnlund, Judith Rae *nutrition scientist*
Von Behren, Ruth Lechner *adult day health care specialist, retired*

Downey
Hart-Duling, Jean Macaulay *clinical social worker*
Rose, Susan M. *rehabilitation nurse*

Duarte
Sollenberger, Donna Kay Fitzpatrick *hospital and clinics executive*

El Cajon
Brown, Marilynne Joyce *emergency nurse*

El Cerrito
Cooper, William Clark *physician*
Schilling, Janet Naomi *nutritionist, consultant*

El Monte
Glass, Jean Ann *special education services professional*

Emeryville
Finney, Lee *negotiator, social worker*
Greene, Albert Lawrence *hospital administrator*
Lewis, Martha Nell *expressive arts therapist, massage therapist, instructor*

Encino
Bekey, Shirley White *psychotherapist*
House-Hendrick, Karen Sue *nursing consultant*
Vogel, Susan Carol *nursing administrator*

Escondido
Gentile, Robert Dale *optometrist, consultant*
Rich, Elizabeth Marie *nursing educator*

Santa Rosa
Cornett, Donna J. *counselor, alcohol moderation administrator*
Lewis, Marion Elizabeth *social worker*
Nickens, Catherine Arlene *retired nurse, freelance writer*
Pearson, Susan Rose *psychotherapist, fine arts educator, artist*
Provost, Rhonda Marie *nurse anesthetist*

Santa Ynez
Walker, Burton Leith *psychotherapist, engineering writer*

Santee
Schenk, Susan Kirkpatrick *geriatric psychiatry nurse, educator, consultant, business owner*

Saratoga
Heaney, Dorothy Phelps *nurse, nursing administrator*

Sausalito
Groah, Linda Kay *nursing administrator, educator*
Seymour, Richard Burt *health educator*

Seal Beach
Stillwell, Kathleen Ann Swanger *healthcare consultant*

Sepulveda
Burton, Paul Floyd *social worker*

Sherman Oaks
Peplau, Hildegard Elizabeth *nursing educator*
Silberman, Irwin Alan *retired public health physician*

Sonoma
Markey, William Alan *health care administrator*

Stanford
Basch, Paul Frederick *international health educator, parasitologist*
Mc Namara, Joseph Donald *researcher, retired police chief, novelist*

Studio City
Herrman, Marcia Kutz *child development specialist*

Sunnyvale
Gordon, Marc Stewart *pharmacist, scientist*

Tarzana
Evans, Colleen Marie *home health administrator*
Rinsch, Maryann Elizabeth *occupational therapist*

Thousand Oaks
Emerson, Alton Calvin *retired physical therapist*
Herman, Joan Elizabeth *healthcare company executive*
Schaeffer, Leonard David *healthcare executive*

Torrance
Harmon Brown, Valarie Jean *hospital laboratory director, information systems executive*
Hoagland, Albert Joseph, Jr. *psychotherapist, hypnotherapist, minister*
Medley, Nancy May *nurse*
Prell, Joel James *medical group administrator*

Trabuco Canyon
Jessup, R. Judd *health care executive*

Upland
Boswell, Dan Alan *health maintenance organization executive, health care consultant*

Vacaville
Dailey, Dawn Elaine *public health service official*

Van Nuys
Westbrook, G. Jay *hospice nurse, grief counselor*

Ventura
Bircher, Andrea Ursula *psychiatric-mental health nurse, educator, clinical nurse specialist*

Visalia
Madden, Wanda Lois *nurse*

Walnut Creek
Ausenbaum, Helen Evelyn *social worker, psychologist*
Williams, Michael James *health care services consultant*

West Covina
Adams, Sarah Virginia *family counselor*
Collins, Beverly Ann *obstetrical, gynecological nurse practitioner*
Franden, Blanche M. *nursing educator*

Westminster
Begg, Cynthia I. *health facility administrator*

Windsor
Gomez, Edward Casimiro *physician, educator, vintner*

Woodlake
Lippmann, Bruce Allan *rehabilitative services professional, educator*

Woodland
Butler, Patricia Lacky *mental health nurse, educator, consultant*
Stormont, Clyde Junior *laboratory company executive*

Woodland Hills
†Funari, Robert Glenn *health care services executive*
†Yates, Gary L. *marriage and family therapist*

Yountville
Helzer, James Dennis *hospital executive*
Jones, Thomas Robert *social worker*

COLORADO

Aurora
Brinkmeyer, Dotty Stewart *maternal/child nurse*
†Brown, Anne Sherwin *speech pathologist*
Gardner, Sandra Lee *nurse, outreach consultant*
Nora, Audrey Hart *physician*
Starr, Nancy Barber *pediatric nurse practitioner*
Vessels, Kevin Daryl *mental health clinician, inventor*

Boulder
Copeland, Poppy Carlson *psychotherapist*
Kelley, Bruce Dutton *pharmacist*
Middleton-Downing, Laura *psychiatric social worker, artist, small business owner*
Sedei Rodden, Pamela Jean *therapist*

Broomfield
Lybarger, Marjorie Kathryn *nurse*
Von Star, Brenda Lee *primary care family nurse practitioner*

Buena Vista
Herb, Edmund Michael *optometrist, educator*

Canon City
Honaker, Charles Ray *health facility administrator*
Romano, Rebecca Kay *counselor*
Trogden, Kathy Ann *nursing administrator*

Colorado Springs
Cameron, Paul Drummond *research facility administrator*
Driscoll, David Lee *chiropractor*
Lokken, Steven Lee *chiropractor, nutritionist*
Moltzan, Nicoline G. *nurse, administrator*
Moorhouse, Mary Frances *rehabilitation nurse*
Roach, Cynthia Whittig *nursing educator*
Trimble, Donna Denise *clinical therapist*
Vayhinger, John Monroe *psychotherapist, minister*

Cortez
Meredith, Richard Stephen *psycotherapist, educator*

Denver
Allen, Robert Edward, Jr. *physician assistant*
Arp, Elizabeth Kench *psychotherapist, social worker*
Barkman, Debra Rae *nephrology nurse*
†Biester, Doris J. *hospital executive*
Boylan, Michelle Marie Obie *medical surgical nurse, hospital administrator*
Burns, Alexandra Darrow (Sandra Burns) *health program administrator*
Edelman, Joel *medical center executive*
Hand, Dale L. *pharmacist*
Harvan, Robin Ann *health professions educator*
Jennett, Shirley Shimmick *home care management executive, nurse*
Jordan, Karin Balten-Babkowski *health facility administrator*
Judson, Franklyn Nevin *physician, educator*
King Calkins, Carol Coleman *health sciences administrator*
Kirkpatrick, Charles Harvey *physician, immunology researcher*
Kraizer, Sherryll A. *health services and interpersonal violence prevention educator*
Mastrini, Jane Reed *social worker, consultant*
McDonnell, Barbara *health facility administrator*
Miller, Jill Marie *psychoanalyst*
Parker, Catherine Susanne *psychotherapist*
Rael, Henry Sylvester *retired health administrator, financial and management consultant*
Rizzi, Teresa Marie *bilingual speech and language pathologist*
Schaubman, Averi Lyn *social worker*
Taussig, Lynn Max *healthcare administrator, pulmonologist, pediatrician, educator*
Warren, Loretta A. Carlson *nursing consultant*
Witt, Catherine Lewis *neonatal nurse practitioner, writer*

Durango
Stetina, Pamela Eleanor *nursing educator*

Florissant
McCaslin, Kathleen Denise *child abuse educator*

Fort Collins
Daniel, Janis Sue *women's health nurse*
Gubler, Duane J. *research scientist, administrator*
Hu, Edna Gertrude Fenske *pediatrics nurse*
Smith, Nina Maria *mental health nurse, administrator, consultant*
Thies, Margaret Diane *nurse*

Glenwood Springs
Reinisch, Nancy Rae *therapist, consultant*

Golden
Leonard, Mary Jo *occupational health nurse*
Napier, Anne Hess *psychotherapist, mental health nurse*

Grand Junction
Pantenburg, Michel *hospital administrator, health educator, holistic health coordinator*

Greeley
Engle, Cindy *medical transcriptionist*
Hart, Milford E. *psychotherapist, counselor*
Linde, Lucille Mae (Jacobson) *motor-perceptual specialist*
Ross, Rosann Mary *psychotherapist, educator*

Idledale
Brown, Gerri Ann *physical therapist*

Lakewood
Babel, Deborah Jean *social worker, paralegal*
Cambio, Irma Darlene *nursing consultant*

Littleton
Benkert, Mary Russell *pediatrics nurse, researcher*
Hammerschmidt, Marilyn Kay *health services administrator*
Miller, Betty Sue *counselor*
Panasci, Nancy Ervin *speech pathologist, cookbook writer, communications consultant*

Longmont
Jones, Beverly Ann Miller *nursing administrator, retired patient services administrator*
Ralston, Paula Jane *nurse*
Walker, Kathleen Mae *health facility administrator*

Louisville
Shively, Merrick Lee *pharmaceutical scientist, consultant*

Parker
Lembeck, James Peter *nutritionist, writer, consultant*

Pueblo
Avery, Julia May *speech pathologist, organizational volunteer*
Hawkins, Robert Lee *health facility administrator*

Swink
Rockwell, Virginia Considine *school counselor*

Thornton
Hendren, Debra Mae *critical care nurse*

Wheat Ridge
LaMendola, Walter Franklin *human services, information technology consultant*

CONNECTICUT

Ansonia
Rubin, Larry Jeffrey *occupational rehabilitation professional*

Bridgeport
Lymm, Peter Jay *hospital administrator*
Trefry, Robert J. *healthcare administrator*

Bristol
Hickingbotham, Nancy Bennett *nursing case manager*

Central Village
Wilson, Aurele Paula *mental health nurse*

Cheshire
Pettine, Linda Faye *physical therapist*

Clinton
Harris, Doris Ann *nurse*

Cromwell
Darius, Franklin Alexander, Jr. (Chip Darius) *health administrator, educator, consultant*

Danbury
Burns, Jacqueline Mary *laboratory administrator*
Pankulis, Pauline Johnson *nursing administrator, geriatrics nurse*

Durham
Russell, Thomas James *critical care supervisor*

East Hartford
Dutka, Linda Semrow *psychiatric and addictions nurse*
Pudlo, Virginia Mary *medical surgical nurse*

Fairfield
Mead, Philomena *mental health nurse*

Farmington
Miller, Crystal C. *intravenous therapy nurse*

Glastonbury
Hamlin, Kathryn F. *geriatrics nurse, administrator*
Schneiderman, Joan Ellen *psychotherapist*

Greenwich
Cretan, Donna *neonatal nurse, lactation consultant*
Gagnon, John Harvey *psychotherapist, educator*
Harrison, Therese Wyka *school nurse*
Krauser, Robert Stanley *health care executive*
Langley, Patricia Coffroth *psychiatric social worker*
Smith, Lisa Ann Peter *nursing administrator*

Groton
Girotti, Robert Bernard *medical and surgical nurse*

Guilford
Eustice, David C. *pharmaceutical researcher*
Hayes, Michael Ernest *psychotherapist, educator*
Rotnem, Diane Louise *clinical social worker, educator, researcher*

Hartford
Bruner, Robert B. *hospital consultant*
Gillmor, Rogene Godding *medical technologist*
Hamilton, Thomas Stewart *physician, hospital administrator*
†Hugg, Geraldine Bertha *retired gerontology specialist, journalist*
Young, Sara Ann *women's health nurse*

Higganum
Twachtman-Cullen, Diane *communication disorders and autism specialist*

Lebanon
Ajemian, Cheryl Bloom *audit consultant*

Madison
Passero, Virginia Ann *retired nursing educator*

Meriden
Molder, Sybil Ailene *occupational health nurse*
Mule, Donna Kemish *human services coordinator*
Pepe, Richard Kane *nurse anesthetist*
Smits, Helen Lida *physician, administrator, educator*

Milford
Antosz, Candace Elizabeth *health promotion educator*
Muth, Eric Peter *ophthalmic optician*

Monroe
Roberge, Cecelia Ament *nursing administrator, rehabilitation nurse*

Moodus
Steinkamp, Dorothy DeMauro *nursing educator*

New Haven
Benfer, David William *hospital administrator*
Cadman, Edwin Clarence *health facility administrator, medical educator*
Cofrancesco, Donald George *health facility administrator*
Condon, Thomas Brian *hospital executive*
Diers, Donna Kaye *nurse educator*
Griffith, Ezra Edward Holman *health facility administrator, educator*
Jekel, James Franklin *physician, public health educator*
Krauss, Judith Belliveau *nursing educator*
Lyder, Courtney *nursing educator, consultant*
McCorkle, Ruth *oncological nurse, educator*
Pāquin, Trudy *gerontological nurse*
Parker, Vineta *social worker*
Reyes, Marcia Stygles *medical technologist*
Vicenzi, Angela Elizabeth *nursing researcher*
Williams, Ena Mae *registered nurse, nursing educator, consultant*
†Zarrangnino, Joseph *hospital executive*

New Milford
DaCunha, Susan Elizabeth *school nurse*

North Branford
Landino, Daniel *speech pathologist*
Womer, Charles Berry *retired hospital executive, management consultant*

North Haven
Hogan, James Carroll, Jr. *public health administrator, research biologist*

Norwalk
Baez, Manuel *health care executive*
Potluri, Venkateswara Rao *medical facility administrator*

Norwich
Houchin, John Frederick, Sr. *human services administrator*

Old Greenwich
Nelson, Norma Randy deKadt *psychotherapist, consultant*

Orange
Douskey, Theresa Kathryn *health facility administrator*

Riverside
Otto, Charles Edward *health care administrator*

Rocky Hill
Hoffman, Penny Joan *adult nurse practitioner, administrator*

Simsbury
Long, Ann Marie *health facility administrator*

Southbury
Wilson, Carolyn Elizabeth *nursing administrator*

Southington
Kassey, Jacquelyn Marie Bonafonte *pediatrics nurse*

Stamford
Haber, Judith Ellen *nursing educator*
Schechter, Audrey *medical, surgical nurse*

Storrs Mansfield
Chinn, Peggy Lois *nursing educator, editor*
Jensen, Helene Wickstrom *retired nutritionist, educator*
Perez-Escamilla, Rafael *nutritionist*

Suffield
Bianchi, Maria *critical care specialist, adult nurse practitioner, acute care nurse practitioner*

Vernon Rockville
Polifroni, Elizabeth Carol *nurse, educator*

Wallingford
Spero, Barry Melvin *medical center executive*

Waterbury
Fischbein, Charles Alan *pediatrician*
Holub, Barbara Ann *rehabilitation nurse*
Oliver, Eugene Alex *speech and language pathologist*
Zasada, Mary Eileen *nursing project leader*

West Hartford
†Ivey, Elizabeth S. *acoustician, physicist*
Leshem, Osnat Alice *institutional resource clinician*

Westbrook
Douglas, Hope M. *psychotherapist, forensic hypnotist*

Weston
Laikind, Donna *psychotherapist, consultant*

Wilton
Kriss, Patricia Anne *health services executive*
Paulson, Loretta Nancy *psychoanalyst*

Wolcott
Regan, Michael Frederick *school psychologist*

DELAWARE

Delmar
Madden, Cynthia Ann *pediatric and family nurse practitioner, educator*

Dover
Richman, Joseph Herbert *public health services official*
Wisneski, Sharon Marie *critical care nurse, educator*

Lewes
Fried, Jeffrey Michael *health care administrator*

Lincoln
Ashley, Linda Ann *nurse*

Milford
Sherman, Jane Ehlinger *nursing educator*
†Wilkerson, Pamela Helen *nurse*
Yindra, Meredith Kaye *nursing administrator, realtor*

Millville
McCabe, Margaret Clark *family practice nurse*

Newark
Doberenz, Alexander R. *nutrition educator, chemist*
Protokowicz, Nora Jane *nursing administrator*

Wilmington
Amsler, Karen Marie *medical technologist, scientist*
Kohler, Frederick William, Jr. *pharmacist*
Maxwell, Audrey L. *healthcare administrator*
McDonough, Kenneth Lee *disease management company executive*

DISTRICT OF COLUMBIA

Washington
Ackerman, F. Kenneth, Jr. *health facility administrator*
Alward, Ruth Rosendall *nursing consultant*
Arapian, Linda *pediatrics nurse*
Arling, Donna Dickson *social worker*
Benica, Sherry Lynn *pediatric critical care nurse*
Bentley, James Daniel *hospital association executive*
Bristo, Marca *healthcare executive*
Carmody, Margaret Jean *retired social worker*
Chilman, Catherine Earles Street *social welfare educator, author*
Cushman, Margaret Jane *home care executive, nurse*
Delgado, Jane *health executive, writer*
†DeParle, Nancy-Ann Min *federal agency administrator, lawyer*
Eckenhoff, Edward Alvin *health care administrator*
Engle, Jane *research nurse*
Francke, Gloria Niemeyer *pharmacist, editor, publisher*
Gibbons, Martha Blechar *psychotherapist, educator, consultant*
†Golden, Olivia A. *health and science agency administrator*
Goldstein, Murray *health organization official*
Gray, Judith Lynn *adult nurse practitioner, rehabilitation nurse*
Grob, George Frederick *health, social services association administrator*
Hammond-Allen, Jeanette Carol *operating room nurse*
Hannett, Frederick James *healthcare consulting company executive*
Hudec, Mary Suzanne *nursing and patient services administrator*
Jones, Stanley Boyd *health policy analyst, priest*
Lash, Myles Perry *hospital administrator, consultant*
Lee, Shew Kuhn *retired optometrist*
Levin, Peter J. *hospital administrator, public health professor*
LLubién, Joseph Herman *psychotherapist, counselor*
Lombardo, Fredric Alan *pharmacist, educator*
Lotze, Evie Daniel *psychodramatist*
Lurding, Donald Scott *business executive*
Masi, Dale A. *research company executive, social work educator*
†May, Sterling Randolph *health association executive*
†McCarthy, John F. *healthcare administrator*
McShane, Franklin John, III *nurse anesthetist, army officer*
Peart, Laverne T. *retired nursing assistant, poet*
Rader, Paul MacFarland *healthcare administrator*
Rheintgen, Laura Dale *research center official*
Rosenblum, Donald Jerome *health facility administrator*
Rouson, Vivian Reissland *alcohol and drug abuse services professional, journalist*
Samet, Kenneth Alan *hospital administrator*
Satcher, David *public health service officer, federal official*
Schorr, Lisbeth Bamberger *child and family policy analyst, author, educator*
Sheavly, Robert Bruce *social worker*
†Soutter, Catherine Patricia *nurse*
Stark, Nathan J. *medical administrator, consultant, lawyer*
†Stombler, Robin E. *medical society executive*
†Tarplin, Richard J. *federal agency administrator*
Tracy, Thomas Miles *international health organization official*
Wargo, Andrea Ann *public health official, commissioned officer*
Wells, Samuel Fogle, Jr. *research center administrator*
Williamson, Darlene Swanson *speech pathologist*
Woteki, Catherine Ellen *nutritionist*
Yoder, Mary Jane Warwick *psychotherapist*
Zechman, Edwin Kerper, Jr. *medical facility administrator*

FLORIDA

Altamonte Springs
Seykora, Margaret S. *psychotherapist*

Apopka
Webb, Erma Lee *nurse educator*

Aventura
McRoberts, Jeffrey Alan *nursing administrator*

Bay Pines
Weaver, Thomas Harold *health facility administrator*

Boca Raton
Baumgarten, Diana Virginia *gerontological nurse*

Douglas, Andrew *legal nurse*
Fels, Robert Alan *psychotherapist*
Gale, Marla *social worker*
Greenfield-Moore, Wilma Louise *social worker, educator*
Guillama-Alvarez, Noel Jesus *healthcare company executive*
Marrese, Barbara Ann *nurse, educator, program planner*
Morris, Jill Carole *psychotherapist*
Perlick, Lillian *counselor, therapist*
Rothberg, June Simmonds *retired nursing educator, psychotherapist, psychoanalyst*
Van Alstine, Ruth Louise *medical language specialist, writer*

Boynton Beach
Berman, Ruth Sharon *chiropractor*
Peltzie, Kenneth Gerald *hospital administrator, educator*

Bradenton
Aerts, Cindy Sue *nurse*
Myette, Jeré Curry *nursing administrator*
Rehmann, Elizabeth Schultz *health system executive*
Taylor, Carol *rehabilitation nurse*
Tilbe, Linda MacLauchlan *nursing administrator*

Brooksville
Smith, Margaret Ann *health care executive*

Cape Coral
Buthman, Nancy Smith *nurse practitioner, critical care nurse*

Cassadaga
Haydu, John N. *psychic counselor*

Chattahoochee
Ivory, Peter B. C. B. *medical administrator*

Clearwater
Conover, Dorothy Nancy Lever *medical practice administrator, nurse*
Houtz, Duane Talbott *hospital administrator*
Keyes, Benjamin B. *therapist*
Sutton, Sharon Jean *surgical nurse*
Whedon, George Donald *medical administrator, researcher*

Coconut Creek
Yormark, Alanna Katherine *pediatrics nurse*

Coral Springs
Carrington, J(oseph) P(eter) (Jossif Peter Bartolotti) *nutritionist, psychoanalyst, research scientist, educator*

Daytona Beach
Cardwell, Harold Douglas, Sr. *rehabilitation specialist*
Salter, Leo Guilford *mental health services professional*
Smith, Ann Marie *nurse educator*

Deerfield Beach
Areskog, Donald Clinton *retired chiropractor*
Solomon, Barry Jason *healthcare administrator, consultant*

Deland
Wilson, Susan *geriatrics nurse*

Delray Beach
Erenstein, Alan *emergency room nurse, medical education consultant*
Haros, Joann *critical care nurse*
Rowland, Robert Charles *writer, clinical psychotherapist, researcher*

Dunedin
Simmons, Patricia Ann *pharmacist, consultant*
Weber, Ellen Schmoyer *pediatric speech pathologist*

Ellenton
Edson, Herbert Robbins *retired foundation and hospital executive*
Murray, Constance Yvonne *gerontology and geropsychiatric nurse, administrator*

Englewood
Curtis, Caroline A. S. *community health and oncology nurse*
Dowdell, Michael Francis *critical care and anesthesia nurse practitioner*
Lahiff, Marilyn J. *nursing administrator*

Fernandina Beach
Kurtz, Myers Richard *hospital administrator*

Fort Lauderdale
Alpert, Martin Jeffrey *chiropractic physician*
Dean, Marilyn Ferwerda *nursing consultant, administrator*
Easton, Robert Morrell, Jr. *optometric physician*
Geronemus, Diann Fox *social work consultant*
Huysman, James David *healthcare executive, consultant*
Kaplan, Elissa *social worker, children's counselor, consultant*
Kurzenberger, Dick *health services executive*
Lister, Mark Wayne *clinical laboratory scientist*
McGinnis, Patrick Bryan *mental health counselor*
Price, Judith *nursing educator*
Rentoumis, Ann Mastroianni *psychotherapist*
Sutton, Douglas Hoyt *nurse*

Fort Myers
Hopple, Jeanne M. *adult nurse practitioner*
Housel, Natalie Rae Norman *physical therapist*
Johnson, Sally A. *nurse, educator*
Newland, Jane Lou *nursing educator*
Williams, Suzanne *pediatric nurse practitioner*
Workman, Susan Barnett *mental health center administrator*

Fort Walton Beach
†Buckroth, Mari Beth *counselor*
Villecco, Judy Diana *substance abuse, mental health counselor, director*

Gainesville
Baker, Bonnie Barbara *mental health and school counselor, educator*
Bzoch, Kenneth Rudolph *speech and language educator, department chairman*
Conner, Kathryn Gamble *nurse*
Coordsen, Karen Gail *medical/surgical nurse*
†Gaintner, Richard J. *health facility administrator*
Houchen, Constance Elaine *nursing administrator*
Malasanos, Lois Julanne Fosse *nursing educator*
McCluskey, Charles James, Jr. *physician assistant*
McFarlane, Neil Frazer *health administrator*
Randall, Malcom *health care administrator*
Schwartz, Michael Averill *pharmacy educator, consultant*
Small, Natalie Settimelli *pediatric mental health counselor*
Thompson, Neal Philip *food science and nutrition educator*
Watson, Robert Joe *hospital administrator, retired career officer*

Havana
Whitehead, Lucy Grace *health facility administrator*

Hollywood
Shane, Doris Jean *respiratory therapist, administrator*
Staller, Aileen J. *neurosurgical nurse clinician*
Tucker, Nina Angella *hospital administrator*

Homosassa
Acton, Norman *international organization executive*

Hudson
Stash, Janet *nursing consultant*

Hurlburt Field
Ingram, Shirley Jean *social worker*

Indian Harbor Beach
†Wagner, Susan Preston *nursing educator*

Inverness
Mavros, George S. *clinical laboratory director*
Nichols, Sally Jo *geriatrics nurse*
Stone, Fred Lyndon *human resources administrator*

Jacksonville
Akers, James Eric *medical practice marketing executive*
†Corcoran, James Joseph, Jr. *health plan administrator, physician*
Frazier, Rosa Mae *medical/surgical and hemodialysis nurse*
Fulton-Quindoza, Debra Ann *nurse practitioner*
Helganz, Beverly Buzhardt *counselor*
Leapley, Patricia Murray *dietitian*
Longino, Theresa Childers *nurse*
Mason, William Cordell, III *hospital administrator*
Pavlick, Pamela Kay *nurse, consultant*
Rubens, Linda Marcia *home health services administrator*
Sanders, Marion Yvonne *geriatrics nurse*
Scales, Marjorie Lahr *pastoral counselor*
Townsend, Heather Marie *family nurse practitioner*
Wilson, C. Nick *health educator, consultant, researcher, lecturer*
Yamane, Stanley Joel *optometrist*

Key West
Burton, Anna Marjorie *nurse*

Kissimmee
Pinellas, Xavier Clinton *counselor, consultant*

Lake Butler
Staggs, Dean, Jr. *surgical nurse*

Lake City
Lundy, Elizabeth Anne *community health nurse*
Norman, Alline L. *health facility administrator*

Lake Helen
Hess, Janice Burdette *nursing administrator*

Lake Wales
Rynear, Nina Cox *retired registered nurse, author, artist*

Lakeland
DiMura, Linda Hart *healthcare organization administrator*
Gaddy, Norma Smith *nursing administrator*
Herendeen, Carol Denise *dietitian*
LaComb-Williams, Linda Lou *community health nurse*

Land O'Lakes
McKee-Dudley, Sandra Irene *correctional health care professional*

Largo
Hamlin, Robert Henry *public health educator, management consultant*
Haumschild, Mark James *pharmacist*
Woodruff, Debra A. *occupational health nurse*

Laud Lakes
Stern, Edith Lois *counselor hypno-therapist*
Wilson, Charles Edward *medical records administrator*

Lauderhill
Schultz, Howard Michael *registered nurse*

Lehigh Acres
†Vodev, Eugene D. *hospital management consultant*

Lighthouse Point
Frock, Terri Lyn *nursing educator and consultant*

Lk Forest
Tarkington, Steven Edward *nursing administrator*

Longwood
Andrews, Diane Randall *nursing administrator, critical care nurse*

Lutz
Money, Joy Ann Fuentes *healthcare consultant*

Madeira Beach
Newton, V. Miller *medical psychotherapist, neuropsychologist, writer*

Maitland
Taylor, Lindsay David, Jr. *health care executive*

Melbourne
Hughes, Ann Nolen *psychotherapist*
MacDonald, Michael Joseph *physician, administrator*

Miami
Albright, John D. *emergency room and telemetry nurse*
Cherry, Andrew Lawrence, Jr. *social work educator, researcher*
Chisholm, Martha Maria *dietitian*
Clark, Ira C. *hospital association administrator, educator*
Dann, Oliver Townsend *psychoanalyst, psychiatrist, educator*
Fitzgerald, Lynne Marie Leslie *family therapist*
Himburg, Susan Phillips *dietitian, educator*
†Jaouhari-McCune, Cynthia *nurse, childbirth educator*
Kassewitz, Ruth Eileen Blower *retired hospital executive*
Kooima, Linda Kay *neonatal and pediatrics nurse*
Kunce, Avon Estes *vocational rehabilitation counselor*
Marcus, Joy John *pharmacist, consultant, educator*
McKeehan, Mildred Hope *nurse*
Morphonios, Martha Monsalve *pharmacist*
Osinski, Martin Henry *healthcare consultant*
Perry, E. Elizabeth *social worker, real estate manager*
Saland, Deborah *psychotherapist, educator*
Schor, Olga Seemann *mental health counselor, real estate broker*
Sonenreich, Steven Douglas *hospital administrator*
Stuchins, Carol Mayberry *nursing executive*
Tamayo, Raquel *medical/surgical nurse*
Whitaker, Cynthia Ellen *managed healthcare nurse*
Yaffa, Jack Ber *healthcare administrator, educator, surgeon*

Miramar
Gauwitz, Donna Faye *nursing educator*

Montverde
Bloder, Lisa W. *critical care nurse, mental health nurse*

Mount Dora
Moretto, Jane Ann *nurse, public health officer, consultant*
Shyers, Larry Edward *mental health counselor, educator*

Naples
Barkley, Marlene A. Nyhuis *nursing administrator*
Brown, Cindy Lynn *critical care nurse, emergency nurse, family nurse practitioner*
Ghorayeb, Fay Elizabeth *nurse educator, secondary education educator*
Lewis, Marianne H. *psychiatric nurse practitioner*
Megee, Geraldine Hess *social worker*
Terenzio, Peter Bernard *hospital administrator*
Walker, Patricia D. *critical care nurse*

New Port Richey
Hlad, Gregory Michael *psychometrist, assessment services coordinator*

North Fort Myers
†Woodbridge, Norma Jean *registered nurse, writer*

North Port
Galterio, Louis *healthcare information executive*

Ocala
Lamon, Kathy Lynn *nursing administrator*
Layton, William Gene *emergency medical service administrator*

Orange Park
Brown, Linda Lockett *nutrition management executive, nutrition consultant*
Holloman, Marilyn Leona Davis *nurse nonprofit administrator*
Reemelin, Angela Norville *dietitian consultant*
Rice, Ronald James *hospital administrator*

Orlando
Bridgett, Noel William *convalescent center administrator*
Hedrick, Steve Brian *psychotherapist*
†Hillenmeyer, John *medical center executive*
Krouse, Helene June *nursing educator*
Mallette, Phyllis Spencer Cooper *medical/surgical nurse*
Reis, Melanie Jacobs *women's health nurse, educator*
Safcsak, Karen *medical/surgical nurse*
Scott, Kathy Lynn *peri-operative nurse*
Witty, John Barber *health care executive*
Woodard, Clara Veronica *nursing home official*

Palm Harbor
Ruskin, Les D. *chiropractor*
Smith, W. James *health facility administrator*

Panama City
Smith, Erlinda Fay *occupational therapist*

Parkland
Brancaleone, Salvatore Joseph *nutritionist, consultant*

Pembroke Pines
Kater, Kathryn M. *critical care nurse*
Mason, Mitchell Gary *emergency nurse*

Pensacola
McCann, Mary Cheri *medical technologist, horse breeder and trainer*
Serangeli, Deborah S. *healthcare facility administrator*
Shimmin, Margaret Ann *women's health nurse*

Taggart, Linda Diane *women's health nurse*

Pineland
Donlon, Josephine A. *diagnostic and evaluation counseling therapist, educator*

Pinellas Park
Tower, Alton G., Jr. *pharmacist*

Placida
Wood, Yvonne McMurray *nursing educator*

Plant City
Hixon, Andrea Kaye *healthcare quality specialist*
Mathis-Sales, Helen *nurse*

Plantation
Gonshak, Isabelle Lee *nurse*
Newburge, Idelle Block *psychotherapist*
Sterling, Carol Barbara *social worker, psychotherapist*

Pompano Beach
Forman, Harriet *nursing publication executive*

Port Charlotte
Gendzwill, Joyce Annette *retired health officer*
Sheahan, Joan A. *long term care nursing administrator*

Port Orange
Parish, Lynn Race *medical technologist*

Port Salerno
Martin, Dale *vocational rehabilitation executive*

Princeton
Cottrill, Mary Elsie *family nurse practitioner*

Punta Gorda
O'Donnell, Mary Murphy *nurse epidemiologist, consultant*
Wood, Emma S. *nurse practitioner*

Ridge Manor
Cameron, Kristen Ellen Schmidt *nurse, construction company executive, educator, writer*

Saint Petersburg
Bailey, Robin Keith *physician assistant, perfusionist*
Clark, Carolyn Chambers *nurse, author, educator*
Cole, Sally Ann *critical care nurse*
Galucki, Frances Jane *nursing educator, medical/surgical nurse*
Jordan, William Reynier, Sr. *therapist, poet*

Sarasota
Benedick, James Michael *psychotherapist*
Bernfield, Lynne *psychotherapist*
Carr, Patricia Ann *community health nurse*
Covert, Michael Henri *healthcare facility administrator*
Dearden, Robert James *retired pharmacist*
Fawks, David Robert *psychiatric clinical nurse specialist*
Kozma, Karen Jean *nurse, educator*
Middleton, Norman Graham *social worker, psychotherapist*
†Steenfatt, Gertraude *community health nursing administrator*
Tucci, Steven Michael *health facility administrator, physician, recording industry executive*

Sebastian
Mauke, Leah Rachel *counselor*

Seminole
Jarrard, Marilyn Mae *nursing consultant, nursing researcher*

Stuart
Lysen, Lucinda Katherine *nutrition support nurse, dietitian*
Proctor, Gail Louise Borrowman *home health nurse, educator, women's health nurse*

Tallahassee
†Bailey, Suzanne K. *health care consultant*
Hedstrom, Susan Lynne *maternal women's health nurse*
†Holtzclaw, Mark Alexander *social worker*
Mustian, Middleton Truett *hospital administrator*
Sprouse, James Dean *nurse anesthetist*

Tamarac
†Krause, John L. *optometrist*

Tampa
Arfsten, Betty-Jane *nurse*
Bittle, Polly Ann *nephrology nurse, researcher*
Boutros, Linda Nelene Wiley *medical/surgical nurse*
Ferlita, Theresa Ann *clinical social worker*
Liller, Karen DeSafey *public health educator*
Mahan, Charles Samuel *public health service officer*
Price, Douglas Armstrong *chiropractor*
Russell, Diane Elizabeth Henrikson *career counselor*
Scott, Charles Francis *health facility administrator*

Tarpon Springs
Georgiou, Ruth Schwab *retired social worker*

Titusville
Hartung, Patricia McEntee *therapist*

Venice
Baga, Margaret Fitzpatrick *nurse, medical office manager*
Barritt, Evelyn Ruth Berryman *nurse, educator, university dean*

Vero Beach
Burdette, Carol Janice *gerontology nursing administrator*
McCrystal, Ann Marie *community health nurse, administrator*
Whitney, J. Lee *home health care administrator, retired*

West Palm Beach
Abernathy, Barbara Eubanks *counselor*
Ackerman, Paul Adam *pharmacist*
Bohn, Barbara Ann *laboratory director*
Davis, Shirley Harriet *social worker, editor*
Glinski, Helen Elizabeth *operating room nurse*
Holloway, Edward Olin *human services manager*
Rafaidus, David Martin *health and human services planner*

Weston
Gordon, Lori Heyman *psychotherapist, author, educator*

Winter Haven
Porter, Howard Leonard, III *health and education policy consultant*
Trickett, Jennifer Beatrice *medical and surgical nurse*
West, Mary Elizabeth *psychiatric management professional*

Winter Park
Blair, Mardian John *hospital management executive*
DiBacco, Richard Paul *vocational case manager*
Douglas, Kathleen Mary Harrigan *psychotherapist, educator*
Granzig, William Walker *clinical sexologist, educator*
Velazquez, Anabel *medical services executive*
Wisler, Willard Eugene *retired health care management executive*

Winter Springs
San Miguel, Sandra Bonilla *social worker*

GEORGIA

Alpharetta
Mock, Melinda Smith *orthopedic nurse specialist, consultant*

Americus
Worrell, Billy Frank *health facility administrator*

Athens
Boudinot, Frank Douglas *pharmaceutics educator*
Lawson, Bonnie Hulsey *retired psychotherapist*
Levine, David Lawrence *social work educator*
Posey, Loran Michael *pharmacist, editor*
Yegidis, Bonnie Lee *social work educator, university dean*

Atlanta
Bales, Virginia Shankle *health administration*
Barker, William Daniel *hospital administrator*
Butte, Anthony Jeffrey *healthcare executive*
Chandler, Robert Charles *healthcare consultant*
Crutchfield, Carolyn Ann *physical therapy educator*
Dobrzyn, Janet Elaine *quality management professional*
Finley, Sarah Maude Merritt *social worker*
Foerster, David Wendel, Jr. *counselor, consultant, human resources specialist*
Gerst, Steven Richard *healthcare director, physician*
Hardegree, Gloria Jean Fore *health services administrator*
Honaman, J. Craig *health facility administrator*
Hopkins, Donald Roswell *public health physician*
Johnson, Carl Frederick *marriage and family therapist*
Leipold, Cynthia A. Ney *critical care nurse, nursing administrator*
†Macomson, Eric David *pharmacist*
Marks, James S. *public health service administrator*
Martin, David Edward *health sciences educator*
Martin, Virve Paul *licensed professional counselor*
Moore, Melinda *public health physician*
Orenstein, Walter A. *health facility administrator*
Phillips, Debbie Jean *managed care nurse*
Renford, Edward J. *hospital administrator*
Riddle, Marnita Marie *medical nurse*
Rosenberg, Mark L. *health facility administrator*
Seffrin, John Reese *health science association administrator, educator*
Stegall, Marbury Taylor *psychiatric, mental health nurse*
Verner, Linda Hogan *manager cardiac surgery operating room*
Walton, Carole Lorraine *clinical social worker*
Weed, Roger Oren *rehabilitation services professional, educator*

Augusta
Feldman, Elaine Bossak *medical nutritionist, educator*
Gillespie, Edward Malcolm *hospital administrator*
Grigsby, R. Kevin *social work and psychiatry educator*
Hilson, Diane Niedling *nursing administrator*
Sansbury, Barbara Ann Pettigrew *nursing administrator*
Whittemore, Ronald Paul *hospital administrator, retired army officer, nursing educator*

Berkeley Lake
†Cooke, Marguerite K. *nurse, mayor*

Brunswick
Crowe, Hal Scott *chiropractor*
Hopwood, Vicki Jeane *medical center official*
Mills, Margie Batley *home health care executive*
Mitchell, Dorothy Harvey *healthcare administrator*
Thomas, Versie Lee *nursing educator*

Cairo
Jordan, Randall Warren *optometrist*

Calhoun
Smith, Janice Self *family nurse practitioner*

Canton
Sperin, Amelia Harrison *medical/surgical and pediatric nurse*

Carrollton
Barron, Purificacion Capulong *nursing administrator, educator*

Clayton
English, Cheryl Ann *medical technologist*

College Park
†Kirk, Thomas *chiropractor*

Decatur
Gregory, Sharon E. *neonatal clinical nurse specialist*
Hagood, Susan Stewart Hahn *clinical dietitian*
Hawkins, Janice Edith *medical/surgical clinical nurse specialist*
Hinman, Alan Richard *public health administrator, epidemiologist*
Ross, Valdor Wendell *operating room nurse*

Douglasville
Henley, Lila Jo *school social worker, consultant, retired*

Dublin
Doster, Daniel Harris *retired counselor, minister*
Folsom, Roger Lee *healthcare administrator*
Sumner, Lorene Knowles Hart *retired medical/surgical and rehabilitation nurse*

Duluth
Hibben, Celia Lynn *psychiatric mental health nurse practitioner*

Dunwoody
Hanna, Vail Deadwyler *critical care nurse*

East Point
Fuller, Ora *nursing administrator, health care executive*

Fayetteville
Harris, Glenda Stange *medical transcriptionist, writer*

Fremont
Macaluso, Mary Margaret *nurse, educator*

Gainesville
†McDade, Dina Catherine *nursing educator*
Thompson, Jeffery Elders *health care administrator, minister*

Glynco
Church, Barbara Ryan *organizational psychologist*

Grayson
Hollinger, Charlotte Elizabeth *medical technologist, tree farmer*
Mitchell, Laura Anne Gilbert *family nurse practitioner*
Nease, Judith Allgood *marriage and family therapist*

Jasper
Ledford, Shirley Louise *practical nurse*

Jonesboro
Dame, Laureen Eva *nursing administrator*

Kathleen
Galeazzo, Constance Jane *neonatal nurse practitioner*

La Fayette
Lim, Esteban, Jr. *medical facility administrator, physician*

Lagrange
Rhodes, Eddie, Jr. *medical technologist, phlebotomy technician, educator*

Lawrenceville
Meehan, Patrick John *public health officer*
Stempler, Benj L. *clinical social worker*

Lilburn
Elixson, E. Marsha *pediatric cardiovascular consultant*
Hammond, Kathleen Ann *nutrition support dietitian and nurse*

Mableton
Ayres, Jayne Lynn Ankrum *community health nurse*

Macon
Brown, Nancy Childs *marriage and family therapist*
Fickling, William Arthur, Jr. *health care manager*
Landry, Sara Griffin *social worker*

Marietta
Billingsley, Judith Ann Seavey *oncology nurse*
DeWolf, Susan Ulmer *operating room nurse*
Felteau, Anne L. *patient care consultant*
Hudson, Linda *health care executive*
Petit, Parker Holmes *health care corporation executive*

Norcross
Irons, Isie Iona *retired nursing administrator*

Odum
Manus, Nancy Manning *social services director, writer*

Plainville
Mealor, Phyllis Jayne *nurse, infection control practitioner*

Quitman
McElroy, Annie Laurie *nursing educator, administrator*

Rex
Bales, Avary *nurse*

Ringgold
Sharp Evans, Dianna K. *gerontology nurse*

Rockmart
Holley, Tammy D. Fennell *critical care nurse*

Rossville
Dodd, Virginia *medical/surgical and endoscopy nurse*

Roswell
Baird, Marianne Saunorus *critical care clinical specialist*
Bastianello, Sandra Crews *therapist*
Beaton, Rebecca Andrea *psychotherapist*

Savannah
DiClaudio, Janet Alberta *health information administrator*

Shannon
Williams, Thresia Wayne Matthews *occupational health nurse*

Sharpsburg
Wooten, Tina Helen Wilhelm *medical/surgical and oncological nurse*

Statesboro
Davenport, Ann Adele Mayfield *home care agency administrator*
Wilhoite, Laura J. *occupational health nurse*

Suwanee
Shihady, Diane Divis *speech pathologist*

Thomaston
Smith, Debra Joan *informatics nurse, critical care nurse*

Toccoa
Scott, Louyse Hulsey *school social worker*

Tucker
Reed, Barbara Alford *pain management nurse, consultant*

Valdosta
Marinelli, Linda Floyd *nurse educator*
Vincent, Kay Louise *community health nursing director*
Waldrop, Mary Louise *nursing educator*

Vidalia
Joyner, Jo Ann *geriatrics nurse*

HAWAII

Hilo
Clark, Janet *retired health services executive*

Honolulu
Fischer, Joel *social work educator*
Flannelly, Laura T. *mental health nurse, nursing educator, researcher*
Gormley, Francis Xavier, Jr. *social worker*
Kadohiro, Jane Kay *educator, nurse, diabetes consultant*
Katz, Alan Roy *public health educator*
Kroll, Sandra L. *healthcare facility administrator*
Loh, Edith Kwok-Yuen *oncology nurse, health education specialist*
Lum, Jean Loui Jin *nurse educator*
Miike, Lawrence Hiroshi *public health officer*
Moccia, Mary Kathryn *social worker*
Roberson, Kelley Cleve *health care financial executive*
Roehr, Kathleen Marie *nursing administrator*
Thomas, Verneda Estella *retired perfusionist*
Wilson, William James *healthcare executive*
Yoshihara, Elva *nursing educator*

Kaaawa
Baldridge, Melinda E. *psychiatric nurse specialist*

Kailua
Lundquist, Dana Richard *healthcare executive*

Kaneohe
Lange-Otsuka, Patricia Ann *nursing educator*
Westerdahl, John Brian *nutritionist, health educator*

Mililani
Kiley, Thomas *rehabilitation counselor*
Neff, Pamela Marie *medical/surgical nurse*

Pahoa
Satterwhite, Sharon *mental health nurse*

Tripler Army Medical Center
Adams, Nancy R. *nurse, military officer*

IDAHO

Bonners Ferry
McClintock, William Thomas *health care administrator*

Burley
King, Janet Felland *family nurse practitioner*

Idaho Falls
Leverett, Margaret Ann *women's health nurse practitioner*

Kimberly
Maschek, Roger Alan *counselor*

Lewiston
Smith, Phyllis Mae *healthcare consultant, educator*

Pocatello
Bott-Graham, Michelle Lynn *behavior therapist*

ILLINOIS

Abbott Park
Fath, Michael John *pharmaceutical/health care stategic planner*

Alvin
Story, Judith K. *adult day care owner, administrator*

Argonne
Masek, Mark Joseph *laboratory administrator*

Arlington Heights
Burdsall, Deborah Patterson *geriatrics nurse, educator*

Aurora
†Kheshgi-Genovese, Zareena *psychotherapist, educator*

Barrington
Schaefer, Mary Ann *health facility administrator, consultant*
Stoutenburg, Jane Sue Williamson *nurse practitioner, fund raiser, actress*

Belleville
Taylor, Lynne M. *medical/surgical nurse*

Bellwood
McCullough-Wiggins, Lydia Statoria *pharmacist, consultant*

Berwyn
Gordon, Dolores Joan *retired emergency medical technician*
Lofquist, Lisa Willson *occupational therapist, business owner*

Bloomington
Dickson, Robert Frank *nursing home executive*
Lauritson, Judy Marie *nursing consultant*

Bolingbrook
Price, Theodora Hadzisteliou *individual and family therapist*

Bradley
Marsh, Carla A. *document control group leader*

Carbondale
Buckley, John Joseph, Jr. *health care executive*
Livengood, Joanne Desler *healthcare administrator*

Carthage
Moore, Richard Alan *optometrist*

Catlin
Phillips, Diana Dawn *nurse*

Champaign
Nesbitt, Juanita *occupational health nurse, medical and surgical nurse*

Charleston
†Hedges, Edith Rittenhouse *nutrition and home economics educator*

Chatham
Chew, Keith Elvin *healthcare services administrator*

Chicago
Anderson, Laurel Alma *nursing educator*
Bailar, John Christian, III *public health educator, physician, statistician*
Baptist, Allwyn J. *health care consultant*
Benson, Irene M. *nurse*
Betz, Ronald Philip *pharmacist*
Bowman, Tina Marie Davis *pediatric nurse*
Bracken, Kathleen Ann *nurse*
Braddock, David Lawrence *health science educator*
Brown, Charles Eric *health facility administrator, biochemist*
Campbell, Bruce Crichton *hospital administrator*
Conlon, Patrick C. *family nurse practitioner*
Crawford, Jean Andre *clinical therapist*
Davis, Concelor Dominquez *mental health therapist, counselor*
Dickerson, Martha Ann *health facility administrator*
Dombkowski, Thomas Raymond *public health administrator*
Edelsberg, Sally C. *physical therapy educator and administrator*
Franklin, Cory Michael *medical administrator, educator*
Goldsmith, Ethel Frank *medical social worker*
Hahn, David Bennett *hospital administrator, marketing professional*
Hickcox, Leslie Kay *health educator, consultant, counselor*
Hirsch, Syrola Ruth *gerontology rehabilitation nurse*
Hudik, Martin Francis *hospital administrator, educator, consultant*
Kaufman, Edward Phillip *psychotherapist*
†Lerner, Wayne *health care executive*
Levin, Arnold Murray *social worker, psychotherapist*
Levitan, Valerie F. *medical research facility executive*
Lim, Len Gui Remolona (Mark Lim) *critical care and emergency nurse*
Ling, Kathryn Wrolstad *health association administrator*
Lubawski, James Lawrence *health care consultant*
Lyne, Sheila *public health commissioner, sister*
†Magoon, Patrick M. *healthcare executive*
Marsh, Jeanne Cay *social welfare educator, researcher*
Massura, Eileen Kathleen *family therapist*
Maynard, George Fleming, III *consultant to philanthropy organizations*
Mecklenburg, Gary Alan *hospital executive*
Menon, Siva Kumar *physical therapist*
Messner, Leonard Vincent *optometrist, educator*
Mikovich, Terry *home health facility administrator*
Muthuswamy, Petham Padayatchi *pulmonary medicine and critical care specialist*
Palmer, Martha H. *counseling educator*
Pond, Joel Patrick *veterinary technician*
Preisler, Harvey D. *medical facility administrator, medical educator*
Reed, Vastina Kathryn (Tina Reed) *child psychotherapist, educator*
Reilly, Joan Rita *nurse practitioner, educator, school nurse*
Rosenheim, Margaret Keeney *social welfare policy educator*
Rudnick, Ellen Ava *health care executive*
Russell, Lillian *medical, surgical nurse*
Schwartz, John Norman *health care executive*
Shannon, Iris Reed *nursing educator*
Simon, Bernece Kern *social work educator*
Smrcina, Catherine Marie *nursing administrator, researcher*
Strauss, Jeffrey Lewis *healthcare executive*
Udeani, George Ogbonna *pharmacist, educator*
Winkelman, Lois Anaya *womens health nurse*
Witrod, Sister Mary Rosalita *nursing home administrator*
Zimmermann, Polly Gerber *emergency nurse*

Crestwood
Morissette, Carol Lynne *healthcare consultant*

Danville
Kettling, Virginia *health facility administrator*

Darien
Klassek, Christine Paulette *behavioral scientist*

Decatur
Morrison, Barbara *nursing educator*
Perry, Anthony John *retired hospital executive*

Deerfield
Sanner, John Harper *retired pharmacologist*

Dekalb
†Banovetz, James M. *public administration educator, consultant*
Bukonda, Ngoyi K. Zacharie *health care management educator*
Crosser, Carmen Lynn *marriage and family therapist, clinical social worker, consultant*

Downers Grove
†Capek, Brenda Joyce *social worker*
Melesio, Kathryn Mary *oncological nurse, educator*

Dunlap
Hanard, Patricia Ann *family nurse practitioner*

Dupo
Gallamore, Betty Lou *nurse*

East Saint Louis
Martin, Betty J. *speech, language pathologist*

Edwardsville
Nehring, Wendy Marie *pediatrics nurse*

Effingham
Heth, Diana Sue *therapist*

Elgin
Beyer, Karen Haynes *social worker*
Eineke, Alvina Marie *public health nurse*
Nelson, John Thilgen *retired hospital administrator, physician*

Elmhurst
Dallas, Daniel George *social worker*
Moffitt, Ray *social worker, consultant*

Evanston
Hennessy, Margaret Barrett *health care executive*
White, Sylvia Frances *gerontology home care nurse, consultant*

Forest Park
Hatch, Edward William (Ted Hatch) *health care executive*

Freeport
Weaver, Michael Glenn *pharmacist*

Galena
Alexander, Barbara Leah Shapiro *clinical social worker*

Galesburg
Kowalski, Richard Sheldon *hospital administrator*
Sandborg, Shirlee J. *health science facility professional*

Glenview
Coulson, Elizabeth Anne *physical therapy educator, state representative*

Grand Ridge
Goodchild, Rosina Ann *community health nurse*

Granite City
Raczkiewicz, Paul Edward *hospital administrator*

Hampshire
Hirn, Doris Dreyer *health service administrator*

Hanover Park
Michel, Lynn Francine *critical care nurse*

Harrisburg
Endsley, Jane Ruth *nursing educator*
Rushing, Philip Dale *retired social worker*

Highland Park
Liebow, Phoebe Augusta Recht *nursing educator, school nurse*
Zywicki, Cindy Mary *nurse*

Hillsboro
Herrmann, Jane Marie *physical therapist*

Hines
Hagarty, Eileen Mary *pulmonary clinical nurse specialist*
Wetherald, Dawn Margaret *surgical nurse*

Hinsdale
Lavine, Lorette Pauline *nursing educator, maternal/women's health nurse*

Homewood
Bultema, Janice Kay *healthcare executive*

Hoyleton
Schnake, Betty Berniece *nursing educator, retired*

Joliet
Cochran, Mary Ann *nurse educator*
Russow, Cheryl Ann *nurse*

Kankakee
Schroeder, David Harold *healthcare facility executive*

Lake Villa
Sikora, Evelyn Marie *psychiatric and substance abuse nurse*

Lewistown
Shank, Glenna Kaye *medical/surgical nurse, educator*

Litchfield
Deaton, Beverly Jean *nursing administrator, educator*

Lombard
Beideman, Ronald Paul *chiropractic physician, college dean*
Holgers-Awana, Rita Marie *electrodiagnosis specialist*

Long Grove
Freeland, Marcia Stephan *nursing educator*

Macomb
Hopper, Stephen Rodger *hospital administrator*

Manteno
Balgeman, Richard Vernon *radiology administrator, alcoholism counselor*

Mapleton
Hayes, Debra Troxell *family nurse practitioner*

Marion
Wilkins, Sondra Ann *mental health nurse, educator*

Maywood
Hindle, Paula Alice *nursing administrator*

Melrose Park
White, Linda Sue *cardiology technician*

Mount Carmel
Wheatley, Joan Mercedese *telemetry care nurse*

Mount Prospect
O'Connor, Nan G. *social worker*

Mundelein
Meehan, Jean Marie Ross *occupational health and safety management consultant*

Naperville
Frizelis, Karen Lynn *adult nurse practitioner*

Normal
Parton, Thomas Albert *speech-language pathologist*

North Chicago
Kringel, John G. *health products company executive*

Northbrook
Hecker, Lawrence Harris *industrial hygienist*
Hicks, Judith Eileen *nursing administrator*
Huebner, Emily Ann *home healthcare administrator, consultant*
Kahn, Sandra S. *psychotherapist*
Lever, Alvin *health science association administrator*
Noeth, Carolyn Frances *speech and language pathologist*

Oak Brook
Baker, Robert J(ohn) *hospital administrator*
Noel, Tallulah Ann *healthcare industry executive*
Risk, Richard Robert *health care executive*

Oak Park
Goold, Florence Wilson *occupational therapist*
Varchmin, Thomas Edward *environmental health administrator*

Oakbrook Terrace
Berry, Lynn Marina *healthcare administrator*

Okawville
Pomeroy, Bruce Marcel *critical care nurse, educator*

Olympia Fields
Haley, David Alan *preferred provider organization executive*

Onarga
Wilken, Caroline Doane *critical care, emergency, recovery room, and medical/surgical nurse*

Orland Park
Rasmason, Frederick Charles, III *emergency nurse*

Oswego
Van Etten, Edythe Augusta *retired occupational health nurse*

Palatine
Aleksandras, Deloris Niles *retired nursing educator*

Park Forest
Steinmetz, Jon David *mental health executive, psychologist*

Park Ridge
Boe, Gerard Patrick *health science association administrator, educator*
Cochin, Rita R. *nurse*
Jennrich, Judith A. *critical care nurse, nursing educator*
Rojek, Kenneth John *health facility administrator, hospital*

Peoria
Anglin, Linda Tannert *community health nurse, geriatrics nurse, educator*
Gard, Carol Lee *nurse educator*
Hungate, Carolyn Wolf *health and public services administrator*
McCollum, Jean Hubble *medical assistant*
Walker, Philip Chamberlain, II *health care executive*

Philo
Martin, Earl Dean *physical therapist*

Plainfield
Schinderle, Robert Frank *retired hospital administrator*

River Forest
Puthenveetil, Jos Anthony *laboratory executive*

River Grove
Hill-Hulslander, Jacquelyne L. *nursing educator and consultant*

Rock Island
Hartsock, Jane Marie *nurse, educator*

Rockford
Cadigan, Elise *social worker*
Cohen, Phyllis Joanne *nurse*
Mahlburg, Norine Elizabeth *retired nurse*
Maysent, Harold Wayne *hospital administrator*
Moehling, Kathryn S. *mental health nurse, counselor*

Saint Anne
Heckman, Patricia A. *geriatrics nurse, educator*

Saint Charles
Carpenter, Mary Laure *hospital administrator*

Schaumburg
Uhrik, Steven Brian *clinical social worker, psychotherapist, employee assistance professional, behavioral science consultant*

Shorewood
Petrella, Mary Therese *community health and women's health nurse*

Skokie
Fan, Tai-Shen Liu *dietitian*
McCarthy, Michael Shawn *health care company executive, lawyer*

Sparta
Pritchett, Allen Monroe, III *healthcare administrator*

Springfield
Campbell, Kathleen Charlotte Murphey *audiology educator, administrator, researcher*
Evans, Marsha Jo Anne *nursing administrator*
Mazzotti, Richard Rene *pharmacist*
O'Connor, Sister Gertrude Theresa *clinical nurse specialist in surgery and anesthesia*
Strow, Marcia Ann *critical care nurse*
Voycheck, Gerald Louis *nursing home administrator, social worker*

Streamwood
Samuelson, Rita Michelle *speech language pathologist*

Tinley Park
Daniels, Kurt R. *speech and language pathologist*

Tremont
Luick, Barbara Jean *physical therapist assistant*

University Park
Leftwich, Robert Eugene *oncological nursing educator*

Urbana
Baker, David Hiram *nutritionist, nutrition educator*
Siedler, Arthur James *nutrition and food science educator*
Visek, Willard James *nutritionist, animal scientist, physician, educator*

Waukegan
Paulsen, Noreen *legal nurse consultant*

Westchester
Clarke, Richard Lewis *health science association administrator*

Western Springs
Tiefenthal, Marguerite Aurand *school social worker*

Westville
Hammer, John Henry, II *hospital administrator*

Wheaton
Boudreau, Beverly Ann *health care professional*
Koenigsmark, Joyce Elyn Sladek *geriatrics nurse*

Wilmette
Ellis, Helene Rita *social worker*

Wood River
Cox, Mary Linda *maintenance industry executive*

INDIANA

Anderson
Pleninger, Susan Elaine *women's health and pediatrics nurse*
Whitaker, Audie Dale *hospital laboratory medical technologist*

Bloomington
Engs, Ruth Clifford *health educator*
Kohr, Roland Ellsworth *retired hospital administrator*
†Mack, P.A., Jr. *manager health network, state commissioner*
Torabi, Mohammad R. *health education educator*

Bluffton
Brockmann, William Frank *medical facility administrator*

Brownsburg
Weddell, Linda Anne *speech and language pathologist*

Clinton
Shew, Rose Jean *nurse*

Columbia City
Behrens, Diane R. *nursing educator*

Crown Point
Randazzo, Rebecca Ann *nursing administrator*

DePauw
Baggett, Alice Diane *critical care nurse*

East Chicago
Psaltis, Helen *medical and surgical nurse*

Evansville
Cox, Vande Lee *critical care nurse*
Francis, Lorna Jean *nutritionist*
Ragsdale, Rex H. *health facility administrator, physician*

Fishers
Chojnacki, Paul Ervin *pharmacist, pharmaceutical company official*

Floyds Knobs
Vernia-Amend, Leah Nadine *counselor*

Fort Wayne
Flynn, Pauline T. *speech pathologist, educator*
Kennedy, Elizabeth *health facility administrator*
Sims, Debbie Deann *psychotherapist*
Smith, Stephen Ralph *health facility administrator*

Franklin
Taylor, Carla Marie *critical care nurse*

Gary
Beamer, Laura *women's health and genetic health nurse*
Bennett, Richard Carl *social worker*
Hull, Grafton Hazard, Jr. *social work educator*

Goshen
Loomis, Norma Irene *marriage and family therapist*

Greencastle
Cole, Joanne W. *women's health nurse, researcher*

Highland
Lacera, Jana L. *critical care nurse, administrator*

Hobart
McKee, Denise Arlene *neonatal intensive care nurse*

Hope
Golden, Eloise Elizabeth *community health nurse*
Miller, David Kent *nursing administrator*

Indianapolis
Aschen, Sharon Ruth *genetic counselor, psychotherapist, nurse*
†Balt, Christine Ann *family nurse practitioner*
Barker, Orel O'Brien *retired activity and social service director*
Brady, Mary Sue *nutrition and dietetics educator*
Buhner, Byron Bevis *health science facility administrator*
†Capone, Vince *health system administrator*
Davis, Edgar Glenn *science and health policy executive*
Fox, Donald Lee *mental health counselor, consultant*
Glendenning, John Armand *registered nurse*
Haddad, Freddie Duke, Jr. *hospital development administrator*
Handel, David Jonathan *health care administrator*
Hayes, John Robert *health care executive, psychiatrist*
Hicks, Allen Morley *hospital administrator*
Holmberg, Sharon K. *psychiatric mental health and geriatrics nurse, researcher, educator*
Loveday, William John *hospital administrator*
Murray, Theresa Marie *critical care nurse, nursing consultant*
Riegsecker, Marvin Dean *pharmacist, state senator*
Rust, Jo Ellen *pediatric and neurosurgical nurse*
SerVaas, Cory *health sciences association administrator*
Smith, Donald Eugene *healthcare facility management administrator owner*
Stookey, George Kenneth *research institute administrator, dental educator*
Strong, Amanda L. *community health nurse*
Walther, Joseph Edward *health facility administrator, retired physician*
Young, Katherine Tratebas *occupational health nurse*

Jasper
Aronoff, Donald Matthew *mental health facility administrator*

Kokomo
Coppock, Janet Elaine *mental health nurse*

La Porte
Morris, Leigh Edward *hospital executive officer*

Lafayette
Geddes, LaNelle Evelyn *nurse, physiologist*
McBride, Angela Barron *nursing educator*
Messman, Bobette Marie (Harman) *nursing administrator*

Leo
Ridderheim, Mary Margaret *psychotherapist*

Madison
Cutschall, John Ray *hospital administrator*

Merrillville
Ledbetter, Brenda LaVerne *women's health nurse*

Michigan City
Brown, Arnold *physical therapy consultant*

Muncie
Bonneau, Sue Ellen *advancement researcher*
Freestone, Jeannette Warren *nurse practitioner*
Hoffman, Mary Catherine *nurse anesthetist*
Irvine, Phyllis Eleanor *nursing educator, administrator*
Terrell, Pamela Sue *pharmacist*

Munster
Nidetz, Myron Philip *health care delivery systems consultant, medical*
Palmer, Marcia Ann *healthcare management consultant, pharmacist*

New Albany
Yeager, Lillian Elizabeth *nurse educator*

New Castle
Ford-Catron, Mary Elaine *nurse*

Noblesville
Tank, Rod Gaillard *orthopaedic physical therapist*

North Manchester
Seward, Steven Le Mar *optometrist*

Orleans
Mapes, Mary Etta *critical care and emergency room nurse*

Richmond
†Anderson, Claudia W. *oncology nurse*

Rockport
Parker, Mary Anne *retired critical care nurse*

South Bend
Greenberg, Bruce Loren *health facility administrator*
Plunkett, Phyllis Jean *nursing administrator*
Szigeti, Michelle Marie *critical care nurse*

Terre Haute
Coe, Michual William *physical therapist*
Frank, Paula Elizabeth *nursing educator*

Upland
Koontz, Lisa Elaine *speech-language pathologist*

Valparaiso
Carr, Wiley Nelson *hospital administrator*

Wabash
Leach, Elaine Kay *speech clinician*

West Lafayette
Belcastro, Patrick Frank *pharmaceutical scientist*
Christian, John Edward *health science educator*
Evanson, Robert Verne *pharmacy educator*
Kirksey, Avanelle *nutrition educator*
Nichols, David Earl *pharmacy educator, researcher, consultant*
Peck, Garnet Edward *pharmacist, educator*
Steer, Max David *speech pathologist, educator*

Westville
Van Cauwenbergh, Janice Topp *mental health and clinical nurse specialist, educator*

Winchester
Tanner, Judith Ann *retired speech-language pathologist*

Windfall
Cooper, Joyce Beatrice *medical/surgical nurse*

IOWA

Ainsworth
Osterkamp-Sellars, Arlene Judy *gerontology nurse*

Anamosa
Haas, Lu Ann *counselor*

Cedar Rapids
Sueppel, Carralee Ann *medical/surgical nurse*
Ziese, Nancylee Hanson *social worker*

Council Bluffs
Blum, Vicky Jolene *medical/surgical nurse*

Davenport
Caffery, Lisa Kaye *nurse*
Melissano, Rita Rosaria *social work educator, marriage, family therapist*

Des Moines
Burgess, Donna Elaine *clinical social worker*
Dawson, Armetta K. *mental health and geriatric nurse*
Eichner, Kay Marie *mental health nurse*
Hall, Donald Vincent *social worker*
Kramer, Mary Elizabeth *health services executive, state legislator*
Molden, A(nna) Jane *retired counselor*
Moos, Pamela Sue *family development specialist*
Waldon, Marja Parker *mental health nurse*

Dubuque
Barker, Barbara Yvonne *nursing home administrator*

Fort Dodge
Sutton, Melle Renee *laboratory technician*

Glenwood
Campbell, William Edward *mental hospital administrator*

Ida Grove
Glisson, Melissa Ann *dietitian*

Inwood
Jacobs, Patricia Louise *geriatrics nurse*

Iowa City
Banker, Gilbert Stephen *industrial and physical pharmacy educator, administrator*
Colloton, John William *university health care executive*
Craft-Rosenberg, Martha Jane *nursing educator*
Cyphert, Stacey Todd *health facilities administrator*
Groves, William Arthur *industrial hygiene educator*
Howell, Robert Edward *hospital administrator*
Muir, Ruth Brooks *counselor, substance abuse service coordinator*
Nesbitt, John Arthur *recreation service educator, recreation therapy educator*
†Schlueter, Mary Sue *nurse*
Wurster, Dale Eric *pharmacy educator*
Wurster, Dale Erwin *pharmacy educator, university dean emeritus*

Jesup
Loeb, DeAnn Jean *nurse*

Johnston
Schumacher, Larry P. *health facility administrator*

Keokuk
Fecht, Lorene *surgical nurse*

Knoxville
Just, Jennie Martha *mental health nurse*
Taylor, Mary Kay *medical, surgical nurse*

Lake Mills
Knudtson, Nancy Ann *family nurse practitioner*
Thompson, Jeannine Lucille *community health nurse*

Manchester
†Sherman, Jane Candace *nurse*

Ottumwa
Lanman, Brenda Kay *operating room nurse*

Shenandoah
Hanna, Suzanne Louise *nurse*

Sioux City
Anderson, Paula D.J. *pharmacist*
Motz, Debra Sue *critical care nurse*
Tronvold, Linda Jean *occupational therapist*

Walford
Brooks, Debra Lynn *neuromuscular therapist, educator*

Waverly
Juhl, Dorothy Helen *social worker, retired*

West Des Moines
Zimmerman, Jo Ann *health services and educational consultant, former lieutenant governor*

KANSAS

Bonner Springs
Elliott-Watson, Doris Jean *psychiatric, mental health and gerontological nurse educator*

Colby
†Flanagin, Luetta Mae *family and pediatric nurse practitioner*

Courtland
Johnson, Dorothy Phyllis *retired counselor, art therapist*

El Dorado
Edwards, Alisyn Arden *marriage and family therapist*

Fort Leavenworth
Oliver, Thornal Goodloe *health care executive*

Goddard
Picotte, Susan Gaynel *geriatrics nurse, nursing educator, rehabilitation nurse*

Hays
Champion, Michael Edward *physician assistant, clinical perfusionist*
Curl, Eileen Deges *nursing educator*
Hassett, Mary Ruth *nursing educator*
Zerr, Dean A. *family nurse practitioner*

Hutchinson
Schmidt, Gene Earl *hospital administrator*

Iuka
Bryan, Cynthia Joan *emergency medical science educator, special education educator*

Junction City
Lacey, Roberta Balaam *emergency room nurse*

Kansas City
Davidson, Laura Janette *nurse practitioner, educator*
Gilliland, Marcia Ann *nurse clinician, infection control specialist*
Godwin, Harold Norman *pharmacist, educator*
Jerome, Norge Winifred *nutritionist, anthropologist*
Kenyon, Elinor Ann *social worker*
Klingele, Janine Marie *nursing administrator*
Peddicord, Tom E. *pharmacist*
Taunton, Roma Lee *nurse educator*
Ternus, Jean Ann *nursing educator*

Larned
Davis, Mary Elizabeth *speech pathologist, educator, counselor*
Zook, Martha Frances Harris *retired nursing administrator*

Lawrence
Frick, John William *health industry executive*
Loudon, Karen Lee *physical therapist*
Mc Coin, John Mack *social worker*
Searles, Lynn Marie *nurse*

Leawood
Tonkens, Rebecca Annette *maternal women's health nurse*

Lenexa
Laven, David Lawrence *nuclear and radiologic pharmacist, consultant*

Manhattan
Chance-Reay, Michaeline K. *educator, psychotherapist*
Moss, Larry W. *nursing administrator, quality management consultant*
Spears, Marian Caddy *dietetics and institutional management educator*

Newton
Westerhaus, Catherine K. *social worker*

North Newton
Schroeder, Gregg LeRoy *critical care nurse*

Olathe
Jones, Robert Lyle *emergency medical services leader, educator*

Overland Park
Bleich, Michael Robert *healthcare administrator and consultant*
Bronaugh, Deanne Rae *home health care administrator, consultant*
Hagemaster, Julia Nelson *nursing educator*
Hudson, Tajquah Jaye *managed health care executive*
Japp, Nyla F. *infection control services administrator*

Quinter
Brooks, Joyce Julianna *gerontological nurse*

Shawnee Mission
Breen, Katherine Anne *speech and language pathologist*
Jones, George Humphrey *retired healthcare executive, hospital facilities and communications consultant*
Wallace, Sherry Lynn *speech-language pathologist*

Sterling
Rogers, Rita Doris Luck *family nurse practitioner*

Topeka
Covington-Kent, Dawna Marie *chemical dependency counselor, continuing care and outpatient coordinator, writer*
Frogge, Beverly Ann *nurse, consultant*
Heim, Dixie Sharp *family practice nurse clinician*
Sheffel, Irving Eugene *psychiatric institution executive*
Varner, Charleen LaVerne McClanahan (Mrs. Robert B. Varner) *nutritionist, educator, administrator, dietitian*

Valley Center
Bryan, Paul Edward *pharmacist*

Wellington
Winn, Robert Cheever *rehabilitation services professional*

Wichita
Arnold, Donald Raymond *addiction consultant*
Ceradsky, Shirley Ann *psychiatric nursing*
Danuatmodjo, Cheryl Lynn *home healthcare nurse*
Guthrie, Diana Fern *nursing educator*
Healy, Patricia Colleen *social worker*
Hicks, M. Elizabeth (Liz Hicks) *pharmacist*
Stewart, John G., III *health science association administrator*

Winfield
Hall, Lydia Jane *geriatrics nurse*
Laws, Carolyn Marie Roderick *medical surgical nurse, pediatrics nurse*

KENTUCKY

Berea
Schaffer, Susan D. *nursing educator, family nurse practitioner*

Bowling Green
Pierce, Verlon Lane *pharmacist, small business owner*

Calvert City
Butler, Sheila Morris *occupational health nurse*

Campbellsville
Dickens, Michele *registered nurse, educator*
Martin, Mary Lois *nursing director, critical care nurse*

Corbin
Mahan, Shirley Jean *nursing educator*

Cynthiana
Dorton, Truda Lou *medical, surgical and geriatrics nurse*

Edgewood
Sansone, Susan Mary *nursing administrator*

Elizabethtown
Ball, Randall *physician assistant, medical technologist*
Morgan, Mary Dan *social worker*

Lexington
†Bell, Marcia Malone *marriage and family therapist, researcher*
Davis, George A. *pharmacologist, medical researcher*
DeLuca, Patrick Phillip *pharmaceutical scientist, educator, administrator*
Farrar, Donna Beatrice *hospital official*
Kelso, Lynn A. *acute care nurse practitioner*
Langford, Sheila Brandise *nurse*
Leukefeld, Carl George *researcher, educator*

Walize, Reuben Thompson, III *health research administrator*

London
Arekapudi, Kumar Vijaya Vasantha *compliance consultant, real estate agent*

Louisville
Arnold, Claire Groemling *health care analyst*
Berger, Barbara Paull *social worker, marriage and family therapist*
DeKay, Barbara Ann *social worker*
Harpring, Linda Jean *critical care and psychiatric nurse*
Holmes, Gary Lee *medical/surgical nurse*
Jones, David Allen *health facility executive*
Lake, Nancy Jean *nursing educator, operating room nurse*
Lofton, Kevin Eugene *medical facility administrator*
Martin, Shirley Bogard *maternal/women's health nurse administrator*
O'Bryan, Mary Louise *nursing administrator, consultant*
Rose, Judy Hardin *nursing administrator*
Rowe, Melinda Grace *public health service officer*
Scott, Lolita Jean *social worker*

Morehead
Johnson, Charlene Denise Logan *medical/surgical and pediatric nurse*

Mount Vernon
Nielsen, Lu Ed *retired community health nurse, civic worker*

Paducah
Cloyd, Bonita Gail Largent *rehabilitation nurse, educator*
Wurth, Susan Winsett *health facility manager*

Prestonsburg
Elliott, Myra Turner *nursing educator*

Rousseau
Bach, Betty Jean *health services educator*

Russellville
Harper, Shirley Fay *nutritionist, educator, consultant, lecturer*

Southgate
Miller, Catherine Ann *nursing administrator*

Whitesburg
Williams, Debbie Kaye *optometrist*

Wilmore
Abbott, Edna Eleanor *nurse, retired*

LOUISIANA

Alexandria
Bradford, Louise Mathilde *social services administrator*
†Jones, Syble Thornhill *dietitian*
Slipman, (Samuel) Ronald *hospital administrator*
Sneed, Ellouise Bruce *nursing educator*

Baton Rouge
Cahill, Marion Frances *nursing and psychology educator*
Chastant, Ledoux J., III *medical clinic administrator*
Davidge, Robert Cunninghame, Jr. *hospital administrator*
Estevens, Ellen Munsil *healthcare professional*
Palmer, Curtis Dwayne *cardiopulmonary practitioner, microbiologist, researcher, builder*
Vaeth, Agatha Min-Chun Fang *clinical nurse, nursing administrator*
Winkler, Steven Robert *hospital administrator*

Bossier City
Fry, Randy Dale *emergency medical technician, paramedic*
Jaeger, Kathleen Rae *pediatrics nurse*

Cut Off
Adams, Laura Ann *critical care nurse*

Deridder
Stailey, Janie Ruth *occupational health nurse*

Hall Summit
Wimberly, Evelyn Louise Russell *nursing coordinator*

Hammond
Emerson, Peter Michael *counselor*

Harahan
Ryan, Teresa Weaver *obstetrical and clinical nurse specialist*

Harrisonburg
Alexander, Lisa D. *nursing administrator*

Houma
Davis, Cheryl Suzanne *critical care nurse*
Gillespie, Betty Glover *critical care nurse*

Jackson
Payne, Mary Alice McGill *behavior management healthcare quality consultant*

Jeanerette
Derise, Nellie Louise *nutritionist, educator, researcher*

La Place
Lodwick, Judith Lynne *nursing educator*

Lafayette
Boudreaux, Gloria Marie *nurse, educator*
Logan, Effie Tanner *mental health nurse*
†Mizelle, William Donner *optometrist*

Lake Charles
Briggs, Arleen Frances *mental health nurse, educator*
†Daigle, Cynthia Coffey *speech and language pathologist*
Dilks, Sattaria S. *mental health nurse, therapist*
Leonard, Sherry Ann *critical care nurse*

Lecompte
Clark, Mary Machen *community health nurse*

Mandeville
Bartee, Roberta P. *nursing educator*
Treuting, Edna Gannon *retired nursing administrator*

Metairie
Evans, Carol Rockwell *nursing administrator*
Friedman, Lynn Joseph *counselor*
Mayo, Edwin M. *physical therapist*
McVay, Mary Ruth *speech pathologist*

Natchitoches
Egan, Shirley Anne *retired nursing educator*

New Orleans
Belsom, John Anton (Jack) *writer, researcher*
†Brown, Mary Willoughby *health facilities administrator*
Burton, Barbara Able *psychotherapist*
Butler, Shirley Ann *social worker*
Cusimano, Cheryll Ann *nursing administrator*
Grace, Marcellus *pharmacy educator, university dean*
Hackman, Gwendolyn Ann *private duty nurse*
Hudzinski, Leonard Gerard *social worker*
Kuerley-Schaffer, Dawn Renee *medical/surgical nurse*
Martof, Mary Taylor *nursing educator*
Oliver, Ronald *retired medical technologist*
Price, Addie Marie Carter *healthcare consultant*
Remley, Theodore Phant, Jr. *counseling educator, lawyer*
Rigby, Perry Gardner *medical center administrator, educator, former university dean, physician*
Rodriguez, Susan Miller *nurse administrator*
Weiner, Roy Samuel *medical educator, health facility administrator*

Pineville
Adams, Jane Miller *retired psychotherapist*

Ruston
Phillips, Kathye *critical care, emergency nurse*

Shreveport
Angermeier, Ingo *hospital administrator, educator*
Carter, Louvenia McGee *nursing educator*
Heacock, Donald Dee *social worker*
Hummel, Kay Jean *physical therapist*
Launius, Beatrice Kay *critical care nurse, educator*
Schneider, Thomas Richard *hospital administrator*

Slidell
Hall, Ogden Henderson *retired allied health educator*

Terrytown
Olson, Sandra Dittman *medical and surgical nurse*

Thibodaux
Risch, Patricia Ann *critical care nurse, administrator*

West Monroe
White, Karen Jo *nurse*
Williams, Sandra Ward *critical care nurse*

MAINE

Auburn
Rausch, Shanti Jo Vogell *mental health nurse*

Augusta
Sotir, Thomas Alfred *healthcare executive, retired shipbuilder*

Bangor
Ballesteros, Paula M. *nurse*
Beaupain, Elaine Shapiro *psychiatric social worker*
Johnson, Sharon Marguerite *social worker, clinical hypnotherapist*
McGuigan, Charles James *rehabilitation therapist*

Brewer
Steele, Teresa Willett *psychiatric clinical nurse specialist, nursing educator*

Brunswick
Cotton, Joyce E. Doherty *mental health nurse*

Caribou
Swanson, Shirley June *registered nurse, adult education educator*

Cumberland Center
Brewster, Linda Jean *family nurse practitioner*

Dresden
Elvin, Peter Wayne *healthcare executive, consultant*

East Boothbay
Eldred, Kenneth McKechnie *acoustical consultant*

Falmouth
Grondin, Jerry Rene *marriage and family therapist*
Nickerson, Bruce Donald *case manager*

Fort Fairfield
Shapiro, Joan Isabelle *laboratory administrator, nurse*

Kittery
Clark, Sandra Ann *clinical social worker*

Mount Desert
Straus, Donald Blun *retired company executive*

New Gloucester
Kuhrt, Sharon Lee *nursing administrator*

Portland
Brigham, Christopher Roy *occupational medicine physician*
McDowell, Donald L. *hospital administrator*

Presque Isle
Barrett, Paul J. *pharmacist*

Scarborough
Berardelli, Catherine Marie *women's health nurse, nurse educator*
Hothersall, Loretta Anne *family nurse practitioner*

South Paris
Creighton, Elizabeth Gaston *counselor*

Waterville
Tormollan, Gary Gordon *health facility administrator, physical therapist*

Yarmouth
Smith, Gayle Muriel *medical/surgical nurse*

MARYLAND

Aberdeen Proving Ground
LaBar, Valerie Kulis *occupational health nurse*

Andrews Air Force Base
Wong, Ruth Ann *nursing administrator*

Annapolis
†Achenback, Nancy Banks *pediatric nurse*
Kushner, Jack *physician executive*
Libby, Jane Elliott *retired dietitian*

Arnold
Brandimore, Wadie Miller *retired pediatrics nurse*

Baltimore
Abeloff, Martin David *medical administrator, educator, researcher*
Applebaum, Gary E. *medical director, executive*
Beilenson, Peter Lowell *public health official*
Block, James A. *hospital administrator, pediatrician*
Boston, Wallace Ellsworth, Jr. *healthcare executive, financial consultant*
Brieger, Gert Henry *medical historian, educator*
Cunningham, Terence Thomas, III *hospital administrator*
Dickler, Howard Byron *biomedical administrator, research physician*
Evans, Judy Anne *health center administrator*
Feldman, Deborah Karpoff *nursing education consultant*
Frazier, Elaine C. *public health nurse*
Gisriel-Bradford, Barbara Ann *nurse administrator*
Gross, Kathleen Albright *interventional radiology nurse, educator*
Howard, Bettie Jean *surgical nurse*
Ingle, Joan Marie *nurse practitioner*
Jenkins, Louise Sherman *nursing researcher*
Knapp, David Allan *pharmaceutical educator, researcher*
Larch, Sara Margaret *chief operating officer*
Lashley, Mark Alan *physician assistant*
Lee, Carlton K. K. *clinical pharmacist, consultant, educator*
Lurie, Shelly Fern *therapist*
Palumbo, Francis Xavier Bernard *pharmacy educator*
Piotrow, Phyllis Tilson *public health educator, international development specialist*
Ryan, Judith W. *geriatrics nurse, adult nurse practitioner, educator, researcher*
Sachs, Murray B. *audiologist, educator*
Sallese, Paula Marie *critical care, resuscitation nurse*
Santamaria, Barbara Matheny *nurse practitioner*
Scheel, Paul Joseph, Jr. *health facility administrator, physician*
Shapiro, Sam *health care analyst, biostatistician*
Sharfstein, Steven Samuel *health care executive, medical director*
Stark, Brian Alan *nurse anesthetist, nursing administrator*
Steinwachs, Donald Michael *public health educator*
Sudia, Mary Eileen *nurse*
Swinson, Angela Anthony *physician*
Walker, Erda Theresa *nursing administrator*
Walton, Kimberly Ann *medical laboratory technician*
Wieczorek, Patricia Christine *medical/surgical nurse*
Williams, Anna M. *social worker*

Bel Air
Kwetkauskie, John A. *medical technologist*

Beltsville
Levin, Gilbert Victor *health information, services and products*
Rupp, Monica Cecilia *nursing administrator*

Berlin
Peters, Charity Nöel *health facility administrator*
Roche, Kathleen Anne *nursing administrator*

Berwyn Heights
†Kirchknopf, Matthew Bela *research laboratory manager*

Bethesda
Atwell, Constance Woodruff *health services executive, researcher*
Coelho, Anthony Mendes, Jr. *health science administrator*
Cotter, Dennis Joseph *health services company executive*
Dyer, Doris Anne *nursing consultant*
Ehrenfeld, Ellie (Elvera Ehrenfeld) *health science association administrator*
Fauci, Anthony Stephen *health facility administrator, physician*
Gaston, Marilyn Hughes *health facility administrator*
Geller, Ronald Gene *health administrator*
Hoyer, Mary Louise *social worker, educator*
Jonas, Gary Fred *health care center executive*
Koslow, Stephen Hugh *science administrator, pharmacologist*
Marino, Pamela Anne *health sciences administrator*
Metzger, Henry *federal research institution administrator*
Nee, Linda Elizabeth *social science analyst*
Obrams, Gunta Iris *research administrator*
Quraishi, Mohammed Sayeed *health scientist, administrator*
Sich, Jeffrey John *health education analyst*
Summers, Donald Fredrick *cancer research center administrator*
Talbot, Bernard *government medical research facility official, physician*
Vaitukaitis, Judith Louise *medical research administrator*
Varricchio, Claudette Goulet *health science administrator, researcher*

Bowie
Boland, Gerald Lee *health facility financial executive*

Burtonsville
Toussaint, Rose Marie *holistic physician, organ transplant surgeon*

Cheverly
Murphy, Kathy Jean *nursing administrator*
Wilkes, Deborah Ann *neonatal intensive care nurse*

Clarksville
Hung, Mei-Jong Chow *social worker*

Clinton
Ward, Sue Elleanore Fryer *social worker, state agency administrator*

College Park
Greenberg, Jerrold Selig *health education educator*
Younger, Deirdre Ann *pharmacist*

Columbia
Beaudin, Christy Louise *health care administrator, consultant*
Margolis, Vivienne O. *psychotherapist*
McDaniel, John Perry *health care company executive*
Sneck, William Joseph *counseling educator, researcher*
Stanek, Gena Stiver *critical care clinical nurse specialist*

Cumberland
Mazzocco, Gail O'Sullivan *nursing educator*
Wolford, Nancy Lou *medical and surgical nurse*

Denton
Camper, Michelle Gwen *community health nurse*

Edgewood
Tucker, Terry L. *critical care clinical nurse specialist*

Elkridge
Szilagyi, Sherry Ann *psychotherapist, lawyer*

Fallston
Lewis, Howard Franklin *chiropractor*

Frederick
Kung, Hsiang-fu *health facility administrator*

Gaithersburg
Bingham, Raymond Joseph *newborn intensive care nurse*
Golden, Thomas Rutledge *psychotherapist, author*
Peele, Roger *hospital administrator*
Tenney, Lisa Christine Gray *healthcare administrator*

Greenbelt
Morris, Joseph Anthony *health science association administrator*

Hagerstown
Harrison, Lois Smith *hospital executive, educator*
Rickard, Edythe *registered nurse, consumer advocate*

Hughesville
Ignatavicius, Donna Dennis *geriatrics and case management consultant*

Hyattsville
Bender, Randi Laine *occupational therapist*
Sondik, Edward J. *health science administrator*

Kensington
Hayunga, Mary Ann *women's health nurse*
Schmerling, Erwin Robert *counselor, retired physicist*

Lanham Seabrook
Cook, Linda Kay *critical care nurse*

Largo
Isom, Virginia Annette Veazey *nursing educator*

Laurel
Landis, Donna Marie *nursing administrator, women's health nurse*

Lutherville
Goodman, Valerie Dawson *psychiatric social worker*

Monkton
Kernan, Pamela Lynne *critical care nurse*

Mount Lake Park
McClintock, Donna Mae *social worker*

North Bethesda
Trachtenberg, Alan I. *public health physician*

Olney
Michael, Jerrold Mark *public health specialist, former university dean, educator*
Weller, Jane Kathleen *emergency nurse*
Westerman, Rosemary Matzzie *nurse, administrator*

Owings Mills
Hubley, Carole Fierro *family nurse practitioner*
Kelly-Jones, Denise Marie *critical care nurse*

Parsonsburg
Holley, Marie Theresa *medical/surgical nurse*

Perry Point
Yackley, Luke Eugene *nursing administrator, mental health nurse*

Potomac
Cohen, Trudy Ornstein *adult nurse practitioner, educator*
Heller, Peggy Osna *psychotherapist, poetry therapist*
Higgins, Nancy Branscome *management and counseling educator*
Leva, Neil Irwin *psychotherapist, hypnotherapist*
Leva, Susan Mary *social worker*
Millonig, Virginia Layng *health education and publishing company executive*
Reynolds, Frank Miller *retired government administrator*

Rockville
Bloch, Bobbie Ann *nurse, educator*
Caswell, Steven James *health care administrator*
Conner, Susan Gordon *nurse, organization official, consultant*
Gabelnick, Henry Lewis *medical research director*
Gleich, Carol S. *health professions education executive*
Howard, Lee Milton *international health consultant*
Hsia, David *health services researcher, administrator*
Kimzey, Lorene Miller *endocrinology nurse*
Lewis, Benjamin Pershing, Jr. *pharmacist, public health service officer*
Long, Cedric William *health research executive*
McCormick, Kathleen Ann Krym *geriatrics nurse, computer information specialist, federal agency science administrator*
Mealy, J. Burke () *psychological services administrator*
Milner, Max *food and nutrition consultant*
Nightingale, Stuart Lester *physician, public health officer*
O'Donnell, James Francis *retired health science administrator*
†Pappas, Gregory *health agency administrator*
Plaut, Thomas F.A. *psychologist*
Smith, Shelagh Alison *public health educator*
Tabibi, S. Esmail *pharmaceutical researcher, educator*
Trujillo, Michael H. *administrator*

Sabillasville
McCulloch, Anna Mary Knott *pharmacy technician*

Saint Michaels
Young, Donald Roy *pharmacist*

Silver Spring
Basinger, Karen Lynn *renal dietitian*
†McLean, Scotia Lee *healthcare administrator*
Munson, John Christian *acoustician*
O'Connell, Mary Ita *psychotherapist*
O'Connor, Elizabeth Ann *enterostomal therapy rehabilitation nurse*
Ow, Elizabeth *women's health nurse*
Waldmann, Katharine Spreng *public health physician*

Towson
Sheredos, Carol Ann *rehabilitation clinical specialist*

Westminster
Lippy, Karen Dorothy Fethe *nurse psychotherapist*

MASSACHUSETTS

Acton
Brody, Leslie Gary *social worker, sociologist*
Buck-Moore, Joanne Rose *nursing administrator, educator*

Attleboro
Bischoff, Marilyn Brett *clinical social worker*

Ayer
Falter, Robert Gary *correctional health care administrator, educator*

Bedford
Castaldi, David Lawrence *health care company executive*

Belmont
Junger, Miguel Chapero *acoustics researcher*
Rassulo, Donna Marie *nurse, poet, writer, television producer*

Berkley
Mills, Carol Andrews *mental health administrator*

Boston
Andrews, Sally May *healthcare administrator*
Avakian, Laura Ann *hospital administrator*
†Bannan, Patricia Mary *nutrition specialist, public relations consultant*
Blendon, Robert Jay *health policy educator*
Brackett, Sharon (Elaine) *medical/surgical nurse*
Brown, Ellen Hynes *nursing administrator*
Deane, Sally Jan *health services administrator, consultant*
Drought, James Henry *healthcare business owner, exercise physiologist*
Fein, Rashi *health sciences educator*
Forman-Bello, Judith *clinical social worker*
Foster, Frances Barrett *advanced nurse practitioner*
Hemenway, David *public health educator*
Keyes, Carol Jane *nurse manager, surgical nurse*
Lamond, Sharon Ann *health facility administrator*
Liang, Matthew H. *medical director*
MacKay, Karel Lee *cancer institue administrator*
Markowitz, Phyllis Frances *mental health services administrator, psychologist*
Millar, Sally Gray *nurse*
†Noble, Mildred M. *retired social worker*
Otten, Jeffrey *health facility administrator*
†Reinertsen, James L. *healthcare executive*
Reinherz, Helen Zarsky *social services educator*
†Robbins, Catherine *healthcare executive*
Santos, Brenda Ann *community health clinical specialist*
Schottland, Edward Morrow *hospital adminstrator*
Scrimshaw, Nevin Stewart *physician, nutrition and health educator*

Stare, Fredrick John *nutritionist, biochemist, physician*
†Ullian, Elaine S. *health facility administrator*
Weinstein, Milton Charles *health policy educator*
Winkelman, James Warren *hospital administrator, pathology educator*
Wirth, Dyann Fergus *public health educator, microbiologist*

Boxford
Hoover, Lynn Di Shong *psychotherapist, health care consultant*

Brighton
†Novack, Sandy Alissa *social worker*

Brockton
Sherman, Beverly Robin *medical/surgical, pediatric nurse*

Brookline
Erick, Miriam Anna *dietitian, medical writer*
Kibrick, Anne *nursing educator, university dean*

Cambridge
Clifton, Anne Rutenber *psychotherapist*
Young, Vernon Robert *nutrition, biochemistry educator*

Canton
Bihldorff, John Pearson *hospital director*
Sawtelle, Carl S. *psychiatric social worker*

Centerville
Rieber, Jesse Alvin *psychotherapist*

Cheshire
Frye-Moquin, Marsha Marie *social worker*

Chestnut Hill
Hawkins, Joellen Margaret Beck *nursing educator*

Chicopee
Dame, Catherine Elaine *acupuncturist*

Concord
Liljestrand, James Stratton *physician administrator, internist*

Danvers
Baures, Mary Margaret *psychotherapist, author*

Dracut
Brousseau, Catherine F. *school health services director*
Medor, Janice Elizabeth *healthcare administrator*

Fall River
King, Paula Jean *nursing administrator*

Foxboro
Aubert, Kenneth Stephen *guidance and counseling administrator, educator*

Framingham
Austin, Sandra Ikenberry *nurse educator, consultant*
O'Bannon, Jacqueline Michele *geriatrics and mental health nurse*
Vermette, Raymond Edward *clinical laboratories administrator*

Gloucester
Johnson, Anne Elisabeth *medical assistant*

Grafton
Hayes, Jacqueline M. *geriatrics nurse*

Greenfield
Curtiss, Carol Perry *nursing consultant*

Hanson
Norris, John Anthony *health sciences executive, lawyer, educator*

Harvard
Evdokimoff, Merrily Weber *nursing administrator, community health nurse*
Larson, Roland Elmer *health care executive*

Holden
Owoc, CherylAnn Smith *geriatrics nurse, educator*

Holyoke
Bilsky, Edward Gerald *clinical social worker*
Chapdelaine, Lorraine Elder *gerontology nurse*
Florek, Leona *nursing educator*
Lambert, Jean Marjorie *health care executive*

Hopedale
Breault, Jean Winsor *nursing consultant*

Hyannis
Nicholson, Ellen Ellis *clinical social worker*
White, Allen Jordan *nursing home adminstrator, consultant*

Jamaica Plain
Brown, Mary Jean *public health nurse*
Manzo, David William *human services administrator*

Lanesboro
Wheeler, Kathleen Marie *emergency nurse*

Lawrence
Mosca, Anthony John *substance abuse professional*

Leominster
Lorente, Roderick Dana *optometrist*

Lexington
Bombardieri, Merle Ann *psychotherapist*
Densmore, Ann *speech pathologist, audiologist, writer*
Perez, Carol Anne *rehabilitation services professional*
Powers, Martha Mary *nursing consultant, education specialist*

Strange, Donald Ernest *health care company executive*

Littleton
Miller, Debra *psychiatric nurse therapist*
Pradas, Nanci Mara *social worker*

Lowell
Richards, Constance Ellen *nursing school administrator, consultant*
Sakellarios, Gertrude Edith *retired office nurse*

Ludlow
Budnick, Thomas Peter *social worker*

Manchester
Moody, Marianna S. *dietitian*

Marblehead
Plakans, Shelley Swift *social worker, psychotherapist*

Marion
McPartland, Patricia Ann *health educator*
Verni, Mary L. *medical/surgical and orthopedics nurse*

Mashpee
Rockett-Bolduc, Agnes Mary *nurse*

Mattapoisett
Perry, Blanche Belle *physical therapist*

Methuen
Jean, Patricia Anne *medical center administrator*

Middleboro
Sylvia, Constance Miriam *family nurse practitioner, clinical specialist*

Nantucket
Bartlett, Cheryl Ann *public health service administrator*

Natick
Bower, Kathleen Anne *nurse consultant*
Stack, Diane Virginia *social service agency officer*

Needham
Gormley, Gail F. *mental health nurse*

New Bedford
LaPorte, Adrienne Aroxie *nursing administrator*
Merolla, Michele Edward *chiropractor, broadcaster*
Raposo, Deborah F. *nursing administrator*

Newburyport
Appleton, Daniel Randolph, Jr. *optometrist*

Newton
Benedict, Mary-Anne *educator*

Newtonville
Monroe, Ramona Frey *nurse*

North Andover
Riendeau, Theresa Frances *rehabilitation nurse*

North Attleboro
Bordeleau, Lisa Marie *human services professional, consultant*
Williams, Ruth L. *rehabilitation counselor, consultant*

North Easton
Dyer, Marsha Jean *critical care nurse*

Norwood
Malay, Marcella Mary *nursing educator, administrator*

Osterville
Weber, Adelheid Lisa *former nurse, chemist*
Williams, Ann Meagher *retired hospital administrator*

Palmer
Holland, Joseph Daniel *psychologist, counselor*

Pembroke
Egan, Denise *home health nurse*
Khoylian, Carol J. *nurse*

Pittsfield
†Blodgett, Ruth *medical executive*

Plymouth
Reid, Nanci Glick *health care professional*

Roxbury
Kelley, Ruth M. *nurse, alcohol, drug abuse services professional*

Salem
Loftis, Rebecca Hope *psychotherapist*
Wathne, Carl Norman *hospital administrator*

Sandwich
Terrill, Robert Carl *hospital administrator*

Sharon
Reilley, Dennen *research agency administrator, educator*

Shutesbury
Gilliam, Charles Lamb, Jr. *body therapist*

Somerset
Fletcher, Dorothy *community health and primary home care nurse*

Somerville
Levensaler, Walter Louis *human resources consultant*

South Attleboro
Shaw, Paul Duane *mental health administrator, social worker, psychotherapist*

South Dennis
Stiefvater, Pamela Jean *chiropractor*

South Yarmouth
McGill, Grace Anita *retired occupational health nurse*

Southborough
Hegsted, David Mark *nutritionist*

Southbridge
Anderson, Ross Barrett *healthcare environmental services manager*
Mangion, Richard Michael *health care executive*
Paszkowski, Susan P. *critical care, office and home care nurse*

Springfield
Moore, Janet Ruth *nurse, educator*
Murphy, Jeanne S. *retired nursing administrator*
Stano, Joseph Francis *rehabilitation counseling educator*

Stoughton
Koffman, Alexandra *medical/surgical nurse*

Sudbury
Murphy, Ann Marie *nurse consultant and educator*

Swampscott
Smith, Carl Dean, Jr. *counselor, young adult advocate, basketball coach*

Swansea
Butler, Ethel Vieira *utilization review nurse*

Taunton
Davis, Lynn Karen *health facility administrator*

Tewksbury
Herlihy-Chevalier, Barbara Doyle *mental health nurse*
Scipione, Diana Sue *psychiatric and mental health nurse*

Vineyard Haven
Knowles, Christopher Allan *healthcare executive*
Rose, Kathleen Nolan *health facility administrator*

Wakefield
McKenna, Mary Elizabeth *nursing educator*

Walpole
Cotter, Douglas Adrian *healthcare executive*

Waltham
Mitchell, Janet Brew *health services researcher*

Watertown
Pellegrom, Daniel Earl *international health and development executive*

Wellesley
Montague, Joel Gedney *public health consultant*
Sutter, Linda Diane *health services administrator*

Westborough
Badenhausen, John Phillips, II *mental health facility administrator*
Gordon, Betty L. *health services administrator*

Weston
Van Keuren, Korinne Suzanne *pediatrics and orthopedics nurse practitioner*
Walker, Marsha *lactation consultant*

Westwood
Donahue, Charles Lee, Jr. *health network executive*

Whitinsville
DiVitto, Sharon Faith *mental health nurse, administrator*

Wilmington
Freeman, Donald Chester, Jr. *health care company executive*

Woburn
Goela, Jitendra Singh *researcher, consultant*
Smith, Judith Ann *retired geriatrics nurse*

Worcester
Capriole, Sister Carmen Maria *geriatric nurse*
Cashman, Suzanne Boyer *health services administrator, educator*
Hatstat, Judy Anne *nursing administrator*
Walker, Gail Flanagan *maternal/child nurse, administrator*

Yarmouth Port
Phelps, Judson Hewett *therapist, counselor, marketing sales executive*

MICHIGAN

Ada
Bandemer, Norman John *healthcare consulting executive*

Allen Park
Kirby, Dorothy Manville *social worker*

Allendale
Haller, Kathleen *nursing educator, family nurse practitioner*

Ann Arbor
Clark, Noreen Morrison *behavioral science educator, researcher*
Depew, Charles Gardner *research company executive*
Gordinier, Terri Klein *speech-language pathologist*
Griffith, John Randall *health services administrator, educator*
Kalisch, Beatrice Jean *nursing educator, consultant*
Ketefian, Shaké *nursing educator*
Romani, John Henry *health administration educator*

PROFESSIONAL INDEX 5993 HEALTHCARE: HEALTH SERVICES

Rupp, Ralph Russell *audiologist, educator, author*
Sasaki, Joseph Donald *optometrist*
Schweitzer, Pamela Bifano *psychiatric and mental health nurse practitioner*
Waldecker, Thomas Raymond *social worker*
Warner, Kenneth E. *public health educator, consultant*
†Warren, Larry *healthcare executive*

Berrien Center
Dunbar, Mable Cleone *counselor education, family*

Big Rapids
Lowther, Gerald Eugene *optometry educator*

Bloomfield Hills
Millsap, Barbara Ann *clinical social worker*
Schoenhals, Katherine Viola *social worker*

Central Lake
Hocking, Marian Ruth *women's health nurse*

Charlotte
Herrick, Kathleen Magara *social worker*

Chesterfield
Burnett, Gary Main *social work administrator, crisis counselor*

Croswell
Cannaday, Paul Benjamin-Dielman *handicap resources educator, consultant*

Dearborn
Suchy, Susanne N. *nursing educator*

Detroit
Berke, Amy Turner *health science association administrator*
Garriott, Lois Jean *clinical social worker, educator*
Heppner, Gloria Hill *medical science administrator, educator*
Jacox, Ada Kathryn *nurse, educator*
Mack, Robert Emmet *hospital administrator*
Marsh, Harold Michael *administrator*
†Marshall, Douglas W. *medical administrator, educxator*
Merritt, Danna Wray *social worker*
Miller Davis, Mary-Agnes *social worker*
Prasad, Ananda Shiva *medical educator*
Redman, Barbara Klug *nursing educator*
Tisdale, James Edward *pharmacy educator, pharmacotherapy researcher*
†Velick, Stephen H. *medical facility administrator*
Warden, Gail Lee *health care executive*

Farmington Hills
Abrams, Roberta Busky *hospital administrator, nurse*
Burns, Sister Elizabeth Mary *hospital administrator*
Cooper, Elaine Janice *physical therapist*

Fenton
Anas, Julianne Kay *retired administrative laboratory director*

Flint
Alarie-Anderson, Peggy Sue *physician assistant*
Millon, Delecta Gay *nursing educator*
Palinsky, Constance Genevieve *hypnotherapist, educator*
Stafford, Marjorie *emergency department nurse*
Williams, JoAnn Lucille *nurse*

Franklin
DeBrincat, Susan Jeanne *nutritionist*

Fruitport
Anderson, Frances Swem *nuclear medical technologist*

Grand Ledge
Evert, Sandra Florence (Wheeler) *medical/surgical nurse*

Grand Rapids
Brent, Helen Teressa *school nurse*
Chase, Sandra Lee *clinical pharmacist, consultant*
Jackson, Wendy S Lewis *social worker*
Kramer, Carol Gertrude *marriage and family counselor*
Miller, Barbara Jean *nephrology home care nurse*

Gregory
Zarley, Karlta Rae *nurse consultant*

Grosse Pointe
Cartmill, George Edwin, Jr. *retired hospital administrator*
Knapp, Mildred Florence *retired social worker*

Hastings
Adrounie, V. Harry *public health administrator, scientist, educator, environmentalist*

Holland
Franken, Darrell *counselor, writer, publisher*

Houghton Lake
Marra, Samuel Patrick *retired pharmacist, small business owner*

Howell
Korsgren, Mary Louise *home care nurse*

Jackson
Richard, Lyle Elmore *retired school social worker, consultant*

Kalamazoo
Bennett, Arlie Joyce *clinical social worker emeritus*
†Lacey, Bernardine M. *nursing administrator, educator*
Lander, Joyce Ann *nursing educator, medical/surgical nurse*
Ortiz-Button, Olga *social worker*

Lansing
Terry, Russell, Jr. *home health aide*

Livonia
Gaipa, Nancy Christine *pharmacist*

Marlette
Brabant, Lori Ann *nursing administrator*

Marquette
Hill, Betty Jean *nursing educator, academic administator*
†Pentland, Karen Jean *mental health facility administrator*
Poindexter, Kathleen A. Krause *nursing educator, critical care nurse*
Sherony, Cheryl Anne *dietitian*

Marysville
Ledtke, Kathryn Ann *community health nurse*

Mason
Frappier, Cara Munshaw *school social worker*

Monroe
Knezevich, Janice A. *critical care nurse*

Muskegon
Heyen, Beatrice J. *psychotherapist*
Mercer, Betty Deborah *electrologist, poet, writer, proofreader*

Negaunee
Matero, Janet Louise *counselor, educator*

Ortonville
Coffel, Patricia K. *retired clinical social worker*

Paw Paw
Walker, Kay S. *geropsychiatric nurse*

Petoskey
Hoshield, Susan Lynn *pediatric nurse practitioner*

Plymouth
McClendon, Edwin James *health science educator*
Stewart, Katherine Hewitt *advanced practice nurse*

Portage
Brown, John Wilford *surgical/medical company executive*

Rochester
†Rauch, Angelika Maria *psychoanalyst, educator*

Royal Oak
Lechner, Jon Robert *nursing administrator, educator*
Matzick, Kenneth John *hospital administrator*

Saginaw
Bosco, Jay William *optometrist*
Shackelford, Martin Robert *social worker*

Southfield
Denes, Michel Janet *physical therapist, consultant in rehabilitation*
Fennell, Christine Elizabeth *healthcare system executive*
Swartz, William John *managed care company executive*

Sterling Heights
Hammond-Kominsky, Cynthia Cecelia *optometrist*

Troy
Hunter, Lorie Ann *women's health nurse*
Kulich, Roman Theodore *healthcare administrator*
Lohrmann, David Kurt *curriculum director*
Potts, Anthony Vincent *optometrist, orthokeratologist*
White, James, Jr. *psychiatric, mental health nurse, consultant*

Warren
Arking, Lucille Musser *nurse epidemiologist*

West Bloomfield
Barr, Martin *health care and higher education adminstrator*
Myers, Kenneth Ellis *hospital administrator*
Romero, Josefino Tabernilla *nurse anesthetist*

Westland
Coates, Dianne Kay *social worker*
Shaw, Randy Lee *human services administrator*

Wyandotte
Consiglio, Helen *nursing educator and consultant*

Ypsilanti
Lucy, Dlorah Rae *medical/surgical nurse*

MINNESOTA

Bloomington
Hulbert, James Richard *health care educator, researcher*

Cokao
Weber, Rebecca Guenigsman *occupational health nurse*

Cottage Grove
Glazebrook, Rita Susan *nursing educator*

Duluth
Dillon, Herb Lester *critical care and emergency room nurse*
Stoddard, Patricia Florence Coulter *psychologist*

Eden Prairie
Skeie, Philip *health plan administrator*

Elysian
Thayer, Edna Louise *medical facility administrator, nurse*

Fairmont
McMurtry, Donna *multiarea nurse*

Georgetown
Thomas, Noreen Jo *healthcare system educator, writer*

Grand Rapids
Johnson, Janis Kay *pharmacist*

Hastings
Blackie, Spencer David *physical therapist, administrator*

Houston
Euler, Diana Leone *nursing educator*

Lilydale
Kilbourne, Barbara Jean *health and human services consultant*

Maple Grove
Manthei, Robin Dickey *research technician*

Maplewood
Gerber, Sandra Elaine *neonatal nurse practitioner*

Minneapolis
Appel, William Frank *pharmacist*
Dahl, Gerald LuVern *psychotherapist, educator, consultant, writer*
Erie, Gretchen Ann *cardiovascular clinician*
Farr, Leonard Alfred *hospital administrator*
Grant, David James William *pharmacy educator*
Hanson, A. Stuart *health facility administrator, physician*
Heston, Renate *nursing administrator*
Kennon, Rozmond Herron *physical therapist*
Kralewski, John Edward *health service administration educator*
Ledin Moser, Debra Joan *occupational health nurse practitioner*
Moncharsh, Jane Kline *rehabilitation counselor, vocational specialist, mediator, case manager*
†Ohanian, Valerie Gay *homeopathic practitioner*
Phelps, Dorothy Rose *critical care nurse*
Steen-Hinderlie, Diane Evelyn *social worker, musician*
Suryanarayanan, Raj Gopalan *researcher, consultant, educator*
Toscano, James Vincent *medical institute administration*
Travis, Marlene O. *healthcare management executive*
Walker, Elva Mae Dawson *health consultant*
Ziegenhagen, David Mackenzie *healthcare company executive*

Moorhead
Ritz, Eugene Frederick *therapist*

Mound
Rosdahl, Caroline Bunker *nurse, educator, author*

Park Rapids
Hansen, Marion Joyce *nursing administrator*

Plainview
Reincke, Rhonda Lea *nursing educator*

Prior Lake
O'Brochta-Woodward, Ruby Catherine *orthopedic nurse*

Robbinsdale
Anderson, Scott Robbins *hospital administrator*

Rochester
Frusti, Doreen Kaye *nursing administrator*
Gervais, Sister Generose *hospital consultant*
Johnson, Ruth Jeannette *nursing administrator*
Lichte, DeAnn *critical care nurse, educator*
†Poppen, Carroll Fredrick *physician assistant, educator*
Prendergast, Franklyn G. *health facility administrator, medical educator*
Stewart, Karen Meyer *pediatrics nurse, nursing manager*
Suelto, Consuelo Quilao *retired nursing educator*
Verbout, James Paul *recreational therapist*

Saint Paul
Ashton, Sister Mary Madonna *healthcare administrator*
†Barry, Anne M. *public health officer*
Feldman, Nancy Jane *health organization executive*
Gilgun, Jane Frances *social work educator*
Hoxmeier, Marlette Marie *nurse educator*
Murphy, Edrie Lee *hospital laboratory administrator*
†Varin, Jason Ashley *community pharmacist, educator*

Sandstone
Muth, William Henry Harrison, Jr. *medical/surgical nurse*

Springfield
Haseleu, Roseann Marie *medical/surgical nurse*

Stillwater
Francis, D. Max *healthcare management executive*
Rescigno, Aldo *pharmacokinetics educator*

Two Harbors
Carlson, Brian Jay *health facility executive*

Vergas
Joyce, Michael Daniel *personal resource management therapist and consultant, neurolearning therapist*

Warren
Kruger, Virginia Joy *health facility administrator, lecturer*

MISSISSIPPI

Biloxi
Erickson, Georganne Morris *nursing administrator, nursing educator, psychiatric-mental health consultant*

Brandon
Burch, Sharron Lee Stewart *woman's health nurse*

Cleveland
Taylor, Donna Buescher *marriage and family therapist*

Clinton
Jarnagin, Teresa Ellis *educator, nursing administrator*
Teague, Karen Lee Hawkins *nurse, administrator*

Gulfport
Perez, Jeffrey Joseph *optometrist*

Hattiesburg
Bilbo, Linda Sue Holston *home health nurse*

Jackson
King, Kenneth Vernon, Jr. *pharmacist*
Lilley, Evelyn Lewis *operating room nurse*
Malloy, James Matthew *managed care executive, health care consultant*
Tchounwou, Paul Bernard *environmental health specialist, educator*
Thornton, Larry Lee *psychotherapist, author, educator*
Williams, Jerrie Sue Dockery *nurse, administrator*

Macon
Johnson, Rolanda Lanetta *medical/surgical nurse, educator*

Mc Cool
Miller, Charlotte Faye *speech pathologist*

Meridian
Dear, Dana Lovorn *critical care nurse*

Natchez
Hutchins, Georgia Cameron *critical care nurse, nursing educator*

Nesbit
Berti, Phyllis Mae *health information management specialist*

Ocean Springs
Lee, Kathleen Mary *administration and nursing executive*
McNulty, Matthew Francis, Jr. *health sciences and health services administrator, educator, university administrator, consultant, horse and cattle breeder*
Parker, Rebecca Mary *special education facility administrator, educator*

Raleigh
Price, Tommye Jo Ensminger *community health nurse*

Tupelo
Zurawski, Jeanette *rehabilitation services professional*

Vicksburg
Hoover, Deborah *critical care, medical and surgical nurse*

Walls
Jones, Yvonne Dolores *social worker*

Waynesboro
Dickerson, Marie Harvison *nurse anesthetist*

Whitfield
Morton, James Irwin *hospital administrator*

MISSOURI

Arnold
Freukes, Patricia E. *pediatrics nurse, nursing supervisor*

Ballwin
Stevens, Julie Ann *peri-operative nurse*

Branson
Burch, Lori Ann *obstetrics nurse*

Brookfield
Wild, Stacie Ann *vocational counselor*

Camdenton
DeShazo, Marjorie White *occupational therapist*

Cameron
Ervans, Mary Sue (Tripolino) *health facility administrator*

Carrollton
Lysne, Allen Bruce *laboratory director*

Carthage
Coffield, Mary Eleanor *speech clinician, educator*

Cassville
Bates, Reitta Ione *retired mental health nurse*

Chesterfield
Allen, Linda Graves *air medical transport company executive*
Baumann, Carol Kay *clinical nurse specialist*
Robinson, Patricia Elaine *women's health nurse practitioner*

Columbia
Blaine, Edward H. *health science administrator, educator*

Brinegar, Elizabeth Anne *critical care nurse, educator*
†Cotton, Karen Theresa *audiologist*
Hensley, Elizabeth Catherine *nutritionist, educator*
Kilgore, Randall Freeman *health information services administrator*
McDonald, Annette Howard *mental health nurse*
†Reahr, Terrye Lee *nurse*
Stewart, Bobby Gene *laboratory director*

Crane
Rose, Terri Kaye *obstetrical gynecological nurse practitioner, forensic exam nurse*

Crystal City
Parish, Brenda Louise *telemetry nurse*

Dexter
Owens, Debra Ann *chiropractor*

Ellisville
Meiner, Sue Ellen Thompson *gerontologist, nursing educator and researcher*

Fayette
Burres, Carla Anne *medical technologist*

Fulton
Garrett, Marilyn Ruth *nurse*

Grandin
Wallace, Louise Margaret *nurse*

Hannibal
Beshears, Brenda K. *nursing educator*

Imperial
Hughes, Barbara Bradford *nurse, real estate manager*

Independence
Sturges, Sidney James *pharmacist, educator, investment and development company executive*
Vigen, Kathryn L. Voss *nursing administrator, educator*

Jackson
Schott, Marilyn Job *patient review auditor*

Jefferson City
Dey, Charlotte Jane *retired community health nurse*
Melton, June Marie *nursing educator*
Strifler, Vivian Elsie *health facilities nursing consultant*
Vieweg, Bruce Wayne *mental health researcher*

Joplin
Ferson, Lu Ann *medical and surgical nurse*

Kansas City
Butler, Alice Claire *rehabilitation nurse*
Collins, John W. *nurse practitioner, lecturer*
Dahl, Andrew Wilbur *health services executive*
Eddy, Charles Alan *chiropractor*
Johnson, Vicki Kristine *rehabilitation nurse*
Kendall, Earnest James *mental health nurse*
Kingsley, James Gordon *healthcare executive*
Lannigan, James William *voluntary service officer*
†Magee, Jon Dirk *health facility administrator, psychologist*
Oliver, Pauline *community health and geriatrics nurse*
Piepho, Robert Walter *pharmacy educator, researcher*
Steffens, John Howard *cytotechnologist*
Tansey, Robert Paul, Sr. *pharmaceutical chemist*
Thompson, Catherine Rush *physical therapist, educator*
†Williams, Arthur Ross *health service administrator*
Williams, Thelma Jean *social worker*
Zechman, David Mark *health system executive, educator*

Lebanon
Caplinger, Patricia E. *family nurse practitioner*

Lees Summit
Couch, Daniel Michael *healthcare executive*

Liberty
Samuel, Robert Thompson *optometrist*

Marshall
Miller, Toni M. Andrews *critical care nurse, educator*

Marshfield
Gloe, Donna *nursing administrator*

Neosho
Guthery, Carolyn J. *pediatrics nurse*

New Haven
Roth, Nancy Louise *former nurse, veterinarian*

Osborn
Findley, Delpha Yoder *retired public health nurse*

Osceola
Dysart, Diana Marie *women's health nurse, medical/surgical nurse*

Potosi
Duing, Edna Irene *women's health nurse, nurse educator*

Rogersville
Dowdy, Linda Katherine *psychiatric and geriatric nurse*

Saint Ann
Farrow, Julie Anne *retired geriatrics nurse, administrator*

Saint Charles
Humphries, Pamela Jean *women's health nurse*

Saint Joseph
Brown, Jean Gayle *social worker*
Johnson, Robert Charles *medical administrator*

Saint Louis
Austrin, Michael Steven *health care consultant, strategic planner*
Brewer, Elizabeth *family therapist*
Brown, Frederick Lee *health care executive*
Bryan, Jean Marie Wehmueller *nurse*
Clark, Jeanenne Frances *community health nurse specialist*
†DiTiberio, John Kesley *psychotherapist, educator, consultant*
Drucker, Barry Jules *environmental health specialist*
Ezenwa, Josephine Nwabuoku *social worker*
Farrell, John Timothy *hospital administrator*
†Fink, Tracey Marks *chiropractor*
Fitch, Rachel Farr *health policy analyst*
†Fleming, Susan *social worker*
Friedel, Helen Brangenberg *counselor, therapist*
Gacem, Debra Ann *critical care nurse*
Greenwalt, Mary Susan *counselor*
Harris, Roberta Lucas *social worker*
Hernandez-Ledezma, Jose Juan *laboratory administrator*
Herzfeld-Kimbrough, Ciby *mental health educator*
Horwitz, Rita *outpatient surgery nurse, educator*
Johnson, Gloria Jean *counseling professional*
Jones, Ronald Vance *health science association administrator*
Kiser, Karen Maureen *medical technologist, educator*
Koesterer, Larry J. *pharmacist*
Kolar, Janet Brostron *physician assistant, medical technologist*
LaBruyere, Thomas Edward *health facility administrator*
Leek, Diane Webb *nurse*
Magill, Gerard *health services educator*
Meyersick, Sharon Kay *nurse, insurance administrator*
Molloff, Florence Jeanine *speech and language therapist*
Ozawa, Martha Naoko *social work educator*
Rodenbaugh, Lisa Pyle *nurse*
Schoenhard, William Charles, Jr. *health care executive*
Sita, Michael John *pharmacist, educator*
†Slavin, Peter *hospital administrator*
Stratton, Sharon Elizabeth Spahn *mental and women's health nurse, nurse supervisor*
Stretch, John Joseph *social work educator, management and evaluation consultant*
Virgo, Katherine Sue *health services researcher*
Wood, Denise P. *clinical nurse specialist*

Smithville
Marzinski, Lynn Rose *oncological nurse*

Springfield
Byers, Thomas William *optometrist*
Feazell, Johnny Ray *physicians assistant*
Johnstone, Paula Sue *medical technologist*
McCullough, V. Beth *pharmacist, educator*
O'Block, Robert *behavioral scientist*
Prayson, Stephen Alexander *pharmacist*
Staudte, Diane Elaine *medical-surgical, cardiac nurse*
Williams, Juanita (Tudie Williams) *home health care nurse, administrator*

Steelville
Hagemeier, Juanita Elizabeth *human services administrator*

Warrensburg
Lewis, Marcile Reneé *nursing educator*

MONTANA

Billings
Glenn, Lucia Howarth *retired mental health services professional*

Great Falls
Annau, Raymone Jeanine *cardiovascular nurse*
Downer, William John, Jr. *retired hospital administrator*

Helena
Cordingley, Mary Jeanette Bowles (Mrs. William Andrew Cordingley) *social worker, psychologist, artist, writer*

Poplar
Gabrielson, Shirley Gail *nurse*

NEBRASKA

Danbury
Drullinger, Leona Pearl Blair *obstetrics nurse*

Fremont
Winans, Anna Jane *dietitian*

Grand Island
Etheridge, Margaret Dwyer *medical center director*
Ward, Kenneth Lee *recreation therapist*

Gretna
Hintz, Norma A. *cardiac care nurse*

Hastings
Bloyd, Beverly *nurse*

Kearney
Glatter, Kathleen Mary *medical/surgical nurse*
Wittman, Connie Susan *oncology clinical nurse specialist*

Lincoln
Hamilton, David Wendell *medical services executive*
Oman, Deborah Sue *health science facility administrator*

North Platte
Kockrow, Elaine Oden *nurse educator, medical/surgical nurse, obstetrical nursing*

Omaha
Baldwin, Jeffrey Nathan *pharmacy educator*
Christensen, Mari Alice *nursing auditor, medicolegal analyst, consultant*
Dash, Alekha K. *pharmaceutical scientist, educator*
†Hageman, Patricia Ann *physical therapy educator*
Johnson, Christine Ann *nurse*
Johnson, Opal M. *retired nurse assistant*
Lee, Carla Ann Bouska *nursing health care educator*
Leininger, Madeleine Monica *nurse, anthropologist, administrator, consultant, editor, author, educator*
Omer, Robert Wendell *hospital administrator*

Scottsbluff
Hippe, Anne Elaine *nursing educator*
Liakos, Angeline G. *retired nurse practitioner*
Olson, Ernestine Lee *nurse*

South Sioux City
Graves, Maureen Ann *counselor, minister*

West Point
Woodbury, Joyce Carol *office nurse*

Wilcox
Ziebarth, Lisa Marie *medical/surgical nurse*

NEVADA

Carson City
Roelke, Ada (Knock-Leveen) *retired psychotherapist*

Las Vegas
Beglinger, Susan Marie *marriage and family therapist, rehabilitation counselor*
Close, Jack Dean, Sr. *physical therapist*
DiOrio, Robert Joseph *psychotherapist, consultant*
Francis, Timothy Duane *chiropractor*
Gilchrist, Ann Roundey *hospice nurse*
Hallas, Evelyn Margaret *physical therapist*
Jagodzinski, Ruth Clark *nursing administrator*
Law, Flora Elizabeth (Libby Law) *retired community health and pediatrics nurse*
Leake, Brenda Gail *enterostomal therapist nurse practitioner*
Michel, Mary Ann Kedzuf *nursing educator*
Smith, Mary B. *medical and surgical nurse*
Van Noy, Terry Willard *health care executive*

Reno
Bramwell, Marvel Lynnette *nurse, social worker*
Graham, Denis David *marriage and family therapist, educational consultant*
Martinson, Julia Ellenor *health science administrator*
McDaniel, Susan Irene *nursing educator*
Middlebrooks, Deloris Jeanette *nurse, educator*
Pinson, Larry Lee *pharmacist*

NEW HAMPSHIRE

Brookline
Buff, Margaret Anne *psychiatric nurse*

Concord
Kalipolites, June Eleanor Turner *rehabilitation professional*
Mac Kay, James Robert *psychiatric social worker, mayor*
Teschner, Douglass Paul *mental health services executive*

Derry
Graff, David Austin *chiropractor*

Dover
Bergeron, Tracey Anne *mental health nurse, educator*

East Rochester
Zemojtel, Alexander Michael *corporate executive*

Enfield
Gamache, Kathleen Smith *retired psychotherapist*

Exeter
Sewitch, Deborah E. *health science association administrator, educator, sleep researcher*

Goffstown
Engebretson, Kathleen Mary Murray *women's health nurse, psychiatric nurse*

Greenfield
Wheelock, Major William, Jr. *health care adminstrator*

Hudson
Rice, Annie Laura Kempton *medical, surgical and rehabilitation nurse*

Keene
Lowell, Janet Ann *nurse*

Laconia
Mulloy, Paula Irene *nursing administrator*

Lebanon
†Oseid, Mary M. *health facility administrator*
Varnum, James William *hospital administrator*

Manchester
Ehlers, Eileen Spratt *family therapist*
Mailloux, Raymond Victor *health services administrator*

Nashua
MacPhail, Estelle R. *nursing administrator*

North Conway
Schmidt, Lynda Wheelwright *Jungian analyst*

Ossipee
Bartlett, Diane Sue *clinical mental health counselor, family therapist*

Sandown
Densen, Paul Maximillian *former health administrator, educator*

Tilton
Wolf, Sharon Ann *psychotherapist*

Webster
Blackey, Pamela Ann Conley *medical/surgical nurse*

Wilmot
Lambert, Elaine L. *surgical nurse, administrator*

Winnisquam
Ricker, Frances Margaret *nursing administrator*

NEW JERSEY

Ancora
Valo, Martha Ann *hospital dietary executive, consultant*

Asbury
Gardner, Janette Lynn *critical care nurse, educator*

Atlantic Highlands
Royce, Paul Chadwick *medical administrator*

Avalon
Beatrice, Ruth Hadfield *hypnotherapist, retired educator, financial administrator*

Bayonne
Blecher, Carol Stein *oncology clinical nurse specialist*
Scudder, Carol Ann *speech and language educator*

Belle Mead
Sarle, Charles Richard *health facility executive*
Wilson, Nancy Jeanne *laboratory director, medical technologist*

Blackwood
Breve, Franklin Stephen *pharmacist*

Bloomfield
Dickson, Geri Lenzen *nursing educator, researcher*

Bordentown
Blackson, Benjamin F(ranklin) *clinical social worker*

Bound Brook
Borah, Kripanath *pharmacist*

Brick
Rusoff, Irving Isadore *industrial food scientist, consultant*

Brigantine
Holl, James Andrew *prehospital care administrator*

Browns Mills
Backman, Alan Gregory *health sciences technologist*
Cholette, Maureen Theresa *geriatrics nurse, nursing administrator*

Burlington
Britt, Donna Marie *school nurse*
Rowlette, Henry Allen, Jr. *social worker*

Camden
Abbott, Ann Augustine *social worker, educator*
Dayer-Berenson, Linda *adult and critical care nurse, educator*
Elkind, Elizabeth C. *perinatal clinical specialist*
Lewis, Michael Seth *health care executive*
Wood, Martha Oakwell *obstetrical and gynecological nurse practitioner*

Chatham
Murphy, Joseph James *chiropractic physician*

Cherry Hill
Betchen, Stephen J. *marital, family and sex therapist*
Grado-Wolynies, Evelyn (Evelyn Wolynies) *clinical nurse specialist, educator*
Israelsky, Roberta Schwartz *speech pathologist, audiologist*
McCormick, Donna Lynn *social worker*
McDonald, Mary Ellen *retired nursing educator*

Clark
Kinley, David *physical therapist, acupuncturist*

Clifton
Adelsberg, Harvey *hospital administrator*
Colflesh, Gertrude Patterson (Trudy Colflesh) *psychotherapist, author*
Epstein, William Eric *health care executive*

East Hanover
Baillie, Stuart Gordon *research technician*
Joseph, Jannan Marie *school social worker*

Eatontown
O'Hare-VanMeerbeke, Anne Marie *dietitian*

Edison
Blumengold, Jeffrey Gene *health care financial and reimbursement expert*

Elmer
†Magnan, Ruthann *registered nurse, social worker*

Englewood
Koch, Randall Glory *hospital administrator*

Fanwood
Butler, Grace Caroline *medical administrator*

Florham Park
Atal, Bishnu Saroop *speech research executive*
Oths, Richard Philip *health systems administrator*
Sniffen, Michael Joseph *hospital administrator*

Forked River
Rudolph, Linda Louise *social worker, legal advocate*

Fort Lee
Welfeld, Joseph Alan *healthcare executive*

Freehold
Dillon, Patricia Harrington *medical/surgical nurse*

Glassboro
Fails, Donna Gail *mental health services professional*

Green Brook
Spoeri, Randall Keith *healthcare company executive*

Hackensack
Baker, Andrew Hartill *clinical laboratory executive*
Ferguson, John Patrick *medical center executive*
Michaelson, Richard Aaron *health science facility administrator*
Shapiro, Sylvia *psychotherapist*
Shaw, Julie Ann *addiction counselor*

Haddonfield
Payne, Deborah Anne *medical company officer*

Highlands
Saad, Valerie Ann *nursing administrator, naval officer*

Hightstown
Decker, Christine Marie *healthcare administrator*
Hart, Patricia Anne *public health officer*

Hillsdale
Kohan, Lois Rae *community health nurse*

Hillside
Patell, Mahesh *pharmacist, researcher*
Webb, Joyce *critical care nurse, educator, legal nurse consult*

Hopatcong
Caddigan, Mary *health facility administrator*
Wolahan, Caryle Goldsack *nursing educator*

Howell
Feinen, Cynthia Lucille *pediatric nurse*

Jersey City
Catalano, James Anthony *social worker*
Giorgio, Marilyn *social worker*
Giuffra, Lawrence John *hospital administrator, medical educator*

Kinnelon
Preston, Andrew Joseph *pharmacist, drug company executive*

Lakewood
Biasini, Virginia *social worker*

Lawrenceville
Griffith, Barbara E. *social worker, political activist*

Linden
Banda, Geraldine Marie *chiropractic physician*

Linwood
Cohen, Diana Louise *private practice, consultation, psychology, educator, psychotherapist, consultant*

Little Falls
Brophy, Debra Elisse *rehabilitation and orthopaedics nurse*

Livingston
Machlin, Lawrence Judah *nutritionist, biochemist, educator*

Long Branch
Shine, Daniel I. *hospital administrator*
†Zizzi, Catherine Sandra *metaphysical educator, counselor*

Madison
Ellenbogen, Leon *nutritionist, pharmaceutical company executive*

Magnolia
Holt, James Theodore *nursing educator*

Medford
Ferris, Violette Irene *nursing educator*

Milltown
Rickards, Cheryl Ann *counselor, minister, educator*

Montclair
DiGeronimo, Diane Mary *nursing educator, psychotherapist*
Kayser, Mary Ellen H. *nursing consultant and educator*
O'Malley, Eileen (Ann) *medical/surgical nurse*

Montville
Leeson, Lewis Joseph *research pharmacist, scientist*

Morristown
Hager, Mary Hastings *nutritionist, educator, consultant*
Morse, Joyce Solomon *nursing administrator*
Watson, Esther Elizabeth *medical/surgical and critical care nurse, retired*

Mountainside
Glassman, Ronald Jay *public health advocate*
Kozberg, Donna Walters *rehabilitation administration executive*

New Brunswick
Boehm, Werner William *social work educator*
Burman, Sondra *social work educator*
Dunn, Patricia C. *social work educator*
Lister, David Alfred *healthcare administrator*
Momah, Ethel Chukwuekwe *women's health nurse*
Spears, Marcia Hopp *nursing educator, health facility administrator*

Newark
Rutan, Thomas Carl *nurse*
Savage, Joseph George *hospital administrator*
Stevenson, Joanne Sabol *older adults care provider, educator, researcher*

Nutley
McLellan, Kathleen Claire *speech therapist*
Romanoski, Barbara Ann *neonatology nurse*

Old Bridge
Gulko, Edward *health care executive, consultant*

Paramus
Blake, Mary Ellen *medical/surgical and home care nurse, educator*

Parsippany
Agostini, Rosemarie Coniglio *human services administrator*

Paterson
Daniels, Cheryl Lynn *pediatrics nurse, case manager*
McEvoy, Lorraine Katherine *oncology nurse*

Pennington
Rodriguez, Noreen Barbara *occupational health nurse*

Piscataway
Goldstein, Bernard David *physician, educator*

Pittsgrove
Burt, Diane Mae *women's health nurse*

Plainfield
Mattson, Joy Louise *oncological nurse*

Pomona
Lyons, Paul Harold *social work educator*
Reid-Merritt, Patricia Ann *social worker, educator, author, performing artist*

Princeton
DeMarco, David G. *registered nurse, pharmaceuticals researcher*
Kidd, Lynden Louise *healthcare consultant*
Logue, Judith R. *psychoanalyst, educator*
Meade, Dale Michael *laboratory director, researcher*

Rahway
Tice, Kirk Clifford *health care facility executive*

Randolph
Allen, B. Marc *managed care executive*

Red Bank
Brown, Valerie Anne *psychiatric social worker, educator*
Gutentag, Patricia Richmond *social worker, family counselor, occupational therapist*
Howson, Agnes Wagner *health educator*
Murray, Abby Darlington Boyd *psychiatric clinical specialist, educator*

Ridgefield Park
Hiemier, Paige Dana *nurse*

Ridgewood
Clements, Lynne Fleming *family therapist, programmer*

Roseland
Malafronte, Donald *health executive*

Rutherford
Suarez, Sally Ann Tevis *health care administrator, nurse, consultant*

Saddle Brook
Clifton, Nelida *social worker*

Scotch Plains
Palmer, Teresa Anne *nurse practitioner*
Touretzky, Muriel Walter *nursing educator*

Secaucus
Mitchell, Peter William *addictions counselor*

Sewell
Aldover-Ayon, Marta *critical care nurse*

Ship Bottom
Adams, Jeanne Masters *community health nurse, consultant*

Shrewsbury
Alburtus, Mary Jo *social worker, consultant, trainer*

Skillman
†Prestbo, (Martha) Darlene *clinical social worker*

Somers Point
Biswas, Linda Joyce *midwife*
Sikora, Sally Marie *nursing administrator*

Somerset
Bieber, Mark Allan *nutrition scientist, researcher*

Teaneck
Alperin, Richard Martin *clinical social worker, psychoanalyst*
Brown, Shirley Ann *speech-language pathologist*
Fanshel, David *social worker*
Hollman, Barbara Carol *psychoanalyst, psychotherapist, consultant*

Toms River
Hines, Patricia *social worker, educator*
Jones, Nancy Patricia *psychotherapist, consultant*

Trenton
Bishop, Ann Shorey *mental health nurse*
DeMontigney, James Morgan *health services administrator*
Ferenchak, Suzanne Mary *counselor*
Majofsky, Karen M. *critical care nurse, mental health nurse*
Schirber, Annamarie Riddering *speech and language pathologist, educator*
Terrill, Thomas Edward *health facility administrator*

Turnersville
Cammarota, Marie Elizabeth *nursing administrator, nursing educator*

Union
Fabyanski, Mary Irene *nursing administrator*
Kramer, Paula Lee *occupational therapist, educator*
Muller, Gregory Alan *health facilities administrator, mayor*
Williams, Carol Jorgensen *social work educator*

Ventnor City
Panico, Elaine Hartman *nurse*

Vineland
Popp, Charlotte Louise *health development center administrator, nurse*

Wayne
Tanzman-Bock, Maxine M. *psychotherapist, hypnotherapist, consultant*

West Caldwell
Schiff, Robert *healthcare consultancy company executive*

West New York
Kelly, Lucie Stirm Young *nursing educator*

West Orange
†Aitchison, Kenneth W. *health facility administrator*
Bornstein, Lester Milton *retired medical center executive*
De Lisa, Joel Alan *rehabilitation physician, rehabilitation facility executive*
Katz, Alix Martha *respiratory care practitioner*

Westfield
†Kozlowski, Dorothy *health center administrator*
Mc Fadden, G. Bruce *hospital administrator*

Westwood
Bilz, Laurie S. *nursing educator*

Whitehouse Station
Gilmartin, Raymond V. *health care products company executive*

Winfield Park
James, Barbara Frances *school nurse, special education educator*

NEW MEXICO

Albuquerque
Andrade, Joseph J., III *counselor, educator*
Boshier, Maureen Louise *health facilities administrator*
Clark, Teresa Watkins *psychotherapist, clinical counselor*
Falcon, Patricia *educator, health psychologist*
Mateju, Joseph Frank *hospital administrator*
Rodriguez, William Joseph *vocational counselor, mental health professional*
Sanderlin, Terry Keith *counselor*
Solomon, Arthur Charles *pharmacist*

Cannon AFB
Chrisman, Lilly Belle *medical/surgical nurse, educator*

Carlsbad
Carpenter, Sheila H. *critical care and medical/surgical nurse*
Moore, Bobbie Fay *geriatrics nurse practitioner, nurse administrator*
Speed, Lynn Elizabeth *nurse practitioner*

Farmington
MacCallum, (Edythe) Lorene *pharmacist*

Gallup
Fuhs, Terry Lynn *emergency room nurse, educator*

Las Cruces
Welsh, Mary McAnaw *educator, family mediator*

Los Alamos
Moore, Tom O. *program administrator*

Milan
Kanesta, Nellie Rose *chemical dependency counselor*

Roswell
Johnston, Mary Ellen *nursing educator*
Miller, Candi *critical care nurse*

Ruidoso
Wade, Pamela Sue *women's health nurse*

Santa Fe
LaTourrette, Kathryn *family therapist, counselor, artist*
Melnick, Alice Jean (AJ Melnick) *counselor*
Nuckolls, Leonard Arnold *retired hospital administrator*
Phipps, Claude Raymond *research scientist*
Ruybalid, Louis Arthur *social worker, community development consultant*

Shiprock
West, Dorcas Joy *women's health nurse*

NEW YORK

Albany
DeNuzzo, Rinaldo Vincent *pharmacy educator*
Kim, Paul David *emergency medical administrator*
Lane, Nancy Lucille *mental health and critical care nurse*
†Loneck, Barry Martin *social work researcher, educator*
Reid, William James *social work educator*
Weiss, Linda Wolff *health systems administrator*

Alfred
Rand, Joella Mae *nursing educator, counselor*

Ardsley
Mohl, Allan S. *social worker*

Astoria
Matheson, Linda *retired clinical social worker*

Baldwin
Nicoleau, Mireille *patient service coordinator, nurse, case manager*

Batavia
Small, Bruce Michael *health facility administrator*

Bedford
Margolin, Carl M. *psychotherapist*

Blasdell
McNierney, Lisa Marie *critical care nurse*

Brockport
Herrmann, Kenneth John, Jr. *social work educator*

Bronx
Bennett, Keith George *nurse*
Clary, Roy *hospital administration executive*
Connor, Paul Eugene *social worker*
Dunn, Ann-Margaret *pediatrics nurse*
Emanuel, Evelyn Louise *nurse*
Han, Timothy Wayne *drug abuse professional, public health educator*
Joseph, Stephen *nephrology and dialysis nurse*
McDonald, Mary *pediatric nurse practitioner*
Orlando, Mary Jean *community health and medical/surgical nurse*
Reilly, Margaret Mary *retired therapist*
Shames, Jordan Nelson *health care executive, consultant health services*
Smith-Alhimer, Marie Margaret Cella *mental health nurse*
Sylvester, John Edward *social worker*
Weiner, Richard Lenard *hospital administrator, educator, pediatrician*
Yadeka, Theophilus Adeniyi *administrator*

Bronxville
Broas, Donald Sanford *hospital executive*
Dvorak, Roger Gran *health facility executive*

Brooklyn
Adasko, Mary Hardy *speech pathologist*
Allen, George Desmond *epidemiology nurse, surgical nurse*
Alywahby, Nancy *geriatric and adult nurse practitioner*
Astwood, William Peter *psychotherapist*
Balogun, Joseph A. *physical therapist, educator, researcher*
Duke-Masters, Velma Regina *pediatrics and psychiatric-mental health nurse*
Eisenberg, Karen Sue Byer *nurse*
Eschen, Albert Herman *optometrist*
Gross, Stephen Mark *pharmacist, academic dean*
Gustin, Mark Douglas *hospital executive*
Harris, Fred *orthotist, prosthetist*
Hird, Mary *nursing administrator*
Houston, Sandra Lee *nurse educator, medical/surgical nurse, ambulatory surgical nurse*
LaCosta, Cosmo Joseph *health facility administrator*
Marsala-Cervasio, Kathleen Ann *medical/surgical nurse, administrator*
Mesiha, Mounir Sobhy *industrial pharmacy educator*
Murillo-Rohde, Ildaura Maria *marriage and family therapist, consultant, educator, dean*
Orsini, Gail *social worker*
Patel, Nagin Keshavbhai *industrial pharmacy educator*
Peters, Mercedes *psychoanalyst*
Pine, Bessie Miriam *social worker, editor, columnist*
†Solomon, Lyn S. *art therapist*
Strauss, Dorothy Brandfon *marital, family, and sex therapist*
Thompson, Theodis *healthcare executive, health management consultant*
Twining, Lynne Dianne *psychotherapist, professional society administrator, writer*
Wilson, Veta Emily *community health nurse*
Yeaton, Cecelia E(mma) *healthcare administration executive*
Zukowski, Barbara Wanda *clinical social work psychotherapist*

Buffalo
Blane, Howard Thomas *research institute administrator*
†Canfield, Holly Beth *legal nurse consultant*
Casper, Bernadette Marie *critical care nurse*
Collins, Catherine *health administrator, educator*
Dispenza, Joan Marie *ambulatory care nurse, administrator*
†Hohn, David C. *healthcare executive*
Hunter, Juanita K. *nurse, educator*
Katz, Jack *audiology educator*
Krol, Nancy Ann *critical care nurse*
Perry, J. Warren *health sciences educator, administrator*
Reboy, Diane L. *medical/surgical and community health nurse*
Richmond, Allen Martin *speech pathologist, educator*
Ryan, Diane Phyllis *nurse*
Silver, Kathleen Frances *rehabilitation counselor*
Tornatore-Morse, Kathleen Mary *pharmacy educator*

Canandaigua
Chappelle, Lou Jo *physical therapist assistant*

Canisteo
Florence, Sally A. *retired school nurse educator, nurse practitioner*

Castle Point
Laubscher, Leeann *medical and surgical nurse*

Cedarhurst
Lipsky, Linda Ethel *business executive*

Claverack
Haus, Ruthann Elizabeth *geriatrics, community health nurse*

Clinton Corners
McDermott, Patricia Ann *nursing administrator*

Cohoes
Kennedy, Kathleen Ann *faculty/nursing consultant*

Colonie
Mallory, Doris Ann *social worker, counselor*

Commack
Kruger, Barbara *audiologist, speech and language pathologist*

Cooperstown
Fullington, Cynthia Janette *pediatric nurse*

Cornwall On Hudson
Holstein, David *psychotherapist, management consultant, educator*

Delmar
Erlich, Fredrick William *human services administrator*

Dix Hills
Katzberg, Jane Michaels *health care administrator, consultant, educator*

Dobbs Ferry
Comizio-Assante, Delva Maria *nurse, clinical nurse specialist*

Dunkirk
Bergmann, Dennis William *health facility administrator*
Huels, Steven Mark *laboratory analyst*

East Aurora
Speller, Kerstin G. Rinta *psychologist*

Eastport
Oliveri, Robert Peter *retired social worker*
Wruck, Michelle Mingino *pediatric nurse practitioner*

Elmira
Swartz, Melanie Lynn *nurse*

Elmont
Brancaleone Kenna, Laurie Ann *social worker*

Fairport
Paul, Thomas Wayne *psychotherapist*

Farmingdale
Thomas, Patrick N. *physical therapist*

Fayetteville
Paul, Linda Baum *geriatrics nurse, toy business owner*

Flushing
Hui, William Man Wai *chiropractor*
Matheis, Vickie Lynne *nurse*

Forest Hills
Alsapiedi, Consuelo Veronica *psychoanalytic psychotherapist, consultant*

Garden City
Festa, Jo Ann V. *nursing educator*
Nicklin, George Leslie, Jr. *psychoanalyst, educator, physician*

Glen Head
Cohen, Lawrence N. *health care management consultant*

Glendale
Linekin, Patricia Landi *clinical nurse specialist*

Goshen
†Warren, Sheila Deveney *nurse administrator, educator*

Grand Island
Deutsch, Anne *clinical nurse specialist*

Great Neck
Dantzker, David Roy *health facility executive*
Feldman, Gary Marc *nutritionist, consultant*

Greenfield Center
Templin, John Leon, Jr. *healthcare consulting executive*

Guilderland
†Bawa, Rubina *pharmacist*

Hamburg
Kuhn, Merrily A. *nursing educator*

Harris
Buonanni, Brian Francis *health care facility administrator, consultant*

Hawthorne
Carlucci, Marie Ann *nursing administrator, nurse*

Hemlock
Doty, Dale Vance *psychotherapist, hypnotherapist*

Hempstead
DiLuoffo, Santina *chiropractor*
Wilkes, David Ross *therapist, social worker*

Hicksville
Ruiz, Gerard *alcohol and drug abuse services professional*

Huntington
Sheil, Wilma Rohloff *psychiatry, mental health nurse*

Huntington Station
Williams, Una Joyce *psychiatric social worker*

Inwood
Jaiswal, Dinesh Kumar *pharmaceutical scientist, educator*

Islip Terrace
Mancuso, Elisa Alvarez *pediatrics nurse, educator, neonatal nurse practitioner*

Ithaca
Haas, Jere Douglas *nutritional sciences educator, researcher*
Habicht, Jean-Pierre *public health researcher, educator, consultant*
Mueller, Betty Jeanne *social work educator*
Pagliarulo, Michael Anthony *physical therapy educator*
Rasmussen, Kathleen Maher *nutritional sciences educator*
Zall, Robert Rouben *food scientist, educator*

Jackson Heights
Chang, Lydia Liang-Hwa *school social worker, educator*

Jamaica
Ahmed, Jimmie *health facility administrator*
†Donnelly, Anna *hospital administrator*
Lassiter, Katrina Ann *medical/surgical nurse*
McDuffie, Minnie *nursing administrator, community health nurse*
McGuire, William Dennis *health care system executive*
Morrill, Joyce Marie *social worker*
Sossi, Anthony James *medical administrator*

Keuka Park
Wilson, Levonne Baldwin *nurse*

Kingston
Ione, Carole *psychotherapist, writer, playwright, director*
Petruski, Jennifer Andrea *speech and language pathologist*
Soltanoff, Jack *nutritionist, chiropractor*

Lake George
Stafford, Dorothy Brooks *private duty nurse*

Lakewood
McConnon, Virginia Fix *dietitian*

Latham
Agard, Nancey Patricia *nursing administrator*
Caruso, Aileen Smith *managed care consultant*
Chase-Dooley, Johanna Anne *medical/surgical and critical care nurse*
Mathews, Susan McKiernan *health care executive*

Lewiston
O'Neil, Mary Agnes *health science facility administrator*

Lincolndale
Morton, Mary Madeline *family nurse practitioner*

Little Falls
Feeney, Mary Katherine O'Shea *retired public health nurse*

Liverpool
Emmert, Roberta Rita *health facility administrator*

Livingston Manor
Zagoren, Joy Carroll *health facility director, researcher*

Lockport
Segarra, Tyrone Marcus *pharmacist, medicinal chemist*

Loudonville
Ribley-Borck, Joan Grace *medical/surgical rehabiliation nurse*

Malone
Kelley, Sister Helen *hospital executive*

Malverne
Ryan, Suzanne Irene *nursing educator*

Manlius
Vasile, Gennaro James *health care executive*

Massapequa
Margulies, Andrew Michael *chiropractor*
Ting, Mark E. *sex researcher, consultant*
Witt, Denise Lindgren *operating room nurse, educator*

Massena
DeLarm, Joan Sharon *social worker, psychotherapist*

Medford
Brower, Robert Charles *rehabilitation counselor, small business owner*

Medina
Berry, Cecilia Anne *nephrology nurse practitioner*

Millerton
DeShields Brooks, DeLora, Sr. *medical technologist, medical writer*

Mineola
Anana-Lind, Elenita M. *critical care and medical/ surgical nurse*
Hinson, Gale Mitchell *social worker*

Montrose
Faden-Qureshi, Betsy Bruzzese *activity director, volunteer coordinator, recreation therapist*

Mount Kisco
Gudanek, Lois Bassolino *clinical social worker*

Mount Vernon
Williams, Patricia Helen *substance abuse services administrator*

New City
†Golden, Gail K. *social worker*

New Hartford
Benzo-Bonacci, Rosemary Anne *health facility administrator*

New Rochelle
Thornton, Elaine Seretha *oncology nurse, clinical nurse specialist*
Wolf, Robert Irwin *psychoanalyst, art and art therapy educator*

New York
Ablow, Ronald Charles *hospital executive*
Alvarado, Sandra Edga *nurse practitioner, psychotherapist*
Barker, Sylvia Margaret *nurse*
Barnum, Barbara Stevens *retired nursing educator*
Barrett, Elizabeth Ann Manhart *nursing educator, psychotherapist, consultant*
Beach, Diana Lee *psychotherapist, priest*
Binkert, Alvin John *hospital administrator*
Buehler, Thomas *psychotherapist, expressive therapist*
Burkhardt, Ann *occupational therapist, clinical educator*
Caroff, Phyllis M. *social work educator*
Cavanagh-McKee, Kathryn *nurse*
Cloward, Richard Andrew *social work educator*
Costa, Max *health facility administrator, pharmacology educator, environmental medicine educator*
Daugherty, Marcus Vincent *mental health administrator*
Dinerman, Miriam *social work educator*
Dobrof, Rose Wiesman *professor*
Dorn, Sue Bricker *consultant, retired hospital administrator*
Dropkin, Mary Jo *nursing researcher, educator*
Edelstein, Joan Erback *physical therapy educator*
Ethan, Carol Baehr *psychotherapist*
†Farber, Barry Alan *psychotherapist, educator*
Feldman, Ronald Arthur *social work educator, researcher*
Fenchel, Gerd H(erman) *psychoanalyst*
Fewell, Christine Huff *psychoanalyst, alcohol counselor*
Fiorillo, John A(nthony) *health care executive*
Franze, Anthony James *pharmacist, lawyer*
†Fuchs, Jonathan M. *health care administrator*
Fuld, Robert O'Connor *social worker*
Gelman, Elaine Edith *nurse*
Giorlando, Jeanne A. *labor and delivery nurse*
Gitterman, Alex *social work educator*
Goff, Robert Edward *health plan executive*
Gold, William Elliott *health care management consultant*
Goldberg, Jane G. *psychoanalyst*
Goldrich, Stanley Gilbert *optometrist*
Goodwill, George Walton *hospital administrator*
Grandizio, Lenore *social worker*
Grant, James Deneale *health care company executive*
Gray, Bradford Hitch *health policy researcher*
Gregori, Maria Isabel *critical care nurse*
Hershcopf, Berta Ruth *psychotherapist, writer*
†Holloman, Patricia Leo *nurse*
Kalayjian, Anie *psychotherapist, nurse, educator, consultant*
Kamerman, Sheila Brody *educator, social worker*
Kassel, Catherine M. *community and maternal-women's health nurse*
Kaufman, Michele Beth *clinical pharmacist, educator*
Kent, Deborah Warren *hypnotherapist, consultant, lecturer*
King, Sheldon Selig *medical center administrator, educator*
Labovitz, Deborah Rose Rubin *occupational therapist, educator*
Lambertsen, Eleanor C. *nursing consultant*
Latimer, Hugh Scot *healthcare consultant, architect*
Lawrence, Lauren *psychoanalytical theorist, psychoanalyst*
Lawry, Sylvia (Mrs. Stanley Englander) *health association administrator*
Lederman, Sally Ann *nutrition educator and researcher*
Leone, Rose Marie *psychotherapist*
Leung, Betty Brigid *nursing administrator*
Levinson, Rascha *psychotherapist*
Maloney, Elizabeth Mary *psychiatric-mental health nurse*
Mandracchia, Violet Ann Palermo *psychotherapist, educator*
Markle, Cheri Virginia Cummins *nurse*
Marshak, Hilary Wallach *psychotherapist, owner*
Mattson, Marlin Roy Albin *health facility administrator, psychiatry educator*
Miller, Linda Sarah *critical care, emergency room nurse*
Morris, Lynne Louise *psychotherapist*
Morris, Thomas Quinlan *hospital administrator, physician*
Mundinger, Mary O'Neil *nursing educator*
Naegle, Madeline Anne *mental health nurse, educator*
Neubauer, Peter Bela *psychoanalyst*
O'Brien, Patricia G. *psychiatric clinical nurse, administrator*
O'Neill, Mary Jane *health agency executive*
O'Neill McGivern, Diane *nursing educator*
Pakter, Jean *medical consultant*
Palmer, John M. *medical administrator*
Pesola, Helen Rostata *nursing administrator*
Piemonte, Robert Victor *association executive*
Pilcz, Maleta *psychotherapist*
Purcell, Karen Barlar *naturopathic physician*
Resnick, Rhoda Brodowsky *psychotherapist*
Richard, Elaine *educational therapist*
Roglieri, John Louis *health facility administrator*
Rosenthal, Donna Myra *social worker*
Rumore, Martha Mary *pharmacist, educator*
Serdans, Rebecca Sybille *nurse*
Shohen, Saundra Anne *health care communications and public relations executive*
Sigety, Cornelius Edward *family office manager*
Solender, Sanford *social worker*
Spada, Dominick *pharmacist*
Spivey, Bruce E. *integrated healthcare delivery systems management executive*
Spriggs, David Randall *healthcare administrator, educator*
Stark, Robin Caryl *psychotherapist, consultant*
Stepherson, Brian Edward *psychological social worker, artist, writer*
Stocker, Beatrice *speech pathologist*
†Trent, Charles H., Jr. *social work educator*
Ungvarski, Peter J. *nursing administrator*
Vladeck, Bruce Charney *health services administrator, policy educator*
Wachtel, Steven Edward *social worker*
Walman, Jerome *psychotherapist, publisher, consultant, critic*
Wessler, Sheenah Hankin *psychotherapist, consultant*
Witkin, Mildred Hope Fisher *psychotherapist, educator*
Wolfert, Ruth *Gestalt therapist*
Wood, Paul F. *national health agency executive*
York, Janet Brewster *nurse, family and sex therapist, sculptor*
Zazula, Bernard Meyer *physician administrator*

Newburgh
Flemming, Arlene Joan Dannenberg *social worker, psychotherapist*

North Bellmore
Klumpp, Barbara Anne *quality assurance and utilization review executive*

North Syracuse
Brophy, Mary O'Reilly *industrial hygienist*

North Tonawanda
Coleman, Kimberlee Michele *critical care nurse*

Norwich
Garzione, John Edward *physical therapist*

Oceanside
Hoffnung, Audrey Sonia *speech and language pathologist, educator*

Olean
Peters, Susan Mary *mental health nurse*

Oneida
Hicks, Phyllis Ann *medical, surgical nurse*

Oneonta
Grappone, William Eugene *clinical social worker, gerontologist, consultant*
Lapidus, Patricia Jean *social worker*

Ontario
Nevil, Linda *nursing administrator*

Orangeburg
Furlong, Patrick Louis *health science association administrator*
Penney, Dixianne McCall *mental health services researcher, administrator*

Orchard Park
Bergmann, Cynthia *pediatrics nurse, lawyer*
Fronckowiak, Felicia Ann *retired surgical services director*

Ozone Park
Catalfo, Betty Marie *health service executive, nutritionist*

Palmyra
Frontuto, Penelope Kerr *mental health administrator*

Patchogue
Lee-Valenti, Renee Ling Mee Bernadette *optometrist*

Pittsford
Taub, Aaron Myron *healthcare administrator, consultant*

Plainview
Ginsberg, Carol Kerre *women's health nurse practitioner*
Warrack, Maria Perini *psychotherapist*

Pomona
Masters, Robert Edward Lee *psychotherapist, neural researcher, human potential educator*

Port Washington
Aronstein, Jacqueline Bluestone *psychoanalyst, counselor, educator*

Poughkeepsie
Borschel, Valerie Lynn *medical/surgical nurse*
Carino, Aurora Lao *psychiatrist, hospital administrator*
Gennaro, Richard Francis, Jr. *chiropractor*
Gordon, Carolann *oncological nurse, community health nurse*
Heller, Mary Bernita *psychotherapist*
Henley, Richard James *health facility administrator*
Weiner, Marc V. *health services facility executive*

Purchase
Berman, Richard Angel *health and educational administrator*

Rego Park
Connington, Mary Ellen *health facility administrator*
Stumpf, Mary Rita *administrator, executive director*

Rochester
Aydelotte, Myrtle Kitchell *nursing administrator, educator, consultant*
Brideau, Leo Paul *healthcare executive*
Chiulli, Michael Richard *laboratory technician*

Hill, Edith Marie *medical/surgical nurse*
Hunt, Roger Schermerhorn *healthcare administrator*
Hurlbut, Robert Harold *health care services executive*
Johnson, Jean Elaine *nursing educator*
LaSpagnoletta, Susan Ann *nurse*
McClurg, Robert James *emergency nurse practitioner*
Moore, Duncan Thomas *optics educator*
Pincus, Patricia Hogan *nurse*
Schaffner, Robert Jay, Jr. *nurse practitioner*

Rockville Centre
Bajaj, Celine Cosme *medical/surgical and pediatric nurse*
Erland, Shirley May *nurse*
Fassetta, Mary Elizabeth *nursing educator*
Marohn, Ann Elizabeth *health information professional*

Roslyn
Epstein, Arthur Barry *optometrist*
Freedman, Joseph Mark *optometrist*
Scollard, Patrick John *hospital executive*

Rushville
Carpenter, Florence Erika *retired human services adminstrator*

Rye
Davis, Samuel *hospital administrator, educator, consultant*
Newburger, Howard Martin *psychoanalyst*

Sag Harbor
Brathwaite, Harriet Louisa *nursing educator*

Salt Point
Lackey, Mary Michele *physician assistant*

Saranac Lake
Caguiat, Carlos Jose *health care administrator, episcopal priest*

Saratoga Springs
Higgins, Marika O'Baire *registered nurse, philosophy educator, novelist, entrepreneur*
Leary, Eileen Marie *psychotherapist*

Scarsdale
Rogalski, Lois Ann *speech and language pathologist*

Schenectady
Oliker, David William *healthcare management administrator*
Pasquariello, Julius Anthony *pharmacist*
Sager, Robert Wendell *retired social work administrator*

Schoharie
Decker, Cynthia J. Schafer *community and occupational health nurse*

Seaford
Waage, Elaine *community health nurse*

Sleepy Hollow
Safian, Keith Franklin *hospital administrator*

Smithtown
Landau, Dorothy *psychotherapist, consultant*

Speculator
Mulleedy, Joyce Elaine *nursing service administrator, educator*

Springfield Gardens
†McFarquhar, Claudette Viviene *nurse, educator*

Staten Island
Camarda, Edith *nurse educator*
Dunne, Desma *medical/surgical nurse*
†Gordon, Benjamin *physical therapist*
Sabido, Almeda Alice *mental health facility administrator*

Stony Brook
Mundie, Gene E. *nursing educator*

Suffern
Monahan, Frances Donovan *nursing educator*

Syracuse
Carlton, Carole Gassett *medical/surgical nurse*
Horn, Doreen T. *critical care nurse*
Kelley, Johnnie L. *mental health nurse*
Mudrick, Nancy Ruth *social work educator*
Pirozzi, Mildred Jean *nursing administrator*
Shedlock, Kathleen Joan Petrouskie *community health and research nurse*

Tillson
Giordano, Sondra *nursing educator, medical and surgical nurse*

Truxton
Schultz, Helen Welkley *marriage and family therapist, minister*

Utica
Fay, Nancy Elizabeth *nurse*

Valhalla
Radeboldt-Daly, Karen Elaine *medical nurse*
Smith-Young, Anne Victoria *health services coordinator*

Wading River
Bolger, Virginia Joan *nursing administrator*

Wantagh
Kushner, Aileen *medical/surgical nurse*

Webster
Liebert, Arthur Edgar *retired hospital administrator*

West Bloomfield
Charron, Helene Kay Shetler *retired nursing educator*

Westbury
Lelonek, David *optometrist*

White Plains
Boese, Geraldine Florence *nurse administrator*
Bostin, Marvin Jay *hospital and health services consultant*
Fowlkes, Nancy Lanetta Pinkard *social worker*

Woodmere
Cohen, Lawrence Alan *health facility administrator*
Natow, Annette Baum *nutritionist, author, consultant*

Woodside
VanArsdale, Diana Cort *social worker*

Yonkers
Alpert, Caroline Evelyn *nurse*
†Carman, Gary O. *hospital administrator*

Youngstown
Micieli, Karen Krisher *geriatrics nurse*

NORTH CAROLINA

Aberdeen
Marcham, Timothy Victor *pharmacist*

Advance
Walser, Sandra Teresa Johnson *rehabilitation nurse, preceptor*

Arden
Adams, Pamela Jeanne *nurse, flight nurse*

Asheville
Korb, Elizabeth Grace *nurse midwife*
Weil, Thomas P. *health services consultant*
Weinhagen, Susan Pouch *emergency care nurse*

Ayden
Nobles, Lorraine Biddle *dietitian*

Benson
Taylor, Martha McClintock *marriage and family therapist, researcher*

Boone
Brown, Jane Comfort Brennan *educator, language and movement therapist*
Pollitt, Phoebe Ann *school nurse*

Burlington
Kernodle, Lucy Hendrick *school system nurse*
Knesel, Ernest Arthur, Jr. *diagnostic company executive*
Mason, James Michael *biomedical laboratories executive*
Powell, James Bobbitt *biomedical laboratories executive, pathologist*

Butner
Ostby, Sandra Josephine *dietitian*

Calabash
Colvin-Herron, Gayle Ann *mental health consultant, psychotherapist, health facility administrator, columnist writer*

Candler
Crowder, Julian Anthony *optometrist*

Chapel Hill
Bland, Annie Ruth (Ann Bland) *nursing educator*
Konsler, Gwen Kline *oncology and pediatrics nurse*
Martikainen, A(une) Helen *retired health education specialist*
Munson, Eric Bruce *hospital administrator*
Nolting, Mavis Williams *critical care and pediatrics nurse*
Palmer, Gary Stephen *health services administrator*
Tolley, Aubrey Granville *hospital administrator*
Zeisel, Steven H. *nutritionist, scientist, educator*

Charlotte
Brink, Arthur M. *hospital administrator*
Doyle, Esther Piazza *critical care nurse, educator*
Hallowell Schemmer, Shannon *nurse anesthetist*
†Holbrook, Patricia Houston *counselor, psychotherapist*
Latimer, Ben William *healthcare executive*
Lowrance, Pamela Kay *medical/surgical nurse*
Martin, James Grubbs *medical research executive, former governor*
†McIntyre, Jane London *healthcare administrator*
Philippe, Scott Louis *optometrist*
Roberts, Joyce Ann (Nichols) *critical care nurse*
Shaul, Roger Louis, Jr. *health care consultant, executive, researcher*
Smith, Elizabeth Hegeman *mental health therapist, hypnotherapist*

Chinquapin
Brown, Anita Lanier *women's health nurse*

Cullowhee
Koons, Eleanor (Peggy Koons) *clinical social worker*

Davidson
Plyler, John Laney, Jr. *retired healthcare management professional*

Dobson
Atkins, Dixie Lee *critical care nurse*

Durham
Burgess, Paula Lashenske *health facility administrator*
Colvin, O. Michael *medical director, medical educator*
Cotten, Catheryn Deon *medical center international advisor*
Donker, Richard Bruce *health care administrator*
Frazier, Ann Lynette *medical/surgical nurse*
†Houchin, Laura Braxton *oncology nurse clinician*
Israel, Michael David *healthcare executive*
Menning, Karen Corinne *occupational therapist*
Taylor, Martha Croll *nursing adminstrator*
Wilson, Ruby Leila *nurse, educator*

Elizabeth City
Hall, Pamela Bright *school health nurse*

Elm City
Morris, Sharon Louise Stewart *emergency medical technician*

Fayetteville
Baltz, Richard Jay *health care company executive*
Jansen, Michael John *hospital administrator*
Schaefer, Lewis George *physicians assistant*

Fort Bragg
McMillan, William B. *counselor, military science educator*

Fremont
Overman, Betty Skeens *critical care and pediatrics nurse*

Garner
Upchurch, Lisa Carole D. *women's health nurse, clinical educator*

Gastonia
Morris, Joseph Wesley *physician assistant*

Goldsboro
Harper, Linda Ruth *disabilities educator, consultant*

Granite Falls
Estes, Shirley Reid *medical/surgical nurse*

Greensboro
Covington, Gail Lynn *nurse practitioner*
Ritter, Sandra Helen *psychotherapist, counselor*
Schwenn, Lee William *retired medical center executive*
Shotwell, Sheila Murray *medical/surgical nurse*

Greenville
Pakowski, Montie Early *critical care nurse*
Parks, Suzanne Lowry *psychiatric nurse, educator*
Tripp, Linda Lynn *nutritition counselor*

Hendersonville
Heil, Mary Ruth *former counselor*

Hickory
Loehr, Arthur William, Jr. *healthcare executive, nurse*
Ryan Billingsley, Joanne *medical/surgical and orthopedic nurse*

Lenoir
Moore, Mary Ellen *community health, hospice nurse*

Matthews
Rusho, Karen G. *critical care and community health nurse, educator*

Morrisville
Stokes, George Clive *healthcare administrator*

New Bern
Forrester, Ann *nurse*
Smith, Larry Wayne *medical/surgical nurse*

Newland
Lustig, Susan Gardner *occupational therapist*
Singleton, Stella Wood *personal care supervisor*

Pinehurst
Fleming, Doris Aven *mental health nurse*

Raleigh
Berry, Joni Ingram *hospice pharmacist, educator*
Ciraulo, Stephen Joseph *nurse, anesthetist*
Eaddy, Paula Johnson *women's health nurse*
Ferguson, Susan Katharine Stover *nurse, psychotherapist, consultant*
Geller, Janice Grace *nurse*
Malling, Martha Hale Shackford *clinical social worker, educator*
Meelheim, Helen Diane *nursing administrator*
Slaton, Joseph Guilford *social worker*
Stewart, D. Jane *nursing educator, researcher*
Taylor, Patricia Kramer *nurse*

Research Triangle Park
Batey, Sharyn Rebecca *clinical research scientist*
Olden, Kenneth *science administrator, researcher*

Rougemont
Cooney, M(uriel) Sharon Taylor *medical/surgical nurse, educator*

Salisbury
Baines, Rhunell (Nell Baines) *nurse*
Logan, David Bruce *health care administrator*

Semora
Williams, Pauline M. *psychiatric-mental and community health nurse*

Tarboro
Andrews, Claude Leonard *psychotherapist*

Vale
Miller, Barbara Sims *health promotion coordinator*

Weaverville
Hauschild, Douglas Carey *optometrist*

Whiteville
Gilmore, Robin Harris *nursing administrator*

Wilmington
Dixon, N(orman) Rex *speech and hearing scientist, educator*
Israel, Margie Olanoff *psychotherapist*

Wilson
Lee, Jayne Frances Peacock *nursing administrator, critical care nurse, infection control practitioner*

Winston Salem
Dawson, Paula Dayl *oncological nurse*
Hutcherson, Karen Fulghum *healthcare executive*
Moskowitz, Jay *public health sciences educator*
Weeks, Sandra Kenney *healthcare facilitator*

NORTH DAKOTA

Bismarck
Bosch, Donna *home health nurse administrator*
Oldenburger, Norma Jane *medical surgical nurse*

Fargo
Haakenson, Philip Niel *pharmacist, educator*
Nickel, Janet Marlene Milton *geriatrics nurse*
Orr, Steven R. *health facility administrator*
Revell, Dorothy Evangeline Tompkins *dietitian*

Grand Forks
Nielsen, Forrest Harold *research nutritionist*

Minot
Mohler, Marie Elaine *nurse educator*

OHIO

Akron
West, Michael Alan *hospital administrator*

Ashtabula
Hornbeck, Harold Douglas *psychotherapist*

Austintown
Nithoo, Rovindranath *pharmacist*

Bath
Hoffer, Alma Jeanne *nursing educator*

Beachwood
Wilson, Sandra Lee *school nurse*

Beavercreek
Sivert, Sharon Lynn *critical care nurse*

Berea
Bersin, Susan Joyce-Heather (Reignbeaux Joyce-Heather Bersin) *critical care nurse, police officer*
Matej, Elaine Diane *critical care nurse*

Boardman
Donatelli, Daniel Dominic, Jr. *medical/surgical and oncological nurse*

Bowling Green
Fallon, L(ouis) Fleming, Jr. *public health consultant, researcher*
Marston-Scott, Mary Vesta *nurse, educator*

Brecksville
Meyer, Karin Zumwalt *pharmacist*

Brookville
Howett, Mark William *kinesiotherapy*

Canfield
Itts, Elizabeth Ann Dunham *psychotherapist, consultant, designer*

Canton
Barr, Dixie Lou *geriatrics nurse*
Rodriques, Pamela S. *orthopedics nurse*
Traveria, Beth M. *mental health counselor*

Cardington
Hart, Elizabeth Ann *surgical nurse supervisor*

Cedarville
Firmin, Michael Wayne *counselor educator*

Centerville
Fulk, Paul Frederick *chiropractor*

Chagrin Falls
Downing, Cynthia Hurst *therapist, addiction and abuse specialist*
Miller, Kimberly Clarke *human services manager*

Cincinnati
Beamon, Mary Ann *retired nursing administrator*
Carney, Robert Alfred *health care administrator*
Curtin, Leah Louise *publisher, editor, author, nurse*
Derstadt, Ronald Theodore *health care administrator*
Dickman, Gloria Joyce *geriatrics nurse*
Frazier, Todd Mearl *retired health science administrator, epidemiologist*
Gillespie, Anita Wright *nursing administrator*
Goldstein, Sidney *pharmaceutical scientist*
Greenwald, Theresa McGowan *medical administrator, nurse*
Harjo, Jeanne *pediatrics nurse*
Heekin, Mary Ann *oncology social worker*
Hensgen, Herbert Thomas *medical technologist*
Jackobs, Miriam Ann *dietitian*
Koebel, Sister Celestia *health care system executive*
Lang, Jackie Ann *nursing consultant*
Lichtin, (Judah) Leon *pharmacist*
Lippincott, Jonathan Ramsay *healthcare executive*
Morgan, John Bruce *hospital care consultant*
Norman, Eric Jesse *laboratory director, medical researcher*
†Oclander, Mónica Silvia *women's health nurse practitioner*
Powley, Elizabeth Ann *health facility administrator*
Reeb, Patricia A. *nursing educator, administrator*
St. John, Maria Ann *nurse anesthetist*
Smith, Beverly Ann *community health nurse*
Weinrich, Alan Jeffrey *occupational hygienist*

Cleveland
Anders, Claudia Dee *occupational therapist*
Bailey, Darlyne *social worker, educator*
Barrat-Gordon, Rene *social worker*
Beamer, Yvonne Marie *psychotherapist, counselor*
Blum, Arthur *social work educator*
Boswell, Nathalie Spence *speech pathologist*
Carrol, Edward Nicholas *psychologist*
Cartier, Charles Ernest *alcohol and drug abuse services professional*
Douglas, Janice Green *physician, educator*
Farone, Brigid Ann *nursing administrator*
Fitzpatrick, Joyce J. *nursing educator, former dean*
Frank, Robert Donald *flight nurse*
Freire, Gloria Medonis *social worker*
Gallienne, Robert Lee *nursing educator*
Gonet, Judith Janu *pediatric nurse, consultant*
Hamilton, Dorothy Jean *acute care nurse practitioner in cardiology*
Hokenstad, Merl Clifford, Jr. *social work educator*
Hulme, Mary Ann K. *women's health nurse, administrator*
Huston, Samuel Richard *health facility executive*
Jackson, Marcia Lynette *women's health, pediatrics and geriatrics nurse*
Kuerti, Rosi *educator*
†Latham, Deborah K. *research nurse*
Mantzell, Betty Lou *school health administrator*
Miller, Randal Howard *health science association administrator*
Neuhauser, Duncan von Briesen *health services educator*
Schlotfeldt, Rozella May *nursing educator*
Schmidt, Patricia Jean *medical lab technician*
Schrott, Norman *clinical social worker*
Schultz, Jeffrey Eric *optometrist*
Shakno, Robert Julian *hospital administrator*
Simmons, Clinton Craig *human resources executive*
Spottsville, Sharon Ann *counselor*
Stark, George Robert *health science association administrator*
Walters, Farah M. *hospital administrator*
Waters, Gwendolyn *human services administrator*

Coldwater
Bladen, Laurie Ann *women's health nurse*

Columbus
Anderson, Carole Ann *nursing educator*
Banasik, Robert Casmer *nursing home administrator, educator*
Beckholt, Alice *clinical nurse specialist*
Bilderback, George Garrison, III *chemical dependency counselor*
Carter, Christine Sue *cardiac recovery nurse*
Conley, Sarah Ann *health facility administrator*
Cross, April Lee *geriatrics nurse, nursing educator*
†Haskell, Brenton Ernest *health facility administrator*
Herron, Holly Lynn *flight nurse, educator*
Keith, Barry Allen *clinical social worker*
Lux, Kathleen Mary *community health educator, nurse*
McCloud, Laurie *critical care nurse*
Pitzer, Martha Seares *nursing educator*
Rudmann, Sally Vander Linden *medical technology educator*
Schuller, David Edward *cancer center administrator, otolaryngology*
†Shea, Mary Pharo *health education program administrator*
Sims, Richard Lee *hospital administrator*
Smith, Ann Marie *rehabilitation nurse*
Tornes, Virginia L. *retired nurse*
Walker, Jewel Lee *health facility administrator, consultant*
Woods, Jo Ellen *medical technologist*

Concord
Schremp, Pamela S. *nurse, risk manager, lawyer*

Copley
Pasini, Debbie Dobbins *nutrition support nurse*

Cuyahoga Falls
Rothkin, Marilyn Mae *psychotherapist*

Dayton
Cordasco, Martha Ann *therapist, social worker, consultant*
Croyle, Barbara Ann *health care management executive*
Gillen, Patrick Bernard *flight nurse*
†McCormick, Patti Leona *holistic health educator, nurse*
Nixon, Charles William *bioacoustician*
Paden, Kimbra Lea Kahle *medical/surgical nurse*
Stefanics, Charlotte Louise *clinical nurse specialist, retired*

Dover
Hamilton, Beverly Edith *former nurse educator*

Duncan Falls
Cooper, April Helen *nurse*

Euclid
Taylor, Theresa Evereth *registered nurse, artist*

Fairborn
Davis, Kathy *critical care nurse*

Findlay
Stephani, Nancy Jean *social worker, journalist*

Franklin
Withrow, Sheila Kay *school nurse*

Gahanna
Kaye, Gail Leslie *healthcare consultant, educator*

Gallipolis
Niehm, Bernard Frank *mental health center administrator, retired*

Granville
Pollard, Jeffrey Wallace *college counseling, health services director*

Hamilton
Fein, Linda Ann *nurse anesthetist, consultant*
Sebastian, Sandra Mary Thompson *clinical counselor, social worker*

Hudson
Gardiner, Stephanie Joann *staff office nurse, endoscopy nurse*
Wooldredge, William Dunbar *health facility administrator*

Lakewood
Schultz, Joann Thomas *clinical nurse specialist*

Lancaster
Phillips, Karen Ann *psychiatric-mental health nurse*
Rusk, Karla Marie *nurse practitioner*
Varney, Richard Alan *medical office manager*

Lebanon
Osborne, Quinton Albert *psychiatric social worker, inspector of institutional services*

Lima
Couts, Rose Marie *medical radiographer, sonographer*
Miller, Roy Raymond *optician, ocularist*
Palmer, Arthur Eugene *nursing home administrator*

Lorain
Buzas, John William *hospital administrator, surgical nurse*
Shimandle, Sharon Anne *critical care nurse*

Mansfield
Reese, Wina Harner *speech pathologist, consultant*

Marietta
O'Connor, Ginger Hobba *speech pathologist*

Marysville
Covault, LLoyd R., Jr. *retired hospital administrator, psychiatrist*

Mason
Clements, Michael Craig *health services consulting executive, retired renal dialysis technician*
Erbe, Janet Sue *medical surgical, orthopedics and pediatrics nurse*
Liedhegner, Barbara Griffin *pediatrics and surgical nurse*

Massillon
Fogle, Marilyn Louise Kiplinger *hospital administrator*

Medina
Walcott, Robert *healthcare executive, priest*

Mentor
Core, Harry Michael *psychiatric social worker, mental health therapist and administrator*
Russell, Brenda Sue *critical care nurse*

Miamisburg
Lucius, Mary Albus *dietitian*

Middleburg Heights
Hazlett, Paul Edward *realtor, information systems executive*

Middletown
Gordon, Sandy Gale Combs *medical surgical nurse, community health nurse*

Milford
Fite, Myra J. Cropper *critical care nurse*
Humbert, Cheryl Ann *field nurse*
Kenner, Carole Ann *nursing educator*

New Carlisle
Leffler, Carole Elizabeth *mental health nurse, women's health nurse*

North Canton
Patton, June G. *oncology nurse, educator*
Watkins, Carolyn A. *retired nursing administrator, nursing educator*

Owensville
Seifert, Caroline Hamilton *community health nurse, school nurse*

Perrysburg
Reider, Marlyn *nursing educator*
Scherer, Clarene Mae *occupational health nurse*

Portsmouth
Christensen, Margaret Anna *nurse, health management educator*

Ravenna
Turcotte, Margaret Jane *retired nurse*

Reynoldsburg
Odor, Richard Lane *mental health administrator, psychologist*

Richfield
Buzzelli, Michael John *critical care nurse*

Russell
Spring, Nicole Marie *legal nurse consultant*

Saint Clairsville
Sidon, Claudia Marie *psychiatric and mental health nursing educator*

Sandusky
Freehling, Harold George, Jr. *respiratory therapist, consultant*
Sokol, Dennis Allen *hospital administrator*

Seville
Webb, Adele Ann *pediatric nurse practitioner*

Spencer
Snyder, Teresa Ann *medical surgical nurse*

Springfield
Parks, Brenda K. *geriatrics nurse*
Whaley-Buckel, Marnie *social service administrator*

Sylvania
Verhesen, Anna Maria Hubertina *counselor*

Toledo
†Brass, Alan W. *healthcare executive*
Davis-Hartenstein, Sharon Lynne *juvenile parole officer, human services program consultant*
Holmes, Debbie *nurse*
Kneen, James Russell *health care administrator*
Kuhlman, Kimberly Ann *clinical dietician*
Rickus, Mary Ann *school nurse*
Talmage, Lance Allen *obstetrician/gynecologist, career military officer*
Toczynski, Janet Marie *oncological nurse*
Weikel, Malcolm Keith *health care company executive*
West, Ann Lee *clinical nurse specialist, educator, trauma nurse coordinator*
Woods, Doris A. *kinesiotherapist*

Troy
Enright, Georgann McGee *mental health nurse*

University Heights
†Klema, Mary Kulifay *nurse*

Upper Arlington
Williams, Cathy Lynn *nurse*

Van Wert
Greve, Diana Lee *community health nurse*

Wadsworth
Hughes, Karen Sue *geriatrics nurse*

Warren
Gianakos, Patricia Ann *social services supervisor*
Storozuk, Barbara Sue *obstetric and pediatric nurse*

Waynesville
Parks, Janice Jean *critical care nurse, legal nurse consultant*

Westerville
Rummell, Helen Mary *critical care and pediatrics nurse*
Strapp, Naomi Ann *women's health nurse*
Williams, John Michael *physical therapist, sports medicine educator*

Westlake
†Coeling, Harriet V. *nursing educator, editor*

Whipple
Carney Stalnaker, Lisa Ann *gerontological and home health nurse*

Whitehall
Pieri, Sharon Ann *rehabilitation nurse administrator*

Willshire
Myers, Janet L(ouise) *geriatrics nurse, educator*

Wooster
Albright, Mindy Sue *college health and geriatrics nurse*

Worthington
Castner, Linda Jane *instructional technologist, nurse educator*
Lentz, Edward Allen *consultant, retired health administrator*

Yellow Springs
Economos, Nikkiann *physical therapist*

Youngstown
Howe, Kimberly Palazzo *critical care nurse*
Ward, Linda V. *nursing administrator*

OKLAHOMA

Antlers
Caves, Peggy *medical/surgical nurse*

Bartlesville
Tayrien, Dorothy Pauline *retired nurse educator*

Bethany
Keeth, Betty Louise *geriatrics nursing director*
Wire, Teddy Kermit *psychotherapist*

Claremore
Cesario, Sandra Kay *women's health nurse, educator*

Cushing
Cruzan, Clarah Catherine *dietitian*

Edmond
Nelson, Laurence Clyde *pastoral psychotherapist*

El Reno
Buendia, Imelda Bernardo *clinical director, physician*

Elgin
Gault, Jeannie Farmer *gerontological nurse, nursing home administrator*

Enid
Lopez, Francisco, IV *health care administrator*

Frederick
Stone, Voye Lynne *women's health nurse practitioner*

Healdton
Eck, Kenneth Frank *pharmacist*

Lawton
Hooper, Roy B. *home health consultant, insurance broker, lobbyist*
Mayes, Glenn *social worker*
Sparkman, Mary M. *medical, surgical and rehabilitation nurse*

Moore
Grider, John Anthony *child and family therapist, consultant*

Newkirk
Newport, L. Joan *consultant, retired psychotherapist*

Norman
Donahue, Patricia Toothaker *retired social worker, administrator*
Gaskins-Clark, Patricia Renae *dietitian*
Weber, Jerome Charles *education and human relations educator, former academic dean and provost*

Oklahoma City
Arbuckle, Averil Dorothy (Cookie Arbuckle) *healthcare facility administrator*
Buckley, Stephanie Denise *health care executive*
Coleman-Portell, Bi Bi *women's health and high risk perinatal nurse*
Jones, Renee Kauerauf *health care administrator*
Lowell, Jeanne *nursing educator, psychiatric-mental health nurse*
Macer, Dan Johnstone *retired hospital administrator*
Maxey, Wanda Jean *geriatrics nurse practitioner, consultant*
McClellan, Mary Ann *pediatrics nurse, educator*
McEwen, Irene Ruble *physical therapy educator*
Mulvihill, John Joseph *medical geneticist*
O'Steen, Randy A. *nursing administrator*
Paris, Wayne *social worker, researcher*
Schwemin, Joseph *retired pharmacist*
Sookne, Herman Solomon (Hank Sookne) *retirement services executive*
Spencer, Melvin Joe *hospital administrator, lawyer*
†Tillinghast, Jon Dalton *public health physician*
Welden, Mary Clare *nurse*

Tahlequah
Edmondson, Linda Louise *optometrist*
Wickham, M(arvin) Gary *optometry educator*

Tulsa
Davis, Annalee Ruth Conyers *clinical social worker*
Gustavson, Cynthia Marie *social worker, writer*
Hannah, Barbara Ann *nurse, educator*
Hill, Delinda Jean *medical/surgical nurse, enterostomal therapy nurse*
Joice, Nora Lee *clinical dietitian*
Klein, Deborah Rae *health facility administrator*
Langenkamp, Sandra Carroll *retired healthcare policy executive*
Walton, Corinne Hemeter *psychotherapist, educator*

OREGON

Albany
Chowning, Orr-Lyda Brown *dietitian*

Azalea
Massy, Patricia Graham Bibbs (Mrs. Richard Outram Massy) *social worker, author*

Beaverton
Little, Gayle Anne *neonatal nurse, educator*

Bend
Thompson, Mari Hildenbrand *medical, legal and administrative consultant*

Clackamas
Cole, June Ann *safety, health and emergency manager*

Corvallis
Cerklewski, Florian Lee *human nutrition educator, nutritional biochemistry researcher*
Oldfield, James Edmund *nutrition educator*
Storvick, Clara Amanda *nutrition educator emerita*

Cove
Kerper, Meike *family violence, sex abuse and addiction educator, consultant*

Eugene
Acker, Martin Herbert *psychotherapist, educator*
Camp, Delpha Jeanne *counselor*
Watson, Mary Ellen *ophthalmic technologist*

Florence
Corless, Dorothy Alice *nurse educator*

Forest Grove
Randolph, Harry (Randy) Franklin, III *health facility administrator, educator, physician assistant*

Grand Junction
Van Horn, O. Frank *retired counselor, consultant*

Grants Pass
Davis, Maxine Mollie *nurse*

Gresham
Davis Lash, Cynthia *public health nurse*

Klamath Falls
Klepper, Carol Herdman *mental health therapist*

Lake Oswego
Silbert, Amy Foxman *clinical art therapist*

Lebanon
Pearson, Dennis Lee *optometrist*

Medford
Linn, Carole Anne *dietitian*
Vinyard, Roy George, II *hospital administrator*

Oregon City
Lareau, Virginia Ruth *counselor*

PROFESSIONAL INDEX 5999 HEALTHCARE: HEALTH SERVICES

Pendleton
Jensen, Judy Dianne *psychotherapist*

Phoenix
Dodd, Darlene Mae *nurse, retired air force officer*

Portland
Baker, Timothy Alan *healthcare administrator, educator, consultant*
Baldwin-Halvorsen, Lisa Rogene *community health and critical care nurse*
Barnes, Lynne Hanawalt *nurse, educator*
Bither, Marilyn Kaye *emergency nurse, educator*
Bowyer, Joan Elizabeth *medical technologist, realtor*
Cereghino, James Joseph *health facility administrator, neurologist*
Cichoke, Anthony Joseph, Jr. *chiropractor, writer, health consultant, researcher, lecturer*
De Roest, Jan Marie *mental health counselor*
Fritz, Barbara Jean *occupational health nurse*
Giffin, Sandra Lee *nursing administrator*
Goldfarb, Timothy Moore *hospital administrator*
Greenlick, Merwyn Ronald *health services researcher*
Gunnels, Mary Dahlgren *trauma coordinator*
Mason, Sara Smith *managed healthcare consultant*
McDaniel, Rickey David *senior living executive*
McDonald, Robert Wayne *cardiac sonographer*
Meighan, Stuart Spence *hospital consultant, internist, writer*
Olson, Roger Norman *health service administrator*
Pfeifer, Larry Alan *public health service coordinator*
Rooks, Judith Pence *family planning, maternal health care, midwifery consultant*
Salibello, Cosmo *optometrist, medical products executive, industrial ergonomist*
Shireman, Joan Foster *social work educator*
Toth, Shirley Louise *health facility administrator*
Ward, Michael Dean *marriage and family therapist, minister*

Redmond
Kuehnert, Deborah Anne *medical center administrator*

Salem
Callahan, Marilyn Joy *social worker*
Edge, James Edward *health care administrator*
Fisher, William G.E. *nursing home owner and operator, state senator*
Fore, Ann *counselor, educator, country dance instructor*
Zumwalt, Roger Carl *hospital administrator*

Silverton
Gantz, Nancy Rollins *nursing administrator, consultant*

Springfield
Baker, Edith Madean *counselor*

Tigard
Kupel, Frederick John *counselor*

PENNSYLVANIA

Abington
Roediger, Paul Margerum *hospital administrator*
Shaughnessy, Kathleen *critical care nurse practitioner*

Acme
Babcock, Marguerite Lockwood *addictions treatment therapist, educator, writer*

Allentown
Berman, Muriel Mallin *optometrist, humanities lecturer*
Dolan, Michael John *psychologist*
Flores, Robin Ann *social worker, social services administrator*
Saylor, Kathleen Marie *pediatric nurse practitioner*
†Sussman, Elliot *hospital executive*

Altoona
Clark, Threese Anne *occupational therapist, disability analyst*
Miller, Mary Lois *retired nurse midwife*

Ambler
Frizzell, Joan Parker *critical care nurse, educator*

Apollo
Kautz, Bonnie Mitchell *school nurse*

Archbald
Drozdis, Lori *medical/surgical nurse*

Aston
Cadorette, Lisa Roberts *medical, surgical nurse*

Auburn
Johnson, Barbara Jean *rehabilitation nurse, gerontology nurse*

Bairdford
Lewetag, Bonita Louise *education manager*

Bala Cynwyd
Cawthorn, Robert Elston *health care executive*
Peret, Karen Krzyminski *health service administrator*

Bart
Scaccia, Leo Ralph, III *nurse*

Berwyn
Base, Carol Cunningham *occupational health nurse, clinical research scientist*

Bethel Park
Buyny, Marianne Jo *eating disorders therapist, addictions counselor*

Bethlehem
Corriere, Julie Anne *family therapist*
†Herrenkohl, Roy Cecil *psychology educator*

Blue Bell
Baine, Richard Joseph *vocational rehabilitation counselor*
Cherry, John Paul *science research center director, researcher*

Brodbecks
McMenamin, Helen Marie Foran *home health care, pediatric, and maternal nurse*

Bryn Mawr
†Applegate, Jeffrey Scott *social work educator*

Buffalo Mills
Braendel, Douglas Arthur *healthcare executive*

Camp Hill
Nowak, Jacquelyn Louise *administrator, realtor, consultant, artist*
Parry-Solá, Cheryl Lee *critical care nurse*
Roach, Ralph Lee *human services and rehabilitation consultant*
Wagner, Tanya Suzanne *health facility administrator*

Carlisle
Powell, Mary Arthur *adult and family nurse practitioner, administrator*

Carnegie
Chambers, Lisa M. *psychiatric and mental health nurse*

Chester
Fisher, M. Janice *hospital administrator*
Leach, Lynne E. *nursing educator*

Clearfield
Wriglesworth, Vicki Lee *nurse*

Clifton Heights
Bonaduce, Judith *medical/surgical nurse, community health nurse*

Cochranville
Procyson, Mary G. Walton *critical care nurse*

Collegeville
Howard, Michael Earl *clinical research specialist*

Columbia
Gillmore, Vicki Longenecker *health care administrator*

Connellsville
Benzio, Donna Marie *cardiopulmonary rehabilitation nurse, educator*

Coopersburg
Kohler, Deborah Diamond *dietitian, food service executive*

Dallas
Moran, Michael Lee *physical therapist, computer consultant*

Danville
Dirienzo, Margaret Helen *nursing administrator*
Knouse, Brenda Lee (Weikel) *critical care, medical/surgical nurse*

Downingtown
Skrajewski, Dennis John *health care informatics executive*

Doylestown
King, Robert Edward *retired pharmacy educator*
Miller, Lynne Marie *critical care nurse, administrator*

Drexel Hill
Heilig, Margaret Cramer *nurse, educator*
Ligenza, Andrea Angela *nurse*

Du Bois
Pyle, Debora L. *critical care nurse*

Dushore
Getz, Mary E. *medical/surgical nurse*

East Norriton
O'Connor, Sheryl Ann *medical services administrator*

Easton
DiMatteo, Rhonda Lynn *speech-language pathologist, audiologist*
Tomaino, George Peter, Jr. *pharmacist*

Ebensburg
Rolt, Holly Lavonne *nursing educator, geriatrics nurse*

Edinboro
Paul, Charlotte P. *nursing educator*

Erie
McMahon, Patricia Pasky *family nurse practitioner*
Nihill, Karen Bailey *nursing home executive, nurse clinician*
Sensor, Mary Delores *hospital official, consultant*

Everett
Gibbons, Janet M. *home health services admininstrator*

Export
Robinette, Teresa Louise *oncology nurse*

Fort Washington
†Minniti, Martha Jean *home healthcare company executive*

Germansville
Vittorio Phillips, Mary Lou *pediatric nurse practitioner, educator*

Gladwyne
Cathcart, Harold Robert *hospital administrator*

Gouldsboro
West, Daniel Jones, Jr. *hospital administrator, rehabilitaton counselor, health care consultant, educator*

Gwynedd Valley
Giordano, Patricia J. *radiation therapist*

Hamburg
Schappell, Abigail Susan *speech, language, hearing and massage therapist*

Hanover
Davis, Ruth Carol *pharmacy educator*
Martin, Levona Ann *women's health nurse*
Wallen, Carol Stonesifer *social worker*

Harrisburg
Comoss, Patricia B. *cardiac rehabilitation nurse, consultant*
Gallaher, William Marshall *dental laboratory technician*
Gardner, Judith Sturgen *nursing administrator, educator*
Hamory, Bruce Hill *health facility administrator*
Heney, Lysle Joseph, III *pharmacist*
Minckler, Pamela Sue *psychiatric and mental health nurse*
O'Donnell, John Joseph, Jr. *optometrist*
Ozereko-deCoen, Mary T. (Mary T. Ozereko deCoen) *therapeutic recreation specialist and therapist*
Stuckey, Susan Jane *perioperative nurse, consultant*
Tyson, Gail L. *health federation administrator*
Walck, Patricia Nelson *nursing educator, consultant*
Weiss, Stephen Max *healthcare administrator, surgeon, educator*

Harveys Lake
Wolensky, Joan *occupational therapist, interfaith minister*

Hatfield
Taylor, Alan Charles *counselor, educational researcher, consultant, chaplain assistant*

Hazleton
Bumbulsky, Mae Alberta *medical/surgical nurse*
Merrigan, Mary Ann Tamone *nursing educator*
Weaver, Sharon Ann *medical/surgical nurse, educator*

Hermitage
Mayne, Ruth E. *medical nurse*

Hershey
Anderson, Allan Crosby *hospital executive*
Lindenberg, Steven Phillip *counselor, consultant*

Homestead
Boshears, James Ray *health system payroll administrator*

Hooversville
Yoder, Linda S. *emergency and trauma nurse*

Horsham
Neff, P. Sherrill *health care executive*

Hulmeville
Jackson, Mary L. *health services executive*

Hunker
Bromke, Cindy Rose *geriatrics nurse, rehabilitation nurse*

Huntingdon Valley
†Isard, Phillip Isaac *medical nutritionist*

Indiana
Nelson, Linda Shearer *child development and family relations educator*

Jermyn
Miller, Jane Lucille *critical care nurse*

Johnstown
Hull, Patricia Ann *nursing administrator*
Huston, Heidi Lynn *medical/surgical nurse*
Schultz, Carolyn Joyce *nursing educator*

King Of Prussia
Janoski, Regina Jane *nursing educator*
Miller, Alan B. *hospital management executive*

Lancaster
Brunner, Lillian Sholtis *nurse, author*
Gingerich, Naomi R. *emergency room nurse*
Rothermel, Joan Marie *occupational health nurse*

Lansdale
Habecker, Sandra K. *retired nurse*
Lovelace, Robert Frank *health facility administrator, researcher*
Reast, Deborah Stanek *ophthalmology center administrator*

Lansdowne
Nolan, Barbara Lee *critical care nurse*

Latrobe
Zanotti, Marie Louise *hospital admininstrator*

Leola
Wedel, Paul George *retired hospital administrator*

Library
Kokowski, Palma Anna *nurse consultant*

Limerick
Monte, Wendy Houser *rehabilitation services professional, counselor*

Lincoln University
Racine, Linda Jean *college health nurse*

Loretto
Sackin, Claire *emerita social work educator*

Martinsburg
Clemens, Tammy Leah *geriatrics nurse*

Mc Keesport
Kaufer, Virginia Gross *family therapist, mental health program, manager*

Media
Bettner, Betty Lou *psychotherapist*
Smith, Eleanor Cowan *social worker*

Mercersburg
Coffman, Patricia JoAnne *school nurse, counselor*

Midland
Vosler Petrella, Brenda Gayle *family nurse practitioner, educator, researcher*

Monaca
Jaskiewicz, David Walter *optometrist*

Monongahela
Fisher Prutz, Mary Louise *coronary care nurse*

Nanticoke
Shelton, Elisabeth Nesbitt *pediatric nurse and educator*

New Brighton
Rodney, Claudette Cecilie *hospital program director*

New Castle
Flannery, Wilbur Eugene *health science association administrator, internist*
Peterson, Janet Ruth *medical/surgical and rehabilitation nurse*

New Kensington
Blair, Karen Elaine *respiratory care practitioner, health educator*

Newton Square
Sacks, Susan Bendersky *mental health clinical specialist, educator*

North Wales
Dorney, Paulette Sue *critical care nurse, consultant, educator*

Oil City
Loring, Richard William *psychotherapist*

Orefield
†Yost, Brenda Ann *therapist*

Orwigsburg
Ketchledge, Kathleen A. *nurse*

Pen Argyl
Cali-Ascani, Mary Ann *oncology nurse*

Penn Valley
Pedersen, Darlene Delcourt *health science publishing consultant, psychotherapist*

Perkasie
Laincz, Betsy Ann *nurse*

Philadelphia
Ackerman, Franklin Kenneth *health services administrator*
Aiken, Linda Harman *nurse, sociologist, educator*
Baessler, Christina A. *medical/surgical nurse*
Baldino-Gloster, Tara *critical coronary care nurse*
Bamberger-Herrmann, Julia Kathryn *social worker*
Beukers, Karen Viola (Karen Viola) *cardiac nurse*
Borislow, Alan Jerome *hospital dental department chairman*
Brown-Gatta, Linda Marion *women's health nurse*
Brunner, Janet Lee *physician assistant*
Burgess, Ann Wolbert *nursing educator*
Byrd, Malcolm Todd *public health administrator*
Caputo, Richard Kevin *social work educator, researcher*
Casey, Rita Jo Ann *nursing administrator*
Clarkin, John Francis *health care management executive*
D'Este, Mary Ernestine *investment group executive*
Fagin, Claire Mintzer *nursing educator, administrator*
†Flynn, Kevin *healthcare company executive*
†Glusman, David H. *healthcare consultant*
Groves, Dorothy Frances *nursing education specialist*
Haignere, Clara Sue *health education educator*
Hand, Virginia Saxton *home health nurse*
Hussar, Daniel Alexander *pharmacy educator*
Kwortnick, Linda Marie *emergency nurse*
Laino-Curran, Donna Marie *pediatrics and public health nurse, educator, healing touch practitioner*
Lauck, Donna L. *adult psychiatric and mental health nurse*
Lawton, Lois *health facility administrator*
Lowery, Barbara J. *psychiatric nurse, educator*
†Malmud, Leon S. *health facility administrator*
Maplesden, Carol Harper *marital and family therapist, music educator*
Maratea, James Michael *healthcare administrator, editor, consultant*
Micozzi, Marc Stephen *health executive, physician, educator*
Miller Calandra, Linda Marguerita *pediatrics nurse*
Paulewicz, Stephanie Victoria *critical care nurse*
Piccolo, Joseph Anthony *hospital administrator*
Potter, Alice Catherine *clinical laboratory scientist*
Reese, Beverly Jean *critical care nurse*
Rim, Thomas B. *healthcare administrator*
Rozarto, Denise *nurse*
Salmon, Marla E. *nursing educator, dean*
Schaffner, Roberta Irene *medical, surgical nurse*
Schultz, Jane Schwartz *health research administrator*
Solomon, Phyllis Linda *social work educator, researcher*
Souders, Beryl V. *medical/surgical and rehabilitation-detox nurse*
Sovie, Margaret Doe *nursing administrator, educator, clinician, researcher*
†Uhlhorn, Ray *healthcare executive*

Velos Weiss, Joan Claire adult/geriatric nurse practitioner
Walsh, Patricia Regina trauma nurse, coordinator, educator
Warnick, Patricia Ann healthcare consultant, nurse ethicist
Weber, Janet M. retired nurse
Williams, Sankey Vaughan health services researcher, internist

Philadephia
Kumanyika, Shiriki K. nutrition epidemiology researcher, educator

Pittsburgh
Bauccio, Lisa Ruth obstetric nurse, high-risk perinatal nurse
Bell, Lori Jo crisis counselor, psychiatric nurse
Berman, Malcolm Frank health facility administrator
Brennen, Carole J. researcher in human services
Clemence, Bonnie J. pediatrics nurse
Connolly, Ruth Carol urological nurse practitioner
Cunningham, Leah Vota medical/surgical nursing educator
Dato, Virginia Marie public health physician
Daube, Patricia Barrett health facility administrator
Doerfler, Leo G. audiology educator
Ferrara-Love, Roseann nurse
Flynn, Bridget Mary transplant coordinator
†Frizzi, Mary Elizabeth rehabilitation specialist
†Gaskey-Spear, Nancy Jane nurse anesthetist
George, John Anthony health corporation executive
Germanowski, Janet women's health and medical surgical nurse, educator, researcher
†Goertzen, Irma hospital executive
Heinecke, Deborah Ann pediatrics nurse
Herleman, Laura Ann nursing administrator
Jakopac-Miller, Kim Ann mental health nurse
†Kapucu, Naim researcher
Kirker, William George health facility administrator
Longest, Beaufort Brown health services administration educator, research director
Lucas, Deborah Ann nurse, administrator
Machtiger, Harriet Gordon psychoanalyst
McCall, Dorothy Kay social worker, psychotherapist
Missiriotis, Irene artist
Moore, Pearl B. nurse
Omiros, George James medical foundation executive
Pacifico, Diane Alane ophthalmic nurse
Romoff, Jeffrey Alan health care executive
Rudy, Ellen Beam nursing educator
Sanzo, Anthony Michael health care executive
Slayton, Val Warren health services executive
Steele, Cheryl A. oncology nurse
Sullivan, Dorothy Louise nurse
Tripodi, Tony social worker, educator
Zanardelli, John Joseph healthcare services executive
Ziegler, Janet Cassaro holistic health nurse

Port Matilda
Henshaw, Beverly Ann Harsh women's health nurse, consultant

Pottsville
Steffan, Nancy Marie cardiothoracic/intensive care nurse
Walsh, James William mental health professional

Punxsutawney
Klohr, Joanne Carol nurse

Quakertown
Ambrus, Lorna medical, surgical and geriatrics nurse

Reading
Bell, Frances Louise medical technologist
Stevens, Jennifer Roehl critical care nurse

Scranton
Farrell, Marian L. nursing educator
†Lepore, Marie Ann home care nurse
Maislin, Isidore hospital administrator
O'Hora, Eileen Rita emergency care nurse
Shovlin, Joseph P. optometrist, consultant
Turock, Jane Parsick nutritionist
Walsh, Denise Ann Jessup critical care nurse

Shohola
Harding, Linda Otto gerontological nurse

Somerset
Watson, Frances Margaret critical care nurse, case manager

Souderton
Moyer, June Faye critical care nurse

Spring Grove
Alcon, Sonja Lee de Bey Gebhardt Ryan retired medical social worker

Springfield
Meahl, Barbara occupational health nurse

Stroudsburg
Miller, Nancy A. nursing administrator

Summerhill
McCoy, Patrick J. family therapist, educator

Temple
VonNieda, Jean Lorayne medical/surgical nurse

Transfer
Larson, Sharon Lynn oncological nurse

Tyrone
Stoner, Philip James hospital administrator

Uniontown
Carder, Mary Alice dietitian

University Park
Cavanagh, Peter Robert science educator, researcher
Mayers, Stanley Penrose, Jr. public health educator
Rolls, Barbara Jean nutrition educator, laboratory director
Taleff, Michael James chemical dependency educator, consultant

Upland
Graves, Maxine medical and surgical nurse

Valencia
Hill, Ellen Brown emergency medicine/gerontology professional, nurse

Villanova
Beletz, Elaine Ethel nurse, educator

Wallingford
Daly, Charles Arthur health services administrator
McCarthy, Carol A. pediatric nurse practitioner

Warren
Crone, John Rossman pharmacist

Washington
Robinson, Jennifer Lynn nursing educator

Wayne
Grace, Thomas Lee healthcare administrator, nurse
Rolleri, Denise Marie business owner, radiation therapist

West Chester
Dong, Gangyi acupunturist, medical researcher

West Point
Ball, William Austin health facility director, researcher
Chen, I-Wu pharmaceutical researcher

Wilkes Barre
Brady, Patricia Marie nurse
Curry, Dianne Swetz school nurse
Olerta, Leslie Anne nuclear medicine technologist

Wyndmoor
Uemura, Teruki child brain developmentalist

Yardley
Thomas, Nora R. neonatal critical care nurse

York
Bartels, Bruce Michael health care executive
Chronister, Virginia Ann school nurse, educator
Greisler, David Scott healthcare executive
Hamilton, Shirley Ann nursing administrator
Keiser, Paul Harold hospital administrator
Moore, Christine Helen nurse anesthetist
Page, Sean Edward emergency medical care provider, educator
Rosen, Raymond health facility executive

RHODE ISLAND

Cranston
Kane, Steven Michael psychotherapist, educator

East Providence
McGee, Mary Alice health science research administrator

Kingston
Katzanek, Robin Jean physical therapy educator

Newport
Michael, Dorothy Ann nursing administrator, naval officer
Mullaney, Joann Barnes nursing educator

North Kingstown
Kenty, Janet Rogers nursing educator

North Smithfield
Muratori, Janice Anne nurse

Pawtucket
Roy, Gail Florine nursing administrator
Tarpy, Eleanor Kathleen social worker

Providence
Aflague, John M. mental health nurse, educator, administrator
Boekelheide, Kim pathologist
Edens, Myra Jim health facility nursing administrator
Graziano, Catherine Elizabeth retired nursing educator
Metrey, George David social work educator, academic administrator
Monteiro, Lois Ann medical science educator
Parris, Thomas Godfrey, Jr. medical facility administrator
Pivin, Jeanette Eva psychotherapist

Smithfield
Baker, Ruth Sharon nurse

Wakefield
Lanni, Lorette Marie nursing manager

SOUTH CAROLINA

Aiken
Voss, Terence J. human factors scientist, educator

Anderson
Cheatham, Valerie Meador clinical dietitian
George-Lepkowski, Sue Ann echocardiographic technologist
Harllee, Mary Beth social worker, educator

Charleston
Austin, Charles John health services educator
Calhoun, Deborah Lynn emergency room nurse, consultant
Cheng, Kenneth Tat-Chiu pharmacy educator
Hollis, Bruce Warren experimental nutritionist, industrial consultant
Infinger, Gloria Altman nursing administrator
Johnston, Stephen Edward clinical information systems coordinator, educator
Keating, Thomas Patrick health care administrator, educator
Robinson, Jakie Lee human services administrator
Smith, W. Stuart strategic planning director

Columbia
Amidon, Roger Lyman health administration educator
Bradham, Tamala Selke audiologist
Bryant, Douglas E. public health service official
Ginsberg, Leon Herman social work educator
Luckes, Mary Helen B. mental health nurse
Ramsey, Bonnie Jeanne mental health facility administrator, psychiatrist
Richardson, Gwendolyn E. medical/surgical nurse
Smith, Susan Arlene nursing educator
Walters, Rebecca Russell Yarborough medical technologist

Conway
Nale, Julia Ann nursing educator

Florence
Isgett, Donna Carmichael critical care nurse, administrator

Fort Mill
Fogle O'Keefe, Maureen Ann nursing administrator

Georgetown
Williams, Rynn Mobley community health nurse

Greenville
Day, Angela Riddle occupational health nurse, educator
Gresham, James Steve health service administrator

Greenwood
Bateman, Carol Vaughan pharmacist
Scales, Carol Jean nursing educator

Hilton Head Island
Wesselmann, Glenn Allen retired hospital executive

Irmo
Stewart, Alexander Constantine medical technologist

Lexington
Maranville, June Kimberly speech language pathologist

Marion
Inabinet, Lawrence Elliott retired pharmacist

Moncks Corner
Deavers, James Frederick optometrist

Mount Pleasant
Krupa, Patricia Ann retired nurse, consultant

Myrtle Beach
Madory, James Richard hospital administrator, former air force officer

Newberry
Pollard, Wendy Higgins counselor

Pendleton
Fehler, Polly Diane neonatal nurse, educator
Kline, Priscilla Mackenzie nursing educator

Pickens
Gilman, Nancy Ellen Helgeson medical and surgical nurse

Simpsonville
Hall, Marilyn Margaret occupational health nurse

Spartanburg
†Jackson, Tracey Leigh health care organization administrator

Summerville
Young, Margaret Aletha McMullen (Mrs. Herbert Wilson Young) social worker

Walhalla
Watson, Jean Vaughn critical care nurse, ambulatory surgery nurse

Ware Shoals
Webb, Patricia Dyan W. speech and language pathologist, sign language educator

West Columbia
Brown, Opal Diann medical technologist, nurse
Palmer, Susan Smith dietitian

SOUTH DAKOTA

Brookings
Jamerson, Patricia Ann Locandro pediatrics nurse, nursing educator
Spease, Loren William chiropractor

Huron
Kuhler, Deborah Gail grief therapist, former state legislator

Rapid City
Buum, Mary Kay dialysis nurse
Corwin, Bert Clark optometrist

Sioux Falls
Danielson, David Gordon health science facility administrator, general legal counsel
Nygaard, Lance Corey nurse, data processing consultant
Richards, LaClaire Lissetta Jones (Mrs. George A. Richards) social worker
VanDemark, Michelle Volin critical care, neuroscience nurse
VanHeerde, Carolyn Kay program manager

Sturgis
Baldwin, Judy critical care nurse
Daane, Kathryn D. retired nursing administrator

Vermillion
Rotert, Denise Anne occupational therapist, army officer, educator

TENNESSEE

Alcoa
Disney, Karen C. critical care nurse

Antioch
Sandlin, Debbie Crowe critical care nurse

Brentwood
Dalton, James Edgar, Jr. health facility administrator
German, Ronald Stephen health care facility administrator
Pruett, James William psychotherapist

Bristol
Moore, Marilyn Patricia community counselor

Camden
Burchum, Jacqueline Rosenjack family nurse practitioner

Chattanooga
Beach, Hazel Elizabeth nurse
†Hendrick, Diane Goza psychiatric nurse
Parker, Christine Wright medical director
Saeger, Dixie Forester dietitian
Scott, Mark Alden hospital network executive
Weinmann, Judy Munger nurse
Young, Sandra Joyce nursing administrator, consultant

Cleveland
Watson, S. Michele home health nurse

Clinton
Seib, Billie McGhee Rushing nursing administrator, consultant

Collegedale
Crosby, Ellen Louise counselor

Collierville
Golden, Eddie Lee optometrist

Cookeville
Musacchio, Marilyn Jean nurse midwife, educator
Richards, Melinda Lou speech and language pathologist

Fayetteville
Dickey, Nancy Eagar social worker

Franklin
Woodside, Donna J. nursing educator

Germantown
†Mitchell, Sheila Lankford pharmacy executive
Nolly, Robert J. hospital administrator, pharmaceutical science educator

Harrogate
Money, Max Lee family nurse practitioner

Hartsville
Linville, Mary Todd family nurse practitioner

Hendersonville
Davis, Robert Norman hospital administrator

Huntingdon
Spain, Joyce Hicks nurse

Huntsville
Boardman, Maureen Bell community health nurse

Jackson
†Lovett, Marilyn Denise social services educator
Smith, Geri Garrett nurse educator
Stutts, Gary Thomas clinical analyst auditor
Tims, Ramona Faye medical and surgical nurse
Woodall, Gilbert Earl, Jr. medical administrator

Jefferson City
Huff, Cynthia Owen nursing educator, nurse practitioner

Jellico
Hausman, Keith Lynn hospital administrator, physical therapist

Kingsport
Coffman, Wilma Martin women's health nurse, educator
Messamore, Michael Miller pharmacist

Knoxville
Cloud, Gary Lynn food and nutrition services administrator
McGuire, Sandra Lynn nursing educator
Menefee-Greene, Laura S. psychiatric nurse
Parker-Conrad, Jane E. occupational health nurse consultant
Phillips, Kenneth D. nursing educator
Plaas, Kristina Maria neonatal nurse specialist, registered nurse
Smith, Vicky Lynn nurse, geriatrics nurse
Swanson, Lorna Ellen physical therapist, athletic trainer, researcher
Taylor, Lee organization development practitioner
Trout, Monroe Eugene hospital systems executive
Young, Peter Bernhart neuropsychologist
Zimmer, Willie Mae medical/surgical nurse

Kodak
Kreider, Sandra Anne Miller medical/surgical nurse

La Follette
Justice, Melissa Morris family nurse practitioner

Lewisburg
Gonzalez, Raquel Maria *pharmacist*

Linden
Mitchell, Elizabeth Marelle *nursing educator, medical, surgical nurse*

Loudon
Wilks, Kimberly Susan *occupational health nurse, educator*

Louisville
McReynolds, David Hobert *hospital administrator*

Martin
Black, Ruby L. *nursing educator*

Memphis
Collins, Earline Brown *medical and surgical and nephrology nurse*
Crain, Frances Utterback *retired dietitian*
Crisman, D'Etta Marie *nursing administrator, chemical dependency and psychiatric nurse*
Diggs, Walter Whitley *health science facilty administrator*
Edwards, William Harold, Jr. *nursing administrator, consultant*
Elfervig, Lucie Theresa Savoie *independent ophthalmic nursing consultant*
Garland, Linda M. *nursing case manager*
Graham, Tina Tucker *psychiatric and pediatrics nurse*
Jarvis, Daphne Eloise *laboratory administrator*
Lawson, Virginia King *nutritionist, consultant*
McBride, Juanita Loyce *oncological nurse*
Mendel, Maurice *audiologist, educator*
Miller, Beverly McDonald *geriatric nurse practitioner*
Mirvis, David Marc *health administrator, cardiologist, educator*
Mulholland, Kenneth Leo, Jr. *health care facility administrator*
Winters, Darcy LaFountain *medical management company executive*

Millington
Lee, Diane *obstetrics/gynecology nurse practitioner*

Morristown
Harmon, David Eugene *optometrist, geneticist*

Murfreesboro
Lasater, Sandra Jo *nurse*

Nashville
Bolian, George Clement *health care executive, physician*
Carpenter, Janet Sharkey *nursing researcher*
†Chapdelaine, Perry Anthony, Jr. *public health physician, educator*
Dale, Kathy Gail *rehabilitation rheumatology nurse*
†Frist, Thomas Fearn, Jr. *hospital management company executive*
Graves, Rebecca O. *public health nurse, consultant*
Harrison, Connie Day *cardiovascular clinical nurse specialist, nursing administrator, consultant*
Johnson, David *medical administrator*
Jones, Evelyn Gloria *medical technologist, educator*
Land, Rebekah Ruth *marriage and family therapist*
Manning, David Lee *health care executive*
McPhee, Scott Douglas *occupational therapist, academic administrator*
Mosely, Marcella-M. *speech pathology educator*
Ragsdale, Richard Elliot *healthcare management executive*
Rose, Don Garry *social worker*
Sanders, Jay William *audiology educator*
Sloan, Reba Faye *dietitian, consultant*
Speller-Brown, Barbara Jean *pediatric nurse practitioner*
Stringfield, Charles David *hospital administrator*
Urmy, Norman B. *hospital administrator*
Watts, Carolyn Sue *nurse*
White, Michael James *healthcare facilities administrator*

Normandy
Stockton, Kim Welch *nurse practitioner*

Oak Ridge
Foust, Donna Elaine Marshall *women's health nurse*
Jones, Virginia McClurkin *social worker*

Old Hickory
Davis, Fred Donald, Jr. *optometrist*

Rockvale
Ferguson, Piete Jackson *home health nurse*

Trenton
McCullough, Kathryn T. Baker *social worker*

Tullahoma
Scalf, Jean A. Keele *medical/surgical, geriatrics and home health nurse*

Winchester
Cashion, Joe Mason *home health care administrator*

TEXAS

Amarillo
Anderson, Allan Curtis *pharmaceuticals researcher*
Arnold, Winnie Jo *retired mental health nurse, nursing administrator*
Bowling, Joyce Blankenchip *retired critical care nurse*
Burrows, Emily Ann *nurse*
McGaughy, Rebecca Lynn *nursing administrator, consultant*
St. Clair, Shelley *music therapist*
†Smith, John Paul *counselor, university official*

Anson
Godsey, Martha Sue *speech-language pathologist*

Arlington
McCuistion, Peg Orem *hospice administrator*
McCuistion, Robert Wiley *lawyer, hospital administrator, management consultant*
McNairn, Peggi Jean *speech pathologist, educator*
Watkins, Ted Ross *social work educator*
Wiig, Elisabeth Hemmersam *speech language pathologist, educator*

Austin
Acker, Virginia Margaret *nursing educator*
Attal, Gene (Fred Eugene Attal) *hospital executive*
Austin, David Mayo *social work educator*
Avant, Patricia *nursing educator*
Davis, Donald Robert *nutritionist, researcher, consultant*
Doerr, Barbara Ann *health facility director*
Doluisio, James Thomas *pharmacy educator*
Durbin, Richard Louis, Sr. *healthcare admnistration consultant*
Easley, Christa Birgit *nurse, researcher*
Gardner, Joan *medical, surgical nurse*
Girling, Bettie Joyce Moore *home health executive*
Golden, Kimberly Kay *critical care, flight nurse*
Hall, Beverly Adele *nursing educator*
Hayes, Patricia Ann *health facility administrator*
Heffley, James Dickey *nutrition counselor*
Hurley, Laurence Harold *medicinal chemistry educator*
Johnson, Mildred Snowden *retired nursing educator*
Larkam, Beverley McCosham *clinical social worker, family therapist*
Martin, Frederick Noel *audiology educator*
Richardson, Betty Kehl *nursing educator, administrator, counselor, researcher*
Riggs, Deborah Kay *critical care, pediatrics nurse*
Taylor, Mildred Lois *nursing home administrator*

Baytown
Coker, Mary Shannon *surgical nurse*

Bedford
Collins, Stephen Barksdale *retired health care executive*
Donnelly, Barbara Schettler *medical technologist, retired*
Flaherty, Carole L. *medical, surgical and mental health nurse*

Bellaire
Knolle, Mary Anne Ericson *psychotherapist, business communications consultant*
Smeal, Janis Lea *operating room nurse, health facility administrator*

Bonham
Phillips, Don Lee *nursing administrator*
Seale, Mary Louise *medical, surgical and geriatrics nurse*

Brenham
Dalrymple, Christopher Guy *chiropractor*

Brownsville
Godinez, Magdalena *cardiology nurse*

Bryan
Bement, Jill Leigh *occupational therapist*
Sulik, Edwin (Pete Sulik) *health care administrator*

Canyon
Kirby, Brenda Jean *critical care nurse*

Carrollton
Sherman, Lisa Le Ellen *pharmacist*
Withrow, Lucille Monnot *nursing home administrator*

Castroville
Strickland, Sandra Jean Heinrich *nursing educator*

Cedar Hill
Findley, Milla Jean *nutritionist*
Kincaid, Sherrie Lynn *clinical research and surgical intensive care unit nurse*

Chillicothe
Brock, Helen Rachel McCoy *retired mental health and community health nurse*

Commerce
Ridgeway, Glenda S. *mental health nurse, educator*

Conroe
Bruce, Rachel Mary Condon *nurse practitioner*
Shepherd, Elizabeth Poole *health science facility administrator*

Converse
Droneburg, Nancy Marie *geriatrics nurse*

Copperas Cove
Sullivan, Theresa Maria *maternal and child health care nurse*

Corpus Christi
Clark, Joyce Naomi Johnson *nurse*
Duarte, Eduardo Adolfo *nursing home administrator*
Jones, Audrey Beyer *dietitian*
Jones, Rebecca Alvina Patronis *nurse*

Cotulla
Gonzales, Pablo *pharmacist*

Dallas
Anderson, Ron Joe *hospital administrator, physician, educator*
Barnett, Peter Ralph *health science facility administrator, dentist*
Bell-Tolliver, LaVerne *social worker*
Bollinger, Pamela Beemer *health facilities administrator*
Bradley, John Andrew *hospital management company executive*
Bryant, L. Gerald *health care administrator*
Champion, Michael Ray *health facility administrator*
Collins, Lynn M. *oncology clinical nurse specialist*
Farrington, Bertha Louise *nursing administrator*
France, Newell Edwin *former hospital administrator, consultant*
Fritze, Julius Arnold *marriage counselor*
Goldmann, James Allen *healthcare consultant*
Gouge, Betty Merle *family therapist*
Heatherley, Melody Ann *nursing administrator*
Hitt, David Hamilton *retired hospital executive*
Holl-Matthews, Dee Lynn *career counselor, psychotherapist, personal development and success coach*
Johnson, Murray H. *optometrist, researcher, consultant, lecturer*
King, Clarence Carleton, II *healthcare executive*
Laramore, Evelyn K. *nursing supervisor*
Miller, Jo Carolyn Dendy *family and marriage counselor, educator*
Nelson, Jill E. *health care consultant, health facility administrator, researcher*
O'Bannion, Mindy Martha Martin *nurse*
Powell, Boone, Jr. *hospital administrator*
†Preston, Donna Joan *dietitian, consultant*
Purkey, Thomas Eugene *social worker*
Smith, William Randolph (Randy Smith) *health care management executive*
Stump, Ann Louise B. *nurse*
†Waterston, Judy C. *healthcare administrator*

Denton
Cissell, William Bernard *health studies educator*
Gershon, Elaine A. *medical and surgical nurse, nursing administrator*
Killeen, JoAnn *community health and critical care nurse*
Levisay, Suzanne Baker *counselor*
Mathes, Dorothy Jean Holden *occupational therapist*
Riddle, Carol Ann *counselor*
Surprise, Juanee *chiropractor, nutrition consultant*
Talley, Linda Jean *food scientist, dietitian*

Donna
Turner, David B. *health facility administrator*

Dripping Springs
Nicholas, Nickie Lee *retired industrial hygienist*

Dublin
Corta, Nancy Ruth *nurse*

Edinburg
Johnson, Barbara Ann *health services educator*
Wilson, Bruce Keith *men's health nurse*

El Paso
Allen, Anna Jean *chiropractor*
Hedrick, Wyatt Smith *pharmacist*
Hornberger, Susan J. *critical care nurse, educator*
Juarez, Antonio *psychotherapist, consultant, counselor, educator*
Monsivais, Diane B. *surgical nurse, writer*
Roark, Charles Elvis *healthcare executive*
Staeger, Earl *nurse*

Eustace
Sheffield, Sue *nursing educator*

Fort Hood
Shuler, George Nixon, Jr. *social worker, writer*

Fort Worth
Brockman, Leslie Richard *social worker*
Brodale, Louise Lado *medical, post surgery and geriatrics nurse*
Dotson, Libby *foundation executive*
Greenstone, James Lynn *psychotherapist, police psychologist, mediator, consultant, author, educator*
Pruitt, Mary Ann *chiropractor*
Smaistrla, Jean Ann *family therapist*
Strength, Danna Elliott *nursing educator*

Galveston
Cabanas, Elizabeth Ann *nutritionist*
†Hargraves, Martha Ann *health services administrator, educator*
Ivy, Berrynell Baker *critical care nurse*
Lawrence, Kathy *medical, surgical, and radiology nurse*
Shannon, Mary Lou *adult health nursing educator*

Graham
Cagle, Paulette Bernice *mental health administrator and psychologist*

Groesbeck
Gilbert, Edith Harmon *medical, surgical and occupational health nurse*

Hearne
Helpert-Nunez, Ruth Anne *clinical social worker, psychotherapist*

Highland Village
Wiedemann, Ramona Diane *occupational therapist*

Houston
Armentrout, Debra Catherine *neonatal nurse practitioner*
Bahl, Saroj Mehta *nutritionist, educator*
Battin, R(osabell) Ray (Rosabell Harriet Ray) *audiologist, neuropsychologist*
Becker, Frederick Fenimore *cancer center administrator, pathologist*
Bellinger, Patricia McHugh *oncology and adult nurse practitioner*
Booker, Ronald Joseph *physician practice management*
Bottoms, Barbara Ann *nurse*
Brown, Patricia Tilley *pharmacist*
Brucker, Janet Mary *nurse*
Burdine, John A. *hospital administrator, nuclear medicine educator*
Callender, Norma Anne *psychology educator, counselor*
Crisp, Jennifer Ann Clair *neurosurgical nurse*
†Dimachkie, Mazen Mohammad *health care educator*
Duncan, Cheryl L. *critical care/cardiac catherization nurse*
Gerhart, Glenna Lee *pharmacist*
Gunn, Joan Marie *health care administrator*
Hodge, Etta Lee *director of surgical services, nurse*
Holmes, Harry Dadisman *health facility administrator*
Hrna, Daniel Joseph *pharmacist, lawyer*
Hudson, W. Gail *social worker*
Janes, Joseph Anthony, Jr. *optometrist*
Jhin, Michael Kontien *health care executive*
Lewis, Wanda Howell *health facility administrator*
Mathis, Sharon Ann *home health nurse, mental health nurse, consultant, columnist, entrepreneur*
McGuire, Dianne Marie *psychotherapist*
Minton, Melanie Sue *neuroscience nurse*
Montgomery, Denise Karen *nurse*
Moore, Lois Jean *health science facility administrator*
Nasser, Moes Roshanali *optometrist*
Orner, Linda Price *family therapist*
Park, Cheryl Antoinette *women's health nurse, educator*
Pate, Patricia Ann *women's health nurse*
Patterson, Ronald R(oy) *health care systems executive*
Piech, Ruth Diane *nursing administrator*
Raber, Martin *health facility administrator, medical educator*
Reed, Kathlyn Louise *occupational therapist, educator*
Richardson, Deborah Kaye *clinical nurse specialist, educator*
Ruppert, Susan Donna *critical care nursing educator, family adult nurse practitioner*
Schiflett, Mary Fletcher Cavender *retired health facility executive, researcher, educator*
Schneider, Karen Lee *psychotherapist*
†Schneider, Pamela Jean *psychotherapist*
Shapiro, Carrie Kimberly *epidemiologist, researcher*
Smith, J. Thomas *mental health consultant*
Tucker, Gary Wilson *nurse educator*
Turner, Kelley Bailey *volunteer program administrator*
Wagner, Donald Bert *health care consultant*
Wallace, Mark Allen *hospital executive*
Wieber, Sandra Jean *pediatric critical care nurse*
Wisecup, Barbara Jean *retired medical/surgical nurse*
Wolinsky, Ira *nutritionist*

Hughes Springs
Koelker, Gail *family nurse practitioner*

Huntsville
Budge, Marcia Charlene *family nurse practitioner*
Vick, Marie *retired health science educator*

Katy
Paden, Carolyn Eileen Belknap *dietitian*
Thorne, Melvin Quentin, Jr. *managed healthcare executive*

Kerrville
Rhodes, James Devers *psychotherapist*

Killeen
Crawford, Norma Vivian *nurse*

Kingsland
Johnson, Vicki Valeen *paramedic, technical advisor movie studios*

Lackland AFB
Winn, Vicki Elaine *nurse, consultant*

Lago Vista
Garcia y Carrillo, Martha Xochitl *pharmacist*

Lancaster
Goelden-Bowen, Michelle Marie *occupational therapist*

Laredo
Qualey, Thomas Leo, Jr. *human services administrator*

Lewisville
Browne, M. Lynne *artist, optician*

Livingston
Jones, Janet Valeria *psychiatric nurse, clinical nurse educators*

Lorena
Mc Call, Charles Barnard *health facility executive, educator*

Los Fresnos
†Sterling, William Carlisle *physician assistant*

Lubbock
Broselow, Linda Latt *medical office technician, aviculturist*
Dersch, Charette Alyse *marriage and family therapist*
Elder, Bessie Ruth *pharmacist*
Gibson, David Roger *optometrist*
McBeath, Don B. *health administrator*
Reeves, A. Sue Windsor *healthcare administrator*
Smith, Doris Corinne Kemp *retired nurse*
Wampler, Richard Scotten *marriage and family therapy educator*
Warren, Jennifer Elizabeth *neonatal nurse*
Young, Teri Ann Butler *pharmacist*

Mc Kinney
Kincaid, Elsie Elizabeth *educational therapist*
Merritt, Linda Ann *neonatal nurse*

Mesquite
Williamson, Barbara Jo *retired community health nurse, educator*

Midland
Best, Alynda Kay *conflict resolution mediator*
Sullivan, Patricia G. *maternal, child and women's health nursing educator*

Mineral Wells
Scott, Geneva Lee Smith *nursing educator*

Mission
Rapp, Joanna A. *retired geriatrics nurse, mental health nurse*

Montgomery
Gooch, Carol Ann *psychotherapist consultant*

Nacogdoches
Migl, Donald Raymond *therapeutic optometrist, pharmacist*

Nashville
†Casey, Marsha *hospital executive*

New Braunfels
Bullard, Bruce Lynn *critical care nurse*
Hooker, Renée Michelle *postanesthesia and perinatal nurse*

Newton
Hopkins, Sallye F. *women's health nurse*

North Richland Hills
Cook, Peggy Jo *psychotherapist, consultant*

Odessa
Pokky, Eric Jon *clinical pharmacist*

Panhandle
Sherrod, Lloyd Bruce *nutritionist*

Paris
Sawyer, Mary Catherine *hospital administrator*

Pasadena
Smith, Oscar William *nursing home administrator*

Pflugerville
Bull, John P. *critical care nurse, electrophysiology nurse*
Schroer, Jane Hastings *nurse practitioner*

Plano
Carmicle, Linda Harper *psychotherapist*

Ponder
Barnett, Janice Elaine *critical care nurse*

Port Arthur
Vinecour, Oneida Agnes *nurse*

Post
Miller, Darwin Leon *healthcare administrator*

Richardson
Byrd, Ellen Stoesser *dermatology nurse*
Loubert, Linda M. *medical technologist*

Roanoke
Kleinkort, Joseph Alexius *physical therapist, consultant*

Rockdale
Brown, Rubye Ellen *retired nursing administrator*

Rowlett
Newkirk, Trixie Darnell *critical care nurse*

Rusk
Cart-Rogers, Katherine Cooper *emergency nurse*

Sam Rayburn
Shabaaz, Ahia *family nurse practitioner*

San Antonio
Adcox, Mary Sandra *dietitian, consultant*
Barnes, Betty Rae *counselor*
Clark, Lady Ellen Marie *occupational health nurse, consultant*
Crabtree, Ben C. *home health care agency administrator*
Crabtree, Tania Oylan *home health nurse, administrator, consultant*
Davis, Yolette Marie Toussaint *home nursing administrator, parish nurse, camp nurse*
Fraley, Debra Lee *critical care nurse*
Gonzalez, Hector Hugo *nurse, educator, consultant*
Hawken, Patty Lynn *retired nursing educator, dean of faculty*
Hopper, Vanessa J. *oncological nurse*
Jackson, Brenda S. *nursing educator*
Jackson, Earl, Jr. *medical technologist, retired*
Jackson, Steve Glen *health services administrator*
Johnson, Katherine Anne *health research administrator, lawyer*
Kossaeth, Tammy Gale *intensive care nurse*
Martinez, Ruben *critical care nurse*
Paris, Karen Marie *nurse, educator*
Pixley, Beryl Kay *nursing educator*
Rosenow, Doris Jane *critical care nurse, nursing consultant*
Schultz, Marilyn Ann *medical/surgical nurse*
Simmons, Cecelia E. *quality improvement, infection control and employee health nurse, researcher*
Soucy, Mark D. *psychiatric-mental health clinical nurse specialist, educator*
Swansburg, Russell Chester *medical administrator educator*
Tucker, Stephen Lawrence *health administration educator, consultant*
Walker, Mary Erline *critical care nurse*
Wilson, Janie Menchaca *nursing educator, researcher*

San Marcos
Mooney, Robert Thurston *health care educator*
Wetter-Kubeck, Daisy Fisher *dietitian, consultant*

Sheppard AFB
Daskal, Paul Linn *psychiatric and mental health professional*

Sherman
†Tonelli, Mary Jo *public health physician*

Southlake
Gelinas, Marc Adrien *healthcare administrator*

Temple
Frost, Juanita Corbitt *retired hospital foundation coordinator*
Tobin, Margaret Ann *cardiac medical critical care nurse*

Texarkana
Bertrand, Betty Harleen *nurse*
Turner, Paige Lea *cardiac telemetry nurse*

The Woodlands
Frison, Paul Maurice *health care executive*

Martineau, Julie Peperone *social worker*

Tomball
†Burgoyne, Mojie Adler *clinical social worker*

Tyler
Deardorff, Kathleen Umbeck *nursing educator, researcher*
Smith, Janna Hogan *nursing administrator, surgical nurse*

Van Horn
Dodson, Hersha Rhee *psychiatric-mental health nurse*

Vernon
Bearden, Jeff R. *hospital official*

Victoria
Craft, Sheryl McArthur *rehabilitation nurse*
Spicak, Doris Elizabeth *health services company executive*

Waco
Corley, Carol Lee *school nurse*
Kahn, Alan Harvey *therapist, administrator, consultant*

Wichita Falls
Cleary, Thomas J. *social worker, administrator*

UTAH

Bountiful
Dowling, Lona Buchanan *nurse*
Rowland, Ruth Gailey *retired hospital official*

Draper
Schutz, Roberta Maria (Bobbi) *social worker*

Holladay
Reinkoester, Robert William, Jr. *critical care nurse*

Hooper
Atwater, Julie Demers *critical care nurse*

Kaysville
Ashmead, Allez Morrill *speech, hearing, and language pathologist, orofacial myologist, consultant*

Logan
Eldredge, Garth Melvin *rehabilitation counseling educator*

Murray
Webster, Linda Jane *clinical social worker, consultant*

Ogden
Jones, Galen Ray *physician assistant*
Palmer, Kim Michaele *mental health counselor, consultant*

Orderville
Goddard, David Benjamin *physician assistant, clinical perfusionist*

Orem
Sauter, Gail Louise *speech pathologist*

Park City
Zaharia, Eric Stafford *developmental disabilities program administrator*

Saint George
Chilow, Barbara Gail *social worker*
Hauenstein, Karen *physician's assistant, critical care nurse*
Violet, Woodrow Wilson, Jr. *retired chiropractor*

Salt Lake City
†Bulkeley, Brooke *healthcare administratrator, small business owner*
Good, Rebecca Mae Wertman *learning and behavior counselor, grief and loss counselor, hospice nurse, therapeutic touch practitioner, educator*
Grabarz, Donald Francis *pharmacist*
Johanson, Orin William *social worker, school counselor, consultant*
Kelen, Joyce Arlene *social worker*
Lee, Glenn Richard *medical administrator, educator*
Lindsay, Elena Margaret *nurse*
Martineau, Holly Low *dietitian*
Mason, James Ostermann *public health administrator*
Reeves, Bruce *social worker*
Sinclair, Sara Voris *health facility administrator, nurse*
Talbot, Steven Richards *vascular technologist, consultant, writer*
Wolf, Harold Herbert *pharmacy educator*

VERMONT

Brattleboro
Gregg, Michael B. *health science association administrator, epidemiologist*

Bridport
Wagner, Barbara Anne Beebe *critical care nurse*

Burlington
Mead, Philip Bartlett *healthcare administrator, physician*
Milliard, Aline *social worker*

Essex Junction
Coffey, Jean Sheerin *pediatric nurse, educator*

Montpelier
Griswold, David James *therapist and physician's assistant*

North Troy
Rosenberger, Janice Whitehill *speech and language pathologist*

Orleans
Floersheim, Sandra Kelton *community health nurse*

Rochester
†Weisfeld, Jay Stanley *public health physician*

South Burlington
Perrine, Mervyn William Bud *alcohol center director, forensic consultant*

Thetford
Morgan, Susan McGuire McGrath *psychotherapist*

Williston
†Coleman, Dale Lynn *health facility administrator, educator*

VIRGINIA

Alexandria
Daniel, Dorothy Isom *nurse specialist, consultant*
Fairchild, Lillie McKeen *nurse, educator*
Fisher, Donald Wayne *medical association executive*
Girouard, Shirley Ann *nurse, policy analyst*
Graham, John H. IV *health science association administrator*

Annandale
Abdellah, Faye Glenn *retired public health service executive*

Arlington
Adreon, Beatrice Marie Rice *pharmacist*
Behney, Clyde Joseph *health services researcher*
Contis, George *medical services company executive*
Kent, Jill Elspeth *academic healthcare adminstrator, lawyer*
Papadopoulos, Patricia Marie *healthcare professional*
Schneider, Clara Garbus *dietitian, nursing consultant*

Aroda
Nisly, Loretta Lynn *medical and surgical nurse, geriatrics nurse*

Ashburn
Walsh, Geraldine Frances *nursing administrator*

Big Island
Durham, Betty Bethea *therapist*

Boones Mill
Oyler, Amy Elizabeth *medical/surgical nurse*

Burkeville
Stiles, Anne Plum *healthcare specialist*

Charlottesville
Bouchard, Ronald A. *health care administrator*
Cook, Lynn J. *nursing educator*
Drake, Emily E. *nurse*
Halseth, Michael James *medical center administrator*
Hanft, Ruth S. Samuels (Mrs. Herbert Hanft) *health care consultant, educator, economist*
Hawkins, Deborah Craun *community health nurse*
Hinnant, Clarence Henry, III *health care executive*
Pate, Robert Hewitt, Jr. *counselor educator*

Chesapeake
Martin, Angela Carter *nursing educator*
Skrip, Linda Jean *nursing administrator, case manager*
†Welch, Nancy M. *public health administrator*

Deltaville
Crittenden, Katherine Lucina *nurse*

Duffield
Orr, Emma Jane *pharmacist, educator*

Fairfax
Harper, Doreen C. *nursing educator*
Madison-Colmore, Octavia Dianne *adult education educator*
Malouff, Frank Joseph *health care association executive*
Nidiffer, Sheri Lynn *medical/surgical nurse*
Priesman, Elinor Lee Soll *family dynamics administrator, mediator, educator*
Robertson, Patricia Aileen *adult and geriatric nurse*
Turjanica, Mary Ann *clinical nurse specialist, consultant*
Wu, Chien-yun (Jennie Wu) *nursing educator*

Fairfax Station
Johansen, Eivind Herbert *special education services executive, former army officer*

Falls Church
Blanck, Ronald Ray *hospital administrator, internist, career officer*
Seifert, Patricia Clark *cardiac surgery nurse, educator, consultant*
†Singleton, John Knox *hospital executive*

Fishersville
Matthews, Judith Nygaard *nursing administrator, home health nurse*
Ward, Kathryn Elizabeth Kurek *nursing case manager*

Fort Belvoir
Humphreys-Heckler, Maureen Kelly *nursing home administrator*

Fredericksburg
Karpiscak, Linda Sue *pediatrics nurse*
Nichols, Mary Reid *community and parent-child health nursing educator*
Speirs, Carol Lucille *nurse, naval officer*

Hampton
Kulp, Eileen Bodnar *social worker*

Wagstaff, Deborah A. *geriatrics and mental health nurse, family nurse practitioner*

Leesburg
Ecker, G. T. Dunlop *hospital administration executive*

Lynchburg
Weimar, Robert Henry *clinical hypnotherapist*

Manassas
Lytton, Linda Rountree *marriage and family therapist, test consultant*
Thompson, Sandy Maria *health and staff development coordinator*
Twitchel, Nancy Lou *medical/surgical and emergency room nurse*

Mc Lean
Cuffe, Robin Jean *nursing educator*
Dean, Lydia Margaret Carter (Mrs. Halsey Albert Dean) *nutrition coordinator, author, consultant*
Eckman, Dianne Ingeborg *critical care nurse*
Filerman, Gary Lewis *health education executive*
Gladeck, Susan Odell *social worker*
Harmon, Robert Gerald *health company administrator, educator*
Smith, Dorothy Louise *pharmacy consultant, author*
Walsh, Marie Leclerc *nurse*

Midlothian
Andrako, John *health sciences educator*

Newport News
Phillips, Denise *critical care nurse*
Warren, Daniel Churchman *health facility administrator*

Norfolk
Fox, Thomas George *health science educator*
Knox, Richard Douglas, Jr. *healthcare executive*
Lidstrom, Peggy Ray *mental health administrator, psychotherapist*
Martin, Wayne A. *clinical social worker*
McMurray, Jennifer Lee *pediatric nurse practitioner*
Pedone, Mary Ann Garcia *adult and geriatric nurse practitioner*
Stallings, Valerie A. *health director*
Vaughan, Linda Ann *hospital administrator, nurse*
Wilson, Angela Saburn *nursing educator*

Petersburg
Edmunds, Cecelia Powers *health facility administrator*
Northrop, Mary Ruth *mental retardation nurse*
Watkins, Sherry Ligon *medical facility data executive, nurse*

Portsmouth
Barnes, Judith P. *nursing administrator*
Glasson, Linda *hospital security and safety official*

Powhatan
Unison, Wendy Jane *critical care nurse*

Radford
Reed, Helen Inez *medical-clinical resource nurse*
Southern, Ann Gayle *nurse, educator*

Reston
Cornette, William Magnus *scientist, technical advisor*
Kader, Nancy Stowe *nurse, consultant, bioethicist*

Richmond
Barker, Thomas Carl *retired health care administration educator, executive*
Edloe, Leonard Levi *pharmacist*
†Fischer, Carl R. *hospital executive*
Fischer, Carl Robert *health care facility administrator*
Freund, Emma Frances *medical technologist*
Geraghty, Patrick James *organ transplant coordinator*
Gilchrist, Eunice Bass *nursing educator*
Hardy, Richard Earl *rehabilitation counseling educator, clinical psychologist*
Jarrard Mahayni, Mary Melissa *psychiatric nurse*
Neal, Gail Fallon *physical therapist, educator*
Vartanian, Isabel Sylvia *dietitian*
White, Kenneth Ray *health administration educator, consultant*
Winter, Joan Elizabeth *psychotherapist*

Roanoke
Dagenhart, Betty Jane Mahaffey *nursing educator, administrator*
Duff, Doris Eileen (Shull) *critical care nurse*
†Karnes, Daniel Elmo *clinical social worker*

Rockville
Smith, Lucy Anselmo *mental health nurse*

Saint Charles
Matlock, Anita Kay *family nurse practitioner*

Shawsville
Murray, Lynda Beran *counselor*

Smithfield
Lauder, Robert Scott *health education coordinator*

South Hill
Clay, Carol Ann *family nurse practitioner*

Springfield
Dake, Marcia Allene *retired nursing educator, university dean*
†Gaffney, Theresa Adcock *nursing administrator*
Gresham, Dorothy Ann *operating room nurse, educator*

Stafford
Collins, Vicki Tichené *critical care and emergency room nurse*

Staunton
†Carter, Sandra Jo *art therapist, costume designer, consultant*

Vienna
Rovis, Christopher Patrick *clinical social worker, psychotherapist*

Virginia Beach
Abbott, Regina A. *neurodiagnostic technologist, consultant, business owner*
Newsome, Moses *social work educator*
Radford, Gloria Jane *retired medical/surgical nurse*
Stockard, Joe Lee *public health service officer, consultant*

Warrenton
Rodgers, Lynne Saunders *women's health nurse*

Williamsburg
Farrar, John Thruston *health facility administrator*
Rosche, Loretta G. *medical, surgical nurse*
Sutton, Karen *nurse, historian*

Winchester
Wagner, Carolyn A(nn) *adult and gerontological nurse practitioner*

Woodbridge
Flori, Anna Marie DiBlasi *nurse anesthetist, educational administrator*
Graham, Reina Lynn *rehabilitation counselor*
Woods, Barbara A. Shell *psychotherapist*

Woodstock
Kabriel, Marcia Gail *psychotherapist*

WASHINGTON

Anacortes
Kuure, Bojan Marlena *operating room nurse*

Auburn
Blum, Sarah Leah *nurse psychotherapist*
Ketchersid, Wayne Lester, Jr. *medical technologist*

Bellingham
Johnson, Jennifer Lucky *psychotherapist*
Parker, Diana L. *nurse, consultant*

Bothell
McDonald, Michael Lee *clinic administrator, retired naval officer*

Chehalis
Burrows, Robert Paul *optometrist*

Clarkston
McCullough, Yvonne *counselor, educator*

Concrete
Mincin, Karl John *nutritionist, educator*

Everett
Miller, Robert Scott *mental health administrator, social worker*

Everson
McGulpin, Elizabeth Jane *nurse*

Federal Way
Mail, Patricia Davison *public health specialist*

Greenacres
Panter, Sara Jane *medical/surgical nurse*

Lacey
Jones, Kelley Simmons *therapist, social worker*
Shkurkin, Ekaterina Vladimirovna (Katia Shkurkin) *social worker*

Lakewood
Monk, Gordon Ray *recreation therapist*

Leavenworth
Bergren, Helen Duffey *retired nurse*

Longview
Moosburner, Nancy *nutritionist*

Mercer Island
Adams, Belinda Jeanette Spain *nursing administrator*

Mount Vernon
Poppe, Patricia Lee *clinical social worker, consultant*

Napavine
Morgan-Fadness, Corrina May *staff charge nurse*

Olympia
Boruchowitz, Stephen Alan *health policy analyst*
Coolen, Phyllis Rose *community health nurse*
Inverso, Marlene Joy *optometrist*

Port Angeles
Muller, Carolyn Bue *physical therapist, volunteer*

Poulsbo
Carle, Harry Lloyd *social worker*

Pullman
Mitchell, Madeleine Enid *nutritionist, educator*

Redmond
Oaks, Lucy Moberley *retired social worker*
Sasenick, Joseph Anthony *healthcare company executive*

Rollingbay
Ringland, Elinor *geriatrics nurse, consultant*

Seattle
Barnard, Kathryn Elaine *nursing educator, researcher*
Blissitt, Patricia Ann *nurse*
Carlson, Margaret Eileen (Peggy Carlson) *counselor, hypnotherapist*
Carlyon, Diane Claire *nurse*

Cates, Coral J. Hansen *nurse practitioner, respiratory therapist*
Dear, Ronald Bruce *social work educator*
de Tornyay, Rheba *nurse, former university dean, educator*
Dorpat, Theodore Lorenz *psychoanalyst*
Everett, Virginia Sauerbrun *counselor*
Golston, Joan Carol *psychotherapist*
Gunter, Laurie M. *retired nurse educator*
Huey, Constance Anne Berner *mental health counselor*
Johnston, William Frederick *emergency services administrator*
Monsen, Elaine Ranker *nutritionist, educator, editor*
Muilenburg, Robert Henry *hospital administrator*
Perkin, Gordon Wesley *international health agency executive*
Perrin, Edward Burton *health services researcher, biostatistician, public health educator*
Portuesi, Donna Rae *psychotherapist, consultant*
Prins, David *speech pathologist, educator*
Thompson, Arlene Rita *nursing educator*

Seaview
McNeil, Helen Jo Connolly *nursing educator, administrator*

Shoreline
Treseler, Kathleen Morrison *retired nursing educator*

Snohomish
Hill, Valerie Charlotte *nurse*

Spanaway
Campbell, Thomas J. *chiropractor, legislator*

Spokane
Burkhead, Virginia Ruth *rehabilitation nurse*
Hendershot, Carol Miller *physical therapist*
Paulsen, Richard Wallace *counselor*
Paulsen, Susan Steenbakkers *counselor*
Rice, Michael John *psychiatric mental health nurse*
Shaw, Brenda Carol *cardiac nurse*

Tacoma
Hendley, Ashley Preston, Jr. *clinical social worker*
Mohler, Georgia Ann *geriatrics nurse practitioner*
Neff Balch, Betty Marie *nursing educator*
Norwood, Paula Kay *medical and surgical nurse*
Sackmann, Margaret E. *geriatric nurse practitioner*
Stailey, Heather Ann *health facility administrator*

Vancouver
Gordon, Ingrid Thorngren *gerontology, home health nurse*
Simontacchi, Carol Nadine *nutritionist*
Simpson, Carolyn Marie *critical care nurse*

Wallula
Hodge, Ida Lee *physical therapist assistant*

Yakima
Simonson, Susan Kay *hospital administrator*

WEST VIRGINIA

Bluefield
Davenport, Dorothy Dean *retired nurse*

Charleston
Goodwin, Phillip Hugh *hospital administrator*

Huntington
Engle, Jeannette Cranfill *medical technologist*
Stultz, Patricia Adkins *health care risk administrator*

Hurricane
Nance, Martha McGhee *rehabilitation nurse*

Kingwood
Rock, Gail Ann *obstetrical/gynecological nurse*

Lewisburg
Fowler, Linda McKeever *hospital administrator, management educator*

Martinsburg
Coyle, Geraldine Anne *nursing administrator*

Morgantown
Barba, Roberta Ashburn *retired social worker*
Leslie, Nan S. *nursing educator, womens' health nurse*
Massey, W(ilmet) Annette *nurse, former educator*
Ponte, Charles Dennis *pharmacist, educator*
Yanero, Lisa Joyce *medical and surgical nurse*

Pratt
Terrell-McDaniel, Robin F. *cardiac rehabilitation and critical care nurse*

Princeton
Knowles, Virginia Lynn *gerontology services educator*

Rainelle
Scott, Pamela Moyers *physician assistant*

Saint Albans
Alderson, Gloria Frances Dale *rehabilitation specialist*

Wardensville
Vance, Dama Lee *obstetrical/gynecological nurse, ultrasound sonographer*

Wayne
Crockett, Patricia Jo Fry *psychiatric-mental health nurse*

Wheeling
Poland, Michelle Lind *medical-surgical and critical care nurse, educator*
Stidd, Linda Marie *rehabilitation nurse*
Urval, Krishna Raj *health facility administrator, educator*

WISCONSIN

Appleton
Leahy, Patricia M. *speech-language pathologist*

Baraboo
Baymiller, Lynda Doern *social worker*

Bear Creek
Schleicher, Susan Lea *critical care nurse*

Beloit
Savage, Christine Dadez *women's health nurse, educator*

Black River Falls
†Lahmayer, Albert T. *optometrist*

Brookfield
Murphy, Josephine Mancuso *critical care nurse, adult nurse practitioner*

Chippewa Falls
Copeland, Christine Susan *therapist*

Columbus
Brinkman, Michael Owen *health care consultant, educator*

Eau Claire
Biegel, Eileen Mae *hospital executive*

Fort Atkinson
Albaugh, John Charles *hospital executive*

Franklin
Czaplewski, Lynn Marie *intravenous nurse, educator*

Green Bay
Manske, Lynn Darlene *surgical nurse*
Mervilde, Michael John *clinical social worker*

Highland
Kreul, Carol Ann *nurse*

Hudson
Christenson, Garth Neil *optometrist*

Jackson
Brunner, Elizabeth King *health facility administrator, consultant*

Madison
Corcoran, Mary Alice *retired medical surgical nurse, educator*
Derzon, Gordon M. *hospital administrator*
Gurney, Mary Kathleen *pharmacist*
Littlefield, Vivian Moore *nursing educator, administrator*
Russell Harrsch, Patricia Eileen *healthcare rules writer*
Schmidt, Cheryl A. Zeise *acute care nurse*
Schoeller, Dale Alan *nutrition research educator*
Wegenke, Rolf *educational association administrator*

Manitowoc
Shimek, Rosemary Geralyn *medical/surgical nurse*

Marshfield
David, Barbara Marie *medical, surgical nurse*
Jaye, David Robert, Jr. *retired hospital administrator*

Menomonie
Naland, Patricia Mae *psychotherapist*

Milwaukee
Beaudry, Diane Fay Puta *quality management executive*
Cohn, Lucile *psychotherapist, nurse*
Coogan, Frank Neil *health and social services administrator*
Fiorelli, Karen Lynn *nurse*
Grochowski, Mary Ann *psychotherapist*
Harvieux, Anne Marie *psychotherapist*
Headlee, Raymond *psychoanalyst, educator*
Heim, Kathryn Marie *psychiatric nurse, author*
Janzen, Norine Madelyn Quinlan *medical technologist*
Lange, Marilyn *social worker*
Mancuso, Joseph Edward *medical psychotherapist*
Nortman, M. Judith Haworth *geriatrics nurse*
Shields, James Richard *alcohol and drug counselor, consultant*
Silverman, Franklin Harold *speech pathologist, educator*
Vice, Jon Earl *hospital executive*
Vos, Theresa Carmella *nurse*
Wake, Madeline Musante *nursing educator, university dean*
Weifbecker, Robert T. *healthcare administrator*
White, Jill Mary *nursing educator*
Winston, Maxine Spears *social worker*

Neenah
Crouch-Smolarek, Judith Ann *community health nurse*

New Berlin
Fishburn, Kay Maurine *nurse*
Kuglitsch, Maureen Rose *maternal/child health nurse*
Winkler, Dolores Eugenia *retired hospital administrator*

Oconomowoc
Schacht, Ruth Elaine *nursing educator*

Oshkosh
†Larson, Vicki Lord *communication disorders educator*

Racine
Fouse, Sarah Virginia *geriatrics nurse*
Singh, Susan Marie *critical care, maternal, women's health nurse*

Rhinelander
Van Brunt, Marcia Adele *social worker*

Shawano
Wilson, Douglas *genetics company executive*

Suamico
Roddan, Ray Gene *chiropractor*

Verona
Hartjes, Laurie Beth *pediatric nurse practitioner, woman's health nurse*

Watertown
Degnitz, Dorothy Elsie *nurse*

Whitehall
Nordhagen, Hallie Huerth *nursing home administrator*

Whitewater
Kirk, Constance Carroll *health educator*

Winnebago
Hable, Steven James *recreational therapist, track coach*

WYOMING

Bonduant
Ellwood, Paul Murdock, Jr. *health policy analyst, consultant*

Cheyenne
Hardway, James Edward *vocational and rehabilitative specialist*
Milton, Wayne Alvin *health services administrator*

Jackson Hole
Farkas, Carol Garner *nurse, administrator*

Powell
Voege, Jean *nursing educator*

TERRITORIES OF THE UNITED STATES

GUAM

Santa Rita
Bradner, Diana Jean *psychiatric and pediatric nurse*

Tamuning
Cahinhinan, Nelia Agbada *retired public health nurse, administrator*

PUERTO RICO

Luquillo
Pinney, Frances Bailey *art therapist, artist, consultant*

San Juan
de Taboas, Hilda Rivera *occupational health nurse*
Febo, Nilda Luz *pediatrics and psychiatric-mental health nurse*

Yauco
Artiles, Nemuel Othniel *hospital executive*

MILITARY ADDRESSES OF THE UNITED STATES

EUROPE

APO
Gibbs, Oscar Keith *physician assistant*
King, Daniel Carleton *physician assistant, air force officer, consultant*
Thon, Patricia Frances *pediatrics nurse, medical and surgical nurse*

CANADA

ALBERTA

Edmonton
Fields, Anthony Lindsay Austin *health facility administrator, oncologist, educator*
Hislop, Mervyn Warren *health advocate administrator, psychologist*

BRITISH COLUMBIA

New Westminster
Fair, James Stanley *hospital administrator*

Vancouver
Gilbert, John Humphrey Victor *speech scientist, educator*
Riedel, Bernard Edward *retired pharmaceutical sciences educator*

MANITOBA

Winnipeg
Seifert, Blair Wayne *clinical pharmacist*
Thorfinnson, A. Rodney *hospital administrator*

NEW BRUNSWICK

Sussex

Secord, Lloyd Douglas *healthcare administrator*

ONTARIO

Brantford

Inns, Harry Douglas Ellis *optometrist*
Woodcock, Richard Beverley *health facility administrator*

Burlington

McGeorge, Ronald Kenneth *hospital executive*

Elgin

Lafave, Hugh Gordon John *medical association executive, psychiatrist, educator, consultant*

Keswick

Macdonald, John Barfoot *research foundation executive*

Kingston

Glynn, Peter Alexander Richard *hospital administrator*
McGeer, James Peter *research executive, consultant*

Markham

Calkin, Joy Durfée *healthcare executive, consultant, educator*

North York

MacKenzie, Donald Murray *hospital administrator*

Ottawa

Langill, George Francis *hospital administrator, educator*

Owen Sound

Jones, Phyllis Edith *nursing educator*

Toronto

Freedman, Theodore Jarrell *healthcare executive*
Herbert, Stephen W. *hospital executive*
Scholefield, Peter Gordon *health agency executive*
Turner, Gerald Phillip *hospital administrator*

QUEBEC

Montreal

Messing, Karen *occupational health researcher*
Scriver, Charles Robert *medical scientist, human geneticist*
Sirois, Gerard *pharmacy educator*

ENGLAND

Stedham

Wheatley, George Milholland *medical administrator*

ISRAEL

Tel Aviv

Manheim, Alan A. *rehabilitation agency executive, psychologist*

REPUBLIC OF KOREA

Kyung

†Kim, Doohie *public health educator*

SAUDI ARABIA

Riyadh

Palmer, Leslie Ellen *registered nurse*

SWITZERLAND

Cologny

Maglacas, A. Mangay *nursing researcher, educator*

Versoix

Mahler, Halfdan Theodor *physician, health organization executive*

ZAMBIA

Mumbwa

Hansen, Florence Marie Congiolosi (Mrs. James S. Hansen) *social worker*

ADDRESS UNPUBLISHED

Abate, Frank Salvatore, Jr. *mental health services professional*
Ackerson, Barry James *social worker*
Adams, Corlyn Holbrook *nursing facility administrator*
Adducci, Regina Marie *medical/surgical nurse*
Addy, Jan Arlene *clinical nurse, educator*
Aehlert, Barbara June *health services executive*
Alfonso, Roberta Jean *emergency room nurse*
Allison, Mary Moon Southwell *community health nurse, nursing administrator*
Altstock, Marsha Marie *pediatrics nurse*
Ambrosio, Deborah Ann *critical care nurse*
Ammons, Barbara Ellen *gerontological, oncological, medical/surgical nurse*
Anaple, Elsie Mae *medical, surgical and geriatrics nurse*
Anderson, Lois D. *nursing administrator, mental health nurse*
Anderson, Shalor Maria *medical/surgical and pediatrics nurse*
Andes, Phoebe Cabotaje *women's health nurse, educator*
Andrau, Maya Hedda *physical therapist*
Andruzzi, Ellen Adamson *nurse, marital and family therapist*
Angst, Karen K. *mental health nurse*
Angus, Robert Carlyle, Jr. *health facility administrator*
Antonellis, Patricia Annette *community health nurse*
Ardire, Linda Lea *critical care nurse*
Arnold, Deborrah Ann *human services director*
Artinian, Nancy Trygar *critical care nurse, researcher*
†Arumugham, Gayathri Shakthi *healthcare activist, educator*
Arvisais, Kari Lynn *marriage and family therapist*
Ashcraft, Kimberly M. *nursing administrator*
Atsberger, Deborah Brown *clinical nurse specialist*
Augustus, Susan J. *nurse anesthetist*
Babitzke, Theresa Angeline *health facility administrator*
Badeaux, Diane Marie *mental health nurse*
Baier, Edward John *former public health official, industrial hygiene engineer, consultant*
Bain, Diane Martha D'Andrea *clinical nurse specialist in critical care*
Baker, Judith J. *nurse manager*
Baker, Nadine Lois *medical technician*
Baldwin, Deanna Louise *dietitian*
Baldwin, William Russell *optometrist, foundation executive*
Ballard, Diane E. *nursing administrator*
Barber, Laura Elizabeth *medical/surgical nurse*
Barker, Virginia Lee *nursing educator*
Barrett, Lisa Marie *acupuncture physician, herbologist*
Barron, Sara *nurse manager*
†Barry, Camille T. *health and human services director*
Bartels, Betty J. *nurse*
Barton, Nancy Shover *nursing administrator*
Baruch, Monica Lobo-Filho *psychological counselor*
Bass, Lynda D. *medical/surgical nurse, educator*
Bast, Kenneth George *healthcare executive*
Batalden, Paul Bennett *pediatrician, health care educator*
Battle, Dolores Elaine *speech, language pathologist, educator*
Baumann-Sinacore, Patricia Lynn *nursing administrator*
Becich, Raymond Brice *healthcare consultant, mediator, trainer, educator*
Belay, Brenda May *emergency room nurse*
Belco, Karen Marie *cardiology nurse*
Bell, Susan Jane *nurse*
Belles, Donald Arnold *pastoral therapist, mental health counselor*
Belmont, Larry Miller *retired public health executive*
Belonick, Cynthia Ann *psychiatric-mental health nurse*
Benford, Anne Michele *pediatric nurse practitioner, clinical nurse specialist*
Bennett, Michele Margulis *women's health nurse*
Berger, Anita Hazel *psychotherapist, adult educator, organizational consultant*
Berger, Marleda Carter *student health nurse practitioner*
Bering, Eva *healthcare executiver*
Berke, Sarah Ballard *geriatrics nurse, mental health nurse*
Bermack, Elaine *speech educator*
Bern, Lynda Kaplan *women's health and pediatric nurse*
Berry, Laurie Ann *critical care nurse*
Berry, Leora Mary *school nurse*
Bertram, Susan *rehabilitation counselor*
Betsinger, Peggy Ann *oncological nurse*
Biegel, David Eli *social worker, educator*
Billingsley, Florence Ilona *nurse, case manager*
Bishop, Linda Baxter *critical care nurse*
Bishop, Maureen E. *critical care nurse, clinical nurse specialist*
Bishop, Nancy Stephanie *nurse, health educator*
†Blackstone, Dara *music educator*
Blanchard, Louis A. *medical/surgical nurse, educator*
Blethen, Shirley E. *dialysis nurse, administrator*
Blomstrom, Bruce A. *healthcare executive*
Blumberg, Mark Stuart *consultant*
Blumenau, Iris Warech *nursing consultant*
Boatman, Deborah Ann *hospice nurse*
Bockius, Ruth Bear *nursing educator*
Bodnar, Elisabeth M. *occupational health consultant*
Boggs, Robert Wayne *healthcare administrator*
Boland, Catherine A. Benning *quality assurance specialist*
Boles, Thomas Lee *medical technician*
Boltz, Christine *community health and emergency nurse*
Bonds, Sophia Jane Riddle *geriatrics, medical/surgical nurse*
Boniey, Emily Ann *critical care nurse, anesthesist nurse*
Boone, Karen *nutritionist, oriental medicine physician*
Borg, Ruth I. *home nursing care provider*
Borgstahl, Kaylene Denise *health facility administrator*
Bottone, JoAnn *health services executive*
Bougalis, Katherine G. *medical surgical nurse, educator*
Boyett, Dorothy Eleanor Anderson *dietitian, educator*
Bozzolo, Donna Louise *family nurse practitioner*
Bradley, Kathryn *health facility administrator*
Bradley, Sandra Lynn Grant *nursing administrator*
Bragenzer, June Anna Ruth Grimm *community health nurse*
†Brandon, Tabitha A. *health service administrator*
Breen, Janice DeYoung *health services executive, community health nurse*
Breslin, Evalynne Louise Wood-Robertson *retired psychiatric nurse*
Brigance, Marcelena *critical care nurse*
Briggs, Janet Marie Louise *nurse practitioner*
Brinkley, Glenda Willis *medical/surgical nurse, women's health nurse*
Brodie, Alice Velma *health and ethics advocate*
Broggini, Carolyn *orthopedics and neuroscience nurse*
Brosz, Margaret Headley *pediatrics nurse*
Brower, Forrest Allen *retired health facility administrator*
Brown, Barbara June *hospital and nursing administrator*
Brown, Billye Jean *retired nursing educator*
Brown, Dorothy Howard *medical practice administrator*
Brown, Geraldine *nurse, freelance writer*
Brown, Hardin *occupational health nurse*
Bruno, Barbara Altman *social worker*
Bryant, Bertha Estelle *retired nurse*
Bryer, Lena Dorothy *nursing educator*
Buchbinder, Sharon Bell *health care management educator*
Buell, Diana E. *nursing administrator, special education professional*
Bullough, Vern LeRoy *nursing educator, historian, sexologist, researcher*
Bundy, Mary Lothrop *retired clinical social worker*
Burchiel, Susan Marguerite *nurse educator*
Burd, Shirley Farley *clinical specialist, mental health nurse*
Burnett, Glenda Morris *community health nurse*
Burris-Schnur, Catherine *medical/surgical nurse, educator, minister, pastoral psychologist*
Büsch, Annemarie *retired mental health nurse*
Butcher, Vanessa Jean *critical care nurse*
Buzard, James Albert *healthcare management consultant*
Byrd, Lorenda Sue *nursing administrator*
Caddeo, Maria Elizabeth *critical care nurse*
†Call, Elizabeth Ann *mental health counselor*
Callison, Nancy Fowler *nurse administrator*
Camayd-Freixas, Yoel *management, strategy & planning consultant*
Cameron, David Brian *health service administrator*
Camp, Virginia Ann *medical/surgical nurse*
Campbell, Jean *retired human services organization administrator*
Campbell, Margaret M. *retired social work educator*
Cantrell, Stephanie Ann *nurse*
Caples, Anne L. *healthcare consultant, former nursing educator*
Capobianco, Anna Theresa *retired patient education specialist*
Carman, Susan Hufert *nurse coordinator*
Carpenter, Phyllis Jean *medical/surgical nurse*
Carruthers, Claudelle Ann *occupational and physical therapist*
Carson, Mary Silvano *career counselor, educator*
Caruana, Joan *educator, psychotherapist, nurse*
Cash, Deanna Gail *nursing educator, retired*
Cason, Nica Virginia *nursing educator*
Cassano, Valerie *women's health nurse*
Castor, Christina Pelayo *critical care nurse*
Castro, Amuerfina Tantiongco *geriatrics nurse*
Cather, Phyllis Baker *pediatrics nurse*
Cauthorne-Burnette, Tamera Dianne *family nurse practitioner, healthcare consultant*
Ceasor, Augusta Casey *medical technologist, microbiologist*
Cecil, Maxine *critical care nurse*
Centafont, Lucy Ann Alexander *occupational therapy consultant*
Challela, Mary Scahill *maternal, child health nurse*
Chambers, Judith Tarnpoll *speech pathologist, audiologist*
Chamings, Patricia Ann *nurse, educator*
Charron, Susan E. *mental health nurse*
Chase, Alison M. *adult nurse practitioner*
Chciuk, Zofia *women's health nurse, neonatal nurse*
Cheney, Lois Sweet *infection control nurse*
Cherry, Carol Jean *health educator*
Child, Carroll Cadell *research nursing administrator*
Chow, Rita Kathleen *nurse consultant*
Christensen, Maria *emergency room nurse*
Cipparone, Josephine Magnino *medical/surgical and community health nurse*
Clark, Barbara Walsh *nurse educator, administrator, clinical specialist*
Clark, Patricia Ryan *crisis intervention specialist*
Clauser, Angela Frances *medical surgical, pediatrics and geriatrics nurse*
Clayton, Paul Douglas *medical facility director*
Clecak, Dvera Vivian Bozman *psychotherapist*
Cleveland, Charlene S. *community health nurse*
Coffey, Joanne Christine *dietitian*
Cohen, Evelyn L. *nursing educator, author*
Colangelo, James Joseph *psychotherapist*
Coleman, Jean Black *nurse, physician assistant*
Coleson, Sarrah Lynn *women's health nurse, critical care nurse*
Coll, Kathleen M. *home care manager*
Collins, Melissa Ann *oncological nurse*
Condie, Vicki Cook *nurse, educator*
Condry, Robert Stewart *retired hospital administrator*
Connolly, John Joseph *health care company executive*
Cooper, Diann Caryn *critical care nurse, staff development specialist*
Cooper, Eugene Bruce *speech, language pathologist, educator*
Cooper, Sarah Jean *nursing educator*
Cornell, David Roger *health care executive*
Couchman, Robert George James *human services consultant*
Cox, Carol A. *oncological nurse*
Cox, J. William *retired physician, health services administrator*
Cox, John Curtis *healthcare and educational administrator*
Cox, William Frederick *hospital executive*
Craine, Diane M. *nursing educator*
Cramer, John Sanderson *health care executive*
Crawford, Pamela J. *critical care nurse*
Crocker, Barbara Jean *infection control practitioner*
Cromwell, Florence Stevens *occupational therapist*
Cross, Charlotte Lord *social worker*
Crossland, Ann Elizabeth *retired psychotherapist*
Croteau, Joan M. *nursing administrator, educator*
Crump, Lisa M. *rehabilitation nurse*
Culley, June Elizabeth *clinical reviewer, quality improvement specialist*
Cumber, Sherry G. *psychotherapist, research consultant*
Cummings, Lucille Maud *geriatrics, psychiatric mental health nurse*
Daddario, Diane Kay *nurse, educator*
Dale Riikonen, Charlene Boothe *international health administrator*
Danhof, Vicki Spicher *maternal/women's health nurse*
Darkovich, Sharon Marie *nurse administrator*
Daus, Victoria Lynn *nurse midwife*
Davidow, Jenny Jean *counselor, writer*
Davis, Carolyne Kahle *health care consultant*
Davis, Gay Ruth *psychotherapist, social welfare educator, author, researcher, consultant*
Davis, Gloria Jean *gerontology clinical specialist*
Davis, Margaret Thacker *critical care, medical and surgical nurse*
Davis, Russell Haden *pastoral psychotherapist*
Dawson, Karen Oltmanns *school health nurse, womens health nurse, educator*
Deam, Connie Marie *school nurse*
DeBello, Marguerite Catherine *oncological nurse*
Deck, Judith Z. *adult nurse practitioner*
Deely, Maureen Cecelia *community health nurse*
Delgado, Gloria Eneida *medical nurse*
Dell, Thomas Charles *nurse anesthetist*
DeLoach, (Elise) Debra *critical care nurse, administrator*
Delwiche, Patricia Ellen *family nurse practitioner*
Dema-ala, Relie L. *medical/surgical nurse*
DeMillion, Julianne *health and fitness specialist, personal trainer, rehabilitation therapist, consultant*
†Denzler, James Wyatt *pharmacist*
Desmond, Patricia Lorraine *psychotherapist, writer, publisher*
Devers, Susan Marie *clinical nurse specialist, researcher*
Dey, Marlene Melchiorre *nursing educator, critical care nurse*
Diáz, Elena R. *community health nurse*
DiCarlo, Laurette Mary *nurse*
Didich, Jan *hospice consultant*
DiMaria, Rose Ann *nursing educator*
DiMauro, Nancy Marion *nursing administrator*
Diorio, Eileen Patricia *medical technologist, retired, philosophy educator*
Dishong, Diane Elizabeth *medical/surgical nurse, rehabilitation nurse*
Dixon, Marguerite Anderson *retired nursing educator*
Dodds, Brenda Kay *nurse*
Dodds, Christine J. *nursing administrator*
Dolan, June Ann *health facility administrator*
Donnelly-Kempf, Moira Ann *nursing administrator*
Donovan, Dorothy Diane *adult nurse practitioner*
Donovan, Marion Conran *school social worker*
Doucette, Betty *public and community health and geriatrics nurse*
Douglass, Laura Lee *pharmaceutical company official*
Dove, Lorraine Faye *gerontology nurse*
Dozier, Nancy Kerns *retired geriatrics nurse*
Dressel, Irene Emma Ringwald *alcoholism and family therapist*
Drews, Jürgen *pharmaceutical researcher*
Dudash, Karen Shreffler *community health nurse*
Duffy, Mary Kathleen *neonatal nurse*
Duncan, Elizabeth Charlotte *marriage and family therapist, educational therapist, educator*
Dungan, Gloria Kronbeck *critical care nurse*
Dunmeyer, Sarah Louise Fisher *retired health care consultant*
Dunning, Kenneth Owen *mental health counselor*
Dutton, Karen Vander Wall *critical care nurse*
Dye, Sharon Elizabeth Herndon *speech pathologist*
Dyer, Rita Frances *medical/surgical and oncology nurse*
Dyer, Wayne Walter *psychologist, author, radio and television personality*
Eaves, Sandra Austra *social worker*
Edelstein, Rosemarie *nurse educator, medical-legal consultant*
Edrington, Sue Ellen *critical care nurse*
†Eggleton, Elizabeth *gerontologist, educator*
Eitel, Dolores J. *healthcare consultant, educator*
Ekery, Adriana Teresa *healthcare administrator, oncology nurse*
Emma, Lynne Anne *healthcare administrator*
English, Jujuan Bondman *women's health nurse, educator*
Erdman, Terri Sue *pediatric and neonatal nurse, consultant*
Ernzen, Mary Anne *women's health nurse, clinical nurse specialist*
Ervin, Rita Ann *occupational health nurse*
Etchells, Joyce Lynn *peri-operative nurse*
Evans, Jeanette Marie *operating room nurse*
Everette, Marlene Miller *nursing administrator, surgical nurse*
Eversull, Janna Bacon *pediatrics nurse, emergency room nurse*
Ewell, Charles Muse *health care industry executive, consultant, publisher, educator*
Falconer, Judith Ann *public health and occupational therapist, educator*
Faub, Kenneth James *school nurse practitioner*
Fehr, Lola Mae *nursing association director*
Felhofer, Marylouise Katherine *nursing administrator*
Fennema, Betty Jane *nurse*
Ferreira, Linda Doreen *long term, acute care and rehabilitation nurse*
Feryo, Catherine M. Lescosky *home health nurse, educator*
Fischer, Linda Marie *nursing educator*
FitzSimons, Corinne Marie *medical/surgical nurse*
Flashburg, Marsha Lynne *community health nurse*
Fletcher, J. S. *health educator*
Fondiller, Shirley Hope Alperin *nursing educator, journalist, historian*
Forman-Mason, Monica N. *speech and language pathologist*
Fountain, Linda Kathleen *health science association executive*
†Fox, Terry Lynn *art psychotherapist*
Franciosa, Joseph Anthony *health care consultant*
†Franklin, Raymond A. *medical facility administrator*
Frederich, Kathy W. *social worker*
Freese, Barbara T. *nursing educator*
Frost, James Hamner *health facility administrator*
Fry, Shirley Ann Mills *nursing administrator, educator*
Fuller, Margaret Jane *medical technologist*
Fusciardi, Katherine *nursing administrator*
Gaede, Ruth Ann *nursing manager*
Gandy, Bonnie Sergiacomi *oncological and intravenous therapy nurse*
Garbacz, Patricia Frances *school social worker, therapist*
Garnett, Linda Kopec *nurse, researcher*
Garrett, Roberta Kampschulte *nurse*
Gatewood, Barbara J. *medical legal consultant, lawyer*
Gaylor, Barbara Gail Davis *geriatric nurse*
Geary, Pamela Blalack *community health and medical/surgical nurse*
Geitgey, Doris Arlene *retired nursing educator, dean*
Gendreau, Bernice Marie *retired women's health nurse*
George, Sharon A. *nurse educator, nurse practitioner*
George, Susan E. Gould *health facility administrator*
Gerald, Michael Charles *pharmacy educator, college dean*

Gerbehy, Christine Petric *medical/surgical and mental health nurse*
Gerry, Debra Prue *psychotherapist, recording artist, writer*
Gerstner, Mary Jane *nurse*
Giannella, Susanne R. *maternal/women's health nurse, medical/surgical nurse*
Gibbons, Doria Desaix *gastroenterology nurse*
Gibson, Scott Russell *nurse*
Gilbertson, Susan *nurse manager*
Giles, Walter Edmund *alcohol and drug treatment executive*
Girvin-Quirk, Susan *nursing administrator*
Gleason, Carol Ann *rehabilitation nurse*
Goddard, Thelma Taylor *critical care nurse, nursing educator*
Gollings, Ruth Erickson *community health nurse*
Golomb, Myra J. *nurse*
Gordon, Ruby Daniels *retired nursing educator, counselor*
Gorr, Elaine Gray *therapist, elementary education educator*
Goslawski, Violet Ann *nurse, substance abuse counselor*
Govan, Gladys Vernita Mosley *retired critical care and medical/surgical nurse*
Graham, Brenda J. *nurse*
Grandstrand, Ruth Helena *retired community health and gerontology nurse*
Grant, Eileen Gerard *medical/surgical nurse*
Grant, Linda Susan *nursing consultant*
Grantham, Shonnette Denise *mental health nurse, care facility supervisor*
Gray, Darlene Agnes *nurse*
Gray, Susanne Marie Hartman *ambulatory care nurse*
Green, Beth Ingber *intuitive practitioner, counselor, musician, composer*
Green, Daphne Kelly *mental health nurse*
Green, Karen Danielle *psychotherapist*
Greenberg, Nancy Ward *school health consultant*
Greenemeier, Cheryl S. *women's health nurse*
Grejtak, Gena Renee *critical care nurse*
Grey, Elizabeth K. *critical care nurse, retired*
Griffin, Annette L. *critical care nurse, educator*
Griffin, Christopher Oakley *hospital professional, humanities educator*
Griffin, Eren G. *retired nursing educator*
Griffin, Myrna McIntosh *critical care nurse*
Grogan, Debby Elaine *geriatric and intensive care nurse*
Guerrero, Lilia *school nurse*
Hackstadt, Chiquita Darleen *medical/surgical nurse*
Hadley, Jane Byington *psychotherapist*
Hagelston, Karman Weatherly *speech pathologist*
Hagen, Edna Mae *retired medical nurse*
Hager, Paula Michele *critical care nurse*
Halden, Martha Ann *pediatrics nurse, educator*
Hall, Julie Jane *community health nurse, administrator*
Hall, Kendra Jean *neuroscience nurse, researcher, educator*
Halleck, Lois Renee *critical care and emergency room nurse*
Hamilton, Nancy Richey *critical care nurse, educator*
Hammond, Judith Anne *family nurse practitioner*
Hand, Janet L. *medical, surgical and critical care nurse, educator*
Hanna, Lee Ann *critical care nurse*
Hanrahan, Lawrence Martin *healthcare consultant*
Hansen, Alan Edward *mental health nurse*
Hanson, Ann M. *women's health care nurse practitioner*
Hanson, Dennis Michael *medical imaging executive*
Hardy, James Chester *speech pathologist, educator*
Harper, Christine Johnson *psychiatric clinical nurse, administrator*
Harrell, Ina Perry *maternal/women's and medical/surgical nurse*
Harrington, Michael Ballou *health economist, systems engineer*
Hartford, Shaun Alison *pediatrics nurse, educator*
†Hassell, Mark Joseph *counselor*
Hasselmeyer, Eileen Grace *medical research administrator*
Havice, Pamela Ann *maternal/women's health nurse, nurse educator*
Hawryluk, Christine Joanne *school nurse*
Hayes, Judy Diane *medical/surgical and ophthalmological nurse, nursing administrator*
Healy, Sonya Ainslie *health facility administrator*
Heath, Alice Privé *women's health nurse, educator*
Heath, Richard Murray *retired hospital administrator*
Heckley, Teresa JoAnn *health facility administrator*
Held, Barbara Kay *pediatric nurse*
Held, Nancy B. *perinatal nurse, lactation consultant*
Hellwig, Eileen Marie *critical care nurse*
Helms Guba, Lisa Marie *nursing administrator*
Hendricks, Deborah J. *medical/surgical and oncological nurse*
Henneman, Stephen Charles *counselor*
Henry, Olga Elaine *nursing educator, health care trainer*
Hensley, Mary Susan Mask *emergency room nurse*
Herd, Joanne May Beers *intravenous therapy nurse, educator*
Herkner, Bernadette Kay *occupational health nurse*
Heronen, Marie F. *nursing administrator, medical/surgical nurse*
Herrin, Frances E. *critical care nurse*
Herrmann, Walter *retired laboratory administrator*
Hertz, Kenneth Theodore *health care executive*
Heyssel, Robert Morris *physician, retired hospital executive*
Higdon, Shirley A. *medical/surgical nurse*
Hille, Robert Arthur *healthcare executive*
Hilli, Mary Elizabeth *rehabilitation nurse, administrator*
Hiner, Elizabeth Ellen *pharmacist*
Hirst, Joanne Flip *community health nurse*
Hoaglund, Leora Mae *emergency nurse, radiology nurse*
Hobson, Alesa *medical/surgical nurse*
Hodge, Patricia Marie Cascio *nurse practitioner in psychiatry*
Hodnicak, Victoria Christine *pediatric nurse*
Hofmann, Paul Bernard *healthcare consultant*
Hogstel, Mildred Onelle *gerontology nursing consultant*
Holland, Rosemary Sheridan *program evaluation consultant*
Hollis, Mary Fern Caudill *nurse educator, music educator*
Holloway, Richard Lawrence *marriage-family therapist, college official*
Holtz, Carolyn A. *medical/surgical nurse*
Homb, Scott Michael *rehabilitation services professional*
Homestead, Susan (Susan Freedlender) *psychotherapist*
Honea, Joyce Clayton *critical care nurse*
Hooper, Marcia Sarita *pediatric critical care nurse*
Horn, Vickie Lynn *medical/surgical nurse, educator*
Hough, M. Catherine *nursing educator*
Howard, Charlene *community health nurse, administrator*
Howe, John Prentice, III *health science center executive, physician*
Howell, Connie Rae *critical care nurse*
Howell, Embry Martin *researcher*
Howell, Mary Ellen Helms *nursing educator, neonatal nurse*
Huber, Ann Cervin *nurse*
Huber, Vida S. *nursing educator*
Huckaby, Mark Anson *paramedic, educator, emergency medical services specialist*
Hughes, Charles R., Jr. *health facility administrator*
Huibregtse, Jayne Lynnor *medical surgical nurse*
Hukins-Rodrigue, Dana Ann *community health nurse*
Hunter, Mattie Sue (Moore) *health facility administrator*
Hunter, Sarah Ann *community health nurse*
Hunter-McLean, Elana M. *critical care and trauma nurse*
Hutchison, Deborah L. *critical care nurse*
Hutzler, Lisa Ann *mental health nurse, adult clinical psychologist*
Ihde, Daniel Carlyle *health science executive*
Ingraham, Jeanne *pediatric nurse practitioner*
Intihar-Hogue, Cynthia Ann *nursing administrator*
Jackson, Erin Denise *speech therapist*
Jackson, M. Dorothy *medical surgical nurse, researcher*
Jacobi, Veronica Ann *community health nurse, educator*
Jacobs, Arthur Dietrich *educator, researcher, health services executive*
Jacobs, Sister Margaret Mary *nurse*
James, Nadine H. *psychiatric nurse, occupational health and home care nurse, nursing administrator, educator*
Jaskula, Janet *pediatrics nurse, educator*
Jaszarowski, Kelly Ann *nurse, enterostomal therapy specialist*
Jennings, Reba Maxine *critical care nurse*
Jernigan, Madeleine Annetta *medical/surgical nurse*
Jew, Henry *pharmacist*
Jobson, Kathleen Miller *nurse midwife*
John, Gerald Warren *hospital pharmacist, educator*
Johnson, Beth Ann *pediatric nurse, gerontology nurse*
†Johnson, Henry Breavoid *occupational therapist, career officer*
Johnson, Naomi Bowers *nurse*
Johnson-Brown, Hazel Winfred *nurse, retired army officer*
Jones, Brenda K. *health facility administrator*
Jones, Daniel Hamilton *optometrist*
Jones, Donna Lee Noble *emergency nurse*
Joustra, Barbara Lynn *nurse*
Juenemann, Sister Jean *hospital executive*
Kacprowicz, Donna Marie (Leonetti) *staff nurse*
Kacur, Lois Marie *obstetric and pediatric nurse*
Kampf, Marilyn Jeanne *medical analyst*
Kapitan, Mary L. *retired nursing administrator, educator*
Karp, Rosanne *medical/surgical nurse*
Kathan, Joyce C. *social worker, administrator*
Kaufmann, Caroline Elizabeth *surgical technologist, critical care nurse*
Kepner, Jane Ellen *psychotherapist, educator, minister*
Kerrigan, Mabel Baisley *retired peri-operative nurse, educator*
Kieffer, Joyce Loretta *health science facility administrator, educator*
Kiel, Brenda Kay *medical/surgical nurse*
King, Rosemary Kranyak *pediatrics nurse*
Kirby, Priscilla Crosby *dietitian*
Kirkpatrick, Dorothy Ann *early childhood education educator, former nurse*
Kison, Carol *nursing educator, critical care nurse*
Kleer, Norma Vesta *retired critical care nurse*
Klein, Fay Magid *health administrator*
Klein, Rosalyn Finkelstein *social worker*
Kline, Barbara A. *nursing case manager*
Klinetob, Carson Wayne *retired physical therapist*
Knies, Robert Carl, Jr. *critical care nurse*
Knuth, Mona May *nursing administrator, educator*
Koerber, Marilynn Eleanor *gerontology nursing educator, consultant, nurse*
Kohlman, Nancy Ann (Zeigenfuse) *medical/surgical nurse*
Kohn, Jean Gatewood *medical facility administrator, physician, retired*
Kono, Jean E. *nursing educator*
Kopf, Randi *family/oncology nurse practitioner, lawyer*
Kovach, Doris Anne *critical care nurse*
Krebs, Mary Jane Schirger *psychiatric nurse specialist*
Krehtinkoff-Yarlovsky, Nina *nursing administrator*
†Krell, Susan Marie *hospital administrator*
Krellwitz, Margit C. *nursing consultant*
Krugle, Marie *health facility administrator*
Kruse, Cynthia Sara *nursing consultant*
Kufner, Sharon Kay *women's health nurse*
Kuzmowych, Chrystyna Prytula *optometrist*
Labbe, Patrick Charles *legal nursing consultant*
Ladly, Frederick Bernard *health services and financial services company executive*
Lajiness-Polosky, Danine Theresa *psychiatric-mental health nurse, pediatric nurse*
Lambert, Wilma S. *medical/surgical nurse*
Landgarten, Helen Barbara *art psychotherapist, educator*
Landreneau, Betty C. *nursing educator, medical/surgical nurse*
Larsen-Denning, Lorie *critical care nurse, risk management professional, insurance broker*
Lasswell, Anita Diane *nutrition educator*
Lawson, Nancy Katherine *medical/surgical nurse*
Lay, Elizabeth Marian *health association administrator*
Leach, Kay T. *critical care nurse, administrator*
Leddy, Susan *nursing educator*
Lee, Barbara Catherine *career counselor*
Lee, Ginger *discharge planning supervisor, administrator*
Lee, Nancy T. *healthcare administrator, educator*
Lee, Susan Ann *social worker, therapist*
Leigh, Vincenta M. *health administrator*
Leihgeber, Katherine L. *retired nursing administrator*
Lemon, Sharon Kay *rehabilitation nurse*
Lentz, Sandra M. *family nurse practitioner*
Leonetti, Evangeline Phillips *retired nursing educator*
L'Eplattenier, Nora Sweeny Hickey *nursing educator*
Lerit, Delia Tumulak *school nurse*
Leslie, Cynthia *mental health nurse*
Levine, Ellen (Sunni) Silverberg *pediatric nurse practitioner*
Lewis, Jacquelyn Rochelle *nursing consultant*
Lewis, Lois A. *health services administrator*
Lewis, Russell Carl, Jr. *family nurse practitioner*
Linto, Nancy *medical unit director*
Lloyd, Michael L. *nursing administrator, educator*
Localio, Marcia Judith *medical/surgical nurse*
Lopez, Constance R. *mental health facility administrator*
Lopez-Boyd, Linda Sue *geriatrics nurse, educator, consultant*
Lubbers, Alice Dianne *operating room nurse*
Lucas, Rebecca Leigh *community health nurse*
Lucchese, Eugene Frank *EMS educator, emergency medicine/critical care*
Lynch, Michael Edward *medical facility administrator*
Lyngbye, Jørgen *hospital administrator, researcher*
Lyon, Mary Kuehlewind *childbirth educator*
Lyons, Natalie Beller *family counselor*
MacDougall, Ingeborg Reibling *mental health nurse*
Mackenzie, Linda Alice *alternative medicine and awareness company executive, entertainer, educator, hypnotherapist, motivational speaker*
Mackety, Carolyn Jean *laser medicine and nursing consultant*
MacMullen, Jean Alexandria Stewart *nurse, administrator*
Magafas, Diania Lee *geriatrics nurse consultant, administrator*
Magee, Karen Strope *nurse, health facility administrator*
Magill, Rosalind May *psychotherapist*
Magnuson, Robert Martin *retired hospital administrator*
Mali, Bradley James Michael *geriatrics service professional*
Mallis, Sophia G. *nurse, educator*
Maloney, Diane Marie *legal nurse consultant*
Manasse, Arlynn H. *pediatric nurse practitioner*
Maness, Diane Mease *pediatrics nurse*
Manganiello, Janice Marie *peri-operative nurse*
Markham, Richard Glover *research executive*
Marks-DeMourelle, Karen *diabetes nurse*
Maroon, Mickey *clinical social worker*
Marquis, Harriet Hill *social worker*
Marsh, Denise A. *critical care and medical/surgical nurse*
Marshall, Brenda Lebowitz *health educator*
Marshall, Donald Thomas *medical technologist*
Marshall, Odessa Josephine *mental health nurse*
Martin, Cheri Christian *health services administrator*
Martin, Ione Edwards *social worker*
Martin, William Collier *hospital administrator*
Marvel, Wanda Faye *home health clinical consultant*
Matherlee, Thomas Ray *health care consultant*
Matsuda, Fujio *technology research center administrator*
Matterson, Joan McDevitt *physical therapist*
Maurer, Geraldine Marie *perinatal nurse, consultant*
Mayer, Patricia Lynn Sorci *mental health nurse, educator*
McAndrews, Daryl Lynn *community health nurse*
McBride, Sandra Teague *psychiatric nurse*
McCabe, Patricia *medical/surgical and intensive care nurse*
McCluskey, Jean Ashford *nursing educator, retired*
McCrary, Sharon Hash *medical and surgical nurse*
McDougall, Jacquelyn Marie Horan *therapist*
McElwee, Doris Ryan *psychotherapist*
McFadden, Irene Frances *medical/surgical nurse, educator*
McFadden, Millidene Kathleen *nurse educator*
McFarland, Constance Anne *nursing educator*
McGhee, Lori Jean Vote *medical/surgical nurse*
McGill, Karleen A. *family nurse practitioner*
McGregor, Darren James *counselor, researcher, mediator*
McHugh, Elizabeth Ann *infection control occupational health nurse*
McLaren, Susan Smith *therapist, healing touch practitioner, instructor*
McNulty, Kathleen Anne *clinical social worker, psychotherapist, business consultant*
McPherson, Geraldine June *medical and surgical nurse*
McQueen-Gibson, Ethlyn *diabetes clinical nurse specialist*
McSain, Tara Jacqueline *medical/surgical nurse, oncological nurse, infusion nurse*
Meaders, Nobuko Yoshizawa *therapist, psychoanalyst*
Meadows, Lois *mental health nursing clinician and educator*
Means-Enoch, Barbara Ann *critical care nurse*
Meehan, John Joseph, Jr. *hospital administrator*
Meeks, Linda Mae *women's health nurse, educator*
Melanson, Susan C. *herbalist*
†Melville, R. Jerrold *mental health services professional*
Meo, Roxanne Marie *critical care nurse*
Merilh, Marietta Paula *critical care nurse*
Merriman, Mary Ann *psychiatric nurse*
Meyer, Harry Martin, Jr. *retired health science facility administrator*
Meyer, Roberta *mediator, communication consultant*
Mich, Connie Rita *mental health nurse, educator*
Middleton, Ellen Long *family nurse practitioner, educator*
Mikel, Thomas Kelly, Jr. *laboratory administrator*
Miknis, Lisa L. *neuroscience intensive care nurse*
Miles, Kimberly Joy *critical care nurse*
Miller, Dolores (Dee Miller) *intensive care nurse*
Miller, Janet Dawn Hoover *nursing educator*
Miller, Lenore Wolf Daniels *speech-language pathologist*
Miller, Lillie M. *nursing educator*
Miller, Roberta Ann *gastroenterology nurse*
Miller, Terry W. *academic adminstrator, legal consultant*
Milligan, Reneé Ann *nursing educator, researcher*
Miltner, Rebecca Suzanne *women's health nurse, pediatrics nurse*
Mincy, Lisa Jo *nurse*
Misner, Lorraine *laboratory technologist*
Mitchell, Adele Dickinson *health facility administrator*
Moak, Elizabeth *critical care and operating room nurse, legal nurse consultant*
Moffatt, Hugh McCulloch, Jr. *hospital administrator, physical therapist*
Moffatt, Laura L. *critical care nurse*
Moffitt, Susan Raye *critical care nurse*
Moliere, Jeffrey Michael *cardiopulmonary administrator*
Molitoris, Sallyann *eye care nurse*
Moller, Mary Denise *psychiatric nurse practitioner*
Moon, Katie Parmley *critical care nurse, home health care nurse*
Morahan, Stephanie *nursing administrator*
Morandi, John Arthur, Jr. *nursing administrator, educator, nurse*
Morehead, Annette Marie *disabled children's facility administrator, child advocate*
Morelli, Laura Baedor *nursing administrator*
Moreno, Jeanne Simonne *telemetry nurse*
Morey, Nancy H. *medical/surgical nurse*
Morgan, Evelyn Buck *nursing educator*
Mosher, D. Russell *cancer therapist*
Mosqueira, Charlotte Marianne *dietitian*
Mould, Joan Powell *social worker*
Mudloff, Barbara *medical/surgical nurse*
Mueller, Barbara Stewart (Bobbie Mueller) *youth drug use prevention specialist, volunteer*
Muhammad, Farid Ilyas *social science educator*
Muico-Mercurio, Luisa *critical care nurse*
Mullikin, Steven Milton *critical care nurse*
Munic, Rachelle Ethel *health services administrator*
Munier, William Boss *medical service executive*
Murphy, Bette Jane M. *retired geriatrics nurse, nursing administrator*
Murphy, Cindy L. *medical/surgical and pediatrics nurse*
Murphy, Margaret A. *nursing educator, adult nurse practitioner*
Murphy, Mary Kathleen *family nurse practitioner, nursing educator*
Murphy, Sheryl Warren *rehabilitation nurse, consultant*
Mutch, James Donald *health therapist*
Nabholz, Mary Vaughan *rehabilitation nurse*
Nakagawa, Allen Donald *radiologic technologist*
Nash, Janet Rae *geriatrics nurse*
Nattras, Ruth A(nn) *school nurse*
Naugle, Jean Marie *legal nurse consultant*
Navarro, Karen Ann *women's health care nurse practitioner*
Nelson, Kaye Lynn *healthcare consultant*
Neumann, Forrest Karl *retired hospital administrator*
Neville-Babst, Lisa Ann *medical/surgical nurse*
Nevins, Sara Ann *retired counselor*
Newell, William Talman, Jr. *hospital administrator*
Nichols, Sandra Lee *community health nurse*
Nicholson, June C. Daniels *speech pathologist*
Nicolette, Lillian H. *nursing administrator, consultant, educator*
Niehaus, Deborah Ann *post-anesthesia care nurse*
Nigro, Ann K. *geriatrics nurse, educator*
Nolde, Shari Ann *pediatrics, critical care nurse*
Nordel, Patricia A. Olmstead *medical/surgical, critical care, and obstetrical nurse*
Norkin, Cynthia Clair *physical therapist*
Norman, Dudley Kent *hospital administrator, nurse*
Nouriel, Margaret Cowan *occupational health nurse*
Novinc, Judith Kaye *medical/surgical nurse, administrator*
Nusbaum, Geoffrey Dean *psychotherapist*
Oakes, Ellen Ruth *psychotherapist, health institute administrator*
O'Brien, Mary Blichfeldt *nursing consultant*
O'Brien, MaryAnn Antoinette *nursing educator*
Okolski, Cynthia Antonia *psychotherapist, social worker*
Oliver, Marian Marie *nurse*
O'Quinn, Nancy Diane *nurse, educator*
Oreluk, Mary M. *critical care nurse*
Orem, Cassandra Elizabeth *health systems administrator, educator, author, holistic health practitioner, entrepreneur*
Otis, Jack *social work educator*
Owano, Mary Beth *pediatrics intensive care unit nurse*
Owens, John Franklin *health care administrator, consultant, nurse*
Oxyer, Mina Jane Stevens *nurse*
Page, Nancy Ellen *pediatrics nurse, nursing consultant*
Panas, Sonya Lee Sawaya *retired gerontology and pediatrics nurse*
Pandya, Deanna Mears *family counselor, addiction counselor*
Pankratz, Carol Joyce *medical/surgical clinical nurse specialist*
Pappachristou, Joyce Flores *dietitian, educator*
Parkman, Cynthia Ann *medical/surgical nurse, nurse educator*
Pate, Joseph Michael *family nurse practitioner*
Patrick, Brenda Jean *educational consultant*
Patterson, F. Ellen *social worker*
Paul, Evelyn Rose *critical care nurse*
Paulson-Schiefelbein, Cindy Patrice *occupational therapist*
Peat, Wanda Jean *critical care nurse*
Peel, Mary Ann *nursing educator*
Penachio, Anthony Joseph, Jr. *psychotherapist, hypnotherapist, behavioral therapist*
Penke, Cynthia Marie *critical care nurse*
Penn, William Robert *critical care nurse*
Pepper, Dorothy Mae *nurse*
Perinelli, Marguerite Rose *women's health nurse, educator*
Peters, Douglas Alan *nurse, case manager*
Peters, Elizabeth *nursing manager*
Peters, Shirley Ann *pediatrics nurse*
Peterson, Sharon L. *community health nurse*
Petree, Betty Chapman *anesthetist*
Petrikas, Regina Marija *acute care nurse practitioner*
Pettit, John W. *administrator*
Phillips, Juanita M. *maternal/women's health and neonatal nurse*
Pignataro, Evelyn Dorothy *trauma clinician, operating room nurse*
Pilcher, Ellen Louise *rehabilitation counselor*
Pilgrim, Deborah Annice *psychotherapist*
Pipchick, Margaret Hopkins *clinical specialist psychiatric nursing, therapist, consultant*
Piperno, Sherry Lynn *psychotherapist*
Pippin, James Rex *health care management consultant*
Pippin, Linda Sue *pediatrics nurse*
Pitasi, Judy *nurse*
Plummer, Leone Poindexter *marriage and family therapist, nursing educator, nurse practitioner*
Polacek, Deborah Jean *nursing consultant*
Polucci, Ashley Victor *emergency staff nurse*
Pooley-Richards, Robin Lee *critical care nurse*

Porte, Patricia Francis Skypeck *geriatrics nursing administrator*
Porter, Marie Ann *neonatal nurse, labor and delivery nurse*
Poston, Ann Genevieve *psychotherapist, nurse*
Poston, Iona *nursing educator*
Poulton, Roberta Doris *nurse, consultant*
Prescott, Tamy A. *nurse practitioner*
Preszler, Sharon Marie *psychiatric home health nurse*
Prettyman-Baker, Sheila *pediatrics, neonatal nurse*
Price, Ann Laurie *senior health program manager*
Principe, Helen Mary *medical case manager*
Pring, Janice *medical/surgical nurse*
Prisco, Frank J. *psychotherapist*
Prominski, Eileen Alice *school nurse, educator*
†Provost, Scott Edward *social worker*
Przybylski, Sandra Marie *speech pathologist*
Ptasinski, Carol Mary *nurse, educator*
Pucek, Anthony J. *psychiatric nurse practitioner*
Puderbaugh, Kathleen Annette *maternal/women's health nurse practitioner*
Quattrone-Carroll, Diane Rose *clinical social worker*
Quinn, Irene S. *critical care nurse*
Quiroz, Carole Elizabeth *critical care nurse*
Ragland, Terry Eugene *emergency physician*
Rainey, Claude Gladwin *retired health care executive*
Rainier, Ellen F. *nurse*
Rairdon, Julia Agee *nursing administrator*
Ramsey, Sandra Lynn *psychotherapist*
Randolph, Nancy Adele *nutritionist, consultant*
Raper, Julia Taylor *pediatric and neonatal nurse*
Rawls, Nancy Lee Stirk *nursing educator*
Ray, Marilyn Anne *nursing educator, nursing researcher*
Reber, Cheryl Ann *consultant, social worker, program developer*
Redburn, Amber Lynne *nurse*
Reece, David Bryson *information systems administrator*
Reeves, Nancy Alice *critical care nurse*
Reilly, Robert Joseph *counselor*
Requénez, Eunice Loida *medical/surgical and community health nurse*
Reynolds, Ellen Aaker *pediatrics and trauma nurse*
Ricards, June Elaine *nursing consultant, administrator*
Ricci, Mary Jean *community health nurse, educator*
Richardson, Wanda Louise Gibson *nurse*
Richburg, Kathryn Schaller *nurse, educator*
Richburg, W. Edward *nurse educator*
Richter, Susan Mary *medical and surgical nurse*
Ries, Barbara Ellen *alcohol and drug abuse services professional*
Risse, Diana Marie *medical/surgical nurse, educator*
Rittgers, Nancy J. *nurse*
Roberts, Karen L(ee) *geriatrics nurse*
Robick, Candace M. Younginger *geriatrics nurse, educator*
Robinette, Betty Lou *occupational health and infection control nurse*
Robinson, Angela Tomei *clinical laboratory technologist*
Robinson, Gail Patricia *mental health counselor, retired*
Robinson, Glenda Carole *pharmacist*
Robinson, Karen Sue *psychiatric nurse*
Robinson, Kathy S. *trauma/emergency nurse*
Robinson, Lisa Gale Langley *community health nurse, educator*
Robinson, William Andrew *health service executive, physician*
Rochette, Ann Robinson *clinical manager*
Rock, Barry David *social work educator*
Roesler, Rose Pieper *retired geriatrics nurse*
Rogers, Laura M. *medical/surgical nurse*
Rohde, Tamera Annette *oncological nurse*
Rohlfing, Linda Anne *physical therapist*
Roper, Sally Ann *health facility coordinator*
Rosa, Vicky Lynn *health facility administrator*
Rose, Joan Marie *medical-surgical nurse*
Rosenstein, Mary Elisabeth Mallory *retired clinical social worker*
Rosenthal, Carla *medical/surgical nurse*
Rossman, Peggy Eyre Elrod *retired nursing administrator, gerontology nurse*
Royal, Alice Calbert *school health nurse*
Rubell, Bonnie Levine *occupational therapist*
Rudan, Vincent Thaddeus *nursing educator, administrator*
Runde, Kathryn Joy *oncology nurse*
Runyon, Elizabeth Behr *mental health nurse*
Russell, Anita S. Garber *maternal/women's health, medical/surgical nurse*
Saad, Barbara T. *occupational health nurse, administrator*
Sacaccio, Margaret Mary *critical care, geriatrics nurse*
Saccente, Cary T. *nurse*
Sadler, Sallie Inglis *psychotherapist*
St. Pierre, Cathy M. *family nurse practitioner*
Salatino, David *critical care nurse*
Salerno, Sister Maria *nursing educator, adult and gerontological nurse*
Salisbury, Jane Jefford *nursing educator*
Salts, Nancy Lee *critical care, emergency nurse*
Sampson, Cindy Kathleen Stewart *school social worker, educator*
†Sanchez-Hartwet, Miguel Enrique *health care program manager*
Sanders, Augusta Swann *retired nurse*
Sandor, Janet Kwarta *nursing educator*
Sansone, Carol Irene *nursing educator*
Santos, Lisa Wells *critical care nurse*
Sappington, Andrew Arnold, III *clinical psychologist*
Sastrowardoyo, Teresita Manejar *nurse*
Sauvage, Lester Rosaire *health facility administrator, cardiovascular surgeon*
Sauvage, Timothy Raymond *nurse anesthetist*
Savage, Dixie Lee Kinney *nursing administrator*
Scala, James *health care industry consultant, author*
Scanlon, Deralee Rose *dietitian, educator, author*
Scheinblum, Anita Franusiszin *pediatrics nurse*
Schellhaas, Robert Wesley *counselor, songwriter, theologian*
Scher, Harry Edward *critical care nurse, adult nurse practitioner*
Schlachter, Kathleen *community health administrator, director*
Schock, Carl Dennis *hospital administrator, mental health nurse*
Schoemaker, Ann Maureen Postorino *pediatrics nurse*
Schoenberg, April Mindy *nursing administrator*
Schultz, Janet K. *nursing consultant, business executive*
Schwartz, Doris Ruhbel *nursing educator, consultant*
Schwartz, Ilene *psychotherapist*
Schwartz, Michael Robinson *health administrator*
Schwartz, Stephen Wayne *critical care, emergency and recovery room nurse*
Scott, Amy Annette Holloway *nursing educator*
Scott, Julia Kim *school nurse*
Scott, Vicki Ann *critical care nurse*
Sebastian, Cynthia Marie *therapy nurse*
Sewer, Doris E. *critical care nurse, educator*
Sgriccia, Mary A. *nurse*
Shafer-Graff, Katherine Michelle *nursing administrator*
Shane, Donea Lynne *retired nursing educator*
Sharrotta, Angela *medical/surgical and neuroscience nurse*
Sheaffer-Jones, Jeanne *pediatrics and critical care nurse*
Sherman, Michael Scott *healthcare executive, anesthesiologist*
Sievers, Ann Elisabeth Furiel *clinical nurse specialist in otolaryngology*
Simon, Jolene Marie *nurse, educator*
Simonson, Steven Neil *psychotherapist*
Simpson, Jack Benjamin *medical technologist, business executive*
Simpson, John Noel *healthcare administrator*
†Slaughter, Djuanique Naté *healthcare analyst, consultant*
Sloane, Arlene Loupus *rehabilitation nurse, specialist*
Smith, Arthur, Jr. *pharmacist, pharmacy company executive*
Smith, Barbara Dail *school nurse*
Smith, Geraldine Field *medical/surgical nurse*
Smith, Leonard, Jr. *medical/surgical and oncology nurse*
Smith, Melissa Christine-Mary *mental health nurse*
Smith, Michele Kathleen *marriage and family therapist*
Smith, Paula Marion *urology and medical/surgical nurse*
Smith, Ronald Lynn *health system executive*
Smith, Virginia *critical care nurse*
Smuk, Kathy Ann *community health nurse, educator*
Soebbing, Janice Bromert *occupational health nurse*
Solomon, Risa Greenberg *clinical social worker, child-family therapist*
Soukup, Jeanne D'Arcy *public health nurse*
Sousa, Barbara Jane *community and school health nurse*
Spagnolo, Lucy W. *hospice nurse*
Spelios, Lisa Garone *nurse, educator*
Spence, Marjorie A. *medical/surgical nurse*
Spero, Maddalena Ann *nurse*
Splane, Richard Beverley *social work educator*
Splitstone, George Dale *retired hospital administrator*
Stacy, Cheryl Anne *critical care nurse*
Stacy, Kathleen Mary *critical care nurse*
Stanley, Melinda Louise *mental health nurse*
Stansil, Sheryl *medical-surgical nurse*
Stash, Susan Michele *medical/surgical nurse*
Stauber, Cynthia B. *medical/surgical nurse*
Steele, Vickie M. *mental health nurse, nursing researcher*
Stein, Ellyn Beth *mental health services professional*
Stein, Gordon Edward *mental health and chemical dependency nurse*
Stevens, Elizabeth *psychotherapist, consultant*
Stevens, Kathleen M. *nurse*
Stoesz, David Paul *social work educator*
Stohlman, Connie Suzanne *obstetrical gynecological nurse*
Stone, Annette Elizabeth Calkins *medical/surgical and occupational health nurse*
†Stow, Gerald Lynn *human services executive, speaker*
Stratton, Mariann *retired naval nursing administrator*
Stratton-Whitcraft, Cathleen Sue *critical care and pediatrics nurse*
Stutzman, Sandra Louise *advanced nurse practitioner*
Su, Hui-I Chen *occupational therapist*
Suber, Robin Hall *former medical and surgical nurse*
Suhr, Geraldine M. *medical/surgical nurse*
Summers, Amy Elder *neonatal nurse*
Sutherland, Debbora *gerontological nurse practitioner*
Svoboda, Janice June *nurse*
Swanson, Jennie Elizabeth Williams *healthcare association administrator, church mentor, antique dealer*
Swaters, Cherie Lynn Butler *retired nurse*
Sweeny, Mary Ellen *nursing administrator, educator*
Swenson, Lucyann *medical/surgical and community health nurse*
Switzman, Jessica (Heimberg) *maternal/women's health nurse, medical/surgical nurse*
Szantai, Linda Marie *speech and language therapist*
Tack, Theresa Rose *women's health nurse*
Talbott, Mary Ann *critical care nurse*
Tarnow, Malva May Wescoe *post-anesthesia care nurse*
Tauber, Sonya Lynn *nurse*
Taylor, Edna Jane *retired employment program counselor*
Taylor, Nathalee Britton *nutritionist*
Tejada, Louis, Jr. *emergency medicine nurse, paramedic*
Tennyson, Andala Mae *nurse*
Terry, Wayne Gilbert *healthcare executive, hospital administrator, consultant and mediator in health services management*
Thomson, James Adolph *medical group practice administrator*
Thornton, Mary Elizabeth Wells *critical care nurse, educator*
Thrasher, Rose Marie *critical care and community health nurse*
Todd, Deborah J. *public health advisor*
Torkelson, Rita Katherine *medical/surgical nurse*
Torre, Carolyn Talley *pediatric nurse practitioner*
Torres, Ophelia Alvina Powell *pediatric and medical/surgical nurse, educator*
Torresyap, Pearl Marie *surgical nurse*
Trafton, E. Joan *nursing educator*
Travers, Rose Elaine *nursing supervisor*
Tremko Housel, Laurie Ann *critical care nurse*
Trippet, Susan Elaine *nursing educator*
Tronolone, Tracey Ann *social worker*
Truitt, Barbara Ann *nurse*
Tucci, Janis A(nn) *health unit administrator*
Tuck, Mary Beth *nutritionist, educator*
Tucker, Constance A. *critical care nurse*
Tucker-Osborne, Annette La Verne *legal nurse consultant, nursing home administrator*
Turner, Nancy Kay *nurse*
Tuttle, Laura Shive *healthcare educator, administrator*
Tuttle, Tammy Lynn *medical/surgical and pediatrics nurse*
Uhrich, Richard Beckley *hospital executive, physician*
Ulrich-Weaver, Judith L. *medical/surgical nurse, educator*
Umpleby, Hannah Barbara Bennett *family therapist*
Usinger, Martha Putnam *counselor, educator*
Valfre, Michelle Williams *nursing educator, administrator, author*
Vangieri, Louis C. *counselor, educator*
Vann, Diane E. Swanson *nursing educator*
Van Wagoner, Ammon Kim *health facility administrator*
Varney, Suzanne Glaab *health facility administrator*
Verney, Judith La Baie *retired health program administrator*
Vestweber, Susan Diane *operating room nurse*
Vierra, Deborah *critical care, community health nurse*
Villareal, Roland *nurse*
Voelker, Margaret Irene (Meg Voelker) *gerontology, medical, surgical nurse*
Vohs, James Arthur *health care program executive*
Voss, Carolyn Jean *nursing educator, consultant*
Wadsworth, Beverly Jane *retired nursing administrator*
Walling, Sally Ann *health system administrator*
Walston, Lola Inge *dietitian*
Walters, Jo Lynn Blackburn *nursing administrator, psychiatric nurse*
Ward, Vicki Dawne *family nurse practitioner, rural health specialist*
Ware, Leigh Ann Carter *neonatal critical care nurse*
Washburn, Caryl Anne *occupational therapist*
Watson, Deborah Lynn *women's health nurse*
Watson, Rosemarie Memie *emergency medical technician*
Weaver, Esther Ruth *medical and surgical, geriatrics and oncology nurse*
Weber, Linda Diane *occupational health nurse*
Webster, John Kingsley Ohl, II *health administrator, rehabilitation manager*
Webster, Susan Jean *medical/surgical nurse*
Wedeen, Marvin Meyer *hospital executive*
Weichler, Nancy Karen *pediatric nurse*
Weightman, Esther Lynn *emergency trauma nurse*
Weimer, Gary W. *university development executive, consultant*
Weiner, Susan Marks *perinatal clinical nurse specialist, educator*
Weitzel, Marilyn Lee *nursing educator*
Welch, Madeleine Lauretta *medical/surgical and occupational health nurse*
Welch, Robyn Perlman *pediatric critical care nurse*
Wendland, Claire *nursing administrator, geriatrics nurse*
Werlein, Donna Dabeck *community health care administrator*
Wessler, Richard Lee *psychology educator, psychotherapist*
West, Raymond L. *nurse*
Westall, Thomas George *pastoral counselor*
Westwick, Carmen Rose *retired nursing educator, consultant*
Whalen, Alberta Dean *retired community health nurse*
Whalen, Jane Claire *nurse, clinical specialist*
Wheaton, Mary Edwina *health facility administrator, educator*
Whildin, Donna *medical/surgical nurse*
White, Eugene Vaden *retired pharmacist*
White, Juanita M. *staff nurse*
White, Sarah Jowilliard *counselor*
Whitehead, John Jed *healthcare and biotech company executive*
Wiebe, Leonard Irving *radiopharmacist, educator*
Wieber, Patricia McNally *medical/surgical nurse, orthopaedics nurse*
Wiedenhoeft, Ann Marie *psychotherapist, consultant*
Wiersma, Peggy Ann *nurse*
Wilamowski, Doris *psychotherapist*
Williams-Barnard, Carol Lou *mental health nurse*
Williams-Maddox, Janice Helen *nurse*
Williamson, William Allen *retired optometrist*
Willingham, Ozella M. *medical/surgical and cardiac nurse*
Willis, Bettina Bentley *oncology nurse*
Wilmoth, Margaret Chamberlain *oncology nurse, researcher*
Wilson, Linda Ann *renal dialysis nurse*
Wilson, Mary Elizabeth *geriatrics nurse*
Wilwerding, Kati Anne *critical care nurse*
Wing, Lilly Kelly Raynor *health services administrator*
Winkler, Margaret Ann *geriatrics nurse, nursing administrator*
Winters, Sheila *family nurse practitioner*
Winton, Howard Phillip *retired optometrist*
†Wolf, Melinda Susan *social worker, poet*
Wolfberg, Melvin Donald *optometrist, educational administrator, consultant*
Wood, Norma J. *nurse practitioner*
Woods, Geraldine Pittman *health education consultant, educational consultant*
Worcester, Peggy Jean *medical/surgical nurse*
Worrell, Cynthia Celeste *school nurse*
Wrenn, Diane Marie *medical/surgical nurse*
Wright, Cathleen R. *administrator*
†Wright, Vera *social worker*
Wurst, Michael H. *critical care nurse, administrator*
Wyatt, Rose Marie *clinical social worker*
Wyche, Ruth Skyler *rehabilitation contractor, researcher*
Wylie, Laurie Jean *nursing administrator*
Yarris, Elizabeth Lester *critical care nurse*
Yates, Linda Fae *women's health nurse*
Yearwood, Jimette Berry *critical care nurse*
Yother, Anthony Wayne *critical care nurse*
Young, Gary A. *rehabilitation counselor*
Young, Kim Ann *health facility administrator*
Younger, Betty Nichols *social worker*
Yousef, Mona Lee *psychotherapist*
Yurman, Maria Anne *critical care nurse*
Zambrano, Debra Kay *community health nurse*
Zevola, Donna Ruth *critical care nurse, educator*
Zierath, Marilyn Jean *adult medical, surgical and pediatrics nurse*
Zinner-Kemp, Susan Elizabeth *medical educator*
Zomber, Beverly Louise *medical, surgical, geriatric and psychiatric nurse, educator*
Zube-Miles, Barbara J. *rehabilitation nurse*
Zweck, Ruth Edna Feeney *human services administrator, psychiatric nurse*

HEALTHCARE: MEDICINE

UNITED STATES

ALABAMA

Alexander City
Powers, Runas, Jr. *rheumatologist*

Auburn
McEldowney, Rene *health care educator, consultant*
Parsons, Daniel Lankester *pharmaceutics educator*

Birmingham
Allman, Richard Mark *physician, gerontologist*
Avent, Charles Kirk *medical educator*
Bridgers, William Frank *physician, educator*
Bueschen, Anton Joslyn *physician, educator*
Caldwell, Tom O. *pediatric physician*
Callahan, Alston *physician, author*
Casebeer, Linda Louise *medical educator*
Caulfield, James Benjamin *pathologist, educator*
†Clayton, Orville Woolford *surgeon*
Cooper, John Allen Dicks *medical educator*
Cooper, Max Dale *physician, medical educator, researcher*
Crenshaw, James Faulkner *physician*
Curtis, John J. *medical educator*
Diethelm, Arnold Gillespie *surgeon*
Dowdey, Benjamin Charles *physician*
Dubovsky, Eva Vitkova *nuclear medicine physician, educator*
Elmets, Craig Allan *dermatologist*
Fallon, Harold Joseph *physician, pharmacology and biochemistry educator*
†Fix, R. Jobe *plastic and reconstructive and hand surgeon*
Fraser, Robert Gordon *diagnostic radiologist*
Friedel, Robert Oliver *physician*
Friedlander, Michael J. *neuroscientist, animal physiologist, medical educator*
Goldenberg, Robert L. *obstetrician*
Hill, Samuel Richardson, Jr. *retired medical educator*
Hirschowitz, Basil Isaac *physician*
†Joseph, David B. *pediatric urologist*
Kapanka, Heidi *emergency physician*
Kelly, David Reid *pathologist*
Kirklin, John Webster *surgeon*
Koopman, William James *medical educator, internist, immunologist*
†Kuzniecky, Ruben Itamar *neurologist, educator*
Lloyd, Lewis Keith, Jr. *surgery and urology educator*
Lochridge, Stanley Keith *cardiovascular and thoracic surgeon*
McLain, David Andrew *internist, rheumatologist*
Meezan, Elias *pharmacologist, educator*
Nepomuceno, Cecil Santos *physician*
Nielsen, Leonard Maurice *physician assistant*
Oakes, Walter Jerry *pediatric neurosurgeon*
Omura, George Adolf *medical oncologist*
Oparil, Suzanne *cardiologist, educator, researcher*
Pacifico, Albert Dominick *cardiovascular surgeon*
Pfister, Roswell Robert *ophthalmologist*
Pittman, Constance Shen *physician, educator*
Pittman, James Allen, Jr. *physician, educator*
Pohost, Gerald Michael *cardiologist, medical educator*
Russell, Richard Olney, Jr. *cardiologist, educator*
Schroeder, Harry William, Jr. *physician, scientist*
Skalka, Harold Walter *ophthalmologist, educator*
Stevenson, Edward Ward *retired physician, surgeon, otolaryngologist*
Tieszen, Ralph Leland, Sr. *internist*
Warnock, David Gene *nephrologist*
Zeiger, Herbert Evan, Jr. *neurosurgeon*

Fairfield
Hamrick, Leon Columbus *surgeon, medical director*

Fairhope
Ottensmeyer, David Joseph *retired neurosurgeon, retired healthcare executive*

Florence
Burford, Alexander Mitchell, Jr. *retired physician*
Eich, Wilbur Foster, III *pediatrician*

Fort Rucker
Glushko, Gail Marie *physician, military officer*

Hoover
Crater, Timothy Andrews *physician*

Huntsville
Huber, Donald Simon *physician*
Loux, Peter Charles *anesthesiologist*
Nuessle, William Raymond *surgeon*

Mobile
Atkinson, William James, Jr. *retired cardiologist*
†Bodie, Belin Frederick *dermatologist*
Brandon, Jeffrey Campbell *physician, interventional radiologist, educator*
Brogdon, Byron Gilliam *physician, radiology educator*
Conrad, Marcel Edward *hematologist, educator*
Cummings, James M. *urology educator*
DeBakey, Ernest George *physician, surgeon*
Durizch, Mary Lou *radiology educator*
Eichold, Samuel *medical educator, medical museum curator*
Guarino, Anthony Michael *pharmacologist, educator, consultant, counselor*
Parmley, Loren Francis, Jr. *medical educator*
Rodning, Charles Bernard *surgeon*
Smith, Jesse Graham, Jr. *dermatologist, educator*
Thomas, Joseph Paul *psychiatrist*

Montgomery
Frazer, David Hugh, Jr. *allergist*
Givhan, Edgar Gilmore *physician*
Hunker, Fred Dominic *internist, medical educator*
Lee, Harry Antonius *allergist, immunologist*
Maya, Ivan Dario *internist*

Ozark
Covin, Theron Michael *psychotherapist*

Tuscaloosa
Aldridge, Kenneth William *physician*
Keeton, J. E. *retired psychiatrist*
Moody, Maxwell, Jr. *retired physician*
Mozley, Paul David *obstetrics and gynecology educator*
Nevels, Charles Thomas *psychiatrist*
Pieroni, Robert Edward *internist, educator, military officer*
†Smith, W. Omar *urologist*

ALASKA

Anchorage
†Beller, Michael *epidemiologist*
Wolf, Aron S. *medical director, psychiatrist*

Juneau
Robinson, David B. *psychiatrist*

Valdez
Todd, Kathleen Gail *physician*

ARIZONA

Carefree
Hook, William Franklin *retired radiologist*

Casa Grande
Houle, Joseph Adrien *orthopedic surgeon*

Chandler
Bies, Roger David *cardiologist*
Robrock, James Lawrence *plastic surgeon*

Flagstaff
†Weston, Laurie Beth *psychiatrist*

Fountain Hills
Gifford, Ray Wallace, Jr. *physician, educator*
Herzberger, Eugene E. *retired neurosurgeon*

Glendale
Trejos, Franklin Anthony *physician assistant*

Mesa
Fiorino, John Wayne *podiatrist*
Hagen, Nicholas Stewart *medical educator, consultant*
Sanders, Aaron Perry *radiation biophysics educator*

Paradise Valley
†Meland, N. Bradley *plastic surgeon*
Polson, Donald Allan *surgeon*
Targovnik, Selma E. Kaplan *physician*

Phoenix
Benach, Sharon Ann *physician assistant*
†Blum, David Elias *neurlogist*
Borel, James David *anesthesiologist*
†Buffmire, Donald K. *internist*
Burgoyne, David Sidney *psychiatrist*
Butler, Byron Clinton *obstetrician, gynecologist*
Charlton, John Kipp *pediatrician*
Desser, Kenneth Barry *cardiologist, educator*
Fishburne, John Ingram, Jr. *obstetrician-gynecologist, educator*
†Garcia-Buñuel, Luis *neurologist*
Goldberg, Morris *internist*
Goldenthal, Nathan David *physician*
Jacobson, Albert Dale *pediatrician, accountant*
Kail, Konrad *physician*
Kandell, Howard Noel *pediatrician*
Kuivinen, Ned Allan *pathologist*
Kurtz, Joan Helene *pediatrician*
Laufer, Nathan *cardiologist*
Lawrence, William Doran *physician*
Merlin Kearfott, DuVal *health consultant*
Palmer, Alice Eugenia *retired physician, educator*
Prieto, Vicente *chiropractor*
Reed, Wallace Allison *physician*
Rowley, Beverley Davies *medical sociologist*
Singer, Jeffrey Alan *surgeon*
Stern, Stanley *psychiatrist*
Steward, Lester Howard *psychiatrist, academic administrator, educator*
Vu, Eric Tin *neurobiologist, researcher*
Wright, Richard Oscar, III *pathologist, educator*
Zerella, Joseph T. *pediatric surgeon*

Scottsdale
Bragg, David Gordon *physician, radiology educator*
Clement, Richard William *plastic and reconstructive surgeon*
Evans, Tommy Nicholas *physician, educator*
Fink, Joel Charles *dermatologist, retired*
Friedman, Shelly Arnold *cosmetic surgeon*
Harrison, Harold Henry *physician, scientist, educator*
Kjellberg, Betty J. *association administrator*
Kübler-Ross, Elisabeth *physician*
†Leighton, William D. *plastic and reconstructive surgeon*
Lillo, Joseph Leonard *osteopath, family practice physician*
Nadler, Henry Louis *pediatrician, geneticist, medical educator*
†Novicki, Donald Edward *urologic surgeon*
Olwin, John Hurst *retired surgeon*
Orford, Robert Raymond *consulting physician*
Reznick, Richard Howard *pediatrician*
Sanderson, David R. *physician*
Scherzer, Joseph Martin *dermatologist*
Sirven, Joseph Ignatius *neurologist*
Starr, Phillip Henry *psychiatrist, educator*
†Trojanowski, Deborah A. *plastic surgeon*

Sedona
Hawkins, David Ramon *psychiatrist, writer, researcher*
Reno, Joseph Harry *retired orthopedic surgeon*
Shors, Clayton Marion *cardiologist*

Sun City
Pallin, Samuel Lear *ophthalmologist, educator*

Sun City West
Calderwood, William Arthur *physician*
Forbes, Kenneth Albert Faucher *urological surgeon*
Wasmuth, Carl Erwin *physician, lawyer*

Sun Lakes
Houser, Harold Byron *epidemiologist*

Tempe
Anand, Suresh Chandra *physician*
Schneller, Eugene Stuart *health adminstration and policy educator*

Tucson
Abrams, Herbert Kerman *physician, educator*
Alberts, David Samuel *physician, pharmacologist, educator*
Alpert, Joseph Stephen *physician, educator*
Ben-Asher, M. David *physician*
Boyse, Edward Arthur *research physician*
Brosin, Henry Walter *psychiatrist, educator*
Burrows, Benjamin *retired physician, educator*
Capp, Michael Paul *physician, educator*
Citron, David Sanford *physician*
Dalen, James Eugene *physician, educator*
Deluca, Dominick *medical educator, researcher*
Ewy, Gordon Allen *cardiologist, researcher, educator*
Giesser, Barbara Susan *neurologist, educator*
Graham, Anna Regina *pathologist, educator*
Harris, David Thomas *immunology educator*
Hildebrand, John G(rant) *neurobiologist, educator*
Katakkar, Suresh Balaji *hematologist, oncologist*
Kotin, Paul *pathologist*
Labelle, James William *retired pediatrician*
Labiner, David M. *neurologist*
Levenson, Alan Ira *psychiatrist, physician, educator*
Marcus, Frank Isadore *physician, educator*
Masters, William Howell *physician, educator*
Nugent, Charles Arter *physician*
Reinmuth, Oscar MacNaughton *physician, educator*
Salmon, Sydney Elias *medical educator, director*
Semm, Kurt Karl *obstetrics and gynecology researcher*
Sibley, William Austin *neurologist, educator*
Smith, Josef Riley *internist*
Stearns, Elliott Edmund, Jr. *retired surgeon*
Weil, Andrew Thomas *physician, educator*
Weinstein, Ronald S. *physician, pathologist, educator*
Witte, Marlys Hearst *internist, educator*
Witten, Mark Lee *lung injury research scientist, educator*
Woolfenden, James Manning *nuclear medicine physician, educator*

Vail
Reichlin, Seymour *physician, educator*

Yuma
Martin, James Franklin *physician, lawyer*

ARKANSAS

Bella Vista
Rose, Donald L. *physician, educator*

Fayetteville
Brown, Craig Jay *ophthalmologist*

Fort Smith
Coleman, Michael Dortch *nephrologist*
Drolshagen, Leo Francis, III *radiologist, physician*
Howell, James Tennyson *allergist, immunologist, pediatrician*
Snider, James Rhodes *radiologist*

Jefferson
Hart, Ronald Wilson *radiobiologist, toxicologist, government research executive*

Jonesboro
Jones, Kenneth Bruce *surgeon*
†Kumar, Bangaroswamy Vijaya *neurologist*

Little Rock
Bates, Joseph Henry *physician, educator*
Brodsky, Michael Carroll *ophthalmologist, educator*
Bruce, Thomas Allen *retired physician, philanthropist, educator*
Bynum, Ann Bailey *medical educator*
Campbell, Gilbert Sadler *surgery educator, surgeon*
Cave, Mac Donald *anatomy educator*
Deer, Philip James, Jr. *ophthalmologist*
Elbein, Alan David *medical science educator*
Ferris, Ernest Joseph *radiology educator*
Garcia-Rill, Edgar Enrique *neuroscientist*
Guggenheim, Frederick Gibson *psychiatry educator*
Hough, Aubrey Johnston, Jr. *pathologist, physician, educator*
Jansen, G. Thomas *dermatologist*
Kemp, Stephen Frank *pediatric endocrinologist, educator, composer*
Lang, Nicholas Paul *surgeon*
Lucy, Dennis Durwood, Jr. *neurologist*
McMillan, Donald Edgar *pharmacologist*
Mrak, Robert Emil *neuropathologist, educator, electron microscopist*
Previte, Joseph Peter *pediatric anesthesiologist*
†Simmons, Debra Lynn *physician, educator*
Sotomora-von Ahn, Ricardo Federico *pediatrician, educator*
Stead, William White *physician, educator, public health administrator*
Strode, Steven Wayne *physician*
Suen, James Yee *otolaryngologist, educator*
Ward, Harry Pfeffer *physician, university chancellor*
†Yuen, James Chui Ping *surgeon, educator*

Marked Tree
†Moissidis, John A. *pediatrician*

North Little Rock
Biondo, Raymond Vitus *dermatologist*

Rogers
Summerlin, William Talley *allergist, immunologist, dermatologist*

Scranton
Uzman, Betty Ben Geren *pathologist, retired educator*

Springdale
Haws, Karl Wayne *physician, consultant*

CALIFORNIA

Agoura Hills
deCiutiis, Alfred Charles Maria *medical oncologist, television producer*

Alameda
Whorton, M. Donald *occupational and environmental health physician, epidemiologist*

Alamo
†Fortuin, Floyd D. *neurologist*

Anaheim
Carvajal, Jorge Armando *endocrinologist, internist*

Arcadia
Sleeter, John William Higgs *physician, health service administrator*

Atherton
†Oakes, David Duane *medical educator*

Auburn
Hanowell, Ernest Goddin *physician*

Bakersfield
Grabski, Daniel Alexis *psychiatrist*

Baldwin Park
Barry(Branks), Diane Dolores *podiatrist*

Belvedere Tiburon
Behrman, Richard Elliot *pediatrician, neonatologist, university dean*

Berkeley
Abel, Carlos Alberto *immunologist*
Budinger, Thomas Francis *radiologist, educator*
Buffler, Patricia Ann *epidemiology educator, retired dean*
†Cedars, Michael G. *plastic surgeon*
Diamond, Marian Cleeves *anatomy educator*
Duhl, Leonard *psychiatrist, educator*
Falkner, Frank Tardrew *physician, educator*
Goodman, Corey Scott *neurobiology educator, researcher*
Grossman, Elmer Roy *pediatrician*
Policoff, Leonard David *physician, educator*
Poor, Clarence Alexander *retired physician*
Shortell, Stephen M. *health services researcher*
Syme, Sherman Leonard *epidemiology educator*
Tempelis, Constantine Harry *immunologist, educator*
Thygeson, Nels Marcus *physician*
Winkelstein, Warren, Jr. *physician, educator*

Beverly Hills
†Berkman, Samuel Abba *internist*
Catz, Boris *endocrinologist, educator*
Goodman, Mark Paul *physician*
Karpman, Harold Lew *cardiologist, educator, author*
Klein, Arnold William *dermatologist*
Kravitz, Hilard L(eonard) *physician*
Lesser, Gershon Melvin *physician, lawyer, medical and legal media commentator*
Menkes, John Hans *pediatric neurologist*
Moelleken, Brent Roderick Wilfred *surgeon*
†Monosson, Ira Howard *physician*
†Moser, Franklin George *neuroradiologist, researcher*
Rodman, Francis Robert *psychoanalyst, writer*
Seiff, Stephen S. *ophthalmologist*
Yuan, Robin Tsu-Wang *plastic surgeon*

Bolinas
Remen, Rachel Naomi *pediatrician, psycho-oncologist*

Brawley
Jaquith, George Oakes *opthalmologist*

Burbank
Renner, Andrew Ihor *surgeon*

Burlingame
Gradinger, Gilbert Paul *plastic surgeon*
Nadell, Andrew Thomas *psychiatrist*

Camarillo
Street, Dana Morris *orthopedic surgeon*

Campbell
Tseng, Alexander *medical oncologist*

Carlsbad
Dziewanowska, Zofia Elizabeth *neuropsychiatrist, pharmaceutical executive, researcher, educator*

Carmel
Felch, William Campbell *internist, editor*

Carmichael
Wagner, Carruth John *physician*

Carson
Hope, Ellen *clinical sciences educator*

Century City
Spirt, Mitchell Jeffrey *internist, gastroenterologist, medical consultant*

Chatsworth
Hage, Stephen John *radiology administrator, consultant*

Chula Vista
Allen, Henry Wesley *biomedical researcher*
Cohen, Elaine Helena *pediatrician, pediatric cardiologist*

Claremont
Gabriel, Earl A. *osteopathic physician*
Johnson, Jerome Linné *cardiologist*

Clovis
Terrell, Howard Bruce *psychiatrist*

Concord
†Robert, Cavett McNeill, Jr. *neurosurgeon*

Covina
Takei, Toshihisa *otolaryngologist*

Culver City
Rose, Margarete Erika *pathologist*

Daly City
†Baladi, Naoum Abboud *surgeon*
Shaw, Richard Eugene *cardiovascular researcher*

Davis
Cardiff, Robert Darrell *pathology educator*
Enders, Allen Coffin *anatomy educator*
Gardner, Murray Briggs *pathologist, educator*
Hollinger, Mannfred Alan *pharmacologist, educator, toxicologist*
Jones, Edward George *neuroscience professor, department chairman*
Lazarus, Gerald Sylvan *physician, university dean*
Palmer, Philip Edward Stephen *radiologist*
Plopper, Charles George *anatomist, cell biologist*
Richman, David Paul *neurologist, researcher*
Schenker, Marc Benet *preventive medicine educator*
Stowell, Robert Eugene *pathologist, retired educator*
Williams, Hibbard Earl *medical educator, physician*

Deer Park
Hodgkin, John E. *pulmonologist*

Del Mar
Lesko, Ronald Michael *osteopathic physician*

Downey
†Diaz, Consuleo *medical executive*
Gong, Henry, Jr. *physician, researcher*
Hackney, Jack Dean *physician*
Magnes, Harry Alan *physician*

Duarte
Comings, David Edward *physician, medical genetics scientist*
Kovach, John Stephen *oncologist, research center administrator*

El Macero
†Andrews, Neil Corbly *surgeon*
Raventos, Antolin *radiology educator*

Emeryville
Hurst, Deborah *pediatric hematologist*

Encinitas
Chavez, Cesar T. *ophthalmologist, cosmetic surgeon*
Satur, Nancy Marlene *dermatologist*

Encino
Costea, Nicolas Vincent *physician, researcher*

Escondido
Everton, Marta Ve *retired ophthalmologist*

Fairfield
Atiba, Joshua Olajide O. *internist, pharmacologist, oncologist, educator*
†Suga, Steven Hidenori *neurologist*

Folsom
Anderson, Jeffrey Lee *physician, anesthesiologist, consultant*
Ewing, Russell Charles, II *physician*

Fremont
Steinmetz, Seymour *pediatrician*

Fresno
Chandler, Bruce Frederick *internist*
Falcone, Alfonso Benjamin *physician and biochemist*
Holmes, Albert William, Jr. *physician*
Leigh, Hoyle *psychiatrist, educator, writer*
Patton, Jack Thomas *family practice physician*
Smith, V. Roy *neurosurgeon*
Thompson, Leonard Russell *pediatrician*

Fullerton
Aston, Edward Ernest, IV *dermatologist*
Nitta, Douglas *family practice physician*
Steward, Marsh, Jr. *obstetrician, gynecologist*
Sugarman, Michael *physician, rheumatologist*

Gardena
Rubin, Lawrence Ira *podiatrist*

Glendale
Garcia, Serafin Montealto *physician*

Glendora
Lasko, Allen Howard *pharmacist*

Greenbrae
Levy, S. William *dermatologist*
Parnell, Francis William, Jr. *physician*
†Ramirez, Archimedes *neurosurgeon*

Gualala
Ring, Alice Ruth Bishop *retired physician*

Half Moon Bay
Robertson, Abel L., Jr. *pathologist*

Harbor City
Ackerson, Bradley Kent *physician*
Kwan, Benjamin Ching Kee *ophthalmologist*

Hillsborough
Kraft, Robert Arnold *retired medical educator, physician*

Hollywood
†Wald, Harlan Ira *plastic surgeon, lawyer*

Huntington Beach
†Nichter, Larry Steven *medical educator, plastic surgeon*

Irvine
Connolly, John Earle *surgeon, educator*
Felton, Jean Spencer *physician*
Gupta, Sudhir *immunologist, educator*
Hubbell, Floyd Allan *physician, educator*
Korc, Murray *endocrinologist*
Miledi, Ricardo *neurobiologist*
Quilligan, Edward James *obstetrician, gynecologist, educator*
Ross, Amy Ann *experimental pathologist*
Steward, Oswald *neuroscience educator, researcher*
Tobis, Jerome Sanford *physician*
van-den-Noort, Stanley *physician, educator*
Weinstein, Gerald D. *dermatology educator*
Yin, Hong Zhen *neuropathologist, researcher*

Kentfield
Bruyn, Henry Bicker *physician*

La Jolla
Barrett-Connor, Elizabeth Louise *epidemiologist, educator*
Bergan, John Jerome *vascular surgeon*
Beutler, Ernest *physician, research scientist*
Block, Melvin August *surgeon, educator*
Brown, Stuart I. *ophthalmologist, educator*
Carmichael, David Burton *physician*
Churg, Jacob *pathologist*
Dalessio, Donald John *physician, neurologist, educator*
Diamant, Joel Charles *internist*
Dixon, Frank James *medical scientist, educator*
Edgington, Thomas S. *pathologist, educator, molecular biologist*
Edwards, Charles Cornell *physician, research administrator*
Friedmann, Theodore *physician*
Garland, Cedric Frank *epidemiologist, educator*
Gill, Gordon N. *medical educator*
Gittes, Ruben Foster *urological surgeon*
Glass, Christopher Kevin *physician*
Hamburger, Robert N. *pediatrics educator, consultant*
Han, Jiahuai *medical researcher*
Johnson, Allen Dress *cardiologist*
Judd, Lewis Lund *psychiatrist, educator*
Katzman, Robert *medical educator, neurologist*
Keeney, Edmund Ludlow *physician*
Klinman, Norman Ralph *immunologist, medical educator*
Malhotra, Vivek *medical educator*
Mathews, Kenneth Pine *physician, educator*
Miller, Stephen Herschel *surgery educator*
Nakamura, Robert Motoharu *pathologist*
Nyhan, William Leo *pediatrician, educator*
Oldstone, Michael Beaureguard Alan *immunologist*
Peebles, Carol Lynn *immunology researcher*
Rearden, Carole Ann *clinical pathologist, educator*
Resnik, Robert *medical educator*
Rights, Clyde Siewers *obstetrician and gynecologist*
Rosenfeld, Michael G. *medical educator*
Ruoslahti, Erkki *medical research administrator*
Silverstone, Leon Martin *cariologist, neuroscientist, educator, researcher*
Spiegelberg, Hans Leonhard *medical educator*
Squire, Larry Ryan *neuroscientist, psychologist, educator*
Steinberg, Daniel *preventive medicine physician, educator*
Tan, Eng Meng *immunologist, biomedical scientist*
Teirstein, Paul Shepherd *physician, health facility administrator*
Terry, Robert Davis *neuropathologist, educator*
Thal, Leon Joel *neuroscientist*
Walker, Richard Hugh *orthopaedic surgeon*
Weigle, William Oliver *immunologist, educator*
Yen, Samuel S(how)-C(hih) *obstetrics and gynecology educator, reproductive endocrinologist*

La Mesa
Wohl, Armand Jeffrey *cardiologist*

La Puente
Goldberg, David Bryan *biomedical researcher*

La Quinta
†Calvin, James Willard *thoracic and vascular surgeon*

La Verne
McDonough-Treichler, Judith Dianne *medical educator, consultant*

Laguna Hills
Ierardi, Stephen John *physician*
Widyolar, Sheila Gayle *dermatologist*

Laguna Niguel
Sturdevant, Charles Oliver *physician, neuropsychiatrist*

Laguna Woods
Ross, Mathew *psychiatry educator*

Lake Forest
Larsen, Robert Ray *healthcare executive, surgeon*

Lake Isabella
Fraser, Eleanor Ruth *radiologist, administrator*

Livermore
Seward, James Pickett *internist, educator*

Loma Linda
Aloia, Roland Craig *scientist, administrator, educator*
Behrens, Berel Lyn *physician, academic administrator*
Brandstater, Murray Everett *physiatrist*
Bull, Brian Stanley *pathology educator, medical consultant, business executive*
Chan, Philip J. *medical educator*
Coggin, Charlotte Joan *cardiologist, educator*
Green, Lora Murray *immunologist, researcher, educator*
Hinshaw, David B., Jr. *radiologist*
Kirk, Gerald Arthur *nuclear radiologist*
†Krick, Edwin Harry, Sr. *medical educator, preventive medicine physician*
Llaurado, Josep G. *nuclear medicine physician, scientist*
Mace, John Weldon *pediatrician*
Rendell-Baker, Leslie *anesthesiologist, educator*
Roberts, Walter Herbert Beatty *anatomist*
Slater, James Munro *radiation oncologist*
Stilson, Walter Leslie *radiologist, educator*
Strother, Allen *biochemical pharmacologist, researcher*
Young, Lionel Wesley *radiologist*

Long Beach
Alkon, Ellen Skillen *physician*
Anderson, Garry Michael *diagnostic radiologist*
Berke, Irving *obstetrician-gynecologist, military officer*
Crivaro, John Pete *family practice physician*
Friis, Robert Harold *epidemiologist, health science educator*
Kurnick, Nathaniel Bertrand *oncologist-hematologist, educator, researcher*
Kwaan, Jack Hau Ming *retired physician*
Loganbill, G. Bruce *logopedic pathologist*
Looney, Gerald Lee *medical educator, administrator*
Macer, George Armen, Jr. *orthopedic hand surgeon*
Moran, Edgar M. *physician, educator*
Pineda, Anselmo *neurosurgery educator*
Stemmer, Edward Alan *surgeon, educator*
Tabrisky, Phyllis Page *physiatrist, educator*
Todd, Malcolm Clifford *surgeon*
†Van Gorder, Chris *medical executive*
White, Katherine Elizabeth *retired pediatrician*

Los Altos
Abrams, Arthur Jay *physician*
Castellino, Ronald Augustus Dietrich *radiologist*
Garman, Jon Kent *anesthesiologist*
Martin, Leonardo San Juan *urologist, surgeon*
Orman, Nanette Hector *psychiatrist*

Los Angeles
Alkana, Ronald Lee *neuropsychopharmacologist, psychobiologist*
Anderson, Kathryn D. *surgeon*
Apt, Leonard *physician*
Archie, Carol Louise *obstetrician and gynecologist, educator*
Ashley, Sharon Anita *pediatric anesthesiologist*
Askanas-Engel, Valerie *neurologist, educator, researcher*
Barrett, Cynthia Townsend *neonatologist*
Beart, Robert W., Jr. *surgeon, educator*
Beck, John Christian *physician, educator*
Becker, Donald Paul *surgeon, neurosurgeon*
Bernstein, Sol *cardiologist, educator*
Bessman, Samuel Paul *pediatrician, biochemist*
Biles, John Alexander *pharmacology educator, chemistry educator*
Blahd, William Henry *physician*
Bluestone, David Allan *pediatrician*
Bodey, Bela *immunomorphologist*
Bondareff, William *psychiatry educator*
Borenstein, Daniel Bernard *physician, educator*
Bowman, C. Michael *physician*
Braunstein, Glenn David *physician, educator*
Breslow, Lester *physician, educator*
Burgess, J. Wesley *neuropsychiatrist*
Caprioli, Joseph *ophthalmologist*
Chandor, Stebbins Bryant *pathologist*
Cherry, James Donald *physician*
Cicciarelli, James Carl *immunology educator*
Clemente, Carmine Domenic *anatomist, educator*
Cooper, Edwin Lowell *anatomy educator*
Corman, Marvin Leonard *surgeon, educator*
Cote, Richard James *pathologist, researcher*
Dann, Francis Joseph *dermatologist, educator*
Davidson, Ezra C., Jr. *physician, educator*
De Cherney, Alan Hersh *obstetrics and gynecology educator*
Detels, Roger *epidemiologist, physician, former university dean*
Dignam, William Joseph *obstetrician, gynecologist, educator*
Edgerton, Bradford Wheatly *plastic surgeon*
Engel, William King *neurologist, educator*
Enstrom, James Eugene *cancer epidemiologist*
Ettenger, Robert Bruce *physician, nephrologist*
Fahey, John Leslie *immunologist*
Feig, Stephen Arthur *pediatrics educator, hematologist, oncologist*
Fielding, Jonathan E. *pediatrician*
Figlin, Robert Alan *physician, hematologist, oncologist*
Fish, Barbara *psychiatrist, educator*
Fleming, Arthur Wallace *physician, surgeon*
Fogelman, Alan Marcus *internist*
Fowler, Vincent R. *dermatologist*
Fox, Saul Lourie *physician, researcher*
Frasier, S. Douglas *medical educator*
Friedman, Nathan Baruch *physician*
Fukushima, Teiichiro *obstetrician and gynecologist, educator*
†Gabriel, Ronald Samuel *child neurologist*
Gale, Robert Peter *physician, scientist, researcher*
Gambino, Jerome James *nuclear medicine educator*
Geller, Stephen Arthur *pathologist, educator*
Giannotta, Steven Louis *neurosurgery educator*
Gonick, Harvey Craig *nephrologist, educator*
Gorney, Roderic *psychiatry educator*
Gorski, Roger Anthony *neuroendocrinologist, educator*
Grinnell, Alan Dale *neurobiologist, educator, researcher*
Guze, Phyllis Arlene *internist, educator, academic administrator*
Haughton, James Gray *medical facility administrator, municipal health department administrator, consultant, physician*
Haywood, L. Julian *physician, educator*
Helsper, James Thomas *surgical oncologist, researcher, educator*
Henriksen MacLean, Eva Hansine *former anesthesiology educator*
Hershman, Jerome Marshall *endocrinologist*
Hoang, Duc Van *theoretical pathologist, educator*
Holland, Gary Norman *ophthalmologist, educator*
Horwitz, David A. *physician, scientist, educator*
House, John William *otologist*
Hsiao, Chie-Fang *neuroscientist*
Ignarro, Louis J. *pharmacology educator*
Jacobson, Edwin James *medical educator*
Jalali, Behnaz *psychiatrist, educator*
Jarvik, Lissy F. *psychiatrist*
†Jarvik, Murray Elias *psychiatry, pharmacology educator*
Jelliffe, Roger Woodham *cardiologist, clinical pharmacologist*
Johnson, Cage Saul *hematologist, educator*
Johnson, John Patrick *neurosurgeon, educator*
Kamil, Elaine Scheiner *physician, educator*
Kaplan, Samuel *pediatric cardiologist*
Katz, Roger *pediatrician, educator*
Katz, Ronald Lewis *physician, educator*
Kelly, Arthur Paul *physician*
Kerman, Barry Martin *ophthalmologist, educator*
†Kerndt, Peter Reynolds *physician*
Kilburn, Kaye Hatch *medical educator*
Kleeman, Charles Richard *medical educator, nephrologist, researcher*
Koch, Richard *pediatrician, educator*
Korsch, Barbara M. *pediatrician*
Kramer, Barry Alan *psychiatrist*
Kreitenberg, Arthur *orthopedic surgeon, consultant*
Labiner, Gerald Wilk *physician, medical educator*
Landing, Benjamin Harrison *pathologist, educator*
Levey, Gerald Saul *physician, educator*
Levy, Michael Lee *neurosurgeon*
Lewin, Klaus J. *pathologist, educator*
Lewis, Charles Edwin *physician, educator*
Liang, Jing *pharmacologist*
Lim, David Jong-Jai *otolaryngology educator, researcher*
Liu, Don *ophthalmologist, medical researcher*
Longmire, William Polk, Jr. *physician, surgeon*
Lubman, Richard Levi *physician, educator, research scientist*
Mabee, John Richard *physician assistant, educator*
Malcolm, Dawn Grace *family physician*
Maloney, Robert Keller *ophthalmologist, medical educator*
Markham, Charles Henry *neurologist*
Marmor, Judd *psychiatrist, educator*
Maronde, Robert Francis *internist, clinical pharmacologist, educator*
Martinez, Miguel Acevedo *urologist, consultant, lecturer*
Mellinkoff, Sherman Mussoff *medical educator*
Mihan, Richard *retired dermatologist*
Mishell, Daniel R., Jr. *physician, educator*
Moxley, John Howard, III *physician*
Moy, Ronald Leonard *dermatologist, surgeon*
Nathwani, Bharat Narottam *pathologist, consultant*
Neufeld, Naomi Das *pediatric endocrinologist*
Newman, Anita Nadine *surgeon*
Nissenson, Allen Richard *physician, educator*
Noble, Ernest Pascal *physician, biochemist, educator*
Parker, John William *pathology educator, investigator*
Parker, Robert George *radiation oncology educator, academic administrator*
Parmelee, Arthur Hawley, Jr. *pediatric medical educator*
Passaro, Edward, Jr. *surgeon, educator*
Perloff, Joseph Kayle *cardiologist*
Pike, Malcolm Cecil *preventive medicine educator*
Pulec, Jack Lee *otolaryngologist*
Rachelefsky, Gary Stuart *medical educator*
Raghavan, Derek *oncologist, medical researcher and educator*
†Reuben, David Burt *medical educator*
Rimoin, David Lawrence *physician, geneticist*
Ritvo, Edward Ross *psychiatrist*
†Rodriguez, Ensor *physician, scientist*
Roemer, Milton Irwin *physician, educator*
Ryan, Stephen Joseph, Jr. *ophthalmology educator, university dean*
Sager, Philip Travis *academic physician, cardiac electrophysiologist*
†Salem, Hadi *thoracic surgeon*
Sarnat, Bernard George *plastic surgeon, educator, researcher*
Sawyer, Charles Henry *anatomist, educator*
Scheibel, Arnold Bernard *psychiatrist, educator, research director*
Schelbert, Heinrich Ruediger *nuclear medicine physician*
Schiff, Martin *physician, surgeon*
Schneider, Edward Lewis *medicine educator, research administrator*
Schwabe, Arthur David *physician, educator*
Schwartz, William Benjamin *educator, physician*
Siegel, Michael Elliot *nuclear medicine physician, educator*
Siegel, Sheldon C. *physician*
Solomon, George Freeman *psychiatrist, retired educator*
Steckel, Richard J. *radiologist, academic administrator*
†Stein, Jay Joseph *urologist*
Stern, Walter Eugene *neurosurgeon, educator*
Straatsma, Bradley Ralph *ophthalmologist, educator*
Tabachnick, Norman Donald *psychiatrist, educator*
Tan, Zhiqun *biomedical scientist*
Titus, Edward Depue *psychiatrist, administrator*
Tompkins, Ronald K. *surgeon*
Tourtellotte, Wallace William *neurologist, educator*
Van Der Meulen, Joseph Pierre *neurologist*
Villablanca, Jaime Rolando *medical neuroscientist, educator*
Vredevoe, Donna Lou *research immunologist, microbiologist, educator*
Wallach, Howard Frederic *psychiatrist*
Walsh, John Harley *medical educator*
Weiner, Leslie Philip *neurology educator, researcher*
Weinstein, Irwin Marshall *internist, hematologist*
Weiss, Martin Harvey *neurosurgeon, educator*
Wilkinson, Alan Herbert *nephrologist, medical educator*
Wilson, Miriam Geisendorfer *retired physician, educator*
Wilson, Myron Robert, Jr. *retired psychiatrist*
Withers, Hubert Rodney *radiotherapist, radiobiologist, educator*
Woodley, David Timothy *dermatology educator*
Woolf, Nancy Jean *neuroscientist, educator*
†Wright, Joan Frances *surgeon*
Wu, Ching-Fong *gastroenterologist*
Yamamoto, Joe *psychiatrist, educator*
Zawacki, Bruce Edwin *surgeon, ethicist*

Los Gatos
Cohen, James Robert *oncologist, hematologist*
Naughten, Robert Norman *pediatrician*

Los Osos
Allison, Ralph Brewster *psychiatrist*

Malibu
Jenden, Donald James *pharmacologist, educator*
Moore, John George, Jr. *medical educator*
Morgenstern, Leon *surgeon*

Mammoth Lakes
Shekhar, Stephen S. *obstetrician, gynecologist*

Marina Del Rey
†Sehdeva, Jagjit S. *surgeon*
Stiess, Walter George *retired surgeon*
Strum, Stephen B. *oncologist*

Martinez
McKnight, Lenore Ravin *child psychiatrist*

Menlo Park
Chin, Albert Kae *research physician*
Glaser, Robert Joy *retired physician, foundation executive*
Hoffman, Thomas Edward *dermatologist*
Kovachy, Edward Miklos, Jr. *psychiatrist*
Sparks, Robert Dean *medical administrator, physician*

Mill Valley
Harris, Jeffrey Saul *physician executive, consultant*
Wallerstein, Robert Solomon *psychiatrist*

Modesto
Goldberg, Robert Lewis *preventive and occupational medicine physician*

Monterey
Black, Robert Lincoln *pediatrician*
†Sunde, Douglas *plastic surgeon*

Monterey Park
Chang, Jonathan Lee *orthopedist, educator*

Moraga
Frey, William Rayburn *healthcare educator, consultant*

Morro Bay
Eggertsen, Paul Fred *psychiatrist*

Mountain View
Emmons, Victoria Ann *hospital administrator, marketing consultant*
†Pearl, Samuel N. *plastice surgery*
†Seidman, Saul William *neurology surgeon*
Warren, Richard Wayne *obstetrician and gynecologist*

Murrieta
Froelich, Wolfgang Andreas *neurologist*

Napa
Price, John James, Jr. *retired orthopaedic surgeon, forensic reporter*
Zimmermann, John Paul *plastic surgeon*

National City
Morgan, Jacob Richard *cardiologist*

Newbury Park
Bleiberg, Leon William *surgical podiatrist*

Newport Beach
†Chong, John Kenneth *plastic surgeon*
†Nitta, Katharine *plastic surgeon*
Robinson, Hurley *surgeon*
Shamoun, John Milam *plastic surgeon*
†Wendt, James Robert *plastic surgeon*
Zalta, Edward *otorhinolaryngologist, physician*

Northridge
†Yasuda, Roderick K. *cardiothoracic surgeon*

Norwalk
Armstrong, David Ligon *psychiatrist*

Novato
Danse, Ilene Homnick Raisfeld *physician, educator, toxicologist*

Oakland
Burdick, Claude Owen *pathologist*
Collen, Morris Frank *physician*
Killebrew, Ellen Jane (Mrs. Edward S. Graves) *cardiologist*
Ng, Lawrence Ming-Loy *pediatrician*
Sharpton, Thomas *physician*

Oceanside
Curtin, Thomas Lee *ophthalmologist*
Haley, Thomas John *retired pharmacologist*

Orange
Achauer, Bruce Michael *plastic surgeon*
Anzel, Sanford Harold *orthopedic surgeon*
Armentrout, Steven Alexander *oncologist*
Barr, Ronald Jeffrey *dermatologist, pathologist*
Berk, Jack Edward *physician, educator*
Crumley, Roger Lee *surgeon, educator*
DiSaia, Philip John *gynecologist, obstetrician, radiology educator*
Eagan, Robert T. *oncologist*
Fisher, Mark Jay *neurologist, neuroscientist, educator*
†Foltz, Eldon Lercy *neurosurgeon, educator*
Furnas, David William *plastic surgeon*
Gardin, Julius Markus *cardiologist, educator*
Kim, Moon Hyun *physician, educator*
Lott, Ira Totz *pediatric neurologist*
MacArthur, Carol Jeanne *pediatric otolaryngology educator*
Morgan, Beverly Carver *physician, educator*
Mosier, Harry David, Jr. *physician, educator*
Rowen, Marshall *radiologist*
Thompson, William Benbow, Jr. *obstetrician, gynecologist, educator*
Vatcher, James Gordon *retired physician*
Vaziri, Nosratola Dabir *internist, nephrologist, educator*
Wilson, Archie Fredric *medical educator*
Yu, Jen *medical educator*

Oxnard
Niesluchowski, Witold S. *cardiovascular and thoracic surgeon*

Pacific Palisades
Claes, Daniel John *physician*
Dignam, Robert Joseph *retired orthopaedic surgeon*
Greene, Warren W. *anesthesiologist*

Palm Desert
McKissock, Paul Kendrick *plastic surgeon*

Palm Springs
Lunde, Donald Theodore *physician*
Weil, Max Harry *physician, medical educator, medical scientist*

Palo Alto
Amylon, Michael David *physician, educator*
Bagshaw, Malcolm A. *radiation oncologist, educator*
Bensch, Klaus George *pathology educator*
Britton, M(elvin) C(reed), Jr. *physician, rheumatologist*
Chase, Robert Arthur *surgeon, educator*
Chen, Stephen Shi-hua *pathologist, biochemist*
Cooke, John P. *cardiologist, medical educator, medical researcher*
Dafoe, Donald Cameron *surgeon, educator*
Date, Elaine Satomi *physician*
Dement, William Charles *sleep researcher, medical educator*
Desai, Kavin Hirendra *pediatrician*
Donaldson, Sarah Susan *radiologist*
Fann, James Ilin *cardiothoracic surgeon*
Farber, Eugene Mark *psoriasis research institute administrator*
Farquhar, John William *physician, educator*
Fries, James Franklin *internal medicine educator*
Goldstein, Avram *pharmacology educator*
Goldstein, Mary Kane *physician*
Harris, Edward D., Jr. *physician*
Hays, Marguerite Thompson *physician*
Holman, Halsted Reid *medical educator*
Hubert, Helen Betty *epidemiologist*
Jamison, Rex Lindsay *medical educator*
Jamplis, Robert Warren *surgeon, medical foundation executive*
Kelly, Charles Eugene, II *gastroenterologist, researcher*
Lane, Alfred Thomas *medical educator*
Lane, William Kenneth *physician*
Linna, Timo Juhani *immunologist, researcher, educator*
Litt, Iris Figarsky *pediatrics educator*
Maffly, Roy Herrick *medical educator, retired*
Mansour, Tag Eldin *pharmacologist, educator*
Michie, Sara H. *pathologist, educator*
Polan, Mary Lake *obstetrics and gynecology educator*
Salvatierra, Oscar, Jr. *transplant surgeon, urologist, educator*
Sawyer, Wilbur Henderson *pharmacologist, educator*
Schrier, Stanley Leonard *physician, educator*
Schurman, David Jay *orthopedic surgeon, educator*
Shuer, Lawrence Mendel *neurosurgery educator*
Strober, Samuel *immunologist, educator*
Thom, David Hinton *family physician, medical educator*
Tune, Bruce Malcolm *pediatrics educator, renal toxicologist*
Urquhart, John *medical researcher, educator*
Weng, Wen-Kai *physician, medical researcher*
Winkleby, Marilyn A. *medical researcher*
Zarins, Christopher Kristaps *surgery educator, vascular surgeon*

Palos Verdes Estates
Wisdom, William Russell *radiologist*

Palos Verdes Peninsula
Haynes, Moses Alfred *physician*
Thomas, Claudewell Sidney *psychiatry educator*

Paradise
†Haws, Hale Louis *medical consultant*

Paramount
Cohn, Lawrence Steven *physician, educator*

Pasadena
Barnard, William Marion *psychiatrist*
Buck, Francis Scott *pathologist, educator*
Caillouette, James Clyde *physician*
†Dyck, Peter *neurosurgeon*
Giem, Ross Nye, Jr. *surgeon*
Girod, Erwin Ernest *internist*
Harvey, Joseph Paul, Jr. *orthopedist, educator*
Konishi, Masakazu *neurobiologist, educator*
Mathies, Allen Wray, Jr. *physician, hospital administrator*
Miklusak, Thomas Alan *psychiatrist, psychoanalyst*
Opel, William *medical research administrator*
Pitts, Ferris Newcomb *physician, psychiatry educator*
†Rosenfeld, Harold Lee *plastic surgeon*
Shalack, Joan Helen *psychiatrist*
Yeager, Caroline Hale *radiologist, consultant*

Piedmont
Hughes, James Paul *physician*

Pinole
Harvey, Elinor B. *child psychiatrist*
Naughton, James Lee *internist*

Pomona
Vo, Huu Dinh *pediatrician, educator*

Rancho Mirage
Lacey, Beatrice Cates *psychophysiologist*

Rancho Santa Fe
Affeldt, John Ellsworth *physician*
Rockoff, S. David *radiologist, physician, educator*

Redding
Shadish, William Raymond *plastic surgeon, retired*

Redlands
Adey, William Ross *physician*
Bangasser, Ronald Paul *physician*
Richardson, A(rthur) Leslie *former medical group consultant*
Wang, Colleen Iona *medical association administrator, writer*

Redondo Beach
Davis, Lowell Livingston *cardiovascular surgeon*

Redwood City
Ellis, Eldon Eugene *surgeon*

Riverside
Bricker, Neal S. *physician, educator*
Childs, Donald Richard *pediatric endocrinologist*
Jung, Timothy Tae Kun *otolaryngologist*
Linaweaver, Walter Ellsworth, Jr. *physician*
Seyfert, Howard Bentley, Jr. *podiatrist*

Rolling Hills Estates
Kline, Frank Menefee *psychiatrist*
Leake, Rosemary Dobson *physician*

Roseville
†Cohen, Michael Wayne *physician*

Ross
Way, Walter Lee *anesthetist, pharmacologist, educator*

Rowland Heights
Allen, Delmas James *anatomist, educator, university administrator*

Sacramento
Achtel, Robert Andrew *pediatric cardiologist*
Benfield, John Richard *surgeon*
Chapman, Michael William *orthopedist, educator*
Frey, Charles Frederick *surgeon, educator*
Lippold, Roland Will *surgeon*
Lynch, Peter John *dermatologist*
†Powers, William Edwards, Jr. *hand surgeon*
Reiber, Gregory Duane *forensic pathologist*
Rounds, Barbara Lynn *psychiatrist*
Shapero, Harris Joel *pediatrician*
Sharma, Arjun Dutta *cardiologist*
Stevenson, Thomas Ray *plastic surgeon*
Styne, Dennis Michael *physician*
†Whetzel, Thomas Porter *plastic surgeon*
Wolfman, Earl Frank, Jr. *surgeon, educator*
Zil, J. S. *psychiatrist, physiologist*

Saint Helena
Herber, Steven Carlton *physician*

Salinas
Phillips, John P(aul) *retired neurosurgeon*

San Bernardino
De Haas, David Dana *emergency physician*
Kuehn, Klaus Karl Albert *ophthalmologist*

San Bruno
Bradley, Charles William *podiatrist, educator*

San Diego
Abrams, Reid Allen *surgeon, educator*
Akeson, Wayne Henry *orthopedic surgeon, educator*
Backer, Matthias, Jr. *obstetrician-gynecologist*
Bailey, David Nelson *pathologist, educator*
Binmoeller, Kenneth Frank *physician, surgeon*
Blum, John Alan *urologist, educator*
Chambers, Henry George *orthopedic surgeon*
Cowen, Donald Eugene *retired physician*
DeMaria, Anthony Nicholas *cardiologist, educator*
Demeter, Steven *neurologist, publishing company executive*
Edwards-Tate, Laurie Ellen *homecare services company executive, educator*
Friedenberg, Richard Myron *radiology educator, physician*
Friedman, Paul Jay *radiologist, chest radiologist, educator*
Goltz, Robert William *physician, educator*
Halasz, Nicholas Alexis *surgeon*
Hamburg, Marian Virginia *health science educator*
Harwood, Ivan Richmond *pediatric pulmonologist*
Hourani, Laurel Lockwood *epidemiologist*
Hunt, Robert Gary *medical consultant, oral and maxillofacial surgeon*
Intriere, Anthony Donald *physician*
Jacoby, Irving *physician*
Jamieson, Stuart William *surgeon, educator*
Jones, Clyde William *anesthesiologist*
Kaback, Michael *medical educator*
Kaplan, George Willard *urologist*
Leopold, George Robert *radiologist*
Levy, Jerome *dermatologist, retired naval officer*
†Marshall, Lawrence F. *neurologist, surgeon*
Mendoza, Stanley Atran *pediatric nephrologist, educator*
Moossa, A. R. *surgery educator*
Neuman, Tom S. *emergency medical physician, educator*
†Olichney, John Michael *neurosciences educator*
Oliphant, Charles Romig *physician*
O'Malley, Edward *physician, consultant*
Owsia, Nasrin Akbarnia *pediatrician*
†Panos, Reed Gregory *plastic surgeon*
Parthemore, Jacqueline Gail *physician, educator*
Pitt, William Alexander *cardiologist*
Radke, Jan Rodger *pulmonologist, physician executive*
Ranney, Helen Margaret *physician, educator*
Ray, Albert *family physician*
Rodin, Alvin Eli *retired pathologist, medical educator, author*
Schmidt, Joseph David *urologist*
Schorr, Martin Mark *forensic examiner, psychologist, educator, screenwriter*
Seagren, Stephen Linner *oncologist*
†Sohn, Steven S. *physician*
Wallace, Helen Margaret *physician, educator*
Wasserman, Stephen Ira *physician, educator*
Welch, Arnold DeMerritt *pharmacologist, biochemist*
Wight, Nancy Elizabeth *neonatologist, educator*

San Fernando
Chiu, Dorothy *pediatrician*

San Francisco
Amend, William John Conrad, Jr. *physician, educator*
Bainton, Dorothy Ford *pathology educator, researcher*
Barondes, Samuel Herbert *psychiatrist, educator*
Benet, Leslie Zachary *pharmacokineticist*
Bishop, John Michael *biomedical research scientist, educator*
Boles, Roger *otolaryngologist*
Brown, Eric Joel *biomedical researcher*
Carson, Jay Wilmer *pathologist, educator*
Castro, Joseph Ronald *physician, oncology researcher, educator*
Cheitlin, Melvin Donald *physician, educator*
Clever, Linda Hawes *physician*
Cobbs, Price Mashaw *social psychiatrist*
Curtis, David Lambert *rheumatologist, educator*
David, George *psychiatrist, economic theory lecturer*
Dawson, Chandler Robert *ophthalmologist, educator*
Debas, Haile T. *gastrointestinal surgeon, physiologist, educator*
Deicken, Raymond Friedrich *neuropsychiatrist, clinical neuroscientist*
Engleman, Ephraim Philip *rheumatologist*
Epstein, Charles Joseph *physician, medical geneticist, pediatrics and biochemistry educator*
Epstein, John Howard *dermatologist*
Epstein, Leon Joseph *psychiatrist*
Finberg, Laurence *pediatrician, educator, dean*
Fishman, Robert Allen *neurologist, educator*
Foye, Laurance Vincent *physician, hospital administrator*
Frick, Oscar Lionel *physician, educator*
Friedman, Meyer *physician*
Fu, Karen King-Wah *radiation oncologist*
Gellin, Gerald Alan *dermatologist*
Gibbs, Patricia Hellman *physician*
Glassberg, Alan Burnett *physician*
Goode, Erica Tucker *internist*
Gooding, Charles Arthur *radiologist, physician, educator*
Greenspan, Francis S. *physician*
Greyson, Clifford Russell *internist*
Grossman, William *medical researcher, educator*
Grumbach, Melvin Malcolm *physician, educator*
Havel, Richard Joseph *physician, educator*
Herbert, Chesley C. *psychiatrist, educator*
Hering, William Marshall *medical organization executive*
Heyman, Melvin Bernard *pediatric gastroenterologist*
Higashida, Randall Takeo *radiologist, neurosurgeon, medical educator*
Hinman, Frank, Jr. *urologist, educator*
Hoffman, Julien Ivor Ellis *pediatric cardiologist, educator*
Hsu, John Chao-Chun *retired pediatrician*
Jaffe, Robert Benton *obstetrician, gynecologist, reproductive endocrinologist*
Jensen, Ronald H. *medical educator*
Kan, Yuet Wai *physician, investigator*
Katz, Hilliard Joel *physician*
Kiefer, Renata Gertrud *physician, epidemiologist, economist, international health management consultant*
†Kilgore, Eugene Sterling, Jr. *surgeon*
†Kind, Gabriel Matthew *plastic surgeon*
Kline, Howard Jay *cardiologist, educator*
Kolb, Felix Oscar *physician*
Kramer, Steven G. *ophthalmologist*
Larsen, Loren Joseph *retired pediatric orthopedic surgeon*
Lee, Philip Randolph *medical educator*
Lim, Robert Cheong, Jr. *surgeon, educator*
Low, Randall *internist, cardiologist*
Lucia, Marilyn Reed *physician*
Lull, Robert John *nuclear medicine physician, educator*
Maibach, Howard I. *dermatologist*
Margulis, Alexander Rafailo *physician, educator*
Mason, Dean Towle *cardiologist*
Mathes, Stephen John *plastic and reconstructive surgeon, educator*
McAninch, Jack Weldon *urological surgeon, educator*
†McClure, Thomas Allan *physician*
McCorkle, Horace Jackson *physician, educator*
Mills, Thomas Cooke *psychiatrist*
Muench, Marcus Oliver *hematologist*
Mustacchi, Piero *physician, educator*
Myers, Howard Milton *pharmacologist, educator*
O'Connor, G(eorge) Richard *ophthalmologist*
Perkins, Herbert Asa *physician*
Petrakis, Nicholas Louis *physician, medical researcher, educator*
Phillips, Theodore Locke *radiation oncologist, educator*
Piel, Carolyn Forman *pediatrician, educator*
Ralston, Henry James, III *neurobiologist, anatomist, educator*
†Raskin, Neil Hugh *neurology educator*
Risse, Guenter Bernhard *physician, historian, educator*
Roe, Benson Bertheau *surgeon, educator*
Rosenbaum, Ernest Harold *internist, oncologist, educator*
Rosinski, Edwin Francis *health sciences educator*
Rudolph, Abraham Morris *physician, educator*
Schiller, Francis *neurologist, medical historian*
Schmid, Rudi (Rudolf Schmid) *internist, educator, scientist*
Schmidt, Robert Milton *physician, scientist, educator, administrator*
Scholten, Paul *obstetrician, gynecologist, educator*
Schrock, Theodore R. *surgeon*
Seebach, Lydia Marie *physician*
Shapiro, Larry Jay *pediatrician, scientist, educator*
Shinefield, Henry Robert *pediatrician*
Smith, David Elvin *physician*
Smith, Lloyd Hollingsworth *physician*
Sokolow, Maurice *physician, educator*
†Solomon, Gina Michelle *physician*
Spencer, William H. *ophthalmologist*
Stamper, Robert Lewis *ophthalmologist, educator*
Steinman, John Francis *psychiatrist*
Terr, Abba Israel *allergist, immunologist*
Terr, Lenore Cagen *psychiatrist, writer*
Thompson, Charlotte Ellis *pediatrician, educator, author*
Trejo, JoAnn *medical researcher*
Van Dyke, Craig *psychiatrist*
Volpe, Peter Anthony *surgeon*
Wallerstein, Ralph Oliver *physician*
Watts, Malcolm S(tuart) M(cNeal) *physician, medical educator*
Way, E(dward) Leong *pharmacologist, toxicologist, educator*
Wescott, William Burnham *oral maxillofacial pathologist, educator*
Wilson, Charles B. *neurosurgeon, educator*
Wintroub, Bruce Urich *dermatologist, educator, researcher*
Wolff, Sheldon *radiobiologist, educator*
†Yao, John Sen *physician*
Zippin, Calvin *epidemiologist, educator*

San Gabriel
Chen, John Calvin *child and adolescent psychiatrist*
Terry, Roger *pathologist, consultant*
Wong, John Wing-Chung *psychiatrist*

San Jose
Avakoff, Joseph Carnegie *medical and legal consultant*
Gale, Arnold David *pediatric neurologist, consultant*
Joshi, Janardan Shantilal *surgeon*
Karin, Mardi Ross *surgeon*
Kramer, Richard Jay *gastroenterologist*
Mendenhall, Carrol Clay *physician*
Nguyen, Thinh Van *physician*
Okita, George Torao *pharmacologist educator*
†Ourmazdi, Behzad *physician, educator*
Piazza, Duane Eugene *biomedical researcher, college official*
Press, Barry Harris Jay *plastic surgeon, educator*
Sidener, Margaret Weil Leathers *foundation administrator*
Stein, Arthur Oscar *pediatrician*
Weeker, Ellis *emergency physician*

San Juan Capistrano
Fisher, Delbert Arthur *physician, educator*

San Marino
Benzer, Seymour *neuroscience educator*

San Mateo
Bell, Leo S. *retired physician*
†Brink, Robert Ross *plastic surgeon*
Kidera, George Jerome *physician*
Van Kirk, John Ellsworth *cardiologist*
von Doepp, Christian Ernest *psychiatrist*
Wong, Otto *epidemiologist*

San Pablo
Woodruff, Kay Herrin *pathologist, educator*

San Ramon
Litman, Robert Barry *physician, author, television and radio commentator*

Santa Ana
†Haldeman, Scott *neurology educator*
Myers, Marilyn Gladys *pediatric hematologist and oncologist*
Pratt, Lawrence Arthur *thoracic surgeon, foreign service officer*

Santa Barbara
Aijian, Haig Schuyler *pathologist, educator*
Bischel, Margaret DeMeritt *physician, managed care consultant*
Enelow, Allen Jay *psychiatrist, educator*
Fisher, Steven Kay *neurobiology educator*
Klakeg, Clayton Harold *cardiologist*
Kohn, Roger Alan *surgeon*
†Mosely, Jack Meredith *thoracic surgeon*
Prager, Elliot David *surgeon, educator*
Rockwell, Don Arthur *psychiatrist*
Shackman, Daniel Robert *psychiatrist*

Santa Clara
de la Roza, Gustavo Luis *pathologist*
Fernbach, Stephen Alton *pediatrician*

Santa Cruz
Shorenstein, Rosalind Greenberg *physician*

Santa Monica
Bohn, Paul Bradley *psychiatrist, psychoanalyst*
Rand, Robert Wheeler *neurosurgeon, educator*
Schultz, Victor M. *physician*
Singer, Frederick Raphael *medical researcher, educator*
Solomon, David Harris *physician, educator*
Thompson, Dennis Peters *plastic surgeon*
Waltzer, Kenneth Brian *physician, company executive*
Warick, Lawrence Herbert *psychiatrist*

Santa Rosa
Bozdech, Marek Jiri *physician*
†Gerst, Jerald Robert *physician*
Leuty, Gerald Johnston *osteopathic physician and surgeon*
Resch, Joseph Anthony *neurologist*

Sebastopol
Delgado, Roger R. *surgeon, educator*

Sepulveda
Wasterlain, Claude Guy *neurologist*

Sherman Oaks
King, Peter D. *psychiatrist, educator, real estate developer*
Zemplenyi, Tibor Karol *cardiologist*

Sierra Madre
Nation, Earl F. *retired urologist, educator*

Sonoma
†Canan, Janine Burford *psychiatrist, poet*

Sonora
Erich, Louis Richard *physician*

South San Francisco
Blethen, Sandra Lee *pediatric endocrinologist*
Dixit, Vishva M. *pathology educator*
Rodriguez, Roman *physician, child psychiatrist, educator*

Spring Valley
Long, David Michael, Jr. *biomedical researcher, cardiothoracic surgeon*
Roberts, Carolyn June *medical school department manager*

Stanford
Abrams, Herbert LeRoy *radiologist, educator*
Bauer, Eugene Andrew *dermatologist, educator*
Baylor, Denis Aristide *neurobiology educator*
Blaschke, Terrence Francis *medicine and molecular pharmacology educator*
Blau, Helen Margaret *molecular pharmacology educator*
Blumenkranz, Mark Scott *surgeon, researcher, educator*
Carlson, Robert Wells *physician, educator*
Cohen, Harvey Joel *pediatric hematology and oncology educator*

Egbert, Peter R. *ophthalmologist, educator*
Fee, Willard Edward, Jr. *otolaryngologist*
Friedman, Gary David *epidemiologist*
Gibson, Count Dillon, Jr. *physician, educator*
Glazer, Gary Mark *radiology educator*
Goldstein, Dora Benedict *pharmacologist, educator*
Hentz, Vincent R. *surgeon*
Herzenberg, Leonard Arthur *medical educator*
Hlatky, Mark Andrew *cardiologist, health services researcher*
Jardetzky, Oleg *medical educator, scientist*
Kendig, Joan Johnston *neurobiology educator*
Klima, Roger Radim *physiatrist*
Mark, James B. D. *surgeon*
Marmor, Michael Franklin *ophthalmologist, educator*
McDevitt, Hugh O'Neill *immunology educator, physician*
McDougall, Iain Ross *nuclear medicine educator*
Melmon, Kenneth Lloyd *physician, biologist, pharmacologist, consultant*
Merigan, Thomas Charles, Jr. *physician, medical researcher, educator*
Moss, Richard B. *pediatrician*
Oberhelman, Harry Alvin, Jr. *surgeon, educator*
Payne, Anita Hart *reproductive endocrinologist, researcher*
Raffin, Thomas A. *physician*
Reitz, Bruce Arnold *cardiac surgeon, educator*
Rosenberg, Saul Allen *oncologist, educator*
Rosenthal, Myer Hyman *anesthesiologist*
Rubenstein, Edward *physician, educator*
Rudd, Peter *physician, medical educator*
Schatzberg, Alan Frederic *psychiatrist, researcher*
Schendel, Stephen Alfred *plastic surgery educator, craniofacial surgeon*
Shortliffe, Edward Hance *internist, medical informatics educator*
Silverman, Frederic Noah *physician*
Spiegel, David *psychiatrist*
Stamey, Thomas Alexander *physician, urology educator*
Weissman, Irving L. *medical scientist*
†Wilson, John Long *physician*

Sylmar
Corry, Dalila Boudjellal *internist*
Munro, Malcolm Gordon *obstetrician, gynecologist, educator*
Shaw, Anthony *physician, pediatric surgeon*
Tully, Susan Balsley *pediatrician, educator*
Ziment, Irwin *medical educator*

Tarzana
Handelsman, Yehuda *endocrinologist, internal medicine physician*

Tehachapi
Badgley, Theodore McBride *psychiatrist, neurologist*

Temecula
†Overman, John W.J. *physician*

Temple City
Costa, George George (Adel George Costandy) *physician*

Thousand Oaks
Buyalos, Richard Paul, Jr. *physician*
Klein, Jeffrey Howard *oncologist, internist*
Walker, Lorenzo Giles *surgeon, educator*

Torrance
Brasel, Jo Anne *physician*
Emmanouilides, George Christos *physician, educator*
Grollman, Julius Harry, Jr. *cardiovascular and interventional radiologist*
Hammer, Terence Michael *physician*
Hollander, Daniel *gastroenterologist, medical educator*
Itabashi, Hideo Henry *neuropathologist, neurologist*
Krout, Boyd Merrill *psychiatrist*
Mehringer, Charles Mark *medical educator*
Myhre, Byron Arnold *pathologist, educator*
Stabile, Bruce Edward *surgeon*
Tabrisky, Joseph *radiologist, educator*
Tanaka, Kouichi Robert *physician, educator*
†Yu, Kian-Ti Tiu *pediatrician, educator*

Ukiah
McClintock, Richard Polson *dermatologist*

Vallejo
Kleinrock, Robert Allen *physician*

Van Nuys
Fox, James Michael *orthopedic surgeon*

Ventura
Abul-Haj, Suleiman Kahil *pathologist*
Lovell, Frederick Warren *pathologist, medical legal consultant*
Villaveces, James Walter *allergist, immunologist*
Zuber, William Frederick *thoracic and vascular surgeon*

Visalia
Riegel, Byron William *ophthalmologist*

Walnut Creek
Acosta, Julio Bernard *obstetrician, gynecologist*
Bristow, Lonnie Robert *physician*
Kang, Isamu Yong *nuclear medicine physician*
Sheen, Portia Yunn-ling *retired physician*

Watsonville
Alfaro, Felix Benjamin *physician*

Weimar
Ing, Clarence Sinn Fook *preventive medicine physician, ophthalmic surgeon*

West Covina
Pollak, Erich Walter *surgeon, educator*

West Hills
†Davidorf, Jonathan Michael *ophthalmologist*

Westminster
Luong, Khanh Vinh Quoc *nephrologist, researcher*
†Salaymeh, Muhammad Tawfik *surgeon*

Whitley Heights
Lawrence, Sanford Hull *physician, immunochemist*

Whittier
Arcadi, John Albert *urologist*
Briney, Allan King *retired radiologist*
Prickett, David Clinton *physician*
Welsh, William Daniel *family practitioner,*

Woodland Hills
Herdeg, Howard Brian *physician*

Woodside
Blum, Richard Hosmer Adams *educator, writer*
†Miller, John Johnston *pediatric rheumatologist*
Spitzer, Walter Oswald *epidemiologist, educator*

Yuba City
Lefever, Eric Bruce *anesthesiologist*
†Skiles, Margaret S. *plastic surgeon*

COLORADO

Aspen
Oden, Robert Rudolph *surgeon*

Aurora
Battaglia, Frederick Camillo *physician*
Bennion, Scott Desmond *physician*
†Slater, Dick Dale *radiologist*

Basalt
Weill, Hans *physician, educator*

Boulder
Dubin, Mark William *educator, neuroscientist*
Lattes, Raffaele *physician, educator*
Warner, Richard *psychiatrist*

Canon City
Mohr, Gary Alan *physician*

Castle Rock
Thornbury, John Rousseau *radiologist, physician*

Colorado Springs
Anderson, Paul Nathaniel *oncologist, educator*
Lewey, Scot Michael *gastroenterologist*
†Manning, George Weston *psychiatrist*
Sceats, D(onald) James, Jr. *neurological surgeon*
†Speirs, Alfred C. *plastic and reconstructive surgeon*
Todd, Harold Wade *association executive, retired air force officer*
Watz, Hallet N. *emergency physician*

Denver
Adler, Charles Spencer *psychiatrist*
Aikawa, Jerry Kazuo *physician, educator*
Atkins, Dale Morrell *retired physician*
Brantigan, Charles Otto *surgeon*
Briney, Walter George *rheumatologist*
Bunn, Paul A., Jr. *oncologist, educator*
Campbell, David Neil *physician, educator*
Churchill, Mair Elisa Annabelle *medical educator*
Clayton, Mack Louis *surgeon, educator*
Cohn, Aaron I. *anesthesiologist, educator*
Deitrich, Richard Adam *pharmacology educator*
Eickhoff, Theodore Carl *physician*
Fennessey, Paul Vincent *pediatrics and pharmacology, educator, research administrator*
Filley, Christopher Mark *neurologist*
Gabow, Patricia Anne *internist*
Gibbs, Ronald Steven *obstetrician-gynecologist*
Golitz, Loren Eugene *dermatologist, pathologist, clinical administrator, educator*
Green, Larry Alton *physician, educator*
Harken, Alden Hood *surgeon, thoracic surgeon*
Imber, Richard Joseph *physician, dermatologist*
Jafek, Bruce William *otolaryngologist, educator*
Johnson, Candice Elaine Brown *pediatrics educator*
Johnston, Richard Boles, Jr. *pediatrician, educator, biomedical researcher*
Jones, M. Douglas Jr., Jr. *pediatrics educator*
Kauvar, Abraham J. *gastroenterologist, medical administrator*
Kinzie, Jeannie Jones *radiation oncologist, nuclear medicine physician*
Kluck, Clarence Joseph *physician*
Krikos, George Alexander *pathologist, educator*
Krugman, Richard David *physician, university administrator, educator*
Larsen, Gary Loy *physician, researcher*
†Loomis, Lucy Williams *physician*
Martin, Richard Jay *medical educator*
McAtee, Patricia Anne Rooney *medical educator*
Meldrum, Daniel Richard *general surgeon, physician*
Moore, Ernest Eugene, Jr. *surgeon, educator*
Moore, George Eugene *surgeon*
Nelson, Nancy Eleanor *pediatrician, educator*
Nutting, Paul Albert *medical educator, medical science administrator*
Petty, Thomas Lee *physician, educator*
Pomerantz, Marvin *thoracic surgeon*
Rainer, William Gerald *cardiac surgeon*
Repine, John Edward *internist, educator*
†Rosen, Paul R. *physician executive*
Rosenwasser, Lanny Jeffrey *allergist, immunologist*
Ruge, Daniel August *retired neurosurgeon, educator*
Sanders, Richard Jeremiah *vascular surgeon, medical educator*
Schiff, Donald Wilfred *pediatrician, educator*
Schrier, Robert William *physician, educator*
Shimm, David Stuart *oncologist, educator*
Shore, James H(enry) *psychiatrist*
Silverman, Arnold *physician*
Sniadach, Milton Steve, Jr. *anesthesiologist*
Sujansky, Eva Borska *physician, educator*
Szefler, Stanley James *pediatrics and pharmacology educator*
Taylor, Edward Stewart *physician, educator*
†Tyler, Kenneth Laurence *neurologist, researcher*
Washington, Reginald Louis *pediatric cardiologist*
Weatherley-White, Roy Christopher Anthony *surgeon, consultant*
Weston, William Lee *dermatologist*
Wiggs, Eugene Overbey *ophthalmologist, educator*
Woodcock, Jonathan Hugh *neurologist*

Dillon
Becker, Quinn Henderson *orthopedic surgeon, army officer*

Durango
Wigton, Chester Mahlon *family physician*

Englewood
Aarestad, Norman O. *oncologist*
Kelsall, David Charles *otologist*
†McCrary, Brian Fountain *physician*

Fort Collins
Gillette, Edward LeRoy *radiation oncology educator*

Fort Garland
Leighninger, David Scott *cardiovascular surgeon*

Fort Morgan
Gibbs, Denis Laurel *radiologist*

Golden
Tegtmeier, Ronald Eugene *physician, surgeon*

Greenwood Village
Arenberg, Irving Kaufman Karchmer *ear surgeon, educator, entrepeneur*

Highlands Ranch
Bublitz, Deborah Keirstead *pediatrician*

Lakewood
Bettinghaus, Erwin Paul *cancer research center administrator*
Karlin, Joel Marvin *allergist*

Littleton
Bachman, David Christian *orthopedic surgeon*
Forstot, Stephan Lance *ophthalmologist*

Pueblo
Lewallen, William Marvin, Jr. *ophthalmologist*
Mou, Thomas William *physician, medical educator and consultant*

Vail
Bevan, William Arnold, Jr. *emergency physician*
†McFadden, Joseph Tedford *retired neurosurgeon, writer*

Westminster
Liard, Jean-Francois *cardiovascular physiologist, researcher, educator*

Wheat Ridge
Brown, Steven Brien *radiologist*
Hashimoto, Christine L. *physician*

CONNECTICUT

Ansonia
Dvoretzky, Israel *dermatologist*
Yale, Jeffrey Franklin *podiatrist*

Bloomfield
Wetstone, Howard Jerome *physician, administrator*

Branford
Vietzke, Wesley Maunder *internist, educator*

Bridgeport
†Mijensohn, Daniel E. *neurosurgeon*
Skowron, Tadeusz Adam *physician*

Cos Cob
Duncalf, Deryck *retired anesthesiologist*

Cromwell
Trowbridge, Phillip Edmund *surgeon, educator*

Danbury
Edmunds, Robert Thomas *retired surgeon*
Kurien, Santha T. *psychiatrist*
†Walker, Michael James *surgeon*
Zirn, Jonathan Russell *dermatologist, dermatopathologist*

East Haven
Conn, Harold O. *physician, educator*

Easton
Pendagast, Edward Leslie Jr. *physician*

Essex
Burris, Harriet Louise *emergency physician*
Goff, Christopher Wallick *pediatrician*

Fairfield
Burd, Robert Meyer *hematologist, oncologist, educator*
Rosenman, Stephen David *obstetrician and gynecologist*

Farmington
Besdine, Richard William *medical educator, scientist*
Cooperstein, Sherwin Jerome *medical educator*
Donaldson, James Oswell, III *neurology educator*
Gossling, Harry Robert *orthopaedic surgeon, educator*
Grunnet, Margaret Louise *pathology educator*
Hinz, Carl Frederick, Jr. *physician, educator*
Katz, Arnold Martin *medical educator*
†Lasser, Jay Andrew *psychiatrist*
Liebowitz, Neil Robert *psychiatrist*
Massey, Robert Unruh *physician, university dean*
Raisz, Lawrence Gideon *medical educator, consultant*
Rothfield, Naomi Fox *physician*
Schenkman, John Boris *pharmacologist, educator*
Testa, John Anthony *medical researcher, consultant*
Walker, James Elliot Cabot *physician*

Glastonbury
Juda, Richard John *anesthesiologist*
Singer, Paul Richard *ophthalmologist*

Greenwich
Blumberg, Joel Myron *cardiologist*
†Camel, Mark Howard *neurological surgeon*
Gordon, Neil Alan *facial plastic surgeon*
Hart, Sidney *physician*
Kopenhaver, Patricia Ellsworth *podiatrist*
Scarpa, Frank Joseph *surgeon*

Groton
Harrigan, Edmund Patrick *physician, researcher*
Holt, Edward Thomas Robert *retired physician*

Guilford
Springgate, Clark Franklin *physician, researcher*

Hamden
Nuland, Sherwin *surgeon, author*

Hartford
Blair, Charles Lee *physician*
Brauer, Rima Lois *psychiatrist*
†Duffy, James Desmond *neopsychiatrist, palliative care physician*
Dworkin, Paul Howard *pediatrician*
Gibbons, John Martin, Jr. *physician, educator*
Gillam, Linda Dawn *cardiologist, researcher*
Humphrey, Chester Bowden *cardio-thoracic surgeon*
Jagjivan, Bipin *radiologist*
Jung, Betty Chin *health program associate, epidemiologist, educator*
Kang, Juliana Haeng-Cha *anesthesiologist*
†Kaplan, Bruce Michael *oncologist*
Kirton, Orlando Cecilio *surgeon, educator*
Mayer, Allan Reed *osteopath, gynecologic oncologist*
Powers, Robert David *physician*
Robinson, Kenneth John *emergency medicine physician*
Sanders, William Michael *emergency physician*
†Schreiber, Jonathan Scot *plastic and reconstructive surgeon*
Silver, Herbert *physician*
†Viets, Douglas Hartley *surgeon*
Welch, John Paton *surgeon, educator*

Lyme
Bloom, Barry Malcolm *pharmaceutical consultant*

Madison
Langdon, Robert Colin *dermatologist, educator*
Snell, Richard Saxon *anatomist*

Manchester
†Jacobson, Charles Edward, Jr. *urologist*

Meriden
Giosa, Richard Peter *pulmonary medicine physician*
Horton, Paul Chester *psychiatrist*

Middlebury
Arnold, William Parsons, Jr. *retired internist*

Middletown
Narad, Joan Stern *psychiatrist*
Osborne, Raymond Lester, Jr. *radiologist*

Milford
Fischer, David Seymour *internist, consultant*

New Haven
Aghajanian, George Kevork *medical educator*
†Ariyan, Stephen *surgeon*
†Arons, Marvin Shield *plastic and hand surgeon*
Askenase, Philip William *medicine and pathology educator*
Barash, Paul George *anesthesiologist, educator*
Beardsley, G(eorge) Peter *pediatric oncologist, biochemical pharmacologist*
Behrman, Harold Richard *endocrinologist, physiologist, educator*
Berliner, Robert William *physician, medical educator*
Bolognia, Jean Lynn *academic dermatologist*
Boyer, James Lorenzen *physician, educator*
Braverman, Irwin Merton *dermatologist, educator*
Brown, Thomas Huntington *neuroscientist*
Bunney, Benjamin Stephenson *psychiatrist*
Burrow, Gerard Noel *physician, educator*
Byck, Robert Samuel *psychiatrist, educator*
Cohen, Donald Jay *pediatrics, psychiatry and psychology educator, administrator*
Cohen, Lawrence Sorel *physician, educator*
Collins, William F., Jr. *neurosurgery educator*
Comer, James Pierpont *psychiatrist, educator*
Cooney, Leo Mathias, Jr. *geriatrician, educator*
Cooper, Dennis Lawrence *oncologist, educator*
Cooper, Jack Ross *pharmacology educator, researcher*
Davey, Lycurgus Michael *neurosurgeon*
Donaldson, Robert Macartney, Jr. *physician*
Edelson, Marshall *psychiatry educator, psychoanalyst*
Feinstein, Alvan Richard *physician, educator*
Ferholt, J. Deborah Lott *pediatrician*
Fikrig, Erol *rheumatologist, medical educator*
Fleck, Stephen *psychiatrist*
Freedman, Gerald Stanley *radiologist, healthcare administrator, educator*
Friedlaender, Gary Elliott *orthopedist, educator*
Genel, Myron *pediatrician, educator*
Glaser, Gilbert Herbert *neuroscientist, physician, educator*
Goldman-Rakic, Patricia Shoer *neuroscience educator*
Goodrich, Isaac *neurosurgeon, educator*
Gross, Ian *academic pediatrician, neonatologist*
Haddad, Gabriel G. *physician, pediatrics educator*
Heninger, George Robert *psychiatry educator, researcher*
Herbert, Peter Noel *physician, medical educator*
Hines, Roberta Leigh *medical educator*
Hoffer, Paul B. *nuclear medicine physician, educator*
Horstmann, Dorothy Millicent *retired physician, educator*
Igarashi, Peter *nephrologist, educator, researcher*
Jackson, Stanley Webber *psychiatrist, medical historian*
Jacoby, Robert Ottinger *comparative medicine educator*
Jatlow, Peter I. *pathologist, medical educator, researcher*
Kashgarian, Michael *pathologist, physician*
Katz, Jay *psychiatry and law educator*
Kirchner, John Albert *retired otolaryngology educator*
Kleinman, Charles Stephan *physician, medical educator*
Kushlan, Samuel Daniel *physician, educator, hospital administrator*

Leffell, David Joel surgeon, medical administrator, dermatologist, educator, researcher
Lentz, Thomas Lawrence biomedical educator, dean, researcher
Levine, Robert John physician, educator
Lewis, Melvin psychiatrist, pediatrician, psychoanalyst
Mark, Harry Horst ophthalmologist, researcher
McCarthy, Paul Louis pediatrics educator
McGoldrick, Kathryn Elizabeth anesthesiologist, educator, writer
Mermann, Alan Cameron pediatrics educator, chaplain
Merrell, Ronald Clifton surgeon, educator
Merritt, John Augustus geriatrician, educator
Musto, David Franklin physician, educator, historian, consultant
Naftolin, Frederick physician, reproductive biologist educator
Newman, Harry Rudolph urologist, educator
Niederman, James Corson physician, educator
Ostfeld, Adrian Michael physician
Pruett, Kyle Dean psychiatrist, writer, educator, musician
Prusoff, William Herman biochemical pharmacologist, educator
Rakic, Pasko neuroscientist, educator
Redmond, Donald Eugene, Jr. neuroscientist, educator
Reiser, Morton Francis psychiatrist, educator
Ritchie, J. Murdoch pharmacologist, educator
Sartorelli, Alan Clayton pharmacology educator
Sasaki, Clarence Takashi surgeon, medical educator
Schowalter, John Erwin child and adolescent psychiatry educator
Schriver, John Allen emergency medicine physician
Schwartz, Peter Edward physician, gynecologic oncology educator
Seashore, Margretta Reed physician
Seigel, Arthur Michael neurologist, educator
Shulman, Gerald I. clinical investigator
Siegel, Norman Joseph pediatrician, educator
Silver, George Albert physician, educator
Silverstone, David Edward ophthalmologist
Smith, Brian Richard hematologist, oncologist, pathologist
Solnit, Albert Jay physician, commissioner, educator
Spiro, Howard Marget physician, educator
Stern, Robert psychiatrist
Tamborlane, William V., Jr. physician, biomedical researcher, pediatrics educator
Taylor, Hugh Smith physician, researcher
Taylor, Kenneth J. diagnostic sonologist
Thome, Johannes Ulrich Vinzenz psychiatrist researcher
Warshaw, Joseph Bennett pediatrician, educator
Waxman, Stephen George neurologist, neuroscientist
Wedgwood, Josiah Francis pediatrician, immunologist
Wright, Hastings Kemper surgeon, educator
Zaret, Barry Lewis cardiologist, medical educator

New London
Schoenberger, Steven Harris physician, research consultant
Urbanetti, John Sutherland internist, consultant

North Haven
McCarthy, Charles Patrick Noel physician

Norwalk
Dakofsky, LaDonna Jung radiation oncologist, educator
Floch, Martin Herbert physician
Greenberg, Sheldon Burt plastic and reconstructive surgeon
Huskins, Dennis G. internist
Reder, Robert Frank physician
Tracey, Edward John physician, surgeon
Vris, Thomas W. surgeon

Old Lyme
Cook, Charles Davenport pediatrician, educator

Old Saybrook
Peszke, Michael Alfred psychiatrist, educator

Orange
Fasanella, Rocko Michael ophthalmologist

Ridgefield
Byrne, Daniel William biomedical research consultant, biostatistician, computer specialist, educator
Colen, Helen Sass plastic surgeon
Sobol, Bruce J. internist, educator, researcher

Sharon
Gottlieb, Richard Matthew psychiatrist, consultant

Simsbury
Roman, Robin anesthesiologist

Stamford
Cook, Colin Burford psychiatrist
Gagnon, Monique Francine pediatrician
Goodhue, Peter Ames obstetrician and gynecologist, educator
Gromults, Joseph Michael, Jr. internist
Klein, Neil Charles physician
Klenk, Rosemary Ellen pediatrician
Shapiro, Bruce psychiatrist
Walsh, Thomas Joseph neuro-ophthalmologist
†Waxberg, Jonathan Abel urologic surgeon, oncologist

Storrs Mansfield
Skauen, Donald Matthew retired pharmaceutical educator

Stratford
Feinberg, Dennis Lowell dermatologist
Russell, Cynthia Pincus social worker, educator

Vernon Rockville
Brooks, Neil H. physician
Marmer, Ellen Lucille pediatric cardiologist

Wallingford
Dunkle, Lisa Marie clinical research executive
Kaplan, Harold Paul physician, health science facility administrator

Waterbury
Dudrick, Stanley John surgeon, scientist, educator
†Eisen, Steven Leslie neurologist
Ostrov, Melvyn R. physician
Peterson, W(alter) Scott ophthalmic surgeon
Sherwood, James Alan physician, scientist, educator

West Haven
Ezekowitz, Michael David physician
Perlmutter, Lynn Susan neuroscientist

West Simsbury
Morest, Donald Kent neuroscientist, educator

Westport
Burns, John Joseph pharmacology educator
Clausman, Gilbert Joseph medical librarian
Densen-Gerber, Judianne psychiatrist, lawyer, educator
Lopker, Anita Mae psychiatrist
Meinke, Alan Kurt surgeon
Sacks, Herbert Simeon psychiatrist, educator, consultant

Woodbridge
Bondy, Philip Kramer physician, educator

DELAWARE

Claymont
†Morra, Daniel Rocco physician

Dover
Wilson, Samuel Mayhew surgeon

Lewes
Adams, John Pletch orthopaedic surgeon

Milford
Trott, Edward Ashley reproductive endocrinologist

Newark
†Desi, Laurence physician
Lemole, Gerald Michael surgeon

Rockland
Levinson, John Milton obstetrician, gynecologist

Wilmington
Athreya, Balu H. pediatrics educator
Benes, Solomon biomedical scientist, physician
Cornelison, Floyd Shovington, Jr. retired psychiatrist, former educator
Frelick, Robert Westcott physician
Goldberg, Morton Edward pharmacologist
Harley, Robison Dooling physician, educator
Ikeda, Satoshi thoracic and cardiovascular surgeon
Inselman, Laura Sue pediatrician
Kaye, Neil Scott psychiatrist
Kerr, Janet Spence physiologist, pharmacologist
Morgan, Craig Douglas orthopaedic surgeon
Nelson, Dewey Allen neurologist, educator
Pell, Sidney epidemiologist
Schwartz, Marshall Zane pediatric surgeon
Smith, S(tewart) Gregory ophthalmologist, inventor, product developer, consultant, author
Stein, Robert Benjamin biomedical researcher, physician
Wallace, Jesse Wyatt pharmaceutical scientist

DISTRICT OF COLUMBIA

Washington
Akhter, Mohammad Nasir physician, government public health administrator
Anthony, Virginia Quinn Bausch medical association executive
Apud, Jose Antonio psychiatrist, psychopharmacologist, educator
Arling, Bryan Jeremy internist
Armaly, Mansour F(arid) ophthalmologist, educator
Bachman, David M. ophthalmologist
Bachman, Leonard physician, retired federal official
Banta, James Elmer physician, epidemiologist, university dean
Beard, Lillian B. McLean physician, consultant
Belman, A. Barry pediatric urologist
Berger, Robert Martin urologist
Bernstein, Lionel M. gastroenterologist, educator
Borenstein, David Gilbert physician, author
Bourne, Peter Geoffrey physician, educator, author
Bryant, Thomas Edward physician, lawyer
Burris, Boyd Lee psychiatrist, psychoanalyst, physician, educator
Buss, Patricia Arnold plastic surgeon
Callaway, Clifford Wayne physician
Callender, Clive Orville surgeon
Catoe, Bette Lorrina physician, health educator
Cheng, Tsung O. cardiologist, educator
Chiapella, Anne Page epidemiologist
Cohen, Jordan Jay medical association executive
Collins, Robert Ellwood surgeon
Curfman, David Ralph neurological surgeon, musician
Davidson, Richard J. medical association administrator
Davis, David Oliver radiologist, educator
Dawson, Nancy Ann hematologist, oncologist
Dell, Ralph Bishop pediatrician, researcher
Dennis, Gary C. neurosurgeon, educator
Deutsch, Stanley anesthesiologist, educator
Dey, Radheshyam Chandra cytologist
Didisheim, Paul internist, hematologist
†Drakes, Duan Anthony surgeon
Dublin, Thomas David retired physician
Duvall, Charles Patton internist, oncologist
Dym, Martin medical educator
Earll, Jerry Miller internist, educator
Edwards, Maureen Crittenden neonatologist, educator
Ein, Daniel allergist
Elgart, Mervyn L. dermatologist, educator
Epps, Charles Harry, Jr. orthopaedic surgery educator
Epps, Roselyn Elizabeth Payne pediatrician, educator
Etzel, Ruth Ann pediatrician, epidemiologist
Evans, Charles Hawes, Jr. immunologist, health science administrator
Fairbanks, David Nathaniel Fox physician, surgeon, educator
Feldman, Bruce Allen otolaryngologist
Finkelstein, James David physician
Fromm, Hans gastroenterologist, educator, researcher
Galson, Steven Kenneth preventive medicine specialist
Gelmann, Edward Paul oncologist, educator
Gilbert, Charles Richard Alsop physician, medical educator
Goldson, Alfred Lloyd oncologist, educator
Goodwin, Frederick King psychiatrist
Gordon, James Samuel psychiatrist
Gray, Sheila Hafter psychiatrist, psychoanalyst
Griner, Paul Francis physician
Grossman, John Henry, III obstetrician, gynecologist, educator
Grundfast, Kenneth Martin otolaryngologist
Hark, William Henry medical executive, retired military officer
Harvey, John Collins physician, educator
Henry, James M. physician, neuropathologist
Holden, Raymond Thomas physician, educator
Hollinshead, Ariel Cahill research oncologist, educator
Hussain, Syed Taseer biomedical educator, researcher
Jani, Sushma Niranjan pediatrics and child and adolescent psychiatrist
Johnston, Gerald Samuel physician, educator
†Kak, Neeraj public health specialist
Kant, Gloria Jean neuroscientist, researcher
†Kaplan, Keith Jacob physician
Karcher, Donald Steven medical educator
Kizer, Kenneth Wayne physician, educator, administrator
Koering, Marilyn Jean anatomy educator, researcher
Korn, David educator, pathologist
Kung, David Shean-Guang plastic surgeon
Kurtzke, John Francis, Sr. neurologist, epidemiologist
Leffall, LaSalle D(oheny), Jr. surgeon
Lessin, Lawrence Stephen hematologist, oncologist, educator
Ling, Geoffrey Shiu Fei neurologist, pharmacologist, educator
Little, John William plastic surgeon, educator
Luessenhop, Alfred John neurosurgeon, educator
Luhrs, Caro Elise internal medicine physician, administrator, educator
Lynn, D. Joanne physician, ethicist, health services researcher
Mann, Marion physician, educator
Martuza, Robert L. neurosurgeon
McGinnis, James Michael physician
McGrath, Mary Helena plastic surgeon, educator
Meekers, Dominique Armand health and demographics researcher
Meyerhoff, James Lester medical researcher
Mrazek, David Allen pediatric psychiatrist
Murray, Robert Fulton, Jr. physician
Nelson, Alan Ray internist, medical assocation executive
Neviaser, Robert Jon orthopaedic surgeon, educator
Newman, Kurt Douglas pediatric surgeon
Novitch, Mark physician, educator, retired pharmaceutical executive
Nowak, Judith Ann psychiatrist
Oertel, Yolanda Castillo pathologist, educator, diagnostician
Paulson, Jerome Avrom pediatrician
Pawlson, Leonard Gregory physician
Pearse, Warren Harland obstetrician and gynecologist, association executive
Pellegrino, Edmund Daniel physician, educator, former university president
Pincus, Jonathan Henry neurologist, educator
Pollack, Murray Michael physician, medical services administrator
Potter, John Francis surgical oncologist, educator
Rall, David Platt pharmacologist, environmentalist
Reaman, Gregory Harold pediatric hematologist, oncologist
Redman, Robert Shelton pathologist, dentist
Robertson, William Wright, Jr. orthopedic surgeon educator
Robinowitz, Carolyn Bauer psychiatrist, educator
Rodriguez, William Julio physician
Ross, Allan Michael physician, medical educator
Ruckman, Roger Norris pediatric cardiologist
Ruehle, Charles Joseph pathologist, military officer
†Rushton, H. Gil pediatrician, urologist, educator
Sabshin, Melvin psychiatrist, educator, medical association administrator
Sanchez, Jose Luis, Jr. physician researcher, army officer
Sandler, Sumner Gerald medical educator
Schechter, Geraldine Poppa hematologist
Seneff, Michael Geren critical care physician
Shanahan, Sheila Ann pediatrician, educator
Shine, Kenneth Irwin cardiologist, educator
Shrier, Diane Kesler psychiatrist
Sidransky, Herschel pathologist
†Silverman, Harold M. pharmacologist, healthcare executive, educator
Simon, Gary Leonard internist, educator
Sly, Ridge Michael physician, educator
Smith, Lee Elton surgery educator, retired military officer
Spagnolo, Samuel Vincent internist, pulmonary specialist, educator
Steel, R. Knight geriatrician, educator
Steinberg, Paul Jay psychiatrist
Stephenson, Patricia Ann public health researcher, educator
Tosi, Laura Lowe orthopaedic surgeon
Vittone, Bernard John psychiatrist, researcher
Warchol, Richard James physician
Wartofsky, Leonard medical educator
Webster, Thomas Glenn psychiatrist
Weingold, Allan B. obstetrician, gynecologist, educator
†Welch, Laura Stewart physician, internist
Werkman, Sidney Lee psychiatry educator
White, Martha Vetter allergy and immunology physician, researcher
Wiener, Jerry M. psychiatrist
Willis, Arnold Jay urologic surgeon, educator
Woosley, Raymond pharmacology and medical educator
Worth, Melvin H. surgeon, educator
Young, Donald Alan physician
Zukowska-Grojec, Zofia Maria cardiovascular physiologist, educator

FLORIDA

Altamonte Springs
Siddiqui, Farooq Ahmad protein biochemist
†Woods, Abraham Lincoln, III urologist

Anna Maria
Dielman, Ray Walter radiologic scientist, clinical herbalist

Atlantic Beach
Walker, Richard Harold pathologist, educator

Atlantis
Stone, Ross Gluck orthopaedic surgeon

Bay Pines
Johnson, David Porter infectious diseases physician
Keskiner, Ali psychiatrist
Law, David Hillis physician
Stewart, Jonathan Taylor psychiatrist, educator

Belleair
Lasley, Charles Haden cardiovascular surgeon, health and fitness consultant

Boca Raton
Cohn, Jess Victor psychiatrist
Friend, Harold Charles neurologist
Gagliardi, Raymond Alfred physician
†Keusch, Cristina Frexes plastic surgeon
Kramer, Cecile E. retired medical librarian
Levenson, David Irwin endocrinologist
Levine, Richard A. physician
Stein, Irvin orthopedic surgeon, educator
†Weiner, Howard Marc physician
Zaleznak, Bernard D. physician
Zuckerman, Sidney retired allergist, immunologist

Boynton Beach
Glickman, Franklin Sheldon dermatologist, educator
Pataky, Paul Eric ophthalmologist
†Rosenstein, David Alan plastic surgeon
Srinath, Latha physician

Bradenton
Mandell, Marshall physician, allergist, consultant
Sprenger, Thomas Robert retired orthopedic surgeon

Brandon
Lafferty, Beverly Lou Brookover retired physician, consultant

Cape Coral
Martin, Benjamin Gaufman ophthalmologist

Casselberry
Pollack, Robert William psychiatrist

Clearwater
†Brown, Richard Christopher epidemiologist
Horowitz, Harry I. podiatrist
Lokys, Linda J. dermatologist
McAllister, Charles John nephrologist, medical administrator
Rinde, John Jacques internist

Coral Gables
Dunn, Charles Anthony family physician
Perez, Josephine psychiatrist, educator
Quillian, Warren Wilson, II pediatrician, educator
Suarez, George Michael urologist
Wolf, Aizik Loft neurosurgeon

Coral Springs
†Dajani, Badr Mustafa neurologist
Swiller, Randolph Jacob internist
†Yalamanchi, Bose surgeon

Dade City
Feld, Harvey Joel pathologist

Daytona Beach
Di Nicolo, Roberto allergist
Goldberg, Paul Bernard gastroenterologist, clinical researcher

Delray Beach
Rosenfeld, Steven Ira ophthalmologist

Dunedin
Gambone, Victor Emmanuel, Jr. internist

Fernandina Beach
Barlow, Anne Louise pediatrician, medical research administrator

Fort Lauderdale
†Catinella, Frank Peter cardiovascular and thoracic surgeon
Cox, Linda Susan allergist, immunologist
Enriquez, Cristino Catud radiologist, internist, cardiologist
Galvez-Jimenez, Nestor neurologist
Lodwick, Gwilym Savage radiologist, educator
Mannino, Robert medical educator
Rendon-Pellerano, Marta Ines dermatologist
†Salanga, Virgilio Dizon neurologist, educator
Whitmore, Douglas Michael physician
†Zlatkin, Michael Brian physician

Fort Myers
Arnall, Robert Esric physician, medical administrator
†Demers, Nora Egan immunologist, biologist, educator
†Pascotto, Robert Daniel cardiovascular/thoracic surgeon
Simmons, Vaughan Pippen medical consultant
Steier, Michael Edward cardiac surgeon

Fort Pierce
Partenheimer, Robert Chapin emergency physician

Fort Walton Beach
†Muehlberger, Gerald L. physician

Gainesville
Anderson, Richard McLemore internist

Berns, Kenneth Ira *physician*
Cluff, Leighton Eggertsen *physician*
Copeland, Edward Meadors, III *surgery educator*
Gravenstein, Joachim Stefan *anesthesiologist, educator*
Greer, Melvin *medical educator*
Iasemidis, Leonidas D. *neuroscience educator*
Lampotang, Samsun *medical educator*
Limacher, Marian Cecile *cardiologist*
Mahla, Michael E. *anesthesiologist, educator*
†Maria, Bernard L. *pediatric neurologist*
Modell, Jerome Herbert *anesthesiologist, educator*
Neiberger, Richard Eugene *pediatrician, nephrologist, educator*
Palovcik, Reinhard Anton *research neurophysiologist*
Pfaff, William Wallace *medical educator*
Reynolds, Richard Clyde *physician, educator*
Rhoton, Albert Loren, Jr. *neurological surgery educator*
Rosenbloom, Arlan Lee *physician, educator*
Rubin, Melvin Lynne *ophthalmologist, educator*
Schiebler, Gerold Ludwig *physician, educator*
Small, Parker Adams, Jr. *pediatrician, educator*
Suzuki, Howard Kazuro *retired anatomist, educator*
Talbert, James Lewis *pediatric surgeon, educator*
Taylor, William Jape *physician*
Walker, Robert Dixon, III *surgeon, urologist, educator*

Hallandale
Haspel, Arthur Carl *podiatrist, surgeon*

Hialeah
Economides, Christopher George *pathologist*
Koreman, Dorothy Goldstein *physician, dermatologist*

Hollywood
†Carter, Richard Leland *neurosurgeon*
Duffner, Lee R. *ophthalmologist*
†Perryman, Richard Allan *cardiac surgeon*

Inverness
Esquibel, Edward V. *psychiatrist, clinical medical program developer*

Jacksonville
Agnew, Samuel Gerard *orthopaedic traumatologist*
Boylan, Kevin Bernard *neurologist*
†Brott, Thomas Gordon *neurologist*
Carithers, Hugh Alfred *physician, retired*
Dorsher, Peter T. *physician*
Feinglass, Neil Gordon *anesthesiologist*
†Goldman, Stephen Lewis *occupational physician*
Groom, Dale *physician, educator*
Hecht, Frederick *physician, researcher, author, educator, consultant*
Huddleston, John Franklin *obstetrics and gynecology educator*
Johnson, Douglas William *physician, radiologist, oncologist*
Kelalis, Panayotis *pediatric urologist*
Lewis, Richard Harlow *urologist*
Lipkovic, Peter *chief medical examiner*
Mass, M. F. *allergist, immunologist*
Mizrahi, Edward Alan *allergist*
Paryani, Shyam Bhojraj *radiologist*
Rice, James Philip *surgeon*
Siegel, Steven Douglas *oncologist*
Simpson, Charles Eugene *physician, military officer*
Stephenson, Samuel Edward, Jr. *retired physician*
Thorsteinsson, Gudni *physiatrist*
Toker, Karen Harkavy *physician*
Wallizada, Wassy A. *physician*

Kennedy Space Center
†Darwood, John Joseph *physician*
†Myers, Kenneth Jeffrey *physician*

Key Biscayne
Palmer, Roger Farley *pharmacology educator*

Key Largo
Manning, John Warren, III *retired surgeon, medical educator*

Lakeland
Fessenden, Stephen Francis *anesthesiologist*
†Moore, Wistar *cardiovascular surgeon*
Schreiber, Fred James, III *oncologist, hematologist*
Spoto, Angelo Peter, Jr. *internist, allergist*

Largo
Brown, Warren Joseph *physician*
Grove, Jeffrey Scott *family practice physician*

Longboat Key
Cummings, Martin Marc *medical educator, physician, scientific administrator*
Kabara, Jon Joseph *biochemical pharmacology educator*

Longwood
†Jankauskas, Saulius Jurgis *plastic surgeon*

Madeira Beach
†Medins, Gunars *surgeon*

Margate
Ory, Steven Jay *physician, educator*

Melbourne
MacDonald, Stephen Hugh *physician, reserve naval officer*

Miami
Alvarez, Raul Alberto *internist*
Anderson, Douglas Richard *ophthalmologist, educator, scientist, researcher*
Beck, Morris *allergist*
Bolooki, Hooshang *cardiac surgeon*
Borstelmann, Stephen Matthew *radiologist*
Cagen, Edward Leslie *surgeon, physician*
Casariego, Jorge Isaac *psychiatrist, psychoanalyst, educator*
Cassel, John Michael *plastic surgeon*
Cassileth, Peter Anthony *internist*
Cohen, Sanford Irwin *physician, educator*
†Concha, Mauricio *epidemiologist, educator, neurologist*
Davis, Richard Edmund *facial plastic surgeon*
Dean, Stanley Rochelle *psychiatrist*

Eaglstein, William Howard *dermatologist, educator*
Eftekhari, Nasser *physiatrist*
Eisdorfer, Carl *psychiatrist, health care executive*
Engle, Mary Allen English *physician*
Engle, Ralph Landis, Jr. *internist, educator*
Freshwater, Michael Felix *surgeon, educator*
Furst, Alex Julian *thoracic and cardiovascular surgeon*
Ganz, William Israel *radiology educator, medical director, researcher*
Gaylis, Norman Brian *internist, rheumatologist, educator*
Gelband, Henry *pediatric cardiologist*
Ginsberg, Myron David *neurologist*
Gittelson, George *physician*
Goldstein, Burton Jack *psychiatrist*
Goodnick, Paul Joel *psychiatrist*
†Goodwin, Jarrad *otolaryngologist, educator*
Hicks, Dorothy Jane *obstetrician and gynecologist, educator*
Howell, Ralph Rodney *pediatrician, educator, geneticist*
Karl, Robert Harry *cardiologist*
Kim, James Jupyung *surgeon, orthopedist, medical educator*
†Kitsos, Constantine Nicholas *plastic surgeon*
Koller, William Carl *neurology educator*
Lasseter, Kenneth Carlyle *pharmacologist*
Layton, Robert Glenn *radiologist*
Lemberg, Louis *cardiologist, educator*
Malinin, Theodore *medical educator, researcher*
Martinez, Luis Osvaldo *radiologist, educator*
Mc Kenzie, John Maxwell *physician*
Mintz, Daniel Harvey *diabetologist, educator, academic administrator*
Page, Larry Keith *neurosurgeon, educator*
Papper, Emanuel Martin *anesthesiologist*
Parrish, Richard Kenneth, II *medical educator*
Patarca, Roberto *immunologist, molecular biologist, physician*
Pham, Si Mai *cadiothoracic surgeon, medical educator*
Potter, James Douglas *pharmacology educator*
Raines, Jeff *biomedical scientist, medical research director*
Sackner, Marvin Arthur *physician*
Scerpella, Ernesto Guillermo *physician researcher*
Scheinberg, Peritz *neurologist*
Schiff, Eugene Roger *medical educator, hepatologist*
†Serure, Alan *plastic and reconstructive surgeon*
†Shebert, Robert T. *neurologist, pathologist*
Smith, Stanley Bertram *clinical pathologist, allergist, immunologist, anatomic pathologist*
Sugarbaker, Everett Van Dyke *surgical oncologist*
Sussex, James Neil *psychiatrist, educator*
Tejada, Francisco *physician, educator*
Temple, Jack Donald, Jr. *physician, medical educator*
Wheeler, Steve Dereal *neurologist*
Wolff, Grace Susan *pediatrician*
Zand, Lloyd Craig *radiologist*
Zwerling, Leonard Joseph *physician, educator*

Miami Beach
Barroso, Eduardo Guillermo *surgeon, educator*
Carmichael, Lynn Paul *family practice physician*
Krieger, Bruce Phillip *medical educator*
Lazović, Gavrilo *internist*
Lehrman, David *orthopedic surgeon*
†Makovsky, Randy D. *urologist*
Mandri, Daniel Francisco *psychiatrist*
Maulion, Richard Peter *psychiatrist*
Nixon, Daniel David. *physician*
Ratzan, Kenneth Roy *physician*
Sayfie, Eugene Joe *cardiologist, internist, educator*
Tiller, J. Howell *physician*

Miami Lakes
Rodriguez, Manuel Alvarez *pathologist*

Miramar
Militello, Lawrence *nursing home adminstrator*

Morriston
Adams, Kelly Lynn *emergency physician*

Naples
Barter, Robert Henry *physician, retired educator*
Brooks, Joae Graham *psychiatrist*
†Carneiro, Ronaldo Dos Santos *surgeon*
Gaskins, William Darrell *ophthalmologist*
Grove, William Johnson *physician, surgery educator*
Kempers, Roger Dyke *obstetrics and gynecology educator*
†Kibria, Eshan *neurologist, engineer*

New Port Richey
Hauber, Frederick August *ophthalmologist*
Hu, Chen-Sien *surgeon*

North Palm Beach
Stein, Mark Rodger *allergist*

Ocala
Altenburger, Karl Marion *allergist, immunologist*
Hunter, Oregon K., Jr. *physiatrist*
Pimpinella, Ronald Joseph *retired surgeon*

Oldsmar
Rogers, James Virgil, Jr. *retired radiologist and educator*

Orlando
Hornick, Richard Bernard *physician*
Layish, Daniel T. *internist*
Okun, Neil Jeffrey *vitreoretinal surgeon*
†Ramos Fonseca, Luis A. *neurological surgeon*
Shub, Harvey Allen *surgeon*
Taitt, Earl Paul *psychiatrist, army officer*
†Trumble, Eric R. *pediatric neurosurgeon*
Whitworth, Hall Baker, Jr. *cardiologist*

Ormond Beach
Cromartie, Robert Samuel, III *thoracic surgeon*
Raimondo, Louis John *psychiatrist*

Osprey
Gross, James Dehnert *pathologist*
Lin, Edward Daniel *anesthesiologist, inventor*

Palm Beach
Simon, Harold *radiologist*

Palm Beach Gardens
Shapiro, Steven David *dermatologist*

Palm Harbor
†Ross, Jay Howard *plastic surgeon*
Thomas, Patrick Robert Maxwell *oncology educator, academic administrator*

Panama City
Schuler, Burton Silverman *podiatrist*
Walters, George John *oral and maxillofacial surgeon*

Pembroke Pines
†Robinson, Howard Neil *plastic surgeon*

Pensacola
Andrews, Edson James, Jr. *radiologist*
Dauser, Kimberly Ann *physician assistant*
Dillard, Robert Perkins *pediatrician, educator*
Hanline, Manning Harold *internist*
Love, Robert William, Jr. *retired physician, government administrator*
†Symonds, Ronald Delbert *retired military physician*
Vuksta, Michael Joseph *surgeon*
White, William Clinton *pathologist*

Plantation
Ramos, Manuel Antonio, Jr. *pulmonologist*
Tingley, Floyd Warren *physician*

Pompano Beach
Bliznakov, Emile George *biomedical research scientist*
Miller, A. Edgar, Jr. *dermatologist*

Ponte Vedra Beach
Nadler, Sigmond Harold *physician, surgeon*
ReMine, William Hervey, Jr. *surgeon*
Weinstein, George William *retired ophthalmology educator*

Saint Pete Beach
Bauman, Tatjana *pathologist, consultant*

Saint Petersburg
Bercu, Barry B. *pediatric endocrinologist*
Betzer, Susan Elizabeth Beers *family physician, geriatrician*
Collins, Paul Steven *vascular surgeon*
Donovan, Denis Miller *psychiatrist, author, lecturer*
Good, Robert Alan *physician, educator*
†Hamilton, John McFarland *plastic surgeon, bank director*
Kaiser, Greg Christopher *pediatric gastroenterologist*
†Krause, James R. *urologist*
Linhart, Joseph Wayland *retired cardiologist, educational administrator*
Pardoll, Peter Michael *gastroenterologist*
Root, Allen William *pediatrician, educator*
Rosenblum, Martin Jerome *ophthalmologist*
White, Charles Ronald *psychiatrist*
Williams, Larry Ross *surgeon*

Sanford
Oostwouder, Peter Henry *family physician*

Sarasota
Aull, Susan *physician*
Giordano, David Alfred *internist, gastroenterologist*
†Graham, Braun H. *plastic surgeon*
†Graper, William Peter *cardiac surgeon*
Jelks, Mary Larson *retired pediatrician*
Magenheim, Mark Joseph *physician, epidemiologist, educator*
O'Malley, Thomas Anthony *gastroenterologist, internist*
Schmidt, James Harvey *plastic surgeon*
†Schumacher, James Matthew *neurosurgeon*
Sturtevant, Ruthann Patterson *anatomy educator*
Welch, John Dana *urologist, arts association executive*
Yonker, Richard Aaron *rheumatologist*
†Zentner, Arnold Stuart *psychiatrist*

Seminole
Schwartzberg, Roger Kerry *osteopath, internist*

Stuart
Campazzi, Earl James *physician*
Delagi, Edward Francis *physician, retired educator*
Haserick, John Roger *retired dermatologist*
Patterson, Robert Arthur *physician, health care consultant, retired health care company executive, retired air force officer*

Sun City Center
Crow, Harold Eugene *physician, family medicine educator*

Tallahassee
Conti, Lisa Ann *epidemiologist, veterinarian*
Maguire, Charlotte Edwards *retired physician*

Tampa
Afield, Walter Edward *psychiatrist, service executive*
Barness, Lewis Abraham *physician*
Bedford, Robert Forrest *anesthesiologist*
Behnke, Roy Herbert *physician, educator*
Bowen, Thomas Edwin *cardiothoracic surgeon, retired army officer*
Branch, William Terrell *urologist, educator*
†Brooks, Stuart Merrill *medical educator*
Bukantz, Samuel Charles *physician, educator*
Bunker-Soler, Antonio Luis *physician*
Cavanagh, Denis *physician, educator*
Donelan, Peter Andrew *dermatologist*
Eichberg, Rodolfo David *physician, educator*
Flynn, Michael Patrick *radiologist*
Frias, Jaime Luis *pediatrician, educator*
Gilbert-Barness, Enid F. *pathologist, pathology and pediatrics educator*
Greenfield, George B. *radiologist*
Grendys, Edward Charles *obstetrician-gynecologist, gynecologic oncologist*
Hadden, John Winthrop *immunopharmacology educator*
Hartmann, William Herman *pathologist, educator*
Hillman, James V. *pediatrician*
Holfelder, Lawrence Andrew *pediatrician, allergist*
Hubbell, David Smith *surgeon, educator*
Jacobs, Timothy Andrew *epidemiologist, international health consultant, medical missionary*

Kaufman, Ronald Paul *physician, school official*
Lakdawala, Sharad R. *psychiatrist*
Lockey, Richard Funk *allergist, educator*
Lozner, Eugene Leonard *internal medicine educator, consultant*
Lyman, Gary Herbert *epidemiologist, cancer researcher, educator*
Malone, John I. *pediatrics educator, biomedical researcher*
Muroff, Lawrence Ross *nuclear medicine physician, educator*
Murtagh, Frederick Reed *neuroradiologist, educator*
Nagera, Humberto *psychiatrist, psychoanalyst, educator, author*
Olson, Robert Eugene *physician, biochemist, educator*
Pfeiffer, Eric Armin *psychiatrist, gerontologist*
Pollara, Bernard *immunologist, educator, pediatrician*
Posner, Gary Philip *physician, medical software company executive*
Powers, Pauline Smith *psychiatrist, educator, researcher*
Reading, Anthony John *physician*
Rogal, Philip James *physician*
Rowlands, David Thomas *pathology educator*
†Ruas, Ernesto Jose *plastic surgeon*
†Sanchez-Ramos, Juan R. *physician, medical educator*
Schmidt, Paul Joseph *physician, educator*
Schnitzlein, Harold Norman *anatomy educator*
Schonwetter, Ronald Scott *physician, educator*
†Sergay, Stephen Michael *neurologist*
Sheridan, Richard *neonatologist*
Shons, Alan Rance *plastic surgeon, educator*
Siegel, Richard Lawrence *allergist, immunologist, pediatrician*
Silbiger, Martin L. *radiologist, medical educator, college dean*
Sinnott, John Thomas *internist, educator*
Smith, Mark A. *physician, educator*
Spellacy, William Nelson *obstetrician, gynecologist, educator*
Tatum, William Otis, IV *neurologist*
Theodoropoulos, Demetrios *medical geneticist, allergist*
Trunnell, Thomas Newton *dermatologist*
Walling, Arthur Knight *orthopedist*
Watkins, Joan Marie *osteopath, occupational medicine physician*
Wells, Karen Elaine *plastic surgeon, educator*

Tarpon Springs
Mueller, Willys Francis, Jr. *retired pathologist*

Tequesta
Seaman, William Bernard *physician, radiology educator*

Venice
Freibott, George August *physician, chemist, priest*
Hrachovina, Frederick Vincent *osteopathic physician and surgeon*
†Liang, Daniel S. *surgeon*
†Ross, Robert Roy, Jr. *urologic surgeon*

Vero Beach
Christy, Nicholas Pierson *physician*
Cooke, Robert Edmond *physician, educator, former college president*
Mosier, William Arthur *psychologist, medical educator, medical administrator*
Schulman, Harold *obstetrician, gynecologist, perinatologist*
Schwarz, Berthold Eric *psychiatrist*

Wellington
†Elmquist, John Gunnar *plastic surgeon, general surgeon*
Reddy, Vardhan Jonnala *surgeon*

West Palm Beach
Alea, Jorge Antonio *physician*
Brumback, Clarence Landen *physician*
Craft, Jerome Walter *plastic surgeon, health facility administrator*
Kapnick, S. Jason *oncologist*
Khouri, George George *ophthalmologist*
Mendelow, Gary N. *physician, emergency consultant*
Newmark, Emanuel *ophthalmologist*
Pottash, A. Carter *psychiatrist, hospital executive*
Wisnicki, Jeffrey Leonard *plastic surgeon*

Winter Haven
Honer, Richard Joseph *surgeon*

Winter Park
Pineless, Hal Steven *neurologist*

GEORGIA

Albany
Peach, Paul E. *physician, medical facility administrator*

Atlanta
Alexander, Robert Wayne *medical educator*
Ambrose, Samuel Sheridan, Jr. *urologist*
Bakay, Roy Arpad Earle *neurosurgeon, educator*
Baker, Edward L., Jr. *physician, science facility executive*
Ballard, Wiley Perry III *hematologist, oncologist*
Barnett, Crawford Fannin, Jr. *internist, educator, cardiologist, travel medicine specialist*
†Beegle, Philip H., Jr. *plastic and reconstructive surgeon*
†Blount, Benroe Wayne *physician*
Brandenburg, David Saul *gastroenterologist, educator*
Broome, Claire Veronica *epidemiologist, researcher*
Capone, Antonio *psychiatrist*
Casarella, William Joseph *physician*
Clements, James David *retired psychiatry educator, physician*
Cooper, Gerald Rice *clinical pathologist*
Curran, James W. *epidemiologist, educator, academic administrator*
Davis, Lawrence William *radiation oncologist*
Davis, Michael *medical educator*
Dean, Andrew Griswold *epidemiologist*
Dobes, William Lamar, Jr. *dermatologist*
Dowda, William F. *internist*

Edelhauser, Henry F. physiologist, ophthalmic researcher, educator
Elliott, Lester Franklyn plastic surgeon
Elsas, Louis Jacob, II medical educator
Fleming, Sidney Howell psychiatrist, educator
Foster, Roger Sherman, Jr. surgeon, educator, health facility administrator
Franco, Ramon S. plastic surgeon
Frank, Erica preventive medicine physician
Galambos, John Thomas medical educator, internist
Ganaway, George Kenneth psychiatrist, psychoanalyst
Gayles, Joseph Nathan, Jr. administrator, fund raising consultant
Gaylor, James Leroy biomedical research director
Goldman, John Abner rheumatologist, immunologist, educator
Gonzalez, Emilio Bustamante rheumatologist, educator
Gordon, Frank Jeffrey medical educator
Hall, Wilbur Dallas, Jr. medical educator
Harris, Econ Nigel rheumatologist, internist
†Harris, Mark I. neurologist
Hatcher, Charles Ross, Jr. cardiothoracic surgeon, medical center executive
Heimburger, Elizabeth Morgan psychiatrist
Hogue, Carol Jane Rowland epidemiologist, educator
Horowitz, Ira R. gynecologic oncologist
Hug, Carl Casimir, Jr. pharmacology and anesthesiology educator
Hughes, James Mitchell epidemiologist
Ingram, Roland Harrison, Jr. physician, educator
Israili, Zafar Hasan scientist, clinical pharmacologist, educator
Jackson, Richard Joseph epidemiologist, public health physician, educator
Johns, Michael Marieb Edward otolaryngologist, academic administrator
Jones, Herbert Cornelius, III otolaryngologist
Jones, Mark Mitchell plastic surgeon
Jurkiewicz, Maurice John surgeon, educator
Karp, Herbert Rubin neurologist, educator
King, Frederick Alexander neuroscientist, educator
Klein, Luella Voogd obstetrics-gynecology educator
Kokko, Juha Pekka physician, educator
Koplan, Jeffrey Powell physician
Ku, David Nelson medical educator
Lee, John Everett physician
Lipman, Bernard internist, cardiologist
Lubin, Michael Frederick physician, educator
Lybarger, Jeffrey Allen epidemiology research administrator
McDuffie, Frederic Clement physician
Mitch, William Evans nephrologist
Nemeroff, Charles Barnet neurobiology and psychiatry educator
Neylan, John Francis, III nephrologist, educator
Nichols, Joseph J., Sr. surgeon
O'Brien, Mark Stephen pediatric neurosurgeon
Payne, Nettleton Switzer, II neurosurgeon
Peacock, Lamar Batts retired physician
†Philen, Rossanne McElroy medical epidemiologist
Pratt, Michael Francis physician and surgeon, otolaryngologist
Reed, James Whitfield physician, educator
Rich, Robert Regier immunology educator, physician
Rock, John Aubrey gynecologist and obstetrician, educator
Salomone, Jeffrey Paul surgeon, educator
†Sanders, Keith Alan neurologist
Sexson, William Robert pediatrician, educator
Sherman, Roger Talbot surgeon, educator
Smith, Michael Vincent surgeon
Smith, Robert Boulware, III vascular surgeon, educator
Spangler, Dennis Lee physician
Steinhaus, John Edward physician, medical educator
Thacker, Stephen Brady medical association administrator, epidemiologist
Thomas, Kenneth Eastman cardiothoracic surgeon
Tissue, Mike medical educator, respiratory therapist
Van Assendelft, Onno Willem hematologist
Waters, William Carter, III internist, educator
Wertheim, Steven Blake orthopedist
White, Perry Merrill, Jr. orthopedic surgeon
Willis, Isaac dermatologist, educator
Wilson, Frank Lyndall surgeon
Woodard, John Roger urologist
Yancey, Asa Greenwood, Sr. physician

Augusta
Chandler, Arthur Bleakley pathologist, educator
Cundey, Paul Edward, Jr. cardiologist
Dolen, William Kennedy allergist, immunologist, pediatrician, educator
Gadacz, Thomas Roman surgery educator
Gambrell, Richard Donald, Jr. endocrinologist, educator
Given, Kenna Sidney surgeon, educator
Guill, Margaret Frank pediatrics educator, medical researcher
Hakim, Fares Samih physician
†Hauenstein, Jill Pledger Hodges psychiatrist
Hooks, Vendie Hudson, III surgeon
Loomis, Earl Alfred, Jr. psychiatrist
Loring, David William neuropsychologist, researcher
Luxenberg, Malcolm Neuwahl ophthalmologist, educator
Mahesh,,Virendra Bhushan endocrinologist
Mansberger, Arlie Roland, Jr. surgeon
Meyer, Carol Frances pediatrician, allergist
Miller, Jerry Allan, Jr. pediatrician
†Mode, Donald G. urologist, medical director
Ownby, Dennis Randall pediatrician, allergist, educator, researcher
Pallas, Christopher William cardiologist
Parrish, Robert Alton retired pediatric surgeon, educator
Prisant, L(ouis) Michael cardiologist
Pryor, Carol Graham obstetrician, gynecologist
Rasmussen, Howard medical educator, medical institute executive
Ryan, James Walter physician, medical researcher
Wray, Betty Beasley allergist, immunologist, pediatrician

Austell
Halwig, J. Michael allergist

Buford
Byrd, Larry Donald behavioral pharmacologist

Columbus
Chan, Philip dermatologist, army officer

Decatur
Bain, James Arthur pharmacologist, educator
Brown, W. Virgil internal medicine educator
Hill, Thomas Glenn, III dermatologist
Rausher, David Benjamin internist, gastroenterologist
Whitesides, Thomas Edward, Jr. orthopaedic surgeon

East Point
Cheves, Harry Langdon, Jr. physician

Fort Benning
†Martinez-Lopez, Lester physician, commander

Fort Valley
†Swartwout, Joseph Rodolph obstetrics and gynecology educator, administrator

Gainesville
Turner, John Sidney, Jr. otolaryngologist, educator

Hapeville
†Dhara, Venkata Ramana physician, educator

Lagrange
Copeland, Robert Bodine internist, cardiologist
West, John Thomas retired surgeon

Lawrenceville
Fetner, Robert Henry radiation biologist

Macon
†Mayville, Christina Lynn neurologist
Robinson, Joe Sam neurosurgeon
Skelton, William Douglas physician
Young, Henry E. medical educator

Marietta
Biggs, Barbara Conner internist
Goldberg, Robert Howard forensic pathologist
Hagood, M. Felton surgeon
Holland, Amy Jeanette psychiatrist
Krug, Douglas Edward emergency physician
Wheatley, Joseph Kevin physician, urologist

Martinez
McKenzie, Harry James surgeon, surgical researcher
Xenakis, Stephen Nicholas psychiatrist, army officer

Norcross
Nardelli-Olkowska, Krystyna Maria ophthalmologist, educator

Roswell
Rudert, Cynthia Sue gastroenterologist

Savannah
†Clary, Warren Upton neurosurgeon
†Greco, Richard Jude plastic and reconstructive surgeon
†Hemphill, John Michael neurologist
Horan, Leo Gallaspy physician, educator
Jenkins, Mark Guerry cardiologist
Krahl, Enzo retired surgeon
Ramage, James Everett, Jr. respiratory and critical care physician, educator
Wirth, Fremont Philip, Jr. neurosurgeon, educator
Zoller, Michael otolaryngologist, head and neck surgeon, educator

Snellville
Brueckner, Lawrence Terence orthopedic surgeon

Stockbridge
Friedman, Robert Barry physician

Thomasville
Watt, William Vance surgeon

Tifton
Dorminey, Henry Clayton, Jr. allergist

Valdosta
Sherman, Henry Thomas retired physician

Watkinsville
Johnson, Norman James physician, lawyer, medicological consultant

HAWAII

Ewa Beach
Neudorf, Howard Fred family physician

Honolulu
Brady, Stephen R.P.K. physician
Camara, Jorge de Guzman ophthalmologist, humanitarian, educator
Chesne, Edward Leonard physician
Chock, Clifford Yet-Chong family practice physician
Fitz-Patrick, David endocrinologist, educator
Gallup, James Donald physician
Goldstein, Sir Norman dermatologist
Ho, Reginald Chi Shing medical educator
Kane, Thomas Jay, III orthopaedic surgeon, educator
Lau, H. Lorrin physician, inventor
Lee, Yeu-Tsu Margaret surgeon, educator
Linman, James William retired physician, educator
Meagher, Michael radiologist
Moreno-Cabral, Carlos Eduardo cardiac surgeon
Nelson, Marita Lee anatomist
Oishi, Stephen Masato physician
Pang, Herbert George ophthalmologist
Pien, Francis D. internist, microbiologist
†Popper, Jordan S. physician
Schatz, Irwin Jacob cardiologist
Sharma, Santosh Devraj obstetrician, gynecologist, educator
Shen, Edward Nin-Da cardiologist, educator
†Strode, Walter Sterling urologist
Sugiki, Shigemi ophthalmologist, educator
Terminella, Luigi critical care physician, educator
Vogel, Carl-Wilhelm Ernst biomedical scientist, clinical pathologist
Wallach, Stephen Joseph cardiologist

Kamuela
Mc Dermott, John Francis, Jr. psychiatrist, physician

Mililani
Gardner, Sheryl Paige gynecologist

Waianae
Kakugawa, Terri Etsumi osteopath

Wailuku
Savona, Michael Richard physician

IDAHO

Boise
Benavides, Mary Kathleen anesthesiologist, nutritional consultant
Hoffman, William Kenneth retired obstetrician, gynecologist
Khatain, Kenneth George psychiatrist, former air force officer
Olson, Richard Dean researcher, pharmacology educator

Coeur D Alene
Strimas, John Howard allergist, immunologist, pediatrician
West, Robert Sumner surgeon

Nampa
Botimer, Allen Ray retired surgeon, retirement center owner

Pocatello
Hillyard, Ira William pharmacologist, educator

Sun Valley
†Bieker, Fred William plastic surgeon

Twin Falls
Shuss, John Logan surgeon

ILLINOIS

Abbott Park
Bush, Eugene Nyle pharmacologist, research scientist

Alton
Kisabeth, Tim Charles obstetrician, gynecologist

Arlington Heights
DeDonato, Donald Michael obstetrician/ gynecologist
Lobo, Philip Anthony radiation oncologist
†Placik, Otto Joseph plastic surgeon
Pochyly, Donald Frederick physician, hospital administrator
†Ruder, John Regan physician
Shetty, Mulki Radhakrishna oncologist, consultant

Belleville
Franks, David Bryan internist, emergency physician

Berwyn
Misurec, Rudolf physician, surgeon

Bloomington
Trefzger, Richard Charles surgeon

Bolingbrook
Malicay, Manuel Alaban physician

Cahokia
Trikha, Ajit psychiatrist

Carol Stream
Schmerold, Wilfried Lothar dermatologist
Trafimow, Jordan Herman orthopedist

Champaign
Freedman, Philip physician, educator
Klausner, Robert David facial, plastic and cosmetic surgeon
Rosenblatt, Karin Ann cancer epidemiologist
Smith, Stanley Edward, Jr. obstetrician-gynecologist

Chicago
Abcarian, Herand surgeon, educator
Abelson, Herbert Traub pediatrician, educator
Andersen, Burton Robert physician, educator
Applebaum, Edward Leon otolaryngologist, educator
Arekapudi, Vijayalakshmi obstetrician-gynecologist
Astrachan, Boris Morton psychiatry educator, consultant
Balk, Robert A. medical educator
Balsam, Theodore physician
Barker, Walter Lee thoracic surgeon
Barton, John Joseph obstetrician, gynecologist, educator, researcher
Bassiouny, Hishan Salah surgeon, educator
Batlle, Daniel nephrologist
Baughman, Verna Lee anesthesiologist
Beck, Robert N. nuclear medicine educator
Becker, Michael Allen physician, educator
Benzon, Honorio Tabal anesthesiologist
Berendi, Erlinda Bayaua physician surgeon
†Berger, Jack Chandler retired physician, surgeon, psychiatrist, educator
Betts, Henry Brognard physician, health facility administrator, educator
†Bluestone, Jeffrey Allen immunology educator, researcher
Boggs, Joseph Dodridge pediatric pathologist, educator
Bonow, Robert Ogden medical educator
Boshes, Louis D. physician, scientist, educator
Bowman, James Edward physician, educator
Bransfield, James Joseph surgeon
†Brendler, Charles Burgess urologist
Bresnahan, James Francis medical ethics educator
Brueschke, Erich Edward physician, researcher, educator
Bunn, William Bernice, III physician, lawyer, epidemiologist
Calenoff, Leonid radiologist
Caro, William Allan physician
Charles, Allan G. physician, educator
Chatterton, Robert Treat, Jr. reproductive endocrinology educator
Cho, Wonhwa biomedical researcher
Clark, John Whitcomb diagnostic radiologist
Coe, Fredric L. physician, educator, researcher
Cohen, Melvin R. physician, educator
Colley, Karen J. medical educator, medical researcher
Colten, Harvey Radin pediatrician, educator
Conway, James Joseph physician
Costa, Erminio pharmacologist, cell biology educator
Cui, Ke-hui embryologist, obstetrician, gynecologist
†Davis, Floyd Asher neurologist
Davison, Richard physician, educator
Degroot, Leslie Jacob medical educator
Deorio, Anthony Joseph surgeon
Derlacki, Eugene L(ubin) otolaryngologist, physician
Deutsch, Thomas Alan ophthalmologist, educator
Diamond, Seymour physician
Diamond, Shari Seidman psychology educator, law researcher
Dunea, George nephrologist, educator
Dyrud, Jarl Edvard psychiatrist
Erdös, Ervin George pharmacology and biochemistry educator
Espat, N. Joseph surgeon
Espinosa, Gustavo Adolfo radiologist, educator
Evans, Thelma Jean Mathis internist
Fagan, Elizabeth Ann medical researcher, hepatologist
Feingold, Daniel Leon anesthesiologist
Fennessy, John James radiologist, educator
Ferguson, Donald John surgeon, educator
†Fiks, Arsen Phillip physician, researcher
Fitch, Frank Wesley pathologist educator, immunologist, educator, administrator
Flaherty, Emalee Gottbrath pediatrician
Freitag, Frederick Gerald osteopathic physician
Frohman, Lawrence Asher endocrinology educator, scientist
Galante, Jorge Osvaldo orthopedic surgeon, educator
Gecht, Martin Louis physician, bank executive
Geha, Alexander Salim cardiothoracic surgeon, educator
Gerbie, Albert Bernard obstetrician, gynecologist, educator
Gewertz, Bruce Labe surgeon, educator
Ginsberg, Norman Arthur physician
Giovacchini, Peter Louis psychoanalyst
Goldberg, Arnold Irving psychoanalyst, educator
Golomb, Harvey Morris oncologist, educator
Gould, Samuel Halpert pediatrics educator
Grayhack, John Thomas urologist, educator
Hambrick, Ernestine retired colon and rectal surgeon
Hanlon, Cyril Rollins physician, educator
Harris, Jules Eli medical educator, physician, clinical scientist, administrator
Hast, Malcolm Howard medical educator, biomedical scientist
Head, Louis Rollin surgeon
Heller, Paul medical educator
Hellman, Samuel radiologist, physician, educator
Hendrix, Ronald Wayne physician, radiologist
Herbst, Arthur Lee obstetrician, gynecologist
Hier, Daniel Barnet neurologist
Hinojosa, Raul physician, ear pathology researcher, educator
Honig, George Raymond pediatrician
Horwitz, Irwin Daniel otolaryngologist, educator
Huckman, Michael Saul neuroradiologist, educator
Hughes, John Russell physician, educator
Jensen, Harold Leroy physician
Jilhewar, Ashok gastroenterologist
Joehl, Raymond Joseph surgeon, educator
Johnson, Maryl Rae cardiologist
Jonasson, Olga surgeon, educator
Jones, Richard Jeffery physician, educator
Kahrilas, Peter James medical educator, researcher
Katz, Adrian Izhack physician, educator
Kirschner, Barbara Starrels pediatric gastroenterologist
Kirsner, Joseph Barnett physician, educator
Kitt, Walter psychiatrist
Kittle, Charles Frederick surgeon
Kohrman, Arthur Fisher pediatrics educator
†La Franco, Frank Paul ophthalmologist, educator
†Lara-Valle, Julio medical educator, physician
Laumann, Anne Elizabeth dermatologist
LaVelle, Arthur anatomy educator
Lazar, Richard Beck physician, medical administrator
Lee, Raphael Carl plastic surgeon, biomedical engineer
Leff, Alan Richard medical educator, researcher
Leventhal, Bennett Lee psychiatry and pediatrics educator, administrator
†Lichtor, Terry neurosurgeon, neuro-oncologist
Lin, Chin-Chu physician, educator, researcher
Loomis, Salora Dale psychiatrist
†Lumpkin, John Robert public health physician, state official
Lurain, John Robert, III gynecologic oncologist
Marcus, Joseph child psychiatrist
Martin, Gary Joseph medical educator
Matsuda, Takayoshi surgeon, biomedical researcher
†McKinney, Peter plastic surgeon
Metz, Charles Edgar radiology educator
Millichap, Joseph Gordon neurologist, educator
Mirkin, Bernard Leo clinical pharmacologist, pediatrician
Mittendorf, Robert physician, epidemiologist
Moawad, Atef obstetrician, gynecologist, educator
Moore, Vernon John, Jr. pediatrician, lawyer, medical consultant
Morris, Naomi Carolyn Minner medical educator, administrator, researcher, consultant
Morris, Ralph William chronopharmacologist
Mullan, John Francis (Sean Mullan) neurosurgeon, educator
Mullen, Charles Frederick health educator
Mustoe, Thomas Anthony physician, plastic surgeon
Naclerio, Robert Michael otolaryngologist, educator
Nahrwold, David Lange surgeon, educator
Narahashi, Toshio pharmacology educator
Nyhus, Lloyd Milton surgeon, educator
Oryshkevich, Roman Sviatoslav physician, physiatrist, dentist, educator
Osiyoye, Adekunle obstetrician, attorney medical and legal consultant, gynecologist, educator
Owens, Charles A. cardiovascular and interventional radiologist
Pachman, Daniel J. physician, educator
Page, Ernest medical educator
Pappas, George Demetrios anatomy and cell biology educator, scientist
Patterson, Roy physician, educator

Peruzzi, William Theodore *anesthesiologist, intensivist, educator*
Pinsky, Steven Michael *radiologist, educator*
Pollak, Raymond *general and transplant surgeon*
Pollock, George Howard *psychiatrist, psychoanalyst*
Pope, Richard M. *rheumatologist*
Poznanski, Andrew Karol *pediatric radiologist*
Prinz, Richard Allen *surgeon*
Ramsey-Goldman, Rosalind *physician*
Reddy, Janardan K. *medical educator*
Replogle, Robert L. *cardiovascular and thoracic surgeon*
Rice, Charles Lane *surgical educator*
Robinson, June Kerswell *dermatologist, educator*
Roizen, Nancy J. *physician, educator*
Rosen, Steven Terry *oncologist, hematologist*
Rosenfield, Robert Lee *pediatric endocrinologist, educator*
Rosenthal, Ira Maurice *pediatrician, educator*
Roth, Sanford Irwin *pathologist, educator*
Rotman, Carlotta Hayes Hill *physician*
Rowley, Janet Davison *physician*
Rudy, Lester Howard *psychiatrist*
Sabbagha, Rudy E. *obstetrician, gynecologist, educator*
Sandlow, Leslie Jordan *physician, educator*
Schade, Stanley Greinert, Jr. *hematologist, educator*
Schafer, Michael Frederick *orthopedic surgeon*
Schilsky, Richard Lewis *oncologist, researcher*
Schneider, Jorge *psychiatrist, dean*
Schuler, James Joseph *vascular surgeon*
Schulman, Sidney *neurologist, educator*
Schumer, William *surgeon, educator*
Schwartzberg, Joanne Gilbert *physician*
Sciarra, John J. *physician, educator*
Scommegna, Antonio *physician, educator*
Scotti, Michael John, Jr. *medical association executive*
Seeler, Ruth Andrea *pediatrician, educator*
Shambaugh, George Elmer, III *internist*
Shields, Thomas William *surgeon, educator*
Short, Marion Priscilla *neurology educator*
Siegler, Mark *internist, educator*
Singh, Manmohan *orthopedic surgeon, educator*
Smith, David Waldo Edward *pathology and gerontology educator, physician*
Smith, Earl Charles *nephrologist, educator*
Socol, Michael Lee *obstetrician, gynecologist, educator*
Sorensen, Leif Boge *physician, educator*
Sparberg, Marshall Stuart *gastroenterologist, educator*
Spargo, Benjamin H. *educator, renal pathologist*
Steele, Glenn Daniel, Jr. *surgical oncologist*
Sternberg, Paul *retired ophthalmologist*
Storb, Ursula Beate *molecular genetics and cell biology educator*
Strauch, Gerald Otto *surgeon*
Stumpf, David Allen *pediatric neurologist*
Svanborg, Alvar *geriatrics educator, researcher*
Swerdlow, Martin Abraham *physician, pathologist, educator*
Taraszkiewicz, Waldemar *physician*
Tardy, Medney Eugene, Jr. *otolaryngologist, facial plastic surgeon*
Telfer, Margaret Clare *internist, hematologist, oncologist*
Temple, Donald *retired allergist and dermatologist*
Teruya, Jun *hematologist, clinical pathologist*
Thomas, Leona Marlene *health information educator*
Tomita, Tadanori *neurosurgeon*
Ultmann, John Ernest *physician, educator*
Vanecko, Robert Michael *surgeon, educator*
Visotsky, Harold Meryle *psychiatrist, educator*
Von Roenn, Kelvin Alexander *neurosurgeon*
Waxler, Beverly Jean *anesthesiologist, physician*
Webster, James Randolph, Jr. *physician*
Weir, Bryce Keith Alexander *neurosurgeon, neurology educator*
Weis, Mervyn J. *physician, gastroenterologist*
Weiss, Robert Alan *surgeon*
Weldon-Linne, C. Michael *pathologist, microbiologist*
Wells, Samuel Alonzo, Jr. *surgeon, educator*
Werner, William Norman *internist, hospital administrator*
Wetzel, Franklin Todd *spinal surgeon, educator, researcher*
Whitington, Peter Frank *pediatrics educator, pediatric hepatologist*
Wied, George Ludwig *physician*
Wilber, David James *cardiologist*
Willoughby, William Franklin, II *physician, researcher*
Winnie, Alon Palm *anesthesiologist, educator*
Wolpert, Edward Alan *psychiatrist*
Yao, Tito Go *pediatrician*
Zisman, Lawrence S. *internist*

Columbia
Megahy, Diane Alaire *physician*

Danville
Prabhudesai, Mukund M. *pathology educator, laboratory director, researcher, administrator*

Darien
Gardner, Howard Garry *pediatrician, educator*

Decatur
Requarth, William Henry *surgeon*
Sweet, Arthur *orthopedist*

Deerfield
Kingdon, Henry Shannon *physician, biochemist, educator, executive*
Scheiber, Stephen Carl *psychiatrist*

Des Plaines
Cucco, Ulisse P. *obstetrician, gynecologist*
Quintanilla, Antonio Paulet *physician, educator*
Zamirowski, Thaddeus Andrew, Jr. *family physician*

Dixon
Polascik, Mary Ann *ophthalmologist*

Downers Grove
Colbert, Marvin Jay *retired internist, educator*

Edwardsville
Hulbert, Linda Ann *health sciences librarian*

Elk Grove Village
Sanders, Joe Maxwell, Jr. *pediatrician, association administrator*

Elmhurst
Blain, Charlotte Marie *physician, educator*
Fornatto, Elio Joseph *otolaryngologist, educator*
Webster, Douglas Peter *emergency physician*

Evanston
Bashook, Philip G. *medical association executive, educator*
Beatty, William Kaye *medical bibliography educator*
Crawford, James Weldon *psychiatrist, educator, administrator*
Enroth-Cugell, Christina Alma Elisabeth *neurophysiologist, educator*
Haring, Olga Munk *retired medical educator, physician*
Hughes, Edward F. X. *physician, educator*
Khandekar, Janardan Dinkar *oncologist, educator*
Langsley, Donald Gene *psychiatrist, medical board executive*
Langsley, Pauline Royal *psychiatrist*
Schwartz, Theodore B. *physician, educator*
Sprang, Milton LeRoy *obstetrician, gynecologist, educator*
Takahashi, Joseph S. *neuroscientist*
Traisman, Howard Sevin *pediatrician*
Vick, Nicholas A. *neurologist*

Evergreen Park
Zumerchik, John *urologist*

Flossmoor
Lis, Edward Francis *pediatrician, consultant*

Freeport
Phillips, Spencer Kleckner *retired surgeon*

Glen Ellyn
Agruss, Neil Stuart *cardiologist*
Dieter, Raymond Andrew, Jr. *physician, surgeon*

Glencoe
†Blonsky, Eugene Richard *neurologist*
Milloy, Frank Joseph, Jr. *surgeon*

Glendale Heights
Pimental, Patricia Ann *neuropsychologist, consulting company executive, author*

Glenview
Goldmann, Morton Aaron *cardiologist*

Greenville
Junod, Daniel August *podiatrist*

Harvey
Heilicser, Bernard Jay *emergency physician*

Herrin
Tibrewala, Sushil *physician*

Highland Park
Bluefarb, Samuel Mitchell *physician*
Saltzberg, Eugene Ernest *physician, educator*

Hillsboro
Mulch, Robert F., Jr. *physician*

Hines
Best, William Robert *physician, educator, university official*
Folk, Frank Anton *surgeon, educator*
Zvetina, James Raymond *pulmonary physician*

Hinsdale
Beatty, Robert Alfred (R. Alfred) *surgeon*
Finley, Robert Coe, III *interventional cardiologist, consultant, educator*
Kazan, Robert Peter *neurosurgeon*
Paloyan, Edward *physician, educator, researcher*

Indianhead Park
Johnson, (Mary) Anita *physician, medical service administrator*

Jacksonville
Scott, Fred Dacon *surgeon*

Joliet
Layman, Dale Pierre *medical educator, author, researcher*
†Lewis, Gregory Austin *urologist*
Ring, Alvin Manuel *pathologist, educator*

Kankakee
Wasser, Larry Paul *hematologist, oncologist*

Lake Forest
Jones, Philip Newton *physician, medical educator*
Levy, Nelson Louis *physician, scientist, corporate executive*
Pawl, Ronald Phillip *neurosurgery educator*
Salter, Edwin Carroll *retired physician*
Wilbur, Richard Sloan *physician, executive*

Lincolnshire
Hughes, William Franklin, Jr. *ophthalmologist, emeritus educator*

Lombard
Kasprow, Barbara Anne *biomedical scientist, writer*

Long Grove
Ausman, Robert K. *surgeon, research executive*
Dajani, Esam Zapher *pharmacologist*

Louisville
Edwards, Ian Keith *retired obstetrician, gynecologist*

Macomb
Dexter, Donald Harvey *surgeon*

Marion
†Munas, Fil A. *psychiatric physician*

Marshall
Mitchell, George Trice *physician*

Mattoon
Maris, Charles Robert *surgeon, otolaryngologist*

Maywood
†Anderson, Douglas E. *neurosurgeon*
Canning, John Rafton *urologist*
Celesia, Gastone Guglielmo *neurologist, neurophysiologist, researcher*
Freeark, Robert James *surgeon, educator*
Hanin, Israel *pharmacologist, educator*
Hart, Cecil William Joseph *otolaryngologist, head and neck surgeon*
Light, Terry Richard *orthopedic hand surgeon*
Newman, Barry Marc *pediatric surgeon*
Pickleman, Jack R. *surgeon*
Slogoff, Stephen *anesthesiologist, educator*
Tobin, Martin John *pulmonary and critical care physician*
†Woody, Lisa Ellen *occuational medicine physician*

Mc Gaw Park
Wolfson, Marsha *internist, nephrologist*

Millstadt
Fowler-Dixon, Deborah Lea *family physician*

Moline
Arnell, Richard Anthony *radiologist*

Normal
Cooley, William Emory, Jr. *radiologist*

North Chicago
†Barsano, Charles P. *medical educator, dean*
Beer, Alan Earl *physician, medical educator*
Ehrenpreis, Seymour *pharmacology educator*
Freese, Uwe Ernest *physician, educator*
Gall, Eric Papineau *physician, educator*
Hawkins, Richard Albert *medical educator, administrator*
Kim, Yoon Berm *immunologist, educator*
Kyncl, John Jaroslav *pharmacologist*
Nair, Velayudhan *pharmacologist, medical educator*
Rogers, Eugene Jack *medical educator*
Rudy, David Robert *physician, educator*
Schneider, Arthur Sanford *physician, educator*
Sierles, Frederick Stephen *psychiatrist, educator*
Taylor, Michael Alan *psychiatrist*
Wiesner, Dallas Charles *immunologist, researcher*

Northbrook
Day, Emerson *physician*
Hirsch, Lawrence Leonard *physician, retired educator*
Scanlon, Edward F. *surgeon, educator*

Northfield
Giffin, Mary Elizabeth *psychiatrist, educator*

Oak Brook
Christian, Joseph Ralph *physician*
Dmowski, W. Paul *obstetrician, gynecologist*
Hand, Roger *physician, educator*
Loughead, Jeffrey Lee *physician*
Rathi, Manohar Lal *pediatrician, neonatologist*

Oak Forest
Lee, David Chang *physician*

Oak Park
Brackett, Edward Boone, III *orthopedic surgeon*

Oakbrook Terrace
Becker, Robert Jerome *allergist, health care consultant*

Olympia Fields
Kasimos, John Nicholas *pathologist*

Park Ridge
Bitran, Jacob David *internist*
Fried, Walter *hematologist, educator*
Mangun, Clarke Wilson, Jr. *public health physician, consultant*

Peoria
Gross, Thomas Lester *obstetrician, gynecologist, researcher*
Miller, Rick Frey *emergency physician*
Stine, Robert Howard *pediatrician*

Peru
Lee, Wayland Sherrod *otolaryngologist*

Pinckneyville
Cawvey, Clarence Eugene *physician*

Rock Island
Bradley, Walter James *emergency physician*
Forlini, Frank John, Jr. *cardiologist*

Rockford
Baptist, Errol Christopher *pediatrician, educator*
Frakes, James Terry *physician, gastroenterologist, educator*
Heerens, Robert Edward *physician*

Saint Charles
McCartney, Charles Price *retired obstetrician-gynecologist*

Skokie
Bellows, Randall Trueblood *ophthalmologist, educator*
Braun, Bennett George *psychiatrist*
Lass, Nancy Anne *physician*

Springfield
Feldman, Bruce Alan *psychiatrist*
Frank, Stuart *cardiologist*
Holland, John Madison *family practice physician*
†Mayersdorf, Assa *neurologist*
Minocha, Anil *physician, educator, researcher*
Myers, Phillip Ward *otolaryngologist*
Rabinovich, Sergio *physician, educator*
Schiller, William Richard *surgeon*
Stauffer, Edward Shannon *orthopedic surgeon, educator*
Sumner, David Spurgeon *surgery educator*
Yaffe, Stuart Allen *physician*
Zook, Elvin Glenn *plastic surgeon, educator*

Urbana
Austin, Jean Philippe *medical educator, radiologist*
Cranston, Robert Earl *neurologist*
Kaufman, Jerome Benzion *neurosurgeon*
Kocheril, Abraham George *physician, educator*
Krock, Curtis Josselyn *pulmonologist*
Nelson, Ralph Alfred *physician*
Oliphant, Uretz John *physician, surgeon*
O'Morchoe, Charles Christopher Creagh *administrator, anatomical sciences educator*
O'Morchoe, Patricia Jean *pathologist, educator*
†Picchietti, Daniel Leigh *neurologist*
Voss, Edward William, Jr. *immunologist, educator*
Welch, William Ben *emergency physician*

Vernon Hills
Keller, Richard Loran *physician*

West Chicago
Paulissen, James Peter *retired physician, county official*

Wheaton
†Christensen, John Gary *urologic surgeon*

Winnetka
Carrow, Leon Albert *physician*
Earle, David Prince, Jr. *physician, educator*
Huff, Stanley Eugene *dermatologist*
Rossi, Ennio C. *physician, educator*

INDIANA

Alexandria
Irwin, Gerald Port *physician*

Anderson
King, Charles Ross *physician*

Bloomington
Bishop, Michael D. *emergency physician*
Crane, David Goodrich *psychiatrist, attorney, educator*
Moore, Ward Wilfred *medical educator*
Rebec, George Vincent *neuroscience researcher, educator, administrator*
Rink, Lawrence Donald *cardiologist*

Bluffton
Pitts, Neal Chase *rheumatologist*

Carmel
Hammond, Isaac William *physician, epidemiologist*
Malik, Muhammad Iqbal *retired pathologist*

Chesterton
Martino, Robert Salvatore *orthopedic surgeon*

Evansville
Faw, Melvin Lee *retired physician*
Penkava, Robert Ray *radiologist, educator*
Rusche, Herman Frederick *gastroenterologist*

Fort Wayne
Donesa, Antonio Braganza *neurosurgeon*
Lee, Shuishih Sage *pathologist*

Gary
Iatridis, Panayotis George *medical educator*
Zunich, Janice *pediatrician, geneticist, educator, administrator*

Hanover
†Voris, David Clarence *retired neurosurgeon*

Highland
Murovic, Judith Ann *neurosurgeon*

Hobart
Mason, Earl James, Jr. *pathologist, educator*

Huntington
Doermann, Paul Edmund *retired surgeon*

Indianapolis
Allen, Stephen D(ean) *pathologist, microbiologist*
Atkins, Clayton H. *family physician, epidemiologist, educator*
Bauer, Dietrich Charles *medical educator*
Bergstein, Jerry Michael *pediatric nephrology*
Besch, Henry Roland, Jr. *pharmacologist, educator*
Biller, Jose *neurologist*
Bonaventura, Leo Mark *gynecologist, educator*
Braddom, Randall L. *physician, medical educator*
Brandt, Ira Kive *pediatrician, medical geneticist*
Braunstein, Ethan Malcolm *skeletal radiologist, paleopathologist, educator*
Brickley, Richard Agar *retired surgeon*
Broadie, Thomas Allen *surgeon, educator*
Brown, Edwin Wilson, Jr. *physician, educator*
Broxmeyer, Hal Edward *medical educator*
Burr, David Bentley *anatomy educator*
†Buzzetti, Lori Ebbers *obstetrician and gynecologist*
Campbell, Judith Lowe *child psychiatrist*
Chernish, Stanley Michael *physician*
Chuang, Tsu-Yi *dermatologist, epidemiologist, educator*
Cleary, Robert Emmet *gynecologist, infertility specialist*
Daly, Walter Joseph *physician, educator*
Dere, Willard Honglen *internist, educator*
Dillon, Francis Xavier *anesthesiologist*
Eigen, Howard *pediatrician, educator*
Eisenberg, Paul Richard *cardiologist, consultant, educator*
Elkins, James Paul *physician*
Farlow, Martin Rhys *neurologist, researcher, educator*
Faulk, Ward Page *immunologist*
Feigenbaum, Harvey *cardiologist, educator*
Feng, Gen-sheng *medical educator, researcher*
Fisch, Charles *physician, educator*
Galvin, Matthew Reppert *psychiatry educator*

Ghetti, Bernardino Francesco neuropathologist, neurobiology researcher
Green, Morris physician, educator
Greist, Mary Coffey dermatologist
Grosfeld, Jay Lazar pediatric surgeon, educator
Hansell, Richard Stanley obstetrician, gynecologist, educator
Helveston, Eugene McGillis pediatric ophthalmologist, educator
Holden, Robert Watson radiologist, educator, university dean
Irwin, Glenn Ward, Jr. medical educator, physician, university official
Jackson, Valerie Pascuzzi radiologist, educator
Johnston, Cyrus Conrad, Jr. medical educator
Joyner, John Erwin medical educator, neurological surgeon
Kaye, Gordon Israel pathologist, anatomist, educator
King, Lucy Jane psychiatrist, health facility administrator
Klug, Michael Gregory scientist
Knoebel, Suzanne Buckner cardiologist, medical educator
Lahiri, Debomoy Kumar molecular neurobiologist, educator
Lamkin, E(ugene) Henry, Jr. internist, medical management executive
Lemberger, Louis pharmacologist, physician
Lumeng, Lawrence physician, educator
MacDougall, John Duncan surgeon
Madura, James Anthony surgical educator
Manders, Karl Lee neurosurgeon
McGarvey, William K. otolaryngologist, surgeon
Miyamoto, Richard Takashi otolaryngologist
Molitoris, Bruce Albert nephrologist, educator
†Mosbaugh, Phillip George urologist, educator
Norins, Arthur Leonard physician, educator
Nurnberger, John I., Jr. psychiatrist, educator
†Ramadan, Nabih M. medical director pharmaceutical company
†Rink, Richard Carlos pediatric urologist, educator
Rogers, Robert Ernest medical educator
Ross, Edward cardiologist
Roth, Lawrence Max pathologist, educator
Ryder, Kenneth William pathologist, educator
Schmetzer, Alan David psychiatrist
Sherman, Stuart internist, gastroenterologist
Small, Joyce Graham psychiatrist, educator
Smith, James Warren pathologist, microbiologist, parasitologist
Stehman, Frederick Bates gynecologic oncologist, educator
Sutton, Gregory Paul obstetrician, gynecologist
Watanabe, August Masaru physician, scientist, medical educator, corporate executive
Weber, George oncology and pharmacology researcher, educator
Weinberger, Myron Hilmar medical educator
White, Arthur Clinton physician
Wilson, Fred M., II ophthalmologist, educator
Woolling, Kenneth Rau internist
Yee, Robert Donald ophthalmologist
Yune, Heun Yung radiologist, educator
Zipes, Douglas Peter cardiologist, researcher

Lafayette
Frey, Harley Harrison, Jr. anesthesiologist
Gordon, Irene Marlow radiology educator
Maickel, Roger Philip pharmacologist, educator
†Pfaff, Dana urologist

Logansport
Brewer, Robert Allen physician

Marion
Fisher, Pierre James, Jr. physician

Merrillville
Nguyen, Thach Ngoc cardiologist

Michigan City
Mothkur, Sridhar Rao radiologist
Nasr, Suhayl Joseph psychiatrist

Monrovia
Bennett, James Edward retired plastic surgeon, educator

Muncie
Roch, Lewis Marshall, II ophthalmic surgeon, medical entrepreneur

Nappanee
Borger, Michael Hinton Ivers osteopathic physician, educator

New Albany
Chowhan, Naveed Mahfooz oncologist

Noblesville
Gatza, Louise Ruth freelance medical writer, small business owner

Portland
Martig, John Frederick anesthesiologist

Rensselaer
Ahler, Kenneth James physician

Rockville
Swaim, John Franklin physician, health care executive

Rushville
†Morrell, Douglas Wayne family practice physician

Scottsburg
Kho, Eusebio surgeon

South Bend
Anderson, Kenneth Paul nephrologist, administrator
Moore-Riesbeck, Susan osteopathic physician
White, Robert Dennis pediatrician

Syracuse
Simmons, Frederick Harrison retired otolaryngologist

Terre Haute
Kunkler, Arnold William retired surgeon
Siebenmorgen, Paul physician, lay church worker
†Stephanian, Erick neurosurgeon

Valparaiso
Kobak, Alfred Julian, Jr. obstetrician, gynecologist

Walton
Chu, Johnson Chin Sheng retired physician

West Lafayette
Borch, Richard Frederic pharmacology and chemistry educator
Borowitz, Joseph Leo pharmacologist
Johns, Janet Susan physician
Robinson, Farrel Richard pathologist, toxicologist
Rutledge, Charles Ozwin pharmacologist, educator
Shaw, Stanley Miner nuclear pharmacy scientist

IOWA

Ames
†Ajax, Ernest Todd neurologist

Bettendorf
Edgerton, Winfield Dow gynecologist

Burlington
Paragas, Rolando G. physician

Cedar Rapids
Houmes, Blaine V. emergency physician
Krivit, Jeffrey Scot surgeon
Norris, Albert Stanley psychiatrist, educator
Reinertson, James Wayne pediatrician

Clinton
Woodman, Grey Musgrave psychiatrist

Davenport
Giudici, Michael Charles cardiac electrophysiologist
†Mobley, William Clifford urologist
Shammas, Nicolas Wahib internist, cardiologist

Des Moines
Brown, Loren Dennis internist, educator
Elmets, Harry Barnard osteopath, dermatologist
Ely, Lawrence Orlo retired surgeon
Rodgers, Louis Dean retired surgeon
Song, Joseph pathologist, educator
Stubbs, David H. vascular surgeon
Thoman, Mark Edward pediatrician

Dubuque
†Stenberg, Michael Donald physician

Fort Dodge
DeLucca, Leopoldo Eloy otolaryngologist, head and neck surgeon

Iowa City
Abboud, Francois Mitry physician, educator
Afifi, Adel Kassim physician
Andreasen, Nancy Coover psychiatrist, educator, neuroscientist
Apicella, Michael Allen physician, educator
Baron, Jeffrey pharmacologist, educator
Bedell, George Noble physician, educator
Buckwalter, Joseph Addison orthopedic surgeon, educator
Burns, C(harles) Patrick hematologist-oncologist
†Caplan, Richard Melvin retired medical educator, musician, author
Clifton, James Albert physician, educator
Cooper, Reginald Rudyard orthopedic surgeon, educator
Damasio, Antonio R. physician, neurologist
Eckstein, John William physician, educator
Erkonen, William E. radiologist, medical educator
Fellows, Robert Ellis medical educator, medical scientist
Galask, Rudolph Peter obstetrician and gynecologist
Gantz, Bruce Jay otolaryngologist, educator
Gergis, Samir Danial anesthesiologist, educator
Grose, Charles Frederick pediatrician, infectious disease specialist
Hein, Herman August physician
Heistad, Donald Dean cardiologist
†Helms, Charles Milton medical educator, consultant
Kardon, Randy H. ophthalmologist
Kelch, Robert Paul pediatric endocrinologist
Kerber, Richard E. cardiologist
Kisker, Carl Thomas physician, medical educator
Knapp, Howard Raymond internist, clinical pharmacologist
Lamping, Kathryn G. medical educator, medical researcher
Lauer, Ronald Martin pediatric cardiologist, researcher
LeBlond, Richard Foard internist, educator
Lim, Ramon (Khe-Siong) neuroscience educator, researcher
Long, John Paul pharmacologist, educator
Mason, Edward Eaton surgeon
Morriss, Frank Howard, Jr. pediatrics educator
Nelson, Herbert Leroy psychiatrist
Nelson, Richard Philip medical educator, dean
Noyes, Russell, Jr. psychiatrist
Ponseti, Ignacio Vives orthopaedic surgery educator
Richenbacher, Wayne Edward cardiothoracic surgeon
Richerson, Hal Bates physician, internist, allergist, immunologist, educator
Robinson, Robert George psychiatry educator
See, William A. urology educator
Snyder, Peter M. medical educator, medical researcher
Strauss, John Steinert dermatologist, educator
Tephly, Thomas Robert pharmacologist, toxicologist, educator
Thompson, Herbert Stanley neuro-ophthalmologist
Traynelis, Vincent Charles neurosurgeon
Van Gilder, John Corley neurosurgeon, educator
Weinberger, Miles M. physician, pediatric educator
Weingeist, Thomas Alan ophthalmology educator
Weinstock, Joel Vincent immunologist
Weintraub, Neal L. medical educator, cardiologist
Ziegler, Ekhard Erich pediatrics educator

Marshalltown
Packer, Karen Gilliland cancer patient educator, researcher

Sioux City
Redwine, John Newland physician

Story City
Wattleworth, Roberta Ann family practice physician, health facility administrator

West Des Moines
Alberts, Marion Edward physician
Cunningham, Kevin James internist

Williamsburg
Bruse, Kristy Dean cardiovascular pharmacologist

KANSAS

Concordia
Fowler, Wayne Lewis, Sr. internist

Great Bend
Jones, Edward physician, pathologist

Hutchinson
Graves, Kathryn Louise dermatologist

Kansas City
Anderson, Harrison Clarke pathologist, educator, biomedical researcher
Arakawa, Kasumi physician, educator
Ardinger, Robert Hall, Jr. physician, educator
Calkins, David Ross physician, medical educator
Cheng, Chiachun medical educator
Cho, Cheng Tsung pediatrician, educator
Cuppage, Francis Edward retired physician, educator
Damjanov, Ivan pathologist, educator
Dunn, Marvin Irvin physician
Godfrey, Robert Gordon physician
Grantham, Jared James nephrologist, educator
Greenberger, Norton Jerald physician
Holmes, Grace Elinor pediatrician
Hudson, Robert Paul medical educator
Johnson, Joy Ann diagnostic radiologist
Krantz, Kermit Edward physician, educator
Lee, Kyo Rak radiology educator
Mathewson, Hugh Spalding anesthesiologist, educator
McCallum, Richard Warwick medical researcher, clinician, educator
Meyers, David George internist, cardiologist, educator
Mohn, Melvin Paul anatomist, educator
Pretz, James Bernard retired family physician
Samson, Frederick Eugene, Jr. neuroscientist, educator
Schloerb, Paul Richard surgeon, educator
Sciolaro, Charles Michael cardiac surgeon
Suzuki, Tsuneo molecular immunologist
Voogt, James Leonard medical educator
Walaszek, Edward Joseph pharmacology educator
Waxman, David physician, university consultant
Ziegler, Dewey Kiper neurologist

Kiowa
Drewry, Marcia Ann physician

Lawrence
Meerson, Felix Zalmanovich cardiologist
Miller, Don Robert surgeon
†Thellman, Scott Thomas physician

Leavenworth
Mengel, Charles Edmund physician, medical educator
Poulose, Kuttikatt Paul neurologist

Lenexa
Fotopoulos, Sophia Stathopoulos medical scientist, administrator

Manhattan
Durkee, William Robert retired physician
Oehme, Frederick Wolfgang medical researcher and educator

Overland Park
Landry, Mark Edward podiatrist, researcher

Rose Hill
Chapman, Randell Barkley family and emergency physician, medical educator

Salina
Richards, Jon Frederick physician

Shawnee Mission
Bell, Deloris Wiley physician
Fairchild, Robert Charles pediatrician
Hartzler, Geoffrey Oliver retired cardiologist
Price, James Gordon physician
Thomas, Christopher Yancey, III surgeon, educator

Topeka
Gabbard, Glen Owens psychiatrist, psychoanalyst
Jacoby, Robert Edward, II family practice physician
Lacoursiere, Roy Barnaby psychiatrist
Menninger, William Walter psychiatrist
Roy, William Robert physician, lawyer, former congressman
Simpson, William Stewart retired psychiatrist, sex therapist
Thoms, Norman Wells cardiovascular and thoracic surgeon
Wallace, Brett E. orthopedic surgeon
Zerbe, Kathryn J. psychiatrist

Westwood
Hart, Paul Vincent, Jr. emergency and family medicine physician, inventor

Wichita
Brada, Donald Robert psychiatrist
Burket, George Edward, Jr. retired family physician
Cummings, Richard J. otologist
Guthrie, Richard Alan physician
Hawley, Raymond Glen pathologist
North, Doris Griffin retired physician, educator
Oxley, Dwight K(ahala) pathologist
Rosenberg, Thomas Frederick physician
Rumisek, John David surgeon, medical educator

KENTUCKY

Ashland
Roth, Oliver Ralph radiologist

Bowling Green
Dewhurst, William Harvey psychiatrist
Jhamb, Indar Mohan physician
Martin, Jerry W. family physician

Cynthiana
Harpel, Gerald Robert obstetrician-gynecologist

Elizabethtown
DeVries, William Castle surgeon, educator
Rahman, Rafiq Ur oncologist, educator

Fort Campbell
Swann, Steven Walter physician, army officer

Henderson
Esser, James Mark cardiovascular and interventional radiologist

Lexington
†Abou-Khalil, Bassam Michael cardiothoracic surgeon
Anderson, James Wingo physician
Avant, Robert Frank physician, educator
Baumann, Robert Jay child neurology educator
Clawson, David Kay orthopedic surgeon
Dalton, Waller Lisle obstetrician and gynecologist
Glenn, James Francis urologist, educator
Griffen, Ward O., Jr. surgeon, educator, medical board executive
Hagen, Michael Dale family physician educator
Hamburg, Joseph physician, educator
Holsinger, James Wilson, Jr. physician
Kang, Bann C. immunologist
Kaplan, Martin P. allergist, immunologist, pediatrician
Mayer, Lloyd D. allergist, immunologist, physician, medical educator
Noonan, Jacqueline Anne pediatrics educator
Poundstone, John Walker preventive medicine physician
†Prevel, Christopher Dean plastic surgeon, hand surgeon
†Purcell, Marguerite Mary diagnostic radiologist, consultant
†Saha, Sibu Pada surgeon, educator
Schwarcz, Thomas H. surgeon
Tollison, Joseph W. family practice physician
Villaran, Yuri physician, medical educator
Young, Paul Ray medical board executive, physician

Louisville
Adamkin, David Howard pediatric medicine educator
Adams, Christine Beate Lieber psychiatrist, educator
Amin, Mohammad urology educator
Andrews, Billy Franklin pediatrician, educator
Bertolone, Salvatore J. pediatric medicine educator
Callen, Jeffrey Phillip dermatologist, educator
Chien, Sufan surgeon, educator
†Cook, Larry Norman pediatrician, neonatologist, educator
Danzl, Daniel Frank emergency physician
Elin, Ronald John pathologist
Farman, Allan George radiologist, oral pathologist, educator
Galandiuk, Susan colon and rectal surgeon, educator
Gall, Stanley Adolph physician, immunology researcher
Garretson, Henry David neurosurgeon
Gleis, Linda Hood physician
Gray, Laman A., Jr. thoracic surgeon, educator
Haynes, Douglas Martin physician, educator
Hobson, Douglas Paul psychiatrist
†Holt, Homer A., Jr. urologist, educator
Jacob, Robert Allen surgeon
Karibo, John Michael allergist, immunologist, pediatrician
King, William Bradley emergency medicine physician
La Rocca, Renato Vincenzo medical oncologist, clinical researcher
Olson, Walter Lewis, Jr. neurology educator
Parker, Joseph Corbin, Jr. pathologist
Pence, Hobert Lee physician
Polk, Hiram Carey, Jr. surgeon, educator
†Richardson, J. David surgeon
Schwab, John Joseph psychiatrist, educator
Scott, Ralph Mason physician, radiation oncology educator
†Shields, Christopher Brian neurosurgeon
Slung, Hilton B. surgeon
Spinnato, Joseph Anthony, II obstetrician
Spratt, John Stricklin surgeon, educator, researcher
†Sundine, Michael James plastic surgeon
Syed, Ibrahim Bijli medical educator and physicist, writer, philosopher, theologist, public speaker
Tasman, Allan psychiatry educator
Tsai, Tsu-Min surgeon
†Uhlenhuth, Eric R. urologist
Waddell, William Joseph pharmacologist, toxicologist
†Weiner, Leonard Jay surgery educator
Weisskopf, Bernard pediatrician, child behavior, development and genetics specialist, educator
Winland, Denise Lynn physician
Wright, Jesse Hartzell psychiatrist, educator
Zimmerman, Thom Jay ophthalmologist, educator

Morehead
Miller, Jon William emergency physician

Richmond
McQuaide, Benjamin Homer radiologist

LOUISIANA

Alexandria
Butler, Robert Moore, Jr. podiatrist

Arcadia
Cummings, Kenneth Ila writer, retired dermatologist

Baton Rouge
Bray, George August physician, scientist, educator
Cherry, William Ashley surgeon, state health officer
Dunlap, Wallace Hart pediatrician

†Hollman, Charlotte Anderson *pediatric neurologist*
Kidd, James Marion, III *allergist, immunologist, naturalist, educator*
†Kisner, Wendell Howard, Jr. *plastic surgeon*
Le Vine, Jerome Edward *retired ophthalmologist*
Lucas, Fred Vance *pathology educator, university administrator*
Parra, Pamela Ann *physician, educator*
Perone, Thomas Patrick *neurosurgeon*
Puyau, Francis Albert *retired physician, radiology educator*
Robichaux, Alfred Godfrey, III *obstetrician and gynecologist*

Covington
Roberts, James Allen *urologist*

Franklinton
Alvarado, Luis Manuel *physician*

Harahan
Maclaren, Noel Keith *pathologist, pediatrician, educator*

Houma
Conrad, Harold Theodore *psychiatrist*
Ferguson, Thomas Glen *internist*

Jackson
Morrison, Francine Darlene *psychiatrist, massage therapist, herbal simplist*

Kenner
White, Charles Albert, Jr. *medical educator, obstetrician-gynecologist*

La Place
Outlaw, Kitti Kiattikunvivat *surgeon*

Lafayette
Jolissaint, Stephen Lacy *pathologist*
†Wyatt, Charles H. *cardiovascular surgeon*

Lake Charles
Drez, David Jacob, Jr. *orthopedic surgeon, educator*
Gunderson, Clark Alan *orthopedic surgeon*
Yadalam, Kashinath Gangadhara *psychiatrist*

Mandeville
Ray, Charles Jackson *retired surgeon*
Wales, John Henry *physician, consultant*

Metairie
Conway, James Donald *internist, educator*
Edisen, Clayton Byron *physician*
Harell, George S. *radiologist*
†Johnston, William J., Jr. *neurosurgeon*
Lake, Wesley Wayne, Jr. *internist, allergist, educator*
Mando, Wagih Rufaat *surgeon*
Ochsner, Seymour Fiske *radiologist, editor*
Spruiell, Vann *psychoanalyst, educator, editor, researcher*

Monroe
Blondin, Joan *nephrologist educator*
Ifediora, Okechukwu Chigozie *nephrologist, educator*

Morgan City
†Denduluri, Ramarao M. *urologist*

New Orleans
Agrawal, Krishna Chandra *pharmacology educator*
Arshad, M. Kaleem *psychiatrist*
Bautista, Abraham Parana *immunologist*
Beck, David Edward *surgeon*
Bertrand, William Ellis *public health educator, academic administrator*
Caldwell, Delmar Ray *ophthalmologist, educator*
Cohn, Isidore, Jr. *surgeon, educator*
Connolly, Edward S. *neurological surgeon*
Corrigan, James John, Jr. *pediatrician, dean*
Daniels, Robert Sanford *psychiatrist, administrator*
†Diaz, James Henry *public health physician*
Domingue, Gerald James *medical scientist, microbiology, immunology and urology educator, researcher, clinical bacteriologist*
Duncan, Margaret Caroline *physician*
Easson, William McAlpine *psychiatrist*
England, John David *neurologist*
Ensenat, Louis Albert *surgeon*
Epstein, Arthur William *physician, educator*
Espinoza, Luis Rolan *rheumatologist*
Fisher, James William *medical educator, pharmacologist*
Frohlich, Edward David *medical educator*
Fuselier, Harold Anthony, Jr. *physician, urologist*
Gatipon, Betty Becker *medical educator, consultant*
Ginsberg, Harley Glen *pediatrician*
Gottlieb, A(braham) Arthur *medical educator*
Hartz, Renee Semo *cardiothoracic surgeon*
Hicks, Terrell Cohlman *surgeon, educator, health facility administrator, academic administrator*
Howard, Richard Ralston, II *medical health advisor, researcher, financier*
Hyman, Albert Lewis *cardiologist*
Hyman, Edward Sidney *physician, consultant*
Imig, John David *medical educator*
Incaprera, Frank Philip *internist*
Jaffe, Bernard Michael *surgeon*
†Jung, Rodney C. *internist, academic administrator*
Kewalramani, Laxman Sunderdas *surgeon, consultant*
Kline, David Gellinger *neurosurgery educator*
Kolinsky, Michael Allen *emergency physician*
Lang, Erich Karl *physician, radiologist*
Le Blanc, Alice Isabelle *public health educator, health program grants and contracts administrator*
Le Jeune, Francis Ernest, Jr. *otolaryngologist*
Lewy, John Edwin *pediatric nephrologist*
Locke, William *endocrinologist*
Lopez, Manuel *immunology and allergy educator*
Martin, David Hubert *physician, educator*
Martin, Louis Frank *surgery and physiology educator*
Massare, John Steve *medical association administrator, educator*
McKinley, Kevin L. *neurologist*
Miller, Robert Harold *otolaryngologist, educator*
Millikan, Larry Edward *dermatologist*
Mogabgab, William Joseph *physician, virologist, educator*
Nelson, James Smith *pathologist, educator*
Nichols, Ronald Lee *surgeon, educator*
Ochsner, John Lockwood *thoracic-cardiovascular surgeon*
Pankey, George Atkinson *physician, educator*
Pfister, Richard Charles *physician, radiology educator*
Plavsic, Branko Milenko *radiology educator*
†Postels, Douglas George *neurologist*
Puschett, Jules B. *medical educator, nephrologist, researcher*
Re, Richard Noel *endocrinologist*
Reyes, Raul Gregorio *surgeon*
Riddick, Frank Adams, Jr. *physician, health care facility administrator*
Rietschel, Robert Louis *dermatologist*
Schally, Andrew Victor *endocrinologist, researcher*
Schmidt-Sommerfeld, Eberhard *pediatrician*
Schneider, George T. *obstetrician-gynecologist*
Stewart, Gregory Wallace *physician*
Straumanis, John Janis, Jr. *psychiatry educator*
†Strub, Richard Lester *neurologist*
Svenson, Ernest Olander *psychiatrist, psychoanalyst*
Timmcke, Alan Edward *physician and surgeon*
Usdin, Gene Leonard *physician, psychiatrist*
Ventura, Hector Osvaldo *cardiologist*
Waring, William Winburn *pediatric pulmonologist, educator*
Webb, Watts Rankin *surgeon*
Weiss, Thomas Edward *physician*
Welsh, Ronald Arthur *physician, educator*
Winstead, Daniel Keith *psychiatrist*
Yates, Robert Doyle *anatomy educator*

Opelousas
Pinac, André Louis, III *obstetrician, gynecologist*

Scott
Bergeron, Wilton Lee *physician*

Shreveport
Albright, James Aaron *orthopedist, surgeon*
Bradley, Ronald James *neuroscientist*
Conrad, Steven Allen *physician, biomedical engineer, educator, researcher*
Dhanireddy, Ramasubbareddy *neonatologist, researcher*
Dilworth, Edwin Earle *retired obstetrician, gynecologist*
Fort, Arthur Tomlinson, III *physician, educator*
Freeman, Arthur Merrimon, III *psychiatry educator, dean*
Ganley, James Powell *ophthalmologist, educator*
George, Ronald Baylis *physician, educator*
Griffith, Robert Charles *allergist, educator, planter*
Levy, Harold Bernard *pediatrician*
Mancini, Mary Catherine *cardiothoracic surgeon, researcher*
McDonald, John Clifton *surgeon*
†O'Neal, Barron Johns *surgeon*
Shelby, James Stanford *cardiovascular surgeon*
Tenney, William Frank *pediatrician*

Slidell
McBurney, Elizabeth Innes *physician, educator*
Muller, Robert Joseph *gynecologist*

Thibodaux
Hebert, Leo Placide *physician*

MAINE

Bangor
†Shubert, Dennis L. *neurosurgeon, medical administrator*
Watt, Thomas Lorne *dermatologist*

Chebeague Island
Middleton, Elliott, Jr. *physician*

Deer Isle
Smith, Gardner Watkins *physician*

Fairfield
Pratt, Loring Withee *otolaryngologist*

Friendship
Walker, Douglass Willey *retired pediatrician, medical center administrator*

Jackman
Thomas, Paulette Suzanne *holistic health practitioner, physician assistant*

Kennebunk
Sholl, John Gurney, III *physician*

Kingfield
Collins, H(erschel) Douglas *retired physician*

Lewiston
Christie, Donald Melvin, Jr. *physician*

Machias
Hayes, Ernest M. *podiatrist*

Orono
Weiss, Robert Jerome *psychiatrist, educator*

Portland
†Brown, Linda M. *neurologist*
Clark, Gordon Hostetter, Jr. *physician*
Mullen, John Reagan *radiation oncologist*

Togus
Hussey, John Francis *physician, geriatrician*

Windham
†Hiebert, Clement Arthur *surgeon, consultant, educator*

York
Lauter, M. David *family physician*

MARYLAND

Annapolis
Brown-Christopher, Cheryl Denise *physician*
Calabrese, Anthony Joseph *gastroenterologist*
Graze, Peter Robert *physician*
Halpern, Joseph Alan *physician*
†Hamill, Peter VanVechten *physician, epidemiologist, consultant*
Holtgrewe, Henry Logan *urologist*
O'Toole, Tara Jeanne *physician*

Arnold
Harris, Roger Clark *psychiatrist, consultant*

Baltimore
†Achuff, Stephen Charles *physician*
Adkinson, N. Franklin, Jr. *clinical immunologist*
Albuquerque, Edson Xavier *pharmacology educator*
Andres, Reubin *gerontologist*
Asper, Samuel Philips *medical administrator, educator*
Bachur, Nicholas Robert, Sr. *research physician*
Baker, R. Robinson *surgeon*
Baker, Susan P. *public health educator*
Baker, Timothy Danforth *physician, educator*
Ball, Marion J. *health information professional*
Bartlett, John Gill *infectious disease physician*
Baughman, Kenneth Lee *cardiologist, educator*
Baumgartner, William Anthony *cardiac surgeon*
Bayless, Theodore M(orris) *gastroenterologist, educator, researcher*
Benz, Edward John, Jr. *physician, educator*
Berlin, Fred Saul *psychiatrist, educator*
Bever, Christopher Theodore, Jr. *neurologist*
Bhardwaj, Anish *neuroscientist, medical educator*
Bigelow, George E. *psychology and pharmacology scientist*
Brody, Eugene B. *psychiatrist, educator*
Brody, William Ralph *radiologist, educator*
Brusilow, Saul *pediatrics researcher*
Bundick, William Ross *retired dermatologist*
†Burnham, Gilbert Miracle *physician, educator*
Cameron, Duke Edward *cardiac surgeon, educator*
Carson, Benjamin Solomon *neurosurgeon*
†Chen, Yu *acupuncturist, Chinese herbologist*
Chernow, Bart *critical care physician*
Childs, Barton *retired, physician, educator*
Conley, Carroll Lockard *physician, emeritus educator*
Covi, Lino *psychiatrist*
Cummings, Charles William *physician, educator*
Dang, Chi Van *hematology and oncology educator*
Daniels, Worth Bagley, Jr. *retired internist*
Dannenberg, Arthur Milton, Jr. *experimental pathologist, immunologist, educator*
DeAngelis, Catherine D. *pediatrics educator*
DeLateur, Barbara Jane *medical educator*
Drachman, Daniel Bruce *neurologist*
Eisenberg, Howard Michael *neurosurgeon*
Eldefrawi, Amira Toppozada *medical educator, toxicologist, pharmacologist*
Elma, Bayani Borja *physician*
Faden, Ruth R. *medical educator, ethicist, researcher*
Felsenthal, Gerald *physiatrist, educator*
Ferencz, Charlotte *pediatrician, epidemiology and preventive medicine educator*
Fox, Harold Edward *obstetrician, gynecologist, educator, researcher*
Freeman, John Mark *pediatric neurologist*
Friedman, Marion *internist, family physician, medical administrator, medical editor*
Gambert, Steven Ross *geriatrician, internist*
Gimenez, Luis Fernando *physician, educator*
Godenne, Ghislaine Dudley *physician, psychoanalyst, educator*
Goldberg, Morton Falk *ophthalmologist, educator*
Goldman, Lynn Rose *medical educator*
Gordis, Leon *physician*
Graham, George Gordon *physician*
Greenough, William Bates, III *medical educator*
Griffin, Diane Edmund *research physician, virologist, educator*
Griffith, Lawrence Stacey Cameron *cardiologist*
Grumbine, Francis *gynecologic oncologist, educator*
Hart, John, Jr. *behavioral neurologist, neuroscientist, educator*
Hellmann, David Bruce *medical educator*
Henderson, Donald Ainslie *public health educator*
Hobbins, Thomas Eben *physician*
Hofkin, Gerald Alan *gastroenterologist*
Hungerford, David Samuel *orthopedic surgeon, educator*
Imboden, John Baskerville *psychiatry educator*
Johns, Richard James *physician, educator*
Johnson, Kenneth Peter *neurologist, medical researcher*
Johnson, Richard T. *neurology, microbiology and neuroscience educator, research virologist*
Karp, Judith Esther *oncologist, science administrator*
Kastor, John Alfred *cardiologist, educator*
Kinnard, William James, Jr. *retired pharmacy educator*
Kowarski, Allen Avinoam *endocrinologist, educator*
Kuppusamy, Periannan *medical educator, medical researcher*
Kwon, Chul Soo *psychiatrist*
Lakatta, Edward Gerard *biomedical researcher*
Lawrence, Robert Swan *physician, educator, academic administrator*
Lawson, Edward Earle *neonatologist*
Levine, Myron Max *medical administrator*
Lewison, Edward Frederick *surgeon*
Lichtenstein, Lawrence Mark *allergy, immunology educator, physician*
Litrenta, Frances Marie *psychiatrist*
Long, Donlin Martin *surgeon, educator*
Mansfield, Carl Major *radiation oncology educator*
Manson, Paul Nellis *plastic surgeon*
Markowska, Alicja Lidia *neuroscientist, researcher*
Massof, Robert William *neuroscientist, educator*
Matheson, Nina W. *medical researcher*
Matjasko, M. Jane *anesthesiologist, educator*
Maumenee, Irene H. *ophthalmology educator*
McHugh, Paul R. *psychiatrist, neurologist, educator*
McKhann, Guy Mead *physician, educator*
†Melville, Kraig Arthur *emergency medicine physician*
Meny, Robert George *medical research administrator*
Migeon, Barbara Ruben *pediatrician, geneticist*
Migeon, Claude Jean *pediatrics educator*
Miller, Edward Doring *anesthesiologist*
Miller, Stanley Joseph *dermatologic surgeon*
Milnor, William Robert *physician*
Moser, Hugo Wolfgang *physician*
Mosley, Wiley Henry *medical educator*
Mulholland, John Henry *internist, educator*
Munster, Andrew Michael *medical educator, surgeon*
Mysko, William Kiefer *emergency physician, educator*
Myslinski, Norbert Raymond *medical educator*
Nagey, David Augustus *physician, researcher*
Norman, Philip Sidney *physician*
Pass, Carolyn Joan *dermatologist*
Patz, Arnall *ophthalmologist*
Pimental, Laura *emergency physician*
Proctor, Donald Frederick *otolaryngology educator, physician*
Provost, Thomas Taylor *dermatology educator, researcher*
†Rabin, Bruce Arlan *neurologist*
†Rapoport, Morton I. *medical educator, university administrator*
Rayson, Glendon Ennes *internist, preventive medicine specialist, writer*
Rennels, Marshall Leigh *neuroanatomist, biomedical scientist, educator*
Rose, Noel Richard *immunologist, microbiologist, educator*
Samet, Jonathan Michael *epidemiologist, educator*
Sanchez Alvarado, Alejandro *embryologist, molecular biologist*
Sanfilippo, Alfred Paul *pathologist, educator*
Schimpff, Stephen Callender *internist, oncologist*
Schoenrich, Edyth Hull *internal and preventive medicine physician*
Schuster, Marvin Meier *physician, educator*
Shuldiner, Alan Rodney *physician, endocrinologist, educator*
Silbergeld, Ellen Kovner *environmental epidemiologist and toxicologist*
Silverstein, Arthur Matthew *ophthalmic immunologist, educator, historian*
Simpson, Thomas William *physician*
Sinno, Fady A. *surgeon*
Snyder, Solomon Halbert *psychiatrist, pharmacologist*
Sommer, Alfred *medical educator, scientist, ophthalmologist*
Starfield, Barbara Helen *physician, educator*
Stolley, Paul David *medical educator, researcher*
Strickland, George Thomas, Jr. *physician, researcher, educator*
Talalay, Paul *pharmacologist, physician*
Tamminga, Carol Ann *neuroscientist*
Taylor, Carl Ernest *physician, educator*
†Theda, Christiane *pediatrics educator*
Vogelstein, Bert *oncology educator*
Wagner, Henry Nicholas, Jr. *physician*
Walker, Wilbur Gordon *physician, educator*
Wallach, Edward Eliot *physician, educator*
Walser, Mackenzie *physician, educator*
Walsh, Patrick Craig *urologist*
Waterbury, Larry *physician, educator*
Weiss, James Lloyd *cardiology educator*
Welch, Robert Bond *ophthalmologist, educator*
Williams, G(eorge) Melville *surgeon, medical educator*
Wilson, Donald Edward *physician, educator*
Woodward, Theodore Englar *medical educator, internist*
Wu, Albert W. *medical educator*
Ye, Shui Qing *medical researcher*
Yossif, George *psychiatrist*
Young, Barbara *psychiatrist, psychoanalyst, psychiatry educator, photographer*
†Zito, Julie Magno *psychopharmacologist, pharmacist, educator*
Zizic, Thomas Michael *physician, educator*

Bethesda
Akin, Cem *internist*
Alexander, Duane Frederick *pediatrician, research administrator*
Atkinson, Arthur John, Jr. *clinical pharmacologist, educator*
Axelrod, Julius *pharmacologist, biochemist*
Berendes, Heinz Werner *medical epidemiologist, pediatrician*
Breman, Joel Gordon *epidemiologist, science administrator*
Brodine, Charles Edward *physician*
Brown, Dudley Earl, Jr. *psychiatrist, educator, health executive, former federal agency administrator, former naval officer*
Brunell, Philip Alfred *physician*
Carney, William Patrick *medical educator*
Chanock, Robert Merritt *pediatrician*
Chase, Thomas Newell *neurologist, researcher, educator*
Cheever, Allen Williams *pathologist*
Chretien, Jane Henkel *internist*
Cohen, Robert Abraham *retired physician*
Cohen, Sheldon Gilbert *physician, historian, immunology educator*
Crout, J(ohn) Richard *physician, pharmaceutical researcher*
Danforth, David Newton, Jr. *physician, scientist*
Dean, Jurrien *biomedical researcher, physician*
Dietrich, Robert Anthony *pathologist, medical administrator, consultant*
Farmer, Richard Gilbert *physician, foundation administrator, medical advisor, health care consultant*
Feller, William Frank *surgery educator*
Fischbach, Gerald D. *neurobiology educator*
Fleisher, Thomas Arthur *physician*
Gibson, Sam Thompson *internist, educator*
Greenwald, Peter *physician, government medical research director*
Haffner, William H.J. *obstetrician-gynecologist*
Hallett, Mark *physician, neurologist, health research institute administrator*
Harris, Curtis C. *physician*
Haseltine, Florence Pat *research administrator, obstetrician, gynecologist*
Herman, Mary Margaret *neuropathologist*
Hrynkow, Sharon Hemond *federal government administrator, researcher*
Hutton, John Evans, Jr. *surgery educator, retired military officer*
†Jabbari, Bahman *neurologist, educator*
†Jabs, Arthur Dean *plastic surgeon*
Javitt, Jonathan C. *physician, health policy analyst, writer*
Jensen, Peter Scott *psychiatrist, public health service officer*
Jiang, He *biomedical scientist, entrepreneur*
Johnson, Joyce Marie *psychiatrist, epidemiologist, public health officer*
Joy, Robert John Thomas *medical history educator*
Katz, Stephen I. *dermatologist*
Katz, Stephen Ira *dermatologist*
Keiser, Harry Robert *physician*
Kirschstein, Ruth Lillian *physician*
Klee, Claude Blenc *medical researcher*
Kramer, Barnett Sheldon *oncologist*
Krause, Richard Michael *medical scientist, government official, educator*
Kupfer, Carl *ophthalmologist, science administrator*

†Lee, Leamon M. federal agency administrator
Lenfant, Claude Jean-Marie physician
Leonard, James Joseph physician, educator
Leppert, Phyllis Carolyn obstetrician, gynecologist
Linehan, William Marston urologic surgeon, cancer researcher
Liotta, Lance Allen pathologist
London, Gary Wayne neurologist
Lu, Bai neurobiologist
MacLean, Paul Donald government institute medical research official
Macnamara, Thomas Edward physician, educator
Magrath, Ian Trevor physician
†Marini, Ann Marie medical researcher, educator
Masur, Henry internist
McCurdy, Harry Ward otolaryngologist
Metcalfe, Dean Darrel medical research physician
Mills, James Louis medical researcher, pediatric epidemiologist
Mullan, Fitzhugh public health physician
Nelson, Stuart James internist, medical informatician
Neumann, Ronald Daniel nuclear medicine physician, educator
Neva, Franklin Allen physician, educator
Nyirjesy, Istvan obstetrician, gynecologist
Ommaya, Ayub Khan neurosurgeon
Paul, William Erwin immunologist, researcher
Perlin, Seymour psychiatrist, educator
Perry, Seymour Monroe physician
Peterson, Charles Marquis medical educator
Pinn, Vivian W. pathologist, federal agency administrator
Pluta, Ryszard Marek neurosurgeon, scientist
Pollard, Harvey B. physician, neuroscientist
Post, Robert Morton psychiatrist
Quon, Michael James medical scientist, physician
Rabson, Alan Saul physician, educator
Rall, Joseph Edward physician
Rapoport, Judith psychiatrist
Reid, Clarice Delores retired physician
Rennert, Owen Murray physician, educator
Resnik, Harvey Lewis Paul psychiatrist
Rhim, Johng Sik physician, educator, medical researcher
Robbins, John Bennett medical researcher
Roberts, Doris Emma epidemiologist, consultant
Rosenberg, Steven Aaron surgeon, medical researcher
Saffiotti, Umberto pathologist
†Sawhney, Roger Anu consultant, physician
Schwartz, Judy Ellen cardiothoracic surgeon
Sheridan, Philp Henry pediatrician, neurologist
Short, Elizabeth M. physician, educator, federal agency administrator
Silverman, Charlotte epidemiologist, educator
†Simon, Robert Isaac psychiatrist
Sontag, James Mitchell cancer researcher
Stetler-Stevenson, William George pathologist
Stoner, Gerald Lee neurovirologist, medical researcher
Sturtz, Donald Lee physician, naval officer
Ursano, Robert Joseph psychiatrist
Waldmann, Thomas Alexander medical research scientist, physician
Webster, Henry deForest neuroscientist
Western, Karl August physician, epidemiologist
Work, Henry Harcus physician, educator
Wu, Changyou immunologist, educator
Wurtz, Robert Henry neuroscientist
Wysocki, Annette B. nurse scientist, educator
Yaffe, Sumner Jason pediatrician, research center administrator, educator

Brooklandville
Kolodny, Abraham Lewis physician

Capitol Heights
Onyejekwe, Chike Onyekachi physician, medical director

Chevy Chase
Ellis, Sydney pharmacological scientist, former pharmacology educator
Gottlieb, H. David podiatrist
Greenberg, Robert Milton retired psychiatrist
Harlan, William Robert, Jr. physician, educator, researcher
Kullen, Shirley Robinowitz psychiatric epidemiologist, consultant
Murphy, Robert Patrick physician, ophthalmic researcher
Pogue, John Marshall physician, editor, researcher
Posnick, Jeffrey Craig plastic surgeon
Romansky, Monroe James physician, educator
Rose, John Charles physician, educator
Williams, Charles Laval, Jr. physician, international organization official

Clinton
Cruz, Wilhelmina Mangahas nephrologist educator
†Grace, René Earle physician

Cockeysville
Breitenecker, Rudiger pathologist
De Hoff, John Burling physician, consultant

Cockeysville Hunt Valley
Dans, Peter Emanuel medical educator
Futcher, Palmer Howard physician, educator

Colesville
Peterson, William Frank retired physician, administrator

Columbia
Carr, Charles Jelleff pharmacologist, educator, toxicology consultant
†Grill, Stephen Elliott neuroscientist, neurologist, educator
Harrison, Elza Stanley medical association executive
Pounds, Moses Belt medical anthropologist
Riddle, Mark Alan child psychiatrist

Darnestown
Gottlieb, Julius Judah podiatrist

Denton
†Jensen, Christian Edward family practice physician

Easton
Snow, James Byron, Jr. physician, research administrator

Fort George G Meade
Kwik-Kostek, Christine Irene physician, air force officer

Frederick
Anderson, Arthur Osmund pathologist, immunologist, army officer

Gaithersburg
Hegyeli, Ruth Ingeborg Elisabeth Johnsson pathologist, government official
Johnson, W. Taylor physician
Liau, Gene medical educator
Mella, Gordon Weed physician
Rosenstein, Marvin public health administrator
Watanabe, Kyoichi A(loysius) chemist, researcher, pharmacology educator

Garrett Park
Lincicome, David Richard biomedical and animal scientist
Silbergeld, Sam psychiatrist

Germantown
Kirchner, Peter Thomas nuclear medicine physician, educator, consultant

Glen Burnie
Oldfield, Allison Lee physician, radiologist, educator

Grasonville
Prout, George Russell, Jr. medical educator, urologist

Greenbelt
Obamogie, Mercy A. physician

Hagerstown
†Cost, Francis Howard, Jr. physician
†Monzur, Mohammed Ali nephrologist

Hollywood
Hertz, Roy physician, educator, researcher

Hyattsville
Smith, Irving gerontologist

Kensington
†Kelley, Patrick Alan neurologist, educator

Laurel
Highman, Barbara dermatologist
Zhang, Jun pathologist, researcher

Lutherville
†Buchholz, David W. neurologist, headache specialist, educator
†Moses, Howard neurologist

Lutherville Timonium
Miller, John E. cardiovascular surgeon
Park, Lee Crandall psychiatrist
Sternberger, Ludwig Amadeus neurologist, educator

Millersville
Martin, Donald William psychiatrist

Monkton
Mountcastle, Vernon Benjamin neurophysiologist

North Bethesda
Halstead, Scott Barker medical research administrator

Parkville
Munson, Paul Lewis pharmacologist

Potomac
Haddy, Francis John physician, educator
Ventry, Paul Guerin physician, government official
Waugaman, Richard Merle psychiatrist, psychoanalyst, educator

Reisterstown
†Seth, Deepak internist

Riverdale
†Kumar, Shailendra urologist, educator
†Shah, Navic C. urologist, educator

Rockville
Arons, Bernard S. psychiatrist, educator, health services director
Barr, Solomon Efrem allergist
Birns, Mark Theodore physician
Boice, John Dunning, Jr. epidemiologist, science administrator
Brown, Martin Howard physician
Calkins, Jerry Milan anesthesiologist, educator, administrator, biomedical engineer
Cannon, Grace Bert immunologist
Decker, John Laws physician
Eisenberg, John Meyer physician, educator
Epstein, Jay Stuart medical researcher
Fratantoni, Joseph Charles medical researcher, hematologist, medical and regulatory consultant
Gulya, Aina Julianna neurotologist, surgeon, educator
Hanna, Michael George, Jr. immunologist, institute administrator
Haudenschild, Christian Charles pathologist, educator, inventor
Hoyer, Leon William physician, educator
Johnson, Emery Allen physician
Kafka, Marian Stern neuroscientist
Kamerow, Douglas Biron epidemiologist, family physician, assistant surgeon general
†Leithauser, Lance plastic surgeon
Ley, Herbert Leonard, Jr. retired epidemiologist
Lloyd, Douglas Seward physician, public health administrator
†Mohan, Aparna Krishna epidemiologist, researcher
Moritsugu, Kenneth Paul physician, government official
Naunton, Ralph Frederick surgeon, educator
Saljinska-Markovic, Olivera T. oncology researcher, educator
Seltser, Raymond epidemiologist, educator
Shuren, Jeffrey Eliot behavioral neurology researcher, lawyer
Tabor, Edward physician, researcher
Vincent, Michael Paul plastic surgeon

Salisbury
†Buchness, Michael Patrick cardiologist, surgeon
Houlihan, Hilda Imelio physician

Severna Park
Greulich, Richard Curtice anatomist, gerontologist

Silver Spring
Adams, Diane Loretta physician
Cornely, Paul Bertau retired physician, educator
Cruze, Kenneth retired surgeon
Eig, Blair Mitchell pediatrician
Grossberg, David Burton cardiologist
Gulbrandsen, Patricia Hughes physician
Lippman, Muriel Marianne biomedical scientist
Monaghan, W(illiam) Patrick immunohematologist, retired naval officer, health educator, consultant
Onyewu, Chukwuemeka A. physician
Waldrop, Francis Neil physician
Weiss, Andre psychiatrist

Stevenson
Hendler, Nelson Howard physician, medical clinic director

Timonium
Pierpont, Ross Z. retired surgeon

Towson
Fitzpatrick, Vincent de Paul, Jr. gynecologist
Mc Indoe, Darrell Winfred nuclear medicine physician, former air force officer
Mordes, Marvin neurologist
Spodak, Michael Kenneth forensic psychiatrist

Waldorf
Berger, Robert Steven dermatologist
Wiggins, Stephen Edward family practice physician, medical administrator

MASSACHUSETTS

Amherst
Fleischman, Paul Robert psychiatrist, writer
Ralph, James R. physician
Ratner, James Henry dermatologist

Andover
Sampson, Robert Carl, Jr. psychiatrist
Seggev, Meir radiologist, educator

Bedford
Alarcon, Rogelio Alfonso physician, researcher
Elkinton, Joseph Russell medical educator
†Hurwitz, Joshua Jacob physician
Letts, Lindsay Gordon pharmacologist, educator
Steinberg, James Jonah physician, medical administrator, educator
Volicer, Ladislav physician, educator

Belmont
Cohen, Bruce Michael psychiatrist, educator, scientist
Coyle, Joseph Thomas psychiatrist
de Marneffe, Francis psychiatrist, hospital administrator
Ewing, Scott Edwin physician, psychiatrist, educator, researcher
Onesti, Silvio Joseph psychiatrist
Ottenstein, Donald psychiatrist
Pope, Harrison Graham, Jr. psychiatrist, educator
Sifneos, Peter Emanuel psychiatrist

Boston
Adams, Douglass Franklin radiologist, educator, medical ethicist
Adelstein, S(tanley) James physician, educator
Aisenberg, Alan C. physician, educator, researcher
Alpert, Joel Jacobs medical educator, pediatrician
Alt, Frederick W. geneticist, pediatrician
Amos, Harold retired biomedical researcher, educator
Ampola, Mary G. pediatrician, geneticist
Arky, Ronald Alfred medical educator
Austen, K(arl) Frank physician, educator
Austen, W(illiam) Gerald surgeon, educator
Barnett, Guy Octo physician, educator
†Bauer, Stuart Barry urologist
Beck, William Samson physician, educator, biochemist
Becker, James Murdoch surgeon, educator
Bellows, A. Robert ophthalmologist
Benacerraf, Baruj pathologist, educator
Berenberg, William physician, educator
Bern, Murray Morris hematologist, oncologist
Bernfield, Merton Ronald pediatrician, scientist, educator
Berson, Eliot Lawrence ophthalmologist, medical educator
Black, Paul Henry medical educator, researcher
Bloch, Kurt Julius physician
Bougas, James Andrew physician, surgeon
Brain, Joseph David biomedical scientist
Braunwald, Eugene physician, educator
Brazelton, Thomas Berry pediatrician, educator
Brenner, Barry Morton physician
Buckley, Mortimer Joseph physician
Burakoff, Steven James immunologist, educator
Buxbaum, Robert C(ourtney) internist
Callow, Allan Dana surgeon
Caplan, Louis Robert neurology educator
Carr, Daniel Barry anesthesiologist, endocrinologist, medical researcher
Clouse, Melvin E. radiologist
Coffman, Jay Denton physician, educator
Cohen, Alan Seymour internist
Collins, Tucker pathologist, molecular biologist
Cotran, Ramzi S. pathologist, educator
Crocker, Allen Carrol pediatrician
†Cua, Christopher Lee thoracic surgeon
David, John R. internist, educator
Delbanco, Thomas Lewis medical educator, researcher
DeSanctis, Roman William cardiologist
Desforges, Jane Fay medical educator, physician
Deuel, Thomas Franklin physician
Dluhy, Robert George physician
Doyle, Jennifer surgical educator, scholar
Duong, Thieu anesthesiologist
Dvorak, Harold F. pathologist, educator, scientist
Earls, Felton child psychiatrist
Egdahl, Richard Harrison surgeon, medical educator, health science administrator
Eisenberg, Leon psychiatrist, educator
Ellis, Franklin Henry, Jr. surgeon, educator
Ellison, R. Curtis medicine and public health educator
†Epler, Gary Robert physician, writer, educator
Epstein, Franklin Harold physician, educator
Estes, Nathan Anthony Mark, III cardiologist, medical educator
Farrer, Lindsay Ames genetic epidemiologist
Federman, Daniel David medical educator, educational administrator, endocrinologist
Feldman, Robert George neurologist, medical educator
Field, James Bernard internist, educator
Fitzpatrick, Thomas Bernard dermatologist, educator
Fletcher, Robert Hillman medical educator
Fletcher, Suzanne Wright physician, educator
Folkman, Moses Judah surgeon
Frantz, Ivan D., III pediatrician
Frazier, Howard Stanley physician
Freedberg, A. Stone physician
Frei, Emil, III physician, medical researcher, educator
Freiman, David Galland pathologist, educator
Fried, Marvin Peter physician
Friedler, Gladys psychiatry and pharmacology educator, scientist
Gelfand, Jeffrey Alan physician, educator
Gellis, Sydney Saul physician
Gilchrest, Barbara Ann dermatologist
Gimbrone, Michael Anthony, Jr. research scientist, pathologist, educator
Glimcher, Melvin Jacob orthopedic surgeon
Goldberg, Irving Hyman molecular pharmacology and biochemistry educator
Goldman, Peter nutrition and clinical pharmacology educator
Goldstein, Jill M. psychiatric epidemiologist, clinical neuroscientist, psychiatry educator
Gottlieb, Leonard Solomon pathology educator
Goumnerova, Liliana Christova physician, neurosurgeon, educator
Green, Alan Ivan psychiatrist
Green, Gareth Montraville physician, educator, scientist
Greenblatt, David J. pharmacologist, educator
Greenfield, Sheldon epidimiologist
Greiner, Jack Volker ophthalmologist, physician, surgeon, research scientist
Guenin, Louis Maurice ethics scholar
Hall, John Emmett orthopedic surgeon, educator
Harris, Jay Robert radiation oncologist
Harris, William Hamilton orthopedic surgeon
Hay, Elizabeth Dexter embryology researcher, educator
Herndon, James Henry orthopedic surgeon, educator
Hiatt, Howard H. physician, educator
Hickey, Paul Robert anesthesiologist , educator
Hingson, Ralph W. medical educator
Hobson, John Allan psychiatrist, researcher, educator
Howley, Peter Maxwell pathology educator
†Hunt, Robert Bridger gynecologist
Hutchinson, Bernard Thomas ophthalmologist
Hutter, Adolph Matthew, Jr. cardiologist, educator
Huvos, Andrew internist, cardiologist, educator
Ingber, Donald Elliot pathology and cell biology educator, bioengineer
Jadvar, Hossein nuclear medicine physician, biomedical engineer
Jandl, James Harriman physician, educator
Jellinek, Michael Steven psychiatrist, pediatrician
Johnson, Willard Chapin surgeon, researcher
Jonas, Richard Andrew medical educator
Kandarian, Susan Christine medical educator
Karnovsky, Morris John pathologist, biologist
Kassirer, Jerome Paul medical educator, editor-in-chief
Kaye, Kenneth Marc physician, educator, scientist
Kazemi, Homayoun physician, medical educator
Kieff, Elliott Dan medical educator
Kitz, Richard John anesthesiologist, educator
Klein, Jerome Osias pediatrician, educator
Klempner, Mark Steven Joel physician, research scientist, educator
Klingenstein, R. James physician
Komaroff, Anthony Leader physician
Korsmeyer, Stanley Joel pathologist, educator
Krane, Stephen Martin physician, educator
Kravitz, Edward Arthur neuroscientist
Kressel, Herbert Yehude medical educator
Krupnik, Valery Efimovich embryologist, writer
Lasagna, Louis Cesare medical educator
Leeman, Susan Epstein neuroscientist, educator
Levenson, James William physician
Levine, Ruth Rothenberg biomedical science educator
Levinsky, Norman George physician, educator
Little, John Bertram physician, radiobiology educator, researcher
Liu, Brian Cheong-Seng urology and oncology educator, researcher
Livingston, David Morse biomedical scientist, physician, internist
Loscalzo, Joseph cardiologist, biochemist
Loughlin, Kevin Raymond urological surgeon, researcher
Maher, Timothy John pharmacologist, educator
†Mandel, Jess physician, educator
Mankin, Henry Jay physician, educator
Mannick, John Anthony surgeon
Martin, Joseph Boyd neurologist, educator
†Matheson, Jean King neurologist, educator
Maynard, Kenneth Irwin medical educator, researcher
Mc Dermott, William Vincent, Jr. physician, educator
McDougal, William Scott urology educator
McNeil, Barbara Joyce radiologist, educator
Meenan, Robert Francis academician, rheumatologist, researcher
Mellins, Harry Zachary radiologist, educator
Merk, Frederick Bannister biomedical educator, medical researcher
Messerle, Judith Rose medical librarian, public relations director
Michel, Thomas Mark internal medicine educator, scientist, physician
Mizel, Mark Stuart orthopedic surgeon
Moellering, Robert Charles, Jr. internist, educator
Monaco, Anthony Peter surgery educator, medical institute administrator
Mongan, James John physician, hospital administrator

Montgomery, William Wayne *surgeon*
Moore, Francis Daniels *surgeon*
Morgan, James Philip *pharmacologist, cardiologist, educator*
Morgentaler, Abraham *urologist, researcher*
†Moses, Robert David *cardiothoracic surgeon*
Nadas, Alexander Sandor *pediatric cardiologist, educator*
Nathan, David Gordon *physician, educator*
Node, Koichi *cardiologist, researcher*
O'Donnell, Thomas Francis *vascular surgeon, health facility administrator*
†Osei, Suzette Y. *endocrinologist*
Papageorgiou, Panagiotis *medical educator*
Pauker, Susan Perlmutter *clinical geneticist, pediatrician*
Paul, Oglesby *cardiologist*
Petersen, Robert Allen *pediatric ophthalmologist*
Pierce, Donald Shelton *orthopedic surgeon, educator*
Pochi, Peter Ernest *physician*
Poser, Charles Marcel *neurology educator*
Poussaint, Alvin Francis *psychiatrist, educator*
Prout, Curtis *internist, educator*
Puliafito, Carmen Anthony *ophthalmologist, healthcare executive*
Rabkin, Mitchell Thornton *physician, hospital administrator, educator*
Ransil, Bernard J(erome) *research physician, methodologist, consultant, educator*
Ravid, Katya *medical educator*
Reid, Lynne McArthur *pathologist*
Relman, Arnold Seymour *physician, educator, editor*
Reppert, Steven Marion *pediatrician, scientist, educator*
Richie, Jerome Paul *surgeon, educator*
Rockoff, Mark Alan *pediatric anesthesiologist*
Rohrer, Richard Jeffrey *surgeon, educator*
Rosen, Fred Saul *pediatrics educator*
Rosenberg, Irwin Harold *physician, educator*
Russell, Paul Snowden *surgeon, educator*
Ryan, Kenneth John *physician, educator*
Ryser, Hugues Jean-Paul *pharmacologist, medical educator, cell biologist*
Sachs, David Howard *surgery and immunology educator, researcher*
Sadeghi-Nejad, Abdollah *pediatrician, educator*
Sallan, Stephen E. *pediatrician*
Sant, Grannum Remy *urology educator*
Saper, Clifford Baird *neurobiology and neurology educator*
Sax, Daniel Saul *neurologist*
†Schalick, Walton Orvyl, III *pediatrician*
Schaller, Jane Green *pediatrician*
Schlossman, Stuart Franklin *physician, educator, researcher*
Schwartz, Bernard *physician*
Scott, James Arthur *radiologist, educator*
Seddon, Johanna Margaret *ophthalmologist, epidemiologist*
Seely, Ellen Wells *endocrinologist*
Selkoe, Dennis Jesse *neurologist, researcher, educator*
Sexton, John Joseph *oral and maxillofacial surgeon*
Shader, Richard Irwin *psychiatrist, pharmacologist, educator*
Shapiro, Jerome Herbert *radiologist, educator*
†Shemin, Richard Jay *cardiothoracic surgeon, educator*
Shields, Lawrence Thornton *orthopedic surgeon, educator*
Silen, William *physician, surgery educator*
Simovic, Drasko *neurologist*
Sledge, Clement Blount *orthopedic surgeon, educator*
Snydman, David Richard *infectious diseases specialist, educator*
Solomon, Caren Grossbard *internist*
Spellman, Mitchell Wright *surgeon, academic administrator*
Stair, Thomas Osborne *physician, educator*
Steere, Allen Caruthers, Jr. *physician, educator*
Stossel, Thomas Peter *medical educator, medical research director*
Surman, Owen Stanley *psychiatrist*
Swartz, Morton Norman *medical educator*
Tauber, Alfred Imre *hematologist, immunologist, philosopher of science*
Taubman, Martin Arnold *immunologist*
Taveras, Juan Manuel *physician, educator*
Thorn, George Widmer *physician, educator*
Tilney, Nicholas Lechmere *surgery educator*
Trichopoulos, Dimitrios Vassilios *epidemiologist, educator*
Trier, Jerry Steven *gastroenterologist, educator*
Vachon, Louis *psychiatrist, educator*
Vaillant, George Eman *psychiatrist*
Wang, Helen Hai-ling *pathologist*
Warshaw, Andrew Louis *surgeon, researcher*
Weber, Georg Franz *immunologist*
Weisman, Avery Danto *psychiatrist*
Weiss, Earle Burton *physician*
Williams, Gordon Harold *internist, medical educator, researcher*
Wolfsdorf, Joseph Isadore *pediatrician, endocrinologist*
Woog, John J. *eye plastic surgeon*
Young, Anne B. *neurologist, educator*
Yuan, Junying *medical educator, researcher*
Zaleznik, Abraham *psychoanalyst, management specialist, educator*
Zarins, Bertram *orthopaedic surgeon*
Zervas, Nicholas Themistocles *neurosurgeon*
Zinner, Michael Jeffrey *surgeon, educator*

Brockton
Carlson, Desiree Anice *pathologist*
Kligler, Roger Michael *physician*

Brookline
Creasey, David Edward *physician, psychiatrist, educator*
Gray, Seymour *medical educator, author*
Jakab, Irene *psychiatrist*
Jordan, Ruth Ann *physician*
Koretsky, Sidney *internist, educator, paper historian*
Kraut, Joel Arthur *ophthalmologist*
Lown, Bernard *cardiologist, educator*
Nadelson, Carol Cooperman *psychiatrist, educator*
†Ostfeld, Robert Jonathan *physician*
Rachlin, William Selig *surgeon*
Tyler, H. Richard *physician*

Burlington
Birk, Lee (Carl Birk) *psychiatrist, educator*
Clerkin, Eugene Patrick *physician*
Fager, Charles Anthony *physician, neurosurgeon*
Jones, Harvey Royden, Jr. *neurologist*
McLellan, Robert *gynecologist, oncologist, educator*
Moschella, Samuel L. *dermatology educator*
Schoetz, David John, Jr. *colon and rectal surgeon*
Seckel, Brooke Rutledge *plastic surgeon*
Wise, Robert Edward *radiologist*

Cambridge
Anderson, William Henry *psychobiologist, educator*
Bartus, Raymond Thomas *neuroscientist, pharmaceutical executive, writer*
Bizzi, Emilio *neurophysiologist, educator*
Brandt, John Henry *physician*
Brusch, John Lynch *physician*
Buchwald, Jed Zachary *environmental health researcher, science history educator*
Coles, Robert *child psychiatrist, educator, author*
Davidson, Charles Sprecher *physician*
Davie, Joseph Myrten *physician, pathology and immunology educator, science administrator*
Dryja, Thaddeus P. *opthalmologist, educator*
Eisen, Herman Nathaniel *immunology researcher, medical educator*
Eisenberg, Carola *psychiatry educator*
Goldstein, Mark Allan *pediatrician, adolescent medicine specialist*
Havens, Leston Laycock *psychiatrist, educator*
Homburger, Freddy *physician, scientist, artist*
Hsiao, Jack Nai-Chang *physician*
Johnson, Michael Lewis *psychiatrist*
Kirshner, Lewis A. *psychiatrist*
Lander, Eric Steven *medical researcher*
London, Irving Myer *physician, educator*
Mathews, Joan Helene *pediatrician*
Nathanson, Larry *medical educator, physician*
Ris, Howard Clinton, Jr. *nonprofit public policy organization administrator*
†Sacknoff, Eric Jon *urologic surgeon*
Shore, Miles Frederick *psychiatrist, educator*
Wacker, Warren Ernest Clyde *physician, educator*
Wurtman, Richard Jay *physician, educator, inventor*

Charlestown
Ackerman, Jerome Leonard *radiology educator*
Gross, Jerome *physician, biologist, educator*
Harlow, Edward E., Jr. *oncologist*
Isselbacher, Kurt Julius *physician, educator*
Lamont-Havers, Ronald William *physician, research administrator*
Leaf, Alexander *physician, educator*
Moskowitz, Michael Arthur *neuroscientist, neurologist*
Potts, John Thomas, Jr. *physician, educator*
Zamecnik, Paul Charles *oncologist, medical research scientist*

Chelmsford
Howard, Terry Thomas *obstetrician/gynecologist*

Chelsea
Ablow, Keith Russell *psychiatrist, journalist, author*
Gold, Matthew David *physician, neurologist*

Chestnut Hill
Baum, Jules Leonard *ophthalmologist, educator*
Cohen, David Joel *medical educator*
Courtiss, Eugene Howard *plastic surgeon, educator*
Flax, Martin Howard *pathologist, retired educator*
Franklin, Morton Jerome *emergency physician*
Kosasky, Harold Jack *fertility researcher*
Purvez, Akhtar *otolaryngologist, researcher*
Stanbury, John Bruton *physician, educator*
Thier, Samuel Osiah *physician, educator*

Concord
Caro, Jesus Jaime *medical researcher*
†Dawson, David M. *neurologist*
Palay, Sanford Louis *retired scientist, educator*

Danvers
Rubinstein, Sidney Jacob *orthopedic technologist*

East Boston
Moore, Kerry Duane *mental health association administrator*

East Dennis
†Phillips, Clay Edison *surgeon*

Falmouth
Sato, Kazuyoshi *pathologist*

Gardner
Du Buske, Lawrence M. *immunologist, allergist, rheumotologist*

Gloucester
White, Harold Jack *pathologist*

Hamilton
†Ceballos, Ruben Alberto *nursing researcher*

Haverhill
MacMillan, Francis Philip *physician*
Niccolini, Drew George *gastroenterologist*

Hingham
Calnan, Arthur Francis *ophthalmologist*

Jamaica Plain
Arbeit, Robert David *physician*
Hartley, Robert Milton *internist, rheumatologist, medical director*
Murphy, Raymond Leo Harrington, Jr. *pulmonologist*
Pierce, Chester Middlebrook *psychiatrist, educator*
Snider, Gordon Lloyd *physician*

Lexington
Paul, Norman Leo *psychiatrist, educator*

Lincoln
Kulka, J(ohannes) Peter *retired physician, pathologist*

Lowell
Dubner, Daniel William *pediatrician*
†Wegman, David Howe *health science educator, consultant*

Ludlow
Roberge, Lawrence Francis *neuroscientist, biotechnology consultant, writer, bioethicist, educator*

Malden
Fox, Bernard Hayman *cancer epidemiologist, educator*

Medfield
Woolston-Catlin, Marian *psychiatrist*

Medford
Burke, Edward Newell *radiologist*

Natick
Schott, John William *psychiatrist*

Needham
Mc Arthur, Janet Ward *endocrinologist, educator*
Weller, Thomas Huckle *physician, former educator*

New Bedford
Shapiro, Gilbert Lawrence *orthopedist*

New Salem
Lenherr, Frederick Keith *neurophysiologist, computer scientist*

Newton
Bassuk, Ellen Linda *psychiatrist*
Blacher, Richard Stanley *psychiatrist*
†Dangond, Fernando *neurologist, educator*
Sasahara, Arthur Asao *cardiologist, educator, researcher*

North Andover
Coleman, Daniel Eugene *physician*

North Billerica
Witover, Stephen Barry *pediatrician*

North Dighton
Cserr, Robert *psychiatrist, physician, hospital administrator*

North Falmouth
Bass, Norman Herbert *physician, scientist, university and hospital administrator, health care executive*

Northborough
Fulmer, Hugh Scott *physician, educator*

Norwood
Berliner, Allen Irwin *dermatologist*

Petersham
Chivian, Eric Seth *psychiatrist, environmental scientist, educator*

Pittsfield
Fanelli, Robert Drew *surgeon*
†Michaels, Basil M. *plastic surgeon, educator*

Revere
Jay, Michael Eliot *radiologist*

Roxbury
Berman, Marlene Oscar *neuropsychologist, educator*
Peters, Alan *anatomy educator*
Resnick, Oscar *neuroscientist*

Salem
Piro, Anthony John *radiologist*

Shrewsbury
Charney, Evan *pediatrician, educator*
Magee, Bernard Dale *obstetrician, gynecologist*

South Harwich
Rigg, Charles Andrew *pediatrician*

South Wellfleet
Blau, Monte *retired radiology educator*

South Weymouth
Young, Michael Chung-En *allergist, immunologist, pediatrician*

Southborough
Dews, P(eter) B(ooth) *medical scientist, educator*
Sidman, Richard Leon *neuroscientist*

Springfield
Andrzejewski, Chester, Jr. *immunologist, research scientist*
Dastgeer, Ghulam Mohammad *surgeon*
Farkas, Paul Stephen *gastroenterologist*
Frankel, Kenneth Mark *thoracic surgeon*
Friedmann, Paul *surgeon, educator*
Kirkwood, John Robert *neuroradiologist*
Liptzin, Benjamin *psychiatrist*
McGee, William Tobin *intensive care physician*
Navab, Farhad *medical educator*
†Paasch, Ron *physical medicine physician*
†Pleet, Albert Bernard *neurologist, internist*
Reed, William Piper, Jr. *surgeon, educator*
†Shaker, Leonard Howard *urologist*
Smith, James Almer, Jr. *psychiatrist*

Stockbridge
Shapiro, Edward Robert *psychiatrist, administrator educator psychoanalyst*

Stoughton
Corcoran, Paul John *physician*

Swampscott
Rubin, Harold Sydney *internist*

Taunton
Bornstein, Myer Sidney *obstetrician, gynecologist*

Vineyard Haven
Jacobs, Gretchen Huntley *psychiatrist*

Waltham
Lackner, James Robert *aerospace medicine educator*
Leach, Robert Ellis *physician, educator*

Wellesley
Avery, Mary Ellen *pediatrician, educator*
Jovanovic, Miodrag Stevana *surgeon, educator*
Landaw, Stephen Arthur *physician, educator*
McAlpine, Frederick Sennett *anesthesiologist*
Murray, Joseph Edward *retired plastic surgeon*

Wellesley Hills
Spierings, Egilius Leonardus Hendricus *pharmacologist, neurologist, headache specialist*

West Falmouth
Holz, George G., IV *research scientist, medicine educator*

West Roxbury
Cohen, Carolyn Alta *health educator*
Goyal, Raj Kumar *medical educator*
Hedley-Whyte, John *anesthesiologist, educator*

West Springfield
Desai, Veena Balvantrai *obstetrician and gynecologist, educator*

Weston
Draskoczy, Paul R. *psychiatrist*
Wells, Lionelle Dudley *psychiatrist, educator*

Weymouth
Iacovo, Michael Jamaal *medical consultant, small business owner*

Williamstown
Payne, Michael Clarence *gastroenterologist*
Stuebner, Erwin August, Jr. *internist*
Wilkins, Earle Wayne, Jr. *surgery educator emeritus*
Williams, Heather *neuroethologist, educator*

Wilmington
Patterson, William B. *occupational and environmental medicine physician*

Winchester
Smith, Robert Moors *anesthesiologist*

Woods Hole
Rafferty, Nancy Schwarz *anatomy educator*

Worcester
Appelbaum, Paul Stuart *psychiatrist, educator*
†Balarajan, Yogarajah *electrophysiologist, cardiologist*
Bernhard, Jeffrey David *dermatologist, editor, educator*
Drachman, David Alexander *neurologist*
Dunlop, George Rodgers *retired surgeon*
Hanshaw, James Barry *physician, educator*
Hunter, Richard Edward *physician*
Kaplan, Melvin Hyman *immunology, rheumatology, medical educator*
Lanza, Robert Paul *medical scientist*
Laster, Leonard *physician, consultant, author*
Lawrence, Walter Thomas *plastic surgeon*
Levine, Peter Hughes *physician, health facility administrator*
Ludlum, David Blodgett *pharmacologist, educator*
†Maloney, Mary Elizabeth *dermatologist, educator*
Marcus, Elliott Meyer *neurologist, educator*
Och, Mohamad Rachid *psychiatrist, consultant*
Ravnikar, Veronika A. *medical educator*
Rothschild, Anthony Joseph *psychiatrist*
Smith, Edward Herbert *radiologist, educator*
†Sodha, Naren B. *neurologist*
Wheeler, Hewitt Brownell *surgeon, educator*
Yankauer, Alfred *physician, educator*
Zurier, Robert Burton *medical educator, clinical investigator*

Yarmouth Port
†Cloutier, Wilfrid Amédée *retired surgeon*
Gordon, Benjamin Dichter *medical executive, pediatrician*

MICHIGAN

Allen Park
Victor, Jay *dermatologist*

Alma
Sanders, Jack Ford *physician*

Ann Arbor
Abrams, Gerald David *physician, educator*
Akil, Huda *neuroscientist, educator, researcher*
Ansbacher, Rudi *physician*
Bacon, George Edgar *pediatrician, educator*
Baker, Laurence Howard *oncology educator*
Bloom, David Alan *pediatric urology educator*
Bloom, Jane Maginnis *emergency physician*
Bole, Giles G. *physician, researcher, medical educator*
Bowdler, Anthony John *physician, educator*
Burdi, Alphonse Rocco *anatomist*
Burke, Robert Harry *surgeon, educator*
Cameron, Oliver Gene *psychiatrist, educator psychobiology reseacher*
Carlson, Bruce Martin *anatomist*
Casey, Kenneth Lyman *neurologist*
†Chandler, William Frederick *physician, neurosurgeon*
†Cho, Kyung Jae *physician, radiologist, educator*
Christensen, A(lbert) Kent *anatomy educator*
Coran, Arnold Gerald *pediatric surgeon*
Craig, Clifford Lindley *orthopaedic pediatric surgery educator*
Curtis, George Clifton *psychiatry educator, clinical research investigator*
De La Iglesia, Felix Alberto *pathologist, toxicologist*
DeWeese, Marion Spencer *educator, surgeon*
Donabedian, Avedis *physician*
†Dong, Qian *radiologist, researcher*
Dubin, Howard Victor *dermatologist*
Fajans, Stefan Stanislaus *internist, retired educator*
Fekety, Robert *physician, educator*
Fox, David Alan *rheumatologist, immunologist*
Frueh, Bartley Richard *surgeon*
Gikas, Paul William *medical educator*
Gilman, Sid *neurologist*
Goldstein, Irwin Joseph *medical research executive*
Goldstein, Steven Alan *medical and engineering educator*
Greden, John Francis *psychiatrist, educator*
Greene, Douglas A. *internist, educator*

Greenfield, Lazar John *surgeon, educator*
Halter, Jeffrey Brian *internal medicine educator, geriatrician*
Hawthorne, Victor Morrison *epidemiologist, educator*
Heidelberger, Kathleen Patricia *physician*
Hiss, Roland Graham *physician, medical educator*
Hoff, Julian Theodore *physician, educator*
Hollenberg, Paul Frederick *pharmacology educator*
Huang, Milton Peechuan *physician, researcher, educator*
Humes, H(arvey) David *nephrologist, educator*
†Kannan, Srimathi *environmental and occupational health educator*
Kramer, Charles Henry *psychiatrist*
Krause, Charles Joseph *otolaryngologist*
Kronfol, Ziad Anis *psychiatrist, educator, researcher*
Kuhl, David Edmund *physician, nuclear medicine educator*
La Du, Bert Nichols, Jr. *pharmacology educator, physician*
Lichter, Paul Richard *ophthalmology educator*
Lockwood, Dean H. *physician, pharmaceutical executive*
Lozoff, Betsy *pediatrician*
Margolis, Philip Marcus *psychiatrist, educator*
†Markel, Howard *medical educator*
Martel, William *radiologist, educator*
Midgley, A(lvin) Rees, Jr. *reproductive endocrinology educator, researcher*
Modell, Stephen Mark *medical researcher, educator*
Monto, Arnold Simon *epidemiology educator*
Morley, George William *gynecologist*
Nelson, Virginia Simson *pediatrician, physiatrist, educator*
Oliver, William John *pediatrician, educator*
†Oneal, Robert Moore *plastic surgeon, educator*
Orringer, Mark Burton *surgeon, educator*
Owyang, Chung *gastroenterologist, researcher*
Pitt, Bertram *cardiologist, educator, consultant*
Reddy, Venkat Narsimha *ophthalmologist, researcher*
Rosenthal, Amnon *pediatric cardiologist*
Schnitzer, Bertram *hematopathologist*
Schottenfeld, David *epidemiologist, educator*
Shayman, James Alan *nephrologist, educator*
Sloan, Herbert Elias *physician, surgeon*
Smith, David John, Jr. *plastic surgeon*
Smith, Donald Cameron *physician, educator*
Strang, Ruth Hancock *pediatric educator, pediatric cardiologist, priest*
Stross, Jeoffrey Knight *physician, educator*
Tandon, Rajiv *psychiatrist, educator*
Thompson, Norman Winslow *surgeon, educator*
Todd, Robert Franklin, III *oncologist, educator*
Turcotte, Jeremiah George *physician, surgery educator*
†Wahl, Richard Leo *radiologist, educator, nuclear medicine researcher*
Ward, Peter Allan *pathologist, educator*
Weber, Wendell William *pharmacologist*
Weg, John Gerard *physician*
Wiggins, Roger C. *internist, educator, researcher*
Yamada, Tadataka *internist*

Bay City
Nicholson, William Noel *clinical neuropsychologist*

Beverly Hills
Edwards, Michael Gerard *physician*

Birmingham
†Kass, Evan J. *pediatric urologist*
Shiener, Gerald Alan *psychiatrist*

Bloomfield Hills
Chason, Jacob (Leon Chason) *retired neuropathologist*
Dean, George Arthur *physician, art educator*
Kaufman, Jerome Seymour *retired ophthalmologist*
Rosenfeld, Joel *ophthalmologist, lawyer*
Stunz, John Henry, Jr. *retired physician*
Wydra, Frank Thomas *healthcare executive*

Brooklyn
Baumann, Gregory William *physician, consultant*

Burton
†Tabbaa, Abdul H. *physician*

Clinton Township
Brown, Ronald Delano *endocrinologist*
Waldmann, Robert *hematologist*

Coldwater
Nomicos, Nicholas Eugene *emergency medicine physician*

Dearborn
Coburn, Ronald Murray *ophthalmic surgeon, researcher*
Fordyce, James George *physician*
†Huebl, Hubert C. *surgeon*
Katz, Sidney Franklin *obstetrician, gynecologist*
Myers, Woodrow Augustus, Jr. *physician, health care management director*
Salazar, Omar Mauricio *radiation oncologist, educator*
†Washington, Bruce Clifford *surgeon*

Detroit
†Abella Dominicis, Esteban Martin *hematologist, oncologist, pediatrician*
Abramson, Hanley Norman *pharmacy educator*
Amirikia, Hassan *obstetrician, gynecologist*
Anderson, John Albert *physician*
Berkelhamer, Jay Ellis *pediatrician*
Cerny, Joseph Charles *urologist, educator*
†Chen, Leilei *ophthalmologist*
†Coffey, C(harles) Edward *physician*
Cohen, Sanford Ned *pediatrics educator, academic administrator*
Diaz, Fernando Gustavo *neurosurgeon*
Dombrowski, Mitchell Paul *physician, inventor, researcher*
Enam, Syed Ather *neurosurgeon, researcher*
Evans, Mark Ira *obstetrician, geneticist*
Fromm, David *surgeon*
Gallick, Harold Lynn *cardiac surgeon*
Gonzalez, Ricardo *surgeon, educator*
Hashimoto, Ken *dermatology educator*
Hayashi, Hajime *immunologist*
Kantrowitz, Adrian *surgeon, educator*
Kaplan, Joseph *pediatrician*
Krull, Edward Alexander *dermatologist*
Lim, Henry Wan-Peng *physician*
Lupulescu, Aurel Peter *medical educator, researcher, physician*
Lusher, Jeanne Marie *pediatric hematologist, educator*
Maiese, Kenneth *neurologist*
†Malik, Ghaus Muhammad *neurosurgeon*
Mayes, Maureen Davidica *physician, educator*
McCarroll, Kathleen Ann *radiologist, educator*
†Michael, Daniel Bernard *neurosurgeon*
Miller, Orlando Jack *physician, educator*
†Minanov, Kristijan George *cardiothoracic surgeon*
Newton, Kenneth Kurt *internist*
Perry, Burton Lars *retired pediatrician*
Peters, William P. *oncologist, science administrator, educator*
Peterson, Patti Lynn *neurologist*
Phillips, Eduardo *surgeon, educator*
Porter, Arthur T. *oncologist, educator*
Reide, Jerome L. *social sciences educator, lawyer*
†Rosenblum, Mark L. *neurosurgeon*
Segel, Mark Calvin *diagnostic radiologist*
†Shaffrey, Christopher Ignatius *spinal surgeon*
Shah, Aashit K *neurologist*
†Shankaran, Seetha *physician, educator, researcher, administrator*
Silverman, Norman Alan *cardiac surgeon*
Sima, Anders Adolph Fredrik *neuropathologist, neurosciences researcher, educator*
Sloan, Andrew Edward *neurosurgeon*
Smith, Wilbur Lazear *radiologist, educator*
Sokol, Robert James *obstetrician, gynecologist, educator*
Stein, Paul David *cardiologist*
Tolia, Vasundhara K. *pediatric gastroenterologist, educator*
Uhde, Thomas Whitley *psychiatry educator, psychiatrist*
Voudoukis, Ignatios John *internist, cardiologist*
Whitehouse, Fred Waite *endocrinologist, researcher*
Wiener, Joseph *pathologist*

East Lansing
Brody, Theodore Meyer *pharmacologist, educator*
Gottschalk, Alexander *radiologist, diagnostic radiology educator*
Johnson, John Irwin, Jr. *neuroscientist*
Magen, Myron Shimin *osteopathic physician, educator, university dean*
Moore, Kenneth Edwin *pharmacology educator*
Murray, Raymond Harold *physician*
Netzloff, Michael Lawrence *pediatric educator, endocrinologist, geneticist*
Paneth, Nigel Sefton *epidemiologist, pediatrician*
Potchen, E. James *radiology educator*
Ristow, George Edward *neurologist, educator*
Rosenman, Kenneth D. *medical educator*
Rovner, David Richard *endocrinology educator*
Sato, Paul Hisashi *pharmacologist*
Waite, Donald Eugene *medical educator, consultant*
Walker, Bruce Edward *anatomy educator*

Farmington Hills
Blum, Jon H. *dermatologist*
Gordon, Craig Jeffrey *oncologist, educator*
Lewis, Barry Kent *cardiologist*
McQuiggan, Mark C. *urologist*

Fife Lake
Knecht, Richard Arden *family practitioner*

Flint
Farrehi, Cyrus *cardiologist, educator*
Jayabalan, Vemblaserry *nuclear medicine physician, radiologist*
Johnson, Gary Keith *pediatrician*
†Sayyid, Samiullah N. *physician*
Soderstrom, Robert Merriner *dermatologist*
Tauscher, John Walter *retired pediatrician, emeritus educator*

Frankenmuth
Shetlar, James Francis *physician*

Grand Blanc
Wasfie, Tarik Jawad *surgeon, educator*

Grand Rapids
Bartek, Gordon Luke *radiologist*
Daniels, Joseph *neuropsychiatrist*
†Grin, Oliver Daniel Woodhouse *neurosurgeon*
Maurer, John Raymond *internist, educator*
†Murphy, Edward Thomas *cardiothoracic surgeon*
Verdier, David D'Ooge *ophthalmologist, educator*
Wilt, Jeffrey Lynn *pulmonary and critical care physician*

Grosse Pointe
Beierwaltes, William Henry *physician, educator*
†Dzul, Paul J. *physician, medical journal editor*
Powsner, Edward Raphael *physician*
Sphire, Raymond Daniel *anesthesiologist*

Grosse Pointe Woods
†Sul, Yi Chul *neurologist*

Harper Woods
DeGiusti, Dominic Lawrence *medical science educator, academic administrator*

Hartford
†Spriegel, John R. *internist, medical association administrator*

Holland
Zuidema, George Dale *surgeon*

Kalamazoo
Chodos, Dale David Jerome *physician, consumer advocate*
†Dorner, Kenneth R. *plastic surgeon*
Fisher, George *gerontological educator*
Gladstone, William Sheldon, Jr. *radiologist*
Taylor, Duncan Paul *research neuropharmacologist*

Kalkaska
Batsakis, John George *pathology educator*

Kentwood
†Scott, Helen Patricia *family physician*

Lake Angelus
Kresge, Bruce Anderson *retired physician*

Lansing
Sauer, Harold John *physician, educator*
Vincent, Frederick Michael, Sr. *neurologist, educational administrator*

Livonia
Sobel, Howard Bernard *osteopath*

Madison Heights
†Metropoulos, George E. *occupational medicine physician*

Mancelona
Whelan, Joseph L. *neurologist*

Marquette
†Gupta, Pratap Chandra *neurologist, educator*

Midland
McCarty, Leslie Paul *pharmacologist, chemist*
Snyder, Robert Lee *anesthesiologist*

Newberry
Summersett, Kenneth George *psychiatric social worker, educator*

Northport
Schultz, Richard Carlton *plastic surgeon*

Northville
Abbasi, Tariq Afzal *psychiatrist, educator*

Oak Park
Borovoy, Marc Allen *podiatrist*
Kaplan, Randy Kaye *podiatrist*

Okemos
Monson, Carol Lynn *osteopath, psychotherapist*

Otsego
Berneis, Kenneth Stanley *physician, educator*

Pleasant Ridge
Krabbenhoft, Kenneth Lester *radiologist, educator*

Pontiac
James, Reese Joseph *physician*

Portage
†Toledo-Pereyra, Luis Horacio *transplant surgeon, researcher, historian educator*

Rochester Hills
Badalament, Robert Anthony *urologic oncologist*
Bartunek, James Scott *psychiatrist*

Royal Oak
Bernstein, Jay *pathologist, researcher, educator*
†Diokno, Ananias C. *urologic surgeon, educator*
Dworkin, Howard Jerry *nuclear physician, educator*
†Ernstoff, Raina Marcia *neurologist*
LaBan, Myron Miles *physician, administrator*
O'Neill, William Walter *physician, educator*
Ryan, Jack *physician, retired hospital corporation executive*

Saginaw
La Londe, Lawrence Lee *family practice physician*
Oesterling, Joseph Edwin *urologic surgeon*

Saint Clair Shores
Walker, Frank Banghart *pathologist*

Saint Joseph
Ahmad, Anwar *radiologist*

Saugatuck
Telder, Thomas Van Doorn *medical educator*

Shelby Township
Miller, Aileen Etta Martha *medical association administrator, consultant, metabolic nutritionist, therapeutic touch practitioner*

Southfield
Dobritt, Dennis William *physician, researcher, pain management specialist*
Duvernoy, Wolf F.C. *cardiologist*
Giles, Conrad Leslie *ophthalmic surgeon*
Green, Henry Leonard *physician*
Mathog, Robert Henry *otolaryngologist, educator*
Newman, Steven E. *neurologist*
O'Hara, John Paul, III *orthopaedic surgeon*
Rosenzweig, Norman *psychiatry educator*
Zubroff, Leonard Saul *surgeon*

Sterling Heights
Frank, Michael Sanford *dermatologist*

Sturgis
Cabansag, Vicente Dacanay, Jr. *medical association administrator*
Reiff, James Stanley *addictions, psychiatric, and osteopathic physician, surgeon*

Traverse City
†Gillett, Ward Robert *urologist*

Troy
Golusin, Millard R. *obstetrician and gynecologist*
Schafer, Sharon Marie *anesthesiologist*

Warren
Yakes, Barbara Lee *occupational and preventive medicine physician, former nurse*

West Bloomfield
†Jones, Lewis Arnold *physician, radiologist*
Joseph, Ramon Rafael *physician, educator*
Sarwer-Foner, Gerald Jacob *physician, educator*
Sawyer, Howard Jerome *physician*
Seidman, Michael David *surgeon, educator*

Ypsilanti
Hildebrandt, H(enry) M(ark) *pediatrician*
†Kirkpatrick, Garland Penn *pediatrician*
Ritter, Frank Nicholas *otolaryngologist, educator*
Sealy, Vernol St. Clair *scientist*

MINNESOTA

Apple Valley
Doyle, O'Brien John, Jr. *emergency medical services consultant, lobbyist, writer*

Billings
†Schwidde, Jess T. *neurological surgeon*

Bloomington
Lakin, James Dennis *allergist, immunologist, director*

Duluth
Aufderheide, Arthur Carl *pathologist*
Eisenberg, Richard Martin *pharmacology educator*
Sebastian, James Albert *obstetrician, gynecologist, educator*
†Wickstrom, Per Henrik *surgeon*

Eden Prairie
Harris, Jean Louise *physician*

Edina
†Fasching, Michael Cloud *plastic surgeon*

Excelsior
Anderson, William Robert *pathologist, educator*
Bilka, Paul Joseph *physician*

Golden Valley
†Mindrum, Gerald Gene *physician*

Minneapolis
Blackburn, Henry Webster, Jr. *retired physician*
Bolman, Ralph Morton, III (Chip Bolman) *cardiac surgeon*
†Bonnabeau, Raymond C. *physician*
Boudreau, Robert James *nuclear medicine physician, researcher*
Brown, David M. *physician, educator, dean*
Buchwald, Henry *surgeon, educator, researcher*
Burton, Charles Victor *physician, surgeon, inventor*
Carson, Linda Frances *gynecologic oncologist*
Cavert, Henry Mead *physician, retired educator*
Chavers, Blanche Marie *pediatrician, educator, reseacher*
Chester, Thomas Jay *physician*
Chisholm, Tague Clement *pediatric surgeon, educator*
Chou, Shelley Nien-chun *neurosurgeon, university official, educator*
Craig, James Lynn *physician, consumer products company executive*
†Cunningham, Bruce L. *plastic and reconstructive surgeon, educator*
Dykstra, Dennis Dale *physiatrist*
Fisch, Robert Otto *medical educator*
Gajl-Peczalska, Kazimiera J. *surgical pathologist, pathology educator*
Gorlin, Robert James *medical educator*
Gullickson, Glenn, Jr. *physician, educator*
Horns, Howard Lowell *physician, educator*
Kane, Robert Lewis *public health educator*
Kaplan, Manuel E. *physician, educator*
Keane, William Francis *nephrology educator, research foundation executive*
Kennedy, B(yrl) J(ames) *medicine and oncology educator*
Knopman, David S. *neurologist*
Kump, Warren Lee *diagnostic radiologist*
LaPrade, Robert F. *orthopedic surgeon, educator*
Leon, Arthur Sol *research cardiologist, exercise physiologist*
Leppik, Ilo E. *neurologist, educator*
Levitt, Seymour Herbert *physician, radiology educator*
Luepker, Russell Vincent *epidemiology educator*
†Mandel, Jack Sheldon *epidemiologist, educator*
Mazze, Roger Steven *medical educator, researcher*
McQuarrie, Donald Gray *surgeon, educator*
Michael, Alfred Frederick, Jr. *physician, medical educator*
Najarian, John Sarkis *surgeon, educator*
Nelson, Charles Alexander III *medical education educator*
Palahniuk, Richard John *anesthesiology educator, researcher*
Peterson, Douglas Arthur *physician*
Peterson, Oliver H. *retired obstetrician/gynecologist*
Phibbs, Clifford Matthew *surgeon, educator*
Prem, Konald Arthur *physician, educator*
Quie, Paul Gerhardt *physician, educator*
Ray, Charles Dean *neurosurgeon, spine surgeon, bioengineer, inventor*
†Rockswold, Gaylan Lee *neurosurgeon*
†Rottenberg, David Allan *neurologist*
Sawchuk, Ronald John *pharmaceutical sciences educator*
Schultz, Alvin Leroy *retired internist, endocrinologist, retired university health science facility administrator*
Staba, Emil John *pharmacognosy and medicinal chemistry educator*
Stenwick, Michael William *internist, geriatric medicine consultant*
Tagatz, George Elmo *obstetrician, gynecologist, educator*
†Tamzarian, Armin Petrovich *physician*
Thompson, Roby Calvin, Jr. *orthopedic surgeon, educator*
Thompson, Theodore Robert *pediatric educator*
Thompson, William Moreau *radiologist, educator*
Ulstrom, Robert A. *pediatrician, educator*
†Wester, M(ary) Sue Hiebert *occupational medicine physician*
Wild, John Julian *surgeon, director medical research institute*
Wilson, Robert Foster *cardiologist, educator*
Wirtschafter, Jonathan Dine *neuro-ophthalmology educator, scientist*

Minnetonka
Shapiro, Fred Louis *physician, educator*

Olivia
Cosgriff, James Arthur *physician*

Plymouth
Berlinger, Norman Thomas *physician, author*

Rochester
Bartholomew, Lloyd Gibson *physician*
†Bastron, James Arthur *retired neurologist*
Beahrs, Oliver Howard *surgeon, educator*
Beckett, Victoria Ling *physician*
Brimijoin, William Stephen *pharmacology educator, neuroscience researcher*
Cascino, Terrence *neurologist*
†Clay, Ricky Perry *plastic surgeon, consultant, medical educator*
Corbin, Kendall Brooks *physician, scientist*
Danielson, Gordon Kenneth, Jr. *cardiovascular surgeon, educator*
DeRemee, Richard Arthur *physician, educator, researcher*
Dickson, Edgar Rolland *gastroenterologist*
Douglass, Bruce E. *physician*
Du Shane, James William *physician, educator*
Engel, Andrew George *neurologist*
Feldt, Robert Hewitt *pediatric cardiologist, educator*
Gilchrist, Gerald Seymour *pediatric hematologist, oncologist, educator*
Gleich, Gerald Joseph *immunologist, medical scientist*
Gomez, Manuel Rodriguez *physician*
Gracey, Douglas Robert *physician, physiologist, educator*
Hattery, Robert R. *radiologist, educator*
Hunder, Gene Gerald *physician, educator*
Krom, Ruud Arne Finco *surgeon*
Kurland, Leonard Terry *epidemiologist educator*
Kyle, Robert Arthur *medical educator, oncologist*
LaRusso, Nicholas F. *gastroenterologist, educator, scientist*
†Liebow, Mark *physician*
Lofgren, Karl Adolph *surgeon*
Lucas, Alexander Ralph *child psychiatrist, educator, writer*
MacCarty, Collin Stewart *neurosurgeon*
Malkasian, George Durand, Jr. *physician, educator*
Michenfelder, John Donahue *anesthesiology educator*
†Miller, Daniel Lee *surgeon*
Morlock, Carl Grismore *physician, medical educator*
Mulder, Donald William *physician, educator*
Neel, Harry Bryan, III *surgeon, scientist, educator*
Nichols, Donald Richardson *medical educator*
Olsen, Arthur Martin *physician, educator*
Payne, W(illiam) Spencer *retired surgeon*
Perry, Harold Otto *dermatologist*
Phillips, Sidney Frederick *gastroenterologist*
Pittelkow, Mark Robert *physician, dermatology educator, researcher*
Porter, Louis II *medical development officer, writer*
Pratt, Joseph Hyde, Jr. *surgeon*
Reitemeier, Richard Joseph *physician*
Rogers, Roy Steele, III *dermatology educator, dean*
Rosenow, Edward Carl, III *medical educator*
Scott, John Paul *medical educator*
Segura, Joseph Weston *urologist, educator*
Siekert, Robert George *neurologist*
Stegall, Mark D. *surgeon, medical educator*
Stillwell, G(eorge) Keith *physician*
Symmonds, Richard Earl *gynecologist*
Whisnant, Jack Page *neurologist*
Woods, John Elmer *plastic surgeon*

Roseville
†Mann, Orrin *preventive medicine physician, health facility administrator*

Saint Cloud
Olson, Barbara Ford *physician*

Saint Louis Park
Galbraith, Richard Frederick *physician, neurologist*
†Stein, Steven David *neurologist*

Saint Paul
Burchell, Howard Bertram *retired physician, educator*
Crabb, Kenneth Wayne *obstetrician, gynecologist*
Edwards, Jesse Efrem *physician, educator*
†Eyunni, Vijay Raghavan *occupational medicine physician*
Hays, Thomas S. *medical educator, medical researcher*
Hodgson, Jane Elizabeth *obstetrician and gynecologist, consultant*
†Ley, Carol Ann *preventative and occupational medicine physician*
Rothenberger, David Albert *surgeon*
Sher, Phyllis Kammerman *pediatric neurology educator*
Swaiman, Kenneth Fred *pediatric neurologist, educator*
Titus, Jack L. *pathologist, educator*
Uckun, Fatih *research scientist, pediatric medicine educator*
Wilson, Leonard Gilchrist *history of medicine educator*
Zander, Janet Adele *psychiatrist*
Zenker, Paul Nicolas *epidemiologist, pediatrician, medical director*

Starbuck
Rapp, Gregory Paul *physician assistant*

Virginia
Knabe, George William, Jr. *pathologist, educator*

Willmar
Vander Aarde, Stanley Bernard *retired otolaryngologist*

MISSISSIPPI

Gautier
Egerton, Charles Pickford *anatomy and physiology educator*

Houston
Griffin, T. David *family physician, pharmacist*

Jackson
Achord, James Lee *gastroenterologist, educator*
Ball, Carroll Raybourne *anatomist, medical educator, researcher*
Bloom, Sherman *pathologist, educator*
Boronow, Richard Carlton *gynecologist, educator*
Burrow, William Hollis, II *dermatologist*
Cruse, Julius Major, Jr. *pathologist, educator*
Currier, Robert David *neurologist*
Freeland, Alan Edward *orthopedic surgery educator, physician*
Guyton, Arthur Clifton *physician, educator*
Houston, Gerry Ann *oncologist*
Howard, William Percy *physician*
Khansur, Tawfiq Iftekhar *physician, researcher, educator*
Lewis, Robert Edwin, Jr. *pathology immunology educator, researcher*
Poole, Galen Vincent *surgeon, educator, researcher*
Russell, Robert Pritchard *ophthalmologist*
†Shearin, Robert Patrick Noel *physician, medical administrator*
Shirley, Aaron *pediatrician*
Sneed, Raphael Corcoran *physiatrist, pediatrician*
Suess, James Francis *retired psychiatry educator*
Thigpen, James Tate *physician, oncology educator*
Tourney, Garfield *psychiatrist, educator*
Walcott, Dexter Winn *allergist*

Laurel
Lacey, Peeler Grayson *diagnostic radiologist*

Madison
Morrison, Francis Secrest *physician*

Magnolia
Lampton, Lucius Marion *physician, editor*

Pascagoula
†Horowitz, Michael Dory *cardiothoracic surgeon*

Ruleville
Cosue, Lamberto Gutierrez, III *internist*

Tupelo
Bullard, Rickey Howard *podiatric physician, surgeon*

Whitfield
Kliesch, William Frank *physician*

MISSOURI

Belton
Blim, Richard Don *retired pediatrician*

Bridgeton
Johnson, Kevin Todd *physician*

Caruthersville
Puangsuvan, Somporn *surgeon, consultant*

Chesterfield
Frawley, Thomas Francis *retired physician*
Hunter, Harlen Charles *orthopedic surgeon*
Johnston, Marilyn Frances-Meyers *physician, medical educator*
Levin, Marvin Edgar *physician*

Clayton
Onken, Henry Dralle *plastic surgeon*

Columbia
Allen, William Cecil *physician, educator*
Boedeker, Ben Harold *anesthesiologist, educator*
Colwill, Jack Marshall *physician, educator*
Cunningham, Milamari Antoinella *anesthesiologist*
Eggers, George William Nordholtz, Jr. *anesthesiologist, educator*
Frey, Jeffery Paul *internist, geriatrician*
Hardin, Christopher Demarest *medical educator*
Hess, Darla Baltersmith *cardiologist, educator*
Hess, Leonard Wayne *obstetrician gynecologist, perinatologist*
Hillman, Richard Ephraim *pediatrician, educator*
James, Elizabeth Joan Plogsted *pediatrician, educator*
Jones, James Wilson *physician, cell biologist, ethicist*
Khojasteh, Ali *medical oncologist, hematologist*
Longo, Daniel Robert *health services researcher, medical educator*
Nichols, Walter Kirt *surgeon*
†Oro, John J. *neurosurgeon*
Perkoff, Gerald Thomas *physician, educator*
Perry, Michael Clinton *physician, medical educator, academic administrator*
Puckett, C. Lin *plastic surgeon, educator*
See, William Mitchel (W. Mike See) *cardiovascular and thoracic surgeon*
Silver, Donald *surgeon, educator*
Southwick, Christopher Lyn *anesthesiologist*
Weiss, James Moses Aaron *psychiatrist, educator*
Witten, David Melvin *radiology educator*

Florissant
Owen, Robert Frederick *internist, rheumatologist*

Fort Leonard Wood
†Hewitson, William Craig *physician, career officer*

Fulton
Gish, Edward Rutledge *surgeon*

Gravois Mills
Dunn, Floyd Emryl *psychiatrist, neurologist, consultant*

Jefferson City
Sugarbaker, Stephen Philip *surgeon, educator*

Joplin
Crumpacker, Rex K. *anesthesiologist*
Daus, Arthur Steven *neurological surgeon*
Singleton, Marvin Ayers *otolaryngologist, senator*

Kansas City
Abdou, Nabih I. *physician, educator*
Butler, Merlin Gene *physician, medical geneticist, educator*
Crayton, Billy Gene *physician*
Crockett, James Edwin *physician, educator*
Dimond, Edmunds Grey *medical educator*
Dixon, George David *radiologist*
Godfrey, William Ashley *ophthalmologist*
Graham, Robert *medical association executive*
Hagan, John Charles, III *ophthalmologist*
†Hunkeler, John Douglas *ophthalmologist*
Hunzicker, Warren John *research consultant, physician, cardiologist*
Jarka, Dale Elizabeth *surgeon*
Kagan, Stuart Michael *pediatrician*
Kirila, Carol Elizabeth *osteopathic physician*
Lofland, Gary Kenneth *cardiac surgeon*
Long, Edwin Tutt *surgeon*
Massey, Vickie Lea *radiologist*
McCoy, Frederick John *retired plastic surgeon*
McPhee, Mark Steven *medical educator, physician, gastroenterologist*
Mebust, Winston Keith *surgeon, educator*
Morrison, David Campbell *immunology educator*
Noback, Richardson Kilbourne *medical educator*
Rengachary, Setti Subbiyer *neurosurgeon, educator*
Sauer, Gordon Chenoweth *physician, educator*
Stelmach, Walter Jack *physician, medical education administrator*
Strain, Herbert Arthur, III *plastic surgeon*
†Willsie, Sandra K. *physician, educator*
†Wu, William Quokan *neurologist, writer*

Kirksville
Kuchera, Michael Louis *osteopathic physician, educator, author*

Lees Summit
†Rathbun, Katharine Cady *preventive medicine physician*

Osage Beach
East, Mark David *physician*

Osceola
†Mathew, Stanley *physician*

Pilot Kove
deCastro, Fernando Jose *pediatrics educator*

Poplar Bluff
Lotuaco, Luisa Go *pathologist*
Piland, Donald Spencer *internist*

Saint Charles
Dieterich, Russell Burks *obstetrician, gynecologist*

Saint Louis
Agrawal, Harish Chandra *neurobiologist, researcher, educator*
Alpers, David Hershel *physician, educator*
Arrington, Barbara *public health educator*
Bacon, Bruce Raymond *physician*
Ballinger, Walter Francis *surgeon, educator*
Baue, Arthur Edward *surgeon, educator, administrator*
Berg, Leonard *neurologist, educator, researcher*
Berland, David I. *psychiatrist, educator*
Blumenthal, Herman Theodore *physician, educator*
Brodeur, Armand Edward *pediatric radiologist*
Brown, Wendy Weinstock *nephrologist, educator*
Cabbabe, Edmond Bechir *plastic and hand surgeon*
Chaplin, David Dunbar *medical research specialist, medical educator*
Chaplin, Hugh, Jr. *physician, educator*
Chole, Richard Arthur *otolaryngologist, educator*
Cloninger, Claude Robert *psychiatric researcher, educator, genetic epidemiologist*
Coe, Rodney Michael *medical educator*
Cryer, Philip Eugene *medical educator, scientist, endocrinologist*
Dagogo-Jack, Samuel E. *medical educator, physician scientist, endocrinologist*
Dewald, Paul Adolph *psychiatrist, educator*
Dodge, Philip Rogers *physician, educator*
Dodson, W(illiam) Edwin *child neurology educator*
Donati, Robert Mario *physician, educational administrator*
Dougherty, Charles Hamilton *pediatrician*
Drews, Robert Carrel *retired physician*
Evens, Ronald Gene *radiologist, medical center administrator*
†Fischer, Keith C. *nuclear medicine physician, radiology educator*
Fitch, Coy Dean *physician, educator*
Fletcher, James Warren *physician*
Flye, M. Wayne *surgeon, immunologist, educator, writer*
Friedman, William Hersh *otolaryngologist, educator*
Gay, William Arthur, Jr. *thoracic surgeon, educator*
Geltman, Edward Mark *cardiologist, educator*
Goldberg, Anne Carol *physician, educator*
Goodenberger, Daniel Marvin *medical educator*
Grigsby, Perry Wayne *physician*
Grossberg, George Thomas *psychiatrist, educator*
Grubb, Robert L., Jr. *neurosurgeon*
Guze, Samuel Barry *psychiatrist, educator*
Hall, William Kearney *retired dermatologist*
Hammerman, Marc Randall *nephrologist, educator*
Hanley, Thomas Patrick *obstetrician, gynecologist*
Heiken, Jay Paul *physician*
Hofstatter, Leopold *psychiatrist, researcher*
Holmes, Nancy Elizabeth *pediatrician*
†Huddleston, Charles B. *surgeon, educator*
Hyers, Thomas Morgan *physician, biomedical researcher*
Kaminski, Donald Leon *medical educator, surgeon, gastrointestinal physiologist*
Kang, Juan *pathologist*
Kaplan, Henry Jerrold *ophthalmologist, educator*
Karl, Michael M. *endocrinology professor*
Kelly, Daniel P. *cardiologist, molecular biologist*
Kimmey, James Richard, Jr. *medical educator, consultant*
Kincaid, Marilyn Coburn *medical educator*
Kinsella, Ralph Aloysius, Jr. *physician*
Kipnis, David Morris *physician, educator*
Kivikoski, Asko Ilmari *obstetrician/gynecologist*
Klahr, Saulo *physician, educator*
Knutsen, Alan Paul *pediatrician, allergist, immunologist*
Kolker, Allan Erwin *ophthalmologist*
Kornfeld, Stuart A. *hematology educator*
Kouchoukos, Nicholas Thomas *surgeon*
Lacy, Paul Eston *pathologist*
Lagunoff, David *physician, educator*
Lewis, Robert David *ophthalmologist, educator*
Loeb, Virgil, Jr. *oncologist, hematologist*
Lustman, Patrick J. *psychiatrist*
Majerus, Philip Warren *physician*
Mangelsdorf, Thomas Kelly *psychiatrist, consultant*
Manske, Paul Robert *orthopedic hand surgeon, educator*
Mantovani, John F. *pediatric neurologist*
Martin, Kevin John *nephrologist, educator*
†McDonald, Josh William *surgical pathologist*
McFadden, James Frederick, Jr. *surgeon*
Middelkamp, John Neal *pediatrician, educator*
Mooradian, Arshag Dertad *physician, educator*
Morales-Galarreta, Julio *psychiatrist, child psychoanalyst*
Morley, John Edward *physician*
Morris, John Carl *neurologist, researcher*
Myerson, Robert J. *radiation oncologist, educator*
Owens, William Don *anesthesiology educator*
Payne, Meredith Jorstad *physician*
Peck, William Arno *physician, educator, university official and dean*
Perez, Carlos A. *radiation oncologist, educator*
Perlmutter, David H. *physician, educator*
†Pertmutter, Joel S. *physician*
Prensky, Arthur Lawrence *pediatric neurologist, educator*
Purkerson, Mabel Louise *physician, physiologist, educator*
Radford, Diane Mary *surgeon, surgical oncologist*
Rao, Dabeeru C. *epidemiologist*
Riner, Ronald Nathan *cardiologist, business consultant*
Robins, Lee Nelken *medical educator*
Royal, Henry Duval *nuclear medicine physician*
Royce, Robert Killian *physician*
Schonfeld, Gustav *medical educator, researcher*
Schreiber, James Ralph *obstetrics, gynecology researcher*
Schwartz, Alan Leigh *pediatrician, educator*
Shank, Robert Ely *physician, preventive medicine educator, retired*
Siegel, Barry Alan *nuclear radiologist*
Slavin, Raymond Granam *allergist, immunologist*
Spector, Gershon Jerry *physician, educator, researcher*
Stoneman, William, III *physician, educator*
Strunk, Robert Charles *physician*
Sutter, Richard Anthony *physician*
Takes, Peter Arthur *immunologist*
Teitelbaum, Steven Lazarus *pathology educator*
†Tempel, Lee W. *neurologist*
Ternberg, Jessie Lamoin *pediatric surgeon*
Ulett, George Andrew *psychiatrist*
Unanue, Emil Raphael *immunopathologist*
Walentik, Corinne Anne *pediatrician*
Walz, Bruce James *radiation oncologist*
†Weber, Mark F. *medical executive*
Whyte, Michael Peter *medicine, pediatrics and genetics educator, research director*
Wickline, Samuel Alan *cardiologist, educator*
Willman, Vallee Louis *physician, surgery educator*
Willmore, Luther James, Jr. *neurologist, academic administrator, educator*
Young, Paul Andrew *anatomist*

Springfield
Geter, Rodney Keith *plastic surgeon*
Hackett, Earl Randolph *neurologist*
H'Doubler, Francis Todd, Jr. *surgeon*
McCorcle, Marcus Duane *obstetrician, gynecologist*

University City
Shen, Jerome Tseng Yung *retired pediatrician*

Warson Woods
†Barnes, Walter C., Jr. *physician*

MONTANA

Billings
Glenn, Guy Charles *pathologist*
Kohler, William Curtis *sleep specialist, neurologist*
Rich, Joseph David *psychiatrist*

Helena
Strickler, Jeffrey Harold *pediatrician*

Missoula
Fawcett, Don Wayne *anatomist*
†Harlan, John W. *physician*

Whitefish
Miller, Ronald Alfred *family physician*

NEBRASKA

Hastings
Dungan, John Russell, Jr. (Titular Viscount Dungan of Clane and Hereditary Prince of Ara) *anesthesiologist*

Lincoln
Clyne, Dianna Marie *psychiatrist*
Hirai, Denitsu *surgeon*
Metz, Philip Steven *surgeon, educator*
Wilson, Charles Stephen *cardiologist*

Omaha
Casey, Murray Joseph *physician, educator*
Dominguez, Edward Anthony *physician, medical educator, consultant*
Eilts, Susanne Elizabeth *physician*
Fleming, William Hare *surgeon*
Frey, Donald Ray *medical association administrator*
Fusaro, Ramon Michael *dermatologist*
Gendelman, Howard Eliot *biomedical researcher, physician*
Hankins, Katherine Elizabeth *obstetrician-gynecologist*
Hartman, Herbert Arthur, Jr. *oncologist*
†Hellbusch, Leslie Carl *neurosurgeon*
Hodgson, Paul Edmund *surgeon*
Imray, Thomas John *radiologist, educator*
Kessinger, Margaret Anne *medical educator*
Korbitz, Bernard Carl *retired oncologist, hematologist, educator, consultant*
Mardis, Hal Kennedy *urological surgeon, educator, researcher*
Maurer, Harold Maurice *pediatrician*
Millatmal, Tajuddin *physician*
Mohiuddin, Syed Maqdoom *cardiologist, educator*
Muelleman, Robert Leo *physician, researcher medical educator*
Neibel, Oliver Joseph, Jr. *retired medical services executive*
O'Donohue, Walter John, Jr. *medical educator*
†Patil, Arun Angelo *neurosurgery educator*
Pearson, Paul Hammond *physician*
Pfeiffer, Ronald Frederick *neurologist, researcher*

Roffman, Blaine Yale pathologist
Rupp, Mark Edmund medical educator
Sanders, W(illiam) Eugene, Jr. physician, educator
Sheehan, John Francis cytopathologist, educator
Shilling, Kay Marlene psychiatrist
Skoog, Donald Paul retired physician, educator
Tinker, John Heath anesthesiologist, educator
Townley, Robert Gordon medical educator
Truhlsen, Stanley Marshall physician, educator
Waggener, Ronald Edgar radiologist
Ward, Vernon Graves internist

Papillion
Casale, Thomas Bruce medical educator
Dvorak, Allen Dale radiologist

Scottsbluff
Kabalin, John Nicholas urologist

NEVADA

Carson City
Meyer, Roger Paul physician

Las Vegas
Amirana, M. T. surgeon
Capanna, Albert Howard neurosurgeon, neuroscientist
†Cooper, Matthew Marc cardiothoracic surgeon
Davidson, Joel surgeon
Fennel, Peter J., Sr. retired anesthesiologist
Hanson, Gerald Eugene oral and maxillofacial surgeon
Kurlinski, John Parker physician
McAnelly, Robert D. physiatrist, researcher
Merkin, Albert Charles pediatrician, allergist
Moritz, Timothy Bovie psychiatrist
Murray, Kevin Dennis surgeon
Shires, George Thomas surgeon, educator
Speck, Eugene Lewis internist
Sullivan, Walter Gerard plastic surgeon, lawyer
Wax, Arnold physician
Zuspan, Frederick Paul obstetrician, gynecologist, educator

Reno
Barnet, Robert Joseph cardiologist, ethicist
Bigley, George Kim, Jr. neurologist
Blake-Inada, Louis Michael cardiologist, researcher
†Eaton, John Monroe neurologist, educator
MacKintosh, Frederick Roy oncologist
Shapiro, Leonard immunologist, allergist

Sparks
Lee, Richard Scott neurologist

NEW HAMPSHIRE

Bedford
Khazei, Amir Mohsen surgeon, oncologist

Bethlehem
Worner, Theresa Marie physician

Canterbury
Chamberlin, Robert West medical educator

Concord
Bagan, Merwyn neurological surgeon
de Nesnera, Alexander Peter psychiatrist

Dover
†Winkler, Peter Alexander plastic surgeon

Etna
Ferm, Vergil Harkness anatomist, embryologist

Franklin
†Dean, Shervin Christopher emergency medicine physician

Grantham
Behrle, Franklin Charles retired pediatrician and educator
Knights, Edwin Munroe pathologist
MacNeill, Arthur Edson physician, science consultant

Hanover
Almy, Thomas Pattison physician, educator
Baldwin, John Charles surgeon, researcher
Koop, Charles Everett surgeon, educator, former surgeon general
Moeschler, John Boyer physician, educator
Rawnsley, Howard Melody physician, educator
Rolett, Ellis Lawrence medical educator, cardiologist
Rueckert, Frederic plastic and reconstructive surgeon
Sporn, Michael Benjamin cancer researcher
Staples, O. Sherwin orthopedic surgeon
Wallace, Andrew Grover physician, educator, medical school dean
Zubkoff, Michael medical educator

Keene
Fuld, Gilbert Lloyd pediatrician

Lebanon
Barney, Christine Anne psychiatrist, educator
Clendenning, William Edmund dermatologist
Cornwell, Gibbons Gray, III physician, medical educator
Cronenwett, Jack LeMoyne vascular surgeon educator
Fanger, Michael W. medical educator
Fiering, Steven medical educator
Foote, Robert Stephens physician
Galton, Valerie Anne endocrinology educator
McCollum, Robert Wayne physician, educator
Shorter, Nicholas Andrew pediatric surgeon
Smith, Barry David obstetrician-gynecologist, educator
Sox, Harold Carleton, Jr. physician, educator
†Stommel, Elijah W. neurologist
von Reyn, C. Fordham infectious disease physician

Lee
Young, James Morningstar physician, naval officer

Lyme
McIntyre, Oswald Ross physician

Manchester
Angoff, Gerald Harvey cardiologist
Feder, Robert Elliot psychiatrist
Khouzam, Hani Raoul psychiatrist, physician, educator

Portsmouth
Lauzé, Karen Prudence physician, neurologist

NEW JERSEY

Avon By The Sea
O'Neill, James Paul psychiatrist

Basking Ridge
Panzarino, Saverio Joseph physician

Bayonne
Rogow, Louis Michael oncologist, educator

Belleville
Caputo, Wayne James surgeon, podiatrist
Goldenberg, David Milton experimental pathologist, oncologist
Sales, Clifford M. surgeon

Bernardsville
Dixon, Rosina Berry physician, pharmaceutical development consultant
Sullivan, Timothy Patrick ophthalmologist

Bridgewater
Feldman, Arthur Edward urologist
Hirsch, Paul J. orthopedic surgeon, medical executive, educator
Mondadori, Cesare neurobiologist, researcher

Browns Mills
Cha, Se Do internist
De Berardinis, Charles Anthony Joseph physician
Lumia, Francis James internist

Camden
Ances, I. G(eorge) obstetrician, gynecologist, educator
Camishion, Rudolph Carmen physician
Goldberg, Jack hematologist
Stahl, Gary Edward neonatologist
†Zaontz, Mark Randall pediatric urologist

Cherry Hill
Amsterdam, Jay D. psychiatrist, educator
Kahn, Sigmund Benham retired internist and dean
†Lipsius, Bruce David neurologist
Olearchyk, Andrew cardiothoracic surgeon, educator
Werbitt, Warren gastroenterologist, educator

Clifton
Kirrer, Ernest Douglas physician
Silber, Judy G. dermatologist

Cranbury
Sofia, R. D. pharmacologist

Cresskill
Gardner, Richard Alan psychiatrist, writer

Demarest
Dornfest, Burton Saul anatomy educator

Denville
Casper, Ephraim Saul medical oncologist
Husar, Walter Gene neurologist, neuroscientist, educator
Marfuggi, Richard Anthony plastic surgeon

Dover
Chung, Tae-Soo physician

East Brunswick
†Miller, Andrew David physician
Rosenberg, Norman surgeon

East Hanover
Anderson, Gary William physician
Zhou, Honghui clinical pharmacokineticist

East Orange
Yoo, James H. radiation oncologist, nuclear medicine physician

Eatontown
Granet, Kenneth M. internist
Orlando, Carl medical research and development executive

Edgewater
Karol, Cecilia Kalijman psychiatrist, psychoanalyst

Edison
Donahue, John Edward physician
Jacobey, John Arthur, III surgeon, educator
Kopidakis, Emmanuel G. general surgeon
Walters, Arthur Scott neurologist, educator, clinical research scientist

Elizabeth
Berger, Harold Richard physician
Rosenstein, Neil surgeon, genealogical researcher
Verret, Joseph Marc psychiatrist
Watson, Rita Marie internist, cardio vascular specialist

Elmer
Ventrella, Gerard physician

Englewood
Masland, Richard Lambert neurologist, educator
Wuhl, Charles Michael psychiatrist

Flanders
Huang, Jacob Chen-ya physician, city official

Forked River
Novak, Dennis E. family practice physician

Fort Lee
Chessler, Richard Kenneth gastroenterologist, endoscopist
Goldfischer, Jerome D. cardiologist
†Tesoriero, John Salvatore physician

Franklin Park
Perry, Arthur William plastic surgeon, educator

Glen Ridge
Clemente, Celestino physician, surgeon
Swerdlow, Dave Baer surgeon
Zbar, Lloyd Irwin Stanley otolaryngologist, educator

Green Brook
Hertzberg, Henry radiologist, educator

Hackensack
Davies, Richard John oncologist
De Groote, Robert David general and vascular surgeon
Rauscher, Gregory E. plastic surgeon
Riegel, Norman physician

Haddonfield
Capelli, John Placido nephrologist

Hamilton
Kane, Michael Joel physician

Hammonton
Pellegrino, Peter surgeon

Highland Park
Plaut, Eric Alfred retired psychiatrist, educator

Hillsdale
Copeland, Lois Jacqueline (Mrs. Richard A. Sperling) physician

Hillside
Fox, Sheldon retired radiologist, medical educator

Holmdel
†Samra, Said A. plastic surgeon

Hopatcong
Oken, Robert neuroscientist, researcher, consultant

Jersey City
Demos, Nicholas John physician, surgeon, researcher
Nissenbaum, Gerald physician, educator, inventor
†Rhodes, George Anthony plastic surgeon
Winters, Robert Wayne medical educator, pediatrician

Kendall Park
Berger, Richard Stanton dermatologist

Kenilworth
Scott, Mary Celine pharmacologist

Lakewood
Bowers, John Zimmerman physician, scientist, educator

Lawrenceville
Pouleur, Hubert Gustave cardiologist

Livingston
Cohn, Joseph David surgeon
Conde, Miguel A. hematologist, oncologist
Duberstein, Joel Lawrence physician
Eisenstein, Theodore Donald pediatrician
†Frankel, Jeffrey neurologist
Hill, George James physician, educator
Krieger, Abbott Joel neurosurgeon
Maron, Arthur pediatrician, medical administrator
Rickert, Robert Richard pathologist, educator
Rommer, James Andrew physician
Templeton, Hilda B. psychiatrist, educator

Long Branch
Barnett, Lester Alfred surgeon
Fox, Howard Alan physician, medical educator
Poch, Herbert Edward pediatrician, educator

Madison
Levy, Robert Isaac physician, educator, research director

Manalapan
Harrison-Johnson, Yvonne Elois pharmacologist

Manasquan
Topilow, Arthur Alan internist

Maplewood
Shuttleworth, Anne Margaret psychiatrist

Margate City
Videll, Jared Steven cardiologist

Metuchen
Slobodien, Howard David surgeon

Middletown
Anania, William Christian podiatrist

Millburn
Corwin, Andrew David physician

Moorestown
Cervantes, Luis Augusto neurosurgeon
Margolis, Gerald Joseph psychiatrist, psychoanalyst

Morganville
†Choy-Kwong, Maria neurologist

Morris Plains
Fielding, Stuart psychopharmacologist

Morristown
Bernson, Marcella Shelley psychiatrist
Casale, Alfred Stanley thoracic and cardiovascular surgeon
Finkel, Marion Judith physician, pharmaceutical company administrator
Jacobowitz, Walter Erwin obstetrician, gynecologist
Pan, Henry Yue-Ming clinical pharmacologist
Parr, Grant Van Siclen surgeon
Smith, Thomas J. surgeon, educator
Thornton, Yvonne Shirley physician, author, musician

Mount Holly
Hurlbut, Terry Allison pathologist

Mountainside
Lissenden, Carol Kay pediatrician
†Lombardi, Neil pediatric neurologist
†Sussman, Neil M(ark) neurologist

Neptune
Baro, Susan Marie surgeon
Boak, Joseph Gordon cardiologist
†Crosley, Powel A. physician
Harrigan, John Thomas, Jr. physician, obstetrician-gynecologist
†Rhee, Richard Sanchul physician, neurologist
Rice, Stephen Gary medical educator, sports medicine physician

New Brunswick
Aisner, Joseph oncologist, physician
Corbett, Siobhan Aiden surgeon
Ettinger, Lawrence Jay pediatric hematologist and oncologist, educator
Gocke, David Joseph immunology educator, physician, medical scientist
Graham, Alan Morrison surgeon
Greco, Ralph Steven surgeon, researcher, medical educator
Laraya-Cuasay, Lourdes Redublo pediatric pulmonologist, educator
Mandelbaum, David Ezra pediatric neurologist
Nosko, Michael Gerrik neurosurgeon
Paz, Harold Louis internist and educator
†Saidi, Parvin hematologist, medical educator
Scully, John Thomas obstetrician, gynecologist, educator
Seibold, James Richard physician, researcher

Newark
Apuzzio, Joseph J. obstetrician-gynecologist
Baker, Herman medical educator, author
Chen, Chunguang cardiologist
Cherniack, Neil Stanley physician, medical educator
Cohen, Stanley pathologist, educator
Cook, Stuart Donald physician, educator
Donahoo, James Saunders cardiothoracic surgeon
Evans, Hugh E. pediatrician
Haycock, Christine Elizabeth medical educator emeritus, health educator
Herman, Steven Douglas cardiothoracic surgeon, educator
Hobson, Robert Wayne, II surgeon
Iffy, Leslie medical educator
Leevy, Carroll Moton medical educator, hepatology researcher
Little, Alan Brian obstetrician, gynecologist, educator
Lourenco, Ruy Valentim physician, educator
Materna, Thomas Walter ophthalmologist
†Oleske, James M. pediatrician, allergist, immunologist, educator
Raveché, Elizabeth Scott immunologist
Reichman, Lee Brodersohn physician
Shain-Alvaro, Judith Carol physician assistant
Weinshenker, Naomi Joyce clinical psychiatrist, educator, researcher
Weiss, Gerson physician, educator
Weiss, Stanley H. physician, epidemiologist, educator, researcher, consultant
Zarbin, Marco Attilio ophthalmologist, surgeon, educator

Nutley
Gordon, Robert Dana transplant surgeon
Mostillo, Ralph medical association executive

Ocean
Kreider, Clement Horst, Jr. neurosurgeon

Ocean City
Altman, Brian David pediatric ophthalmologist

Old Tappan
Howard, Clifton Merton psychiatrist

Paramus
†Basuk, Richard physician
Greenberg, William Michael psychiatrist
Liva, Edward Louis eye surgeon
†Schiffman, Erica Rae psychiatrist

Parlin
Flick, Ferdinand Herman surgeon, prevention medicine physician

Passaic
Haddad, Jamil Raouf physician
Pino, Robert Salvatore radiologist

Paterson
Correa, Alonso Velez neurosurgeon
DeBari, Vincent Anthony medical researcher, educator

Phillipsburg
Kim, Ih Chin pediatrician
Rosenthal, Marvin Bernard pediatrician, educator

Piscataway
Conney, Allan Howard pharmacologist
†Leibowitz, Michael J. medical educator
Pollack, Irwin William psychiatrist, educator
Rhoads, George Grant medical epidemiologist
Shea, Stephen Michael physician, educator
Upton, Arthur Canfield experimental pathologist, educator

Plainsboro
Royds, Robert Bruce physician

Point Pleasant
Monaco, Robert Anthony *radiologist*

Pomona
Sung, Edward *physician*

Princeton
Carver, David Harold *physician, educator*
Chandler, James John *surgeon*
Conn, Hadley Lewis, Jr. *physician, educator*
†Cross, Richard James *physician, educator*
Gomoll, Allen Warren *cardiovascular pharmacologist*
Haynes, William Forby, Jr. *retired internist, cardiologist, educator*
May, Graham Stirling *physician*
Mayhew, Eric George *cancer researcher, educator*
Mueller, Peter Sterling *psychiatrist, educator*
Rosen, Arye *microwave, optoelectronics and medicine researcher*
Sandy, Lewis Gordon *physician, foundation executive*
Scasta, David Lynn *forensic psychiatrist*
Schroeder, Steven Alfred *medical educator, researcher, foundation executive*
Sugerman, Abraham Arthur *psychiatrist*
†von der Schmidt, Edward, III *neurosurgeon*
Wei, Fong *nephrologist*

Ridgewood
Baddoura, Rashid Joseph *emergency medicine physician*
Sumers, Anne Ricks *ophthalmologist, museum director*

Roseland
Schneider, George *internist, endocrinoligist*

Roselle Park
Margolin, Michael Leonard *gastroenterologist*
Wilchins, Sidney A. *gynecologist*

Rumson
Pflum, William John *physician*

Shamong
Kahn, Marc Leslie *orthopedic surgeon*

Short Hills
Chaiken, Bernard Henry *internist, gastroenterologist*

Somerset
De Salva, Salvatore Joseph *retired pharmacologist, toxicologist*
†Ilogu, Noel Obiajulu *internist*

South Amboy
Gupta, Suresh K. *pathologist*

South Orange
Weierman, Robert Joseph *orthopaedic surgeon*

Stratford
†McAbee, Gary N. *osteopath, lawyer*

Summit
Carniol, Paul J. *plastic and reconstructive surgeon, otolaryngologist*
O'Byrne, Elizabeth Milikin *pharmacologist, researcher, endocrinologist*

Teaneck
Ngai, Shih Hsun *physician*
Scotti, Dennis Joseph *educator, researcher, consultant*

Tenafly
Cosgriff, Stuart Worcester *internist, consultant, medical educator*
Katzman, Merle Hershel *orthopaedic surgeon*

Tinton Falls
Macdonald Jr., Donald Arthur *physician, surgeon*

Toms River
Clancy, Kevin F. *cardiologist*
Marchese, Michael James, Jr. *radiation oncologist*
Spedick, Michael John *ophthalmologist*

Trenton
Chappen, Edward Peter *physician*
Paul, Sindy Michelle *preventive medicine physician*
Roman, Cecelia Florence *cardiologist*
Rubin, Bernard *pharmacologist, biomedical writer, consultant*
Sporn, Aaron Adolph *physician*
Tolan, Robert Warren *pediatric infectious disease specialist*
Weinberg, Martin Herbert *retired psychiatrist*
Zanna, Martin Thomas *physician*

Turnersville
DePace, Nicholas Louis *physician*

Union
Rokosz, Gregory Joseph *emergency medicine physician, educator*

Ventnor City
Mason, James Henry, IV *retired surgeon*
Zuckerman, Stuart *psychiatrist, forensic examiner, educator*

Vineland
†Gupta, Vipin K. *neurologist*

Voorhees
†Kuchler, Joseph Albert *surgeon*
†Siddiqi, Tariq Sifat *neurosurgeon*

Washington
Drago, Joseph Rosario *urologist, educator*

Watchung
Murphree, Henry Bernard Scott *psychiatry and pharmacology educator, consultant*

Wayne
Eisenstein, Elliot Martin *pediatrician*
Gollance, Robert Barnett *ophthalmologist*
Sgroi, Donald Angelo *obstetrician, gynecologist*
Siepser, Stuart Lewis *cardiologist, internist*

West Long Branch
Shagan, Bernard Pellman *endocrinologist, educator*

West Orange
Ghali, Anwar Youssef *psychiatrist, educator*
Langsner, Alan Michael *pediatric cardiologist*
Panagides, John *pharmacologist*

Whitehouse Station
Douglas, Robert Gordon, Jr. *physician*

Woodbury
Gehring, David Austin *physician, administrator, cardiologist*
Stambaugh, John Edgar *oncologist, hematologist, pharmacologist, educator*

Wyckoff
Bauer, Theodore James *physician*
Marcus, Linda Susan *dermatologist*
Stahl, Alice Slater *psychiatrist*

NEW MEXICO

Alamogordo
Ashdown, Franklin Donald *physician, composer*
Stapp, John Paul *flight surgeon, retired air force officer*

Albuquerque
Cobb, John Candler *medical educator*
Edwards, William Sterling, III *cardiovascular surgeon*
Goss, Jerome Eldon *cardiologist*
Heffron, Warren A. *medical educator, physician*
Janis, Kenneth M. *physician*
King, Lowell Restell *pediatric urologist*
Knospe, William Herbert *medical educator*
Mora, Federico *neurosurgeon*
Napolitano, Leonard Michael *anatomist, university administrator*
Omer, George Elbert, Jr. *orthopaedic surgeon, hand surgeon, educator*
Saland, Linda Carol *anatomy educator, neuroscience researcher*
Stevenson, James Richard *radiologist, lawyer*
Turner, William Joseph *retired psychiatrist*
Uhlenhuth, Eberhard Henry *psychiatrist, educator*
Waitzkin, Howard Bruce *physician, sociologist, educator*
Winslow, Walter William *psychiatrist*
Wong, Phillip Allen *osteopathic physician*
Worrell, Richard Vernon *orthopedic surgeon, college dean*
Zumwalt, Ross Eugene *forensic pathologist, educator*

Carlsbad
Markle, George Bushar, IV *surgeon*

Chama
Moser, Robert Harlan *physician, educator, writer*

Farmington
Neidhart, James Allen *physician, educator*

Las Cruces
Jacobs, Kent Frederick *dermatologist*
Reeves, Billy Dean *obstetrics and gynecology educator emeritus*
Talamantes, Roberto *developmental pediatrician*

Los Alamos
Smith, Fredrica Emrich *rheumatologist, internist*
Wadstrom, Ann Kennedy *retired anesthesiologist*

Portales
Goodwin, Martin Brune *radiologist*

Rodeo
Scholes, Robert Thornton *physician, research administrator*

Roswell
Jennings, Emmit M. *surgeon*

Santa Fe
Gilmour, Edward Ellis *psychiatrist*
Hoffmann, Louis Gerhard *immunologist, educator, sex therapist*
Schwartz, George R. *physician*
Williams, Ralph Chester, Jr. *physician, educator*

NEW YORK

Albany
Barron, Kevin Delgado *physician, educator*
Bennett, Edward Virdell, Jr. *surgeon*
Bradley, Wesley Holmes *physician*
Burkart, Peter Thomas *hematologist*
Capone, Robert Joseph *physician, educator*
Davis, Paul Joseph *endocrinologist*
†DeBuono, Barbara Ann *physician, state official*
DeFelice, Eugene Anthony *physician, medical educator, consultant, magician*
Dougherty, James *orthopedic surgeon, educator, author*
Doyle, Joseph Theobald *physician, educator*
Hoffmeister, Jana Marie *cardiologist*
Howard, Lyn Jennifer *medical educator*
†Kennedy, Debbie A. *plastic surgeon*
†King, Joshua Adam *plastic surgeon*
Macario, Alberto Juan Lorenzo *physician*
Risemberg, Herman Mario *pediatrician, educator*
Sturman, Lawrence Stuart *health research administrator*
Swartz, Donald Percy *physician*
Tepper, Clifford *allergist, immunologist, educator*
Uhl, Richard Laurence *physician, medical educator*
Unger, Gere Nathan *physician, lawyer*
Ushkow, Bruce Scott *emergency physician*

Amherst
Levy, Gerhard *pharmacologist*

Amityville
Liang, Vera Beh-Yuin Tsai *psychiatrist, educator*
Serpe, Salvatore John *internist*
Upadhyay, Yogendra Nath *physician, educator*

Amsterdam
†Tasher, Jacob *otolaryngologist*

Ardsley
Kuntzman, Ronald *pharmacology research executive*
Utermohlen, Herbert Georg *dermatologist*

Argyle
Bruce, David Lionel *retired anesthesiologist, educator*

Armonk
Mellors, Robert Charles *physician, scientist, educator*

Babylon
Epstein, Jeffrey Mark *neurosurgeon*

Bay Shore
Sampino, Anthony F. *physician, obstetrician and gynecologist*

Bayside
Gavencak, John Richard *pediatrician, allergist*

Bethpage
Brodie, Sheldon J. *physician*

Binghamton
Bethje, Robert *retired general surgeon*
Michael, Sandra Dale *reproductive endocrinology educator, researcher*
Michaels, Robert M. *physician, medical educator*
Peterson, Alfred Edward *family physician*

Briarcliff Manor
Glassman, Jerome Martin *clinical pharmacologist, educator*
†Housman, Arno David *urologist*
†Lowe, James Edward, Jr. *plastic and reconstructive surgeon*
Weintraub, Michael Ira *neurologist*

Bronx
Aldrich, Thomas Knight *physician, scientist*
Aronow, Wilbert Solomon *physician, educator*
Bennett, Michael Vander Laan *neuroscience educator*
Blaufox, Morton Donald *physician, educator*
Burde, Ronald Marshall *neuro-ophthalmologist*
Buschke, Herman *neurologist*
Chiaramida, Salvatore *cardiologist, educator, health facility adminstrator*
Cohen, Herbert Jesse *physician, educator*
Cohen, Michael I. *pediatrician*
Coupey, Susan McGuire *pediatrician, educator*
DeMartino, Anthony Gabriel *cardiologist, internist*
Dutcher, Janice Jean Phillips *oncologist*
Eder, Howard Abram *physician*
Elkin, Milton *radiologist, physician, educator*
Eng, Calvin *cardiologist, researcher*
Fernandez-Pol, Blanca Dora *psychiatrist, researcher*
Fleischer, Norman Samuel *director of endocrinology, medical educator*
Foreman, Spencer *pulmonary specialist, hospital executive*
Freeman, Leonard Murray *radiologist, nuclear medicine physician, educator*
Gerst, Paul Howard *physician*
Gillman, Arthur Emanuel *psychiatrist*
Gliedman, Marvin L. *surgeon, educator*
Goldberg, Marcia B. *medical educator*
†Goldstein, Robert David *plastic surgeon, educator*
Goodrich, James Tait *neuroscientist, pediatric neurosurgeon*
Herbert, Victor Daniel *medical educator*
Hirano, Asao *neuropathologist*
Hodgson, W(alter) John B(arry) *surgeon*
Jacobson, Harold Gordon *radiologist, educator*
Jaffé, Ernst Richard *medical educator and administrator*
Kadish, Anna Stein *pathologist, educator, researcher*
Kahn, Thomas *medical educator*
Kanofsky, Jacob Daniel *psychiatrist, educator*
Karasu, T(oksoz) Byram *psychiatry educator*
Karkanias, George B. *neurologist, educator*
†Karwa, Gattu Lal *urologist*
Koss, Leopold G. *physician, pathologist, educator*
Lieber, Charles Saul *physician, educator*
†Marantz, Paul Russell *medical educator*
Muschel, Louis Henry *immunologist, educator*
Nagler, Arnold Leon *pathologist, scientist, educator*
Nathenson, Stanley Gail *immunology educator*
Nitowsky, Harold Martin *physician, educator*
Okpalanma, Chika *psychiatrist*
Orkin, Louis Richard *physician, educator*
†Patel, Mahendrakumar P. *plastic surgeon*
Pitchumoni, Capecomorin Sankar *gastroenterologist, educator*
Plimpton, Calvin Hastings *physician, university president*
Purpura, Dominick P. *neuroscientist, university dean*
Radel, Eva *pediatrician, hematologist*
Rapin, Isabelle *physician*
†Razani, Babak *medical researcher*
Reynolds, Benedict Michael *surgeon*
Robinson, Bernard Pahl *retired thoracic surgeon, educator*
Romney, Seymour Leonard *physician, educator*
Rosenbaum, David Herbert *neurologist*
Ruben, Robert Joel *physician, educator*
Rubinstein, Arye *pediatrician, microbiology and immunology educator*
Sable, Robert Allen *gastroenterologist*
Satir, Birgit H. *medical educator, medical researcher*
Scharff, Matthew Daniel *immunologist, cell biologist, educator*
Schaumburg, Herbert Howard *neurology educator*
†Segan, Scott Marshall *neurologist*
Senturia, Yvonne Dreyfus *pediatrician, epidemiologist*
Shafritz, David Andrew *physician, research scientist*
Shapiro, Nella Irene *surgeon*
Shatin, Harry *medical educator, dermatologist*
Spitzer, Adrian *pediatrician, medical educator*
Stein, Ruth Elizabeth Klein *physician*
†Strauch, Berish *plastic surgeon, hand surgeon*
Surks, Martin I. *medical educator, endocrinologist*
Tellis, Vivian Anthony *transplant surgeon, administrator*
Tetrokalashvili, Mikhail S. *physician*
Waltz, Joseph McKendree *neurosurgeon, educator*
Wiernik, Peter Harris *oncologist, educator*
Williams, Marshall Henry, Jr. *physician, educator*

Bronxville
Kaplan, Sanford Allen *internist, allergist*
Levitt, Miriam *pediatrician*
Rizzo, Thomas Dignan *orthopedic surgeon*

Brooklyn
Alfonso, Antonio Escolar *surgeon*
Barth, Robert Henry *nephrologist, educator*
Biro, David Eric *dermatologist*
Biro, Laszlo *dermatologist*
Clark, Luther Theopolis *physician, educator, researcher*
Cohn, Steven Lawrence *internist, medical educator*
Cracco, Roger Quinlan *medical educator, neurologist*
Crum, Albert Byrd *psychiatrist, consultant*
†Cunningham, Joseph Newton, Jr. *cardiothoracic and vascular surgeon*
Davidson, Steven J. *emergency physician*
Dimant, Jacob *internist*
Edemeka, Udo Edemeka *surgeon*
El Kodsi, Baroukh *gastroenterologist, educator*
Erber, William Franklin *gastroenterologist*
Feinbaum, George *internist, endocrinologist*
Friedman, Eli Arnold *nephrologist*
Furchgott, Robert Francis *pharmacologist, educator*
Gintautas, Jonas *physician, scientist, administrator*
Gotta, Alexander Walter *anesthesiologist, educator*
Imperato, Pascal James *physician, health administrator, author, editor, medical educator*
Jaffe, Eric Allen *physician, educator, researcher*
Kaggen, Elias *physician*
Kirshenbaum, Richard Irving *public health physician*
Leff, Sanford Erwin *cardiologist*
Levendoglu, Hulya *gastroenterologist, educator*
Levy, Norman B. *psychiatrist, educator*
Lindo, J. Trevor *psychiatrist, consultant*
Marcus, Harold *retired physician, health facility administrator*
Mark, Richard Kushakow *internist*
Mayer, Ira Edward *gastroenterologist*
McIntyre, John S. *oral and maxillofacial surgeon*
Mendez, Hermann Armando *pediatrician, educator*
Milhorat, Thomas Herrick *neurosurgeon*
Mirra, Suzanne Samuels *neuropathologist, researcher*
Norstrand, Iris Fletcher *psychiatrist, neurologist, educator*
Nurhussein, Mohammed Alamin *internist, geriatrician, educator*
Pertschuk, Louis Philip *pathologist*
Plotz, Charles Mindell *physician*
Price, Ely *dermatologist*
Rabinowitz, Simon S. *pediatric gastroenterologist, scientist*
Reich, Nathaniel Edwin *physician, poet, artist, educator, explorer*
†Salgado, Miran *neurologist*
Savits, Barry Sorrel *surgeon*
Sawyer, Philip Nicholas *surgeon, educator, health science facility administrator*
Schwarz, Richard Howard *obstetrician, gynecologist, educator*
Shalita, Alan Remi *dermatologist*
Stern, Leon *psychiatrist*
Traube, Charles *internist, cardiologist*
Viswanathan, Ramaswamy *physician, educator*
Wolintz, Arthur Harry *physician, neuro-ophthalmologist*

Buffalo
Ambrus, Clara Maria *physician*
Ambrus, Julian L. *physician, medical educator*
Aquilina, Alan T. *physician*
Batt, Ronald Elmer *gynecologist, scientist*
Brody, Harold *neuroanatomist, gerontologist*
Brooks, John Samuel Joseph *pathologist, researcher*
Calkins, Evan *physician, educator*
Chu, Tsann Ming *immunochemist, educator*
Chutkow, Jerry Grant *neurologist, educator*
Coles, William Henry *ophthalmologist, educator*
Creaven, Patrick Joseph *physician, research oncologist*
Dwoskin, Joseph Y. *pediatric urologist*
Enhorning, Goran *obstetrician, gynecologist, educator*
Fallavollita, James A. *cardiologist, educator, researcher*
Genco, Robert Joseph *scientist, immunologist, periodontist, educator*
Graham, (Lloyd) Saxon *epidemiology educator*
Gresham, Glen Edward *physician*
Gugino, Lawrence James *medical educator*
Hershey, Linda Ann *neurology and pharmacology educator*
Hohn, David *physician*
Horoszewicz, Juliusz Stanislaw *oncologist, cancer researcher, laboratory administrator*
Kipping, Hans F. *dermatologist*
Lele, Amol Shashikant *obstetrician and gynecologist*
Levy, Harold James *physician, psychiatrist*
Mihich, Enrico *medical researcher*
Milgrom, Felix *immunologist, educator*
Miller, Kennon Sewall *urologist*
Mindell, Eugene Robert *surgeon, educator*
Mirand, Edwin Albert *medical scientist*
Naughton, John Patrick *cardiologist*
Nolan, James Paul *medical educator, scientist*
Pentney, Roberta Jean *neuroanatomist, educator*
Pincus, Stephanie Hoyer *dermatologist, educator*
Piver, M. Steven *gynecologic oncologist*
Regan, Peter Francis, III *physician, psychiatry educator*
Rekate, Albert C. *physician*
†Salerno, Tomas A. *cardiothoracic surgeon*
Seller, Robert Herman *cardiologist, family physician*
Shedd, Donald Pomroy *surgeon*
Simpson, George True *surgeon, educator*
Stoddard, Elizabeth Jane *physician assistant, artist*
Stoll, Howard Lester, Jr. *dermatologist*
Trevisan, Maurizio *epidemiologist, researcher*
Wright, John Robert *pathologist, educator*

Canaan
Rothenberg, Albert *psychiatrist, educator*

Castle Point
Mehta, Rakesh Kumar *physician, consultant*

Cazenovia
Muschenheim, Frederick *retired pathologist*

Cedarhurst
Cohen, Harris L. *diagnostic radiologist, consultant*

Centerport
Fischel, Edward Elliot *physician, educator*

Cheektowaga
Woldman, Sherman *pediatrician*

Chestnut Ridge
Day, Stacey Biswas *physician, educator*

Clifton Park
Adomfeh, Charles N. *internist*
Buhac, Ivo *gastroenterologist*

Clinton
Stowens, Daniel *pathologist*

Cohocton
Frame, Paul Sutherland *medical educator, physician*

Cooperstown
Bordley, James, IV *surgeon*
Franck, Walter Alfred *rheumatologist, medical administrator, educator*
Steinberg, Paul *allergist, immunologist*
†Whelan, Mary Anne *pediatrician, neurologist, educator*

Corning
Lin, Min-Chung *obstetrician, gynecologist*

Cortland
Malakar, Jagadish Chandra *internist*

Croton On Hudson
Werman, David Sanford *psychiatrist, psychoanalyst, educator*

Dix Hills
†Ivy, Edward Joseph *plastic surgeon*
Mastrogiannis, Dimitrios S. *obstetrician/ gynecologist, perinatologist*

East Hampton
Paton, David *ophthalmologist, educator*

East Islip
Delman, Michael Robert *physician*

East Meadow
De Santis, Mark *osteopathic physician*

East Northport
Haggerty, Arthur Daniel *stress and chronic pain management specialist*

Elmhurst
Barron, Charles Thomas *psychiatrist*
Byun, Hang S. *neurosurgeon, educator*
Masci, Joseph Richard *medical educator, physician*
Schwartz, Evan Gary *orthopedist*

Elmira
Graham, David Richard *orthopedic surgeon*
Quintos, Elias Rilloraza *cardiac surgeon, thoracic surgeon*

Fairport
Herz, Marvin Ira *psychiatrist, educator*

Far Rockaway
Farron, Robert *physician, family practice*
Madhusoodanan, Subramoniam *psychiatrist, educator*

Fayetteville
Chevli, Renate Naren *obstetrician, gynecologist*
Pirodsky, Donald Max *psychiatrist, educator*

Fishkill
Brocks, Eric Randy *ophthalmologist, surgeon*

Flushing
Castro, Robert R. *retired surgeon*
Hon, John Wingsun *physician*
Kresic, Eva *pediatrician*
Nori, Dattatreyudu *oncologist, researcher*
Nussbaum, Michel Ernest *physician*
Stark, Joel *speech language pathologist*

Forest Hills
Eden, Alvin Noam *pediatrician, author*
Narasimhan, Parthasarathy *physician*

Freeport
Burstein, Stephen David *neurosurgeon*
Dimancescu, Mihai D. *neurosurgeon, researcher, educator*
†McCally, Daniel S. *urologist*

Fresh Meadows
Kaplan, Barry Hubert *physician*

Garden City
Deane, Leland Marc *plastic surgeon*
Good, Larry Irwin *physician, consultant*
†Zelman, Warren Henry *otolaryngologist, surgeon*

Garrison
Callahan, Daniel John *biomedical researcher*

Geneva
Dickson, James Edwin, II *obstetrician, gynecologist*
Givelber, Harry Michael *pathologist*

Glens Falls
†Brender, William Charles *plastic and reconstructive surgeon, artist*
Wurzberger, Bezalel *psychiatrist*

Goshen
Roncal, Rogelio *psychiatrist*

Great Neck
Arlow, Jacob A. *psychiatrist, educator*
Bungarz, William Robert *pediatrician*
Goldman, Ira Steven *gastroenterologist*
Gross, Lillian *psychiatrist*
Kechijian, Paul *dermatologist, educator*
†Keller, Alex Jay *plastic and reconstructive surgeon*
Kodsi, Sylvia Rose *ophthalmologist*
†Oberby, M. Chris *physician, neurosurgeon*
Rosenberg, Richard F. *physician, radiologist*
Simon, Arthur *pharmacologist, research laboratory executive*
Tosheff, Julij Gospodinoff *psychiatrist*
Wolff, Edward *physician*

Guilderland
Yunich, Albert Mansfeld *physician*

Hartsdale
Cantor, Morton B. *psychiatrist*
Chait, Maxwell Mani *physician*

Hauppauge
Graham, David Gregory *preventive medicine physician, psychiatrist*

Hempstead
Laano, Archie Bienvenido Maaño *cardiologist*

Hewlett
Cohen, David Leon *physician*
Steinfeld, Philip Sheldon *pediatrician*

Hudson
Mustapha, Tamton *gastroenterologist*

Huntington
†Allis, Barbara A. *physician*
†Engstrand, Beatrice C. *neurologist, educator*
Joseph, Richard Saul *cardiologist*
Salcedo-Dovi, Hector Eduardo *anatomist, educator*
Trager, Gary Alan *endocrinologist, diabetologist*
Vale, Margo Rose *physician*
†Weissberg, David J. *orthopaedic surgeon*

Irving
†Lee-Kwen, Peterkin *physician, neurologist*

Ithaca
Dietert, Rodney Reynolds *immunology and toxicology educator*
Quimby, Fred William *pathology educator, veterinarian*
Whitaker, Susanne Kanis *veterinary medical librarian*

Jackson Heights
Fischbarg, Zulema F. *pediatrician, educator*

Jamaica
Alberts, Alan Richard *rheumatologist*
†Barley, Linda R. *health education and gerontology educator*
Rosner, Fred *physician, educator*

Jericho
Schell, Norman Barnett *physician, consultant*

Johnson City
McGovern, Thomas Boardman *physician, pediatrician*

Kenmore
Elibol, Tarik *gastroenterologist*

Kingston
Johnson, Marie-Louise Tully *dermatologist, educator*

Lansing
Thomas, John Melvin *retired surgeon*

Larchmont
Holleb, Arthur Irving *surgeon*

Latham
†Silverman, Warren *physician*

Laurens
Spoor, John Edward *physician*

Lawrence
Sklarin, Burton S. *endocrinologist*

Lewiston
Zavon, Mitchell Ralph *physician*

Lockport
Carr, Edward Albert, Jr. *medical educator, physician*

Long Beach
†Brontoli, Margreth J. *ophthalmologist*
Chaudhry, Humayun Javaid *physician, medical educator, writer*

Lowville
Becker, Robert Otto *orthopedic surgery educator*

Lyndonville
Bell, David Sheffield *physician*

Mamaroneck
Halpern, Abraham Leon *psychiatrist*
Hoffert, Paul Washington *surgeon*
Rosenthal, Elizabeth Robbins *physician*

Manhasset
Elkowitz, Sheryl Sue *radiologist*
Feinsilver, Steven Henry *physician, educator*
Fenton, Arnold N. *obstetrician, gynecologist, educator*
Kreis, Willi *physician*
†Lukash, Frederick Neil *plastic surgeon*
Nelson, Roy Leslie *cardiac surgeon, researcher, educator*
Samuel, Paul *cardiologist*
Scherr, Lawrence *physician, educator*
†Vishnubhakat, Surya Murthy *neurologist*

Manlius
Prior, John Thompson *pathology educator*

Massapequa
Zwanger, Jerome *physician*

Merrick
Copperman, Stuart Morton *pediatrician*

Millerton
Green, George Edward *surgeon*

Mineola
Feinstein, Robert P. *dermatologist*
Hines, George Lawrence *surgeon*
Hull, Magdalen Eleanor *reproductive medicine physician, educator*
Mofenson, Howard C. *pediatrician, toxicologist*
Molho, Laura *pathologist*
Twist, Paul Francis, Jr. *neonatologist*

Monroe
Werzberger, Alan *pediatrician*

Monticello
Lauterstein, Joseph *cardiologist*

Mount Kisco
Mooney, Robert Michael *ophthalmologist*
†Riechers, Roger Neil *urologist, surgeon*
Schneider, Robert Jay *oncologist*
Stillman, Michael Allen *dermatologist*

Mount Sinai
Feinberg, Sheldon Norman *pediatrician*

Mount Vernon
Zucker, Arnold Harris *psychiatrist*

Mountainville
Johns, Margaret Bush *neuroendocrinologist, researcher, educator*

Nanuet
Savitz, Martin Harold *neurosurgeon*

Naples
Beal, Myron Clarence *osteopathic physician*

New City
Esser, Aristide Henri *psychiatrist*

New Hartford
†Arastu, Jameel Husain *neurologist*
Eidelhoch, Lester Philip *physician, educator, surgeon*

New Hyde Park
Armstrong, Denise Grace *medical association administrator*
Eviatar, Lydia *pediatric neurologist*
Lee, Won Jay *radiologist*
†McKinley, Matthew John *gastroenterologist*
Mealie, Carl A. *physician, educator*
Prisco, Douglas Louis *physician*
Seltzer, Vicki Lynn *obstetrician, gynecologist*
Shenker, Ira Ronald *physician*
†Smith, Arthur David *urologist*
Wolf, Julius *medical educator*

New Rochelle
Glassman, George Morton *dermatologist*
Hayes, Arthur Hull, Jr. *physician, clinical pharmacology educator, medical school dean, business executive, consultant*
†Kleinman, Andrew Young *plastic surgeon*
Lin, Joseph Pen-Tze *retired neuroradiologist*
Rovinsky, Joseph Judah *obstetrician, gynecologist*

New Windsor
†Antony, Ajit Ivan *urologist*

New York
Abramson, Sara Jane *radiologist, educator*
Adler, Karl Paul *medical educator, academic administrator*
Ahrens, Edward Hamblin, Jr. *physician*
Albom, Michael Jonathan *surgeon, educator*
Alderson, Philip Otis *radiologist, educator*
Altman, Lawrence Kimball *physician, journalist*
Altman, Roy Peter *pediatric surgeon*
Ames, Richard Pollard *physician, educator, lecturer*
Angelakos, Evangelos Theodorou *physician, physiologist, pharmacologist, educator*
Antell, Darrick Eugene *plastic surgeon*
April, Max Michael *otolaryngologist*
Archibald, Reginald Mac Gregor *physician, chemist, educator*
Armenakas, Noel Anthony *medical educator*
Arnold, Charles Burle, Jr. *psychiatrist, writer*
Aronoff, Michael Stephen *psychiatrist*
Asanuma, Hiroshi *physician, educator*
†Ascherman, Jeffrey Alan *plastic and reconstructive surgeon*
Atkinson, Holly Gail *physician, journalist, business executive, author, lecturer, human rights activist*
Aufses, Arthur H(arold), Jr. *surgeon, medical educator*
Aviv, Jonathan Enoch *otolaryngologist, educator*
Axel, Richard *pathology and biochemistry educator*
Baer, Rudolf Lewis *dermatologist, educator*
Baldwin, David Shepard *physician*
Barber, Ann McDonald *physician*
Barchas, Jack David *psychiatrist, educator*
Barie, Philip Steven *surgeon, educator*
Barish, Julian I. *psychiatrist*
Barker, Barbara Ann *ophthalmologist*
Barnett, Henry Lewis *pediatrician, medical educator*
Barondess, Jeremiah Abraham *physician*
†Becker, Glenn Adam *plastic surgeon*
†Bederson, Joshua Benjamin *neurosurgeon*
Beerman, Joseph *health educator*
Behrens, Myles Michael *neuro-ophthalmologist*
Bellin, Howard Theodore *plastic surgeon*
†Belok, Lennart C. *neurologist*
Bendixen, Henrik Holt *physician, educator, dean*
Ben-Zvi, Jeffrey Stuart *gastroenterologist, internist*
Berger, Frank Milan *biomedical researcher, scientist, former pharmaceutical company executive*
Berk, Paul David *physician, scientist, educator*
Bertino, Joseph Rocco *physician, educator*
Bickers, David Rinsey *physician, educator*
Biel, Leonard, Jr. *urologist*
Birbari, Adil Elias *physician, educator*
Bogdonoff, Morton David *physician, educator*
Borer, Jeffrey Stephen *cardiologist*
Brand, Leonard *physician, educator*
†Brandt-Rauf, Paul Wesley *public health educator*
Braude, Robert Michael *medical library administrator*
Breinin, Goodwin M. *physician*
Brennan, Murray Frederick *surgeon, oncologist*
Breslow, Jan Leslie *scientist, educator, physician*
Brook, David William *psychiatrist, researcher*
Brook, Judith Suzanne *psychiatry and psychology researcher and educator*
Brown, Jason Walter *neurologist, educator, researcher*
Burke, Michael Desmond *pathologist*
Bush, Harry Leonard, Jr. *surgery educator*
Butler, Robert Neil *gerontologist, psychiatrist, writer, educator*
Butler, Vincent Paul, Jr. *physician, educator*
Bystryn, Jean-Claude *dermatologist, educator*
Cahan, William George *surgeon, educator*
†Camins, Martin B. *neurosurgeon*
Cammisa, Frank P., Jr. *surgeon, educator*
Cancro, Robert *psychiatrist, educator*
Carr, Ronald Edward *ophthalmologist, educator*
Casals-Ariet, Jordi *physician*
†Cassel, Christine Karen *physician*
Cassell, Eric Jonathan *physician*
Chan, W. Y. *pharmacologist, educator*
Chaney, Verne Edward, Jr. *surgeon, foundation executive, educator*
Chase, Merrill Wallace *immunologist, educator*
Chase, Norman Eli *radiologist, educator*
Chiu, David Tak Wai *surgeon*
Chou, Ting-Chao *pharmacology educator*
Ciobanu, Niculae *oncologist, researcher*
Close, Lanny Garth *otolaryngologist, educator*
Cohen, David Harris *neurobiology educator, university official*
†Cohen, Elliot L. *urologist, educator*
Cohen, Noel Lee *otolaryngologist, educator*
Coleman, D. Jackson *ophthalmologist, educator*
Coleman, John William *urologist*
Coleman, Lester Laudy *otolaryngologist*
Coleman, Morton *oncologist, hematologist*
Cooper, Norman Streich *pathologist, medical educator*
†Cutting, Court Baldwin *plastic surgeon, computer graphics researcher*
Davis, Kenneth Leon *psychiatrist, pharmacologist, medical educator*
Defendi, Vittorio *medical research administrator, pathologist*
Deuschle, Kurt Walter *physician, educator*
De Vivo, Darryl Claude *pediatric neurologist*
Dick, Harold Michael *orthopedic surgeon*
Dieterich, Douglas Thomas *gastroenterologist, researcher*
†DiGiacinto, George Vincent *neurosurgeon*
Distenfeld, Ariel *hematologist, educator*
Dixon, Shirley Lee *emergency physician*
Dohrenwend, Bruce Philip *psychiatric epidemiologist, social psychologist, educator*
Dole, Vincent Paul *medical research executive, educator*
Dolgin, Martin *cardiologist*
Dorfman, Howard David *pathologist, educator*
Downey, John Alexander *physician, educator*
Doyle, Eugenie Fleri *pediatric cardiologist, educator*
Drescher, Jack *psychoanalyst, psychiatrist*
Du Mont, Nicolas *psychiatrist, educator*
Dworetzky, Murray *physician, educator*
Eaton, Richard Gillette *surgeon, educator*
Ebin, Leonard Ned *radiologist, educator, consultant*
Edwards, Adrian L. *medical educator*
Edwards, Niloo Mario *surgeon*
Ehlers, Kathryn Hawes (Mrs. James D. Gabler) *physician*
Eidsvold, Gary Mason *physician, public health officer, medical educator*
English, Joseph Thomas *physician, medical administrator*
Epstein, Seth Paul *immunologist, infectious disease researcher*
Ergas, Enrique *orthopedic surgeon*
Fahn, Stanley *neurologist, educator*
Farber, Saul Joseph *physician, educator*
Feldman, Samuel Mitchell *neuroscientist, educator*
Field, Michael *gastroenterologist*
Fisher, Edward Abraham *cardiologist, educator*
Flach, Frederic Francis *psychiatrist*
Foley, Kathleen M. *neurologist, educator, researcher*
Fondo, Edwin Young *surgical oncologist*
†Foo, Sun-Hoo *physician*
Foraste, Roland *psychiatrist*
†Forley, Bryan G. *plastic surgeon*
Forrest, David Vickers *psychiatrist, educator*
Fortner, Joseph Gerald *surgeon, educator*
Foscarinis, Rosa *pediatrician, allergist*
Fountain, Karen Schueler *physician*
Fox, Arthur Charles *physician, educator*
Francis, Charles K. *medical educator*
Frantz, Andrew Gibson *physician, educator*
Freedberg, Irwin Mark *dermatologist*
Freedman, Aaron David *medical educator, former university dean*
Freedman, Michael Leonard *geriatrician, educator*
Friedewald, William Thomas *physician*
Friedhoff, Arnold J. *psychiatrist, medical scientist*
Friedman, Alan Herbert *ophthalmologist*
Friedman, Arnold Carl *diagnostic radiologist*
Friedman, Emanuel A. *medical educator*
Friedman, Howard Samuel *cardiologist, educator, researcher*
Friedman, Ira Hugh *surgeon*
Fuchs, Anna-Riitta *medical educator, scientist*
Fuks, Zvi Y. *medical educator*
Furmanski, Philip *cancer research scientist*
Fuster, Valentin *cardiologist, educator*
Gable, Carol Brignoli *health economics researcher*
Gabrilove, Jacques Lester *physician*
Galanter, Marc *psychiatrist, educator*
Galin, Miles A. *ophthalmologist, educator*
Gaylin, Willard *physician, educator*
Gebbie, Kristine Moore *health science educator, health official*
Geiger, H. Jack *medical educator*
Gellhorn, Alfred *physician, educator*
Genkins, Gabriel *physician*
Gershengorn, Marvin Carl *physician, scientist, educator*
Gersony, Welton Mark *physician, pediatric cardiologist, educator*
Gertler, Menard M. *physician, educator*
Ghebrehiwet, Berhane *immunologist, educator*

Giancotti, Filippo Giusto *cell and molecular biologist*
Ginsberg, Robert Jason *thoracic surgeon*
Glasberg, Scot Bradley *plastic surgeon*
Glassman, Alexander Howard *psychiatrist, researcher*
Godman, Gabriel Charles *pathology educator*
†Goldberg, Ira Jay *internist, educator*
Golde, David William *physician, educator*
Goldenberg, Marvin Manus *pharmacologist, pharmaceutical developer*
Goldfarb, Lisa Michele *psychiatrist*
Goldfrank, Lewis Robert *physician*
Goldsmith, Michael Allen *oncologist, educator*
Goldsmith, Stanley Joseph *nuclear medicine physician, educator*
Goldstein, Marc *microsurgeon, urology educator, administrator*
Golomb, Frederick Martin *surgeon, educator*
Gordon, Alan Lee *psychiatrist*
Gordon, Alvin Joseph *cardiologist*
Gotschlich, Emil Claus *physician, educator*
Gotto, Antonio Marion, Jr. *internist, educator*
Graber, Edward Alex *obstetrician, gynecologist, educator*
Green, Jack Peter *pharmacology educator, medical scientist*
Greenberg, Carolyn Phyllis *anesthesiologist, educator*
Greengard, Paul *neuroscientist*
Griffiths, Sylvia Preston *physician*
Grossman, Ruth Kostik *medical education company executive*
Guida, Peter Matthew *surgeon, educator*
Gusberg, Saul Bernard *physician, educator*
Guthrie, Randolph Hobson, Jr. *plastic surgeon, consultant*
Haddad, Heskel Marshall *ophthalmologist*
†Hagstrom, Jack Walter Carl Kling *retired pathology educator*
Haines, Kathleen Ann *physician, educator*
Hambrick, George Walter, Jr. *dermatologist, educator*
Hamburg, Beatrix Ann *medical educator, researcher*
Hamburg, David A. *psychiatrist, foundation executive*
Harley, Naomi Hallden *radiation specialist, environmental medicine educator*
Harris, Henry William *physician*
Harris, Matthew Nathan *surgeon, educator*
Hayes, Constance J. *pediatric cardiologist*
Heagarty, Margaret Caroline *pediatric physician*
Hecht, Alan Jay *cardiologist*
Heimarck, Gregory James *psychoanalyst, child psychiatrist*
Hein, Karen Kramer *pediatrician, epidemiologist*
Hennessey, N. Patrick *physician, clinical researcher*
Hilgartner, Margaret Wehr *pediatric hematologist, educator*
Hirsch, Jules *physician, scientist*
Hirschhorn, Kurt *pediatrics educator*
Ho, David D. *research physician, virologist*
Hochlerin, Diane *pediatrician, educator*
Hofer, Myron A(rms) *psychiatrist, researcher*
Holland, Jimmie C. *psychiatrist, educator*
Holt, Peter Rolf *physician, educator*
Hoskins, William John *obstetrician, gynecologist, educator*
Hugo, Norman Eliot *plastic surgeon, medical educator*
Hunter, John Gerard *plastic surgeon*
Hymes, Norma *internist*
†Imber, Gerald *plastic surgeon*
Imparato, Anthony Michael *vascular surgeon, medical educator, researcher*
Imperato-McGinley, Julianne Leonore *endocrinologist, educator*
†Ingram, Douglas Howard *psychoanalyst*
Isay, Richard Alexander *psychiatrist*
Jacobs, Allan Joel *gynecologist, administrator*
†Jacobs, Elliot William *plastic surgery*
Javitt, Norman B. *medical educator, researcher*
†Jelks, Glenn William *plastic surgeon*
Johnson, Horton Anton *pathologist*
Jonas, Saran *neurologist, educator*
Jones, Ronald Arthur *physician, composer*
Jurka, Edith Mila *psychiatrist, researcher*
Kabat, Elvin Abraham *immunologist*
Kadar, Avraham *immunologist*
Kahn, Norman *pharmacology and dentistry educator*
Kandel, Eric Richard *neuroscience educator*
Kanick, Virginia *radiologist*
Kanof, Norman B. *dermatologist*
Kapelman, Barbara Ann *physician, educator*
Kappas, Attallah *physician, medical scientist*
Katz, Lois Anne *internist, nephrologist*
Katz, Sidney *medical educator*
Kaufman, David Marc *pediatric neurologist*
Kaufmann, Charles Arthur *psychiatrist, educator*
Kaufmann, Horacio Carlos *neurologist, educator*
Kauth, Benjamin *podiatrist consultant*
Keefe, Deborah Lynn *cardiologist, educator*
†Keegan, Leo Martin *plastic surgeon, educator*
Keill, Stuart Langdon *psychiatrist*
Kelman, Charles D. *ophthalmologist, educator*
Kemether, Eileen *psychiatrist*
King, Thomas *physician, physiology educator*
Kleber, Herbert David *psychiatrist, educator*
Klein, Donald Franklin *psychiatrist, scientist, educator*
Klein, Harvey *physician, educator*
Kligfield, Paul David *physician, medicine educator*
†Knapp, Albert Bruce *gastroenterologist*
Knapp, Robert Charles *retired obstetrics and gynecology educator*
Kolodny, Edwin Hillel *neurologist, geneticist, medical administrator*
Koplewicz, Harold Samuel *child and adolescent psychiatrist*
Kosovich, Dushan Radovan *psychiatrist*
Kourides, Ione Anne *endocrinologist, researcher, educator*
Kramer, Elissa Lipcon *nuclear medicine physician, educator*
Kreek, Mary Jeanne *physician*
Kushner, Brian Harris *pediatric oncologist*
Lamparello, Patrick John *surgeon, educator*
Landrigan, Philip John *epidemiologist*
Lane, Joseph M. *orthopedic surgeon, educator, oncologist*
Lang, Enid Asher *psychiatrist*
Langan, Marie-Noelle Suzanne *cardiologist, educator*
Laragh, John Henry *physician, scientist, educator*
Larson, Steven Mark *physician*
Lauersen, Niels Helth *physician, educator*
Laufer, Ira Jerome *physician*
Laufman, Harold *surgeon*
Laurence, Jeffrey Conrad *immunologist*
Lawrence, Henry Sherwood *physician, educator*
Lawson, William *otolargyngologist, educator*
Ledger, William Joe *physician, educator*
Lee, Mathew Hung Mun *physiatrist*
†Lepor, Herbert *urologist*
Levere, Richard David *physician, academic administrator, educator*
Levin, Warren Mayer *family practice physician*
Levitan, Max Fishel *geneticist, anatomy educator*
Levy, Albert *family physician*
Lewis, Jonathan Joseph *surgical oncologist, molecular biologist, educator*
Lewy, Robert Max *physician*
Lieberman, James S. *physiatrist, neurologist*
Lifton, Robert Jay *psychiatrist, author*
Lipkin, Martin *physician, scientist*
Lipton, Lester *ophthalmologist, entrepreneur*
Liu, Si-kwang *veterinary pathologist*
Llinás, Rodolfo Riascos *medical educator, researcher*
Localio, S. Arthur *retired surgeon, educator*
Lockshin, Michael Dan *rheumatologist*
Loo, Marcus H. *physician, educator*
Lubkin, Virginia Leila *ophthalmologist*
Luntz, Maurice Harold *ophthalmologist*
Macdonald, John Stephen *oncologist, educator*
Macken, Daniel Loos *physician, educator*
MacKinnon, Roger Alan *psychiatrist, educator*
Malitz, Sidney *psychiatrist, educator, researcher*
Manger, William Muir *internist*
Marcus, Eric Robert *psychiatrist*
Mark, Laurence Peter *anesthesiology educator*
Marks, Paul Alan *oncologist, cell biologist, educator*
Masterson, James Francis *psychiatrist*
Mauskop, Alexander *physician*
Mazzia, Valentino Don Bosco *physician, educator, lawyer*
McCarty, Maclyn *medical scientist*
Mc Crory, Wallace Willard *pediatrician, educator*
Mc Murtry, James Gilmer, III *neurosurgeon*
Mellins, Robert B. *pediatrician, educator*
Mesia, Augusto Fajardo *pathologist*
Mesnikoff, Alvin Murray *psychiatry educator*
Michels, Robert *psychiatrist, educator*
Michelsen, Christopher Bruce Hermann *surgeon*
Mildvan, Donna *infectious diseases physician*
Mohr, Jay Preston *neurologist*
Moore, Anne *physician*
Moss, Melvin Lionel *anatomist, educator*
Moss-Salentijn, Letty (Aleida Moss-Salentijn) *anatomist*
Muchnick, Richard Stuart *ophthalmologist*
Murphy, Brian Stuart *internist, consultant*
Murphy, Ramon Jeremiah Castroviejo *physician, pediatrician*
Muszynski, Cheryl Ann *neurosurgeon*
Nachman, Ralph Louis *physician, educator*
Nahas, Gabriel Georges *pharmacologist, educator, writer*
Nazir, Tabinda *physician*
Neuspiel, Daniel Robert *pediatrician, epidemiologist*
Neuwirth, Robert Samuel *obstetrician, gynecologist*
New, Maria Iandolo *physician, educator*
Newbold, Herbert Leon, Jr. *psychiatrist, writer*
Newman, Robert Gabriel *physician*
Nicholas, James A. *surgeon, consultant, educator*
Nisce, Lourdes *radiologist*
Nivarthi, Raju Naga *anesthesiology educator*
Noback, Charles Robert *anatomist, educator*
Ochoa, Manuel, Jr. *oncologist*
Oettgen, Herbert Friedrich *physician*
Oldham, John Michael *physician, psychiatrist, educator*
Olsson, Carl Alfred *urologist*
Orazi, Attilio *anatomic pathologist, researcher, educator*
Ordorica, Steven Anthony *obstetrician, gynecologist, educator*
O'Reilly, Richard John *pediatrician*
Osborn, June Elaine *pediatrician, microbiologist, educator, foundation administrator*
Osborne, Michael Piers *surgeon, researcher, health facility administrator*
Oster, Martin William *oncologist*
Pacella, Bernard Leonardo *psychiatrist*
Pardes, Herbert *psychiatrist, educator*
Pastores, Gregory McCarthy *physician, researcher*
Pedley, Timothy Asbury, IV *neurologist, educator, researcher*
†Petito, Frank A. *neurologist*
Pfaff, Donald W. *neurobiology and behavior educator*
Phillips, Gerald Baer *internal medicine scientist, educator*
Phoon, Colin Kit-Lun *pediatric cardiologist*
Pierri, Mary Kathryn Madeline *cardiologist, critical care physician, educator*
Pirani, Conrad Levi *pathologist, educator*
Pi-Sunyer, F. Xavier *medical educator, medical investigator*
Pitt, Jane *medical educator*
Plum, Fred *neurologist*
Polenz, Joanna Magda *psychiatrist*
Posner, Jerome Beebe *neurologist, educator*
Quraishi, Nisar Ali *internist*
Rabbani, LeRoy Elazar *physician, researcher*
Rabinowitz, Jack Grant *radiologist, educator*
Rainess, Alan Edward *psychiatrist, neurologist, educator*
Ramsay, David Leslie *physician, dermatologist, medical educator*
Raskin, Noel Michael *thoracic surgeon*
Redo, S(averio) Frank *surgeon*
Reidenberg, Marcus Milton *physician, educator*
Reis, Donald Jeffery *neurologist, neurobiologist, educator*
Reisberg, Barry *geropsychiatrist, neuropsychopharmacologist*
Reiss, Robert Francis *physician*
Rendon, Mario Ivan *psychiatrist*
Rifkind, Arleen B. *physician, researcher*
Ristich, Miodrag *psychiatrist*
Ritch, Robert Harry *ophthalmologist, educator*
Rodriguez-Sains, Rene S. *physician, surgeon, educator*
Roen, Philip Ruben *urologist, surgeon, medical educator*
Rogers, Mark Charles *physician, educator*
Rom, William Nicholas *physician*
Roman, Stanford Augustus, Jr. *medical educator, dean*
Romano, John Francis *physician*
Rosenberg, Victor I. *plastic surgeon*
Rosendorff, Clive *cardiologist*
Rosenfield, Allan *physician*
†Rosenthal, Richard Nelson *psychiatrist*
Rothenberg, Robert Edward *physician, surgeon, author*
Roufa, Arnold *gynecologist, obstetrician*
Rovit, Richard Lee *neurological surgeon*
Rowland, Lewis Phillip *neurologist, medical editor, educator*
Rubin, Albert Louis *physician, educator*
Rubin, Theodore Isaac *psychiatrist*
Rubinstein, Alina Anna *psychiatrist*
Sachar, David Bernard *gastroenterologist, medical educator*
Sachdev, Ved Parkash *neurosurgeon*
Sacks, Oliver Wolf *neurologist, writer*
Sadock, Benjamin James *psychiatrist, educator*
Sager, Clifford J(ulius) *psychiatrist, educator*
Salans, Lester Barry *physician, scientist, educator*
Salgo, Peter Lloyd *internist, anesthesiologist, broadcaster, jounalist, lecturer, consultant*
Samman, Juan M. *prosthodontist*
Sanchez, Miguel Ramon *dermatologist, educator*
Saphir, Richard Louis *pediatrician*
Schaffner, Bertram Henry *psychiatrist*
Schiff, Andrew Newman *physician, venture capitalist*
Schley, William Shain *otorhinolaryngologist*
Schneck, Jerome M. *psychiatrist, medical historian, educator*
Schneier, Harvey Allen *physician, pharmaceutical researcher*
Schuker, Eleanor Sheila *psychiatrist, educator*
Schuster, Carlotta Lief *psychiatrist*
Schwartz, Irving Leon *physician, scientist, educator*
Schwartz, Roselind Shirley Grant *podiatrist*
†Sciarra, Daniel *physician, consultant in neurology*
†Sclafani, Anthony Paul *plastic surgeon, educator, biomedical researcher*
Sedlin, Elias David *physician, orthopedic researcher, educator*
Seely, Robert Daniel *physician, medical educator*
Sessions, Roy Brumby *otolaryngologist, educator*
Shainess, Natalie *psychiatrist, educator*
Shapiro, Theodore *psychiatrist, educator*
Shatan, Chaim Felix *psychiatrist, medical educator, expert on Vietnam veterans, traumatic stress pioneer*
Shepherd, Gillian Mary *physician*
Siffert, Robert Spencer *orthopedic surgeon*
Silver, Richard Tobias *physician, educator*
Siris, Ethel Silverman *endocrinologist*
Sitarz, Anneliese Lotte *pediatrics educator, physician*
Skinner, David Bernt *surgeon, educator, administrator*
Snyderman, Selma Eleanore *pediatrician, educator*
Soave, Rosemary *internist*
Solomon, Gail Ellen *physician*
Sorrel, William Edwin *psychiatrist, educator, psychoanalyst*
Spaide, Richard Frederick *ophthalmologist*
Spencer, Frank Cole *medical educator*
Spiera, Harry *rheumatologist*
Stark, Richard Boies *surgeon, artist*
Stein, Marvin *psychiatrist, historian*
Steinglass, Peter Joseph *psychiatrist, educator*
Steinherz, Laurel Judith *pediatric cardiologist*
Stellman, Steven Dale *epidemiologist*
Stenzel, Kurt Hodgson *physician, nephrologist, educator*
Stern, Claudio Daniel *medical educator, embryological researcher*
Stern, Marvin *psychiatrist, educator*
Stimmel, Barry *cardiologist, internist, educator, university dean*
Stoopler, Mark Benjamin *physician*
Sulkowicz, Kerry J. *psychiatrist, psychoanalyst, consultant*
Sullivan, Stephen Gene *psychiatrist, pharmacologist, administrator*
Sun, Tung-Tien *medical science educator*
Sverdlik, Samuel Simon *physiatrist, physician*
†Swistel, Daniel George *surgeon*
Temple, Donald Edward *medical association executive*
Thomas, Stephen Jay *anesthesiologist*
Thomashow, Byron Martin *pulmonary physician*
Thomson, Gerald Edmund *physician, educator*
Tilley, Shermaine Ann *molecular immunologist, educator*
Tolchin, Joan Gubin *psychiatrist, educator*
Tourlitsas, John Constantine *radiologist*
Turino, Gerard Michael *physician, medical scientist, educator*
Turndorf, Herman *anesthesiologist, educator*
Tzimas, Nicholas Achilles *orthopedic surgeon, educator*
Vaughan, Edwin Darracott, Jr. *urologist, surgeon*
Vidovich, Danko Victor *neurosurgeon, neuroradiologist, researcher*
Vilcek, Jan Tomas *medical educator*
Vivera, Arsenio Bondoc *allergist*
Waksman, Byron Halsted *neuroimmunologist, experimental pathologist, educator, medical association administrator*
Wallace, Joyce Irene Malakoff *internist*
Walsh, Joseph Brennan *ophthalmologist*
Wang, Frederick Mark *pediatric ophthalmologist, medical educator*
Warshaw, Leon J(oseph) *physician*
Wasserman, Louis Robert *physician, educator*
Waugh, Theodore Rogers *orthopedic surgeon*
Wazen, Jack Joseph *otolaryngologist, educator*
Weber, Carol Martinez *physician*
†Weiland, Andrew J. *orthopaedic surgeon*
Weinstein, I. Bernard *oncologist, geneticist, research administrator*
Weisfeldt, Myron Lee *physician, educator*
Weiss, Paul Richard *plastic surgeon*
Weissmann, Gerald *medical educator, researcher, writer, editor*
Weksler, Marc Edward *physician, educator*
Werner, Andrew Joseph *physician, endocrinologist, musicologist*
Wharton, Ralph Nathaniel *psychiatrist, educator*
Whelan, Elizabeth Ann Murphy *epidemiologist*
Whitehead, Edgar Douglas *urology educator*
Whitsell, John Crawford, II *retired general surgeon*
Wiesel, Torsten Nils *neurobiologist, educator*
Wilson, Philip Duncan, Jr. *orthopedic surgeon*
†Wilson, Victor J. *neuroscientist*
Winawer, Sidney Jerome *physician, clinical investigator, educator*
Wishnick, Marcia Margolis *pediatrician, geneticist, educator*
Worman, Howard Jay *physician, educator*
Wright, Jane Cooke *physician, educator, consultant*
Yahr, Melvin David *physician*
Yeh, Hsu-Chong *radiology educator*
Yeh, Ming-Neng *obstetrician, gynecologist*
Yurt, Roger William *surgeon, educator*
Zatlin, Gabriel Stanley *physician*
Zimmerman, Sol Shea *pediatrician*
Zinn, Keith Marshall *ophthalmologist, educator*
†Zisfein, James *physician*
Zitrin, Arthur *physician*
Zonszein, Joel *endocrinologist*
Zucker, Howard Alan *pediatric cardiologist, intensivist, anesthesiologist*

Niskayuna
Zepp, Ann-Marie *rehabilitation nurse, adult nurse practitioner*

North Tonawanda
†Megahed, Mohamed Salah *neurologist, educator*

Nyack
Rossi, Harald Hermann *retired radiation biophysicist, educator, administrator*

Old Westbury
DiGiovanna, Eileen Landenberger *osteopathic physician, educator*

Olean
Catalano, Robert Anthony *ophthalmologist, physician, hospital administrator, writer*
Gupta, Sanjay *psychiatrist*

Oneonta
Bucove, Arnold David *psychiatrist*
†Falco, Gennaro Anthony *urologist, surgeon*
†Lusins, John *neurologist*

Ontario
Loomis, Norman Richard *physician*

Orangeburg
Levine, Jerome *psychiatrist, educator*
Nixon, Ralph Angus *psychiatrist, educator, research neuroscientist*

Orchard Park
Lee, Richard Vaille *physician, educator*

Ossining
Wolfe, Mary Joan *physician*

Pittsford
Faloon, William Wassell *physician, educator*

Plainview
Kelemen, John *neurologist, educator*
Krauss, Leo *urologist, educator*
Lieberman, Elliott *urologist*
†Shoen, Steven Lloyd *plastic surgeon*

Plattsburgh
Bedworth, David Albert *health educator*
Kuehl, Alexander Edward *physician, health facility administrator, medical educator, writer*
Medearis, Kenneth Robert *medical products manufactoring company executive*
Rech, Susan Anita *obstetrician, gynecologist*
Virostek, Robert Joseph *physician*

Pleasantville
Waletzky, Lucy R. *psychiatrist*

Pomona
Glassman, Lawrence S. *plastic surgeon*
Zugibe, Frederick Thomas *pathologist*

Port Ewen
Ausubel, David Paul *retired psychiatrist, author*

Port Jefferson
Dranitzke, Richard J. *surgeon*

Port Jefferson Station
Kaplan, Martin Paul *pediatrician, educator*

Port Washington
Brownstein, Martin Herbert *dermatopathologist*

Poughkeepsie
Berlin, Doris Ada *psychiatrist*

Rego Park
Gudeon, Arthur *podiatrist*

Rochester
Akiyama, Toshio *cardiologist, educator, researcher*
Baum, John *physician*
Bennett, John Morrison *medical oncologist*
Berg, Robert Lewis *physician, educator*
Bessey, Palmer Quintard *surgeon*
Bonfiglio, Thomas Albert *pathologist, educator*
Brody, Bernard B. *physician, educator*
Brooks, Walter S. *dermatologist*
Burgener, Francis André *radiology educator*
Burton, Richard Irving *orthopedist, educator*
Bushinsky, David Allen *nephrologist, educator, researcher*
Chey, William Yoon *physician*
Cohen, Nicholas *immunologist, educator*
†Condemi, John J. *physician*
Crino, Marjanne Helen *anesthesiologist*
Danforth-Morningstar, Elizabeth *obstetrician/ gynecologist*
de Papp, Zsolt George *endocrinologist*
Doty, Robert William *neurophysiologist, educator*
†Drepaul, Loris Omesh *infectious diseases physician*
Dreyfuss, Eric Martin *allergist*
DuBeshter, Brent *physician*
Forbes, Gilbert Burnett *physician, educator*
Frazer, John Paul *surgeon*
Golden, Reynold Stephen *geriatrician*
Goldstein, Marvin Norman *physician*
Griggs, Robert Charles *physician*
Haywood, Anne Mowbray *pediatrics, virology, and biochemistry educator*
Heinle, Robert Alan *physician*
Jacobs, Laurence Stanton *physician, educator*
†Kieburtz, Karl David *physician, educator, researcher*
Lawrence, Ruth Anderson *pediatrician, clinical toxicologist*
Lichtman, Marshall Albert *medical educator, physician, scientist*
McDonald, Joseph Valentine *neurosurgeon*
McMeekin, Thomas Owen *dermatologist*
McQuillen, Michael Paul *neurologist, educator*
Morgan, William Lionel, Jr. *physician, educator*
Moss, Arthur Jay *physician*

Mundorff Shrestha, Sheila Ann *cariologist*
Nazarian, Lawrence Fred *pediatrician*
Okunieff, Paul *radiation oncologist, physician*
O'Mara, Robert Edmund George *radiologist, educator*
Panner, Bernard J. *pathologist, educator*
Papadakos, Peter John *critical care physician, educator*
Pearson, Thomas Arthur *epidemiologist, educator*
Powers, James Matthew *neuropathologist*
Risher, William Henry *cardiothoracic surgeon, educator*
Rowley, Peter Templeton *physician, educator*
Schmidt, John Gerhard *neurologist, educator, researcher*
Schwartz, Seymour Ira *surgeon, educator*
Sherman, Charles Daniel, Jr. *surgeon*
Smith, Julia Ladd *medical oncologist, hospice physician*
Sparks, Charles Edward *pathologist, educator*
Toribara, Taft Yutaka *radiation biologist, biophysicist, chemist, toxicologist*
Utell, Mark Jeffrey *medical educator*
†Waugh, Richard E. *biomedical engineering educator*
Wax, Paul Matthew *emergency medicine physician, educator, medical toxicologist*
Williams, Thomas Franklin *physician, educator*
Wynne, Lyman Carroll *psychiatrist*

Rome
†Dela Cruz, Pablito Sulit *pediatrician, neurologist*

Roslyn
Damus, Paul Shibli *cardiac surgeon*

Roslyn Heights
Rogatz, Peter *physician*

Rye
Barker, Harold Grant *surgeon, educator*
Marcus, Joel David *pediatrician*
Reader, George Gordon *physician, educator*
Wessler, Stanford *physician, educator*
Wilmot, Irvin Gorsage *former hospital administrator, educator, consultant*

Sands Point
Goodman, Edmund Nathan *surgeon, pain management consultant*
Lear, Erwin *anesthesiologist, educator*

Scarsdale
Edis, Gloria Toby *pediatrician*
Moser, Marvin *physician, educator, author*
Newman, Fredric Alan *plastic surgeon, educator*
Perez, Louis Anthony *radiologist*
Scheinberg, Labe Charles *physician, educator*

Schenectady
†Bentrovato, Donald A. *genito-urinary surgeon*
de la Rocha, Carlos A. *retired physician*
Schenck, John Frederic *physician*

Silver Creek
Schenk, Worthington George, Jr. *surgeon, educator*

Sleepy Hollow
Hershman, Jack Ira *urologist*

Slingerlands
†Elliott, Ray Andrew, Jr. *retired surgeon, consultant*

Smithtown
Dvorkin, Ronald Alan *emergency physician*
Pearl, Richard Alan *neurologist, educator*
†Zippin, Allen Gerald *neurosurgeon*

Somers
Bauman, William Allen *pediatrician, educator, health systems consultant*
Rubin, Samuel Harold *physician, consultant*

Spring Valley
†Ganchrow, Mandell I. *surgeon*

Staten Island
Banner, Burton *pediatrician*
Bruckstein, Alex Harry *internist, gastroenterologist, geriatrician*
O'Connor, Robert James *gynecologist, consultant*
Raz, Lois Katz *speech-language pathologist, writer*
Stathopoulos, Peter *internist*
Winter, Steven *internist, cardiologist*

Stony Brook
Bilfinger, Thomas Victor *surgeon, educator*
Cottrell, Thomas Sylvester *pathology educator, university dean*
†Coulehan, John Leo *physician educator, poet*
Davis, James Norman *neurologist, neurobiology researcher*
Edelman, Norman Herman *medical educator, university dean and official*
†Epstein, Mark Daniel *plastic surgeon*
Fritts, Harry Washington, Jr. *physician, educator*
Jasiewicz, Ronald Clarence *anesthesiologist, educator*
Jonas, Steven *public health physician, medical educator, writer*
Kuchner, Eugene Frederick *neurosurgeon, educator*
Lane, Dorothy Spiegel *physician*
Meyers, Morton Allen *physician, radiology educator*
Miller, Frederick *pathologist*
Poppers, Paul Jules *anesthesiologist, educator*
Priebe, Cedric Joseph, Jr. *pediatric surgeon*
Rapaport, Felix Theodosius *surgeon, editor, researcher, educator*
Ricotta, John Joseph *vascular surgeon, educator*
Schoenfeld, Elinor Randi *epidemiologist*
Steigbigel, Roy Theodore *infectious disease physician and scientist, educator*
Steinberg, Amy Wishner *dermatologist*
Volkman, David J. *immunology educator*

Suffern
Codispoti, Andre John *allergist, immunologist*
Fogelman, Harold Hugo *psychiatrist*
Oppenheim, Jeffrey Sable *neurosurgeon*

Syracuse
Baker, Bruce Edward *orthopedic surgeon, consultant*
Bellanger, Barbara Doris Hoysak *biomedical research technologist*
Clausen, Jerry Lee *psychiatrist*
Cohen, William Nathan *radiologist*
Daly, Robert W. *psychiatrist, medical educator*
Farah, Fuad Salim *dermatologist*
Gold, Joseph *medical researcher*
Horst, Pamela Sue *medical educator, family physician*
Irwin, Martin *psychiatrist*
Kieffer, Stephen Aaron *radiologist, educator*
Murray, David George *orthopedic surgeon, educator*
Nast, Edward Paul *cardiac surgeon*
Rabuzzi, Daniel D. *medical educator*
Ratner, Michael Harvey *pediatric surgeon*
Rogers, Sherry Anne *physician*
Sagerman, Robert Howard *radiation oncologist*
Scheinman, Steven Jay *medical educator*
Smith, Robert L. *medical research administrator*
Szasz, Thomas Stephen *psychiatrist, educator, writer*
Threatte, Gregory Allen *pathology educator, academic director*
Verrillo, Ronald Thomas *neuroscience educator, researcher*
Weiner, Irwin M. *retired medical educator/ researcher, college dean,*
Williams, William Joseph *physician, educator*

Tarrytown
Baum, Carol Grossman *physician*
Field, Barry Elliot *internist, gastroenterologist*
Panitz, Lawrence *physician*

Tuckahoe
Curtin, Brian Joseph *ophthalmologist*

Tuxedo Park
Regan, Ellen Frances (Mrs. Walston Shepard Brown) *ophthalmologist*

Upton
Hamilton, Leonard Derwent *physician, molecular biologist*

Utica
Bowers, Roger Paul *radiologist*
Millet, John Bradford *retired surgeon*

Valhalla
Accardo, Pasquale J. *pediatrician, educator*
†Ahluwalia, Brij M. Singh *neurologist, educator*
Cimino, Joseph Anthony *physician, educator*
Couldwell, William Tupper *neurosurgeon, educator*
Del Guercio, Louis Richard Maurice *surgeon, educator, company executive*
Fink, Raymond *medical educator*
Frishman, William Howard *cardiology educator, cardiovasular pharmacologist, gerontologist*
Frost, Elizabeth Ann McArthur *physician*
Kline, Susan Anderson *medical school official and dean, internist*
Madden, Robert Edward *surgeon, educator*
Masdeu, Jose Cruz *neurologist, medical school administrator*
McGiff, John C(harles) *pharmacologist*
Reed, George Elliott *surgery educator*
Valsamis, Marius Peter *neuropathologist, educator*
Weisburger, John Hans *medical researcher*
Williams, Gary Murray *medical researcher, pathology educator*

Warsaw
Dy-Ang, Anita C. *pediatrician*

Washington Mills
†Wei, Wen Chen *neurosurgeon*

Watertown
Ebbels, Bruce Jeffery *physician, health facility administrator*
Fredriksen, Maryellen *physician assistant*
†Innes, George Michael *emergency medicine physician*

West Nyack
†Katz, S. Sheldon *neurolosurgeon*

Westbury
Ente, Gerald *pediatrician*

White Plains
Alcena, Valiere *internist, hematologist, educator, television producer, broadcast journalist*
†Bernard, Robert William *plastic surgeon*
Bertles, John Francis *physician, educator*
Biers, Martin Henry *physician*
Blass, John Paul *medical educator, physician*
†Blau, Morocai *plastic surgeon*
Canepa, Cathy *psychiatrist*
Katz, Michael *pediatrician, educator*
Liebert, Peter Selig *pediatric surgeon, consultant*
Marano, Anthony Joseph *cardiologist*
Marrero, Vito Anthony *surgeon*
McDowell, Fletcher Hughes *physician, educator*
Monteferrante, Judith Catherine *cardiologist*
Morello, Daniel Conway *plastic surgeon*
Morris, Robert Warren *physician assistant*
Pfeffer, Cynthia Roberta *psychiatrist, educator*
Samii, Abdol Hossein *physician, educator*
Smith, Gerard Peter *neuroscientist*
Soley, Robert Lawrence *plastic surgeon*

Whitestone
Rosmarin, Leonard Alan *dermatologist*

Williamsville
Ogra, Pearay L. *physician, educator*
Reisman, Robert E. *physician, educator*
Stein, Alfred Marvin *hematologist*

Woodstock
Dolamore, Michael John *physician*

Yonkers
Daman, Harlan Richard *allergist*
Hirschman, Shalom Zarach *physician*
Mennin, Gerald Stanley *ophthalmologist*
†Rosch, Elliott Carl *internist*

NORTH CAROLINA

Aberdeen
Jacobson, Peter Lars *neurologist, educator*

Asheboro
Helsabeck, Eric H. *emergency physician*

Asheville
Enriquez, Manuel Hipolito *physician*
White, Terry Edward *physician*

Banner Elk
Littlejohn, Mark Hays *radiologist*

Boone
Domer, Floyd Ray *pharmacologist, educator*

Burlington
†Clarke, Peter Randolph Hasche *neurologist*
Wilson, William Preston *psychiatrist, emeritus educator*

Chapel Hill
Azar, Henry Amin *medical historian, educator*
Baerg, Richard Henry *podiatrist, surgeon*
Bondurant, Stuart *physician, educational administrator*
Boone, Franklin Delanor Roosevelt, Sr. *cardiovascular perfusionist, realtor*
Briggaman, Robert Alan *dermatologist, medical educator*
Brinkhous, Kenneth Merle *retired pathologist, educator*
Bromberg, Philip Allan *internist, educator*
Brownlee, Robert Calvin *pediatrician, educator*
Cance, William George *surgeon*
Carson, Culley Clyde, III *urologist*
Cefalo, Robert Charles *obstetrician, gynecologist*
Clemmons, David Robert *internist, educator*
Collier, Albert M. *pediatric educator, child development center director*
Cromartie, William James *medical educator, researcher*
De Friese, Gordon H. *health services researcher*
Denny, Floyd Wolfe, Jr. *pediatrician*
De Rosa, Guy Paul *orthopedic surgery educator*
Earley, Laurence Elliott *medical educator*
Easterling, William Ewart, Jr. *obstetrician, gynecologist*
Eifrig, David Eric *ophthalmologist, educator*
Farmer, Thomas Wohlsen *neurologist, educator*
Fowler, Wesley Caswell, Jr. *obstetrician, gynecologist*
Goyer, Robert Andrew *pathology educator*
Graham, John Borden *pathologist, writer, educator*
Greganti, Mac Andrew *physician, medical educator*
Grisham, Joe Wheeler *pathologist, educator*
Hawkins, David Rollo, Sr. *psychiatrist*
Henson, Anna Miriam *otolaryngology researcher, medical educator*
Henson, O'Dell Williams, Jr. *anatomy educator*
Hirsch, Philip Francis *pharmacologist, educator*
Hollister, William Gray *psychiatrist*
Houpt, Jeffrey Lyle *psychiatrist, educator*
Hulka, Barbara Sorenson *epidemiology educator*
Hulka, Jaroslav Fabian *obstetrician, gynecologist*
Johnson, Andrew Myron *pediatric immunologist, educator*
Johnson, George, Jr. *physician, educator*
Juliano, Rudolph L. *medical educator*
Keagy, Blair Allen *surgery educator*
McMillan, Campbell White *pediatric hematologist*
Miller, C. Arden *physician, educator*
Nebel, William Arthur *obstetrician, gynecologist*
Ontjes, David Ainsworth *medicine and pharmacology educator*
Pagano, Joseph Stephen *physician, researcher, educator*
Palmer, Jeffress Gary *hematologist, educator*
Pillsbury, Harold Crockett, III *otolaryngologist*
Pollitzer, William Sprott *anatomy educator*
Prange, Arthur Jergen, Jr. *psychiatrist, neurobiologist, educator*
Prather, Donna Lynn *psychiatrist*
Roper, William Lee *dean, physician*
Runyan, Desmond Kimo *medical educator, researcher*
Sheldon, George F. *medical educator*
Sheps, Cecil George *physician*
Sorenson, James Roger *public health educator*
Spencer, Roger Felix *psychiatrist, psychoanalyst, medical educator*
Stockman, James Anthony, III *pediatrician*
Suzuki, Kunihiko *biomedical educator, researcher*
Tunnessen, Walter William, Jr. *pediatrician*
Tyroler, Herman Alfred *epidemiologist*
Van Wyk, Judson John *endocrinologist, pediatric educator*
Wheeler, Clayton Eugene, Jr. *dermatologist, educator*
Wilcox, Benson Reid *cardiothoracic surgeon, educator*
Williams, Roberta Gay *pediatric cardiologist, educator*
Winfield, John Buckner *rheumatologist, educator*
†Zenn, Michael Robert *plastic and reconstructive surgeon*

Charlotte
†Andrews, David Scott *thoracic and cardiovascular surgeon*
Bosse, Michael Joseph *orthopedic trauma surgeon, retired medical officer*
Duffy, John Charles *psychiatric educator*
Freeman, Tyler Ira *physician*
Hutcheson, J. Sterling *allergist, immunologist, physician*
Lapp, Charles Warren *internal medicine physician, pediatrician*
McLanahan, Charles Scott *neurosurgeon*
Nicholson, Henry Hale, Jr. *surgeon*
Shah, Nandlal Chimanlal *physiatrist*
Thompson, John Albert, Jr. *dermatologist*
Tillett, Grace Montana *ophthalmologist, real estate developer*
Visser, Valya Elizabeth *physician*
Watkins, Carlton Gunter *retired pediatrician*

Durham
Alexander, C. Alex *physician*
Amos, Dennis B. *immunologist*
Anderson, Robert W. *surgeon*
Anderson, William Banks, Jr. *ophthalmology educator*
Anlyan, William George *surgeon, university administrator*
Barry, David Walter *infectious diseases physician, researcher*
Bennett, Peter Brian *researcher, hyperbaric medicine*
Blazer, Dan German *psychiatrist, epidemiologist*
Blazing, Michael August *internist*
Bradford, William Dalton *pathologist, educator*
Brodie, Harlow Keith Hammond *psychiatrist, educator, past university president*
Buckley, Charles Edward, III *physician, educator*
Buckley, Rebecca Hatcher *physician, educator*
Busse, Ewald William *psychiatrist, educator*
Carter, James Harvey *psychiatrist, educator*
Christmas, William Anthony *internist, educator*
Cohen, Harvey Jay *physician, educator*
†Cokgor, Ilkcan *neuro-oncologist, neurologist*
Coleman, Ralph Edward *nuclear medicine physician*
Dees, Susan Coons *physician, educator*
Estes, Edward Harvey, Jr. *medical educator*
Falletta, John Matthew *pediatrician, educator*
Feldman, Jerome Myron *physician*
Foreman, John William *pediatrician, educator*
Freemark, Michael Scott *pediatric endocrinologist and educator*
Frothingham, Thomas Eliot *pediatrician*
Gaede, Jane Taylor *pathologist, educator*
Georgiade, Nicholas George *plastic and oral surgeon, educator*
Greenfield, Joseph Cholmondeley, Jr. *physician, educator*
Hamilton, Michael A. *medical educator*
Hammond, Charles Bessellieu *obstetrician, gynecologist, educator*
Harmel, Merel Hilber *anesthesiologist, educator*
Harris, Jerome Sylvan *pediatrician, pediatrics and biochemistry educator*
Heinz, E(dward) Ralph *neuroradiologist, educator*
†Husain, Aatif Mairaj *neurologist*
Jennings, Robert Burgess *experimental pathologist, medical educator*
Kaprielian, Victoria Susan *medical educator*
Katz, Samuel Lawrence *pediatrician, scientist*
Kaufman, Russell Eugene *hematologist, oncologist*
Kirshner, Norman *pharmacologist, researcher, educator*
Klitzman, Bruce *physiologist, plastic surgery educator, researcher*
Koepke, John Arthur *hematologist, clinical pathologist*
Krishnan, Krishnaswamy Ranga Rama *psychiatrist*
Lack, Leon *pharmacology and biochemistry educator*
Lee, Paul P. *physician, educator, consultant, lawyer*
Lefkowitz, Robert Joseph *physician, educator*
London, William Lord *pediatrician*
Marchuk, Douglas Alan *medical educator*
Michener, James Lloyd *medical educator*
Moon, Samuel David *medical educator*
Moore, John Wilson *neurophysiologist, educator*
Murphy, Barbara Anne *emergency physician, surgery educator*
Murphy, Thomas Miles *pediatrician*
Nevins, Joseph Roy *medical educator*
Odom, Guy Leary *retired physician*
Osterhout, Suydam *physician, educator*
Pinnell, Sheldon Richard *physician, medical educator*
Pizzo, Salvatore Vincent *pathologist*
Pratt, Philip Chase *pathologist, educator*
Putman, Charles E(d) *medical educator, clinician, academic administrator, radiologist*
†Radtke, Radney A. *neurologist*
Reves, Joseph Gerald *anesthesiology educator*
Roulidis, Zeses Chris *medical educator*
Sabiston, David Coston, Jr. *surgeon, educator*
Schanberg, Saul Murray *pharmacology educator*
Serafin, Donald *plastic surgeon*
Severance, Harry Wells *emergency medicine educator*
Shelburne, John Daniel *pathologist*
Shetty, Ashok K. *neuroscientist*
Snyderman, Ralph *medical educator, physician*
Spach, Madison Stockton *cardiologist*
Stead, Eugene Anson, Jr. *physician*
Stiles, Gary Lester *cardiologist, molecular pharmacologist, educator*
Strauss, Harold Carl *cardiology educator*
Sum-Ping, Sam Thio *anesthesiologist, hospital administrator*
Swaim, Mark Wendell *hepatologist, molecular biologist, gastroenterologist, educator, photographer*
Tedder, Thomas Fletcher *immunology educator, researcher*
Weiner, Richard David *psychiatrist*
Wilkins, Robert Henry *neurosurgeon, editor*
Williams, Redford Brown *medical educator*
Yancy, William Samuel *pediatrician*

Emerald Isle
†Gates, Herbert Stelwyn *retired obstetrician-gynecologist*

Fairview
Gaffney, Thomas Edward *retired physician*

Fayetteville
Chipman, Martin *neurologist, retired army officer*
Jones, James Curtiss *surgeon*

Fort Bragg
Abreu, Sue Hudson *physician, army officer*

Gastonia
Prince, George Edward *retired pediatrician*

Greensboro
Baird, Haynes Wallace *pathologist*
Cotter, John Burley *ophthalmologist, corneal specialist*
Houston, Frank Matt *dermatologist*
Stevens, Elliott Walker, Jr. *allergist, pulmonologist*
Truesdale, Gerald Lynn *plastic and reconstructive surgeon*

Greenville
Cunningham, Paul Raymond Goldwyn *surgery educator*
Drury, James Anthony Bartholomew *psychiatrist, psychoanalyst*
Hallock, James Anthony *pediatrician, school dean*
Lannin, Donald Rowe *oncologist*
Laupus, William Edward *physician, educator*
Lee, Tung-Kwang *pathologist, cancer researcher*
Meggs, William Joel *internist, emergency physician, educator*
Metzger, W. James, Jr. *physician, researcher, educator*

Norris, H. Thomas *retired pathologist, academic administrator*
Pories, Walter Julius *surgeon, educator*
Tingelstad, Jon Bunde *physician*
Volkman, Alvin *pathologist, researcher, educator*
Winn, Francis John, Jr. *medical educator*
Wortmann, Dorothy Woodward *physician*

Hampstead
Solomon, Robert Douglas *pathology educator*

Hendersonville
Reinhart, John Belvin *child and adolescent psychiatrist, educator*

Hickory
Lefler, Wade Hampton, Jr. *ophthalmologist*

High Point
Bardelas, Jose Antonio *allergist*
Blazek, F. Douglas *surgeon*
Draelos, Zoe Diana *dermatologist, consultant*
Kandt, Raymond S. *neurologist*

Hillsborough
Johnston, William Webb *pathologist, educator*
Marzluff, William Frank *medical educator*

Indian Beach
Wiley, Albert Lee, Jr. *physician, engineer, educator*

Lenoir
Carswell, Jane Triplett *family physician*

Mebane
Langley, Ricky Lee *occupational medicine physician*

Mooresville
Herring, Ralph McNeely *nurse*

Morehead City
Graham, Gloria Flippin *dermatologist*

Murphy
Khan, Rashid Hussain *physician, researcher*

New Bern
Finnerty, Frances Martin *medical administrator*
Futch, William Stewart, Jr. *gastroenterologist*
Hunt, William B. *cardiopulmonary physician*
Sinning, Mark Alan *thoracic and vascular surgeon*

Raleigh
†Ammon, John Richard *anesthesiologist*
Barish, Charles Franklin *internist, gastroenterologist, educator*
Boone, Stephen Christopher *neurosurgeon*
Garrett, Leland Earl *nephrologist, educator*
Gremillion, David H(enry) *internist, educator*
Hughes, Francis P. *medical researcher*
Kimbrell, Odell Culp, Jr. *physician*
†Levine, Ronald H. *physician, state official*
Peacock, Erle Ewart, Jr. *surgeon, lawyer, educator*
Stratas, Nicholas Emanuel *psychiatrist*
Veenhuis, Philip Edward *psychiatrist, educator, administrator*

Research Triangle Park
Barrett, J. Carl *cancer researcher, molecular biologist*
Golden, Carole Ann *immunologist, microbiologist*
Panas, Raymond Michael *pharmaceutical researcher*
Qualls, Charles Wayne, Jr. *research pathologist*
Roses, Allen David *neurologist, educator*

Salisbury
Kiser, Glenn Augustus *retired pediatrician, investor*
Lomax, Donald Henry *physician*

Sneads Ferry
†LaMar, James Edward *preventive medicine physician, marine officer*

Statesville
Deddens, Alan Eugene *otolaryngologist, head and neck surgeon*
Lorentzen, James Clifford *radiologist*

Thomasville
Sprinkle, Robert Lee, Jr. *podiatrist*

Waxhaw
Edwards, Irene Elizabeth (Libby Edwards) *dermatologist, educator, researcher*

Waynesville
McKinney, Alexander Stuart *neurologist, retired*

Whisper Pines
Enlow, Donald Hugh *anatomist, educator, university dean*

Wilmington
Bachman, David *neurologist, pediatric neurologist*
Gillen, Howard William *neurologist, medical historian*
Kesler, James L. *ophthalmologist*
Penick, George Dial *pathologist*
Perko, Mike A. *health education and health promotion educator*

Wilson
Kushner, Michael James *neurologist, consultant*
Ladwig, Harold Allen *neurologist*

Winston Salem
Alexander, Eben, Jr. *neurological surgeon*
Cheng, Che Ping *cardiologist, researcher, educator*
Clarkson, Thomas Boston *comparative medicine educator*
Cordell, A(lfred) Robert *cardiothoracic surgeon, educator*
Cowan, Robert Jenkins *radiologist, educator*
Dean, Richard Henry *surgeon, educator*
Donofrio, Peter Daniel *neurology educator*
Ferree, Carolyn Ruth *radiation oncologist, educator*
Georgitis, John *allergist, educator*
Hazzard, William Russell *geriatrician, educator*
Henrichs, W(alter) Dean *dermatologist*
Hopkins, Judith Owen *oncologist*
Howell, Charles Maitland *dermatologist*
Howell, Julius Ammons *plastic surgeon*
Ibrahim, Mounir Labib *physician, psychiatrist*
James, Francis Marshall, III *anesthesiologist*
Jorizzo, Joseph L. *dermatology educator*
Kaufman, William *internist*
Kelly, David Lee, Jr. *neurosurgeon, educator*
Kohut, Robert Irwin *otolaryngologist, educator*
Lawless, Michael Rhodes *pediatrics educator*
Maynard, Charles Douglas *radiologist*
Meis, Paul Jean *obstetrics and gynecology educator*
Mueller-Heubach, Eberhard *medical educator*
O'Steen, Wendall Keith *neurobiology and anatomy educator*
Podgorny, George *emergency physician*
Rogers, Lee Frank *radiologist*
Simon, Jimmy Louis *pediatrician, educator*
Stein, Barry Edward *medical educator*
Toole, James Francis *medical educator*
Veille, Jean-Claude *maternal-fetal medicine physician, educator*
Walker, John Samuel *retired pediatrician*
Woods, James Watson, Jr. *cardiologist*
Yeatts, Robert Patrick *ophthalmologist*

NORTH DAKOTA

Fargo
Taylor, Doris Denice *physician, entrepreneur*

Grand Forks
Carlson, Edward C. *anatomy educator*
Sobus, Kerstin MaryLouise *physician, physical therapist*

Minot
Rioux, Pierre August *psychiatrist*

Williston
Adducci, Joseph Edward *obstetrician, gynecologist*

OHIO

Ada
Elliott, Robert Betzel *retired physician*

Akron
Evans, Douglas McCullough *surgeon, educator*
Gallagher, Mortimer Anthony *surgeon*
†Houston, Alma Faye *psychiatrist*
Kraus, Henry *retired physician, educator*
Levy, Richard Philip *physician, educator*
Milsted, Amy *medical educator*
Rothmann, Bruce Franklin *pediatric surgeon*
Tan, James *physician*
Timmons, Gerald Dean *pediatric neurologist*

Athens
Chila, Anthony George *osteopathic educator*
Hedges, Richard Houston *epidemiologist, lawyer*

Bowling Green
Shehata, Said Ahmed *surgeon, researcher*

Brunswick
Kuchynski, Marie *physician*

Bryan
Carrico, Virgil Norman *physician*

Bucyrus
Solt, Robert Lee, Jr. *surgeon*

Canal Winchester
Burrier, Gail Warren *physician*

Canton
†Ahmad, Mirza Nasir *plastic and reconstructive surgeon*
†Carp, Steven Scott *plastic surgery*
Di Simone, Robert Nicholas *radiologist, educator*
Howland, Willard J. *radiologist, educator*
Kellermeyer, Robert William *physician, educator*
Maioriello, Richard Patrick *otolaryngologist*
Nadas, John Adalbert *psychiatrist*
Rubin, Patricia *internist*
Sicard, Guillermo Rafael *dermatologist*

Celina
Heinrichs, Timothy Arnold *family practice physician*

Centerville
Kelso, Harold Glen *family practice physician*

Chagrin Falls
Cusumano, Philip Anthony *physician*
Lingl, Friedrich Albert *psychiatrist*

Chardon
Dobyns, Brown McIlvaine *surgeon, educator*
Kellis, Michael John *osteopathic physician*

Cincinnati
Adolph, Robert J. *physician, medical educator*
Alamin, Khosrow *pathologist*
Alexander, James Wesley *surgeon, educator*
Azizkhan, Richard George *pediatric surgeon, educator*
Baughman, Robert Phillip *physician*
Beary, John Francis, III *physician, pharmaceutical executive*
Boat, Thomas Frederick *physician, educator, researcher*
Bridenbaugh, Phillip Owen *anesthesiologist, physician*
Buchman, Elwood *internist, pharmaceutical company medical director*
†Buckley, Donald Charles *cardiac thoracic surgeon*
Buncher, Charles Ralph *epidemiologist, educator*
Carothers, Charles Omsted *retired orthopedic surgeon*
Chin, Nee Oo Wong *reproductive endocrinologist*
Cudkowicz, Leon *medical educator*
Fenoglio-Preiser, Cecilia Mettler *pathologist, educator*
Fischer, Carl G. *anesthesiologist*
Fowler, Noble Owen *physician, university administrator*
Greenwalt, Tibor Jack *physician, educator*
Harshman, Morton Leonard *physician, business executive*
Heaton, Charles Lloyd *dermatologist, educator*
Heimlich, Henry Jay *physician, surgeon*
Hess, Evelyn Victorine (Mrs. Michael Howett) *medical educator*
Hogg, Stephen P. *otolaryngologist*
Hollerman, Charles Edward *pediatrician*
†Ireland, Gene E. *surgeon*
Loggie, Jennifer Mary Hildreth *medical educator, physician*
Lucas, Stanley Jerome *radiologist, physician*
Lucky, Anne Weissman *dermatologist*
Macpherson, Colin R(obertson) *pathologist, educator*
Maltz, Robert *surgeon*
Meese, Ernest Harold *thoracic and cardiovascular surgeon*
Neale, Henry Whitehead *plastic surgery educator*
Rapoport, Robert Morton *medical educator*
Rashkin, Mitchell Carl *internist, pulmonary medicine specialist*
Schreiner, Albert William *physician, educator*
†Shani, Hezekiah Gyunda Pyuza *surgeon*
Smith, Roger Dean *pathologist*
Suskind, Raymond Robert *physician, educator*
†Tobler, William D. *neurosurgeon*
†van Lovern, Harry R. *neurosurgeon*
Vilter, Richard William *physician, educator*
Weber, Fredrick Louis, Jr. *hepatologist, medical researcher*
West, Clark Darwin *pediatric nephrologist, educator*
Wilson, James Miller, IV *cardiovascular surgeon, educator*
Wiot, Jerome Francis *radiologist*
Wood, Robert Emerson *pediatrics educator*
Woodward, James Kenneth *pharmacologist*
Wright, Creighton Bolter *cardiovascular surgeon, educator*
†Yee, Leslie Mitchell *physician executive, educator*

Cleveland
Alfidi, Ralph Joseph *radiologist, educator*
Altose, Murray David *physician*
Awais, George Musa *obstetrician, gynecologist*
Badal, Daniel Walter *psychiatrist, educator*
Baker, Saul Phillip *geriatrician, cardiologist, internist*
Bambakidis, Peter *neurologist, educator*
Barnett, Gene Henry *neurosurgeon*
Bass, Jonathan *dermatologist*
Bause, George Stephen *anesthesiologist*
Bella, Jonathan Noriega *internist*
Berger, Melvin *allergist, immunologist*
Bloser, Dieter *radiologist*
Bowerfind, Edgar Sihler, Jr. *physician, medical administrator*
Boyd, Arthur Bernette, Jr. *surgeon, clergyman, beverage company executive*
Bronson, David Leigh *physician, educator*
Carter, James Rose, Jr. *medical educator*
Cascorbi, Helmut Freimund *anesthesiologist, educator*
Castele, Theodore John *radiologist*
Cole, Christopher Robert *cardiologist*
Cole, Monroe *neurologist, educator*
Collis, John Stanley *neurosurgeon*
Daroff, Robert Barry *neurologist*
Davis, Pamela Bowes *pediatric pulmonologist*
Dell'Osso, Louis Frank *neuroscience educator*
Denko, Joanne D. *psychiatrist, writer*
Doershuk, Carl Frederick *physician, professor of pediatrics*
Eiben, Robert Michael *pediatric neurologist, educator*
Elewski, Boni Elizabeth *dermatologist, educator*
Ellis, Lloyd H., Jr. *emergency physician*
Elston, Robert C. *medical educator*
Fazio, Victor Warren *physician, colon and rectal surgeon*
Friedman, Ernest Harvey *physician, psychiatrist*
Geho, Walter Blair *biomedical research executive*
Harris, John William *physician, educator*
Hermann, Robert Ewald *surgeon*
Holzbach, Raymond Thomas *gastroenterologist, author, educator*
Izant, Robert James, Jr. *pediatric surgeon*
Jackson, Edgar B., Jr. *medical educator*
Judge, Nancy Elizabeth *obstetrician, gynecologist*
Kass, Lawrence *hematologist, oncologist, hematopathologist*
Katzman, Richard A. *cardiologist, consultant*
†Kay, Robert *physician*
†Klein, Eric Alan *surgical oncologist, urologist*
†Konstan, Michael William *pediatric pulmonologist, researcher*
Lamm, Michael Emanuel *pathologist, immunologist, educator*
†Landis, Dennis Michael Doyle *neurologist, researcher*
Lazo, John, Jr. *physician*
Lefferts, William Geoffrey *physician, educator*
Lenkoski, Leo Douglas *psychiatrist, educator*
Lytle, Bruce Whitney *cardiovascular surgeon*
Macklis, Roger Miton *physician, educator, researcher*
†Marks, Kenneth Edward *orthopaedic surgeon*
McCrae, Keith R. *medical educator, researcher*
McHenry, Martin Christopher *physician, educator*
Medalie, Jack Harvey *physician*
Montague, Drogo K. *urologist*
Moravec, Christine D. Schomis *medical educator*
Moskowitz, Roland Wallace *internist*
Novick, Andrew Carl *urologist*
Olness, Karen Norma *pediatrics and international health educator*
Perez, Dianne M. *medical researcher*
Perry, George *neuroscientist, educator*
Pomeranz, Jerome Raphael *dermatopathologist*
Pretlow, Thomas Garrett *physician, pathology educator, researcher*
Raaf, John Hart *surgeon, health facility administrator, educator*
Rakita, Louis *cardiologist, educator*
Ransohoff, Richard Milton *neurologist, researcher*
Ratnoff, Oscar Davis *physician, educator*
Rogers, Douglas George *endocrinologist*
†Rothner, A. David *pediatric neurologist*
Ruff, Robert Louis *neurologist, physiology researcher*
Samodelov, Leonid Feodor *anesthesiologist*
Scarpa, Antonio *medicine educator, biomedical scientist*
Schneider, Edward Martin *retired physician*
Schumacher, O. Peter *physician, educator*
Schwartz, Howard Julius *allergy educator*
Schwartz, Michael Alan *physician*
Shuck, Jerry Mark *surgeon, educator*
Sila, Cathy Ann *neurologist*
Stanton-Hicks, Michael D'Arcy *anesthesiologist, educator*
Stavitsky, Abram Benjamin *immunologist, educator*
Stern, Robert C. *physician, educator*
Strome, Marshall *otolaryngologist, educator*
Utian, Wulf Hessel *gynecologist, endocrinologist*
Washington, John Augustine *retired physician, pathologist*
Webster, Leslie Tillotson, Jr. *pharmacologist, educator*
Weiner, George David *medical association executive, researcher*
Whittlesey, Diana *surgeon*
Wish, Jay Barry *nephrologist, specialist*
Wolfman, Alan *medical educator, researcher*
Wolinsky, Emanuel *physician, educator*
Young, Jess Ray *physician*
†Zollinger, Robert Milton, Jr. *surgery educator*

Columbus
Ackerman, John Henry *health services consultant, physician*
Bachman, Sister Janice *health care executive*
Barth, Rolf Frederick *pathologist, educator*
Bell, George Edwin *retired physician, insurance company executive*
Beversdorf, David Quentin *neurologist, researcher*
Billings, Charles Edgar *physician*
Boudoulas, Harisios *physician, educator, researcher*
Boué, Daniel Robert *pathologist*
Bowman, Louis L. *emergency physician*
Bullock, Joseph Daniel *pediatrician, educator*
Christoforidis, A. John *radiologist, educator*
Clark, Robert Wesley *neurologist*
Copeland, William Edgar, Sr. *physician*
Cramblett, Henry Gaylord *pediatrician, virologist, educator*
†Duff, Steven Barron *cardiovascular surgeon*
Ellison, Edwin Christopher *physician, surgeon*
Falcone, Robert Edward *surgeon*
Ferguson, Ronald Morris *surgeon, educator*
Furste, Wesley Leonard, II *surgeon, educator*
Hansen, Thomas Nanastad *pediatrician, health facility administrator*
Huheey, Marilyn Jane *ophthalmologist*
Inglis, William Darling *internist, health facility administrator*
Kakos, Gerard Stephen *thoracic and cardiovascular surgeon*
†Kissel, John Thomas *neurologist*
Lander, Ruth A. *medical group and association administrator*
Laufman, Leslie Rodgers *hematologist, oncologist*
Leier, Carl Victor *internist, cardiologist*
Lewis, Richard Phelps *physician, educator*
Litvak, Ronald *psychiatrist*
Lombardi, Adolph Vincent, Jr. *orthopaedic surgeon*
Long, Sarah Elizabeth Brackney *physician*
†Matkovic, Velimir *physical medicine and rehabilitation educator*
Mazzaferri, Ernest Louis *physician, educator*
Morrow, Grant, III *medical research director, physician*
Moser, Debra Kay *medical educator*
Mueller, Charles Frederick *radiologist, educator*
†Nappi, James Francis *hand surgeon, educator*
Nasrallah, Henry Ata *psychiatry researcher, educator*
Newton, William Allen, Jr. *pediatric pathologist*
†Nobrega, Fred Thomas *hospital executive*
Penn, Gerald Melville *pathologist*
Ruberg, Robert Lionel *surgery educator*
Rund, Douglas Andrew *emergency physician, educator*
St. Pierre, Ronald Leslie *anatomy educator, university administrator*
Sayers, Martin Peter *pediatric neurosurgeon*
Senhauser, Donald A(lbert) *pathologist, educator*
Shepard, Kirk Van, Sr. *physician, researcher*
Skillman, Thomas Grant *endocrinology consultant, former educator*
Slivka, Andrew Paul Jr. *neurologist, physician*
Speicher, Carl Eugene *pathologist*
Stephens, Sheryl Lynne *family practice physician*
Stoner, Gary David *cancer researcher*
†Tsao, Chang Yong *pediatric neurologist*
Tzagournis, Manuel *physician, educator, university administrator*
Vogel, Thomas Timothy *surgeon, health care consultant, lay church worker*
Whitacre, Caroline Clement *immunologist, researcher*
Yashon, David *neurosurgeon, educator*

Dayton
Chang, Jae Chan *hematologist, oncologist, educator*
Cruikshank, Stephen Herrick *physician, consultant*
DeWall, Richard Allison *retired surgeon*
Dunn, Margaret M. *general surgeon*
Elliott, Daniel Whitacre *surgeon, retired educator*
Gardner, Charles Clifford, Jr. *colorectal surgeon*
Heller, Abraham *psychiatrist, educator*
Hewes, Robert Charles *radiologist*
Lechner, George William *surgeon*
Mandal, Anil Kumar *nephrologist, medical educator*
Mohler, Stanley Ross *physician, educator*
Monk, Susan Marie *physician, pediatrician*
Nanagas, Maria Teresita Cruz *pediatrician, educator*
Pflum, Barbara Ann *pediatric allergist*
Savage, Joseph Scott *physician*
Von Gierke, Henning Edgar *biomedical science educator, former government official, researcher*
Weinberg, Sylvan Lee *cardiologist, educator, author, editor*
Wilson, William C.M. *gastroenterologist*

Defiance
Kane, Jack Allison *physician, county administrator*

Delaware
Faerber, Abigail Hobbs *physician, farm manager*

Edgerton
Wu, Lawrence Mg Hla Myin *physician*

Elyria
Burrell, Joel Brion *neurologist, researcher, clinician*
Eady, Carol Murphy (Mrs. Karl Ernest Eady) *retired medical association administrator*

Euclid
Convery, Patrick George *orthopedic surgeon*

Gahanna
Robbins, Darryl Andrew *pediatrician*

Gallipolis
Clarke, Oscar Withers *physician*
Senthil Nathan, Selvaraj *internist, geriatrician*

Garfield Heights
De Piero, Nicholas Gabriel *anesthesiologist*

Girard
Gaylord, Sanford Fred *physician*

Grove City
Kilman, James William *surgeon, educator*

Holland
Sippo, Arthur Carmine *occupational medicine physician*

Huron
†Brownlow, Wilfred J. *retired physician*

Jefferson
Macklin, Martin Rodbell *psychiatrist*

Kettering
Kwiatek, Kim David *emergency physician*
Mantil, Joseph Chacko *nuclear medicine physician, researcher*

Lima
Becker, Dwight Lowell *physician*
Collins, William Thomas *retired pathologist*

Madison
Stafford, Arthur Charles *medical association administrator*

Mansfield
Adair, Charles Valloyd *retired physician*
Bogart, Keith Charles *neurologist*
Capaldo, Guy *obstetrician, gynecologist*
Houston, William Robert Montgomery *ophthalmic surgeon*

Marion
Lim, Shun Ping *cardiologist*

Mason
†Meyer, Joan M. *drug researcher*

Massillon
Vaughn, Lisa Dawn *physician, educator*

Maumee
Musa, Mahmoud Nimir *psychiatry educator*

Medina
Noreika, Joseph Casimir *ophthalmologist*

New Richmond
Reynolds, Ronald Davison *family physician*

Norwalk
Gutowicz, Matthew Francis, Jr. *radiologist*
Holman, William Baker *surgeon, coroner*

Pepper Pike
Solomon, Glen David *physician, researcher*

Rootstown
Blacklow, Robert Stanley *physician, medical college administrator*
Brodell, Robert Thomas *internal medicine educator*
Campbell, Colin *obstetrician, gynecologist, school dean*

Springfield
Kurian, Pius *nephrologist, educator*
Wood, Dirk Gregory *surgeon, physician, forensic consultant*

Toledo
Barrett, Michael John *anesthesiologist*
Bedell, Archie William *family physician, educator*
Ferguson-Rayport, Shirley Martha *psychiatrist*
Kim, E. Kitai *pathologist*
Knotts, Frank Barry *physician, surgeon*
Lawrence, Edmund Pond, Jr. *neurosurgeon*
Martin, John Thomas *physician, author, educator*
Mulrow, Patrick Joseph *medical educator*
Pawelczak, Mark A. *health department investigator*
Rejent, Marian Magdalen *pediatrician*
Senour, Connie Lee *internist*
†Shelley, E. Dorinda *dermatologist*
Shelley, Walter Brown *physician, educator*

Troy
Davies, Alfred Robert *physician, educator*

Twinsburg
Morris, Jeffrey Selman *orthopedic surgeon*

Uniontown
Krabill, Robert Elmer *osteopathic physician*

Warren
Rizer, Franklin Morris *physician, otolarynogologist*

West Chester
Loughman, Barbara Ellen *immunologist researcher*

West Farmington
Hardesty, Hiram Haines *ophthalmologist, educator*

West Milton
Dallura, Sal Anthony *physician*

Westerville
Dadmehr, Nahid *neurologist*

Whitehouse
Howard, John Malone *surgeon, educator*

Willoughby
Carter, John Robert *physician*
Combs, Steven Paul *orthopedic surgeon*

Wooster
Kuffner, George Henry *dermatologist, educator*

Worthington
Stone, Linda Chapman *physician, consultant, medical educator*
Winter, Chester Caldwell *physician, surgery educator*

Wright Patterson AFB
Bohanon, Kathleen Sue *neonatologist, educator*
Frazier, John W. *physiologist, researcher*

Yellow Springs
Webb, Paul *physician, researcher, consultant, educator*

Youngstown
Buckley, John Joseph *obstetrician, gynecologist*
Rubin, Jeffrey Reed *vascular surgeon*

Zanesfield
Tetirick, Jack E. *retired surgeon*

Zanesville
Camma, Albert John *neurosurgeon*
Kopf, George Michael *ophthalmologist*
Ray, John Walker *otolaryngologist, educator, broadcast commentator*
Whitacre, Vicki Ann *emergency physician*

OKLAHOMA

Ada
Van Burkleo, Bill Ben *osteopath, emergency physician*

Ardmore
Mynatt, Cecil Ferrell *psychiatrist*

Edmond
Nelson, John Woolard *neurology educator, physician*

Enid
Dandridge, William Shelton *orthopedic surgeon*

Hobart
Ball, William James *pediatrician*

Kingfisher
Buswell, Arthur Wilcox *physician, surgeon*

Lawton
Hensley, Ross Charles *dermatologist*
Webb, O(rville) Lynn *physician, pharmacologist, educator*

Midwest City
Bogardus, Carl Robert, Jr. *radiologist, educator*

Muskogee
Kent, Bartis Milton *physician*

Norman
Cochran, Gloria Grimes *pediatrician, retired*
Dille, John Robert *physician*

Oklahoma City
Bahr, Carman Bloedow *internist*
Bozalis, John Russell *physician*
Bradford, Reagan Howard, Jr. *ophthalmology educator*
Brandt, Edward Newman, Jr. *physician, educator*
Brumback, Roger Alan *neuropathologist, researcher*
Claflin, James Robert *pediatrician, allergist*
Comp, Philip Cinnamon *medical researcher*
Couch, James Russell, Jr. *neurology educator*
Ellis, Robert Smith *allergist, immunologist*
Everett, Mark Allen *dermatologist, educator*
Felton, Warren Locker, II *surgeon*
Filley, Warren Vernon *allergist, immunologist*
Gavaler, Judith Ann Stohr Van Thiel *bio-epidemiologist*
George, James Noel *hematologist-oncologist, educator*
Gilchrist, John Mark *otolaryngologist*
Halverstadt, Donald Bruce *urologist, educator*
Haywood, B(etty) J(ean) *anesthesiologist*
Hill, Robert Fred *medical educator*
Hough, Jack Van Doren *otologist*
Kimerer, Neil Banard, Sr. *retired psychiatrist, educator*
Kinasewitz, Gary Theodore *medical educator*
Lambird, Perry Albert *pathologist*
McFadden, Robert Stetson *hepatologist*
Moore, Joanne Iweita *pharmacologist, educator*
Neuenschwander, Pierre Fernand *medical educator*
Parke, David Wilkin, II *ophthalmologist, educator, healthcare executive*
Perez-Cruet, Jorge *physician, psychiatrist, psychopharmacologist, psychophysiologist, educator*
Rahhal, Donald K. *obstetrician, gynecologist*
†Raulston, Robert Owen *urologist, educator*
†Reynolds, Charles Lee, Jr. *urologist*
†Rix, Robert Alvin, Jr. *retired neurosurgeon*
Robison, Clarence, Jr. *surgeon*
Shurley, Jay Talmadge *psychiatrist, medical educator, administrator, behavioral sciences researcher, polar explorer, author, genealogist*
Srouji, Elias Salim *retired pediatrician, educator*
Thadani, Udho *physician, cardiologist*
Thurman, William Gentry *medical research foundation executive, pediatric hematology and oncology physician, educator*
†Tyndall, Robert James *neurologist*
†Wisdom, Peggy J. *neurologist*
Worsham, Bertrand Ray *psychiatrist*
Zuhdi, Nazih *surgeon, administrator*

Owasso
Reed, Walter George, Jr. *osteopathic physician*

Shawnee
Wilson, Robert Godfrey *radiologist*

Stillwater
Cooper, Donald Lee *physician*

Tulsa
Allen, Thomas Wesley *medical educator, dean*
†Berry, Charles Miles *cardiac surgeon*
Brunk, Samuel Frederick *oncologist*
Calvert, Jon Channing *family practice physician*
Friedman, Mark Joel *cardiologist, educator*
Gregg, Lawrence J. *physician*
Kalbfleisch, John McDowell *cardiologist, educator*
Martin, Edward Thomas *cardiologist*
Miller, Gerald Cecil *immunologist, laboratory administrator, educator*
Nettles, John Barnwell *obstetrics and gynecology educator*
Okada, Robert Dean *cardiologist*
Plunket, Daniel Clark *pediatrician*
Say, Burhan *physician*
Shane, John Marder *endocrinologist*
Stearns, Frederic William *dermatologist*
Stone, William Charles *surgeon*
Tompkins, Robert George *retired physician*

Vinita
Neer, Charles Sumner, II *orthopedic surgeon, educator*

Woodward
Keith, Howard Barton *surgeon*

OREGON

Ashland
Kirschner, Richard Michael *naturopathic physician, speaker, author*

Athena
Mengis, Chris Ludwig *retired internist*

Beaverton
Swank, Roy Laver *physician, educator, inventor*

Corvallis
Engle, Molly *program evaluator, preventive medicine researcher, medical educator*
Hafner-Eaton, Chris *health services researcher, educator*
†Lafrance, Richard Arthur *neurologist*
Steele, Robert Edwin *orthopedic surgeon*

Eugene
Algra, Ronald James *dermatologist*
Biglan, Anthony *medical educator*
†Goins, Steven Carter *pediatric neurologist*
Loescher, Richard Alvin *gastroenterologist*
†McMillen, Shannon M. *urologist*
Roe, Thomas Leroy Willis *pediatrician*
Schroeder, Donald J. *orthopedic surgeon*
Starr, Grier Forsythe *retired pathologist*

Grants Pass
Petersen, Michael Kevin *internist,endoscopist, osteopathic physician*

Klamath Falls
Bohnen, Robert Frank *hematologist, oncologist, educator*

Lake Oswego
Thong, Tran *biomedical company executive*

Lebanon
Girod, Frank Paul *retired surgeon*

Medford
†Worland, Ronald Glenn *plastic surgeon*

Ontario
Tyler, Donald Earl *urologist*

Portland
Baker, Diane R.H. *dermatologist*
Barmack, Neal Herbert *neuroscientist*
Bennett, William Michael *physician*
Benson, John Alexander, Jr. *physician, educator*
Campbell, John Richard *pediatric surgeon*
Collins, Michael Sean *obstetrician and gynecologist, educator*
Connor, William Elliott *physician, educator*
Crawshaw, Ralph *psychiatrist*
DeMots, Henry *cardiologist*
Fraunfelder, Frederick Theodore *ophthalmologist, educator*
Greer, Monte Arnold *physician, educator*
Hagmeier, Clarence Howard *retired anesthesiologist*
Hutchens, Tyra Thornton *physician, educator*
Jacob, Stanley Wallace *surgeon, educator*
Janzen, Timothy Paul *family practice physician*
Johnson, Martin Clifton *physician*
Julien, Robert Michael *anesthesiologist, author*
Kendall, John Walker, Jr. *medical educator, researcher, university dean*
Kohler, Peter Ogden *physician, educator, university president*
Martinez-Maldonado, Manuel *medical service administrator, physician*
Noonan, William Donald *physician, lawyer*
Palmer, Earl A. *ophthalmologist, educator*
Patterson, James Randolph *physician*
Robertson, Joseph E., Jr. *ophthalmologist, educator*
Schmidt, Waldemar Adrian *pathologist, educator*
Scott, John D. *pharmacologist*
Sklovsky, Robert Joel *naturopathic physician, pharmacist, educator*
Stevens, Wendell Claire *retired anesthesiology educator*
Swan, Kenneth Carl *surgeon*
Taylor, Robert Brown *medical educator*
Zimmerman, Gail Marie *medical foundation executive*

Roseburg
Jones, Henry Earl *dermatologist, direct patient care educator*
Romero, José Diego *anesthesiologist, educator*

Wilsonville
Bernard, Richard Montgomery *retired physician*

PENNSYLVANIA

Abington
Redmond, John *oncologist*
†Slavin, James William *plastic surgeon*

Allentown
Chang, Chris C.N. *physician, pediatric surgeon*
Fitzgibbons, John P. *nephrologist*
Gaylor, Donald Hughes *surgeon, educator*
†Lusser, Martha Ann *neurologist*
Mackin, Glenn Alexander *neurologist*
Maffeo, Alphonse A. *anesthesiologist*

Altoona
McKinney, Henry Daniel *dermatologist*

Bala Cynwyd
Cander, Leon *physician, educator*
Chiusano, Michael Augustus *urologic surgeon, mechanical engineer*
Marden, Philip Ayer *physician, educator*

Bangor
Wolf, Stewart George, Jr. *physician, medical educator*

Berwick
Crake, Roger F. *general surgeon*

Bethlehem
Benz, Edward John *clinical pathologist*
Cole, Jack Eli *physician*

Blue Bell
Flaherty, Lois Talbot *psychiatrist, educator*

Bridgeville
Keddie, Roland Thomas *physician, hospital administrator, lawyer*

Bryn Mawr
Gruenberg, Alan Mark *psychiatrist*
Harkins, Herbert Perrin *otolaryngologist, educator*
Hermann, George Arthur *pathologist, educator*
Hoopes, Janet Louise *educator, psychologist*
Huth, Edward Janavel *physician, editor*
Levitt, Robert E. *gastroenterologist*
†Nast, Philip Robert *gastroenterologist*
Noone, Robert Barrett *plastic surgeon*
Widzer, Steven J. *pediatric gastroenterologist*

Carlisle
Gorby, William Guy *anesthesiologist*
Graham, William Patton, III *plastic surgeon, educator*

Chester Springs
Scheer, R. Scott *physician*

Coatesville
Ainslie, George William *psychiatrist, behavioral economist*

Conneaut Lake
Piroch, Joseph Gregory *internist, cardiologist*

Cranberry Township
Walsh, Arthur Campbell *psychiatrist*

Danville
Cochran, William John *physician, pediatrician, gastroenterologist, nutritionist, consultant*
Kazem, Ismail *radiation oncologist, educator, health science facility administrator*
Pierce, James Clarence *surgeon*
Randall, Neil Warren *gastroenterologist*

Devon
Burget, Dean Edwin, Jr. *plastic surgeon*

Dillsburg
Jackson, George Lyman *nuclear medicine physician*

Downingtown
Newman, Richard August *psychiatrist, educator*

Doylestown
Blewitt, George Augustine *physician, consultant*
Shaddinger, Dawn Elizabeth *medical researcher*

Drexel Hill
Bomberger, John Henry Augustus *pediatrician*

Dunmore
Culliney, John James *radiologist, educator*
Sebastianelli, Mario Joseph *internist, nephrologist, health services administrator*

East Berlin
Greer, Robert Bruce, III *orthopedic surgeon, educator*

East Stroudsburg
†Cohen, Beth Ann *neurologist*

Easton
Grunberg, Robert Leon Willy *nephrologist*

Elkins Park
Glijansky, Alex *psychiatrist, psychoanalyst*
Rosen, Rhoda *obstetrician and gynecologist*
Serber, William *radiation oncologist, educator*
Yun, Daniel Duwhan *physician, foundation administrator*

Erie
Brunner, Kirstin Ellen *pediatrician, psychiatrist*
†Chorazy, Zdzislaw J. *surgeon*
Diefenbach, William Paul *neurosurgeon*
†Flamini, John Anthony *physician*
Kalkhof, Thomas Corrigan *physician*
Kish, George Franklin *thoracic and cardiovascular surgeon*
Mainzer, Francis Kirkwood *neurosurgeon, health facility administrator*
Mason, Gregg Claude *orthopedic surgeon, researcher*

Michaelides, Doros Nikita *internist, medical educator*

Fairview
Weckesser, Elden Christian *surgery educator*

Fort Washington
Pappas, Charles Engelos *plastic surgeon*
Urbach, Frederick *physician, educator*

Gaines
Beller, Martin Leonard *retired orthopaedic surgeon*

Gladwyne
Gilbert, Robert Pettibone *retired physician, educator*
Gonick, Paul *retired urologist*

Glenside
Johnson, Waine Cecil *dermatologist*
Reiss, George Russell, Jr. *physician*

Greensburg
Lisowitz, Gerald Myron *neuropsychiatrist*

Harrisburg
Cadieux, Roger Joseph *physician, mental health care executive*
Chernicoff, David Paul *osteopathic physician, educator*
Jeffries, Richard Haley *physician, broadcasting company executive*
Jones, David John, III *preventive medicine physician, medical executive*
†Leber, David Clair *plastic surgeon*
Logue, James Nicholas *epidemiologist*
†Lurie, Perrianne *public health physician, epidemiologist*
Margo, Katherine Lane *family physician, educator*
Rudy, Frank R. *pathologist*

Haverford
Aronson, Carl Edward *pharmacology and toxicology educator*
Rosefsky, Jonathan Benensohn *pediatrician*

Havertown
Prevoznik, Stephen Joseph *retired anesthesiologist*

Hershey
Berlin, Cheston Milton, Jr. *pediatrician, educator*
Caputo, Gregory Michael *physician, educator*
Davis, Dwight *cardiologist, educator*
Eyster, Mary Elaine *hematologist, educator*
Ferriss, John Alden III *medical educator*
Geder, Laszlo *neurologist, educator*
†Helm, Klaus F. *dermatology educator*
Kauffman, Gordon Lee, Jr. *surgeon, educator*
Leaman, David Martin *cardiologist*
Madewell, John Edward *radiologist*
Marks, James Garfield, Jr. *dermatologist*
Naeye, Richard L. *pathologist, educator*
Pierce, William Schuler *cardiac surgeon, educator*
Reynolds, Herbert Young *physician, internist*
Rohner, Thomas John, Jr. *urologist*
Schuller, Diane Ethel *allergist, immunologist, educator*
Severs, Walter Bruce *pharmacology educator, researcher*
Tan, Tjiauw-Ling *psychiatrist, educator*
Vesell, Elliot Saul *pharmacologist, educator*
Waldhausen, John Anton *surgeon, editor*
Wassner, Steven Joel *pediatric nephrologist, educator*
Zelis, Robert Felix *cardiologist, educator*

Hollidaysburg
Mariano, Ana Virginia *pathologist*

Huntingdon
Schock, William Wallace *pediatrician*

Huntingdon Valley
Spector, Larry Wayne *osteopath*

Jenkintown
Donner, William Troutman *psychiatrist*
Sadoff, Robert Leslie *psychiatrist*

Johnstown
Fritz, William Thomas *anesthesiologist*
Green, James Matthew *anesthesiologist*
Kolff, Willem Johan *internist, educator*
McNiesh, Lawrence Melvin *radiologist*
Untracht, Steven Harris *surgeon*

Kingston
Kopen, Dan Francis *surgeon, consultant*

Lancaster
Brod, Roy David *ophthalmologist, educator*
Falk, Robert Barclay, Jr. *anesthesiologist, educator*
Lu, Milton Ming-Deh *plastic surgeon, consultant*

Langhorne
Barbetta, Maria Ann *health information management consultant*
Byrne, Jeffrey Edward *pharmacology researcher, educator, consultant*
Lamonsoff, Norman Charles *psychiatrist*

Lansdale
Ladman, A(aron) J(ulius) *anatomist, educator*
Schwartz, Louis Winn *ophthalmologist*

Latrobe
Berardi, Ronald Stephen *pathologist, educator*

Lemoyne
Klein, Michael Elihu *physician*
†Vickery, Jon Livingstone *neurologist*

Lower Gwynedd
Pendleton, Robert Grubb *pharmacologist*

Meadowbrook
Kiesel, Harry Alexander *internist*

Mechanicsburg
Scher, David Lee *cardiac electrophysiologist*

Media
Kessler, Woodrow Bertram *family practice physician, geriatrician, educator*
Valdes-Dapena, Marie Agnes *retired pediatric pathologist, educator*

Millersville
Kendall, Leigh Wakefield *surgeon*

Mohnton
Hildreth, Eugene A. *physician, educator*

Monongahela
Brandon, John Mitchell *physician*
†Yovanof, Silvana *physician*

Monroeville
Stanger, Robert Henry *psychiatrist, educator*

Narberth
Luscombe, Herbert Alfred *physician, educator*
Madow, Leo *psychiatrist, educator*
Strom, Brian Leslie *internist, educator*

New Hope
Lee, Robert Earl *retired physician*
Raabe, Gerhard Karl *epidemiologist*

Newtown
Somers, Anne Ramsay *medical educator*

Norristown
Hunter, Patricia Phelps *physician assistant*
Tornetta, Frank Joseph *anesthesiologist, educator, consultant*
Tsou, Walter Hai-tze *physician*

Orwigsburg
Garloff, Samuel John *psychiatrist*

Paoli
LeWitt, Michael Herman *physician, educator*

Pennsburg
Shuhler, Phyllis Marie *physician*

Philadelphia
Abrahm, Janet Lee *hematologist, oncologist, educator*
Agus, Zalman S. *physician, educator*
Alexander, John Dewey *internist*
Amexo, Kwaku *internist*
Arce, A. Anthony *psychiatrist*
Asbury, Arthur Knight *neurologist, educator*
Atkinson, Barbara Frajola *pathologist*
Austrian, Robert *physician, educator*
Baker, Lester *physician, educator, research administrator*
Baldwin, Harold Scott *pediatrician*
Barchi, Robert Lawrence *clinical neurologist, neuroscientist, educator*
Barker, Clyde Frederick *surgeon, educator*
Baum, Stanley *radiologist, educator*
Baxt, William G. *medical educator*
Bearn, Alexander Gordon *physician scientist, former pharmaceutical company executive*
Bergelson, Jeffrey Michael *pediatrician , educator*
Bernstein, Joseph *orthopedic surgeon, philosopher*
Bianchi, Carmine Paul *pharmacologist*
Bibbo, Marluce *physician, educator*
Black, Perry *neurological surgeon, educator*
Boden, Guenther *endocrinologist*
Bove, Alfred Anthony *medical educator*
Bowles, L. Thompson *medical executive*
Brady, Luther W., Jr. *physician, radiation oncology educator*
Bridger, Wagner H. *psychiatrist, educator*
Brighton, Carl Theodore *orthopedic surgery educator*
†Buchheit, William A. *neurosurgeon, educator*
Burns, Rosalie Annette *neurologist, educator*
Capizzi, Robert Lawrence *physician*
Casey, Kenneth G. *neurosurgeon, educator*
Chait, Arnold *radiologist*
Chu, Mon-Li Hsiung *dermatology educator*
Chung, Edward Kooyoung *cardiologist, educator, author*
Clarke, John Rodney *surgeon*
Clearfield, Harris Reynold *physician*
Cohen, Marc *cardiologist*
Cohen, Sidney *medical educator*
Cohn, Herbert Edward *surgeon, educator*
Colman, Robert Wolf *physician, medical educator, researcher*
Comer, Nathan Lawrence *psychiatrist, educator*
Comerota, Anthony James *vascular surgeon, biomedical researcher*
Conn, Rex Boland, Jr. *physician, educator*
Cook-Sather, Scott Douglas *pediatric anesthesiology educator*
Cooper, Edward Sawyer *cardiovascular internist, educator*
Cortner, Jean Alexander *physician, educator*
Dalinka, Murray Kenneth *radiologist, educator*
D'Angio, Giulio John *radiologist, educator*
Danzon, Patricia M. *medical educator*
DeHoratius, Raphael Joseph *rheumatologist*
De La Cadena, Raul Alvarez *physician, physiology and thrombosis educator*
Depp, (O.) Richard, III *obstetrician-gynecologist, educator*
Dinoso, Vicente Pescador, Jr. *physician, educator*
DiPalma, Joseph Rupert *pharmacology educator*
Djerassi, Isaac *physician, medical researcher*
Doty, Richard Leroy *medical researcher*
Ecker, Paul Gerard *physician, educator*
Ehrlich, George Edward *rheumatologist, international pharmaceutical consultant*
Eisen, Howard Joel *physician, researcher*
Ernst, Calvin Bradley *vascular surgeon, surgery educator*
Eskin, Bernard Abraham *obstetrics and gynecology educator, medical researcher*
Esterhai, John Louis, Jr. *surgeon, medical educator*
Evans, Audrey Elizabeth *physician, educator*
†Farrar, John T. *physician, researcher*
Fisher, Robert *gastroenterologist, health facility administrator*
Fishman, Alfred Paul *physician*
FitzGerald, Garret Adare *medical educator*
Fitzgerald, Robert Hannon, Jr. *orthopedic surgeon*
†Frank, Leonard Arnold *physician*
Frankl, William Stewart *cardiologist, educator*
Fraser, David William *epidemiologist*
Freese, Andrew *neurosurgeon, educator, scientist*
Friedman, Harvey Michael *infectious diseases educator*
Gabrielson, Ira Wilson *physician, educator*
Garcia, Celso-Ramón *obstetrician and gynecologist*
Gardiner, Geoffrey Alexander, Jr. *radiologist, educator*
Gartland, John Joseph *physician, writer*
Gary, Nancy Elizabeth *nephrologist, academic administrator*
Gault, Janice Ann *ophthalmologist, educator*
Gerner, Edward William *medical educator*
Ginsberg, Phillip Carl *physician*
Giordano, Antonio *medical educator*
Glick, John H. *oncologist, medical educator*
Goldberg, Martin *physician, educator*
Golden, Gerald Samuel *national medical board executive*
Goldfarb, Stanley *internist, educator*
Goldhamer, David J. *medical educator, researcher*
Gonnella, Joseph Salvator *medical educator, university dean and official, consultant, researcher*
Gonzalez-Scarano, Francisco Antonio *neurologist*
Goodman, David Barry Poliakoff *physician, educator*
Gozum, Marvin Enriquez *internist*
Graessle, William Rudolf *pediatrician, educator*
Graziani, Leonard Joseph *pediatric neurologist, researcher*
Greenfield, Val Shea *ophthalmologist*
Greenstein, Jeffrey Ian *neurologist*
Gueson, Emerita Torres *obstetrician, gynecologist*
†Halpern, Marcia Lynn *neurologist*
Hanks, Gerald E. *oncologist*
Hansen-Flaschen, John Hyman *medical educator, researcher*
Haugaard, Niels *pharmacologist*
Heitz, James W. *anesthesiologist, internist*
Hillman, Alan L. *internist, educator, researcher*
Holzbaur, Erika L. *medical educator*
Hussain, M. Mahmood *medical educator*
Iannotti, Joseph Patrick *orthopedic surgeon*
Jackson, Laird Gray *physician, educator*
Jacobs, Eugene Gardner, Jr. *psychiatrist, psychoanalyst, educator*
Jensh, Ronald Paul *anatomist, educator*
Jimenez, Sergio A. *internist, science educator*
Johnson, Joseph Eggleston, III *physician, educator*
Johnson, Mark Paul *obstetrics and gynecology educator, geneticist*
Joseph, Rosaline Resnick *hematologist and oncologist*
Kaji, Hideko Katayama *pharmacology educator*
Kauffman, Leon A. *internist, educator*
Kaye, Donald *physician, educator*
Kaye, Robert *pediatrics educator*
Kazazian, Haig Hagop, Jr. *medical scientist, physician, educator*
Kefalides, Nicholas Alexander *physician, educator*
Kelley, Mark Albert *internal medicine educator, university official*
Kelley, William Nimmons *physician, educator*
Kennedy, David William *otolaryngologist, educator*
Kimball, Harry Raymond *medical association executive, educator*
Kligerman, Morton M. *radiologist*
Klinghoffer, June Florence *physician, educator*
Koenigsberg, Robert Alan *neuroradiologist*
Kotler, Ronald Lee *physician, educator*
Kurtz, Alfred Bernard *radiologist*
Lambertsen, Christian James *environmental physiologist, physician, educator*
†LaRossa, Don *plastic surgeon, medical educator*
Legido, Agustin *pediatric neurologist*
Leventhal, Lawrence Jay *rheumatologist, educator*
Levine, Rhea Joy Cottler *anatomy educator*
Levinson, Arnold Irving *allergist, immunologist*
Levit, Edithe Judith *physician, medical association administrator*
Levitt, Jerry David *medical educator*
Li, Weiye *ophthalmologist, biochemist, educator*
†Lieben, Jan *environmental and occupational health physician*
Long, Sarah Sundborg *pediatrician, educator*
Longnecker, David Eugene *anesthesiologist, educator*
†Low, David Wei-Wen *plastic surgeon*
Malis, Bernard Jay *pharmacologist*
Mancall, Elliott Lee *neurologist, educator*
†Marcotte, Paul John *neurosurgeon, educator*
Mascarenhas, Maria Rebello *pediatrician*
Mastroianni, Luigi, Jr. *physician, educator*
Matsumoto, Teruo *surgeon, educator*
McClurken, James Bartholomew *surgeon*
Ming, Si-Chun *pathologist, educator*
Monos, Dimitrios *medical educator, researcher*
†Moore, John Harlan *plastic surgeon*
Mulholland, S. Grant *urologist*
Murphey, Sheila Ann *infectious diseases physician, educator, researcher*
Myers, Allen Richard *rheumatologist*
Nimoityn, Philip *cardiologist*
Nowell, Peter Carey *pathologist, educator*
O'Brien, Charles P. *psychiatrist, educator*
Olenginski, Jan Anthony *surgeon*
Platsoucas, Chris Dimitrios *immunologist*
Potsic, William Paul *physician, educator*
Price, Trevor Robert Pryce *psychiatrist, educator*
Pugliese, Maria Alessandra *psychiatrist*
Rabinowitz, Howard K. *physician, educator*
Reece, E. Albert *obstetrician, gynecologist, perinatologist*
Reinecke, Robert Dale *ophthalmologist*
Ren, Jian-Fang *echocardiologist, medical educator*
Rhoads, Jonathan Evans *surgeon*
Rickels, Karl *psychiatrist, physician, educator*
Ritchie, Wallace Parks, Jr. *surgeon, educator*
Ritter, Deborah Elizabeth *anesthesiologist, educator*
Roberts, Jay *pharmacologist, educator*
Rogers, Fred Baker *medical educator*
Rorke, Lucy Balian *neuropathologist*
Ross, Leonard Lester *anatomist*
Rothrock, Robert William *physician assistant*
Rovera, Giovanni Aurelio *medical educator, scientist*
Rubin, Emanuel *pathologist, educator*
Rubin, Stephen Curtis *gynecologic oncologist, educator*
Rudley, Lloyd Dave *psychiatrist*
Russo, Irma Haydee Alvarez de *pathologist*
Sabili, Erlinda Asa *physician*
Saunders, James C. *neuroscientist, educator*
Savage, Michael Paul *medicine educator, interventional cardiologist*
Schimmer, Barry Michael *rheumatologist*
Schneider, Jan *obstetrics and gynecology educator*
Schotland, Donald Lewis *retired medical educator, neurologist*
Schumacher, H(arry) Ralph *internist, rheumatologist, medical educator*
Schwartz, Gordon Francis *surgeon, educator*
Segal, Bernard Louis *physician, educator*
Sevy, Roger Warren *retired pharmacology educator*
Silberberg, Donald H. *neurologist*
Simpkins, Henry *medical educator*
Sloviter, Henry Allan *medical educator*
Smith, David Stuart *anesthesiology educator, physician*
Smith, Randall Norman *orthopedist*
Spaeth, George Link *physician, ophthalmology educator, writer*
Sprague, James Mather *medical scientist, educator*
Steinberg, Marvin Edward *orthopaedic surgeon, educator*
Strauss, Jerome Frank, III *physician, educator*
Stunkard, Albert James *psychiatrist, educator*
Sudak, Howard Stanley *physician, psychiatry educator*
Sunderman, Frederick William *physician, educator, author, musician*
Taichman, Norton Stanley *pathology educator*
Tasman, William Samuel *ophthalmologist, medical association executive*
Thomas, Carmen Christine *physician, consultant administrator*
Torg, Joseph Steven *orthopaedic surgeon, educator*
Tortella, Bartholomew Joseph *trauma surgeon*
Tourtellotte, Charles Dee *physician, educator*
Tsykalov, Eugene *neuroscientist, researcher*
†Van Arsdalen, Keith Norman *urologist*
Walinsky, Paul *cardiology educator*
Webber, John Bentley *orthopedic surgeon*
Weese, James Leighton *surgical oncologist*
Wein, Alan Jerome *urologist, educator, researcher*
Weiss, William *retired pulmonary medicine and epidemiology educator*
Weller, Elizabeth Boghossian *child and adolescent psychiatrist*
Whelan, Gerald Patrick *emergency physician*
Whitaker, Linton Andin *plastic surgeon*
Wivel, Nelson Auburn *physician, medical researcher, educator*
Wolf, Nelson Marc *cardiologist*
Xu, Gang *medical educator*
Yanoff, Myron *ophthalmologist*
Young, Donald Stirling *clinical pathology educator*
Yunginger, John W. *allergist*
Zweiman, Burton *physician, scientist, educator*

Pittsburgh
†Bellinger, Mark F. *urology educator*
Bentz, Michael Lloyd *plastic and reconstructive surgeon*
Berga, Sarah Lee *women's health physician, educator*
Burke, Leah Weyerts *physician*
Cockerham, Kimberly Peele *ophthalmologist*
Cooper, William Marion *physician*
†Crumrine, Patricia K. *physician, educator*
Cutler, John Charles *physician, educator*
deGroat, William Chesney *pharmacology educator*
DeKosky, Steven Trent *neurologist*
Detre, Katherine Maria *physician*
Detre, Thomas *psychiatrist, educator*
Dixit, Balwant Narayan *pharmacology and toxicology educator*
Donaldson, William Fielding, Jr. *orthopedic surgeon*
Einhorn, Jerzy *internist, endocrinologist, consultant*
Feczko, William Albert *radiologist*
Ferguson, Donald Guffey *radiologist*
Fireman, Philip *pediatrician, allergist, immunologist, medical association executive*
Fisher, Bernard *surgeon, educator*
Fleming, Arthur William *ophthalmologist*
Friday, Gilbert Anthony, Jr. *pediatrician*
Gaffney, Paul Cotter *retired physician*
Hardesty, Robert Lynch *surgeon, educator*
Harrold, Ronald Thomas *research scientist*
†Hassouri, Hassan *neurologist*
Heckler, Frederick Roger *plastic surgeon*
Jannetta, Peter Joseph *neurosurgeon, educator*
Janosko, Rudolph E. M. *psychiatrist*
Johnson, Jonas Talmadge *otolaryngology educator*
Joyner, Claude Reuben, Jr. *physician, medical educator*
Karol, Meryl Helene *immunotoxicology educator*
Kent, Georgia L. *obstetrician-gynecologist, healthcare executive*
Keshavan, Matcheri *psychiatrist*
Kochanek, Patrick Michael *pediatrician, educator*
Krause, Helen Fox *physician, otolaryngologist*
Kupfer, David J. *psychiatry educator*
Levine, Arthur Samuel *physician, scientist*
Levine, Macy Irving *physician*
Lewis, Jessica Helen (Mrs. Jack D. Myers) *physician, educator*
Lotze, Michael Thomas *surgeon*
Lowery, Willa Dean *obstetrician, gynecologist*
Lyjak Chorazy, Anna Julia *pediatrician, medical administrator, educator*
MacLeod, Gordon Kenneth *physician, educator*
Marino, Ignazio Roberto *transplant surgeon, researcher*
Moore, Robert Yates *neuroscience educator*
Myers, Eugene Nicholas *otolaryngologist, otolaryngology educator*
Needleman, Herbert Leroy *psychiatrist, pediatrician*
Pepe, Paul Ernest *emergency physician, educator*
Planinsic, Raymond M. *anesthesiologist, educator*
Pollock, Bruce Godfrey *psychiatrist, educator*
Portman, Mary Ann *gynecologist*
Pyeritz, Reed Edwin *medical geneticist, educator, research director*
Rabin, Bruce Stuart *immunologist, physician, educator*
Roche, Karen Ruth *plastic surgeon*
Rogers, Robert Mark *physician*
Roth, Loren H. *psychiatrist*
Rubin, Robert Terry *physician, researcher, educator*
Sanfilippo, Joseph Salvatore *physician, reproductive endocrinologist, educator*
Schade, Robert Richard *medical educator, researcher*
Siker, Ephraim S. *anesthesiologist*
Simmons, Richard L. *surgeon*
Totten, Mary Anne *internist*
Troen, Philip *physician, educator*
Vogel, Victor Gerald *medical educator, researcher*
Wald, Niel *public health educator*
†Welch, William Charles *neurosurgeon*
Winnie, Glenna Barbara *pediatric pulmonologist*
Winter, Peter Michael *physician, anesthesiologist, educator*
†Zimmerman, Richard Kent *family physician, preventive medicine specialist*

Plymouth Meeting
Nobel, Joel J. *biomedical researcher*

PROFESSIONAL INDEX 6029 HEALTHCARE: MEDICINE

Pottsville
Boran, Robert Paul, Jr. *orthopedic surgeon*

Radnor
Merchenthaler, Istvan Jozsef *anatomist, neuroscientist*
Templeton, John Marks, Jr. *pediatric surgeon, foundation executive*

Reading
Lusch, Charles Jack *oncologist*

Sayre
Moody, Robert Adams *neurosurgeon*

Scranton
Denaro, Anthony Thomas *psychiatrist*
Meredick, Richard Thomas *podiatrist*
O'Leary, Robert Thomas *physiatrist*
Rhiew, Francis Changnam *physician*

Sellersville
Loux, Norman Landis *psychiatrist*
Rilling, David Carl *surgeon*

Somerset
Nair, Velupillai Krishnan *cardiologist*

Sunbury
Hetrick, Theodore Lewis, Jr. *emergency medicine physician*

Swarthmore
Carey, William Bacon *pediatrician, educator*
Sing, Robert Fong *physician*

Swiftwater
Woods, Walter Earl *biomedical research and development executive*

Thorndale
Hodess, Arthur Bart *cardiologist*

Tyrone
Lewis, Kathryn Huxtable *pediatrician*

University Park
Fedoroff, Nina Vsevolod *research scientist, consultant, educator*

Upland
Green, Lawrence *neurologist, educator*

Upper Darby
Hurley, Harry James, Jr. *dermatologist*

Vandergrift
Bullard, Ray Elva, Jr. *retired psychiatrist, hospital administrator*

Villanova
Hafkenschiel, Joseph Henry, Jr. *cardiologist, educator*
Tepper, Lloyd Barton *physician*

Washington
Diamond, Daniel Lloyd *surgeon*

Wayne
de Rivas, Carmela Foderaro *psychiatrist, hospital administrator*
Horwitz, Orville *cardiologist, educator*
Lief, Harold Isaiah *psychiatrist*

Waynesboro
Stefenelli, George Edward *physician*

Wescosville
Rienzo, Robert James *radiologist*

West Chester
Flood, Dorothy Garnett *neuroscientist*
Harrington, Anne Wilson *medical librarian*

West Mifflin
Goldstein, Keith Stuart *family practice physician, emergency physician*

West Point
Sherwood, Louis Maier *physician, scientist, pharmaceutical company executive*
Vickers, Stanley *biochemical pharmacologist*

White Oak
Lebovitz, Charles Neal *surgeon*

Wilkes Barre
Bali, Ajay Kumar *cardiologist*

Williamsport
Lattimer, Gary Lee *physician*

Wynnewood
Alter, Milton *neurologist, educator*
Brady, John Paul *psychiatrist*
Hodges, John Hendricks *physician, educator*
Koprowska, Irena *cytopathologist, cancer researcher*

Wyomissing
Henry, John Martin *urologist*

Yardley
Somma, Beverly Kathleen *medical and marriage educator*

York
†Rhoads, Jonathan Evan, Jr. *surgeon, medical educator*

RHODE ISLAND

Barrington
Carpenter, Charles Colcock Jones *physician, educator*

Block Island
Gasner, Walter Gilbert *retired dermatologist*

East Greenwich
Soderberg, Clarence Harold, Jr. *surgeon, artist*

Lincoln
Magendantz, Henry Guenther *physician*

Newport
Turner, Numa Fletcher, III *family physician, military officer*

North Providence
Stankiewicz, Andrzej Jerzy *physician, biochemistry educator*

Pawtucket
Carleton, Richard Allyn *cardiologist*
Glicksman, Arvin S(igmund) *radiation oncologist*
Kiessling, Louise Sadler *pediatrician, medical educator*

Providence
Aronson, Stanley Maynard *physician, educator*
Biron, Christine Anne *medical science educator, researcher*
Block, Stanley Hoyt *pediatrician, allergist*
†Brown, William Douglas *pediatric neurologist*
Calabresi, Paul *oncologist, educator, pharmacologist*
Conway, Paul Gary *neuropharmacologist*
Crowley, James Patrick *hematologist, medical educator*
Davis, Robert Paul *physician, educator*
Dowben, Robert Morris *physician, scientist*
Easton, J(ohn) Donald *neurologist, educator*
Erikson, G(eorge) E(mil) (Erik Erikson) *anatomist, archivist, historian, educator, information specialist*
Feng, William Ching-lih *cardiothoracic surgeon*
Gilmore, Judith Marie *physician*
Hamolsky, Milton William *physician*
Jackson, Benjamin Taylor *retired surgeon, educator, medical facility administrator*
Kahn, Douglas Marc *osteopath*
Kane, Agnes Brezak *pathologist, educator*
†Kaufman, Joel M. *physician executive, neurologist*
Lewis, David Carleton *medical educator, university center director*
Marchant, Douglas Jeffery *surgeon, obstetrician, gynecologist, educator*
Mates, Susan Onthank *physician, medical educator, writer, violinist*
Mc Donald, Charles J. *physician, educator*
Merlino, Anthony Frank *orthopedic surgeon*
Nichols, David Harry *gynecologic surgeon, obstetrics and gynecology educator, author*
Oh, William *physician*
Parks, Robert Emmett, Jr. *medical science educator*
Patinkin, Terry Allan *physician*
Plotz, Richard Douglas *pathologist*
Pueschel, Siegfried M. *pediatrician, educator*
Souney, Paul Frederick *pharmacist*
†Sullivan, Patrick K. *surgeon*
Swift, Robert Michael *psychiatrist, educator*
Thayer, Walter Raymond *internist*
Vezeridis, Michael Panagiotis *surgeon, educator*
Wang, Ping *biomedical researcher, medical educator*

Riverside
Lekas, Mary Despina *retired otolaryngologist*

Wakefield
†Fair, Charles Maitland *neuroscientist, author*

Warwick
†L'Europa, Gary A. *neurologist*

Westerly
Bachmann, William Thompson *dermatologist*

SOUTH CAROLINA

Charleston
Beale, Mark Douglas *psychiatrist, educator*
Bell, Norman Howard *physician, endocrinologist, educator*
Brewerton, Timothy David *psychiatrist*
Carek, Donald J(ohn) *child psychiatry educator*
Carter, James Folger *obstetrician-gynecologist, consultant*
†Chambers, Joe Carroll *physician, consultant, educator*
Cuddy, Brian Gerard *neurosurgeon*
Daniell, Herman Burch *pharmacologist*
Dobson, Richard Lawrence *dermatologist, educator*
Favaro, Mary Kaye Asperheim (Mrs. Biagino Philip Favaro) *pediatrician*
Finn, Albert Frank, Jr. *physician*
Gettys, Thomas Wigington *medical researcher*
Grush, Owen Charles *psychiatry educator*
Haines, Stephen John *neurological surgeon*
Hoffman, Brenda Joyce *gastroenterology educator*
Hogan, Edward Leo *neurologist*
Jaffa, Ayad A. *medical educator, medical researcher*
Jaffe, Murray Sherwood *surgeon, retired*
Jenrette, Joseph Malphus, III *radiation oncologist*
Kaplan, Allen P. *physician, educator, researcher*
Key, Janice Dixon *physician, medical educator*
Langdale, Emory Lawrence *physician*
LeRoy, Edward Carwile *rheumatologist*
Lutz, Myron Howard *obstetrician, gynecologist, surgeon, educator*
†Maize, John Christopher *dermatology educator*
Margolius, Harry Stephen *pharmacologist, physician*
†Markland, Alan Colin *medical educator*
McCurdy, Layton *medical educator*
Mohr, Lawrence Charles *physician*
O'Brien, Paul Herbert *surgeon*
Ogawa, Makio *physician*
Othersen, Henry Biemann, Jr. *pediatric surgeon, physician, educator*
Roof, Betty Sams *internist*
Rustin, Rudolph Byrd, III *physician*
Schuman, Stanley H. *epidemiologist, educator*
Shealy, Ralph McKeetha *emergency physician, educator*
Underwood, Paul Benjamin *obstetrician, educator*
Willi, Steven Matthew *physician, educator, researcher*
Wilson, Frederick Allen *medical educator, medical center administrator, gastroenterologist*

Columbia
Abel, Anne Elizabeth Sutherland *pediatrician*
Adcock, David Filmore *radiologist, educator*
Almond, Carl Herman *surgeon, physician, educator*
†Brugh, Rex *urologist*
da Silva, Ercio Mario *physician*
Donald, Alexander Grant *psychiatrist, educator*
Flanagan, Clyde Harvey, Jr. *psychiatrist, psychoanalyst, educator*
Horger, Edgar Olin, III *obstetrics and gynecology educator*
Humphries, John O'Neal *physician, educator, university dean*
Jervey, Harold Edward, Jr. *medical education consultant, retired*
Lin, Tu *endocrinologist, educator, researcher, academic administrator*
Neff, Linda Joy *epidemiologist, researcher*
Rowland, Thomas C., Jr. *obstetrician/gynecologist*
Schwarz, Ferdinand (Fred Schwarz) *ophthalmologist, ophthalmic plastic surgeon*
Sheppe, Joseph Andrew *surgeon*
Shmunes, Edward *dermatologist*
Stewart, Nathaniel Johnson *emergency medicine physician*
Still, Charles Neal *neurologist, consultant*
Wallace, Edwin Ruthven, IV *psychiatrist, neuropsychiatrist psychotherapist*
Wright, Harry Hercules *psychiatrist*

Florence
Imbeau, Stephen Alan *allergist*
Windham, Nancy Quintero *obstetrician, gynecologist*

Gaffney
Wheeler, William Earl *general surgeon*

Greenville
Bonner, Jack Wilbur, III *psychiatrist, educator, administrator*
DeLoache, William Redding *pediatrician*
Kilgore, Donald Gibson, Jr. *pathologist*
Price, Thomas M. *reproductive endocrinologist*

Greenwood
Abercrombie, Stoney Alton *family physician*

Hilton Head Island
Birk, Robert Eugene *retired physician, educator*
Engelman, Karl *physician*
Humphrey, Edward William *surgeon, medical educator*
Lindner, Joseph, Jr. *physician, medical administrator*
Margileth, Andrew Menges *physician, former naval officer*
Santos, George Wesley *physician, educator*

Isle Of Palms
Elliott, Larry Paul *cardiac radiologist, educator*
Wohltmann, Hulda Justine *pediatric endocrinologist*

Loris
Logan, Alexander C., III *pathologist*

Myrtle Beach
Schwartz, Steve Wendelin *physician*

Rock Hill
Hull, William Martin, Jr. *ophthalmologist*
†Sweet, Robert Michael *plastic surgeon, dentist*

Seneca
Uden, David Elliott *cardiologist, educator*

Spartanburg
Chauhan, Suneet Bhushan *medical educator*
Fowler, Paul Raymond *physician, lawyer*
†Fudenberg, Herman Hugh *immunologist, educator*
Sovenyhazy, Gabor Ferenc *surgeon*

Summerville
Orvin, George Henry *psychiatrist*

SOUTH DAKOTA

Aberdeen
Gruca, Pawel Piotr *neuroradiologist*

Brookings
Singh, Yadhu Nand *pharmacology educator, researcher*

Mitchell
Gaede, James Ernest *physician, medical educator*

Mobridge
Lucek, Donald Walter *surgeon*

Rapid City
Croyle, Robert Harold *physician assistant*

Sioux Falls
Carpenter, Paul Lynn *cardiologist*
Fenton, Lawrence Jules *pediatric educator*
Flora, George Claude *retired neurology educator, neurologist*
Jaqua, Richard Allen *pathologist*
Kontos, George John, Jr. *cardiothoracic surgeon*
Morse, Peter Hodges *ophthalmologist, educator*
†Richards, George Alvarez *psychiatrist, educator*
Trujillo, Angelina *endocrinologist*
Wegner, Karl Heinrich *physician, educator*
Zawada, Edward Thaddeus, Jr. *physician, educator*

TENNESSEE

Bolivar
Wingate, Robert Lee, Jr. *internist*

Bristol
McIlwain, William Anthony *orthopedic surgeon*
Patel, Ashvin Ambalal *psychiatrist*

Chattanooga
Fody, Edward Paul *pathologist*
Shuck, Edwin Haywood, III *surgeon*
Thow, George Bruce *surgeon*

Cordova
Lieberman, Phillip Louis *allergist, educator*

Dunlap
†Nelson, Roger T. *surgeon*

Franklin
Moessner, Harold Frederic *allergist*

Germantown
†Vastagh, George Frederick *physician*

Gray
Combs, Stephen Paul *pediatrician, health facility administrator*

Hermitage
†Kreegel, Drew A. *plastic and reconstructive surgeon*

Jackson
Hazlehurst, George Edward *physician*
Misulis, Karl Edward *physician*
†Spruill, James H. *neurologist*
Taylor, Ronald Fulford *physician*
Torstrick, Robert Frederick *hand surgeon, orthopaedic surgeon*

Johnson City
Adebonojo, Festus O. *medical educator*
Coogan, Philip Shields *pathologist*
†Cupp, Horace Ballard *surgeon, educator*
Kostrzewa, Richard Michael *pharmacology educator*
†Pumariega, Andres Julio *medical educator, administrator*
Schueller, William Alan *dermatologist*
Shurbaji, M. Salah *pathologist*
Skalko, Richard Gallant *anatomist, educator*

Knoxville
Acker, Joseph Edington *retired cardiology educator*
Adams, Linas Jonas *gastroenterologist*
Burkhart, John Henry *retired physician*
DePersio, Richard John *otolaryngologist, plastic surgeon*
Filston, Howard Church *pediatric surgeon, educator*
Gould, Howard Richard *physician*
Henderson, R(ichard) Winn *physician*
Howard, George Turner, Jr. *retired surgeon*
Kliefoth, A(rthur) Bernhard, III *neurosurgeon*
Turner, John Charles *physician*

Maryville
Howard, Cecil Byron *pediatrician*
Lucas, Melinda Ann *pediatrician, educator*

Memphis
†Butler, Darel Anthony *neurologist*
Chesney, Russell Wallace *pediatrician*
Christopher, Robert Paul *physician*
Cicala, Roger Stephen *physician, educator*
Cox, Clair Edward, II *urologist, medical educator*
†De Saussure, Richard Laurens, Jr. *retired neurosurgery educator*
Doherty, Peter Charles *immunologist*
Gerald, Barry *radiology educator, neuroradiologist*
Godsey, William Cole *physician*
Green, Joseph Barnet *neurologist, educator*
Hamada, Omar Louis *physician*
Heimberg, Murray *pharmacologist, biochemist, physician, educator*
Herrod, Henry Grady, III *allergist, immunologist*
Hughes, Walter Thompson *physician, pediatrics educator*
Iannaccone, Alessandro *ophthalmologist, clinical scientist*
Ingram, Alvin John *surgeon*
Kitabchi, Abbas Eqbal *medical educator*
Korones, Sheldon Bernarr *physician, educator*
Kudsk, Kenneth Allan *surgeon*
Latta, George Haworth, III *neonatologist*
Lazar, Rande Harris *otolaryngologist*
†Leal, Gumersindo R. *physician*
Mauer, Alvin Marx *physician, medical educator*
Morreim, E. Haavi *medical ethics educator*
Neely, Charles Lea, Jr. *retired physician*
Nienhuis, Arthur Wesley *physician, researcher*
Riely, Caroline Armistead *physician, medical educator*
Shanklin, Douglas Radford *physician*
Shochat, Stephen Jay *pediatric surgeon*
Smolenski, Lisabeth Ann *family practice physician*
Sullivan, Jay Michael *medical educator*
Tutko, Robert Joseph *radiology administrator, law enforcement officer*
Waller, Robert Rex *ophthalmologist, educator, foundation executive*
Wilcox, Harry Hammond *retired medical educator*
Woodson, Gayle Ellen *otolaryngologist*

Mountain Home
McCoy, Sue *surgeon, biochemist*

Nashville
Allen, George Sewell *neurosurgery educator*
Allison, Fred, Jr. *physician, educator*
Barnett, Joey Victor *pharmacologist, educator, researcher*
Bates, George William *obstetrician, gynecologist, educator*
Bender, Harvey W., Jr. *cardiac and thoracic surgeon*
Bernard, Louis Joseph *surgeon, educator*
Brigham, Kenneth Larry *medical educator*
Brill, Aaron Bertrand *nuclear medicine educator*
Burk, Raymond Franklin, Jr. *physician, educator, researcher*
Burnett, Lonnie Sheldon *obstetrics and gynecology educator*
Burt, Alvin Miller, III *anatomist, cell biologist, educator, writer*
Butler, Javed *cardiologist*
Byrd, Benjamin Franklin, Jr. *surgeon, educator*
Fazio, Sergio *medical educator, researcher*
Fenichel, Gerald Mervin *neurologist, educator*
†Fisher, Jack *medical educator, plastic surgeon*
Foster, Henry Wendell *medical educator*
Franks, John Julian *anesthesiology educator, medical investigator*
George, Alfred L., Jr. *medical educator, researcher*
Graham, Thomas Pegram, Jr. *pediatric cardiologist*
†Hamberg, Marcelle Robert *retired urologist*
Huffman, William Raymond *emergency physician*
Jennings, Henry Smith, III *cardiologist*

Kaplan, Peter Robert *cardiologist*
Konrad, Peter Erich *neurosurgeon*
Krantz, Sanford Burton *physician*
Lawton, Alexander Robert, III *immunologist, educator*
Leftwich, Russell Bryant *allergist, immunologist, consultant*
Lynch, John Brown *plastic surgeon, educator*
Marney, Samuel Rowe, Jr. *physician, educator*
Martin, Peter Robert *psychiatrist, pharmacologist*
May, James M. *medical educator, medical researcher*
Meltzer, Herbert Yale *psychiatry educator*
Morrow, Jason Drew *medical and pharmacology educator*
Neilson, Eric Grant *physician, educator, health facility administrator*
Oates, John Alexander, III *medical educator*
O'Day, Denis Michael *ophthalmologist, educator*
O'Neill, James Anthony, Jr. *pediatric surgeon, educator*
Ossoff, Robert Henry *otolaryngological surgeon*
Partain, Clarence Leon *radiologist, nuclear medicine physician, educator, administrator*
Pendergrass, Henry Pancoast *physician, radiology educator*
†Petrie, William Marshall *psychiatrist*
Pinson, Charles Wright *transplant surgeon, educator*
Ray, Wayne Allen *epidemiologist*
Riley, Harris DeWitt, Jr. *pediatrician, medical educator*
Robertson, David *physician, scientist, educator*
Robinson, Roscoe Ross *nephrologist, educator*
Roden, Dan Mark *cardiologist, medical educator*
Ross, Joseph Comer *physician, educator, academic administrator*
Ryan, Sean Patrick *physician*
Shack, R. Bruce *plastic surgeon*
Sharp, Vernon Hibbett *psychiatrist*
Smith, Joseph A. *urologic surgeon*
Smith, William Barney *allergist*
Spengler, Dan Michael *orthopedic surgery educator, researcher, surgeon*
Stahlman, Mildred Thornton *pediatrics and pathology educator, researcher*
Strupp, John Allen *oncologist*
Thornton, Spencer P. *ophthalmologist, educator*
van Eys, Jan *retired pediatrician, educator, administrator*
Wasserman, David H. *medical educator, researcher*
Whetsell, William Otto, Jr. *neuropathologist*
Wilkinson, Grant Robert *pharmacology educator*
Williams, Lester Frederick, Jr. *general surgeon*
Wolraich, Mark Lee *pediatrician*

Oak Ridge
Clapp, Neal Keith *experimental pathologist*
Spray, Paul Ellsworth *surgeon*
Stevens, George M., III *surgeon*
Wise, Edmund Joseph *physician assistant, industrial hygienist*

Smyrna
†Moore, Wesley Boyd *occupational physician*

Williamsport
Dysinger, Paul William *physician, educator, health consultant*

TEXAS

Abilene
Morgan, Clyde Nathaniel *dermatologist*
Richert, Harvey Miller, II *ophthalmologist*
Russell, Byron Edward *physical therapy educator*

Alice
†Shalhoub, Issam Toufic *urologist*

Amarillo
Berry, Rita Kay *medical technologist*
†Kelleher, John Charles, Jr. *plastic surgeon*
Laur, William Edward *retired dermatologist*
Marupudi, Sambasiva Rao *surgeon, educator*
Norrid, Henry Gail *osteopathic physician and surgeon, biologist, researcher, human anatomy and physiology educator*
Parker, Gerald M. *physician, researcher*
Pratt, Donald George *physician*
Saadeh, Constantine Khalil *internist, health facility administrator, educator*

Aransas Pass
Stehn, Lorraine Strelnick *physician*

Arlington
Chong, Vernon *surgeon, physician, Air Force officer*
Gorski, Timothy N. *obstetrician-gynecologist, educator*

Austin
Bernstein, Robert *retired physician, state official, former army officer*
Brender, Jean Diane *epidemiologist, nurse*
Elequin, Cleto, Jr. *retired physician*
Ersek, Robert Allen *plastic surgeon, inventor*
Fleeger, David Clark *colon and rectal surgeon*
Ivy, John L. *medical educator, researcher*
Mullins, Charles Brown *physician, academic administrator*
Painter, Theophilus Shickel, Jr. *physician*
Schleuse, William *psychiatrist, psychoanalyst*
Shaw, Frederic Elijah *epidemiologist*

Baytown
Williams, Drew Davis *surgeon*

Beaumont
Lozano, Jose *nephrologist*

Bellaire
Haywood, Theodore Joseph *physician, educator*
Holmquest, Donald Lee *physician, astronaut, lawyer*
Pokorny, Alex Daniel *psychiatrist*
Thorne, Lawrence George *allergist, immunologist, pediatrician*

Bellville
Neely, Robert Allen *ophthalmologist*

Boerne
Wittmer, James Frederick *preventive medicine physician, educator*

Brooks AFB
Balldin, Ulf Ingemar *medical researcher*

Brownsville
Walss, Rodolfo J. *obstetrician-gynecologist, artist*

Bryan
Dirks, Kenneth Ray *pathologist, medical educator, army officer*

Camp Wood
Triplett, William Carryl *physician, researcher*

Carrollton
Kelly, Ralph Whitley *emergency physician, health facility administrator*

Cibolo
Jensen, Andrew Oden *retired obstetrician, gynecologist*

College Station
Kuo, Lih *medical educator*
Lemanski, Larry Fredrick *medical educator, university administrator*

Conroe
Cecil, Linda Marie *obstetrician/gynecologist*

Corpus Christi
Appel, Truman Frank *surgeon*
Cox, William Andrew *cardiovascular thoracic surgeon*
Kylstra, Johannes Arnold *physician*
Pinkel, Donald Paul *pediatrician*

Dallas
Allen, Terry Devereux *urologist, educator*
†Barton, Fritz Engel *plastic surgeon, educator*
Bashour, Fouad Anis *cardiology educator*
Bick, Rodger Lee *hematologist, oncologist, researcher, educator*
Blomqist, Carl Gunnar *cardiologist*
Bonte, Frederick James *radiology educator, physician*
Boswell, George Marion, Jr. *orthopedist, health care facility administrator*
Burnside, John Wayne *medical educator, university official*
Caetano, Raul *psychiatrist, educator*
Carman, George Henry *retired physician*
Cavanagh, Harrison Dwight *ophthalmic surgeon, medical educator*
Cloud, Robert Royce *surgeon*
Cox, Rody P(owell) *medical educator, internist*
Cullum, Colin Munro *psychiatry and neurology educator*
Dees, Tom Moore, II *internist*
Dutta, Paritosh Chandra *immunologist*
Edwards, George Alva *physician, educator*
Eichenwald, Heinz Felix *physician*
Einspruch, Burton Cyril *psychiatrist*
Emmett, Michael *physician*
Fagan, Peter Gail *occupational medicine physician*
†Fearon, Jeffrey Archer *surgeon*
Flatt, Adrian Ede *surgeon*
Foster, Daniel W. *medical educator*
Frenkel, Eugene Phillip *physician*
Friedberg, Errol Clive *pathology educator, researcher*
Fyfe, Alistair Ian *cardiologist, scientist, educator*
Gage, Tommy Wilton *pharmacologist, dentist, pharmacist, educator*
Gant, Norman Ferrell, Jr. *obstetrician, gynecologist*
Gantt, James Raiford *thoracic surgeon*
Gilman, Alfred Goodman *pharmacologist, educator*
Goldstein, Joseph Leonard *physician, medical educator, molecular genetics scientist*
Gonwa, Thomas Arthur *nephrologist, transplant physician*
Griffith, Rachel *neonatologist*
Gross, Gary Neil *allergist, physician*
Grundy, Scott Montgomery *physician, medical educator*
Harper, John Frank *cardiologist*
Harrington, Marion Ray *ophthalmologist*
Helm, Phala Aniece *physiatrist*
Hilgemann, Donald William *medical educator*
Holman, James *allergist, immunologist*
Hughes, Waunell McDonald (Mrs. Delbert E. Hughes) *retired psychiatrist*
Hurd, Eric Ray *rheumatologist, internist, educator*
Jialal, Ishwarlal *medical educator*
Johnson, Robert Lee, Jr. *physician, educator, researcher*
Kindberg, Shirley Jane *pediatrician*
Kollmeyer, Kenneth Robert *surgeon*
Lakhanpal, Sharad *physician*
Lewis, Jerry M. *psychiatrist, educator*
Lichliter, Warren Eugene *surgeon, educator*
Lumry, William Raymond *physician, allergist*
Maddrey, Willis Crocker *medical educator, internist, academic administrator, consultant, researcher*
Margolin, Solomon Begelfor *pharmacologist*
Martin, Jack *physician*
Mc Clelland, Robert Nelson *surgeon, educator*
Menter, M(artin) Alan *dermatologist*
Mitchell, Teddy Lee *physician*
Montgomery, Philip O'Bryan, Jr. *pathologist*
New, William Neil *physician, retired naval officer*
Odom, Floyd Clark *surgeon*
Page, Richard Leighton *cardiologist, medical educator, researcher*
Parkey, Robert Wayne *radiology and nuclear medicine educator, research radiologist*
Perry, Malcolm Oliver *vascular surgeon*
Phillips, Margaret A. *pharmacology educator*
Pippin, John Joseph *cardiologist*
Race, George Justice *pathology educator*
Rainey, William E., II *medical educator*
Richardson, Dennise Marie *physician assistant*
Rohrich, Rodney James *plastic surgeon, educator*
Romero, Jorge Antonio *neurologist, educator*
Rosenberg, Roger Newman *neurologist, educator*
Ross, Elliott M. *pharmacology, researcher, educator*
†Samson, Duke Staples *neurosurgeon*
Schecter, Arnold Joel *preventive medicine educator*
Seldin, Donald Wayne *physician, educator*
Silverman, Alan Kenneth *dermatologist, consultant*
Simmang, Clifford Liles *surgeon*
Simon, Theodore Ronald *physician, medical educator*
Smith, Barry Samuel *physiatrist*
Stage, Key Hutchinson *urologist*
Stembridge, Vernie A(lbert) *pathologist, educator*
Stone, Marvin Jules *physician, educator*
Talmadge, John Mills *physician*
Thompson, Jesse Eldon *vascular surgeon*
Tong, Alex Waiming *immunologist*
Turner, Ralph James *obstetrician-gynecologist*
Uhr, Jonathan William *immunologist, educator, researcher*
Wasserman, Richard Lawrence *pediatrician, educator*
Wildenthal, C(laud) Kern *physician, educator*
Wilson, Jean Donald *endocrinologist, educator*
Ziff, Morris *internist, rheumatologist, educator*

Dickinson
Smith, Jerome Hazen *retired pathologist*

Eden
Boyd, John Hamilton *osteopath*

El Paso
Crossen, John Jacob *radiologist, educator*
Foley, John Donald *physician*
Gainer, Barbara Jeanne *radiology educator*
Huchton, Paul Joseph, Jr. *pediatrician*
Levine, Johanan Sidney *neurologist*
Magana, Jorge Carlos *pediatrician*
Mrochek, Michael J. *physician*
Naghmi, Rifat Pervaiz *internist, educator*
Silberg, Louise Barbara *physician, anesthesiologist*
Simpson, Michael Homer *dermatologist*
Verghese, Abraham Cheeran *internist, writer, educator*
Williams, Darryl Marlowe *medical educator*
Zaloznik, Arlene Joyce *oncologist, retired army officer*

Fort Sam Houston
Battafarano, Daniel Francis *rheumatologist*
Bauman, Wendall Carter, Jr. *ophthalmologist, career officer*
Cohen, David John *cardiothoracic surgeon*
†Halliday, Alan Wood *neurologist*

Fort Worth
Ahmed, M. Basheer *psychiatrist, educator*
Cox, James Sidney *physician*
de Sousa, Byron Nagib *physician, anesthesiologist, clinical pharmacologist, educator*
Dewar, Thomas Norman *gastroenterologist*
Gillette, Paul Crawford *pediatric cardiologist*
Lorenzetti, Ole John *pharmaceutical research executive, ophthalmic research and development executive*
Oakford, Lawrence Xavier *electron microscopist, laboratory administrator*
Tobey, Martin Alan *cardiologist*
Treviño, Fernando Manuel *medical educator*
Weyandt, Linda Jane *anesthetist, physician*
Wynn, Susan Rudd *physician*
Yanni, John Michael *pharmacologist*

Galveston
Arens, James F. *anesthesiologist, educator*
†Avery, A. Nelson *physician, medical educator*
Bailey, Byron James *otolaryngologist, medical association executive*
Bernier, George Matthew, Jr. *physician, medical educator, medical school dean*
Brasier, Allan R. *medical educator*
Bryan, George Thomas *pediatrician, academic administrator*
Bungo, Michael William *physician, educator, science administrator*
Burns, Chester Ray *medical history educator*
Calverley, John Robert *physician, educator*
Chonmaitree, Tasnee *pediatrician, educator, infectious disease specialist*
Dawson, Earl Bliss *obstetrics and gynecology educator*
Goodwin, Jean McClung *psychiatrist*
Herndon, David N. *surgeon*
Hillman, Gilbert Rothschild *medical educator*
Hilton, James Gorton *pharmacologist*
James, Thomas Naum *cardiologist, educator*
Levin, William Cohn *hematologist, former university president*
Luo, Hong Yuan *biomedical scientist, educator*
Luthra, Gurinder Kumar *osteopath*
Pearl, William Richard Emden *pediatric cardiologist*
Phillips, Linda Goluch *plastic surgeon, educator, researcher*
†Rice, James Carter *medical educator*
Sandstead, Harold Hilton *medical educator*
Schreiber, Melvyn Hirsh *radiologist*
Shope, Robert Ellis *epidemiology educator*
Smith, Edgar Benton *physician*
Stobo, John David *physician, educator*
Suzuki, Fujio *immunologist, educator, researcher*
White, Robert Brown *medical educator*
Willis, William Darrell, Jr. *neurophysiologist, educator*

Garland
Duren, Michael *cardiologist*
Haynsworth, Robert F., Jr. *anesthesiologist*

Georgetown
Manning, Robert Thomas *physician, educator*
Sawyer, William Dale *physician, educator, university dean, foundation administrator*

Harlingen
Klein, Garner Franklin *cardiologist, internist*

Houston
Abbruzzese, James Lewis *medical oncologist*
Adams, James Mervyn, Jr. *pediatrician, neonatologist, educator*
Aguilar-Bryan, Lydia *medical educator, medical researcher*
Alexanian, Raymond *hematologist*
Alford, Bobby Ray *physician, educator, university official*
Appel, Stanley Hersh *neurologist*
Aslam, Muhammed Javed *physician*
Baig, Mukarram *internist*
Bailey, Harold Randolph *surgeon*
Ballantyne, Christie Mitchell *medical educator*
Barrett, Bernard Morris, Jr. *plastic and reconstructive surgeon*
Baskin, David Stuart *neurosurgeon, educator*
Bast, Robert Clinton, Jr. *medical researcher, medical educator*
Beasley, Robert Palmer *epidemiologist, dean, educator*
Beck, John Robert *pathologist, information scientist*
Berry, Michael A. *physician, consultant*
Bethea, Louise Huffman *allergist*
Bevers, Therese Bartholomew *physician, medical educator*
Bowman, Jeffrey Neil *podiatrist*
Brown, Dale, Jr. *obstetrician, educator, health facility adminstrator*
Burdette, Walter James *surgeon, educator*
Burzynski, Stanislaw Rajmund *internist*
Busch, Harris *medical educator*
Buster, John Edmond *gynecologist, medical researcher*
Butler, Ian John *neurologist*
†Callender, David L. *medical educator, administrator*
Campbell, Andrew William *immunotoxicology physician*
Cantrell, William Allen *psychiatrist, educator*
Carabello, Blase Anthony *cardiology educator*
Cardus, David *physician*
Casscells, Samuel Ward, III *cardiologist, educator*
Catlin, Francis Irving *physician*
Collins, Vincent Patrick *radiologist, physician, educator*
Cooley, Denton Arthur *surgeon, educator*
†Cooper, Timothy Robert *neonatologist, pediatrician, educator, consultant*
Corriere, Joseph N., Jr. *urologist, educator*
Couch, Robert Barnard *physician, scientist, educator*
Daily, Louis *ophthalmologist*
Dawood, Mohamed Yusoff *obstetrician, gynecologist*
DeBakey, Michael Ellis *cardiovascular surgeon, educator, scientist*
Delpassand, Ebrahim Seyed *pathologist, nuclear medicine physician*
Doubleday, Charles William *dermatologist, educator*
†Driver, Larry C. *medical educator*
Drutz, Jan Edwin *pediatrics educator*
DuPont, Herbert Lancashire *medical educator, researcher*
Eisner, Diana *pediatrician*
Elwood, William Norelli *medical researcher*
Evans, Harry Launius *pathology educator*
Ferrendelli, James Anthony *neurologist, educator*
Fischer, Craig Leland *physician*
Fishman, Marvin Allen *pediatrician, neurologist, educator*
Freireich, Emil J *hematologist, educator*
Fritsch, Derek Adrian *nurse anesthetist*
Giesecke, Noel Martin *cardiovascular anesthesiologist*
Gigli, Irma *physician, educator, academic administrator*
Gildenberg, Philip Leon *neurosurgeon*
Glassman, Armand Barry *physician, pathologist, scientist, educator, administrator*
Goldman, Stanford Milton *medical educator*
Gorry, G. Anthony *medical educator*
Graham, David Yates *gastroenterologist*
†Greenberg, Stephen Baruch *physician, educator*
Grossman, Herbert Barton *urologist, researcher*
Grossman, Robert George *physician, educator*
Gunn, Albert Edward, Jr. *internist, educator, lawyer, administrator*
Gupta, Kaushal Kumar *internist*
Guynn, Robert William *psychiatrist, educator*
Hall, Robert Joseph *physician, medical educator*
Hamilton, Carlos Robert, Jr. *internist, endocrinologist*
Hanania, Nicola Alexander *physician*
Harrell, James Earl, Sr. *radiologist, educator*
Harris, John H. *radiologist*
Haynie, Thomas Powell, III *physician*
Hicks, John Bernard *internist*
Hollister, Leo Edward *physician, educator*
Hong, Waun Ki *medical oncologist, clinical investigator*
Jackson, Gilchrist L. *surgeon*
Jankovic, Joseph *neurologist, educator, scientist*
Johnson, Thomas David *pharmacologist*
Jones, Dan Brigman *ophthalmologist, educator*
Jones, Edith Irby *physician*
Jordon, Robert Earl *physician*
Kahan, Barry Donald *surgeon, educator*
Kaplan, Alan Leslie *gynecology educator, oncologist*
Kaufman, Raymond Henry *physician*
Kavanagh, John Joseph *medical educator*
Kellaway, Peter *neurophysiologist, researcher*
Key, James Everett *ophthalmologist*
Kitowski, Vincent Joseph *medical consultant, former physical medicine and rehabilitation physician*
Knight, J. Vernon *medicine and microbiology educator*
Koch, Douglas Donald *ophthalmologist*
Kraft, Irvin Alan *psychiatrist*
Kutka, Nicholas *nuclear medicine physician*
†Laurent, John Paul *neurosurgeon*
Lechago, Juan *pathologist, educator*
Levin, Bernard *physician*
†Linn, Heather *neurologist*
Low, Morton David *physician, educator*
Malorzo Waller, Amy Lynn *physician assistant in pediatric neurosurgery*
†Martin, Raymond Anthony *neurologist, educator*
Max, Ernest *surgeon*
†McCollum, Charles H. *surgeon*
McKechnie, John Charles *gastroenterologist, educator*
McPherson, Alice Ruth *ophthalmologist, educator*
†Mendelsohn, John *oncologist, hematologist, educator*
Meyer, John Stirling *neurologist, educator*
Milam, John Daniel *pathologist, educator*
Miller, Gary Evan *psychiatrist, mental health services administrator*
†Miller, Geoffrey *child neurologist*
Miner, Michael E. *neurosurgery educator*
Morgenstern, Lewis B. *medical educator*
Munk, Zev Moshe *allergist, researcher*
Murad, Ferid *physician*
Murphy, William Alexander, Jr. *diagnostic radiologist, educator*
Ordonez, Nelson Gonzalo *pathologist*
Phung, Nguyen Dinh *medical educator*
Portman, Ronald Jay *pediatric nephrologist, researcher*
Poston, Walker Seward, II *medical educator, researcher*
†Powers, William Edward *emergency physician, educator*
Raijman, Isaac *gastroenterologist, endoscopist, educator*

Ray, Priscilla physician
Raymer, Warren Joseph retired allergist
Ribble, John Charles medical educator
Riley, William John neurologist
Romsdahl, Marvin Magnus surgeon, educator
Rosenthal, Morris William pediatrician
†Ross, Michael Wallis public health educator
Rudolph, Andrew Henry dermatologist, educator
Schachtel, Barbara Harriet Levin epidemiologist, educator
Scharold, Mary Louise psychoanalyst, educator
Schoolar, Joseph Clayton psychiatrist, pharmacologist, educator
Selke, Oscar O., Jr. physiatrist, educator
Shearer, William Thomas pediatrician, educator
Shulman, Robert Jay physician
Simpson, Joe Leigh obstetrics and gynecology educator
Sirbasku, David Andrew medical educator
Spira, Melvin plastic surgeon
Stehlin, John Sebastian, Jr. surgeon
Tanous, Helene Mary physician
Thomas, Orville C. physician
Tulloch, Brian Robert endocrinologist
Tullos, Hugh Simpson orthopedic surgeon, educator
Vallbona, Carlos physician
Vanderploeg, James M. preventive medicine physician
Vassilopoulou-Sellin, Rena medical educator
†Vindekilde, Soren John physician
Walker, William Easton surgeon, educator, lawyer
Wall, Matthew J., Jr. surgeon, scientist
Wheless, James Warren neurologist
Wiemer, David Robert plastic surgeon
Williams, Temple Weatherly, Jr. internist, educator
Yang, Zhong-Jing physician assistant
†Zoghbi, Huda Y. pediatric neurology and genetics educator

Humble
Trowbridge, John Parks physician

Huntsville
Conwell, Halford Roger physician

Irving
Garcia, Raymond Lloyd dermatologist

Kemp
Wurlitzer, Fred Pabst surgeon

Kermit
Gremmel, Gilbert Carl family physician

Killeen
Vancura, Stephen Joseph radiologist

League City
Moore, Walter D., Jr. retired pathologist

Lubbock
Beck, George Preston anesthesiologist, educator
Bricker, Donald Lee surgeon
Buesseler, John Aure ophthalmologist, management consultant
†Homan, Richard Warren physician, educator
Jackson, Francis Charles physician, surgeon
Kaye, Alan David anesthesiologist, researcher
Kimbrough, Robert Cooke, III infectious diseases physician
Kurtzman, Neil A. medical educator
May, Donald Robert Lee ophthalmologist, retina and vitreous surgeon, educator, farmer
Mittemeyer, Bernhard Theodore urology and surgery educator
Sabatini, Sandra physician
Schiffer, Randolph Brenton physician
Way, Barbara Haight dermatologist
Wolpmann, Michael Joseph physician
Woolam, Gerald Lynn surgeon

Lufkin
Perry, Lewis Charles emergency medicine physician, osteopath

Marshall
Sudhivoraseth, Niphon pediatrician, allergist, immunologist

Mcallen
Ramirez, Mario Efrain physician

Midland
Lohmann, George Young, Jr. neurosurgeon, hospital executive, artist

Nacogdoches
Mallot, Michael E. gastroenterologist

Odessa
Lane, Daniel McNeel pediatric hematologist, lipidologist

Pampa
Mohan, Vijay Krishnan surgeon

Pasadena
D'Andrea, Mark radiation oncologist
Mullins, Jack Allen cardiologist, educator
Shapiro, Edward Muray dermatologist

Plano
Ahmad, Syeda Sultana physician
Vengrow, Michael Ian neurologist

Raymondville
Montgomery-Davis, Joseph osteopathic physician

Richardson
†Munoz, Shanan Brinson neurologist
Wheeler, Clarence Joseph, Jr. physician
Wood, Joseph George neurobiologist, educator

Rockport
Johnson, Marilyn obstetrician, gynecologist

Salado
Wilmer, Harry Aron psychiatrist

San Angelo
Fischer, Duncan Kinnear neurosurgeon

San Antonio
Aust, Joe Bradley surgeon, educator
Baker, Floyd Wilmer surgeon, retired army officer
Croft, Harry Allen psychiatrist
Davis, Steven Andrew dermatologist
Dobie, Robert Alan otologist
Fornos, Peter Secundino pulmonary medicine physician
Freeman, Theodore Monroe physician
†Garza, Jaime Ruperto plastic/reconstructive surgeon
Hall, Brad Bailey orthopaedic surgeon, health care administrator
Horton, Granville Eugene occupational medicine physician, retired air force officer
Huff, Robert Whitley obstetrician, gynecologist, educator
Jorgensen, James H. pathologist, educator, microbiologist
Kamada-Cole, Mika M. allergist, immunologist, medical educator
Kotas, Robert Vincent research physician, educator
Kreisberg, Jeffrey I. medical educator, researcher
Le Maistre, Charles Aubrey internist, epidemiologist, educator
Leon, Robert Leonard psychiatrist, educator
McFee, Arthur Storer physician
McGill, Henry Coleman, Jr. physician, educator, researcher
Mercado, Mary Gonzales cardiologist
Mitchell, George Washington, Jr. physician, educator
Neel, Spurgeon Hart, Jr. physician, retired army officer
New, Pamela Zyman neurologist
Ognibene, Andre J(ohn) physician, army officer, educator
Persellin, Robert Harold physician
Pestana, Carlos physician, educator
Pruitt, Basil Arthur, Jr. surgeon, retired army officer
Ramos, Raul surgeon
Randall, Charles Wilson gastroenterologist
Reuter, Stewart Ralston radiologist, lawyer, educator
Rhodes, Linda Jane psychiatrist
Schenker, Steven physician, educator
Smith, Reginald Brian Furness anesthesiologist, educator
†Solomon, Diane Hurst neurologist
Townsend, Frank Marion pathology educator
†Walsh, Nicolas Eugene rehabilitation medicine physician, educator
Wiedeman, Geoffrey Paul physician, air force officer
†Wolff, Hugh Lipman urologist, educator
Zilveti, Carlos B. preventive medicine physician, pediatrician

Seabrook
Patten, Bernard Michael neurologist, writer, educator

Sherman
†Swamy, Ponnuswamy T. plastic surgeon

Stafford
Polinger, Iris Sandra dermatologist

Sugarland
†DeVere, Ronald neurologist

Temple
Bailey, William Harold medical educator
Brasher, George Walter physician
Knudsen, Kermit Bruce physician
Stoebner, John Martin physician
Watson, Linley Everett cardiologist
†Waxman, Jeffrey Alan urologist

Terrell
Makowski, John Jaroslaw, Jr. psychiatrist

Texarkana
Harrison, James Wilburn gynecologist
Selby, Roy Clifton, Jr. neurosurgeon

Tow
Shepherd, Donald Ray pathologist

Tyler
Kronenberg, Richard Samuel physician, educator
Pinkenburg, Ronald Joseph ophthalmologist

Vernon
Casimir, Kenneth Charles adolescent forensic psychiatrist, educator

Victoria
Lorenzen, Janice Ruth physician

Waco
Dow, David Sontag retired ophthalmologist
Richie, Rodney Charles critical care and pulmonary medicine physician

Webster
Farnam, Jafar allergist, immunologist, pediatrician

West
Eisma, Jose A. physician
Smith, George Norvell physician

Wichita Falls
Harvey, Peter Marshall podiatrist

UTAH

Layton
Yates, Jay Reese physician

Ogden
Maughan, Willard Zinn dermatologist
Spencer, LaVal Wing physician

Park City
Wardell, Joe Russell, Jr. retired pharmacologist

Provo
Roberts, Stanley Dwayne physician, medical educator

Salt Lake City
Abildskov, J. A. cardiologist, educator
Bauer, A(ugust) Robert, Jr. surgeon, educator
Carey, John Clayton pediatrician
Davis, Brian Adam physician
Davis, Roy Kim otolaryngologist, health facility administrator
†Fowler, James Raymond surgeon
Fujinami, Robert Shin neurology educator
Goldstein, Michael L. neurologist
Grosser, Bernard Irving psychiatry educator
Iverius, Per-Henrik physician, biochemist, educator
Linardakis, Nikos Michalis physician, publisher
Lloyd, Ray Dix health physicist, consultant
Matsuo, Fumisuke physician, educator
Middleton, Anthony Wayne, Jr. urologist, educator
Moser, Royce, Jr. physician, medical educator
Nelson, Russell Marion surgeon, educator
Odell, William Douglas physician, scientist, educator
Petersen, Finn Bo oncologist, educator
Renzetti, Attilio David physician
Vanderhooft, Jan Eric orthopedic surgeon, educator
Ward, John Robert physician, educator
Wong, Kuang Chung anesthesiology and pharmacology educator

VERMONT

Bennington
Wallace, Harold James, Jr. physician

Bradford
Kaplow, Leonard Samuel pathologist, educator

Brattleboro
Ames, Adelbert, III neurophysiologist, educator
Cole, Stephen Adams psychiatrist

Burlington
Ciongoli, Alfred Kenneth neurologist
Cooper, Sheldon Mark medical educator, immunology researcher, rheumatologist
Craighead, John Edward pathology educator
Davis, John Herschel surgeon, educator
Galbraith, Richard Anthony physician, hospital administrator
Hong, Richard pediatrician, educator
LeWinter, Martin M. cardiologist
Lidofsky, Steven David medical educator
Lucey, Jerold Francis pediatrician
Riddick, Daniel Howison obstetrics and gynecology educator, priest
Sobel, Burton Elias physician, educator
Tampas, John P. radiologist
Waterman, Gerald Scott psychiatrist, physician educator

Colchester
Danielson, Ursel Rehding psychiatrist

Dorset
Bamford, Joseph Charles, Jr. gynecologist, obstetrician, educator, medical missionary

Essex Junction
Dustan, Harriet Pearson former physician, educator

Norwich
Chapman, Robert James clinical psychiatrist, educator

Rutland
†Corbett, Joseph Edward neurosurgeon

Saint Johnsbury
Toll, David pediatrician

Stowe
Fagan, William Thomas, Jr. urologist

Underhill
Danforth, Elliot, Jr. medical educator

West Dover
Humphreys, George H., II surgery educator

White River Junction
Barton, Gail Melinda psychiatrist, educator
Myers, Warren Powers Laird physician, educator
Rous, Stephen Norman urologist, educator

Woodstock
Killian, Edward James pediatrician
Lash, James William (Jay Lash) embryology educator
Wollman, Harry health care and executive search consultant

VIRGINIA

Alexandria
†Akukwe, Chinua public health physician, health service executive
Buhain, Wilfrido Javier medical educator
Chapman, Anthony Bradley psychiatrist
Hurtado, Rodrigo Claudio allergist, immunologist
Maves, Michael Donald medical association executive

Annandale
Binder, Richard Allen hematologist, oncologist
Kiernan, Paul Darlington thoracic surgeon, educator
Lefrak, Edward Arthur cardiovascular and thoracic surgeon
Scott, Hugh Patrick physician, naval officer
Shamburek, Roland Howard physician
Simonian, Simon John surgeon, scientist, educator

Arlington
†Banks, Willie J. orthopaedic surgeon, educator
Corley, Sarah Taylor physician
Dolan, William David, Jr. physician
Ferraz, Francisco Marconi neurological surgeon
Harper, Michael John Kennedy obstetrics and gynecology educator
Healy, Bernadine P. physician, educator, federal agency administrator, scientist
Highsmith, Wanda Law retired association executive
Iqbal, Zafar biochemist, neurochemist
Keeve, Jack Philip physician, educator, retired
Werbos, Paul John neural net research director

Charlottesville
Barnett, Benjamin Lewis, Jr. physician
Beller, George Allan medical educator
Cantrell, Robert Wendell otolaryngologist, head and neck surgeon, educator
Chevalier, Robert Louis pediatric nephrologist, educator, researcher
Conway, Brian Peter ophthalmologist, educator
Craig, James William physician, educator, university dean
Dalton, Claudette Ellis Harloe anesthesiologist, educator, university official
DeSilvey, Dennis Lee cardiologist, educator, university administrator
Epstein, Robert Marvin anesthesiologist, educator
Ferguson, James Edward, II obstetrician, gynecologist
Fernbach, Louise Oftedal physician, educator
Flickinger, Charles John anatomist, educator
Gillenwater, Jay Young urologist, educator
Harbert, Guy Morley, Jr. retired obstetrician, gynecologist
Howards, Stuart S. physician, educator
Jane, John Anthony neurosurgeon, educator
Jones, Rayford Scott surgeon, medical educator
Kassell, Neal Frederic neurosurgery educator
Kattwinkel, John physician, pediatrics educator
Keats, Theodore Eliot physician, radiology educator
Kitchin, James D., III obstetrician-gynecologist, educator
Larner, Joseph pharmacology educator
Mandell, Gerald Lee physician, medicine educator
Marshall, Victor Fray physician, educator
Morgan, Raymond F. plastic surgeon
Muller, William Henry, Jr. surgeon, educator
Nolan, Stanton Peelle surgeon, educator
Owen, John Atkinson, Jr. physician, educator
Peterson, Kent Wright physician
Phillips, Lawrence H., II neurologist, educator
Platts-Mills, Thomas Alexander E. immunologist, educator, researcher
Pullen, Edwin Wesley anatomist, university dean
Rowlingson, John Clyde anesthesiologist, educator, physician
Sarembock, Ian Joseph internist
Stevenson, Ian psychiatrist, educator
Taylor, Peyton Troy, Jr. gynecologic oncologist, educator
Teates, Charles David radiologist, educator
Thorner, Michael Oliver medical educator
Tillack, Thomas Warner pathologist
Tuttle, Jeremy Ballou neurobiologist
Villar-Palasi, Carlos pharmacology educator
Wang, Gwo Jaw orthopaedic surgery educator
Weary, Peyton Edwin medical educator
Wills, Michael Ralph medical educator

Chesapeake
Kovalcik, Paul Jerome surgeon

Christiansburg
Hershey, Jody Henry public health physician

Colonial Heights
†Thompson, Louis M., III obstetrician-gynecologist

Danville
Kovarsky, Joel Severin rheumatologist, small business owner

Fairfax
Dettinger, Garth Bryant surgeon, physician, retired air force officer, county health officer
DuRocher, Frances Antoinette physician, educator
†Johnson, Clarion Ellis physician
Rubin, Robert Joseph physician, health care consultant
Stage, Thomas Benton psychiatrist

Falls Church
Anderson, George Kenneth physician, foundation executive, retired air force officer
Elliott, Virginia F. Harrison retired anatomist, kinesiologist and educator, investment advisor, publisher, philanthropist
Evans, Peter Yoshio ophthalmologist, educator
Golomb, Herbert Stanley dermatologist
Ho, Hien Van pediatrician
Inglefield, Joseph T., Jr. allergist, immunologist, pediatrician
†John, Sarah A. emergency medicine physician
Mushtaq, Ednan physician
Wise, Thomas Nathan psychiatrist
†Withers, Benjamin G. preventive medicine physician, career officer

Fredericksburg
†Daniel, James Richard surgeon, oncologist

Great Falls
Schreiner, George E. nephrologist, educator, writer

Hampton
Brown, Loretta Ann Port physician, geneticist

Harrisonburg
McNamara, Joseph Gerard physician

Herndon
Lynch, George Michael family practice physician
Payne, Fred J. physician, educator

Kenbridge
Walton, G. Clifford family practice physician

Langley AFB
Dawson, Robert A. physician assistant

Leesburg
Mitchell, Russell Harry dermatologist

Locust Grove
Sjogren, Robert William internist

Lynchburg
Cooper, Alan Michael psychiatrist
Lane, Richard Allan physician, health sciences educator

Maidens
Adams, Jimmy Wayne *osteopath*

Manassas
Sehn, James Thomas *urological surgeon*

Marion
Armbrister, Douglas Kenley *surgeon*

Martinsville
Eller, M. Edward, Jr. *physician*

Mc Lean
Buck, Alfred Andreas *physician, epidemiologist*
Felts, William Robert, Jr. *physician*
Gerson, Elliot Francis *health care executive*
Laning, Robert Comegys *retired physician, former naval officer*
Wallace, Robert Bruce *surgeon, retired*
Wright, William Evan *physician*

Midlothian
Jones, John Evan *medical educator*

Moneta
Singleton, Samuel Winston *physician, pharmaceutical company executive*

Monterey
Tabatznik, Bernard *retired physician, educator*

Newport News
†Bobbitt, John Maxwell *surgeon, medical educator*
†Han, D(ongyeon) Peter *urologist*

Norfolk
Andrews, William Cooke *physician*
Dandoy, Suzanne Eggleston *physician, academic administrator, educator*
†Devine, Patrick Campbell *urologist, educator*
Faulconer, Robert Jamieson *pathologist, educator*
Lester, Richard Garrison *radiologist, educator*
Lind, James Forest *surgeon, educator*
Morrison, Ashton Byrom *pathologist, medical school official*
Oelberg, David George *neonatologist, educator, researcher*
Schneider, Daniel Scott *pediatric cardiologist*
Wolcott, Hugh Dixon *obstetrics and gynecology educator*

North Garden
Moses, Hamilton, III *medical educator, hospital executive, management consultant*

Norton
Vest, Gayle Southworth *obstetrician and gynecologist*
Vest, Steven Lee *gastroenterologist, hepatologist, internist*

Portsmouth
†Clare, Frank Brian *neurosurgeon, neurologist*
Wolf, Jeffrey Stephen *physician*

Reston
Ryan, Mary Catherine *pediatrician*

Richmond
Ayres, Stephen McClintock *physician, educator*
Balster, Robert Louis *pharmacologist*
Bates, Hampton Robert, Jr. *pathologist*
Blumberg, Michael Zangwill *allergist*
Burke, Arthur Wade *retired physician*
Carr, David Turner *physician*
David, Ronald Brian *child neurologist*
Dessypris, Emmanuel Nicholas *hematologist-oncologist*
†Dunn, Leo James *obstetrician, gynecologist, educator*
Franko, Bernard Vincent *pharmacologist*
†Graham, Sam Dixon *urologist*
Harris, Louis Selig *pharmacologist, researcher*
Howell, Talmadge Rudolph *radiologist*
Kaplowitz, Lisa Glauser *physician, educator*
Kendig, Edwin Lawrence, Jr. *physician, educator*
Lawrence, Walter, Jr. *surgeon*
Marshall, Wayne Keith *anesthesiology educator*
Mauck, Henry Page, Jr. *medical and pediatrics educator*
†Mehrhof, Austin Irving *plastic surgery educator*
Mellette, M. Susan Jackson *physician, educator, researcher*
Mollen, Edward Leigh *pediatrician, allergist and clinical immunologist*
Mullinax, Perry Franklin *rheumatologist, allergist, immunologist*
Owen, Duncan Shaw, Jr. *physician, medical educator*
Richardson, David Walthall *cardiologist, educator, consultant*
Sirica, Alphonse Eugene *pathology educator*
Smoker, Wendy Rue Kartinos *neuroradiologist, consultant, educator*
Towne, Alan Raymond *neurologist, educator*
Tunner, William Sams *urological surgeon*
Turner, Elaine S. *allergist, immunologist*
Ward, John Wesley *retired pharmacologist*
Young, Estelle Irene *dermatologist*

Roanoke
Enright, Michael Joseph *radiologist*
Hutcheson, Jack Robert *hematologist, medical oncologist*
Kennedy, Stephen Smith *hematologist, oncologist, educator*
Moore, Richard Carroll, Jr. *family physician*

Roseland
Stemmler, Edward Joseph *physician, retired association executive, retired academic dean*
Wood, Maurice *medical educator*

Salem
Chakravorty, Ranes Chandra *surgeon, educator*

Springfield
Luisada, Paul Victor *psychiatrist*

Staunton
Lossing, Wallace William *inventor, minister*

Sterling
Jaffe, Russell Merritt *pathologist, research director*

Suffolk
Carroll, George Joseph *pathologist, educator*

Vienna
Mitchell, John David *ophthalmologist*
Moen, Ahmed Abdul *national and international health educator*
Penrose, Cynthia C. *health plan administrator, consultant*
Schwartz, Richard Harvey *pediatrician*

Virginia Beach
Carlston, John A. *allergist*
Fischer, Daniel Edward *psychiatrist*
Heuser, George Kelly *physician*
Kornylak, Harold John *osteopathic physician*
McDaniel, David Henry *physician*
Onsanit, Tawachai *physician*

Williamsburg
Connell, Alastair McCrae *physician*
Davis, Richard Bradley *internal medicine, pathology educator, physician*
Dhillon, Avtar Singh *psychiatrist*
Jacoby, William Jerome, Jr. *internist, retired military officer*
Maloney, Milford Charles *retired internal medicine educator*
Schwartz, Miles Joseph *cardiologist*
Voorhess, Mary Louise *pediatric endocrinologist*

Winchester
Bechamps, Gerald Joseph *surgeon*

Woodbridge
†Soyer, Aysegul *neurologist*

Wytheville
McConnell, James Joseph *internist*

WASHINGTON

Auburn
†Anderson, Brian Lynn *urologist*
Sata, Lindbergh Saburo *psychiatrist, physician, educator*

Bellevue
Hackett, Carol Ann Hedden *physician*
Matsumoto, Shinichi *surgeon, researcher*
Phillips, Zaiga Alksnis *pediatrician*

Bellingham
Howe, Warren Billings *physician*
Wayne, Marvin Alan *emergency medicine physician*

Bremerton
Genuit, David Walter *podiatrist*

Camas
Liem, Annie *pediatrician*

Centralia
Miller, James McCalmont *pediatrician*

Chehalis
Neal-Parker, Shirley Anita *obstetrician and gynecologist*

Clyde Hill
Condon, Robert Edward *surgeon, educator, consultant*

Colville
Higginbotham, Edith Arleane *radiologist, researcher*

Edmonds
Crone, Richard Allan *cardiologist, educator*
Kim, Sang U. *gastroenterologist*
Yoon, Jay Myoung *oncologist, hematologist, internist*

Everett
Beegle, Earl Dennis *family physician*
Valentine, Mark Conrad *dermatologist*

Federal Way
Dorman, Thomas Alfred *internist, orthopaedist*

Fircrest
Martin, Robert Joseph *dermatologist*

Fort Lewis
Maher, Cornelius Creedon, III *neurologist, toxicologist, army officer*

Gig Harbor
McGill, Charles Morris *physician, consultant*

Issaquah
Barchet, Stephen *physician, former naval officer*

Kent
†Brannen, George Elsdon *surgeon*
O'Bara, Kenneth J. *physician*

Kirkland
Barto, Deborah Ann *physician*
Dunn, Jeffrey Edward *neurologist*

Longview
Kirkpatrick, Richard Alan *internist*
Sandstrom, Robert Edward *physician, pathologist*

Mazama
Hogness, John Rusten *physician, academic administrator*

Mercer Island
Coe, Robert Campbell *retired surgeon*
Elgee, Neil Johnson *retired internist and endocrinologist, educator*

Olympia
Hayes, Maxine Delores *physician*
†Milham, Samuel *epidemiologist*
Wales, Bryan Douglas *anesthesiologist*
†Yung, Edward Vance *retired preventive medicine physician*

Point Roberts
†Hepworth, Richard Gordon *surgeon, writer*

Port Ludlow
Ward, Louis Emmerson *retired physician*

Puyallup
Salzman, Keith Lawrence *family practice physician, military officer*

Redmond
Beeson, Paul Bruce *physician*
Ransdell, Tod Elliot *pharmaceutical, parenteral and in vitro diagnostics validation specialist*

Richland
Bair, William J. *radiation biologist*
Yang, I-Yen *internist, acupuncturist*
Zirkle, Lewis Greer *physician, executive*

Seattle
†Aigner, B. Robert *neurologist*
Ansell, Julian S. *physician, retired urology educator*
Beavo, Joseph A. *pharmacology professor*
Benirschke, Stephen Kurt *orthopedic surgeon*
Bezruchka, Stephen Anthony *emergency physician, writer*
Bierman, Charles Warren *physician, educator*
Bornstein, Paul *physician, biochemist*
Bowden, Douglas McHose *neuropsychiatric scientist, educator, research center administrator*
Boyko, Edward John *internist, medical researcher*
Brockenbrough, Edwin Chamberlayne *surgeon*
Bush, Mark Robert *physician*
Cardenas, Diana Delia *physician, educator*
Catterall, William A. *pharmacology, neurobiology educator*
Couser, William Griffith *medical educator, academic administrator, nephrologist*
Cullen, Bruce F. *anesthesiologist*
Dale, David C. *physician, medical educator*
Dawson, Patricia Lucille *surgeon*
Day, Robert Winsor *cancer researcher*
Dunner, David Louis *medicine educator*
Eschbach, Joseph Wetherill *nephrology educator*
Figley, Melvin Morgan *radiologist, physician, educator*
Fine, James Stephen *physician*
Freeny, Patrick Clinton *radiology educator, consultant*
Gabbe, Steven Glenn *physician, educator*
Geyman, John Payne *physician, educator*
Giblett, Eloise Rosalie *hematology educator*
†Glass, Stephen Tolman *pediatric neurologist*
Grayston, J. Thomas *medical and public health educator*
Greene, Martin Lee *internist*
Guntheroth, Warren Gaden *physician*
Hackett, John Peter *dermatologist*
Han, Mao-Tang *surgeon, researcher*
Hargiss, James Leonard *ophthalmologist*
†Helgerson, Steven Dale *epidemiologist, educator*
Henderson, Maureen McGrath *medical educator*
Holm, Vanja Adele *developmental pediatrician, educator*
Holmes, King Kennard *medical educator*
Hornbein, Thomas Frederic *anesthesiologist*
†Hsiang, John *neurosurgeon*
Hudson, Leonard Dean *physician*
Jonsen, Albert R. *retired medical ethics educator*
Kahn, Steven Emanuel *medical educator*
Kalina, Robert Edward *physician, educator*
King, Mary-Claire *geneticist, educator*
Klebanoff, Seymour Joseph *medical educator*
Kraft, George Howard *physician, educator*
Krohn, Kenneth Albert *radiology educator*
Mankoff, David Abraham *nuclear medicine physician*
Martin, George M. *pathologist, gerontologist, educator*
Matsen, Frederick Albert, III *orthopedic educator*
Merendino, K. Alvin *surgical educator*
Mohai, Peter *internist, rheumatologist, research administrator*
Moore, Daniel Charles *physician*
Mottet, Norman Karle *pathologist, educator*
Nelson, James Alonzo *radiologist, educator*
Orcutt, James Craig *ophthalmologist*
Petersdorf, Robert George *physician, medical educator*
Phillips, William Robert *physician*
Plorde, James Joseph *physician, educator*
Ramsey, Paul Glenn *internist*
Ravenholt, Reimert Thorolf *epidemiologist*
†Rho, Jong Min *physician, educator*
Rosenblatt, Roger Alan *physician, educator*
Ross, Russell *pathologist, educator*
Sale, George Edgar *physician*
Schilling, John Albert *surgeon*
Schimmelbusch, Werner Helmut *psychiatrist*
Scribner, Belding Hibbard *medical educator, nephrologist*
Shepard, Thomas Hill *physician, educator*
Simkin, Peter Anthony *physician, educator*
Stenchever, Morton Albert *physician, educator*
Stolov, Walter Charles *physician, rehabilitation educator, physiatrist*
Strahilevitz, Meir *inventor, researcher, psychiatry educator*
Strandjord, Paul Edphil *physician, educator*
Strandness, Donald Eugene, Jr. *surgeon*
Swanson, August George *physician, retired association executive*
Swanson, Phillip Dean *neurologist*
Tapper, David *pediatric surgeon*
Thomas, Edward Donnall *physician, researcher*
Todaro, George Joseph *pathologist*
Tucker, Gary Jay *physician, educator*
Van Citters, Robert Lee *medical educator, physician*
Weiss, Noel S. *epidemiologist*
Wilske, Kenneth Ray *internist, rheumatologist, researcher*
Winn, H. Richard *surgeon*
Yee, Kuo Chiang *neuroscientist, neurologist*
Yue, Agnes Kau-Wah *otolaryngologist*

Silverdale
Walcott, William Oliver *family practice physician*

Spokane
Bakker, Cornelis B. *psychiatrist, educator*
Cohen, Arnold Norman *gastroenterologist*
Genung, Sharon Rose *pediatrician*
Lee, Hi Young *physician, acupuncturist*
McClellan, David Lawrence *physician*
Schlicke, Carl Paul *retired surgeon*

Tacoma
†Collins, George J., Jr. *surgeon*
Nazaire, Michel Harry *physician*

Tracyton
Pliskow, Vita Sari *anesthesiologist*

University Place
Flemming, Stanley Lalit Kumar *family practice physician, mayor, state legislator*

Vashon
†Vallarta, Josefina M. *retired child neurologist*

Walla Walla
Johnson, Robert Arnold *physician, cardiologist, poet*

Wenatchee
Knecht, Ben Harrold *surgeon*
Sorom, Terry Allen *ophthalmic surgeon*

Yakima
Newstead, Robert Richard *urologist*
Wolf, John Arthur, Jr. *urologist*

WEST VIRGINIA

Beckley
Dinh, Anthony Tung *internist*

Bluefield
†Pujari, Bhasker Rao *physician*

Charleston
Heck, Albert Frank *neurologist*
Ukoha, Ozuru Ochu *surgeon, educator*

Clarksburg
Ona-Sarino, Milagros Felix *physician, pathologist*
Sarino, Edgardo Formantes *physician*

Fairmont
Goodwin, Andrew Wirt, II *radiologist*

Huntington
Bateman, Mildred Mitchell *psychiatrist*
Cocke, William Marvin, Jr. *plastic surgeon, educator*
Edwards, Roy Alvin *physician, psychiatrist, educator*
Leppla, David Charles *pathology educator*
†Molina, Rafael Evencio *urologist*
Morabito, Rocco Anthony *urologist*
Mufson, Maurice Albert *physician, educator*

Kingwood
Moyers, Sylvia Dean *retired medical record librarian*

Lewisburg
Hooper, Anne Dodge *pathologist, educator*
Mazzio-Moore, Joan L. *radiology educator, physician*
Willard, Ralph Lawrence *surgery educator, physician, former college president*

Martinsburg
Malin, Howard Gerald *podiatrist*

Morgantown
Bergstein, Jack Marshall *surgeon*
Ducatman, Alan Marc *physician*
Fleming, William Wright, Jr. *pharmacology educator*
Hill, Ronald Charles *surgeon, educator*
Iammarino, Richard Michael *pathologist, student support services director*
Mansmann, Paris Taylor *medical educator*
Martin, James Douglas *neurologist*
Poland, Alan Paul *oncology educator*
Sikora, Rosanna Dawn *emergency physician, educator*
Warden, Herbert Edgar *surgeon, educator*

Ranson
Rudacille, Sharon Victoria *medical technologist*

WISCONSIN

Appleton
Boren, Clark Henry, Jr. *general and vascular surgeon*
Luther, Thomas William *retired physician*

Boulder Junction
†Russell, John Robert *neurosurgeon*

Brookfield
Hardman, Harold Francis *pharmacology educator*
Kortebein, Stuart Rowland *orthopedic surgeon*
Scheving, Lawrence Einar *anatomy educator, scientist*

Fond Du Lac
Lambert, Eugene Kent *oncologist, hematologist*
Stein, Michael Alan *cardiologist, medical educator*
Treffert, Darold Allen *psychiatrist, author, hospital director*

Green Bay
†Baek, Paul *neurological surgeon*
Finesilver, Alan George *rheumatologist*
Sehring, Frederick George *obstetrician/gynecologist*
Taillon, James Howard *orthotist*
von Heimburg, Roger Lyle *surgeon*

Hales Corners
Kuwayama, S. Paul *physician, allergist, immunologist*

Hartford
Babbitt, Donald Patrick *radiologist*

Janesville
†Fuiks, Kimball Sands *neurosurgeon*
Gianitsos, Anestis Nicholas *surgeon*

La Crosse
Corser, David Hewson *pediatrician, retired*
Lindesmith, Larry Alan *physician, administrator*
Silva, Paul Douglas *reproductive endocrinologist*
Smith, Martin Jay *physician, biomedical research scientist*
Webster, Stephen Burtis *physician, educator*

Lake Geneva
Liebman, Monte Harris *retired psychiatrist*
Petersen, Edward Schmidt *retired physician*

Madison
Albert, Daniel Myron *ophthalmologist, educator*
Atkinson, Richard Lee, Jr. *internal medicine educator*
Bass, Paul *pharmacology educator*
Bloodworth, J(ames) M(organ) Bartow, Jr. *physician, educator*
Boutwell, Roswell Knight *oncology educator*
Brown, Arnold Lanehart, Jr. *pathologist, educator, university dean*
Budzak, Kathryn Sue (Mrs. Arthur Budzak) *physician*
Burgess, Richard Ray *oncology educator, molecular biology researcher, biotechnology consultant*
Carbone, Paul Peter *oncologist, educator, administrator*
Cohen, Marcus *allergist, immunologist*
Dodson, Vernon Nathan *physician, educator*
Fahien, Leonard August *physician, educator*
Ford, Charles Nathaniel *otolaryngologist, educator*
Forster, Francis Michael *physician, educator*
Graziano, Frank Michael *medical educator, researcher*
Guillery, Rainer Walter *anatomy educator*
Harkness, Donald Richard *retired hematologist, educator*
Javid, Manucher J. *retired neurosurgery educator*
Jefferson, James Walter *psychiatry educator*
Kepecs, Joseph Goodman *physician, educator*
Kindig, David A. *medical educator*
Laessig, Ronald Harold *preventive medicine and pathology educator, state official*
Leavitt, Lewis A. *pediatrician, medical educator*
Lemanske, Robert F., Jr. *allergist, immunologist*
MacKinney, Archie Allen, Jr. *physician*
Maki, Dennis G. *medical educator, researcher, clinician*
Malter, James Samuel *pathologist, educator*
Marton, Laurence Jay *clinical pathologist, educator, researcher*
McBeath, Andrew Alan *orthopedic surgery educator*
Miller, James Alexander *oncologist, educator*
Myers, Franklin Lewis, II *ophthalmologist*
Niederhuber, John Edward *surgical oncologist and molecular immunologist, university educator and administrator*
Onsager, David Ralph *cardiothoracic surgeon, educator*
Peters, Henry Augustus *neuropsychiatrist*
Pitot, Henry Clement, III *physician, educator*
Potter, Van Rensselaer *cancer researcher, author*
Reynolds, Ernest West *retired physician, educator*
Robins, H(enry) Ian *medical oncologist*
Rowe, George Giles *cardiologist, educator*
Schutta, Henry Szczesny *neurologist, educator*
Smith, Morton Edward *ophthalmology educator, dean*
Sobkowicz, Hanna Maria *neurology researcher*
Sondel, Paul Mark *pediatric oncologist, educator*
Sonnedecker, Glenn Allen *pharmaceutical historian, pharmaceutical educator*
Tomar, Russell Herman *pathologist, educator, researcher*
Valdivia, Hector Horacio *medical educator*
Wenger, Ronald David *surgeon*
Westman, Jack Conrad *child psychiatrist, educator*
Whiffen, James Douglass *surgeon, educator*
Wilson, Pamela Aird *physician*
Zografi, George *pharmacologist, educator*

Manitowoc
Trader, Joseph Edgar *orthopedic surgeon*

Marshfield
Fye, W. Bruce, III *cardiologist*
Stueland, Dean Theodore *emergency physician*

Middleton
Lobeck, Charles Champlin, Jr. *pediatrics educator*

Milwaukee
Adamson, John William *hematologist*
Alexander, Janice Hoehner *physician, educator*
Atlee, John Light *physician*
Carballo, Fernando Anthony *gastroenterologist, hepatologist*
Chan, Carlyle Hung-lun *psychiatrist, educator*
Cooper, Richard Alan *hematologist, college dean, health policy analyst*
†Deacon, John Stanley Raymond *physician*
Esterly, Nancy Burton *physician*
Gonnering, Russell Stephen *ophthalmic plastic surgeon*
Hosenpud, Jeffrey *cardiovascular physician*
Hur, Su-Ryong *physician, anesthesiologist*
Kampine, John P. *anesthesiologist*
Kirby, Russell Stephen *epidemiologist, statistician, geographer*
Kloehn, Ralph Anthony *plastic surgeon*
Kochar, Mahendr Singh *physician, educator, administrator, scientist, writer, consultant*
Krausen, Anthony Sharnik *surgeon*
Larson, David Lee *surgeon*
Miller, Edward Carl William *physician*
Pisciotta, Anthony Vito *physician, educator*
Schultz, Richard Otto *ophthalmologist, educator*
Shetty, Kaup Rajmohan *endocrinologist, educator*
Shindell, Sidney *medical educator, physician*
Siegesmund, Kenneth August *retired forensic, scientist, anatomist, consultant, and educator*
Soergel, Konrad Hermann *physician*
Stokes, Kathleen Sarah *dermatologist*
Taylor, Robert *oncologist*
Terry, Leon Cass *neurologist, educator*
Towne, Jonathan Baker *vascular surgeon*
Tweddell, James Scott *surgeon*
Wagner, Marvin *general and vascular surgeon, educator*
Youker, James Edward *radiologist*

Minocqua
Van Howe, Robert Storms *pediatrician*

Monroe
Kindschi, George William *pathologist*

Oak Creek
Kim, Zaezeung *allergist, immunologist, educator*

Onalaska
Waite, Lawrence Wesley *osteopathic physician*

Oshkosh
Cooper, Janelle Lunette *neurologist, educator*
†Siepmann, James Patrick *family practice physician*

Racine
†Phillips, Robert Derrick *psychiatrist*
Stewart, Richard Donald *internist, educator*

Sheboygan
Gore, Donald Ray *orthopedic surgeon*

Tomah
Due, James M. *pharmacist*
Odiet, Fred Michael *family practice physician assistant*

Wauwatosa
Hollister, Winston Ned *pathologist*

Woodruff
Agre, James Courtland *physical medicine and rehabilitation educator*

WYOMING

Buffalo
Watkins, Eugene Leonard *surgeon, educator*

Centennial
Nord, Thomas Allison *healthcare consultant*

Gillette
Naramore, James Joseph *family practice physician, educator*

Laramie
Kelley, Robert Otis *medical science educator*

TERRITORIES OF THE UNITED STATES

GUAM

Agana
Espaldon, Ernesto Mercader *former senator, plastic surgeon*

PUERTO RICO

Mayaguez
Sahai, Hardeo *medical statistics educator*

Ponce
Cummings, Luis Emilio *anesthesiologist, consultant*

San Juan
Bonilla-Felix, Melvin A. *pediatrician, educator*
Ghaly, Evone Shehata *pharmaceutics and industrial pharmacy educator*
Rodriguez, Agustin Antonio *surgeon*
Rodriguez Arroyo, Jesus *gynecologic oncologist*
Rosario-Guardiola, Reinaldo *dermatologist*

VIRGIN ISLANDS

Saint Thomas
Mattsson, Ake *psychiatrist, physician*

MILITARY ADDRESSES OF THE UNITED STATES

EUROPE

APO
Scriggins, Alan Lee *developmental pediatrician*

CANADA

Hamilton
Collins, John Alfred *obstetrician-gynecologist, educator*

Winnipeg
†Barwinsky, Jaroslaw *cardiac surgeon*

ALBERTA

Calgary
Lederis, Karolis Paul (Karl Lederis) *pharmacologist, educator, researcher*
Melvill-Jones, Geoffrey *physician, educator*
Rewcastle, Neill Barry *neuropathology educator*
Smith, Eldon *cardiologist, physiology and biophysics educator*
Stell, William Kenyon *neuroscientist, educator*

Edmonton
Cook, David Alastair *pharmacology educator*
Miller, Jack David R. *radiologist, physician, educator*

BRITISH COLUMBIA

Vancouver
Baird, Patricia Ann *physician, educator*
Bates, David Vincent *physician, medical educator*
Chow, Anthony Wei-Chik *physician*
Doyle, Patrick John *otolaryngologist*
Eaves, Allen Charles Edward *hematologist, medical agency administrator*
Friedman, Sydney M. *anatomy educator, medical researcher*
Hardwick, David Francis *pathologist*
Knobloch, Ferdinand J. *psychiatrist, educator*
McGeer, Edith Graef *neurological science educator emerita*
Mizgala, Henry F. *physician, consultant, retired medical educator*
Paty, Donald Winston *neurologist*
Rootman, Jack *ophthalmologist, surgeon, pathologist, oncologist, artist*
Roy, Chunilal *psychiatrist*
Slonecker, Charles Edward *anatomist, medical educator, author*
Sutter, Morley Carman *medical scientist*
Tingle, Aubrey James *pediatric immunologist, research administrator*
Tyers, Geddes Frank Owen *surgeon*

Victoria
Mac Diarmid, William Donald *physician*

MANITOBA

Winnipeg
Angel, Aubie *physician, academic administrator*
Haworth, James Chilton *pediatrics educator*
Israels, Lyonel Garry *hematologist, medical educator*
Naimark, Arnold *medical educator, physiologist, educator*
Persaud, Trivedi Vidhya Nandan *anatomy educator, researcher, consultant*
Ronald, Allan Ross *internal medicine and medical microbiology educator, researcher*
Ross, Robert Thomas *neurologist, educator*
Schacter, Brent Allan *oncologist, health facility administrator*

NOVA SCOTIA

Halifax
Casson, Alan Graham *thoracic surgeon, researcher*
Gold, Judith Hammerling *psychiatrist*
Goldbloom, Richard Ballon *pediatrics educator*
Langley, George Ross *medical educator*
Stewart, Ronald Daniel *medical educator, government official*
Tonks, Robert Stanley *pharmacology and therapeutics educator, former university dean*

ONTARIO

Greely
Smith, Stuart Lyon *psychiatrist, corporate executive*

Hamilton
Basmajian, John Varoujan *medical scientist, educator, physician*
Bienenstock, John *physician, educator*
Mueller, Charles Barber *surgeon, educator*
Roland, Charles Gordon *physician, medical historian, educator*
Uchida, Irene Ayako *cytogenetics educator, researcher*

Kingston
Kaufman, Nathan *pathology educator, physician*
Low, James A. *physician*

London
Buck, Carol Kathleen *medical educator*
Carruthers, S. George *medical educator, physician*
Lala, Peeyush Kanti *medical scientist, educator*
Marotta, Joseph Thomas *medical educator*
McWhinney, Ian Renwick *physician, medical educator*

North York
Regan, David *brain researcher, psychology and biology educator*
Turnbull, John Cameron *pharmacist, consultant*

Ottawa
de Bold, Adolfo J. *pathology and physiology educator, research scientist*
Hagen, Paul Beo *physician, medical scientist*
Hurteau, Gilles David *retired obstetrician, gynecologist, educator, dean*
Jackson, W. Bruce *ophthalmology educator, researcher*
Lavoie, Lionel A. *physician, medical executive*
Losos, Joseph Zbigniew *epidemiologist*

Toronto
Alberti, Peter William *otolaryngologist*
Brown, Gregory Michael *psychiatrist, educator, researcher*
Bruce, William Robert *physician, educator*
Carlen, Peter Louis *neuroscientist educator, science administrator*
Cinader, Bernhard *immunologist, gerontologist, scientist, educator*
Eisenberg, Howard Edward *physician, psychotherapist, educator, consultant, author*
Hudson, Alan Roy *neurosurgeon, medical educator, hospital administrator*
Kalant, Harold *pharmacology educator, physician*
Kalow, Werner *pharmacologist, toxicologist*
Lindsay, William Kerr *surgeon*
Mc Culloch, Ernest Armstrong *physician, educator*
Miller, Anthony Bernard *physician, medical researcher*
Ogilvie, Richard Ian *clinical pharmacologist*
Page, Linda Jewel *mental health care educator*
Rakoff, Vivian Morris *psychiatrist, writer*
Silverman, Melvin *medical research administrator*
Sole, Michael Joseph *cardiologist*
Till, James Edgar *medical educator, researcher*
Turner, Robert Edward *psychiatrist, educator*
Volpé, Robert *endocrinologist, researcher, educator*
Wadenberg, Marie-Louise Gertrud *psychopharmacologist, researcher*

Windsor
Ferguson, John Duncan *medical researcher*

QUEBEC

Beauport
Parent, André *neurobiology educator, researcher*

Montpellier
Poirier, Louis Joseph *neurology educator*

Montreal
Aguayo, Albert Juan *neuroscientist*
Baxter, Donald William *physician, educator, retired*
Beardmore, Harvey Ernest *retired physician, educator*
Becklake, Margaret Rigsby *physician, educator*
Burgess, John Herbert *physician, educator*
Clermont, Yves Wilfrid *anatomy educator, researcher*
Cruess, Richard Leigh *surgeon, university dean*
Cuello, Augusto Claudio Guillermo *medical research scientist, author*
Feindel, William Howard *neurosurgeon, consultant*
Freeman, Carolyn Ruth *radiation oncologist*
Genest, Jacques *physician, researcher, administrator*
Gold, Phil *immunologist, educator, researcher*
Goltzman, David *endocrinologist, educator, researcher*
Jasmin, Gaetan *pathologist, retired educator*
Karpati, George *neurologist, neuroscientist*
Kramer, Michael Stuart *pediatric epidemiologist*
Leblond, Charles Philippe *anatomy educator, researcher*
MacDonald, R(onald Angus) Neil *physician, educator*
Mac Lean, Lloyd Douglas *surgeon*
McGregor, Maurice *cardiologist, medical educator*
Milic-Emili, Joseph *physician, educator*
Moore, Sean *pathologist, educator*
Mulder, David S. *cardiovascular surgeon*
Nadeau, Reginald Antoine *medical educator*
Nattel, Stanley *cardiologist, research scientist*
Osmond, Dennis Gordon *medical educator, researcher*
Pelletier, Louis Conrad *surgeon, educator*
†Snell, Linda S. *physician, medical educator*

Quebec
Couture, Jean G. *retired surgeon, educator*
Labrie, Fernand *physician, researcher*

Sainte Foy
Dussault, Jean H. *endocrinologist, medical educator*

Sherbrooke
Bureau, Michel André *pediatrician, pulmonologist*

Verdun
Gauthier, Serge Gaston *neurologist*

SASKATCHEWAN

Saskatoon
Houston, C(larence) Stuart *radiologist, educator*

ARGENTINA

Buenos Aires
Bergel, Meny *physician, researcher*

AUSTRALIA

Melbourne
Metcalf, Donald *biomedical researcher*

Nedlands
Oxnard, Charles Ernest *anatomist, anthropologist, human biologist, educator*

Parkville
Denton, Derek Ashworth *medical researcher, foundation administrator*

Subiaco Perth
Newnham, John Phillipps *obstetrician*

CHINA

Shanghai
Ng, Lorenz K. *neurologist, educator*

ENGLAND

Cambridge
Acheson, Roy Malcolm *epidemiologist, educator*
Detmer, Don Eugene *health management and policy researcher, medical educator, surgeon*

Hayes
Hounsfield, Godfrey Newbold *radiation scientist*

London
Nurse, Paul M. *cancer researcher*
Rutter, Michael Llewellyn *child psychiatry educator*
Vane, John Robert *pharmacologist*

Oxon
Comfort, Alexander *physician, author*

Wiltshire
Symon, Lindsay *retired neurological educator*

FINLAND

Tampere
Pöntinen, Pekka Juhani *anesthesiologist, consultant*

FRANCE

Chartres
†Benoit, Jean-Pierre Robert *pneumologist, consultant*

Neuilly Sur Seine
Hewes, Thomas Francis *physician*

Paris
Chachques, Juan Carlos *cardiac surgeon, researcher*
Dausset, Jean *immunologist*
Degos, Laurent *hematologist, educator*
Gontier, Jean Roger *medicine and physiology educator*
Levy, David Alfred *immunology educator, physician, scientist*

GERMANY

Bremen
Fahle, Manfred *ophthalmology researcher*

Halle
Schmoll, Hans Joachim *internal medicine, hematology, oncology educator*

Mannheim
Henn, Fritz Albert *psychiatrist*

Salzwedel
Nowack, Nicolas Sebastian *psychotherapist, psychiatrist*

Tübingen
Nüsslein-Volhard, Christiane *medical researcher*

Wuppertal
Schubert, Guenther Erich *pathologist*

GRENADA

Saint George's
Barrett, James Thomas *immunologist, educator*

ISRAEL

Jerusalem
Kornel, Ludwig *medical educator, physician, scientist*

ITALY

Sestri Levante
Barlascini, Cornelius Ottavio, Jr. *physician*

JAPAN

Gummaken
Okada, Ryozo *educator, clinician and researcher*

Hiyoshicho Tkorozawa
Nakamura, Hiroshi *urology educator*

Ishikawa
Mukawa, Akio *pathology educator*

Nagoya
Maeda, Kenji *medical educator*

Nishi ku
Nakagawa, Koji *endocrinologist, educator*

Okazaki
Ebashi, Setsuro *scientist, educator*

Omiya
Hozumi, Motoo *medical educator, medical researcher*

Tochigi
Hyodo, Haruo *radiologist, educator*

Tokyo
Akera, Tai *pharmacologist*
Sakuta, Manabu *neurologist, educator*
Terao, Toshio *physician, educator*
Yagyu, Kuniyoshi *surgeon*

Yokohama
Kaneko, Yoshihiro *cardiologist, researcher*

KOREA

Seoul
Kim, Geun-Eun *surgeon, educator*

MALAYSIA

Kuala Lumpur
Chee, Chee Pin *neurosurgeon, consultant*
Looi, Lai-Meng *pathology educator*

THE NETHERLANDS

Groningen
Gips, Christiaan Hendrik *medical educator*

Leiden
Banta, Henry David *physician, researcher*

Maastricht
Van Praag, Herman Meir *psychiatrist, educator*

NIGERIA

Sagamu
†Adetoro, Olalekan Olayiwola *obstetrician, gynecologist, educator*

PANAMA

Panama
Fletcher Arancibia, Pablo Enrique *internal medicine endocrinology physician, educator*

PORTUGAL

Coimbra
dos Reis, Luciano Sérgio Lemos *surgeon*

REPUBLIC OF KOREA

Kuri
Kim, Kwang-Iel *psychiatrist, educator*

Seoul
Surh, Young-Joon *medical educator*

Taegu
Park, Soong-Kook *internist, researcher*

SCOTLAND

Dundee
Black, Sir James (Whyte) *pharmacologist*

SINGAPORE

Singapore
Ho, Yik Hong *colon and rectal surgeon*

SOUTH AFRICA

Capetown
Benatar, Solomon Robert *internist*

SWEDEN

Göteborg
Carlsson, Per Arvid Emil *pharmacologist, educator*
Norrby, Klas Carl Vilhelm *pathology educator*

Uppsala
Ahlstedt, N. Staffan *immunologist*

SWITZERLAND

Arzier
Wilson, Ronald Gene *physician*

Bern
Reuter, Harald *pharmacologist*

Busingen
Friede, Reinhard L. *neuropathologist, educator*

Geneva
Henderson, Ralph Hale *physician*
Piot, Peter *United Nations official, public health official*

Zurich
†Siegenthaler, Walter Ernst *internal medicine educator*
Zinkernagel, Rolf Martin *immunology educator*

TAIWAN

Taipei
Ho, Low-Tone *physician, researcher, educator*

WEST INDIES

Grenada
†Taylor, Keith Breden *physician, educator*

ADDRESS UNPUBLISHED

Abell, Murray Richardson *retired medical association administrator*
Ablin, Richard Joel *immunologist, educator*
Adams, James Thomas *surgeon*
Adkisson, Gregory Hugh *anesthesiologist*
†Ajax, Ernest Theodore *neurology educator*
Aldrich, Franklin Dalton *research physician*
Alexander, Jonathan *cardiologist, consultant*
Allinson, Carl *radiologist*
Allums, James A. *retired cardiovascular surgeon*
Altekruse, Joan Morrissey *retired preventive medicine educator*
Altman, Adele Rosenhain *radiologist*
Altshuler, Kenneth Z. *psychiatrist*
Anderson, Carolyn Harvey *retired pediatrician*
Angel, Armando Carlos *rheumatologist, internist*
Angelov, George Angel *pediatrician, anatomist, teratologist*
†Appel, Robert A. *urologist*
Appenzeller, Otto *neurologist, researcher*
Arat, Metin *retired psychiatrist*
Arnaud, Claude Donald, Jr. *physician, educator*
Bahr, Sheila Kay *physician*
Baird, William David *retired anesthesiologist*
Baldwin, DeWitt Clair, Jr. *physician, educator*
Ball, John Robert *healthcare executive*
Baney, Richard Neil *physician, internist*
Bardin, Clyde Wayne *biomedical researcher*
Barlow, John Sutton *neurophysiologist, electroencephalographer, lexicographer*
Barner, John L. *radiologist*
Barnett, Margaret Edwina *nephrologist, researcher, business consultant*
Barrickman, Les L. *psychiatrist*
Barricks, Michael Eli *retinal surgeon*
Bartlett, James Williams *psychiatrist, educator*
Beattie, Edward James *surgeon, educator*
Becker, Bruce Carl, II *physician, educator*
Belanger, Luc *oncologist*
Benjamin, Georges Curtis *emergency physician, consultant*
Bercel, Nicholas Anthony *neurologist, neurophysiologist*
Berg, Alfred Oren *epidemiology and famiy practice medicine educator*
Bergin, Colleen Joan *medical educator*
Berglund, Robin G. *child psychiatrist, former corporate executive*
Bergquist, Sandra Lee *medical and legal consultant, nurse*
†Berkowitz, Robert *psychiatrist*
†Bernbeck, Volkert Joachim *retired plastic surgeon*
†Bhargava, Dinesh *plastic and reconstructive surgeon*
Bick, Katherine Livingstone *scientist, international liaison, consultant*
Bird, Harrie Waldo, Jr. *psychiatrist, educator*
Blatt, Philip Mark *hematologist, educator*
Blazina, Janice Fay *transfusion medicine physician*
†Boczko, Stanley *urologist*
Boddie, Lewis Franklin *obstetrics and gynecology educator*
Bolliger, Eugene Frederick *retired surgeon*
Bonn, Ethel May *psychiatrist, educator*
†Bonner, William P. *physician*
Bonnet, John David *physician, medical facility administrator*
Bowie, E(dward) J(ohn) Walter *hematologist, researcher*
Brackett, Tracy Ann *science journalist, consultant*
Brent, Robert Leonard *radiology and pediatrics educator*
†Brewer, Keith F. *plastic surgeon*
Brohammer, Richard Frederic *psychiatrist*
Brown, Eli Matthew *anesthesiologist*
†Brown, Henry *surgeon*
Browne, Thomas Reed *neurologist, researcher, educator*
Brunt, Harry Herman, Jr. *psychiatrist*
Bubrick, Melvin Phillip *surgeon*
†Budnick, Lawrence David *physician, medical educator*
Budoff, Penny Wise *physician, author, researcher*
Buenaventura, Milagros Paez *psychiatrist*
Burch, Robert Emmett *retired physician, educator*
Burger, Leslie Morton *physician, army officer*
Bussey, George Davis *psychiatrist*
Bussman, John Wood *physician, health care administrator*
Bynes, Frank Howard, Jr. *physician*
Calvert, William Preston *radiologist*
Camm, Gertrude Elizabeth *physician, writer*
Carpenter, Anne Betts *pathologist, physician, immunologist*
Carrison, Dale Mitchell *emergency medicine physician*
†Casa, Douglas James *sports medicine educator*
Caston, J(esse) Douglas *medical educator*
Cawood, Charles David *urologist*
Chafkin, Rita M. *physician, dermatologist*
Chaikof, Elliot Lorne *vascular surgeon*
†Chang, David Woosuk *medical educator*
Chassin, Mark R. *health policy educator*
Chen, Stephen Shau-tsi *retired psychiatrist, physiologist*
Cherenzia, Bradley James *radiologist*
Chernoff, Amoz Immanuel *hematologist, consultant*
Chiu, William Chien-Chen *surgeon*
Chow, John Lap Hong *physician, biomedical engineer*
Christenson, William Newcome *retired physician*
Christman, Robert Alan *podiatric radiologist*
Cimino, James Ernest *physician*
Cioczek, Henryk Antoni *medical oncologist, internist*
Clark, Jeffrey Ray *surgeon*
Clayton, Bruce David *pharmacology educator*
Cleaver, James Edward *radiologist, educator*
Clemendor, Anthony Arnold *obstetrician, gynecologist, educator*
Clemetson, Charles Alan Blake *physician*
Clifford, Maurice Cecil *physician, former college president, foundation executive*
Cline, Carolyn Joan *plastic and reconstructive surgeon*
Colburn, Harold Lewis *dermatologist, state legislator*
Collins, Allen Howard *psychiatrist*
Colonnier, Marc Leopold *neuroanatomist, educator*
Conant, Steven George *psychiatrist*
†Concannon, Matthew Jerome *plastic surgeon*
Connelly, Margery Annette *research pathologist, educator*
Conrad-England, Roberta Lee *pathologist*
Convery, Fredrick Richard *retired surgeon, orthopedist*
Conway, Gene Farris *cardiologist*
Coppolecchia, Rosa *internist*
Cortes, Dennis Alfredo *internist*
Cotsonas, Nicholas John, Jr. *physician, medical educator*
†Covington, Faith Henrietta *health educator*
Covintree, George E. *retired physician*
Cox, John Michael *cardiologist*
Cozen, Lewis *orthopedic surgeon*
Crabtree, Gerald R. *pathology and biology educator*
Cronkite, Eugene Pitcher *physician, retired*
Cross, Brian Gregory *internist*
Cross, Harold Dick *physician*
Cross, Robert Lawrence *retired surgeon*
Cuetter, Albert Cayetano *neurologist*
Dailey, Thomas Hammond *retired surgeon*
Dane, Steven Howard *neurologist, educator*
Danilowicz, Delores Ann *pediatric cardiologist, pediatrics educator*
Davidson, Mayer B. *medical educator, researcher*
†DeConti, Robert W. *plastic surgeon*
DeFlorio, Mary Lucy *physician, psychiatrist*
Degann, Sona Irene *obstetrician-gynecologist, educator*
De Laney, Allen Young *retired surgeon*
de la Piedra, Jorge *orthopedic surgeon*
†Dellaportas, George *physician, medical facility administrator*
†Dennis, Rodney L. *physician*
DePalma, Ralph George *surgeon, educator*
DeVita, Vincent Theodore, Jr. *oncologist*
Dewhurst, William George *psychiatrist, educator, research director*
de Zoeten, Gustaaf Adolf *plant pathologist*
Dickes, Robert *psychiatrist*
Dickson, James Francis, III *surgeon*
Diehl, Louis F. *hematologist*
Diener, Erwin *immunologist*
†Divon, Michael Y. *obstetrician and gynecologist*
Dmochowski, Jan Rafal *surgeon, researcher*
Doane, Woolson Whitney *internist*
Dockery, J. Lee *retired medical school administrator*
Dracker, Robert Albert *physician*
Draper, Edgar *psychiatrist*
Duarte, Cristobal G. *nephrologist, educator*
Duffy, Brian Francis *immunologist, educator*
Dumont, Allan Eliot *retired physician, educator*
Durant, John Ridgeway *physician*
Durell, Jack *psychiatrist*
Eastman, Wilfred W. *retired surgeon*
Eaton, Merrill Thomas *psychiatrist, educator*
Edwards, Charles *neuroscientist, educator*
Edwards, Larry David *internist*
Eisenberg, Mickey Stewart *municipal medical services director*
Eisenstat, Theodore Ellis *colon and rectal surgeon, educator*
Eisinger, Robert Peter *nephrologist, educator*
El-Mahdi, Anas Morsi *retired radiation oncologist*
†Emery, Frank (Michael) *plastic surgeon*
Engel-Arieli, Susan Lee *physician*
Engle, Howard A. *retired pediatrician*
Enna, Salvatore Joseph *research pharmacologist, pharmaceutical company executive*
Etzwiler, Donnell Dencil *pediatrician*
†Evarts, Charles McCollister *orthopaedic surgeon*
Fanos, Kathleen Hilaire *osteopathic physician, podiatrist*
Faris, James Vannoy *cardiology educator, hospital executive*
Fariss, Bruce Lindsay *endocrinologist, educator*
Felgar, Raymond E(ugene) *pathologist, medical educator*
Ferguson, Earl Wilson *cardiologist, physiologist, medical executive*
Ferguson, Emmet Fewell, Jr. *surgeon*
†Fermanis, Ernest George *urologic surgeon*
Ferstenfeld, Julian Erwin *internist, educator*
Fischer, A(lbert) Alan *family physician*
Fisher, Herbert Calvin *retired surgeon*
Fisher, Linda Alice *physician*
Fisher, Richard H. *retired orthopaedic surgeon*
Fishman, Glenn I. *medical educator*
Fishman, Marc Judah *physician, researcher*
Flanigan, Robert Charles *urologist, educator*
Fomon, Samuel Joseph *physician, educator*
Fox, William Richard *retired physician*
Fredrickson, Donald Sharp *physician, scientist*
Friedman, Eugene Warren *surgeon*
Frost, J. Ormond *otolaryngologist, educator*
†Furlow, Thomas William, Jr. *neurologist*
Galbraith, William Bruce *physician, educator*
Gangarosa, Raymond Eugene *epidemiologist, engineer*
Garcia, Alexander *orthopedic surgeon*
Gardner, John Howland, III *neurologist*
Gardner, Lee Robbins *psychiatrist*
Garell, Paul Charles *family practice physician*
Gartner, Lawrence Mitchel *pediatrician, medical college educator*
Gathright, John Byron, Jr. *colon and rectal surgeon, educator*
Gelpi, Armand Philippe *internist*
Gemell, Nicholas I. *retired radiologist*
Gerard, Gary *neurologist*
Gill, Thomas James, III *physician, educator*
Giordano, James Joseph *neuroscientist, aeromedical engineer, educator*
Glasauer, Franz Ernst *neurosurgeon*
Glass, Dorothea Daniels *physiatrist, educator*
Gleaton, Harriet E. *retired anesthesiologist*
Glenn, Jules *psychiatrist*
Goffman, Thomas Edward *radiation oncologist, researcher*
Goldberg, Mark Arthur *neurologist*
Goldstein, Naomi *psychiatrist*
Gordan, Gilbert Saul *physician, educator*
Gordon, Ann Marie *pharmacist*
Goss, J.B. *psychopharmacologist*
Gottfried, Eugene Leslie *physician, educator*
Graham, James Herbert *dermatologist*
Greene, Barnett Alan *anesthesiologist*
Greene, Laurence Whitridge, Jr. *surgical educator*
Griffin, John Henry *medical researcher*
Griffith, B(ezaleel) Herold *physician, educator, plastic surgeon*
Grimes, Hugh Gavin *physician*
Gross, Ruth Taubenhaus *physician*
Groves, Sheridon Hale *orthopedic surgeon*
Gusdon, John Paul, Jr. *obstetrics and gynecology educator, physician*
Guyer, Bernard *maternal and child health educator*
Haft, Gail Klein *pediatrician*
Haggerty, Robert Johns *physician, educator*
Halbert, Ronald Joel *preventive medicine physician, educator*
Halliday, William Ross *retired physician, speleologist, writer*
Hansell, John Royer *retired physician*
Hanson, David Gordon *otolaryngologist, surgeon*
Hardman, Joel Griffeth *pharmacologist*
Harris, Burton H. *surgeon*
Harris, Elaine K. *medical consultant*
Harris, Pamela Sue *rehabilitation physician*
Hartman, James Theodore *physician, educator*
Harvey, Birt *retired pediatrician, educator*
†Hastaacca, Alfredo Xavier *medical researcher*
Hathaway, David Roger *physician, medical educator, scientist*
Hayes, George J. *retired neurosurgeon*
Head, Henry Buchen *physician*
Hecht, Harold Arthur *orchidologist, chiropractor*
Heiman, Deborah Reid *medical and legal consultant, rehabilitation consultant*

Heimburger, Irvin LeRoy *retired surgeon*
Henderson, Melford J. *epidemiologist, molecular biologist, chemist*
Hendricks, Leonard D. *emergency medicine physician, consultant*
Hennessey, William Joseph *physician*
Heptinstall, Robert Hodgson *physician*
Herman, Chester Joseph *physician*
Herman, Martin Neal *neurologist, educator*
Himes, John Harter *medical researcher, educator*
Hirose, Teruo Terry *surgeon, educator*
Hirsch, Bruce Elliot *anatomy educator*
†Hirsch, Stuart *orthopaedic surgeon*
Hoch, Frederic Louis *medical educator*
Hoeprich, Paul Daniel *physician educator*
Holland, Robert Campbell *anatomist, educator*
Holoubek, Joe *physician*
Hood, William Boyd, Jr. *cardiologist, educator*
Hooper, Billy Ernest *retired medical association administrator*
Hoskins, John Howard *urologist, educator*
Howell, Joel DuBose *physician, educator*
Huber, Douglas Crawford *pathologist*
Huggins, Charles Edward *obstetrician-gynecologist, educator*
Hunt, William Edward *neurosurgeon, educator*
Huntley, Robert Ross *physician, educator*
Hurd, Suzanne Sheldon *federal agency health science director*
Inui, Thomas Spencer *physician, educator*
Irizarry, Michael Carl *neurologist, neuroscientist, educator*
Irwin, Peter John *orthopaedic surgeon*
Izenstark, Joseph Louis *radiologist, physician, educator*
Jackman, Jay M. *psychiatrist*
Jackson, Carmault Benjamin, Jr. *physician*
Jackson, Rudolph Ellsworth *pediatrician, educator*
Janowitz, Henry David *gastroenterologist, researcher, medical educator*
Jefferies, William McKendree *internist, educator*
Jenkins, James William *osteopath, medical consultant*
Jensen, Robert Travis *physician, educator, researcher*
Johnson, Leonard Morris *pediatric surgeon*
Johnson, Theodore *retired physician*
Jones, Billy Ernest *dermatology educator*
Jones, Walton Linton *internist, former government official*
†Joyce, Stephen Thomas *occupational and preventive medicine physician*
Kamenar, Elizabeth *neurologist, neuropathologist*
Karam, Naji E. *cardiologist*
Karpilow, Craig *physician*
Karpinos, Robert Douglas *anesthesiologist*
†Karwacki, Jerome John *physician*
Kashani, Javad Hassan-Nejad *physician*
Kellerman, Jonathan Seth *pediatric psychologist, writer*
Kelly, Douglas Elliott *retired biomedical researcher, association administrator*
Kendall, Harry Ovid *internist*
†Kennedy, Charles *retired medical educator*
Kent, Howard Lees *obstetrician, gynecologist*
Kern, Donald Michael *internist*
Kettelkamp, Donald Benjamin *retired surgeon and educator*
Khachadurian, Avedis *physician*
Khan, Arfa *radiologist, educator*
Kiang, Barbara Norris *scientific research assistant*
Kiefer, Helen Chilton *neurologist, psychiatrist*
†Klindt, Joyce Ann *plastic surgeon*
Klitzman, Robert Lloyd *physician, author*
Klombers, Norman *retired podiatrist, association executive*
Kogut, Maurice David *pediatric endocrinologist*
Kolansky, Harold *physician, psychiatrist, psychoanalyst*
Kough, Robert Hamilton *retired clinical hematologist, consultant*
Krentzman, Ben Z. *family physician*
Krippaehne, Marion Larsen *medicine educator*
Kundel, Harold Louis *radiologist, educator*
Kurk, Mitchell *physician*
Kyger, Edgar Ross *surgeon, educator*
Landau, Judith *psychiatrist*
Langfitt, Thomas William *neurosurgeon, foundation administrator*
Larson, Richard Smith *pathologist, researcher*
†Latov, Norman *neurologist, educator*
Lauterbach, Edward Charles *psychiatric educator*
Leis, Henry Patrick, Jr. *surgeon, educator*
†Leivy, David Mayer *neurosurgeon*
Leslie, Gerrie Allen *immunologist*
LeVay, Simon *neuroscientist, writer, educator*
Levien, David Harold *surgeon*
Lewis, Ceylon Smith, Jr. *physician, educator*
Lipkin, David Lawrence *physician*
Lipton, Judith Eve *psychiatrist*
Little, Brian W. *pathology educator, administrator*
Livezey, Mark Douglas *physician*
Lobdell, Kevin Wallace *cardiothoracic surgeon*
LoIudice, Thomas Anthony *gastroenterologist, researcher*
Long, Charles William *child and adolescent psychiatrist*
†Lopez-Cuenca, Victor *emergency medicine physician*
Loube, Samuel Dennis *physician*
Lovy, Andrew *osteopathic physician, psychiatrist*
Lutz, Lawrence Joseph *family practice physician*
Maas, Anthony Ernst *pathologist*
†Macmillan, Carol *neurologist*
Madlang, Rodolfo Mojica *retired urologic surgeon*
Mair, Douglas Dean *medical educator, consultant*
Makowski, Edgar Leonard *obstetrician and gynecologist*
Malach, Monte *physician*
Malis, Leonard Irving *neurosurgeon*
Malkinson, Frederick David *dermatologist*
Malloy, Craig Riggs *physician, educator*
Manning, John Joseph *retired physician, healthcare administrator*
Margolis, Harold Stephen *epidemiologist*
Mark, Saralyn *endocrinologist*
Markovic, Nenad S. *internist, hematologist, oncologist, educator*
Marks, James Frederic *pediatric endocrinologist, educator*
Marshall, John Crook *internal medicine educator, researcher*
Martino, Silvana *osteopath, medical oncologist*
Materson, Richard Stephen *physician, educator*
Mattson, Richard Henry *neurologist, educator*
May, Robert M. *retired obstetrician, gynecologist, educator*
Mayerson, Peter *psychiatrist, educator*
Mazzetti, Robert F. *real estate manager, retired orthopedic surgeon*
McCartney, James Robert *psychiatrist*
McCormack, Marjorie Guth *psychology educator, career counselor, communications educator, public relations consultant*
McCormick, Kenneth L. *pediatrics educator, researcher*
McCullough, David L. *urologist*
McDonagh, Thomas Joseph *physician*
McEwen, Bruce S. *neuroendocrinology educator*
McGuire, Hunter Holmes, Jr. *surgeon, educator*
McLeskey, Charles Hamilton *anesthesiology educator*
Mead, Beverley Tupper *physician, educator*
Meilman, Edward *physician*
Mendels, Joseph *psychiatrist, educator*
Mendez, C. Beatriz *obstetrician, gynecologist, educator*
Messamore, Andrew Karl *anesthesiologist, pharmacist*
Meyer, George Wilbur *internist, health facility administrator*
Meyer, Greg Charles *psychiatrist*
Michelsen, W(olfgang) Jost *neurosurgeon, educator, retired*
Miller, Ross Hays *retired neurosurgeon*
†Miller, Stuart Henry *radiologist, inventor*
Millikan, Clark Harold *physician*
Molson, Robert Henry *obstetrician, gynecologist*
Monninger, Robert Harold George *ophthalmologist, educator*
Moore, Emily Allyn *pharmacologist*
Moos, Daniel James *retired surgeon, educator*
Moossy, John *neuropathologist, neurologist, consultant*
Morgan, Elizabeth *plastic and reconstructive surgeon*
Motto, Jerome Arthur *psychiatry educator*
Mountain, Clifton Fletcher *surgeon, educator*
Munger, Bryce Leon *physician, educator*
†Murphy, M(ichael) John *neurologist, educator*
Murray, James D. *physician*
Myerowitz, P. David *cardiologist, cardiac surgeon*
Nabrit, Samuel Milton *retired embryologist*
Needleman, Philip *cardiologist, pharmacologist*
Nicholas, Peter *medical educator*
Norman, Matthew West *psychiatrist*
Nostrant, Timothy Thomas *internist, gastroenterologist*
Novack, Alvin John *physician*
†Nusbaum, Margaret R.H. *physician*
Oates, Joyce Marie *psychiatrist*
Olds, Jacqueline *psychiatrist, educator*
O'Leary, Denis Joseph *retired physician, insurance company executive*
O'Leary, Dennis Sophian *medical organization executive*
Ornston, Darius Gray, Jr. *psychiatrist*
Osment, Lamar Sutton *retired dermatologist, educator*
Overcash, Shelia Ann *nurse*
Packard, John Mallory *physician*
Padberg, Frank Thomas, Jr. *surgeon, educator*
Painter, Robert Lowell *surgeon, educator*
Palmer, Raymond Alfred *administrator, librarian, consultant*
†Pantzer, John G. *retired physician*
Pardue, A. Michael *retired plastic and reconstructive surgeon*
Parker, Brent Mershon *retired medical educator, internist, cardiologist*
Parker, Gerald William *physician, medical administrator, retired*
Parrish, Matthew Denwood *psychiatrist*
Parsa, Brian Bahram *surgeon, military officer*
Parsons, Harry Glenwood *retired surgeon*
Paskawicz, Jeanne Frances *pain specialist*
Pastorek, Norman Joseph *facial plastic surgeon*
Paul, Frank Allen *physician*
Pauly, John Edward *anatomist*
Payne, Douglas DeFrees *cardiothoracic surgeon, educator*
Peete, William Pettway Jones *surgeon*
Peixoto, Jose Ulysses *internist, researcher*
Pelz, Herman H. *physician*
Pennardt, Andre M. *emergency physician*
Perez-Borja, Carlos M. *neurologist, hospital executive*
Perlman, Morton Henry *retired surgeon and educator*
Pesola, Gene Raymond *physician, educator*
Peters, Kurt James *retired obstetrician, gynecologist*
Peterson, Ann Sullivan *physician, health care consultant*
Pick, Anthony J. *physician, educator*
Pick, Robert Yehuda *orthopedic surgeon, consultant*
Pickens, Samuel C. *family physician, educator*
Pirro, Alfred Anthony, Jr. *physician*
Pomeroy, Kent Lytle *physical medicine and rehabilitation physician*
Porter, Herbert M. *retired pediatrician*
Potts, Douglas Gordon *retired neuroradiologist*
Powell, Clinton Cobb *radiologist, physician, former university administrator*
Prange, Hilmar Walter *neurology educator*
Price, Fredric Victor *physician*
Prusiner, Stanley Ben *neurology and biochemistry educator, researcher*
Quetglas, Moll Juan *plastic and maxillofacial surgeon*
Rachkova, Mariana Ilieva *physician, researcher*
Ragucci, John Albert *family practice physician*
Raichle, Marcus Edward *radiology, neurology educator*
Ram, Chitta Venkata *physician*
Ramirez-Rivera, Jose *physician*
Ramos, Eleanor Lacson *transplant nephrologist*
Randolph, Judson Graves *pediatric surgeon*
Redlich, Fredrick Carl (Fritz) *psychiatrist, educator*
Reich, Harvey S. *critical care physician*
Reynolds, Pamela Preston *physician, historian*
Richmond, Julius Benjamin *retired physician, health policy educator emeritus*
Riehle, Robert Arthur, Jr. *medical director, surgeon*
Riker, Walter F., Jr. *pharmacologist, physician*
Riker, William Kay *pharmacologist, educator*
Rimpila, Charles Robert *physician*
Rinaldi, Renee Zaira *physician*
Robbins, Frederick Chapman *retired physician, medical school dean emeritus*
Roberts, Alan Silverman *orthopedic surgeon*
Roberts, Albert Dee *internist*
Roberts, (Ruth) Eleanor Sterett *osteopathic physician*
Robinson, David Adair *neurophysiologist*
Robson, Martin Cecil *surgery educator, plastic surgeon*
Rodgers, Lawrence Rodney *physician, educator*
Roehrig, C(harles) Burns *internist, health policy consultant, editor*
Rollins, Arlen Jeffery *osteopathic physician*
Rosemberg, Eugenia *physician, educator, medical research administrator*
Rosen, Paul Peter *pathologist*
Rosenberg, Leon Emanuel *medical educator, geneticist, university dean*
Rosenblum, Mindy Fleischer *pediatrician*
Rossavik, Ivar Kristian *obstetrician, gynecologist*
Rubnitz, Myron Ethan *pathologist, educator*
Rui, Hallgeir *cancer researcher*
Ruoho, Arnold Eino *pharmacology educator*
Russo, Jose *pathologist*
Ruzicka, Francis F., Jr. *radiologist*
Sacerdote, Alan Scott *endocrinologist*
Sacha, Robert Frank *osteopathic physician*
Sackellares, James Chris *neurology educator*
St. Cyr, John Albert, II *cardiovascular and thoracic surgeon*
†Saltzman, Brian *physician, surgeon, educator*
†Sampson, Christian Edward *surgeon, educator*
Sanchez, Rafael Camilo *physician*
Sandt, John Joseph *psychiatrist, educator*
Sanfelippo, Peter Michael *cardiac, thoracic and vascular surgeon*
Saravolatz, Louis Donald *epidemiologist, physician educator*
Sargent, William Winston *retired anesthesiologist*
Sawlani, Tulsi C. *radiologist*
Scardino, Peter T. *urology educator*
Schecter, William Palmer *surgeon*
Schell, Catherine Louise *family practice physician*
Scheuerman, Eleanor Joyce Miller *medical association administrator*
Schneck, Stuart Austin *retired neurologist, educator*
Schneider, Eleonora Frey *retired physician*
Sessions, Roger Carl *emergency physician*
Sever, John Louis *medical researcher and educator*
Sewell, Robert Dalton *pediatrician*
†Shanklin, Kenneth Dale *plastic and reconstructive surgeon*
Shaw, Ronald Ahrend *physician, educator*
Sher, Paul Phillip *physician, pathologist*
Sherman, John Foord *biomedical consultant*
Sherman, Joseph Owen *pediatric surgeon*
†Sherman, Sterling Scott *surgeon, career officer*
Shils, Maurice Edward *physician, scientist, educator*
Shumacker, Harris B., Jr. *surgeon, educator, author*
Shuster, Frederick *retired internist*
Siegel, Wilma Bulkin *oncologist, educator, artist*
Sifontes, Jose E. *pediatrics educator*
Silberberg, Inga *dermatologist*
Silva, Omega Logan *physician*
Silver, Malcolm David *pathologist, educator*
Silverstein, Martin Elliot *surgeon, author, consultant*
Simmons, Geoffrey Stuart *physician*
Skinner, Shari L. *dermatologist*
Skolnick, Lawrence *neonatologist, medical administrator*
Slavit, David Hal *otolaryngologist*
Smith, John Wallace *surgeon, educator*
Smith, Jonathan David *medical educator*
Smith, Martin Henry *pediatrician*
Smith, Martin Lane *biomedical researcher*
Smith, Ronald Edward *ophthalmologist*
Smith, Vestal Beecher, Sr. *physician*
Smyth, Nicholas Patrick D. *surgeon*
Soltero-Harrington, Luis Rubén *surgeon, educator*
Soyke, Jennifer Mae *emergency and family physician*
Spackman, Thomas James *radiologist*
Spencer, Richard Glenn Stevens *physician, nuclear magnetic resonance spectroscopist*
Sperry, Len Thomas *psychiatry and preventive medicine educator*
Sprague, Charles Cameron *medical foundation president*
Steele, Clarence Hart *retired otolaryngologist*
Stein, Bennett Mueller *neurosurgeon*
Steiner, Michael Louis *pediatrician*
Stickler, Gunnar Brynolf *pediatrician*
Stoken, Jacqueline Marie *physician*
Stollerman, Gene Howard *physician, educator*
Stonnington, Henry Herbert *physician, medical executive, educator*
Strain, James Ellsworth *pediatrician, retired association administrator*
Stringham, Renée *physician*
Strongin, Jonathan David *physician*
Sullivan, Colleen Anne *physician, educator*
Sung, James Pang-Chieh *surgeon*
Svensson, Lars Georg *cardiovascular and thoracic surgeon*
Tagiuri, Consuelo Keller *child psychiatrist, educator*
Tan, Veronica Y. *psychiatrist*
Tanner, Anita Louise *physician assistant*
Taren, James Arthur *neurosurgeon, educator*
Terris, Susan *physician, cardiologist*
Thompson, Joseph Warren *osteopathic physician*
Thorsen, Marie Kristin *radiologist, educator*
Threefoot, Sam Abraham *physician, educator*
Towers, Bernard Leonard *medical educator*
Tranquada, Robert Ernest *medical educator, physician*
Troost, Bradley Todd *neurologist, educator*
Tropez-Sims, Susanne *pediatrician, educator*
Tsay, Ching Sow *anesthesiologist*
Turk, Richard Errington *retired psychiatrist*
Turner, H(arry) Spencer *preventive medicine physician, educator*
Turrill, Fred Lovejoy *surgeon*
Tyler, Carl Walter, Jr. *physician, health research administrator, retired*
Unger, Albert Howard *allergist, immunologist*
Unger, Roger Harold *physician, scientist*
Vachher, Prehlad Singh *psychiatrist*
Valentine, William Newton *physician, educator*
Van Brunt, Edmund Ewing *physician*
†Vitolo, Robert V. *plastic and reconstructive surgeon*
Vore, Mary Edith *pharmacology educator, researcher*
Walenga, Jeanine Marie *medical educator, researcher*
†Wallman, Lester Julian *retired medical educator*
Walrath, Daniel Laurens *physician*
Ware, James Latané *plastic surgeon*
Ware, John E. *psychiatry educator, medical laboratory executive*
Wawrose, Frederick Eugene *psychiatrist*
Weil, Inga Frenkel *psychiatrist*
Weinberg, Sidney R. *physician*
Weiner, Gershon Ralph *physician*
Weiner, Harold M. *retired radiologist*
†Weintraub, William H. *pediatric surgeon, educator*
Weiss, Robert M. *urologist, educator*
Weissmann, Heidi Seitelblum *radiologist, educator*
Wenzel, Richard Putnam *internist*
Wescoe, W(illiam) Clarke *physician*
Wessel, Morris Arthur *retired pediatrics educator*
West, Gregory Alan *physician*
Westmoreland, Barbara Fenn *neurologist, electroencephalographer, educator*
White, Augustus Aaron, III *orthopedic surgeon*
White, Kerr Lachlan *retired physician, foundation director*
White, Richard Thomas *radiologist*
Wiegenstein, John Gerald *physician*
Wilhelm, Morton *retired surgery educator*
Williams, George Doyne, Jr. *cardiovascular surgeon*
Williams, Robert Leon *psychiatrist, neurologist, educator*
Williams, Roger Stewart *physician*
Williams, Ronald Lee *pharmacologist*
Williams, Thomas Lloyd *psychiatrist*
Wilmore, Douglas Wayne *surgeon, educator*
Wilner, Freeman Marvin *retired hematologist, oncologist*
Wilson, Almon Chapman *surgeon, physician, retired naval officer*
Winter, Harland Steven *pediatric gastroenterologist*
Witkowski, Joseph Albin *dermatologist*
Wolfe, Frances Diane *medical secretary, artist*
Wolfgang, Gary L. *orthopaedic surgeon*
†Woodwork, Bruce E. *physician, urologist*
Wyer, Peter Charles *emergency physician*
Wyngaarden, James Barnes *physician*
Yamane, George Mitsuyoshi *oral medicine and radiology educator*
Yarington, Charles Thomas, Jr. *surgeon, administrator*
Yee, Henry Chan Myint *cardiologist*
Yielding, K. Lemone *physician*
Yodaiken, Ralph E. *pathologist, occupational medicine physician*
Yollick, Bernard Lawrence *otolaryngologic surgeon*
Yoshimoto, Tetsuyuki *neurosurgeon*
Youmans, Julian Ray *neurosurgeon, educator*
†Young, Mary Eming *physician*
†Zacarias, Fernando Raul Kahlil *physician*
Zacks, Sumner Irwin *pathologist*
†Zeidan, Hissam Issa A. *family physician, air force officer, researcher*
Zimmerman, James Robert *radiologist, engineer*
Zukin, Paul *retired health research educator*
Zwislocki, Jozef John *neuroscience educator, researcher*

HUMANITIES: LIBERAL STUDIES

UNITED STATES

ALABAMA

Auburn
Amacher, Richard Earl *literature educator*
Andelson, Robert Vernon *social philosopher, educator*
Lewis, Walter David *historian*
Littleton, Taylor Dowe *humanities educator*

Birmingham
Allen, Lee Norcross *historian, educator*
Benditt, Theodore Matthew *humanities educator*
†Brouwer, Bert *art educator*
Burden, Cedric Jerome *English educator*
†Glosecki, Stephen Orin *English educator, folklorist*
Hamilton, Virginia Van der Veer *historian, educator*
Irons, George Vernon, Sr. *history educator*
Morton, Marilyn Miller *genealogy and history educator, lecturer, researcher, travel executive, director*

Brewton
†Reynolds, Harold Mark *language educator*

Decatur
Simmons, Robert Burns *history and political science educator*

Dothan
Ameter, Brenda K. *English educator*

Florence
Gartman, Max Dillon *language educator*

Huntsville
Robb, David Metheny, Jr. *art historian*
Roberts, Frances Cabaniss *history educator*
Spor, Mary W. *English educator*
White, John Charles *historian*

Jacksonville
Horton, Gloria Ann *English educator*

Loachapoka
Schafer, Elizabeth Diane *historian, writer*

Mobile
Hamner, Eugenie Lambert *English educator*
†Sauer, David Kennedy *English educator*

Montgomery
Cornett, Lloyd Harvey, Jr. *retired historian*
Futrell, Robert Frank *military historian, consultant*
Gribben, Alan *English language educator, research consultant*
Harmon, David Andrew *historian, researcher*
McIntyre, Linda Robbins *language professional/educator, English*
Napier, Cameron Mayson Freeman *historic preservationist*
†Richburg, Terri Scroggins *English educator*
Robinson, Ella Scales *language educator*
Whitt, Mary F. *reading educator, consultant*

Ramer
Napier, John Hawkins, III *historian*

Troy
McPherson, Milton Monroe *history educator*
†Mitchell, Norma Taylor *history educator*

Tuscaloosa
Bell, Robert Fred *German language educator*
Hocutt, Max Oliver *philosophy educator*
Lockett, James *history educator*

Marvin, Roberta Montemorra *musicologist*
McDonald, Forrest *historian, educator*
Mills, Elizabeth Shown *genealogist editor, writer*
Mills, Gary Bernard *history educator*
Nadine, Claudia *French educator*
†Ruiz-Fornells, Enrique *history educator*
†Williford, Lex A. *educator*

ALASKA

Anchorage
Crawford, Ronald Merritt *history and geography educator*
†Crosman, Robert True *English language educator*

Fairbanks
Falk, Marvin William *historian, bibliographer*
Krauss, Michael Edward *linguist*

Gakona
†Ainsworth, Cynthea Lee *folklorist*

Juneau
Ruotsala, James Alfred *historian, writer*

Ketchikan
†Dunning, David Michael *history educator*

Sterling
Frusetta, James Walter *historian*

ARIZONA

Apache Junction
Bracken, Harry McFarland *philosophy educator*
Ransom, Evelyn Naill *language educator, linguist*

Davis Monthan A F B
Miller, Charles Wallace *historian, environmental geologist*

Glendale
Galletti, Marie Ann *English language and linguistics educator*
Tuman, Walter Vladimir *Russian language educator, researcher*

Green Valley
Brewington, Arthur William *retired English language educator*
Dmytryshyn, Basil *historian, educator*

Holbrook
†O'Hop, Suzanne Elizabeth *educator*

Mesa
Hiatt, Holly Marlane *history educator*

Phoenix
Cristiano, Marilyn Jean *speech communication educator*
Kupel, Douglas Edward *historian*
Land, George A. *philosopher, writer, educator, consultant*
Maimon, Elaine Plaskow *English educator, university provost*
Rister, Gene Arnold *humanities educator*

Prescott
Brown, James Isaac *rhetoric educator*
Moses, Elbert Raymond, Jr. *speech and dramatic arts educator*

Scottsdale
Bonner, Thomas Neville *history and higher education educator*
Donaldson, Scott *English language educator, writer*
Mousseux, Renate *language educator*

Sun City
Oppenheimer, Max, Jr. *foreign language educator, consultant*

Surprise
Clark, Lloyd *historian, educator*

Tempe
Adelson, Roger Dean *history educator, editor, historian*
Bjork, Robert Eric *language professional educator*
Brack, O. M., Jr. *English language educator*
†Chambers, Anthony Hook *Literature educator*
Doebler, Bettie Anne *language educator, researcher, writer*
†Gruzinska, Aleksandra *language educator*
Harris, Mark *English educator, author*
Iverson, Peter James *historian, educator*
MacKinnon, Stephen R. *Asian studies administrator, educator*
Ruiz, Vicki Lynn *history educator*
†Taylor, Nora Annesley *humanities educator, art historian*

Tucson
Austin, John Norman *classics educator*
†Briggs, Laura *humanities*
†Canfield, John Douglas *English educator, writer, consultant*
†Chalmers, David J. *philosophy educator*
Dahood, Roger *English literature educator*
Dinnerstein, Leonard *historian, educator*
Dufner, Max *retired German language educator*
Furlow, Mary Beverley *English language educator*
Herrnstadt, Richard Lawrence *American literature educator*
Hogle, Jerrold Edwin *English language educator*
†Kiefer, Frederick P. *English educator*
Langendoen, Donald Terence *linguistics educator*
Negley, Floyd Rollin *genealogist, retired army officer and civilian military employee*
†Penner, Jonathan David *English educator, writer*
Rabuck, Donna Fontanarose *English writing educator*

ARKANSAS

Arkadelphia
Bass, Carol Ann (Mitzi Bass) *English language educator*
Halaby, Raouf Jamil *English and art educator, consultant*

Bella Vista
Fite, Gilbert Courtland *historian, educator, retired*

Conway
†Knipscheer, Carol S. *English language educator*

Fayetteville
Gatewood, Willard Badgett, Jr. *historian*
Levine, Daniel Blank *classical studies educator*
†Restrepo, Luis Fernando *Latin-American literature educator*

Hot Springs National Park
Hutchison, Donna McAnulty *humanities educator*

Jonesboro
Elkins, Francis Clark *history educator, university official*

Little Rock
Ferguson, John Lewis *state historian*

Magnolia
Davis, Elizabeth Hawk *English language educator*

Monticello
Babin, Claude Hunter *history educator*

Mountain Home
Easley, June Ellen Price *genealogist*

Russellville
†Jenkins, Ellen Janet (Jan Jenkins) *historian, history educator*

State University
Schichler, Robert Lawrence *English language educator*

Van Buren
Bradberry, Karen Lynn *English educator*

CALIFORNIA

Arcadia
Yen, Wen-Hsiung *language and music professional educator*

Arroyo Grande
Nay, Joan McNeilly *retired English educator, university administrator*

Atherton
Bales, Royal Eugene *philosophy educator*

Bakersfield
Boyd, William Harland *historian*
Kegley, Jacquelyn Ann *philosophy educator*
Peterson, Pamela Carmelle *English language educator*
Schmidt, Joanne (Josephine Anne Schmidt) *language educator*

Berkeley
Alter, Robert B. *comparative literature educator and critic*
Anderson, William Scovil *classics educator*
Baas, Jacquelynn *art historian, museum administrator*
Bloom, Robert *language professional educator*
Bronstein, Arthur J. *linguistics educator*
Costa, Gustavo *Italian language educator*
Crews, Frederick Campbell *humanities educator, writer*
Davidson, Donald Herbert *philosophy educator*
Herr, Richard *history educator*
Karlinsky, Simon *language educator, author*
Kay, Paul de Young *linguist*
Kerman, Joseph Wilfred *musicologist, critic*
Landauer, Elvie Ann Whitney *humanities educator, writer*
Lichterman, Martin *history educator*
Litwack, Leon Frank *historian, educator*
Long, Anthony Arthur *classics educator*
Mace, Susan Lidgate *comparative literature educator, researcher*
Middlekauff, Robert Lawrence *history educator, administrator*
Muscatine, Charles *English educator, author*
Rauch, Irmengard *linguist, educator*
†Rex, Walter Edwin, III *humanities educator*
Selz, Peter Howard *art historian, educator*
Sloane, Thomas O. *speech educator*
Tracy, Robert (Edward) *English language educator, poetry translator*
Wakeman, Frederic Evans, Jr. *historian educator*
Wang, William Shi-Yuan *linguistics educator*
Wilson, W(illiam) Daniel *language professional educator*
Zwerdling, Alex *English educator*

Beverly Hills
Kravitz, Ellen King *musicologist, educator*
Novak, Maximillian Erwin *English language educator*

Cambria
Salaverria, Helena Clara *educator*

Carmel
Chung, Kyung Cho *Korean specialist, scholar, educator, author*

Chico
Moore, Brooke Noel *philosophy educator*

Claremont
Ackerman, Gerald Martin *art historian, consultant*
Atlas, Jay David *philosopher, consultant, linguist*
Barnes, Richard Gordon *English literature educator, poet*
Burns, Richard Dean *history educator, publisher, author*
†Chávez-Silverman, Suzanne *Latin American studies educator*
Davis, Nathaniel *humanities educator*
Fossum, Robert H(eyerdahl) *retired English literature educator*
Goodrich, Norma Lorre (Mrs. John H. Howard) *French and comparative literature educator*
Lofgren, Charles Augustin *legal and constitutional historian, history educator*
Macaulay, Ronald Kerr Steven *linguistics educator, former college dean*
McKirahan, Richard Duncan, Jr. *classics and philosophy educator*
Moss, Myra Ellen (Myra Moss Rolle) *philosophy educator*
Pinney, Thomas Clive *retired English language educator*
Roth, John King *philosopher, educator*
Sontag, Frederick Earl *philosophy educator*
†Ulitin, Vladimir Gregor *retired Russian language and literature educator*
Wheeler, Geraldine Hartshorn *historian*
Woodress, James Leslie, Jr. *English language educator*
Young, Howard Thomas *foreign language educator*

Cool
Sheridan, George Groh *English and history educator*

Covina
Straw, Ellen Katrina *English educator, writer*

Culver City
Clodius, Albert Howard *history educator*

Cupertino
Tice, Bradley Scott *humanities educator*

Davis
Hayden, John Olin *English literature educator, author*
Hoffman, Michael Jerome *humanities educator*
Manoliu, Maria *linguist, educator*
Rothstein, Morton *historian, retired educator*
Tinney, Thomas Milton, Sr. *genealogical research specialist*
Waddington, Raymond Bruce, Jr. *English language educator*
Williamson, Alan Bacher *English literature educator, poet, writer*
Willis, Frank Roy *history educator*

El Cerrito
Kuo, Ping-chia *historian, educator*

Fresno
Genini, Ronald Walter *history educator, historian*
Kouymjian, Dickran *art historian, Orientalist, educator*

Glendale
de Grassi di Santa Cristina, Leonardo *art historian, educator*

Gualala
Gaustad, Edwin Scott *historian*

Happy Camp
†Jefferson, Peggy Lee *English educator*

Irvine
Clark, Michael Phillip *English educator*
Fukui, Naoki *theoretical linguist*
Hine, Robert Van Norden, Jr. *historian, educator*
Hufbauer, Karl George *historian of science*
Key, Mary Ritchie (Mrs. Audley E. Patton) *linguist, author, educator*
Kluger, Ruth *German language educator, editor*
Krieger, Murray *English language educator, author*
Lillyman, William John *German language educator, academic administrator*
Maddy, Penelope Jo *philosopher*
Mc Culloch, Samuel Clyde *history educator*
Sutton, Dana Ferrin *classics educator*
Wiener, Jon *history educator*

La Jolla
Bernstein, Michael Alan *history educator, department chairman*
Langacker, Ronald Wayne *linguistics educator*
†Levinsky, Frieda Libby *language educator*
McDonald, Marianne *classicist*
Miyoshi, Masao *English literature educator, writer*
Newmark, Leonard Daniel *linguistics educator*
†Nicolaides, Becky Marianna *history educator*
Olafson, Frederick Arlan *philosophy educator*
Oreskes, Naomi *science historian*
Wesling, Donald Truman *English literature educator*
Wright, Andrew *English literature educator*

La Verne
Chu, Esther Briney *retired history educator*

Laguna Beach
Calderwood, James Lee *former English literature educator, writer*

Livermore
Hiskes, Dolores G. *educator*

Long Beach
Beebe, Sandra E. *retired English language educator, artist, writer*
†Domingo-Forasté, Douglas *classics educator*
Nguyen, Huong Tran *English language professional, federal agency official*
Schneider, Duane Bernard *English literature educator, publisher*
†Snider, Clifton Mark *English educator, writer, poet*
Yousef, Fathi Salaama *communication studies educator, management consultant*

Los Altos
Nivison, David Shepherd *Chinese and philosophy educator*

Los Angeles
Alkon, Paul Kent *English language educator*
Allen, Michael John Bridgman *English educator*
Alpers, Edward Alter *history educator*
Appleby, Joyce Oldham *historian*
Bahr, Ehrhard *Germanic languages and literature educator*
Bauml, Franz Heinrich *German language educator*
Berst, Charles Ashton *English educator*
Boime, Albert Isaac *art history educator*
Bradshaw, Murray Charles *musicologist*
Bruneau, Marie-Florine *French educator*
Burns, Robert Ignatius *historian, educator, clergyman*
†Caram, Eve La Salle *English educator, writer*
Cherkin, Adina *interpreter, translator*
†Chrzanowski, Joseph *language educator*
Cohen, S(tephen) Marshall *philosophy educator*
Cortinez, Veronica *literature educator*
Davidson, Herbert Alan *Near Eastern languages and cultures educator*
Dyck, Andrew Roy *philologist, educator*
Fromkin, Victoria Alexandra *linguist, phonetician, educator*
Fry, Michael Graham *historian, educator*
Göllner, Marie Louise *musicologist, educator*
Gómez, Ricardo Juan *philosophy educator*
†Handley, William Ross *English educator*
Hospers, John *philosophy educator*
Hovannisian, Richard G. *Armenian and Near East history educator*
†Hsu, Kylie *language educator*
Hundley, Norris Cecil, Jr. *history educator*
Jorgensen, Paul Alfred *English language educator emeritus*
Kelly, Henry Ansgar *English language educator*
Kemp, Anthony Maynard *English educator*
Kirsner, Robert Shneider *Dutch and Afrikaans educator*
Klein, Snira L(ubovsky) *Hebrew language and literature educator*
Kolve, V. A. *English literature educator*
Laird, David *humanities educator emeritus*
†Lal, Vinay *history educator*
Lehan, Richard D'Aubin *English language educator, writer*
Levine, Philip *classics educator*
†Lionnet, Francoise *educator*
Löfstedt, Bengt Torkel Magnus *classics educator*
Marc, David *American studies educator*
Mellor, Ronald John *history educator*
Miles, Richard Robert *art historian, writer*
Nakanishi, Don Toshiaki *Asian American studies educator, writer*
†Pedroarias, Ricardo Jose *Spanish educator*
Rabinovitz, Jason *film and television consultant*
Rathbun, John Wilbert *American studies educator*
Rogger, Hans Jack *history educator*
Rouse, Richard Hunter *historian, educator*
Sarris, Greg *Native American educator*
Schaefer, William David *English language educator*
Schipper, Merle *art historian and critic, exhibition curator*
Schutz, John Adolph *historian, educator, former university dean*
Schwartz, Leon *foreign language educator*
See, Carolyn *English language educator, novelist, book critic*
Sellin, Paul Roland *retired English literature educator*
†Shammas, Carole *historian, educator*
Shideler, Ross Patrick *foreign language and comparative literature educator, author, translator, poet*
Stockwell, Robert Paul *linguist, educator*
Toulmin, Stephen Edelston *humanities educator*
†Troy, Nancy J. *art history educator*
Weber, Eugen *historian, educator, author*
Wills, John Elliot, Jr. *history educator, writer*
Winterowd, Walter Ross *English educator*
Wortham, Thomas Richard *English language educator*
Wu, Qingyun *Chinese language and literature educator*

Los Gatos
Rogers, Franklin Robert *former language educator, writer*
Tinsley, Barbara Sher *historian, educator, writer*

Menlo Park
Craig, Gordon Alexander *historian, educator*

Mill Valley
†Smith, Karen Randlev *educator, writer*

Millbrae
Palmer, Patricia Ann Texter *English language educator*

Mission Viejo
Teitelbaum, Harry *English educator*

Modesto
†Sill, Anna Laura *retired language educator*

Monterey
Kennedy-Minott, Rodney *international relations educator, former ambassador*
Peet, Phyllis Irene *women's studies educator*
Shropshire, Helen Mae *retired historian*

Moorpark
Hall, Elton Arthur *philosophy educator*

Moraga
Lester, Jacob Franklin *liberal arts educator*

Newport Beach
Brown, Giles Tyler *history educator, lecturer*

Northridge
Chen, Joseph Tao *historian, educator*
Flores, William Vincent *Latin American studies educator*
†Hall, Donald E. *English educator*
Watson, Julia *women's studies and liberal studies educator*

Oak Park
Connolly, Thomas Edmund *educator*

Oakland
Mayers, Eugene David *philosopher, educator*
†Serin, Judith Ann *English educator*

Orange
Yeager, Myron Dean *English language educator, business writing consultant*

Pacific Palisades
Garwood, Victor Paul *retired speech communication educator*
Georges, Robert Augustus *emeritus professor, researcher, writer*
Nash, Gary Baring *historian, educator*

Palo Alto
Eitner, Lorenz Edwin Alfred *art historian, educator*
Mommsen, Katharina *retired German language and literature educator*
Walker, Carolyn Peyton *English language educator*

Palos Verdes Estates
Sun, Teresa Chi-Ching *foreign languages and literature educator*

Pasadena
Elliot, David Clephan *historian, educator*
Fay, Peter Ward *history educator*
†Gerber, Merrill Joan *writing educator*
Kevles, Daniel Jerome *history educator, writer*
Kousser, J(oseph) Morgan *history educator*
Mandel, Oscar *literature educator, writer*

Petaluma
†Knight, Arthur Winfield *English educator*

Piedmont
Putter, Irving *French language educator*

Placerville
Nesbitt, Paul Edward *historian, author, educator*

Pleasant Hill
Ashby, Denise Stewart *speech educator, communication consultant*

Rancho Cordova
Darlington, Ronald Lawrence *English language educator*

Rancho Santa Fe
Ruiz, Ramon Eduardo *history educator*

Redlands
†McAllister, Bruce Hugh *writer and educator*
Stuart, Robert Lee *English language educator*

Rialto
Walker, Jeanne Claire *retired English educator, writer*

Riverside
Cavers-Huff, Dasiea Yvonne *philosopher*
Decker, Catherine Helen *English language educator*
Elliott, Emory Bernard *English language educator, educational adminstrator*
Fagundo, Ana Maria *creative writing and Spanish literature educator*
†Kronenfeld, Judy Zahler *humanities educator, writer*
Ross, Delmer Gerrard *historian, educator*
Snyder, Henry Leonard *history educator, bibliographer*

Rowland Heights
†Shear, Walter L. *retired English educator*

Sacramento
Bankowsky, Richard James *English educator*
Carr, Gerald Francis *German educator*
Schmitz, Dennis Mathew *English language educator*

San Bernardino
Ruml, Treadwell *English language educator*

San Diego
Brandes, Raymond Stewart *history educator*
Chamberlin, Eugene Keith *historian, educator*
Coox, Alvin David *history educator*
Daley, Arthur Stuart *retired humanities educator*
†Savvas, Minas *English educator*
Vanderbilt, Kermit *English language educator*
Wood, Hadley Hesse *French language educator*

San Francisco
Batchelor, Karen Lee *English language educator*
Cherny, Robert Wallace *history educator*
Costa-Zalessow, Natalia *foreign language educator*
Langton, Daniel Joseph *English, writing educator, poet*
Marmysz, John Alexander *philosophy educator, consultant*
Needleman, Jacob *philosophy educator, writer*
Satin, Joseph *language professional, university administrator*
Schlesinger, Norma Honig *art historian, writer*

San Jose
Gillett, Paula *humanities educator*
Hodgson, Peter John *music educator, composer*

San Marcos
†O'Doherty, Fergal Columba *English educator, researcher*
Rolle-Rissetto, Silvia Maria *foreign languages educator, writer, artist*
†Yuan, Yuan *English educator, translator*

San Marino
Karlstrom, Paul Johnson *art historian*
Ridge, Martin *historian, educator*
Rolle, Andrew F. *historian, educator, author*
Steadman, John Marcellus, III *English educator*
Zall, Paul Maxwell *retired English language educator, consultant*

San Mateo
Fellows, Ward Jay *philosophy educator, minister*
Petit, Susan Yount *French and English educator*

San Rafael
Eekman, Thomas Adam *Slavic languages educator*

Santa Barbara
Bliss, Lee *English language educator*
Brownlee, Wilson Elliot, Jr. *history educator*
Cathcart, Linda *art historian*
Chafe, Wallace LeSeur *linguist, educator*
Collins, Robert Oakley *history educator*
Crawford, Donald Wesley *philosophy educator, university official*
Dauer, Francis Watanabe *philosophy educator*
Delaney, Paul William *English language educator*
Del Chiaro, Mario Aldo *art historian, archeologist, etruscologist, educator*
Duffy, Andrew Enda *language educator*
†Enders, Jody *French educator*
Erickson, Robert Allen *English literature educator*
Fingarette, Herbert *philosopher, educator*
Fleming, Brice Noel *retired philosophy educator*
Gordon, Helen Heightsman *English language educator, writer, publisher*
Gunn, Giles Buckingham *English educator, religion educator*
Helgerson, Richard *English literature educator*
Hsu, Immanuel Chung Yueh *history educator*
Lim, Shirley Geok Lin *English language educator, author*
Marcuse, Harold *history educator*
McGee, James Sears *historian*
Renehan, Robert Francis Xavier *Greek and Latin educator*
Rose, Mark Allen *humanities educator*
Russell, Jeffrey Burton *historian, educator*
VanderMey, Randall John *English language educator*
Wilkins, Burleigh Taylor *philosophy educator*
Zimmerman, Everett Lee *English educator, academic administrator*

Santa Clara
Meier, Matthias S(ebastian) *historian*
Mori, Maryellen Toman *language educator, translator, literature educator*

Santa Cruz
Lieberman, Fredric *ethnomusicologist, educator*
Stevens, Stanley David *local history researcher, retired librarian*
Suckiel, Ellen Kappy *philosophy educator*

Santa Monica
†Aghabegian, Diana E. Bortnowsky *English language educator, publisher*
Heimann-Hast, Sybil Dorothea *language arts and literature educator*

Santa Rosa
Aman, Reinhold Albert *philologist, publisher*

Stanford
Baker, Keith Michael *history educator*
Carnochan, Walter Bliss *retired humanities educator*
Dekker, George Gilbert *literature educator, literary scholar, writer*
Dunlop, John Barrett *foreign language educator, research institution scholar*
Duus, Peter *history educator*
Frank, Joseph Nathaniel *comparative literature educator*
Fredrickson, George Marsh *history educator*
Gelpi, Albert Joseph *English educator, literary critic*
Giraud, Raymond Dorner *retired language professional*
Guerard, Albert Joseph *retired modern literature educator, author*
Johnson, John J. *historian, educator*
Kennedy, David Michael *historian, educator*
L'Heureux, John Clarke *English language educator*
Loftis, John (Clyde), Jr. *English language educator*
Lohnes, Walter F. W. *German language and literature educator*
Middlebrook, Diane Wood *English language educator*
Moravcsik, Julius Matthew *philosophy educator*
Newman-Gordon, Pauline *French language and literature educator*
Perloff, Marjorie Gabrielle *English and comparative literature educator*
Perry, John Richard *philosophy educator*
Robinson, Paul Arnold *historian, educator, author*
Sheehan, James John *historian, educator*
Simons, Thomas W., Jr. *history educator*
Sorrentino, Gilbert *English language educator, novelist, poet*
Spitz, Lewis William *historian, educator*
Stansky, Peter David Lyman *historian*
Steidle, Edward *humanities educator*
Traugott, Elizabeth Closs *linguistics educator and researcher*

Stockton
Limbaugh, Ronald Hadley *history educator, history center director*
Lutz, Reinhart *English language educator, writer*

Ukiah
Lohrli, Anne *retired English language educator, author*

Union City
Cobos, Josè Manuel *Spanish language educator*

Van Nuys
†Freeman, Margaret H. *English educator*
Zucker, Alfred John *English language educator, academic administrator*

Walnut
Dibell, Marta Lee *foreign language educator*

Woodland Hills
Pickard, Dean *philosophy and humanities educator*

COLORADO

Aurora
Johnson, Geraldine Esch *language specialist*

Boulder
Barchilon, Jacques *foreign language educator, researcher, writer*
Frey, Julia Bloch *French language educator*
Gonzalez-del-Valle, Luis Tomas *Spanish language educator*
Hawkins, David *philosophy and history of science, educator*
Hill, Boyd H., Jr. *medieval history educator*
†Krysl, Marilyn *English educator*
Limerick, Patricia Nelson *history educator*
Maier, Edward Karl *foreign language educator*
Main, Gloria Jean Lund *history educator*
Main, Jackson Turner *history educator*
Menn, Lise *linguistics educator*
Rood, David S. *linguistics educator*
Taylor, Allan Ross *linguist, educator*

Colorado Springs
Blackburn, Alexander Lambert *author, English literature educator*
Cramer, Owen Carver *classics educator*
Hallenbeck, Kenneth Luster *numismatist*
Stavig, Mark Luther *English language educator*
Watkins, Lois Irene *English educator*

Denver
Chapman, Gerald Wester *educator*
Espenlaub, Margo Linn *women's studies educator, artist*
Hughes, J(ohnson) Donald *history educator, editor*
Pfnister, Allan Orel *humanities educator*
Porter, Donna Jean *genealogist*
Ronning, Charlotte Jean *foreign language educator*
Storey, Brit Allan *historian*

Dolores
Kreyche, Gerald Francis *retired philosophy educator*

Englewood
Bardsley, Kay *historian, archivist, dance professional*

Erie
Dilly, Marian Jeanette *humanities educator*

Fort Collins
Berwanger, Eugene Harley *history educator*
Tremblay, William Andrew *English language educator*

Glenwood Springs
Walker, Robert Harris *historian, author, editor*

Golden
Eckley, Wilton Earl, Jr. *humanities educator*
Quirke, Terence Thomas, Jr. *genealogist, retired geologist*
Sneed, Joseph Donald *philosophy educator, author*

Grand Junction
Fay, Abbott Eastman *history educator*

Greeley
†Embry, Marcus *English educator*
Worley, Lloyd Douglas *English language educator*

Gunnison
Myers, Rex Charles *history educator, retired college dean*

Lakewood
Joy, Carla Marie *history educator*
Woodruff, Kathryn Elaine *English language educator*

Littleton
Dolan, Patrick Thomas *English educator*

Palmer Lake
Harrington, Judith Regina *English language educator*

Sterling
Christian, Roland Carl (Bud Christian) *retired English language and speech communications educator*

U S A F Academy
Newmiller, William Ernest *English educator*

CONNECTICUT

Branford
Whitaker, Thomas Russell *English literature educator*

Bridgeport
Allen, Richard Stanley (Dick Allen) *English language educator, author*

Colebrook
Mc Neill, William Hardy *retired history educator, writer*

Danbury
Edelstein, David Simeon *historian, educator*
Toland, John Willard *historian, writer*

Deep River
Hieatt, Allen Kent *language professional, educator*
Hieatt, Constance Bartlett *English language educator*

East Granby
Scanlon, Lawrence Eugene *English language educator*

Enfield
Folmsbee, Patricia Hurley *reading consultant*

Fairfield
Newton, Lisa Haenlein *philosophy educator*
†Rinaldi, Nicholas M. *educator in English language*

Falls Village
Collins, Robert G(eorge) *literature educator, writer*

Hamden
Gay, Peter *history educator, author*
McClellan, Edwin *Japanese literature educator*
Pelikan, Jaroslav Jan *history educator*
St Aubyn, Frederic Chase *French language educator*
Woodward, Comer Vann *historian*

Hampton
†Trecker, Janice Law *English educator*

Hartford
Chiarenza, Frank John *English language educator*
Decker, Robert Owen *history educator, clergyman*
†Hunter, Dianne M. *English educator*

Ivoryton
Osborne, John Walter *historian, educator, author*

Middletown
Abelove, Henry *historian, literary critic*
Arnold, Herbert Anton *German language educator*
Buel, Richard Van Wyck, Jr. *history educator, writer, editor*
Gillmor, Charles Stewart *history and science educator, researcher*
Meyer, Priscilla Ann *Russian language and literature educator*
Pomper, Philip *history educator*
Reed, Joseph Wayne *American studies educator, artist*
†Schwarcz, Vera *history educator*
Shapiro, Norman Richard *Romance languages and literatures educator*
Slotkin, Richard Sidney *American studies educator, writer*
Wensinger, Arthur Stevens *language and literature educator, author*
Winston, Krishna Ricarda *foreign language professional*

New Britain
Emeagwali, Gloria Thomas *humanities educator*
Rohinsky, Marie-Claire *modern languages educator*

New Canaan
Thacher, Barbara Auchincloss *history educator*

New Haven
Alexandrov, Vladimir Eugene *Russian literature educator*
Bartlett, Beatrice Sturgis *modern China historian, educator*
Bloom, Harold *humanities educator*
Blum, John Morton *historian*
Borroff, Marie *English language educator*
Brooks, Peter (Preston) *French and comparative literature educator, writer*
Demos, John Putnam *history educator, writer, consultant*
Dupré, Louis *retired philosopher, educator*
Dworski, Sylvia *modern languages educator*
English, Mark Edward *Latin educator*
Erlich, Victor *Slavic languages educator*
Gilbert, Creighton Eddy *art historian*
Glier, Ingeborg Johanna *German language and literature educator*
Górniak-Kocikowska, Krystyna Stefania *philosopher, educator*
Greene, Liliane *French educator, editor*
Hallo, William Wolfgang *Assyriologist*
Harries, Karsten *philosophy educator, researcher*
Hartman, Geoffrey H. *language professional, educator*
Hersey, George Leonard *art history educator, retired*
Hollander, John *humanities educator, poet*
Holmes, Frederic Lawrence *science historian*
Holquist, James Michael *Russian and comparative literature educator*
Hyman, Paula E(llen) *history educator*
Insler, Stanley *philologist, educator*
Kagan, Donald *historian, educator*
Kennedy, Paul Michael *history educator*
†Laroussi, Farid *educator*
Lord, George deForest *English educator*
Mack, Maynard *English language educator, writer*
MacMullen, Ramsay *retired history educator*
Marcus, Ruth Barcan *philosopher, educator, writer, lecturer*
Martz, Louis Lohr *English literature educator*
Palisca, Claude Victor *musicologist, educator*
Peterson, Linda H. *English language and literature educator*
†Pinzka, Lauren Cecile *french educator, literary critic*
Pollitt, Jerome Jordan *art history educator*
Prown, Jules David *art historian educator*
Rawson, Claude Julien *English educator*
Robinson, Fred Colson *English language educator*
Schenker, Alexander Marian *Slavic linguistics educator*
Smith, John Edwin *philosophy educator*
Spence, Jonathan Dermot *historian, educator*
†Targoff, Ramie *English educator*
Totman, Conrad Davis *history educator*
Turner, Frank Miller *historian, educator*
Underdown, David Edward *historian, educator*
van Altena, Alicia Mora *language educator*
Wandycz, Piotr Stefan *history educator*
Winks, Robin William *history educator*

New London
Burlingame, Michael Ashton *historian, educator*
Taranow, Gerda *English language educator, researcher, author*
Willauer, George Jacob *English literature educator*

North Haven
Culler, Arthur Dwight *English language educator*

Old Greenwich
Baritz, Loren *history educator*

Old Lyme
Pepe, Joy *art history educator*

Old Saybrook
Knobelsdorff, Kristina Louise Marie *English language educator*

Orange
†Davis, David Brion *historian, educator*

Salisbury
Kilner, Ursula Blanche *genealogist, writer*

Storrs Mansfield
Abramson, Arthur Seymour *linguistics educator, researcher*
Charters, Ann *biographer, editor, educator*
Coons, Ronald Edward *historian, educator*

Reed, Howard Alexander *historian, educator*
Rosen, William *English language educator*
Shaffer, Jerome Arthur *philosophy educator*

Washington
Leab, Daniel Joseph *history educator*

Waterbury
MacLeod, Glen Gary *English language educator*
Meyer, Judith Chandler Pugh *history educator*

West Hartford
†Collins, Alma Jones *English educator, writer*
†Jamil, S. Selina *eduator*

West Haven
Glen, Robert Allan *history educator*

Woodbridge
Ecklund, Constance Cryer *French language educator*
Kleiner, Diana Elizabeth Edelman *art history educator, administrator*

Woodstock
Susla, Jeffrey Jonathan *English language educator*

DELAWARE

Dover
Angstadt, F. V. *language arts and theatre arts educator*
Flayhart, William Henry *history educator*
Pelzer, Linda Lee *English language educator*

New Castle
Cope, Maurice Erwin *art history educator*

Newark
Bergström, Anna *foreign language educator*
Day, Robert Androus *English language educator, former library director, editor, publisher*
†Gates, Barbara T. *English literature educator*
Goodman, Susan *English language educator*
†Grossman, Jonathan Hamilton *English literature educator, researcher*
Halio, Jay Leon *language professional, educator*
Homer, William Innes *art history educator, art expert, author*
Jenkins, McKay Bradley *English language educator, journalist*
Lathrop, Thomas Albert *language educator*
Roselle, David Paul *university president, mathematics educator*
Satinoff, Evelyn *educator*
Steiner, Roger Jacob *linguistics educator, author, researcher*
Tolles, Bryant Franklin, Jr. *history and art history educator*
Venezky, Richard Lawrence *English language educator*
Walker, Jeanne Murray *English educator*
Wolters, Raymond *historian, educator*

Wilmington
Chipman, Bruce Lewis *English language educator*
Kneavel, Ann Callanan *humanities educator, communications consultant*
Lahvis, Sylvia Leistyna *art historian, educator, curator*

DISTRICT OF COLUMBIA

Bolling AFB
Hallion, Richard Paul *aerospace historian, museum consultant*

Washington
Albrecht, Kathe Hicks *art historian, visual resources manager*
†Babb, Valerie M. *English educator, writer*
Bader, William Banks *historian, foundation executive, former corporate executive*
Bedini, Silvio A. *historian, author*
Bellamy, Joe David *English language educator, writer*
†Benedict, Carol Ann *educator*
Bennett, Betty T. *English language educator, university dean, writer*
Billington, James Hadley *historian, librarian*
Bloomfield, Maxwell Herron, III *history and law educator*
Boorstin, Daniel Joseph *historian, lecturer, educator, author, editor*
Bowen, Margareta Maria *interpretation and translation educator*
†Breitman, Richard David *historian, educator, writer*
Broun, Elizabeth *art historian, museum administrator*
Cafritz, Robert Conrad *art historian, critic, consultant*
Caws, Peter James *philosopher, educator*
Cheney, Lynne V. *humanities educator, writer*
†Cima, Gay Gibson *English educator*
Craig, Peter Stebbins *historian*
Cua, Antonio S. *philosophy educator*
Curran, Robert Emmett *history educator*
DeVorkin, David Hyam *historian, curator*
Dudley, William Sheldon *historian*
†Duncan, Richard Ray *history educator*
Durfee, Harold Allen *philosophy educator*
Fain, Cheryl Ann *translator, editor*
Farr, Judith Banzer *writer, literature educator*
Fern, Alan Maxwell *art historian, museum director*
Fink, Lois Marie *art historian*
†Frost, Molly Spitzer *Chinese culture educator*
Hamarneh, Sami Khalaf *historian of pharmacy, medicine and science, author*
Heelan, Patrick Aidan *philosophy educator*
Howland, Richard Hubbard *architectural historian*
Huber, Richard Miller *American studies consultant*
Irizarry, Estelle Diane *foreign language educator, author, editor*
Kazin, Michael *history educator, writer*
Kennedy, Robert Emmet, Jr. *history educator*
Kreidler, Charles W(illiam) *linguist, educator*
Kreinheder, Hazel Fuller *genealogist, historian*
Laqueur, Walter *history educator*
Lewis, Douglas *art historian*
Lichtman, Allan Jay *historian, educator, consultant*
Lucas, George Ramsdell, Jr. *philosophy educator*
Marr, Phebe Ann *historian, educator*
Menard, Edith *English language educator, artist, poet, actress*
Miller, Jeanne-Marie Anderson (Mrs. Nathan J. Miller) *English language educator, academic administrator*
Minnich, Nelson Hubert Joseph *historian, educator*
Morse, Richard McGee *historian*
Mujica, Barbara Louise *foreign language educator, author*
Park, Alice Mary Crandall *genealogist*
†Pireddu, Nicoletta *educator in Italian and comparative literature*
Raaflaub, Kurt Arnold *classics educator*
Rand, Harry Zvi *art historian, poet*
Reed, Berenice Anne *art historian, artist, government official*
Reilly, John Marsden *English language educator*
Robb, James Willis *Romance languages educator*
Roberts, Jeanne Addison *retired literature educator*
Rosenblatt, Jason Philip *English language educator*
Ross, Bernard Harvey *humanities educator*
†Ruf, Frederick John *humanities educator*
Schlagel, Richard H. *philosophy educator*
Scott, Gary Thomas *historian*
Seagrave, Pia Seija *English language educator, editor, poet*
Severino, Roberto *foreign language educator, academic administration executive*
Sha, Richard Chih-Tung *literature educator*
Sherman, Nancy *philosophy educator*
†Sklarew, Myra *humanities educator, poet*
Smith, Bruce R. *English language educator*
Solomon, Julie Robin *language educator*
Stine, Jeffrey Kim *science historian, curator*
Taylor, Estelle Wormley *English educator, college dean*
Taylor, Henry Splawn *literature educator, poet, writer*
Thompson, Wayne Wray *historian*
Van Cleve, John Vickrey *history educator, university official*
Veatch, Robert Marlin *philosophy educator, medical ethics researcher*
Ver Eecke, Wilfried Camiel *philosopher, educator*
Voll, John Obert *history educator*
Waite, Robert George *historian, historic preservation consultant*
†Walsh, Thomas J. *Spanish language educator*
Webb, Robert Kiefer *history educator*
Weiss, Paul *philosopher, educator*
Wheelock, Arthur Kingsland, Jr. *art historian*
Winslow, Rosemary *English language educator*
Wippel, John Francis *philosophy educator*
Yochelson, Kathryn Mersey *art researcher*

FLORIDA

Beverly Hills
Larsen, Erik *art history educator*

Boca Raton
Collins, Robert Arnold *English language educator*
†Engle, Stephen Douglas *history educator*
Parker, Kim Anne *English educator*

Bradenton
Stewart, Priscilla Ann Mabie *art historian, educator*

Coral Gables
Roy, Joaquin *humanities and international affairs educator*

Davie
Speiller-Morris, Joyce *English educator*

Daytona Beach
Braim, Paul Francis *history educator, writer*
Carmona, José Antonio *Spanish language educator, English language educator*

Dunedin
Espy, Charles Clifford *English language educator, author, consultant, lecturer, administrator*

Fort Myers
Brown, Earl Kent *historian, clergyman*
Miner, Thelma Smith *retired American literature educator*

Fort Pierce
Bynum, Henri Sue *education and French educator*

Gainesville
Abbott, Thomas Benjamin *speech educator*
Brown, William Samuel, Jr. *communication sciences and disorders educator*
Der-Houssikian, Haig *linguistics educator*
†Gilbert, Pamela Katherine *literature educator*
Haring, Ellen Stone (Mrs. E. S. Haring) *philosophy educator*
†Johnston, Otto William *German language and literature educator*
Proctor, Samuel *history educator*
Schmeling, Gareth *classics educator*
Stephan, Alexander F. *German language and literature educator*
†Wyatt-Brown, Anne Marbury *linguistics educator*
Wyatt-Brown, Bertram *historian, educator*

Green Cove Springs
Norton, Joan Jennings *English language educator*

Gulf Breeze
†Twiss, Dorothy Gleason *English educator, poet*

Gulfport
Davis, Ann Caldwell *history educator*

Hernando
Cooper, Harry Edwin *historian*

Highland Beach
Stimson, Frederick Sparks *Hispanist, educator*

Hillsboro Beach
McGarry, Carmen Racine *historian, artist*

Jacksonville
Joos, Olga Martín-Ballestero de *language educator*
Short, Howard Elmo *church history educator*

Marathon
Mc Cormick, Edward Allen *foreign language educator*
Wiecha, Joseph Augustine *linguist, educator*

Melbourne
Jones, Elaine Hancock *humanities educator*

Miami
†Chung, Bongkil *Asian studies educator*
†Gray, Christopher John *history educator, human rights activist*
Mendez, Jesus *history educator, education administrator*

Naples
Siddall, Patricia Ann *retired English language educator*
Wemple Kinder, Suzanne Fonay *historian, educator*

Oldsmar
Thompson, Mack Eugene *history educator*

Orange Park
Gadapee, Brett Ronald *English language educator, coach*

Orlando
†Lopez Cruz, Humberto J. *foreign language educator*
†Moriarty, Michael Eugene *retired humanities educator*
Pauley, Bruce Frederick *history educator*
†Velez, Diana *historian, educator*

Palm Bay
Simpson, Philip Lockwood *English educator*

Panama City
†McWhorter, Susan Carol *English language educator*
Wallace, Arnold Lynn *English educator, writer*

Pensacola
Coker, William Sidney *historian, educator*
Maddock, Lawrence Hill *retired language educator*

Pomona Park
Garcia, Mary Elizabeth *Spanish and English as second language educator*

Port Charlotte
Mulligan, Louise Eleanore *retired English literature educator*

Port Saint Lucie
Wedzicha, Walter *foreign language educator*

Saint Augustine
Adams, William Roger *historian*
Keys, Leslee Frances *historic preservation planner*

Saint Petersburg
Reilly, Tracy Lynn *language professional/educator, English*
Walker, Brigitte Maria *translator, linguistic consultant*

Sanford
Wright, Stephen Caldwell *English language educator*

Sarasota
†Doenecke, Justus D. *history educator*
Ebitz, David MacKinnon *art historian, museum director*
†Ihde, Aaron John *history of science educator emeritus*
Lengyel, Alfonz *art history, archeology and museology educator*
Taplin, Winn Lowell *historian, retired senior intelligence operations officer*

Sebastian
Becker, Jim *gem historian, jeweler*

Tallahassee
Allaire, Joseph Leo *French educator*
Beck, Earl Ray *historian, educator*
Davis, Bertram Hylton *retired English educator*
Dillingham, Marjorie Carter *foreign language educator*
Dorn, Charles Meeker *art education educator*
Garretson, Peter P. *historian, educator*
Golden, Leon *classicist, educator*
Halpern, Paul G. *history educator*
Harper, George Mills *English language educator*
Hunt, Mary Alice *library science educator*
Jenks, Frederick Lynn *English educator, university program administrator*
Laird, Doris Anne Marley *humanities educator, musician*
†Moore, Dennis D. *English educator*

Tampa
Anton, John Peter *philosopher, educator*
Mitchell, Mozella Gordon *English language educator, minister*
Preto-Rodas, Richard A. *retired foreign language educator*
†Rubin, Steven J. *English studies educator, academic administrator*

Temple Terrace
DeHainaut, Raymond Kirk *international studies educator*
†Scruggs, Charles Eugene *language linguistics educator*

Winter Garden
Earls, Irene Anne *art history educator*

Winter Haven
Small, Norman Morton *speech and humanities educator, theater producer*

Winter Park
Benedict, Dorothy Jones *genealogist, researcher*
Mason, Aimee Hunnicutt Romberger *retired philosophy and humanities educator*
Seymour, Thaddeus *English educator*

GEORGIA

Albany
†Hollis, Lois B. *history and political science educator*

Americus
Bearden, Denise G(odwin) *humanities educator, secondary education educator*
Isaacs, Harold *history educator*

Andersonville
Boyles, Frederick Holdren *historian*

Athens
†Franklin, Rosemary F. *English educator*
Freer, Coburn *English language educator*
Hellerstein, Nina Salant *French literature and language educator*
Kretzschmar, William Addison, Jr. *English language educator*
Mamatey, Victor Samuel *history educator*
Miller, Ronald Baxter *English language educator, author*
Moore, Rayburn Sabatzky *American literature educator*
†Morrow, John H., Jr. *history educator*
Nute, Donald E., Jr. *philosophy educator*
Teague, Frances Nicol *English language educator*

Atlanta
Benario, Herbert William *classics educator*
Blumenthal, Anna Catherine *English educator*
Burns, Thomas Samuel *history educator*
†Eidecker, Martina Elisabeth *foreign language educator*
†Evans, Dorinda *art history educator*
Fox-Genovese, Elizabeth Ann Teresa *humanities educator*
Garrett, Franklin Miller *historian*
Garrow, David Jeffries *historian, author*
Hartle, Robert Wyman *retired foreign language and literature educator*
Kuntz, Marion Lucile Leathers *classicist, historian, educator*
Luker, Ralph Edlin *history educator*
Mafico, Temba Levi Jackson *Old Testament and Semitic languages educator, clergy*
Manley, Frank *English language educator*
Richtarik, Marilynn Josephine *English language educator*
Rojas, Carlos *Spanish literature educator*
Sitter, John Edward *English literature educator*
†Slater, Niall Ward *classics educator*
Spivey, Ted Ray *English educator*
Tuschhoff, Christian *liberal studies educator, paramedic*

Bainbridge
Chambers, Heidi Kniskern *English educator*

Carrollton
Noe, Kenneth William *historian, educator*

Dalton
Hutcheson, John Ambrose, Jr. *history educator*

Decatur
Dillingham, William Byron *literature educator, author*
Major, James Russell Richards *historian, educator*
Young, James Harvey *historian, educator*

Demorest
Lytle, Timothy Fenner *philosophy educator*

Dublin
Claxton, Harriett Maroy Jones *retired English language educator*

Epworth
Walker, Sarah Harriet *English educator, administrator*

Griffin
Canup, Sherrie Margaret *foreign languages educator*

Lithonia
Williams, Emily Allen *English language educator*

Macon
Hennecy, Bobbie Bobo *English language educator*
Huffman, Joan Brewer *history educator*

Marietta
Rainey, Kenneth Tyler *English language educator*

Oxford
Carpenter, Lucas Adams, III *English educator, writer*

Plains
†Bagwell, James Emmett *history educator*

Robins AFB
Head, William Pace *historian, educator*

Savannah
†Jones, William Randolph *history educator*

Statesboro
†Flynn, Richard McDonnell *English educator*
Rodell, Paul Arthur *history educator*

Tifton
Johnson, Edith Scott *English educator, writing consultant*

Toccoa
van der Veur, Paul W. *humanities educator*

Toccoa Falls
Williams, Donald T. *English educator*

Tucker
Twining, Henrietta Stover *retired English language educator*

HAWAII

Honolulu
Aung-Thwin, Michael Arthur *history educator*
†Ball, Robert Jerome *classics educator*
Bender, Byron Wilbur *linguistics educator*
Dyen, Isidore *linguistic scientist, educator*
Howes, William Craig *English educator*
†Kellogg, Judith Lillian *English educator*
Knowlton, Edgar Colby, Jr. *linguist, educator*
Moody, Raymond Albert *foreign language educator*
Moore, Willis Henry Allphin *history and geography educator*
Rapson, Richard L. *history educator*
Rehg, Kenneth Lee *linguistics educator*
Seidensticker, Edward George *Japanese language and literature educator*
Stephan, John Jason *historian, educator*
Topping, Donald M. *English language professional, educator*
Varley, Herbert Paul *Japanese language and cultural history educator*
Vroom, Jennifer Galleher *history educator*

Pearl City
Roberts, Norman Frank *English composition and linguistics educator*

IDAHO

Boise
Wells, Merle William *historian, state archivist*

Caldwell
Attebery, Louie Wayne *English language educator, folklorist*

Jerome
†Ricketts, Virginia Lee *historian, researcher*

Moscow
Greever, William St. Clair *educator, historian*
Harris, Robert Dalton *history educator, researcher, writer*

Pocatello
Smith, Evelyn Elaine *language educator*
Van Pelt, Tamise Jo *English educator*
†Wahl, Russell Edward *philosphy educator*

ILLINOIS

Bloomington
Lord, Timothy Charles *philosophy educator*

Carbondale
Ammon, Harry *history educator*
†Chavasse, Philippe *foreign languages educator*
Gilbert, Glenn Gordon *linguistics educator*
Hahn, Lewis Edwin *philosopher, retired educator*
Little, Judy Ruth *English educator*
Molino, Michael Robert *English educator*
Webb, Howard William, Jr. *retired humanities educator, university official*

Champaign
Friedberg, Maurice *Russian literature educator*
Koenker, Diane P. *history educator*
O'Neill, John Joseph *speech educator*
†Searsmith, Kelly Lin *English language educator, writer*
Smith, Ralph Alexander *cultural and educational policy educator*

Charleston
Jones, George Hilton *retired history educator, writer*
Lee, Young Sook *philosopher, educator*
McCormick, Frank Grady *English educator*
†Young, Bailey Kilbourne *history educator*

Chicago
Adler, Mortimer Jerome *philosopher, author*
Aronson, Howard Isaac *linguist, educator*
Baird, Ellen Taylor *art historian, educator*
Berk, Harlan Joseph *numismatist, writer, antiquarian*
Bevington, David Martin *English literature educator*
Biggs, Robert Dale *Near Eastern studies educator*
Booth, Wayne Clayson *English literature and rhetoric educator, author*
†Bouson, J. Brooks *English educator*
†Bregoli-Russo, Mauda Rita *language educator*
Brinkman, John Anthony *historian, educator*
Burt-Bradley, Della Ann *English educator, consultant*
Chinitz, David Evan *literature educator*
†Clarke, Jay A. *art historian, curator*
Cohen, Ted *philosophy educator*
Cullen, Charles Thomas *historian, librarian*
†Cumings, Bruce *history educator, writer*
Debus, Allen George *history educator*
Dembowski, Peter Florian *foreign language educator*
Edelstein, Teri J. *art history educator, art federation administrator*
†Elshtain, Jean Bethke *social and political ethics educator*
Erlebacher, Albert *history educator*
Farr, Marcia Elizabeth *English and Linguistics educator*
Fleischer, Cornell Hugh *history educator*
Gannon, Sister Ann Ida *retired philosophy educator, former college administrator*
Garber, Daniel Elliot *philosophy educator*
Gardiner, Judith Kegan *English language and women's studies educator*
†Gilfoyle, Timothy Joseph *historian*
Gilman, Sander Lawrence *German language educator*
Golden, Lily Oliver *educator*
Goldsmith, John Anton *linguist, educator*
Gossett, Philip *musicologist*
Grant, Robert McQueen *humanities educator*
Gray, Hanna Holborn *history educator*
Gross, Hanns *history educator*
Haley, George *Romance languages educator*
Harris, Neil *history educator*
†Harris, Rivkah *liberal arts educator*
Headrick, Daniel Richard *history and social sciences educator*
Heller, Reinhold August *art educator, consultant*
Hellie, Richard *Russian history educator, researcher*
Helmbold, Nancy Pearce *classical languages educator*
Holli, Melvin George *history educator*
Hunter, J(ames) Paul *English language educator, literary critic, historian*
Ingham, Norman William *Russian literature educator, genealogist*
Karanikas, Alexander *English language educator, author, actor*
Keenan, James George *classics educator*
Kolb, Gwin Jackson *language professional, educator*
Lach, Donald F. *history educator, author*
Lawler, James Ronald *French language educator*
Lichtenbert, Robert Henry *philosopher educator and writer*
Lieb, Michael *English educator, humanities educator*
Liebenow, Franklin Eastburn, Jr. *English literature educator*
†Love, Richard H. *art historian, art gallery executive*
Makkai, Adam *linguistics educator, poet*
Marshall, Donald Glenn *English language and literature educator*
Meltzer, Sharon Bittenson *English language and humanities educator*
Miller, Angela Perez *bilingual and special education educator*
†Moore, Nancy Gaye *dance historian*
Najita, Tetsuo *history educator*
Neff, John Hallmark *art historian*
Nussbaum, Martha Craven *philosophy and classics educator*
Osborne, Karen Lee *educator*
Phillips, Gene Daniel *English language educator*
†Phillips, Keith *Spanish language educator*
Pollock, Sheldon Ivan *language professional, educator*
Poston, Carol Hoaglan *English educator, writer*
Rosenheim, Edward Weil *English educator*
Roy, David Tod *Chinese literature educator*
Saller, Richard Paul *classics educator*
Scherman, Timothy Harris *language educator*
Shaughnessy, Edward Louis *Chinese language educator*
Shen, Virginia Shiang-lan *Spanish language educator*
Sochen, June *history educator*
†Spangehl, Stephen Douglas *educator, accrediting agency administrtor*
Tanner, Helen Hornbeck *historian*
Thaden, Edward Carl *history educator*
Vertreace, Martha Modena *English educator, poet*
Weinberg, Meyer *humanities educator*
Wingfield-Hyrams, Carlene *English educator*

Danville
Colwell, Sue Ellen *English educator*

Deerfield
Woodbridge, John Dunning *history and church history educator*

Dekalb
Baker, William *British literature educator*
Kind, Joshua B. *history educator*

Dorsey
Hinkle, Jo Ann *English language educator*

Edwardsville
Swalley, Gary William *history educator*

Elgin
Duffy, John Lewis *retired Latin, English and reading educator*
Parks, Patrick *English language educator, humanities educator*

Evanston
Buchbinder-Green, Barbara Joyce *art and architectural historian*
Cole, Douglas *retired English literature educator*
Fine, Arthur I. *philosopher*
Greenberg, Douglas Stuart *history educator*
Jennings, Francis P. *historian, writer*
Johnson, David Kenneth *historian*
Jones, Dorothy Vincent *diplomatic historian*
Laff, Ned Scott *English educator, university administrator*
†Lems, Kristin *English language educator, songwriter*
Seeskin, Kenneth Robert *philosophy educator*
Sheridan, James Edward *history educator*
Sundquist, Eric John *American studies educator*
Ver Steeg, Clarence Lester *historian, educator*
Weil, Irwin *Slavic languages and literature educator*
Well, Irwin *language educator*
Wright, John *classics educator*

Flat Rock
Marx, Michael William *English educator*

Galesburg
†Bailey, Stephen *history educator*
Hane, Mikiso *history educator*

Glen Ellyn
Georgalas, Robert Nicholas *English language educator*

Glenview
†Nelson, Paul Alfred *philosopher, editor*

Griggsville
†Dunham, Charlotte Ann *English language educator*

Gurnee
†Theard, Clausel *language educator*

Joliet
Chamberlain, Jeffrey Scott *history educator*

Lake Bluff
Sweetser, Marie-Odile Gauny *retired foreign language educator*

Lisle
Fortier, Mardelle LaDonna *English educator*

Macomb
†Colvin, Daniel L. *English educator*
Hallwas, John Edward *English language educator*

Moline
Badur, Diana Isabel *English language educator*

Normal
†Brosnahan, Leger Nicholas *English educator*
†Elledge, Jim *poet, literature educator*
Fry, Terry L. *English educator*
Hesse, Douglas Dean *English educator*

Northbrook
Young, Susan Jean *music specialist*

Orland Park
Capstaff, Genevieve MacKeeby *humanities educator*

Palatine
†Fleenor, Juliann Evans *English language educator, writer*
Keres, Karen Lynne *English language educator*

Peoria
Ballowe, James *English educator, author*
Brill de Ramirez, Susan Berry *English educator*
Tondeur, Claire Lise *French educator*

Quincy
Anderson, Peggy Joan *English educator*
†Klein, Mary Ann *English educator*

River Forest
†Stadtwald, Kurt Werner *historian*

Rockford
Carlson, Allan Constantine *historian*
Den Adel, Raymond Lee *classics educator*
Hoshaw, Lloyd *historian, educator*
Provo, Wade Arden *foreign language educator*
Sylvester, Nancy Katherine *speech educator, management consultant*

Rolling Meadows
Strongin, Bonnie Lynn *English language educator*

Romeoville
Lifka, Mary Lauranne *history educator*

Salem
Basnett, C. Jan *English educator*

Springfield
Davis, George Cullom *historian*
Fischoff, Ephraim *humanities educator, sociologist, social worker*
Temple, Wayne Calhoun *historian*

Sugar Grove
Kanwar, Anju *English educator*

Urbana
Aldridge, Alfred Owen *English language educator*
Antonsen, Elmer Harold *Germanic languages and literature educator*
Arnstein, Walter Leonard *historian, educator*
Bateman, John Jay *classics educator*
Baym, Nina *English educator*
†Burton, Orville Vernon *history educator*
Dawn, Clarence Ernest *history educator*
†Guibbory, Achsah *English educator, writer*
Haile, H. G. *German language and literature educator*
Hendrick, George *English language educator*
†Hoxie, Frederick Eugene *history educator*
Hurt, James Riggins *English language educator*
Jacobson, Howard *classics educator*
Kaufmann, Urlin Milo *English literature educator*
Lasersohn, Peter Nathan *linguist, educator*
Love, Joseph L. *history educator, cultural studies center administrator*
Mall, Laurence S. *French language educator*
Manning, Sylvia *English studies educator*
Marcovich, Miroslav *classics educator*
McColley, Robert McNair *history educator*
McGlathery, James Melville *foreign language educator*
†Mortimer, Armine Kotin *literature educator*
†Murdoch, H. Adlai *literature educator*
Nelson, Cary Robert *English educator*
Newman, John Kevin *classics educator*
Scanlan, Richard Thomas *classics educator*
Schacht, Richard Lawrence *philosopher, educator*
Solberg, Winton Udell *history educator*
Spence, Mary Lee *historian*
Sullivan, Zohreh T. *English educator*
Talbot, Emile Joseph *French language educator*
Watts, Emily Stipes *English language educator*
Zgusta, Ladislav *linguist, educator*

Westchester
Masterson, John Patrick *retired English language educator*

Wilmette
Fries, Robert Francis *historian, educator*

INDIANA

Arcadia
Travison, John A. *English educator*

Bloomington
Anderson, Judith Helena *English language educator*
Barnstone, Willis (Robert Barnstone) *language literature educator, poet, scholar*
Bernhardt-Kabisch, Ernest Karl-Heinz *English and comparative literature educator*
†Brottman, Mikita *humanities educator, writer*
Buelow, George John *musicologist, educator*
Calinescu, Matei Alexe *literature educator*
Choksy, Jamsheed Kairshasp *historian, religious scholar, language professional, humanities educator*
Cohen, William Benjamin *historian, educator*
Cole, Bruce Milan *art historian*
Dunn, Jon Michael *philosophy educator*
Edgerton, William B. *foreign language educator*
Ferrell, Robert Hugh *historian, educator*
Frederick, Robert Allen *history educator*
Hanson, Karen *philosopher, educator*
Johnson, Sidney Malcolm *foreign language educator*
Juergens, George Ivar *history educator*
Knudsen, Laura Georgia *linguist*
Martins, Heitor Miranda *foreign language educator*
Mathiesen, Thomas James *musicology educator*
McCluskey, John Asberry, Jr. *literature educator, writer*
Mickel, Emanuel John *foreign language educator*
Pletcher, David Mitchell *history educator*
Rieselbach, Helen Funk *English educator*
Rosenberg, Samuel Nathan *French and Italian language educator*
Sebeok, Thomas Albert *linguistics educator*
Sinor, Denis *Orientalist, educator*

Carmel
Hayashi, Tetsumaro *English and American literature educator, author*

Charlestown
Schmidt, Jakob Edward *medical and medicolegal lexicographer, physician, author, inventor*

Columbus
Spector, Judith Ann *English educator*

Crawfordsville
Barnes, James John *history educator*

Ellettsville
Matson, Donald Keith *genealogist*

Evansville
†Blevins, James Richard *English educator, academic administrator*
Humphrey, Lois M. *English educator*
Perkins, R. Wayne *philosophy, religion educator*

Fairmount
Cowling, Judy Kathleen *historic preservation consultant, nurse*

Fort Wayne
Essig, Erhardt Herbert *English educator*
Fairchild, David Lawrence *philosophy educator*
†Fox, Linda Chodosh *Spanish educator*
†Ramsey, Yvonne Akers *English language educator*
Scheetz, Sister Mary JoEllen *English language educator*

Franklin
Nugent, Helen Jean *history educator*

Goshen
Sterling-Hellenbrand, Alexandra Christina *language educator*

Greencastle
Dittmer, John Avery *history educator*
†Shumaker, Arthur Wesley *English educator*
Spicer, Harold Otis *retired English educator, communications educator*
Weiss, Robert Orr *speech educator*

Indianapolis
Baetzhold, Howard George *English language educator*
Beyer, Werner William *retired English educator*
Davis, Kenneth Wayne *English language educator, business communication consultant*
†Franken, Lynn *English educator*
Gentry, Marshall Bruce *English educator*
Gooldy, Walter Raymond *genealogist*
Henning, Teresa Beth *English educator*
Houser, Nathan *philosophy educator*
Krasean, Thomas Karl *historian*
Lovejoy, Kim Brian *English educator*
Mason, Thomas Alexander *historian, educator, author*
Plater, William Marmaduke *English language educator, academic administrator*
Shaughnessy, Edward Lawrence *English educator*

Muncie
Hozeski, Bruce William *English language and literature educator*
†Trimmer, Joseph F. *English educator*

North Liberty
Lowery, Joanne *English educator, writer, editor*

Notre Dame
Delaney, Cornelius Francis *philosophy educator*
Fallon, Stephen Michael *humanities educator*
†Gleason, (John) Philip *history educator*
Klene, Mary Jean *English educator*
Lanzinger, Klaus *language educator*
Matthias, John Edward *English literature educator*
McInerny, Ralph Matthew *philosophy educator, author*
Mc Mullin, Ernan Vincent *philosophy educator*
Moevs, Christian Robert *literature educator*
Nugent, Walter Terry King *historian*
Quinn, Philip Lawrence *philosophy educator*
Rosenberg, Charles Michael *art historian, educator*
Slabey, Robert McKeon *English educator*
Vasta, Edward *humanities educator*
Walicki, Andrzej Stanislaw *history of ideas educator*

Purdue University
Zou, Zhen *English and Chinese educator, translator and critic, computer technologist*

Richmond
Southard, Robert Fairbairn *history educator*

South Bend
†Furlong, Patrick J. *historian, educator, university administrator*
van Inwagen, Peter Jan *philosophy educator*

Terre Haute
Baker, Ronald Lee *English educator*
Brennan, Matthew Cannon *English literature educator, poet*
Carmony, Marvin Dale *linguist, educator*
De Marr, Mary Jean *English language educator*
Jennermann, Donald L. *humanities educator*

Kleiner, Elaine Laura *English literature educator*
Montañez, Carmen Lydia *Spanish language educator, literature researcher, lawyer*
Pickett, William Beatty *history educator*
Pierard, Richard Victor *history educator*

Upland
Dayton, Nancy Cheryl *English educator*

Valparaiso
†Duvick, Randa Jane *French language educator*
Morgan, David A. *art history educator*
Peters, Howard Nevin *foreign language educator*

Vincennes
†Rogers, John Headley *educator*

West Lafayette
Bertolet, Rodney Jay *philosophy educator*
Contreni, John Joseph, Jr. *humanities educator*
Cutter, Charles Ross *historian, educator*
†DiGiulio, Cinzia *Italian language educator*
Garfinkel, Alan *Spanish language and education educator*
Gottfried, Leon Albert *English language educator*
Kirby, John Thomas *comparative literature educator*
Mc Bride, William Leon *philosopher, educator*
Mork, Gordon Robert *historian, educator*
Rothenberg, Gunther Erich *history educator*
Saunders, James Robert *English educator*
Woodman, Harold David *historian*

IOWA

Ames
Berry, Jay Robert, Jr. *English educator*
Bruner, Charlotte Hughes *French language educator*
Dial, Eleanore Maxwell *foreign language educator*

Avoca
Hardisty, William Lee *English language educator*

Cedar Falls
Clohesy, William Warren *philosophy educator*
Wang, Jennie *literature educator*
Wilson, Robley Conant, Jr. *English educator, editor, author*

Cedar Rapids
Heller, Terry L(ynn) *English literature educator, writer*
Lisio, Donald John *historian, educator*

Clinton
Hicok, Bethany Faith *English educator*

Davenport
†Bradley, Ritamary *retired English educator*
Stauff, Jon William *history educator*

Decorah
†Nelson, Harland Stanley *retired English educator*

Dubuque
Brimeyer, James Leon *English educator*
Fischer, Katherine Mary *English educator*
†McAlpin, Sara Ann *English educator*
Perry, E. Eugene *humanities educator*
Swiderski, Suzanne Marie *English educator*

Fairfield
Aubrey, Bryan *educator, writer, editor*

Grinnell
Irving, Donald C. *English educator*
Kaiser, Daniel Hugh *historian, educator*
Kintner, Philip L. *history educator*
Michaels, Jennifer Tonks *foreign language educator*
Schrift, Alan Douglas *philosophy educator*
†Smith, Don Alan *educator*

Iowa City
Addis, Laird Clark, Jr. *philosopher, educator, musician*
†Aikin, Judith Popovich *languages educator, academic administrator*
†Baynton, Douglas Cameron *historian*
Butchvarov, Panayot Krustev *philosophy educator*
Coolidge, Archibald Cary, Jr. *English language educator, literature researcher*
Ertl, Wolfgang *German language and literature educator*
Folsom, Lowell Edwin *English language educator*
Fumerton, Richard Anthony *philosopher educator*
Gelfand, Lawrence Emerson *historian, educator*
Gerber, John Christian *English language educator*
Goldstein, Jonathan Amos *ancient history and classics educator*
Green, Peter Morris *classics educator, writer, translator*
Haravon Collins, Leslea *women's studies educator*
Hawley, Ellis Wayne *historian, educator*
Kerber, Linda Kaufman *historian, educator*
Kinsey, Joni Louise *art history educator*
†McCloskey, Deirdre Nansen *economics and history educator*
†McDowell, Frederick Peter Woll *retired English educator*
Percas de Ponseti, Helena *foreign language and literature educator*
Raeburn, John Hay *English language educator*
Ringen, Catherine Oleson *linguistics educator*
Sayre, Robert Freeman *English language educator*
Solbrig, Ingeborg Hildegard *German literature educator, author*
Steele, Oliver *English educator*
Trank, Douglas Monty *rhetoric and speech communications educator*
Wachal, Robert Stanley *linguistics educator, consultant*

Lamoni
Wight, Darlene *retired speech educator, emerita educator*

Peosta
Kelly, Kathleen Ann *humanities educator*

Sioux City
Emmons, Jeanne Carter *English educator*

Waterloo
Holub, Jeanne Helen *English language educator*
†Jaeger, Kathleen Grace *French educator*

KANSAS

Chanute
Dillard, Dean Innes *English language educator*

Cimarron
Wiseman, susan J. *English educator*

Dighton
Stanley, Ellen May *historian, consultant*

Easton
Rebarchek, Sherri Lynne *reading educator*

Emporia
Heldrich, Philip Joseph *English educator, academic administrator, writer*
Hoy, James F. *folklorist*

Lawrence
Alexander, John Thorndike *historian, educator*
Debicki, Andrew Peter *foreign language educator*
Devitt, Amy Joanne *English educator*
Eldredge, Charles Child, III *art history educator*
Gunn, James E. *English language educator*
Hanson, Anne Marie LaLonde *speech and theatre educator*
Kuntz, Dieter Kurt *history educator, researcher, translator*
Li, Chu-Tsing *art history educator*
Pasco, Allan Humphrey *literature educator*
Quinn, Dennis B. *English language and literature educator*
Saul, Norman Eugene *history educator*
Schoeck, Richard J(oseph) *English and humanities scholar*
Spires, Robert Cecil *foreign language educator*
Tuttle, William McCullough, Jr. *history educator*
Woelfel, James Warren *philosophy and humanities educator*
Worth, George John *English literature educator*

Leavenworth
†Novak, Michael Paul *English language educator*

Manhattan
†Kremer, S. Lillian *English educator*
McCulloh, John Marshall *historian*

North Newton
Juhnke, James Carlton *humanities educator*

Ottawa
Tyler, Priscilla *retired English language and education educator*

Pittsburg
Franklin, John Thomas Ikeda *English educator*
†Harmon, Stephen Albert *history educator*

Wichita
†Dietrich, Bryan David *english educator, poet*
Goodpasture, Judy Gail Ashmore *English language educator, administrator*

KENTUCKY

Bowling Green
Minton, John Dean *historian, educator*
†Rose, Ferrel Victoria *humanities educator, translator*

Burgin
†Bradshaw, Phyllis Bowman *historian, historic site staff member*

Georgetown
Klotter, James C. *historian, educator*

Lebanon
Benningfield, Troy Lee *language arts educator*

Lexington
†Allen, John Jay *Spanish language educator*
†Banning, Lance Gilbert *historian, educator*
Bryant, Joseph Allen, Jr. *English language educator*
Coffman, Edward McKenzie *history educator*
Madden, Edward Harry *philosopher, educator*
Warth, Robert Douglas *history educator*

Louisville
Ford, Gordon Buell, Jr. *English language, linguistics, and medieval studies educator, author, retired hospital industry accounting financial management executive*
†Green, Catherine C. *foreign language educator*
†Pennington, Royce Lee *English educator, writer*
†Villiger, Martha Ann *English educator*

Madisonville
†Werner, Mary Beth *English educator*

Midway
Minister, Kristina *speech communication educator*

Morehead
Thomas, Malayilmelathethil *English language educator*

Murray
†Aguiar, Sarah Appleton *English language educator, writer*

Owensboro
†Schoenbachler, Matthew G. *historian, educator*

Radcliff
Cranston, John Welch *historian, educator*

Richmond
Myers, Marshall Dean *English educator*

Shearon, Forrest Bedford *humanities educator*

Southgate
Glenn, Jerry Hosmer, Jr. *foreign language educator*

Williamsburg
Faught, Jolly Kay *English language educator*
Fish, Thomas Edward *English language and literature educator*

LOUISIANA

Baton Rouge
Arceneaux, William *historian, educator, association official*
Cooper, William James, Jr. *history educator*
†Crosby, Janice Celia *language and literature educator*
Hardy, John Edward *English language educator, author*
†Lazzaro-Weis, Carol Marie *foreign languages educator*
†Loveland, Anne Carol *history educator*
Moreland, Richard Clayton *English educator*
Olney, James *English language educator*
Ricapito, Joseph Virgil (Giuseppe) *Spanish and comparative literature educator*
Smith, David Jeddie *American literature educator*
Wheeler, Otis Bullard *retired English educator and university official*

Dubach
Lindsay, Robby Lane *English educator*

Hammond
Broussard, Francis Peter *English educator*
Thorburn, James Alexander *humanities educator*

Lafayette
†Raffel, Burton Nathan *educator, poet, writer, translator*

Leesville
Norman, Paralee Frances *English language educator, researcher*

Metairie
Baisier, Maria Davis *English language educator, theater director*

New Orleans
Brosman, Catharine Savage *French language educator, poet*
†Collins, Richard Wayne *English literature educator*
Holditch, William Kenneth *American literature educator*
Kilroy, James Francis *educator*
Kukla, Jon (Keith) *historian, museum director*
Luza, Radomir Vaclav *historian, educator*
Paolini, Gilberto *literature and science educator*
Poesch, Jessie Jean *art historian*
Qian, Zhaoming *critic, literature educator*
Reck, Andrew Joseph *philosophy educator*
Robert, Phyllis Ann *English educator*
Roberts, Louise Nisbet *philosopher*
Sellin, Eric *linguist, poet, educator*

Pineville
Howell, Thomas *history educator*

Ruston
†Dodge Robbins, Dorothy Ellin *English educator*

Ville Platte
De Ville, Winston *genealogist*

MAINE

Bar Harbor
Carpenter, William Morton *English educator, writer*

Brunswick
Hodge, James Lee *German language educator*

Bucksport
Ives, Edward Dawson *folklore educator*

Castine
Berleant, Arnold *philosopher*
Hoople, Sally Crosby *retired humanities and communications educator*

Dresden
Turco, Lewis Putnam *English educator*

Lubec
†Tanney, Rick Willard *philosophy educator, computer sciences educator*

Orono
Cruikshank, Margaret Louise *humanities educator, writer*
Hatlen, Burton Norval *English educator*
Rogers, Deborah Dee *English language educator*

Portland
Louden, Robert Burton *philosopher, educator*
†McDaniel, Dana Irene *linguistics educator*
Schwanauer, Francis *philosopher, educator*

Sanford
†Allan, Jonathan David *autograph dealer, pop culture historian*

Scarborough
Martin, Harold Clark *humanities educator*
Sadik, Marvin Sherwood *art consultant, former museum director*

Waterville
Bassett, Charles Walker *English language educator*
Hudson, Yeager *philosophy educator, minister*
Roisman, Hanna Maslovski *classics educator*

MARYLAND

Annapolis
Cooper, Sherod Monroe, Jr. *retired English language educator*
Corredor, Eva Livia *foreign language educator*
†Fleming, Bruce E. *English literature educator, writer*
Good, Jane Elizabeth *history educator*
Jason, Philip Kenneth *English language educator*

Baltimore
Achinstein, Peter Jacob *philosopher, educator*
Baldwin, John Wesley *history educator*
Bardaglio, Peter Winthrop *humanities educator*
Basile, Joseph John *art history educator, archaeologist*
Bett, Richard Arnot Home *philosophy educator*
Castro-Klaren, Sara *Latin American literature educator*
Chapelle, Suzanne Ellery Greene *history educator*
†Child-Olmsted, Gisèle Alexandra *language educator*
Cohen, Warren I. *history educator*
Cooper, Jerrold Stephen *historian, educator*
DeLuna, D.N. *literary educator*
Forster, Robert *history educator*
Higham, John *history educator*
Hillers, Delbert Roy *Near East language educator*
Irwin, John Thomas *humanities educator*
Johnson, Michael Paul *history educator*
Judson, Horace Freeland *history of science, writer, educator*
Kessler, Herbert Leon *art historian, educator, university administrator*
Knight, Franklin W. *history educator*
Kurth, Lieselotte *foreign language educator*
Lidtke, Vernon LeRoy *history educator*
Luck, Georg Hans Bhawani *classics educator*
McCarter, P(ete) Kyle, Jr. *Near Eastern studies educator*
†McKusick, James Chase *English educator*
Moorjani, Angela *foreign languages educator*
Paulson, Ronald Howard *English and humanities educator*
Peirce, Carol Marshall *English educator*
Ranum, Orest Allen *historian, educator*
Russell-Wood, Anthony John R. *history educator*
Schneewind, Jerome Borges *philosophy educator*
Sedlak, Valerie Frances *English language educator, university administrator*
Terborg-Penn, Rosalyn Marian *historian, educator*
†Varga, Nicholas *historian, archivist, retired educator*
Walker, Mack *historian, educator*
Ziff, Larzer *English language educator*

Bel Air
Lu, David John *history educator, writer*

Bethesda
Benson, Elizabeth Polk *Pre-Columbian art specialist*
Duncan, Francis *historian, government official*
Highfill, Philip Henry, Jr. *retired language educator*
Raffini, Renee Kathleen *foreign language professional, educator*
Serlin, David H. *history educator*
van der Linden, Frank Morris *historian*

Bowie
Miller, M. Sammye *history educator*
Sterling, Richard Leroy *English and foreign language educator*
Vidal, Pedro Jose *foreign language educator*

Brunswick
Quesada, Bernard *English educator*

Catonsville
Loerke, William Carl *art history educator*

Chestertown
Trout, Charles Hathaway *historian, educator*

Cockeysville
Peirce, Brooke *English language educator*

College Park
Bouvier, Virginia Marie *foreign language educator, researcher, writer*
†Collins, Merle *English educator*
De Lorenzo, William E. *foreign language educator*
Fraistat, Neil Richard *English language educator*
Holton, William Milne *English language and literature educator*
Lightfoot, David William *linguistics educator*
McGinnis, Scott Gary *language and linguistics educator*
Olson, Keith Waldemar *history educator*
Oster, Rose Marie Gunhild *foreign language professional, educator*
Pasch, Alan *philosopher, educator*
Spear, Richard Edmund *art history educator*
Turner, Mark Bernard *English language educator*
Weart, Spencer Richard *historian*
Yaney, George *history educator*

Columbia
†Mack, Kibibi Voloria *history educator*
Marshall, Linda Murphy *linguist, government official*

Emmitsburg
Collinge, William Joseph *humanities educator*
Stay, Byron Lee *rhetoric educator, college administrator*

Frederick
Hamilton, Rhoda Lillian Rosen *guidance counselor, language educator, consultant*
Pyne, Frederick Wallace *genealogist, clergyman, retired civil engineer, retired mathematics educator*

Frostburg
Allen, Philip Mark *arts and humanities educator, dean, writer*
Coward, Patricia Ann *language educator*

Gaithersburg
Shull, Michael Slade *lecturer, writer, researcher*

Glencoe
Weeks, Anne Macleod *English language eductor, education director*

Hagerstown
Shuttleworth, Rebecca Scott *English language educator*

Lanham Seabrook
Kari, Daven Michael *religion educator*

Lusby
Eshelman, Ralph Ellsworth *maritime historian, educator, consultant*

Mitchellville
Embree, Ainslie Thomas *history educator*

Pasadena
De Pauw, Linda Grant *history educator, publisher*

Potomac
Sceery, Beverly Davis *genealogist, writer, educator*

Rockville
Brown, David Harry *speech educator*
Cantelon, Philip Louis *historian*
Goldenberg, Myrna Gallant *English language and literature educator*
Hewlett, Richard Greening *historian*
Moran, Sean Farrell *historian*
†Phillips, John K. *philosophy educator*

Saint Michaels
Marshall, Robert Gerald *language educator*

Salisbury
Cubbage, Elinor Phillips *English language educator*

Severna Park
Schick, Edgar Brehob *German literature educator*

Silver Spring
Borkovec, Vera Z. *Russian studies educator*
Calinger, Ronald Steve *historian*
Cole, Wayne Stanley *historian, educator*
Price, Victoria Louise *history lecturer, storyteller*

Takoma Park
Bevin, Teresa *educator, psychotherapist, writer*

Temple Hills
†Mikesh, Robert Clement *aviation historian, writer, museum consultant*

Towson
Avery, Evelyn Madeline *English language educator*
Baker, Jean Harvey *history educator*
†Mruck, Armin Einhard *history educator emeritus*
Romero, Patricia Watkins *historian, educator, researcher*

University Park
†Walker, John Samuel *historian*

Upper Marlboro
LeValley, Guy Glenn *speech communication educator*

Waldorf
Morrison, Jennifer Lyn Dydo *English language educator, coach*

Williamsport
†Nycum, Debra Wetzel *English language educator*

MASSACHUSETTS

Amesbury
Labaree, Benjamin Woods *history educator*

Amherst
Baker, Lynne Rudder *philosophy educator*
Bezucha, Robert Joseph *history educator*
Chappell, Vere Claiborne *philosophy educator*
Ciruti, Joan Estelle *Spanish language and literature educator*
Gibson, Walker *retired English language educator, poet, writer*
Haven, Richard *English language educator*
Hernon, Joseph Martin, Jr. *history educator*
Kinney, Arthur Frederick *literary history educator, author, editor*
†Lowance, Mason I. *American literature educator*
Oates, Stephen Baery *history educator*
Partee, Barbara Hall *linguist, educator*
Rosbottom, Ronald Carlisle *French, arts and humanities educator*
Skerrett, Joseph Taylor *literature educator*
†Stavans, Ilan *professor, writer*
Taubman, Jane Andelman *Russian literature educator*
Taylor, Robert Edward *foreign language educator*
Trahan, Elizabeth Welt *retired comparative literature educator*
Wideman, John Edgar *English literature educator, novelist*
Wolff, Robert Paul *philosophy educator*
Wyman, David Sword *historian, educator*

Attleboro
Stevens, E(lizabeth) Kathleen *English language educator*

Auburndale
Lindgren, Charlotte Holt *English language educator*
†Winslow, Donald James *retired English educator, archivist*

Belmont
Barsam, Joyce Lorna *language educator, classicist*
Bloch, Herbert *classicist, medievalist, historian, educator*
Buckley, Jerome Hamilton *English language educator*

Boston
Bartley, Scott Andrew *genealogist, archivist*
Blaisdell, Charmarie Jenkins *historian, educator*
Brandt, Allan M. *medical history educator*
Bromsen, Maury Austin *historian, bibliographer, antiquarian bookseller*
Cardona, Rodolfo *Spanish language and literature educator*
Dallek, Robert *history educator*
Foss, Clive Frank Wilson *history educator*
Freeman, Robert Schofield *musicologist, educator, pianist*
Green, Harvey *history educator*
Henry, DeWitt Pawling, II *creative writing educator, writer, arts administrator*
Hintikka, Jaakko *philosopher, educator*
†Jones, Caroline Ann *art historian, educator, curator*
Jones, Robert Emmet *French language educator*
Kafker, Frank A. *historian, educator*
Keylor, William Robert *humanities educator*
Kleiner, Fred Scott *art historian, archaeologist, educator, editor*
Langer, Lawrence Lee *English educator, writer*
Lowry, Bates *art historian, museum director*
Lyons, David Barry *philosophy and law educator*
Ness, Arthur Joseph *musicologist*
Petronella, Vincent F. *English educator, researcher*
Phillips, William *English language educator, editor, author*
Riely, John Cabell *english educator, art historian, consultant*
Rosen, Stanley Howard *humanities educator*
Sanborn, George Freeman, Jr. *genealogist*
Scanlon, Dorothy Therese *history educator*
†Sullivan, Megan Mary *English educator*
Vasaly, Ann Carol *classical studies educator*
Weitzman, Arthur Joshua *English educator*
Wermuth, Paul Charles *retired English educator*
Wiseman, James Richard *classicist, archaeologist, educator*

Bradford
†Murphy, Rich *educator in English language*

Bridgewater
Hurley, Mike *English language educator*

Brockton
†Helfrich, Theodora Thompson *spanish educator, academic administrator*

Brookline
†Golden, Herbert Hershel *retired Romance languages educator*

Cambridge
Badian, Ernst *history educator*
Bailyn, Bernard *historian, educator*
Bate, Walter Jackson *English literature educator*
Bolster, Arthur Stanley, Jr. *history educator*
Brustein, Robert Sanford *English language educator, theatre director, author*
Chomsky, Avram Noam *linguistics and philosophy educator*
Clausen, Wendell Vernon *classics educator*
Coatsworth, John Henry *history educator*
Conley, Tom Clark *literature educator*
Cross, Frank Moore, Jr. *foreign language educator*
Donaldson, Peter Samuel *humanities educator*
Dunn, Charles William *Celtic languages and literature educator, author*
Dyck, Arthur James *ethicist, educator*
Engell, James Theodore *English educator*
†Erdmann, Andrew Patrick Nicholas *historian*
Fanger, Donald Lee *Slavic language and literature educator*
Flier, Michael Stephen *Slavic languages educator*
Fogelson, Robert Michael *history educator, writer, consultant*
Ford, Franklin Lewis *history educator, historian*
Ford, Patrick Kildea *Celtic studies educator*
Gates, Henry Louis, Jr. *English language educator*
Gienapp, William Eugene *history educator*
Gilman, Todd Seacrist *language educator, musician*
Goldfarb, Warren (David) *philosophy educator*
Graham, Loren Raymond *historian, educator*
Graubard, Stephen Richards *history educator, editor*
Greenblatt, Stephen J. *English language educator*
Guthke, Karl Siegfried *foreign language educator*
Halle, Morris *linguist, educator*
Hanan, Patrick Dewes *foreign language professional, educator*
Harrington, Anne *science historian*
Heimert, Alan Edward *humanities educator*
Henrichs, Albert Maximinus *classicist, educator*
Hungness, Lisa Sue *English language educator, consultant*
Iriye, Akira *historian, educator*
Jones, Christopher Prestige *classicist, historian*
Kalb, Marvin *public policy and government educator*
Karl, Barry Dean *historian, educator*
Keller, Evelyn Fox *history and philosophy educator*
Keyser, Samuel Jay *linguistics educator, university official*
Ladjevardi, Habib *historian*
Laiou, Angeliki Evangelos *history educator*
Linsky, Martin Alan *public policy educator, consultant*
Lunt, Horace Gray *linguist, educator*
MacMaster, Robert Ellsworth *historian, educator*
Maier, Charles Steven *history educator*
Maier, Pauline *history educator*
Malmstad, John Earl *Slavic languages and literatures, educator*
Nozick, Robert *philosophy educator, author*
Nykrog, Per *French literature educator*
O'Neil, Wayne *linguist, educator*
Ozment, Steven *historian, educator*
Pannapacker, William Albert III *humanities educator*
Perkins, David *English language educator*
†Perry, Ruth *literature educator*
Pian, Rulan Chao *musicologist, scholar*
Quine, Willard Van Orman *philosophy educator*
Rosenkrantz, Barbara Gutmann *retired history educator*
Rotberg, Robert Irwin *historian, political economist, educator, editor*
Ryan, Judith Lyndal *German language and literature educator*
Scheffler, Israel *philosopher, educator*
Segal, Charles Paul *classics educator, author*
Sevcenko, Ihor *history and literature educator*
Shinagel, Michael *English literature educator*
Simon, Eckehard (Peter) *foreign language educator*
Singer, Irving *philosophy educator*
Smith, Merritt Roe *history educator*
Sollors, Werner *English language, literature and American studies educator*
Spaethling, Robert Herbert *retired German language educator*
†Stauffer, John William *cultural historian*
Tarrant, R(ichard) J(ohn) *classicist, educator*
Thernstrom, Stephan *historian, educator*
Thorburn, David *literature educator*
Tu, Wei-Ming *historian, philosopher, writer*
Ulrich, Laurel Thatcher *historian, educator*
Vanger, Milton Isadore *history educator*
Vendler, Helen Hennessy *literature educator, poetry critic*
Wolff, Christoph Johannes *music historian, educator*
Ziolkowski, Jan Michael *medievalist educator*

Canton
Parker, Virginia Marie *English language educator*

Chestnut Hill
Barth, John Robert *English educator, priest*
Blanchette, Oliva *philosophy educator*
Casper, Leonard Ralph *American literature educator*
Duhamel, Pierre Albert *English language professional*
Mahoney, John L. *English literature educator*
McAleer, John Joseph *English literature educator*
Reed, James Eldin *historian, educator, consultant, publisher*
Valette, Rebecca Marianne *Romance languages educator*

Danvers
†Hodgin, Jean *English educator*

Fall River
Powers, Alan William *literature educator*
†Tinberg, Howard *English educator*

Fitchburg
Keough, William Richard *English language educator*

Framingham
Finn, Gary *educator, entrepreneur*
Horn, Bernard *English language educator, writer*
Lipton, Leah *art historian, educator, museum curator*
†McCarthy, Desmond Fergus *English literature educator*
†Nolin, Anna Patricia *English language educator*

Franklin
Pano, Gregory James *history educator*

Great Barrington
Filkins, Peter Joel *English language educator*

Greenfield
Ruiz, Lillian *English language educator*

Holden
Jareckie, Gretchen Kinsman Fillmore *retired English language educator*

Holyoke
†Dutcher, James Marshall *English language educator*

Lowell
Aste, Mario Andrea *foreign language educator*

Medford
Bedau, Hugo Adam *philosophy educator*
Brooke, John L. *history educator*
Dennett, Daniel Clement *philosopher, author, educator*
Fyler, John Morgan *English language educator*
Giordano, Donna Langone *foreign language and ESL educator*
Laurent, Pierre-Henri *history educator*
Marcopoulos, George John *history educator*
Ueda, Reed Takashi *historian, educator*

Milford
Barrs, James Thomas *linguistics educator*

Milton
Frazier, Marie Dunn *speech educator, public relations and human resources specialist*

Needham
Bottiglia, William Filbert *humanities educator*
Criscenti, Joseph Thomas *retired history educator*

New Bedford
Messier, Gerald Roland *genealogist*

North Andover
Longsworth, Ellen Louise *art historian, consultant*

North Dartmouth
Yoken, Mel B(arton) *French language educator, author*

North Eastham
Masterson, Dianne Johnson *English language educator*

North Easton
†Wolf-Devine, Celia Curtis *philosophy educator*

Northampton
Birkett, Mary Ellen *humanities educator*
Elkins, Stanley Maurice *historian, educator*
Ellis, Frank Hale *English literature educator*
Hoyt, Nelly Schargo (Mrs. N. Deming Hoyt) *history educator*
Pickrel, Paul *English educator*
Seelig, Sharon Cadman *English educator*
Smith, Malcolm Barry Estes *philosophy educator, lawyer*
Vaget, Hans Rudolf *language professional, educator*
von Klemperer, Klemens *historian, educator*

Norton
Dahl, Curtis *English literature educator*
†Evans, Nancy Ann *classics educator*
Taylor, Robert Sundling *English educator, art critic*

Plymouth
Jones, Cheryl Bromley *English language and humanities educator*

Randolph
Morrissey, Edmond Joseph *classical philologist*

Rockport
Delakas, Daniel Liudviko *retired foreign language educator*
Walen, Harry Leonard *historian, lecturer, author*

Salem
Flibbert, Joseph Thomas *English language educator*
Gozemba, Patrica Andrea *women's studies and English language educator, writer*

Sharon
†Smuts, R. Malcolm *historian, educator*

Shrewsbury
†Cronin, Laura Aileen *English language educator*

Shutesbury
Creed, Robert Payson, Sr. *retired literature educator*

Somerville
Feld, Marjorie Nan *history educator*
†Phelps, Cassandra Deirdre *independent scholar*

South Hadley
Berek, Peter *English educator*
Brownlow, Frank Walsh *English language educator*
Doezema, Marianne *art historian*
Farnham, Anthony Edward *English language educator*
Herbert, Robert Louis *art history educator*
Johnson, Richard August *English language educator*

Springfield
Garabedian-Urbanowski, Martha Ann *foreign language educator*
Habermehl, Lawrence LeRoy *philosophy educator*
Porter, Burton Frederick *philosophy educator, author, dean*

Stoughton
Hall, Roger Lee *musicologist, educator, composer*

Truro
Fader, Daniel Nelson *English language educator*

Waltham
†Gendzier, Stephen J. *foreign language educator*
Harth, Erica *French language and comparative literature educator*
Jackendoff, Ray Saul *linguistics educator*
Marshall, Robert Lewis *musicologist, educator*
Staves, Susan *English educator*

Watertown
Goodheart, Eugene *English language educator*
Rivers, Wilga Marie *foreign language educator*

Wayland
Clogan, Paul Maurice *English language and literature educator*

Wellesley
Bidart, Frank *English educator, poet*
Wilson, Elaine Louise *English language educator*

Wellfleet
Mc Feely, William Shield *historian, writer*

Wenham
Flint-Ferguson, Janis Deane *English language educator*

Weston
Higgins, Sister Therese *English educator, former college president*
Vetterling, Mary-Anne *Spanish language and literature educator*

Westwood
Burrell, Sidney Alexander *history educator*

Williamstown
Bell-Villada, Gene H. *literature educator, writer*
Bundtzen, Lynda Kathryn *English and women's studies educator*
Dalzell, Robert Fenton, Jr. *historian*
Dew, Charles Burgess *historian, educator*
Fuqua, Charles John *classics educator*
Graver, Lawrence Stanley *English language professional*
Horan, Patrick M. *English educator*
Oakley, Francis Christopher *history educator, former college president*
Payne, Harry Charles *historian, educator*
Raab, Lawrence Edward *English educator*
Rudolph, Frederick *history educator*
Stamelman, Richard Howard *French and humanities educator*

Worcester
Billias, George Athan *history educator*
Cary, Noel Demetri *history educator*
†Grad, Bonnie L. *art historian, educator*
Koelsch, William Alvin *history educator*
Langevin, Edgar Louis *retired humanities educator*
†Pakaluk, Michael *philosophy educator*
†Shary, Timothy Matthew *communication educator, critic*
Vaughan, Alden True *history educator*
Von Laue, Theodore Herman *historian, educator*
Whall, Helen Marie *classicist, writer*
Zeugner, John Finn *history educator, writer*

MICHIGAN

Adrian
Peeradina, Saleem *English educator, poet*

Allendale
†Persoon, James Leo *English educator*

Ann Arbor
Aldridge, John Watson *English language educator, author*
Bailey, Richard Weld *English language educator*
Baker, Sheridan *English educator, author*
Becker, Marvin Burton *historian*
Blouin, Francis Xavier, Jr. *history educator*
Bornstein, George Jay *literary educator*
Brown, Deming Bronson *Slavic languages and literature educator*
Burbank, Jane Richardson *Russian and European studies educator*
Cowen, Roy Chadwell, Jr. *German language educator*
Curley, Edwin Munson *philosophy educator*
†Dann, John Christie *historian, library director*
†Delbanco, Nicholas Franklin *English educator, writer*
Dunnigan, Brian Leigh *military historian, curator*
Eisenberg, Marvin Julius *art history educator*
Eisenstein, Elizabeth Lewisohn *historian, educator*
Feuerwerker, Albert *history educator*
Forsyth, Ilene Haering *art historian*
†Garbaty, Thomas Jay *retired English language educator*
Gomez, Luis Oscar *Asian and religious studies educator*
Hackett, Roger Fleming *history educator*
Knott, John Ray, Jr. *language professional, educator*
Lewis, David Lanier *business history educator*
Lewis, Robert Enzer *lexicographer, educator*
Mersereau, John, Jr. *Slavic languages and literatures educator*
Munro, Donald Jacques *philosopher, educator*
†Palmer, Stephanie Candace *English educator, literary critic*
Perkins, Barbara M. *English educator*
Potter, David Stone *Greek and Latin educator*
Pulgram, Ernst *linguist, philologist, Romance and classical linguistics educator, writer*
†Saddik, Annette Joy *English literature educator*
Steinhoff, William Richard *English literature educator*
Stolz, Benjamin Armond *foreign language educator*
Trautmann, Thomas Roger *history and anthropology educator*
Vander, Judith Rose *ethnomusicologist*
Woodcock, Leonard *humanities educator, former ambassador*
†Zurier, Rebecca *art history educator*
Zwiep, Mary Nelva *humanities educator*

Benton Harbor
Atwood, Harold Ashley *retired historian*

Berrien Springs
†Land, Gary Gene *history educator*

Big Rapids
†Ding, Dan Xiong *English educator*
Mehler, Barry Alan *humanities educator, journalist, consultant*

Bloomfield Hills
Gossett, Kathryn Myers *language professional, educator*

Cassopolis
Hall, Janet Foresman *retired English language, science educator*

Clinton Township
Crawford, Betty Elizabeth *English and computer science educator*

Dearborn
†Spinelli, Emily *Spanish language educator*
†Summers, Claude Joseph *humanities educator*

Detroit
Abt, Jeffrey *art and art history educator, artist, writer*
Brill, Lesley *literature and film studies educator*
†Chauderlot, Fabienne-Sophie *foreign language educator*
Finkenbine, Roy Eugene *history educator*
†Fitzgibbons, Eleanor Elizabeth *retired English educator*
†Leland, Christopher Towne *English educator*
Lombard, Lawrence Brian *philosopher, educator*
Madigan, Brian Christopher *art historian, educator*
Schindler, Marvin Samuel *foreign language educator*
Small, Melvin *history educator*
†Spickermann, Roland *history educator*
van der Marck, Jan *art historian*

East Lansing
Anderson, David Daniel *retired humanities educator, writer, editor*
Eadie, John William *history educator*
Falk, Julia S. *linguist, educator*
Fisher, Alan Washburn *historian, educator*
Francese, Joseph *Italian language and literature educator*
Granger, Bruce Ingham *retired English language educator*
Huzar, Eleanor Goltz *history educator*
Kronegger, Maria Elisabeth *French and comparative literature educator*
Mansour, George P. *Spanish language and literature educator*
Mead, Carl David *retired educator*
Natoli, Joseph *English language educator*
Paananen, Victor Niles *English educator*
Platt, Franklin Dewitt *retired history educator*
Pollack, Norman *history educator*
Silverman, Henry Jacob *history educator*
Thomas, Franklin Richard *American studies and language educator, writer*
Thomas, Samuel Joseph *history educator*
Whallon, William *literature educator*

Farmington
Ellens, J(ay) Harold *philosopher, educator, psychotherapist*
Moehlman, Ruth *historian, writer*

Flint
Stuckey, Janice Faith *English educator, sales executive*

Grand Blanc
Lemke, Laura Ann *foreign language educator, assistant principal*

Grand Rapids
†Hardy, Lee Patrick *humanities educator*
Zuidervaart, Lambert Paul *philosophy educator*

Grosse Pointe
Peters, Thomas Robert *English language educator, writer*

Harbert
Morrissette, Bruce Archer *Romance languages educator*

Harper Woods
Havrilcsak, Gregory Michael *history educator*

Howell
†Eiss, Harry Edwin *English educator*

Huntington Woods
Gutmann, Joseph *art history educator*
Smith, Edwin Burrows *language educator, academic administrator*

Jackson
Feldmann, Judith Gail *language professional, educator*

Kalamazoo
Blickle, Peter *German educator*
Breisach, Ernst A. *historian, educator*
Callan, Edward Thomas *English educator*
†Digby-Junger, Richard A *educator in English*
Dybek, Stuart *English educator, writer*
Heller, Janet Ruth *English language, writing and literature educator*
Raaberg, Gloria Gwen *literature educator*
†Sauret, Martine *French educator*

Livonia
Hassan, Lois Mary *English language educator*
Holtzman, Roberta Lee *French and Spanish language educator*

Marquette
Choate, Jean Marie *history educator*
Heldreth, Leonard Guy *English educator, university official*
†Mitchell, David Thomas *humanities educator, filmmaker*

North Branch
†Mims, Sarah Patricia *English language educator*

Okemos
Huddleston, Eugene Lee *retired American studies educator*
†Marcus, Harold G. *history educator*

Rochester
Arrathoon, Leigh Adelaide *medievalist, editor, writer*
Eberwein, Jane Donahue *English educator*
Nakao, Seigo *Japanese language, culture and literature educator*

Rochester Hills
Matthews, George Tennyson *history educator*

Shelby
Glerum, Sally Jane *English educator*

Southfield
Papazian, Dennis Richard *history educator, political commentator*

Sterling Heights
Ice, Orva Lee, Jr. *history educator, retired*

University Center
†Haynes, Margaret Elizabeth *English educator*

Waterford
Adler, Raphael *educator emeritus, speech pathologist*

Wayne
†Cobbs, Alfred Leon *German language educator*

West Bloomfield
Williamson, Marilyn Lammert *English educator, university adminstrator*

Ypsilanti
Cere, Ronald Carl *languages educator, consultant, researcher*
Perkins, Bradford *history educator*

MINNESOTA

Brandon
Hansen, Richard Buddie *English educator, chef*

Duluth
Fischer, Roger Adrian *retired history educator*
Jankofsky, Klaus Peter *medieval studies educator*
Schroeder, Fred Erich Harald *humanities educator*

Elk River
Sandusky, Christine Ann *English language educator*

Faribault
Strand, Melvin LeRoy *English educator*

Fergus Falls
Lundburg, Paul Wesley *English educator*

Minneapolis
Anderson, Chester Grant *English educator*
Bales, Kent Roslyn *English language educator*
Bashiri, Iraj *Central Asian studies educator*
Boylan, Brian Richard *author, historian, director, photographer, literary agent*
Browne, Donald Roger *speech communication educator*
Campbell, Karlyn Kohrs *speech and communication educator*
†Clayton, Thomas Swoverland *English educator*
Erickson, Gerald Meyer *classical studies educator*
Farah, Caesar Elie *Middle Eastern and Islamic studies educator*
Firchow, Evelyn Scherabon *German educator, author*
Firchow, Peter Edgerly *language professional, educator, author*
Hauch, Valerie Catherine *historian, educator, researcher*
Jewell, H. Richard *English language educator*
Klee, Carol Anne *foreign language educator*
Kohlstedt, Sally Gregory *history educator*
Krause, Timothy Gilbert *English educator*
Marling, Karal Ann *art history and social sciences educator, curator*
Monson, Dianne Lynn *literacy educator*
†Mowitt, John William *humanities educator*
Noonan, Thomas Schaub *history educator, Russian studies educator*
Norberg, Arthur Lawrence, Jr. *historian, physicist educator*
Pazandak, Carol Hendrickson *liberal arts educator*
†Peterson, Sandra Lynne *philosophy educator*
†Rabinowitz, Paula *writer, educator*
Ross, Donald, Jr. *English language educator, university administrator*
Sarles, Harvey B. *humanities educator*
Scott, Robert Lee *speech educator*
Seidel, Robert Wayne *science historian, educator, institute administrator*
Tracy, James Donald *historian*
Weiss, Gerhard Hans *German language educator*
†Zahareas, Anthony Nicholas *Spanish language educator*

Moorhead
Anderson, Jerry Maynard *speech educator*
†Bense, Charles James *English educator*
†Glasrud, Clarence Arthur *English educator*

Northfield
Clark, Clifford Edward, Jr. *history educator*
Iseminger, Gary Hudson *philosophy educator*
Mason, Perry Carter *philosophy educator*
Rippley, LaVern J. *German educator, real estate developer*
Sipfle, David Arthur *retired philosophy educator*
Soule, George Alan *literature educator, writer*
Yandell, Cathy Marleen *foreign language educator*
Zelliot, Eleanor Mae *history educator*

Owatonna
McGuire, David Ottis *history educator*

Plymouth
Klobuchar, Myrna Nilan *English educator*

Rochester
Maristuen-Rodakowski, Julie *English language educator*
Robbins, Thomas Landau *humanities researcher*

Saint Cloud
Falk, Armand Elroy *retired English educator, writer*
Hofsommer, Donovan Lowell *history educator*
Litterst, Judith K. *speech communication educator*
†Sheppard, Lois Arleen *English educator*
Specht-Jarvis, Roland Hubert *fine arts and humanities educator, dean*
Van Buren, Phyllis Eileen *Spanish and German language educator*

Saint Paul
Barker-Nunn, Jeanne Beverly *English educator*
†Johnson, Feng-Ling Margaret *English educator*
†Litecky, Larry Paul *humanities educator, academic administrator*
Mather, Richard Burroughs *retired Chinese language and literature educator*
†May, S. Rachel *Russian language educator, foundation executive*
McDougal, Stuart Yeatman *comparative literature educator, author*
Murray, Peter Bryant *English language educator*
Stewart, James Brewer *historian, author, college administrator*

Saint Peter
Kyoore, Paschal Baylon *foreign language educator*
Voight, Phillip Anthony *forensics educator*

Vadnais Heights
Polakiewicz, Leonard Anthony *foreign language and literature educator*

White Bear Lake
Mulcahy, Greg *English educator, writer*

Winona
Ramos, Lilian Eva Maria *foreign language educator*

MISSISSIPPI

Clinton
Bigelow, Martha Mitchell *retired historian*
Eaves, Richard Glen *history educator, dean*

Gulfport
Swetman, Glenn Robert *English language educator, poet*

Hattiesburg
†Barthelme, Steven *English educator*

Itta Bena
Washington, Barbara J. *English educator*

Jackson
Mitchell, Dennis Jerrell *history educator, humanities consultant*

Magnolia
Coney, Elaine Marie *English and foreign languages educator*

Mississippi State
Lowery, Charles Douglas *history educator, academic administrator*

Pascagoula
Irving, Thomas Ballantine *retired Spanish language educator, consultant*

Starkville
Wolverton, Robert Earl *classics educator*

Tougaloo
Johnson, Richard Carl *philosophy educator, humanities educator*
†Ward, Jerry Washington *English language educator*

University
Golding, Alan Charles *English educator*
Hall, J(ames) R(obert) *English educator*
Jordan, Winthrop Donaldson *historian, educator*
Kiger, Joseph Charles *history educator*
Landon, Michael de Laval *historian, educator*

MISSOURI

Cape Girardeau
†Hilty, Peter Daniel *retired English educator, poet*
Hoffman, Steven James *historian, educator*
†Jedan, Dieter *language educator*
Nickell, Franklin Delano *historian*
†Raschlee, Debrah *English educator*

Chesterfield
Matros, Larisa Grigoryevna *medical philosophy researcher, writer*

Columbia
Alexander, Thomas Benjamin *history educator*
Anderson, Donald Kennedy, Jr. *English educator*
Bien, Joseph Julius *philosophy educator*
Goodrich, James William *historian, association executive*
Horner, Winifred Bryan *humanities educator, researcher, consultant, writer*
Jones, William McKendrey *language professional, educator*
†Koditschek, Theodore *historian, educator*
Lago, Mary McClelland *English language educator, author*
Miller, Kerby A. *history educator*
Mullen, Edward John, Jr. *Spanish language educator*
†Muratore, Mary Jo *humanities educator*
Overby, Osmund Rudolf *art historian, educator*
†Pierce, Glenn Palen *language educator*
†Rueda, Ana M. *Spanish literature educator*
Schwartz, Richard Brenton *English language educator, university dean, writer*
Strickland, Arvarh Eunice *history educator*
Timberlake, Charles Edward *history educator*
Wallach, Barbara Price *classicist, educator*
Zguta, Russell *history educator*

Fayette
Melnyk, Julie Ann *english educator*

Florissant
Ashhurst, Anna Wayne *foreign language educator*

Fulton
Blair, Rebecca Sue *English educator, lay minister*

Higginsville
Allison, Sandy *genealogist, appraiser, political consultant*

Joplin
†Boudreaux, Marjory Ann *English language educator, consultant*
Laas, Virginia Jeans *historian*
Merriam, Allen Hayes *speech communication educator*
Weber, Maryann *language educator*

Kansas City
Hoffmann, Donald *architectural historian*

Kirksville
Davis, Adam Brooke *English educator*
Engber, Cheryl Ann *language educator, linguist*
†Iles, Lawrence Irvine *liberal arts educator*
Siewert, Gregg Hunter *language professional educator*

Maryville
Heusel, Barbara Stevens *English scholar and educator*

Nevada
†Campbell, Catherine Ellen *French language educator*

Rolla
Cohen, Gerald Leonard *foreign language educator*

Saint Joseph
Chelline, Warren Herman *English educator, clergy member*

Saint Louis
Barmann, Lawrence Francis *history educator*
Boyd, Robert Cotton *English language educator*
†Burkholder, Mark Alan *historian, educator*
Critchlow, Donald Thomas *history educator*
Dezon-Jones, Elyane Agnes *French language educator, writer*
Jones, Ellen Carol *English educator*
Krukowski, Lucian *philosophy educator, artist*
Montesi, Albert Joseph *retired English educator*
†Pautrot, Jean-Louis Jacques *educator*
Perry, Lewis Curtis *historian, educator*
Pitelka, Linda Pacini *history educator*
Ruland, Richard Eugene *English and American literature educator, critic, literary historian*
Sale, Merritt *classicist, comparatist, educator*
Schwarz, Egon *humanities and German language educator, author, literary critic*
Shea, Daniel Bartholomew, Jr. *English language educator, actor*
Ullian, Joseph Silbert *philosophy educator*

Watson, Richard Allan *philosophy educator, writer*
Wellman, Carl Pierce *philosophy educator*
Wu, Nelson Ikon *art history educator, author, artist*
Zlobin, Nikolai V. *history educator*

Salem
Wood, Thomas Wesley *humanities educator, editor*

Springfield
Burgess, Ruth Lenora Vassar *speech and language educator*
Costabile-Heming, Carol Anne *humanities educator*

University City
Adams, Joseph Lee, Jr. *history educator, mayor*

Warrensburg
Robbins, Dorothy Ann *foreign language educator*

Wildwood
Brawner, Patricia Ann *English educator*

Windyville
Blosser, Pamela Elizabeth *metaphysics educator, counselor, minister*

MONTANA

Big Arm
†Dale, David Wilson *English educator, poet*

Bozeman
Mentzer, Raymond Albert *history educator*

Butte
†Reardon, Stephen James, Jr. *retired English speech educator*

Great Falls
†Bobbitt, Curtis Wayne *English educator*

Missoula
Brenner, Gerry *English educator*
†Chacón, Hipólito Rafael *art historian, educator, art critic*

NEBRASKA

Callaway
Maring, Glady Marie *English educator, poet*

Kearney
Luscher, Robert Michael *English educator, department chair*
Schuyler, Michael W. *historian, educator*
Young, Ann Elizabeth O'Quinn *historian, educator*

Lincoln
Buhler, Stephen Michael *English educator*
†Knoll, Robert Edwin *English educator*
Leinieks, Valdis *classicist, educator*
Levin, Carole *history educator*
Luebke, Frederick Carl *retired humanities educator*
Pratt, Linda Ray *English language educator*
Rawley, James Albert *history educator*
Sawyer, Robert McLaran *history educator*
†Smith, Delores Kay *secondary English educator*
Stover, John Ford *railroad historian, educator*

Omaha
Bergman, Roger Charles *ethics educator*
†LeBeau, Bryan F. *history educator*
Okhamafe, Imafedia *English literature and philosophy educator*
†Spencer, Brent Avery *English literature educator, writer*
Tate, Michael Lynn *history educator*

NEVADA

Henderson
McCafferty, Steven Garth *English educator*

Las Vegas
Adams, Charles Lynford *English language educator*
Strauss, Paul Edward *English language educator*
†Unrue, Darlene Harbour *English educator, writer*

North Las Vegas
Beachley, DeAnna Eileen *history educator*
Green, Michael Scott *history educator, columnist*
Miller, Eleanor *English language and literature educator*

Reno
Branch, Michael Paul *humanities educator*
Hulse, James Warren *history educator, writer*
Simonian, Lane Peter *history educator*
White, Linda Louise *literture educator, writer*

NEW HAMPSHIRE

Barrington
Olivier, Julien L. *translator, consultant*

Derry
†Wixson, Kellie Donovan *English educator*

Durham
†Diller, Karl Conrad *linguistics educator*
Hapgood, Robert Derry *English educator*
Wheeler, Douglas Lanphier *history educator, author*

Exeter
Dunleavy, Janet Frank Egleson *English language educator*

Freedom
Kucera, Henry *linguistics educator*

Hanover
Arndt, Walter W. *Slavic scholar, linguist, writer, translator*
Bien, Peter Adolph *English language educator, author*
Conley, Katharine *language educator*
Cook, William Wilbert *English language educator*
Daniell, Jere Rogers, II *history educator, consultant, public lecturer*
Doney, Willis Frederick *philosophy educator*
†Foelsche, Otmar Karl Ernst *German language educator*
Garthwaite, Gene Ralph *historian, educator*
Gert, Bernard *philosopher, educator*
Heffernan, James Anthony Walsh *English language and literature educator*
Kritzman, Lawrence David *humanities educator*
Low, Victor N. *historian*
Lyon, Bryce Dale *historian, educator*
Mansell, Darrel Lee, Jr. *English educator*
Oxenhandler, Neal *language educator, writer*
Penner, Hans Henry *historian*
Russell, Robert Hilton *Romance languages and literature educator*
Scher, Steven Paul *literature educator*
Scherr, Barry Paul *foreign language educator*
Sheldon, Richard Robert *Russian language and literature educator*
Shewmaker, Kenneth Earl *history educator*
Wood, Charles Tuttle *history educator*

Keene
Long, Mark Chistopher *English educator*

Laconia
Heald, Bruce Day *English and music educator, historian*

Madbury
Bruce, Robert Vance *historian, educator*

Nashua
Light, James Forest *English educator*

Orford
Beale, Georgia Robison *historian, educator*

Penacook
Szoverffy, Joseph *educator, medieval scholar*

Portsmouth
Brage, Carl Willis *genealogist*

Strafford
Simic, Charles *English language educator, poet*

NEW JERSEY

Atco
Lowe, Thomas Joseph *history educator*

Avon By The Sea
Potter, Emma Josephine Hill *language educator*

Caldwell
Jennings, Sister Vivien Ann *English language educator*
†Mullaney, Marie Marmo *history and political science educator*

Camden
Scranton, Philip Brown *history educator*
Showalter, English, Jr. *French language educator*

Cape May
Lassner, Franz George *educator*

Clifton
Ressetar, Nancy *foreign language educator*
Stalbaum, Bernardine Ann *English language educator*

Demarest
Brody, Saul Nathaniel *English literature educator*

Edgewater
Meier, August *historian, educator*

Edison
Frary, John Newton *history educator*

Fort Monmouth
Ignoffo, Matthew Frederick *English language educator, writer, counselor*

Glassboro
†Johnson, Frances Swigon *English educator*

Hewitt
Mollenkott, Virginia Ramey *English language educator, author, guest lecturer*

Highland Lakes
Kiraly, Béla Kálmán *retired history educator, Hungarian army officer*

Highland Park
Pane, Remigio Ugo *Romance languages educator*

Jersey City
†Coreil, Raymond Clyde *English educator*
Daane, Mary Constance *English language educator*
Lane, Ted *literacy education educator*

Lawrenceville
O'Reilly, Mary Irby *literature educator, composition consultant*

Lincroft
Jones, Floresta D. *English educator*

Madison
Mc Mullen, Edwin Wallace, Jr. *English language educator*

Manasquan
Mangan, Judith Ann *English language educator*

Mays Landing
Benner, Richard Byron *philosophy educator*

Metuchen
†Rodriguez-Laguna, Asela *Spanish educator*

New Brunswick
Chambers, John Whiteclay, II *history educator*
Derbyshire, William Wadleigh *language educator, translator*
Gardner, Lloyd Calvin, Jr. *history educator*
Gillette, William *historian, educator*
Grob, Gerald N. *historian, educator*
Hartman, Mary S. *historian*
Kelley, Donald Reed *historian*
Levine, George Lewis *English language educator, literature critic*
Lewis, David Levering *history educator*
Lyons, Bridget Gellert *English educator*
†Marder, Tod A. *art historian, educator*
O'Neill, William Lawrence *history educator*
Reed, James Wesley *social historian, educator*
Serafini, Tina *English and reading educator*
Smith, Bonnie Gene *historian, educator*
Stich, Stephen Peter *philosophy educator*
Tripolitis, Antonia *religion, classics and comparative literature educator*
Walker, Steven F. *comparative literature educator*
†Welsh, Andrew *English educator*
†Westermann, Martine Henriëtte *art historian, educator, curator*

Newark
Diner, Steven Jay *history educator*
Franklin, H. Bruce *language educator, writer*
Gironda, Marie Grace *English language educator*
Schweizer, Karl Wolfgang *historian, writer*
Sher, Richard B. *historian*
Stiller, Nikki *English language educator*

Newton
Ancona, Francesco Aristide *humanities and mythology educator, writer*

Paramus
Lenk, Richard William, Jr. *history educator*
†Ryan, Steven D. *English language educator*

Parsippany
Donaghy, Christine Ann *English language educator*

Piscataway
Martinez-Fernandez, Luis *history educator, writer*
Mc Cormick, Richard Patrick *history educator*

Pomona
†Mench, Fred Charles *classics educator*

Princeton
Aarsleff, Hans *linguistics educator*
Bermann, Sandra Lekas *English language educator*
Bowersock, Glen Warren *historian*
Brombert, Victor Henri *literature educator, author*
Brown, Leon Carl *history educator*
Cahill, James Francis *retired art history educator*
Champlin, Edward James *classics educator*
Coffin, David Robbins *art historian, educator*
Cooper, John Madison *philosophy educator*
Corngold, Stanley Alan *German and comparative literature educator, writer*
Curschmann, Michael Johann Hendrik *German language and literature educator*
Darnton, Robert Choate *history educator*
Ermolaev, Herman Sergei *Slavic languages educator*
Feria, Bernabe Francis *linguist*
Goheen, Robert Francis *classicist, educator, former ambassador*
Grafton, Anthony Thomas *history educator*
Gutmann, Amy *political science and philosophy educator*
Habicht, Christian Herbert *history educator*
Harman, Gilbert Helms *philosophy educator*
Hollander, Robert B., Jr. *Romance languages educator*
Hynes, Samuel *English language educator, author*
Itzkowitz, Norman *history educator*
Jeffery, Peter Grant *musicologist, fine arts educator*
Jeffrey, Richard Carl *philosophy educator*
Jenson, Pauline Alvino *retired speech and hearing educator*
Jordan, William Chester *history educator*
Knoepflmacher, Ulrich Camillus *literature educator*
Lewis, Bernard *Near Eastern studies educator*
Lewis, David Kellogg *philosopher, educator*
Mahoney, Michael Sean *history educator*
Marks, John Henry *Near Eastern studies educator*
McFarland, Thomas *English educator*
Mc Pherson, James Munro *history educator*
Miner, Earl Roy *literature educator*
Moote, A. Lloyd *history educator*
Morrison, Simon Alexander *musicologist, educator*
Moynahan, Julian Lane *English language educator, author*
Nehamas, Alexander *philosophy educator*
Oberg, Barbara Bowen *historian, educator, scholarly writer*
†Obi, Chinwe I *French language educator*
Paret, Peter *historian*
Rabb, Theodore K. *historian, educator*
Rigolot, François *French literature educator, literary critic*
Rodgers, Daniel Tracy *history educator*
Schofield, Robert E(dwin) *history educator, academic administrator*
Schorske, Carl Emil *historian, educator*
Shimizu, Yoshiaki *art historian, educator*
Showalter, Elaine *humanities educator*
Walter, Hugo Günther *humanities educator*
White, Morton Gabriel *philosopher, author*
Wightman, Ludmilla G. Popova *language educator, foreign educator, translator*
Woolf, Harry *historian, educator*
Ziolkowski, Theodore Joseph *comparative literature educator*

Red Bank
†Stansbury, Kevin Bradley *English educator, educational consultant*

Ridgewood
Hinckley, Deborah Clark *language services professional*

Sewell
†Hart, Robert Lee *English educator*

Teaneck
Dowd, Janice Lee *foreign language educator*
Gordon, Lois Goldfein *English language educator*
Rudy, Willis *historian*
Soletsky, Albert *language educator*
Walensky, Dorothy Charlotte *foreign language educator*

Trenton
Cole, Robert Carlton *English and journalism educator*
George, Emery Edward *foreign language and studies educator*

Upper Saddle River
Cullen, Thomas Joseph *history educator*

Wayne
Bowles, Suzanne Geissler *history educator*
Kolak, Daniel *philosopher*
O'Connor, John Morris, III *philosophy educator*
Rogoff, Paula Drimmer *English and foreign language educator*

West Long Branch
Dvoichenko-Markov, Demetrius *history educator*
†Garvey, Brian Thomas *educator in English, university administrator*

Westfield
McDevitt, Brian Peter *history educator, educational consultant*

NEW MEXICO

Albuquerque
Cully, Suzanne Maria *modern language educator*
DePalo, William Anthony, Jr. *Latin American studies educator*
†Etulain, Richard Wayne *historian, educator*
Frings, Manfred Servatius *philosophy educator*
Fuller, Anne Elizabeth Havens *English language and literature educator, consultant*
Gaines, Barry Joseph *English literature educator*
Gatlin, Karen Christensen *English language educator*
Hutton, Paul Andrew *history educator, writer*
Lind, Levi Robert *classics educator, author*
Nash, Gerald David *historian*
Peña, Juan José *interpreter*
Thorson, James Llewellyn *English language educator*

Las Cruces
Bloom, John Porter *historian, editor, administrator, archivist*
†Erhard, Thomas Agnew *English educator*
†Graham, Kenneth John Emerson *English language educator*
Newman, Edgar Leon *historian, educator*
Wilson, Keith Charles *retired English educator, poet, short story writer*

Las Vegas
Croxton, Dorothy Audrey Simpson *speech educator*

Santa Fe
Lehmberg, Stanford Eugene *historian, educator*
Maehl, William Henry *historian, university administrator, educational consultant*

Socorro
†McKee, John DeWitt *retired English educator*

NEW YORK

Albany
†Cohen, Tom F. *critic*
Creegan, Robert Francis *philosophy educator, writer*
Donovan, Robert Alan *English educator*
Eckstein, Jerome *philosopher, educator*
Frank, Francine Harriet *language educator, linguist*
Hahner, June Edith *history educator*
Kekes, John *philosopher, educator*
Mastrangelo, Lisa Siobhan *humanities educator*
Pohlsander, Hans Achim *classics educator*
Pryse, Marjorie Lee *American literature educator, researcher*
Reese, William Lewis *philosophy educator*
Roberts, Louis William *classics and humanities educator*
Zacek, Joseph Frederick *history educator, international studies consultant, East European culture and affairs specialist*

Alfred
†Tolhurst, Fiona *English language educator*

Amherst
Kibby, Michael William *reading educator*
†Wickert, Max Albrecht *English educator*

Annandale On Hudson
Mullen, William Cocke *classics educator*

Auburn
Patterson, John Edward *language educator*

Ballston Spa
†MacDonald, Bonney *English educator*

Bayside
Testa, Lauren *English educator*

Bear Mountain
Smith, Andrew Josef *historian, publishing executive, naturalist, writer*

Binghamton
Dublin, Thomas Louis *history educator*
Gaddis Rose, Marilyn *comparative literature educator, translator*

Kessler, Milton *English language educator, poet*
Quataert, Donald *history educator*
Sklar, Kathryn Kish *historian, educator*
Stein, George Henry *historian, educator, administrator*

Brentwood
Kelly, Margaret Frances *English language educator*

Briarcliff Manor
Leiser, Burton Myron *philosophy and law educator*

Brockport
Bucholz, Arden Kingsbury *historian, educator*
Leslie, William Bruce *history educator*
Marcus, Robert D. *historian, educator*

Bronx
Asare, Karen Michelle Gilliam *reading, math and English language educator*
†Bernstein, Martin *musicologist, bassist*
†Boon, Kevin Alexander *English educator, writer*
Bowers, Francis Robert *literature educator*
Bullaro, Grace Russo *literature, film and foreign language educator, speaker*
Castora, Joseph Charles *history educator*
†Conley, John Joseph *philosophy educator, priest*
Dobson, Joanne Abele *English language educator*
Hallett, Charles Arthur, Jr. *English and humanities educator*
Hilfstein, Erna *science historian, educator*
Himmelberg, Robert Franklin *historian, educator*
†Isaacs, Diane S. *English educator*
Macklin, Ruth *bioethics educator*
Pietarinen, George *English language educator*
Pita, Marianne D'Arcy *English language educator*
Ultan, Lloyd *historian*

Bronxville
Peters, Sarah Whitaker *art historian, writer, lecturer*
Randall, Francis Ballard *historian, educator, writer*
Sluberski, Thomas Richard *international educator, journalist*
Woodard, Komozi *American history educator*

Brookhaven
Reeves, John Drummond *English language professional, writer*

Brooklyn
Berger, David *history educator*
Blasi, Alberto *Romance languages educator, writer*
†Bloom, Leonard *language educator*
Brownstone, Paul Lotan *retired speech communications and drama educator*
†Cardinale, Drew Anthony *language educator*
Contino, Rosalie Helene *drama educator, costume designer and historian, playwright*
Everdell, William Romeyn *humanities educator*
Flam, Jack Donald *art historian, educator*
Jaffe, Louise *English language educator, creative writer*
Jofen, Jean *foreign language educator*
King, Margaret Leah *history educator*
Langiulli, Nino F. *philosophy educator*
Lobron, Barbara L. *speech educator, writer, editor, photographer*
†McCrary, Donald *English language educator*
Morrison, Barbara Sheffield *Japanese translator and interpreter, consultant*
Morton, Marsha Lee *art history educator*
Olson, Robert Goodwin *philosophy educator*
†Rittner, Leona Phyllis *comparative literature scholar*
Seiden, Morton Irving *humanities educator*
†Sparrow, Jennifer Ruth *English language educator*
Spector, Robert Donald *language professional, educator*
†Templeton, Joan *educator English*
Vidal, Maureen Eris *English language educator, actress*
†Yin, Kenneth Joseph *language educator*

Buffalo
Allen, William Sheridan *history educator*
Doyno, Victor Anthony *literature educator*
Drew, Fraser Bragg Robert *English language educator*
Fiedler, Leslie Aaron *English educator, actor, author*
†Fisher, Jane Elizabeth *English educator*
Gallagher, Shaun Andrew *philosophy educator, writer*
Gracia, Jorge Jesus Emiliano *philosopher, educator*
Hare, Peter Hewitt *philosophy educator*
Iggers, Georg Gerson *history educator*
Kearns, John Thomas *philosophy educator*
LaHood, Marvin John *English educator*
Levine, George Richard *English language educator*
Merini, Rafika *foreign language and literature and women's studies educator*
Milligan, John Drane *historian, educator*
Mitchell, William I. *historian, social studies educator*
O'Donnell, William Edward *Spanish language educator*
†Ousley, Laurie Marie *English educator*
Payne, Frances Anne *literature educator, researcher*
Peradotto, John Joseph *classics educator, editor*
Richards, David Gleyre *German language educator*
Riepe, Dale Maurice *philosopher, writer, illustrator, educator, Asian art dealer*
Saveth, Edward Norman *history educator*
†Shimojo, Mitsuaki *linguist, educator*
Siedlecki, Peter Anthony *English language and literature educator*
†Stinger, Charles L. *history educator*
Tall, Emily *foreign language educator*
Wolck, Wolfgang Hans-Joachim *linguist, educator*

Canton
Goldberg, Rita Maria *foreign language educator*

Castleton
†Kienzle, John Fred *history educator*
VanVliet, Mary Lynne *English language educator, photographer's assistant*

Clinton
†Doubleday, Simon Richard *historian*
Wagner, Frederick Reese *language professional*

Cooperstown
Tripp, Wendell *historian, publications director*

Cortland
Anderson, Donna Kay *musicologist, educator*
Kaminsky, Alice Richkin *English language educator*
†Wright, Donald R. *history educator*

Delmar
†Brewer, Floyd I. *history consultant*
Schwartz, Louise A. *musicologist*

Dobbs Ferry
LeRoy, Karen Leslie *English language educator*
Poian, Edward Licio *historian*

East Amherst
Ernest, Welden Arenas *retired history educator*

East Hampton
Swerdlow, Amy *historian, educator, writer*
†Thompson, William Irwin *humanities educator, author*

Fairport
Carlton, Charles Merritt *linguistics educator*
†Graham, Susette Ryan *retired English educator*

Flushing
Bird, Thomas Edward *foreign language and literature educator*
Hirshson, Stanley Philip *history educator*
Kinsbruner, Jay *history educator*
Lonigan, Paul Raymond *language professional educator*
†Low, Frederick Emerson *English educator*
Rabassa, Gregory *Romance languages educator, translator, poet*
Ranald, Margaret Loftus *English literature educator, author*
Richter, David Henry *English language educator, writer*
†Slatkes, Leonard Joseph *art history educator*
Tai, Emily Sohmer *history educator, writer*
Tytell, John *humanities educator, writer*

Forest Hills
Kra, Pauline Skornicki *French language educator*

Fredonia
Belliotti, Raymond Angelo *philosopher, educator, lawyer*
Browder, George Clark *history educator, writer*
Sonnenfeld, Marion *linguist, educator*
†Steinberg, Theodore Louis *English educator*

Garden City
†Falk, Patricia *English language educator*
Jenkins, Kenneth Vincent *literature educator, writer*
Korshak, Yvonne *art historian*
Shneidman, J. Lee *historian, educator*

Gardiner
Mabee, Carleton *historian, educator*

Geneseo
Edgar, William John *philosophy educator*
†Lutkus, Alan H. *English educator*
†Nassif, Maggie N. *educator in English and literature, translator*

Geneva
Singal, Daniel Joseph *historian*

Glen Cove
Petrovich, Peter Yurosh *English and foreign language educator, writer*

Greenvale
†Dinan, Susan Eileen *history educator*
Dircks, Phyllis Toal *English language educator*

Hamburg
Falkner, Noreen Margaret *English language educator*

Hamilton
†Balakian, Peter *English educator*
Blackton, Charles S(tuart) *history educator*
Busch, Briton Cooper *historian, educator*
Garland, Robert Sandford John *classical studies educator*
Hathaway, Robert Lawton *Romance languages educator*
†Johnson, Anita *Spanish language educator*
Levy, Jacques *educator, theater director, lyricist, writer*
Soderberg, Dale LeRoy *English language educator, drama director, producer*
Staley, Lynn *English educator*
Van Schaack, Eric *art historian, educator*

Hempstead
†Pugliese, Stanislao *history educator, researhcer*

Herkimer
Martin, Lorraine B. *humanities educator*

Ithaca
Abrams, Meyer Howard *English language educator*
Brown, Theodore Morey *art history educator*
Colby-Hall, Alice Mary *Romance studies educator*
Culler, Jonathan Dwight *English language educator*
Duhig, Susan C. *English language and literature educator*
Eddy, Donald Davis *English language educator*
Gibian, George *Russian and comparative literature educator*
Groos, Arthur Bernhard, Jr. *German literature educator*
Hohendahl, Peter Uwe *German language and literature educator*
Kammen, Carol Koyen *historian, educator*
†Kim, Youngmin *English educator*
†Kline, Ronald R. *history and technology educator*
Koschmann, J. Victor *history educator, academic program director*
Kronik, John William *Romance studies educator*
LaCapra, Dominick Charles *historian*
LaFeber, Walter Frederick *history educator, author*
McConkey, James Rodney *English educator, writer*
†Najemy, John Michael *history educator*
Norton, Mary Beth *history educator, author*
Porte, Joel Miles *English educator*
†Pucci, Pietro *humanities educator*

Radzinowicz, Mary Ann *language educator*
Schwarz, Daniel Roger *English language educator*
Shoemaker, Sydney S. *philosophy educator*
Silbey, Joel Henry *history educator*

Jamaica
Dircks, Richard Joseph *English language educator, writer*
Fay, Thomas A. *philosopher, educator*
Harmond, Richard Peter *historian, educator*
Kitts, Thomas Michael *English language educator, writer*
Maertz, Gregory *English language educator*
Wintergerst, Ann Charlotte *language educator*

Jericho
Astuto, Philip Louis *retired Spanish educator*

Johnson City
Bernardo, Aldo Sisto *foreign language educator, retired*

Katonah
†Baker, Ian Archbald *explorer, educator, writer, photographer*

Kenmore
Dumych, Daniel Martin *historian*

Lake George
Foulke, Robert Dana *English educator, travel writer*

Lockwood
Keating, Keith Anthony *English language educator*

Long Island City
†Ard, Patricia *English language educator*
Pender, Karen Imelda *humanities educator*

Loudonville
†Fiore, Peter Amadeus *English educator, clergy*
Van Hook, John Edward *philosophy educator*

Melville
Feindler, Joan La Garde *foreign language educator*
Kennedy, Nancy Macri *English language educator*

Middle Village
Walter, John Frederick *historical researcher, genealogist*

Monsey
Erickson, Barbara Martha *historian, writer, florist*

New Paltz
Fakler, Mary Edith *English educator*
Hathaway, Richard Dean *language professional, educator*
Hauptman, Laurence Marc *history educator*
Ryan, Marleigh Grayer *Japanese language educator*

New Rochelle
Fitch, Nancy Elizabeth *historian*
Noone, Katherine A. *English language educator*
†Pendleton, Thomas A. *English educator*

New York
Adams, Barbara *English language educator, poet, writer*
†Adams, Rachel Elizabeth *English language educator*
†Adenaike, Carolyn Keyes *historian, educator*
Alazraki, Jaime *Romance languages educator*
Allentuck, Marcia Epstein *English language and art history educator*
Andreopoulos, George John *history educator, lawyer, political science educator*
Ashbery, John Lawrence *language educator, poet, playwright*
Baker, Paul Raymond *history educator*
Barickman, Richard Bruce *English educator, writer*
†Barkan, Leonard *humanities educator*
Baron, Robert *folklorist*
Belknap, Robert Lamont *Russian and comparative literature educator*
Bender, Thomas *history and humanities educator, writer*
Berghahn, Volker Rolf *history educator*
Bielenstein, Hans Henrik August *Oriental studies educator*
†Birns, Nicholas Boe *educator, editor*
Bishop, Thomas Walter *French language and literature educator*
Block, Ned *philosophy educator*
Bonfante, Larissa *classics educator*
Boudreau, A. Allan *historian, writer, educator*
Brilliant, Richard *art history educator*
Brooks, Jerome Bernard *English and Afro-American literature educator*
Brown, Jonathan *art historian, fine arts educator*
Brush, Craig Balcombe *retired French language and computer educator*
Bulliet, Richard Williams *history educator, novelist*
Burrill, Kathleen R. F. (Kathleen R. F. Griffin-Burrill) *Turkologist, educator*
Cahn, Steven Mark *philosopher, educator*
†Campbell, Margarette Monjoa *interpreter, translator*
Cavallo, Jo Ann *Italian language educator*
Caws, Mary Ann *French language and comparative literature educator, critic*
†Cohen, Morton Norton *English educator, writer*
Compagnon, Antoine Marcel *French language educator*
Cook, Blanche Wiesen *history educator, journalist*
Czerwinski, Edward Joseph *foreign language educator*
Danisi, John J. *philosopher, educator*
D'Arms, John Haughton *association executive, classics educator*
Dawson, Philip *history educator*
Deak, Istvan *historian, educator*
de Menil, Lois Pattison *historian, philanthropist*
Diggins, John Patrick *history educator*
Discorfano, Sharon Marie *English literature educator*
Dore, Anita Wilkes *English language educator*
Driver, Martha Westcott *English language educator, writer, researcher*
Duberman, Martin *historian*
Eisler, Colin Tobias *art historian, curator*
Ferrante, Joan Marguerite *English and comparative literature educator*
Foner, Eric *historian, educator*

Freedberg, David Adrian *art educator, historian*
Freeman, James Beaumont *philosophy educator*
Gallo, Pia *art historian*
Gerdts, William Henry *art history educator*
Ginter, Valerian Alexius *urban historian, educator*
Gluck, Carol *history educator*
Gromada, Thaddeus V. *historian, administrator*
†Haac, Oscar Alfred *retired French educator*
Harris, Frederick John *foreign language and literature educator*
Harris, Katherine Safford *speech and hearing educator*
Harris, William Vernon *history educator*
Harvey, Donald Joseph *history educator*
Heffner, Richard Douglas *historian, educator, communications consultant, television producer*
Heilbrun, Carolyn Gold *English literature educator*
Held, George *English educator*
Hoeflin, Ronald Kent *philosopher, test designer, newsletter publisher*
†Howard, Jean E. *English educator*
Howe, Florence *English educator, writer, publisher*
Hunter-Stiebel, Penelope *art historian, art dealer*
Hyman, Arthur *philosopher, educator, dean*
Jackson, Kenneth Terry *historian, educator*
Johnson, Samuel Frederick *English and literature educator emeritus*
Kalmus, Ellin *art historian, educator*
Karsen, Sonja Petra *retired American-Spanish literature educator*
Kastan, David Scott *university educator, writer*
Kivette, Ruth Montgomery *English language educator*
Kneller, John William *retired French language and literature educator*
Krinsky, Carol Herselle *art history educator*
Kroeber, Karl *English language educator*
Lamont, Rosette Clementine *Romance languages educator, theatre journalist, translator*
La Rue, (Adrian) Jan (Pieters) *musicologist, educator, author*
Leavitt, Charles Loyal *English language educator, administrator*
Leibowitz, Herbert Akiba *English language educator, author*
Lemisch, Jesse *history educator, writer*
Lencek, Rado Ludovik *Slavic languages educator*
Levi, Isaac *philosophy educator*
Lewyn, Ann Salfeld *English as a second language educator*
London, Herbert Ira *humanities educator, institute executive*
Long, Rose-Carol Washton *art historian*
Lorch, Maristella De Panizza *medieval and Renaissance scholar, writer*
Low, Anthony *English language educator*
Lowenthal, Constance *art historian*
Malefakis, Edward E. *history educator*
Malin, Irving *English literature educator, literary critic*
Mapp, Edward Charles *speech educator*
Marrin, Albert *history educator, writer*
Mayerson, Philip *classics educator*
Maynard, John Rogers *English educator*
†McAleer, Edward Cornelius *retired Englishliterature educator*
Mc Kitrick, Eric Louis *historian, educator*
Meisel, Martin *English and comparative literature educator*
Meisel, Perry *English educator*
Middendorf, John Harlan *English literature educator*
Miller, Walter James *English and humanities educator, writer*
Minkoff, Harvey Allen *English educator*
Mintz, Samuel Isaiah *English language educator, writer*
Monfasani, John *historian, educator*
Myers, Gerald E. *humanities educator*
Olivares, Rene Eugenio *translator*
Paxton, Robert Owen *historian, educator*
Plottel, Jeanine Parisier *foreign language educator*
Podracky, John Robert *police and law enforcement historian, curator*
Poirier, Richard *English educator, literary critic*
Posner, Donald *art historian*
†Quiñones Keber, Eloise *art historian, educator*
Ravitch, Diane Silvers *historian, educator, author, government official*
†Read, Allen Walker *retired English educator, researcher*
Rebay, Luciano *Italian literature educator, literary critic*
Reiman, Donald Henry *English language educator*
Reynolds, David Spencer *humanities educator*
Richtman, Jack *French language educator*
†Roden, Frederick Scott *English educator*
Rodriguez, Maria Pilar *foreign language educator*
Rosand, David *art history educator*
Rosenberg, John David *English educator, literary critic*
Rosenblum, Robert *art historian, educator*
†Roth, Robert Joseph *philosophy educator*
Rothman, David J. *history and medical educator*
Rowen, Ruth Halle *musicologist, educator*
†Sacca, Annalisa *Italian literature educator*
Sandler, Lucy Freeman *art history educator*
Scammell, Michael *writer, translator*
Schama, Simon *historian, educator, author*
Scheindlin, Raymond Paul *Hebrew literature educator, translator*
†Schrecker, Ellen Wolf *historian, educator, editor*
Schult, Frederick Charles, Jr. *history educator*
Seigel, Jerrold Edward *historian, writer*
Selig, Karl-Ludwig *language and literature educator*
†Silver, Carole Greta *English language educator*
Silverman, Kenneth Eugene *English educator, writer*
†Sitruk, Michel Maurice *foreign language educator*
Stade, George Gustav *humanities educator*
Steinberg, Leo *art historian, educator*
Stempleski, Susan *English language professional, writer*
Stern, Fritz Richard *historian, educator*
Stimpson, Catharine Roslyn *English language educator, writer*
Tanselle, George Thomas *English language educator, foundation executive*
Taran, Leonardo *classicist, educator*
Travers, Scott Andrew *numismatist*
Turner, Almon Richard *art historian, educator*
Tusiani, Joseph *foreign language educator, author*
Ulanov, Alexander *classics and comparative literature educator*
Unger, Irwin *historian, educator*
Unger, Peter Kenneth *philosophy educator*
†Ward, Aileen *retired humanities educator*
Wasser, Henry *retired American literature and sociology educator*
Wehrmann, Renee Fainas *french professor*

Weil-Garris Brandt, Kathleen (Kathleen Brandt) *art historian*
Weinberg, H. Barbara *art historian, educator, curator paintings and sculpture*
Wiseman, Cynthia Sue *language educator*
Wixom, William David *art historian, museum administrator, educator*
Wortman, Richard S. *historian, educator*
Yerushalmi, Yosef Hayim *historian, educator*
Yurchenco, Henrietta Weiss *ethnomusicologist, writer*
Zirin, Ronald Andrew *classics educator, psychoanalyst*

Niagara University
Martin, William Joseph *English language educator*

Niskayuna
Beharriell, Frederick John *German and comparative literature educator*

Oakdale
Lu, Yuxin *historian, linguist*

Oneonta
Malhotra, Ashok Kumar *philosophy educator*
†Shrader, Douglas Wall, Jr. *philosophy educator*

Orangeburg
Stiles, Stephanie Johnson *English educator*

Oswego
Smiley, Marilynn Jean *musicologist*

Owego
Davis, Joan *English language educator*

Penn Yan
Stiles, Leon Noble *genealogist*

Plattsburgh
Henning, Sylvie Debevec *French language educator*

Potsdam
Cross, John William *foreign language educator*
Harder, Kelsie Brown *retired language professional, educator*

Poughkeepsie
Bartlett, Lynn Conant *English literature educator*
Bergon, Frank *English language educator, writer*
Daniels, Elizabeth Adams *English language educator*
DeMaria, Robert, Jr. *English language educator*
Griffen, Clyde Chesterman *retired history educator*
Hytier, Adrienne Doris *French language educator*
†Johnson, Charles Colton *English educator, dean*
†Kane, Paul *English language educator, poet*
Kelley, David Christopher *philosopher*
Van Norden, Bryan William *Asian studies educator*

Purchase
Redkey, Edwin Storer *history educator*

Rensselaer
Semowich, Charles John *art historian, art dealer and appraiser, curator, artist*

Riverdale
†Di Lascia, Alfred Paul *philosophy educator*

Rochester
Abrams, Sam *humanities educator*
†Albright, Daniel *English educator*
†Bauman, M. Garrett *English educator*
Berman, Milton *history educator*
Brown, Theodore M. *history educator, curator, historical consultant*
Chiarenza, Carl *art historian, critic, artist, educator*
Dohanian, Diran Kavork *art historian, educator*
Eaves, Morris Emery *English language educator*
†Ganley, Beatrice *English educator, writer*
Hauser, William Barry *history educator, historian*
Herminghouse, Patricia Anne *foreign language educator*
Howard, Hubert Wendell *English language educator, academic administrator, choral conductor*
Hoy, Cyrus Henry *language professional, educator*
Johnson, Bruce Marvin *English language educator*
Johnson, James William *English educator, author*
Mann, Alfred *musicology educator, choral conductor*
Ramsey, Jarold William *English language educator, author*
Sanders, John Theodore *philosophy educator*
†Skinner-Linnenberg, Virginia *English educator*
Watanabe, Ruth Taiko *music historian, library science educator*
†Wechsler, Harold Stuart *history educator, consultant*
Young, Mary Elizabeth *history educator*
Zagorin, Perez *historian, educator*

Rockville Centre
Fitzgerald, Sister Janet Anne *philosophy educator, college president emeritus*

Rome
Widrick, Lynn S. *English language educator*

Sag Harbor
Cantor, Norman Frank *history educator, writer*

Saint Bonaventure
Wood, Paul William *language educator*

Sayville
Lippman, Sharon Rochelle *art historian, curator, art therapist, writer*

Scarsdale
Graff, Henry Franklin *historian, educator*

Schenectady
Jonas, Manfred *historian, educator*
Morris, John Selwyn *philosophy educator, college president emeritus*
Murphy, William Michael *literature educator, biographer*

Schenevus
Green, Margaret Mildred *English language educator*

Setauket
Simpson, Louis Aston Marantz *English educator, author*

Sound Beach
Everett, Graham *English language educator, poet, publisher*

Southampton
Brophy, James David, Jr. *humanities educator*

Staten Island
†Bernardo, Susan Marie *English educator*
Fried, Stephen William *English language educator, poet*
†Stearns, Stephen Jerold *history educator, writer*
Urbanc, Katica *language educator*

Stony Brook
Aronoff, Mark H. *linguistics educator, author, consultant*
Crease, Robert Poole, Jr. *philosopher, writer, educator*
Davidson, Cynthia Ann *English language educator, poet*
Goldberg, Homer Beryl *English language educator*
Ihde, Don *philosophy educator, university administrator*
Kuspit, Donald Burton *art historian, art critic, educator*
Levin, Richard Louis *English language educator*
Mignone, Mario B. *Italian studies educator*
Silverman, Hugh J. *philosophy educator*
Spector, Marshall *philosophy educator*
†Wang, Ban *comparative literature educator, writer*

Stuyvesant
Tripp, David Enders *numismatist, art historian, cartoonist*

Suffern
Commanday, Sue Nancy Shair *English language educator*
Harvey, Emily Dennis *art history educator*
Walsh, James Jerome *philosophy educator*

Syracuse
Alston, William Payne *philosophy educator*
Crowley, John W(illiam) *English language educator*
Denise, Theodore Cullom *philosophy educator*
Field, Daniel *history educator*
†Gregory, Robert Granville *historian*
Hoffman, Arthur Wolf *English language educator*
†Novelli, Cornelius *educator, drama critic*
Powell, James Matthew *history educator*
†Schneider, Gerd Klaus *German language educator*
Sternlicht, Sanford *English and theater arts educator, writer*
Sutton, Walter *English educator*
Tatham, David Frederic *art historian, educator*
Waddy, Patricia A. *architectural history educator*

Troy
Ahlers, Rolf Willi *philosopher, theologian*
†Gil-Gomez, Ellen Marie *English language educator*
Whitburn, Merrill Duane *English literature educator*

Valhalla
Leone, Stephen Joseph *English language educator, computer technology consultant*

Vestal
Carpenter, Charles Albert *English language educator*

Waterford
†Madigan, Francis Vincent *English educator*

West Nyack
†Cunneen, Sally McDevitt *English language educator, editor, writer*

West Point
Hilferty, Bryan Carey *English language educator*

White Plains
†Sax, Boria *educator, writer*

Yonkers
Agli, Stephen Michael *English language educator, literature educator*

NORTH CAROLINA

Boone
†Simon, Stephen Joseph *history educator*
Williamson, Jerry Wayne *history educator, editor*

Brevard
McDowell, Laura *music educator*

Cary
Mata, Elizabeth Adams *language educator, land investor*

Chapel Hill
Baron, Samuel Haskell *historian*
Bister-Broosen, Helga *German linguistics educator*
Churchill, Larry Raymond *ethics educator*
Debreczeny, Paul *Slavic language educator, author*
Falk, Eugene Hannes *foreign language educator emeritus*
Flora, Joseph M(artin) *English language educator*
Folda, Jaroslav Thayer, III *art historian*
Garrett, Don James *philosophy educator*
Grendler, Paul Frederick *history educator*
Harlan, Louis Rudolph *history educator, writer*
Heninger, Simeon Kahn, Jr. *English language educator*
Jackson, Blyden *English language educator*
Jones, Houston Gwynne *history educator*
Kohn, Richard H. *historian, educator*
Lee, Sherman Emery *art historian, curator*
Levine, Madeline Geltman *Slavic literatures educator, translator*
Long, Douglas Clark *philosophy educator*
Ludington, Townsend *English and American studies educator*
†McGowan, John Patrick *English language and literature educator*

Munsat, Stanley Morris *philosopher, educator*
Nelson, Philip Francis *musicology educator, consultant, choral conductor*
Rabil, Albert, Jr. *humanities educator*
Schier, Donald Stephen *language educator*
Smith, Sidney Rufus, Jr. *linguist, educator*
Stadter, Philip Austin *classicist, educator*
Stanberry, D(osi) Elaine *English literature educator, writer*
Stephens, Laurence David, Jr. *linguist, investor, oil industry executive*
Tindall, George Brown *historian, educator*
Vogler, Frederick Wright *French language educator*
Weinberg, Gerhard Ludwig *history educator*
Williamson, Joel Rudolph *humanities educator*
Ziff, Paul *philosophy educator*

Charlotte
Hill, Ruth Foell *language consultant*
Myers, Robert Manson *English educator, author*
Preyer, Norris Watson *history educator*

Cullowhee
Farwell, Harold Frederick, Jr. *English language educator*

Davidson
Cole, Richard Cargill *English language educator*
†McMillen, Sally Gregory *history educator*
Mele, Alfred R. *philosophy educator*
†Toumazou, Michael K. *classics educator*
Williams, Robert Chadwell *history educator*
Zimmermann, T. C. Price *historian, educator*

Durham
Budd, Louis John *English language educator*
Butters, Ronald Richard *English language educator*
Cady, Edwin Harrison *English language educator, author*
Chafe, William Henry *history educator*
Colton, Joel *historian, educator*
Davis, Calvin De Armond *historian, educator*
Franklin, John Hope *historian, educator, author*
Gleckner, Robert Francis *English language professional, educator*
Golding, Martin Philip *law and philosophy educator*
Holley, Irving Brinton, Jr. *historian, educator*
Lerner, Warren *historian*
Mauskopf, Seymour Harold *history educator*
Oates, John Francis *classics educator*
Porter, Joseph A. (Joe Ashby Porter) *English language educator, fiction writer*
Preston, Richard Arthur *historian*
Richardson, Lawrence, Jr. *Latin language educator, archeologist*
Roland, Alex Frederick *history educator*
Sanford, David Hawley *philosophy educator*
Scott, Anne Byrd Firor *history educator*
Smith, Grover C(leveland) *English language educator*
Thompson, John Herd *history educator*
Wilder, Alma Ann *English educator*
Williams, George Walton *English educator*

Fayetteville
McMillan, Bettie Barney *English language educator*

Greenmountain
Smith, Kearney Isaac *retired language educator*

Greensboro
Almeida, José Agustin *romance languages educator*
Bardolph, Richard *historian, educator*
Chappell, Fred Davis *English language educator, poet*
MacKenzie, David *history educator, researcher, writer*
†Moraru, Christian *English educator*
†Porter, Thomas Earl *history educator*
Thompson, James Howard *historian, library administrator*

Greenville
Runyan, Timothy Jack *historian, educator*
Shields, Edgar Thomson, Jr. *American literature educator*
Snyder, Harold Michael *language educator*

Hendersonville
Schwarz, Richard William *historian, educator*

High Point
McCaslin, Richard Bryan *history educator*

Hillsborough
Idol, John Lane, Jr. *English language educator, writer, editor*

Jacksonville
Kimball, Lynn Jerome *historian*

Laurinburg
Bayes, Ronald Homer *English language educator, author*

Louisburg
Davis, Sarah Irwin *retired English language educator*

New Bern
Fegely, Eugene Leroy *retired humanities educator*

Pittsboro
Noether, Emiliana Pasca *historian, educator*

Pope AFB
Conley, Raymond Leslie *English language educator*

Raleigh
Durant, Frederick Clark, III *aerospace history and space art consultant*
Jones, Frederick Claudius *English language and linguistics educator*
†Katz, Steven Barry *English educator, writer*
Rhodes, Donald Robert *musicologist, retired electrical engineer*
Ryan, Bryan *language educator, writer, editor*

Reno
†Seib, Kenneth Allen *English educator*

Research Triangle Park
Connor, Walter Robert *classics educator, humanities center administrator*

Shelby
Bolich, Gregory Gordon *humanities educator*

Wilkesboro
†Carroll, Elizabeth Lee *educator English*

Wilmington
Graham, Otis Livingston, Jr. *history educator*
†Habibi, Don A. *philosophy educator*

Winston Salem
Barnett, Richard Chambers *historian, educator*
Hendricks, J(ames) Edwin *historian, educator, consultant, author*
†Oczkowicz, Edyta Katarzyna *English educator*
Shapere, Dudley *philosophy educator*
†Weyler, Karen Ann *English educator*

NORTH DAKOTA

Bismarck
†Brudvig, Jon Larsen *educator, historian*
Newborg, Gerald Gordon *state archives administrator*
Severson, Lynn Kathleen *English educator*

Fargo
Anderson, Gerald Dwight *history educator*
†Cosgrove, William E. *English literature educator*
Danbom, David Byers *history educator*
†O'Connor, Robert Harold *English educator*
Peet, Howard David *English educator, writer*

Grand Forks
Clingan, Charles Edmund *historian*
Coleman, Joyce Kit *English literature educator, literary historian*
Dixon, Kathleen Grace *English educator*

Jamestown
†Lorenzo, David Joseph *history and political science educator*

Mayville
Batesel, Billy Paul *English language educator*

Rolla
†Jacobsen-Theel, Hazel M. *historian*

Williston
†Landes, Daniel Warren *English language educator*

OHIO

Akron
Bryant, Keith Lynn, Jr. *history educator*
Fischer, Jennifer Welsh *English educator*
Knepper, George W. *history educator*
†Sakezles, Priscilla Kathleen *philosophy educator*

Athens
Booth, Alan Rundlett *history educator*
Borchert, Donald Marvin *philosopher, educator*
Crowl, Samuel Renninger *former university dean, english language educator*
Flannagan, Roy Catesby, Jr. *English literature educator, editor*
Matthews, Jack (John Harold Matthews) *English educator, writer*
Perdreau, Cornelia Ruth Whitener (Connie Perdreau) *English as a second language educator, international exchange specialist*
Ping, Charles Jackson *philosophy educator, retired university president*
Whealey, Robert Howard *historian*

Batavia
†Dial, John Elbert *foreign language educator*

Berea
Blumer, Frederick Elwin *philosophy educator*
Lingswiler, Robert Dayton *philosophy educator*
Martin, Terry Jon *English educator*

Bluffton
Gundy, Jeffrey Gene *English educator*

Bowling Green
Browne, Ray Broadus *popular culture educator*
Foell, Kristie Ann *foreign language educator*
†Green, Cecilia Anne *humanities educator*
Hernandez, Mark Alan *educator in Spanish*
†Hess, Gary Ray *historian*
Lavezzi, John Charles *art history educator, archaeologist*

Brecksville
Pappas, Effie Vamis *English and business educator, writer*

Canton
Dickens, Sheila Jeanne *family preservation educator*
Doriani, Beth Maclay *English language educator*
†McLaughlin, Joseph David *English educator, poet, writer*
†Pahlau, Randi Christine *English language educator*

Chagrin Falls
Rawski, Conrad H(enry) *humanities educator, medievalist*

Cincinnati
Bleznick, Donald William *Romance languages educator*
Brod, Evelyn Fay *foreign language educator*
Ciani, Alfred Joseph *language professional, associate dean*
Lewis, Gene Dale *historian, educator*
Michelini, Ann Norris *classics educator*
Muntz, Ernest Gordon *historian, educator*
Schrier, Arnold *historian, educator*

Cleveland
Anderson, David Gaskill, Jr. *Spanish language educator*
Beatie, Bruce Alan *comparative and medieval studies educator*
Benseler, David Price *foreign language educator*
Camden, Vera Jean *psychoanalyst*
†Curnow, Kathy *art historian, educator*
Ferguson, Suzanne Carol *English educator*
Friedman, Barton Robert *English educator*
Greppin, John Aird Coutts *philologist, editor, educator*
Heald, Morrell *humanities educator*
Juhlin, Doris Arlene *French language educator*
Miller, Genevieve *retired medical historian*
Olszewski, Edward John *art history educator*
Pursell, Carroll Wirth *history educator*
Roth, Jack Joseph *historian, educator*
Salomon, Roger Blaine *English language educator*
Spencer, James Calvin, Sr. *humanities educator*
Taylor, Margaret Wischmeyer *retired English language and journalism educator*
Zupancic, Anthony *English and communication educator*

Columbus
Babcock, Charles Luther *classics educator*
†Baishanski, Jacqueline Marie *foreign language educator*
Battersby, James Lyons, Jr. *English language educator*
Beja, Morris *English literature educator*
Boh, Ivan *philosophy educator*
Burnham, John Chynoweth *historian, educator*
DeSando, John Anthony *humanities educator*
Dillon, Merton Lynn *historian, educator*
Gribble, Charles Edward *editor, Slavic languages educator*
Hahm, David Edgar *classics educator*
Hare, Robert Yates *music history educator*
Hoffmann, Charles Wesley *retired foreign language educator*
Jarvis, Gilbert Andrew *humanities educator, writer*
Kasulis, Thomas Patrick *humanities educator*
Kuhn, Albert Joseph *English educator*
Nakayama, Mineharu *language professional/educator Japanese*
Peterson, Gale Eugene *historian*
†Riede, David George *English educator*
Rule, John Corwin *history educator*
Scanlan, James Patrick *philosophy and Slavic studies educator*
Shikina, Seiji *educator, consultant*
Silbajoris, Frank Rimvydas *Slavic languages educator*

Conneaut
Strawbridge, Mary Elizabeth *English educator*

Dayton
Alexander, Roberta Sue *history educator*
Escalón Delgado, Clara S. *English language education specialist*
†Garrison, David Lee *language educator*
Harden, Oleta Elizabeth *English educator, university administrator*
†Martin, Herbert Woodward *English educator, poet*
Vice, Roy Lee *history educator*

Delaware
Lewes, Ulle Erika *English educator*

Dublin
Brooks, Keith *retired speech communication educator*

Galion
Ross, Shirley S. *retired English educator*

Gambier
Guiney, Mortimer Martin *French educator*
Sharp, Ronald Alan *English literature educator, author*

Granville
Lisska, Anthony Joseph *humanities educator, philosopher*
Santoni, Ronald Ernest *philosophy educator*

Grove City
Jackson, Steven Donald *English educator*

Hamilton
†Krafft, John M. *English educator, editor*

Harrison
Coakley, Janet Marie *English educator, consultant creative arts theater*

Huron
Ruble, Ronald Merlin *humanities and theater communications educator*

Kent
Beer, Barrett Lynn *historian, educator*
Byrne, Frank Loyola *history educator*
Dzeda, Bruce Michael *history educator*
†Floyd, Kevin R. *English educator*
Fontes, Manuel Da Costa *foreign language educator*
†Hakutani, Yoshinobu *English educator*
Hassler, Donald Mackey, II *English language educator, writer*
James, Patricia Ann *philosophy educator*
Reid, Sidney Webb *English educator*
†Remley, R. Dirk *English educator, consultant*

Kirtland
Rebolj, Joan Kaletta *language educator*

Logan
Conner, Leland Lavon *Indian lorist*

Mansfield
†Dominick, Raymond Hunter, III *history educator*

Marietta
Wilbanks, Jan Joseph *philosopher*

New Philadelphia
Lazar, Mary Diane *English educator*

Oberlin
Blodgett, Geoffrey Thomas *history educator*
Care, Norman Sydney *philosophy educator*
Colish, Marcia Lillian *history educator*
Collins, Martha *English language educator, writer*
†Hernton, Calvin Coolidge *African American studies educator, artist, writer*
Young, David Pollock *humanities educator, author*

Oxford
†Bauer, Steven Albert *English educator, writer*
Jeep, John Michael *German studies educator*
Parks, John Gordon *English educator*
Siatra, Eleni *English educator*

Parma Heights
Cook, Jeanne Garn *historian, genealogist*

Rio Grande
†Hart, Jack Wayne *English language educator*

Saint Clairsville
Fisher, Sandra Irene *English educator*

Salem
Rice, Douglas Francis *English educator*

Solon
Gallo, Donald Robert *retired English educator*

Springfield
Cantrell, John L. *language educator*

Tiffin
Davison, Kenneth Edwin *American studies educator*
Kramer, Frank Raymond *classicist, educator*
†Norton, Holly Louise *English literature educator*

Toledo
†Barden, Thomas Earl *English literature educator*
†Baumgartner, Holly Lynn *educator in English language and literature*
Cave, Alfred Alexander *history educator, writer*
Nowatzki, Robert Carl *English educator*

University Heights
Aggor, Francis Komla *language educator*
Gatto, Katherine Gyékényesi *modern languages and literatures educator*

Warren
†Dudley, Joseph Michael *English educator*
Yoke, Carl Bernard *English language educator, critic*

Willard
Fritz, Melissa Jane *English educator*

Wooster
Shostak, Debra Beth *English educator*

Yellow Springs
Fogarty, Robert Stephen *historian, educator, editor*

Youngstown
Bowers, Bege K. *English educator*
Brothers, Barbara *English language educator*

OKLAHOMA

Ada
Daniel, Arlie Verl *speech education educator*

Alva
Hardaway, Roger Dale *historian, educator*
Yates, James Newton *English educator*

Chickasha
Meredith, Howard Lynn *American Indian studies educator*

Edmond
†Hamilton, Carol Jean *English educator, writer, storyteller*

Norman
Fears, Jesse Rufus *historian, educator, academic dean*
Gilje, Paul Arn *history educator*
Hagan, William Thomas *history educator*
Hassrick, Peter Heyl *art historian*
Hobbs, Catherine Lynn *English language and literature educator*
Lowitt, Richard *history educator*
Palmer, Marilyn Joan *English composition educator*

Oklahoma City
Foster, Victor Lynn *translator*
Lestina, Roger Henry *English language educator*
Owens, Barbara Ann *English educator*
Todd, Joe Lee *historian*

Stillwater
Agnew, Theodore Lee, Jr. *historian, educator*
Fischer, LeRoy Henry *historian, educator*
Luebke, Neil Robert *philosophy educator*

Tulsa
Buckley, Thomas Hugh *historian, educator*
Faingold, Eduardo Daniel *language and linguistics educator, researcher*

OREGON

Ashland
Bornet, Vaughn Davis *former history and social science educator, research historian*
Levy, Leonard Williams *history educator, author*
Weeks, Roger Wolcott, Jr. *retired German and Russian language educator*

Bend
Donohue, Stacey Lee *English language and literature educator*

Eugene
Albert-Galtier, Alexandre *literature and language educator*
Donnelly, Marian Card *art historian, educator*
Li, David Leiwei *English and Asian American studies educator*
Pascal, C(ecil) Bennett *classics educator*
Wickes, George *English language educator, writer*

Forest Grove
Boersema, David Brian *philosopher, educator*

Hermiston
Ortiz, James George *educator*

North Bend
Shepard, Robert Carlton *English language educator*
†Vendler, Zeno *retired philosophy educator*

Port Orford
Drinnon, Richard *history educator*

Portland
Englert, Walter George *classics and humanities educator*
Ferrua, Pietro Michele Stefano *foreign language educator, writer*
Harris, Frederick Philip *retired philosophy educator*
Kimbrell, Leonard Buell *retired art history educator, art appraiser*
Sacks, David Harris *historian, humanities educator*
Schmidt, Stanley Eugene *retired speech educator*
Steinman, Lisa Malinowski *English literature educator, writer*
Vaughan, Thomas James Gregory *historian*

Waldport
Harrison, Ruth Feuerborn *retired literature and writing educator*

PENNSYLVANIA

Allentown
Kipa, Albert Alexander *foreign language and literature educator*

Ardmore
Gutwirth, Marcel Marc *French literature educator*

Beaver Falls
Lambert, Lynda Jeanne *humanities, arts educator, artist*

Bensalem
Burtt, James *humanities educator*

Bethlehem
Beidler, Peter Grant *English educator*
Dowling, Joseph Albert *historian, educator*
Haynes, Thomas Morris *philosophy educator*
Lindgren, John Ralph *philosophy educator*
Roberts, Leonard Robert *English language educator, poet*

Bloomsburg
Salas Elorza, Jesús *language educator*

Brodheadsville
†Smith, Wanda Lou *English educator*

Bryn Mawr
Bober, Phyllis Pray *humanities educator, art historian*
Brand, Charles Macy *history educator*
Dostal, Robert Joseph *philosophy educator*
Dudden, Arthur Power *historian, educator*
Gaisser, Julia Haig *classics educator*
King, Willard Fahrenkamp (Mrs. Edmund Ludwig King) *Spanish language educator*
Krausz, Michael *philosopher, educator*
Lane, Barbara Miller (Barbara Miller-Lane) *humanities educator*
Lang, Mabel Louise *classics educator*

Carlisle
Fox, Arturo Angel *Spanish language educator*
†Grier, Philip Todd *philosophy educator*
†Moffat, Wendy *English educator*
Nichols, Brooks Ashton *English language educator*
Schiffman, Joseph Harris *literary historian, educator*
Shrader, Charles Reginald *historian*

Clarion
Thomas, Joe Alan *art historian*

Colmar
Weber-Roochvarg, Lynn *English second language adult educator, communications consultant*

Duncansville
Huntley-Speare, Anne *language educator*

East Stroudsburg
Crackel, Theodore Joseph *historian*

Easton
Bonanni, Marc A. *English language educator, newscaster*
†Lusardi, James Proctor *English language and literature educator*
Schlueter, June Mayer *English educator, author*

Edinboro
Jones, Jean Grace *speech educator*

Elizabethtown
†Winpenny, Thomas Reese, III *history educator*

Elkins Park
Davidson, Abraham Aba *art historian, educator, photographer*

Erie
Allshouse, Robert Harold *history educator*
Minot, Walter S. *English language educator*

Fairfield
†Freund, John Richard *former English educator*

Ford City
†Smits, Ronald Francis *English educator, poet*

Forty Fort
Meeker, Robert Gardner *English language educator*

Gettysburg
†Birkner, Michael J. *history educator*

Glenside
†Grady, Hugh H. *English educator*
Splawn, P. Jane *English language educator*

Grantham
Sider, E(arl) Morris *English language and history educator, archivist*

Grove City
Smith, Gary Scott *historian, educator, clergyman*
Wentworth, Theodore Oscar, Jr. *Spanish language educator*

Gwynedd Valley
Duclow, Donald Francis *philosophy educator, researcher*

Harrisburg
Bello, Shere Capparella *foreign language educator*
Britton, Wesley Alan *English language educator*
†Khanzina, Helen P. *English educator, translator*
†Qi, Shouhua *English educator*

Haverford
Jorden, Eleanor Harz *linguist, educator*

Holtwood
†Carter, Jennifer Lyn *English language educator*

Indiana
†Broad, Peter G. *Spanish educator*
Roumm, Phyllis Evelyn Gensbigler *English language educator, writer*

Johnstown
Mock, Michele L. *literature educator, author*

Kennett Square
Beddall, Barbara Gould *science historian, writer*

King Of Prussia
Mielke, Andreas *German language, literature and culture educator*

Kutztown
†Dewey, Sylvie Pascale *French and Spanish language educator*

Lancaster
Andrew, John Alfred, III *history educator*
†Harman, Mark *English educator*
†Mongia, Padmini *English language educator*
Rupp, Theodore Hanna *retired French language educator*
Schuyler, David P. *historian, educator*
Steiner, Robert Lisle *language consultant, retired*

Leesport
Jackson, Eric Allen *philatelist*

Lehighton
Levis, Cynthia Ann *English language educator, German language educator*

Lewisburg
Little, Daniel Eastman *philosophy educator, university program director*

Lock Haven
Podol, Peter L. *foreign language educator*

Loretto
Woznak, John Francis *English language educator*

Lumberville
Fallon, Robert Thomas *English language educator*

Macungie
†Paulson, Michael George *foreign language educator*

Meadville
Helmreich, Jonathan Ernst *history educator*
Katope, Christopher George *English language educator*

Media
Beeman, Richard Roy *historian, educator*
†Sorkin, Adam J. *English educator*

Melrose Park
Steinlauf, Michael Charles *historian*

Merion Station
Littell, Marcia Sachs *Holocaust educator*
Ueland, Elizabeth Pritchard *English language educator*

Millersville
Craven, Roberta Jill *educator in literature and film*

Mont Alto
Russo, Peggy Anne *English language educator*

Moon Township
†Farley, Glen David *English educator*

New Castle
Sands, Christine Louise *English educator*

New Kensington
†Krochalis, Jeanne Elizabeth *English language educator*

New Tripoli
Fritzinger, Rebecca Ann *English language educator*

New Wilmington
Perkins, James Ashbrook *English language educator*

Newtown
Palmer, Robert Roswell *historian, educator*

Norristown
Feeny, Margaret A. *English language educator, real estate agent*

Orefield
Tannery, Charles N. *language educator*

Philadelphia
Angelini, Eileen Marie *foreign languages educator*
Davis, Allen Freeman *history educator, author*
DeLaura, David Joseph *English language educator*
Duclow, Geraldine *historian, theatre and film librarian*
†Goldin, Paul Rakita *history educator*
†Hadlock, Philip G. *French language educator*
Hines, Susan Carol *English language educator*
Hoenigswald, Henry Max *linguist, educator*
Hoffman, Daniel (Gerard) *literature educator, poet*
†Holod, Renata *historian*
†Kennedy, Richard Sylvester *English educator*
Keto, C. Tsehloane *historian*
Knauer, Georg Nicolaus *classical philologist*
Lowry, Ralph James, Sr. *retired history educator*
Lucid, Robert Francis *English educator*
Marzik, Thomas David *historian, educator*
Means, John Barkley *foreign language educator, association executive*
Morello, Celeste Anne *historian, criminologist*
Moss, Roger William, Jr. *historian, writer, administrator*
Murphey, Murray Griffin *history educator*
Peters, Edward Murray *history educator*
Prince, Gerald Joseph *Romance languages educator*
Quann, Joan Louise *English language educator, real estate broker*
Regan, Robert Charles *English language educator*
Rosenberg, Charles Ernest *historian, educator*
†Rudnytzky, Leo Dennis *educator, journalist*
Schiffman, Harold Fosdick *Asian language educator*
Sebold, Russell Perry, III *Romance languages educator, author*
Sivin, Nathan *historian, educator*
†Steiner, Wendy Lois *English educator*
Tigay, Jeffrey H(oward) *foreign language, literature, religion educator*
Varkonyi, Istvan Laszlo *language educator*
Watt, David Harrington *history educator*
Weigley, Russell Frank *history educator*
Welch, Charles Edgar, Jr. *retired English language educator, writer*
†Williams, Ronald Leander *English educator*

Phoenixville
Lukacs, John Adalbert *historian, retired educator*

Pittsburgh
Anthony, Edward Mason *linguistics educator*
Arnett, Ronald Charles *communication educator*
†Brignano, Russell Carl *English educator, research specialist*
†Bruckner, Lynne Dickson *English educator*
Buchanan, James Junkin *classics educator*
Clack, Jerry *classics educator*
Di Medio, Gregory Lawrence *writer, English language educator, information analyst*
Drescher, Seymour *history educator, writer*
Gale, Robert Lee *retired American literature educator and critic*
Goldstein, Donald Maurice *historian, educator*
Grunbaum, Adolf *philosophy educator, author*
Harris, Ann Birgitta Sutherland *art historian*
Hicks, Wendell Leon *history educator, publisher, political scientist*
Hsu, Cho-yun *history educator*
Kurland, Stuart M. *English language educator*
Looney, Dennis Oscar *foreign language educator*
Miller, David William *historian, educator*
Paulston, Christina Bratt *linguistics educator*
Rawski, Evelyn Sakakida *history educator*
Rescher, Nicholas *philosophy educator*
Rimer, John Thomas *foreign language educator, academic administrator, writer, translator*
Rosen, Robert Stephen *theatre arts, humanities and English educator*
Seligson, Mitchell A. *Latin American studies educator*
Sheon, Aaron *art historian, educator*
Stearns, Peter Nathaniel *history educator*
Tarr, Joel Arthur *history and public policy educator*
Toker, Franklin K. *art history educator, archaeologist, foundation executive*
Weingartner, Rudolph Herbert *philosophy educator*
West, Michael Davidson *English educator*
†Wright, Michelle Maria *English language educator*

Reading
De Syon, Guillaume Paul Sam *history educator*

Rosemont
Bolger, Stephen Garrett *English and American studies educator*

Schuylkill Haven
Vickers, Anita Marissa *English language and literature educator*

Scranton
Bourcier, Richard Joseph *French language and literature educator*
Gougeon, Len Girard *literature educator*
Zaydon, Jemille Ann *English language and communications educator*

Selinsgrove
†Fincke, Gary W. *educator*
Kolbert, Jack *foreign language educator, French literature educator, humanities educator*
Whitman, Jeffrey Paul *philosophy educator*

Sharpsville
Durek, Dorothy Mary *retired English language educator*

Slippery Rock
†Boggs, William O. *English educator*

Springtown
Hunt, John Wesley *English language educator*

State College
Darnell, Doris Hastings *storyteller, antique costume collector*
Redford, Donald Bruce *historian, archaeologist*
Robinett, Betty Wallace *linguist*
Strasser, Gerhard Friedrich *German language and comparative literature educator*

Swarthmore
Anderson, Margaret Lavinia *history educator*
Bannister, Robert Corwin, Jr. *history educator*
Blackburn, Thomas Harold *English language professional, educator*
Gelzer, David Georg *English educator, missionary*
Kitao, T. Kaori *art history educator*
Lacey, Hugh Matthew *philosophy educator*
North, Helen Florence *classicist, educator*
Ostwald, Martin *classics educator emeritus*

Titusville
Hall, Mary Ann *English language educator*

Topton
Haskell, Ellery Bickford *retired philosophy educator*

University Park
Ameringer, Charles D. *history educator*
Anderson, John Mueller *retired philosophy educator*
Brault, Gerard Joseph *French language educator*
De Armas, Frederick Alfred *foreign language educator*
Frank, Robert Worth, Jr. *English language educator*
Gannon, Robert Haines *writing educator, writer*
Goldschmidt, Arthur Eduard, Jr. *history educator, author*
†Grosholz, Emily Rolfe *philosophy educator, poet*
Halsey, Martha Taliaferro *Spanish language educator*
†Holmes, Charlotte Amalie *English educator*
†Lantolf, James Paul *linguistics educator*
Lima, Robert *Hispanic studies and comparative literature educator*
†Sanchez, Victoria E. *English educator*
Schmalstieg, William Riegel *Slavic languages educator*
Spanier, Sandra Whipple *English language educator*
Weintraub, Stanley *arts and humanities educator, author*
Weiss, Beno *Italian language educator*
Williams, Edward Vinson *music history educator*

Villanova
Bergquist, James Manning *history educator*
Caputo, John David *philosophy educator*
Hunt, John Mortimer, Jr. *classical studies educator*
McDiarmid, Lucy *English educator, author*
Salmon, John Hearsey McMillan *historian, educator*

Washington
Troost, Linda Veronika *English language educator*

Wayne
Frye, Roland Mushat *literary historian, theologian*

West Chester
Gougher, Ronald Lee *foreign language educator and administrator*

Wilkes Barre
†Hupchick, Dennis Paul *history educator, writer*

Williamsport
Feinstein, Sascha *English language educator*
Griffith, Stephen Ray *philosophy educator*
Kingery, Sandra Lynn *Spanish language educator, translator*

York
Jackson, Renée Bernadette *English language educator*

RHODE ISLAND

Cranston
Morrissey, Elizabeth A. Schwimer *language educator, writer*

East Greenwich
†White, Sidney Howard *English educator*

Kingston
†Aronian, Suna *Russian and women's studies educator*
Kim, Yong Choon *philosopher, theologian, educator*
MacLaine, Allan Hugh *English language educator*
Schwegler, Robert Andrew *English language educator*

Newport
Brennan, Joseph Gerard *philosophy educator*
Haas, William Paul *humanities educator, former college president*

Providence
Almeida, Onésimo Teotónio *foreign language educator*
Anderson, James Arthur *humanities educator, academic director*
Arant, Patricia *Slavic languages and literature educator*
Bensmaia, Reda *French studies educator, researcher*
Boegehold, Alan Lindley *classics educator*
Bryan, Elizabeth Johnson *English language educator*
Cook, Albert Spaulding *comparative literature and classics educator, writer*
Donovan, Bruce Elliot *classics educator, university dean*
Enteman, Willard Finley *philosophy educator*
†Esolen, Anthony Michael *English educator*
Fornara, Charles William *historian, classicist, educator*
Gleason, Abbott *history educator*
Harleman, Ann *English educator, writer*
Honig, Edwin *comparative literature educator, poet*

Kim, Jaegwon *philosophy educator*
†Kirschenbaum, Blossom S. *educator of English language*
Kniesche, Thomas Werner *German language educator*
Konstan, David *classics and comparative literature educator, researcher*
Lesko, Leonard Henry *Egyptologist, educator, publisher*
Monteiro, George *English educator, writer*
Neu, Charles Eric *historian, educator*
Neumann, Dietrich *architectural historian*
†Ortega, Julio *humanities educator, writer*
Putnam, Michael Courtney Jenkins *classics educator*
Ribbans, Geoffrey Wilfrid *Spanish educator*
Rohr, Donald Gerard *history educator*
Rosenberg, Bruce Alan *English language educator, author*
Saint-Amand, Pierre Nemours *humanities educator*
Scharf, Peter Mark *Sanskrit and Indian studies educator*
Schulz, Juergen *art history educator*
Sosa, Ernest *philosopher, educator*
Spilka, Mark *retired English language educator*
Terras, Victor *Slavic languages and comparative literature educator*
Trueblood, Alan Stubbs *former modern language educator*
Williams, Lea Everard *history educator*
Wood, Gordon Stewart *historian, educator*
Wrenn, James Joseph *East Asian studies educator*

Wakefield
†Coffin, Tristram Potter *retired English educator, writer*

SOUTH CAROLINA

Beaufort
Rowland, Lawrence Sanders *history educator*

Bluffton
Brown, Dallas Coverdale, Jr. *retired army officer, retired history educator*

Charleston
†Coates, Timothy Joel *historian*
Dulaney, William Marvin *history educator, curator*
Lally, Margaret Mates *English educator, poet*

Clemson
Grant, H(arry) Roger *history educator*
Moran, Ronald Wesson *retired English educator, dean, writer*
Morrissey, Lee *language educator*
Underwood, Richard Allan *English language educator*

Cleveland
†Sinclair, Bennie Lee *English educator*

Columbia
Ashley, Perry Jonathan *journalism educator*
Baird, Davis W. *philosophy educator*
Belasco, Simon *French language and linguistics educator*
Bruccoli, Matthew Joseph *English educator, publisher*
Edgar, Walter Bellingrath *historian*
†Edwards, Kathryn A. *history educator*
Geckle, George Leo, III *English language educator*
Hardin, James Neal *German and comparative literature educator, publisher*
Hatch, Mary Gies *German language educator*
Howard-Hill, Trevor Howard *English language educator*
Johnson, Herbert Alan *history and law educator, lawyer, chaplain*
Joiner, Elizabeth Garner *French language educator*
Kay, Carol McGinnis *literature educator*
Long, Eugene Thomas, III *philosophy educator, administrator*
Mackey, Peter Francis *English educator, university official*
Madden, Norman Edward, Jr. *English educator*
Meriwether, James Babcock *retired English language educator*
Myerson, Joel Arthur *English language educator, researcher*
Nolte, William Henry *English language educator*
†Norman, George Buford, Jr. *foreign language educator*
Reeves, George McMillan, Jr. *comparative literature educator, educational administrator*
†Siebert, Donald Tate, Jr. *English educator*
Sproat, John Gerald *historian*
Timmons, Judith Herring *English educator*

Conway
Talbert, Roy, Jr. *history educator*

Florence
White, Victor Daniel, III *English educator*

Greenwood
Smith, Sara Elizabeth Cushing *English language educator, writer*

Hilton Head Island
Male, Roy Raymond *English language educator*

Irmo
Hric, Joan Esther *English educator, writer*

Mullins
Stonesifer, Richard James *humanities and social science educator*

Orangeburg
Johnson, Alex Claudius *English language educator*

Pawleys Island
Ford, Anna Marie *language professional*

Rock Hill
†Tarvers, Josephine Koster *English language educator*

Spartanburg
Clark, Elizabeth Adams (Liz Clark) *genealogy educator*

Sumter
Arl, Ellen Marie *English educator, television producer and host*
†Maness, Dinford Gray *English educator*

West Columbia
Ochs, Robert David *history educator*
Parker, Harold Talbot *history educator*

SOUTH DAKOTA

Aberdeen
Hastings, Albert Waller *English and journalism educator, consultant*

Brookings
Miller, John Edward *history educator*
Ryder, Mary Ruth *English language educator*

Sioux Falls
Huseboe, Arthur Robert *American literature educator*
Olson, Gary Duane *history educator*
Staggers, Kermit LeMoyne, II *history and political science educator, state senator*

Vermillion
Cunningham, Frank Robert *humanities educator, researcher*
Gasque, Thomas James *English educator*
Klein, Dennis Allan *language educator, writer*

TENNESSEE

Big Sandy
Chastain, Kenneth Duane *retired foreign language educator*

Bristol
Macione, Beatriz Huarte-Irujo *Spanish language educator*

Cleveland
†Washick, James Stewart *English educator*

Collierville
†Beaudette, Michele J. *language educator*

Columbia
Curry, Beatrice Chesrown *retired English educator*

Cookeville
Campana, Phillip Joseph *German language educator*

Jackson
McMillin, Barbara Ann *English educator*

Jefferson City
Baumgardner, James Lewis *history educator*

Johnson City
Hendricks, Miriam Joan *English educator*
Schneider, Valerie Lois *speech educator*
Stanley, Isabel Bonnyman *English educator*
Wyatt, Doris Fay Chapman *English language educator*
Zayas-Bazan, Eduardo *foreign language educator*

Knoxville
Adams, David Parrish *historian, educator*
Brady, Patrick *French literature educator, novelist*
Ensor, Allison Rash *English language educator*
Fisher, John Hurt *English language educator*
Ford, Harriet-Lynn *English educator*
Gallo, Louis *historian, educator*
Heizer, Ruth Bradfute *philosophy educator*
Klein, Milton Martin *history educator*
Moser, Harold Dean *historian*
Wier, Allen *english educator*

Martin
†Depta, Victor Marshall *English educator, editor*
†Norton, Dorotha Oliver *speech educator*

Maryville
†Lewis, Wallace L. *history educator*
†Wright, Nathalia *retired English educator*

Memphis
†Bigelow, Gordon Stinson *English educator*
Copper, John Franklin *Asian studies educator, consultant*
Jolly, William Thomas *foreign language educator*
Kitts, Judith Pate *English educator*
Stagg, Louis Charles *English language and literature educator*
Tuggle, Melvin *philosophy educator, publisher*
Vinson, Mark Alan *English language and literature educator*

Murfreesboro
Lowe, Larry Veazey *retired speech educator, consultant*
Rupprecht, Nancy Ellen *historian, educator*

Nashville
Boorman, Howard Lyon *history educator*
†Bracks, Lean'tin LaVerne *African-American literature educator*
Collier, Simon *history educator*
Compton, John Joseph *philosophy educator*
Conkin, Paul Keith *history educator*
Cook, Ann Jennalie *English language educator*
Dickerson, Dennis Clark *history educator*
Doody, Margaret Anne *English language educator*
Doyle, Don Harrison *history educator*
Fox, Edward Inman *education administrator and Spanish educator*
Fryd, Vivien Green *art history educator, researcher*
Girgus, Sam B. *English literature educator*
Graham, Hugh Davis *history educator*
Grantham, Dewey Wesley *historian, educator*
Halperin, John William *English literature educator*

Harris, Alice Carmichael *linguist, educator*
Hassel, Rudolph Christopher *English language educator*
Lombardy, Anthony Michael *classics educator*
†Nzabatsinda, Anthere *French language educator*
Smith, Samuel Boyd *history educator*
Voegeli, Victor Jacque *history educator, dean*
von Raffler-Engel, Walburga (Walburga Engel) *linguist, cross-cultural communications specialist, lecturer, writer*

Sewanee
Chitty, (Mary) Elizabeth Nickinson *university historian*
Flynn, John Francis *historian, educator*
Williamson, Samuel Ruthven, Jr. *historian, university president*

Shiloh
Hawke, Paul Henry *historian*

Trezevant
Blanks, Naomi Mai *retired English language educator*

Tullahoma
Majors, Betty-Joyce Moore *genealogist, writer*

TEXAS

Abilene
†Tippens, Darryl L. *educator in English, writer*

Alvin
Crider, Allen Billy *English educator, novelist*

Arlington
Anguizola, Gustav (Antonio) *historian, educator, writer, consultant*

Austin
Bonevac, Daniel Albert *philosopher, author*
Bordie, John George *linguistics educator*
Boyd, Carolyn Patricia *history educator*
Brown, Norman Donald *history educator*
Carleton, Don Edward *history center administrator, educator, writer*
Causey, Robert Louis *philosopher, educator, consultant*
Divine, Robert Alexander *history educator*
Dulles, John Watson Foster *history educator*
Falola, Toyin *history educator*
Farrell, Edmund James *retired English language educator, author*
Fishkin, Shelley Fisher *English language educator*
Friedman, Alan Warren *humanities educator*
Galinsky, Gotthard Karl *classicist, educator*
Gutiérrez, Elisa de León *languages educator*
Hancock, Ian Francis (O Yanko le Redžosko) *linguistics educator*
Harms, Robert Thomas *linguist, educator*
†Hess, Peter Andreas *German language educator*
Hinojosa-Smith, Roland *English language educator, writer*
†Hull, Richard Thompson *retired philosophy educator, non-profit executive*
Jazayery, Mohammad Ali *foreign languages and literature educator emeritus*
Kendall, Dorothy Helen *retired art historian*
Lehmann, Ruth Preston Miller *literature educator*
Lehmann, Winfred Philipp *linguistics educator*
Lockett, Landon Johnson *retired linguistic educator, researcher*
Louis, William Roger *historian, educator, editor*
Mackey, Louis Henry *philosophy educator*
Marcus, Leah S. *English educator*
Megaw, Robert Neill Ellison *English educator*
Middleton, Christopher *Germanic languages and literature educator*
Moag, Rodney Frank *language educator, country music singer*
†Newburger, Caryn Lason *English educator*
Polomé, Edgar Charles *foreign language and linguistics educator*
Rebhorn, Wayne Alexander *literature educator*
Rich, John Martin *humanities educator, researcher*
Seung, Thomas Kaehao *philosophy educator*
†Shumway, Nicolas *Spanish American literature educator*
Staley, Thomas Fabian *language professional, academic administrator*
Sutherland, William Owen Sheppard *English language educator*
Tyler, Ronnie Curtis *historian*
Wadlington, Warwick Paul *English language educator*
Werbow, Stanley Newman *language educator*
Whitbread, Thomas Bacon *English educator, author*
Williams, Diane Elizabeth *architectural historian*

Beaumont
Hawkins, Emma B. *humanities educator*
Saur, Pamela S. *English and German educator*

Brownwood
Murphy, Justin Duane *history educator*

Canyon
†Dudt, Charmazel *classics educator*
†Teichmann, Sandra Gail *English educator*

College Station
Cannon, Garland *English language educator*
†Christensen, Paul Norman *English educator, writer*
Cockroft, Jeannette Wimmer *historian educator*
Davenport, Manuel Manson *philosophy educator*
Dethloff, Henry Clay *history educator*
Kallendorf, Craig William *English, speech and classical languages educator*
Knobel, Dale Thomas *history educator, university administrator*
Unterberger, Betty Miller *history educator, writer*

Commerce
Linck, Charles Edward, Jr. *English language educator*
†Linck, Ernestine Porcher *English educator, writer*
Perry, Thomas Amherst *English literature and language educator*

Corpus Christi
Wooster, Robert *history educator*

Dallas
Chawner, Lucia Martha *English educator*
Comini, Alessandra *art historian, educator*
Countryman, Edward Francis *historian, educator*
Crain, John Walter *historian*
Davis, Daisy Sidney *history educator*
Hunter, Robert Grams *retired English language educator*
Martin, Carol Jacquelyn *educator, artist*
May, William Francis *ethicist, educator*
Perry, Anne Gordon *arts and humanities educator, writer*
Pike, Kenneth Lee *linguist, educator*
Terry, Marshall Northway, Jr. *English language educator, author*

Denton
†Emery, Sarah Martha Watson *retired philosophy educator, writer*
Kamman, William *historian, educator*
Kesterson, David Bert *English language educator*
Oxford, Jeffrey Thomas *foreign language educator*
Palmer, Leslie Howard *literature educator*
Preston, Thomas Ronald *English language educator, researcher*
Snapp, Harry Franklin *historian*
Vaughn, William Preston *historian, educator*

Edinburg
Barrera, Eduardo *Spanish language and literature educator*

El Paso
Bailey, Kenneth Kyle *history educator*
Landy, Ricardo Lopez *humanities educator*
Lujan, Rosa Emma *bilingual specialist, trainer, consultant*
Metz, Leon Claire *historical speaker*

Flower Mound
Jones, Nancy Jane *English educator*

Fort Worth
Boller, Paul Franklin, Jr. *retired American history educator, writer*
Dale, Eric Michael *philosopher of religion*
Durham, Carolyn Richardson *foreign language and literature educator*
McWhiney, Grady *history educator*
Reuter, Frank Theodore *history educator*
†Smith, Gene A. *history educator, writer*
Wertz, Spencer K. *philosophy educator*
Woodward, Ralph Lee, Jr. *historian, educator*
Worcester, Donald Emmet *history educator, author*

Friendswood
†White, John Albert *retired history educator*

Galveston
Ryan, James Gilbert *historian, educator, writer*

Grapevine
Stack, George Joseph *philosopher, writer*

Harlingen
Martin, Leland Morris (Pappy Martin) *history educator*

Hewitt
Pickens, Lee *history educator*

Houston
Castañeda, James Agustin *Spanish language educator, university golf coach*
Chance, Jane *English literature educator*
de Kanter, Ellen Ann *English language professional, educator*
Drew, Katherine Fischer *history educator*
Folk, Katherine Pinkston *English language educator, writer, journalist*
Galvani, Christiane Mesch *English as a second language educator, translator*
Gos, Michael Walter *English educator, author*
Gruber, Ira Dempsey *historian, educator*
Haskell, Thomas Langdon *history educator*
Hult, Susan Freda *history educator*
Huston, John Dennis *English educator*
Hyman, Harold M. *history educator, consultant*
†Kastely, James Louis *English language educator*
Lamb, Sydney MacDonald *linguistics and cognitive science educator*
Martin, James Kirby *historian, educator*
Mayo, Marti *art historian, curator*
Mc Fadden, Joseph Michael *history educator*
Minter, David Lee *English literature educator*
Patten, Robert Lowry *English language educator*
†Petrovich, Alisa Vladimira *historian, educator*
Pryor, William Daniel Lee *humanities educator*
Sher, George Allen *philosophy educator*
Smith, Richard Joseph *history educator*
†Southwell, Samuel Beall *English educator*
Temkin, Larry Scott *philosopher, educator*
Thompson, Ewa M. *foreign language educator*
Urbina, Manuel, II *legal research historian, history educator*
White, Craig Alan *history educator, consultant*
Wiener, Martin Joel *historian*
Wyschogrod, Edith *philosophy educator*

Huntsville
†Policarpo, Alcibiades G. *educator Spanish language and literature*
Raymond, Kay E(ngelmann) *Spanish language educator, consultant*
Schwetman, John William *English language professional educator*

Irving
Sommerfeldt, John Robert *historian*

Kerrville
†Tran, Qui-Phiet *English educator*

Laredo
†Mitchell, Thomas Reagan *English educator*

Levelland
Sears, Edward L. *English language educator, real estate investor*

Lubbock
Butterworth, Daniel Drew *humanities educator, consultant*
Connor, Seymour Vaughan *historian, educator, writer*
Hurst, Mary Jane *English language educator*
Kelsey, Clyde Eastman, Jr. *philosophy and psychology educator*
Ketner, Kenneth Laine *philosopher, educator*
Pelley, Patricia Marie *Asian history specialist*
Purinton, Marjean D. *English language educator, researcher*
Stoll, Mark Richard *humanities educator*
Walker, Warren Stanley *English educator*

Mason
Ponder, Jerry Wayne *historian*

Paris
Proctor, Richard Owen *historian, public health administrator, army officer*

Plano
Levy, Ralph David *translator, researcher*

Richardson
Redman, Timothy Paul *English language educator, author, chess federation administrator*

Round Top
Lentz, Edwin Lamar *art historian*

Salado
Veninga, James Frank *humanities educator, editor, author*

San Antonio
Almeida, Michael James *philosophy educator*
Fite, Patricia Paulette *English educator*
Leighton, Albert Chester *history educator*
Matthews, Rebecca Jan *English educator*
Passty, Jeanette Nyda *English language educator*
Reesman, Jeanne Campbell *English language educator*
Sauer, James Benson *philosopher, educator*
†Shelton-Colangelo, Sharon *English educator*
Williams, James David *history educator*
Woodson, Linda Townley *English educator, writer*

San Marcos
Beebe, Susan Jane *English language educator*
†Wilson, Steven Michael *English educator, poet*

Seguin
Moline, Jon Nelson *philosopher, educator, college president*

Stafford
Orman, Helen Belton *humanities educator, artist*

Stephenville
Christopher, Joe Randell *English language educator*

Tyler
†Turman, Judith Jenkins *English educator*

Uvalde
Wood, James Albert *foreign language educator*

Waco
Andrist, Debra Diane *Spanish language educator*
Baird, Robert Malcolm *philosophy educator, researcher*
Collmer, Robert George *English language educator*
Goode, Clement Tyson *retired English language educator*
Herring, Jack William *retired English language educator*
†Hunt, Maurice Arthur *English educator, researcher*
†Lahaie, Ute S. *language educator*

Wharton
†Johnson, Alan Gerhard *English educator*

Wichita Falls
Bourland, D(elphus) David, Jr. *linguist*
Hoggard, Lynn *French and English language educator*

UTAH

Brigham City
Huchel, Frederick M. *historian, writer, consultant, speaker, educator*

Cedar City
†Bostick, Curtis Van *history educator*

Hurricane
Christensen, Steven J. *foreign language educator*

Logan
Crumbley, Paul James *English language educator*
Milner, Clyde A., II *historian*

Paradise
Bremer, Ronald Allan *genealogist, editor*

Provo
Clark, Bruce Budge *humanities educator*
Cracroft, Richard Holton *English literature educator*
Forster, Merlin Henry *foreign languages educator, author, researcher*
†Lawrence, Keith *American literature educator*
Lyon, James Karl *German language educator*
†Murphy, John Joseph *educator in English literature, critic, editor*

Salt Lake City
†Miller, Susan Jane Passler *English and writing educator*
Olpin, Robert Spencer *art history educator*
†Sajé, Natasha *educator, poet*
Sillars, Malcolm Osgood *communication educator*

Tremonton
Eakle, Arlene Haslam *genealogist*

VERMONT

Burlington
Daniels, Robert Vincent *history educator, former state senator*
Flores, Yolanda *literature educator*
Hall, Robert William *philosophy and religion educator*
Metcalfe, William Craig *retired history educator*
Nunley, Gayle Roof *language educator*

East Middlebury
†Gavin, Thomas Michael *retired English educator, writer*

East Ryegate
Martland, T(homas) R(odolphe) *philosophy educator*

Middlebury
Jacobs, Travis Beal *historian, educator*
Katz, Michael Ray *Slavic languages educator*
Lamberti, Marjorie *history educator*
Nunley, Charles Arthur *language educator*
Vail, Van Horn *German language educator*

Montpelier
Facos, James Francis *English language educator, author*

Newfane
Reed, John Addison Jr. *European studies educator*

Northfield
†Chevalier, Frances Sikola *French language educator*

Rutland
Wiles, William Patrick *English language educator*

Shelburne
Weiger, John George *foreign language educator*

VIRGINIA

Alexandria
Byrne, John Edward (JEB Byrne) *writer, retired government official*
Seale, William *historian*

Annandale
Henretty, Donald Bruce *history educator*

Arlington
Allard, Dean Conrad *historian, retired naval history center director*
French, Mary B. *English educator*
Wilcox, Shirley Jean Langdon *genealogist*

Ashland
Inge, Milton Thomas *American literature and culture educator, author*

Blacksburg
Baehr, Stephen Lessing *Russian langauge educator, researcher*
Doswald, Herman Kenneth *German language educator, academic administrator*
Landen, Robert Geran *retired historian, educator, university administrator*
†Sullivan, Ernest Walter, II *English educator*

Burlington
†Kete, Mary Louise *English and American Literature educator*

Charlottesville
Abbot, William Wright *history educator*
Arnold, Albert James *foreign language educator*
Barolsky, Paul *art history educator*
Battestin, Martin Carey *English language educator*
Cano-Ballesta, Juan *Spanish language educator*
Cherno, Melvin *humanities educator*
†Childress, Marcia Day *humanities educator*
Courtney, Edward *classics educator*
†Davidson, Hugh MacCullough *French language and literature educator*
Denommé, Robert Thomas *foreign language educator*
Forbes, John Douglas *architectural and economic historian*
Garrett, George Palmer, Jr. *creative writing and English language educator, writer*
Gianniny, Omer Allan, Jr. *retired humanities educator*
Gies, David Thatcher *language educator*
Graebner, Norman Arthur *history educator*
Heath, Peter Lauchlan *philosophy educator*
Hirsch, Eric Donald, Jr. *English language educator, educational reformer*
Hopkins, P. Jeffrey *Asian studies educator, author, translator*
Humphreys, Paul William *philosophy educator, consultant*
Kellogg, Robert Leland *English language educator*
Kett, Joseph Francis *historian, educator*
Kolb, Harold Hutchinson, Jr. *English language educator*
Kraehe, Enno Edward *history educator*
Lang, Cecil Yelverton *English language educator*
Langbaum, Robert Woodrow *English language educator, author*
Leffler, Melvyn P. *history educator*
Levenson, Jacob Clavner *English language educator*
Little, W(illia)m A(lfred) *foreign language educator, researcher*
Lyons, John David *French, Italian and comparative literature educator*
McGann, Jerome John *English language educator*
Megill, Allan D. *historian, educator*
Midelfort, Hans Christian Erik *history educator*
Mikalson, Jon Dennis *classics educator*
Nelson, Raymond John *English literature educator, university dean, author*
Nohrnberg, James Carson *English language educator*
Oliver, Charles Montgomery *retired English educator*
Perkowski, Jan Louis *language and literature educator*
Peterson, Merrill Daniel *history educator*
Rubin, David Lee *French literature educator, critic, editor, publisher*
Sedgwick, Alexander *historian, educator*

Shackelford, George Green *historian*
Shaw, Donald Leslie *Spanish language educator*
Simmons, Alan John *philosophy educator*
Spacks, Patricia Meyer *English educator*
Spearing, Anthony Colin *English literature educator*
Stocker, Arthur Frederick *classics educator*
†Wall, Cynthia Sundberg *English literature educator*
Wright, Charles Penzel, Jr. *English language educator*
Zunz, Olivier Jean *history educator*

Cross Junction
Stephenson, Richard Walter *librarian, historian, geographer*

Danville
Hayes, Jack Irby *historian*

Deltaville
White, Gordon Eliot *historian*

Emory
†Chamberlain, Kathleen Reuter *English educator, dean*
†Reid, Suzanne Elziabeth *English educator*

Fairfax
Bailey, Helen McShane *historian*
Censer, Jack Richard *history educator*
King, James Cecil *Medievalist, educator*
Lavine, Thelma Zeno *philosophy educator*

Ferrum
†Obiechina, Emmanuel Nwanonye *humanities educator*

Fort Lee
Sterling, Keir Brooks *historian, educator*

Fredericksburg
Bourdon, Roger Joseph *history educator*
Dorman, John Frederick *genealogist*
Nails, Debra *philosophy educator*

Glen Allen
†Hinkle, Douglas Paddock *retired languages educator*

Hampden Sydney
Bagby, George Franklin, Jr. *English language educator*
†Weese, Katherine Jane *English educator*

Hampton
Maher, Kim Leverton *museum administrator*
Whittenburg, Carolyn Sparks *history educator*

Harrisonburg
Alotta, Robert Ignatius *historian, educator, writer*
Geary, Robert Francis, Jr. *English educator*
Morey, Ann-Janine *English educator*
†Nickels, Cameron Charles *English educator*

Kingstowne
Hixson, Stanley G. *speech, language and computer technology educator*

Lexington
Brooke, George Mercer, Jr. *historian, educator*
Ryan, Halford Ross *speech educator*
Sessions, William Lad *philosophy educator, administrator*

Lynchburg
†Carwile, Billie Newman *history educator*
†Kimball, Anne Spofford *French language educator*

Manassas
†Adamson, Heidi Beth *English educator*

Mc Lean
García-Godoy, Cristián *historian, educator*

Newport News
†Keeling, Kara Kay *English literature educator*
Santoro, Anthony Richard *history educator*

Norfolk
†Greene, Douglas George *humanities educator, author, publisher*
Pope, Stephanie Marie *classicist, educator*
Rutyna, Richard Albert *history educator*

Onancock
Verrill, John Howard *museum director*

Petersburg
Calkins, Christopher Miles *historian*

Portsmouth
Jackson, Cheryl K. *English educator*
Williams, Lena Harding *English language educator*

Radford
Jervey, Edward Drewry *retired history educator*

Richmond
Ciulla, Joanne Bridgett *business ethics educator*
†Fuller, Kathryn Helgesen *historian, educator*
Gordon, John L., Jr. *historian, educator*
Gray, Clarence Jones *foreign language educator, dean emeritus*
†Nelson, Robert McDowell *English educator*
Rilling, John Robert *history educator*
Robert, Joseph Clarke *historian, consultant*
Shapiro, Gary Michael *philosophy educator*
Urofsky, Melvin Irving *historian, educator, director*
Vallentyne, Peter Lloyd *philosophy educator*

Roanoke
Dillard, Richard Henry Wilde *English language professional, educator, author*
Moriarty, Marilyn Frances *English educator, writer*

Schuyler
Mastromarino, Mark Anthony *historian*

Suffolk
Derby, Shelah Ann Novak *English language educator*

Sumerduck
McCamy, Sharon Lynn *English educator*

Surry
Wachsmann, Elizabeth Rideout *reading specialist*

Sweet Briar
Grubbs, Judith Evans *classical studies educator*
Piepho, (Edward) Lee *humanities educator*

Topping
Willett, Albert James, Jr. *family historian*

University Of Richmond
Hall, James H(errick), Jr. *philosophy educator, author*
Terry, Robert Meredith *foreign language educator*

Virginia Beach
Alexander, Christina Anamaria *translator, performing company executive*

Williamsburg
Axtell, James Lewis *history educator*
Ball, Donald Lewis *retired English language educator*
Becker, Lawrence Carlyle *philosopher, educator, author*
Cell, Gillian Townsend *historian, educator*
Chappell, Miles Linwood, Jr. *art history educator*
Crapol, Edward P. *history educator*
Esler, Anthony James *historian, novelist, educator*
Gross, Robert Alan *history educator*
Hoffman, Ronald *historical institute administrator, educator*
McGiffert, Michael *retired history educator, editor*
McLane, Henry Earl, Jr. *philosophy educator*
Nettels, Elsa *English language educator*
Oakley, John Howard *humanities educator*
Tate, Thaddeus W(ilbur), Jr. (Thad Tate) *history educator, historical institute executive, historian*
Wallach, Alan *art historian, educator*

Winchester
Meschutt, David Randolph *historian, curator*

Woodbridge
Hood, Ronald Chalmers, III *historian, writer*

WASHINGTON

Auburn
Sims, Marcie Lynne *English language educator, writer*

Bellingham
Fiero, Petra Schug *language professional educator*
Whisenhunt, Donald Wayne *history educator*

Ellensburg
Cadello, James Peter *philosopher, educator*

Enumclaw
Vernier, Richard *educator, author*

Federal Way
Boling, Joseph Edward *numismatist, retired military officer*

Lacey
Edwards, Margaret H. *English as second language instructor*

Olympia
Beck, Gordon Eugene *art history educator, consultant*
Nesbit, Robert Carrington *historian*

Port Angeles
de Broux, Peggy C. *English educator, French educator, publisher*

Pullman
Burbick, Joan *English educator*
Swan, Susan Linda *history educator*

Renton
Hill, Alice Lorraine *history, genealogy and social researcher, educator*

Seattle
Adams, Hazard Simeon *English educator, author*
Brand, Gerhard *retired English educator*
Brandauer, Frederick Paul *Asian language educator*
Bultmann, William Arnold *historian*
Burgess, Charles Orville *history educator*
Butow, Robert Joseph Charles *history educator*
Coburn, Robert Craig *philosopher*
Coldewey, John Christopher *English literature educator*
Ellison, Herbert Jay *history educator*
Gerstenberger, Donna Lorine *humanities educator*
Harmon, Daniel Patrick *classics educator*
Heer, Nicholas Lawson *Arabist and Islamist educator*
Jones, Edward Louis *historian, educator*
Keyt, David *philosophy and classics educator*
Korg, Jacob *English literature educator*
Matchett, William H(enry) *English literature educator*
Moore, Ronald Melville *Philosophy educator*
Newmeyer, Frederick Jaret *linguist, educator*
Oldknow, Constantina W. *art historian*
Pressly, Thomas James *history educator*
Pyle, Kenneth Birger *historian, educator*
Silbergeld, Jerome Leslie *art historian, educator*
Snow-Smith, Joanne Inloes *art history educator*
Sugar, Peter Frigyes *historian*
VanArsdel, Rosemary Thorstenson *English studies educator*
van den Berg, Sara Jane *English educator*
Webb, Eugene *English language educator*
Ziadeh, Farhat J. *Middle Eastern studies educator*

Sedro Woolley
Hinckley, Ted C. *historian, educator, writer*

Spokane
Carriker, Robert Charles *history educator*
Kossel, Clifford George *retired philosophy educator, clergyman*
†Minkler, James Elton *humanities educator, academic administrator*
Stackelberg, John Roderick *history educator*

Tacoma
Barnett, Suzanne Wilson *history educator*
Browning, Christopher R. *historian, educator*
Collier, Richard Bangs *philosopher, foundation executive*
Jensen, Mark Kevin *foreign language educator*
Le Roy, Bruce Murdock *historian*
Sloane, Sarah Jane *English educator*

Walla Walla
Carlsen, James Caldwell *musicologist, educator*
Edwards, Glenn Thomas *history educator*
Stratton, Jon *philosophy educator*

Yakima
Meshke, George Lewis *drama and humanities educator*

WEST VIRGINIA

Charles Town
Na, (Terry) Tsung Shun *Chinese studies educator, writer*

Institute
Garrett, Naomi Mills *foreign language educator, retired*

Morgantown
Blaydes, Sophia Boyatzies *English language educator*
†Bruner, Jeffrey Benham *foreign language educator*
Davis, Leonard McCutchan *speech educator*
Schlunk, Jurgen Eckart *German language educator*
Singer, Armand Edwards *foreign language educator*

Reedsville
Williford, Drury Fisher, Jr. *historical researcher*

WISCONSIN

Appleton
Chaney, William Albert *historian, educator*
Goldgar, Bertrand Alvin *literary historian, educator*

Chetek
Erspamer, Peter Roy *humanities educator, writer*

Chippewa Falls
†Schmider, Mary Ellen Heian *American studies educator, academic administrator*

Eau Claire
†Sen, Asha *English educator*

Elcho
Doran, Kay JoAnn *Spanish language educator*

Ferryville
Tedeschi, John Alfred *historian, librarian*

Fond Du Lac
Kraus, Michael John *English language and literature educator*

Green Bay
Toonen, Linda Marie *composition educator*

Kenosha
†Kummings, Donald Dale *English educator*
†Lenard, Mary Kathleen *English educator*

La Crosse
Boudreau, Richard Owen *retired English educator, freelance writer*
†Provencher, Denis Michael *French language educator*
Rausch, Joan Mary *art historian*
†White-Parks, Annette *English educator*

Lodi
Schereck, William John *retired historian, consultant*

Madison
Ammerman, Robert Ray *philosopher, educator*
Berg, William James *French language educator, writer, translator*
Berghahn, Klaus Leo *German and Jewish studies educator*
Bogue, Allan George *history educator*
Ciplijauskaite, Birute *humanities educator*
Cronon, William *history educator*
Dembo, Lawrence Sanford *English educator*
Dubrow, Heather *English educator*
Filipowicz, Halina *literature educator*
Fowler, Barbara Hughes *classics educator*
Frykenberg, Robert Eric *historian*
†Gamble, Vanessa N. *historian*
Goodkin, Richard Elliot *French educator, writer*
Hamalainen, Pekka Kalevi *historian, educator*
Hamerow, Theodore Stephen *history educator*
Hutchison, Jane Campbell *art history educator, researcher*
Klein, Sheldon *computational linguist, educator*
Kleinhenz, Christopher *foreign language educator, researcher*
Knowles, Richard Alan John *English language educator*
Kutler, Stanley Ira *history and law educator, author*
Leavitt, Judith Walzer *history of medicine educator*
Marks, Elaine *French language educator*
O'Brien, James Aloysius *foreign language educator*
Powell, Barry Bruce *classicist*
Rideout, Walter Bates *English educator*
Sewell, Richard Herbert *historian, educator*
Spear, Thomas Turner *history educator*
Vowles, Richard Beckman *literature educator*
Weinbrot, Howard David *English educator*

Menomonie
Levy, Michael Marc *English educator*

Milwaukee
Bicha, Karel Denis *historian, educator*
Carozza, Davy Angelo *Italian language educator*
Gallop, Jane (Anne) *women's studies educator, writer*
Hachey, Thomas Eugene *British and Irish history educator, consultant*
Hay, Robert Pettus *history educator*
Liddy, James Daniel Reeves *English educator*
McCanles, Michael Frederick *English language educator*
Olson, Frederick Irving *retired history educator*
Rivero, Albert J. *English educator*
Roeming, Robert Frederick *foreign language educator*
Rosenblum, Martin Jack *historian*
Schwartz, Joseph *English language educator*
Swanson, Roy Arthur *classicist, educator*
Waldbaum, Jane Cohn *art history educator*

Randolph
Belongie, Michael Eugene *English language educator, poet*

Ripon
Miller, George H. *historian, educator*

River Falls
Karolides, Nicholas J. *English educator*

Stevens Point
Ackley, Katherine Anne *English educator, writer*
Morrison, Clifford August *history educator*

Superior
Bischoff, Joan *English educator*

Waukesha
Dukes, Jack Richard *history educator*

Wausau
†Whitney, John Denison *English educator, writer*

West Allis
Aderman, Ralph Merl *English educator*

Whitewater
Gulgowski, Paul William *German language, social science, and history educator*
Ritterbusch, Dale E. *English educator*

WYOMING

Gillette
Garry, James B. *historian, storyteller, researcher, writer*

Laramie
Bantjes, Adrian Alexander *history educator*
Chisum, Emmett Dewain *historian, archeologist, researcher*
Frye, Susan Caroline *English literature educator*
Hardy, Deborah Welles *history educator*
Roberts, Philip John *history educator, editor*
Williams, Roger Lawrence *historian, educator*

Sheridan
Aguirre-Batty, Mercedes *Spanish and English language and literature educator*
Goodwin, Doris Helen Kearns *history educator, writer*

TERRITORIES OF THE UNITED STATES

PUERTO RICO

Rio Piedras
†Arrillaga, Maria *foreign language educator*

San Juan
Ocasio-Melendez, Marcial Enrique *history educator*

CANADA

ALBERTA

Calgary
Izzo, Herbert John *language and linguistics educator, researcher*

Edmonton
McMaster, Juliet Sylvia *English language educator*

BRITISH COLUMBIA

Burnaby
Buitenhuis, Peter Martinus *language professional, educator*
Kitchen, John Martin *historian, educator*

Sidney
Saddlemyer, Ann (Eleanor Saddlemyer) *educator, critic, theater historian*

Vancouver
Batts, Michael Stanley *German language educator*
Bentley, Thomas Roy *educator, writer, consultant*
Conway, John S. *history educator*
Durrant, Geoffrey Hugh *retired English language educator*
Overmyer, Daniel Lee *Asian studies educator*
Pacheco-Ransanz, Arsenio *Hispanic and Italian studies educator*

Saint-Jacques, Bernard *linguistics educator*
Unger, Richard Watson *history educator*

MANITOBA

Winnipeg
Wolfart, H.C. *linguistics scholar, author, editor*

NEW BRUNSWICK

Douglas
Cogswell, Frederick William *English language educator, poet, editor, publisher*

Saint John
Condon, Thomas Joseph *university historian*

NOVA SCOTIA

Halifax
Carrigan, David Owen *history educator*
Gray, James *English literature educator*

Wolfville
Zeman, Jarold Knox *history educator*

ONTARIO

Downsview
Thomas, Clara McCandless *retired English language educator, biographer*

Hamilton
Blewett, David Lambert *English literature educator*
Lee, Alvin A. *literary educator, scholar, author*
McKay, Alexander Gordon *classics educator*

Kingston
Akenson, Donald Harman *historian, educator*
Dick, Susan Marie *English language educator*
Hamilton, Albert Charles *English language educator*
Riley, Anthony William *German language and literature educator*

London
Collins, Thomas Joseph *English language educator*
Gerber, Douglas Earl *classics educator*
Groden, Michael Lewis *English literature educator*

Nepean
Kallmann, Helmut Max *music historian, retired music librarian*

North York
Adelman, Howard *philosophy educator*

Ottawa
Dray, William Herbert *philosophy educator*
Hamelin, Marcel *historian, educator*
Staines, David McKenzie *English educator*

Rockwood
Eichner, Hans *German language and literature educator*

Thornbury
Keyes, Gordon Lincoln *history educator*

Toronto
Blissett, William Frank *English literature educator*
Dryer, Douglas Poole *retired philosophy educator*
Elkhadem, Saad Eldin Amin *foreign language and literature educator, author, editor, publisher*
Frank, Roberta *English language educator*
Goffart, Walter André *history educator*
Graham, Victor Ernest *French language educator*
Granatstein, Jack Lawrence *history educator*
Johnson, Robert Eugene *historian, academic administrator*
Mann, Susan *history educator*
McAuliffe, Jane Dammen *religious studies and Islamic studies educator*
Millgate, Jane *language professional*
Millgate, Michael (Henry) *retired English educator*
Morey, Carl Reginald *musicologist, academic administrator*
Schogt, Henry Gilius *foreign language educator*
Skvorecky, Josef Vaclav *English literature educator, novelist*
Webster, Jill Rosemary *historian, educator*
Wetzel, Heinz *foreign language educator*
Wevers, John William *retired Semitic languages educator*

Waterloo
Haworth, Lawrence Lindley *philosophy educator*

QUEBEC

Montreal
Beugnot, Bernard Andre Henri *French literature educator*
Brown, Peter Gilbert *philosopher, educator, tree farmer*
Duquette, Jean-Pierre *French language and literature educator*
Hoffmann, Peter Conrad Werner *history educator*
Kinsley, William Benton *literature educator*
Morin, Yves-Charles *linguistics educator, researcher*
†O'Toole, Tess *English educator*
Paikowsky, Sandra Roslyn *art historian*
Silverthorne, Michael James *classics educator*

North Hatley
Jones, Douglas Gordon *retired literature educator*

Outremont
Domaradzki, Theodore Felix *Slavic studies educator, editor*

Sainte Foy
Murray, Warren James *philosophy educator*

MEXICO

Cuernavaca
Illich, Ivan *educator, researcher*

Mexico City
Leon-Portilla, Miguel *historian, educator*

Morelia
Warren, J. Benedict *retired history educator*

AUSTRIA

Graz
Weisstein, Ulrich Werner *English literature educator*

Vienna
Steinbruckner, Bruno Friedrich *foreign language educator*

BELGIUM

Brussels
Labio, Catherine Marie Bernadette Henriette *humanities educator, researcher, international organization administrator*

COLOMBIA

Cali
Keppel, Timothy Anderson *humanities educator, writer*

ENGLAND

Eastbourne
Baylen, Joseph O. *retired history educator*

Liverpool
Reilly, Thomas *humanities educator*

London
Allan, Sarah Katherine *Oriental studies educator*
Elson, Sarah Lee *art historian and consultant*
Martines, Lauro *historian, writer*
Perkin, Harold James *retired social historian, educator*
†Rubin, Patricia Lee *art historian*

Milford on Sea
Styan, John Louis *English literature and theater educator*

Oxford
Carey, John *English language educator, literary critic*
Heilbron, John L. *historian*
Howe, Daniel Walker *historian, educator*

Oxfordshire
Rousseau, George Sebastian *eighteenth century studies educator, chamber musician*

FRANCE

Strasbourg
Shea, William Rene *historian, science philosopher, educator*

Toulouse
Courtés, Joseph Jean-Marie *humanities educator, writer, semiotician*

Vence
Polk, William Roe *historian*

Villeneuve d'Ascq
Allain, Louis *literature educator, scientific advisor*

GERMANY

Münster
Spevack, Marvin *English educator*

Nuremberg
Doerries, Reinhard René *modern history educator*

Stuttgart
Bettisch, Johann *linguist, researcher*

HONG KONG

Pokfulam
McNaughton, William Frank *translator, educator*

ITALY

Florence
Kaiser, Walter *English language educator*

Milan
Bolognesi, Giancarlo *linguist, orientalist, educator*

JAPAN

Bunkyo
Kobayashi, Seiei *English literature educator*

Fukuoka
Fukumoto, Yasunobu *American history educator*

Izumi
Hagiwara, Naoyuki *English language and literature educator*

Kanagawa-ken
Fukatsu, Tanefusa *retired Chinese classics educator*

Kumamoto
Fukuda, Shohachi *English language educator*

Mito
Kobayashi, Susumu *supercomputer company executive*

Nagasaki
Lorenz, Loretta Rose *English language educator*

Nago
Senaha, Eiki *English literature educator, university administrator*

Nagoya
Tanaka, Harumi *linguist, educator*

THE NETHERLANDS

Amsterdam
Bal, Mieke *literature educator, cultural critic and theorist*
Kolko, Gabriel *historian, educator*

PORTUGAL

Coimbra
Holm, John Alexander *linguist, educator*

SCOTLAND

Cellardyke
Roff, William Robert *history educator, writer*

Saint Andrews
Lenman, Bruce Philip *historian, educator*

SINGAPORE

Singapore
McDonough, Richard Michael *philosophy educator*

SOUTH AFRICA

Gauteng Province
Ntlola, Peter Makhwenkwe *retired translator*

SWEDEN

Lerum
Borei, Sven Hans Emil *translator*

TAIWAN

Taichung
Lu, Shih-Peng *history educator*

ZAMBIA

Lusaka
Hipple, Walter John *English language educator*

ADDRESS UNPUBLISHED

Adams, Harlene *speech communications educator*
Allaire, Gloria Kaun *Italian language educator*
Allington, Richard Lloyd *literacy studies educator*
Angell, Richard Bradshaw *philosophy educator*
Aptheker, Herbert *historian, lecturer*
Arbelbide, C(indy) L(ea) *historian, author*
Aubrey, James Reynolds *English educator*
Bahre, Jeannette *English language educator, education educator, librarian*
Bailey, Charles-James Nice *linguistics educator*
Bailey, David Roy Shackleton *classics educator*
Baker, Ronald James *English language educator, university administrator*
Baxter, Stephen Bartow *retired history educator*
†Bayer, Gregory D. *historian, researcher*
Belnap, Nuel Dinsmore, Jr. *philosophy educator*
†Belton, John *English educator*
Benc, Tamara Susan *reading and language arts educator*
Bercovitch, Sacvan *English language professional, educator*
Berkhofer, Robert Frederick, Jr. *retired history educator*
†Bhattacharya, Nandini *English educator, researcher, writer*
Bickford, Shirley Verna Williams *retired English educator*
Blackbourn, David Gordon *history educator*
†Blumenfeld-Kosinski, Renate *French educator*
Bok, Sissela *philosopher, writer*
Bolsterli, Margaret Jones *English educator, farmer*
Booker, Michael James *philosophy educator*
Bosmajian, Haig Aram *speech communication educator*
Bosse, Malcolm Joseph, Jr. *professional language educator, author*
†Boyle, Kathleen Marie *English educator, soccer coach*
Brettell, Richard Robson *art historian, museum consultant, educator*
Brewster, Elizabeth Winifred *English language educator, poet, novelist*
Brody, Jacob Jerome *art history educator*
Bryant, Paul Thompson *English language educator*
Bush, Sarah Lillian *historian*

Byard, Vicki Faye *English educator*
Cachia, Pierre Jacques *Middle East languages and culture educator, researcher*
Carls, Alice Catherine *history educator*
Caswell, Frances Pratt *retired English language educator*
Chandler, Alfred Dupont, Jr. *historian, educator*
Chandra, Pramod *art history educator*
Chellas, Brian Farrell *retired philosophy educator, author*
Chesson, Michael Bedout *history educator*
†Clayson, Susan Hollis *art historian, educator*
Coffman, Stanley Knight, Jr. *English educator, former college president*
Cohen, Henry *historian, retired educator*
Collins, Jean Katherine *English educator*
†Cook, Pamela Margaret *French educator*
Cooper, John Milton, Jr. *history educator, author*
Cooper, Rebecca *art dealer*
†Cordova, Denise A. *foreign language educator*
Costa, Albert Bernard *retired science history educator*
Covino, William Anthony *English language educator*
Culverwell, Albert Henry *historian*
Cunningham, William Francis, Jr. *English language educator, university administrator*
†Cuppo Csaki, Luciana *foreign language educator, writer*
Cutler, Maxine Gordon *French language and literature educator*
de Grazia, Sebastian *political philosopher, author*
†de la Torre Falzon, Alicia Maria *Spanish language educator*
Deligiorgis, Stavros G. *retired literature educator*
Demenchonok, Edward Vasilevich *philosopher, linguist, researcher, educator*
Dias, Kathleen R. Bruni-Kerrigan *foreign language educator*
Di Paolo, Maria Grazia *language educator, writer*
Djordjevic, Dimitrije *historian, educator*
Dorsey, Loraine *English educator*
Dosé, Frederick Philip, Jr. *art historian, art and antiques appraiser, consultant, liquidator*
Douglass, Ellen Heather *humanities educator*
Duncan, Carol Greene *art historian, educator*
†Eby, Carl Peter *English educator*
Eby, Cecil DeGrotte *English language educator, writer*
Edel, Abraham *philosophy educator*
Edmunds, (Arthur) Lowell *philology educator*
Ellis, John Martin *German literature educator*
Farina, Donna Marie *languages and linguistics educator*
Fleck, Stephen Harlan *French language educator*
Fleischauer, John Frederick *retired English language educator*
Flint, John E. *historian, educator*
Fodor, Sarah Joan *writer, English educator*
Folker, Cathleen Ann *humanities educator*
†Fong, Wen Chih *art historian, educator, author, museum curator*
†Ford, William D. *English educator*
†Foulkes, Julia Lawrence *historian*
Frederick, Lizetta Mary *educator, counselor*
Friedman, Victor Allen *linguist, eduator*
Froberg, Brent Malcolm *classics educator*
†Gac-Artigas, Priscilla *foreign language educator, publisher*
Gaddis, John Lewis *history educator*
Galbraith, John Semple *history educator*
Gambone, Philip Arthur *English language educator*
Gardner, Barbara Rogers *humanities educator, writer*
Geiselhart, Lorene Annetta *English language educator*
Geist, Kathe Sternbach *art history, cinema and English educator, writer*
Gendre, Michael *philosophy educator*
Gentry, Francis G. *German language educator*
Gerlach, Jeanne Elaine *English language educator*
Ghymn, Esther Mikyung *English educator, writer*
Gilb, Corinne Lathrop *history educator*
Gillespie, Gerald Ernest Paul *comparative literature educator, writer*
Gillett, Mary Caperton *military historian*
†Gingher, Marianne B. *English educator*
Glancy, Diane *English educator*
Goldberg, Maxwell Henry *retired humanities educator*
Goldstein, Phyllis Ann *art historian, educator*
Gonzalez-Vales, Luis Ernesto *historian, educational administrator*
Gordon, Cyrus Herzl *Orientalist, educator*
Greene, Elinore Aschah *speech and drama professional, writer*
Greene, John Colton *retired history educator*
Greider, John Calhoun *English educator*
Greve, Sally Doane *English educator*
Grinnell, Helen Dunn *musicologist, arts administrator*
Gromen, Richard John *historian, educator*
Gumpel, Liselotte *German language educator*
†Gunderson, Keith Robert *philosophy educator*
†Guo, Sheng Ming *retired history educator*
Haag, Walter M(onroe), Jr. *philatelist*
†Halmer, Judith R. *writing and literature educator*
Harris, John M. *historian*
Hart, Arthur Alvin *historian, author*
†Harter, Hugh Anthony *foreign language educator*
Havran, Martin Joseph *historian, educator, author*
Haworth, Dale Keith *art history educator, gallery director*
Hemlow, Joyce *language and literature educator, author*
Herbst, Jurgen *history and education educator*
Hill, William Frank *history educator*
Hoart, Gladys Gallagher *English language educator*
Holloway, Julia Bolton *professor emerita, theologian*
†Hoover, Oliver D. *classics scholar*
Howard, Michael Eliot *historian, educator*
Hubbell, Elizabeth Wolfe *English language educator*
Hughes, Thomas Parke *history educator*
†Hume, Beverly Ann *English and linguistics educator*
Hungerford, Edward Arthur *humanities professional educator*
Hutcheon, Linda Ann *English language educator*
Hutchinson, Joseph Candler *retired foreign language educator*
Ingham, Charles Andrew *literature and English language educator*
Irwin, Anna Mae *English language educator*
Ivry, Alfred Lyon *history of, Jewish and Islamic philosophy educator*
Jacobs, William Jay *historian, writer*
†Jaren, Courtney Bates *historian, lawyer, consultant*
†Jiménez, Onilda A. *Spanish educator*
†John, Judith A. *literature educator*

Johnson, John Prescott *philosophy educator*
Johnson, Vernon Eugene *history educator, educational administrator*
Jones, Peter d'Alroy *historian, writer, retired educator*
Jordan, William Bryan, Jr. *art historian*
Kagan, Constance Henderson *philosopher, educator, consultant*
Kane, Loana *foreign language educator*
Kane, Patricia Lanegran *language professional, educator*
Kaplan, Robert B. *linguistics educator, consultant, researcher*
Kares, Robin Lee *English educator*
Kastor, Frank Sullivan *English language educator*
Keeter, Lynn Carpenter *English educator*
Kessler-Harris, Alice *historian, educator*
†Kirby, Carol Bingham *Spanish language educator*
Kissane, James Donald *English literature educator*
Knight, Doris Rathbun *retired government and history educator*
Kochhar-Lindgren, Gray Meredith *humanities educator*
Korsgaard, Christine Marion *philosophy educator*
Kramer, Dale Vernon *retired English language educator*
Lambert, Edythe Rutherford *retired language educator, civic volunteer*
Lance, Donald Max *linguistics educator, retired*
Latner, Helen Stambler *former English educator*
Lawson Donadio, Carolina Anna *foreign language educator, translator*
†Lee, James Wade *humanities educator, writer, actor*
Levin, Gerald Henry *English educator*
Levy, Andrew Alan *literature educator, curator, editor*
Levy, Debra S. *humanities educator*
Lewis, Arthur Orcutt, Jr. *retired English language educator, dean*
Lightburn, Faye Marie *genealogist*
†Lindner, Carl Martin *English educator*
Lindsey, Roberta Lewise *music researcher, historian*
Lingenfelter, Andrea Diane *translator, writer*
†Lipton, Eunice *art history, writer*
Loughran, James Newman *philosophy educator, college administrator*
†Low, Lisa Elaine *English educator*
Maehl, William Harvey *historian, educator*
Mahoney, Michael Robert Taylor *art historian, educator*
Manogue, Ralph Anthony *English language educator*
†Manso, Leira A. *Latin American literature educator*
Marchant, JoAnn Reviczky *English language educator, actress*
Marion, Marjorie Anne *English language educator, education consultant*
Marshall, Richard *art historian, curator*
Martin, John William *educator, antiquarian bookseller*
Mathews, Barbara Jean *genealogist*
Mattis, Olivia *musicologist*
†Matzky, Karl Frederick, Jr. *history educator*
McCaffrey, Phillip *English language educator*
†McCarthy, Jeffrey Mathes *English educator*
McCormick, John Owen *retired comparative literature educator*
†McCoy, Nancy Jeanne *history educator, writer*
McDermott, Agnes Charlene Senape *philosophy educator*
McEvoy-Jamil, Patricia Ann *English language educator*
McGann, Lisa B. Napoli *language educator*
McSpadden, Katherine Frances *English language educator*
Meintsma, Peter Evans *history and political science educator*
†Mendoza, Nydia *language arts educator*
Metcalf, Pauline Cabot *architectural historian*
Meyer, Kathleen Marie *English educator, editor, writer*
Miner-Farra, Tess Antoinette *English language educator, dean*
†Mirabelli, Eugene *English educator*
Miscella, Maria Diana *humanities educator*
Molloy, Sylvia *Latin American literature educator, writer*
Morgan, Ann Lee *art historian, writer*
Morgan, Edmund Sears *history educator*
Morreale, Ben *retired history educator, novelist*
Morrill, Penny Chittim *art historian*
†Morrisard-Larkin, Mary Angela *foreign language educator*
Morrissey, Charles Thomas *historian, educator*
Morrow, Ralph Ernest *historian, educator*
Mosca, Virginia *retired language educator*
Moser, Gerald M. *emeritus educator*
Murdock, Mary-Elizabeth *history educator*
Murphy, Francis *English language educator*
Nagel, Thomas *philosopher, educator*
Nix, Nancy Jean *librarian, designer*
Nochman, Lois Wood Kivi (Mrs. Marvin Nochman) *educator*
Nostrand, Howard Lee *humanities educator*
Novak, Barbara *art history educator*
†O'Kane, Karen Ann *English educator*
Olson, James Clifton *historian, university president*
Olson, Paul Richard *Spanish literature educator, editor*
Outka, Gene Harold *philosophy and Christian ethics educator*
†Padrón, Ricardo *foreign language educator*
Paige, Anita Parker *retired English language educator*
Palter, Robert Monroe *philosophy and history educator*
Parrish, T. Michael *historian*
Patton, John Joseph *retired literature educator*
Paxton, Laura Belle-Kent *English language educator, management professional*
Perdigó, Luisa Marina *foreign language and literature educator*
†Peterson, Barbara Ann Bennett *history educator, television personality*
Peyser, Joseph Leonard *author, translator, historial researcher*
Pflanze, Otto Paul *history educator*
Pincus-Witten, Robert A. *art history educator, art gallery director, critic*
†Plumly, Stanley *English educator, poet*
Purtill, Richard Lawrence *philosopher, writer*
Rabiola, Samuel Charles *English educator*
Radycki, Diane Josephine *art historian, writer*
Ranieri, Joseph John *English language educator*
Ransom, Nancy Alderman *sociology and women's studies educator, university administrator*
†Rappaport, Susan Elizabeth *English language educator*
Reiss, Timothy James *comparative literature educator, writer*
Riasanovsky, Nicholas Valentine *historian, educator*
Richardson, Robert Dale, Jr. *English language educator*
Rickard, Ruth David *retired history and political science educator*
Robinson, Carmen Delores *educator*
†Robinson, Mary Frances *retired French language educator*
Rollins, Alfred Brooks, Jr. *historian, educator*
Romeo, Luigi *linguist, educator*
Rosenberg, David Alan *military historian, educator*
Rossi, Mary Ann *research scholar*
Rouman, John Christ *classics educator*
Ruoff, A. LaVonne Brown *English language educator*
Sabat-Rivers, Georgina *Latin American literature educator*
†Salladay, John R. *historian, sociologist, educator*
Sanborn, Melinde Lutz *genealogist, writer*
†Sandoval, Chela *humanities educator*
Schlossman, Beryl Fern *literature educator*
Schoen, Carol Bronston *retired English language educator*
†Severin, Laura R. *English educator*
†Sharp, Floyd Montgomery *historian, educator*
Sices, David *language educator, translator*
†Siemon, James *English language educator*
†Simpson, Mona Elizabeth *English educator, writer*
Smith, Charlotte Reed *retired music educator*
†Smith, Gerrit Bruce *foreign language educator*
Smith, Susan Lee *history educator*
Smither, Howard Elbert *musicologist*
Smock, Raymond William *historian*
Snyder, Susan Brooke *retired English literature educator*
Solomon, Robert Charles *philosopher, educator*
Sonkowsky, Robert Paul *classicist, educator, actor*
†Spink, Walter Milton *art historian, educator*
Sprowl, Dale Rae *English educator*
Stokstad, Marilyn Jane *art history educator, curator*
Stolarik, M. Mark *history educator*
Straulman, Ann Therese *retired English language educator*
Street, John Charles *linguistics educator*
Stringer, Mary Evelyn *art historian, educator*
Styne, Marlys Marshall *retired English educator*
Suits, Bernard Herbert *philosophy educator*
Sullivan, Mary Rose *English language educator*
Sutton, Julia Sumberg *musicologist, dance historian*
Svrcek, Debbie M. *English educator*
Swanson, Georgia May *retired speech communication educator*
Tallet, Jorge Antonio *philosopher, writer*
†Tarozzi-Goldsmith, Marcella I. *philosopher, writer*
Tayler, Irene *English literature educator*
Tedesco, Paul Herbert *humanities educator*
Thackray, Arnold Wilfrid *historian, foundation executive*
†Thurin, Susan Schoenbauer *English educator*
Tong, Rosemarie *medical humanities and philosophy educator, consultant and researcher*
Topik, Steven Curtis *history educator*
Tracy, James *history educator*
Trelease, Allen William *historian, educator*
†Turkkan-Wille, Fatma *art historian*
†Vargas, Margarita *modern languages educator*
Vermeule, Emily Townsend (Mrs. Cornelius C. Vermeule, III) *classicist, educator*
†Viswanathan, Meera Sushila *comparative literature and East Asian studies educator*
von Hoffman, Alexander *historian*
Wagner, Diana Mae *English language educator*
Wallace, William Augustine *philosophy and history educator*
Waller, Gary Fredric *English language educator, administrator, poet*
Walters, David Wayne *history and government educator, tennis coach*
Weisbuch, Robert Alan *English educator*
Wheeler, Burton M. *literature educator, higher education consultant, college dean*
†Wickliffe, Mary *art historian*
Williams, Patrice Dale *linguist, educator*
Wishnia, Kenneth J.A. *writer, translator, language educator*
Wolff, Cynthia Griffin *humanities educator, author*
Wolters, Oliver William *history educator*
Woodman, Jean Wilson *educator, consultant*
Wright, Beth Segal *art historian, educator*
Wruck, Erich-Oskar *retired foreign language educator*
Wuellner, Kathleen D. *English educator*
Wyatt, Marcia Jean *fine arts educator, administrative assistant*
Yolton, John William *philosopher, educator*
Zaferson, William S. *philosophy educator, publisher*
†Zolov, Eric S. *historian, educator*

HUMANITIES: LIBRARIES

UNITED STATES

ALABAMA

Athens
Williams, Timothy Dale *reference librarian*

Auburn
Havens, Carolyn Clarice *librarian*
Straiton, T(homas) Harmon, Jr. *librarian*

Bay Minette
†Cabaniss, Charlotte Jones *library services director*

Birmingham
Bulow, Jack Faye *library director*
Clemmons, Nancy Washington *library administrator*
Murrell, Susan DeBrecht *librarian*
Spence, Paul Herbert *librarian*
Stephens, Jerry Wayne *librarian, library director*

Fairhope
†Suddeth, Betty Fisher *librarian*

Huntsville
Miller, Carol Lynn *librarian*

Jacksonville
Hubbard, William James *library director*

Mobile
Jones, Daniel Hare *librarian, consultant*
Parsley, Brantley Hamilton *librarian*
Peplowski, Celia Ceslawa *librarian*
†Rodgers, Patricia Mansfield *librarian*

Montgomery
Owes, Juanita *library director*

Orange Beach
†Owens, Marsha *library director*

Pelham
Stewart, George Ray *association executive, librarian*

Thomaston
Counselman, Anne *librarian*

ALASKA

Anchorage
Rollins, Alden Milton *documents librarian*

Juneau
Crane, Karen R. *director Alaska State Library*
Schorr, Alan Edward *librarian, publisher*

ARIZONA

Chandler
Miller, Robert Carl *retired library director*

Green Valley
White, Herbert Spencer *research library educator, university dean*

Mesa
Anderson, Herschel Vincent *librarian*

Phoenix
Hanley, Fred William *librarian, educator*

Scottsdale
Biglin, Karen Eileen *library director*

Sun City West
Williams, William Harrison *retired librarian*

Tempe
Matthews, Gertrude Ann Urch *retired librarian, writer*
Maynard, Michael *librarian*
Weiler, Dorothy Esser *librarian*

Tucson
Anderson, Rachael Keller *library administrator*
Griffen, Agnes Marthe *library administrator*
†Kruse, Diane Viewing *college library director*
Wolfe, William Jerome *librarian, English language educator*

Winslow
Kaliher, Michael Dennis *librarian, historian*

ARKANSAS

Fayetteville
Simpson, Ethel Chachere *archivist*

Little Rock
Baker, Russell Pierce *archivist*
Berry, Janet Claire *librarian*
Jones, Philip Lindsey *librarian*
Mulkey, Jack Clarendon *library director*

Pine Bluff
Burdick, David *library director*

CALIFORNIA

Altadena
Dutton, Pauline Mae *fine arts librarian*

Anaheim
Miller, Jean Ruth *retired librarian*

Aptos
Heron, David Winston *librarian*

Berkeley
Bacon, Elizabeth Morrow *librarian, writer, editor, educator*
Buckland, Michael Keeble *librarian, educator*
Danton, Joseph Periam *librarian, educator*
Harlan, Robert Dale *information studies educator, academic administrator*
Levin, Marc Alan *library assistant director*
Minudri, Regina Ursula *librarian, consultant*

Camarillo
Kiser, Nagiko Sato *retired librarian*

Carlsbad
Lange, Clifford E. *librarian*
Weiss, Egon Arthur *retired library administrator*

Chula Vista
Vess, Ronald Wayne *librarian*

Cupertino
Fletcher, Homer Lee *librarian*

Davis
Grossman, George Stefan *library director, law eductor*
Sharrow, Marilyn Jane *library administrator*

El Cerrito
Smith, Eldred Reid *library educator*

Foster City
Josephine, Helen Bowden *librarian*

Fresno
Gorman, Michael Joseph *library director, educator*
Kallenberg, John Kenneth *librarian*

Fullerton
Ayala, John *librarian, dean*
†Milo, Albert J. *librarian*

Hayward
Ramsdell, Kristin Romeis *librarian, researcher*

Huntington Beach
Hayden, Ron L. *library director*

Inglewood
Alaniz, Miguel José Castañeda *library director*

Irvine
Laird, Wilbur David, Jr. *bookseller, editor*

La Jolla
Mirsky, Phyllis Simon *librarian*

La Mesa
Freeland, Robert Frederick *retired librarian*

Livermore
Love, Sandra Rae *information specialist*
Schalit, Michael *research librarian*

Los Angeles
Bates, Marcia Jeanne *information scientist educator*
Borko, Harold *information scientist, psychologist, educator*
Brecht, Albert Odell *library and information technology administrator*
Chang, Henry Chung-Lien *library administrator*
Ciccone, Amy Navratil *art librarian*
Cuadra, Carlos Albert *information scientist, management executive*
Gilman, Nelson Jay *library director*
Helgeson, Duane Marcellus *retired librarian*
Kent, Susan *library director, consultant*
Patron, Susan Hall *librarian, writer*
Richardson, John Vinson, Jr. *library and information science educator*
Shank, Russell *librarian, educator*
Steele, Victoria Lee *librarian*
Sutherland, Michael Cruise *librarian*
Werner, Gloria S. *librarian*

Menlo Park
White, Cecil Ray *librarian, consultant*

Mission Hills
Weber, Francis Joseph *archivist, museum director*

Monterey
Reneker, Maxine Hohman *librarian*

Monterey Park
Wilson, Linda *librarian*

Mountain View
Di Muccio, Mary-Jo *retired librarian*
Michalko, James Paul *library association administrator*

Napa
Meredith, Joseph Charlton *retired military officer, librarian, tree farmer*

Newport Beach
Kienitz, LaDonna Trapp *city librarian, city official*

North Hollywood
Schlosser, Anne Griffin *librarian*

Oakland
MacKay, Nancy *librarian, oral historian*

Oceanside
†Aponte, Jose A. *library director*

Palmdale
Moore, Everett LeRoy *library administrator*

Pasadena
Buck, Anne Marie *library director, consultant*
Harmsen, Tyrus George *librarian*

Placerville
Wickline, Marian Elizabeth *former corporate librarian*

Pollock Pines
Rickard, Margaret Lynn *library consultant, former library director*

Redlands
Burgess, Larry Eugene *library director, history educator*
Musmann, Klaus *librarian*

Riverside
Auth, Judith *library director*

Sacramento
Killian, Richard M. *library director*
Liberty, John Joseph *librarian*
Starr, Kevin *librarian, educator*

Salinas
Spinks, Paul *retired library director*

San Bernardino
Burgess, Michael *library science educator, publisher*
†Roop, Ophelia Georgiev *library director*

San Diego
Ling, David Chang *international book dealer*

Sannwald, William Walter *librarian*

San Francisco
Shadwick, VirginiaAnn Greer *librarian*

San Jose
Light, Jane Ellen *librarian*
Schmidt, Cyril James *librarian*
Woolls, Esther Blanche *library science educator*

San Juan Capistrano
Brown, Stephanie Cecile *librarian, writer*
Peterson, Fred McCrae *retired librarian*

San Marcos
Cater, Judy Jerstad *librarian*
Ciurczak, Alexis *librarian*

San Marino
Robertson, Mary Louise *archivist, historian*
Thorpe, James *humanities researcher*

San Rafael
Morehouse, Valerie Jeanne *librarian*

Santa Ana
Adams, John M. *library director*
Richard, Robert John *library director*

Santa Barbara
Keator, Carol Lynne *library director*

Santa Clara
Hopkinson, Shirley Lois *library and information science educator*

Santa Clarita
Gardner, Frederick Boyce *library director*

Santa Cruz
Dyson, Allan Judge *librarian*

Santa Monica
Ackerman, Helen Page *librarian, educator*

Santa Rosa
Pearson, Roger Lee *library director*

Sausalito
Glaser, Edwin Victor *rare book dealer*

Sebastopol
Sabsay, David *library consultant*

Sherman Oaks
Miller, Margaret Haigh *librarian*

South Pasadena
†Maguire, Theresa Louise *library director*

Stanford
Derksen, Charlotte Ruth Meynink *librarian*
Keller, Michael Alan *librarian, educator, musicologist*

Stockton
Foster, Colleen *library director*

Torrance
Buckley, James W. *librarian*

Turlock
Parker, John Carlyle *retired librarian and archivist, editor*

Westminster
Gylseth, Doris (Lillian) Hanson *retired librarian*

Yorba Linda
Naulty, Susan Louise *archivist*

COLORADO

Aurora
Miller, Sarah Pearl *librarian*
Nicholas, Thomas Peter *library administrator, community television consultant, producer*

Canon City
Cochran, Susan Mills *librarian*

Colorado Springs
Budington, William Stone *retired librarian*

Denver
Ashton, Rick James *librarian*
Garcia, Joan Marie *library director*
Phillips, Dorothy Reid *retired library technician*

Edwards
Chambers, Joan Louise *retired librarian, retired university educator and dean*

Englewood
Wynar, Bohdan Stephen *librarian, author, editor*

Fort Collins
Ernest, Douglas Jerome *librarian*
Mc Clellan, William Monson *library administrator, retired*

Golden
Mathews, Anne Jones *consultant, library educator and administrator*

Lakewood
Knott, William Alan *library director, library management and building consultant*

Loveland
Carter, Laura Lee *academic librarian, psychotherapist*

New Castle
†Spuhler, Jacilyn E. *librarian*

Pueblo
Bates, Charles Emerson *library administrator*
Cress, Cecile Colleen *retired librarian*

CONNECTICUT

Branford
De Gennaro, Richard *retired library director, library advisor*

Bridgeport
Sheridan, Eileen *librarian*

Chester
Harwood, Eleanor Cash *librarian*

Derby
†Augusta, Judith Wood *librarian*

Fairfield
Bryan, Barbara Day *retired librarian*
Dunham, Christopher Scott *librarian*

Hartford
Kaimowitz, Jeffrey Hugh *librarian*
Posteraro, Catherine Hammond *librarian, gerontology educator*

Middletown
Meyers, Arthur Solomon *library director*

Milford
Fontaine, Ronald Gerard *librarian*

Mystic
Rogers, Brian Deane *retired librarian*

New Britain
Sohn, Jeanne *librarian*
Tomaiuolo, Nicholas Gregory *librarian, educator*

New Haven
Bennett, Scott Boyce *librarian*
†McGinn, Howard Francis *library director, educator*
Oliver-Warren, Mary Elizabeth *retired library science educator*
Peterson, Sandra Kay *librarian*
Stuehrenberg, Paul Frederick *librarian*

New London
Daragan, Patricia Ann *librarian*

Niantic
Deakyne, William John *library director, musician*

Rockville
†Ciparelli, Peter Francis *library director*

Simsbury
Roberts, Celia Ann *librarian*

Southington
Burkhardt, Dolores Ann *library consultant*

Storrs Mansfield
Stevens, Norman Dennison *retired library director*

Willimantic
†Perch, Theodore Lesco *library director, artist*

Wilton
Poundstone, Sally *library director*

DELAWARE

Dover
Wetherall, Robert Shaw *librarian*

Wilmington
Newell, Katherine Claiborne *librarian*
Williams, Richmond Dean *library appraiser, consultant*

DISTRICT OF COLUMBIA

Washington
†Adam, Nancy Elizabeth *library and information manager*
Augustyn, Frederick John, Jr. *librarian*
Baker, Emily Lind *editor, digital library specialist*
Carlin, John William *archivist, former governor*
†Carlson, Melinda Suzanne *librarian*
Carr, Timothy Bernard *librarian*
Chin, Cecilia Hui-Hsin *librarian*
Clemmer, Dan Orr *librarian*
Converse, Joseph Thomas *archivist, records manager*
Craig, Susan Lyons *library director*
Cylke, Frank Kurt *librarian*
Daffron, MaryEllen *librarian*
Elder, Mary Louise *librarian*
Emperado, Mercedes Lopez *librarian*
†Falk, Diane M. *research director, librarian, editor, writer*
Fifer Canby, Susan Melinda *library administrator*
Franklin, Hardy R. *retired library director*
Gifford, Prosser *library administrator*
Gregory, John Forrest *information technology consultant, writer*
Gruhl, Andrea Morris *librarian*
Haley, Roger Kendall *librarian*
Harlem, Susan Lynn *librarian*
Hedges, Kamla King *library director*
Heiss, Harry Glen *archivist*
Higbee, Joan Florence *librarian*
†Jackson, Mary Ellen *librarian, consultant*
Knezo, Genevieve Johanna *science and technology policy researcher*
Lewis, Robert John Cornelius Koons *university library director, consultant*
Marcum, Deanna Bowling *library administrator*
Martin, Susan Katherine *librarian*

Missar, Charles Donald *librarian*
Moulton, David Aubin *library director*
Mulhollan, Daniel Patrick *research director*
Murphy, Kathryn Marguerite *archivist*
Newton, Virginia *archivist, historian, librarian*
Pinkett, Harold Thomas *archivist, historian*
Player, Thelma B. *librarian*
Renninger, Mary Karen *librarian*
Rovelstad, Mathilde Verner *library science educator*
Thomas, Mary Augusta *library administrator*
Turtell, Neal Timothy *librarian*
Wand, Patricia Ann *librarian*
Wasserman, Krystyna *librarian, art historian*
Wattenmaker, Richard Joel *archive director, art scholar*
Young, Peter Robert *librarian*

FLORIDA

Atlantis
Gough, Carolyn Harley *library director*

Beverly Hills
†Denis, Heidi Anfinson *library administrator*

Boca Raton
Miller, William *library administrator*
Sarna, Helen Horowitz *retired librarian, educator*

Boynton Beach
Farace, Virginia Kapes *librarian*

Clearwater
Moore, Matthew Stafford *librarian*

Coleman
Crenshaw, Tena Lula *librarian*

Deland
Caccamise, Genevra Louise Ball (Mrs. Alfred E. Caccamise) *retired librarian*

Dunedin
†Foley, Wendy H. *library director*

Fort Lauderdale
Bethel, Marilyn Joyce *librarian*
Hershenson, Miriam Hannah *librarian*
Riggs, Donald Eugene *librarian, university official*

Fort Myers
Rose, Susan A. Schultz *retired theological librarian*

Fort Walton Beach
†Hill, Carol Jean *library director*

Gainesville
Brown, Myra Suzanne *librarian*
Willocks, Robert Max *retired librarian*

Graceville
Murrell, Irvin Henry, Jr. *librarian, minister*

Jacksonville
Farkas, Andrew *library director, educator, writer*
Marion, Gail Elaine *reference librarian*

Kissimmee
†Lambert, Wendy Ecklund *library information specialist, social studies educator*

Lakeland
Reich, David Lee *library director*

Maitland
Westall, Marta Susan Wolf *librarian*

Melbourne
Regis, Nina *librarian, educator*

Naples
Chartrand, Robert Lee *information scientist*
Hainsworth, Melody May *information professional, researcher*

Oakland Park
Kilpatrick, Clifton Wayne *book dealer*

Opa Locka
Conner, Laban Calvin *retired librarian*

Orlando
Allison, Anne Marie *retired librarian*
Green, Joal Fekete Stafford *library media specialist*

Oviedo
Hyslop, Gary Lee *librarian*

Palm Harbor
†Paolilli, Almonte Louis *librarian*

Saint Petersburg
Kent, Allen *library and information sciences educator*

Sarasota
Hummel, Dana D. Mallett *librarian*
Retzer, Mary Elizabeth Helm *retired librarian*

Tallahassee
Robbins, Jane Borsch *library science educator, information science educator*
†Sapp, Lauren B. *librarian, educator*
Summers, Frank William *librarian*
Summers, Lorraine Dey Schaeffer *librarian*
Thompson, Jean Tanner *retired librarian*
Wilkins, (George) Barratt *librarian*
Zachert, Martha Jane *retired librarian*

Venice
†Pike, Nancy M. *librarian*

West Palm Beach
†Smith, Pamela Sandlian *library director*
Storch, Barbara Jean Cohen *librarian*
Terwillegar, Jane Cusack *librarian, educator*

Winter Park
Rogers, Rutherford David *librarian*

Zephyrhills
Martindale, Carla Joy *librarian*

GEORGIA

Athens
Potter, William Gray, Jr. *library director*

Atlanta
Brown, Lorene B(yron) *library educator, educational administrator*
†Cravey, Pamela J. *librarian*
Drake, Miriam Anna *librarian, educator*
Lawson, A(bram) Venable *retired librarian*
Roberts, Edward Graham *librarian*
Robison, Carolyn Love *retired librarian*
Schewe, Donald Bruce *archivist, library director*
Thaxton, Mary Lynwood *librarian*
Yates, Ella Gaines *library consultant*

Augusta
Rowland, Arthur Ray *librarian*

Carrollton
Beard, Charles Edward *library director, consultant*
Goodson, Carol Faye *librarian*

Dalton
Forsee, Joe Brown *library director*

Marietta
Rogers, Gail Elizabeth *library director*

Rome
Mosley, Mary Mac *retired librarian*

Savannah
Amin, Shamima *library and media services director, university professor*
Dickerson, Lon Richard *library administrator*

Smarr
Evans, Rosemary King (Mrs. Howell Dexter Evans) *librarian, educator*

HAWAII

Aiea
Uyehara, Harry Yoshimi *library educator*

Honolulu
Flynn, Joan Mayhew *librarian*
Masuchika, Glenn Norio *librarian, university official, book reviewer*
Wageman, Lynette Mena *librarian*

Lahaina
Conover, Robert Warren *retired librarian*

Lihue
Stevens, Robert David *librarian, educator*

IDAHO

Boise
Bolles, Charles Avery *librarian*

Moscow
Force, Ronald Wayne *librarian*

ILLINOIS

Alton
Fortado, Robert Joseph *librarian, educator*

Argenta
†Bowman, Cynthia D. *library director*

Aurora
Cochran, William Michael *librarian*

Bloomington
Olson, Rue Eileen *librarian*

Bradford
†Jason, Mary L. *librarian*

Carbondale
Bauner, Ruth Elizabeth *library administrator, reference librarian*
Koch, David Victor *librarian, administrator*
Koch, Loretta Peterson *librarian, educator*

Chicago
Brown, Richard Holbrook *library administrator, historian*
Dempsey, Mary A. *library commissioner, lawyer*
Elbaz, Sohair Wastawy *library director, consultant*
Feiner, Arlene Marie *librarian, researcher, consultant*
Funk, Carla Jean *library association executive*
Gerdes, Neil Wayne *library director*
Hanrath, Linda Carol *librarian, archivist*
†John, Nancy R. *librarian, writer*
Knoblauch, Mark George *librarian, consultant*
Kosokoff, Jeffrey Eugene *librarian*
Marco, Guy Anthony *librarian, educator*
Miletich, Ivo *library and information scientist, bibliographer, educator, linguist, literature research specialist*
Runkle, Martin Davey *library director*
Shedlock, James *library director, consultant*
†Snow, Randy J. *librarian, English educator*
Sullivan, Peggy (Anne) *librarian*
Vondruska, Eloise Marie *librarian*
Wagner, Rose Mary *librarian*

Coal City
†Franciskovich, Jolene Ann *library administrator*

Decatur
Moorman, John A. *librarian*

Dekalb
Studwell, William Emmett *librarian, writer*

Downers Grove
Saricks, Joyce Goering *librarian*

Elgin
Zack, Daniel Gerard *library director*

Evanston
Bishop, David Fulton *library administrator*
Cates, Jo Ann *library administrator, writer*
Crawford, Susan *library director, educator, author*
Wright, Donald Eugene *retired librarian*

Franklin Park
†Watson, Robert Edward *librarian, information specialist*

Galva
†Heck, Melody Ann *library director*

Grayslake
†Thomas, Roberta M. *librarian*

Joliet
Johnston, James Robert *library director*

La Grange
Mikolyzk, Thomas Andrew *librarian*
†Moskal, Stephen L., Jr. *librarian*

Lake Forest
Miller, Arthur Hawks, Jr. *librarian, consultant*

Mattoon
†Bays, Mona Rae *librarian*

Maywood
Ellington, Mildred L. *librarian*

Monmouth
Kirk, Sherwood *librarian*

Oak Lawn
†Casey, James B. *librarian*

Quincy
Tyer, Travis Earl *library consultant*

Richton Park
†Nevins, Patrick Fredrick *librarian*

River Grove
†Jurkowski, Orion Lech *librarian*

Rochester
Petterchak, Janice A. *researcher, writer*

Rockford
Chitwood, Julius Richard *librarian*

Rolling Meadows
†Medal, Carole Ann *library director*

Roselle
Lueder, Dianne Carol *library director*

Schaumburg
Adrianopoli, Barbara Catherine *librarian*

Shorewood
†Thomas, Mary Faith *library director*

Springfield
Coss, John Edward *archivist*
Kaige, Alice Tubb *retired librarian*

Sycamore
Young, Arthur Price *librarian, educator*

Urbana
Brichford, Maynard Jay *archivist*
Choldin, Marianna Tax *librarian, educator*
O'Brien, Nancy Patricia *librarian, educator*
Shtohryn, Dmytro Michael *librarian, educator*
Watson, Paula D. *library administrator*
†Woodard, Beth Stuckey *librarian, educator*

Wauconda
Kramer, Pamela Kostenko *librarian*

Western Springs
Carroll, Aileen *retired librarian*

Wheaton
Thompson, Bert Allen *retired librarian*

Wheeling
Hammer, Donald Price *librarian*
Long, Sarah Ann *librarian*
Mc Clarren, Robert Royce *librarian*
†Meehan, Tamiye Marcia *library director*

INDIANA

Auburn
Mountz, Louise Carson Smith *retired librarian*

Bloomington
Browar, Lisa Muriel *librarian*
Legler, April Arington *librarian, educator*
Martin, Fenton Strickland *librarian, writer*
Rudolph, Lavere Christian *library director*

Bluffton
Elliott, Barbara Jean *librarian*

Brookville
†Ariens, Karla Rae *library director*

Fort Wayne
Krull, Jeffrey Robert *library director*

Gary
Moran, Robert Francis, Jr. *library director*

Goshen
Chenoweth, Rose Marie *librarian*

Greensburg
†Porter, Kimberly Michelle *library director*

Huntington
Smith, Mary Lou *librarian*

Indianapolis
Bundy, David Dale *librarian, educator*
Ewick, Charles Ray *librarian*
Fellers, Frederick Paul *librarian*
Gnat, Raymond Earl *librarian*
Tucker, Dennis Carl *library executive*
Young, Philip Howard *library director*

Logansport
†Shih, Philip C. *library administrator*

Markle
†Hamilton, Rhonda Lynn *librarian*

Merrillville
†Derner, Carol A. *librarian*

Muncie
Schaefer, Patricia *librarian*
Yeamans, George Thomas *librarian, educator*

Notre Dame
Hayes, Stephen Matthew *librarian*

Plymouth
Sherwood, Lillian Anna *librarian, retired*

Purdue University
Mobley, Emily Ruth *library dean, educator*

Richmond
Farber, Evan Ira *librarian*
Kirk, Thomas Garrett, Jr. *librarian*

Saint Meinrad
Daly, Simeon Philip John *librarian*

West Lafayette
†Anderson, Kristine Jo *librarian*
Andrews, Theodora Anne *retired librarian, educator*
Markee, Katherine Madigan *librarian, educator*
Nixon, Judith May *librarian*
Pask, Judith Marie *librarian educator*
Tucker, John Mark *librarian, educator*

IOWA

Ames
Hill, Fay Gish *librarian*

Armstrong
†Jensen, Gertrude Eileen *librarian*

Carlisle
Berning, Robert William *librarian*

Cedar Falls
Kuethe-Strudthoff, Denise LaRae *librarian*

Cedar Rapids
Armitage, Thomas Edward *library director*

Council Bluffs
†Godsey, James Mark *library director*

Davenport
Potter, Corinne Jean *retired librarian*
Runge, Kay Kretschmar *library director*

Decorah
Kalsow, Kathryn Ellen *library clerk*

Des Moines
Isenstein, Laura *library director*
Rittmer, Elaine Heneke *library media specialist*
Smith, Sharman Bridges *state librarian*

Grinnell
McKee, Christopher Fulton *librarian, naval historian, educator*

Iowa City
Bentz, Dale Monroe *librarian*
Huttner, Sidney Frederick *librarian*

Kalona
†Skaden, Anne M. *library director*

Mason City
Iverson, Carol Jean *retired library media specialist*

North Liberty
†Crowner, Dee Kay *library administrator*

Waverly
Schroeder, Randall Lee *librarian*

West Bend
Wuebker, Colleen Marie *librarian*

West Branch
Mather, Mildred Eunice *retired archivist*
Miller, Dwight Merrick *archivist, historian*
Walch, Timothy George *library administrator*

KANSAS

Atchison
†Donaldson, Penny L. *library director*
McDonald, Joseph Andrew *information services director, consultant, writer*

Enterprise
Wickman, John Edward *librarian, historian*

Fort Leavenworth
Burgess, Edwin Bond *librarian, archivist*

Goodland
Warren, Janet Elaine *librarian*

Great Bend
Swan, James Albert *library administrator, writer*

Lawrence
Crowe, William Joseph *librarian*
Koepp, Donna Pauline Petersen *librarian*

Topeka
Marvin, James Conway *librarian, consultant*

Wichita
Berner Harris, Cynthia Kay *librarian*
Rademacher, Richard Joseph *librarian*

KENTUCKY

Danville
Campbell, Stanley Richard *library services director*

Hopkinsville
†Satterwhite, Robert Lee *library director*

Lexington
Bishop, Kay *media educator*
Mason, Ellsworth Goodwin *librarian*
Sineath, Timothy Wayne *library educator, university dean*
Steensland, Ronald Paul *librarian*
Willis, Paul Allen *librarian*

Louisville
Coalter, Milton J, Jr. *library director, educator*
Deering, Ronald Franklin *librarian, minister*
Poston, Janice Lynn *librarian*
VanMeter, Vandelia L. *library director*

Morehead
Besant, Larry Xon *librarian, administrator, consultant*

Summer Shade
Smith, Ruby Lucille *librarian*

Williamsburg
Burch, John Russell, Jr. *technical services librarian*

LOUISIANA

Baton Rouge
†Anjier, Jennifer J.M. *librarian*
Jaques, Thomas Francis *librarian*
Lane, Margaret Beynon Taylor *librarian*
Patterson, Charles Darold *librarian, educator*

Jennings
Patterson, Trudy Jenkins *librarian*

Lafayette
Branch, Sonya Meyer *library director*
Carstens, Jane Ellen *retired library science educator*

Lake Charles
Curol, Helen Ruth *librarian, English language educator*

New Orleans
Leinbach, Philip Eaton *retired librarian*
Skinner, Robert Earle *university librarian, writer*
Somers, Sally West *librarian*

Plaquemine
Mc Cray, Evelina Williams *librarian, researcher*

Shreveport
Colón, Carlos Wildo *librarian*

Slidell
Hendricks, Donald Duane *librarian*

Ville Platte
†Saunders, Wesley Hugh *librarian*

MAINE

Bangor
Rea, Ann W. *librarian*

Bar Harbor
Dworak, Marcia Lynn *library director, library building consultant*

Camden
†Moran, Elizabeth Ames *library director*

Searsport
Cagle, William Rea *librarian*

Waterville
Muehlner, Suanne Wilson *library director*

Westbrook
Parks, George Richard *librarian*

MARYLAND

Annapolis
Kozlowski, Ronald Stephan *librarian*
Papenfuse, Edward Carl, Jr. *archivist, state official*
Werking, Richard Hume *librarian, historian, academic administrator*

Ashton
Tabler, Shirley May *retired librarian, artist*

Baltimore
Allen, Norma Ann *librarian*
Blumberg, David Russell *librarian*
Hayden, Carla *library director*
†Hollowak, Thomas Leo *architist, historian*
Magnuson, Nancy *librarian*

Beltsville
Andre, Pamela Q. J. *library director*

Bethesda
Knachel, Philip Atherton *librarian*
Lindberg, Donald Allan Bror *library administrator, pathologist, educator*
Tilley, Carolyn Bittner *technical information specialist*

California
Avram, Henriette Davidson *librarian, government official*

College Park
Burke, Frank Gerard *archivist*
Wasserman, Paul *library and information science educator*

Columbia
Hill, Norma Louise *librarian*
Klein, Sami Weiner *librarian*

Easton
Bronson, John Orville, Jr. *librarian*

Fort Washington
Cross, Rita Faye *librarian, early childhood educator, writer*

Gaithersburg
Smith, Ruth Lillian Schluchter *librarian*

Greenbelt
Auerbach, Bob Shipley *librarian*
Hogensen, Margaret Hiner *librarian, consultant*

Hunt Valley
Tull, Willis Clayton, Jr. *librarian*

Kensington
Rather, Lucia Porcher Johnson *library administrator*

La Plata
†Johnson, Diane Jones *librarian*

Lanham Seabrook
Banks, William Ashton *librarian*

Laurel
Brandhorst, Wesley Theodore *information manager*

Potomac
Broderick, John Caruthers *retired librarian, educator*

Rockville
Henderson, Harriet *librarian*
Kohlhorst, Gail Lewis *librarian*

Salisbury
House, Charletta *librarian*

Savage
Filby, Percy William *library consultant*

Silver Spring
Liu, Rhonda Louise *librarian*

Solomons
Heil, Kathleen Ann *librarian*

Stevensville
Marquis, Rollin Park *retired librarian*

Takoma Park
von Hake, Margaret Joan *librarian*

Towson
Fish, James Henry *library director*

Wheaton
Negro, Sandra Elizabeth *librarian*

MASSACHUSETTS

Amesbury
Dowd, Frances Connelly *librarian*

Amherst
Bridegam, Willis Edward, Jr. *librarian*
Tenenbaum, Jeffrey Mark *academic librarian*

Boston
Armstrong, Rodney *librarian*
Chen, Ching-chih *information science educator, consultant*
Desnoyers, Megan Floyd *archivist, educator*
Gerratt, Bradley Scott *presidential library director*
Kowal, Ruth Elizabeth *library administrator*
Lawrence, Mary Josephine (Josie Lawrence) *library official, artist*
Lucker, Jay K. *library education educator*
Maciora, Joseph Gerard Vincent *reference librarian*
Margolis, Bernard Allen *library administrator*
†McKain, Joshua Van Kirk *library director*
Peek, Robin Patricia *library and information science educator*

von Fettweis, Yvonne Caché *archivist, historian*
Wendorf, Richard Harold *library director, scholar*

Bridgewater
Zilonis, Mary Frances *information science educator, consultant*

Brookline
Tuchman, Maurice Simon *library director*
Wertsman, Vladimir Filip *librarian, information specialist, author, translator*

Cambridge
Bond, William Henry *librarian, educator*
Bourneuf, Henri Joseph, Jr. *librarian*
Cole, Heather Ellen *librarian*
Collins, John William, III *librarian*
Dunn, Mary Maples *library director*
Flannery, Susan Marie *library administrator*
Hamilton, Malcolm Cowan *librarian, editor, indexer, personnel professional*
Horrell, Jeffrey Lanier *library administrator*
Stoddard, Roger Eliot *librarian*
Willard, Louis Charles *librarian*

Carver
Neubauer, Richard A. *library science educator, consultant*

Chestnut Hill
Mellins, Judith Weiss *archivist*

Eastham
Gross, Dorothy-Ellen *library director, dean*

Fall River
Sullivan, Ruth Anne *librarian*

Lexington
Davis, Barbara M(ae) *librarian*
Freitag, Wolfgang Martin *librarian, educator*
Preve, Roberta Jean *librarian, researcher*

Lunenburg
†Tallman, Susan Porri *library director*

Middleboro
†Judd, Marjorie Lois *librarian, consultant*

Monson
†De Santis, Sylvia *library director*

Natick
Rendell, Kenneth William *rare and historical documents dealer, consultant*

Needham
Mills, Elizabeth Ann *librarian*

Newton
Glick-Weil, Kathy *library director*

North Andover
Holmes, Sue Ellen *library director*

Northampton
Piccinino, Rocco Michael *librarian*

Norton
Deekle, Peter Van *library director*

Paxton
Kuklinski, Joan Lindsey *librarian*

Sharon
Roberson, Kip Michael *library director, librarian*

Springfield
Stack, May Elizabeth *library director*

Turners Falls
†SanSoucie, Susan A. *librarian*

Upton
Hoar, Susan Remillard *library media specialist*

Waltham
Hahn, Bessie King *library administrator, lecturer*

Williamstown
Erickson, Peter Brown *librarian, scholar, writer*
Wikander, Lawrence Einar *librarian*

Worcester
Dunlap, Ellen S. *library administrator*
McCorison, Marcus Allen *librarian, cultural organization administrator*

MICHIGAN

Albion
†Seidl, James C. *librarian*

Allendale
Murray, Diane Elizabeth *librarian*

Ann Arbor
Beaubien, Anne Kathleen *librarian*
Bidlack, Russell Eugene *librarian, educator, former dean*
Carlen, Sister Claudia *librarian*
Daub, Peggy Ellen *library administrator*
Dougherty, Richard Martin *library and information science educator*
Dunlap, Connie *librarian*
Hessler, David William *information and multimedia systems educator*
Hodel, Mary Anne *library director*
Slavens, Thomas Paul *library science educator*
Williams, John Troy *librarian, educator*

Auburn Hills
Williams, Calvin *librarian, consultant*

Big Rapids
Weber, Joseph Edwin *librarian, educator*

Bloomfield Hills
Coir, Mark Allen *archivist*

Brighton
†Huget, Charlene Dorothy *library director*

Clinton Township
Hage, Christine Lind *library administrator*

Coldwater
†Hutchins, Mary Louise *library director*

Detroit
Mika, Joseph John *library director, consultant*
Spyers-Duran, Peter *librarian, educator*
Sutton, Lynn Sorensen *librarian*
Wheeler, Maurice B. *librarian*

East Lansing
Chapin, Richard Earl *librarian*

Ecorse
†Williams, Reginald Bernard *library director*

Farmington Hills
Papai, Beverly Daffern *library director*

Flint
Heymoss, Jennifer Marie *librarian*

Flushing
Gordon, Reva Jo *retired librarian*

Garden City
†Elmouchi, Joan Leslie *library director*

Grand Rapids
Jacobsen, Arnold *archivist*

Kalamazoo
Amdursky, Saul Jack *library director*
Carlson, Sharon Lee *archivist*
Grotzinger, Laurel Ann *university librarian*

Marshall
†Garypie, Rudolph Renwick *library director*

Owosso
Bentley, Margaret Ann *librarian*

Plymouth
deBear, Richard Stephen *library planning consultant*

Port Huron
Wu, Harry Pao-Tung *retired librarian*

Redford
Karpinski, Huberta Elaine *library trustee*
Lamb, Michael John *librarian, consultant*

Saginaw
†Maas, Norman Lewis *library director*

Saint Clair Shores
Woodford, Arthur MacKinnon *library director, historian*

Saint Joseph
Anderson, Mary Jane *public library director*

Saline
†Niethammer, Leslee *library administrator*

Thompsonville
Perry, Margaret *librarian, writer*

MINNESOTA

Circle Pines
†Young, Jerry Francis *librarian*

Collegeville
Haile, Getatchew *archivist, educator*

Duluth
Pearce, Donald Joslin *retired librarian*

Mankato
Descy, Don Edmond *library media technology educator, writer, editor*

Minneapolis
Asp, William George *librarian*
Johnson, Donald Clay *librarian, curator*
Johnson, Margaret Ann (Peggy) *library administrator*
Kukla, Edward Richard *rare books and special collections librarian, lecturer*
Ostrem, Walter Martin *librarian, educator, consultant*
Shaughnessy, Thomas William *librarian, consultant*

Northfield
Hong, Howard Vincent *library administrator, philosophy educator, editor, translator*

Rochester
Homan, J. Michael *library administrator*
Key, Jack Dayton *librarian*
Leachman, Roger Mack *librarian*
Main, Michael Dee *information developer*

Saint Cloud
Peterson, Patricia Elizabeth *library network administrator, educator*

Saint Paul
†Broding, Marilyn A. *librarian*
Brudvig, Glenn Lowell *retired library director*
Kane, Lucile Marie *retired archivist, historian*
Lineweaver, Joe Reherd *information scientist*

Magnuson, Norris Alden *librarian, history educator*
Wagner, Mary Margaret *library and information science educator*
Zietlow, Ruth Ann *reference librarian*

Zumbrota
Post, Diana Constance *retired librarian*

MISSISSIPPI

Biloxi
†Hastings, Stanley *librarian, organist*

Brookhaven
†Ledet, Henry Joseph *librarian*

Natchez
Barnett, James F., Jr. *historic properties and archives administrator*

Sunflower
Powell, Anice Carpenter *retired librarian*

MISSOURI

Albany
Noble, Cheryl A. *library director*

Canton
†Howe, Sandra Jo *library director*

Chesterfield
Landram, Christina Louella *librarian*

Columbia
Alexander, Martha Sue *librarian*
Almony, Robert Allen, Jr. *librarian, businessman*

Fulton
Roettger, Margaret Begley *library director*

Independence
Johnson, Niel Melvin *archivist, historian*

Jefferson City
Parker, Sara Ann *librarian*

Kansas City
Bradbury, Daniel Joseph *library administrator*
La Budde, Kenneth James *librarian*
Miller, William Charles *theological librarian, educator*
Pedram, Marilyn Beth *reference librarian*
Sheldon, Ted Preston *library director*

Lake Lotawana
Zobrist, Benedict Karl *library director, historian*

North Kansas City
†Hartmetz, Walter Judson *library director*

Parkville
†Schultis, G. Ann *library director*

Portageville
†Dial, Marshall Reece *library director*

Saint Louis
Heiser, Walter Charles *librarian, priest, educator*
Holt, Glen Edward *library administrator*
Holt, Leslie Edmonds *librarian*
Krasney, Rina Susan *school librarian*
†Shipman, Charles Andrew *librarian*

Springfield
Bohnenkamper, Katherine Elizabeth *library science educator*
Busch, Annie *library director*
Maltby, Florence Helen *library science educator*
†Moore, Neal Worden *archivist*

MONTANA

Bozeman
†Meister, Alice Marie *librarian*

Great Falls
†Heckel, James John *library director*

Helena
Fitzpatrick, Lois Ann *library administrator*

NEBRASKA

Hastings
Bush, Marjorie Evelynn Tower-Tooker *educator, media specialist, librarian*

Lincoln
Connor, Carol J. *library director*
Montag, John Joseph, II *librarian*
Wagner, Rod *library director*

Rushville
Plantz, Christine Marie *librarian, union officer*

NEVADA

Carson City
Rocha, Guy Louis *archivist, historian*

Las Vegas
Gray, Phyllis Anne *librarian*
Honsa, Vlasta *retired librarian*

Reno
Ross, Robert Donald *librarian*

NEW HAMPSHIRE

Berlin
Doherty, Katherine Mann *librarian, writer*

Concord
McCracken, Linda *librarian, commercial artist*
Wajenberg, Arnold Sherman *retired librarian, educator*
York, Michael Charest *librarian*

Hampton
Morton, Donald John *librarian*

Hanover
Hunter, Marie Hope *library media generalist*
Otto, Margaret Amelia *librarian*

Keene
Martin, Vernon Emil *librarian*

Newmarket
Getchell, Sylvia Fitts *librarian*

Rindge
†Gardenour, Diane Leslie *library director*

NEW JERSEY

Budd Lake
Hilbert, Rita L. *librarian*

Clark
Kolaya, Margaret Helen Boutwell *librarian*

East Brunswick
Karmazin, Sharon Elyse *library director*

East Orange
Amadei, Deborah Lisa *librarian*

Emerson
†Hannon, Patricia Ann *library director*

Garfield
Nickles, I. MacArthur *librarian*

Glassboro
Martin, Marilyn Joan *library director*

Highland Park
Coughlin, Caroline Mary *library consultant, educator*

Hightstown
Brodman, Estelle *librarian, retired educator*

Hoboken
Mintz, Kenneth Andrew *librarian*
Widdicombe, Richard Palmer *librarian*

Jersey City
Hayes, Dennis Joseph *library director*

Laurel Springs
Cleveland, Susan Elizabeth *library administrator, researcher*

Lawrenceville
Petronio, Bruce J. *librarian, writer*

Livingston
Sikora, Barbara Jean *library director*

Long Branch
Pachman, Frederic Charles *library director*

Lyndhurst
Sieger, Charles *librarian*

Mendham
Chatfield, Mary Van Abshoven *librarian*

New Brunswick
Becker, Ronald Leonard *archivist*
Nash, Stanley Dana *librarian*
Polelle, Mark Robert *librarian, historian*
Reeling, Patricia Glueck *library studies educator, educational consultant*
Turock, Betty Jane *library and information science educator*

Newark
Slutsky, Bruce *technical reference librarian*

North Haledon
Dougherty, June Eileen *librarian*

Nutley
Tropiano, JoAnn Alma *librarian, library director*

Oakland
†Brechtel, Unda Jurka *library director*

Palisades Park
†Chelariu, Ana Radu *library director*

Princeton
Fox, Mary Ann Williams *librarian*
Joyce, William Leonard *librarian*
†Noble, Stephen Lloyd *information scientist*
Woodward, Daniel Holt *librarian, researcher*

Rahway
†McCoy, William Keith *library director*

Rockaway
Kelsey, Ann Lee *library administrator*

Roselle
Riley, Barbara Polk *retired librarian*

PROFESSIONAL INDEX 6055 HUMANITIES: LIBRARIES

Rutherford
†Sawyer, Miriam library director

Sewell
Wright, William Cook archivist, historian, researcher

Trenton
Butorac, Frank George librarian, educator
Falzini, Mark William archivist
Russell, Joyce Anne Rogers librarian

Union
Darden, Barbara L. library director

Upper Montclair
†Stock, Norman librarian

Williamstown
†Bogis, Nana Eileen librarian

NEW MEXICO

Alamogordo
Flanary, Kathy Venita Moore librarian

Albuquerque
Freeman, Patricia Elizabeth library and education specialist
Ross, Marie Heise retired librarian
Snell, Patricia Poldervaart librarian, consultant
Wilkinson, Frances Catherine librarian, educator

Carlsbad
Regan, Muriel librarian

Gallup
Fellin, Octavia Antoinette retired librarian

Las Cruces
Myers, R. David library director, dean

Los Alamos
Orndoff, Elizabeth Carlson retired reference librarian, educator
Sayre, Edward Charles librarian

Portales
Romo, Jose León library consultant

NEW YORK

Albany
Aceto, Vincent John librarian, educator
Katz, William A. library science educator
Mancuso, J(ohn) James librarian
Paulson, Peter John librarian, publishing company executive
Shubert, Joseph Francis librarian
Van Nortwick, Barbara Louise library director
Welch, Janet Martin librarian

Beechhurst
Cooke, Constance Blandy librarian

Bellmore
Andrews, Charles Rolland library administrator
†Bregman, Steven Howard library director

Bohemia
Manley, Gertrude Ella librarian, media specialist

Brightwaters
†Kavanagh, Eileen J. librarian

Bronx
Humphry, James, III librarian, publishing executive
McCabe, James Patrick library director
†Padnos, Mark reference librarian, literary translator
Skurdenis, Juliann Veronica librarian, educator, writer, editor

Brooklyn
Corry, Emmett Brother librarian, educator, researcher, archivist
Eriksen, Norman John librarian, research historian
Hill, Leda Katherine librarian
Karkhanis, Sharad librarian, political science educator
Lawrence, Deirdre Elizabeth librarian, coordinator research services
Schneider, Adele Goldberg librarian, educator
Sharify, Nasser educator, author, librarian
Tsai, Bor-sheng educator

Buffalo
Bobinski, George Sylvan librarian, educator
Chrisman, Diane J. librarian
Stelzle, James Joseph library administrator
Zimmerman, Nancy Picciano library science educator

Canandaigua
†Stocker, Patricia Marilyn library administrator

Canton
Thompson, Jean Alling librarian

Cazenovia
Pavese, Jacqueline Marie librarian

Chappaqua
Whittingham, Charles Arthur publisher, library administrator

Chautauqua
†Yurth, Helene Louise librarian

Clifton Park
Farley, John Joseph library science educator emeritus

Clinton
Anthony, Donald Charles librarian, educator

Corona
Jackson, Andrew Preston library director

Delmar
Nitecki, Joseph Zbigniew librarian

Flushing
†Ausubel, Hillel librarian

Great Neck
Pohl, Gunther Erich retired library administrator

Greenport
†Richland, Lisa library director

Hempstead
Freese, Melanie Louise librarian, professor

Huntington
Rosar, Virginia Wiley librarian

Ithaca
Finch, C. Herbert retired archivist, library administrator, historian
Law, Gordon Theodore, Jr. library director
Szasz, Suzy librarian, writer

Jamaica
†Cerny, Rosanne librarian
Daubenas, Jean Dorothy Tenbrinck librarian, educator
Strong, Gary Eugene librarian

Kings Point
Billy, George John library director

Lackawanna
†Bordonaro, Salvatore librarian

Lake Ronkonkoma
Delaney, Robert Patrick librarian, writer

Lewiston
Domzella, Janet library director

Loudonville
Haverly, Douglas Lindsay librarian, historian

New Hyde Park
Hammer, Deborah Marie librarian, paralegal

New York
Ashton, Jean Willoughby library director
†Augenbraum, Harold library director, editor
†Bakinowski, Carol Ann journalist
Belliveau, Gerard Joseph, Jr. librarian
Berger, Pearl library director
Berliner, Barbara librarian, consultant
Berner, Andrew Jay library director, writer
Birnbaum, Henry librarian
Bourke, Thomas Anthony librarian, writer
Bowen, Jean librarian, consultant
Brewer, Karen librarian
Bristah, Pamela Jean librarian
Buckwald, Joel David archivist
Cassell, Kay Ann librarian
Castleberry, May Lewis librarian, curator, editor
Cohen, Selma reference librarian, researcher
Colby, Robert Alan retired library science educator
Ellenbogen, Rudolph Solomon library curator
Fletcher, Harry George, III library director
Gelfand, Morris Arthur librarian, publisher
Gossage, Wayne library director, management consultant, entrepreneur, executive recruiter
Graves, Fred Hill librarian
Green, David Edward librarian, priest, translator
Hewitt, Vivian Ann Davidson (Mrs. John Hamilton Hewitt, Jr.) librarian
Isaacson, Melvin Stuart library director
Jones, Anne librarian
Kasinec, Edward Joseph library administrator
†Langstaff, Eleanor Marguerite library science educator
LeClerc, Paul library director
Little, Robert David library science educator
Lohf, Kenneth A. librarian, writer
LoSchiavo, Linda Bosco library director
Lowe, Ida Brandwayn library administrator, systems administrator
Lubetski, Edith Esther librarian
Lundquist, John Milton librarian, author, travel writer, photographer
Mackey, Patricia Elaine university librarian
Mattson, Francis Oscar retired librarian and rare books curator
Matyas, Charles Julian retired archivist
McCormick, Donald E. librarian, archivist
Meyerhoff, Erich librarian, administrator
Miller, Philip Efrem librarian
Moore, Jane Ross librarian
†North, Michael Jefferson librarian
Palmer, Paul Richard librarian, archivist
Palmer, Robert Baylis librarian
Pierce, Charles Eliot, Jr. library director, educator
Pollard, Bobbie Jean librarian, educator
Rabinowitz, Mayer Elya librarian, educator
Rachow, Louis A(ugust) librarian
Richmond, Eero composer, music librarian
Root, Nina J. librarian
†Rosenthal, Faigi librarian
Siefert-Kazanjian, Donna corporate librarian
Slawsky Leon, Donna Susan librarian, singer
Smith, John Brewster library administrator
Stoops, Louise information services administrator
†Vaughan, David George archivist

Oneonta
†Bulson, Christine E. academic librarian
Johnson, Richard David retired librarian

Patchogue
Gibbard, Judith R. library director

Port Washington
Ciccariello, Priscilla Chloe librarian

Poughkeepsie
Van Zanten, Frank Veldhuyzen retired library system director

Richmond Hill
Hamroff, Michael Scott archives executive

Rochester
Dow, Ronald F. librarian
Matzek, Richard Allan library director
Panz, Richard library director
Swanton, Susan Irene library director

Sayville
Edelman, Hendrik library and information science educator

Scarborough
Stigall, Phyllis Graham retired librarian

Somers
Lane, David Oliver retired librarian

Staten Island
Auh, Yang John librarian, educational administrator
Butler, Tyrone G. records manager
Mayer, Andrew Mark librarian, journalist

Stony Brook
Cook, Jeannine Salvo library consultant
Stalker, Dianne Sylvia librarian

Syracuse
Abbott, George Lindell librarian
Coppola, Elaine Marie librarian
†Frank, Lawrence J. library administrator
Luft, Eric v.d. librarian, educator
Stam, David Harry librarian

Tarrytown
Bowen, Christopher Edward library director

Tuxedo Park
Friedman, Rodger antiquarian bookseller, consultant

Vails Gate
Fife, Betty H. librarian

Wantagh
†Kappenberg, Marilyn Lorrin library director

West Point
Watson, Georgianna librarian

Westbury
†Krampitz, Barbara E.M. library director

White Plains
Manville, Stewart Roebling archivist

Williamsville
Cloudsley, Donald Hugh library administrator

NORTH CAROLINA

Chapel Hill
Holley, Edward Gailon library science educator, former university dean
Kilgour, Frederick Gridley librarian, educator
Moran, Barbara Burns librarian, educator
Pruett, James Worrell librarian, musicologist

Charlotte
Cannon, Robert Eugene librarian, public administrator, fund raiser
Sintz, Edward Francis librarian
Smith, Edith Joan librarian, writer

Davidson
Jones, Arthur Edwin, Jr. library administrator, English and American literature educator
Park, Leland Madison librarian

Dunn
†Guldan, Janice Marie librarian

Durham
Canada, Mary Whitfield librarian
Feinglos, Susan Jean library director

Eden
Williams, Sue Darden library director

Elkin
Sawyer, Michael E. library director

Fayetteville
Ross, Bernadette Marie-Teresa librarian

Greensboro
Carmichael, James Vinson, Jr. library and information science educator
Kovacs, Beatrice library studies educator
Wright, Kieth Carter librarian, educator

Hayesville
Parch, Grace Dolores librarian

Hillsborough
Stephens, Brenda Wilson librarian

Kings Mountain
Turner, Marguerite Rose Cowles library administrator

Louisburg
†Fish, Hilda Jean Barker library director

Pembroke
Sexton, Jean Elizabeth librarian

Raleigh
Littleton, Isaac Thomas, III retired university library administrator, consultant
Moore, Thomas Lloyd librarian

Spring Creek
†Jones, Sara Sue Fisher library director

Washington
Timour, John Arnold retired librarian, medical bibliography and library science educator

Wilmington
Mc Cabe, Gerard Benedict retired library administrator
Oakley, Carolyn Cobb library director, academic administrator

Winston Salem
Berthrong, Merrill Gray retired library director

NORTH DAKOTA

Bismarck
†Ott, Doris Ann librarian

Mayville
Karaim, Betty June librarian, retired

Minot
Iversen, David Stewart librarian

Valley City
Fischer, Mary Elizabeth library director

OHIO

Ada
Herr, Sharon Marie librarian

Akron
Friedman, Richard Everett librarian
Konkel, Mary Susan library administrator
Rebenack, John Henry retired librarian

Alexandria
†Hannahs, Dorothy Gene library director

Alliance
Clem, Harriet Frances library director

Athens
Lee, Hwa-Wei librarian, educator

Bluffton
Dudley, Durand Stowell librarian

Bowerston
†Spencer, Dawn Joyce librarian, educator

Bucyrus
Herold, Jeffrey Roy Martin library director

Cadiz
†Thompson, Sandra Lee library administrator

Chardon
†O'Connor, Deborah Frances library director

Cincinnati
Bestehorn, Ute Wiltrud retired librarian
Bluestein, Barbara Ann librarian
Brestel, Mary Beth librarian
Dahmann, Rosemary Gaiser librarian
Everett, Karen Joan retired librarian, genealogy educator
Proffitt, Kevin archivist
Schutzius, Lucy Jean librarian
Wellington, Jean Susorney librarian
Zafren, Herbert Cecil librarian, educator

Cleveland
Abid, Ann B. art librarian
Gardner, Richard Kent retired librarian, educator, consultant
Mason, Marilyn Gell library administrator, writer, consultant
Pike, Kermit Jerome library director
Smythe Zǎjc, M. Catherine library administrator, development officer

Columbiana
†Geary, Amy Jo librarian

Columbus
Black, Larry David library director
Branscomb, Lewis Capers, Jr. librarian, educator
Donovan, Maureen Hildegarde librarian, educator
Goerler, Raimund Erhard archivist
Meredith, Meri Hill reference librarian, educator
Olson, Carol Ann librarian
Sawyers, Elizabeth Joan librarian, administrator
Studer, William Joseph library director

Dayton
Chait, William librarian, consultant
Klinck, Cynthia Anne library director
Wichman, Edna Carol media specialist, librarian

Delaware
Schlichting, Catherine Fletcher Nicholson librarian, educator

Dublin
Childress, Eric Rogers librarian, consultant, metadata specialist

Elmore
†Huizenga, Georgiana R. public library director, storyteller

Fairview Park
Bellamy, John Stark, II librarian

Hudson
Antonucci, Ron librarian, editor

Kenton
Petty, Sue Wright

Miamisburg
Yakura, Thelma Pauline *retired library director, consultant, writer*

Middleburg Heights
Maciuszko, Kathleen Lynn *librarian, educator*

Middletown
Schaefer, Patricia Ann *retired librarian*

Oberlin
English, Ray *library administrator*

Oxford
Sessions, Judith Ann *librarian, university library dean*
Wortman, William Allen *librarian*

Pemberville
King, Laura Jane *librarian, genealogist*

Portsmouth
†Cain, Beverly Lynn *library director*

Riverside
Wyllie, Stanley Clarke *retired librarian*

Steubenville
Hall, Alan Craig *library director*

Tiffin
Hillmer, Margaret Patricia *library director*

Wadsworth
†Nichols, C. Allen *librarian*

Westerville
Tiefel, Virginia May *librarian*

Wickliffe
†Fisher, Nancy DeButts *library director*

Wooster
Hickey, Damon Douglas *library director*

Worthington
Meyer, Betty Jane *former librarian*

OKLAHOMA

Altus
†Smith, Donna Jean *librarian*

Bartlesville
†Sanders, Jan W. *librarian*

Hodgen
Brower, Janice Kathleen *library technician*

Marlow
†Bannister, Lois Ann *library director*

Norman
Hodges, Thompson Gene *librarian, retired university dean*
Kemp, Betty Ruth *librarian*
Lee, Sul Hi *library administrator*
Lester, June *library information studies educator*

Oklahoma City
Brawner, Lee Basil *librarian*
Clark, Robert Lloyd, Jr. *librarian*
Simpson, Jerome Dean *librarian*

Okmulgee
Doan, Patricia Nan *librarian*

Stillwater
Johnson, Edward Roy *library director*

Tulsa
Saferite, Linda Lee *library director*

Welling
Varner, Joyce Ehrhardt *librarian*

OREGON

Beaverton
Pond, Patricia Brown *library science educator, university administrator*

Bend
†Gaston, Michael *library director*

Corvallis
Landers, Teresa Price *librarian*

Eugene
Edwards, Ralph M. *librarian*
Hildebrand, Carol Ilene *librarian*
Morrison, Perry David *librarian, educator*

Klamath Falls
Leonhardt, Thomas Wilburn *librarian, library director*

Ontario
Edwards, Dale Leon *library director*

Portland
Browne, Joseph Peter *retired librarian*
Cooper, Ginnie *library director*
Eshelman, William Robert *librarian, editor*
Morgan, James Earl *librarian, administrator*

Salem
Kenyon, Carleton Weller *librarian*
Oberg, Larry Reynold *librarian*
Turnbaugh, Roy Carroll *archivist*

PENNSYLVANIA

Allentown
Sacks, Patricia Ann *librarian, consultant*
Sautter, Carolyn Huber *librarian*

Altoona
Kinney, Janis Marie *librarian, consultant, storyteller*

Barto
†Knight, Cheryl DuBois *library director*

Beaver Falls
†Focer-Richards, Linda Jean *library director*

Bethel Park
Marrs, Sharon Carter *librarian*

Birdsboro
†Shipe, Susan Louise *librarian*

Brownsville
†Blaine, Barry Richard *library director*

Bryn Mawr
Fletcher, Marjorie Amos *librarian*
Tanis, James Robert *library director, history educator, clergyman*

Cranberry Township
Lorenz, John George *librarian, consultant*

Doylestown
Wolfinger, Audrey Jane *retired librarian*

Du Bois
Williams, Kathryn Blake *librarian*

East Stroudsburg
Kratz, Charles E., Jr. *library director*

Greensburg
Duck, Patricia Mary *librarian*

Havertown
†Hoffman, Elizabeth Parkinson *librarian*

Irwin
†Mignogna, Jacalyn Corrine *library director, librarian*

Lancaster
Filler, Mary Ann *librarian*
Zeager, Lloyd *librarian*

Langhorne
†Fitzgerald, Dorothy Stickle *librarian*

Lebanon
Bard, Judy Kay *librarian*

Lock Haven
†Chang, Shirley Lin (Hsiu-Chu Chang) *librarian*

Milton
†Brandau, Susan Carol *library director*

New Kensington
Miller, Albert Jay *retired library and information sciences director*

New Tripoli
Fiedler, Kathy Lou *library media specialist*

Philadelphia
Arnold, Lee *library scientist*
Azzolina, David Sean *librarian*
Gendron, Michèle Marguerite Madeleine *librarian*
Lemley, Bernice R. *retired archivist*
Levitt, Martin Lee *library administrator, historian*
Roth, Marilyn Dorothy *law library coordinator*
Schaeffer-Young, Judith *library director*
Shelkrot, Elliot L. *library director*

Pittsburgh
Carbo, Toni (Toni Carbo Bearman) *information scientist, university dean*
Josey, E(lonnie) J(unius) *librarian, educator, former state administrator*
Minnigh, Joel Douglas *library director*
Wohleber, Lynne Farr *archivist, librarian*
Yourison, Karola Maria *information specialist, librarian*

Radnor
Fisher, Ellen Roop *librarian, educator*

Riegelsville
Banko, Ruth Caroline *retired library director*

Saint Davids
Sauer, James Leslie *librarian, educator*

Saltsburg
Kyle, Diane Wagman *librarian*

State College
Forth, Stuart *librarian*

University Park
Eaton, Nancy Ruth Linton *librarian, university dean*

Villanova
Mullins, James Lee *library director*

Wayne
Carter, Edward Carlos, II *librarian, historian*
Garrison, Guy Grady *librarian, educator*
Townsend, Philip W., Jr. *library director*

Wilkes Barre
Mech, Terrence Francis *library director*

Yardley
Soultoukis, Donna Zoccola *library director*

RHODE ISLAND

Cranston
†Gallo, Adrienne Arline *librarian*

Jamestown
Logan, Nancy Allen *library media specialist*

Newport
Schnare, Robert Edey, Jr. *library director*

Providence
Caldwell, Naomi Rachel *library media specialist*
Hamerly, Michael T. *librarian, historian*
Weaver, Barbara Frances *librarian*

Warwick
Charette, Sharon Juliette *library administrator*

SOUTH CAROLINA

Charleston
Basler, Thomas G. *librarian, administrator, educator*
Buvinger, Jan *library director*

Clemson
Boykin, Joseph Floyd, Jr. *librarian*

Columbia
Duggan, Carol Cook *research director*
Griffin, Mary Frances *retired library media consultant*
Helsley, Alexia Jones *archivist*
Johnson, James Bek, Jr. *library director*
Olsgaard, John Newman *library science educator, university official*
Rawlinson, Helen Ann *librarian*
Toombs, Kenneth Eldridge *librarian*
Warren, Charles David *library administrator*

Darlington
†Rainey, Nettie Sue *library director*

Greenville
Belk, F. Norman *librarian*

Greenwood
Townsend, Catherine Anne Morgan *information specialist*

Hilton Head Island
Kadar, Karin Patricia *librarian*

Laurens
†Cooper, William Copeland *public library director*

Orangeburg
Caldwell, Rossie Juanita Brower *retired library service educator*

Rock Hill
Du Bois, Paul Zinkhan *library director*

SOUTH DAKOTA

Brookings
†Landau, Enita Ann *library director*
Marquardt, Steve Robert *library director*

Freeman
†Koller, Berneda Joleen *library administrator*

Gettysburg
†Williams, Peggy A. *library director*

Sioux Falls
Dertien, James LeRoy *librarian*
Thompson, Ronelle Kay Hildebrandt *library director*

TENNESSEE

Chattanooga
Clapp, David Foster *library administrator*
McFarland, Jane Elizabeth *librarian*

Clarksville
Hester, Bruce Edward *library media specialist, lay worker*

Cleveland
Nicol, Jessie Thompson *librarian*

Collegedale
Bennett, Peggy Elizabeth *librarian, library director, educator*

Crossville
Sweetland, Loraine Fern *librarian, educator*

Dresden
Powell, Wanda Garner *librarian*

Greeneville
Smith, Myron John, Jr. *librarian, author*

Jonesborough
Kozsuch, Mildred Jeannette *librarian, archivist*

Knoxville
Cottrell, Jeannette Elizabeth *retired librarian*
Watson, Patricia L. *library director*

Memphis
Drescher, Judith Altman *library director*
Meredith, Donald Lloyd *librarian*
Pourciau, Lester John *librarian*
Wallis, Carlton Lamar *librarian*

Murfreesboro
Marshall, John David *retired librarian, author*

Nashville
Lyle, Virginia Reavis *retired archivist, genealogist*
Shockley, Ann Allen *librarian*
Stewart, David Marshall *librarian*

Paris
McNutt, Gwyn Bellamy *archivist*

Sewanee
Dunkly, James Warren *theological librarian*

TEXAS

Abilene
Anderson, John Thomas *librarian, historian*

Arlington
Burson, Betsy Lee *librarian*

Austin
Billings, Harold Wayne *librarian, editor*
Branch, Brenda Sue *library director*
Davis, Donald Gordon, Jr. *librarian, educator*
Felsted, Carla Martindell *librarian, travel writer*
Fox, Beth Wheeler *library director*
Gracy, David Bergen, II *archivist, information science educator, writer*
Jackson, Eugene Bernard *librarian*
Jackson, William Vernon *library science and Latin American studies educator*
Middleton, Harry Joseph *library administrator*
Oram, Robert W. *library administrator*
Rascoe, Paul Stephen *librarian, researcher*
Smith, Dorothy Brand *retired librarian*

Batson
Johnston, Maxine *retired librarian*

Breckenridge
†Fox, Grady Harrison *library director*

Brownwood
Roby, Annie Beth Brian *librarian*

Cedar Hill
Hickman, Traphene Parramore *library director, storyteller, library and library building consultant*

Coldspring
Bunch, Robert Craig *librarian*

College Station
Wilson, Don Whitman *retired archivist, historian*

Corsicana
Roberts, Nancy Mize *retired librarian, composer, pianist*

Dallas
Bradshaw, Lillian Moore *retired library director*
†Eatenson, Ervin Theodore *retired librarian*
Howell, Bradley Sue *librarian*
Ibach, Robert Daniel, Jr. *library director*
Roach-Reeves, Catharyn Petitt *librarian, educator*
Salazar, Ramiro S. *library administrator*
Young, Julia Anne *librarian, elementary education educator*

Denton
Poole, Eva Duraine *librarian*
Snapp, Elizabeth *librarian, educator*

El Paso
Freeman, Mary Anna *librarian*
Gardner, Kerry Ann *librarian*
†Hooker, Mary Katherine *librarian*
Ramsey, Donna Elaine *librarian*
Strait, Viola Edwina Washington *librarian*

Fairfield
†Thornton, Sue Bonner *former librarian*

Fort Davis
†Gadberry, Vicki Lynn Himes *librarian*

Fort Worth
Allmand, Linda F(aith) *retired library director*
Ard, Harold Jacob *library administrator*
†Boger, David L *librarian*
de Tonnancour, Paul Roger Godefroy *library administrator*

Fredericksburg
Thompson, Glenn Judean *retired library science educator*

Hidalgo
McKelvy, Nicole Andrée *librarian*

Houston
Henington, David Mead *library director*
Hornak, Anna Frances *library administrator*
Miles, Ruby A. Branch *librarian, consultant*
Newbold, Benjamin Millard, Jr. *library manager, education consultant*
Radoff, Leonard Irving *librarian, consultant*
Russell, John Francis *retired librarian*
Suter, Jon Michael *academic library director, educator*
Tong, Louis Lik-Fu *information scientist*
Wilson, Patricia Potter *library science and reading educator, educational and library consultant*

Huntsville
Hoffmann, Frank William *library science educator, writer*

Katy
Bradshaw, Melissa Webb *librarian*

Kilgore
Pipkin, Wade Lemual, Jr. *reference librarian*

Laredo
Weber, Janice Ann *library director, grant writer*

Levelland
Pearson, Dana Bart *librarian*

Livingston
Wolter, John Amadeus *librarian, government official*

Lubbock
Murrah, David J. *archivist, historian*
Wood, Richard Courtney *library director, educator*

Mansfield
Icenhower, Della Maude *retired school librarian*

Marshall
Magrill, Rose Mary *library director*

Mcallen
McGee, William Howard John *library system coordinator*

Odessa
†Ciallella, Emil Anthony *library director, consultant*

Richardson
Lovelace, Julianne *library director*

San Antonio
Kozuch, Julianna Bernadette *librarian, educator*
Lussky, Warren Alfred *librarian, educator, consultant*
Wallace, James Oldham *retired librarian*
Young, Olivia Knowles *retired librarian*

Tyler
Albertson, Christopher Adam *librarian*
Arps, Joyce Ann *librarian*
Cleveland, Mary Louise *librarian, media specialist*

Van Alstyne
†Hazelton, Juanita Louise *librarian*

Waco
Bonnell, Pamela Gay *library administrator*
Davis, Mary Duesterberg (Mimi) *librarian, publisher*
Progar, Dorothy *retired library director*

UTAH

Orem
Hall, Blaine Hill *retired librarian*

Provo
Jensen, Richard Dennis *librarian*
Smith, Nathan McKay *library and information sciences educator*

Richfield
†Fields, Linda Jean *library director*

Riverside
Reveal, Arlene Hadfield *librarian, consultant*

Salt Lake City
Buttars, Gerald Anderson *librarian*
Kraus, Peter Leo *librarian*
Mogren, Paul Andrew *librarian*

VERMONT

Essex Junction
†Pillsbury, Penelope DeLaire *library director*

Pownal
Gibson, Sarah Ann Scott *art librarian*

South Burlington
Kebabian, Paul Blakeslee *librarian*

VIRGINIA

Alexandria
Berger, Patricia Wilson *retired librarian*
Budde, Mitzi Marie Jarrett *librarian*
Deel, Frances Quinn *retired librarian*
Emery, Vicki Morris *school library media specialist*
Gray, Dorothy Louise Allman Pollet *librarian*
O'Brien, Patrick Michael *library administrator*
Strickland, Nellie B. *library program director*

Bristol
Muller, William Albert, III *library director*

Castleton
Hahn, James Maglorie *former librarian, farmer*

Charlottesville
Berkeley, Edmund, Jr. *retired archivist, educator*
Berkeley, Francis Lewis, Jr. *retired archivist*
Frantz, Ray William, Jr. *retired librarian*
Frieden, Charles Leroy *university library administrator*
Self, James Reed *librarian*
Stubbs, Kendon Lee *librarian*

Farmville
Boyer, Calvin James *librarian*

Fort Story
Smail, Leslie Anne *librarian*

Franklin
Culpepper, Jo Long *librarian*

Fredericksburg
Dennis, Donald Daly *retired librarian*

Harrisonburg
Gill, Gerald Lawson *librarian*
Maxfield, Sandra Lynn *librarian, educator*

Hudgins
Story, Martha vanBeuren *librarian*

Lexington
Gaines, James Edwin, Jr. *retired librarian*
†Krantz, Linda Law *librarian*

Norfolk
Reed, Sally Gardner *library director*

Poquoson
†Tai, Elizabeth Shi-Jue Lee *library director*

Rapidan
Grimm, Ben Emmet *former library director and consultant*

Riner
Foster, Joy Via *library media specialist*

Spotsylvania
†Todd, Deborah Kathleen *library media specialist*

Vienna
Mulvihill, John Gary *retired information services administrator*

Williamsburg
Parham, Annette Relaford *librarian*

Winchester
Hughes, Donna Jean *librarian*

WASHINGTON

Auburn
Willson, David Allen *reference librarian, writer*

Bellevue
Mutschler, Herbert Frederick *retired librarian*

Bremerton
Schuyler, Michael Robert *librarian*

Ellensburg
†Kline, Celeste Marie *librarian*

Mount Vernon
Havist, Marjorie Victoria *librarian, educator*

Olympia
†Kruse, Thelma Merle *library director*
Rider, Diane Elizabeth *librarian*

Port Townsend
Hiatt, Peter *retired librarian studies educator*

Seattle
Bishop, Virginia Wakeman *retired librarian and humanities educator*
Blase, Nancy Gross *librarian*
Boylan, Merle Nelson *librarian*
Chisholm, Margaret Elizabeth *retired library education administrator*
Euster, Joanne Reed *retired librarian*
Kruse, Paul Robert *retired librarian, educator*
Stroup, Elizabeth Faye *librarian*

Shoreline
Privat, Jeannette Mary *librarian*

Spokane
Bender, Betty Wion *librarian*
Burr, Robert Lyndon *information services specialist*
George, Aubrey Westmoreland *director Spokane public library*
Wirt, Michael James *library director*

Tacoma
Crisman, Mary Frances Borden *librarian*
†Parikh, Neel *library director*

Walla Walla
Jonish, Arley Duane *retired bibliographer*
Yaple, Henry Mack *library director*

WEST VIRGINIA

Charleston
†Smith, Ingrid I. *librarian*

Glenville
Tubesing, Richard Lee *library director*

Huntington
†Rule, Judy K. *library director*

Morgantown
Pyles, Rodney Allen *archivist, county official*

New Cumberland
†Mehaffey, Oplas Jane *librarian*

Shepherdstown
Elliott, Jean Ann *librarian emeritus*

WISCONSIN

Franklin
Roark, Barbara Ann *librarian*

Hartland
†Moses, D. James (Jim) (Jim Moses) *public library director*

Kenosha
Baker, Douglas Finley *library director*

La Crosse
†Polodna, David Lee *library director*

Madison
Bunge, Charles Albert *library science educator*
†Larson, Ronald Jon *library director*
Maloney, Thomas Peter *library services professional*

Milwaukee
Huston, Kathleen Marie *library administrator*
Valance, Marsha Jeanne *library director, story teller*

Oshkosh
Blake, Frank Burgay *librarian, writer*
Jones, Norma Louise *librarian, educator*

Portage
†Jensen, Hans William *library director*

Richland Center
Gollata, James Anthony *library director*

Thiensville
Roselle, William Charles *librarian*

Waupun
Norman, Steve Ronald *librarian*

WYOMING

Cheyenne
Johnson, Wayne Harold *librarian, county official*
Rounds, Linnea Paula *library administrator*

Laramie
Cottam, Keith M. *librarian, educator, administrator*

TERRITORIES OF THE UNITED STATES

PUERTO RICO

San Juan
Muñoz-Solá, Haydeé Socorro *library administrator*

MILITARY ADDRESSES OF THE UNITED STATES

EUROPE

APO
Wakefield, Marie Annette *librarian*

CANADA

ALBERTA

Calgary
MacDonald, Alan Hugh *librarian, university administrator*

Lethbridge
Rand, Duncan D. *librarian*

BRITISH COLUMBIA

Vancouver
Aalto, Madeleine *library director*
Piternick, Anne Brearley *librarian, educator*
Rothstein, Samuel *librarian, educator*

Victoria
Richards, Vincent Philip Haslewood *librarian*

MANITOBA

Winnipeg
Converse, William Rawson Mackenzie *retired librarian*

NOVA SCOTIA

Dartmouth
Horrocks, Norman *library science educator, editor*

Halifax
Birdsall, William Forest *librarian*
Dykstra Lynch, Mary Elizabeth *library and information science educator*

ONTARIO

Guelph
Land, Reginald Brian *library administrator*

Hamilton
Hill, Graham Roderick *librarian*

Mississauga
Mills, Donald McKenzie *librarian*
Ryan, Noel *librarian, consultant*

Ottawa
Scott, Marianne Florence *librarian, educator*
Sylvestre, Jean Guy *former national librarian*
Wallot, Jean-Pierre *archivist, historian*

Scarborough
Bassnett, Peter James *retired librarian*

Toronto
Bryant, Josephine Harriet *library executive*

Moore, Carole Irene *librarian*
Packer, Katherine Helen *retired library educator*

QUEBEC

Charlesbourg
Paradis, Andre *librarian*

Laval
Adrian, Donna Jean *librarian*

Montreal
Large, John Andrew *library and information service educator*
Ormsby, Eric Linn *educator, researcher, writer*
Panneton, Jacques *librarian*
Sauvageau, Philippe *library director*
Sykes, Stephanie Lynn *library director, archivist, museum director*

SASKATCHEWAN

Regina
Powell, Trevor John David *archivist*

Saskatoon
Kennedy, Marjorie Ellen *librarian*

AUSTRALIA

Belair
Briggs, Geoffrey Hugh *retired librarian*

Sydney
Rayward, Warden Boyd *librarian, educator*

CZECH REPUBLIC

Prague
Kalkus, Stanley *librarian, administrator, consultant*

DENMARK

Copenhagen
Larsen, Poul Steen *library educator*

GUATEMALA

Antigua
Rodgers, Frank *librarian*

SWITZERLAND

Geneva
Peterson, Trudy Huskamp *archivist*

ADDRESS UNPUBLISHED

Adkins, Thomas Samuel *library director*
Baker, Zachary Moshe *librarian*
Balog, Rita Jean *retired librarian*
Bino, Marial Desolyn *librarian, educator, psychologist*
†Bolluyt, Linda Beth *library director*
Brady, Jean Stein *retired librarian*
Bullard, Sharon Welch *librarian*
†Byrd, Joan Eda *film librarian*
Campbell, Henry Cummings *librarian*
†Carlson, Elizabeth Anne *library director*
Cartier, Celine Paule *librarian, administrator, consultant*
Chu, Ellin Resnick *librarian, consultant*
Clement, Hope Elizabeth Anna *librarian*
Cochran, Carolyn *library director*
Cooke, Eileen Delores *retired librarian*
Dickinson, Donald Charles *library science educator*
Diehl, Carol Lou *library director, retired, library consultant*
Dillon-McHugh, Cathleen Theresa *librarian, consultant*
Dixon, Ann Renee *writer*
†Dolan, Ellen Marie *library director*
Driver, Lottie Elizabeth *librarian*
Edmonds, Anne Carey *librarian*
Ellis, Kem Byron *public library administrator*
Else, Carolyn Joan *library system administrator*
Erickson, Alan Eric *librarian*
Estes, Elaine Rose Graham *retired librarian*
Fasick, Adele Mongan *information services consultant*
Fawcett, John Thomas *archivist*
Felts, Margaret Davis *librarian, bibliographer*
Flinner, Beatrice Eileen *retired library and media sciences educator*
Flug, Janice *librarian*
Funk, Vicki Jane *librarian*
Gaertner, Donell John *retired library director*
†Gallucci, Robert R. *librarian*
Galvin, Thomas John *retired information science policy educator, retired librarian, retired information scientist*
Gatch, Milton McCormick, Jr. *library administrator, clergyman, educator*
Gauthier, Mary Elizabeth *librarian, researcher, secondary education educator*
Giebel, Miriam Catherine *librarian, genealogist*
Gilbert, Nancy Louise *librarian*
Gold, Leonard Singer *librarian, translator*
Gould, Martha Bernice *retired librarian*
Greenberg, Hinda Feige *library director*
Gregor, Dorothy Deborah *librarian*
†Guldner, Joel Raymond *librarian*
†Habich, Elizabeth Chamberlain *librarian*
Hazekamp, Phyllis Wanda Alberts *library director*
Hempleman, Barbara Florence *archivist*
Henry, Charles Jay *library director*
Hicks, Jack Alan *library director*
†Higginson, Karen Ann Dorothy *librarian*
Hoke, Sheila Wilder *retired librarian*

Howard, Joseph Harvey *retired librarian*
Jacob, Rosamond Tryon *librarian*
Jenkins, Darrell Lee *librarian*
Kaser, David *retired librarian, educator, consultant*
Kaufman, Paula T. *librarian*
Leather, Victoria Potts *college librarian*
Lee, Harrison Hon *naval architecture librarian, consultant*
Lehner-Quam, Alison Lynn *library administrator*
Levin-Wixman, Irene Staub *librarian*
Lewis, Emanuel Raymond *historian, psychologist, retired librarian*
Lindgren, William Dale *librarian*
†Long, Patricia A. *librarian*
McBurney, Margot B. *librarian*
McDougall, Donald Blake *retired government official, librarian*
McGrath, Anna Fields *retired librarian*
McLain, Thelma Louise *retired college librarian, artist*
Merlini, Sandra Ann *librarian, writer*
†Mesenbrink, Shawna *library director*
Metz, T(heodore) John *librarian, consultant*
Miele, Anthony William *retired librarian*
Miller, Charles Edmond *library administrator*
Miller, Jacqueline Winslow *library director*
Miller, Marilyn Lea *library science educator*
Moody, Roland Herbert *retired librarian*
Morgan, Jane Hale *retired library director*
†Morgan, Janet Carol *library director*
Nelson, Helen Martha *retired library director*
O'Brien, Betty Alice *theological librarian, researcher*
Patterson, Robert Hudson *retired university library director*
Pitman, LaVern Frank *retired librarian*
Poad, Flora Virginia *retired librarian and educator*
Rhoads, James Berton *archivist, former government official, consultant, educator*
Ricketts, Sondra Lou *librarian*
Robinson, Verna Cotten *retired librarian, property management owner*
Rouse, Roscoe, Jr. *librarian, educator*
Sadler, Graham Hydrick *library administrator*
Scoles, Clyde Sheldon *library director*
Scott, Alice H. *retired librarian*
Scott, Catherine Dorothy *librarian, information consultant*
Shirley, Wayne Douglas *music librarian*
Shultz, Linda Joyce *retired library director*
Silvia, Raymond Alan *librarian*
Smith, Barbara Jeanne *retired librarian*
Smith, Dentye M. *library media specialist*
Smith, Howard McQueen *librarian*
Spaulding, Frank Henry *librarian*
Suput, Ray Radoslav *librarian*
Teeple, Fiona Diane *librarian, lawyer*
Thorn, Rosemary Kost *former librarian*
Tower, Kathleen Ruth *librarian, consultant*
Townsend, Jerrie Lynne *librarian*
Trenery, Mary Ellen *librarian*
Trezza, Alphonse Fiore *librarian, educator*
†Turner, Joyce May *librarian*
UmBayemake, Linda *librarian*
Van Orden, Phyllis Jeanne *librarian, educator*
Vickery, Byrdean Eyvonne Hughes (Mrs. Charles Everett Vickery, Jr.) *retired library services administrator*
Waite, Frances W. *librarian, professional genealogist*
Wartluft, David Jonathan *librarian, clergyman*
Whitmore, Menandra M. *librarian*
Williams, Richard Clarence *retired librarian*
Wilson, C. Daniel, Jr. *library director*
Wingate, Bettye Faye *librarian, educator*
Woodrum, Patricia Ann *librarian*
Yeo, Ronald Frederick *librarian*
Young, Susan Babson *retired library director*
Zoelle, Andrea Marie *reference librarian*

HUMANITIES: MUSEUMS

UNITED STATES

ALABAMA

Birmingham
Dodd, Donald Bradford *museum administrator, historian*
†Morin, Bode Joseph *curator, historian, industrial archeologist*
Schloder, John E. *museum director*

Mc Calla
Gentry, Vicki Paulette *museum director*

Mobile
†Delaney, Caldwell *museum director*
Richelson, Paul William *curator*

Montgomery
Johnson, Mark Matthew *museum administrator*

Tuscaloosa
Jones, Douglas Epps *natural history museum director*

ALASKA

Anchorage
Spencer, Ted *museum director*
Wolf, Patricia B. *museum director*

Fairbanks
Jonaitis, Aldona Claire *museum administrator, art historian*

Juneau
Kato, Bruce *curator*

ARIZONA

Bisbee
Gustavson, Carrie *museum director*

Flagstaff
Eide, Joel S. *museum director*
Fox, Michael J. *museum director*

Ganado
Chamberlin, Ed *curator*

Mesa
Mead, Tray C. *museum director*

Phoenix
Grinell, Sheila *museum director*
Johnson, Mary *museum director*
Lidman, Roger Wayne *museum director*
Myers, Cindy L. *museum director*
Sullivan, Martin Edward *museum director*

Portal
Zweifel, Richard George *curator*

Tonalea
Francisco, Irving *landmark administrator*

Tucson
Brown, Don *museum director*
Yassin, Robert Alan *museum administrator, curator*

ARKANSAS

Little Rock
Bradshaw, William C. *museum director*
DuBois, Alan Beekman *art museum curator*
Wolfe, Townsend Durant, III *art museum director, curator*
Worthen, William Booker, Jr. *museum director*

Prairie Grove
Smith, Ed *historic site administrator*

CALIFORNIA

Arcata
Zielinski, Melissa L. *museum director*

Bakersfield
Enriquez, Carola Rupert *museum director*

Berkeley
Benedict, Burton *retired museum director, anthropology educator*

Beverly Hills
Berman, Jerome *museum director, curator*
†Gabriel, Jeanette Hanisee *curator, art historian*
†Korn, Henry *museum administrator*

Bodega Bay
Cohen, Daniel Morris *museum administrator, marine biology researcher*

Burlingame
Stofflet, Mary Kirk *museum curator, writer*

Carmel Valley
Wolfe, Maurice Raymond *retired museum director, educator*

Carson
Zimmerer, Kathy Louise *university art gallery director*

Costa Mesa
Botello, Troy James *arts administrator, educator*

Escondido
Killmar, Lawrence E. *wild animal park site curator*

Hollywood
Byrnes, James Bernard *museum director emeritus*

La Jolla
†Armstrong, Elizabeth Neilson *curator*
Beebe, Mary Livingstone *curator*
Davies, Hugh Marlais *museum director*

Long Beach
Glenn, Constance White *art museum director, educator, consultant*
Nelson, Harold Bernhard *museum director*

Los Angeles
†Barron, Stephanie *museum curator*
Beal, Graham William John *museum director*
Fontenote-Jamerson, Belinda *museum director*
Henderson, Jai *museum director*
Hopkins, Henry Tyler *museum director, art educator*
King, Duane Harold *museum administrator*
Kuwayama, George *retired curator*
Mulryan, Lenore Hoag *author, art curator*
Naef, Weston John *museum curator*
Powell, James Lawrence *museum director*
Rich, Andrea Louise *museum executive*
Rudolph, Jeffrey N. *museum director*
Walsh, John *museum director*
Wittmann, Otto *art museum executive*

Montara
Wall, Glennie Murray *historic preservation professional*

Oakland
Power, Dennis Michael *museum director*

Orinda
Dorn, Virginia Alice *artist, art gallery director*

Pacific Grove
Adams, Margaret Bernice *retired museum official*
Bailey, Stephen Fairchild *museum director and curator, ornithologist*

Redlands
Griesemer, Allan David *retired museum director*

Riverside
Green, Jonathan William *museum administrator and educator, artist, author*
Korzec, Patricia Ann *museum administrator*
Warren, Katherine Virginia *art gallery director*

Sacramento
Gray, Walter P., III *archivist, consultant*

San Carlos
Schumacher, Henry Jerold *museum administrator, former career officer, business executive*

San Diego
Longenecker, Martha W. *museum director*
Petersen, Martin Eugene *museum curator*

San Francisco
Aldrich, Michael Ray *library curator, health educator*
Berggruen, John Henry *art gallery executive*
†Boas, Nancy M. *curator*
Delacote, Goery *museum director*
Leviton, Alan Edward *museum curator*
Lindsay, George Edmund *museum director*
Parker, Harry S., III *art museum administrator*
Ross, David A. *art museum director*
Sano, Emily Joy *museum director*
Thomas, William Geraint *museum administrator*

San Jose
Callan, Josi Irene *museum director*

San Luis Obispo
Mette, Joe *museum director*

San Marino
Skotheim, Robert Allen *museum administrator*
Wark, Robert Rodger *art curator*

Santa Barbara
Karpeles, David *museum director*

Sausalito
Elliott, James Heyer *retired university art museum curator, fine arts consultant*

Simi Valley
Hunt, Mark Alan *museum director*

Stanford
Seligman, Thomas Knowles *museum administrator*

Stockton
Hepper, Iona Lydia *gallery owner*

Studio City
Bull, David *fine art conservator*

Venice
Davis, Kimberly Brooke *art gallery director*

Watsonville
Hernandez, Jo Farb *museum curator, consultant*

Yosemite National Park
Forgang, David M. *museum curator*

COLORADO

Boulder
Danilov, Victor Joseph *museum management program director, consultant, writer, educator*
Meier, Thomas Joseph *museum director, author*

Colorado Springs
LeMieux, Linda Dailey *museum director*

Cripple Creek
Swanson, Erik Christian *museum director*

Denver
Maytham, Thomas Northrup *art and museum consultant*

Evergreen
Lang, Brian Joseph *museum curator*

Golden
Fahey, Barbara Stewart Doe *public agency administrator*

Pueblo
Henning, William Thomas *museum director*

CONNECTICUT

Greenwich
Sturges, Hollister, III *museum director*

Hartford
Faude, Wilson Hinsdale *museum director*
White, David Oliver *museum executive*

Mystic
Carr, James Revell *museum executive, curator*
Johnston, Waldo Cory Melrose *museum director*

New Haven
Hickey, Leo J(oseph) *museum curator, educator*

Norwalk
Luongo, Janet Duffy *curator, art educator, writer, artist*

Norwich
Gualtieri, Joseph Peter *museum director*

Old Lyme
Dangremond, David W. *museum administrator, educator*

Stamford
Kinsman, Robert Donald *art museum administrator, cartoonist*

Waterbury
Smith, Ann Youngdahl *museum administrator*

Weston
Daniel, James *curator, business executive, writer, former editor,*
Oliver, Sandra *art dealer, painter*

DELAWARE

Odessa
Pulinka, Steven M. *historic site director*

Wilmington
Bruni, Stephen Thomas *art museum director*

Winterthur
Hummel, Charles Frederick *museum official*
Lanmon, Dwight Pierson *museum director*

DISTRICT OF COLUMBIA

Washington
Beach, Milo C. *art museum director*
Bloomfield, Sara *museum director*
Brannan, Beverly Wood *curator of photography*
Bretzfelder, Deborah May *museum exhibit designer, photographer*
Carr, Carolyn Kinder *deputy director National Portrait Gallery*
Cikovsky, Nicolai, Jr. *curator, art history educator*
Crew, Spencer *museum administrator*
Demetrion, James Thomas *art museum director*
Evelyn, Douglas Everett *museum executive*
Fauntleroy, Carma Cecil *arts administration executive*
Fetters, J. Michael *museum administrator*
Fisher, Wesley Andrew *research administrator, Eurasian studies specialist*
Furgol, Edward Mackie *museum curator, historian*
Goler, Robert I. *museum curator*
Grasselli, Margaret Morgan *curator*
Hand, John Oliver *museum curator*
Hanle, Robert V. *museum administrator*
Hoffmann, Robert Shaw *museum administrator, educator*
Ketchum, James Roe *curator*
Kornicker, Louis S. *museum curator*
Kurin, Richard *museum program director*
Lapp, Douglas Martin *director national science resource center*
†LaRiche, Jeffrey T. *museum administrator*
Levy, David Corcos *museum director*
Lowe, Harry *museum director*
Marsh, Caryl Amsterdam *museum exhibitions curator, psychologist, advisor*
Monkman, Betty Claire *curator*
Neufeld, Michael John *curator, historian*
Newsome, Steven Cameron *museum director*
Panzer, Mary Caroline *museum curator*
Phillips, Laughlin *art museum chairman, former magazine editor*
Quick, Edward Raymond *museum director, educator, curator*
Reber, Paul *museum director*
Ritchie, Charles Morton, Jr. *artist, curator*
Robertson, Charles James *museum director*
Robison, Andrew Cliffe, Jr. *museum curator*
Samuels Lasner, Mark *book and art collector*
Sheehan, Michael Terrence *arts administrator, historian, consultant*
Shestack, Alan *museum administrator*
Solinger, Janet W. *museum executive*
Stanton, Robert *historic site director*
Stevenson, Frances Kellogg *museum program director, inventor*
Sullivan, Robert D. *museum program director*
Sultan, Terrie Frances *curator*
Trapp, Kenneth R. *gallery curator*
Walker, Roslyn Adele *director National Museum African Art*
Weil, Stephen Edward *museum official*
Withuhn, William Lawrence *museum curator, railroad economics and management consultant*
Wolanin, Barbara Ann Boese *art curator, art historian*
Wulff, Roger LaVern *museum administrator*

FLORIDA

Daytona Beach
Libby, Gary Russell *museum director*

Delray Beach
Shute, Melodie Ann *community services administrator*

Fort Lauderdale
Rosen, Barry Howard *museum director, history educator*

Gainesville
Dickinson, Joshua Clifton, Jr. *museum director, educator*
Wing, Elizabeth Schwarz *museum curator, educator*

Jacksonville
Dundon, Margo Elaine *museum director*
Schlageter, Robert William *museum administrator*

Lakeland
Stetson, Daniel Everett *museum director*

Miami
Dursum, Brian A. *museum curator, art educator*
Etling, Russell Hull *museum executive, production company executive*
Morgan, Dahlia *museum director*

Orlando
Morrisey, Marena Grant *art museum administrator*

Palm Beach
Blades, John Michael *museum director*

Pensacola
Rasmussen, Robert *museum director*

Port Orange
Horváth, Michael Joseph *curator*

Saint Augustine
Dale, Chuck *landmark staff member*

Saint Petersburg
Connelly, David O'Brien *museum administrator, journalist*

Sarasota
Graham, Douglas John *museum curator, banker, artist, poet*

Tallahassee
Palladino-Craig, Allys *museum director*

Tampa
Kass, Emily *art museum administrator*

West Palm Beach
Borchers, Karen Lily *museum administrator*
Orr-Cahall, Christina *art museum director, art historian*

Winter Park
Ruggiero, Laurence Joseph *museum director*

GEORGIA

Atlanta
Bibb, Daniel Roland *antique painting restorer and conservator*
Davis, Eleanor Kay *museum administrator*
Hiers, Mary A. *museum director*
Vigtel, Gudmund *museum director emeritus*

Columbus
Butler, Charles Thomas *museum director, curator*

Jekyll Island
Hicks, Leslie Elizabeth *museum curator*
Murphy, F. Warren *museum director*

Marietta
Gaudieri, Alexander V. J. *museum director*

Roswell
Forbes, John Ripley *museum executive, educator, naturalist*

Saint Simons
King, Linda Orr *museum director*

Savannah
Brandner, Christine Marie *curator, artist*
Harold, Fran Powell *historic site director*

HAWAII

Honolulu
Ellis, George Richard *museum administrator*
Klobe, Tom *art gallery director*

Kalaupapa
Alexander, Dean *museum director*

Lihue
Lovell, Carol *museum director*

Mililani
Magee, Donald Edward *retired national park service administrator*

Puunene
Kubota, Gaylord *museum director*

IDAHO

Boise
Swanson, Kenneth J. *museum administrator*

Coeur D Alene
Dahlgren, Dorothy *museum director*

Pocatello
Jackson, Allen Keith *museum administrator*

Salmon
Wiederrick, Robert *museum director*

Twin Falls
Woods, James C. *museum director*

ILLINOIS

Carbondale
Whitlock, John Joseph *museum director*

Chicago
Balzekas, Stanley, Jr. *museum director*
Consey, Kevin Edward *museum administrator*
Flynn, John J. *museum curator*
Heltne, Paul Gregory *museum executive*
Jakstas, Alfred John *museum conservator, consultant*
Kamyszew, Christopher D. *museum curator, executive educator, art consultant*
Kubida, Judith Ann *museum administrator*
Lewis, Phillip Harold *museum curator*
Mc Carter, John Wilbur, Jr. *museum executive*
Nordland, Gerald *art museum administrator, historian, consultant*
†Strick, Jeremy *curator*
Wardropper, Ian Bruce *museum curator, educator*

Weisberg, Lois *arts administrator, city official*
Wood, James Nowell *museum director and executive*
Zukowsky, John Robert *curator*

Collinsville
Pallozola, Christine *non-profit historic site administrator*

Evanston
Frazer, Ricardo Amando *program director*

Homewood
MacMaster, Daniel Miller *retired museum official*

Kampsville
Sutton, Cynthia Ann *executive director museum*

Mahomet
Kennedy, Cheryl Lynn *museum director*

Springfield
Hallmark, Donald Parker *museum director, lecturer*
Mc Millan, R(obert) Bruce *museum executive, anthropologist*
Wynn, Nan L. *historic site administrator*

INDIANA

Bloomington
Calinescu, Adriana Gabriela *museum curator, art historian*
Carroll, David Lee *museum administrator*
Gealt, Adelheid Maria *museum director*

Dana
Bray, Rick *curator*

Elkhart
Burns, B(illye) Jane *museum director*

Evansville
Alexander, Mary L. *historic site adminstrator*
Streetman, John William, III *museum official*

Fort Wayne
Anderson, Jim *zoo director*
Watkinson, Patricia Grieve *museum director*

Indianapolis
Gantz, Richard Alan *museum administrator*
Waller, Aaron Bret, III *museum director*

Muncie
Joyaux, Alain Georges *art museum director*

Rochester
Willard, Shirley Ann Ogle *museum director, editor*

Terre Haute
Ondish, Andrea *museum coordinator*

IOWA

Iowa City
Prokopoff, Stephen Stephen *art museum director, educator*
Smothers, Ann E. *museum director*

West Branch
Kohan, Carol E. *historial site administrator*

KANSAS

Dodge City
Clifton-Smith, Rhonda Darleen *art center director*

Larned
Linderer, Steve *historic site executive*

Lawrence
Norris, Andrea Spaulding *art museum director*

Manhattan
Walker Schlageck, Kathrine L. *museum educational administrator, educator*

Salina
Douglass, Mary Clement *retired curator, historian*

KENTUCKY

Ashland
Maxwell, Donald Robert *museum director*

Louisville
Becker, Gail Roselyn *museum director*
Morrin, Peter Patrick *museum director*

Paducah
Faoro, Victoria Anna *museum director, magazine editor*

LOUISIANA

Deridder
Mallory, Patricia Jody *museum curator*

New Orleans
Bullard, Edgar John, III *museum director*
Casellas, Joachim *art gallery executive*
Fagaly, William Arthur *curator*
Owen, Kenneth Emerson *museum director, retired librarian*
Sefcik, James Francis *museum director*

MAINE

Augusta
Phillips, Joseph Robert *museum director*

Hancock
Silvestro, Clement Mario *museum director, historian*

Kennebunk
Escalet, Frank Diaz *art gallery owner, artist, educator*

Orono
Hartgen, Vincent Andrew *museum director, educator, artist*
Whittington, Stephen Lunn *museum director*

Portland
Hull, William Floyd, Jr. *former museum director, ceramic consultant*

MARYLAND

Annapolis
Cheevers, James William *museum curator*
Fligsten, Ann M. *historic foundation director*

Baltimore
Kellett, John M. *museum director*
Lamp, Frederick John *museum curator*
Mogilensky, Emma Sarah *museum educator*
Ott, John Harlow *museum administrator*
Somerville, Romaine Stec *arts administrator*

Bethesda
Fri, Robert Wheeler *museum director*

Clinton
Verge, Laurie *museum director, historian*

Edgewater
Hines, Anson H. *museum director*
Simons, Ross B. *environmental center director*

Friendship
Clagett, Diana Wharton Sinkler *museum docent*

West Bethesda
Wegner, Dana Marc *museum curator, historian*

MASSACHUSETTS

Acton
Gilpin, Deborah J. *museum administrator*

Amherst
Parkhurst, Charles *retired museum director, art historian*

Boston
Curran, Emily Katherine *museum director*
Ellis, David Wertz *museum director*
Fairbanks, Jonathan Leo *museum curator*
Freed, Rita Evelyn *curator, Egyptologist, educator*
Hills, Patricia Gorton Schulze *curator*
Howlett, D(onald) Roger *art gallery executive, art historian*
Logan, Lox Albert, Jr. *museum director*
Meister, Mark Jay *museum director, professional society administrator*
Nylander, Jane Louise *museum director*
Rogers, Malcolm Austin *museum director, art historian*
Vermeule, Cornelius Clarkson, III *museum curator*
Washburn, Bradford (Henry B. Washburn, Jr.) *museum administrator, cartographer, photographer*
Wentworth, Michael Justin *curator*
Wu, Tung *curator, art historian, art educator, artist*

Brockton
Hyland, Douglas K. S. *museum administrator, educator*

Cambridge
Cohn, Marjorie Benedict *curator, art historian, educator*
Cuno, James *art museum director*
Gaskell, Ivan George Alexander De Wend *art museum curator*
Rathbone, Perry Townsend *art museum director*
Seamans, Warren Arthur *museum director*
Slive, Seymour *museum director, fine arts educator*

Concord
Kehoe, Dorrie Bonner *museum educator*

Fitchburg
Jareckie, Stephen Barlow *museum curator*

Jamaica Plain
Zahn, Carl Frederick *museum publications director, designer, photographer*

Lenox
Kochta, Ruth Martha *art gallery owner*

Milton
Randall, Lilian Maria Charlotte *museum curator*

Salem
Finamore, Daniel Robert *museum curator*
Neel, Thomas Harris *museum director*

Southfield
Melvin, Ronald McKnight *retired museum director*

Springfield
Muhlberger, Richard Charles *former museum administrator, writer, educator*
Zaik, Carol Ford *museum director, art historian, educator*

Waltham
Arena, Albert A. *museum director*

MICHIGAN

Ann Arbor
Bailey, Reeve Maclaren *museum curator*
Sawyer, Charles Henry *art educator, art museum director emeritus*

Detroit
Darr, Alan Phipps *curator, historian*
Edwards, Esther G. *museum administrator, former record, film and entertainment company executive*
Parrish, Maurice Drue *museum executive*
†Peck, Elsie Holmes *museum curator*
Peck, William Henry *museum curator, art historian, archaeologist, author, lecturer*

East Lansing
Bandes, Susan Jane *museum director, educator*
Dewhurst, Charles Kurt *museum director, curator, folklorist, English language educator*

Flint
Germann, Steven James *museum director*

Grand Rapids
Chester, Timothy J. *museum director*
Frankforter, Weldon DeLoss *retired museum administrator*

Kalamazoo
Norris, Richard Patrick *museum director, history educator*

MINNESOTA

Grand Marais
Cochrane, Tim *landmark administrator*

Minneapolis
King, Lyndel Irene Saunders *art museum director*
†Lanyon, Scott Merrill *museum director, educator*
Zakian, Michael *museum director*

Saint Paul
Osman, Stephen Eugene *historic site administrator*

MISSISSIPPI

Madison
Hiatt, Jane Crater *arts agency administrator*

MISSOURI

Boonville
McVicker, Mary Ellen Harshbarger *museum director, art history educator*

Florissant
Luebke, Martin Frederick *retired curator*

Fort Leonard Wood
Combs, Robert Kimbal *museum director*

Hannibal
Sweets, Henry Hayes, III *museum director*

Independence
Hackman, Larry J. *program director*
Lambertson, John Mark *museum director, historian*

Kansas City
McKenna, George LaVerne *art museum curator*
Scott, Deborah Emont *curator*
Svadlenak, Jean Hayden *museum administrator, consultant*
Ucko, David Alan *museum director*
Wilson, Marc Fraser *art museum administrator and curator*

Lexington
Fuller, Janae *historic site administrator*

Saint Joseph
Chilcote, Gary M. *museum director, reporter*

Saint Louis
Burke, James Donald *museum administrator*
Crandell, Dwight Samuel *museum executive*

Springfield
Berger, Jerry Allen *museum director*

MONTANA

Billings
Towe, A. Ruth *museum director*

Butte
Thompson, John *museum director*

Crow Agency
Deernose, Kitty *museum curator*

Deer Lodge
McWright, Michael J. *historic site administrator*

Missoula
Brown, Robert Munro *museum director*
Millin, Laura Jeanne *museum director*

NEBRASKA

Boys Town
Lynch, Thomas Joseph *museum and historic house manager*

Chadron
Lecher, Belvadine (Reeves) *museum curator*

North Platte
Morrison, Thomas B. *historic site administrator*

Omaha
Schmidt, Wayne William *museum director, curator*

NEVADA

Elko
Seymour, Lisa *museum director*

Las Vegas
Gillespie, Marilyn *museum administrator*
Lewis, Oli Parepa *curator*
Naegle, Shirl R. *museum director*

Reno
Bandurraga, Peter Louis *museum director, historian*
Feinhandler, Edward Sanford *writer, photographer, art dealer, sports mentor, consultant, educator*

NEW HAMPSHIRE

Cornish
Duffy, Henry J. *museum curator, consultant*

Keene
Ahern, Maureen Jeanne *museum director, artist*

Manchester
Coleman, Linda Lee Devoe *museum educator*

NEW JERSEY

Holmdel
Smith, Sibley Judson, Jr. *historic site administrator, educator*

Morristown
Klindt, Steven *art museum director*

New Brunswick
Cate, Phillip Dennis *art museum director*

Newark
Reynolds, Valrae *museum curator*

Park Ridge
Maurer, C(harles) F(rederick) William, III *museum director*

Princeton
Welton, Donna Ann *curator, translator*

Wayne
Einreinhofer, Nancy Anne *art gallery director*

West Cape May
Cadge, William Fleming *gallery owner, photographer*

Wildwood
Scully, Robert *museum director, curator*

NEW MEXICO

Abiquiu
Martinez, Ray *museum director*

Albuquerque
Moore, James C. *museum director*
Smartt, Richard A. *museum director*
Walch, Peter Sanborn *museum director, publisher*

Grants
Lujan, John *landmark administrator*

Las Cruces
Lovell, Charles Muir *museum curator, photographer*

Placitas
Smith, Richard Bowen *retired national park superintendent*

Ruidoso Downs
Eldredge, Bruce Beard *museum director*

Santa Fe
Ashman, Stuart *museum director*
Cerny, Charlene Ann *museum director*
DiMaio, Virginia Sue *gallery owner*
Enyeart, James L. *museum director*
Kennedy, Roger George *museum director, park service executive*
Livesay, Thomas Andrew *museum administrator, lecturer*
Way, Jacob Edson, III *museum director*

Silver City
Bettison, Cynthia Ann *museum director, archaeologist*

Taos
Ebie, William D. *museum director*
Witt, David L. *curator, writer*

NEW YORK

Albany
Levine, Louis David *museum director, archaeologist*
Miles, Christine Marie *museum director*

Blue Mountain Lake
Day, Jacqueline Frances *museum director*

Brooklyn
Ferber, Linda S. *museum curator*
Lehman, Arnold Lester *museum official, art historian*

Buffalo
Bayles, Jennifer Lucene *museum education curator*
Day, Richard *museum administrator*
Metz, Donald *art center director, musician*
Schultz, Douglas George *art museum director*

Cold Spring Harbor
MacKay, Robert Battin *museum director*

Corning
Spillman, Jane Shadel *curator, researcher, writer*
Whitehouse, David Bryn *museum director*

East Hampton
Vered, Ruth *art gallery director*

Flushing
Friedman, Alan Jacob *museum director*

Ithaca
Robinson, Franklin Westcott *museum director, art historian*

Keene Valley
Lanyon, Wesley Edwin *retired museum curator, ornithologist*

Miller Place
Sanger, Eileen *gallery owner, artist*

New York
Anderson, Maxwell L. *museum director*
Arnot, Andrew H. *art gallery director*
Bandy, Mary Lea *museum official*
Baragwanath, Albert Kingsmill *curator*
Barnett, Vivian Endicott *curator*
Bates, Michael Lawrence *curator*
Batscha, Robert Michael *museum executive*
Biddle, Flora Miller *art museum administrator*
Bothmer, Dietrich Felix von *museum curator, archaeologist*
Brooks, Diana B. *auction house executive*
Brown, Eric *art gallery director, art dealer*
Buck, Robert Treat, Jr. *gallery director, former museum director, educator*
Burge, Christopher *auction house executive*
Celant, Germano *curator*
Cohen, Mildred Thaler *art gallery director*
Coll, Jim *gallery director*
Cooper, Steve Neil *art gallery owner, photographer*
De Ferrari, Gabriella *curator, writer*
de Montebello, Philippe Lannes *museum administrator*
Draper, James David *art museum curator*
Elam, Leslie Albert *museum administrator*
Emmerich, Andre *art gallery executive, author*
Esman, Rosa Mencher *art gallery executive*
Esmerian, Ralph O. *museum administrator*
Faunce, Sarah Cushing *former museum curator*
Feldman, Ronald *art gallery director*
Freed, Stanley Arthur *museum curator*
Futter, Ellen Victoria *museum administrator*
Ginsburg, Sigmund G. *museum administrator*
Glimcher, Arnold B. *art gallery executive*
†Gumpert, Lynn *gallery director*
Hambrecht, Patricia G. *auction house administrator*
Haskell, Barbara *curator*
†Hotchner, Holly *curator, museum director*
Hoving, Thomas *museum and cultural affairs consultant, author*
Howat, John Keith *museum executive*
Hutton, Anne Moore *museum consultant*
Ives, Colta Feller *museum curator, educator*
Kallir, Jane Katherine *art gallery director, author*
Kardon, Janet *museum director, curator, educator*
Kind, Phyllis *art gallery owner*
†Kleeblatt, Norman L. *museum curator*
Kramer, Linda Konheim *curator, art historian*
Krens, Thomas *museum director*
Kuchta, Ronald Andrew *art museum director, magazine editor, curator*
Kujawski, Elizabeth Szancer *art curator, consultant*
Leff, Sandra H. *gallery director, consultant*
Lerner, Martin *museum curator*
Levai, Pierre Alexandre *art gallery executive*
Lowry, Glenn David *art museum director*
Macdonald, Robert Rigg, Jr. *museum director*
Martegani Luini, Micaela *curator, art critic*
Martin, Mary-Anne *art gallery owner*
Martin, Richard Harrison *curator, art historian*
McFadden, David Revere *museum curator*
McGovern, Maureen Ann *curator*
Mc Shine, Kynaston Leigh *curator*
Mertens, Joan R. *museum curator, art historian*
Messer, Thomas Maria *museum director*
Metcalf, William Edwards *museum curator*
Moffett, Charles Simonton *museum director, curator, writer*
Munhall, Edgar *curator, art history educator*
Murdock, Robert Mead *art consultant, curator*
O'Brien, Catherine Louise *museum administrator*
Oldenburg, Richard Erik *auction house executive*
Parker, James *retired curator*
Pesner, Carole Manishin *art gallery owner*
Pilgrim, Dianne Hauserman *art museum director*
Pisano, Ronald George *art consultant*
Platnick, Norman I. *curator, arachnologist*
Rosenbaum, Joan Hannah *museum director*
Rosenthal, Nan *curator, author*
Schuster, Karen Sutton *administrator*
†Senouf, Yvonne Gabrielle *art gallery administrator*
Sidamon-Eristoff, Anne Phipps *museum official*
Simon, Ronald Charles *curator*
Sragow, Ellen *gallery owner*
Storr, Robert *curator painting and sculpture, artist, writer*
Tobach, Ethel *retired curator*
Toll, Barbara Elizabeth *art gallery director*
Varnedoe, John Kirk Train *museum curator*
Vuilleumier, François *curator, biology and ornithology educator*
Wright, Gwendolyn *art center director, writer, educator*

Purchase
Gedeon, Lucinda Heyel *museum director*

Rochester
Adams, G. Rollie *museum executive*
Bannon, Anthony Leo *museum director*
Hall, Donald S. *former planetarium administrator, pottery expert*
Holcomb, Grant, III *museum director*

Schenectady
Roselli, Bart A. *museum director*

Southampton
Lerner, Abram *retired museum director, artist*

Staten Island
Botwinick, Michael *museum director*
Gasteyer, Carlin Evans *museum administrator, museum studies educator*

Stuyvesant
Tripp, Susan Gerwe *museum director*

Syracuse
Skoler, Celia Rebecca *art gallery director*

Troy
Pascale, Ralph *museum director*

Tupper Lake
Welsh, Peter Corbett *museum consultant, historian*

Utica
Schweizer, Paul Douglas *museum director*

Wantagh
Smits, Edward John *museum consultant*

Waterford
Gold, James Paul *museum director*

Willow
Cox, James David *art gallery executive*

NORTH CAROLINA

Asheville
Cecil, William A.V. *landmark director*

Chapel Hill
Bolas, Gerald Douglas *art museum administrator, art history educator*
Riggs, Timothy Allan *museum curator*

Charlotte
Boggs, Willene Graythen *property manager, oil and gas broker, consultant*
Evans, Bruce Haselton *art museum director*
Nicholson, Freda Hyams *museum executive, medical educator*
Perry, Barbara Ann *museum curator*
Shuford, Jill Renee *museum educator, art educator*

Durham
Krakauer, Thomas Henry *museum director*

Fort Bragg
Merritt, Roxanne Marie *museum curator*

Kure Beach
Hoppe, Barbara G. *historic site administrator*

Manteo
Berry, Russell W. *historic site administrator*

Raleigh
Hansley, Lee *art gallery owner, curator*
Kuhler, Renaldo Gillet *museum official, scientific illustrator*
McNutt, James Charles *museum director*
Wheeler, Lawrence Jefferson *art museum director*

Salisbury
Shalkop, Robert Leroy *retired museum director*

Stanfield
Dysart, John *historic site administrator*

Wilmington
Seapker, Janet Kay *museum director*

Winston Salem
Cawood, Hobart Guy *historic site administrator*
Rauschenberg, Bradford Lee *museum research director*

OHIO

Akron
Kahan, Mitchell Douglas *art museum director*

Athens
Ahrens, Kent *museum director, art historian*

Cincinnati
Brown, Daniel *independent art consultant, critic, writer*
Desmarais, Charles Joseph *museum director, writer, editor*
†Henry, Laurie Jayne *writer, educator*
Hessler, Gene Joseph *retired musician, retired museum curator*
Long, Phillip Clifford *museum director*
Rogers, Millard Foster, Jr. *retired art museum director*
Timpano, Anne *museum director, art historian*
Tolzmann, Don Heinrich *curator, educator*

Cleveland
Bergman, Robert Paul *museum administrator, art historian, educator, lecturer*
King, James Edward *museum director*
Ward, William Edward *museum exhibition designer*

Dayton
Nyerges, Alexander Lee *museum director*
Ruffer, David Gray *museum director, former college president*

Fremont
Bridges, Roger Dean *historical agency administrator*

Gnadenhutten
McKeown, Barbara *curator*

Kirtland
Johnston, Stanley Howard, Jr. *curator of rare books, bibliographer*

Mentor
Miller, Frances Suzanne *historic site curator*

Toledo
Steadman, David Wilton *museum official*

University Heights
Cook, Alexander Burns *museum curator, artist, educator*

Vandalia
Smith, Marjorie Aileen Matthews *museum director*

Wright Patterson AFB
Metcalf, Charles David *museum director, retired military officer*

Youngstown
Zona, Louis A. *art institute director*

OKLAHOMA

Fort Sill
Spivey, Towana *museum director*

Tulsa
Joyner, John Brooks *museum director*
Manhart, Marcia Y(ockey) *art museum director*
Wyckoff, Lydia Lloyd *art curator*

OREGON

Bend
Moore, Jerry N. *museum director*

Portland
Buchanan, John E., Jr. *museum director*
Eichinger, Marilynne H. *museum administrator*
Gilkey, Gordon Waverly *curator, artist*
Jenkins, Donald John *art museum administrator*
Kinley, Loren Dhue *museum director*
Lacrosse, Patrick *museum administrator*
Taylor, J(ocelyn) Mary *museum administrator, zoologist, educator*

PENNSYLVANIA

Allentown
Blume, Peter Frederick *museum director*
†Fishman, Bernard Philip *museum director*

Birdsboro
Lewars, James A. *historic site director*

Camp Hill
McGeary, Clyde Mills *artist, educator, advisor*

Chadds Ford
Duff, James Henry *museum director, environmental administrator*

Erie
Vanco, John L. *art museum director*

Fort Washington
Wint, Dennis Michael *museum director*

Gettysburg
Cisneros, Jose A. *historical site administrator*
Latschar, John A. *historic site administrator*

Harrisburg
Mahey, John Andrew *retired museum director*

Kennett Square
Naeve, Milo Merle *museum curator and trustee*

Merion Station
Camp, Kimberly N. *museum administrator, artist*

New Hope
Purpura, Peter Joseph *museum curator, exhibition designer*

Philadelphia
Bantel, Linda Mae *museum curatorial consultant*
Carter, John Swain *museum administrator, consultant*
d'Harnoncourt, Anne *museum director, executive*
Dyson, Robert Harris *museum director emeritus, archaeologist, educator*

INDUSTRY: MANUFACTURING. See also FINANCE: FINANCIAL SERVICES.

UNITED STATES

ALABAMA

Albertville
†Rice, Fuhrman D. (Runt) *retired paper executive*

Alexander City
Gade, Marvin Francis *retired paper company executive*

Andalusia
Taylor, James Marion, II *automotive wholesale executive*

Birmingham
Bennett, Joe Claude *pharmaceutical executive*
Campbell, Charles Alton *manufacturing corporate executive*
Chrencik, Frank *chemical company executive*
Daniel, Kenneth Rule *former iron and steel manufacturing company executive*
Goldberg, Edward Jay *general contractor*
Harbert, Bill Lebold *construction corporation executive*
Holton, J(erry) Thomas *concrete company executive*
McMahon, John J., Jr. *metal processing company executive*
Neal, Phil Hudson, Jr. *manufacturing company executive*
Richey, V. L. *steel company executive*
Sklenar, Herbert Anthony *industrial products manufacturing company executive*
Styslinger, Lee Joseph, Jr. *manufacturing company executive*

Dothan
Singletary, William Barry *manufacturing company executive*

Gadsden
Young, Fredda Florine *steel manufacturing manager*

Huntsville
King, Olin B. *electronics systems company executive*

Montgomery
Blount, Winton Malcolm, Jr. *manufacturing company executive*
†Caddell, John Allen *construction and engineering company executive*

Opelika
Jenkins, Richard Lee *manufacturing company executive*

Theodore
Mc Coy, Lee Berard *paint company executive*

Tuscaloosa
Fowler, Conrad Murphree *retired manufacturing company executive*

ALASKA

Anchorage
DeLoach, Robert Edgar *corporate executive*
Easley, George Washington *construction executive*

Haines
Kaufman, David Graham *construction company executive*

Juneau
Lauber, Mignon Diane *food processing company executive*
Smith, Charles Anthony *businessman*

ARIZONA

Carefree
Alexander, Judd Harris *retired paper company executive*
Byrom, Fletcher Lauman *chemical manufacturing company executive*

Chandler
Farley, James Newton *manufacturing executive, engineer*

Flagstaff
Giovale, Virginia Gore *medical products ecexutive, civic leader*

Gilbert
Earnhardt, Hal J., III *automotive executive*

Glendale
Lopez, Steven Richard *small business owner, consultant*

Green Valley
Blickwede, Donald Johnson *retired steel company executive*

Lake Havasu City
Barbieri, Arthur Robert *insurance agent, former chemical company official*

Mesa
DeRosa, Francis Dominic *chemical company executive*
Frisk, Jack Eugene *recreational vehicle manufacturing company executive*
Luth, William Clair *retired research manager*

Paradise Valley
Unruh, James Arlen *former business machines company executive*

Phoenix
Anderson, Milada Filko *manufacturing company executive*
Carter, Ronald Martin, Sr. *pharmaceutical company executive*
Cook, Mary Margaret *steamfitter*
Dewane, John Richard *retired manufacturing company executive, consultan*
Franke, William Augustus *corporate executive*
Giedt, Bruce Alan *paper company executive*
Kopp, David Eugene *manufacturing company executive*
McClelland, Norman P. *food products executive*
Sebold, Duane David *food manufacturing executive*
Solheim, Karsten *golf equipment company executive*
Van Horssen, Charles Arden *manufacturing executive*
White, Edward Allen *electronics company executive*

Prescott
Parkhurst, Charles Lloyd *electronics company executive*
White, Brittan Romeo *manufacturing company executive*

Scottsdale
Buel, Jeffrey A. *pharmaceutical executive*
Freedman, Stanley Marvin *manufacturing company executive*
Gans, Eugene Howard *cosmetic and pharmaceutical company executive*
Grenell, James Henry *retired manufacturing company executive*
Howard, William Gates, Jr. *electronics company executive*
Lloyd, Eugene Walter *retired construction company executive*
Malsack, James Thomas *retired manufacturing company executive*
Reins, Ralph Erich *automotive components supply company executive*
Roe, Richard C. *industry consultant, former home furnishings manufacturing executive*
Walsh, Edward Joseph *toiletries and food company executive*
Wong, Astria Wor *cosmetic business consultant*

Sedona
Bolton, Robert Floyd *construction executive*

Sun City
Van Horssen, Arden Darrell *retired manufacturing executive*

Surprise
Eriksen, Otto Louis *retired manufacturing company executive*

Tucson
Acker, Loren Calvin *medical instrument company executive*
Eckdahl, Donald Edward *manufacturing company executive*
Meeker, Robert Eldon *retired manufacturing company executive*
Mullikin, Vernon Eugene *aerospace executive*
Sundt, Harry Wilson *construction company executive*

ARKANSAS

Bella Vista
Sutherland, Gail Russell *retired industrial equipment manufacturing company executive*

Conway
Morgan, Charles Donald, Jr. *manufacturing executive*

Fayetteville
Marquardt, Stephen Alan *ironworks company executive*

Fort Smith
†Banks, David R. *health products executive*
Flanders, Donald Hargis *manufacturing company executive*
Qualls, Robert L. *manufacturing executive, banker, former state official, educator*

Hot Springs National Park
Schroeder, Donald Perry *retired food products company executive*

Little Rock
Hickingbotham, Frank D. *food product executive*
McCoy, Stuart Sherman *manufacturing executive*
McMullin, Carleton Eugene *automotive business executive*

North Little Rock
Givens, John Kenneth *manufacturing executive*
†Harrison, Angela Eve *industrial company executive*
Harrison, Stephen Earle *manufacturing executive*
†Moore, Helen Lucille *cosmetics company human resources executive*

Siloam Springs
McMennamy, Roger Neal *automobile dealership executive*

Springdale
Tollett, Leland Edward *food company executive*
Tyson, Donald John *food company executive*

Stuttgart
Bell, Richard Eugene *grain and food company executive*

CALIFORNIA

Agoura Hills
Currie, Malcolm Roderick *aerospace and automotive executive, scientist*

Alamo
Liggett, Lawrence Melvin *vacuum equipment manufacturing company executive*

Alhambra
Fried, Elaine June *business executive*

Aliso Viejo
Baumgartner, Anton Edward *automotive sales professional*

Anaheim
Rubenstein, David H. *media manufacturing executive*
Valdez, James Gerald *automotive aftermarket executive*

Aptos
Mechlin, George Francis *electrical manufacturing company executive*

Arcadia
Dodds, Dale Irvin *chemicals executive*

Atherton
Goodman, Sam Richard *electronics company executive*

Bakersfield
Akers, Tom, Jr. *cotton broker, consultant*
Hart, Donald Milton *automotive and ranching executive, former mayor*
Lundquist, Gene Alan *cotton company executive*

Berkeley
Cutter, David Lee *pharmaceutical company executive*

Beverly Hills
Brann, Alton Joseph *manufacturing company executive*
Colburn, Richard Dunton *business executive*
†Mohajer, Dineh *cosmetics company executive*
Willson, James Douglas *aerospace executive*
Winthrop, John *wines and spirits company executive*

Bishop
Naso, Valerie Joan *automotive dealership executive, travel company operator*

Buena Park
Parker, Larry Lee *electronics company executive, consultant*

Burbank
Joseff, Joan Castle *manufacturing executive*
Raulinaitis, Pranas Algis *electronics executive*

Burlingame
Hepler, Kenneth Russel *manufacturing executive*

Calabasas
Iacobellis, Sam Frank *retired aerospace company executive*
Laney, Michael L. *manufacturing executive*
†Sperber, Burton S. *construction executive*

Calistoga
Ogg, Robert Danforth *corporate executive*

Camarillo
Cleary, Thomas Charles *technology company executive*
Denmark, Bernhardt *manufacturing executive*
Weiss, Carl *aerospace company executive*

Carlsbad
Anderson, Paul Irving *management executive*
Bartok, Michelle *cosmetic company executive*
Crooke, Stanley Thomas *pharmaceutical company executive*

Carmichael
Rich, Albert Clark *solar energy manufacturing executive*

Chino
Goodman, Lindsey Alan *furniture manufacturing executive, architect*

Chula Vista
Manary, Richard Deane *manufacturing executive*

City Of Industry
Scritsmier, Jerome Lorenzo *manufacturing company executive*

Colusa
Carter, Jane Foster *agriculture industry executive*

Compton
Golleher, George *food company executive*

Concord
Thompson, Jeremiah Beiseker *international medical business executive*

Corona Del Mar
Wolf, Karl Everett *aerospace and communications corporation executive*

Coronado
Brunton, Paul Edward *retired diversified industry executive*
Dalton, Matt *retired foundry executive*
Sack, Edgar Albert *electronics company executive*

Costa Mesa
Brady, John Patrick, Jr. *electronics educator, consultant*
Davis, Don H. *electronics executive*
Trivelpiece, Craig Evan *computer electronics executive*

Covina
Fillius, Milton Franklin, Jr. *food products company executive*

Culver City
Leve, Alan Donald *electronic materials manufacturing company owner, executive*

Cupertino
Burg, John Parker *signal processing executive*
Mishelevich, David Jacob *medical company executive, consultant*

Cypress
Barman, Robert John *home electronics company executive*

Danville
Amon, William Frederick, Jr. *biotechnology company executive*

Del Mar
Cooper, Martin *electronics company executive*

Dublin
Whetten, John D. *food products executive*

El Cajon
McClure, Donald Edwin *electrical construction executive, consultant*

El Segundo
Criss, William Sotelo *electronics company executive*
McDonald, Rosa Nell *federal research and budgets manager*
Mo, Roger Shih-Yah *electronics engineering manager*

El Sobrante
Withrow-Gallanter, Sherrie Anne *construction and audio company executive*

Emeryville
McEachern, Alexander *electronics company executive*
Nady, John *electronics company executive*
Penhoet, Edward *biochemicals company executive*

Encino
Davenport, Alfred Larue, Jr. *manufacturing company executive*
Roderick, Robert Lee *aerospace executive*

Escalon
Barton, Gerald Lee *farming company executive*

Fair Oaks
Chernev, Melvin *retired beverage company executive*

Fallbrook
Higbee, Donald William *electronics company executive*

Fontana
De Tomaso, Ernest Pat *general building contractor, developer*

Foster City
†McManus, Dana C. *construction company executive*

Fremont
Lahri, Rajeeva *electronics executive*
Torian, Henry *automotive executive*
Wang, Stanley *electronics executive*
Zajac, John *semiconductor equipment company executive*

Fullerton
Miller, Arnold *electronics executive*

Gardena
Kanner, Edwin Benjamin *electrical manufacturing company executive*

Glendora
Cahn, David Stephen *cement company executive*

Goleta
Thom, Richard David *aerospace executive*

Granite Bay
Manzo, Salvatore Edward *retired business developer*

Greenfield
Munoz, John Joseph *retired transportation company executive*

Gridley
Tanimoto, George *agricultural executive, farmer*

Hawthorne
Roberts, George Christopher *manufacturing executive*

Hayward
Minzner, Dean Frederick *aviation company executive*

Hesperia
Butcher, Jack Robert (Jack Risin) *manufacturing executive*

Hillsborough
Keller, John Francis *retired wine company executive, mayor*
Schapiro, George A. *electronics company executive*

Hollywood
Parks, Robert Myers *appliance manufacturing company executive*

Huntington Beach
Kovach, Ronald *footwear manufacturing executive*
Licata, Paul James *health products executive*
Thomas-Cote, Nancy Denece *office products manufacturing company executive*
Wolzinger, Renah *medical products executive, music company executive*

Indian Wells
Harris, Milton M. *distributing company executive*

PROFESSIONAL INDEX 6063 INDUSTRY: MANUFACTURING

Reed, A(lfred) Byron retired apparel and textile manufacturing company

Indio
York, Douglas Arthur manufacturing and construction company executive

Irvine
Alspach, Philip Halliday manufacturing company executive
Basler, Richard Alan medical consultant
Beckman, Arnold Orville analytical instrument manufacturing company executive
†Click, James H. automotive executive
†Haggerty, Charles A. electronics executive
Herbert, Gavin Shearer health care products company executive
†Manian, Vahid manufacturing operations executive
Ruttencutter, Brian Boyle manufacturing company executive
Salesky, William Jeffrey corporate executive
Stricklin, Guy Michael construction company executive
Thornton, Robert Lee aircraft manufacturing company executive
Webb, Louis automotive company executive
Williams, James E. food products manufacturing company executive
Zack, James G(ordon), Jr. construction claims executive, consultant

La Jolla
Drake, Hudson Billings aerospace and electronics company executive
Geckler, Richard Delph metal products company executive
Stevens, Paul Irving manufacturing company executive
Todd, Harry Williams aircraft propulsion system company executive

La Mesa
Bourke, Lyle James electronics company executive, small business owner
Reiff, Theodore Curtis construction executive

La Puente
Hitchcock, Fritz automotive company executive

Lafayette
Lewis, Sheldon Noah technology consultant

Laguna Beach
Bezar, Gilbert Edward retired aerospace company executive, volunteer

Laguna Hills
Rossiter, Bryant William chemistry consultant

Laguna Niguel
Meyers, Theda Maria textile company executive
Nelson, Alfred John retired pharmaceutical company executive

Livermore
Bennett, Alan Jerome electronics executive, physicist

Livingston
Fox, Robert August food company executive

Long Beach
Bos, John Arthur retired aircraft manufacturing executive
Crane, Steven financial company executive
McGuire, James Charles aircraft company executive

Los Alamitos
Hanson, Larry Keith plastics company executive

Los Altos
Beer, Clara Louise Johnson retired electronics executive

Los Angeles
Ash, Roy Lawrence business executive
Borneman, John Paul Jay pharmaceutical executive
Campion, Robert Thomas manufacturing company executive
Davidson, Robert C., Jr. manufacturing executive
Hutchins, Joan Morthland manufacturing executive, farmer
Irani, Ray R. oil and gas and chemical company executive
Johnson, Keith Liddell chemical company executive
Karatz, Bruce E. business executive
Korn, Lester Bernard business executive, diplomat
†Little, Carole women's apparel company executive
Mager, Artur retired aerospace company executive, consultant
Mall, William John, Jr. aerospace executive, retired air force officer
Marciano, Maurice apparel executive
Mathias, Alice Irene health plan company executive
Perry, William Joseph food processing company executive
†Pinkus, Steve roofing contractor
Preston, Martha Sue pharmaceutical company executive
Ramer, Lawrence Jerome corporation executive
Segil, Larraine Diane materials company executive
Settles, F. Stan, Jr. engineering educator, manufacturing executive
Spindler, Paul corporate executive, consultant
Stern, Ruth Szold business executive, artist
Sudarsky, Jerry M. industrialist
Tamkin, S. Jerome business executive, consultant
Watkins, Sydney Lynn pharmaceutical sales consultant
Wyatt, James Luther drapery hardware company executive

Malibu
Krueger, Kenneth John corporate executive, nutritionist, educator
Smith, George Foster retired aerospace company executive

Marina Del Rey
Dankanyin, Robert John international business executive
Goldaper, Gabriele Gay clothing executive, consultant

Mckinleyville
Thueson, David Orel pharmaceutical executive, researcher, educator, writer

Menlo Park
Bremser, George, Jr. electronics company executive
Cook, Paul Maxwell technology company executive
Evans, Bob Overton electronics executive
Schnebly, F(rancis) David aerospace and electronics company executive
Taft, David Dakin chemical executive
Westcott, Brian John manufacturing executive

Mill Valley
Winskill, Robert Wallace manufacturing executive

Milpitas
Berkley, Stephen Mark computer peripherals manufacturing company executive
†Brown, Michael A. computer hardware company executive
Granchelli, Ralph S. company executive
Nishimura, Koichi electronics manufacturing company executive
Roddick, David Bruce construction company executive

Mission Viejo
Faley, Robert Lawrence retired instruments company executive
Gilbert, Heather Campbell manufacturing company executive

Monrovia
Adler, Fred Peter electronics company executive

Montebello
Meeker, Arlene Dorothy Hallin (Mrs. William Maurice Meeker) manufacturing company executive

Montecito
Meghreblian, Robert Vartan manufacturing executive, physicist

Moorpark
Kavli, Fred manufacturing executive

Mountain View
†Beaudry, Guy G. company executive, lawyer
Casey, Richard L. pharmaceutical executive
Cusumano, James Anthony pharmaceutical company executive
Smith, Lonnie Max diversified industries executive

Newport Beach
Bennett, Bruce W. construction company executive, civil engineer
Chihorek, John Paul electronics company executive
Crean, John C. retired housing and recreational vehicles manufacturing company executive
Jones, Roger Wayne electronics executive
†Laidlaw, Victor D. construction executive
Rogers, Robert Reed manufacturing company executive

North Hills
Boeckmann, H. F. automotive executive

Northridge
dePaolis, Potito Umberto food company executive

Oakland
Koplin, Donald Leroy health products executive, consumer advocate
Saunders, Ward Bishop, Jr. retired aluminum company executive
Sidney, William Wright retired aerospace company executive
Sullivan, G. Craig household products executive

Oceanside
Garruto, John Anthony cosmetics executive

Ojai
Weill, Samuel, Jr. automobile company executive

Ontario
Carlson, Ralph William, Jr. food products company executive

Orange
Roden, Donald R. medical products executive

Oxnard
Poole, Henry Joe, Jr. business executive

Palm Desert
Gullander, Werner Paul retired consultant, retired corporate executive

Palo Alto
Chow, Winston engineering research executive
DeLustro, Frank Anthony biomedical company executive, research immunologist
Early, James Michael electronics research consultant
Goff, Harry Russell retired manufacturing company executive
Halperin, Robert Milton retired electrical machinery company executive
Hewlett, William (Redington) manufacturing company executive, electrical engineer
Johnson, Horace Richard electronics company executive
Kennedy, W(ilbert) Keith, Jr. electronics company executive
Kung, Frank F. biotechnology and life sciences venture capital investor
Lau, John Hon Shing manufacturing executive
Mario, Ernest pharmaceutical company executive
Neil, Gary Lawrence pharmaceutical company research executive, biochemical pharmacologist
Smith, Pamela Iris consulting company executive
Staprans, Armand electronics executive
Watkins, Dean Allen electronics executive, educator
†Whitfield, Roy A. pharmaceutical executive

Palos Verdes Estates
Mackenbach, Frederick W. welding products manufacturing company executive

Palos Verdes Peninsula
Grant, Robert Ulysses retired manufacturing company executive
Leone, William Charles retired manufacturing executive
Pfund, Edward Theodore, Jr. electronics company executive
Thomas, Hayward manufacturing company executive
Wilson, Theodore Henry retired electronics company executive, aerospace engineer

Pasadena
Caldwell, William Mackay, III business executive
Chamberlain, Willard Thomas retired metals company executive
Falick, Abraham Johnson printing company executive
Marlen, James S. chemical-plastics-building materials manufacturing company executive
Miller, Charles Daly self-adhesive materials company executive
Neal, Philip Mark diversified manufacturing executive
Smith, Howard Russell manufacturing company executive
Tollenaere, Lawrence Robert retired industrial products company executive

Pebble Beach
Rivette, Gerard Bertram manufacturing company executive

Piedmont
Solomon, Neal Edward management consultant, executive recruiter, social theorist, author

Pleasanton
Weiss, Robert Stephen medical manufacturing company financial executive

Portola Valley
Graham, William James packaging company executive
Millard, Stephens Fillmore electronics company executive
Purl, O. Thomas retired electronics company executive

Ramona
Vaughn, Robert Lockard aerospace and astronautics company executive

Rancho Cordova
†Martin, Rafael M., Sr. construction company executive

Rancho Dominguez
Janura, Jan Arol apparel manufacturing executive

Rancho Mirage
Foster, David Ramsey soap company executive
Greenbaum, James Richard liquor distributing company executive, real estate developer

Rancho Murieta
Irelan, Robert Withers retired metal products executive

Rancho Santa Fe
Jordan, Charles Morrell retired automotive designer
Step, Eugene Lee retired pharmaceutical company executive

Redding
Emmerson, Red sawmill owner
†Shea, John F. construction executive, contractor

Redlands
Skomal, Edward Nelson aerospace company executive, consultant

Redondo Beach
Kagiwada, Reynold Shigeru advanced technology manager
Sabin, Jack Charles engineering and construction firm executive

Redwood City
Tooley, Terry L(ee) software company executive
Wang, Chen Chi electronics company, real estate, finance company, investment services, and international trade executive

Rescue
Ackerly, Wendy Saunders construction company executive

Richmond
Dolberg, David Spencer business executive, lawyer, scientist
Kaune, James Edward ship repair company executive, former naval officer

Riverside
Kummer, Glenn F. manufactured housing executive

Sacramento
Aldrich, Thomas Albert former brewing executive, consultant
Baccigaluppi, Roger John agricultural company executive
Mack, Edward Gibson retired business executive

Salinas
Taylor, Steven Bruce agriculture company executive

San Bruno
Corbett, Gerard Francis electronics executive

San Carlos
Gutow, Bernard Sidney packaging manufacturing company executive

San Clemente
Clark, Earnest Hubert, Jr. tool company executive

San Diego
Baird, Mellon Campbell, Jr. electronics industry executive
†Barnhart, Douglas E. construction company executive
Cobianchi, Thomas Theodore engineering and marketing executive, educator
Darmstandler, Harry Max real estate executive, retired air force officer
Devine, Brian Kiernan pet food and supplies company executive
Duddles, Charles Weller food company executive
Garcia, Stephanie Brown aerospace company pricing manager
Goode, John Martin manufacturing company executive
Ivans, William Stanley electronics company executive
Jones, Ronald H. computer information systems executive
Keith, Norman Thomas aerospace company administrator
Lewis, Alan James pharmaceutical executive, pharmacologist
Maier, Paul Victor pharmaceutical executive
Nassif, Thomas Anthony business executive, former ambassador
Piskor, Chrystal Lea service company owner
Ray, Gene Wells industrial executive
Rice, Clare I. electronics company executive
Tidwell, Geoffrey Morgan medical company executive

San Francisco
Broadway, Nancy Ruth landscape design and construction company executive, consultant, model and actress
Chiaverini, John Edward construction company executive
Clark, Richard Ward trust company executive, consultant
Gaut, Norman Eugene software firm executive
Grubb, David H. construction company executive
Haas, Robert Douglas apparel manufacturing company executive
Hull, Cordell William business executive
James, George Barker, II apparel industry executive
Jewett, George Frederick, Jr. forest products company executive
Kreitzberg, Fred Charles construction management company executive
Marcus, Robert aluminum company executive
Merrill, Harvie Martin manufacturing executive
Monson, Arch, Jr. fire alarm manufacturing company executive
Nicholson, William Joseph forest products company executive
Pulido, Mark A. pharmaceutical and cosmetics company executive
Shackley, Douglas John fire alarm company executive
Thacher, Carter Pomeroy diversified manufacturing company executive
Wertheimer, Robert E. paper company executive
Wilson, Ian Robert food company executive
Zellerbach, William Joseph retired paper company executive

San Jose
Faggin, Federico electronics executive
Hill, Anna Marie manufacturing executive
Hind, Harry William pharmaceutical company executive
Jacobson, Raymond Earl electronics company entrepreneur and executive
Leavy, Paul Matthew management consultant
Pausa, Clements Edward electronics company executive
Rosendin, Raymond Joseph electrical contracting company executive
Schroeder, William John electronics executive
Scifres, Donald Ray semiconductor laser, fiber optics and electronics company executive
Smith, Rodney electronics executive
Steinberg, Charles Allan electronics manufacturing company executive

San Luis Obispo
Sullivan, Thomas James retired manufacturing company executive

San Marcos
Andersen, Robert health products, business executive

San Mateo
Graham, Howard Holmes financial executive
Grammater, Rudolf Dimitri retired construction executive
Rollo, F. David hospital management company executive, health care educator

San Pedro
†Berg, Deborah Jean construction management owner

Santa Ana
Baugh, Coy Franklin corporate executive
Hoops, Alan health care company executive
Yuen, Andy Tak Sing electronics executive

Santa Barbara
Blasingame, Benjamin Paul electronics company executive
Bongiorno, James William electronics company executive
Potter, David Samuel former automotive company executive
Prindle, William Roscoe consultant, retired glass company executive
Silverander, Carol Weinstock manufacturing executive
Zaleski, James Vincent electronics executive

Santa Clara
Elkus, Richard J., Jr. electronics company executive
Grove, Andrew S. electronics company executive
Halla, Brian electronics company executive
House, David L. electronics components company executive
Moore, Gordon E. electronics company executive
Morgan, James C. electronics executive
Stockton, Anderson Berrian electronics company executive, consultant, genealogist

Santa Cruz
Marks, Peter Amasa technical consulting company administrator

Santa Fe Springs
Lovatt, Arthur Kingsbury, Jr. *manufacturing company executive*

Santa Monica
Deckert, Harlan Kennedy, Jr. *manufacturing company official*
O'Gara, Barbara Ann *soap company executive*
Rive, Sarelle Roselyn *retired manufacturing company executive*

Saratoga
Houston, Joseph Brantley, Jr. *optical instrument company executive*
Reagan, Joseph Bernard *retired aerospace executive, management consultant*

Sausalito
Katz, Bruce R. *company executive*

Seal Beach
Beall, Donald Ray *multi-industry high-technology company executive*

Sherman Oaks
Reiner, Thomas Karl *manufacturing company executive*

Simi Valley
Weiser, Paul David *manufacturing company executive*

Solana Beach
Arledge, Charles Stone *former aerospace executive, entrepreneur*
Brody, Arthur *industrial executive*
Derbes, Daniel William *manufacturing executive*

South Pasadena
White-Thomson, Ian Leonard *mining company executive*

Sun Valley
†Kamins, Philip E. *diversified manufacturing company executive*

Sunnyvale
Alich, John Arthur, Jr. *manufacturing company executive*
Evans, Barton, Jr. *analytical instrument company executive*
Fairweather, Edwin Arthur *electronics company executive*
Green, Marjorie *automotive distribution, import and manufacturing company executive*
Kempf, Martine *voice control device manufacturing company executive*
Lewis, John Clark, Jr. *manufacturing company executive*
Sanders, Walter Jeremiah, III *electronics company executive*
Simon, Ralph E. *electronics executive*
Woolsey, Roy Blakeney *electronics company executive*

Tarzana
†Haberkorn, John G. *small business owner*

Thousand Oaks
Binder, Gordon M. *health and medical products executive*

Torrance
†Burnham, Daniel Patrick *manufacturing company executive*
Lee, James King *technology corporation executive*
Mann, Michael Martin *electronics company executive*
Perrish, Albert *steel company executive*

Tustin
Hester, Norman Eric *chemical company technical executive, chemist*

Ukiah
McAllister, (Ronald) Eric *pharmaceutical executive, physician, software developer*

Universal City
Kay, Kenneth Jeffrey *entertainment company executive*

Upland
Goodman, John M. *construction executive*
Porrero, Henry, Jr. *construction company executive*

Valley Ford
†Clowes, Garth Anthony *electronics executive, consultant*

Walnut Creek
Hamlin, Kenneth Eldred, Jr. *retired pharmaceutical company executive*
Palmer, Vincent Allan *construction consultant*
Shastid, Jon Barton *wine company executive*

Watsonville
Solari, R. C. *retired heavy construction company executive*
†Watts, David H. *construction company executive*

West Sacramento
Teel, Michael J. *supermarket chain executive*

Westlake Village
Colburn, Keith W. *electronics executive*
DeLorenzo, David A. *food products executive*
Troxell, Lucy Davis *consulting firm executive*
Weisman, Martin Jerome *manufacturing company executive*

Willits
Handley, Margie Lee *business executive*

Woodland Hills
Firestone, Morton H. *business management executive*
Halamandaris, Harry *aerospace executive*
Hoch, Orion Lindel *corporate executive*

Morishita, Akihiko *trading company executive*

Woodside
Gates, Milo Sedgwick *retired construction company executive*

Yorba Linda
Forth, Kevin Bernard *beverage distributing industry consultant*

COLORADO

Arvada
Holden, George Fredric *brewing company executive, policy specialist, author*

Aspen
Hansen, Steven Alan *construction executive*

Boulder
Clark, Melvin Eugene *chemical company executive*
Malone, Michael William *electronics executive, software engineer*
Mancino, John Gregory *software company executive*
Secunda, David Abraham *outdoor products sales executive*

Broomfield
Sissel, George Allen *manufacturing executive*

Colorado Springs
Cimino, Jay *automotive company executive*
Ehrhorn, Richard William *electronics company executive*
Robinson, Robert James *retired manufacturing executive*
Robinson, Ronald Alan *manufacturing executive*

Denver
†Alvarado, Linda G. *construction company executive*
Cooper, Larry S. *carpet industry consultant*
Gates, Charles Cassius *rubber company executive*
Hohner, Kenneth Dwayne *retired fodder company executive*
Johnson, James Gibson, Jr. *community recycling specialist*
Lee, Richard Kenneth *building products company executive*
Livingston, Johnston Redmond *manufacturing executive*
Marcum, Walter Phillip *manufacturing executive, heavy*
Martin, J. Landis *manufacturing company executive, lawyer*
Perlmutter, Leonard Michael *concrete construction company executive*
Shreve, Theodore Norris *construction company executive*
Weil, Jack Baum *clothing manufacturing company executive*

Englewood
†Chavez, Lloyd G. *automotive executive*
Mahoney, Gerald Francis *manufacturing company executive*
Runice, Robert E. *retired corporate executive*
Saliba, Jacob *manufacturing executive*

Estes Park
Arnold, Leonard J. *construction executive*

Glendale
Childs, John David *computer hardware and services company executive*

Golden
Coors, William K. *brewery executive*
Woods, Sandra Kay *manufacturing executive*

Greeley
Morgensen, Jerry Lynn *construction company executive*

Highlands Ranch
Breuer, Werner Alfred *retired plastics company executive*

Lakewood
Heath, Gary Brian *manufacturing firm executive, engineer*
Rosa, Fredric David *construction company executive*

Littleton
Gertz, David Lee *homebuilding company executive*
Plusk, Ronald Frank *manufacturing company executive*
Price, Gayl Baader *residential construction company administrator*

Lone Tree
Bauer, Randy Mark *management training firm executive*

Monument
Karasa, Norman Lukas *home builder, developer, geologist*

Morrison
Routson, Clell Dennis *manufacturing company executive*

Snowmass Village
Mattis, Louis Price *pharmaceutical and consumer products company executive*

CONNECTICUT

Bloomfield
Kaman, Charles Huron *diversified technologies corporation executive*

Branford
McCurdy, Larry Wayne *automotive parts company executive*

Bridgeport
Semple, Cecil Snowdon *retired manufacturing company executive*

Bristol
Barnes, Carlyle Fuller *manufacturing executive*
Barnes, Wallace *manufacturing executive*

Broad Brook
Kement, Isabella Viniconis *retired construction company executive*

Danbury
Baker, Leonard Morton *manufacturing company executive*
Lichtenberger, H(orst) William *chemical company executive*
Soviero, Joseph C. *chemical company executive*

Darien
Britton, Robert Austin *manufacturing company executive*
Dordelman, William Forsyth *food company executive*
Sprole, Frank Arnott *retired pharmaceutical company executive, lawyer*
Ziegler, William, III *diversified industry executive*

East Hartford
Zampiello, Richard Sidney *metals and trading company executive*

Enfield
Dyer, Joseph Edward *company executive*

Fairfield
Bunt, James Richard *electric company executive*
Harkrader, Milton Keene, Jr. *corporate executive*
Levine, Stanley Walter *chemical company executive*
Sutphen, Harold Amerman, Jr. *retired paper company executive*
Welch, John Francis, Jr. (Jack Welch) *electrical manufacturing company executive*

Farmington
Hermann, Robert Jay *manufacturing company engineering executive, consultant*
Moran, John Joseph *retired food and beverage company executive*

Greenwich
Barber, Charles Finch *retired metals company executive, financial services company executive*
Cameron, Dort *electronics executive*
Case, Richard Paul *electronics executive*
Combe, Ivan DeBlois *drug company executive*
Dettmer, Robert Gerhart *retired beverage company executive*
Dorme, Patrick John *electronic company executive*
Holten, John V. *food products executive*
Ix, Robert Edward *food company executive*
Kelly, David Austin *investment counselor*
Mead, Dana George *diversified industrial manufacturing company executive*
Squier, David Louis *manufacturing executive*
Wearly, William Levi *business executive*

Hartford
Clear, Albert F., Jr. *retired hardware manufacturing company executive*
David, George Alfred Lawrence *industrial company executive*
Raffay, Stephen Joseph *manufacturing company executive*

Madison
Golembeski, Jerome John *wire and cable company executive*

Meriden
Reitz, H(oward) Wesley *construction company executive*

Middletown
Gerber, Murray A. *molding manufacturing company executive*
Smith, Brian Condray *manufacturing executive*

Milford
Hanlon, James Allison *confectionery products company executive*

Naugatuck
Flannery, Joseph Patrick *manufacturing company executive*

New Britain
Weddle, Stephen Shields *manufacturing company executive*

New Canaan
Bartlett, Dede Thompson *company executive*
Burns, Ivan Alfred *grocery products and industrial company executive*
Hodgson, Richard *electronics company executive*
Kennedy, John Raymond *pulp and paper company executive*
Oatway, Francis Carlyle *corporate executive*
Rutledge, John William *former watch company executive*
Sachs, John Peter *carbon company executive*

Newtown
Farrell, Edgar Henry *building components manufacturing executive, lawyer*

North Branford
Mead, Lawrence Myers, Jr. *retired aerospace executive*

North Haven
Seton, Fenmore Roger *manufacturing company executive, civic worker*

Norwalk
Griffin, Donald Wayne *diversified chemical company executive*
Harris, Holton Edwin *plastics machinery manufacturing executive*

Mintz, Lenore Chaice (Lea Mintz) *personnel company executive*
Peltz, Alan Howard *manufacturing company executive*
Ruggiero, Anthony William *chemical company executive*
Vanderbilt, Hugh Bedford, Sr. *mineral and chemical company executive*

Old Greenwich
Mc Donough, Richard Doyle *retired paper company executive*
Rukeyser, Robert James *manufacturing executive*
Viscardi, Peter G. *consumer products and services executive*

Old Saybrook
Huftalen, Lisa Freeman *corporate executive, graphic designer*

Orange
Randall, Arthur Raymond *building contractor*

Plainville
Glassman, Gerald Seymour *metal finishing company executive*

Ridgefield
Knortz, Herbert Charles *retired conglomerate company executive*
Levine, Paul Michael *paper industry executive, consultant*
Sadow, Harvey S. *health care company executive*

Shelton
†Coughlin, Karen A. *health care company executive*

Somers
Blake, Stewart Prestley *retired ice cream company executive*

South Kent
Samartini, James Rogers *retired appliance company executive*

Southport
Wheeler, Wilmot Fitch, Jr. *diversified manufacturing company executive*

Stamford
Allaire, Paul Arthur *office equipment company executive*
Anderson, Susan Stuebing *business equipment company executive*
Burston, Richard Mervin *business executive*
Calarco, Vincent Anthony *specialty chemicals company executive*
Caldwell, Philip *retired automobile manufacturing company executive, retired financial services company executive*
Cassetta, Sebastian Ernest *industry executive*
Coleman, Ernest Albert *plastics and materials consultant*
Evans, Robert Sheldon *manufacturing executive*
Fickenscher, Gerald H. *chemicals company executive*
Filter, E. Margie *business equipment manufacturing executive*
Gladstone, Herbert Jack *manufacturing company executive*
Gross, Ronald Martin *forest products executive*
Hedge, Arthur Joseph, Jr. *corporate executive*
Hollander, Milton Bernard *corporate executive*
Hood, Edward Exum, Jr. *retired electrical manufacturing company executive*
Kingsley, John McCall, Jr. *manufacturing company executive*
Lennard, Gerald *metal products executive*
Maarbjerg, Mary Penzold *office equipment company executive*
Martin, Patrick *business equipment company executive*
Motroni, Hector John *manufacturing executive*
Munera, Gerard Emmanuel *manufacturing company executive*
Nevans, Roy Norman *food products executive, producer*
O'Malley, Thomas D. *diversified company executive*
Parker, Jack Steele *retired manufacturing company executive*
Peterson, Carl Eric *metals company executive, banker*
Silver, R. Philip *metal products executive*

Stratford
Salzberg, Emmett Russell *new product developer*
Weisz, Sandor Ferenc *business machines company executive, industrial designer, educator, consultant*

Thomaston
Mühlanger, Erich *ski manufacturing company executive*

Trumbull
Reeves, Edmund Hoffman, III *food products executive*
Schmitt, William Howard *cosmetics company executive*

Vernon Rockville
McKeever, Brian Edward *general contractor*

Wallingford
Cohen, Gordon S. *health products executive*
Fleming, James Stuart, Jr. *pharmaceutial company manager*

Waterbury
Leever, Harold *chemical company executive*
Luedke, Frederick Lee *manufacturing company executive*
Tomaszek, Thomas Richard *manufacturing executive*

West Hartford
Doran, James Martin *retired food products company executive*

Westport
†Fash, Victoria R. *Healthcare company executive*
McKane, David Bennett *business executive*
Stashower, Michael David *retired manufacturing company executive*

Morris, Gordon James *financial company executive, consultant*
Mullane, John Francis *pharmaceutical company executive*
Pollack, Joseph *diversified company executive*
Roth, James Frank *manufacturing company executive, chemist*
Slocum, Donald Hillman *product development executive*
Venit, William Bennett *electrical products company executive, consultant*

Spring Hill
Martin, Gary J. *retired business executive, mayor*

Stuart
Conklin, George Melville *retired food company executive*
Jaffe, Jeff Hugh *retired food products executive*
Leibson, Irving *retired industrial executive*
McKenna, Sidney F. *retired technical company executive*
Snider, Harlan Tanner *former manufacturing company executive*

Tallahassee
Leeper, Zane H. *company executive, consultant*
Skagfield, Hilmar Sigurdsson *business executive*

Tamarac
Auletta, Joan Miglorisi *construction company executive, mortgage and insurance broker*

Tampa
Brown, Troy Anderson, Jr. *electrical distributing company executive*
Cohen, Frank Burton *wholesale novelty company executive*
Flom, Edward Leonard *retired steel company executive*
Fritzsche, R. Wayne *corporate executive*
Genter, John Robert *grocery industry executive*
Johnson, Ewell Calvin *research and engineering executive*
†McKinney, Patricia J. *automobile company executive*
†Shawkey, Gary Alan *manufacturing executive, consultant*

Tarpon Springs
Jackel, Simon Samuel *food products company executive*
Wilson, Robert William *aerospace/defense systems company executive*

Tequesta
Peterson, James Robert *retired writing instrument manufacturing executive*

Vero Beach
Allik, Michael *diversified industry executive*
Cartwright, Alton Stuart *electrical manufacturing company executive*
Cochrane, William Henry *municipal administration executive*
Furrer, John Rudolf *retired manufacturing business executive*
Janicki, Robert Stephen *retired pharmaceutical company executive*
MacTaggart, Barry *retired corporate executive*
Reed, Sherman Kennedy *chemical consultant*
Ritterhoff, C(harles) William *retired steel company executive*
Wiegner, Edward Alex *multi-industry executive*
Wilcox, Harry Wilbur, Jr. *retired corporate executive*

Village Of Golf
Boer, F. Peter *chemical company executive*

West Palm Beach
Nelson, Richard Henry *manufacturing company executive*
Oppenheim, Justin Sable *business executive*
Saraf, Shevach *electronics executive*
Stern, Harold Peter *business executive*
Vecellio, Leo Arthur, Jr. *construction company executive*

Weston
Casey, George Edward, Jr. *construction executive*

Windermere
Hylton, Hannelore Menke *retired manufacturing executive*

Winter Haven
O'Connor, R. D. *retired health care executive*

Winter Park
Kost, Wayne L. *business executive*

GEORGIA

Alpharetta
Brands, James Edwin *finance executive*

Atlanta
Abrams, Bernard William *construction manufacturing and property development executive*
Abrams, Edward Marvin *construction company executive*
Anderson, Ray C. *carpet company executive*
Benatar, Leo *packaging company executive*
Bevington, E(dmund) Milton *electrical machinery manufacturing company executive*
Boeke, Eugene H., Jr. *construction executive*
Corr, James Vanis *furniture manufacturing executive, investor, lawyer, accountant*
Correll, Alston Dayton, Jr. *forest products company executive*
Edwards, Louis Ward, Jr. *diversified manufacturing company executive*
Emerson, James Larry *beverage company executive*
French, Michael Bruce *beverage company executive*
Ivester, Melvin Douglas *beverage company executive*
Johnston, Summerfield K., Jr. *food products executive*
Kenney, Belinda Jill Forseman *electronics executive*
Kuse, James Russell *chemical company executive*
Lee, R(aymond) William, Jr. *retired apparel company executive*
Liebmann, Seymour W. *construction consultant*
†Love, Gay *manufacturing executive*
Millikan, James Rolens *cleaning service executive, musician, composer*
Mitchell, Stephen Milton *manufacturing executive*
Murphy, James Jeffrey *electronics executive*
Nie, Zenon Stanley *manufacturing company executive*
Petersen-Frey, Roland *manufacturing executive*
Prince, Larry L. *automotive parts and supplies company executive*
Reith, Carl Joseph *apparel industry executive*
Robinson, Jeffery Herbert *design and building company executive*
Schimberg, Henry Aaron *soft drink company executive*
Seretean, Martin B. (Bud Seretean) *carpet manufacturing company executive*
Sutton, Berrien Daniel *beverage company executive*
Thorp, Benjamin A., III *paper manufacturing company executive*

Augusta
Barton, Raymond Oscar, III *concrete company executive*

Baxley
Reddy, Yenamala Ramachandra *metal processing executive*

Brunswick
Brubaker, Robert Paul *food products executive*
Iannicelli, Joseph *chemical company executive, consultant*

Carrollton
Richards, Roy, Jr. *wire and cable manufacturing company executive*

College Park
Fahy, Nancy Lee *food products marketing executive*

Columbus
Andrews, Gerald Bruce *retired textile executive*
Carmack, Comer Aston, Jr. *steel company executive*
Heard, William T. *automotive executive*
Leebern, Donald M. *distilled beverage executive*

Conley
Marcus, James Elbert *manufacturing company executive*

Conyers
Burman, Marsha Linkwald *lighting manufacturing executive, manpower development professional*
Mc Clung, Jim Hill *light manufacturing company executive*

Dalton
Bouckaert, Carl *manufacturing executive*
Shaw, Robert E. *carpeting company executive*

Jasper
Dewey, Edward Allen *retired construction company executive*

Mableton
Brannon, Winona Eileen *electrical contractor*

Macon
Mc Farland, Terry Lynn *construction company executive*

Marietta
Lewis, William Headley, Jr. *manufacturing company executive*

Milledgeville
Williamson, John Thomas, Sr. *minerals company executive*

Monroe
Felker, G(eorge) Stephen *textile company executive*

Moultrie
Vereen, William Jerome *uniform manufacturing company executive*

Norcross
Adams, Kenneth Francis *automobile maufacturing company executive*
Thomas, Robert L. *manufacturing company executive*

Oakwood
Smith, David Claiborne *construction company executive*

Roswell
Diercks, Chester William, Jr. *capital goods manufacturing company executive*
Tucker, Robert Dennard *health care products executive*

Savannah
Cartledge, Raymond Eugene *retired paper company executive*
Davis, Chris *aerospace company executive*
Gillespie, Daniel Curtis, Sr. *retired non-profit company executive, consultant*
Granger, Harvey, Jr. *retired manufacturing company executive*
Peer, George Joseph *metals company executive*
Roth, Richard Harrison *petrochemical inspection company executive*
Scott, Walter Coke *retired sugar company executive, lawyer*
Spitz, Seymour James, Jr. *retired fragrance company executive*
Sprague, William Wallace, Jr. *retired food company executive*

Smyrna
Lubker, John William, II *manufacturing executive, civil engineer*
Mc Kenzie, Harold Cantrell, Jr. *retired manufacturing executive*

Thomasville
Flowers, Langdon Strong *foods company executive*
Flowers, William Howard, Jr. *food company executive*
Mc Mullian, Amos Ryals *food company executive*

West Point
Glover, Clifford Clarke *retired construction company executive*

HAWAII

Honolulu
Couch, John Charles *diversified company executive*
Gary, James Frederick *business and energy advising company executive*
Hughes, Robert Harrison *former agricultural products executive*
Loeffler, Richard Harlan *retail and technology company executive*
Usui, Leslie Raymond *retired clothing executive*

Papaikou
Andrasick, James Stephen *agribusiness company executive*
Buyers, John William Amerman *agribusiness and specialty foods company executive*

IDAHO

Boise
Appleton, Steven R. *electronics executive*
Beebe, Stephen A. *agricultural products company executive*
Cleary, Edward William *retired diversified forest products company executive*
Harad, George Jay *manufacturing company executive*
Kemp, J. Robert *beef industry consultant, food company executive*
Littman, Irving *forest products company executive*
McClary, James Daly *retired contractor*
Michael, Gary G. *retail supermarket and drug chain executive*
Sullivan, James Kirk *retired forest products company executive*

Hayden Lake
Wogsland, James Willard *retired heavy machinery manufacturing executive*

Salmon
Snook, Quinton *construction company executive*

ILLINOIS

Abbott Park
Coughlan, Gary Patrick *pharmaceutical company executive*
Lussen, John Frederick *pharmaceutical laboratory executive*
†Robbins, Paul LaVerne *pharmaceutical executive*
Young, Jay Maitland *product manager health care products*

Addison
Brunken, Gerald Walter, Sr. *manufacturing company executive*
Nedza, Sandra Louise *manufacturing executive*

Arlington Heights
Church, Herbert Stephen, Jr. *retired construction company executive*
Hughes, John *chemical company executive*
Li, Norman N. *chemicals executive*

Aurora
Belcher, La Jeune *automotive parts company executive*
†Cano, Juventino *manufacturing company executive*

Barrington
Furst, Warren Arthur *retired holding company executive*
Kroha, Bradford King *electronics manufacturing corporation executive*

Bartonville
Graves, Carol Kenney *construction company executive*

Bedford Park
Wenstrup, H. Daniel *chemical company executive*

Belvidere
Britt, Ronald Leroy *manufacturing company executive*

Bloomington
Hoyt, Don, Sr. *home builder, former association executive*

Bourbonnais
Bahls, Gene Charles *agricultural products company executive*

Buffalo Grove
Wigodner, Byron I. *pharmaceutical executive*

Calumet City
Self, Madison Allen *chemical company executive*

Carbondale
Riley, Peter Christopher *aeronautics company official*

Champaign
Lyon, James Cyril *chemical society executive*
Richards, Daniel Wells *company executive*

Chester
Welge, Donald Edward *food manufacturing executive*

Chicago
Barber, Edward Bruce *medical products executive*
Borenstine, Alvin Jerome *search company executive*
Brake, Cecil Clifford *retired diversified manufacturing executive*
Bryan, John Henry *food and consumer products company executive*
Burt, Robert Norcross *diversified manufacturing company executive*
Callahan, Michael J. *chemicals and manufacturing company executive*
Conant, Howard Rosset *steel company executive*
Cooper, Charles Gilbert *toiletries and cosmetics company executive*
Cotter, Daniel A. *diversified company executive*
Covalt, Robert Byron *chemicals executive*
Crawford, William F. *corporate executive, consultant*
Crown, Lester *manufacturing company executive*
Darnall, Robert J. *steel company executive*
Donnelley, James Russell *printing company executive*
Drexler, Richard Allan *manufacturing company executive*
Eastman, Dean Eric *science research executive*
Falkof, Melvin Milton *food products executive*
Francois, William Armand *packaging company executive, lawyer*
Giesen, Richard Allyn *business executive*
Gordon, Ellen Rubin *candy company executive*
Haas, Howard Green *retired bedding manufacturing company executive*
Hamister, Donald Bruce *retired electronics company executive*
Harris, Irving Brooks *cosmetics executive*
Hatton, Stephen Barth *chemical company executive, information executive*
Holland, Eugene, Jr. *lumber company executive*
Horne, John R. *farm equipment company executive*
Jezuit, Leslie James *manufacturing company executive*
Kelly, Gerald Wayne *chemical coatings company executive*
Kirby, William Joseph *corporation executive*
Kuchta, John Albert *manufacturing executive*
Lannert, Robert Cornelius *manufacturing company executive*
Lennes, Gregory *manufacturing and financing company executive*
Lichten, Nancy G. *chemical company executive*
Linde, Ronald Keith *corporate executive, private investor*
†Mason, Earl Leonard *food products executive*
McKee, Keith Earl *manufacturing technology executive*
Murphy, Michael Emmett *retired food company executive*
Nichol, Norman J. *manufacturing executive*
Parrish, Overton Burgin, Jr. *pharmaceutical corporation executive*
Patel, Homi Burjor *apparel company executive*
Pritzker, Robert Alan *manufacturing company executive*
Richards, Linda *pharmaceutical company executive*
Rollhaus, Philip Edward, Jr. *manufacturing company executive*
Rosenberg, Gary Aron *real estate development executive, lawyer*
Schmitz, Edward Henry *distribution company executive*
Schwartz, Charles Phineas, Jr. *financial and business consultant, lawyer*
Smithburg, William Dean *food manufacturing company executive, retired*
Sopranos, Orpheus Javaras *manufacturing company executive*
Stack, Stephen S. *manufacturing company executive*
Steinfeld, Manfred *furniture manufacturing executive*
Stewart, S. Jay *chemical company executive*
Stone, Alan *container company executive*
Stone, Roger Warren *container company executive*
Stotler, Edith Ann *grain company executive*
Strubel, Richard Perry *manufacturing company executive*
Toll, Daniel Roger *corporate executive, civic leader*
Wellington, Robert Hall *manufacturing company executive*
Williams, Richard Lucas, III *electronics company executive, lawyer*
Yapoujian, Nerses Nick *manufacturing executive*
Zeid, Philip L. *metal recycling executive*
Zimny, Robert Walter *metal processing executive*

Crystal Lake
Althoff, J(ames) L. *construction company executive*
Anderson, Lyle Arthur *manufacturing company executive*
Pearson, Nels Kenneth *retired manufacturing company executive*
Smyth, Joseph Vincent *manufacturing company executive*

Darien
†Beardon, Richard *beverage company executive*

Decatur
Andreas, Glenn Allen, Jr. *agricultural company executive*
Kraft, Burnell D. *agricultural products company executive*
Staley, Henry Mueller *manufacturing company executive*

Deerfield
Graham, William B. *pharmaceutical company executive*
Loucks, Vernon R., Jr. *medical technologies executive*
Marsh, Miles L. *paper company executive*
Ringler, James M. *cookware company executive*
Wolf, Andrew *food manufacturing company executive*
Zywicki, Robert Albert *electrical distribution company executive*

Dekalb
Bickner, Bruce *food products executive*
Troyer, Alvah Forrest *seed corn company executive, plant breeder*

Des Plaines
Carroll, Barry Joseph *manufacturing and real estate executive*
Frank, James S. *automotive executive*
Larrimore, Randall Walter *manufacturing company executive*

Meinert, John Raymond *clothing manufacturing and retailing executive, investment banker*

Downers Grove
†Cantu, Carlos *holding company executive*
Kellum, Carmen Kaye *apparel company executive*

Dunlap
Leetz, John Richard *health care executive*

Elgin
Wilson, Robert Byron *manufacturing executive*

Elk Grove Village
Field, Larry *paper company executive*
Nadig, Gerald George *manufacturing executive*

Elmhurst
Duchossois, Richard Louis *manufacturing executive, racetrack executive*

Evanston
†Goldman, Lawrence H. *construction company executive*

Franklin Park
Dean, Howard M., Jr. *food company executive*
Simpson, Michael *metals service center executive*

Genoa
Naden, Vernon Dewitt *manufacturing executive*

Glen Ellyn
Cvengros, Joseph Michael *manufacturing company executive*

Glencoe
Hickey, John Thomas *retired electronics company executive*

Glenview
Farrell, W. James *manufacturing company executive*
Nichols, John Doane *diversified manufacturing corporation executive*
Ptak, Frank S. *manufacturing executive*
Smith, Harold B. *manufacturing executive*
Winett, Samuel Joseph *manufacturing company executive*

Grayslake
Johnson, Margaret H *welding company executive*

Highland Park
Rudo, Milton *retired manufacturing company executive, consultant*
Smith, Malcolm Norman *manufacturing company executive*

Hinsdale
Gallagher, John Pirie *retired corporation executive*
Lowenstine, Maurice Richard, Jr. *retired steel executive*

Hoffman Estates
Dennis, Steven P. *retail executive*
Nicholas, Arthur Soterios *manufacturing company executive*

Huntley
Plunkett, Melba Kathleen *manufacturing company executive*

Indianhead Park
Frisque, Alvin Joseph *retired chemical company executive*

Itasca
Boler, John *manufacturing executive*
Ellis, Harold Donald *auto repair company executive*
Garratt, Reginald George *electronics executive*

Kenilworth
Weiner, Joel David *retired consumer packaged goods products executive*

Kildeer
Harrod, Scott *consulting manufacturing executive*

La Grange
Hubert, Jean-Luc *chemicals executive*

Lake Forest
Bernthal, Harold George *healthcare company executive*
Brown, Sharon Gail *company executive, consultant*
Burnham, Duane Lee *retired pharmaceutical company executive*
Deters, James Raymond *retired manufacturing and services company executive*
Dur, Philip Alphonse *automotive executive, retired naval officer*
Hamilton, Peter Bannerman *business executive, lawyer*
Hammar, Lester Everett *health care manufacturing company executive*
Holzman, Esther Rose *perfume company executive*
Hough, Richard T. *chemical company executive*
Keyser, Richard Lee *distribution company executive*
Larsen, Peter N. *leisure products manufacturing executive*
Larson, Peter N. *company executive*
O'Mara, Thomas Patrick *manufacturing company executive*
Reichert, Jack Frank *manufacturing company executive*

Lake Villa
Anderson, Milton Andrew *chemical executive*

Lansing
Stuart, Robert *container manufacturing executive*

Lemont
Dillon, Phillip Michael *construction company executive*

Libertyville
Baske, C. Alan *manufacturing company executive*

Bell, Robert Matthew *pharmaceutical company consultant*
Burrows, Brian William *research and development manufacturing executive*
Rancourt, John Herbert *pharmaceutical company executive*

Lincolnshire
Bayly, George V. *manufacturing executive*
Simes, Stephen Mark *pharmaceutical products executive*

Lincolnwood
†Lewis, Harriet Gerber *plumbing fixtures manufacturing company executive*

Lisle
Birck, Michael John *manufacturing company executive, electrical engineer*
Koford, Stuart Keith *electronics executive*
Krehbiel, Frederick August, II *electronics company executive*
Reum, W. Robert *manufacturing executive*

Lombard
Miczuga, Mark Norbert *metal products executive*

Long Grove
Liuzzi, Robert C. *chemical company executive*

Mahomet
Bosworth, Douglas LeRoy *international company executive, educator*

Mc Gaw Park
Knight, Lester B. *healthcare company executive*

Mchenry
McKinley, James Frank, Jr. *manufacturing executive*

Melrose Park
†Bernick, Carol Lavin *corporate executive*
Bernick, Howard Barry *manufacturing company executive*
Cernugel, William John *consumer products and special retail executive*
Douglas, Kenneth Jay *food products executive*
†Lavin, Bernice E. *cosmetics executive*
Shturmakov, Alexander Joseph *automotive industry executive*
Umans, Alvin Robert *manufacturing company executive*

Mokena
Maiotti, Dennis Paul *manufacturing company executive*

Moline
Becherer, Hans Walter *agricultural equipment manufacturing executive*

Mount Prospect
Rogers, Richard F. *construction company executive, architect, engineer*

Mundelein
Mills, James Stephen *medical supply company executive*

Naperville
†Hellmuth, John S. *healthcare executive*
Katai, Andrew Andras *chemical company executive*
Schaack, Philip Anthony *retired beverage company executive*
Wake, Richard W. *food products executive*
Wake, Thomas G. *food products executive*

Niles
†Herb, Marvin J. *food products executive*

Northbrook
Bueche, Wendell Francis *agricultural products company executive*
Fowler, Robert Edward, Jr. *agricultural products company executive*
†Fowler, Robert F., Jr. *chemicals executive*
Green, David *manufacturing company executive*
Harris, Neison *manufacturing company executive*
Lenon, Richard Allen *chemical corporation executive*
Sayatovic, Wayne Peter *manufacturing company executive*
Schmidt, Arthur Irwin *steel fabricating company executive*
Singer, Norman Sol *food products executive, inventor*

Northfield
Carlin, Donald Walter *retired food products executive, consultant*
Hadley, Stanton Thomas *international manufacturing and marketing company executive, lawyer*
Smeds, Edward William *retired food company executive*
Stepan, Frank Quinn *chemical company executive*

Oak Brook
†Greenberg, Jack M. *food products executive*

Oak Park
Burhoe, Brian Walter *automotive service executive*

Oregon
Abbott, David Henry *manufacturing company executive*

Orland Park
Gittelman, Marc Jeffrey *manufacturing and financial executive*
Kahn, Jan Edward *manufacturing company executive*

Palos Park
Nelson, Lawrence Evan *business consultant*

Park Ridge
Bales, Edward Wagner *consultant, former manufacturing executive*
Herting, Robert Leslie *pharmaceutical executive*
Weber, Philip Joseph *retired manufacturing company executive*

Peoria
Fites, Donald Vester *tractor company executive*
Thorstenson, Terry N. *construction equipment company executive*

Prospect Heights
Byrne, Michael Joseph *business executive*

Quincy
Walters, Tom Frederick *manufacturing company official*

Riverwoods
Kushner, Jeffrey L. *manufacturing company executive*

Rockford
Gloyd, Lawrence Eugene *diversified manufacturing company executive*
Horst, Bruce Everett *manufacturing company executive*
Kimball, Donald Robert *food company executive*
O'Donnell, William David *retired construction firm executive*

Rolling Meadows
Brennan, Charles Martin, III *construction company executive*
Buchanan, Richard Kent *electronics company executive*
Cash, Alan Sherwin *electronics assembly specialist*
Kuhar, June Carolynn *retired fiberglass manufacturing company executive*

Rosemont
Isenberg, Howard Lee *manufacturing company executive*

Saint Charles
Stone, John McWilliams, Jr. *electronics executive*

Schaumburg
Dibos, Dennis Robert *electronics industry executive*
Galvin, Christopher B. *electronics company executive*
Galvin, Robert W. *electronics executive*
Tooker, Gary Lamarr *electronics company executive*
Tucker, Frederick Thomas *electronics company executive*

Skokie
Alexander, John Charles *pharmaceutical company executive, physician*
Caldwell, Wiley North *retired distribution company executive*

Sterling
Conway, John Paul *retired steel executive*

Tinley Park
Leeson, Janet Caroline Tollefson *cake specialties company executive*

Union
Perlick, Richard Allan *steel company executive*

Wadsworth
Bannick, Janice Carol *automotive dealerships executive*

Waukegan
Cherry, Peter Ballard *electrical products corporation executive*

Westmont
†Kuhn, Robert Mitchell *rubber company executive*

Wheaton
Spedale, Vincent John *manufacturing executive*

Wheeling
Keats, Glenn Arthur *manufacturing company executive*

Wilmette
Barth, David Keck *industrial distribution industry consultant*
Bro, Kenneth Arthur *plastic manufacturing company executive*
Egloff, Fred Robert *manufacturers representative, writer, historian*
Pearlman, Jerry Kent *electronics company executive*

Winnetka
Gavin, James John, Jr. *diversified company executive*
Hartman, Robert S. *retired paper company executive*
Kennedy, George Danner *chemical company executive*
Menke, Allen Carl *industrial corporation executive*
Puth, John Wells *consulting company executive*

Woodridge
Stall, Alan David *packaging company executive*

INDIANA

Anderson
Carrell, Terry Eugene *manufacturing company executive*

Angola
Young, James E. *business executive, engineer*

Bloomington
Haeberle, William Leroy *corporate director, business educator, entrepreneur*

Bluffton
Lawson, William Hogan, III *electrical motor manufacturing executive*

Brownsburg
Riggs, Anna Claire *metals company executive*

Brownstown
Robertson, Joseph Edmond *grain processing company executive*

Butler
Longardner, Craig Theodor *manufacturing executive*

Carmel
Risdon, Michael Paul *manufacturing executive*
Shoup, Charles Samuel, Jr. *chemicals and materials executive*
Walsh, John Charles *metallurgical company executive*

Chesterton
Brown, Gene W. *steel company executive*

Churubusco
Morgan, Gretna Faye *retired automotive executive*

Columbus
Boll, Charles Raymond *engine company executive*
Henderson, James Alan *engine company executive*
Miller, Joseph Irwin *automotive manufacturing company executive*

Elkhart
Corson, Thomas Harold *manufacturing company executive*
Decio, Arthur Julius *manufacturing company executive*
Groom, Gary Lee *recreational vehicle manufacturing executive*
Holtz, Glenn Edward *band instrument manufacturing executive*
Hunsberger, Ruby Moore *electronics manufacturing corporation executive, religious organization representative*
Kloska, Ronald Frank *manufacturing company executive*
Leader, Christopher Robert *manufacturing executive*
Martin, Rex *manufacturing executive*
Mathias, Margaret Grossman *manufacturing company executive, leasing company executive*
Mischke, Frederick Charles *manufacturing company executive*

Evansville
Koch, Robert Louis, II *manufacturing company executive, mechanical engineer*
Muehlbauer, James Herman *manufacturing executive*

Fairmount
Boswell, Larry Ray *electronics company executive*

Fort Wayne
Burns, Thagrus Asher *manufacturing company executive, former life insurance company executive*
Grogg, Terrie Lynn *factory assembler*
Latz, G. Irving, II *manufacturing company executive*
Marine, Clyde Lockwood *agricultural business consultant*
Molfenter, David P. *electronics executive*
Rifkin, Leonard *metals company executive*

Franklin
Janis, F. Timothy *technology company executive*

Gary
Washington, Wilma Jeanne *business executive*

Goshen
Schrock, Harold Arthur *manufacturing company executive*

Granger
Miller, Callix Edwin *manufacturing executive, consultant*

Greenwood
Smith, Donald Archie *retired religion and business executive, consultant*

Hammond
Ash, Frederick Melvin *manufacturing company executive*

Indianapolis
Be Sant, Craig *company executive*
Bindley, William Edward *pharmaceutical executive*
Burkhart, John *manufacturing company executive*
Carlino, Guy Thomas *construction executive*
Dollens, Ronald W. *pharmaceuticals company executive*
Gay, David Earl *chemicals executive, chemist*
Greer, Charles Eugene *company executive, lawyer*
Harmon, Tim James *construction executive*
Hunt, Robert Chester *construction company executive*
Justice, Brady Richmond, Jr. *medical services executive*
King, J. B. *medical device company executive, lawyer*
Kirkham, James Alvin *manufacturing executive*
Lacy, Andre Balz *industrial executive*
Lanford, Luke Dean *electronics company executive*
Long, William Allan *retired forest products company executive*
†Mays, William G. *chemical company executive*
Mc Farland, H. Richard *food company executive*
Pettinga, Cornelius Wesley *pharmaceutical company executive*
Powdrill, Gary Leo *production operations manager*
Reeve, Ronald Cropper, Jr. *manufacturing executive*
Richmond, James Ellis *restaurant company executive*
Salentine, Thomas James *pharmaceutical company executive*
Smith, K. Clay *machinery transport company executive*
Stewart, Paul Arthur *pharmaceutical company executive*
Tobias, Randall Lee *pharmaceutical company executive*
Tomlinson, Joseph Ernest *manufacturing company executive*
Zapapas, James Richard *pharmaceutical company executive*

Lafayette
Meyer, Brud Richard *retired pharmaceutical company executive*

Loogootee
Burcham, Eva Helen (Pat Burcham) *retired electronics technician*

Middlebury
Guequierre, John Phillip *manufacturing company executive*

Mishawaka
Kapson, Jordan *automotive executive*
Rubenstein, Pamela Silver *precision machinery executive*
Silver, Neil Marvin *manufacturing executive*

Muncie
Fisher, John Wesley *manufacturing company executive*

Munster
Corsiglia, Robert Joseph *electrical construction company executive*
Luerssen, Frank Wonson *retired steel company executive*

Nappanee
Shea, James F. *manufacturing executive*

Nashville
Stackhouse, David William, Jr. *retired furniture systems installation contractor*

Newburgh
Reavis, Hubert Gray, Jr. *metal products executive*

Noblesville
Almquist, Donald John *retired electronics company executive*

Portage
Popp, Joseph Bruce *manufacturing executive*

Seymour
†Rust, Lois *food company executive*

South Bend
Altman, Arnold David *business executive*

South Whitley
†Fox, Alan Hugo *musical instrument manufacturing company executive*

Washington
Graham, David Bolden *food products executive*

Waterloo
Snyder, Joseph James *steel construction company executive*

West Lafayette
Lacci, John *chemical company executive*
St. John, Charles Virgil *retired pharmaceutical company executive*

Zionsville
Schlensker, Gary Chris *landscaping company executive*

IOWA

Birmingham
Goudy, James Joseph Ralph *electronics executive, educator*

Boone
Beckwith, F. W. *food products executive*

Cedar Falls
Silverson, Rex *autos and homes builder, educator*

Davenport
Juckem, Wilfred Philip *manufacturing company executive*

Dubuque
Crahan, Jack Bertsch *manufacturing company executive*
Tully, Thomas Alois *building materials executive, consultant, educator*

Fairfield
Schaefer, Jimmie Wayne, Jr. *agricultural company executive*

Fort Dodge
Tursso, Dennis Joseph *business executive*

Iowa City
Sulg, Madis *corporation executive*

Marion
Starr, Dave *corporate executive*

Marshalltown
Foote, Sherril Lynne *retired manufacturing company technician*

Mason City
Murphy, David McGregor *manufacturing executive*

Muscatine
Dahl, Arthur Ernest *former manufacturing executive, consultant*

New Hampton
Boge, Arnold Joseph *builder, contractor*

Newton
Hadley, Leonard Anson *appliance manufacturing corporation executive*
Ward, Dean Morris *appliance manufacturing executive*
Ward, Lloyd D. *appliance company executive*

Okoboji
Pearson, Gerald Leon *food company executive*

Pella
Farver, Mary Joan *building products company executive*

Saint Ansgar
Kleinworth, Edward J. *agricultural company executive*

Springville
Nyquist, John Davis *retired radio manufacturing company executive*

West Des Moines
Pomerantz, Marvin Alvin *container corporation executive*

KANSAS

Colby
Baldwin, Irene S. *corporate executive, real estate investor*

Dodge City
Chaffin, Gary Roger *business executive*

Goddard
Peterman, Bruce Edgar *aircraft company executive, retired*

Hesston
Yost, Lyle Edgar *farm equipment manufacturing company executive*

Hutchinson
Dick, Harold Latham *manufacturing executive*

Kansas City
Olofson, Tom William *computer executive*

Leawood
Marcy, Charles Frederick *food company executive*

Lenexa
Ascher, James John *pharmaceutical executive*
Pierson, John Theodore, Jr. *manufacturer*

Mcpherson
Darting, Edith Anne *pharmaceutical company administrator*

Mission Hills
Smith, DeLancey Allan *retired business executive*

Overland Park
Callahan, Michael Thomas *construction consultant, lawyer*
Derr, Lee E. *chemical company executive*
Kopac, Andrew Joseph *manufacturing executive*
Randolph, Scott Howard *chemical company executive*

Salina
Cosco, John Anthony *health care executive, educator, consultant*

Shawnee
Goldberg, Nolan Hilliard *automotive company official*

Shawnee Mission
Arneson, George Stephen *manufacturing company executive, management consultant*
Dougherty, Robert Anthony *manufacturing company executive*
Fuller, David Scott *construction and investment company executive*
Gamet, Donald Max *appliance company executive*

Silver Lake
Rueck, Jon Michael *manufacturing executive*

Topeka
Gatewood, Judith Anne *roofing company administrator*
Plummer, Mary Elizabeth *cosmetologist*
Stoner, Leonard D. *automotive parts company executive*

Wichita
Eby, Martin Keller, Jr. *construction company executive*
Fink, Richard H. *manufacturing company executive*
Johnson, George Taylor *training and manufacturing executive*
Loux, Richard Charles *retired research executive, accountant*
Meyer, Russell William, Jr. *aircraft company executive*
Nienke, Steven A. *construction company executive*

KENTUCKY

Bowling Green
Holland, John Ben *clothing manufacturing company executive*

Erlanger
Cuneo, Dennis Clifford *automotive company executive*

Georgetown
Moffat, MaryBeth *automotive company executive*

Lexington
†Shannon, Susan G. *manufacturing company executive*

Louisville
Berry, Phillip Reid *beverage distribution executive*
Bujake, John Edward, Jr. *beverage company executive*
Clayton, Marvin Courtland *engineering, manufacturing sourcing and health wellness consultant*
Heiden, Charles Kenneth *former army officer, metals company executive*
James, Virginia Lynn *contracts executive*
Lunsford, W. Bruce *company executive*

Mountz, Wade *retired health service management executive*
Niblock, William Robert *manufacturing executive*
Rapp, Christian Ferree *textile home furnishings company executive*
Street, William May *beverage company executive*
Vogel, Werner Paul *retired machine company executive*

Morehead
Huber, John Michael *lumber executive*

Murray
Faihst, Michael Ernest *plastics engineer*

Owensboro
Hulse, George Althouse *retired steel company executive*

Rineyville
Jackson, Charles Wayne *food products executive, former telecommunications industry executive*

LOUISIANA

Baton Rouge
Turner, Bert S. *construction executive*

Calhoun
Robbins, Marion LeRon *agricultural research executive*

Lafayette
Mallet, Alexis, Jr. *construction company executive*

Mandeville
Napier, William James, Jr. *marine oil and gas construction consultant*

Many
Byles, Robert Valmore *manufacturing company executive*

Metairie
Newman, Claire Poe *corporate executive*

New Orleans
Collins, Harry David *construction consultant, forensic engineering specialist, mechanical and nuclear engineer, retired army officer*
Cospolich, James Donald *electrical engineering executive, consultant*
Crumley, Martha Ann *company executive*
Deasy, William John *construction, marine dredging, engineering and mining company executive*
Gaubert, Lloyd Francis *shipboard and industrial cable distribution executive*

Slidell
†Stroud, Robert Arlen *medical equipment company executive*

MAINE

Andover
Kaltsos, Angelo John *electronics executive, educator, photographer*

Bath
Simone, Gail Elisabeth *manfacturing administrator*

Ellsworth
Goodyear, Austin *electronics and retail company executive*

Falmouth
Cabot, Lewis Pickering *manufacturing company executive, art consultant*

Kennebunk
Damon, Edmund Holcombe *retired plastics company executive*

New Vineyard
Smith, Frederick Orville, II *wood products manufacturer, retired naval officer*

Pittsfield
†Cianchette, Alton E. *construction company executive*

Portland
Whedon, Ralph Gibbs *manufacturing executive*

South Bristol
Wells, Arthur Stanton *retired manufacturing company executive*

Winthrop
Saunders, Joseph Arthur *office products manufacturing company executive*

MARYLAND

Annapolis
Hyde, Lawrence Henry, Jr. *industrial company executive*

Arbutus
Maloney, Charles Wayne *gunsmith*

Baltimore
Bowe, Peter Armistead *manufacturing executive*
Deoul, Neal *electronics company executive*
Foster, Lester Anderson, Jr. *retired steel company executive*
Glassgold, Israel Leon *construction company executive, engineer, consultant*
Legum, Jeffrey David *automobile company executive*
Reeder, Oliver Howard *paint products manufacturing executive*
Scheeler, Charles *construction company executive*
Strull, Gene *technology consultant, retired electrical manufacturing company executive*

Walker, Kenneth Adley *aluminum fabricating company executive*

Beltsville
Seyfried, Donna Marie *biomedical company executive*

Bethesda
Augustine, Norman Ralph *industrial executive, educator*
Baird, Charles Fitz *retired mining and metals company executive*
Blanchette, Robert Wilfred *business executive, lawyer*
Bregman, Jacob Israel *environmental consulting company executive*
Brunson, Burlie Allen *aerospace executive*
†Choquette, William H. *construction company executive*
Evans, John Vaughan *communications satellite executive, physicist*
Weinberger, Alan David *corporate executive*

Bozman
Peterson, H(arry) William *chemicals executive, consultant*

Burtonsville
Frederick, George Francis *manufacturing executive*

Chevy Chase
Bissinger, Frederick Lewis *retired manufacturing executive, consultant*
Roberts, Clyde Francis *business executive*

Columbia
Levner, Louis Jules *contract administrator*
Peck, Charles Edward *retired construction and mortgage executive*

Easton
Peterson, James Kenneth *manufacturing company executive*

Elkridge
Slatkin, Murray *paint sundry distribution executive*

Frederick
Carnochan, John Low, Jr. *retired aluminum company executive, consultant*

Gaithersburg
Chin, James Ying *corporate executive*
Ewing, Frank Marion *lumber company executive, industrial land developer*
Grecich, Daryl George *marketing communications executive*

Germantown
Hill-Fessenden, Anne Lynn *multi-faceted food and beverage consultant*

La Plata
†Wyman, Kenneth F. *construction executive*

Lutherville
Revelle, Donald Gene *manufacturing and health care company executive, consultant*

Mount Airy
McCoskey, William L. *automotive executive*

Reisterstown
Bond, Nelson Leighton, Jr. *health care executive*

Rockville
Halperin, Jerome Arthur *pharmaceutical executive*

Saint Michaels
Jones, Raymond Edward, Jr. *brewing executive*
Meendsen, Fred Charles *retired food company executive*

Salisbury
Perdue, Franklin P. *retired poultry products company executive*

Severna Park
Kumm, William Howard *energy products company executive*

Silver Spring
Coates, Robert Jay *retired electronic scientist*
Schneider, William Charles *aerospace consultant*

Sparks
Mulligan, Martin Frederick *clothing executive, professional tennis player*

Towson
Day, John Charles *chemical company executive*
Ryker, Norman J., Jr. *retired manufacturing company executive*

Upper Marlboro
Bowles, Liza K. *construction executive*

MASSACHUSETTS

Acton
Wade, Samuel David *medical products company executive*

Attleboro
Hammerle, Fredric Joseph *metal processing executive*
Stahl, Robert Alan *manufacturing executive, consultant*

Barnstable
Langhans, Lester Frank, III *construction company executive*

Bedford
Ellenbogen, S. David *electronics company executive*

Belmont
Lewis, Henry Rafalsky *manufacturing company executive*

Billerica
Gray, Charles Agustus *chemical company research executive*
Kronick, Barry *lumber company executive*
McCaffrey, Robert Henry, Jr. *retired manufacturing company executive*

Boston
Alie, Alleyn A. *construction and engineering company executive*
Bodman, Samuel Wright, III *specialty chemicals and materials company executive*
Chizauskas, Cathleen Jo *manufacturing company executive*
Connell, William Francis *diversified company executive*
Glass, Milton Louis *retired manufacturing company executive*
Hoskins, William Keller *pharmaceutical executive, mediator/arbitrator, lawyer*
Jarvis, Edward Curtis *manufacturing and distribution company executive, international business consultant*
Kames, Kenneth F. *manufacturing company executive*
Leaman, J. Richard, Jr. *paper company executive*
Macomber, John D. *construction executive*
Schorr, Marvin G. *technology company executive*
Spilhaus, Karl Henry *textiles executive, lawyer*
Swift, Humphrey Hathaway *manufacturing executive*
Tremblay, Joan Louise *perishables administrator*
Zabriskie, John L. *healthcare and agricultural products manufacturing company executive*

Boxford
Glass, John Sheldon *manufacturing executive*

Braintree
Latham, Allen, Jr. *manufacturing company consultant*

Brighton
†Yurovich, Daniel J. *manufacturing company executive*

Burlington
Bright, Willard Mead *manufacturing company executive*
Sproull, Robert Fletcher *research and development executive*

Cambridge
Ancona, Henry *software company executive*
Bullock, Francis Jeremiah *pharmaceutical research executive*
†D'Arbeloff, Alexander V. *electronics company executive*
DiCamillo, Gary Thomas *manufacturing executive*
Epstein, Henry David *electronics company executive*
†Fantone, Stephen D. *company executive*
Forney, G(eorge) David, Jr. *retired electronics company executive*
Frosch, Robert Alan *retired automobile manufacturing executive, physicist*
Kalelkar, Ashok Satish *consulting company executive*
Sunderman, Deborah Ann *clothing designer and manufacturer*
Termeer, Henricus Adrianus *biotechnology company executive*

Charlestown
Waldfogel, Morton Sumner *prefabricated housing/plywood company executive*

Chelsea
Dunn, Norman Samuel *plastics and textiles company executive*

Chestnut Hill
Bender, Harold *beverage company consultant*

Cohasset
Rabstejnek, George John *electronics executive*

Danvers
Langford, Dean Ted *lighting and precision materials company executive*
Waite, Charles Morrison *food company executive*

Dedham
Naughton, Marie Ann *corporate executive*

Dennis Port
Hebert, Donna Marie *food product executive*

Easthampton
Perkins, Homer Guy *manufacturing company executive*

Falmouth
Litschgi, Richard John *computer manufacturing company executive*

Framingham
Deutsch, Marshall E(manuel) *medical products company executive, inventor*
Merser, Francis Gerard *manufacturing company executive, consultant*
Silverman, Harold Irving *pharmaceutical executive*
Waters, James Logan *analytical instrument manufacturing executive*

Franklin
Lowrie, Kathryn Yanacek *high technology recruiter*

Gloucester
Lanzkron, Rolf Wolfgang *manufacturing company executive*

Harvard
Matson, Stephen L. *technology industry executive*

Hopkinton
Harris, Jeffrey Sherman *technology company executive*

Ipswich
Barth, Elmer Ernest *wire and cable company executive*

Lexington
Berstein, Irving Aaron *biotechnology and medical technology executive*
Bilow, Howard L. *health care company executive*
Picard, Dennis J. *retired electronics company executive*
Smith, Robert Louis *construction company executive*

Lincoln
Green, David Henry *manufacturing company executive*
Tobin, James Robert *biomedical device manufacturing company executive*

Littleton
Patel, Mahendra Rambhai *electronics executive*

Lowell
Clark, Richard Paul *electronics company executive*

Marblehead
Kleiman, Macklen *manufacturing company executive*
†Thompson, Michael Laurie *food manufacturing executive*
Zeo, Frank James *health products company professional*

Marion
Walsh, William Egan, Jr. *electronics executive*

Marlborough
Otto, Jeffrey Bruce *industrial research and development executive*
Shobert, Benjamin Andrew *manufacturing executive*
Wiedeman, Richard Lawrence *electronics executive*

Methuen
Pollack, Herbert William *electronics executive*

Middleboro
Llewellyn, John Schofield, Jr. *food company executive*

Middleton
Daniels, William Albert *food products executive*

Nantucket
Ingram, George *business executive*

Needham
Kung, Patrick Chung-Shu *biotechnology executive*

Newton
Balsamo, Salvatore Anthony *technical and temporary employment companies executive*
Chubb, Stephen Darrow *medical corporation executive*
Clarkson, Cheryl Lee *healthcare executive*
Gerrity, J(ames) Frank, II *building materials company executive*
Stein, Seymour *electronics scientist*

North Andover
Jannini, Ralph Humbert, III *electronics executive*

Nutting Lake
Furman, John Rockwell *wholesale lumber company executive*

Peabody
†Hedrick, Hunt R(andolph), Jr. *sportswear company official*

Sharon
Paolino, Richard Francis *manufacturing company executive*

Springfield
D'Amour, Donald H. *supermarket chain executive*
Gallup, John Gardiner *retired paper company executive*

Stoughton
Fireman, Paul B. *footwear and apparel company executive*

Sturbridge
Belforte, David Arthur *company president*

Tewksbury
DeMoulas, Telemachus A. *retail grocery company executive*

Waltham
Bernstein, Stanley Joseph *manufacturing executive*
Weinert, Henry M. *biomedical company executive*

Wellesley
Aall, Christian Bergengren *software company executive*
Gailius, Gilbert Keistutis *manufacturing company executive*
Marcus, William Michael *rubber and vinyl products manufacturing company executive*

West Boylston
Cummings, Henry Savage Chase *manufacturing executive*

West Bridgewater
Wyner, Justin L. *laminating company executive*

Westborough
Skates, Ronald Louis *computer manufacturing executive*

Weston
Chu, Jeffrey Chuan *business executive, consultant*
Saad, Theodore Shafick *retired microwave company executive*
Smick, Susan Schnee *tile designer and manufacturer, airline strategic, marketing planner*

Wilbraham
Dailey, Franklyn Edward, Jr. *electronic image technology company executive, analyst, consultant*

Williamstown
McGill, Robert Ernest, III *retired manufacturing company executive*

Wilmington
Altschuler, Samuel *electronics company executive*
Rosenzweig, Mark Richard *semiconductor equipment executive*

Woburn
Cox, Terrence Guy *manufacturing automation executive*

Worcester
Goldberg, Marc Evan *biotechnology executive*
Nelson, John Martin *corporate executive*

Wrentham
Teplow, Theodore Herzl *valve company executive*

MICHIGAN

Addison
Knight, V. C. *manufacturing executive*

Ann Arbor
Decker, Raymond Frank *scientist, technology transfer executive*
Eberbach, Steven John *consumer electronics company executive*
Herzig, David Jacob *pharmaceutical company executive, immunopharmacologist*
Lutz, Robert Anthony *automotive company executive*
Moss, Cruse Watson *automobile company executive*
Oliver, Marguerite Bertoni *food service executive*
Powers, William Francis *automobile manufacturing company executive*
Winbury, Martin Maurice *pharmaceutical executive, educator*

Auburn Hills
Davidson, William M. *diversified company executive, professional basketball executive*
Eaton, Robert James *automotive company executive*
Farrar, Stephen Prescott *glass products manufacturing executive*
†Gerson, Ralph Joseph *corporate executive*
Lapadot, Sonee Spinner *automobile manufacturing company official*
Stegmayer, Joseph Henry *housing industry executive*

Battle Creek
Langbo, Arnold Gordon *food company executive*
McKay, Eugene Henry, Jr. *food company executive*

Bay City
Greve, Lucius, II *metals company executive*

Benton Harbor
Fernando, J. Anicetus P. *manufacturing executive*
Hopp, Daniel Frederick *manufacturing company executive, lawyer*
Whitwam, David Ray *appliance manufacturing company executive*

Benzonia
Frostic, Gwen *paper company executive*

Beulah
Edwards, Wallace Winfield *retired automotive company executive*

Birmingham
Nicholson, Robert D. *manufacturing executive*
VanDeusen, Bruce Dudley *company executive*

Bloomfield Hills
Frey, Stuart Macklin *automobile manufacturing company executive*
Hagenlocker, Edward E. *retired automobile company executive*
Lauer, Clinton Dillman *automotive executive*
Maxwell, Jack Erwin *manufacturing company executive*

Brighton
Crabtree, John David *manufacturing company executive*

Cass City
Althaver, Lambert Ewing *manufacturing company executive*
Walpole, Robert *heavy manufacturing executive*

Dearborn
Avila, Fernando *automotive company executive*
Baldwin, Charles Franklin, Jr. *automotive executive*
Bixby, Harold Glenn *manufacturing company executive*
Ford, William Clay *automotive company executive*
Lundy, J(oseph) Edward *retired automobile company executive*
Milton, Robert Mitchell *chemical company executive*
†Nasser, Jacques *automotive company executive*
Scott, David William *automotive company executive*
Trotman, Alexander J. *automobile manufacturing company executive*

Detroit
†Aguirre, Pamela A. *manufacturing executive*
Chapin, Roy Dikeman, Jr. *automobile company executive*
Dauch, Richard E. *automobile manufacturing company executive*
†Dodd, Geralda *metal products executive*
Engelhardt, Regina *cosmetologist, artist, art restorer*
Ferguson, James Peter *distilling company executive*
Kalman, Andrew *manufacturing company executive*
Kantrowitz, Jean Rosensaft *research program administrator medical products*
Levy, Edward Charles, Jr. *manufacturing company executive*
Rakolta, John, Sr. *construction company executive*
Smith, John Francis, Jr. *automobile company executive*
Stella, Frank Dante *food service and dining equipment executive*

East Lansing
Stanley, Kurt Edward *auto parts executive*

Farmington Hills
Holmes, Tyrone Anthony *performance consulting company executive, educator*
Landry, Thomas Henry *construction executive*
Mackey, Robert Joseph *business executive*

Flint
Goodstein, Sanders Abraham *scrap iron company executive*
Spencer, Dianne S. *electronics executive, educator*

Galesburg
Lawrence, John Warren *business and broadcasting executive*

Grand Haven
Sabolcik, Gene *manufacturing executive*

Grand Rapids
Baker, Hollis MacLure *furniture manufacturing company executive*
Dykstra, William Dwight *business executive, consultant*
Hackett, James P. *manufacturing executive*
Helder, Bruce Alan *metal products executive*
Hooker, Robert *automotive executive*
Pew, Robert Cunningham, II *office equipment manufacturing company executive*
Rougier-Chapman, Alwyn Spencer Douglas *furniture manufacturing company executive*
Van Andel, Betty Jean *retired direct selling company executive*
Woodrick, Robert *food products executive*

Grawn
Clous, James M. *electrical equipment company executive, engineer*

Grosse Pointe
Krebs, William Hoyt *company executive, industrial hygienist*
Obolensky, Marilyn Wall (Mrs. Serge Obolensky) *metals company executive*
Valk, Robert Earl *corporate executive*
Wilkinson, Warren Scripps *manufacturing company executive*

Grosse Pointe Farms
Allen, Lee Harrison *industrial consultant, wholesale company executive*

Harrison Township
McGregor, Theodore Anthony *chemical company executive*

Holland
Haworth, Gerrard Wendell *office systems manufacturing company executive*
Haworth, Richard G. *office furniture manufacturer*
Johanneson, Gerald Benedict *office products company executive*

Howell
Cattani, Luis Carlos *manufacturing engineer*

Huntington Woods
†Hassig, Gordon L. *automotive sales executive*

Jackson
Kelly, Robert Vincent, Jr. *metal company executive*
Vischer, Harold Harry *manufacturing company executive*

Kalamazoo
Connable, Alfred Barnes *retired business executive*
Edmondson, Keith Henry *chemical company executive, retired*
Hite, Judson Cary *retired pharmaceutical company executive*
Hubbard, William Neill, Jr. *pharmaceutical company executive*
Hudson, Roy Davage *retired pharmaceutical company executive*
Jones, Eugene Gordon *pharmaceutical company executive*
Markin, David Robert *motor company executive*
Vescovi, Selvi *pharmaceutical company executive*
Wilson, James Rodney *air equipment company executive*

Laingsburg
Scripter, Frank C. *manufacturing company executive*

Lansing
Hines, Marshall *construction engineering company executive*
Wimmer, Billie Kops *association executive*

Livonia
Crundwell, Duncan James *electronics executive*

Madison Heights
Kafarski, Mitchell I. *chemical processing company executive*

Midland
Birdsall, Arthur Anthony *chemical executive*
Cuthbert, Robert Lowell *product specialist*
Hampton, Leroy *retired chemical company executive*
Hazleton, Richard A. *chemicals executive*
Popoff, Frank Peter *chemical company executive*
Schmidt, William C. *chemical company executive*
Stavropoulos, William S. *chemical executive*
Weiler, Scott Michael *machine tool manufacturing company executive*

Muskegon
Anderson, Harvey Gregg *pattern company executive*
Turner, Peter Merrick *retired manufacturing company executive*

Oak Park
Brann, Donald Treasurer *manufacturing executive*
Moilanen, Thomas Alfred *construction equipment distributor*

Plymouth
Massey, Donald E. *automotive executiv*
Merrill, Kenneth Coleman *retired automobile company executive*
Vlcek, Donald Joseph, Jr. *food distribution company executive, consultant, business author*

Pontiac
Mahone, Barbara Jean *automotive company executive*

Rochester
Gouldey, Glenn Charles *manufacturing company executive*
Rossio, Richard Dominic *automobile company executive*

Rochester Hills
Akeel, Hadi Abu *robotics executive*

Romulus
Scannell, Thomas John *cold metal forming company executive*

Royal Oak
Cook, Noel Robert *manufacturing company executive*

Saint Joseph
King, George Raleigh *manufacturing company executive*

Saranac
Herbrucks, Stephen *food products executive*

South Haven
Nequist, John Leonard *retired food company executive*

Southfield
Gulda, Edward James *automotive executive*
Maibach, Ben C., III *construction company executive*
Ponka, Lawrence John *automotive executive*
Raden, Louis *tape and label corporation executive*
Way, Kenneth L. *seat company executive*
Wisne, Lawrence A. *metal products executive*

Sparta
Fairchild, Henry Brant, III *manufacturing executive*

Spring Arbor
Dowley, Joel Edward *manufacturing executive, lawyer*

Taylor
Manoogian, Richard Alexander *manufacturing company executive*
Rosowski, Robert Bernard *manufacturing company executive*

Tecumseh
†Herrick, Kenneth Gilbert *manufacturing company executive*
Herrick, Todd W. *manufacturing company executive*

Traverse City
Parsons, John Thoren *corporate executive, inventor*

Troy
Acton, David L(awrence) *automobile company executive*
Aksoy, Zeynel *manufacturing professional*
Buschmann, Siegfried *manufacturing executive*
Corace, Joseph Russell *automotive parts company executive*
†Elder, Irma *automotive company executive*
Given, Kerry Wade *plastics industry executive*
Hamilton, Edward Tedjasukmana *automotive executive, small business owner*
Martin, Raymond Bruce *plumbing equipment manufacturing company executive*
Parker, Richard E. *building products manufacturing company executive*
Serafyn, Alexander Jaroslav *retired automotive executive*
Sharf, Stephan *automotive company executive*
Sloan, Hugh Walter, Jr. *automotive industry executive*
Williams, David Perry *manufacturing company executive*

Warren
Ableson, Donald William *automobile industry executive*
Viano, David Charles *automotive safety research scientist*

Washington
Gothard, Donald Lee *retired auto company executive*

Williamsburg
Harlan, John Marshall *construction company executive*

Wixom
Saussele, Charles William *marking systems company executive*

Ypsilanti
†Edwards, Gerald *plastics company executive*

MINNESOTA

Alexandria
Templin, Kenneth Elwood *paper company executive*

Anoka
Sliefert, Paula Rhea *manufacturing company executive*

Austin
Anderson, Jeffrey Lynn *stone company executive*
Hodapp, Don Joseph *food company executive*
Johnson, Joel W. *food products executive*

Bayport
†Garofalo, Donald R. *window manufacturing executive*
†Johnson, Alan *retired window/patio door manufacturer*

Brooklyn Park
Rogers, David *apparel executive*

Detroit Lakes
Super, William Alan *manufacturing executive*

Duluth
Whitney, Gwin Richard *brick distribution company executive*

Eagan
Clemens, T. Pat *manufacturing company executive*

Edina
Brown, Charles Eugene *retired electronics company executive*
Prince, Robb Lincoln *manufacturing company executive*
Sampson, John Eugene *consulting company executive*

Fairmont
Rosen, Thomas J. *food and agricultural products executive*

Golden Valley
Tracey, Timothy Neal *medical device, data processing executive*

Hopkins
Rappaport, Gary Burton *defense equipment and software company executive*

Lindstrom
Messin, Marlene Ann *plastics company executive*

Marshall
Schwan, Alfred *food products executive*

Mendota Heights
Frechette, Peter Loren *dental products executive*

Minneapolis
Anderson, Davin Charles *business representative, labor consultant*
Asplin, Edward William *retired packaging company executive*
Benson, Donald Erick *holding company executive*
Bonsignore, Michael Robert *electronics company executive*
Book, William Joseph *manufacturing executive*
Carlson, Curtis LeRoy *corporate executive*
Findorff, Robert Lewis *retired air filtration equipment company executive*
George, William Wallace *manufacturing company executive*
Gockel, John Raymond *construction executive*
Goldberger, Robert D. *food products company executive*
†Grazzini, Gregory Paul *construction company executive*
Hale, Roger Loucks *manufacturing company executive*
Hodder, William Alan *fabricated metal products company executive*
Jacobs, Irwin Lawrence *diversified corporate executive*
Johnson, Sankey Anton *manufacturing company executive*
Lupient, James *automotive executive*
Luthringshauser, Daniel Rene *manufacturing company executive*
MacMillan, Whitney *food products and import/export company executive*
McCune, Thomas *construction executive contractor*
Micek, Ernest S. *food products executive*
Nelson, Glen David *medical products executive, physician*
Paulu, Frances Brown *international center administrator*
Rauenhorst, Gerald *architectural, construction and development*
Scott, Andrew *retired corporate executive*
Spoor, William Howard *food company executive*
†Staley, Warren *food products company executive*
Sullivan, Austin Padraic, Jr. *diversified food company executive*
Toupin, Harold Ovid *retired chemical company executive*
Van Dyke, William Grant *manufacturing company executive*
Walsh, Paul S. *food products executive*
Wurtele, Christopher Angus *paint and coatings company executive*

Minnetonka
Henningsen, Peter, Jr. *diversified industry executive*
Macfarlane, Alastair Iain Robert *business executive*
McGuire, William W. *health service organization executive*

North Oaks
Swanson, Thomas Richard *manufacturing, supply chain and systems executive*

Oakdale
Brullo, Robert Angelo *chemical company executive*

Plymouth
Friswold, Fred Ravndahl *manufacturing executive*
Kahler, Herbert Frederick *diversified business executive*
Rusch, Thomas William *manufacturing executive*

Richfield
McGraw, Vincent DePaul *manufacturing executive*

Rochester
Carlson, Roger Allan *manufacturing company executive, accountant*

Saint Paul
Andersen, Elmer Lee *manufacturing and publishing executive, former governor of Minnesota*
Baukol, Ronald Oliver *company executive*
Burd, Francis John *packaging executive*
Cohen, Robert *medical device manufacturing-marketing executive*
Desimone, Livio Diego *diversified manufacturing company executive*
Ferkingstad, Susanne M. *cosmetics executive*
Garretson, Donald Everett *retired manufacturing company executive*
Gherty, John E. *food products and agricultural products company executive*
Kuhrmeyer, Carl Albert *manufacturing company executive*
Lehr, Lewis Wylie *diversified manufacturing company executive*
Ling, Joseph Tso-Ti *manufacturing company executive, environmental engineer*
Maas, Duane Harris *distilling company executive*
Ostby, Ronald *dairy and food products company executive*
Shannon, Michael Edward *specialty chemical company executive*
Wollner, Thomas Edward *manufacturing company executive*

Shorewood
Rotunda, Joseph L. *retail and service company executive*

Spring Park
Haun, James William *retired food company executive, consultant, chemical engineer*

Wayzata
Blodgett, Frank Caleb *retired food company executive*
Hoffman, Gene D. *food company executive, consultant*
Swanson, Donald Frederick *retired food company executive*

MISSISSIPPI

Hattiesburg
Chain, Bobby Lee *electrical contractor, former mayor*

Hurley
Ross, Donald Paul, Jr. *robotics design executive*

Jackson
Irby, Stuart Charles, Jr. *construction company executive*
Julian, Michael *grocery company executive*

Ocean Springs
Lorenz, Ronald Theodore *manufacturing executive*
Sims, Thomas Auburn *retired shipbuilding company executive*

Yazoo City
Arnold, David Walker *chemical company executive, engineer*

MISSOURI

Blue Springs
Heller, John L., II *food products executive*
Olsson, Björn Eskil *railroad supply company executive*

Boonville
Gehm, David Eugene *construction and environmental management executive*

Bridgeton
Brauer, Stephen Franklin *manufacturing company executive*

Carthage
Jefferies, Robert Aaron, Jr. *diversified manufacturing executive, lawyer*

Chesterfield
Carpenter, Will Dockery *chemical company executive*
King, William Terry *retired manufacturing company executive*
Malvern, Donald *retired aircraft manufacturing company executive*
McCarthy, Paul Fenton *aerospace executive, former naval officer*
Palazzi, Joseph L(azarro) *manufacturing executive*
Pylipow, Stanley Ross *retired manufacturing company executive*

Clayton
Ball, Kenneth Leon *manufacturing company executive, organizational development consultant*
Beracha, Barry Harris *food company executive*
Buechler, Bradley Bruce *plastic processing company executive, accountant*
Heininger, S(amuel) Allen *retired chemical company executive*
Keyes, Marion Alvah, IV *manufacturing company executive*

Columbia
Thompson, John Edward *small appliance manufacturing company executive*

Creve Coeur
Helfrich, Thomas Stough *healthcare company executive*

Hannibal
Coleman, Gloria Jean *chemical manufacturing company professional*

Kansas City
Bartlett, Paul Dana, Jr. *agribusiness executive*
Bass, Lee Marshall *food products company executive*
Berkley, Eugene Bertram (Bert Berkley) *envelope company executive*
Cleberg, Harry C. *food products company executive*
Dees, Stephen Phillip *agricultural finance executive, lawyer*
Hebenstreit, James Bryant *agricultural products executive, bank and venture capital executive*
Johnson, Richard Dean *pharmaceutical consultant, educator*
Kronschnabel, Robert James *manufacturing company executive*
†O'Dell, Jane *automotive company executive*
†Pearson, Donna Sutherland *lumber company executive*
Sullivan, Charles A. *food products executive*

Mexico
Stover, Harry M. *corporate executive*

North Kansas City
Stout, Edward Irvin *medical manufacturing company executive*

Saint Charles
Brahmbhatt, Sudhirkumar *chemical company executive*
Pundmann, Ed John, Jr. *automotive company executive*

Saint Louis
Abelov, Stephen Lawrence *uniform clothing company executive, consultant*
Adams, Albert Willie, Jr. *lubrication company executive*
Beare, Gene Kerwin *electric company executive*
Bock, Edward John *retired chemical manufacturing company executive*
Brodsky, Philip Hyman *chemical executive, research director*
Browde, Anatole *electronics company executive, consultant*
Brown, JoBeth Goode *food products executive, lawyer*
Brubaker, James Clark *construction executive*
Busch, August Adolphus, III *brewery executive*
Conerly, Richard Pugh *retired corporation executive*
Cunningham, Charles Baker, III *manufacturing company executive*
Davis, Christopher Kevin *equipment company executive*
Dill, Charles Anthony *manufacturing and computer company executive*
Faught, Harold Franklin *electrical equipment manufacturing company executive*
Gilbert, Allan Arthur *manufacturing executive*
Gomes, Edward Clayton, Jr. *construction company executive*
Graff, George Stephen *aerospace company executive*
Gupta, Surendra Kumar *chemical firm executive*
Hirsch, Raymond Robert *chemical company executive, lawyer*
Kaestner, John Thomas *beverage company executive*
Kummer, Fred S. *construction company executive*
Langness, David Gordon *manufacturing executive*
†McCoole, Robert *construction company executive*
McDonnell, Sanford Noyes *aircraft company executive*
McGuinness, Barbara Sue *food products executive*
McKenna, William John *textile products executive*
Monroe, Thomas Edward *industrial corporation executive*
Rich, Harry Earl *financial executive*
Sanders, Fred Joseph *aerospace company executive*
Sathe, Sharad Somnath *chemical company executive*
Shapiro, Robert B. *manufacturing executive*
Stearley, Robert Jay *retired packaging company executive*
Stiritz, William P. *food company executive*
Suter, Albert Edward *manufacturing company executive*
Throdahl, Monte Corden *former chemical company executive*
Tober, Lester Victor *shoe company executive*
Winter, William Earl *retired beverage company executive*

Springfield
Stern, Roy Dalton *manufacturing financial executive*
Witherspoon, John Thomas *water treatment company executive*
†Wooten, Rosalie *automotive company executive*

Sullivan
Penn, Ronald Hulen *manufacturing executive*

Windsor
Boarman, Marjorie Ruth *manufacturing company executive, consultant*

MONTANA

Great Falls
Sletten, John Robert *construction company executive*

Helena
Morrison, John Haddow, Jr. *engineering company executive*
Warren, Christopher Charles *electronics executive*

Missoula
Washington, Dennis *construction executive*

Stevensville
Derrick, William Dennis *physical plant administrator, consultant*

NEBRASKA

Columbus
Keller, Harry Allan *electronics technician*

Lincoln
Fisher, Calvin David *food manufacturing company executive*
Tinstman, Dale Clinton *food products company consultant*

Omaha
†Campos, Robert *construction company executive*
Faith, Marshall E. *grain company executive*
Fletcher, Philip B. *food products company executive*
Harper, Charles Michel *food company executive*

Lindsay, James Wiley *agricultural company executive*
Nogg, Donald Irwin *paper distribution executive, population researcher*
Norton, Robert R., Jr. *food products executive*
Regan, Timothy James *grain company executive*
†Rohde, Bruce *food products executive*
Rohde, Bruce C. *food company executive, lawyer*
Scott, Walter, Jr. *construction company executive*
†Stinson, Kenneth E. *construction company executive*

NEVADA

Carson City
Burns, Dan W. *manufacturing company executive*
Noland, Robert LeRoy *retired manufacturing company executive*

Fallon
Tedford, Jack Nowlan, III *construction executive, small business owner*

Incline Village
Strack, Harold Arthur *retired electronics company executive, retired air force officer, planner, analyst, author, musician*
Wahl, Howard Wayne *retired construction company executive, engineer*
Yount, George Stuart *paper company executive*

Las Vegas
Bernard, Thelma Rene *property management professional*
Jones, Fletcher, Jr. *automotive company executive*
Kaiser, Glen David *construction company executive*
Opfer, Neil David *construction educator, consultant*
Peck, Gaillard Ray, Jr. *defense contractor, aerospace and business consultant, business owner*
Regazzi, John Henry *retired electronic distributor executive*
Root, Alan Charles *diversified manufacturing company executive*
Strahan, Julia Celestine *electronics company executive*

Sparks
Corbin, Krestine Margaret *manufacturing company executive, fashion designer, columnist*
Kramer, Gordon Edward *manufacturing executive*
Root, William Dixon *construction company executive*

NEW HAMPSHIRE

Bennington
Verney, Richard Greville *paper company executive*

Concord
Slusser, Eugene Alvin *electronics manufacturing executive*

Exeter
Beck, Albert *manufacturing company executive*
Kenick, Joseph Louis, III *construction executive*
Kozlowski, L. Dennis *manufacturing company executive*

Georges Mills
Dulude, Richard *glass manufacturing company executive*

Hampton
Russell, Richard R. *chemicals executive*

Keene
Burkart, Walter Mark *manufacturing company executive*

Lisbon
Trelfa, Richard Thomas *paper company executive*

Manchester
Keillor, Sharon Ann *electronics company executive*

Meredith
Hatch, Frederick Tasker *chemicals consultant*

Milford
Morison, John Hopkins *casting manufacturing company executive*

Nashua
Gregg, Hugh *former cabinet manufacturing company executive, former governor New Hampshire*
Hippauf, Georgette Laurin *company executive*

Newport
Ruger, William Batterman *firearms manufacturing company executive*

North Hampton
Taylor, Donald *retired manufacturing company executive*
White, Ralph Paul *automotive executive, consultant*

Sunapee
Rauh, John David *manufacturing company executive*

NEW JERSEY

Alpine
Raasch, Ernest Martin *company executive*

Annandale
Drakeman, Lisa N. *biotechnology company executive*

Avenel
Sansone, Paul J. *automotive executive*

Basking Ridge
Abeles, James David *manufacturing company executive*
Conklin, Donald Ransford *retired pharmaceutical company executive*
Darrow, William Richard *pharmaceutical company executive, consultant*
Munch, Douglas Francis *pharmaceutical and health industry consultant*
Riesenberger, John Richard *pharmaceutical company executive*

Bedminster
Vagelos, Pindaros Roy *pharmaceutical company executive*
Yannuzzi, Elaine Victoria *food and home products executive*

Bridgewater
Allen, Randy Lee *corporate executive*
†Hassan, Fred *pharmaceutical executive*
Kennedy, James Andrew *chemical company executive*
†Olson, Margaret Smith *food services professional*
Rothwell, Timothy Gordon *pharmaceutical company executive*

Budd Lake
Havens, Edwin Wallace *manufacturing executive*
Pollack, Jordan Ellis *pharmaceutical company executive*

Butler
Klaas, Nicholas Paul *management and technical consultant*

Camden
Johnson, David Willis *food products executive*
†Morrison, Dale F. *food company executive*

Carteret
Donald, James *supermarket chain executive*
Goldberg, Arthur M. *gaming and fitness company executive, food products executive, lawyer*

Cedar Knolls
Blake, Richard F. *transistor devices company executive*

Cherry Hill
Keele, Lyndon Alan *electronic company executive*
Marsh, Robert Harry *chemical company executive*

Chester
Cameron, Nicholas Allen *diversified corporation executive*

Clark
Glatman-Stein, Marcia *executive search company executive*
Meilan, Celia *food products executive*

Clinton
Acerra, Michele (Mike Acerra) *engineering and construction company executive*
DeGhetto, Kenneth Anselm *engineering and construction company executive*
Hansen, Arthur Magne *engineering and manufacturing executive*

Cranbury
Barcus, Gilbert Martin *medical products executive, business educator*
Daoust, Donald Roger *pharmaceutical and toiletries company executive, microbiologist*
Perhach, James Lawrence *pharmaceutical company executive*

Cranford
Cleaver, William Pennington *retired sugar refining company executive, consultant*
Mullen, Edward K. *paper company executive*

Denville
Minter, Jerry Burnett *electronic component company executive, engineer*

Dover
Mc Donald, John Joseph *electronics executive*

East Brunswick
Marshall, Keith *pharmaceutical consultant*

East Hanover
Kent, Bruce Jonathan *pharmaceutical executive*

East Rutherford
Gerstein, David Brown *hardware manufacturing company executive, professional basketball team executive*

Edison
Andreasen, Charles Peter *retired electronics executive*
Jones, James Thomas, Jr. *tobacco company executive*

Elizabeth
Finder, Robert Andrew *pharmaceutical company executive*

Elmwood Park
Wygod, Martin J. *pharmaceuticals executive*

Englewood
Neis, Arnold Hayward *pharmaceutical company executive*

Englewood Cliffs
Feuerstein, Herbert *food company executive*
Shoemate, Charles R. *food company executive*
Shrem, Charles Joseph *metals corporation executive*

Fair Haven
McKissock, David Lee *retired manufacturing company executive*

Fairfield
Stein, Robert Alan *electronics company executive*

Fairview
Anton, Bruce Norman *textile company executive*

Fanwood
Butler, William Langdon *manufacturing company representative*

Farmingdale
Martin, Robert Francis *roof maintenance systems company executive*
Schluter, Peter Mueller *electronics company executive*

Florham Park
Sperber, Martin *pharmaceutical company executive, pharmacist*

Fords
Kaufman, Alex *chemicals executive*

Fort Lee
Vignolo, Biagio Nickolas, Jr. *chemical company executive*

Fort Monmouth
Schwering, Felix Karl *electronics engineer, researcher*
Thornton, Clarence Gould *electronics engineering executive*

Franklin Lakes
Castellini, Clateo *medical technology company executive*
Friedman, Martin Burton *chemical company executive*
Throdahl, Mark Crandall *medical technology company executive*

Freehold
Shapiro, Michael *supermarket corporate officer*

Garfield
Kodaka, Kunio *plastics company executive*

Glen Gardner
Epstein, Edward Joseph *textile company executive*

Hackensack
Markey, Jonathan H. *printing company executive*

Hainesport
Sylk, Leonard Allen *housing company executive, real estate developer*

Hazlet
Miller, Duane King *health and beauty care company executive*

Highlands
Hansen, Christian Andreas, Jr. *plastics and chemical company executive*

Hillsborough
Kenyhercz, Thomas Michael *pharmaceutical company executive*

Hoboken
Rubin, Irvin I. *plastics company executive*

Holmdel
Kogelnik, Herwig Werner *electronics company executive*

Hopatcong
Reese, Harry Edwin, Jr. *electronics executive*

Iselin
Clarke, David H. *industrial products executive*
Smith, Orin Robert *chemical company executive*
Wolynic, Edward Thomas *specialty chemicals technology executive*

Jersey City
Bowen, Linda Florence *pharmaceutical executive*
Pietrini, Andrew Gabriel *automotive aftermarket executive*
Zuckerberg, David Alan *pharmaceutical company executive*

Kendall Park
Hershenov, Bernard Zion *electronics research and development company executive*

Kenilworth
Gen, Martin *corporate executive*

Kirkwood Voorhees
Cohen, Mark N. *business executive*

Laurence Harbor
Goodwin, Douglas Ira *steel trading company executive*

Lawrenceville
O'Brien, James Jerome *construction management consultant*
†Steele, Ryan Edward *chemical company executive*

Lebanon
Hakes, Thomas Brion *manufacturing company executive, physician*

Linden
Covino, Charles Peter *chemicals executive*
Tamarelli, Alan Wayne *chemical company executive*

Livingston
†Candido, A. Michael *contracting company executive, real estate manager*
Martin, Daniel Richard *pharmaceutical company executive*

Long Beach
Warren, Craig Bishop *flavor and fragrance company executive, researcher*

Lyndhurst
Benschip, Gary John *manufacturing company executive*

Madison
Kogan, Richard Jay *pharmaceutical company executive*
Luciano, Robert Peter *pharmaceutical company executive*
Stafford, John Rogers *pharmaceutical and household products company executive*
Whitley, Arthur Francis *retired international consulting company executive, engineer, lawyer*

Mahwah
†Cevetillo, Gerri Marie *manufacturing company executive*

Marlton
Gottfried, Benjamin Frank *retired manufacturing executive*
Samek, Edward Lasker *service company executive*

Matawan
Amato, Vincent Vito *business executive*

Medford
Kesty, Robert Edward *chemical manufacturing company executive*
Vereb, Michael Joseph *retired pharmaceutical and cosmetic executive*

Mercerville
Yeager, Arthur Leonard *health company executive*

Middletown
Rosen, Beth Dee *travel agency executive*

Montclair
Dubrow, Marsha Ann *high technology company executive, composer*

Montvale
Corrado, Fred *food company executive*
Roob, Richard *manufacturing executive*

Moorestown
Springer, Douglas Hyde *retired food company executive, lawyer*

Morris Plains
Caveney, William John *pharmaceutical company executive, lawyer*
Goodes, Melvin Russell *retired manufacturing company executive*
Otani, Mike *optical company executive*

Morristown
†Barpal, Isaac Ruben *retired technology and operations executive*
Bossidy, Lawrence Arthur *industrial manufacturing executive*
DiSerio, Frank Joseph *pharmaceutical company executive, consultant*
Herman, Robert Lewis *cork company executive*
Hittinger, William Charles *electronics company executive*
Huck, John Lloyd *pharmaceutical company executive*
Kirby, Fred Morgan, II *corporation executive*
Mazur, Leonard L. *pharmaceutical company executive*
Williams, Joseph Dalton *pharmaceutical company executive*

Mount Laurel
Instone, John Clifford *manufacturing company executive*

Murray Hill
†McGinn, Richard A. *telecommunications company executive*

New Brunswick
Bern, Ronald Lawrence *consulting company executive*
Campbell, Robert Emmett *retired health care products company executive*
Fine, Roger Seth *pharmaceutical executive, lawyer*
Griffin, Gary Arthur *technological products executive*
Haines, William Joseph *pharmaceutical company executive*
Larsen, Ralph S(tanley) *health care company executive*
McGuire, John Lawrence *pharmaceuticals executive*
†Mondschein, Lawrence Geoffrey *medical products executive*

New Providence
Chatterji, Debajyoti *manufacturing company executive*
Longfield, William Herman *health care company executive*

North Bergen
†Choi, Jay Lee *women's apparel executive*
Miller, Samuel Martin *apparel company finance executive*

Northvale
Barna, Richard Allen *lighting company executive, broadcasting executive*
Di Mino, André Anthony *manufacturing executive, consultant*

Nutley
English, Robert Joseph *electronic corporation executive*
Seyffarth, Linda Jean Wilcox *corporate executive*

Old Tappan
Dubnick, Bernard *retired pharmaceutical company administrator*

Paramus
Forman, Beth Rosalyne *specialty food trade executive*
Maclin, Ernest *biomedical diagnostics company executive*

Parsippany
Bunin, Jeffrey Howard *manufacturing company executive*

Deones, Jack E. *corporate executive*
Fleisher, Seymour *manufacturing company executive*

Paterson
Danziger, Glenn Norman *chemical sales company executive*
Welles, Ernest I. *chemical company executive*

Pennington
Brandinger, Jay Jerome *electronics executive*

Pennsauken
†Kolb, John *automotive executive*

Piscataway
Kalaher, Richard A. *company executive*
Kampouris, Emmanuel Andrew *corporate executive*

Point Pleasant Beach
Beno-Clark, Candice Lynn *chemical company executive*

Princeton
Barker, Richard Gordon *corporate research and development executive*
Becker, Ivan Endre *retired plastics company executive*
Carnes, James Edward *electronics executive*
Cavanaugh, James Henry *medical corporate executive, former government official*
Cryer, Dennis Robert *pharmaceutical company executive, researcher*
Dovey, Brian Hugh *health care products company executive, venture capitalist*
Hayes, Edwin Junius, Jr. *business executive*
Hendrickson, Robert Frederick *pharmaceutical company executive*
Jacobson, Herbert Leonard *licensing executive*
Kuebler, Christopher Allen *pharmaceutical executive*
Liao, Paul Foo-Hung *electronics executive*
Minton, Dwight Church *manufacturing company executive*
Sapoff, Meyer *electronics component manufacturer*
Villafranca, Joseph J. *pharmaceutical executive, chemistry educator*
Wavle, James Edward, Jr. *pharmaceutical company executive, lawyer*
Wildnauer, Richard Harry *pharmaceutical company executive*

Rahway
Mandel, Lewis Richard *pharmaceutical company executive*

Raritan
Frank, David Stanley *medical diagnostics company executive*
Hahn, Dowon *pharmaceutical researcher, educator*

Red Bank
†Pohl, Anna Lise *executive*
Sgaramella, Peter *chemical products executive, technical consultant*
Tan, Nianxiong *electronics professional*

Ridgefield
†Riggs, Rory *pharmaceutical executive*

Ridgewood
Healey, Frank Henry *retired research executive*

Riverdale
Fremund, Zdenek Anthony *manufacturing company executive*

Rochelle Park
Laskey, Richard Anthony *biomedical device executive*
Schapiro, Jerome Bentley *chemical company executive*

Roseland
Mitschele, Michael Douglas *concrete and aggregate company executive*

Rumson
Brennan, William Joseph *manufacturing company executive*

Saddle River
McClelland, William Craig *paper company executive*
†Pak, Dongtak *business executive*

Salem
Seabrook, John Martin *retired food products executive, chemical engineer*

Secaucus
Stern, Leonard Norman *pet supply manufacturing company executive*
Unanue, Joseph *food products executive*

Short Hills
Jackson, William Ward *chemical company executive*

Skillman
Goldblatt, Barry Lance *manufacturing executive*
Wang, Jonas Chia-Tsung *pharmaceutical executive*

Somerset
Aronson, Louis Vincent, II *manufacturing executive*

South Hackensack
Cohen, Brett I. *health products executive*

South Orange
†Wilson, Theodore Louis *construction executive*

South Plainfield
Hunsinger, Doyle J. *electronics executive*
Schlossman, Mitchell Lloyd *cosmetics and chemical specialties executive*

Springfield
Adams, James Mills *retired chemicals executive*
Toresco, Donald *automotive executive*

Summit
Pawelec, William John *retired electronics company executive*

Teaneck
Feinberg, Robert S. *plastics manufacturing company executive, marketing consultant*
Gordon, Maxwell *pharmaceutical company executive*
Woerner, Alfred Ira *medical device manufacturer, educator*

Trenton
Devine, James Joseph *chemical products manufacturing company executive*
Roshon, George Kenneth *manufacturing company executive*

Union
Lapidus, Norman Israel *food broker*

Wall
Jost, Wesley William *automotive executive, mayor*

Warren
Jackson, John Wyant *medical products executive*

Watchung
Knudson, Harry Edward, Jr. *retired electrical manufacturing company executive*

Wayne
Cordover, Ronald Harvey *business executive, venture capitalist*
Heyman, Samuel J. *chemicals and building materials manufacturing company executive*
Jeffrey, Robert George, Jr. *industrial company executive*
Nicastro, Francis Efisio *defense electronics and retailing executive*
Schwartz, Robert *automotive manufacturing company executive, marketing executive*

West Orange
Chin, Carolyn Sue *business executive*
Johnson, Clarice P. *materials procurement executive*

West Windsor
Giddings, Clifford Frederick *retired corporate executive*

Westfield
Connell, Grover *food company executive*
Keyko, George John *electronics company executive*
McLean, Vincent Ronald *former manufacturing company financial executive*

Westwood
Black, Theodore Halsey *retired manufacturing company executive*

Whippany
Golden, John F. *packaging company executive*

Whitehouse Station
Lewent, Judy Carol *pharmaceutical executive*

Woodbridge
Mount, Karl A. *manufacturing executive*

Woodcliff Lake
Perrella, James Elbert *manufacturing company executive*

Wyckoff
Brown, James Joseph *manufacturing company executive*

NEW MEXICO

Albuquerque
Friberg, George Joseph *electronics company executive*
King, James Nedwed *construction company executive, lawyer*
Korman, Nathaniel Irving *research and development company executive*
Mayes, Richard Adolphus *electronics executive*
Minahan, Daniel Francis *manufacturing company executive, lawyer*
†Pohl, Elizabeth *contracting company executive*
Stamm, Robert Jenne *building contractor, construction company executive*
Sullivan, Terry Brian *semiconductor plant executive*
Swenka, Arthur John *food products executive*
Thomas, Douglas Graham *technology company executive, communications consultant*

Farmington
Webb, Marlo L. *automobile executive, banking executive*

Roswell
Armstrong, Billie Bert *retired highway contractor*

Sandia Park
Wilczynski, Janusz S. *packaging technology executive, physicist*

Santa Fe
Odell, John H. *construction company executive*
Robinson, Charles Wesley *energy company executive*

NEW YORK

Albany
Naumann, Hans J. *manufacturing company executive*
Standish, John Spencer *textile manufacturing company executive*

Amityville
†Curri, Joanne M. *pharmaceutical company executive*

Armonk
Sydney, Doris S. *sports touring company executive, interior designer*

Athens
Lew, Roger Alan *manufacturing company executive*

Baldwin
Sarnoff, Paul *metals consultant, author, editor*

Bay Shore
Shreve, Sue Ann Gardner *retired health products company administrator*

Bethpage
Murphy, Susan Lynn Jaycox *construction executive*

Blauvelt
Citardi, Mattio H. *business analyst, project manager, researcher*

Bohemia
Hausman, Howard *electronics executive*

Briarcliff Manor
Bingham, J. Peter *electronics research executive*

Bronx
Draeger, Wayne Harold *manufacturing company executive*

Brooklyn
Hood, Ernest Alva, Sr. *pharmaceutical company executive*
Oussani, James John *stapling company executive*
Zisser, Martin Shepherd *fur apparel manufacturer, investor and trader*

Buffalo
Ping, Douglas Edward *food and beverage company executive*
Rice, Victor Albert *manufacturing executive, heavy*
Rich, Robert E., Jr. *food products company executive*
Starks, Fred William *chemical company executive*
Timmerman, Leon Bernard *pump industry consultant*

Cedarhurst
Cohen, David B. *optical company executive*

Clifton Park
Fell, Samuel Kennedy (Ken Fell) *infosystems executive*
Scher, Robert Sander *instrument design company executive*

Cooperstown
Tilton, Webster, Jr. *contractor*

Corning
Behm, Forrest Edwin *glass manufacturing company executive*
Booth, C(hesley) Peter Washburn *manufacturing company executive*
Ecklin, Robert Luther *materials company executive*
Houghton, James Richardson *retired glass manufacturing company executive*
Peck, Arthur John, Jr. *diversified manufacturing executive, lawyer*

Cortland
Miller, John David *manufacturing company executive*

Dearby
Goodell, Joseph Edward *manufacturing executive*

Dix Hills
Meyers, George Edward *plastics company executive*

East Amherst
†Haltam, Michael Patrick *medical device manufacturing executive*

East Aurora
Hawk, George Wayne *retired electronics company executive*

East Hampton
Karp, Harvey Lawrence *metal products manufacturing company executive*

East Meadow
Cymbler, Murray Joel *corporate professional*

Elmsford
De Nicola, Peter Francis *photographic manufacturer*
Fachnie, H(ugh) Douglas *film manufacturing company official*

Falconer
Ruhlman, Herman C(loyd), Jr. *manufacturing company executive*

Farmingdale
Blum, Melvin *chemical company executive, researcher*

Fayetteville
Pachter, Irwin Jacob *pharmaceutical consultant*

Flushing
Georghiou, Michael *construction and development executive*
Henshel, Harry Bulova *watch manufacturer*

Glen Cove
Burnham, Harold Arthur *pharmaceutical company executive, physician*
Maxwell, J. Douglas, Jr. *chemical service company executive*

Hauppauge
Arams, Frank Robert *electronics company executive*
Artzt, Russell M. *computer software company executive*

Hicksville
Tucci, Gerald Frank *manufacturing company executive*

Holtsville
Miller, Ronald M. *manufacturing executive*

Honeoye
Stone, Alan John *manufacturing company executive, real estate executive*

Hoosick Falls
Dodge, Cleveland Earl, Jr. *manufacturing executive*

Horseheads
Tanner, David Harold *professional roof consultant*

Ithaca
Howard, Rustin Ray *corporate executive*
Moore, Charles Hewes, Jr. *industrial and engineered products executive*

Jamestown
Anderson, Raymond Quintus *diversified company executive*
Leising, Mary Kathleen *manufacturing executive*
Wellman, Barclay Ormes *furniture company executive*

Lansing
Gage, George H(enry) *retired high technology company executive*

Latham
Stallman, Donald Lee *corporate executive*

Levittown
Ahmad, Naseer *pharmaceutical sales executive*

Lewiston
Waters, William Ernest *microelectronics executive*

Lindenhurst
Boltz, Mary Ann *aerospace materials company executive, travel agency executive*
Levy, (Alexandra) Susan *construction company executive*

Liverpool
Greenway, William Charles *electronics executive, design engineer*
Morabito, Bruno Paul *machinery manufacturing executive*

Lockport
Hoyme, Chad Earl *packaging company executive*
Schultz, Gerald Alfred *chemical company executive*

Locust Valley
Schor, Joseph Martin *pharmaceutical executive, biochemist*

Mamaroneck
Holz, Harold A. *chemical and plastics manufacturing company executive*
Mizrahi, Abraham Mordechay *retired cosmetics and health care company executive, physician*

Manhasset
Keen, Constantine *retired manufacturing company executive*

Melville
Kaufman, Stephen P. *electronics company executive*
Kissinger, Walter Bernhard *automotive test and service equipment manufacturing executive*

Mount Kisco
Laster, Richard *biotechnology executive, consultant*
Marwell, Edward Marvin *instrument company executive*

New Hyde Park
Hinerfeld, Norman Martin *manufacturing company executive*

New Rochelle
Goodman, Joan Frances *avionics manufacturing executive*
Miller, Rita *personnel consultant, diecasting companyexecutive*
Tassone, Gelsomina (Gessie Tassone) *metal processing executive*

New York
†Azrielant, Aya *jewelry manufacturing executive*
Barth, Richard *pharmaceutical executive*
Barton, Lewis *consultant*
Bennett, Joel Herbert *construction company executive*
Bertuccioli, Bruno *petrochemical company executive*
Bible, Geoffrey Cyril *tobacco company executive*
Blinken, Robert James *manufacturing and communications company executive*
Bordiga, Benno *automotive parts manufacturing company executive*
Boyer, Robert Allan *business executive*
Bresani, Federico Fernando *business executive*
Bronfman, Edgar Miles *beverage company executive*
Brown, Kenneth Charles *manufacturing company executive*
Bryan, Katherine Byram *healthcare executive*
Call, Neil Judson *corporate executive*
Campbell, Robert David *minerals and metals executive*
Cavanna, Dino Francesco *chemicals executive*
Charron, Paul Richard *apparel company executive*
Clark, Robert Henry, Jr. *holding company executive*
Clarke, Kenneth Kingsley *electrical equipment company executive*
Coffin, Dwight Clay *grain company executive*
Coleman, Martin Stone *retired office furniture company executive*
Collamore, Thomas Jones *corporate executive*
†Cripps, Kathy Hickey *public relations company official*
Daniel, Richard Nicholas *fabricated metals manufacturing company executive*
Day, John W. *international corporation executive*
D'Lower, Del *manufacturing executive*

Edmands, Susan Banks *consulting company executive*
Farber, John J. *chemical company executive*
Flaherty, William E. *chemicals and metals company executive*
Fletcher, Mary Lee *business executive*
French, Harold Stanley *food company executive*
Fribourg, Michel *international agribusiness executive*
Fribourg, Paul J. *grain company executive*
Furlaud, Richard Mortimer *pharmaceutical company executive*
Gelb, Harold Seymour *industrial company executive, investor*
Glaubinger, Lawrence David *manufacturing company executive, consultant*
Goldstone, Steven F. *consumer products company executive*
Goodale, Toni Krissel *development consultant*
Gould, Harry Edward, Jr. *industrialist*
Greenfield, Gordon Kraus *software company executive*
Haas, Frederick Carl *paper and chemical company executive*
Harder, Lewis Bradley *ore bodies development company executive*
Heimbold, Charles Andreas, Jr. *pharmaceutical company executive*
Helpern, David Moses *shoe corporation executive*
Isogai, Masaharu *women's apparel executive*
Jordan, Michael Hugh *retired broadcasting and media company executive*
Juliber, Lois *manufacturing executive*
Kann, Peter R. *publishing executive*
Karcher, John Drake *textile and apparel company executive*
Kito, Teruo *former international trading company executive*
Koch, David Hamilton *chemical company executive*
Koenig, Marvin *heavy manufacturing executive*
Koplik, Michael R. *durable goods company executive*
Koplik, Perry H. *durable goods company executive*
Krominga, Lynn *cosmetic and health care company executive, lawyer*
Kropf, Susan J. *cosmetics company executive*
Lala, Dominick J. *manufacturing company executive*
Landegger, Carl Clement *machinery and pulp manufacturing executive*
Lauder, Estee *cosmetics company executive*
Lauder, Leonard Alan *cosmetic and fragrance company executive*
Levin, Michael Stuart *steel company executive*
Levinson, Robert Alan *textile company executive*
Lewis, Loida Nicolas *food products holding company executive*
Lifton, Robert Kenneth *diversified companies executive*
Lord, Marvin *apparel company executive*
Luftglass, Murray Arnold *manufacturing company executive*
Luke, John Anderson, Jr. *paper, packaging and chemical company executive*
Mango, Wilfred Gilbert, Jr. *real estate and construction company executive*
Marcus, Hyman *business executive*
Margolis, David I(srael) *industrial manufacturing executive*
May, William Frederick *manufacturing executive*
McFadden, Mary Josephine *fashion industry executive*
Meyaart, Paul Jan *distilling company executive*
Miller, Morgan Lincoln *textile manufacturing company executive*
Munroe, George Barber *former mining and manufacturing company executive*
Murdolo, Frank Joseph *pharmaceutical company executive*
Murphy, John Arthur *tobacco, food and brewing company executive*
Natori, Josie Cruz *apparel executive*
Norwick, Braham *textile specialist, consultant, columnist*
Nussbaumer, Gerhard Karl *metals company executive*
Opel, John R. *business machines company executive*
Paalz, Anthony L. *beverage company executive*
Palitz, Anka A. Kriser *manufacturing and distributing company executive*
Philipp, Elizabeth R. *manufacturing company executive, lawyer*
Plaskitt, Piers *sales and marketing executive*
Preston, James E. *cosmetics company executive*
Puschel, Philip P. *textiles executive*
Reece, Thomas L. *manufacturing executive*
Rennert, Ira Leon *heavy manufacturing executive*
Riley, William *corporate executive, writer*
†Roberts, Dorothy Hyman *accessory company executive*
Rochlis, James Joseph *manufacturing company executive*
Rosenberg, Robert Charles *housing corporation executive*
Rosenthal, Milton Frederick *minerals and chemical company executive*
Roubos, Gary Lynn *diversified manufacturing company executive*
Rubin, Joel Edward *consulting company executive*
Sacks, David G. *retired distilling company executive, lawyer*
Sarnelle, Joseph R. *electronic publishing specialist, magazine and newspaper editor*
†Schacht, Henry Brewer *retired manufacturing executive*
Schmitter, Charles Harry *electronics manufacturing company executive, lawyer*
Schulhof, Michael Peter *entertainment, electronics company executive*
Schwartz, Bernard Leon *space and communications company executive*
Shineman, Edward William, Jr. *retired pharmaceutical executive*
Silverman, Jeffrey Stuart *manufacturing executive*
Skule, John L. *pharmaceutical company executive*
Slavin, Rosanne Singer *textile converter*
Smolinski, Edward Albert *holding company executive, lawyer, accountant, deacon*
Solomon, Howard *pharmaceutical company executive*
Solomon, Zachary Leon *apparel manufacturing company executive*
Sowder, Donald Dillard *pharmaceutical executive*
Steere, William Campbell, Jr. *pharmaceutical company executive*
Steiner, Jeffrey Josef *industrial manufacturing company executive*
Sullivan, Eugene John Joseph *manufacturing company executive*
Swanson, David Heath *agricultural company executive*

Tapella, Gary Louis *manufacturing company executive*
Tsai, Cynthia Ekberg *entertainment executive*
Tse, Charles Yung Chang *drug company executive*
Valles, Jean-Paul *manufacturing company executive*
Wachner, Linda Joy *apparel marketing and manufacturing executive*
Wacker, Susan Regina *cosmetic design director*
Weinstein, Martin *aerospace manufacturing executive, materials scientist*
Windelev, Claus *engine manufacturing company executive*
†Woods, Emily *apparel executive*
Yates, Marypaul *textile company executive*

Niskayuna
Adler, Michael S. *control systems and electronic technologies executive*
Mangan, John Leo *retired electrical manufacturing company executive, international trade and trade policy specialist*

North Point
Kohrt, Carl Fredrick *manufacturing executive, scientist*

Northport
†Blume, Richard Stephen *medical company executive, physician*
Reinertsen, Norman *retired aircraft systems company executive*

Oneida
Stevens, James Walter *manufacturing representative*

Orchard Park
Franklin, Murray Joseph *retired steel foundry executive*

Patterson
Black, Charles Catus *industrial company executive*

Plattsburgh
Cooper, Richard Francis *computer company executive*

Port Washington
†Korez, John Joseph *chemical executive*

Poughkeepsie
Slade, Bernard Newton *electronics company executive*

Poughquag
LaRussa, Joseph Anthony *optical company executive*

Purchase
Casey, Gerard William *food products company executive, lawyer*
Deering, Allan Brooks *soft drink company executive*
Dillon, John T. *paper company executive*
Enrico, Roger A. *soft drink company executive*
Finnerty, Louise Hoppe *beverage and food company executive*
†Nooyi, Indra K. *food products company executive*
Thomas, Dennis *paper company executive, former government official*
von der Heyden, Karl Ingolf Mueller *manufacturing company executive*
Wright, David L. *food and beverage company executive*

Rego Park
LeFrak, Samuel J. *housing and building corporation executive*
†Weinstein, Gerald *housing and building corporation executive*

Rhinebeck
McGuire, John Francis, Jr. *construction company executive*

Rhinecliff
Conklin, John Roger *retired electronics company executive*

Rochester
Corio, Mark Andrew *electronics executive*
Fisher, George Myles Cordell *photographic imaging company executive, mathematician, engineer*
Gustin, Carl E., Jr. *manufacturing company executive*
Harvey, Douglass Coate *retired photographic company executive*
Lewis, Charles Spencer *professional business manager*
Miller, Richard Bruce *electronics company executive*
Oberlies, John William *physician organization executive*
Pollicove, Harvey Myles *manufacturing executive*
Sieg, Albert Louis *photographic company executive*

Rye Brook
Masson, Robert Henry *paper company executive*

Sands Point
Tane, Susan Jaffe *retired manufacturing company executive*
Wurzel, Leonard *retired candy manufacturing company executive*

Scarsdale
Blitman, Howard Norton *construction company executive*
Fortune, Philip Robert *retired metal manufacturing company executive*
Johnson, Boine Theodore *instruments company executive, mayor*

Schenectady
Grant, Ian Stanley *engineering company executive*
Wilson, Delano Dee *consultant*

Seaford
Setzler, William Edward *chemical company executive*

Smithtown
Sporn, Stanley Robert *retired electronic company executive*

Somers
†Siegel, Sarah Ellin *electronics executive*
Sora, Sebastian Antony *business machines manufacturing executive, educator*

Suffern
Jaffe, Elliot Stanley *women's clothing retail chain founder, executive*
Sutherland, George Leslie *retired chemical company executive*

Syosset
Guthart, Leo A. *electronics executive*

Syracuse
Frazier, J(ohn) Phillip *manufacturing company executive*
Steigerwald, Louis John, III *corporate executive*

Tarrytown
Kane, Stanley Bruce *food products executive*

Tonawanda
Kulp, J. Robert *metal company executive*

Troy
Doremus, Robert Heward *glass and ceramics processing educator*

Valley Stream
Ferares, Kenneth *automobile executive*
Wollman, June Rose *clothing executive*

Van Hornesville
†Durham, Ormonde George, III *manufacturing executive*

Webster
Dea, Donald Don *business executive*
Duke, Charles Bryan *research and development manufacturing executive, physics educator*
Przybylowicz, Edwin Paul *chemical company executive, retired research director*

Westbury
Rosenberg, Rudy *chemical company executive*

White Plains
Greene, Leonard Michael *aerospace manufacturing executive, institute executive*
Krasne, Charles A. *food products executive*
Lapidus, Herbert *medical products executive*
Orisek, Ivan *business executive, consultant*
Sanford, Linda S. *computer manufacturing executive*

Whitestone
Feinberg, Irwin L. *retired manufacturing company executive*
Rahr, Stewart *health medical products executive*

Williamsville
Krzyzan, Judy Lynn *automotive executive*

Williston Park
Segel, J. Norman *garment manufacturing company executive*

Woodbury
Guttenplan, Harold Esau *retired food company executive*

Yonkers
Lukach, Arthur S., Jr. *manufacturing executive*

Youngstown
Alpert, Norman *chemical company executive*

NORTH CAROLINA

Advance
Huber, Thomas Martin *container company executive*

Asheboro
Davis, J. B. *furniture manufacturing executive*

Asheville
Coli, Guido John *chemical company executive*
Johnson, John Andrew *construction executive*
Vander Voort, Dale Gilbert *textile company executive*

Beaufort
Cullman, Hugh *retired tobacco company executive*

Belmont
Stowe, Robert Lee, III *textile company executive*

Blowing Rock
Barnebey, Kenneth Alan *food company executive*

Burnsville
Gouge, Ruby Lee *textiles company administrator*

Cary
Alstadt, Donald Martin *business executive*
Nyce, David Scott *electronics company executive*

Chapel Hill
Drutz, David Jules *biotechnology executive*
Morgan, G. Kenneth *association executive*
Thakor, Haren Bhaskerrao *manufacturing company executive*

Charlotte
Bowden, James Alvin *construction company financial executive*
Dalton, Robert Issac, Jr. *textile executive, consultant, researcher*
Diamond, Harvey Jerome *machinery manufacturing company executive*
Iverson, Francis Kenneth *metals company executive*
Jenkins, John Edward, Jr. *electronics executive, engineering educator*
Lea, Scott Carter *retired packaging company executive*

McVerry, Thomas Leo *manufacturing company executive*
Peacock, A(lvin) Ward *textile company executive*
Perkins, Jim C. *automotive executive*
Rathke, Dieter B. *construction company executive*
Regelbrugge, Roger Rafael *steel company executive*
Siegel, Samuel *metals company executive*
Squires, James Ralph *development company executive*
Walker, Kenneth Dale *automotive service company executive*
Weisenburger, Randall *company executive*
Wiggins, Jerome Meyer *apparel textile industry financial executive*

Cherry Point
Laviolette, Bruce Edward *industrial manufacturing management*

Durham
Althaus, David Steven *chemicals executive, controller*
Burger, Robert Mercer *semiconductor device research executive*
Dennehy, Leisa Jeanotta *company executive*
De Vone, James Milton *manufacturing company owner, entrepreneur*
Fair, Richard Barton *electronics executive, educator*

Elon College
Powell, William Council, Sr. *service company executive*

Fayetteville
Richardson, Emilie White *manufacturing company executive, investment company executive, lecturer*

Flat Rock
Demartini, Robert John *textile company executive*

Gastonia
Kimbrell, Willard Duke *textile company executive*
Lawson, William David, III *retired cotton company executive*

Greensboro
Brecht, Blaine Richard *manufacturing company executive*
Englar, John David *textile company executive, lawyer*
Fenn, Ormon William, Jr. *furniture company executive*
Howard, Richard Turner *construction company executive*
Korb, William Brown, Jr. *manufacturing company executive*
Mann, Lowell Kimsey *retired manufacturing executive*
Peterson, John Edgar, Jr. *retired agricultural executive, textile executive*
Staab, Thomas Robert *consumer product company financial executive*

Hendersonville
Stepkoski, Robert John *automobile dealership executive*

Hickory
Nye, John Robert *furniture company executive, transportation consultant*
Shuford, Harley Ferguson, Jr. *furniture manufacturing executive*

High Point
†Lyon, Wayne Barton *manufacturing company executive*
Marsden, Lawrence Albert *retired textile company executive*

Hillsborough
Moore, Edward Towson *electronics company executive, electrical engineer*

Kannapolis
Ridenhour, Joseph Conrad *textile company executive*

Maiden
Pruitt, Thomas P., Jr. *textiles executive*

Mocksville
Smith, Mark Eugene *architectural engineering service company executive*

Mount Airy
Woltz, Howard Osler, Jr. *steel and wire products company executive*

Oriental
Sutter, John Richard *manufacturer, investor*

Pine Knoll Shores
Benson, Kenneth Victor *manufacturing company executive, lawyer*

Pinehurst
O'Neill, John Joseph, Jr. *business consultant, former chemical company executive*

Raleigh
Cresimore, James Leonard *food broker*
Klein, Verle Wesley *corporate executive, retired naval officer*
Prior, William Allen *electronics company executive*
Sloan, O. Temple, Jr. *automotive equipment executive*

Research Triangle Park
†Gaither, John Stokes *chemical company executive*
Jarrell, Donald Ray *laboratory administrator*
Key, Karen Letisha *pharmaceutical executive*
Maar, Rosina *medical organization executive*
Niedel, James E. *pharmaceuticals executive*
Wilson, Donald Hurst, III *biopharmaceutical industry executive*

Sanford
Kilmartin, Joseph Francis, Jr. *business executive, consultant*
Walker, Gary Linn *materials and logistics executive, consultant*

Weldon
Barringer, Paul Brandon, II *lumber company executive*

Wilkesboro
Tillman, Robert L. *construction executive*

Wilmington
Silloway, Benton, Jr. *food products executive*
Thompson, Donald Charles *electronics company executive, former coast guard officer*

Winston Salem
Hanes, Ralph Philip, Jr. *former textiles executive, arts patron, cattle farmer*
Maselli, John Anthony *food products company executive*
Smith, Zachary Taylor, II *retired tobacco company executive*
Sticht, J. Paul *retired food products and tobacco company executive*
Wallace, Roanne *hosiery company executive*

NORTH DAKOTA

Fargo
†McCormick, Thomas Duncan *construction company executive*

Grand Forks
Gjovig, Bruce Quentin *manufacturing consultant, entreprenuer*

OHIO

Akron
Bonsky, Jack Alan *chemical company executive, lawyer*
Bosley, Ronald Edmund *retired aircraft executive*
Gibara, Samir S. G. *manufacturing executive*
Hackbirth, David William *aluminum company executive*
Kaufman, Donald Leroy *building products executive*
Shaffer, Oren George *manufacturing company executive*

Athens
Werner, R(ichard) Budd *retired business executive*

Aurora
Braude, Edwin Simon *manufacturing company executive*
Lefebvre, Gabriel Felicien *retired chemical company executive*
Toomey, William Shenberger *retired wire manufacturing company executive*

Beachwood
Van Aken, William J. *construction executive*
Weatherhead, Albert John, III *business executive*

Berea
Soppelsa, John Joseph *decal manufacturing company executive*

Bratenahl
Jones, Trevor Owen *biomedical products and automobile supply company executive, management consultant*

Brecksville
Usalis, George Jerome *metal processing executive*

Canton
Birkholz, Raymond James *metal products manufacturing company executive*
†Davis, Henry Arnold *healthcare company executive*
Elsaesser, Robert James *retired manufacturing executive*
Karabasz, Felix Francois "Sam" *engineering and manufacturing company executive*

Cedarville
Gordin, Dean Lackey *retired agricultural products executive*

Chagrin Falls
Brophy, Jere Hall *manufacturing company executive*
Callahan, Francis Joseph *manufacturing company executive*
Heckman, Henry Trevennen Shick *steel company executive*

Chardon
Jones, Sandra *electronics executive*
Seidemann, Robert Simon *manufacturing company executive*

Cincinnati
Ackermann, Russell Albert *manufacturing company executive*
Anderson, Jerry William, Jr. *technical and business consulting executive, educator*
Christensen, Paul Walter, Jr. *gear manufacturing company executive*
Coombe, V. Anderson *valve manufacturing company executive*
Farmer, Richard T. *uniform rental and sales executive*
Harrell, Samuel Macy *agribusiness executive*
Leyda, James Perkins *retired pharmaceutical company executive*
Mates, Lawrence A., II *medical company executive, consultant*
Meyer, Daniel Joseph *machinery company executive*
Meyer, Walter H. *retired food safety executive, consultant*
Pichler, Joseph Anton *food products executive*
Price, Jay E. *consumer products company executive*
Ruthman, Thomas Robert *manufacturing executive*
Schulman, Melvin Louis *food processing company executive*
Shepherd, Elsbeth Weichsel *supply chain consultant*
Smale, John Gray *diversified industry executive*
Stern, Joseph Smith, Jr. *former footwear manufacturing company executive*
Thompson, Morley Punshon *textile company executive*

Cleveland
Anderson, Harold Albert *engineering and building executive*
Bersticker, Albert Charles *chemical company executive*
Bissett, Barbara Anne *steel distribution company executive*
Bollenbacher, Herbert Kenneth *steel company official*
Breen, John Gerald *manufacturing company executive*
Callsen, Christian Edward *medical device company executive*
Coleman, George Michael *chemical company executive*
Collins, Duane E. *manufacturing executive*
Cutler, Alexander MacDonald *manufacturing company executive*
Decker, John William *steel company executive*
Gray, James Patrick *business executive, consultant, educator*
Hamilton, William Milton *manufacturing executive*
Hardis, Stephen Roger *manufacturing company executive*
Hedrick, Hal Clemons *company executive*
Hellman, Peter Stuart *technical manufacturing executive*
Henning, George Thomas, Jr. *steel company executive*
Hushen, John Wallace *manufacturing company executive*
Jameson, J(ames) Larry *chemical company executive*
Kamm, Christian Philip *manufacturing company executive*
Kay, Albert Joseph *textile executive*
Loop, Floyd D. *health, medical executive*
Luke, Randall Dan *retired tire and rubber company executive, lawyer*
Mac Laren, David Sergeant *manufacturing corporation executive, inventor*
Mandel, Jack N. *manufacturing company executive*
McFadden, John Volney *retired manufacturing company executive*
Moll, Curtis E. *manufacturing executive*
Mullally, Pierce Harry *retired steel company executive*
Myers, David N. *construction executive*
Nelson, Richard Alan *financial executive*
Oesterling, Thomas Ovid *pharmaceutical company executive*
Parker, Patrick Streeter *manufacturing executive*
Reid, James Sims, Jr. *automobile parts manufacturer*
Rich, Lawrence Vincent *manufacturing and engineering company executive*
Rosenthal, Leighton A. *aviation company executive*
Sabo, Richard Steven *electrical company executive*
Stone, Harry H. *business executive*
Tomsich, Robert J. *heavy machinery manufacturing executive*
Tracht, Allen Eric *electronics executive*
Unger, Paul A. *packaging executive*
Wright, Marshall *retired manufacturing executive, former diplomat*

Columbus
Alban, Roger Charles *construction equipment distribution executive*
Anderson, Kerrii B. *construction company executive*
†Baker, John *electronics executive*
Berndt, Ellen German *company executive*
Cottingham, Richard Sumner *paper company executive*
Crane, Jameson *plastics manufacturing company executive*
Curtis, Loretta O'Ellen *retired construction executive*
Daab-Krzykowski, Andre *pharmaceutical and nutritional manufacturing company administrator*
Evans, Daniel E. *sausage manufacturing and restaurant chain company executive*
Gardner, Robert Meade *retired building contractor*
Kidder, C. Robert *food products executive*
Knilans, Michael Jerome *supermarkets executive*
Lazar, Theodore Aaron *retired manufacturing company executive, lawyer*
Pfening, Frederic Denver, III *manufacturing company executive*
Post, Natalie Jenkins *recreational vehicle executive*
Rohrbaugh, Wayne Joseph *chemical company executive*
Smith, Eric Craig *construction executive*
Stratton, James Edward *construction educator*
Wigington, Ronald Lee *retired chemical information services executive*
Wolf, John Steven *construction executive, land developer*
Yenkin, Bernard Kalman *coatings and resins company executive*

Dayton
Diggs, Matthew O'Brien, Jr. *air conditioning and refrigeration manufacturing executive*
Duval, Daniel Webster *manufacturing company executive*
Enouen, William Albert *paper corporation executive*
Harlan, Norman Ralph *construction executive*
Ladehoff, Leo William *metal products manufacturing executive*
Mathile, Clayton Lee *corporate executive*
Mc Swiney, James Wilmer *retired pulp and paper manufacturing company executive*
Poseidon, Pantelis Lee *marketing and product executive*
Shuey, John Henry *diversified products company executive*

Delaware
Eells, William Hastings *retired automobile company executive*

Dublin
Borror, Donald A. *construction company executive*
Borror, Douglas G. *construction company executive*
Clement, Henry Joseph, Jr. *diversified building products executive*
Lamp, Benson J. *tractor company executive*

Fairlawn
Brubaker, Karen Sue *manufacturing executive*

Garrettsville
Diskin, Michael Edward *plastics industry executive*

Gates Mills
Reitman, Robert Stanley *manufacturing and marketing executive*

Veale, Tinkham, II *former chemical company executive, engineer*

Greenville
King, Charles Homer *manufacturing executive*

Grove City
Lok, Silmond Ray *pharmaceutical executive*

Groveport
Ricart, Fred *automotive company executive*

Hilliard
Rahal, Robert W. *automotive company executive*

Holland
D'Anniballe, Priscilla Lucille *contracting company executive*
Hirsch, Carl Herbert *retired manufacturing company executive*

Holmesville
Bolender, James Henry *tire and rubber manufacturing executive*

Hudson
Galloway, Ethan Charles *technology development executive, former chemicals executive*

Jackson Center
Thompson, Wade Francis Bruce *manufacturing company executive*

Kettering
Purdy, John Edgar *manufacturing company executive*

Lakewood
Bradley, J. F., Jr. *retired manufacturing company executive*

Lancaster
Fox, Robert Kriegbaum *manufacturing company executive*
Sulick, Robert John *general contractor*

Lima
Pranses, Anthony Louis *retired electric company executive, organization executive*

Lorain
Bado, Kenneth Steve *automotive company administrator*

Mansfield
Gorman, James Carvill *pump manufacturing company executive*
Hooker, James Todd *manufacturing executive*

Mantua
Ray, James Allen *research consultant*

Marysville
Berger, Charles Martin *food company executive*

Masonnnati
Wilson, Frederic Sandford *pharmaceutical company executive*

Massillon
Snyder, Rachel Ann *manufacturing company specialist*

Maumee
Anderson, Richard Paul *agricultural company executive*

Mayfield Heights
Rankin, Alfred Marshall, Jr. *business executive*

Medina
Smith, Richey *chemical company executive*
Sullivan, Thomas Christopher *coatings company executive*

Milan
Henry, Joseph Patrick *chemical company executive*

Milford
Donahue, John Lawrence, Jr. *paper company executive*
Klosterman, Albert Leonard *technical development business executive, mechanical engineer*

New Bremen
Dicke, James Frederick, II *manufacturing company executive*

New Philadelphia
Mears, Orum Glenn, III *automotive executive*

North Ridgeville
Baughman, Dennis John *director of operations service*
Rehm, John Edwin *manufacturing company executive*

Painesville
Humphrey, George Magoffin, II *plastic molding company executive*
†Spencer, Elden A. *retired manufacturing company executive*

Pepper Pike
Grabner, George John *manufacturing executive*

Perrysburg
Eastman, John Richard *retired manufacturing company executive*
King, John Joseph *manufacturing company executive*

Pickerington
Zacks, Gordon Benjamin *manufacturing company executive*

Plain City
Kinman, Gary *company executive*

Powell
Funk, John William *emergency vehicle manufacturing executive, packaging company executive, lawyer*

Randolph
Pecano, Donald Carl *truck trailer manufacturing executive*

Reynoldsburg
Woodward, Greta Charmaine *construction company executive*

Richfield
Tobler, D. Lee *retired chemical and aerospace company executive*

Sandusky
Amos, Janice Rae *automotive executive*

Solon
Rosica, Gabriel Adam *corporate executive, engineer*

Streetsboro
Kearns, Warren Kenneth *business executive*

Sylvania
Lock, Richard William *packaging company executive*

Tipp City
Panayirci, Sharon Lorraine *textiles executive, design engineer*
Tighe-Moore, Barbara Jeanne *electronics executive*

Toledo
†Abeln, Maura *plastics company executive*
Boller, Ronald Cecil *glass company executive*
Hiner, Glen Harold, Jr. *materials company executive*
Lemieux, Joseph Henry *manufacturing company executive*
Morcott, Southwood J. *automotive parts manufacturing company executive*
Romanoff, Milford Martin *building contractor*
Strobel, Martin Jack *lawyer, motor vehicle and industrial component manufacturing and distribution company executive*

Twinsburg
Novak, Harry R. *manufacturing company executive*

University Heights
Epstein, Marvin Morris *retired construction company executive*

Walbridge
†Rudolph, Frederick William *contractor*

Warren
Thompson, Eric Thomas *manufacturing company executive*

Wheelersburg
Hulse, Dexter Curtis *manufacturing executive*

Willoughby
Manning, William Dudley, Jr. *retired specialty chemical company executive*

Wooster
Basford, James Orlando *container manufacturing company executive*
Degnan, Martin J. *rubber products corporation executive, lawyer*

Worthington
Trevor, Alexander Bruen *computer company executive*

Youngstown
Courtney, William Francis *food and vending service company executive*
Powers, Paul J. *manufacturing company executive*

OKLAHOMA

Bixby
Garrett, James Lowell *contractor*

Edmond
Morgan, Ralph Rexford *manufacturing company executive*

Enid
Berry, Robert Bass *construction executive*

Guthrie
†Cleek, Clifford R. *power assembly company executive*

Oklahoma City
Batenic, Mark K. *manufacturing company executive*
Horner, Russell Grant, Jr. *energy and chemical company executive*
Jonsson, Skuli *construction company executive*
Smith, Robert Walter *food company executive*
Turner, Eugene Andrew *manufacturing executive*
Worthington, J.B. *chemical company executive*

Sand Springs
Ackerman, Robert Wallace *steel company executive*
Ray, Eddye Robert *occupational safety and health professional*

Skiatook
Hoy, Charles William, III *electrical controls company executive*

Tulsa
Calvert, Delbert William *chemical company executive*
Dearmon, Thomas Alfred *automotive industry and life insurance executive*
Narwold, Lewis Lammers *paper products manufacturer*
Primeaux, Henry, III *automotive executive, author, speaker*
Riggs, David Lynn *company executive*

Thomas, Robert Eggleston *former corporate executive*
Tomer, Mark John *manufacturing/research and development executive*

OREGON

Beaverton
Barnes, Keith Lee *electronics executive*
†Dinh, Thin Van *electronics specialist*
Donahue, Richard King *athletic apparel executive, lawyer*
Knight, Philip H(ampson) *shoe manufacturing company executive*

Cottage Grove
Nordin, Donald Marion *manufacturing industry executive*

Eugene
Leeds, Elizabeth Louise *miniature collectibles executive*

Klamath Falls
Wendt, Richard L. *manufacturing executive*

Medford
Barnes, Joseph Curtis *aircraft development executive*
Hannum, Gerald Luther (Lou Hannum) *retired tire manufacturing company official*

Portland
Abbott, Robert Carl *management company executive*
Eberwein, Barton Douglas *construction company executive, consultant*
Flowerree, Robert Edmund *retired forest products company executive*
Foehl, Edward Albert *chemical company executive*
Gray, John Delton *retired manufacturing company executive*
Leineweber, Peter Anthony *forest products company executive*
McKennon, Keith Robert *chemical company executive*
Nagel, Stanley Blair *retired construction and investment executive*
Pamplin, Robert Boisseau, Sr. *textile manufacturing executive, retired*
Pamplin, Robert Boisseau, Jr. *manufacturing company executive, minister, writer*
Steinfeld, Ray, Jr. *food products executive*
Stott, Peter Walter *forest products company executive*
Swindells, William, Jr. *lumber and paper company executive*
Thomason, Scott *automobile executive*
Walker, Daphine Broadhead *construction executive*
Watkins, Charles Reynolds *medical equipment company executive*
Whitsell, Helen Jo *lumber executive*

Sisters
Baxter, John Lincoln, Jr. *manufacturing company executive*

Springfield
Detlefsen, William David, Jr. *chemicals executive*

Tigard
Berglund, Carl Neil *electronics company executive*

Wilsonville
Meyer, Jerome J. *diversified technology company executive*

PENNSYLVANIA

Adamstown
Milner, Charles Fremont, Jr. *manufacturing company executive*

Allentown
Armor, John N. *chemical company scientist and research manager*
Baker, Dexter Farrington *manufacturing company executive*
Donley, Edward *manufacturing company executive*
Foster, Edward Paul (Ted Foster) *process industries executive*
Lovett, John Robert *retired chemical company executive*
Samuels, Abram *stage equipment manufacturing company executive*
Shire, Donald Thomas *retired air products and chemicals executive, lawyer*

Allison Park
Backus, John King *former chemical company research administrator*

Altoona
Yohn, Sharon A. *manufacturing executive*

Ambler
Zane, William Anthony *chemicals executive*

Avondale
Friel, Daniel Denwood, Sr. *manufacturing executive*

Bala Cynwyd
Driscoll, Edward Carroll *construction management firm executive*
Furlong, Edward V., Jr. *paper company executive*
Lotman, Herbert *food processing executive*
Rines, John Randolph *automotive company executive*

Beaver
Price, Ronald James *electrical products company executive*

Belle Vernon
Wapiennik, Carl Francis *manufacturing firm executive, planetarium and science institute executive*

Bensalem
Sergey, John Michael, Jr. *distribution company executive*

Berwyn
Burch, John Walter *mining equipment company executive*
Gockley, Barbara Jean *corporate professional*
Silverman, Stanley Wayne *chemical company executive*

Bethlehem
Barnette, Curtis Handley *steel company executive, lawyer*
Church, Thomas Trowbridge *former steel company executive*
Hartmann, Robert Elliott *manufacturing company executive, retired*
Rushton, Brian Mandel *chemical company executive*

Blue Bell
Barry, Lei *medical equipment manufacturing executive*
Theis, Steven Thomas *executive safety director*

Boswell
Straw, Gary Lee *construction company executive*

Bradford
Rice, Lester *electronics company executive*

Bradfordwoods
Allardice, John McCarrell *coatings manufacturing company executive*

Butler
Artz, Frederick James *diversified manufacturing company executive*

Canonsburg
Harker, Joseph Edward *construction, industrial and steel company executive*
Piatt, Jack Boyd *manufacturing executive*

Central City
Brown, Robert Alan *retired construction materials company executive*

Chambersburg
Rumler, Robert Hoke *agricultural consultant, retired association executive*

Clarks Summit
Alperin, Irwin Ephraim *clothing company executive*
Ross, Adrian E. *drilling manufacturing company executive*

Clifton Heights
Rothermel, Rodman Schantz *manufacturing company executive*

Collegeville
De Rosen, Michel *pharmaceutical company executive*
Kun, Kenneth A. *business executive*
McCairns, Regina Carfagno *pharmaceutical executive*

Colmar
Taylor, Robert Morgan *electronics executive*

Conshohocken
Gibson, Thomas Richard *automobile import company executive*
Naples, Ronald James *manufacturing company executive*
Spaeth, Karl Henry *retired chemical company executive, lawyer*

Coopersburg
Spira, Joel Solon *electronics company executive*

Coraopolis
†Luffy, Robert H. *construction company executive*

Corry
Rathinavelu, Madi *manufacturing executive*

Cranberry Township
Hogberg, Carl Gustav *retired steel company executive*

Doylestown
McNulty, Carrell Stewart, Jr. *retired manufacturing company executive, architect*
McNutt, Richard Hunt *manufacturing company executive*

East Stroudsburg
Bishop, Gerald Iveson *pharmaceutical executive*

Easton
Stipe, Edwin, III *mechanical contracting company executive*
Sun, Robert Zu Jei *inventor, manufacturing company executive*

Edinboro
Tramontano, John Patrick, Jr. *electrical products company executive*

Eighty Four
Capone, Alphonse William *retired industrial executive*
†Magerko, Maggie Hardy *lumber company executive*

Emmaus
Bowers, Klaus D(ieter) *retired electronics research development company executive*

Erie
Duval, Albert Frank *paper company executive*

Exton
Dorsey, Jeremiah Edmund *pharmaceutical company executive*
Lewis, Thomas B. *specialty chemical company executive*

Feasterville Trevose
Liberati, Maria Theresa *fashion production company executive*

Fort Washington
Meyer, Andrew R. *manufacturing executive*

Greentown
Forcheskie, Carl S. *former apparel company executive*

Greenville
Stuver, Francis Edward *former railway car company executive*

Halifax
Stauffer, Joanne Rogan *steel company official*

Hanover
Antonaccio, Mario Americo *retired manufacturing executive*

Harrisburg
Goell, James Emanuel *electronics company executive*
Hudson, William Jeffrey, Jr. *manufacturing company executive*
Marley, James Earl *manufacturing company executive*

Hatboro
Hull, Lewis Woodruff *manufacturing company executive*

Haverford
Talucci, Samuel James *retired chemical company executive*

Havertown
Tassone, Bruce Anthony *chemical company executive*

Hazleton
Stamatopoulos, Steven John *automotive industry executive, consultant*

Hershey
Blouch, Timothy Craig *food company executive*
Duncan, Charles Lee *food products company executive*
Wolfe, Kenneth L. *food products manufacturing company executive*

Hollidaysburg
Bloom, Lawrence Stephen *retired clothing company executive*

Horsham
Hook, Jerry B. *pharmaceutical company executive*

Jenkintown
Reese, Francis Edward *retired chemical company executive, consultant*

Kennett Square
May, Harold Edward *chemical company executive*

King Of Prussia
Dee, Robert Forrest *retired pharmaceutical company executive*
McLane, James Woods *healthcare executive*
Poste, George Henry *pharmaceutical company executive*
Wachs, David V. *retired apparel executive*
Winkhaus, Hans-Dietrich *chemicals executive*

Kingston
Fierman, Gerald Shea *electrical distribution company executive*

Lancaster
Case, Edward Ralph *manufacturing executive*
Dodge, Arthur Byron, Jr. *business executive*
Hess, Donald F. *retired manufacturing executive, accountant*
High, S. Dale *diversified company executive*
Hoover, Donald Leroy *construction executive*
Liddell, W. Kirk *specialty contracting company executive*
Lorch, George A. *manufacturing company executive*
†Needleman, Alvin D. *research and development company executive*

Large
Dick, Douglas Patrick *construction company executive*

Latrobe
Daughenbaugh, Terry Lee *steel industry executive*

Lebanon
McMindes, Roy James *aggregate company executive*
Paul, Herman Louis, Jr. *valve manufacturing company executive*

Lemoyne
Deeg, Emil Wolfgang *manufacturing company executive, physicist*
Kirkwood, James Mace *pharmaceutical benefit management company executive*

Ligonier
Pilz, Alfred Norman *manufacturing company executive*

Lower Gwynedd
Torok, Raymond Patrick *steel and aluminum company executive*

Lyon Station
Breidegam, DeLight Edgar, Jr. *battery company executive*

Malvern
Weisman, Harlan Frederick *pharmaceutical company executive*
†Yost, R. David *healthcare manufacturing company administrator*

Mc Murray
Langenberg, Frederick Charles *business executive*

Meadville
Foster, Catherine Rierson *manufacturing company executive*

Media
Garrison, Walter R. *corporate executive*
Resnick, Stewart Allen *diversified company executive*

Mohnton
Bowers, Richard Philip *manufacturing executive*

Monroeville
Maclay, William Nevin *retired manufacturing and construction company executive*

Montgomeryville
Seal, John S., Jr. *manufacturing company executive*

Moylan
Peabody, William Tyler, Jr. *retired paper manufacturing company executive*

New Hope
Williamson, Frederick Beasley, III *rubber company executive*

Newtown
Henshaw, Jonathan Cook *manufacturing company executive*
Ross, Edwin William *rubber company executive*

Newtown Square
Benenson, James, Jr. *manufacturer*
Traynor, Sean Gabrial *manufacturing executive*

Oakmont
DeFazio, John Lorenzo *retired manufacturing executive*

Paoli
Blankley, Walter Elwood *manufacturing company executive*

Peach Glen
Carey, Dean Lavere *fruit canning company executive*

Philadelphia
Avery, William Joseph *packaging manufacturing company executive*
Azoulay, Bernard *chemicals company executive*
Berwind, C. G., Jr. *manufacturing executive*
Callé, Craig R.L. *packaging executive*
Driscoll, Lee Francis, Jr. *corporate director, lawyer*
Katherine, Robert Andrew *chemical company executive*
Kiefer, J. Richard, Jr. *retired corporate executive*
Lien, Eric L. *pharmaceutical executive*
†Llewellyn, J. Bruce *food products executive*
McKenna, Michael Joseph *manufacturing company executive*
Potamkin, Robert *automotive executive*
Rost, Peter *pharmaceutical company executive*
Sorgenti, Harold Andrew *petroleum and chemical company executive*
Stetson, John Batterson, IV *construction executive*
Wilson, James Lawrence *chemical company executive*

Pittsburgh
Burnham, Donald Clemens *manufacturing company executive*
Courtsal, Donald Preston *manufacturing company executive, financial consultant*
Dick, David E. *construction company executive*
Dinman, Bertram David *consultant, retired aluminum company executive*
Edelman, Harry Rollings, III *engineering and construction company executive*
Fairbanks, Frank Bates *manufacturing company executive*
†Fischer, Richard Lawrence *metal products executive*
Foxen, Richard William *manufacturing company executive*
Frank, Alan I W *manufacturing company executive*
Giel, James Arthur, Jr. *steel company executive*
Huntington, James Cantine, Jr. *equipment manufacturing company executive*
LaRusso, Anthony Carl *company executive, educator*
Lauterbach, Robert Emil *steel company executive*
Lego, Paul Edward *retired corporation executive*
Limbach, Walter F. *construction company executive*
Mason, Robert Thomas *chemical company executive*
Mulloney, Peter Black *retired steel, oil and gas executive*
O'Neill, Paul Henry *aluminum company executive*
O'Reilly, Anthony John Francis *food company executive*
Paul, Robert Arthur *steel company executive*
Paxton, Harold William *educator, former steel company executive*
Puskar, Milan *pharmaceuticals executive*
Rust, William James *retired steel company executive*
Simmons, Richard P. *steel company executive*
Thomas, W(illiam) Bruce *retired steel, oil, gas company executive*
Turnbull, Gordon Keith *metal company executive, metallurgical engineer*
Usher, Thomas James *steel executive, energy executive*
Will, James Fredrick *steel company executive*

Plains
Pugliese, Frank Anthony, Jr. *health executive*

Pocopson
Mulligan, James Francis *retired business executive, lawyer*

Portland
Hutton, William Michael *manufacturing company owner*

Reading
Beaver, Howard Oscar, Jr. *retired alloys manufacturing company executive*
Ehlerman, Paul Michael *industrial battery manufacturing company executive*

Fiore, Nicholas Francis *special alloys and materials company executive*
Pugliese, Anthony Paul *construction company executive, educator*

Saint Davids
Smalley, Christopher Joseph *pharmaceutical company professional*

Saint Marys
Johnson, J. M. Hamlin *manufacturing company executive*

Sewickley
Bouchard, James Paul *steel manufacturing and planning executive*
Rastogi, Anil Kumar *medical device manufacturer executive*
Snyder, William Penn, III *manufacturing company executive*
Thorbecke, Willem Henry *international company executive, consultant*

Sharon
Myers, Ronald Kosty *manufacturing executive, inventor*

Shippensburg
Collier, Duaine Alden *manufacturing and distribution company executive*
Luhrs, H. Ric *toy manufacturing company executive*

Shiremanstown
Denison, Richard Eugene *retired agricultural services company executive*

Shoemakersville
Graeff, David Wayne *maintenance executive, consultant*

Souderton
†Delp, R. Lee *meat packing company executive*

Southampton
DaCosta, Edward Hoban *plastics and electronics manufacturing company executive*
Zocholl, Stanley Ernest *electronics executive*

Spring House
Herb, Samuel Martin *manufacturing company executive*
Payn, Clyde Francis *technology company executive, consultant*

Springfield
Linker, Frank Vincent, II *manufacturing executive, consultant*

Swarthmore
Heaps, Marvin Dale *food services company executive*
Kaufman, Antoinette D. *business services company executive*

Trevose
Faulkner, Henry, III *automotive executive*

Unionville
Forney, Robert Clyde *retired chemical industry executive*
Irwin, Robert Hugh Crawford *manufacturing company executive*

Valley Forge
Dachowski, Peter Richard *manufacturing executive*

Washington
Kastelic, Robert Frank *aerospace company executive*

Wayne
Agersborg, Helmer Pareli K. *pharmaceutical company executive, researcher*
Curry, Thomas James *manufacturers representative*
Wolcott, Robert Wilson, Jr. *consulting company executive*

Waynesboro
Benchoff, James Martin *manufacturing company executive*

West Chester
Aiken, Robert McCutchen *retired chemical company executive, management consultant*
Gadsby, Robin Edward *chemical company executive*
†Kim, James Joo-Jin *electronics company executive*
Merion, Richard Donald *retired onstruction company executive*

West Conshohocken
†Ball, John H. *construction executive*

West Point
Keyser, Janet Marie *pharmaceutical industry executive*

Wexford
Efaw, Cary Ross *manufacturing company executive*

Willow Grove
Kulicke, C(harles) Scott *business executive*

Worcester
McAdam, Will *electronics consultant*

Wynnewood
Connor, James Edward, Jr. *retired chemical company executive*

Wyomissing
Cottrell, G. Walton *manufacturing executive*
Garr, Carl Robert *manufacturing company executive*

Yardley
Spector, Ira Charles *pharmaceutical research executive, consultant*

York
Macdonald, Andrew *entrepreneur*

Pokelwaldt, Robert N. *manufacturing company executive*
Schmitt, Ralph George *manufacturing company executive*

Zionsville
Fleming, Richard *chemical company executive*

RHODE ISLAND

Cranston
MacGunnigle, Bruce Campbell *manufacturing company executive*

Newport
Nash, Karen Marsteller Myers *sculptor, designer, systems analyst*

North Kingstown
Sharpe, Henry Dexter, Jr. *retired manufacturing company executive*

Pawtucket
Gordon, Harold P. *manufacturing executive*
Reed, Cynthia S. *manufacturing eecutive*

Providence
Ames, Robert San *retired manufacturing company executive*
Choquette, Paul Joseph, Jr. *construction company executive*
Geckle, Robert Alan *manufacturing company executive*
Gilbane, Jean Ann (Mrs. Thomas F. Gilbane) *construction company executive*
Hardymon, James Franklin *retired diversified products company executive*
Resnik, David Alan *manufacturing company executive*

West Warwick
Galkin, Robert Theodore *company executive*

SOUTH CAROLINA

Arcadia
Dent, Frederick Baily *mill executive, former ambassador, former secretary of commerce*

Beaufort
Richards, Charlene Anna *computer manufacturing company executive*

Camden
Daniels, John Hancock *agricultural products company executive*

Charleston
Addlestone, Nathan Sidney *metals company executive*
Geentiens, Gaston Petrus, Jr. *former construction management consultant company executive*
Harding, Enoch, Jr. *clothing executive*
Kent, Harry Ross *construction executive, lay worker*
Mackaness, George Bellamy *retired pharmaceutical company executive*
Martin, Roblee Boettcher *retired cement manufacturing executive*
Thompson, W(ilmer) Leigh *pharmaceutical company executive, physician, pharmacologist*

Clinton
Cornelson, George Henry, IV *retired textile company executive*
Vance, Robert Mercer *textile manufacturing company executive, banker*

Columbia
†Lolas, Anthony Joseph, Sr. *health and environmental business executive*
Robinson, Robert Earl *chemical company executive*

Florence
Dixon, Gale Harllee *drug company executive*

Fort Mill
Horten, Carl Frank *textile manufacturing company executive*

Greenville
Dobson, Robert Albertus, IV *corporate executive*
Friedman, Steven M. *textile company executive*
Roe, Thomas Anderson *building supply company executive*

Greenwood
Self, W. M. *textile company executive*

Greer
Gallman, Clarence Hunter *textile executive*
Lane, James Garland, Jr. *diversified industry executive*

Hartsville
Browning, Peter Crane *packaging company executive*
Coker, Charles Westfield *diversified manufacturing company executive*

Hilton Head Island
Cunningham, William Henry *retired food products executive*
Harty, James D. *former manufacturing company executive*
Mersereau, Hiram Stipe *wood products company consultant*
Pritchard, Dalton Harold *retired electronics research engineer*
Rulis, Raymond Joseph *manufacturing company executive, consultant*
Russell, Allen Stevenson *retired aluminum company executive*
Stoll, Richard Edmund *retired manufacturing executive*

North Charleston
Zucker, Jerry *energy systems manufacturing executive*

Reidville
Armstrong, Thomas Gliem *steel company executive*

Simpsonville
Maguire, D.E. *electronics executive*

Spartanburg
Mahanes, Michael Wayne *audio-visual electronics company executive*
Milliken, Roger *textile company executive*

Townville
Wright, George Cullen *electronics company executive*

SOUTH DAKOTA

Dakota Dunes
Peterson, Robert L. *meat processing executive*

Sioux Falls
Christensen, David Allen *manufacturing company executive*
Reynolds, Leo Thomas *electronics company executive*
†Rosenthal, Joel *manufacturing executive*

TENNESSEE

Antioch
Nelson, Richard Alver *contractor*

Chattanooga
St. Goar, Herbert *retired food corporation executive*

Collegedale
McKee, Ellsworth R. *food products executive*

Cordova
Colbert, Robert B., Jr. *apparel company executive*
Dean, Jimmy *meat processing company executive, entertainer*

Crossville
Lawrence, Ralph Waldo *manufacturing company executive*

Dandridge
Comer, Evan Philip *manufacturing company executive*

Gallatin
Crutcher, Dimetrec Artez *electronics technician*

Greeneville
Renner, Glenn Delmar *agricultural products executive*

Kingsport
Coover, Harry Wesley *manufacturing company executive*
Deavenport, Earnest W., Jr. *chemical executive*
Findley, Don Aaron *manufacturing company executive*
Head, William Iverson, Sr. *retired chemical company executive*

Knoxville
Faires, Ross Norbert *manufacturing company executive*
Klingerman, Robert Harvey *manufacturing company executive*
Lobins, Christine Marie *accounts sales administrator*
Martin, James Robert *identification company executive*
Stringfield, Hezz, Jr. *contractor, financial consultant*
Wesley, Stephen Harrison *pharmaceutical company executive*

Lookout Mountain
Rymer, S. Bradford, Jr. *retired appliance manufacturing company executive*

Memphis
Andrews, William Eugene *construction products manufacturing executive*
Ballou, Howard Burgess *commercial plumbing designer*
Duke, Gary James *electronics executive*
Dunavant, William Buchanan, Jr. *textiles executive*
Dunnigan, T. Kevin *electrical and electronics manufacturing company executive*
Hurley, Jeffrey Scott *fabric company administrator*
Jenkins, Ruben Lee *chemical company executive*
Mantey, Elmer Martin *food company executive*

Nashville
Fitzgerald, Edmund Bacon *electronics industry executive*
Gulmi, James Singleton *apparel manufacturing company executive*
Harris, J(acob) George *health care company executive*
Hass, Joseph Monroe *automotive executive*
Hofstead, James Warner *laundry machinery company executive, lawyer*
Mahanes, David James, Jr. *retired distillery executive*
Mizell, Yolanda Mattei *ornamental plaster company executive*
Shipley Biddy, Shelia *artist management executive*
Thompson, Anthony *retired corporate executive*
Wire, William Shidaker, II *retired apparel and footwear manufacturing company executive*

Oak Ridge
Poutsma, Marvin L. *chemical research administrator*

Union City
Graham, R(ichard) Newell *soft drink bottling company executive*

TEXAS

Addison
†Anderson, Jack Roy *health care company executive*

Alamo
Pritchett, Thomas Ronald *retired metal and chemical company executive*

Arlington
Gates, Richard Daniel *retired manufacturing company executive*
Kemp, Thomas Joseph *electronics company executive*
Mansen, Steven Robert *manufacturing company executive*

Austin
†Allen, Glenn T. *manufacturing executive*
Brager, Walter S. *retired food products corporation executive*
Cook, Chauncey William Wallace *retired food products company executive*
Culp, Joe C(arl) *electronics executive*
Edwards, Wayne Forrest *paper company executive*
McBee, Frank Wilkins, Jr. *industrial manufacturing executive*
Nelson, Steven Douglas *construction company executive*
Sullivan, Jerry Stephen *electronics company executive*
Thompson, Larry Flack *semiconductor equipment company executive*
†Ulibarri, River Cecilia *construction company executive*
Van Buren, William Benjamin, III *retired pharmaceutical company executive*
Vykukal, Eugene Lawrence *wholesale drug company executive*
Watkins, Sarah Frances Ashford *electronic manufacturing company executive*

Beaumont
Ware, John David *valve and hydrant company executive*

Bryan
Lusas, Edmund William *food processing research executive*

Carrollton
Heath, Jinger L. *cosmetics executive*
Hulbert, Paul William, Jr. *paper, lumber company executive*

College Station
†Kainthla, Ramesh Chand *manufacturing company executive*

Coppell
Minyard, Liz *food products executive*
†Williams, Gretchen Minyard *food store executive*

Corpus Christi
Heinz, Walter Ernst Edward *retired chemical executive*
Kane, Sam *meat company executive*

Dallas
Adams, James R. *electronics company executive*
Ash, Mary Kay *cosmetics company executive*
Barnes, Robert Vertreese, Jr. *masonry contractor executive*
Bartley, David Anthony *electronics executive*
Bartos, Jerry Garland *corporate executive, mechanical engineer*
Bradford, William Edward *oil field equipment manufacturing company executive*
Calado, Miguel Maria *food company executive*
Dawson, Edward Joseph *merger and acquisition executive*
Dorris, Carlos Eugene *chemicals executive*
Engels, Lawrence Arthur *metals company executive*
Forward, Gordon E. *manufacturing executive*
†Gentry, Jerry L. *manufacturing executive*
Gifford, Porter William *retired construction materials manufacturing company executive*
Gray, James Larry *metals company executive*
Guerin, Dean Patrick *executive*
Hirsch, Laurence Eliot *construction executive, mortgage banker*
Hirsh, Bernard *supply company executive, consultant*
Margerison, Richard Wayne *diversified industrial company executive*
McCally, Charles Richard *construction company executive*
Murphy, John Joseph *manufacturing company executive*
O'Brien, George Aloysius, Jr. *paper company executive*
Pearce, Ronald *retired cosmetic company executive*
Roach, John D. C. *manufacturing company executive*
Robbins, Ray Charles *manufacturing company executive*
Robertson, Beverly Carruth *retired steel company executive*
Rochon, John Philip *cosmetics company executive*
Rosson, Glenn Richard *building products and furniture company executive*
St. John, Bill Dean *diversified equipment and services company executive*
Sammons, Elaine D. *corporate executive*
Schenkel, Pete *food company executive*
Solomon, William Tarver *general construction company executive*
Thompson, Charles Kerry *company executive*
Yanagisawa, Samuel Tsuguo *electronics executive*
Zumwalt, Richard Dowling *flour mill executive*

Denton
Brown, John Fred *steel company executive*

Diboll
Grum, Clifford J. *manufacturing company executive*
Harbordt, Charles Michael *forest products executive*

El Paso
Peinado, Arnold Benicio, Jr. *consulting engineer*

Falfurrias
Gonzalez, Salvador Hinojosa *electronics executive, municipal official*

Floydada
Carthel, Anne Fawver *food products executive*

PROFESSIONAL INDEX 6077 INDUSTRY: MANUFACTURING

Fort Mc Kavett
Stokes, Charles Eugene, Jr. *retired wool merchant*

Fort Worth
Arena, M. Scott *retired pharmaceutical company executive*
Cummings, Patrick Henry *manufacturing executive*
Leone, George Frank *pharmaceutical executive*
Roberts, Leonard H. *retail executive*
Thornton, Charles Victor *metals executive*
Williamson, Philip *apparel executive*

Houston
Ahart, Jan Fredrick *electrical manufacturing company executive*
Austin, Harry Guiden *engineering and construction company executive*
Boren, William Meredith *manufacturing executive*
Buchanan, Dennis Michael *manufacturing and holding company executive*
Cizik, Robert *manufacturing company executive*
Dean, Warren Michael *construction company executive*
De Wree, Eugene Ernest *manufacturing company executive*
Dodson, D. Keith *engineering and construction company executive*
Friedkin, Thomas H. *automotive executive*
Goff, Robert Burnside *retired food company executive*
Hafner, Joseph A., Jr. *food company executive*
Harman, Angela Diane *construction company executive*
Hartsfield, Henry Warren, Jr. *electronics company executive, retired astronaut*
Huffington, Roy Michael *business executive, former ambassador*
†Hurwitz, Charles Edwin *manufacturing company executive*
Jacobson, Charles Allen *aerospace company executive*
Kaptopodis, Louis *supermarket chain executive*
Klausmeyer, David Michael *scientific instruments manufacturing company executive*
Lukens, Max L. *manufacturing company executive*
Mangapit, Conrado, Jr. *manufacturing company executive*
Mason, Franklin Rogers *retired automotive executive*
Menscher, Barnet Gary *steel company executive*
Munisteri, Joseph George *construction executive*
†Murray, Frank *heating, air conditioning manufacturing executive*
Nuss, Eldon Paul *casket manufacturer*
Peterkin, George Alexander, Jr. *marine transportation company executive*
Pognonec, Yves Maurice *steel products executive*
Pyle, Jerry *automotive executive*
Riedel, Alan Ellis *retired manufacturing company executive, lawyer*
Rock, Douglas Lawrence *manufacturing executive*
Roorda, John Francis, Jr. *business consultant*
Smith, Michael William *construction and consulting company executive*
Temple, Robert Winfield *chemical company executive*
Templeton, Robert Earl *engineering and construction company executive*
†Thompson-Draper, Cheryl L. *electronics executive, real estate executive*
Waggoner, James Virgil *chemicals company executive*
Waycaster, Bill *chemicals executive*
White, David Alan, Jr. *manufacturing company executive*
Wilsmann, Edward Charles *chemical company executive, educator*
Wilson, Carl Weldon, Jr. *construction company executive, civil engineer*
Wnuk, Wade Joseph *manufacturing and service company executive*
Wuensche, Vernon Edgar *construction company executive*

Hurst
Mc Keen, Chester M., Jr. *business executive*

Irving
Barber, Jerry Randel *medical device company executive*
Rethore, Bernard Gabriel *diversified manufacturing and mining company executive*

League City
Burns, Richard Robert *chemicals executive*

Liberty Hill
Adams, Christopher Steve, Jr. *retired defense electronics corporation executive, former air force officer*

Longview
Mann, Jack Matthewson *bottling company executive*

Lubbock
Hester, Ross Wyatt *retired business forms manufacturing executive*
†Mitchell, Gary W. *molding company executive*

Mansfield
†Simeus, Dumas *food products executive*

Mcallen
†Garcia, David P. *construction company executive*

Pasadena
Gross, Cynthia Sue *patreochemicals maintenance manager*
Stephens, Sidney Dee *chemical manufacturing company executive*

Plano
Bain, Travis Whitsett, II *manufacturing and retail executive*
Bivona, Virginia Siena *acquisitions editor*
Cumming, Marilee *apparel company executive*
Gibson, Ernest L., III *healthcare consultant*

Port Lavaca
Fisher, (Mary) Jewel Tanner *retired construction company executive*

Richardson
Richards, Frederick Francis, Jr. *manufacturing company executive*

Richmond
Barratt, Cynthia Louise *pharmaceutical company executive*

Roanoke
Hamilton, Kimberly Darlene *diversified service company executive*

Rockwall
Fisher, Gene Jordan *retired chemical company executive*

Round Rock
Dell, Michael S. *manufacturing executive*
Whitlock, Darrell Dean *manufacturing company executive*

San Antonio
Baker, Helen Marie *health services executive*
Berg, Thomas *manufacturing executive*
Cloud, Bruce Benjamin, Sr. *construction company executive*
†Davila, Rodolfo G. *pharmaceutical company executive*
Moore, Kurt W. *pharmaceuticals company executive*
Zachry, Henry Bartell, Jr. *construction company executive*

Sugar Land
Kempner, Isaac Herbert, III *sugar company executive*

Sweeny
Griffin, Stanley Ray *machinist*

Texas City
Chen, Yuan James *chemical company executive*

The Woodlands
†Oubari, Dalal *pharmaceutical executive*

Tyler
Smith, Howard Thompson *business executive*
Warner, John Andrew *foundry executive*

Weatherford
Trigg, George Leon *construction executive*

UTAH

Heber City
Day, Gerald W. *wholesale grocery company executive*

Ogden
Klepinger, John William *trailer manufacturing company executive*
Nickerson, Guy Robert *lumber company executive*

Provo
Newitt, Jay *construction management educator*

Salt Lake City
Anderson, Joseph Andrew, Jr. *retired apparel company executive, retail consultant*
Clark, Jeffrey Raphiel *research and development company executive*
Gregory, Herold La Mar *chemical company administrator*
Hembree, James D. *retired chemical company executive*
Huntsman, Jon Meade *chemical company executive*
Motter, Thomas Franklin *medical products executive*
Norton, Delmar Lynn *candy company executive, video executive*

Sandy
Kille, Willard Bronson, III *business executive*

VERMONT

Arlington
Nowicki, George Lucian *retired chemical company executive*

Bennington
Killen, Carroll Gorden *electronics company executive*

Brattleboro
Cohen, Richard B. *grocery company executive*

Brownsville
Olderman, Gerald *retired medical device company executive*

South Burlington
Pizzagalli, James *construction executive*

Williamstown
Dickinson, Charles Arthur *manufacturing company executive*

Windsor
Furnas, Howard Earl *business executive, educator, retired government official*

VIRGINIA

Alexandria
Cicolani, Angelo George *research company executive, operating engineer*
Cooper, Kenneth Banks *business executive, former army officer*
Haas, Ward John *research and development executive*
Lantz, Phillip Edward *corporate executive, consultant*
Marshall, Maryann Chorba *office administrator*
McKinney, James Clayton *electronics executive, electrical engineer*
Mc Lucas, John Luther *aerospace company executive*
Stempler, Jack Leon *government and aerospace company executive*
Vander Myde, Paul Arthur *technology and engineering services executive*
Wynn, Robert E. *electronics executive, retired career officer*

Arlington
Bennett, John Joseph *professional services company executive*
Cox, Henry *research company executive, research engineer*
Gracey, James Steele *corporate director, retired coast guard officer, consultant*
Mylonakis, Stamatios Gregory *chemicals company executive*
†Nash, Henry G. *company executive*
Otstott, Charles Paddock *company executive, retired army officer*
Pollock, Neal Jay *electronics executive*
Yarymovych, Michael Ihor *retired manufacturing company executive*

Ashburn
Cuteri, Frank R., Jr. *automotive executive*

Blacksburg
Kincade, Doris Helsing *apparel marketing educator*

Bristol
Shean, Timothy Joseph *manufacturing company executive*

Broad Run
Hinkle, Barton Leslie *retired electronics company executive*

Broadway
Keeler, James Leonard *food products company executive*

Catlett
Scheer, Julian Weisel *business executive, author*

Chantilly
Miller, Donald Eugene *aerospace electronics executive*

Charlottesville
MacAvoy, Thomas Coleman *glass manufacturing executive, educator*
Rader, Louis T. *corporation executive, educator*

Deltaville
Koedel, John Gilbert, Jr. *retired forge company executive*

Dulles
Persavich, Warren Dale *diversified manufacturing company executive*

Edinburg
Rhodes, Stephen Michael *poultry company executive*

Fairfax
Edwards, James Owen *engineering and construction company executive*
Sheehan, Edward James *technical consultant, former government official*
Sheehy, Vincent *automotive executive*
†Stringfellow, Charles *automotive executive*

Fairfax Station
Starry, Donn Albert *former aerospace company executive, former army officer*

Franklin
Minor, Edward Colquitt *paper company executive, lawyer*

Glen Allen
Fife, William Franklin *retired drug company executive*
Minor, George Gilmer, III *drug and hospital supply company executive*
Murphey, Robert Stafford *pharmaceutical company executive*

Heathsville
Winkel, Raymond Norman *aerospace industry consultant, avionics manufacturing executive*

Herndon
Guerreri, Carl Natale *electronic company executive*
Guirguis, Raouf Albert *health science executive*

Keswick
Norgren, C. Neil *retired manufacturing company executive*

Kilmarnock
Moore, William Black, Jr. *retired aluminum company executive*

Manassas
Geerdes, James D(ivine) *chemical company executive*
Parrish, Frank Jennings *food company executive*

Marion
†Grinstead, Paul Lee *materials company official*

Mc Lean
Dempsey, James Raymon *industrial executive*
Franklin, Jude Eric *electronics executive*
Graf, Dorothy Ann *business executive*
Levy, Michael Howard *environmental management professional*
Mars, Forrest E., Jr. *candy company executive*
Mars, John F. *candy company executive*
Mehuron, William Otto *electronics company executive*
Perry, Stephen Clayton *manufacturing executive*

Newport News
Banks, Charles Augustus, III *manufacturing executive*
Fricks, William Peavy *shipbuilding company executive*
Salvatori, Vincent Louis *corporate executive*

Norfolk
White, Ira Beauregard, III *pro audio company executive*

Reston
Christ, Thomas Warren *electronics research and development company executive, sociologist*
Gorog, William Francis *corporate executive*

Richmond
Blumberg, Peter Steven *manufacturing company executive*
Bunzl, Rudolph Hans *retired diversified manufacturing company executive*
Dent, Edward Eugene *manufacturing company specialist*
Gottwald, Bruce Cobb *chemical company executive*
Gottwald, Floyd Dewey, Jr. *chemical company executive*
Helwig, Arthur Woods *chemical company executive*
Jordan, Henry Preston, Jr. *manufacturer's representative*
O'Keeffe, Charles B. *pharmaceutical executive*
Pauley, Stanley Frank *manufacturing company executive*
Rogers, James Edward *paper company executive*
Rudnick, Alan A. *management company executive, corporate lawyer*
Sheehan, Jeremiah J. *metal company executive*
Sweeney, Arthur Hamilton, Jr. *metal manufacturing executive, retired army officer*
Totten, Arthur Irving, Jr. *retired metals company executive, consultant*
Watts, Robert Glenn *retired pharmaceutical company executive*

Smithfield
Baxter, Raoul *meat packing company executive*
†Luter, Joseph Williamson, III *meat packing and processing company executive*

Sterling
Lewis, Gene Evans *retired medical equipment company executive*

Suffolk
Birdsong, George Yancy *manufacturing company executive*

Virginia Beach
Toth, Stephen Michael *electronics specialist*

Williamsburg
Wehrly, Jack R. *chemical company executive*

Winchester
Holland, James Tulley *plastic products company executive*
Jolly, Bruce Dwight *manufacturing company executive*
Murtagh, John Edward *alcohol production consultant*

Yorktown
Gross, Leroy *sugar company executive*

WASHINGTON

Anacortes
Holtby, Kenneth Fraser *manufacturing executive*
Randolph, Carl Lowell *chemical company executive*

Bainbridge Island
Blumenthal, Richard Cary *construction executive, consultant*

Bellevue
Hovind, David J. *manufacturing company executive*
Meeker, Milton Shy *manufacturing company executive*
Nowik, Dorothy Adam *medical equipment company executive*
Pigott, Charles McGee *transportation equipment manufacturing executive*
Pigott, Mark C. *automotive executive*

Bellingham
Bestwick, Warren William *retired construction company executive*
Haggen, Donald E. *food products executive*

Biemerton
McClung, J(ames) David *corporate executive, lawyer*

Eastsound
Anders, William Alison *aerospace and defense manufacturing executive*

Edmonds
Parrish, John Brett *business executive*

Gig Harbor
Hedman, Janice Lee *business executive*

Issaquah
Tenenbaum, Michael *steel company executive*
Wainwright, Paul Edward Blech *construction company executive*

Kent
Goo, Abraham Meu Sen *retired aircraft company executive*
Hebeler, Henry Koester *retired aerospace and electronics executive*

Kirkland
Biggs, Thomas Wylie *chemical company executive*
Puckett, Allen Weare *health care information systems executive*

Liberty Lake
Anderson, Gregory Martin *medical company representative*

Longview
Wollenberg, Richard Peter *paper manufacturing company executive*

Manson
Stager, Donald K. *construction company executive, retired*

Maple Valley
Brown, Thomas Andrew *retired aircraft/weaponry manufacturing executive*

Medina
Schlotterbeck, Walter Albert *manufacturing company executive, lawyer*

Mercer Island
Gould, Alvin R. *international business executive*

Pasco
Wright, Tim Eugene *packaging development executive*
Yoshino, George *food products executive*

Puyallup
†Absher, Dan *construction executive*
Stover, Miles Ronald *manufacturing executive*

Richland
Nolan, John Edward *retired electrical corporation executive*

Roche Harbor
Daum, David Ernest *machinery manufacturing company executive*

Seattle
Albrecht, Richard Raymond *airplane manufacturing company executive, lawyer*
Behnke, Carl Gilbert *beverage franchise executive*
Farrell, Anne Van Ness *foundation executive*
McFarland, Lynne Vernice *pharmaceutical executive*
Mennella, Vincent Alfred *automotive manufacturing and airplane company executive*
Schoenfeld, Walter Edwin *manufacturing company executive*
Shrontz, Frank Anderson *airplane manufacturing executive*
Stonecipher, Harry Curtis *manufacturing company executive*
Whitacre, John *apparel executive*

Spokane
Fosseen, Neal Randolph *business executive, former banker, former mayor*
Powell, Sandra Theresa *timber company executive*
Siegel, Louis Pendleton *forest products executive*

Tacoma
Hutchings, George Henry *food company executive*
Rogel, Steven R. *forest products company executive*

Vancouver
†Vogel, Ronald Bruce *food products executive*

WEST VIRGINIA

Alloy
Wymer, Robert Ernest *metals company executive*

Charleston
Gunnoe, Nancy Lavenia *food executive, artist*
†Manning, Sherry Fischer *college president emerita, business executive*

Huntington
deBarbadillo, John Joseph *metallurgist, management executive*

Shepherdstown
Parmesano, Vincent, III *construction executive, mayor*

Wheeling
Clarke, S. Bruce *paper company executive*
Exley, Ben, III *retired pharmaceutical company executive*
Good, Laurance Frederic *office director*

WISCONSIN

Appleton
Barlow, F(rank) John *mechanical contracting company executive*
Boldt, Oscar Charles *construction company executive*
Rankin, Arthur David *paper company executive*
Spiegelberg, Harry Lester *retired paper products company executive*

Beloit
Kaplan, Kenneth Franklin *manufacturing company financial executive*

Brookfield
Grove, Richard Charles *power tool company executive*

Cedarburg
Schaefer, Gordon Emory *food company executive*

Eau Claire
Menard, John R. *lumber company executive*

Fort Atkinson
Jones, Alan Porter, Jr. *food manufacturing executive*

Grafton
Kacmarcik, Thomas *manufacturing company executive*
Yarger, James Gregory *chemical company executive*

Green Bay
Kress, William F. *manufacturing company executive*
Kuehne, Carl W. *food products executive*
Meng, Jack *food products executive*

Vesta, Richard V. *meat packing company executive*

Hartland
Vitek, Richard Kenneth *scientific instrument company executive*

Kenosha
Huml, Donald Scott *manufacturing company executive*
Infusino, Achille Francis *construction company executive*
Steigerwaldt, Donna Wolf *clothing manufacturing company executive*

Kohler
Kohler, Herbert Vollrath, Jr. *diversified manufacturing company executive*

La Crosse
Gelatt, Charles Daniel *manufacturing company executive*

Madison
Klodt, Gerald Joseph *office product development executive*
Lonnebotn, Trygve *battery company executive*
Shain, Irving *retired chemical company executive and university chancellor*

Manitowish Waters
Laidig, William Rupert *retired paper company executive*

Marathon
Natzke, Paulette Ann *manufacturing executive*

Marion
Simpson, Vinson Raleigh *manufacturing company executive*

Markesan
Chamberlain, Robert Glenn *retired tool manfacturing executive*

Mequon
Dohmen, Frederick Hoeger *retired wholesale drug company executive*

Middleton
†Rowland, Pleasant *publisher, toy company executive*

Milwaukee
Beals, Vaughn Le Roy, Jr. *retired motorcycle manufacturing company executive*
Bishop, Charles Joseph *manufacturing company executive*
Corby, Francis Michael, Jr. *manufacturing company executive*
Hudson, Katherine Mary *manufacturing company executive*
Keuler, Roland Leo *retired shoe company executive*
Keyes, James Henry *manufacturing company executive*
Killian, William Paul *industrial corporate executive*
Manning, Kenneth Paul *food company executive*
Marringa, Jacques Louis *manufacturing company executive*
Martin, Vincent Lionel *manufacturing company executive*
Morris, G. Ronald *industrial executive*
Parker, Charles Walter, Jr. *consultant, retired equipment company executive*
Rich, Robert C. *manufacturing executive*
Sante, William Arthur, II *electronics manufacturing executive*
Sterner, Frank Maurice *industrial executive*
Yontz, Kenneth Fredric *medical and chemical company executive*

Neenah
Bergstrom, Dedric Waldemar *retired paper company executive*
Bero, R.D. *manufacturing executive*
Hanson, Charles R(ichard) *manufacturing company executive*

Oshkosh
Drebus, Richard William *pharmaceutical company executive*
Hulsebosch, Charles Joseph *truck manufacturing company executive*
Zuern, Rosemary Lucile *manufacturing executive, treasurer*

Pleasant Prairie
Morrone, Frank *electronic manufacturing executive*

Racine
Campbell, Edward Joseph *retired machinery company executive*
Gunnerson, Robert Mark *manufacturing company executive, accountant, lawyer*
Henley, Joseph Oliver *manufacturing company executive*
Johnson, Samuel Curtis *wax company executive*
Konz, Gerald Keith *retired manufacturing company executive*
Kunz, Charles Alphonse *farm machinery manufacturing executive*
†Perez, William D. *chemical company executive*
†Rosso, Jean-Pierre *electronics company executive*
†Vinakmens, Andris *manufacturing executive*

Saint Francis
Grade, Jeffery T. *manufacturing company executive*

Sussex
Losee, John Frederick, Jr. *manufacturing executive*
Stromberg, Gregory *printing ink company executive*

Union Grove
Swanson, William Fredin, III *manufacturing executive*

Waterloo
Burke, Richard A. *manufacturing executive*

Watertown
Peebles, Allene Kay *manufactured housing company executive*

Wausau
Slayton, John Arthur *electric motor manufacturing executive*

Wisconsin Rapids
Engelhardt, LeRoy A. *retired paper company executive*
Mead, George Wilson, II *paper company executive*

WYOMING

Casper
Jozwik, Francis Xavier *agricultural business executive*

Jackson
Gordon, Stephen Maurice *manufacturing company executive, rancher*

TERRITORIES OF THE UNITED STATES

PUERTO RICO

Dorado
Spector, Michael Joseph *agribusiness executive*

San Juan
Abella, Marisela Carlota *business executive*

CANADA

ALBERTA

Calgary
Holman, J(ohn) Leonard *retired manufacturing corporation executive*
†Lipton, Jeffrey M. *chemical company executive*

Edmonton
Bateman, William Maxwell *retired construction company executive*
Stollery, Robert *construction company executive*

BRITISH COLUMBIA

North Vancouver
Gibbs, David George *retired food processing company executive*

Vancouver
Bentley, Peter John Gerald *forest industry company executive*
Solloway, C. Robert *forest products company executive*

MANITOBA

Winnipeg
MacKenzie, George Allan *diversified company executive*

NEW BRUNSWICK

Fredericton
Grotterod, Knut *retired paper company executive*

NOVA SCOTIA

Halifax
Pincock, Douglas George *electronics company executive*

North Sydney
Nickerson, Jerry Edgar Alan *manufacturing executive*

Stellarton
Sobey, David Frank *food company executive*

ONTARIO

Agincourt
Lutgens, Harry Gerardus *food company executive*

Aurora
Lanthier, Ronald Ross *retired manufacturing company executive*
Stronach, Frank *automobile parts manufacturing executive*

Brampton
Greenough, John Hardman *business forms company executive*
Toole, David George *pulp and paper products executive*

Burlington
McMulkin, Francis John *retired steel company executive*

Cambridge
Turnbull, Robert Scott *manufacturing company executive*
White, Joseph Charles *manufacturing and retailing company executive*

Fort Erie
Watson, Stewart Charles *construction company executive*

Galt
Dobbie, George Herbert *retired textile manufacturing executive*

Hamilton
Telmer, Frederick Harold *steel products manufacturing executive*

Hanover
Adams, John David Vessot *manufacturing company executive*

Kitchener
Pollock, John Albon *broadcasting and manufacturing company executive*

Markham
Burns, H(erbert) Michael *corporate director*

Mississauga
Barkin, Martin *pharmaceutical company executive, physician*
Lewis, William Leonard *food products executive*

Toronto
Blundell, William Richard Charles *electric company executive*
Connell, Philip Francis *food industry executive*
Dale, Robert Gordon *business executive*
Eagles, Stuart Ernest *business executive*
Knowlton, Thomas A. *retired food products executive*
Mercier, Eileen Ann *management consultant*
Van Houten, Stephen H. *manufacturing company executive*
Wleugel, John Peter *manufacturing company executive*

Willowdale
McDonald, William Henry *financial executive*

QUEBEC

Longueuil
Caplan, L(azarus) David *manufacturing company executive*
Smith, Elvie Lawrence *retired corporate director*

Montreal
Bougie, Jacques *aluminum company executive*
Gouin, Serge *corporate executive*
Herling, Michael *steel company executive*
Ivanier, Paul *steel products manufacturing company executive*
Molson, Eric H. *beverage company executive*
Nadeau, Bertin Felix *diversified company executive*
Pal, Prabir Kumar *aluminium company executive*
Pinard, Raymond R. *pulp and paper executive*
Plourde, Gerard *corporate executive*
Redfern, John D. *manufacturing company executive*
Rolland, Lucien Gilbert *paper company executive*

Outremont
Larose, Roger *former pharmaceutical company executive, former university administrator*

Verdun
Ferguson, Michael John *electronics and communications educator*

SASKATCHEWAN

Regina
Dalla-Vicenza, Mario Joseph *steel company executive*
Phillips, Roger *steel company executive*

Saskatoon
Carr, Roy Arthur *agricultural products applied research, development and commercialization processing organization executive*
Steck, Warren Franklin *chemical company executive, former biochemistry researcher*

BAHAMAS

Nassau
Dingman, Michael David *industrial company executive, international investor*

BRAZIL

Sao Paulo
Reigrod, Robert Hull *manufacturing executive*

CHINA

Shanghai
Jackson, Robert Keith *manufacturing company executive*

ENGLAND

Ascot Berkshire
Grubman, Wallace Karl *chemical company executive*

London
Greener, Anthony *food and beverage company executive*

Malmesbury
Shober, Edward Wharton *bioscience company executive*

Poole
Stokes, Donald Gresham *vehicle company executive*

FRANCE

Antony
†Reinhoudt, Johannes Feike *pharmaceutical industry executive*

Paris
Collomb, Bertrand Pierre *cement company executive*
Jones, Dennis Paul *food and consumer goods company executive*
Lecerf, Olivier Maurice Marie *construction company executive*

GERMANY

Eschborn
Fozzati, Aldo *automobile manufacturing company executive*

Schleusingen-Gethles
Frank, Dieter *technical consultant, retired chemical company executive*

GREECE

Athens
Larounis, George Philip *manufacturing company executive*

HUNGARY

Dunaharszti
Hope, Mark Alan *soft drink company executive*

ITALY

Turin
Agnelli, Giovanni *industrial executive*

JAPAN

Kanagawa-ken
Hoshino, Yoshiro *industrial technology critic*

Tokyo
Baba, Isamu *construction company executive*
Makino, Shojiro (Mike Makino) *chemicals executive*
Ohga, Norio *electronics and entertainment executive*
Saba, Shoichi *manufacturing company executive*
Wakumoto, Yoshihiko *electronics company executive, grants executive*

Toyota
Toyoda, Shoichiro *automobile company executive*

LUXEMBOURG

Luxembourg
Kasperczyk, Jürgen *business executive, government official, educator*

MALAYSIA

Penang
†Ang, Hooi Hoon *pharmaceutical educator*

THE NETHERLANDS

Sittard
van Raalte, John A. *research and engineering management executive*

RUSSIA

Moscow
Knaus, Jonathan Charles *manufacturing executive*

SCOTLAND

Edinburgh
Miller, James *construction company executive*

SPAIN

Madrid
Feltenstein, Harry David, Jr. *chemical executive*

SWEDEN

Stockholm
Schröder, Harald Bertel *aerospace industry executive*

SWITZERLAND

Zurich
Barnevik, Percy Nils *electrical company executive*

TAIWAN

Taipei
O'Hearn, James Francis *chemical company executive*

ADDRESS UNPUBLISHED

Adams, William White *retired manufacturing company executive*
Adelman, Robert Paul *retired construction company executive, lawyer*
Alagem, Beny *former electronics executive*
Albino, George Robert *business executive*
Alig, Frank Douglas Stalnaker *retired construction company executive*
Ammon, R. Theodore *food products executive*
Anastole, Dorothy Jean *retired electronics company executive*
Anderer, Joseph Henry *textile company executive*
Anderson, Fletcher Neal *chemical executive*
Anderson, Joseph Norman *executive consultant, former food company executive, former college president*
Andersson, Craig Remington *retired chemical company executive*
Andreas, Dwayne Orville *business executive*
Andrews, William Frederick *manufacturing executive*
Anspach, Herbert Kephart *retired appliance company executive, patent attorney*
Archer, Sarah Ellen *public health consultant*
Archibald, Nolan D. *household and industrial products company executive*
Armstrong, John Allan *business machine company research executive*
Aschauer, Charles Joseph, Jr. *corporate director, former company executive*
Ashton, Harris John *business executive*
Askins, Wallace Boyd *manufacturing company executive*
Azarnoff, Daniel Lester *pharmaceutical company consultant*
Baker, Charles DeWitt *research and development company executive*
Bannister, Dan R. *professional and technical services company executive*
Barber, Marsha *company executive*
Barron, Charles Elliott *retired electronics executive*
†Barton, Glen A. *manufacturing company executive*
Bass, Robert Olin *manufacturing executive*
Batterden, James Edward *business executive*
Battistelli, Joseph John *electronics executive*
Batts, Warren Leighton *retired diversified industry executive*
Bauman, Robert Patten *diversified company executive*
Beadle, John Grant *retired manufacturing company executive*
Beighey, Lawrence Jerome *packaging company executive*
Bennett, Jay Brett *medical device company executive*
Bennett, Richard Thomas *retired manufacturing executive*
Bergmann, Donald Gerald *pharmaceutical company executive*
Berry, Robert Vaughan *retired electrical manufacturing company executive*
Beutler, Arthur Julius *manufacturing company executive*
Bierwirth, John Cocks *retired aerospace manufacturing executive*
Biggers, William Joseph *retired manufacturing company executive*
Biggs, Arthur Edward *retired chemical manufacturing company executive*
Birkenstock, James Warren *business machine manufacturing company executive*
Bixler, Margaret Triplett *former manufacturing executive*
Blanchard, Richard Frederick *construction executive*
†Blum, Betty Ann *footwear company executive*
Borten, William H. *research company executive*
Bourke, William Oliver *retired metal company executive*
Boyle, R. Emmett *metal products executive*
Brancato, Leo John *manufacturing company executive*
Bratton, William Edward *electronics executive, management consultant*
Brewer, Gail Lee *pre-cast concrete company executive, banker*
†Bridenbaugh, Peter Reese *industrial research executive*
Brinckerhoff, Richard Charles *retired manufacturing company executive*
Broadhurst, Norman Neil *foods company executive*
Brooker, Robert Elton, Jr. *retired manufacturing company executive*
Bruinsma, Theodore August *retired business executive*
Bull, Bergen Ira *retired equipment manufacturing company executive*
Burch, Hamlin Doughty, III *retired sheet metal professional*
Burkett, Thomas O. *manufacturing executive*
Burns, Ward *textile company executive*
Butler, Jack Fairchild *semiconductors company executive*
Buxton, Winslow Hurlbert *manufacturing company executive*
Calcaterra, Edward Lee *construction company executive*
Calvert, James Francis *manufacturing company executive, retired admiral*
Campbell, Richard Alden *electronics company executive*
Candlish, Malcolm *manufacturing company executive*
Carpenter, Myron Arthur *manufacturing company executive*
Carter, Joseph Edwin *former nickel company executive, writer*
Cassidy, James Mark *construction company executive*
Castberg, Eileen Sue *construction company owner*
Chamberlain, George Arthur, III *manufacturing company executive, venture capitalist*
Chaykin, Robert Leroy *manufacturing and marketing executive*
Chen, Di *electro-optic company executive, consultant*
Chmielinski, Edward Alexander *retired electronics company executive*
Clouston, Ross Neal *retired food and related products company executive*
Coffey, Dennis James *performance technology consultant*
Cohn, Leonard Allan *retired chemical company executive*
Cook, Charles William, Jr. *manufacturing executive*
Cook, M(elvin) Garfield *chemical company executive*
Cooley, James William *retired executive researcher*
Cooper, Norton J. (Sky Cooper) *liquor, wine and food company executive*
Correnti, John David *steel company executive*
Costello, James Joseph *retired electrical manufacturing company executive*
Cotting, James Charles *manufacturing company executive*
Cowan, Mark Douglas *government relations executive, lawyer*
Cox, John Francis *retired cosmetic company executive*
Cox, Wilford Donald *retired food company executive*
Craft, Edmund Coleman *automotive parts manufacturing company executive*
Crawford, William David *office equipment company executive*
Cross, Alexander Dennis *business consultant, former chemical and pharmaceutical executive*
Cull, Robert Robinette *electric products manufacturing company executive*
Culwell, Charles Louis *retired manufacturing company executive*
Curtis, Arnold Bennett *lumber company executive*
Cushing, Ralph Harvey *chemical company executive*
Cushwa, William Wallace *retired machinery parts company executive*
D'Agostino, Stephen Ignatius *bottling company executive*
Daly, William James *retired health industry distributing company executive*
Danziger, Gertrude Seelig *metal fabricating executive*
Davis, Bobby Eugene *business owner*
Davis, Darrell L. *automotive executive*
Decker, Gilbert Felton *manufacturing company executive*
Dempsey, David Allan *company official, small business owner*
Denegall, John Palmer, Jr. *construction company executive*
Denise, Robert Phillips *consultant*
Diener, Royce *corporate director, retired healthcare services company executive*
Dobelis, George *manufacturing company executive*
Dohrmann, Russell William *manufacturing company executive*
Dolan, Peter Robert *company executive*
Dole, Robert Paul *retired appliance manufacturing company executive*
Doran, Charles Edward *textile manufacturing executive*
Doyle, Irene Elizabeth *electronic sales executive, nurse*
Doyle, John Laurence *manufacturing company executive*
Dragon, William, Jr. *footwear and apparel company executive*
Dressler, David Charles *retired aerospace company executive*
Drew, Walter Harlow *retired paper industry executive*
Droukas, Ann Hantis *management executive*
Durr, Robert Joseph *construction firm executive, mechanical engineer*
Dye, Robert Harris *retired manufacturing company executive*
Earle, Arthur Percival *textile company executive, airport executive*
Eberle, Charles Edward *paper and consumer products executive*
Egan, John Frederick *retired electronics executive*
Ehrlich, Grant C(onklin) *business consultant*
Eisen, Leonard *food and retail company executive*
Eissmann, Walter James *consulting company executive*
Elverum, Gerard William, Jr. *retired electronic and diversified company executive*
Elwell, Robert H. *manufacturing executive*
Ely, Paul C., Jr. *electronics company executive*
Erdeljac, Daniel Joseph *retired manufacturing company executive*
Evanoff, George C. *retired business executive*
Fatzinger, James A. S. *construction educator, estimator*
Fein, Seymour Howard *pharmaceutical executive*
Feinberg, Herbert *apparel and beverage executive*
Finlay, Robert Derek *food company executive*
Fitch, Robert McLellan *business and technology consultant*
Fite, Robert Carroll *retired cosmetics industry executive*
Flaschen, Steward Samuel *high technology company executive*
Flaten, Alfred N. *retired food and consumer products executive*
Flitcraft, Richard Kirby, II *former chemical company executive*
Flynn, Robert James *electronic commerce executive*
Fogg, Richard Lloyd *food products company executive*
Ford, Jerry Lee *service company executive*
Fossier, Mike Walter *consultant, retired electronics company executive*
Fraser, Campbell *business consultant*
French, Clarence Levi, Jr. *retired shipbuilding company executive*
Friedman, Richard Lee *lumberyard owner*
Frieling, Gerald Harvey, Jr. *specialty steel company executive*
Fries, Raymond Sebastian *manufacturing company executive*
Frisco, Louis Joseph *retired materials science company executive, electrical engineer*
Fritz, Rene Eugene, Jr. *manufacturing executive*
Frohock, Sylvanus E. *food company executive*
Fuller, James Chester Eedy *retired chemical company executive*
Fullerton, Jymie Luie *pharmaceutical company executive*
Gardner, Clyde Edward *healthcare executive, consultant, educator*
Garrison, Paul Cornell *retired office products company executive*
Gates, Martina Marie *food products company executive*
Gee, Irene *food products executive, school administrator*
Gidwitz, Gerald *retired hair care company executive*
Gifford, John Irving *retired agricultural equipment company executive*
Gillespie, Robert James *manufacturing company executive*
Gilreath, Warren Dean *retired packaging company executive*
Goldberg, Lee Winicki *furniture company executive*
Gorman, Joseph Tolle *corporate executive*
Gorman, Michael Stephen *construction executive*
Grass, George Mitchell, IV *pharmaceutical executive*
Gray, Richard Alexander, Jr. *retired chemical company executive*
Greenberg, Milton *corporation executive*
†Grieve, Pierson MacDonald *retired specialty chemicals and services company executive*
Grossman, Jerrold B. *pharmaceutical executive*
Grubbs, Christopher Andrew *electronics company executive*
Guiliano, Francis James *office products manufacturing company executive*
Guillemette, Gloria Vivian *dressmaker, designer*
Gulcher, Robert Harry *aircraft company executive*
Gurney, Daniel Sexton *race car manufacturing company executive, racing team executive*
Hager, Robert Worth *retired aerospace company executive*
Hahn, Lucille Denise *paper company executive, retired*
Hakimoglu, Ayhan *electronics company executive*
Hammond, Robert Lee *retired feed company executive*
Hansen, Donald Curtis *retired manufacturing executive*
Hare, LeRoy, Jr. *pharmaceutical company executive*
Harrell, Henry Howze *tobacco company executive*
Hartmann, George Herman *retired manufacturing company executive*
Hartwick, Thomas Stanley *technical management consultant*
Harvey, Joseph Emmett *construction executive*
Hashimi, Caren Sue *food service manager*
Hauptli, Barbara Beatrice *program administrator*
Hausman, Arthur Herbert *electronics company executive*
Hayes, John Patrick *retired manufacturing company executive*
Heckel, John Louis (Jack Heckel) *aerospace company executive*
Heilmann, Christian Flemming *corporate executive*
Heit, Ivan *packaging equipment company executive*
Heller, Ronald Gary *manufacturing company executive, lawyer*
Hiatt, Arnold *shoe manufacturer, importer, retailer*
Higman, Sally Lee *company executive*
†Hilburn, Hedwig Alison *electrician*
Hines, Anthony Loring *automotive executive*
Hirsch, Horst Eberhard *business consultant in metals and semiconductors*
Hodge, Mary Gretchen Farnam *manufacturing company distributor, manager and executive*
Hoerig, Gerald Lee *retired chemical company executive*
Holder, Richard Gibson *retired metal products executive*
Holland, Charles Edward *medical products corporate executive*
Hornak, Thomas *retired electronics company executive*
Horovitz, Zola Philip *pharmaceutical company executive*
Howe, Wesley Jackson *medical supplies company executive*
Hubbard, Paul Leonard *company executive*
Hudson, Franklin Donald *diversified company executive, consultant*
Hurd, Richard Nelson *pharmaceutical company executive*
†Jackson, Jeanne Pellegren *apparel executive*
Jackson, Robbi Jo *non-hazardous agricultural products company executive, lawyer*
Jenkins, Royal Gregory *manufacturing executivve*
Jensen, Anne Turner *automobile service company executive*
Jensen, Erik Hugo *pharmaceutical quality control consultant*
Johnson, Irving Stanley *pharmaceutical company executive, scientist*
Johnson, Katherine Holthaus *health care marketing professional*
Johnson, Rogers Bruce *retired chemical company executive*
Johnson, Warren Donald *retired pharmaceutical executive, former air force officer*
Johnstone, John William, Jr. *retired chemical company executive*
Jones, Christine Massey *retired furniture company executive*
Joyce, William Robert *textile machinery company executive*
Judelson, David N. *company executive*
Kapcsandy, Louis Endre *building construction and manufacturing executive, chemical engineering consultant*
Karrh, Bruce Wakefield *retired industrial company executive*
Karson, Emile *international business executive*
Keith, Brian Thomas *automobile executive*
Kellgren, George Lars *manufacturing company executive*
Kelly, Anthony Odrian *flooring manufacturing company executive*
Kennedy, Earle James *retired steel manufacturing company executive*
Kerber, Ronald Lee *industrial corporation executive*
Kern, Irving John *retired food company executive*
Kerstetter, Michael James *retired manufacturing company executive*
King, Susan Bennett *retired glass company executive*
Kleinberg, Lawrence H. *food industry executive*
Klocek, Mark C. *manufacturing specialist*
Knight, Herbert Borwell *manufacturing company executive*
Krause, Werner William *plastics company executive*
Kulik, Rosalyn Franta *food company executive, consultant*
Labrecque, Richard Joseph *industrial executive*
Landon, Robert Gray *retired manufacturing company executive*
Lane, Bernard Bell *furniture company executive*
Lane, Marvin Maskall, Jr. *retired electronics company executive*
Lane, William W. *electronics executive*
Langer, Dennis Henry *pharmaceutical company executive*
Langford, Walter Martin *retired greeting card and gift wrap manufacturing executive*
Lathlaen, Robert Frank *retired construction company executive*
Laughlin, Christine Nelson *manufacturing company executive*
Laurenzo, Vincent Dennis *industrial management company executive*
Lavington, Michael Richard *venture capital company executive*
Leff, Joseph Norman *yarn manufacturing company executive*
Lehman, John F., Jr. *industrialist*
Lennox, Donald D(uane) *automotive and housing components company executive*
Leonard, Guy Meyers, Jr. *international holding company executive*

Leveille, Gilbert Antonio food products executive
Lewis, Arthur Dee corporation executive
Lewis, Martin R. paper company executive, consultant
Liebler, Arthur C. automotive executive
Liffers, William Albert retired chemical company executive
Lindars, Laurence Edward retired health care products executive
Lindsay, Franklin Anthony business executive, author
Lippincott, Philip Edward retired paper products company executive
Logan, John Francis electronics company executive, management consultant
Loggins, Bobby Gene meat company executive
Long, Robert Livingston retired photographic equipment executive
Lowden, John L. retired corporate executive
Lowndes, Jeffrey Dennis auto mechanic
Lucas, William Ray aerospace consultant
Luke, David Lincoln, III retired paper company executive
Lynch, Charles Andrew chemical industry consultant
Madden, Richard Blaine forest products executive
Manchester, Kenneth Edward electronics executive, consultant
Martin, Albert Charles manufacturing executive, lawyer
Marvin, Roy Mack retired foundry executive
Mason, Frank Henry, III automobile company executive, leasing company executive
Matasovic, Marilyn Estelle business executive
May, Kenneth Nathaniel food industry consultant
McCabe, Charles Law retired manufacturing company executive, management consultant
McCaskill, Dean Morgan manufacturing industry executive
McGillivray, Donald Dean seed company executive, agronomist
McMullin, Joyce Anne general contractor
McNeeley, Donald Robert steel company executive
Mc Pherson, Frank Alfred retired manufacturing corporate executive
McTague, John Paul automobile manufacturing company executive, chemist
Merrick, George Boesch aerospace company executive
Miles, John Frederick retired manufacturing company executive
Millard, Charles Phillip manufacturing company executive
Miller, Harold Edward retired manufacturing conglomerate executive, consultant
Miskowski, Lee R. retired automobile executive
Moens, David Brian manufacturing company executive
Moore, John Ronald manufacturing executive
Moore, Malcolm Frederick manufacturing executive
Moore, Vernon Lee agricultural consultant, retired food products company executive
Morelli, Peter Richard electronic executive
Morris, Albert Jerome medical company executive
Mott, Stewart Rawlings business executive, political activist
Moylan, Jay Richard medical products executive
Mudd, Sidney Peter former beverage company executive
Mueller, Robert Louis business executive
Mukamal, David Samier sign manufacturing company executive
Neff, Jack Kenneth apparel manufacturing company executive
Nelson, John Howard food company research executive
Nesheim, Robert Olaf food products executive
Nord, Eric Thomas retired manufacturing executive
Nordlund, Donald Elmer manufacturing company executive
Novak, Alan Lee retired pharmaceutical company executive
Nuckols, William Marshall electrical goods manufacturing executive
O'Donnell, Kevin retired metal working company executive
Oelman, Robert Schantz retired manufacturing executive
Ordal, Caspar Reuben business executive
Oster, Lewis Henry manufacturing executive, engineering consultant
Parker, George retired pen manufacturing company executive
Pearce, Paul Francis retired aerospace electronics company executive
Peck, Daniel Farnum chemical company executive
Perelman, Leon Joseph paper manufacturing executive, university president
Peters, Robert Allen retired drug company executive
Peterson, Robert Austin manufacturing company executive retired
Petok, Samuel retired manufacturing company executive
Pettigrew, Steven Lee healthcare management consultant
†Pitman, Lemoine sheet metal worker, trade union director
Platt, Lewis Emmett electronics company executive
Poplawski, Joseph Walter retired glass manufacturing company executive
Potts, Gerald Neal manufacturing company executive
Powell, Thomas Edward, III biological supply company executive, physician
Precopio, Frank Mario chemical company executive
Preston, Seymour Stotler, III manufacturing company executive
Prevost, Edward James paint manufacturing executive
Price, Robert electronics consultant
Pruis, John J. business executive
Raker, Gilbert Dunkin manufacturing executive, financial investor
Rao, Rama Krishna R. pharmaceutical company executive
Raymond, Lloyd W. machinery company executive
Regan, Paul Jerome, Jr. manufacturing company executive, consultant
Rhodes, Peter Edward label company executive
Rice, Otis LaVerne nursing home builder and developer
Richard, Edward H. manufacturing company executive, former municipal government official
Richardson, Thomas Andrew business executive, educator
Richman, Paul semiconductor industry executive, educator
Richman, Peter electronics executive
Rider, Robert Farrington agribusiness executive
Riklis, Meshulam manufacturing and retail executive
Riley, Michael Joseph manufacturing company executive
Robbins, Charles Dudley, III manufacturing executive
Robertson, Melvina construction company executive
Rodgers, Nancy Lucille corporate executive
Rodgers, Nancy Lucille corporate executive
Roesner, Peter Lowell manufacturing company executive
Romanos, Nabil Elias business development manager
Romans, Donald Bishop corporate executive
Rooke, David Lee retired chemical company executive
Roper, John Lonsdale, III shipyard executive
Rosen, Ana Beatriz electronics executive
Rothman, Deanna electroplating company executive
Rubinovitz, Samuel diversified manufacturing company executive
Rudy, Raymond Bruce, Jr. retired food company executive
Ryan, Raymond D. retired steel company executive, insurance and marketing firm executive
Rymar, Julian W. manufacturing company executive
Salathe, John, Jr. manufacturing company executive
Salbaing, Pierre Alcee retired chemical company executive
Salvador, Richard Anthony pharmaceutical company executive
Samek, Michael Johann corporation executive
Samper, Joseph Phillip retired photographic products company executive
Sanders, Wayne R. manufacturing executive
Saute, Robert Emile drug and cosmetic consultant
Sauvey, Donald (Robert) retired musical instrument company executive
Savin, Ronald Richard chemical company executive, inventor
Scheele, Paul Drake former hospital supply corporate executive
Schilling, Dean William manufacturing executive
Schrader, Peter Harmon contractor
Schultz, Robert J. retired automobile company executive
Schwartz, Samuel retired chemical company executive, business consultant
Schwartzberg, Martin M. chemical company executive
Seachrist, William Earl holding company executive
Seligman, David M. apparel executive, secondary education educator
Serenbetz, Robert retired manufacturing executive
Sharkey, Leonard Arthur automobile company executive
Shaw, Richard Melvin gemologist, gold company executive
Shea, Bernard Charles retired pharmaceutical company executive
Shepherd, Mark, Jr. retired electronics company executive
Shirley, George Milton, Jr. chemicals executive
Shuster, Robert G. electronics company executive, consultant
Siegel, Jack Morton retired biotechnology company executive
Silver, George metal trading and processing company executive
Simeral, William Goodrich retired chemical company executive
Simmons, Marguerite Saffold pharmaceutical sales professional
Simon, Michael Paul general contractor, realtor
Singhvi, Virendra Singh consumer products company executive
Smith, Charles Conard refractory company executive
Smith, Frederick Coe manufacturing executive
Smith, Goff industrial equipment manufacturing executive
Smith, James Alexander metal processing executive
Smith, Maurice R. food products executive
Smith, Robert Hugh engineering construction company executive
Somers, Louis Robert retired food company executive
Sommer, Howard Ellsworth textile executive
Southerland, S. Duane manufacturing company executive
Spliethoff, William Ludwig chemical company executive
Starr, Leon retired chemical research company executive
Stern, Arthur Paul electronics company executive
Stern, Milton chemical company executive
Stewart, Daniel Robert retired glass company executive
Stewart, Joseph Turner, Jr. retired pharmaceutical company executive
Stewart, Peter Beaufort retired beverage company executive
Stickler, Fred Charles manufacturing company executive
Stivers, William Charles forest products company executive
Stoneham, Edward Bryant technical company executive
Strohm, Raymond William laboratory equipment manufacturing company executive
Studebaker, Glenn Wayne steel company executive
Swaim, David Dee diversified company financial executive
Swanger, Sterling Orville appliance manufacturing company executive
†Switzer, Daniel Lewis construction company administrator
†Szydlowski, Ralph die maker, formability consultant
Talley, Robert Morrell aerospace company executive
Tannenberg, Dieter E. A. retired manufacturing company executive
Taylor, Dennis J. retired steel company executive
Taylor, Randall William quality assurance administrator
Temple, Joseph George, Jr. retired pharmaceutical company executive
Terry, Kay Adell marketing executive
Tew, E. James, Jr. electronics company executive
Thomas, Leo J. retired imaging company executive
Thomas, Tom retired plastics company executive
Thompson, Ralph Newell former chemical corporation executive
Tombros, Peter George pharmaceutical company executive
Traher, William George automotive model maker, retired
Trice, William Henry paper company executive
Tucker, Charles Ray metalworking company executive, sales and service engineer
Turnbull, John Neil retired chemical company executive
Uffelman, Malcolm Rucj electronics company executive, electrical engineer
Vanaltenburg, Betty Marie lumber company executive
Van Tassel, James Henry retired electronics executive
Verderber, Joseph Anthony capital equipment company executive
Vitt, David Aaron medical manufacturing company executive
Volkhardt, John Malcolm food company executive
Wallace, Michael Arthur aerospace executive
Warner, Walter Duke corporate executive
Wasson, James Walter aircraft manufacturing company executive
†Watkins, James David food products executive
Weaver, William Charles retired industrial executive
Wechsler, Sergio automotive executive, consultant
Weiss, Max Tibor retired aerospace company executive
White, Bertram Milton chemicals executive
White, Gerald Andrew retired chemical company executive
White, John Kiernan lighting company executive
Wieland, William Dean health care consulting executive
Wiesen, Donald Guy retired diversified manufacturing company executive
Wiley, Carl Ross timber company executive
Will, Joanne Marie food and consumer services executive, communications consultant, writer
Williams, Ernest Going retired paper company executive
Winston, Michael G. corporate executive
Witcher, Daniel Dougherty retired pharmaceutical company executive
Witt, Hugh Ernest technology consultant
Wolf, Hans Abraham retired pharmaceutical company executive
Wolff, Brian Richard metal manufacturing company executive
Wollert, Gerald Dale retired food company executive, investor
Woloshen, Jeffrey Lawrence automobile executive, consultant, accountant
Wolotkiewicz, Marian M. household products company official
Yen, Duen Hsi corporate executive, physicist
Ying, John L. manufacturing executive
Yoh, Harold Lionel, Jr. retired engineering, construction and management company executive
Young, John Alan electronics company executive
Zachary, Louis George chemical company consultant
Zanetti, Joseph Maurice, Jr. corporate executive
Zehnder, Frederick John retired automotive executive

INDUSTRY: SERVICE

UNITED STATES

ALABAMA

Auburn
Zallen, Harold corporate executive, scientist, former university official

Birmingham
Agee, Claudia clerk, receptionist, tax consultant
Bruno, Ronald G. food service executive
Floyd, John Alex, Jr. editor, marketing executive, horticulturist
Goodner, Jacob B., Jr. (Jay Goodner) marketing professional
Harris, Aaron management consultant
Luckie, Robert Ervin, Jr. advertising executive
Parker, John Malcolm management and financial consultant
Smitherman, David Conrad medical marketing professional
Spahn, James Francis marketing professional
Young, Thomas Richard sales professional

Dadeville
Barnes, Ben Blair company executive, electrical engineer

Hayden
Graves, Marie Maxine public relations executive, OSHA consultant

Huntsville
Bendickson, Marcus J. company executive
Burns, Pat Ackerman Gonia information systems specialist, software engineer
Childs, Rand Hampton data processing executive
Gray, Ronald W. business executive
McIntyre-Ivy, Joan Carol data processing executive
Richter, William, Jr. technical management consulting executive
Shafer, Roberta W. Crow (Robbie Shafer) human resources executive, career marketing consultant, venture capital consultant

Hurtsboro
Bouilliant-Linet, Francis Jacques global management consultant

Jacksonville
Fairleigh, Marlane Paxson retired business consultant, educator

Mobile
Tunnell, William Newton, Jr. tourism executive

Montgomery
Dillon, Jean Katherine executive secretary, small business owner
Murkett, Philip Tillotson human resource executive
Robinson, Peter Clark general management executive
†Russell, Houston Roy, II managment educator
Schloss, Samuel Leopold, Jr. retired food service executive, consultant

Point Clear
Williams, Willie John, II marketing consultant

Tuscaloosa
Barban, Arnold Melvin advertising educator

Union Springs
Anthony, Lance Coleman marketing professional, social worker, counselor, researcher

ALASKA

Anchorage
Brady, Carl Franklin retired aircraft charter company executive
Gottstein, Barnard Jacob retail and wholesale food company executive, real estate executive
Porcaro, Michael Francis advertising agency executive

Fairbanks
Thompson, Daniel Emerson vending machine service company executive

Ketchikan
Laurance, Leonard Clark marketing researcher, educator and consultant

Talkeetna
Stubblefield, Bobette Lynn business administrator

Wrangell
Kraft, Richard Joe sales executive

ARIZONA

Apache Junction
Cameron, Janice Carol executive assistant

Benson
Collmer, Russell Cravener data processing executive, educator

Carefree
Giolito, Caesar Augustus public relations executive, consultant

Casa Grande
Rutherford, Linda Marie corporate recruiter

Cave Creek
O'Reilly, Thomas Eugene human resources consultant

Chandler
†Barrett, Craig R. computer company executive
Brunello-McCay, Rosanne sales executive
†Eckstat, Arthur Gene consultant
Goyer, Robert Stanton communication educator

Cortaro
Fossland, Joeann Jones professional speaker, personal coach

Flagstaff
Bolin, Richard Luddington industrial development consultant
Evans, Ronald Allen lodging chain executive

Glendale
Baum, Phyllis Gardner travel management consultant
Shimek, John Anton legal investigation business owner, educator

Green Valley
Crystall, Joseph N. communications company executive
Gilliam, Mary travel executive

Mesa
Johnson, Doug advertising and public relations executive
Murphy, Edward Francis sales executive
Tindle, Charles Dwight Wood broadcasting company executive

Paradise Valley
Denning, Michael Marion entrepreneur, computer company executive
De Shazor, Ashley Dunn business consultant
Grimm, James R. (Ronald Grimm) multi-industry executive
Turner, William Cochrane international management consultant

Peoria
Saunders, James management and training consultant
Schindler, William Stanley retired public relations executive, consultant

Phoenix
Armstrong, Nelson William, Jr. gaming company executive
Bellus, Ronald Joseph marketing and communications executive
Brown, James Carrington, III (Bing Brown) public relations and communications executive
Buscha, Ralph Victor security firm executive
Carpenter, Carol Settle communications executive
Conway, David Antony management executive, marketing professional
DeWall-Owens, Karen Marie marketing consultant
Drain, Albert Sterling business management consultant
DuMoulin, Diana Cristaudo marketing professional
Gossell, Terry Rae advertising agency executive, small business owner
†Holdsworth, John H. marketing professional
Komando, Kimberly Ann computer company executive, radio and television host
Lemon, Leslie Gene retired diversified services company executive
McCoy-Shay, Donna Carol telecommunication manager
Newman, Lois Mae marketing executive
Simpson, Charles Robert marketing professional
Snell, Richard holding company executive
Subach, James Alan information systems company executive, consultant
Teets, John William retired diversified company executive

Prescott
Palmer, Robert Arthur *private investigator*

Prescott Valley
Cole, Susie Cleora *retired government employee relations official*

Scottsdale
Adams, Robert Granville *marketing professional*
Blinder, Martin S. *business consultant, art dealer*
Comfort, Clifton C. *management consultant, fraud examiner*
Doglione, Arthur George *data processing executive*
Draeger, Kenneth W. *high technology company executive*
Garfield, Ernest *bank consultant*
Grier, James Edward *hotel company executive, lawyer*
†Grimm, Phillip Henry *electronic security company executive*
Gwinn, Mary Dolores *business developer, philosopher, writer, speaker*
Lillestol, Jane Brush *career development company executive*
O'Donnell, William Thomas *management consultant*
Perry, David Niles *public relations executive*
Ralston, Joanne Smoot *public relations counseling firm executive*
Swanson, Robert Killen *management consultant*
Weil, John David *teleservices executive*
Wolf, Anne K. *sales and marketing executive*

Sedona
Wolfe, Al *marketing and advertising consultant*

Sun City West
Berkenkamp, Fred Julius *management consultant*
Forti, Lenore Steimle *business consultant*
Stevens, George Richard *business consultant, public policy commentator*
Suttles, Virginia Grant *advertising executive*

Tempe
Arters, Linda Bromley *public relations consultant, writer, lecturer*
Guinouard, Philip Andre *restaurant executive*
Mathews, Wilma Kendrick *public relations executive*
McKeever, Jeffrey D. *computer company executive*
Sackton, Frank Joseph *public affairs educator*
Williams, James Eugene *management consultant*

Tucson
Barton, Stanley Faulkner *management consultant*
Bergamo, Ron *marketing executive*
†Bryan, Judith Hager *travel consultant, educator*
Cain, Shannon Margaret *fundraising executive*
Cogut, Theodore Louis *environmental specialist, meteorologist*
Cox, Robert Gene *management consultant*
Harinck, John Gordon *sales executive, hydraulics engineer*
Hoyt, Charlee Van Cleve *management executive*
Jones, Frank Wyman *management consultant, mechanical engineer*
King, Marcia *management consultant*
Lewis, Wilbur H. *educational management consultant*
Rose, Hugh *management consultant*
Sankovich, Joseph Bernard *cemetery management consultant*
Sarlat, Gladys *public relations consultant*
Sohnen-Moe, Cherie Marilyn *business consultant*
Toland, Florence Winifred *printing company executive, retired business educator*
Vanatta, Chester B. *retired business executive, educator*
Williams, John Charles, II *data processing executive*

Yuma
Hilgert, Arnie *management and marketing educator*

ARKANSAS

Bentonville
Higham, Paul H. *marketing professional*
Ingram, Dale *consumer products company executive*

Clarksville
Mooney, Robbi Gail *operations officer*

Conway
Hatcher, Joe Branch *executive search consulting company executive*

Fayetteville
Bennett, Sonja Quinn *administrative assistant*
Brady, Robert *communications educator*
Webb, Lynne McGovern *communication educator, consultant*

Fort Smith
Harper, S. Birnie *business brokerage company owner*

Hot Springs National Park
†Clontz, Jerry Michael *sales administrator*

Jonesboro
Tims, Robert Austin *data processing official, pilot*

Leachville
Adams, Eddie *company executive*

Little Rock
Babin, Claude Hunter, Jr. *marketing executive*
Burnett, Crystal Blythe *marketing professional*
Clark, Ouida Ouijella *public relations executive, educator*
Klein, Reynold Anthony *marketing professional*
McCaleb, Annette Watts *executive secretary*
†McQuary, Vaughn *management company executive*
†Nelson, Rex *communications executive*

Little Rock AFB
Lawrence-Cox, Nancy Nell *executive secretary, artist*

Mabelvale
Hacker, Larry E. *advertising executive*

Monticello
Webster, Linda Jean *communication educator, media consultant*

Pine Bluff
Long, Edward Arlo *business consultant, retired manufacturing company executive*

Springdale
Smith, Danny Leon *sales executive*

CALIFORNIA

Agoura Hills
Gressak, Anthony Raymond, Jr. *sales executive*
Landau, Thomas C. *marketing professional*
Powers, J. D., III *marketing executive*
Schmidt, Frank Broaker *executive recruiter*

Alameda
Billings, Thomas Neal *computer and publishing executive, management consultant*
Ejabat, Mory *communications executive*

Alamo
da Roza, Victoria Cecilia *human resources administrator*
Shiffer, James David *retired utility executive*
Whalen, John Sydney *management consultant*

Aliso Viejo
Harder, Wendy Wetzel *communications executive*

Altadena
Fairbanks, Mary Kathleen *data analyst, researcher*
†McKnight, Ralph William, Jr. *computer company executive, advertising consultant*

Anaheim
Kallay, Michael Frank, II *medical devices company official*
Keller, Kent Eugene *advertising and public relations executive*
Noorda, Raymond J. *computer software company executive*

Arcadia
Gallup, Janet Louise *human resources development executive*

Atherton
Amdahl, Gene Myron *computer company executive*
Baran, Paul *computer executive*
Lowry, Larry Lorn *management consulting company executive*

Atwater
DeVoe, Kenneth Nickolas *food service executive*

Avila Beach
McLaren, Archie Campbell, Jr. *marketing executive*

Bakersfield
Weygand, Leroy Charles *service executive*

Belvedere Tiburon
Denton, Charles Mandaville *corporate consultant*
Hudnut, David Beecher *retired leasing company executive, lawyer*

Berkeley
†Gable, Cate M. *communications company executive*
Poulos-Woolley, Paige M. *public relations executive*
Rippe, Lynn E. *contract administrator*

Beverly Hills
Berg, Jeffrey Spencer *talent agency executive*
Cantor, Alan Bruce *management consultant, computer software engineer*
David, Clive *event planning executive*
Fenimore, George Wiley *management consultant*
Fickinger, Wayne Joseph *communications executive*
Florence, Verena Magdalena *business and computer consultant*
Goldman, Larry *public relations executive*
Hilton, Barron *hotel executive*
Litman, Brian David *communications executive*
†Nyman, Michael S. *company executive*
Ovitz, Michael S. *communications executive*
Riess, Gordon Sanderson *management consultant*
Rowan, Keith Patterson *communications executive, consultant*
St John, Martin *marketing consultant*
Shepard, Kathryn Irene *public relations executive*
Toffel, Alvin Eugene *corporate executive, business and governmental consultant*
Zarem, Abe Mordecai *management consulting executive*

Brea
Herzing, Alfred Roy *computer executive*

Buena Park
Underwood, Thomas Woodbrook *communications company executive*

Burbank
Cook, Richard W. *motion picture company executive*
Cooke, John F. *entertainment company executive*
Dargan, John Henry *strategic planner*
†Green, Judson C. *marketing agency executive*
Mather, Ann *international entertainment company executive*
Schwartz, Allen Marvin *production company executive*

Burlingame
†Garnett, Katrina A. *information technology executive*

Calabasas
Larese, Edward John *company executive*

Camarillo
Cobb, Roy Lampkin, Jr. *retired computer sciences corporation executive*
Faulconer, Kay Anne *communications executive, dean*
Frayssinet, Daniel Fernand *software company executive*
Parker, Allan Leslie *marketing executive*

Cambria
Morse, Richard Jay *human resources and organizational development consultant, manufacturers' representative company executive*

Cardiff By The Sea
Karr, Marie Aline Christensen *executive*

Carlsbad
Mitchell, Thomas Edward, Jr. *communications cabling executive*
Moore, Terry Wayne *high technology venture management consultant*
Peckham, Donald *computer company executive*
Tompane, Mary Beth *management consultant*
Wilson, Donald Grey *management consultant*

Carmel
Allan, Robert Moffat, Jr. *corporate executive, educator*
Evans, Charlotte Mortimer *communications consultant, writer*
Krugman, Stanley Lee *international management consultant*
Smith, Gordon Paul *management consulting company executive*

Castro Valley
Denning, Eileen Bonar *management consultant*

Cerritos
Rice, Barbara Pollak *advertising and marketing executive*

Chatsworth
Sherman, Robert *communications executive, producer*
Weisbrod, Ken (Joseph Louis Weisbrod) *marketing professional*

Chino
Yochem, Barbara June (Runyan) *sales executive, lecturer*

Chula Vista
Tilden, Kevin Archer *communications executive*

City Of Industry
†Requeno, Nestor Danilo *strategic planner*

Compton
Janeway, Barbara *public relations executive*

Concord
Crocker, Kenneth Franklin *data processing consultant*
Padget, John E. *management professional*
Travers, Judith Lynnette *human resources executive*

Corona
Wetsch, Peggy A. *information systems specialist, publisher, educator, nurse*

Corona Del Mar
Bird-Porto, Patricia Anne *personnel director*
Freeman, Richard Dean *new business start-up service company executive*
Menke, Cathleen Vejsicky *management executive, educator*
Terrell, A. John *university telecommunications director*

Coronado
Perrill, Frederick Eugene *information systems executive*

Costa Mesa
Damsky, Robert Philip *communications executive*
Lopata, Martin Barry *business executive*
Paine, David M. *public relations executive*

Coyote
Keeshen, Kathleen Kearney *public relations consultant*

Crescent City
Hight, Harold Philip *retired security company executive*

Crestline
Merrill, Steven William *research and development executive*

Culver City
Berland, James Fred *software company executive*
Boonshaft, Hope Judith *public relations executive*
Davis, George Osmond *communications executive*
†Litewka, Albert Bernard *communications and publishing company executive*
Mehlman, Lon Douglas *information systems specialist*
Williams, Kenneth Scott *entertainment company executive*

Cupertino
Baab, Carlton *advertising executive*
Cleary, William T. *marketing executive*
Flynn, Ralph Melvin, Jr. *sales executive, marketing consultant*
Kvamme, Mark D. *marketing professional*
Mattathil, George Paul *communications specialist, consultant*
Suiter, Thomas *advertising executive*

Daly City
Hargrave, Sarah Quesenberry *consulting company executive*

Dana Point
Mardian, Robert Charles, Jr. *restaurateur*

Danville
Gorman, Russell William *marketing executive, consultant*
Mattoon, Henry Amasa, Jr. *advertising and marketing consultant, writer*
Randolph, Kevin H. *marketing executive*

Del Mar
Comrie, Sandra Melton *human resource executive*

Downey
Huff, Ricky Wayne *sales executive*

El Cajon
Silverberg, Lewis Henry *legal consultant*

El Cerrito
Addison, Alonzo Church *graphics visualization executive, educator, consultant*

El Dorado Hills
Davies, William Ralph *service executive*

El Segundo
Autolitano, Astrid *consumer products executive*
Barad, Jill Elikann *family products company executive*
Brown, Lorraine Ann *office manager*
Cordner, Tom *advertising executive*
Honeycutt, Van B. *computer services company executive*
Katz, Lew *advertising executive*
McQuillin, Richard Ross *management consultant*

Elk Grove
Crapo, Sheila Anne *telecommunications company professional, artist*

Emeryville
Smith, Christopher Allen *technology company executive, marketing professional*

Encinitas
Deuble, John L., Jr. *environmental science and engineering services consultant*

Encino
Greenberg, Allan *advertising and marketing research consultant*
Woskow, Robert Marshall *management consultant*

Escondido
Daniels, Richard Martin *public relations executive*
Kilmer, Maurice Douglas *marketing executive*
Sampson, Richard Arnim *security professional*

Fair Oaks
Nolan, Mark Gregory *advertising executive*

Fallbrook
Cralley, Lester Vincent *retired industrial hygienist, editor*

Fort Bragg
Galli, Darrell Joseph *management consultant*

Foster City
Lutvak, Mark Allen *computer company executive*
†McHenry, Julie *communications executive*

Fountain Valley
Lonegan, Thomas Lee *retired restaurant corporation executive*

Fremont
Tribus, Myron *retired quality counselor, engineer, educator*
†Weinstein, Marta *packaging services company executive*

Fresno
Ganulin, Judy *public relations professional*
Levy, Joseph William *department stores executive*
Shmavonian, Gerald S. *entertainment executive*

Fullerton
Hollander, Gerhard Ludwig *computer company executive*

Garden Grove
McKee, Kathryn Dian Grant *human resources consultant*

Gilroy
Katemopoulos, Mildred Josephine *executive secretary*

Glen Ellen
Hurlbert, Roger William *information service industry executive*

Glendale
Dohring, Doug *marketing executive*
Dohring, Laurie *marketing executive*
Herzer, Richard Kimball *franchising company executive*
Horton, Kathryn Lynne *marketing executive*
Lathe, Robert Edward *management and financial consultant*
Misa, Kenneth Franklin *management consultant*
†Smith, Robert A., II *leasing executive, foundation administrator*

Glendora
Barrett, Thomas Joseph *sales executive, computer systems consultant*

Gold River
Milani, Diva *marketing and communications executive*

Granada Hills
Shoemaker, Harold Lloyd *infosystem specialist*

Grass Valley
Hutcherson, Christopher Alfred *marketing, recruiting and educational fundraising executive*
McDonnell, MaryAnn Margaret *medical marketing executive*

Grover Beach
Edwards, Patrick Michael *sales consultant*

Guerneville
Weese, Bruce Eric *pharmaceutical sales executive*

Half Moon Bay
Fennell, Diane Marie *marketing executive, process engineer*
Hinthorn, Micky Terzagian *volunteer, retired*

Harbor City
Lee, Grace Tze *information services company executive*

Hawthorne
Perry, James Gregory *sales and marketing executive*

Healdsburg
Canfield, Grant Wellington, Jr. *management consultant*

Hercules
†Guevara, A.P. *network consultant*

Hermosa Beach
†McQuiggan, David K. *computer company executive*

Highlands
Lee, Robert Erich *information technology consultant*

Hillsborough
Westerfield, Putney *management consulting executive*

Huntington Beach
†Lieberman, Phillip E. *data company executive*
Wing, Roger *management consultant*

Indian Wells
Kelley, John Paul *communications consultant*

Irvine
Alcone, Matt *advertising executive*
†Buenavista, Joseph Constante *sales manager*
†Colombatto, Martin J. *technology company executive*
Dossett, Lawrence Sherman *professional services company official*
†Fernandez, Aurelio *sales executive*
Garretson, Steven Michael *PC support manager*
Jordan, Michelle Henrietta *public relations company executive*
†Lightburn, Jeffrey Caldwell *corporate communications executive*
†Lindenfelser, Timothy L. *marketing professional*
Rollans, James O. *service company executive*
†Ruehle, William J. *technology company executive*
Schuetz, John Michael *sales executive*
Seller, Gregory Erol *marketing executive, writer, consultant*
Sowder, Kathleen Adams *marketing executive*

La Crescenta
Sanders, David Clyde *management and marketing consultant*

La Habra
Chase, Cochrane *advertising agency executive*

La Jolla
Bardwick, Judith Marcia *management consultant*
Bavasi, Peter Joseph *angling service executive*
†Craig, Jenny *weight management executive*
Kent, Paula *public relations, marketing and management consultant, lecturer*
Levenstein, Roslyn M. *advertising consultant, writer*
Morse, Jack Hatton *management consultant*
Nelson, Craig Alan *management consultant*
Reed, James Anthony *hotel industry executive, consultant*
Wertheim, Robert Halley *national security consultant*

La Puente
Ogden, Jean Lucille *sales executive*
Sheridan, Christopher Frederick *human resources executive*

La Quinta
Peden, Lynn Ellen *marketing executive*

Lafayette
Hemphill, Norma Jo *special event planning and tour company executive*
Kahn, Robert Irving *management consultant*

Laguna Beach
Segard, Hubert J. *international marketing company executive, consultant*

Laguna Hills
Miller, Eldon Earl *corporate business publications consultant, retired manufacturing company executive*

Laguna Niguel
Greenberg, Lenore *public relations professional*
†King, Richard Maurice, Jr. *consultant*

Larkspur
Finkelstein, James Arthur *management consultant*

Livermore
Brieger, Stephen Gustave *management consultant*
Williams, David Michael *manufacturing executive*

Long Beach
Aldrich, David Lawrence *public relations executive*
Johnson, William Harry *international management consultant*
†Nuiry, Octavio Emilio *advertising executive*
Sosoka, John Richard *consulting firm executive, engineer*

Los Altos
Hammond, Donald Leroy *computer company executive*
Heymann, Stephen *marketing management consultant*

Los Altos Hills
Esber, Edward Michael, Jr. *software company executive*

Los Angeles
Bakeman, Carol Ann *travel and administrative services manager, singer*
Bartoletti, Barbara Marie *corporate secretary*
Beam, William Washington, III *data coordinator*
Beltramo, Michael Norman *management consultant*
Bender, Dean *public relations executive*
Berman, Geoffrey Louis *turnaround management company executive*
Berman, Saul Jay *strategic consultant*
Bloch, Paul *public relations executive*
Bohle, Sue *public relations executive*
Byrd, Marc Robert *florist*
Carter, Janice Joene *telecommunications executive*
Crosby, Peter Alan *management consultant*
Davis, Paul Milton *communications administrator*
†DeDominic, Patty (Lee DeDominic) *personnel executive*
DeMartini, Frank Thomas *film company executive, lawyer*
Doll, Lynne Marie *public relations agency executive*
Duffy, Patrick Sean *television production executive*
Edwards, William H., Sr. *retired hotel corporation executive*
Engoron, Edward David *food service consultant, television and radio broadcaster*
†Farrell, Joseph *movie market analyst, producer, entertainment research company executive, writer, sculptor, designer*
Ferry, Richard Michael *executive search firm executive*
Fishman, Arnie *marketing executive, consultant, film producer*
Flynn, Elizabeth Anne *advertising and public relations company executive*
Garland, G(arfield) Garrett *sales executive, golf professional*
Georgesco, Victor *printing company executive*
Giffin, Margaret Ethel (Peggy Giffin) *management consultant*
Gorman, Lillian R. *human resources executive*
Gottfried, Ira Sidney *management consulting executive*
Greene, Alvin *service company executive, management consultant*
Grossman, Dorothea G. *consulting services administrator, poet*
Hale, Kaycee *research marketing professional*
Hartsough, Gayla Anne Kraetsch *management consultant*
Helper, Lee *public relations executive*
Hill, Bonnie Guiton *company executive*
Hodal, Melanie *public relations executive*
Hofert, Jack *consulting company executive, lawyer*
Holt, James Franklin *retired numerical analyst, scientific programmer analyst*
Hotchkiss, Vivian Evelyn *employment agency executive*
Humphreys, Robert Lee *advertising agency executive*
Irving, Jack Howard *technical consultant*
Jarc, Frank Robert *printing company executive*
Katz, Jerry Paul *corporate executive*
†Klein, Jim *company executive*
Kleiner, Arnold Joel *television station executive*
Kline, Richard Stephen *public relations executive*
Krueger, Robert William *management consultant*
Kupchick, Alan Charles *advertising executive*
Laba, Marvin *management consultant*
Lee, Burns Wells *public relations executive*
Lee, James Jui-Chang *public relations executive*
Leibert, Richard William *special events producer*
Leiweke, Timothy *sports executive, marketing professional*
Levine, Michael *public relations executive, author*
†Madwin, Paul M. *retired sales executive*
Margol, Irving *personnel consultant*
Mishkin, Marjorie Wong *aviation and marketing consultant*
Murray, Alice Pearl *data processing company executive*
Newman, Craig Alan *media executive, lawyer*
Patel, Chandra Kumar Naranbhai *communications company executive, educator, researcher*
Pearce, Joan DeLap *research company executive*
†Pondel, Roger S. *public relations executive*
Quinn, Tom *communications executive*
†Resnick, Lynda *art company executive*
†Roberts, Norman C. *company executive*
Rust, Patricia Joan *television production company executive, writer/producer*
Sackman, Dave *marketing executive*
Silverman, Bruce Gary *advertising executive*
Spitzer, Peter George *information systems executive, consultant*
Spofford, Robert Houston *advertising agency executive*
Stergion, Monica Lee *information technology management consultant*
Strawn, Judy C. *public relations professional*
Sylvester, Richard Russell *economist, management executive*
Tardio, Thomas A. *public relations executive*
Tatum, Jackie *parks and recreation manager, municipal official*
Tellem, Susan Mary *public relations executive*
Tennant, John Randall *management advisory company executive*
Tomash, Erwin *retired computer equipment company executive*
von Neumeyer Hull, LeAnne *public relations and communication executive, research consultant, writer*
Wade, Michael Robert Alexander *marketing specialist*
Webster, Jeffery Norman *science and technology policy analyst*
Zelikow, Howard Monroe *management and financial consultant*

Los Gatos
Pfeiffer, Gerald G. *human resources specialist*

Malibu
Fulton, Norman Robert *credit manager*
Hill, Lawrence Sidney *management educator*
Jeffrey, Francis *software developer, forecaster*
Ratliff, James Conway *hospitality consultant*

Mammoth Lakes
Buchanan, Lee Ann *public relations executive*

Manhattan Beach
Curran, Janet S. *advertising executive*
Deutsch, Barry Joseph *consulting and development company executive*
Stern, Daniel Alan *business management consultant*
Trager, Russell Harlan *advertising consultant*

Marina Del Rey
Collins, Russell Ambrose *advertising executive, creative director*
Frank, Ann-Marie *sales administration executive*
†Glen, Paul Michael *management consultant, educator*
Gold, Carol Sapin *international management consultant, speaker*
Holland, Robin Jean *personnel company executive*
Lott, Davis Newton *advertising agency executive, publisher*

Menlo Park
Alsop, Stewart *communications executive*
Arthur, Greer Martin *maritime container leasing firm executive*
Creswell, Donald Creston *management consultant*
Lockton, David Ballard *business executive*
Phipps, Allen Mayhew *management consultant*
†Root, Jonathan David *company executive*
Saffo, Paul *communications executive*
Shows, Winnie M. *speaker, author, consultant*
Steiger, Bettie Alexander *information industry specialist*

Mill Valley
Baker, Malcolm *marketing executive*
Gianturco, Paola *management consulting company executive*
McFarlane, William John *management consultant*

Millbrae
Mank, Edward Warren *marketing professional*

Milpitas
Corrigan, Wilfred J. *data processing and computer company executive*
Fenner, Peter David *communications executive*
Sobeck, Gerald Robert *quality assurance professional, professional baseball scout*

Mission Hills
McFarland-Esposito, Carla Rae *nursing executive*

Mission Viejo
Corey, Jo Ann *senior management analyst*
Dillon, Francis Patrick *human resources executive, management and sales consultant*
Sanz, Kathleen Marie *management consultant*

Modesto
Cofer, Berdette Henry *public management consulting company executive*

Monrovia
Jemelian, John Nazar *management consultant*

Montebello
Norkin, Mark Mitchell *sales executive*

Monterey
Cutino, Bert Paul *restaurant co-founder, chef*

Moraga
Haag, Carol Ann Gunderson *marketing professional, consultant*

Mountain View
Andreessen, Marc *communications company executive*
Barksdale, James Love *communications company executive*
†Belluzzo, Richard E. *computer company executive*
Boyd, Dean Weldon *management consultant*
Castor, Jon Stuart *electronics company executive*
Clark, Jim *communications executive*
Clinton, John Philip Martin *communications executive*
de Urioste, George Adolfo, IV *software company executive*
Feld, Donald H. *network consultant*
Hamilton, Judith Hall *computer company executive*
Koo, George Ping Shan *business consultant*
†Kriens, Scott G. *information technology executive*
Lee, Murlin E. *solutions manager*
Maas, Joan Louise *training and development consultant*
Mc Nealy, Scott *computer company executive*
Polese, Kim *software company executive*
Qureishi, A. Salam *computer software and services company executive*
†Watson, Ian *telecommunications company executive, investor*

Napa
Buchanan, Teri Bailey *communications executive*

Newhall
Heekin, Valerie Anne *telecommunications technician*

Newport Beach
†de Garcia, Lucia *marketing professional*
Garra, Raymond Hamilton, II *marketing executive*
Gellman, Gloria Gae Seeburger Schick *marketing professional*
Joyce, Stephen Francis *human resource executive*
†Lee, Christopher Michael *information technology specialist*
Lipson, Melvin Alan *technology and business management consultant*
Mayfield, Lori Jayne *marketing professional*
McCue, Dennis Michael *management consultant*
Shonk, Albert Davenport, Jr. *advertising executive*
Spisak, John Francis *environmental company executive*

North Highlands
Hope, Gerri Danette *telecommunications management executive*

Novato
†Fraser, Margot *consumer products company executive*

Oakland
Crane, Robert Meredith *health care executive*
Hoffman, George Alan *consulting company executive*
Howard, Bradford Reuel *travel company executive*
Patton, Warren Andre *public relations executive, journalist*
Potash, Jeremy Warner *public relations executive*
Potash, Stephen Jon *public relations executive*
Warrick, Brooke *marketing executive*
Wendlinger, Robert Matthew *communications and memory consultant*

Oceanside
Asato, Susan Pearce *business executive, educator*
Burney, Victoria Kalgaard *corporate business executive, consultant, civic worker*

Oildale
Gallagher, Joseph Francis *marketing executive*

Ontario
Kahn, Mario Santamaria *international marketing executive*
Wright, Charles Lee *information systems consultant*

Orange
Maier, John Mark *organizational leadership educator*

Orinda
Somerset, Harold Richard *retired business executive*
Woolsey, David Arthur *leasing company executive*

Oxnard
Snasdell, Susan Kathleen *computer company executive*
Zigman, Paul Edmond *environmental consultant, executive*

Palm Desert
Kern, Paul Alfred *advertising company executive, research consultant, realtor, financial analyst*

Palm Springs
Arnold, Stanley Norman *manufacturing consultant*
Seale, Robert McMillan *office services company executive*

Palo Alto
Allen, Louis Alexander *management consultant*
Allen, Vicky *sales and marketing professional*
Colligan, John C. (Bud Colligan) *multimedia company executive*
Davis, Glenn *communications company executive*
Eleccion, Marcelino *security executive, computer consultant, music consultant, editor, writer, lecturer, artist*
Fox, Lorraine Susan *marketing professional*
Fried, Louis Lester *information technology and management consultant*
Grubb, William Francis X. *consumer software executive, marketing executive*
†Hamilton, Joe *executive*
Hecht, Lee *software company executive*
Joy, Bill *computer company executive*
Koomen, Cornelis Jan *telecommunications, micro and consumer electronics executive*
Levinson, Kathy *multimedia executive*
Oshman, M. Kenneth *computer company executive*
Quraishi, Marghoob A. *management consultant*
Rheingold, Howard *multimedia executive*
Roberts, Lawrence Gilman *telecommunications company executive*
Rulifson, Johns Frederick *computer company executive, computer scientist*
Seethaler, William Charles *international business executive, consultant*
Waller, Peter William *public affairs executive*
Wohlmut, Thomas Arthur *communications executive*
Wolf, Christopher Robin *biotechnology executive*

Pasadena
Berger, Jay Vari *executive recruiter*
Caine, Stephen Howard *data processing executive*
Dayton, Sky *communications company executive*
Garrett, Duane David *hospitality executive*
Griesche, Robert Price *hospital purchasing executive*
Hanson, Noel Rodger *management consultant*
Kaplan, Gary *executive recruiter*
Koenig, Marie Harriet King *public relations director, fund raising executive*
Little, Paul Edward *communications executive, city official*
Ott, George William, Jr. *management consulting executive*
Pattie, Steven Norris *advertising executive, artist, author*
†Schaller, Anthony Josef *technology management executive*
Soloway, Jay Stephen *consulting firm executive*
Stevens, Roy W. *sales and marketing executive*
Strick, Ruth Cochran *career counselor*
Watkins, John Francis *management consultant*

Paso Robles
Boxer, Jerome Harvey *computer and management consultant, vintner, accountant*

Pebble Beach
Harvie, J. Jason *administrative aide, private secretary*

Petaluma
McKibben, James Denis *marketing and sales executive*

Piedmont
Hurley, Morris Elmer, Jr. *management consultant*

Playa Del Rey
Clow, Lee *advertising agency executive*
Coots, Laurie *advertising executive*
Kuperman, Robert Ian *advertising agency executive*
Weir, Alexander, Jr. *utility consultant, inventor*

Pleasant Hill
Gardner, Nord Arling *management consultant administrator*
Newkirk, Raymond Leslie *management consultant*

Pleasanton
Burd, Steve *food service executive*
Petrone, Joseph Anthony *business consultant, writer*

PROFESSIONAL INDEX 6083 INDUSTRY: SERVICE

Ruppert, Paul Richard *telecommunications executive*
Smith, Gary *marketing executive*

Port Hueneme
Haddad, Edmonde Alex *public affairs executive*
Hedvig, Michael Elliott *management consultant*

Portola Valley
Moses, Franklin Maxwell *retired chemical marketing executive*

Poway
Berger, Newell James, Jr. *security professional*
Rudolph, Charles Herman *computer software development executive*

Rancho Cucamonga
Southard, Burton M. *political and public affairs consultant*

Rancho La Costa
Handel, William Keating *advertising and sales executive*

Rancho Mirage
Rotman, Morris Bernard *public relations consultant*

Rancho Murieta
Ragsdale, Christina Ann *public relations executive, consultant*

Rancho Palos Verdes
Marlett, De Otis Loring *retired management consultant*
Rubenstein, Leonard Samuel *communications executive, ceramist, painter, sculptor, photographer*
Savage, Terry Richard *information systems executive*

Rancho Santa Fe
Baker, Charles Lynn *management consultant*
Best, Jacob Hilmer (Jerry), Jr. *hotel chain executive*
Gruenwald, George Henry *new products development management consultant, writer*
LaBonté, C(larence) Joseph *financial and marketing executive*
Matthews, Leonard Sarver *advertising and marketing executive*
Rible, Morton *financial services and manufacturing executive*
Schirra, Walter Marty, Jr. *business consultant, former astronaut*

Rancho Santa Margarita
†Butte, Kenneth Michael *executive*

Redwood City
Ellison, Lawrence J. *computer software company executive*
Gagarin, Dennis Paul *advertising agency executive*
Kovacevic, Brenda L. *sales administrator*
Oppel, Andrew John *computer systems consultant*
Rohde, James Vincent *software systems company executive*
Sollman, George Henry *telecommunications company executive*
Stone, Herbert Allen *management consultant*

Redwood Shores
Howard, Karen Lynn *marketing executive*
Kertzman, Mitchell E. *software company executive*
Martin-O'Neill, Mary Evelyn *advertising, marketing, business writing, sales training consultant*

Reseda
†Brooks, Robert Eugene *management consultant*
Leahy, T. Liam *marketing and management consultant*

Richmond
Jobs, Steven Paul *computer corporation executive*

Riverbank
Ingram, Robert M. *communications company executive*

Riverside
Gordon, Jerry Arthur *retired family services organization administrator*

Rocklin
Gans, Dennis Joseph *information technology solutions specialist*

Rosemead
Rosenblum, Richard Mark *utility executive*

Ross
Goulet, William Dawson *marketing professional*

Rutherford
Staglin, Garen Kent *finance and computer service company executive*

Sacramento
Capps, Cindy M. *computer systems analyst*
Franz, Jennifer Danton *public opinion and marketing researcher*
Hackett, Louise *personnel services company executive, consultant*
Hunt, Dennis *public relations executive*
Kline, Fred Walter *retired communications company executive*
†Lucas, Donna *communications executive*
McElroy, Leo Francis *communications consultant, journalist*
Swatt, Stephen Benton *communications executive, consultant*
Wilks-Owens, Dixie Rae *conference/meeting planner, workforce preparation specialist*

Saint Helena
Spann, Katharine Doyle *marketing and communications executive*

Salinas
†Bans, Phil *retired corporate security professional*

San Bernardino
Seitz, Victoria Ann *apparel merchandising and marketing educator*

San Carlos
Eby, Michael John *marketing research and technology consultant*
Fleishman, Alan Michael *marketing consultant*

San Clemente
†Alter, Robert A. *hotel executive*
Anderson, Michael Robert *marketing representative*
Fall, John Robert *management and information technology consultant*
†Hulce, Randy C. *hotel executive*
Stenzel, William A. *consulting services executive*

San Diego
Adams, Loretta *marketing executive*
†Birnbaum, Aaron S *marketing professional*
Bryan, John Rodney *management consultant*
†Coulter, Borden McKee *retired management consultant*
Davis, John Warren *program integrator*
Davis, William Albert *theme park director*
DiRuscio, Lawrence William *advertising executive*
Evans, John Joseph *management professional, writer, consultant*
Fauchier, Dan R(ay) *construction management consultant, mediator, arbitrator, educator*
Goodall, Jackson Wallace, Jr. *restaurant company executive*
Hale, David Fredrick *health care company executive*
Johnson, Michael Edward *communication consultant, magician*
Jong, Theresa Ann *human resource executive*
Larson, Mark Devin *communications executive*
Mosteller, James Wilbur, III *data processing executive*
Murray, Colette Morgan *executive search executive*
Neumann, Linda Kay *marketing executive*
†North, Robert L. *computer software executvie*
Nugent, Robert J., Jr. *fast food company executive*
O'Leary, John Joseph *security firm executive*
Ortiz, Antonio Ignacio *public relations executive*
Partida, Gilbert A. *executive*
Stoorza Gill, Gail *corporate professional*
Taylor, George Allen *advertising agency executive*
Tillinghast, Charles Carpenter, III *marketing company executive*
Vallbona, Marisa *public relations counselor*
Waitt, Ted W. *computer company executive*
Warner, John Hilliard, Jr. *technical services, military and commercial systems and software company executive*
Ziegaus, Alan James *public relations executive*

San Fernando
Douglass, Ramona Elizabeth *medical sales professional*

San Francisco
Bancel, Marilyn *fund raising management consultant*
†Bernstein, Gerald William *management consultant, researcher*
Blanc, Maureen *public relations executive*
Bliss, Marian Alice *information systems professional*
†Boehlke, Christine *public relations executive*
†Boehlke, William Fredrick *public relations executive*
Boyle, Antonia Barnes *audio producer, writer*
†Brown, Cabot *private equity investor*
Burgess, Robert *software company executive*
Butenhoff, Susan *public relations executive*
Calvin, Dorothy Ver Strate *computer company executive*
Cavanagh, John Charles *advertising agency executive*
Davis, J. Steve *advertising agency executive*
deWilde, David Michael *executive search consultant, financial services executive, lawyer*
Doan, Mary Frances *advertising executive*
Edgar, James Macmillan, Jr. *management consultant*
Faron, Fay Cheryl *private investigator, writer*
Goldberg, Fred Sellmann *advertising executive*
Gordon, Judith *communications consultant, writer*
Grayson, Ellison Capers, Jr. *human resources executive*
†Green, Bartley Crocker *advertising executive*
Gyani, Mohan *communications company executive*
Haas, Peter E., Sr. *company executive*
Handlery, Paul Robert *hotel executive*
Hara, George *software company executive*
Harlan, Neil Eugene *retired healthcare company executive*
Henderson, Nancy Grace *marketing and technical documentation executive*
†Henshaw, Guy Runals *management consultant*
†Hoffman, Auren *company executive*
Holmes, Irvin R., Jr. *marketing professional*
Horne, Grant Nelson *public relations consultant*
Howitt, David Andrew *human resources executive*
Howley, Peter Anthony *communications executive*
Johnson, Camille *media executive*
Jones, J. Gilbert *research consultant*
Jones, Stanton William *management consultant*
Kahle, Brewster *communications executive*
†Kamer, Larry *public relations executive*
Kaufman, Jonathan Allan (Jon) *public relations executive*
Keeney, Ralph Lyons *information systems specialist, educator*
Kemp, Jeanne Frances *office manager*
Kielarowski, Henry Edward *marketing executive*
†Kimpton, Bill *hotel executive*
Klammer, Joseph Francis *management consultant*
Kurtz, Larry *corporate communications executive*
Landis, Richard Gordon *retired food company executive*
†LaTour, Thomas W. *hotel executive*
Lee, Ivy, Jr. *public relations consultant*
Maneatis, George A. *retired utility company executive*
†Mao, Stephen Tsing *executive*
Marshall, Scott *advertising agency executive*
Massaro, Mike *advertising executive*
Meyer, Keith John *marketing professional*
Minor, Halsey *multimedia company executive*
Minor, Halsey M. *computer company executive*
Muegge, Lyn *advertising executive*
Murphy, Kathleen Anne Foley *advertising agency executive*
Nelson, Jonathan *computer communications company executive*
Nelson, Matthew Sherwood *computer communications company executive*
Ninkovich, Thomas *owner research firm, consultant*
O'Rourke, Dennis *advertising executive*
Otus, Simone *public relations executive*
Parker, Diana Lynne *restaurant manager, special events director*
Pollack, Jeffrey Lee *restaurateur*
Probert, Colin *advertising executive*
Riney, Hal Patrick *advertising executive*
Rutschke, Annamarie *administrative technician*
Siegel, Patricia Ann *association management specialist*
Silverstein, Richard *advertising agency executive*
Sproul, John Allan *retired public utility executive*
Sweet, Cynthia Kay *business administrator*
Tonini, Leon Richard *sales professional*
Torme, Margaret Anne *public relations executive, communications consultant*
Vick, Edward Hoge, Jr. *advertising executive*
Weaver, Sara Lee *sales executive*
Wentz, Jeffrey Lee *information systems consultant*
Wernick, Sandra Margot *advertising and public relations executive*
Whitaker, Clem, Jr. *advertising and public relations executive*
Wilbur, Brayton, Jr. *distribution company executive*
Willner, Jay R. *consulting company executive*

San Jose
Beverett, Andrew Jackson *marketing executive*
Brough, Bruce Alvin *public relations and communications executive*
Bunn, Charles Nixon *strategic business planning consultant*
Castagnetto, Perry Michael *retail sales executive*
Chambers, John T. *computer company executive*
Dougherty, John James *computer software company executive, consultant*
Hutcheson, Jerry Dee *manufacturing company executive*
Kiggins, Mildred L. *telemarketing firm executive*
Monia, Joan *management consultant*
Mulvey, Gerald John *telecommunication engineering administrator, meteorologist educator*
Nguyen, Lam Duc *business executive, consultant*
†Orr, Dominic *information technology company executive*
Ostrom, Philip Gardner *computer company executive*
Rostoker, Michael David *micro-electronics company executive, lawyer*
Scott, Edward William, Jr. *computer software company executive*
Smith, Charles Richard *high technology marketing executive*
Warnock, John Edward *computer company executive*

San Juan Capistrano
Grayson, Robert Allen *marketing executive, educator*

San Lorenzo
Morrison, Martin (Earl) *computer systems analyst*

San Luis Obispo
Vanderspek, Peter George *management consultant, writer*

San Marcos
Barnes, Howard G. *communications executive, film and video producer*

San Marino
Babcock, Catherine Marly *public relations executive*

San Mateo
Helfert, Erich Anton *management consultant, author, educator*
Leong, Carol Jean *electrologist*
Nazzaro, David Alfred *sales executive*

San Rafael
Bartz, Carol *software company executive*
Dykstra, Edie M. *human resource director*
Gould, R(ichard) Martin (Richard Martin Goldman) *marketing consultant, researcher*
Kennedy, James Waite *management consultant, author*
Ligare, Kathleen Meredith *strategy and marketing executive*
Nelson, James Carmer, Jr. *writer, advertising executive*
Saunders, Kathryn A. *retired data processing administrator*
Thompson, John William *international management consultant*

San Ramon
Dickerson, Cynthia Rowe *marketing firm executive, consultant*
Garcia, Michael Joseph *telecommunications company executive*
Moore, Justin Edward *data processing executive*
Rogula, James Leroy *consumer products company executive*

Santa Ana
Boynton, William Lewis *electronic manufacturing company official*
Holtz, Joseph Norman *marketing executive*
Smith, Keith Larue *research company executive*
Tanaka, Richard I. *computer products company executive*

Santa Barbara
†Adizes, Ichak *management consultant, author*
Boehm, Eric Hartzell *information management executive*
Cooper, Saul *producer, public relations executive*
Dennison, Richard Leon *entertainment company executive*
Emmons, Robert John *corporate executive*
Hanley, Kevin Lance *maintenance manager*
†Morgan, Alfred Vance *management consulting company executive*
Schultz, Arthur Warren *communications company executive*

Santa Clara
Benhamou, Eric A. *computer company executive*
Carter, Dennis Lee *marketing professional*
Filo, David *computer communications executive*
Koogle, Tim *communications executive*
Kwong, Donald *contracts administrator, consultant*
Menkin, Christopher (Kit Menkin) *leasing company executive*
Mizer, Richard Anthony *technology company executive*
Rudolph, Ronald Alvin *human resources executive*
Vincent, David Ridgely *management consulting executive*
Warmenhoven, Daniel John *communications equipment executive*
Yang, Jerry *online computer services executive*
Young, Douglas Ryan *technology company executive*

Santa Cruz
†Edwards, Susan M. *hotel executive*

Santa Fe Springs
Hammond, Judy McLain *business services executive*

Santa Monica
Bachrach, Charles Lewis *advertising agency executive*
Janulaitis, M. Victor *consulting company executive*
Katinsky, Steven *communications company executive*
Kessler, Robert Allen *data processing executive*
Krakower, Bernard Hyman *management consultant*
Lempert, Philip *advertising executive, author, syndicated columnist, television correspondent*
McVay, John D. *human resources executive*
Naulin, John Arthur *entertainment company executive*
Postaer, Larry *advertising executive*
Price, David *recreational facilities executive*
Roberts, Kevin *recreational facility executive*
Salveson, Melvin Erwin *business executive, educator*
Seymour, Jeffrey Alan *governmental relations consultant*
Weinberger, Martin Andrew *computer company executive*

Santa Rosa
Christopher, Linda Ellen *consultant, association executive*
Howard, Victor *management consultant*
Schudel, Hansjoerg *international business consultant*

Santa Ynez
Krug, Fred Roy *film and television director and producer*

Saratoga
Lynch, Milton Terrence *retired advertising agency executive*

Sausalito
Pryor, Lois Marie *management consultant*
Treat, John Elting *management consultant*

Scotts Valley
McClymonds, Jean Ellen *marketing professional*

Sebastopol
Dorr, Daniel Alan *personal and professional development facilitator*
†McCarthy, Thomas Edward *retired telecommunications executive*
O'Reilly, Tim *company executive*
Slater, Michael *communications executive*

Sherman Oaks
Dawson, David Smith *television executive*
Holst, Sanford *strategic consulting executive, author*
Lindgren, Timothy Joseph *supply company executive*
Strauss, John *public relations executive*
Winkler, Lee B. *business consultant*

Sierra Madre
MacGillivray, MaryAnn Leverone *marketing professional*

Signal Hill
Jarman, Donald Ray *retired public relations professional, minister*

Sonora
Mathias, Betty Jane *communications and community affairs consultant, writer, editor, lecturer*

South Pasadena
Lowe, Richard Gerald, Jr. *computer programming manager*

South San Francisco
Grannuci, Leo *marketing professional*
Lewis, Jason Alvert, Jr. *communications executive*
Walsh, Gary L. *consumer products company executive*

Stanford
Fuller, Joseph Barry *company executive*
Martin, Roger Lloyd *educator, management consultant*
Miller, William Frederick *research company executive, educator, business consultant*

Stockton
Dolgow, Allan Bentley *consulting company executive*
Gallagher, Tim *parks and recreation director*
Jacobs, Marian *advertising agency owner*
†Lawrence, James Russell *information systems specialist*
Viscovich, Sir Andrew John *educational management consultant*

Studio City
Chambers, Clytia Montllor *public relations consultant*
Kaye, Lori *travel academy executive, consultant*

Sunnyvale
Armistead, Robert Ashby, Jr. *scientific research company executive*

Tehachapi
Smith-Thompson, Patricia Ann *public relations consultant, educator*

Temecula
Buzbee, John Duffie, Jr. *sales executive*
Coram, David James *marketing professional*

Thousand Oaks
Cobb, Shirley Ann *public relations specialist, journalist*

Forti, Corinne Ann *corporate communications executive*
Lark, M. Ann *management consultant, strategic planner, naturalist*
Noonan, Daniel Christopher *consultant*

Toluca Lake
Mracky, Ronald Sydney *marketing and promotion executive, travel consultant*

Torrance
Gilbert, Scott *advertising executive*
†Howroyd, Janice Bryant *personnel placement executive*
Kasari, Leonard Samuel *quality control professional, concrete consultant*
Signorovitch, Dennis J. *communications executive*
Sloan, Michael Dana *information systems specialist*

Tracy
Green, Brian Gerald *marketing executive*

Tustin
Bartlett, Arthur Eugene *franchise executive*

Twentynine Palms
Fultz, Philip Nathaniel *management analyst*

Ukiah
Eversole, Walter Robert *funeral director*

Universal City
Costello, Richard Neumann *advertising agency executive*

Upland
Deppisch, Paul Vincent *data communications executive*

Valley Glen
Ghent, Peer *management consultant*

Valley Springs
Vitrac, Jean-Jacques Charles *international business consultant*

Van Nuys
Cochran, Anne Westfall *public relations executive*
Josephs, Alice Ruth *retired executive secretary*
Kagan, Stephen Bruce (Sandy Kagan) *network marketing executive*
Simon, David Harold *retired public relations executive*

Villa Park
Britton, Thomas Warren, Jr. *management consultant*
Hawe, David Lee *consultant*

Walnut
Tan, Colleen Woo *communications educator*

Walnut Creek
Garlough, William Glenn *marketing executive*
Kuhl, Ronald Webster *marketing executive*
Moore, John D. *management consultant*
Stover, W. Robert *temporary services executive*
Wilkins, Sheila Scanlon *management consultant*

Washington
Gonzales, Daniel Richard *defense and technology analyst*

West Covina
Musich, Robert Lorin *motivational speaker*
West, Edward Alan *graphics communications executive*

West Hills
Tennen, Ken *lawyer*

West Hollywood
Einstein, Clifford Jay *advertising executive*
Feidelson, Marc *advertising executive*
Gates, Lisa *private chef, caterer*
Holt, Dennis F. *media buying company executive*
Kingsley, Patricia *public relations executive*
McGaughey, Emmett Connell *advertising agency executive*

West Sacramento
Lloyd, Sharon *marketing professional*
McGagin, Nancy *public affairs executive*
†Teal, Joyce Raley *grocery chain executive*

Westlake Village
Catrambone, Eugene Dominic *magazine editor*
Murdock, David H. *diversified company executive*
Smyth, Glen Miller *management consultant*
†Swink, Greg *computer software executive*

Woodland Hills
Burke, Tamara Lynn *marketing professional*
Ennis, Thomas Michael *management consultant*
†Gray, Laura *human resources specialist*
Parrott, Dennis Beecher *sales executive*
Randall, Craig *financial and business management consultant, accountant, computer specialist*
Stoll, Leonard Peter *aerospace business administrator, consultant*

Yorba Linda
Hutchins, James Leigh *quality assurance professional*

Yountville
Kay, Douglas Casey *leasing consultant*
†Paquet, Gary Michael Sebastian *company executive*

Yreka
Fiock, Shari Lee *event planner, entrepreneur, publishing executive*

COLORADO

Arvada
Deere, Cyril Thomas *retired computer company executive*
Williams, Marsha Kay *data processing executive*

Aspen
Finster, Brent Edwin *public safety communications administrator*
McDade, James Russell *management consultant*

Aurora
Bobrick, Steven Aaron *marketing executive*
Harlan, Raymond Carter *communication executive, computer application developer*
Reitan, Harold Theodore *management consultant*
Welch, Richard LeRoy *personal improvement company executive*

Bailey
Van Dusen, Donna Bayne *communication consultant, educator, researcher*

Boulder
Bryson, Gary Spath *cable television and telephone company executive*
Fisher, Joseph Stewart *management consultant*
†Hatfield, Steven Michael *data processing executive*
Jerritts, Stephen G. *management consultant*
Oromaner, Daniel Stuart *marketing consultant*
Shumick, Diana Lynn *computer executive*

Breckenridge
Sbragia, Gary W. *communications company executive*

Broomfield
Lybarger, John Steven *human resources development consultant, trainer*

Carbondale
Linden, Susan Pyles *marketing executive*

Colorado Springs
Fahey, Henry Martin *information technology executive*
Ford, James Carlton *human resources executive*
Fortune, James Michael *network analyst*
Hall, Nechie Tesitor *advertising and public relations executive*
Loux, Jonathan Dale *business development consultant*
Mitchell, John Henderson *management consultant, retired career officer*
†Valdez, Troy *business executive*

Denver
Baca, Kelly Mae *marketing communications director*
Blatter, Frank Edward *travel agency executive*
Browne, Spencer I. *mortgage company executive*
Clinch, Nicholas Bayard, III *business executive*
Cotherman, Audrey Mathews *management and policy consultant, administrator*
DeVine, B. Mack *management consultant*
†Dunham, Joan Roberts *administrative assistant*
†Fassler, Karen Kay *human resources specialist*
Giesen, John William *advertising executive*
Greenberg, David Ethan *communications consultant*
Greenberg, Pamela Thayer *public policy specialist*
Harris, Howard Jeffrey *marketing and printing company executive*
Henry, David Allen *advertising executive*
Isenberg, Walter L. *recreational facility executive*
Karsh, Philip Howard *advertising executive*
Kurtz, Maxine *personnel consultant, lawyer*
Lazarus, Steven S. *management consultant, marketing consultant*
Lutsky, Sheldon Jay *financial and marketing consultant, writer*
Mackinnon, Peggy Louise *public relations executive*
Mahadev, Rajesh *strategic marketing professional*
Marcus, Jeffrey Howard *electronic security system company executive*
Martin, Robert Burton *management and marketing consultant*
Michaels, Alan J. *safety, occupational health and training executive*
Muftic, Felicia Anne Boillot *consumer relations professional*
Murdock, Pamela Ervilla *travel and advertising company executive*
Murray, James Alan *urban and environmental consultant, investor*
Myhren, Trygve Edward *communications company executive*
†Nacchio, Joseph P. *communications executive*
Neu, Carl Herbert, Jr. *management consultant*
Neumeyer, Zachary T. *hotel executive*
Notari, Paul Celestin *communications executive*
†Perington, Philip *management investment company executive*
Schiell, Charles Randall *leasing company executive*
Schmidt-Nelson, Martha Alice *communications and training executive, ergonomist*
†Stanford, Gully *public affairs administrator*
Welchert, Steven Joseph *political and public affairs consultant*
Wessler, Mary Hraha *marketing and management executive*
†West, Deborah Ellen *administrator*
Williams, Sue M. *corporate communications specialist, writer*
†Young, Clifford W. *food service executive, consultant*

Durango
Foster, James Henry *advertising and public relations executive*

Englewood
Cooper, Sharon Marsha *marketing, advertising executive*
Cooper, Steven Jon *healthcare management consultant, educator*
Greenagel, Debra *travel agency executive*
Harding, Wayne Edward, III *software company executive, accountant*
Hindery, Leo Joseph, Jr. *media company executive*
Joffe, Barbara Lynne *computer applications systems manager, computer artist, project management professional*
Jones, Glenn Robert *cable systems executive*
Lake, Stanley James *security consulting company executive, motel chain executive, locksmith*
Murdock, Michelle Marie *marketing executive*
Neiser, Brent Allen *public affairs consultant*
†Peck, Charles *hotel executive*
Shaddock, Paul Franklin, Sr. *human resources director*

Evergreen
Rodolff, Dale Ward *sales executive, consultant*

Fort Collins
Fletcher, Charles Rickey *public affairs specialist*
Hinz, Shirley Sorensen *administrative secretary*
Lameiro, Gerard Francis *corporate strategist*
†Marecaux, Marie Laure *consultant*
Newlin, Douglas Randal *learning products engineer*

Franktown
Smith, James Micheal *marketing executive*

Fraser
Hibbs, John David *software executive, engineer, business owner*

Grand Junction
Freeman, Neil *accounting and computer consulting firm executive*

Greeley
Mader, Douglas Paul *quality engineering manager*
Miller, Diane Wilmarth *human resources director*

Lafayette
†Kelly, John Fitzgerald *software developer*

Lakewood
Allen, Sam Raymond *organization development specialist*
Boyd, John Garth *manufacturing production and operations consultant*
Porter, Lael Frances *communication consultant, educator*
Rhamy, Jennifer Frances *marketing professional*
Richards, Robert Charles *management consultant*
Wolfe, Brian Augustus *retired sales executive, small business owner*

Littleton
Fisher, Louis McLane, Jr. *management consultant*
Hopping, William Russell *hospitality industry consultant and appraiser*
Smith, Derrin Ray *information systems company executive*
Treybig, Edwina Hall *sales executive*

Longmont
Nevling, Harry Reed *health care human resources executive*

Louisville
Ferguson, Gary L. *public relations executive*
Slater, Shelley *telecommunications company administrator*
Sontag, Peter Michael *travel management company executive*

Loveland
Hughes, Edwin Strode *public relations executive*

Northglenn
Peters, LeRoy Richard *materials management consulting company executive*

Pagosa Springs
Howard, Carole Margaret Munroe *retired public relations executive*

Parker
Jankura, Donald Eugene *hotel executive, educator*

Pueblo
Noblit, Betty Jean *publishing technician*

Rollinsville
Burandt, Gary Edward *advertising agency executive*

Sterling
Jones, Daniel Lee *software development company executive*
Jones, Laurie Ganong *sales and marketing executive*

Thornton
†Roberts, Steven L. *human resources specialist*

CONNECTICUT

Bloomfield
Handel, Morton Emanuel *management consultation executive*
Mackey, William Arthur Godfrey *analytical testing company executive*

Bridgeport
†Bruner, Evans *management consultant*

Cheshire
Burton, Robert William *retired office products executive*

Cos Cob
Yudain, Carole Gewirtz *public relations consultant, writer, editor, historian, photojournalist, audio-visual producer, educator*

Danbury
Baruch, Eduard *management consultant*
Izzo, Lucille Anne *sales representative*
McNabb, Frank William *consumer products company executive*
Perun, John Joseph, Jr. *information systems professional*
Williamson, Brian David *information systems executive, consultant*

Darien
Chyung, Chi Han *management consultant*
Cowherd, Edwin Russell *management consultant*
Kobak, James Benedict *management consultant*
†Welsh, John Francis *retired advertising executive*

Devon
Spinelli, Viola June *healthcare management consultant*

East Berlin
†Pelton, Timothy Noble *management consultant*

East Haddam
Clarke, Cordelia Kay Knight Mazuy *managment executive, consultant*
Clarke, Logan, Jr. *management consultant*

East Hartford
Milo, George Thomas *administrator*
Pudlo, Frances Theresa *executive assistant*

Enfield
Oliver, Bruce Lawrence *information systems specialist, educator*

Essex
Thompson, George Lee *consulting company executive*

Fairfield
Ambrosino, Ralph Thomas, Jr. *retired telecommunications executive*
Booth, George Keefer *finanical service executive*
Cole, Richard John *marketing executive*
Dean, George Alden *advertising executive*
Hodgkinson, William James *marketing company executive*
Koutas, Samuel Demetrios *human resources executive*
Luther, David Byron *energy company executive*

Farmington
LaGanga, Donna Brandeis *sales and marketing executive*
Murphy, Joanne M. *computer company executive*

Glastonbury
†Andrews, Bryant Aylesworth *software company executive*
†Guzzi, R. James, Jr. *health care fraud consultant*
Tomlinson, Richard Giles *author, consultant*

Greens Farms
McManus, John Francis, III *advertising executive*

Greenwich
Amen, Robert Anthony *investor and corporate relations consultant*
Ball, John Fleming *advertising and film production executive*
Bollman, Mark Brooks, Jr. *communications executive*
Burton, Robert Gene *printing and publishing executive*
Carmichael, William Daniel *consultant, educator*
Chisholm, William Hardenbergh *management consultant*
Davidson, Thomas Maxwell *international management company executive*
Donley, James Walton *management consultant*
†Harrigan, Kelly A. *human resources professional*
Harrington, Robert Dudley, Jr. *printing company executive*
Keegan, Richard John *advertising agency executive*
Kestnbaum, Albert S. *advertising executive*
Landman, Fred *communications executive*
Lipner, William E. *information systems executive*
MacDonald, Gordon Chalmers *management consultant*
Meek, Phillip Joseph *communications executive*
Morano, Gerard John *marketing executive*
Pappas, Alceste Thetis *consulting company executive, educator*
Paulson, Paul Joseph *advertising executive*
Rizzo, Raymond S. *advertising executive*
Roberts, James Carl *communications executive, engineer*
Rozelle, Mark Albert *company executive*
Schlafly, Hubert Joseph, Jr. *communications executive*
Scott, John Constante *marketing company executive*
Srere, Benson M. *communications company executive, consultant*
†Trainor, Deborah Anne *sales and marketing executive*
Wallach, Philip C(harles) *financial, public relations consultant*
Whitmore, George Merle, Jr. *management consulting company executive*
Wyman, Ralph Mark *corporate executive*

Guilford
Mick, Margaret Anne *communications executive*
Ragan, James Thomas *communications executive*

Hartford
Coleman, Winifred Ellen *administrator*
Faruolo, Edward A. *marketing professional*
Hudson, Jane Duclos *management consultant, writer*
†Micklus, Donna Jane *communications executive*
Reynolds, Tom *communications executive*
Whaley, Charles Henry, IV *communications company executive*

Madison
Keim, Robert Phillip *retired advertising executive, consultant*

Mansfield Center
Petrus, Robert Thomas *internet distribution executive, real estate executive*

Marion
Perkins, James Winslow *international business consultant, builder, contractor*

Milford
Khoury, Robert John *international leadership management consultant*
Olson, Harold Roy *computer company executive*

Monroe
Magazian, Victor Edward *private investigator*

Mystic
†McCabe, Edward Owen *photoprocessing executive*

New Britain
Brownstein, Julian M. *advertising and public relations executive*

Bruemmer, Lorraine Venskunas *funeral director, real estate broker, nurse*

New Canaan
†Batchelor, David Henry Lowe *marketing consultant*
Crossman, William Whittard *retired wire cable and communications executive*
Lione, Susan Garrett *consultant*
McClure, Grover Benjamin *management consultant*
Mc Mennamin, George Barry *advertising agency executive*
Means, David Hammond *retired advertising executive*
Silbey, Paula J. *public relations consultant, writer*
Stack, J. William, Jr. *management consultant*
Ward, Richard Vance, Jr. *management executive*
White, Richard Booth *management consultant*

New Haven
Huwiler, Joan P. *public relations executive, consultant*
McPike, Martin John, III *market research analyst*
Waters, Donald Joseph *information services administrator*

Newtown
Coates, John Peter *technical executive*

Norfolk
Burrows, John Edward *communications company executive*

North Haven
Ungerleider, Alex *marketing professional*

Norwalk
Ahlers, Douglas *communications company executive*
Allen, Robert *communications company executive*
Czajkowski-Barrett, Karen Angela *human resources management executive*
Klink, Karin Elizabeth *medical communications company executive, writer*
†Kulick, Elliot David *information technology specialist*
Manning, James Forrest *computer executive*
Mundt, Barry Maynard *management consultant*
Neuman, Curtis William *computer systems company executive*
Rezek, Geoffrey Robert *management consultant*
Weiner, Sandra Joan *computer catalog reseller company executive*

Old Greenwich
Fernous, Louis Ferdinand, Jr. *consumer products company executive*
Robinson, Hobart Krum *management consulting company executive*

Old Lyme
Nuhn, Charles Kelsey *advertising executive*

Old Saybrook
Dewdney, Anthony Edward *quality assurance professional, auditor*
Phillips, William E. *advertising agency executive*

Ridgefield
Lodewick, Philip Hughes *equipment leasing company executive*

Riverside
Battat, Emile A. *management executive*
Geismar, Richard Lee *communications executive*
McSpadden, Peter Ford *retired advertising agency executive*
Olshan, Kenneth S. *business executive, advisor, writer*

Salisbury
Block, Zenas *management consultant, educator*

Sharon
Kahn, Paul Frederick *executive search company executive*

Sherman
Cohn, Jane Shapiro *public relations executive*

Somers
Hooper, Donald Robert *retired corporate chief executive*

South Windsor
Coullard, Chad *information systems specialist*
Famiglietti, Nancy Zima *computer executive*

Southbury
Leonard, John Harry *advertising executive*
Marchese, Ellen *consultant*

Southport
Schadt, James Phillip *investment company executive*

Stamford
Ast, Steven Todd *executive search firm executive*
Breakstone, Robert Albert *consumer products, information technology and consulting executive*
Broadhurst, Austin, Jr. *executive recruiter*
Brown, W. Michael *publishing company executive*
Cochran, David MacDuffie *management consultant*
Collins, Joseph Jameson *communications executive*
Daleo, Robert *communications executive*
Dell, Warren Frank, II *management consultant*
Di Maria, Valerie Theresa *public relations executive*
Everhart, Judd *public relations executive*
Fuchs, Hanno *communications consultant, lawyer*
Kerr, Ian *public relations executive*
Lynch, John T. *management consultant*
Marlowe, Edward *research company executive*
Miklovic, Daniel Thomas *research director*
Miller, Wilbur Hobart *business diversification consultant*
Murphy, Robert Blair *management consulting company executive*
Nightingale, William Joslyn *management consultant*
Ogden, Dayton *executive search consultant*
†Peppers, Donald Alan *marketing consultant, writer*
Pollock, Duncan *advertising executive*
Rapp, James Allen *marketing executive*
Reade, Lewis Pollock *business executive, retired diplomat, engineer*
Sadove, Stephen Irving *consumer products company executive*
Sarbin, Hershel Benjamin *management consultant, business publisher, lawyer*
Sherman, Norman Mark *advertising agency executive*
Silver, Charles Morton *communications company executive*
Steeneck, Regina Aultice *information systems specialist*
Sveda, Michael *management and research consultant*
Thoman, G. Richard *computer company executive*
Tierney, Patrick John *information services executive*
Trivisonno, Nicholas Louis *communications company executive, accountant*
Vos, Frank *advertising and marketing executive*
Wallfesh, Henry Maurice *business communications company executive, editor, writer*
Yardis, Pamela Hintz *computer consulting company executive*

Storrs Mansfield
Deb, Somnath *software company executive*
Glasser, Joseph *manufacturing and marketing executive*

Stratford
Kaufman, Jess *communication, financial and marketing consultant*

Torrington
Sexton, Diana Elizabeth *communications company executive*

Trumbull
London, Michael Jeffrey *public relations executive*

Uncasville
†Bunnel, Charles Franklin *personnel director, lobbyist*

West Hartford
Glotzer, Mortimer M. *quality assurance consultant*
Scott, Mary Elizabeth *management consultant*

West Haven
Borrell, Paul Nicholas *sales executive*

Weston
Levien, Roger Eli *strategy and innovation consultant*
Murray, Thomas Joseph *advertising executive*

Westport
Aasen, Lawrence Obert *public relations executive*
†Allen, Michael G. *management consultant*
Blau, Barry *marketing executive, financial investor*
Brandt, Kathy A. *public relations and events management executive, secondary school educator*
Gallagher, Michael Robert *consumer products company executive*
Gold, Richard N. *management consultant*
Kurz, Mitchell Howard *marketing communications executive*
McFarland, Richard M. *executive recruiting consultant*
Nathan, Irwin *business systems company executive*
Schriever, Fred Martin *management consultant, financial investor*
Weissman, Robert Evan *information services company executive*

Wethersfield
Franco, Carole Ann *international consultant*
Karwic, Richard A. *management consultant, educator*

Wilton
Bishop, William Wade *advertising executive*
Black, Rita Ann *communications executive*
Caravatt, Paul Joseph, Jr. *communications company executive*
Cassidy, George Thomas *international business development consultant*
Eisen, Glenn Philip *management consultant, teacher*
Flesher, Margaret Covington *corporate communications consultant*
Kovak, Ellen B. *public relations firm executive*
†McCracken, Douglas M. *consultant company executive*
Mc Dannald, Clyde Elliott, Jr. *management consultation company executive*
Nickel, Albert George *advertising agency executive*
†Parrett, William G. *consultant company executive*
Pethley, Lowell Sherman *management consultant*
Sideroff, Barry *advertising executive*
Weiland, Juliette Marie *public relations executive, freelance writer and photographer*

Windsor
Kamerschen, Robert Jerome *consumer products company executive*

Windsor Locks
Heisler, Elwood Douglas *hotel executive*

Woodbridge
Ostfeld, Alexander Marion *advertising agency executive*
Van Sinderen, Alfred White *former telephone company executive*

Woodstock
Boote, Alfred Shepard *marketing researcher, educator*

DELAWARE

Fenwick Island
Dickerson, Joseph Alfred *retired sales executive*

Montchanin
†Melloy, Joseph Patrick, Sr. *consulting company executive*

Newark
†Gore, Genevieve Walton *company executive*

Wilmington
D'Angelo, Arthur E. *advertising agency executive*
Elliott, Roxanne Snelling *educational consultant to independent schools*
Emanuel, Abraham Gabriel *photo processing company executive, consultant*
Maggard, Woodrow Wilson, Jr. *management consultant*
Perse, Aria Leon *international business advanced technologies executive*
Shipley, Samuel Lynn *advertising and public relations executive*
Sly, John Eugene *advertising and marketing consultant*

DISTRICT OF COLUMBIA

Washington
†Abbott, Ernest B. *emergency management administrator*
Adams, A. John Bertrand *public affairs consultant*
Aguirre-Sacasa, Rafael Eugenio *marketing executive*
Akey, Steven John *public relations executive*
Allen, Richard Vincent *international business consultant, bank executive*
Allnutt, Robert Frederick *management consultant, corporate director*
†Baker, Jennifer L. *strategic communications consultant*
Balfour, Ana Maria *office manager*
Barrett, Laurence Irwin *public relations executive, writer*
Baruch, Jordan Jay *management consultant*
Berman, Ellen Sue *energy and telecommunications executive, theatre producer*
†Biltchik, David Ellis *business consultant*
†Bloom, Bruce *hotel executive*
†Bolden, Betty *labor relations administrator*
Borwick, Richard *management consultant*
Bradley, Melvin LeRoy *communications company executive*
†Bramucci, Raymond L. *employment and training executive*
Brewster, Bill K. *business executive, former congressman*
†Brown, Jeanette L. *environmental protection administrator*
†Buckley, Jill *legislative and public affairs administrator*
Campbell, James Albert Barton *association executive, retired marketing executive*
†Carey, Wilhelmina Cole *management consultant*
†Cicotello, Thomas Matthew *property manager*
Clay, Don Richard *environmental consulting firm executive*
Cohen, Perry D. *management consultant*
Coin, Sheila Regan *organization and management development consultant*
†Conley, Jeff *company executive*
Coons, Barbara Lynn *public relations executive, librarian*
Cope, Jeannette Naylor *executive search consultant*
†Cox, Courtland *minority business administrator*
†Crackett, Delores *womens bureau administrator*
Culley-Foster, Anthony Robert *international business consultant*
Dach, Leslie Alan *public relations company executive*
Dasch, Pat (Anne) *society executive*
Davidow, Malcolm Hartley *management consultant*
Davis, Preston Augustus *management consultant*
Davis, Rex Darwin *business consultant*
Dawson, Mimi Weyforth *government affairs consultant*
†de la Guardia, Pablo Antonio *marketing administrator*
Denysyk, Bohdan *marketing professional*
Dessaso, Deborah Ann *online communication specialist*
Deuschl, Dennis Erwin *communications executive*
†Dolan, Kay Frances *human resources administrator*
Donoghue, John *communications executive*
†Duggan, Joseph Patrick *public affairs executive*
Dyck, Wesley James *personnel director*
†Eckles, Susan *management executive*
Edmonds, Thomas Nelson *advertising executive*
Ellis, Steven George *public relations/corporate communication executive*
Erumsele, Andrew Akhigbe *development policy analyst*
Fairchild, Samuel Wilson *professional services company executive, former federal agency administrator*
†Farrell, Richard T. *human resources administrator*
Fenn, Peter Huntington *political consultant, media producer, educator*
Fertig-Dykes, Susan Beatrice *communications executive, human resourses professional*
Fields, Stuart Howard *labor relations specialist*
Flanagan, Francis Dennis *retired corporate executive*
Foer, Sara *public relations spokesperson, consultant*
†Franklin, Cabe Gerard *information systems specialist*
Fuller, Edwin Daniel *hotel executive*
Gibbons, Sam Melville (Sam Gibbons) *business executive, former congressman*
†Goetz, Peter *safety board director*
Golden, John Joseph, Jr. *information systems executive*
Gottlieb, Anita Faye *management consultant*
Grant, Carl N. *communications executive*
†Green, Amy Elizabeth *administrator*
Grossman, Steven *company executive, political party executive*
Guzda, Henry Peter *industrial relations specialist*
Hanback, Hazel Marie Smallwood *management consultant*
Hannaford, Peter Dor *public relations executive, writer*
†Hardin, Sara Jane *consumer products company executive*
Havlicek, Franklin J. *communications executive*
Hecht, Susan Elizabeth *consulting executive*
Helms, Richard McGarrah *international consultant, former ambassador*
Herrett, Richard Allison *agricultural research institute administrator*
†Hezir, Joseph S. *energy and environmental company executive*
Higgins, James Henry, III *marketing executive*
†Hirning, Katie *information officer*
Hoffmann, Melane Kinney *marketing and public relations executive, writer*
Holland, James Ricks *public relations executive, association executive*
Hoving, John Hannes Forester *consulting firm executive*
Howard, Jack *labor relations consultant*
Howe, Fisher *management consultant, former government official*
Huberman, Benjamin *technology consultant*
Ibañez, Alvaro *patent design company executive, artist*
Jagoda, Barry Lionel *media adviser, communications consultant*
Jordan, Sandra *public relations professional*
Kaludis, George *management consultant, book company executive, educator*
Kanuk, Leslie Lazar *management consultant, educator*
†Katz, Mitchell Jay *public affairs specialist*
Kavulich, John Steven, II *international marketing executive*
Kimmitt, Joseph Stanley *political consultant*
†Kraus, Margery *management consultant*
Lane, Herman Eugene *human resource manager*
Lasko, Joel *company executive*
†Lattimore, Patricia *administration and management administrator*
Leibach, Dale W. *public relations executive*
Levinson, Nanette Segal *international relations educator, administrator*
Lewis, William Walker *management consultant*
Lisboa-Farrow, Elizabeth Oliver *public and government relations consultant*
Lombard, Judith Marie *human resource policy specialist*
†Longest, Henry L., II *research and development administrator*
Luikart, Fordyce Whitney *management consultant*
Maddock, Jerome Torrence *information services specialist*
†Majak, Roger *administration executive*
Manatos, Andrew Emanuel *public relations executive*
Mann, Roger Ellis *food service and real estate and business development executive*
Mansfield, Edward Patrick, Jr. *advertising executive*
Marriott, John Willard, Jr. *lodging and senior living executive*
Marumoto, William Hideo *management consultant*
†Mayer, Susan *telecommunications company executive*
McBride, Jonathan Evans *executive search consultant*
McCann, Michael F. *industrial hygienist*
McLaughlin, John *broadcast executive, television producer, political commentator, journalist*
McMahon, Debra Brylawski *management consultant*
Miller, Robert Allen *hotel executive*
Millian, Kenneth Young *public policy consultant*
Moe, Ronald Chesney *public administration researcher*
Moore, Bob Stahly *communications executive*
Morris, Craig Allen *international marketing specialist*
Newton, Hugh C. *public relations executive*
Norman, William Stanley *travel and tourism executive*
†Novak, Vicki A. *human resources specialist*
O'Brien, Richard Francis *advertising agency executive*
O'Connor, Tom *corporate executive, management consultant*
Oliver-Simon, Gloria Craig *human resources advisor, consultant, lawyer*
Olson, Walter Justus, Jr. *management consultant*
Orski, C. Kenneth *consulting company executive, lawyer, publisher*
Palumbo, Benjamin Lewis *public affairs consulting company executive*
†Pass, Jeffrey Ryan *researcher*
Patrick, Janet Cline *personnel company executive*
Payne, Michael Lee *association management executive*
Pedersen, Wesley Niels *public relations and public affairs executive*
Petito, Margaret L. *public relations executive, consultant*
Petrou, David Michael *marketing and communications executive*
Pfenninger, Leslie J. *management consultant, writer, artist*
Phillips, Jean Crider *employee communications specialist*
Pines, Wayne Lloyd *public relations counselor*
†Powell, Jody L. *public relations executive*
Powell, Joseph Lester (Jody Powell) *public relations executive*
Pucie, Charles R., Jr. *public affairs executive*
Pyle, Robert Noble *public relations executive*
Rainey, Jean Osgood *public relations executive*
Rausch, Howard *information service executive*
Reed, Travis Dean *public relations executive*
Rice, Lois Dickson *former computer company executive*
†Roessel, Faith *Indian arts and crafts administrator*
Rose, Elizabeth *public relations executive*
Rosebush, James Scott *international management and public affairs consultant, former government official*
Rosenthal, Aaron *management consultant*
Rotunda, Donald Theodore *public relations consultant*
†Rubin, James P. *public affairs administrator*
Satterlee, Peter Hamilton *communications executive, military officer*
Schick, Michael William *public affairs consultant*
Schriever, Bernard Adolph *management consultant*
Scott, Evelyn Fuller *customer service professional*
Seats, Peggy Chisolm *marketing executive*
Sharples, Ruth Lissak *public relations specialist, video producer*
Shaw, Anesther O(live) *university administrative staff member*
†Shaw, William J. *hotel facility executive*
Shear, Natalie Pickus *public relations executive*
†Signer, William Alan *consultant*
Silverman, Marcia *public relations executive*
Simpkins, Robert Allyn *business consultant*
Sisco, Joseph John *management consultant, corporation director, educator, government official*
Skol, Michael *management consultant*
Slagle, Larry B. *human resources specialist*
Smith, Richard Hewlett, II *senior analyst*
†Smulkstys, Inga *operations and management executive*
†Soule, Robert R. *program analysis administrator*
Stauffer, Thomas George *hotel executive, retired*
†Stewart, Roy J. *communications executive*
†Stillman, Neil J. *information resources administrator*
Stowe, Ronald Floyd *telecommunications executive*
Stringer, Dann Pollard *executive search firm executive*
Tanham, George Kilpatrick *retired research company executive*

Tate, Sheila Burke *public relations executive*
Taylor, Sandra E. *public relations executive*
Tiefel, William Reginald *hotel company executive*
Timmons, William Evan *corporate executive*
Trowbridge, Alexander Buel, Jr. *business consultant*
†Tychan, Terrence J. *grants and acquisitions administrator*
Vickery, Raymond Ezekiel, Jr. *management consultant, educator*
Walker, Ronald Hugh *executive search company executive*
Walker, Savannah T. *executive assistant, legislative assistant*
†Ward, H. Marshall *special programs administrator*
Weiss, Paul Thomas *management consultant, editor-in-chief, public manager*
Welles, Judith *public affairs executive*
Wertheim, Mitzi Mallina *technology company executive*
Wheeler, Thomas Edgar *communications technology executive*
†White, Evelyn *human resources administrator*
Whittlesey, Judith Holloway *public relations executive*
†Wiggins, Sandra Lynn *human resources executive*
Wilhide, Peggy C. *public affairs administrator*
Winner, Lara E. *database manager*
Young, Vincent Arron *publicist*
Yulish, Charles Barry *public relations executive*
Zimmerman, Carole Lee *public relations professional*
Zulberti, Carlos Alberto *planning executive*

FLORIDA

Apopka
Leslie, John William *public relations and advertising executive*

Atlantic Beach
Buell, Victor Paul *marketing educator, author, editor*
Filips, Nicholas Joseph *management consultant*

Bartow
Andress, Lucretia Ann King *health care executive*

Boca Grande
Dyche, David Bennett, Jr. *retired management consultant*

Boca Raton
Beck, Louis S. *hotel executive*
†Cope, Daniel *package good industry executive*
Dolan, Dan *communications executive*
Dorfman, Allen Bernard *international management consultant*
Dunhill, Robert W. *advertising direct mail executive*
Frank, William Edward, Jr. *executive recruitment company executive*
Houraney, William George *marketing and public relations executive*
Kewley, Sharon Lynn *systems analyst, consultant*
Langbort, Polly *retired advertising executive*
Monroe, William Lewis *human resources executive*
Rosner, M. Norton *business systems and financial services company executive*
Saffir, Leonard *public relations executive*
Schechterman, Lawrence *business consultant*
Spencer, James Gray *marketing professional*

Bokeelia
Winterer, Victoria Thompson *hospitality executive*
Winterer, William G. *hotel executive*

Bonita Springs
Snedden, James Douglas *retired health service management consultant*

Boynton Beach
Ashley, James MacGregor *management consultant*
Ganz, Samuel *human resource and management professional*
Koteen, Jack *management consultant, writer*
Lentin, Dennis Henry *communications executive*
Sterman, Gail K. Mendelson *public relations specialist*

Bradenton
Doyle, William Jay, II *business consultant*
Robinson, Hugh R. *retired marketing executive*
Roehl, Nancy Leary *marketing professional, educator*

Cape Coral
Brevoort, Richard William *public relations executive*

Casselberry
Lucas, Robert William *human resources consultant, writer*
Medin, A. Louis *computer company executive*

Celebration
Renard, Meredith Anne *marketing and advertising professional*

Clearwater
Chisholm, William DeWayne *retired contract manager*
Devoe, Charles Louis, II *sales and marketing consultant*
Hallam, Arlita Warrick *quality of life administrator*
Raymund, Steven A. *computer company executive*

Coconut Grove
La Forge, Raymond Bernard, Jr. *marketing and sales consultant*
Softness, John *public relations executive*
Taylor, J(ames) Bennett *management consultant*

Cooper City
Waganheim, Arthur Brian *marketing executive*

Coral Gables
Bishopric, Susan Ehrlich *public relations executive*
Groome, Kimberly VonGonten *administrative assistant*
Hertz, Arthur Herman *business executive*
Lomonosoff, James Marc *marketing executive*
Nacknouck, James D. *management executive*

Coral Springs
Bosted, Dorothy Stack *public relations executive*

Davie
†Gonzalez, Richard *quality performance professional*

Debary
Schaeffer, Barbara Hamilton *retired rental leasing company executive, writer*

Deerfield Beach
Moran, James M. *automotive sales executive*

Delray Beach
Gaffey, Thomas Michael, Jr. *retired consumer products executive*
Mueller, Gerry *retired computer company executive*
Randall, Priscilla Richmond *travel executive*
†Scott, James Lawrence *retired human resources executive, consultant*
Sondak, Arthur *management consultant*

Deltona
Morgan, Shirley Ann *information systems executive*

Dunedin
Metcalf, Robert John Elmer *industrial consultant*
Samson, Jerome *communications executive, software engineer*

Fernandina Beach
D'Agnese, John Joseph *sanitation, public health and pest management consultant*

Fisher Island
Bandler, Richard *advertising executive*
Ventura, Richard Eugene *human resources executive*

Floral City
Wise, Lawrence George *human resources executive*

Fort Lauderdale
Barnes, William Douglas *advertising executive*
Cantwell, John Walsh *advertising executive*
Costello, John H., III *business and marketing executive*
Danzig, Sheila Ring *marketing and direct mail executive*
Danzig, William Harold *marketing executive*
†Faust, Charles *hotel executive*
Fine, Howard Alan *travel industry executive*
Gerbino, John *advertising executive*
Goodstein, Richard George *sales executive*
Honahan, H(enry) Robert *motion picture theatre executive*
Horowitz, Kenneth A. *communications executive, entrepreneur*
Jotcham, Thomas Denis *marketing communications consultant*
Koch, Katherine Rose *communications executive*
Lobeck, William E. *rental company executive*
Olen, Milton William, Jr. *marketing executive*
Page, Earl Michael *management specialist*
Sorensen, Allan Chresten *service company executive*
Stadtmiller, Marguerita W. *advertising executive*
Tanner, Travis *travel company executive*
†Valliere, Flora Lee *law firm official*
Williams, Roslyn Patrice *marketing executive*

Fort Myers
Antonic, James Paul *international marketing consultant*
Fromm, Winfield Eric *retired corporate executive, engineering consultant and investor*
†Fulker, Edmund *management consultant*
Milaski, John Joseph *business transformation industry consultant*
Ranney, Mary Elizabeth *business executive*

Fort Myers Beach
Oerter, Al *motivational speaker*

Fort Pierce
Arnold, Donna F. *business educator*
Thoma, Richard William *chemical safety and waste management consultant*

Fort Walton Beach
Fallin, Barbara Moore *human resources director*

Gainesville
Siegel, Robert James *communications executive*

Gulf Breeze
MacKenzie, Malcolm Robert *personnel management consultant*
Milford, Stephen Alan *management consultant*
Strength, Janis Grace *management executive, educator*

Hialeah
Edelcup, Norman Scott *management and financial consultant*
Grahm, Charles Morton *sales executive*
Proctor, Thomas F. Goldsmith *sales executive, publishing executive*

Highland Beach
Karp, Richard M. *advertising and communication executive*
Summers, James Irvin *retired advertising executive*

Hollywood
Angstrom, Wayne Raymond *communications executive*
Cowan, Irving *real estate owner, developer*
Ladin, Eugene *communications company executive*
Shapiro, Samuel Bernard *management consultant*

Hutchinson Island
Wegman, Harold Hugh *management consultant*

Indian Harbor Beach
Harrington, Peter Tyrus *emergency management company executive, public relations consultant, author, photographer*
Koenig, Harold Paul *management consultant, ecologist, evangelist, writer*

Islamorada
Pritchard, Robert Jerome *resort owner, retired*

Jacksonville
Bodkin, Ruby Pate *corporate executive, real estate broker, educator*
Constantini, JoAnn M. *information management consultant*
Davis, A. Dano *grocery store chain executive*
Hatch, Donald James (Jim Hatch) *business leadership and planning executive*
†Hearle, Edward F.R. *retired management consultant*
Motsett, Charles Bourke *sales and marketing executive*
Rinehart, Harry Elmer *retired sales executive*
Schramm, Bernard Charles, Jr. *advertising agency executive*
Sederbaum, William *marketing executive*
Shoup, James Raymond *computer systems consultant*

Jacksonville Beach
Jones, Herman Otto, Jr. *corporate professional*

Juno Beach
Pingel, John Spencer *retired advertising executive*

Jupiter
†Migdol, Kenneth M. *labor relations consultant, industrial psychologist*
Van Allen, Veronica E. *marketing and public relations professional*

Key Biscayne
Duffy, Earl Gavin *hotel executive*

Key Colony Beach
Crenshaw, Patricia Shryack *sales executive, consultant*

Key Largo
Chevins, Anthony Charles *retired advertising agency executive*

Kissimmee
Casler, Janice Loreen *marketing professional, public relations executive*
Johnston, Nancy Dahl *data processing specialist, paralegal*

Lady Lake
Langevin, Thomas Harvey *higher education consultant*

Lake Buena Vista
†Griswold, John A. *hotel executive*
Norsworthy, Josef Lawrence *marketing professional*
Parke, Robert Leon *communications executive*

Lake Mary
Sucher, Cynthia Clayton Crumb *communications executive*

Lake Worth
Diener, Bert *former food broker, artist*

Lakeland
Huggins, Richard Leonard *development director*
Jackson, Elijah, Jr. *communication executive*
Jenkins, Howard M. *supermarket executive*
Meads, Walter Frederick *executive recruitment consultant*
Rhodes, Jim *human resources professional*
Siedle, Robert Douglas *management consultant*

Land O'Lakes
Johnson, Tesla Francis *data processing executive, educator*

Largo
Chambers, Ray Wayne *security and loss control consultant*
Gould, Glenn Hunting *marketing professional, consultant*
†May, Andrew *technology company executive*
Ray, Roger Buchanan *retired communications executive, lawyer*

Leesburg
Entorf, Richard Carl *retired management consultant*

Longboat Key
Holcomb, Constance L. *sales and marketing management executive*
Moulton, Katherine Klauber *hotel executive*
Schoenberg, Lawrence Joseph *computer services company executive*
Valle, Vicente *management consultant*

Longwood
Bernabei, Raymond *management consultant*
Faller, Donald E. *marketing and operations executive*
Manjura, Bonnie Doreen *marketing and advertising executive, educator*

Maitland
Stephens, Patricia Ann *marketing professional*

Melbourne
Farmer, Phillip W. *company executive*
Gabriel, Roger Eugene *management consulting executive*
Hughes, Edwin Lawson *retired information systems company executive*
Ott, James Forgan *financial executive*

Melbourne Beach
Costa, Manuel Antone *recreational facility manager*

Miami
Amos, Betty Giles *restaurant company executive, accountant*
Argibay, Jorge Luis *information systems firm executive and founder*
Arison, Micky *cruise line company executive, sports team executive*
Batista, Alberto Entimio *marketing professional*
Carter, Harriet Vanessa *public relations specialist, congressional aide*
Cole, Todd Godwin *management consultant transportation*
Collins, Susan Ford *leadership consultant*
Cubas, Jose M(anuel) *advertising agency executive*
D'Gabriel, Carlos Leonardo *retired travel executive*
Dye, H. Michael *marketing executive*
Evans, Peter Kenneth *advertising executive*
Fernandez, Isabel Lidia *human resources specialist*
Fromkin, Ava Lynda *management consultant, healthcare risk management services*
Haar, Ana Maria Fernández *advertising and public relations executive*
†Hewitt, Thomas F. *hotel executive*
Howard, Elsie Sterling *marketing executive*
Knight, Kenneth Vincent *leisure company executive, entrepreneur, venture capitalist*
LeBow, Bennett S. *communications executive*
Le Duc, Albert Louis, Jr. *management consultant*
Lefton, Donald E. *hotel executive*
Levitt, Ronald Larry *public relations consulting executive*
Llanes, José Ramón *corporate professional, educator*
Neuman, Susan Catherine *public relations and marketing consultant*
Newman, Terrie Lynne *advertising and marketing executive*
Ortiz, Loida A. *communications executive*
Polen-Dorn, Linda Frances *communications executive*
Porter, Charles King *advertising executive*
Portland, Charles Denis *publishing executive*
Prussin, Jeffrey A. *management consultant*
Rothchild, Howard Leslie *advertising executive*
Rubin, Bruce Stuart *public relations executive*
Schwartz, Gerald *public relations and fundraising agency executive*
†Valdes, Juan Carlos *marketing executive*
Villarreal, Juan De Dios *management consultant*
Weiser, Ralph Raphael *business executive*
Weiser, Sherwood Manuel *hotel and corporation executive, lawyer*
Whittington, Robert Wallace *corporate professional, pianist*

Miami Beach
Crisci, Mathew G. *marketing executive, writer*
Paresky, David S. *travel company executive*
†Sharlach, Jeffrey *public relations executive*

Mount Dora
Hensinger, Margaret Elizabeth *horticultural and agricultural advertising and marketing executive*

Naples
Berman, Robert S. *marketing consultant*
Censits, Richard John *business consultant*
Franco, Anthony M. *public relations executive*
Johnson, Kennett Conrad *advertising agency executive*
Kleinrock, Virginia Barry *public relations executive*
Marshall, Charles *communications company executive*
Mehaffey, John Allen *marketing, newspaper management and advertising executive*
Moore, Mechlin Dongan *communications executive, marketing consultant*
Pancero, Jack Blocher *restaurant executive*
Savage, Robert Heath *advertising executive*
Shields, Bruce Maclean *management consultant*
Tarbutton, Lloyd Tilghman *motel executive, franchise consultant*
†Tymann, Jack T. *technology company executive*

Navarre
Wesley, Stephen Burton *training professional*

Newberry
Smith, Michael Steven *data processing executive*

North Bay Village
Solomon, Norman Frank *finance company executive*

North Miami
Roslow, Sydney *marketing educator*

Ocala
Leek, Jay Wilbur *management consultant*

Oldsmar
Brunner, George Matthew *management consultant, former business executive*
MacLeod, Donald Martin *corporate professional*

Orlando
†Andrew, Brian J. *information technology company executive*
Butler, John Paul *sales professional*
Connolly, Joseph Francis, II *educational executive, government consultant*
Davis, Duane Lee *marketing educator*
Hall, Lawrie Platt *consumer products executive, public community corporate philanthropy executive*
Lee, Joe R. *food service executive*
Moltzon, Richard Francis *manufacturing executive*
Neiman, Norman *aerospace business and marketing executive*
Pantuso, Vincent Joseph *food service consultant*
Polite, Edmonia Allen *consultant*
†Rosen, Harris *hotel company executive*
Yesawich, Peter Charles *advertising executive*

Ormond Beach
Coke, C(hauncey) Eugene *consulting company executive, scientist, educator, author*
Shepard, Janie Ray (J. R. Shepard) *software development executive*
Stogner, William Louis *pharmaceutical company sales executive*

Osprey
Halladay, Laurie Ann *public relations consultant, former franchise executive*

Palm Bay
Bigda, Rudolph A. *business and financial consultant*
Herro, John Joseph *software specialist*

Palm Beach
Baum, Selma *customer relations consultant*
Halmos, Peter *entrepreneur*

Tremain, Alan *hotel executive*

Palm Beach Gardens
Druck, Kalman Breschel *public relations counselor*
Mendelson, Richard Donald *former communications company executive*
Merritt, Jean *consulting firm executive*
Robb, David Buzby, Jr. *financial services company executive, lawyer*
Rosenfeld, Carson *retired leasing company executive*
Wackenhut, Richard Russell *security company executive*

Palm Harbor
McDonald, Peggy Ann Stimmel *retired automobile company official*

Panama City
Shelton, Karl Mason *management consultant*

Pembroke Pines
Motes, Joseph Mark *cruise and convention promotion company executive*

Pensacola
Arnold, Barry Raynor *philosophy educator, minister, ethicist, counselor*

Placida
Grissom, Joseph Carol *retired leasing and investments business executive*

Pompano Beach
Brands, Robert Franciscus *marketing executive*
Calevas, Harry Powell *management consultant*
Danziger, Terry Leblang *public relations and marketing consultant*
Donnelly, Michael Joseph *management consultant*
†Slovin, Bruce *diversified holding company executive*

Ponte Vedra Beach
Gold, Keith Dean *advertising and design executive*
Ramsey, William Dale, Jr. *marketing and technology consultant*

Port Charlotte
Reynolds, Helen Elizabeth *management services consultant*

Port Orange
Willhoit-Rudt, Marilyn Jean *medical resources company executive*

Port Saint Joe
Burke, Sabrina Nelson *sales and marketing professional*

Port Saint Lucie
Hambel, Henry Peter *clinical hypnotherapist, forensic security consultant, educator*

Punta Gorda
Harrington, John Vincent *retired communications company executive, engineer, educator*
Truby, John Louis *computer, management and trucking consultant*

Riverview
Till, Beatriz Maria *international business consultant, translator*

Safety Harbor
Fay, Carolyn M. *education marketing business owner*

Saint Augustine
Tuseo, Norbert Joseph John *marketing executive, consultant*

Saint Pete Beach
DeLorenzo, David Joseph *retired public relations executive*

Saint Petersburg
Kubiet, Leo Lawrence *newspaper advertising and marketing executive*
Lanitis, Tony Andrew *market researcher*
Metz, Robert Edward *quality assurance executive*
Metzger, Kathleen Ann *computer systems specialist*
Silver, Lawrence Alan *marketing executive*

Sanibel
Bailey, John Turner *public relations executive*
Brodbeck, William Jan *marketing consultant, speaker*
Lautenbach, Terry Robert *information systems and communications executive*

Sarasota
Beck, Robert Alfred *hotel administration educator*
Blanchard, Leonard Albert *management consultant, writer*
Feder, Allan Appel *management executive, consultant*
Fendrick, Alan Burton *retired advertising executive*
Gittelson, Bernard *public relations consultant, author, lecturer*
Huff, Russell Joseph *public relations and publishing executive*
Kelly, John Love *public relations executive*
Landis, Edgar David *retired services business company executive*
Mattran, Donald Albert *management consultant, educator*
Minette, Dennis Jerome *financial computing consultant*
Poppel, Harvey Lee *strategic management consultant, investment banker*
Shulman, Arthur *communications executive*
Simon, Joseph Patrick *food services executive*
Skelton, Howard Clifton *advertising and public relations executive*
Skelton, Winifred Karger *advertising agency executive, painter*
Stickler, Daniel Lee *health care management consultant*
White, Will Walter, III *public relations consultant, writer*

Silver Springs
Sundstrom, Harold Walter *public relations executive*

Stuart
Donohue, Edith M. *human resources specialist, educator*

Sun City Center
Steele, Richard J. *management consultant*

Tallahassee
Mason, Robert McSpadden *technology management educator, consultant*
Penson, Edward Martin *management consulting company executive*
†Wilson, Damian Michael *management analyst*

Tampa
Brackin, Phyllis Jean *recruiting professional*
Brown, Steven Thomas *communications company official*
Callen, David H. *hotel executive*
Christopher, Wilford Scott *public relations consultant*
Greenhalgh, Terry Lamont *marketing executive*
Grimes, David Lynn *communications company executive*
Hadden, John Randolph *sales and marketing executive*
Heuer, Martin *temporary services executive*
Highsmith, Jasper Habersham *sales executive*
Jablonski, Carol Jean *communication professional, educator*
Luber, Amanda Kimmer *public relations executive, marketing professional*
Mangiapane, Joseph Arthur *consulting company executive, applied mechanics consultant*
Miller, Bonnie Sewell *marketing professional, writer*
Ortinau, David Joseph *marketing specialist, educator*
Silver, Paul Robert *marketing executive, consultant*
Taylor, Austin Randall *sales executive*
Tewksbury, Russell Baird *Internet and new media consultant, educator*
Veasey, Byron Keith *information systems consultant*
Williams, Yvonne G. *corporate trainer*
Wyman, Richard Thomas *information services consultant*

Tarpon Springs
Crismond, Linda Fry *public relations executive*

Tequesta
Vollmer, James E. *high technology management executive*

Titusville
Bartley, Larry Durand *computer systems planner, mayor*

Treasure Island
Foote, Frances Catherine *association executive, living trust consultant*

Valrico
Foster, Michael Paul *sales and marketing representative*

Venice
Bluhm, Barbara Jean *communications agency executive*
McEntee, Robert Edward *management consultant*
Ogan, Russell Griffith *business executive, retired air force officer*

Vero Beach
Binney, Jan Jarrell *publishing executive*
Fisher, Andrew *management consultant*
Hubner, Robert Wilmore *retired business machines company executive, consultant*
McNamara, John J(oseph) *advertising executive, writer*
Menk, Carl William *executive search company executive*
Nichols, Carl Wheeler *retired advertising agency executive*

West Palm Beach
Alimanestianu, Calin *retired hotel consultant*
Ronan, William John *management consultant*
Stauderman, Bruce Ford *advertising executive, writer*

Weston
Boles, Eric Paul *staffing company executive*

GEORGIA

Albany
Ezeamii, Hyacinth Chinedum *public administration educator*

Alpharetta
Ashley, John Bryan *software executive, management consultant*
Bobo, Genelle Tant (Nell Bobo) *office administrator*
Butts, Carol Henderson *personnel consultant*
Esher, Brian Richard *environmental company executive*
Eubanks, Omer Lafayette *data communications consultant, systems engineer*

Americus
Mecke, William Moyn *public affairs consultant*

Athens
Hofer, Charles Warren *strategic management, entrepreneurship educator, consultant*
Jackson, Thomas Harold, Jr. *public relations administrator*
Thomas, Howard Lamar *chef, consultant, writer*

Atlanta
†Ahlquist, Jeffrey *strategy consultant*
Baker, Jerry Herbert *executive search consultant*
Bergonzi, Al *company executive*
Bevington, Paula Lawton *facilities management consulting executive*
†Blank, Arthur M. *home and lumber retail chain executive*
Bowers, Patricia Newsome *communications executive*
Boyle, Robert Daniel *management consultant, program management and business process reengineering*
Braswell, Cruse C., Jr. *public relations executive*
Brooks, Jeffrey Martin *marketing and sales executive*
Brothers, June Esternaux Scott *forest products company executive*
Brown-Olmstead, Amanda *public relations executive*
Bump, Gerald Jack *executive recruiter*
Buoch, William Thomas *corporate executive*
Burge, William Lee *retired business information executive*
Bush, John Kendall *management consultant*
Carlos, Michael C. *wine, spirits and linen service wholesale executive*
Chasen, Sylvan Herbert *computer applications consultant, investment advisor*
Choa, Walter Kong *technical service professional*
Cohn, Bob *public relations executive*
†Cole, Robert S. *hotel executive*
Cone, Frances McFadden *data processing consultant*
Cooper, Thomas Luther *retired printing company executive*
Copen, Melvyn Robert *management educator, university administrator*
Curtiss, Jeffery Steven *organizational development executive*
Darden, Claibourne Henry, Jr. *marketing research professional*
Delahanty, Edward Lawrence *management consultant*
Dudley, Perry, Jr. *wireless communications administrator*
†Duffey, Lee *communications company executive*
Dunlap, Donald Kelder *rental company executive*
Dysart, Benjamin Clay, III *environmental consultant, conservationist, engineer*
Ehrlich, Jeffrey *data processing company executive*
†Ellis, U. Bertram, Jr. *information technology company executive*
Farley, Charles P. *public relations executive*
Fredo, Peter W. *public relations executive*
Frizzell, Rick Dale *corporate creative director*
Gelardi, Robert Charles *trade association executive, consultant*
Goldstein, Burton Benjamin, Jr. *communications executive*
Goodwin, George Evans *public relations executive*
Hammill, Dick *advertising and marketing executive*
Healy, Maureen *marketing executive*
Hill, Donald Dee *management consultant, lecturer, writer*
Hodgson, Reginald Hutchins, Jr. *corporate executive*
Hoffman, Fred L. *human resources professional*
House, Donald Lee, Sr. *software executive, private investor, management consultant*
Howell, Hilton Hatchett, Jr. *business executive*
Hunter, Douglas Lee *media executive, former elevator company executive*
Hyle, Charles Thomas *marketing specialist*
Jones, Walter Edward *communications executive*
Kelly, Carol White *company executive*
Kent, Philip *communications executive*
Kolb, Derek Andrew *information systems specialist*
Laubscher, Robert James *consumer products company executive*
Lnenicka, Wade Sheridan *purchasing official, councilman*
Mahan, James S. *communications company executive*
Malhotra, Naresh Kumar *management educator*
†Malone, Richard Harlan *consultant*
Manley, Lance Filson *data processing consultant*
Marks, Marilyn *company executive*
Mashburn, Guerry Leonard *marketing professional*
Mashburn, Sylvia Anita Smith *communications executive, state official*
Massey, Charles Knox, Jr. *advertising agency executive*
†Matlock, Kent *company executive*
Mauldin, Earle *communications company executive*
McChesney, Michael C. *computer network security company executive*
McLean, Ephraim Rankin *information systems educator*
Minner, Thomas *marketing executive*
†Murnane, George, III *business executive*
Nelson, Linda Carol *corporate chief executive*
Newkirk, Isaac L. *communications executive*
†Oliver, Thomas *hotel executive*
†Ortman, Mary Fallon *public relations company official*
Overstreet, Jim *public relations executive*
Pace, Wayne H. *communications executive*
Pucci, Mark Leonard *public relations professional*
Raper, Charles Albert *retired management consultant*
Reda, James Francis *business consultant*
Reedy, Edward K. *research operations administrator*
Rink, Christopher Lee *information technology consultant, photographer*
Roberson, Timothy Randall *public relations professional*
†Rountree, Neva B. *business executive*
Ryan, J. Bruce *health care management consulting executive*
Salay, Cindy Rolston *technical specialist, nurse*
Schadl, John Scott *marketing consultant*
Schulze, Horst H. *hotel company executive*
Sherry, Henry Ivan *marketing consultant*
Sherwood, Deborah Grace *travel executive*
Smith, David Doyle *international management consultant, consulting engineer*
Söderberg, Bo Sigfrid *business executive*
Stormont, Richard Mansfield *hotel executive*
Summerlin, Glenn Wood *advertising executive*
Thomas, Mable *communications company executive, former state legislator, councilwoman*
Tomaszewski, Richard Paul *market representation manager*
Turner, Michael Griswold *advertising executive, writer*
Verrill, F. Glenn *advertising executive*
Walker, Betsy Ellen *consulting and systems integration company executive*
†Ward, Jackie M. *computer company executive*
West, Benjamin B. *advertising executive*
White, Ronald Leon *financial management consultant*
Yarnell, Jeffrey Alan *retired regional credit executive*
Zunde, Pranas *information science educator, researcher*

Augusta
Ingham, Robert Francis *marketing professional*
Morgante, John-Paul *management consultant*

Bainbridge
Hodges, Benjamin, Jr. *management consultant*

Carrollton
Sullivan, Robert R. *marketing professional*

Columbus
Tate, Charles W. *information system specialist, municipal official*

Conyers
Smith, William Lester *sales executive*

Dalton
Alexander, Burt Edward *management executive*
Evans, Thomas Passmore *business and product licensing consultant*

Dawsonville
Jorgensen, Alfred H. *computer software and data communications executive*

Fort Benning
Alles, Rodney Neal, Sr. *information management executive*

Griffin
Marshall, Allen Wright, III *communications executive, financial consultant*

La Fayette
Thompson, Arthur Raymond *marketing professional*

Lavonia
Masterson Raines, Judith Amanda *marketing executive*

Macon
Gurley, Steven Harrison *sales executive*

Marietta
Bradshaw, Rod Eric *personnel consultant*
Flinn, Michael Joseph *marketing executive*
Gamblin, James E. *quality assurance specialist*
Johnson, Herbert Frederick *sales executive, former university administrator, librarian*
Sherrington, Paul William *marketing communications executive*
Smith, Baker Armstrong *management executive, lawyer*
Smith, Beverly Ann Evans *management consultant, small business owner*
Spann, George William *management consultant*
Spann, Laura Nason *data processing executive*

Mineral Bluff
Alexander, Patricia Ross *administrative assistant*

Moreland
Andrews, Rowena *public relations executive*

Norcross
†Bender, Paul S. *management consultant*
Bennett, Catherine June *data processing manager, educator, consultant*
Cole, David Winslow *personal care industry executive*
Cramer, James Perry *management consultant, publisher*
Emanuele, R.M. *business executive*
Jondahl, Terri Elise *importing and distribution company executive, medical equipment company executive*
Shain, Kenneth Stephen *software company executive*
Sherwood, Kenneth Wesley *information systems executive, consultant*

Oxford
Stamps, George Moreland *communications consultant, facsimile pioneer*

Pine Mountain
Callaway, Howard Hollis *business executive*

Powder Springs
Zoda, Suzanne Marie *environmental public relations consultant*

Roswell
Burgess, John Frank *management consultant, former utility executive, former army officer*
Jordan, DuPree, Jr. *management consultant, educator, journalist, publisher, business executive*
Strong-Tidman, Virginia Adele *marketing and advertising executive*

Saint Simmons Island
Riedeburg, Theodore *management consultant*

Saint Simons
Clay, Ryburn Glover, Jr. *resort executive*
Dressner, Paul Robert *outside sales and customer service representative*
Sullivan, Barbara Boyle *management consultant*

Savannah
Lindqvist, Gunnar Jan *management consultant, international trade consultant*
Otter, John Martin, III *television advertising consultant, retired*
†Samir, Sami A. *food service executive*
Schafer, Thomas Wilson *advertising agency executive*
Sheehy, Barry Maurice *management consultant*

Snellville
Elleby, Gail *management consultant*

Stone Mountain
†Moseley, Clifford Longstaff *industrial hygienist*

Sugar Hill
Jordan, Henry Hellmut, Jr. *management consultant*

Tucker
Baker, Russ *executive search firm owner*
Broucek, William Samuel *printing plant executive*
†Brown, Betsy S. *hotel executive*
†Guimbellot, Bobby E. *hotel executive*

HAWAII

Fort Shafter
Maruoka, Jo Ann Elizabeth *information systems manager*

Honolulu
Bossert, Philip Joseph *information systems executive*
†Carey, W. David P. *hotel executive*
DeVilbiss, Jonathan Frederick *airline analyst*
Dougherty, Raleigh Gordon *manufacturer's representative*
Kelley, Richard Roy *hotel executive*
Keogh, Richard John *firearms and explosives consultant*
Miyamoto, Craig Toyoki *public relations executive*
O'Neill, Charles Kelly *marketing executive, former advertising agency executive*
Rogers, Dwane Leslie *retired management consultant*
Shimabukuro, Elton Ichio *sales professional*
Singer, Hersh *marketing executive*
Smales, Fred Benson *corporate executive*
Sorenson, Perry *resort facility executive*
Tatibouet, Andre Stephan *condominium and resort management firm executive*
Yamato, Kei C. *international business consultant*
Yang, David Chie-Hwa *business administration educator*

Kihei
†McCullough-Dieter, Carol Mae *database administrator*

Lanai City
Keenan-Abilay, Georgia Ann *service representative*

Waikoloa
Switaj, Carmen Marie *administrative assistant*

IDAHO

American Falls
Newlin, L. Max *parks and recreation director*

Bellevue
Pearson, Robert Greenlees *writing services company executive*

Boise
Beaumont, Pamela Jo *marketing professional*
†Eastland, Larry L. *entertainment and theme park development executive*
†Ewing, Jack *communications executive*
†Gellert, Edward Bradford *advertising agency executive*
†Orien, Harold Andrew *customer service representative*
Pon-Brown, Kay Migyoku *research and development project administrator*
Saldin, Thomas R. *lawyer, consumer products company executive*

Eagle
Kenyon, Kendra Sue *organizational consultant*

Ketchum
Ziebarth, Robert Charles *management consultant*

Plummer
Matheson, Donna Jane *communications executive, editor*

Post Falls
Grassi, James Edward *Christian ministry executive director*

ILLINOIS

Addison
†Christopher, Doris *consumer products executive*
McDonald, David Eugene *package car driver*

Aledo
Prosser, Wesley Lewis *advertising and public relations executive*

Antioch
Dahl, Laurel Jean *human services administrator*

Arlington Heights
Crawford, Robert W., Jr. *furniture rental company executive*
Gabrielsen, Carol Ann *employment consulting company executive*
Payne, Thomas, II *market research company executive*
Pollin, Pierre Louis *executive chef*
Spohr, Frederick Stephen *sales professional*

Aurora
Lee, Robert Hugh *management executive*
Nelson, Kay Hoyle *communication educator*

Bannockburn
Slavin, Craig Steven *management and franchising consultant*

Barrington
Francis, Philip Hamilton *management consultant*
Groesch, John William, Jr. *marketing research consultant*
Koten, John A. *retired communications executive*
Mathis, Jack David *advertising executive*
Murphy, Robert *search firm executive*
Ross, Frank Howard, III *management consultant*
Stephens, Norval Blair, Jr. *marketing consultant*
Sturm, Sherri Charisse *marketing and developmental researcher, actuary*

Bartlett
Robinson, Lois Hart *retired public relations executive*

Bloomingdale
Konopinski, Virgil James *industrial hygienist*

Bloomington
Daily, Jean A. *marketing executive, spokesperson*

Bolingbrook
Willadsen, Michael Chris *marketing professional, sales executive*

Brookfield
Dornhecker, Sandra Lee *human resources executive, consultant*

Buffalo Grove
Tracy, Allen Wayne *management consultant*

Burr Ridge
Bottom, Dale Coyle *management consultant*

Calumet City
Kovach, Joseph William *management consultant, psychologist, educator*

Carbondale
Jugenheimer, Donald Wayne *advertising and communications educator, university administrator*
Stetter, John *publishing executive*

Carol Stream
Kearns, Janet Catherine *corporate secretary*

Champaign
Aniello, Anthony Joseph *information system executive*
Knox, Charles Milton *purchasing agent, consultant*
Mies, John Charles *internet industry executive*

Charleston
†Kunkel, Robert Anthony *business educator*

Chicago
Allen, Belle *management consulting firm executive, communications company executive*
Amberg, Thomas L. *public relations executive*
Baglivo, Mary L. *client services administrator*
Bailey, Robert, Jr. *advertising executive*
Ball, Neal *management consultant, philanthropist*
Bard, John Franklin *consumer products executive*
†Barry, Richard A. *public relations executive*
Bayer, Gary Richard *advertising executive*
Becker, Robert Allen *data processing executive*
Bell, David Arthur *advertising agency executive*
Bensinger, Peter Benjamin *consulting firm executive*
Bess, Ronald W. *advertising executive*
Beugen, Joan Beth *communications company executive*
Biggles, Richard Robert *marketing executive*
Boatman, Elizabeth Artle *information systems specialist, municipal official*
Bowen, William Joseph *management consultant*
Boyda, Debora *advertising executive*
Brady, Catherine Rawson *software company executive*
Brandt, William Arthur, Jr. *consulting executive*
Brown, Faith A. *communications executive*
Buckley, Joseph Paul, III *polygraph specialist*
Bueschel, David Alan *management consultant*
Burack, Elmer Howard *management educator*
Cary, Arlene D. *retired hotel company sales executive*
Cass, Edward Roberts (Peter) *hotel and travel marketing professional*
Castorino, Sue *communications executive*
Chang, Sung-Jin James *management consultant*
†Chorengel, Bernd *international hotel corporation executive*
Conidi, Daniel Joseph *private investigation agency executive*
Corbett, Frank Joseph *advertising executive*
Cornell, Rob *hotel executive*
Cox, Allan James *management consultant and sports executive*
†Cox, Daniel T. *management consultant*
Coyle, Thomas *marketing executive*
De Francesco, John Blaze, Jr. *public relations company executive*
Digangi, Al *marketing executive*
Dobrick, Jo-Anne *business executive, environmental consultant*
Doetsch, Virginia Lamb *former advertising executive, writer*
Draft, Howard Craig *advertising executive*
Dwyer, Dennis D. *information technology executive*
Eastham, Dennis Michael *advertising executive*
Echols, M(ary) Evelyn *travel consultant*
Edelman, Daniel Joseph *public relations executive*
Ferguson, Leonard Price (Bear Ferguson) *advertising executive, consultant*
Fisher, Eugene *marketing executive*
Fisher, Lawrence Edgar *market research executive, anthropologist*
Fizdale, Richard *advertising agency executive*
Flagg, Michael James *communications and graphics company executive*
Flanagan, Joseph Patrick *advertising executive*
Foley, Joseph Lawrence *sales executive*
†Frangipane, Amy Christina *media planner*
Frankel, Bernard *advertising executive*
Freedman, Walter G. *corporate services executive*
Freidheim, Cyrus F., Jr. *management consultant*
Friedlander, Patricia Ann *marketing professional*
Fulgoni, Gian Marc *market research company executive*
Fullmer, Paul *public relations counselor*
Furcon, John Edward *management and organizational consultant*
Furth, Yvonne *advertising executive*
Gardner, Howard Alan *travel marketing executive, travel writer and editor*
Garr, Daniel Frank *restaurateur*
Gerber, Phillip *advertising executive*
†Giustino, Maryanne *public relations executive*
Gladden, Robert Wiley *corporate executive*
Glasser, James J. *leasing company executive, retired*
Goldring, Norman Max *advertising executive*
Golter, Christina Rita *marketing specialist, consultant*
Gordon, Howard Lyon *advertising and marketing executive*
Gray, Dawn Plambeck *work-family consultant*
Green, RuthAnn *marketing and management consultant*
Grosso, James Alan *information technology executive*
Haffner, Charles Christian, III *retired printing company executive*
Hanika, Stephen D. *advertising executive*
Hansen, Carl R. *management consultant*
Harris, Gregory Scott *management services executive*
Haupt, Roger A. *advertising executive*
Hayden, Harrold Harrison *information company executive*
†Healy, Sondra Anita *consumer products company executive*
Heidrick, Robert Lindsay *management consultant*
†Height, David Joseph *consumer products executive, lawyer*
Hochhalter, Gordon Ray *advertising communications executive*
Hoey, Rita Marie *public relations executive*
Holmes, Colgate Frederick *hotel executive*
Holzer, Edwin *advertising executive*
Husting, Peter Marden *advertising consultant*
Isaacs, Roger David *public relations executive*
Jernstedt, Richard Don *public relations executive*
Johnson, Shirley Elaine *management consultant*
Johnston, Sheryl L. *communications executive*
Kaplan, Jonathan Harris *healthcare business transformation and information technology specialist*
Kathrein, Michael Lee *leasing company executive, real estate company executive*
Kazenas, Susan Jean *consultant*
Keroff, William B. *advertising agency executive*
Kindzred, Diana *communications company executive*
Kipper, Barbara Levy *corporate executive*
Klues, Jack *communications executive*
Knight, James Atwood *consulting executive*
Kobs, James Fred *advertising agency executive*
Koch, Carole Jackson *human resources executive*
Kos, Heather Anne *management consultant*
Kraus, Herbert Myron *public relations executive*
Krivkovich, Peter George *advertising executive*
Kuczmarski, Susan Smith *management consulting company executive*
Lane, Kenneth Edwin *retired advertising agency executive*
Larson, Paul William *public relations executive*
Leavitt, Victoria Seyferth *marketing professional*
Lehman, George Morgan *food sales executive*
Leigh, Sherren *communications executive, editor, publisher*
Lewy, Ralph I. *hotel executive*
Lowery, Sharon A. *travel industry executive*
Lowry, James Hamilton *management consultant*
Lynch, William Thomas, Jr. *advertising agency executive*
Lynnes, R. Milton *advertising executive*
Maczulski, Margaret Louise *marketing event professional, meeting manager*
Mahaffey, John Christopher *association executive*
Marin, Vincent Arul *infosystems executive*
Martin, Robert C. *marketing professional*
Martinez, Josemaria Espino *computer services administrator*
McCallister, Richard Anthony *business consulting company executive*
McConnell, E. Hoy, II *advertising/public policy executive*
McCullough, Richard Lawrence *advertising agency executive*
Mendelsohn, Zehavah Whitney *data processing executive*
Miller, Bernard J., III *advertising executive*
Miller, Bernard Joseph, Jr. *advertising executive*
Miller, Ellen *advertising executive*
Mitchell, Lee Mark *communications executive, investment fund manager, lawyer*
Modesto, Mark *advertising professional*
Morgan, Wesley James *personnel executive*
†Myers, Mary A. *public relations executive, consultant*
Nelson, Harry Donald *telecommunications executive*
Oates, James G. *advertising executive*
O'Connor, William Michael *executive search company executive*
Olins, Robert Abbot *communications research executive*
Pacchini, Mark *advertising executive*
Paitich, Olivia *executive assistant*
Paul, Ronald Neale *management consultant*
†Petrillo, Nancy *public relations executive*
Pincus, Theodore Henry *public relations executive*
Plank, Betsy Ann (Mrs. Sherman V. Rosenfield) *public relations counsel*
Plotkin, Manuel D. *management consultant, educator, former corporate executive and government official*
Poe, Gertie LaVerne *sales executive*
Pritzker, Thomas Jay *lawyer, business executive*
Proctor, Barbara Gardner *advertising agency executive*
Provus, Barbara Lee *executive search consultant*
Rabin, Joseph Harry *marketing research company executive*
Raphaelson, Joel *retired advertising agency executive*
Reid, Daniel James *public relations executive*
Reilly, Robert Frederick *valuation consultant*
Reitman, Jerry Irving *advertising agency executive*
Rich, S. Judith *public relations executive*
Robbins, Henry Zane *public relations and marketing executive*
Robinson, Samira E. Watson *marketing executive, writer*
Rosenthal, Albert Jay *advertising agency executive*
†Rowe, John W. *company executive*
Rozran, Jack Louis *courier service executive*
Sacks, Terence Julius *writer, editor, consultant*
Sampson, Ronald Alvin *advertising executive*
Saul, Bradley Scott *communications, advertising and entertainment executive*
Schneider, Wesley Clair *marketing communications company executive*
Schubert, Helen Celia *public relations executive*
Schuster, Bertram *recruiter, management consultant, publisher*
Seaman, Irving, Jr. *public relations consultant*
Seebert, Kathleen Anne *international sales and marketing executive*
Seifert, Timothy Michael *infosystems specialist*
Senior, Richard John Lane *textile rental service executive*
Shepherd, Daniel Marston *executive recruiter*
Shirley, Virginia Lee *advertising executive*
Singer, Emel *staffing industry executive*
Siska, Richard Stanly *marketing professional*
Sive, Rebecca Anne *public affairs company executive*
Smith, Scott Clybourn *media company executive*
Soto, Ramona *training specialist*
Steingraber, Frederick George *management consultant*
Stern, Carl William, Jr. *management consultant*
Stone, James Howard *management consultant*
Streeto, Joseph Michael *catering company official*
Strubel, Ella Doyle *advertising and public relations executive*
Struggles, John Edward *management consultant*
Sweet, Charles Wheeler *executive recruiter*
Talbot, Pamela *public relations executive*
Teichner, Lester *management consulting executive*
Thomas, Bertha Sophia *office manager, paralegal*
Thomas, John Thieme *management consultant*
Thompson, Kenneth Roy *management educator*
Tobaccowala, Rishad *marketing professional*
Tripp, Marian Barlow Loofe *retired public relations company executive*
Turner, La Ferria Maria *business consultant, financial consultant*
Van Den Hende, Fred J(oseph) *human resources executive*
Van Eron, Kevin Joseph *organizational development consultant*
Wackerle, Frederick William *management consultant*
Wade, Suzanne *management consultant*
†Walker, Joan H. *public relations executive*
Walters, Lawrence Charles *advertising executive*
Watson, MaryFrances Elizabeth *management consultant, librarian*
Weaver, Donna Rae *company executive*
Weber, Donald B. *advertising and marketing executive*
Webster, Ronald D. *communications company executive*
†Westcott, Robert Frederick *consultant*
Wiecek, Barbara Harriet *advertising executive*
Williams, Elynor A. *public affairs specialist*
Williams, Mark H. *marketing communications executive*
Wilson, Thomas W. *market research company executive*
†Winninghoff, Albert C. M. *advertising company executive*
Wolf, Linda *advertising executive*
Wooldridge, Patrice Marie *marketing professional, martial arts and meditation educator*
Young, James Eugene *management consultant*

Chicago Heights
Dowden, Craig Phillips *human resources executive*

Crete
Langer, Steven *human resources management consultant and industrial psychologist*

Crystal Lake
Halperin, Richard George *information technology executive*

Decatur
Bluhm, Myron Dean *sales professional*
Heisler, Harold Reinhart *management consultant*

Deerfield
Benjamin, Lawrence *food service executive*
Berman-Hammer, Susan *public relations executive*
Dennison, Terry Alan *management consultant*
Karp, Gary *marketing and public relations executive*
Wallace, Rick *marketing professional*

Dekalb
†Merwin, Donald Miles *retired phone worker, politician*
Stoia, Dennis Vasile *industrial management educator*

Des Plaines
†Baerenklau, Alan H. *hotel executive*
Holtz, Michael P. *hotel executive*
Mueller, Kurt M. *hotel executive*
Torchia, H. Andrew *hotel executive*

Downers Grove
Beres, Michael John *plant engineer*
†Canitz, Henry Charles *food company executive*
Clement, Paul Platts, Jr. *performance technologist, educator*
Pollard, C. William *environmental services administrator*
Pollard, Charles William *diversified services company executive*
Powers, Anthony Richard, Jr. *educational sales professional*
Schwemm, John Butler *printing company executive, lawyer*

Edwardsville
Dietrich, Suzanne Claire *instructional designer, communications consultant*

Elburn
Hansen, H. Jack *management consultant*

Elgin
Rogers, Carleton Carson, Jr. *trade show and convention executive*

Elk Grove Village
Flaherty, John Joseph *quality assurance company executive*

Elmhurst
Baker, Robert I. *business executive*
Choyke, Phyllis May Ford (Mrs. Arthur Davis Choyke, Jr.) *management executive, editor, poet*

Evanston
Crook, Stephen Richard *sales and marketing management consultant*
Durst, Gary Michael *management trainer, speaker*
Fryburger, Vernon Ray, Jr. *advertising and marketing educator*
Goodyear, Julie Ann *marketing and fundraising specialist*
Keith, Thomas Warren, Jr. *marketing executive*
Miller, Deborah Jean *computer training and document consultant*
Neuschel, Robert Percy *management consultant, educator*
Rolfe, Michael N. *management consulting firm executive*
Sims, William Ronald *advertising executive*
Tornabene, Russell C. *communications executive*

Galesburg
Conway, Lowava Denise *data processing administrator*

Gibson City
Welch, Melanie Gay *administrative assistant*

Glen Ellyn
Parkhurst, Edwin Wallace, Jr. *healthcare management consultant*
Taylor, Robert Rowe *communications executive, consultant*

Glencoe
Cole, Kathleen Ann *advertising agency executive, retired social worker*
Joseph, Donald Louis *management consultant*
Niefeld, Jaye Sutter *advertising executive*

Glendale Heights
Silver, Marc Laurence *marketing and advertising executive*

Glenview
Feldman, Burton Gordon *printing company executive*
Franklin, Lynne *business communications consultant, writer*

Gurnee
Murgatroyd, Eric Neal *data processing executive*
Weber, James Stuart *management educator*

Highland Park
Bakalar, John Stephen *printing and publishing company executive*
Burman, Diane Berger *organization development consultant*
Harris, Thomas L. *public relations executive*
Herbert, Edward Franklin *public relations executive*

Hillside
†Payton, Roger *logistics company executive*

Hinsdale
Bloom, Stephen Joel *distribution company executive*
Carlini, James *management consultant*
Cohen, Burton David *franchising executive, lawyer*
Lebedow, Aaron Louis *consulting company executive*
Whitney, William Elliot, Jr. *advertising agency executive*
Zaccone, Suzanne Maria *sales executive*

Hoffman Estates
Martinez, Arthur C. *retail company executive*
Schulz, Michael John *fire and explosion analyst, consultant*

Hudson
Mills, Lois Jean *company executive, former legislative aide, former education educator*

Inverness
Hetzel, William Gelal *executive search consultant*

Itasca
Carter, Eleanor Elizabeth *business manager*

Joliet
Starner, Barbara Kazmark *marketing, advertising and export sales executive*

Kankakee
Kanouse, Donald Lee *wastewater treatment executive*

Kenilworth
Guelich, Robert Vernon *retired management consultant*

La Grange Park
Carroll, Thomas John *retired advertising executive*

Lake Bluff
Preschlack, John Edward *management consultant*

Lake Forest
Carter, Donald Patton *advertising executive*
Chieger, Kathryn Jean *recreation company executive*
Davidson, Richard Alan *data communications company executive*
Fromm, Henry Gordon *retired manufacturing and marketing executive*
Kenly, Granger Farwell *marketing consultant, college official*
Kenzenkovic, Kevin G. *management consultant*
Kozitka, Richard Eugene *retired consumer products company executive*
Mitchell, Richard Charles *human resources executive*
Mohr, Roger John *advertising agency executive*
Rand, Kathy Sue *public relations executive*
Raudabaugh, Joseph Luther *management consultant*
Tyler, W(illiam) Ed *printing company executive*

Lake Zurich
Schmitz, Shirley Gertrude *marketing and sales executive*

Lansing
Kaplan, Huette Myra *business educator, training consultant*

Libertyville
Conklin, Mara Loraine *public relations executive*

Lincolnshire
Goldin, Sol *marketing consultant*
Hebda, Lawrence John *data processing executive, consultant*
Stern, Gerald Joseph *advertising executive*

Lincolnwood
Donovan, John Vincent *consulting company executive*
Grant, Paul Bernard *industrial relations educator, arbitrator*

Lindenhurst
Rose, William *retired business executive*

Lisle
Kubo, Gary Michael *advertising executive*

Long, Charles Franklin *corporate communications executive*
Smith, Sydney David *data processing executive*
Tyson, Kirk W. M. *management consultant*

Litchfield
Talley, Hayward Leroy *communications executive*

Lombard
Burdett, James Richard *golf products innovator*

Mapleton
†Dailey, Alice Beatrice *postmaster*

Matteson
Goyak, Elizabeth Fairbairn *retired public relations executive*

Mattoon
†Keown, Michele L. *computer training specialist, business educator*

Mchenry
Sheft, Mark David *market analyst, consultant, product manager*

Moline
†Schwiebert, Deborah Johnson *marketing executive*

Mount Prospect
Gerlitz, Curtis Neal *business executive*
Pulsifer, Edgar Darling *leasing service and sales executive*
†Sayers, Gale *computer company executive, retired professional football player*

Mount Vernon
Wittmeyer, Richard Arthur *management consulting company executive*

Mundelein
Smith McKee, Maureen Jacquelene *marketing professional*

Naperville
Fritz, Roger Jay *management consultant*
Fuhrer, Larry *management consultant, finance company executive*
Modery, Richard Gillman *marketing and sales executive*
Sellers, Lucia Sunhee *marketing professional*

Northbrook
†Abbott, Boyce *temporary help company executive*
Clarey, John Robert *executive search consultant*
Lewis, Evelyn *management consultant*
Milligan, Robert Lee, Jr. *computer company executive*
†Rijos, John P. *hospitality company executive*
Ross, Debra Benita *jewelry designer, marketing executive*
Sudbrink, Jane Marie *sales and marketing executive*
Turner, Lee *travel company executive*
Wajer, Ronald Edward *management consultant*
Weinstein, Ira Phillip *advertising executive*
Young, R. James *marketing executive*

Northfield
Heise, Marilyn Beardsley *public relations company executive*
Larson, Donald Harold *information systems executive*
Pratt, Murray Lester *information systems specialist*
Smart, Jackson Wyman, Jr. *business executive*

Oak Brook
Cannon, Patrick Francis *public relations executive*
DeLorey, John Alfred *printing company executive*
Higgens, William John, III (Trey Higgens) *sales executive*
Michelsen, John Ernest *software and internet services company executive*
Nelson, Robert Eddinger *management and development consultant*
Quinlan, Michael Robert *fast food franchise company executive*
Turner, Fred L. *fast food company executive*
Wigginton, Adam *marketing professional*

Oak Lawn
Gordon, Edward Earl *management consultant*

Oak Park
Andre, L. Aumund *management consultant*
Devereux, Timothy Edward *advertising agency executive*

Oakbrook Terrace
Buntrock, Dean Lewis *waste management company executive*
Singhal, Vivek Kumar *management consultant*

Oswego
Weilert, Ronald Lee *data processing executive*

Palatine
Compton, David Bruce *international management consultant*
Medin, Lowell Ansgard *management executive*

Peoria
Clough, Barry *marketing executive*
Lund, Thomas C. *advertising executive*

Peoria Heights
Bro, William Price *communications executive*

Plainfield
Chase, Maria Elaine Garoufalis *publishing company executive*
Glenn, Gerald Marvin *marketing, engineering and construction executive*

Prospect Heights
Kosinski, Richard Andrew *public relations executive*

Quincy
Adams, Beejay (Meredith Elisabeth Jane J. Adams) *sales executive*

Kallner, Norman Gust *management information systems manager*

Rock Island
Crisp, Sandra Sue *contract specialist*

Rockford
Anderson, Max Elliot *television and film production company executive*
Liebovich, Samuel David *warehouse executive*

Rolling Meadows
Cain, R. Wayne *sales, finance and leasing company executive*
†Cataldo, C. A. *hotel executive*
†Cataldo, Robert J. *hotel executive*
Padgitt, David G. *corporate executive*
Podgorski, Robert Paul *human resources executive*

Roselle
Laughlin, Terry Xavier *management consultant*

Rosemont
Moster, Mary Clare *public relations executive*
Myers, Michael Charles *marketing executive*
Stabler, Nancy Rae *infosystems specialist*

Round Lake
Laskowski, Richard E. *retail hardware company executive*

Saint Charles
Frank, Ruby Merinda *employment agency executive*
Markham, John Phillip, Jr. *research analyst*

Schaumburg
Hill, Raymond Joseph *packaging company executive*
Huff, Gayle Compton *advertising/marketing executive*
Littel Zdon, Laura *communications executive*
Sandler, Norman *business executive*
Stabej, Rudolph John *computer consultant*

Skokie
Finkel, Bernard *public relations, communications and association management consultant, radio host*
Haben, John William *funeral director*
Johansson, Nils A. *information services executive*
Roemer, James Paul *data processing executive*
Seeder, Richard Owen *infosystems specialist*

Springfield
Weinhoeft, John Joseph *data processing executive*

Sullivan
Harshman, Milton Moore *sales and marketing professional*

Urbana
Rotzoll, Kim Brewer *advertising and communications educator*

Vernon Hills
Claassen, W(alter) Marshall *employment company executive*

West Dundee
†Woltz, Kenneth Allen *consulting executive*

Westchester
Anderson, Carol Lee *communications executive*

Western Springs
Carroll, Jeanne *public relations executive*
Frommelt, Jeffrey James *management consulting firm executive*

Wheeling
Raney, David Elliot *computer professional*

Wilmette
Blair, Virginia Ann *public relations executive*
Chiaro, A. William *management consultant*
Snyder, Mary-Jane Ryan *communications executive*

Wood Dale
Sorensen, Jimmy Louis *management consultant*

Woodridge
Zucchero, Rocco *communications specialist*

Zion
†Gardner, Adrienne Moore *public relations specialist*

INDIANA

Auburn
Adair, Leslie Gayle *marketing professional*

Bloomington
Burton, Philip Ward *advertising executive, educator*
Henson, Jane Elizabeth *information management professional, adult educati*
Kravchuk, Robert Sacha *management educator, financial consultant*
Patterson, James Milton *marketing specialist, educator*
Sears, Everett Maurice *personnel executive*
Sullivan, Michael Francis, III *executive*

Brazil
Jones, Carole Moody-Anderson *retired outreach representative*

Carmel
Goldberg, John Robert *information specialist, historian, advocate*
Mahoney, Margaret Ellis *executive assistant*

Columbus
DeLorenzo, David W. J. *human resources manager, health consultant*
Kirkpatrick, Robert Hugh *communications executive*
Tucker, Thomas Randall *public relations executive*

Crown Point
Retort, Valerie Carmel *public relations executive, educator*

Elkhart
Chism, James Arthur *information systems executive, business consultant*

Evansville
Hampel, Robert Edward *advertising executive*
Kitch, Frederick David *advertising executive*
Zion, Roger Herschel *consulting firm executive, former congressman*

Fort Wayne
Collins, Linda Lou Powell *manager of contracts*
†Lucenta, Dominic A. *human resources executive*
Schweickart, Jim *advertising executive, broadcast consultant*
Taritas, Karen Joyce *telemarketing executive*
Waters, Wayne Arthur *conference and travel service agency executive*
Wolf, Don Allen *hardware wholesale executive*

Franklin
Grossnickle, Ted Richard *non-profit consulting company executive*

Greenwood
†Du Bois, William, Jr. *retired public relations professional*
†Egold, Thomas A. *electronics company administrator*
Saint-Pierre, Michael Robert *funeral director, consultant*

Hammond
Habzansky, Andrew Melvin *quality manager, maintenance manager, trainer*

Hobart
Harrigan, Richard George *salesperson*

Huntington
†Brown, Robert Clark, Jr. *sales executive*

Indianapolis
Abbott, Verlin Leroy *sales executive*
Ahlrichs, Nancy Surratt *marketing professional*
Boggs, John Steven *sales and development executive*
Boner, Donald Leslie *information systems executive*
Bryant, Maxine L(eona) *training consultant, entrepreneur*
Carr, William H(enry) A. *public relations executive, author*
Clary, Keith Uhl *retired industrial relations executive*
Cunningham, Karen Lee *marketing professional*
Damin, David E. *technology integration company executive*
Dedert, Steven Ray *marketing professional, consultant*
†Diehm, Jamie Renee *company official*
Durbin, Robert Cain *retired hotel executive*
Gilman, Alan B. *restaurant company executive*
Hancock, Joan Herrin *retired executive search company executive*
Hillman, Charlene Hamilton *public relations executive*
Kacek, Don J. *management consultant, business owner*
Knutson, Roger Craig *marketing and sales professional, inventor*
Krueger, Alan Douglas *communications company executive*
Landis, Larry Seabrook *marketing and communications consultant*
Manley, Karen Ann *human resources director*
Meyer, Fred William, Jr. *memorial parks executive*
Miniear, J. Dederick *software company executive, consultant*
Moore, Judy Kay *marketing communications consultant*
Morris, Greg James *advertising executive*
Poinsette, Donald Eugene *business executive, value management consultant*
Quiring, Patti Lee *human resource consulting company executive*
Rati, Robert Dean *data processing executive*
Robinson, Clifford Fossett *human resources administrator*
Ruben, Gary A. *marketing and communications consultant*
Simmons, Roberta Johnson *public relations firm executive*
Slaymaker, Gene Arthur *public relations executive*
Spanogle, Robert William *marketing and advertising company executive, association administrator*
Thompson, Roland *marketing professional*
Walker, Frank Dilling *market research executive*
Walker, Steven Frank *management consultant*

Kokomo
Lowther, Roberta Wynn *information security analyst*

Lafayette
Lazarus, Bruce I. *restaurant and hotel management educator*

Linden
Eutsler, Mark Leslie *business services executive, real estate broker*

Marion
Hall, Charles Adams *information systems specialist*

Merrillville
White, Dean *advertising executive*

Michigan City
Komp, Barbara Ann *marketing communications executive*
Pecze, David Emery *marketing professional*

Milltown
†Pesek, James Robert *management consultant*

Monroeville
Ray, Annette D. *business executive*

Muncie
Barber, Earl Eugene *consulting firm executive*
†Clark, Catherine Kay *human recources specialist*
Kuratko, Donald F. *business management educator, consultant*
Norris, Tracy Hopkins *retired public relations executive*

Munster
†Witting, Marie A. *management consultant*

Nashville
Rogers, Frank Andrew *restaurant, hotel executive*

North Vernon
Hicks, Gregory Steven *marketing professional*

Osceola
Tatum, Rita *communications executive*

Santa Claus
Edwards, James Dallas, III *consulting company executive*

Schererville
Hendricks, Stanley Marshall, II *executive recruiter, consultant*
Pettit, Wendy Jean *management company executive*

Seymour
Bollinger, Don Mills *retired grocery company executive*

South Bend
Brennen, William Elbert *management consultant*
Murphy, William Host *sales executive, retired*

Valparaiso
Schlender, William Elmer *management sciences educator*
Taylor, Kenard Lyle, Jr. *director training*

Wabash
Scales, Richard Lewis *sales representative*

Warsaw
Holbrook, Stephen Eugene *printing executive*

West Lafayette
Laskowitz, Kate *labor relations educator*
†Oates, William Matthew *communication consultant*
Schendel, Dan Eldon *management consultant, business educator*

IOWA

Ames
Bonomi, Ferne Gater *public relations executive*

Ankeny
Creswell, Dorothy Anne *computer consultant*
Rivers, Donald Lee *marketing professional*

Arnolds Park
Ritzer, Karen Rae *executive secretary, office administrator*

Bettendorf
Kucharo, Donald Dennis, Jr. *manufacturer's representative*

Cedar Falls
Sweet, Cynthia Rae *office administrator*

Cedar Rapids
Baker, Frank C. (Buzz Baker) *advertising executive*
Damrow, Richard G. *marketing executive*
Richardson, Robert Edward *data processing analyst*
Stolte, Larry Gene *marketing executive, former computer and publishing company executive*
Vanderpool, Ward Melvin *management and marketing consultant*
Wiese, Daniel Edward *marketing and communications researcher*

Cherokee
Simonsen, Robert Alan *marketing executive*

Clinton
Baker, Gilbert Jens *management consultant*

Council Bluffs
Duquette, Diana Marie *company official*

Des Moines
†Bodensteiner, Carol A. *public relations executive*
Proudfoot, James Mark *custodian*

Fairfield
Hawthorne, Timothy Robert *direct response advertising and communications company executive*
Wright, Max *information processing executive, consultant, youth leadership corporate training executive*

George
Symens, Maxine Brinkert Tanner *restaurant owner*

Glenwood
Hoogestraat, Thomas John *human services professional*

Hiawatha
Robertson, Florence Winkler *advertising and public relations agency executive*

Iowa City
Turner, James Daniel *computer company executive*

Kellogg
Anderson, Dale C. *state agency professional, travel consultant*

Knoxville
Ribar, Dixie Lee *marketing coordinator*

Marshalltown
Reitenbaugh, Luann Rose *quality assurance professional*

Milford
Fontaine, Sue (Jeane Fontaine) *public relations professional*

Newton
Cooper, Janis Campbell *public relations executive*

Orange City
Fynaardt, Tamara Dianne *public relations professional, educator*
Schulte, Linda F. *faculty assistant, office manager*

Urbandale
Lucas, Dale Adrian *grounds supervisor*

Waterloo
†Stewart, Margaret Faye *executive*

West Des Moines
Bamford, Carol Marie *marketing executive*

KANSAS

Basehor
Franklin, Shirley Marie *marketing consultant*

Emporia
Hedstrom, Cora Zaletel *public relations director*

Great Bend
McLaughlin, Deborah Ann *public relations and marketing executive*

Kansas City
Freund, Ronald S. *management consultant, marketing company executive*

Lawrence
†Dietz, Paul T. *company executive*
Mackenzie, Kenneth Donald *management consultant, educator*

Manhattan
Streeter, John Willis *information systems manager*

Olathe
Bruski, Paul Steven *marketing executive*
Burke, Paul E., Jr. *governmental relations consultant*

Overbrook
Dale, Kenneth Ray *computer executive*

Overland Park
Click, Marianne Jane *credit manager*
Hanson, Patti Lynn *human resources administrator*
Intrater, Cheryl Watson Waylor *career marketing consultant*
†Molz, Philip Jack *management consultant*
Rayburn, George Marvin *business executive, investment executive*
Voska, Kathryn Caples *consultant, facilitator*

Saint John
Hathaway, Michael Jerry *personal care assistant, editor, publisher*

Salina
Ryan, Stephen Collister *funeral director*

Shawnee Mission
Hagans, Robert Frank *industrial clothing cleaning company executive*
Hill, W. Clayton *management consultant*
Mealman, Glenn *corporate marketing executive*
Mooney, Justin David *motel executive*
Putman, Dale Cornelius *management consultant, lawyer*

Stilwell
Keith, Dale Martin *management consultant*

Topeka
Vidricksen, Ben Eugene *food service executive, state legislator*
Volpert, Mary Katherine *administrative assistant, revenue specialist*

Wichita
Angel, Larry *business professional*
George, David Bruce *hotel executive*
Herr, Peter Helmut Friederich *sales executive*
Lair, Robert Louis *catering company executive*
Lerman, Kenneth Barry *marketing professional*
McIntyre, Darla Jean *sales executive, merchandiser*
Menefee, Frederick Lewis *advertising executive*

KENTUCKY

Ashland
Carter, David Edward *communications executive*

Campbellsville
Whitt, Marcus Calvin *development and public relations executive*

Covington
Sampson, Susan J. *marketing communications consultant, writer, television producer*
Surber, David Francis *public affairs consultant, syndicated television producer*

Hopkinsville
Neville, Thomas Lee *food service company executive*

Lexington
Blanchard, Richard Emile, Sr. *management services executive, consultant*
Carney, Robert Arthur *restaurant executive*
Charley, Nancy Jean *communications professional*
Dorio, Martin Matthew *material handling company executive*
†Lockard, Paula Lynn *human resources specialist*
Millard, James Kemper *marketing executive*
Mitchell, John Charles *business executive*
Scharlatt, Harold *management company executive*

Louisa
†Compton, Hazel Louise *office administrator*

Louisville
Everett, Elbert Kyle *marketing executive, consultant*
†Fullenlove, Carmen (Kit) Millay *public relations executive*
Hughes, J. Deborah *quality management consultant*
Lumley, Thomas Dewey *travel professional, real estate investor*
Peden, Katherine Graham *industrial consultant*
Pelfrey, Deanna Kaye Wedmore *public relations and marketing executive, educator*
Pepples, Ernest *tobacco company executive*
Sutton, John Schuhmann, Jr. *retired purchasing consultant*

Nicholasville
Bender, Betty Barbee *food service professional*

Versailles
Preston, Thomas Lyter *crisis management, anti-terrorism and workplace violence consultant*

LOUISIANA

Baton Rouge
Crusemann, F(rederick) Ross *advertising agency official*
Finney, Clifton Donald *publishing executive*
Williams-Daly, Angelia Evette *marketing executive, small business owner*

Lafayette
Baudoin, Peter *family business consultant*
Sides, Larry Eugene *advertising executive*

Lake Charles
†Prater, Michael Albert *security executive*
Premeaux, Shane Richard *marketing educator*

Mandeville
Klein, Bernard Joseph *management specialist*

Metairie
Feran, Russell G. *sales executive*
Gereighty, Andrea Saunders *polling company executive, poet*
Goss, Donald Davis *consultant, author, lecturer*
Goyette, Geoffrey Robert *sales executive*
Grimm, John Lloyd *business executive, marketing professional*

New Iberia
Grubbs, Conway E. *marine company executive*

New Orleans
Allerton, William, III *public relations executive*
Bacot, Marie *management consultant, researcher*
Barden, Janice Kindler *personnel company executive*
Bridges, Elizabeth Ann *marketing consultant*
Cook, Victor Joseph, Jr. *marketing educator, consultant*
Creppel, Claire Binet *hotel owner*
Fertel, Ruth U. *restaurant owner*
Johnson, Arnold Ray *public relations executive*
Tahir, Mary Elizabeth *retail marketing and management consultant*
†Williams, Ronald David *telecommunications executive*

Pineville
Cummings, Karen Sue *corrections classification administrator*

Shreveport
Sandifer, Kevin Wayne *archival services executive*
Tullis, John Ledbetter *retired wholesale distributing company executive*
Wright, Marie Beulah Battey *retired advertising executive*

Westwego
Reyes, Shirley Norflin *computer learning center educator*

MAINE

Auburn
†Lord, Michael Clark *executive secretary*

Augusta
Blais, Helen Christine *daycare operator*
Roberts, Donald Albert *advertising, public relations, marketing and media consultant*

Brooklin
Schmidt, Klaus Dieter *management consultant, university administrator, marketing and management educator*

Brunswick
Horton, Michael *public affairs executive, information specialist*

Camden
Lavenson, Susan Barker *hotel corporate executive, consultant*
†Rourke, Bradley Kevin *public affairs executive*

Center Lovell
Adams, Herbert Ryan *management consultant, retired clergyman, actor, director, educator, publishing executive*

Gouldsboro
Eustice, Russell Clifford *consulting company executive, academic director*

Hartland
Larochelle, Richard C. *tanning company executive*

Kennebunk
Peterson, Karen Ida *marketing research company executive*
Schofield, John Emerson *consultant*

Kittery Point
Burgard, Ralph *cultural/education planner*

Lamoine
Becker, Ray Everett *management consultant*

Lewiston
Cutter, David L. *advertising specialty executive*

Portland
Becker, Seymour *hazardous materials and wastes specialist*
Bride, John W(illiam) *communications executive, entrepreneur*
Brown, Andrea Lynn *executive recruiter*
Caswell, Robert Stearns *public relations director*
End, William Thomas *business executive*
Hall, Christopher George Longden *management consultant*
Kendrick, Peter Murray *communications executive, investor*

South Portland
Fetteroll, Eugene Carl, Jr. *human resources professional*

MARYLAND

Aberdeen Proving Ground
Starnes, Edward Clinton *public relations executive*

Annapolis
Carman, Anne *management consultant*
Crosby, Ralph Wolf *communications executive*
Jefferson, Ralph Harvey *international affairs consultant*
Pillsbury, Leland Clark *service executive*

Arnold
Barrett, John Anthony *publishing and printing company financial executive*

Baldwin
Decker, James Ludlow *management consultant*

Baltimore
†Blair, Timothy Daniel *quality assurance specialist*
Edlund, Timothy Wendell *management educator, consultant, researcher*
Eisner, Henry Wolfgang *advertising agency executive*
Fried, Herbert Daniel *advertising executive*
Friedman, Maria Andre *public relations executive*
Hillman, Sandra Schwartz *public relations executive, marketing professional*
Holton, Helen Lara *city official, marketing professional*
Hug, Richard Ernest *environmental company executive*
Kim, Lillian G. Lee *retired administrative assistant*
List, Douglass William *management consultant, investment adviser, civil engineer*
Lowenthal, Henry *retired greeting card company executive*
Orwig, Larry Gordon *human resource professional*
Park, Mary Woodfill *information consultant*
Passano, E. Magruder, Jr. *corporate philanthropist*
Robinson, Brooks Calbert, Jr. *former professional baseball player, TV commentator, business consultant*
Robinson, Florine Samantha *marketing executive*
Roland, Donald Edward *printing company executive*
Rolland, Donald F. *printing company executive*
Rosen, Wendy Workman *marketing professional*
Shaper, Christopher Thorne *sales executive*
Talbot, Donald Roy *consulting services executive*
Yellin, Judith *electrologist*
Zehler, Edward Joseph *occupational safety and health consultant*

Beltsville
Quirk, Frank Joseph *management consulting company executive*
Sickles, Carlton Ralph *employee benefit consultant*

Bethesda
†Angelo, Robert M. *advertising executive*
†Augustine, Hilton H., Jr. *computer company executive*
†Begala, Kathleen *consumer safety organization administrator*
Belak, Michael James *information systems executive*
Brown, Earle Palmer *advertising agency executive*
Carberry, Michael Glen *advertising executive*
Cody, Thomas Gerald *management consultant, writer*
Craig, Douglas Warren *food service industry executive*
Estrin, Melvyn J. *computer products company executive*
†Flaherty, Barbara A. *marketing professional, artist*
Fowler, Emil Eugene *nuclear technology consultant*
†Garrison, Howard H. *public relations executive*
Goldschmidt, Peter Graham *physician executive, business development consultant*
†Howard, Frank Joseph, Jr. *public relations company executive*
Johnson, Eugene Clare *data processing company executive*
Levin, Carl *public and government relations consultant*
McClure, Brooks *management consultant*
Mc Gurn, Barrett *communications executive, writer*
Miller, Judith Wolfe Cohen *consultant*
Moseley, Chris Rosser *marketing executive*
†Sauer, Michael James *business consultant*
†Scanlon, Thomas J. *consulting company executive*
Schmidt, Randall David *information technology and business consultant*
Shellow, Robert *management service company executive, consultant*
Southwick, Paul *retired public relations executive*
Spector, Melbourne Louis *management consultant*
Spivak, Alvin A. *retired public relations executive*

Terragno, Paul James *information industry executive*
Van Dyke, Joseph Gary Owen *computer consulting executive*
Wertheimer, Franc *retired corporate executive*

Bowie
Purcell, Steven Richard *international management consultant, engineer, economist*
Tobin, Charles Fulton, Jr. *information technology executive*

Brooklandville
Miller, Paul George *computer company executive*

Catonsville
Ahalt, Mary Jane *management consultant*

Chestertown
Parke, Jo Anne Mark *marketing executive*
Schreiber, Harry, Jr. *management consultant*

Chevy Chase
Broide, Mace Irwin *public affairs consultant*
Corrigan, Robert Foster *business consultant, retired diplomat*
Michaelis, Michael *management and technical consultant*
†Neiberger, Ami Dawn *public relations executive*
Schlegel, John Frederick *management consultant, speaker, trainer*
Zurkowski, Paul George *information company executive*

Clinton
†Usher, Marcella Denise *management consultant*

Cockeysville
Donaho, John Albert *consultant*
Shepard, George Leo *sales and marketing executive, consultant*

Cockeysville Hunt Valley
Elkin, Lois Shanman *business systems company executive*
Simms, Charles Averill *environmental management company executive*
Somerville, Warren Thomas, II *management consultant*
Whitehurst, William Wilfred, Jr. *management consultant*

College Park
Holder, Sallie Lou *training and meeting management consultant*

Columbia
Letaw, Harry, Jr. *technology corporation executive*
Madison, Anne Conway *public relations and marketing professional*
Vassar, John Dixie, Jr. *environmental, radiological, and information technology consultant*

Davidsonville
Montague, Brian John *consulting company executive*

Easton
Burns, Michael Joseph *operations and sales-marketing executive*

Elkton
Jasinski-Caldwell, Mary L. *company executive*

Ellicott City
Gleaves, Leon Rogers *marketing and sales executive*

Forest Hill
†Ferretti, Kevin Michael *human resource director*
Klein, Michael Jeffrey *consumer products company executive*

Fort George G Meade
Schmitt, Robert Lee *computer scientist*

Frederick
Boyd, Joseph Aubrey *communications company executive*
Docksteader, Karen Kemp *marketing executive*
Schricker, Ethel Killingsworth *retired business management consultant*

Gaithersburg
Carey, John Edward *information services executive*
Ehrlich, Clifford John *hotel executive*
Flickinger, Harry Harner *organization and business executive, management consultant*
Kemmerer, Sharon Jean *computer systems analyst*
†Pine, Martin E. *management consultant, technology consultant*

Germantown
Shaw, Jack Allen *communications company executive*

Glen Arm
Lotz, George Michael *retired computer graphics executive, graphic designer, photographer*

Hyattsville
Rooney, Peggy Ann *executive secretary*

Indian Head
Wamsley, Barbara Simborski *public administration educator*

Kensington
Hum, Vance York *technology consulting executive*

Landover
Fortson-Rivers, Tina E. (Thomasena Elizabeth Fortson-Rivers) *information technology specialist*

Lanham Seabrook
Barnes, Margaret Anderson *business consultant*

Laurel
Brubaker, Lou Ann *advertising executive, consultant*
Fox, Dawne Marie *safety scientist*

Linthicum
Ramachandran, Anand *operations management executive*

Millersville
†Schulmeyer, G(eorge) Gordon *information systems executive, consultant*

Odenton
Mucha, John Frank *information systems professional*

Olney
Brady, Anita Kelley *training and organizational development executive*

Oxon Hill
Dunleavy, Kristie Lyn *direct marketing and advertising executive*

Pasadena
†Dalton, Frances Marlene *business consultant*

Phoenix
Byrd, Harvey Clifford, III *information management company executive*

Potomac
Benton, Kay Myers *sales executive*
Fink, Daniel Julien *management consultant*
Rhode, Alfred Shimon *business consultant, educator*

Reisterstown
Daley, Peter Edmund *business and human resources company executive*

Riverdale
Gonzalez Arias, Victor Hugo *management executive*

Rockville
Bainum, Stewart William, Jr. *health care and lodging company executive*
Boyle, Lisa C. *marketing and communications executive*
Campbell, R. Nelson *financial executive*
Gardner, David John *communications executive, recording engineer*
Haas, Suzanne Newhouse *human resources generalist*
Hanes, Donald Keith *cooperative executive*
Hazard, Robert Culver, Jr. *hotel executive*
Isbister, James David *pharmaceutical business executive*
Leslie, John Walter *development consultant*
Smith, Mark Alan *management consultant*
Ward, Neil Anthony *corporate communications specialist*
Wolf, Marilyn *consumer safety officer*

Salisbury
Kettinger, David John *broadcast executive*
Wanzer, Mary Kathryn *computer company executive, consultant*

Severna Park
Fraser, Robert Carson *business consultant*

Silver Spring
Burke, Gerard Patrick *business executive, lawyer*
†Dollar, Alison Cathleen *business official*
Hersey, David Floyd *information resources management consultant, retired government official*
Hubbell, Katherine Jean *marketing consultant*
Kendrick, James Earl *business consultant*
Kenner, Mary Ellen *marketing and communications executive*
Kolodny, Debra Ruth *labor management consultant*
†Ledsinger, Charles A. *hotel executive*
Lett, Cynthia Ellen Wein *marketing executive*
Perlmutter, Jerome Herbert *communications specialist*
Raphael, Coleman *business consultant*
Zakheim, Barbara Jane *information management, marketing*

Sparks Glencoe
Smith, Rodney Russell *operations executive*

Stevensville
Kepley, Thomas Alvin *management consultant*

Sykesville
Leizear, Charles William *retired information services executive*

Tall Timbers
Jensen, Paul Erik *marketing executive*

Waldorf
Stokely, Mary Curry *marketing specialist*

Warwick
Wilkinson, Janet Worman *advertising/marketing consultant, reading tutor*

West Bethesda
Vogelgesang, Sandra Louise *business executive, writer*

West River
Bower, Catherine Downes *communications and public relations executive*

MASSACHUSETTS

Acton
Webber, Howard Rodney *computer company executive*

Arlington
Nahigian, Alma Louise *technical documentation administrator*

Babson Park
Goldberg, Pamela Winer *business manager*

Bedford
Brawley, Margaret Wacker *communications executive*
Rudzinsky, David Michael *information systems director*

Belmont
Klein, Martin Samuel *management consulting executive*

Beverly
Barger, Richard Wilson *hotel executive*

Bolton
Langenwalter, Gary Allan *manufacturing and management consulting company executive*
Leighton, Charles Milton *specialty consumer products executive*

Boston
Andrews, Kenneth Richmond *business administration educator*
Arnold, John David *management counselor, catalyst*
Ashkin, Ronald Evan *international executive*
Bacon, A(delaide) Smoki *public relations consultant, television host*
Berenson, Paul Stewart *advertising executive*
†Berger, Jerome Morris *communications executive*
Berman, Lisa *advertising executive*
†Bertino, Fred *advertising executive*
†Biro, Kathy *advertising executive*
Bronner, Michael *advertising executive*
Buchin, Stanley Ira *management consultant, educator*
Budd, Eric Merrill *company official, writer, consultant*
†Burnham, David Henderson *management consultant*
Chandler, Harriette Levy *management consultant, educator, legislator*
Clarke, Terence Michael *public relations and advertising executive*
†Cone, Carol Lynn *public relations executive*
Connors, John Michael, Jr. *advertising agency executive*
†Copithorne, David A. *public relations executive*
†Cornwall, Deborah Joyce *consulting firm executive, management consultant*
†Coutermarsh, Eva Marina *personnel executive*
Cutter, Curtis Carly *consulting company executive*
Delaney, Brian *communication executive, educator*
†Domini, Amy Lee *trustee*
†Doorley, Thomas Lawrence, III *management consulting firm executive*
Dowd, Peter Jerome *public relations executive*
Dutile, Robert Arthur *management consultant*
Emerson, Richard B. *marketing company executive*
Eskandarian, Edward *advertising agency executive*
Ferson, Scott Melbourne *public relations executive*
†Finucane, Anne M. *communications and marketing executive*
Flaschen, David Jenkin Steward *marketing executive*
Gould, John Joseph *communications executive*
Hayes, Andrew Wallace, II *consumer products company executive*
†Hoar, Frederick M. *public relations executive*
Hoffman, S. Joseph *advertising agency executive*
Hunter, Durant Adams *executive search company executive*
Hurd, J. Nicholas *executive recruiting consultant, former banker*
Judson, Arnold Sidney *management consultant*
Kelly, Francis J., III *marketing company executive*
Kenny, David *communications company professional*
Kincaid, Steven Randall *marketing professional*
Laspada, Mary Anne *medical assistant*
Lawner, Ron *advertising executive*
Lawson, Thomas Elsworth *advertising agency executive*
Lowe, Alfred Mifflin, III *advertising agency executive, writer*
Luongo, C. Paul *public relations executive*
McArdle, Patricia Anne *security company executive*
McGovern, Patrick J. *communications executive*
Merullo-Boaz, Lisa Helen *marketing and fundraising executive*
Metcalfe, Robert *communications executive*
Nuzzo, Anthony Gerald *banking executive*
O'Block, Robert Paul *management consultant*
†Pantano, Dick *advertising executive*
Peirce, Georgia Wilson *public relations executive*
Rhinesmith, Stephen Headley *global management consultant*
Riccelli, Richard Joseph *advertising agency executive*
†Rosen, Mark *management consultant*
Roston, Arnold *information specialist, educator, advertising executive, artist, editor*
Saunders, Roger Alfred *hotel group executive*
†Schneider, Joan *company executive*
Schrager, Mindy Rae *business professional*
Singer, Thomas Eric *industrial company executive*
Smith, Raoul Normand *computer science educator*
†Sonnabend, Roger Philip *hotel company executive*
†Spaienza, Tony *public relations executive*
Sullivan, John Louis, Jr. *retired search company executive*
Tarantino, Louis Gerald *business consultant, lawyer*
Turillo, Michael Joseph, Jr. *management consultant*
Tyszkowski, Robert *business executive, cell biologist*
Vannasse, Dana Edward *corporation executive*
Verrochi, Paul M. *executive training company executive*
Volk, Kristin *advertising agency executive*
White, Jan Tuttle (Mrs. Benjamin Winthrop White) *information systems executive*
Wilkes, Brent Ames *management consultant*
Wilson, Robert Gould *management consultant*
Zeien, Alfred M. *consumer products company executive*

Bourne
Roper, Burns Worthington *retired opinion research company executive*

Brighton
Mahoney, Kathleen Mary *event planning company executive, consultant*

Brookline
Dubrovsky, Ben *communications executive*

Burlington
Bhathena, Firdaus *software company executive, consultant*
Hampl, Mary Notermann *program manager*
Randall, Patricia Mary *consulting firm executive*
Smith, Derek Armand *consulting company executive*

Cambridge
Altshuler, David T. *software company executive*
Aspinall, Mara Glickman *marketing and general management professional*
Bloom, Kathryn Ruth *public relations executive*
Boghani, Ashok Balvantrai *consulting firm executive*
Brynjolfsson, Erik *management educator, researcher*
Burger, Todd Oliver *management consultant*
Caswell, Rex Ace *sales executive*
†Clark, Maynard Stephen *vegetarian resource center administrator*
†Connaughton, David Michael *management consultant*
Cooper, Mary Campbell *information services executive*
Dennis, Jack Bonnell *computer scientist*
Forrester, Jay Wright *management specialist, educator*
Fox, Gretchen Hovemeyer *staff assistant, freelance editor, genealogical consultant*
Hermes, Frank *marketing executive*
Knickrehm, Glenn Allen *management executive*
†Knox, Wendall J. *management consultant*
LaMantia, Charles Robert *management consulting company executive*
Levy, Stephen Raymond *high technology company executive*
Littlefield, Paul Damon *management consultant*
Marolda, Anthony Joseph *management consulting company executive*
Mueller, Robert Kirk *management consulting company executive*
Paresky, Linda K. *travel company executive*
Schumacher, Bill *information services company executive*
†Shine, Daniel Joseph, Jr. *management consultant*
Turner, Stephen *software executive*
Weber, Larry *public relations executive*

Canton
Ferrera, Arthur Rocco *food distribution company executive*
Pitts, Virginia M. *human resources executive*

Carlisle
†Taylor, Ferris Willard *marketing and planning executive*
Tema-Lyn, Laurie *management consultant*

Centerville
Donaldson, John Cecil, Jr. *consumer products company executive*

Chatham
Escalante, Judson Robert *business consultant*
Tucker, Jo-Von *marketing executive*

Chestnut Hill
Addis, Deborah Jane *management consultant, editor*

Concord
Daltas, Arthur John *management consultant*
Eberle, William Denman *international management consultant*
Keane, Thomas Edward *management consultant*
Rarich, Anne Lippitt *management and organizational development consultant*
Two Feathers, Morwen *event coordinating company executive*

Dedham
Daley, Charles Mike *vehicle recovery company executive*
†Hogan, Frances L. *executive*
Magner, Jerome Allen *entertainment company executive*
Redstone, Sumner Murray *entertainment company executive, lawyer*

Dennis
Weilbacher, William Manning *advertising and marketing consultant*

Dover
Bonis, Laszlo Joseph *business executive, scientist*
Edwards, Carl Normand *lawyer*

Essex
†Lawson, Judith Carroll *corporation executive, administrator*

Fitchburg
Flinkstrom, Henry Allan *sales executive*

Foxboro
Hershman, Judith *advertising executive*

Framingham
Donovan, R. Michael *management consultant*
Hillman, Carol Barbara *communications executive*
Leppo, Tamara Elizabeth Marks *account manager*
Margolis, Bruce Lewis *human resources executive*
Meador, Charles Lawrence *management and systems consultant, educator*
Wulf, Sharon Ann *management consultant*

Gloucester
†Brady, Patrick *advertising executive*
Hausman, William Ray *fund raising and management consultant*
†Mammola, Dominic *advertising executive*

Great Barrington
Porteous, Skipp *private investigator, writer*

Hopkinton
Nickerson, Richard Gorham *research company executive*
†Ruettgers, Michael C. *computer company executive*

Hull
Anderson, Timothy Christopher *consulting company executive*

Lakeville
Colcord, Herbert Nathaniel, III *food company executive*

†Washburn, Stewart Alexander *management consultant*

Lexington
Brick, Donald Bernard *consulting company executive*
Fray, Lionel Louis *management consultant*
Kluczynski, Janet *computer company marketing executive*
Monash, Curt Alfred *software industry executive*
Ross, Douglas Taylor *retired software company executive*
Spero, Rand Kevin *management consultant*
White, Gary Francis *investigation professional*

Longmeadow
Locklin, Wilbert Edwin *management consultant*

Lynnfield
Solomon, Jerry Lawrence *sports marketing executive*

Manchester
Conley, Patrick *clinic administrator*

Marlborough
Carpenter, Elizabeth Jane *communications executive*

Marstons Mills
Martin, Vincent George *management consultant*

Maynard
Gerroir, Richard Ernest *retired computer industry executive*

Medford
Garrett, John R. *communication executive*

Milton
†Gerring, Clifton, III *corporate executive*
Sgarlat, Mary Anne E. A. *marketing, public relations professional*

Nantucket
Mercer, Richard Joseph *retired advertising executive, freelance writer*

Natick
Gregory, Thomas Raymond *management consultant*
Strayton, Robert Gerard *public communications executive*
Wheeler, Mary Harrison (Mardy Wheeler) *human resources development specialist, consultant*

New Bedford
Anderson, James Linwood *pharmaceutical sales official*

Newburyport
Russell, David Francis *management consultant, utilities executive*

Newton
Kosowsky, David I. *retired biotechnical company executive*

North Andover
Briggs, David Melvin *information systems executive*
McCarthy, Albert Henry *executive search consultant*

North Reading
Day, Ronald Elwin *consulting executive*

Norwell
Case, David Knowlton *management consultant*
Sostilio, Robert Francis *office equipment marketing executive*

Norwood
Pytka, Stephen Milton *office equipment executive*
Tritter, Richard Paul *strategic planning consulting executive*

Orleans
Hiscock, Richard Carson *marine safety investigator*

Palmer
Dupuis, Robert Simeon *sales executive*

Peabody
Gordon, Bernard M. *computer company executive*
Torkildsen, Peter G. *consulting company executive*

Pittsfield
Wenner, Gene Charles *arts management executive*

Quincy
Bierman, George William *technical consulting executive, food technologist*
Chung, Cynthia Norton *communications specialist*
Hall, John Raymond, Jr. *fire protection executive*
Levin, Robert Joseph *retail grocery chain store executive*
Young, Richard William *corporate director*

Randolph
Margolin, Milton *sales and marketing professional*

Reading
Donald, John Hepburn, II *quality assurance professional, consultant*
White, Karen Ruth Jones *information systems executive*

Revere
Kirby, Brendan Timothy *security system specialist, entrepreneur*

Rockport
Wiberg, Lars-Erik *occupational compatibility consultant*

Salem
Ettinger, Mort *marketing educator*

Scituate
Lane, Barbara Ann *environmental company official, systems analyst*

Sheffield
Velmans, Loet Abraham *retired public relations executive*

Shrewsbury
†Manzoli, Joseph William, Jr. *computer company executive*

Somerville
McKenzie, Gwendolyn V. *public relations, marketing and business development executive*

Stoughton
Snyder, Mark Irwin *marketing and public relations executive*

Stow
Kulas, Frederick John *computer company executive*

Sudbury
McCree, Paul William, Jr. *systems design and engineering company executive*

Swansea
Holmes, Henry *literary agent, book publicist, writer and editor, advertising and marketing consultant*

Townsend
Smith, Denise Groleau *data processing professional*

Waban
Portuondo, Jose Francisco *management consultant*
Rossolimo, Alexander Nicholas *management consultant, corporate director*

Waltham
Buchholz, William James *communications specialist, educator*
Hancock, William Marvin *computer security and network engineering executive*
Kalba, Kas *international telecommunications consultant*
Kasputys, Joseph Edward *corporate executive, economist*
†Kawasaki, Gregory Yukio *communications consultant*
Mitchell, Donald Wayne *management consultant, investment manager, lawyer*
Poduska, John William, Sr. *computer company executive*
†Schwartz, Steven Mark *marketing executive*
Wilsey, Naomi Yanaga *marketing professional, communications executive*

Watertown
Goldstein, Arthur Louis *liquid purification company executive*

Wayland
Caristo-Verrill, Janet Rose *international management consultant*

Wellesley
†Allen, Michael W *management consultant*
Arnold, Peter Gordon *communications consultant*
Nagler, Leon Gregory *management consultant, business executive*
Numata, Nobuo *software company executive, consultant, engineer*

Wellesley Hills
Coco, Samuel Barbin *venture consultant*
Grimes, Howard Ray *management consultant*

Wenham
Johnson, Alan B. *advertising executive*
Roberts, David E. *marketing professional*

West Barnstable
Field, Richard Albert *sales and marketing professional*

West Newbury
Collins, John Joseph *communications consultant*

Weston
Stambaugh, Armstrong A., Jr. *restaurant and hotel executive*

Westport
Norcross, Alvin Watt *retired personnel administrator, consultant*

Wilbraham
Nakashian, Craig Meran *sales professional*

Williamstown
Driscoll, Genevieve Bosson (Jeanne Bosson Driscoll) *management and organization development consultant*
Sprague, John Louis *management consultant*

Wilmington
D'Alene, Alixandria Frances *human resources professional*

Winchester
Brown, David A.B. *strategy consultant*
Ingari, Frank A. *communications executive*
Taggart, Ganson Powers *management consultant*

Winthrop
Brown, Alan Anthony *marketing executive*

Woburn
Mehra, Raman Kumar *data processing executive, automation and control engineering researcher*
Neville, Elisabeth *quality assurance professional*
Philbrook, Maureen *small business owner*

Worcester
Camougis, George *health, safety and environmental consultant*
Candib, Murray A. *business executive, retail management consultant*
Heman, Robert Jerome, Jr. *printing company executive, association executive*

MICHIGAN

Ada
Brenner, David H. *marketing executive*
DeVos, Douglas Lee *sales company executive*
DeVos, Richard Marvin, Jr. (Dick DeVos) *direct sales company executive, sports team executive*
Van Andel, Jay *direct selling company executive*

Ann Arbor
Agno, John G. *management consultant*
Belcher, Louis David *marketing and operations executive, former mayor*
Foley, Daniel Ronald *business and personnel executive*
†Fornell, Claes *management consultant, marketing educator*
Hartley, Terry L. *management consultant*
Hofmann, Hubert Franz *management consultant*
Martin, Claude Raymond, Jr. *marketing consultant, educator*
Pritts, Bradley Arthur, Jr. *management systems consultant*
Sprandel, Dennis Steuart *management consulting company executive*

Auburn Hills
MacDonald, John *marketing executive*
Wagner, Bruce Stanley *marketing communications executive*

Bloomfield Hills
Abel Horowitz, Michelle Susan *advertising executive*
Adams, Charles Francis *advertising and real estate executive*
Benton, William Pettigrew *advertising agency executive*
Berline, James H. *advertising executive, public relations agency executive*
Bissell, John Howard *marketing executive*
Husband, William Swire *computer industry executive*
Sandy, William Haskell *training and communication systems executive*
Weil, John William *technology management consultant*

Brighton
Bitten, Mary Josephine *quality consultant, municipal official*
Veno, Glen Corey *management consultant*

Cadillac
Krafve, Allen Horton *management consultant*

Charlotte
Young, Everett J. *management consultant, agricultural economist*

Dearborn
Ahmed, Saleem *management consultant*
Friedman, Hal Marc *history educator*
Jelinek, John Joseph *public relations executive*
†Nguyen, Nhon T. *business analyst*

Dearborn Heights
Darin, Frank Victor John *management consultant*
Simpkin, Lawrence James *company executive*

Detroit
Barden, Don H. *communications executive*
Bassett, Tina *communications executive*
Czarnecki, Walter P. *truck rental company executive*
De Haan-Puls, Joyce Elaine *sales account representative*
Demos, Dave *marketing executive*
Go, Robert A. *management consultant*
Henry, William Lockwood *sales and marketing executive*
Phillips, Charles Albert *market analyst, accountant*
Roberts, Seymour M. (Skip Roberts) *advertising agency executive*
Salter, Linda Lee *security officer*
Schweitzer, Peter *advertising agency executive*
†Spearman-Leach, Anthony Maurice Paul *communications executive*
Tallet, Margaret Anne *theatre executive*
Werba, Gabriel *public relations consultant*
Zoubareff, Kathy Olga *administrative assistant*

East Lansing
Hilbert, Virginia Lois *computer consultant and training executive*

Escanaba
Schnesk, Elizabeth Ann *office manager, small business owner*

Evart
Fatum, Russ Allen *human resources professional, educator*

Farmington Hills
Bricker, Gerald Wayne *marketing executive*
Frederick, Raymond Joseph *sales engineering executive*

Ferndale
Gienapp, Helen Fischer *jewelry company owner*

Franklin
Vanderlaan, Richard B. *marketing company executive*

Grand Rapids
Becker, Robert Joseph *database consultant, computer science specialist, database software developer and educator*
Bissell, Mark *consumer products company executive*
†Gordon, Dan *food service executive*
Hahn, H. Michael *advertising executive*
Hakala, Judyth Ann *data processing executive*
Kranz, Kenneth Louis *human resources company executive, entrepreneur*
†Mbah, Chris H.N. *business educator*
Messner, James W. *advertising executive*
Portelli, Vincent George *business consultant and executive*
Sadler, David Gary *management executive*
Schwartz, Garry Albert *advertising executive*
Sebastian, James Rae, Jr. *management consultant*
Smith, Bill *advertising and marketing executive*
Zimmerman, John *public relations executive*

Grosse Ile
Kohn, Julieanne *travel agent*

Grosse Pointe
Blevins, William Edward *management consultant*
Caldwell, John Thomas, Jr. *communications executive*

Grosse Pointe Park
Coe, John William *management consultant*
Wilson, Henry Arthur, Jr. *management consultant*

Hastings
Jones, Kensinger *advertising executive*

Holland
Johnson, Robert Dale *marketing technology administrator*
Mc Gurk, James Henry *consultant company executive*
Spoelhof, John *consumer products company executive*

Interlochen
Stolley, Alexander *advertising executive*

Jackson
Osborn, Janet Lynn *information systems executive*

Kalamazoo
Gilchrist, James A. *communication educator*
Lawrence, William Joseph, Jr. *retired corporate executive*

Lansing
†Trezise, Robert Lewis *economic development administrator*

Lincoln Park
Bredell, Frank Fulston *public relations company executive*

Livonia
†Chowdhury, Subir *business executive, author, researcher*

Manchester
Nikoui, Hossein Reza *quality assurance professional*
Spencer, Mark Edward *management consultant*

Marquette
Earle, Mary Margaret *marketing executive*
†LaJoie, James Alan *public relations professional*
Pesola, William Ernest *restaurant management executive*

Midland
†Doan, Herbert Dow *technical business consultant*
Maneri, Remo R. *management consultant*
Sira, Craig John *data coordinator*
Sosville, Dick *sales and marketing executive*

Mount Clemens
Robinson, Earl, Jr. *marketing and economic research executive, transportation executive, business educator, retired air force officer*

Northport
Munro, Roderick Anthony *quality assurance professional, human performance technologist*

Novi
O'Mara, Marilyn Mae *communications executive*

Orchard Lake
Casey, John Patrick (Jack Casey) *public relations executive, political analyst*

Oxford
Hubbard, John Morris *golf course executive*

Plymouth
Moore, Joan Elizabeth *human resources executive, lawyer*

Pontiac
†Auch, Fred H., Jr. *company executive*
Popadak, Geraldine L. *organizational development consultant, educator*

Portage
Seely, Robert Eugene *management consultant*

Portland
Anesi, Michael Richard *restaurant executive*

Rapid City
Coulson, John Selden *retired marketing executive*

Redford
Flint, H. Howard, II *printing company executive*

Reed City
Devendorf, Louise Marie *promoter, writer*

Rochester Hills
Pfister, Karl Anton *industrial company executive*

Royal Oak
Stanalajczo, Greg Charles *computer and technology company executive*

Saginaw
Scharffe, William Granville *academic administrator, educator*

Saint Ignace
Dodson, Bruce J. *funeral director*

Saline
Low, Louise Anderson *consulting company executive*

Saranac
LaVean, Michael Gilbert *advertising agency executive, political consultant*

Southfield
Barnett, Marilyn advertising agency executive
Decerchio, John advertising company executive
Howard, Michael Joseph communications executive, real estate developer
Jackson, William Gene computer company executive
Kalter, Alan advertising agency executive
Maibach, Ben C., Jr. service executive
†Serra, Barbara Josephine community relations administrator
Smith, Nancy Hohendorf sales and marketing executive

Stockbridge
†Macdonald, Guy Allen telecommunications company executive

Troy
Adderley, Terence E. corporate executive
Baker, Ernest Waldo, Jr. advertising executive
Baker, Michael Howard sales executive
Harrison, Christine Delane company executive
Hill, Richard A. advertising executive
†Horton, Gary J. advertising executive
McLaren, Karen Lynn advertising executive
Meyers, Christine Laine marketing and media executive, consultant
Ranney, Richard William electronic data systems company official
Wilson, Duane Isaac executive search consultant

Walled Lake
Gillespie, J. Martin sales and distribution company executive

Warren
Belles, Christine Fugiel office administration educator
Gervason, Robert J advertising executive
Gilbert, Suzanne Harris advertising executive
Hopp, Anthony James advertising agency executive
Ludwig, William John advertising executive
Schultz, Louis Michael advertising agency executive
Wisz, Joseph A., Jr. management consultant

Waterford
Land, Robert Donald business consultant

West Bloomfield
Beck, Jerry Gunther development company executive, consultant
Considine, John Joseph advertising executive
Rosenfeld, Martin Jerome executive recruiter, educator

Whitmore Lake
Stanny, Gary infosystems specialist, rocket scientist

MINNESOTA

Apple Valley
Kettle, Sally Anne consulting company executive, educator

Austin
Budd, Jim communications manager

Babbitt
†Marks, Dawn Marie excavating contractor

Bloomington
Thickins, Graeme Richard marketing consultant

Burnsville
Ringquist, Lynn Anne micrographics company executive

Chaska
Knapp, Peggy Durda international company administrator

Cottage Grove
Briggs, Robert Henry infosystems specialist

Duluth
Bailey, Charles William management consultant, researcher
Smith, Robert Francis synthesist
†Stender, Bruce William business executive

Eden Prairie
Carlson, Kenneth George data processing executive
†Erickson, Kim consumer products company executive
Johnson, Howard Arthur, Jr. corporate executive, operations analyst, financial officer
McClure, Alvin Bruce information systems manager
Platt, Ann animal care company executive
Roth, Thomas marketing executive
Schulze, Richard M. consumer products executive
Thompsen, Joyce Ann organizational consultant
Verdoorn, Sid food service executive

Edina
Burdick, Lou Brum public relations executive
Hunt, David Claude sales and marketing executive
Polsfuss, Craig Lyle leadership specialist, psychologist, social worker
Slocum, Rosemarie physician management search consultant
Wurdeman, Lew Edward data processing corporation consultant

Hastings
†Avent, Sharon H. consumer products company executive

Lake Crystal
Pawlitschek, Donald Paul business consultant

Lakeville
Krueger, Richard Arnold technology executive

Le Roy
Erickson, Larry Alvin electronics sales and marketing executive

Mahtomedi
Brainerd, Richard Charles human resources executive, consultant, educator

Mendota Heights
Newman, Donald John marketing executive

Minneapolis
Anderson, Ron advertising executive
Beardsley, John Ray public relations firm executive
Bergeson, James advertising executive
Bileydi, Sumer advertising agency executive
Bird, Dick sign painter
Brooks, Gladys Sinclair public affairs consultant
Bush, David H. management consultant
Cardozo, Richard Nunez marketing, entrepreneurship and business educator
†Carlson, Marilyn C. travel service company executive
†Carlson-Nelson, Marilyn advertising executive
Chakravarthy, Balaji Srinivasan strategic management educator, consultant
Cowles, John, III management consultant, investor
Diemand, Kim Eugene human resources executive
Dunlap, William DeWayne, Jr. advertising agency executive
Eich, Susan public relations executive
Eisenberg, Jay Lynn marketing professional
Fallon, Patrick R. advertising executive
Ferner, David Charles non-profit management and development consultant
Fiedler, Robert Max management consultant
Floren, David D. advertising executive
Gage, Edwin C., III (Skip Gage) travel and marketing services executive
Gavin, Sara public relations executive
Healton, Bruce Carney data processing executive
Hesslund, Bradley Harry product manager
Johnson, Lola Norine advertising and public relations executive, educator
Koutsky, Dean Roger advertising executive
Kruegel, Patrick Ferdinand purchasing agent
Liszt, Howard Paul advertising executive
Moore, Tanna Lynn business development executive
Mouser, Les broadcasting executive
Mulligan, Michael L. sales and marketing executive
Nee, Kay Bonner advertising executive
Olson, Clifford Larry management consultant, entrepreneur
Owens, Scott Andrew sales executive
Perlman, Lawrence business executive
Petersen, Maureen Jeanette Miller management information consultant, former nurse
†Peterson, Michael business executive
Read, John Conyers industrial management
Retzler, Kurt Egon diversified management company merger and acquisition and financial executive, retired hospitality, travel and marketing company executive
Sanger, Stephen W. consumer products company executive
Schultz, Louis Edwin management consultant
Simmer, Rita public relations executive
†Stage, Brian hotel facility executive
Stricklin, James Thomas, II sales executive
Sullivan, Michael Patrick food service executive
Tandon, Rajiv training company executive
Toren, Brian Keith futures multimedia, management consultant
Tree, David L. advertising agency executive
†Tunheim, Kathryn H. public relations executive
Valder, Zachary Evans communications project administrator
Walton, Gloria Jean secretary
Westbrook, Bill advertising executive
Weyl, Tom F. advertising executive
Wickesberg, Albert Klumb retired management educator
Yourzak, Robert Joseph management consultant, engineer, educator
Zimmermann, Robert Laurence marketing professional
Zoberi, Nadim Bin-Asad management consultant

Minnetonka
Boubelik, Henry Fredrick, Jr. travel company executive
Gillies, Donald Richard advertising agency and marketing consultant
Gottier, Richard Chalmers retired computer company executive
Kostka, Ronald Wayne marketing consultant
Schmidt, Russel Alan, II sales executive
Schuett, Carol Ann travel industry business analyst
Veblen, Thomas Clayton management consultant

New Brighton
Grieman, John Joseph communications executive

Plymouth
†Selbo, Ray Gordon public speaker

Prior Lake
Hatcher, Thomas Fountain management consultant, publisher

Rochester
Belau, Jane Carol Gullickson marketing, government affairs and public relations company executive

Saint Cloud
†Gangopadhyay, Partha management educator
McIntyre, Vicky Joyce business owner

Saint Louis Park
Kuregel, Patrick Ferdinand buyer

Saint Paul
Bell-Brown, Brenda Yvette arts administrator
Clawson, John Thomas government relations professional
Esposito, Bonnie Lou marketing professional
Feinberg, David Erwin publishing company executive
Forshay, Steven R. marketing professional, consultant
Hill, James Stanley computer consulting company executive
Killorin Caswell, Mary Katherine management consultant
Lendt, Harold Hanford manufacturing representative
Zimmerman, Susan G. sales executive

Saint Peter
Taylor, Scott Maxfield sales and marketing executive

Savage
Luth, James Curtis systems consultant

Scandia
Speer, David James retired public relations executive

Victoria
Courtney, Eugene Whitmal computer company executive

Wayzata
Andrews, Dennis customer service professional
Waldera, Wayne Eugene crisis management specialist

Willmar
Norling, Rayburn food service executive

MISSISSIPPI

Bay Saint Louis
Torguson, Marlin F. entertainment company executive

Biloxi
Love, James Sanford, III communications executive

Brandon
McCreery, James Allan retired business services company executive

Carriere
Woodmansee, Glenn Edward employee relations executive

Columbus
Holt, Robert Ezel data processing executive
Hudnall, Jarrett, Jr. management and marketing educator
†Labensky, Sarah Ross culinary educator

Greenwood
Jones, Carolyn Ellis publisher, retired employment agency and business service company executive

Gulfport
Slade, Jeannye Zo public relations executive

Hattiesburg
Martin, Matthew E. advertising and marketing executive
Watkins, Cathy Collins corporate purchasing agent

Jackson
Ebbers, Bernard J. communications executive
Lewis, Larry Lisle human resources specialist company executive
Palmer, John N. communications executive
Sullivan, Scott D. communications executive

Moss Point
Reynolds, Margaret Jensen quality assurance professional

Olive Branch
Frischenmeyer, Michael Leo sales executive

Philadelphia
Molpus, Dick H. resource management company executive

Starkville
Wakeman, Olivia Van Horn marketing professional

Stennis Space Center
Sprouse, Susan Rae Moore human resources specialist

Tishomingo
Poole, Wanda Sue quality control inspector

Vicksburg
Bagby, Rose Mary pollution control administrator, chemist

MISSOURI

Bolivar
†Coen, Cheryl Lynn secretary

Bridgeton
Campbell, Anita Joyce computer company executive
†Piacentino, Marcia advertising executive

Burlington Junction
McLaughlin, Lana Gale business educator, office manager

Cape Girardeau
Bir, Michelle Marie sales executive
Smallwood, Glenn Walter, Jr. utility marketing management executive

Chesterfield
Handelman, Alice Samuels public relations professional, writer, former social worker
Kelly, James Joseph printing company executive

Clayton
Malnassy, Louis Sturges public relations counselor
Preuss, James Eugene human resources professional
Vecchiotti, Robert Anthony management and organizational consultant

Excelsior Springs
Loomis, Robert Arthur retired sales executive

Fenton
Maritz, William E. communications company executive
Mix, GeGe Simmonds marketing professional

Fulton
Archuleta, Laura Lynn marketing executive

Independence
Booz, Gretchen Arlene marketing executive
Evans, Margaret Ann human resources administrator, business owner
Grover, Robert LaVern retired auto worker

Kansas City
Adams, Beverly Josephine data processing specialist
Baker, Ronald Phillip service company executive
Belzer, Ellen J. negotiations and communications consultant
Benner, Richard Edward, Jr. management and marketing consultant, investor
Bernstein, Robert advertising executive
Courson, Marna B.P. public relations executive
Dillingham, John Allen marketing professional
Gilbert, John Robert advertising and public relations agency executive
Grossman, Jerome Barnett retired service firm executive
Hall, Donald Joyce greeting card company executive
Hockaday, Irvine O., Jr. greeting card company executive
Hoffman, Gloria Levy communications executive
Howlett, Stephanie Ann home care equipment sales representative, nurse
Krause, Heather Dawn data processing executive
Lynch, Bob David retired business agent
Neely, Susanne J. marketing professional, director
Robertson, Leon H. management consultant, educator
Schwab, Mark marketing executive
Smiley, David Bruce administrative director
Solberg, Elizabeth Transou public relations executive
Stevens, Jane advertising executive
Stowers, James, III data processing company executive
VanAuken, Alan Bradley management consultant
Venable, William Ralph, III marketing executive, banking executive
Woodson, Stephen William collection agency executive

Lake Saint Louis
Dommermuth, William Peter marketing consultant, educator

Lees Summit
Letterman, Ernest Eugene manufacturers representative company executive
Williams, Kenneth Eugene advertising, marketing and sales professional

Liberty
McCaslin, WC products and packaging executive

Nixa
Aduddle, Larry Steven marketing and sales executive, consultant

Park Hills
Sebastian, Phylis Sue real estate broker

Parkville
Jacobs, Carl Eugene printing company official

Perryville
Johnson, Charles Joseph telecommunications executive, computer engineer

Rolla
Datz, Israel Mortimer information systems specialist

Saint Ann
Drury, Charles Louis, Jr. hotel executive

Saint Charles
Gross, Charles Robert personnel executive, legislator, appraiser
Nickisch, Willard Wayne funeral director

Saint Joseph
Huff, David Richard funeral home executive

Saint Louis
Barney, Steven Matthew human resources executive
Brown, Stella Chaney advertising agency executive
Cooper, Robert James purchasing consultant
Davis, Irvin advertising, public relations, broadcast executive
Devantier, Paul W. communications executive, broadcaster
Epner, Steven Arthur computer consultant
Evans, Pamela R. marketing executive
Finnie, William C. consulting company executive, educator
Finnigan, Joseph Townsend public relations executive
Foster, Scarlett Lee public relations executive
Gers, Harvey marketing professional
Graham, John Dalby public relations executive
Heck, Debra Upchurch information technology, procurement professional
Hilgert, Raymond Lewis management and industrial relations educator, consultant, arbitrator
Hillard, Robert Ellsworth public relations consultant
Hollingsworth, Gary Mayes Internet access provider company
Jamison, Frederick William data processing executive
Khoury, George Gilbert printing company executive, baseball association executive
Lents, Peggy Iglauer marketing executive
Loynd, Richard Birkett consumer products company executive
Lyons, Gordon marketing executive
Macauley, Edward C. company executive
Moseley, Marc Robards sales executive
Musial, Stan(ley) (Frank Musial) hotel and restaurant executive, former baseball team executive, former baseball player
Nadeau, John marketing and corporate communications consultant
†Nelson, Barbara Jeanne sales executive
Provost, Cheryl Louise Winters account executive
Saligman, Harvey consumer products and services company executive
Schnuck, Scott C. grocery store executive
Seemann, Rosalie Mary international business and foreign policy association executive
Sibbald, John Ristow management consultant

Siemer, Paul Jennings *public relations executive*
Stork, Donald Arthur *advertising executive*
Taylor, Andrew C. *rental leasing company executive*
Taylor, Jack C. *rental and leasing company executive*
Tyler, William Howard, Jr. *advertising executive, educator*
Van Luven, William Robert *management consultant*
Ward, Richard Compton *management consultant*
Wassell, Loren W. *public affairs administrator, writer*
Weaver, Charles Lyndell, Jr. *institutional and manufacturing facilities administrator, management and marketing systems consultant*
Weaver, William Clair, Jr. *(Mike Weaver) human resources development executive*
†Weppelman, Roger Michael *regulatory compliance officer*

Saint Peters
Meier, Donald James *marketing executive*

Salisbury
†Head, Shane Everett *animal nutrition company executive, consultant*

Springfield
Cooper, J. Michael *advertising executive*
Denton, D. Keith *management educator*
†Hammons, John Q. *hotel executive*
Hignite, Michael Anthony *computer information systems educator, researcher, writer, consultant*
Jones, Sheryl Leanne *retail sales executive*
Kincaid, Paul Kent *public relations professional*

Town And Country
Lachenicht-Berkeley, Angela Marie *marketing professional*

Washington
†Bauer, Carl Jonathan *public relations executive*

Waynesville
†Taylor, Lee Edward *quality control engineer*

MONTANA

Butte
Ouellette, Debra Lee *association administrator, consultant*

Helena
Hays, Rick F. *public policy executive*
Manuel, Vivian *public relations company executive*

Missoula
Egley, Thomas Arthur *computer services executive, accountant*

NEBRASKA

Bellevue
Moore, Alan Frank *management consultant*
Nicholsen, James Therman *computer company executive*

Fort Calhoun
†Herman, Theresa Joan (Terri) *quality assurance professional*

Lincoln
†Brownson, E. Ramona Lidstone Brady *secretary*
Clifton, James K. *market research company executive*
†Donovan, Gregory Stearn *human services administrator*
Fleharty, Mary Sue *secretary*

Omaha
Brailey, Susan Louise *quality analyst, educator*
Eggers, James Wesley *executive search consultant*
Frazier, Chet June *advertising agency executive*
Lietzen, John Hervy *human resources executive, health agency volunteer*
Phares, Lynn Levisay *public relations communications executive*
Roskens, Ronald William *international business consultant*

Papillion
Scott, Raymond Gerald *management executive*

NEVADA

Boulder City
Ferraro, Robert *customer service executive*

Carson City
†Rhodes, Karren *public information officer*

Henderson
Cohan, George Sheldon *advertising and public relations executive*
Grembowski, Eugene *retired leasing company executive*
Henry, Philip Lawrence *marketing professional*

Incline Village
Mitton, Michael Anthony *environmental technology company executive*
Moore, Patricia Ann *medical technology investor, consultant*

Las Vegas
Arce, Phillip William *hotel and casino executive*
Basile, Richard Emanuel *retired management consultant, educator*
Beagles, Dorothy Boetticher *office administrator, homeopathic consultant*
Boyle, Carolyn Moore *public relations executive, marketing communications manager*
†Boynton, Peter G. *hotel executive*
Collis, Kay Lynn *professional beauty consultant*
Goldstein, Morris *entertainment company executive*
Goodwin, Nancy Lee *corporate executive*
Koon, Ray Harold *management and security consultant*

Landau, Ellis *gaming company executive*
Marcella, Joseph *information system administrator*
Mataseje, Veronica Julia *sales executive*
Pringle, Thomas Hivick *sales executive*
Rossin, Herbert Yale *business executive*
Rowe, Carl Osborn *business consultant*
Schaeffer, Glenn William *casino corporate financial executive*
†Schwartz, Robert John *landscape contractor, landscape designer*
Shipper, Todd Jeffrey *communications executive*
Shively, Judith Carolyn (Judy Shively) *contract administrator*
Thill, John Val *communications professional, writer, consultant*
Welter, William Michael *marketing and advertising executive*

North Las Vegas
Folden, Norman C. (Skip Folden) *information systems executive, consultant*

Pahrump
Marsh, Mary Elizabeth Taylor *recreation administrator, dietician, nutritionist*

Park City
Milner, Harold William *hotel executive*

Reno
Adams, Kenneth Robert *gaming analyst, writer, consultant, historian*
Johnson, Richard Karl *hospitality company executive*
Perry, Anthony Frank *entertainment company executive, printing company executive, graphic designer*
Strauss, Judy *marketing educator, consultant, writer*

NEW HAMPSHIRE

Atkinson
Trotter, William John *sales professional*

Bedford
Alderman, Walter Arthur, Jr. *computer company and corporate rescue executive*
Cronin, Timothy Cornelius, III *computer manufacturing executive*
Hall, Pamela S. *environmental consulting firm executive*
Manocchi, James Charles *marketing professional*

Center Harbor
Shaw, Robert William, Jr. *management consultant, venture capitalist*

Claremont
Middleton, John Albert *retired communications executive*

Concord
Mahon, Thomas James *management consultant*
Roberts, George Bernard, Jr. *business and government affairs consultant, former state legislator*
White, Jeffrey George *healthcare consultant, educator*

Cornish Flat
Lawton, Jacqueline Agnes *retired communications company executive, management consultant*

Derry
Lazinsky, Jo Anne Marie *advertising executive*

Dublin
Biklen, Paul *retired advertising executive*

Enfield
Gamache, Richard Donald *retired business development executive*

Exeter
Gray, Christopher Donald *software researcher, author, consultant*
Harmon, Richard Wingate *management consultant*
Jackson, Patrick John *public relations counsel, editor, author, public speaker*

Fitzwilliam
Cooper, Marshall *information company executive*

Franconia
Schaffer, David Edwin *retired management systems executive*

Freedom
Stolz, Alan Jay *youth camp executive*

Hillsboro
Marsh, Richard J. *strategic management consultant*

Jackson
Synnott, William Raymond *retired management consultant*

Jaffrey
Schott, John (Robert) *international consultant, educator*

Lebanon
Sadler, Barbara Ann *quality assurance professional*

Litchfield
Darlington, David William *management consultant*

Manchester
†Morse, Joshua Lin *advertising and communication executive*
Prew, Diane Schmidt *information systems executive*

Merrimack
†Gallup, Patricia *computer company executive*

Milton Mills
Kramer, Sherri Marcelle *business and community development consultant*

Nashua
Garbacz, Gerald George *information services company executive*
Hargreaves, David William *communications company executive*
Piper, Linda Ammann *personnel consulting firm executive*
Weinstein, Jeffrey Allen *consumer products company executive, lawyer*

New Castle
Brink, Marion Alice *employee assistance professional*

New London
Gepfert, Alan Harry *management consultant, business educator, author*
Wheaton, Perry Lee *management consultant*
Zuehlke, Richard William *technical communications consultant, writer*

Portsmouth
Akridge, William David *hotel management company executive*
Greene, Douglas Edward *hotel executive*
Pearson, Timothy Alfred *sales executive, marketing professional*

Rochester
Scott, Elaine Theresa *business development administrator*
Waterhouse, Trenton Dean *marketing director*

Rye
MacRury, King *management counselor*
Sullivan, James Ash *visitor information service executive*

Salem
Snierson, Lynne Wendy *communications executive*

Somersworth
Gow, Linda Yvonne Cherwin *travel executive*

Windham
Arvai, Ernest Stephen *consulting executive*

NEW JERSEY

Aberdeen
Stillwagon, Wesley William *corporate professional*

Absecon
Steinruck, Charles Francis, Jr. *management consultant, lawyer*

Allendale
Bisanzo, Mark Thomas *sales executive*
Petersen, Martin Ross *public affairs executive*

Allenhurst
Hinson, Robert William *advertising executive, consultant*

Asbury Park
Rosenthal, Robert Irwin *consultant*

Atlantic Highlands
Dellosso, Roy J. *sales executive*

Avalon
Johnson, Adele Cunningham *marina executive*
Yochum, Philip Theodore *retired motel and cafeteria chain executive*

Barnegat
Lowe, Angela Maria *business owner*

Basking Ridge
Armstrong, C. Michael *communications company executive*
Atkyns, Robert Lee *communications research professional*
Grimes-Frederick, Dorothea D. *communications executive*
Medley, Marc Allen *marketing executive*
Schmidt, William Max *management consultant, business executive*
†Zeglis, John D. *communications company executive, lawyer*

Bayonne
Obernauer, Marne *corporate executive*

Bedminster
Albert, Jack *communications company executive*
Hart, Terry Jonathan *communications executive*

Bellmawr
Sibley, Robert Whitman *printing company executive*

Bergenfield
Janow, Lydia Frances *meeting planner*
Phelan, Thomas Anthony *private investigator*

Bernardsville
Dixon, Richard Wayne *retired communications company executive*

Bloomfield
Peizer, Maurice Samuel *retired medical advertising consultant*

Boonton
Bona, Frederick Emil *public relations executive*

Bound Brook
Aloisi, Carol Ann *marketing executive*

Brick
Alpiar, Hal *management and marketing consultant, author*
Pistolakis, Nicholas Stelios *advertising executive*

Roache, Patrick Michael, Jr. *management consultant*
Shortess, Edwin Steevin *marketing consultant*

Bridgewater
†Chamorro, Juan Pablo *financial analyst, marketing professional*
Hulse, Robert Douglas *high technology executive*
Mencher, Stuart Alan *sales and marketing executive*
Pedone, Joseph Lawrence *advertising executive*
Pickett, Doyle Clay *employment and training counselor, consultant*
Skidmore, James Albert, Jr. *management, computer technology and engineering services company executive*
Wieschenberg, Klaus *management consultant*

Caldwell
Chatlos, William Edward *management consultant*

Camden
Gans, Samuel Myer *temporary employment service executive*
Meyers, Gilliard E. *sales executive*

Cedar Grove
Carlozzi, Catherine L. *corporate communications consultant, writer*

Cedar Knolls
Stewart, Terry Gifford *computer company executive*

Chatham
Lenz, Henry Paul *management consultant*

Cherry Hill
Bashkin, Lloyd Scott *marketing and management consultant*
Doherty, Evelyn Marie *data processing consultant*
Sax, Robert Edward *food service equipment company executive*
Schelm, Roger Leonard *information systems specialist*

Clifton
Bronkesh, Annette Cylia *public relations executive*
Burke, Bruce Lowell *consumer products company executive*

Convent Station
Tintle, Carmel Joseph *public relations executive*

Denville
Dudrow, Peter Warren *human resources executive, consultant*
Pan, Maria Weiyei *company executive*
Trukenbrod, Sharon Lightbody *day care provider*

East Brunswick
Meshowski, Frank Robert *business consultant*

East Hanover
Elam, Karen Morgan *food company executive, consultant*
Knight, Frank James *pharmaceutical marketing professional*

East Rutherford
Kluge, John Werner *broadcasting and advertising executive*

Eatontown
DeMarinis, Bernard Daniel *engineering management consultant*

Edison
D'Agostino, Matthew Paul *bakery executive*
Haberman, Louise Shelly *consulting company executive*
Kumar, Krishan *management consultant company executive*
Marash, Stanley Albert *consulting company executive*

Emerson
Cheslik, Francis Edward *management consultant*

Englewood
Kreston, Martin Howard *advertising, marketing, public relations, and publishing executive*
Miles, Virginia (Mrs. Fred C. Miles) *marketing consultant*

Fair Lawn
Hayden, Neil Steven *communications company executive*

Fairfield
Guida, Pat *information broker, literature chemist*
Hower, Paul H. *hotel executive*
Kull, Bryan Paul *business information/technology executive, real estate investor*
Mills, Gloria Adams *energy service company executive*
†Petrocelli, A. F. *hotel executive*

Far Hills
Alexandre, Kristin Kuhns *public relations executive, writer*
Bruett, Karen Diesl *sales and fundraising consultant*

Farmingdale
†Edwards, Ann Concetta *human resources manager, writer*

Flemington
†Thomas, Anne Moreau *newspaper owner*

Florham Park
Kovach, Andrew Louis *administrative executive*
Naimark, George Modell *marketing and management consultant*
Russell, Jesse E. *communications executive*

Fort Lee
Seitel, Fraser Paul *public relations executive*

Franklin Lakes
†Marcelina, Louis Alan *company executive*

PROFESSIONAL INDEX 6095 INDUSTRY: SERVICE

Freehold
Schockaert, Barbara Ann *operations executive*

Gladstone
Close, Donald Pembroke *management consultant*
Holt, Jonathan Turner *public relations executive*

Glassboro
†Lewis, Phillip Allen *business administration educator*

Glen Ridge
Agnew, Peter Tomlin *employee benefit consultant*

Green Brook
Bohanan, David John *management consultant*

Hackensack
Borg, Malcolm Austin *communications company executive*
Carra, Andrew Joseph *advertising executive*
Timmins, Michael Joseph *communications services company executive*

Hackettstown
Fremon, Richard C. *retired infosystems specialist*
Passantino, Benjamin Arthur *marketing executive*

Haddonfield
Bauer, Raymond Gale *sales professional*

Hamburg
Buist, Richardson *corporate executive, retired banker*

Hamilton
Holmes, Bradley Paul *information technology management consultant*

Hampton
Yates, Michael Francis *management consultant*

Hasbrouck Heights
Kloepper, David Alan *management consultant*

Holmdel
Hudson, Wendy Joy *software manager*
Vitullo, Anthony Joseph *communications industry executive*

Iselin
Whelpley, William Albert *management consultant, educator*

Jackson
†LaBollita, Sharon Ann *retired executive secretary*

Jersey City
Christensen, Walter Frederick, Jr. *information, telecommunications and financial systems specialist*
Dupey, Michele Mary *communications specialist*
Frank, William Fielding *computer systems design executive, consultant*
Maguire-Krupp, Marjorie Anne *corporate executive*

Kearny
†Antunes, Daniel L. *sales consultant, camera operator*

Kendall Park
Cua, Florence *consultant*

Kenilworth
Johnson Velazco, Nancy Ruth *marketing professional*

Kingston
Gross, Steven *medical marketing communications and device company executive*

Kinnelon
†D'Arcy, Michael Patrick *public relations professional*

Lakewood
Nasr, Salah *sales executive*
Woodman, G. Roger *management consultant*

Lavallette
Tesoriero, Philip James *human resource consultant*

Lawrenceville
Adams, Christine Hanson *advertising executive*
Coleman, Wade Hampton, III *management consultant, mechanical engineer, former banker*
Cox, Teri P. *public relations executive*
Williams, Brown F *television media services company executive*

Little Silver
Finch, Rogers Burton *association management consultant*
Morrison, James Frederick *management consultant*

Livingston
Burns, Edward Charles *infosystems specialist*
Grant, Daniel Gordon *information services company executive*
Greenberg, Aaron Rosmarin *public relations executive*
Mandelbaum, Howard Arnold *marketing and management consultant*
Sethi, Deepak *leadership development/marketing executive*

Long Valley
Cross, Thomas Gary *executive search consultant*
Ward, David F. *business executive*

Lyndhurst
Herndon, John Laird *consulting firm executive*

Madison
Byrd, Stephen Fred *human resource consultant*
Goodman, Michael B(arry) *communications educator*
Markowski, John Joseph *human resources executive*
O'Brien, Mary Devon *communications executive, consultant*
Shelby, Bryan Rohrer *information systems consultant*
Siegel, George Henry *international business development consultant*
†Van Story, Joseph Cleveland *facilities consultant, management consultant*
Weiner, Lowell B. *corporate communications executive*

Mahwah
Wagner, Susan Jane *sales and marketing consulting company executive*

Mantoloking
Mehta, Narinder Kumar *marketing executive*

Maplewood
Hamburger, Mary Ann *medical management consultant*
Safian, Gail Robyn *public relations executive*

Margate City
Stoolman, Herbert Leonard *public relations executive*

Marlton
Farwell, Nancy Larraine *public relations executive*
Klein, Gerhart Leopold *public relations executive*
McCullen, Michael John *advertising executive*

Matawan
Katz, Irwin *marketing executive*

Mercerville
Migliaccio, Patrick Frank *salesman*

Metuchen
Rakov, Barbara Streem *marketing executive*

Middletown
Heng, Siang Gek *communications executive*
Jaros, Robert James *data processing executive*

Millburn
Erenburg, Steven Alan *retired communications executive*

Mine Hill
Nadeau, Michael Joseph *college service assistant*

Monmouth Junction
Lancaster, Barbara Mae *management consulting company executive*

Montclair
Barnard, Kurt *retail trend/consumer spending forecaster, publisher*
†Gaines Nelson, Tami Camari *management consultant*

Montvale
Giambalvo, Vincent *training and career development executive*
Mackerodt, Fred *public relations specialist*

Moorestown
Carson, William Charles *sales and marketing executive*
Condax, Kate Delano (Kate Delano Condax Decker) *marketing and public relations executive*
Schwerin, Horace S. *marketing research executive*

Morganville
Marder, Carol *advertising specialist and premium firm executive*

Morristown
Bockian, James Bernard *computer systems executive*
Cucco, Judith Elene *international marketing professional*
Haselmann, John Philip *marketing executive*
Levy, Joel Howard *marketing research executive*
Mammola, George Charles *air pollution control executive*
McClung, Kenneth Austin, Jr. *training executive, performance consultant*
McConnell, John Howard *personnel management consultant, writer*
Musa, John Davis *computer and infosystems executive, software reliability engineering researcher and expert, independent consultant*
Nalewako, Mary Anne *corporate secretary*
Smith, Richard C. Jr. *public relations executive, quality assurance professional*
Weber, Joseph H. *communications company executive*

Mount Laurel
Hart, Larry Edward *communications company executive*
Li, Pearl Nei-Chien Chu *information specialist, executive*
Turner, John Carl *internet development company executive*

Mountainside
DiPietro, Ralph Anthony *marketing and management consultant, educator*
Lingle, Kathleen McCall *consultant, marketing executive, entrepreneur*

Murray Hill
DiFrancesco, Jeffrey James *telecommunication and media executive*
Doescher, William Frederick *communications executive*
Taylor, Volney *information company executive*

Neshanic Station
Castellon, Christine New *information systems specialist, real estate agent*

New Brunswick
Burke, James Edward *consumer products company executive*
†Edson, Paul Lynwood *quality assurance professional*
Ruben, Brent David *communication educator, university administrator*
Wilson, Robert Nathan *health care company executive*

New Providence
Netravali, Arun N. *communications executive*
Reynolds, Robert Webster *public relations executive*
†Russo, Patricia F. *communications executive*
Sundberg, Carl-Erik Wilhelm *telecommunications executive, researcher*

Newark
Baldassarro, Anthony *human resources professional*
Bohannon, Jean Andrea *research company executive*
Fox, Sandra Gail *insurance marketing executive*
Kaltenbacher, Philip D(avid) *industrialist, former public official*
Reddy, Gerard Anthony *corporate training executive*

North Arlington
Borowski, Jennifer Lucile *corporate administrator*

North Brunswick
Livingston, Lee Franklin *recreation industry executive, real estate and finance consultant*
Sims, Gregory Michael *purchasing agent*

North Haledon
Anstatt, Peter Jan *marketing services executive*

Northvale
Goodman, Stanley Leonard *advertising executive*

Nyack
Flood, Diane Lucy *marketing communications specialist*

Oak Ridge
Sacerdote, Craig R. *management consultant, engineering consultant*

Old Bridge
Engel, John Jacob *communications executive*

Oldwick
Griggs, Stephen Layng *management consultant*

Paramus
Fader, Seymour Jeremiah *management and engineering consulting company executive*

Park Ridge
Kennedy, Brian James *marketing executive*
Olson, Frank Albert *car rental company executive*

Parsippany
Azzarone, Carol Ann *marketing executive*
Belmonte, Steven Joseph *hotel chain executive*
Brady, Philip T. *marketing professional*
Chinitz, Jody Anne Kolb *data processing manager*
Derr, Debra Hulse *advertising executive, publisher, editor*
Ferguson, Thomas George *retired healthcare advertising agency executive*
Lezny, Christopher Adalbert *computer systems specialist*
†Mahoney, Mary *hotel executive*
McNicholas, David Paul *franchise company executive*
Weller, Robert N(orman) *hotel executive*

Passaic
Stagen, Mary-Patricia Healy *marketing executive*

Pennington
†Bertone, Thomas Lee *management consultant*

Pennsauken
Holman, Joseph S. *automotive sales executive*

Phillipsburg
King, Michael John *sanitarian*

Piscataway
Wagner-Westbrook, Bonnie Joan *management professional*

Pitman
Kephart, Wilmer Atkinson, Jr. *industrial management executive*

Plainsboro
Devine, Hugh James, Jr. *marketing executive, consultant*
Spiegel, Phyllis *public relations consultant, journalist*

Pleasantville
Andes, Derien Romaric *retired purchasing specialist*
Freeman, Lillie Brooks *communications company administrator*

Princeton
Barkocy, Andrew Bernard *executive search firm executive*
Bishop, James Francis *executive search consulting company executive*
Boyd, John Howard *corporate location consultant*
Connelly, John F. *communications executive*
Crespi, Irving *public opinion and market research consultant*
†Evslin, Tom *internet telephone service executive*
Hillier, James *technology management executive, researcher*
Hollander, Lawrence Jay *marketing executive*
Kelble, William Francis *information services editor*
Kornhauser, Henry *advertising executive*
Lincoln, Anna *company executive, foreign languages educator*
Makadok, Stanley *management consultant*
Morris, Mac Glenn *advertising bureau executive*
O'Connor, Neal William *former advertising agency executive*
O'Neill, Harry William *survey research company executive*
Sethi, Shyam Sunder *management consultant*
Spitzer, T. Quinn *management consultant company executive*
Weinstein, Stephen Brant *communications executive, researcher, writer*

Randolph
Charm, Joel Barry *management consultant executive*
Chen, Kevin Sangone *corporate executive, consultant*
Stoskus, Joanna Jorzysta *computer information systems educator*

Red Bank
Cataldo, Patrick A., Jr. *corporate training executive*
Haskell, Barry Geoffry *communications company research administrator*
Lukacs, Michael Edward *communications researcher*
Reinhart, Peter Sargent *corporate executive, lawyer*

Ridgewood
Warner, John Edward *advertising executive*

River Edge
†Davis, Alison B. *company executive*

Rockleigh
Siracusano, Louis H. *communications company executive*

Roseland
Lafer, Fred Seymour *data processing company executive*
Sokalski, Debra Ann *computer systems developer, programming consultant*
Taub, Henry *retired computer services company executive*
Weinbach, Arthur Frederic *computing services company executive*

Saddle River
Farrand, George Nixon, Jr. *marketing professional*
O'Connor, Denise Lynn *marketing communications executive*
Roes, Nicholas A. *communications executive*

Scotch Plains
Buckridee, Patricia Ilona *international marketing/strategy consultant*

Sea Girt
Pace, Thomas *information services executive, lawyer*

Secaucus
Schenck, Frederick A. *business executive*

Short Hills
Harwood, Jerry *market research executive*
Schaefer, Charles James, III *advertising agency executive, consultant*
†Spector, Shelly *company executive*

Shrewsbury
Jones, George Edwin *private investigator*

Somerset
Bockian, Donna Marie *data processing executive*
Lau, John Tze *computers and communications executive*

Somerville
Dobrinsky, Susan Elizabeth *human resources director*
Mattei, Marianne *consumer affairs director*

South Orange
Lapinski, Frances Constance *data processing systems executive*
Long, Philip Lee *information systems executive*
Williams, Veronica Ann *marketing and business consultant*

Spring Lake
Ernst, John Louis *management consultant*

Summit
Bostwick, Randell A. *retired retail food company executive*
Eisner, Philip Nathan *management consultant*
Fuess, Billings Sibley, Jr. *advertising executive*
Nessen, Ward Henry *typographer, lawyer*
Pace, Leonard *retired management consultant*

Teaneck
Allen, Brenda Joyce *management consultant, editor-in-chief*

Tenafly
Gibbons, Robert Philip *management consultant*

Three Bridges
Lawrence, Gerald Graham *management consultant*

Titusville
Marden, Kenneth Allen *advertising executive*

Toms River
Dorn, Norman Philip *management consulting firm executive*
Parker, John Osmyn *management consultant*

Towaco
Gasperini, Elizabeth Carmela (Lisa Gasperini) *marketing professional, graphic designer*

Trenton
Himm, Emilie Gina *records and information manager, consultant*
Losi, Maxim John *medical communications executive*
Robinson, Susan Mittleman *data processing executive*

Union
Donovan, Craig Poulenez *public administration educator*
Stern, Marianne *advertising agency executive*

Upper Saddle River
Ross, Deborah Ann *customer relations professional, philatelist*

Ventnor City
Bolton, Kenneth Albert *management consultant*

Verona
Greenwald, Robert *public relations executive*

Voorhees
†Cohen, Gregory Leighton *computer operations executive*
Gottschalk, Milton Joe *management consultant*

Warren
Blass, Walter Paul *consultant, management educator*
Chesney, Robert Henry *communications executive, consultant*
Earle, Jean Buist *computer company executive*
Kozberg, Ronald Paul *health and human services administrator*
†Wallace, Lorna H. *market strategy researcher*

Watchung
Grey, Ruthann E. *management consultant*

Wayne
Donald, Robert Graham *retail food chain human resources executive*
Freimark, Jeffrey Philip *retail supermarket executive*
Powell, Richard Cortland *advertising executive*
Salloum, Salim George *sales executive*
Vaillancourt, Donald Charles *public affairs executive, lawyer*

West Caldwell
Dixon, Jo-Ann Conte *management consultant*
Page, Frederick West *business consultant*

West Long Branch
Hedlund, Dennis M. *film company executive*
Kovacs, Aimee *conference speaker, minister*

West Milford
Ferguson, Harley Robert *service company executive*

West Orange
Ficks, F. Lawrence *communications executive*
Kyle, Corinne Silverman *management consultant*
Petrokubi, Marilyn *film company executive, researcher, producer*

Westfield
Cushman, Helen Merle Baker *retired management consultant*
Kababik, Dana Lynne *health communications executive*
Mazzarese, Michael Louis *executive coach, consultant*

Whippany
Scroggs, Deb Lee *communications professional*

Whitehouse Station
Nulman, Philip Roy *advertising executive*

Whiting
Husselman, Grace *retired innkeeper, educator*

Williamstown
Morrison, Howard Irwin *computer services executive*

Woodbridge
Kuchta, John Andrew *management consultant*

Woodcliff Lake
Morrione, Melchior S. *management consultant, accountant*

Wyckoff
Lavery, Daniel P. *management consultant*

NEW MEXICO

Albuquerque
DeWitt, Mary Therese *consultant*
Geary, David Leslie *communications executive, educator, consultant*
Golden, Julius *advertising and public relations executive, lobbyist, investor*
Hale, Bruce Donald *retired marketing professional*
Hancock, Don Ray *researcher*
Hayo, George Edward *management consultant*
Horner, Harry Charles, Jr. *sales executive, theatrical and film consultant*
Keyler, Robert Gordon *material handling company executive*
Leach, Richard Maxwell, Jr. (Max Leach, Jr.) *corporate professional*
Myers, Carol McClary *retired sales administrator, editor*
Ofte, Donald *retired environmental executive, consultant*
Oppedahl, Phillip Edward *computer company executive*
Smith, Katherine Theresa *human resources specialist, small business owner*

Bosque Farms
Kelly, Brian Matthew *industrial hygienist*

Los Alamos
Foryst, Carole *computer electronics executive*
Goldberg, David Charles *computer company executive*
Greene Lloyd, Nancy Ellen *infosystems specialist, physicist*

Portales
Edwards, Carolyn Mullenax *public relations executive*

Rio Rancho
Young, Frederic Hisgin *information systems executive, data processing consultant*

Sandia Park
Greenwell, Ronald Everett *communications executive*

Santa Fe
Allio, Robert John *management consultant, educator*
Alsaker, Robert John *information systems specialist*
Brandt, Richard Paul *communications and entertainment company executive*
Mercer, James Lee *management consultant*
Merrin, Seymour *computer marketing company executive*
Robinson, Richard Gary *management consultant, accountant*
Taylor, Beverly Lacy *stringed instrument restorer, classical guitarist*

Watrous
Myers, Harry Charles *national monument administrator*

White Sands
Molander, Glenn M. *human resources executive*

NEW YORK

Lipinsky de Orlov, Lucian Christopher *consultant*

Albany
†Angelis, Janet Ives *executive*
†Brown, David P. *public relations executive*
Favreau, Susan Debra *management consultant*
Gaw, James Richard *corporate manager*
Holmes, Walter John *public relations consultant, author*
†Pardo, Theresa Ann *project director*

Amherst
Cohen, Herman Nathan *private investigator*
†Ross-Stefanie, Bonnie Jean *information systems company executive*
Sobolewski, Timothy Richard *marketing executive*

Armonk
Bolduc, Ernest Joseph *association management consultant*
Harreld, James Bruce *computer company executive*
Kohnstamm, Abby E. *marketing executive*
Levy, Kenneth James *advertising executive*
McGroddy, James Cleary *retired computer company executive, consultant*

Astoria
Fassoulis, Satiris Galahad *communications company executive*
Sheridan, Ruth Stewart *business development consultant*

Averill Park
Traver, Robert William, Sr. *management consultant, author, lecturer, engineer*

Babylon
Meirowitz, Claire Cecile *editor, public relations executive*

Ballston Lake
Miller, Clark Alvin *human resource and organization management consultant*

Bayside
Shainis, Murray Joseph *management consultant*

Bedford Corners
Singer, Craig *broker, consultant, investor*

Berlin
Pelz, Caroline Duncombe *retired educational administrator*

Bethpage
Marrone, Daniel Scott *business, production and quality management educator*
Rolston, Richard Gerard *industrial welding and heating company executive*

Briarcliff Manor
Dolmatch, Theodore Bieley *management consultant*
Driver, Sharon Humphreys *marketing executive*

Bronx
Aronowitz, Julian *management consultant*
Griffin, Kelly Ann *public relations executive, consultant*
Lane, Elizabeth Nilaja Hannah *information analyst, educator*

Bronxville
Ellinghaus, William Maurice *communications executive*
Lawrence, Ruddick Carpenter *public relations executive*
Ryan, Frank James, Jr. *advertising executive*

Brooklyn
Ahrens, Thomas H. *production company executive*
Aspenberg, Gary Alan *personnel and labor relations professional*
De Lisi, Joanne *communications executive, educator*
Frisch, Ivan Thomas *computer and communications company executive*
Hendra, Barbara Jane *public relations executive*
Moehring, Fred Adolf *fastener distribution company executive*
†Morris, Sandra Winsome *administrative assistant*
†Smith, John W(esley), Jr. *data processing executive, consultant*

Buffalo
Blessing, Gary Albert *technical communications executive*
Fryer, Appleton *publisher, sales executive, lecturer, diplomat*
†Garland, Simon Greville *service technician*
Goralski, Donald John *public relations executive, counselor*
Halt, James George *advertising executive, graphic designer*
Hudson, Stanton Harold, Jr. *public relations executive, educator*
Levite, Laurence A. *communications executive*
Pegels, C. Carl *management science and systems educator*
Rowell, David Benton *sales and marketing company executive, consultant*

Carmel
Iglehart, Patricia Ann *strategy and market planning executive*

Cheektowaga
Mruk, Eugene Robert *retired marketing professional, urban planner*

Cooperstown
Deysenroth, Peter Albin *funeral director*

Corning
Youst, David Bennett *career development educator*

Cornwall
Loeffel, Bruce *software company executive, consultant*

Croton On Hudson
Plotch, Walter *management consultant, fund raising counselor*

Deer Park
Sacco, Russell *community employment coordinator, clergyman*

Delmar
Button, Rena Pritsker *public affairs executive*

Dewitt
Stefano, Ross William *business executive*

Dix Hills
Fisher, Fenimore *business development consultant*
Kornhauser, Kenneth Richard *funeral director, executive*

Dundee
Pfendt, Henry George *retired information systems executive, management consultant*

East Fishkill
Poschmann, Andrew William *information systems and management consultant*

East Hampton
†Duffy, Francis J. *public relations executive*
Munson, Lawrence Shipley *management consultant*

East Meadow
Bunshaft, Marilyn Janosy *community services specialist*
†Fernandes, Carla Michelle *advertising assistant*
Fuchs, Jerome Herbert *management consultant*

Elmira
Paul, Christopher Donald *carpenter, author*

Elmont
Butera, Ann Michele *consulting company executive*

Elmsford
Clutter, Bertley Allen, III *management company executive*

Farmingdale
Doucette, David Robert *computer systems company executive*

Fayetteville
Wallace, Spencer Miller, Jr. *hotel executive*

Floral Park
Dudek, Henry Thomas *management consultant*
Heyderman, Mark Baron *sales and marketing company executive*

Forest Hills
Miller, Donald Ross *management consultant*
Torrence-Thompson, Juanita Lee *public relations executive*
Van Westering, James Francis *management consultant, educator*

Fredonia
Krohn, Franklin Bernard *marketing specialist, educator*

Frewsburg
Burgeson, Joyce Ann *travel agency official*

Garden City
Conlon, Brian Thomas *promotion executive*
Conlon, Thomas James *marketing executive*
Crom, James Oliver *professional training company executive*
Doucette, Mary-Alyce *computer company executive*

Glen Cove
Tecce, Jacqueline *office manager*

Goshen
Seidman, A(bram) Alan *marketing representative, county official*

Great Neck
Donenfeld, Kenneth Jay *management consultant*
Friedland, Louis N. *retired communications executive*
Goldberg, Melvin Arthur *communications executive*
†Means, Rosaline *business executive, business educator*
Rubenstein, Stanley Ellis *public relations consultant*
†Schwartz, Alan Paul *corporate executive*
Vignola, Andrew Michael, Sr. *systems management executive*

Hancock
DeLuca, Ronald *former advertising agency executive, consultant*

Harrison
Krantz, Melissa Marianne *public relations company executive*
Wilson, William James *marketing professional*

Hastings On Hudson
Cooper, Doris Jean *market research executive*

Haverstraw
Motin, Revell Judith *retired data processing executive*

Hawthorne
Turk, Stanley Martin *advertising agency executive*

Hempstead
Pell, Arthur Robert *human resources development consultant, author*
Vissicchio, Andrew John, Jr. *linen service company executive*

Hopewell Junction
Hayden, Spencer James *management consultant*

Howard Beach
Krein, Catherine Cecilia *public relations professional, educator*

Huntington
Emery, Howard Ivan, Jr. *management consultant, telecommunications specialist*
Mandelbaum, Frank *software company executive*
Ruppert, Mary Frances *management consultant, school counselor*

Huntington Station
Miller, Sally *public relations professional*

Hyde Park
Metz, Ferdinand *chef, educator, academic administrator*
Smith, Lewis Motter, Jr. *advertising and direct marketing executive*

Islandia
Wang, Charles B. *computer software company executive*

Ithaca
Farley, Jennie Tiffany Towle *industrial and labor relations educator*
Merle, H. Etienne *specialty foods broker, restaurateur*
Park, Roy Hampton, Jr. *advertising executive*
Stevens, James Thomas *English educator*
Whyte, William Foote *industrial relations educator, author*

Jamaica
Capellan, Angel *small business executive*
Greenblatt, Fred Harold *data processing consultant*

Jamestown
Elofson, Nancy Meyer *retired office equipment company executive*

Jericho
Freedman, Mark *marketing executive*
†Rosen, Robert Arnold *management company executive, real estate investor*

Johnson City
Barber, Kenneth W. *funeral director*

Katonah
Hamilton, Kathryn Borys *marketing communications consultant*
Herbert, Marilynne *public relations executive, freelance photographer*

Kingston
Rypczyk, Candice Leigh *employee relations executive*

Lake Luzerne
Goldstein, Manfred *retired consultant*

Lake Success
Ponzi Kay, Marylou *human resources specialist*

Lancaster
Neumaier, Gerhard John *environment consulting company executive*

Larchmont
Gould, Douglas C(hester) *communications executive*
Greenwald, Carol Schiro *professional services marketing research executive*
Levy, Walter Kahn *management consultant executive*
Plumez, Jean Paul *advertising agency executive, consultant*
Steinberg, Lois Saxelby *marketing executive*
Wielgus, Charles Joseph *information services company executive*

Latham
Schwartz, Robert William *management consultant*

Long Beach
Siegel, Herbert Bernard *certified professional management consultant*

Long Island City
Craig, Elizabeth Coyne *marketing executive*
Schoenberg, David Arthur *business educator*
Shyer, Christopher Dean *optical company executive, writer*

Loudonville
Ferguson, Henry *international management consultant*

Malverne
Freund, Richard L. *communications company executive, consultant, lawyer*

Mamaroneck
Korn, Barry Paul *equipment and vehicle leasing company executive*
New, Anne Latrobe *public relations, fund raising executive*

Manhasset
Mindin, Vladimir Yudovich *information systems specialist, chemist, educator*

Malgieri, Nick *chef, author, educator*
Mallozzi, Cos M. *public relations executive*
Manoff, Richard Kalman *advertising executive, public health consultant, author*
Mansi, Joseph Anneillo *public relations company executive*
Marcosson, Thomas I. *service company executive*
†Mariam, Thomas Fred *public relations executive, radio producer*
Mark, Reuben *consumer products company executive*
†Maroun, Mary *advertising executive*
Marshall, Gary Charles *mailing list company executive*
Marshall, Michael Borden *marketing executive*
Marston, Robert Andrew *public relations executive*
Martino, Donna Frances *newspaper sales administrator*
Masi, Jane Virginia *marketing and sales consultant*
†McCandless, Carolyn Keller *human resources executive*
McCartin, Thomas Joseph *advertising executive*
McCaslin, Teresa Eve *human resources executive*
McCourt, Robert D. *marketing and creative services executive*
McDonough, Mamie *public relations executive*
McGarry, John Patrick, Jr. *retired advertising agency executive*
†McGlynn, Brian *public relations executive*
McGrath, Patrick J. *advertising agency executive*
McKelvey, Andrew J. *advertising executive*
McKelvey, Gerald *public relations executive*
McKenna, William Michael *advertising executive*
McNamara, John Jeffrey *advertising executive*
McNamee, Louise *advertising agency executive*
Medney, Tania Levy *advertising agency executive*
Meehan, Robert Henry *human resources executive, business educator*
Meehan, Sandra Gotham *advertising executive, communications consultant*
Meigher, S. Christopher, III *communications and media executive, publisher*
†Meily, Rene S. *communications executive*
Mele, Gregg Charles *management consultant, attorney*
Meranus, Arthur Richard *advertising agency executive*
Messner, Thomas G. *advertising executive, copywriter*
Mew, Calvin Marshall *advertising executive*
Meyer, Edward Henry *advertising agency executive*
Meyer, Fred Josef *advertising executive*
Meyer, Pearl *executive compensation consultant*
Miano, Louis Stephen *arts advisor*
†Michels, William Charles *management consultant*
Michenfelder, Joseph Francis *public relations executive*
†Middleberg, Don *company executive*
Mihailescu, Manuela *marketing executive*
Miller, Alan *software executive, management specialist*
†Miller, Andrew Kenneth *management consultant*
Miller, Ernest Charles *management consultant*
Miller, Lawrence *communications executive*
Miller, Robert *advertising executive*
Miller, William Jacob *public relations executive*
Mines, Herbert Thomas *executive recruiter*
Minicucci, Robert A. *business executive*
Mitchell, Jerry *public affairs educator*
Mitchell, Richard Boyle *advertising executive*
†Moed, Edward *company executive*
†Moore, Thomas A. *consumer products company executive*
Moreira, Marcio Martins *advertising executive*
Morgen, Lynn *public relations executive*
Morin, George Wilson *advertising agency executive*
Morley, Michael B. *public relations executive*
Morris, Stephen Burritt *marketing information executive*
Moss, Charles *advertising agency executive*
Moyer, David S. *executive search consultant*
Mulhearn, Patrick F.X. *telecommunications company executive*
Mulligan, David Keith *consulting company executive, securities arbitrator*
Mulligan, Deanna Marie *management consultant*
Murphy, Elva Glenn *executive assistant*
Murphy, James E. *public relations and marketing executive*
Murphy, Mark Joseph *enterprise sales executive*
Murphy, Nora Sharkey *public relations executive*
†Musham, Bettye Martin *consumer products executive*
Nash, Edward L. *advertising agency executive*
Neff, Thomas Joseph *executive search firm executive*
Nelson, Bruce Sherman *advertising agency executive*
Nelson, Wayne K. *advertising executive*
Nesbit, Robert Grover *management consultant*
Nicholson, Shelia Elaine *senior print production manager*
Niles, Nicholas Hemelright *travel company executive*
Nisenholtz, Martin Abram *telecommunications executive, educator*
Nixon, Shirnette *pharmaceutical company administrator*
Noonan, Susan Abert *public relations executive*
Norcia, Stephen William *advertising executive*
Novak, Gregory *marketing professional*
Obermayer, Michael Erik Max *management consultant*
Olbrick, Valerie Lyn *management consultant, information technologist*
Oldfield, Barney *entertainment executive*
Olinger, Carla D(ragan) *medical advertising executive*
Olsen, David George *executive search consultant*
Olson, Thomas Francis, II *communications company executive*
Orell, Lawrence *advertising executive*
Orlov, Darlene *management consultant*
Orovitz, Marcia Carol *publishing executive*
Osnos, Gilbert Charles *management consultant*
Ostrow, Joseph W. *advertising executive*
O'Sullivan, Eugene Henry *retired advertising executive*
Pagano, Michael Pro *advertising executive*
Palmiere, Catherine Emilia *executive recruiter*
Paltos, Robert Nicholas *sales executive*
Parlato, Charles *advertising executive*
†Parsons, Richard Dean *communications company executive*
Paster, Howard G. *public relations, public affairs company executive*
Patton, Joanna *advertising agency owner*
Paul, Robert David *management consultant*
Pauley, Rhoda Anne *communications and marketing executive*
Paulus, Eleanor Bock *professional speaker, author*
†Paz, Alberto *advertising executive*
Pearson, Clarence Edward *management consultant*
Peasback, David R. *recruiting company executive*
Peebler, Charles David, Jr. *advertising executive*
Perelman, Ronald Owen *diversified holding company executive*
Perless, Ellen *advertising executive*
Perlmutter, Diane F. *communications executive*
Phillips, Elizabeth Joan *marketing executive*
†Phillips, Graham Holmes *retired advertising executive*
Phillips, Joyce Martha *human resources executive*
Pickholz, Jerome Walter *advertising agency executive*
Pinkard, Lee S. *marketing and communications executive*
Pittman, Preston Lawrence *executive assistant*
Pollock-O'Brien, Louise Mary *public relations executive*
Pompadur, I. Martin *communications executive*
Potvin, William Tracey *management consultant*
Powell, Timothy Wood *information executive, consultant*
Primi, Don Alexis *advertising and public relations executive, railroad transportation executive*
†Profili, Guido *telecommunications executive, consultant*
Propp, Gail Dane Gomberg *computer consulting company executive*
†Puglisi, John Richard *advertising executive*
†Quella, James Andrew *management consultant*
Quinlan, Mary Lou *advertising executive*
Quintero, Ronald Gary *management consultant*
Radice, Frank J. *communications executive*
Rasor, Richard Drew, Jr. *advertising sales professional*
Ratcliffe, Sandra M(arguerite) *convention manager*
Rathke, Sheila Wells *advertising and public relations executive*
Rauch, Arthur Irving *management consultant*
Reges, Marianna Alice *marketing executive*
Reichel, Walter Emil *advertising executive*
Reichert, Maureen *advertising executive*
Reinhard, Keith Leon *advertising executive*
Resnick, Rosalind *multimedia executive*
Reuben, Alvin Bernard *entertainment executive*
Reynolds, James *management consultant*
Rice, Glenn T.C. *sales executive, marketing consultant, distributor*
Rice, Regina Kelly *marketing executive*
Rickin, Sheila Anne *personnel professional*
Rider, Joseph Kuntzman *information systems specialist*
Riordan, James Quentin *retired company executive*
Ritchie, Richard Lee *media company executive*
Robbins, John Clapp *management consultant*
Roberts, Francis Stone *advertising executive*
Roche, Gerard Raymond *management consultant*
†Rodriguez, Julio *information technology executive*
Rogers, Thomas Sydney *communications executive*
Roman, Kenneth, Jr. *corporate communications executive*
Romano, Joseph Anthony *marketing and consulting executive*
Ronson, Susan *administrative assistant*
Rose, Merrill *public relations counselor*
Rosen, David Michael *public relations director, public affairs consultant*
Rosenberg, George A. *public relations company executive*
Rosenfeld, Naomi Eve *corporate communications specialist*
Rosensaft, Lester Jay *management consultant, lawyer, business executive*
Rosenshine, Allen Gilbert *advertising agency executive*
Rosenthal, Peter *public relations executive*
Ross, Randolph Ernest *management consultant*
Ross, Thomas Bernard *communications company executive*
Rothenberg, Robert Philip *public relations counselor*
Rothholz, Peter Lutz *public relations executive*
Rotter, Steven Jeffrey *company executive*
Ruben, William Samuel *marketing consultant*
Rubenstein, Howard Joseph *public relations executive*
Rudd, Nicholas *marketing communications company executive*
Ruder, William *public relations executive*
Russo, Anthony Joseph *public relations professional*
Sacks, Temi J. *public relations executive*
†St. Pierre, Nakia Catherine *consultant*
Sakai, Hiroko *trading company executive*
Samet, Michael *communications executive*
Sandler, Kenneth Bruce *advertising executive*
Sarkis, J. Ziad *management consultant*
Sauerhaft, Stan *public relations executive, consultant*
Savas, Emanuel S. *public management and public policy educator*
Savory, Mark *management consultant, insurance company executive*
Sayre, Linda Damaris *human resources professional*
Schaffer, Kenneth B. *communications executive, satellite engineer, inventor, consultant*
Schaub, Sherwood Anhder, Jr. *management consultant*
†Scheer, Linda Canfield *staff development specialist*
†Scherry, Howard Jay *hotel reservation agent*
Schnall, David Jay *management and administration educator*
Schoonover, Jean Way *public relations consultant*
Schulman, Mark Allen *market research company executive*
Schupak, Leslie Allen *public relations company executive*
Schur, Jeffrey *advertising executive*
Schwab, Frank, Jr. *management consultant*
Schwartz, Alan Victor *advertising agency executive*
Schwartz, Kenneth Ernst *communications executive*
Schwartz, Lois C. *instructional technologist, consultant*
Schweitzer, George *communications executive*
Scott, William Clement, III *entertainment industry executive*
Scotti, Gavin A. *advertising executive*
Seadler, Stephen Edward *business and computer consultant, social scientist*
Seaman, Alfred Jarvis *retired advertising agency executive*
Secunda, Eugene *marketing communications executive, educator*
Seid, Lynne *advertising agency executive*
Seiden, Henry (Hank Seiden) *advertising executive*
Seiden, Steven Arnold *executive search consultant*
Seligson, Carl H. *management consultant*
Selkowitz, Arthur *advertising agency executive*
†Seltzer, Bob *public relations executive*
Shaffer, Richard *communications executive*
Shaheen, George T. *management consultant*
†Shahid, Sam N. *advertising executive*
Shair, David Ira *human resources executive*
Shapiro, Marvin Lincoln *communications company executive*
Sherman, Aliza *computer communications specialist*
Sherman, Eugene Jay *retired marketing executive, economist*
Shevack, Brett David *advertising agency executive*
†Siegel, Herbert Jay *communications executive*
Siegel, Lucy Boswell *public relations executive*
Silverman, Marylin A. *advertising agency executive*
Sinclair, Daisy *advertising executive, casting director*
Slosberg, Mike *advertising executive*
Smith, George S., Jr. *communications financial executive*
Smith, Martin Jay *advertising and marketing executive*
Sorell, Kitty Julia *public relations executive*
Sorensen, Robert C. *marketing executive, educator*
†Soriano, Marcy Jill *circulation coordinator*
Soter, George Nicholas *advertising executive*
Souham, Gérard *communications executive*
Sparkes, Cheryl Flowers *management consultant*
†Spence, Gene Lyle *executive recruiter*
Spiegel, Elwyn *advertising agency executive, creative director*
Spivak, Joan Carol *healthcare communications specialist*
Sprague, Peter Julian *software company executive, lecturer*
†Spring, Chris N. *company executive*
Springer, John Shipman *public relations executive*
†Srere, Linda Jean *advertising executive*
Stack, Edward William *business management and foundation executive*
†Stanton, Alex *public relations executive*
Stauffer, Michael Kirk *communications executive, consultant*
Stein, Elliot, Jr. *media executive*
Stepanek, Daniel P. *public relations executive*
Stetler, Russell Dearnley, Jr. *private investigator*
Stevens, Art *public relations executive*
Stevens, Jerome Hebert *management consultant*
Stewart, Jeff *advertising agency executive*
Stolfi, Thomas Edward *advertising executive*
Strand, Curt Robert *hotel executive*
Stratigos, William Narge *computer company executive*
Strear, Joseph D. *public relations executive*
Stroock, Mark Edwin, II *public relations company executive*
Stuart, Lori Ames *public relations executive*
Sturges, John Siebrand *management consultant*
Sulcer, Frederick Durham *advertising executive*
Sussman, Jeffrey Bruce *public relations and marketing executive*
Svinkelstin, Abraham Joshua *information technology executive*
Swanzey, Robert Joseph *data processing executive*
Swid, Stephen Claar *business executive*
Swift, John Francis *health care advertising company executive*
Sykes, John *communications company executive*
Tanaka, Patrice Aiko *public relations executive*
Tarter, Fred Barry *advertising executive*
Taylor, Barbara Alden *public relations executive*
Taylor, Humphrey John Fausitt *information services executive*
Tayson, Richard Allan *office management director, writer, educator*
Temin, Davia B. *marketing executive*
Teran, Timothy Eric Alba *marketing professional*
Thompson, Gary W. *public relations executive*
Thompson, Page *advertising executive*
Tilson, Dorothy Ruth *word processing executive*
Tisch, James Solomon *diversified holding company executive*
Tisch, Jonathan Mark *hotel company executive*
Tisch, Laurence Alan *diversified manufacturing and service executive*
Tofel, Richard Jeffrey *communication executive*
†Tom, Howard S. *company executive*
Torrenzano, Richard *public affairs executive*
Tortorello, Nicholas John *public opinion and market research company executive*
Towers, Robert *restaurant executive*
Trencher, Lewis *advertising company executive*
Trinkaus, John William *management educator*
Turkel, Stanley *hotel consultant, management executive*
Turso, Vito Anthony *public relations executive*
Upson, Stuart Barnard *advertising agency executive*
Van Allen, Barbara Martz *marketing professional*
Van Brunt, Albert Daniel *advertising agency executive*
Veru, Theodore *advertising agency executive*
†Vick, Edward H. *advertising executive*
†Vickers, John A. *hotel executive*
Volpe, Thomas J. *advertising executive*
†Vosloo, Paul *public relations executive*
†Wachalter, Terry *advertising executive*
Wachter, Susan Cohen *advertising executive*
Waite, David Allen *software development executive*
Waldman, Robert Charles *corporate entertainment executive*
Walke, David Michael *public relations executive*
Waller, Tom *marketing executive*
Walsh, Annmarie Hauck *research firm executive*
Wanek, William Charles *public relations executive*
Washburn, Michael *management consultant*
Waterhouse, Stephen Lee *management consultant*
Wax, Edward L. *advertising executive*
Weida, Lewis Dixon *marketing analyst, consultant*
Weiner, Richard *public relations executive*
Weinstein, Sharon Schlein *corporate communications executive, educator*
Weiss, Mark *public relations executive*
Wells, Peter Scoville *marketing executive*
Werfelman, William Herman, Jr. *public relations executive*
†Whiting, Charles S(pencer), Jr. *company executive, software consultant*
Willett, Roslyn Leonore *public relations executive, food service consultant, writer*
Wilson, James Reid, Jr. *advertising executive*
Winkleman, John Sandler *public relations executive*
†Winston, Stanley S. *advertising executive*
Winters, Mark Bennett *personnel company executive*
Wit, David Edmund *software and test preparation company executive*
Wolff, Richard Joseph *public relations executive, consultant, historian*
Woodrum, Robert Lee *executive search consultant*
†Wren, John *advertising executive*
Wright, Michael Kearney *retired public relations executive*
Wunderman, Lester *advertising agency executive*
Wyse, Lois *advertising executive, author*
Yoder, Patricia Doherty *public relations executive*
Zelnick, Strauss *entertainment company executive*

Newburgh
Cornell, Ryan Scott Michael *communications company executive*

North Salem
Sloves, Marvin *retired advertising agency executive*

North Tonawanda
†Whitbeck, Scott J. *business association executive*

Nyack
Karp, Peter Simon *marketing executive*
Keil, John Mullan *advertising agency executive*

Old Chatham
Wright, Margaret Taylor *marketing consultant, publisher*

Old Westbury
Galatianos, Gus A. *computer executive, information systems consultant, educator*

Orangeburg
Ulrich, Max Marsh *executive search consultant*

Ossining
Reynolds, Calvin *management consultant, business educator*

Oswego
†Sherman, Christopher Peter *customer service representative, musician*

Park Slope
Reisler, Helen Barbara *public relations consultant, publicity and product promotion*

Pearl River
Griffith, Clark Dexter *consultant*
Jackson, Phillip Ellis *cause-related marketing executive, writer*

Peekskill
Fishkind, Lawrence *marketing consultant*

Pelham
Hearle, Douglas Geoffrey *public relations consultant*

Penfield
Perkins-Carpenter, Betty Lou *fitness company executive*

Pittsford
Estin-Klein, Libbyada *advertising executive, medical writer*
Saini, Vasant Durgadas *computer software company executive*

Plattsburgh
Hanton, E(mile) Michael *public and personnel relations consultant*

Pleasantville
Keller, Mary Beth *consumer research consultant*

Port Chester
Ailloni-Charas, Dan *marketing executive*

Port Washington
Hackett, John Byron *advertising agency executive, lawyer*
Johnson, Tod Stuart *market research company executive*
Sonnenfeldt, Richard Wolfgang *management consultant*

Poughkeepsie
Agerwala, Tilak Krishna Mahesh *computer company executive*
Mareth, Paul David *communications consultant*

Pound Ridge
Rubino, John Anthony *management and human resources consultant*
Throckmorton, Joan Helen *direct marketing consultant*

Purchase
Cohen, Alan Norman *business executive*

Quogue
Lyons, Jude (Anne Lyons) *advertising agency executive*

Rego Park
Cortese, Edward *marketing and public relations executive*

Rensselaer
Hull, Raymond Whitford *public relations executive*

Richmond Hill
Velazco, Julio E. *security specialist*

Rochester
Adiletta, Debra Jean Olson *business analyst consultant*
Belgiorno, John *career consultant, educator*
Briggs, James T. *marketing executive*
Degraff, David Charles *purchasing executive*
Edson, Marian Louise *communications executive*
†Fallesen, Elaine Gertrude *public relations professional*
Fowler, Robert Archibald *infosystems company executive*
Goldberg-Schaible, Jocelyn Hope Schnier *market research consultant*
Harris, Diane Carol *merger and acquisition consulting firm executive*
Hutchins, Frank McAllister *advertising executive*
LaSpagnoletta, Benjamin Joseph *infosystems specialist*
McCall, Thomas Donald *marketing communications company executive*
McKie, W. Gilmore *human resources executive*

Nace, Morton Oliver, Jr. human resources professional, performance consultant
Parke, John Shepard marketing consultant
Sawyer, William Curtis pest control company executive
Sharp, Alfred Jay retired personnel relations executive
Wegman, Robert B. food service executive
Wiedrick-Kozlowski, Jan Barbara communications executive

Rockville Centre
Beyer, Suzanne advertising agency executive

Roslyn
Arstark, Lester D. advertising agency executive
Ulanoff, Stanley M. communications executive

Roslyn Heights
Saridakis, Andrew Peter international trader and business consultant

Rye
†Clyatt, Robert Lee executive distance learning firm
Gurfein, Stuart James data processing executive
Kaulakis, Arnold Francis management consultant
McDonnell, Mary Theresa travel service executive
Metzger, Frank management consultant
Mittelstadt, Charles Anthony advertising executive
Vauclair, Marguerite Renée communications executive, sales executive
Vernon, Lillian mail order company executive

Rye Brook
McKenna, John computer company executive
†McKenna, John A., Jr. data processing executive

Saratoga Springs
Davis, John Eugene restaurant owner, disc jockey
Masie, Elliott training executive
Stanley, Karen Francine Mary Lesniewski human resources professional

Scarsdale
Blinder, Abe Lionel management consultant
Bloomfield, Keith Martin management executive
Callaghan, Georgann Mary management consultant
Kaufman, Robert Jules communications consultant, lawyer
Schultz, Harley consulting company executive
Winkler, Katherine Maurine management consultant, educator

Schenectady
Golub, Lewis supermarket company executive

Skaneateles
Huxford, J. David retired sales representative

Sleepy Hollow
Schmidt, Klaus Franz advertising executive

Slingerlands
Childs, Rhonda Louise motivational speaker, consultant

Smithtown
†Guthrie, James Russell data system analyst
Jonassen, Gaylord D. computer company executive, new products and market development
†Nielsen-Jones, Ian Richard lottery and gaming executive

Somers
Banik, Douglas Heil marketing executive
Elix, Douglas Thorne computer company executive
Wladawsky-Berger, Irving communications executive

Southampton
Lieberman, Carol healthcare marketing communications consultant

Staten Island
Fafian, Joseph, Jr. management consultant
Fernandes, Richard Louis retired advertising firm executive
†McGee, Sean-Reed advertising official

Stony Brook
Katz, Victoria Manuela public relations executive, educator, consultant
Ohannessian, Harry Haroutune travel agency executive

Syosset
Heller, Al marketing consultant, business journalist
Roche, John Edward human resources management consultant, educator

Syracuse
Berinstein, William Paul business executive
Boghosian, Paula der computer business consultant
Gartner, Joseph Charles business systems administrator
Higbee, Ann G. public relations executive, consultant
Ramsey, Dan Steven consultant, business executive

Syyosset
Gorenstein, Edward employment services executive

Tallman
Strasser, Joel A. public relations executive, engineer, producer

Tappan
Fox, Muriel public relations executive

Tarrytown
Fudge, Ann Marie marketing executive
Kenney, Dion Patrick business strategist, entrepreneur

Thornwood
Bassett, Lawrence C management consultant

Tuckahoe
Brecher, Bernd management consultant
Elliott, Dennis Dawson communications executive

Unadilla
Compton, John Robinson rake company executive

Upper Nyack
†Seife, Agie information technologist

Valhalla
Warakomski, Alphonse Walter Joseph, Jr. sales executive

Watervliet
Alber, Richard Lawrence quality assurance professional

West Islip
Softness, Donald Gabriel marketing and manufacturing executive

West Nyack
Oppenheim, Robert beauty industry executive

Westbury
O'Mara, Sharyn advertising executive

Westhampton Beach
Maas, Jane Brown advertising executive

White Plains
Allen, Ralph Dean diversified company corporate executive
Aron, Eve Glicka Serenson personal care industry executive
Bartels, Juergen E. hotel company executive
Cohen, Joseph Michael communications executive
Colwell, Howard Otis advertising executive
DeMond, Jeffrey Stuart cable television and telecommunications executive
Gill, Patricia Jane human resources executive
Kleisner, Fred hotel executive
Lukaszewski, James Edmund communications executive
Martin, Thomas Rhodes communications executive, writer
Otten, Michael data processing executive
Roll, Irwin Clifford (Win Roll) advertising, marketing and publishing executive
Winterton, Joseph Henry computer software executive
Woody, Carol Clayman data processing executive

Whitesboro
Bulman, William Patrick data processing executive

Williamsville
De Gasper, Edgar Eugene food services consultant
Stoeckl, Shelley Joan marketing professional

Woodhaven
Bolster, Jacqueline Neben (Mrs. John A. Bolster) communications consultant

Woodside
Wynne, Linda Marie administrative assistant, artist

Yonkers
Miller, Karl A. management counselor
Newman, Suzanne Dinkes web site development executive
†Wen, Sheree computer compancy executive, president

Yorktown Heights
Kessler, Bernard Milton organizational and human resources development specialist
Rosenblatt, Stephen Paul marketing and sales promotion company executive

NORTH CAROLINA

Asheville
Etter, Robert Miller retired consumer products executive, chemist
Summey, Steven Michael advertising company executive
Turcot, Marguerite Hogan innkeeper, medical researcher

Beaufort
Mackenzie, James fire protection and industrial safety executive

Boone
Parker, William Dale management consultant, political adviser

Burlington
Eddins, James William, Jr. marketing executive
McCrickard, Eric Eugene customer service representative

Canton
Dixon, Shirley Juanita restaurant owner

Cary
†Meyer, William Eugene marketing consultant
Smith, Janet Sue systems specialist
Sussenguth, Edward Henry computer company executive, computer network designer
Wait, George William sales executive

Cashiers
Yates, Linda Snow communications, marketing executive

Chapel Hill
Hill, Robert Folwell, Jr. information systems specialist
Jerdee, Thomas Harlan business administration educator, organization psychology researcher and consultant
Lauterborn, Robert F. advertising educator, consultant
†Orsini, Peter F. graphics company executive
Swanson, Michael Alan sales and marketing executive
Williams, John Trent public policy company executive

Charlotte
Bradshaw, Howard Holt management consulting company executive
Burke, Steven Charles healthcare administration executive
Butler, Carol King advertising executive
Carino, Linda Susan business consultant
Coffey, Darren Kemper planner
Doherty, Barbara Whitehurst chemical purchasing manager
Eppes, Thomas Evans advertising executive, public relations executive
Gerber, Charles M. sales and marketing executive
Hudgins, Catherine Harding business executive
Ignozzi, Bryan K. management consultant
Kallman, Kathleen Barbara marketing and business development professional
Loeffler, William George, Jr. advertising executive
Lyerly, Elaine Myrick advertising executive
Mascavage, Joseph Peter training executive
Risko, James Richard business executive
Rivenbark, Jan Meredith corporate executive
Suter, George August management and marketing consultant
Wallsh, Bonnie Elaine meeting management consultant, educator
†Wayer, Glen Patrick information and technology specialist
Wood, Donald Craig retired marketing professional
†Zampieri, Robert P. business consultant

Clayton
Silberman, H. Lee public relations executive

Clinton
Fetterman, Annabelle packing company executive

Conover
†Wallace, Terri Goodman communications executive, sales executive

Durham
Byers, Garland Franklin, Jr. private investigator, security firm executive
Fogle, G. Lee credit union executive, consultant
Gunter, Emily Diane communications executive, marketing professional, real estate developer, author, educator
Ladd, Marcia Lee medical equipment and supplies company executive
†McDonald, Trevy Ann communications educator, writer
Oakley, Wanda Faye management consultant, educator
Otterbourg, Robert Kenneth public relations consultant, writer
Squire, Alexander management consultant
Taylor, James Francis marketing professional

Elizabeth City
†Irvin, James Samuel company executive

Fort Bragg
Rinehart, James Forrest educator

Garner
Barbour, Charlene management firm executive

Gastonia
Eads, Ronald Preston management consultant

Goldsboro
Barkley, Monika Johanna general contracting professional

Greensboro
Allen, Jesse Owen, III management development and organizational behavior
Ertel, Ross Steven printing sales executive
Formo, Brenda Terrell travel company executive
†Hilliard, Kelly McCollum employment manager
Kerley, Janice Johnson personnel executive
Sanders, William Eugene marketing executive
Spears, Alexander White, III tobacco company executive

Hickory
George, Boyd Lee consumer products company executive
Hilton, Deanie Herman human resources executive, telecommunications manager

High Point
Winn, Walter Garnett, Jr. marketing strategist, advertising executive

Jefferson
†Van Arnam, Mark Stephen sales executive

Lake Toxaway
Morgan, Marianne corporate professional

North Wilkesboro
Ashworth, Robert Vincent data processing executive
Parsons, Irene management consultant

Oak Ridge
Johnson, Willie Spoon quality management consultant

Pine Knoll Shores
Griffin, Thomas Lee, Jr. industrial and federal government specialist

Pinehurst
Gilmore, Voit travel executive
Grantham, Joseph Michael, Jr. hotel executive, management and marketing consultant
Nuzzo, Salvatore Joseph defense, electronics company executive
Paquette, Dean Richard retired computer company executive, consultant

Pinetops
Robertson, Richard Blake management consultant

Raleigh
Cook, Norma Baker consulting company executive
Doherty, Robert Cunningham advertising executive, retired
Eberly, Harry Landis retired communications company executive
Grubb, Donald Hartman paper industry company executive
Larsen, Eric Lyle information technology executive, writer, consultant, farmer
Leak, Robert E. economic development consultant
McLaurin, Martha Regina parking service company executive
Ofner, J(ames) Alan management consultant
Robinson, Keith sales and marketing executive
Roisler, Glenn Harvey quality assurance professional
Sharpe, Donald Charles service manager
Shaw, Robert Gilbert restaurant executive, senator
†Winston, Robert W., III hotel facility executive

Research Triangle Park
Clark, Kevin Anthony marketing executive, communications executive
Hamner, Charles company executive

Rocky Mount
Polk, Ronald Thomas marketing executive

Rural Hall
Wager, Michael company executive

Sanford
Schneider, Steven L. company executive

Southern Pines
Owings, Malcolm William retired management consultant

Sparta
Allen, Robert English business development executive, consultant

Statesville
Grogan, David R. company executive

Supply
Pollard, Joseph Augustine advertising and public relations consultant

Vass
Glassman, Edward public relations management creativity consultant

Weaverville
Parsons, Vinson Adair retired computer software company executive

Wilkesboro
Boyd, Robert Giddings, Jr. health facility administrator

Wilmington
Burton, Richard Greene retired marketing executive
Flohr, Daniel P. company executive
†Foster, Amy Nicole television station sales administrator
Lees, Anthony Philip business consultant

Wilson
Dean, Thomas A. research laboratory executive
Mercer, Danny Thomas sales representative

Winston Salem
Atkinson, G. Douglas, Sr. marketing executive, consultant
Evans, Lisbeth business networking executive, political party official
Griswold, George marketing, advertising and public relations executive
Gunzenhauser, Gerard Ralph, Jr. management consultant, investor
Hamlin, Edwin Cliburn sales consultant
Jackson, Mae Boger executive administrative assistant, office manager
Johnston, James Wesley retired tobacco company executive
Kaufman, Charlotte S. communications executive
MacKinnon, Sally Anne retired fast food company executive
Walker, Wendy K. marketing executive

Zebulon
Kirkland, Gerry Paul sales executive

NORTH DAKOTA

Bismarck
†Keller, Kent Kyle computer technician

Bottineau
Gorder, Steven F. business executive

Fargo
†Tharaldson, Gary hotel executive
Wallwork, William Wilson, III automobile executive

Grand Forks
Rolshoven, Ross William legal investigator, art photographer

Mandan
Heick, Leon Joseph data processing executive

OHIO

Akron
Hochschwender, Herman Karl international consultant
Jasso, William Gattis public relations executive
Johnson, Joyce Marie marketing and communications executive
Meeker, David Anthony public relations executive
Molinari, Marco marketing executive
Sonnecken, Edwin Herbert management consultant
Walker, Debra May marketing professional
Zeno, Jo Ann sales executive

Bay Village
Berger, James (Hank) business broker

Bowling Green
Varney, Glenn Herbert *management educator*

Broadview Heights
Sternlieb, Lawrence Jay *marketing professional*

Bryan
Benedict, Gregory Bruce *business administration/ finance professional, legal consultant*

Canton
Goldwater, Leslie Rachel *business communications consultant*
Suarez, Benjamin *consumer products company executive*

Chagrin Falls
Church, Irene Zaboly *personnel services company executive*
Eastburn, Richard A. *consulting firm executive*
Fisher, Will Stratton *illumination consultant*

Chesterland
Spitz, Arnoldt John *international trade professional, consultant*
Ullery, Richard Frank *sales executive*

Cincinnati
Artzt, Edwin Lewis *consumer products company executive*
Bernish, Paul *public relations executive, consultant*
Brown, Dale Patrick *retired advertising executive*
Bull, Louis Antal (Tony) *sales executive*
Dillon, David Brian *retail grocery executive*
Eager, William Earl *information systems corporation executive*
Freshwater, Paul Ross *consumer goods company executive*
Groth, Jon Quentin *management consultant*
Hawkins, Lawrence Charles *management consultant, educator*
Henry, J(ohn) Porter, Jr. *sales consultant*
Hicks, Irle Raymond *retail food chain executive*
Howe, John Kingman *manufacturing, sales and marketing executive*
Hutton, Edward Luke *diversified public corporation executive*
†Jager, Durk I. *marketing agency executive*
Jennings, James Norbert, Jr. *marketing executive, entrepreneur*
Kollstedt, Paula Lubke *communications executive, writer*
Lange, Scott Leslie *communications company executive, voice professional*
Levine, Aaron *executive*
Levy, Sam Malcolm *advertising executive*
Liss, Herbert Myron *communications executive, educator, journalist*
Lockhart, John Mallery *management consultant*
Maier, Craig Frisch *restaurant executive*
Maxfield, Anne M. *sales executive*
McNulty, John William *retired public relations executive, automobile company executive*
Meixner, Helmut *consumer products company executive*
Million, Kenneth Rhea *management consultant*
Monroe, William Frederick *marketing professional*
Moore, John Edward *marketing professional, freelance writer*
Morris, Margaret E. *marketing professional*
Pedrick, Dwayne Ellis, Sr. *information systems specialist*
Pepper, John Ennis, Jr. *consumer products company executive*
Rice, Maurice Ainsworth *management consultant*
Sperzel, George E., Jr. *personal care industry executive*
Sullivan, Dennis James, Jr. *public relations executive*
Wehling, Robert Louis *household products company executive*
White, Joy Mieko *communications executive*

Cleveland
Benghiat, Russell *advertising agency executive*
Bersoux, Henri Robert *marketing executive*
Buchstein, Frederick David *public relations executive*
Byron, Rita Ellen Cooney *travel executive, publisher, real estate agent, civic leader, photojournalist, writer*
Cargile, Michael Edward *advertising agency executive*
Connelly, Diane Cecile *communications executive*
†Cook, Ron A. *management company executive*
Danco, Léon Antoine *management consultant, educator*
Dougherty, Ursel Thielbeule *communications and marketing executive*
Dunbar, Mary Asmundson *communications executive, investor and public relations consultant*
Eaton, Henry Felix *public relations executive*
Eichhorn, Bradford Reese *management consultant*
Fountain, Ronald Glenn *management consultant, finance/marketing executive*
Frisman, Roger Lawrence *industrial sales executive*
Gallagher, Patrick Francis Xavier *public relations executive*
Graham, John W. *advertising executive*
Gund, Gordon *advertising executive, sports team executive*
Hamilton, Nancy Beth *business executive*
Hastie, Ronald Leslie *sales executive*
Henry, Edward Frank *computer accounting service executive*
†Lee, Inmoo *business educator*
Lowry, Dennis Martin *training executive*
Luce, Priscilla Mark *public relations executive*
Lyatkher, Victor Mikhailovich *seismology research, hydropower/windpower designer*
Marcus, Donald Howard *advertising agency executive*
Miller, John Robert *environmental recycling company executive*
Nagel, William Lee *management consultant*
Olson, Barry Gay *advertising executive, creative director*
O'Shea, Lynne Edeen *marketing executive, educator*
Perkovic, Robert Branko *international management consultant*
Pollack, Florence K.Z. *management consultant*
Roop, James John *public relations executive*
Schonberg, Alan Robert *management recruiting executive*
Stefunek, Paul Christopher *executive search company executive*

Sudow, Thomas Nisan *marketing services company executive, broadcaster*
Taw, Dudley Joseph *sales executive*
Wangermann, John Paul *management consultant*

Columbus
Barker, Llyle James, Jr. *management consultant, jounalism educator*
Bosworth, Jeffrey Willson *emerging technologies consultant, client/server specialist*
Brown, Rowland Chauncey Widrig *information systems, strategic planning and ethics consultant*
Burke, Kenneth Andrew *advertising executive*
Chapman, John William, Jr. *marketing executive*
†Fechtor, Steve *advertising executive*
†Garner, Carol Lynn *executive*
Gower, Cindy Elaine Lones *electronic technician*
Iammartino, Nicholas R. *corporate communications executive*
Keller, Kenneth Christen *advertising executive*
†Lomax, Howard *security officer*
Mangum, Stephen L. *business educator*
†Matthews, Terina Joann *human resources specialist*
McCoy, William Earl, Jr. *economic development training consultant*
†Milenthal, David *advertising executive*
†Milenthal, Rick *advertising executive*
Muller, Mervin Edgar *information systems educator, consultant*
Reed, Constance Louise *materials management and purchasing consultant*
Ress, Charles William *management consultant*
Ryan, Robert *consulting company executive*
Schoedinger, David Stanton *funeral director*
Sullivan, Ernest Lee *human resources director*
Taylor, Celianna Isley *information systems specialist*
Tipton, Clyde Raymond, Jr. *communications and resources development consultant*
†Upchurch, Carl Douglass *lecturer, consultant, columnist*
†Yeo, Augustus C. *business and systems consultant*
Zapp, David Edwin *infosystems specialist, investment consultant*

Dayton
Daoud, George Jamil *hotel and motel consultant*
Henley, Terry Lew *computer company executive*
Kegerreis, Robert James *management consultant, marketing educator*
Maher, Frank Aloysius *research and development executive, psychologist*
Morris, John Steven *marketing professional*
Nevin, Robert Charles *information systems executive*
Nyberg, Lars *company executive*
Reading, Anthony John *business executive, accountant*
Riley, David Richard *management consultant, retired military officer*
Robinson, Gregory Alan *practice management executive*
Schnier, David Christian *marketing executive, author*
Tatar, Jerome F. *business products executive*
Walusis, Eric M. *product developer, consultant*
Wilson, Jack *advertising executive*

Dover
Miller, Mary Katherine *management consultant*

Dublin
Freytag, Donald Ashe *management consultant*
McCauley, William Albert *business executive*
McCormick, William Edward *environmental consultant*
Smith, K(ermit) Wayne *computer company executive*
Spies, Phyllis Bova *information services company executive*

Elyria
Patton, Thomas James *sales and marketing executive*
Schrott, Janet Ann *human resources specialist, consultant*

Euclid
Arko, John David *transportation company driver*

Fairborn
Beer, Daniel Jackson *sales executive*

Fairfield
Rafalowski, Raymond Victor *printing and publishing executive*

Findlay
Moore, Nick Alan *information systems specialist, consultant*

Fostoria
Howard, Kathleen *computer company executive*

Franklin
Murray, Thomas Dwight *advertising agency executive*

Fulton
McCloskey, Katherine Mary *retired office manager*

Gates Mills
Abbott, James Samuel, III *marketing executive*

Geneva
†Reed, Roger Duane *maintenance technician*

Georgetown
Frame, Lawrence Milven, Jr. *inventor*

Germantown
Lansaw, Charles Ray *sales industry executive*

Grand River
Abel, Mary Ellen Kathryn *quality control executive, chemist*

Granville
†Oliva, Maurizio *computer technologist*

Hamilton
Ferng, Douglas Ming-Haw *infosystems executive*

Heath
Gregorich, Penny Denise *purchasing agent*

Hilliard
Cash, Francis Winford *hotel industry executive*
Price, Virginia Ashbaugh *technical service director, workers compensation c*

Hudson
Bell, Harry Edward *quality consulting company executive*
Wilfong, Brenda A. *telecommunications executive*

Independence
Pesec, David John *data systems executive*

Jackson
Benson, Steven Clark *management and engineering executive*

Kent
Aleman, Mindy R. *advertising and public relations consultant, marketing and development executive, newspaper columnist, freelance writer*
Bancik, Steven Charles *information specialist, researcher*
Bissler, Richard Thomas *mortician*
Stevenson, Thomas Herbert *management consultant, writer*

Kettering
Seto, Ken Hon *consultant, small business owner*

Lancaster
Katlic, John Edward *management consultant*
Phillips, Edward John *consulting firm executive*

London
Wiley, Jerold Wayne *environmental services executive, retired air force officer*

Loveland
Dalambakis, Christopher A. *workplace performance consultant*

Macedonia
Szczurek, Thomas Eugene *marketing executive*

Maineville
Collins, Larry Wayne *small business owner, information systems specialist*

Mansfield
Crittenden, Sophie Marie *communications executive*
Ellison, Lorin Bruce *management consultant*
Granter, Sharon Savoy *restaurateur, caterer*
Nordstrom, Walter Erick *communications consultant*

Marysville
Jones-Morton, Pamela *human resources specialist*

Maumee
Nowak, Patricia Rose *advertising executive*
Sacksteder, Thomas M. *corporate executive, entrepreneur, writer*

Mayfield Heights
Newman, Joseph Herzl *advertising consultant*

Medina
Prakup, Barbara Lynn *communications executive*

Miamisburg
Dalrymple, Cheryl *online information company executive*
Davies, Tim *online information company executive*

Middletown
Rhein, Thomas Anthony *recreational facility administrator*

Milford
Shipley, Tony L(ee) *software company executive*

North Olmsted
Galysh, Robert Alan *information systems analyst*

Oxford
Pringle, Lewis Gordon *marketing professional, educator*
Yen, David Chi-Chung *management information systems educator*

Peninsula
Ludwig, Richard Joseph *ski resort executive*

Perrysburg
Kovacik, Neal Stephen *hotel and restaurant executive*

Pickerington
Basinger, Cheryl Kathryn Ricketts *organizational development executive*

Port Clinton
Subler, Edward Pierre *advertising executive*

Rocky River
Hosek, John Jude *planning organization executive*

Saint Clairsville
Dankworth, Margaret Anne *management consultant*

Salem
Fehr, Kenneth Manbeck *retired computer systems company executive*

Seven Hills
Kuznik, Susan Marie *management consultant*

Shaker Heights
Kaplan, Norman Charles *industrialist, philanthropist*

Solon
Johnson, Madeline Mitchell *retired administrative assistant*

Streetsboro
Weiss, Joseph Joel *consulting company executive*

Sylvania
Ring, Herbert Everett *management executive*

Toledo
Block, Allan James *communications executive*
Cummings, Erwin Karl *information technology executive*
Kimble, James A. *management consultant, accountant*
Paquette, Jack Kenneth *management consultant, antiques dealer*
Root, David Leigh *advertising company executive*
Vicary, William Charles, Jr. *director sales and marketing*

Warren
Westman, Robert Allan *management consultant*

West Alexandria
Scoville, George Richard *marketing professional*

West Chester
Neiheisel, Thomas Henry *marketing research consultant*

Westerville
Kerner, Joseph Frank, Jr. *management consultant, educator*
O'Meara, John Richard *park district director*

Willoughby
Sherman, Francis George Harry *advertising agency executive*

Wooster
Schmitt, Wolfgang Rudolf *consumer products executive*

Wright Patterson AFB
†Parr, Sharon E. *purchasing executive*
Szucs, Andrew Eric *training manager*

Wyoming
Cooley, William Edward *regulatory affairs manager*

Yellow Springs
Schulsinger, Michael Alan *data processing executive*

OKLAHOMA

Altus
Wilcoxen, Joan Heeren *fitness company executive*

Broken Arrow
Miller, Robert Elmer *management consultant*

Edmond
Keckel, Peter J. *advertising executive*

Miami
Dicharry, James Paul *company official, retired air force officer*

Mustang
Laurent, J(erry) Suzanna *technical communications specialist*

Oklahoma City
Ackerman, Raymond Basil *advertising agency executive*
Adams, Warren Lynn *publisher, business consultant*
Bailey, Clark Trammell, II *public relations/public affairs professional*
Crow, Charles Delmar *human resources manager, consultant*
Grupe, Robert Charles *corporate training consultant*
Hulseberg, Paul David *financial executive, educator*
LaMotte, Janet Allison *retired management specialist*
Mildren, Jack *oil/gas company executive, former state official*

Perkins
Sasser, William David *advertising company executive*

Tahlequah
Hare, Jerry Wayne *communications executive*

Tulsa
†Bartmann, Kathryn *collections management executive*
Boyle, Lester Joseph *marketing and broadcast executive*
Davis, Lourie Irene Bell *computer education and information systems specialist*
Gentry, Bern Leon, Sr. *minority consulting company executive*
†Jensen, Joli *communicatons educator*
Stephens, C. Michael *service executive*
Wagner, Ann Louise *management consultant, public relations executive*

OREGON

Astoria
Holcom, Floyd Everett *international business consultant*

Baker City
Graham, Beardsley *management consultant*

Beavercreek
Filener, Millard Lee *wholesale and retail distribution company executive*

Beaverton
Murray, Jean Rupp *communications executive, author, speaker*
Stewart, Kirk T. *public relations executive*
†Wilskey, Mike *marketing professional*

Bend
Wonser, Michael Dean *retired public affairs director*

Canby
Flinn, Roberta Jeanne *management, computer applications consultant*

Eugene
Bennett, Robert Royce *engineering and management consultant*
Chambers, Carolyn Silva *communications company executive*
Miner, John Burnham *industrial relations educator, writer*
Peterson, Donna Rae *marketing professional*

Forest Grove
Carson, William Morris *manpower planning and development advisor*

Hubbard
Hick, Kenneth William *business executive*

Lake Oswego
†Waggener, Melissa *public relations executive*

Mcminnville
Naylor-Jackson, Jerry *public relations consultant, retired, entertainer, broadcaster*

Medford
Hennion, Reeve Lawrence *communications executive*
Keener, John Wesley *management consultant*

Newberg
†Austin, Joan D. *personal care industry executive*

Otis
Haralson, Linda Jane *communications executive*

Pendleton
Bedford, Amy Aldrich *public relations executive, corporation secretary*

Portland
Anderegg, Karen Klok *management and marketing consultant*
Bosch, Samuel Henry *computer company executive*
Boyle, Gertrude *sportswear company executive*
Boynton, Robert Granville *computer systems analyst*
Butler, Leslie Ann *advertising agency owner, artist, writer, editor*
Conkling, Roger Linton *consultant, business administration educator, retired utility executive*
Day, L. B. *management consultant*
Griggs, Gail *marketing executive*
†Hemstreet, Mark S. *hotel executive*
†Lee, Susan E. *public affairs coordinator*
Linstone, Harold Adrian *management and systems science educator*
Maclean, Charles (Bernard Maclean) *philanthropy researcher, consultant, coach*
Robbins, Jeanette Lee *sales and manufacturing executive*
Rotzien, Frederick William, III *marketing executive*
Rusunen, Robert Lee *purchasing manager*
Skiens, William Eugene *electrical interconnect systems scientist, polymer engineer*
Suwyn, Mark A. *building products executive*
Thenell, Janice Catherine *public relations director, educator*
Urbanowski, John Richard *lighting systems company official*
VanSickle, Sharon Dee *public relations executive*
Wieden, Dan G. *advertising executive*

Roseburg
Plunkett, Marvin Wayne *data processing company executive*

Salem
Baker, Edwin Stuart *retired computer consultant*
Garcia, Michael Ralph *funeral director*
Milbrath, Mary Merrill Lemke *quality assurance professional*

Tualatin
Peters, Robert Wayne *direct mail and catalog sales specialist*

West Linn
Parrick, Gerald Hathaway *communications and marketing executive*

Wilsonville
Neun, Carl *communications executive*

Yachats
Korgan, Michelle Lee *restaurateur*

PENNSYLVANIA

Allentown
Ehrlich, Geraldine Elizabeth *management consultant*

Altoona
Johnopolos, Stephen Gary *commission representative*

Ambler
Learnard, William Ewing *marketing executive*

Ambridge
Diakiwsky, Nicholas Metro *account executive*

Ardmore
Lockett-Egan, Marian Workman *advertising executive*
Luther, Judy *management consultant*

Baden
†Stuban, Michael L. *management professional*

Bala Cynwyd
Albertini, Stephen Anthony *public relations and advertising executive*
DuBois, Ruth Harberg *human service agency executive*
Frankel, Andrew Joel *management consultant*

Berwyn
Greene, Ronald D. *advertising executive*
Guenther, George Carpenter *travel company executive, retired*
Mauch, Robert Carl *service industry executive, venture capitalist*

Bethel Park
Willard, John Gerard *consultant, author, lecturer*

Bethlehem
Felix, Patricia Jean *steel company purchasing professional*
Penny, Roger Pratt *management executive*

Blue Bell
Faden, Lee Jeffrey *technical advisory service executive*
Miniutti, John Roberts *software services executive*
Nichols, James Lee *advertising executive*

Brentwood
Swanson, Fred A. *retired communications designer, former councilman*

Broomall
Czuj, Chester Francis, Jr. *food service professional*

Bryn Mawr
Kraftson, Raymond Harry *business executive*

Buckingham
Altier, William John *management consultant*

Butler
†Meals, Cynthia *management analyst*

Camp Hill
Crist, Christine Myers *consulting executive*

Carlisle
†Rhoads, Philip R., Sr. *safety director*

Chadds Ford
Reddish, John Joseph *management consulting company executive*
Sanford, Richard D. *computer company executive*

Chambersburg
Neilson, Winthrop Cunningham, III *communications executive, financial communications consultant*

Conestoga
Gochnauer, Elisa Anne *marketing executive*

Delmont
Thompson, Paul A. *business consultant, performance improvement expert*

East Earl
Kass, Howard R. *information systems consultant*

Emmaus
Caton, Timothy Charles *marketing professional*
Zahradnik, Fredric Douglas *marketing professional*

Erie
Lund, Edwin Harrison *business accounting systems executive*

Exton
Amichetti, Dennis Joseph *advertising executive*

Ferndale
Folk, James *sales executive*

Ford City
Ursiak, David Allen *operations executive, consultant*

Fort Washington
Blumberg, Donald Freed *management consultant*
Cassel, Neil Jonathon *business owner*
Fulton, Cheryl Lynn *customer service administrator*

Frazer
Stirling, Douglas Bleecker, Jr. *human resources specialist*

Freeport
Chvala, Kathleen Ann *administrative assistant*

Gettysburg
Hallberg, Budd Jaye *management consulting firm executive*

Glenmoore
Walish, Geralyn Rose *business consultant, analyst*

Greensburg
Boyd, Robert Wright, III *lamp company executive*

Gwynedd Valley
O'Connell, Antoinette Kathleen *training executive, consultant, artist*

Harrisburg
Edwards, JoAnn Louise *human resources executive*
†Granzow, Robert Frederick, III *security firm executive*
Pressler, Philip Bernard *advertising executive, educator*
Wolfe, Steven Scott *technical recruiter*
†Yenchko, Suzanne *government relations executive*

Hatfield
Fetterman, Alan Roy *equipment sales executive*

Hummelstown
Smedley, Elizabeth *researcher, codifier, consultant, historian, writer*

Huntingdon Valley
Vollum, Robert Boone *management consultant*

Jamison
Thorne, John Watson, III *advertising and marketing executive*

Kennett Square
Hennes, Robert Taft *former management consultant, investment executive*

Kersey
Shobert, Erle Irwin, II *management consultant*

King Of Prussia
Clauson, Sharyn Ferne *consulting company executive, educator*
Rhoads, Michael Dennis *sales executive*

Lafayette Hill
Green, Raymond Ferguson St. John *marketing and advertising executive*

Lancaster
Dunlap, Hallowell *data processing executive*
Kelly, Robert Lynn *advertising agency executive*
Veitch, Boyer Lewis *printing company executive*

Lansdale
Campman, Christopher Kuller *consulting company executive*

Lemoyne
Powell, Fredrick Charles *business executive*

Lewisburg
Rote, Nelle Fairchild Hefty *business consultant*

Lock Haven
†Little, Robert Owens *administration and technology executive*

Lower Burrell
Kinosz, Donald Lee *quality consultant*

Macungie
Nikischer, Frank William, Sr. *retired restaurant owner and operator*

Media
Garvin, Florence Ward *management consultant*

Merion Station
Mayer, Charles Arthur *management consultant, musician*

Middletown
Dhir, Krishna Swaroop *business administration educator*
Yucelt, Ugur *marketing professional, educator*

Millersville
†Renfroe, Aubrey Vance *company executive*

Monroeville
Valentine, Ruthann Loretta *counseling company executive*

Morrisville
Robinson, Lorna Jane *marketing executive*

Newtown Square
Pacini, Renee Annette *consulting company executive*
Tomlinson, Charles Wesley, Jr. *advertising executive*

Norristown
Breckenridge, Betty Gayle *management development consultant*

North Andover
†Walker, Lawrence Gordon *technology company executive*

Nottingham
White, Richard Edmund *marketing executive*

Orwigsburg
Bemiller, C. Richard, II *consultant*

Philadelphia
Anderson, Barbara Graham *philanthropic resources development consultant*
Barnett, Samuel Treutlen *international company executive*
Barrett, James Edward, Jr. *management consultant*
Barrett, Thomas Leon Francis *information technology software executive*
Blades, Herbert William *diversified consumer products company executive*
Bodner, Susan R. *marketing and communications executive*
Boyd, Larry Chester *recruitment manager*
Cabot, Diana Marie *marketing professional, travel and transportation executive*
†Clark, Paul J. *management consultant*
Coulson, Zoe Elizabeth *retired consumer marketing executive*
Dickerson, Rita M. *human resources professional*
Estrin, Deborah Perry *human resources executive*
Feninger, Claude *industry management services company executive*
Finney, Graham Stanley *management consultant*
Fuller, John Garsed Campbell *food and drug company executive*
Gilbert, Harry Ephraim, Jr. *hotel executive*
Jordan, Clifford Henry *management consultant*
Kaser, Richard Todd *communications executive*
Mangol, Leona Alvina *public broadcasting administrator*
Neubauer, Joseph *food services company executive*
Oliva, Terence Anthony *marketing educator*
Roberts, Brian Leon *communications executive*
Roberts, Ralph Joel *telecommunications, cable broadcast executive*
Salometo, Peter James Morgan *marketing consultant, lawyer*
Soslow, Arnold *quality consultant*
Tierney, Brian Patrick *advertising and public relations executive*
Waite, Helen Eleanor *funeral director*
Walker, Allen Lyon *logistics analyst*

Whelan, Daniel J. *communications company executive*
Wiksten, Barry Frank *communications executive*
Wilder, Robert George *advertising and public relations executive*
Williams, Robert Benjamin *convention center executive*
Wright, Yvette V. *termination contracting officer*
Yaffe, Peter Marc *public policy executive*

Phoenixville
Brundage, Russell Archibald *retired data processing executive*
Gillie, Michelle Francoise *industrial hygienist*

Pittsburgh
Arbutina, Petra *advertising executive*
Bartlett, Byron Robert *consumer products company marketing executive*
Bender, Charles Christian *retail home center executive*
†Bolster, Ronald Hugh *company executive*
Bonner, Shirley Harrold *business communications educator*
Boyd, William, Jr. *business advisor, banker*
Burger, Herbert Francis *advertising agency executive*
Dempsey, Jerry Edward *retired service company executive*
Dieter, Richard Charles *marketing and management professional*
Espy, Siri Norine *marketing professional*
Fine, Milton *hotel company executive, lawyer*
Fisher, James Aiken *industrial marketing executive*
Genge, William Harrison *advertising executive, writer*
Hershey, Colin Harry *management consultant*
Humphrey, Watts Sherman *technical executive, author*
†Kilkeary, Kevin P. *hospitality executive*
Marts, Terri Louise *management executive*
Mason, Craig Watson *corporate planning executive*
Meyers, Gerald Carl *educator, author, expert witness, consultant*
Miner, Mark Alan *public relations professional*
Neel, John Dodd *memorial park executive*
Patten, Charles Anthony *management consultant, retired manufacturing company executive, author*
Paugh, Patricia Lou *business consultant*
†Paul, John *company executive*
Reich, Deborah Ziskind *public relations and legal marketing executive*
Reichblum, Audrey Rosenthal *public relations executive*
Richards, Aleta Williams *marketing and quality professional*
†Richardson, J. William *hotel executive*
Ruddock, Ellen Sylves *business consultant*
Shane, Charles William *communication company executive, marketing consultant*
Sheehan, Robert James, II *management and market research consultant*
Simmermon, James Everett *credit bureau executive*
Siporin, David *human resources specialist*
Victor, Ronald Joseph, Jr. *banking professional*
Wink, John Joseph *project manager*

Plymouth Meeting
Siegal, Jacob J. *management and financial consultant*
Thomsen, Thomas Richard *retired communications company executive*

Port Royal
Wert, Jonathan Maxwell, II *management consultant*

Radnor
Harrison, Robert Drew *management consultant*
Paier, Adolf Arthur *computer software and services company executive*

Reading
Dersh, Rhoda E. *management consultant, business executive*
Hackenberg, Barbara Jean Collar *retired advertising and public relations executive*
Kraras, Gust C. *hotel executive*
Lysakowski, Linda Suzanne *fund raising consulting company executive*

Ridley Park
Walls, William Walton, Jr. *management consultant*

Saint Davids
McCarthy, Justin Milton *marketing professional*

Scranton
†Wiese, Marjorie Ann *administrative assistant*
Williams, Holly Thomas *business executive*

Sellersville
Fluck, J. Stephen *disability issues information specialist, writer, educator, poet*

Shippensburg
Stone, Susan Ridgaway *marketing educator*

Solebury
Gart, Herbert Steven *communications executive, producer*

Southeastern
Hawley, Linda Donovan *advertising executive*

State College
†Shaner, Frederick J. *hotel company executive*
†Shaner, Lance T. *hotel executive*

Sunbury
Weis, Robert Freeman *supermarket company executive*

Swarthmore
Kaufman, John Robert *marketing and information management consultant*
Krattenmaker, Thomas John *public relations executive*

Tannersville
Moore, James Alfred *ski company executive, lawyer*

Temple
Stump, Richard Carl *environmental services administrator, consultant*

Unionville
De Marino, Donald Nicholson *international business executive, former federal agency administrator*

University Park
Gouran, Dennis Stephen *communications educator*
†Jackson, Ronald Lee, II *communications educator*

Upper Saint Clair
Anderson, Catherine M. *consulting company executive*

Valley Forge
Boreen, Henry Isaac *computer company executive*
LaBoon, Lawrence Joseph *personnel consultant*
Rassbach, Herbert David *marketing executive*

Warrendale
Buckley, Deborah Jeanne Morey *manager of process*
Cooper, Eric *multimedia executive*

Warrington
Shaw, Milton Herbert *conglomerate executive*

Washington
Grimm, Donald Lee *executive*

Waterford
Kelley, Betty Marie *office manager*

Wayne
Carroll, Robert W. *retired business executive*
†Higgs, Jon Scott *computer company executive, researcher*
Kopelman, Joshua Marc *information company executive*
†Manas, Gerald Bennett *systems consultant*
Murray, Pamela Alison *business executive*

West Chester
Briggs, Douglas D. *communications executive*
Dunlop, Edward Arthur *computer company executive*
Hanna, Colin Arthur *county official, management and computer consultant*
Hanson, Diane Charske *management consultant*
Murray, Lawrence *management consultant*

West Conshohocken
Mullen, Eileen Anne *human resources executive*

Willow Grove
Asplundh, Christopher B. *tree service company executive*
Emory, Thomas Mercer, Jr. *data communications equipment manufacturing executive*
Schiffman, Louis F. *management consultant*

Woolrich
Himes, Kenneth Alan *retired marketing executive*

Wynnewood
Belinger, Harry Robert *business executive, retired*
Squires, Bonnie Stein *fundraising consultant*

Wyomissing
Blessing, Scott Francis *marketing executive*
Williams-Wennell, Kathi *human resources consultant*

Yardley
Kubilus, Norbert John *information technology executive*
Minter, Philip Clayton *retired communications company executive*
Newsom, Carolyn Cardall *management consultant*

York
Hake, Theodore Lowell *auction house owner, writer*
Horn, Russell Eugene, Jr. *business executive*
Livingston, Pamela Anna *corporate image and marketing management consultant*
Roetenberg, Aaron David *retail implementation specialist*

RHODE ISLAND

Barrington
Mihaly, Eugene Bramer *corporate executive, consultant, writer, educator*

Block Island
Coxe, Weld *management consultant*

Bristol
Esty, David Cameron *marketing and communications executive*

East Greenwich
†Weiss, Alan *management consultant, author*

North Kingstown
Kullberg, Gary Walter *advertising agency executive*

Pawtucket
Baum, Herbert Merrill *toy company executive*
Davison, C. Hamilton *greeting card executive*
DeWerth, Gordon Henry *management consultant*
Hassenfeld, Alan Geoffrey *toy company executive*
O'Neill, John T. *toy company executive*
†Riches, Wendy *advertising executive*

Providence
Andrews, Sue E. *park director*
Baar, James A. *public relations and corporate communications executive, author, consultant, internet publisher, software developer*
†Gilbane, William James *construction executive*
Grasso, James Anthony *public relations executive, educator*
Roussel, Normand Lucien *advertising executive*

Rumford
Sullivan, Stephanie *information services professional*

Smithfield
Fischman, Burton Lloyd *communications educator, management consultant*

Wakefield
Doody, Agnes G. *communications educator, management and communication consultant*

Warwick
Groh, Susan Laurel *public relations consultant*
Pagliarini, John Raymond *public affairs executive*
Patchis, Pauline *handwriting expert, consultant*

SOUTH CAROLINA

Aiken
Perdunn, Richard Francis *management consultant*

Beaufort
Day, John Sidney *management sciences educator*

Camden
Davis, Paul Michael *sales executive, transportation company executive*

Charleston
De Wolff, Louis *management consultant*
Dowell, Richard Patrick *technology company executive*

Clemson
†Nicholas, Davis M. *history educator*

Columbia
Ferillo, Charles Traynor, Jr. *public relations executive*
Fischer, Robert Andrew *computer executive*
Goble, Robert Thomas *planning consultant*
Grimball, Caroline Gordon *sales professional*
Krantz, Palmer E., III *parks and recreation director*
Quinn, Michael William *public affairs educator*

Greenville
Becker, Cheri A(nn) *marketing professional, business consultant*
†Cundiff, Kathleen Jean *business executive*
†Dorsey, Benjamin William *engineering/construction company executive*
Fitzgerald, Eugene Francis *management consultant*
Gerretsen, Gilbert Wynand (Gil Gerretsen) *marketing consultant, coach*
Townes, Bobby Joe *travel agency executive*

Hilton Head Island
Coble, Paul Ishler *advertising agency executive*
Haley, Cain Calmes *computer consultant*
†Hill, Courtney King *marketing professional*
Little, Thomas Mayer *public relations executive*
Martin, Donald James *marketing professional*
McDowell, Theodore Noyes *public relations consultant*
McKeldin, William Evans *management consultant*
Patton, Joseph Donald, Jr. *management consultant*
Thompson, David Charles, Sr. *retired management executive*
†Wolf, Dona *management consultant*

Lake Wylie
Buggie, Frederick Denman *management consultant*

Laurens
Williams-Tims, Lillie Althea *distribution administrator, genealogist*

Mauldin
Frank, Myra Linden *consultant*

Mount Pleasant
Cantwell, John Dalzell, Jr. *management consultant*
Hill, Larkin Payne *real estate company data processing executive*

Prosperity
†Jennings, Wirt Holman, Jr. *retired marketing executive*

Ridgeland
Gardner, James *recreational management executive, personal care industry executive*

Rock Hill
Click, John William *communication educator*

Spartanburg
Adamson, James B. *business executive*
Dillard, Richard *director of public affairs*
King, David Steven *quality control executive*
Lambert, Kurt *marketing executive*

SOUTH DAKOTA

Lennox
Courey, Fred Samuel *management consultant, former mayor*

Rapid City
Johnson, William Jennings *marketing consultant, entrepreneur, estate planner*

Sioux Falls
Weeks, M. J. *international management consultant*

TENNESSEE

Antioch
Morris, Jeannine Eddings *administrative assistant*

Brentwood
Cline, Judy Butler *human resources executive*
Power, Elizabeth Henry *consultant*

Camden
Brown, John Robert *computer company executive*

Chattanooga
De Riemer, Daniel Louis *leasing company executive*
Knight, Ralph H. *consumer products company executive*

Tosteson, Heather *communications specialist, writer*

Cleveland
†Rhodes, Arthur Delano *benefits administrator*

Collierville
Bentley, Sheila Carver *communication consultant, education educator*
Ludwig, Charles T. *technical company executive*

Cordova
Hamilton, David John *business systems/technology manager*
McKinney, William Douthitt, Jr. *sales and engineering company executive*

Cowan
Yates, Patricia England *human resources company executive*

Crossville
Roe, Michael Henry *computer specialist, business manager*

Dickson
Auchterlonie, David Thomas *quality assurance professional*

Dyersburg
Scearce, Janna Luebkemann *sales professional*

Franklin
Dorland, John Howard *international management consultant*

Gallatin
Bradley, Nolen Eugene, Jr. *personnel executive, educator*
Ellis, Joseph Newlin *retired distribution company executive*

Gatlinburg
Flanagan, Judy *marketing specialist, entertainment manager, university official*

Germantown
†Koerber, Robert Conrad *company executive*

Hendersonville
Ambrose, Charles Stuart *sales executive*
†Buttolph, John *company executive*

Knoxville
Cox, Anna Lee *retired administrative assistant*
Haslam, James A., III *petroleum sales executive*
Herndon, Anne Harkness *sales executive*
Mayfield, T. Brient, IV *media and computer executive*
Sansom, William E. *consumer products executive*
Siler, Susan Reeder *communications educator*
Vaughan, Gary David *governmental and public relations executive*

Lebanon
Davis, Julie Kramer *communications executive*

Maryville
Davis, William Walter *recruiter, trainer*

Memphis
Abston, Dunbar, Jr. *management executive*
†Blake, Norman *hotel executive*
Edwards, Doris Porter *computer specialist*
Ellis, Stephen Walker *corporate executive*
Krieger, Robert Lee, Jr. *human resource/management consultant, educator, writer, travel/meeting planner, political analyst*
†Lovelace, J. William *hotel executive*
Mann, Donald Cameron *marketing company executive*
Romanoff, Stanley M., Jr. *human resource specialist*
†Satre, Philip Glen *casino entertainment executive, lawyer*
†Solmson, Robert M. *hotel executive*
Sullivan, Eugene Joseph *food service company executive*

Mount Juliet
Varallo, Deborah Garr *marketing executive*

Murfreesboro
Mitchell, Jerry Calvin *environmental company executive*

Nashville
Baines, Gwendolyn L. *university office manager*
Brown, Tony Ersic *record company executive*
Cawthon, William Connell *operations management consultant*
Dobbs, George Albert *funeral director, embalmer*
†Dye, Henry C. *public relations firm executive*
Faust, A. Donovan *communications executive*
Ingram, Martha Rivers *company executive*
James, Kay Louise *management consultant, healthcare executive*
Lawrence, Thomas Patterson *public relations executive*
Meredith, Owen Nichols *public relations executive, genealogist*
Moore, William Grover, Jr. *management consultant, former air freight executive, former air force officer*
Murray, Richard Keith *marketing executive*
†Pitts, J. Kenneth *information systems specialist*
Reuther, Rosann White *advertising agency executive*
Stockell, Albert W., III *information systems analyst, accountant*
†Van Mol, Louis John *public relations firm executive*
Van Mol, Louis John, Jr. *public relations executive*
†Waters, Raymond *hotel executive*

Oak Ridge
Arnold, Jamie K. *program management, safety and health, and training professional*
Fricke, Martin Paul *science company executive*

Old Hickory
Brett, John Brendan, Jr. *corporate advertising and public relations executive*

Pulaski
Baker, Kerry Allen *management consultant*

Puryear
Stephenson, Jerry Coleman *mail carrier*

Shelbyville
Nelson, Clara Singleton *human resources consultant*

Soddy Daisy
Dall, Peter Andrew *management and organizational consultant*

Toone
Slaughter, Phillip Howard *computer company executive*

Tullahoma
Gossick, Lee Van *consultant, executive, retired air force officer*

TEXAS

Addison
Grote, Richard Charles *management consultant, educator, radio commentator*
Kline, J. Peter *hotel executive*

Amarillo
Borchardt, Paul Douglas *recreational executive*
Dunn, Jim Edward *sales executive*
Peck, Kay Chandler *resource development consultant*
Stubben, Dolus Jane (D. J. Stubben) *advertising executive*

Argyle
Merritt, Joe Frank *industrial supply executive*

Arlington
English, Marlene Cabral *management consultant*
Hammond, Karen Smith *marketing professional, paralegal*
Harris, Vera Evelyn *personnel recruiting and search firm executive*
Henderson, Arvis Burl *data processing executive, biochemist*
Lombard, Mitchell Monte *marketing professional*
Sawyer, Dolores *motel chain executive*
Spears, Georgann Wimbish *marketing executive*
Wiig, Karl Martin *knowledge management expert and consultant*

Austin
Baysinger, Stephen Michael *quality assurance professional*
Belle-Isle, David Richard *organization and management consultant*
Blankenbeker, Joan Winifred *communications, computer, and information management executive*
†Canter, Jamie A. *web designer, marketing consultant*
Casey, James Francis *management consultant*
Chavarria, Ernest Montes, Jr. *international trade, business and finance consultant, lecturer*
Craig, James Norman *marketing executive, Internet consultant*
Curle, Robin Lea *computer software industry executive*
Dabbs Riley, Jeanne Kernodle *retired public relations executive*
†Gazzaway, Kenneth M. *information systems consultant, educator*
Gurasich, Stephen William, Jr. *advertising executive*
Hammer, Katherine Gonet *software company executive*
Hart, Roderick P. *communications educator, researcher, author*
Jorgeson, Brent Wilson *management executive*
Kam, Mitchell M.T. *international career specialist*
Knapp, Mark Lane *communications educator, consultant*
Lundgren, Clara Eloise *public affairs administrator, journalist*
Maguire, Kevin *travel management consultant*
Martinez, Ernesto, III *sales professional*
Moore, Rebecca Ann Rucker *marketing executive*
Onstead, Randall *consumer goods company executive*
Payne, John Ross *rare books and archives appraisal consulting company executive, library science educator*
†Peters, Gregory A. *technology company executive*
Rector, Clark Ellsworth *advertising executive*
†Roe, Emily Matthews *recruiting coordinator*
Shipley, George Corless *political consultant*
Smith, Barry Alan *hotel executive*
Spence, Roy *advertising executive*
Sturdevant, Wayne Alan *computer executive*
Trabulsi, Judy *advertising and marketing executive*
Vande Hey, James Michael *corporate executive, former air force officer*
Vandel, Diana Geis *performance consultant*
Walls, Carl Edward, Jr. *communications company official*
Winegar, Albert Lee *computer systems company executive*
†Woods, Charles Thomas *public service executive*

Bedford
Champney, Raymond Joseph *advertising and marketing executive, consultant*
Rosene, Linda Roberts *organizational consultant, researcher*
Rosene, Ralph Walfred *consulting company executive*

Blanco
Holmes, Darrell *travel consultant*

Bryan
Pearce, Stephen Lamar *management consultant*

Buda
Levinson, Joseph *computer company executive, marketing and sales consultant*

Burleson
Prior, Boyd Thelman *management consultant*

Carrollton
Goodman, Thomas Blackburn, III *regional processor specialist*
Plummer, Paul James *software company executive*
Primas, Vinson Bernardi *management consultant*

Cedar Hill
Garrett, C. Lynn *researcher, business consultant*

Cleveland
Rice, J. Andrew *management consultant, tree farmer*

College Station
Gunn, Clare Alward *travel consultant, writer, retired educator*

Colleyville
Compo, Lawrence Judd *sales and marketing executive*
Thompson, James Richard *human resources management consultant*

Coppell
Owen, Cynthia Carol *sales executive*

Corpus Christi
Benn, Douglas Frank *information technology and computer science executive*
Muniz, Eva Vera *English educator*

Dallas
Alvey, David Lynn *advertising executive, artist, curator, poet*
Arnold, George Lawrence *retired advertising company executive*
†Azcarraga, Gaston *hotel executive*
Bartlett, Richard Chalkley *business executive, writer, conservationist*
Bearden, Fred B(urnette), Jr. *marketing executive*
Bennett, Verna Green *employee relations executive*
Bolton, Kevin Michael *human resources executive*
†Brown, Timothy Allen *executive search consulting company executive*
Buickerood, Richard W. *park and recreation director*
Carl, Robert E. *retired marketing company executive*
Cave, Skip *company executive*
Dao, Khanh Phuong Thi *automotive executive, sales professional*
Dedman, Robert Henry *sales executive*
Dillon, Donald Ward *management consultant*
Dodson, George Wayne *computer company executive, consultant*
Dozier, David Charles, Jr. *marketing public relations and advertising executive*
Durham, Michael Jonathan *information technology company executive*
Dykeman, Alice Marie *public relations executive*
Ellis, June B. *human resource consultant*
†Evans, William Will *hospitality executive*
Friedheim, Stephen Bailey *public relations executive*
Fullingim, John Powers *consulting firm executive*
Geddie, Tom *business communications consultant*
Gilder, Richard Earl *clinical information system administrator, data analyst*
Gossen, Emmett Joseph, Jr. *motel chain executive, lawyer*
Harkness, R. Kenneth *restaurant chain executive*
Heydrick, Linda Carol *consulting company executive, editor*
Horchow, S(amuel) Roger *marketing consultant*
†Jaksa, David M. *wireless network company official*
†Johnson, David W. (Dave) *hotel facility executive*
Jones, Rosemarie Frieda *service executive*
Keath, (Martin) Travis *business valuation consultant*
Korba, Robert W. *communications executive*
Lane, Alvin Huey, Jr. *management consultant*
†Langdale, Mark *hotel executive*
Leigh-Manuell, Robert Allen *training executive, educator*
Levenson, Stanley Richard *public relations and advertising executive*
Levinson, Mark Bradley *corporate professional*
†Lippe, George L. *company executive*
MacMahon, Paul *advertising executive*
†Mays, Edwin David *technical consulting company executive*
McCarthy, Michael Joseph *communications company executive*
†Meltzer, Larry Alan *public relations executive*
Miles, Ray *telecommunications executive, educator*
Mong, Robert William, Jr. *media executive*
Murphy, Randall Kent *training consultant*
Naor, Daniel *management consultant*
†Nussbaum, Paul A. *hospitality executive*
Osborn, Jacqueline Elizabeth *water treatment systems company executive*
Osen, Gregory Alan *water conditioning company executive*
Parmerlee, Mark S. *food service executive*
†Pearson, Robert Lawrence *executive recruiter*
†Price, Steve *advertising executive*
Pruzzo-Hawkins, Judith Josephine *office manager*
†Puente-Brancato, Gina I. *concession company executive*
Richards, Stanford Harvey *advertising agency executive, design studio executive*
Robertson, Jane Ryding *marketing executive*
Robinson, Hugh Granville *consulting management company executive*
†Romero, John *computer game company executive*
Routman, Daniel Glenn *business development executive, lawyer*
†Rubin, Warren Lloyd *retail sales executive*
Salerno, Philip Adams *information systems specialist*
Sheinberg, Israel *computer company executive*
Snead, Richard Thomas *restaurant company executive*
Spiegel, Lawrence Howard *advertising executive*
Staber, Dorothee Beatrice *administrative assistant*
†Stern, Andrew Milton *public relations executive*
†Thomas, Philip Robinson *management consulting company executive*
Treasure, Suzanne Marie *marketing and sales professional, writer, poet*
Vanderveld, John, Jr. *international business development specialist*
Waters, Rollie Odell *management consultant*
Weinberger, Blanche Raphael *public relations executive*
Werner, Seth Mitchell *advertising executive*
Wilber, Robert Edwin *corporate executive*
Wilde, Patrick Joseph *administrator*
†Williams, Sterling L. *computer software executive*
Wyly, Charles Joseph, Jr. *corporate executive*

De Soto
Aars, Rallin James *management, business development, marketing communications executive, consultant*

Del Rio
Prather, Gerald Luther *management consultant, retired air force officer, judge*

Dripping Springs
Ballard, Mary Melinda *financial communications and investment banking firm executive, consumer advocate*

Early
Cupp, Marilyn Marie *sales executive*

El Paso
Cassidy, Richard Thomas *hotel executive, defense industry consultant, retired army officer*
Deerman, Ruth Gillett *sales professional, flying instructor*
Roberts, Ernst Edward *marketing consultant*

Elgin
Cole, Aubrey Louis *management consultant, forest products company executive*

Euless
Self, Dianne Logan *communications company executive*
Self, Mark Edward *communications consultant*

Fair Oaks
Jack, Nancy Rayford *supplemental resource company executive, consultant*

Fort Worth
Appel, Bernard Sidney *marketing consultant, former electronic company executive*
Bonderman, David *company executive*
Bradshaw, James Edward (Jim) *consultant*
Brown, Janet McNalley *retirement plan consultant*
Jeffreys, Charles Wayne *advertising executive*
Johnson, J. Mitchell *communications executive*
Michalski, Jeanne Ann *human resources professional*
Poole, Anita Joyce *marketing and publishing company executive*
Ray, Paul Richard, Jr. *executive search consultant*
Shannon, Larry Redding *public relations professional*
Turner, Loyd Leonard *advertising executive, public relations executive*
Turner, R(alph) Chip *public relations and telecommunications executive, religious studies educator*
Webb, James Robert *strategic management consultant*

Galveston
May, Joy Elaine *recreational facility executive*

Garland
Sims, Judy *software company executive*

Grapevine
Holley, Cyrus Helmer *management consulting service executive*

Helotes
Kuba, John Albert *mortician*

Hemphill
Dutton, Frank Elroy *data processing executive*

Hico
Blankenship, Jenny Mary *public relations executive, publisher, editor-in-chief*

Highland Village
Richardson, K. Scott *sales executive*

Houston
Adams, C. Lee *marketing executive*
Arledge, David A. *business executive*
Baysal, Edip *executive*
Bazelides, Diane *public relations executive*
Blackburn, Sadie Gwin Allen *executive*
Bodner, Emanuel *industrial recycling company executive*
Combs, Janet Louise *sales and advertising company executive*
Crystal, Jonathan Andrew *executive recruiter*
Dewing, Henry Woods, Sr. *telecommunications executive*
Dobbs, Rita Marie *travel company executive*
†Eggen, Svein *company executive*
†Ehsani, Michael *quality assurance executive*
Engel, James Harry *computer company executive*
Ferguson, Arlen Gary *human resources specialist*
Flato, William Roeder, Jr. *software development company executive*
Gaucher, Donald Holman *public opinion research company executive*
Giddens, Paul Joseph *human resources executive*
Gilbert, Harold Stanley *warehousing company executive*
†Harrell, Michael V. *hospitality company executive*
†Harris, Courteney Franchelle *program manager*
Hart, James Whitfield, Jr. *retired corporate public affairs executive, lawyer*
†Heiker, Vincent Edward *information systems executive*
Helland, George Archibald, Jr. *management consultant, manufacturing executive, former government official*
Herrington, James Benjamin, Jr. *job recruiting executive*
Holmes, Roscette Yvonne Lewis *organizational development and training consultant*
Hughes, William Joseph *management consultant*
Hutcheson, Thad Thomson, Jr. *international executive*
Ifft, Lewis George, III *company administrator*
Jeanneret, Paul Richard *management consultant*
Jenkins, Linda Faye *executive secretary*
†Jenkins, Margie Little *human relations specialist, psychotherapist*
Jones, Sonia Josephine *advertising agency executive*
Keller, Robert Bounds *marketing professional, consultant, inventor*
King, Carl Edward *employee screening executive*
Kors, R. Paul *search company executive*
Kramm, Deborah Ann *data processing executive*
Krueger, Artur W. G. *international business consultant*
Larkin, William Vincent, Jr. *service company executive*
Levit, Max *food service executive*
Marcus, Jerry *broadcasting executive*
Margotta, Maurice Howard, Jr. *management consultant*
Mauck, William M., Jr. *executive recruiter, small business owner*
McCollam, Marion Andrus *consulting firm executive, educator*
McKim, Paul Arthur *management consultant, retired petroleum executive*
Myers, James Clark *advertising and public relations executive*
Myers, Norman Allan *marketing professional*
O'Brient, David Warren *sales executive, consultant*
Onstead, Robert R. *consumer goods company executive*
Palmer, James Edward *public relations executive*
Phillippi, Elmer Joseph, Jr. *data communications consultant*
Ranck, Bruce E. *waste management executive*
Ribble, Anne Hoerner *communications executive*
Riley, Harold John, Jr. *business executive*
Saunders, William Arthur *management consultant*
Sill, Gerald de Schrenck *hotel executive*
Slack, Karen Kershner *advertising agency executive*
Solymosy, Edmond Sigmond Albert *international marketing executive, retired army officer*
Sperber, Matthew Arnold *direct marketing company executive*
Tatarinov, Kirill *computer software company executive*
Tilney, Elizabeth A. *marketing executive*
Untermeyer, Charles Graves (Chase) *computer company executive*
Watson, Max P., Jr. *computer software company executive*
Welch, Byron Eugene *communications educator*
Welch, Kathy Jane *information technology executive*
†Wise, Linda *marketing executive, consultant*
Woods, Stephanie Elise *computer professional*
Yuen, Benson Bolden *airline management consultant, software executive*

Humble
†Gruman, Robert Richard *energy management consultant*
Hahne, C. E. (Gene Hahne) *computer services executive*

Huntsville
Jenkin, Douglas Alan *computer consultant*
Smyth, Joseph Philip *travel industry executive*
Stowe, Charles Robinson Beecher *management consultant, educator, lawyer*

Hurst
Bishara, Amin Tawadros *management and consulting firm executive, technical services executive*
Buford, Evelyn Claudene Shilling *jewelry specialist, merchandising professional*

Irving
Anderson, Greg R. *communications company executive*
Appel, John C. *communications company executive*
†Caldwell, James D. *hospitality company executive*
Corcoran, Thomas Joseph *hotel executive*
Dinicola, Robert *consumer products company executive*
Gibson, Colvin Donald *human resources specialist*
†Gilbert, Glen Stuart *marketing executive*
Gretzinger, Ralph Edwin, III *management consultant*
Jorns, Steven D. *hotel executive*
Lifson, Kalman Alan *management consultant, retail executive*
Masterton, Craig William *management consultant*
McClain, Dennis Douglas *advertising executive*
Nugent, John Hilliard *communications executive*
†Rowling, Robert B. *hotel executive*
Savage, Richard Mark *quality manager*
†Sidu, Sanjiv *computer software executive*
Siefkin, William Charles *investor, Internet sales executive, consultant*
White, Thomas W. *telecommunications company executive*
Wicks, William Withington *retired public relations executive*

Joshua
Hoggard, William Zack, Jr. *amusement park executive*

Junction
Evans, Jo Burt *communications executive*

Kilgore
Garvin, Wilford L. *sales and marketing manager*

Kingwood
Hawk, Phillip Michael *service corporation executive*
†Wigglesworth, David Cunningham *business and management consultant*

Laredo
Lakshmana, Viswanath *computer and information systems executive*

Lewisville
Mebane, Barbara Margot *service company executive, studio owner*
Tucker, Phyllis Anita *sales representative, guidance counselor*

Lubbock
†Davis, Alvin G. *company executive*
Fontenot, Andrea Dean *communications executive*
†Martinez-Flores, Sylvia Alicia *management consultant*
Miller, Stephen Laurence *responsive services executive*

Midland
Roberts, David Glen *regional marketing director, investor*
Roomberg, Susan Kelly *management consultant*

Montgomery
Snider, Robert Larry *management consultant*

Pasadena
McClay, Harvey Curtis *data processing executive*

Plainview
Ticer, Terri Jean *sales executive*

Plano
Collumb, Peter John *communications company executive*
Dougherty, F(rancis) Kelly *data processing executive*
Duff-Bloom, Gale *marketing executive*
Grogan, Timothy James *information technology executive*
Hahn, Cathy Ann Clifford *sales executive*
James, Michael Thames *information technology executive, consultant*
Kriegler, Arnold Matthew *management consultant*
Perry, Randall A. *business executive*
Scott, Terry Lee *communications company executive*

Port Aransas
Peters, Jean Theresa *sales executive*

Quinlan
Gross, Paul Allan *health service executive*

Richardson
Anderson, John Kerby *writer, radio talk show host*
Chlamtac, Imrich *computer company executive, educator*
Fahrlander, Henry William, Jr. *management consultant*
Madden, Marie Frances *marketing professional*
O'Shea, Karen *public relations executive*
Yang, Yueh Sam *electronics company executive*

Round Rock
Morrison, Scott David *computer company executive*
Pearson, Jim Berry, Jr. *human resources specialist*

San Angelo
Baker, Samuel Garrard *advertising agency executive*
Coe, Robert Stanford *retired management educator*

San Antonio
†Brown, Thomas Edward *information systems executive*
Bruff, Beverly Olive *public relations consultant*
Butt, Charles Clarence *food service executive*
†Carr, Cassandra Colvin *communications company executive*
Cory, William Eugene *retired consulting company executive*
Davis, Walter Barry *quality assurance professional*
Ellis, James D. *communications executive, corporate lawyer*
Fasano, Anthony John *marketing consultant*
Ferrin, Marshall Sims *telecommunications executive*
Foster, Charles F. *communications executive*
Franklin, Larry Daniel *communications company executive*
Garcia, Henry Frank *finance and administration executive*
Hargrave, Robert Warren *hair styling salon chain executive*
Harte, Houston Harriman *marketing executive*
Kehl, Randall Herman *executive, consultant, lawyer*
Labenz-Hough, Marlene *dispute resolution professional*
Mills, Linda S. *public relations executive*
Montemayor, Carlos Rene *advertising executive*
Orr, Joseph Newton *recreational guide, outdoor educator*
Schonhoff, Robert Lee *marketing and advertising executive*
Schultz, Steven T. *hotel executive*
Shirley, Graham Edward *management executive*
Simpson, Andrea Lynn *energy communications executive*
Ullmer, (R.) John *computer company executive, retired educator*
Weatherston, George Douglas, Jr. *food service executive*
Whitesell, Stephen Ernest *parks and recreation director*
Wickstrom, Jon Alan *telecommunications executive, consultant*
Wilson, Bennie James, III *human resource executive, educator*
Wimpress, Gordon Duncan, Jr. *corporate consultant, foundation executive*

San Marcos
Moore, Patsy Sites *food service consultant*
Taylor, Ruth Arleen Lesher *marketing educator*

Sherman
†Evans, Sarah Nell *information technology administrator*

Southlake
Alford, Stephen Clark *communications executive, multi image programmer*
Sorge, Karen Lee *commercial printing company executive, consultant*

Spring
Cooley, Andrew Lyman *corporation executive, former army officer*
Maxfield, Mary Constance *management consultant*

Sugar Land
Preng, David Edward *management consultant*

Temple
Cone, Thomas Conrad *communications executive*
Mathis, Marsha Debra *software company executive*
Odem, Joyce Marie *human resources specialist*

The Woodlands
Jones, Susan Chafin *management consultant*

Trophy Club
Caffee, Virginia Maureen *executive administrative associate*
Haerer, Deane Norman *marketing and public relations executive*

Tyler
Resnik, Linda Ilene *marketing and information executive, consultant*

Victoria
Logan, Mary Calkin *development and public relations consultant*

Weatherford
McMahon, Robert Lee, Jr. (Bob McMahon) *information systems executive*

UTAH

Boulder
Davis, Larry *park director*

Heber City
McLean, Hugh Angus *management consultant*

Logan
Burke, Lee Hall *administrative assistant*
Drozdeck, Steven Richard *management consultant*

Midvale
Kitto, Franklin Curtis *computer systems specialist*

Ogden
†Ogden, Melvin J. *retire purchaser*

Orem
Morey, Robert Hardy *communications executive*
Sawyer, Thomas Edgar *management consultant*
Schulz, Raymond Alexander *medical marketing professional, consultant*

Park City
Weight, Alec Charles *retired management consultant*

Provo
Bartlett, Leonard Lee *communications educator, retired advertising agency executive, advertising historian*
Herrera, Shirley Mae *personnel and security executive*
Soter, Nicholas Gregory *advertising agency executive*

Salt Lake City
Burkle, Ronald W. *food service executive*
Campbell, Stewart Clawson *retired sales executive, artist*
†Clinesmith, Frederick Clinton *business executive*
Corley, Jean Arnette Leister *infosystems executive*
Elkins, Glen Ray *service company executive*
Hansen, Kent *public relations professional, consultant*
Howell, Kevin L. *hotel executive*
Jensen, Rodney H. *hotel executive*
Johnson, Jon L. *advertising executive*
Lund, Victor L. *retail food company executive*
Maher, David L. *drug store company executive*
Mills, Carol Margaret *business consultant, public relations consultant*
Nixon, Carol Holladay *park and recreation director*
Steiner, Richard Russell *company executive*

Sandy
Skidmore, Joyce Thorum *public relations and communication executive*

West Valley City
Mickelson, Elliot Spencer *quality assurance professional*

VERMONT

Alburg
Schallert, Patrick James *bed and breakfast owner, importer*

Burlington
Heffernan, Patricia Conner *management consultant*

East Burke
Burnham, Patricia White *consultant advocate, writer on aging, business executive, author*

East Montpelier
Christiansen, Andrew P. *Internet consulting business executive*

Essex Junction
Sweetser, Gene Gillman *quality assurance professional, state legislator*

Montpelier
Fitzhugh, William Wyvill, Jr. *printing company executive*

Newfane
Farber, Lillian *retired photography equipment company executive*

Rutland
Ferraro, Betty Ann *corporate administrator, state senator*

South Royalton
Chang, David Ping-Chung *business consultant, architect*

Stowe
Fiddler, Barbara Dillow *sales and marketing professional*

Waitsfield
Parrish, Thomas Kirkpatrick, III *marketing consultant*

VIRGINIA

Abingdon
Ramos-Cano, Hazel Balatero *caterer, chef, innkeeper, entrepreneur*

Alexandria
Alloway, Robert Malcombe *computer consulting executive*
Amiri, Afsaneh *computer professional*
Ancell, Robert Manning *leadership organization executive*
Battocletti, Elizabeth Carmel *marketing executive*
Bernsen, Harold John *marketing executive, political affairs consultant, retired naval officer*
Borden, Enid A. *public relations executive*
Bozell, L. Brent, III *communications executive*
Burch, Michael Ira *public relations executive, former government official*
Bussler, Robert Bruce *management consultant*
Cooper, B. Jay *public relations executive*
Cooper, Roger Merlin *information technology executive, federal government official, school administrator*
Davis, Ruth Margaret (Mrs. Benjamin Franklin Lohr) *technology management executive*
Del Fosse, Claude Marie *aerospace software executive*
Devine, Donald J. *management and political consultant*
Harris, David Ford *management consultant, retired government official*
Hartsock, Linda Sue *educational and management association executive*
Hazard, Christopher Wedvik *international business executive*
†Heath, Ross Bradley *consulting company executive*
Laurent, Lawrence Bell *communications executive, former journalist*
†Lightner, Candace Lynne *management consultant*
Locigno, Paul Robert *public affairs executive*
Loving, William Rush, Jr. *public relations company executive, consultant*
McMillan, Charles William *consulting company executive*
McMiller, Anita Williams *entrepreneur, management consultant, public*
Nelson, David Leonard *process management systems company executive*
Simmons, Richard De Lacey *mass media executive*
†Starr, James Edward *logistics management executive*
Trent, Darrell M. *academic and corporate executive*
Widner, Ralph Randolph *civic executive*
Wilding, James Anthony *airport administrator*

Annandale
Greinke, Everett Donald *corporate executive, international programs consultant*
Jarvis, Elbert, II (Jay Jarvis) *employee benefits specialist*
Khim, Jay Wook *high technology systems integration executive*
Samuelson, Douglas Alan *information systems company executive*

Arlington
Anderson, Steven Hunter *media relations professional*
Blankinship, Henry Massie *management consultant*
Bloomer, William Arthur *security industry executive*
Cocolis, Peter Konstantine *business development executive*
Erwin, Frank William *personnel research and publishing executive*
Freeman, Neal Blackwell *communications corporation executive*
Gianturco, Delio E. *management consultant*
Golden, James Leslie *information technology executive*
Gunderson, Steve Craig *consultant, former congressman*
Hill, Donna Marie *communications executive*
Ingrassia, Anthony Frank *human resource specialist*
Johnson, John A. *communications company executive*
Johnson, Rosemary Wrucke *personnel management specialist*
Kanter, L. Erick *public relations executive*
Kilduff, Bonnie Elizabeth *director of expositions*
Klosk, Russell Martin *human resources executive*
McFarland, Walter Gerard *management consultant*
McLeer, Laureen Dorothy *drug development, pharmaceutical professional*
Morris, John Woodland, II *businessman, former army officer*
Pan, Gary George *information technology executive, consultant*
Pensmith, Sharyn Elaine *communications executive*
Plevyak, Thomas Joseph *communications executive*
Riegel, Kurt Wetherhold *environmental protection executive*
Samburg, A. Gene *security company executive*
Shaker, William Haygood *marketing professional, public policy reformer*
†Woods, Willie E. *information specialist*
Zirkle, William Vernon *philanthropist*
Zorthian, Barry *communications executive*

Ashburn
Waetjen, Daniel G. *information technology executive*

Boones Mill
Sumpter, James Hardee, III *sales executive*

Centreville
Hanson, Lowell Knute *seminar developer and leader, information systems consultant*
James, Louis Meredith *personnel executive*

Charlottesville
Dunn, Mary Jarratt *public relations executive*
Friedman, Susan Lynn Bell *non-profit association executive*
Ruggieri, Elaine *public relations administrator*
Wolcott, John Winthrop, III *retired corporate executive*

Chesterfield
Hoffman, Mitchell Wade *corporate executive*

Dulles
Case, Stephen M. *business executive*
Leonsis, Ted *media executive*

Fairfax
Anderson, Maynard Carlyle *national and international security executive*
Baker, Daniel Richard *computer company executive, consultant*
Bluitt, Karen *software engineering director*
Brehm, William Keith *information systems company executive*
Gross, Patrick Walter *business executive, management consultant*
Hess, Milton Siegmund *computer company executive*
McCormick, Robert Junior *company executive, former government official*
†Merrick, Phillip *technology company executive*
Palmer, James Daniel *information technology educator*
Rosenburgh, Stephen Aruthur *executive*
Saverot, Pierre-Michel *nuclear waste management company executive*
Sullivan, Penelope Dietz *computer software development company executive*
Witek, James Eugene *retired public relations executive*

Falls Church
Bingman, Charles Franklin *public administration educator*
Bonzagni, Vincent Francis *lawyer, program administrator, analyst, researcher*
Boyd, Lynne Kaplan *software company executive*
Brown, Gerald Curtis *retired army officer, engineering executive*
Cain, David Lee *corporate executive*
Carney, Daniel L. *program and financial management consultant*
Cetron, Marvin Jerome *management executive*
Glass, Lawrence *business executive*
Hamor, Kathy Virginia *consultant*
Lindholm, Lori Ann *program manager, naval officer*
Miller, Mary Jeannette *office management specialist*
Nashman, Alvin Eli *computer company executive*
Orkand, Donald Saul *management consultant*

Farnham
Durham, James Michael, Sr. *marketing consultant*

Franklin
Atkinson, Sandra Miller *marketing educator*

Fredericksburg
Geary, Patrick Joseph *naval security administrator*
Hickman, Richard Lonnie *advertising executive*

Glen Allen
Lloyd, Christopher Donald *consultant*

Hampton
Bhuiyan, Mohammad Ali *university administrator, educator, consultant*
Drummond, James Everman *defense technology transfer consultant, former army officer*
Schauer, Catharine Guberman *public affairs specialist*

Hardy
Harriett, Rebecca *park director*

Haymarket
Douglas, Clarence James, Jr. *corporation executive, management consultant*

Herndon
Abbott, Gayle Elizabeth *human resources consultant*
Harris, Shelley Follansbee *proposal manager*
Schrader, William *communications company executive*
Stanton, Patricia Lynn Noboa *management and consulting executive*
Ulvila, Jacob Walter *management consultant*

Kilmarnock
Maxwell, W(ilbur) Richard *management consultant*
Smith, Raymond Francis *company executive*

Lexington
Dunlap, Kathleen Jane *public relations executive*

Lightfoot
Morris, Robert Louis *management consultant*

Lynchburg
Shircliff, James Vanderburgh *communications executive*

Manassas
Sutton, Robert K. *park administrator*

Mc Lean
Adler, Larry *marketing executive*
†Armistead, William Spencer *communications executive, political organization executive, political writer*
Bartlett, John Wesley *consulting firm executive*
Blanchard, Townsend Eugene *retired service companies executive*
Capone, Lucien, Jr. *management consultant, former naval officer*
Donahue, Timothy M. *communications executive*
Estren, Mark James *business and media consultant, TV producer, author*
Frostic, Frederick Lee *strategic planning and defense policy consultant*
Gallagher, Anne Porter *business executive*
Garnes, Ronald Vincent *marketing executive, finance broker, consultant*
Horowitz, Barry Martin *systems research and engineering company executive*
James, Daniel J. *management consultant*
Jennings, Jerry D. *communications company executive*
Lane-Maher, Maureen Dorothea *marketing educator, consultant*
McLennan, Barbara Nancy *management consultant*
McNichols, Gerald Robert *consulting company executive*
Miller, Christine Marie *marketing executive, public relations executive*
Newman, William Bernard, Jr. *telecommunications executive*
O'Brien, Morgan Edward *communications executive, lawyer*

Paschall, Lee McQuerter *retired communications consultant*
Smith, Esther Thomas *communications executive*
Somers, James Wilford *information management company executive*
Sowle, Donald Edgar *management consultant*
Steventon, Robert Wesley *marketing executive*
Tuttle, William G(ilbert) T(ownsend), Jr. *research executive*

Melfa
†Hickman, John Norwood *marketing executive*

Merrifield
Nelson, Ruth Naomi *marketing professional*

Midlothian
Doumlele, Ruth Hailey *communications company executive, broadcast accounting consultant*
Wadsworth, Robert David *advertising agency executive*

Moneta
Ulmer, Walter Francis, Jr. *consultant, former army officer*

Newington
Bowen, Harry Ernest *management consultant*

Newport News
Behlmar, Cindy Lee *business manager, consultant*
Fisher, Denise Butterfield *marketing executive*
Guastaferro, Angelo *company executive*
†Thomas, Lawsey Shyrone *safety and training administrator*

Norfolk
Bland, Gilbert Tyrone *foodservice executive*
Blount, Robert Haddock *corporate executive, retired naval officer*

Portsmouth
†Hoggard, Sharon Riddick *public relations executive*

Reston
Brooker, Susan Gay *employment consulting firm executive*
Easton, Glenn Hanson, Jr. *management and insurance consultant, federal official, naval officer*
Foster, William Anthony *management consultant, educator*
†Fusco, Barbara Leigh *communications executive, editor*
Gemma, Peter Benedict, Jr. *political, public relations and fund raising consultant*
†Johnson, Thea Jean *internet and intranet security service provider*
Lynch, Daniel C. *multimedia executive*
Mendelsohn, Stuart *management consultant, environmental engineer, lawyer*
Mowbray, Robert Norman *natural resource management consultant*
Salisbury, Alan Blanchard *information systems executive*
Schleede, Glenn Roy *energy market and policy consultant*

Richmond
Baar, Diane *advertising executive*
Hanzak, Gary A. John *credit and leasing executive*
Hoskie, Lorraine *consumer products representative, poet*
Hughes, Mike *advertising executive*
Kennedy, James Bruce *operations administrator*
King, Allen B. *company executive*
Laverge, Jan *tobacco company executive*
McKee, Paul Vincent *advertising agency executive*
Newbrand, Charles Michael *advertising firm executive*
Roop, Ralph Goodwin *retired oil marketing company executive*
Roper, Hartwell H. *tobacco company executive*
Thornhill, Barbara Cole *marketing executive*
Trott, Sabert Scott, II *marketing professional*
Tuszynski, Daniel J., Jr. *sales, management and marketing consultant*

Roanoke
Shaftman, Fredrick Krisch *telephone communications executive, lawyer*

Seaford
Jenkins, Margaret Bunting *human resources executive*

Springfield
Bruen, John Dermot *business management consultant*
Gallagher, Matthew Philip, Jr. *advertising agency executive*
Nodeen, Janey Price *company executive*
†Rothschild, Susy Schaflander *data analyst*

Stafford
Kline, Denny Lee *hazardous devices and explosives consultant*

Sterling
Bennett, William Leo, Jr. *management consultant*

Vienna
Cantus, H. Hollister *government relations consultant*
Feld, Kenneth J. *entertainment executive*
Jandreau, James Lawrence *information systems executive*
Jayne, Edward Randolph, II *executive search consultant*
Oleson, Ray Jerome *computer service company executive*
†Poulos, Stephen Paul *information systems specialist*
Rothery, Chet *business executive*
Sheinbaum, Gilbert Harold *international management consultant*
Steele, Carol D. *information processing coordinator*
Syence Kennedy, Karen *advertising agency executive*
Van Stavoren, William David *investor, retired government official*
Walker, Edward Keith, Jr. *business executive, retired naval officer*

Virginia Beach
Alexander, William Powell *business advisor*

Allen, Elizabeth Maresca *marketing and telecommunications executive*
Burgess, Marvin Franklin *human resources, management specialist, consultant*
Dean, Edwin Becton *business owner*
Dixon, John Spencer *international executive*
†Godsey, James Paul (J.P. Godsey) *security firm executive*
Goffigan, Christopher Wayne *research associate*
Goodwin, Robert *human resources specialist*
Hilgers, John Jack William *management and transportation consultant*
Kodis, Mary Caroline *marketing consultant*
Wick, Robert Thomas *retired supermarket executive*

Washingtons Birthplace
Donahue, John Joseph *park and recreation director*

White Stone
Wroth, James Melvin *former army officer, computer company executive*

Williamsburg
Aaron, Bertram Donald *corporation executive*
Ackerman, Lennis Campbell *management consultant retired*
†Andrews, Timothy William *public relations executive*
Coffman, Orene Burton *hotel executive*

Winchester
Bonometti, Robert John *technology management and strategy executive*
Engelage, James Roland *business executive, consultant*
Gaither, George Manney *marketing consultant*

Woodbridge
Richardson, Sharon Young *marketing professional*

WASHINGTON

Auburn
Howard, George Harmon *management consultant*

Bainbridge Island
Schmidt, Karen Anne *travel company executive, state legislator*

Bellevue
†Bondarook, Nina *public relations consultant*
Evans, Robert Vincent *sales and marketing executive*
†Frei, Brent R. *computer software executive*
Hall, Eleanor Williams *public relations executive*
Johnson, Gary Kent *management education company executive*
Lauver, Lydia Monserrat Ollis *public relations executive*
†Otterholt, Barry L. *technology management consultant*
†Pool, David *software executive*

Burlington
Herbaugh, Roger Duane *computer and software company executive*

Carnation
Beshur, Jacqueline E. *pet training consultant, writer*

Colfax
Beckmann, Michele Lillian *secretary*

Des Moines
Brandmeir, Christopher Lee *hospitality and food service consultant*

Edmonds
Brinton, Richard Kirk *marketing executive*
Johnson, LuAn *disaster management consultant*

Federal Way
Muzyka-McGuire, Amy *marketing professional, nutrition consultant*

Gig Harbor
Robinson, James William *retired management consultant*
Wissmann, Carol Reneé *sales executive*

Issaquah
Stanley, James Gordon *retired engineering marketing executive, writer*

Kirkland
Hooper, Steven W. *communications executive*
Ladd, James Roger *international business executive and consultant*

Langley
Kenny, Robert Martin *organizational development consultant*

Littlerock
Gunderson, Cleon Henry *management consultant corporation executive*

Malaga
Nanto, Roxanna Lynn *marketing professional, management consultant*

Mercer Island
Dykstra, David Charles *management executive, consultant, accountant, author, educator*
Herres, Phillip Benjamin *computer software executive*

Mill Creek
†Nelson, Elinor S. *human resources consultant, labor mediator*

Newcastle
†Meshke, Paul John *business consultant*

Olympia
Adkins, Ben Frank *management and engineering consultant*
Calkins, Bruce Edgar *computer company executive*
Marcelynas, Richard Chadwick *management consultant*
Ogden, Valeria Munson *management consultant, state representative*
Petersen, Donald Felix *consultant*
†Zimmerman, Michael Phillip *administrative assistant*

Port Angeles
Smithson, Michael *parks director*

Port Ludlow
Scott, Louis Edward *advertising agency executive*

Redmond
Addams, Robert Jean *finance executive*
Ballmer, Steve *software company executive*
Gates, William Henry, III *software company executive*
Herbold, Robert J. *communications company executive*
Myhrvold, Nathan *communications executive*

Renton
Bates, Charles Walter *human resources executive, lawyer*
Jones, Stanley R. *government contracts business consultant*

Richland
Towner, Larry Edwin *consulting company executive*

Seattle
Adams, Donald Elwin *cultural and organization development consultant*
Beer, Joseph Ernest *telecommunications manager*
Beetham, Stanley Williams *international management consultant*
Bezos, Jeffrey P. *multimedia executive*
Bryant, Arthur Steven *public relations executive*
Buck, Gene *graphics company executive, satirist, historian*
Chang, Taiping *marketing executive, magazine publisher*
Dagnon, James Bernard *human resources executive*
Dederer, Michael Eugene *public relations company executive*
Duryee, David Anthony *management consultant*
†Eastham, John D. *business executive*
Gerwick-Brodeur, Madeline Carol *marketing and timing professional*
Gilder, George *communications executive, writer*
Gist, Marilyn Elaine *organizational behavior and human resource management educator*
Glaser, Rob *communications company executive*
Gormèzano, Keith *arbitrator, writer, marketer*
Griffin, William R. *consulting company executive*
†Helgath, Sheila Fay *environmental company executive*
Hough, John Dennis *public relations executive*
Kelly, Dennis Ray *sales executive*
Kraft, Donald Bowman *advertising agency executive*
Kraft, Elaine Joy *community relations and communications official*
MacDonald, Andrew Stephen *management consulting firm executive*
McConnell, J. Daniel *sports marketing professional*
McReynolds, Neil Lawrence *management consultant*
Mitchum, Beth *bookstore manager*
Miyata, Keijiro *culinary arts educator*
Palmer, Hollis Marie *public relations executive*
Patten, Richard E. *personnel company owner*
Porad, Laurie Jo *jewelry company official*
Ray, Sankar *communication network research and development professional*
Reis, Jean Stevenson *administrative secretary*
Ruckelshaus, William Doyle *investment group executive*
Ruff, Lorraine Marie *public relations executive*
Stumbles, James Rubidge Washington *multinational service company executive*
Williams, Kenneth A. *food service executive*
Wilson, Emily Marie *sales executive*

Spokane
Ballinger, Charles Kenneth *information specialist*
Geraghty, John Vincent *public relations consultant*
Higgins, Shaun O'Leary *media executive*
Perry, Lois Wanda *safety and health administrator*
Storey, Francis Harold *business consultant, retired bank executive*
Tsutakawa, Edward Masao *management consultant*

Tacoma
Bartlett, Norma Thyra *retired administrative assistant*
Brevik, J. Albert *communications consultant*
Hudson, Edward Voyle *linen supply company executive*
Metsker, Thomas Charles *map company executive*
Robinson, Richard Allen, Jr. *human resources development trainer, consultant*

Vancouver
Guenther, Sheila Walsh *sales and promotion executive*
Hixon, Robin Ray *food service executive, writer*
Middlewood, Martin Eugene *technical communications specialist, writer, consultant*
Smith, Milton Ray *computer company executive, lawyer*
Wiita, Kathryn Carpenter *public relations company executive*

Walla Walla
Potts, Charles Aaron *management executive, writer*

Woodinville
Herron, Sidney Earl *sales executive*
Newlands, Sheila Ann *consumer products company executive, controller*

Yakima
Myers, Elizabeth Rouse *management consultant*
Vujovic, Mary Jane *education and employment training planner*

WEST VIRGINIA

Charleston
†Etter, Alan Yancy *legal administration executive*
Isabella, Mark Douglas *communication consultant*
Mc Gee, John Frampton *communications company executive*

Clarksburg
Huber, Clayton Lloyd *marketing professional, engineer*

Great Cacapon
Chapple, Abby *consumer communications consultant*

Huntington
McSorley, Danny Eugene *sales executive*

Parkersburg
Crooks, Dorena May (Dee Crooks) *administrative assistant, social worker*
Fahlgren, H(erbert) Smoot *advertising agency executive*

Summit Point
Taylor, Harold Allen, Jr. *industrial mineral marketing consultant*

Sylvester
Mace, Mary Alice *coal company administrator*

Triadelphia
McCullough, John Phillip *management consultant, educator*

West Union
Howes, Melinda Sue *marketing executive*

WISCONSIN

Algoma
Golomski, William Arthur *consulting company executive*

Appleton
McManus, John Francis *association executive, writer*

Blue Mounds
Winner, Scott *company executive*

Brookfield
Bader, Ronald L. *advertising executive*
Brown, Edward Sherman *computer company executive*
Huss, William Lee *computer consultant*
Nickerson, Greg *public relations executive*
Saam, Robert Harry *human resources consultant*
Welnetz, David Charles *human resources executive*

Cedarburg
King, Frederic *health services management executive, educator*

Darien
Miller, Malcolm Henry *manufacturing sales executive, real estate developer*

Delavan
Armstrong, Kevin William *marketing executive, researcher*

Dodgeville
Eisenberg, Lee B. *communications executive, author*
Rux, Paul Philip *management consultant, educator*

Eau Claire
Leary, Robin Janell *administrative secretary, county government official*

Germantown
Tietyen, David Earl *marketing professional*

Glendale
Chait, Jon Frederick *corporate executive, lawyer*

Green Bay
Bush, Robert G. *food service executive*
Poppenhagen, Ronald William *advertising agency executive*
Promis, Brenda *parks director*

Hayward
Peterson, Louis Robert *retired consumer products company executive*

Janesville
Butters, John Patrick *educator, tour director*

Jefferson
Morgan, Gaylin F. *public relations consultant*
†Myers, Gary *public relations executive*

Kewaunee
Allen, Gerald Campbell Forrest *management consulting company owner*

Kohler
Kohler, Laura E. *public relations executive*

La Crosse
Ruyle, Kim Ernest *training and software development executive*

Lake Geneva
Weed, Edward Reilly *marketing executive*

Madison
Dunham, Michael Herman *human services executive*
McMillan, Reed John *sales executive*
Opitz, David Wilmer *corporate executive, state political party executi*
Scheidler, James Edward *business executive*
Stites, Susan Kay *human resources consultant*

Mequon
Diesem, John Lawrence *business executive*
Elias, Paul S. *marketing executive*
Miller, Scott Joseph *software executive*

Middleton
Lee, Leslie Warren *marketing executive, public speaker*
Senn, Richard Allan *environmental safety professional*

Milwaukee
Arbit, Bruce *direct marketing executive, consultant*
Balbach, George Charles *technology company executive*
Bergmann, Linda J. *marketing professional*
Colbert, Virgis William *brewery company executive*
Constable, John *advertising executive*
Counsell, Paul S. *advertising executive*
Davis, Thomas William *computer company executive*
Felde, Martin Lee *advertising agency executive, accountant*
Fromstein, Mitchell S. *temporary office services company executive*
Gerlach, Frederick Herman *international business consultant*
Hunter, Victor Lee *marketing executive, consultant*
Joseph, Jules K. *retired public relations executive*
King, William Stewart, II *public relations executive*
Larson, Marlene Louise *educator, hotel consultant*
Laughlin, Steven L. *advertising executive*
Mahler, Stephanie Irene *executive assistant*
Marcus, Stephen Howard *hospitality and entertainment company executive*
Paul, Mary Melchior *human resources professional*
Randall, William Seymour *leasing company executive*
Roozen, Mary Louise *public relations executive*
Scheinfeld, James David *travel agency executive*
Shapiro, Robert Donald *management consultant*
Shiely, John Stephen *company executive, lawyer*
Teuschler, Michael Alexander *computer consultant*
Walthers, Bruce Julius *hobby industry executive*
Wilde, Anne Marie *sales executive, artist*

Monroe
Bean, Virginia Ann *marketing executive*
Bishop, Carolyn Benkert *public relations counselor*
Wilcox, Winton Wilfred, Jr. *computer specialist, consultant*

New Berlin
Peck, Curtiss Steven *organization development consultant, author*
Weinzierl, Thomas Allen *data processing and data communications manager*

Oak Creek
Harris, R(ichard) Steven *data processing executive, consultant, educator*

Pewaukee
Quadracci, Harry V. *printing company executive, lawyer*

Pleasant Prairie
Ziccarelli, Joan Mary *secretary*

Plymouth
Gentine, Lee Michael *marketing professional*

Racine
Klein, Gabriella Sonja *retired communications executive*

South Milwaukee
Kitzke, Eugene David *research management executive*

Thiensville
Dickow, James Fred *management consultant*

Waterford
Karraker, Louis Rendleman *retired corporate executive*

Waunakee
Kronschnabel, Gerald Leo *sales executive*

Wauwatosa
Wright, Isaac Wilson, Jr. *quality assurance professional*

West Bend
Lenz, Dave N. *safety administrator*

Weyauwega
Hanneman, Elaine Esther *salesperson*

Williams Bay
Morava, Alice Jean *corporate executive*

Wisconsin Rapids
Knuteson, Miles Gene *advertising executive*

WYOMING

Alpine
Cittone, Henry Aron *hotel and restaurant management educator*

Cheyenne
Grothaus, Pamela Sue *marketing professional*
†Houston, Janice Lynn *employment counselor*
†Wagner, Samuel Albin Mar *records management executive, educator*

Cody
Keenan, Beverly Owen *entrepreneur*

Fort Laramie
Mack, James A. *parks director*

Jackson
Herrick, Gregory Evans *technology corporation executive*

Mills
Kennerknecht, Richard Eugene *marketing executive*

Riverton
Hudson, Gary Michael *corporate executive*

Wilson
Fritz, Jack Wayne *communications and marketing company executive*

TERRITORIES OF THE UNITED STATES

GUAM

Mangilao
Colfax, Richard Schuyler *business management and human resources educator*

PUERTO RICO

San Juan
†Callen, Tarquin M. *hotel executive*

VIRGIN ISLANDS

Saint Thomas
†O'Bryan, James A. *communications specialist*

MILITARY ADDRESSES OF THE UNITED STATES

EUROPE

FPO
Bailey, Steven Scott *operations research analyst*

CANADA

Toronto
†Sharp, Isadore *hotel facility executive*

ALBERTA

Calgary
Hume, James Borden *corporate professional, foundation executive*
Shaw, JR *communications executive*

De Winton
Shutiak, James *management consultant*

Edmonton
Forsyth, Joseph *privacy and information management consultant*

BRITISH COLUMBIA

North Vancouver
†Francis, Norm *computer software executive, accountant*

Vancouver
Campbell, Bruce Alan *market research consultant*
Collins, Mary *management consultant, former Canadian legislator*
Cormier, Jean G. *communications company executive*
†O'Neill, John *hotel executive*
†O'Neill, Rob *hotel executive*

Victoria
Nuttall, Richard Norris *management consultant, physician*

West Vancouver
Rae, Barbara Joyce *former employee placement company executive*

MANITOBA

Winnipeg
Fraser, John Foster *management company executive*

NEWFOUNDLAND

Saint John's
Russell, Frederick William *travel company executive, former Canadian provincial official*

NOVA SCOTIA

Halifax
Gratwick, John *management consulting executive, writer, consultant*

Stellarton
Rowe, Allan Duncan *company executive*

ONTARIO

Downsview
Burton, Ian *environmentalist, consultant, scholar, writer*

Etobicoke
†Cooper, Simon F. *hotel executive*

Freelton
Sonnenberg, Hardy *data processing company research and development executive, engineer*

Gloucester
Boisvert, Laurier Joseph *communications executive*

Markham
Nelson, William George, IV *software company executive*

Mississauga
Beckley, Michael John *hotel executive*
Farrell, Craig *hotel executive*
†Jackson, Michael I. *hospitality company executive*
Roth, John Andrew *communications executive*
Thibault, J(oseph) Laurent *service company executive*

North York
Denham, Frederick Ronald *management consultant*
Jacob, Ellis *entertainment company executive*

Oakville
Barlow, Kenneth James *management consultant*

Ottawa
Hoyles, John D.V. *company executive*
Ouellet, André *business executive*
Sharp, Mitchell William *advisor to prime minister*

Toronto
Bandeen, Robert Angus *management corporation executive*
†Cahill, Chris J. *hotel executive*
†Cieszkowski, Edward D. *marketing and management professional*
Curlook, Walter *management consultant*
DeMone, Robert Stephen *hotel company executive*
†Fatt, William R. *hospitality company executive*
Fierheller, George Alfred *corporate director*
Godfrey, Paul Victor *communications company executive*
Gregor, Tibor Philip *management consultant*
Harvey, George Edwin *communications company executive*
Irwin, Samuel Macdonald *toy company executive*
Lowe, Donald Cameron *consulting company executive*
Marshall, Donald Stewart *computer systems company executive*
McCoubrey, R. James *advertising and broadcast executive*
Meadows, George Lee *communications company executive*
Miller, Kenneth Merrill *computing services company executive*
Morden, John Reid *security-business intelligence company executive*
Rogers, Edward Samuel *communications company executive*
†Sharpe, John L. *hotel executive*
Singleton-Wood, Allan James *communications executive*
Tanaka, Ron S. *hotel executive*

Unionville
Nichols, Harold Neil *corporate executive, former pipeline company executive*

Willowdale
MacDonald, Brian Scott *management consultant*

QUEBEC

Leclercville
Morin, Pierre Jean *retired management consultant*

Montreal
Audet, Henri *retired communications executive*
Beauregard, Luc *public relations executive*
Bouthillier, André *public relations executive, consultant*
†Cavell, Charles G. *printing company executive*
Des Marais, Pierre, II *communications holding company executive*
†Monty, Jean C. *communications executive*
Neveu, Jean *company executive*
Saint-Jacques, Madeleine *advertising agency executive*
Sirois, Charles *communications executive*
Tousignant, Jacques *human resources executive, lawyer*

Mount Royal
Chauvette, Claude R. *building materials company administrator*
Glezos, Matthews *consumer products and services company executive*

Quebec
Courtois, Bernard Andre *communications executive*

Saint Sauveur
Dunsky, Menahem *retired advertising agency executive, communications consultant, painter*

SASKATCHEWAN

Regina
Clayton, Raymond Edward *government official*

MEXICO

Coahuila
Whelan, James Robert *communications executive, international trade and investment consultant, author, educator, mining executive*

Mexico City
†Nicholas, Ronald Wayde *business consultant*

AUSTRALIA

Richmond
Conomikes, Melanie Remington *marketing executive*

BELGIUM

Lens
Peat, Randall Dean *defense analysis company executive, retired air force officer*

Strombeek Bever
Mancel, Claude Paul *household product company executive*

BULGARIA

Sofia
Franken, Martin *public relations company executive*

CHINA

Hong Kong
Pisanko, Henry Jonathan *command and control communications company executive*

DENMARK

Hoersholm
Sørensen, Erik *international company executive*

ENGLAND

London
Habgood, Anthony John *corporate executive*
Hallissey, Michael *strategic consultant*
Leaf, Robert Stephen *public relations executive*
Sainsbury of Preston Candover, Lord (John Davan Sainsbury) *food retailer executive, art patron*
Sorrell, Martin Stuart *advertising and marketing executive*

Richmond
Treasure, John Albert Penberthy *advertising executive*

Stroud
Robinson, John Beckwith *development management consultant*

Windsor Berkshire
Ehmann, Carl William *consumer products executive, researcher*

FRANCE

Alpes Maritimes
Morley, Roger Hubert *company executive, consultant*

Levallois-Perret
de Pouzilhac, Alain Duplessis *advertising executive*

Paris
Marcus, Claude *advertising executive*

IRELAND

Dublin
Voss, Katherine Evelyn *international management consultant*

ISRAEL

Herzliyya
Warshavsky, Eli Samuel *media company chief executive*

JAPAN

Meguroku
Miura, Akio *quality assurance management professional*

Tokyo
Wada, Yutaka *patent information executive*

THE NETHERLANDS

Amsterdam
Dornbush, K. Terry *former ambassador, consulting company executive*

SINGAPORE

Singapore
†Umehara, Ichigo *hotel executive*

SOUTH AFRICA

Johannesburg
Crockett, Noluthando Phyllis *communications executive*

SPAIN

Madrid
Muniain, Javier P. *computer company executive, theoretical physicist, researcher*

Santiago de Compostela
Balseiro Gonzalez, Manuel *management executive, consultant*

SWEDEN

Stockholm
Johnson, Antonia Axson *corporate executive*

SWITZERLAND

Bern
Braun, Reto *computer systems company executive*

Lyss
Scheftner, Gerold *marketing executive*

THAILAND

Bangkok
McInerney, Joseph Aloysius *hotel executive*

TURKEY

Ankara
Camlibel, Dizdar *marketing professional, advertising consultant*

ZIMBABWE

Borrowdale
Rooney, John Patrick *company executive*

ADDRESS UNPUBLISHED

Albert, Margaret Cook *communications executive*
Allen, Paul *computer executive, professional sports team owner*
†Alm, Alvin Leroy *retired technical services executive*
Amancio, Ruth Carson *safety professional*
Ambrose, James Richard *consultant, retired government official*
Ambrose, Thomas Cleary *communications executive*
Amparado, Keith D. *communications company executive*
Anders, Brenda Michelle *communications professional*
Anderson, Donald Lloyd *weapon systems consultant*
Anderson, Mark Robert *data processing executive, biochemist*
Anderson, Vernon Russell *technology company executive, entrepreneur*
Andriole, Stephen John *information systems executive*
Appell, Kathleen Marie *management consultant, legal administrator*
Appell, Louise Sophia *consulting company executive*
Ashkin, Rajasperi Maliapen *marketing executive*
Asokan, Unisa *information professional*
†Atkinson, Donna Durant *research and evaluation consultant*
Avery, Stephen Goodrich *marketing professional, consultant*
Baglio, Vincent Paul *management consultant*
Balder, James Ellsworth *infosystems specialist*
Balick, Kenneth D. *international real estate finance executive*
Bamberger, Gerald Francis *plastics marketing consultant*
Barger, William James *management consultant, educator*
Barnes, Judith Anne *communications executive*
Barnes, Wesley Edward *energy and environmental executive*
Barron, Peggy Pennisi *management consultant*
Bartholomew, Charles R. *advertising executive*
Bartizal, Robert George *computer systems company executive, business consultant*
Barton, Peter Richard, III *communications executive*
†Barton, Tina Roxanne *technical information specialist, writer*
Battle, Emery Alford, Jr. *sales executive*
Bauer, Barbara Ann *marketing consultant*
Beasley, Barbara Starin *sales executive, marketing professional*
Beaumont, Richard Austin *management consultant*
Beck, Timothy Daniel *human resources specialist, consultant*
†Bedford, Danielle *public relations specialist*
Bell, P. Jackson *computer executive*
Bennett, Robert LeRoy *computer software development company executive*
Bennett, Saul *public relations agency executive*
Berger, Frank Stanley *management executive*
Bergstein, Stanley Francis *horse racing executive*
†Bermard, Theodore G. *marketing executive*
Berra, Robert Louis *human resources consultant*
Bey, Joan S. *retired public information specialist, writer*
Bicofsky, David Marc *public relations executive*
Binks, Rebecca Anne *communications executive*
Birk, John R. *marketing/financial services consultant*
Black, Susan *public relations consultant*
Blacker, Harriet *public relations executive*
Blackston, Brenda Joyce *computer software company manager*
Blaine, Davis Robert *valuation consultant executive*
Blake, John Edward *retired car rental company executive*
Blomgren, Ronald Walter *business executive*
Blount, Kerry Andrew *defense analyst*
Bloustein, Peter Edward *entertainment management consultant, producer*
Boatwright, Charlotte Jeanne *hospital marketing and public relations executive*
Bogart, Judith Saunders *public relations executive*
Bohannan, Jules Kirby *printing company executive*

Matthew, Lyn *sales and marketing executive consultant*
Matthews, Gail Thunberg *marketing executive*
Matthiesen, David Karl *consultant*
Mazzarella, Rosemary Louise *business administration executive*
McCann, Joseph F. *retired public relations executive*
McCarthy, Daniel William *management consultant*
McCaw, Craig O. *communications executive*
McCormick, Elaine Alice *former nurse, retired fundraising executive*
McGuire, John W., Sr. *advertising executive, marketing professional, author*
McInnis, Susan Musé *corporate communications manager*
McKeown, Lorraine Laredo *travel company executive, writer*
McKinney, John Gage *purchasing agent, writer*
McQuarrie, Terry Scott *technical director*
McVeigh-Pettigrew, Sharon Christine *communications consultant*
Meads, Donald Edward *management services company executive*
Meis, Nancy Ruth *marketing and development executive*
Mellendorf, Patricia Jean *retired personnel professional*
Melsheimer, Mel P(owell) *consumer products business executive*
Merrill, Frank Harrison *data processing executive, consultant*
Metz, Frank Andrew, Jr. *data processing executive*
Michael, Harold Kaye (Bud Michael) *sales and marketing executive*
Mikhail, Mary Attalla *computer systems development executive*
Mikiewicz, Anna Daniella *marketing and sales representative*
Miller, Diane Doris *executive search consultant*
Miller, Ellen S. *marketing communications executive*
†Miller, Jennifer Ann *cleaning service owner*
Mitelman, Bonnie Cossman *editor, writer, lecturer*
Mitrany, Devora *marketing consultant, writer*
Mitzelfeld, Lisa Grayson *public relations executive*
Moeller, Robert John *management consultant*
Molloy, Angela Margaret *advertising executive*
Moltzau, Hughitt Gregory *retired management training specialist*
Monaghan, Thomas Stephen *retired restaurant chain executive*
Monda, Marilyn *quality improvement consultant*
Montero, Fernan Gonzalo *retired advertising executive*
Montgomery, James Morton *public relations, marketing executive, association executive*
Moore, Richard Earl *communications creative director*
Moosbruker, Jane Barbara *organization development consultant*
Moradi, Ahmad F. *software company executive, consultant*
†Morrell, Kim Irving *sales and marketing professional*
Morris, Dorothy Kay *credit executive*
Moszkowicz, Virginia Marie *quality administrator*
Mulcahy, Robert Edward *management consultant*
Mull, Charles Leroy, II *retired naval officer and travel agency executive*
Murdza, Deanna Carol *database administrator*
Nason, Dolores Irene *computer company executive, counselor, eucharistic minister*
Neish, Francis Edward *advertising agency executive*
Neswald, Barbara Anne *advertising executive, writer*
Neuman, Robert Harold *communication executive*
†Neuwirth, Matthew Anthony *marketing executive*
Niemann, Lewis Keith *lamp manufacturing company executive*
Noolan, Julie Anne Carroll *management consultant*
Norris, Katharine Eileen *communications professional, educator*
Norton, Nathaniel Goodwin *marketing executive*
Novas, Joseph, Jr. *advertising agency executive*
Novotny, Deborah Ann *management consultant*
O'Connor, John Joseph *operations executive*
Ogden, Denise Theresa *marketing professional, educator*
Okada, Takuya *retail executive*
Olson, Dale C. *public relations executive*
O'Neil, Cleora Tanner *personnel specialist*
O'Shea, Catherine Large *marketing and public relations consultant*
O'Sullivan, Paul Kevin *business executive, management and instructional systems consultant*
Ott, Joseph John *computer specialist, writer*
Oviedo, Tamara Lenore *management consultant, photojournalist*
Owens, Charles Vincent, Jr. *diagnostic company executive and consultant*
Palumbo, Matthew Aloysius *marketing executive*
†Panagakos, Michael Joseph *sales executive*
Parenti, Kathy Ann *sales professional*
Parker, George Anthony *computer leasing company executive*
Parker, Lee Fischer *sales executive*
Parker, Scott Lane *management consultant*
Partridge, Connie R. *advertising executive*
Patterson, Dennis Joseph *management consultant*
Patton, David Wayne *health care executive*
Paul, Frank *retired consulting company executive*
Pazdera, John Paul *regulatory services executive*
Pearson, Wayman J. *waste management executive*
Perlov, Dadie *management consultant*
Perraud, Pamela Brooks *human resources professional*
†Perry, Chris Nicholas *advertising executive*
Perry, James DeWolf *management consultant*
Peterman, Donna Cole *communications executive*
Plottel, Gloria Susanne Stone *marketing professional*
Polich, John Elliott *global marketing executive*
Posner, Sidney *advertising executive*
Post, Richard Bennett *retired human resources executive*
†Potempa Niedosik, Kim Marie *sales executive*
Potter, James Earl *retired international hotel management company executive*
Poulsen, Fern Sue *special events and public relations consultant*
Powers, Eldon Nathaniel *computer mapping executive*
Pride, Benjamin David *advertising executive*
Priester, Horace Richard, Jr. *retired quality assurance professional*
Probasco, Dale Richard *management consultant*
Prokopis, Emmanuel Charles *computer company executive*
Provenzano, Dominic *information specialist*
Pruett, Jo Ann *marketing professional, special events coordinator*
Puetz, Pamela Ann *human resources executive*
Pugliese, Karen Olsen *freelance public relations counsel*
Radabaugh, Michele Jo *sales executive*
Radkowsky, Karen *research and marketing consultant*
Rairdin, Craig Allen *software company executive, software developer*
Rank, Larry Gene *management consultant*
†Raven, Sheila Sherece *management consultant*
Rayl, India *marketing executive*
Reed, David Patrick *infosystems specialist*
Rennekamp, Rose Greeley *marketing professional*
Retsky, Sidney Gerald *retired company executive*
Riccardi, Robert *advertising executive*
Richard, Susan Mathis *communications executive, screenwriter*
Richards, Carmeleete A. *computer training executive, network administrator*
Richards, Susan R. *management consultant*
Richey, Thomas Adam *advertising executive*
Richter, Carol Dean *sales representative*
Robins, Norman Alan *strategic planning consultant, former steel company executive*
Robinson, Henry, III *office manager, legal consultant*
Robinson, Linda Gosden *communications executive*
Roby, Christina Yen *data processing specialist, educator*
Roebuck, Joseph Chester *leasing company executive*
Roiz, Myriam *foreign trade marketing executive*
Rolof, Marcia Christine *sales executive*
Roman, Ernan *marketing executive*
Ropes, David Gardner *advertising executive*
Roseman, Jack *computer services company executive*
Rosen, Arthur Marvin *advertising executive*
Rosenfield, James Harold *communications executive*
†Ross, Alan *management consultant*
Royston, Lloyd Leonard *educational marketing consultant*
Rubin, Martin N. *meeting planner, consultant*
Ryan, William Joseph *communications company executive*
Rydholm, Ralph Williams *advertising agency executive*
Saiola, Frances *retired corporate administrator*
Sandage, Elizabeth Anthea *retired market research executive*
Saul, Ann *medical writer, public relations executive*
Saunders, Brian Keith *consulting company executive*
Savage, Neve Richard *marketing executive*
Sawyer, Raymond Lee, Jr. *motel chain executive*
Scaglione, Cecil Frank *marketing executive, publisher*
Schmid, Andrew Michael, Jr. *advertising executive*
Schmidt, Richard Alan *management company executive*
Schneider, Sharon M. *systems administrator, information technologist*
Schreckinger, Sy Edward *advertising executive, consultant*
Schulberg, Jay William *advertising agency executive*
Schulman, Tammy Beth *communications executive*
Schult, Dain Leslie *broadcast executive, consultant*
Schur, Susan Dorfman *public affairs consultant*
Schuster, Gary Francis *public relations executive*
Schwartz, Stephen Blair *retired information industry executive*
Scutt, Cheryl Lynn *marketing communications executive*
Sease, Gene Elwood *public relations company executive*
Seelig, Gerard Leo *management consultant*
Semos, William *management consultant, educator*
Senske, Marlowe Orlyn *healthcare executive, hospital administrator*
Serocky, William Howard *retired sales professional*
Seteroff, Sviatoslav Steve *management and logistics company executive*
Severino, Elizabeth Forrest *consulting company executive*
Shafran, Hank *public relations executive*
Shalhoup, Judy Lynn *marketing communications executive*
Shapira, David S. *food chain executive*
Shapiro, Richard Charles *sales and marketing executive*
Sheeline, Paul Cushing *hotel executive*
Shikuma, Eugene Yujin *travel agency executive*
Sidebottom, William George *communications executive*
Sincoff, Michael Z. *human resources and marketing professional*
Singer, David Michael *marketing and public relations company executive*
†Smaardyk, Sarah Lynn *management professional*
Smiley, Ronald Michael *communications executive*
†Smith, Daniel Leroy *computer company executive*
Smith, Jack C. *food service executive*
Smith, Joban Jonathan *security consultant*
Smith, Kathryn Ann *advertising executive*
Smith, Michael Elwin *film company executive, director, producer*
Smith, Thomas Winston *cotton marketing executive*
Smyth, Cornelius Edmonston *retired hotel executive*
Snow, Claude Henry, Jr. *information services executive, consultant*
Sollender, Joel David *management consultant, financial executive*
Solow, Martha S. *nonprofit management consultant, state legislator*
Sommers, William Paul *management consultant, research and development institute executive*
Sooter, Will James *executive search consultant*
Sorgi, Deborah Bernadette *educational software company executive*
Souder, Howard R., Jr. *customer support representative*
Souveroff, Vernon William, Jr. *business executive*
Speakes, Larry Melvin *public relations executive*
Spellman, Douglas Toby *advertising executive*
Spingarn, Joel William *small business owner*
Spoehel, Ronald Ross *communications company executive*
Spoor, James Edward *human resources executive, entrepreneur*
Springer, Gerald William *sales executive*
Sroge, Maxwell Harold *marketing consultant, publishing executive*
Srygley, Paul Dean *marketing manager*
Stark, Diana *public relations and promotion executive*
Stauber, Brandon Frederick *consultant information technology and communications*
Stengel, Ronald Francis *management consultant*
Stentz, Steven Thomas *researcher, project consultant*
Stepanski, Anthony Francis, Jr. *computer company executive*
Stephenson, Toni Edwards *publisher, investment management executive, communications executive*
†Steris, Charles William *sales executive*
Stern, S(eesa) Beatrice *executive secretary, registered nurse*
†Sterne, Rosanne L.P. *consultant to nonprofit organizations*
Stettler, Carla Rice *marketing executive*
Stevens, Berton Louis, Jr. *data processing manager*
Stewart, Arthur Irving, III (Art Stewart) *marketing communications executive*
Stewart, Miriam *utilization review professional*
Stewart, Richard Alfred *business executive*
Stone, Lloyd *corporate executive, state political party official*
Strasser, Gabor *management consultant*
Straub, Linda Catherine *administrative assistant*
Straus, Jerry Alan *management consultant*
Strother, Patrick Joseph *public relations executive*
Stults, Walter Black *management consultant, former trade organization executive*
Sturgeon, Charles Edwin *management consultant*
Subotnick, Stuart *food service executive*
Sullivan, Nell Inklebarger *administrative official, counselor*
Sullivan, Patrick Raney *labor management consultant*
Sullivan, Sarah Louise *management and technology consultant*
Sutlin, Vivian *advertising executive*
Swanson, William Russell *marketing professional*
†Szabo, Yurika Lin *marketing executive, advertising executive*
Taplett, Lloyd Melvin *human resources management consultant*
Tarar, Afzal Muhammad *management consultant*
Tarjan, Robert Wegg *retired information services executive, part-time math teacher*
Tarr, Curtis W. *business executive*
Temerlin, Liener *advertising agency executive*
Tenney, Frank Putnam *marketing executive*
Terry, Richard Frank *data transcriber*
Tesarek, Dennis George *retired business consultant, writer, educator*
Tetelman, Alice Fran *consultant*
Thomas, Joe Carroll *retired human resources director*
Thomas, Rhonda Robbins *marketing educator, consultant*
Thompson, Craig Snover *corporate communications executive*
Thompson, Joyce Lurine *retired information systems specialist*
Thompson, Lawrence D. *marketing and sales executive*
Thompson, Richard Stephen *management consultant*
Thongsak, Vajeeprasee Thomas *business planning executive*
Thorn, Brian Earl *retail company executive*
Thurman, Jimmy Cline *sales executive*
Toevs, Alden Louis *management consultant*
Togerson, John Dennis *computer software company executive, retired*
Toirac, S(eth) Thomas *engineering executive, consultant*
Toole, Linda Jernigan *quality control technician, cosmetics company admininstrator*
Tooley, Charles Frederick *communications executive, consultant*
Traxler, Eva Maria *marketing administrator*
Triolo, Peter *advertising agency executive, marketing educator, consultant*
Tuft, Mary Ann *executive search firm executive*
Tulley, Monica Elaine *marketing professional*
Tytler, Linda Jean *communications and public affairs executive, retired state legislator*
Underwood, Ralph Edward *computer systems engineer*
Ussery, Luanne *retired communications consultant*
Uvena, Frank John *retired printing company executive, lawyer*
Valeskie-Hamner, Gail Yvonne *information systems specialist*
Vallerand, Philippe Georges *sales executive*
Van Dine, Alan Charles *advertising agency executive, writer*
Van Every, Kathleen Mary *contracts manager*
Van Houten, Elizabeth Ann *corporate communications executive*
Varley, Michael Chris *communications executive*
Viscelli, Therese Rauth *materials management consultant*
Volans, Ronald Paul *marketing professional*
von Linsowe, Marina Dorothy *information systems consultant*
Vytal, James Alfred *printing company executive*
†Wachtel, Jeffrey M. *management educator, management consultant*
Wadley, M. Richard *consumer products executive*
†Walser, Clarke L. *management consultant*
Walsh, Michael Joseph *special operations consulting company executive*
Walsh, William Albert *management consultant, former naval officer*
Warren, Richard Ernest *advertising executive*
†Warren, Winnifred Patricia *human resources manager*
Washow, Paula Burnette *security company and investigation agency executive*
Wasserman, Anthony Ira *software company executive, educator*
Weismantel, Gregory Nelson *management consultant and software executive*
Wellman, Anthony Donald Emerson *advertising executive*
Wells, Victor Hugh, Jr. *retired advertising agency executive*
Weston, Josh S. *retired data processing company executive*
Wheaton, Alice Alshuler *administrative assistant*
Wheeler, Barbara J. *management consultant*
Whitaker, Shirley Ann *telecommunications company marketing executive*
White, Bonnie Yvonne *management consultant, retired educator*
White, Erskine Norman, Jr. *management company executive*
White, Loray Betty *public relations executive, writer, actress, producer*
Whittaker, Mary Frances *educational and industrial company official*
Whyte, Bruce Lincoln *management executive, marketing professional*
Wikarski, Nancy Susan *information technology consultant*
Williams, Alfred Blythe *business communication educator*
Williams, Earle Carter *retired professional services company executive*
Williams, Harry Edward *management consultant*
Williams, Louis Clair, Jr. *public relations executive*
Williams, Ross Arnold *computer systems engineer*
Willig, Karl Victor *computer firm executive*
Wilson, Michael Dean *business executive*
Winsor, David John *cost consultant*
Wise, Susan Tamsberg *management and communications consultant, speaker*
Woods, Reginald Foster *management consulting executive*
Wozniak, Joyce Marie *sales executive*
Wujciak, Sandra Criscuolo *personnel executive*
Yaeger, Therese Francis *management professional*
Yakich, David Eli *international sales executive*
Yetto, John Henry *company executive*
Yocam, Delbert Wayne *software products company executive*
Yool, George Richard *consultant*
Yost, Bernice *detective agency owner*
Young, Anna Lucia *communications professional*
Zajas, J. Jonathan R. *management consulting company executive, principal*
Zehring, Karen *information executive*
Zeller, Joseph Paul *advertising executive*
Zinnen, Robert Oliver *general management executive*
Zuckerman, Martin Harvey *personnel director*

INDUSTRY: TRADE

UNITED STATES

ALABAMA

Birmingham
George, Frank Wade *small business owner, antiquarian book dealer*
Pizitz, Richard Alan *retail and real estate group executive*

Cullman
Freeman, Chester Willie *small business owner*

Foley
Breed, Eileen Judith *small business owner*

Montgomery
Grewelle, Larry Allan *travel agency owner*

Pelham
Walker, William W, III *wholesale distribution executive*

Tuscaloosa
Blackburn, John Leslie *small business owner*

ALASKA

Anchorage
Schnell, Roger Thomas *business owner, state official, retired career officer*

ARIZONA

Phoenix
Pasholk, Paul Douglas *retail executive, government official*

Scottsdale
Boat, Ronald Allen *business executive*
Cunningham, Gilbert Earl *business owner*

Sun City
Thompson, Betty Jane *small business owner*

ARKANSAS

Bentonville
Glass, David D. *department store company executive, professional baseball team executive*
Walton, S. Robson *discount department store chain executive*
†White, Nick *retail executive*

Hot Springs National Park
Tanenbaum, Bernard Jerome, Jr. *corporate executive*

Little Rock
Dillard, William T. *department store chain executive*

Pine Bluff
Watts, James Carter *carpenter, writer*

CALIFORNIA

Aliso Viejo
Purdy, Alan MacGregor *financial executive*

Big Bear Lake
Hendler, Rosemary Nielsen *business owner, digital artist*

Brisbane
Orban, Kurt *foreign trade company executive*

Burbank
Rosen, Eden Ruth *promoter, merchandiser, consultant, writer*
Wise, Woodrow Wilson, Jr. *small business owner*

Cathedral City
Jackman, Robert Alan *retail executive*

Colton
Brown, Jack H. *supermarket company executive*

Downieville
Forbes, Cynthia Ann *small business owner, marketing educator*

Dublin
Cope, Kenneth Wayne *chain store executive*

El Segundo
Williams, Theodore Earle *industrial distribution company executive*

Emeryville
Weaver, Velather Edwards *small business owner*

Encino
Vigdor, James Scott *distribution executive*

Fremont
Buswell, Debra Sue *small business owner, programmer, analyst*
†Liang, Christine *import company executive*

Fresno
Blum, Gerald Henry *department store executive*
Redmond-Stewart, Audrey A. *small business owner*

Garden Grove
Virgo, Muriel Agnes *swimming school owner*

Glendora
O'Hagan, William Gordon *state agency administrator*

Goleta
Winslow, Norman Eldon *business executive*

La Quinta
Atkins, Honey Jean *retired business executive*

Lafayette
Koetser, David *export company executive*

Laguna Beach
Pelton, Virginia Lue *small business owner*

Laguna Hills
Bell, Sharon Kaye *small business owner*

Long Beach
Shoji, June Midori *import and export trading executive*

Los Angeles
Blodgett, Julian Robert *small business owner*
Hawley, Philip Metschan *retired retail executive, consultant*
Lynch, Martin Andrew *retail company executive*
Roeder, Richard Kenneth *business owner, lawyer*
Sinay, Joseph *retail executive*
Triqueneaux, Laurent E. *photography agency owner*
Tuthill, Walter Warren *retail and financial executive*
Vander Naald Egenes, Joan Elizabeth *business owner, educator*
†Wylie, Pamela Jane *writer, producer, consultant, small business owner*

Modesto
Piccinini, Robert M. *grocery store chain executive*

Newark
Ferber, Norman Alan *retail executive*

Newport Coast
Pavony, William H. *retail executive, consultant*

Oakland
Spitzer, Matthew L. *retired retail store executive*

Orange
Andrews, Charles *wholesale distribution executive*
Underwood, Vernon O., Jr. *grocery stores executive*

Pacific Palisades
Diehl, Richard Kurth *retail business consultant*

Pacoima
†Buzzetti, George Howard *small business owner, chemical miller*

Palos Verdes Peninsula
Slayden, James Bragdon *retired department store executive*

Paradise
†Likley, Katherine *retail executive*

Pasadena
Cappello, Eve *international business consultant*
Olson, Diana Craft *image and etiquette consultant*

Petaluma
Herlihy, James Edward *retail executive*

Pleasanton
†Plaisance, Melissa *retail executive*

Quartz Hill
Noble, Sunny A. *business owner*

Redding
Streiff, Arlyne Bastunas *business owner, educator*

Riverside
Anderson, Jolene Slover *small business owner, publishing executive, consultant*
White, Clara Jo *graphoanalyst*

San Diego
Lehrer, Merrill Clark *retail store executive*
Saito, Frank Kiyoji *import-export firm executive*

San Francisco
Draper, William Henry, III *business executive*
†Ermatinger, John *apparel executive*
Fisher, Donald G. *casual apparel chain stores executive*

Seelenfreund, Alan *distribution company executive*
Ullman, Myron Edward, III *retail executive*

San Jose
Finnigan, Robert Emmet *business owner*

San Marino
Meyer, William Danielson *retired department store executive*

Santa Ana
Shahin, Thomas John *dry cleaning wholesale supply company executive*

Santa Paula
Anderson, William *retail company executive, business education educator*

South San Francisco
Allen, Robert *wholesale distribution executive*

Stockton
Dornbush, Vicky Jean *medical billing systems executive*

Thousand Oaks
Knight, Jeffrey Richard *small business owner*

Upland
Graw, LeRoy Harry *purchasing-contract management company executive*

Walnut Creek
Long, Robert Merrill *retail drug company executive*

Watsonville
Pye, David Thomas *specialty retail company executive*

West Sacramento
Solomon, Russell *retail products executive*
Teel, James E. *supermarket and drug store retail executive*
Teel, Joyce *supermarket and drugstore retail executive*

Westminster
Rupel, Daniel Patrick *retailing excutive*

Woodland Hills
Weider, Joseph *wholesale distribution executive*

COLORADO

Aurora
Magalnick, Elliott Ben *retail medical supply company executive*

Boulder
Johnson, Maryanna Morse *business owner*
Meyer, Andrea Peroutka *small business owner*

Colorado Springs
Artl, Karen Ann *business owner, author*
Noyes, Richard Hall *bookseller*

Denver
Cashman, Michael Richard *small business owner*
Cheris, Elaine Gayle Ingram *business owner*
Nelson, LeAnn Lindbeck *small business owner*
Newberry, Elizabeth Carter *greenhouse and floral company owner*
Oakes, Terry Louis *retail clothing store executive*

Littleton
Bowe, Roger Lee *small business owner*

Loveland
Rodman, Alpine C. *arts and crafts company executive*
Rodman, Sue A. *wholesale Indian crafts company executive, artist, writer*

CONNECTICUT

Avon
Kling, Phradie (Phradie Kling Gold) *small business owner*

Cheshire
Bozzuto, Michael Adam *wholesale grocery company executive*

Enfield
Squires, William Allen *distribution company executive*

Fairfield
Wexler, Herbert Ira *retail company executive*

Glastonbury
Goodwin, Rodney Keith Grove *international bank and trade company executive*

Greenwich
Pivirotto, Richard Roy *former retail executive*

New Britain
Davidson, Phillip Thomas *retail company executive*

New London
Lumadue, Donald Dean *hobby and crafts company executive*

Norwalk
Bennett, Carl *retired discount department store executive*

Old Lyme
Johnson, Diana Atwood *business owner, innkeeper*

Shelton
Pagliaro, Frank Carl, Jr. *collection agency executive, city official*

Windsor
Goldman, Ethan Harris *retail executive*

DELAWARE

Wilmington
Uffner, Michael S. *retail automotive executive*

DISTRICT OF COLUMBIA

Washington
Brown, Doreen Leah Hurwitz *development company executive*
Carr, Marie Pinak *book distribution company executive*
Chalkley, Jacqueline Ann *retail company executive*
†DeBusk, F. Amanda *export administration executive*
Howell, Joseph Toy *company owner*
Kelso, Gwendolyn Lee *silver appraiser, consultant*
Lessard, Arnold Fred *international business executive*
McGraw, Lavinia Morgan *retired retail company executive*
†Mezo, Ronald S. *retail executive, small business consultant*
†Pelavin, Diane Christine *small business owner, research analyst*
Smith, Jack Carl *foreign trade consultant*
Wurtzel, Alan Leon *retail company executive*

FLORIDA

Aventura
Golden, Alfred *business owner*

Bradenton
Beall, Robert Matthews, II *retail chain executive*
Blankenship, Dwight David *business owner*
Corey, Kay Janis *business owner, designer, nurse*

Brandon
Pomeroy, Wyman Burdette *business owner, consultant*

Clearwater
Hoornstra, Edward H. *retail company executive*
Maxwell, Richard Anthony *retail executive*
Stettner, Jerald W. *retail drugs stores executive*
Turley, Stewart *retired retail company executive*

Coral Gables
†Currier, Susan Anne *computer software company executive*
Freedman, Anne Beller *public speaking and marketing consultant*

Deerfield Beach
Moran, Patricia Genevieve *corporate executive*

Englewood
Heintz, Mary Ethel *business owner*

Fort Lauderdale
†Dworin, Micki (Maxine) *automobile dealership executive*
Kropp, Stacy Anne *small business owner*
Loos, John Thompson *business owner*
Palmer, Marcia Stibal *food and wine retailer, interior designer, real estate investor*
Wojcik, Cass *decorative supply company executive, former city official*

Fort Myers
Colgate, Doris Eleanor *retailer, sailing school owner and adminstrator*

Fort Myers Beach
Tatarian, Mary Linda *retailer, real estate broker*

Gainesville
McClellan, Richard Augustus *small business owner*

Highland Beach
Frager, Albert S. *retired retail food company executive*

Jacksonville
Mann, Timothy *corporate executive*
Stein, Jay *retail executive*

Jupiter
Peters, S. Jeffrey *small business owner, foundation administrator*

Lakeland
Luther, George Albert *truck brokerage executive*

Longboat Key
Goldsmith, Jack Landman *former retail company executive*

Marco Island
Lesser, Joseph M. *retired business executive, retail store executive*

Melbourne
Smith, Willis Ballard (Milton Smith) *business owner*

Merritt Island
Smith, David Edward *business executive*

Miami
Chaplin, Harvey *wine and liquor wholesale executive*
Liebes, Raquel *import/export company executive, educator*
Newlin, Kimrey Dayton *international trade consultant, political consultant, personal computer analyst*
Risi, Louis J., Jr. *business executive*
Urban, Alan Gene *painter, art executive*

Miami Beach
Katzenstein, Thea *retail executive, jewelry designer*

Naples
McCarthy, Joseph Harold *consultant, former retail food company executive*
White, Warren Wurtele *retired retailing executive*

Orlando
Kindlund, Newton Carlton *retail executive*

Palm Beach
Black, Leonard Julius *retail store consultant*

Saint Augustine
Bishop, Claire DeArment *small business owner, former librarian*

Sanibel
Perkinson, Diana Agnes Zouzelka *interior design firm import company executive*

Sarasota
Meyer, B. Fred *small business executive, home designer and builder, product designer*

Sunrise
Groover, Sandra Mae *business executive*

Tampa
Davis, Blondell Gilliam *business manager, evangelist, artist, author*
Eddy, Colette Ann *aerial photography studio owner, photographer*

West Melbourne
Fetner, Suzanne *small business owner*

GEORGIA

Alpharetta
Watts, William David *corporate executive, business owner*

Atlanta
Allen, Ivan, Jr. *office products company owner*
Cabey, Alfred Arthur, Jr. *business owner, publisher*
Farmer, Mary Bauder *small business owner, artist, painter*
Haverty, Rawson *retail furniture company executive*
Kalafut, George Wendell *distribution company executive, retired naval officer*
Marcus, Bernard *retail executive*

Brunswick
Hicks, Virginia Hobson *bookstore owner, educator*

Dalton
Saul, Julian *retail executive*

Decatur
Solomon, Hilda Pearl *wholesale executive*

Fort Valley
Stumbo, Helen Luce *retail executive*

Lavonia
Raines, Stephen Samuel *franchising, consulting and development firm executive, lawyer*

Macon
Jones, Carolyn Evans *speaker, writer, small business owner*

Smyrna
Head, John Francis, Jr. *distributing company executive*

Social Circle
Penland, John Thomas *import and export and development companies executive*

Statesboro
Bacon, Martha Brantley *small business owner*

Tunnel Hill
†McNelley, Judy Anne *small business owner*

Valdosta
Halter, H(enry) James, Jr. (Diamond Jim Halter) *retail executive*

Vidalia
Fortner, Billie Jean *small business owner*

HAWAII

Honolulu
†Hays, John Tennyson, III *import, export company executive*
Lee, Candie Ching Wah *retail executive*
Nakabayashi, Nicholas Takateru *retired retail executive*
Niles, Geddes Leroy *private investigator*

Kailua Kona
Luizzi, Ronald *wholesale distribution executive*

IDAHO

Boise
Long, William D. *grocery store executive*

ILLINOIS

Auburn
Burtle, Debra Ann *needlework and gift shop owner*

Bensenville
Leach, Donald Paul *small business owner*
Lewis, Darrell L. *retail executive*
Naker, Mary Leslie *export transportation company executive*

Bloomingdale
Pelant, Barney Frank *international business consulting executive*

Champaign
Flora, Kent Allen *small business owner*

Chicago
Al-Chalabi, Margery Lee *economic development services company executive*
Beck, Robert Lee *bookstore owner*
Christianson, Stanley David *corporate executive*
Doolittle, Sidney Newing *retail executive*
Gall, Betty Bluebaum *office services company executive*
Gingiss, Benjamin Jack *retired formal clothing stores executive*
Goddu, Roger *retail executive*
Robins, Joel *company executive*
Tomaino, Joseph Carmine *former retail executive, former postal inspector*
Vrablik, Edward Robert *import/export company executive*
Vyn, Kathleen A. *small business owner*
Will, Jon Nicholson *small business owner, financial consultant*

Crystal Lake
Wood, Leslie Ann *retail administrator*

Danville
Brumaghim, Paul *small business owner*

Decatur
Bradshaw, Billy Dean *retail executive*
Cain, Richard Duane *small business owner*

Deerfield
†Jorndt, Louis Daniel *retail drug store chain executive*

Evanston
Markowitz, Judith Ann *owner small business*

Glen Ellyn
Baloun, John Charles *wholesale grocery company executive, retired*

Glencoe
Nebenzahl, Kenneth *rare book and map dealer, author*

Glenview
Schulman, Alan Michael *small business owner*

Jacksonville
†Ware, Jon Dean *retail executive*

Lisle
Bradna, Joanne Justice *manufacturer's representative*

Morton Grove
McKenna, Andrew James *paper distribution and printing company executive, baseball club executive*

Naperville
Wake, William S. *wholesale distribution executive*

Niles
Fillicaro, Barbara Jean *business owner, consultant*

Oak Brook
Hodnik, David F. *retail company executive*
Holsinger, Wayne Townsend *retail executive, retired*

Oak Park
Spartz, Alice Anne Lenore *retired retail executive*

Palatine
Cesario, Robert Charles *franchise executive, consultant*

Riverwoods
Ferkenhoff, Robert J. *retail executive*

Steger
Carpenter, Kenneth Russell *international trading executive*

Wheeling
Hestad, Bjorn Mark *metal distributing company executive*
Ochsner, Othon Henry, II *importer, restaurant critic*

Wilmette
Mc Nitt, Willard Charles *business executive*
Williams, Emory *former retail company executive, banker*

Winnetka
Person, Paula (Mrs. P. Barry Person) *social skills organization executive, entrepreneur*

INDIANA

Bicknell
Risley, Gregory Byron *furniture company executive, interior designer*

Elkhart
Drexler, Rudy Matthew, Jr. *professional law enforcement dog trainer*

Evansville
Blesch, K(athy) Suzann *small business owner*
Craig, Martha Ann *retail store owner*

Fort Wayne
Cast, Anita Hursh *small business owner*
Cummings, William Robert, Jr. *business executive*
Curtis, Douglas Homer *small business owner*

Indianapolis
Fredrickson, William Robert *scientist, company executive*

La Crosse, James *retail executive*
Norwalk, Kelli Curran *retail executive, entrepreneur*
Pyle, R. Michael *wholesale distribution executive*
Seitz, Melvin Christian, Jr. *distributing company executive*
Seneff, Smiley Howard *business owner*
Stout, William Jewell *department store executive*

Jasper
Newman, Leonard Jay *retail jewel merchant, gemologist*

Marion
Simons, Richard Stuart *retailer, owner*

Terre Haute
Cary, Walter Ray *small business owner*

IOWA

Cedar Rapids
Baldwin, George Koehler *retail executive*

Des Moines
Westphal, Deborah Louise *retail executive, choreographer*

Keosauqua
Murphy, Donna Lee *retired dance school owner*

Marshalltown
Shawstad, Raymond Vernon *retired business owner/ computer specialist*

Orange City
Korver, Gerry R(ozeboom) *purchasing executive*

West Des Moines
Pearson, Ronald Dale *retail food stores corporation executive*

West Union
Hansen, Ruth Lucille Hofer *business owner, consultant*

KANSAS

Kansas City
Baska, James Louis *wholesale grocery company executive*
Carolan, Douglas *wholesale company executive*

Olathe
Cordell, Steven Mark *small business owner*

Osawatomie
Jimenez, Bettie Eileen *retired small business owner*

Shawnee Mission
Minkoff, Jill S. *business owner, entrepreneur*

Wichita
Gates, Walter Edward *small business owner*
Trombold, Walter Stevenson *supply company executive*

KENTUCKY

Berea
Brosi, George Ralph *small business owner*

Glasgow
Lessenberry, Robert Adams *retail executive*

Lancaster
Arnold, Cecil Benjamin *former small business owner*

Louisville
Smith, Donald Ray *magazine dealer*

Olive Hill
Anderson, Melissa Eva *small business owner*

Owensboro
Edge, Marianne Smith *business owner*

Winchester
Book, John Kenneth (Kenny Book) *retail store owner*

LOUISIANA

Bossier City
Johnson, Ruby LaVerne *retail executive*

Houma
Rhodes, Gene Paul *small business owner*

Lafayette
Guidry, Rodney-Lee Joseph *small business owner*
Zuschlag, Richard Emery *small business owner*

Shreveport
Dickson, Markham Allen *wholesale company executive*

MAINE

Fairfield
Massaua, John Roger *retail executive*

Freeport
Gorman, Leon A. *mail order company executive*

Kennebunk
Ward, Nina Gillson *jewelry store executive*

Scarborough
Farrington, Hugh G. *wholesale food and retail drug company executive*

Sedgwick
Donnell, William Ray *small business owner, communications executive*

MARYLAND

Annapolis
Cann, Nancy Timanus *retail yacht sales executive*

Baltimore
Durham, J(ames) Michael *retail executive*
Hoffberger, Jerold Charles *corporation executive*
Schilling, Franklin Charles, Jr. *retail management professional*
Stein, Bernard Alvin *business consultant*

Ellicott City
Huey, J(oseph) Wistar, III *import/export executive*

Frederick
Rock, Sandra Kaye *retail executive*

Gaithersburg
Nemecek, Albert Duncan, Jr. *retail company executive, investment banker, management consultant*

Largo
†Adams, Mark *retail executive*
†Schwartz, Mark *home improvement stores executive*

Potomac
Shapiro, Richard Gerald *retired department store executive, consultant*

Riva
Barto, Bradley Edward *small business owner, educator*

Rockville
Kamerow, Norman Warren *business owner, financial services executive*

Severn
†Wions, Steven Paul *small business owner*

Sykesville
Gubernatis, Thomas Frank, Sr. *electrical buyer*

MASSACHUSETTS

Auburn
Baker, David Arthur *small business owner, manufacturer*

Bernardston
Fullerton, Albert Louis, Jr. *bookstore owner*

Boston
Diener, Betty Jane *business educator*
†Giargiari, Michelle *retail executive, artist*
Kane, Louis Isaac *merchant*
Kwasnick, Paul Jack *retail executive*
Rosenberg, Manuel *retail company executive*
Rutstein, Stanley Harold *apparel retailing company executive*
Zaldastani, Guivy *business consultant*

Cambridge
Lazarus, Maurice *retired retail executive*

Canton
Bentas, Lily H. *retail executive*

Dudley
Van de Workeen, Priscilla Townsend *small business owner and executive*

Framingham
Cammarata, Bernard *retail company executive*
Feldberg, Sumner Lee *retired retail company executive*
Wishner, Steven R. *retail executive*

Hingham
Cooke, Gordon Richard *retail executive*
†Larsen, Edward Lee *retail executive*

Marlborough
Palihnich, Nicholas Joseph, Jr. *retail executive*

Medfield
McQuillen, Jeremiah Joseph *distribution executive*

Milton
Huban, Christopher M. *retail buyer, manager*

Natick
Nugent, John J. *wholesale distribution executive*
Zarkin, Herbert *retail company executive*

Needham
DerMarderosian, Diran Robert *rug cleaning company executive*

North Eastham
York, Elizabeth Jane *innkeeper*

Plympton
O'Connell, Philip Edward *retired retail business owner*

Quincy
Tobin, Robert G. *supermarket chain executive*

Somerville
Fryatt, Richard Paul *import distribution executive*

South Dartmouth
Hodgson, James Stanley *antiquarian bookseller*

MICHIGAN

Ann Arbor
Quinnell, Bruce Andrew *retail book chain executive*

Bad Axe
Sullivan, James Gerald *business owner, postal letter carrier*

Battle Creek
Hazel, James R. C., Jr. *small business owner, civic volunteer*

Bloomfield Hills
Robinson, Jack Albert *retail drug stores executive*

Dearborn
Younis, Mahmoud Rachid *business owner, electrical engineer*

Detroit
Tushman, J. Lawrence *wholesale distribution executive*

Farmington Hills
Pargoff, Robert Michael *small business owner*

Grand Blanc
Hicks, Susan Lynn Bowman *small business owner*

Grand Rapids
DeLapa, Judith Anne *business owner*
Meijer, Douglas *retail company executive*
Meijer, Frederik *retail company executive*
Meijer, Hendrik *retail company executive*
Meijer, Mark *retail executive*
Morin, William Raymond *bookstore chain executive*
†Riley, Robert E. *retail executive, lawyer*

Lansing
LaHaine, Gilbert Eugene *retail lumber company executive*

Midland
Huntress, Betty Ann *former music store proprietor, educator*

Naubinway
Beaudoin, Robert Lawrence *small business owner*

Oscoda
Shackleton, Mary Jane *small business owner*

Paw Paw
Warner, James John *small business owner*

Richmond
Huvaere, Richard Floyd *auto dealer*

Royal Oak
Corwin, Vera-Anne Versfelt *small business owner, consultant*

Saint Clair Shores
Seppala, Katherine Seaman (Mrs. Leslie W. Seppala) *retail company executive*

Saint Joseph
McCoy, Richard James *jeweler, real estate developer, broker*
Renwick, Ken *retail executive*

Saline
†Ottum, Brian Douglas *research and marketing consulting executive*

Southfield
Portnoy, Lynn A. *fashion retailer*

Troy
†Cooper, Warren F. *retail executive*
Hall, Floyd *retail executive*
Strome, Stephen *distribution company executive*

MINNESOTA

Edina
Emmerich, Karol Denise *foundation executive, former retail executive*

Grand Rapids
Crane, Faye *small business owner*

Minneapolis
†Bogdan, Joann *retail executive*
Erickson, Ronald A. *retail executive*
Gilpin, Larry Vincent *retail executive*
Hale, James Thomas *retail company executive, lawyer*
Logan, Veryle Jean *retail executive, realtor*
Mammel, Russell Norman *retired food distribution company executive*
Ruff, Dureen Anne *small business owner, operater*
†Stephenson, Vivian M. *retail executive*
Trestman, Frank D. *distribution company executive*
Ulrich, Robert J. *retail discount chain stores executive*
Wright, Michael William *wholesale distribution, retailing executive*

Minnetonka
Beeler, Donald Daryl *retail executive*

Saint Paul
Nash, Nicholas David *retailing executive*
Sykes, Philip Kimbark *retail executive*

Walker
Collins, Thomas William *caterer, consultant*

West Saint Paul
Sittard, Herman Joseph *public relations executive, editor, retired*

MISSOURI

Charleston
Cassell, Lucille Richardson *small business owner*

Chesterfield
Schwind, Wanda Ruth *retail executive*

Clayton
Hall, Carl Loren *electrical distribution executive*
Ross, E. Earl *small business owner*

Cuba
Work, Bruce Van Syoc *business consultant*

Franklin
Becker, Barbara Ann Stulac (Bobbie Becker) *small business owner*

Independence
Lundy, Sadie Allen *small business owner*

Joplin
Logsdon, Cindy Ann *small business owner*

Kansas City
Stueck, William Noble *small business owner*
Truitt, Kenneth Ray *owner*

Lebanon
Louderback, Kevin Wayne *business owner*

Maryland Heights
Marcus, John *wholesale distribution executive*

Saint Charles
Dauphinais, George Arthur *import company executive*

Saint Louis
Bridgewater, Bernard Adolphus, Jr. *footwear company executive*
Edison, Bernard Alan *retired retail apparel company executive*
Fish, Michele Loyd *retailer*
Hartenbach, Stephen Charles *small business owner*
Loeb, Jerome Thomas *retail executive*
Newman, Andrew Edison *restaurant executive*
Schnuck, Craig D. *grocery stores company executive*
Upbin, Hal Jay *consumer products executive*
Van Dover, Donald *business owner, consultant*

Saint Peters
Krey, Mary Ann Reynolds *beer wholesaler executive*

Springfield
Wishard, Mary Lee *small business operator*

MONTANA

Butte
Shipham, Mark Roger *small business owner, artist*

Helena
Brown, Jan Whitney *small business owner*

NEBRASKA

Lincoln
Rawley, Ann Keyser *small business owner, picture framer*

NEVADA

Las Vegas
Marcovitz, Leonard Edward *retail executive*

NEW HAMPSHIRE

New Castle
Friese, George Ralph *retail executive*

New London
Thoma, Kurt Michael *business owner*

North Salem
Stone, Robert Eldred *small business owner, museum director*

Northwood
Macri, Stephan Anthony *seafood export company executive*

Warner
Face, Wayne Bruce *small business owner*

NEW JERSEY

Brookside
†Keyes, Richard Paul *small business owner*

Carteret
†Jemal, Lawrence *retail executive*

Chatham
Manning, Frederick William *retired retail executive*

Elizabeth
Gellert, George Geza *food importing company executive*

Englewood
Rawl, Arthur Julian (Lord of Cursons) *retail executive, accountant, consultant, author*
Solomon, Edward David *consultant*

Franklin Lakes
Kapr, John Robert *operations executive*

Freehold
Foster, Eric Harold, Jr. *retail executive*

Mahwah
Inserra, Lawrence R. *retail executive*

Manasquan
†Giuffrida, Thomas S. *telecommunications executive*

Montvale
Wood, James *supermarket executive*

Moonachie
Toscano, Samuel, Jr. *wholesale distribution executive*

New Milford
Walsh, Joseph Michael *magazine distribution executive*

New Monmouth
Donnelly, Gerard Kevin *marketing and retail executive*

North Bergen
Karp, Roberta S. *wholesale apparel and accessories executive*

Paramus
Goldstein, Michael *retail executive*
Nakasone, Robert C. *retail toy and game company executive*

Princeton
Hochschwender, Karl Albert *international trade and government relations consultant*
Simmons, Warren Hathaway, Jr. *retired retail executive*

Princeton Junction
Payne, Linda Cohen *business owner*

Seaside Park
Tweed, John Louis *consultant, association executive, lecturer, small business owner*

Secaucus
†Syms, Marcy *retail executive*

Somerville
Campbell, Mildred Corum *business owner, nurse*

South Orange
Teetsell, Janice Marie Newman *business owner, lawyer*

South River
Fontaine, Bernard Leo, Jr. *small business owner*

Teaneck
Lawrence, Brian David *wedding professional*

Verona
Brightman, Robert Lloyd *importer, textile company executive, consultant*

Wayne
Lang, William Charles *financial executive*

NEW YORK

Appleton
Singer, Thomas Kenyon *international business consultant, farmer*

Bellport
Regalmuto, Nancy Marie *small business owner, psychic consultant, therapist*

Binghamton
Florance, Douglas Allan *wholesale distributor*

Brooklyn
Levine, Neil *small business owner*
Magliocco, John *wholesale distribution executive*
Rosen, Stuart Morris *wholesale distributor*
Zelin, Jerome *retail executive*

Buffalo
Cozzi, Ronald Lee *antiquarian book seller, rare book appraiser*
Jerge, Dale Robert *small business owner*

Hunter
Jaeckel, Christopher Carol *memorabilia company executive, antiquarian*

Katonah
Levine, Pamela Gail *business owner*

Lewiston
Simonson, Lee J. *small business owner*

Lockport
†Bontempi, Gail Diane *small business owner*

Mattituck
Marquardt, Ann Marie *small business administrator*

New York
Becker, Isidore A. *business executive*
Brown, Andreas Le *book store and art gallery executive*
Caputo, Lucio *trade company executive*
Catsimatidis, John Andreas *retail chain executive, airline executive*
Farah, Roger *retail company executive*
Finkelstein, Edward Sydney *department store executive*
Fortgang, Charles *wholesale distribution executive*
†Friedman, Rachelle *music retail executive*
Gilinsky, Stanley Ellis *department store executive*
Ho, Weifan Lee *merchandise executive*
Matthews, Norman Stuart *department store executive*
Michelson, Gertrude Geraldine *retired retail company executive*
Mondlin, Marvin *retail executive, antiquarian book dealer*
Pressman, Robert *retail executive*
Quint, Ira *retail executive*
Ramer, Richard C. *bookseller, antiquarian*
Seegal, Herbert Leonard *retired department store executive*
Spector, Anita Frohmann *buyer*
Stanton, Ronald P. *export company executive*
Stern, Madeleine Bettina *rare books dealer, author*
Strauss, Edward Robert *carpet company executive*
Tendler, David *international trade company executive*
Tutun, Edward H. *retired retail executive*
Vander Heyden, Marsha Ann *business owner*
Washburn, Joan Thomas *business owner, art gallery director*

North Syracuse
Smith, Gail B. *small business owner*

Ossining
Getts, Nino *studio owner*

Rochester
McCurdy, Gilbert Geier *retired retailer*

Sag Harbor
Barry, Nada Davies *retail business owner*

Scarsdale
Sandell, Richard Arnold *international trade executive, economist*

Stony Brook
†Grudens, Richard William *retail executive, writer*

Syracuse
Fisher, Joseph V. *retail executive*

Whitestone
Caldwell, David Bruce *music store executive*

Yonkers
Friend, Miriam Ruth *personnel company executive*

NORTH CAROLINA

Asheville
Pine, Charles *retail executive*

Charlotte
Belk, Irwin *retail executive*
Belk, John M. *retail company executive*
Gambrell, Sarah Belk *retail executive*
Graham, Sylvia Angelenia *wholesale distributor, retail buyer*
Richards, Craig M. *wholesale distribution executive*

Durham
Civello, Anthony Ned *retail drug company executive, pharmacist*

Greensboro
Goulder, Gerald Polster *retail executive, management consultant, lawyer*
Kennedy, Charles G. *wholesale distribution executive*
Kiser, Mose, III *small business owner*
Orlowsky, Martin L. *executive manager*

Highlands
Shaffner, Randolph Preston *shop owner, educator, writer*

Pisgah Forest
Pulliam, Steve Cameron *business owner*

Rocky Mount
Rabon, Ronald Ray *retail jewelry store chain executive*
Wordsworth, Jerry L. *wholesale distribution executive*

Shelby
Arey, Robert Jackson, Jr. *small business owner*

Spindale
Howard, Elizabeth Ann Blanton *courier service executive*

Statesville
Lawson, Willard Francis, Jr. *paper company owner, sales executive*

NORTH DAKOTA

Stanley
Patrick, Dennis M. *theology book dealer*

OHIO

Bellevue
Davenport, Thomas Herbert *small business owner*

Cambridge
Tostenson, Beverly Ann *book store owner*

Chardon
†Takacs, Cris Clair *bookbinder*

Cincinnati
Arnett, Louise Eva *information records management executive*
Hodge, Robert Joseph *retail executive*
Price, Thomas Emile *investment company executive*
†Zimmerman, James M. *retail company executive*

Cleveland
Anderson, Warren *distribution company executive*
Crosby, Fred McClellan *retail home and office furnishings executive*
Milgrim, Franklin Marshall *merchant*

Columbus
Callander, Kay Eileen Paisley *business owner, retired gifted talented education educator, writer*
Hollis-Allbritton, Cheryl Dawn *retail paper supply store executive*
Schottenstein, Jay L. *retail executive*
Traver, Noel Allen *small business owner, creative director*
Unverferth, Barbara Patten *small business owner*
Wexner, Leslie Herbert *retail executive*

Dublin
Walter, Robert D. *wholesale pharmaceutical distribution executive*

Galion
Butterfield, James T. *small business owner*

Helena
Moss, Clifton Michael *factory laborer, small business owner*

Hudson
Duchon, Roseann Marie *business owner, consultant*

Lima
Fisher, Glenn Duane *small business executive*

Lodi
Bock, Carolyn A. *author, consultant, trainer, small business owner*

Mansfield
Amadio-Backowski, Therese Marie *small business owner*
Benham, Lelia *small business owner, social/political activist*

Milford
Conover, Nellie Coburn *retail furniture company executive*

Shaker Heights
Feuer, Michael *office products superstore executive*

Strongsville
Nekola, Louis William *utility line clearance executive*

Toledo
Fuhrman, Charles Andrew *country club proprietor, real estate management executive, lawyer*

West Jefferson
Puckett, Helen Louise *tax consulting company executive*

Westerville
Goh, Anthony Li-Shing *business owner, consultant*

Willoughby
Oldham, Lea Leever *business owner, author*

Youngstown
Catoline-Ackerman, Pauline Dessie *small business owner*
Gottron, Francis Robert, III *small business owner*

OKLAHOMA

Bixby
Brown, James Roy *retail executive*

Oklahoma City
Davis, Emery Stephen *wholesale food company executive*
Howeth, Lynda Carol *small business owner*
Werries, E. Dean *food distribution company executive*
Williams, Richard Donald *retired wholesale food company executive*

Tulsa
Rippley, Robert *wholesale distribution executive*

OREGON

Applegate
Pursglove, Betty Merle *computer-software quality assurance tester*

Eugene
Gillespie, Penny Hannig *business owner*

Klamath Falls
Pastega, Richard Louis *retail specialist*

Medford
Stong, John Elliott *retail music and electronic company executive*

Myrtle Creek
Shirtcliff, John Delzell *business owner, oil jobber*

Portland
Bauer, Louis Edward *retail bookstore executive, educator*
Miller, Robert G. *retail company executive*
Tomjack, T.J. *wholesale distribution executive*

Prineville
Wick, Philip *wholesale distribution executive*

PENNSYLVANIA

Allison Park
Rust, S. Murray, III *building contractor*
Thomson, Douglas Craig *retail executive*

Altoona
Kaufman, Harry *retail executive*
Sheetz, Stanton R. *retail executive*

Berwyn
Fry, Clarence Herbert *retail executive*

Blue Bell
Drye, William James *business owner*

Camp Hill
Grass, Alexander *retail company executive*

Chambersburg
LaBorde, Terrence Lee *small business owner, negotiator*

Cheltenham
Oflazian, Paul Sarkis *small business owner*

Eighty Four
Hardy, Joseph A., Sr. *wholesale distribution executive*

Grover
†Shedden, Lynette Karen *small business owner*

Hawley
Kanzer, Larry *small business owner, food service director*

Hummelstown
Murphy, S(usan) (Jane Murphy) *small business owner*

Lewisburg
Ondrusek, David Francis *discount store chain executive*

Littlestown
Plunkert, Donna Mae *business owner*

Media
Wood, Richard D., Jr. *retail executive*

Mifflintown
Lauver, Nelson Charles *narrator, voice-over, small business owner*

Norristown
Genuardi, Charles A. *retail executive*

Philadelphia
Carter, Irene Lavenia *greeting card company owner, poet*
Visconto, Anthony J. *small business owner*

Pittsburgh
Gerhard, Harry E., Jr. *counter trader, management and trade consultant*

Reading
Boscov, Albert *retail executive*

Sharon
Epstein, Louis Ralph *retired wholesale grocery executive*
Rosenblum, Harold Arthur *grocery distribution executive*

Shippensburg
Thompson, Elizabeth Jane *small business owner*

Shiremanstown
Nesbit, William Terry *small business owner, consultant*

Villanova
Vander Veer, Suzanne *aupair business executive*

West Sunbury
Stewart, Mark Thomas *compressed gas company executive*

Whitehall
Collina, Kathleen Alice *corrugated box company executive*

Williamsport
Largen, Joseph *retailer, furniture manufacturer, book wholesaler*

RHODE ISLAND

Westerly
Hirsch, Larry Joseph *retail executive, lawyer*

Woonsocket
Goldstein, Stanley P. *retail company executive*
†Ryan, Thomas M. *drug store chain executive*

SOUTH CAROLINA

Columbia
Clark, David Randolph *wholesale grocer*

Fort Mill
Morris, John *trading company executive*

Greenville
Bauknight, Clarence Brock *consultant*

Seneca
Caperton, Richard Walton *automobile repair company executive, educator, consultant*

Union
Denton, David Thomas *small business owner*

Yemassee
Olendorf, William Carr, Jr. *small business owner*

TENNESSEE

Bristol
Cauthen, Charles Edward, Jr. *retail executive, business consultant*

Dandridge
Trent, Wendell Campbell *business owner*

Johnson City
Sell, Joan Isobel *mobile home company owner*

Kingsport
Ice, Billie Oberta *retail executive*

Knoxville
Harris, Charles Edgar *retired wholesale distribution company executive*
Jenkins, Frances Owens *retired small business owner*

Lafayette
Crowder, Bonnie Walton *small business owner, composer*

Maryville
Hendren, Jo Ann *small business owner*

Memphis
Johnson, Robert Lewis, Jr. *retail company executive*
Schaefgen, Philip P. *business owner, consultant, accountant*

Nashville
Reid, Donna Joyce *small business owner*
Zibart, Michael Alan *wholesale book company executive*
Zimmerman, Raymond *retail chain executive*

Sevierville
Koff, Shirley Irene *writer, church administrator*

TEXAS

Arlington
Burnett, Paul David *small business owner*
Satterlee, Warren Sanford, II *retail management professional*

Athens
Geddie, Thomas Edwin *retired small business owner*

Austin
Beaman, Margarine Gaynell *scrap metal broker*
Girling, Robert George William, III *business owner*
Lenoir, Gloria Cisneros *small business owner, educator*
Wilson, Margaret Scarbrough *retail executive*

Beaumont
Alter, Nelson Tobias *jewelry retailer and wholesaler*
Alter, Shirley Jacobs *jewelry store owner*
Everett, John Howard *diving business owner, paramedic*

Bellaire
Teas, John Frederick *small business owner*

Boerne
Morton, Michael Ray *retail company consultant*

Brenham
Lubbock, Mildred Marcelle (Midge Lubbock) *former small business owner*

Bryan
Smith, Elouise Beard *restaurant owner*

Carthage
Cooke, Walta Pippen *automobile dealership owner*

Corpus Christi
DuVall, Lorraine *recreation center owner*
Finley, George Alvin, III *wholesale executive*
Salem, Joseph John *jeweler, real estate developer*

Dallas
Augur, Marilyn Hussman *distribution executive*
Callahan, Rickey Don *business owner*
Carter, Donald J. *wholesale distribution, manufacturing executive*
Day, Maurice Jerome *automobile parts distributing company executive*
†Gardner, Ricki *retail store official, minister*
Hallam, Robert G. *wholesale distribution executive*
Halpin, James *retail computer stores executive*
Matthews, Clark J(io), II *retail executive, lawyer*
Stone, Donald James *retired retail executive*

El Paso
Froemming, Herbert Dean *retail executive*
Harden, Doyle Benjamin *import-export company executive*

Fort Worth
Conrad, Craig Edward *electronic distribution executive*
Michero, William Henderson *retired retail trade executive*
Roach, John Vinson, II *retail company executive*
Thompson, Carson R. *retail and manufacturing company executive*

Hitchcock
†Lampl, Lee A. *small business owner*
Shaffer, Richard Paul *business owner, retired career military officer*

Houston
Baysal, Fatih Dogan *trading company executive*

†Gaucher, Jane Heyck *retail executive*
Hughes, James Baker, Jr. *retail executive, consultant*
Levit, Milton *grocery supply company executive*
Lindig, Bill M. *food distribution company executive*
†Oshman, Marilyn *retail executive*
Schmeal, Jacqueline Andre *art store owner*
Tooker, Carl E. *department store executive*
Wagner, Charlene Brook *small business owner, retired middle school educator, consultant*
Wike, D. Elaine *business executive*
Williams, Robert Lyle *corporate executive, consultant*
Woodhouse, John Frederick *food distribution company executive*

Irving
Skinner, John Vernon *retail credit executive*

Levelland
Harrell, Wanda Faye *retail executive*

Longview
Sonnier, David Joseph *wholesale distributing executive*

Lubbock
Snell, Robert *retail executive*
Willingham, Mary Maxine *fashion retailer*

Marble Falls
Simpson, H. Richard (Dick Simpson) *retailer*

Mc Kinney
Fairman, Jarrett Sylvester *retail company executive*

Odessa
Brumelle, Kenneth Coy *retail store owner*

Plano
McKay, Donald A. *retail company executive*
Neppl, Walter Joseph *retired retail store executive*
Oesterreicher, James E. *department stores executive*
Samford, Karen Elaine *small business owner, consultant*

Sulphur Springs
McKenzie, Michael K. *wholesale executive*
Tiegiser, Donald P. *business owner*

Terrell
Wolfe, Tracey Dianne *distributing company executive*

Tyler
Edwards, D. M. *retail, wholesale distribution and commercial real estate investment executive*
Hardin, James *retail food company executive*
Seeber, Joseph Oliver, IV *small business owner, lawyer*
Winskie, Richard Clay *retail executive, songwriter*

Wimberley
Ellis, John *small business owner*

UTAH

Logan
Watterson, Scott *home fitness equipment manufacturer*

Saint George
Day, John Denton *retired company executive, cattle and horse rancher, trainer, wrangler, actor, educator*

Salt Lake City
McDermott, Kathleen E. *retail executive*
Miller, Lorraine *business owner*
†Spalding, Barbara *small business owner*

VERMONT

Brattleboro
Edgerton, Brenda Evans *soup company executive*

Brookfield
Gerard, James Wilson *book distributor*

Colchester
Lawton, Lorilee Ann *pipeline supply company owner, accountant*

Danby
Rudy, Kathleen Vermeulen *small business owner*

Montpelier
Stevens, Allyssa Elizabeth *retail executive*

VIRGINIA

Arlington
Scarborough, Robert Henry, Jr. *enterpreneur*

Bristol
McGlothlin, James W. *wholesale distribution executive*

Charlottesville
Lupton, Mary Hosmer *retired small business owner*

Fairfax
Pugh, Arthur James (Jay Pugh) *retired department store executive, consultant*
Schrock, Simon *retail executive*

Glen Allen
Bennett, Donald Dalton *grocery stores executive*

Mc Lean
Hagar, James Thomas *retail executive*
Vandemark, Robert Goodyear *retired retail company executive*

Norfolk
DeVenny, Lillian Nickell *trophy company executive*

Purcellville
Sharples, Winston Singleton *automobile importer and distributor*

Richmond
Ackman, Paul Jeffrey *wholesale distribution executive, researcher*
Gresham, Ann Elizabeth *retailer, horticulturist executive, consultant*
Sharp, Richard L. *retail company executive*
Sniffin, John Harrison *retail executive*
Ukrop, James E. *retail executive*

Salem
Brand, Edward Cabell *retail executive*

Staunton
Hammaker, Paul M. *retail executive, business educator, author*

Sterling
Moulton, James Roger *small business owner*

WASHINGTON

Bellingham
Olsen, Mark Norman *small business owner*

Buckley
Christensen, Doris Ann *antique dealer, researcher, writer*

Ellensburg
Shults, Mary J. *retail store owner*

Issaquah
Brotman, Jeffrey H. *variety stores executive*
Sinegal, James D. *variety store wholesale business executive*

Lynnwood
Stocking, Sherl Dee *retail executive*

Monroe
Kirwan, Katharyn Grace (Mrs. Gerald Bourke Kirwan, Jr.) *retail executive*

Redmond
Nagel, Daryl David *retail executive*

Seattle
Bridge, Herbert Marvin *jewelry executive*
Denniston, Martha Kent *business owner, author*
Farrington-Hopf, Susan Kay *plumbing and heating contractor*
Fix, Wilbur James *department store executive*
Leale, Olivia Mason *import marketing company executive*
Read, Charles Raymond, Sr. *business executive*
Smith, Mara A. *small business owner, artist*
Stearns, Susan Tracey *lighting design company executive, lawyer*
Stewart, Thomas J. *wholesale distribution executive*

Spokane
Krueger, Larry Eugene *import export company executive, lawyer*
Leighton, Jack Richard *small business owner, former educator*
Sines, Randy Dwain *business executive*
Wagner, Teresa Ann *business owner*

Yakima
Newland, Ruth Laura *small business owner*

WISCONSIN

Argyle
Davis, Jane Strauss *business owner*

Beloit
Hendricks, Kenneth *wholesale distribution executive*

Hatley
Bartholomaus, Brett William *small business owner*

Hurley
Nicholls, Thomas Maurice *business owner*

Menomonee Falls
Kellogg, William S. *retail executive*

Milwaukee
†Choban, Glenwood T. *business owner*
Papas, George Nick *bakery company executive*
Wucherer, Ruth Marie *small business owner*

Pewaukee
Lestina, Gerald F. *wholesale grocery executive*

Rhinelander
Kovala, Kathleen Ann *small business owner, educator*

Stevens Point
Copps, Michael William *retail and wholesale company executive*

Warrens
Potter, June Anita *small business owner*

Wausau
Builer, Dorothy Marion *business owner*

WYOMING

Douglas
Harrop, Diane Glaser *shop owner, mayor*

Jackson
Law, Clarene Alta innkeeper, state legislator

CANADA

MANITOBA

Winnipeg
Cohen, Albert Diamond retail executive

ONTARIO

London
Crncich, Tony Joseph retired pharmacy chain executive

Toronto
†Bachand, Stephen E. retail company executive
Ryan, James Franklin retail executive

Willowdale
Binder, Herbert R. drug store chain executive
Bloom, David Ronald retail drug company executive

MEXICO

Mexico City
Kim, Earnest Jae-Hyun import and export company executive

DEM REPUBLIC OF CONGO, AFRICA

Kinshasha
†Musafiri, Ngongo Elongo import-export executive, agricultural consultant

ADDRESS UNPUBLISHED

Alexakos, Frances Marie business owner, psychology educator, researcher, producer, editor
†Antioco, John F. entertainment company executive
Aspen, Alfred William international trading company executive
Aved, Barry retail executive, consultant
Baker, Edward Kevin retail executive
Barrett, Yvonne Laughlin retail manager
Baugh, John Frank wholesale company executive, retired
Bayard, Susan Shapiro educator, small business owner
Biagi, Richard Charles retail executive, real estate consultant
Bice, Michael David retail and wholesale executive, marketing consultant, insurance consultant
Binder, Madeline Dotti retail professional
Birne, Cindy Frank business owner
Bogart, Carol Lynn writer, media consultant
Bolotin, Lora M. retired business owner, electronics executive
Brabec, Rosemary Jean retail executive
†Bradshaw, John Robert internet service company executive
Bravo, Rose Marie retail executive
Brewer, Stanley R. wholesale grocery executive
Broth, Ray retail executive
Busch, Joyce Ida small business owner
Chevalier, Paul Edward retired retail executive, lawyer
Clark, Maxine retail executive
†Clark, Sue Janet business owner
Claus, Carol Jean small business owner
Colgate, Stephen small business owner
Conte, Andrea retail executive, health care consultant, community activist
†Corcoran, Philip E. wholesale distribution executive
Cross, Betty Felt small business owner
Dealy, Janette Diane marketing consultant
Depkovich, Francis John retired retail chain executive
DeVivo, Ange former small business owner
†Dooley, Timothy Kevin retail professional
Dwight, Harvey Alpheus retired small business owner
Dyer, Arlene Thelma retail company owner
Edgerton, Richard restaurant and hotel owner
Edwards, Patricia Burr small business owner, counselor, consultant
Edwards, Patrick Ross former retail company executive, lawyer, management consultant
Ellis, Patricia Weathers small business owner, electronic technician
Evans, Robert George, Jr. retail and mail order executive
Fehr, Gregory Paris marketing and distribution company executive
Fields, Douglas Philip building supply and home furnishings wholesale company executive
Fields, Leo former jewelry company executive, investor
Firster, D. James small business owner
Folkman, David H. retail, wholesale and consumer products consultant
Gagen, J. Wilfrid business owner, marketing and public relations executive, consultant
Galvao, Louis Alberto import and export corporation executive, consultant
Gamroth, Arthur Paul small business owner
†Garza, Fernando Raul small business owner
Geoffroy, Charles Henry retired business executive
Goldman, Gerald Hillis beverage distribution company executive
Goldner, Sheldon Herbert export-import company executive
Goldstein, Alfred George retail and consumer products executive
Goldstein, Norman Ray international trading company executive, consultant
Gray, Deborah Mary wine importer
Hawk, Robert Dooley wholesale grocery company executive
Henderson, Deirdre Healy interior decorating, leasing company executive
Hoving, Raymond Howard consultant
Howell, William Robert retail company executive
Huron, Roderick Eugene small business owner
Jirousek, Charles Edward small business owner
Kay, Patricia Kremer business owner
Kittlitz, Linda Gale small business owner
Kogut, John Anthony retail/wholesale executive
Lape, Michael John small business owner
Lebor, John F(rancis) retired department store executive
LeMonnier, Daniel Brian small business owner, entertainer
Lowry, Marilyn Jean horticultural retail company executive
Marshall, George Dwire retired supermarket chain executive
Martini, Robert Edward wholesale pharmaceutical and medical supplies company executive
McGaw, Kenneth Roy wholesale distribution executive
McIntosh, Calvin Eugene retired small business owner
†McLaurin, Cathy Reneé small business owner, artist, educator
Meek, Forrest Burns trading company executive
Melnikoff, Sarah Ann gem importer, jewelry designer
Mench, John William retail store executive, electrical engineer
Metz, Steven William small business owner
Meyer, Lasker Marcel retail executive
†Molinari, Ana Maria salon owner
†Montoya, Michael Evaristo small busniess owner
Moy, Audrey retired retail buyer
Murphy, Donna Mae small business owner, social worker, lawyer
Napoleon, Donald Paul grocery store executive
Nicholas, Lawrence Bruce import company executive
Nicolas, Kenneth Lee international financial business executive
Nishimura, Joseph Yo retired retail executive, accountant
Paterson, Robert E. trading stamp company executive
Pearl, B. Michael business owner
Phillips, Darrell retail executive
Polichino, Joseph Anthony, Jr. wholesale company executive
Raab, Herbert Norman retail executive
Ramsey, Lucie Avra small business owner
Ransome, Ernest Leslie, III retail company executive
Raskin, Michael A. retail company executive
†Rickard, Norman Edward office equipment company executive
Rizzolo, Robert Steven small business owner, historian
Rodbell, Clyde Armand distribution executive
Rohner, Bonnie-Jean small business owner, computer consultant
Rosenbaum, Irving M. retail store executive
Ruland, Midlred Ardelia retail executive, retail buyer
Runge, Donald Edward food wholesale company executive
Samson, Alvin former distributing company executive, consultant
Sewell, Phyllis Shapiro retail chain executive
Sherwood, (Peter) Louis retail executive
Smith, Shelly Gerald, Jr. small business owner, author
Stemberg, Thomas George retail executive
Stern, Charles retired foreign trade company executive
Substad Lokensgard-Schimmelpfennig, Kathryn Ann small business owner, career consultant
Swiff, Kelly small business owner, civic volunteer, author
Tate, Fran M. small business owner
Thayer, Martha Ann small business owner
Tielke, James Clemens retail and manufacturing management consultant
Tomkiel, Judith Irene small business owner
Trutter, John Thomas consulting company executive
Vernon, Carl Atlee, Jr. retired wholesale food distributor executive
Vila, Adis Maria corporate executive, former government official, lawyer
Violette, Diane Marie small business owner, consultant, editor
Waddle, John Frederick former retail chain executive
White, Bruce Emerson, Jr. business chain executive
Wien, Stuart Lewis retired supermarket chain executive
Wiesner, John Joseph retail chain store executive
Williams, Leona Rae lingerie shop owner, consultant
Winter, Richard Samuel, Jr. computer training company owner, writer
Wolfe, Jonathan A. food wholesaler, retailer
Wood, Arthur MacDougall retired retail executive
Zamansky, Jeffrey Ira small business owner
Zodl, Joseph Arthur international trade executive, consultant

INDUSTRY: TRANSPORTATION

UNITED STATES

ALABAMA

Athens
†Ruf, Donnie Lee delivery service driver

Birmingham
Brough, James A. airport terminal executive

Gulf Shores
Wallace, John Loys aviation services executive

Huntsville
Heidish, Louise Oridge-Schwallie transportation specialist, marketing professional
Olstead, Christopher Eric aerospace executive, talent manager

Meridianville
Oberhausen, Joyce Ann Wynn aircraft company executive, artist

ALASKA

Anchorage
†Bowers, Paul D. transportation company executive
Sullivan, George Murray transportation consultant, former mayor

Fairbanks
†Ruff, Doyle C. airport manager

Juneau
†Miller, David C. airport manager

Ketchikan
†Chenhall, Donald R. airport manager

ARIZONA

Bullhead City
†Bettendorf, Jerry airport administrator
†Hicks, Norm airport operations executive

Grand Canyon
Bryant, Leland Marshal business and nonprofit executive

Phoenix
Amoako, James Kwaku transportation services executive, financial analyst
Aybar, Charles Anton aviation executive
Elien, Mona Marie air transportation professional
Solomon, John Davis aviation executive
Woods, Bobby Joe transportation executive

Prescott
Morrison, Gladys Mae pilot training firm executive

Tucson
Ballou, Kenneth Walter retired transportation executive, university dean
Burg, Walter A. airport terminal executive
Mercker, Mary Alice aviation school administrator
Smith, Gordon Eugene pilot

ARKANSAS

Bella Vista
Pogue, William Reid former astronaut, foundation executive, business and aerospace consultant

Conway
Petersen, Laddian Walter flight operations director

Fort Smith
Young, Robert A., III freight systems executive

Huntsville
Carr, Gerald Paul former astronaut, business executive, former marine officer

Little Rock
†Knight, John K. aeronautics director

Lowell
Hunt, J. B. transportation executive

Pine Bluff
Seawell, William Thomas former airline executive

Warren
†Harper, David Virgil water system operator

CALIFORNIA

Burbank
Volk, Robert Harkins aviation company executive

Edwards
Brand, Vance Devoe astronaut, government official
Deets, Dwain Aaron aerospace technology executive

El Segundo
Gregg, Lucius Perry, Jr. aerospace executive

Encino
Aaronson, Robert Jay aviation executive
Gasich, Welko Elton retired aerospace executive, management consultant
O'Donnell, Scott Richard aviation administrator

Fountain Valley
Mauldin, Jean Humphries aviation company executive

Gilroy
Borton, George Robert retired airline captain

Hawthorne
Hunt, Brian L. program manager

Healdsburg
Kamm, Thomas Allen air transportation company executive

Inyokern
Bass, Nancy Agnes airport executive

Irvine
Crowley, Daniel Francis, Jr. transportation and logistics executive

La Mesa
Hansen, Grant Lewis retired aerospace and information systems executive

Laguna Beach
Linhart, Eddie Gene aerospace executive

Long Beach
Anderson, Gerald Verne retired aerospace company executive
Moss, Elizabeth Lucille (Betty Moss) transportation company executive
Myers, John Wescott aviation executive
Williams, David Alexander pilot

Los Angeles
Anderson, Roy A. aerospace company executive
†Bruce, William A. airport executive
Coln, William Alexander, III pilot
Kresa, Kent aerospace executive
Miller, Gary Douglas aerospace company executive, former urban planning consultant
Moore, Walter Dengel rapid transit system professional
Park, Sam-Koo transportation executive
Welborne, John Howard railway company executive, lawyer
Williams, Walter David aerospace executive, consultant

Malibu
Ensign, Richard Papworth transportation executive

Menlo Park
Morrison, David Fred freight company executive
O'Brien, Raymond Francis transportation executive

Murrieta
Steiling, Daniel Paul retired railroad conductor, writer

Oakland
Crowley, Thomas B., Jr. water transportation executive
Haskell, Arthur Jacob retired steamship company executive
Reynolds, Kathleen Diane Foy (KDF Reynolds) transportation executive
Rhein, Timothy J. transportation company executive
Wade, Bill airport executive

Ontario
†Drinkwater, Peter L. airport executive

Palo Alto
Kott, Joseph transportation executive, consultant, educator
Moffitt, Donald Eugene transportation company executive

Palos Verdes Estates
Smith, Stephen Randolph aerospace executive

Palos Verdes Peninsula
Slusser, Robert Wyman aerospace company executive

Ramona
Hoffman, Wayne Melvin retired airline official

Rancho Cucamonga
Bucks, Charles Alan airline industry consultant, former executive

Redwood City
Foley, Patrick air courier company executive
Waller, Stephen air transportation executive

Rosamond
Trippensee, Gary Alan aerospace executive

San Diego
†Bowens, Thella senior aviation director
Reading, James Edward transportation executive

San Francisco
Anschutz, Philip F. transportation executive, communications executive
Martin, John L. airport executive
van Hoften, James Dougal Adrianus business executive, former astronaut

San Jose
Stapleton, Beverly Cooper aerospace company executive
Tonseth, Ralph G. airport executive

San Mateo
Trabitz, Eugene Leonard aerospace company executive

Santa Ana
Dean, William Evans aerospace industry executive

Stockton
Biddle, Donald Ray aerospace company executive

Temecula
Kinsler, Bruce Whitney air traffic controller, consultant, air traffic control engineer, air defense engineer, air traffic control automation specialist, branch manager

Torrance
Savitz, Maxine Lazarus aerospace company executive

Van Nuys
Stender, Charles Frederick test pilot

Walnut Creek
DeBoer, David James transportation executive

Westlake Village
Caren, Robert Poston aerospace company executive

Woodland Hills
Richards, Benness Melvin airline pilot

COLORADO

Aurora
Munro, Michael Donald air transportation executive, retired military officer

Colorado Springs
Davis, Richard Shermer, Jr. *aerospace company operations manager*
Freeman, J. P. Ladyhawk *underwater exploration, security and transportation executive, educator, fashion model*
Pickett, David Franklin, Jr. *technology company executive*
Stienmier, Saundra Kay Young *aviation educator*

Denver
†Baumgartner, Bruce *airport administrator*
Boyd, Dawn Andrea Williams *airline employee, artist*
McMorris, Jerry *transportation company executive, sports team executive*

Golden
Lindsay, Nathan James *aerospace company executive, retired career officer*

Littleton
Bragg, Albert Forsey *retired airline captain*
Kleinknecht, Kenneth Samuel *retired aerospace company executive, former federal space agency official*

Trinidad
Potter, William Bartlett *business executive*

CONNECTICUT

Bloomfield
Ervin, Billy Maxwell *aerospace executive*

Darien
Hartong, Hendrik J., Jr. *transportation company executive*

Deep River
Zack, Steven Jeffrey *master automotive instructor*

Fairfield
Murphy, Eugene F. *aerospace, communications and electronics executive*

Greenwich
Roitsch, Paul Albert *pilot*

Newington
†Juliano, Robert F. *bureau chief*
Leeds, Robin Leigh *transportation executive*
Robert, Kenneth J. *airport administrator*

Ridgefield
†Swartout, Torin Sherwin Roberts *transportation executive, real estate broker*

Southport
Taylor, James Blackstone *aviation company executive*

Stamford
Barker, James Rex *water transportation executive*
Tregurtha, Paul Richard *marine transportation and construction materials company executive*

DELAWARE

Dagsboro
Lally, Richard Francis *aviation security consultant, former association executive, former government official*

DISTRICT OF COLUMBIA

Washington
Altschul, Alfred Samuel *airline executive*
Burwell, David Gates *transportation executive*
†Carlton, Bruce J. *transportation company executive*
Cocke, Erle, Jr. *international business consultant*
Donovan, George Joseph *industry executive, consultant*
Downey, Mortimer Leo, III *transportation executive*
Farrell, Joseph Michael *steamship company executive*
Hallett, Carol Boyd *air transportation executive*
Hargrove, Michael B. *transportation executive*
Hinson, David Russell *airline company executive, federal agency administrator*
Mederos, Carolina Luisa *transportation policy consultant*
Meurlin, Keith W. *airport manager*
†Morgan, Ronald E. *federal air traffic director*
Olcott, John Whiting *aviation executive*
Overbeck, Gene Edward *retired airline executive, lawyer*
†Tranyham, David *United States Government administrator*
Troutman, George Glenn *retired aerospace executive, retired military officer*
†Warrington, George D. *rail transportation executive*

FLORIDA

Boca Raton
Garelick, Martin *retired transportation executive*

Clearwater
Howes, James Guerdon *airport director*

Daytona Beach
†Kane, Lorie *professional golfer*
Simatos, Nicholas Jerry *aerospace company executive, consultant*

Fort Myers
†Manning, John E. *port authority chairman*
Mc Grath, William Restore *transportation planner, traffic engineer*

Jacksonville
Aftoora, Patricia Joan *transportation executive*

Anderson, John Quentin *rail transportation executive*
Hamilton, Susan Owens *transportation company executive, lawyer*
Kilbourne, Krystal Hewett *rail transportation executive*

Kissimmee
Musgrave, Story *astronaut, surgeon, pilot, physiologist, educator*

Lake Mary
Curboy, Robert Edward *aviation safety consultant*

Largo
Manty, Brian Alan *high technology company executive*

Miami
Bastian, James Harold *air transport company executive, lawyer*
Burns, M. Anthony *transportation services company executive*
Dellapa, Gary J. *airport terminal executive*
Fain, Richard David *cruise line executive*
Pubillones, Jorge *transit adminstration administrator*
Trippe, Kenneth Alvin Battershill *shipping industry executive*

Montverde
Harris, Martin Harvey *aerospace company executive*

Naples
Bush, John William *federal transportation official*
Johnson, Walter L. *transportation company executive*

Oldsmar
Burrows, William Claude *aerospace executive, retired air force officer*

Orlando
Davis, H. Alan *retired airline captain, consultant*
Pearlman, Louis Jay *aviation and promotion company executive*

Palm Beach Gardens
Colussy, Dan Alfred *aviation executive*

Ponte Vedra Beach
Fiorentino, Thomas Martin *transportation executive, lawyer*
Hamilton, William Berry, Jr. *shipping company executive*

Sanibel
Hasselman, Richard B. *retired transportation company executive*

Sarasota
†Gurney, Frank Irving *transportation executive*
Lindsay, David Breed, Jr. *aircraft company executive, former editor and publisher*

Tallahassee
Thagard, Norman E. *astronaut, physician, engineer, educator*

Tampa
Johnson, James E. *airport executive*

GEORGIA

Atlanta
Connor, Charles William *airline pilot*
Cook, Christopher Dixon *communications company executive*
†Cousins, William Luke *transportation administrator*
†Decosta, Benjamin *airport administrator*
Ferguson, Erik Tillman *transportation consultant*
Kelly, James P. *delivery service executive*
†Mullin, Leo Francis *airline executive*
Oppenlander, Robert *retired airline executive*

Lawrenceville
Lane, Pearce Allen *military pilot*

Macon
Hails, Robert Emmet *aerospace consultant, business executive, former air force officer*

Savannah
†Graham, Patrick Samuel *air transportation executive*

HAWAII

Honolulu
Pfeiffer, Robert John *business executive*
†Wilson, Charles Robert *port captain, harbor master*

IDAHO

Boise
Ilett, Frank, Jr. *trucking company executive, educator*

Idaho Falls
Thorsen, James Hugh *aviation director, airport manager, retired*

ILLINOIS

AMF Ohare
Kalcevic, Timothy Francis *airline pilot, educator*

Argonne
Saricks, Christopher Lee *transportation analyst*

Arlington Heights
Hudson, Ronald Morgan *aviation planner*

Broadview
Christopher, Alexander George *transportation company executive*

Chicago
†al-Chalabi, Suhail Abdul-Jabbar *transportation executive*
Barriger, John Walker, IV *transportation executive*
Burton, Raymond Charles, Jr. *transportation company executive*
Heineman, Ben Walter *corporation executive*
Loney, Mary Rose *airport administrator*
Nord, Henry J. *transportation executive*
Reed, John Shedd *former railway executive*
Zell, Samuel *transportation leasing company executive*

Geneva
Barney, Charles Richard *transportation company executive*

Glen Ellyn
Logan, Henry Vincent *transportation executive*

Kankakee
Call, Cary C. *transportation specialist*

Lansing
Ansary, Hassan Jaber *transportation executive*

Lombard
Yeager, Phillip Charles *transportation company exeuctive*

Marion
Crane, Hugh Wingate *railroad executive*

Oak Brook
Duerinck, Louis T. *retired railroad executive, attorney*
Veno, Ronald James, Jr. *travel industry executive*

Park Ridge
Carr, Gilbert Randle *retired railroad executive*

Pecatonica
Merkel, Richard Eugene *retired pilot*

Rolling Meadows
Hassert, Elizabeth Anne *transportation executive*

Rosemont
Burkhardt, Edward Arnold *transportation company executive*
Currie, Earl James *transportation company executive*

Springfield
†Blake, William L. *airport company executive*

Union
Hilbert, Elroy E. "Buck" *retired airline pilot*

Wood River
Copeland, Benny James *transportation agent*

INDIANA

Fishers
Ruzbasan, Anthony *distribution executive*

Griffith
Johnson, Mary Susan *transportation company professional*

Indianapolis
Mikelsons, J. George *air aerospace transportation executive*
Roberts, David *airport executive*

Lawrenceburg
Dickey, Julia Edwards *aviation consultant*

Noblesville
Morrison, Joseph Young *transportation consultant*

Plymouth
Miller, Philip William *sales executive*

West Lafayette
Drake, John Warren *aviation consultant*

KANSAS

Overland Park
Myers, A. Maurice *transportation executive*

Topeka
Uhler, William Grant, IV *freight company administrator*

Wichita
Bell, Baillis F. *airport terminal executive*
Rosendale, George William *aircraft company executive*

KENTUCKY

Elizabethtown
Robey, John Dudley *transportation executive*

Franklin
Clark, James Benton *railroad industry consultant, former executive*

Louisville
DeLong, James Clifford *air transportation executive*
Dunman, Leonard Joe, III *trucking company executive*
Hayes, William Meredith *pilot, retired career officer*

LOUISIANA

New Orleans
Amoss, W. James, Jr. *shipping company executive*
Johnson, Peter Forbes *transportation executive, business owner*

MAINE

Bangor
Ziegelaar, Bob W. *terminal executive*

Portland
†Schultes, Jeffrey *transportation manager*

MARYLAND

Annapolis
Moellering, John Henry *aviation maintenance company executive*

Baltimore
†Mathison, Theodore E. *air transportation executive*

Bethesda
†Coffman, Vance D. *aerospace company executive*
Mineta, Norman Yoshio *aerospace transportation executive, former congressman*
Rymarcsuk, Jim Arthur *aerospace industry executive, consultant*

Columbia
Gottfeld, Gunther Max *retired urban mass transit official, consultant*

Rockville
Fthenakis, Emanuel John *diversified aerospace company executive*
Phillips, Mark Douglas *information technology executive*
Porter, John Robert, Jr. *space technology company executive, geochemist*

Stevensville
Deen, Thomas Blackburn *retired transportation research executive*

Westminster
Davis, Michael Chase *aerospace industry executive, consultant, retired naval officer*

MASSACHUSETTS

Boston
Davis, David William *transportation consultant*
Doherty, Robert Francis, Jr. *aerospace industry professional*
Klotz, Charles Rodger *shipping company executive*
Tocco, Stephen *former airport administrator*

Brookline
Frankel, Ernst Gabriel *shipping and aviation business executive, educator*

Cambridge
John, Richard Rodda *transportation executive*
Schwartz, William Lee *transportation consultant*

Concord
Smith, Eric Parkman *retired railroad executive*

East Boston
Blute, Peter I. *transportation executive, former congressman*

Jamaica Plain
Laudato, Gaetano Joseph, Jr. *retired locomotive engineer*

Marlborough
Birstein, Seymour Joseph *aerospace company executive*
Brower, David Charles *transportation executive*

North Billerica
Mellon, Timothy *transportation executive*

Stow
Shrader, William Whitney *radar consulting scientist*

MICHIGAN

Ann Arbor
Waller, Patricia Fossum *transportation executive, researcher, psychologist*

Dearborn
Boulos, Edward Nashed *transportation specialist*

Detroit
†Katz, David M. *airport administrator*
Trout, Michael Gerald *airport administrator*

Farmington Hills
Karolak, Dale Walter *aerospace company executive*

Flat Rock
Wright, Arthur Franklin *transportation executive, municipal official*

Grand Rapids
Auwers, Stanley John *motor carrier executive*

Lansing
Schmidt, Thomas Walter *airport executive*

Saint Joseph
Hoyt, J. Brian *light manufacturing company logistics executive*

Warren
Morelli, William Annibale, Sr. *aerospace manufacturing company executive*

Waterford
Randall, Karl W. *aviation executive, lawyer*

MINNESOTA

Duluth
Hartley, Alan Haselton *lexicographer, stevedoring administrator*

Edina
Foret, Mickey Phillip *air transportation company executive*

Minneapolis
Anderson, Tim *airport terminal executive*
Harper, Donald Victor *transportation and logistics educator*
Nyrop, Donald William *airline executive*
Olson, James Richard *retired transportation company executive*

Red Wing
Lindquist, Everett Carlton *retired air traffic controller*

Saint Paul
Checchi, Alfred A. *airline company executive*
Engle, Donald Edward *retired railway executive, lawyer*
Gehrz, Robert Gustave *retired railroad executive*
†Washburn, Donald Arthur *business executive*

MISSISSIPPI

Iuka
Crawford, Robert Roy *rail company executive*

Jackson
Vanderleest, Dirk *airport executive*

Pass Christian
Clark, John Walter, Jr. *shipping company executive*

MISSOURI

Blue Springs
Reed, Tony Norman *aviation company executive*

Bridgeton
Delaney, Robert Vernon *logistics and transportation executive*

Fenton
Baer, Robert J. *transportation and relocation services company executive*
Greenblatt, Maurice Theodore *transportation executive*

Kansas City
Baisden, Eleanor Marguerite *airline compensation executive, consultant*
Malecki, David Michael *airport manager*
Wallis, Elizabeth Susan *air traffic control specialist*

Lake Saint Louis
German, John George *retired transportation consultant*

Saint Louis
Gitner, Gerald L. *aviation and investment banking executive*
O'Neill, John Robert *airline executive*

Webster Groves
Forry, John Emerson *retired aerospace company executive*

MONTANA

Missoula
†Van Pelt, Peter J. *airport terminal executive*

NEBRASKA

Lincoln
Wood, John *air transportation executive*

Omaha
Davidson, Richard K. *railroad company executive*
Davis, Jerry Ray *retired railroad company executive*
Smithey, Donald Leon *airport authority director*
Stuart, Gary Miller *railroad executive*

NEVADA

Las Vegas
Walker, Randall H. *air transportation executive*

Reno
White, Robert C. *air transportation executive*

NEW HAMPSHIRE

Dover
Nelson, Michael Underhill *association executive*

Sunapee
Cary, Charles Oswald *aviation executive*

NEW JERSEY

Alpine
Vandersteel, William *transportation executive*

Cherry Hill
Holfeld, Donald Rae *railroad consultant*

Edison
Cronin, John Joseph *airline pilot, poet, author*

Egg Harbor Township
Raftner, Thomas *airport terminal executive*

Flemington
Kettler, Carl Frederick *airline executive*

Hammonton
†Crawford, James A. *transportation authority executive*

Mahwah
†Coley, Elliot Edward *delivery service executive*

Morristown
Sugahara, Byron Masahiko *transportation company executive*

Mount Arlington
Krosser, Howard S. *aerospace company executive, retired congressman*

Mount Laurel
Buchan, Alan Bradley *rail transportation executive, consultant*

New Brunswick
†Gambaccini, Louis John *transportation executive, educational*

Newark
Baer, Susan M. *airport executive*
†Fitzpatrick, Robert J. *transit company executive*

Peapack
Weiss, Allan Joseph *transport company executive, lawyer*

Pennington
Dickerson, John Joseph, Jr. *airport manager*

Raritan
Alatzas, George *delivery service company executive*

Roselle
Mahadeshwar, Sanjay Sakharam *marine consultant*

Teterboro
Jennings, Robert Lee *aircraft maintenance executive*

Union
White, Robert L. G., Jr. *aerospace company executive*

Willingboro
Collard, Thomas Albert *transportation executive*

NEW MEXICO

Albuquerque
Weh, Allen Edward *airline executive*

Farmington
Anderson, Mark Eugene *specialized truck driver, safety inspector*

Las Cruces
Borman, Frank *former astronaut, laser patent company executive*

Santa Fe
Swartz, William John *retired transportation resources company executive*

NEW YORK

Babylon
Collis, Charles *aircraft company executive*

Buffalo
Stone, Robert A. *airport administrator*

Carmel
Shen, Chia Theng *former steamship company executive, religious institute official*

Centerport
†Trotta, Ric Charles *aerospace company executive, consultant*

Cooperstown
Rich, Walter George *railroad transportation executive*

Garden City
Campbell, James R. *transportation executive*

Great Neck
Pollack, Paul Robert *airline service company executive*
Satinskas, Henry Anthony *airline services company executive*

Huntington
Jackson, Richard Montgomery *former airline executive*
Myers, Robert Jay *retired aerospace company executive*

Jamaica
Feldman, Arlene Butler *aviation industry executive*
Mc Kinnon, Clinton Dan *aerospace transportation executive*

Prendergast, Thomas Francis *railroad executive*
†Seliga, Charles G. *airport administrator*

Kingston
McGuire, Thomas Peter *show boat captain, secondary school educator*

New York
Apostolakis, James John *shipping company executive*
Ascher, Michael Charles *transportation executive*
Borrone, Lillian C. *transportation executive*
Chao, James S. C. *maritime executive*
Danaher, Frank Erwin *transportation technologist*
Evans, James Hurlburt *retired transportation and natural resources executive*
Evans, Mary Johnston *corporate director*
Gilliam, Paula Hutter *transportation company executive*
Hyman, Morton Peter *shipping company executive*
Johnsen, Niels Winchester *ocean shipping company executive*
†Kallakis, Achilleas Michalis S. *shipping company executive*
Kelly, Robert *airport executive*
Marinakis, Markos K. *water transportation executive*
Matalon, Norma *travel and public relations executive*
Recanati, Elias Isaac *shipping company executive*
Thayer, Russell, III *airlines executive*
Wright, Joseph Robert, Jr. *corporate executive*

Niagara Falls
Napolitano, Ralph E. *airport administrator*

Ogdensburg
Belgard, Stephen L. *airport administrator*

Patchogue
Ihne, Edward Alan *railroad official, city official*

Peekskill
Harte, Andrew Dennis *transportation company executive, travel agent*

Syracuse
Carlson, William Clifford *defense company executive*
Everett, Charles Roosevelt, Jr. *airport executive*

West Islip
Cassell, Dean George *retired aerospace executive, management consultant*

NORTH CAROLINA

Chapel Hill
Bauer, Frederick Christian *motor carrier executive*

Charlotte
Hutchinson, Olin Fulmer, Jr. *transportation executive, data processing consultant*
Miller, James Alfred Locke, Jr. (Jim Miller) *aircraft maintenance technician*
Orr, T(homas) J(erome) (Jerry Orr) *airport terminal executive*
Tolan, David Joseph *transportation executive*

Cherryville
Mayhew, Kenneth Edwin, Jr. *transportation company executive*

High Point
Berrier, J. Alan *transportation executive, entrepreneur*

Kannapolis
Thigpen, Alton Hill *motor transportation company executive*

Winston Salem
Davis, Thomas Henry *airline executive*

NORTH DAKOTA

Grand Forks
Lindseth, Paul Douglas *aerospace educator, flight instructor, farmer*
Skroch, Larry Eugene *railway conductor*

OHIO

Cincinnati
George, Allen Van *manufacturing company executive*
Torbush, Robert Daniel *transportation executive*

Cleveland
Hill, Robert John *aviation executive*
Lawrence, Estelene Yvonne *transportation executive, musician*

Columbus
Hedrick, Larry Willis *airport executive*
Mason, Raymond E., Jr. *distributing company executive*

Dayton
Vaughan, David Kirk *aviation educator*

Granville
†Sinsabaugh, Joseph Charles *airline pilot*

Painesville
Lulita, Caroline Naumann *airport manager, flight educator*

Piqua
Disbrow, Michael Ray *aerospace supplier company executive*

Rocky River
Shively, Daniel Jerome *retired transportation executive*

Toledo
Hartung, James H. *airport authority executive*

Wilmington
Lundblad, John Ladd *airline pilot, flight instructor*

OKLAHOMA

Enid
Deunk, N. Howard, III *flying educator*

Oklahoma City
Trent, Luther E. *airport executive, state agency executive*

Tulsa
Collins, John Roger *transportation company executive*
Eaton, Leonard James, Jr. *aerospace executive*
Kitchen, Brent A. *airport executive*
Kruse, David Louis, II *transportation company executive*

OREGON

Aloha
Jones, Charles J. *transportation executive, firefighter*

Oakland
Smelt, Ronald *retired aircraft company executive*

Portland
Lewis, Kenneth *shipping executive*

PENNSYLVANIA

Allentown
Doughty, George Franklin *airport administrator*

Avoca
Centini, Barry J. *airport administrator*

Bethlehem
Lewis, Andrew Lindsay, Jr. (Drew Lewis) *former transportation and natural resources executive*

Bristol
Shenefelt, Arthur B. *transportation executive, consultant*

Conshohocken
Cunningham, James Gerald, Jr. *transportation company executive*

Essington
Piasecki, Frank Nicholas *aircraft corporation executive, aeronautics engineer*

Fogelsville
Young, Richard Robert *logistics and transportation educator*

King Of Prussia
Fleming, Hubert Loy *water systems company executive*

Philadelphia
Fisher, Allan Campbell *railway executive*
Terry, John Joseph *transportation investor*

Reading
Hard, Brian *truck leasing company executive*

Trout Run
McKissick, Michael Landon *transportation consultant*

University Park
Williams, Lisa Rochelle *logistics and transportation educator*

Wayne
Wilson, Bruce Brighton *retired transportation executive*

York
Grossman, Robert Allen *transportation executive*
Rebert, Jephrey Lee *transportation planner, musician*

RHODE ISLAND

Warwick
Roberts, Elaine *airport terminal executive*

SOUTH CAROLINA

Charleston
Chapin, Fred *airport executive*

Columbia
Conrad, Paul Ernest *transportation consultant*

Hilton Head Island
Love, Richard Emerson *equipment manufacturing company executive*

SOUTH DAKOTA

Sioux Falls
Smith, Murray Thomas *transportation company executive*

TENNESSEE

Chattanooga
Quinn, Patrick *tranportation executive*

Knoxville
Igoe, Terence B. *airport terminal executive*

Memphis
Cox, Larry D. *airport terminal executive*
Smith, Frederick Wallace *transportation company executive*

Morristown
Johnson, Evelyn Bryan *flying service executive*

Nashville
†Claverie, Roy E. *water transportation executive, transportation exec*
Ingram, Orrin Henry, II *transportation executive*
Zierdt, John Graham, Jr. *transportation company executive*

Soddy Daisy
Frazier, Douglas Almeda McRee *former energy facility analyst*

TEXAS

Bridge City
Smith, Phillip Carl *marine and ship pilot, rancher*

Dallas
†Baker, Robert Woodward *airline executive*
Carty, Donald J. *airline company executive*
Fegan, Jeffrey P. *airport executive*
Keck, Philip Walter *transportation executive*
Kelleher, Herbert David *airline executive, lawyer*
Kelly, Robert Vincent, III *transportation executive*
Megredy, Millard Howard *retired aviation director, realtor, consultant*
Taylor, Herman Ivan, Jr. *defense company manager*

Dickinson
Bush, Robert Thomas *shipping company executive*

Euless
Tunnell, Clida Diane *air transportation specialist*

Fort Worth
Krebs, Robert Duncan *transportation company executive*
Morland, Jeff R. *railroad company executive*
Shoemaker, Sandra Kaye *aerospace executive*

Georgetown
Aadnesen, Christopher *railroad company executive, consultant*

Granbury
Mainord, William Ronald *pilot*

Houston
Acree, G. Hardy *airport executive*
Bethune, Gordon *airline executive*
Brandenstein, Daniel Charles *astronaut, retired naval officer*
Vacar, Richard M. *airport executive*
Young, John Watts *astronaut*

Irving
Plaskett, Thomas G. *transportation company executive*

Lindale
Carter, Thomas Smith, Jr. *retired railroad executive*

Mc Queeney
Gunter, Edwin Dale, Jr. *pilot*

Port Lavaca
Fisher, King *retired marine contracting company executive*

Roanoke
Steward, Jerry Wayne *air transportation executive, consultant*

San Antonio
Billingsley, Charles Edward *retired transportation company executive*
Gonzalez, Efren *airport executive*
Kutchins, Michael Joseph *aviation consultant, former airport executive*
Lowry, A. Robert *federal government railroad arbitrator*

Thorndale
Fish, Howard Math *aerospace industry executive*

UTAH

Brigham City
Pflug, Andrew Knox *aerospace company executive*

Ogden
Dilley, William Gregory *aviation company executive*

Orem
Snow, Marlon O. *trucking executive, state agency administrator*

Salt Lake City
Bouley, Joseph Richard *pilot*

VERMONT

Burlington
Bergesen, Robert Nelson *transportation company executive*

Northfield
†Batra, N.D. *communications educator*

South Burlington
Hamilton, John J., Jr. *airport executive*

Woodstock
Hoyt, Coleman Williams *postal consultant*

VIRGINIA

Alexandria
Carpenter, Stanley Hammack *retired military aviation organization executive*
Coyne, James Kitchenman, III *association executive, congressman, aviator*
Langstaff, David Hamilton *aerospace industry executive*
Matthews, Sir Stuart *aviation industry executive*

Arlington
Beyer, Barbara Lynn *aviation consultant*
†Chung, Caroline *airline executive, aerobics instructor*
Hochstein, Anatoly Boris *maritime ports and waterways educator, researcher, consultant*
Luffsey, Walter Stith *transportation executive*
Mason, Phillip Howard *aircraft company executive, retired army officer*
Shortal, Terence Michael *systems company executive*
Spooner, Richard Edward *aerospace company executive*
Stokes, B. R. *retired transportation consultant*
Wolf, Stephen M. *airline executive*

Burke
Forster, William Hull *aerospace executive*

Cape Charles
Brookshire, James Knox, Jr. *transportation facility administrator*

Catlett
Broderick, Anthony James *air transportation executive*

Chantilly
Harris, Paul Lynwood *aerospace transportation executive*

Chesterfield
Congdon, John Rhodes *transportation executive*

Fairfax
Whitcomb, Darrel Dean *pilot*

Independence
Hurst, John Emory, Jr. *retired airline executive*

Newport News
†Smith, James Robert *airport terminal executive*

Norfolk
Goode, David Ronald *transportation company executive*
McKinnon, Arnold Borden *transportation company executive*
Ruehlmann, William John *communications educator*
Rump, Kendall E. *air transportation executive*
Scott, Kenneth R. *transportation executive*

Poquoson
Holloway, Paul Fayette *retired aerospace executive*

Purcellville
Mainwaring, Thomas Lloyd *motor freight company executive*

Reston
Crawford, Lawrence Robert *aviation and aerospace consultant*
Kreyling, Edward George, Jr. *railroad executive*

Richmond
Fisher, Todd Rogers *transportation executive*
Hintz, Robert Louis *transportation company executive*
Watkins, Hays Thomas *retired railroad executive*

Winchester
Jamison, Richard Bryan *airport consultant*

WASHINGTON

Bainbridge Island
Cioc, Charles Gregory *information systems executive*

Bellevue
Salerno, Joseph Michael *retired air cargo company executive*

Kirkland
Clarkson, Lawrence William *airplane company executive*

Medina
Waldmann, Raymond John *aerospace executive*

Port Orchard
Newport, Cris *publications editor*

Seattle
Cella, John J. *freight company executive*
Chittick, Arden Boone *steamship agency executive*
Cline, Robert Stanley *air freight company executive*
Condit, Philip Murray *aerospace executive, engineer*
Givan, Boyd Eugene *aircraft company executive*
Grinstein, Gerald *transportation executive*
Kelley, John F. *airline executive*
Liljebeck, Roy C. *transportation company executive*
Lindsey, Gina Marie *airport executive*
Miller, Paige *port executive*
Rose, Carol Ann *air transportation executive*
Schmidt, Peter Gustav *shipbuilding industry executive*
Strombom, Cathy Jean *transportation planner, consultant*
Thornton, Dean Dickson *retired airplane company executive*

Spanaway
Loete, Steven Donald *pilot*

WEST VIRGINIA

Moorefield
Hedrick, John O. *railroad executive*

WISCONSIN

Appleton
Crowley, Geoffrey Thomas *airline executive*
Petinga, Charles Michael *transportation executive*

Green Bay
Schneider, Donald J. *trucking company executive*

Milwaukee
Bateman, C. Barry *airport terminal executive*
Rinnemaki, William Allen *transportation executive*

Oshkosh
Schoenrock, Tracy Allen *airline pilot, securities trader*

Waupaca
Schoofs, Gerald Joseph *pilot*

WYOMING

Casper
True, Diemer D. *trucking company executive, former state senator*

Worland
Woods, Lawrence Milton *airline company executive*

CANADA

ALBERTA

Calgary
Caron, Ernie Matthew *airport executive*
McCaig, Jeffrey James *transportation company executive*
McCaig, John Robert *transportation executive*

Edmonton
Marcotte, Brian *transportation executive*

BRITISH COLUMBIA

Sidney
Paquette, Richard *airport executive*

NOVA SCOTIA

Elsmdale
Shrieves, Janet *airport terminal executive*

Halifax
Renouf, Harold Augustus *business consultant, retired*

Lower Sackville
Ortlepp, Bruno *marine navigation educator, master mariner*

ONTARIO

Almonte
Morrison, Angus Curran *aviation executive*

Brampton
Savoie, Leonard Norman *transportation company executive*

London
Baker, Steve J. *airport executive*

Markham
Dayment, David *airport executive*

Mississauga
Tobias, Kal *transportation executive*

Ottawa
Coleman, John Morley *transportation engineering executive*
Sheflin, Michael John Edward *environment and transportation official*

Sault Sainte Marie
Calce, Brenda V. *airport executive*

Toronto
Turpen, Louis A. *airport terminal executive*

QUEBEC

Montreal
Beaudoin, Laurent *industrial, recreational and transportation company executive*
Bourgeault, Jean-Jacques *air transportation executive*
Labelle, Eugene Jean-Marc *airport director general*
Taddeo, Dominic *transportation executive*
Tellier, Paul M. *Canadian railway transportation executive*

Saint Anne Des Lacs
Rochette, Louis *retired shipowner and shipbuilder*

Saint Sauveur
Hanigan, Lawrence *retired railway executive*

AUSTRALIA

Stirling, ACT
Keith, Leroy Allen *aviation safety executive*

CHINA

Beijing
Pinoli, Burt Arthur *airline executive*

DENMARK

Vedbaek
Nordqvist, Erik Askbo *shipping company executive*

ENGLAND

Burford
Blackney, Arthur Bruce *Middle East defense and aviation consultant*

ADDRESS UNPUBLISHED

Ames, Donald Paul *retired aerospace company executive, researcher*
Armstrong, Neil A. *former astronaut*
Baddour, Anne Bridge *pilot*
†Beckwith, Marlin *aeronautics program manager*
Blanchard, David Lawrence *aerospace executive, real estate developer, consultant*
Brazier, Don Roland *retired railroad executive*
Brown, Donald Douglas *transportation company executive, retired air force officer, consultant*
†Coleman, Robert Wayne *airline company executive*
Collins, Eileen Marie *astronaut*
Cook, Stephen Champlin *retired shipping company executive*
Crowder, Richard Morgan *pilot*
Culbertson, Philip Edgar, Sr. *aerospace company executive, consultant*
Dasburg, John Harold *airline executive*
Dely, Steven *aerospace company executive*
Dini, Joseph J. *aircraft leasing and finance executive*
Donohue, George L. *federal aviation educator, former government official, mechanical engineer*
Eischen, Michael Hugh *retired railroad executive*
Falzone, Joseph Sam *retired airlines company crew chief*
Ferreira, Jo Ann Jeanette Chanoux *time-definite transportation industry executive*
Fetzer, Edward Frank *transportation company executive*
Fischbach, Charles Peter *railway executive consultant, lawyer, arbitrator, mediator*
Foss, Charles R. *transportation operations specialist*
Glennon, Harrison Randolph, Jr. *retired shipping company executive*
Goldstein, Bernard *transportation and casino gaming company executive*
Graebner, James Herbert *transportation executive*
Greenwald, Gerald *air transportation executive*
Harp, Solomon, III *former airport executive*
Hawkins, Willis Moore *aerospace and astronautical consultant*
Hayward, Charles Winthrop *retired railroad company executive*
Heitz, Edward Fred *freight traffic consultant*
Hickerson, Glenn Lindsey *leasing company executive*
Hidalgo, Miguel *transportation company executive*
Horton, Sir Robert Baynes *railroad company executive*
Kerbs, Wayne Allan *transportation executive*
King, Edward William *retired transportation executive*
Lerner-Lam, Eva I-Hwa *transportation executive*
Lesko, Harry Joseph *transportation company executive*
Lewis, Martin Edward *shipping company executive, foreign government concessionary*
Lillibridge, John Lee *retired airline executive*
†Linenger, Jerry Michael *astronaut*
†Lorenzo, Francisco A. *airline companies executive*
Macormic, William Dean *railway company executive*
Marshall, Charles Noble *railroad executive*
Masiello, Rocco Joseph *airlines and aerospace manufacturing executive*
Mast, Stewart Dale *retired airport manager*
Matthews, L. White, III *railroad executive*
†McGrail, Christopher W. *aerospace machinist*
Mowatt-Larssen, Erling *transportation consultant*
Murray, Leonard Hugh *railroad executive*
Orton, Patricia Osborn *marina owner, real estate investor*
Pai, Suren *telecommunications company executive*
Peete, Russell Fitch, Jr. *aircraft appraiser*
Regalado, Raul Leo *airport and parking consultant*
Reid, George Harrison *marine consultant, writer*
Renda, Dominic Phillip *airline executive*
Rose, James Turner *aerospace consultant*
Ruegg, Donald George *retired railway company executive*
Schaefer, C. Barry *railroad executive, lawyer, investment banker*
Shockley, Edward Julian *retired aerospace company executive*
Smith, Russell Francis *transportation executive*
Snow, John William *railroad executive*
Snowden, Lawrence Fontaine *retired aircraft company executive, retired marine corps general officer*
Swanson, Ralph William *aerospace executive, consultant, engineer*
†Theis, Stuart H. *water transport executive*
†Tracy, Sean Michael *pilot*
Valine, Delmar Edmond, Sr. *corporate executive*
Vecci, Raymond Joseph *airline industry consultant*
Voss, Omer Gerald *truck company executive*
Wallace, F. Blake *aerospace executive, mechanical engineer*
Weiss, Rita Sandra *transportation executive*

INDUSTRY: UTILITIES, ENERGY, RESOURCES

UNITED STATES

ALABAMA

Birmingham
Barker, Thomas Watson, Jr. *energy company executive*
Bowron, Richard Anderson *retired utilities executive*
Drummond, Garry N. *mining company executive*
Harris, Elmer Beseler *electric utility executive*
Hutchins, William Bruce, III *utility company executive*
Kuehn, Ronald L., Jr. *natural resources company executive*
Rubright, James Alfred *oil and gas company executive, lawyer*

Foley
St. John, Henry Sewell, Jr. *utility company executive*

Shoal Creek
Ahearn, John Francis, Jr. *retired oil and gas company executive*

ALASKA

Anchorage
Shultz, Delray Franklin (Lucky Shultz) *management consultant*

Fairbanks
Beistline, Earl Hoover *mining consultant*

ARIZONA

Carefree
Birkelbach, Albert Ottmar *retired oil company executive*

Cave Creek
LeNeau, Thomas Ervin *retired gas company executive*

Phoenix
De Michele, O. Mark *utility company executive*
Huffman, Edgar Joseph *oil company executive*
St. Clair, Thomas McBryar *mining and manufacturing company executive*
Yearley, Douglas Cain *mining and manufacturing company executive*

Scottsdale
Baker, Jeffrey Charles *telecommunications executive*
Doyle, Michael Joseph *mining executive*
Holliger, Fred Lee *oil company executive*
Swetnam, Monte Newton *petroleum exploration executive*

Sun City West
O'Brien, Gerald James *utilities executive*

Surprise
Black, Robert Frederick *former oil company executive*

Tempe
Clevenger, Jeffrey Griswold *mining company executive*
Hickson, Robin Julian *mining company executive*

Tucson
Davis, James Luther *retired utilities executive, lawyer*
Heller, Frederick *retired mining company executive*
Jamison, Harrison Clyde *former oil company executive, petroleum exploration consultant*
Peeler, Stuart Thorne *petroleum industry executive and independent oil operator*
Peters, Charles William *research and development company manager*

Vail
Saul, Kenneth Louis *retired utility company executive*

ARKANSAS

El Dorado
Vaughan, Odie Frank *oil company executive*
Watkins, Jerry West *retired oil company executive, lawyer*

Fayetteville
Scharlau, Charles Edward, III *natural gas company executive*

Little Rock
Ferra, Dennis J. *telecommunications company executive*
Ford, Joe Thomas *telephone company executive, former state senator*
Ford, Scott T. *telecommunications company executive*
Gardner, Kathleen D. *gas company executive, lawyer*
Orsini, Tom *telecommunications company executive*

Russellville
Jones, James Rees *retired oil company executive*

CALIFORNIA

Anaheim
Fenton, Donald Mason *retired oil company executive*

Beverly Hills
Levingston, John Colville Bowring *telecommunications executive*

Brea
Stegemeier, Richard Joseph *oil company executive*

Camarillo
MacAlister, Robert Stuart *oil company executive*

Carmel
Aurner, Robert Ray, II *oil company, auto diagnostic, restaurant franchise and company development executive*
Loper, D. Roger *retired oil company executive*

Corona Del Mar
Hill, Melvin James *oil company executive*

El Segundo
Beach, Roger C. *oil company executive*

Flintridge
Read, William McClain *retired oil company executive*

Hillsborough
Willoughby, Rodney Erwin *retired oil company executive*

Los Altos
Sun, Bill Kawo-Hwa *energy consulting company executive*

Los Angeles
Bowlin, Michael Ray *oil company executive*
†Chazen, Stephen I. *oil company executive*
Davis, Marvin *petroleum company executive, entrepreneur*
Van Horne, R. Richard *oil company executive*

Martinez
Meyer, Jarold Alan *oil company research executive*

Menlo Park
Quigley, Philip J. *telecommunications industry executive*

Mill Valley
Premo, Paul Mark *oil company executive*

Mission Viejo
Dergarabedian, Paul *energy and environmental company executive*

Monterey Park
Montag, David Moses *telecommunications company executive*

Newport Beach
Armstrong, Robert Arnold *petroleum company executive*

Pacific Palisades
Klein, Joseph Mark *retired mining company executive*
Middleton, James Arthur *oil and gas company executive*
Mulryan, Henry Trist *mineral company executive, consultant*

Palo Alto
Gouraud, Jackson S. *energy company executive*

Palos Verdes Peninsula
Christie, Hans Frederick *retired utility company subsidiaries executive, consultant*

Pasadena
Finnell, Michael Hartman *corporate executive*
Mc Duffie, Malcolm *oil company executive*

Petaluma
Frederickson, Arman Frederick *minerals company executive*

Piedmont
Willrich, Mason *energy industry executive*

Rosemead
Bryson, John E. *utilities company executive*
Bushey, Richard Kenneth *utility executive*

Sacramento
Crabbe, John Crozier *telecommunications consultant*
Sequeira, Jim *utilites administrator, municipal official*
Wickland, J. Al, Jr. *petroleum product executive, real estate executive*

San Diego
Cota, John Francis *utility executive*
Gray-Bussard, Dolly H. *energy company executive*

San Francisco
Brandin, Alf Elvin *retired mining and shipping company executive*
Caccamo, Aldo M. *oil industry executive*
Carter, George Kent *oil company executive*
Clarke, Richard Alan *electric and gas utility company executive, lawyer*
Derr, Kenneth T. *oil company executive*
Flittie, Clifford Gilliland *retired petroleum company executive*
Ginn, Sam L. *telephone company executive*
Glynn, Robert D., Jr. *energy-based holding company*
High, Thomas W. *energy-services executive*
Kleeman, Michael Jeffrey *telecommunications and computer consultant*
Littlefield, Edmund Wattis *mining company executive*
Savage, Michael John Kirkness *oil company and arts management executive*
Sullivan, James N. *fuel company executive*
Wall, James Edward *telecommunications, petroleum and pharmaceutical executive*

San Jose
†Takizawa, Gregory Hidaeki *telecommunication industry executive*

San Rafael
Latno, Arthur Clement, Jr. *telephone company executive*

Santa Barbara
†Warner, John Jeffrey *mining executive*

Santa Fe Springs
Orden, Ted *gasoline service stations executive*

Santa Rosa
Hinch, Stephen Walter *telecommunications industry executive*

Stanford
Brinegar, Claude Stout *retired oil company executive*

Thousand Oaks
Monis, Antonio, Jr. (Tony Monis) *electric industry executive*

Turlock
Williams, Delwyn Charles *telephone company executive*

Van Nuys
Fisher, Earl Monty *utilities executive*

Villa Grande
Shirilau, Mark Steven *utilities executive*

Walnut Creek
Conger, Harry Milton *mining company executive*

COLORADO

Broomfield
Steinhauser, John Stuart (Jack Steinhauser) *oil company executive*

Colorado Springs
King, Peter Joseph, Jr. *retired gas company executive*
O'Shields, Richard Lee *retired natural gas company executive*
Russel, Richard Allen *telecommunications consultant, aerospace engineer, nuclear engineer, electrical engineer, retired naval officer*
Stoen, J. Thomas *energy company executive, land developer, investor*

Denver
Danos, Robert McClure *retired oil company executive*
Fagin, David Kyle *natural resource company executive*
Fryt, Monte Stanislaus *petroleum company executive, speaker, advisor*
†Helton, Bill D. *utilities company executive*
†Johnston, Van Robert *management educator*
Lewis, Jerome A. *petroleum company executive, investment banker*
Macey, William Blackmore *oil company executive*
McCormick, Richard *telecommunications company executive*
McFadden, Michael J. *utilities industry consultant*
Owens, Marvin Franklin, Jr. *oil company executive*
Pepper, John Roy *oil and gas executive*
Rendu, Jean-Michel Marie *mining executive*
Taylor, Leslie George *mining and financial company executive*
Thompson, Lohren Matthew *oil company executive*
Trueblood, Harry Albert, Jr. *oil company executive*
†Trujillo, Solomon D. *telecommunications executive*
Vickery, Robert Bruce *oil industry executive, consultant*
Vostiar, John *telecommunications industry executive*

Durango
Thurston, William Richardson *oil and gas industry executive, geologist*

Englewood
Malone, John C. *telecommunications executive*
Ward, Milton Hawkins *mining company executive*

Evergreen
McEldowney, Roland Conant *gold mining company executive*

Fort Collins
Kleinschnitz, Barbara Joy *oil company executive, consultant*

Golden
Coakley, William Thomas *utilities executive*
O'Connor, Patricia Eryl *telecommunications consultant*

Lakewood
Hall, Larry D. *energy company executive, lawyer*

Larkspur
Bierbaum, J. Armin *petroleum company executive, consultant*

Littleton
Haley, John David *petroleum consulting company executive*
VanderLinden, Camilla Denice Dunn *telecommunications industry manager*

CONNECTICUT

Danbury
Rafferty, James Paul *telecommunications executive*

Darien
Kutz, Kenneth John *retired mining executive*
Smith, Elwin Earl *mining and oil company executive*

Greenwich
Bennett, Jack Franklin *oil company executive*
DeCrane, Alfred Charles, Jr. *petroleum company executive*
Lawi, David Steven *energy, oil and gas, entertainment, agriservice and thermoplastic resins industries executive, merchant banker*
Nelson, Don Harris *gas and oil industry executive*
Schmidt, Herman J. *former oil company executive*
Tell, William Kirn, Jr. *oil company executive, lawyer, retired*

Guilford
Morgan, Leon Alford *retired utility executive*

Hartford
Dixon, Robert F. *telecommunications executive*

New Canaan
McIvor, Donald Kenneth *retired petroleum company executive*

New Haven
Miglio, Daniel Joseph *telecommunications company executive*

Norwalk
†Quartarone, John Anthony *abrasives industry company executive*

Old Greenwich
Hittle, Richard Howard *corporate executive, international affairs consultant*

Southport
Damson, Barrie Morton *oil and gas exploration company executive*

Stamford
Donahue, Donald Jordan *mining company executive*
Jacobson, Ishier *retired utility executive*
Kinnear, James Wesley, III *retired petroleum company executive*
Mc Kinley, John Key *retired oil company executive*

West Haven
Bowerman, Richard Henry *utility company executive, lawyer*

Westport
Nedom, H. Arthur *petroleum consultant*

DELAWARE

Wilmington
Connelly, Donald Preston *electric and gas utility company executive*

DISTRICT OF COLUMBIA

Washington
Barrett, Lake H. *energy industry executive*
†Boergers, David Paul *energy executive*
Buchan, Douglas Charles *petroleum company executive, government official*
Deland, Michael Reeves *energy executive*
Derrick, John Martin, Jr. *electric company executive*
†Felder, Richard Bruce *pipeline safety administrator*
†Friedman, Gregory H. *energy administrator*
Friend, William L. *oil industry executive*
†Gee, Robert W. *energy administrator*
King, Gwendolyn S. *retired utility company executive, former federal official*
†Kripowicz, Robert S. *energy administrator*
Maher, Patrick Joseph *retired utility company executive*
McCollam, William, Jr. *utility company executive*
Modiano, Albert Louis *gas, oil industry executive*
Money, Arthur Lewis *electronics executive*
Paige, Hilliard Wegner *corporate director, consultant*
Roberts, Bert C., Jr. *telecommunications company executive*
Seidenberg, Ivan G. *telecommunications company executive*
Smith, James Michael *telecommunications executive, lawyer*
†Sullivan, Mary Anne *energy professional, lawyer*
Thompson, William Reid *public utility executive, lawyer*
Wraase, Dennis Richard *utilities company executive, accountant*

FLORIDA

Boca Raton
Gralla, Eugene *natural gas company executive*

Boynton Beach
Babler, Wayne E. *retired telephone company executive, lawyer*

Bradenton
Gurian, Mal *telecommunications executive*

Captiva
Ronald, Peter *utility executive*

Deerfield Beach
Laser, Charles, Jr. *oil company executive*

Delray Beach
Reef, Arthur *industry business consultant*

Jacksonville
Francis, James Delbert *oil company executive*
Milbrath, Robert Henry *retired petroleum executive*
Rue, Douglas Michael *technical application consultant*

Juno Beach
Broadhead, James Lowell *electrical power industry executive*

Lake Wales
Deaver, Darwin Holloway *former utility executive*

Largo
Dolan, John E. *consultant, retired utility executive*
Loader, Jay Gordon *retired utility company executive*
Stein, Ronald Marc *telecommunications executive*

Longwood
Scoates, Wesley Marvin *mining company executive*

Naples
Ivancevic, Walter Charles *former gas distribution company executive*
Johnson, Zane Quentin *retired petroleum company executive*
Kay, Herbert *retired natural resources company executive*
Rowe, Jack Field *retired electric utility executive*

Orlando
Cirello, John *utility and engineering company executive*
Ispass, Alan Benjamin *utilities executive*

Palm Beach
Donnell, John Randolph *retired petroleum executive*
Smith, Lloyd Hilton *independent oil and gas producer*

Palm Beach Gardens
Harnett, Joseph Durham *oil company executive*

Palm Coast
Farrell, Joseph Christopher *retired mining executive, services executive*

Pinellas Park
Perry, Paul Alverson *utility executive*

Ponte Vedra
Wood, Quentin Eugene *oil company executive*

Ponte Vedra Beach
Green, Norman Kenneth *retired oil industry executive, former naval officer*

Quincy
Laughlin, William Eugene *electric power industry executive*

Saint Petersburg
Fassett, John D. *retired utility executive, consultant*
Hines, Andrew Hampton, Jr. *utilities executive*
Houser, Ruth G. *data communications manager*
Moneypenny, Edward William *petroleum exploration and production executive*

Sun City Center
McGrath, John Francis *utility executive*

Tampa
Campbell, David Ned *retired electric utility executive, business consultant*
Daks, Peter A. *telecommunications company executive*
Leavengood, Victor Price *telephone company executive*

Venice
Torrey, Richard Frank *utility executive*

Wesley Chapel
Donovan, Brian Joseph *oil industry executive*

West Palm Beach
Koch, William I. *energy company executive*
Smith, Betsy Keiser *telecommunications company executive*

Winter Park
Spake, Ned Bernarr *energy company executive*

Yalaha
Brown, Paula Kinney *heating and air conditioning contractor*

GEORGIA

Alpharetta
Adams, Rex M. *telecommunications executive*

Atlanta
Ackerman, F. Duane *utility company executive*
Bolch, Carl Edward, Jr. *corporation executive, lawyer*
Chilton, Horace Thomas *pipeline company executive*
Clemons, Julie Payne *telephone company manager*
Dahlberg, Alfred William *electric company executive*
Drummond, Jere A. *telecommunications company executive*
Duques, Ric *information services executive*
Frost, Norman Cooper *retired telephone company executive*
Hamm, (Charles) Stan(ley) *telecommunications company executive*
Ramsey, Ira Clayton *retired pipeline company executive*
Robbins, James *communications executive*

Big Canoe
†Helms, Vernon Lamar *telecommunications executive*

Conyers
Kilkelly, Brian Holten *lighting company executive*

Dalton
Bundros, Thomas Anthony *utilities executive*

Decatur
Bullock, George Daniel *energy consultant*

Dunwoody
†Whitt, Jeffrey E. *nuclear energy industry executive*

Gainesville
Ferguson, David Robert *energy research manager*
Leet, Richard Hale *oil company executive*

Lawrenceville
McClure, David H. *utilities company analyst*

Lithonia
Keyes, David Taylor *telecommunications company administrator*

Newnan
McBroom, Thomas William, Sr. *consultant, lawyer*

Norcross
Salazar, Andres C. *communications company executive*
Shaver, Edwards Boone *telephone company executive*

Savannah
Croom, John Henry, III *utility company executive*

HAWAII

Honolulu
Clarke, Robert F. *utilities company executive*
Williams, Carl Harwell *utilities executive*

IDAHO

Boise
†Stead, Jerre L. *telecommunications company executive*

Coeur D Alene
Griffith, William Alexander *former mining company executive*

Mountain Home
Hiddleston, Ronal Eugene *drilling and pump company executive*

ILLINOIS

Argonne
Mattas, Richard Frank *nuclear energy industry executive*

Barrington
Perry, I. Chet *petroleum company executive*

Bridgeport
Legg, Ronald Otis *oil company executive*

Chicago
Ban, Stephen Dennis *natural gas industry research institute executive*
Batlivala, Robert Bomi D. *oil company executive, economics educator*
Brooker, Thomas Kimball *oil company executive*
Carlson, LeRoy Theodore, Jr. *telecommunications industry executive*
Conrad, John R. *corporate executive*
Fligg, James Edward *retired oil company executive*
Fuller, Harry Laurance *oil company executive*
Kaye, Richard William *utility company executive*
Lowrie, William G. *oil company executive*
Mc Gimpsey, Ronald Alan *oil company executive*
Morrow, Richard Martin *retired oil company executive*
Notebaert, Richard C. *telecommunications industry executive*
O'Connor, James John *retired utility company executive*
Rogers, Desiree Glapion *utilities executive*
Rowe, John William *utility executive*
Skala, Gary Dennis *electric and gas utilities executive management consultant*
Smith, J. Clarke *telecommunications industry executive*

Decatur
Womeldorff, Porter John *utilities executive*

Flossmoor
Pierce, Shelby Crawford *management and oil industry consultant*

Forsyth
Dreyer, Alec Gilbert *independent power producer*

Geneva
Pershing, Robert George *telecommunications company executive*

Glen Ellyn
Lischer, Ludwig Frederick *retired consultant, former utility company executive*
†Rusnack, William *petroleum company executive*

Hinsdale
Brandt, John Ashworth *fuel company executive*

Lake Bluff
Marino, William Francis *telecommunications industry executive, consultant*

Libertyville
Rucker, Dennis Morton Arthur *telecommunications executive*

Naperville
†Bremer, Michael Stewart *management consultant*

Orland Park
English, Floyd Leroy *telecommunications company executive*

Peoria
DuBois, Mark Benjamin *utilities executive*
Sheehan, Michael Gilbert *utilities executive*
Sprowls, Robert Joseph *energy company executive*
Viets, Robert O. *utilities executive*

Rock Island
Whitmore, Charles Horace *utility executive, lawyer, management consultant*

West Frankfort
Williams, Joseph Scott *energy and natural resources company executive, city commissioner*

INDIANA

Brownsburg
Diasio, Richard Leonard *power transmission executive, sports facility executive*

Evansville
Able, Warren Walter *natural resource company executive, physician*
Kiechlin, Robert Jerome *retired coal company executive, financial consultant*

Frankfort
Stonehill, Lloyd Herschel *gas company executive, mechanical engineer*

Greensburg
Schilling, Don Russell *electric utility executive*

Hammond
Schroer, Edmund Armin *utility company executive*

Highland
Purcell, James Francis *former utility executive, consultant*

Indianapolis
Griffiths, David Neal *utility executive*
Husted, Ralph Waldo *former utility executive*
Todd, Zane Grey *retired utilities executive*

Lawrenceburg
Dautel, Charles Shreve *retired mining company executive*

Merrillville
Adik, Stephen Peter *energy company executive*
Lynn, Robert William *gas and electric utility official*

IOWA

Cedar Rapids
†Schmidt, Joel Joseph *energy company executive*

Sioux City
Wharton, Beverly Ann *utility company executive*

KANSAS

Council Grove
Coffin, Bertha Louise *telephone company executive*

Eskridge
Taylor, Russell Benton *mining executive*

Independence
Swearingen, Harold Lyndon *oil company executive*

Lenexa
Gressel, Gary Lee *telecommunications professional*

Overland Park
Stein, Allison *media specialist*

Pittsburg
Nettels, George Edward, Jr. *mining executive*

Topeka
Spencer, William Edwin *telephone company executive, engineer*

Westwood
Esrey, William Todd *telecommunications company executive*
LeMay, Ronald T. *telecommunications industry executive*

Wichita
Cadman, Wilson Kennedy *retired utility company executive*
†Elliott, Donald Harris *utility executive*
Koch, Charles de Ganahl *oil industry executive*
Varner, Sterling Verl *retired oil company executive*

KENTUCKY

Ashland
Dansby, John Walter *retired oil company executive*
Quin, Joseph Marvin *oil company executive*
Weaver, Carlton Davis *retired oil company executive*

Covington
Boyd, James Robert *oil company executive*
Brothers, John Alfred *oil company executive*
Chellgren, Paul Wilbur *industrial company executive*

Glasgow
Duvo, Mechelle Louise *oil company executive, consultant*

Louisville
Royer, Robert Lewis *retired utility company executive*

LOUISIANA

Lafayette
Gaubert, Ronald Joseph *gas and oil industry executive, management consultant*

New Orleans
Bachmann, Richard Arthur *oil company executive*
Lind, Thomas Otto *barge transportation company executive*
Lupberger, Edwin Adolph *retired utility executive*

Murrish, Charles Howard *oil and gas exploration company executive, geologist*
Regan, William Joseph, Jr. *energy company executive*
Smith, John Webster *retired energy industry executive, consultant*
Stephens, Richard Bernard *natural resource company executive*

MAINE

Portland
Haynes, Peter Lancaster *utility holding company executive*

South Paris
Barlow, Walter John, Jr. *utilities executive, consultant*

Surry
Kilgore, John Edward, Jr. *former petroleum company executive*

MARYLAND

Annapolis
Ellis, George Fitzallen, Jr. *retired energy services company executive*

Baltimore
Harvey, Keiko Takeuchi *telephone company executive*
Higgins, Kenneth Michael *electrician*
Ihrie, Robert *oil, gas and real estate company executive*
McGowan, George Vincent *public utility executive*
Poindexter, Christian Herndon *utility company executive*
Rosenberg, Henry A., Jr. *petroleum executive*

Bethesda
Ikle, Doris Margret *energy efficiency company executive*
McMurphy, Michael Allen *energy company executive, lawyer*
Olmsted, Jerauld Lockwood *telephone company executive*

Cabin John
Dragoumis, Paul *electric utility company executive*

Chevy Chase
Bodman, Richard Stockwell *telecommunications executive*

Ellicott City
Perry, Nancy Trotter *former telecommunications company executive*

Glen Arm
Jackson, Theodore Marshall *retired oil company executive*

Hagerstown
†Noia, Alan James *utility company executive*

Kensington
Marienthal, George *telecommunications company executive*

Lanham
†Parker, William H., Jr. *telecommunications industry executive*

Rockville
Hyde, Geoffrey *satellite communications research executive*
†Vietti-Cook, Annette *nuclear energy administrator*

Silver Spring
Jacobs, George *broadcast engineering consulting company executive*
Melnick, Jack *retired telecommunications company executive*

Suitland
Asbell, Fred Thomas *government executive*

MASSACHUSETTS

Andover
Maguire, Robert Edward *retired public utility executive*

Boston
Bok, Joan Toland *utility executive*
†Grimes, Calvin M., Jr. *oil industry executive*
Pardus, Donald Gene *utility executive*

Burlington
Reno, John F. *communications equipment company executive*

Cambridge
Buckler, Sheldon A. *energy company executive*

Centerville
Anderson, Gerald Edwin *utilities executive*
Scherer, Harold Nicholas, Jr. *electric utility company executive, engineer*

Chelsea
Kaneb, Gary *oil industry executive*

Danvers
Dolan, John Ralph *retired corporation executive*
Keppler, Richard Rudolph *consultant, former oil company executive*

Harwich Port
Staszesky, Francis Myron *independent energy consultant*

Melrose
Brown, Ronald Osborne *telecommunications and computer systems consultant*

Needham
Cogswell, John Heyland *retired telecommunications executive, financial consultant*

North Andover
†Jain, Anant Kumar *data communications and telecommunications consultant*

Waltham
Slifka, Alfred A. *oil corporation executive*

Watham
Lee, Charles Robert *telecommunications company executive*

Westborough
Houston, Alfred Dearborn *energy company executive*
Young, Roger Austin *natural gas distribution company executive*

Weston
Raskin, Fred Charles *transportation and utility holding company executive*

MICHIGAN

Birmingham
†Harter, Roger Karr *retired telecommunications executive*

Dearborn
Boulanger, Rodney Edmund *energy company executive*
McCormick, William Thomas, Jr. *electric and gas company executive*

Detroit
Garberding, Larry Gilbert *utilities companies executive*
Glancy, Alfred Robinson, III *public utility company executive*

East Detroit
Cattaneo, Michael S. *heating and cooling company executive*

Owosso
Hoddy, George Warren *electric company executive, electrical engineer*

Port Huron
Thomson, Robert James *natural gas distribution company executive*

Shelby Township
Fillbrook, Thomas George *telephone company executive*

MINNESOTA

Eden Prairie
Emison, James Wade *petroleum company executive*

Fergus Falls
MacFarlane, John Charles *utility company executive*

Minneapolis
Gudorf, Kenneth Francis *business executive*
Wyman, James Thomas *petroleum company executive*

Saint Paul
Estenson, Noel K. *refining and fertilizer company executive*
Robertson, Jerry Earl *retired manufacturing company executive*

MISSOURI

Ballwin
Anderson, James Donald *mining company executive*

Kansas City
Baker, John Russell *utilities executive*
Jennings, A. Drue *utility company executive*
Potter, George William, Jr. *mining executive*

Lebanon
Beavers, Roy Lackey *retired utility executive, essayist, activist*

Saint Louis
Elliott, Howard, Jr. *gas distribution company executive*
†Engelhardt, Irl F. *coal company executive*
Moten, John, Jr. *gas industry executive, chemist*
Mueller, Charles William *electric utility company executive*
Quenon, Robert Hagerty *retired mining consultant and holding company executive*

Springfield
Jura, James J. *electric utility executive*

MONTANA

Bigfork
Shennum, Robert Herman *retired telephone company executive*

Billings
Nance, Robert Lewis *oil company executive*
Reed, Kenneth G. *petroleum company executive*

Butte
Bishop, Robert Charles *architect, metals and minerals company executive*
Burke, John James *utility executive*

Mc Elwain, Joseph Arthur *retired power company executive*

Missoula
Brumit, Lawrence Edward, III *oil field service company executive*

NEBRASKA

Lincoln
Tavlin, Michael John *telecommunications company executive*

NEVADA

Henderson
Trimble, Thomas James *retired utility company executive, lawyer*

Las Vegas
Grace, John William *electrical company executive*
Laub, William Murray *retired utility executive*

Reno
Busig, Rick Harold *mining executive*

Winnemucca
Hesse, Martha O. *natural gas company executive*

Zephyr Cove
Proctor, Robert Swope *retired petroleum company executive*

NEW HAMPSHIRE

Concord
Tomajczyk, S(tephen) F(rancis) *communications company executive, author*

Portsmouth
Powers, Henry Martin, Jr. *oil company executive*
Tillinghast, John Avery *utilities executive*

Rindge
Emerson, Susan *oil company executive*

NEW JERSEY

Basking Ridge
Collis, Sidney Robert *retired telephone company executive*

Bedminster
Robinson, Paul Barry *telecommunications executive*

Collingswood
Mohrfeld, Richard Gentel *heating oil distributing company executive*

East Rutherford
Golashesky, Chrysa Zofia *telecommunications company executive*

Edison
Avery, James Stephen *oil company executive*
Francis, Peter T. *gas and oil industry executive*

Florham Park
MacMillan, David Paul *oil company executive*

Fort Lee
Schiessler, Robert Walter *retired chemical and oil company executive*

Lakehurst
Sherwood, Harold DeWitt *oil industry executive, consultant*

Middletown
Scott, Stephen Gregory *telecommunications company executive*

Mount Laurel
Rabbe, David Ellsworth *oil company executive*

New Providence
Cohen, Melvin Irwin *communications systems and technology executive*

Newark
Ferland, E. James *electric utility executive*

Nutley
Mallard, Stephen Anthony *retired utility company executive*

Parsippany
Hafer, Frederick Douglass *utility executive*

Peapack
Walsh, Philip Cornelius *retired mining executive*

Piscataway
Kelly, Robert Emmett *telecommunications company administrator*
Lewis, Peter A. *energy consultant*

Princeton
Farley, Edward Raymond, Jr. *mining and manufacturing company executive*
McCullough, John Price *retired oil company executive*

Red Bank
Chynoweth, Alan Gerald *retired telecommunications research executive, consultant*

South Orange
Joel, Amos Edward, Jr. *telecommunications consultant*

Summit
Pollak, Henry Otto *retired utility research executive, educator*

Toms River
Janiak, Cathy Lynn *telecommunications industry executive*

Union
Lewandowski, Andrew Anthony *utilities executive, consultant*

Wall
Colford, Francis Xavier *gas industry executive*

Warren
Starr, Miriam Carolyn *telecommunications company executive*

Westfield
DeMarco, Annemarie Bridgeman *telecommunications company manager*
Specht, Gordon Dean *retired petroleum executive*

NEW MEXICO

Albuquerque
Gorham, Frank DeVore, Jr. *petroleum company executive*

Hobbs
Garey, Donald Lee *pipeline and oil company executive*

Mora
Mossavar-Rahmani, Bijan *oil and gas company executive*

Roswell
Anderson, Donald Bernard *oil company executive*
Robinson, Mark Leighton *oil company executive, petroleum geologist, horse farm owner*

Santa Fe
Pickrell, Thomas Richard *retired oil company executive*

NEW YORK

Albany
von Schack, Wesley W. *energy services company executive*

Babylon
Lopez, Joseph Jack *oil company executive, consultant*

Bardonia
†DiCarlo, Bernard *telecommunication executive*

Bethpage
Dolan, James *communications executive*
Lusgarten, Marc A. *communications executive*

Binghamton
Carrigg, James A. *retired utility company executive*
Farley, Daniel W. *utility company executive, lawyer*

Blauvelt
Gillespie, John Fagan *mining executive*

Brooklyn
Bisbee, Joyce Evelyn *utility company manager*
Catell, Robert Barry *gas utility executive*
Matthews, Craig Gerard *gas company executive*

Buffalo
Ackerman, Philip Charles *utility executive, lawyer*
Kennedy, Bernard Joseph *utility executive*

Cazenovia
Fleming, William Sloan *energy, environmental and technology company executive*

Flushing
Parascos, Edward Themistocles *retired utilities executive*

Grand Island
Schenck, Henry Paul *telecommunications executive*

Huntington Station
Pierce, Charles R. *electric company consultant*

Jericho
Fitteron, John Joseph *real estate/petroleum products company executive*

Latham
Rosner, Carl H. *energy executive*

Little Valley
Anastasia, David Jon *state legislator*

Manhasset
Anderson, Arthur N. *retired utility company executive*

New Hyde Park
Bocchino, Frances Lucia *retired oil company official*

New York
Alonzo, Martin Vincent *mining and aluminum company executive, investor, financial consultant*
Alpert, Warren *oil company executive, philanthropist*
Atigbi, Kofitunde Jolomi *telecommunications professional*
Baird, Dugald Euan *oil field service company executive*
Belknap, Norton *petroleum company consultant*
Bernstein, Alan Arthur *oil company executive*
Brown, Edward James, Sr. *utility executive*
Carey, Edward John *utility executive*
Case, Hadley *oil company executive*

Delaney, Robert Vincent *former gas company executive, economic development consultant*
Douglas, Paul Wolff *retired mining executive*
Duke, Robert Dominick *mining executive, lawyer*
Freilich, Joan Sherman *utilities executive*
Gelfand, Neal *oil company executive*
Greene, Carl William *financial consultant, former utility company executive*
Hess, John B. *oil industry executive*
Host, Stig *oil company executive*
Luce, Charles Franklin *former utilities executive, lawyer*
Lyons, John Matthew *telecommunications executive, broadcasting executive*
McGrath, Eugene R. *utility company executive*
Morse, Edward Lewis *petroleum industry executive*
Murray, Allen Edward *retired oil company executive*
Osborne, Richard de Jongh *mining and metals company executive*
Paret, Dominique *petroleum company executive*
Passage, Stephen Scott *energy company executive*
Salerno, Frederic V. *telecommunications company executive*
Silverman, Henry Richard *diversified business executive, lawyer*
Smith, Stanton Kinnie, Jr. *utility executive*
Staley, Delbert C. *telecommunications executive*
Underweiser, Irwin Philip *mining company executive, lawyer*
Warner, Rawleigh, Jr. *oil company executive*

Niskayuna
Fitzroy, Nancy deLoye *technology executive, engineer*

Pearl River
Caliendo, G. D. (Jerry Caliendo) *public utility executive*

Poughkeepsie
Mack, John Edward, III *utility company executive*

Rochester
Richards, Thomas Savidge *utility company executive*

Schenectady
Robb, Walter Lee *retired electric company executive, management company executive*

Somers
Davidson, Carl B. *retired oil company executive*

Syosset
Vermylen, Paul Anthony, Jr. *oil company executive*

Syracuse
Davis, William E. *utility executive*

Tonawanda
Dillman, Joseph John Thomas *electric utility executive*

White Plains
Araskog, Rand Vincent *diversified telecommunications multinational company executive*
Bijur, Peter I. *petroleum company executive*
Brazell, James Ervin *oil company executive, lawyer*
Engen, D(onald) Travis *diversified telecommunications company executive*
Smith, Elizabeth Patience *oil industry executive, lawyer*

NORTH CAROLINA

Black Mountain
Cody, Hiram Sedgwick, Jr. *retired telephone company executive*

Cary
Jones, James Arthur *retired utilities executive*

Charlotte
Grigg, William Humphrey *utility executive*
Osborne, Richard Jay *electric utility company executive*
Priory, Richard Baldwin *electric utility executive*
†Shaw, Ruth G. *energy company executive*
Spangler, Clemmie Dixon, Jr. *business executive*
Thies, Austin Cole *retired utility company executive*

Hendersonville
Haynes, John Mabin *retired utilities executive*

Mooresville
Cox, Herbert Bartle *natural gas company executive*

Morrisville
Hardin, George Cecil, Jr. *petroleum consultant*

Pinehurst
Amspoker, James Mack *retired gas company executive*

Raleigh
Johnson, William Dean *power company executive*
Nelson, Cynthia Kaye *network engineer*
Smith, Sherwood Hubbard, Jr. *utilities executive*

NORTH DAKOTA

Bismarck
Schuchart, John Albert, Jr. *utility company executive*

OHIO

Akron
†Alexander, Anthony J. *electric power industry executive*
Holland, Willard Raymond, Jr. *electric utility executive*
Spetrino, Russell John *retired utility company executive, lawyer*

Bannock
Gentile, Anthony *coal company executive*

Bexley
Maloney, Gerald P. *retired utility executive*

Canton
Stage, Richard Lee *consultant, retired utilities executive*

Cincinnati
Colwell, Christopher Scott *telecommunications industry executive*
Ehrnschwender, Arthur Robert *former utility company executive*
Foley, Cheryl M. *company executive*
Henry, Brian C. *telephone company executive*
Randolph, Jackson Harold *utility company executive*
Rogers, James Eugene *electric and gas utility executive*
Victor, William Weir *retired telephone company executive, consultant*

Cleveland
Ayers, Richard Wayne *electrical company official*
Blodgett, Omer William *electric company design consultant*
Ginn, Robert Martin *retired utility company executive*
Kuehn, Richard Arthur *telecommunications consultant*
Sheffler, Dudley *telecommunications industry executive*
†Woods, Jacqueline F. *telecommunications industry executive*

Columbus
Draper, E(rnest) Linn, Jr. *electric utility executive*
Feck, Luke Matthew *utility executive*
Kanwar, Deepak Vineet *telecommunications company executive*
Massey, Robert John *telecommunications executive*
Schafer, William Harry *loss prevention consultant*
Vassell, Gregory S. *electric utility consultant*

Findlay
Yammine, Riad Nassif *retired oil company executive*

Massillon
Dawson, Robert Earle *utilities executive*

Pepper Pike
Bray, Pierce *business consultant*
Hauserman, Jacquita Knight *electricity company executive*

Perrysburg
Williamson, John Pritchard *utility executive*

Westlake
Connelly, John James *retired oil company technical specialist*

OKLAHOMA

Bartlesville
Allen, W. Wayne *oil industry executive*
Cox, Glenn Andrew, Jr. *petroleum company executive*
Hedrick, Kirby L. *petroleum company executive*
Silas, Cecil Jesse *retired petroleum company executive*
†Whitworth, J. Bryan, Jr. *oil company executive, lawyer*

Edmond
Schader, Billy Wayne *oil company executive*

Enid
Dolezal, Leo Thomas *telecommunications executive*
Ward, Llewellyn Orcutt, III *oil company executive*

Fairview
†Swearingen, David Eugene *oil industry executive*

Oklahoma City
Campbell, David Gwynne *petroleum executive, geologist*
†Harlan, Ross Edgar *retired utility company executive, writer, lecturer, consultant*
Kirkpatrick, John Elson *oil company executive, retired naval reserve officer*
Nichols, J. Larry *energy company executive, lawyer*
Peace, H. W., II *oil company executive*
Wilkerson, Matha Ann *oil company executive*

Ponca City
Leonard, Samuel Wallace *oil company and bank executive*

Seminole
Moran, Melvin Robert *oil industry executive*

Tulsa
Bailey, Keith E. *petroleum pipeline company executive*
Braumiller, Allen Spooner *oil and gas exploration company executive, geologist*
Brolick, Henry John *energy company executive*
Cadieux, Chester *gas industry executive*
Dotson, George Stephen *drilling company executive*
Helmerich, Hans Christian *oil company executive*
Horkey, William Richard *retired diversified oil company executive*
Hulings, Norman McDermott, Jr. *energy consultant, former company executive*
Ingram, Charles Clark, Jr. *energy company executive*
King, Peter Cotterill *former utilities executive*
O'Toole, Allan Thomas *electric utility executive*
Parker, Robert Lee, Jr. *drilling company executive*
Repasky, Mark Edward *oil and gas company executive*
Schaechterle, Gordon Everett *retail propane executive*
Warren, W. K., Jr. *oil industry executive*

Wetumka
Hughes, Steven Bryan *gas measurement company executive*

OREGON

Portland
Bacon, Vicky Lee *lighting services executive*
Frisbee, Don Calvin *retired utilities executive*
Jungers, Francis *oil consultant*
Reiten, Richard G. *natural gas industry executive*
Short, Robert Henry *retired utility executive*

PENNSYLVANIA

Allentown
Campbell, William Leroy *retired public utility executive, consultant*
Gadomski, Robert Eugene *chemical and industrial gas company executive*
Hecht, William F. *electric power industry executive*
Wagner, Harold A. *industrial gas and chemical company executive*
Walton, David P. *utility company executive*

Bloomsburg
Lowthert, William Hughes, III *utility company executive*

Bryn Mawr
Ballam, Samuel Humes, Jr. *retired corporate director*
Braha, Thomas I. *business executive*

Coraopolis
Koepfinger, Joseph Leo *utilities executive*

Gladwyne
Patten, Lanny Ray *industrial gas industry executive*

Haverford
Boyer, Vincent Saull *energy consultant*
Olson, Robert Edward *coal mining executive*

Indiana
Kegel, William George *mining company executive*

Johnstown
Simmons, Elroy, Jr. *retired utility executive*
Wise, Robert Lester *utilities executive*

King Of Prussia
Greenberg, Lon Richard *energy company executive, lawyer*

Lancaster
Sware, Richard Michael, Jr. *electric company executive*

Philadelphia
Albertini, William Oliver *telecommunications industry executive*
Calman, Robert Frederick *mining executive*
Heilig, William Wright *coal and manufacturing company executive*
McNeill, Corbin Asahel, Jr. *utility executive*
Thompson, Sheldon Lee *refining company executive*

Pittsburgh
†Banerjee, Sujata *telecommunications educator*
Bartley, Burnett Graham, Jr. *oil company and manufacturing executive*
Brown, Bobby R. *retired coal company executive*
Davidson, George A., Jr. *utility company executive*
Froehlich, Fritz Edgar *telecommunications educator and scientist*
Gernert, Eric Vincent *telecommunications analyst*
Hammer, Harold Harlan *oil company financial executive*
La Rue, Henry Aldred *consultant, former oil company executive*
Mc Featters, Dale Stitt *retired electric company executive*
Moeller, Audrey Carolyn *energy company executive, corporate secretary*
Murphy, John Nolan *mining executive, researcher, electrical engineer*
Stern, Theodore *electric company executive*
Stirewalt, John Newman *coal company executive*
Warsaw, Rand A. *energy/financial services company executive*
Welfer, Thomas, Jr. *utility company executive*

Radnor
Castle, Joseph Lanktree, II *energy company executive, consultant*

Strasburg
Ware, Marilyn *water company executive*
Ware, Paul W. *gas industry executive*

Uniontown
Eberly, Robert Edward *oil and gas production company executive*

Wayne
Lefevre, Thomas Vernon *retired utility company executive, lawyer*
Wang, Stephen *oil company executive*

RHODE ISLAND

Barrington
O'Toole, John Dudley *retired utility executive, consultant*

Middletown
Watkins, William, Jr. *electric power industry executive*

SOUTH CAROLINA

Columbia
Gressette, Lawrence M., Jr. *utilities executive*

Hilton Head Island
Simpson, John Wistar *energy consultant, former manufacturing company executive*

Johns Island
Behnke, Wallace Blanchard, Jr. *consultant, engineer, retired utility executive*

Kiawah Island
Reed, Rex Raymond *retired telephone company executive*

SOUTH DAKOTA

Pierre
Dunn, James Bernard *mining company executive, state legislator*

Rapid City
Lien, Bruce Hawkins *minerals and oil company executive*

TENNESSEE

Brentwood
Goodwin, William Dean *consulting company executive*

Chattanooga
†Scalice, John A. *nuclear energy executive*

Knoxville
†Prosser, George T. *utilities executive*

Nashville
Adams, Kenneth Stanley, Jr. (Bud Adams) *energy company executive, football executive*
Cordaro, Matthew Charles *utility executive, energy developer, engineer*

Oak Ridge
Jasny, George Roman *retired energy company executive*

TEXAS

Abilene
Tindell, William Norman *oil company executive, petroleum geologist*

Austin
Deisler, Paul Frederick, Jr. *retired oil company executive*
Haas, Joseph Marshall *petroleum consultant*
Larkam, Peter Howard *electric utility executive, entrepreneur*
†Taute, Barbara Ehli *telecommunications company official*

Beaumont
Long, Alfred B. *former oil company executive, consultant*
Smith, Floyd Rodenback *retired utilities executive*

Chandler
Sanders, Sharon Raye (Sharri Sanders) *telecommunications executive, educator*

Channelview
Gower, Bob G. *gas and oil industry executive*

Corpus Christi
Benner, Richard Walter *oil company executive, geologist, engineer*
Haas, Paul Raymond *petroleum company executive*
Paulson, Bernard Arthur *oil company executive, consultant*

Crane
Crawford, Judy Carol *energy services company executive*
Dohlman, Dennis Raye *oil company executive*

Cypress
Day, Robert Michael *oil company executive*

Dallas
Brachman, Malcolm K. *oil company executive*
Brooks, E. R. (Dick Brooks) *utility company executive*
Carson, Virginia Hill *oil and gas executive*
Ellison, Luther Frederick *oil company executive*
Farrington, Jerry S. *utility holding company executive*
Fielder, Charles Robert *oil industry executive*
Goss, James Walter *oil company executive*
Gratton, Patrick John Francis *oil company executive*
Griffitts, Keith Loyd *oil industry executive*
Hunt, Ray L. *petroleum company executive*
Jackson, Alphonso *utility company executive*
Jones, Everett Riley, Jr. *oil company executive*
Keiser, Robert Lee *gas and oil industry executive*
Killam, Jill Minervini *oil and gas company executive*
†Mackenzie, Nanci *gas company executive*
Mandeville, Hubert Turner, Jr. *oil company executive*
Montgomery, Kathy MacLean *international business consultant*
Nye, Erle Allen *utilities executive, lawyer*
Perry, George Wilson *oil and gas company executive*
Pryor, Richard Walter *telecommunications executive, retired air force officer*
Robinson, Edgar Allen *retired oil company executive*
Shahsavari, Darius *oil and gas company executive*
Shoup, Andrew James, Jr. *oil company executive*
Sizer, Phillip Spelman *consultant, retired oil field services executive*
Winters, J. Otis *oil industry consultant*

Duncanville
Bilhartz, James Rohn, Jr. *independent oil producer*

Fort Worth
Armiger, Gene Gibbon *telecommunications executive, consultant*
Bass, Perry Richardson *oil company executive*
†Hudson, Edward Randall, Jr. *gas, oil industry executive*
Hyde, Clarence Brodie, II *oil company executive*
Johnson, Dennis Ray *utility supply executive*
McInnes, Donald Gordon *railroad executive*
Messman, Jack L. *oil executive*
Moncrief, William Alvin, Jr. *oil and gas producer*
Munn, John William *telecommunications executive*

Fredericksburg
Malec, William Frank *utilities company executive*

Frisco
Larsen, David Wayne *telecommunications industry executive*

Galveston
Ewing, George H. *pipeline company executive*

Granbury
Carder, Thomas Allen *nuclear energy industry emergency planner, educator*

Hockley
Sweeney, George Bernard *petrochemical industry executive, investor, broadcast executive, travel agency executive*

Horseshoe Bay
Jorden, James Roy *oil company engineering executive, consultant*

Houston
Barracano, Henry Ralph *retired oil company executive, consultant*
Barrow, Thomas Davies *oil and mining company executive*
Blanton, Jack Sawtelle *oil company executive*
Bonneville, Richard Briggs *retired petroleum exploration and production executive*
Bowen, W. J. *retired gas company executive*
Brown, Benjamin A. *gas, oil industry executive*
Bryan, James Lee *oil field service company executive*
Burke, Michael Donald *oil and gas company executive*
Campbell, Carl David *oil industry executive*
Capps, Ethan LeRoy *oil company executive*
Carameros, George Demitrius, Jr. *natural gas company executive*
Carter, James Sumter *oil company executive, tree farmer*
Carter, John Boyd, Jr. *oil operator, bank executive*
Chalmers, David B. *petroleum executive*
Cofran, George Lee *telecommunication consultant*
Cox, Frank D. (Buddy Cox) *oil company executive, exploration consultant*
Crimmins, Sean T(homas) *oil company executive*
DeVault, John Lee *oil company executive, geophysicist*
de Vries, Douwe *oil company executive*
Dice, Bruce Burton *exploration company executive*
DiCorcia, Edward Thomas *oil industry executive*
Drury, Leonard Leroy *retired oil company executive*
Duncan, Dan L. *gas company executive*
Edens, Donald Keith *oil company executive*
†Farley, Claire S. *petroleum company executive*
Ferrand, Jean C. *oil company executive*
Foster, Joe B. *oil company executive*
Frost, John Elliott *minerals company executive*
Fulwiler, Robert Neal *oil company executive*
Giacalone, Frank Thomas *energy and environmental company executive*
Gibson, Jerry Leigh *oil company executive*
Goodman, Herbert Irwin *petroleum company executive*
Halbouty, Michel Thomas *geologist, petroleum engineer, petroleum operator*
Hoglund, Forrest Eugene *petroleum company executive*
Howell, Paul Neilson *oil company executive*
Irwin, John Robert *oil and gas drilling executive*
Johnson, Kenneth Oscar *oil company executive*
Johnson, Wayne D. *gas industry executive*
Jones, Larry Leroy *oil company executive*
Kerr, Baine Perkins *oil company executive*
Kirkland, John David *oil and gas company executive, lawyer*
Kuntz, Hal Goggan *petroleum exploration company executive*
Lay, Kenneth Lee *diversified energy company executive*
†Lehne, Kathy Prasnicki *gas industry executive*
Leonard, Gilbert Stanley *oil company executive*
Little, Jack Edward *petroleum company executive*
Long, William Everett *retired utility executive*
Loveland, Eugene Franklin *petroleum executive*
†Luckner, Robert Clark *oil industry executive*
Luigs, Charles Russell *gas and oil drilling industry executive*
Mathis, James Forrest *retired petroleum company executive*
Miller, Michael Jaye *energy executive*
Nanz, Robert Hamilton *petroleum consultant*
Nicandros, Constantine Stavros *retired oil company executive*
Nyberg, Donald Arvid *oil company executive*
Pate, James Leonard *oil company executive*
Prentice, James Stuart *energy company executive, chemical engineer*
Reynolds, John Terrence *oil industry executive*
Robbins, Earl L. *oil operator*
Roff, J(ohn) Hugh, Jr. *energy company executive*
Rossler, Willis Kenneth, Jr. *petroleum company executive*
Segner, Edmund Peter, III *natural gas company executive*
Smith, David Kingman *retired oil company executive, consultant*
Spincic, Wesley James *oil company executive, consultant*
Sullivan, Neil Maxwell *oil and gas company executive*
Swanson, Charles Richard *accountant, oil and gas consultant*
Thorn, Terence Hastings *international energy industry executive*
†Watson, Chuck *electric power industry executive*
Williams, Robert Henry *oil company executive*
Wilson, Edward Converse, Jr. *oil and natural gas production company executive*
Wilson, Walter Clinton *gas, oil industry executive*
Wise, William Allan *oil company executive, lawyer*
Wyatt, Oscar Sherman, Jr. *retired energy company executive*

Ingram
Hughes, David Michael *oil service company executive, rancher*

Inglis, James *telecommunications company executive*
Jackson, Robert William *utility company executive, retired*
Jones, Jack Dellis *oil company executive*
Judge, Rosemary Ann *oil company executive*
Kaufman, Raymond L. *energy company executive*
Kebblish, John Basil *retired coal company executive, consultant*
Kettel, Edward Joseph *oil company executive, retired*
†King, Karen Kay *petroleum company executive*
King, William Collins *oil company executive*
Kinzer, James Raymond *retired pipeline company executive*
Kirkby, Maurice Anthony *oil company executive*
Kousparis, Dimitrios *oil consulting company executive*
Krempel, Roger Ernest *public works management consultant*
Kruizenga, Richard John *retired energy company executive*
Kurnit, Scott *telecommunications industry executive*
Kush, Charles Andrew, III *telecommunications executive, entrepreneur*
Land, Kenneth Dean *test and balance agency executive, energy and environmental consultant*
Leva, James Robert *retired electric utility company executive*
Lewis, Alexander, Jr. *oil company executive*
Lewis, Floyd Wallace *former electric utility executive*
Lilly, Edward Guerrant, Jr. *retired utility company executive*
Lively, Edwin Lester *retired oil company executive*
Macdonald, Sheila de Marillac *transaction management company executive*
Markle, Roger A(llan) *retired oil company executive*
Mastin, Wayne Alan *consumer education administrator*
Maycock, Ian David *retired oil executive*
Mc Carthy, Walter John, Jr. *retired utility executive*
McCready, Kenneth Frank *past electric utility executive*
McSweeny, William Francis *petroleum company executive, author*
Meek, Paul Derald *oil and chemical company executive*
Melvin, Ben Watson, Jr. *petroleum and chemical manufacturing executive*
Mitchell, Claybourne, Jr. *retired utilities executive*
Montgomery, Roy Delbert *retired gas utility company executive*
Monty, Charles Embert *utility company executive*
Moran, John Arthur *oil company executive*
Morrell, Gene Paul *liquid terminal company executive*
Morrow, George Lester *retired oil and gas executive*
Munsey, Virdell Everard, Jr. *retired utility executive*
Murrill, Paul Whitfield *former utility executive, former university administrator*
Nicholson, Leland Ross *retired utilities company executive, energy consultant*
Nurenberg, David *retired oil company executive*
O'Hare, James Raymond *energy company executive*
Ormasa, John *retired utility executive, lawyer*
Osterhoff, James Marvin *retired telecommunications company executive*
Pack, Allen S. *retired coal company executive*
Peckham, Donald Eugene *retired utilities company executive*
Perkins, Thomas Keeble *oil company researcher*
Perry, Kenneth Walter *retired integrated oil company executive*
Petrina, Anthony J. *retired mining executive*
Portal, Gilbert Marcel Adrien *oil company executive*
Quillen, Lloyd Douglas *oil and gas executive*
Ralston, Roy B. *petroleum consultant*
Raymond, Lee R. *oil company executive*
Reynolds, Jack W. *retired utility company executive*
Richard, Oliver, III (Rick Richard) *energy company executive*
Roe, Thomas Coombe *former utility company executive*
Rogers, Justin Towner, Jr. *retired utility company executive*
Samuels, John Stockwell, III *mining company executive, financier*
Sanders, Charles Franklin *management and engineering consultant*
Schenck, Jack Lee *retired electric utility executive*
Schenker, Leo *retired utility company executive*
Schumacher, Robert Joseph *petroleum company executive*
†Schwolsky, Peter M. *gas industry executive, lawyer, partner*
Scott, Isadore Meyer *former energy company executive*
†Sheibani, Sasan Banisoleiman *oil company official*
Smith, Paul Vergon, Jr. *corporate executive, retired oil company executive*
Smith, William Bridges *diversified company executive*
Stratman, Joseph Lee *petroleum refining company executive, consultant, chemical engineer*
Sugarman, Samuel Louis *retired oil transportation and trading company executive, horse breeder*
Templeton, John Alexander, II *coal company executive*
Thomas, Hilary Bryn *telecommunications executive, interactivist, writer, speaker*
Thompson, Jack Edward *mining company executive*
Threet, Jack Curtis *oil company executive*
Tonkyn, Richard George *retired oil and gas company executive, researcher, consultant*
Tucker, H. Richard *oil company executive*
Turner, Thomas Marshall *telecommunications executive, consultant*
Ward, Edward Wells *telecommunications executive*
Werth, Andrew M. *telecommunications executive*
Wheeler, John Charles *telecommunications professional*
White, Willis Sheridan, Jr. *retired utilities company executive*
Whitehouse, Alton Winslow, Jr. *retired oil company executive*
Williams, Joseph Theodore *oil and gas company executive*
†Wilson, Sandra Thomason *utility company executive*
Witte, Merlin Michael *oil company executive*
Wood, Willis Bowne, Jr. *retired utility holding company executive*
Wright, Mae A. *engineering/nuclear waste management specialist*
Wright, Randolph Earle *retired petroleum company executive*

LAW: JUDICIAL ADMINISTRATION

UNITED STATES

ALABAMA

Albertville
Johnson, Clark Everette, Jr. *judge*

Anniston
Harwell, Edwin Whitley *judge*

Ashland
Ingram, Kenneth Frank *retired state supreme court justice*

Birmingham
Acker, William Marsh, Jr. *federal judge*
†Armstrong, Robert R., Jr. *federal judge*
†Bennett, Thomas B. *federal judge*
Blackburn, Sharon Lovelace *federal judge*
Campbell, Elizabeth Todd *judge*
Clemon, U. W. *federal judge*
†Cohen, Benjamin *federal judge*
Goldstein, Debra Holly *judge*
Guin, Junius Foy, Jr. *federal judge*
Lynne, Seybourn Harris *federal judge*
Mitchell, Tamara O. *judge*
Nelson, Edwin L. *federal judge*
Pointer, Sam Clyde, Jr. *federal judge*
Propst, Robert Bruce *federal judge*
†Putnam, Terry Michael *magistrate judge*
Shores, Janie Ledlow *retired state supreme court justice*
Smith, Edward Samuel *federal judge*

Florence
Tease, James Edward *judge*

Gadsden
Sledge, James Scott *judge*

Huntsville
†Greene, Paul W. *federal judge*

Mobile
Butler, Charles Randolph, Jr. *federal judge*
†Cassady, William E. *federal judge*
Cox, Emmett Ripley *federal judge*
Hand, William Brevard *federal judge*
Howard, Alex T., Jr. *federal judge*
Kahn, Gordon Barry *retired federal bankruptcy judge*
†Mahoney, Margaret A. *federal judge*
McCall, Daniel Thompson, Jr. *retired judge*
†Milling, Bert William, Jr. *magistrate judge*
Pittman, Virgil *federal judge*
†Steele, William H. *federal judge*
Thomas, Daniel Holcombe *federal judge*

Montgomery
Albritton, William Harold, III *federal judge*
Almon, Reneau Pearson *state supreme court justice*
Black, Robert Coleman *judge, lawyer*
Carnes, Edward E. *federal judge*
†Carroll, John L. *federal judge*
†Coody, Charles S. *federal judge*
Cook, Ralph D. *state supreme court justice*
De Ment, Ira *judge*
Dubina, Joel Fredrick *federal judge*
Godbold, John Cooper *federal judge*
†Gordon, A. Pope *federal judge*
Hobbs, Truman McGill *federal judge, lawyer*
Houston, James Gorman, Jr. *state supreme court justice*
Kennedy, (Henry) Mark *former state supreme court judge*
Maddox, Alva Hugh *state supreme court justice*
Maddox, Hugh *state supreme court justice*
†McPherson, Vanzetta Penn *magistrate judge*
Steele, Rodney Redfearn *judge*
Thompson, Myron H. *federal judge*
Torbert, Clement Clay, Jr. *state supreme court justice*
Varner, Robert Edward *federal judge*

Tuscaloosa
†Stilson, C. Michael *federal judge*

ALASKA

Anchorage
Branson, Albert Harold (Harry Branson) *magistrate judge, educator*
Compton, Allen T. *state supreme court justice*
Eastaugh, Robert L. *state supreme court justice*
Fabe, Dana Anderson *judge*
Fitzgerald, James Michael *federal judge*
Holland, H. Russel *federal judge*
†MacDonald, Donald, IV *federal judge*
†Ross, Herbert A. *federal judge*
Sedwick, John W. *judge*
Singleton, James Keith *federal judge*
von der Heydt, James Arnold *federal judge, lawyer*

Fairbanks
†Fenton, Thomas E., Jr. *federal judge*
Kleinfeld, Andrew Jay *federal judge*

ARIZONA

Flagstaff
†Verkamp, Stephen L. *federal judge*

Phoenix
†Baum, Redfield T., Sr. *federal judge*
Broomfield, Robert Cameron *federal judge*
Canby, William Cameron, Jr. *federal judge*
Carroll, Earl Hamblin *federal judge*
Copple, William Perry *federal judge*
Curley, Sarah Sharer *federal bankruptcy judge*
Feldman, Stanley George *state supreme court justice*
Gerber, Rudolph Joseph *judge, educator*
Hardy, Charles Leach *federal judge*
Hicks, Bethany Gribben *judge, lawyer, commissioner*
Kaufman, Roger Wayne *state judge*
Martone, Frederick J. *state supreme court justice*
†Mathis, Virginia *federal judge*
McClennen, Crane *judge*
McNamee, Stephen M. *federal judge*
†Mooreman, Robert G. *federal judge*
Myers, Robert David *judge*
Rosenblatt, Paul Gerhardt *judge*
Schroeder, Mary Murphy *federal judge*
Silver, Roslyn O. *judge, federal*
†Silverman, Barry G. *federal judge*
†Sitver, Morton *federal judge*
Strand, Roger Gordon *federal judge*

Springerville
Geisler, Sherry Lynn *magistrate*

Tucson
Bilby, Richard Mansfield *federal judge*
Browning, William Docker *federal judge*
†Fiora, Nancy *federal judge*
Lacagnina, Michael Anthony *judge*
†Marlar, James M. *federal judge*
Marquez, Alfredo C. *federal judge*
†Ollason, Lawrence *federal judge*
Roll, John McCarthy *judge*
†Terlizzi, Raymond T. *federal judge*
†Zapata, Frank *federal judge*

Yuma
†Irwin, Jay R. *federal judge*

ARKANSAS

Batesville
Harkey, John Norman *judge*

Conway
Hays, Steele *retired state supreme court judge*

El Dorado
Barnes, Harry F. *federal judge*
†Shepherd, Bobby E. *federal judge*

Fayetteville
Hendren, Jimm Larry *federal judge*
Waters, H. Franklin *federal judge*

Fort Smith
Stites, Beverly R. *judge*

Little Rock
Arnold, Morris Sheppard *judge*
Arnold, Richard Sheppard *federal judge*
†Cavaneau, Jerry W. *federal judge*
Corbin, Donald L. *state supreme court justice*
Eisele, Garnett Thomas *federal judge*
†Forster, John, Jr. *federal judge*
†Fussell, Robert F. *federal judge*
Glaze, Thomas A. *state supreme court justice*
†Jones, Henry L., Jr. *federal judge*
†Mixon, James G. *federal judge*
Moody, James Maxwell *judge, federal*
†Penix, William R., III *federal judge*
Reasoner, Stephen M. *federal judge*
Roaf, Andree Layton *state appellate court judge*
Roy, Elsijane Trimble *federal judge*
†Scott, Mary Davies *federal judge*
Stroud, John Fred, Jr. *judge*
Thornton, Ray *state supreme court justice, former congressman*
Wilson, William R., Jr. *judge*
Woods, Henry *federal judge*
Wright, Susan Webber *judge*
†Young, H. David *federal judge*

CALIFORNIA

Alameda
Bartalini, C. Richard *judge*

Arroyo Grande
†del Campo, Robert A. *federal judge, lawyer*

Bakersfield
†Etcheverry, Louis P. *federal judge*

Barstow
†Mahlum, Kirtland L. *federal judge*

Beverly Hills
Jaffe, F. Filmore *lawyer, retired judge*

El Centro
†Schmitt, Joseph E. *federal judge*

Eureka
†Nord, Larry B. *federal judge*

Fort Bragg
Lehan, Jonathan Michael *judge*

Fresno
†Beck, Dennis L. *magistrate judge*
†Best, Hollis G. *federal judge*
Coyle, Robert Everett *federal judge*
Crocker, Myron Donovan *federal judge*
†Dorian, Brett J. *federal judge*
†Ishii, Anthony W. *judge*
†Rimel, Whitney *federal judge*
†Snyder, Sandra M. *federal magistrate judge*
Wanger, Oliver Winston *federal judge*

Hollywood
Fischer, Dale Susan *judge*

Irvine
Curtis, Jesse William, Jr. *retired federal judge*

Los Angeles
†Ahart, Alan M. *bankruptcy judge*
Alarcon, Arthur Lawrence *federal judge*
Armstrong, Orville *judge*
Baird, Lourdes G. *federal judge*
†Block, Robert N. *federal judge*
Bufford, Samuel Lawrence *federal judge*
Byrne, William Matthew, Jr. *federal judge*
†Chapman, Rosalyn M. *federal judge*
Chavez, Victor Edwin *judge*
Collins, Audrey B. *judge*
Curry, Daniel Arthur *judge*
Donovan, Thomas B. *judge*
†Eick, Charles F. *federal judge*
Fenning, Lisa Hill *federal judge*
Fleming, Macklin *judge, author*
Gold, Arnold Henry *judge*
Hatter, Terry Julius, Jr. *federal judge*
Hauk, A. Andrew *federal judge*
†Hillman, Stephen J. *federal judge*
Hupp, Harry L. *federal judge*
Ideman, James M. *federal judge*
†Johnson, Earl, Jr. *judge, author*
Johnson, Michael Marion *judge*
Kelleher, Robert Joseph *federal judge*
Keller, William D. *federal judge*
Kenyon, David V. *federal judge*
†King, George H. *judge*
Klein, Joan Dempsey *judge*
Letts, J. Spencer *federal judge*
Lew, Ronald S. W. *federal judge*
†March, Kathleen Patricia *bankruptcy judge*
Marshall, Consuelo Bland *federal judge*
Masterson, William A. *judge*
†McMahon, James W. *federal magistrate judge*
Norris, William Albert *former federal judge*
Paez, Richard A. *judge*
Pfaelzer, Mariana R. *federal judge*
†Phillips, Virginia A. *federal judge*
Rafeedie, Edward, Sr. *federal judge*
Rea, William J. *judge*
Real, Manuel Lawrence *federal judge*
†Robbins, Brian Quinn *federal judge*
†Robles, Ernest *federal judge*
†Russell, Barry *federal judge*
Takasugi, Robert Mitsuhiro *federal judge*
Tevrizian, Dickran M., Jr. *federal judge*
Turchin, Carolyn *judge*
Waters, Laughlin Edward *federal judge*
Williams, David Welford *federal judge*
Wilson, Stephen Victor *federal judge*
†Wistrich, Andrew J. *federal judge*
†Zurzulo, Vincent P. *federal judge*

Modesto
Mayhew, William A. *judge*
†McManus, Michael S. *federal judge*

Monterey
†Garrett, William L. *federal judge*

Oakland
Armstrong, Saundra Brown *federal judge*
†Brazil, Wayne D. *federal judge*
†Jellen, Edward D. *federal judge*
Jensen, D. Lowell *federal judge, lawyer, government official*
Newsome, Randall Jackson *judge*
†Tchaikovsky, Leslie J. *bankruptcy judge*
Wilken, Claudia *judge*

Pacific Palisades
†Anwyl-Davies, Marcus John *judge, arbitrator*

Pasadena
Boochever, Robert *federal judge*
Fernandez, Ferdinand Francis *federal judge*
Goodwin, Alfred Theodore *federal judge*
Hall, Cynthia Holcomb *federal judge*
Johnson, Barbara Jean *retired lawyer, judge*
Kozinski, Alex *federal judge*
Nelson, Dorothy Wright (Mrs. James F. Nelson) *federal judge*
Rymer, Pamela Ann *federal judge*
Tashima, Atsushi Wallace *federal judge*
Wardlaw, Kim A.M. *federal judge*

Ramona
Jordan, David Francis, Jr. *retired judge*

Redding
†Bay, Richard M. *federal judge*

Redwood City
Harrington, Walter Howard, Jr. *judge*

Riverside
†Alberts, Robert W. *federal judge*
†Goldberg, Mitchel R. *federal judge*
†Jury, Meredith A. *federal judge*
†Naugle, David N. *federal judge*
Timlin, Robert J. *judge*

Sacramento
Burrell, Garland E., Jr. *federal judge*
Dahl, Loren Silvester *retired federal judge*
†Damrell, Frank C., Jr. *judge*
Garcia, Edward J. *federal judge*
†Hollows, Gregory G. *federal judge*
Karlton, Lawrence K. *federal judge*
†Klein, Christopher M. *federal judge*
Kolkey, Daniel Miles *judge*
Levi, David F. *federal judge*
McKeag, Jane Dickson *judge*
Moulds, John F. *federal judge*
†Nowinski, Peter A. *federal judge*
Russell, David E. *judge*
Schwartz, Milton Lewis *federal judge*
Van Camp, Brian Ralph *judge*

San Diego
Aaron, Cynthia G. *judge*
†Adler, Louise DeCarl *bankruptcy judge*
†Battaglia, Anthony J. *federal judge*
Bowie, Peter Wentworth *judge, educator*
Brewster, Rudi Milton *state judge*
†Brooks, Reuben B. *federal judge*
Enright, William Benner *judge*
Gilliam, Earl B. *federal judge*
Gonzalez, Irma Elsa *federal judge*
†Hargrove, John James *bankruptcy judge*
Huff, Marilyn L. *federal judge*
Jones, Napoleon A., Jr. *judge*
Keep, Judith N. *federal judge*
Lewis, Gerald Jorgensen *judge*
Meyers, James William *federal judge*
†Moskowitz, Barry T. *judge*
Nielsen, Leland C. *federal judge*
†Papas, Leo S. *federal judge*
†Porter, Louisa S. *federal judge*
Rhoades, John Skylstead, Sr. *federal judge*
Schwartz, Edward J. *federal judge*

Thompson, David Renwick *federal judge*
Thompson, Gordon, Jr. *federal judge*
Turrentine, Howard Boyd *federal judge*
Wallace, J. Clifford *federal judge*

San Francisco
Baxter, Marvin Ray *state supreme court justice*
†Brennan, Joan Stevenson *federal judge*
Brown, Janice Rogers *state supreme court justice*
Browning, James Robert *federal judge*
†Carlson, Thomas Edward *bankruptcy judge*
Chesney, Maxine M. *judge*
Chin, Ming *state supreme court justice*
Conti, Samuel *federal judge*
George, Ronald M. *state supreme court chief justice*
Haerle, Paul Raymond *judge*
Henderson, Thelton Eugene *federal judge*
Illston, Susan Y. *judge*
†James, Maria-Elena *federal judge*
Kennard, Joyce L. *state supreme court justice*
†Langford, F. Steele *federal judge*
Legge, Charles Alexander *federal judge*
Montali, Dennis *federal judge*
Mosk, Stanley *state supreme court justice*
Noonan, John T., Jr. *federal judge, legal educator*
Orrick, William Horsley, Jr. *federal judge*
Patel, Marilyn Hall *judge*
Robertson, Armand James, II *judge*
Schwarzer, William W *federal judge*
Sneed, Joseph Tyree, III *federal judge*
Walker, Vaughn R. *federal judge*
Werdegar, Kathryn Mickle *state supreme court justice*
Zimmerman, Bernard *judge*

San Jose
†Grube, James R. *federal judge*
†Infante, Edward A. *federal judge*
Ingram, William Austin *federal judge*
Morgan, Marilyn *federal judge*
Panelli, Edward Alexander *retired state supreme court justice*
Stewart, Melinda Jane *judge*
†Trumbull, Patricia V. *federal judge*
Ware, James W. *federal judge*
†Weissbradt, Arthur S. *federal judge*
Whyte, Ronald M. *federal judge*
Williams, Spencer Mortimer *federal judge*

San Marino
Mortimer, Wendell Reed, Jr. *judge*

Santa Ana
Barr, James Norman *federal judge*
†Edwards, Elgin C. *federal judge*
Ferguson, Warren John *federal judge*
Riddle, Lynne *judge*
Ryan, John Edward *federal judge*
Stotler, Alicemarie Huber *judge*
Taylor, Gary L. *federal judge*
†Wilson, John James *federal judge*

Santa Barbara
Aldisert, Ruggero John *federal judge*
Riblet, Robin L. *judge*

Santa Monica
Vega, Benjamin Urbizo *retired judge, television producer*

Santa Rosa
Jaroslovsky, Alan *judge*

Solana Beach
Watson, Jack Crozier *retired state supreme court justice*

South Lake Tahoe
†Reece, Monte M. *federal judge*

Studio City
Lasarow, William Julius *retired federal judge*

Susanville
†Kellison, Craig M. *federal judge*

Van Nuys
Mohr, Anthony James *judge*

Woodland Hills
†Greenwald, Arthur M. *federal judge*
†Lax, Kathleen Thompson *bankruptcy judge*
Mund, Geraldine *judge*
Pregerson, Harry *federal judge*

Yucca Valley
†Martin, George Leonard *federal judge*

COLORADO

Denver
Abram, Donald Eugene *federal magistrate judge*
Babcock, Lewis Thornton *federal judge*
†Borchers, Richard M. *federal judge*
†Brooks, Sidney B. *bankruptcy judge*
†Brumbaugh, Roland John *bankruptcy judge*
Clark, Patricia Ann *federal judge*
Ebel, David M. *federal judge*
Felter, Edwin Lester, Jr. *judge*
Hobbs, Gregory James, Jr. *state supreme court justice*
Kane, John Lawrence, Jr. *federal judge*
Kirshbaum, Howard M. *judge, arbitrator*
Kourlis, Rebecca Love *judge*
Krieger, Marcia Smith *judge*
Lucero, Carlos *federal judge*
†Matheson, Charles E. *federal judge*
Matsch, Richard P. *judge*
McWilliams, Robert Hugh *federal judge*
Miller, Walker David *judge*
Mullarkey, Mary J. *state supreme court justice*
Nottingham, Edward Willis, Jr. *federal judge*
Porfilio, John Carbone *federal judge*
Pringle, Bruce D. *federal magistrate*
Rovira, Luis Dario *state supreme court justice*
Satter, Raymond Nathan *judge*
Schlatter, O. Edward *judge*
Scott, Gregory Kellam *state supreme court justice*
Sparr, Daniel Beattie *federal judge*
Stacy, Richard A. *judge*
Swihart, Steven Taylor *judge*
Vollack, Anthony F. *former state supreme court justice*
Weinshienk, Zita Leeson *federal judge*

Durango
†West, David L. *federal judge*

Englewood
Erickson, William Hurt *retired state supreme court justice*

Fort Collins
Gandy, Hoke Conway *judge, state official*

Golden
Jackson, Richard Brooke *judge*

Grand Junction
†Robb, James M. *federal judge*

CONNECTICUT

Bridgeport
Eginton, Warren William *federal judge*
†Fitzsimmons, Holly B. *federal judge, educator*
Nevas, Alan Harris *federal judge*
Shiff, Alan Howard William *federal judge*

Fairfield
Lumbard, Joseph Edward, Jr. *federal judge*

Guilford
Ross, Michael Frederick *magistrate, lawyer*

Hartford
Berdon, Robert Irwin *state supreme court justice*
Borden, David M. *state supreme court justice*
Callahan, Robert Jeremiah *state supreme court justice*
Chatigny, Robert Neil *judge*
Covello, Alfred Vincent *federal judge*
Droney, Christopher F. *judge*
Katz, Joette *state supreme court justice*
Killian, Robert Kenneth, Jr. *judge, lawyer*
†Krechevsky, Robert L. *federal judge*
Newman, Jon O. *federal judge*
Norcott, Fleming L., Jr. *state supreme court justice*
Peters, Ellen Ash *state supreme court justice*
Shea, David Michael *state supreme court justice*
†Smith, Thomas P. *federal judge*
†Squatrito, Dominic J. *judge*
Thompson, Alvin W. *judge*
Wright, Douglass Brownell *judge, lawyer*

Milford
Grogins, Jack Lawrence *state judge*

New Britain
Meskill, Thomas J. *federal judge*

New Haven
Arterton, Janet Bond *judge*
Burns, Ellen Bree *federal judge*
Cabranes, José Alberto *federal judge*
Calabresi, Guido *federal judge, law educator*
†Dabrowski, Albert S. *federal judge*
Dorsey, Peter Collins *federal judge*
†Margolis, Joan G. *federal judge*
†Martinez, Donna F. *federal judge*
Walker, John Mercer, Jr. *federal judge*
Winter, Ralph Karl, Jr. *federal judge*

New London
Santaniello, Angelo Gary *retired state supreme court justice*

Waterbury
Glass, Robert Davis *judge*
Goettel, Gerard Louis *federal judge*

DELAWARE

Dover
Hartnett, Maurice A., III *judge*

Georgetown
Holland, Randy James *state supreme court justice*

Wilmington
Balick, Helen Shaffer *retired judge*
Del Pesco, Susan Marie Carr *state judge*
Farnan, Joseph James, Jr. *federal judge*
Gebelein, Richard Stephen *judge, former state attorney general*
Jacobs, Jack Bernard *judge*
Latchum, James Levin *federal judge*
Longobardi, Joseph J. *federal judge*
McKelvie, Roderick R. *federal judge*
Robinson, Sue L(ewis) *federal judge*
Roth, Jane Richards *federal judge*
Schwartz, Murray Merle *federal judge*
Stapleton, Walter King *federal judge*
Trostle, Mary Pat *judge*
Veasey, Eugene Norman *chief justice*
Walsh, Joseph Thomas *state supreme court justice*
†Walsh, Peter J. *federal judge*
Wright, Caleb Merrill *federal judge*

DISTRICT OF COLUMBIA

Washington
Andewelt, Roger B. *federal judge*
Archer, Glenn LeRoy, Jr. *federal circuit judge*
†Attridge, Patrick J. *federal judge*
Bartnoff, Judith *judge*
Bayly, John Henry, Jr. *judge*
Beddow, Richard Harold *judge*
Beghe, Renato *federal judge*
Belson, James Anthony *judge*
Bernstein, Edwin S. *judge*
Blair, Warren Emerson *retired federal judge*
Breyer, Stephen Gerald *United States supreme court justice*
Bruggink, Eric G. *federal judge*
Bryant, William B. *federal judge*
Bryson, William Curtis *federal judge*
Buckley, James Lane *federal judge*
Burnett, Arthur Louis, Sr. *judge*
Chabot, Herbert L. *judge*
†Chaitovitz, Samuel *judge*
Chiechi, Carolyn Phyllis *federal judge*
†Clapp, Charles E., II *senior judge*
Clevenger, Raymond C., III *federal judge*
Cohen, Mary Ann *judge*
Colvin, John O. *federal judge*
Cooper, Jean Saralee *judge*
Cowen, Wilson *federal judge*
Cox, Walter Thompson, III *federal judge*
Crawford, Susan Jean *federal judge, lawyer*
Dawson, Howard Athalone, Jr. *federal judge*
Edwards, Harry T. *federal judge*
†Effron, Andrew S. *federal judge*
Everett, Robinson Oscar *federal judge, law educator*
Farley, John Joseph, III *federal judge*
Farrell, Michael W. *state supreme court justice*
Fay, William Michael *federal judge*
†Foley, Maurice B. *federal judge*
Friedman, Daniel Mortimer *federal judge*
Futey, Bohdan A. *federal judge*
Gajarsa, Arthur J. *judge*
Gale, Joseph H. *federal judge*
Gallagher, George R. *judge*
Garland, Merrick Brian *federal judge*
Gasch, Oliver *judge*
Gerber, Joel *federal judge*
Gibson, Reginald Walker *federal judge*
Gierke, Herman Fredrick, III *federal judge*
Ginsburg, Douglas Howard *federal judge, educator*
Ginsburg, Ruth Bader *United States supreme court justice*
Goodrich, George Herbert *judge*
Green, Joyce Hens *federal judge*
Green, June Lazenby *federal judge*
Greene, Harold H. *federal judge*
Halpern, James S. *federal judge*
Hamblen, Lapsley Walker, Jr. *judge*
Harkins, Kenneth R. *federal judge*
Harris, Stanley S. *judge*
Heifetz, Alan William *federal judge*
Henderson, Karen LeCraft *federal judge*
Hodges, Robert H., Jr. *federal judge*
†Holdaway, Ronald M. *federal judge*
Horn, Marian Blank *federal judge*
Ivers, Donald Louis *judge*
Jackson, Thomas Penfield *federal judge*
Jacobs, Julian I. *federal judge*
Johnson, Norma Holloway *federal judge*
Kennedy, Anthony McLeod *United States supreme court justice*
†Kennedy, Henry H. *judge*
Kern, John Worth, III *judge*
Kessler, Gladys *federal judge*
King, Warren R. *judge*
Kline, Norman Douglas *federal judge*
†Kollar-Kotelly, Colleen *district judge*
†Korner, Jules Gilmer, III *senior judge*
Kramer, Kenneth Bentley *federal judge, former congressman*
Lamberth, Royce C. *federal judge*
Laro, David *judge*
Lourie, Alan David *federal judge*
Lydon, Thomas J. *federal judge*
Mack, Julia Cooper *judge*
Margolis, Lawrence Stanley *federal judge*
Marvel, L. Paige *judge, lawyer*
Mayer, Haldane Robert *federal chief judge*
Mencher, Bruce Stephan *judge*
Merow, James F. *federal judge*
Michel, Paul Redmond *federal judge*
Miller, Christine Odell Cook *judge*
Nangle, John Francis *federal judge*
Nebeker, Frank Quill *federal judge*
Newman, Pauline *federal judge*
Oberdorfer, Louis F. *federal judge*
O'Connor, Sandra Day *United States supreme court justice*
Parr, Carolyn Miller *federal judge*
Penn, John Garrett *federal judge*
Plager, S. Jay *federal judge*
Pryor, William C. *judge*
Queen, Evelyn E. Crawford *judge, law educator*
Rader, Randall Ray *federal judge*
Randolph, Arthur Raymond *federal judge, lawyer*
Raum, Arnold *federal judge*
Rehnquist, William Hubbs *United States supreme court chief justice*
Reid, Inez Smith *lawyer, educator*
Robertson, James *judge*
Robinson, Aubrey Eugene, Jr. *federal judge*
Robinson, Deborah A. *judge*
Robinson, Wilkes Coleman *retired federal judge*
Rogers, Judith W. *federal judge*
Ruiz, Vanessa *state judge*
Ruwe, Robert P. *federal judge*
Scalia, Antonin *United States supreme court justice*
Schall, Alvin Anthony *federal judge*
Schwelb, Frank Ernest *court of appeals judge*
Sentelle, David Bryan *federal judge*
Simpson, Charles Reagan *retired judge*
Smith, Roy Philip *judge*
Sporkin, Stanley *federal judge*
Steadman, John Montague *appellate judge*
Steinberg, Jonathan Robert *judge*
Stevens, John Paul *United States supreme court justice*
†Streb, Paul Gerard *federal judge*
Sullivan, Emmet G. *judge*
Sullivan, Eugene Raymond *federal judge*
Swift, Stephen Jensen *federal judge*
†Tannenwald, Theodore, Jr. *federal judge*
Tatel, David Stephen *federal judge*
†Teel, S. Martin, Jr. *federal judge*
Terry, John Alfred *state supreme court judge*
Thomas, Clarence *United States supreme court justice*
†Thornton, Michael B. *federal judge*
Tidwell, Moody Rudolph *federal judge*
Turner, James Thomas *judge*
Urbina, Ricardo M. *judge*
Van Doren, Emerson Barclay *administrative judge*
†Vasquez, Juan Flores *judge*
Wagner, Annice McBryde *supreme court justice*
Wagner, Curtis Lee, Jr. *judge*
Wald, Patricia McGowan *federal judge*
Weinstein, Diane Gilbert *federal judge, lawyer*
Wells, Thomas B. *federal judge*
Whalen, Laurence J. *federal judge*
White, Byron R. *former United States supreme court justice*
Wiese, John Paul *federal judge*
Williams, Stephen Fain *federal judge*
Wright, Lawrence A. *federal judge*
Yock, Robert John *federal judge*
Yoder, Ronnie A. *judge*
Zobel, Rya Weickert *federal judge, legal administrator*

FLORIDA

Deland
Sanders, Edwin Perry Bartley *judge*

Fort Lauderdale
Gonzalez, Jose Alejandro, Jr. *federal judge*
†Hymann, Paul G., Jr. *federal judge*
†Ray, Raymond B. *federal judge*
Roettger, Norman Charles, Jr. *federal judge*
†Seltzer, Barry S. *federal judge*
Snow, Lurana S. *judge*
Zloch, William J. *federal judge*

Fort Myers
Schoonover, Jack Ronald *judge*
Shafer, Robert Tinsley, Jr. *judge*
†Swartz, George T. *federal judge*

Fort Pierce
†Lynch, Frank J. *federal judge*

Gainesville
†Belz, Richard A. *federal judge*
Coleman, Mary Stallings *retired chief justice*
Paul, Maurice M. *federal judge*

Jacksonville
Black, Susan Harrell *federal judge*
†Funk, Jerry A. *federal judge*
Hill, James Clinkscales *federal judge*
Hodges, William Terrell *federal judge*
Melton, Howell Webster, Sr. *federal judge*
Moore, John Henry, II *federal judge*
Nimmons, Ralph Wilson, Jr. *federal judge*
†Proctor, George L. *federal judge*
Schlesinger, Harvey Erwin *judge*
†Snyder, Howard T. *federal judge*
†Steele, John E. *federal judge*
Tjoflat, Gerald Bard *federal judge*

Key Biscayne
Kraft, C. William, Jr. *federal judge*

Merritt Island
Johnson, Clarence Traylor, Jr. *circuit court judge*

Miami
Atkins, C(arl) Clyde *federal judge*
†Bandstra, Ted E. *federal judge*
Barkett, Rosemary *federal judge*
Brown, Stephen Thomas *magistrate judge*
Cristol, A. Jay *federal judge*
Davis, Edward Bertrand *federal judge*
†Dube, Robert L. *federal judge*
Fay, Peter Thorp *federal judge*
Fletcher, John Greenwood II *state judge*
Freeman, Gill Sherryl *judge*
†Garber, Barry L. *magistrate judge*
†Gold, Alan Stephen *judge, lawyer, educator*
Graham, Donald Lynn *federal judge*
Highsmith, Shelby *federal judge*
Hoeveler, William M. *federal judge*
†Johnson, Linnea Ruth *federal judge*
Karlan, Sandy Ellen *judge*
Kehoe, James W. *federal judge*
King, James Lawrence *federal judge*
Marcus, Stanley *federal judge*
†Mark, Robert A. *federal judge*
Moore, Kevin Michael *federal judge*
Moreno, Federico Antonio *federal judge*
Nesbitt, Lenore Carrero *federal judge*
†Palermo, Peter R. *federal judge*
Rosinek, Jeffrey *judge*
Shevin, Robert Lewis *judge*
†Sorrentino, Charlene H. *federal judge*
Ungaro-Benages, Ursula Mancusi *federal judge*

Orlando
†Baker, David A. *federal judge*
†Briskman, Arthur B. *federal judge*
Conway, Anne Callaghan *federal judge*
Fawsett, Patricia Combs *federal judge*
†Glazebrook, James G. *federal judge*
†Jenneman, Karen S. *federal judge*
Sharp, George Kendall *federal judge*
Young, George Cressler *federal judge*

Panama City
Smith, Larry Glenn *retired state judge*

Pensacola
Collier, Lacey Alexander *federal judge*
Novotny, Susan M. *judge*
Vinson, C. Roger *federal judge*

Saint Petersburg
Grube, Karl Bertram *judge*
Roney, Paul H(itch) *federal judge*

Sarasota
Burdick, Eugene Allan *retired judge, lawyer, surrogate judge*

Sebring
Shinholser, Olin Wilson *judge*

Tallahassee
Anstead, Harry Lee *state supreme court justice*
Grimes, Stephen Henry *retired state supreme court justice*
Harding, Major Best *state supreme court chief justice*
Hatchett, Joseph Woodrow *federal judge*
Kogan, Gerald *state supreme court justice*
McCord, Guyte Pierce, Jr. *retired judge*
Overton, Benjamin Frederick *state supreme court justice*
Shaw, Leander Jerry, Jr. *state supreme court justice*
†Sherill, William C. *federal judge*
Stafford, William Henry, Jr. *federal judge*
Sundberg, Alan Carl *former state supreme court justice, lawyer*
Webster, Peter David *judge*
Wells, Charles Talley *state supreme court justice*

Tampa
Adams, Henry Lee, Jr. *federal judge*
Baynes, Thomas Edward, Jr. *judge, lawyer, educator*
Bucklew, Susan Cawthon *federal judge*
†Corcoran, Clement Timothy, III *bankruptcy judge*
Dail, Joseph Garner, Jr. *judge*
†Glenn, Paul M. *federal judge*
†Jenkins, Elizabeth A. *federal judge*
Kovachevich, Elizabeth Anne *federal judge*
†McCoun, Thomas B., III *federal judge*
Menendez, Manuel, Jr. *judge*
Merryday, Steven D. *federal judge*
Paskay, Alexander L. *federal judge, law educator*
†Pizzo, Mark A. *federal judge*
†Wilson, Thomas G. *federal judge*

West Palm Beach
Eschbach, Jesse Ernest *federal judge*
†Friedman, Steven H. *federal judge*
Hurley, Daniel T. K. *federal judge*
Paine, James Carriger *federal judge*
Ryskamp, Kenneth Lee *federal judge*
Vitunac, Ann E. *judge*

GEORGIA

Albany
†Hodge, Richard L. *federal judge*
Sands, W. Louis *federal judge*

Atlanta
Benham, Robert *state supreme court justice*
Bihary, Joyce *federal judge*
Birch, Stanley Francis, Jr. *federal judge*
†Brill, Gerrilyn G. *federal judge*
†Brizendine, Robert E. *federal judge*
†Byington, William W., Jr. *federal judge*
Camp, Jack Tarpley, Jr. *federal judge*
Carley, George H. *state supreme court justice*
Carnes, Julie Elizabeth *federal judge*
Cooper, Clarence *federal judge*
†Cotton, Stacey W. *federal judge*
†Deane, Richard H., Jr. *federal judge*
Dougherty, John Ernest *judge*
Edmondson, James Larry *federal judge*
Evans, Orinda D. *federal judge*
Feldman, Joel Martin *magistrate judge*
Fletcher, Norman S. *state supreme court justice*
Forrester, J. Owen *federal judge*
Freeman, Richard Cameron *federal judge*
†Harper, William Lloyd *federal judge*
Henderson, Albert John *federal judge*
Hines, Preston Harris *state supreme court justice*
Hull, Frank Mays *federal judge*
Hunstein, Carol *state supreme court justice*
Hunt, Willis B., Jr. *federal judge*
†Kahn, A. David *federal judge*
Kravitch, Phyllis A. *federal judge*
†Massey, James E. *federal judge*
Moye, Charles Allen, Jr. *federal judge*
Murphy, Margaret Hackett *federal judge*
O'Kelley, William Clark *federal judge*
†Robinson, Hugh, Jr. *federal judge*
Sears, Leah J. *state supreme court justice*
Shoob, Marvin H. *federal judge*
Thompson, Hugh P *state supreme court justice*
Tidwell, George Ernest *federal judge*
Ward, Horace Taliaferro *federal judge*

Augusta
†Barfield, W. Leon *federal judge*
Bowen, Dudley Hollingsworth, Jr. *federal judge*
†Dalis, John S. *federal judge*

Brunswick
Alaimo, Anthony A. *federal judge*
†Graham, James E. *federal judge*

Cleveland
Barrett, David Eugene *judge*

Columbus
Elliott, James Robert *federal judge*
Laney, John Thomas, III *federal judge*
†Slaughter, William L. *federal judge*

Decatur
Shulman, Arnold *judge, lawyer*

Gainesville
†Strother, John R., Jr. *federal judge*

Lawrenceville
Reeves, Gene *judge*

Macon
Anderson, Robert Lanier, III *federal judge*
Fitzpatrick, Duross *federal judge*
Gerson, Robert Walthall *judge, retired lawyer*
Hershner, Robert Franklin, Jr. *judge*
†Hicks, Claude W., Jr. *federal judge*
Owens, Wilbur Dawson, Jr. *federal judge*
†Walker, James D., Jr. *federal judge*

Marietta
Smith, George Thornewell *retired state supreme court justice*

Newnan
†Drake, W. Homer, Jr. *federal judge*

Rome
Murphy, Harold Loyd *federal judge*
Vining, Robert Luke, Jr. *federal judge*

Savannah
Edenfield, Berry Avant *federal judge*
†Lamar, W. Davis, Jr. *federal judge*
Moore, William Theodore, Jr. *judge*

HAWAII

Honolulu
Acoba, Simeon Rivera, Jr. *judge*
Ashford, Clinton Rutledge *judge*
†Blair, Robert C. *federal judge*
Choy, Herbert Young Cho *federal judge*
Ezra, David Alan *federal judge*
†Faucher, David F. *federal judge*
Gillmor, Helen *federal judge*
†Heen, Walter Meheula *retired judge, political party executive*
Kay, Alan Cooke *federal judge*
†King, Lloyd *federal judge*
†Kurren, Barry M. *federal judge*
Levinson, Steven Henry *state supreme court justice*
Moon, Ronald T. Y. *state supreme court justice*
Nakayama, Paula Aiko *state supreme court justice*
Pence, Martin *federal judge*
†Yamashita, Francis Isami *magistrate judge*

IDAHO

Boise
Boyle, Larry Monroe *federal judge*
Lodge, Edward James *federal judge*
McDevitt, Charles Francis *state supreme court justice*
Mc Quade, Henry Ford *state justice*
Nelson, Thomas G. *federal judge*
†Pappas, Jim D. *chief bankruptcy judge*
Trott, Stephen Spangler *federal judge, musician*
†Williams, Mikel H. *magistrate judge*
Winmill, B. Lynn *judge*

ILLINOIS

Barrington
Wynn, Thomas Joseph *judge, educator*

Belleville
Ferguson, John Marshall *retired federal magistrate judge*

Benton
Foreman, James Louis *retired judge*
†Frazier, Phillip M. *federal judge*
Gilbert, J. Phil *federal judge*

Chicago
Alesia, James H(enry) *judge*
Andersen, Wayne R. *federal judge*
†Ashman, Martin C. *federal judge*
Aspen, Marvin Edward *federal judge*
†Barliant, Ronald *federal judge*
Bauer, William Joseph *federal judge*
Bilandic, Michael A. *state supreme court justice, former mayor*
†Bobrick, Edward A. *federal judge*
Bua, Nicholas John *retired federal judge*
Bucklo, Elaine Edwards *United States district court judge*
Castillo, Ruben *judge*
Coar, David H. *federal judge*
Conlon, Suzanne B. *federal judge*
Cudahy, Richard D. *federal judge*
†Denlow, Morton *federal judge*
Duff, Brian Barnett *federal judge*
Easterbrook, Frank Hoover *federal judge*
Fairchild, Thomas E. *federal judge*
Flaum, Joel Martin *federal judge*
Freeman, Charles E. *state supreme court justice*
Gettleman, Robert William *judge*
Gottschall, Joan B. *judge*
Grady, John F. *federal judge*
†Guzman, Ronald A. *federal judge*
Hart, William Thomas *federal judge*
Holderman, James F., Jr. *federal judge*
†James, Thomas W. *federal judge*
Johnson, Glenn Thompson *judge*
Jones, Dorothy F. *judge*
Kanne, Michael Stephen *federal judge*
†Katz, Erwin I. *federal judge*
†Keys, Arlander *federal judge*
Kocoras, Charles Petros *federal judge*
†Lefkow, Joan H. *federal judge*
Lefkow, Joan Humphrey *judge*
Leighton, George Neves *retired federal judge*
Leinenweber, Harry D. *federal judge*
Lindberg, George W. *federal judge*
Manning, Blanche M. *federal judge*
Marovich, George M. *federal judge*
McGarr, Frank James *retired federal judge, dispute resolution consultant*
Moran, James Byron *federal judge*
Morrissey, George Michael *judge*
Nickels, John L. *state supreme court justice*
Nordberg, John Albert *federal judge*
Norgle, Charles Ronald, Sr. *federal judge*
Pallmeyer, Rebecca Ruth *federal judge*
Pell, Wilbur Frank, Jr. *federal judge*
Plunkett, Paul Edmund *federal judge*
Posner, Richard Allen *federal judge*
†Rosemond, Thomas W., Jr. *federal judge*
Rovner, Ilana Kara Diamond *federal judge*
Schmetterer, Jack Baer *federal judge*
†Schwartz, John David *federal judge*
Shadur, Milton I. *judge*
Sonderby, Susan Pierson *chief federal bankruptcy judge*
Squires, John Henry *judge*
†Wedoff, Eugene R. *federal judge*
Williams, Ann Claire *federal judge*
Zagel, James Block *federal judge*

Danville
†Fines, Gerald D. *federal judge*

East Saint Louis
Beatty, William Louis *federal judge*
†Cohn, Gerald B. *federal judge*
†Meyers, Kenneth J. *federal judge*
Proud, Clifford J. *judge*
Riley, Paul E. *judge*
Stiehl, William D. *federal judge*

Edwardsville
Crowder, Barbara Lynn *judge*

Elgin
Kirkland, Alfred Younges, Sr. *federal judge*

Fairview Heights
Harrison, Moses W., II *state supreme court justice*

Hennepin
Bumgarner, James McNabb *judge*

Homewood
Dietch, Henry Xerxes *judge*

Kankakee
Elliott, Kathy Bradshaw *judge*

Peoria
†Altenberger, William V. *federal judge*
Kauffman, Robert Joseph *magistrate*
McDade, Joe Billy *federal judge*
Mihm, Michael Martin *federal judge*

Pontiac
Glennon, Charles Edward *judge, lawyer*

Rock Island
Telleen, John Martin *retired judge*

Rockford
†Mahoney, Patrick M. *federal judge*
Reinhard, Philip G. *federal judge*

Springfield
†Coutrakon, Basil H. *federal judge*
†Evans, Charles H. *federa; judge*
Lessen, Larry Lee *federal judge*
Miller, Benjamin K. *state supreme court justice*
Mills, Richard Henry *federal judge*
Wood, Harlington, Jr. *federal judge*

Tonica
Ryan, Howard Chris *retired state supreme court justice*

Urbana
Baker, Harold Albert *federal judge*
†Bernthal, David G. *federal judge*

Waukegan
Brady, Terrence Joseph *judge*

Wheaton
Leston, Patrick John *judge*

Wilmette
Bowman, George Arthur, Jr. *judge*

INDIANA

Boonville
Campbell, Edward Adolph *judge, electrical engineer*

Evansville
Capshaw, Tommie Dean *judge*
†Hussmann, William G., Jr. *federal judge*

Fort Wayne
†Cosbey, Roger B. *federal judge*
†Grant, Robert E. *federal judge*
Lee, William Charles *judge*

Gary
†Lindquist, Kent *federal judge*

Hammond
Dywan, Jeffery Joseph *judge*
Lozano, Rudolpho *federal judge*
Moody, James T(yne) *federal judge*
Rodovich, Andrew Paul *lawyer, federal magistrate*
†Springham, Theresa L. *federal judge*

Indianapolis
Barker, Sarah Evans *judge*
†Bayt, Robert L. *federal judge*
Dickson, Brent E(llis) *state supreme court justice*
Dillin, S. Hugh *federal judge*
Fisher, Thomas Graham *judge*
†Foster, Kennard P. *federal judge*
Givan, Richard Martin *state supreme court justice, retired*
Godich, John Paul *federal magistrate judge*
Hamilton, David F. *judge*
McKinney, Larry J. *federal judge*
†Metz, Anthony J., III *federal judge*
†Otte, Frank J. *federal judge*
Sharpnack, John Trent *judge*
Shepard, Randall Terry *state supreme court justice*
†Shields, V. Sue *federal magistrate judge*
Tinder, John Daniel *federal judge*

Jeffersonville
Barthold, Clementine B. *retired judge*

Kokomo
Stein, Eleanor Bankoff *judge*

Lagrange
Brown, George E. *judge, educator*

New Albany
†Lorch, Basil H., III *federal judge*

South Bend
Brueseke, Harold Edward *magistrate*
†Dees, Harry C., Jr. *federal judge*
Manion, Daniel Anthony *federal judge*
Miller, Robert L., Jr. *federal judge*
†Pierce, Robin D. *federal judge*
Ripple, Kenneth Francis *federal judge*
Rodibaugh, Robert Kurtz *judge*
Sharp, Allen *federal judge*

Terre Haute
†Lewis, Jordan D. *federal judge*

IOWA

Algona
Andreasen, James Hallis *retired state supreme court judge*

Cedar Rapids
Hansen, David Rasmussen *federal judge*
†Jarvey, John A. *federal judge*
†Kilburg, Paul J. *federal judge*
Mc Manus, Edward Joseph *federal judge*
Melloy, Michael J. *federal judge*

Chariton
Stuart, William Corwin *federal judge*

Council Bluffs
Peterson, Richard William *magistrate judge, lawyer*

Davenport
Neuman, Linda Kinney *state supreme court justice*

Des Moines
Bremer, Celeste F. *judge*
Carter, James H. *state supreme court justice*
Fagg, George Gardner *federal judge*
Harris, K. David *state supreme court justice*
†Hill, Russell J. *federal judge*
†Jackwig, Lee M. *federal judge*
Larson, Jerry Leroy *state supreme court justice*
Lavorato, Louis A. *state supreme court justice*
Longstaff, Ronald E. *federal judge*
McGiverin, Arthur A. *state supreme court chief justice*
Ternus, Marsha K. *state supreme court justice*
Vietor, Harold Duane *federal judge*
†Walters, Ross A. *federal judge*
Wolle, Charles Robert *federal judge*

Osceola
Reynoldson, Walter Ward *state supreme court chief justice*

Sioux City
†Deck, Paul Wayne, Jr. *federal judge*
†Edmonds, William L. *federal judge*
O'Brien, Donald Eugene *federal judge*

KANSAS

Kansas City
†Flanagan, John T. *federal judge*
Lungstrum, John W. *federal judge*
†Rushfelt, Gerald Lloyd *magistrate judge*
VanBebber, George Thomas *federal judge*
Vratil, Kathryn Hoefer *federal judge*

Lawrence
Briscoe, Mary Beck *federal judge*
Tacha, Deanell Reece *federal judge*

Leavenworth
Stanley, Arthur Jehu, Jr. *retired federal judge*
†Tillotson, John C. *federal judge, lawyer*

Olathe
Chipman, Marion Walter *judge*

Topeka
Abbott, Bob *state supreme court justice*
Allegrucci, Donald Lee *state supreme court justice*
Cox, Joseph Lawrence *judge*
Crow, Sam Alfred *federal judge*
Davis, Robert Edward *state supreme court justice*
Herd, Harold Shields *state supreme court justice*
Lockett, Tyler Charles *state supreme court justice*
Macnish, James Martin, Jr. *judge*
Marquardt, Christel Elisabeth *judge*
McFarland, Kay Eleanor *state supreme court chief justice*
Miller, Robert Haskins *retired state chief justice*
†Newman, Ronald C. *federal judge*
Pusateri, James Anthony *judge*
†Robinson, Julie Ann *federal judge*
Rogers, Richard Dean *federal judge*
Saffels, Dale Emerson *federal judge*
Six, Fred N. *state supreme court justice*

Wichita
Bell, Charles Robert, Jr. *judge*
Brown, Wesley Ernest *federal judge*
Humphreys, Karen M. *judge*
†Marten, J. Thomas *judge*
†Reid, John T. *federal judge*

KENTUCKY

Ashland
Patterson, Peggy *judge*
Wilhoit, Henry Rupert, Jr. *federal judge*

Bowling Green
Huddleston, Joseph Russell *judge*

Covington
†Wehrman, James Gregory *federal judge*

Frankfort
Hood, Joseph M. *federal judge*
Lambert, Joseph Earl *state supreme court chief justice*
Stephens, Robert F. *state supreme court chief justice*
Stumbo, Janet Lynn *state supreme court justice*
Wintersheimer, Donald Carl *state supreme court justice*

Lexington
Forester, Karl S. *federal judge*
†Howard, William S. *federal judge*
Lee, Joe *federal judge*
†Todd, James Black *federal judge*

London
Coffman, Jennifer B. *federal judge*
Siler, Eugene Edward, Jr. *federal judge*
Unthank, G. Wix *federal judge*

Louisville
Allen, Charles Mengel *federal judge*
Boggs, Danny Julian *federal judge*
†Dickinson, Henry H. *federal judge*
†Gambill, C. Cleveland *federal judge*
Heyburn, John Gilpin, II *federal judge*
Martin, Boyce Ficklen, Jr. *federal judge*
†Roberts, J. Wendell *federal judge*
Simpson, Charles R., III *judge*
Stosberg, David Thomas *bankruptcy judge*
Strause, Randall Scott *judge, lawyer*

Paducah
Johnstone, Edward Huggins *federal judge*
†King, W. David *federal judge*
Russell, Thomas B. *judge*

Wickliffe
Shadoan, William Lewis *judge*

Williamsburg
†Johnson, J. B., Jr. *federal judge*

LOUISIANA

Alexandria
Little, F. A., Jr. *federal judge*
†Simon, John F. *federal judge*

Baton Rouge
Cole, Luther Francis *former state supreme court associate justice*
Kelley, Timothy Edward *state judge*
†Noland, Christine A. *magistrate judge*
Parker, John Victor *federal judge*
†Phillips, Louis M. *federal judge*
Polozola, Frank Joseph *federal judge*
†Riedlinger, Stephen C. *federal judge*

Covington
†Ellis, Frederick Stephen *retired judge*

Crowley
Harrington, Thomas Barrett *judge*

Denham Springs
Kuhn, James E. *judge*

Gretna
Wicker, Thomas Carey, Jr. *judge*

Lafayette
Davis, William Eugene *federal judge*
Doherty, Rebecca Feeney *federal judge*
Duhe, John Malcolm, Jr. *federal judge*
Haik, Richard T., Sr. *federal judge*
Melançon, Tucker Lee *judge*
Methvin, Mildred E. *judge*
Putnam, Richard Johnson *federal judge*
Tynes, Pamela Anne *federal magistrate*

Lake Charles
Hunter, Edwin Ford, Jr. *federal judge*
McLeod, William Lasater, Jr. *judge, former state legislator*
Trimble, James T., Jr. *federal judge*
†Wilson, Alonzo P. *federal judge*

New Orleans
†Africk, Lance M. *federal judge*
Alarcon, Terry Quentin *judge*
Beer, Peter Hill *federal judge*
Berrigan, Helen Ginger *federal judge*
†Brahney, Thomas J., III *federal judge*
†Brown, Jerry A. *federal judge*
Calogero, Pascal Frank, Jr. *state supreme court chief justice*
†Chasez, Alma L. *federal judge*
Clement, Edith Brown *federal judge*
Dennis, James Leon *federal judge*
Duplantier, Adrian Guy *federal judge*
Duval, Stanwood Richardson, Jr. *judge*
Feldman, Martin L. C. *federal judge*
†Fonseca, Ronald A. *federal judge*
Johnson, Bernette Joshua *state supreme court justice*
Kimball, Catherine D. *state supreme court justice*
†Kingsmill, T. Hartley, Jr. *federal judge*
†Lemelle, Ivan L.R. *federal judge*
Lemmon, Harry Thomas *state supreme court justice*
Livaudais, Marcel, Jr. *federal judge*
Marcus, Walter F., Jr. *state supreme court justice*
McNamara, A. J. *federal judge*
Mentz, Henry Alvan, Jr. *federal judge*
Mitchell, Lansing Leroy *federal judge*
†Moore, Louis, Jr. *federal judge*
Porteous, G. Thomas, Jr. *judge*
Schwartz, Charles, Jr. *federal judge*
Sear, Morey Leonard *federal judge, educator*
Vance, Sarah S. *federal judge*
Wiener, Jacques Loeb, Jr. *federal judge*

Norco
Marino, Ruche Joseph *retired district court judge*

Opelousas
†Schiff, Gerald H. *federal judge*

Shreveport
†Callaway, Stephen V. *federal judge*
Payne, Roy Steven *judge*
Politz, Henry Anthony *federal judge*
†Shemwell, Robert H. *federal judge*
Stagg, Tom *federal judge*
Stewart, Carl E. *federal judge*
Walter, Donald Ellsworth *federal judge*

MAINE

Auburn
Clifford, Robert William *state supreme court justice*

Bangor
†Bequlieu, Eugene W. *federal judge*
Brody, Morton Aaron *federal judge*
†Haines, James B., Jr. *federal judge*
Rudman, Paul Lewis *state supreme court justice*

Portland
Bradford, Carl O. *judge*
†Brownell, William S. *federal judge*
Carter, Gene *federal judge*
Coffin, Frank Morey *federal judge*
Cohen, David Michael *federal magistrate judge*
Dana, Howard H., Jr. *state supreme court justice*
Glassman, Caroline Duby *state supreme court justice*
Goodman, James A. *federal judge*
Hornby, David Brock *federal judge*
Lipez, Kermit V. *federal judge, former state supreme court justice*
McKusick, Vincent Lee *former state supreme court justice, lawyer, arbitrator, mediator*

Rockland
Collins, Samuel W., Jr. *judge*

MARYLAND

Annapolis
Eldridge, John Cole *judge*

Baltimore
Bell, Robert M. *state court chief judge*
Black, Walter Evan, Jr. *federal judge*
Blake, Catherine C. *judge*
Davis, Andre Maurice *judge, educator*
Derby, Ernest Stephen *federal judge*
Garbis, Marvin Joseph *judge*
Gauvey, Susan K. *judge*
Goetz, Clarence Edward *retired judge, retired chief magistrate judge*
Harvey, Alexander, II *federal judge*
†Klein, Daniel E., Jr. *federal judge*
Legg, Benson Everett *federal judge*
Levin, Marshall Abbott *judge, educator*
Maletz, Herbert Naaman *federal judge*
Motz, Diana Gribbon *federal judge*
Motz, John Frederick *federal judge*
Murnaghan, Francis Dominic, Jr. *federal judge*
Nickerson, William Milnor *federal judge*
Niemeyer, Paul Victor *federal judge*
Northrop, Edward Skottowe *federal judge*
Rodowsky, Lawrence Francis *state judge*
†Rosenberg, Paul M. *federal judge*
†Schneider, James Frederick *federal judge*
Smalkin, Frederic N. *federal judge*
Young, Joseph H. *federal judge*

Bethesda
Nejelski, Paul Arthur *retired judge, freelance writer*

Greenbelt
Chasanow, Deborah K. *federal judge*
†Keir, Duncan W. *federal judge*
†Mannes, Paul *chief bankruptcy judge*
Messitte, Peter Jo *judge*
†Schulze, Jillyn K. *federal judge*
Williams, Alexander, Jr. *judge*

Hagerstown
†Beachley, Donald E. *federal judge*

Rockville
McAuliffe, John F. *retired judge*
Megan, Thomas Ignatius *retired judge*

Towson
Eyler, James R. *judge*

Upper Marlboro
Chasanow, Howard Stuart *judge, lecturer*

MASSACHUSETTS

Boston
Abrams, Ruth Ida *state supreme court justice*
Aldrich, Bailey *federal judge*
Alexander, Joyce London *judge*
Boudin, Michael *federal judge*
Bowler, Marianne Bianca *judge*
Bownes, Hugh Henry *federal judge*
Campbell, Levin Hicks *federal judge*
†Cohen, Lawrence P. *federal judge*
†Collings, Robert Biddlecombe *judge*
Connolly, Thomas Edward *judge*
Dacey, Kathleen Ryan *judge*
Dreben, Raya Spiegel *judge*
†Feeney, Joan N. *judge*
Garrity, Wendell Arthur, Jr. *federal judge*
Gertner, Nancy *federal judge, educator*
Greaney, John M. *state supreme court justice*
Harrington, Edward F. *federal judge*
Hillman, William Chernick *federal bankruptcy judge, educator*
†Karol, Zachary R. *judge*
Keeton, Robert Ernest *federal judge*
†Kenner, Carol J. *federal judge*
Lasker, Morris E. *judge*
Lindsay, Reginald Carl *lawyer*
Lynch, Neil L(awrence) *state supreme court justice*
Lynch, Sandra Lea *judge*
Mazzone, A. David *federal judge*
Nelson, David S. *federal judge*
O'Connor, Francis Patrick *state supreme court justice*
O'Toole, George A., Jr. *judge*
Saris, Patti Barbara *federal judge*
Skinner, Walter Jay *federal judge*
Stearns, Richard Gaylore *judge*
Tauro, Joseph Louis *federal judge*
Wolf, Mark Lawrence *federal judge*
Woodlock, Douglas Preston *judge*
Young, William Glover *federal judge*
Zobel, Hiller Bellin *judge*

Cambridge
Boorstein, Beverly Weinger *judge*
Kaplan, Benjamin *judge*

Longmeadow
Keady, George Cregan, Jr. *judge*

Newburyport
Allard, David Henry *judge*

Newton
Wilkins, Herbert Putnam *state supreme court chief justice, retired*

Springfield
Freedman, Frank Harlan *federal judge*
†Neiman, Kenneth Paul *judge*
Ponsor, Michael Adrian *federal judge*

Worcester
†Boroff, Henry Jack *federal judge, educator*
Gorton, Nathaniel M. *federal judge, lawyer*
†Queenan, James F., Jr. *judge*
†Swartwood, Charles B., III *federal judge*

MICHIGAN

Ann Arbor
Guy, Ralph B., Jr. *federal judge*
Hackett, Barbara (Kloka) *federal judge*
Pepe, Steven Douglas *federal magistrate judge*

Bay City
†Binder, Charles E. *federal judge*
Cleland, Robert Hardy *federal judge*
†Shapero, Walter *federal judge*
Spector, Arthur Jay *federal judge*

Birmingham
La Plata, George *federal judge*

Bloomfield Hills
Kaufman, Ira Gladstone *judge*

Dearborn
Runco, William Joseph *judge*

Detroit
Borman, Paul David *judge*
Boyle, Patricia Jean *state supreme court justice, retired*
†Carlson, Thomas A. *federal judge*
Clay, Eric L. *judge*
Duggan, Patrick James *federal judge*
Edmunds, Nancy Garlock *federal judge*
Feikens, John *federal judge*
Friedman, Bernard Alvin *federal judge*
Gilmore, Horace Weldon *federal judge*
Graves, Ray Reynolds *judge*
Hood, Denise Page *federal judge*
†Hooe, Lynn V. *federal judge*
Keith, Damon Jerome *federal judge*
Kennedy, Cornelia Groefsema *federal judge*
†Komives, Paul J. *federal judge*
Lloyd, Leona Loretta *judge*
Mallett, Conrad LeRoy, Jr. *state supreme court chief justice*
Morgan, Virginia *magistrate judge*
O'Meara, John Corbett *federal judge*
†Rhodes, Steven William *judge*
Rosen, Gerald Ellis *federal judge*
Ryan, James Leo *federal judge*
†Scheer, Donald A. *federal judge*
Sullivan, Joseph B. *retired judge*
Taylor, Anna Diggs *judge*
Woods, George Edward *judge*
Zatkoff, Lawrence P. *federal judge*

East Lansing
Bladen, Edwin Mark *lawyer, judge*

Flint
Gadola, Paul V. *federal judge*
†Goldman, Marc L. *federal judge*

Glen Arbor
Newblatt, Stewart Albert *federal judge*

Grand Rapids
Bell, Robert Holmes *federal judge*
†Gregg, James D. *federal judge*
Hillman, Douglas Woodruff *federal judge*
†Howard, Lawrence E. *federal judge*
Miles, Wendell A. *federal judge*
Quist, Gordon Jay *federal judge*
†Scoville, Joseph G. *federal judge*
†Stevenson, Jo Ann C. *federal judge*

Grayling
Davis, Alton Thomas *judge, lawyer*

Kalamazoo
Enslen, Richard Alan *federal judge*
Rowland, Doyle Alfred *federal judge*

Kentwood
Kelly, William Garrett *judge*

Lansing
Burns, Marshall Shelby *retired judge, lawyer, arbitrator*
Cavanagh, Michael Francis *state supreme court justice*
Hollenshead, Robert Earl *judge*
McKeague, David William *judge*
Spence, Howard Tee Devon *administrative law judge, arbitrator, lawyer, consultant, insurance executive, government official*
Suhrheinrich, Richard Fred *federal judge*

Marquette
†Greeley, Timothy P. *federal judge*

Mason
Harrison, Michael Gregory *judge*

Monroe
Costello, Joseph Anthony, Jr. *circuit court judge, educator*

Pontiac
Grant, Barry M(arvin) *judge*

Saint Clair Shores
Hausner, John Herman *judge*
Stanczyk, Benjamin Conrad *judge*

Southfield
Doctoroff, Martin Myles *judge*

Traverse City
Brickley, James H. *state supreme court justice*
Weaver, Elizabeth A. *state supreme court chief justice*

MINNESOTA

Albert Lea
Sturtz, William Rosenberg *retired judge*

Anoka
Quinn, R. Joseph *judge*

Bemidji
†Burg, Randall K. *federal judge*

Duluth
Heaney, Gerald William *federal judge*

Minneapolis
Amdahl, Douglas Kenneth *retired state supreme court justice*
Arthur, Lindsay Grier *retired judge, author, editor*
†Cudd, J. Earl *federal judge*
Davis, Michael J. *judge*
Doty, David Singleton *federal judge*
Dreher, Nancy C. *federal judge*
Larson, Earl Richard *federal judge*
Lebedoff, Jonathan Galanter *federal judge*
MacLaughlin, Harry Hunter *federal judge*
Montgomery, Ann D. *judge, federal, educator*
Murphy, Diana E. *federal judge*
Noel, Franklin Linwood *federal chief magistrate judge*
Rosenbaum, James Michael *judge*

Minnetonka
Rogers, James Devitt *judge*

Rochester
Keith, Alexander Macdonald *retired state supreme court chief justice, lawyer*

Saint Paul
Alsop, Donald Douglas *federal judge*
Anderson, Paul Holden *state supreme court justice*
Kishel, Gregory Francis *federal judge*
Kyle, Richard House *federal judge*
Lay, Donald Pomeroy *federal judge*
Loken, James Burton *federal judge*
†Mason, John M. (Jack Mason) *federal judge*
Mason, John Milton (Jack Mason) *judge*
†O'Brien, Dennis D. *federal judge*
Renner, Robert George *federal judge*
Stringer, Edward Charles *state supreme court justice*
Tomljanovich, Esther M. *state supreme court justice*
Willis, Bruce Donald *judge*

MISSISSIPPI

Aberdeen
Davidson, Glen Harris *federal judge*
Davis, Jerry Arnold *judge*
†Houston, David Winston *federal judge*
Senter, Lyonel Thomas, Jr. *federal judge*

Biloxi
†Gaines, Edward R. *federal judge*
Gex, Walter Joseph, III *federal judge*
Roper, John Marlin, Sr. *federal magistrate judge*

Greenville
†Bogen, Eugene M. *federal judge*

Gulfport
Russell, Dan M., Jr. *federal judge*

Hattiesburg
†Guirola, Louis, Jr. *federal judge*
Pickering, Charles W., Sr. *federal judge*

Jackson
Barbour, William H., Jr. *federal judge*
Barksdale, Rhesa Hawkins *federal judge*
†Ellington, Edward *federal judge*
Jolly, E. Grady *federal judge*
Lee, Tom Stewart *judge*
McRae, Charles R. *state supreme court justice*
†Nicols, Alfred G., Jr. *federal judge*
Payne, Mary Libby *judge*
Pittman, Edwin Lloyd *state supreme court justice*
Prather, Lenore Loving *state supreme court chief justice*
Roberts, James L., Jr. *state supreme court justice*
Smith, James W., Jr. *state supreme court justice*
Sugg, Robert Perkins *former state supreme court justice*
Sullivan, Michael David *state supreme court justice*
†Sumner, James C. *federal judge*
Wingate, Henry Travillion *federal judge*

Natchez
Bramlette, David C., III *federal judge*

Oxford
Biggers, Neal Brooks, Jr. *federal judge*

MISSOURI

Cape Girardeau
†Blanton, Lewis M. *federal judge*

Excelsior Springs
Berrey, Robert Wilson, III *retired judge, lawyer*

Hannibal
Reinhard, James Richard *retired judge*

Jefferson City
Benton, W. Duane *judge*
Blackmar, Charles Blakey *state supreme court justice*
Covington, Ann K. *state supreme court justice*
Donnelly, Robert True *retired state supreme court justice*
Holstein, John Charles *state supreme court judge*
†Knox, William Arthur *judge*
Price, William Ray, Jr. *state supreme court judge*
Robertson, Edward D., Jr. *state supreme court justice*

Kansas City
Bartlett, D. Brook *federal judge*
Bowman, Pasco Middleton, II *federal judge*
†Federman, Arthur *federal judge*
Gaitan, Fernando J., Jr. *federal judge*
Gibson, Floyd Robert *federal judge*
Gibson, John Robert *federal judge*
†Hays, Sarah W. *federal judge*
Hunter, Elmo Bolton *federal judge*
Koger, Frank Williams *federal judge*
†Larsen, Robert Emmett *federal judge*

Laughrey, Nanette K. *judge, federal*
Maughmer, John Townsend *federal judge*
Sachs, Howard F(rederic) *federal judge*
†See, Karen Mason *federal judge*
Smith, Ortrie D. *judge*
†Smith, Ortrie Dale *judge*
Ulrich, Robert Gene *judge*
Whipple, Dean *federal judge*
Wright, Scott Olin *federal judge*

Saint Louis
†Adelman, Terry I. *federal judge*
Ahrens, Clifford H. *judge*
Barta, James Joseph *judge*
†Buckles, Frederick R. *federal judge*
Cahill, Clyde S. *retired federal judge*
†Davis, Lawrence O. *federal judge*
Filippine, Edward Louis *federal judge*
Gaertner, Gary M. *judge*
Hamilton, Jean Constance *judge*
Jackson, Carol E. *federal judge*
Limbaugh, Stephen Nathaniel *federal judge*
McDonald, David P. *federal judge*
McMillian, Theodore *federal judge*
†Medler, Mary Ann L. *federal judge*
†Mummert, Thomas C., III *federal judge*
†Noce, David D. *federal judge*
Perry, Catherine D. *judge*
†Schermer, Barry S. *federal judge*
Shaw, Charles Alexander *judge*
Stohr, Donald J. *federal judge*
Webber, E. Richard, Jr. *judge*

Springfield
Clark, Russell Gentry *federal judge*
†England, James C. *federal judge*

West Plains
Dunlap, David Houston *judge*

MONTANA

Billings
†Anderson, Richard W. *federal judge*
Fagg, Russell *judge, lawyer*
Shanstrom, Jack D. *federal judge*
†Thomas, Sidney R. *federal court judge*

Circle
McDonough, Russell Charles *retired state supreme court justice*

Great Falls
Hatfield, Paul Gerhart *federal judge, lawyer*
†Holter, Robert M. *federal judge*

Helena
Gray, Karla Marie *state supreme court justice*
Harrison, John Conway *state supreme court justice*
Hunt, William E., Sr. *state supreme court justice*
Leaphart, W. William *state supreme court justice*
Lovell, Charles C. *federal judge*
Nelson, James C *state supreme court justice*
Trieweiler, Terry Nicholas *state supreme court justice*
Turnage, Jean A. *state supreme court justice*

Missoula
†Erickson, Leif B. *federal judge*

NEBRASKA

Lincoln
Beam, Clarence Arlen *federal judge*
Connolly, William M. *state supreme court justice*
Gerrard, John M. *state supreme court justice*
Hastings, William Charles *retired state supreme court chief justice*
Kopf, Richard G. *federal judge*
†Minahan, John C., Jr. *federal judge*
Piester, David L(ee) *magistrate judge*
Urbom, Warren Keith *federal judge*
White, C. Thomas *state supreme court justice*

Omaha
Cambridge, William G. *federal judge*
Grant, John Thomas *retired state supreme court justice*
Jaudzemis, Kathleen A. *judge*
†Mahoney, Timothy J. *federal judge*
Shanahan, Thomas M. *judge*
Strom, Lyle Elmer *federal judge*
†Thalken, Thomas D. *federal judge*

NEVADA

Carson City
†Becker, Nancy Anne *state supreme court justice*
Gunderson, Elmer Millard *state supreme court justice, law educator*
Maupin, Bill *state supreme court justice*
Rose, Robert E(dgar) *state supreme court justice*
Springer, Charles Edward *retired state supreme court chief justice*
Young, C. Clifton *state supreme court justice*

Las Vegas
George, Lloyd D. *federal judge*
†Hunt, Roger Lee *judge*
Johnston, Robert Jake *federal magistrate judge*
†Jones, Robert Clive *judge*
Karau, Jon Olin *judge*
†Leavitt, Lawrence R. *federal judge*
Pro, Philip Martin *judge*
Riegle, Linda B. *federal judge*
Steffen, Thomas Lee *lawyer, former state supreme court justice*

Reno
†Atkins, Phyllis Halsey *federal judge*
Brunetti, Melvin T. *federal judge*
†Goldwater, Bert M. *federal judge*
Hagen, David Warner *judge*
Hug, Procter Ralph, Jr. *federal judge*
McKibben, Howard D. *federal judge*
†McQuaid, Robert A., Jr. *federal judge*
Reed, Edward Cornelius, Jr. *federal judge*

NEW HAMPSHIRE

Concord
Barbadoro, Paul J. *federal judge*
Brock, David Allen *state supreme court chief justice*
Broderick, John T., Jr. *state supreme court justice*
Cann, William Francis *judge*
Devine, Shane *federal judge*
DiClerico, Joseph Anthony, Jr. *federal judge*
Horton, Sherman D., Jr. *state supreme court justice*
Johnson, William R. *state supreme court justice*
McAuliffe, Steven James *federal judge*
†Muirhead, James R. *federal judge*
Stahl, Norman H. *federal judge*
Thayer, W(alter) Stephen, III *state supreme court justice*

Manchester
†Vaughn, Mark W. *federal judge*

Nashua
Barry, William Henry, Jr. *federal judge*

NEW JERSEY

Atlantic City
Knight, Edward R. *judge, lawyer, educator, psychologist*

Camden
Brotman, Stanley Seymour *federal judge*
Burns, Gloria M. *judge*
Irenas, Joseph Eron *judge*
†Kugler, Robert B. *federal judge*
Laskin, Lee B. *laywer, state senator*
Rodriguez, Joseph H. *federal judge*
†Rosen, Joel B. *federal judge*
Simandle, Jerome B. *federal judge*
Wizmur, Judith H. *federal judge*

Freehold
Fisher, Clarkson Sherman, Jr. *judge*
Newman, James Michael *lawyer, judge*

Hackensack
Kestin, Howard H. *judge*
Stein, Gary S. *state supreme court justice*

Long Branch
†Manna, John C. *federal judge*

Moorestown
Kearney, John Francis, III *lawyer*

Morristown
Pollock, Stewart Glasson *former state supreme court justice, lawyer*

New Brunswick
Ferencz, Bradley *judge*

Newark
Ackerman, Harold A. *federal judge*
Alito, Samuel Anthony, Jr. *federal judge*
Barry, Maryanne Trump *federal judge*
Bassler, William G. *federal judge*
Bissell, John W. *federal judge*
†Cavanaugh, Dennis M. *federal judge*
Chesler, Stanley Richard *federal judge*
Debevoise, Dickinson Richards *federal judge*
Gambardella, Rosemary *federal judge*
Garth, Leonard I. *federal judge*
Greenaway, Joseph Anthony, Jr. *judge*
†Haneke, G. Donald *federal judge*
†Hedges, Ronald J. *federal judge*
Lechner, Alfred James, Jr. *judge*
Lifland, John C. *federal judge*
†Pisano, Joel A. *federal judge*
Politan, Nicholas H. *federal judge*
Tuohey, William F. *federal judge*
Walls, William Hamilton *judge*
Winfield, Novalyn L. *federal bankruptcy judge*
Wolin, Alfred M. *federal judge*

Red Bank
O'Hern, Daniel Joseph *state supreme court justice*

Somerville
Yurasko, Frank Noel *judge*

Trenton
†Cooper, Mary L. *judge*
Cooper, Mary Little *federal judge, former banking commissioner*
Cowen, Robert E. *federal judge*
Ferguson, Kathryn Cuccia *judge*
Gindin, William Howard *judge*
Greenberg, Morton Ira *federal judge*
Handler, Alan B. *state supreme court justice*
†Hughes, John J. *federal judge, educator*
Poritz, Deborah T. *state supreme court chief justice, former attorney general*
Thompson, Anne Elise *federal judge*
Wolfson, Freda L. *judge*

Warren
Coleman, James H., Jr. *state supreme court justice*

NEW MEXICO

Albuquerque
†Black, Bruce D. *judge*
Conway, John E. *federal judge*
Dal Santo, Diane *judge, writer*
†Deaton, William W., Jr. *federal judge*
†DeGiacomo, Robert J. *federal judge*
†Garcia, Lorenzo F. *federal judge*
†Hansen, C. Leroy *judge*
Hansen, Curtis LeRoy *federal judge*
McFeeley, Mark B. *federal judge*
Parker, James Aubrey *federal judge*
†Puglisi, Richard L. *federal judge*
†Rose, Stewart *federal judge*
†Svet, Don J. *federal judge*

Clovis
†Tharp, Fred C., Jr. *federal judge, lawyer*

Gallup
†Ionta, Robert W. *federal judge, lawyer*

Las Cruces
Bratton, Howard Calvin *federal judge*
†Galvan, Joe H. *federal judge*
†Smith, Leslie C. *federal judge*

Los Lunas
Pope, John William *judge, law educator*

Roswell
Baldock, Bobby Ray *federal judge*

Santa Fe
Baca, Joseph Francis *state supreme court justice*
Campos, Santiago E. *federal judge*
Franchini, Gene Edward *state supreme court justice*
Kelly, Paul Joseph, Jr. *judge*
Minzner, Pamela B. *state supreme court justice*
Serna, Patricio *state supreme court justice*
Vazquez, Martha Alicia *judge*
Yalman, Ann *lawyer*

Silver City
†Hodges, Norman *retired district judge*

NEW YORK

Albany
Bellacosa, Joseph W. *state supreme court justice*
†Homer, David Robert *federal judge*
†Kahn, Lawrence E. *judge*
Kahn, Lawrence Edwin *judge*
Kaye, Judith Smith *state supreme court chief justice*
†Littlefield, Robert E., Jr. *federal judge*
Meader, John Daniel *judge*
Miner, Roger Jeffrey *federal judge*
Smith, Ralph Wesley, Jr. *federal judge*

Bath
†Latham, Joseph William *judge*

Binghamton
McAvoy, Thomas James *federal judge*

Bronx
†DiFede, Joseph *retired judge*

Brooklyn
Amon, Carol Bagley *federal judge*
Azrack, Joan M. *judge*
Block, Frederic *judge*
Bramwell, Henry *federal judge*
†Caden, John L. *federal judge*
†Cherin, Aaron Simon *federal judge*
Dearie, Raymond Joseph *federal judge*
Duberstein, Conrad B. *federal judge*
†Feller, Jerome *federal judge*
Gershon, Nina *federal judge*
Glasser, Israel Leo *federal judge*
Gleeson, John *judge, educator*
†Go, Marilyn D. *federal judge*
†Holland, Marvin A. *federal judge*
Hurley, Denis R. *federal judge*
Johnson, Sterling, Jr. *federal judge*
Korman, Edward R. *federal judge*
†Levy, Robert Morris *judge*
†Mann, Roanne L. *federal judge*
Nickerson, Eugene H. *federal judge*
†Pollak, Cheryl L. *federal judge*
Raggi, Reena *federal judge*
Ross, Allyne R. *federal judge*
Ryan, Leonard Eames *administrative law judge*
Sifton, Charles Proctor *federal judge*
Solomon, Martin M. *judge*
Trager, David G. *federal judge*
Weinstein, Jack Bertrand *federal judge*

Buffalo
Arcara, Richard Joseph *federal judge*
†Bucki, Carl L. *federal judge*
Curtin, John T. *federal judge*
Elfvin, John Thomas *federal judge*
Heckman, Carol E. *judge*
Jasen, Matthew Joseph *state justice*
†Kaplan, Michael J. *federal judge*
†Maxwell, Edmund F. *federal judge*
Pietruszka, Michael F. *judge*
†Scott, Hugh B. *federal judge*
Skretny, William Marion *federal judge*

Garden City
Harwood, Stanley *retired judge, lawyer*

Hauppauge
†Cyganowski, Melanie L. *bankruptcy judge*
†Lindsay, Arlene Rosario *federal judge*
Wexler, Leonard D. *federal judge*

Jamaica
Grayshaw, James Raymond *judge*

Lake George
Austin, John DeLong *judge*

Little Valley
Himelein, Larry M. *judge*

Mineola
Burstein, Beatrice S. *judicial administrator, retired judge*

New York
Aquilino, Thomas Joseph, Jr. *federal judge, law educator*
Baer, Harold, Jr. *judge*
Batts, Deborah A. *judge*
†Beatty, Prudence Carter *federal judge*
Berman, Richard Miles *judge*
†Bernikow, Leonard *federal judge*
†Bernstein, Stuart M. *federal judge*
†Blackshear, Cornelius *federal judge*
Blinder, Albert Allan *judge*
Brozman, Tina L. *federal judge*
Buchwald, Naomi Reice *judge*
Carman, Gregory Wright *federal judge*
†Casey, Richard Conway *judge*
Cedarbaum, Miriam Goldman *federal judge*
Chin, Denny *judge*
Ciparick, Carmen Beauchamp *state judge*
Cote, Denise Louise *federal judge*
DiCarlo, Dominick L. *federal judge*
†Dolinger, Michael H. *federal judge*
Duffy, Kevin Thomas *federal judge*
Edelstein, David Northon *federal judge*
†Ellis, Ronald L. *federal judge*
Feinberg, Wilfred *federal judge*
†Francis, James Clark, IV *judge*
Freedman, Helen Edelstein *justice*
†Garrity, James, Jr. *federal judge*
Goldberg, Richard W. *federal judge*
†Gonzalez, Arthur J. *federal judge*
Griesa, Thomas Poole *federal judge*
†Grubin, Sharon E. *federal judge*
Haight, Charles Sherman, Jr. *federal judge*
Jacobs, Dennis *federal judge*
Kaplan, Lewis A. *judge*
†Katz, Theodore H. *federal judge*
Kearse, Amalya Lyle *federal judge*
Keenan, John Fontaine *federal judge*
Knapp, Whitman *federal judge*
Koeltl, John George *judge*
Kram, Shirley Wohl *federal judge*
Kupferman, Theodore R. *former state justice, lawyer*
Leisure, Peter Keeton *federal judge*
Leval, Pierre Nelson *federal judge*
†Lifland, Burton R. *federal judge*
Lowe, Mary Johnson *federal judge*
Martin, John Sherwood, Jr. *federal judge*
McKenna, Lawrence M. *federal judge*
McLaughlin, Joseph Michael *federal judge, law educator*
Motley, Constance Baker (Mrs. Joel Wilson Motley) *federal judge, former city official*
Mukasey, Michael B. *federal judge*
Musgrave, R. Kenton *federal judge*
Nelson, Barbara Anne *judge*
Newman, Bernard *federal judge*
Owen, Richard *federal judge*
Patterson, Robert Porter, Jr. *federal judge*
†Peck, Andrew Jay *federal judge*
†Pogue, Donald C. *federal judge*
Pollack, Milton *federal judge*
Preska, Loretta A. *federal judge*
Rakoff, Jed Saul *federal judge, author*
Restani, Jane A. *federal judge*
Rosenberger, Ernst Hey *judge*
Sack, Robert David *judge*
Sand, Leonard B. *federal judge*
Scheindlin, Shira A. *federal judge*
Schwartz, Allen G. *federal judge*
Smith, George Bundy *state supreme court justice*
Sotomayor, Sonia *judge*
Sprizzo, John Emilio *federal judge*
Stein, Sidney H. *judge*
Titone, Vito Joseph *state supreme court justice*
Tsoucalas, Nicholas *federal judge*
Ward, Robert Joseph *federal judge*
Watson, James Lopez *federal judge*
Wood, Kimba M. *judge*

Newburgh
†Goldberg, Martin L. *federal judge*

Oswego
Jansen, Lambertus *judge*

Penn Yan
Falvey, W(illiam) Patrick *judge*

Port Washington
Jones, Farrell *judge*

Poughkeepsie
†Berk, Jeremiah E. *federal judge*
Dolan, Thomas Joseph *judge*
Rosenblatt, Albert Martin *judge*

Rochester
Kehoe, L. Paul *state judge*
Larimer, David George *federal judge*
†Siragusa, Charles J. *judge*
Telesca, Michael Anthony *federal judge*
Van Graafeiland, Ellsworth Alfred *federal judge*

Rome
Simons, Richard Duncan *lawyer, retired state judge*

Rouses Point
†Van Acker, Henry C., Jr. *federal judge*

Sag Harbor
Pierce, Lawrence Warren *retired federal judge*

Schenectady
Levine, Howard Arnold *state supreme court justice*

Syracuse
†DiBianco, Gustave J. *federal judge, eductor*
Hancock, Stewart F., Jr. *state judge*
Johnson, Marc Jay *judge*
McCurn, Neal Peters *federal judge*
Munson, Howard G. *federal judge*
Pooler, Rosemary S. *federal judge*
Scullin, Frederick James, Jr. *federal judge*

Uniondale
†Boyle, E. Thomas *federal judge*
Mishler, Jacob *federal judge*
†Orenstein, Michael L. *federal judge*
Platt, Thomas Collier, Jr. *federal judge*
†Pohorelsky, Viktor Vaclav *federal magistrate judge*
Seybert, Joanna *federal judge*
Spatt, Arthur Donald *federal judge*

Utica
Cardamone, Richard J. *federal judge*
†Gerling, Stephen P. *federal judge*
†Hurd, David N. *federal judge*

Watertown
†Scanlon, Daniel, Jr. *federal judge*

Webster
Witmer, G. Robert *retired state supreme court justice*

Westbury
†Bernstein, Stan *federal judge*
†Conrad, Francis G. *federal judge*

SOUTH CAROLINA

Aiken
Simons, Charles Earl, Jr. *federal judge*

Anderson
Anderson, George Ross, Jr. *federal judge*

Charleston
Blatt, Solomon, Jr. *federal judge*
†Carr, Robert S. *federal judge*
Duffy, Patrick Michael *judge, federal*
Hawkins, Falcon Black, Jr. *federal judge*
Norton, David C. *federal judge*

Columbia
Anderson, Joseph Fletcher, Jr. *federal judge*
†Bishop, William Thurmond *federal judge*
Bristow, Walter James, Jr. *retired judge*
†Buchanan, Robert L., Jr. *federal judge, lawyer*
Chapman, Robert Foster *federal judge*
†Davis, J. Bratton *federal judge*
Finney, Ernest Adolphus, Jr. *state supreme court chief justice*
Hamilton, Clyde Henry *federal judge*
†McCrorey, Joseph R. *federal judge*
Perry, Matthew J., Jr. *federal judge*
Shedd, Dennis W. *federal judge*
Toal, Jean Hoefer *state supreme court justice, lawyer*
†Waites, John E. *federal judge*

Florence
Currie, Cameron McGowan *judge*
Houck, Charles Weston *federal judge*
†Swearingen, Ervin S. *federal judge*

Greenville
†Catoe, William M., Jr. *federal judge*
Herlong, Henry Michael, Jr. *federal judge*
Smith, Willie Tesreau, Jr. *retired judge, lawyer*
Traxler, William Byrd, Jr. *federal judge*
Wilkins, William Walter, Jr. *federal judge*

Greenwood
Moore, James E. *state supreme court justice*

Marion
Waller, John Henry, Jr. *state supreme court justice*

Myrtle Beach
Harwell, David Walker *retired state supreme court chief justice*

Orangeburg
Williams, Karen Johnson *federal judge*

Spartanburg
Burnett, E. C., III *state supreme court justice*

SOUTH DAKOTA

Aberdeen
Richards, Carlyle Edward *magistrate judge*

Fort Pierre
Hoyt, Irvin N. *judge*

Pierre
Amundson, Robert A. *state supreme court justice*
Gilbertson, David *state supreme court justice*
Miller, Robert Arthur *state supreme court chief justice*
†Moreno, Mark A. *federal judge*
Sabers, Richard Wayne *state supreme court justice*

Rapid City
Battey, Richard Howard *judge*
Bogue, Andrew Wendell *federal judge*
†Young, Marshall P. *federal judge*

Sioux Falls
Ecker, Peder Kaloides *former judge*
Jones, John Bailey *federal judge*
†Marshall, Mark F. *federal judge*
Piersol, Lawrence L. *federal judge*
†Srstka, William J., Jr. *judge*
Wollman, Roger Leland *federal judge*

TENNESSEE

Chattanooga
Edgar, R(obert) Allan *federal judge*
Franks, Herschel Pickens *judge*
†Kelley, Ralph Houston *judge*
Milburn, Herbert Theodore *federal judge*
Powers, John Y. *federal judge*
†Stinnett, R. Thomas *federal judge*
Summitt, Robert Murray *circuit judge*

Greeneville
Hull, Thomas Gray *federal judge*
†Inman, Dennis H. *federal judge*
Parsons, Marcia Phillips *judge*

Jackson
†Boswell, G(eorge) Harvey *federal judge*
†Breen, J. Daniel *federal judge*
Todd, James Dale *federal judge*

Johnson City
Kiener, John Leslie *judge*

Knoxville
Anderson, Edward Riley *state supreme court chief justice*
Jarvis, James Howard, II *judge*
Jordan, Robert Leon *federal judge*
Murrian, Robert Phillip *magistrate, judge, educator*
Phillips, Thomas Wade *judge, lawyer*
†Stair, Richard, Jr. *federal judge*

Memphis
Allen, James Henry *magistrate*
Brown, Bailey *federal judge*
Donald, Bernice B. *judge*
Gibbons, Julia Smith *federal judge*
Gilman, Ronald Lee *judge*
Kennedy, David Stewart *federal judge*
McCalla, Jon P. *federal judge*
McRae, Robert Malcolm, Jr. *federal judge*
Turner, Jerome *federal judge*
†Vescovo, Diane K. *federal judge*
Wellford, Harry Walker *federal judge*

Nashville
Birch, Adolpho A., Jr. *state supreme court justice*
Brown, Joe Blackburn *judge*
Daughtrey, Martha Craig *federal judge*
Drowota, Frank F., III *state supreme court justice*
Echols, Robert L. *federal judge*
†Griffen, Juliet E. *federal judge*
Higgins, Thomas A. *federal judge*
†Lundin, Keith M. *federal judge*
Merritt, Gilbert Stroud *federal judge*
Nixon, John Trice *judge*
†Paine, George C., II *federal judge*
Reid, Lyle *former state supreme court justice*
Trauger, Aleta Arthur *judge*
Wiseman, Thomas Anderton, Jr. *federal judge*

Pigeon Forge
Brackett, Colquitt Prater, Jr. *judge, lawyer*

Signal Mountain
Cooper, Robert Elbert *state supreme court justice*

TEXAS

Alpine
†Baker, Katherine H. *federal judge*

Amarillo
†Averitte, Clinton E. *federal judge*
Johnson, Philip Wayne *judge*
Robinson, Mary Lou *federal judge*

Arlington
Wright, James Edward *judge*

Austin
†Albright, Alan D. *federal judge*
Baird, Charles F. *state supreme court justice*
Baker, James A. *state supreme court justice*
Benavides, Fortunato Pedro (Pete Benavides) *federal judge*
†Capelle, Stephen H. *federal judge*
Enoch, Craig Trively *state supreme court justice*
Garwood, William Lockhart *federal judge*
Gonzalez, Raul A. *state supreme court justice*
Greenhill, Joe Robert *former chief justice state supreme court, lawyer*
Hecht, Nathan Lincoln *state supreme court justice*
Johnson, Sam D. *federal judge*
Justice, William Wayne *United States district judge*
†Kelly, Larry E. *federal judge*
Maloney, Frank *judge, lawyer*
Mansfield, Stephen W. *state supreme court justice*
McCormick, Michael Jerry *judge*
Meyers, Lawrence Edward *state judge*
†Miller, Charles (Chuck) E. *judge*
†Monroe, Frank R. *federal judge*
Nowlin, James Robertson *federal judge*
Overstreet, Morris L. *state supreme court justice*
Owen, Priscilla Richman *state supreme court justice*
Phillips, Thomas Royal *state supreme court chief justice*
Pope, Andrew Jackson, Jr. (Jack Pope) *retired judge*
Ray, Cread L., Jr. *retired state supreme court justice*
Reavley, Thomas Morrow *federal judge*
Sparks, Sam *federal judge*
Spector, Rose *state supreme court justice*
Williams, Mary Pearl *judge, lawyer*

Bastrop
Eskew, Benton *judge*

Beaumont
Cobb, Howell *federal judge*
Fisher, Joseph Jefferson *federal judge*
Heartfield, Thad *judge*
†Hines, Earl S. *federal judge*
†Radford, Wendell C. *federal judge*
Schell, Richard A. *federal judge*

Brownsville
†Black, John W. *federal judge*
†Garza, Fidencio C., Jr. *federal judge*
Garza, Reynaldo G. *federal judge*
Vela, Filemon B. *federal judge*

Corpus Christi
Brazell, Ida Hernandez *judge*
Head, Hayden Wilson, Jr. *judge*
Jack, Janis Graham *judge*
Schmidt, Richard S. *federal judge*

Dallas
†Abramson, Harold C. *federal judge*
†Boyle, Jane J. *federal judge*
Buchmeyer, Jerry *federal judge*
Fish, A. Joe *federal judge*
Fitzwater, Sidney Allen *federal judge*
†Haydar, Ziad Rafic *geriatrician*
Higginbotham, Patrick Errol *federal judge*
†Kaplan, Jeffrey A. *federal judge*
Kendall, Joe *federal judge*
Maloney, Robert B. *federal judge*
†McGuire, Robert C. *federal judge*
Price, Robert Eben *judge*
Robertson, Ted Zanderson *judge*
Sanders, Harold Barefoot, Jr. *federal judge*
Sanderson, William Fletcher, Jr. *federal judge*
Solis, Jorge Antonio *federal judge*
Stewart, Wesley Holmgreen *judge, lawyer*
†Tolle, John B. *federal judge*

Del Rio
†Edwards, Durwood *federal judge*
Thurmond, George Murat *judge*

Edinburg
Hinojosa, Federico Gustavo, Jr. *judge*

El Paso
Briones, David *judge*
Dinsmoor, Robert Davidson *judge*
Hudspeth, Harry Lee *federal judge*
†Mesa, Richard P. *federal judge*

Fort Worth
King, Steve Mason *judge, lawyer*
†Lessis, James W. *judge*
Mahon, Eldon Brooks *federal judge*
McBryde, John Henry *federal judge*
Means, Terry Robert *federal judge*
Tillman, Massie Monroe *federal judge*

Galveston
†Froeschner, John R. *federal judge*
Kent, Samuel B. *federal judge*

Houston
Atlas, Nancy Friedman *judge*
†Brown, Karen K. *federal judge*
Bue, Carl Olaf, Jr. *retired federal judge*
Clark, Letitia Z. *federal judge*
DeMoss, Harold Raymond, Jr. *federal judge*
Gilmore, Vanessa D. *federal judge*
†Greendyke, William R. *federal judge*
Harmon, Melinda Furche *federal judge*
Hittner, David *federal judge*
Hoyt, Kenneth M. *federal judge*
Hughes, Lynn Nettleton *federal judge*
Johnson, Nancy K. *judge*
Jones, Edith Hollan *federal judge*
King, Carolyn Dineen *federal judge*
Lake, Sim *federal judge*
†Leal, Manuel D. *federal judge*
Milloy, Maryrose *judge*
Rainey, John David *federal judge*
Rendon, Josefina Muniz *judge, mediator, arbitrator*
Rosenthal, Lee H. *federal judge*
Singleton, John Virgil, Jr. *retired federal judge, lawyer*
Smith, Jerry Edwin *federal judge*
†Stacy, Frances H. *judge*
†Steen, Wesley Wilson *bankruptcy judge, lawyer*
Werlein, Ewing, Jr. *federal judge*
†Wheless, Randolph F. *federal judge*
York, James Martin *judge*

Laredo
Kazen, George Philip *federal judge*
†Notzon, Marcel C. *federal judge*

Levelland
Walker, James Kenneth *judge*

Lubbock
†Akard, John C. *federal judge*
Cummings, Sam R. *federal judge*
†Warnick, J.Q., Jr. *federal judge*

Lufkin
Hannah, John Henry, Jr. *judge*

Mcallen
Hinojosa, Ricardo H. *federal judge*
†Ormsby, Peter E. *federal judge*

Midland
Furgeson, William Royal *federal judge*

Pampa
Cain, Donald Ezell *judge*

Plano
†Sharp, Donald R. *federal judge*

San Angelo
†Lane, Philip R. *federal judge*
Sutton, John Ewing *judge*

San Antonio
Biery, Fred *judge*
†Clark, Leif Michael *federal judge*
Garcia, Hipolito Frank (Hippo Garcia) *federal judge*
Garcia, Orlando Luis *judge*
Garza, Emilio M(iller) *federal judge*
Hardberger, Phillip Duane *judge, lawyer, journalist*
King, Ronald Baker *federal judge*
Nowak, Nancy Stein *judge*
†O'Connor, Robert B. *federal judge*
Prado, Edward Charles *federal judge*
†Primono, John W. *federal judge*
Suttle, Dorwin Wallace *federal judge*

Sherman
Brown, Paul Neeley *federal judge*
†Faulkner, Robert W. *federal judge*

Temple
Skelton, Byron George *federal judge*

Texarkana
Folsom, David *judge*

Tyler
†Abel, C. Houston *federal judge*
Guthrie, Judith K. *federal judge*
†McKee, Harry W. *federal judge*
Parker, Robert M. *federal judge*
Steger, William Merritt *federal judge*

Vernon
Streit, Gary Bernard *judge*

Waco
†Green, Dennis G. *federal judge*
Smith, Walter S., Jr. *federal judge*

Wichita Falls
†Roach, Robert K. *federal judge*

UTAH

Monticello
†Redd, F. Bennion *federal judge*

Provo
Bullock, J(ames) Robert *judge*
Harding, Ray Murray, Jr. *judge*

Saint George
†Nuffer, David O. *federal judge*

Salt Lake City
†Alba, Samuel *federal judge*
Anderson, Stephen Hale *federal judge*
Benson, Dee Vance *federal judge*
†Boyce, Ronald N. *federal judge*
Campbell, Tena *judge*
†Clark, Glen Edward *judge*
Durham, Christine Meaders *state supreme court justice*
Greene, John Thomas *judge*
Hall, Gordon R. *retired state supreme court chief justice*
Howe, Richard Cuddy *state supreme court chief justice*
Jenkins, Bruce Sterling *federal judge*
McKay, Monroe Gunn *federal judge*
Murphy, Michael R. *federal judge*
Rigtrup, Kenneth *state judge, arbitrator, mediator*
Russon, Leonard H. *state supreme court justice*
Sam, David *federal judge*
Stewart, Isaac Daniel, Jr. *state supreme court justice*
Winder, David Kent *federal judge*
Zimmerman, Michael David *state supreme court justice*

VERMONT

Brattleboro
Murtha, J. Garvan *federal judge*
Oakes, James L. *federal judge*

Burlington
†Niedermeier, Jerome J. *federal judge*
Parker, Fred I. *federal judge*
Sessions, William K., III *judge, federal*

Manchester
Gagliardi, Lee Parsons *federal judge*

Montpelier
Dooley, John Augustine, III *state supreme court justice*
Gibson, Ernest Willard, III *retired state supreme court justice*
Johnson, Denise Reinka *state supreme court justice*
Morse, James L. *state supreme court justice*

Rutland
Marro, Charles John *retired bankruptcy judge*

Waterbury Center
Amestoy, Jeffrey Lee *state supreme court chief justice*

Woodstock
Billings, Franklin Swift, Jr. *federal judge*

VIRGINIA

Abingdon
Jones, James Parker *federal judge*
Widener, Hiram Emory, Jr. *federal judge*
Williams, Glen Morgan *federal judge*

Alexandria
Brinkema, Leonie Milhomme *federal judge*
Bryan, Albert V., Jr. *federal judge*
Cacheris, James C. *federal judge*
Ellis, Thomas Selby, III *federal judge*
Hilton, Claude Meredith *federal judge*
†Hunter, Henley A. *federal judge*
†Jones, Thomas Rawles, Jr. *federal judge*
Luttig, J. Michael *federal judge*
†Mitchell, Stephen Scott *federal judge*
†Poretz, Barry R. *federal judge*
†Sewell, W. Curtis *federal judge*

Annandale
Hollis, Daryl Joseph *judge*

Charlottesville
Crigler, B. Waugh *federal judge*
Michael, James Harry, Jr. *federal judge*
Wilkinson, James Harvie, III *federal judge*

Chesterfield
Davis, Bonnie Christell *judge*

Clifton
Gales, Robert Robinson *judge*

Covington
Stephenson, Roscoe Bolar, Jr. *state supreme court justice*

Danville
Kiser, Jackson L. *federal judge*

Fairfax
Stitt, David Tillman *judge*
Williams, Marcus Doyle *judge*

Falls Church
Gruggel, John Stuart, Jr. *judge*
Morse, Marvin Henry *judge*
Spector, Louis *retired federal judge, lawyer, arbitrator, consultant*

Harrisonburg
†Krumm, Ross W. *federal judge*

King George
Revercomb, Horace Austin, III *judge*

Lynchburg
†Anderson, William E. *federal judge*
†Moon, Norman K. *judge*

Newport News
†Bradberry, James E. *federal judge*

Norfolk
Bonney, Hal James, Jr. *federal judge*
Clarke, J. Calvitt, Jr. *federal judge*
Doumar, Robert George *judge*
Jackson, Raymond A. *federal judge*

†Miller, Tommy Eugene *federal judge*
Morgan, Henry Coke, Jr. *judge*
Prince, William Taliaferro *federal judge*
†St. John, Stephen C. *federal judge*
Smith, Rebecca Beach *federal judge*

Pennington Gap
†Kinser, Cynthia D. *state supreme court justice*

Richmond
Carrico, Harry Lee *state supreme court chief justice*
Compton, Asbury Christian *state supreme court justice*
Gordon, Thomas Christian, Jr. *former justice*
Hassell, Leroy Rountree, Sr. *state supreme court justice*
Keenan, Barbara Milano *state supreme court justice*
†King, Robert Bruce *federal judge*
†Lowe, David G. *federal judge*
Payne, Robert E. *federal judge*
Poff, Richard Harding *state supreme court justice*
†Shelley, Blackwell N. *federal judge*
Spencer, James R. *federal judge*
Tice, Douglas Oscar, Jr. *federal judge*
Whiting, Henry H. *state supreme court justice*
Williams, Richard Leroy *federal judge*

Roanoke
†Conrad, Glen E. *federal judge*
Turk, James Clinton *federal judge*
Wilson, Samuel Grayson *federal judge*

Salem
Koontz, Lawrence L., Jr. *state supreme court justice*
Pearson, Henry Clyde *judge*
Willett, Roy Baldwin *judge*

Stafford
Brown, Harold Eugene *magistrate*

WASHINGTON

Bellevue
Andersen, James A. *retired state supreme court justice*

Ephrata
Fitterer, Richard Clarence *judge*

Mount Vernon
Meyer, John Michael *judge*

Olympia
Alexander, Gerry L. *state supreme court justice*
Durham, Barbara *state supreme court justice*
Guy, Richard P. *state supreme court justice*
Harrison, William Alan *judge, arbitrator*
†Ireland, Faith *judge*
Sanders, Richard Browning *state supreme court justice*
Smith, Charles Z. *state supreme court justice*

Seattle
Beezer, Robert Renaut *federal judge*
Coughenour, John Clare *federal judge*
Dimmick, Carolyn Reaber *federal judge*
Dwyer, William L. *federal judge*
Farris, Jerome *federal judge*
Fletcher, Betty B. *federal judge*
†Glover, Thomas T. *federal judge*
Mc Govern, Walter T. *federal judge*
†McKeown, Mary Margaret *judge*
Overstreet, Karen A. *federal bankruptcy judge*
Pekelis, Rosselle *judge*
Rothstein, Barbara Jacobs *federal judge*
†Steiner, Samuel J. *bankruptcy judge*
†Sweigert, Philip K. *federal judge*
Weinberg, John Lee *federal judge*
Wilson, David Eugene *magistrate judge*
Wright, Eugene Allen *federal judge*
Zilly, Thomas Samuel *federal judge*

Spokane
Green, Dale Monte *retired judge*
†Imbrogno, Cynthia *magistrate judge*
Nielsen, William Fremming *federal judge*
Quackenbush, Justin Lowe *federal judge*
Van Sickle, Frederick L. *federal judge*
Whaley, Robert Hamilton *judge*

Tacoma
†Arnold, J. Kelley *federal judge*
†Brandt, Philip H. *federal judge*
Bryan, Robert J. *federal judge*
Burgess, Franklin Douglas *judge*
†Snyder, Paul *federal judge*
Tanner, Jack Edward *federal judge*

Yakima
McDonald, Alan Angus *federal judge*
†Rossmeissl, John A. *federal judge*
Suko, Lonny Ray *judge*
†Williams, Patricia C. *federal judge*

WEST VIRGINIA

Bluefield
Faber, David Alan *federal judge*
Feinberg, Mary Stanley *judge*

Charleston
Copenhaver, John Thomas, Jr. *federal judge*
Goodwin, Joseph R. *judge*
Haden, Charles Harold, II *federal judge*
Hallanan, Elizabeth V. *federal judge*
†Hogg, Jerry D. *federal judge*
Knapp, Dennis Raymond *federal judge*
Marland, Melissa Kaye *judge*
McHugh, Thomas Edward *state supreme court justice*
Michael, M. Blane *federal judge*
†Pearson, Ronald G. *federal judge*
Workman, Margaret Lee *state supreme court justice*

Clarksburg
Keeley, Irene Patricia Murphy *federal judge*

Elkins
†Core, David L. *federal judge*
Maxwell, Robert Earl *federal judge*

Huntington
†Taylor, Maurice G., Jr. *federal judge*

Union
Sprouse, James Marshall *retired federal judge*

Wheeling
†Friend, L. Edward *federal judge*
Recht, Arthur *former state supreme court justice*
Seibert, James E. *lawyer, magistrate judge*

WISCONSIN

Appleton
Bayorgeon, James Thomas *judge*
Froehlich, Harold Vernon *judge, former congressman*

Dodgeville
Dyke, William Daniel *circuit court judge*

Eau Claire
†Utschig, Thomas S. *federal judge*

Green Bay
†Sickel, James *federal judge*

Madison
Abrahamson, Shirley Schlanger *state supreme court chief justice*
Bablitch, William A. *state supreme court justice*
Bradley, Ann Walsh *state supreme court justice*
Crabb, Barbara Brandriff *federal judge*
†Crocker, Stephen L. *federal judge*
Deininger, David George *judge*
Fiedler, Patrick James *circuit court judge*
Heffernan, Nathan Stewart *retired state supreme court chief justice*
Martin, Robert David *judge, educator*
Shabaz, John C. *federal judge*
†Skupniewitz, Joseph W. *federal judge*
Steinmetz, Donald Walter *state supreme court justice*
Wilcox, Jon P. *state supreme court justice*

Milwaukee
†Callahan, William E., Jr. *federal judge*
Curran, Thomas J. *federal judge*
†Eisenberg, Russell A. *federal judge*
Evans, Terence Thomas *federal judge*
Goodstein, Aaron E. *federal magistrate judge*
Gordon, Myron L. *federal judge*
†McGarity, Margaret Dee *federal judge*
Randa, Rudolph Thomas *judge*
Reynolds, John W. *federal judge*
Shapiro, James Edward *judge*
Stadtmueller, Joseph Peter *federal judge*

Mukwonago
†Adelman, Lynn S. *United States district judge*

Sheboygan
Buchen, John Gustave *retired judge*

WYOMING

Casper
Downes, William F. *judge*

Cheyenne
Barrett, James Emmett *federal judge*
†Beaman, William C. *federal judge*
Brimmer, Clarence Addison *federal judge*
†Brooks, John C. *federal judge*
Brorby, Wade *federal judge*
Golden, T. Michael *state supreme court justice*
Hill, William U. *state supreme court justice*
Johnson, Alan Bond *federal judge*
Lehman, Larry L. *state supreme court justice*
Macy, Richard J. *state supreme court justice*
†McNiff, Peter J. *federal judge*
Schrader, Robert Wesley *judge*
Taylor, William Al *state supreme court justice*

Cody
Patrick, H. Hunter *lawyer, judge*

Green River
Marty, Lawrence A. *magistrate*

Lander
†Gist, Richard D. *federal judge*

Sheridan
†Connor, Robert W., Jr. *federal judge*

Story
Mc Ewan, Leonard *former judge*

Yellowstone National Park
†Cole, Stephen E. *federal judge*

TERRITORIES OF THE UNITED STATES

FEDERATED STATES OF MICRONESIA

Pohnpei
King, Edward C. *judge*

GUAM

Agana
Lamorena, Alberto C., III *supreme court justice guam*
Maraman, Katherine Ann *judge*
Unpingco, John Walter Sablan *federal judge*
Weeks, Janet Healy *supreme court justice*

NORTHERN MARIANA ISLANDS

Saipan
Dela Cruz, Jose Santos *retired state supreme court chief justice*
Munson, Alex Robert *judge*

PUERTO RICO

Hato Rey
Cerezo, Carmen Consuelo *federal judge*
†DeJesus-Kellogg, Sara E. *federal judge*
Laffitte, Hector Manuel *federal judge*
†Lamoutte, Enrique S. *federal judge*

San Juan
Acosta, Raymond Luis *federal judge*
Andreu-Garcia, Jose Antonio *territory supreme court chief justice*
†Arenas, Justo *federal judge*
†Carlo-Altieri, Gerardo A. *federal judge*
Casellas, Salvador E. *judge*
†Castellanos, Jesus Antonio *federal judge*
Corrada del Rio, Baltasar *supreme court justice*
†Delgado-Colon, Aida M. *federal judge*
de Rodon, Miriam Naveira *supreme court justice*
Dominguez, Daniel R. *judge*
Fusté, José Antonio *federal judge*
Fuster, Jaime B. *supreme court justice*
Gierbolini-Ortiz, Gilberto *federal judge*
Hernandez-Denton, Federico *supreme court justice*
Torruella, Juan R. *federal judge*

VIRGIN ISLANDS

Charlotte Amalie
†Barnard, Geoffrey W. *federal judge*

Christiansted
Finch, Raymond Lawrence *judge*
Resnick, Jeffrey Lance *federal magistrate judge*

Saint Thomas
Caffee, Lorren Dale *judge*
Hodge, Verne Antonio *judge*
Moore, Thomas Kail *chief judge supreme court VI*

CANADA

ALBERTA

Edmonton
Fraser, Catherine Anne *Canadian chief justice*
Stevenson, William Alexander *retired justice of Supreme Court of Canada*

BRITISH COLUMBIA

Vancouver
de Weerdt, Mark Murray *retired judge*
Lysyk, Kenneth Martin *judge*
McEachern, Allan *Canadian justice*

MANITOBA

Winnipeg
Lyon, Sterling Rufus Webster *justice*

NEW BRUNSWICK

Fredericton
Strange, Henry Hazen *judge*

Westfield
Logan, Rodman Emmason *retired jurist*

NOVA SCOTIA

Halifax
Glube, Constance Rachelle *Canadian chief justice*

ONTARIO

Bracebridge
Evans, John David Daniel *judge*

North York
Harris, Sydney Malcolm *retired judge*

Ottawa
Archambault, Pierre Guy *judge*
Cullen, Jack Sydney George Bud *federal judge*
Décary, Robert *judge*
Gonthier, Charles Doherty *Canadian supreme court justice*
Heald, Darrel Verner *retired Canadian federal judge*
Hugessen, James K. *judge*
Lamer, Antonio *Canadian supreme court chief justice*
L'Heureux-Dubé, Claire *judge*
MacKay, William Andrew *judge*
Major, John Charles *judge*
Margeson, Theodore Earl *judge*
McKeown, William Philip *judge*
McLachlin, Beverley *supreme court judge*
Muldoon, Francis Creighton *Canadian federal judge*
Rip, Gerald J. *federal judge*
Strayer, Barry Lee *federal judge*

Toronto
Boland, Janet Lang *judge*
McMurtry, R. Roy *chief justice*

PRINCE EDWARD ISLAND

Charlottetown
Carruthers, Norman Harry *Canadian province supreme court justice*

QUEBEC

Montreal
Bisson, Claude *retired chief justice of Quebec*
Gold, Alan B. *former Canadian chief justice*
Mailhot, Louise *judge*
Rothman, Melvin L. *judge*

Quebec
Morin, Louis *judge*

SASKATCHEWAN

Regina
Bayda, Edward Dmytro *judge*

ADDRESS UNPUBLISHED

Aaroe, Paul Morris *retired superior court judge*
Askey, William Hartman *magistrate, lawyer*
Bertelsman, William Odis *federal judge*
Bootle, William Augustus *retired federal judge*
Boslaugh, Leslie *retired judge*
†Boulden, Judith Ann *bankruptcy judge*
Boyle, Francis Joseph *retired federal judge*
Brown, Robert Laidlaw *state supreme court justice*
Bunton, Lucius Desha, III *federal judge*
Burke, Edmond Wayne *retired judge, lawyer*
Butzner, John Decker, Jr. *federal judge*
Callow, Keith McLean *judge*
Callow, William Grant *retired state supreme court justice*
Castagna, William John *federal judge*
Ceci, Louis J. *former state supreme court justice*
Clark, Thomas Alonzo *federal judge*
Cochran, George Moffett *retired judge*
Coffey, John Louis *federal judge*
Cohn, Avern Levin *federal judge*
Colaianni, Joseph Vincent *judge*
Cole, Betty Lou McDonel Shelton (Mrs. Dewey G. Cole, Jr.) *judge*
Cook, Julian Abele, Jr. *federal judge*
Cory, Peter de Carteret *retired Canadian supreme court justice*
Cyr, Conrad Keefe *federal judge*
Daugherty, Frederick Alvin *federal judge*
Day, Roland Bernard *retired chief justice state supreme court*
Dolliver, James Morgan *retired state supreme court justice*
Easley, Mack *retired state supreme court chief justice*
Eaton, Joe Oscar *federal judge*
Edwards, Ninian Murry *judge*
Fahrnbruch, Dale E. *retired state supreme court justice*
Fisk, Merlin Edgar *judge*
Foster, Robert Lawson *retired judge, deacon*
Fremont-Smith, Thayer *judge*
Garibaldi, Marie Louise *state supreme court justice*
Gibson, Benjamin F. *federal judge*
Gillette, W. Michael *state supreme court justice*
Golden, Elliott *judge*
Gorence, Patricia Josetta *judge*
Griffin, Robert Paul *former United States senator, state supreme court justice*
Grimes, William Alvan *retired state supreme court chief justice*
Haltom, Elbert Bertram, Jr. *retired federal judge*
Harris, Ed Jerome *retired judge*
Hawkins, Armis Eugene *former state supreme court chief justice*
Hawkins, Michael Daly *federal judge*
Hayek, Carolyn Jean *retired judge, former church administrator*
Hellerstein, Alvin Kenneth *judge*
Hightower, Jack English *former state supreme court justice, congressman*
Hogan, Thomas Francis *federal judge*
Horton, Odell *federal judge*
Howard, George, Jr. *federal judge*
Hoyt, William Lloyd *chief justice*
Johnson, Byron Jerald *retired state supreme court judge*
Joiner, Charles Wycliffe *judge*
Jones, Phyllis Gene *judge*
Karwacki, Robert Lee *judge*
Kauger, Yvonne *state supreme court chief justice*
Kelly, Aurel Maxey *retired judge*
Krupansky, Blanche *retired judge*
Langley, Jimmy Don *judge*
Laycraft, James Herbert *judge*
Lee, Barbara A. *retired federal magistrate judge*
Lee, Dan M. *retired state supreme court justice*
Liacos, Paul Julian *retired state supreme judicial court chief justice*
Linde, Hans Arthur *state supreme court justice*
Lively, Pierce *federal judge*
Logan, James Kenneth *lawyer, former federal judge*
Love, Miron Anderson *retired judge*
Low, Harry William *judge*
Magnuson, Paul Arthur *federal judge*
Matthews, Warren Wayne *state supreme court justice*
McCown, Hale *retired judge*
McKee, Roger Curtis *retired federal magistrate judge*
Meschke, Herbert Leonard *retired state supreme court justice*
Metzner, Charles Miller *federal judge*
Meyer, Louis B. *judge, retired state supreme court justice*
Montgomery, Seth David *retired state supreme court chief justice*
Muecke, Charles Andrew (Carl Muecke) *federal judge*
Murray, Florence Kerins *retired state supreme court justice*
Mydland, Gordon James *judge*
Nesbit, Phyllis Schneider *judge*
Newbern, William David *retired state supreme court justice*
Newman, Theodore Roosevelt, Jr. *judge*
Papadakos, Nicholas Peter *retired state supreme court justice*

Pascale, Daniel Richard *circuit judge*
Perez-Gimenez, Juan Manuel *federal judge*
Phillips, James Dickson, Jr. *federal judge*
Pokras, Sheila Frances *retired judge*
†Powers, Richard Augustine, III *judge*
Prager, David *retired state supreme court chief justice*
Quillen, William Tatem *judge, lawyer, educator*
Ransom, Richard Edward *state supreme court justice*
Reinhardt, Stephen Roy *federal judge*
Rice, Walter Herbert *federal judge*
Rivers, Kenneth Jay *retired judicial administrator, consultant*
Ross, Donald Roe *federal judge*
Roszkowski, Stanley Julian *retired federal judge*
Royse, Mary Kay *judge*
Sarokin, H. Lee *retired federal judge*
Schroeder, Gerald Frank *state supreme court justice*
Schultz, Louis William *judge*
Schwebel, Stephen Myron *judge, arbitrator*
Shearing, Miriam *state supreme court justice*
Sheedy, Patrick Thomas *judge*
Shubb, William Barnet *judge*
Silberman, Laurence Hirsch *federal judge*
Sinclair, Virgil Lee, Jr. *judge, writer*
Smith, Fern M. *judge*
Smith, Loren Allan *federal judge*
Souter, David Hackett *United States supreme court justice*
Stahl, Madonna *retired judge*
Staker, Robert Jackson *federal judge*
Stamos, John James *judge*
Stamp, Frederick Pfarr, Jr. *federal judge*
Stanton, Louis Lee *federal judge*
Sweet, Robert Workman *federal judge*
Talmadge, Philip Albert *state supreme court justice, former state senator*
Thomas, William Kernahan *retired federal judge*
Torres, Edwin *state judge, writer*
Trout, Linda Copple *state supreme court justice*
†Turnoff, William Charles *magistrate judge*
Utter, Robert French *retired state supreme court justice*
Vittone, John Michael *federal judge*
Vollmer, Richard Wade *federal judge*
Wathen, Daniel Everett *state supreme court chief justice*
Weber, Fred J. *retired state supreme court justice*
†White, Helene Nita *federal judge*
White, Renee Allyn *judge*
Wiggins, Charles Edward *judge*
Wood, Diane Pamela *judge*
Wyman, Louis Crosby *judge, former senator, former congressman*
†Zive, Gregg William *judge*

LAW: LAW PRACTICE AND ADMINISTRATION

UNITED STATES

ALABAMA

Andalusia
Albritton, William Harold, IV *lawyer*
Fuller, William Sidney *lawyer*

Anniston
Klinefelter, James Louis *lawyer*
Woodrow, Randall Mark *lawyer*

Auburn
Samford, Thomas Drake, III *lawyer*

Bay Minette
Granade, Fred King *lawyer*

Birmingham
Akers, Ottie Clay *lawyer, publisher*
Alford, Margie Searcy *lawyer*
Baker, David Remember *lawyer*
Berg, Thomas Charles *law educator*
Blan, Ollie Lionel, Jr. *lawyer*
Boardman, Mark Seymour *lawyer*
Braswell, Walter E. *prosecutor*
Brown, Ephraim Taylor, Jr. *lawyer*
Carlton, Eric L. *lawyer*
Carruthers, Thomas Neely, Jr. *lawyer*
Coleman, Brittin Turner *lawyer*
Cooper, Jerome A. *lawyer*
Cooper, N. Lee *lawyer*
Cullen, William Zachary *lawyer*
Davis, Julian Mason, Jr. *lawyer*
DeGaris, Annesley Hodges *lawyer, educator*
Denson, William Frank, III *lawyer*
Farley, Joseph McConnell *lawyer*
Foster, Arthur Key, Jr. *lawyer*
Friend, Edward Malcolm, III *lawyer, educator*
Gale, Fournier Joseph, III *lawyer*
Garner, Robert Edward Lee *lawyer*
Givhan, Robert Marcus *lawyer*
Goodrich, Thomas Michael *lawyer, engineering and construction executive*
Grant, Walter Matthews *lawyer, corporate executive*
Greenwood, P. Nicholas *lawyer*
Hinton, James Forrest, Jr. *lawyer*
Howell, William Ashley, III *lawyer*
Irons, William Lee *lawyer*
Johnson, Joseph H., Jr. *lawyer*
†Jones, G. Douglas *prosecutor*
Kracke, Robert Russell *lawyer*
Lacy, Alexander Shelton *lawyer*
Logan, J. Patrick *lawyer*
Long, Thad Gladden *lawyer*
Max, Rodney Andrew *lawyer, mediator*
Mc Millan, George Duncan Hastie, Jr. *lawyer, former state official*
McWhorter, Hobart Amory, Jr. *lawyer*
Mills, William Hayes *lawyer*
Molen, John Klauminzer *lawyer*
Nettles, Bert Sheffield *lawyer*
Newton, Alexander Worthy *lawyer*
Norris, Robert Wheeler *lawyer, military officer*
Palmer, Robert Leslie *lawyer*
Pearson, Richard L. *lawyer*
Privett, Caryl Penney *lawyer*
Redden, Lawrence Drew *lawyer*
Robin, Theodore Tydings, Jr. *lawyer, engineer, consultant*
Rogers, Ernest Mabry *lawyer*
Rotch, James E. *lawyer*
Rountree, Asa *lawyer*
Selfe, Edward Milton *lawyer*
Smith, John Joseph *lawyer*
Stabler, Lewis Vastine, Jr. *lawyer*
Stewart, Joseph Grier *lawyer*
Sydnor, Edgar Starke *lawyer*
Timberlake, Marshall *lawyer*
Todd, Judith F. *lawyer*
Vinson, Laurence Duncan, Jr. *lawyer*
Weeks, Arthur Andrew *lawyer, law educator*
Wrinkle, John Newton *lawyer*

Clayton
Jackson, Lynn Robertson *lawyer*

Cullman
Poston, Beverly Paschal *lawyer*

Dadeville
Adair, Charles Robert, Jr. *lawyer*
Oliver, John Percy, II *lawyer*

Daphne
Hilley, Joseph Henry *lawyer*

Decatur
Blackburn, John Gilmer *lawyer*
Caddell, John A. *lawyer*

Demopolis
Dinning, Woodford Wyndham, Jr. *lawyer*
Lloyd, Hugh Adams *lawyer*

Hoover
Cole, Charles DuBose, II *law educator*

Huntsville
Accardi, James Roy *prosecutor*
Huckaby, Gary Carlton *lawyer*
Morgan, Timothy Wayne, Sr. *district attorney*
Potter, Ernest Luther *lawyer*
Stephens, (Holman) Harold *lawyer*

Mobile
Armbrecht, William Henry, III *retired lawyer*
Ballard, Michael Eugene *lawyer*
Braswell, Louis Erskine *lawyer*
Foster, J. Don *lawyer*
Harris, Benjamin Harte, Jr. *lawyer*
Helmsing, Frederick George *lawyer*
Holland, Lyman Faith, Jr. *lawyer*
Holmes, Broox Garrett *lawyer*
Kimbrough, William Adams, Jr. *lawyer*
Lyons, George Sage *lawyer, oil industry executive, former state legislator*
†Miller, John C. H., Jr. *lawyer*
Murchison, David Roderick *lawyer*
Roedder, William Chapman, Jr. *lawyer*
Vulevich, Edward, Jr. *prosecutor*

Montgomery
Byars, Walter Ryland, Jr. *lawyer*
Clement, Frances Roberts *lawyer, mediator, nurse, consultant*
Eubanks, Ronald W. *lawyer, broadcaster*
Franco, Ralph Abraham *lawyer*
Gooden, Pamela Joyce *lawyer*
Graddick, Charles Allen *lawyer*
Gregory, William Stanley *lawyer*
Hamner, Reginald Turner *lawyer*
Hawthorne, Frank Howard *lawyer*
Hester, Douglas Benjamin *lawyer, federal official*
Hill, Thomas Bowen, III *lawyer*
Howell, Allen Windsor *lawyer*
Kloess, Lawrence Herman, Jr. *lawyer*
Laurie, Robin Garrett *lawyer*
Lawson, Thomas Seay, Jr. *lawyer*
Leslie, Henry Arthur *lawyer, retired banker*
McFadden, Frank Hampton *lawyer, business executive, former judge*
Nachman, Merton Roland, Jr. *lawyer*
Pitt, Redding *lawyer*
Prestwood, Alvin Tennyson *lawyer*
Salmon, Joseph Thaddeus *lawyer*
Volz, Charles Harvie, Jr. *lawyer*
Wood, James Jerry *lawyer*

Opelika
Samford, Yetta Glenn, Jr. *lawyer*

Orange Beach
Adams, Daniel Fenton *law educator*

Tuscaloosa
Christopher, Thomas Weldon *legal educator, administrator*
Cook, Camille Wright *law educator*
Hoff, Timothy *law educator, priest*
Smith, James Dwight *lawyer*
Williams, Roger Courtland *lawyer*

ALASKA

Anchorage
Anderson, Kathleen Gay *consultant mediator, hearing officer, arbitrator*
Bundy, Robert Charles *prosecutor*
Butler, Rex Lamont *lawyer*
Cantor, James Elliot *lawyer*
De Lisio, Stephen Scott *lawyer*
Ealy, Jonathan Bruce *lawyer*
Edwards, George Kent *lawyer*
Hayes, George Nicholas *lawyer*
Hughes, Mary Katherine *lawyer*
Linxwiler, James David *lawyer*
Lowe, Robert Charles *lawyer, banker*
Munson, Vivian Ruth *lawyer*
Owens, Robert Patrick *lawyer*
Perkins, Joseph John, Jr. *lawyer*
Roberts, John Derham *lawyer*
Ross, Wayne Anthony *lawyer*
Teal, Gilbert Earle, II *lawyer, coast guard officer*
Wagstaff, Robert Hall *lawyer*
Weinig, Richard Arthur *lawyer*
Wohlforth, Eric Evans *lawyer*

Bethel
McMahon, Craig Roger *lawyer*

Juneau
Cole, Charles Edward *lawyer, former state attorney general*
†Collins, Patricia A. *lawyer, judge*
Nave, Thomas George *lawyer*

Kodiak
Jamin, Matthew Daniel *lawyer, magistrate judge*
Ott, Andrew Eduard *lawyer*

Nondalton
Gay, Sarah Elizabeth *lawyer*

ARIZONA

Carefree
Hutchison, Stanley Philip *lawyer, retired*

Chandler
Markey, James Kevin *lawyer*

Flagstaff
Bertoldo, Joseph Ramon *lawyer*
Cowser, Danny Lee *lawyer, mental health specialist*
Gliege, John Gerhardt *lawyer*
Stoops, Daniel J. *lawyer*

Gilbert
Handy, Robert Maxwell *patent lawyer*

Glendale
Bellah, C. Richard *lawyer*

Green Valley
Friedman, Edward David *lawyer, arbitrator*

Mesa
Shelley, James LaMar *lawyer*
Squire, Bruce M. *lawyer*

Nogales
Castro, Raul Hector *lawyer, former ambassador, former governor*

Paradise Valley
Levetown, Robert Alexander *lawyer*

Peoria
Keesling, Karen Ruth *lawyer*
Moshier, Mary Baluk *patent lawyer*

Phoenix
Allen, Robert Eugene Barton *lawyer*
Alsentzer, William James, Jr. *lawyer*
Arbetman, Jeffrey Farrell *lawyer*
Bain, C. Randall *lawyer*
Baker, William Dunlap *lawyer*
Bakker, Thomas Gordon *lawyer*
Begam, Robert George *lawyer*
†Bivens, Donald Wayne *lawyer, judge*
Bodney, David Jeremy *lawyer*
Bouma, John Jacob *lawyer*
Burke, Timothy John *lawyer*
Case, David Leon *lawyer*
Cohen, Jon Stephan *lawyer*
Colburn, Donald D. *lawyer*
Cole, George Thomas *lawyer*
Condo, James Robert *lawyer*
Conrad, John Regis *lawyer, engineering executive*
Cooledge, Richard Calvin *lawyer*
Coppersmith, Sam *lawyer*
Crockett, Clyll Webb *lawyer*
Daughton, Donald *lawyer*
Davies, David George *lawyer*
Deeny, Robert Joseph *lawyer*
Derdenger, Patrick *lawyer*
Derouin, James G. *lawyer*
Dunipace, Ian Douglas *lawyer*
Durrant, Dan Martin *lawyer*
Eaton, Berrien Clark *retired lawyer, author*
Ehmann, Anthony Valentine *lawyer*
Esahak, George Michael *lawyer*
Everett, James Joseph *lawyer*
Everroad, John David *lawyer*
Feinstein, Allen Lewis *lawyer*
Fenzl, Terry Earle *lawyer*
Fine, Charles Leon *lawyer*
Flickinger, Don Jacob *patent agent*
Frank, John Paul *lawyer, author*
Gaffney, Donald Lee *lawyer*
Gaines, Francis Pendleton, III *lawyer*
Gilbert, Donald Roy *lawyer*
Gladner, Marc Stefan *lawyer*
Goldstein, Stuart Wolf *lawyer*
Griller, Gordon Moore *court administrator*
Halpern, Barry David *lawyer*
Harrison, Mark Isaac *lawyer*
Hayden, William Robert *lawyer*
Hicks, William Albert, III *lawyer*
Hienton, James Robert *lawyer*
Hoecker, Thomas Ralph *lawyer*
Hoxie, Joel P. *lawyer*
Huntwork, James Roden *lawyer*
Jacobson, (Julian) Edward *lawyer*
James, Charles E., Jr. *lawyer*
Jansen, Donald William *lawyer, legislative administrator*
Jirauch, Charles W. *lawyer*
Johnston, Logan Truax, III *lawyer*
King, Jack A. *lawyer*
Klahr, Gary Peter *lawyer*
Klausner, Jack Daniel *lawyer*
Knoller, Guy David *lawyer*
Koester, Berthold Karl *lawyer, law educator, retired honorary German consul*
Kreutzberg, David W. *lawyer*
Kurn, Neal *lawyer*
Le Clair, Douglas Marvin *lawyer, educator, judge*
Lee, Richard H(arlo) *lawyer*
Leonard, Jeffrey S. *lawyer*
Lowry, Edward Francis, Jr. *lawyer*
Lubin, Stanley *lawyer*
Madden, Paul Robert *lawyer*
Marks, Merton Eleazer *lawyer*
Martori, Joseph Peter *lawyer*
Mc Clennen, Louis *lawyer, educator*
McDougall, Roderick Gregory *lawyer*
McRae, Hamilton Eugene, III *lawyer*
Merritt, Nancy-Jo *lawyer*
Meschkow, Jordan Mark *patent lawyer*
Meyers, Howard Craig *lawyer*
Meyerson, Bruce Elliot *lawyer*
Miller, Eleanor Louise *lawyer*
Miller, Louis Rice *lawyer*
Mousel, Craig Lawrence *lawyer*
Moya, Patrick Robert *lawyer*
Olsen, Alfred Jon *lawyer*
Olson, Robert Howard *lawyer*
O'Steen, Van *lawyer*
Perry, Lee Rowan *retired lawyer*
Platt, Warren E. *lawyer*
Plattner, Richard Serber *lawyer*
Pogson, Stephen Walter *lawyer*
Price, Charles Steven *lawyer*
Quayle, Marilyn Tucker *lawyer, wife of former vice president of United States*
Rathwell, Peter John *lawyer*
Refo, Patricia Lee *lawyer*
Romley, Richard M. *lawyer*
Rosen, Sidney Marvin *lawyer*
Rudolph, Gilbert Lawrence *lawyer*
Savage, Stephen Michael *lawyer*
Seamons, Quinton Frank *lawyer*
Sherk, Kenneth John *lawyer*
Silverman, Alan Henry *lawyer*
Sliger, Herbert Jacquemin, Jr. *lawyer*
Smock, Timothy Robert *lawyer*
Stahl, Louis A. *lawyer*
Storey, Lee A. *lawyer*
Storey, Norman C. *lawyer*
Thompson, Joel Erik *lawyer*
Thompson, Terence William *lawyer*
Udall, Calvin Hunt *lawyer*
Ulrich, Paul Graham *lawyer, author, publisher, editor*
Walker, Richard K. *lawyer*
Wall, Donald Arthur *lawyer*
Wheeler, Steven M. *lawyer*
Whisler, James Steven *lawyer, mining and manufacturing executive*
Williams, Quinn Patrick *lawyer*
Winthrop, Lawrence Fredrick *lawyer*
Wolf, G. Van Velsor, Jr. *lawyer*
Woods, Grant *lawyer, former state attorney general*
Woolf, Michael E. *lawyer*
Yarnell, Michael Allan *lawyer*

Prescott
Goodman, Mark N. *lawyer*
Gose, Richard Vernie *lawyer*
Kleindienst, Richard Gordon *lawyer*

Scottsdale
Angle, Margaret Susan *lawyer*
Berry, Charles Richard *lawyer*
Buri, Charles Edward *lawyer*
Burke, Richard Kitchens *lawyer, educator*
Fennelly, Jane Corey *lawyer*
Inman, William Peter *lawyer*
Itkin, Robert Jeffrey *lawyer*
Krupp, Clarence William *lawyer, personnel and hospital administrator*
Mybeck, Richard Raymond *lawyer*
Peshkin, Samuel David *lawyer*
Roberts, Jean Reed *lawyer*
Sears, Alan Edward *lawyer*
Swartz, Melvin Jay *lawyer, author*
Titus, Jon Alan *lawyer*

Sun City
Treece, James Lyle *lawyer*

Tempe
†Bucklin, Leonard Herbert *lawyer*
Evans, Lawrence Jack, Jr. *lawyer*
Matheson, Alan Adams *law educator*
Shimpock, Kathy Elizabeth *lawyer, writer*
Spritzer, Ralph Simon *lawyer, educator*

Tucson
Bell, Alan *lawyer, environmental health activist*
Betteridge, Frances Carpenter *retired lawyer, mediator*
D'Antonio, James Joseph *lawyer*
Dobbs, Dan Byron *lawyer, educator*
Dolph, Wilbert Emery *lawyer*
Eckhardt, August Gottlieb *law educator*
Fortman, Marvin *law educator, consultant*
Froman, Sandra Sue *lawyer*
Gantz, David Alfred *lawyer, university official*
Glaser, Steven Jay *lawyer*
Hyams, Harold *lawyer*
Kaucher, James William *lawyer*
Kimble, William Earl *lawyer*
Lesher, Robert Overton *lawyer*
Lombard, Richard Spencer *lawyer*
Mc Donald, John Richard *lawyer*
Meehan, Michael Joseph *lawyer*
Morrow, James Franklin *lawyer*
Pace, Thomas M. *lawyer*
Polan, David Jay *lawyer*
Schorr, S. L. *lawyer*
Strong, John William *lawyer, educator*
Tindall, Robert Emmett *lawyer, educator*
Tretschok, Dale Deege *lawyer*
Waterman, David Moore *lawyer*

Yuma
Hossler, David Joseph *lawyer, law educator*

ARKANSAS

Bentonville
Rhoads, Robert K. *lawyer, retail executive*

Blytheville
Fendler, Oscar *lawyer*

Conway
Johnson, James Douglas (Jim Johnson) *lawyer*

Crossett
Hubbell, Billy James *lawyer*

Fayetteville
Ahlers, Glen-Peter, Sr. *law library director, educator, consultant*
Bassett, Woodson William, Jr. *lawyer*
Copeland, John Dewayne *law educator*
Davis, Wylie Herman *lawyer, educator*

Pearson, Charles Thomas, Jr. *lawyer*
VanWinkle, John Ragan *lawyer*

Fort Smith
Dotson, Donald L. *lawyer*
Holmes, Paul Kinloch, III *prosecutor*

Harrison
Pinson, Jerry D. *lawyer*

Helena
Roscopf, Charles Buford *lawyer*

Holiday Island
Epley, Lewis Everett, Jr. *lawyer*

Little Rock
Anderson, Philip Sidney *lawyer*
Campbell, George Emerson *lawyer*
Casey, Paula Jean *prosecutor*
Creasman, William Paul *lawyer*
Cross, J. Bruce *lawyer*
Culp, Nathan Craig *lawyer*
Dillahunty, Wilbur Harris *lawyer*
Drummond, Winslow *lawyer*
Fogleman, John Albert *lawyer, retired judge*
Gunter, Russell Allen *lawyer*
Haley, John Harvey *lawyer*
Hall, John Wesley, Jr. *lawyer*
Haught, William Dixon *lawyer*
Heuer, Sam Tate *lawyer*
Jennings, Alston *lawyer*
Johnson, Michael Dennis *lawyer*
Jones, Stephen Witsell *lawyer*
Julian, Jim Lee *lawyer*
Lipe, Linda Bon *lawyer*
May, Ronald Alan *lawyer*
†McMath, Phillip *lawyer, writer*
Murphey, Arthur Gage, Jr. *law educator*
Nelson, Edward Sheffield *lawyer, former utility company executive*
†Phillips, Kay *legal assistant*
†Ronnel, Jennifer Averbuch *lawyer*
Warner, Cecil Randolph, Jr. *lawyer*
Witherspoon, Carolyn Brack *lawyer*
Wright, Robert Ross, III *law educator*

Mena
Thrailkill, Daniel B. *lawyer*

Monticello
Ball, William Kenneth *lawyer*

North Little Rock
Patty, Claibourne Watkins, Jr. *lawyer*

Osceola
Wilson, Ralph Edwin *lawyer, justice*

Pine Bluff
Jones, John Harris *lawyer, banker*
Moon, Deborah Joan *paralegal*
Ramsay, Louis Lafayette, Jr. *lawyer, banker*
Strode, Joseph Arlin *lawyer*

Rogers
Myers, Dane Jacob *lawyer, podiatrist*

Sheridan
†Nichols, J. Christopher *lawyer*

Springdale
Cypert, Jimmy Dean *lawyer*

Warren
Claycomb, Hugh Murray *lawyer, author*

West Memphis
Fogleman, Julian Barton *lawyer*

CALIFORNIA

Alameda
Stonehouse, James Adam *lawyer*

Alamo
Madden, Palmer Brown *lawyer*

Antioch
Richards, Gerald Thomas *lawyer, consultant, educator*

Arcadia
Forward, Dorothy Elizabeth *legal assistant*
Gelber, Louise C(arp) *lawyer*
Mc Cormack, Francis Xavier *lawyer, former oil company executive*

Atherton
Ferris, Robert Albert *lawyer, venture capitalist*

Bakersfield
Barmann, Bernard Charles, Sr. *lawyer*
Clark, Thomas Sullivan *lawyer*
Farr, G(ardner) Neil *lawyer*
Kind, Kenneth Wayne *lawyer, real estate broker*
Martin, George Francis *lawyer*
Tornstrom, Robert Ernest *lawyer, oil company executive*
Young, John Byron *retired lawyer*

Belvedere Tiburon
Buell, Edward Rick, II *lawyer*

Berkeley
Barton, Babette B. *lawyer, educator*
Bond, Thomas Moore, Jr. *labor mediation and arbitration executive*
Buxbaum, Richard M. *law educator, lawyer*
Choper, Jesse Herbert *law educator, university dean*
De Goff, Victoria Joan *lawyer*
Eisenberg, Melvin A. *law educator*
Feeley, Malcolm M. *law educator, political scientist*
Feller, David E. *law educator, arbitrator*
Gordley, James Russell *law educator*
Halbach, Edward Christian, Jr. *legal educator*
Haley, George Patrick *lawyer*
Kadish, Sanford Harold *law educator*

McNulty, John Kent *lawyer, educator*
Messinger, Sheldon L(eopold) *law educator*
Mishkin, Paul J. *lawyer, educator*
Ogg, Wilson Reid *lawyer, poet, retired judge, lyricist, curator, publisher, educator, philosopher, social scientist, parapsychologist*
Petty, George Oliver *lawyer*
Post, Robert Charles *law educator*
Reilley, Kathleen Patricia *lawyer*
Scheiber, Harry N. *law educator*
Shapiro, Martin *law educator*
Woodhouse, Thomas Edwin *lawyer*
Zimring, Franklin E. *legal educator, lawyer*

Beverly Hills
Amado, Honey Kessler *lawyer*
Bloom, Jacob A. *lawyer*
Bordy, Michael Jeffrey *lawyer*
Brown, Hermione Kopp *lawyer*
Casey, Thomas J. *lawyer*
Clark, Marcia Rachel *prosecutor*
†Cook, Melanie *lawyer*
Haile, Lawrence Barclay *lawyer*
†Hansen, Tom *lawyer*
†Hergott, Alan *laywer*
Hogan, Steven L. *lawyer*
Horwin, Leonard *lawyer*
†Jacobson, Craig *lawyer*
†Levy, Richard Brian *lawyer*
Nicholas, Frederick M. *lawyer*
Ramer, Bruce M. *lawyer*
Rosky, Burton Seymour *lawyer*
Russell, Irwin Emanuel *lawyer*
Schaefer, Susan G. *lawyer*
Sobelle, Richard E. *lawyer*

Brea
Pearson, April Virginia *lawyer*

Burbank
Cunningham, Robert D. *lawyer*
Litvack, Sanford Martin *lawyer*
Noddings, Sarah Ellen *lawyer*

Burlingame
Cotchett, Joseph Winters *lawyer, author*
Ocheltree, Richard Lawrence *lawyer, retired forest products company executive*
Peel, Fred Welch, Jr. *law educator, writer*
Ziegler, R. W., Jr. *lawyer, consultant*

Carlsbad
McCracken, Steven Carl *lawyer*

Carmel
Robinson, John Minor *lawyer, retired business executive*

Carmichael
Halpenny, Diana Doris *lawyer*
Jarrett, Ronald Douglas *lawyer, nurse*

Cerritos
Sarno, Maria Erlinda *lawyer, scientist*

China Lake Nwc
Long, Andre Edwin *law educator, lawyer*

Chino
Determan, John David *lawyer*

Chula Vista
Allen, David Russell *lawyer*
Santee, Dale William *lawyer, air force officer*

City Of Industry
Churchill, James Allen *lawyer*

Claremont
Ansell, Edward Orin *lawyer*

Coalinga
Frame, Ted Ronald *lawyer*

Corona Del Mar
†Quinlan, Francis E. *lawyer*

Coronado
Raushenbush, Walter Brandeis *law educator*

Costa Mesa
Anderson, Jon David *lawyer*
Caldwell, Courtney Lynn *lawyer, real estate consultant*
Calise, William Joseph, Jr. *lawyer*
Currie, Robert Emil *lawyer*
Daniels, James Walter *lawyer*
Frieden, Clifford E. *lawyer*
Goldstein, Michael Gerald *lawyer*
Hamilton, James William *lawyer*
Hamilton, Phillip Douglas *lawyer*
Hay, Howard Clinton *lawyer*
Jansen, Allan W. *lawyer*
Jones, H(arold) Gilbert, Jr. *lawyer*
Reveal, Ernest Ira, III *lawyer*
Rudolph, George Cooper *lawyer*
Schaaf, Douglas Allan *lawyer*
Tanner, R. Marshall *lawyer*
Tennyson, Peter Joseph *lawyer*
Thurston, Morris Ashcroft *lawyer*

Culver City
Pavitt, William Hesser, Jr. *lawyer*

Cupertino
Adams, Jo-Ann Marie *lawyer*
Simon, Nancy Ruth *lawyer*

Cypress
Olschwang, Alan Paul *lawyer*

Daly City
Boccia, Barbara *lawyer*

Davis
Bartosic, Florian *lawyer, arbitrator, educator*
Bruch, Carol Sophie *lawyer, educator*
Dykstra, Daniel James *lawyer, educator*
Feeney, Floyd Fulton *legal educator*
Henderson, Mark Gordy *lawyer*

Imwinkelried, Edward John *law educator*
Johnson, Kevin Raymond *lawyer, educator*
Juenger, Friedrich Klaus *lawyer, educator*
Oakley, John Bilyeu *law educator, lawyer, judicial consultant*
Wolk, Bruce Alan *law educator*
Wydick, Richard Crews *lawyer, educator*

Del Mar
Seitman, John Michael *lawyer, arbitrator, mediator*

Downey
Duzey, Robert Lindsey *lawyer*

El Cerrito
Garbarino, Joseph William *labor arbitrator, economics and business educator*

El Segundo
†Codon, Dennis P. *lawyer*

Elverta
Betts, Barbara Lang *lawyer, rancher, realtor*

Emeryville
Chilvers, Robert Merritt *lawyer*
Taylor, William James (Zak Taylor) *lawyer*

Encinitas
Williams, Michael Edward *lawyer*

Encino
Hoefflin, Richard Michael *lawyer, judicial administrator, contractor*
Kent, Thomas Edward *lawyer*
Luna, Barbara Carole *financial analyst, accountant, appraiser*
Smith, Selma Moidel *lawyer, composer*
Sperber, David Sol *lawyer*

Fairfield
Honeychurch, Denis Arthur *lawyer*
Moore, Marianna Gay *law librarian, consultant*

Felton
Kulzick, Kenneth Edmund *retired lawyer, writer*

Folsom
Emery, Nancy Beth *lawyer*

Foster City
Lonnquist, George Eric *lawyer*

Fremont
Cummings, John Patrick *lawyer*

Fresno
Ewell, A. Ben, Jr. *lawyer, businessman*
Jamison, Oliver Morton *retired lawyer*
Lambe, James Patrick *lawyer*
Palmer, Samuel Copeland, III *lawyer*
Sherr, Morris Max *lawyer*

Fullerton
Bakken, Gordon Morris *law educator*
Everett, Pamela Irene *legal management company executive, educator*
Goldstein, Edward David *lawyer, former glass company executive*
Moerbeek, Stanley Leonard *lawyer*
Parsons, Rodney Hunter *lawyer*
Roberts, Mark Scott *lawyer*

Glendale
Hoffman, Donald M. *lawyer*
Kazanjian, Phillip Carl *lawyer, business executive*
MacDonald, Kirk Stewart *lawyer*
Martin, John Hugh *lawyer, retired*
Martinetti, Ronald Anthony *lawyer*
Scott, A. Timothy *lawyer*
Simpson, Allyson Bilich *lawyer*
Toscano, Oscar Ernesto *lawyer*

Gold River
Andrew, John Henry *lawyer, retail corporation executive*

Granite Bay
Holtz, Sara *lawyer, consultant*

Grass Valley
Hawkins, Richard Michael *lawyer*

Half Moon Bay
Lambert, Frederick William *lawyer, educator*

Hayward
Smith, John Kerwin *lawyer*

Hillsborough
Zimmerman, Bryant Kable *retired lawyer*

Imperial
O'Leary, Thomas Michael *lawyer*

Imperial Beach
Merkin, William Leslie *lawyer*

Irvine
Bastiaanse, Gerard C. *lawyer*
Cahill, Richard Frederick *lawyer*
Clark, Karen Heath *lawyer*
Fisher, Lawrence N. *lawyer*
Fybel, Richard D. *lawyer*
Gauntlett, David Allan *lawyer*
Jeffers, Michael Bogue *lawyer*
Muller, Edward Robert *lawyer*
Petrasich, John Moris *lawyer*
Puzder, Andrew F. *lawyer*
Ristau, Kenneth Eugene, Jr. *lawyer*
Specter, Richard Bruce *lawyer*
Thomas, Joseph Edward *lawyer*
Toledano, James *lawyer*
Weissbard, Samuel Held *lawyer*
Weissenberger, Harry George *lawyer*
Williams, S. Linn *lawyer*
Wintrode, Ralph Charles *lawyer*

King City
Bolles, Donald Scott *lawyer*

La Canada Flintridge
Costello, Francis William *lawyer*
Wallace, James Wendell *lawyer*

La Habra
Kent, Jeffrey Donald *lawyer*

La Jolla
Kirchheimer, Arthur E(dward) *lawyer, business executive*
Siegan, Bernard Herbert *lawyer, educator*
Wilkins, Floyd, Jr. *retired lawyer, consultant*

Laguna Beach
Simons, Barry Thomas *lawyer*

Laguna Hills
Reinglass, Michelle Annette *lawyer*

Larkspur
Greenberg, Myron Silver *lawyer*
Maier, Peter Klaus *business executive*
Ratner, David Louis *retired law educator*

Long Beach
Boccia Rosado, Ann Marie *paralegal*
Calhoun, John R. *lawyer*
Johnson, Philip Leslie *lawyer*
Lodwick, Michael Wayne *lawyer*
Russell, Thomas Arthur *lawyer*
Taylor, Reese Hale, Jr. *lawyer, former government administrator*
Vander Lans, John Anthony *city prosecutor*
Wise, George Edward *lawyer*

Los Alamitos
Peters, Samuel Anthony *lawyer*

Los Altos
Bell, Richard G. *lawyer*
Weir, Robert H. *lawyer*

Los Altos Hills
Alexander, Katharine Violet *lawyer*

Los Angeles
†Aaron, Benjamin *law educator, arbitrator*
Abrams, Norman *law educator, university administrator*
Adamek, Charles Andrew *lawyer*
Adams, Thomas Merritt *lawyer*
Adell, Hirsch *lawyer*
Adler, Erwin Ellery *lawyer*
Adler, Sara *arbitrator, mediator*
Antin, Michael *lawyer*
Apfel, Gary *lawyer*
April, Rand Scott *lawyer*
Arbit, Beryl Ellen *legal assistant*
Arnold, Dennis B. *lawyer*
Barrett, Jane Hayes *lawyer*
Barton, Alan Joel *lawyer*
Barza, Harold A. *lawyer*
Baum, Michael Lin *lawyer*
Bauman, John Andrew *law educator*
Baumann, Richard Gordon *lawyer*
Beard, Ronald Stratton *lawyer*
Belleville, Philip Frederick *lawyer*
†Bender, Charles William *lawyer*
Bendix, Helen Irene *lawyer*
Bennett, Fred Gilbert *lawyer*
Berman, Myles Lee *lawyer*
Bernacchi, Richard Lloyd *lawyer*
Bernhard, Herbert Ashley *lawyer*
Bice, Scott Haas *lawyer, educator*
Biederman, Donald Ellis *lawyer*
Bierstedt, Peter Richard *lawyer, entertainment industry consultant*
Bishop, Sidney Willard *lawyer*
Black, Donna Ruth *lawyer*
Blackman, Lee L. *lawyer*
Blencowe, Paul Sherwood *lawyer*
Blumberg, Grace Ganz *law educator, lawyer*
Bodkin, Henry Grattan, Jr. *lawyer*
Bogaard, William Joseph *lawyer*
Bogen, Andrew E. *lawyer*
Bomes, Stephen D. *lawyer*
Bonner, Robert Cleve *lawyer*
Borenstein, Mark A. *lawyer*
Bortman, David *lawyer*
Bosl, Phillip L. *lawyer*
Bradley, Lawrence D., Jr. *lawyer*
Branca, John Gregory *lawyer, consultant*
Brandler, Jonathan M. *lawyer*
Braun, David A(dlai) *lawyer*
Breidenbach, Francis Anthony *lawyer*
Bressan, Paul Louis *lawyer*
Brickwood, Susan Callaghan *lawyer*
Bringardner, John Michael *lawyer, clergyman*
Brittenham, Skip *lawyer*
Broussard, Thomas Rollins *lawyer*
Burch, Robert Dale *lawyer*
Burke, Robert Bertram *lawyer, political consultant, lobbyist*
Burns, Marvin Gerald *lawyer*
Byrd, Christine Waterman Swent *lawyer*
Byrne, Jerome Camillus *lawyer*
Capron, Alexander Morgan *lawyer, educator*
Carlson, Robert Edwin *lawyer*
Carr, James Patrick *lawyer*
Carr, Willard Zeller, Jr. *lawyer*
Carrey, Neil *lawyer, educator*
Cartwright, Brian Grant *lawyer*
Castro, Leonard Edward *lawyer*
Cathcart, David Arthur *lawyer*
Chiate, Kenneth Reed *lawyer*
Chin, Llewellyn Philip *lawyer*
Christol, Carl Q(uimby) *lawyer, political science educator*
Chu, Morgan *lawyer*
Clark, Rufus Bradbury *lawyer*
Cleary, William Joseph, Jr. *lawyer*
Cochran, Johnnie L., Jr. *lawyer*
Cohan, John Robert *retired lawyer*
Cohen, Cynthia Marylyn *lawyer*
Coleman, Rexford Lee *lawyer, educator*
Collier, Charles Arthur, Jr. *lawyer*
Cooper, Leon Melvin *lawyer*
Dana, Lauren Elizabeth *lawyer*
Daniels, John Peter *lawyer*
Darby, G(eorge) Harrison *lawyer*
Darden, Christopher A. *lawyer, actor, writer*

Davis, Edmond Ray *lawyer*
De Brier, Donald Paul *lawyer*
de Castro, Hugo Daniel *lawyer*
DeLuce, Richard David *lawyer*
Denham, Robert Edwin *lawyer, investment company executive*
Deukmejian, George *lawyer, former governor*
Diamond, Stanley Jay *lawyer*
Dickson, Robert Lee *lawyer*
Donovan, John Arthur *lawyer*
Dryden, Mary Elizabeth *law librarian, writer, actress*
Dudziak, Mary Louise *law educator, lecturer*
Eckardt, Richard William *lawyer*
Emanuel, William Joseph *lawyer*
English, Stephen Raymond *lawyer*
Etra, Donald *lawyer*
Faal, Edi M. O. *lawyer*
Fairbank, Robert Harold *lawyer*
Farmer, Robert Lindsay *lawyer*
Feigen, Brenda S. *literary manager, lawyer, motion picture producer*
Field, Richard Clark *lawyer*
Fields, Bertram Harris *lawyer*
Fisher, Richard N. *lawyer*
Fohrman, Burton H. *lawyer*
Follick, Edwin Duane *law educator, chiropractic physician*
Ford, Donald Hainline *lawyer*
Frackman, Russell Jay *lawyer*
Fragner, Matthew Charles *lawyer*
Franceschi, Ernest Joseph, Jr. *lawyer*
Francis, Merrill Richard *lawyer*
Fredman, Howard S *lawyer*
Friedman, Alan E. *lawyer*
Frimmer, Paul Norman *lawyer*
Gallo, Jon Joseph *lawyer*
Galton, Stephen Harold *lawyer*
Garcetti, Gilbert I. *prosecutor*
Gebb, Sheldon Alexander *lawyer*
Gentile, Joseph F. *lawyer, educator*
Gest, Howard David *lawyer*
Gilbert, Robert Wolfe *lawyer*
Glazer, Michael *lawyer*
Glick, Earl A. *lawyer*
Glushien, Morris P. *lawyer, arbitrator*
Goldman, Allan Bailey *lawyer*
Goldman, Benjamin Edward *lawyer*
Goodman, Max A. *lawyer, educator*
Gordon, David Eliot *lawyer*
Gorman, Joseph Gregory, Jr. *lawyer*
Gould, Charles Perry *lawyer*
Gould, David *lawyer*
Grausam, Jeffrey Leonard *lawyer*
Green, Kenneth Norton *law educator*
Green, William Porter *lawyer*
Griffey, Linda Boyd *lawyer*
Grimwade, Richard Llewellyn *lawyer*
Grobe, Charles Stephen *lawyer, accountant*
Gross, Allen Jeffrey *lawyer*
Grosz, Philip J. *lawyer*
Gurfein, Peter J. *lawyer*
Gyemant, Robert Ernest *lawyer*
Hahn, James Kenneth *lawyer*
Halkett, Alan Neilson *lawyer*
Handzlik, Jan Lawrence *lawyer*
Hansell, Dean *lawyer*
Hanson, John J. *lawyer*
Havel, Richard W. *lawyer*
Hayes, Byron Jackson, Jr. *retired lawyer*
Hayutin, David Lionel *lawyer*
Hedlund, Paul James *lawyer*
Heinke, Rex S. *lawyer*
Heller, Philip *lawyer*
Hemminger, Pamela Lynn *lawyer*
Heyck, Theodore Daly *lawyer*
Heyler, Grover Ross *retired lawyer*
Hieronymus, Edward Whittlesey *lawyer*
Highberger, William Foster *lawyer*
Hight, B. Boyd *lawyer*
Hinerfeld, Robert Elliot *lawyer*
Hirsch, Barry L. *lawyer*
Holliday, Thomas Edgar *lawyer*
Holtzman, Robert Arthur *lawyer*
Hough, Steven Hedges *lawyer*
Howard, Nancy E. *lawyer*
Huben, Brian David *lawyer*
Hudson, Jeffrey Reid *lawyer*
Hufstedler, Seth Martin *lawyer*
Hufstedler, Shirley Mount (Mrs. Seth M. Hufstedler) *lawyer, former federal judge*
Hyman, Milton Bernard *lawyer*
Iamele, Richard Thomas *law librarian*
Irwin, Philip Donnan *lawyer*
Jacobs, Randall Brian *lawyer*
James, William J. *lawyer*
Janofsky, Leonard S. *lawyer, association executive*
Johnson, Jonathan Edwin, II *lawyer*
Jordan, Robert Leon *lawyer, educator*
Kadison, Stuart *lawyer and educator*
Kamine, Bernard Samuel *lawyer*
Karst, Kenneth Leslie *legal educator*
Kendig, Ellsworth Harold, Jr. *retired corporate lawyer*
Kiekhofer, William Henry *lawyer*
Kindel, James Horace, Jr. *lawyer*
Kirwan, R. DeWitt *lawyer*
Klein, Jeffrey S. *lawyer, media executive*
Kleinberg, Marvin H. *lawyer*
Klinger, Marilyn Sydney *lawyer*
Klowden, Michael Louis *lawyer*
Koelzer, George Joseph *lawyer*
Kuechle, John Merrill *lawyer*
Kupietzky, Moshe J. *lawyer*
Kupperman, Henry John *lawyer*
Lappen, Chester I. *lawyer*
Latham, Joseph Al, Jr. *lawyer*
Lauchengco, Jose Yujuico, Jr. *lawyer*
Lavin, Laurence Michael *lawyer*
Lawton, Eric *lawyer, photographer, visual artist, writer*
Le Berthon, Adam *lawyer*
Leibow, Ronald Louis *lawyer*
Lesser, Joan L. *lawyer*
Letwin, Leon *legal educator*
Leung, Frankie Fook-Lun *lawyer*
Levine, C. Bruce *lawyer*
Levine, Thomas Jeffrey Pello *lawyer*
Liebeler, Wesley J. *law educator, lawyer*
Lindholm, Dwight Henry *lawyer*
Link, George Hamilton *lawyer*
Lipsig, Ethan *lawyer*
Loeb, Ronald Marvin *lawyer*
Long, Gregory Alan *lawyer*
Lublinski, Michael *lawyer*
Lund, James Louis *lawyer*
Lynch, Patrick *lawyer*
MacLaughlin, Francis Joseph *lawyer*
Manatt, Charles Taylor *lawyer*
Mancino, Douglas Michael *lawyer*
Manella, Nora M. *US district judge*
Marcus, Stephen Howard *lawyer*
Marshall, Arthur K. *lawyer, judge, arbitrator, educator, writer*
May, Lawrence Edward *lawyer*
McAniff, Edward John *lawyer*
McDermott, John E. *lawyer*
McDermott, Thomas John, Jr. *lawyer*
McKinzie, Carl Wayne *lawyer*
McKnight, Frederick L. *lawyer*
McLane, Frederick Berg *lawyer*
Medearis, Miller *lawyer*
Mellinkoff, David *lawyer, educator*
Metzger, Robert Streicher *lawyer*
Meyer, Michael Edwin *lawyer*
Millard, Neal Steven *lawyer*
Miller, Milton Allen *lawyer*
Mintz, Marshall Gary *lawyer*
Mintz, Ronald Steven *lawyer, photojournalist*
Molleur, Richard Raymond *lawyer*
Moloney, Stephen Michael *lawyer*
Morgenthaler, Alisa Marie *lawyer*
Mosk, Richard Mitchell *lawyer*
Moskowitz, Joel Steven *lawyer*
Moyer, Craig Alan *lawyer*
Neely, Sally Schultz *lawyer*
Neiter, Gerald Irving *lawyer*
Nelson, Grant Steel *lawyer, educator*
Newman, David Wheeler *lawyer*
Newman, Michael Rodney *lawyer*
Nibley, Robert Ricks *retired lawyer*
Nicholas, William Richard *lawyer*
Niemeth, Charles Frederick *lawyer*
Niese, William A. *lawyer, newspaper publishing executive*
Niles, John Gilbert *lawyer*
Noble, Richard Lloyd *lawyer*
Nocas, Andrew James *lawyer*
Nochimson, David *lawyer*
O'Connell, Kevin *lawyer*
O'Donnell, Pierce Henry *lawyer*
Olivas, Daniel A. *lawyer*
Olsen, Frances Elisabeth *law educator, theorist*
Ordin, Andrea Sheridan *lawyer*
Owen, Michael Lee *lawyer*
Packard, Robert Charles *lawyer*
Palazzo, Robert P. *lawyer, accountant*
Papiano, Neil Leo *lawyer*
Parsky, Gerald Lawrence *lawyer*
Pasich, Kirk Alan *lawyer*
Peck, Austin H., Jr. *lawyer*
Pedersen, Norman A. *lawyer*
Perry, Ralph Barton, III *lawyer*
Peters, Aulana Louise *lawyer, former government agency commissioner*
Peters, Richard T. *lawyer*
Pircher, Leo Joseph *lawyer*
Poindexter, William Mersereau *lawyer*
Polley, Terry Lee *lawyer*
Pollock, John Phleger *lawyer*
Porter, Verna Louise *lawyer*
Power, John Bruce *lawyer*
Preonas, George Elias *lawyer*
Presant, Sanford Calvin *lawyer, educator, author, lecturer*
Pritsker, Keith Wayne *lawyer*
Pugsley, Robert Adrian *law educator*
Rabinovitz, Joel *lawyer, educator*
Rae, Matthew Sanderson, Jr. *lawyer*
Rappeport, Ira J. *lawyer*
Rath, Howard Grant, Jr. *lawyer*
Ray, Gilbert T. *lawyer*
Reeves, Barbara Ann *lawyer*
Renwick, Edward S. *lawyer*
Reynoso, Cruz *lawyer, educator*
Richardson, Arthur Wilhelm *lawyer*
Richardson, Douglas Fielding *lawyer*
Ring, Michael Wilson *lawyer*
Robison, William Robert *lawyer*
Roney, John Harvey *lawyer, consultant*
Rosenthal, Sol *lawyer*
Rosett, Arthur Irwin *lawyer, educator*
Rothenberg, Alan I. *lawyer, professional sports association executive*
Rothman, Frank *lawyer, motion picture company executive*
Rutter, Marshall Anthony *lawyer*
Salvaty, Benjamin Benedict *lawyer*
Samet, Jack I. *lawyer*
Saxe, Deborah Crandall *lawyer*
Schmidt, Karl A. *lawyer*
Scoular, Robert Frank *lawyer*
Shanks, Patricia L. *lawyer*
Shapiro, Marvin Seymour *lawyer*
Shapiro, Robert Leslie *lawyer*
Sheehan, Lawrence James *lawyer*
Shortz, Richard Alan *lawyer*
Shultz, John David *lawyer*
Silbergeld, Arthur F. *lawyer*
Slavitt, Earl Benton *lawyer*
Snyder, Arthur Kress *lawyer*
Snyder, Christina A. *lawyer*
Stamm, Alan *lawyer*
Stephens, George Edward, Jr. *lawyer*
Stone, Lawrence Maurice *lawyer, educator*
Straw, Lawrence Joseph, Jr. *lawyer*
Streiker, Susan L. *law librarian*
Stromberg, Ross Ernest *lawyer*
Strong, George Gordon, Jr. *litigation and management consultant*
Stuppi, Craig *lawyer*
Sullivan, Peter Meredith *lawyer*
Sumner, James DuPre, Jr. *lawyer, educator*
Tarr, Ralph William *lawyer, former federal government official*
Taylor, Minna *lawyer*
Teele, Cynthia Lombard *lawyer*
Thoren-Peden, Deborah Suzanne *lawyer*
Thorpe, Douglas L. *lawyer*
Tinsley, Walton Eugene *retired lawyer*
Title, Gail Migdal *lawyer*
Tobisman, Stuart Paul *lawyer*
Treister, George Marvin *lawyer*
Trimble, Phillip Richard *law educator*
Troy, Joseph Freed *lawyer*
Trygstad, Lawrence Benson *lawyer*
Ukropina, James R. *lawyer*
Valenzuela, Manuel Anthony, Jr. *lawyer*
Van de Kamp, John Kalar *lawyer*
Vanderet, Robert Charles *lawyer*
Vaughn, William Weaver *lawyer*
Volpert, Richard Sidney *lawyer*
von Kalinowski, Julian Onesime *lawyer*
Wagner, Darryl William *lawyer*
Wainess, Marcia Watson *legal management consultant*
Walcher, Alan Ernest *lawyer*
Walker, Charles Montgomery *lawyer*
†Wallock, Terrence J. *corporate lawyer*
Wayte, (Paul) Alan *lawyer*
Weil, Robert Irving *arbitrator, mediator, retired judge*
Weinman, Glenn Alan *lawyer*
Weinstock, Harold *lawyer*
Weiss, Walter Stanley *lawyer*
Wessling, Robert Bruce *lawyer*
Wheat, Francis Millspaugh *retired lawyer*
White, Robert Joel *lawyer*
Whitmore, Bruce G. *lawyer*
Wigmore, John Grant *lawyer*
Williams, Donald Clyde *lawyer*
Williams, Richard Thomas *lawyer*
Wilson, Donald Kenneth, Jr. *lawyer, publisher*
Wilson, Mable Jean *paralegal*
Windham, Timothy Ray *lawyer*
Wine, Mark Philip *lawyer*
Wolfen, Werner F. *lawyer*
Woodland, Irwin Francis *lawyer*
Wright, Kenneth Brooks *lawyer*
York, Gary Alan *lawyer*
Zelon, Laurie Dee *lawyer*
Ziffren, Kenneth *lawyer*

Los Gatos
Seligmann, William Robert *lawyer, author*

Malibu
Darraby, Jessica L. *lawyer, educator, writer*

Marina Del Rey
Orr, Ronald Stewart *lawyer*
Wineman, Paul Raymond, Jr. *contract negotiator*

Martinez
Bray, Absalom Francis, Jr. *lawyer*
Williams, Charles Judson *lawyer*

Mendocino
Rappaport, Stuart Ramon *lawyer*

Menlo Park
Bader, W(illiam) Reece *lawyer*
Coats, William Sloan, III *lawyer*
Crandall, Nelson David, III *lawyer*
Ehrlich, Thomas *educator*
Gunderson, Robert Vernon, Jr. *lawyer*
Kaufman, Christopher Lee *lawyer*
Kirk, Cassius Lamb, Jr. *lawyer, investor*
Madison, James Raymond *lawyer*
Millard, Richard Steven *lawyer*
Sauers, William Dale *lawyer, playwright*
Scott, Michael Dennis *lawyer*
Taylor, Robert P. *lawyer*
Wegner, Judith Welch *law educator, dean*

Middletown
Downing, James Christie *lawyer*

Mill Valley
Nemir, Donald Philip *lawyer*

Millbrae
Lande, James Avra *lawyer, contracts manager*
Rosenthal, Herbert Marshall *lawyer*

Mission Viejo
Sessions, Don David *lawyer*

Modesto
Owens, Jack Byron *lawyer*

Monte Rio
Pemberton, John de Jarnette, Jr. *lawyer, educator*

Monterey
Bomberger, Russell Branson *lawyer, writer*
Fenton, Lewis Lowry *lawyer*
Haddad, Louis Nicholas *paralegal*
Stern, Gerald Daniel *lawyer*

Monterey Park
Groce, Ewin Petty *lawyer*

Morgan Hill
Foster, John Robert *lawyer*

Napa
Kuntz, Charles Powers *lawyer*

Newport Beach
Adams, William Gillette *lawyer*
Allen, Russell G. *lawyer*
Baskin, Scott David *lawyer*
Black, William Rea *lawyer*
Cano, Kristin Maria *lawyer*
Clark, Thomas P., Jr. *lawyer*
Copenbarger, Lloyd Gaylord *lawyer*
Hancock, S. Lee *lawyer*
Johnson, Thomas Webber, Jr. *lawyer*
Katayama, Arthur Shoji *lawyer*
Knobbe, Louis Joseph *lawyer*
Logan, April Charise *lawyer*
Mallory, Frank Linus *lawyer*
Mandel, Maurice, II *lawyer, educator*
McEvers, Duff Steven *lawyer*
McGee, James Francis *lawyer*
Millar, Richard William, Jr. *lawyer*
Pepe, Stephen Phillip *lawyer*
Phillips, Layn R. *lawyer*
Rooklidge, William Charles *lawyer*
Schnapp, Roger Herbert *lawyer*
Wagner, John Leo *lawyer, former magistrate judge*
Wentworth, Theodore Sumner *lawyer*
Wolf, Alan Steven *lawyer*

North Fork
Flanagan, James Henry, Jr. *lawyer*

Novato
Lewin, Werner Siegfried, Jr. *lawyer*

Oakland
Allen, Jeffrey Michael *lawyer*
Bjork, Robert David, Jr. *lawyer*
Burnison, Boyd Edward *lawyer*
Deming, Willis Riley *lawyer*
Drexel, Baron Jerome *lawyer*
Heywood, Robert Gilmour *lawyer*
Johnson, Kenneth F. *lawyer*
Leslie, Robert Lorne *lawyer*
McCarthy, Steven Michael *lawyer*
Mendelson, Steven Earle *lawyer*
Miller, Kirk Edward *lawyer, health foundation executive*
Miller, Thomas Robbins *lawyer, publisher*
O'Connor, Paul Daniel *lawyer*
Patton, Roger William *lawyer, educator*
Quinby, William Albert *lawyer, mediator, arbitrator*
Skaff, Andrew Joseph *lawyer, public utilities, energy and transportation executive*
Stromme, Gary L. *law librarian*
Thompson Stanley, Trina *lawyer*
Wallace, Elaine Wendy *lawyer*
Wallis, Eric G. *lawyer*
Wood, James Michael *lawyer*

Orange
Batchelor, James Kent *lawyer*
†Sawdei, Milan A. *lawyer*

Orinda
Welch, Thomas Andrew *retired lawyer, arbitrator*

Oxnard
O'Hearn, Michael John *lawyer*

Pacific Palisades
Cale, Charles Griffin *lawyer, investor*
Dean, Ronald Glenn *lawyer*
Flattery, Thomas Long *lawyer, legal administrator*
Lagle, John Franklin *lawyer*
Rothenberg, Leslie Steven *lawyer, ethicist*
Schwartz, Murray Louis *lawyer, educator, academic administrator*
Sevilla, Stanley *lawyer*

Palm Desert
Singer, Gerald Michael *lawyer, educator, author, arbitrator and mediator*
Spirtos, Nicholas George *lawyer, financial company executive*

Palm Springs
FitzGerald, John Edward, III *lawyer*
Kimberling, John Farrell *retired lawyer*

Palmdale
Reichman, Dawn Leslie *lawyer, educator, deputy sheriff*

Palo Alto
Bradley, Donald Edward *lawyer*
Brigham, Samuel Townsend Jack, III *lawyer*
Climan, Richard Elliot *lawyer*
Donnally, Robert Andrew *lawyer, real estate broker*
Furbush, David Malcolm *lawyer*
Haslam, Robert Thomas, III *lawyer*
Klotsche, John Chester *lawyer*
Laurie, Ronald Sheldon *lawyer*
Lesser, Henry *lawyer*
Massey, Henry P., Jr. *lawyer*
Mendelson, Alan Charles *lawyer*
Miller, Michael Patiky *lawyer*
Moretti, August Joseph *lawyer*
Nau, Charles John *lawyer*
Nopar, Alan Scott *lawyer*
Nordlund, Donald Craig *corporate lawyer*
Nycum, Susan Hubbell *lawyer*
O'Rourke, C. Larry *lawyer*
Pasahow, Lynn H(arold) *lawyer*
Patterson, Robert Edward *lawyer*
Phair, Joseph Baschon *lawyer*
Pooley, James *lawyer, author*
Ragan, Charles Ransom *lawyer*
Rinsky, Arthur C. *lawyer*
Small, Jonathan Andrew *lawyer*
Smith, Glenn A. *lawyer*
Tiffany, Joseph Raymond, II *lawyer*
Van Atta, David Murray *lawyer*
Walker, Ann Yvonne *lawyer*
Wheeler, Raymond Louis *lawyer*

Palos Verdes Estates
Toftness, Cecil Gillman *lawyer, consultant*

Palos Verdes Peninsula
Yeomans, Russell Allen *lawyer, translator*

Pasadena
Ammirato, Vincent Anthony *lawyer*
Ashley-Farrand, Margalo *lawyer, mediator, private judge*
Bakaly, Charles George, Jr. *lawyer, mediator*
Bunt Smith, Helen Marguerite *lawyer*
Calleton, Theodore Edward *lawyer*
Chan, Daniel Chung-Yin *lawyer*
D'Angelo, Robert William *lawyer*
Epstein, Bruce Howard *lawyer, real estate broker*
Haight, James Theron *lawyer, corporate executive*
Hale, Charles Russell *lawyer*
Hunt, Gordon *lawyer*
Koch, Albin Cooper *lawyer*
Linstedt, Walter Griffiths *lawyer, banker*
Lisoni, Gail Marie Landtbom *lawyer*
Logan, Francis Dummer *lawyer*
Mosher, Sally Ekenberg *lawyer, musician*
Mueth, Joseph Edward *lawyer*
Myers, R(alph) Chandler *lawyer*
Pianko, Theodore A. *lawyer*
Talt, Alan R. *lawyer*
Tanner, Dee Boshard *retired lawyer*
van Schoonenberg, Robert G. *corporate lawyer*
Wyatt, Joseph Lucian, Jr. *lawyer, author*
Yohalem, Harry Morton *lawyer*

Paso Robles
Knecht, James Herbert *lawyer*

Pebble Beach
Maxeiner, Clarence William *lawyer, construction company executive*

Piedmont
McCormick, Timothy Brian Beer *lawyer*

Pleasant Hill
†McQueen, Geoffrey Pierce *lawyer*

Pleasanton
Scott, G. Judson, Jr. *lawyer*

Staley, John Fredric *lawyer*

Plymouth
Andreason, John Christian *lawyer*

Pomona
Palmer, Robert Alan *lawyer, educator*

Portola Valley
Cooper, John Joseph *lawyer*

Rancho Cordova
Lynch, Robert Berger *lawyer*

Rancho Mirage
Goldie, Ray Robert *lawyer*
Leydorf, Frederick Leroy *lawyer*
Reuben, Don Harold *lawyer*
Vaughan, Joseph Robert *lawyer*

Rancho Santa Fe
Peterson, Nad A. *lawyer, retired corporate executive*
†Woolley, Roger Swire *lawyer*

Rancho Santa Margarita
Curtis, John Joseph *lawyer*

Redwood City
Heuman, Donna Rena *lawyer*
Rowland, John Arthur *lawyer*
Silvestri, Philip Salvatore *lawyer*
Tight, Dexter Corwin *lawyer*
Wilhelm, Robert Oscar *lawyer, civil engineer, developer*

Richmond
Kirk-Duggan, Michael Allan *retired law and computer sciences educator*
Quenneville, Kathleen *lawyer*

Rio Linda
Lebrato, Mary Theresa *lawyer, psychologist*

Riverside
Aderton, Jane Reynolds *lawyer*
Chang, Janice May *lawyer, administrator, notary public*
Darling, Scott Edward *lawyer*
Graves, Patrick Lee *lawyer*
Marlatt, Michael James *lawyer*
Schwartz, Bernard Julian *lawyer*
Yamamoto, Stanly Tokio *city attorney*

Rolling Hills Estates
Rumbaugh, Charles Earl *arbitrator, mediator, educator, lawyer, speaker*

Rosemead
Danner, Bryant Craig *lawyer*

Sacramento
Blackman, David Michael *lawyer*
Blake, D. Steven *lawyer*
Bobrow, Susan Lukin *lawyer*
Brookman, Anthony Raymond *lawyer*
Burton, Randall James *lawyer*
Carrel, Marc Louis *lawyer, policy advisor*
Felderstein, Steven Howard *lawyer*
Friedman, Morton Lee *lawyer*
Gray-Fuson, Joan Lorraine *lawyer*
Houpt, James Edward *lawyer*
James, Robert William *lawyer, government executive*
Janigian, Bruce Jasper *lawyer, educator*
Keiner, Christian Mark *lawyer*
Malloy, Michael Patrick *law educator, author, consultant*
Phillips, Dana Wayne *lawyer*
Robbins, Stephen J. M. *lawyer*
Root, Gerald Edward *planning and operational support administrator*
†Seave, Paul L. *prosecutor*
Shelley, Susanne Mary *lawyer, mathematics educator*
Soble, Mark Richard *lawyer*
Stevens, Charles J. *former prosecutor, lawyer*
Twiss, Robert Manning *prosecutor*
Waks, Dennis Stanford *lawyer*
Wishek, Michael Bradley *lawyer*
Wroten, Walter Thomas *lawyer*
Zeff, Ophelia Hope *lawyer*

San Andreas
Arkin, Michael Barry *lawyer, arbitrator, writer*

San Anselmo
Murphy, Barry Ames *lawyer*

San Bernardino
Stout, Dennis Lee *district attorney*
Whitney, David *prosecutor*

San Diego
Alpert, Michael Edward *lawyer*
Andreos, George Phillip *lawyer*
Asaro, V. Frank *lawyer*
Brooks, John White *lawyer*
Buzunis, Constantine Dino *lawyer*
Chatroo, Arthur Jay *lawyer*
Copeland, Robert Glenn *lawyer*
Cox, Kim Carroll *lawyer, broadcaster*
Damoose, George Lynn *lawyer*
Dyer, Charles Richard *law librarian, law educator*
Frasch, Brian Bernard *lawyer*
Guinn, Stanley Willis *lawyer*
Howard, William Matthew *educator, lawyer, arbitrator, author*
Hutcheson, J(ames) Sterling *lawyer*
Klinedinst, John David *lawyer*
Kripke, Kenneth Norman *lawyer*
Lathrop, Mitchell Lee *lawyer*
LeBeau, Charles Paul *lawyer*
Mayer, James Hock *mediator, lawyer*
McGinnis, Robert E. *lawyer*
Meyer, Paul I. *lawyer*
Miller, William Charles *lawyer*
Mittermiller, James Joseph *lawyer*
Morris, Grant Harold *law educator*
Morris, Sandra Joan *lawyer*
Noziska, Charles Brant *lawyer*
O'Malley, James Terence *lawyer*
Payne, Margaret Anne *lawyer*
Peterson, Paul Ames *lawyer*
†Philipp, Adam Lief Kakimoto *lawyer*
Pray, Ralph Marble, III *lawyer*
Preston, David Raymond *lawyer*
Pugh, Richard Crawford *lawyer*
Roseman, Charles Sanford *lawyer*
Ross, Terry D. *lawyer*
St. George, William Ross *lawyer, retired naval officer, consultant*
Samuelson, Derrick William *lawyer*
Sceper, Duane Harold *lawyer*
Schuck, Carl Joseph *lawyer*
Shapiro, Philip Alan *lawyer*
Shearer, William Kennedy *lawyer, publisher*
Shelton, Dorothy Diehl Rees *lawyer*
Slomanson, William Reed *law educator, legal writer*
Smith, Steven Ray *law educator*
Snaid, Leon Jeffrey *lawyer*
Snyder, David Richard *lawyer*
Sterrett, James Kelley, II *lawyer*
Stiska, John Charles *lawyer*
Sullivan, Michelle Cornejo *lawyer*
Sullivan, William Francis *lawyer*
Underwood, Anthony Paul *lawyer*
Valliant, James Stevens *lawyer*
†Varela, José Hector *public defender*
Whitmore, Sharp *lawyer*
Witt, John William *lawyer*
Zakarin, Keith *lawyer*

San Francisco
Alexander, Mary Elsie *lawyer*
Alexander, Robert C. *lawyer*
Allen, Jose R. *lawyer*
Allen, Paul Alfred *lawyer, educator*
Alsup, William *lawyer*
Arbuthnot, Robert Murray *lawyer*
Archer, Richard Joseph *lawyer*
Baker, Cameron *lawyer*
Bancroft, James Ramsey *lawyer, business executive*
Barbagelata, Robert Dominic *lawyer*
Barber, James P. *lawyer*
Bates, William, III *lawyer*
Baxter, Ralph H., Jr. *lawyer*
Beck, Edward William *lawyer*
Bedford, Daniel Ross *lawyer*
Benvenutti, Peter J. *lawyer*
Bertain, G(eorge) Joseph, Jr. *lawyer*
Bertram, Phyllis Ann *lawyer, communications executive*
Bonapart, Alan David *lawyer*
Bondoc, Rommel *lawyer*
Bookin, Daniel Henry *lawyer*
Booth, Forrest *lawyer*
Borowsky, Philip *lawyer*
Boucher, Harold Irving *retired lawyer*
Boutin, Peter Rucker *lawyer*
Boyd, William Sprott *lawyer*
Bridges, Robert Lysle *retired lawyer*
Bridgman, Richard Darrell *lawyer*
Briggs, Susan Shadinger *lawyer*
Briscoe, John *lawyer*
Bromley, Dennis Karl *lawyer*
Brown, Donald Wesley *lawyer*
Brown, Geoffrey Francis *public defender, lawyer*
†Brown, Robert Elliott *lawyer*
Bruen, James A. *lawyer*
Burden, James Ewers *lawyer*
Burns, Brian Patrick *lawyer, business executive*
Bushnell, Roderick Paul *lawyer*
Callison, Russell James *lawyer*
Campbell, Scott Robert *lawyer, former food company executive*
Campisi, Dominic John *lawyer*
Carlson, John Earl *lawyer*
Carter, John Douglas *lawyer*
Cartmell, Nathaniel Madison, III *lawyer*
Chao, Cedric C. *lawyer*
Cheatham, Robert William *lawyer*
Chong, Rachelle B. *lawyer, federal communications commissioner*
Clopton, Karen Valentia *lawyer, president civil services commission*
Coffin, Judy Sue *lawyer*
Cohn, Nathan *lawyer*
Coleman, Thomas Young *lawyer*
Collas, Juan Garduño, Jr. *lawyer*
Cook, John C. *lawyer*
Coombe, George William, Jr. *lawyer, retired banker*
Corcoran, Maureen Elizabeth *lawyer*
Crawford, Roy Edgington, III *lawyer*
Cumming, George Anderson, Jr. *lawyer*
Davies, Paul Lewis, Jr. *retired lawyer*
Davis, Roger Lewis *lawyer*
†Dell, Robert Michael *lawyer*
DeMuro, Paul Robert *lawyer*
Diamond, Philip Ernest *lawyer*
Diekmann, Gilmore Frederick, Jr. *lawyer*
Donnici, Peter Joseph *lawyer, law educator, consultant*
Donovan, Charles Stephen *lawyer*
Drozd, Leon Frank, Jr. *lawyer*
Dryden, Robert Eugene *lawyer*
Dunne, Kevin Joseph *lawyer*
Dupree, Stanley M. *lawyer*
Edginton, John Arthur *lawyer*
Edwards, Robin Morse *lawyer*
Elderkin, E(dwin) Judge *retired lawyer*
Ericson, Bruce Alan *lawyer*
Fergus, Gary Scott *lawyer*
Finberg, James Michael *lawyer*
Finck, Kevin William *lawyer*
Fine, Marjorie Lynn *lawyer*
Fogel, Paul David *lawyer*
Folberg, Harold Jay *lawyer, mediator, educator, university dean*
Forsythe, Janet Winifred *lawyer*
Foster, David Scott *lawyer*
Fredericks, Dale Edward *lawyer*
Freeman, Tom M. *lawyer*
Freud, Nicholas S. *lawyer*
Friedman, K. Bruce *lawyer*
Friese, Robert Charles *lawyer*
Furth, Frederick Paul *lawyer*
Gaither, James C. *lawyer*
Garvey, Joanne Marie *lawyer*
Gelhaus, Robert Joseph *lawyer, publisher*
Glazer, Jack Henry *lawyer*
†Goode, Barry Paul *lawyer*
Gowdy, Franklin Brockway *lawyer*
Gresham, Zane Oliver *lawyer*
Guggenhime, Richard Johnson *lawyer*
Hall, Paul J. *lawyer*
Halloran, Michael James *lawyer*
Hannawalt, Willis Dale *retired lawyer*
Hanschen, Peter Walter *lawyer*
Haven, Thomas Edward *lawyer*
Heafey, Edwin Austin, Jr. *lawyer*
Heilbron, David M(ichael) *lawyer*
Henderson, Dan Fenno *lawyer, law educator*
Heng, Donald James, Jr. *lawyer*
Henson, Ray David *legal educator, consultant*
Herlihy, Thomas Mortimer *lawyer*
Hilton, Stanley Goumas *lawyer, educator, writer*
Hinman, Harvey DeForest *lawyer*
Hofmann, John Richard, Jr. *lawyer*
Holden, Frederick Douglass, Jr. *lawyer*
Homer, Barry Wayne *lawyer*
†Hor, Johnson *contractor*
Howard, Carl (Michael) *lawyer*
Howe, Drayton Ford, Jr. *lawyer*
Hudner, Philip *lawyer, rancher*
Hudson, Mark Woodbridge *lawyer*
Hunt, James L. *lawyer*
Hunter, William Dennis *lawyer*
Hurabiell, John Philip, Sr. *lawyer*
Irwin, William Rankin *lawyer*
James, David Lee *lawyer, international advisor, author*
Johns, Richard Seth Ellis *lawyer*
Johnson, Martin Wayne *lawyer*
Johnson, Reverdy *lawyer*
Joseph, Allan Jay *lawyer*
Jung, David Joseph *law educator*
Kallgren, Edward Eugene *lawyer*
Kane, Mary Kay *law educator, college dean*
Kaplan, Alvin Irving *lawyer, adjudicator, investigator*
Kasanin, Mark Owen *lawyer*
Kelly, J. Michael *lawyer*
Kemp, Alson Remington, Jr. *lawyer, legal educator*
Kennedy, Raoul Dion *lawyer*
Kern, John McDougall *lawyer*
Kerner, Michael Philip *lawyer*
Kimport, David Lloyd *lawyer*
Klott, David Lee *lawyer*
Knapp, Charles Lincoln *law educator*
Knebel, Jack Gillen *lawyer*
Knutzen, Martha Lorraine *lawyer*
Koeppel, John A. *lawyer*
Kuhl, Paul Beach *lawyer*
Ladar, Jerrold Morton *lawyer*
Lane, Fielding H. *lawyer*
Larson, John William *lawyer*
Lasky, Moses *lawyer*
Lee, John Jin *lawyer*
Levit, Victor Bert *lawyer, foreign representative, civic worker*
Libbin, Anne Edna *lawyer*
Lindstrom, Gregory P. *lawyer*
Livsey, Robert Callister *lawyer*
Lombardi, David Ennis, Jr. *lawyer, lecturer, mediator*
Lotito, Michael Joseph *lawyer*
MacGowan, Eugenia *lawyer*
Mann, Bruce Alan *lawyer*
Manning, Jerome Alan *lawyer*
Marchant, David Judson *lawyer*
Marcus, Richard Leon *lawyer, educator*
Martel, John Sheldon *lawyer, author*
Mason, Cheryl White *lawyer*
Mattes, Martin Anthony *lawyer*
McElhinny, Harold John *lawyer*
McGuckin, John Hugh, Jr. *lawyer*
McKelvey, Judith Grant *lawyer, educator, university dean*
Mc Laughlin, Jerome Michael *lawyer, shipping company executive*
McNally, Thomas Charles, III *lawyer*
McNamara, Thomas Neal *lawyer*
Meadows, John Frederick *lawyer*
Mellor, Michael Lawton *lawyer*
Metzler, Roger James, Jr. *lawyer*
Mihan, Ralph George *lawyer*
Miller, William Napier Cripps *lawyer*
Millstein, David J. *lawyer*
Minnick, Malcolm David *lawyer*
Mitchell, Bruce Tyson *lawyer*
Moore, Scott Michael *lawyer*
Morrissey, John Carroll, Sr. *lawyer*
Musfelt, Duane Clark *lawyer*
Musser, Sandra G. *retired lawyer*
Mussman, William Edward, III *lawyer*
Odgers, Richard William *lawyer*
Offer, Stuart Jay *lawyer*
Olejko, Mitchell J. *lawyer*
Olson, Walter Gilbert *lawyer*
Penskar, Mark Howard *lawyer*
Philipsborn, John Timothy *lawyer, author*
Phillips, Steve *lawyer, past president board of education*
Poole, Gordon Leicester *lawyer*
Popofsky, Melvin Laurence *lawyer*
Ramey, Drucilla Stender *legal association executive*
Raven, Robert Dunbar *lawyer*
Reding, John Anthony *lawyer*
Reese, John Robert *lawyer*
Rembe, Toni *lawyer*
Renfrew, Charles Byron *lawyer*
Renne, Louise Hornbeck *lawyer*
Rice, Denis Timlin *lawyer*
Richards, Norman Blanchard *lawyer*
Riley, Benjamin Kneeland *lawyer*
Robertson, J. Martin *lawyer*
Roethe, James Norton *lawyer*
Roman, Stan G. *lawyer*
Rosch, John Thomas *lawyer*
Rosen, Sanford Jay *lawyer*
Rossmann, Antonio *lawyer, educator*
Rubin, Michael *lawyer*
Russoniello, Joseph Pascal *lawyer*
Ryland, David Ronald *lawyer*
Salomon, Darrell Joseph *lawyer*
†Sarti, Edward R. *lawyer, accountant*
Scarlett, Randall H. *lawyer*
Schaffer, Jeffrey L. *lawyer*
Schwartz, Louis Brown *legal educator*
Seabolt, Richard L. *lawyer*
Seavey, William Arthur *lawyer, vintner*
Seegal, John Franklin *lawyer*
Seneker, Carl James, II (Kim Seneker) *lawyer*
Sevier, Ernest Youle *lawyer*
Shenk, George H. *lawyer*
Shepherd, John Michael *lawyer*
Sherry, Robert Joseph *lawyer*
Silk, Thomas *lawyer*
Singer, Allen Morris *lawyer*
Small, Marshall Lee *lawyer*
Smegal, Thomas Frank, Jr. *lawyer*
Smith, Kerry Clark *lawyer*
Snow, Tower Charles, Jr. *lawyer*
Soberon, Presentacion Zablan *state bar administrator*
Sparks, John Edward *lawyer*
Sparks, Thomas E., Jr. *lawyer*
Spiegel, Hart Hunter *retired lawyer*
Stanzler, Jordan *lawyer*
Staring, Graydon Shaw *lawyer*
Steer, Reginald David *lawyer*
Stephenson, Charles Gayley *lawyer*
Stinnett, Terrance Lloyd *lawyer*
Stotter, Lawrence Henry *lawyer*
Stratton, Richard James *lawyer*
Stroup, Stanley Stephenson *lawyer, educator*
Sugarman, Myron George *lawyer*
Sullivan, Robert Edward *lawyer*
Sutcliffe, Eric *lawyer*
Suter, Ben *lawyer*
Sutton, John Paul *lawyer*
Thompson, Robert Charles *lawyer*
Thornton, D. Whitney, II *lawyer*
Tingle, James O'Malley *lawyer*
Tobin, James Michael *lawyer*
Trautman, William Ellsworth *lawyer*
Traynor, John Michael *lawyer*
Truett, Harold Joseph, III (Tim Truett) *lawyer*
Venning, Robert Stanley *lawyer*
Walker, Ralph Clifford *lawyer*
Walker, Walter Herbert, III *lawyer, writer*
Walsh, Francis Richard *law educator, lawyer, arbitrator*
Wang, William Kai-Sheng *law educator*
Warmer, Richard Craig *lawyer*
Weber, Arnold I. *lawyer*
Weiner, Peter H. *lawyer*
Whelan, John William *lawyer, law educator, consultant*
Whitehead, David Barry *lawyer*
Wild, Nelson Hopkins *lawyer*
Willson, Prentiss, Jr. *lawyer*
Wingate, C. Keith *legal educator*
Wolfe, Cameron Withgot, Jr. *lawyer*
Wood, Robert Warren *lawyer*
Woods, James Robert *lawyer*
Worthington, Bruce R. *lawyer*
Wyle, Frederick S. *lawyer*
Yamakawa, David Kiyoshi, Jr. *lawyer*
Young, Bryant Llewellyn *lawyer, business executive*
Ziering, William Mark *lawyer*

San Jose
Anderson, Edward Virgil *lawyer*
Beizer, Lance Kurt *lawyer*
Bohn, Robert Herbert *lawyer*
Clark, William Frederick *lawyer*
Cummins, Charles Fitch, Jr. *lawyer*
Doan, Xuyen Van *lawyer*
Goldstein, Robin *lawyer*
Granneman, Vernon Henry *lawyer*
Greenstein, Martin Richard *lawyer*
Hannon, Timothy Patrick *lawyer, educator*
Hernández, Fernando Vargas *lawyer*
Katzman, Irwin *lawyer*
Kennedy, George Wendell *prosecutor*
Kraw, George Martin *lawyer, essayist*
McManis, James *lawyer*
Mitchell, David Walker *lawyer*
Morgan, Robert Hall *lawyer*
Nielsen, Christian Bayard *lawyer*
Towery, James E. *lawyer*

San Juan Capistrano
Brown, Robert G. *lawyer*

San Leandro
Newacheck, David John *lawyer*

San Marino
Baldwin, James William *lawyer*
Cranston, Howard Stephen *lawyer, management consultant*
Galbraith, James Marshall *lawyer, business executive*
Tomich, Lillian *lawyer*

San Mateo
Bell, Frank Ouray, Jr. *lawyer*
Grill, Lawrence J. *lawyer, accountant, corporate/banking executive*
Kenney, William Fitzgerald *lawyer*
Monaco, Daniel Joseph *lawyer*

San Rafael
Freitas, David Prince *lawyer*

San Ramon
Davis, John Albert *lawyer*
Freed, Kenneth Alan *lawyer*

Santa Ana
Capizzi, Michael Robert *prosecutor*
Dillard, John Martin *lawyer, pilot*
Dunn, Edward Thomas, Jr. *lawyer, educator*
Fay-Schmidt, Patricia Ann *paralegal*
Frost, Winston Lyle *lawyer, educator*
Harley, Robison Dooling, Jr. *lawyer, educator*
Schiff, Laurie *lawyer*
Storer, Maryruth *law librarian*
Zaenglein, William George, Jr. *lawyer*

Santa Barbara
Ah-Tye, Kirk Thomas *lawyer*
Bridges, B. Ried *lawyer*
Carlson, Arthur W. *lawyer*
Egenolf, Robert F. *lawyer*
Falstrom, Kenneth Edward *lawyer*
Gaines, Howard Clarke *retired lawyer*
Israel, Barry John *lawyer*
McEwen, Willard Winfield, Jr. *lawyer, judge*
Metzinger, Timothy Edward *lawyer*
Nelson, Sonja Bea *paralegal*
Shames, Henry Joseph *lawyer*
Simpson, Curtis Chapman, III *lawyer*
Stirling, Clark Tillman *lawyer*

Santa Clara
Alexander, George Jonathon *law educator, former dean*
Dunlap, F. Thomas, Jr. *lawyer, electronics company executive*
Kaner, Cem *lawyer, computer software consultant*
Wehde, Albert Edward *lawyer*

Santa Cruz
Kato, Pamela Kiyomi *lawyer*

Santa Monica
Boltz, Gerald Edmund *lawyer*
Bonesteel, Michael John *lawyer*
Bower, Allan Maxwell *lawyer*
Hirsch, Richard Gary *lawyer*
Jones, William Allen *lawyer, entertainment company executive*
Kanner, Gideon *lawyer*

Landay, Andrew Herbert *lawyer*
Loo, Thomas S. *lawyer*
McGovern, David Carr *lawyer*
McMillan, M. Sean *lawyer*
Prewoznik, Jerome Frank *lawyer*
Risman, Michael *lawyer, business executive, securities company executive*
Sheller, John Willard *lawyer*
Sperling, George Elmer, Jr. *lawyer*
Weatherup, Roy Garfield *lawyer*

Santa Rosa
Henderson, Joe H. *lawyer, mediator, arbitrator, college dean*

Saratoga
Stephens, Lawrence Keith *lawyer*

Sausalito
Berkman, William Roger *lawyer, army reserve officer*
Selman, Roland Wooten, III *lawyer*
Trimmer, Harold Sharp, Jr. *lawyer, international telecommunications consultant*

Seal Beach
Weitzman, Marc Herschel *lawyer*

Seaside
Weingarten, Saul Myer *lawyer*

Sherman Oaks
Gotcher, James Ronald *lawyer*
†Nemetz, Joseph C. *lawyer, plastic surgeon*

Solana Beach
Zwick, Shelly Crittendon *lawyer*

Solvang
Morrow, Richard Towson *lawyer*

Stanford
Babcock, Barbara Allen *lawyer, educator*
Brest, Paul A. *law educator*
Cohen, William *law educator*
Donohue, John Joseph *law educator*
Franklin, Marc Adam *law educator*
Friedman, Lawrence M. *law educator*
Goldstein, Paul *lawyer, educator*
Gunther, Gerald *lawyer, educator*
Mann, J. Keith *arbitrator, law educator, lawyer*
Roster, Michael *lawyer*
Scott, Kenneth Eugene *lawyer, educator*
Sofaer, Abraham David *lawyer, legal advisor, federal judge, law educator*

Stockton
Blewett, Robert Noall *lawyer*
Curtis, Orlie Lindsey, Jr. *lawyer*

Studio City
Miller, Charles Maurice *lawyer*

Sunnyvale
Ludgus, Nancy Lucke *lawyer*
McReynolds, Stephen Paul *lawyer*
Zahrt, William Dietrich, II *lawyer*

Temecula
Rosenstein, Robert Bryce *lawyer, financial advisor*

Thousand Oaks
Dougherty, Gerard Michael *lawyer*
Geiser, Thomas Christopher *lawyer*
Jessup, Warren T. *retired lawyer*
Trover, Ellen Lloyd *lawyer*

Tiburon
Bauch, Thomas Jay *lawyer, educator, former apparel company executive*
Widman, Gary Lee *lawyer, former government official*

Toluca Lake
Runquist, Lisa A. *lawyer*

Torrance
Deason, Edward Joseph *lawyer*
†Hennig, Alfred W. *lawyer*
Johnson, Einar William *lawyer*
Kaufman, Sanford Paul *lawyer*
Matsunaga, Geoffrey Dean *lawyer*
Moore, Christopher Minor *lawyer*

Tracy
Hay, Dennis Lee *lawyer*

Tustin
Kraft, Henry R. *lawyer*
Madory, Richard Eugene *lawyer*

Van Nuys
Arabian, Armand *arbitrator, mediator, lawyer*
Boyd, Harry Dalton *lawyer, former insurance company executive*

Ventura
Arant, Eugene Wesley *lawyer*
Bray, Laurack Doyle *lawyer*
English, Woodrow Douglas *lawyer*
Gartner, Harold Henry, III *lawyer*
Robinson, William Franklin *retired legal consultant*

Victorville
Quadri, Fazle Rab *lawyer, government official*

Visalia
Crowe, John T. *lawyer*
Hart, Timothy Ray *lawyer, dean*

Walnut
McKee, Catherine Lynch *law educator, lawyer*

Walnut Creek
Curtin, Daniel Joseph, Jr. *lawyer*
De Benedictis, Dario *arbitrator, mediator*
Epstein, Judith Ann *lawyer*
Garrett, James Joseph *lawyer, partner*
Ginsburg, Gerald J. *lawyer, business executive*
Jones, Orlo Dow *lawyer, drug store executive*

Medak, Walter Hans *lawyer*
Mitgang, Iris Feldman *lawyer, educator*
Nolan, David Charles *lawyer, mediator*
Pagter, Carl Richard *lawyer*
Skaggs, Sanford Merle *lawyer*

West Covina
McHale, Edward Robertson *retired lawyer*

West Hollywood
Finstad, Suzanne Elaine *writer, producer, lawyer*

Westlake Village
Vinson, William Theodore *lawyer, diversified corporation executive*

Whittier
Scheifly, John Edward *retired lawyer*

Woodland
†Breeden, Michael Edward *defender*

Woodland Hills
Barrett, Robert Matthew *lawyer, law educator*
Gill, Keith Hubert *lawyer*
Johnson-Champ, Debra Sue *lawyer, educator, writer, artist*
†Preston, John Elwood *lawyer*
Robertson, Alexander, IV *lawyer*
Strote, Joel Richard *lawyer*

Woodside
Martin, Joseph, Jr. *retired lawyer, former ambassador*

COLORADO

Arvada
Peck, Kenneth E. *lawyer*

Aspen
McGrath, J. Nicholas *lawyer*
Peirce, Frederick Fairbanks *lawyer*
Shipp, Dan Shackelford *lawyer*

Aurora
Halford, Sharon Lee *legal studies administrator, victimologist, educator*
Richardson, Charles H. *lawyer*
Schilling, Edwin Carlyle, III *lawyer*

Boulder
Bintliff, Barbara Ann *law librarian, educator*
Corbridge, James Noel, Jr. *law educator*
Dubofsky, Jean Eberhart *lawyer, retired state supreme court justice*
Dumas, Jeffrey Mack *lawyer*
DuVivier, Katharine Keyes *lawyer, educator*
Echohawk, John Ernest *lawyer*
Fenster, Herbert Lawrence *lawyer*
Fiflis, Ted James *lawyer, educator*
Flowers, William Harold, Jr. *lawyer*
Gray, William R. *lawyer*
LaVelle, Betty Sullivan Dougherty *legal professional*
Moses, Raphael Jacob *lawyer*
Peterson, Courtland Harry *law educator*
Porzak, Glenn E. *lawyer*

Breckenridge
Katz, Jeri Beth *lawyer*

Castle Rock
Bell, Brian Mayes *lawyer*

Cherry Hills Village
Meyer, Milton Edward, Jr. *lawyer, artist*

Colorado Springs
Adams, Deborah Rowland *lawyer*
Buell, Bruce Temple *lawyer*
Campbell, Frederick Hollister *retired lawyer, historian*
Everson, Steven Lee *lawyer, real estate executive*
Fisher, Robert Scott *lawyer*
Kendall, Phillip Alan *lawyer*
Kubida, William Joseph *lawyer*
MacDougall, Malcolm Edward *lawyer*
Palermo, Norman Anthony *lawyer*
Purvis, Randall W. B. *lawyer*
Rhodes, Eric Foster *arbitrator, employee relations consultant, writer*
Rouss, Ruth *lawyer*
Wheeler, Stephen Frederick *municipal court administrator*
White, Deborah Sue Youngblood *lawyer*

Commerce City
Trujillo, Lorenzo A. *lawyer, educator*

Delta
Wendt, John Arthur Frederic, Jr. *lawyer*

Denver
Abramovitz, Michael John *lawyer*
†Aisenberg, Bennett S. *lawyer*
Alfers, Stephen Douglas *lawyer*
Archibold, John Ewing *lawyer, consultant*
Austin, H(arry) Gregory *lawyer*
Bain, Donald Knight *lawyer*
Bain, James William *lawyer*
Beatty, Michael L. *lawyer*
Belitz, Paul Edward *lawyer*
Benson, Robert Eugene *lawyer*
Benton, Auburn Edgar *lawyer*
Blair, Andrew Lane, Jr. *lawyer, educator*
Blitz, Stephen M. *lawyer*
Blunk, Forrest Stewart *lawyer*
Brega, Charles Franklin *lawyer*
Burford, Anne McGill *lawyer*
Burke, Kenneth John *lawyer*
Butler, David *lawyer*
Bye, James Edward *lawyer*
Byrne, Thomas J. *lawyer*
Cain, Douglas Mylchreest *lawyer*
Campbell, Leonard Martin *lawyer*
Carr, James Francis *lawyer*
Carraher, John Bernard *lawyer*
Carrigan, Jim R. *arbitrator, mediator, retired federal judge*
Carver, Craig R. *lawyer*

Cassidy, Samuel H. *lawyer, lieutenant governor, state legislator*
Cheroutes, Michael Louis *lawyer*
Christopher, Daniel Roy *lawyer*
Cockrell, Richard Carter *retired lawyer*
Commander, Eugene R. *lawyer*
Cooper, Paul Douglas *lawyer*
Cope, Thomas Field *lawyer*
Cordova, Donald E. *lawyer*
Crow, Nancy Rebecca *lawyer*
Daniel, Wiley Y. *lawyer*
Dauer, Edward Arnold *law educator*
Dean, James Benwell *lawyer*
De Gette, Diana Louise *lawyer, congresswoman*
DeLaney, Herbert Wade, Jr. *lawyer*
Dempsey, Howard Stanley *lawyer, mining executive, investment banker*
DeMuth, Alan Cornelius *lawyer*
Donder, Pauline Veronica *legal secretary*
Dorr, Robert Charles *lawyer*
Dowdle, Patrick Dennis *lawyer*
†Dunham, Stephen Sampson *lawyer*
Dunn, Randy Edwin *lawyer*
Edwards, Daniel Walden *lawyer*
Eiberger, Carl Frederick *trial lawyer*
Eklund, Carl Andrew *lawyer*
Faxon, Thomas Baker *lawyer*
Featherstone, Bruce Alan *lawyer*
Finegan, Cole *lawyer*
Fortune, Lowell *lawyer*
Gallegos, Larry Duayne *lawyer*
Grant, Patrick Alexander *lawyer, association administrator*
Grissom, Garth Clyde *lawyer*
Gustus, Stacey A. *legal secretary*
Hagen, Glenn W(illiam) *lawyer*
Harris, Dale Ray *lawyer*
Hartley, James Edward *lawyer*
Hendrix, Lynn Parker *lawyer*
Hensen, Stephen Jerome *lawyer*
Hilbert, Otto Karl, II *lawyer*
Hoagland, Donald Wright *lawyer*
Hobson, Harry Lee, Jr. *lawyer*
Hoffman, Daniel Steven *lawyer, legal educator*
Holder, Holly Irene *lawyer*
Holleman, Paul Douglas *lawyer*
Holme, Richard Phillips *lawyer*
Hopfenbeck, George Martin, Jr. *lawyer*
Hopkins, Donald J. *lawyer*
Husband, John Michael *lawyer*
Imig, William Graff *lawyer, lobbyist*
Irwin, R. Robert *lawyer*
Jablonski, James Arthur *lawyer*
Jacobs, Paul Alan *lawyer*
Jones, Richard Michael *lawyer*
Jonsen, Eric R. *lawyer*
Kaczanowska, Laurie Hyson Smith *lawyer*
†Kaufman, Richard C. *federal lawyer*
Keatinge, Robert Reed *lawyer*
Keller, Glen Elven, Jr. *lawyer*
Kintzele, John Alfred *lawyer*
Levy, Mark Ray *lawyer*
Low, John Wayland *lawyer*
Lutz, John Shafroth *lawyer*
Malatesta, Mary Anne *lawyer*
Marquess, Lawrence Wade *lawyer*
Martin, Raymond Walter *lawyer*
Martz, Clyde Ollen *lawyer, educator*
Mauro, Richard Frank *lawyer, investment manager*
McCabe, John L. *lawyer*
McDowell, Karen Ann *lawyer*
McGuane, Frank L., Jr. *lawyer*
McKendree, John W. *lawyer*
McMichael, Donald Earl *lawyer*
Merker, Steven Joseph *lawyer*
Miller, Gale Timothy *lawyer*
Miller, Robert Nolen *lawyer*
Molling, Charles Francis *lawyer*
Muldoon, Brian *retired lawyer*
Murane, William Edward *lawyer*
Nanda, Ved Prakash *law educator, university official*
Nathan, J(ay) Andrew *lawyer*
Nelson, John Gustaf *lawyer*
Newton, James Quigg, Jr. *lawyer*
Norton, Gale Ann *lawyer*
O'Keefe, Edward Franklin *lawyer*
Olsen, M. Kent *lawyer, educator*
Palmer, David Gilbert *lawyer*
Peloquin, Louis Omer *lawyer*
Petros, Raymond Louis, Jr. *lawyer*
Pope, David Bruce *lawyer*
Poulson, Robert Dean *lawyer*
Pringle, Edward E. *law educator, former state supreme court chief justice*
Prochnow, James R. *lawyer*
Quiat, Gerald M. *lawyer*
Rich, Robert Stephen *lawyer*
Ris, William Krakow *lawyer*
Ritsema, Fredric A. *lawyer*
Rockwood, Linda Lee *lawyer*
Roesler, John Bruce *lawyer*
Ruppert, John Lawrence *lawyer*
Sayre, John Marshall *lawyer, former government official*
Schauer, Tone Terjesen *lawyer*
Schindler, Ronald Irvin *lawyer*
Scott, Peter Bryan *lawyer*
Shannon, Malcolm Lloyd, Jr. *lawyer*
Shea, Kevin Michael *lawyer*
Smead, Burton Armstrong, Jr. *retired lawyer*
Smith, Daniel Timothy *lawyer*
Spencer, Margaret Gilliam *lawyer*
Springer, Jeffrey Alan *lawyer*
Starrs, Elizabeth Anne *lawyer*
Stockmar, Ted P. *lawyer*
Sutton, Leonard v. B. *lawyer*
Thomasch, Roger Paul *lawyer*
Timmins, Edward Patrick *lawyer*
Tomlinson, Warren Leon *lawyer*
Ulrich, Theodore Albert *lawyer*
Wedgle, Richard Jay *lawyer*
Welch, Carol Mae *lawyer*
Welton, Charles Ephraim *lawyer*
Wheeler, Malcolm Edward *lawyer, law educator*
Williams, Michael Anthony *lawyer*
Wohlgenant, Richard Glen *lawyer*
Wollins, David Hart *lawyer*
Woodward, Lester Ray *lawyer*
Yegge, Robert Bernard *law educator, dean*

Durango
Burnham, Bryson Paine *retired lawyer*
Sherman, Lester Ivan *retired lawyer*

Englewood
†Brett, Stephen M. *lawyer, entertainment company executive*

Burg, Michael S. *lawyer*
Figa, Phillip Sam *lawyer*
Karr, David Dean *lawyer*
Katz, Michael Jeffery *lawyer*
Lidstone, Herrick Kenley, Jr. *lawyer*
McReynolds, Gregg Clyde *lawyer*
Rodin, Mike *lawyer, corporate*
Steinhauser, John William *retired lawyer*
Syke, Cameron John *lawyer*
Wagner, David James *lawyer*
Wiegand, Robert, II *lawyer*

Fort Collins
Brown, Ronald Laming *lawyer*
Fromm, Jeffery Bernard *lawyer*
Gilmore, Timothy Jonathan *paralegal*

Golden
Carney, Deborah Leah Turner *lawyer*
Hughes, Marcia Marie *lawyer, mediator, trainer*
Snead, Kathleen Marie *lawyer*
Wilson, James Robert *lawyer*

Greeley
Conway, Rebecca Ann Koppes *lawyer*
Houtchens, Barnard *lawyer*
Kerr, Robert James *mediator, educational consultant*

Green Mountain Falls
Faber, Michael Warren *lawyer*

Greenwood Village
Bowen, Peter Geoffrey *arbitrator, investment advisor, business management lecturer*
Dymond, Lewis Wandell *lawyer, mediator, educator*
Poe, Robert Alan *lawyer*
Ramsey, John Arthur *lawyer*

Highlands Ranch
Mierzwa, Joseph William *lawyer, legal communications consultant*

Lakewood
Downey, Arthur Harold, Jr. *lawyer, mediator*
Guyton, Samuel Percy *retired lawyer*
Isely, Henry Philip *association executive, integrative engineer, writer, educator*
McElwee, Dennis John *lawyer, former pharmaceutical company executive*
Thome, Dennis Wesley *lawyer*

Littleton
Eberhardt, Gretchen Ann *lawyer, hearing officer*
Keely, George Clayton *lawyer*
Spelts, Richard John *lawyer*
Truhlar, Doris Broaddus *lawyer*

Louisville
Raymond, Dorothy Gill *lawyer*
†Spagnola, Robert G. *lawyer, business management educator*

Lyons
Brown, Michael DeWayne *lawyer*

Manitou Spgs
Slivka, Michael Andrew *lawyer*

Parker
Greenberg, Morton Paul *lawyer, consultant, insurance broker, underwriter*

Placerville
Reagan, Harry Edwin, III *lawyer*

Pueblo
Altman, Leo Sidney *lawyer*
Farley, Thomas T. *lawyer*
Geisel, Henry Jules *lawyer*
Humes, James Calhoun *lawyer, communications consultant, author, professor*
O'Callaghan, Robert Patrick *lawyer*
White, Rodney Curtis *paralegal, legal assistant*

Rocky Ford
†Mendenhall, Harry Barton *lawyer*

CONNECTICUT

Avon
Wiechmann, Eric Watt *lawyer*

Bloomfield
Day, John G. *lawyer*
Mark, Henry Allen *lawyer*
Reid, Hoch *lawyer*

Bridgeport
Williams, Ronald Doherty *lawyer*

Brooklyn
Dune, Steve Charles *lawyer*

Canaan
Capecelatro, Mark John *lawyer*

City Place
Nolan, John Blanchard *lawyer*

Clinton
Hershatter, Richard Lawrence *lawyer, author*

Danbury
Chaifetz, David Harvey *lawyer*
Dornfeld, Sharon Wicks *lawyer*
Geoghan, Joseph Edward *lawyer, chemical company executive*
Murray, Stephen James *lawyer*
Skolan-Logue, Amanda Nicole *lawyer, consultant*

Darien
Beach, Stephen Holbrook *lawyer*
Brown, James Shelly *lawyer*
Dale, Erwin Randolph *lawyer, author*
Prince, Kenneth Stephen *lawyer*

PROFESSIONAL INDEX 6135 LAW: LAW PRACTICE AND ADMINISTRATION

East Hartford
Whiston, Richard Michael *lawyer*

Enfield
Berger, Robert Bertram *lawyer*

Fairfield
Caruso, Daniel F. *lawyer, judge, former state legislator*
Daley, Pamela *lawyer*
Denniston, Brackett Badger, III *lawyer*
Heineman, Benjamin Walter, Jr. *lawyer*
LaFollette, Ernest Carlton *lawyer*

Farmington
Anderson, Buist Murfee *lawyer*
Mandell, Joel *lawyer*
McCann, John Joseph *lawyer*

Glastonbury
Schroth, Peter W(illiam) *lawyer, management and law educator*

Greenwich
Auerbach, Ernest Sigmund *lawyer, company executive, writer*
Bam, Foster *lawyer*
Behren, Robert Alan *lawyer, accountant*
Bentley, Peter *lawyer*
Berk, Alan S. *law firm executive*
Cantor, Samuel C. *lawyer, company executive*
Cantwell, Robert *lawyer*
Coleman, Joel Clifford *lawyer*
Forrow, Brian Derek *lawyer, corporation executive*
Jones, Edwin Michael *lawyer, former insurance company executive*
Kurtz, Melvin H. *lawyer, cosmetics company executive*
Laudone, Anita Helene *lawyer*
Lochner, Philip Raymond, Jr. *lawyer, communications executive*
Lowenstein, Peter David *lawyer*
Lynch, William Redington *lawyer*
McDonald, Paul Kimball *lawyer, investment executive*
Mendenhall, John Ryan *retired lawyer, transportation executive*
More, Douglas McLochlan *lawyer*
†Pascarella, Henry William *lawyer*
Paul, Roland Arthur *lawyer*
Schoonmaker, Samuel Vail, III *lawyer*
Steinmetz, Richard Bird, Jr. *lawyer*
Storms, Clifford Beekman *lawyer*
Tetzlaff, Theodore R. *lawyer*
†Teztlaff, Theodore R. *lawyer*

Groton
Kalkstein, Joshua Adam *lawyer*
Nelson, Janice Eileen *paralegal*

Hamden
Bix, Brian *law educator*
Margulies, Martin B. *lawyer, educator*
Peterson, George Emanuel, Jr. *lawyer, business executive*

Hartford
Alfano, Charles Thomas, Sr. *lawyer*
Anthony, J(ulian) Danford, Jr. *lawyer*
Appel, Robert Eugene *lawyer, educator*
Bennett, Jessie F. *lawyer*
Berall, Frank Stewart *lawyer*
Berlage, Jan Ingham *lawyer*
Blumberg, Phillip Irvin *law educator*
Blumenthal, Jeffrey Michael *lawyer*
Buckingham, Harold Canute, Jr. *lawyer*
Cain, George Harvey *lawyer, business executive*
Cantor, Donald Jerome *lawyer*
Cole, William Kaufman *lawyer*
Cullina, William Michael *lawyer*
Dempsey, Edward Joseph *lawyer*
Dennis, Anthony James *lawyer*
Dowling, Vincent John *lawyer*
Elliot, Ralph Gregory *lawyer*
Fain, Joel Maurice *lawyer*
Flaschen, Evan Daniel *lawyer*
Garfield, Gerald *lawyer*
Godfrey, Robert Douglas *lawyer*
Hall, Janet C. *lawyer*
Harrison, Thomas Flatley *lawyer*
Johnson, Dwight Alan *lawyer*
Kennedy, Jack S. *lawyer*
Knickerbocker, Robert Platt, Jr. *lawyer*
Korzenik, Armand Alexander *lawyer*
Libassi, Frank Peter *lawyer*
Lloyd, Alex *lawyer*
Lyon, James Burroughs *lawyer*
Margulies, Beth Zeldes *assistant attorney general*
Martocchio, Louis Joseph *lawyer, educator*
McCarthy, Patrice Ann *lawyer*
Merriam, Dwight Haines *lawyer, land use planner*
Metzler, Robert J., II *lawyer*
Middlebrook, Stephen Beach *lawyer*
Miller, Jeffrey Clark *lawyer*
Milliken, Charles Buckland *lawyer*
Murtha, John Stephen *lawyer*
Pepe, Louis Robert *lawyer*
Pinney, Sidney Dillingham, Jr. *lawyer*
Quinn, Andrew Peter, Jr. *lawyer, insurance executive*
Richter, Donald Paul *lawyer*
Rome, Donald Lee *lawyer*
Ryan, David Thomas *lawyer*
Schatzki, George *law educator*
See, Edmund M. *lawyer*
Shaw, L. Edward, Jr. *lawyer*
Space, Theodore Maxwell *lawyer*
Spear, H(enry) Dyke N(ewcome), Jr. *lawyer*
Speziale, John Albert *lawyer*
Sussman, Mark Richard *lawyer*
Tancredi, James J. *lawyer*
Taylor, Allan Bert *lawyer*
Thomas, Calvert *lawyer*
Trachsel, William Henry *corporate lawyer*
Voigt, Richard *lawyer*
Webster, Arthur Edward *lawyer*
Wetzler, Monte Edwin *lawyer*
Wilson-Coker, Patricia Anne *lawyer, social service administrator, educator*
Wolman, Martin *lawyer*
Young, Dona Davis Gagliano *lawyer, insurance executive*
Young, Roland Frederic, III *lawyer*
Zakarian, Albert *lawyer*

Lakeville
Jones, Ronald David *lawyer*

Madison
Clendenen, William Herbert, Jr. *lawyer*

Manchester
Gaines, Robert Martin *lawyer*

Meriden
Lowry, Houston Putnam *lawyer*

Middlebury
Davis, Joanne Fatse *lawyer*

Middletown
Quattro, Mark Henry *lawyer, developer*

Milford
Berchem, Robert Lee, Sr. *lawyer*

Mystic
Antipas, Constantine George *lawyer, civil engineer*

New Britain
Pearl, Helen Zalkan *lawyer*

New Canaan
Vasta, Vincent Joseph, Jr. *lawyer*
Wallace, Kenneth Donald *lawyer*

New Haven
Ackerman, Bruce Arnold *lawyer, educator*
Belt, David Levin *lawyer*
Birnbaum, Irwin Morton *lawyer*
Burt, Robert Amsterdam *lawyer, educator*
Carr, Cynthia *lawyer*
Clark, Elias *law educator*
Cohen, Morris Leo *retired law librarian and educator*
Craig, William Emerson *lawyer*
Days, Drew S., III *lawyer, law educator*
De Lio, Anthony Peter *lawyer*
Duke, Steven Barry *law educator*
Ellickson, Robert Chester *law educator*
Fiss, Owen M. *law educator*
Freed, Daniel Josef *law educator*
Gildea, Brian Michael *lawyer*
Goldstein, Abraham Samuel *lawyer, educator*
Greenfield, James Robert *lawyer*
Hansmann, Henry Baethke *law educator*
Holder, Angela Roddey *lawyer, educator*
Johnstone, Quintin *law educator*
Krinsky, Mary McInerney *lawyer*
Kronman, Anthony Townsend *law educator, dean*
Langbein, John Harriss *lawyer, educator*
Logue, Frank *arbitrator, mediator, urban consultant, former mayor New Haven*
Marcus, Edward Leonard *lawyer*
Marshall, Burke *law educator*
Priest, George L. *law educator*
Reisman, William M. *lawyer, educator*
Robinson, Dorothy K. *lawyer*
†Robinson, Stephen C. *lawyer*
Rose-Ackerman, Susan *law and political economy educator*
Schloss, Irving Steven *lawyer*
Simon, John Gerald *law educator*
Sullivan, Shaun Stuart *lawyer*
Tilson, John Quillin *lawyer*
Wagoner, Walter Dray, Jr. *lawyer*
Wedgwood, Ruth *law educator, international affairs expert*
Wenig, Mary Moers *law educator*

New London
Dupont, Ralph Paul *lawyer, educator*
Johnstone, Philip MacLaren *lawyer*

New Milford
Edmondson, John Richard *lawyer, pharmaceutical manufacturing company executive*
Friedman, John Maxwell, Jr. *lawyer*

Norfolk
Lambros, Lambros John *lawyer, petroleum company executive*

Norwalk
Feinstein, Stephen Michael *lawyer*
Jacobs, Mark Randolph *lawyer*

Norwich
Masters, Barbara J. *lawyer*

Old Greenwich
Klemann, Gilbert Lacy, II *lawyer*
Peters, Joan Schlump *lawyer*

Redding
Russell, Allan David *lawyer*

Ridgefield
Fricke, Richard John *lawyer*

Rowayton
Raikes, Charles FitzGerald *retired lawyer*

Shelton
Asija, S(atya) Pal *lawyer*

Simsbury
†Mogck, Derek Leonard

Southport
Moore, Roy Worsham, III *lawyer*

Stamford
Amarilios, John Alexander *lawyer, real estate consultant*
Apfelbaum, Marc *lawyer*
†Barr, Charles F. *lawyer, reinsurance company executive*
Barreca, Christopher Anthony *lawyer*
Birenbaum, Jonathan *lawyer*
Bowen, Patrick Harvey *lawyer, consultant*
†Brown, Stephen Bernard *corporate lawyer*
Carten, Francis Noel *lawyer*
Casper, Stewart Michael *lawyer*
Critelli, Michael J. *lawyer, manufacturing executive*
Dederick, Ronald Osburn *lawyer*
Della Rocco, Kenneth Anthony *lawyer*
Dolian, Robert Paul *lawyer*
Knag, Paul Everett *lawyer*
Kweskin, Edward Michael *lawyer*
Livolsi, Frank William, Jr. *lawyer*
Lowman, George Frederick *lawyer*
Margolis, Emanuel *lawyer, educator*
†McClave, Wilkes, III *business executive*
McGrath, Richard Paul *lawyer*
Merritt, William Alfred, Jr. *lawyer, telecommunications company executive*
Nichols, Ralph Arthur *lawyer*
Padilla, James Earl *lawyer*
Paul, Richard Stanley *lawyer*
Perle, Eugene Gabriel *lawyer*
Rose, Richard Loomis *lawyer*
Sarner, Richard Alan *lawyer*
Sisley, G. William *lawyer*
Skidd, Thomas Patrick, Jr. *lawyer*
Spindler, John Frederick *lawyer*
Stapleton, James Francis *lawyer*
Teitell, Conrad Laurence *lawyer, author*
Weitzel, William Conrad, Jr. *lawyer*
Wilhelm, Gayle Brian *lawyer*
Yonkman, Fredrick Albers *lawyer, management consultant*
Younskevicius, Adriana *law librarian*

Stonington
Van Rees, Cornelius S. *lawyer*

Storrs Mansfield
Tucker, Edwin Wallace *law educator*

Suffield
†Alfano, Charles T., Jr. *lawyer*

Torrington
Leard, David Carl *lawyer*
Lippincott, Walter Edward *law educator*
Wall, Robert Anthony, Jr. *lawyer*

Waterbury
Marano, Richard Michael *lawyer*
Titus, Curtis Vest *lawyer*

West Hartford
Conard, Frederick Underwood, Jr. *lawyer*
Storm, Robert Warren *lawyer*
Swerdloff, Ileen Pollock *lawyer*

Westbrook
Dundas, Philip Blair, Jr. *lawyer*

Weston
Cohen, Fred Howard *lawyer, investment company executive*

Westport
Albani, Suzanne Beardsley *lawyer*
Barton, James Miller *lawyer, international business consultant*
Cramer, Allan P. *lawyer*
Daw, Harold John *lawyer*
Jacobs, Jeffrey Lee *lawyer, education network company executive*
Kosakow, James Matthew *lawyer*
Mc Bride, Thomas Frederick *lawyer, former university dean, government official*
Razzano, Pasquale Angelo *lawyer*
Saxl, Richard Hildreth *lawyer*
Sheiman, Ronald Lee *lawyer*
Swiggart, Carolyn Clay *lawyer*

White Plains
Turner, Stephen Miller *lawyer, oil company executive*

Wilton
Adams, Thomas Tilley *lawyer*
Healy, James Casey *lawyer*
Lamb, Frederic Davis *retired lawyer*
Slater, Ralph Evan *lawyer*

Windsor
Morelli, Carmen *lawyer*

Winsted
†Finch, Frank Herschel, Jr. *lawyer*

Woodbury
Fiederowicz, Walter Michael *lawyer*
Marsching, Ronald Lionel *lawyer, former precision instrument company executive*

DELAWARE

Dover
Ennis, Bruce Clifford *lawyer*
Stone, F. L. Peter *lawyer*
Twilley, Joshua Marion *lawyer*

New Castle
Brzoska, Denise Jeanne *paralegal*

Wilmington
Bader, John Merwin *lawyer*
Baumann, Julian Henry, Jr. *lawyer*
Carey, John Patrick, III *lawyer*
Carpenter, Edmund Nelson, II *retired lawyer*
Clark, Esther Frances *law educator*
Curran, Barbara Sanson *lawyer*
Devine, Donn *lawyer, genealogist, former city official*
DiLiberto, Richard Anthony, Jr. *lawyer*
Du Pont, Pierre Samuel, IV *lawyer, former governor of Delaware*
Fenton, Wendell *lawyer*
Gilliam, James H., Jr. *lawyer, private investor, consultant*
Goldstein, Jack Charles *lawyer*
Green, James Samuel *lawyer*
Grossman, Jerome Kent *lawyer, accountant*
Herdeg, John Andrew *lawyer*
Kimmel, Morton Richard *lawyer*
Kirk, Richard Dillon *lawyer*
Kirkpatrick, Andrew Booth, Jr. *lawyer*
Klayman, Barry Martin *lawyer*
Kristol, Daniel Marvin *lawyer*
Macel, Stanley Charles, III *lawyer*
Magee, Thomas Hugh *lawyer*
Malik, John Stephen *lawyer*
McBride, David Clinton *lawyer*
Meitner, Pamela *lawyer, educator*
Mekler, Arlen B. *lawyer, chemist*
Patton, James Leeland, Jr. *lawyer*
†Rodgers, Stephen John *lawyer, consultant*
Rothschild, Steven James *lawyer*
Rudge, Howard J. *corporate lawyer*
Salinger, Frank Max *lawyer*
Shapiro, Irving Saul *lawyer*
Sleet, Gregory M. *lawyer*
Smith, Craig Bennett *lawyer*
Tigani, Bruce William *lawyer*
Ward, Rodman, Jr. *lawyer*
Wier, Richard Royal, Jr. *lawyer, inventor*
Willard, John Martin *lawyer*

DISTRICT OF COLUMBIA

Washington
Aaronson, David Ernest *lawyer, educator*
Abbott, Alden Francis *lawyer, government official, educator*
Abeles, Charles Calvert *retired lawyer*
Ablard, Charles David *lawyer*
Acheson, David Campion *lawyer, author, policy analyst*
Ackerson, Nels J(ohn) *lawyer*
Adams, Lee Stephen *lawyer, banker*
†Adams, Roger C. *lawyer*
Adler, Howard, Jr. *lawyer*
Adler, Howard Bruce *lawyer*
Adler, Robert Martin *lawyer*
Ain, Sanford King *lawyer*
Aisenberg, Irwin Morton *lawyer*
Albertson, Terry L. *lawyer*
Alexander, Clifford Joseph *lawyer*
Alexander, Donald Crichton *lawyer*
Allan, Richmond Frederick *lawyer*
Allard, Nicholas W. *lawyer*
Allen, William Hayes *lawyer*
Ambrose, Myles Joseph *lawyer*
Anderson, Frederick Randolph, Jr. *lawyer, law educator*
Anderson, John Bayard *lawyer, educator, former congressman*
Andrew, Joseph Jerald *lawyer, political party official*
Andrews, Mark Joseph *lawyer*
Apperson, Bernard James *lawyer*
Applebaum, Harvey Milton *lawyer*
Arbit, Terry Steven *lawyer*
Arent, Albert Ezra *lawyer*
Ashton, Richard M. *federal lawyer*
Atwood, James R. *lawyer*
Avil, Richard D., Jr. *lawyer*
Axelrod, Jonathan Gans *lawyer*
Ayer, Donald Belton *lawyer*
Ayres, Richard Edward *lawyer*
Babby, Lon S. *lawyer*
Bachman, Kenneth Leroy, Jr. *lawyer*
Bachrach, Eve Elizabeth *lawyer*
†Baer, William J. *lawyer*
Ball, (Robert) Markham *lawyer*
Ballard, Frederic Lyman, Jr. *lawyer*
Banzhaf, John F., III *legal association executive, lawyer*
Baran, Jan Witold *lawyer, educator*
Bardin, David J. *lawyer*
Barnes, Dennis Norman *lawyer*
Barnes, Donald Michael *lawyer*
Barnes, Mark James *lawyer*
Barnes, Michael Darr *lawyer, think tank executive*
Barnes, Peter *lawyer*
Barnett, Robert Bruce *lawyer*
Barr, Michael Blanton *lawyer*
Barr, William Pelham *lawyer, former attorney general of United States*
Barron, Jerome Aure *law educator*
Bartlett, John Laurence *lawyer*
Bartlett, Michael John *lawyer*
Basseches, Robert Treinis *lawyer*
Bates, John Cecil, Jr. *lawyer*
Batla, Raymond John, Jr. *lawyer*
Beatty, Richard Scrivener *lawyer*
Becker, Brandon *lawyer*
Beckwith, Edward Jay *lawyer*
Beisner, John Herbert *lawyer*
Beizer, Robert A. *lawyer*
†Bekhechi, Mohammed Abdelwahab *lawyer*
Bell, James Frederick *retired lawyer*
Bell, Stephen Robert *lawyer*
Beller, Herbert N. *lawyer*
Bellinger, Edgar Thomson *lawyer*
Bello, Judith Hippler *lawyer*
Belman, Murray Joel *lawyer*
Bennett, Alexander Elliot *lawyer*
Bercovici, Martin William *lawyer*
Beresford, Douglas Lincoln *lawyer*
Berger, Melvin Gerald *lawyer*
Berger, Paul S. *lawyer*
Berl, Joseph M. *lawyer*
Berlack, Evan Raden *lawyer*
Berman, Marshall Fox *lawyer*
Berner, Frederic George, Jr. *lawyer*
Bernhard, Berl *lawyer*
Bernstein, Mitchell Harris *lawyer*
Berrington, Craig Anthony *lawyer*
Berryman, Richard Byron *lawyer*
Berz, David R. *lawyer*
Besozzi, Paul Charles *lawyer*
Best, Judah *lawyer*
Biddle, Timothy Maurice *lawyer*
Bierman, James Norman *lawyer*
Birnbaum, S. Elizabeth *lawyer*
Birnkrant, Henry Joseph *lawyer*
Biro, Susan Lori *lawyer*
Bishop, James Dodson *lawyer, mediator*
Bishop, Wayne Staton *lawyer*
Bittman, William Omar *lawyer*
Black, Stephen Franklin *lawyer*
Blair, Robert Allen *business executive, lawyer*
Blair, William McCormick, Jr. *lawyer*
Blake, Jonathan Dewey *lawyer*
Blanchard, Charles Alan *lawyer, former state senator*
Blazek-White, Doris *lawyer*
Bleakley, Peter Kimberley *lawyer*
Bleicher, Samuel Abram *lawyer*
Bliss, Donald Tiffany, Jr. *lawyer*
Bloch, Richard Isaac *labor arbitrator*
Bloch, Stuart Marshall *lawyer*
Blumenfeld, Jeffrey *lawyer, educator*
Blumenthal, Ronnie *lawyer*
†Blumer, Dennis Hull *lawyer*
Bodansky, Robert Lee *lawyer*

Bodner, John, Jr. *lawyer*
Boehm, Steven Bruce *lawyer*
Bogard, Lawrence Joseph *lawyer*
Boggs, George Trenholm *lawyer*
Boggs, Thomas Hale, Jr. *lawyer*
Bohlke, Gary Lee *lawyer, playwright*
Boland, Christopher Thomas, II *lawyer*
Bolton, John Robert *lawyer, former government official*
Bonner, Walter Joseph *lawyer*
Bonvillian, William Boone *lawyer*
Boone, Theodore Sebastian *lawyer*
Borsari, George Robert, Jr. *lawyer, broadcaster*
Boskey, Bennett *lawyer*
Boss, Lenard Barrett *lawyer*
Boyd, Stephen Mather *arbitrator, mediator, lawyer*
Boyette, Van Roy *lawyer, consultant*
Bradford, William Allen, Jr. *lawyer*
Bradford, William Hollis, Jr. *lawyer*
Bradley, Amelia Jane *lawyer*
Brame, Joseph Robert, III *lawyer*
Bregman, Arthur Randolph *lawyer, educator*
Brenner, Daniel Leslie *lawyer*
Brenner, Janet Maybin Walker *lawyer*
Brick, Barrett Lee *lawyer*
Briggs, Alan Leonard *lawyer*
Brinkmann, Robert Joseph *lawyer*
Britton, Katherine Lela Quainton *lawyer*
Bronstein, Alvin J. *lawyer*
Brooke, Edward William *lawyer, former senator*
Brooks, Daniel Townley *lawyer*
Brown, Charles Freeman, II *lawyer*
Brown, David Nelson *lawyer*
Brown, Donald Arthur *lawyer*
Brown, George Leslie *legislative affairs and business development consultant, former manufacturing company executive, former lieutenant governor*
Brown, Michael Arthur *lawyer*
Brown, Preston *lawyer*
Browne, Richard Cullen *lawyer*
Brownstein, Philip Nathan *lawyer*
Bruce, E(stel) Edward *lawyer*
Brunsvold, Brian Garrett *lawyer, educator*
Bryant, Arthur H. *lawyer*
Buc, Nancy Lillian *lawyer*
Bucholtz, Harold Ronald *lawyer*
Buckley, Jeremiah Stephen *lawyer*
Buckley, John Joseph, Jr. *lawyer*
Buechner, Jack W(illiam) *lawyer, government affairs consultant*
Buergenthal, Thomas *lawyer, educator, international judge*
Burack, Michael Leonard *lawyer*
Burchfield, Bobby Roy *lawyer*
Burdette, Robert Bruce *lawyer*
Burgess, David *lawyer*
Burka, Robert Alan *lawyer*
Burns, Stephen Gilbert *lawyer*
Burt, Jeffrey Amsterdam *lawyer*
Busby, David *lawyer*
Buscemi, Peter *lawyer*
Butler, J. Bradway *lawyer*
Butler, Michael Francis *lawyer*
Calamaro, Raymond Stuart *lawyer*
Calhoun-Senghor, Keith *lawyer*
Calvani, Terry *lawyer, former government official*
Cameron, Duncan Hume *lawyer*
Campbell, James Sargent *lawyer*
Canfield, Edward Francis *lawyer, business executive*
Cantor, Herbert I. *lawyer*
Caplin, Mortimer Maxwell *lawyer, educator*
Carey, Sarah Collins *lawyer*
Carliner, David *lawyer*
Carneal, George Upshur *lawyer*
Carney, Robert Thomas *lawyer*
Carome, Patrick Joseph *lawyer*
Carpenter, Sheila Jane *lawyer*
Carr, Lawrence Edward, Jr. *lawyer*
Carroll, J. Speed *lawyer, financial executive*
Carrow, Milton Michael *lawyer, educator*
Carter, Barry Edward *lawyer, educator, administrator*
Carter, William Joseph *lawyer*
Carver, George Allen, Jr. *lawyer*
Casey, Bernard J. *lawyer*
Cashen, Henry Christopher, II *lawyer, former government official*
Casserly, James Lund *lawyer*
Cassidy, Robert Charles, Jr. *lawyer*
Chabot, Elliot Charles *lawyer*
Chafetz, Marc Edward *lawyer*
Chameides, Steven B. *lawyer*
Chanin, Michael Henry *lawyer*
Chanin, Robert Howard *lawyer*
Chapoton, John Edgar *lawyer, government official*
Charles, Robert Bruce *lawyer*
Cheston, Sheila Carol *lawyer*
Chierichella, John W. *lawyer*
Cho, Sung Yoon *law librarian*
Chopko, Mark E. *lawyer*
Christaldi, Brian *lawyer*
Christian, Betty Jo *lawyer*
Christian, Ernest Silsbee, Jr. *lawyer*
Chused, Richard Harris *law educator*
Cicconi, James William *lawyer*
Clagett, Brice McAdoo *lawyer, writer*
Clark, John Franklin *lawyer*
Clark, LeRoy D. *legal educator, lawyer*
Clark, Robert William, III *lawyer*
Clegg, Roger Burton *lawyer*
Close, David Palmer *lawyer*
Cobb, Calvin Hayes, Jr. *lawyer*
Cobbs, Nicholas Hammer *lawyer*
Coerper, Milo George *lawyer, priest*
Coffield, Shirley Ann *lawyer, educator*
Cohen, Edward Barth *lawyer*
Cohen, Louis Richard *lawyer*
Cohen, Nelson Craig *lawyer*
Cohn, Sherman Louis *lawyer, educator*
Cole, Charles Glaston *lawyer*
Cole, John Pope, Jr. *lawyer*
Coleman, William Thaddeus, Jr. *lawyer*
Coleman, William Thaddeus, III *federal official*
Collins, Daniel Francis *lawyer*
Colman, Richard Thomas *lawyer*
Colson, Earl Morton *lawyer*
Columbus, R. Timothy *lawyer*
Constandy, John Peter *lawyer*
Cook, Harry Clayton, Jr. *lawyer*
Cooper, Alan Samuel *lawyer, educator*
Cooper, Clement Theodore *lawyer*
Cope, John R(obert) *lawyer*
Coppelman, Peter David *lawyer, government official*
†Corprew, Barbara Anne *lawyer*
Cortese, Alfred William, Jr. *lawyer, consultant*
Cox, Chapman Beecher *lawyer, corporate executive*
Cox, Kenneth Allen *lawyer, communications consultant*
Craft, Robert Homan, Jr. *lawyer*
Cragin, Charles Langmaid *lawyer*
†Craig, Gregory Bestor *lawyer, government official*
Crampton, Scott Paul *lawyer*
Craven, Donald B. *lawyer*
Crocker, Saone Baron *lawyer*
Crosby, William Duncan, Jr. *lawyer*
Crump, Lynn *lawyer*
Crump, Ronald Cordell *lawyer*
Culvahouse, Arthur Boggess, Jr. *lawyer*
Cumberland, William Edwin *lawyer*
Cummings, Frank *lawyer*
Cummins, Howard Wallace *lawyer*
Cutler, Lloyd Norton *lawyer, company director*
Cymrot, Mark Alan *lawyer*
Cys, Richard L. *lawyer*
Czarra, Edgar F., Jr. *lawyer*
Daddario, Emilio Quincy *lawyer*
Dalley, George Albert *lawyer*
Damico, Nicholas Peter *lawyer*
Damus, Robert George *lawyer, goverment official*
Danas, Andrew Michael *lawyer*
Daniel, Aubrey Marshall, III *lawyer*
Daniels, Diana M. *lawyer*
Davidow, Joel *lawyer*
Davidson, Daniel Ira *lawyer*
Davidson, Daniel Morton *lawyer*
Davidson, Tom William *lawyer*
†Davies, Charles R. *lawyer*
Davison, Calvin *retired lawyer*
Dean, Paul Regis *law educator*
Deckelbaum, Nelson *lawyer*
Dees, C. Stanley *lawyer*
DeGrandi, Joseph Anthony *lawyer*
de Leon, Sylvia A. *lawyer*
Dembling, Paul Gerald *lawyer, former government official*
DeMuth, Christopher Clay *lawyer, foundation executive*
Denger, Michael L. *lawyer*
Dennin, Joseph Francis *lawyer, former government official*
Denny, Judith Ann *retired lawyer*
Derrick, Butler Carson, Jr. *lawyer, former congressman*
Dewey, Anne Elizabeth Marie *lawyer*
Dicello, Francis P. *lawyer*
Dickstein, Sidney *lawyer*
Diercks, Walter Elmer *lawyer*
diGenova, Joseph E. *lawyer*
Dillon-Ridgley, Dianne Granville *mediator, consultant, association executive*
Dinan, Donald Robert *lawyer*
†Dinerstein, Robert David *lawyer*
Disheroon, Fred Russell *lawyer*
Dobkin, James Allen *lawyer, engineer, artist*
Docter, Charles Alfred *lawyer, former state legislator*
Dolan, Edward Charles *lawyer*
Dolan, Michael William *lawyer*
Dole, Robert J. *lawyer, former senator*
Donegan, Charles Edward *lawyer, educator*
Doolittle, Jesse William, Jr. *lawyer*
Dowd, John Maguire *lawyer*
Dowley, Joseph Kyran *lawyer, member congressional staff*
Downey, Arthur Thomas, III *lawyer*
Doyle, Justin Emmett *lawyer, government official*
Drabkin, Murray *lawyer*
Drinan, Robert Frederick *lawyer, former congressman, educator, clergyman*
DuBoff, Scott M. *lawyer*
Duke, Paul Robert *lawyer*
Duncan, John Dean, Jr. *lawyer*
Dunn, H. Stewart, Jr. *lawyer*
Dunn, Herbert Irvin *lawyer*
Dunner, Donald Robert *lawyer*
Durney, Michael Cavalier *lawyer*
Durnil, Gordon Kay *lawyer, diplomat, arbitrator, political party official*
Dwyer, John Charles *lawyer*
Dye, Stuart S. *lawyer*
Dyk, Timothy Belcher *lawyer, educator*
Earle, Ralph, II *lawyer*
Easton, John Jay, Jr. *lawyer*
Eckart, Dennis Edward *lawyer, former congressman*
Edelman, Alan Irwin *lawyer*
Edelman, Marian Wright (Mrs. Peter B. Edelman) *lawyer*
Edelman, Peter Benjamin *lawyer*
Edson, Charles Louis *lawyer, educator*
Edwards, Tony M. *lawyer*
Efros, Ellen Ann *lawyer*
Ehrenhaft, Peter David *lawyer*
Eisenberg, Meyer *lawyer*
Eisner, Neil Robert *lawyer*
†Elcano, Mary S. *lawyer, federal agency administrator*
Ellicott, John LeMoyne *lawyer*
Elliott, Edwin Donald, Jr. *law educator, federal administrator, environmental lawyer*
Elliott, Robert John *lawyer*
†Elliott, Warren G. *lawyer*
Ellis, Courtenay *lawyer*
Elmer, Brian Christian *lawyer*
Elrod, Eugene Richard *lawyer*
Emmett, Robert Addis, III *lawyer*
Engel, John *lawyer*
Epstein, Gary Marvin *lawyer*
Epstein, Lionel Charles *lawyer*
Epstien, Jay Alan *lawyer*
Esslinger, John Thomas *lawyer*
Etters, Ronald Milton *lawyer, government official*
Evans, Thomas William *lawyer*
Everett, Ralph Bernard *lawyer*
†Everly, Rebecca D. *lawyer*
Ewing, Kevin Andrew *lawyer*
Ewing, Ky Pepper, Jr. *lawyer*
Fahrenkopf, Frank Joseph, Jr. *lawyer*
Fairbanks, Richard Monroe, III *lawyer, former ambassador at large*
Faley, R(ichard) Scott *lawyer*
Falk, David Benjamin *lawyer, professional athletic representative*
Falk, James Harvey, Sr. *lawyer*
Falk, John Mansfield *shareholder*
Farabow, Ford Franklin, Jr. *lawyer*
Farmer, Donald A(rthur), Jr. *lawyer*
Fasman, Zachary Dean *lawyer*
Faust, Marcus G. *lawyer*
Fedders, John Michael *lawyer*
Feffer, Gerald Alan *lawyer*
Feinberg, Kenneth Roy *lawyer, law educator*
†Feinstein, Frederick Lee *lawyer*
Feldhaus, Stephen Martin *lawyer*
Feldman, Clarice Rochelle *lawyer*
Feldman, Mark B. *lawyer*
Feldman, Roger David *lawyer*
Fels, Nicholas Wolff *lawyer*
Fendrich, Roger Paul *lawyer*
Ferguson, Thomas Crooks *lawyer*
Ferrand, Louis George *lawyer*
Ferrara, Ralph C. *lawyer*
Feuerstein, Donald Martin *lawyer*
Field, Andrea Bear *lawyer*
Fielding, Fred Fisher *lawyer*
Fields, Wendy Lynn *lawyer*
Finelsen, Libbi June *lawyer*
Finkel, Eugene Jay *lawyer*
Fiorini, John E., III *lawyer*
Fishburne, Benjamin P., III *lawyer*
Fisher, Bart Steven *lawyer, educator, investment banker*
Fisher, Benjamin Chatburn *lawyer*
Fisher, Raymond Corley *lawyer*
Fitzpatrick, James Franklin *lawyer*
Flagg, Ronald Simon *lawyer*
Flannery, Ellen Joanne *lawyer*
Flannery, John Philip *lawyer*
Fleischaker, Marc L. *lawyer*
Fleit, Martin *lawyer*
Flowe, Carol Connor *lawyer*
Fogarty, John Patrick Cody *lawyer*
Fogel, J(oan) Cathy *lawyer*
Fois, Andrew *lawyer, educator*
Foley, Robert Matthew *lawyer*
Fontheim, Claude G.B. *lawyer, advisor*
Forester, John Gordon, Jr. *lawyer*
Forrest, Herbert Emerson *lawyer*
Foscarinis, Maria *lawyer*
Foster, C(harles) Allen *lawyer*
Fowler, J. Edward *lawyer*
Fox, Sarah *lawyer*
Frank, Arthur J. *lawyer*
Frank, Richard Asher *lawyer, health products executive*
Frank, Theodore David *lawyer*
Frankle, Edward Alan *lawyer*
†Franzel, Brent Steven *lawyer*
Freedman, Jay Weil *lawyer*
Freedman, Walter *lawyer*
Freeman, Milton Victor *lawyer*
Freer, Robert Elliott, Jr. *lawyer*
Freije, Philip Charles *lawyer*
Friedlander, James Stuart *lawyer*
Friedman, Alvin *lawyer*
Friedman, Frank Bennett *lawyer*
†Friedman, Paul Lawrence *lawyer*
Frost, Edmund Bowen *lawyer*
Futrell, John William *legal association administrator, lawyer*
Fygi, Eric J. *federal government lawyer*
Gable, Edward Brennan, Jr. *lawyer*
Gaguine, Benito *lawyer*
Gainer, Ronald Lee *lawyer*
Garrett, Theodore Louis *lawyer*
Garrish, Theodore John *lawyer*
Garvey, John Leo *lawyer, educator*
Gelb, Joseph Donald *lawyer*
Geller, Kenneth Steven *lawyer*
Gellhorn, Ernest Albert Eugene *lawyer*
Geniesse, Robert John *lawyer*
Genz, Michael Andrew *lawyer*
George, Joey Russell *lawyer*
George, W. Peyton *lawyer*
Gerson, Stuart Michael *lawyer*
Gertzman, Stephen F. *lawyer*
Gibbs, Lawrence B. *lawyer*
Gideon, Kenneth Wayne *lawyer*
Gildenhorn, Joseph Bernard *lawyer, businessman, former diplomat*
Gilfoyle, Nathalie Floyd Preston *lawyer*
Ginsburg, Charles David *lawyer*
Ginsburg, Gilbert J. *lawyer, law educator*
Ginsburg, Martin David *lawyer, educator*
Glancz, Ronald Robert *lawyer*
Glaser, Howard B. *lawyer*
Glasgow, Norman Milton *lawyer*
Glick, Leslie Alan *lawyer*
†Glover, Jere Walton *lawyer*
Goelzer, Daniel Lee *lawyer*
Gold, Peter Frederick *lawyer*
Goldberg, Seth A. *lawyer*
Goldblatt, Steven Harris *law educator*
Golden, Cornelius Joseph, Jr. *lawyer*
Golden, Gregg Hannan Stewart *lawyer*
Goldfarb, Ronald Lawrence *lawyer*
Goldschmid, Harvey Jerome *law educator*
Goldsmith, Willis Jay *lawyer*
Goldson, Amy Robertson *lawyer*
Goldstein, Frank Robert *lawyer*
Goldstein, Michael B. *lawyer*
Goodman, Alfred Nelson *lawyer*
Goodman, Sherri Wasserman *lawyer*
Gorelick, Jamie Shona *lawyer*
Gorinson, Stanley M. *lawyer*
Gorman, Joyce J(ohanna) *lawyer*
Gostin, Lawrence *lawyer, educator*
Gould, William Benjamin, IV *lawyer, educator, federal agency administrator*
Grady, Gregory *lawyer, banker*
†Graham, John Stuart, III *lawyer*
Graham, Thomas, Jr. *lawyer*
Graham, Thomas Richard *lawyer*
Grant, Paula DiMeo *lawyer, nursing educator*
Gray, Clayland Boyden *lawyer*
Green, Donald Hugh *lawyer*
Green, Richard Alan *lawyer*
Greenberg, Robert E. *lawyer*
Greenberger, I. Michael *lawyer*
Greenebaum, Leonard Charles *lawyer*
Greenspan, Michael Alan *lawyer*
Greenstone, Adam Franklin *lawyer*
Greenwald, Gerald Bernard *lawyer*
Greif, Joseph *lawyer*
Grenier, Edward Joseph, Jr. *lawyer*
Gribbon, Daniel McNamara *lawyer*
Grier, Phillip Michael *lawyer, former association executive*
Grimes, Larry Bruce *lawyer*
Groner, Samuel Brian *lawyer*
Gross, Richard Alan *lawyer*
Gross, Roberta Lee *inspector general*
Gulland, Eugene D. *lawyer*
Guttman, Egon *law educator*
Haft, Robert J. *law educator*
Haines, Martha Mahan *lawyer*
Halpern, James Bladen *lawyer*
Halvorson, Newman Thorbus, Jr. *lawyer*
Hanlon, R(obert) Timothy *lawyer*
Hansen, Orval *lawyer, former congressman, think tank executive*
Harman, William Boys, Jr. *lawyer*
Harper, Emery Walter *lawyer*
Harrington, Anthony Stephen *lawyer*
Harris, Don Victor, Jr. *lawyer*
Harris, Jeffrey *lawyer*
Harris, Scott Blake *lawyer*
Harris, Steven Brown *lawyer*
Harrison, Earl David *lawyer, real estate executive*
Harrison, Marion Edwyn *lawyer*
Hart, Christopher Alvin *lawyer*
Hassett, Joseph Mark *lawyer*
Hastings, Douglas Alfred *lawyer*
Hauser, Richard Alan *lawyer*
Havens, Charles W., III *lawyer*
Hawke, John Daniel, Jr. *lawyer*
Hawkins, Edward Jackson *lawyer*
Hawkins, Lisa Lynne *lawyer, municipal official*
Haynes, R. Michael *lawyer*
Haynes, William J(ames), II *lawyer*
Heckman, Jerome Harold *lawyer*
Heffernan, James Vincent *lawyer*
Hefter, Laurence Roy *lawyer*
Heintz, John Edward *lawyer*
Helfer, Michael Stevens *lawyer*
Heller, Jack Isaac *lawyer*
Heller, John Roderick, III *lawyer, business executive*
Henderson, Douglas Boyd *lawyer*
Henderson, Thomas Henry, Jr. *lawyer, legal association executive*
Henke, Michael John *lawyer, educator*
Henneberger, Lawrence Francis *lawyer*
Hennessy, Ellen Anne *lawyer, benefits compensation analyst, educator*
Heron, Julian Briscoe, Jr. *lawyer*
Herzstein, Robert Erwin *lawyer*
Hewitt, Emily Clark *lawyer, minister*
Hewitt, Paul Buck *lawyer*
Hibbert, Robert George *lawyer, food company executive*
Higgins, John Edward, Jr. *lawyer*
Hill, David Lamar *lawyer*
Hill, Eleanor Jean *lawyer*
Hills, Carla Anderson *lawyer, former federal official*
Hills, Roderick M. *lawyer, business executive, former government official*
Hirsch, Michael *lawyer*
Hirschhorn, Eric Leonard *lawyer*
Hobbs, J. Timothy, Sr. *lawyer*
Hobelman, Carl Donald *lawyer*
Hobson, James Richmond *lawyer*
†Hoecker, James John *lawyer*
Hoffman, E. Leslie *lawyer*
Hoffman, Joel Elihu *lawyer*
Hoffmann, Martin Richard *lawyer*
Ho-Gonzalez, William *lawyer*
Holder, Eric H. *prosecutor*
Hollis, Sheila Slocum *lawyer*
Holmstead, Jeffrey Ralph *lawyer*
Holtz, Edgar Wolfe *lawyer*
Hoppel, Robert Gerald, Jr. *lawyer*
Horahan, Edward Bernard, III *lawyer*
Horlick, Gary Norman *lawyer, legal educator*
Horn, Charles M. *lawyer*
Horn, Donald Herbert *lawyer*
Horne, Michael Stewart *lawyer*
House, W(illiam) Michael *lawyer*
Howard, Jeffrey Hjalmar *lawyer*
Huddleson, Edwin Emmett, III *lawyer*
Hughes, Marija Matich *law librarian*
Hugler, Edward C. *lawyer, federal and state government*
Hunnicutt, Charles Alvin *lawyer*
Huntsman, Lawrence Darrow *lawyer*
Hutt, Peter Barton *lawyer*
Hyde, Howard Laurence *lawyer*
Hyman, Lester Samuel *lawyer*
Hynes, Terence Michael *lawyer*
Irish, Leon Eugene *lawyer, educator, non-profit executive*
Isbell, David Bradford *lawyer, legal educator*
Isenbergh, Max *lawyer, musician, educator*
Jackson, Jimmy Joe *litigation consultant*
Jackson, John Howard *lawyer, educator*
Jackson, Neal A. *lawyer*
†Jacobsen, Magdalena Gretchen *mediator, federal agency executive*
Jacobsen, Raymond Alfred, Jr. *lawyer*
Jacobson, David Edward *lawyer*
Jamar, Steven Dwight *law educator*
Jameson, Paula Ann *lawyer*
Javits, Joshua Moses *lawyer*
Jehani, Ahmed *lawyer*
Jepsen, Peter Lee *court reporter*
Jessup, Philip Caryl, Jr. *lawyer, museum executive*
Jeweler, Robin *lawyer*
Johnson, David Raymond *lawyer*
Johnson, Oliver Thomas, Jr. *lawyer*
Johnson, Philip McBride *lawyer*
Johnson, Richard Clark *lawyer*
Johnson, Richard Tenney *lawyer*
Jones, Aidan Drexel *lawyer*
Jones, Boisfeuillet, Jr. *lawyer, newspaper executive*
Jordan, Robert Elijah, III *lawyer*
Jordan, Vernon Eulion, Jr. *lawyer, former association official*
Joseph, Daniel Mordecai *lawyer*
Journey, Drexel Dahlke *lawyer*
Kabel, Robert James *lawyer*
Kafka, Gerald Andrew *lawyer*
Kahn, Edwin Leonard *lawyer*
Kapp, Robert Harris *lawyer*
Kass, Benny Lee *lawyer*
Katz, John W. *lawyer, state official*
Katz, Sherman E. *lawyer*
Katzen, Sally *lawyer, government official*
Katzmann, Robert Allen *law educator, non-profit association executive, political scientist*
Keeney, John C. *lawyer*
Keeney, John Christopher, Jr. *lawyer*
Keiner, R(obert) Bruce, Jr. *lawyer*
Kellison, James Bruce *lawyer*
Kelly, William Charles, Jr. *lawyer*
Kendall, David E. *lawyer*
Kennard, Mary Elizabeth *lawyer*
Kennedy, Jerry Wayne *lawyer*
Kenney, Robert James, Jr. *lawyer*
Kent, M. Elizabeth *lawyer*
Kerr, Stuart H. *lawyer, think tank executive*
Kessler, Judd Lewis *lawyer*
Kies, Kenneth J. *lawyer*
Kiko, Philip George *lawyer*
Kilburn, Edwin Allen *lawyer*
Kimmitt, Robert Michael *lawyer, banker, diplomat*
King, Patricia Ann *law educator*
King, Rufus *lawyer*
Kirsch, Laurence Stephen *lawyer*
Kissel, Peter Charles *lawyer*
Kittrie, Nicholas N(orbert Nehemiah) *law educator, international consultant, author*
Klarfeld, Peter James *lawyer*
Klawiter, Donald Casimir *lawyer*
Klein, Michael Roger *lawyer, business executive*
Knapp, George M. *lawyer*

Tauber, Mark J. *lawyer*
Taylor, James, Jr. *lawyer*
Taylor, Ralph Arthur, Jr. *lawyer*
Taylor, Richard Powell *lawyer*
Taylor, William Woodruff, III *lawyer*
Teague, Randal Cornell, Sr. *lawyer*
Temko, Stanley Leonard *lawyer*
Thaler, Paul Sanders *lawyer, mediator*
Theroux, Eugene *lawyer*
Thomas, Ritchie Tucker *lawyer*
Thornburgh, Richard L. (Dick Thornburgh) *lawyer, former United Nations official, former United States attorney general, former governor*
Tigar, Michael Edward *law educator*
Timberg, Sigmund *lawyer*
Tirana, Bardyl Rifat *lawyer*
Tomar, Richard Thomas *lawyer*
Tompert, James Emil *lawyer*
Tompkins, Joseph Buford, Jr. *lawyer*
Topelius, Kathleen Ellis *lawyer*
Townsend, John Michael *lawyer*
Toy, Charles David *lawyer*
Trinder, Rachel Bandele *lawyer*
Troy, Daniel E. *lawyer, scholar*
Troyer, Thomas Alfred *lawyer*
Tufaro, Richard Chase *lawyer*
Tuohey, Mark Henry, III *lawyer*
Turnage, Fred Douglas *lawyer*
Tushnet, Mark Victor *law educator*
Tyler, Peggy Lynne Bailey *lawyer*
Tyner, Lee Reichelderfer *lawyer*
Uehlein, E(dward) Carl, Jr. *lawyer*
Unger, Laura S. *lawyer*
Vacketta, Carl Lee *lawyer, educator*
Valentine, Debra A. *govenment attorney*
Valentine, Steven Richards *lawyer*
Vander Clute, Norman Roland *lawyer*
Vanderstar, John *lawyer*
Vanderver, Timothy Arthur, Jr. *lawyer*
Vardaman, John Wesley *lawyer*
Verner, James Melton *lawyer*
Verrill, Charles Owen, Jr. *lawyer*
Vickery, Ann Morgan *lawyer*
Vieth, G. Duane *lawyer*
Villa, John Kazar *lawyer*
Vince, Clinton Andrew *lawyer*
Vinyard, Walter Darnall *lawyer*
Violante, Joseph Anthony *lawyer*
Vodra, William Wilson *lawyer*
Wade, Robert Paul *lawyer*
Waits, John A. *lawyer*
Wald, Robert Lewis *lawyer*
Wallace, Don, Jr. *law educator*
Wallace, James Harold, Jr. *lawyer*
Walsh, Michael J. *lawyer*
Walter, Sheryl Lynn *lawyer*
Ward, Alan S. *lawyer*
Warin, Roger E. *lawyer*
Warnke, Paul Culliton *lawyer*
Wasserman, Michael Francis *lawyer*
Waters, Jennifer Nash *lawyer*
Watkins, Charles Morgan *lawyer*
Watson, Jack H., Jr. *lawyer*
Waxman, Seth Paul *lawyer*
Weadon, Donald Alford, Jr. *lawyer*
Webber, Richard John *lawyer*
Webster, Robert Kenly *lawyer*
Webster, William Hedgcock *lawyer*
Wegener, Mark Douglas *lawyer*
Weidenfeld, Edward Lee *lawyer*
Weiner, Kenneth Brian *lawyer*
Weinman, Howard Mark *lawyer*
Weinmann, Eric *retired lawyer*
Weinstein, Harris *lawyer*
Weisgall, Jonathan Michael *lawyer*
Weiss, Arnold Hans *lawyer, consultant*
Weiss, Mark Anschel *lawyer*
Weiss, Stephen J. *lawyer*
Weissman, William R. *lawyer*
Weiswasser, Stephen Anthony *lawyer, broadcast executive*
Wellen, Robert Howard *lawyer*
Wenner, Charles Roderick *lawyer*
West, Gail Berry *lawyer*
Whelan, Roger Michael *lawyer, educator*
Whitaker, A(lbert) Duncan *lawyer*
White, Lee Calvin *lawyer*
Whiting, Richard Albert *lawyer*
Wides, Burton V. *lawyer*
Wilcher, Shirley J. *lawyer*
Wilderotter, James Arthur *lawyer*
Wiley, Richard Emerson *lawyer*
Willard, Richard Kennon *lawyer*
Williams, B. John, Jr. *lawyer, former federal judge*
Williams, John Edward *lawyer*
Williams, Julie Lloyd *lawyer*
Williams, Karen Hastie *lawyer, think tank executive*
Williams, Thomas Raymond *lawyer*
Williams, Wesley Samuel, Jr. *lawyer*
Williamson, Thomas Samuel, Jr. *lawyer*
Willmore, Robert Louis *lawyer*
Wilner, Thomas Bernard *lawyer*
Wilson, Gary Dean *lawyer*
Wilson, Michael Moureau *lawyer, physician*
Wine, L. Mark *lawyer*
Winston, Judith Ann *lawyer*
Winter, Douglas E. *lawyer, writer*
Wintrol, John Patrick *lawyer*
Wirtz, William Willard *lawyer*
Wise, Sandra Casber *lawyer*
Wiseman, Alan M(itchell) *lawyer*
Wiss, Marcia A. *lawyer*
Wolff, Alan William *lawyer*
Wolff, Elroy Harris *lawyer*
Wolff, Paul Martin *lawyer*
Wolin, Neal Steven *lawyer*
Wollenberg, J. Roger *lawyer*
Wood, John Martin *lawyer*
Woodall, Samuel Roy, Jr. *lawyer*
Woodfin, Jane Dee *lawyer, legislative director*
Woodworth, Ramsey Lloyd *lawyer*
Work, Charles Robert *lawyer*
Worsley, James Randolph, Jr. *lawyer*
Worthy, K(enneth) Martin *lawyer*
Wray, Robert *lawyer*
Wright, Wiley Reed, Jr. *lawyer, retired judge, mediator*
Wu, Frank H. *law educator, journalist*
Wyss, John Benedict *lawyer*
Yablon, Jeffery Lee *lawyer*
Yambrusic, Edward Slavko *lawyer, consultant*
Yerick, Martin R. *lawyer*
Yoskowitz, Irving Benjamin *merchant banker*
Yurow, John Jesse *lawyer*
Zausner, L. Andrew *lawyer*
Zax, Leonard A. *lawyer*
Zeidman, Philip Fisher *lawyer*
Zeifang, Donald Paul *lawyer*

Zimmerman, Edwin Morton *lawyer*
Zipp, Joel Frederick *lawyer*
Zollar, Carolyn Catherine *lawyer*
Zuckman, Harvey Lyle *law educator*
Zweben, Murray *lawyer, consultant*

FLORIDA

Alachua
Gaines, Weaver Henderson *lawyer*

Altamonte Springs
Heindl, Phares Matthews *lawyer*
Hoogland, Robert Frederics *lawyer*

Aventura
Fishman, Barry Stuart *lawyer*

Bay Harbor Islands
Patrick, Marty *lawyer*

Boca Grande
Baldwin, William Howard *lawyer, retired foundation executive*
Brock, Mitchell *lawyer*

Boca Raton
Beber, Robert H. *lawyer, financial services executive*
Buckstein, Mark Aaron *lawyer, educator*
Camilleri, Michael *lawyer, educator*
Comisky, Ian Michael *lawyer*
Erdman, Joseph *lawyer*
Golis, Paul Robert *lawyer*
Kassner, Herbert Seymore *lawyer*
Kauffman, Alan Charles *lawyer*
Kitzes, William Fredric *lawyer, safety analyst, consultant*
MacFarland, Richard B. *lawyer*
Racine, Brian August *intellectual property lawyer*
Reinstein, Joel *lawyer*
Siegel, David Burton *lawyer*
Wichinsky, Glenn Ellis *lawyer*
Willis, John Alexander *lawyer*

Bonita Springs
Olander, Ray Gunnar *retired lawyer*

Boynton Beach
Armstrong, Jack Gilliland *lawyer*
Miller, Emanuel *retired lawyer, banker*
Saxbe, William Bart *lawyer, former government official*

Bradenton
Lopacki, Edward Joseph, Jr. *lawyer*

Brandon
Curry, Clifton Conrad, Jr. *lawyer*
Tittsworth, Clayton (Magness) *lawyer*

Casselberry
Sokol, I. Scott *political and fundraising executive*

Clearwater
Bairstow, Frances Kanevsky *labor arbitrator, mediator, educator*
Birmingham, Richard Gregory *lawyer*
Cheek, Michael Carroll *lawyer*
Fine, A(rthur) Kenneth *lawyer*
Free, E. LeBron *lawyer*
Hopen, Anton John *lawyer*
Johnson, Timothy Augustin, Jr. *lawyer*
Peters, Robert Timothy *circuit judge*
Pope, Fred Wallace, Jr. *lawyer*
Sandefer, G(eorge) Larry *lawyer*
Tragos, George Euripedes *lawyer*

Coconut Creek
Godofsky, Stanley *lawyer*

Coconut Grove
Denaro, Gregory *lawyer*
Katz, Lawrence Sheldon *lawyer*
McAmis, Edwin Earl *lawyer*

Coral Gables
Buell, Rodd Russell *lawyer*
Cano, Mario Stephen *lawyer*
Ely, John Hart *lawyer, university dean*
Feiler, Michael Benjamin *lawyer*
Hoffman, Carl H(enry) *lawyer*
Kniskern, Joseph Warren *lawyer*
Lott, Leslie Jean *lawyer*
Mitchell, David Benjamin *lawyer, mediator, arbitrator*
Pastoriza, Julio *lawyer*
Rosenn, Keith Samuel *lawyer, educator*
Sacasas, Rene *lawyer*
Telepas, George Peter *lawyer*
Thornton, John William, Sr. *lawyer*

Coral Springs
Polin, Alan Jay *lawyer*

Daytona Beach
Dunagan, Walter Benton *lawyer, educator*
Gewirtz, Jeffrey Brian *lawyer*
Neitzke, Eric Karl *lawyer*

Deerfield Beach
Brown, Colin W(egand) *lawyer, diversified company executive*
Levitan, David M(aurice) *lawyer, educator*
Rung, Richard Allen *lawyer, retired air force officer, retired educator*

Delray Beach
Larry, R. Heath *lawyer*
Seder, Arthur Raymond, Jr. *lawyer*
Shister, Joseph *arbitrator, educator*

Dunedin
Zschau, Julius James *lawyer*

Fort Lauderdale
Adams, Daniel Lee *lawyer*
Adams, Salvatore Charles *lawyer, speaker, financial consultant, radio and television commentator*
Austin, Scott Raymond *lawyer*

Barnard, George Smith *lawyer, former federal agency official*
Bogenschutz, J. David *lawyer*
Brawer, Marc Harris *lawyer*
Bunnell, George Eli *lawyer*
Bustamante, Nestor *lawyer*
Caulkins, Charles S. *lawyer*
Ceasar, Mitchell *lawyer*
Cooney, David Francis *lawyer*
Dressler, Robert A. *lawyer*
Dutko, Michael Edward *lawyer*
Ephraim, Charles *lawyer*
Glantz, Wendy Newman *lawyer*
Golden, E(dward) Scott *lawyer*
Hargrove, John Russell *lawyer*
Heath, Thomas Clark *lawyer*
Hess, George Franklin, II *lawyer*
Hester, Julia A. *lawyer*
Hirsch, Jeffrey Allan *lawyer*
Hoines, David Alan *lawyer*
James, Gordon, III *lawyer*
Krathen, David Howard *lawyer*
Kreizinger, Loreen I. *lawyer, nurse*
Kubler, Frank Lawrence *lawyer*
†LaMarr, Jack Paul *lawyer*
Lataif, Lawrence P. *lawyer*
Magrino, Peter Frank *lawyer*
Mastronardi, Corinne Marie *lawyer*
Meeks, William Herman, III *lawyer*
Mintz, Joel Alan *law educator*
Moss, Stephen B. *lawyer*
Nyce, John Daniel *lawyer*
Richmond, Gail Levin *law educator*
Rose, Norman *retired lawyer, retired accountant*
Roselli, Richard Joseph *lawyer*
Satz, Michael *lawyer*
Schrader, Robert George *lawyer*
Schreiber, Alan Hickman *lawyer*
Sherman, Richard Allen *lawyer*
Spann, Ronald Thomas *mediator*
Stankee, Glen Allen *lawyer*
Tripp, Norman Densmore *lawyer*
Turner, Hugh Joseph, Jr. *lawyer*
Wich, Donald Anthony, Jr. *lawyer*

Fort Myers
Allen, Richard Chester *retired lawyer, educator*
Colasurd, Richard Michael *lawyer*
Dalton, Anne *lawyer*
Fisher, Michael Bruce *lawyer*
Medvecky, Robert Stephen *lawyer*
Morse, John Harleigh *lawyer*
Peterson, Rodney Delos *mediator, forensic economist*

Fort Walton Beach
Day, George Everette *lawyer, retired military officer*

Gainesville
Boyes, Patrice Flinchbaugh *lawyer, environmental executive*
Freeland, James M. Jackson *lawyer, educator*
Huszar, Arlene Celia *lawyer, mediator*
Israel, Jerold Harvey *law educator*
Kaimowitz, Gabe Hillel *civil rights lawyer*
Kurrus, Thomas William *lawyer*
Maurer, Virginia Gallaher *law educator*
Smith, David Thornton *lawyer, educator*
Tillman, Michael Gerard *lawyer*
Van Alstyne, W. Scott, Jr. *lawyer, educator*
Weyrauch, Walter Otto *law educator*
White, Jill Carolyn *lawyer*

Haines City
Mc Dougall, Dugald Stewart *retired lawyer*

Hialeah
Dominik, Jack Edward *lawyer*

Highland Beach
Zagoria, Sam D(avid) *arbitrator, author, educator*

Hobe Sound
Etherington, Edwin Deacon *lawyer, business executive, educator*
Havens, Oliver Hershman *lawyer, consultant*
Markoe, Frank, Jr. *lawyer, business and hospital executive*
Matheson, William Lyon *lawyer*
Simpson, Russell Gordon *lawyer, mayor, counselor to not-for-profit organizations*

Hollywood
Fischler, Shirley Balter *retired lawyer*
Roseman, Mark Alan *lawyer*
Tannen, Ricki Lewis *lawyer, depth psychologist/analyst, educator*

Jacksonville
Ansbacher, Lewis *lawyer*
Beytagh, Francis Xavier, Jr. *law educator*
Boyer, Tyrie Alvis *lawyer*
Bradford, Dana Gibson, II *lawyer*
Bryan, Joseph Shepard, Jr. *lawyer*
Commander, Charles Edward *lawyer, real estate consultant*
Criser, Marshall M. *lawyer, retired university president*
Dornan, Kevin William *lawyer*
Ehrlich, Raymond *lawyer*
Farmer, Guy Otto, II *lawyer*
Fawbush, Andrew Jackson *lawyer*
Getman, Willard Etheridge *lawyer, mediator*
Gooding, David Michael *lawyer, mediator*
Halverson, Steven Thomas *lawyer, construction executive*
Held, Edwin Walter, Jr. *lawyer*
Keefe, Kenneth M., Jr. *lawyer*
Kelso, Linda Yayoi *lawyer*
Kent, John Bradford *lawyer*
Korn, Michael Jeffrey *lawyer*
Legler, Mitchell Wooten *lawyer*
McBurney, Charles Walker, Jr. *lawyer*
McWilliams, John Lawrence, III *lawyer*
Milton, Joseph Payne *lawyer*
Moseley, James Francis *lawyer*
Mullaney, Richard A. *lawyer*
Phillips, Mary Kleyla *lawyer*
Pillans, Charles Palmer, III *lawyer*
Rinaman, James Curtis, Jr. *lawyer*
Sadler, Luther Fuller, Jr. *lawyer*
Slade, Thomas Bog, III *lawyer, investment banker*
Stone, Dennis J. *law educator, dean, lawyer*
Vane, Terence G., Jr. *mortgage company executive, lawyer*
Wallis, Donald Wills *lawyer*

White, Edward Alfred *lawyer*
Zahra, Ellis E. *lawyer*

Jasper
McCormick, John Hoyle *lawyer*

Jensen Beach
Stuart, Harold Cutliff *lawyer, business executive*

Jupiter
Brophy, Gilbert Thomas *lawyer*
Click, David Forrest *lawyer*
del Russo, Alessandra Luini *law educator*

Key West
Eden, Nathan E. *lawyer*
Smith, Wayne LaRue *lawyer, consultant*

Lady Lake
Clements, Allen, Jr. *lawyer*

Lake Buena Vista
Schmudde, Lee Gene *corporate lawyer*

Lake Wales
Adams, Paul Winfrey *lawyer, business executive*

Lakeland
Artigliere, Ralph *lawyer, educator*
Dufoe, William Stewart *lawyer*
Harris, Christy Franklin *lawyer*
Kibler, David Burke, III *lawyer*
Kittleson, Henry Marshall *lawyer*
Knowlton, Kevin Charles *lawyer*
Koren, Edward Franz *lawyer*
McClurg, E. Vane *lawyer*
Schott, Clifford Joseph *lawyer*

Largo
Trevena, John Harry *lawyer*

Leesburg
Austin, Robert Eugene, Jr. *lawyer*
Fechtel, Vincent John *legal administrator*

Live Oak
Peters, Lee Ira, Jr. *public defender*

Longboat Key
Freeman, Richard Merrell *lawyer, corporate director*
Heitler, George *lawyer*
Pulvermacher, Louis Cecil *lawyer*

Longwood
Cordes, Alexander Charles *lawyer*
Dicks, Jack William *lawyer*
Simon, James Lowell *lawyer*
Tomasulo, Virginia Merrills *retired lawyer*

Lutz
Hayes, Timothy George *lawyer, consultant*

Melbourne
Ballantyne, Richard Lee *lawyer*
Cacciatore, S. Sammy, Jr. *lawyer*
Gougelman, Paul Reina *lawyer*
Trachtman, Jerry H. *lawyer*

Miami
Alonso, Antonio Enrique *lawyer*
Armstrong, James Louden, III *lawyer*
Astigarraga, Jose I(gnacio) *lawyer*
Baumberger, Charles Henry *lawyer*
Beckham, Walter Hull, Jr. *lawyer, educator*
Berger, Steven R. *lawyer*
Berley, David Richard *lawyer*
Berman, Bruce Judson *lawyer*
Blackburn, Roger Lloyd *lawyer*
Blumberg, Edward Robert *lawyer*
Brady, Steven Michael *lawyer*
Bronis, Stephen J. *lawyer*
Burnett, Henry *lawyer*
Clarke, Mercer Kaye *lawyer*
Cohen, Jeffrey Michael *lawyer*
Colsky, Andrew Evan *lawyer, mediator, arbitrator*
Dady, Robert Edward *lawyer*
David, Christopher Mark *lawyer*
Deaktor, Darryl Barnett *lawyer*
de Leon, John Louis *public defender*
Dribin, Michael A. *lawyer*
Dyer, John Martin *lawyer, marketing educator*
England, Arthur Jay, Jr. *lawyer, former state justice*
Ersek, Gregory Joseph Mark *lawyer, business administrator*
Ferrell, Milton Morgan, Jr. *lawyer*
Fishman, Lewis Warren *lawyer, educator*
Fontes, J. Mario F., Jr. *lawyer*
Fox, Gary Devenow *lawyer*
Garrett, Richard G. *lawyer*
Godofsky, Lawrence *lawyer*
Gomez, Ivan A. *lawyer*
Gong, Edmond Joseph *lawyer*
Gragg, Karl Lawrence *lawyer*
Granata, Linda M. *lawyer*
Greenleaf, Walter Franklin *lawyer*
Greer, Alan Graham *lawyer*
Gross, Leslie Jay *lawyer*
Grossman, Robert Louis *lawyer*
Hall, Andrew Clifford *lawyer*
Hall, Miles Lewis, Jr. *lawyer*
Halsey, Douglas Martin *lawyer*
Hartz, Steven Edward Marshall *lawyer*
Hector, Louis Julius *lawyer*
Hickey, John Heyward *lawyer*
Hirsch, Milton Charles *lawyer*
Hoffman, Larry J. *lawyer*
Houlihan, Gerald John *lawyer*
Hudson, Robert Franklin, Jr. *lawyer*
Imperato, Joseph John *lawyer, composer*
Kenin, David S. *lawyer*
Klein, Peter William *lawyer, corporate officer, investment company executive*
Klock, Joseph Peter, Jr. *lawyer*
Korchin, Judith Miriam *lawyer*
Kuehne, Benedict P. *lawyer*
Kurzban, Ira Jay *lawyer*
Lampen, Richard Jay *lawyer, investment banker*
Landy, Burton Aaron *lawyer*
Lipcon, Charles Roy *lawyer*
Long, Maxine Master *lawyer*
Louis, Paul Adolph *lawyer*
Maher, Stephen Trivett *lawyer, educator*

DuBose, Charles Wilson *lawyer*
Duffey, William Simon, Jr. *lawyer*
Durrett, James Frazer, Jr. *lawyer*
Eason, William Everette, Jr. *lawyer*
Eckl, William Wray *lawyer*
Edwards, Stephen Allen *lawyer*
Egan, Michael Joseph *retired lawyer, state legislator*
Eidson, James Anthony *lawyer*
England, John Melvin *lawyer, clergyman*
Epstein, David Gustav *lawyer*
Etheridge, Jack Paul *arbitrator, mediator, former judge*
Farnham, Clayton Henson *lawyer*
Fellows, Henry David, Jr. *lawyer*
Felton, Jule Wimberly, Jr. *lawyer*
Fernandez, Henry A. *lawyer, consultant*
Fiorentino, Carmine *lawyer*
Fleming, Julian Denver, Jr. *lawyer*
Forbes, Theodore McCoy, Jr. *arbitrator, mediator, retired lawyer*
Foreman, Edward Rawson *lawyer*
Fortin, Raymond D. *lawyer*
Franklin, Charles Scothern *lawyer*
Gambrell, David Henry *lawyer*
Genberg, Ira *lawyer*
Girth, Marjorie Louisa *lawyer, educator*
Gladden, Joseph Rhea, Jr. *lawyer*
Glaser, Arthur Henry *lawyer*
Goldstein, Elliott *lawyer*
Gonzalez-Pita, J. Alberto *lawyer*
Grady, Kevin E. *lawyer*
Greenblatt, Edward Lande *lawyer*
Greer, Bernard Lewis, Jr. *lawyer*
Haas, George Aaron *lawyer*
Harkey, Robert Shelton *lawyer*
Harness, William Walter *lawyer*
Harney, Thomas C. *lawyer*
Hassett, Robert William *lawyer*
Hasson, James Keith, Jr. *lawyer, law educator*
Head, William Carl *lawyer, author*
Henson, Howard Kirk *lawyer*
Henwood, William Scott *lawyer*
Hill, Paul Drennen *lawyer, banker*
Hoff, Gerhardt Michael *lawyer, insurance company executive*
Hoffman, Michael William *lawyer, accountant*
Hopkins, George Mathews Marks *lawyer, business executive*
Howard, Harry Clay *lawyer*
Hunter, Forrest Walker *lawyer*
Isaf, Fred Thomas *lawyer*
Izard, John *lawyer*
Janney, Donald Wayne *lawyer*
Jenkins, Albert Felton, Jr. *lawyer*
Johnson, Weyman Thompson, Jr. *lawyer*
Jones, Frank Cater *lawyer*
Katz, Joel Abraham *lawyer, music consultant*
Kelley, James Francis *lawyer*
Kelly, James Michael *lawyer*
Killorin, Edward Wylly *lawyer, tree farmer*
Killorin, Robert Ware *lawyer*
Kinzer, William Luther *lawyer*
Kitchens, Joyce Ellen *lawyer, assistant county guardian*
Kitchens, William H. *lawyer*
Klamon, Lawrence Paine *lawyer*
†Kline, Lowry F. *lawyer*
Kneisel, Edmund M. *lawyer*
Knight, W. Donald, Jr. *lawyer*
Knowles, Marjorie Fine *lawyer, educator, dean*
Lackland, Theodore Howard *lawyer*
Lamon, Harry Vincent, Jr. *lawyer*
Landau, Michael B. *law educator, musician, author*
Landon, James Henry *lawyer*
Lanier, George H. *lawyer*
Leonard, David Morse *lawyer*
Lester, Charles Turner, Jr. *lawyer*
Levy, David *lawyer*
Linkous, William Joseph, Jr. *lawyer*
Lipshutz, Robert Jerome *lawyer, former government official*
Lotito, Nicholas Anthony *lawyer*
Lower, Robert Cassel *lawyer, educator*
Marshall, John Treutlen *lawyer*
Marshall, Thomas Oliver, Jr. *lawyer*
Marvin, Charles Arthur *law educator*
McNeill, Thomas Ray *lawyer*
McVey, Walter Lewis *lawyer, educator*
†Meltz, David Barry *law educator*
Mobley, John Homer, II *lawyer*
Moderow, Joseph Robert *lawyer, package distribution company executive*
Moeling, Walter Goos, IV *lawyer*
Moss, Sandra Hughes *legal administrator*
Mull, Gale W. *lawyer*
Muller, William Manning *corporate lawyer*
Murphy, Richard Patrick *lawyer*
Newton, Floyd Childs, III *lawyer*
Ortiz, Jay Richard Gentry *lawyer*
Owen, Robert Hubert *lawyer, former real estate broker*
Pannell, Robert D. *lawyer*
Paquin, Jeffrey Dean *lawyer*
Partain, Eugene Gartly *lawyer*
Patterson, William Robert *lawyer*
Phillips, Barry *lawyer*
Phillips, William Russell, Sr. *lawyer*
Piassick, Joel Bernard *lawyer*
Pike, Larry Samuel *lawyer*
Pilcher, James Brownie *lawyer*
Pless, Laurance Davidson *lawyer*
Podgor, Ellen Sue *law educator*
Poe, H. Sadler *lawyer*
Prince, David Cannon *lawyer*
Pryor, Shepherd Green, III *lawyer*
Raby, Kenneth Alan *lawyer, retired army officer*
Reed, Glen Alfred *lawyer*
Rhodes, Thomas Willard *lawyer*
Richey, Thomas S. *lawyer*
Riggs, Gregory Lynn *lawyer*
Rogers, C. B. *lawyer*
Rusher, Derwood H., II *lawyer*
Salo, Ann Sexton Distler *lawyer*
Sands, Robert O. *lawyer*
Savell, Edward Lupo *lawyer*
Schroder, Jack Spalding, Jr. *lawyer*
Schulte, Jeffrey Lewis *lawyer*
Schwartz, Arthur Jay *lawyer*
Sibley, Horace Holden *lawyer*
Sibley, James Malcolm *retired lawyer*
Smith, Alexander Wyly, Jr. *lawyer*
Smith, Eleanor Van Law *paralegal*
Smith, James Louis, III *lawyer*
Smith, Jeffrey Michael *lawyer*
Smith, Lawrence A. *lawyer*
Smith, Sidney Oslin, Jr. *lawyer*
Somers, Fred Leonard, Jr. *lawyer*
Spalten, David Elliot *lawyer*

Stallings, Ronald Denis *lawyer*
Stamps, Thomas Paty *lawyer, consultant*
Stephenson, Mason Williams *lawyer*
Stewart, Jeffrey B. *lawyer, commodity trading advisor*
Stone, Matthew Peter *lawyer*
Strauss, Robert David *lawyer*
Sullivan, Terrance Charles *lawyer*
Swann, Jerre Bailey *lawyer*
Sweeney, Neal James *lawyer*
Swift, Frank Meador *lawyer*
Tanner, W(alter) Rhett *lawyer*
Taylor, George Kimbrough, Jr. *lawyer*
Tennant, Thomas Michael *lawyer*
Thompson, Larry Dean *lawyer*
Togut, Torin Dana *lawyer*
Varner, Chilton Davis *lawyer*
Volentine, Richard J., Jr. *lawyer*
Wakefield, Stephen Alan *lawyer*
Walsh, W. Terence *lawyer*
Weisz, Peter R. *lawyer*
Whitley, Joe Dally *lawyer*
Williams, David Howard *lawyer*
Williams, Neil, Jr. *lawyer*
Wilson, James Hargrove, Jr. *lawyer*
Withrow, William N., Jr. *lawyer*
Wolensky, Michael K. *lawyer*
Womack, Mary Pauline *lawyer*
†Worley, David *lawyer*
Wright, Peter Meldrim *lawyer*
Young, Michael Anthony *lawyer*
Zink, Charles Talbott *lawyer*

Augusta
Cooney, William J. *lawyer*
Woods, Gerald Wayne *lawyer*

Barnesville
Kennedy, Harvey John, Jr. *lawyer*

Buford
Rowe, Audrey *paralegal*

Canton
Hasty, William Grady, Jr. *lawyer*

Columbus
Brinkley, Jack Thomas *lawyer, former congressman*
Brinkley, Jack Thomas, Jr. *lawyer*
Harp, John Anderson *lawyer*
Lasseter, Earle Forrest *lawyer*
Page, William Marion *lawyer*
Polleys, Hardwick, Jr. *lawyer*

Dallas
Williams, Gary Randall *lawyer*

Dalton
†Laughter, Bennie M. *corporate lawyer*

Decatur
Apolinsky, Stephen Douglas *lawyer*
Middleton, James Boland *lawyer*
Williams, Rita Tucker *lawyer*

Dillard
Wilkinson, Albert Mims, Jr. *lawyer*

Douglas
Sims, Rebecca Littleton *lawyer*

Dublin
Greene, Jule Blounte *lawyer*

Duluth
Sloan, Donnie Robert, Jr. *lawyer*

Dunwoody
Callison, James W. *former lawyer, consultant, airline executive*

Eastman
Wiggins, James L. *lawyer*

Fayetteville
Johnson, Donald Wayne *lawyer*

Gainesville
Schuder, Raymond Francis *lawyer*

Hamilton
Byrd, Gary Ellis *lawyer*
Chewning, Martha Frances MacMillan *lawyer*

Jasper
Marger, Edwin *lawyer*

Lilburn
West, Stephen Allan *lawyer*

Lookout Mountain
Hitching, Harry James *retired lawyer*

Macon
†Aderhold, H. Randolph *prosecutor*
Ennis, Edgar William, Jr. *lawyer*
Robinson, W. Lee *lawyer*
Snow, Cubbedge, Jr. *lawyer*
Woody, Thomas Clifton II *assistant district attorney*

Marietta
Ahlstrom, Michael Joseph *lawyer*
†Barnes, Roy Eugene *lawyer*
Bentley, Fred Douglas, Sr. *lawyer*
Ingram, George Conley *judge*
Nowland, James Ferrell *lawyer*

Mcdonough
Meadows, Rod G. *lawyer*

Milledgeville
Buice, Bonnie Carl *lawyer, priest*

Newnan
Franklin, Bruce Walter *lawyer*

Norcross
Anderson, Albert Sydney, III *lawyer*
Hahn, Stanley Robert, Jr. *lawyer, financial executive*

Winkler, Allen Warren *lawyer*

Perry
Geiger, James Norman *lawyer*

Roswell
†Burkey, Frederick D. *lawyer*

Savannah
Bowman, Catherine McKenzie *lawyer*
Dixon, Harry D., Jr. (Donnie Dixon) *prosecutor*
Forbes, Morton Gerald *lawyer*
Painter, Paul Wain, Jr. *lawyer*
Rawson, William Robert *lawyer, retired manufacturing company executive*
Stillwell, Walter Brooks, III *lawyer*
Trosten, Leonard Morse *lawyer*

Sea Island
Leisure, George Stanley, Jr. *lawyer*
Revoile, Charles Patrick *lawyer*

Statesboro
Stone, Ralph Kenny *lawyer*

Summerville
Connelly, Lewis Branch Sutton *lawyer*

Tucker
Armstrong, Edwin Alan *lawyer*

Valdosta
Bright, Joseph Converse *lawyer*

Winder
McLemore, Michael Kerr *lawyer, minister*

Zebulon
Watson, Forrest Albert, Jr. *lawyer, bank executive*

HAWAII

Honolulu
Akinaka, Asa Masayoshi *lawyer*
Alm, Steve *prosecutor*
Asai-Sato, Carol Yuki *lawyer*
Bloede, Victor Carl *lawyer, academic executive*
Boas, Frank *lawyer*
Boggs, Steven Eugene *lawyer*
Callies, David Lee *lawyer, educator*
Case, James Hebard *lawyer*
Char, Vernon Fook Leong *lawyer*
Chuck, Walter G(oonsun) *lawyer*
Cowan, Stuart Marshall *lawyer*
Deaver, Phillip Lester *lawyer*
Devens, Paul *lawyer*
Dreher, Nicholas C. *lawyer*
Gay, E(mil) Laurence *lawyer*
Gelber, Don Jeffrey *lawyer*
Gillin, Malvin James, Jr. *lawyer*
Heller, Ronald Ian *lawyer*
Hipp, Kenneth Byron *lawyer*
Katayama, Robert Nobuichi *lawyer*
Kawachika, James Akio *lawyer*
Kupchak, Kenneth Roy *lawyer*
Lau, Eugene Wing Iu *lawyer*
Lau, Jeffrey Daniel *lawyer*
Lilly, Michael Alexander *lawyer, author*
Louie, David Mark *lawyer*
Matayoshi, Coralie Chun *lawyer, bar association executive*
†Mattoch, Ian L. *lawyer*
†Mau-Shimizu, Patricia Ann *lawyer*
Miller, Clifford Joel *lawyer*
Miller, Richard Sherwin *law educator*
Miyasaki, Shuichi *lawyer*
Moore, Ernest Carroll, III *lawyer*
Moroney, Michael John *lawyer*
Okinaga, Lawrence Shoji *lawyer*
Potts, Dennis Walker *lawyer*
Quinn, William Francis *lawyer*
Reber, David James *lawyer*
Reinke, Stefan Michael *lawyer*
Sato, Glenn Kenji *lawyer*
Shigetomi, Keith Shigeo *lawyer*
Sumida, Kevin P.H. *lawyer*
Tharp, James Wilson *lawyer*
Turbin, Richard *lawyer*
Weight, Michael Anthony *lawyer, former judge*
Wong, Alfred Mun Kong *lawyer*
Woo, Vernon Ying-Tsai *lawyer, real estate developer, judge*
Yamada, Stephen Kinichi *lawyer, real estate developer*
Yap, Frank, Jr. *lawyer*

Kahului
Richardson, Robert Allen *lawyer, educator*

Kailua Kona
Martin, William Charles *retired lawyer, law educator*
Zimmerman, William Irving *lawyer*
Zola, Michael S. *lawyer*

Kaneohe
Donahoe, Peter Aloysius *lawyer*

Kihei
Burns, Richard Gordon *retired lawyer, writer, consultant*

Kula
Rohlfing, Frederick William *lawyer, travel executive, political consultant, retired judge*

Laie
Allen, Merle Maeser, Jr. *lawyer*

Lihue
Tanaka, Leila Chiyako *lawyer*

Wailuku
Kinaka, William Tatsuo *lawyer*

IDAHO

Boise
Barber, Phillip Mark *lawyer*
Doolittle, Michael Jim *lawyer*
Erickson, Robert Stanley *lawyer*
Geston, Mark Symington *lawyer*
Hoagland, Samuel Albert *lawyer, pharmacist*
Holleran, John W. *lawyer*
Leroy, David Henry *lawyer, state and federal official*
Meyer, Christopher Hawkins *lawyer*
Minnich, Diane Kay *state bar executive*
Myers, William Gerry, III *lawyer*
Noack, Harold Quincy, Jr. *lawyer*
†Park, William Anthony (Tony) *lawyer*
Richardson, Betty H. *prosecutor*
Risch, James E. *lawyer*
Shurtliff, Marvin Karl *lawyer*
VanHole, William Remi *lawyer*

Caldwell
Kerrick, David Ellsworth *lawyer*

Driggs
Cantwell, William Patterson *lawyer*

Idaho Falls
Whittier, Monte Ray *lawyer*

Lewiston
Aherin, Darrel William *lawyer*
Peterson, Philip Everett *legal educator*
Tait, John Reid *lawyer*

Moscow
Vincenti, Sheldon Arnold *law educator, lawyer*

Twin Falls
Hohnhorst, John Charles *lawyer*
Tolman, Steven Kay *lawyer*

ILLINOIS

Alton
Hoagland, Karl King, Jr. *lawyer*
Struif, L. James *lawyer*
Talbert, Hugh Mathis *lawyer*

Argo
Castellano, Christine Marie *lawyer*

Arlington Heights
Biestek, John Paul *lawyer*

Aurora
Alschuler, Sam *retired lawyer*
Camic, David Edward *lawyer*
McCleary, Scott Fitzgerald *lawyer*

Barrington
Cass, Robert Michael *lawyer, consultant*
Lee, William Marshall *lawyer*
Lessman, Robert Edward *lawyer*
Tobin, Dennis Michael *lawyer*
White, Jeffrey Paul *lawyer*
Wyatt, James Frank, Jr. *lawyer*

Batavia
Thompson, Juul Harold *lawyer, educator*

Belleville
Bauman, John Duane *lawyer*
Boyle, Richard Edward *lawyer*
Coghill, William Thomas, Jr. *lawyer*
Heiligenstein, Christian E. *lawyer*
Hess, Frederick J. *lawyer*
James, Ernest Wilbur *lawyer*
Parham, James Robert *lawyer*
Waller, Paul Pressley, Jr. *lawyer*

Bensenville
Demouth, Robin Madison *lawyer, corporate executive*

Bloomington
Bragg, Michael Ellis *lawyer, insurance company executive*
Goebel, William Mathers *lawyer*
Kelly, Timothy William *lawyer*
Sullivan, Laura Patricia *lawyer, insurance company executive*

Buffalo Grove
Kole, Julius S. *lawyer*

Carbondale
Clemons, John Robert *lawyer*
Guernsey, Thomas Franklin *law educator*

Carrollton
Strickland, Hugh Alfred *lawyer*

Carthage
Glidden, John Redmond *lawyer*

Champaign
Cribbet, John Edward *law educator, former university chancellor*
Frampton, George Thomas, Sr. *legal educator*
Johnson, Lawrence Eugene *lawyer*
Kindt, John Warren, Sr. *lawyer, educator, consultant*
Krause, Harry Dieter *law educator*
Maggs, Peter Blount *lawyer, educator*
Mamer, Stuart Mies *lawyer*
Mc Cord, John Harrison *lawyer, educator*
Miller, Harold Arthur *lawyer*
Nowak, John E. *law educator*
Rawles, Edward Hugh *lawyer*
Rotunda, Ronald Daniel *law educator, consultant*
Stone, Victor J. *law educator*

Chicago
Abrams, Lee Norman *lawyer*
Abt, Ralph Edwin *lawyer*
Acker, Ann *lawyer*
Acker, Frederick George *lawyer*
Adair, Wendell Hinton, Jr. *lawyer*
Adelman, Stanley Joseph *lawyer*

Adelman, Steven Herbert *lawyer*
Allard, Jean *lawyer, urban planner*
Allen, Ronald Jay *law educator*
Allen, Thomas Draper *lawyer*
Anderson, David Albert *lawyer*
Anderson, J. Trent *lawyer*
Anderson, John Thomas *lawyer*
Anderson, Kimball Richard *lawyer*
Anderson, William Cornelius, III *lawyer*
Angst, Gerald L. *lawyer*
Anthony, Michael Francis *lawyer*
Antonio, Douglas John *lawyer*
Anvaripour, M. A. *lawyer*
Appel, Nina Schick *law educator, dean*
Argeros, Anthony George *lawyer*
Armstrong, Edwin Richard *lawyer, publisher, editor*
Aronson, Virginia L. *lawyer*
Athas, Gus James *lawyer*
Auerbach, Marshall Jay *lawyer*
Augustynski, Adam J. *lawyer*
Avery, Robert Dean *lawyer*
Axley, Frederick William *lawyer*
Badel, Julie *lawyer*
Baer, John Richard Frederick *lawyer*
Baetz, W. Timothy *lawyer*
Bailey, Robert Short *lawyer*
Baker, Bruce Jay *lawyer*
Baker, James Edward Sproul *retired lawyer*
Baker, Pamela *lawyer*
Baldwin, Shaun McParland *lawyer*
Banoff, Sheldon Irwin *lawyer*
Barker, William Thomas *lawyer*
Barnard, Robert N. *lawyer*
Barnes, James Garland, Jr. *lawyer*
Barr, John Robert *lawyer*
Barrett, Roger Watson *lawyer*
Barron, Howard Robert *lawyer*
Barry, Norman J., Jr. *lawyer*
Baruch, Hurd *lawyer, arbitrator*
Bashwiner, Steven Lacelle *lawyer*
Baugher, Peter V. *lawyer*
Beck, Philip S. *lawyer*
Becker, Theodore Michaelson *lawyer*
Beem, Jack Darrel *lawyer*
Benak, James Donald *lawyer*
Bennett, Robert William *law educator*
Berens, Mark Harry *lawyer*
Berenzweig, Jack Charles *lawyer*
Berger, Robert Michael *lawyer*
Berkoff, Mark Andrew *lawyer*
Berland, Abel Edward *lawyer, realtor*
Berner, Robert Lee, Jr. *lawyer*
Berning, Larry D. *lawyer*
Bernstein, H. Bruce *lawyer*
Berolzheimer, Karl *lawyer*
Biebel, Paul Philip, Jr. *lawyer*
Biederman, Jerry H. *lawyer*
Bierig, Jack R. *lawyer, educator*
Bitner, John Howard *lawyer*
Bixby, Frank Lyman *lawyer*
Blatt, Richard Lee *lawyer*
Block, Neal Jay *lawyer*
Blount, Michael Eugene *lawyer*
Blume, Paul Chiappe *lawyer*
Blust, Larry D. *lawyer*
Boardman, Robert A. *lawyer*
Boardman, William Penniman *lawyer, banker*
Bockelman, John Richard *lawyer*
Bodenstein, Ira *federal government lawyer*
Bodine, Laurence *lawyer, editor, marketer*
Boehnen, Daniel A. *lawyer*
Bolaños, Anita Marie *lawyer*
Bowe, William John *lawyer*
Bower, Glen Landis *lawyer*
Bramnik, Robert Paul *lawyer*
Brennan, James Joseph *lawyer, banking and financial services*
Brice, Roger Thomas *lawyer*
Bridewell, David Alexander *lawyer*
Bridgman, Thomas Francis *lawyer*
Brizzolara, Charles Anthony *lawyer*
Brown, Alan Crawford *lawyer*
Brown, Donald James, Jr. *lawyer*
Brown, Gregory K. *lawyer*
Brown, Steven Spencer *lawyer*
Bruner, Stephen C. *lawyer*
Bulger, Brian Wegg *lawyer*
Burditt, George Miller, Jr. *lawyer*
Burgdoerfer, Jerry *lawyer*
Burke, Thomas Joseph, Jr. *lawyer*
Burkey, Lee Melville *lawyer*
Burns, James B. *prosecutor*
Burns, Terrence Michael *lawyer*
Busey, Roxane C. *lawyer*
Bush, Crystal Reed *lawyer*
Bussman, Donald Herbert *lawyer*
Carlin, Dennis J. *lawyer*
Carlson, Stephen Curtis *lawyer*
Carlson, Walter Carl *lawyer*
Carpenter, David William *lawyer*
Carren, Jeffrey P. *lawyer*
Carroll, James J. *lawyer*
Carroll, William Kenneth *law educator, psychologist, theologian*
Cascino, Anthony Elmo, Jr. *lawyer, insurance executive*
Cassel, Douglass Watts, Jr. *lawyer, educator, journalist*
Chandler, Kent, Jr. *lawyer*
Cheely, Daniel Joseph *lawyer*
Chefitz, Joel Gerald *lawyer*
Chemers, Robert Marc *lawyer*
Cherney, James Alan *lawyer*
Chico, Gery J. *lawyer, school system administrator*
Chiles, Stephen Michael *lawyer*
Christian, John M. *lawyer*
Chudzinski, Mark Adam *lawyer*
Cipinko, Scott J. *lawyer, general counsel, secretary*
Clark, James Allen *lawyer, educator*
Clemens, Richard Glenn *lawyer*
Clinton, Edward Xavier *lawyer*
Closen, Michael Lee *law educator*
Cohen, Christopher B. *lawyer*
Cohen, Melanie Rovner *lawyer*
Collen, Sheldon Orrin *lawyer*
Comiskey, Michael Peter *lawyer*
Conklin, Thomas William *lawyer*
Connelly, Mary Jo *lawyer*
Conviser, Richard James *law educator, lawyer, publications company executive*
Conway, Michael Maurice *lawyer*
Copeland, Edward Jerome *lawyer*
Corcoran, James Martin, Jr. *lawyer, writer, lecturer*
Corwin, Sherman Phillip *lawyer*
Costello, John William *lawyer*
Coughlan, Kenneth Lewis *lawyer*
Coulson, William Roy *lawyer*
Covey, Frank Michael, Jr. *lawyer, educator*
Crane, Mark *lawyer*
Craven, George W. *lawyer*
Crawford, Dewey Byers *lawyer*
Cremin, Susan Elizabeth *lawyer*
Cressey, Bryan Charles *lawyer*
Crihfield, Philip J. *lawyer*
Crisham, Thomas Michael *lawyer*
Cross, Chester Joseph *lawyer, accountant*
Crossan, John Robert *lawyer*
Csar, Michael F. *lawyer*
Cunningham, Robert James *lawyer*
Cunningham, Thomas Justin *lawyer*
Curran, Barbara Adell *retired law foundation administrator, lawyer, writer*
Currie, David Park *lawyer, educator*
Cusack, John Thomas *lawyer*
Custer, Charles Francis *lawyer*
Dam, Kenneth W. *lawyer, law educator*
Daniels, John Draper *lawyer*
Davidson, Stanley J. *lawyer*
Davis, Michael W. *lawyer*
Davis, Muller *lawyer*
Davis, Scott Jonathan *lawyer*
DeCarlo, William S. *lawyer*
Decker, Richard Knore *lawyer*
†de Hoyos, Debora M. *lawyer*
Deitrick, William Edgar *lawyer*
Delp, Wilbur Charles, Jr. *lawyer*
Dent, Thomas G. *lawyer*
D'Esposito, Julian C., Jr. *lawyer*
Despres, Leon Mathis *lawyer, former city official*
Detuno, Joseph Edward *lawyer*
DeWolfe, John Chauncey, Jr. *lawyer*
Ditkowsky, Kenneth K. *lawyer*
Dixon, Stewart Strawn *lawyer*
Dockterman, Michael *lawyer*
Donlevy, John Dearden *lawyer*
Donohoe, Jerome Francis *lawyer*
Dorman, Jeffrey Lawrence *lawyer*
†Douglas, Charles W. *lawyer*
Downing, Robert Allan *lawyer*
Doyle, John Robert *lawyer*
Dropkin, Allen Hodes *lawyer*
Drymalski, Raymond Hibner *lawyer, banker*
Duhl, Michael Foster *lawyer*
Duncan, John Patrick Cavanaugh *lawyer*
Durchslag, Stephen P. *lawyer*
Dykstra, Paul Hopkins *lawyer*
Early, Bert Hylton *lawyer, legal search consultant*
Edelman, Alvin *lawyer*
Egan, Kevin James *lawyer*
Eggert, Russell Raymond *lawyer*
Eimer, Nathan Philip *lawyer*
Ekdahl, Jon Nels *lawyer, corporate secretary*
Elden, Gary Michael *lawyer*
Ellwood, Scott *lawyer*
Elson, Alex *lawyer, educator, arbitrator*
English, John Dwight *lawyer*
Epstein, Richard A. *law educator*
Erens, Jay Allan *lawyer*
Esrick, Jerald Paul *lawyer*
Even, Francis Alphonse *lawyer*
Fahner, Tyrone C. *lawyer, former state attorney general*
Farber, Bernard John *lawyer*
Fazio, Peter Victor, Jr. *lawyer*
Fein, Roger Gary *lawyer*
Feinstein, Fred Ira *lawyer*
Feldman, Scott M. *lawyer*
Fellows, Jerry Kenneth *lawyer*
Felsenthal, Steven Altus *lawyer*
Ferencz, Robert Arnold *lawyer*
Ferguson, Bradford Lee *lawyer*
Ferrini, James Thomas *lawyer*
Field, Robert Edward *lawyer*
Filpi, Robert Alan *lawyer*
Fina, Paul Joseph *lawyer*
Finke, Robert Forge *lawyer*
Fisher, Herbert Hirsh *lawyer*
Fitch, Morgan Lewis, Jr. *intellectual property lawyer*
Fitzpatrick, Christine Morris *legal administrator, former television executive*
Flanagin, Neil *lawyer*
Formeller, Daniel Richard *lawyer*
Fort, Jeffrey C. *lawyer*
Foster, Teree E. *law educator, dean*
Foudree, Bruce William *lawyer*
Fox, Elaine Saphier *lawyer*
Fox, Paul T. *lawyer*
Franch, Richard Thomas *lawyer*
Franklin, Richard Mark *lawyer*
Frano, Andrew Joseph *lawyer, civil engineer*
Fraumann, Willard George *lawyer*
Freed, Mayer Goodman *law educator*
Freeman, Lee Allen, Jr. *lawyer*
Freeman, Louis S. *lawyer*
Friedman, Lawrence Milton *lawyer*
Friedman, Roselyn L. *lawyer*
Fross, Roger Raymond *lawyer*
Fullagar, William Watts *lawyer*
Fuller, Perry Lucian *lawyer*
Furlane, Mark Elliott *lawyer*
Garber, Samuel Baugh *lawyer, retail company executive*
Garth, Bryant Geoffrey *law educator, foundation executive*
Gearen, John Joseph *lawyer*
Geiman, J. Robert *lawyer*
Gelman, Andrew Richard *lawyer*
Geraldson, Raymond I. *lawyer*
Geraldson, Raymond I., Jr. *lawyer*
†Gerber, Lawrence *lawyer*
Geren, Gerald S. *lawyer*
Gerlits, Francis Joseph *lawyer*
Gerske, Janet Fay *lawyer*
Gerstman, George Henry *lawyer*
Gertz, Elmer *lawyer, author, educator*
Gertz, Theodore Gerson *lawyer*
Giampietro, Wayne Bruce *lawyer*
Gibbons, William John *lawyer*
Gilbert, Howard N(orman) *lawyer*
Gilford, Steven Ross *lawyer*
Gilson, Jerome *lawyer, writer*
Gladden, James Walter, Jr. *lawyer*
Gleeson, Paul Francis *lawyer*
Glenn, Cleta Mae *lawyer*
Glieberman, Herbert Allen *lawyer*
Golan, Stephen Leonard *lawyer*
Goldblatt, Stanford Jay *lawyer*
Golden, Bruce Paul *lawyer*
Golden, William C. *lawyer*
Goldman, Louis Budwig *lawyer*
Goldman, Michael P. *lawyer*
Goldschmidt, Lynn Harvey *lawyer*
Goodman, Gary Alan *lawyer*
Gordon, James S. *lawyer*
Gordon, William A. *lawyer*
Gottlieb, Gidon Alain Guy *law educator*
Graham, David F. *lawyer*
Gralen, Donald John *lawyer*
Grant, Burton Fred *lawyer*
Grant, Robert Nathan *lawyer*
Gray, Milton Hefter *lawyer*
Grayck, Marcus Daniel *lawyer*
Greenberger, Ernest *lawyer*
Greenfield, Michael C. *lawyer*
Griffin, Lawrence Joseph *lawyer*
Griffith, Donald Kendall *lawyer*
Grossi, Francis Xavier, Jr. *lawyer, educator*
Grossman, Robert Mayer *lawyer*
Grund, David Ira *lawyer*
Guthman, Jack *lawyer*
Gutstein, Solomon *lawyer*
Haderlein, Thomas M. *lawyer*
Hahn, Frederic Louis *lawyer*
Hales, Daniel B. *lawyer*
Hall, Joan M. *lawyer*
Halloran, Michael John *lawyer*
Hammesfahr, Robert Winter *lawyer*
Hannah, Wayne Robertson, Jr. *lawyer*
Hannay, William Mouat, III *lawyer*
Hanson, Ronald William *lawyer*
Hardgrove, James Alan *lawyer*
Harrington, Carol A. *lawyer*
Harrington, James Timothy *lawyer*
Harris, Donald Ray *lawyer*
Harrold, Bernard *lawyer*
Harvey, Elizabeth Schroer *lawyer*
Hayes, David John Arthur, Jr. *legal association executive*
Hayes, John T. *lawyer, accountant*
Hayward, Thomas Zander, Jr. *lawyer*
Head, Patrick James *lawyer*
Heatwole, Mark M. *lawyer*
Heindl, Warren Anton *law educator, retired*
Heinz, John Peter *lawyer, educator*
Heinz, William Denby *lawyer*
Heisler, Quentin George, Jr. *lawyer*
Helman, Robert Alan *lawyer*
Helmholz, R(ichard) H(enry) *law educator*
Henning, Joel Frank *lawyer, author, publisher, consultant*
Henry, Brian Thomas *lawyer*
Henry, Frederick Edward *lawyer*
Herbert, William Carlisle *lawyer*
Herman, Sidney N. *lawyer*
Herman, Stephen Charles *lawyer*
Hermann, Donald Harold James *lawyer, educator*
Herzog, Fred F. *law educator*
Hess, Sidney J., Jr. *lawyer*
Hester, Thomas Patrick *lawyer, business executive*
Hickey, John Thomas, Jr. *lawyer*
Hickman, Frederic W. *lawyer*
Hilliard, David Craig *lawyer, educator*
Hillman, Jordan Jay *law educator*
Hirshman, Harold Carl *lawyer*
Hoban, George Savre *lawyer*
Hodes, Scott *lawyer*
Hofer, Roy Ellis *lawyer*
Hoff, John Scott *lawyer*
Hoffman, Richard Bruce *lawyer*
Hoffman, Valerie Jane *lawyer*
Hollins, Mitchell Leslie *lawyer*
Horwich, Allan *lawyer*
Hoseman, Daniel *lawyer*
Hoskins, Richard Jerold *lawyer*
Howe, Jonathan Thomas *lawyer*
Howell, R(obert) Thomas, Jr. *lawyer, former food company executive*
Hubbard, Elizabeth Louise *lawyer*
Hummel, Gregory William *lawyer*
Hunt, Lawrence Halley, Jr. *lawyer*
Hunter, James Galbraith, Jr. *lawyer*
Huston, DeVerille Anne *lawyer*
Huston, Steven Craig *lawyer*
Hyman, Michael Bruce *lawyer*
Jackowiak, Patricia *lawyer*
Jacobson, Harold LeLand *lawyer*
Jacobson, Marian Slutz *lawyer*
Jacobson, Richard Joseph *lawyer*
Jacover, Jerold Alan *lawyer*
Jager, Melvin Francis *lawyer*
Jahns, Jeffrey *lawyer*
Jambor, Robert Vernon *lawyer*
Jersild, Thomas Nielsen *lawyer*
Jester, Jack D. *lawyer*
Jock, Paul F., II *lawyer*
Johnson, Douglas Wells *lawyer*
Johnson, Gary Thomas *lawyer*
Johnson, Lael Frederic *lawyer*
Johnson, Richard Fred *lawyer*
Jordan, Michelle Denise *lawyer*
Joseph, Robert Thomas *lawyer*
Joslin, Rodney Dean *lawyer*
Junewicz, James J. *lawyer*
Kallick, David A. *lawyer*
Kamerick, Eileen Ann *financial executive, lawyer*
Kamin, Chester Thomas *lawyer*
Kaminsky, Richard Alan *lawyer*
Kanter, Burton Wallace *lawyer*
Kaplan, Jared *lawyer*
Kaplan, Sidney Mountbatten *lawyer*
Karu, Gilda M(all) *lawyer, government official*
Kastel, Howard L. *lawyer, business executive*
Katz, Stuart Charles *lawyer, concert jazz musician*
Kawitt, Alan *lawyer*
Kelly, Charles Arthur *lawyer*
†Kelly, Janet Langford *lawyer*
Kempf, Donald G., Jr. *lawyer*
Kenney, Frank Deming *lawyer*
Kenny, Edmund Joyce *lawyer*
Kikoler, Stephen Philip *lawyer*
Kim, Michael Charles *lawyer*
King, Clark Chapman, Jr. *lawyer*
King, Michael Howard *lawyer*
King, Sharon Louise *lawyer*
Kins, Juris *lawyer*
Kirkland, John Leonard *lawyer*
Kissel, Richard John *lawyer*
Kite, Steven B. *lawyer*
Klein, Melvyn Norman *lawyer, investment executive*
Klein, Robert Marshall *lawyer*
Klenk, James Andrew *lawyer*
Klenk, Timothy Carver *lawyer*
Knight, Christopher Nichols *lawyer*
Knox, James Edwin *lawyer*
Knox, James Marshall *lawyer*
Kohlstedt, James August *lawyer*
Kohn, Shalom L. *lawyer*
Kohn, William Irwin *lawyer*
Kolek, Robert Edward *lawyer*
Kolmin, Kenneth Guy *lawyer*
Kozak, John W. *lawyer*
Kramm, Deborah Lucille *lawyer*
Kravitt, Jason Harris Paperno *lawyer*
Kriss, Robert J. *lawyer*
Kroll, Barry Lewis *lawyer*
Kunkle, William Joseph, Jr. *lawyer*
Kuta, Jeffrey Theodore *lawyer*
Laidlaw, Andrew R. *lawyer*
Lampert, Steven A. *lawyer*
Landes, William M. *law educator*
Landow-Esser, Janine Marise *lawyer*
Landsberg, Jill Warren *lawyer, consultant to government agencies*
Lane, Ronald Alan *lawyer*
Laner, Richard Warren *lawyer*
†Lassar, Scott R. *lawyer*
Latimer, Kenneth Alan *lawyer*
Lauderdale, Katherine Sue *lawyer*
LeBaron, Charles Frederick, Jr. *lawyer*
Leisten, Arthur Gaynor *lawyer*
Levenfeld, Milton Arthur *lawyer*
Levi, John G. *lawyer*
Levin, Charles Edward *lawyer*
Levin, Jack S. *lawyer*
Levin, Michael David *lawyer*
Levine, Laurence Harvey *lawyer*
Leyhane, Francis John, III *lawyer*
Liggio, Carl Donald *lawyer*
Lind, Jon Robert *lawyer*
Linklater, William Joseph *lawyer*
Lippe, Melvin Karl *lawyer*
Lipton, Lois Jean *lawyer*
Lipton, Richard M. *lawyer*
Litwin, Burton Howard *lawyer*
Lloyd, William F. *lawyer*
Lochbihler, Frederick Vincent *lawyer*
Lockwood, Gary Lee *lawyer*
Looman, James R. *lawyer*
Lorch, Kenneth F. *lawyer*
Loughnane, David J. *lawyer*
Lowry, Donald Michael *retired lawyer*
Lubin, Donald G. *lawyer*
Lundergan, Barbara Keough *lawyer*
Luning, Thomas P. *lawyer*
Lutter, Paul Allen *lawyer*
Lyerla, Bradford Peter *lawyer*
Lynch, John Peter *lawyer*
MacCarthy, Terence Francis *lawyer*
Maher, David Willard *lawyer*
Malinowski, Arthur Anthony *lawyer, labor arbitrator*
Malkin, Cary Jay *lawyer*
Mancoff, Neal Alan *lawyer*
Mandly, Charles Robert, Jr. *lawyer*
Mansfield, Karen Lee *lawyer*
Manzo, Edward David *patent lawyer*
Marick, Michael Miron *lawyer*
Marks, Jerome *lawyer*
Marovitz, James Lee *lawyer*
Marroquin-Merino, Victor Miguel *lawyer*
Marshall, John David *lawyer*
Martin, Arthur Mead *lawyer*
Marvel, Kenneth Robert *lawyer, corporate executive*
Marwedel, Warren John *lawyer*
Marx, David, Jr. *lawyer*
Mason, Henry Lowell, III *lawyer*
Mason, Richard J. *lawyer*
Matanky, Robert William *lawyer*
Mattos Neto, Sebastiao De Souza *lawyer*
Mattson, Stephen Joseph *lawyer*
Mayer, Frank D., Jr. *lawyer*
McCabe, Charles Kevin *lawyer, author*
McCaleb, Malcolm, Jr. *lawyer*
McClain, Lee Bert *corporate lawyer, insurance executive*
McClure, James Julius, Jr. *lawyer, former city official*
McConnell, James Guy *lawyer*
McCracken, Thomas James, Jr. *lawyer*
McCrohon, Craig *lawyer*
McCue, Judith W. *lawyer*
McDermott, John H(enry) *lawyer*
McDermott, Robert B. *lawyer*
McDonald, Thomas Alexander *lawyer*
McDonough, John Michael *lawyer*
McKenzie, Robert Ernest *lawyer*
McLaughlin, T. Mark *lawyer*
McLees, John Alan *lawyer*
McMenamin, John Robert *lawyer*
McNeill, Thomas B. *retired lawyer*
McVisk, William Kilburn *lawyer*
McWhirter, Bruce J. *lawyer*
McWilliams, Dennis Michael *lawyer*
Mehlman, Mark Franklin *lawyer*
Melton, David Reuben *lawyer*
Meltzer, Bernard David *law educator*
Meltzer, Robert Craig *lawyer, educator*
Merrill, Thomas Wendell *lawyer, law educator*
Meyer, Michael Louis *lawyer*
Michaels, Richard Edward *lawyer*
Michalak, Edward Francis *lawyer*
Mikva, Abner Joseph *lawyer, retired federal judge*
Miller, Edward Boone *lawyer*
Miller, John Leed *lawyer*
Miller, Paul J. *lawyer*
Miller, Stephen Ralph *lawyer*
Millner, Robert B. *lawyer*
Milnikel, Robert Saxon *lawyer*
Minichello, Dennis *lawyer*
Minow, Newton Norman *lawyer, educator*
Mobbs, Michael Hall *lawyer*
Montgomery, Charles Barry *lawyer*
Montgomery, William Adam *lawyer*
Moran, John Thomas, Jr. *lawyer*
Morency, Paula J. *lawyer*
Morris, Norval *criminologist, educator*
Morrison, Portia Owen *lawyer*
Morsch, Thomas Harvey *lawyer*
Muchin, Allan B. *lawyer*
Mullen, J. Thomas *lawyer*
Muller, Kurt Alexander *lawyer*
Mumford, Manly Whitman *lawyer*
Murdock, Charles William *lawyer, educator*
Murray, Daniel Richard *lawyer*
Murtaugh, Christopher David *lawyer*
Myers, Lonn William *lawyer*
Nachman, Norman Harry *lawyer*
Napleton, Robert Joseph *lawyer*
Nechin, Herbert Benjamin *lawyer*
Nelson, Richard David *lawyer*
Neumeier, Matthew Michael *lawyer*
Newey, Paul Davis *lawyer*
Newlin, Charles Fremont *lawyer*
Nissen, William John *lawyer*
Nitikman, Franklin W. *lawyer*
Nora, Gerald Ernest *lawyer*
Nord, Robert Eamor *lawyer*
Notz, John Kranz, Jr. *arbitrator and mediator, retired lawyer*
Novak, Mark *lawyer*
Nowacki, James Nelson *lawyer*
Nussbaum, Bernard J. *lawyer*

O'Brien, James Phillip *lawyer*
O'Brien, Patrick William *lawyer*
Oesterle, Eric Adam *lawyer*
O'Flaherty, Paul Benedict *lawyer*
O'Hagan, James Joseph *lawyer*
O'Leary, Daniel Vincent, Jr. *lawyer*
Olian, Robert Martin *lawyer*
Oliver, Roseann *lawyer*
O'Malley, John Daniel *law educator, banker*
O'Neill, Timothy P. *law educator*
Orin, Stuart I. *lawyer*
Overgaard, Mitchell Jersild *lawyer*
Overton, George Washington *lawyer*
Pallasch, B. Michael *lawyer*
Palmer, John Bernard, III *lawyer*
Palmer, Robert Towne *lawyer*
Panich, Danuta Bembenista *lawyer*
Paprocki, Thomas John *lawyer, priest*
Parkhurst, Todd Sheldon *lawyer*
Partridge, Mark Van Buren *lawyer, educator, writer*
Pascal, Roger *lawyer*
Pattishall, Beverly Wyckliffe *lawyer*
Pavalon, Eugene Irving *lawyer*
Pelton, Russell Meredith, Jr. *lawyer*
Perlberg, Jules Martin *lawyer*
Petersen, Donald Sondergaard *lawyer*
Petersen, William Otto *lawyer*
Peterson, Bradley Laurits *lawyer*
Peterson, Ronald Roger *lawyer*
Piecewicz, Walter Michael *lawyer*
Piekarski, Victor J. *lawyer*
Pimentel, Julio Gumeresindo *lawyer, accountant*
Pinsky, Michael S. *lawyer*
Pitt, George *lawyer, investment banker*
Polaski, Anne Spencer *lawyer*
Polk, Lee Thomas *lawyer*
Pollock, Earl Edward *lawyer*
Pope, Daniel James *lawyer*
Pope, Michael Arthur *lawyer*
†Porento, Gerald John *lawyer*
Preece, Lynn Sylvia *lawyer*
Presser, Stephen Bruce *lawyer, educator*
Price, Paul L. *lawyer*
Price, William S. *lawyer*
Prior, Gary L. *lawyer*
Prochnow, Douglas Lee *lawyer*
Prochnow, Herbert Victor, Jr. *lawyer*
Rankin, James Winton *lawyer*
Ranney, George A., Jr. *lawyer*
Ratner, Gerald *lawyer*
Reda, Robert Salvatore *lawyer*
Redmond, Richard Anthony *lawyer*
Reed, Keith Allen *lawyer*
Reich, Allan J. *lawyer*
Reicin, Ronald Ian *lawyer*
Reiter, Michael A. *lawyer, educator*
Relias, John Alexis *lawyer*
Resnick, Donald Ira *lawyer*
Reum, James Michael *lawyer*
Rhind, James Thomas *lawyer*
Rhodes, Charles Harker, Jr. *lawyer*
Richardson, William F. *lawyer*
Richman, John Marshall *retired lawyer, business executive*
Richmond, James G. *lawyer*
Richmond, William Patrick *lawyer*
Rieger, Mitchell Sheridan *lawyer*
Riley, Jack T., Jr. *lawyer*
Rissman, Burton Richard *lawyer*
Ritchie, Albert *lawyer*
Rizowy, Carlos Guillermo *lawyer, educator, political analyst*
Rizzo, Ronald Stephen *lawyer*
Roberts, John Charles *law school educator*
Robin, Richard C. *lawyer*
Robinson, Theodore Curtis, Jr. *lawyer*
Roche, James McMillan *lawyer*
Rohrman, Douglass Frederick *lawyer*
Rooney, Matthew A. *lawyer*
Ropski, Gary Melchior *lawyer*
Rosemarin, Carey Stephen *lawyer*
Rosenbloom, Lewis Stanley *lawyer*
Rosso, Christine Hehmeyer *lawyer*
Roston, David Charles *lawyer*
Roustan, Yvon Dominique *lawyer, real estate broker*
Rovell, Michael Jay *lawyer*
Rovner, Jack Alan *lawyer*
Rowder, William Louis *lawyer*
Rubin, Robert J. *lawyer*
Rudnick, Paul David *lawyer*
Rudstein, David Stewart *law educator*
Rundio, Louis Michael, Jr. *lawyer*
Rupert, Donald William *lawyer*
Russell, Paul Frederick *lawyer*
Rutkoff, Alan Stuart *lawyer*
Ruxin, Paul Theodore *lawyer*
Ryan, Thomas F. *lawyer*
Sanders, David P. *lawyer*
Sanders, Richard Henry *lawyer*
Sarauskas, Paul Justas *lawyer*
Saunders, George Lawton, Jr. *lawyer*
Saunders, Terry Rose *lawyer*
Sawyier, David R. *lawyer*
Schar, Stephen L. *lawyer*
Schiller, Donald Charles *lawyer*
Schiller, Eric M. *lawyer*
Schimberg, A(rmand) Bruce *retired lawyer*
Schindel, Donald Marvin *lawyer*
Schink, James Harvey *lawyer*
Schippers, David Philip *lawyer*
Schlickman, J. Andrew *lawyer*
Schlitter, Stanley Allen *lawyer*
Schneider, Dan W. *lawyer, consultant*
Schneider, Robert E., II *lawyer*
Schneider, Robert Jerome *lawyer*
Schoonhoven, Ray James *retired lawyer*
Schoumacher, Bruce Herbert *lawyer*
Schreck, Robert A., Jr. *lawyer*
Schriver, John T., III *lawyer*
Schulhofer, Stephen Joseph *law educator, consultant*
Schulte, Bruce John *lawyer*
Schulte, Stephen Charles *lawyer*
Schulz, Keith Donald *corporate lawyer*
Schwartz, Donald Lee *lawyer*
Schwartzberg, Hugh Joel *lawyer, corporate executive, educator*
Scogland, William Lee *lawyer*
Selfridge, Calvin *lawyer*
Serritella, James Anthony *lawyer*
Serritella, William David *lawyer*
Serwer, Alan Michael *lawyer*
Sfikas, Peter Michael *lawyer, educator*
Shadur, Robert H. *lawyer*
Shank, William O. *lawyer*
Shannon, Peter Michael, Jr. *lawyer*
Shapiro, Harold David *lawyer, educator*
Shapiro, Stephen Michael *lawyer*
Shapo, Marshall Schambelan *lawyer, educator*
Shepherd, Stewart Robert *lawyer*
Shields, Thomas Charles *lawyer*
Shindler, Donald A. *lawyer*
Siegel, Howard Jerome *lawyer*
Sigal, Michael Stephen *lawyer*
Silberman, Alan Harvey *lawyer*
Simon, John Bern *lawyer*
Simon, Seymour *lawyer, former state supreme court justice*
Siske, Roger Charles *lawyer*
Skilling, Raymond Inwood *lawyer*
Sklarsky, Charles B. *lawyer*
Smith, Gordon Howell *lawyer*
Smith, John Gelston *lawyer*
Smith, Michele *lawyer*
Smith, Tefft Weldon *lawyer*
Snider, Lawrence K. *lawyer*
Snyder, Jean Maclean *lawyer*
†Solomon, Jack Avrum *lawyer, automotive distributor, art dealer*
Solovy, Jerold Sherwin *lawyer*
Spain, Richard Colby *lawyer*
Spector, David M. *lawyer*
Spellmire, George W. *lawyer*
Spindler, George S. *lawyer, oil industry executive*
Spiotto, James Ernest *lawyer*
Sproger, Charles Edmund *lawyer*
Stack, John Wallace *retired lawyer*
Stack, Paul Francis *lawyer*
Starkman, Gary Lee *lawyer*
Stein, Robert Allen *legal association executive, law educator*
Steinberg, Morton M. *lawyer*
Sternstein, Allan J. *lawyer*
Stetler, David J. *lawyer*
Stevenson, Adlai Ewing, III *lawyer, former senator*
Stillman, Nina Gidden *lawyer*
Stoll, John Robert *lawyer, educator*
Stone, Geoffrey Richard *law educator, lawyer*
Streff, William Albert, Jr. *lawyer*
Sullivan, Marcia Waite *lawyer*
Sullivan, Thomas Patrick *lawyer*
Sussman, Arthur Melvin *law educator*
Sutter, William Paul *lawyer*
Swaney, Thomas Edward *lawyer*
Sweeney, James Raymond *lawyer*
Swibel, Steven Warren *lawyer*
Szczepanski, Slawomir Zbigniew Steven *lawyer*
Tabin, Julius *patent lawyer, physicist*
Tarun, Robert Walter *lawyer*
Taylor, Roger Lee *lawyer*
Theobald, Edward Robert *lawyer*
Thies, Richard Brian *lawyer*
Thomas, Dale E. *lawyer*
Thomas, Frederick Bradley *lawyer*
Thomas, Stephen Paul *lawyer*
Thompson, James Robert, Jr. *lawyer, former governor*
Thorne-Thomsen, Thomas *lawyer*
Tobin, Thomas F. *lawyer*
Toohey, James Kevin *lawyer*
Torshen, Jerome Harold *lawyer*
Trapp, James McCreery *lawyer*
Trienens, Howard Joseph *lawyer*
Trost, Eileen Bannon *lawyer*
Truskowski, John Budd *lawyer*
Tryban, Esther Elizabeth *lawyer*
Tucker, Bowen Hayward *lawyer*
Turow, Scott F. *lawyer, author*
Ungaretti, Richard Anthony *lawyer*
Van Demark, Ruth Elaine *lawyer*
Veverka, Donald John *lawyer*
Vree, Roger Allen *lawyer*
Wade, Edwin Lee *writer, lawyer*
Wahlen, Edwin Alfred *lawyer*
Waintroob, Andrea Ruth *lawyer*
Waite, Norman, Jr. *lawyer*
Wall, Robert F. *lawyer*
Walsh, Michael S. *lawyer*
Walter, Priscilla Anne *lawyer*
Waltz, Jon Richard *lawyer, educator, author*
Wander, Herbert Stanton *lawyer*
Wanke, Ronald Lee *lawyer*
Ward, Michael W. *lawyer*
Watson, Robert R. *lawyer*
Weaver, Timothy Allan *lawyer*
Webb, Dan K. *lawyer*
Webster, David Macpherson *lawyer*
Weinberg, David B. *investor*
Weinkopf, Friedrich J. *lawyer*
Weinsheimer, William Cyrus *lawyer*
Weissman, Michael Lewis *lawyer*
Welsh, Kelly Raymond *lawyer, telecommunications company executive*
Wexler, Richard Lewis *lawyer*
Whalen, Wayne W. *lawyer*
White, Linda Diane *lawyer*
White, R. Quincy *lawyer*
Wick, Lawrence Scott *lawyer*
Wiggins, Charles Henry, Jr. *lawyer*
Wilcox, Mark Dean *lawyer*
Wildman, Max Edward *lawyer*
Williams, George Howard *lawyer, association executive*
Williamson, Richard Salisbury *lawyer*
Wilson, Clarence Sylvester, Jr. *lawyer, educator*
Wine-Banks, Jill Susan *lawyer*
Winkler, Charles Howard *lawyer, investment management company executive*
Winton, Jeffrey Blake *arbitrator*
Witcoff, Sheldon William *lawyer*
Witwer, Samuel Weiler, Jr. *lawyer*
Wolf, Charles Benno *lawyer*
Wolfe, David Louis *lawyer*
Wolfson, Larry Marshall *lawyer*
Wright, Judith Margaret *law librarian, educator*
Young, Keith Lawrence *lawyer*
Zabel, Sheldon Alter *lawyer, law educator*
Zaremski, Miles Jay *lawyer*
Zemm, Sandra Phyllis *lawyer*
Zenner, Sheldon Toby *lawyer*
Zolno, Mark S. *lawyer*

Chicago Heights
Cifelli, John Louis *lawyer*

Crystal Lake
Bishop, James Francis *lawyer*
Knox, Susan Marie *paralegal*

Danville
Blan, Kennith William, Jr. *lawyer*

Decatur
Dunn, John Francis *lawyer, state representative*
Reising, Richard P. *lawyer*
Vigneri, Joseph William *lawyer*

Deerfield
Abbey, G(eorge) Marshall *lawyer, former health care company executive, general counsel*
Cutchins, Clifford Armstrong, IV *lawyer*
Dawson, Suzanne Stockus *lawyer*
Gaither, John F. *lawyer*
Gash, Lauren Beth *lawyer, state legislator*
Oettinger, Julian Alan *lawyer, pharmacy company executive*
Scott, Theodore R. *lawyer*
Staubitz, Arthur Frederick *lawyer, healthcare products company executive*
Vollen, Robert Jay *lawyer*

Dekalb
Davidson, Kenneth Lawrence *lawyer, educator*
Tucker, Watson Billopp *lawyer*
Witmer, John Harper, Jr. *lawyer*

Des Plaines
Brodl, Raymond Frank *lawyer, former lumber company executive*
Jacobs, William Russell, II *lawyer*

Downers Grove
Martan, Joseph Rudolf *lawyer*

Du Quoin
Atkins, Aaron Ardene *lawyer*

East Moline
Silliman, Richard George *retired lawyer, retired farm machinery company executive*

Edwardsville
Rikli, Donald Carl *lawyer*

Elgin
Juergensmeyer, John Eli *lawyer*
Roeser, Ronald O. *lawyer, consultant*

Elmhurst
Berry, James Frederick *lawyer, biology educator*

Evanston
Gormley, R(obert) James *retired lawyer*
Morrison, John Horton *lawyer*
Vanneman, Edgar, Jr. *retired lawyer*

Fairview Heights
Grace, (Walter) Charles *prosecutor*

Flossmoor
Gevers, Marcia Bonita *lawyer, lecturer, mediator, consultant*

Franklin Park
Blanchard, Eric Alan *lawyer*

Galesburg
McCrery, David Neil, III *lawyer*

Geneseo
Brown, Mabel Welton *lawyer*

Genoa
Cromley, Jon Lowell *lawyer*

Glen Ellyn
Barrett, Carolyn Hernly *paralegal*
Hudson, Dennis Lee *lawyer, retired government official, arbitrator, educator*
Ulrich, Werner *patent lawyer*

Glencoe
Baer, Joseph Winslow *retired lawyer, mediator, arbitrator*

Glenview
Berkman, Michael G. *lawyer, chemical consultant*
Marmet, Gottlieb John *lawyer*

Gurnee
Southern, Robert Allen *lawyer*

Hanover
Bleveans, John *lawyer*

Highland Park
Karol, Nathaniel H. *lawyer, consultant*
Ruder, David Sturtevant *lawyer, educator, government official*

Indianhead Park
†Strojny, Ronald P. *lawyer*

Inverness
Victor, Michael Gary *lawyer, physician*

Joliet
Boyer, Andrew Ben *lawyer*
Copeland, Charlene Carole *lawyer*
Lenard, George Dean *lawyer*

Kenilworth
Dixon, Carl Franklin *lawyer*
McKittrick, William Wood *lawyer*

La Grange
Kerr, Alexander Duncan, Jr. *lawyer*

Lafox
Seils, William George *lawyer*

Lake Bluff
Burns, Kenneth Jones, Jr. *lawyer, consultant*

Lake Forest
Covington, George Morse *lawyer*
Emerson, William Harry *lawyer, retired, oil company executive*
Palmer, Ann Therese Darin *lawyer*
Sikorovsky, Eugene Frank *retired lawyer*

Lansing
Hill, Philip *retired lawyer*

Libertyville
Beeler, Thomas Joseph *lawyer, general management consultant*
Rallo, Douglas *lawyer*
Ranney, George Alfred *lawyer, former steel company executive*

Lincolnshire
Galatz, Henry Francis *lawyer*
Giza, David Alan *lawyer*

Lisle
Myers, Daniel N. *lawyer, association executive*
Sandrok, Richard William *lawyer*

Litchfield
Best, Karen Magdalene *legal secretary*

Lombard
Goodman, Elliott I(rvin) *lawyer*
O'Shea, Patrick Joseph *lawyer, electrical engineer*
Sheehan, Dennis William, Sr. *lawyer, business executive*
Willis, Douglas Alan *lawyer*

Long Grove
Conway, John K. *lawyer*
Obert, Paul Richard *lawyer, manufacturing company executive*

Macomb
Hogan, Kenneth James *lawyer*

Marengo
Franks, Herbert Hoover *lawyer*

Marion
Powless, Kenneth Barnett *lawyer*

Mattoon
Horsley, Jack Everett *lawyer, author*

Mc Gaw Park
†Feather, William L. *corporate lawyer*

Mokena
Sangmeister, George Edward *lawyer, consultant, former congressman*

Moline
Cleaver, William Lehn *lawyer*
Cottrell, Frank Stewart *lawyer, manufacturing executive*
Morrison, Deborah Jean *lawyer*

Mount Carroll
Leemon, John Allen *lawyer*

Mount Prospect
Cohn, Bradley M. *lawyer*

Mount Vernon
Harvey, Morris Lane *lawyer*

Mundelein
Ackley, Robert O. *lawyer*

Murphysboro
McCann, Maurice Joseph *lawyer*

Naperville
Fawell, Harris W. *lawyer former congressman*
Larson, Mark Edward, Jr. *lawyer, educator, financial advisor*
Shaw, Michael Allan *lawyer, mail order company executive*

Normal
Spears, Larry Jonell *lawyer*

North Chicago
†de Lasa, José M. *lawyer*

Northbrook
Dilling, Kirkpatrick Wallwick *lawyer*
Lapin, Harvey I. *lawyer*
McGinn, Mary Jovita *lawyer, insurance company executive*
Pollak, Jay Mitchell *lawyer*
Rotchford, Patricia Kathleen *lawyer*
Sernett, Richard Patrick *lawyer*
Stewart, Charles Leslie *lawyer*
Wallace, Harry Leland *lawyer*

Northfield
Porter, Helen Viney (Mrs. Lewis M. Porter, Jr.) *lawyer*
Wise, William Jerrard *lawyer*

Oak Brook
Barnes, Karen Kay *lawyer*
Bennett, Margaret Airola *lawyer*
Congalton, Susan Tichenor *lawyer*
Getz, Herbert A. *lawyer*
Johnson, Grant Lester *lawyer, retired manufacturing company executive*
Mlsna, Kathryn Kimura *lawyer*
Ring, Leonard M. *lawyer*
Warnock, William Reid *lawyer*

Oak Lawn
Kenny, Mary Alice *lawyer, law librarian*

Oak Park
Schubert, Blake H. *lawyer, investor*

Oakbrook Terrace
Fenech, Joseph Charles *lawyer*
LaForte, George Francis, Jr. *lawyer*
O'Brien, Walter Joseph, II *lawyer*
Tibble, Douglas Clair *lawyer*

Oregon
Cargerman, Alan William *lawyer*

Palatine
Castle, Grace Eleanor *legal investigator*

Palos Heights
Swanson, Warren Lloyd *lawyer*

Park Forest
Goodrich, John Bernard *lawyer, consultant*

Park Ridge
Hegarty, Mary Frances *lawyer*
LaRue, Paul Hubert *lawyer*

Peoria
Allen, Lyle Wallace *lawyer*
†Atterbury, Robert Rennie, III *lawyer*
Christison, William Henry, III *lawyer*
Coletta, Ralph John *lawyer*
Prusak, Maximilian Michael *lawyer*
Ryan, Michael Beecher *lawyer, former government official*
Strodel, Robert Carl *lawyer*
Winget, Walter Winfield *lawyer*

Pinckneyville
Johnson, Don Edwin *lawyer*

Princeton
Johnson, Watts Carey *lawyer*

Prospect Heights
Leopold, Mark F. *lawyer*

River Forest
Li, Tze-chung *lawyer, educator*

Rock Island
Wallace, Franklin Sherwood *lawyer*

Rockford
Anderson, LaVerne Eric *lawyer*
Barrick, William Henry *lawyer*
Canfield, Elizabeth Frances *lawyer*
†Gaziano, Mary J. *lawyer, educator*
Hunsaker, Richard Kendall *lawyer*
Johnson, Thomas Stuart *lawyer*
Logli, Paul Albert *lawyer*
Matschullat, Dale Lewis *lawyer*
Reno, Roger *lawyer*
Rudy, Elmer Clyde *lawyer*
Sullivan, Peter Thomas, III *lawyer*

Saint Charles
Mc Kay, Thomas, Jr. *lawyer*

Schaumburg
Meltzer, Brian *lawyer*
Shapiro, Edwin Henry *lawyer*

Schiller Park
Congalton, Christopher William *lawyer*

Skokie
Greenspan, Jeffrey Dov *lawyer*
Plotnick, Paul William *lawyer*
Salit, Gary *lawyer*

Springfield
Davis, Thomas Edward *prosecutor*
Dodge, James William *lawyer, educator*
Heckenkamp, Robert Glenn *lawyer*
Hulin, Frances C. *prosecutor*
Immke, Keith Henry *lawyer*
Kerr, Gary Enrico *lawyer, educator*
Malany, Le Grand Lynn *lawyer, engineer, bank executive*
Mathewson, Mark Stuart *lawyer, editor*
Narmont, John Stephen *lawyer*
Rowe, Max L. *lawyer, corporate executive, management and political consultant, writer, judge*
†Ryan, Jim *Illinois attorney general*
Van Meter, Abram DeBois *lawyer, retired banker*

Sterling
Brooks, Terry *lawyer, author*

Taylorville
Austin, Daniel William *lawyer*

Toledo
Prather, William C. III *lawyer, writer*

Urbana
Balbach, Stanley Byron *lawyer*
†Van Ness, Phillip R. *lawyer*

Waterloo
Coffee, Richard Jerome, II *lawyer*

Watseka
Tungate, James Lester *lawyer*

Waukegan
Bairstow, Richard Raymond *retired lawyer*
Decker, David Alfred *lawyer*
Hall, Albert L. *lawyer, retired*
Henrick, Michael Francis *lawyer*
Leibowitz, David Perry *lawyer*

Western Springs
Hanson, Heidi Elizabeth *lawyer*
Rhoads, Paul Kelly *lawyer*

Wheaton
Butt, Edward Thomas, Jr. *lawyer*
May, Frank Brendan, Jr. *lawyer*
O'Reilly, Roger Kevin *lawyer*
Stein, Lawrence A. *lawyer*

Willowbrook
Walton, Stanley Anthony, III *lawyer*

Wilmette
Frick, Robert Hathaway *lawyer*
Lieberman, Eugene *lawyer*
Simon, Thelma Brook *lawyer, educator*

Winnetka
Abell, David Robert *lawyer*
Barnard, Morton John *lawyer*
Crowe, Robert William *lawyer, mediator*

Davis, Britton Anthony *retired lawyer*
Greenblatt, Ray Harris *lawyer*

Winthrop Harbor
Getz, James Edward *legal association administrator*

Wonder Lake
McNamara, Joseph Burk *lawyer, corporate executive*

Woodridge
Conti, Lee Ann *lawyer*

INDIANA

Anderson
Woodruff, Randall Lee *lawyer*

Beech Grove
Brown, Richard Lawrence *lawyer*

Bloomington
Dilts, Jon Paul *law educator*
†Rodwin, Marc Andre *law educator*
Shreve, Gene Russell *law educator*

Carmel
Sabl, John J. *lawyer*
Stein, Richard Paul *lawyer*

Columbus
Fairchild, Raymond Francis *lawyer*
Harrison, Patrick Woods *lawyer*

Connersville
Kuntz, William Henry *lawyer, mediator*

Danville
Baldwin, Jeffrey Kenton *lawyer, educator*

Dyer
DeGuilio, Jon E. *lawyer*

Elkhart
Gassere, Eugene Arthur *lawyer, business executive*
Harman, John Royden *lawyer*
Treckelo, Richard M. *lawyer*

Evansville
Baugh, Jerry Phelps *lawyer*
Berger, Charles Lee *lawyer*
Clouse, John Daniel *lawyer*
Knight, Jeffrey Lin *lawyer, corporation executive*
Liberty, Arthur Andrew *judge*
Wallace, Keith M. *lawyer*

Fort Wayne
Baker, Carl Leroy *lawyer*
Fink, Thomas Michael *lawyer*
Fleck, John R. *lawyer*
Gehring, Ronald Kent *lawyer*
Keefer, J(ames) Michael *lawyer*

Franklin
Hamner, Lance Dalton *prosecutor*

Ft Wayne
Spielman, Kim Morgan *lawyer, educator*

Greenwood
Van Valer, Joe Ned *lawyer, land developer*

Hammond
Diamond, Eugene Christopher *lawyer, hospital administrator*
Ruman, Saul I. *lawyer*

Hartford City
Ford, David Clayton *lawyer, Indiana state senator*

Highland
Forsythe, Randall Newman *paralegal, educator*

Indianapolis
Albright, Terrill D. *lawyer*
Allen, David James *lawyer*
Aschleman, James Allan *lawyer*
Badger, David Harry *lawyer*
Baird, John Michael *lawyer, non-profit organization executive*
Beckwith, Lewis Daniel *lawyer*
Beeler, Virgil L. *lawyer*
Boldt, Michael Herbert *lawyer*
Born, Samuel Roydon, II *lawyer*
Buttrey, Donald Wayne *lawyer*
Capehart, Craig Earl *lawyer*
Carney, Joseph Buckingham *lawyer*
Choplin, John M., II *lawyer*
Conour, William Frederick *lawyer*
Deer, Richard Elliott *lawyer*
Dorocke, Lawrence Francis *lawyer*
Downs, Thomas K. *lawyer*
Due, Danford Royce *lawyer*
Dutton, Clarence Benjamin *lawyer*
Dutton, Stephen James *lawyer*
Evans, Daniel Fraley, Jr. *lawyer*
Ewbank, Thomas Peters *lawyer, retired banker*
Fisher, James R. *lawyer*
FitzGibbon, Daniel Harvey *lawyer*
Fruehwald, Kristin G. *lawyer*
Fuller, Samuel Ashby *lawyer, mining company executive*
Funk, David Albert *retired law educator*
†Goss, Rebecca O. *lawyer, pharmaceutical company executive*
Grayson, John Allan *lawyer*
Hammel, John Wingate *lawyer*
Heerens, Joseph Robert *lawyer*
†Heise, Michael Richard *law educator*
Hetzner, Marc Andrew *lawyer*
Holt, John Manly *retired corporate lawyer*
Horn, Brenda Sue *lawyer*
Huffman, Rosemary Adams *lawyer, corporate executive*
Huston, Michael Joe *lawyer*
Jegen, Lawrence A., III *law educator*
Johnstone, Robert Philip *lawyer*
Johnting, Wendell *law librarian*
Kahlenbeck, Howard, Jr. *lawyer*
Kappes, Philip Spangler *lawyer*

Kautzman, John Fredrick *lawyer*
Kemper, James Dee *lawyer*
Kerr, William Andrew *lawyer, educator*
King, J. Bradley *lawyer*
Kirk, Carol *lawyer*
Klaper, Martin Jay *lawyer*
Kleiman, David Harold *lawyer*
Knebel, Donald Earl *lawyer*
Koch, Edna Mae *lawyer, nurse*
Koeller, Robert Marion *lawyer*
Lamkin, Martha Dampf *lawyer*
Lee, Stephen W. *lawyer*
Lobley, Alan Haigh *retired lawyer*
Lofton, Thomas Milton *lawyer*
Lowe, Louis Robert, Jr. *lawyer*
McCarthy, Kevin Bart *lawyer*
McKinney, Dennis Keith *lawyer*
Miller, David W. *lawyer*
Moffatt, Michael Alan *lawyer*
Nolan, Alan Tucker *retired lawyer, labor artibrator, writer*
Padgett, Gregory Lee *lawyer*
Paul, Stephen Howard *lawyer*
Polston, Ronald Wayne *law educator*
Ponder, Lester McConnico *lawyer, educator*
Powlen, David Michael *lawyer*
Price, Henry J. *lawyer*
Reuben, Lawrence Mark *lawyer*
Reynolds, Robert Hugh *lawyer*
Roberts, William Everett *lawyer*
Russell, David Williams *lawyer*
Ryder, Henry C(lay) *lawyer*
Scaletta, Phillip Ralph, III *lawyer*
Scanlon, Thomas Michael *lawyer*
Schlegel, Fred Eugene *lawyer*
Schreckengast, William Owen *lawyer*
Scism, Daniel Reed *lawyer*
Shideler, Shirley Ann Williams *lawyer*
Shula, Robert Joseph *lawyer*
Stayton, Thomas George *lawyer*
Steger, Evan Evans, III *lawyer*
Stewart, Judith A. *lawyer*
Stieff, John Joseph *legislative lawyer, educator*
Sutherland, Donald Gray *lawyer*
Tabler, Bryan G. *lawyer*
Tabler, Norman Gardner, Jr. *lawyer*
Talesnick, Stanley *lawyer*
Townsend, Earl C., Jr. *lawyer, writer*
Tuchman, Steven Leslie *lawyer, theatre critic*
Wampler, Lloyd Charles *retired lawyer*
Wampler, Robert Joseph *lawyer*
Wellnitz, Craig Otto *lawyer, English language educator*
Whale, Arthur Richard *lawyer*
White, James Patrick *law educator*
Wishard, Gordon Davis *lawyer*
Wood, William Jerome *lawyer*
Woodard, Harold Raymond *lawyer*
Yeager, Joseph Heizer, Jr. *lawyer*

Jeffersonville
Hoehn, Elmer Louis *lawyer, state and federal agency administrator, educator, consultant*

Kokomo
Maugans, John Conrad *lawyer*

Lafayette
Branigin, Roger D., Jr. *lawyer*
Gerde, Carlyle Noyes (Cy Gerde) *lawyer*
O'Callaghan, Patti Louise *court program administrator*

Lagrange
Glick, Cynthia Susan *lawyer*

Marion
Ryan, Patrick Nelson *lawyer*

Merrillville
Brenman, Stephen Morris *lawyer*
Kinney, Richard Gordon *lawyer, educator*
Miller, Richard Allen *lawyer*

Mount Vernon
Bach, Steve Crawford *lawyer*

Muncie
Kelly, Eric Damian *lawyer, educator*
Radcliff, William Franklin *lawyer*

Munster
Amber, Douglas George *lawyer*

New Albany
Naville, Michael Gerard *lawyer*

Notre Dame
Grazin, Igor Nikolai *law educator, state official*
Gunn, Alan *law educator*
Payne, Lucy Ann Salsbury *law librarian, educator, lawyer*

South Bend
Carey, John Leo *lawyer*
†Carrington, Michael Davis *criminal justice administrator, educator, consultant*
Ford, George Burt *lawyer*
Lambert, George Robert *lawyer, realtor*
McGill, Warren Everett *lawyer, consultant*
Reinke, William John *lawyer*
Seall, Stephen Albert *lawyer*
Shaffer, Thomas Lindsay *lawyer, educator*
Vogel, Nelson J., Jr. *lawyer*

Terre Haute
Bitzegaio, Harold James *retired lawyer*
Kesler, John A. *lawyer, land developer*

Valparaiso
Gaffney, Edward McGlynn *law educator, university administrator*
Johnson, Shelli Wright *lawyer*
Koeppen, Raymond Bradley *lawyer*
Persyn, Mary Geraldine *law librarian, law educator*

Vincennes
Emison, Ewing Rabb, Jr. *lawyer*

Warsaw
Walmer, James L. *lawyer*

West Lafayette
Scaletta, Phillip Jasper *lawyer, educator*

Zionsville
Bruess, Charles Edward *lawyer*

IOWA

Burlington
Hoth, Steven Sergey *lawyer*

Carroll
Neu, Arthur Alan *lawyer*

Cedar Rapids
Albright, Justin W. *lawyer*
Faches, William George *lawyer*
Nazette, Richard Follett *lawyer*
Riley, Tom Joseph *lawyer*
Wilson, Robert Foster *lawyer*

Charles City
Mc Cartney, Ralph Farnham *lawyer*

Dallas Center
McDonald, John Cecil *lawyer*

Davenport
Bush, Michael Kevin *lawyer*
Halligan, Kevin Leo *lawyer*
Lathrop, Roger Alan *lawyer*
Le Grand, Clay *lawyer, former state justice*
Shaw, Donald Hardy *lawyer*
Shaw, Elizabeth Orr *lawyer*
Skora, Susan Sundman *lawyer*

Des Moines
Baybayan, Ronald Alan *lawyer*
Bittle, Edgar H. *lawyer*
†Brauch, William Leland *lawyer*
Brown, Paul Edmondson *lawyer*
Burns, Bernard John, III *public defender*
Campbell, Bruce Irving *lawyer*
Carroll, Frank James *lawyer, educator*
Claypool, David L. *lawyer*
Conlin, Roxanne Barton *lawyer*
Cortese, Joseph Samuel, II *lawyer*
Doyle, Richard Henry, IV *lawyer*
Duckworth, Marvin E. *lawyer, educator*
Edwards, John Duncan *law educator, librarian*
Fisher, Thomas George *lawyer, retired media company executive*
Fisher, Thomas George, Jr. *lawyer*
Flynn, Thomas Lee *lawyer*
Foxhoven, Jerry Ray *lawyer*
Frederici, C. Carleton *lawyer*
Graziano, Craig Frank *lawyer*
Grefe, Rolland Eugene *lawyer*
Hansell, Edgar Frank *lawyer*
Harris, Charles Elmer *lawyer*
Hill, Luther Lyons, Jr. *lawyer*
Hockenberg, Harlan David *lawyer*
Hoffmann, Michael Richard *lawyer*
Jensen, Dick Leroy *lawyer*
Koehn, William James *lawyer*
Langdon, Herschel Garrett *lawyer*
Lawyer, Vivian Jury *lawyer*
Narber, Gregg Ross *lawyer*
Neiman, John Hammond *lawyer*
Nickerson, Don C. *lawyer*
Peddicord, Roland Dale *lawyer*
Power, Joseph Edward *lawyer*
Shors, John D. *lawyer*
Simpson, Lyle Lee *lawyer*
Stork, Frank James *lawyer*
Wanek, Jerrold *lawyer*
Wine, Donald Arthur *lawyer*

Dubuque
Ernst, Daniel Pearson *lawyer*
Hammer, David Lindley *lawyer, author*

Fort Madison
Sallen, David Urban *lawyer*

Indianola
Ouderkirk, Mason James *lawyer*

Iowa City
Bonfield, Arthur Earl *lawyer, educator*
Downer, Robert Nelson *lawyer*
Kurtz, Sheldon Francis *lawyer, educator*
McAndrew, Paul Joseph, Jr. *lawyer*
Spies, Leon Fred *lawyer*
Tomkovicz, James Joseph *law educator*
Vernon, David Harvey *lawyer, educator*
Widiss, Alan I. *lawyer, educator*
Wing, Adrien Katherine *law educator*

Johnston
Leitner, David Larry *lawyer*

Keokuk
Hoffman, James Paul *lawyer, hypnotist*

Marshalltown
Brennecke, Allen Eugene *lawyer*
Brooks, Patrick William *lawyer*
Geffe, Kent Lyndon *lawyer, educator*

Mason City
Heiny, James Ray *lawyer*

Mount Pleasant
Vance, Michael Charles *lawyer*

Muscatine
Coulter, Charles Roy *lawyer*
Nepple, James Anthony *lawyer*

Nevada
Countryman, Dayton Wendell *lawyer*

New Hampton
Kennedy, Michael Kelly *attorney, state representative*

Ottumwa
Krafka, Mary Baird *lawyer*

Sioux City
Bennett, Mark Warren *lawyer, educator*
Giles, William Jefferson, III *lawyer*
Marks, Bernard Bailin *lawyer*
Mayne, Wiley Edward *lawyer*
Nymann, P. L. *lawyer*
Peterson, Delaine Charles *lawyer, bank executive*

Stuart
Bump, Wilbur Neil *retired lawyer*

Washington
Day, John Robert *lawyer*

Waterloo
Rapp, Stephen John *prosecutor*

Winfield
Carty, John Wesley *lawyer*

KANSAS

Augusta
Richardson, Myrtle *abstractor, former judge*

Ellsworth
Aylward, Paul Leon *lawyer, banker, rancher*

Gardner
Webb, William Duncan *lawyer, mediator*

Hugoton
Nordling, Bernard Erick *lawyer*

Hutchinson
Hayes, John Francis *lawyer*
Swearer, William Brooks *lawyer*

Iola
Toland, Clyde William *lawyer*

Kansas City
Case, Rosemary Podrebarac *lawyer*
Jurcyk, John Joseph, Jr. *lawyer*

Lawrence
Casad, Robert Clair *legal educator*
Hoeflich, Michael Harlan *law school dean*
Kautsch, M(ike) A. *law educator*
Murray, Thomas Veatch *lawyer*
Smith, Glee Sidney, Jr. *lawyer*
Turnbull, H. Rutherford, III *law educator, lawyer*

Leawood
Johnston, Jocelyn Stanwell *paralegal*

Lenexa
Scott, Robert Gene *lawyer*

Lyons
Hodgson, Arthur Clay *lawyer*

Olathe
Haskin, J. Michael *lawyer*

Overland Park
Bennett, Robert Frederick *lawyer, former governor*
Cole, Elsa Kircher *lawyer*
Cole, Roland Jay *lawyer*
Keim, Robert Bruce *lawyer*
Keplinger, (Donald) Bruce *lawyer*
Krauss, Carl F. *lawyer*
Sampson, William Roth *lawyer*
Smith, Daniel Lynn *lawyer*
Smith, Edwin Dudley *lawyer*
Van Dyke, Thomas Wesley *lawyer*
Waxse, David John *lawyer*
Westerhaus, Douglas Bernard *lawyer*

Prairie Village
Stanton, Roger D. *lawyer*

Salina
Conner, Fred L. *lawyer*

Shawnee Mission
Badgerow, John Nicholas *lawyer*
Biggs, J. O. *lawyer, general industry company executive*
Bond, Richard Lee *lawyer, state senator*
Cahal, Mac Fullerton *lawyer, publisher*
Nulton, William Clements *lawyer*
Rubin, Charles Elliott *lawyer, sports agent*
Shank, Suzanne Adams *lawyer*
Sparks, Billy Schley *lawyer*

Topeka
Concannon, James M. *law educator, university dean*
Dimmitt, Lawrence Andrew *lawyer*
Elrod, Linda Diane Henry *lawyer, educator*
Harwick, Dennis Patrick *lawyer*
Hejtmanek, Danton Charles *lawyer*
Holmes, Richard Winn *lawyer, retired state supreme court justice*
Marshall, Herbert A. *lawyer*
Moots, Jeffrey Alan *lawyer*
Rainey, William Joel *lawyer*
Schroer, Gene Eldon *lawyer*
Spring, Raymond Lewis *legal educator*

Wellington
Ferguson, William McDonald *retired lawyer, rancher, author, banker, former state official*

Westwood
Devlin, James Richard *lawyer*

Wichita
Arabia, Paul *lawyer*
Ayres, Ted Dean *lawyer, academic counsel*
Curfman, Lawrence Everett *retired lawyer*
Docking, Thomas Robert *lawyer, former state lieutenant governor*
Grace, Brian Guiles *lawyer*

Kennedy, Joseph Winston *lawyer*
†Moore, Tim J. *lawyer*
Sorensen, Harvey R. *lawyer*
Stark, Stephen M. *lawyer*
Stephenson, Richard Ismert *lawyer*
Thompson, (Morris) Lee *lawyer*
†Williams, Jackie N. *prosecutor*
Winkler, Dana John *lawyer*

Winfield
Andreas, Warren Dale *lawyer*

KENTUCKY

Ashland
Compton, Robert H. *lawyer*

Bowling Green
†Dixon, John Morris, Jr. *lawyer*

Covington
Wolnitzek, Stephen Dale *lawyer*

Crestwood
Ray, Ronald Dudley *lawyer*

Florence
Frohlich, Anthony William *lawyer, master commissioner*

Fort Thomas
Whalen, Paul Lewellin *lawyer, educator, MEDIATOR*

Frankfort
Carroll, Julian Morton *lawyer, former governor*
Chadwick, Robert *lawyer, judge*
Palmore, John Stanley, Jr. *retired lawyer*

Glasgow
Baker, Walter Arnold *lawyer*
Dickinson, Temple *lawyer*

Highland Heights
Brewer, Edward Cage, III *law educator*
Jones, William Rex *law educator*

Lexington
Baesler, Scotty *lawyer, former congressman*
Bagby, William Rardin *lawyer*
Beshear, Steven L. *lawyer*
Breathitt, Edward Thompson, Jr. *lawyer, railroad executive, former governor*
Daniel, Marilyn S. *lawyer*
Detjen, Ann L. *retired legal assistant*
Famularo, Joseph L. *prosecutor*
Fryman, Virgil Thomas, Jr. *lawyer*
Garmer, William Robert *lawyer*
Goldman, Alvin Lee *lawyer, educator*
Hinkle, Buckner, Jr. *lawyer*
Lewis, Thomas Proctor *law educator*
Miller, Harry B(enjamin) *lawyer*
Newberry, James Henry, Jr. *lawyer*
Oberst, Paul *law educator*
Schaeffer, Edwin Frank, Jr. *lawyer, finance company executive*
Turley, Robert Joe *lawyer*

London
Keller, John Warren *lawyer*

Louisville
Aberson, Leslie Donald *lawyer*
Allen, Charles Ethelbert, III *lawyer*
Apperson, Jeffrey A. *lawyer*
Ardery, Philip Pendleton *lawyer*
Ballantine, John Tilden *lawyer*
Barr, James Houston, III *lawyer*
Benfield, Ann Kolb *lawyer*
Blaine, Steven Robert *lawyer*
Brown, Bonnie Maryetta *lawyer*
Buckaway, William Allen, Jr. *lawyer*
Chauvin, Leonard Stanley, Jr. *lawyer*
Conner, Stewart Edmund *lawyer*
Cowan, Frederic Joseph *lawyer*
Davidson, Gordon Byron *lawyer*
Dolt, Frederick Corrance *lawyer*
Dudley, George Ellsworth *lawyer*
Duffy, Martin Patrick *lawyer*
Edwards, Steven Alan *lawyer*
Faller, Rhoda Dianne Grossberg *lawyer*
Fenton, Thomas Conner *lawyer*
Ferguson, Jo McCown *lawyer*
Fuchs, Olivia Anne Morris *lawyer*
Gilman, Sheldon Glenn *lawyer*
Gorman, Chris *lawyer*
Guethlein, William O. *lawyer*
Hallenberg, Robert Lewis *lawyer*
Helm, Thomas Kennedy, Jr. *retired lawyer*
Hopson, Edwin Sharp *lawyer*
Hunter, William Jay, Jr. *lawyer*
Keeney, Steven Harris *lawyer*
Klotter, John Charles *retired legal educator*
Lay, Norvie Lee *law educator*
Lyndrup, Peggy B. *lawyer*
Macdonald, Lenna Ruth *lawyer*
Maddox, Robert Lytton *lawyer*
Maggiolo, Allison Joseph *lawyer*
Manly, Samuel *lawyer*
Maple, Mary Alice *lawyer*
†McCall, John Richard *lawyer*
Mellen, Francis Joseph, Jr. *lawyer*
Metzger, Gregory Scott *lawyer*
Morreau, James Earl, Jr. *lawyer, entrepreneur*
Morris, Benjamin Hume *lawyer*
Osborn, John Simcoe, Jr. *lawyer*
Pelfrey, D. Patton *lawyer*
Pettyjohn, Shirley Ellis *lawyer, real estate executive*
Reed, D. Gary *lawyer*
Reed, John Squires, II *lawyer*
Runyon, Keith Leslie *lawyer, newspaper editor*
Shaikun, Michael Gary *lawyer*
Skees, William Edward *lawyer*
Skees, William Leonard, Jr. *lawyer*
Talbott, Ben Johnson, Jr. *lawyer*
Troop, (Walter) Michael *prosecutor*
Vincenti, Michael Baxter *lawyer*
Welsh, Alfred John *lawyer, consultant*
Willenbrink, Rose Ann *lawyer*
Wren, Harold Gwyn *arbitrator, lawyer, legal educator*
Zingman, Edgar Alan *lawyer*

Madisonville
Monhollon, Leland *lawyer*

Mount Sterling
Moore, George William *lawyer*

Munfordville
Lang, George Edward *lawyer*

Newport
Halloran, Brian Paul *lawyer*

Owensboro
Miller, James Monroe *lawyer*

Paducah
Nickell, Christopher Shea *lawyer*
Westberry, Billy Murry *lawyer*

Scottsville
Secrest, James Seaton, Sr. *lawyer*
Wilcher, Larry K. *lawyer*

Somerset
Prather, John Gideon, Jr. *lawyer*

LOUISIANA

Alexandria
Gist, Howard Battle, Jr. *lawyer*

Baton Rouge
Baer, Michael Shellman, III *lawyer, Louisiana Senate secretary*
Blackman, John Calhoun, IV *lawyer*
Byrd, Warren Edgar, II *lawyer*
Giglio, Steven Rene *lawyer*
Hymel, L(ezin) J(oseph) *prosecutor*
Johnson, Joseph Clayton, Jr. *lawyer*
Karns, Barry Wayne *lawyer*
Lamonica, P(aul) Raymond *lawyer, educator*
LeBlanc, J. Burton, IV *lawyer*
LeClere, David Anthony *lawyer*
Leonard, Paul Haralson *retired lawyer*
Mc Clendon, William Hutchinson, III *lawyer*
Pugh, George Willard *law educator*
†Pyle, Susan H. *legal association official*
Riddick, Winston Wade, Sr. *lawyer*
Schroeder, Leila Obier *retired law educator*
Unglesby, Lewis O. *lawyer*
Walsh, Milton O'Neal *lawyer*
Wittenbrink, Jeffrey Scott *lawyer*

Chalmette
†Zelaya, Carlos Alberto, II *lawyer*

Covington
Paddison, David Robert *lawyer*

Franklin
McClelland, James Ray *lawyer*

Hammond
Matheny, Tom Harrell *lawyer*

Jefferson
Conino, Joseph Aloysius *lawyer*

Kenner
Valvo, Barbara-Ann *lawyer, surgeon*

Lafayette
Breaux, Paul Joseph *lawyer, pharmacist*
Davidson, James Joseph, III *lawyer*
Judice, Marc Wayne *lawyer*
Mansfield, James Norman, III *lawyer*
Myers, Stephen Hawley *lawyer*
Revels, Richard W., Jr. *lawyer*
Saloom, Kaliste Joseph, Jr. *lawyer, retired judge*
Swift, John Goulding *lawyer*

Lake Charles
Clements, Robert W. *lawyer*
Everett, John Prentis, Jr. *lawyer*
Hanchey, James Clinton *lawyer*
Ortego, Jim *lawyer, legal educator*
Sanchez, Walter Marshall *lawyer*
Shaddock, William Edward, Jr. *lawyer*
Veron, J. Michael *lawyer*

Mandeville
Christian, John Catlett, Jr. *lawyer*
Deano, Edward Joseph, Jr. *lawyer, state legislator*

Metairie
Album, Jerald Lewis *lawyer*
Butcher, Bruce Cameron *lawyer*
Derbes, Albert Joseph, III *lawyer, accountant*
Hardy, Ashton Richard *lawyer*
McMahon, Robert Albert, Jr. *lawyer*
Nehrbass, Seth Martin *patent lawyer*
Olivier, Jason Thomas *lawyer*
Ostendorf, Lance Stephen *lawyer, investor, financial consultant and planner*
Perlis, Sharon A. *lawyer*

Monroe
Sartor, Daniel Ryan, Jr. *lawyer*

New Orleans
Abaunza, Donald Richard *lawyer*
Abbott, Hirschel Theron, Jr. *lawyer*
Acomb, Robert Bailey, Jr. *lawyer, educator*
Allen, F(rank) C(linton), Jr. *lawyer, retired manufacturing executive*
Alsobrook, Henry Bernis, Jr. *lawyer*
Backstrom, William M., Jr. *lawyer*
Barham, Mack Elwin *lawyer, educator*
Barry, Francis Julian, Jr. *lawyer*
Beahm, Franklin D. *lawyer*
Beck, William Harold, Jr. *lawyer*
Benjamin, Edward Bernard, Jr. *lawyer*
Bieck, Robert Barton, Jr. *lawyer*
Bronfin, Fred *lawyer*
Burr, Timothy Fuller *lawyer*
Cheatwood, Roy Clifton *lawyer*
Childress, Steven Alan *law educator*
Claverie, Philip deVilliers *lawyer*

Coleman, James Julian *lawyer*
Coleman, James Julian, Jr. *lawyer, industrialist, real estate executive*
Combe, John Clifford, Jr. *lawyer*
Correro, Anthony James, III *lawyer*
Crusto, Mitchell Ferdinand *lawyer, educator*
Denegre, George *lawyer*
Dwyer, Ralph Daniel, Jr. *lawyer*
Esman, Marjorie Ruth *lawyer*
Eustis, Richmond Minor *lawyer*
Fallon, Eldon E. *lawyer, educator, judge*
Fantaci, James Michael *lawyer*
Fierke, Thomas Garner *lawyer*
Force, Robert *law educator*
Friedman, Joel William *law educator*
Garcia, Patricia A. *lawyer*
Haygood, Paul M. *lawyer*
Healy, George William, III *lawyer, mediator*
Henderson, Helena Naughton *legal association administrator*
Hoffman, Robert Dean, Jr. *lawyer*
Johnson, Beth Exum *lawyer*
Johnson, Patrick, Jr. *lawyer*
Jones, Philip Kirkpatrick, Jr. *lawyer*
Jordan, Eddie J. *prosecutor*
Judell, Harold Benn *lawyer*
Keller, Thomas Clements *lawyer*
Kemp, James Bradley, Jr. *lawyer*
Kupperman, Stephen Henry *lawyer*
Lavelle, Paul Michael *lawyer*
Lemann, Thomas Berthelot *lawyer*
Lowe, Robert Charles *lawyer*
Marcus, Bernard *lawyer*
Masinter, Paul James *lawyer*
McGlone, Michael Anthony *lawyer*
McMillan, Lee Richards, II *lawyer*
Miller, Gary H. *lawyer*
Mintz, Albert *lawyer*
Molony, Michael Janssens, Jr. *lawyer*
Morrell, Arthur Anthony *lawyer, state legislator*
Norwood, Colvin Gamble, Jr. *lawyer*
Nuzum, Robert Weston *lawyer*
Palmer, Vernon Valentine *law educator*
Pearce, John Y. *lawyer*
Perez, Luis Alberto *lawyer*
Phelps, Esmond, II *lawyer*
Poitevent, Edward Butts, II *lawyer*
Ponoroff, Lawrence *law educator, legal consultant*
Pugh, William Whitmell Hill *lawyer*
Rawls, John D. *lawyer*
Rice, Winston Edward *lawyer*
Riess, George Febiger *lawyer, educator*
Rodriguez, Antonio Jose *lawyer*
Rosen, Charles, II *lawyer*
Rosen, William Warren *lawyer*
Serio, Charles V. *United States marshal*
Simon, H(uey) Paul *lawyer*
Sims, John William *lawyer*
Sinor, Howard Earl, Jr. *lawyer*
Slater, Benjamin Richard, Jr. *lawyer*
Snyder, Charles Aubrey *lawyer*
Stapp, Dan Ernest *retired lawyer, utility executive*
Tarver, Michael Keith *lawyer*
†Thompson, Michael Greenwood *lawyer*
Vance, Robert Patrick *lawyer*
Vaudry, J. William, Jr. *lawyer*
Waechter, Arthur Joseph, Jr. *lawyer*
Wedig, Regina Scotto *lawyer*
Weinmann, John Giffen *lawyer, diplomat*
Weiss, Kenneth Andrew *lawyer, law educator*
Wilkinson, Joseph C. *lawyer*
Willems, Constance Charles *lawyer*

Shreveport
Achee, Roland Joseph *lawyer*
Bryant, J(ames) Bruce *lawyer*
Carmody, Arthur Roderick, Jr. *lawyer*
Cox, John Thomas, Jr. *lawyer*
Hall, Pike, Jr. *lawyer*
Hetherwick, Gilbert Lewis *lawyer*
Jeter, Katherine Leslie Brash *lawyer*
Perlman, Jerald Lee *lawyer*
Politz, Nyle Anthony *lawyer*
Ramey, Cecil Edward, Jr. *lawyer*
Ratcliff, John Garrett *lawyer*
Rigby, Kenneth *lawyer*
Roberts, Robert, III *lawyer*
Skinner, Michael David *lawyer*
Smith, Brian David *lawyer, educator*

Slidell
Eiermann-Wegener, Darlene Mae *paralegal*
Hammond, Margaret *lawyer*

Sunset
Brinkhaus, Armand J. *lawyer*

MAINE

Augusta
Adelberg, Arthur William *lawyer*

Bangor
Ebitz, Elizabeth Kelly *lawyer*
Woodcock, John Alden *lawyer*

Brunswick
Owen, H. Martyn *lawyer*

Castine
Wiswall, Frank Lawrence, Jr. *lawyer, educator*

Hallowell
Crawford, Linda Sibery *lawyer, educator*

Portland
Bohan, Thomas Lynch *lawyer, physicist*
Coggeshall, Bruce Amsden *lawyer*
Concepción, David Alden *arbitrator, educator*
Coughlan, Patrick Campbell *lawyer*
Culley, Peter William *lawyer*
Graffam, Ward Irving *lawyer*
Hirshon, Robert Edward *lawyer*
Lancaster, Ralph Ivan, Jr. *lawyer*
LeBlanc, Richard Philip *lawyer*
McCloskey, Jay P. *prosecutor*
†Munch, James C., Jr. *lawyer*
Philbrick, Donald Lockey *lawyer*
Piombino, Alfred Ernest *law consultant, writer*
Rundlett, Ellsworth Turner, III *lawyer*
Smith, William Charles *lawyer*
Stauffer, Eric P. *lawyer*
Tierney, Kevin Joseph *lawyer*

White, Jeffrey Munroe *lawyer*
Zarr, Melvyn *lawyer, law educator*

Sanford
Nadeau, Robert Maurice Auclair *lawyer*

Waterville
Sandy, Robert Edward, Jr. *lawyer*

Wells
Carleton, Joseph George, Jr. *lawyer, state legislator*

Yarmouth
Webster, Peter Bridgman *lawyer*

York
Berlew, Frank Kingston *lawyer*

MARYLAND

Abingdon
Wolf, Martin Eugene *lawyer*

Annapolis
Dembrow, Dana Lee *lawyer*
Duncan, Charles Tignor *lawyer*
Ferris, William Michael *lawyer*
Jones, Sylvanus Benson *adjudicator, consultant*
Levin, David Alan *lawyer*
Levitan, Laurence *lawyer, former state senator*
Michaelson, Benjamin, Jr. *lawyer*
Perkins, Roger Allan *lawyer*

Annapolis Junction
Woodard, Mark Davis *lawyer, association executive, lobbyist*

Baltimore
Adkins, Edward James *lawyer*
Archibald, James Kenway *lawyer*
Arnick, John Stephen *lawyer, legislator*
Ayres, Jeffrey Peabody *lawyer*
Bailey, James (Jim Bailey) *lawyer, professional football team executive*
Bair, Robert Rippel *lawyer*
Barnhouse, Robert Bolon *lawyer*
Battaglia, Lynne Ann *prosecutor*
Beall, George *lawyer*
Bernhardt, Herbert Nelson *law educator, labor arbitrator*
Blanton, Edward Lee, Jr. *lawyer*
Boone, Harold Thomas *retired lawyer*
Bowen, Lowell Reed *lawyer*
Brumbaugh, John Maynard *lawyer, educator*
Bruner, William Gwathmey, III *lawyer*
Burch, Francis Boucher, Jr. *lawyer*
Byrd, Ronald Dicky *lawyer*
Carbine, James Edmond *lawyer*
Carey, Anthony Morris *lawyer*
Carey, Jana Howard *lawyer*
Chaplin, Peggy Fannon *lawyer*
Chernow, Jeffrey Scott *lawyer, educator, author*
Chiarello, Donald Frederick *lawyer*
Chiu, Hungdah *lawyer, legal educator*
Chriss, Timothy D. A. *lawyer*
Cook, Bryson Leitch *lawyer*
Crowe, Thomas Leonard *lawyer*
Devan, Deborah Hunt *lawyer*
Digges, Edward S(imms), Jr. *business management consultant*
Dilloff, Neil Joel *lawyer*
Dubé, Lawrence Edward, Jr. *lawyer*
Ellin, Marvin *lawyer*
Engel, Paul Bernard *lawyer*
Evans, Nolly Seymour *lawyer*
Eveleth, Janet Stidman *law association administrator*
Fergenson, Arthur Friend *lawyer*
Ferro, Elizabeth Krams *lawyer*
Fisher, Morton Poe, Jr. *lawyer*
†Fried, Arthur *lawyer*
Friedman, Louis Frank *lawyer*
Gately, Mark Donohue *lawyer*
Gilbert, Blaine Louis *lawyer*
Gillece, James Patrick, Jr. *lawyer*
Goldman, Brian Arthur *lawyer, accountant*
Gray, Frank Truan *lawyer*
Gray, Oscar Shalom *lawyer*
Hafets, Richard Jay *lawyer*
Haines, Thomas W. W. *lawyer*
Hanks, James Judge, Jr. *lawyer*
Herr, Stanley Sholom *law educator*
Herschman, Jeffrey D. *lawyer*
Hirsh, Theodore William *lawyer*
Hochberg, Bayard Zabdial *lawyer*
Honemann, Daniel Henry *lawyer*
Howell, Harley Thomas *lawyer*
Hubbard, Herbert Hendrix *lawyer*
Immelt, Stephen J. *lawyer*
Jenkins, Robert Rowe *lawyer*
Johnston, Edward Allan *lawyer*
Johnston, George W. *lawyer*
Jones, John Martin, Jr. *lawyer*
Kallina, Emanuel John, II *lawyer*
Kandel, Nelson Robert *lawyer*
Kandel, Peter Thomas *lawyer*
Katz, Martha Lessman *lawyer*
Kershaw, Robert Barnsley *lawyer*
Kramer, Paul R. *lawyer*
Kuryk, David Neal *lawyer*
Levin, Edward Jesse *lawyer*
Levine, Richard E. *lawyer*
Lewis, Alexander Ingersoll, III *lawyer*
Liebmann, George W(illiam) *lawyer*
Lohr, Walter George, Jr. *lawyer*
Lundy, Audie Lee, Jr. *lawyer*
MacColl, J. A. *lawyer*
Machen, Arthur Webster, Jr. *lawyer*
McClung, A(lexander) Keith, Jr. *lawyer*
McPherson, Donald Paxton, III *lawyer*
McWilliams, John Michael *lawyer*
Melvin, Norman Cecil *lawyer*
Messina, Bonnie Lynn *lawyer*
Miliman, David Jay *lawyer*
Milio, Louis Romolo *law educator (retired), social worker*
Miller, Decatur Howard *lawyer*
Moser, M(artin) Peter *lawyer*
Neil, Benjamin Arthur *lawyer, educator*
Orman, Leonard Arnold *lawyer*
Owen, Stephen Lee *lawyer*
Pappas, George Frank *lawyer*
Peacock, James Daniel *lawyer*
Plant, Albin MacDonough *lawyer*
Plummer, Risque Wilson *retired lawyer*
Pokempner, Joseph Kres *lawyer*
Pollak, Joanne E. *lawyer*
Pollak, Mark *lawyer*
Putzel, Constance Kellner *lawyer*
Radding, Andrew *lawyer*
Redden, Roger Duffey *lawyer*
Reed, Gregory *lawyer*
Reno, Russell Ronald, Jr. *lawyer*
Reynolds, William Leroy *lawyer, educator*
Ritter, Jeffrey Blake *lawyer*
Robinson, Zelig *lawyer*
Rose, Rudolph L. *lawyer*
Rosenthal, William J. *lawyer*
Sack, Sylvan Hanan *lawyer*
Schaefer, William Goerman *lawyer*
Schochor, Jonathan *lawyer*
Scriggins, Larry Palmer *lawyer*
Sfekas, Stephen James *lawyer, educator*
Shapiro, Harry Dean *lawyer*
Sharkey, Robert Emmett *lawyer*
Short, Alexander Campbell *lawyer*
Smith, Robert G. *lawyer*
Speed, Leslie Bokee *lawyer*
Stalfort, John Arthur *lawyer*
Stewart, C(ornelius) Van Leuven *lawyer*
Sykes, Melvin Julius *lawyer*
Thompson, Otho M. *city solicitor*
Trimble, William Cattell, Jr. *lawyer*
†Urick, Kevin *lawyer*
Walker, Irving Edward *lawyer*
Wasserman, Richard Leo *lawyer*
White, Pamela Janice *lawyer*
White, William Nelson *lawyer*
Whitman, Marland Hamilton, Jr. *lawyer*
Wilson, Thomas Matthew, III *lawyer*
Winn, James Julius, Jr. *lawyer*
Woods, William Ellis *lawyer, pharmacist, association executive*
Yarmolinsky, Adam *lawyer, educator*
Zinkham, W. Robert *lawyer*

Bethesda
Allen, Toni K. *lawyer*
Alper, Jerome Milton *lawyer*
Baird, Bruce Allen *lawyer*
Bauersfeld, Carl Frederick *lawyer*
Brown, Thomas Philip, III *lawyer*
Burton, Charles Henning *lawyer*
Calvert, Gordon Lee *retired legal association executive*
Eisen, Eric Anshel *lawyer*
English, William deShay *lawyer*
Eule, Norman L. *lawyer*
Goldstone, Mark Lewis *lawyer*
Goodwin, Robert Cronin *lawyer, consultant*
Hagberg, Viola Wilgus *lawyer*
Herman, Stephen Allen *lawyer*
Hill, Hugh Francis, III *lawyer, physician*
Himelfarb, Stephen Roy *lawyer*
Jayson, Lester Samuel *lawyer, educator*
Mannix, Charles Raymond *law educator*
Meier, Louis Leonard, Jr. *lawyer*
Morgan, Jo Valentine, Jr. *lawyer*
Nelson, William Eugene *lawyer*
Pankopf, Arthur, Jr. *lawyer*
Poppleton, Miller John *lawyer*
Rosenberg, Mark Louis *lawyer*
Ross, William Warfield *lawyer*
Rubin, Allan Avrom *lawyer, regulatory agency consultant*
Schoem, Alan Howard *lawyer*
Scully, Roger Tehan *lawyer*
Strickler, Scott Michael *lawyer*
Toomey, Thomas Murray *lawyer*
Wasilewski, Vincent Thomas *retired lawyer*

Bowie
Lower, Philip Edward *lawyer*

Brookeville
Johns, Warren LeRoi *lawyer*

Burtonsville
Covington, Marlow Stanley *retired lawyer*

Cambridge
†Eckel, Grason John-Allen *lawyer*

Catonsville
Zumbrun, Alvin John Thomas *law and criminology educator*

Chestertown
Mowell, George Mitchell *lawyer*

Chevy Chase
Bruder, George Frederick *lawyer*
Chase, Nicholas Joseph *lawyer, educator*
Elliott, R Lance *lawyer*
Ikenberry, Henry Cephas, Jr. *lawyer*
Ketcham, Orman Weston *lawyer, former judge*
Klain, Ronald Alan *lawyer*
Lyons, Ellis *retired lawyer*
Montedonico, Joseph *lawyer*
Paul, Carl Frederick *lawyer, former judge*

Cockeysville Hunt Valley
Edgett, William Maloy *lawyer, labor arbitrator*

College Park
Neal, Edward Garrison *lawyer*

Columbia
Maseritz, Guy B. *lawyer*
Ulman, Louis Jay *lawyer*

Easton
Jacobs, Michael Joseph *lawyer*
Kehoe, Stephen H. *lawyer*
Maffitt, James Strawbridge *lawyer*

Ellicott City
Closson, Walter Franklin *prosecutor*
Henry, Edwin Maurice, Jr. *lawyer, electrical engineer, consultant*
Raum, Bernard Anthony *lawyer, county court official, educator*

Fort Washington
Alexander, Gary R. *lawyer, state legislator, lobbyist*

Frederick
Duncan, Stephen Mack *lawyer*
Hogan, Ilona Modly *lawyer*

Gaithersburg
Phillips, Leo Harold, Jr. *lawyer*

Glen Burnie
Cole, Ronald Clark *lawyer*
Smith, John Stanley *lawyer, mediator*

Greenbelt
Brugger, George Albert *lawyer*
Greenwald, Andrew Eric *lawyer*
Jascourt, Hugh D. *lawyer, arbitrator, mediator*

Hagerstown
Berkson, Jacob Benjamin *lawyer, author, conservationist*

Hyattsville
Rummel, Edgar Ferrand *retired lawyer*
Spiegel, Robert Alan *lawyer*

Kensington
Daisley, William Prescott *lawyer*
Dauster, William Gary *lawyer, economist*
Mathias, Joseph Marshall *lawyer, judge*

Lanham Seabrook
McCarthy, Kevin John *lawyer*

Largo
†Krauser, Peter B. *lawyer, political party executive*

Laytonsville
McDowell, Donna Schultz *lawyer*

Lexington Park
Lacer, Alfred Antonio *lawyer, educator*

Linthicum Heights
Fanseen, James Foster *lawyer*

Lutherville
Mc Kenney, Walter Gibbs, Jr. *lawyer, publishing company executive*

Lutherville Timonium
Levasseur, William Ryan *lawyer*

North Bethesda
Schwinn, Steven David *lawyer, mediator*

North Potomac
Kehoe, Patrick Emmett *law librarian, law educator*

Ocean City
Wimbrow, Peter Ayers, III *lawyer*

Oxon Hill
Serrette, Cathy Hollenberg *lawyer*

Parkville
Hill, Milton King, Jr. *lawyer*

Patuxent River
Fitzhugh, David Michael *lawyer*

Potomac
Conner, Troy Blaine, Jr. *retired lawyer, writer*
Feldman, Myer *lawyer*
Hall, William Darlington *lawyer*
Latham, Patricia Horan *lawyer*
Meyer, Lawrence George *lawyer*
Mullenbach, Linda Herman *lawyer*
Muntzing, L(ewis) Manning *lawyer*
Neuman, Robert Henry *lawyer*
Peter, Phillips Smith *lawyer*
Powell, Robert Dominick *lawyer*
Stetler, C. Joseph *retired lawyer*
Troffkin, Howard Julian *lawyer*

Reisterstown
Frank, Robert Louis *lawyer*

Rockville
Avery, Bruce Edward *lawyer*
Barkley, Brian Evan *lawyer, political consultant*
Bolle, Robert L. *lawyer, administrator*
Byrne, Olivia Sherrill *lawyer*
†Cyr, Karen D. *lawyer*
De Jong, David Samuel *lawyer, educator*
Frye, Roland Mushat, Jr. *lawyer*
Gordon, Joan Irma *lawyer*
†Horton, Linda Rae *lawyer*
Kadish, Richard L. *lawyer*
Katz, Steven Martin *lawyer, accountant*
Kerxton, Alan Smith *lawyer*
McGuire, Edward David, Jr. *lawyer*
Molitor, Graham Thomas Tate *lawyer*
Pensinger, John Lynn *lawyer*
Shadoan, George Woodson *lawyer*
Titus, Roger Warren *lawyer*
Van Grack, Steven *lawyer*
Yale, Kenneth P. *lawyer, dentist*
Zaphiriou, George Aristotle *lawyer, educator*

Saint Michaels
Brown, Omer Forrest, II *lawyer*

Silver Spring
Carter, Glenn Thomas *lawyer, clergyman*
Craig, Paul Max, Jr. *retired lawyer*
Gingell, Robert Arthur *lawyer*
McDermitt, Edward Vincent *lawyer, educator*
Mitchell, Milton *retired lawyer*
†Witkin, James B. *lawyer*

Solomons
Whitaker, Mary Fernan *lawyer*

Suitland
Bea, Barbara Ann *legal secretary*

Towson
Carney, Bradford George Yost *lawyer, educator*
Comeau, Michael Gerard *lawyer*
Hansen, Christopher Agnew *lawyer*
Murphy, Edward D. *company lawyer*
Proctor, Kenneth Donald *lawyer*

Upper Marlboro
Parker, Ellis Jackson, III *lawyer, broadcaster*

Westminster
Blakeslee, Wesley Daniel *lawyer, consultant*
Dulany, William Bevard *lawyer*
†Preston, Charles Michael *lawyer*
Staples, Lyle Newton *lawyer*

Wheaton
Kirchman, Charles Vincent *lawyer*
Kirchman, Eric Hans *lawyer*

MASSACHUSETTS

Abington
Tuttle, William Roger *lawyer, financial advisor*

Amherst
Howland, Richard Moulton *lawyer*
Katsh, M. Ethan *law educator*
Mazor, Lester Jay *law educator*

Andover
Boumil, Marcia Mobilia *legal educator, mediator, writer*
Gaff, Brian Michael *attorney, electrical engineer*
Lakin, John Francis *lawyer*

Arlington
Keshian, Richard *lawyer*

Ashfield
Pepyne, Edward Walter *lawyer, psychologist, former educator*

Belmont
Luick, Robert Burns *lawyer*
Simpson, Russell Avington *retired law firm administrator*

Boston
Abraham, Nicholas Albert *lawyer, real estate developer*
Achatz, John *lawyer*
Ames, James Barr *lawyer*
Aresty, Jeffrey M. *lawyer*
Auerbach, Joseph *lawyer, educator*
Bae, Frank S. H. *law educator, law librarian*
Bangs, Will Johnston *lawyer*
Beard, Charles Julian *lawyer*
Becker, Fred Ronald *lawyer*
Belin, Gaspard d'Andelot *retired lawyer*
Benjamin, William Chase *lawyer*
Bergen, Kenneth William *lawyer*
Bernhard, Alexander Alfred *lawyer*
Bines, Harvey Ernest *lawyer, educator, writer*
Blodgett, Mark Stephen *legal studies educator, author*
Bodoff, Joseph Samuel Uberman *lawyer*
Bohnen, Michael J. *lawyer*
Bok, John Fairfield *lawyer*
Borenstein, Milton Conrad *lawyer, manufacturing company executive*
Bornheimer, Allen Millard *lawyer*
Brody, Richard Eric *lawyer*
Brountas, Paul Peter *lawyer*
Brown, Judith Olans *lawyer, educator*
Brown, Matthew *lawyer*
Brown, Michael Robert *lawyer*
Browne, Kingsbury *lawyer*
Buchanan, Robert McLeod *lawyer*
Burgess, John Allen *lawyer*
Burleigh, Lewis Albert *lawyer*
Burns, Thomas David *lawyer*
Burr, Francis Hardon *lawyer*
Cabot, Charles Codman, Jr. *lawyer*
Caner, George Colket, Jr. *lawyer*
Carr, Stephen W. *lawyer*
Carroll, James Edward *lawyer*
Casner, Truman Snell *lawyer*
Chapin, Melville *lawyer*
Cherwin, Joel Ira *lawyer*
Chow, Stephen Y(ee) *lawyer*
Cogan, John Francis, Jr. *lawyer*
Cohn, Andrew Howard *lawyer*
Cronin, Philip Mark *lawyer*
Curley, Robert Ambrose, Jr. *lawyer*
Curtin, John Joseph, Jr. *lawyer*
Cushing, George Littleton *lawyer*
Cutler, Arnold Robert *lawyer*
Daley, Paul Patrick *lawyer*
Davis, Joshua Malcolm *lawyer*
Davitt, F. George *lawyer*
Daynard, Richard Alan *law educator*
Delaney, John White *lawyer*
de Rham, Casimir, Jr. *lawyer*
Dignan, Thomas Gregory, Jr. *lawyer*
Dillon, James Joseph *lawyer*
Dineen, John K. *lawyer*
Duffy, James Francis, III *lawyer*
Dusseault, C. Dean *lawyer*
Edwards, Richard Lansing *lawyer*
Ehrlich, M. Gordon *lawyer*
Elfman, Eric Michael *lawyer*
Ellis, Fredric Lee *lawyer*
Engel, David Lewis *lawyer*
Eurich, Richard Rex *lawyer*
Everett, Jonathan Jubal *lawyer*
Fay, Michael Leo *lawyer*
Feinberg, Robert I(ra) *lawyer*
Felter, John Kenneth *lawyer*
Finn, Terrence M. *lawyer*
Fischer, Eric Robert *lawyer, educator*
Fischer, Mark Alan *lawyer, law educator*
Fisher, Champe Andrews *lawyer*
Floor, Richard Earl *lawyer*
Fox, Francis Haney *lawyer*
Frankenheim, Samuel *lawyer*
Fraser, Robert Burchmore *lawyer*
Freehling, Daniel Joseph *law educator, law library director*
Fremont-Smith, Marion R. *lawyer*
Friedman, Michael Phillip *lawyer*
Gabovitch, William *lawyer, accountant*
Galvani, Paul B. *lawyer*
Galvin, Robert J. *lawyer*
†Garber, Paul William *lawyer*
Garcia, Adolfo Ramon *lawyer*

Gargiulo, Andrea W. *lawyer*
Gaudreau, Russell A., Jr. *lawyer, educator*
Gault, Robert Mellor *lawyer*
Gerstmayr, John Wolfgang *lawyer*
Gill, Robert Tucker *lawyer*
Giso, Frank, III *lawyer*
Glosband, Daniel Martin *lawyer*
Goldman, Eric Scot *lawyer*
Goldman, Richard Harris *lawyer*
Goodman, Louis Allan *lawyer*
Greer, Gordon Bruce *lawyer*
Gupta, Paul R. *lawyer*
Haddad, Ernest Mudarri *lawyer*
Hall, David *law educator, dean*
Hall, Henry Lyon, Jr. *lawyer*
Halström, Frederic Norman *lawyer*
Hamel, Louis H., Jr. *lawyer*
Harrington, John Michael, Jr. *lawyer*
Hauser, Harry Raymond *lawyer*
Haussermann, Oscar William, Jr. *lawyer, retired*
Hawkey, G. Michael *lawyer*
Hayes, Robert Francis *lawyer*
Heigham, James Crichton *lawyer*
Hester, Patrick Joseph *lawyer*
Hieken, Charles *lawyer*
Hines, Edward Francis, Jr. *lawyer*
Hoffman, Christian Matthew *lawyer*
Hoffman, David Alan *lawyer*
Holland, Hubert Brian *lawyer*
Hoort, Steven Thomas *lawyer*
Hoover, David Carlson *lawyer*
Hotchkiss, Andra Ruth *lawyer*
Howe, Jas. Murray *lawyer*
Hrones, Stephen Baylis *lawyer, educator*
Huang, Thomas Weishing *lawyer*
Johnston, Richard Alan *lawyer*
Jones, Jeffrey Foster *lawyer*
Jones, Sheldon Atwell *lawyer*
Jordan, Alexander Joseph, Jr. *lawyer*
Kaler, Robert Joseph *lawyer*
Kanin, Dennis Roy *lawyer*
Kaplan, Lawrence Edward *lawyer*
Katzmann, Gary Stephen *lawyer*
Keating, Michael Burns *lawyer*
Kehoe, William Francis *lawyer*
Keller, Stanley *lawyer*
Kenney, Raymond Joseph, Jr. *lawyer*
Kerry, Cameron F. *lawyer*
King, William Bruce *lawyer*
Kirchick, William Dean *lawyer*
Kirk, Paul Grattan, Jr. *lawyer, former political organization official*
Koffel, William Barry *lawyer*
Kopelman, Leonard *lawyer*
Krasnow, Jordan Philip *lawyer*
Krulewich, Leonard M. *lawyer*
Lamb, Kevin Thomas *lawyer*
Lane, Newton Alexander *retired lawyer*
Last, Michael P. *lawyer*
Latham, James David *lawyer*
Lewis, Scott P. *lawyer*
Licata, Arthur Frank *lawyer*
Lockwood, Rhodes Greene *retired lawyer*
Loeser, Hans Ferdinand *lawyer*
Looney, William Francis, Jr. *lawyer*
Loria, Martin A. *lawyer*
Loring, Arthur *lawyer, financial services company executive*
Lukey, Joan A. *lawyer*
Lynch, Francis Charles *lawyer*
Lyons, Paul Vincent *lawyer*
MacFarlane, Maureen Anne *lawyer*
Malt, Ronald Bradford *lawyer*
Mandel, David Michael *lawyer*
Marks, Stephen Paul *law and international affairs educator, international official*
Martin, Stanley A. *lawyer*
Matthews, Roger Hardin *lawyer*
McChesney, S. Elaine *lawyer*
McDonald, John Barry, Jr. *lawyer*
McKittrick, Neil Vincent *lawyer*
McLaughlin, John Joseph, Jr. *lawyer*
Meserve, William George *lawyer*
Metzer, Patricia Ann *lawyer*
Mikels, Richard Eliot *lawyer*
Minkel, Herbert Philip, Jr. *lawyer*
Mokriski, J. Charles *lawyer*
Moncreiff, Robert P. *lawyer*
Mooney, Michael Edward *lawyer*
Moriarty, George Marshall *lawyer*
Muldoon, Robert Joseph, Jr. *lawyer*
Mullare, T(homas) Kenwood, Jr. *lawyer*
Murray, Philip Edmund, Jr. *lawyer*
Mutterperl, William Charles *lawyer*
Neely, Thomas Emerson *lawyer*
Neumeier, Richard L. *lawyer*
Nissenbaum, Gerald L. *lawyer*
Norris, Charles Head *lawyer, manufacturing executive*
Nutt, Robert L. *lawyer*
O'Dell, Edward Thomas, Jr. *lawyer*
O'Donnell, Thomas Lawrence Patrick *lawyer*
Oetheimer, Richard A. *lawyer*
O'Leary, Joseph Evans *lawyer*
O'Neill, Philip Daniel, Jr. *lawyer, educator*
O'Neill, Timothy P. *lawyer*
Packenham, Richard Daniel *lawyer*
Packer, Rekha Desai *lawyer*
Park, William Wynnewood *law educator*
Parker, Christopher William *lawyer*
Partan, Daniel Gordon *lawyer, educator*
Patterson, John de la Roche, Jr. *lawyer*
Pechilis, William John *lawyer*
Perera, Lawrence Thacher *lawyer*
Perkins, James Wood *lawyer*
Perkins, John Allen *lawyer*
Pomeroy, Robert Corttis *lawyer*
Poss, Stephen Daniel *lawyer*
Raish, David Langdon *lawyer*
Rappaport, James Wyant *lawyer, real estate developer*
Reardon, Frank Emond *lawyer*
Redlich, Marc *lawyer*
Remis, Shepard M. *lawyer*
Richmond, Alice Elenor *lawyer*
Ritt, Roger Merrill *lawyer*
Rivlin, Rachel *lawyer*
Rizzo, William Ober *lawyer*
Rose, Alan Douglas *lawyer*
Sapers, Carl Martin *lawyer*
Sargeant, Ernest James *lawyer*
Sawyer, William C. *lawyer*
Schmelzer, Henry Louis Phillip *lawyer, financial company executive*
Schoenfeld, Barbara Braun *lawyer*
Schram, Ronald Byard *lawyer*
Scott, A. Hugh *lawyer*
Sears, John Winthrop *lawyer*
Segal, Robert Mandal *lawyer*
Shapiro, Sandra *lawyer*
Shepard, Henry Bradbury, Jr. *lawyer*
Silberman, Robert A. S. *lawyer*
Sirkin, Joel H. *lawyer*
Skrine, Bruce E. *lawyer*
Smith, Edwin Eric *lawyer*
Smith, Philip Jones *lawyer*
Snyder, John Gorvers *lawyer*
Soden, Richard Allan *lawyer*
Solet, Maxwell David *lawyer*
Sommerfeld, Nicholas Ulrich *lawyer*
Sonnenschein, Adam *lawyer*
Southard, William G. *lawyer*
Spelfogel, Scott David *lawyer*
Spiess, Gary A. *lawyer*
Stein, Marshall David *lawyer*
Steinberg, Laura *lawyer*
Stern, Donald Kenneth *prosecutor*
Stevenson, Philip Davis *lawyer*
Stokes, James Christopher *lawyer*
Storer, Jeffrey B. *lawyer*
Storer, Thomas Perry *lawyer*
Storey, James Moorfield *lawyer*
Streeter, Henry Schofield *lawyer*
Sugarman, Paul Ronald *lawyer, educator, academic administrator*
Surkin, Elliot Mark *lawyer*
Sutherland, John Edward *lawyer, educator*
Swaim, Charles Hall *lawyer*
Swope, Jeffrey Peyton *lawyer*
Taylor, Thomas William *lawyer*
Testa, Richard Joseph *lawyer*
Touster, Saul *law educator*
Trimmier, Roscoe, Jr. *lawyer*
Tuchmann, Robert *lawyer*
Van, Peter *lawyer*
Vance, Verne Widney, Jr. *lawyer*
Vaughan, Herbert Wiley *lawyer*
Walker, Gordon T. *lawyer*
Weiner, Stephen Mark *lawyer*
Weitzel, John Patterson *lawyer*
Wellington, Carol Strong *law librarian*
Weltman, David Lee *lawyer*
White, Barry Bennett *lawyer*
Whitlock, John L. *lawyer*
Whitters, James Payton, III *lawyer, university administrator*
Williams, John Taylor *lawyer*
Winter, Donald Francis *lawyer*
Wolf, David *lawyer*
Woodburn, Ralph Robert, Jr. *lawyer*
Woolsey, John Munro, Jr. *lawyer*
Young, Raymond Henry *lawyer*

Brookline
Burnstein, Daniel *lawyer*

Cambridge
Aldave, Barbara Bader *law educator, lawyer*
Andrews, William Dorey *lawyer, educator*
Bok, Derek *law educator, former university president*
Chapin, Richard *arbitrator, consultant*
Chayes, Abram *law educator, lawyer*
Clark, Robert Charles *law educator, dean*
Connors, Frank Joseph *lawyer*
Cox, Archibald *lawyer, educator*
Dershowitz, Alan Morton *lawyer, educator*
Fallon, Richard H., Jr. *law educator*
Fisher, Roger Dummer *lawyer, educator, negotiation expert*
Fried, Charles *law educator*
Glauner, Alfred William *lawyer, engineering company executive*
Glendon, Mary Ann *law educator*
Gonson, S. Donald *lawyer*
Kaplow, Louis *law educator*
Kaufman, Andrew Lee *law educator*
Kennedy, David W. *law educator*
Mansfield, John H. *lawyer, educator*
Martin, Harry Stratton, III *law librarian*
Meltzer, Daniel J. *law educator*
Merrill, Dale Marie *lawyer*
Michelman, Frank I. *lawyer, educator*
Miller, Arthur Raphael *law educator*
Mnookin, Robert Harris *lawyer, educator*
Patton, Bruce M. *law educator*
Ramseyer, J. Mark *law educator*
Roche, John Jefferson *lawyer*
Ryan, Allan Andrew, Jr. *lawyer, author, lecturer*
Sander, Frank Ernest Arnold *law educator*
Schauer, Frederick Franklin *law educator*
Scott, Hal S. *law educator*
Steiner, Henry Jacob *law and human rights educator*
Stone, Alan A. *law and psychiatry educator, psychiatrist*
Ta, Tai Van *lawyer, researcher*
Vagts, Detlev Frederick *lawyer, educator*
von Mehren, Arthur Taylor *lawyer, educator*
Vorenberg, James *lawyer, educator, university dean*
Weinreb, Lloyd Lobell *law educator*
Westfall, David *lawyer, educator*
Wolfman, Bernard *lawyer, educator*

Canton
Fuller, Robert L(eander) *lawyer*
Masiello, Thomas Philip, Jr. *lawyer, risk manager*

Carlisle
Hensleigh, Howard Edgar *lawyer*

Chatham
Popkin, Alice Brandeis *lawyer*

Chelmsford
Grossman, Debra A. *lawyer, real estate manager, radio talk show host*
Lerer, Neal M. *lawyer*

Chestnut Hill
Batchelder, Samuel Lawrence, Jr. *retired corporate lawyer*
Geller, Eric P. *lawyer, cinema company executive*

Concord
Berger, Raoul *retired law educator, violinist*
White, James Barr *lawyer, real estate investor, consultant*

Dennis Port
Singer, Myer R(ichard) *lawyer*

Dover
Craver, James Bernard *lawyer*

Easton
Segersten, Robert Hagy *lawyer, investment banker*

Framingham
Felper, David Michael *lawyer*
Gatlin, Michael Gerard *lawyer, educator*
Heng, Gerald C. W. *lawyer*
Hunt, Samuel Pancoast, III *lawyer, corporate executive*
Meltzer, Jay H. *lawyer, retail company executive*
Munro, Meredith Vance *lawyer*

Gloucester
Birchfield, John Kermit, Jr. *lawyer*

Greenfield
Lee, Marilyn (Irma) Modarelli *law librarian*

Hingham
Lane, Frederick Stanley *lawyer*

Ipswich
Getchell, Charles Willard, Jr. *lawyer, publisher*

Lexington
Eaton, Allen Ober *lawyer*
Glovsky, Susan G. L. *lawyer*
†Hyde, Thomas D. *lawyer*
Nason, Leonard Yoshimoto *lawyer, writer, publisher*

Lincoln
Gnichtel, William Van Orden *lawyer*
Schwartz, Edward Arthur *lawyer*

Lowell
Curtis, James Theodore *lawyer*
Martin, William Francis, Jr. *lawyer*

Lynnfield
McGivney, John Joseph *lawyer*

Medford
Berman, David *lawyer, poet*
Salacuse, Jeswald William *lawyer, educator*

Milton
Cooperstein, Paul Andrew *lawyer, business consultant*

Nantucket
Lobl, Herbert Max *lawyer*

Natick
Marr, David E *lawyer*

Needham
Coleman, Richard William *lawyer*

New Bedford
Murray, Robert Fox *lawyer*

Newburyport
Maslen, David Peter *lawyer*

Newton
Baron, Charles Hillel *lawyer, educator*
Bernard, Michael Mark *lawyer, city planning consultant*
Coquillette, Daniel Robert *lawyer, educator*
Glazer, Donald Wayne *lawyer, business executive, educator*
Goldweitz, Julie *lawyer*
Huber, Richard Gregory *lawyer, educator*
Messing, Arnold Philip *lawyer*
Monahan, Marie Terry *lawyer*
Norris, Melvin *lawyer*
Peterson, Osler Leopold *lawyer*

North Reading
Green, Jack Allen *lawyer*

Northampton
Park, Beverly Goodman *lawyer*

Norwell
O'Sullivan, James Michael *lawyer*

Otis
Idzik, Daniel Ronald *lawyer*

Pittsfield
Doyle, Anthony Peter *lawyer*

Plymouth
Barreira, Brian Ernest *lawyer*

Quincy
Motejunas, Gerald William *lawyer*
Weischadle, David Emanuel, II *lawyer, literary agent*
Weischadle, Douglas Eric *lawyer, literary agent*

Salem
Griffin, Thomas McLean *retired lawyer*
Moran, Philip David *lawyer*

Somerset
Sabra, Steven Peter *lawyer*

Somerville
†Rajagopal, Balakrishnan *lawyer*

South Chatham
Horton, Elliott Argue, Jr. *lawyer, business consultant*

South Orleans
Parker, Douglas Martin *writer, retired lawyer*

Springfield
Burke, Michael Henry *lawyer*
†Burkett, Lawrence V. *insurance company executive*
Dunn, Donald Jack *law librarian, law educator, dean, lawyer*
Maidman, Stephen Paul *lawyer*
McCarthy, Charles Francis, Jr. *lawyer*
Miller, J(ohn) Wesley, III *lawyer, author*
Milstein, Richard Sherman *lawyer*
Oldershaw, Louis Frederick *lawyer*
Santopietro, Albert Robert *lawyer*
Sullivan, Frederick Lawrence *lawyer*
Sweeney, Kevin Michael *lawyer*

Stoughton
Gabovitch, Steven Alan *lawyer, accountant*
Schepps, Victoria Hayward *lawyer*

Stow
Golder, Leonard Howard *lawyer, writer*

Tewksbury
†Powers, Arthur George *lawyer*

Wakefield
Lucas, Robert Frank *lawyer*

Waltham
Barnes-Brown, Peter Newton *lawyer*

Wellesley
Aldrich, Richard Orth *lawyer*
Carlson, Christopher Tapley *lawyer*
Goglia, Charles A., Jr. *lawyer*
Riley, Michael Hylan *lawyer*
Shea, Robert McConnell *lawyer*

West Chatham
Rowley, Glenn Harry *lawyer*

West Falmouth
Carlson, David Bret *lawyer*

Westborough
Frank, Jacob *lawyer*

Westfield
Pollard, Frank Edward *lawyer*

Weston
Haas, Jacqueline Crawford *lawyer*
Lashman, L. Edward *arbitrator, mediator, consultant*
Thomas, Roger Meriwether *lawyer*

Winchester
Bigelow, Robert P. *lawyer, arbitrator, mediator, journalist*

Winthrop
Brown, Patricia Irene *lawyer, retired law librarian*

Worcester
Bassett, Edward Caldwell, Jr. *lawyer*
Cowan, Fairman Chaffee *lawyer*
Donnelly, James Corcoran, Jr. *lawyer*
Lougee, David Louis *lawyer*
Moschos, Demitrios Mina *lawyer*
Uhl, Christopher Martin *lawyer, educator*

Worthington
Hastings, Wilmot Reed *lawyer*

Yarmouth Port
Paquin, Thomas Christopher *lawyer*

MICHIGAN

Ada
Mc Callum, Charles Edward *lawyer*

Ann Arbor
Allen, Layman Edward *law educator, research scientist*
Bollinger, Lee Carroll *law educator*
Britton, Clarold Lawrence *lawyer, consultant*
Browder, Olin Lorraine *legal educator*
Cooper, Edward Hayes *lawyer, educator*
DeVine, Edmond Francis *lawyer*
Dew, Thomas Edward *lawyer*
Ellmann, Douglas Stanley *lawyer*
Ellmann, William Marshall *lawyer, mediator, arbitrator, researcher*
Ferris, Donald William, Jr. *lawyer*
Frier, Bruce W. *law educator*
Joscelyn, Kent Buckley *lawyer*
Kahn, Douglas Allen *legal educator*
Krier, James Edward *law educator, author*
Krislov, Marvin *federal government lawyer*
Lehman, Jeffrey Sean *law educator, dean*
Lempert, Richard Owen *lawyer, educator*
MacKinnon, Catharine A. *lawyer, law educator, legal scholar, writer*
McHugh, Richard Walker *lawyer*
Niehoff, Leonard Marvin *lawyer*
Phillips, Daniel Miller *lawyer*
Reed, John Wesley *lawyer, educator*
Roach, Thomas Adair *lawyer*
Sandalow, Terrance *law educator*
Schneider, Carl Edward *law educator*
Simpson, A. W. B. *law educator*
Vining, (George) Joseph *law educator*
White, James Boyd *law educator*

Auburn Hills
O'Brien, William J. *lawyer*

Battle Creek
Fisher, James A. *lawyer*

Bay City
Greve, Guy Robert *lawyer*

Bingham Farms
Fershtman, Julie Ilene *lawyer*
Moffitt, David Louis *lawyer, county and state official*
Toth, John Michael *lawyer*

Birmingham
Bromberg, Stephen Aaron *lawyer*
Buesser, Anthony Carpenter *lawyer*
Elsman, James Leonard, Jr. *lawyer*
Gold, Edward David *lawyer*
Harms, Steven Alan *lawyer*
Kienbaum, Thomas Gerd *lawyer*
Lesser, Margo Rogers *legal consultant*

PROFESSIONAL INDEX 6147 LAW: LAW PRACTICE AND ADMINISTRATION

Morganroth, Fred *lawyer*
†Schaefer, John Frederick *lawyer*
Sweeney, Thomas Frederick *lawyer*

Bloomfield Hills
Andrews, Frank Lewis *lawyer*
Baker, Robert Edward *lawyer, retired financial corporation executive*
Baumkel, Mark S. *lawyer*
Berlow, Robert Alan *lawyer*
Brodhead, William McNulty *lawyer, former congressman*
Clippert, Charles Frederick *lawyer*
Cranmer, Thomas William *lawyer*
Cunningham, Gary H. *lawyer*
Dawson, Stephen Everette *lawyer*
Gelder, John William *lawyer*
Googasian, George Ara *lawyer*
Hurlbert, Robert P. *lawyer*
Janover, Robert H. *lawyer*
Kasischke, Louis Walter *lawyer*
Kirk, John Mac Gregor *lawyer*
Lehman, Richard Leroy *lawyer*
LoPrete, James Hugh *lawyer*
McDonald, Patrick Allen *lawyer, arbitrator, educator*
McGarry, Alexander Banting *lawyer*
Meyer, George Herbert *lawyer*
Nolte, Henry R., Jr. *lawyer, former automobile company executive*
Norris, John Hart *lawyer*
Pappas, Edward Harvey *lawyer*
Rader, Ralph Terrance *lawyer*
Simon, Evelyn *lawyer*
Snyder, George Edward *lawyer*
Solomon, Mark Raymond *lawyer, educator*
Thurber, John Alexander *lawyer*
Victor, Richard Steven *lawyer*
Weinstein, William Joseph *lawyer*
Williams, Walter Joseph *lawyer*
Yamin, Joseph Francis *lawyer, counselor*
Ziegler, John Augustus, Jr. *lawyer*

Dearborn
Demorest, Mark Stuart *lawyer*
Gardner, Gary Edward *lawyer*
Kahn, Mark Leo *arbitrator, educator*
Taub, Robert Allan *lawyer*

Detroit
†Acomb, Frederick Allan *lawyer*
Adamany, David Walter *law and political science educator*
Amsden, Ted Thomas *lawyer*
Andreoff, Christopher Andon *lawyer*
Babcock, Charles Witten, Jr. *lawyer*
Banas, C. Leslie *lawyer*
Brady, Edmund Matthew, Jr. *lawyer*
Brand, George Edward, Jr. *lawyer*
Brown, Stratton Shartel *lawyer*
Brustad, Orin Daniel *lawyer*
Burstein, Richard Joel *lawyer*
Bushnell, George Edward, Jr. *lawyer*
Candler, James Nall, Jr. *lawyer*
Charfoos, Lawrence Selig *lawyer*
Charla, Leonard Francis *lawyer*
Christiansen, Roy Hvidkaer *lawyer*
Cohan, Leon Sumner *lawyer, retired electric company executive*
Collier, James Warren *lawyer*
Connor, Laurence Davis *lawyer*
Corrigan, Maura Denise *lawyer, judge*
Cothorn, John Arthur *lawyer*
Darlow, Julia Donovan *lawyer*
Deron, Edward Michael *lawyer*
Devaney, Dennis Martin *lawyer, educator*
Draper, James Wilson *lawyer*
Dudley, John Henry, Jr. *lawyer*
Eggertsen, John Hale *lawyer*
Ettinger, David A. *lawyer*
Faison, W. Mack *lawyer*
Garzia, Samuel Angelo *lawyer*
Getz, Ernest John *lawyer*
Gilbert, Ronald Rhea *lawyer*
Glotta, Ronald Delon *lawyer*
Gottschalk, Thomas A. *lawyer*
†Green, Saul A. *prosecutor*
Gushee, Richard Bordley *lawyer*
Hampton, Verne Churchill, II *lawyer*
Heaphy, John Merrill *lawyer*
Herstein, Carl William *lawyer*
Howbert, Edgar Charles *lawyer*
James, Phyllis A. *lawyer*
Krsul, John Aloysius, Jr. *lawyer*
Kuehn, George E. *lawyer, beverage company executive*
Lamborn, LeRoy Leslie *law educator*
Lawrence, John Kidder *lawyer*
Ledwidge, Patrick Joseph *lawyer*
Lenga, J. Thomas *lawyer*
Lewand, F. Thomas *lawyer*
Lockman, Stuart M. *lawyer*
Longhofer, Ronald Stephen *lawyer*
Lucow, Milton *lawyer*
Mamat, Frank Trustick *lawyer*
Maurer, David Leo *lawyer*
Maycock, Joseph Farwell, Jr. *lawyer*
McKim, Samuel John, III *lawyer*
McNair, Russell Arthur, Jr. *lawyer*
Mitseff, Carl *lawyer*
Myers, Rodman Nathaniel *lawyer*
Nadeau, Steven C. *lawyer*
Nemeth, Patricia Marie *lawyer*
Nix, Robert Royal, II *lawyer*
O'Hair, John D. *lawyer*
Parker, George Edward, III *lawyer*
Pearce, Harry Jonathan *lawyer*
Phillips, Elliott Hunter *lawyer*
Pirtle, H(arold) Edward *lawyer*
Prather, Kenneth Earl *lawyer*
Rasmussen, Douglas John *lawyer*
Rentenbach, Paul Robert *lawyer*
Rohr, Richard David *lawyer*
Rozof, Phyllis Claire *lawyer*
Santo, Ronald Joseph *lawyer*
Saxton, William Marvin *lawyer*
Saylor, Larry James *lawyer*
Scholler, Thomas Peter *lawyer, accountant*
Schwartz, Alan E. *lawyer*
Scott, John Edward Smith *lawyer*
Sedler, Robert Allen *law educator*
Semple, Lloyd Ashby *lawyer*
Shaevsky, Mark *lawyer*
Shannon, Margaret Anne *lawyer*
Shapiro, Michael B. *lawyer*
Skutt, Richard Michael *lawyer*
Sott, Herbert *lawyer*
Sparrow, Herbert George, III *lawyer*
Thelen, Bruce Cyril *lawyer*
Thoms, David Moore *lawyer*
Thurber, Peter Palms *lawyer*
Timm, Roger K. *lawyer*
Toll, Sheldon Samuel *lawyer*
Volz, William Harry *law educator, administrator*
Walsh, James Joseph *lawyer*
Williams, J. Bryan *lawyer*
Wise, John Augustus *lawyer*
Wittlinger, Timothy David *lawyer*

Dexter
†Sharp, Ronald Farrington *lawyer*

East Lansing
Bitensky, Susan Helen *law educator*
Lashbrooke, Elvin Carroll, Jr. *law educator, consultant*
Wilkinson, William Sherwood *lawyer*

Farmington
Torpey, Scott Raymond *lawyer*

Farmington Hills
Birnkrant, Sherwin Maurice *lawyer*
Fenton, Robert Leonard *lawyer*
Haliw, Andrew Jerome, III *lawyer, engineer*

Flint
Hart, Clifford Harvey *lawyer*
Henneke, Edward George *lawyer*
Pelavin, Michael Allen *lawyer*
Powers, Edward Herbert *lawyer*

Frankfort
Gerberding, Miles Carston *lawyer*

Grand Ledge
Smith, Terry J. *lawyer*

Grand Rapids
Barnes, Thomas John *lawyer*
Blackwell, Thomas Francis *lawyer*
Boyden, Joel Michael *lawyer*
Bradshaw, Conrad Allan *lawyer*
Bransdorfer, Stephen Christie *lawyer*
Curtin, Timothy John *lawyer*
Davis, Henry Barnard, Jr. *lawyer*
Deems, Nyal David *lawyer, mayor*
Engbers, James Arend *lawyer*
Kara, Paul Mark *lawyer*
McGarry, John Everett *lawyer*
McNeil, John W. *lawyer*
Mears, Patrick Edward *lawyer*
Oetting, Roger H. *lawyer*
Smith, H(arold) Lawrence *lawyer*
Spies, Frank Stadler *lawyer*
Stadler, James Robert *lawyer*
Sytsma, Fredric A. *lawyer*
Titley, Larry J. *lawyer*
Van Haren, W(illiam) Michael *lawyer*
Van't Hof, William Keith *lawyer*

Grosse Pointe
Avant, Grady, Jr. *lawyer*
Axe, John Randolph *lawyer, financial executive*
Barrows, Ronald Thomas *lawyer*
Brucker, Wilber Marion *retired lawyer*
Goss, James William *lawyer*
King, John Lane *retired lawyer*
McIntyre, Anita Grace Jordan *lawyer*
Mogk, John Edward *law educator, association executive, consultant*
Pytell, Robert Henry *lawyer, former judge*

Grosse Pointe Woods
Darke, Richard Francis *lawyer*

Harbor Springs
Turner, Lester Nathan *lawyer, international trade consultant*

Hickory Corners
Bristol, Norman *lawyer, arbitrator, former food company executive*

Holland
Moritz, John Reid *lawyer*
Murphy, Max Ray *lawyer*

Inkster
Bullock, Steven Carl *lawyer*

Jackson
Jacobs, Wendell Early, Jr. *lawyer*
Marcoux, William Joseph *lawyer*

Kalamazoo
Halpert, Richard Lee *lawyer*
Hilboldt, James Sonnemann *lawyer, investment advisor*
Ritter, Charles Edward *lawyer*

Lansing
Baker, Frederick Milton, Jr. *lawyer*
Bretz, Ronald James *law educator*
Brewer, Mark Courtland *lawyer*
Demlow, Daniel J. *lawyer*
Fink, Joseph Allen *lawyer*
Fitzgerald, John Warner *law educator*
Foster, Joe C., Jr. *lawyer*
Latovick, Paula R(ae) *lawyer, educator*
Lindemer, Lawrence Boyd *lawyer, former utility executive, former state justice*
Marvin, David Edward Shreve *lawyer*
Rasmusson, Thomas Elmo *lawyer*
Tieber, F. Martin *lawyer*
Valade, Alan Michael *lawyer*
Warren, J(ohn) Michael *lawyer*
Winder, Richard Earnest *legal foundation administrator, writer, consultant*

Livonia
Hoffman, Barry Paul *lawyer*
McCuen, John Francis, Jr. *lawyer*
Thompson, Robert Rex *lawyer*

Midland
Battle, Leonard Carroll *lawyer*
†Scriven, John G. *lawyer, chemical company executive*

Monroe
Lipford, Rocque Edward *lawyer, corporate executive*

Muskegon
Briggs, John Mancel, III *lawyer*
Fauri, Eric Joseph *lawyer*
McKendry, John H., Jr. *lawyer, educator*
Nehra, Gerald Peter *lawyer*
Van Leuven, Robert Joseph *lawyer*

Okemos
Schneider, Karen Bush *lawyer, educator*

Owosso
Shulaw, Richard A. *lawyer*

Plymouth
McNish, Susan Kirk *retired lawyer*
Morgan, Donald Crane *lawyer*

Pontiac
Pierson, William George *lawyer*

Rapid City
Ring, Ronald Herman *lawyer*

Saginaw
Martin, Walter *retired lawyer*
McGraw, Patrick John *lawyer*

Saint Clair Shores
Danielson, Gary R. *lawyer*
Shehan, Wayne Charles *lawyer*

Saint Joseph
Gleiss, Henry Weston *lawyer*

Southfield
Antone, Nahil Peter *lawyer, civil engineer*
Dawson, Dennis Ray *lawyer, manufacturing company executive*
Gordon, Arnold Mark *arbitrator, lawyer*
Hanket, Mark John *lawyer*
Hotelling, Harold *law and economics educator*
Jacobs, John Patrick *lawyer*
Kaplow, Robert David *lawyer*
Kippert, Robert John, Jr. *lawyer*
Martin, Joseph Patrick *lawyer*
May, Alan Alfred *lawyer*
McClow, Roger James *labor lawyer*
Morganroth, Mayer *lawyer*
Ritchie, Alexander Buchan *lawyer*
Satovsky, Abraham *lawyer*
Schwartz, Robert H. *lawyer*
Sullivan, Robert Emmet, Jr. *lawyer*
Taravella, Christopher Anthony *lawyer*
Tombers, Evelyn Charlotte *lawyer*

Sterling Heights
Novak, Joseph Anthony *lawyer*

Taylor
Hirsch, David L. *lawyer, corporate executive*
Leekley, John Robert *lawyer*
Pacynski, Rick Alan *corporation lawyer*

Traverse City
Quandt, Joseph Edward *lawyer, educator*
Wolfe, Richard Ratcliffe *lawyer*

Troy
Alterman, Irwin Michael *lawyer*
Cantor, Bernard Jack *patent lawyer*
Chapman, Conrad Daniel *lawyer*
Crane, Louis Arthur *retired labor arbitrator*
Gullen, Christopher Roy *lawyer*
Haron, David Lawrence *lawyer*
Hirschhorn, Austin *lawyer*
Kruse, John Alphonse *lawyer*
LaDuke, Nancie *lawyer, corporate executive*
Lenihan, Robert Joseph, II *lawyer*
McGinnis, Thomas Michael *lawyer*
Ponitz, John Allan *lawyer*

Walled Lake
Seglund, Bruce Richard *lawyer*

Warren
Bridenstine, Louis Henry, Jr. *lawyer*

West Bloomfield
Meyer, Philip Gilbert *lawyer*
†Montera, David John *lawyer*
Robbins, Norman Nelson *lawyer*
Tobin, Bruce Howard *lawyer*

Ypsilanti
Barr, John Monte *lawyer*

MINNESOTA

Anoka
Hicken, Jeffrey Price *lawyer*

Austin
Schneider, Mahlon C. *lawyer*

Bemidji
Kief, Paul Allan *lawyer*
Woodke, Robert Allen *lawyer*

Benson
Wilcox, Donald Alan *lawyer*

Bloomington
Ueland, Sigurd, Jr. *retired lawyer*

Brooklyn Center
Neff, Fred Leonard *lawyer*

Burnsville
Knutson, David Lee *lawyer, state senator*

Cottage Grove
O'Gorman, Patricia Ann *lawyer*

Crystal
Reske, Steven David *lawyer, writer*

Duluth
Burns, Richard Ramsey *lawyer*
Nys, John Nikki *lawyer*
Wade, James Alan *lawyer*

Eagan
Todd, John Joseph *lawyer*

Eden Prairie
†Joyce, Joseph M. *lawyer*
Nilles, John Michael *lawyer*

Edina
Burk, Robert S. *lawyer*
Gurstel, Norman Keith *lawyer*
Lillehaug, David Lee *lawyer*
Weber, Gail Mary *lawyer*

Excelsior
Grathwol, James Norbert *lawyer*

Fridley
Savelkoul, Donald Charles *retired lawyer*

Golden Valley
Hagglund, Clarance Edward *lawyer, publishing company owner*

Grand Rapids
Licke, Wallace John *lawyer*

Hallock
Malm, Roger Charles *lawyer*

Hopkins
Hunter, Donald Forrest *lawyer*

Inver Grove Heights
Kaner, Harvey Sheldon *lawyer, executive*

Kenyon
Peterson, Franklin Delano *lawyer*

Mankato
Gage, Fred Kelton *lawyer*

Maplewood
Nemo, Anthony James *lawyer*

Minneapolis
Ackman, Lauress V. *lawyer*
Adamson, Oscar Charles, II *lawyer*
Aldrich, Stephen Charles *lawyer, judge*
Allers, Marlene Elaine *legal administrator*
Anderson, Alan Marshall *lawyer*
Anderson, Eric Scott *lawyer*
Anderson, Laurence Alexis *lawyer*
Andrews, Albert O'Beirne, Jr. *lawyer*
Barnard, Allen Donald *lawyer*
Bearmon, Lee *lawyer*
Berens, William Joseph *lawyer*
Berg, Thomas Kenneth *lawyer*
Bland, J(ohn) Richard *lawyer*
Blanton, W. C. *lawyer*
Boelter, Philip Floyd *lawyer*
Borger, John Philip *lawyer*
Brand, Steve Aaron *lawyer*
Brehl, James William *lawyer*
Breimayer, Joseph Frederick *patent lawyer*
Bress, Michael E. *retired lawyer*
Brink, David Ryrie *lawyer*
Brosnahan, Roger Paul *lawyer*
Bruner, Philip Lane *lawyer*
Buratti, Dennis P. *lawyer*
Burke, Martin Nicholas *lawyer*
Burns, Robert Arthur *lawyer*
Busdicker, Gordon G. *lawyer*
Carlson, Thomas David *lawyer*
Carpenter, Norman Roblee *retired lawyer*
Champlin, Steven Kirk *lawyer*
Chester, Stephanie Ann *lawyer, banker*
Christiansen, Jay David *lawyer*
Ciresi, Michael Vincent *lawyer*
Clary, Bradley G. *lawyer, educator*
Cohen, Earl Harding *lawyer*
Comstock, Rebecca Ann *lawyer*
Conn, Gordon Brainard, Jr. *lawyer*
Corwin, Gregg Marlowe *lawyer*
Crosby, Thomas Manville, Jr. *lawyer*
Degnan, John Michael *lawyer*
DiPietro, Mark Joseph *lawyer*
Drawz, John Englund *lawyer*
Eck, George Gregory *lawyer*
Eckland, Jeff Howard *lawyer*
Erstad, Leon Robert *lawyer*
Faricy, John Hartnett, Jr. *lawyer*
Feuss, Linda Anne Upsall *lawyer*
Finzen, Bruce Arthur *lawyer*
Flom, Gerald Trossen *lawyer*
Freeman, Orville Lothrop *lawyer, former governor of Minnesota, think tank executive*
Freeman, Todd Ira *lawyer*
French, John Dwyer *lawyer*
Gagnon, Craig William *lawyer*
Garon, Philip Stephen *lawyer*
Garton, Thomas William *lawyer*
Genia, James Michael *lawyer*
Gill, Richard Lawrence *lawyer*
Goodman, Elizabeth Ann *lawyer*
Gordon, Corey Lee *lawyer*
Gottschalk, Stephen Elmer *lawyer*
Grayson, Edward Davis *lawyer, manufacturing company executive*
Greener, Ralph Bertram *lawyer*
Griffith, G. Larry *lawyer*
Hanson, Bruce Eugene *lawyer*
Hanson, Kent Bryan *lawyer*
Harris, John Edward *lawyer*
Hayward, Edward Joseph *lawyer*
Heiberg, Robert Alan *lawyer*
Hendrixson, Peter S. *lawyer*
Henson, Robert Frank *lawyer*
Hibbs, John Stanley *lawyer*
Hippee, William H., Jr. *lawyer*
Hobbins, Robert Leo *lawyer*
Howland, Joan Sidney *law librarian, law educator*

Hudec, Robert Emil *lawyer, educator*
Jarboe, Mark Alan *lawyer*
Johnson, Gary M. *lawyer*
†Johnson, Gary R. *corporate lawyer*
Johnson, Larry Walter *lawyer*
Kaplan, Sheldon *lawyer*
Kelly, A. David *lawyer*
Keppel, William James *lawyer, educator, author*
Keyes, Jeffrey J. *lawyer*
Kilbourn, William Douglas, Jr. *law educator*
Klaas, Paul Barry *lawyer*
Koneck, John Michael *lawyer*
Krohnke, Duane W. *lawyer*
Landry, Paul Leonard *lawyer*
Lareau, Richard George *lawyer*
Lazar, Raymond Michael *lawyer, educator*
Lebedoff, David M. *lawyer, author, investment advisor*
Lebedoff, Randy Miller *lawyer*
Lindgren, D(erbin) Kenneth, Jr. *retired lawyer*
Lofstrom, Mark D. *lawyer, educator, communications executive*
Magnuson, Roger James *lawyer*
Manthey, Thomas Richard *lawyer*
Marshall, Siri Swenson *corporate lawyer*
Martin, Phillip Hammond *lawyer*
Matthews, James Shadley *lawyer*
McGuire, Timothy James *lawyer, editor*
Meller, Robert Louis, Jr. *lawyer*
Mellum, Gale Robert *lawyer*
Meshbesher, Ronald I. *lawyer*
Minish, Robert Arthur *lawyer*
Mooty, Bruce Wilson *lawyer*
Mooty, John William *lawyer*
Munic, Martin Daniel *lawyer*
Myers, Howard Sam *lawyer*
Nelson, Gary Michael *lawyer*
Nelson, Richard Arthur *lawyer*
Nelson, Steven Craig *lawyer*
O'Neill, Brian Boru *lawyer*
Palmer, Brian Eugene *lawyer*
Palmer, Deborah Jean *lawyer*
Parsons, Charles Allan, Jr. *lawyer*
Pluimer, Edward J. *lawyer*
Potuznik, Charles Laddy *lawyer*
Pratte, Robert John *lawyer*
Price, Joseph Michael *lawyer*
Radmer, Michael John *lawyer, educator*
Reilly, George *lawyer*
Rein, Stanley Michael *lawyer*
Reinhart, Robert Rountree, Jr. *lawyer*
Reister, Raymond Alex *retired lawyer*
Reuter, James William *lawyer*
Rockenstein, Walter Harrison, II *lawyer*
Rockwell, Winthrop Adams *lawyer*
Roe, Roger Rolland *lawyer*
Saeks, Allen Irving *lawyer*
Safley, James Robert *lawyer*
Sanner, Royce Norman *lawyer*
Schneider, Elaine Carol *lawyer, researcher, writer*
Schnell, Robert Lee, Jr. *lawyer*
Schnobrich, Roger William *lawyer*
Schoettle, Ferdinand P. *lawyer, educator*
Shnider, Bruce Jay *lawyer*
†Silberfarb, Stephen Russell *lawyer*
Silverman, Robert Joseph *lawyer*
Skare, Robert Martin *lawyer*
Soland, Norman R. *corporate lawyer*
Sortland, Paul Allan *lawyer*
Spaeth, Nicholas John *lawyer, former state attorney general*
Stageberg, Roger V. *lawyer*
Stern, Leo G. *lawyer*
Street, Erica Catherine *lawyer*
Struthers, Margo S. *lawyer*
Struyk, Robert John *lawyer*
Thorson, Steven Greg *lawyer*
Tigue, Randall Davis Bryant *lawyer*
Trucano, Michael *lawyer*
Vander Molen, Thomas Dale *lawyer*
Ventres, Judith Martin *lawyer*
Wahoske, Michael James *lawyer*
Weil, Cass Sargent *lawyer*
Whelpley, Dennis Porter *lawyer*
Wille, Karin L. *lawyer*
Windhorst, John William, Jr. *lawyer*
Witort, Janet Lee *lawyer*
Woods, Robert Edward *lawyer*
Yost, Gerald B. *lawyer*
Younger, Judith Tess *lawyer, educator*
Yudof, Mark George *law educator, university president*
Zalk, Robert H. *lawyer*

Minnetonka
Freeman, Gerald Russell *lawyer*
†Lubben, David J. *lawyer*

Minnetonka Mills
Hoard, Heidi Marie *lawyer*

Moorhead
Miller, Keith Lloyd *lawyer*

North Saint Paul
O'Brien, Daniel William *lawyer, corporation executive*

Pipestone
Scott, William Paul *lawyer*

Rochester
Baker, Gail Dyer *lawyer*
Seeger, Ronald L. *lawyer*
Wicks, John R. *lawyer*

Saint Cloud
Lalor, Edward David Darrell *labor and employment arbitrator, lawyer*

Saint Joseph
Olheiser, Mary David *lawyer, educator*

Saint Louis Park
Paschke, Jerry Bryan *lawyer*
Rothenberg, Elliot Calvin *lawyer, writer*

Saint Paul
Allison, John Robert *lawyer*
Dietz, Charlton Henry *lawyer*
Ebert, Robert Alvin *retired lawyer, retired airline executive*
Failinger, Marie Anita *law educator, editor*
Fisk, Martin H. *lawyer*
Friel, Bernard Preston *lawyer*
Galvin, Michael John, Jr. *lawyer*
†Gehan, Mark William *lawyer*
Geis, Jerome Arthur *lawyer, legal educator*
Hansen, Robyn L. *lawyer*
Hvass, Sheryl Ramstad *lawyer*
Johnson, Carolyn Jean *law librarian*
Johnson, Paul Oren *lawyer*
Jones, C. Paul *lawyer, educator*
Kirwin, Kenneth Francis *law educator*
Larson, David Allen *law educator*
Levinson, Kenneth S. *lawyer, corporate executive*
Maclin, Alan Hall *lawyer*
Maffei, Rocco John *lawyer*
Mahoney, Kathleen Mary *lawyer*
McNeely, John J. *lawyer*
Rebane, John T. *lawyer*
Seymour, McNeil Vernam *lawyer*
†Steenland, Douglas *lawyer*
Ursu, John Joseph *lawyer*
Winthrop, Sherman *lawyer*
Wruble, Bernhardt Karp *lawyer*

South Saint Paul
Pugh, Thomas Wilfred *lawyer*

Wayzata
Bergerson, David Raymond *lawyer*
Johnson, Eugene Laurence *lawyer*
Reutiman, Robert William, Jr. *lawyer*

Willmar
Hulstrand, George Eugene *lawyer*

MISSISSIPPI

Batesville
Cook, William Leslie, Jr. *lawyer*

Bay Saint Louis
Bernstein, Joseph *lawyer*

Biloxi
O'Barr, Bobby Gene, Sr. *lawyer*

Clarksdale
Curtis, Chester Harris *lawyer, retired bank executive*

Cleveland
Alexander, William Brooks *lawyer, former state senator*

Columbus
Davidson, Hubert James, Jr. *lawyer, educator*

Greenville
Martin, Andrew Ayers *lawyer, physician, educator*

Gulfport
Hopkins, Alben Norris *lawyer*

Hernando
Brown, William A. *lawyer*

Jackson
Barnett, Robert Glenn *lawyer*
Black, D(eWitt) Carl(isle), Jr. *lawyer*
Clark, David Wright *lawyer*
Corlew, John Gordon *lawyer*
Currie, Edward Jones, Jr. *lawyer*
Fuselier, Louis Alfred *lawyer*
Hammond, Frank Jefferson, III *lawyer*
Hosemann, C. Delbert, Jr. *lawyer*
Hughes, Byron William *lawyer, oil exploration company executive*
Lilly, Thomas Gerald *lawyer*
Moize, Jerry Dee *lawyer, government official*
Phillips, George Landon *prosecutor*
Pigott, Brad *prosecutor*
Price, Alfred Lee *lawyer, mining company executive*
Ray, H. M. *lawyer*
West, Carol Catherine *law educator*
Wilson, William Roberts, Jr. (Bob Wilson) *lawyer, apparel executive*
Wise, Robert Powell *lawyer*

Lumberton
Tonry, Richard Alvin *lawyer, pecan farmer*

Meridian
Eppes, Walter W., Jr. *lawyer*

Ocean Springs
Luckey, Alwyn Hall *lawyer*

Oxford
Alexander, S. Allan *lawyer*
†Buchanan, Calvin D. (Buck Buchanan) *prosecutor*
Lewis, Ronald Wayne *lawyer*
Rayburn, S. T. *lawyer*

Pascagoula
Krebs, Robert Preston *lawyer*

Ridgeland
Dye, Bradford Johnson, Jr. *lawyer, former state official*

Starkville
Yoste, Charles Todd *lawyer*

Tupelo
Bush, Fred Marshall, Jr. *lawyer*
Moffett, T(errill) K(ay) *lawyer*

Tylertown
Mord, Irving Conrad, II *lawyer*

Vicksburg
Mazzeo-Merkle, Linda Lou *legal administrator*

MISSOURI

Camdenton
Clark, Mark Jeffrey *paralegal, researcher*

Cape Girardeau
Lowes, Albert Charles *lawyer*
McManaman, Kenneth Charles *lawyer*

Chesterfield
Coffin, Richard Keith *lawyer*
Denneen, John Paul *lawyer*
Hier, Marshall David *lawyer*
Pollihan, Thomas Henry *lawyer*

Clayton
Belz, Mark *lawyer*
Klarich, David John *lawyer, state senator*
Mohrman, Henry J(oe), Jr. *lawyer, investment manager*
Ritter, Robert Thornton *lawyer*

Columbia
Fisch, William Bales *lawyer, educator*
Mays, William Gay, II *lawyer, real estate developer*
Parrigin, Elizabeth Ellington *lawyer*
Schwabe, John Bennett, II *lawyer*
Welliver, Warren Dee *lawyer, retired state supreme court justice*
Westbrook, James Edwin *lawyer, educator*
Whitman, Dale Alan *lawyer, law educator*

Creve Coeur
Nicely, Constance Marie *paralegal, physician recruiter, medical consultant*

Fenton
Stolar, Henry Samuel *lawyer*

Grandview
Dietrich, William Gale *lawyer, real estate developer, consultant*

Hannibal
Welch, Joseph Daniel *lawyer*

Hillsboro
Howald, John William *lawyer*

Independence
Cady, Elwyn Loomis, Jr. *medicolegal consultant, educator*
†Farrington, Buford Lee *lawyer*
Lashley, Curtis Dale *lawyer*

Jefferson City
Bartlett, Alex *lawyer*
Deutsch, James Bernard *lawyer*
Gaw, Robert Steven *lawyer, state representative*
Tettlebaum, Harvey M. *lawyer*

Joplin
Guillory, Jeffery Michael *lawyer*
Scott, Robert Haywood, Jr. *lawyer*

Kansas City
Abele, Robert Christopher *lawyer*
Anderson, Christopher James *lawyer*
Ayers, Jeffrey David *lawyer*
†Bacon, Jennifer Gille *lawyer*
Ball, Owen Keith, Jr. *lawyer*
Bartunek, Robert R(ichard), Jr. *lawyer*
Bates, William Hubert *lawyer*
Becker, Thomas Bain *lawyer*
Beckett, Theodore Charles *lawyer*
Beihl, Frederick *lawyer*
Berkowitz, Lawrence M. *lawyer*
Bevan, Robert Lewis *lawyer*
Black, John Sheldon *lawyer*
Blackwell, Menefee Davis *lawyer*
Borel, Steven James *lawyer*
Bradshaw, Jean Paul, II *lawyer*
Brous, Thomas Richard *lawyer*
Bruening, Richard P(atrick) *lawyer*
Canfield, Robert Cleo *lawyer*
Chisholm, Donald Herbert *lawyer*
Clark, Charles Edward *arbitrator*
Clarke, Milton Charles *lawyer*
Crawford, Howard Allen *lawyer*
Cross, William Dennis *lawyer*
Davis, John Charles *lawyer*
Deacy, Thomas Edward, Jr. *lawyer*
Edgar, John M. *lawyer*
Egan, Charles Joseph, Jr. *lawyer, greeting card company executive*
Eldridge, Truman Kermit, Jr. *lawyer*
Field, Lyman *lawyer*
Foster, Mark Stephen *lawyer*
Fox, Byron Neal *lawyer*
Franke, Linda Frederick *lawyer*
Gaines, Robert Darryl *lawyer, food services executive*
Gardner, Brian E. *lawyer*
Glesner Fines, Barbara *law educator*
Gorman, Gerald Warner *lawyer*
Graham, Harold Steven *lawyer*
Greer, Norris E. *lawyer*
Handley, Gerald Matthew *lawyer*
Helder, Jan Pleasant, Jr. *lawyer*
Hill, Stephen L., Jr. *prosecutor*
Hubbell, Ernest *lawyer*
†Jenkins, Melvin Lemuel *lawyer*
Johnson, Leonard James *lawyer*
Johnson, Mark Eugene *lawyer*
Joyce, Michael Patrick *lawyer*
Kaplan, Harvey L. *lawyer*
Kaufman, Michelle Stark *lawyer*
Kilroy, John Muir *lawyer*
Kilroy, William Terrence *lawyer*
King, Richard Allen *lawyer*
Kroenert, Robert Morgan *lawyer*
Langworthy, Robert Burton *lawyer*
Lindsey, David Hosford *lawyer*
Lolli, Don R(ay) *lawyer*
Lombardi, Cornelius Ennis, Jr. *lawyer*
Lotven, Howard Lee *lawyer*
Manka, Ronald Eugene *lawyer*
Margolin, Abraham Eugene *lawyer*
Matheny, Edward Taylor, Jr. *lawyer*
Matzeder, Jean Marie Znidarsic *lawyer*
McKinney, Janet Kay *law librarian*
McManus, James William *lawyer*
Mick, Howard Harold *lawyer*
Milton, Chad Earl *lawyer*
Molzen, Christopher John *lawyer*
Moore, Stephen James *lawyer*
Mordy, James Calvin *lawyer*
Newcom, Jennings Jay *lawyer*
Newsom, James Thomas *lawyer*
Northrip, Robert Earl *lawyer*
Owen, Loyd Eugene, Jr. *lawyer*
Owens, Stephen J. *lawyer*
Palmer, Dennis Dale *lawyer*
Pelofsky, Joel *lawyer*
Pemberton, Bradley Powell *lawyer*
Popper, Robert *law educator, former dean*
Price, James Tucker *lawyer*
Prugh, William Byron *lawyer*
Ralston, Richard H. *lawyer*
Rove, Frances Ann *lawyer*
Sader, Neil Steven *lawyer*
Sands, Darry Gene *lawyer*
Satterlee, Terry Jean *lawyer*
Sauer, Elisabeth Ruth *lawyer*
Scarritt, Richard Winn *lawyer*
Sharp, Rex Arthur *lawyer*
Shaw, John W. *lawyer*
Shay, David E. *lawyer*
Shughart, Donald Louis *lawyer*
Smith, R(onald) Scott *lawyer*
Spalty, Edward Robert *lawyer*
Spencer, Richard Henry *lawyer*
Stoup, Arthur Harry *lawyer*
Suter, Carol J. *non-profit organization executive, lawyer*
†Terry, Robert Brooks *lawyer*
Todd, Stephen Max *lawyer*
Toll, Perry Mark *lawyer*
Vandever, William Dirk *lawyer*
Vering, John Albert *lawyer*
Viani, James Lawrence *lawyer*
Vleisides, Gregory William *lawyer*
Walsh, Rodger John *lawyer*
Whittaker, Judith Ann Cameron *lawyer*
Willy, Thomas Ralph *lawyer*
Wirken, James Charles *lawyer*
Woods, Richard Dale *lawyer*
Wrobley, Ralph Gene *lawyer*
Ziegenhorn, Eric Howard *lawyer, legal writer*

Keytesville
Wheeler, James Julian *lawyer*

Lebanon
Hutson, Don *lawyer*

Macon
Parkinson, Paul K. *lawyer*

Marshall
Peterson, William Allen *lawyer*

Maryland Heights
Sobol, Lawrence Raymond *lawyer*

Nevada
Ewing, Lynn Moore, Jr. *lawyer*

Platte City
Cozad, John Condon *lawyer*

Saint Ann
Johnson, Harold Gene *lawyer*

Saint Charles
Dorsey, Mary Elizabeth *lawyer*

Saint Joseph
Kranitz, Theodore Mitchell *lawyer*
Taylor, Michael Leslie *lawyer*

Saint Louis
Appleton, R. O., Jr. *lawyer*
Arnold, John Fox *lawyer*
Atwood, Hollye Stolz *lawyer*
Aylward, Ronald Lee *lawyer*
Babington, Charles Martin, III *lawyer*
Baldwin, Edwin Steedman *lawyer*
Banks, Eric Kendall *lawyer*
Banstetter, Robert J. *lawyer*
Barken, Bernard Allen *lawyer*
Baum, Gordon Lee *lawyer, non-profit organization administrator*
Beach, Douglas Ryder *lawyer, educator*
Bean, Bourne *lawyer*
Becker, David Mandel *law educator, author, consultant*
Berendt, Robert Tryon *lawyer*
Berger, John Torrey, Jr. *lawyer*
Bernstein, Merton Clay *lawyer, educator, arbitrator*
Blanke, Richard Brian *lawyer*
Boardman, Richard John *lawyer*
Bonacorsi, Mary Catherine *lawyer*
Breece, Robert William, Jr. *lawyer*
Brickey, Kathleen Fitzgerald *law educator*
Brickler, John Weise *lawyer*
Brickson, Richard Alan *lawyer*
Brody, Lawrence *lawyer, educator*
Brownlee, Robert Hammel *lawyer*
Bryan, Henry C(lark), Jr. *lawyer*
Burke, Thomas Michael *lawyer*
Carp, Larry (Larry Carp) *lawyer*
Carr, Gary Thomas *lawyer*
Clear, John Michael *lawyer*
Colagiovanni, Joseph Alfred, Jr. *lawyer*
Conran, Joseph Palmer *lawyer*
Cornfeld, Dave Louis *lawyer*
Crebs, P(aul) Terence *lawyer*
Cullen, James D. *lawyer*
Donohue, Carroll John *lawyer*
Dorwart, Donald Bruce *lawyer*
Dowd, Edward L., Jr. *prosecutor*
Duesenberg, Richard William *lawyer*
Falk, William James *lawyer*
Farris, Clyde C. *lawyer*
Floyd, Walter Leo *lawyer*
Fogle, James Lee *lawyer*
Fryer, Edwin Samuel *lawyer*
Gerard, Jules Bernard *law educator*
Gershenson, Harry *lawyer*
Gilhousen, Brent James *lawyer*
Gillis, John Lamb, Jr. *lawyer*
Gilroy, Tracy Anne Hunsaker *lawyer*
Gladding, Nicholas C. *lawyer*
Godiner, Donald Leonard *lawyer*
Goebel, John J. *lawyer*
Goldstein, Steven *lawyer*
Goodman, Harold S. *lawyer*
Graham, Robert Clare, III *lawyer*
Gray, Charles Elmer *lawyer, rancher, investor*
Green, Dennis Joseph *lawyer*
Guerri, William Grant *lawyer*

Hansen, Charles *lawyer*
Harris, Whitney Robson *lawyer, educator*
Hays, Ruth *lawyer*
Hecker, George Sprake *lawyer*
Hellmuth, Theodore Henning *lawyer*
Hetlage, Robert Owen *lawyer*
Hiles, Bradley Stephen *lawyer*
Hunt, Jeffrey Brian *lawyer*
Inkley, John James, Jr. *lawyer*
Jaudes, Richard Edward *lawyer*
†Jaudes, William E. *retired lawyer*
Keller, Juan Dane *lawyer*
Klobasa, John Anthony *lawyer*
Komen, Leonard *lawyer*
Krehbiel, Robert John *lawyer*
Kuhlmann, Fred Mark *lawyer*
Lane, Frank Joseph, Jr. *lawyer*
Lause, Michael Francis *lawyer*
Lebowitz, Albert *lawyer, author*
Leontsinis, George John *lawyer*
Levin, Ronald Mark *law educator*
Liberman, Keith Gordon *lawyer*
Lieberman, Edward Jay *lawyer*
Logan, Joseph Prescott *lawyer*
Lowenhaupt, Charles Abraham *lawyer*
Lucy, Robert Meredith *lawyer*
Mandelker, Daniel Robert *law educator*
Mandelstamm, Jerome Robert *lawyer*
Marks, Murry Aaron *lawyer*
McCarter, Charles Chase *lawyer*
†McCracken, Ellis W., Jr. *retired lawyer, corporation executive*
McDaniel, James Edwin *lawyer*
McKinnis, Michael B. *lawyer*
Meisel, George Vincent *lawyer*
Merrill, Charles Eugene *lawyer*
Metcalfe, Walter Lee, Jr. *lawyer*
Meyer, John Strauch, Jr. *lawyer*
Mohan, John J. *lawyer*
Moore, McPherson Dorsett *lawyer*
Mulligan, Michael Dennis *lawyer*
Needham, Carol Ann *lawyer, educator*
Neville, James Morton *lawyer, consumer products executive*
Newman, Charles A. *lawyer*
Newman, Joan Meskiel *lawyer*
Noel, Edwin Lawrence *lawyer*
O'Keefe, Michael Daniel *lawyer*
Olson, Robert Grant *lawyer*
Ortbals, Gerald Ray *lawyer*
Palans, Lloyd Alex *lawyer*
Peper, Christian Baird *lawyer*
Perotti, Rose Norma *lawyer*
Pickle, Robert Douglas *lawyer, footwear industry executive*
Poscover, Maury B. *lawyer*
Rataj, Edward William *lawyer*
Reeg, Kurtis Bradford *lawyer*
Riddle, Veryl Lee *lawyer*
Ring, Lucile Wiley *lawyer*
Ritter, Robert Forcier *lawyer*
Ritterskamp, Douglas Dolvin *lawyer*
Rubenstein, Jerome Max *lawyer*
Sachs, Alan Arthur *lawyer, corporate executive*
Sale, Llewellyn, III *lawyer*
Sandberg, John Steven *lawyer*
Sant, John Talbot *lawyer*
Schoene, Kathleen Snyder *lawyer*
Schramm, Paul Howard *lawyer*
Searls, Eileen Haughey *lawyer, librarian, educator*
Sestric, Anthony James *lawyer*
Shands, Courtney, Jr. *lawyer*
Shaw, John Arthur *lawyer*
Smith, Arthur Lee *lawyer*
Sneeringer, Stephen Geddes *lawyer*
Suhre, Walter Anthony, Jr. *retired lawyer and brewery executive*
Sullivan, Edward Lawrence *lawyer*
Switzer, Frederick Michael, III *lawyer, mediator*
Teasdale, Kenneth Fulbright *lawyer*
Tierney, Michael Edward *lawyer*
Turley, Michael Roy *lawyer*
Van Cleve, William Moore *lawyer*
Virtel, James John *lawyer*
Wagner, Raymond Thomas, Jr. *lawyer, corporation executive*
Walsh, Joseph Leo, III *lawyer*
Walsh, Thomas Charles *lawyer*
Watters, Richard Donald *lawyer*
Weiss, Charles Andrew *lawyer*
Welch, David William *lawyer*
Willard, Gregory Dale *lawyer*
Williams, Theodore Joseph, Jr. *lawyer*
Wilson, Margaret Bush *lawyer, civil rights leader*
Wilson, Michael E. *lawyer*
Winning, John Patrick *lawyer*
Withers, W. Wayne *lawyer*
Wolff, Frank Pierce, Jr. *lawyer*
Woodruff, Bruce Emery *lawyer*
Young, Marvin Oscar *lawyer*

Springfield
Carlson, Thomas Joseph *real estate developer, lawyer, former mayor*
†Carmichael, Joe *lawyer*
Clithero, Monte Paul *lawyer*
Hulston, John Kenton *lawyer*
Lowther, Gerald Halbert *lawyer*
McDonald, William Henry *lawyer*
Penninger, William Holt, Jr. *lawyer*
Roberts, Patrick Kent *lawyer*
Starnes, James Wright *lawyer*

Stockton
Hammons, Brian Kent *lawyer, business executive*

MONTANA

Billings
Aldrich, Richard Kingsley *lawyer*
Beiswanger, Gary Lee *lawyer*
†Cromley, Brent Reed *lawyer, legal association administrator*
Gallinger, Lorraine D. *prosecutor*
Hanson, Norman *lawyer*
Haughey, James McCrea *lawyer, artist*
Malee, Thomas Michael *lawyer*
Matteucci, Sherry Scheel *prosecutor*
Thompson, James William *lawyer*
Towe, Thomas Edward *lawyer*

Bozeman
Conover, Richard Corrill *lawyer*
Frohnmayer, John Edward *lawyer, legal scholar, ethicist, writer*

Harris, Christopher Kirk *lawyer*
Nelson, Steven Dwayne *lawyer*
Wylie, Paul Richter, Jr. *lawyer*

Butte
†Peterson, John Leonard *lawyer, judge*

Great Falls
Doherty, Steve *lawyer, state legislator*

Havre
Moog, Mary Ann Pimley *lawyer*

Helena
Meadows, Judith Adams *law librarian, educator*

Kalispell
Robinson, Calvin Stanford *lawyer*

Missoula
George, Alexander Andrew *lawyer*
Haddon, Sam Ellis *lawyer*
Molloy, Donald William *lawyer, partner*
Morales, Julio K. *lawyer*
Mudd, John O. *lawyer*
Poore, James Albert, III *lawyer*
Renz, Jeffrey Thomas *lawyer, educator*

NEBRASKA

Columbus
Schumacher, Paul Maynard *lawyer*

Crete
Panec, William Joseph *lawyer*

Fremont
Gill, Lyle Bennett *retired lawyer*

Grand Island
Busick, Denzel Rex *lawyer*

Holdrege
Klein, Michael Clarence *lawyer*

Kearney
Kelley, Michael Eugene *lawyer*
Munro, Robert Allan *lawyer*
Voigt, Steven Russell *lawyer*

Lincoln
Colleran, Kevin *lawyer*
Cope, Thom K. *lawyer*
Hewitt, James Watt *lawyer*
Lichty, Warren Dewey, Jr. *lawyer*
Luedtke, Roland Alfred *lawyer*
Ogle, Robbin Sue *criminal justice educator*
Perry, Edwin Charles *lawyer*

Omaha
Barmettler, Joseph John *lawyer*
Brownrigg, John Clinton *lawyer*
Caporale, D. Nick *lawyer*
Dolan, James Vincent *lawyer*
Fitzgerald, James Patrick *lawyer*
Forbes, Franklin Sim *lawyer, educator*
Gaines, Tyler Belt *lawyer*
Harr, Lawrence Francis *lawyer*
Jensen, Sam *lawyer*
Kozlik, Michael David *lawyer*
Lee, Dennis Patrick *lawyer, judge*
Monaghan, Thomas Justin *prosecutor*
Niemann, Nicholas Kent *lawyer*
North, John E., Jr. *lawyer*
Riley, William Jay *lawyer*
Rock, Harold L. *lawyer*
Runge, Patrick Richard *lawyer*
Schmidt, Kathleen Marie *lawyer*
von Bernuth, Carl W. *diversified corporation executive, lawyer*
Vosburg, Bruce David *lawyer*
Wilson, Joseph Lopez *lawyer*

Scottsbluff
†Fairbanks, Charles F. *law educator*

NEVADA

Battle Mountain
†Schaeffer, William E. *lawyer*

Carson City
Reid, Joan Evangeline *lawyer, stockbroker*
Rodefer, Jeffrey Robert *lawyer, prosecutor*

Henderson
Bybee, Jay Scott *lawyer, educator*
Dobberstein, Eric *lawyer*

Las Vegas
Arum, Robert *lawyer, sports events promoter*
Brebbia, John Henry *lawyer*
Cardinalli, Marc Patrick *lawyer*
Chesnut, Carol Fitting *lawyer*
Curran, William P. *lawyer*
Ecker, Howard *lawyer*
Faiss, Robert Dean *lawyer*
Galane, Morton Robert *lawyer*
Greene, Addison Kent *lawyer, accountant*
Gubler, John Gray *lawyer*
Han, Ittah *lawyer, political economist, high technology and financial strategist, computer engineer*
Havemann, Michael R. *court administrator*
Hilbrecht, Norman Ty *lawyer*
Hill, Judith Deegan *lawyer*
Jost, Richard Frederic, III *lawyer*
Kennedy, Dennis L. *lawyer*
Landreth, Kathryn E. *prosecutor*
Lovell, Carl Erwin, Jr. *lawyer*
Lukens, John Patrick *lawyer*
Mahan, James Cameron *lawyer*
Riddell, Richard Harry *retired lawyer*
Singer, Michael Howard *lawyer*
†Sklar, Alan Curtis *lawyer*
Solomon, Mark A. *lawyer*
Wilson, Joseph Morris, III *lawyer*

Lovelock
†Evenson, Steve Earle *lawyer*

Reno
Broili, Robert Howard *lawyer*
Denham, Rena Belle *lawyer, educator*
Guild, Clark Joseph, Jr. *lawyer*
Hibbs, Loyal Robert *lawyer*
Kennedy, Jack Edward *lawyer*
Marshall, Robert William *lawyer, rancher*
Shaffer, Wayne Alan *lawyer*

NEW HAMPSHIRE

Concord
Gagnon, Paul Michael *lawyer, former county attorney*
Mekeel, Robert K. *lawyer*
Rath, Thomas David *lawyer, former state attorney general*
Rines, Robert Harvey *lawyer, inventor, educator, composer*

Dover
Catalfo, Alfred, Jr. (Alfio Catalfo) *lawyer*

East Sullivan
Hoffman, John Ernest, Jr. *retired lawyer*

Etna
Mitrano, Peter Paul *lawyer, engineer*

Exeter
Moroze, Marshall Brian *lawyer*
Vogelman, Lawrence Allen *law educator, lawyer*

Franconia
Merwin, John David *retired lawyer, former governor*

Grantham
Goss, Richard Henry *lawyer*

Hanover
Prager, Susan Westerberg *law educator, provost*

Hollis
Lumbard, Eliot Howland *lawyer, educator*
Merritt, Thomas Butler *lawyer*

Hooksett
Rogers, David John *lawyer*

Keene
Bell, Ernest Lorne, III *lawyer*

Manchester
†Burack, Thomas S. *lawyer*
Mc Lane, John Roy *lawyer*
Millimet, Joseph Allen *retired lawyer*
Monson, John Rudolph *lawyer*
Richards, Thomas H. *lawyer, arbitrator*
Zachos, Kimon Stephen *lawyer*

Nashua
Hanson, Arnold Philip *retired lawyer*
Jette, Ernest Arthur *lawyer*

New Durham
Kosko, Susan Uttal *legal administrator*

New London
Plant, David William *lawyer*

Portsmouth
DeGrandpre, Charles Allyson *lawyer*
Doleac, Charles Bartholomew *lawyer*
Volk, Kenneth Hohne *lawyer*
Watson, Thomas Roger *lawyer*

West Lebanon
Isaacs, Robert Charles *retired lawyer*

NEW JERSEY

Atlantic City
Jacobson, Carole Renee *lawyer, educator*

Audubon
Montano, Arthur *lawyer*
Watson, Mark Henry *lawyer, business writer*

Barnegat Light
Gibbs, Frederick Winfield *lawyer, communications company executive*

Bloomfield
Lordi, Katherine Mary *lawyer*

Boonton
Walzer, James Harvey *lawyer, author*

Brick
Cornblatt, Alan Jack *lawyer*
Tivenan, Charles Patrick *lawyer*

Bridgewater
Conroy, Robert John *lawyer*

Camden
Fairbanks, Russell Norman *law educator, university dean*
Kaden, Ellen Oran *lawyer, consumer products company executive*
Pomorski, Stanislaw *lawyer, educator*

Carteret
Strassler, Marc A. *corporate lawyer*

Cherry Hill
Adler, John Herbert *lawyer, state legislator*
Copsetta, Norman George *real estate executive*
Dunfee, Thomas Wylie *law educator*
Garrigle, William Aloysius *lawyer*
Levin, Susan Bass *lawyer*

Myers, Daniel William, II *lawyer*
Rose, Joel Alan *legal consultant*
Tomar, William *lawyer*
Weinstein, Steven David *lawyer*

Cliffside Park
Diktas, Christos James *lawyer*

Clifton
Palma, Nicholas James *lawyer*

Clinton
Kennedy, Harold Edward *lawyer*

Cranbury
Iatesta, John Michael *lawyer*

Cranford
Ascher, David Mark *lawyer*

Denville
Kirna, Hans Christian *lawyer, consultant*

East Brunswick
Burns, Barbara *lawyer*

East Hanover
Davidson, Anne Stowell *lawyer*

East Rutherford
Wadler, Arnold L. *lawyer*

Edgewater
Virelli, Louis James, Jr. *lawyer*

Edison
Applebaum, Charles *lawyer*
Fink, Edward Murray *lawyer, educator*

Elizabeth
Kabak, Douglas Thomas *lawyer*

Englewood
Cherovsky, Erwin Louis *lawyer, writer*

Englewood Cliffs
Fredericks, Barry Irwin *lawyer*
†Heller, Hanes Ayres *lawyer*

Fair Lawn
Hirschklau, Morton *lawyer*

Far Hills
Corash, Richard *lawyer*

Flemington
Miller, Louis H. *lawyer*

Florham Park
Calabrese, Arnold Joseph *lawyer*
Chase, Eric Lewis *lawyer*
Hardin, William Downer *retired lawyer*
Laulicht, Murray Jack *lawyer*
Stanton, Patrick Michael *lawyer*
Witman, Leonard Joel *lawyer*
Wright, Paul William *lawyer, oil company executive*

Fort Lee
Abut, Charles C. *lawyer*
Cox, Melvin Monroe *lawyer*

Franklin Lakes
Galiardo, John William *lawyer*
Hector, Bruce John *lawyer*

Freehold
Brown, Sanford Donald *lawyer*
Littman, Jules Sanford *lawyer*
Lomurro, Donald Michael *lawyer*
Scarola, Susan Margaret *lawyer*

Garfield
Herpst, Robert Dix *lawyer, optics and materials technology executive*

Glen Rock
Markey, Brian Michael *lawyer*

Hackensack
Caminiti, Donald Angelo *lawyer*
Croland, Barry I. *lawyer*
Curtis, Robert Kern *lawyer, physics educator*
D'Alessandro, Dianne Marie *public defender*
Duus, Gordon Cochran *lawyer*
Gallucci, Michael A. *lawyer*
Goldsamt, Bonnie Blume *lawyer*
Greenberg, Steven Morey *lawyer*
Latimer, Stephen Mark *lawyer*
Masi, John Roger *lawyer*
Mullin, Patrick Allen *lawyer*
Navatta, Anna Paula *lawyer*
Pollinger, William Joshua *lawyer*
Spiegel, Linda F. *lawyer*

Hackettstown
Kobert, Joel A. *lawyer*
Mulligan, Elinor Patterson *lawyer*

Haddon Heights
D'Alfonso, Mario Joseph *lawyer*

Haddonfield
Fuoco, Philip Stephen *lawyer*
Iavicoli, Mario Anthony *lawyer*
Suflas, Steven William *lawyer*

Highland Park
Michaels, Jennifer Alman *lawyer*

Hightstown
Bronner, William Roche *lawyer*

Iselin
Dornbusch, Arthur A., II *lawyer*
Gupta, Rajat Kumar *lawyer, accountant*

Jersey City
D'Alessandro, Daniel Anthony *lawyer, educator*
Feder, Arthur A. *lawyer*
Lawatsch, Frank Emil, Jr. *lawyer*
Leff, David *lawyer*
McFadden, Rosemary Theresa *lawyer, mercantile exchange executive*
Signorile, Vincent Anthony *lawyer*

Kearny
Brady, Lawrence Peter *lawyer*

Kenilworth
Hoffman, John Fletcher *lawyer*

Keyport
Colmant, Andrew Robert *lawyer*

Lakewood
Bielory, Abraham Melvin *lawyer, financial executive*
Freitas, Elizabeth Frances *lawyer*

Lawrenceville
Kline, Michael J. *lawyer*
Rudy, James Francis Xavier *lawyer*

Lebanon
Johnstone, Irvine Blakeley, III *lawyer*

Liberty Corner
Edwards, Robert Nelson *lawyer*
McDermott, Frank Xavier *lawyer, lobbyist*

Little Falls
Draper, Daniel Clay *lawyer*

Livingston
Harris, Brian Craig *lawyer*
Hock, Frederick Wyeth *lawyer*
Klein, Peter Martin *lawyer, retired transportation company executive*
Kuller, Jonathan Mark *lawyer*
Pantages, Louis James *lawyer*
Rinsky, Joel Charles *lawyer*

Lyndhurst
Lasky, David *lawyer, corporate executive*

Madison
Connors, Joseph Conlin *lawyer*
Huettner, Richard Alfred *lawyer*
Tramutola, Joseph Louis *lawyer, educator*

Mahwah
Bryan, Thomas Lynn *lawyer, educator*
†Howenstein, Mark Stephen *law educator*

Manalapan
Stone, Fred Michael *lawyer*

Maplewood
Joseph, Susan B. *lawyer*
MacWhorter, Robert Bruce *retired lawyer*

Mc Afee
Fogel, Richard *lawyer*

Millburn
Grosman, Alan M. *lawyer*
Kuttner, Bernard A. *lawyer, former judge*

Montclair
Brown, Geraldine Reed *lawyer, consulting executive*
Mullins, Margaret Ann Frances *lawyer, educator*
Ward, Roger Coursen *lawyer*
Weisert, Kent Albert Frederick *lawyer*

Moorestown
Begley, Thomas D., Jr. *lawyer*
Ewan, David E. *lawyer*
Rabil, Mitchell Joseph *lawyer*

Morris Plains
Bruno, Anthony D. *lawyer*
†Johnson, Gregory L. *lawyer*

Morristown
Aspero, Benedict Vincent *lawyer*
Bartkus, Robert Edward *lawyer*
Berkley, Peter Lee *lawyer*
Bromberg, Myron James *lawyer*
Campion, Thomas Francis *lawyer*
Fishman, Richard Glenn *lawyer, accountant*
Freilich, Irvin M. *lawyer*
Gillen, James Robert *lawyer, insurance company executive*
Greenman, Jane Friedlieb *lawyer*
Handler, Lauren E. *lawyer*
Herzberg, Peter Jay *lawyer*
Humick, Thomas Charles Campbell *lawyer*
Hyland, William Francis *lawyer*
Jolles, Ira Hervey *lawyer*
Kandravy, John *lawyer*
Kastner, Cynthia *lawyer*
Korf, Gene Robert *lawyer*
Kreindler, Peter Michael *lawyer*
Lavey, Stewart Evan *lawyer*
Lunin, Joseph *lawyer*
McDonough, Joseph Richard *lawyer*
Mc Elroy, William Theodore *lawyer*
Newman, John Merle *lawyer*
Nittoly, Paul Gerard *lawyer*
O'Connell, Daniel F. *lawyer*
O'Grady, Dennis Joseph *lawyer*
Pantel, Glenn Steven *lawyer*
Reid, Charles Adams, III *lawyer*
Robertson, William Withers *lawyer*
Rose, Robert Gordon *lawyer*
Rosenthal, Meyer L(ouis) *lawyer*
Scott, Susan *lawyer*
Sharkey, Vincent Joseph *lawyer*
Sherman, Sandra Brown *lawyer*
Stephens, Jay B. *lawyer*
Szuch, Clyde Andrew *lawyer*
Whitmer, Frederick Lee *lawyer*

Mountainside
Jacobson, Gary Steven *lawyer*

Murray Hill
Adler, Nadia C. *lawyer*

New Brunswick
Corman, Randy *lawyer*
Scott, David Rodick *lawyer, legal educator*
Shirtz, Joseph Frank *lawyer, consultant*
Stamato, Linda Ann Lautenschlaeger *legal educator, mediator*
Yorke, Marianne *lawyer, real estate executive*

New Providence
Manthei, Richard Dale *lawyer, health care company executive*

Newark
Abrams, Roger Ian *law educator, arbitrator*
Askin, Frank *law educator*
Bizub, Johanna Catherine *library director*
Blumrosen, Alfred William *law educator*
Blumrosen, Ruth Gerber *lawyer, educator, arbitrator*
Brescher, John B., Jr. *lawyer*
Cahn, Jeffrey Barton *lawyer*
†Caldwell, Toni L. *court official, charitable organization executive*
Callahan, Patrick Michael *lawyer*
Colli, Bart Joseph *lawyer*
Costenbader, Charles Michael *lawyer*
Creenan, Katherine Heras *lawyer*
Cummis, Clive Sanford *lawyer*
Dee, Francis X. *lawyer*
Defeis, Elizabeth Frances *law educator, lawyer*
Del Tufo, Robert J. *lawyer, former US attorney, former state attorney general*
Eittreim, Richard MacNutt *lawyer*
English, Nicholas Conover *lawyer*
Garde, John Charles *lawyer*
Goldstein, Marvin Mark *lawyer*
Gouraige, Hervé *lawyer*
Haring, Eugene Miller *lawyer*
Harrison, Roslyn Siman *lawyer*
Hochberg, Faith S. *prosecutor*
Karp, Donald Mathew *lawyer, banker*
Knee, Stephen H. *lawyer*
Kott, David Russell *lawyer*
Labaj, Pamela Joan *Lawyer*
Laurino, Robert Dennis *prosecutor*
Levin, Simon *lawyer*
Linken, Dennis C. *lawyer*
McGuire, William B(enedict) *lawyer*
McKinney, John Adams, Jr. *lawyer*
Muscato, Andrew *lawyer*
Neuer, Philip David *lawyer, real estate consultant*
Oberdorf, John J. *lawyer*
Paul, James Caverly Newlin *law educator, former university dean*
Rak, Lorraine Karen *lawyer*
Reams, Bernard Dinsmore, Jr. *lawyer, educator*
Reilly, William Thomas *lawyer*
Roth, Allan Robert *lawyer, educator*
Selover, R. Edwin *lawyer*
Siegal, Joel Davis *lawyer*
Simmons, Peter *law and urban planning educator*
Tischman, Michael Bernard *lawyer*
Vajtay, Stephen Michael, Jr. *lawyer*
Wachenfeld, William Thomas *lawyer, foundation executive*
Walker, Linda Lee *lawyer*
Wyer, James Ingersoll *lawyer*
Yamner, Morris *lawyer*

Newton
Cox, William Martin *lawyer, educator*

North Haledon
Harrington, Kevin Paul *lawyer*

Northvale
Seaman, Robert E., III *lawyer*

Oakhurst
Konvitz, Milton Ridbaz *law educator*
Widman, Douglas Jack *lawyer*

Old Bridge
Downs, Thomas Edward, IV *lawyer*

Oldwick
Hitchcock, Ethan Allen *lawyer*

Paramus
Levy, Joseph *lawyer*
Tumolo, Michael L. *corporate lawyer*

Parsippany
Berkowitz, Bernard Joseph *lawyer*
†Buckman, James Edward *lawyer*
Chobot, John Charles *lawyer*
Doherty, Robert Christopher *lawyer*
Haney, James Kevin *lawyer*
Hansbury, Stephan Charles *lawyer*
Shaw, Alan *lawyer, corporate executive*

Pilesgrove Township
Crouse, Farrell R. *lawyer*

Piscataway
Smith, Bob *lawyer, assemblyman, educator*
Wilson, Abraham *lawyer*

Pitman
Cloues, Edward Blanchard, II *lawyer*

Plainsboro
Gorrin, Eugene *lawyer*
Kozlowski, Thomas Joseph, Jr. *lawyer, trust company executive*

Princeton
Ackourey, Peter Paul *lawyer*
Anderson, Ellis Bernard *retired lawyer, pharmaceutical company executive*
Beidler, Marsha Wolf *lawyer*
Bergman, Edward Jonathan *lawyer, educator*
Brennan, William Joseph, III *lawyer*
Connor, Geoffrey Michael *lawyer*
Hill, James Scott *lawyer*
Judge, Marty M. *lawyer*
Katz, Stanley Nider *law history educator*
Katzenbach, Nicholas deBelleville *lawyer*
Picco, Steven Joseph *lawyer*
Souter, Sydney Scull *lawyer*
Sutphin, William Taylor *lawyer*
Ufford, Charles Wilbur, Jr. *lawyer*
Zimmer, Richard Alan *lawyer*

Red Bank
Auerbach, Philip Gary *lawyer*
Duggan, John Peter *lawyer*
†Hempstead, George H., III *lawyer, diversified company executive*
Labrecque, Theodore Joseph *lawyer*
Nucciarone, A. Patrick *lawyer*
Rogers, Lee Jasper *lawyer*

Ridgewood
Seigel, Jan Kearney *lawyer*

River Vale
Falcon, Raymond Jesus, Jr. *lawyer*
Lotito, Joseph Daniel *lawyer*

Rochelle Park
Knopf, Barry Abraham *lawyer*

Roseland
Berkowitz, Bernard Solomon *lawyer*
Eakeley, Douglas Scott *lawyer*
Foster, M. Joan *lawyer*
Greenberg, Stephen Michael *lawyer, businesss executive*
Kohl, Benedict M. *lawyer*
Levithan, Allen B. *lawyer*
Lowenstein, Alan Victor *lawyer*
MacKay, John Robert, II *lawyer*
Newman, Gary *lawyer*
Schenkler, Bernard *lawyer*
Smith, Wendy Hope *lawyer*
Starr, Ira M. *lawyer*
Stern, Herbert Jay *lawyer*
Tarino, Gary Edward *lawyer*
Vanderbilt, Arthur T., II *lawyer*
Wovsaniker, Alan *lawyer, educator*

Saddle Brook
Pearlman, Peter Steven *lawyer*

Scotch Plains
Klock, John Henry *lawyer*

Sea Girt
Crispi, Michele Marie *lawyer*
Wyskowski, Barbara Jean *lawyer*

Secaucus
Castano, Gregory Joseph *lawyer*
Fahy, John J. *lawyer*
Fitzpatrick, Harold Francis *lawyer*
Holt, Michael Bartholomew *lawyer*
McNamara, Patrick James *lawyer*

Ship Bottom
Shackleton, Richard James *lawyer*

Short Hills
Hazlehurst, Robert Purviance, Jr. *lawyer*
Kaye, Marc Mendell *lawyer*
Siegfried, David Charles *retired lawyer*

Somerset
Green, Jeffrey C. *lawyer*
Macey, Scott J. *lawyer*

Somerville
Bernstein, Eric Martin *lawyer*
Fleischman, Joseph Jacob *lawyer*

South Amboy
Moskovitz, Stuart Jeffrey *lawyer*

South Orange
Delo, Ellen Sanderson *lawyer*

Spring Lake
Anderson, James Francis *lawyer*

Springfield
Grayson, Bette Rita *lawyer*
Katz, Jeffrey Harvey *lawyer, mayor*

Stone Harbor
Taylor, Robert Lee *lawyer, former judge*

Summit
Benjamin, Jeff *lawyer, pharmaceutical executive*
Kenyon, Edward Tipton *lawyer*
Parsons, Judson Aspinwall, Jr. *lawyer*
Thompson, Robert L., Jr. *lawyer*
Woller, James Alan *lawyer*

Tenafly
Badr, Gamal Moursi *legal consultant*
Vort, Robert A. *lawyer*

Toms River
Whitman, Russell Wilson *lawyer*

Trenton
Bigham, William J. *lawyer*
Caldwell, Wesley Stuart, III *lawyer, lobbyist*
Gogo, Gregory *lawyer*
Jones, Dale Edwin *public defender*
Metzger, John Mackay *lawyer*
Pellecchia, John Michael *lawyer*
Reldan, Robert Ronald *law educator, psychological consultant*
Sterns, Joel Henry *lawyer*

Union
Rosenberg, A. Irving *lawyer*

Union City
Rondon, Edania Cecilia *lawyer*

Vauxhall
Ross, Mark Samuel *lawyer, educator, funeral director, writer*

Voorhees
Picariello, Pasquale *lawyer*

Wanaque
Jordan, Leo John *lawyer*

Warren
Hurley, Lawrence Joseph *lawyer*
Kasper, Horst Manfred *lawyer*

Watchung
Kraus, Steven Gary *lawyer*

Wayne
Gelman, Jon Leonard *lawyer*

Weehawken
Hayden, Joseph A., Jr. *lawyer*

West Orange
Askin, Marilyn *lawyer, educator*
†Bottitta, Joseph Anthony *lawyer*
Gordon, Harrison J. *lawyer*
Kushen, Allan Stanford *retired lawyer*
Laves, Benjamin Samuel *lawyer*

Westfield
†Decker, Mark Richard *lawyer*
Phillips, John C. *lawyer*

Whitehouse Station
McDonald, Mary M. *lawyer*

Woodbridge
Becker, Frederic Kenneth *lawyer*
Brauth, Marvin Jeffrey *lawyer*
Brown, Morris *lawyer*
Buchsbaum, Peter A. *lawyer*
Cirafesi, Robert J. *lawyer*
Constantinou, Clay *lawyer, ambassador*
Hoberman, Stuart A. *lawyer*
Lepelstat, Martin L. *lawyer*
McCarthy, G. Daniel *lawyer*
Schaff, Michael Frederick *lawyer*

Woodbury
Adler, Lewis Gerard *lawyer*

Woodcliff Lake
Nachtigal, Patricia *lawyer, equipment manufacturing company executive*

NEW MEXICO

Albuquerque
Addis, Richard Barton *lawyer*
Aurbach, Robert Michael *lawyer, consultant, photographer*
Bardacke, Paul Gregory *lawyer, former attorney general*
Baum, Marsha Lynn *law educator*
Beach, Arthur O'Neal *lawyer*
Bova, Vincent Arthur, Jr. *lawyer, consultant, photographer*
Cargo, David Francis *lawyer*
Caruso, Mark John *lawyer*
Ellis, Willis Hill *lawyer, educator*
Farmer, Terry D(wayne) *lawyer*
Hart, Frederick Michael *law educator*
Kelly, John J. *prosecutor*
Loubet, Jeffrey W. *lawyer*
Messersmith, Lanny Dee *lawyer*
Miller, Gardner Hartmann *paralegal*
Mueller, Diane Mayne *lawyer*
Paster, Janice Dubinsky *lawyer, former state legislator*
Ramo, Roberta Cooper *lawyer*
Roehl, Jerrald J. *lawyer*
Romero, Jeff *lawyer*
Schoen, Stevan Jay *lawyer*
Schuler, Alison Kay *lawyer*
Shaw, Mark Howard *lawyer, business owner, entrepreneur*
Sisk, Daniel Arthur *lawyer*
Slade, Lynn Heyer *lawyer*
Thompson, Rufus E. *lawyer*
White, Robert Milton *lawyer*

Deming
Sherman, Frederick Hood *lawyer*

Farmington
Gurley, Curtis Raymond *lawyer*

Las Cruces
Lutz, William Lan *lawyer*
Martin, Connie Ruth *lawyer*
Neumann, Rita *lawyer*
Schweikart, Debora Ellen *lawyer*

Roswell
Bassett, John Walden, Jr. *lawyer*
Haines, Thomas David, Jr. *lawyer*
†Kraft, Richard Lee *lawyer*
Olson, Richard Earl *lawyer, state legislator*

Ruidoso
Thomsen, David Allen *lawyer*

Santa Fe
Besing, Ray Gilbert *lawyer, writer*
Bienvenu, John Charles *lawyer*
Carpenter, Richard Norris *lawyer*
Coffield, Conrad Eugene *lawyer*
Culbert, Peter Van Horn *lawyer*
Dodds, Robert James, III *lawyer*
Farber, Steven Glenn *lawyer*
Hatfield, Christian Andrew *lawyer*
Hickey, John Miller *lawyer*
McClaugherty, Joe L. *lawyer, educator*
Moll, Deborah Adelaide *lawyer*
Noland, Charles Donald *lawyer, educator*
Pound, John Bennett *lawyer*
Schwarz, Michael *lawyer*
Stevens, Ron A. *lawyer, public interest organization administrator*
Weckesser, Susan Oneacre *lawyer*
Zorie, Stephanie Marie *lawyer*

Seneca
Monroe, Kendyl Kurth *retired lawyer*

Silver City
Foy, Thomas Paul *lawyer, retired state legislator, retired banker*

NEW YORK

Albany
Barsamian, J(ohn) Albert *lawyer, lecturer, educator, criminologist, arbitrator*
Beach, John Arthur *lawyer*
Buldrini, George James *lawyer*
Catalano, Jane Donna *lawyer*
Cooke, Lawrence Henry *lawyer, former state chief judge*
Couch, Leslie Franklin *lawyer*
†Doherty, Glen Patrick *lawyer*
Dulin, Thomas N. *lawyer*
†Glasel, David Paul *lawyer*
Hoffman, Nancy E. *lawyer*
Hudson, Paul Stephen *lawyer, consumer advocate*
Koff, Howard Michael *lawyer*
Laird, Edward DeHart, Jr. *lawyer*
Lefkowitz, Jerome *lawyer*
Meacham, Norma Grace *lawyer*
Peaslee, Maurice Keenan *lawyer*
Piedmont, Richard Stuart *lawyer*
Powers, John Kieran *lawyer*
Ruggeri, Robert Edward *lawyer*
Ruzow, Daniel Arthur *lawyer*
Salkin, Patricia E. *law educator*
Santola, Daniel Ralph *lawyer*
Siegel, David Donald *law educator*
Sponsler, Thomas H. *law educator, dean*
Sprow, Howard Thomas *lawyer, educator*
Wallender, Michael Todd *lawyer*
Wukitsch, David John *lawyer*

Albion
Lyman, Nathan Marquis *lawyer*

Amherst
Jones, E. Thomas *lawyer*
Murray, William Michael *lawyer*

Ardsley On Hudson
Stein, Milton Michael *lawyer*

Armonk
Moskowitz, Stuart Stanley *lawyer*
Quinn, James W. *lawyer*
Ricciardi, Lawrence R. *lawyer*
Wood, Teri Wilford *lawyer*

Auburn
Wolczyk, Joseph Michael *lawyer*

Babylon
Hennelly, Edmund Paul *lawyer, oil company executive*

Batavia
Saleh, David John *lawyer*

Bedford
Atkins, Ronald Raymond *lawyer*

Bethpage
Lemle, Robert Spencer *lawyer*

Binghamton
Anderson, Warren Mattice *lawyer*
Axtell, Clayton Morgan, Jr. *lawyer*
Beck, Stephanie G. *lawyer*
Chivers, James Leeds *lawyer*
Gerhart, Eugene Clifton *lawyer*
Price, Paul Marnell *lawyer*

Briarcliff Manor
Maloney, Michael Patrick *lawyer, mediator, arbitrator*

Bronx
Balka, Sigmund Ronell *lawyer*
Calamari, Andrew M. *lawyer*
Cornfield, Melvin *lawyer, university institute director*
Garance, Dominick (D. G. Garan) *lawyer, author*
Hyman, Andrew M. *lawyer*

Bronxville
Cook, Charles David *international lawyer, arbitrator, consultant*
Cutler, Kenneth Burnett *lawyer, investment company executive*
Falvey, Patrick Joseph *lawyer*
Fuller, David Otis, Jr. *lawyer*
Recabo, Jaime Miguel *lawyer*
Veneruso, James John *lawyer*

Brooklyn
Carter, Zachary W. *prosecutor*
Fallek, Andrew Michael *lawyer*
Henderson, Janice Elizabeth *law librarian*
Herzog, Lester Barry *lawyer, educator*
Jacobson, Barry Stephen *lawyer, judge*
Kamins, Barry Michael *lawyer*
Karmel, Roberta Segal *lawyer, educator*
Kramer, Meyer *lawyer, editor, clergyman*
Lewis, Felice Flanery *lawyer, educator*
Lizt, Sara Enid Vanefsky *lawyer, educator*
Nicholson, Michael *lawyer*
Onken, George Marcellus *lawyer*
Poser, Norman Stanley *law educator*
Raskind, Leo Joseph *law educator*
Solan, Lawrence Michael *lawyer*
†Swain, Laura Taylor *judge*

Buffalo
Bailey, Thomas Charles *lawyer*
Barney, Thomas McNamee *lawyer*
Bean, Edwin Temple, Jr. *lawyer*
Bermingham, Joseph Daniel *lawyer*
Blaine, Charles Gillespie *retired lawyer*
Brock, David George *lawyer*
Brown, Jerrold Stanley *lawyer*
Brydges, Thomas Eugene *lawyer*
Carmichael, Donald Scott *lawyer, business executive*
Clemens, David Allen *lawyer*
Day, Donald Sheldon *lawyer*
Feuerstein, Alan Ricky *lawyer, consultant*
†Foschio, Leslie George *lawyer*
Freedman, Maryann Saccomando *lawyer*
Gardner, Arnold Burton *lawyer*
Glanville, Robert Edward *lawyer*
Goldstein, Brian Alan *lawyer, physician*
Grasser, George Robert *lawyer*
Gray, F(rederick) William, III *lawyer*
Hall, David Edward *lawyer*
Halpern, Ralph Lawrence *lawyer*
Hayes, J. Michael *lawyer*
Head, Christopher Alan *lawyer*
Headrick, Thomas Edward *lawyer, educator*
Heilman, Pamela Davis *lawyer*
Kristoff, Karl W. *lawyer*
Lippes, Gerald Sanford *lawyer, business executive*
MacLeod, Gordon Albert *retired lawyer*
Mattar, Lawrence Joseph *lawyer*
Mucci, Gary Louis *lawyer*
Murray, Glenn Edward *lawyer*
†NeMoyer, Patrick H. *prosecutor*
Newman, Stephen Michael *lawyer*
Nichols, F(rederick) Harris *lawyer*
O'Donnell, Denise Ellen *lawyer*
Odza, Randall M. *lawyer*
O'Loughlin, Sandra S. *lawyer*
Oppenheimer, Randolph Carl *lawyer*
Pajak, David Joseph *lawyer, consultant*
Pearson, Paul David *lawyer, mediator*
Ross, Christopher Theodore *lawyer*
Sampson, John David *lawyer*
Schroeder, Harold Kenneth, Jr. *lawyer*
Sherwood, Arthur Morley *lawyer*
Toohey, Philip S. *lawyer*
Wickser, John Philip *lawyer*
Wisbaum, Wayne David *lawyer*

Camillus
Endieveri, Anthony Frank *lawyer*

Campbell Hall
Stone, Peter George *lawyer, publishing company executive*

Canaan
Pennell, William Brooke *lawyer*

Cape Vincent
Stiefel, Linda Shields *lawyer*

Carle Place
Seiden, Steven Jay *lawyer*
Smolev, Terence Elliot *lawyer, educator*

Carmel
Laporte, Cloyd, Jr. *lawyer, retired manufacturing executive*

Catskill
Kingsley, John Piersall *lawyer*

Cazenovia
Dillingham, Ruth Elaine *lawyer, nurse*
Shattuck, George Clement *retired lawyer*

Cedarhurst
Klein, Irwin Grant *lawyer*
Taubenfeld, Harry Samuel *lawyer*

Chappaqua
Graham, Lawrence Otis *lawyer, writer, television personality*
Howard, John Brigham *lawyer, foundation executive*
Pollet, Susan L. *lawyer*

Chestnut Ridge
Burns, Richard Owen *lawyer*

Chittenango
Baum, Peter Alan *lawyer*

Commack
Steindler, Walter G. *retired lawyer*

Corning
Hauselt, Denise Ann *lawyer*
Ughetta, William Casper *lawyer, manufacturing company executive*

Crugers
Walther, Zerita *paralegal*

Cutchogue
O'Connell, Francis Joseph *lawyer, arbitrator*

Dansville
Vogel, John Walter *lawyer*

Delhi
Hamilton, John Thomas, Jr. *lawyer*

Delmar
Eldridge, Douglas Alan *lawyer*
†LaFave, Cynthia S. *lawyer*

Dobbs Ferry
Juettner, Diana D'Amico *lawyer, educator*

Douglaston
Walsh, Sean M. *lawyer, audio-video computer forensics consultant*

Dunkirk
Woodbury, Robert Charles *lawyer*

East Aurora
Brott, Irving Deerin, Jr. *lawyer, judge*

East Hampton
Ehren, Charles Alexander, Jr. *lawyer, educator*

East Meadow
Adler, Ira Jay *lawyer*
Bergman, Bruce Jeffrey *lawyer*
Hyman, Montague Allan *lawyer*

Floral Park
Cardalena, Peter Paul, Jr. *lawyer, educator*
Chatoff, Michael Alan *lawyer*

Flushing
Brown, Kenneth Lloyd *lawyer*
Chang, Lee-Lee *lawyer*
Cheng, Sharon Goon *lawyer*
Pillinger, James J. *lawyer, educator*

Forest Hills
Povman, Morton *lawyer*

Forestville
†Adams, Lee Towne *lawyer*

Garden City
Caputo, Kathryn Mary *paralegal*
†Cohen, Harvey *lawyer*
Cook, George Valentine *lawyer*
Corleto, Raymond Anthony *lawyer*
Corsi, Philip Donald *lawyer*
Di Mascio, John Philip *lawyer*
Fischoff, Gary Charles *lawyer*
Fishberg, Gerard *lawyer*
Gordon, Jay F(isher) *lawyer*
Kaplan, Joel Stuart *lawyer*
Kestenbaum, Harold Lee *lawyer*
Lilly, Thomas Joseph *lawyer*
McCann, Louise Mary *paralegal*
Minicucci, Richard Francis *lawyer, former hospital administrator*
Ostrow, Michael Jay *lawyer*
Tucker, William P. *lawyer, writer*

Glen Cove
Mills, Charles Gardner *lawyer*

Glen Head
Savinetti, Louis Gerard *lawyer*

Glens Falls
Bartlett, Richard James *lawyer, former university dean*

Gouverneur
Leader, Robert John *lawyer*

Great Neck
Gellman, Yale H. *lawyer*
Kawano, Arnold Hubert *lawyer*
Rockowitz, Noah Ezra *lawyer*
Salzman, Stanley P. *lawyer*
Samanowitz, Ronald Arthur *lawyer*
Wachsman, Harvey Frederick *lawyer, neurosurgeon*

Greenvale
Halper, Emanuel B(arry) *real estate lawyer, developer, consultant, author*

Hamburg
Gaughan, Dennis Charles *lawyer*
Hargesheimer, Elbert, III *lawyer*

Hammond
Musselman, Francis Haas *lawyer*

Harrison
†O'Hare, Bernard F. *lawyer*

Hawthorne
Traub, Richard Kenneth *lawyer*

Hempstead
Agata, Burton C. *lawyer, educator*
Mahon, Malachy Thomas, Sr. *lawyer, educator*

Herkimer
Kirk, Patrick Laine *lawyer*

Hicksville
Giuffré, John Joseph *lawyer*
Goldman, Donald Howard *lawyer*

Hillsdale
Lunde, Asbjorn Rudolph *lawyer*

Huntington
Augello, William Joseph *lawyer*
Brettschneider, Rita Roberta Fischman *lawyer*
DeMartin, Charles Peter *lawyer*
Fine, Barry Kenneth *lawyer*
German, June Resnick *lawyer*
Glickstein, Howard Alan *law educator*
Hochberg, Ronald Mark *lawyer*
Levitan, Katherine D. *lawyer*
Morris, Jeffrey Brandon *law educator*
Munson, Nancy Kay *lawyer*
Pratt, George Cheney *law educator, retired federal judge*
Robinson, Kenneth Patrick *lawyer*

Irvington
Bonomi, John Gurnee *retired lawyer*
Goodkind, Louis William *lawyer*

Islandia
Davidow, Lawrence Eric *lawyer*

Islip
Baker, Lloyd Harvey *retired lawyer*

Ithaca
Barcelo, John James, III *law educator*
Barney, John Charles *lawyer*
Fineman, Martha Albertson *law educator*
Germain, Claire Madeleine *law librarian, educator*
Hay, George Alan *law and economics educator*
Hillman, Robert Andrew *law educator, former university dean*
Kent, Robert Brydon *law educator*
Macey, Jonathan R. *law educator*
Martin, Peter William *lawyer, educator*
Palmer, Larry Isaac *lawyer, educator*
Rossi, Faust F. *lawyer, educator*
Summers, Robert Samuel *lawyer, author, educator*
Theisen, Henry William *lawyer*
Thoron, Gray *lawyer, educator*
†Yale-Loehr, Stephen William *lawyer, editor*

Jamaica
Angione, Howard Francis *lawyer, editor*
Tschinkel, Andrew Joseph, Jr. *law librarian*
Vanora, Jerome Patrick *lawyer*

Jamestown
Idzik, Martin Francis *lawyer*

Jamesville
DeCrow, Karen *lawyer, author, lecturer*

Jericho
Blau, Harvey Ronald *lawyer*
Corso, Frank Mitchell *lawyer*
Friedman, David Samuel *lawyer, law review executive*
Rehbock, Richard Alexander *lawyer*

Keeseville
Turetsky, Aaron *lawyer*

Kew Gardens
Adler, David Neil *lawyer*
Reichel, Aaron Israel *lawyer*
Schechter, Donald Robert *lawyer*

Kinderhook
Benamati, Dennis Charles *law librarian, editor, consultant*

Larchmont
Berridge, George Bradford *retired lawyer*
Bloom, Lee Hurley *lawyer, public affairs consultant, retired household products manufacturing executive*
Engel, Ralph Manuel *lawyer*
Pelton, Russell Gilbert *lawyer*
Seton, Charles B. *lawyer*
White, Thomas Edward *lawyer*

Latham
Conway, Robert George, Jr. *lawyer*

Liberty
Eisenberg, Bertram William *lawyer*

Lido Beach
Billauer, Barbara Pfeffer *lawyer, educator*

Long Beach
Levine, Samuel Milton *lawyer*
Solomon, Robert H. *lawyer*

Long Island
Weiner, Alan E. *lawyer*

Long Island City
Alimaras, Gus *lawyer*
Wanderman, Susan Mae *lawyer*

Malverne
Benigno, Thomas Daniel *lawyer*

Manhasset
Benewitz, Maurice Charles *labor arbitrator, educator*
Wachtler, Sol *law educator, retired judge, arbitration corporation executive, writer*

Melville
Klatell, Robert Edward *lawyer, electronics company executive*
McMillan, Robert Ralph *lawyer*
Rathkopf, Daren Anthony *lawyer*

Merrick
Seader, Paul Alan *lawyer*

Mineola
Bartlett, Clifford Adams, Jr. *lawyer*
Block, Martin *lawyer*
Braid, Frederick Donald *lawyer*
Brush, Louis Frederick *lawyer*
Jones, Lawrence Tunnicliffe *lawyer*
Kelly, Edward Joseph *lawyer*
Klein, Arnold Spencer *lawyer*
Kral, William George *lawyer*
Mayer, Renee G. *lawyer*
Meyer, Bernard Stern *lawyer, former judge*
Monaghan, Peter Gerard *lawyer*
Paterson, Basil Alexander *lawyer*
Pogrebin, Bertrand B. *lawyer*
Rossen, Jordan *lawyer*
Sandback, William Arthur *lawyer*
Schaffer, David Irving *lawyer*
Stanisci, Thomas William *lawyer*
Tankoos, Sandra Maxine *court reporting services executive*
Zuckerman, Richard Karl *lawyer*

Mount Kisco
Curran, Maurice Francis *lawyer*
Goodhue, Mary Brier *lawyer, former state senator*

Neponsit
Re, Edward Domenic *law educator, retired federal judge*

New City
Fenster, Robert David *lawyer*

New Hartford
Chapin, Mary Q. *arbitrator, mediator, writer, perfoming artist*

New Hyde Park
Ezersky, William Martin *lawyer*
Jensen, Richard Currie *lawyer*
Offner, Eric Delmonte *lawyer*

New Rochelle
Blotner, Norman David *lawyer, real estate broker, corporate executive*
Gunning, Francis Patrick *lawyer, insurance association executive*
Herzberg, Sydelle Shulman *lawyer, accountant*
Lurie, Alvin David *lawyer*

New York
Abelman, Arthur F. *lawyer*
Abrams, Floyd *lawyer*
Abrams, Robert *lawyer, former state attorney general*

Abramson, Stephanie W. *lawyer*
Adams, George Bell *lawyer*
Adams, John Hamilton *lawyer*
Agranoff, Gerald Neal *lawyer*
Ahmad, Kamal M. *lawyer*
Aibel, Howard J. *lawyer*
Aidinoff, M(erton) Bernard *lawyer*
Aksen, Gerald *lawyer, educator, arbitrator*
Albert, Garett J. *lawyer*
Albert, Neale Malcolm *lawyer*
Alden, Steven Michael *lawyer*
Alessandroni, Venan Joseph *lawyer*
Allen, Leon Arthur, Jr. *lawyer*
Allen, William Thomas *educator, lawyer, judge*
Alter, Andrew William *lawyer*
Alter, David *lawyer*
Alter, Eleanor Breitel *lawyer*
Altieri, Peter Louis *lawyer*
Amabile, John Louis *lawyer*
Amdur, Martin Bennett *lawyer*
Amhowitz, Harris J. *lawyer, educator*
Amsterdam, Anthony Guy *law educator*
Amsterdam, Mark Lemle *lawyer*
Andersen, Richard Esten *lawyer*
Anderson, Eugene Robert *lawyer*
Andresen, Malcolm *lawyer*
Andrews, Gordon Clark *lawyer*
Andrus, Roger Douglas *lawyer*
Angland, Joseph *lawyer*
Anthoine, Robert *lawyer, educator*
Appel, Albert M. *lawyer*
Appelbaum, Ann Harriet *lawyer*
Arenson, Gregory K. *lawyer*
Arkin, Stanley S. *lawyer*
Armstrong, James Sinclair *foundation director, retired lawyer*
Armstrong, Steven Holm *lawyer*
Arouh, Jeffrey Alan *lawyer*
Arquit, Kevin James *lawyer*
Arther, Richard Oberlin *polygraphist, educator*
Ash, Herbert Leonard *lawyer*
Atkins, Peter Allan *lawyer*
Auerbach, William *lawyer*
Axinn, Stephen Mark *lawyer*
Bach, Thomas Handford *lawyer, investor*
Bachelder, Joseph Elmer, III *lawyer*
Backman, Gerald Stephen *lawyer*
Badertscher, David Glen *law librarian, consultant*
Bagger, Richard Hartvig *lawyer*
Bahler, Gary M. *lawyer*
Bainton, J(ohn) Joseph *lawyer*
Baird, Zoë *lawyer, insurance company executive*
Baity, John Cooley *lawyer*
Baker, Stuart David *lawyer*
Ball, John H(anstein) *lawyer*
Bamberger, Michael Albert *lawyer*
Bancroft, Alexander Clerihew *lawyer*
Bancroft, Margaret Armstrong *lawyer*
Bankston, Archie Moore, Jr. *lawyer*
Barandes, Robert *lawyer*
Barasch, Clarence Sylvan *lawyer*
Barasch, Mal Livingston *lawyer*
Barist, Jeffrey A. *lawyer*
Barnabeo, Susan Patricia *lawyer*
Barr, Thomas D. *lawyer*
Barry, David Earl *lawyer*
Barry, Desmond Thomas, Jr. *lawyer*
Barth, Mark Harold *lawyer*
Bartlett, Joseph Warren *lawyer*
Bason, George R., Jr. *lawyer*
Bassen, Ned Henry *lawyer*
Bauer, Douglas F. *lawyer*
Bauer, Ralph Glenn *lawyer, maritime arbitrator*
Baumgardner, John Ellwood, Jr. *lawyer*
Baumgarten, Paul Anthony *lawyer*
†Baumgarten, Sidney *lawyer, company executive*
Baumrin, Bernard Stefan Herbert *lawyer, educator*
Bazerman, Steven Howard *lawyer*
Bear, Donald *law firm executive director*
Bear, Larry Alan *lawyer, educator*
Bearak, Corey B(ecker) *lawyer*
Beatie, Russel Harrison, Jr. *lawyer*
Beck, Andrew James *lawyer*
Beerbower, John Edwin *lawyer*
†Begley, Louis *lawyer, writer*
Behr, Alan Andrew *lawyer, writer*
Beinecke, Candace Krugman *lawyer*
Bell, Derrick Albert *law educator, author, lecturer*
Bell, Jonathan Robert *lawyer*
Beller, Daniel J. *lawyer*
Beller, Gary A. *lawyer, insurance company executive*
Belnick, Mark Alan *lawyer*
Benakis, George James *lawyer*
Bender, John Charles *lawyer*
Benedict, James Nelson *lawyer*
Benenson, Mark Keith *lawyer*
Benkard, James W. B. *lawyer*
Bennett, Scott Lawrence *lawyer*
Bentley, Anthony Miles *lawyer*
Berg, Alan *lawyer, government official*
Bergan, Edmund Paul, Jr. *lawyer*
Berger, George *lawyer*
Bergreen, Morris Harvey *lawyer, business executive, private investor*
Bergstein, Daniel Gerard *lawyer*
Berland, Sanford Neil *lawyer*
Berman, Keith *solicitor, lawyer*
Bernard, Richard Phillip *lawyer*
Bernstein, Bernard *lawyer, corporate executive*
Bernstein, Daniel Lewis *lawyer*
Berry, Loren Curtis *lawyer, consultant*
Berzow, Harold Steven *lawyer*
Beshar, Robert Peter *lawyer*
Bettman, Gary Bruce *lawyer*
Beuchert, Edward William *lawyer*
Bezanson, Thomas Edward *lawyer*
Bialkin, Kenneth Jules *lawyer*
Bialo, Kenneth Marc *lawyer*
Bicks, David Peter *lawyer*
Bidwell, James Truman, Jr. *lawyer*
Bing, Jonathan Lloyd *lawyer*
Birnbaum, Edward Lester *lawyer*
†Birnbaum, Sheila L. *lawyer, educator*
Black, Barbara Aronstein *legal history educator*
Black, James Isaac, III *lawyer*
Black, Jerry Bernard *lawyer*
Blackman, Kenneth Robert *lawyer*
Blakeslee, Edward Eaton *lawyer, insurance executive*
Blanc, Roger David *lawyer*
Blattmachr, Jonathan George *lawyer*
Block, William Kenneth *lawyer*
Bloomer, Harold Franklin, Jr. *lawyer*
Blumberg, Gerald *lawyer*
Blume, Lawrence Dayton *lawyer*
Blumkin, Linda Ruth *lawyer*
Bockstein, Herbert *lawyer*
Boddie, Reginald Alonzo *lawyer*
Bodovitz, James Philip *lawyer*
Boehner, Leonard Bruce *lawyer*
Boes, Lawrence William *lawyer*
Bolan, Thomas Anthony *lawyer*
Bonacquist, Harold Frank, Jr. *lawyer*
Booth, Edgar Hirsch *lawyer*
Booth, Mitchell B. *lawyer*
Bordoff, Jason Eric *consultant*
Borisoff, Richard Stuart *lawyer*
Boros, Jerome S. *lawyer*
Borsody, Robert Peter *lawyer*
Bosses, Stevan J. *lawyer*
Bowden, William P., Jr. *lawyer, banker*
Boxer, Leonard *lawyer*
Bozorth, Squire Newland *lawyer*
Bradley, E. Michael *lawyer*
Brandrup, Douglas Warren *lawyer*
Braun, Jeffrey Louis *lawyer*
Braverman, Alan N. *lawyer*
Brecher, Howard Arthur *lawyer*
Brecker, Jeffrey Ross *lawyer, educator*
Breglio, John F. *lawyer*
Brenner, Frank *lawyer*
Bressler, Bernard *lawyer*
Briggs, Taylor Rastrick *lawyer*
Bring, Murray H. *lawyer*
Briskman, Louis J. *lawyer*
Broadwater, Douglas Dwight *lawyer*
Brock, Charles Lawrence *lawyer, business executive*
Brockway, David Hunt *lawyer*
Broder, Douglas Fisher *lawyer*
Brodsky, Samuel *lawyer*
Brome, Thomas Reed *lawyer*
Bronstein, Richard J. *lawyer*
Brooks, Lorimer Page *patent lawyer*
Bross, Steward Richard, Jr. *lawyer*
Brosterman, Melvin A. *lawyer*
Broude, Richard Frederick *lawyer, educator*
Broughton, Phillip Charles *lawyer*
Browdy, Joseph Eugene *lawyer*
Brown, Charles Dodgson *lawyer*
Brown, Meredith M. *lawyer*
Brown, Paul M. *lawyer*
Brown, Ralph Sawyer, Jr. *retired lawyer, business executive*
Browne, Jeffrey Francis *lawyer*
Brumm, James Earl *lawyer, trading company executive*
Brundige, Robert William, Jr. *lawyer*
Bryan, Barry Richard *lawyer*
Buchbinder, Darrell Bruce *lawyer*
Budd, Thomas Witbeck *lawyer*
Bulliner, P. Alan *corporate lawyer*
Burak, H(oward) Paul *lawyer*
Burgweger, Francis Joseph Dewes, Jr. *lawyer*
Burns, Arnold Irwin *lawyer*
Burrows, Michael Donald *lawyer*
Bursky, Herman Aaron *lawyer*
Bushnell, George Edward, III *lawyer*
Butler, Samuel Coles *lawyer*
Butler, William Joseph *lawyer*
Butowsky, David Martin *lawyer*
Buttenwieser, Lawrence Benjamin *lawyer*
Butterklee, Neil Howard *lawyer*
Caginalp, Aydin S. *lawyer*
Callahan, Joseph Patrick *lawyer*
Campbell, Maria Bouchelle *lawyer, church executive*
Cannell, John Redferne *lawyer*
Canoni, John David *lawyer*
Cantor, Melvyn Leon *retired lawyer*
Carb, Stephen Ames *lawyer*
Cardinali, Albert John *lawyer*
Cardozo, Benjamin Mordecai *lawyer*
Carey, J. Edwin *lawyer*
Carling, Francis *lawyer*
Carlson, Theodore Joshua *lawyer, retired utility company executive*
Carnell, Richard Scott *law educator*
Carter, James Hal, Jr. *lawyer*
Case, Stephen H. *lawyer*
Castel, P. Kevin *lawyer*
Cayea, Donald Joseph *lawyer*
Chaitman, Helen Davis *lawyer*
Chapnick, David B. *lawyer*
Chappell, John Charles *lawyer*
Chase, Edward Thornton *lawyer*
Chasey, Jacqueline *lawyer*
Chazen, Hartley James *lawyer*
Chell, Beverly C. *lawyer*
Chen, Wesley *lawyer*
Chiang, Yung Frank *law educator*
Chiarchiaro, Frank John *lawyer*
Chilstrom, Robert Meade *lawyer*
Chin, Sylvia Fung *lawyer*
Chirls, Richard *lawyer*
Cho, Tai Yong *lawyer*
Christensen, Henry, III *lawyer*
Christy, Arthur Hill *lawyer*
Chromow, Sheri P. *lawyer*
Clapman, Peter Carlyle *lawyer, insurance company executive*
Clark, Carolyn Cochran *lawyer*
Clark, Merrell Edward, Jr. *lawyer*
Clarke, John M. *lawyer*
Clary, Richard Wayland *lawyer*
Clayton, Joe Don *lawyer*
Clemen, John Douglas *lawyer*
Clemente, Robert Stephen *lawyer*
Cliff, Walter Conway *lawyer*
Coffee, John Collins, Jr. *legal educator*
Cohen, Edmund Stephen *lawyer*
Cohen, Edward Herschel *lawyer*
Cohen, Henry Rodgin *lawyer*
Cohen, Joel J. *lawyer, investment banker*
Cohen, Myron *lawyer, educator*
Cohen, Richard Gerard *lawyer*
Cohen, Robert Stephan *lawyer*
Cole, Charles Dewey, Jr. *lawyer*
Cole, Lewis George *lawyer*
Colfin, Bruce Elliott *lawyer, video producer*
Coll, John Peter, Jr. *lawyer*
Collins, J. Barclay, II *lawyer, oil company executive*
Collinson, Dale Stanley *lawyer*
Collyer, Michael *lawyer*
Conboy, Kenneth *lawyer, former federal judge*
Connelly, Albert R. *lawyer*
Connolly, Kevin Jude *lawyer*
Connor, John Thomas, Jr. *lawyer*
Conrad, Winthrop Brown, Jr. *lawyer*
Constantine, Jan Friedman *lawyer*
Conston, Henry Siegismund *lawyer*
Cook, Michael Lewis *lawyer*
Cook, Robert S., Jr. *lawyer*
†Coonelly, Francis X. *lawyer*
Cooney, John Patrick, Jr. *lawyer*
Cooper, Michael Anthony *lawyer*
Cooper, R. John, III *lawyer*
Cooper, Stephen Herbert *lawyer*
Corbin, Sol Neil *lawyer*
Costikyan, Edward N. *lawyer*
Cotter, James Michael *lawyer*
Cotton, Richard *lawyer*
Cowan, Wallace Edgar *lawyer*
Cowen, Edward S. *lawyer*
Cramer, Edward Morton *lawyer, music company executive*
Crane, Benjamin Field *lawyer*
Crane, Roger Ryan, Jr. *lawyer*
Cranney, Marilyn Kanrek *lawyer*
Crary, Miner Dunham, Jr. *lawyer*
Creel, Thomas Leonard *lawyer*
Crisona, James Joseph *lawyer*
Critchlow, Charles Howard *lawyer*
Crowell, Kenneth E. *lawyer, chemical engineer*
Cubitto, Robert J. *lawyer*
Cuiffo, Frank Wayne *lawyer*
Cuneo, Donald Lane *lawyer, educator*
Cunha, Mark Geoffrey *lawyer*
†Cuomo, Mario Matthew *lawyer, former governor*
Curtis, Susan Grace *lawyer*
Dacey, Eileen M. *lawyer*
Dallas, William Moffit, Jr. *lawyer*
D'Amato, Alfonse M. *lawyer, former senator*
Dankner, Jay Warren *lawyer*
†Dannhauser, Stephen J. *lawyer*
Darrell, Norris, Jr. *lawyer*
Darrow, Jill E(llen) *lawyer*
Das, Kalyan *lawyer*
†Davenport, Ronald *lawyer*
David, Reuben *lawyer*
Davidson, George Allan *lawyer*
Davidson, Mark Edward *lawyer*
Davidson, Robert Bruce *lawyer*
Davidson, Sheila Kearney *lawyer*
Davis, Deborah Lynn *lawyer*
Davis, Evan Anderson *lawyer*
Davis, Florence Ann *lawyer*
Davis, Michael S. *lawyer*
Davis, Richard Joel *lawyer, former government official*
Davis, Wendell, Jr. *lawyer*
Debo, Vincent Joseph *lawyer, manufacturing company executive*
Degener, Carol Marie-Laure *lawyer*
Della-Giustina, Jo-Ann Subotin *lawyer*
Demarest, Daniel Anthony *retired lawyer*
De Natale, Andrew Peter *lawyer*
DeOrchis, Vincent Moore *lawyer*
Derwin, Jordan *lawyer, consultant, actor*
de Saint Phalle, Pierre Claude *lawyer*
De Sear, Edward Marshall *lawyer*
Detjen, David Wheeler *lawyer*
Diamond, Bernard Robin *lawyer*
Diamond, David Howard *lawyer*
Dichter, Barry Joel *lawyer*
Diskant, Gregory L. *lawyer*
Doman, Nicholas R. *lawyer*
Donald, Norman Henderson, III *lawyer*
Donnellan, Andrew B., Jr. *lawyer*
Donovan, Maureen Driscoll *lawyer*
Dopf, Glenn William *lawyer*
Dorado, Marianne Gaertner *lawyer*
†Dorkey, Charles Edward, III *lawyer*
Dorsen, Norman *lawyer, educator*
Doyle, Joseph Anthony *retired lawyer*
Doyle, Paul Francis *lawyer*
Drebsky, Dennis Jay *lawyer*
Dreizen, Alison M. *lawyer*
†Dressel, Henry Francis *lawyer*
Drucker, Jacquelin F. *lawyer, arbitrator, mediator, educator, author*
Dubin, James Michael *lawyer*
Duffy, John Fitzgerald *law educator*
DuLaux, Russell Frederick *lawyer*
Dunham, Corydon Busnell *lawyer, broadcasting executive*
Dunham, Wolcott Balestier, Jr. *lawyer*
Dunn, M(orris) Douglas *lawyer*
Dunne, Gerard Francis *lawyer*
Earle, Victor Montagne, III *lawyer*
Edelbaum, Philip R. *lawyer*
Edelman, Paul Sterling *lawyer*
Edelson, Gilbert Seymour *lawyer*
Edgar, Harold Simmons Hull *legal educator*
†Edwards, Christine Annette *lawyer, securities firm executive*
Effel, Laura *lawyer*
Ehrenkranz, Joel S. *lawyer*
Einhorn, David Allen *lawyer*
Eisert, Edward Gaver *lawyer*
Elicker, Gordon Leonard *lawyer*
Elkin, Jeffrey H. *lawyer*
Ellis, Carolyn Terry *lawyer*
Elsen, Sheldon Howard *lawyer*
Emil, Arthur D. *lawyer*
Emrich, Edmund Michael *lawyer*
Epling, Richard Louis *lawyer*
Epstein, Jeremy G. *lawyer*
Epstein, Melvin *lawyer*
Ercklentz, Enno Wilhelm, Jr. *lawyer*
Ericson, Robert Walter *lawyer*
Estes, Richard Martin *lawyer*
Eustice, James Samuel *legal educator, lawyer*
Evans, Douglas Hayward *lawyer*
Evans, John Thomas *lawyer*
Evans, Martin Frederic *lawyer*
Evarts, William Maxwell, Jr. *lawyer*
Faber, Peter Lewis *lawyer*
Fales, Haliburton, II *lawyer*
Farber, Donald Clifford *lawyer, educator*
Farley, Robert Donald *lawyer, business executive*
Farnsworth, E(dward) Allan *lawyer, educator*
Fass, Peter Michael *lawyer, educator*
Faulkner, Walter Thomas *lawyer*
Feder, Saul E. *lawyer*
Feit, Glenn M. *lawyer*
Feldberg, Michael Svetkey *lawyer*
Felder, Myrna *lawyer*
Felder, Raoul Lionel *lawyer*
†Feldman, Eric Adam *law educator, academic administrator*
Feldman, Franklin *lawyer, printmaker*
Feldman, Jerome Ira *lawyer, patent development executive*
Feller, Lloyd Harris *lawyer*
Fensterstock, Blair Courtney *lawyer*
Ferguson, Milton Carr, Jr. *lawyer*
Ferguson, Robert Harry Munro *lawyer*
Fernandez, Jose Walfredo *lawyer*
Feuerstein, Bernard A. *lawyer*
Fewell, Charles Kenneth, Jr. *lawyer*
Fields, Robert Meddin *lawyer*
Fier, Elihu *lawyer*
Filler, Ronald Howard *lawyer*
Finch, Edward Ridley, Jr. *lawyer, diplomat, author, lecturer*
Fink, Robert Steven *lawyer, writer, educator*
Finkelstein, Allen Lewis *lawyer*
Finkelstein, Bernard *lawyer*
Finnerty, Joseph Gregory, Jr. *lawyer*
†Fiorilla, John Leopoldo *lawyer*
First, Harry *law educator*
Fischman, Bernard D. *lawyer*
Fishbein, Peter Melvin *lawyer*
Fisher, Ann Bailen *lawyer*
Fisher, Robert I. *lawyer*
Fishman, Fred Norman *lawyer*
Fishman, James Bart *lawyer*
Fishman, Marshall H. *lawyer*
Fishman, Mitchell Steven *lawyer*
Fishman, Paul J. *lawyer*
Fiske, Robert Bishop, Jr. *lawyer*
†Flaherty, Martin Stephen *law educator*
Flanagan, Deborah Mary *lawyer*
Fleder, Robert Charles *lawyer*
Fleischer, Arthur, Jr. *lawyer*
Fleischman, Edward Hirsh *lawyer*
Fleischman, Keith Martin *lawyer*
Fleming, Peter Emmet, Jr. *lawyer*
Fletcher, Anthony L. *lawyer*
Fletcher, George P. *law educator*
Fletcher, Raymond Russwald, Jr. *lawyer*
Flint, George Squire *lawyer*
Flom, Joseph Harold *lawyer*
Flumenbaum, Martin *lawyer*
Fodor, Susanna Serena *lawyer*
Fogg, Blaine Viles *lawyer*
†Folkenflik, Max *lawyer*
Fontana, Vincent Robert *lawyer*
Forstadt, Joseph Lawrence *lawyer*
Forster, Arnold *lawyer, author*
Fortenbaugh, Samuel Byrod, III *lawyer*
Foster, David Lee *lawyer*
Fox, Donald Thomas *lawyer*
Fox, Jeanne Marie *lawyer*
Fraidin, Stephen *lawyer*
Franck, Thomas Martin *law educator*
Frank, Lloyd *lawyer, retired chemical company executive*
Frankel, Benjamin Harrison *lawyer*
Frankel, Marvin E. *lawyer*
Franklin, Blake Timothy *lawyer*
Frazza, George S. *lawyer, business executive*
Fredericks, Wesley Charles, Jr. *lawyer*
Freedman, Gerald M. *lawyer*
Freeman, David John *lawyer*
Freilicher, Morton *lawyer*
French, John, III *lawyer*
Freund, Fred A. *retired lawyer*
Frey, Andrew Lewis *lawyer*
Fried, Burton Theodore *lawyer*
Fried, Donald David *lawyer*
Fried, Walter Jay *lawyer*
Friedman, Alan Roy *lawyer*
Friedman, Bart *lawyer*
Friedman, Eugene Stuart *lawyer*
Friedman, Robert Laurence *lawyer*
Friedman, Samuel Selig *lawyer*
Friedman, Stephen James *lawyer*
Friedman, Victor Stanley *lawyer*
Friedman, Wilbur Harvey *lawyer*
Frisch, Harry David *lawyer, consultant*
Frischling, Carl *lawyer*
Frohlich, Jack T. *lawyer*
†Fromkin, David Henry *law educator*
Frost, William Lee *lawyer*
Fry, Morton Harrison, II *lawyer*
Fryer, Judith Dorothy *lawyer*
Fuhrer, Arthur K. *lawyer*
Fuld, James Jeffrey *retired lawyer*
Fuzesi, Stephen, Jr. *lawyer, communications executive*
Gabay, Donald David *lawyer*
Galant, Herbert Lewis *lawyer*
Gallagher, Brian John *lawyer*
Gallagher, Terence Joseph *lawyer*
Gallantz, George Gerald *lawyer*
Gamboni, Ciro Anthony *lawyer*
Gams, Aaron Joseph *lawyer*
Ganz, David L. *lawyer*
Ganz, Howard Laurence *lawyer*
Ganzi, Victor Frederick *lawyer*
Garber, Robert Edward *lawyer, insurance company executive*
Gardner, Stephen David *lawyer, law educator*
Garfinkel, Barry Herbert *lawyer*
Garfinkel, Neil B. *lawyer*
Garland, Sylvia Dillof *lawyer*
Gartner, Murray *lawyer*
Garvey, Richard Anthony *lawyer*
Gassel, Philip Michael *lawyer*
Gatting, Carlene J. *lawyer*
Gelb, Judith Anne *lawyer*
Gelfman, Robert William *lawyer*
Genova, Diane Melisano *lawyer*
Genova, Joseph Steven *lawyer*
Geoghegan, Patricia *lawyer*
George, Beauford James, Jr. *lawyer, educator*
Gerard, Whitney Ian *lawyer*
Gerber, Robert Evan *lawyer*
Getnick, Neil Victor *lawyer*
Giannetti, Thomas Leonard *lawyer*
Gifford, William C. *lawyer*
Gill, E. Ann *lawyer*
Gillers, Stephen *law educator*
Gillespie, George Joseph, III *lawyer*
Gilligan, Mary Ann *law librarian*
Ginsberg, Ernest *lawyer, banker*
Gioiella, Russell Michael *lawyer*
Girden, Eugene Lawrence *lawyer*
Gitter, Max *lawyer*
Glanstein, Joel Charles *lawyer*
Glekel, Jeffrey Ives *lawyer*
Glickstein, Steven *lawyer*
†Glocer, Thomas Henry *lawyer*
Glusband, Steven Joseph *lawyer*
Glynn, Robert *lawyer, foundation chairman*
Goetz, Maurice Harold *lawyer*
Gold, Martin Elliot *lawyer, educator*
Gold, Simeon *lawyer*
Goldberg, Jay *lawyer*
Goldberg, Victor Paul *law educator*
Golden, Arthur F. *lawyer*
Goldman, Lawrence Saul *lawyer*
Goldman, Marvin Gerald *lawyer*
Goldsmith, Lee Selig *lawyer, physician*
Goldstein, Alvin *lawyer*
Goldstein, Charles Arthur *lawyer*
Goldstein, Howard Sheldon *lawyer*
Goldstein, Howard Warren *lawyer*
Goldstein, Kenneth B. *lawyer*
Goldstein, Marcia Landweber *lawyer*
Gooch, Anthony Cushing *lawyer*
Goodale, James Campbell *lawyer, media executive, television producer/host*

Goodfriend, Herbert Jay *lawyer*
†Goodman, Carol M. *lawyer*
Goodman, Gary A. *lawyer*
Goodridge, Allan D. *lawyer*
Goott, Alan F(ranklin) *lawyer*
Gordon, Michael Mackin *lawyer*
Gotthoffer, Lance *lawyer*
Gottlieb, Paul Mitchel *lawyer*
Gotts, Ilene Knable *lawyer*
Grad, Frank Paul *law educator, lawyer*
Graff, George Leonard *lawyer*
Graham, Jesse Japhet, II *lawyer*
Graham, Jul Eliot *lawyer, educator*
Granoff, Gary Charles *lawyer, investment company executive*
Grant, Stephen Allen *lawyer*
Grant, Susan Irene *lawyer*
Grashof, August Edward *lawyer*
Gray, Glenn Oliver *lawyer*
Green, Alvin *lawyer, consultant*
Green, Eric Howard *lawyer*
Green, Robert S. *lawyer*
Greenawalt, Robert Kent *lawyer, law educator*
Greenawalt, William Sloan *lawyer*
Greenbaum, Maurice Coleman *lawyer*
Greenberg, Daniel Herbert *lawyer*
Greenberg, Daniel Lawrence *lawyer*
Greenberg, Gary Howard *lawyer*
Greenberg, Ira George *lawyer*
Greenberg, Jack *lawyer, law educator*
Greenberg, Philip Alan *lawyer*
Greenberger, Howard Leroy *lawyer, educator*
Greene, Bernard Harold *lawyer*
Greene, Ira S. *lawyer*
Greenfield, Scott H. *lawyer*
Greenspon, Robert Alan *lawyer*
Greenwald, Harold *lawyer*
Greer, Allen Curtis, II *lawyer*
Greig, Robert Thomson *lawyer*
Greilsheimer, James Gans *lawyer*
Grew, Robert Ralph *lawyer*
Groban, Robert Sidney, Jr. *lawyer*
Groh, Jennifer Calfa *law librarian*
Gropper, Allan Louis *lawyer*
Gross, Richard Benjamin *lawyer*
Gross, Steven Ross *lawyer*
Grossman, Dan Steven *lawyer*
Grossman, Sanford *retired lawyer*
Gruen, Michael Stephan *lawyer*
Grunstein, Leonard *lawyer*
Gruson, Michael *lawyer*
Guggenheim, Martin Franklin *law educator*
Gunther, Jack Disbrow, Jr. *lawyer*
Gurfein, Richard Alan *lawyer*
Gussin, Arnold Marvin *lawyer*
Guth, Paul C. *lawyer*
Hackett, Kevin R. *lawyer*
Haffner, Alfred Loveland, Jr. *lawyer*
Hagendorn, William *lawyer*
Hager, Charles Read *lawyer*
Haig, Robert Leighton *lawyer*
Haims, Bruce David *lawyer*
Halberstam, Malvina *law educator, lawyer*
Halliday, Joseph William *lawyer*
Halperin, Richard E. *lawyer, holding company executive*
Hamburg, Charles Bruce *lawyer*
Hamel, Rodolphe *lawyer, pharmaceutical company executive*
Hamm, David Bernard *lawyer*
†Hammerman, Stephen Lawrence *lawyer, financial services company executive*
Handelsman, Lawrence Marc *lawyer*
Handler, Arthur M. *lawyer*
Hanson, Jean Elizabeth *lawyer*
Harbison, James Wesley, Jr. *lawyer*
Harper, Conrad Kenneth *lawyer, former government official*
Harper, Gerard Edward *lawyer*
Harris, Joel B(ruce) *lawyer*
Hart, Joseph Thomas Campbell *lawyer*
Hart, Robert M. *lawyer*
Hartzell, Andrew Cornelius, Jr. *lawyer, retired*
Hauser, Rita Eleanore Abrams *lawyer*
Hawes, Douglas Wesson *lawyer*
Hawke, Roger Jewett *lawyer*
Hayden, Raymond Paul *lawyer*
Hayes, Gerald Joseph *lawyer*
Head, Elizabeth *lawyer*
Healy, Harold Harris, Jr. *lawyer*
Healy, Nicholas Joseph *lawyer, educator*
Healy, Walter F. X. *lawyer*
Hearn, George Henry *lawyer, steamship corporate executive*
Heftler, Thomas E. *lawyer*
Heineman, Andrew David *lawyer*
Heisler, Stanley Dean *lawyer*
Helander, Robert Charles *lawyer*
Hellawell, Robert *law educator*
Hellenbrand, Samuel Henry *lawyer, diversified industry executive*
Heller, Edwin *lawyer*
Heller, Robert Martin *lawyer*
Hellman, Herbert Martin *lawyer*
Heming, Charles E. *lawyer*
Henderson, Donald Bernard, Jr. *lawyer*
Henderson, Harold Richard, Jr. *lawyer, labor relations executive*
Hendry, Andrew Delaney *lawyer, consumer products company executive*
Henry, Sally McDonald *lawyer*
Herbert Rose, Kathy Lynne *lawyer*
Herman, Kenneth Beaumont *lawyer*
Hernandez, Jacqueline Charmaine *lawyer*
Herold, Karl Guenter *lawyer*
Hersh, Robert Michael *lawyer, insurance company executive*
Hershman, Scott Edward *lawyer*
Herz, Andrew Lee *lawyer*
Herzeca, Lois Friedman *lawyer*
Hess, P. Gregory *lawyer*
Hessellund-Jensen, Peter Lykke *lawyer*
Hetherington, John Warner *lawyer*
Hiden, Robert Battaile, Jr. *lawyer*
Higgs, John H. *lawyer*
Hill, Alfred *lawyer, educator*
Hirsch, Barry *lawyer*
Hirsch, Daniel *lawyer*
Hirsch, Jerome S. *lawyer*
Hirschfeld, Michael *lawyer*
Hirshfield, Stuart *lawyer*
Hodes, Robert Bernard *lawyer*
Hoffman, David Nathaniel *lawyer*
Hoffman, Mathew *lawyer*
Hollyer, A(rthur) Rene *lawyer*
Holman, Bud George *lawyer*
Holmes, Stephen T. *political science and law educator*
Hooker, Wade Stuart, Jr. *lawyer*
Hopper, Walter Everett *lawyer*
Horowitz, Raymond J. *lawyer*
Howard, Susanne C. *lawyer*
Howe, Edwin A(lberts), Jr. *lawyer*
Howe, Richard Rives *lawyer*
Hritz, George F. *lawyer*
Hruska, Alan J. *lawyer*
Hudspeth, Stephen Mason *lawyer*
Hughes, Kevin Peter *lawyer*
Huhs, John I. *international lawyer*
Hulbert, Richard Woodward *lawyer*
Hull, Philip Glasgow *lawyer*
Hunt, Franklin Griggs *lawyer*
Hupper, John Roscoe *lawyer*
Hurlock, James Bickford *lawyer*
Hyde, David Rowley *lawyer*
Hyman, Jerome Elliot *lawyer*
Iannuzzi, John Nicholas *lawyer, author, educator*
Ichel, David W. *lawyer*
Ingram, Samuel William, Jr. *lawyer*
Insel, Michael S. *lawyer*
Intriligator, Marc Steven *lawyer*
Iovenko, Michael *lawyer*
Isaacson, Allen Ira *lawyer*
Iseman, Joseph Seeman *lawyer*
Isquith, Fred Taylor *lawyer*
Issler, Harry *lawyer*
Ivanick, Carol W. Trencher *lawyer*
Jackson, Raymond Sidney, Jr. *lawyer*
Jackson, Thomas Gene *lawyer*
Jackson, William Eldred *lawyer*
Jacob, Edwin J. *lawyer*
Jacob, Marvin Eugene *lawyer*
Jacobowitz, Harold Saul *lawyer*
Jacobs, Arnold Stephen *lawyer*
Jacobs, Robert Alan *lawyer*
Jacobson, Jeffrey Eli *lawyer, consultant*
Jacobson, Jerold Dennis *lawyer*
Jacobson, Sandra W. *lawyer*
Jacqueney, Stephanie A(lice) *lawyer*
Jaffe, Alan Steven *lawyer*
Jaffe, Mark M. *lawyer*
Jaffin, Charles Leonard *lawyer*
Jaglom, Andre Richard *lawyer*
Jander, Klaus Heinrich *lawyer*
Jassy, Everett Lewis *lawyer*
Javits, Eric Moses *lawyer*
Jessup, John Baker *lawyer*
Jeydel, Richard K. *lawyer*
Jiménez, Emilio *corporate lawyer*
Jinnett, Robert Jefferson *lawyer*
Joffe, Robert David *lawyer*
Johnson, Donald Raymond *lawyer*
Johnson, Lynne A. *lawyer*
Jones, Douglas W. *lawyer*
Joseph, Ellen R. *lawyer*
Joseph, Gregory Paul *lawyer*
Joseph, L. Anthony, Jr. *lawyer*
Joseph, Leonard *lawyer*
Josephson, William Howard *lawyer*
Juceam, Robert E. *lawyer*
Kaden, Lewis B. *law educator, lawyer*
Kahn, Alan Edwin *lawyer*
Kahn, Anthony F. *lawyer*
Kahn, Richard Dreyfus *lawyer*
Kailas, Leo George *lawyer*
Kalish, Arthur *lawyer*
Kalish, Myron *lawyer*
Kamin, Sherwin *lawyer*
Kaminsky, Arthur Charles *lawyer*
Kamm, Linda Heller *lawyer*
Kandel, William Lloyd *lawyer, lecturer, author*
Kane, Alice Theresa *lawyer*
Kane, Daniel Hipwell *lawyer*
Kane, Edward K. *lawyer*
Kane, Siegrun Dinklage *lawyer*
Kanner, Frederick W. *lawyer*
Kanusher, Lawrence Allen *lawyer*
Kaplan, Carl Eliot *lawyer*
Kaplan, Joseph Solte *lawyer*
Kaplan, Peter James *lawyer*
Karan, Paul Richard *lawyer*
Karatz, William Warren *lawyer*
Karmali, Rashida Alimahomed *lawyer*
†Kartiganer, Joseph *retired lawyer*
Kasowitz, Marc Elliot *lawyer*
Katsh, Salem Michael *lawyer*
Katsoris, Constantine Nicholas *lawyer, consultant*
Katz, Gregory *lawyer*
Katz, Jerome Charles *lawyer*
Katz, Ronald Scott *lawyer*
Kaufman, Arthur Stephen *lawyer*
Kaufman, Robert Max *lawyer*
Kaufmann, Ed *lawyer*
Kaufmann, Jack *lawyer*
Kavaler, Thomas J. *lawyer*
Kavoukjian, Michael Edward *lawyer*
Kaye, Stephen Rackow *lawyer*
Kazanjian, John Harold *lawyer*
Kean, Hamilton Fish *lawyer*
Keany, Sutton *lawyer*
Kelly, Daniel Grady, Jr. *lawyer*
Kelman, Edward Michael *lawyer*
Kende, Christopher Burgess *lawyer*
Kennedy, Michael John *lawyer*
Kenney, John Joseph *lawyer*
Keogh, Kevin *lawyer*
Kern, George Calvin, Jr. *lawyer*
Kernochan, John Marshall *lawyer, educator*
Kessel, Mark *lawyer*
Kessler, Jeffrey L. *lawyer*
Kheel, Theodore Woodrow *lawyer, arbitrator and mediator*
Kidd, John Edward *lawyer, corporate executive*
Kies, David M. *lawyer*
Kill, Lawrence *lawyer*
Kimball, Richard Arthur, Jr. *lawyer*
King, Henry Lawrence *lawyer*
King, Lawrence Philip *lawyer, educator*
Kinney, Stephen Hoyt, Jr. *lawyer*
Kinsolving, Augustus Blagden *lawyer*
Kinzler, Thomas Benjamin *lawyer*
Kirby, John Joseph, Jr. *lawyer*
Kirschbaum, Myron *lawyer*
Klapper, Molly *lawyer, educator*
Kleckner, Robert George, Jr. *lawyer*
Kleckner, Simone Marie *law librarian*
Kleinbard, Edward D. *lawyer*
Kleinberg, Norman Charles *lawyer*
Kline, Eugene Monroe *lawyer*
Klingsberg, David *lawyer*
Klink, Fredric J. *lawyer*
Klipstein, Robert Alan *lawyer*
Kmiotek-Welsh, Jacqueline *lawyer*
Knight, Townsend Jones *lawyer*
Knutson, David Harry *retired lawyer, banker*
Kober, Jane *lawyer*
Koblenz, Michael Robert *lawyer*
Kobrin, Lawrence Alan *lawyer*
Koch, Edward Richard *lawyer, accountant*
Koegel, William Fisher *lawyer*
Koenigsberg, Roberta Gale *lawyer, non-profit organization administrator*
Kolbe, Karl William, Jr. *lawyer*
Komaroff, Stanley *lawyer*
Koob, Charles Edward *lawyer*
Koral, Alan Max *lawyer*
Korff, Phyllis G. *lawyer*
Kornberg, Alan William *lawyer*
Kornreich, Edward Scott *lawyer*
Korotkin, Michael Paul *lawyer*
Kostelanetz, Boris *lawyer*
Kostelny, Albert Joseph, Jr. *lawyer*
Kourides, Peter Theologos *lawyer*
Kraemer, Lillian Elizabeth *lawyer*
Kramer, Alan Sharfsin *lawyer*
Kramer, Daniel Jonathan *lawyer*
Kramer, George P. *lawyer*
Krane, Steven Charles *lawyer*
Kranwinkle, Conrad Douglas *lawyer*
Krasner, Daniel Walter *lawyer*
Kreitzman, Ralph J. *lawyer*
Krieger, Sanford *lawyer*
Krikorian, Van Z. *lawyer*
Krinsly, Stuart Z. *lawyer, manufacturing company executive*
Kroll, Arthur Herbert *lawyer, educator, consultant*
Kroll, Sol *lawyer*
Kronman, Carol Jane *lawyer*
Krouse, George Raymond, Jr. *lawyer*
Krupman, William Allan *lawyer*
Krupp, Fred D. *lawyer, environmental agency executive*
†Kuby, Ronald L. *lawyer*
Kufeld, William Manuel *lawyer*
Kuh, Richard Henry *lawyer*
Kuhbach, Robert Gerdes *lawyer*
Kuklin, Anthony Bennett *lawyer*
Kumble, Steven Jay *lawyer*
Kuntz, Lee Allan *lawyer*
Kurtz, Jerome *lawyer, educator*
Kury, Bernard Edward *lawyer*
Kurzweil, Harvey *lawyer*
Lacovara, Philip Allen *lawyer*
Lacy, Robinson Burrell *lawyer*
Lambert, Judith A. Ungar *lawyer*
Lamia, Thomas Roger *lawyer*
Lanchner, Bertrand Martin *lawyer, advertising executive*
Landa, Howard Martin *lawyer, business executive*
Landau, Walter Loeber *lawyer*
Lane, Alvin S. *lawyer*
Lane, Arthur Alan *lawyer*
Lang, John Francis *lawyer*
Lange, Marvin Robert *lawyer*
Langer, Bruce Alden *lawyer*
Lantier, Brendan John *lawyer*
La Pointe, Laurence Michael *lawyer*
Larkin, Leo Paul, Jr. *lawyer*
Larose, Lawrence Alfred *lawyer*
La Rossa, James M(ichael) *lawyer*
Larsen, Robert Dhu *lawyer*
Lascher, Alan Alfred *lawyer*
Lasker, Richard S. *lawyer*
Lauer, Eliot *lawyer*
Laufer, Jacob *lawyer*
Laughlin, James Patrick *lawyer*
LeBlang, Skip Alan *lawyer*
Lebow, Mark Denis *lawyer*
Leckie, Gavin Frederick *lawyer, banker*
Lederer, Peter David *lawyer*
Lederman, Lawrence *lawyer, writer, educator*
Lee, In-Young *lawyer*
Lee, Jerome G. *lawyer*
Lee, Paul Lawrence *lawyer*
Leebron, David Wayne *law educator, dean*
Lefkowitz, Howard N. *lawyer*
Lefkowitz, Jerry *lawyer, accountant*
Lehman, Mark E. *lawyer*
Leichtling, Michael Alfred *lawyer*
Leland, Richard G. *lawyer*
Leonard, Edwin Deane *lawyer*
Lerner, Max Kasner *lawyer*
Lesch, Michael Oscar *lawyer*
Lesser, William Melville *lawyer*
Lester, Pamela Robin *lawyer*
Levie, Joseph Henry *lawyer*
Levin, Ezra Gurion *lawyer*
Levin, Michael Joseph *lawyer*
Levine, Alan *lawyer*
Levine, Laurence William *lawyer*
Levine, Lawrence Steven *lawyer*
Levine, Mark Leonard *lawyer*
Levine, Melvin Charles *lawyer*
Levine, Robert Jay *lawyer*
Levinson, Paul Howard *lawyer*
Levitan, James A. *lawyer*
Levy, Stanley Herbert *lawyer*
Lewyn, Thomas Mark *lawyer*
Lidsky, Ella *law librarian*
Liebman, Lance Malcolm *law educator, lawyer*
Lifland, William Thomas *lawyer*
Lin, Maria C. H. *lawyer*
Lindsay, George Peter *lawyer*
Lindskog, David Richard *lawyer*
Linsenmeyer, John Michael *lawyer*
Lipsky, Burton G. *lawyer*
Lipton, Charles Jules *lawyer*
Lipton, Martin *lawyer*
Lipton, Robert Steven *lawyer*
Liss, Norman *lawyer*
Loengard, Richard Otto, Jr. *lawyer*
Longstreth, Bevis *lawyer*
Loprest, Frank James Jr. *special assistant United States Attorney*
Lorch, Ernest Henry *lawyer*
Lore, Martin Maxwell *lawyer*
Loscalzo, Anthony Joseph *lawyer*
Loss, Margaret Ruth *lawyer*
Lowell, Stanley Herbert *lawyer*
Lowenfeld, Andreas Frank *law educator, arbitrator*
Lowenfels, Fred M. *lawyer*
Lowenfels, Lewis David *lawyer*
Lowenstein, Louis *legal educator*
Lowy, George Theodore *lawyer*
Lubell, David G. *lawyer*
Lupert, Leslie Allan *lawyer*
Luria, Mary Mercer *lawyer*
Lustenberger, Louis Charles, Jr. *lawyer*
Lutringer, Richard Emil *lawyer*
Lutzker, Elliot Howard *lawyer*
Lynch, Gerard E. *law educator*
Lynn, Theodore Stanley *lawyer*
Lyon, Carl Francis, Jr. *lawyer*
Macan, William Alexander, IV *lawyer*
Mack, Dennis Wayne *lawyer*
MacKinnon, John Alexander *lawyer*
MacLean, Babcock *lawyer*
MacRae, Cameron Farquhar, III *lawyer*
Macris, Michael *lawyer*
Madden, Donald Paul *lawyer*
Madsen, Stephen Stewart *lawyer*
Magnano, Joseph Sebastian *lawyer*
Mahon, Arthur J. *lawyer*
Maidman, Richard Harvey Mortimer *lawyer*
Maitland, Guy Edison Clay *lawyer*
Malina, Michael *lawyer*
Malkin, Michael M. *lawyer*
Malkin, Peter Laurence *lawyer*
Mandelstam, Charles Lawrence *lawyer*
Maneker, Morton M. *lawyer*
Maney, Michael Mason *lawyer*
Mangia, Angelo James *lawyer*
Mann, Pamela A. *lawyer*
Mantle, Raymond Allan *lawyer*
Marcus, Eric Peter *lawyer*
Marcus, Maria Lenhoff *lawyer, law educator*
Marcus, Norman *lawyer*
Marcusa, Fred Haye *lawyer*
Margulis, Howard Lee *lawyer*
Marino, Michael Frank, III *lawyer*
Marlin, Richard *lawyer*
†Maroney, Thomas Joseph *lawyer*
Marshall, Sheila Hermes *lawyer*
Martin, George J., Jr. *lawyer*
Martin, Malcolm Elliot *lawyer*
Martone, Patricia Ann *lawyer*
†Marx, Herbert Lewis, Jr. *arbitrator*
Marx, Owen Cox *lawyer*
Marzulli, John Anthony, Jr. *lawyer*
Masin, Michael Terry *lawyer*
Maslow, Will *lawyer, association executive*
Masters, Jon Joseph *corporate governance consultant, mediator*
Materna, Joseph Anthony *lawyer*
Mathers, William Harris *lawyer*
Matteson, William Bleecker *lawyer*
Matthews, Edwin Spencer, Jr. *lawyer*
Matus, Wayne Charles *lawyer*
Maulsby, Allen Farish *lawyer*
Maxfield, Guy Budd *lawyer, educator*
Mayerson, Sandra Elaine *lawyer*
Mayesh, Jay Philip *lawyer*
Mazza, Thomas Carmen *lawyer*
McBryde, Thomas Henry *lawyer*
McCarthy, Robert Emmett *lawyer*
McClimon, Timothy John *lawyer*
McClung, Richard Goehring *lawyer*
McCormack, Howard Michael *lawyer*
McCormick, Hugh Thomas *lawyer*
McDavid, William Henry *lawyer*
McDermott, Richard T. *lawyer, educator*
†McDonald, Joel Matthews *lawyer*
McGanney, Thomas *lawyer*
Mc Goldrick, John Gardiner *retired lawyer*
McGoldrick, John Lewis *lawyer*
McGrath, Christopher Thomas *lawyer*
McGrath, Thomas J. *lawyer, writer, film producer*
McGuire, Eugene Guenard *lawyer*
Mc Inerney, Denis *lawyer*
McKenna, Peter Dennis *lawyer*
McLaughlin, Joseph *lawyer*
McMahon, James Charles *lawyer*
McMeen, Elmer Ellsworth, III *lawyer, guitarist*
McNally, John Joseph *lawyer*
McNamara, J(ohn) Donald *retired lawyer, business executive*
Mc Nicol, Donald Edward *lawyer*
McSherry, William John, Jr. *lawyer, consultant*
Medina, Standish Forde, Jr. *lawyer*
Meiklejohn, Donald Stuart *lawyer*
Melnik, Selinda A. *lawyer*
Menack, Steven Boyd *lawyer, mediator*
Mentz, Lawrence *lawyer*
Mercorella, Anthony J. *lawyer, former state supreme court justice*
Meron, Theodor *law educator, researcher*
Merow, John Edward *lawyer*
Merritt, Bruce Gordon *lawyer*
Mestres, Ricardo Angelo, Jr. *lawyer*
Metsch-Ampel, Glenn Randy *lawyer, fundraiser*
Michaelson, Arthur M. *lawyer*
Michel, Clifford Lloyd *lawyer, investment executive*
Middendorf, Henry Stump, Jr. *lawyer*
Milgrim, Roger Michael *lawyer*
Miller, Arthur Madden *lawyer, investment banker*
Miller, Charles Hampton *lawyer*
Miller, David *lawyer, advertising executive*
Miller, Harvey R. *lawyer, bankruptcy reorganization specialist*
Miller, Paul S(amuel) *lawyer*
Miller, Peggy A(nn) *lawyer*
Miller, Phebe Condict *lawyer, financial executive*
Miller, Richard Allan *lawyer*
Miller, Richard Steven *lawyer*
Miller, Sam Scott *lawyer*
Miller, Steven Scott *lawyer*
Millstein, Ira M. *lawyer, lecturer*
Milmed, Paul Kussy *lawyer*
Minkowitz, Martin *lawyer, former state government official*
Minuse, Catherine Jean *lawyer*
Modlin, Howard S. *lawyer*
Moerdler, Charles Gerard *lawyer*
Molnar, Lawrence *lawyer*
Moloney, Thomas Joseph *lawyer*
Monge, Jay Parry *lawyer*
Montgomery, Robert Humphrey, Jr. *lawyer*
Moore, Donald Francis *lawyer*
Moore, Franklin Hall, Jr. *lawyer*
Moore, John Joseph *lawyer*
Moore, Thomas Ronald (Lord Bridestowe) *lawyer*
Morgan, Frank Edward, II *lawyer*
Morgenthau, Robert Morris *prosecutor*
Morphy, James Calvin *lawyer*
Morris, Edward William, Jr. *lawyer*
Morris, Eugene Jerome *lawyer*
Mortimer, Peter Michael *lawyer*
Moskin, Morton *lawyer*
Moss, Lawrence Craig *lawyer*
Moss, William John *lawyer*
Most, Jack Lawrence *lawyer, consultant*
Moy, Mary Anastasia *lawyer*
Muccia, Joseph William *lawyer*
Mukamal, Steven Sasoon *lawyer*
Mullaney, Thomas Joseph *lawyer*
Mullen, Peter P. *lawyer*
Muller, Frank *mediator, arbitrator*
Mulligan, Jeremiah T. *lawyer*
Mullman, Michael S. *lawyer*
Mundheim, Robert Harry *law educator*
Munzer, Stephen Ira *lawyer*
Murase, Jiro *lawyer*

Murphy, Arthur William *lawyer, educator*
Murphy, James Gilmartin *lawyer*
Muskin, Victor Philip *lawyer*
Myerson, Toby Salter *lawyer*
Naftalis, Gary Philip *lawyer, educator*
Nance, Allan Taylor *retired lawyer*
Nash, Paul LeNoir *lawyer*
Nassau, Michael Jay *lawyer*
Nathan, Andrew Jonathan *lawyer, real estate developer*
Nathan, Frederic Solis *lawyer*
Nemser, Earl Harold *lawyer*
Neuwirth, Alan James *lawyer*
Neveloff, Jay A. *lawyer*
Nevins, Arthur Gerard, Jr. *lawyer*
Newcombe, George Michael *lawyer*
Newman, Fredric Samuel *lawyer, business executive*
Newman, Howard Neal *lawyer, educator*
Newman, Lawrence Walker *lawyer*
Nicholls, Richard H. *lawyer*
Nimetz, Matthew *lawyer*
Nimkin, Bernard William *retired lawyer*
Nolan, Terrance Joseph, Jr. *lawyer*
Nonna, John Michael *lawyer*
Nordquist, Stephen Glos *lawyer*
Norfolk, William Ray *lawyer*
North, Steven Edward *lawyer*
Novikoff, Harold Stephen *lawyer*
Nusbacher, Gloria Weinberg *lawyer*
Oberly, Kathryn Anne *lawyer*
Oberman, Michael Stewart *lawyer*
O'Brien, Donal Clare, Jr. *lawyer*
O'Brien, John Graham *lawyer*
O'Brien, Kevin J. *lawyer*
O'Connell, Margaret Sullivan *lawyer*
O'Connor, William Matthew *lawyer*
O'Dea, Dennis Michael *lawyer*
O'Donnell, John Logan *lawyer*
Oechler, Henry John, Jr. *lawyer*
Ogden, Alfred *lawyer*
O'Grady, John Joseph, III *lawyer*
O'Hara, Alfred Peck *lawyer*
Olick, Philip Stewart *lawyer*
Oliensis, Sheldon *lawyer*
O'Neil, John Joseph *lawyer*
Oppenheimer, Martin J. *lawyer*
Orden, Stewart L. *lawyer*
O'Rorke, James Francis, Jr. *lawyer*
Osborn, Donald Robert *lawyer*
Oshima, Michael W. *lawyer*
Ostrager, Barry Robert *lawyer*
O'Sullivan, Thomas J. *lawyer*
Owen, Robert Dewit *lawyer*
Oxman, David Craig *lawyer*
Pack, Leonard Brecher *lawyer*
Packard, Stephen Michael *lawyer*
Paladino, Daniel R. *lawyer, beverage corporation executive*
Paley, Alan H. *lawyer*
Palmieri, Victor Henry *lawyer, business executive*
Panken, Peter Michael *lawyer*
Papernik, Joel Ira *lawyer*
Parish, J. Michael *lawyer, writer*
Parver, Jane W. *lawyer*
Paul, Eve W. *lawyer*
Paul, Herbert Morton *lawyer, accountant, taxation educator*
Paul, James William *lawyer*
Pavia, George M. *lawyer*
Peaslee, James M. *lawyer*
Peet, Charles D., Jr. *lawyer*
Peloso, John Francis Xavier *lawyer*
Pelster, William Charles *lawyer*
Pelz, Robert Leon *lawyer*
Pennoyer, Paul Geddes, Jr. *lawyer*
Pennoyer, Robert M. *lawyer*
Pepper, Allan Michael *lawyer*
Peppers, Jerry P. *lawyer*
Perkiel, Mitchel H. *lawyer*
Perkins, Roswell Burchard *lawyer*
Perlmuth, William Alan *lawyer*
Perschetz, Martin L. *lawyer*
Pershan, Richard Henry *lawyer*
Peters, Alton Emil *lawyer*
Peterson, Charles Gordon *retired lawyer*
Petkanics, Bryan G. *lawyer*
Petraro, Vincent L. *lawyer*
Pettibone, Peter John *lawyer*
Pfeffer, David H. *lawyer*
Phillips, Anthony Francis *lawyer*
Phillips, Barnet, IV *lawyer*
Phillips, Charles Gorham *lawyer*
Phillips, Pamela Kim *lawyer*
Pierce, Morton Allen *lawyer*
Pierpoint, Powell *lawyer*
Pietrzak, Alfred Robert *lawyer*
Pike, Laurence Bruce *retired lawyer*
Pinczower, Kenneth Ephraim *lawyer*
Plottel, Roland *lawyer*
Polak, Werner L. *lawyer*
Polevoy, Nancy Tally *lawyer, social worker, genealogist*
Polisar, Leonard Myers *lawyer*
Pollack, Stanley P. *lawyer*
Pollak, Martin Marshall *lawyer, training company executive*
Pollan, Stephen Michael *lawyer, personal finance expert, speaker, author*
Posen, Susan Orzack *lawyer*
Posner, Louis Joseph *lawyer, accountant*
Powell, James Henry *lawyer*
Powell, Richard Gordon *retired lawyer*
Preble, Laurence George *lawyer*
Preiskel, Barbara Scott *lawyer, association executive*
Prem, F. Herbert, Jr. *lawyer*
Price, Robert *lawyer, media executive, investment banker*
Primps, William Guthrie *lawyer*
Prince, Charles O., III *lawyer*
Puleo, Frank Charles *lawyer*
†Quale, Andrew Christopher, Jr. *lawyer*
†Quarles, Randal Keith *lawyer*
Quillen, Cecil Dyer, III *lawyer*
Quinlan, Guy Christian *lawyer*
Quinn, Francis F. *lawyer*
Quinn, Yvonne Susan *lawyer*
Raab, Sheldon *lawyer*
Rabb, Bruce *lawyer*
Rabb, Maxwell M. *lawyer, former ambassador*
Rabin, Jack *lawyer*
Radon, Jenik Richard *lawyer*
Rahm, David Alan *lawyer*
Rahm, Susan Berkman *lawyer*
Ralli, Constantine Pandia *lawyer*
Rand, Harry Israel *lawyer*
Rand, William *lawyer, former state justice*
Rankin, Clyde Evan, III *lawyer*
Rapoport, Bernard Robert *lawyer*
Rappaport, Charles Owen *lawyer*
Ray, Jeanne Cullinan *lawyer, insurance company executive*
Raylesberg, Alan Ira *lawyer*
Redlich, Norman *lawyer, educator*
Reibstein, Richard Jay *lawyer*
Reicher, Robert Jay *lawyer*
Reid, Edward Snover, III *lawyer*
Reid, John Phillip *law educator*
Reilly, Conor Desmond *lawyer*
Reilly, Edward Arthur *lawyer*
Reinhold, Richard Lawrence *lawyer*
Reinthaler, Richard Walter *lawyer*
Reiss, Steven Alan *lawyer, law educator*
Rembar, Charles (Isaiah) *lawyer, writer*
Resor, Stanley Rogers *lawyer*
Reverdin, Bernard J. *lawyer*
Rice, Donald Sands *lawyer, entreprenuer*
Rice, Joseph Lee, III *lawyer*
Rich, R(obert) Bruce *lawyer*
Richards, David Alan *lawyer*
Richman, Martin Franklin *lawyer*
Rifkind, Robert S(inger) *lawyer*
Rikon, Michael *lawyer*
Ring, Renee Etheline *lawyer*
Ringel, Dean *lawyer*
Ringer, James Milton *lawyer*
Ritter, Ann L. *lawyer*
Rittman, Frank Sears *lawyer*
Roberts, Burton Bennett *lawyer, retired judge*
Roberts, Sidney I. *lawyer*
Robertson, Edwin David *lawyer*
Robinowitz, Stuart *lawyer*
Robinson, Barbara Paul *lawyer*
Robinson, Irwin Jay *lawyer*
Rodman, Leroy Eli *lawyer*
Rodriguez, Vincent Angel *lawyer*
Roe, Mark J. *law educator*
Rogers, Theodore Otto, Jr. *lawyer*
Rohrbach, Heidi A. *lawyer*
Rolfe, Ronald Stuart *lawyer*
Romans, John Niebrugge *lawyer*
Rooney, Paul C., Jr. *lawyer*
Rosa, Margarita *agency chief executive, lawyer*
Rosdeitcher, Sidney Samuel *lawyer*
Rosen, Richard Lewis *lawyer, real estate developer*
Rosenberg, Alan Stewart *lawyer*
Rosenberg, Gary Marc *lawyer*
Rosenberg, Jerome Ira *lawyer*
Rosenberg, Stephen *lawyer*
Rosenblum, Scott S. *lawyer*
†Rosenblum, William F., Jr. *lawyer*
Rosendahl, Roger Wayne *lawyer*
Rosenfeld, Arthur H. *lawyer, publisher*
Rosenfeld, Steven B. *lawyer*
Rosensaft, Menachem Zwi *lawyer, author, foundation executive, community activist*
Rosenzweig, Charles Leonard *lawyer*
Rosenzweig, Theodore B. *lawyer*
Rosow, Stuart L. *lawyer*
Ross, Matthew *lawyer*
Roth, Eric M. *lawyer*
Roth, Judith Shulman *lawyer*
Roth, Paul Norman *lawyer*
Roth, Richard Alan *lawyer*
Rothenberg, Stanley *lawyer*
Rothman, Bernard *lawyer*
Rothman, Henry Isaac *lawyer*
Rotstein, Andrew David *lawyer*
Rover, Edward Frank *lawyer*
Rovine, Arthur William *lawyer*
Rozel, Samuel Joseph *lawyer*
Rubenfeld, Stanley Irwin *lawyer*
Rubenstein, Joshua Seth *lawyer*
Rubin, Howard Jeffrey *lawyer*
Rubin, Jane Lockhart Gregory *lawyer, foundation executive*
Rubin, Richard Allan *lawyer*
Rubinstein, Frederic Armand *lawyer*
Rudoff, Sheldon *lawyer*
Ruebhausen, Oscar Melick *lawyer*
Ruegger, Philip T., III *lawyer*
Rusmisel, Stephen R. *lawyer*
Russo, Gregory Thomas *lawyer*
Russo, Thomas Anthony *lawyer*
Russotti, Philip Anthony *lawyer*
Ryan, J. Richard *lawyer*
Sabel, Bradley Kent *lawyer*
Sachs, David *lawyer*
Sacks, Ira Stephen *lawyer*
Safer, Jay Gerald *lawyer*
Saft, Stuart Mark *lawyer*
Sahid, Joseph Robert *lawyer*
Saiman, Martin S. *lawyer*
Salman, Robert Ronald *lawyer*
Salter, Kevin Thornton *lawyer*
Samuel, Raphael *lawyer*
Samuels, Leslie B. *lawyer*
Sandler, Ross *law educator*
†Sanford, Eric *lawyer*
Sanseverino, Raymond Anthony *lawyer*
Sassoon, Andre Gabriel *lawyer*
Satine, Barry Roy *lawyer*
Saunders, Mark A. *lawyer*
Saunders, Paul Christopher *lawyer*
Savell, Polly Carolyn *lawyer*
Savitt, Susan Schenkel *lawyer*
Savrin, Louis *lawyer*
Schachter, Oscar *lawyer, educator, arbitrator*
Schade, Malcolm Robert *lawyer*
Schallert, Edwin Glenn *lawyer*
Schapiro, Donald *lawyer*
†Scheck, Barry C. *legal association administrator, educator*
Scheiman, Eugene R. *lawyer*
Scheler, Brad Eric *lawyer*
Scher, Irving *lawyer*
Schirmeister, Charles F. *lawyer*
Schizer, Zevie Baruch *lawyer*
Schlesinger, Sanford Joel *lawyer*
Schmertz, Eric Joseph *lawyer, educator*
Schmidt, Charles Edward *lawyer*
Schmidt, Daniel Edward, IV *lawyer*
Schmidt, Joseph W. *lawyer*
Schmolka, Leo Louis *law educator*
Schneider, Harold Lawrence *lawyer*
Schneider, Howard *lawyer*
Schneider, Willys Hope *lawyer*
Schneiderman, Irwin *lawyer*
Schorr, Brian Lewis *lawyer, business executive*
Schreiber, Paul Solomon *lawyer*
Schreyer, Leslie John *lawyer*
Schroeder, Edmund R. *lawyer*
Schueller, Thomas George *lawyer*
Schulte, Stephen John *lawyer, educator*
Schwab, Terrance W. *lawyer*
Schwartz, Barry Fredric *lawyer, diversified holding company executive*
Schwartz, Carol Vivian *lawyer*
Schwartz, Herbert Frederick *lawyer*
Schwartz, James Evan *lawyer*
Schwartz, Marvin *lawyer*
Schwartz, Renee Gerstler *lawyer*
Schwartz, William *lawyer, educator*
Schwarz, Frederick August Otto, Jr. *lawyer*
Schwind, Michael Angelo *law educator*
Sederbaum, Arthur David *lawyer*
Sedgwick, Robert Minturn *lawyer*
Segall, Harold Abraham *lawyer*
Seidel, Selvyn *lawyer, educator*
Seifert, Thomas Lloyd *lawyer*
Seiff, Eric A. *lawyer*
Seigel, Stuart Evan *lawyer*
Seligman, Delice *lawyer*
Seltzer, Richard C. *lawyer*
Selver, Paul Darryl *lawyer*
Semaya, Francine Levitt *lawyer*
Senzel, Martin Lee *lawyer*
Serbaroli, Francis J. *lawyer, educator, writer*
Serota, Susan Perlstadt *lawyer*
Setrakian, Berge *lawyer*
Seward, George Chester *lawyer*
Sexton, John Edward *lawyer, dean, law educator*
Seymour, Everett Hedden, Jr. *lawyer*
†Shaikh, Ayaz R. *lawyer*
Shanman, James Alan *lawyer*
Shapiro, Jerome Gerson *lawyer*
Shaw, Robert Bernard *retired lawyer*
Shays, Rona Joyce *lawyer*
Shea, Edward Emmett *lawyer, educator, author*
Shea, James William *lawyer*
Shechtman, Ronald H. *lawyer*
Sheehan, Robert C. *lawyer*
Sheft, Peter Ian *lawyer*
Shelby, Jerome *lawyer*
Shen, Michael *lawyer*
Sherman, Jonathan Henry *lawyer*
Sherman, Randolph S. *lawyer*
Shientag, Florence Perlow *lawyer*
Shimer, Zachary *lawyer*
Short, Skip *lawyer*
Shorter, James Russell, Jr. *lawyer*
Shoss, Cynthia Renée *lawyer*
Shyer, John D. *lawyer*
Sidamon-Eristoff, Constantine *lawyer*
Siegel, Edward M. *lawyer*
Siegel, Jeffrey Norton *lawyer*
Siegel, Stanley *lawyer, educator*
Siegel, Sylvia *law librarian*
Sigmond, Carol Ann *lawyer*
Silberberg, Richard Howard *lawyer*
Silberman, John Alan *lawyer*
Silkenat, James Robert *lawyer*
Silleck, Harry Garrison *lawyer*
Siller, Stephen I. *lawyer*
Silverberg, Jay L. *lawyer*
Silverberg, Michael Joel *lawyer*
Silverman, Arthur Charles *lawyer*
Silverman, Moses *lawyer*
Silverman, Samuel Joshua *lawyer*
Silvers, Eileen S. *lawyer*
Simon, Michael Scott *lawyer*
Simone, Joseph R. *lawyer*
Simons, Albert, III *lawyer*
Singer, Jeffrey *lawyer*
Sirkin, Michael S. *lawyer*
Siskind, Arthur *lawyer, director*
Siskind, Donald Henry *lawyer*
Sitrick, James Baker *lawyer*
Skigen, Patricia Sue *lawyer*
Skirnick, Robert Andrew *lawyer*
Sklaren, Cary Stewart *lawyer*
Skolnick, Jerome H. *law educator*
Skolnik, Miriam *lawyer*
Sladkus, Harvey Ira *lawyer*
Slonaker, Norman Dale *lawyer*
Small, Jonathan Andrew *lawyer*
Smiley, Guy Ian *lawyer*
Smit, Hans *law educator, academic administrator, lawyer*
Smith, Bradley Youle *lawyer*
Smith, Edward Paul, Jr. *lawyer*
Smith, James Walker *lawyer*
Smith, Morton Alan *lawyer*
Smith, Robert Everett *lawyer*
Smith, Stuart A. *lawyer*
Smith, Vincent Milton *lawyer, designer, consultant*
Snitow, Charles *lawyer*
Sommers, George R. *lawyer*
Sorensen, Theodore Chaikin *lawyer, former special counsel to President of United States*
Sorkin, Laurence Truman *lawyer*
Sovern, Michael Ira *law educator*
Soyster, Margaret Blair *lawyer*
Spanbock, Maurice Samuel *lawyer*
Spear, Harvey M. *lawyer*
Sperling, Allan George *lawyer*
Spivack, Gordon Bernard *lawyer, lecturer*
Springer, David Edward *lawyer*
Squire, Walter Charles *lawyer*
Staffa, Thomas Francis *lawyer*
Stakias, G. Michael *lawyer, merchant banker*
Stamm, Charles H. *lawyer*
Stanger, Abraham M. *lawyer*
Starer, Brian D. *lawyer*
Stathis, Nicholas John *lawyer*
Stein, Stephen William *lawyer*
Steinbach, Harold I. *lawyer*
Steinberg, Howard Eli *lawyer, holding company executive, public official*
Steiner, David Miller *lawyer*
Stephenson, Alan Clements *lawyer*
Sternman, Joel W. *lawyer*
Steuer, Richard Marc *lawyer*
Stewart, Charles Evan *lawyer*
Stewart, Duncan James *lawyer*
Stewart, Richard Burleson *lawyer, educator*
Stoffel, Klaus Peter *lawyer*
Stoll, Neal Richard *lawyer*
Stone, David Philip *lawyer*
Stone, Merrill Brent *lawyer*
Storette, Ronald Frank *lawyer*
Stratton, Walter Love *lawyer*
Straub, Chester John *judge*
Strauss, Gary Joseph *lawyer*
Strickon, Harvey Alan *lawyer*
Strom, Milton Gary *lawyer*
Strossen, Nadine *law educator, human rights activist*
Strougo, Robert Isaac *lawyer*
Strum, Jay Gerson *lawyer*
Struve, Guy Miller *lawyer*
Subin, Florence *lawyer*
Sugarman, Irwin J. *lawyer*
Sugarman, Robert Gary *lawyer*
†Sugden, Samuel M. *lawyer*
Suhr, J. Nicholas *lawyer*
†Sun, Jeffrey C. *legal educator*
Supino, Anthony Martin *lawyer*
Sussman, Alexander Ralph *lawyer*
Sussman, David William *lawyer*
Sutter, Laurence Brener *lawyer*
Sweeney, Thomas Joseph, Jr. *lawyer*
Tancredi, Laurence Richard *law and psychiatry educator, physician*
Taylor, Job, III *lawyer*
Taylor, John Chestnut, III *lawyer*
Taylor, Richard Trelore *retired lawyer*
Teclaff, Ludwik Andrzej *law educator, consultant, author, lawyer*
Teich, Howard Bernard *lawyer, activist, public affairs specialist*
Teiman, Richard B. *lawyer*
Tengi, Frank R. *lawyer, insurance company executive*
Tenney, Dudley Bradstreet *lawyer*
Terrell, J. Anthony *lawyer*
Terry, Frederick Arthur, Jr. *lawyer*
Terry, James Joseph, Jr. *lawyer*
Testa, Michael Harold *lawyer*
Thackeray, Jonathan E. *lawyer*
Thal, Steven Henry *lawyer*
Thalacker, Arbie Robert *lawyer*
Thomas, Robert Morton, Jr. *lawyer*
Thomas, Roger Warren *lawyer*
Thompson, Katherine Genevieve *lawyer*
Thoyer, Judith Reinhardt *lawyer*
Tighe, Maria Theresa *paralegal*
Tillinghast, David Rollhaus *lawyer*
Todd, Ronald Gary *lawyer*
Tondel, Lawrence Chapman *lawyer*
Tract, Marc Mitchell *lawyer*
Tracy, Janet Ruth *legal educator, librarian*
Tramontine, John Orlando *lawyer*
Traube, Victoria Gilbert *lawyer*
Traum, Jerome S. *lawyer*
Treadway, James Curran *lawyer, investment company executive, former government official*
Trost, J. Ronald *lawyer*
Trubin, John *lawyer*
Tuck, Edward Hallam *lawyer*
Tulchin, David Bruce *lawyer*
Tung, Ko-Yung *lawyer*
Turner, E. Deane *lawyer*
Udell, Richard *lawyer*
Ullman, Leo Solomon *lawyer*
Ulrey, Prescott David *lawyer*
Underberg, Mark Alan *lawyer*
Uram, Gerald Robert *lawyer*
Urowsky, Richard J. *lawyer*
Vachss, Andrew Henry *lawyer, author, juvenile justice and child abuse consultant*
Vance, Cyrus Roberts *lawyer, former government official*
Van Gorder, John Frederic *lawyer*
Van Gundy, Gregory Frank *lawyer*
Van Setter, George Gerard *lawyer*
Varet, Michael A. *lawyer*
Vassallo, Edward E. *lawyer*
Vassallo, John A. *lawyer*
Vega, Matias Alfonso *lawyer*
Vernon, Darryl Mitchell *lawyer*
Versfelt, David Scott *lawyer*
Viener, John D. *lawyer*
Vig, Vernon Edward *lawyer*
Vitkowsky, Vincent Joseph *lawyer*
Vittor, Kenneth Mark *lawyer*
Vogel, Eugene Lewis *lawyer*
Volckhausen, William Alexander *lawyer, banker*
Volk, Stephen Richard *lawyer*
von Mehren, Robert Brandt *lawyer, retired*
Vyskocil, Mary Kay *lawyer*
Wachtel, Norman Jay *lawyer*
Wailand, George *lawyer*
Wainwright, Carroll Livingston, Jr. *lawyer*
Waks, Jay Warren *lawyer*
Waksman, Ted Stewart *lawyer*
Wald, Bernard Joseph *lawyer*
Wallace, Nora Ann *lawyer*
Wallace, Walter C. *lawyer, government official*
Wallach, Eric Jean *lawyer*
†Wallach, Evan Jonathan *judge, international law educator*
Wallance, Gregory J. *lawyer*
Wallin, James Peter *lawyer*
Walpin, Gerald *lawyer*
Warden, John L. *lawyer*
Warner, Edward Waide, Jr. *lawyer*
Warren, Irwin Howard *lawyer*
Warren, William Bradford *lawyer*
Warren, William Clements *law educator*
Warshauer, Irene Conrad *lawyer*
Washburn, David Thacher *lawyer*
Watanabe, Roy Noboru *lawyer*
Watson, Solomon Brown, IV *lawyer, business executive*
Watts, David Eide *lawyer*
Wechsler, Herbert *retired legal educator*
Weiksner, Sandra S. *lawyer*
Weil, Gilbert Harry *lawyer*
Weinberg, Herschel Mayer *lawyer*
Weinberger, Harold Paul *lawyer*
Weiner, Andrew Jay *lawyer*
Weiner, Earl David *lawyer*
Weiner, Stephen Arthur *lawyer*
Weinschel, Alan Jay *lawyer*
Weinstein, Mark Michael *lawyer*
Weinstein, Ruth Joseph *lawyer*
Weinstock, Leonard *lawyer*
Weir, John Keeley *lawyer*
Weir, Peter Frank *lawyer*
Weisbrod, Carl *lawyer, public official*
Weisburd, Steven I. *lawyer*
Weiser, Martin Jay *lawyer*
Weiss, Lawrence N. *lawyer*
Weitz, Harvey *lawyer*
Weld, Jonathan Minot *lawyer*
Welikson, Jeffrey Alan *lawyer*
Welles, James Bell, Jr. *lawyer*
Wellington, Harry Hillel *lawyer, educator*
Welt, Philip Stanley *lawyer, consultant*
Wemple, William *lawyer*
Wender, Ira Tensard *lawyer*
Werner, Robert L. *lawyer*
Wesely, Edwin Joseph *lawyer*
Westin, David Lawrence *lawyer*
Wexelbaum, Michael *lawyer*
Weyher, Harry Frederick *lawyer*
Whelan, Stephen Thomas *lawyer*
Whelchel, Betty Anne *lawyer*
White, Harry Edward, Jr. *lawyer*
White, John Patrick *lawyer*
White, Mary Jo *prosecutor*
Whoriskey, Robert Donald *lawyer*
Wiegley, Roger Douglas *lawyer*

Wilcox, John Caven *lawyer, corporate consultant*
Wilder, Charles Willoughby *lawyer, consultant*
Wilkinson, John Hart *lawyer*
Williams, Lowell Craig *lawyer, employee relations executive*
Williams, Michael *lawyer, associate*
Williamson, Douglas Franklin, Jr. *lawyer*
Willis, William Ervin *lawyer*
Willkie, Wendell Lewis, II *lawyer*
Wilson, Paul Holliday, Jr. *lawyer*
Wimpfheimer, Michael Clark *lawyer*
Windels, Paul, Jr. *lawyer*
Wing, John Russell *lawyer*
Winger, Ralph O. *lawyer*
Winterer, Philip Steele *lawyer*
Wise, Aaron Noah *lawyer*
Witmeyer, John Jacob, III *lawyer*
Wohl, Ronald Gene *lawyer*
Wolf, Gary Wickert *lawyer*
Wolfe, James Ronald *lawyer*
Wolff, Jesse David *lawyer*
Wolff, Kurt Jakob *lawyer*
Wolff, Sanford Irving *lawyer*
Wolfson, Michael George *lawyer*
Wolkoff, Eugene Arnold *lawyer*
Wollman, Eric *lawyer*
Wolson, Craig Alan *lawyer*
Worenklein, Jacob Joshua *lawyer*
Wray, Cecil, Jr. *lawyer*
Wulf, Melvin Lawrence *lawyer*
Wyckoff, E. Lisk, Jr. *lawyer*
Yamin, Michael Geoffrey *lawyer*
Yelenick, Mary Therese *lawyer*
Yerman, Fredric Warren *lawyer*
Yodowitz, Edward J. *lawyer*
Young, Alice *lawyer*
†Young, James R. *corporate lawyer*
Young, John Edward *lawyer*
Young, Nancy *lawyer*
Young, William F. *legal educator*
Youngwood, Alfred Donald *lawyer*
Zahnd, Richard H. *professional sports executive, lawyer*
Zaitzeff, Roger Michael *lawyer*
Zammit, Joseph Paul *lawyer*
Zaslowsky, David Paul *lawyer*
Zauderer, Mark Carl *lawyer*
Zedrosser, Joseph John *lawyer*
Zerin, Steven David *lawyer*
Zifchak, William C. *lawyer*
Zimand, Harvey Folks *lawyer*
Zimmerman, Jean *lawyer*
Zimmett, Mark Paul *lawyer*
Zirin, James David *lawyer*
Zirinsky, Bruce R. *lawyer*
Zoeller, Donald J. *lawyer*
Zonana, Victor *lawyer, educator*
Zoogman, Nicholas Jay *lawyer*
Zornow, David M. *lawyer*
Zucker, Howard *lawyer*
Zukerman, Michael *lawyer*
Zweibel, Joel Burton *lawyer*

Newburgh
Liberth, Richard Francis *lawyer*
Milligram, Steven Irwin *lawyer*

Niagara Falls
Levine, David Ethan *lawyer*

North Syracuse
Kasouf, Joseph Chickery *lawyer*

Olean
Heyer, John Henry, II *lawyer*

Oneida
Matthews, William D(oty) *lawyer, consumer products manufacturing company executive*

Oneonta
Hill, Peter Waverly *lawyer*

Ossining
Daly, William Joseph *lawyer*

Oswego
Greene, Stephen Craig *lawyer*

Oyster Bay
Ott, Gilbert Russell, Jr. *lawyer*
Robinson, Edward T., III *lawyer*

Patchogue
Weisberg, David Charles *lawyer*

Peconic
Mitchell, Robert Everitt *lawyer*

Pelham
Hanrahan, Michael G. *lawyer, business consultant*
Simon, Robert G. *lawyer*

Pittsford
Snyder, Donald Edward *corporate executive*
Williams, Henry Ward, Jr. *lawyer*

Plattsburgh
Lewis, Clyde A. *lawyer*

Pleasantville
Ahrensfeld, Thomas Frederick *lawyer*

Port Jefferson
Hindin, Seymour *lawyer*

Port Washington
Adler, Edward Andrew Koeppel *lawyer*
Feldman, Jay Newman *lawyer, telecommunications executive*
Read, Frederick Wilson, Jr. *lawyer, educator*

Poughkeepsie
Dietz, Robert Barron *lawyer*
Kranis, Michael David *lawyer, judge*
Millman, Jode Susan *lawyer*
Ostertag, Robert Louis *lawyer*
Wallace, Herbert Norman *lawyer*

Pound Ridge
Hart, Kenneth Nelson *lawyer*

Purchase
Bowers, James W. *retired lawyer*
Guedry, James Walter *lawyer, paper corporation executive*
Kelly, Edmund Joseph *lawyer, investment banker*
Lytton, William B(ryan) *lawyer*
Melican, James Patrick, Jr. *lawyer*
Sharpe, Robert Francis, Jr. *lawyer*
Wallach, Ira David *lawyer, business executive*

Rego Park
Meruelo, Raul Pablo *lawyer, mortgage brokerage executive*

Riverdale
Itzkoff, Norman Jay *lawyer*

Riverhead
Maggipinto, V. Anthony *lawyer*
Twomey, Thomas A., Jr. *lawyer*

Rochester
Andolina, Lawrence J. *lawyer*
Baker, Bruce J. *lawyer*
Braunsdorf, Paul Raymond *lawyer*
Brovitz, Richard Stuart *lawyer*
Clement, Thomas Earl *lawyer*
Clifford, Eugene Thomas *lawyer*
Doyle, Justin P *lawyer*
Fix, Meyer *lawyer*
Geiger, Alexander *lawyer*
George, Richard Neill *lawyer*
Goldman, Joel J. *retired lawyer*
Gootnick, Margery Fischbein *lawyer*
Hampson, Thomas Meredith *lawyer*
Harris, Wayne Manley *lawyer*
Harter, Ralph Millard Peter *lawyer, educator*
Hoffberg, David Lawrence *lawyer*
Hood, John B. *lawyer*
Jesserer, Henry L., III *lawyer*
Kraus, Sherry Stokes *lawyer*
Kurland, Harold Arthur *lawyer*
Law, Michael R. *lawyer*
Lundback, Staffan Bengt Gunnar *lawyer*
Macko, John *lawyer, farmer*
Mayka, Stephen Paul *lawyer*
McCrory, John Brooks *retired lawyer*
†Moore, James Conklin *lawyer*
Morrison, Patrice B. *lawyer*
Palermo, Anthony Robert *lawyer*
Paley, Gerald Larry *lawyer*
Parsons, George Raymond, Jr. *lawyer*
Reed, James Alexander, Jr. *lawyer*
Robfogel, Susan Salitan *lawyer*
Rosenbaum, Richard Merrill *lawyer*
Rosner, Leonard Allen *lawyer*
Schumacher, Jon Lee *lawyer*
Scutt, Robert Carl *lawyer*
Smith, John Stuart *lawyer*
Smith, Jules Louis *lawyer*
Speranza, Paul Samuel, Jr. *lawyer*
Stewart, Sue S. *lawyer*
Stiller, Sharon Paula *lawyer*
Stonehill, Eric *lawyer*
Trevett, Thomas Neil *lawyer*
Trueheart, Harry Parker, III *lawyer*
Turner, Scott MacNeely *lawyer*
Turri, Joseph A. *lawyer*
Twietmeyer, Don Henry *lawyer*
Tyler, John Randolph *lawyer*
Van Graafeiland, Gary P. *lawyer*
Waite, Stephen Holden *lawyer*
Wild, Robert Warren *lawyer*
Willett, Thomas Edward *lawyer*
Witmer, George Robert, Jr. *lawyer*
Young, Deborah Schwind *lawyer*
Young, Thomas Paul *lawyer*
Zamboni, Helen Attena *lawyer, international telecommunications executive*

Rome
Griffith, Emlyn Irving *lawyer*

Roslyn
Zeitlan, Marilyn Labb *lawyer*

Rye
Dixon, Paul Edward *lawyer, metal products and manufacturing company executive*
Roberts, Thomas Alba *lawyer*

Rye Brook
Garcia C., Elisa Dolores *lawyer*

Salamanca
Brady, Thomas Carl *lawyer*

Sands Point
Busner, Philip H. *retired lawyer*
Hoynes, Louis LeNoir, Jr. *lawyer*

Saratoga Springs
Dorsey, James Baker *lawyer, surgeon*
Studley, Jamienne Shayne *lawyer*

Scarsdale
Angel, Dennis *lawyer*
Gerber, Roger Alan *lawyer, business consultant*
Hoffman, Richard M. *lawyer*
Kanter, Carl Irwin *lawyer*
Keeffe, John Arthur *lawyer, director*
King, Robert Lucien *lawyer*
Korzenik, Sidney S. *lawyer*
Liegl, Joseph Leslie *lawyer*
Macchia, Vincent Michael *lawyer*
O'Brien, Edward Ignatius *lawyer, private investor, corporation director*
Perko, Kenneth Albert, Jr. *lawyer, real estate executive, mathematics researcher*
Sheehan, Larry John *lawyer*
Sinsheimer, Warren Jack *lawyer*

Schenectady
Sokolow, Lloyd Bruce *lawyer, psychotherapist*
Thiele, Leslie Kathleen Larsen *lawyer*

Sea Cliff
McGill, Gilbert William *lawyer*

Silver Bay
Parlin, Charles C., Jr. *retired lawyer*

Smithtown
Dowis, Lenore *lawyer*
Pruzansky, Joshua Murdock *lawyer*
Spellman, Thomas Joseph, Jr. *lawyer*

Snyder
Genrich, Willard Adolph *lawyer*

Somers
Cowles, Frederick Oliver *lawyer*

Southampton
Lopez, David *lawyer*
Platt, Harold Kirby *lawyer*
Platt, Jonathan James *lawyer*

Spencertown
Dunne, John Richard *lawyer*

Staten Island
Ferranti, Thomas, Jr. *lawyer*
Klingle, Philip Anthony *law librarian*
Neuberger, Jerome M. *lawyer*

Suffern
Stack, Daniel *lawyer, financial consultant*

Syosset
Bermas, Stephen *lawyer*

Syracuse
Ackerman, Kenneth Edward *lawyer, educator*
Barclay, H(ugh) Douglas *lawyer, former state senator*
Bogart, William Harry *lawyer*
Cirando, John Anthony *lawyer*
Engel, Richard Lee *lawyer, educator*
Fitzpatrick, James David *lawyer*
Fraser, Henry S. *lawyer*
Gaal, John *lawyer*
Gerber, Edward F. *lawyer, educator*
Gilman, Karen Frenzel *legal assistant*
Gingold, Harlan Bruce *lawyer*
Grizanti, Anthony J. *lawyer*
Hayes, David Michael *lawyer*
Herzog, Peter Emilius *legal educator*
Hildebrandt, George Frederick *lawyer*
Hole, Richard Douglas *lawyer*
Hubbard, Peter Lawrence *lawyer*
Kopp, Robert Walter *lawyer*
Lawton, Joseph J., Jr. *retired lawyer*
†Maroney, Thomas J. *prosecutor*
Melnicoff, Joel Niesen *lawyer, sports agent*
Miller, Philip Charles *lawyer*
Moses, Robert Edward *lawyer*
Regan, Paul Michael *lawyer*
Sager, Jonathan Ward *lawyer*
Wells, Peter Nathaniel *lawyer*
Wladis, Mark Neil *lawyer*
Young, Douglas Howard *lawyer*

Tarrytown
Oelbaum, Harold *lawyer, corporate executive*

Troy
Burch, Mary Seelye Quinn *law librarian, consultant*
Finkel, Sanford Norman *lawyer*
Jones, E. Stewart, Jr. *lawyer*

Tuxedo Park
Brown, Walston Shepard *lawyer*

Uniondale
Cassidy, David Michael *lawyer*
Eilen, Howard Scott *lawyer, mediator*

Utica
Brennan, John Joseph *lawyer, legal administrator*
Jones, Hugh Richard *lawyer*

Valley Stream
Blakeman, Royal Edwin *lawyer*

Waterford
Glavin, A. Rita Chandellier (Mrs. James Henry Glavin, III) *lawyer*

Watervliet
Hilts, Earl T. *lawyer, government official, educator*

Westbury
Nogee, Jeffrey Laurence *lawyer*
Zychick, Joel David *lawyer*

White Plains
Alin, Robert David *lawyer*
Berlin, Alan Daniel *lawyer, international energy and legal consultant*
Bodnar, Peter O. *lawyer*
Carey, John *lawyer, judge*
Feder, Robert *lawyer*
Gjertsen, O. Gerard *lawyer*
Greenspan, Leon Joseph *lawyer*
Halpern, Philip Morgan *lawyer*
Klein, Paul E. *lawyer*
Lalli, Michael Anthony *lawyer*
Levine, Steven Jon *lawyer*
Maffeo, Vincent Anthony *lawyer, executive*
Munneke, Gary Arthur *law educator, consultant*
Mutz, Steven Herbert *lawyer*
Nesci, Vincent Peter *lawyer*
Nolletti, James Joseph *lawyer*
Parker, Barrington D., Jr. *lawyer*
Payson, Martin Fred *lawyer*
Rosenberg, Michael *lawyer*
Ryan, Robert Davis *lawyer*
Serchuk, Ivan *lawyer*
Silverberg, Steven Mark *lawyer*
Sive, David *lawyer*
Sloan, F(rank) Blaine *law educator*
Smith, Lisa Margaret *lawyer*
Taft, Nathaniel Belmont *lawyer*
Topol, Robin April Levitt *lawyer*
Triffin, Nicholas *law librarian, law educator*
Tsamis, Donna Robin *lawyer*
Vogel, Howard Stanley *lawyer*

Wolcott
Bartlett, Cody Blake *lawyer, educator*

Woodmere
Bobroff, Harold *lawyer*

Yonkers
Clark, Celia Rue *lawyer*
Connors, James Patrick *lawyer*
Moonie, William M. *lawyer*

NORTH CAROLINA

Andrews
Steinbronn, Richard Eugene *lawyer*

Asheville
Baldwin, Garza, Jr. *lawyer, manufacturing company executive*
Bissette, Winston Louis, Jr. *lawyer, mayor*
Branch, John Wells (Jack Twig) *lawyer*
†Cogburn, Max Oliver *lawyer*
Hyde, Herbert Lee *lawyer*
Johnston, John Devereaux, Jr. *law educator, retired*
Sharpe, Keith Yount *retired lawyer*

Buies Creek
Whichard, Willis Padgett *law educator, former state supreme court justice*

Cary
Glass, Fred Stephen *lawyer*
Montgomery, Charles Harvey *lawyer*

Chapel Hill
Broun, Kenneth Stanley *lawyer, educator*
Brower, David John *lawyer, urban planner, educator*
Campbell, William Aubrey *law educator*
Crassweller, Robert Doell *retired lawyer, writer*
Crohn, Max Henry, Jr. *lawyer*
Daye, Charles Edward *law educator*
Gressman, Eugene *lawyer*
Haskell, Paul Gershon *retired law educator*
Lawrence, David Michael *lawyer, educator*
Lilley, Albert Frederick *retired lawyer*
Loeb, Ben Fohl, Jr. *lawyer, educator*

Charlotte
Ayscue, Edwin Osborne, Jr. *lawyer*
Beatty, Tina Marie *legal assistant*
Bernstein, Mark R. *retired lawyer*
†Blackburn, Richard Wallace *lawyer*
Brackett, Martin Luther, Jr. *lawyer*
Buchan, Jonathan Edward, Jr. *lawyer*
Buckley, Charles Robinson, III *lawyer*
Calloway, Mark T. *prosecutor*
Campbell, Hugh Brown, Jr. *lawyer*
Cowell, Marion Aubrey, Jr. *lawyer*
Dagenhart, Larry Jones *lawyer*
Davis, William Maxie, Jr. *lawyer*
Grier, Joseph Williamson, Jr. *lawyer*
Hanna, George Verner, III *lawyer*
Harris, Richard Foster, III *lawyer*
McBryde, Neill Gregory *lawyer*
McConnell, David Moffatt *lawyer*
McGill, John Knox *lawyer*
Newitt, John Garwood, Jr. *lawyer*
Polking, Paul J. *lawyer*
Thigpen, Richard Elton, Jr. *lawyer*
Van Allen, William Kent *lawyer*
Van Alstyne, Vance Brownell *arbitration management consultant*
Vinroot, Richard Allen *lawyer, mayor*
Waggoner, William Johnson *lawyer*
Walker, Clarence Wesley *lawyer*
Wood, William McBrayer *lawyer*
Woolard, William Leon *lawyer, electrical distributing company executive*

Cherryville
Huffstetler, Palmer Eugene *lawyer*

Columbus
Bell, Mildred Bailey *lawyer, educator*

Cullowhee
Wilson, LeVon Edward *law educator, lawyer*

Durham
Bartlett, Katharine Tiffany *law educator*
Carpenter, Charles Francis *lawyer*
Carrington, Paul DeWitt *lawyer, educator*
Christie, George Custis *lawyer, educator, author*
Conner, James Leon, II *lawyer, mediator*
Cox, James D. *law educator*
Danner, Richard Allen *law educator, dean*
Dellinger, Walter Estes, III *lawyer, educator*
Fisher, Stewart Wayne *lawyer*
Havighurst, Clark Canfield *law educator*
Horowitz, Donald Leonard *lawyer, educator, researcher, political scientist, arbitrator*
Jenkins, Richard Erik *patent lawyer*
Lange, David L. *law educator*
Markham, Charles Buchanan *lawyer*
Maxwell, Richard Callender *lawyer, educator*
McMahon, John Alexander *law educator*
Mosteller, Robert P. *law educator*
Robertson, Horace Bascomb, Jr. *law educator*
Rowe, Thomas Dudley, Jr. *law educator*
Schwarcz, Steven Lance *law educator, lawyer*
Shimm, Melvin Gerald *law educator*

Elkin
Gillespie, James Davis *lawyer*

Fairview
Rhynedance, Harold Dexter, Jr. *lawyer, consultant*

Fayetteville
Parish, James Riley *lawyer*
Ruppe, Arthur Maxwell *lawyer*
Townsend, William Jackson *lawyer*

Gastonia
Alala, Joseph Basil, Jr. *lawyer, accountant*
Stott, Grady Bernell *lawyer*

Graham
Walker, Daniel Joshua, Jr. *lawyer*

Greensboro
Bell, Haney Hardy, III *lawyer*
Capone, Lucien, III *lawyer*

Clark, David McKenzie *lawyer*
Davidson, Gerard H., Jr. *lawyer*
Davis, Herbert Owen *lawyer*
Floyd, Jack William *lawyer*
Gabriel, Richard Weisner *lawyer*
Gumbiner, Kenneth Jay *lawyer*
Holton, Walter Clinton, Jr. *lawyer*
Hopkins, John David *lawyer*
Hunter, Bynum Merritt *lawyer*
Koonce, Neil Wright *lawyer*
Melvin, Charles Edward, Jr. *lawyer*
Moore, Beverly Cooper *lawyer*
Rowlenson, Richard Charles *lawyer*
St. George, Nicholas James *lawyer, manufactured housing company executive*
Schell, Braxton *lawyer*
†Sitton, Larry Bruce *lawyer*
Smith, John McNeill, Jr. *lawyer*
Smith, Lanty L(loyd) *lawyer, business executive*
Swan, George Steven *law educator*
Turner, James Reginald *lawyer*

Greenville
Burti, Christopher Louis *lawyer*
Clark, John Graham, III *lawyer*
Flanagan, Michael Perkins *lawyer*

Hendersonville
Hull, J(ames) Richard *retired lawyer, business executive*

Hillsborough
Martin, Harry Corpening *lawyer, retired state supreme court justice*

Horse Shoe
Howell, George Washington *lawyer, consultant*

Jacksonville
Taylor, Vaughan Edward *lawyer, educator*

Lenoir
Flaherty, David Thomas, Jr. *lawyer*

Marion
Burgin, Charles Edward *lawyer*

Murphy
Bata, Rudolph Andrew, Jr. *lawyer*

New Bern
Davis, James Lee *lawyer*
Kellum, Norman Bryant, Jr. *lawyer*
Overholt, Hugh Robert *lawyer, retired army officer*
Stoller, David Allen *lawyer*

Oxford
Burnette, James Thomas *lawyer*

Raleigh
Cameron, Christie Speir *lawyer*
Carlton, Alfred Pershing, Jr. *lawyer*
Carter, Jean Gordon *lawyer*
Case, Charles Dixon *lawyer*
Cole, Janice McKenzie *prosecutor*
Dannelly, William David *lawyer*
Davis, Egbert Lawrence, III *lawyer*
Davis, Thomas Hill, Jr. *lawyer*
Dixon, Daniel Roberts, Jr. *retired tax lawyer*
Dixon, Wright Tracy, Jr. *lawyer*
Edwards, Charles Archibald *lawyer*
Ellis, Lester Neal, Jr. *lawyer*
Ellis, Richard W. *lawyer*
Foley, Peter Michael *lawyer*
Givens, George Franklin *lawyer*
Graham, William Edgar, Jr. *lawyer, retired utility company executive*
Graham, William Thomas *lawyer*
Hall, John Thomas *lawyer*
Hensey, Charles McKinnon *retired lawyer*
Homick, Daniel John *lawyer, financial executive*
Huggard, John Parker *lawyer*
Hunter, Richard Samford, Jr. *lawyer*
Jolly, John Russell, Jr. *lawyer*
Joyner, Walton Kitchin *lawyer*
Kapp, Michael Keith *lawyer*
Kaufman, Sarah Hall *legal assistant*
Maupin, Armistead Jones *lawyer*
McCormick, Thomas A., Jr. *city attorney*
Miller, Ralph Bradley *lawyer, state legislator*
Neely, Charles B., Jr. *lawyer*
Pinnix, John Lawrence *lawyer*
Powell, Durwood Royce *lawyer*
Ragsdale, George Robinson *lawyer*
Roach, Wesley Linville *lawyer, insurance executive*
Sasser, Jonathan Drew *lawyer*
Schwab, Carol Ann *law educator*
Simpson, Steven Drexell *lawyer*
Suhr, Paul Augustine *lawyer*
Thomas, Mark Stanton *lawyer*
Wetsch, Laura Johnson *lawyer*
Wilson, Robert Lee, Jr. *lawyer*

Rocky Mount
Zipf, Robert Eugene, Jr. *legal medicine consultant, pathologist*

Sanford
Raisig, Paul Jones, Jr. *lawyer*

Smithfield
Schulz, Bradley Nicholas *lawyer*

Tabor City
Jorgensen, Ralph Gubler *lawyer, accountant*

Tarboro
Hopkins, Grover Prevatte *lawyer*

Tryon
McDermott, James Alexander *retired lawyer*
McDermott, Renée R(assler) *lawyer*
Stinson, George Arthur *lawyer, former steel company executive*

Wilmington
Kaufman, James Jay *lawyer*
McCauley, Cleyburn Lycurgus *lawyer*
Medlock, Donald Larson *lawyer*
Seagle, J. Harold *lawyer*

Winston Salem
Adams, Alfred Gray *lawyer*
Barnhardt, Zeb Elonzo, Jr. *lawyer, independent consultant*
Barnhill, Henry Grady, Jr. *lawyer*
Blynn, Guy Marc *lawyer*
Brunstetter, Peter Samuel *lawyer*
Coffey, Larry B(ruce) *lawyer*
Copenhaver, W. Andrew *lawyer*
Davis, Linwood Layfield *lawyer*
Davis, William Allison, II *lawyer*
Early, James H., Jr. *lawyer*
Farr, Henry Bartow, Jr. *lawyer*
Gitter, Allan Reinhold *lawyer*
Greason, Murray Crossley, Jr. *lawyer*
Herring, Jerone Carson *lawyer, bank executive*
Hopkins, Muriel-Beth Norbrey *lawyer*
Leonard, R. Michael *lawyer*
Loughridge, John Halsted, Jr. *lawyer*
McAllister, Kenneth Wayne *lawyer*
Osborn, Malcolm Everett *lawyer*
Petree, William Horton *lawyer*
Ray, Michael Edwin *lawyer*
Sandridge, William Pendleton, Jr. *lawyer*
Schollander, Wendell Leslie, Jr. *lawyer*
†Thrift, Ashley Ormand *lawyer*
Vance, Charles Fogle, Jr. *lawyer*
Walker, George Kontz *law educator*
Wells, Dewey Wallace *lawyer*
Womble, William Fletcher *lawyer*

Wrightsville Beach
Block, Franklin Lee *retired lawyer*

NORTH DAKOTA

Bismarck
Edin, Charles Thomas *lawyer*
Gilbertson, Joel Warren *lawyer*
Klemin, Lawrence R. *lawyer*
Murry, Charles Emerson *lawyer, official*
Strutz, William A. *lawyer*

Cooperstown
Ratcliffe, Phyllis Ann *lawyer, antique dealer*

Fargo
Schneider, John Thomas *prosecutor*

Grand Forks
Anderson, Damon Ernest *lawyer*
Vogel, Robert *retired lawyer, educator*

Mandan
Bair, Bruce B. *lawyer*

Minot
Armstrong, Phillip Dale *lawyer*

OHIO

Akron
Bartlo, Sam D. *lawyer*
Childs, James William *lawyer, legal educator*
Chrisant, Rosemarie Kathryn *law library administrator*
Fisher, James Lee *lawyer*
Gippin, Robert Malcolm *lawyer*
†Harvie, Crawford Thomas *lawyer*
Holloway, Donald Phillip *lawyer*
Kreek, Louis Francis, Jr. *lawyer*
Lammert, Thomas Edward *lawyer*
Lee, Brant Thomas *lawyer, federal official, educator*
Lombardi, Frederick McKean *lawyer*
Moss, Robert Drexler *lawyer*
Nolfi, Edward Anthony *lawyer*
Richert, Paul *law educator*
Rooney, George Willard *lawyer*
Ruport, Scott Hendricks *lawyer*
Schrader, Alfred Eugene *lawyer*
Tipping, Harry A. *lawyer*
Trotter, Thomas Robert *lawyer*
Weitendorf, Kurt Robert *lawyer*

Amelia
Thoman, Henry Nixon *lawyer*

Aurora
Hermann, Philip J. *lawyer*

Avon Lake
Kitchen, Charles William *lawyer*

Barberton
Stevenson, Scot A. *lawyer, educator*

Beachwood
Donnem, Roland William *board of directors, hotel owner, developer*

Beavercreek
Stadnicar, Joseph William *lawyer*

Berea
Jolles, Janet Kavanaugh Pilling *lawyer*

Bowling Green
Hanna, Martin Shad *lawyer*

Bucyrus
Neff, Robert Clark, Sr. *lawyer*

Canfield
Goldberg, Martin Stanford *lawyer*
Mumaw, James Webster *lawyer*

Canton
Bennington, Ronald Kent *lawyer*
Brannen, John Howard *lawyer*
Brown, Larry R. *lawyer*
Lindamood, John Beyer *lawyer*
Mokodean, Michael John *lawyer, accountant*

Carrollton
Childers, John Charles *lawyer, engineer*

Chagrin Falls
Streicher, James Franklin *lawyer*

Chardon
Karch, George Frederick, Jr. *lawyer*

Chesterland
Durn, Raymond Joseph *lawyer*
Kancelbaum, Joshua Jacob *lawyer*

Cincinnati
Adams, Edmund John *lawyer*
Anderson, James Milton *lawyer*
Anderson, William Hopple *lawyer*
Anthony, Thomas Dale *lawyer*
Ashdown, Charles Coster *lawyer*
Bahlman, William Thorne, Jr. *retired lawyer*
Bissinger, Mark Christian *lawyer*
Black, Stephen L. *lawyer*
Bridgeland, James Ralph, Jr. *lawyer*
Broderick, Dennis John *lawyer, retail company executive*
Bromberg, Robert Sheldon *lawyer*
Buechner, Robert William *lawyer, educator*
Carr, George Francis, Jr. *lawyer*
Case, Douglas Manning *lawyer*
Chesley, Stanley Morris *lawyer*
Christenson, Gordon A. *law educator*
Cioffi, Michael Lawrence *lawyer*
Cissell, James Charles *lawyer*
Cobey, John Geoffrey *lawyer*
Cody, Thomas Gerald *lawyer*
Coffey, Thomas William *lawyer*
Cowan, Jerry Louis *lawyer*
Craig, L. Clifford *lawyer*
Dehner, Joseph Julnes *lawyer*
DeLong, Deborah *lawyer*
Desmond, William J. *lawyer*
Diller, Edward Dietrich *lawyer*
Dornette, W(illiam) Stuart *lawyer, educator*
Elleman, Lawrence Robert *lawyer*
Evans, James E. *lawyer*
Faller, Susan Grogan *lawyer*
Fink, Jerold Albert *lawyer*
Flanagan, John Anthony *lawyer, educator*
Fleming, Lisa L. *lawyer*
Frantz, Robert Wesley *lawyer*
Freedman, William Mark *lawyer*
Garfinkel, Jane E. *lawyer*
Gettler, Benjamin *lawyer, manufacturing company executive*
Goodman, Stanley *lawyer*
Greenberg, Gerald Stephen *lawyer*
Halpert, Douglas Joshua *immigration lawyer*
Hardy, William Robinson *lawyer*
Harris, Irving *lawyer*
Heinlen, Ronald Eugene *lawyer*
Heldman, James Gardner *lawyer*
Heldman, Paul W. *lawyer, grocery store company executive*
Henderson, Stephen Paul *lawyer*
Hermanies, John Hans *lawyer, retired*
Hill, Thomas Clark *lawyer*
Hoffheimer, Daniel Joseph *lawyer*
Holschuh, John David, Jr. *lawyer*
Hust, Bruce Kevin *lawyer*
Johnson, James J. *lawyer*
Kelley, John Joseph, Jr. *lawyer*
Kenrich, John Lewis *lawyer*
Kiel, Frederick Orin *lawyer*
Kite, William McDougall *lawyer*
Lawrence, James Kaufman Lebensburger *lawyer*
Lemke, Judith A. *lawyer*
Levin, Debbe Ann *lawyer*
Longenecker, Mark Hershey, Jr. *lawyer*
Manley, Robert Edward *lawyer, economist*
Mann, David Scott *lawyer*
Maxwell, Robert Wallace, II *lawyer*
McClain, William Andrew *lawyer*
McDowell, John Eugene *lawyer*
McGavran, Frederick Jaeger *lawyer*
Mc Henry, Powell *lawyer*
Meranus, Leonard Stanley *lawyer*
Nechemias, Stephen Murray *lawyer*
Nelson, Frederick Dickson *lawyer*
Neumark, Michael Harry *lawyer*
Olson, Robert Wyrick *lawyer*
Parker, R. Joseph *lawyer*
Petrie, Bruce Inglis *lawyer*
Phillips, T. Stephen *lawyer*
Porter, Robert Carl, Jr. *lawyer*
Reichert, David *lawyer*
Rich, Robert Edward *lawyer*
Rose, Donald McGregor *retired lawyer*
Ryan, James Joseph *lawyer*
Schmidt, Thomas Joseph, Jr. *lawyer*
Schmit, David E. *lawyer*
Schuck, Thomas Robert *lawyer, farmer*
Shea, Joseph William, III *lawyer*
Shore, Thomas Spencer, Jr. *lawyer*
Silbersack, Mark Louis *lawyer*
Sims, Victor Dwayne *lawyer*
Strauss, William Victor *lawyer*
Swigert, James Mack *lawyer*
Terp, Thomas Thomsen *lawyer*
Tobias, Charles Harrison, Jr. *lawyer*
Tobias, Paul Henry *lawyer*
Tomain, Joseph Patrick *law educator, dean*
Townsend, Robert J. *lawyer*
Vander Laan, Mark Alan *lawyer*
Vogel, Cedric Wakelee *lawyer*
Wales, Ross Elliot *lawyer*
Wang, Charleston Cheng-Kung *lawyer, engineer*
Watts, Barbara Gayle *law academic administrator*
Weeks, Steven Wiley *lawyer*
Weseli, Roger William *lawyer*
Whitaker, Glenn Virgil *lawyer*
White, Alfred Kenneth, Jr. *lawyer*
Woodside, Frank C., III *lawyer, educator, physician*
Yurchuck, Roger Alexander *lawyer*
Zavatsky, Michael Joseph *lawyer*
Zealey, Sharon Janine *lawyer*

Cleveland
Adamo, Kenneth R. *lawyer*
Akers-Parry, Deborah *lawyer*
Andorka, Frank Henry *lawyer*
Andrews, Oakley V. *lawyer*
Ashmus, Keith Allen *lawyer*
Asman, Robert Joseph
Austin, Arthur Donald, II *lawyer, educator*
Bacon, Brett Kermit *lawyer*
Bamberger, Richard H. *lawyer*
Bates, Walter Alan *former lawyer*
Baughman, R(obert) Patrick *lawyer*
Bell, Steven Dennis *lawyer*
Berger, Sanford Jason *lawyer, securities dealer, real estate broker*
Berick, James Herschel *lawyer*
Berry, Dean Lester *lawyer*
Besse, Ralph Moore *lawyer*
Bilchik, Gary B. *lawyer*
Binford, Gregory Glenn *lawyer*
Birne, Kenneth Andrew *lawyer*
Blattner, Robert A. *lawyer*
Boyko, Christopher Allan *lawyer, judge*
Braverman, Herbert Leslie *lawyer*
Bravo, Kenneth Allan *lawyer*
Brennan, Maureen *lawyer*
Brown, Seymour R. *lawyer*
Brucken, Robert Matthew *lawyer*
Burke, Kathleen B. *lawyer*
Buzzelli, Laurence Francis *lawyer*
Cairns, James Donald *lawyer*
Calfee, John Beverly *retired lawyer*
Calfee, William Lewis *lawyer*
Campbell, Paul Barton *retired lawyer*
Canary, Nancy Halliday *lawyer*
Carrick, Kathleen Michele *law librarian*
Carter, Daniel Paul *lawyer, educator*
Cherchiglia, Dean Kenneth *lawyer*
Clarke, Charles Fenton *lawyer*
Collin, Thomas James *lawyer*
Coquillette, William Hollis *lawyer*
Coyle, Martin Adolphus, Jr. *lawyer*
Crist, Paul Grant *lawyer*
Currivan, John Daniel *lawyer*
Daroff, William Clayton *lawyer*
Doris, Alan S(anford) *lawyer*
Drinko, John Deaver *lawyer*
Duncan, Ed Eugene *lawyer*
Duvin, Robert Phillip *lawyer*
Fabens, Andrew Lawrie, III *lawyer*
Falsgraf, William Wendell *lawyer*
Fay, Regan Joseph *lawyer*
Fay, Robert Jesse *lawyer*
Fay, Terrence Michael *lawyer*
Feinberg, Paul H. *lawyer*
Fisher, Thomas Edward *lawyer*
Friedman, Harold Edward *lawyer*
Friedman, James Moss *lawyer*
Gerhart, Peter Milton *law educator*
Gherlein, Gerald Lee *lawyer, diversified manufacturing company executive*
Glaser, Robert Edward *lawyer*
Goins, Frances Floriano *lawyer*
Gold, Gerald Seymour *lawyer*
Goldfarb, Bernard Sanford *lawyer*
Goler, Michael David *lawyer*
Graham, David Browning *lawyer*
Groetzinger, Jon, Jr. *lawyer, consumer products executive*
Grossman, Theodore Martin *lawyer*
Grundstein, Nathan David *lawyer, management science educator, management consultant*
Haiman, Irwin Sanford *lawyer*
Hardy, Michael Lynn *lawyer*
Hochman, Kenneth George *lawyer*
Hoerner, Robert Jack *lawyer*
Hollington, Richard Rings, Jr. *lawyer*
Horvitz, Michael John *lawyer*
Inglis, Patricia Marcus *lawyer*
Jacobs, Leslie William *lawyer*
Janke, Ronald Robert *lawyer*
Jeavons, Norman Stone *lawyer*
Jorgenson, Mary Ann *lawyer*
Kahrl, Robert Conley *lawyer*
Kapp, C. Terrence *lawyer*
Katcher, Richard *lawyer*
Katz, Lewis Robert *law educator*
Kelly, Dennis Michael *lawyer*
Kilbane, Catherine M. *lawyer*
Kilbane, Thomas Stanton *lawyer*
Kirchick, Calvin B. *lawyer*
Kola, Arthur Anthony *lawyer*
Kramer, Edward George *lawyer*
Kramer, Eugene Leo *lawyer*
Krotinger, Myron Nathan *lawyer*
Kundtz, John Andrew *lawyer*
Kurit, Neil *lawyer*
Langer, Carlton Earl *lawyer*
Lawniczak, James Michael *lawyer*
Lease, Robert K. *lawyer*
Leidner, Harold Edward *lawyer*
Leiken, Earl Murray *lawyer*
Lenn, Stephen Andrew *lawyer*
Lentz, Mary A. *lawyer, educator*
Lewis, John Bruce *lawyer*
Lewis, John Francis *lawyer*
Lewis, Robert Lawrence *lawyer, educator*
Madsen, H(enry) Stephen *retired lawyer*
Mancuso, John H. *lawyer, bank executive*
Markey, Robert Guy *lawyer*
Marting, Michael G. *lawyer*
Mason, Thomas Albert *lawyer*
McAndrews, James Patrick *lawyer*
†Mc Cartan, Patrick Francis *lawyer*
McCarthy, Mark Francis *lawyer*
McCormack, Mark Hume *lawyer, business management company executive*
Mc Elhaney, James Wilson *lawyer, educator*
McLaughlin, Patrick Michael *lawyer*
Mehlman, Maxwell Jonathan *law educator*
Melsher, Gary W. *lawyer*
Meyer, G. Christopher *lawyer*
Millstone, David J. *lawyer*
Moore, Kenneth Cameron *lawyer*
Morrison, Donald William *lawyer*
Newman, John M., Jr. *lawyer*
Nudelman, Sidney *lawyer*
Oberdank, Lawrence Mark *lawyer, arbitrator*
Ollinger, W. James *lawyer*
Pace, Stanley Dan *lawyer*
Pearlman, Samuel Segel *lawyer*
Podboy, Alvin Michael, Jr. *lawyer, law library director*
Preston, Robert Bruce *retired lawyer*
Price, Charles T. *lawyer*
Putka, Andrew Charles *lawyer*
Pyke, John Secrest, Jr. *lawyer, polymers company executive*
Rains, M. Neal *lawyer*
Rapp, Robert Neil *lawyer*
Rekstis, Walter J., III *lawyer*
Reppert, Richard Levi *lawyer*
Rosenbaum, Jacob I. *lawyer*
Ross, Harold Anthony *lawyer*
Ruben, Alan Miles *law educator*
Ruf, H(arold) William, Jr. *lawyer, corporation executive*
Rydzel, James A. *lawyer*
Sanislo, Paul Steve *lawyer*
Satola, James William *lawyer*
Sawyer, Raymond Terry *lawyer*

PROFESSIONAL INDEX 6157 LAW: LAW PRACTICE AND ADMINISTRATION

Scanlon, Thomas J. *lawyer*
Schiller, James Joseph *lawyer*
Schnell, Carlton Bryce *lawyer*
Shapiro, Fred David *lawyer*
Sharp, Robert Weimer *lawyer*
Shrallow, Dale Phillip *lawyer*
Sicherman, Marvin Allen *lawyer*
Skulina, Thomas Raymond *lawyer*
Slinger, Michael Jeffery *law library director*
Sloan, David W. *lawyer*
Smith, Barbara Jean *lawyer*
Sogg, Wilton Sherman *lawyer*
Solomon, Randall L. *lawyer*
Spero, Keith Erwin *lawyer*
Stanley, Hugh Monroe, Jr. *lawyer*
Steindler, Howard Allen *lawyer*
Stellato, Louis Eugene *lawyer*
Stevens, Thomas Charles *lawyer*
Strauch, John L. *lawyer*
Streeter, Richard Edward *lawyer*
Striefsky, Linda A(nn) *lawyer*
Strimbu, Victor, Jr. *lawyer*
Stuhan, Richard George *lawyer*
Swartzbaugh, Marc L. *lawyer*
Sweeney, Emily Margaret *prosecutor*
Szaller, James Francis *lawyer*
Taft, Seth Chase *retired lawyer*
Toohey, Brian Frederick *lawyer*
Toomajian, William Martin *lawyer*
Trevor, Leigh Barry *lawyer*
von Mehren, George M. *lawyer*
Waldeck, John Walter, Jr. *lawyer*
Wallach, Mark Irwin *lawyer*
Watson, Richard Thomas *lawyer*
Weber, Robert Carl *lawyer*
Weiler, Jeffry Louis *lawyer*
Weinberger, Peter Henry *lawyer*
Whiteman, Joseph David *retired lawyer, manufacturing company executive*
Whitney, Richard Buckner *lawyer*
Williams, Clyde E., Jr. *lawyer*
†Withers, Carl Raymond *lawyer*
Young, James Edward *lawyer*
Zambie, Allan John *lawyer*
Zangerle, John A. *lawyer*

Cleveland Heights
Gutfeld, Norman E. *lawyer*

Columbus
Acker, Frederick Wayne *lawyer*
Adams, John Marshall *lawyer*
Anderson, Jon Mac *lawyer*
Aukland, Duncan Dayton *lawyer*
Bailey, Daniel Allen *lawyer*
Barnes, Wallace Ray *retired lawyer*
Belton, John Thomas *lawyer*
Bennett, Robert Thomas *lawyer*
Bibart, Richard L. *lawyer*
Blickenstaff, Kathleen Mary *lawyer, mental health nurse, nursing educator*
Booker, James Douglas *retired lawyer, government official*
Bowen, John Wesley Edward, IV *lawyer*
Bridgman, G(eorge) Ross *lawyer*
Brinkman, Dale Thomas *lawyer*
Brooks, Richard Dickinson *lawyer*
Brown, Herbert Russell *lawyer, writer*
Brown, Philip Albert *lawyer*
Brubaker, Robert Loring *lawyer*
Buchenroth, Stephen Richard *lawyer*
Burns, Robert Edward *lawyer*
Carnahan, John Anderson *lawyer*
Carpenter, Michael H. *lawyer*
Chesley-Lahm, Diane *lawyer*
Chester, John Jonas *lawyer*
Christensen, John William *lawyer*
Cline, Richard Allen *lawyer*
Cvetanovich, Danny L. *lawyer*
DeRousie, Charles Stuart *lawyer*
Di Lorenzo, John Florio, Jr. *lawyer*
Draper, Gerald Linden *lawyer*
Dreher, Darrell L. *lawyer*
Elam, John Carlton *lawyer*
Fahey, Richard Paul *lawyer*
Ferguson, Gerald Paul *lawyer*
Fisher, Lawrence L. *lawyer*
Fisher, Lloyd Edison, Jr. *lawyer*
Frasier, Ralph Kennedy *lawyer, banker*
Fried, Samuel *lawyer*
Frye, Richard Arthur *lawyer*
Fu, Paul Shan *law librarian, consultant*
Fultz, Robert Edward *lawyer*
Gibson, Rankin MacDougal *lawyer*
Greek, Darold I. *lawyer*
Gross, James Howard *lawyer*
Hardymon, David Wayne *lawyer*
Hollenbaugh, H(enry) Ritchey *lawyer*
Hutson, Jeffrey Woodward *lawyer*
Jackson, Janet Elizabeth *city attorney, association executive*
Jenkins, George L. *lawyer, fast food company executive*
Jenkins, John Anthony *lawyer*
Johnson, Mark Alan *lawyer*
Ketcham, Richard Scott *lawyer*
King, G. Roger *lawyer*
Koblentz, Robert Alan *lawyer*
Kuehnle, Kenton Lee *lawyer*
Kurtz, Charles Jewett, III *lawyer*
Kusma, Kyllikki *lawyer*
Kyte, Susan Janet *lawyer*
Larzelere, Kathy Lynn Heckler *paralegal*
Lehman, Harry Jac *lawyer*
Lindsey, Thomas Kenneth *lawyer, administrator*
Long, Thomas Leslie *lawyer*
Lowry, Bruce Roy *lawyer*
Maloon, Jerry L. *trial lawyer, physician, medicolegal consultant*
Markus, Kent Richard *lawyer*
Martin, William Giese *lawyer*
Maynard, Robert Howell *lawyer*
McAlister, Robert Beaton *lawyer*
McConnaughey, George Carlton, Jr. *lawyer*
McDermott, Kevin R. *lawyer*
McKenna, Alvin James *lawyer*
McMahon, John Patrick *lawyer*
McNealey, J. Jeffrey *lawyer, corporate executive*
Miller, Malcolm Lee *retired lawyer*
Miller, Michael Stratton *lawyer*
Miller, Terry Morrow *lawyer*
Minor, Charles Daniel *lawyer*
Minor, Robert Allen *lawyer*
Mirman, Joel Harvey *lawyer*
Moloney, Thomas E. *lawyer*
Mone, Robert Paul *lawyer*
Morgan, Dennis Richard *lawyer*
Moul, William Charles *lawyer*
Nathan, Jerry E. *lawyer*
Oliphant, James S. *lawyer*
Oman, Richard Heer *lawyer*
O'Reilly, Michael Joseph *lawyer, real estate investor*
Owsiany, David James *lawyer, lobbyist*
Petricoff, M. Howard *lawyer, educator*
Petro, James Michael *lawyer, politician*
Phillips, James Edgar *lawyer*
Pressley, Fred G., Jr. *lawyer*
Quigley, John Bernard *law educator*
Radnor, Alan T. *lawyer*
Ramey, Denny L. *bar association executive director*
Ray, Frank Allen *lawyer*
Reasoner, Willis Irl, III *lawyer*
Rennick, Kyme Elizabeth Wall *lawyer*
Ridgley, Thomas Brennan *lawyer*
Robinson, Barry R. *lawyer*
Robol, Richard Thomas *lawyer*
Rose, Michael Dean *lawyer, educator*
Ryan, Joseph W., Jr. *lawyer*
Schrag, Edward A., Jr. *lawyer*
Shamansky, Robert Norton *lawyer*
Sidman, Robert John *lawyer*
Smith, Norman T. *lawyer*
Smith, R(obert) Michael *lawyer*
Stein, Jay Wobith *legal research and education consultant, mediator arbitrator*
Stern, Geoffrey *lawyer, disciplinary counsel*
Stinehart, Roger Ray *lawyer*
Sully, Ira Bennett *lawyer*
Taft, Sheldon Ashley *lawyer*
Taggart, Thomas Michael *lawyer*
Tait, Robert E. *lawyer*
Tarpy, Thomas Michael *lawyer*
Taylor, Joel Sanford *lawyer*
Thomas, Duke Winston *lawyer*
Todd, William Michael *lawyer*
Treneff, Craig Paul *lawyer*
Tripp, Thomas Neal *lawyer, political consultant*
Turano, David A. *lawyer*
Vorys, Arthur Isaiah *lawyer*
Warner, Charles Collins *lawyer*
Whipps, Edward Franklin *lawyer*
Wightman, Alec *lawyer*
Williams, Gregory Howard *law educator, dean*
Wiseman, Randolph Carson *lawyer*
Wright, Harry, III *retired lawyer*
Yeazel, Keith Arthur *lawyer*

Cuyahoga Falls
Jones, John Frank *retired lawyer*
Thomas, Carol Todd *law firm administrator*

Dayton
Burick, Lawrence T. *lawyer*
Chernesky, Richard John *lawyer*
Conway, Mark Allyn *lawyer*
Faruki, Charles Joseph *lawyer*
Finn, Chester Evans *lawyer*
Gottschlich, Gary William *lawyer*
Hadley, Robert James *lawyer*
Heyman, Ralph Edmond *lawyer*
Jacobs, Richard E. *lawyer*
Jenks, Thomas Edward *lawyer*
Johnson, C. Terry *lawyer*
Kinlin, Donald James *lawyer*
Koeller, Lynn Garver *public defender*
Lockhart, Gregory Gordon *lawyer*
Macklin, Crofford Johnson, Jr. *lawyer*
McSwiney, Charles Ronald *lawyer*
Nicholson, Mark William *lawyer*
Posey, Terry Wayne *lawyer*
Randall, Vernellia *lawyer, nurse, educator*
Rapp, Gerald Duane *lawyer, manufacturing company executive*
Roberts, Brian Michael *lawyer*
Rogers, Richard Hunter *lawyer, business executive*
Saul, Irving Isaac *lawyer*
Sessler, Albert Louis, Jr. *lawyer*
Taronji, Jaime, Jr. *lawyer*
Watts, Steven Richard *lawyer*
Wightman, Ann *lawyer*
Yerkeson, Douglas Alan *lawyer*

Delphos
Clark, Edward Ferdnand *lawyer*

Dublin
†Bennett, George H., Jr. *lawyer, healthcare company executive*
Bennett, Steven Alan *lawyer*
Dugan, Charles Francis, II *lawyer*
Inzetta, Mark Stephen *lawyer*
Tenuta, Luigia *lawyer*

Eaton
Bennett, Herd Leon *lawyer*
Thomas, James William *lawyer*

Fairborn
Roach, B. Randall *lawyer, city council member*

Findlay
Jetton, Girard Reuel, Jr. *lawyer, retired oil company executive*
Kostyo, John Francis *lawyer*

Fremont
Smith, Bradley Jason *lawyer, recreational facility owner*

Howard
Lee, William Johnson *lawyer*

Hudson
Giffen, Daniel Harris *lawyer, educator*
Ong, John Doyle *retired lawyer*

Independence
Schwallie, Daniel Phillip *legal consultant*

Kent
Nome, William Andreas *lawyer*

Lancaster
Libert, Donald Joseph *lawyer*

Lima
Jacobs, Ann Elizabeth *lawyer*
Robenalt, John Alton *lawyer*

Loveland
McCoy, John Joseph *lawyer*

Marietta
Fields, William Albert *lawyer*

Maumee
Kline, James Edward *lawyer*
Marsh, Benjamin Franklin *lawyer*

Medina
Ballard, John Stuart *retired educator, former mayor, former lawyer*
Steinmetz, Robert Francis *lawyer*

Mentor
Driggs, Charles Mulford *lawyer*

Miamisburg
Byrd, James Everett *lawyer*

Middletown
Rathman, William Ernest *lawyer, minister*

Milford
Vorholt, Jeffrey Joseph *lawyer, software company executive*

Minerva
Martin, Robert Dale *lawyer*

Mount Vernon
Turner, Harry Edward *lawyer*

New Richmond
Menke, William Charles *lawyer*

Newark
Mantonya, John Butcher *lawyer*
Reidy, Thomas Anthony *lawyer*

North Royalton
Jungeberg, Thomas Donald *lawyer*

Oxford
Brown, Edward Maurice *retired lawyer, business executive*

Pepper Pike
Leech, John Dale *lawyer, health care/corporate consultant*

Poland
Carlin, Clair Myron *lawyer*

Portsmouth
Gerlach, Franklin Theodore *lawyer*
Horr, William Henry *lawyer*

Richfield
Schulz, Mary Elizabeth *lawyer*

Sagamore Hills
Consilio, Barbara Ann *legal administrator, management consultant*

Saint Marys
Kemp, Barrett George *lawyer*

Salem
Bowman, Scott McMahan *lawyer*

Sandusky
Bailey, K. Ronald *lawyer*

Shaker Heights
Ekelman, Daniel Louis *lawyer*
Messinger, Donald Hathaway *lawyer*
Tubbs Jones, Stephanie *prosecuting attorney*

Springfield
Browne, William Bitner *lawyer*
Lagos, James Harry *lawyer*

The Plains
†Carsey, Tamara *paralegal*

Toledo
Baker, Richard Southworth *lawyer*
Boesel, Milton Charles, Jr. *lawyer, business executive*
Boggs, Ralph Stuart *retired lawyer*
Brown, Charles Earl *lawyer*
Chilton, Bradley Stewart *law educator*
Dalrymple, Thomas Lawrence *retired lawyer*
Dane, Stephen Mark *lawyer*
Doner, Gary William *lawyer*
Fisher, Donald Wiener *lawyer*
Hiett, Edward Emerson *retired lawyer, glass company executive*
Jackson, Reginald Sherman, Jr. *lawyer*
La Rue, Carl Forman *lawyer*
Leech, Charles Russell, Jr. *lawyer*
Machin, Barbara E. *lawyer*
McCormick, Edward James, Jr. *lawyer*
Morgan, James Edward *lawyer*
Nicholson, Brent Bentley *lawyer, educator*
O'Connell, Maurice Daniel *lawyer*
Pletz, Thomas Gregory *lawyer*
Rice, Kollin Lawrence *lawyer*
St. Clair, Donald David *lawyer*
Spitzer, John Brumback *lawyer*
Tuschman, James Marshall *lawyer*
Webb, Thomas Irwin, Jr. *lawyer*
Wicklund, David Wayne *lawyer*
Zychowicz, Ralph Charles *lawyer*

Troy
Bazler, Frank Ellis *retired lawyer*

Twinsburg
Hill, Thomas Allen *lawyer*

Warren
Dennison, David Short, Jr. *lawyer*
Rossi, Anthony Gerald *lawyer*

West Union
Young, Vernon Lewis *lawyer*

Wickliffe
Kidder, Fred Dockstater *lawyer*

Wilmington
Buckley, Frederick Jean *lawyer*
Schutt, Walter Eugene *lawyer*

Wooster
Kennedy, Charles Allen *lawyer*

Xenia
Chappars, Timothy Stephen *lawyer*

Youngstown
Ausnehmer, John Edward *lawyer*
Blair, Richard Bryson *lawyer*
Briach, George Gary *lawyer, consultant*
Matune, Frank Joseph *lawyer*
Melnick, Robert Russell *lawyer*
Nadler, Myron Jay *lawyer*
Roth, Daniel Benjamin *lawyer, business executive*
Stevens, Paul Edward *lawyer*
Tucker, Don Eugene *retired lawyer*
Wellman, Thomas Peter *lawyer*

Zanesville
Micheli, Frank James *lawyer*

OKLAHOMA

Antlers
Stamper, Joe Allen *lawyer*

Bartlesville
Huchteman, Ralph Douglas *lawyer*
Roff, Alan Lee *lawyer, consultant*

Edmond
Lester, Andrew William *lawyer*
Loving, Susan Brimer *lawyer, former state official*

Enid
Jones, Stephen *lawyer*
Martin, Michael Rex *lawyer*
McNaughton, Alexander Bryant *lawyer*
Musser, William Wesley, Jr. *lawyer*
Wyatt, Robert Lee, IV *lawyer*

Fort Sill
Livingston, Douglas Mark *lawyer*

Guymon
Wood, Donald Euriah *lawyer*

Jones
Dean, Bill Verlin, Jr. *lawyer*

Mcalester
Cornish, Richard Pool *lawyer*

Muskogee
†Green, Bruce *lawyer*
Williams, Betty Outhier *lawyer*

Norman
Fairbanks, Robert Alvin *lawyer*
Pain, Betsy M. *lawyer*
Petersen, Catherine Holland *lawyer*
Talley, Richard Bates *lawyer*

Oklahoma City
†Abbamondi, John Gabriel *lawyer*
Allen, Robert Dee *lawyer*
Almond, David Randolph *lawyer, company executive*
Angel, Arthur Ronald *lawyer, consultant*
Beech, Johnny Gale *lawyer*
Boston, William Clayton *lawyer*
Brooks, Norma Newton *legal assistant*
Champlin, Richard H. *lawyer, insurance company executive*
Christiansen, Mark D. *lawyer*
Coats, Andrew Montgomery *lawyer, former mayor, dean*
Conison, Jay *lawyer*
Court, Leonard *lawyer, educator*
Cunningham, Stanley Lloyd *lawyer*
Decker, Michael Lynn *lawyer, judge*
Derrick, Gary Wayne *lawyer*
Durland, Jack Raymond *lawyer*
Elder, James Carl *lawyer*
Enis, Thomas Joseph *lawyer*
Featherly, Henry Frederick *lawyer*
Gordon, Kevin Dell *lawyer*
Hanna, Terry Ross *lawyer, small business owner*
Hemry, Jerome Eldon *lawyer*
Johnson, Robert Max *lawyer*
Kline, David Adam *lawyer, educator, writer*
Kline, Timothy Deal *lawyer*
Lambird, Mona Salyer *lawyer*
Legg, William Jefferson *lawyer*
Mather, Stephanie J. *lawyer*
McCampbell, Robert Garner *lawyer*
Milsten, Robert B. *lawyer*
Mock, Randall Don *lawyer*
Moler, Edward Harold *lawyer*
Necco, Alexander David *lawyer, educator*
Nesbitt, Charles Rudolph *lawyer, energy consultant*
†Parr, Royse Milton *lawyer, writer, book reviewer*
Parrott, Nancy Sharon *lawyer*
Paul, William George *lawyer*
Reynolds, Norman Eben *lawyer*
Rockett, D. Joe *lawyer*
Ross, William Jarboe *lawyer*
Ryan, Patrick M. *prosecutor*
Schwabe, George Blaine, III *lawyer*
Sowers, Wesley Hoyt *lawyer, management consultant*
Steinhorn, Irwin Harry *lawyer, educator, corporate executive*
Stringer, L.E. (Dean Stringer) *lawyer*
Taliaferro, Henry Beauford, Jr. *lawyer*
Thompson, Carolyn Stallings *lawyer*
Tompkins, Raymond Edgar *lawyer*
Towery, Curtis Kent *lawyer, judge*
Tuck-Richmond, Doletta Sue *prosecutor*
Turpen, Michael Craig *lawyer*
Tytanic, Christopher Alan *lawyer*

Walsh, Lawrence Edward *lawyer*
Wheeler, Albert Lee, III *lawyer, legal consultant*
Wood, Paula Davidson *lawyer*
Woods, Harry Arthur, Jr. *lawyer*
Zevnik-Sawatzky, Donna Dee *litigation coordinator*
Zuhdi, Nabil (Bill) *lawyer, litigator, consultant, producer*

Ponca City
Northcutt, Clarence Dewey *lawyer*
Raley, John W., Jr. *lawyer*

Sapulpa
Gardner, Dale Ray *lawyer*
Lane, Tom Cornelius *lawyer*

Stillwater
Fischer, Richard Samuel *lawyer*

Tulsa
Abrahamson, A. Craig *lawyer*
Anderson, Peer LaFollette *lawyer, petroleum corporation executive*
Arrington, John Leslie, Jr. *lawyer*
Belsky, Martin Henry *law educator, lawyer*
Biolchini, Robert Fredrick *lawyer*
Blackstock, LeRoy *lawyer*
Bowman, David Wesley *lawyer*
Brewster, Clark Otto *lawyer*
Bryant, Hubert Hale *lawyer*
Clark, Gary Carl *lawyer*
Clark, Wendell W. *lawyer*
Cooper, Richard Casey *lawyer*
Davenport, Gerald Bruce *lawyer*
Davis, G. Reuben *lawyer*
Eagan, Claire Veronica *magistrate judge*
Eldridge, Richard Mark *lawyer*
Farrell, John L., Jr. *lawyer, business executive*
Gaberino, John Anthony, Jr. *lawyer*
Gable, G. Ellis *retired lawyer*
Graham, Tony M. *lawyer*
Hatfield, Jack Kenton *lawyer, accountant*
Haynie, Tony Wayne *lawyer*
Hood, William Wayne, Jr. *lawyer*
Howard, Gene Claude *lawyer, former state senator*
Huffman, Robert Allen, Jr. *lawyer*
Imel, John Michael *lawyer*
Kellough, William C. *lawyer*
Kihle, Donald Arthur *lawyer*
Killin, Charles Clark *lawyer*
Kothe, Charles Aloysius *lawyer*
La Sorsa, William George *lawyer, educator*
Lewis, Stephen C. *prosecutor*
Luthey, Graydon Dean, Jr. *lawyer*
Marlar, Donald Floyd *lawyer, partner*
Matthies, Mary Constance T. *lawyer*
Nigh, Robert Russell, Jr. *lawyer*
Slicker, Frederick Kent *lawyer*
Steltzlen, Janelle Hicks *lawyer*
Stewart, Murray Baker *lawyer*
Walker, Floyd Lee *lawyer*

Vinita
Johnston, Oscar Black, III *lawyer*

OREGON

Ashland
Fine, J. David *lawyer*

Beaverton
Fulsher, Allan Arthur *lawyer*
Stewart, Lindsay D. *corporate lawyer*

Brookings
Maxwell, William Stirling *retired lawyer*

Camas Valley
Lounsbury, Steven Richard *lawyer*

Canby
Drummond, Gerard Kasper *lawyer, retired minerals company executive*
Thalhofer, Paul Terrance *lawyer*

Cannon Beach
Hillestad, Charles Andrew *lawyer*

Central Point
Richardson, Dennis Michael *lawyer, educator*

Eugene
Clark, Chapin DeWitt *law educator*
DuPriest, Douglas Millhollen *lawyer*
Henner, Martin E. *arbitrator, mediator*
Mumford, William Porter, II *lawyer*
Sahlstrom, E(lmer) B(ernard) *retired lawyer*
Scoles, Eugene Francis *law educator, lawyer*

Lake Oswego
†Bullivant, Rupert Reid *lawyer*
Byczynski, Edward Frank *lawyer, financial executive*

Lebanon
Kuntz, Joel Dubois *lawyer*

Medford
Deatherage, William Vernon *lawyer*
Mansfield, William Amos *lawyer*
O'Connor, Karl William (Goodyear Johnson) *lawyer*

Oregon City
Hill, Gary D. *lawyer*

Portland
Abrams, Marc *lawyer, state political party executive*
Abravanel, Allan Ray *lawyer*
Achterman, Gail Louise *lawyer*
Anderson, Herbert Hatfield *lawyer, farmer*
Arthur, Michael Elbert *lawyer*
Bakkensen, John Reser *lawyer*
Balmer, Thomas Ancil *lawyer*
Berger, Leland Roger *lawyer*
Bernstine, Daniel O'Neal *law educator, university president*
Brenneman, Delbert Jay *lawyer*
Cable, John Franklin *lawyer*
Canaday, Richard A. *lawyer*
Chevis, Cheryl Ann *lawyer*
†Cooke, Roger Anthony *lawyer*
Crowell, John B., Jr. *lawyer, former government official*
Dahl, Joyle Cochran *lawyer*
Dailey, Dianne K. *lawyer*
Deering, Thomas Phillips *lawyer*
Dotten, Michael Chester *lawyer*
Edwards, Richard Alan *lawyer*
Eighmey, George V. *lawyer, state legislator*
English, Stephen F. *lawyer*
Epstein, Edward Louis *lawyer*
Fell, James F. *lawyer*
Feuerstein, Howard M. *lawyer*
Foley, Ridgway Knight, Jr. *lawyer, writer*
Foster, Mark Edward *lawyer, consultant, international lobbyist*
Franzke, Richard Albert *lawyer*
Georges, Maurice Ostrow *retired lawyer*
Glasgow, William Jacob *lawyer, venture capitalist, business executive*
Greene, Herbert Bruce *lawyer, investor*
Hanna, Harry Mitchell *lawyer*
Harrell, Gary Paul *lawyer*
Hart, John Edward *lawyer*
Helmer, M(artha) Christie *lawyer*
Hergenhan, Kenneth William *lawyer*
Hinkle, Charles Frederick *lawyer, clergyman, educator*
Holman, Donald Reid *lawyer*
Howorth, David Bishop *lawyer*
Hurd, Paul Gemmill *lawyer*
Jernstedt, Kenneth Elliott *lawyer*
†Johnson, Mark Andrew *lawyer*
Josephson, Richard Carl *lawyer*
Kennedy, Jack Leland *lawyer*
Kester, Randall Blair *lawyer*
Knoll, James Lewis *lawyer*
Krahmer, Donald Leroy, Jr. *lawyer*
Larpenteur, James Albert, Jr. *lawyer*
Leedy, Robert Allan, Sr. *retired lawyer*
Lindley, Thomas Ernest *environmental and trial lawyer, law educator*
Love, William Edward *lawyer*
Maloney, Robert E., Jr. *lawyer*
Matarazzo, Harris Starr *lawyer*
Miller, William Richey, Jr. *lawyer*
Mowe, Gregory Robert *lawyer*
Nash, Frank Erwin *lawyer*
Nunn, Robert Warne *lawyer*
Purcell, John F. *lawyer*
Rawlinson, Dennis Patrick *lawyer*
Richardson, Campbell *lawyer*
Richter, Peter Christian *lawyer*
Rosenbaum, Lois Omenn *lawyer*
Rubin, Bruce Alan *lawyer*
Rutzick, Mark Charles *lawyer*
Ryan, John Duncan *lawyer*
Sand, Thomas Charles *lawyer*
Savage, John William *lawyer*
Schuster, Philip Frederick, II *lawyer, writer*
Shinn, Michael Robert *lawyer*
Simpson, Robert Glenn *lawyer*
Sokol, Larry Nides *lawyer, educator*
Stewart, Milton Roy *lawyer*
Stone, Richard James *lawyer*
Strader, Timothy Richards *lawyer*
Sullivan, Edward Joseph *lawyer, educator*
Troutwine, Gayle Leone *lawyer*
Van Valkenburg, Edgar Walter *lawyer*
Weaver, Delbert Allen *lawyer*
Westwood, James Nicholson *lawyer*
Whinston, Arthur Lewis *lawyer*
White, Douglas James, Jr. *lawyer*
Wiener, Norman Joseph *lawyer*
Wilson, Owen Meredith, Jr. *lawyer*
Wood, Marcus Andrew *lawyer*
Wright, Charles Edward *lawyer*
Wyse, William Walker *lawyer, real estate executive*
Zalutsky, Morton Herman *lawyer*

Salem
Bailey, Henry John, III *retired lawyer, educator*
Breen, Richard F., Jr. *law librarian, lawyer, educator*
Bulkley, Robert De Groff, Jr. *lawyer*
Gatti, Daniel Jon *lawyer*
Hartley, Karen Jeanette *lawyer, mediator, state official*
Haselton, Rick Thomas *lawyer*
Mannix, Kevin Leese *lawyer*
Nafziger, James Albert Richmond *lawyer, educator*
Walsh, Richard Michael *lawyer*

Springfield
Wilson, Virgil James, III *lawyer*

Tigard
Lowry, David Burton *lawyer*

Wilsonville
Yacob, Yosef *lawyer, economist*

PENNSYLVANIA

Allentown
Agger, James H. *lawyer*
Brown, Robert Wayne *lawyer*
Frank, Bernard *lawyer*
Holt, Leon Conrad, Jr. *lawyer, business executive*
Nagel, Edward McCaul *lawyer, former utilities executive*
Simmons, James Charles *lawyer*

Allison Park
Herrington, John David, III *lawyer*
Ries, William Campbell *lawyer*

Altoona
Serbin, Richard Martin *lawyer*

Annville
Warshaw, Roberta Sue *lawyer, financial specialist*

Bala Cynwyd
Cades, Stewart Russell *lawyer, communications company executive*
Chovanes, Eugene *lawyer*
Ezold, Nancy O'Mara *lawyer*
Garrity, Vincent Francis, Jr. *lawyer*
Gerber, Albert B. *lawyer, former legal association executive*
Kane-Vanni, Patricia Ruth *lawyer, production consultant, educator*
Lasak, John Joseph *lawyer*
Manko, Joseph Martin, Sr. *lawyer*
Odell, Herbert *lawyer*
Wiener, Thomas Eli *lawyer*

Bangor
Spry, Donald Francis, II *lawyer*

Beaver
Ledebur, Linas Vockroth, Jr. *retired lawyer*

Berwyn
Ewing, Joseph Neff, Jr. *lawyer*
Gadsden, Christopher Henry *lawyer*
Huffaker, John Boston *lawyer*
Ledwith, James Robb *lawyer*
Markle, John, Jr. *lawyer*
Watters, Edward McLain, III *lawyer*
Wood, Thomas E. *lawyer*

Bethlehem
Graham, William Henry *lawyer*

Blue Bell
Barron, Harold Sheldon *lawyer*
Elliott, John Michael *lawyer*
Settle, Eric Lawrence *lawyer*
Siedzikowski, Henry Francis *lawyer*
Simon, David Frederick *lawyer*
Swansen, Samuel Theodore *lawyer*
Teklits, Joseph Anthony *lawyer*

Bradford
Hauser, Christopher George *lawyer*

Brookville
Smith, Sharon Louise *lawyer, consultant*

Broomall
Narin, Stephen B. *lawyer*

Bryn Mawr
Hankin, Mitchell Robert *lawyer*

Center Valley
Smillie, Douglas James *lawyer*

Chadds Ford
Cohen, Felix Asher *lawyer*

Charleroi
Savona, Michael Joseph *lawyer*

Churchill Borough
Aronson, Mark Berne *consumer advocate*

Clarks Summit
Beemer, John Barry *lawyer*

Clearfield
Falvo, Mark Anthony *lawyer*

Conshohocken
Bramson, Robert Sherman *lawyer*

Conway
Krebs, Robert Alan *lawyer*

Doylestown
Elliott, Richard Howard *lawyer*
Gathright, Howard T. *lawyer*
Rubenstein, Alan Morris *district attorney*

Drexel Hill
West, Kenneth Edward *lawyer*

Du Bois
Blakley, Benjamin Spencer, III *lawyer*

East Petersburg
Whare, Wanda Snyder *lawyer*

Easton
Brown, Robert Carroll *lawyer*
Noel, Nicholas, III *lawyer*

Elkins Park
Dickstein, Joan Borteck *arbitrator, conflict management consultant*

Exton
Ashton, Mark Randolph *lawyer*
Hedges, Donald Walton *lawyer*

Feasterville Trevose
Osterhout, Richard Cadwallader *lawyer*

Gibsonia
Heilman, Carl Edwin *lawyer*

Gladwyne
Acton, David *lawyer*
Booth, Harold Waverly *lawyer, finance and investment company executive*

Glassport
Lippard, Thomas Eugene *lawyer*

Glenside
†Adelsberger, Donna L. *lawyer, educator*
Mermelstein, Jules Joshua *lawyer, township official*

Greensburg
Galloway, Richard H. *lawyer*
Gounley, Dennis Joseph *lawyer*

Grove City
McBride, Milford Lawrence, Jr. *lawyer*

Harrisburg
Allen, Heath Ledward *lawyer*
Barasch, David M. *prosecutor*
Barto, Charles O., Jr. *lawyer*
Boswell, William Douglas *lawyer*
Burcat, Joel Robin *lawyer*
Cline, Andrew Haley *lawyer*
Cramer, John McNaight *lawyer*
Diehm, James Warren *lawyer, educator*
Frye, Mary Catherine *prosecutor*
Hafer, Joseph Page *lawyer*
Hanson, Robert DeLolle *lawyer*
Howett, John Charles, Jr. *lawyer*
Kane, Yvette *lawyer, federal judge*
Kelly, Robert Edward, Jr. *lawyer*
Klein, Michael D. *lawyer*
Kury, Franklin Leo *lawyer*
Lappas, Spero Thomas *lawyer*
Preski, Brian Joseph *lawyer*
Schore, Niles *lawyer*
Shakely, William Warren *lawyer*
Sheldon, J. Michael *lawyer, educator*
Stefanon, Anthony *lawyer*
Sullivan, John Cornelius, Jr. *lawyer*
Van Zile, Philip Taylor, III *lawyer, educator*
Warshaw, Allen Charles *lawyer*
West, James Joseph *lawyer*

Hatboro
John, Robert McClintock *lawyer*
Nicholson, Bruce Allen *lawyer*

Haverford
Frick, Benjamin Charles *lawyer*
McGlinn, Frank Cresson Potts *lawyer*
Stroud, James Stanley *retired lawyer*
Szabad, George Michael *lawyer, former mayor*

Hazleton
Schiavo, Pasco Louis *lawyer*

Holtwood
Campbell, Paul Gary *lawyer*

Huntingdon Valley
Forman, Howard Irving *lawyer, former government official*

Indiana
Barbor, John Howard *lawyer*

Jenkintown
Michie, Daniel Boorse, Jr. *lawyer*

Jersey Shore
Flayhart, Martin Albert *lawyer*

Johnstown
Glosser, William Louis *lawyer*
Kaharick, Jerome John *lawyer*

Jones Mills
Fish, Paul Waring *lawyer*

Kennett Square
Partnoy, Ronald Allen *lawyer*

Kingston
Meyer, Martin Jay *lawyer*

Lake Harmony
Polansky, Larry Paul *court administrator, consultant*

Lancaster
Duroni, Charles Eugene *retired lawyer, food products executive*
Minney, Michael Jay *lawyer*
Nast, Dianne Martha *lawyer*
Pyfer, John Frederick, Jr. *lawyer*
Zimmerman, D(onald) Patrick *lawyer*

Langhorne
Hillje, Barbara Brown *lawyer*

Lansdale
Sultanik, Jeffrey Ted *lawyer*

Lansdowne
Kyriazis, Arthur John (Athanasios Ioannis Kyriazis) *lawyer*

Lewistown
Levin, Allen Joseph *lawyer*

Ligonier
Walters, Gomer Winston *lawyer*

Lock Haven
Snowiss, Alvin L. *lawyer*

Macungie
Gavin, Austin *retired lawyer*

Malvern
Cameron, John Clifford *lawyer, health science facility administrator*
Moulton, Hugh Geoffrey *lawyer, business executive*
Quay, Thomas Emery *lawyer*

Marietta
Shumaker, Harold Dennis *lawyer*

Mc Keesport
Kessler, Steven Fisher *lawyer*

Mc Murray
Brzustowicz, John Cinq-Mars *lawyer*

Media
Elman, Gerry Jay *lawyer*
Emerson, Sterling Jonathan *lawyer*
Ewing, Robert Clark *lawyer*
Garrison, Susan Kay *lawyer*
Tomlinson, Herbert Weston *lawyer*
Zicherman, David L. *lawyer, educator, financial consultant*

Mendenhall
Reinert, Norbert Frederick *patent lawyer, retired chemical company executive*

Merion
Laddon, Warren Milton *lawyer, arbitrator*

Middletown
Pannebaker, James Boyd *lawyer*

Moon Township
Alstadt, Lynn Jeffery *lawyer*
Lipson, Barry J. *lawyer, columnist*

Morrisville
Glosser, Harry John, Jr. *lawyer*
Heefner, William Frederick *lawyer*

Narberth
Mezvinsky, Edward M. *lawyer*

New Castle
Flannery, Harry Audley *lawyer*
Mangino, Matthew Thomas *lawyer*

Newtown
Godwin, Robert Anthony *lawyer*
Simkanich, John Joseph *lawyer, engineer*

Newtown Square
Bower, Ward Alan *management consultant, lawyer*

Norristown
Aman, George Matthias, III *lawyer*
Gregg, John Pennypacker *lawyer*
Rounick, Jack A. *lawyer, company executive*
Scheffler, Stuart Jay *lawyer*
Williamson, Ronald Thomas *lawyer*

Oakmont
Medonis, Robert Xavier *lawyer*

Paoli
Emory, Hugh Mercer *lawyer*

Philadelphia
Aaron, Kenneth Ellyot *lawyer*
Abbott, Frank Harry *lawyer*
Abraham, Lynne M. *district attorney*
Abramowitz, Robert Leslie *lawyer*
Adams, Arlin Marvin *lawyer, arbitrator, mediator, retired judge*
Anders, Jerrold P. *lawyer*
Aronstein, Martin Joseph *lawyer, educator*
Auten, David Charles *lawyer*
Baccini, Laurance Ellis *lawyer*
Bachman, Arthur *lawyer*
Bales, John Foster, III *lawyer*
Ballengee, James McMorrow *lawyer*
Barrett, John J(ames), Jr. *lawyer*
Baum, E. Harris *lawyer*
Beasley, James Edwin *lawyer*
Berger, David *lawyer*
Berger, Harold *lawyer, engineer*
Berkley, Emily Carolan *lawyer*
Berkman, Richard Lyle *lawyer*
Bernard, John Marley *lawyer, educator*
Bershad, Jack R. *lawyer*
Best, Franklin Luther, Jr. *lawyer*
Bildersee, Robert Alan *lawyer*
Binder, David Franklin *lawyer, author*
Black, Allen Decatur *lawyer*
Black, Creed C., Jr. *lawyer*
Bloom, Michael Anthony *lawyer*
Blumstein, Edward *lawyer*
Bochetto, George Alexander *lawyer*
Boda, Veronica Constance *lawyer*
Bogutz, Jerome Edwin *lawyer*
Boss, Amelia Helen *law educator, lawyer*
Bradley, Raymond Joseph *lawyer*
Bressler, Barry E. *lawyer*
Brown, Richard P., Jr. *lawyer*
Brown, Stephen D. *lawyer*
Brown, William Hill, III *lawyer*
Browne, Stanhope Stryker *lawyer*
Burbank, Stephen Bradner *law educator*
Cabot, Stephen Jay *lawyer*
Calvert, Jay H., Jr. *lawyer*
Cannon, John, III *lawyer*
Carnecchia, Baldo M., Jr. *lawyer*
Carroll, Thomas Colas *lawyer, educator*
Carter, Richard E(itel) *legal association executive*
Casper, Charles B. *lawyer*
Chang, Howard Fenghau *law educator, economist*
Cherken, Harry Sarkis, Jr. *lawyer*
Cheston, George Morris *lawyer*
Chiacchiere, Mark Dominic *lawyer*
Chimples, George *lawyer*
Clark, John Arthur *lawyer*
Clark, William H., Jr. *lawyer*
Clothier, Isaac H., IV *lawyer*
Cohen, David Louis *lawyer*
Cohen, Sylvan M. *lawyer*
Coleman, Robert J. *lawyer*
Collings, Robert L. *lawyer*
Comfort, Robert Dennis *lawyer*
Comisky, Hope A. *lawyer*
Comisky, Marvin *retired lawyer*
Connor, Joseph Patrick, III *lawyer*
Cooney, John Gordon *lawyer*
Cooney, J(ohn) Gordon, Jr. *lawyer*
Cooper, Wendy Fein *lawyer*
Cox, Roger Frazier *lawyer*
Coyne, Charles Cole *lawyer*
Cramer, Harold *lawyer*
Crawford, James Douglas *lawyer*
Crough, Daniel Francis *lawyer, insurance company executive*
Dabrowski, Doris Jane *lawyer*
Damsgaard, Kell Marsh *lawyer*
Darby, Karen Sue *legal education administrator*
Davidson, Stuart West *lawyer*
Davis, Alan Jay *lawyer*
Davis, C. VanLeer, III *lawyer*
Davis, Howard Jeffrey *lawyer*
DeBunda, Salvatore Michael *lawyer*
Del Raso, Joseph Vincent *lawyer*
Deming, Frank Stout *lawyer*
Dennis, Edward S(pencer) G(ale), Jr. *lawyer*
Denworth, Raymond K. *lawyer*
Devlin, John Gerard *lawyer, author*
Diamond, Paul Steven *lawyer*
Diaz, Nelson Angel *lawyer*
Dichter, Mark S. *lawyer*
Dilks, Park Bankert, Jr. *lawyer*
Diver, Colin S. *law educator, dean*
Donahue, John M(ichael) *lawyer*
Donohue, James J. *lawyer*
Donohue, John Patrick *lawyer*
Doran, William Michael *lawyer*
Dorfman, John Charles *lawyer*
Drake, William Frank, Jr. *lawyer*
Dubin, Leonard *lawyer*
Dubin, Stephen Victor *lawyer, holding company executive*
Durant, Marc *lawyer*
Dworetzky, Joseph Anthony *lawyer, city official*
Elkins, S. Gordon *lawyer*
Epstein, Alan Bruce *lawyer*
Esser, Carl Eric *lawyer*
Fader, Henry Conrad *lawyer*
Fala, Herman C. *lawyer*
Falcao, Linda Phyllis *lawyer, former screenwriter*
Feirson, Steven B. *lawyer*
Feldman, Albert Joseph *lawyer*
Ferst, Walter B. *lawyer*
Fickler, Arlene *lawyer*
Fiebach, H. Robert *lawyer*
Fioretti, Michael D. *lawyer*
Fitts, Michael Andrew *law educator*
Flanagan, Joseph Patrick, Jr. *lawyer*
Flaster, Richard Joel *lawyer*
Frank, Barry H. *lawyer*
Frank, Harvey *lawyer, author*
Freedman, Robert Louis *lawyer*
Fritton, Karl Andrew *lawyer*
Garcia, Rudolph *lawyer*
Genkin, Barry Howard *lawyer*
German, Edward Cecil *lawyer*
Gilberg, Kenneth Roy *lawyer*
Glanton, Richard H. *lawyer*
Glassman, Howard Theodore *lawyer*
Glassmoyer, Thomas Parvin *lawyer*
Glazer, Ronald Barry *lawyer*
Goldberg, Marvin Allen *lawyer, business consultant*
Goldman, Gary Craig *lawyer*
Goldman, Jerry Stephen *lawyer*
Goldstein, William Marks *lawyer*
Golomb, Richard Moss *lawyer*
Goodman, Stephen Murry *lawyer*
Goodrich, Herbert Funk, Jr. *lawyer*
Gough, John Francis *lawyer*
Granoff, Gail Patricia *lawyer*
Grant, M. Duncan *lawyer*
Grant, Richard W. *lawyer*
Greenfield, Bruce Harold *lawyer, banker*
Grove, David Lavan *lawyer*
Haley, Vincent Peter *lawyer*
Hanselmann, Fredrick Charles *lawyer*
Harkins, John Graham, Jr. *lawyer*
Harmelin, Stephen Joseph *lawyer*
Hauptfuhrer, George Jost, Jr. *lawyer*
Haviland, Bancroft Dawley *lawyer*
Haydanek, Ronald Edward *lawyer and consultant*
Henrich, William Joseph, Jr. *lawyer*
Hess, Hans Ober *lawyer*
Hoelscher, Robert James *lawyer*
Hoffman, Alan Jay *lawyer*
†Huang, Peter Henry *law educator*
Hunter, Jack Duval *lawyer*
Hunter, James Austen, Jr. *lawyer*
Jellinek, Miles Andrew *lawyer*
Jones, Robert Jeffries *lawyer*
Jones, Robert Mead, Jr. *lawyer*
Justice, Jack Burton *retired lawyer*
Kahn, James Robert *lawyer*
Kaier, Edward John *lawyer*
Kaufman, David Joseph *lawyer*
Kempin, Frederick Gustav, Jr. *lawyer, educator*
Kendall, Robert Louis, Jr. *lawyer*
Kessler, Alan Craig *lawyer*
King, David Roy *lawyer*
Klasko, Herbert Ronald *lawyer, law educator, writer*
Klaus, William Robert *lawyer*
Klein, Howard Bruce *lawyer, law educator*
Klein, Samuel Edwin *lawyer*
Kohn, Harold Elias *lawyer*
Kopp, Charles Gilbert *lawyer*
Kraemer, Michael Frederick *lawyer*
Krampf, John Edward *lawyer*
Krebs, Hope Paula *lawyer*
Krzyzanowski, Richard L(ucien) *lawyer, corporate executive*
Kunnel, Joseph Mathew *lawyer*
Ledwith, John Francis *lawyer*
Leonard, Thomas Aloysius *lawyer*
Levin, A. Leo *law educator, retired government official*
Levin, Murray Simon *lawyer*
Levy, Dale Penneys *lawyer*
Lewis, John Hardy, Jr. *lawyer*
Libonati, Michael Ernest *lawyer, educator, writer*
Lichtenstein, Robert Jay *lawyer*
Lillie, Charisse Ranielle *lawyer, educator*
Lipman, Frederick D. *lawyer, writer, educator*
Loewenstein, Benjamin Steinberg *lawyer*
Lombard, John James, Jr. *lawyer*
Loveless, George Group *lawyer*
Lowery, William Herbert *lawyer*
Lundy, Joseph E. *lawyer*
Luongo, Stephen Earle *lawyer*
Maclay, Donald Merle *lawyer*
Madeira, Edward W(alter), Jr. *lawyer*
Madva, Stephen Alan *lawyer*
Magargee, W(illiam) Scott, III *lawyer*
Magaziner, Fred Thomas *lawyer*
Mann, Theodore R. *lawyer*
Mannino, Edward Francis *lawyer*
Mason, Theodore W. *lawyer*
Mathes, Stephen Jon *lawyer*
Mattoon, Peter Mills *lawyer*
Maxey, David Walker *lawyer*
McHugh, James Joseph *lawyer*
McKeever, John Eugene *lawyer*
McMichael, Lawrence Grover *lawyer*
McQuiston, Robert Earl *lawyer*
Meigs, John Forsyth *lawyer*
Meyers, Howard L. *lawyer*
Milbourne, Walter Robertson *lawyer*
Miller, Henry Franklin *lawyer*
†Milone, Francis Michael *lawyer*
Minisi, Anthony S. *lawyer*
Mirabello, Francis Joseph *lawyer*
Mitchell, Charles Edward *lawyer*
Moss, Arthur Henshey *lawyer*
Mullinix, Edward Wingate *lawyer*
Murphy, Daniel Ignatius *lawyer*
Nofer, George Hancock *lawyer*
Nowak, Gregory Joseph *lawyer, educator*
O'Connor, Joseph A., Jr. *lawyer*
O'Donnell, G. Daniel *lawyer*
O'Leary, Dennis Joseph *lawyer*
Ominsky, Alan Jay *lawyer, medical educator*
Ominsky, Harris *lawyer*
O'Reilly, Timothy Patrick *lawyer*
Oswald, Stanton S. *lawyer*
Pagliaro, James Domenic *lawyer*
Palmer, Richard Ware *lawyer*
Parry, William DeWitt *lawyer*
Phillips, Dorothy Kay *lawyer*
Phillips, Stephen S. *lawyer*
Pollack, Michael *lawyer*
Pollard, Dennis Bernard *lawyer, educator*
Posner, Edward Martin *lawyer*
Poul, Franklin *lawyer*
Powell, Walter Hecht *labor arbitrator*
Presser, Stefan *lawyer, educator*
Price, Robert Stanley *lawyer*
Putney, Paul William *lawyer*
Quinn, Charles Norman *lawyer*
Rabinowitz, Samuel Nathan *lawyer*
Rachofsky, David J. *lawyer*
Rackow, Julian Paul *lawyer*
Rainone, Michael Carmine *lawyer*
Ramsey, Natalie D. *lawyer*
Raymond, Fred Douglas, III *lawyer*
Reed, Michael Haywood *lawyer*
Reich, Abraham Charles *lawyer*
Reiss, John Barlow *lawyer*
Reiter, Joseph Henry *lawyer, retired judge*
Reitz, Curtis Randall *lawyer, educator*
Roberts, Carl Geoffrey *lawyer*
Roomberg, Lila Goldstein *lawyer*
Root, Stanley William, Jr. *lawyer, retired*
Rosenbleeth, Richard Marvin *lawyer*
Rosenbloom, Sanford M. *lawyer*
Rosenstein, James Alfred *lawyer, negotiation facilitator*
Ross, Daniel R. *lawyer*
Rudolph, Andrew J. *lawyer*
Samuel, Ralph David *lawyer*
Satinsky, Barnett *lawyer*
Schaub, Harry Carl *lawyer*
Scher, Howard Dennis *lawyer*
Schneider, Carl William *lawyer*
Schneider, Richard Graham *lawyer*
Schwartz, Robert M. *lawyer*
Scott, Donald Allison *lawyer*
Scott, William Proctor, III *lawyer*
Segal, Irving Randall *lawyer*
Segal, Robert Martin *lawyer*
Shapiro, Raymond L. *lawyer*
Sheils, Denis Francis *lawyer*
Shestack, Jerome Joseph *lawyer*
Shiekman, Laurence Zeid *lawyer*
Shipman, Lynn Karen *lawyer*
Shmukler, Stanford *lawyer*
Siegel, Bernard Louis *lawyer*
Sigmond, Richard Brian *lawyer*
Siskind, Ralph Walter *lawyer*
Solano, Carl Anthony *lawyer*
Somers, Hans Peter *lawyer*
Spaeth, Edmund Benjamin, Jr. *lawyer, law educator, former judge*
Sparrow, Ruth S. *lawyer*
Spector, Martin Wolf *lawyer, business executive*
Speyer, Debra Gail *lawyer*
Steinberg, Robert Philip *lawyer*
Stern, Joan Naomi *lawyer*
Stewart, Robert Forrest, Jr. *lawyer*
Stiles, Michael *prosecutor*
Stiller, Jennifer Anne *lawyer*
Strasbaugh, Wayne Ralph *lawyer*
Strickler, Matthew M. *lawyer*
Stuntebeck, Clinton A. *lawyer*
Subak, John Thomas *lawyer*
Summers, Clyde Wilson *law educator*
Temin, Michael Lehman *lawyer*
Thomas, Lowell Shumway, Jr. *lawyer*
Tiger, Ira Paul *lawyer*
Toll, Seymour Irving *lawyer, writer, educator*
Tractenberg, Craig R. *lawyer*
Tumola, Thomas Joseph *lawyer*
Vaira, Peter Francis *lawyer*
Vogel, Robert Philip *lawyer*
Wagner, Thomas Joseph *lawyer, insurance company executive*
Walker, Kent *lawyer*
Warner, Theodore Kugler, Jr. *lawyer*
Weil, Jeffrey George *lawyer*
Weisberg, Morris L. *retired lawyer*
Wert, Robert Clifton *lawyer*
Whiteside, William Anthony, Jr. *lawyer*
Wild, Richard P. *lawyer*
Wilf, Frederic Marshal *lawyer*
Wittels, Barnaby Caesar *lawyer*
Wolf, Bruce *lawyer*
Wolf, Robert B. *lawyer*
Wolff, Deborah H(orowitz) *lawyer*
Woods, Teri *paralegal, writer*
Wright, Minturn Tatum, III *lawyer*
Wrobleski, Jeanne Pauline *lawyer*
Young, Andrew Brodbeck *lawyer*
Zivitz, Stephen Charles *lawyer*

Pipersville
Sigety, Charles Edward *lawyer, family business consultant*

Pittsburgh
Aaron, Marcus, II *lawyer*
Aderson, Sanford M. *lawyer*
Anderson, Edwyna Goodwin *lawyer*
†Artz, John Curtis *lawyer*
Baldauf, Kent Edward *lawyer*
Basinski, Anthony Joseph *lawyer*
Bellisario, Domenic Anthony *lawyer*
Bleier, Michael E. *lawyer*
Bleil, Walter G. *lawyer*
Blenko, Walter John, Jr. *lawyer*
Bonessa, Dennis R. *lawyer*
Boocock, Stephen William *lawyer*
Boswell, William Paret *lawyer*
Breault, Theodore Edward *lawyer*
Brennan, Carey M. *lawyer*
Brown, Ronald James *lawyer, political consultant*
Burke, Linda Beerbower *lawyer, aluminum manufacturing company executive, mining executive*
Burke, Timothy Francis, Jr. *lawyer*
Candris, Laura A. *lawyer*
Cheever, George Martin *lawyer*
Chipman, Debra Decker *paralegal*
Cohen, Henry C. *lawyer*
Colen, Frederick Haas *lawyer*
Coney, Aims C., Jr. *lawyer, labor-management negotiator*
Connors, Eugene Kenneth *lawyer, educator*
Conti, Joy Flowers *lawyer*
Cooper, Thomas Louis *lawyer*
Corbett, Thomas Wingett, Jr. *lawyer*
Cowan, Barton Zalman *lawyer*
Daniel, Robert Michael *lawyer*
Davis, John Phillips, Jr. *lawyer*
DeForest, Walter Pattison, III *lawyer*
Dell, Ernest Robert *lawyer*
Demmler, John Henry *lawyer*
Denys, Sylvia *lawyer*
Donnelly, Thomas Joseph *lawyer*
Doty, Robert Walter *lawyer*
Dugan, John F. *lawyer*
Ehrenwerth, David Harry *lawyer*
Evans, Bruce Dwight *lawyer*
Ewalt, Henry Ward *lawyer*
Farley, Andrew Newell *lawyer*
Ferguson, Sanford Barnett *lawyer*
Flatley, Lawrence Edward *lawyer*
Flinn, Michael James *lawyer*
Fort, James Tomlinson *lawyer*
Frank, Ronald William *lawyer, financier*
Geeseman, Robert George *lawyer*
Gerlach, G. Donald *lawyer*
Gold, Harold Arthur *lawyer*
Hague, Paul Christian *lawyer*
Halpern, Richard I. *lawyer*
Hardie, James Hiller *lawyer*
Harff, Charles Henry *lawyer, retired diversified industrial company executive*
Harvey, Calvin Rea *lawyer*
Hellman, Arthur David *law educator, consultant*
Helmrich, Joel Marc *lawyer*
Hershey, Dale *lawyer*
Hershey, Nathan *lawyer, educator*
Hess, Emerson Garfield *lawyer*
Hill, John Howard *lawyer*
Hoffstot, Henry Phipps, Jr. *lawyer*
Hollinshead, Earl Darnell, Jr. *lawyer*
Hull, John Daniel, IV *lawyer*
Isabella, Mary Margaret *lawyer*
Johnson, Robert Alan *lawyer*
Jones, Craig Ward *lawyer*
Jordan, Sandra Dickerson *law educator*
Kearns, John J., III *lawyer*
Keenan, C. Robert, III *lawyer*
Kelleher, William Eugene, Jr. *lawyer*
†Kelly, Linda L. *prosecutor*
Kelson, Richard B. *lawyer*
Kenrick, Charles William *lawyer*
Ketter, David Lee *lawyer*
Klett, Edwin Lee *lawyer*
Klodowski, Harry Francis, Jr. *lawyer*
Knox, Charles Graham *lawyer*
Lefkowitz, Alan Zoel *lawyer*
Leibowitz, Marvin *lawyer*
Letwin, Jeffrey William *lawyer*
Litman, Harry Peter *lawyer, educator*
Litman, Roslyn Margolis *lawyer, educator*
Lovisсky, Douglas Charles *lawyer*
Mansmann, J. Jerome *lawyer*
McCabe, Lawrence James *lawyer, food products company executive*
McCartney, Robert Charles *lawyer*
McConomy, James Herbert *lawyer*
McGinley, John Regis, Jr. *lawyer*
McGough, Walter Thomas, Jr. *lawyer*
McKee, Ralph Dyer, Jr. *lawyer*
McLaughlin, John Sherman *lawyer*
Meisel, Alan *law educator*
Mellott, Cloyd Rowe *lawyer*
Messner, Robert Thomas *lawyer, banking executive*
Meyers, Jerry Ivan *lawyer*
Miller, Harbaugh *lawyer*
Mills, Edward James *lawyer, insurance consultant*
Morton, James Davis *lawyer*
Murdoch, David Armor *lawyer*
Murray, John Edward, Jr. *lawyer, educator, university president*
Murrin, Regis Doubet *lawyer*
Nordenberg, Mark Alan *law educator, university official*
Norris, James Harold *lawyer*
Ober, Russell John, Jr. *lawyer*
O'Connor, Donald Thomas *lawyer*
O'Connor, Edward Gearing *lawyer*
Olson, Stephen M(ichael) *lawyer*
Orsatti, Ernest Benjamin *lawyer*
Phillips, Larry Edward *lawyer*
Plowman, Jack Wesley *lawyer*
Pohl, Paul Michael *lawyer*
Pois, Joseph *lawyer, educator*
Powderly, William H., III *lawyer*
Prosperi, Louis Anthony *lawyer*
Pugliese, Robert Francis *lawyer, business executive*
Quinn, Patrick William *lawyer*
Randolph, Robert DeWitt *lawyer*
Reed, W. Franklin *lawyer*
Restivo, James John, Jr. *lawyer*
Ritchey, Patrick William *lawyer*
Roman, Andrew Michael *lawyer, educator*
Rosenberger, Bryan David *lawyer*
Sandman, Dan D. *lawyer*
Scarlata, Charles Francis *lawyer*
Scheinholtz, Leonard Louis *lawyer*
Schliebs, Charles Allan *lawyer*
Schmidt, Edward Craig *lawyer*
Schmidt, Thomas Mellon *lawyer*
Schwab, Arthur James *lawyer*
Schwendeman, Paul William *lawyer*
Scully, Erik Vincent *lawyer, accountant*
Sell, William Edward *legal educator*
Sherry, John Sebastian *lawyer*
Shuman, Joseph Duff *lawyer*
Silverman, Arnold Barry *lawyer*
Sokol, Stephen M. *lawyer*
Stein, Arland Thomas *lawyer*
†Stoner, Eugenia Chambers *lawyer, corporation secretary*
Strader, James David *lawyer*
Sweeney, Clayton Anthony *lawyer, business executive*
Symons, Edward Leonard, Jr. *lawyer, educator, investment advisor*
Tarasi, Louis Michael, Jr. *lawyer*
Thomas, Richard Irwin *lawyer*
Thompson, Thomas Martin *lawyer*
Thurman, Andrew Edward *lawyer*
Tucker, Richard Blackburn, III *lawyer*
Turner, Harry Woodruff *lawyer*
Ubinger, John W., Jr. *lawyer*
Van Kirk, Thomas L. *lawyer*
Vater, Charles J. *lawyer*
Veeder, Peter Greig *lawyer*
von Waldow, Arnd N. *lawyer*
Walton, Jon David *lawyer*
Ward, Thomas Jerome *lawyer*
†Williams, Stephen Edward *corporate lawyer*
Woodward, Thomas Aiken *lawyer*
Wycoff, William Mortimer *lawyer*
Yorsz, Stanley *lawyer*

Plymouth Meeting
Britt, Earl Thomas *lawyer*

Pocono Pines
Hardiman, Therese Anne *lawyer*

Pottsville
Jones, Joseph Hayward *lawyer*
Tamulonis, Frank Louis, Jr. *lawyer*

Reading
Decker, Kurt Hans *lawyer, educator, author*
Kline, Sidney DeLong, Jr. *lawyer*
Rothermel, Daniel Krott *lawyer, holding company executive*
Welty, John Rider *lawyer*

Reynoldsville
Wheeler, Mark Andrew, Sr. *lawyer*

Royersford
Zearfoss, Herbert Keyser *lawyer*

Scranton
Cimini, Joseph Fedele *law educator, lawyer, former magistrate*
Haggerty, James Joseph *lawyer*
Howley, James McAndrew *lawyer*
Myers, Morey Mayer *lawyer*

Solebury
Cross, Robert William *lawyer, venture capital executive*
Valentine, H. Jeffrey *legal association executive*

Somerset
Barkman, Jon Albert *lawyer*
†Kappel, David A. *lawyer*

Spring City
Mayerson, Hy *lawyer*

Spring House
Rosoff, William A. *lawyer, executive*

State College
Nollau, Lee Gordon *lawyer*

Sunbury
Fernsler, John Paul *lawyer*
Saylor, Charles Horace *lawyer*

Swarthmore
Ullman, Roger Roland *lawyer, realtor*

Tannersville
Love, Mark Steven *lawyer*

Trevose
McEvilly, James Patrick, Jr. *lawyer*

Uniontown
Fox, Susan E. *legal assistant*

Valley Forge
Bovaird, Brendan Peter *lawyer*
Walters, Bette Jean *lawyer*

Venetia
Breslin, Elvira Madden *tax lawyer, educator*

Villanova
Bersoff, Donald Neil *lawyer, psychologist*
Cerino, Angela Marie *lawyer, educator*
Maule, James Edward *law educator, lawyer*
Mulroney, Michael *lawyer, law educator, graduate program director*
Termini, Roseann Bridget *lawyer, educator*

Warren
Ristau, Mark Moody *lawyer, petroleum consultant*

Washington
Allison, Jonathan *retired lawyer*
Curran, M(ichael) Scot *lawyer*
Posner, David S. *lawyer*
Richman, Stephen I. *lawyer*

Wayne
Baldwin, Frank Bruce, III *lawyer*
Churchill, Winston John *lawyer, investment firm executive*
Donnella, Michael Andre *lawyer*
Griffith, Edward, II *lawyer*
Kalogredis, Vasilios J. *lawyer, health care management consultant*
Woodbury, Alan Tenney *lawyer*

Wernersville
Worley, Jane Ludwig *lawyer*

West Chester
Casellas, Gilbert F. *lawyer, business executive*
St. Landau, Norman *lawyer*

West Conshohocken
Sharp, M. Rust *lawyer*
Teillon, L. Pierre, Jr. *lawyer*

White Oak
Pribanic, Victor Hunter *lawyer*

Wilkes Barre
Reilly, Michael James *law librarian*
Roth, Eugene *lawyer*
Ufberg, Murray *lawyer*

Williamsport
Ertel, Allen Edward *lawyer, former congressman*
Knecht, William L. *lawyer*

Wormleysburg
Cherewka, Michael *lawyer*

Wynnewood
Carbine, Sharon *lawyer, corporation executive*

York
Davis, Jane G. *corporate lawyer*
Hoffmeyer, William Frederick *lawyer, educator*
Markowitz, Lewis Harrison *lawyer*
Perry, Ronald *lawyer*

RHODE ISLAND

Barrington
Soutter, Thomas Douglas *retired lawyer*

Bristol
Bogus, Carl Thomas *law educator*

Cranston
Cervone, Anthony Louis *lawyer*
†Dillon-Marcotte, Kathryn Anne *Lawyer*
Ferguson, Christine C. *lawyer, state agency administrator*

East Greenwich
Dence, Edward William, Jr. *lawyer, banker*

Little Compton
Caron, Wilfred Rene *lawyer*

Newport
Levie, Howard S(idney) *lawyer, educator, author*
McConnell, David Kelso *lawyer*
Nelligan, Kenneth Egan *lawyer*
Scheck, Frank Foetisch *retired lawyer*

Pawtucket
Kranseler, Lawrence Michael *lawyer*

Providence
Blish, John Harwood *lawyer*
Borod, Richard Melvin *lawyer*
Carlotti, Stephen Jon *lawyer*
Courage, Thomas Roberts *lawyer*
Curran, Joseph Patrick *lawyer*
Donnelly, Kevin William *lawyer*
Esposito, Dennis Harry *lawyer*
Farrell, Margaret Dawson *lawyer*
Field, Noel Macdonald, Jr. *lawyer*
Fogarty, Edward Michael *lawyer*
Furness, Peter John *lawyer*
Gale, Edwin John *prosecutor*
Gasbarro, Pasco, Jr. *lawyer*
Hastings, Edwin H(amilton) *lawyer*
Johnson, Vahe Duncan *lawyer*
†Jones, Lauren Evans *lawyer*
Juchatz, Wayne Warren *lawyer*
Kacir, Barbara Brattin *lawyer*
Kean, John Vaughan *retired lawyer*
Licht, Richard A. *lawyer*
Long, Beverly Glenn *lawyer*
Long, Nicholas Trott *lawyer*
Lynch, William Joseph *lawyer*
McCann, Gail Elizabeth *lawyer*
McIntyre, Jerry L. *lawyer*
Medeiros, Matthew Francis *lawyer*
Olsen, Hans Peter *lawyer*
Parks, Albert Lauriston *lawyer*
Paster, Benjamin G. *lawyer*
Pendergast, John Joseph, III *lawyer*
Pierce, Richard Hilton *lawyer*
Reilly, Charles James *lawyer, educator, accountant*
Robinson, William Philip, III *lawyer*
Salter, Lester Herbert *lawyer*
Sherman, Deming Eliot *lawyer*
Staples, Richard Farnsworth *lawyer*
Svengalis, Kendall Frayne *law librarian*
Walker, Howard Ernest *lawyer*

Scituate
Gorham, Bradford *lawyer*

Slatersville
Pannullo, Deborah Paolino *lawyer, training and consulting company executive*

Wakefield
Rothschild, Donald Phillip *lawyer, arbitrator*

Warwick
Goldman, Steven Jason *lawyer, accountant*
Knowles, Charles Timothy *lawyer, state legislator*
Sholes, David Henry *lawyer, former state senator*

West Warwick
Pollock, Bruce Gerald *lawyer*

SOUTH CAROLINA

Aiken
Maxwell, Ronald A. *lawyer, state political party executive*
Rudnick, Irene Krugman *lawyer, former state legislator, educator*

Anderson
Watkins, William Law *retired lawyer*

Barnwell
Loadholt, Miles *lawyer*

Beaufort
Harvey, William Brantley, Jr. *lawyer, former lieutenant governor*

Camden
Jacobs, Rolly Warren *lawyer*

Charleston
Barker, Douglas Alan *lawyer*
Branham, C. Michael *lawyer*
Cannon, Hugh *lawyer*
Clement, Robert Lebby, Jr. *lawyer*
Darling, Stephen Edward *lawyer*
Good, Joseph Cole, Jr. *lawyer*
Grimball, William Heyward *retired lawyer*
Hood, Robert Holmes *lawyer*
Kahn, Ellis Irvin *lawyer*
Ogier, Alton L. *lawyer*
Patrick, Charles William, Jr. *lawyer*
Spitz, Hugo Max *lawyer*
Warren, John Hertz, III *lawyer*

Clemson
Cox, Headley Morris, Jr. *lawyer, educator*

Columbia
Babcock, Keith Moss *lawyer*

Bailey, George Screven *lawyer*
Blanton, Hoover Clarence *lawyer*
Buchanan, William Jennings *lawyer, judge*
Carpenter, Charles Elford, Jr. *lawyer*
Day, Richard Earl *lawyer, educator*
Finkel, Gerald Michael *lawyer*
Gibbes, William Holman *lawyer*
Handel, Richard Craig *lawyer*
†Harpootlian, Richard Ara *lawyer, political party official*
Johnson, Lawrence Wilbur, Jr. *lawyer*
†Josey, Jon Rene *prosecutor*
Marchant, Bristow *lawyer*
Matthews, Steve Allen *lawyer*
McCullough, Ralph Clayton, II *lawyer, educator*
McMaster, Henry Dargan *lawyer*
Nexsen, Julian Jacobs *lawyer*
Rouse, LeGrand Ariail, II *retired lawyer, educator*
Sloan, Frank Keenan *lawyer, writer*
Strom, J. Preston, Jr. *lawyer*
Strong, Franklin Wallace, Jr. *lawyer*
Tate, Harold Simmons, Jr. *lawyer*
Unger, Richard Mahlon *lawyer*

Dataw Island
Scoville, Laurence McConway, Jr. *arbitrator, mediator*

Denmark
Crum, Henry Hayne *lawyer*

Georgetown
Moore, Albert Cunningham *lawyer, insurance company executive*
Terhune, Jane Howell *legal assistant, educator*

Greenville
Barash, Anthony Harlan *lawyer*
Dobson, Robert Albertus, III *lawyer, executive, volunteer*
Edwards, Harry LaFoy *lawyer*
Foulke, Edwin Gerhart, Jr. *lawyer*
Horton, James Wright *retired lawyer*
Mauldin, John Inglis *public defender*
McKinney, Ronald W. *lawyer*
Oxner, G. Dewey *lawyer*
Phillips, Joseph Brantley, Jr. *lawyer*
Thompson, Robert Thomas *lawyer*
Todd, John Dickerson, Jr. *lawyer*
Walker, Wesley M. *lawyer*
Walters, Johnnie McKeiver *lawyer*
Wyche, Cyril Thomas *lawyer*
Wyche, Madison Baker, III *lawyer*

Greenwood
Nexsen, Julian Jacobs, Jr. *lawyer*

Hartsville
†Shelley, James Herbert *lawyer, paper company executive*

Hilton Head Island
Becker, Karl Martin *lawyer*
Hagoort, Thomas Henry *lawyer*
McKay, John Judson, Jr. *lawyer*
Rose, William Shepard, Jr. *lawyer*
Scarminach, Charles Anthony *lawyer*

Langley
Bell, Robert Morrall *lawyer*

Lexington
Wilkins, Robert Pearce *lawyer*

Mount Pleasant
Laddaga, Lawrence Alexander *lawyer*
McConnell, John William, Jr. *lawyer*

Myrtle Beach
Breen, David Hart *lawyer*

Newberry
Pope, Thomas Harrington, Jr. *lawyer*

Pawleys Island
Daniel, J. Reese *lawyer*

Salem
Everett, C(harles) Curtis *retired lawyer*

Seneca
Fleming, Mack Gerald *lawyer*

Spartanburg
King, Henry Spencer, III *lawyer*

Sumter
†McDougall, John Olin *lawyer*

Union
Dineen, Joseph Lawrence *legal compliance professional, consultant*

Walterboro
Boensch, Arthur Cranwell *lawyer*

West Columbia
Jedziniak, Lee Peter *lawyer, educator, state insurance administrator*

SOUTH DAKOTA

Britton
Farrar, Frank Leroy *lawyer, former governor*

Dakota Dunes
Putney, Mark William *lawyer, utility executive*

Parker
Zimmer, John Herman *lawyer*

Pierre
Johnson, Julie Marie *lawyer/lobbyist*
Miller, Suzanne Marie *law librarian, educator*
Thompson, Charles Murray *lawyer*

Rapid City
Foye, Thomas Harold *lawyer*

Sioux Falls
Haas, Joseph Alan *court administrator, lawyer*
Johnson, Richard Arlo *lawyer*
Schreier, Karen Elizabeth *prosecutor*

Spearfish
Hood, Earl James *lawyer, state legislator*

TENNESSEE

Brentwood
Provine, John C. *lawyer*
Schreiber, Kurt Gilbert *lawyer*

Chattanooga
Adams, Morgan Goodpasture *lawyer*
Akers, Samuel Lee *lawyer*
Campbell, Paul, III *lawyer*
Collier, Curtis Lynn *lawyer*
Cooper, Gary Allan *lawyer*
Copeland, Floyd Dean *lawyer*
Eason, Marcia Jean *lawyer*
Moore, Hugh Jacob, Jr. *lawyer*
Phillips, John Bomar *lawyer*
Proctor, John Franklin *lawyer*
Ragan, Charles Oliver, Jr. *lawyer*
Vital, Patricia Best *lawyer*
Williams, Rosemary Helen *paralegal*

Church Hill
Faulk, Michael Anthony *lawyer*

Clarksville
Love, Michael Joseph *lawyer*
Smith, Gregory Dale *lawyer, judge*

Collierville
Springfield, James Francis *retired lawyer, banker*

Cookeville
Day, David Owen *lawyer*

Dresden
†Swearington, Sheila Holt *parole board official*

Fayetteville
Dickey, John Harwell *lawyer*

Huntsville
Galloway, John W., Jr. *lawyer*

Johnson City
Epps, James Haws, III *lawyer*

Knoxville
Arnett, Foster Deaver *lawyer*
Bly, Robert Maurice *lawyer*
Christenbury, Edward Samuel *lawyer*
Creekmore, David Dickason *lawyer, educator*
Cremins, William Carroll *lawyer*
Dillard, W. Thomas *lawyer*
Giordano, Lawrence Francis *lawyer*
Hagood, Lewis Russell *lawyer*
Howard, Lewis Spilman *lawyer*
Kirkpatrick, Carl Kimmel *prosecutor*
Lloyd, Francis Leon, Jr. *lawyer*
London, James Harry *lawyer*
McCall, Jack Humphreys, Jr. *lawyer*
Midkiff, Kimberly Ann *paralegal*
Murphree, Sharon Ann *lawyer, mediator*
Murphy, Deborah Jane *lawyer*
Ownby, Jere Franklin, III *lawyer*
Phillips, Jerry Juan *law educator*
Rayson, Edwin Hope *lawyer*
Roach, Jon Gilbert *lawyer*
Rodgers, Ralph Emerson *lawyer*
Routh, John William *lawyer*
Smith, Leonard Ware *lawyer*
White, Edward Gibson, II *lawyer*
Worthington, Carole Yard Lynch *lawyer*

Livingston
†Roberts, John M. *law educator, former prosecutor*

Lookout Mountain
Leitner, Paul Revere *lawyer*

Mc Ewen
Williams, John Lee *lawyer*

Memphis
Allen, Newton Perkins *lawyer*
Broadhurst, Jerome Anthony *lawyer*
†Brown, William Houston *lawyer*
Buchignani, Leo Joseph *lawyer*
Carr, Oscar Clark, III *lawyer*
Cody, Walter James Michael *lawyer, former state official*
Coleman, Veronica Freeman *prosecutor*
Cook, August Joseph *lawyer, accountant*
Dann, Alexander William, Jr. *lawyer*
deWitt, Charles Benjamin, III *lawyer, educator*
Friedman, Robert Michael *lawyer*
†Gray, Bruce F(rank) *lawyer*
Haight, Scott Kerr *lawyer*
Harpster, James Erving *lawyer*
Harvey, Albert C. *lawyer*
Latta, Jennie Davidson *lawyer*
Ledbetter, Paul Mark *lawyer, writer*
Manire, James McDonnell *lawyer*
Masterson, Kenneth Rhodes *lawyer*
McLean, Robert Alexander *lawyer*
Monypeny, David Murray *lawyer*
Morgan, Colby Shannon, Jr. *lawyer*
Newman, Charles Forrest *lawyer*
Patton, Charles Henry *lawyer, educator*
Risner, Paul Edward *lawyer*
Rutledge, Roger Keith *lawyer*
Seidman, Phillip Kenneth *lawyer*
Sossaman, William Lynwood *lawyer*
Spore, Richard Roland, III *lawyer, educator*
Steinhauer, Gillian *lawyer*
Summers, James Branson *lawyer*
Tate, Stonewall Shepherd *lawyer*
Terry, Joseph Ray, Jr. *lawyer*
Waddell, Phillip Dean *lawyer*
Wilder, James Sampson, III *lawyer, judge*

Williams, J. Maxwell *lawyer, arbitrator and mediator*

Nashville
Anderson, Charles Hill *lawyer*
Bass, James Orin *lawyer*
Belton, Robert *law educator*
Berry, William Wells *lawyer*
Bloch, Frank Samuel *law educator*
Blumstein, James Franklin *legal educator, lawyer, consultant*
Bostick, Charles Dent *lawyer, educator*
Bramlett, Paul Kent *lawyer*
Burkett, Gerald Arthur *lawyer, musician*
Carr, Davis Haden *lawyer*
Cheek, James Howe, III *lawyer, educator*
Cobb, Stephen A. *lawyer*
Conner, Lewis Homer, Jr. *lawyer*
Covington, Robert Newman *law educator*
Culbertson, Katheryn Campbell *lawyer*
Day, John Arthur *lawyer*
Dean, Karl *public defender*
Edwards, Mark E. *healthcare company lawyer*
Farris, Frank Mitchell, Jr. *retired lawyer*
Freeman, James Atticus, III *lawyer, insurance and business consultant*
Gannon, John Sexton *lawyer, management consultant, arbitrator/mediator*
Gillmor, John Edward *lawyer*
Griffith, James Leigh *lawyer*
Hardin, Hal D. *lawyer, former United States attorney, former judge*
Harris, James Harold, III *lawyer, educator*
Hart, Richard Banner *lawyer*
Lane, William Arthur *lawyer*
Ledyard, Robins Heard *lawyer*
Levinson, L(eslie) Harold *lawyer, educator*
Lyon, Philip K(irkland) *lawyer*
Madu, Leonard Ekwugha *lawyer, human rights officer, newspaper columnist, politician, business executive*
Maier, Harold Geistweit *law educator, lawyer*
May, Joseph Leserman (Jack) *lawyer*
Mayden, Barbara Mendel *lawyer*
Mc Creary, James Franklin *lawyer, mediator*
McNamee, Dennis Patrick *lawyer*
Oldfield, Russell Miller *lawyer*
Parker, Mary Ann *lawyer*
Partlett, David F. *law educator*
Penny, William Lewis *lawyer*
Phillips, W. Alan *entertainment lawyer, educator*
Ramsaur, Allan Fields *lawyer, lobbyist*
Sims, Wilson *lawyer*
Soderquist, Larry Dean *lawyer, educator, consultant, writer*
Trautman, Herman Louis *lawyer, educator*
Tuke, Robert Dudley *lawyer, educator*
White, Bruce David *law and ethics educator*
Winstead, George Alvis *law librarian, biochemist, educator, consultant*
Yuspeh, Alan Ralph *lawyer, healthcare company executive*

Newport
Bell, John Alton *lawyer, judge*

Powell
Hyman, Roger David *lawyer*

Sevierville
Waters, John B. *lawyer*

Signal Mountain
Cook, Arthur John David *labor arbitrator*

Springfield
Wilks, Larry Dean *lawyer*

Trenton
Harrell, Limmie Lee, Jr. *lawyer*

Union City
Graham, Hardy Moore *lawyer*

TEXAS

Abilene
Boone, Billy Warren *lawyer, judge*
Boone, Celia Trimble *lawyer*
Robinson, Vianei Lopez *lawyer*
Surovik, Bob J. *lawyer*
Suttle, Stephen Hungate *lawyer*
Whitten, C. G. *lawyer*
Wilson, Stanley P. *retired lawyer*

Addison
Parr, Richard Arnold, II *lawyer*
Turner, Bruce Edward *lawyer*

Amarillo
Madden, Wales Hendrix, Jr. *lawyer*
Smithee, John True *lawyer, state legislator*
White, Sharon Elizabeth *lawyer*
Woods, John William *retired lawyer*

Arlington
Jensen, John Robert *lawyer*
Pierson, Grey *lawyer*
Rosenberry, William Kenneth *lawyer, educator*

Austin
Allday, Martin Lewis *lawyer*
Anderson, David Arnold *law educator*
Armbrust, David B. *lawyer*
Baade, Hans Wolfgang *legal educator, law expert*
Bobbitt, Philip Chase *lawyer, educator, writer*
Brown, Frank Beverly, IV *lawyer*
Byrd, Linward Tonnett *lawyer, rancher*
Calhoun, Frank Wayne *lawyer, former state legislator*
Cantilo, Patrick Herrera *lawyer*
†Cheng, Michelle Mei-Hsue *lawyer*
Churgin, Michael Jay *law educator*
Cook, J. Rowland *lawyer*
Cunningham, Judy Marie *lawyer*
Dougherty, John Chrysostom, III *lawyer*
Dyer, Cromwell Adair, Jr. *lawyer, international organization official*
Fuller, John William *lawyer*
Furman, James Housley *lawyer*
Gambrell, James Bruton, III *lawyer, educator*
Gammage, Robert Alton (Bob Gammage) *lawyer*
Gangstad, John Erik *lawyer*
Getman, Julius Gerson *law educator, lawyer*
Gibbins, Bob *lawyer*
Gibson, William Willard, Jr. *law educator*
Goldstein, E. Ernest *lawyer*
Golemon, Ronald Kinnan *lawyer*
Graglia, Lino Anthony *lawyer, educator*
Graham, Seldon Bain, Jr. *lawyer, engineer*
Greene, John Joseph *lawyer*
Greig, Brian Strother *lawyer*
Hamilton, Dagmar Strandberg *lawyer, educator*
Hampton, Charles Edwin *lawyer, mathematician, computer programmer*
Harrison, Richard Wayne *lawyer*
Hazel, Joseph Patrick *law educator*
Helburn, Isadore B. *arbitrator, mediator, educator*
Helman, Stephen Jody *lawyer*
Henderson, George Ervin *lawyer*
Ikard, Frank Neville, Jr. *lawyer*
Jennings, John Cecil *lawyer, minister, career officer*
Jentz, Gaylord Adair *law educator*
Johnson, Corwin Waggoner *law educator*
Knight, Gary *lawyer, educator, publisher, trader*
Krueger, William Wayne, III *lawyer*
Laycock, Harold Douglas *law educator, writer*
Livingston, Ann Chambliss *lawyer*
Lochridge, Lloyd Pampell, Jr. *lawyer*
Mauzy, Oscar Holcombe *lawyer, retired state supreme court justice*
McCullough, Frank Witcher, III *lawyer*
McDaniel, Myra Atwell *lawyer, former state official*
Mersky, Roy Martin *law educator, librarian*
Moss, Bill Ralph *lawyer*
Nevola, Roger Paul *lawyer*
Osborne, Duncan Elliott *lawyer*
Patman, Philip Franklin *lawyer*
†Pena, Richard *lawyer*
Pickens, Franklin Ace *lawyer*
Probus, Michael Maurice, Jr. *lawyer*
Prosperi, Wayne Joseph *lawyer, mediator*
Rider, Brian Clayton *lawyer*
Roan, Forrest Calvin, Jr. *lawyer*
Saltmarsh, Sara Elizabeth *lawyer*
Schwartz, Leonard Jay *lawyer*
Shaffer, Roberta Ivy *law librarian*
Shapiro, Sander Wolf *lawyer*
Sims, Robert Barry *lawyer*
Stephen, John Erle *lawyer, consultant*
Strauser, Robert Wayne *lawyer*
Sturley, Michael F. *law educator*
Sullivan, Teresa Ann *law and sociology educator, academic administrator*
Sutton, John F., Jr. *law educator, dean, lawyer*
Temple, Larry Eugene *lawyer*
Terry, Craig Robert *lawyer*
Thomajan, Robert *lawyer, management consultant*
Thompson, G. Gaye *lawyer*
Weddington, Sarah Ragle *lawyer, educator, speaker, writer*
Weinberg, Louise *law educator, author*
Weintraub, Russell Jay *lawyer, educator*
Wellborn, Olin Guy, III *law educator*
Westbrook, Jay Lawrence *law educator*
Wilson, James William *retired lawyer*
Winters, J. Sam *lawyer, federal government official*
Wright, Charles Alan *law educator, author*
Zager, Steven Mark *lawyer*
Zimmerman, Louis Seymour *lawyer*

Bay City
Peden, Robert F., Jr. *retired lawyer*

Beaumont
Black, Robert Allen *lawyer*
†Bradford, J. Michael *prosecutor*
Scofield, Louis M., Jr. *lawyer*

Bellaire
Jacobus, Charles Joseph *lawyer, title company executive, author*

Belton
Miller, Richard Joseph *lawyer*

Borger
Edmonds, Thomas Leon *lawyer, management consultant*

Brownfield
Moore, Bradford L. *lawyer*

Brownsville
Fleming, Tommy Wayne *lawyer*
Ray, Mary Louise Ryan *lawyer*
Weisfeld, Sheldon *lawyer*

Brownwood
Bell, William Woodward *lawyer*

Bryan
Michel, C. Randall *judge, lawyer*
Smith, Steven Lee *lawyer, judge*
Strong, Stephen Andrew *lawyer*

Burleson
Johnstone, Deborah Blackmon *lawyer*

Carrollton
Riggs, Arthur Jordy *retired lawyer*

Cleburne
MacLean, John Ronald *lawyer*

Cleveland
Campbell, Selaura Joy *lawyer*

Corpus Christi
Alberts, Harold *lawyer*
Branscomb, Harvie, Jr. *lawyer*
Carnahan, Robert Narvell *lawyer*
Davis, Martin Clay *lawyer, professor*
Harrison, William Oliver, Jr. *lawyer, small business owner*
Laws, Gordon Derby *lawyer*
Leon, Rolando Luis *lawyer*
Locke, William Henry *lawyer*
Wood, James Allen *retired lawyer*

Corsicana
Sodd, Glenn *lawyer*

Dallas
Abney, Frederick Sherwood *lawyer*
Acker, Rodney *lawyer*
Agnich, Richard John *lawyer, electronics company executive*
Anderson, Barbara McComas *lawyer*
Anderson, E. Karl *lawyer*
Anglin, Michael Williams *lawyer*
Armour, James Lott *lawyer*
Attanasio, John Baptist *law educator*
Baggett, Steven Ray *lawyer*
Baggett, W. Mike *lawyer*
Barbee, Linton E. *lawyer*
Bennett, Paul William *lawyer*
Beuttenmuller, Rudolf William *lawyer*
Bickel, John W., II *lawyer*
Birkeland, Bryan Collier *lawyer*
Blachly, Jack Lee *lawyer*
Bliss, Robert Harms *lawyer*
Blount, Charles William, III *lawyer*
Bonesio, Woodrow Michael *lawyer*
Bonney, Samuel Robert *lawyer*
Brewer, David Madison *lawyer*
Brin, Royal Henry, Jr. *lawyer*
Bromberg, John E. *lawyer*
Brown, Ronald Lee *lawyer*
Bumpas, Stuart Maryman *lawyer*
Burke, William Temple, Jr. *lawyer*
Burns, Sandra *lawyer, educator*
Busbee, Kline Daniel, Jr. *law educator, lawyer, retired*
Carlton, Dean *lawyer*
Carpenter, Gordon Russell *lawyer, banker*
Case, Thomas Louis *lawyer*
Clardy, Thelma Sanders *lawyer*
Clark, John W. *lawyer*
Clark, Robert Murel, Jr. *lawyer*
†Coggins, Paul Edward, Jr. *prosecutor*
Coleman, Lester L. *corporate lawyer*
Coleman, Robert Winston *lawyer*
Conant, Allah B., Jr. *lawyer*
Copley, Edward Alvin *lawyer*
Corman, Jack Bernard *lawyer, investment manager*
Courtney Westfall, Constance *lawyer*
Cox, Richard D. *lawyer*
Crain, Gayla Campbell *lawyer*
Creel, Luther Edward, III *lawyer*
Cromartie, Eric Ross *lawyer*
Crotty, Robert Bell *lawyer*
Crowley, James Worthington *retired lawyer, business consultant, investor*
Curran, Geoffrey Michael *lawyer*
Davis, Clarice McDonald *lawyer*
Demarest, Sylvia M. *lawyer*
Dicus, Brian George *lawyer*
Dillard, Robert Lionel, Jr. *lawyer, former life insurance executive*
Doke, Marshall J., Jr. *lawyer*
Douglass, Frank Russell *lawyer*
Drumm, David Gary *lawyer*
Dutton, Diana Cheryl *lawyer*
Dyess, Bobby Dale *lawyer*
Eaton, Michael William *lawyer, educator*
Eddleman, William Roseman *lawyer*
Elkins-Elliott, Kay *law educator*
Ellis, Alfred Wright (Al Ellis) *lawyer*
Ellis, James Alvis, Jr. *lawyer*
Emery, Herschell Gene *lawyer*
Engleman, Donald James *lawyer, corporate executive*
Everbach, Otto George *lawyer*
Fanning, Barry Hedges *lawyer*
Farquhar, Robert Michael *lawyer*
Feld, Alan David *lawyer*
Feldman, H. Larry *lawyer*
Fenner, Suzan Ellen *lawyer*
Ferguson, Hugh W., III *lawyer*
Fifield, William O. *lawyer*
Flanagan, Christie Stephen *lawyer*
Flanary, Donald Herbert, Jr. *lawyer*
Flegle, Jim L. *lawyer*
Fortado, Michael George *lawyer*
French, Joseph Jordan, Jr. *lawyer*
Freytag, Sharon Nelson *lawyer*
Gilchrist, Henry *lawyer*
Gilmore, Jerry Carl *lawyer*
†Ginsberg, Carl Haralson *lawyer*
Glancy, Walter John *lawyer*
Glass, Carson McElyea *lawyer*
Glendenning, Don Mark *lawyer*
Godfrey, Cullen Michael *lawyer*
Goodell, Sol *retired lawyer*
Goodstein, Barnett Maurice *lawyer*
Gores, Christopher Merrel *lawyer*
Govett, Brett Christopher *lawyer*
Grayson, Walton George, III *retired lawyer*
Grissom, Gerald Homer *lawyer, mediator, arbitrator*
Hammond, Herbert J. *lawyer*
Hamon, Richard Grady *lawyer*
Hartnett, Thomas Robert, III *lawyer, author*
Hartnett, Will Ford *lawyer*
Haworth, Charles Ray *lawyer*
Henkel, Kathryn Gundy *lawyer*
Hennessy, Daniel Kraft *lawyer*
Hicks, Marion Lawrence, Jr. (Larry Hicks) *lawyer*
Hinshaw, Chester John *lawyer*
Holmes, James Hill, III *lawyer*
Honea, Floyd Franklin *lawyer*
Horton, Paul Bradfield *lawyer*
Howie, John Robert *lawyer*
Hranitzky, Rachel Robyn *lawyer*
Huffman, Gregory Scott Combest *lawyer*
Hughes, Vester Thomas, Jr. *lawyer*
Humble, Monty Garfield *lawyer*
Jayson, Melinda Gayle *lawyer*
Jennings, Susan Jane *lawyer*
Johnson, James Joseph Scofield *lawyer, judge, educator, author*
Joplin, Julian Mike *lawyer*
Jordan, William Davis *lawyer*
Kearney, Douglas Charles *lawyer, journalist*
Keithley, Bradford Gene *lawyer*
Kennedy, Marc J. *lawyer*
Kent, David Charles *lawyer*
Kinnebrew, Jackson Metcalfe *lawyer*
Kinser, Katherine Anne *lawyer*
Kirby, Le Grand Carney, III *lawyer, accountant*
Kitner, David N. *lawyer*
Kneipper, Richard Keith *lawyer*
Kobdish, George Charles *lawyer*
Kohl, Kathleen Allison Barnhart *lawyer*
Kuhn, Willis Evan, II *lawyer, mediator*
Lacy, John Ford *lawyer*
Lafving, Brian Douglas *lawyer*
Lan, Donald Paul, Jr. *lawyer*
Lancaster, John Lynch, III *lawyer*
Lang, Douglas Stewart *lawyer*
Lang-Miers, Elizabeth Ann *lawyer*
Laves, Alan Leonard *lawyer*
Leeper, Harold Harris *arbitrator*
Levin, Hervey Phillip *lawyer*
Levin, Richard C. *lawyer*
Levine, Harold *lawyer*
Lotzer, Gerald Balthazar *lawyer*
Lowe, John Stanley *lawyer, educator*
Maguire, Kevin Jerome *lawyer*
Malorzo, Thomas Vincent *lawyer*
Malouf, Edward Wayne *lawyer*
Mankoff, Ronald Morton *lawyer*
Maris, Stephen S. *lawyer, educator*
Martin, Richard Kelley *lawyer*
Massman, Richard Allan *lawyer*
†Mayo, Thomas William *law educator*
McCurley, Mary Johanna *lawyer*
McDonald, Michael Scott *lawyer*
Mc Elhaney, John Hess *lawyer*
McGarry, Charles William *lawyer*
McGowan, Patrick Francis *lawyer*
McKnight, Joseph Webb *law educator, historian*
McLane, David Glenn *lawyer*
†McNamara, Anne H. *lawyer, corporate executive*
McNamara, Lawrence John *lawyer*
McNamara, Martin Burr *lawyer, oil and gas company executive*
McWilliams, Mike C. *lawyer*
Mears, Rona Robbins *lawyer*
Mebus, Robert Gwynne *lawyer*
Menges, John Kenneth, Jr. *lawyer*
Meyer, Ferdinand Charles, Jr. *lawyer*
Mighell, Kenneth John *lawyer*
Mills, Jerry Woodrow *lawyer*
Moore, Stanley Ray *lawyer*
Mow, Robert Henry, Jr. *lawyer*
Mueller, Mark Christopher *lawyer*
Mullinax, Otto B. *retired lawyer*
Nichols, Henry Louis *lawyer*
Owens, Rodney Joe *lawyer*
Palmer, Philip Isham, Jr. *lawyer*
Parker, James Francis *lawyer, airline executive*
Peterson, Edward Adrian *lawyer*
Pettey, Walter Graves, III *lawyer*
Pew, John Glenn, Jr. *lawyer*
Phelan, Robin Eric *lawyer*
Phelps, Robert Frederick, Jr. *lawyer*
Pingree, Bruce Douglas *lawyer*
Pleasant, James Scott *lawyer*
Portman, Glenn Arthur *lawyer*
Powell, Michael Vance *lawyer*
Price, John Aley *lawyer*
Prothro, Jerry Robert *lawyer*
Purnell, Charles Giles *lawyer*
Purnell, Maurice Eugene, Jr. *lawyer*
Raggio, Kenneth Gaylord *lawyer, mediator*
Raggio, Louise Ballerstedt *lawyer*
Rice, Darrel Alan *lawyer*
Roberts, Harry Morris, Jr. *lawyer*
Salazar, Steve *lawyer*
Savage, Wallace Hamilton *lawyer*
Schmid, Frances M. *lawyer, law librarian, nurse*
Schreiber, Sally Ann *lawyer*
Scuro, Joseph E., Jr. *lawyer*
See, Robert Fleming, Jr. *lawyer*
Selinger, Jerry Robin *lawyer*
Sides, Jack Davis, Jr. *lawyer*
Siegel, Mark Jordan *lawyer*
Siegel, Thomas Louis *lawyer*
Sloman, Marvin Sherk *lawyer*
Smith, Brian *lawyer*
Smith, Frank Tupper *lawyer*
Smith, Milton Clark, Jr.
Spears, Robert Fields *lawyer*
Stalcup, Joe Alan *lawyer, clergyman*
Steinberg, Lawrence Edward *lawyer*
Stilwell, John Quincy *lawyer*
Stinnett, Mark Allan *lawyer*
Stockard, James Alfred *lawyer*
Storey, Charles Porter *lawyer*
Sullivan, Thomas Patrick *lawyer*
Thau, William Albert, Jr. *lawyer*
True, Roy Joe *lawyer*
Tubb, James Clarence *lawyer*
Tucker, L. Dan *lawyer*
Tygrett, Howard Volney, Jr. *lawyer*
Verner, Jimmy Lynn, Jr. *lawyer, expert witness*
Vetter, James George, Jr. *lawyer*
Walkowiak, Vincent Steven *lawyer*
Wells, Leonard Nathaniel David, Jr. *lawyer*
White, James Richard *lawyer*
Williams, James Alexander *lawyer*
Willingham, Clark Suttles *lawyer*
Wilson, Claude Raymond, Jr. *lawyer*
Wise, Marvin Jay *lawyer*
Yarbrough, Fletcher Leftwich *lawyer*
Young, Barney Thornton *lawyer*

Denton
Lawhon, John E., III *lawyer, former county official*
Waage, Mervin Bernard *lawyer*

Diboll
Ericson, Roger Delwin *lawyer, forest resource company executive*

Dripping Springs
Gallerano, Andrew John *lawyer*

East Bernard
Boettcher, Armin Schlick *lawyer, banker*

Edinburg
Hunter, Jack Duval, II *lawyer*

El Paso
Ainsa, Francis Swinburne *lawyer*
Cox, Sanford Curtis, Jr. *lawyer*
Feuille, Richard Harlan *lawyer*
McCotter, James Rawson *lawyer*
McDonald, Charles Edward *lawyer*
Yetter, Richard *lawyer*

Eldorado
Kosub, James Albert *lawyer*

Farmers Branch
Hamby, Robert Kevin *lawyer*

Flower Mound
Hunt, David Ford *lawyer*

Fort Worth
Berenson, William Keith *lawyer*
Blair, Sloan Blackmon *lawyer*
Bosser, Steven John *prosecutor*
Brender, Art *lawyer*
Brown, C. Harold *lawyer*

Brown, Richard Lee lawyer
Carr, Thomas Eldridge lawyer
Chalk, John Allen, Sr. lawyer
Collins, Whitfield James lawyer
Curry, Donald Robert lawyer, oil company executive
Dean, Beale lawyer
Elliott, Frank Wallace lawyer, educator
Ganske, Vicki Smith lawyer
Harcrow, E. Earl lawyer
Hart, John Clifton lawyer
Hayes, Larry B. lawyer
Hill, Mark C. lawyer
Kelly, Dee J. lawyer
Langenheim, Roger Allen lawyer
McConnell, Michael Arthur lawyer
Minton, Jerry Davis lawyer, consultant, former banker
†Moreland, Jeffrey R. lawyer
Munn, Cecil Edwin lawyer
Reedom, James Patrick paralegal, educator
Sartain, James Edward lawyer
Shannon, Joe, Jr. lawyer
Tatum, Stephen Lyle lawyer
Tracy, J. David lawyer, educator
Wallach, David Michael lawyer
Watson, Robert Francis lawyer
Wayland, Sharon Morris law librarian
Weekley, Frederick Clay, Jr. lawyer
Whitney, William Bernard lawyer
Zahn, Donald Jack lawyer

Galveston
Caldwell, Garnett Ernest lawyer
Schwartz, Aaron Robert lawyer, former state legislator
Vie, George William, III lawyer

Garland
Hinton, Charles lawyer
Irby, Holt lawyer

Georgetown
Bryce, William Delf lawyer
Wilkerson, James Neill lawyer

Hallettsville
Baber, Wilbur H., Jr. lawyer

Harlingen
Johnson, Orrin Wendell lawyer

Houston
Aarons-Holder, Charmaine Michele lawyer
Abbott, Lawrence E. lawyer
Allender, John Roland lawyer
Anderson, Eric Severin lawyer
Anderson, Thomas Dunaway retired lawyer
Arbuckle, Kurt lawyer
Bambace, Robert Shelly lawyer
Barnett, Edward William lawyer
Bech, Douglas York lawyer, resort executive
Becher, Andrew Clifford lawyer
Beirne, Martin Douglas lawyer
Bellatti, Lawrence Lee lawyer
Berg, David Howard lawyer
Bilger, Bruce R. lawyer
Bistline, F. Walter, Jr. lawyer
Blackmon, Willie Edward Boney lawyer
Blackshear, A. T., Jr. lawyer
Blair, Graham Kerin (Kerry Blair) lawyer
Bland, John L. lawyer
Bliss, Ronald Glenn lawyer
Bluestein, Edwin A., Jr. lawyer
Botley, Calvin lawyer, magistrate judge
Bowersox, Thomas H. lawyer
Bradie, Peter Richard lawyer, engineer
Brann, Richard Roland lawyer
Brantley, John Randolph lawyer
Bridges, David Manning lawyer
Brinsmade, Lyon Louis lawyer
Brinson, Gay Creswell, Jr. lawyer
Brunson, John Soles lawyer
Buckingham, Edwin John, III lawyer
Burch, Voris Reagan retired lawyer, mediator, arbitrator
Bux, William John lawyer
†Cabello, J. David lawyer
Caddy, Michael Douglas lawyer
Caldwell, Rodney Kent lawyer
Campbell, Bert Louis lawyer, mediator, arbitrator
Carmody, James Albert lawyer
Carr, Edward A. lawyer
Carter, Daniel Roland lawyer
Carter, John Francis, II lawyer
Carter, John Loyd lawyer
Chandler, George Francis, III lawyer, naval architect
Chavez, John Anthony lawyer
Clark, Pat English lawyer
Clarke, Robert Logan lawyer
Clemenceau, Paul B. lawyer
Clore, Lawrence Hubert lawyer
Coghlan, Kelly Jack lawyer
Coleman, Bryan Douglas lawyer, educator, arbitrator, mediator
Conlon, Michael William lawyer
Cook, B. Thomas lawyer
Cook, Eugene Augustus lawyer
Corrallo, Carl Anthony lawyer
Cox, James Talley lawyer
Craig, Robert Mark, III lawyer, educator
Crooker, John H., Jr. lawyer
Curry, Alton Frank lawyer
DeAtley, James Harry prosecutor
DeMent, James Alderson, Jr. lawyer
†Derrick, James V., Jr. lawyer
Diaz-Arrastia, George Ravelo lawyer
Dillon, Clifford Brien retired lawyer
Dinkins, Carol Eggert lawyer
Disher, David Alan lawyer, geophysical research consultant
Dunlop, Fred Hurston lawyer
Dykes, Osborne Jefferson, III lawyer
Eastin, Keith E. lawyer
England, Rudy Alan lawyer
Essmyer, Michael Martin lawyer
Eubank, J. Thomas lawyer
Farenthold, Frances Tarlton lawyer
Feldcamp, Larry Bernard lawyer
Fellers, Rhonda Gay lawyer
Fladung, Richard Denis lawyer
Fleming, Michael Paul lawyer
Forbes, Arthur Lee, III lawyer
Fromm, Eva Maria lawyer
Fullenweider, Donn Charles lawyer
Garten, David Burton lawyer
Gayle, Gibson, Jr. lawyer
Gibson, Rex Hilton lawyer
Gissel, L. Henry, Jr. lawyer
Gonynor, Francis James lawyer
Gover, Alan Shore lawyer
Graham, Michael Paul lawyer
Grossberg, Marc Elias lawyer
Hall, Charles Washington lawyer
Harper, Alfred John, II lawyer
Harrington, Bruce Michael lawyer, investor
Harris, Warren Wayne lawyer
Hartrick, Janice Kay lawyer
Harvin, David Tarleton lawyer
Heggen, Ivar Nelson lawyer
Heinrich, Randall Wayne lawyer, investment banker
Hermann, Robert John lawyer, corporate executive
Hewitt, Lester L. lawyer
Hinton, Paula Weems lawyer
Holderness, Algernon Sidney, Jr. lawyer
Holloway, Gordon Arthur lawyer
Hollyfield, John Scoggins lawyer
Holstead, John Burnham lawyer
Hoyt, Mont Powell lawyer
Huck, Lewis Francis lawyer
Hudspeth, Chalmers Mac lawyer, educator
Jamail, Joseph Dahr, Jr. lawyer
Jansen, Donald Orville lawyer
Jennings, Debra Vera lawyer
Jeske, Charles Matthew lawyer
Jewell, George Hiram lawyer
Johnson, James Harold lawyer
Jones, Frank Griffith lawyer
Kaplan, Lee Landa lawyer
Kay, Joel Phillip lawyer
Kelly, Hugh Rice lawyer
Ketchand, Robert Lee lawyer
Kline, Allen Haber, Jr. lawyer
Koenig, Rodney Curtis lawyer, rancher
Kratochvil, L(ouis) Glen lawyer
Krebs, Arno William, Jr. lawyer
Kruse, Charles Thomas lawyer
Kurz, Thomas Patrick lawyer
LaBoon, Robert Bruce lawyer
Lacey, David Morgan lawyer, school administrator
Lackey, S. Allen lawyer, petroleum company executive
Lake, Kathleen Cooper lawyer
Larkin, Lee Roy lawyer
Larson, Peter L. legal assistant, investigator
Lawson, Ben F. lawyer, international legal consultant
Lee, William Gentry lawyer
Locke, Gene L. lawyer
Looper, Donald Ray lawyer
Lopez, David Tiburcio lawyer, educator, arbitrator, mediator
Louck, Lisa Ann lawyer
Lynch, John Edward, Jr. lawyer
Maloney, James Edward lawyer
Marley, Everett Armistead, Jr. lawyer
Marsel, Robert Steven law educator, mediator, arbitrator
Marston, Edgar Jean, III lawyer
Mayor, Richard Blair lawyer
McClure, Daniel M. lawyer
McCormack, David Richard lawyer
McDaniel, Jarrel Dave lawyer
Melamed, Richard lawyer
Mithoff, Richard Warren lawyer
Moehlman, Michael Scott lawyer
Moncure, John Lewis lawyer
Morgan, Richard Greer lawyer
Morris, (William) Carloss lawyer, insurance company executive
Mueller, Carl Gustav, Jr. lawyer
Murphy, Ewell Edward, Jr. lawyer
Myers, Franklin lawyer, oil service company executive
Nacol, Mae lawyer
Nations, Howard Lynn lawyer
Newton, Jon P. lawyer
Nimmer, Raymond T. lawyer, law educator
Nolen, Roy Lemuel lawyer
†O'Donnell, Lawrence, III lawyer
Oldham, Darius Dudley lawyer
Orton, John Stewart lawyer
O'Toole, Austin Martin lawyer
Parker, Dallas Robert lawyer
Paul, Thomas Daniel lawyer
Paulsen, James Walter law educator
Pearson, Michael P. lawyer
Pitts, Gary Benjamin lawyer
Plaeger, Frederick Joseph, II lawyer
Pravel, Bernarr Roe lawyer
Prestridge, Pamela Adair lawyer
Price, Mark Eldredge lawyer
Pruitt, Robert Randall lawyer
Pugsley, Frank Burruss lawyer
Ray, Hugh Massey, Jr. lawyer
Reasoner, Harry Max lawyer
Reif, Louis Raymond lawyer, utilities executive
Robertson, James Woolsey lawyer
Robins, W. Ronald lawyer
Rogers, Arthur Hamilton, III lawyer
Rozzell, Scott Ellis lawyer
Runge, Barbara Kay lawyer, arbitrator, mediator
Ryan, Thomas William lawyer
Ryan, Vince lawyer
Salch, Steven Charles lawyer
Sales, James Bohus lawyer
Sapp, Walter William lawyer, energy company executive
Saunders, Charles Albert lawyer
Schwartz, Brenda Keen lawyer
Schwartz, Charles Walter lawyer
Scott, Ronald lawyer
Secrest, Ronald Dean lawyer
Selke, Charles Richard real estate lawyer
Seymour, Barbara Laverne lawyer
Shaddock, Carroll Sidney lawyer
Shurn, Peter Joseph, III lawyer
Siekman, Thomas Clement lawyer
Simmons, Stephen Judson lawyer
Sing, William Bender lawyer
Smith, Brooke Ellen lawyer
Smith, William Randolph lawyer
Soliz, Joseph Guy lawyer
Sonfield, Robert Leon, Jr. lawyer
Spalding, Andrew Freeman lawyer
Staine, Ross lawyer
Stephens, Delia Marie Lucky lawyer
Stradley, William Jackson lawyer
Streng, William Paul lawyer, educator
Stryker, Steven Charles lawyer
Susman, Morton Lee lawyer
Susman, Stephen Daily lawyer
Sydow, Michael David lawyer
Szalkowski, Charles Conrad lawyer
Toedt, D(ell) C(harles), III lawyer
Touchy, Deborah K. P. lawyer, accountant
Travis, Andrew David lawyer
Tripp, Karen Bryant lawyer
Vance, Carol Stoner lawyer
Van Fleet, George Allan lawyer
Van Kerrebrook, Mary Alice lawyer
Vest, G. Waverly, Jr. lawyer
Wall, Kenneth E., Jr. lawyer
Wallis, Olney Gray lawyer
Waska, Ronald Jerome lawyer
Watson, John Allen lawyer
Webb, Jack M. lawyer
Weber, Fredric Alan lawyer
Weberpal, Michael Andrew lawyer
Welch, Robert Morrow, Jr. lawyer
Wells, Benjamin Gladney lawyer
Westby, Timothy Scott lawyer
Wheelan, R(ichelieu) E(dward) lawyer
Wickliffe, Jerry L. lawyer
Wilde, Carlton D. lawyer
Wilde, William Key lawyer
Williamson, Peter David lawyer
Worthington, William Albert, III lawyer
Wray, Thomas Jefferson lawyer
Yetter, R. Paul lawyer
Yokubaitis, Roger T. lawyer
Zeigler, Ann dePender lawyer

Irving
Glober, George Edward, Jr. lawyer
Lieberman, Mark Joel lawyer
Matthews, Charles W. lawyer
Pitts, Joe W., III (Chip Pitts) lawyer, law educator

Jacksonville
Brewer, Brett lawyer
Thrall, Gordon Fish lawyer

Kaufman
Legg, Reagan Houston lawyer

Kerrville
Parmley, Robert James lawyer, consultant

Kilgore
Rorschach, Richard Gordon lawyer

Lampasas
Harvey, Leigh Kathryn lawyer

Lancaster
Pratt, John Edward law educator

Laredo
Barrett, Bryan Edward prosecutor

Liberty
Wheat, John Nixon lawyer

Longview
Welge, Jack Herman, Jr. lawyer

Lubbock
Cochran, Joseph Wesley law librarian, educator
Crowson, James Lawrence lawyer, financial company executive, academic administrator
Davis, Jimmy Frank assistant attorney general
Purdom, Thomas James lawyer

Lufkin
Garrison, Pitser Hardeman lawyer, mayor emeritus

Mason
Johnson, Rufus Winfield lawyer

Mc Kinney
Roessler, P. Dee lawyer, former judge, educator

Midland
Arizaga, Lavora Spradlin retired lawyer
Bullock, Maurice Randolph lawyer
Stoltz, Michael Rae lawyer
Truitt, Robert Ralph, Jr. lawyer

Missouri City
Hodges, Jot Holiver, Jr. lawyer, business executive

New Braunfels
Benfield, Marion Wilson, Jr. law educator
Nolte, Melvin, Jr. lawyer

Odessa
Ratliff, Janice Kay legal administrator
Rouse, Randall Lyle lawyer

Plano
Bonet, Frank Joseph lawyer
†Dixon-Shomette, Donna M. medical paralegal
Friedlander, D. Gilbert lawyer
†Friedlander, D. Gilbert lawyer
Hemingway, Richard William law educator
Lotter, Charles Robert corporate lawyer, retail company legal executive
Middleton, Linda Jean Greathouse lawyer

Pottsboro
Thomas, Ann Van Wynen law educator

Richardson
Conkel, Robert Dale lawyer, pension consultant
Davis, M. G. lawyer
DeBusk, Manuel Conrad lawyer, business executive
Douglas, John Paul recruiter, lawyer, commercial and family law media
Edwards, Carl Elmo, Jr. lawyer
Ellwanger, J. David lawyer
Hablutzel, Margo Lynn lawyer
Mondul, Donald David patent lawyer
Olson, Dennis Oliver lawyer

Rockport
Benningfield, Carol Ann lawyer

Rockwall
Kolodey, Fred James lawyer

Round Mountain
Moursund, Albert Wadel, III lawyer, rancher

Round Rock
LaShelle, Charles Stanton lawyer, insurance company executive

Rowlett
Lyon, Robert Charles lawyer

Rusk
Phifer, Forrest Keith lawyer

San Angelo
Talley, Pamala Walker lawyer, judicial officer

San Antonio
Armstrong, William Tucker, III lawyer
Barton, James Cary lawyer
Biery, Evelyn Hudson lawyer
†Blagg, James W. prosecutor
Bramble, Ronald Lee lawyer, business and legal consultant
Cabezas-Gil, Rosa M. lawyer
Castleberry, James Newton, Jr. retired law educator, dean
Dazey, William Boyd retired lawyer
Durbin, Richard Louis, Jr. lawyer
Evans, Michelle Lee lawyer, educator
Fox, Michael W. lawyer
Frigerio, Charles Straith lawyer
Guenther, Jack Egon lawyer
Guess, James David lawyer
Hardy, Harvey Louchard lawyer
Henry, Peter York lawyer, mediator
Hollin, Shelby W. lawyer
Javore, Gary William lawyer
Labay, Eugene Benedict lawyer
Lutter, Charles William, Jr. lawyer
Macon, Jane Haun lawyer
Maloney, Marynell lawyer
Montgomery, James Edward, Jr. lawyer
Moynihan, John Bignell lawyer
Patrick, Dane Herman lawyer
Putman, (James) Michael lawyer
Ross, James Ulric lawyer, accountant, educator
Ruttenberg, Frank Z. lawyer
Sakai, Peter A. lawyer
Schlueter, David Arnold law educator
Schuk, Linda Lee legal assistant, business educator
Spears, Sally lawyer
Steen, John Thomas, Jr. lawyer
Wachsmuth, Robert William lawyer
Wallis, Ben Alton, Jr. lawyer
Welmaker, Forrest Nolan lawyer
Williamson, Deborah Daywood lawyer
Yates, Norris William, Jr. lawyer

Spearman
Jarvis, Billy Britt lawyer

Spring
Hearn-Haynes, Theresa lawyer
Hendricks, Randal Arlan lawyer
McGregor, Martin Luther, Jr. lawyer

Sweetwater
Jones, Charles Eric, Jr. lawyer

The Woodlands
Schlacks, Stephen Mark lawyer, educator

Tyler
Ellis, Donald Lee lawyer
Patterson, Donald Ross lawyer, educator

Waco
Bracken, William Earl, Jr. lawyer
Morrison, Michael Dean lawyer, law educator
Page, Jack Randall lawyer
Smith, Cullen lawyer
Wendorf, Hulen Dee law educator, author, lecturer
Wilson, John Ross retired law educator

Wichita Falls
Altman, William Kean lawyer

Yoakum
Williams, Walter Waylon lawyer, pecan grower

UTAH

Logan
Hillyard, Lyle William lawyer
Honaker, Jimmie Joe lawyer, ecologist

Manti
Petersen, Benton Lauritz paralegal

Ogden
Mecham, Glenn Jefferson lawyer, mayor
Richards, Richard lawyer, political consultant
Sullivan, Kevin Patrick lawyer
Warner, Frank Shrake lawyer

Park City
Kennicott, James W. lawyer

Provo
Abbott, Charles Favour lawyer
Hill, Richard Lee lawyer
Kimball, Edward Lawrence law educator, lawyer
Thomas, David Albert law educator

Saint George
Gallian, Russell Joseph lawyer
Terry, Gary A. lawyer, former trade association executive

Salt Lake City
Adams, Joseph Keith lawyer
Anderson, Kent Taylor lawyer
Anderson, Robert Monte lawyer
Atkin, Gary Eugene lawyer
Barusch, Lawrence Roos lawyer
Baucom, Sidney George lawyer
Berman, Daniel Lewis lawyer
Buchi, Mark Keith lawyer
Christensen, Patricia Anne Watkins lawyer
Christensen, Ray Richards lawyer
Clark, Robert Stokes lawyer
Clark, Scott H. lawyer

Colessides, Nick John *lawyer*
Cornaby, Kay Sterling *lawyer, former state senator*
Curtis, LeGrand R., Jr. *lawyer*
Erickson, David Belnap *lawyer*
Gardiner, Lester Raymond, Jr. *lawyer*
Holbrook, Donald Benson *lawyer*
Holtkamp, James Arnold *lawyer, educator*
Hunt, George Andrew *lawyer*
Jensen, Dallin W. *lawyer*
Lochhead, Robert Bruce *lawyer*
Mabey, Ralph R. *lawyer*
Manning, Brent V. *lawyer*
Matsumori, Douglas *lawyer*
McConkie, Oscar Walter *lawyer*
McIntosh, James Albert *lawyer*
McIntosh, Terrie Tuckett *lawyer*
Mills, Lawrence *lawyer, business and transportation consultant*
Mock, Henry Byron *lawyer, writer, consultant*
Moore, James R. *lawyer*
Moore, Larry Gale *lawyer*
Nielsen, Greg Ross *lawyer*
Oaks, Dallin Harris *lawyer, church official*
Purser, Donald Joseph *lawyer*
Rasmussen, Thomas Val, Jr. *lawyer, small business owner*
†Raucci, Francis Joseph *lawyer, business executive*
Reeder, F. Robert *lawyer*
Roberts, Jack Earle *lawyer, ski resort operator, wood products company executive, real estate developer*
Scofield, David Willson *lawyer*
Tateoka, Reid *lawyer*
Teitelbaum, Lee E. *law educator, dean*
Wadsworth, Harold Wayne *lawyer*
Weiss, Loren Elliot *lawyer, law educator*
Wikstrom, Francis M. *lawyer*

Sandy
Bush, Rex Curtis *lawyer*

Spanish Fork
Ashworth, Brent Ferrin *lawyer*

Vernal
Judd, Dennis L. *lawyer*

VERMONT

Bennington
Sternberg, Rolf Max *lawyer*

Bethel
Obuchowski, Raymond Joseph *lawyer*

Burlington
Davis, Christopher Lee *lawyer*
Dinse, John Merrell *lawyer*
Hoff, Philip Henderson *lawyer, former state senator, former governor*
Martin, Allen *lawyer*
Shattuck, Gary G. *lawyer*
Tetzlaff, Charles Robert *prosecutor*
Wick, Hilton Addison *lawyer*

Concord
Norsworthy, Elizabeth Krassovsky *lawyer*

Middlebury
Palmer, Michael Paul *lawyer, mediator, educator*

Montpelier
Brock, James Sidney *lawyer*
Diamond, M. Jerome *lawyer, former state official*
Guild, Alden *retired lawyer*

Morrisville
Simonds, Marshall *lawyer*

Norwich
Lundquist, Weyman Ivan *lawyer*

Randolph
Angell, Philip Alvin, Jr. *lawyer*

Randolph Center
Casson, Richard Frederick *lawyer, travel bureau executive*

Rutland
Faignant, John Paul *lawyer, educator*
Keyser, Frank Ray, Jr. *lawyer, former governor*
Stafford, Robert Theodore *lawyer, former senator*
Taylor, A. Jeffry *lawyer*

Shelburne
Kurrelmeyer, Louis Hayner *retired lawyer*
Ross, Charles Robert *lawyer, consultant*

South Royalton
Wroth, L(awrence) Kinvin *lawyer, educator*

Waitsfield
Raphael, Albert Ash, Jr. *lawyer*

Williston
Adams, Charles Jairus *lawyer*

Woodstock
Sincerbeaux, Robert Abbott *lawyer, preservationist, foundation executive*

VIRGINIA

Alexandria
Abell, Richard Bender *lawyer, federal judicial official*
Alberger, William Relph *lawyer, government official*
Battle, Timothy Joseph *lawyer*
Beach, Barbara Purse *lawyer*
Campbell, Thomas Douglas *lawyer, consultant*
Carlson, J(ohn) Philip *lawyer*
Clubb, Bruce Edwin *retired lawyer*
Cohen, Bernard S. *lawyer*
Costello, Daniel Brian *lawyer, consultant*
D'Amours, Norman Edward *lawyer, former congressman*
Dokurno, Anthony David *lawyer*
Evans, H(arold) Bradley, Jr. *lawyer*
Fahey, Helen F. *prosecutor*
Fugate, Wilbur Lindsay *lawyer*
Georges, Peter John *lawyer*
Hathaway, Fred William *lawyer*
Huckabee, Harlow Maxwell *lawyer, writer*
Hussey, Ward MacLean *lawyer, former government official*
Hutzelman, Martha Louise *lawyer*
Kelly, Nancy Frieda Wolicki *lawyer*
Klewans, Samuel N. *lawyer*
Kopp, Eugene Paul *lawyer*
Mar, Eugene *lawyer, financial consultant*
Mathis, William Lowrey *lawyer*
McClure, Roger John *lawyer*
McDowell, Charles Eager *lawyer, retired military officer*
Montague, Robert Latane, III *lawyer*
O'Hara, John Patrick *lawyer, accountant*
Paturis, E. Michael *lawyer*
Rossi, Eugene Joseph *federal prosecutor, law educator*
Rubin, Burton Jay *lawyer, editor*
Schultz, Franklin M. *retired lawyer*
Sczudlo, Walter Joseph *lawyer*
Sherk, George William *lawyer*
Straub, Peter Thornton *lawyer*
Sturtevant, Brereton *retired lawyer, former government official*
Swinburn, Charles *lawyer*
Thomas, William Griffith *lawyer*
Van Cleve, Ruth Gill *retired lawyer, government official*
Von Drehle, Ramon Arnold *lawyer*
Walkup, Charlotte Lloyd *lawyer*
Wendel, Charles Allen *lawyer*
Wieder, Bruce Terrill *lawyer, electrical engineer*
Wilner, Morton Harrison *retired lawyer*

Annandale
Gaberman, Harry *lawyer, economic analyst*
Hovis, Robert Houston, III *lawyer*

Arlington
Anthony, Robert Armstrong *lawyer, educator*
Brenner, Edgar H. *legal administrator*
Carbaugh, John Edward, Jr. *lawyer*
Chapple, Thomas Leslie *lawyer*
Collins, Philip Reilly *lawyer, educator*
Doyle, Gerard Francis *lawyer*
Drayton, William *lawyer, social entrepreneur, management consultant*
Dunn, Loretta Lynn *lawyer*
Fowler, David Lucas *corporate lawyer*
Frame, Nancy Davis *lawyer*
Hansen, Kenneth D. *lawyer, ophthalmologist*
Hogue, Dale Curtis, Sr. *lawyer*
Jackson, William Paul, Jr. *lawyer*
Kelly, John James *lawyer*
Korman, James William *lawyer*
Kuelbs, John Thomas *lawyer*
†Lash, William Henry *law educator*
Levinson, Lawrence Edward *lawyer, corporation executive*
Litman, Richard Curtis *lawyer*
Malone, William Grady *retired lawyer*
Mathis, Mark Jay *lawyer*
McCorkindale, Douglas Hamilton *lawyer, publishing company executive*
McDermott, Francis Owen *lawyer*
Mossinghoff, Gerald Joseph *patent lawyer, educator*
Muris, Timothy Joseph *law educator*
Rhodes, Alice Graham *lawyer*
Rousselot, Peter Frese *consultant*
Stover, David Frank *lawyer*
Uncapher, Mark Elson *lawyer, trade association administrator*
Van Lare, Wendell John *lawyer*
Walker, Woodrow Wilson *lawyer, cattle and timber farmer*
Wall, Barbara Wartelle *lawyer*

Ashburn
Gold, George Myron *lawyer, editor, writer, consultant*

Ashland
d'Evegnee, Charles Paul *lawyer*

Blackstone
Allen, Jeffrey Rodgers *lawyer*

Bowling Green
Long, Clarence Dickinson, III *lawyer*

Charlottesville
Alford, Neill Herbert, Jr. *retired law educator*
Bonnie, Richard Jeffrey *legal educator, lawyer*
Chandler, Lawrence Bradford, Jr. *lawyer*
Cohen, Edwin Samuel *lawyer, educator*
Dooley, Michael P. *law educator*
Edwards, James Edwin *lawyer*
Henderson, Stanley Dale *lawyer, educator*
Hodous, Robert Power *lawyer*
Howard, Arthur Ellsworth Dick *law educator*
Kitch, Edmund Wells *lawyer, educator, private investor*
Kudravetz, David Waller *lawyer*
Landess, Fred S. *lawyer*
Low, Peter W. *legal educator*
Martin, David Alan *law educator*
McKay, John Douglas *lawyer*
Meador, Daniel John *law educator*
Menefee, Samuel Pyeatt *lawyer, anthropologist*
Middleditch, Leigh Benjamin, Jr. *lawyer, educator*
Monahan, John T. *law educator, psychologist*
Moore, John Norton *lawyer, diplomat, educator*
O'Connell, Jeffrey *law educator*
Scott, Robert Edwin *law educator, dean*
Sinclair, Kent *law educator*
Slaughter, Edward Ratliff, Jr. *lawyer*
†Stuntz, William John *law educator*
Turner, Robert Foster *law educator, former government official, writer*
Wadlington, Walter James *law educator*
Wenger, Larry Bruce *law librarian, law educator*
White, George Edward *law educator, lawyer*
White, Thomas Raeburn, III *law educator, consultant*
Whitehead, John Wayne *law educator, organization administrator, author*
Wyatt, Deborah Chasen *lawyer*

Chesapeake
Jones, John Lou *arbitrator, retired railroad executive*

Chester
Connelly, Colin Charles *lawyer*
Gray, Charles Robert *lawyer*

Chesterfield
Barnes, Edward Dean *lawyer*

Danville
Talbott, Frank, III *lawyer*

Earlysville
Grattan, George Gilmer, IV *lawyer*

Fairfax
Anderson, David Lawrence *lawyer*
Arnold, William McCauley *lawyer*
Arntson, Peter Andrew *lawyer*
Baird, Charles Bruce *lawyer, consultant*
Becker, James Richard *lawyer*
Bloomquist, Dennis Howard *lawyer*
Carretta, Albert Aloysius *lawyer, educator*
Codding, Frederick Hayden *lawyer*
Field, David Ellis *lawyer*
Folk, Thomas Robert *lawyer*
†Gillespie, Samuel H., III *lawyer, oil company executive*
Groves, Hurst Kohler *lawyer, oil company executive*
Kear, Maria Martha Ruscitella *lawyer*
Maiwurm, James John *lawyer*
Sanderson, Douglas Jay *lawyer*
Spitzberg, Irving Joseph, Jr. *lawyer, corporate executive*
Stearns, Frank Warren *lawyer*

Fairfax Station
Bishop, Alfred Chilton, Jr. *lawyer*

Falls Church
Calkins, Gary Nathan *lawyer, retired*
Chabraja, Nicholas D. *lawyer*
Christman, Bruce Lee *lawyer*
Conklin, Kenneth Edward *lawyer, industry executive*
Diamond, Robert Michael *lawyer*
Duesenberg, Robert H. *lawyer*
Ehrlich, Bernard Herbert *lawyer, association executive*
Elderkin, Helaine Grace *lawyer*
Greigg, Ronald Edwin *lawyer*
Honigberg, Carol Crossman *lawyer*
Jennings, Thomas Parks *lawyer*
Kondracki, Edward John *lawyer*
Padgett, Gail Blanchard *lawyer*
Perkins, Jack Edwin *lawyer*
†Pischke, Vail W. *lawyer, Judge*
Redmond, Robert *lawyer, educator*
Rooney, Kevin Davitt *lawyer*
Schmidt, Paul Wickham *lawyer*
Ward, Joe Henry, Jr. *retired lawyer*
Winzer, P.J. *lawyer*

Franklin
Cobb, G. Elliott, Jr. *lawyer*

Fredericksburg
Billingsley, Robert Thaine *lawyer*
Glessner, Thomas Allen *lawyer*

Glen Allen
Batzli, Terrence Raymond *lawyer*
Carneal, Drew St. John *lawyer*
Reed, Austin F. *lawyer*
Weaver, Mollie Little *lawyer*

Gloucester
Powell, Bolling Raines, Jr. *lawyer, educator*

Great Falls
Neidich, George Arthur *lawyer*
Preston, Charles George *lawyer*
Railton, William Scott *lawyer*
Wallman, Steven Mark Harte *lawyer*

Halifax
Greenbacker, John Everett *retired lawyer*

Hampton
McNider, James Small, III *lawyer*
Schon, Alan Wallace *lawyer, actor*

Harrisonburg
Wallinger, M(elvin) Bruce *lawyer*

Heathsville
McKerns, Charles Joseph *lawyer*

Herndon
Kunkel, David Nelson *lawyer*
Vakerics, Thomas Vincent *lawyer*

Ivy
Wilcox, Harvey John *lawyer*

Kilmarnock
Parrett, Sherman O. *lawyer*

Leesburg
Minchew, John Randall *lawyer*

Lexington
Beveridge, Albert Jeremiah, III *lawyer*
Kirgis, Frederic Lee *law educator*
Sullivan, Barry *law educator*
Sundby, Scott Edwin *law educator*
Wiant, Sarah Kirsten *law library director, educator*

Lynchburg
Burnette, Ralph Edwin, Jr. *lawyer*
Healy, Joseph Francis, Jr. *lawyer, arbitrator, retired airline executive*
Packert, G(ayla) Beth *lawyer*
Westenburger, Linda Santner *lawyer*

Madison
Coates, Frederick Ross *lawyer*

Manakin Sabot
Bright, Craig Bartley *lawyer*

Manassas
Foote, John Holland *lawyer*
McGolrick, J. Edward, Jr. *lawyer*
Mitchell, William Graham Champion *lawyer, business executive*
Weimer, Peter Dwight *mediator, lawyer, corporate executive*

Mc Lean
Anthony, Joan Caton *lawyer, writer*
Appler, Thomas L. *lawyer*
Armstrong, C(harles) Torrence *lawyer*
Aucutt, Ronald David *lawyer*
Bardack, Paul Roitman *lawyer, consultant*
Bingaman, Anne K. *lawyer*
Brown, Thomas Cartmel, Jr. *lawyer*
Byrnes, William Joseph *lawyer*
Church, Randolph Warner, Jr. *lawyer*
Cohn, Herbert B. *lawyer*
Corson, J. Jay, IV *lawyer*
Friedlander, Jerome Peyser, II *lawyer*
Gammon, James Alan *lawyer*
Goolrick, Robert Mason *lawyer, consultant*
Greene, Timothy Geddes *lawyer*
Herge, J. Curtis *lawyer*
Kennedy, Cornelius Bryant *retired lawyer*
Klinedinst, Duncan Stewart *lawyer*
Maloof, Farahe Paul *lawyer*
Mater, Maud *lawyer*
Morris, James Malachy *lawyer*
Murphy, Thomas Patrick *lawyer*
Neel, Samuel Ellison *lawyer*
O'Brien, Francis Anthony *retired lawyer*
Peet, Richard Clayton *lawyer, consultant*
Prichard, Edgar Allen *lawyer*
Rau, Lee Arthur *lawyer*
Rhyne, Charles Sylvanus *lawyer*
Shepard, Julian Leigh *lawyer, humanitarian*
Sparks, Robert Ronold, Jr. *lawyer*
Stephens, William Theodore *lawyer, business executive*
Stump, John Sutton *lawyer*
Tansill, Frederick Joseph *lawyer*
Toole, John Harper *lawyer*
Traver, Courtland Lee *lawyer*
Trotter, Haynie Seay *lawyer*
Walton, Edmund Lewis, Jr. *lawyer*

McLean
Alexander, Fred Calvin, Jr. *lawyer*
Brady, Phillip Donley *lawyer*
†Houle, Jeffrey Robert *lawyer*

Midlothian
Shands, William Ridley, Jr. *lawyer*

Mineral
Schelling, John Paul *lawyer, consultant*
Whitlock, Willie Walker *lawyer*

Mosman
Barusch, Ronald Charles *lawyer*

Mount Jackson
Cohen, Lewis Isaac *lawyer*

Mount Vernon
Spiegel, H. Jay *lawyer*

Nellysford
Sims, John Rogers, Jr. *lawyer*

Newport News
Cuthrell, Carl Edward *lawyer, educator, clergyman*
Kamp, Arthur Joseph, Jr. *lawyer*
Martin, Terrence Keech *lawyer, city councilor*
Segall, James Arnold *lawyer*

Norfolk
Achampong, Francis Kofi *law educator, consultant*
Baird, Edward Rouzie, Jr. *lawyer*
Boyd, Robert Friend *lawyer*
Breit, Jeffrey Arnold *lawyer*
Clark, Morton Hutchinson *lawyer*
Corcoran, Andrew Patrick, Jr. *lawyer*
Cranford, Page Deronde *lawyer, educator, executive*
Crenshaw, Francis Nelson *lawyer*
Drescher, John Webb *lawyer*
Parker, Richard Wilson *lawyer*
Pearson, John Y., Jr. *lawyer*
Rephan, Jack *lawyer*
Russell, C. Edward, Jr. *lawyer*
Ryan, John M. *lawyer*
Shannon, John Sanford *retired railway executive, lawyer*
Smith, Richard Muldrow *lawyer*
Tolmie, Donald McEachern *lawyer*
Waldo, Joseph Thomas *lawyer*
Wooldridge, William Charles *lawyer*

Norton
Shortridge, Judy Beth *lawyer*

Palmyra
White, Luther Wesley *retired lawyer*

Petersburg
Baskervill, Charles Thornton *lawyer*
Shell, Louis Calvin *lawyer*
Spero, Morton Bertram *lawyer*

Portsmouth
Bangel, Herbert K. *lawyer*
Blachman, Michael Joel *lawyer*

Radford
Turk, James Clinton, Jr. *lawyer*

Reston
Bredehoft, Elaine Charlson *lawyer*
Humphreys, David John *lawyer, trade association executive*
†Keler, Marianne Martha *lawyer*
Scharff, Joseph Laurent *lawyer*
Spath, Gregg Anthony *lawyer*

Richmond
Ackerly, Benjamin Clarkson *lawyer*
Addison, David Dunham *lawyer*
Allen, George Felix *lawyer*
Aron, Mark G. *lawyer, transportation executive*
Baliles, Gerald L. *lawyer, former governor*

Bates, John Wythe, III *lawyer*
Belcher, Dennis Irl *lawyer*
Bing, Richard McPhail *lawyer*
Booker, Lewis Thomas *lawyer*
Boyd, B(everley) Randolph *lawyer*
Brasfield, Evans Booker *lawyer*
Brissette, Martha Blevins *lawyer*
Brockenbrough, Henry Watkins *lawyer*
Brooks, Robert Franklin, Sr. *lawyer*
Burke, John K(irkland), Jr. *lawyer*
Burrus, Robert Lewis, Jr. *lawyer*
Bush, Thomas Norman *lawyer*
Carrell, Daniel Allan *lawyer*
Carter, Joseph Carlyle, Jr. *lawyer*
Catlett, Richard H., Jr. *retired lawyer*
Clinard, Robert Noel *lawyer*
Cohn, David Stephen *lawyer*
Cullen, Richard *lawyer, former state attorney general*
Dabney, H. Slayton, Jr. *lawyer*
Denny, Collins, III *lawyer*
Dray, Mark S. *lawyer*
Edmonds, Thomas Andrew *state bar executive director*
Ellis, Andrew Jackson, Jr. *lawyer*
Elmore, Edward Whitehead *lawyer*
Epps, Augustus Charles *lawyer*
Fitzsimmons, Ellen Marie *lawyer*
†Fuhr, Edward J. *lawyer*
Gary, Richard David *lawyer*
Goodpasture, Philip Henry *lawyer*
Graves, H. Brice *lawyer*
Hackney, Virginia Howitz *lawyer*
Hall, Stephen Charles *lawyer*
Hettrick, George Harrison *lawyer*
Hicks, C. Flippo *lawyer*
Horsley, Waller Holladay *lawyer*
Howell, George Cook, III *lawyer*
Johnston, Francis Claiborne, Jr. *lawyer*
Kearfott, Joseph Conrad *lawyer*
Ledbetter, David Oscar *lawyer*
Levit, Jay J(oseph) *lawyer*
Mallory, Jean Long *paralegal*
McClard, Jack Edward *lawyer*
McElligott, James Patrick, Jr. *lawyer*
McVey, Henry Hanna, III *lawyer*
Merhige, Robert Reynold, Jr. *lawyer*
Mezzullo, Louis Albert *lawyer*
Miller, Stephen Wiley *lawyer*
Milmoe, Patrick Joseph *lawyer*
Minardi, Richard A., Jr. *lawyer*
Moore, Thurston Roach *lawyer*
Musick, Robert Lawrence, Jr. *lawyer*
Oulton, Richard James *lawyer, entrepreneur*
Palmore, Fred Wharton, III *lawyer*
Pasco, Hansell Merrill *retired lawyer*
Peters, David Frankman *lawyer*
Phillips, Elizabeth Jason *lawyer*
Pinckney, Charles Cotesworth *lawyer*
Pope, Robert Dean *lawyer*
Powell, Lewis Franklin, III *lawyer*
Rainey, Gordon Fryer, Jr. *lawyer*
Rigsby, Linda Flory *lawyer*
Roach, Edgar Mayo, Jr. *lawyer*
Rolfe, Robert Martin *lawyer*
Rubinstein, Phyllis M. *lawyer*
Rucker, Douglas Pendleton, Jr. *lawyer*
Rudlin, David Alan *lawyer*
Sharer, John Daniel *lawyer*
Slater, Thomas Glascock, Jr. *lawyer*
Slaughter, Alexander Hoke *lawyer*
Smith, R. Gordon *lawyer*
Smolla, Rodney Alan *lawyer, educator*
Spahn, Gary Joseph *lawyer*
Spain, Jack Holland, Jr. *lawyer*
Starke, Harold E., Jr. *lawyer*
Stoyko, William Nelson *lawyer*
Strickland, William Jesse *lawyer*
Thomas, John Charles *lawyer, former state supreme court justice*
Thompson, Paul Michael *lawyer*
Troy, Anthony Francis *lawyer*
Walsh, William Arthur, Jr. *lawyer*
Warthen, Harry Justice, III *lawyer*
Watts, Stephen Hurt, II *lawyer*
Weis, Laura Visser *lawyer*
White, Hugh Vernon, Jr. *lawyer*
White, James M., III *lawyer*
†Williams, Steven Robert *lawyer*
Witt, Walter Francis, Jr. *lawyer*

Roanoke
Barnhill, David Stan *lawyer*
Bates, Harold Martin *lawyer*
Butler, Manley Caldwell *retired lawyer*
Crouch, Robert P., Jr. *prosecutor*
Fishwick, John Palmer *lawyer, retired railroad executive*
Hale, Lance Mitchell *lawyer*
Harris, Bayard Easter *lawyer*
Keesee, Roger Neal, Jr. *lawyer*
Lemon, William Jacob *lawyer*
McGarry, Richard Lawrence *lawyer*
Mundy, Gardner Marshall *lawyer*
Woodrum, Clifton A., III *lawyer, state legislator*

Rustburg
Hughes, Deborah Enoch *circuit court clerk*

Salem
Burkart, Francis William, III *lawyer*

Springfield
Englert, Roy Theodore *lawyer*

Sterling
Howard, Angela Kay *lawyer, accountant*
McBarnette, Bruce Olvin *lawyer, corporate executive*

The Plains
Rose, Henry *lawyer*

Tysons Corner
Hicks, C. Thomas, III *lawyer*

Vienna
McCabe, Thomas Edward *lawyer*
Molineaux, Charles Borromeo *lawyer, arbitrator, columnist, poet*
Price, Ilene Rosenberg *lawyer*
Razzano, Frank Charles *lawyer*
Seidman, Paul Joseph *lawyer*
Titus, Bruce Earl *lawyer*
Whitaker, Thomas Patrick *lawyer*

Virginia Beach
Fruit, J. Curtis *municipal court clerk*
Hajek, Francis Paul *lawyer*
Layton, Garland Mason *lawyer*
Sekulow, Jay Alan *lawyer*
Spitzli, Donald Hawkes, Jr. *lawyer*
Swope, Richard McAllister *retired lawyer*
Szto, Mary Christine *law educator*

Warrenton
Howard, Blair Duncan *Lawyer*

Waterford
Harris, Caspa, Jr. *lawyer, educator, association administrator*

Weems
LaPrade, Carter *lawyer*

Williamsburg
Church, Dale Walker *lawyer*
Fisher, Chester Lewis, Jr. *retired lawyer*
Geddy, Vernon Meredith, Jr. *lawyer*
Lund, Wendell Luther *retired lawyer*
Marcus, Paul *law educator*
Rogers, Leo P. *deputy county attorney, educator*
Sullivan, Timothy Jackson *law educator, academic administrator*
Whitehead, James Madison *law librarian*
Whyte, James Primrose, Jr. *former law educator*
Wilson, Paul Lowell *lawyer, mortgage company executive*

Woodstock
Walton, Morgan Lauck, III *lawyer*

WASHINGTON

Bellevue
Boespflug, John Francis, Jr. *lawyer*
Gulick, Peter VanDyke *lawyer*
Kimball, Mark Douglas *lawyer*
Landau, Felix *lawyer*
Morie, G. Glen *lawyer, manufacturing company executive*
Sebris, Robert, Jr. *lawyer*
Treacy, Gerald Bernard, Jr. *lawyer*

Bellingham
Anderson, David Bowen *lawyer*
Packer, Mark Barry *lawyer, financial consultant, foundation official, mediator*
Raas, Daniel Alan *lawyer*
Uhrig, Ira John *attorney, court commissioner*

Centralia
Buzzard, Steven Ray *lawyer*

Colfax
Webster, Ronald B. *lawyer*

Ephrata
Aiken, Michael DeWayne *lawyer*

Everett
Mestel, Mark David *lawyer*

Friday Harbor
Gonser, Thomas Howard *lawyer, former bar association executive*

Gig Harbor
Thompson, Ronald Edward *lawyer*

Hoquiam
Kessler, Keith Leon *lawyer*

Issaquah
Benoliel, Joel *lawyer*

Kennewick
Hames, William Lester *lawyer*

Kirkland
Dorkin, Frederic Eugene *lawyer*
Wolff, Joel Henry *human factors engineer, lawyer*

Mount Vernon
Moser, C. Thomas *lawyer*

Olympia
Edmondson, Frank Kelley, Jr. *lawyer, legal administrator*
Hoglund, John Andrew *lawyer*
Miller, Allen Terry, Jr. *lawyer*
Norwood, Deborah Anne *law librarian*
Wilson, Wesley M. *retired lawyer, writer*

Pasco
Norris, Kenneth Michael *lawyer*

Port Angeles
Gay, Carl Lloyd *lawyer*

Redmond
Erxleben, William Charles *lawyer*
†Neukom, William H. *corporate lawyer*

Renton
Swanson, Arthur Dean *lawyer*
Thompson, George Lewis *lawyer*

Richland
Barr, Carlos Harvey *lawyer*

Seattle
Alkire, John D. *lawyer, mediator, arbitrator*
Anderson, Peter MacArthur *lawyer*
Andreasen, Steven W. *lawyer*
Andrews, J. David *lawyer*
Bagshaw, Bradley Holmes *lawyer*
Barnes, Susan Lewis *lawyer*
Birmingham, Richard Joseph *lawyer*
Black, W. L. Rivers, III *lawyer*
†Blair, Wayne M *lawyer*
Blais, Robert Howard *lawyer*
Blom, Daniel Charles *lawyer, investor*
Blumenfeld, Charles Raban *lawyer*
Boeder, Thomas L. *lawyer*
Bringman, Joseph Edward *lawyer*
Burke, William Thomas *law educator, lawyer*
Burkhart, William Henry *lawyer*
Cavanaugh, Michael Everett *lawyer, arbitrator, mediator*
Char, Patricia Helen *lawyer*
Claflin, Arthur Cary *lawyer*
Clinton, Gordon Stanley *lawyer*
Clinton, Richard M. *lawyer*
Collins, Theodore John *lawyer*
Cornell, Kenneth Lee *lawyer*
Corning, Nicholas F. *lawyer*
Cross, Harry Maybury *retired law educator, consultant*
Cunningham, Joel Dean *lawyer*
Cutler, Philip Edgerton *lawyer*
Dalton, Thomas George *paralegal, social worker, legal consultant*
Davis, John MacDougall *lawyer*
DeVore, Paul Cameron *lawyer*
Diamond, Josef *lawyer*
Diggs, Bradley C. *lawyer*
Dolan, Andrew Kevin *lawyer*
Ebell, C(ecil) Walter *lawyer*
Elliott, Clifton Langsdale *lawyer*
Ellis, James Reed *lawyer*
Emory, Meade *lawyer*
Fitzpatrick, Thomas Mark *lawyer*
Freedman, Bart Joseph *lawyer*
Gandara, Daniel *lawyer*
Giles, Robert Edward, Jr. *lawyer*
Gittinger, D. Wayne *lawyer*
Goeltz, Thomas A. *lawyer*
Gores, Thomas C. *lawyer*
Gottlieb, Daniel Seth *lawyer*
Graham, Stephen Michael *lawyer*
Gray, Marvin Lee, Jr. *lawyer*
Greenan, Thomas J. *lawyer*
Greene, John Burkland *lawyer*
Groff, David Clark, Jr. *lawyer*
Gustafson, Alice Fairleigh *lawyer*
Guy, Andrew A. *lawyer*
Haman, Raymond William *lawyer*
Hansen, Wayne W. *lawyer*
Hanson, William Lewis *lawyer*
Hazelton, Penny Ann *law librarian, educator*
Hecht, Irene Margret *lawyer*
Hill, G. Richard *lawyer*
Hilpert, Edward Theodore, Jr. *lawyer*
Huff, Gary D. *lawyer*
Huston, John Charles *law educator*
Hutcheson, Mark Andrew *lawyer*
Isaki, Lucy Power Slyngstad *lawyer*
Israel, Allen D. *lawyer*
Jackson, Dillon Edward *lawyer*
Johnson, Bruce Edward Humble *lawyer*
Judson, C(harles) James (Jim Judson) *lawyer*
Kane, Alan Henry *lawyer*
Kane, Christopher *lawyer*
Kaplan, Barry Martin *lawyer*
Katz, Charles J., Jr. *lawyer*
Keegan, John E. *lawyer*
Kellogg, Kenyon P. *lawyer*
Klein, Otto G., III *lawyer*
Koehler, Reginald Stafford, III *lawyer*
Kuhrau, Edward W. *lawyer*
Leitzell, Terry Lee *lawyer*
Lemly, Thomas Adger *lawyer*
Loftus, Thomas Daniel *lawyer*
Lombard, David Norman *lawyer*
Lundgren, Gail M. *lawyer*
Maleng, Norm *prosecuting attorney*
Malone, Thomas William *lawyer*
Marshall, David Stanley *lawyer*
McCann, Richard Eugene *lawyer*
McKay, Michael Dennis *lawyer*
McKinstry, Ronald Eugene *lawyer*
Merkle, Alan Ray *lawyer*
Mines, Michael *lawyer*
Moch, Robert Gaston *lawyer*
Murray, Michael Kent *lawyer*
Mussehl, Robert Clarence *lawyer*
Nellermoe, Leslie Carol *lawyer*
Niemi, Janice *lawyer, former state legislator*
Noble, Phillip D. *lawyer*
Oehler, Richard William *lawyer*
Oles, Stuart Gregory *lawyer*
Olsen, Harold Fremont *lawyer*
Palm, Gerald Albert *lawyer*
Palmer, Douglas S., Jr. *lawyer*
Parker, Omar Sigmund, Jr. *lawyer*
Parks, Gerald Thomas, Jr. *lawyer, business executive*
Parks, Patricia Jean *lawyer*
Parsons, A. Peter *lawyer*
Perey, Ron *lawyer*
Peterson, Jan Eric *lawyer*
Petrie, Gregory Steven *lawyer*
Pettigrew, Edward W. *lawyer*
Pflauer, Katrina Campbell *lawyer*
†Pflaumer, Katrina C. *lawyer*
Prentke, Richard Ottesen *lawyer*
Price, John Richard *lawyer, law educator*
Pritchard, Llewelyn G. *lawyer*
Pym, Bruce Michael *lawyer*
Reardon, Mark William *lawyer*
Redman, Eric *lawyer*
Rieke, Paul Victor *lawyer*
Ritter, Daniel Benjamin *lawyer*
Rosen, Jon Howard *lawyer*
Ruddy, James W. *lawyer*
Rummage, Stephen Michael *lawyer*
Sandman, Irvin W(illis) *lawyer*
Scott, Brian David *lawyer*
Sidran, Mark H. *lawyer*
Soltys, John Joseph *lawyer*
Spitzer, Hugh D. *lawyer*
Squires, William Randolph, III *lawyer*
Steers, George W. *lawyer*
Steinberg, Jack *lawyer*
Stoebuck, William Brees *law educator*
Strichartz, James Leonard *lawyer*
Sweeney, David Brian *lawyer*
Tallman, Richard C. *lawyer*
Tessier, Dennis Medward *paralegal, lecturer, legal advisor, consultant*
Thorne, David W. *lawyer*
Thorson, Lee A. *lawyer*
Tousley, Russell Frederick *lawyer*
Treiger, Irwin Louis *lawyer*
Veblen, John Elvidge *lawyer*
Vestal, Josephine Burnet *lawyer*
Wagner, Patricia Hamm *lawyer*
Wagoner, David Everett *lawyer*
Walter, Michael Charles *lawyer*
Wayne, Robert Jonathan *lawyer, educator*
Wechsler, Mary Heyrman *lawyer*
Wells, Christopher Brian *lawyer*
Whalen, Jerome Demaris *lawyer*
White, Rick *lawyer, former congressman*
White, Thomas S. *lawyer*
Whitehead, James Fred, III *lawyer*
Whitford, Joseph P. *lawyer*
Whitson, Lish *lawyer*
Williams, J. Vernon *lawyer*

Spokane
†Connelly, James P. *prosecutor*
Connolly, K. Thomas *lawyer*
Harbaugh, Daniel Paul *lawyer*
Koegen, Roy Jerome *lawyer*
Pontarolo, Michael Joseph *lawyer*
Riherd, John Arthur *lawyer*
Weatherhead, Leslie R. *lawyer*

Tacoma
Chiappinelli, Eric Andrew *law educator*
George, Nicholas *criminal defense lawyer, entrepreneur*
Gordon, Joseph Harold *lawyer*
Graves, Ray *lawyer*
Holt, William E. *lawyer*
Hostnik, Charles Rivoire *lawyer*
Krueger, James A. *lawyer*
Miller, Judson Frederick *lawyer, former military officer*
Mungia, Salvador Alejo, Jr. *lawyer*
Nance, John Joseph *lawyer, writer, air safety analyst, broadcaster, consultant*
Steele, Anita Martin (Margaret Anne Martin) *law librarian, legal educator*
Sterbick, Peter Lawrence *lawyer*
Waldo, James Chandler *lawyer*
Wang, Arthur Ching-li *administrative law judge, law educator*

Tukwila
Gouras, Mark Steven *lawyer*

Vancouver
Kleweno, Gilbert H. *lawyer*

Vashon
Biggs, Barry Hugh *lawyer*

Walla Walla
Hayner, Herman Henry *lawyer*
Hedine, Kristian Einar *lawyer*

Wenatchee
Foreman, Dale Melvin *lawyer, state official*

Yakima
Larson, Paul Martin *lawyer*

WEST VIRGINIA

Beckley
Kennedy, David Tinsley *retired lawyer, labor arbitrator*

Bluefield
Evans, Wayne Lewis *lawyer*

Buckhannon
McCauley, David W. *lawyer, educator*

Charleston
Betts, Rebecca A. *lawyer*
Brown, James Knight *lawyer*
Cline, Michael Robert *lawyer*
Davis, James Hornor, III *lawyer*
Gage, Charles Quincey *lawyer*
Goodwin, Claude Elbert *lawyer, former gas utility executive*
Kizer, John Oscar *lawyer*
Maroney, Thomas P. *lawyer, political party executive*
McClaugherty, John Lewis *lawyer*
Neely, Richard *lawyer*
Stacy, Charles Brecknock *lawyer*
Teare, John Richard, Jr. *lawyer*
Zak, Robert Joseph *lawyer*

Clarksburg
Jarvis, John Cecil *lawyer*

Fairmont
Stanton, George Patrick, Jr. *lawyer*

Fairview
Bunner, Patricia Andrea *lawyer*

Huntington
Bagley, Charles Frank, III *lawyer*
St. Clair, James William *lawyer*

Lewisburg
Ford, Richard Edmond *lawyer*

Martinsburg
Rice, Lacy I., Jr. *lawyer*

Morgantown
Bunner, William Keck *lawyer*
Cleckley, Franklin D. *law educator*
†Fisher, John Welton, II *law educator, magistrate judge, university official*
Fusco, Andrew G. *lawyer*
Morris, William Otis, Jr. *lawyer, educator, author*

Romney
Saville, Royce Blair *lawyer*

Sprague
Rhoades, Marye Frances *paralegal*

Summersville
Yeager, Charles William *lawyer, newspaper publisher*

Wellsburg
Bell, Charles D. *lawyer*
Viderman, Linda Jean *paralegal, corporate executive*

Mercier, Francois *lawyer*
Messier, Pierre *lawyer, manufacturing company executive*
Montcalm, Norman Joseph *lawyer*
Popovici, Adrian *law educator*
Pound, Richard William Duncan *lawyer, accountant*
Régnier, Marc Charles *lawyer, corporate executive*
Robb, James Alexander *lawyer*
Scraire, Jean-Claude *lawyer, investment management executive*
Sheppard, Claude-Armand *lawyer*
Tremblay, Andre Gabriel *lawyer*
Trudeau, Pierre Elliott *lawyer, former Canadian prime minister*
Vennat, Michel *lawyer*

Quebec
LeMay, Jacques *lawyer*
Verge, Pierre *legal educator*

Sainte Foy
Normand, Robert *lawyer*

Sillery
Dinan, Robert Michael *lawyer*

Westmount
Fortier, L. Yves *barrister*

SASKATCHEWAN

Regina
Balfour, Reginald James *retired lawyer*
Laschuk, Roy Bogdan *lawyer*
MacKay, Harold Hugh *lawyer*

Saskatoon
Ish, Daniel Russell *law educator, academic adminstrator*

MEXICO

Santiago Colima
Williams, Wayne De Armond *lawyer*

BELGIUM

Brussels
Barnum, John Wallace *lawyer*
Bustin, George Leo *lawyer*
Glazer, Barry David *lawyer*
Liebman, Howard Mark *lawyer*
Oberreit, Walter William *lawyer*

BERMUDA

Hamilton
Beerbower, Cynthia Gibson *lawyer*

CHINA

Hong Kong
Chu, Franklin Dean *lawyer*
O'Brien, Timothy James *lawyer*
Scown, Michael John *lawyer*
Tanner, Douglas Alan *lawyer*

DENMARK

Copenhagen
Alsted, Peter *lawyer*

ENGLAND

Beverley
Edles, Gary Joel *lawyer*

London
Albert, Robert Alan *lawyer*
Beharrell, Steven Roderic *lawyer*
Bigbie, John Taylor *lawyer, banker*
Brownwood, David Owen *lawyer*
Bruce, Robert Rockwell *lawyer*
Cole, Richard A. *lawyer*
Fabricant, Arthur E. *lawyer, corporate executive*
Fox, Hazel Mary *barrister, editor*
Gaines, Peter Mathew *lawyer*
Gates, Stephen Frye *lawyer, business executive*
Haubold, Samuel Allen *lawyer*
Hudson, Manley O., Jr. *lawyer*
Jalili, Mahir *lawyer*
Kingham, Richard Frank *lawyer*
Montgomery, John Warwick *law educator, theologian*
Morrison, William David *lawyer*
Nelson, Bernard Edward *lawyer*
Phocas, George John *international lawyer, business executive*
Raleigh, Martha Collins *lawyer*
Schoenlaub, Fred Edward *lawyer, retired circuit court judge*
Smalley, David Vincent *lawyer*
Stevens, Robert Bocking *lawyer, educator*
Thomas, Allen Lloyd *lawyer, private investor*

FRANCE

Paris
Baum, Axel Helmuth *lawyer*
Craig, William Laurence *lawyer*
Kammerer, Kelly Christian *lawyer*
Landers, Steven E. *lawyer*
MacCrindle, Robert Alexander *lawyer*
McGurn, William Barrett, III *lawyer*
Rawlings, Boynton Mott *lawyer*
Reeves, Van Kirk *lawyer*
Salans, Carl Fredric *lawyer*
Shapiro, Isaac *lawyer*

GERMANY

Finning
English, Charles Brand *retired lawyer*

Frankfurt
Simitis, Spiros *legal educator*

GRENADA

Saint George's
Helgerson, John Walter *lawyer*

ISRAEL

Jerusalem
Rosenne, Meir *lawyer, government agency administrator*

ITALY

Rome
Alegi, Peter Claude *lawyer*

JAPAN

Hachioji
Kojima, Takeshi *law educator, arbitrator, writer*

Kyoto
Miki, Arata *law educator*

Nagoya
Kato, Masanobu *lawyer, educator*

Osaka
Solberg, Norman Robert *lawyer*

Tokyo
Hunter, Larry Dean *lawyer*
Inoue, Akira *law educator*
Lunding, Christopher Hanna *lawyer*
Nakamura, Hideo *law educator*
Nishi, Osamu *law educator*
Shirai, Shun *law educator, lawyer*
Yamasaki, Yukuzo *lawyer*

NORWAY

Oslo
Fleischer, Carl August *law educator, consultant*

THE PHILIPPINES

Manila
Siguion-Reyna, Leonardo *lawyer, business executive*

POLAND

Warsaw
Romney, Richard Bruce *lawyer*

PORTUGAL

Funchal
Mayda, Jaro *lawyer, educator, author, consultant*

REPUBLIC OF KOREA

Seoul
Rhi, Sang-Kyu *lawyer, educator*

SAUDI ARABIA

Riyadh
Taylor, Frederick William, Jr. (Fritz Taylor) *lawyer*

SCOTLAND

Edinburgh
Macneil, Ian Roderick *lawyer, educator*

SWITZERLAND

Basel
Rosenthal, David *lawyer, publicist*

Fribourg
Gurley, Franklin Louis *lawyer, military historian*

Geneva
Abram, Morris Berthold *lawyer, educator, diplomat*

TURKEY

Camkaya
Wales, Gwynne Huntington *lawyer*

WALES

Wiltshire
Sherwin, James Terry *lawyer*

ADDRESS UNPUBLISHED

Abbott, Gregory Andrew *lawyer*
Adams, David Gray *lawyer*
Adams, Thomas Lawrence *lawyer*
Adams, Thomas Lynch, Jr. *lawyer*
Adcock, Richard Paul *lawyer*
Aikman, Albert Edward *lawyer*
†Alexander, Andrew Lamar (Lamar Alexander) *lawyer, former secretary of education, former governor*
Alfred, Stephen Jay *lawyer*
Allred, Michael Sylvester *lawyer*
Alpern, Andrew *lawyer, architect, architectural historian*
Amar, Akhil Reed *law educator*
Anderson, Geoffrey Allen *retired lawyer*
Anderson, Jon Eric *lawyer*
Anderson, Keith *retired lawyer, retired banker*
Andreozzi, Louis Joseph *lawyer*
Andrews, David Ralph *lawyer*
Ansley, Shepard Bryan *lawyer*
Arnold, Jerome Gilbert *lawyer*
Ashe, Bernard Flemming *arbitrator, educator, lawyer*
Assael, Michael *lawyer, accountant*
Avery, James Thomas, III *lawyer, management consultant*
Babb, Frank Edward *lawyer, executive*
Bagley, William Thompson *lawyer*
Bailey, Francis Lee *lawyer*
Bain, William Donald, Jr. *lawyer, chemical company executive*
Baker, Donald *lawyer*
Baker, William Thompson, Jr. *lawyer*
Bandy, Jack D. *lawyer*
Bangs, John Kendrick *lawyer, foundation executive, former chemical company executive*
Banks, Robert Sherwood *lawyer*
Baskin, Stuart Jay *lawyer*
Bateman, David Alfred *lawyer*
Bates, Charles Turner *lawyer, educator*
Battle, Frank Vincent, Jr. *lawyer*
Baum, Stanley David *lawyer*
Baxter-Smith, Gregory John *shareholder*
Beasley, James W., Jr. *lawyer*
Beattie, Charles Robert, III *lawyer*
Beck, Mary Virginia *lawyer, public official*
Beck, Stuart Edwin *lawyer*
Becker, William Watters *lawyer*
Beldock, Myron *lawyer*
Belmont, Madra Alvis *lawyer*
Ben-Veniste, Richard *lawyer*
Bergan, William Luke *lawyer*
Beringer, William Ernst *mediator, arbitrator, lawyer*
Berle, Peter Adolf Augustus *lawyer, media director*
Berman, Joshua Mordecai *lawyer, manufacturing company executive*
Berman, Richard Bruce *lawyer*
Bernstein, George L. *lawyer, accountant*
Berrey, Robert Forrest *lawyer*
Berry, Robert Worth *lawyer, educator, retired army officer*
Bertram, Manya M. *lawyer*
Beukema, John Frederick *lawyer*
Blatt, Harold Geller *lawyer*
Blazzard, Norse Novar *lawyer*
Blevins, Jeffrey Alexander *lawyer*
Block, Dennis Jeffrey *lawyer*
Block, Richard Raphael *lawyer, economic development arbitrator*
Blow, George *lawyer*
Boho, Dan L. *lawyer*
Bork, Robert Heron *lawyer, author, educator, former federal judge*
Borowitz, Albert Ira *lawyer, author*
Bost, Thomas Glen *lawyer*
Bower, Jean Ramsay *lawyer, writer*
Bowman, Patricia Lynn *lawyer*
Boyd, Thomas Marshall *lawyer*
Bradford, Barbara Reed *lawyer*
Brafford, William Charles *lawyer*
Branagan, James Joseph *lawyer*
Brantz, George Murray *retired lawyer*
Brauer, Rhonda Lyn *lawyer*
Braun, Jerome Irwin *lawyer*
Brechbill, Susan Reynolds *lawyer, educator*
Breidenbach, Cherie Elizabeth *lawyer, accountant*
Brink, Richard Edward *lawyer*
Brodhead, David Crawmer *lawyer*
Brodsky, David M. *lawyer*
Brotman, Stuart Neil *management consultant, lawyer, educator*
Brower, Charles Nelson *lawyer, judge*
Buchanan, William Hobart, Jr. *lawyer, publishing company executive*
Buchmann, Alan Paul *lawyer*
Buechel, William Benjamin *lawyer*
Bujold, Tyrone Patrick *lawyer*
Burcham, Randall Parks *lawyer, farmer*
Burgess, Hayden Fern (Poka Laenui) *lawyer*
Burlingame, John Hunter *lawyer*
Califano, Joseph Anthony, Jr. *lawyer, public health policy educator, writer*
Campos-Orrego, Nora Patricia *lawyer, consultant*
Canan, Michael James *lawyer, author*
Canoff, Karen Huston *lawyer*
Capps, James Leigh, II *lawyer, reserve military career officer*
Carlucci, Joseph P. *lawyer*
Carmack, Mildred Jean *retired lawyer*
Carr, Jesse Metteau, III *lawyer, engineering executive*
Carroll, Joseph J(ohn) *lawyer*
Casella, Peter F(iore) *patent and licensing executive*
Casey, Robert Reisch *lawyer*
Casselman, William E., II *lawyer*
Cassidy, John Harold *lawyer*
Castel, Jean Gabriel *lawyer*
Cattani, Maryellen B. *lawyer*
Catuzzi, J(erome) P(rimo), Jr. *lawyer*
Cazalas, Mary Rebecca Williams *lawyer, nurse*
Chamberlin, Michael Meade *lawyer*
Chase, Seymour M. *lawyer*
Chave, Carolyn Margaret *lawyer, arbitrator*
Clabaugh, Elmer Eugene, Jr. *lawyer*
Clarke, Edward Owen, Jr. *lawyer*
Cobb, Miles Alan *retired lawyer*
Cohen, Seymour *lawyer*
Coleman, John Michael *lawyer, consumer products executive*
Coleman, Robert Lee *retired lawyer*
Coleman, Ronald D. (Ron Coleman) *former congressman*
Collins, James Francis *lawyer, financial consultant*
Colodny, Edwin Irving *lawyer, retired airline executive*
Cologne, Gordon Bennett *lawyer*

Colton, Sterling Don *lawyer, business executive, missionary*
Connelly, Sharon Rudolph *lawyer, federal official*
Cook, Quentin LaMar *lawyer, healthcare executive, church leader*
Cooper, Hal Dean *lawyer*
Coplin, Mark David *lawyer*
Cox, Marshall *lawyer*
Crawford, Muriel Laura *lawyer, author, educator*
Criscuolo, Wendy Laura *lawyer, interior design consultant*
Cronson, Robert Granville *lawyer*
Crook, Donald Martin *lawyer*
Crowe, James Joseph *lawyer*
Crown, Nancy Elizabeth *lawyer*
Culp, Gordon Calvin *retired lawyer*
D'Agusto, Karen Rose *lawyer*
Damaska, Mirjan Radovan *law educator*
Darr, Carol C. *lawyer*
David, Marilyn Hattie *lawyer, retired military officer*
Davis, Frances Kay *lawyer*
Davis, Roger Edwin *lawyer, retired discount chain executive*
Dean, Michael M. *lawyer*
De Concini, Dennis *lawyer, former United States senator, consultant*
DeLaFuente, Charles *lawyer, educator, journalist*
DeMitchell, Terri Ann *law educator*
Deric, Arthur Joseph *lawyer, management consultant, health coop trustee*
†DeVore, Daun Aline *lawyer*
DiBattiste, Carol A. *lawyer*
Dickerman, John Melvin *lawyer*
Diehl, Deborah Hilda *lawyer*
Dietel, James Edwin *lawyer, consultant*
Dimitry, Theodore George *retired lawyer*
Dodds, Lawrence Donald *lawyer*
Doherty, John L. *lawyer*
Dolan, Peter Brown *lawyer*
Dondanville, John Wallace *lawyer*
Doty, James Robert *lawyer*
Douglas, Robert Lee *lawyer*
Dubuc, Carroll Edward *lawyer*
Dudzik, Carol Joanne *lawyer, art educator*
Duncan, Donald William *lawyer*
Duncan, Nora Kathryn *lawyer*
Dunn, Warren Howard *retired lawyer, brewery executive*
Easterling, Charles Armo *lawyer*
Eaton, Larry Ralph *lawyer*
Edwards, Daniel Paul *lawyer, educator*
Edwards, Jerome *lawyer*
Eichhorn, Frederick Foltz, Jr. *retired lawyer*
Ellenberger, Jack Stuart *law librarian*
†Elliott, Diane V. *lawyer*
Elston, Michael James *lawyer, educator*
Embry, Stephen Creston *lawyer*
Emert, Timothy Ray *lawyer*
Engelhardt, John Hugo *lawyer, banker*
Erlebacher, Arlene Cernik *retired lawyer*
Erlenborn, John Neal *lawyer, educator, former congressman*
Esposito, Amy Sklar *lawyer*
Ettinger, Joseph Alan *lawyer*
Eustis, Albert Anthony *lawyer, diversified industry corporate executive*
Evans, Jeffrey Allen *lawyer*
Everdell, William *lawyer*
Falkner, Robert Frank *lawyer*
Fanwick, Ernest *lawyer*
Farmakides, John Basil *lawyer*
Fekete, George Otto *judge, lawyer, pharmacist*
Fernandez, Dennis Sunga *lawyer, electrical engineer, entrepreneur*
Ferraro, Geraldine Anne *lawyer, former congresswoman*
Fetzer, Mark Stephen *lawyer*
Fiala, David Marcus *lawyer*
Field, Arthur Norman *lawyer*
Fink, Norman Stiles *lawyer, educational administrator, fundraising consultant*
Fiorito, Edward Gerald *lawyer*
†Fischer, David Charles *lawyer*
Fischer, David Jon *lawyer*
Flaxman, Howard Richard *lawyer*
Flick, John Edmond *lawyer*
Ford, Ashley Lloyd *lawyer, retired consumer products company executive*
Fowler, Flora Daun *lawyer*
Fox, Eleanor Mae Cohen *lawyer, professor, author*
Franklin, Michael Harold *arbitrator, lawyer, consultant*
Freedman, Monroe Henry *lawyer, educator, columnist*
Freeman, Russell Adams *lawyer*
Friedman, Paul Richard *lawyer*
Fryburger, Lawrence Bruce *lawyer, mediator, writer*
Fuller, Robert Ferrey *lawyer, investor*
Futter, Victor *lawyer*
Gamble, E. James *lawyer, accountant*
Gardner, Anne Lancaster *lawyer*
Gardner, Warner Winslow *lawyer*
Garner, Mary Martin *lawyer*
Garry, John Thomas, II *lawyer*
Gaunt, Janet Lois *arbitrator, mediator*
George, Joyce Jackson *judge emeritus, lawyer*
Gilbride, William Donald *lawyer*
Gilster, Peter Stuart *lawyer*
Gingras, John Richard *lawyer, consultant*
Givens, Richard Ayres *lawyer*
Glasser, Ira Saul *civil liberties organization executive*
Glosser, Jeffrey Mark *lawyer*
Gobel, John Henry *lawyer*
Goldman, Charles Norton *retired corporate lawyer*
Goldstein, Joseph *law educator*
Gomez, David Frederick *lawyer*
Goodrich, Leon Raymond *lawyer*
Goonrey, Charles W. *retired lawyer*
Gora, Daniel Martin *lawyer*
Gordon, David Zevi *retired lawyer*
†Gould, Ronald *lawyer*
Grab, Frederick Charles *lawyer*
Grabemann, Karl W. *lawyer*
Grady, Maureen Frances *lawyer*
Green, Carol H. *lawyer, educator, journalist*
Green, Mark Joseph *lawyer, author*
Greenberg, Joshua F. *lawyer, educator*
Griffin, Campbell Arthur, Jr. *lawyer*
Griffith, James Lewis *lawyer*
Griffith, Steven Franklin, Sr. *lawyer, real estate title insurance agent and investor*
Grodsky, Jamie Anne *lawyer*
Grutman, Jewel Humphrey *lawyer, writer*
Gudenberg, Harry Richard *arbitrator, mediator*
Gustavson, Mark Steven *lawyer*
Gutman, Richard Edward *lawyer*
Guttentag, Joseph Harris *lawyer, educator*

MEDICINE. *See* **HEALTHCARE: MEDICINE.**

MILITARY

UNITED STATES

ALABAMA

Alexander City
Shuler, Ellie Givan, Jr. *retired military officer, military museum administrator*

Auburn
Tolbert, Clinton Jame *machinist, army officer*

Birmingham
Fayne, Gwendolyn Davis *air force officer, English educator*

Camp Hill
Hennies, Clyde Albert (Lou) *military officer, state official, military academy administrator*

Enterprise
Parker, Ellis D. *retired career officer, aviation executive*
Patterson, Albert Love III *career military officer*

Fort Mc Clellan
Baker, Robert Vernon, Jr. *retired military officer, military trainer*
†Ryder, Donald J. *military career officer*
†Wooten, Ralph G. *career officer*

Fort Rucker
†Jones, Anthony Ray *military career officer*

Huntsville
Kuehn, Robert John, Jr. *air force officer*
McClendon, Dennis Edward *retired air force officer*
Watts, William Park *naval officer*
Williamson, Donald Ray *retired career Army officer*

Maxwell AFB
†Ellis, Edward R. (Buster) *career officer*
Kane, Robert Barry *career officer*
Kinnan, Timothy Alan *air force officer*
†Rosa, John William *career officer*

Montgomery
Boston, Hollis Buford, Jr. *retired military officer*
Chamberlain, Kathryn Burns Browning *retired naval officer*
Pickett, George Bibb, Jr. *retired military officer*

Redstone Arsenal
†Gibson, Emmitt E. *career officer*

ALASKA

Anchorage
Overly, Frederick Dean *civilian military employee, entrepreneur*

Eielson AFB
†Crawford, Tommy F. *career officer*

Fort Richardson
†Cash, Dean W. *military career officer*

Kodiak
Croyle, Douglas Eugene *career officer*

ARIZONA

Davis Monthan A F B
†Corley, John D. W. *military officer*

Fort Huachuca
Tyler, Cecilia K. *army officer*

Glendale
Ingham, Edward A. *career officer*

Luke AFB
†Barry, John L. *military officer*

Scottsdale
O'Berry, Carl Gerald *former air force officer, electrical engineer*

Sierra Vista
Smith, Donna Nadine *army noncommissioned officer*

Tucson
Bryan, Gordon Redman, Jr. *retired naval officer*
Guice, John Thompson *retired career officer*
Rutter, George B., Jr. *career officer*
Wickham, John Adams, Jr. *retired army officer*

Yuma
Hudson, John Irvin *retired career officer*

ARKANSAS

Blytheville
Slowik, Richard Andrew *air force officer*

Fort Huachuca
†Sutten, Charles G., Jr. *career military officer*

Mountain Home
Baker, Robert Leon *naval medical officer*

CALIFORNIA

Arroyo Grande
Oseguera, Palma Marie *retired marine corps officer, reservist*

Beale AFB
†Simpson, Charles N. *military officer*

Bonita
Curtis, Richard Earl *former naval officer, former company executive, business consultant*

Camp Pendleton
Admire, John H. *career officer*

Carlsbad
Kauderer, Bernard Marvin *retired naval officer*

Carmichael
McHugh, James Joseph *retired naval officer, retired associate dean*

Coronado
Butcher, Bobby Gene *retired military officer*
Rizza, Joseph Padula *naval officer, former president maritime academy*
Worthington, George Rhodes *retired naval officer*

Edwards AFB
†Reynolds, Richard V. *career officer*

El Segundo
†Hamel, Michael A. *military officer*

Escondido
Briggs, Edward Samuel *naval officer*

Folsom
Aldridge, Donald O'Neal *military officer*

Fort Irwin
Burns, Julian H(all), Jr. *military officer*
Strunz, Kim Carol *military officer*
†Webster, William G., Jr. *army officer*

Healdsburg
Eade, George James *retired air force officer, research executive, defense consultant*

Long Beach
Higginson, John *retired military officer*
VavRosky, Mark James *career officer, educator*

Los Angeles
Chernesky, John Joseph, Jr. *retired naval officer, healthcare executive*
Hernandez, Mike *city official*

Mcclellan AFB
†Wiedemer, Michael P. *military officer*

Monterey
†Frampton, James Scott *career officer*
Matthews, David Fort *military weapon system acquisition specialist*
Schrady, David Alan *operations research educator*

Napa
Smith, Robert Bruce *former security consultant, retired career officer*

Pebble Beach
Carns, Michael Patrick Chamberlain *air force officer*
Mauz, Henry Herrward, Jr. *retired naval officer*

Rancho Cordova
Meigel, David Walter *retired career officer, retired musician*

San Diego
Butler, William H. *military officer*
Froman, Veronica Zasadni *career officer*
Green, Kevin Patrick *career officer*
Magnus, Robert *military officer*
Moore, Edward, Jr. *career officer*
Richards, Thomas R. *military officer*
Stone, Thomas Edward *defense consultant, retired rear admiral*
Tedeschi, Ernest Francis, Jr. *retired naval officer, naval company executive*
Thornton, Wayne Allen *naval officer, engineer*

San Francisco
Moss, Douglas Mabbett *military officer, airline pilot, test pilot*

Santa Barbara
Conley, Philip James, Jr. *retired air force officer*

Santa Maria
Roadarmel, Stanley Bruce *civilian military employee*

Santa Rosa
Andriano-Moore, Richard Graf *naval officer*
Bowen, James Thomas *military officer*

Saratoga
Henderson, William Darryl *army officer, writer*

Seaside
Gales, Samuel Joel *retired civilian military employee, counselor*

South Dos Palos
Hirohata, Derek Kazuyoshi *career officer*

Spring Valley
Blackwell, Garland W(ayne) *retired military officer*

Travis AFB
†Rasmussen, Craig P. *career officer*
†Rodgers, Lee P. *career officer*
†Roser, Steven A. *career officer*

Vandenberg AFB
†Perryman, Gerald F., Jr. *military officer*

COLORADO

Arvada
Eaves, Sally Ann *logistics director, research administrator*

Aurora
Dawes, Douglas Charles *retired career officer*

Cheyenne Mountain Air Station
†Baptiste, Thomas L. *career officer*

Colorado Springs
Bowen, Clotilde Marion Dent *retired army officer, psychiatrist*
Brooks, Timothy Joe *career military officer*
Dinerstein, Marc J. *career military officer*
Forgan, David Waller *retired career officer*
†Lorenz, Stephen R. *career officer*
†Oelstrom, Tad J. *lieutenant general United States Air Force*
Sawyer, Thomas William *air force officer*
Schaeffer, Reiner Horst *career officer, retired librarian, foreign language professional*

Denver
Avrit, Richard Calvin *defense consultant*

Durango
Fogleman, Ronald Robert *retired air force officer, consultant*

Englewood
Nuce, Madonna Marie *career officer*
†Platt, John B. *hotel executive*
Thompson, Robert Frank, Jr. *career officer*

Fort Carson
Boylan, Steven Arthur *career officer*
†Riggs, John M. *army officer*

Fort Collins
Roberts, Archibald Edward *retired career officer, author*

Monument
Breckner, William John, Jr. *retired air force officer, corporate executive, consultant*

Peterson AFB
†Arnold, Brian A. *career officer*
†Drennan, Jerry M. *military officer*
†Hinson, Robert C. *career officer*
†Kelly, Rodney P. *military officer*
†Pettit, Donald *career officer*

Schriever AFB
†Looney, William R., III *career officer*

U S A F Academy
Krise, Thomas Warren *military officer, English language educator*
Morris, Steven Lynn *career officer, aeronautical engineering educator*

Woodland Park
Stewart, Robert Lee *retired army officer, astronaut*

CONNECTICUT

Bloomfield
Less, Anthony Albert *retired naval officer*

Bridgeport
†Menke, Richard Xavier *military officer*

Groton
Fages, Malcom I. *career officer*

New London
Padgett, John B., III *military officer, federal agency executive*

Niantic
Hunt, Francis Howard *retired navy laboratory official*

Rogers
Boomer, Walter Eugene *marine officer*

Windsor Locks
Trubia, Michael Leo *retired army officer, business administrator*

DISTRICT OF COLUMBIA

Bolling AFB
†Dendinger, William J. *career officer, chaplain*
†Jones, Hiram L. (Doc) *career officer, chaplain*
†Mabry, Earl W. *military officer*
Randolph, Leonard McElRoy, Jr. *career officer*
†Wyrick, Michael K. *military officer*

Fort Mcnair
†Chilcoat, Richard Allen *army officer, university president*
†Clodfelter, Mark A. *air force officer, educator*
†Engel, Richard L. *career officer*

Washington
†Ackerman, Michael W. *career officer*
†Adams, Patrick O. *career officer*
Albright, Joseph William *army officer*
†Altenburg, John D., Jr. *career officer*
†Anarde, Russell J. *career officer*
†Anderson, Edward G., III *army officer*
†Anderson, Frank J., Jr. *career officer*
†Andrews, James E. *career officer*
Aultman, William Robert *career officer*
Baca, Edward Dionicio *national guard officer*
†Ballard, Joe N. *career officer*
Beeson, Virginia Reed *naval officer, nurse*
Benken, Eric W. *career officer*
†Bergren, Scott C. *career officer*
Bice, David F. *career officer*
Bolden, Charles F., Jr. *career officer*
†Brooks, John W. *military officer*
†Brown, Richard E., III *military officer*
†Buchholz, Douglas David *military officer*
†Burnette, Thomas N. *career officer*
Byron, Michael J. *career officer*
†Campbell, William H. *career officer*
†Cannon, Charles C., Jr. *military career officer*
Card, James Conrad *coast guard officer*
Carlson, Bruce *career officer*
Carlton, Paul Kendall, Jr. *air force officer, physician*
†Carpenter, Shirley M. (Sam) *career officer*
Casciano, John P. *federal military program director*
†Casey, George W. *military career officer*
Cheney, Stephen A. *career officer*
Cherry, Robert Newton, Jr. *army officer, health physicist*
Christenson, Ronald L. *military officer*
†Claypool, Robert T. *military career officer*
†Clem, Ralph S. *career officer*
†Close, George F., Jr. *career officer*
†Coleman, Richard A., Jr. *career officer*
Craine, John W., Jr. *career officer*
Crawford, Hunt Dorn, Jr. *retired military officer, educator, diplomat*
Dake, Terrence R. *career officer*
Davidson, William A. *career officer*
†Davis, Russell C. *career officer*
DeFilippi, George *career military officer*
†Dekok, Roger Gregory *air force officer*
†DeLuca, Anthony J. *director small and minority business program in United State Air Force*
†Dodgen, Larry J. *career officer*
†Dubia, John Austin *army executive*
Dyke, Charles William *retired army officer*
†Eberhart, Ralph E. *general United States Air Force*
†Egeland, Andrew M., Jr. *military officer*
†Elliott, Carol C. *career officer*
Ellis, Winford G. *career officer*
†Ettenson, Gordon Michael *air force officer*
Falter, Vincent Eugene *retired army officer, consultant*
Finerty, Martin Joseph, Jr. *military officer, researcher, association management executive*
Fisher, Stephen Todd *naval officer*
†Foglesong, Robert H. *lieutenant general United States Air Force*
Franklin, Peter Charles *brigadier general*
Frost, S. David *retired naval officer*
†Fuhrman, Russell L. *career officer*
†Genetti, Albert J., Jr. *army officer*
†Gill, Clair F. *military career officer*
†Gioconda, Thomas F. *career officer*
Goodpaster, Andrew Jackson *retired army officer*
†Goslin, Thomas B. *career officer*
Graves, Ernest, Jr. *retired army officer, engineer*
Gregory, Frederick D. *career officer, space agency administrator*
†Griffin, Benjamin S. *military career officer*
†Guilbeaux, Wilson, Jr. *military officer*
†Gunhus, Gaylord T. *military career officer*
†Hancock, William John *career officer*
†Heebner, David K. *career officer*
†Hessert, Wilfred O. *military officer*
†Hester, Paul V. *career officer*
Hicks, Robert Ruiz, Jr. *army officer*
Holder, Gordon S. *career officer*
Hoskins, Carlton L. *career military officer*
Hudson, Joel B. *civilian military employee*
Hudson, McKinley *retired army officer, zoo deputy director*
†Huffman, Walter B. *army officer*
†Hughes, Patrick M. *career officer*
†Hunter, Milton *army officer*
Huston, John Wilson *air force officer, historian*
Insprucker, Nancy Rhoades *air force officer*
Jacoby, Lowell Edwin *career officer*
†Johnson, Jay L. *career officer*
†Jordan, Larry R. *career officer*
Keaney, Thomas Addis *strategic studies educator*
†Kellogg, Joseph J., Jr. *military career officer*
Kendall, Gene R. *military officer, federal agency administrator*
†Kennedy, Claudia J. *military officer*
†Kerrick, Donald L. *career officer*
†Kievenaar, Henry A. *military career officer*
Koenig, Harold Martin *former United States Navy surgeon general*
Kramek, Robert E. *United States Coast Guard officer*
Krol, Joseph John, Jr. *career officer*
†Krulak, Charles Chandler *marine officer*
†Kudlacz, Michael S. *career officer*
†Lampe, George P. *retired military officer*
Langston, Edward R., Jr. *career officer*
Leaf, Howard Westley *retired air force officer, military official*
†Leahy, Daniel F. *federal agency administrator*
†Lewis, Fred P. *career officer*
Loy, James M. *coast guard officer*
†Lupia, Eugene A. *military officer*
Luti, William Joseph *career officer*
†Maher, John Joseph, III *military career officer*
Marfiak, Thomas F. *career officer*
Marfiak, Thomas Fletcher *naval officer*
†Maude, Timothy J. *career officer*
Mayer, Martin *career officer*
†McCoy, Helen Thomas *civilian military employee*
†McDuffie, John M. *military officer*
McGinley, Edward Stillman, II *former naval officer, engineering executive*
†McKinley, Craig R. *air force officer*
†McMahon, Timothy J. *career officer*
†Menig, Janet *federal government executive*
†Metz, Thomas Frederic *military career officer*
†Moore, William F. *military officer*
†Mosely, Teed M. *career officer*
Murett, Robert B. *career officer*
Mutter, Carol A. *career officer*
†Navas, William Antonio, Jr. *retired military officer, civil engineer*
†Nicogossian, Anrauld E.T. *federal agency administrator*
†Northington, Larry W. *career officer*
Nutting, Wallace Hall *army officer*
†Odgers, Everett G. *career officer*
Odom, William Eldridge *army officer, educator*
†Ohle, David H. *military career officer*
O'Reilly, Kenneth William *military officer*
†Pamerleau, Susan L. *military officer*
†Pasini, Ralph *career officer*
†Pesachowitz, Alvin M. *federal agency administrator*
Peterson, David Glenn *retired career officer*
†Peterson, Quentin L. *career officer*
Pilling, Donald L. *military officer*
Pirie, Robert Burns, Jr. *defense analyst*
Poe, Larry L. *naval officer*
Prendergast, Kenneth Lee Michael, Jr. *career officer*

Cambridge
Felman, Marc David *air force officer*

Dudley
Carney, Roger Francis Xavier *retired army officer*

Hanscom AFB
†McFarland, Ted M. *career officer*

Lexington
Trainor, Bernard Edmund *retired military officer*

Medford
Galvin, John Rogers *educator, retired army officer*

Natick
†Mangual, Jesus A. *army officer*

Osterville
Schwarztrauber, Sayre Archie *former naval officer, maritime consultant*

Pittsfield
Watts, Dennis Lester *retired military officer*

Quincy
Miller, George David *retired air force officer, marketing consultant*

South Hamilton
Patton, George Smith *military officer*

Westford
Stansberry, James Wesley *air force officer*

MICHIGAN

Ann Arbor
Ploger, Robert Riis *retired military officer, engineer*

Detroit
Ivany, Robert Rudolph *military officer, historian*

East Lansing
†Robinson, Michael *protective services official*

Warren
†Beauchamp, Roy E. *career officer*

MINNESOTA

Burnsville
Larson, Doyle Eugene *retired air force officer, consultant*

Minneapolis
Chen, William Shao-Chang *retired army officer*

Rochester
Seligman, Jay Arnold *military officer, public health service officer*

Saint Paul
†Beers, Anne *protective services official*

MISSISSIPPI

Keesler AFB
†Locker, Dan L. *career officer*
†Pelak, Andrew J., Jr. *military officer*
Rigdon, David Tedrick *air force officer, geneticist, director*

Pass Christian
McCardell, James Elton *retired naval officer*

Vicksburg
†Anderson, Phillip R. *career officer*

MISSOURI

Chesterfield
Willis, Frank Edward *retired air force officer*

Fort Leonard Wood
†Flowers, Robert B. *military career officer*
†Rhoades, M. Stephen *career officer*

Kansas City
Magee, Thomas Mark *government official*

Saint Louis
King, Joseph, Jr. *government administrator, educator*
Strevey, Tracy Elmer, Jr. *army officer, surgeon, physician executive*

Whiteman AFB
†Barnidge, Leroy, Jr. *military officer*

NEBRASKA

Bellevue
Wright, John Charles *air force intelligence officer*

Lincoln
Heng, Stanley Mark *national guard officer*

Offutt A F B
Behler, Robert F. *military officer*
Gooch, Stanford Rondall *Air Force Operations research analyst*
†Habiger, Eugene E. *career officer*
†Henderson, Charles R. *major general United States Air Force*
†Sams, Ronald F. *brigadier general United States Air Force*
†Waltman, Glenn C. *military officer*

Omaha
Marsh, Clayton Edward *retired army officer, information systems specialist*

Salon
Beard, Timothy *career officer*

NEVADA

Henderson
Creech, Wilbur Lyman *retired career officer*
Hatfield, Samuel Fay, Jr. *retired military officer, construction consultant*
†Holdaway, Eric John *military officer*

Nellis A F B
†Lay, Theodore W., II *career officer*
†Moorhead, Glen W., III (Wally) *career officer*

NEW HAMPSHIRE

Greenland
Sargent, Douglas Robert *air force officer, engineer*

NEW JERSEY

Dover
†Geis, John P. *military career officer*
†Michitsch, John F. *career officer*

Fort Dix
†Davis, Steven Michael *air force officer, test pilot*
†Welser, William, III *military officer*

Fort Monmouth
†Boutelle, Steven W. *army officer*
†Gust, David R. *military career officer*

Freehold
Hooper, John David *coast guard officer*

Kearny
Badders, Rebecca Susanne *military officer, educator, writer*

Mc Guire AFB
Laramie, Regina Carol *career officer, writer*

Trenton
†Terhune, Jack *government administrator*

NEW MEXICO

Albuquerque
Flournoy, John Charles, Sr. *training specialist, retired military officer*

Belen
Smith, Helen Elizabeth *retired career officer*

Cedar Crest
Sheppard, Jack W. *retired career officer*

Kirtland AFB
†Cliver, Jeffrey G. *career officer*
†Gideon, Francis C., Jr. *military officer*
Henry, Gary Norman *air force officer, astronautical engineer*

Roswell
Miller, Nelson Alvin *retired army officer, public affairs administrator*

Santa Fe
Sumner, Gordon, Jr. *retired military officer*

White Sands
†Gatanas, Harry D. *career officer*

NEW YORK

Brooklyn
†Dukes, Frank Ronald *career military, collections investigator*
†Sinn, Jerry L. *army officer*

Fort Drum
†Kuykendall, Benjamin Loren *military officer*
Magruder, Lawson William, III *military officer*

Hamburg
Markulis, Henryk John *career military officer*

New York
Dugan, Michael Joseph *former air force officer, health agency executive*

Orient
Hanson, Thor *retired health agency executive and naval officer*

Sackets Harbor
†Clancy, Michael Neville *military officer*

West Point
†Abizaid, John P. *career officer*
Burke, Michael Augustus *miliatary officer*
Christman, Daniel William *military officer*
Kingseed, Cole Christian *military officer, history educator*

NORTH CAROLINA

Camp Lejeune
Bedard, Emil R. *career officer*
Blackman, Robert R., Jr. *military officer*
Rollings, Wayne E. *military officer*

Cherry Point
Braaten, Thomas A. *career officer*
Wells, David Patrick *career officer*

Fayetteville
Lungu, Angela Maria *career officer*

Fort Bragg
†Bergman, Mark *non-commissioned officer*
†Bowra, Kenneth R. *career officer*
†Boykin, William C. *career officer*
†Brown, Bryan D. *career officer*
†Dunkle, Keith Allen *military officer*
†Farage, Michael N. *career officer*
Juskowiak, Terry Eugene *career military officer*
†Kernan, William Frank *lieutenant general United States Army*
†McNeill, Dan K. *military career officer*
†Ryneska, John Joseph *military career officer*
†Tangney, William Patrick *military officer*

Pinehurst
Carroll, Kent Jean *retired naval officer*

Raleigh
Robb, Nathaniel Heyward, Jr. *remote sensing company executive*

Seymour Johnson AFB
†Bigum, Randall K. (Randy) *career officer*

Spring Hope
Hildreth, James Robert *retired air force officer*

Swansboro
Juhl, Harold Alexander *retired career officer, construction executive*

Wake Forest
Delaney, Gary Louis *retired military officer, management consultant*

NORTH DAKOTA

Bismarck
†Hughes, James M. *protective services official*

Minot AFB
Savage, Jeffrey Scott *military officer*

OHIO

Columbus
†Marshall, Kenneth B. *protective services agency administrator*
†Saunders, Mary L. *military officer*

Dayton
Halki, John Joseph *retired military officer, physician*
Whitlock, David C. *retired military officer*

Fairborn
Lawlis, Patricia Kite *air force officer, computer consultant*
Miller, Kenneth Gregory *retired air force officer*
Nowak, John Michael *retired air force officer, company executive*

Lebanon
Hollett, Grant T. *career officer*

Tiffin
Einsel, David William, Jr. *retired army officer and consultant*

Wright Patterson AFB
†Babbitt, George T. *career officer*
†Courter, Robert J., Jr. *career officer*
†Herrelko, David A. *career officer*
†Johnson, Charles L., II *military officer*
†Kelley, Joseph E. *career officer*
Maguire, Frank Edward *military officer*
†Mushala, Michael C. *career officer*
†Nielsen, Paul Douglas *Air Force officer, engineering manager*
†Paul, Richard R. *military officer*
†Pearson, Willie D. *career officer*
†Samic, Dennis R. *career officer*
†Sieg, Stanley A. *military official*
†Stewart, Todd I. *military officer*

OKLAHOMA

Altus AFB
†Kelly, Christopher A. *brigadier general United States air force*

Fort Sill
†Adair, Lawrence R. *army officer*
†Baxter, Leo J. *career officer*
Massey, Ronald Florian, Jr. *career officer*

Oklahoma City
†Blount, James Robert *military career officer*
†Luebbert, Stephen P. *career officer*
Vaughn, James Eldon *retired military officer, civic volunteer*

Tinker AFB
Goodman, Ernest Monroe *air force officer*
†McFann, Maurice L., Jr. *career officer*
†Perez, Charles H. *military officer*

Tulsa
Council, Terry Ray *military officer*

OREGON

Lake Oswego
McPeak, Merrill Anthony *business executive, consultant, retired officer*

Portland
†Griffin, Robert H. *army officer*
Sienkiewicz, Raymond Jerome *retired army officer*

Salem
Davis, Harley Cleo *retired military officer*

PENNSYLVANIA

Bethlehem
Rokke, Ervin Jerome *college president*

Carlisle
Kilgore, Joe Everett, Jr. *army officer*
†Tilford, Earl Hawkins, Jr. *defense analyst*

Carlisle Barracks
†Scales, Robert H., Jr. *army officer*

Gettysburg
Coughenour, Kavin Luther *career officer, military historian*

Johnstown
Samples, Jerry Wayne *military officer, educator*

King Of Prussia
Gallis, John Nicholas *naval officer, healthcare executive*

Mechanicsburg
Kinney, Linford Nelson *retired army officer*
Pearsall, Gregory Howard *naval officer*

Philadelphia
Eastwood, James W. *naval officer*
Retz, William Andrew *retired naval officer*

RHODE ISLAND

Narragansett
Apperson, Jack Alfonso *retired army officer, business executive*

Newport
Bergstrom, Albion Andrew *army officer, federal official*
Smith, Bernard J. *military officer*

SOUTH CAROLINA

Aiken
Cutting, Robert Thomas *army officer, physician*

Bluffton
Pendley, William Tyler *naval officer, international relations educator*

Charleston
Watts, Claudius Elmer, III *retired air force officer*

Charleston AFB
Gillespie, Shawn Paul *military pilot*

Columbia
Davidson, Janine Anne *military officer*
Lander, James Albert *retired military officer, comptroller*
Marchant, Trelawney Eston *retired national guard officer, lawyer*

Hilton Head Island
Brown, Arthur Edmon, Jr. *retired army officer*

Seneca
Clausen, Hugh Joseph *retired army officer*

Shaw A F B
†Cameron, Hugh C. *career officer*

Sumter
Olsen, Thomas Richard, Sr. *air force officer*

Wedgefield
McLaurin, Hugh McFaddin, III *military officer, historian consultant*

York
Blackwell, Paul Eugene, Sr. *army officer*

SOUTH DAKOTA

Rapid City
Sykora, Harold James *military officer*

TENNESSEE

Maryville
Forster, Frederick Harwood *air force officer*

Palmyra
Davidson, Robert Donald *civilian military employee*

TEXAS

Amarillo
Taylor, Wesley Bayard, Jr. *retired army officer*

Austin
Eyre, Pamela Catherine *retired army officer*
Graves, Howard Dwayne *army officer, academic administrator, educator*

Belton
Harrison, Benjamin Leslie *retired army officer*
Shoemaker, Robert Morin *retired army officer, county government official*

PROFESSIONAL INDEX 6171 MILITARY

Brooks AFB
Corrigan, Paula Ann *military officer, internist*
†Jernigan, John G. *career officer*

Copperas Cove
London, David Tshombe *military officer*

Corsicana
Batchelor, J. Casey *career military officer*

Dallas
†Bates, Barry D. *career officer*
†Wood, Rodney W. *military officer*

Dublin
Davis, Paul Rick *military career officer*

Dyess AFB
†McMahon, Michael C. *career officer*

El Paso
Murphy, Michael Patrick *military officer*
Riddle, Wesley Allen *army officer, writer*
Shapiro, Stephen Richard *retired air force officer, physician*

Fort Bliss
†Campbell, Kevin T. *military officer*

Fort Hood
†Boyd, Morris J. *military officer*
Burke, Charles Michael *military officer*
†Byrnes, Kevin P. *military officer*
†Cody, Richard A. *army officer*
†Glacel, Robert Allan *military career officer*
Sprabary, Larry Drew *military analyst*

Fort Sam Houston
†DeWitt, Ralph Ogden, Jr. *military career history*
†Peake, James Benjamin *military career officer*

Fort Worth
Lichtman, David Michael *military officer, health care administrator, orthopedist, educator*

Georgetown
Graham, Charles Passmore *retired army officer*
Weyrauch, Paul Turney *retired army officer, educator*

Grand Prairie
Loo, Maritta Louise *military officer, nurse*

Harker Heights
Hughes, William Foster *career officer, surgeon, obstetrician, gynecologist*

Houston
Kline, John William *retired air force officer, management consultant*

Irving
Dykstra, Ronald Joseph *military officer*

Kelly A F B
†Bielowicz, Paul L. *career officer*
†Murdock, Robert M. *career officer*
Murdock, Robert McClellan *air force officer*

Lackland AFB
†Barksdale, Barry W. *career officer*
Charlip, Ralph Blair *career officer*

Plano
Burr, Hiram Hale, Jr. *retired air force officer*

Randolph AFB
†Cook, Sharla J. *military officer*
†Lamontagne, Donald A. *career officer*
†Marr, Richard C. *military officer*
†Mentemeyer, Richard A. *career officer*
†Sutton, Peter U. *military officer*
†Winterberger, Gary A. *military officer*

San Antonio
Bethel, Paulette Martinez *retired military officer, counselor*
†Cook, Harold Rodney *military officer, medical facility administrator*
Hill, William Victor, II *retired army officer, secondary school educator*
†Lebras, Paul J. *career officer*
†Rankin, Karen S. *retired career officer*
†Ware, Joseph Milton *military officer, public administration educator*

San Marcos
Bullock, Jerry McKee *retired military officer, consultant, educator*

The Woodlands
Jones, Lincoln, III *army officer*

Tyler
Gann, Benard Wayne *air force officer*

Wichita Falls
Uzzell-Baggett, Karon Lynette *career officer*

UTAH

Hill Air Force Base
†Oriordan, Thomas A. *career officer*
†Roellig, Richard H. *military officer*

Salt Lake City
†Greenwood, Richard A. *protective services official*

VERMONT

Burlington
Cram, Reginald Maurice *retired air force officer*

VIRGINIA

Alexandria
Adams, Ranald Trevor, Jr. *retired air force officer*
†Barker, Charles Oliver *military officer*
†Benchoff, Dennis L. *career officer*
Bowman, Richard Carl *defense consultant, retired air force officer*
Brown, Frederic Joseph *army officer*
Burke, Kelly Howard *former air force officer, business executive*
†Caldwell, John S. *career officer*
†Coburn, John G. *career officer*
Curtin, Gary Lee *air force officer*
De Graf, William Bradford *career officer*
Downs, Michael Patrick *retired marine corps officer*
Dunn, Bernard Daniel *former naval officer, consultant*
Dyer, Joseph Wendell *career officer*
†Garrett, Thomas W. *career officer*
Kroesen, Frederick James *retired army officer, consultant*
Mc Mullen, Thomas Henry *retired air force officer*
McNair, Carl Herbert, Jr. *army officer, aeronautical engineer*
Minor, Mary Ellen *civilian military employee*
†Mitchell, Howard J. *career officer*
Powell, Colin Luther *retired military officer, author*
†Smith, Larry G. *career military officer*
Sulick, Joseph Edward *military communications administrator*
†Vollrath, Frederick E. *military officer*
Weiler, Todd Alan *army official*
†Whelden, Craig B. *army officer*
†Williams, Norman E. *army officer*
Wilson, Charles H(arrison) *retired air force officer, financial planner, human resource development professional*
†Wilson, Johnnie Edward *military officer*

Annandale
Clayton, William E. *naval officer*
†Evenson, Eric Todd *army officer, public health physician*
McCaffree, Burnham Clough, Jr. *retired naval officer*
McKee, Fran *retired naval officer*
Watts, Helena Roselle *military analyst*
Williams, James Arthur *retired army officer, information systems company executive*

Arlington
Bowman, Frank Lee *admiral and director naval nuclear propulsion*
Carr, Kenneth Monroe *naval officer*
Chapman, Donald D. *retired naval officer, lawyer*
Coady, Philip James, Jr. *retired naval officer*
Davis, John P. *career officer*
†Davison, Michael S., Jr. *military officer*
Elam, Fred Eldon *retired career army officer*
Gaffney, Paul Golden, II *military officer*
Garner, Jay Montgomery *career officer*
Goodwin, Richard Clarke *military analyst*
†Kelley, David J. *military officer*
Kelley, Paul Xavier *retired marine corps officer*
Kem, Richard Samuel *retired army officer*
†Kenne, Leslie F. *military officer*
†Kern, Paul John *army officer*
Lisanby, James Walker *retired naval officer*
Maness, Stephen Ray *manufacturing engineer, retired army officer*
Marini, Elizabeth Ann *civilian military executive*
McCoy, Timothy John *naval officer*
McGann, Barbara E. *career officer*
Merritt, Jack Neil *retired army officer*
Nanos, George P. *career officer, physicist*
Putnam, George W., Jr. *retired army officer*
Quinn, William Wilson *army officer, manufacturing executive*
Saalfeld, Fred Erich *naval researcher*
Sargent, David Putnam, Jr. *career officer*
Schrock, Philip John *army officer*
Seely, James Michael *defense consultant, retired naval officer, small business owner*
Shipway, John Francis *career officer*
Singstock, David John *military officer*
Welch, Jasper Arthur, Jr. *retired air force officer*
Zumwalt, Elmo Russell, Jr. *retired naval officer*

Ashburn
Tice, Raphael Dean *army officer*
Weyman, Steven Aloysius *military officer*

Burke
O'Connor, Edward Cornelius *army officer*

Centreville
†Amerault, James F. *military officer*

Chesapeake
Picotte, Leonard Francis *naval officer*

Clifton
Peay, J.H. Binford, III *retired army officer*

Fairfax
Allen, Gary Wayne *career officer, dentist*
Baer, Robert Jacob *retired army officer*
Bradunas, John Joseph *marine corps officer*
Dawalt, Kenneth Francis *former army officer, former aerospace company executive*
Ginn, Richard Van Ness *retired army officer, health care executive*
Johnson, Wallace *retired army officer*
Rogers, Alan Victor *former career officer*
Rosenkranz, Robert Bernard *military officer*
Tobin, Paul Edward, Jr. *naval officer*

Fairfax Station
Ross, Jimmy Douglas *army officer*

Falls Church
†Cain, Eddie *army officer*
Gray, D'Wayne *retired marine corps officer*
Layman, Lawrence *naval officer*
†Montero, Mario F., Jr. *military career officer*
†Sculley, Patrick David *army officer*
Simokaitis, Frank Joseph *air force officer, lawyer*

Fort Belvoir
†Chamberlin, Edward Robert *career officer, educator*
†Foley, David W. *career officer*
Frizzelle, Charles Delano, Jr. *military officer, educator*
†Glisson, Henry T. *director*
†Noonan, Robert W., Jr. *career officer*
St. John, Adrian, II *retired army officer*
Suycott, Mark Leland *naval flight officer*

Fort Eustis
Brown, Daniel G. *military officer*

Fort Monroe
†Abrams, John N. *career officer*
†Bolt, William J. *military officer*
†Buckley, Edward T., Jr. *career officer*
†Goff, Leroy R. (Rob), III *career officer*
†Morehouse, James W. *career officer*
†Wallace, Stewart S. *career military officer*

Fort Myer
†Costello, John *military officer*

Hampton
Erck, Walter W. *air force officer*

Lancaster
Rowden, William Henry *naval officer*

Langley AFB
†Dylewski, Gary R. *military officer*
†Haines, Dennis G. *military officer*
†Hawley, John W. *military officer*
†Johnston, Lawrence D. *career officer*
†MacGhee, David F. *military officer*
†Meyerrose, Dale William *career officer*
†Modica, Edward S., Jr. *air force officer*
†Moorman, William A. *career officer*
†Peck, William A., Jr. *career officer*
†Rayburn, Bentley B. *career officer*
†Robbins, Earnest O., II *career officer*
†Schafer, Klaus O. *military officer*

Leesburg
McDonough, Joseph Corbett *former army officer, aviation consultant*

Lynchburg
Snead, George Murrell, Jr. *army officer, scientist, consultant*

Mason Neck
Heiberg, Elvin Ragnvald, III *civil engineer, army officer*

Mc Lean
Cowhill, William Joseph *retired naval officer, consultant*
De Lauder, Roy Allen *business administrator*
Fedorochko, William, Jr. *retired army officer, policy analyst*
Haddock, Raymond Earl *career officer*
Hopkins, Thomas Matthews *former naval officer*
Linville, Ray Pate *logistics analyst, editor*
Molino, Thomas Michael *retired military officer*
Oren, John Birdsell *retired coast guard officer*
†Skantze, Lawrence A. *retired military officer*
Strean, Bernard M. *retired naval officer*

Merrifield
Earner, William Anthony, Jr. *naval officer*

Monterey
†Woodson, Albert Tarleton *retired navy enlisted man*

Mount Jackson
Sylvester, George Howard *retired air force officer*

Newport News
Yacavone, David William *military officer, consultant, researcher*

Norfolk
Baker, Stephen H. *career officer*
Boland, James Francis, Jr. *naval officer, helicopter pilot*
Ferriter, Edward Chadwick *naval officer*
Florer, Hayward Stanley *career officer*
Giambastiani, Edmund P., Jr. *military officer, federal agency administrator*
†Gile, Greg L. *military career officer*
Herrera, Henry Francis *career officer*
Hines, Dean Howard *military officer*
†Keane, John M. *career officer*
Knapp, Roland B. *rear admiral United States Navy*
†McElwee, Jerry W. *military career officer*
†Miller, John F. *military officer*
Mobley, Joseph S. *military officer*
†Peppe, Timothy A. *career officer*
Pettigrew, Kenneth W. *career officer*
Rendin, Robert Winter *environmental health officer*
Richard, Ronald Gene *career officer*
Sutton, William G. *military officer*
Train, Harry Depue, II *retired naval officer*
Ziemer, Robert T. *career officer*

Oakton
Anderson, William Robert *career naval officer*

Quantico
Downey, Gary Neil *marine corps officer*
†Howard, Patrick Gene *marine corps officer*
Klimp, Jack W. *military officer*
Palm, Leslie M. *military officer*

Reston
Brown, James Robert *retired air force officer*
Jaynes, Robert Henry, Jr. *retired military officer*
Miller, John Edward *army officer, educational administrator*
Naylon, Michael Edward *retired army officer*
Seiberlich, Carl Joseph *retired naval officer*
†Sikes, Arthur D. *military officer*
Wilkinson, Edward Anderson, Jr. *retired naval officer, business executive*

Richmond
Dilworth, Robert Lexow *career military officer, adult education educator*

Spotsylvania
Orsini, Eric Andrew *army official*

Springfield
†Ha, Dinh Trong *retired air force officer, computer sepcialist*

Suffolk
Berndt, Martin R. *career officer*

Vienna
Chandler, Hubert Thomas *former army officer*
Hatch, Harold Arthur *retired military officer*
Jackson, Dempster McKee *retired naval officer*
Jenkins, Robert Gordon *retired air force officer, technology executive*
Lawing, Charles William *retired naval officer, consultant*
Leonard, Edward Paul *naval officer, dentist, educator*
Webb, William Loyd, Jr. *army officer*
Yarborough, William Glenn, Jr. *military officer, forest farmer, defense and international business executive*

Virginia Beach
Dantone, Joseph John, Jr. *naval officer*
Halpin, Timothy Patrick *former air force officer*
Polley, John Edward *military officer*

WASHINGTON

Anacortes
Higgins, Robert (Walter) *military officer, physician*

Fort Lewis
†Edwards, Warren Chappelle *military career officer*
†Smith, Zannie O. *army officer*

Lynnwood
Jenes, Theodore George, Jr. *retired career officer*

Tacoma
†Hill, Mack *career officer*

WYOMING

Francis E Warren AFB
†Neary, Thomas H. *career officer*

MILITARY ADDRESSES OF THE UNITED STATES

EUROPE

APO
Adams, Ronald Emerson *army officer*
Barry, William Patrick *military officer*
†Begert, William J. *lieutenant general United States Air Force*
†Bell, Burwell Baxter, III *major general United States Army*
Benedict, John Anthony, II *army officer*
†Brady, Roger A. *brigadier general United States Air Force*
†Croom, Charles Edward, Jr. *brigadier general United States Air Force*
†Deptula, David A. *United States Air Force general*
†Hendrix, John Walter *lieutenant general United States Army*
Meigs, Montgomery Cunningham, Jr. *military officer*
†Paddock, John Francis, Jr. *rear admiral United States Navy Reserve*
Ray, Norman Wilson *career officer*
Scholes, Edison Earl *army officer*

FPO
Bryant, Stanley W. *career officer*
Metzger, James W. *military officer*
Murphy, Daniel J., Jr. *military officer*
Naughton, Richard J. *military officer*
Shirk, Keith Byron *US Navy weather specialist*

PPO
Loren, Donald Patrick *naval officer*

PACIFIC

APO
†Dallager, John R. *career officer*
Hobbs, Roy Jerry *military career officer, health services administrator*
Murray, Terrence P. *career officer*
Ormes, Ashton Harrison *career officer*
Pulaski, Lori Jaye *career officer*

FPO
Haskins, Michael Donald *naval officer*
†Murphy, Dennis John *military officer*

CANADA

Winnipeg
†Hodgkins, William F. *career officer*

NORTHWEST TERRITORIES

Yellowknife
LeBlanc, Pierre Gabriel *military officer*

ONTARIO

Bracebridge
MacKenzie, Lewis Wharton *military officer*

Orleans
Murray, Larry *government agency administrator*

Ottawa
Adams, John L. *retired career officer, federal agency administrator*
Baril, Maurice *career officer*
de Chastelain, A(lfred) John G(ardyne) D(rummond) *Canadian army officer, diplomat*

Stittsville
Tellier, Henri *retired Canadian military officer*

EGYPT

Cairo
Callison, Charles Stuart *retired foreign service officer, development economist*

JAPAN

DISTRICT OF COLUMBIA

Tokyo
Wright, William H., IV *military officer, federal official*

ADDRESS UNPUBLISHED

Austin, Robert Clarke *naval officer*
†Baldwin, Miles Arnold *air force officer*
Bartrem, Duane Harvey *retired military officer, designer, building consultant*
Bauman, Richard Arnold *coast guard officer*
Blanchard, George Samuel *retired military officer*
Block, Emil Nathaniel, Jr. *military officer*
Boge, Walter Edward *retired army civilian official, private consultant*
†Bramlett, David A. *retired military officer*
Braye, Rubye Howard *army officer*
Brooks, Thomas Aloysius, III *retired naval officer, telecommunications company executive*
Buker, Robert Hutchinson, Sr. *army officer, thoracic surgeon*
†Burfeindt, Douglas Glenn *civilian military official*
Campbell, Brian Scott *army officer*
Carter, William George, III *career officer*
Chelberg, Robert Douglas *army officer*
Clarke, Una *city official*
Clarke, Walter Sheldon *military consultant, educator*
Cole, Brady Marshall *retired naval officer*
†Crocker, George A. *career officer*
Davis, Dempsie Augustus *former air force officer, educator*
Davis, Henry Jefferson, Jr. *former naval officer*
Decker, Oscar Conrad, Jr. *retired army officer*
†DeFrancisco, Joseph E. *military officer*
Dozier, James Lee *former army officer*
†Dula, Brett M. *retired military officer*
Evans, Jack *city official*
Evans, Marsha Johnson *former naval officer, non-profit executive*
Evans, Roxanne Romack *retired military officer, hospital administrator*
†Fallon, William J. *career officer*
Faulkenberry, Virgil Thomas *retired naval officer, educator*
Ferraro, John *city official*
Fisher, Thomas Scott *army officer, broadcasting network executive*
Foote, Evelyn Patricia *retired army officer, consultant*
Gaugler, Robert Walter *retired career military officer*
Gray, David Lawrence *retired air force officer*
Guthrie, Wallace Nessler, Jr. *naval officer*
Harper, Henry H. *military officer, retired*
Harris, Marcelite Jordan *retired air force officer*
†Hartzog, William W. *retired military officer*
Hays, John Alan *military officer, construction company executive*
Hoover, John Elwood *former military officer, consultant, writer*
Hostettler, Stephen John *naval officer*
Hurd, Veronica Terez *career soldier*
Johnson, Silas R., Jr. *air force officer*
Johnston, James Monroe, III *air force officer*
Jones, David Charles *retired air force officer, former chairman Joint Chiefs of Staff*
Jumper, John Phillip *career officer*
Kather, Gerhard *retired air force base administrator*
†Keenan, Joseph Michael *military officer*
Keene-Burgess, Ruth Frances *army official*
Kelso, Frank Benton, II *naval officer*
Kempf, Cecil Joseph *naval officer*
Kerwin, Walter Thomas, Jr. *career officer, consultant*
Kielt, Raymond John *naval officer, dentist*
King, Charolette Elaine *retired career officer*
King, Chris Allen *military officer*
King, Rosemary Ann *air force officer*
†Kinzer, Joseph W. *military officer*
Klemm, William Raymond *career officer*
Kojac, Jeffrey Stanley *military officer*
Kutyna, Donald Joseph *air force officer*
†Lane, Frances Caroline *retired military officer, national security analyst, volunteer*
Lautenbacher, Conrad Charles, Jr. *naval officer*
Lindquist, Michael Adrian *career military officer*
Lyons, John W(inship) *retired government official, chemist*
Manganaro, Francis Ferdinand *naval officer*
Marlow, Edward A. *retired career officer*
Martin, James Victor, Jr. *foreign service officer, writer*
Mathis, Harry *city official*
Mc Fadden, George Linus *retired army officer*
McKinnon, Daniel Wayne, Jr. *naval officer*
Michels, Stanley E. *city official*
Minners, Howard Alyn *physician, research administrator*
Moloff, Alan Lawrence *army officer, physician*
Moore, William Leroy, Jr. *career officer, physician*
Morgan, Thomas Rowland *retired marine corps officer*
Morton, Richard Lew *retired military officer*
Mullen, William Joseph, III *military analyst, retired army officer*
†Najera, Peter Francisco *military officer*
Nelson, Ben, Jr. *retired air force officer*
Olson, Phillip Roger *naval officer*
Palmer, Dave Richard *retired military officer, academic administrator*
Parent, Rodolphe Jean *Canadian air force official, pilot*
Partington, James Wood *naval officer*
Polatty, David P., III *military officer, federal agency administrator*
Price, Robert Ira *coast guard officer*
Rhame, Thomas Gene *retired army officer*
†Riddell, Richard Anderson *retired naval officer*
Ridley-Thomas, Mark *city official*
Riley, Robert Shean *Colonel, United States Army, retired*
Robinson, David Brooks *retired naval officer*
Rogers, Bernard William *military officer*
Romeo, James Joseph *retired army nurse corps officer, nursing researcher*
Sagan, Stanley Daniel *career officer, retired*
Sanderson, James Richard *naval officer, planning and investment company consultant*
Schulter, Eugene C. *city official*
Schumacher, William Jacob *retired army officer*
Scott, Michael *career officer*
Sekiguchi, June *retired army officer, health professional*
Shalikashvili, John Malchase *retired military career officer*
Shapiro, Sumner *retired naval officer, business executive*
Shaw, John Frederick *retired naval officer*
Slewitzke, Connie Lee *retired army officer*
Smith, Loretta Mae *contracting officer*
Smoker, Roy Ellis *military officer*
Spitze, Steven Clyde *army officer*
Springer, Robert Dale *retired air force officer, consultant, lecturer*
Stiner, Carl Wade *army officer*
Street, John F. *city official*
Sunell, Robert John *retired army officer*
Terrill, W(allace) Andrew *international security analyst, educator*
Traister, Robert Edwin *naval officer, engineer*
Tucker, Pierce Edward *air force officer*
Tuttle, Jerry Owen *retired naval officer, business executive*
Vessey, John William, Jr. *army officer*
†Vigness, Bryan *career officer*
Vincent, Hal Wellman *marine corps officer, investor*
Walden, Joseph Lawrence *career officer*
Watts, Ronald Lester *retired military officer*
Weir, Kenneth Wynn *marine corps officer, experimental test pilot*
Wheeler, Albin Gray *United States Army career officer, educator, retail executive, law firm executive*
Wilhelm, Charles Elliott *military officer*
Williamson, Myrna Hennrich *retired army officer, lecturer, consultant*
Wilson, Dwight Liston *former military officer, investment advisor*

RELIGION

UNITED STATES

ALABAMA

Andalusia
Patterson, Edwin *minister*

Auburn
†Penaskovic, Richard John *religious studies educator*

Birmingham
†Foley, David E. *bishop*
Hull, William Edward *theology educator*
Loftin, Sister Mary Frances *religious organization administrator*
Morrison, Gregg Scott *minister, college administrator*
O'Brien, Dellanna West *religious organization administrator*
Roby, Jasper *bishop*
Savage, Laura Lou *ministry consultant*
Threadcraft, Hal Law, III *pastor, counselor*
Zahl, Paul Francis Matthew *dean*

Camden
Lewis, Robert Henry *lay worker*

Cordova
Anthony, Yancey Lamar *minister*

Decatur
Ragland, Wylheme Harold *minister, health facility administrator*

Gadsden
Arnold, Don Carl *pastor, religious organization executive*

Greensboro
Massey, James Earl *clergyman, educator*

Huntsville
Robinson, Isaiah, Jr. *minister*

Mobile
Lipscomb, Oscar Hugh *archbishop*

Montgomery
Bullard, Mary Ellen *retired religious study center administrator*
Mitchell, Timothy Charles *minister*
Morrison, Troy Lee *religious organization administrator*

Moulton
Nelson, William Hoyt *minister*

Northport
Johnson, Roger Lee *minister*

Tuscaloosa
Doty, William Guy *religious studies/humanities educator*

ALASKA

Anchorage
Clary, William Victor *minister*
Hurley, Francis T. *archbishop*
Rosenfeld, Harry Leonard *rabbi*

Elmendorf AFB
Luckett, Byron Edward, Jr. *chaplain, career officer*

Fairbanks
†Kaniecki, Michael Joseph *bishop*

Juneau
†Warfel, Michael W. *clergy member*

North Pole
Fleming, Carolyn Elizabeth *religious organization administrator, interior designer*

ARIZONA

Arizona City
Ross, Lanson Clifford, Jr. *religion educator, author*

Coolidge
Shih, Marie *metaphysical healer*

Duncan
Ouzts, Eugene Thomas *minister, secondary education educator*

Flagstaff
†Castillo, Diana May *religious organization administrator*

Green Valley
Pike, George Harold, Jr. *religious organization executive, clergyman*

Mesa
Simpson, John Berchman, Jr. *clergy member, chaplain, retired law enforcement officer, retired newspaper editor*

Oro Valley
Tinker, Robert Eugene *minister, educational consultant*

Paradise Valley
Kilgore, L(eRoy) Wilson *minister*

Phoenix
Darby, Wesley Andrew *minister, educator*
Hamilton, Ronald Ray *minister*
Harte, John Joseph Meakins *bishop*
King, Felton *bishop*
†Kuzma, George Martin *bishop*
Morrison, Richard Neely *deacon*
O'Brien, Thomas Joseph *bishop*
Whitlow, William La Fond *minister, theology school planter*

Scottsdale
Jann, Donn Gerard *minister*
Mueller, Gerald Damon Adent *publisher, editor*

Sierra Vista
Ford, Frederick Jay *clergyman*

Sun City
Lapsley, James Norvell, Jr. *minister, pastoral theology educator*
Park, Francis Wood, III *retired minister*
Randall, Claire *church executive*

Tempe
†Wentz, Richard Eugene *religious studies educator*

Tucson
Moreno, Manuel D. *bishop*

ARKANSAS

Conway
Reddin, George *religious organization administrator*

Crofton
Parsley, Robert Charles *minister*

El Dorado
Lee, Vernon Roy *minister*

Fayetteville
Dockery, Robert Gerald *minister*

Greenbrier
Reed, James David *minister, social worker*

Hampton
Copley, Stephen Jean *minister*

Little Rock
Branstetter, Russell Wayne *minister*
Mc Donald, Andrew J. *bishop*
Walker, L. T. *bishop*

Magnolia
†Evans, Thomas Evan *minister*

Marion
Hughes, Michael Randolph *evangelist*

North Little Rock
†Edelman, Sammie (Samm) Kay *theologian, writer*

Pine Bluff
Adair, Toby Warren, Jr. *minister*
Thompson, Robert Jaye *minister*

Russellville
Chesnut, Franklin Gilmore *clergyman*

Siloam Springs
Lewis, Cecil Dwain *minister*

CALIFORNIA

Acton
Butman, Harry Raymond *clergyman, author*

Altadena
Talton, Chester Lovelle *bishop*
Willans, Jean Stone *religious organization executive*
Willans, Richard James *bishop, religious organization executive*

Anaheim
Nguyen, Tai Anh *minister*
Settgast, Leland G. *religion educator, minister*

Antioch
Cakebread, Steven Robert *minister, chef*

Azusa
Shoemaker, Melvin Hugh *religious educator*

Bakersfield
†Johnson, Deborah Valerie Germaine *parish administrator*

Barstow
Jones, Nathaniel *bishop*

Berkeley
Gall, Donald Arthur *minister*
Oliver, Mary Anne McPherson *religion educator*
Welch, Claude (Raymond) *theology educator*

Blythe
Bryant, Gary Jones *minister*

Burbank
Bower, Richard James *minister*
Teague, Jane Lorene *lay worker*

Capo Beach
Hallowell, John H *minister*

Carmichael
Probasco, Calvin Henry Charles *clergyman, college administrator*

Castro Valley
Morrison, Glenn Leslie *minister*

Claremont
Kibler, Ray Franklin, III *minister*
Kroll, C(harles) Douglas *minister*
Kucheman, Clark Arthur *religion educator*
Sanders, James Alvin *minister, biblical studies educator*
Tengbom, Luverne Charles *religion educator*

Clovis
Smith, William Clarke *clergyman*

Concord
Hammond, Blaine Randol *priest*
Jones, Gerald Edward *religion educator*

Culver City
†Ewing, Elisabeth Anne Rooney *priest*
†Ewing, James E. *priest*
†Jacobs, Sidney J. *rabbi, journalist*

Cupertino
Russi, John Joseph *priest, educational administrator*

Davis
Brown, Arthur Carl, Jr. *retired minister*

Del Mar
Randall, Chandler Corydon *church rector*

Duarte
Driskill, James Lawrence *minister*
Probst, John Elwin *chaplain, minister*

El Monte
Hwang, Tzu-Yang *minister*

Elk Grove
Vang, Timothy Teng *church executive*

Escondido
Bergsma, Derke Peter *minister, religious studies educator*
Raher, Richard Ray *minister*

Etna
Auxentios, (Bishop Auxentios) *clergyman*

Fountain Valley
Einstein, Stephen Jan *rabbi*

Fresno
Howe, Ronald Evans *minister*
Lawless, John Howard *minister*
O'Berg, Robert Myron *minister*
Steinbock, John Thomas *bishop*
Xiong, Tousu Saydangnmvang *minister*

Fullerton
Kim, Sang Koo *pastor, educator*

Garden Grove
Ballesteros, Juventino Ray, Jr. *minister*
Clarke, S. Gordon *clergyman*
†Schuller, Robert Harold *clergyman, author*

Glendale
Courtney, Howard Perry *clergyman*

Glendora
Richey, Everett Eldon *religion educator*

Grass Valley
Robbins, Dale Alan *minister*

Hacienda Heights
Sim, John Kim-Chye *minister*

Ione
Sparrowk, Cora Catherine *lay church leader*

Irvine
Christopher, Steven Lee *religious studies educator*
†Johnson, Benjamin Arlen *religious studies educator*
Lindquist, Raymond Irving *clergyman*
Rachlis, Arnold Israel *rabbi, religion educator*

La Crescenta
Peterson, John Edward *minister*

La Jolla
Freedman, David Noel *religion educator*
Waddy, Lawrence Heber *religious writer*
Wyle, Ewart Herbert *clergyman*

Laguna Hills
Wheatley, Melvin Ernest, Jr. *retired bishop*

Lake Forest
Hertweck, Galen Fredric *minister*

Lindsay
Sanchez, Ruben Dario *minister, family counselor, parochial school educator, writer*

Long Beach
Lowentrout, Peter Murray *religious studies educator*
Skelly, John Joshua *retired clergyman, fundraiser*

Los Alamitos
Booth, John Nicholls *minister, magician, writer, photographer*

Los Angeles
Anderson, Robert Marshall *retired bishop*
Borsch, Frederick Houk *bishop*
Boyd, Malcolm *minister, religious author*
Breuer, Stephen Ernest *temple administrator*
†Chedid, John G. *bishop*
Fitzgerald, Tikhon (Lee R. H. Fitzgerald) *bishop*
Freehling, Allen Isaac *rabbi*
Hymers, Robert Leslie, Jr. *pastor*
Mahony, Cardinal Roger M. *archbishop*
Mc Pherson, Rolf Kennedy *clergyman, church official*
Milligan, Sister Mary *theology educator, religious consultant*
Neal, Joseph C., Jr. *church administrator*
Ochoa, Armando *bishop*
O'Connor, Kevin Thomas *archdiocese development official*
Phillips, Keith Wendall *minister*
Pressman, Jacob *rabbi*
†Setian, Nerses Mikail *bishop, former apostolic exarchate*
Williams, Ronald Dean *minister, religious organization executive*
Wolf, Alfred *rabbi*
Wooten, Cecil Aaron *religious organization administrator*

Mill Valley
Crews, William Odell, Jr. *seminary administrator*
DuBose, Francis Marquis *clergyman*
Stubblefield, Jerry Mason *religious educator, minister*

Monrovia
Huffey, Vinton Earl *clergyman*

Monterey
Ryan, Sylvester D. *bishop*

Monterey Park
Szeto, Paul (Cheuk-Ching) *religious mission executive*

Moraga
Lu, Matthias *priest, educator*

Mountain View
Ching, Andy Kwok-yee *minister*

Newport Beach
Huffman, John Abram, Jr. *minister*

North Hollywood
Wannebo, Ode *religious organization executive, opera-concert singer, educator*

Northridge
Dart, John Seward *journalist, author*
†Douglas, Crerar *religious studies educator*

Oakland
Benham, Priscilla Carla *religion educator, college president*
Cummins, John Stephen *bishop*
Patten, Bebe Harrison *minister, chancellor*
Schomer, Howard *retired clergyman, educator, social policy consultant*

Oceanside
Peck, Paul Lachlan *minister*

Orange
Brown, Tod David *bishop*
Buhler, Richard Gerhard *minister*
Mc Farland, Norman Francis *bishop*
Miller, Jay Anthony *minister*

Orangevale
Webb, Andrew Howard *minister*

Oxnard
Oncken, Ellen Lorraine *minister, speaker*

Palm Desert
Ponder, Catherine *clergywoman*

Palo Alto
Brown, Robert McAfee *minister, religion educator*
Forbes, Alfred Dean *religious studies researcher, biomedical consultant*

Palos Verdes Peninsula
Cubillos, Robert Hernan *church administrator, philosophy educator*

Pasadena
Sano, Roy I. *bishop*
Shuster, Marguerite *minister, educator*
Torres, Ralph Chon *minister*

Pleasanton
Davis, Ron Lee *clergyman, author*

Poway
Dollen, Charles Joseph *clergyman, writer*
Wirt, Sherwood Eliot *writer, minister*

Rancho Mirage
Stenhouse, Everett Ray *clergy administrator*

Redding
†Campbell, Barth Lynn *theology educator*
Nicholas, David Robert *minister, college president*
Potter, James Vincent *educator*

Redlands
Langer, Richard Charles *minister*

Redondo Beach
Hawkins, Harold Stanley *pastor, police chaplain, school director*

Reedley
Dick, Henry Henry *minister*

Sacramento
Cole, Glen David *minister*
Quinn, Francis A. *bishop*
Venema, Jon Roger *educator, pastor*
Weigand, William Keith *bishop*

San Anselmo
Mudge, Lewis Seymour *theologian, educator, university dean*

San Bernardino
Barnes, Gerald R. *bishop*

San Diego
Brom, Robert H. *bishop*
Chavez, Gilbert Espinoza *bishop*
Downing, David Charles *minister*
Fleischmann, Paul *youth minister*
Kraft, William Armstrong *retired priest*
Savitripriya, Swami *Hindu religious leader, author*
Scorgie, Glen Given *religious studies educator*

San Francisco
Anthony, Metropolitan, of Sourozh (Anthony Emmanuel Gergiannakis) *bishop*
†Brown, Amos Cleophilus *minister*
Hurley, Mark Joseph *bishop*
Kendall, Robert Daniel *priest, theology educator*
Levada, William Joseph *archbishop*
McGrath, Patrick Joseph *bishop*
Perlman, Susan Gail *organization executive*
Rosen, Moishe *religious organization founder*
Sevilla, Carlos A. *bishop*
Shreibman, Henry M. *religious educator*
Sparer, Malcolm Martin *rabbi*
Swing, William Edwin *bishop*

San Jose
Soos, Richard Anthony *pastor*

San Juan Bautista
Fort, Robert Bradley *minister*

San Rafael
Trepp, Leo *rabbi*

Santa Barbara
Campbell, Robert Charles *minister, theology educator*
Gillquist, Peter Edward *church organization executive*

Santa Clara
DuMaine, R. Pierre *bishop*

Santa Rosa
Ziemann, G. Patrick *bishop*

Seaside
Hamilton, W. W. *church administrator*

Sebastopol
DeMartini, Rodney J. *executive director religious organization, priest*

Simi Valley
Kearns, Albert Osborn *minister*

Solana Beach
Friedman, Maurice Stanley *religious educator*

Solvang
Chandler, E(dwin) Russell *clergyman, author*

Sonora
Patterson, Paul Edward *minister*

Stockton
Mathre, Lawrence Gerhard *minister, federal agency administrator*

Sun Valley
Stitzinger, James Franklin *religion educator, library director*

Temple City
Perkins, Floyd Jerry *retired theology educator*

Turlock
Stensether, John Eldon *minister*

Tustin
Crouch, Paul Franklin *minister, church official*

Upland
Chaney, Robert Galen *religious organization executive*

Vallejo
McGowan, Thomas Randolph *retired religious organization executive*

Walnut Creek
Fuller, Glenn Straith *minister*

West Hills
Godsil, Richard William *minister*

West Hollywood
Eastman, Donald *church officer*
Eger, Denise Leese *rabbi*
Perry, Troy D. *clergyman, church administrator*
Wilson, Nancy Linda *church officer*

Whittier
Connick, Charles Milo *retired religion educator, clergyman*

Williams
Ratzlaff, Ruben Menno *religion educator, minister*

Windsor
Smith, Maynard Dwight *minister*

Yucaipa
Horn, Paul Ervin *minister*

COLORADO

Aurora
†Nichols, Clyde Richard *clergyman, company executive*

Canon City
Williamson, Edward Henry *chaplain, army officer*

Colorado Springs
Bishop, Leo Kenneth *clergyman, educator*
Bridges, Gerald Dean *religious organization executive*
Child, Joseph Alan *minister*
Eyman, Roger Allen *minister*
Fox, Douglas Allan *retired religion educator*
Hanifen, Richard Charles *bishop*
Loux, Gordon Dale *organization executive*

Denver
Barger, Louise Baldwin *religious organization administrator*
Brownlee, Judith Marilyn *priestess, psychotherapist, psychic*
Bukowiecki, Sister Angeline Bernadette *nun*
Burrell, Calvin Archie *minister*
Chaput, Charles J. *archbishop*
Goldberg, Hillel *rabbi, educator*
Gould, Marty Leon *minister, writer, composer*
Hayes, Edward Lee *religious organization administrator*
Lewallen, Elinor Kirby *organization executive, lay church worker*
Meeks, Mark Anthony *minister*
Sheeran, Michael John Leo *priest, college administrator*
Stafford, J. Francis *archbishop*

Fort Collins
Pape, Arnis Weston *minister*
Rolston, Holmes, III *theologian, educator, philosopher*

Lafayette
Short, Ray Everett *minister, sociology educator emeritus, author, lecturer*

Lakewood
Foster, David Mark *retired bishop*
Hickman, Ruth Virginia *Bible educator*
Vogt, Hugh Frederick *minister, college administrator*

Louisville
Willette, Donald Corliss *reverend*

Pueblo
Tafoya, Arthur N. *bishop*

South Fork
Foster, Bruce Dudley *retired clergyman*

Westcliffe
Jones, Daniel Edwin, Jr. *bishop*

Wheat Ridge
Wilcox, Mary Marks *Christian education consultant, educator*

Woodland Park
Sallquist, Gary Ardin *minister, non-profit executive*

CONNECTICUT

Bethany
Childs, Brevard Springs *religious educator*

Bridgeport
Agee, Kevin Jerome *minister*
Byrd, Charles Everett *clergyman*
Egan, Edward M. *bishop*
Rubenstein, Richard Lowell *theologian, educator*

Bristol
Pallotti, Robert Michael *minister*

Danbury
†DiBiccari, Grace *pastor*
Malino, Jerome R. *rabbi*

East Hartford
Henry, Paul Eugene, Jr. *minister*
Scholsky, Martin Joseph *priest*

Fairfield
Regan, Thomas Joseph *Roman Catholic priest*

Greenwich
Lennick, Robert Brent *rabbi*

Hamden
Forman, Charles William *religious studies educator*

Hartford
Cronin, Daniel Anthony *archbishop*
Kirkpatrick, Frank Gloyd *minister, religion educator*
Winter, Miriam Therese (Gloria Frances Winter) *nun, religious education educator*
Zikmund, Barbara Brown *minister, seminary president, church history educator*

Kent
White, Roger Bradley *priest*

Middletown
Crites, Stephen Decatur *religion educator*

New Haven
Dittes, James Edward *psychology of religion educator*
Krey, Andrew Emil Victor *minister*
Malherbe, Abraham Johannes, VI *religion educator, writer*
Meeks, Wayne A. *religious studies educator*
Rosazza, Peter Anthony *bishop*
Sanneh, Lamin *religion educator*
Weinstein, Stanley *Buddhist studies educator*
Wilson, Robert Rutherford *religious studies educator*

New Milford
Johnson, Robert Clyde *theology educator*

Newtown
Wismar, Gregory Just *minister*

North Haven
Hudson, Richard Lloyd *retired educator, clergyman*

Norwich
Hart, Daniel Anthony *bishop*

Plantsville
Roy, Ralph Lord *clergyman*

Torrington
Drobena, Thomas John *minister, educator*
Kucharek, Wilma Samuella *minister*

Woodstock Valley
Allaby, Stanley Reynolds *clergyman*

DELAWARE

Dover
Deuble, Lottie Edwards *missionary, receptionist*

Rehoboth Beach
Johnson, Kermit Douglas *minister, retired military officer*

Wilmington
Gewirtz, Leonard Benjamin *rabbi*
Harris, Robert Laird *minister, theology educator emeritus*
Linderman, Jeanne Herron *priest*
†Saltarelli, Michael A. *priest*

DISTRICT OF COLUMBIA

Washington
Allen, William Jere *minister*
Apostolos-Cappadona, Diane Pan *religion and art educator*
Borelli, John *religious organization professional*
Burke, John *priest*
Cacciavillan, Agostino *archbishop*
Cenkner, William *religion educator, academic administrator*
Clearfield, Sidney *religious organization executive*
Di Lella, Alexander Anthony *biblical studies educator*
Dugan, Robert Perry, Jr. *minister, religious organization administrator*
Dunn, James Milton *religious organization administrator*
Fitzmyer, Joseph Augustine *theology educator, priest*
Godsey, John Drew *minister, theology educator emeritus*
Gros, Jeffrey *ecumenical theologian*
Haines, Ronald H. *bishop*
Hargrove, Jerry Edward, Jr. *minister*
Hickey, James Aloysius Cardinal *archbishop*
Hicks, Sherman Gregory *pastor*
Hotchkin, John Francis *church official, priest*
Hug, James Edward *religious organization administrator*
Irwin, Paul Garfield *former minister, humane society executive*
Kane, Annette Pieslak *religious organization executive*
†Lori, William E. *bishop*
Lynn, Barry William *religious organization executive*
Marshall, Ann Louise *pastoral counselor*
May, Felton Edwin *bishop*
McCrabb, Donald Raymond *lay minister*
Mc Lean, George Francis *philosophy of religion educator, clergyman*
Metz, Ronald Irwin *retired priest, addictions counselor*
Miller, Mary Hotchkiss *lay worker*
Moore, Jerry *retired religious organization administrator*

Novak, Michael (John) *religion educator, author, editor*
†O'Brien, Edwin F. *bishop*
Pitts, Tyrone S. *reverend*
Rabinowitz, Stanley Samuel *rabbi*
Romig, Edgar Dutcher *clergyman*
Roque, Francis Xavier *auxiliary bishop*
†Ryan, Judith Margaret *scripture scholar, educator*
†Saperstein, David Nathan *rabbi, lawyer, educator*
Saperstein, Marc Eli *religious history educator, rabbi*
Shearin, Morris Lee *minister*
Trisco, Robert Frederick *church historian, educator*
Wimberly, John William, Jr. *minister*
Wogaman, John Philip *minister, educator*
†Zuern, Theodore Francis *priest*

FLORIDA

Boca Raton
Agler, Richard Dean *rabbi*
Demes, Dennis Thomas *religious studies educator*
Singer, Merle Elliot *rabbi*

Boynton Beach
Gill, Milton Randall *minister*

Brooksville
Melli, Richard George *bishop*

Bushnell
Panzetta, John Cosmo *clinical chaplain*

Carrollwood
O'Keefe, Fredrick Rea *bishop, consultant, educator, writer*

Crystal River
Hoge, James Cleo *retired priest and school administrator*

Daytona Beach
Bronson, Oswald Perry *religious organization administrator, clergyman*

Deland
Fant, Clyde Edward, Jr. *religion educator*

Englewood
Seeley, David William *minister*

Eustis
Pinkston, Isabel Hay *minister, writer, educator, therapist*

Fort Lauderdale
Eynon, Steven Scott *minister*

Fort Myers
Griffin, Jerry J. *chaplain*
Koehler, Robert Brien *priest*
Massa, Conrad Harry *religious studies educator*
Snelling, Lonie Eugene, Jr. *minister*

Fort Pierce
Garment, Robert James *clergyman*

Gainesville
Creel, Austin Bowman *religion educator*
Owens, Robin Shane *clergyman*

Holiday
Swatos, William Henry, Jr. *sociologist, priest*

Jacksonville
Bartholomew, John Niles *church administrator*
Blackburn, Robert McGrady *retired bishop*
Holliday, Patricia Ruth McKenzie *evangelist*
Snyder, John Joseph *bishop*

Jensen Beach
Smalley, William Richard *priest*

Jupiter
McCall, Duke Kimbrough *clergyman*

Lake Wales
Hayes, Sherrill D. *religious organization administrator*

Longwood
Dalles, John Allan *minister*
Hunter, Joel Carl *clergyman, educator*

Melbourne Beach
Walker, Harriette Katherine *religious administrator*

Miami
Fitzgerald, John Thomas, Jr. *religious studies educator*
Harper, Kenneth Charles *clergyman*
Hoy, William Ivan *minister, religion educator*
Roman, Agustin A. *clergyman*
Schofield, Calvin Onderdonk, Jr. *bishop*
†Wenski, Thomas Gerard *priest*

Miami Beach
Lehrman, Irving *rabbi*
Wernick, Nissim *rabbi*

Miami Shores
Favalora, John Clement *bishop*
McCarthy, Edward Anthony *archbishop*
Sunshine, Edward Robert *theology educator*

Mount Dora
Schnatterly, Michael Dean *priest*

Ocala
Kofink, Wayne Alan *minister*

Orlando
Downs, David Rutherford *minister*
Gokee, Donald LeRoy *clergyman, author*
Grady, Thomas J. *retired bishop*
Howe, John Wadsworth *bishop*

O'Farrell, Mark Theodore *religious organization administrator*
Ponder, James Alton *clergyman, evangelist*
Randall, Roger Paul *religious organization consultant*

Palm Beach
Feldman, Leonid Ariel *rabbi*

Palm Beach Gardens
O'Connell, Anthony J. *bishop*

Palm Harbor
Fischer, John Jules *clergy member, theology educator, writer*

Panama City
Wade, Larry Edward *evangelist, academic administrator*

Penney Farms
Bronkema, Frederick Hollander *retired minister and church official*

Pensacola
Ricard, John H. *bishop, educator*

Port Saint Lucie
Westman, Steven Ronald *rabbi*

Saint Augustine
McCarty, Doran Chester *religious organization administrator*

Saint Petersburg
Erlinger, Melvin Herbert *pastor, educator*
Lamar, William Fred *chaplain, educator*
Walker, Lola H. *religious organization administrator*

Sarasota
Castle-Hasan, Elizabeth E. *religious organization administrator*
Jones, Tracey Kirk, Jr. *minister, educator*
Larsen, Lawrence Bernard, Jr. *priest, pastoral psychotherapist*

Sunrise
Thompson, Yaakov *rabbi*

Tampa
Biles, (Lee) Thomas *religious organization executive, clergyman*
Franzen, Lavern Gerhard *bishop*
Justice, Eunice McGhee *missionary, evangelist*
Neusner, Jacob *humanities and religious studies educator*

Venice
†Nevins, John J. *bishop*

Wellington
Knudsen, Raymond Barnett *clergyman, association executive, author*

West Palm Beach
Nolan, Richard Thomas *clergyman, educator*

Wildwood
†Terry, Ernest Lee *clergyman, international evangelist*

Winter Haven
Gage, Robert Clifford *minister*

GEORGIA

Athens
Logan, Dayton Norris *retired minister*

Atlanta
Coleman, David Michael *religious organization executive*
Donoghue, John Francis *archbishop*
Dunahoo, Charles *religious publisher, religious organization administrator, consultant, human resource director*
Graham, Matt Patrick *minister, librarian*
McMaster, Belle Miller *religious organization administrator*
Skillrud, Harold Clayton *minister, retired bishop*
Stokes, Mack (Marion) Boyd *bishop*
Westerhoff, John Henry, III *clergyman, theologian, educator*
White, Gayle Colquitt *religion writer, journalist*

Augusta
MacLeod, James L. *minister, finance executive, gallery owner*

Brooks
Buzzard, Sir Anthony Farquhar *religion educator*

Covington
Wilson, Guy Harris, Jr. *minister*

Decatur
Cirou, Joseph Philip *priest, organist, educator*
Gericke, Paul William *minister, educator*
Hagood, Thomas Richard, Jr. *minister, publisher*
Hale, Cynthia Lynette *religious organization administrator*

Garfield
Fountain, Edwin Byrd *minister, educator, librarian, poet*

Grovetown
Bledsoe, Tommy Dalton *minister*

Hinesville
Carter, Georgian L. *minister*

Jonesboro
Dawson, Lewis Edward *minister, retired military officer*

Lawrenceville
†Henson, Gene Ethridge *retired legal administrator*

Macon
Franklin, Roosevelt *minister*
Looney, Richard Carl *bishop*
Staton, Cecil Pope, Jr. *religious and academic publisher, educator*

Marietta
Owens, Chandler David *bishop*

Metter
Guido, Michael Anthony *evangelist*

Moultrie
Brown, John Eugene *social science educator, retired minister*

Newnan
Brewster, Daniel Fergerson *minister, religious organization executive*

Norcross
Kyle, John Emery *mission executive*

Rex
Thompson, James Martin *minister, protective services official*

Riverdale
Waters, John W. *minister, educator*

Savannah
Boland, John Kevin *bishop*
Lessard, Raymond William *bishop*
Webb, James Calvin *minister*

South Jesup
Wilcox, Ronald Wayne *minister*

Sylvania
Martin, Charles Wade *pastor*

Tucker
†Giavaras, Faith E. *minister*

Tyrone
Slocum, Sheila Jean *missionary*

Valdosta
Robertson, Dale Wayne *minister*

Woodstock
Collins, David Browning *religious institution administrator*

HAWAII

Honolulu
DiLorenzo, Francis X. *bishop*
Kitagawa, Audrey Emiko *lawyer, retired*
Moody, John Henry *minister, hospital chaplain, clinical pastoral educator*
Scott, David Irvin *minister*
Strickland, John Arthur Van *minister*

Ocean View
Gilliam, Jackson Earle *bishop*

Waianae
Hiapo, Patricia Kamaka *lay worker*

IDAHO

Boise
Caufield, Marie Celine *religious organization administrator*
Driscoll, Michael P. *bishop*
Lawrence, Ralph Alan *minister*
Thornton, John S., IV *retired bishop*

Jerome
Feiss, Hugh Bernard *priest, religious educator*

Nampa
Lodahl, Michael Eugene *religion educator*

ILLINOIS

Addieville
Utke, Robert Ahrens *minister*

Arlington Heights
Dickau, John C. *religious organization executive*
Ricker, Robert S. *religious organization administrator*

Bartlett
Robinson, Jack Fay *clergyman*

Belleville
Gregory, Wilton D. *bishop*
Kramer, Andrew Joseph *clergyman*
Looman, Gary John *minister*
Wittenbrink, Boniface Leo *priest*

Bensenville
Matera, Richard Ernest *minister*

Chicago
Almen, Lowell Gordon *church official*
Anderson, Hugh George *bishop*
Anderson, Philip Vernon *retired pastor*
Andrews, Robert Lee *clergyman, architect*
Bacher, Robert Newell *church official*
Banks, Deirdre Margaret *church organization administrator*
Barbour, Claude Marie *minister*
Baumhart, Raymond Charles *Roman Catholic church administrator*
Berman, Howard Allen *rabbi*
Betz, Hans Dieter *theology educator*

Black, Robert Durward *television producer*
Browning, Don Spencer *religion educator*
Cadieux, Dennis Barry *religious organization administrator, minister*
Doniger, Wendy *history of religions educator*
Farrakhan, Louis *religious leader*
Flanagan, Patrick Sean Liam *priest*
Fortune, Michael Joseph *religion educator*
George, Francis Cardinal *archbishop*
Gorman, John R. *auxiliary bishop*
Hefner, Philip James *theologian*
Homans, Peter *psychology and religious studies educator*
Jakubowski, Thad J. *bishop*
Larsen, Paul Emanuel *religious organization administrator*
Lathon, Sheraine *church administrator*
LeFevre, Perry Deyo *minister, theology educator*
†Lotocky, Innocent Hilarius *bishop*
†Lutzer, Erwin Wesley *clergyman, author*
Magnus, Kathy Jo *religious organization executive*
Marshall, Cody George
†Martin, Dennis Dale *religious studies educator*
Marty, Martin Emil *religion educator, editor*
McAuliffe, Richard L. *church official*
McCulloh, Gerald William *theology educator*
McDonald, Theresa Beatrice Pierce (Mrs. Ollie McDonald) *church official, minister*
McGinn, Bernard John *religious educator*
Miller, Charles S. *clergy member, church administrator*
Minnick, Malcolm L., Jr. *clergy member, church administrator*
Ogui, Koshin *Buddhist minister*
Rajan, Fred E. N. *clergy member, church administrator*
Reynolds, Frank Everett *religious studies educator*
Sagarin, James Leon *rabbi, author, editor*
Schupp, Ronald Irving *clergyman, civil and human rights leader*
Shafer, Eric Christopher *minister*
Simon, Mordecai *religious association administrator, clergyman*
Sorensen, W. Robert *clergy member, church administrator*
Thurston, Stephen John *pastor*
†Unsworth, Richard Timothy *writer*
Wagner, Joseph M. *church administrator*
Wall, James McKendree *minister, editor*
Wiwchar, Michael *bishop*
Yu, Anthony C. *religion and literature educator*

Crystal Lake
Haemmelmann, Keith Alan *minister*

Decatur
†Buck, Christopher George *religion educator, writer*
Morgan, E. A. *church administrator*

Elgin
Nolen, Wilfred E. *church administrator*

Elk Grove Village
Stein, David Timothy *minister*

Evanston
Fisher, Neal Floyd *religious organization administrator*
Moore, Wallace David *minister, religious organization administrator*
Walker, Harold Blake *minister*

Frankfort
Huff, John David *church administrator*

Galena
Burkhart, John Ernest *minister, religion educator*

Glenview
Braun, Eunice Hockspeier *author, religious order executive, lecturer*

Glenwood
Christopher, Claude *minister*

Homewood
Pedersen, Walter *minister*

Jacksonville
Woodworth, Harold G. *minister*

Joliet
†Imesch, Joseph Leopold *bishop*
Kaffer, Roger Louis *bishop*

Kankakee
Dalton, Ronnie Thomas *theology educator*

Kenilworth
Bowen, Gilbert Willard *minister*

Lake Forest
Price, John Edward *religion educator*

Lemont
Galati, Michael Bernard *lay church worker*

Lincoln
Wilson, Robert Allen *religion educator*

Moline
Johnson, Mary Lou *lay worker*

Naperville
Landwehr, Arthur John *minister*
Worden, William Patrick *deacon*

Oak Lawn
Wright, Steven Randall *minister*

Oak Park
Cary, William Sterling *retired church executive*
Gerson, Gary Stanford *rabbi*
Hallstrand, Sarah Laymon *denomination executive*
Lunney, Daniel Thomas *chaplain, bereavement coordinator*

Oregon
Clement, John Edward Strausz *minister, religious organization administrator*

Palos Heights
Nederhood, Joel H. *church organization executive, minister, retired*

Park Ridge
†Joyce, Teri *church organization administrator*

Peoria
Myers, John Joseph *bishop*
Parsons, Donald Keith *retired bishop*
Saxon, Randall Lee *pastor, author, educator*

Rockford
Doran, Thomas George *bishop*
Hanson, Murray Lynn *minister*
McClelland, Patricia G. *minister*
O'Neill, Arthur J. *retired bishop*
Weissbard, David Raymond *minister*

Rolling Meadows
Giese, Robert James *minister*
Rahfeldt, Daryl Gene *minister*

Saint Charles
Nelson, Norman Augustine *minister*

Savoy
Gauger, Randy Jay *minister*

Springfield
Bell, John Perry *minister, religious organization administrator*
Cluney, J(ohn) C(harles) (Jack Cluney) *minister*
Ryan, Daniel Leo *bishop*

Summit Argo
Abramowicz, Alfred L. *retired bishop*

Thornton
Braico, Carmella Elizabeth Lofrano *clergy member*

University Park
McClellan, Larry Allen *educator, writer, minister*

Vandalia
Sussenbach, Ward Virgil *minister*

Westchester
Brushwyler, Lawrence Ronald *minister*

Wheaton
Estep, John Hayes *religious denomination executive, clergyman*
†French, Talmadge L. *clergyman, educator*
Gill, Kenneth Duane *minister, missiologist*
Harris, E(leanor) Lynn(e) *religious studies and literature educator*
Pappas, Barbara Estelle *Biblical studies educator, author*
Tinder, Donald George *theology educator, lecturer*
Vest, R. Lamar *church administrator*

Wilmette
Stockman, Robert Harold *religious organization administrator, educator*

INDIANA

Anderson
Conrad, Harold August *retired religious pension board executive*
Grubbs, J. Perry *church administrator*
Kufeldt, George *biblical educator*
Lambert, Lloyd Laverne *minister*
Lyon, James Donald *minister*

Bloomington
†Choksy, Jamsheed *religious studies educator*
Hicks, Marilyn Sue *lay worker*

Carmel
Swartz, Paul Frederick *clergyman*

Clinton
Keown, William Arvel *minister, educator*

Dayton
Bomgarden, Stanley Ralph *minister*

Evansville
Brenner, Raymond Anthony *priest*
Flowers, Glen Dale *minister*
Gettelfinger, Gerald Andrew *bishop*
Hoy, George Philip *clergyman, food bank executive*
Williams, Jean Marie *religious organization administrator*

Ferdinand
Bilskie, Kathy *religious order administrator, nun*

Fort Wayne
Bunkowske, Eugene Walter *religious studies educator*
D'Arcy, John Michael *bishop*
Kline, Joel D. *pastor*
Mann, David William *minister*
Mather, George Ross *clergy member*
Moran, John *religious organization administrator*

Gary
†LaGrand, James, Jr. *minister*

Huntington
Seilhamer, Ray A. *bishop*

Indianapolis
Bates, Gerald Earl *bishop*
Brannon, Ronald Roy *minister*
Bray, Donald Lawrence *religious organization executive, minister*
Buechlein, Daniel Mark *archbishop*
Caldwell, John William *pastor*
Castle, Howard Blaine *religious organization administrator*
Crow, Paul Abernathy, Jr. *clergyman, religious council executive, educator*
Dickinson, Richard Donald Nye *clergyman, educator, theological seminary administrator*

Haines, Lee Mark, Jr. *religious denomination administrator*
Hamm, Richard L. *church administrator*
Harness, David Keith *pastor*
Johnson, James P. *religious organization executive*
Kempski, Ralph Aloisius *bishop*
Manworren, Donald B. *church administrator*
Marshall, Carolyn Ann M. *church official, executive*
Page, Curtis Matthewson *minister*
Plaster, George Francis *Roman Catholic priest*
Polston, Mark Franklin *minister*
Sindlinger, Verne E. *bishop*
Towne, Edgar Arthur *theologian, educator*
Watkins, Harold Robert *minister*
Welsh, Robert K. *religious organization executive*
Wilson, Earle Lawrence *church administrator*
Woodring, DeWayne Stanley *religion association executive*

Kokomo
Hall, Milton L. *bishop*
Ungerer, Walter John *minister*

Lafayette
Higi, William L. *bishop*
Miller, Larry Joe *evangelist*

Marion
McIntyre, Robert Walter *church official*

Muncie
Granger, Philip Richard *minister*

Noblesville
Wilson, Norman Glenn *church administrator, writer*

Notre Dame
†Blantz, Thomas Edward *Roman Catholic priest, educator*
Blenkinsopp, Joseph *biblical studies educator*
Driscoll, Michael Stephan *priest, liturgy and theology educator*
Hesburgh, Theodore Martin *clergyman, former university president*
Malloy, Edward Aloysius *priest, university administrator, educator*
McBrien, Richard Peter *theology educator*
O'Meara, Thomas Franklin *priest, educator*
Sterling, Gregory Earl *religious studies educator*
†Trembath, Kern Robert *theology educator*
White, James Floyd *theology educator*

Oakland City
Johnson, Ora J. *clergyman*

Peru
Fager, Everett Dean *minister*

Richmond
Maurer, Johan Fredrik *religious denomination administrator*

Russiaville
Knierim, Stephen Dale *minister*

South Bend
Crowley, Joseph R. *bishop*

Terre Haute
Mansfield, Dianne Lynn *minister*

Winona Lake
Ashman, Charles H. *retired minister*
Davis, John James *religion educator*
Julien, Thomas Theodore *religious denomination administrator*
Lewis, Edward Alan *religious organization administrator*
†Soto, Mark Harrison *Biblical studies educator, pastor*
Williams, Ronald Eugene *minister, evangelist*

IOWA

Ames
†Zimmerman, Zora Devrnja *dean, English language educator*

Ankeny
Houghton, Myron James *theology educator*

Cedar Rapids
Frangipane, Francis A. *minister, religious organization executive, writer*

Centerville
Strube, Christopher William *pastor*

Corning
Rummer, Kenneth Dale *pastor*

Corydon
Hopkins, Theodore Mark *minister, guidance counselor*

Davenport
Franklin, William Edwin *bishop*
O'Keefe, Gerald Francis *bishop, retired*

Decorah
Farwell, Elwin D. *minister, educational consultant*

Des Moines
Charron, Joseph L. *bishop*
Epting, C. Christopher *bishop*
Hanusa, George Leonard *minister*
Jordan, Charles Wesley *bishop*

Dubuque
Barta, James Omer *priest, psychology educator, church administrator*
Beck, Robert Raymond *priest*
Bloesch, Donald George *theologian, writer, educator*
Hanus, Jerome George *archbishop*
Nessan, Craig Lee *minister, educator*

Fort Dodge
Hammar, David Bruce *clergyman*

Walsh, Patrick R. *priest, school system administrator*

Grinnell
Mitchell, Orlan E. *clergyman, former college president*

Iowa City
Baird, Robert Dahlen *religious educator*
Forell, George Wolfgang *religion educator*
Holstein, Jay Allen *Judaic studies educator*
Keen, Ralph *religious studies educator*

Orange City
Scorza, Sylvio Joseph *religion educator*

Sioux City
Mack, Thomas Russell *foundation administrator, management consultant*
Soens, Lawrence Donald *bishop*

Storm Lake
Miller, Curtis Herman *bishop*

KANSAS

Atchison
Bryan, Caroline Elizabeth *nun*

Copeland
Birney, Walter Leroy *religious administrator*

Durham
Curtis, Richard Lewis *pastor*

Goodland
Ross, Chester Wheeler *retired clergyman*

Kansas City
Forst, Marion Francis *bishop*
Keleher, James P. *bishop*
†Strecker, Ignatius J. *archbishop*

Leavenworth
Buselt, Clara Irene *religious organization administrator*
McGilley, Sister Mary Janet *nun, educator, writer, academic administrator*

Manhattan
Gillispie, Harold Leon *minister*
Paddock, Wesley Thomas *minister, educator*

North Newton
Fast, Darrell Wayne *minister*

Olathe
Mixer, Ronald Wayne *minister*

Salina
Fitzsimons, George Kinzie *bishop*

Shawnee Mission
Holter, Don Wendell *retired bishop*
Mandl, Herbert Jay *rabbi*
Olsen, Stanley Severn *minister*
Smith, Patricia Ann *religious organization administrator*

Sterling
Kendall, Charles Terry *librarian*

Topeka
Goetz, Roger Melvin *minister*
Mutti, Albert Frederick *minister*
Smalley, William Edward *bishop*
Vaughn, Ima Jean *minister, educator*

Wichita
Armstrong, Hart Reid *minister, editor, publisher*
Essey, Basil *bishop*
Gerber, Eugene J. *bishop*

KENTUCKY

Ashland
Touchton, Bobby Jay *minister*

Covington
†Hughes, William Anthony *bishop*

Crestwood
Roy, Elmon Harold *minister*

Elizabethtown
Phelps, Dennis Lane *minister, educator, author*

Erlanger
Muench, Robert W. *bishop*

Frankfort
Hestand, Joel Dwight *minister, evangelist*

Hopkinsville
Birkhead, Thomas Larry *minister*

Lexington
Williams, James Kendrick *bishop*

Louisville
Blaising, Craig Alan *religious studies educator*
Dale, Judy Ries *religious organization administrator*
Draper, Charles William *religious studies educator*
Granady, Juanita H. *retired religious organization administrator*
Holladay, James Franklin, Jr. *minister*
Jenkins, C(arle) Frederick *religious organization executive, minister, lawyer*
Kelly, Thomas Cajetan *archbishop*
Reed, David Benson *bishop*
Strachan, Gladys *retired religious organization executive*
Zimmerman, Gideon K. *minister*

Owensboro
Bennett, Edith Lillian *lay church worker, radio personality*
McRaith, John Jeremiah *bishop*

Paris
Steffer, Robert Wesley *clergyman*

Pineville
Whittaker, Bill Douglas *minister*

Vine Grove
McNamara, Patricia Rae *religious organization administrator, school system administrator*

Wilmore
Kinlaw, Dennis Franklin *clergyman, society executive*

Winchester
Evans, William Halla *minister*
Hall, Bennett Freeman *minister*

LOUISIANA

Baton Rouge
Hughes, Alfred Clifton *bishop*
Porter, Gary Stephan *minister*
Swaggart, Jimmy Lee *evangelist, gospel singer*
Witcher, Robert Campbell *bishop*

Bossier City
Tice, William Fleet, Jr. *pastor*

Calhoun
Roberts, Thomas Keith *minister*

Crowley
†Foreman, Alfred G. *theologian, philosopher*

Deridder
Magee, Thomas Eston, Jr. *minister*

Donaldsonville
Watson, Stanley Ellis *clergyman, small business owner*

Homer
Anglin, Walter Michael *minister, law enforcement professional$D*

Houma
†Jarrell, Charles Michael *bishop*

Lafayette
Hermes, Mother Theresa Margaret *prioress*
O'Donnell, Edward Joseph *bishop, former editor*

Lake Charles
Speyrer, Jude *bishop*
†Vincent, Amos Joseph, Jr. *priest*

Meraux
Broome, Randall *evangelist*

New Iberia
Henton, Willis Ryan *bishop*

New Orleans
Clancy, Thomas Hanley *seminary administrator*
Hannan, Philip Matthew *bishop*
Schulte, Francis B. *archbishop*
Truehill, Marshall, Jr. *minister*
Warren, William Frampton, Jr. *religion educator*

Pineville
Boswell, Bill Reeser *religious organization executive*

Saint Bernard
Lee, Melvin Joseph *minister*

Shreveport
Friend, William Benedict *bishop*
Stewart, James Joseph *minister, consultant*
Webb, Donald Arthur *minister*

Springhill
Morgan, Larry Ronald *minister*

Tioga
Tenney, Tom Fred *bishop*

MAINE

Brunswick
Ault, James Mase *bishop*
Geoghegan, William Davidson *religion educator, minister*

Cushing
Day, Giles William, Jr. (Bill Day) *religious studies educator*

Friendship
Du Bois, Clarence Hazel, Jr. *clergy member*

Islesboro
Maes, John Leopold *theologian, psychologist, educator*

Portland
†Cote, Michael Richard *bishop*
Gerry, Joseph John *bishop*
O'Leary, Edward Cornelius *former bishop*

Sedgwick
Becker, Robert Clarence *retired clergyman*

Windham
†Small, Richard Leroy *clergyman, sanctuary design consultant*

MARYLAND

Baltimore
†Davish, William Martin *priest, educator*
Eberwein, Granville Allen *lay minister, civil servant*
Houck, John Roland *clergyman*
Macleod, Donald *clergyman, educator*
Margalit, Shlomo *educator*
Mocko, George Paul *minister*
Murphy, Philip Francis *bishop*
Newman, William C. *bishop*
Strickland, Marshall Hayward *bishop*
Talar, Charles John Thomas *priest, educator*
Zaiman, Joel Hirsh *rabbi*

Cambridge
Pierce, Nathaniel W. *minister*

Catonsville
Wynn, John Charles *clergyman, retired religion educator*

Chesapeake City
Smalley, Stephen Mark *priest*

Cockeysville
Hager, Louise Alger *retired chaplain*

Columbia
Davis, Benjamin George *theologian, educator*

Frederick
Hein, David *religion educator*

Gaithersburg
Hall, Arthur Raymond, Jr. *minister*
Rupert, (Lynn) Hoover *minister*

Glen Burnie
Colvin, John Alexander *campus minister*
Kirk, James Graham *pastor*

Hagerstown
Coles, Robert Nelson, Sr. *religious organization administrator*

Hyattsville
Ilogu, Edmund Christopher Onyedum *priest*

Rockville
Luxemburg, Jack Alan *rabbi*
Meade, Kenneth Albert *minister*
Stano, Lester Paul *minister*

Sandy Spring
Moulton, Phillips Prentice *religion and philosophy educator*

Severn
Freeman, Joel Arthur *behavioral consultant*

Silver Spring
Beach, Bert Beverly *clergyman*
Beckmann, David Milton *minister, economist, social activist*
Closter, Sidney Howard *international service organization administrator*
Doerr, Edd *religious liberty organization executive*
†Paulsen, Jan *clergyman, church administrator*
Thompson, George Ralph *church administrator*

Westminster
Koehnlein, John Martin, Sr. *minister, consultant*

MASSACHUSETTS

Amherst
Wills, David Wood *minister, educator*

Andover
Simone, Joseph *clergyman, educator*

Auburn
Bachelder, Robert Stephen *minister*

Boston
Bard, Terry Ross *rabbi*
Dickinson, Charles Cameron, III *theologian, educator*
Harris, Barbara C(lementine) *bishop*
Katz, Steven Theodore *religious studies educator*
Kessler, Diane Cooksey *religious organization administrator, minister*
Korff, Yitzchok Aharon *rabbi*
Mason, Herbert Warren, Jr. *religion and history educator, author*
Rouner, Leroy Stephens *religious studies educator, philosophy educator*
Samaan, John George *nonprofit organization executive*
Shaw, M. Thomas, III *bishop*
Wickenhiser, Sister Mary Mark *religious organization official, nun*
Williams, Rhys *minister*
Worthley, Harold Field *minister, educator*

Brighton
Law, Bernard Francis Cardinal *archbishop*
Murphy, William F. *priest, monsignor, religion educator*

Brockton
Holland, David Vernon *minister*

Brookline
Chryssavgis, John *theology educator, administrator*
Newman, Thomas Daniel *minister, school administrator*

Burlington
O'Brien, John Joseph *theology educator, priest*

Cambridge
Ahmed, Leila Nadine *religious studies educator*
Fiorenza, Francis P. *religion educator*
Gomes, Peter John *clergyman, educator*
Graham, William Albert *religion educator, history educator*
Kaufman, Gordon Dester *theology educator*
Koester, Helmut Heinrich *theologian, educator*
Potter, Ralph Benajah, Jr. *theology and social ethics educator*
Schuessler Fiorenza, Elisabeth *theology educator*
Whitaker, Arthur Luther *retired minister, psychologist*
Williams, Preston Noah *theology educator*

Chestnut Hill
Helmick, Raymond Glen *priest, educator*
Mc Innes, William Charles *priest, academic administrator*
Schatkin, Margaret Amy *theology educator*
Vicini, Andrea *priest, pediatrician*

Dedham
Spoolstra, Linda Carol *minister, educator, religious organization administrator*

Dorchester
†Boles, John P. *bishop*

Fall River
O'Malley, Sean *bishop*
Wolberg, Richard Allen *Cantor*

Harvard
Sutherland, Malcolm Read, Jr. *clergyman, educator*

Haverhill
Korinow, Ira Lee *rabbi*

Hyde Park
Riley, Lawrence Joseph *bishop*

Leeds
Grenz, Linda L. *Episcopal priest*

Lenox
Collins, Oral Edmond *theology educator, archaeologist*

Longmeadow
Stewart, Alexander Doig *bishop*

Lowell
McNamara, John R. *bishop*

Marlborough
Lohr, Harold Russell *bishop*

Natick
Kushner, Harold Samuel *rabbi*

New Bedford
Hartman, Barry David *rabbi*
Kellaway, Richard Allen *minister, art association administrator*

Northampton
Donfried, Karl Paul *minister, theology educator*
Unsworth, Richard Preston *minister, school administrator*

Norwood
†Wolkovich-Valkaviciu, William Lawrence *priest*

Pittsfield
Bostley, Jean Regina *nun, library association administrator*
†Small, David J. *rabbi*

South Hamilton
Kalland, Lloyd Austin *minister*
Tennent, Timothy Craig *theology educator*

Springfield
Dupre, Thomas L. *bishop*

Swampscott
Weinsberg, Edgar James *rabbi, consultant, lecturer*

Waltham
Delaney, Mary Anne *pastoral educator*
Johnson, William Alexander *clergyman, philosophy educator*
Reisman, Bernard *theology educator*

Wellesley
Lazar, Jeffrey Bennett *rabbi, educator*

West Newton
Elya, John Adel *bishop*

Weston
Barry, William Anthony *priest, writer*

Westwood
Bier, Louis Henry Gustav *minister*

Worcester
Covino, Paul Francis Xavier *religious executive, college chaplain, consultant*
Isaksen, Robert L. *bishop*
Parsons, Edwin Spencer *clergyman, educator*
Reilly, Daniel Patrick *bishop*

MICHIGAN

Adrian
Oswald, Harold Nicholas, Jr. *lay worker*

Ann Arbor
Cambers, Philip William *pastor, music minister, music educator*

Berrien Springs
Andreasen, Niels-Erik Albinus *religious educator*
Kis, Miroslav Mirko *minister, religion educator*

Bloomfield Hills
Hertz, Richard Cornell *rabbi*

Cassopolis
Bruneau, William Joseph, Jr. *minister, career counselor*

Clarkston
Keough, James Gillman, Jr. *minister*

Dearborn
Hess, Margaret Johnston *religious writer, educator*

Dearborn Heights
Lorenz, Felix Alfred, Jr. *minister*

Detroit
Adams, Charles Gilchrist *pastor*
†Anderson, Moses B. *bishop*
Gumbleton, Thomas J. *bishop*
Maida, Adam Joseph Cardinal *cardinal*
Mc Gehee, H(arry) Coleman, Jr. *bishop*
Quick, William Kellon *pastor*
Schoenherr, Walter Joseph *bishop*
Ursache, Victorin (His Eminence The Most Reverend Archbishop Victorin) *archbishop*
†Vigneron, Allen Henry *theology educator, rector, auxiliary bishop*
Wood, R. Stewart *bishop*

East Jordan
Donaldson, Robert Frost *minister*

Eastpointe
Andrzejewski, Darryl Lee *clergyman*

Farmington
Wine, Sherwin Theodore *rabbi*

Farmington Hills
Plaut, Jonathan Victor *rabbi*

Flint
Edsall, David Leonard *councillor, religious educator*
McClanahan, Connie Dea *pastoral minister*
Meissner, Suzanne Banks *pastoral associate*

Fort Gratiot
Salt, Alfred Lewis *priest*

Gaylord
Cooney, Patrick Ronald *bishop*

Grand Rapids
Anderson, Roger Gordon *minister*
Beals, Paul Archer *religious studies educator*
Borgdorff, Peter *church adminstrator*
DeVries, Robert K. *religious book publisher*
Hofman, Leonard John *minister*
Rozeboom, John A. *religious organization administrator*
Schwanda, Tom *religious studies educator*
Smith, Edgar Wright, Jr. *editor religious books*
Thompson, John Ross *minister*

Holland
Brouwer, Wayne Allen *clergyman, writer*
Cook, James Ivan *clergyman, religion educator*
Luchies, John Elmer *religion educator*
Van Voorst, Robert E. *theology educator, minister*

Jackson
Nathaniel *bishop*

Jenison
Vunderink, Ralph William *lay minister*

Kalamazoo
Donovan, Paul V. *former bishop*

Livonia
Davis, Lawrence Edward *church official*

Marquette
Burt, John Harris *bishop*
Garland, James H. *bishop*
Ray, Thomas Kreider *bishop*
Skogman, Dale R. *bishop*

Midland
Clarkson, William Morris *children's pastor*

Millersburg
Griffin, Richard Ray *minister*

Montague
Sirotko, Theodore Francis *priest, retired military officer*

Northville
Hess, Bartlett Leonard *clergyman*

Portage
Lee, Edward L. *bishop*

Redford
Gibbons, Gregory Dennis *minister*

Saginaw
Untener, Kenneth E. *bishop*

Southfield
Ibrahim, Ibrahim N. *bishop*
Willingham, Edward Bacon, Jr. *ecumenical minister, administrator*

Spring Arbor
Thompson, Stanley B. *church administrator*

Warren
†Samra, Nicholas James *bishop*

Wayland
Willcox, William Brewster *minister*

Wyandotte
Kirsch, Norman Maynard *clergyman*

Syme, Daniel Bailey *rabbi, institution executive*

MINNESOTA

Alexandria
Hultstrand, Donald Maynard *bishop*

Anoka
Nelson, Duane Juan *minister*

Arden Hills
Hartsoe, James Russell *minister*

Austin
Alcorn, Wallace Arthur *minister*
Morgan, Robert Ashton *minister, ethics and world religions educator*

Bloomington
McDill, Thomas Allison *minister*
Thomas, Margaret Jean *clergywoman, religious research consultant*

Buffalo
Hagen, Ione Carolyn *religion educator*

Cottage Grove
Hudnut, Robert Kilborne *clergyman, author*

Crookston
†Balke, Victor H. *bishop*

Duluth
Aadland, Thomas Vernon *minister*
Andert, David August *minister*
Schwietz, Roger L. *bishop*

Edina
Brown, Laurence David *retired bishop*
Cedar, Paul Arnold *church executive, minister*
Putnam, Frederick Warren, Jr. *bishop*

Excelsior
Fenske, Jerald Allan *minister*

Fergus Falls
Egge, Joel *clergy member, academic administrator*
Jahr, Armin N., II *clergy member, church administrator*
Overgaard, Robert Milton *religious organization administrator*

Hastings
Bzoskie, James Steven *minister*

Inver Grove Heights
Koenig, Robert August *clergyman, educator*

Lake Elmo
Schultz, Clarence John *minister*

Little Falls
Mottram, Richard Donald, Jr. *minister*

Mankato
Orvick, George Myron *church denomination executive, minister*

Minneapolis
†Chemberlin, Peg *clergy, religious organization administrator*
Corts, John Ronald *minister, religious organization executive*
Drahmann, Brother Theodore *religious order official*
Dyrud, Amos Oliver *minister, educator*
Graham, William Franklin (Billy Graham) *evangelist*
Hamel, William John *church administrator, minister*
Klemp, Harold *minister, writer*
Lee, Robert Lloyd *pastor, religious association executive*
Lindberg, Duane R. *minister, historian*
Sawatsky, Ben *church administrator*
†Swan, Wallace Kent *public administrator*
Wang, L. Edwin *church official*

Minnetonka
Parker, Robert Chauncey Humphrey *clergyman, publishing executive, psychic*

Moorhead
Jacobson, Arland Dean *religion educator*

New Brighton
Steckel, Clyde James *retired theology educator, dean, minister*

New Ulm
Lucker, Raymond Alphonse *bishop*

Northfield
Crouter, Richard Earl *religion educator*

Preston
Schommer, Trudy Marie *pastoral minister, religion education*

Robbinsdale
Be Vier, William A. *religious studies educator*

Rochester
Nycklemoe, Glenn Winston *bishop*

Saint Cloud
Kinney, John Francis *bishop*

Saint Paul
Athans, Sister Mary Christine *church history educator*
†Ferris, Paul Wayne, Jr. *religious studies educator*
Flynn, Harry Joseph *bishop*
Hopper, David Henry *religion educator*
†Huffman, Douglas Scott *educator and administrator college level*
Jaberg, Eugene Carl *theology educator, administrator*
McMillan, Mary Bigelow *retired minister, volunteer*
McNamee, Sister Catherine *educator*
Ofstedal, Paul Estrem *clergy member*
Preus, David Walter *bishop, minister*
Roach, John Robert *retired archbishop*

Saint Peter
Jodock, Darrell Harland *minister, religion educator*

Saipan
†Camacho, Tomas Aguon *bishop*

Sandstone
†Laposky, James Edward *pastor*

Winona
Dill, Ellen Renée *minister*

MISSISSIPPI

Bay Saint Louis
Frey, Gerard Louis *retired bishop*

Biloxi
†Howze, Joseph Lawson Edward *bishop*

Clinton
Bryant, William Bruce *minister*

Gulfport
Freret, René Joseph *minister*

Hattiesburg
Taylor, David Neil *minister*

Indianola
Matthews, David *clergyman*

Jackson
Duncan, Jennings Ligon *minister*
Gordon, Granville Hollis *church official*
Gray, Duncan Montgomery, Jr. *retired bishop*
†Houck, William Russell *bishop*
Larsen, Samuel Harry *minister, educator*
McKnight, William Edwin *minister*
†Rankin, William Duncan *theology educator*
Woodward, Wayne William *librarian, minister*

Kosciusko
Kearley, F. Furman *minister, religious educator, magazine editor*

Long Beach
Horton, Jerry Smith *minister*

Myrtle
Pirkle, Estus Washington *minister*

Waveland
Romagosa, Elmo Lawrence *retired clergyman, retired editor*

MISSOURI

Ballwin
Ackerson, Charles Stanley *minister, social worker*

Bridgeton
Asma, Lawrence Francis *priest*

Columbia
†Yonker, John Joseph *clergyman*

Dittmer
Miller, Bertin *priest, social administrator*

Excelsior Springs
Mitchell, Earl Wesley *clergyman*

Fayette
Keeling, Joe Keith *religion educator, college official and dean*

Fordland
Fields, Samuel Preston, Jr. *lay worker*

Hazelwood
Rose, Joseph Hugh *clergyman*
Urshan, Nathaniel Andrew *minister, church administrator*

Highlandville
Pruter, Karl Hugo *bishop*

Independence
Lindgren, A(lan) Bruce *church administrator*
Tyree, Alan Dean *clergyman*

Jefferson City
Kelley, Patrick Michael *minister, state legislator*
King, Robert Henry *minister, church denomination executive, former educator*
Mc Auliffe, Michael F. *retired bishop*

Joplin
Butler, Paul Thurman *retired religious studies educator*
Minor, Ronald Ray *minister*
Wilson, Aaron Martin *religious studies educator, college executive*

Kansas City
Bell, Wallace Edward *minister*
Boland, Raymond James *bishop*
Bowers, Curtis Ray, Jr. *chaplain*
Cunningham, Paul George *minister*
Diehl, James Harvey *church administrator*
Estep, Michael R. *church administrator*
Frank, Eugene Maxwell *bishop*
Friedlander, Edward Robert *pathologist*
Gray, Helen Theresa Gott *religion editor*
Jenkins, Orville Wesley *retired religious administrator*
Juarez, Martin *priest*
Knight, John Allan *clergyman, philosophy and religion educator*
Mazza, Biagio *religious studies educator*
Prince, William J. *church officer*
Rowden, A(lphro) J(ohn) *minister*
Stone, Jack *religious organization administrator*

Sullivan, Bill *church administrator*
Sullivan, John Joseph *bishop*
Vogel, Arthur Anton *clergyman*

Kimberling City
Docherty, Robert Kelliehan, II *minister*

Lees Summit
Demetreon, Daiboune Elayne *minister*
Mosley, Glenn Richard *religious organization administrator, minister*

Marshall
Bunch, Albert William *minister*

Monett
Block, Michael David *minister*

Poplar Bluff
Black, Ronnie Delane *religious organization administrator, mayor*
Carr, Charles Louis *retired religious organization administrator*
Duncan, Leland Ray *retired mission administrator*

Saint Louis
Barry, A. L. *church official*
Brungs, Robert Anthony *theology educator, institute director*
Gottwald, George J. *bishop*
Mahsman, David Lawrence *religious publications editor*
†McClain, Curtis Keith, Jr. *religious studies educator, minister*
Merrell, James Lee *religious editor, clergyman*
Morrison, Barton Douglas *minister*
Muller, Lyle Dean *retired religious organization administrator*
Munger, George Howard, Jr. *pastor, chaplain*
†Naunann, Joseph F. *bishop*
Ong, Walter Jackson *priest, English educator, author*
O'Shoney, Glenn *church administrator*
Poellot, Luther *minister*
Rigali, Justin F. *archbishop*
Rockwell, Hays Hamilton *bishop*
Rosin, Walter L. *retired religious organization administrator*
Rowold, Henry Lawrence *religious studies educator*
Ward, R. J. *bishop*
Wilke, LeRoy *church administrator*

Sedalia
Shelton, Thomas Alfred *Christian education director*

Springfield
Baird, Robert Dean *mission director*
†Gillming, Kenneth *church administrator*
Grams, Betty Jane *minister, educator, writer*
Hobus, Robert Allen *minister*
Leibrecht, John Joseph *bishop*
Trask, Thomas Edward *religious organization administrator*

Tipton
Wazir, Tadar Jihad *chaplain, small business owner*

MONTANA

Great Falls
Milone, Anthony M. *bishop*

Helena
Hart, John William *theology educator*
Jones, Charles Irving *bishop*

Missoula
Wingenbach, Gregory Charles *priest, religious-ecumenical agency director*

NEBRASKA

Bellevue
Elliott, Ronald Dean *minister*

Fremont
Deahl, William Evans, Jr. *minister*

Grand Island
†Mc Namara, Lawrence J. *bishop*
Zichek, Melvin Eddie *retired clergyman, educator*

Hastings
†Watts, James Washington *religion educator*

Kilgore
Olsen, Lester Paul (Les Olsen) *minister*

Lincoln
Bruskewitz, Fabian W. *bishop*
Case, Sylvester Quezada *minister*
Hanway, Donald Grant *Episcopal priest*
Manglitz, Marjorie Joan *religious education director*
Turner, John Douglas *religious studies educator*
Wiersbe, Warren Wendell *clergyman, author, lecturer*

Omaha
Curtiss, Elden F. *bishop*
†Malina, Bruce John *theology educator, author*
Schultenover, David George *theology educator*
Sheehan, Daniel Eugene *bishop*
Zuerlein, Damian Joseph *priest*

Wayne
†Russell, Martin John *minister*

NEVADA

Las Vegas
†Shafe, Michele Wheeler *county administrator*
Walsh, Daniel Francis *bishop*

Minden
Jackson, John Jay *clergyman*

Reno
†Apassa, Cyril Omo-Osagie *clergyman, educator*
Chrystal, William George *minister*
Savoy, Douglas Eugene *bishop, religion educator, explorer, writer*
Straling, Phillip Francis *bishop*
Walrath, Harry Rienzi *minister*
Weld, Roger Bowen *clergyman*

NEW HAMPSHIRE

Center Sandwich
Booty, John Everitt *historiographer*

Concord
Theuner, Douglas Edwin *bishop*

Contoocook
Payne, Paula Marie *minister*

Durham
Frankfurter, David Thomas Munro *religious studies educator*

Freedom
Davidson, George Thomas, Jr. *minister, educator*

Hanover
Green, Ronald Michael *ethics and religious studies educator*

Hillsboro
Gibson, Raymond Eugene *clergyman*

Hollis
Litchfield, Barbara Mae Smith *clergywoman*

Jaffrey
Van Ness, Patricia Wood *religious studies educator, consultant*

Loudon
Moore, Beatrice *religious organization administrator*

Manchester
Christian, Francis Joseph *bishop*
Gendron, Odore Joseph *retired bishop*

Nashua
Dowd, Karl Edmund *priest*

Stratham
Bodine, John Jermain *pastor*

West Chesterfield
Garinger, Louis Daniel *religion educator*

NEW JERSEY

Bernardsville
Baldwin, Frederick Stephen *priest*

Browns Mills
McNabb, Talmadge Ford *religious organization administrator, retired military chaplain*

Burlington
Gunn, Sandra Joyce *musician and church lay leader*

Caldwell
Campbell, Sister Maura *religious studies and philosophy educator*

Cape May Court House
Foley, Eugene Arthur *pastor*

Clifton
Rodimer, Frank Joseph *bishop*

East Brunswick
Lachs, Annie *religious organization administrator*

Edison
Tedesco, Richard Albert *minister*

Englewood
Hertzberg, Arthur *rabbi, educator*
Khouri, Antoun *church administrator*
Saliba, Philip E. *archbishop*

Jersey City
Ashley, Willard Walden C., Sr. *minister*
†Carter, Guy Christopher *theologian*

Lakewood
Levovitz, Pesach Zechariah *rabbi*
Taylor, Robert M. *minister*

Linden
Marconi, Dominic Anthony *clergyman*

Madison
Yrigoyen, Charles, Jr. *church denomination executive*

Mahwah
Boadt, Lawrence Edward *priest, religion educator*
Padovano, Anthony Thomas *theologian, educator*

Metuchen
Breen, Vincent De Paul *bishop*

Montclair
Leggett, Paul Arthur *minister*
Schnitzer, Jeshaia *rabbi, marriage and family therapist*

Morris Plains
Korbman, Jack Soloman *cantor, educator*

Mullica Hill
Demola, James, Sr. *church administrator*

New Brunswick
Bowden, Henry Warner *religion educator*
Coakley, John Wayland *theological historian, educator*

Newark
Garner, Robert F. *bishop*
Mc Carrick, Theodore Edgar *archbishop*
McKelvey, Jack M. *bishop*
Spong, John Shelby *bishop*

Newfield
Hartman, Jeffrey Edward *pastor*

Ocean Grove
Anderson, James Frederick *clergyman*

Orange
Johnson, Anthony Peter *minister*

Pompton Plains
†Scroggs, Robin Jerome *theology educator*

Princeton
Allen, Diogenes *clergyman, philosophy educator*
Armstrong, Richard Stoll *minister, educator, writer, poet*
Belshaw, George Phelps Mellick *bishop*
Douglass, Jane Dempsey *theology educator*
Gordon, Ernest *clergyman*
Metzger, Bruce Manning *clergyman, educator*
Miller, Patrick Dwight, Jr. *religion educator, minister*
Mulder, Edwin George *retired minister, church official*
West, Charles Converse *theologian, educator*
Yun, Samuel *minister, educator*

Ringwood
Edge, Thomas Leslie *minister*

Rochelle Park
Brandt, Robert Barry *lay worker*

Roselle Park
Freeland, Herbert Thomas *minister*

Rutherford
Gerety, Peter Leo *archbishop*

Short Hills
Pilchik, Ely Emanuel *rabbi, writer*

South Orange
Fleming, Edward J. *priest, educator*

Summit
May, Ernest Max *charitable organization official*

Teaneck
Meno, John Peter *chorepiscopus*

Tinton Falls
Priesand, Sally Jane *rabbi*

Toms River
Donaldson, Marcia Jean *lay worker*

Trenton
Medley, Alex Roy *executive minister*
Old, Hughes Oliphant *research theologian, clergyman*

Union
Korbman, Meyer Hyman *rabbi, public school administrator*

Union City
†Younan, Joseph *bishop*

Warren
Jaffe, Howard Lawrence *rabbi*
Wildrick, Kenyon Jones *minister*

Watchung
Miller, John Ronald *minister*

West Milford
Stelpstra, William John *minister*

West New York
Arias, David *bishop*

West Orange
Guthrie, William Anthony *minister*

West Paterson
†Pataki, Andrew *bishop*

Westville
Doughty, A. Glenn *minister*

Willingboro
Bass, Joseph Oscar *minister*

NEW MEXICO

Albuquerque
George, Roy Kenneth *minister*
Sanchez, Robert Fortune *archbishop*
Sheehan, Michael Jarboe *archbishop*

Artesia
Robinson, J. Kenneth *religious organization administrator, minister*

Farmington
Plummer, Steven Tsosie, Sr. *bishop*

Las Cruces
Ramirez, Ricardo *bishop*

Portales
Overton, Edwin Dean *campus minister, educator*

Rio Rancho
†Haney, Kevin Scott *adminitrator*

Roswell
Pretti, Bradford Joseph *lay worker, insurance company executive, retired*

NEW YORK

Adams Center
Hood, Thomas Gregory *minister*

Albany
Bowen, Mary Lu *ecumenical developer, community organizer*
Hubbard, Howard James *bishop*

Angola
Green, Gerard Leo *priest, educator*

Binghamton
Fay, Rowan Hamilton *minister*

Blue Point
†Daly, James Joseph *bishop*

Bronx
Dulles, Avery *priest, theologian*
Fahey, Charles Joseph *priest, gerontology educator*
Hatcher, Baldwin *minister, educator*
Hennessy, Thomas Christopher *clergyman, educator, retired university dean*
Hunt, George William *priest, magazine editor*
Kirmse, Sister Anne-Marie Rose *nun, educator, researcher*
Parker, Everett Carlton *clergyman*
Ruffing, Janet Kathryn *spirituality educator*

Bronxville
L'Huillier, Peter (Peter) *archbishop*
Schneider, David Paul *church administrator*

Brooklyn
Al-Hafeez, Humza *minister, editor*
Baltakis, Paul Antanas *bishop*
†Barbarito, Gerald Michael *bishop*
Bowers, John Carl *minister*
Critchlow, Edith Hope *minister*
Daily, Thomas V. *bishop*
Gross, Abraham *rabbi, educator*
†Henschel, Milton G. *church administrator*
Huneke, John George *minister*
Sorscher, Marvin Loeb *religious studies educator, rabbi*
Sullivan, Joseph M. *bishop*
Williams, Carl E., Sr. *bishop*

Buffalo
Grosz, Edward M. *bishop*
Head, Edward Dennis *bishop*
Jerge, Marie Charlotte *minister*
Mansell, Henry J. *bishop*
Smith, Bennett Walker *minister*
Snyder, Robert Carl *minister*

Canton
O'Connor, Daniel William *retired religious studies and classical languages educator*

Chautauqua
Mackenzie, John Anderson Ross *educator*

Cohoes
Kreutz, Austin Thomas *clergyman*

College Point
Harvey, Joel *chaplain, educator*

Corning
Davis, Francis Raymond *priest*

Douglaston
Valero, René Arnold *clergyman*

Dover Plains
Arnold, Doris Foltz *minister, former health care administrator*

East Aurora
Hayes, Bonaventure Francis *priest*

East Meadow
Grassano, Thomas David *minister*

Far Rockaway
Kelly, George Anthony *clergyman, author, educator*

Garrison
Egan, Daniel Francis *priest*

Geneva
Coon, Penny K. *religious organization official*

Glen Cove
Costa, Thomas Charles *priest*

Gloversville
Rhodes, Alan Charles *minister*

Grand Island
Backus, Kevin Michael *minister*

Hyde Park
Pastrana, Ronald Ray *Christian ministry counselor, theology and biblical studies educator, former school system administrator*

Ithaca
Clarkson, George Edward *theology educator, minister*

Jamaica
†Catanello, Ignatius Anthony *bishop*
Connolly-Weinert, Francis David *theology educator*
Heaney-Hunter, Joann Catherine *theology educator*
Zirkel, Patricia McCormick *theology educator, researcher*

Kingston
Tsirpanlis, Constantine N. *theology, philosophy, classics and history educator*

Lackawanna
McNair McAllister, Hazel *pastor, educator, writer*

Lawrence
Wurzburger, Walter Samuel *rabbi, philosophy educator*

Lily Dale
Merrill, Joseph Hartwell *religious association executive*

Lindenhurst
Hamilton, Daniel Stephen *clergyman*

Maryknoll
Ellsberg, Robert Boyd *religious press editor*
LaVerdiere, Claudette Marie *sister, head religious order*

Mount Vernon
Richardson, W. Franklyn *minister*

Naples
†Flory, Sheldon *retired clergyman, poet*

New Hyde Park
Daley, John Terence *priest*

New Rochelle
Kelly, James Anthony *priest*

New York
Anderson, Fred Richard *minister*
Balter, Bernice *religious organization administrator*
Barsamian, Khajag Sarkis *primate*
Bradsell, Kenneth Raymond *minister*
Caliandro, Arthur *minister*
Chanes, Jerome Alan *non-profit organization administrator, public affairs analyst*
Chinnis, Pamela P. *religion organization administrator*
Church, Frank Forrester *minister, author, columnist*
Ciangio, Sister Donna Lenore *religious organization administrator*
Cohen, Samuel Israel *clergyman, organization executive*
Cone, James Hal *theologian, educator, author*
Corso, Susan Falk *minister*
Dorn, Louis Otto *minister, editor*
Driver, Tom Faw *theologian, writer, justice/peace advocate*
Field, Curtis Lincoln *church elder, library director*
Fretz, Mark Jonathan Hochstetler *editor, religion educator*
Friedman, Herbert A. *rabbi, educator, fund raising executive*
Geer, John Farr *retired religious organization administrator*
Ginsberg, Hersh Meier *rabbi, religious organization executive*
Goldstein, Niles Elliot *rabbi, author*
Greenberg, Irving *rabbi*
Grein, Richard Frank *bishop, pastoral theology educator*
Griswold, Frank Tracy, III *bishop*
Habecker, Eugene Brubaker *religious association executive*
Harman, Robert John *religious organization administrator*
Harris, Lyndon F. *priest*
Hawley, John Stratton *religious studies educator*
Howard, M(oses) William, Jr. *minister, seminary president*
Hughart, Thomas Arthur *minister*
Hunsberger, Alice Chandler *religion educator, human rights activist*
Johnson, Douglas Wayne *church organization official, minister*
Kazanjian, Shant *religious organization administrator*
†Kern, William Bliem, Jr. *minister*
Kraemer, David C. *theology educator*
Kreitman, Benjamin Zvi *rabbi, Judaic studies educator*
Laurus, (Laurus Skurla) *archbishop*
McGeady, Sister Mary Rose *religious organization administrator, psychologist*
Menuez, D. Barry *retired religious organization administrator*
Mestice, Anthony F. *bishop*
Miller, Israel *rabbi, university administrator*
Moore, Paul, Jr. *bishop*
Morris, Clayton Leslie *priest*
Morton, James Parks *priest*
Murphy, Peregine Leigh *priest*
Murray, Bernard Joseph *former theology educator, former municipal government administrator*
Nadich, Judah *rabbi*
Neuhaus, Richard John *priest, research institute president*
Norgren, William Andrew *religious denomination administrator*
O'Connor, John Joseph Cardinal *archbishop, former naval officer*
O'Keefe, Vincent Thomas *clergyman, educational administrator*
Ousley, John Douglas *priest*
Perry, David *priest*
Powers, Edward Alton *minister, educator*
Read, David Haxton Carswell *clergyman*
Riddle, Sturgis Lee *minister*
Rosenberg, Ellen Y. *religious association administrator*
Roth, Sol *rabbi*
Rusch, William Graham *religious organization administrator*
Salisbury, Nancy *convent director*
Schindler, Alexander Moshe *rabbi, organization executive*
Schorsch, Ismar *clergyman, Jewish history educator*
Sharpton, Alfred Charles *minister, political activist*
Shriver, Donald Woods, Jr. *theology educator*
Siegel, Morton Kallos *religious organization administrator, educational administrator*
Sisk, Mark Sean *priest, seminary dean, religious educator, bishop*
Sohl, Joyce Darlene *religious organization administrator*
Solheim, James Edward *church executive, journalist*
†Spivak, Marc *rabbi, health administrator*
†Spyridon, (George C.P. George) *archbishop*
Stock, Ben *religious organization consultant*
Stolper, Pinchas Aryeh *religious organization executive, rabbi*
Tannenbaum, Bernice Salpeter *religious organization executive*
Tertzakian, Hovhannes *bishop*
Thurman, Robert *theology, religious studies educator*
Truesdell, Walter George *minister, librarian*
Twiname, John Dean *minister, health care executive*
Vessup, Jolene Adriel *pastoral counselor*
Wiener, Marvin S. *rabbi, editor, executive*
†Wolneki, Stephen S. *church administrator*
†Yoffie, Erich H. (Rabbi) *church administrator*

Newport
Wilson, Eldon Ray *minister*

Nyack
Mann, Kenneth Walker *retired minister, psychologist*

Pawling
Peale, Ruth Stafford (Mrs. Norman Vincent Peale) *religious leader*
Stonesifer, John DeWitt *Episcopal priest, educator*

Pelham
Gorman, Leo Joseph *priest*

Pine Bush
Wilson, David Palir *evangelist*

Poughkeepsie
Glasse, John Howell *retired philosophy and theology educator*
Harmelink, Herman, III *clergyman, author, educator, ecumenist*

Rochester
Clark, Matthew Harvey *bishop*
Gripe, Alan Gordon *minister*
Hickey, Dennis Walter *retired bishop*
Wehner, Sister Mary B. *pastoral counselor, spiritual director*

Rockville Center
McHugh, James T. *bishop*

Rockville Centre
McGann, John Raymond *bishop*

Rosedale
Chan, Henry Albert *minister*

Rye
Iakovos, (Demetrios A. Coucouzis) *retired archbishop*

Scarsdale
Goodwin, Everett Carlton *minister*
Rubenstein, Jacob Samuel *rabbi*

Setauket
Gard, Richard Abbott *religious institute executive, educator*

Speculator
Kelly, Paul John *priest*

Spencerport
Webster, Gordon Visscher, Jr. *minister*

Spring Valley
Stedge-Fowler, Joyce *retired clergywoman*

Staten Island
Bogholtz, William E. *minister*

Stony Brook
Von Gonten, Kevin Paul *priest, liturgist, theologian*

Syosset
Hull, Gretchen Gaebelein *lay worker, writer, lecturer*
Lazor, Theodosius (His Beatitude Metropolitan Theodosius) *archbishop*
†Theodosius, (Most Blessed Theodosius) *archbishop*

Syracuse
Costello, Thomas Joseph *bishop*
†Moynihan, James M. *bishop*
Schiess, Betty Bone *priest*
Wiggins, James Bryan *religion educator*

Troy
Phelan, Thomas *clergyman, academic administrator, educator*

West Shokan
Mackey, Jeffrey Allen *priest*

Westbury
De Pauw, Gommar Albert *priest, educator*

White Plains
Kabakoff, Jacob *retired religious studies educator*

Williamsville
Jones, Robert Alfred *retired clergyman*

Wolcott
Searle, Robert Ferguson *minister*

Woodside
Vasilachi, Vasile Gheorghe *priest, vicar*

Youngstown
Lamb, Charles F. *minister*

NORTH CAROLINA

Angier
McClain, Gregory David *minister*

Boiling Springs
Arnold, Ernest Woodrow *minister*
Hearne, Stephen Zachary *minister, educator*
Lamb, Robert Lee *religious studies educator*

Brevard
Flory, Margaret Martha *retired religious organization administrator*

Cary
Harvey, Daniel Richard *minister*

Chapel Hill
Dixon, John Wesley, Jr. *retired religion and art educator*
Van Seters, John *biblical literature educator*

Charlotte
Curlin, William G. *bishop*
Grigg, Eddie Garman *minister, educator*
Michael, Caroline Marshall *religious organization administrator*
Oliver, John William Posegate *minister*
Prosser, Bruce Reginal, Jr. (Bo Prosser) *minister, consultant*
Reeves, John Craig *religious studies educator*
Ross, David Edmond *church official*
Sustar, T. David *college president*
Walker, Jewett Lynius *clergyman, church official*

Clyde
Rogers, Garry Lee *minister, medical technician*

Concord
Sloop, Gregory Todd *clergyman*

Dunn
Blackman, Danny *religious organization administrator*
Davis, Dolly *religious organization administrator*
Heath, Preston *clergy member, religious organization administrator*

Durham
Efird, James Michael *theology educator*
Langford, Thomas Anderson *retired theology educator, academic administrator*
McCarthy, David Bruce *minister*
Meyers, Eric Mark *religion educator*
Smith, Harmon Lee, Jr. *clergyman, moral theology educator*
Steinmetz, David Curtis *religion educator, publisher, minister*
Westbrook, Don Arlen *minister*

Elizabethtown
Taylor, David Wyatt Aiken *retired clergyman*

Ellenboro
Burgin, Max Edward *minister, farmer*

Fairview
Eck, David Wilson *minister*

Greensboro
Dziordz, Walter Michael *priest*
Hull, James Ernest *religion and philosophy educator*
Rights, Graham Henry *minister*

Greenville
Heath, Jeffrey Dale *minister*
Jackson, Bobby Rand *minister*
Thompson, Emerson McLean, Jr. *retired clergyman*
Wood, Gerald David *religious organization administrator*

Harrisburg
Helton, Max Edward *minister, consultant, religious organization executive*

Havelock
Lindblade, Eric Norman, Jr. *minister*

Haw River
Poindexter, Richard Grover *minister*

Hendersonville
Sims, Bennett Jones *minister, educator*
Trexler, Edgar Ray *minister, editor*

Hickory
Kyker, Charles Clinton *pastor*
McDaniel, Michael Conway Dixon *bishop, retired theology educator*

High Point
Weatherford, Ronald Jeffrey *minister*

Lake Junaluska
Goodgame, Gordon Clifton *minister*
Hale, Joseph Rice *church organization executive*
Tullis, Edward Lewis *retired bishop*

Manteo
Miller, William Lee, Jr. *minister*

Marshville
Steagald, Thomas Ray *minister*

Mill Spring
Osborn, Christopher Raymoln, Jr. *minister*

Pikeville
Sauls, Don *clergyman*

Raleigh
Gossman, Francis Joseph *bishop*
Huffman, David Curtis *minister*
Johnson, Peter Ray *minister*
Kirkley, James Franklin *religion and ethics educator*
Lolley, William Randall *minister*
†Malone, Elmer Taylor, Jr. *religious organization administrator*

Sapinsley, Elbert Lee *rabbi*

Roanoke Rapids
Alves, Robert Mark *priest*

Robbins
Mac Kenzie, James Donald *clergyman*

Rocky Mount
Smith, Preston *minister*
Weaver, James Paul *retired clergyman*

Shelby
Cagle, Terry Dee *clergyman*

Southport
Harrelson, Walter Joseph *minister, religion educator emeritus*

Steadman
Taylor, David *clergy member, religious administrator*

Wake Forest
Blackmore, James Herrall *clergyman, educator, author*

Wallace
Johnson, James Wilson *pastor*

Waynesville
Lundy, Robert Fielden *minister*

Wilmington
†Conser, Walter Hurley, Jr. *religion and philosophy educator*
Stokes, John Lemacks, II *clergyman, retired university official*

Winston Salem
Beach, Franklin Darrel *minister*
Boger, Richard Edwin, Jr. *minister*
Capps, Richard Henry *minister*
Fitzgerald, Ernest Abner *retired bishop*
Martin, James Alfred, Jr. *religious studies educator*
Spach, Jule Christian *church executive*
Talbert, Charles Harold *retired religion educator*
Winn, Albert Curry *clergyman*

NORTH DAKOTA

Bismarck
Fry, Charles George *theologian, educator*
Montz, Florence Stolte *church official*

Fargo
Foss, Richard John *bishop*
Sullivan, James Stephen *bishop*

OHIO

Ashland
Waters, Ronald W. *educator, church executive, pastor*
Watson, JoAnn Ford *theology educator*

Beavercreek
Bennett, Anna Dell *minister, religion educator, retired elementary school educator*
Clarke, Cornelius Wilder *religious organization administrator, educator*

Bowling Green
Versteeg, Robert John *clergyman, dramatic artist, author*

Canton
Watson, Duane Frederick *religious studies educator*

Chesterland
Ruble, Bernard Roy *educator, minister, labor relations consultant*

Cincinnati
Adams, Mendle Eugene *minister*
Anderson, Joan Balyeat *religion educator, minister*
Bokenkotter, Thomas Stephen *clergyman*
Harrington, Jeremy Thomas *clergyman, publisher*
Linsey, Nathaniel L. *bishop*
Maher, Terry Marina *religious organization administrator*
†Moeddel, Carl K. *bishop*
Molitor, Sister Margaret Anne *nun, former college president, archivist*
Perry, Norman Robert *priest, magazine editor*
Pilarczyk, Daniel Edward *archbishop*
Thompson, Herbert, Jr. *bishop*
Wallace, Betty Louise Dollar *retired religious educator*
Walter, Gerry Henry *rabbi*

Circleville
Norman, Jack Lee *church administrator, consultant*
Tipton, Daniel L. *religious organization executive*

Clayton
Stutzman, L. Lee *pastor*

Cleveland
Abrams, Sylvia Fleck *religious studies educator*
Buhrow, William Carl *religious organization administrator*
Cohen, Armond E. *rabbi*
Dipko, Thomas Earl *minister, national church executive*
Holck, Frederick H. George *priest, educator*
Knull, Erhard *minister*
Osvath, Ludovic Lajos *minister*
Pilla, Anthony Michael *bishop*
Sherry, Paul Henry *minister, religious organization administrator*
Williams, Arthur Benjamin, Jr. *bishop*

Cleveland Heights
Jackson, Cedric Douglas Tyrone, Sr. *minister*
†Zierler, Lawrence Stephen *rabbi, community leader*

Columbus
Darling, George Curtis *minister, administrator*
Donovan, Dennis Dale *priest*
Jackson, David Gordon *religious organization administrator*
Plagenz, George Richard *minister, journalist, columnist*
Simms, Lowelle *synod executive*
Watson, John Allan *clergyman*

Delaware
Lattimore, Vergel Lyronne *minister, educator, counselor*

Dublin
Baker, Mary Evelyn *church librarian, retired academic librarian*

Englewood
Shearer, Velma Miller *clergywoman*

Findlay
Resseguie, James Lynn *theology educator*
Wallen, Raeburn Glenn *religion educator*
Wilkin, Richard Edwin *clergyman, religious organization executive*

Gates Mills
Obloy, Leonard Gerard *priest*

Granville
Woodyard, David Oliver *religious studies educator, clergy member*

Hubbard
Ehrlich, Lawrence *retired cantor, educator*

Ironton
Cremeans, James L. *minister*

Lakeside
Mead, Millard Wilmer *retired minister*

London
Hughes, Clyde Matthew *religious denomination executive*

Lorain
Quinn, Alexander James *bishop*

Loveland
Grimmet, Alex J. *clergyman, school administrator, elementary and secondary education educator*

Maumee
Yeager, Robert Julius *priest, financial consultant*

New Albany
Brown, Michael Richard *minister*

Niles
Cornell, William Harvey *clergyman*

Oberlin
Zinn, Grover Alfonso, Jr. *religion educator*

Oregonia
†McCollister, Cynthia A. *minister*

Pandora
Stucky, Ken *clergy member, church organization administrator, foundation executive*

Parma
Moskal, Robert M. *bishop*

South Euclid
Mehok, Edward Eugene *priest, English and theology educator*

Springfield
Berridge, Paul Thomas *minister*
Fullmer, Lee Wayne *minister*
Moose, Elton LeRoy *minister, counselor, senior center executive*

Steubenville
†Ottenweller, Albert Henry *bishop*
Sheldon, Gilbert Ignatius *clergyman*

Struthers
Sugden, Richard Lee *pastor*

Sunbury
Griffin, Larry Allen *minister, evangelist*

Toledo
Donnelly, Robert William *bishop*
Hoffman, James R. *bishop*
James, William Morgan *bishop*
Matthews, Christian William, Jr. *minister*
White, Polly Sears *religious organization administrator*

Van Wert
McCune, Barry Lynn *minister*

Waverly
Hays, Richard Secrest *minister*

Westerville
Schultz, Arthur LeRoy *clergyman, educator*

Wickliffe
Pevec, Anthony Edward *bishop*

Wilmington
Brindle, David Lowell *minister*

Worthington
Browning, Robert Lynn *educator, clergyman*
Craig, Judith *bishop*

Youngstown
Byrd, Swettie Lee *minister*
Franzetta, Benedict C. *bishop*

OKLAHOMA

Bethany
Johnson, John Randall, Sr. *religious organization administrator*
Leggett, James Daniel *bishop*

Broken Arrow
Janning, Sister Mary Bernadette *nun, retired association executive*

Lawton
Young, J. A. *bishop*

Oklahoma City
Beltran, Eusebius Joseph *archbishop*
Benson, Travis Theo "Doc" *minister, association administrator*
Jones, Charles Edwin *historian, bibliographer, chaplain*
Kuner, Charles Michael *minister*
Moody, Robert M. *bishop*
Neaves, Norman Earl *minister*
Ridley, Betty Ann *educator, church worker*
Sheldon, Eli Howard *minister*
Simmons, Jesse Doyle *retired minister, educator*
Taylor-White-Grigsby, Queen Delores *minister, consultant*
White, James Robert *minister*

Purcell
Lucas, Roy Edward, Jr. *minister*

Seminole
Wantland, William Charles *retired bishop, lawyer*

Stillwater
Lawson, F. D. *bishop*

Tulsa
Cox, William Jackson *bishop*
Gottschalk, Sister Mary Therese *nun, hospital administrator*
Hatfield, William Keith *minister*
McGee, Glorea Hooks *religious organization adminstrator, minister*
Osborn, La Donna Carol *clergywoman*
Rex, Lonnie Royce *religious organization administrator*
Roberts, (Granville) Oral *clergyman*
Slattery, Edward J. *bishop*

Vici
McCoy, Carroll Pierce *retired minister*

OREGON

Beaverton
†Overlund, Ervin Kenneth *pastor*
Palau, Luis *evangelist*

Bend
Connolly, Thomas Joseph *bishop*

Coquille
Potter, Kenneth Roy *retired minister*

Corvallis
Borg, Marcus Joel *theologian, theology educator*
Dennis, John Davison *minister*
McCarthy, William Robert *minister*
Steiner, Kenneth Donald *bishop*

Dallas
Calkins, Loren Gene *church executive, clergyman*

Eugene
Sanders, Jack Thomas *religious studies educator*

Hillsboro
Curry, Everett William, Jr. *minister*
Rice, Richard Lee, Jr. *minister, office manager*

Hood River
Browning, Edmond Lee *retired bishop*

Keizer
Null, Paul Bryan *minister*

Lake Oswego
Ladehoff, Robert Louis *bishop*

Pendleton
Nichols, Albert Myron *minister*

Philomath
Stensvad, Allan Maurice *minister*

Portland
Langrock, Karl Frederick *former academic administrator*
Morgan, Gwendolyn Jean *minister, writer*
Powell, Charles William *coach, former minister*
Richards, Herbert East *minister emeritus, commentator*
Riddle, Earl Waldo *retired church official, small business owner*

Salem
Muntz, J(ohn) Richard *clergyman*

Wilsonville
Gross, Hal Raymond *bishop*

PENNSYLVANIA

Akron
Lapp, John Allen *retired religious organization administrator*

Allentown
†Cullen, Edward Peter *bishop*
Hemmerle, Dave Chris *missionary*

Ardmore
†Maginnis, Robert P. *bishop*

Auburn
Ruof, Richard Alan *clergyman*

Bensalem
Bevan, Norman Edward *religious organization executive*

Bethel Park
Funka, Thomas Howard *minister*

Bethlehem
†Caldwell, Douglas W. *clergyman*
Mraz, John Stephen *Roman Catholic priest*
Steffen, Lloyd Howard *minister, religion educator*

Brackney
Carlson, Paul Robins *Presbyterian minister, author*

Bradford
Cox, J. Arthur *minister*

Camp Hill
Johnston, Thomas McElree, Jr. *church administrator*
McNutt, Charlie Fuller, Jr. *retired bishop*

Carlisle
Reed, David LaRue *minister*

Chambersburg
Fleming, Steven Robert *minister*

Coatesville
Copeland, W(illiam) Joel, Jr. *clergyman*

Confluence
Bower, Roy Donald *minister, counselor*

Cranberry Township
Bashore, George Willis *bishop*
Tiller, Olive Marie *retired church worker*

Doylestown
Maser, Frederick Ernest *clergyman*

Drexel Hill
Thompson, William David *minister, homiletics educator*

Elizabethtown
Brown, Dale Weaver *clergyman, theologian, educator*
Johnson, Clarence Ray *minister*

Elkins Park
Maslin, Simeon Joseph *rabbi*
Shedinger, Robert Frederick *religious studies educator*

Ephrata
Young, David Samuel *minister*

Erie
Rowley, Robert Deane, Jr. *bishop*
Trautman, Donald W. *bishop*

Everett
Weaver, E(lvin) Paul *minister*

Forty Fort
Henderson, Robb Alan *minister*

Greenock
†Swift, James *minister*

Harleysville
Ritchings, Frances Anne *priest*

Harrisburg
Chambers, Clarice Lorraine *clergy, educational consultant*
Dattilo, Nicholas C. *bishop*
Ebaugh, David Paul *minister, school system administrator*
Edmiston, Guy S., Jr. *bishop*
Libert, John Clement *minister, theologian*

Haverford
Kee, Howard Clark *religion educator*

Havertown
Koenig, Robert Emil *clergyman*

Hillsgrove
Cox, Albert Edward *pastor*

Hollidaysburg
Adamec, Joseph Victor *bishop*

Huntingdon
Durnbaugh, Donald Floyd *church history educator, researcher*

Jim Thorpe
Umbehocker, Kenneth Sheldon *priest*

Johnstown
Miloro, Protopresbter Frank *church official, religious studies educator*
Nicholas, (Richard G. Smisko) *bishop*
Smisko, Nicholas Richard *bishop, educator*

Kingston
Evanofski, Bernard Peter *Roman Catholic priest*

Kittanning
†Sehring, Frederick Albert *dean*

Kutztown
Johnson, Nils, Jr. *minister*

Lancaster
Augsburger, Aaron Donald *clergyman*
Carlisle, James Patton *clergyman*

Glick, Garland Wayne *retired theological seminary president*

Lewisburg
Jump, Chester Jackson, Jr. *clergyman, church official*
Main, A. Donald *bishop*

Malvern
Brighton, Ruth Louise *lay worker, educator*

Mendenhall
Lee, Virginia Diane *lay worker*

Merion Station
Littell, Franklin Hamlin *theologian, educator*

Monroeville
Edelstein, Jason Zelig *rabbi, psychologist*

Myerstown
Schwenk, James Lee *minister, educator*

New Holland
West, Daniel Charles *lay worker, dentist*

New Stanton
Black, Cora Jean *evangelist, wedding consultant*

Paoli
Agnew, Christopher Mack *minister, historian*

Perkasie
Ritter, Paul Revere *retired minister*

Philadelphia
Bartlett, Allen Lyman, Jr. *retired bishop*
Bevilacqua, Anthony Joseph Cardinal *archbishop*
Birchard, Bruce *religious organization administrator*
Bracey, Cookie Frances Lee *minister*
Burch, Francis Floyd *clergyman, English educator*
Butz, Geneva Mae *pastor*
Darling, Pamela Ann Wood *religious consultant, educator*
De Simone, Louis A. *bishop*
Evangelista, Allan *clergy member, medical researcher*
Goldin, Judah *Hebrew literature educator*
Hammond, Charles Ainley *clergyman*
Harvey, William J. *religious service organization, religious publication editor*
Hickey, Gregory Joseph *priest, educational administrator*
Jones, O. T. *bishop*
Kraft, Robert Alan *history of religion educator*
Marple, Dorothy Jane *retired church executive*
Ryken, Philip Graham *minister, theologian*
Sangster, Verley Gene *youth ministry executive*
Sulyk, Stephen *archbishop*
Turner, Franklin Delton *bishop*
Wachs, Saul Philip *Jewish education educator*
Wengert, Timothy *church history educator, clergyman*

Pittsburgh
Brauner, Ronald Allan *religion educator*
Collins, Rose Ann *minister*
Drabiska, Frank John *priest, parochial school educator*
Koedel, Robert Craig *minister, historian, educator*
Lu, Sheldon Hsiao-peng *foreign literature educator*
Maximos, Metropolitan (Maximos Demetrios Aghiorgoussis) *bishop, metropolitan*
McCoid, Donald James *bishop*
Mc Dowell, John B. *bishop*
Muto, Susan Annette *religion educator, academic administrator*
Procyk, Judson M. *metropolitan archbishop*
Schaub, Marilyn McNamara *religion educator*
Shaffer, Terry George *pastor*
Wuerl, Donald W. *bishop*

Rebersburg
Kuhns, Nancy Evelyn *minister*

Rochester
Garlathy, Frank Bryan *minister*

Rydal
Black, Thomas Donald *retired religious organization administrator*

Salunga
Landis, Paul Groff *bishop, mission executive*

Scottdale
Schrock, Paul Melvin *editor*

Scranton
†Dougherty, John Martin *bishop*
Morse, Terry Wayne *clergyman*
Timlin, James Clifford *bishop*
Turel, Joan Marie *religious program director*

Selinsgrove
Clark, Beth *minister*

Seneca
Spring, Paull E. *bishop*

Skippack
Rothenberger, Jack Renninger *clergyman*

Souderton
Lapp, James Merrill *clergyman, marriage and family therapist*

Sunbury
Ely, Donald J(ean) *clergyman, secondary school educator*

Swarthmore
Frost, Jerry William *religion and history educator, library administrator*
Swearer, Donald Keeney *Asian religions educator, writer*

Tamaqua
Seifert, William Norman *priest, religion educator*

Tylersport
Raub, Donald Wilmer *minister, author*

Upper Darby
Clemens, David Allen *minister*
Livingston, Margery Elsie *missionary, clinical psychologist*

Valley Forge
Sundquist, John A. *religious organization executive*
Weiss, Daniel Edwin *clergyman, educator*
Wright-Riggins, Aidsand F., III *religious organization executive*

Valley View
Shankweiler, Carl David *minister*

Villanova
Palmer, Donald Curtis *interdenominational missionary society executive*

Warrington
Walker, Edwin Stuart, III *retired missionary organization executive*

Wayne
Rabii, Patricia Berg *church administrator*

Waynesburg
Visser, Richard Edgar *minister*

Willow Grove
Duff, Donald James *religious organization administrator*

Wynnewood
†Martino, Joseph F. *bishop*
McNally, Michael James *priest*
Sider, Ronald J. *theology educator, author*

Wyomissing
Hampton, Richard Clinton, Jr. *clergy member, therapist*

Yardley
Lynch, Sister Francis Xavier *nun, development director*

Yeadon
Logan, Thomas Wilson Stearly, Sr. *priest*

York
Strayer, Gene Paul *lay worker, educator*

RHODE ISLAND

Central Falls
Tajrá, Harry William Michael *theologian, religious writer*

Lincoln
Barlow, August Ralph, Jr. *minister*

Middletown
Demy, Timothy James *military chaplain*

Providence
Frerichs, Ernest Sunley *religious studies educator*
Milhaven, John Giles *religious studies and ethics educator*
Motte, Sister Mary Margaret *missionary*
Mulvee, Robert Edward *bishop*
Pearce, George Hamilton *archbishop*
Taylor, Richard Henry *minister*

Westerly
Looper, George Kirk *religious society executive*

SOUTH CAROLINA

Anderson
Burks, Robert Edward *minister, educator*
Wisler, Darla Lee *pastor*

Blythewood
Moore, Edward Raymond, Jr. *pastor, chaplain, campaign consultant*

Charleston
Donehue, John Douglas *interdenominational ministries executive*
Salmon, Edward Lloyd, Jr. *bishop*
Thompson, David B. *bishop*

Columbia
Adams, John Hurst *bishop*
Aull, James Stroud *retired bishop*
Brubaker, Lauren Edgar *minister, educator*
Gantt, Michael David *business executive*
Jones, Donald Lee *religious studies educator*
McCrory, Sarah Graydon *church lay leader, retired lawyer*
Perrin, K(arl) Eric *minister*

Due West
Farley, Benjamin Wirt *religious studies educator, writer*

Easley
Leith, John Haddon *clergyman, theology educator*

Florence
Baroody, Albert Joseph, Jr. *pastoral counselor*

Gaffney
Harrison, Richard Dean *minister, counselor*

Georgetown
Allison, Christopher FitzSimons *bishop*

Goose Creek
Johnson, Johnnie *bishop*

Greenville
Bell, Robert Daniel *religious studies educator*
McKnight, Edgar Vernon *religion educator*

Greenwood
Armfield, Fred Munger *minister*

Greer
Baldwin, Leroy Franklin *minister*

Heath Springs
Feagin, Eugene Lloyd *pastor*

Leesville
Crumley, James Robert, Jr. *retired clergyman*

Mauldin
Phillips, James Oscar *minister*

Newberry
Martell, Denise Mills *lay worker*

North Myrtle Beach
Kantner, Helen Johnson *church education administrator*

Spartanburg
Bullard, John Moore *religion educator, church musician*
Ely, Elizabeth Wickenberg *priest*
Fogartie, James Eugene *retired clergyman*

Taylors
Smith, Morton Howison *religious organization administrator, educator*
Vaughn, John Carroll *minister, educator*

Winnsboro
McCants, Clyde Taft *retired clergyman*

SOUTH DAKOTA

Freeman
Roussos, Stephen Bernard *minister*

Sioux Falls
Carlson, Robert James *bishop*
Cowles, Ronald Eugene *church administrator*

Watertown
Witcher, Gary Royal *minister, educator*

TENNESSEE

Antioch
Worthington, Melvin Leroy *minister, writer*

Brentwood
Bennett, Harold Clark *clergyman, religious organization administrator*
Porch, James Milton *religious organization administrator*

Chattanooga
Maloney, J. Patrick *minister, educator, seminary administrator*
Mohney, Nell Webb *religion educator, speaker, author*
Ragon, Robert Ronald *clergyman*

Cleveland
Albert, Leonard *religious organization executive*
Alford, Delton Lynol *religious organization executive*
Baker, Michael Lyndon *minister*
Gillum, Perry Eugene *religious organization administrator, minister*
Rayburn, Billy J. *Church administrator*
Reyes, Jose Antonio, Sr. *minister*
Taylor, William Al *church administrator*
Vaughan, Roland *church administrator*
Walker, Donald Murray *minister*

Collierville
Ratzlaff, David Edward *minister*

Cookeville
Adkisson, Randall Lynn *minister*

Franklin
Young, William Edgar *religious organization official*

Greeneville
Starks, Charles Wiley *minister*

Hermitage
Chambers, Curtis Allen *clergyman, church communications executive*

Jackson
Maynard, Terrell Dennis *minister*

Johnson City
Bradford, Michael Lee *religious organization administrator, clergyman*
Phillips, Dorothy Alease *lay church worker, educator, freelance writer*

Kingsport
Robelot, Milton Paul *deacon, architect*

Knoxville
Stooksbury, William Claude *minister*

La Follette
Eads, Ora Wilbert *clergyman, church official*

Loudon
Jones, Robert Gean *religion educator*
†Puckett, Robert Marion *clergyman*

Madison
Spillers, James Andrew *Bible and history educator, minister*

Mc Minnville
Gammon, James Edwin, Sr. *clergyman*

Memphis
Fussell, Keith Baugus *minister*
Magrill, Joe Richard, Jr. *religious organization administrator, minister*
Nichols, William Howard, Jr. *minister*
Steib, James Terry *bishop*
Todd, Virgil Holcomb *clergyman, religion educator*

Milton
Coaker, George Mack *minister*

Mount Juliet
Beeman, Bob Joe *minister*

Murfreesboro
Walker, David Ellis, Jr. *educator, minister, consultant*

Nashville
Baker, Cosette Marlyn *religion writer, editor*
Boucher, Pamela Kay *church consultant, editor*
Chapman, Morris Hines *denominational executive*
Draper, James Thomas, Jr. (Jimmy Draper) *clergyman*
Hall, Richard Clyde, Jr. *religious educational administrator*
Harrod, Howard Lee *religion educator*
Jones, Kathryn Cherie *pastor*
Kmiec, Edward Urban *bishop*
†Land, Richard Dale *minister, religious organization administrator*
Martin, Theodore Halliwell *minister*
McInteer, Jim Bill *minister, publishing executive, farmer*
Mills, Liston Oury *theology educator*
Niedergeses, James D. *bishop*
†Patterson, Paige *church administrator, former seminary president*
Pursell, Cleo Wilburn *church official*
Wray, Harmon Lee *religious organization administrator, religious studies educator*

Sewanee
Hughes, Robert Davis, III *theological educator*
Lytle, Guy Fitch, III *priest, educator, dean*

Signal Mountain
Hall, Thor *religion educator*

Springfield
Fagan, A. Rudolph *minister*

Waverly
Doyle, Lloyd Allen, III *minister*

TEXAS

Abilene
Baird, Larry Don *minister, nurse*

Aledo
Barton, Charles David *religious studies educator, author, researcher, historian*

Amarillo
Klein, Jerry Lee, Sr. *religion educator, minister*
Matthiesen, Leroy Theodore *retired bishop*

Arlington
Lingerfelt, B. Eugene, Jr. *minister*
Machle, Edward Johnstone *emeritus educator*

Austin
Bernard, David Kane *minister, writer, editor*
Gardner, Dan Nobles *deacon, church official*
Mc Carthy, John Edward *bishop*
Wahlberg, Philip Lawrence *former bishop*

Beaumont
†Galante, Joseph A. *bishop*

Brownsville
Fitzpatrick, John J. *bishop*
Pena, Raymundo Joseph *bishop*

Brownwood
Smith, Robert Leonard *pastor, religious studies educator*

Canyon Lake
Reinhardt, Linda Kay *minister*

Cedar Hill
Lang, James Devore, Jr. *ministry executive*

Colleyville
Maddox, Roger Wayne *minister*

Corpus Christi
Doty, James Edward *pastor, psychologist*
Fleischer, Daniel *minister, religious organization administrator*
Lowe, J. Allen *minister*
Pivonka, Leonard Daniel *priest*

Cypress
Drennan, Harry Joseph *minister*

Dallas
Allen, John Carlton *minister*
Blue, J(ohn) Ronald *evangelical mission executive*
†Carnes, Joseph Sydney *clergyman*
Closser, Patrick Denton *radio evangelist, artist*
†Grahmann, Charles V. *bishop*
Gross, Harriet P. Marcus *religious studies and writing educator*
Harrell, Roy Harrison, Jr. *minister*
Haynes, J. Neauell *clergyman, bishop*
Herbener, Mark Basil *bishop*
Holleman, Sandy Lee *religious organization administrator*
Ingram, Osmond Carraway, Jr. *minister*
Kirby, James Edmund, Jr. *theology educator*
Oden, William Bryant *bishop, educator*

Pauley, Shirley Stewart *religious organization executive*
Pinson, William Meredith, Jr. *pastor, writer, administrator*
Robertson, Calvin Coolidge, Sr. *pastor*
†Rollins, Richard A. *religious association administrator*
Smith, James G. *minister, educator*
Valentine, Foy Dan *clergyman*
Wiles, Charles Preston *minister*

De Soto
Jackson, Johnny W. *minister*
Lewis, Paul Wesley *minister*

Deer Park
Deutsch, Lawrence Ira *minister*

Fort Worth
Delaney, Joseph P. *bishop*
Edwards, Samuel Lee *religious organization executive*
Garrett, James Leo, Jr. *theology educator*
Gilbert, James Cayce *minister*
Hendricks, William Lawrence *theology educator*
Huey, F. B., Jr. *minister, theology educator*
Mathis, Robert Rex *church administrator, educator*
Newport, John Paul *philosophy of religion educator, former academic administrator*
Suggs, Marion Jack *minister, college dean*
Teegarden, Kenneth Leroy *clergyman*
Toulouse, Mark Gene *religion educator*

Frisco
Wicker, James Robert *minister*

Galveston
Wells, Robert Louis *priest*

Garland
Brockles, Arge James *pastor, educator*

Grand Prairie
Rose, Douglas Raymond *minister*

Houston
Arnold, James Phillip *religious studies educator, history educator*
Barrett, Michael Joseph *priest*
Bui, Long Van *church custodian, translator*
†Fiorenza, Joseph A. *bishop*
Guillory, Curtis J. *bishop*
Henderson, Nathan H. *bishop*
Hipps, Larry Clay *clergyman, evangelistic association executive*
Joyce, James Daniel *clergyman*
Karff, Samuel Egal *rabbi*
Kelber, Werner Heinz *religious educator*
McGary, Betty Winstead *minister, counselor, individual, marriage, and family therapist*
Meeks, Herbert Lessig, III *pastor, former school system administrator*
Montgomery, Cleothus *minister*
Nelson, John Robert *theology educator, clergyman*
Nielsen, Niels Christian, Jr. *theology educator*
Prokurat, Michael *religious studies educator, pastor*
Sampson, Franklin Delano *minister*
Stephens, Carson Wade *minister*

Jacksonville
Blaylock, James Carl *clergyman, librarian*
Pruitt, William Charles, Jr. *minister, educator*

Lake Whitney
Lawson, Carole Jean *religious educator, author, poet*

League City
Ellis, Walter Leon *minister*

Liberty
Hughes, Paul Anthony *minister, musician, songwriter, author, publisher*

Longview
Turner, Ellis Dale *clergyman, paint manufacturing executive*

Lubbock
Rodriguez, Placido *bishop*
Woodworth, Margo Deane *religious organization administrator*

Mcallen
Sutton, William Blaylock *pastor*

Mineral Wells
Reedy, Thomas Wayne *minister, theologian, educator*

Mount Pleasant
O'Donnell, Robert Patrick *priest*

Plano
Lee, Allan Wren *clergyman*

Quitman
Sutton, Jesse Noel *minister*

Richardson
Conrad, Flavius Leslie, Jr. *minister*
Williams, James Francis, Jr. *religious organization administrator*

San Angelo
Mathews, James Harold *minister*
Pfeifer, Michael David *bishop*

San Antonio
Barajas, Felipe Lara *deacon*
Culver, John Blaine *minister*
Fecher, Vincent John *priest*
Flores, Patrick F. *archbishop*
Fogg, Ernest Leslie *minister, retired*
Iglehart, T. D. *bishop*
Jacobson, David *rabbi*
Knox, Robert Burns *religious organization administrator*
Langlinais, Joseph Willis *educator, chaplain*
Leies, John Alex *theology educator, clergyman*
Mc Allister, Gerald Nicholas *retired bishop, clergyman*

Nix, Robert Lynn *minister*
Teran, Sister Mary Inez *retired nun, educator*

Spring
Hunt, T(homas) W(ebb) *retired religion educator*

The Woodlands
Sudbury, John Dean *religious foundation executive, petroleum chemist*

Tyler
Carmody, Edmond *bishop*
Hardy, William McDonald, Jr. *clergyman, physician assistant*

Van Alstyne
Daves, Don Michael *minister*

Victoria
†Fellhauer, David E. *bishop*

Waco
Chewning, Richard Carter *religious business ethics educator*
Flanders, Henry Jackson, Jr. *religious studies educator*
Wood, James E., Jr. *religion educator, author*

Waxahachie
Tschoepe, Thomas *bishop*

UTAH

Bountiful
Carter, Richard Bert *retired church official, retired government official*

Ogden
Harrington, Mary Evelina Paulson (Polly Harrington) *religious journalist, writer, educator*

Salt Lake City
Eyring, Henry Bennion *bishop*
Faust, James E. *church official*
†Haight, David B. *church official*
Hinckley, Gordon B. *church official*
†Holland, Jeffrey R. *religious organization administrator*
Masters, Lorraine Susanne *religious organization administrator*
Maxwell, Neal A. *church official*
Monson, Thomas Spencer *church official, former publishing company executive*
Niederauer, George H. *bishop*
Packer, Boyd K. *church official*
†Perry, L. Tom *church official, merchant*
†Scott, Richard G. *church official*
Smith, Eldred Gee *church leader*
†Wirthlin, Joseph B. *church official*

VERMONT

Burlington
Angell, Kenneth Anthony *bishop*
Martin, Luther Howard *religious studies educator*

Essex Junction
Davignon, Charles Philias *priest*

Middlebury
Ferm, Robert Livingston *religion educator*

Newport Center
MacKellar, James Marsh *minister*

Northfield
Wick, William Shinn *clergyman, chaplain*

Norwich
Post, Avery Denison *retired church official*

Pawlet
Buechner, Carl Frederick *minister, author*

West Glover
Hadash, Brendan Douglas *minister*

VIRGINIA

Accomac
Plonk, William McGuire *retired minister*

Amherst
Armstrong, Gregory Timon *religious studies educator, minister*

Amissville
Coutu, Charles Arthur *deacon*

Arlington
Loverde, Paul S. *bishop*
Lowe, Jeanne Catherine *pastor*

Big Island
Durham, John I. *retired religious studies educator*

Blacksburg
Grover, Norman LaMotte *theologian, philosopher*

Charlottesville
Childress, James Franklin *theology and medical educator*
Finley, Robert Van Eaton *minister*
Scott, Nathan Alexander, Jr. *minister, literary critic, religious educator*

Chesapeake
Stafford, Kenneth Victor, Sr. *minister*

Christiansburg
Brown, Shelby Jean Bailey *lay worker*

Churchville
Kirkland, Bryant Mays *clergyman*

Clarksville
Westbrook, Walter Winfield *minister*

Dillwyn
Davenport, James Guython *minister*

Fairfax
Southern, Lonnie Steven *minister*

Falls Church
Bankson, Marjory *religious association administrator*

Fincastle
Cummings, Kevin Bryan *minister*

Floyd
Cosby, John Canada *lay professional church worker, retired*

Fredericksburg
Bailey, Amos Purnell *clergyman, syndicated columnist*

Front Royal
Andes, Larry Dale *minister*

Gainesville
Austin, James Grover, Jr. *theologian, pastor, telecommunications manager*

Glen Allen
Collier, Roger Malcolm *minister*

Hampton
Dennis, Walter Decoster *suffragan bishop*
Henderson, Salathiel James *minister, clergy*

Harrisonburg
Burkholder, Owen Eugene *religious organization administrator*
Richardson, John MacLaren, Jr. *clergyman*

Keswick
Massey, Donald Wayne *Disciples of Christ minister, Episcopal minister, small business owner*

Lexington
Hodges, Louis Wendell *religion educator*

Lynchburg
Falwell, Jerry L. *clergyman*
†Morrison, John Douglas *theology and philosophy educator*

Manassas
Gustavson, Brandt *religious association executive*
Lumpkin, Vicki G. *minister*

Martinsville
McCann, Thomas Ryland, Jr. *minister*
Shackleford, William Alton, Sr. *minister*
Torrence, Billy Hubert *minister*

Mc Lean
Lotz, Denton *minister, church official*
Topping, Eva Catafygiotu *writer, lecturer, educator*
Wümpelmann, Knud Aage Abildgaard *clergyman, religious organization administrator*

Middletown
Ibach, Douglas Theodore *minister*

Midlothian
Lee, Jerome Odell *minister*

Mount Crawford
Creswell, Norman Bruce *minister*

North Tazewell
Oldham, William Edward *minister, accountant, educator*

Petersburg
Hart, Donald Purple *bishop*

Portsmouth
Thomas, Ted, Sr. *bishop*

Richmond
Aigner, Emily Burke *lay worker*
Barton, Jonathan Miller *clergyman*
Deekens, Elizabeth Tupman *writer*
De Vries, Dawn Ann *theology educator*
Dombalis, Constantine Nicholas *minister*
†Eutsler, R(alph) Kern *retired bishop, church finance consultant*
Gerrish, Brian Albert *theologian, educator*
Gray, Francis Campbell *bishop*
Gray, Frank C. *bishop*
Lee, Peter James *bishop*
McDonough, Reginald Milton *religious organization executive*
Moore, John Sterling, Jr. *minister*
Rogers, Isabel Wood *religious studies educator*
Smith, Russell Edward *priest*
Sullivan, Walter Francis *bishop*

Roanoke
Harding, Margaret Tyree *minister*
MacLean, Iain Stewart *religion educator*
Marmion, William Henry *retired bishop*

Rockbridge Baths
Patteson, Roy Kinneer, Jr. *retired clergyman, administrator*

Salem
Bansemer, Richard Frederick *bishop*

Staunton
Kopp, George Philip, Jr. *minister*

Sterling
Piper, Thomas Samuel *minister, consultant*

Thaxton
Buchanan, Ray Allen *clergyman*

Virginia Beach
Williams, John Rodman *theologian, educator*
†Windsor, Michael Harold *clergyman, educator*

Williamsburg
Holmes, David L. *religion educator*

Winchester
Kohl, Harold *missionary, educator*

Woodberry Forest
Campbell, Dennis Marion *educator, university administrator, theologian*

Woodbridge
Townsend, Kenneth Ross *retired priest*

Yorktown
Stinnette, Timothy Earl *minister*

WASHINGTON

Auburn
Dillon, Joseph Neil *pastor*
Maier, Anthony Alvin *pastor, counselor*

Camano Island
Blair, Edward Payson *theology educator*

Chehalis
Detrick, Donald Howard *minister*

Des Moines
Tuell, Jack Marvin *retired bishop*

Edmonds
Dunbar, R. Allan *college administrator, clergyman*

Goldendale
Watson, Darrell Valentine, Jr. *church administrator*

Index
Davis, Peter (Peter Pathfinder Davis) *priest*

Montesano
Clausel, Nancy Karen *minister*

Oak Harbor
Corey, Stuart Merton *minister*

Prosser
Cooper, Lynn Dale *retired minister, retired navy chaplain*

Renton
Warren, Larry Michael *clergyman*

Seattle
Brunett, Alexander J. *bishop*
Galvan, Elias Gabriel *bishop*
Hunthausen, Raymond Gerhardt *archbishop*
Mackenzie, Donald Matthew, Jr. *minister*
Pearce, Ann Ruble *minister*
Robb, John Wesley *religion educator*
Stevens, Robert William *church denomination administrator*
Warner, Vincent W. *bishop*
Zehr, Clyde James *church administrator*

Snohomish
Reese, Kerry David *minister*

Spokane
†Lee, Richard Francis James *evangelical clergyman, media consultant*
Skylstad, William S. *bishop*

Tacoma
Peterson, Thomas Charles *minister, pastoral counselor and therapist*
Wiegman, Eugene William *minister, former college administrator*
Wold, David C. *bishop*

Vancouver
Congdon, Roger Douglass *theology educator, minister*

WEST VIRGINIA

Barboursville
Vance, Charles Randall *minister*

Charleston
Ives, Samuel Clifton *minister*
Prichard, John David *minister*

Clarksburg
Reynolds, Lewis Dayton *pastor*

Fairmont
Stevens, Earl Patrick *minister*

Hinton
Glaser, Robert Harvey, Sr. *pastor*

Mannington
Peterson, Kristina J. *religious organization executive*

Morgantown
Cayton, Mary Evelyn *minister*
Hudson, David M. *minister*
Mili, Jude Joseph *priest, religious organization administrator*

Parkersburg
Aebi, Charles Jerry *minister, educator*

West Liberty
†Gold, Jonathan M. *philosophy and religion educator*

Wheeling
Schmitt, Bernard W. *bishop*

WISCONSIN

Bloomer
Prenzlow, Elmer John-Charles, Jr. *minister*

Brookfield
Gia-Russo, A(nthony) Paul *retired minister, lawyer*

Eau Claire
Kirby, H(arry) Scott *priest*

Green Bay
Banks, Robert J. *bishop*
Geisendorfer, James Vernon *author*
Morneau, Robert Fealey *bishop*
Noel, Donald Claude *clergyman, sculptor*

La Crosse
Burke, Raymond L. *bishop*

Lake Geneva
Slocum, Robert Boak *minister, educator*

Madison
Bullock, William Henry *bishop*
Enslin, Jon S. *bishop*
Fox, Michael Vass *Hebrew educator, rabbi*
Gwynne, Rober Harold *minister*
Little, George Daniel *clergyman*
Thomas, J. Mark *research fellow, sociology educator*
Wirz, George O. *bishop*

Mequon
Ratcliffe, Kermit Herman *theology educator*

Middleton
McDermott, Molly *lay minister*

Milwaukee
Hirsch, June Schaut *chaplain*
†Koelpin, Daniel Herbert *religious association administrator*
Radke, Dale Lee *religious organization administrator, deacon, editor, pastor*
Robertson, Michael Swing *church administrator*
Scarvie, Walter Bernard *clergyman*
†Sklba, Richard J. *bishop*
Stubbe, Ray William *minister, chaplain, author*
Wagner, Diane M(argaret) *theology educator*
Weakland, Rembert G. *archbishop*

Nashotah
Kriss, Gary W(ayne) *Episcopal priest*

Oshkosh
Barwig, Regis Norbert James *priest*
Sutter-Olson, Linda Kristine *minister*

Rice Lake
Alho, Sister Bonnie Kathleen *religion educator*

Superior
Fliss, Raphael M. *bishop*

Walworth
Rowland, David Kenneth *religious organization executive*

Watertown
Henry, Carl Ferdinand Howard *theologian*
Thompson, Richard Lloyd *pastor*
Williams, Edward Allen *religious educator, minister*

Waukesha
†Wallace, Stan W. *minister*

Wauwatosa
Wellumson, Douglas R. *religious organization administrator*

Windsor
Baumer, Martha Ann *minister*

WYOMING

Cheyenne
†Hart, Joseph H. *bishop*

Cody
Grimes, Daphne Buchanan *priest, artist*

Worland
Foster, William Silas, Jr. *minister*

TERRITORIES OF THE UNITED STATES

AMERICAN SAMOA

Pago Pago
Weitzel, John Quinn *bishop*

FEDERATED STATES OF MICRONESIA

Chuuk
Neylon, Martin Joseph *retired bishop*
†Samo, Amando *bishop*

GUAM

Agana
Apuron, Anthony Sablan *archbishop*

Yigo
Kio, Stephen Hre *minister*

PUERTO RICO

Caguas
Corrada del Rio, Alvaro *bishop*

Mayaguez
Casiano Vargas, Ulises Aurelio *bishop*

Ponce
Surinach Carreras, Ricardo Antonio *bishop*
Torres Oliver, Juan Fremiot *bishop*

San Juan
Aponte Martinez, Luis Cardinal *archbishop*

VIRGIN ISLANDS

Charlotte Amalie
Thomas, Elliott G. *bishop*

CANADA

ALBERTA

Calgary
Curtis, John Barry *archbishop*

Edmonton
Mac Neil, Joseph Neil *archbishop*

BRITISH COLUMBIA

Kamloops
Sabatini, Lawrence *bishop*

Richmond
Plomp, Teunis (Tony Plomp) *minister*

Vancouver
Exner, Adam *archbishop*
Wakefield, Wesley Halpenny *church official*

Victoria
De Roo, Remi Joseph *bishop*
Hollis, Reginald *archbishop*

MANITOBA

Churchill
Rouleau, Reynald *bishop*

Otterburne
McKinney, Larry *religious organization administrator*

Saint Boniface
Hacault, Antoine Joseph Leon *archbishop*

Winnipeg
Wall, Leonard J. *bishop*

NEW BRUNSWICK

Fredericton
Lemmon, George Colborne *bishop*

Rothesay
Troy, J. Edward *bishop*

NEWFOUNDLAND

Corner Brook
Payne, Sidney Stewart *retired archbishop*

Saint John's
Harvey, Donald Frederick *bishop*

NORTHWEST TERRITORIES

Yellowknife
Croteau, Denis *bishop*

NOVA SCOTIA

Parrsboro
Hatfield, Leonard Fraser *retired bishop*

Yarmouth
Wingle, James Mathew *bishop*

ONTARIO

Brampton
Bastian, Donald Noel *bishop, retired*

Burlington
Karsten, Albert *religious organization administrator*

Cambridge
MacBain, William Halley *minister, theology educator, seminary chancellor*

Campbellville
Georgije, Djokic *bishop*

Cornwall
La Rocque, Eugene Philippe *bishop*

Etobicoke
Coleman, K. Virginia *diaconal minister*

Hamilton
Tonnos, Anthony *bishop*

Kingston
Read, Allan Alexander *minister*
Spence, Francis John *archbishop*

Kitchener
Huras, William David *bishop*
Winger, Roger Elson *church administrator*

London
Peterson, Leslie Ernest *bishop*
Scott, W. Peter *bishop*
Sherlock, John Michael *bishop*

Manitowaning
Hamilton, Donald Gordon *religious association administrator*

Mississauga
Griffin, William Arthur *clergyman, religious organization executive*

Nova Scotia
Hooper, Wayne Nelson *clergy member*

Ottawa
Landriault, Jacques Emile *retired bishop*
Ryan, William Francis *priest*
Squire, Anne Marguerite *religious leader*
Wilson, Lois M. *minister*

Peterborough
Doyle, James Leonard *bishop*
Kristensen, John *church organization administrator*

Saint Catharines
O'Mara, John Aloysius *bishop*

Sault Sainte Marie
Ferris, Ronald Curry *bishop*

Scarborough
Mikloshazy, Attila *bishop*

Schumacher
Lawrence, Caleb James *bishop*

Toronto
Athanassoulas, Sotirios (Sotirios of Toronto) *bishop*
Carter, Gerald Emmett *retired archbishop*
Finlay, Terence Edward *bishop*
Jay, Charles Douglas *religion educator, college administrator, clergyman*
McWilliam, Joanne Elizabeth *retired religion educator*
Novak, David *Judaic studies educator, rabbi*
Plaut, Wolf Gunther *minister, author*
Tindal, Douglas Lorne *religious organization administrator*

Waterloo
Mills (Kutz-Harder), Helga *religious organization executive*

QUEBEC

Chicoutimi
Couture, Jean Guy *bishop*

Hull
Ebacher, Roger *archbishop*

Montreal
Hakim, Michel *religious leader*
Hutchison, Andrew Sandford *bishop*
Turcotte, Jean-Claude Cardinal *archbishop*

Outremont
Derderian, Hovnan *church official*

Quebec
Fortier, Jean-Marie *retired archbishop*
Stavert, Alexander Bruce *bishop*

Quebec City
Noel, Laurent *bishop, educator*

Rimouski
Blanchet, Bertrand *archbishop*

Rouyn
Hamelin, Jean-Guy *bishop*

Saint Jerome
Valois, Charles *retired bishop*

Sillery
Couture, Maurice *archbishop*

Valleyfield
Lebel, Robert *bishop*

SASKATCHEWAN

Muenster
Novecosky, Peter Wilfred *abbot*

Prince Albert
Burton, Anthony John *bishop*
Morand, Blaise E. *bishop*

Regina
Holm, Roy K. *church administrator*
Mallon, Peter *archbishop*

Saskatoon
Epp, Menno Henry *clergyman*
Jacobson, Sverre Theodore *retired minister*
Morgan, Thomas Oliver *bishop*

YUKON TERRITORY

Whitehorse
Lobsinger, Thomas *bishop*

MEXICO

Aguascalientes AGS
Godinez Flores, Ramon *auxiliary bishop*

Guadalajara
Sandoval Iniguez, Juan Cardinal *archbishop*

Mexico DF
†Rivera Carrera, Norberto Cardinal *archbishop*

San Nicolas de Garza
Suarez Rivera, Adolfo Antonio *archbishop*

BELGIUM

Brussels
Jadot, Jean Lambert Octave *clergyman*

BRAZIL

Rio de Janeiro
Sales, Eugenio de Araujo Cardinal *archbishop*

ENGLAND

London
Hornyak, Eugene Augustine *bishop*
Rader, Paul Alexander *minister, administrator*
Van Culin, Samuel *religious organization administrator*

Oxford
Gulbrandsen, Natalie Webber *religious association administrator*

Tunbridge Wells
Howden, Frank Newton *Episcopal priest, humanities educator*

IRAN

Tehran
Dinkha, Mas Kh'nanya, IV *church administrator*

ITALY

Rome
Audet, Leonard *theologian*
Baum, William Wakefield Cardinal *archbishop*
†Gagnon, Edouard Cardinal *ecclesiastic*

JAPAN

Nagano-ken
Wahl, Thomas Peter *priest, monk, educator*

Nara
Miyata, Gen *history of religion educator*

THE PHILIPPINES

Pasay
Lim, Sonia Yii *minister*

REPUBLIC OF KOREA

APO AE
Tille, James Eugene *army chaplain*

Inchon
McNaughton, William John *bishop*

SAINT LUCIA

Castries
Felix, Kelvin Edward *archbishop*

VATICAN CITY

Vatican City
Foley, John Patrick *archbishop*

John Paul, His Holiness Pope, II (Karol Jozef Wojtyla) *bishop of Rome*
†Stafford, James Francis *archbishop*
Szoka, Edmund Casimir Cardinal *archbishop*

ADDRESS UNPUBLISHED

Ambrozic, Aloysius Matthew (His Eminence Aloysius Cardinal Ambrozio) *cardinal archbishop*
Anderson, John Firth *church administrator, librarian*
Arledge-Benko, Patricia *retired minister*
Armstrong, (Arthur) James *educator, consultant, lecturer, writer*
Baehr, Theodore *religious organization administrator, communications executive*
Barker, Verlyn Lloyd *retired minister, educator*
Barnes, Rosemary Lois *minister*
Barnett, James Monroe *rector, author*
Bauer, Judy Marie *minister*
Bayne, David Cowan *priest, legal scholar, law educator*
Bechtol, Larry Owen *pastor*
Bell, Scott Lee *pastor*
Bender, Ross Thomas *minister*
Bensoussan, Abraham *rabbi*
Bersin, Ruth Hargrave *priest, social services administrator*
Bodey, Richard Allen *minister, educator*
Bollback, Anthony George *minister*
Boone, John Lewis *religious organization administrator*
Borecky, Isidore *bishop*
Bosco, Anthony Gerard *bishop*
Bothwell, John Charles *archbishop*
Bryant, Roy, Sr. *bishop*
Bubar, Joseph Bedell, Jr. *church official*
Burkholder, Timothy James *religious organization administrator*
Capon, Edwin Gould *church organization administrator, clergyman*
Cavins, William Robert *deacon, educator*
Charlton, Gordon Taliaferro, Jr. *retired bishop*
Ching, Julia *philosophy and religion educator*
Christopher, Sharon A. Brown *bishop*
Chrysostomos, (González-Alexopoulos) *archbishop, clergyman, psychologist, educator*
Clymer, Wayne Kenton *bishop*
Cobb, John Boswell, Jr. *clergyman, educator*
Cole, Clifford Adair *clergyman*
†Corripio Ahumada, Ernesto Cardinal *retired archbishop*
Crabtree, Davida Foy *minister*
Derickson, Stanley Lewis *minister, writer*
Dirksen, Richard Wayne *canon precentor, organist, choirmaster*
Douty, Robert Watson *minister, educator*
†Dudick, Michael Joseph *retired bishop*
Duecker, Robert Sheldon *retired bishop*
Dunn, Margaret Ann *religious studies educator, administrator, minister*
Eitrheim, Norman Duane *bishop*
Ellis, Howard Woodrow *evangelist, creative agent, clergyman, artist, author*
Ely, Laurence Driggs, III *theoretical Christian astrologer*
Epp, Eldon Jay *religion educator*
Epps, William David *priest*
Erickson, James Huston *clergyman, physician*
Fajen, John Herman *minister*
Farrar, Martha Ann *lay worker, retired gift shop owner*
†Fillman, G. Allan *priest, educator*
Fisher, Robert Bruce *priest*
Fricklas, Anita Alper *religious organization administrator*
Frost, Linda Gail *clergyman, hospital chaplain*
Fry, Malcolm Craig *retired clergyman*
Gandolfo, Lucian John *minister, federal official*
Garmendia, Francisco *bishop*
Gemignani, Michael Caesar *clergyman, retired educator*
Grant, Leonard Tydings *clergyman*
Grasso, Anthony Robert *priest, educator*
Gregory, Myra May *religious organization administrator, educator*
Griffin, James Anthony *bishop*
Gutmann, Reinhart Bruno *clergyman, social worker*
Haberer, John Henry, Jr. *minister*
†Hales, Robert D. *church official*
Hambidge, Douglas Walter *archbishop*
Hamilton, David Eugene *minister, educator*
Hansen, Wendell Jay *clergyman, gospel broadcaster*
Harris, Rogers Sanders *bishop*
Hayes, Charles *religious organization executive, clergyman*
Hernandez, Ramon Robert *retired clergyman and librarian*
Holle, Reginald Henry *retired bishop*
Hoops, William James *clergyman*
Hughes, Edward T. *retired bishop*
Hummel, Gene Maywood *retired bishop*
Hunt, George Nelson *bishop*
Hurn, Raymond Walter *minister, religious order administrator*
Johnson, Alice Elaine *retired academic administrator*
Johnson, Don Robert *religious organization leader, administrator*
Johnson, Gordon Gilbert *religion educator, minister*
Johnson, Jennie *chaplain, social worker*
†Johnson, Jone E. *clergy member*
Jones, Elizabeth Selle *minister*
Jones, William Augustus, Jr. *retired bishop*
Joslin, David Bruce *bishop*
Kalkwarf, Leonard V. *minister*
Keeler, William Henry *cardinal*
Keyser, Charles Lovett, Jr. *bishop*
Kidd, James Lambert *retired minister*
King, Charles Benjamin *minister*
Kucera, Daniel William *retired bishop*
Laha, Robert Randall, Jr. *minister*
Lamar, Martha Lee *chaplain*
Landes, George Miller *biblical studies educator*
Lansdale, H. Parker *minister, historian, non-profit administrator*
Légaré, Henri Francis *archbishop*
Light, Arthur Heath *bishop*
Lohmuller, Martin Nicholas *bishop*
Loppnow, Milo Alvin *clergyman, former church official*
Losten, Basil Harry *bishop*
Lotz, Linda Ann *religious organizer*
Lucas, Bert Albert *pastor, social services administator, consultant*
Luetkehoelter, Gottlieb Werner (Lee) *retired bishop, clergyman*
Mabson, Robert Langley *clergyman, librarian*
Madera, Joseph J. *bishop*
Malone, James William *retired bishop*
Mangham, R. Harold *retired church administrator*
McClinton, Wendell C. *religious organization administrator*
McClurg, Patricia A. *minister*
McConnell, Calvin Dale *retired clergyman*
McElveen, William Henry *minister*
McKee, Adele Dieckmann *retired church music director, educator*
McKelway, Alexander Jeffrey *religion studies educator*
McKinley, Ellen Bacon *priest*
†Mc Kinney, Joseph Crescent *retired bishop*
McNabb, Robert Henry *minister*
McNeill, Douglas Arthur *priest*
McQuilkin, John Robertson *religion educator, academic administrator, writer*
Meier, George Karl, III *pastor, lawyer*
Melczek, Dale J. *bishop*
Melvin, Billy Alfred *clergyman*
Melzer, Barbara Evelyn *minister*
Milhouse, Paul William *bishop*
Miller, Vernon Dallace *retired minister*
Mills, Robert Harry *retired clergyman and church administrator*
Mischke, Carl Herbert *religious association executive, retired*
Mobley, Patricia Ann (Trish Mobley) *lay church worker, church secretary*
Moffett, Samuel Hugh *retired educator, minister*
Montrose, Donald W. *retired bishop*
Muckerman, Norman James *priest, writer*
Mullan, Donald William *archbishop*
Nairn, Charles Edward *librarian, pastor, religious educator*
Nance, David W. *minister*
Netterville, George Bronson *minister*
Norris, June Rudolph *minister*
Nottingham, William Jesse *retired church mission executive, minister*
Nunn, Charles Burgess *religious organization executive*
Nygren, Malcolm Ernest *minister*
Ochs, Carol Rebecca *theologian, philosophy and religion educator*
O'Connell, Brian James *priest, former university president*
Ortiz, Angel Vicente *church administrator*
Osborne, James Alfred *religious organization administrator*
Ostaszewski, Alyce Vitella *religion educator*
Palms, Roger Curtis *educator, editor, clergyman*
Paret, John J. *clergyman*
Parsons, Elmer Earl *retired clergyman*
Patterson, Donis Dean *bishop*
Pease, Sara Gooding *lay worker*
Peers, Michael Geoffrey *archbishop*
Pelotte, Donald Edmond *bishop*
Petersen, James Randall *lay religious leader, writer, theater artist*
Phinney, Frederick Warren *priest*
Pittelko, Roger Dean *clergyman, religious educator*
Pleming-Yocum, Laura Chalker *religion educator*
Poteat, James Donald *diaconal minister, retired military officer*
Povish, Kenneth Joseph *retired bishop*
Procter, John Ernest *former publishing company executive*
Raible, Peter Spilman *minister, religious organization executive*
Raymond, Robert Earl *retired minister*
Reed, Thomas Lee, II *minister, elementary education educator*
Righter, Walter Cameron *bishop*
†Roberson, Linwood John *minister*
Robinson, Clayton David *minister, educator*
Rooks, Charles Shelby *minister*
Rose, Robert John *bishop*
Rosenbaum, Jonathan *theology educator, college administrator*
Rushing, Rayburn Lewis *evangelist*
Russell, Patrick James *priest*
Ryk, Mary A. *retired chaplain*
Salatka, Charles Alexander *archbishop*
Scharlemann, Robert Paul *religious studies educator, clergyman*
Scherch, Richard Otto *minister, consultant*
Schmiel, David Gerhard *clergyman, religious education administrator*
Schmitt, Howard Stanley *minister*
Schuelke, John Paul *religious organization administrator*
Scott, Robert Hal *retired minister*
Scott, Waldron *mission executive*
Seale, James Millard *retired religious organization administrator, clergyman*
Seckel, Carol Ann *Methodist minister*
Setchko, Edward Stephen *minister, theology educator*
Shankel, Jack Eugene *minister*
Shaw, Robert Eugene *retired minister, administrator*
Sherwood, John Martin *rabbi*
Shotwell, Malcolm Green *retired minister*
Shultz, Retha Mills *retired missionary*
Sider, Harvey Ray *retired minister*
Singletary, Patricia Ann *minister*
Sloyan, Gerard Stephen *religious studies educator, priest*
Smith, Ann Hamill *retired religion educator*
Smith, John M. *bishop*
Soderquist, Ronald Bruce *minister, ministry consultant*
Sparks, William Sheral *retired librarian*
Spence, Glen Oscar *clergyman*
Stanley, Myrtle Brooks *minister, educational and religious consultant*
Stendahl, Krister *retired bishop*
Stevens, John Flournoy *priest*
Sullivan, James Lenox *clergyman*
Sullivan, Leon Howard *clergyman*
Swanson, Paul Rubert *minister*
Talley, Jim Allen *minister, counselor*
Tanquary, Oliver Leo *minister*
Taylor, June Ruth *retired minister*
Thompson, Eugene Mayne *retired minister*
Thottupuram, Kurian Cherian *priest, college director, educator*
Vachon, Louis-Albert Cardinal *archbishop*
van Dyck, Nicholas Booraem *minister, foundation official*
†Vlazny, John George *bishop*
Walker, Donald Robert, Jr. *minister*
Waltz, Alan Kent *clergyman, denominational executive*
Ward, John J. *bishop*
Weinhauer, William Gillette *retired bishop*
Weitzel, Harvey M. *minister, counselor*
†Welsh, Thomas J. *retired bishop*
Williams, Ervin Eugene *religious organization administrator*
Wills, Charles Francis *former church executive, retired career officer*
Wilshire, Robert Vidal *priest, theology educator*
Wilson, Warren Samuel *clergyman, bishop*
Wisehart, Mary Ruth *retired religious organization executive*
Witthuhn, Norman Edward *minister*
Wold, Margaret Barth *religion educator, author*
Woods, J. P. *minister*
Yount, William McKinley *minister, librarian, educator*
Zayek, Francis Mansour *retired bishop*
Ziegler, Earl Keller *minister*

SCIENCE: LIFE SCIENCE

UNITED STATES

ALABAMA

Auburn
Bailey, Wilford Sherrill *retired parasitology educator, science administrator, university president*
Ball, Donald Maury *agronomist, consultant*
Klesius, Phillip Harry *microbiologist, researcher*

Birmingham
Bradley, John M(iller), Jr. *forestry executive*
Davenport, Horace Willard *physiologist*
Elgavish, Ada *molecular, cellular biologist*
Finley, Sara Crews *medical geneticist, educator*
Marchase, Richard Banfield *cell biologist, educator*
Oglesby, Sabert, Jr. *retired research institute administrator*
Page, John Gardner *research administrator, scientist*
Rouse, John Wilson, Jr. *technology consultant*
Schafer, James Arthur *physiologist*
Wallace, Carl Jerry *zoo director*

Montgomery
Foster, Paul *zoo director*
Singh, Shree Ram *biology educator*

Normal
Coleman, Tommy Lee *soil science educator, researcher, laboratory director*

Tuscaloosa
Darden, William Howard, Jr. *biology educator*
†Smith, Coralee S. *science educator*
Wetzel, Robert George *botany educator*

Tuskegee Institute
Madison, Willie Clarence *park superintendent*

ALASKA

Anchorage
Davies, Garry *biology educator*
Keffer, Maria Jean *environmental auditor*
Kudenov, Jerry David *zoology educator*
Nielsen, Jennifer Lee *molecular ecologist, researcher*

Fairbanks
Kessel, Brina *ornithologist, educator*
White, Robert Gordon *research director, biology educator*

Juneau
Wilbur, Robert L. *biologist, science editor*

Soldotna
Franzmann, Albert Wilhelm *wildlife veterinarian, consultant*

ARIZONA

Bisbee
Johnson, Heidi Smith *science educator*
Milton, John P. *ecologist, educator, author, photographer*

Flagstaff
Drickamer, Lee Charles *zoology educator*
Phillips, Arthur Morton, III *botanist, consultant*
Price, Peter Wilfrid *ecology educator, researcher*

Glendale
Collins, Richard Francis *microbiologist, educator*

Oracle
Brusca, Richard Charles *zoologist, researcher, educator*

Phoenix
Bolin, Vernon Spencer *microbiologist, consultant*
Kimball, Bruce Arnold *soil scientist*
McKelvey, Tanya Hope *biologist, physical anthropologist*
Papp, Harry *science association administrator*
Saffo, Mary Beth *biologist*
Witherspoon, James Donald *biology educator*
†Wu, Jianguo *ecologist, educator*

Surprise
Veigel, Jon Michael *science administrator*

Tempe
Herald, Cherry Lou *research educator, research director*
Patten, Duncan Theunissen *ecologist educator*
Severe, Salvatore Francis *school psychologist*

Tucson
Acker, Robert Flint *microbiologist*
Baldwin, Ira Lawrence *retired bacteriologist, educator*
Blue, James Guthrie *retired veterinarian*
†Childs, Richard Francis *scientist, educator, retired*
Cortner, Hanna Joan *science administrator, research scientist, educator*
Fritts, Harold Clark *dendrochronology educator, researcher*
Green, Robert Scott *biotechnology company executive*
Hull, Herbert Mitchell *plant physiologist, researcher*
Jeter, Wayburn Stewart *retired microbiology educator, microbiologist*
McCormick, Floyd Guy, Jr. *agricultural educator, college administrator*
Metcalfe, Darrel Seymour *agronomist, educator*
Neuman, Shlomo P. *hydrology educator*
Osterberg, Charles Lamar *marine radioecologist, oceanographer*
Pepper, Ian L. *environmental microbiologist, research scientist, educator*
Shannon, Robert Rennie *optical sciences center administrator, educator*
Strausfeld, Nicholas James *neurobiology and evolutionary biology researcher, educator*
Wheeler, Jeanette Norris *entomologist*
Winfree, Arthur Taylor *biologist, educator*
Yocum, Harrison Gerald *horticulturist, botanist, educator, researcher*
†Zwolinski, Malcolm John *natural resources educator*

Window Rock
Hathaway, Loline *zoo and botanic park curator*

ARKANSAS

Batesville
Logan, Michael J. *veterinary medical officer*

Bella Vista
Musacchia, X(avier) J(oseph) *physiology and biophysics educator*

Cherokee Village
Hollingsworth, John Alexander *retired science and mathematics educator, writer, consultant*

Fayetteville
Brown, Connell Jean *retired animal science educator*
Evans, William Lee *biologist*
Kellogg, David Wayne *agriculture educator, researcher*
Morris, Justin Roy *food scientist, consultant, enologist, research director*
Musick, Gerald Joe *entomology educator*
Riggs, Robert Dale *plant pathology/nematology educator, researcher*
Scifres, Charles Joel *agricultural educator*

Gillett
Wood, Edward Ephraim, Jr. *park administrator*

Jefferson
Casciano, Daniel Anthony *biologist*
Schwetz, Bernard Anthony *toxicologist*

Little Rock
Barron, Almen Leo *microbiologist*
Hinson, Jack Allsbrook *research toxicologist, educator*

Monticello
Cain, Michael Dean *research forester*

State University
Bednarz, James C. *wildlife ecologist educator*

CALIFORNIA

Angwin
Ness, Bryan Douglas *biologist, educator*

Arcata
Barratt, Raymond William *biologist, educator*

Atherton
Starr, Chauncey *research institute executive*

Bakersfield
Anderson, Cliffton *science educator*

Berkeley
Anderson, John Richard *entomologist, educator*
Baldwin, Bruce Gregg *botany educator, researcher*
Barrett, Reginald Haughton *biology educator, wildlife management educator*
Berkner, Klaus Hans *laboratory administrator, physicist*
Bern, Howard Alan *science educator, research biologist*
Burnside, Mary Beth *biology educator, researcher*
Casida, John Edward *entomology educator*
Chemsak, John Andrew *entomologist*
Cline, Thomas Warren *molecular biologist, educator*
Cozzarelli, Nicholas Robert *molecular biologist, educator*
Dahlsten, Donald Lee *entomology educator, university dean*
Duesberg, Peter Heinz Hermann *molecular biology educator*
†Dunbar, Ian Fraser *veterinarian, animal behaviorist*
Fraenkel-Conrat, Heinz Ludwig *cell biology educator*
Getz, Wayne Marcus *biomathematician, researcher, educator*
Harris, Eva *molecular biology educator*
Levine, Michael Steven *science educator*
Licht, Paul *zoologist, educator*
Lidicker, William Zander, Jr. *zoologist, educator*
Ornduff, Robert *botany educator*
Pace, Norman R. *microbiologist, educator*
Pitelka, Frank Alois *zoologist, educator*
Schachman, Howard Kapnek *molecular biologist, educator*
Schekman, Randy W. *molecular biology administrator, biochemist*
Schwimmer, Sigmund *food enzymologist*
Shank, Charles Vernon *science administrator, educator*
Shatz, Carla J. *biology educator*
Spear, Robert Clinton *environmental health educator, consultant*
Teeguarden, Dennis Earl *forest economist, educator*

Vedros, Neylan Anthony *microbiologist*
Wake, David Burton *biology educator*
Wake, Marvalee Hendricks *biology educator*
Willhite, Calvin Campbell *toxicologist*
Wohletz, Leonard Ralph *soil scientist, consultant*
Wood, David L. *entomologist, educator*

Bodega Bay
Allard, Robert Wayne *geneticist, educator*
Clegg, James Standish *physiologist, biochemist, educator*
Hand, Cadet Hammond, Jr. *marine biologist, educator*

Bolinas
Lerner, Michael Albers *educator*

Chico
Ediger, Robert Ike *botanist, educator*
Kistner, David Harold *biology educator*
Vaught, Tony Steven *aquaculturist*

Chino
Pfuntner, Allan Robert *entomologist*

Claremont
Purves, William Kirkwood *biologist, educator*
Taylor, Roy Lewis *botanist, educator*
†Wright, Jonathan Charles *biology educator, researcher*

Coalinga
Harris, John Charles *agriculturalist*

Costa Mesa
Medina-Puerta, Antonio *scientist*

Davis
Addicott, Fredrick Taylor *retired botany educator*
Ardans, Alexander Andrew *veterinarian, laboratory director, educator*
Baldwin, Ransom Leland *animal science educator*
Barbour, Michael G(eorge) *botany educator, ecological consultant*
Baskin, Ronald Joseph *cell biologist, physiologist, biophysicist educator, dean*
Bruening, George E. *virologist*
Cliver, Dean Otis *microbiologist, educator*
Colvin, Harry Walter, Jr. *physiology educator*
Epstein, Emanuel *plant physiologist*
Ernst, Ralph Ambrose *poultry specialist*
Freedland, Richard Allan *retired biologist, educator*
Gifford, Ernest Milton *biologist, educator*
Green, Melvin Martin *geneticist*
†He, Pingnian *physiologist, researcher*
Hess, Charles Edward *environmental horticulture educator*
Horwitz, Barbara Ann *physiologist, educator, consultant*
Kado, Clarence Isao *molecular biologist*
Kester, Dale Emmert *pomologist, educator*
Kofranek, Anton Miles *floriculturist, educator*
Laidlaw, Harry Hyde, Jr. *entomology educator*
Learn, Elmer Warner *agricultural economics educator, retired*
Meyer, Margaret Eleanor *microbiologist, educator*
Moyle, Peter Briggs *fisheries and biology educator*
Murphy, Terence Martin *biology educator*
Qualset, Calvin O. *plant genetics and agronomy educator*
Rhode, Edward Albert *veterinary medicine educator, veterinary cardiologist*
Rick, Charles Madeira, Jr. *geneticist, educator*
Rost, Thomas Lowell *plant biology educator*
Schoener, Thomas William *zoology educator, researcher*
Sillman, Arnold Joel *physiologist, educator*
Steffey, Eugene Paul *veterinary medicine educator*
Uyemoto, Jerry Kazumitsu *plant pathologist, educator*
Vermeij, Geerat Jacobus *marine biologist, educator*
Watt, Kenneth Edmund Ferguson *zoology educator*
Williams, William Arnold *agronomy educator*

Del Mar
Farquhar, Marilyn Gist *cell biology and pathology educator*

Duarte
Balon, Thomas William *exercise physiologist*
Lundblad, Roger Lauren *research director*
Ohno, Susumu *research scientist*
Smith, Steven Sidney *molecular biologist*
Vaughn, James English, Jr. *neurobiologist*

El Centro
Flock, Robert Ashby *retired entomologist*

El Sobrante
Gilbert, William Marshall *retired biologist, educator*

Encinitas
Motoyama, Hiroshi *science association administrator*

Foster City
Miller, Jon Philip *research and development organization executive*

Fullerton
Brattstrom, Bayard Holmes *biology educator*
Jones, Claris Eugene, Jr. *botanist, educator*

Gilroy
McGrogan, Michael Patrick *molecular and cell biologist*

Granite Bay
Flora, Edward Benjamin *research and development company executive, mechanical engineer*

Grass Valley
Pasten, Laura Jean *veterinarian*

Hopland
Jones, Milton Bennion *agronomist, educator*

Industry
†Osuala, Chima Iheanyichukwu *microbiologist*

Irvine
Ayala, Francisco José *geneticist, educator*
Demetrescu, Mihai Constantin *research scientist, educator, computer company executive*
Fan, Hung Y. *virology educator, consultant*
Fitch, Walter M(onroe) *molecular biologist, educator, evolutionist*
Larson, Kirk David *pomologist and extension specialist*
Lawton, Michael James *entomologist, pest management specialist*
Lenhoff, Howard Maer *biological sciences educator, academic administrator, activist*
Silverman, Paul Hyman *science administrator, former university official*

Kelseyville
Sandmeyer, E. E. *toxicologist, consultant*

Kensington
Stent, Gunther Siegmund *molecular biologist, educator*

La Jolla
Alvariño De Leira, Angeles (Angeles Alvariño) *biologist, oceanographer*
Bloom, Floyd Elliott *physician, research scientist*
Brooks, Charles Lee, III *computational biophysicist, educator*
Cheverton, William Kearns *science corporation executive, consultant*
Chrispeels, Maarten Jan *biology educator*
Fishman, William Harold *cancer research foundation executive, biochemist*
Goel, Ajay *molecular biophysicist, researcher*
Guillemin, Roger C. L. *physiologist*
Haxo, Francis Theodore *marine biologist*
Helinski, Donald Raymond *biologist, educator*
Knowlton, Nancy *biologist*
Lewin, Ralph Arnold *biologist*
Pollard, Thomas Dean *cell biologist, educator*
Saier, Milton H., Jr. *biology educator*
Verma, Inder M. *biochemist*
West, John Burnard *physiologist, physicuan, educator*
Wilkie, Donald Walter *biologist, aquarium museum director*

La Verne
Neher, Robert Trostle *biology educator*

Laguna Hills
Mirman, Irving R. *scientific adviser*

Laguna Niguel
Coleman, Roger Dixon *bacteriologist*

Lewiston
McColm, George Lester *international agricultural consultant, journalist*

Livermore
Alcock, Charles Roger *science educator*

Loma Linda
Longo, Lawrence Daniel *physiologist, obstetrician-gynecologist*

Long Beach
Small, Richard David *research scientist*
Swatek, Frank Edward *microbiology educator*

Los Angeles
Bailey, Julia Nancy *geneticist*
Baker, Robert Frank *molecular biologist, educator*
Birren, James Emmett *university research center executive*
Bodnar, Jackie Sue *molecular biologist, geneticist*
Bok, Dean *cell biologist, educator*
Brown, Sally Ann *research scientist*
Collias, Nicholas Elias *zoology educator, ornithologist*
Craft, Cheryl Mae *neurobiologist, anatomist, researcher*
Davies, Kelvin James Anthony *research scientist, educator, consultant, author*
Diamond, Jared Mason *biologist*
Eisenberg, David Samuel *molecular biologist, educator*
Finch, Caleb Ellicott *neurobiologist, educator*
Finegold, Sydney Martin *microbiology educator*
Gilman, John Joseph *research scientist*
Gordon, Malcolm Stephen *biology educator*
Haglund, Thomas Roy *research biologist, consultant, educator*
Kadner, Carl George *biology educator emeritus*
Lu, John Kuew-Hsiung *physiology educator, endocrinologist*
McClure, William Owen *biologist*
Mockary, Peter Ernest *clinical laboratory scientist, researcher, medical writer*
Mohr, John Luther *biologist, environmental consultant*
Phinney, Bernard O. *research scientist, educator*
Shi, Wenyuan *microbiologist*
Sonnenschein, Ralph Robert *physiologist*
Storms, Lester C. (C Storms) *retired veterinarian*
Sullivan, Cornelius Wayne *marine biology educator, university research foundation,government agency administrator*
Szego, Clara Marian *cell biologist, educator*
Taylor, Charles Ellett *biologist*
Wei, Jen Yu *physiologist, researcher, educator*
Yang, Yang *science educator*

Los Banos
Castellano, Valen Edward *biologist*

Menlo Park
Crane, Hewitt David *science advisor*
Fuhrman, Frederick Alexander *physiology educator*
Jorgensen, Paul J. *research company executive*
Pake, George Edward *research executive, physicist*
Paustenbach, Dennis James *environmental toxicologist*

Merced
Olsen, David Magnor *chemistry and astronomy educator*

Modesto
Moe, Andrew Irving *veterinarian*

Moffett Field
Greenleaf, John Edward *research physiologist*
McDonald, Henry (Harry McDonald) *research center administrator*
Morrison, David *science administrator*
Strawa, Anthony Walter *research scientist*

Monrovia
Kimnach, Myron William *botanist, horticulturist, consultant*

Mountain View
Klein, Harold Paul *microbiologist*

Napa
Jones, Wayne Ross *agronomist*

Newport Coast
Swan, Peer Alden *scientific company executive, bank director*

Oakland
Cherry, Lee Otis *scientific institute administrator*
Collins, James Francis *toxicologist*
Earle, Sylvia Alice *research biologist, oceanographer*
Firoozabady, Ebrahim *plant scientist*
Parrott, Joel *zoo director*
Whitsel, Richard Harry *biologist, entomologist*

Pacific Grove
Epel, David *biologist, educator*

Palm Desert
Sausman, Karen *zoological park administrator*

Palo Alto
Anderson, Charles Arthur *former research institute administrator*
Balzhiser, Richard Earl *research and development company executive*
Botstein, David *geneticist, educator*
Briggs, Winslow Russell *plant biologist, educator*
Eggers, Alfred John, Jr. *research corporation executive*
Garland, Harry Thomas *research administrator*
Johnson, Noble Marshall *research scientist*
Sanders, William John *research scientist*
Scoledes, Aristotle Georgius Michale *retired science and technology educator, research consultant*
Tsien, Richard Winyu *biology educator*

Pasadena
Abelson, John Norman *biology educator*
Beer, Reinhard *atmospheric scientist*
†Bertani, Lillian Elizabeth T. *biologist, researcher, educator*
Davidson, Eric Harris *molecular and developmental biologist, educator*
Lewis, Edward B. *biology educator*
Meyerowitz, Elliot Martin *biologist, educator*
North, Wheeler James *marine ecologist, educator*
Owen, Ray David *biology educator*
Revel, Jean-Paul *biology educator*
Tirrell, David A. *research scientist, educator*
Varshavsky, Alexander Jacob *molecular biologist*
Wayland, J(ames) Harold *biomedical scientist, educator*

Pleasanton
Choy, Clement Kin-Man *research scientist*
Eby, Frank Shilling *retired research scientist*

Pomona
Keating, Eugene Kneeland *animal scientist, educator*

Redwood City
Neville, Roy Gerald *scientist, chemical management and environmental consultant*

Richmond
Beall, Frank Carroll *science director and educator*

Riverside
Barnes, Martin McRae *entomologist*
Bartnicki-Garcia, Salomon *microbiologist, educator*
Clegg, Michael Tran *genetics educator, researcher*
Erwin, Donald Carroll *plant pathology educator*
Hall, Anthony Elmitt *crop ecologist*
Keen, Noel Thomas *plant pathology educator*
Moore, John Alexander *biologist*
Page, Albert Lee *soil science educator, researcher*
Sherman, Irwin William *biological sciences educator*
Spencer, William Franklin, Sr. *soil scientist, researcher*
Talbot, Prue *biology educator*
Van Gundy, Seymour Dean *nematologist, plant pathologist, educator*
Zentmyer, George Aubrey *plant pathology educator*

Rohnert Park
Schafer, John Francis *retired plant pathologist*

Sacramento
Booze, Thomas Franklin *toxicologist*
Hackney, Robert Ward *plant pathologist, nematologist, parasitologist, molecular geneticist, commercial arbitrator*
Rosenberg, Dan Yale *retired plant pathologist*

San Bernardino
Mian, Lal Shah *entomologist, educator*

San Diego
Archibald, James David *biology educator, paleontologist*
Bernstein, Sanford Irwin *biology educator*
Bieler, Charles Linford *development director, zoo executive director emeritus*
Crick, Francis Harry Compton *science educator, researcher*
Eckhart, Walter *molecular biologist, educator*
Georgakakos, Konstantine Peter *research hydrologist*
Greenspan, Ralph Jay *biologist*
Gulliver, Edward Quentin *marine consultant, writer*
McGraw, Donald Jesse *biologist, historian of science, writer*
Myers, Douglas George *zoological society administrator*
Nordt, Sean Patrick *clinical toxicologist*
Pyatt, Kedar Davis, Jr. *research and development company executive*
Risser, Arthur Crane, Jr. *zoo administrator*
Schaechter, Moselio *microbiology educator*
Taylor, Tony S. *research scientist*
Thomas, Charles Allen, Jr. *molecular biologist, educator*
Vause, Edwin Hamilton *research foundation administrator*
Wehrli, John Erich *biotechnology executive*
Whitehead, Marvin Delbert *plant pathologist*

San Francisco
Anderson, David E. *zoological park administrator*
Blackburn, Elizabeth Helen *molecular biologist*
Brown, Walter Creighton *biologist*
Cape, Ronald Elliot *retired biotechnology company executive*
Dallman, Mary F. *physiology educator*
de Hostos, Eugenio Luis *cell biologist*
Eschmeyer, William Neil *marine scientist*
Furst, Arthur *toxicologist, educator*
Ganong, William F(rancis) *physiologist, physician*
Handler, Evelyn *science administrator*
Herskowitz, Ira *educator, molecular geneticist*
Heyneman, Donald *parasitology and tropical medicine educator*
Iacono, James Michael *research center administrator, nutrition educator*
Jan, Lily Yeh *physiology, biochemist*
†Lyon, David William *research executive*
Nichols, Richard Alan *ecologist*
Werb, Zena *cell biologist, educator*
Wyse, Roger Earl *physiologist*
Yamamoto, Keith Robert *molecular biologist, educator*

San Jacinto
Jones, Marshall Edward, Jr. *retired environmental educator*

San Jose
Moates, Betty Carolyn *microbiologist, computer consultant*
Taylor, Kendrick Jay *microbiologist*
Zaro, Brad A. *research company executive, biologist*

San Juan Capistrano
White, Beverly Jane *cytogeneticist*

San Mateo
Potts, David Malcolm *population specialist, administrator*

San Simeon
Jennings, Mark Russell *biologist*

Santa Ana
Glazier, Ron *zoological park administrator*
Wang, Jian-Ming *research scientist*

Santa Barbara
Badash, Lawrence *science history educator*
Doutt, Richard Leroy *entomologist, lawyer, educator*
Kryter, Karl David *research scientist*
Lambrecht, Frank Laurent *medical entomologist, parasitology researcher*
Lennox Buchthal, Margaret Agnes *retired neurophysiologist*
Philbrick, Ralph *botanist*
Schneider, Edward Lee *botanic garden administrator*
Tucker, Shirley Lois Cotter *botany educator, researcher*

Santa Clara
Mansfield, Elaine Schultz *molecular geneticist, automation specialist*

Santa Cruz
Beevers, Harry *biologist*
Dasmann, Raymond Fredric *ecologist*
Flegal, A(rthur) Russell, Jr. *toxicologist, geochemist, educator*
Langenheim, Jean Harmon *biology educator*

Santa Monica
Augenstein, Bruno W. *research scientist*
Shubert, Gustave Harry *research executive, consultant, social scientist*

South San Francisco
Levinson, Arthur David *molecular biologist*

Stanford
Atkin, J. Myron *science educator*
Bjorkman, Olle Erik *plant biologist, educator*
Campbell, Allan McCulloch *bacteriology educator*
Cohen, Stanley Norman *geneticist, educator*
Cork, Linda Katherine *veterinary pathologist, educator*
Davis, Mark M. *microbiologist, educator*
Davis, Ronald Wayne *genetics researcher, biochemistry educator*
Ehrlich, Anne Howland *research biologist*
Ehrlich, Paul Ralph *biology educator*
Elliott, David Duncan, III *science research company executive*
Falkow, Stanley *microbiologist, educator*
Francke, Uta *medical geneticist, genetics researcher, educator*
Hanawalt, Philip Courtland *biology educator, researcher*
Long, Sharon Rugel *molecular biologist, plant biology educator*
Mooney, Harold Alfred *plant ecologist*
Perkins, David D(exter) *geneticist, educator*
Scheller, Richard H. *molecular and cellular physiology educator*
Shapiro, Lucille *molecular biology educator*
Shooter, Eric Manvers *neurobiology educator, consultant*
Somerville, Chris *plant biologist, educator*
Spudich, James A. *biology educator*
Strena, Robert Victor *university research laboratory manager*
Vitousek, Peter M. *botany educator, research ecologist*
Yanofsky, Charles *biology educator*

Stockton
McNeal, Dale William, Jr. *biological sciences educator*

Sun Valley
Dergrigorian, Ronald *water microbiologist*

Terra Bella
Gletne, Jeffrey Scott *forester*

The Sea Ranch
Hayflick, Leonard *microbiologist, cell biologist, gerontologist, educator, writer*

Thousand Oaks
Malmuth, Norman David *scientist, program manager*

Tiburon
Harary, Keith *research scientist, writer, science journalist*

Torrance
Cai, Khiem Van *technologist, researcher, administrator*

Tulare
Vickrey, Herta Miller *microbiologist*

Tustin
Sinnette, John Townsend, Jr. *research scientist, consultant*

Ventura
Arita, George Shiro *biology educator*

Vista
Hofmann, Frieder Karl *biotechnologist, consultant*

Walnut
Shannon, Cynthia Jean *biology educator*

Walnut Creek
Seaborg, David Michael *evolutionary biologist*

West Hills
Centorino, James Rocco *science educator, composer*

Westminster
Allen, Merrill James *marine biologist*

Woodland Hills
Fox, Stuart Ira *physiologist*

COLORADO

Arvada
Reynolds-Sakowski, Dana Renee *science educator*

Aurora
Dooley, J. Gordon *food scientist*

Boulder
Armstrong, David Michael *biology educator*
Breed, Michael Dallam *environmental, population, organismic biology educator*
Byerly, Radford, Jr. *science policy official*
Clifford, Steven Francis *science research director*
De Fries, John Clarence *behavioral genetics educator, institute administrator*
Derr, Vernon Ellsworth *retired government research administrator*
Hanley, Howard James Mason *research scientist*
Mc Intosh, J(ohn) Richard *biologist, educator*
Meier, Mark Frederick *research scientist, glaciologist, educator*
†Mitchell, David S. *writer, editor, publisher, educator*
Prescott, David Marshall *biology educator*
Roble, Raymond Gerald *science administrator*
Serafin, Robert Joseph *science center administrator, electrical engineer*
Staehelin, Lucas Andrew *cell biology educator*
Thomas, Gary Edward *science educator, researcher*

Brush
Gabriel, Donald Eugene *science educator*

Carbondale
Cowgill, Ursula Moser *biologist, educator, environmental consultant*

Colorado Springs
Bybee, Rodger Wayne *science education administrator*
Clifford, Walter Jess *microbiologist, immunologist*
Comes, Robert George *research scientist*
Markert, Clement Lawrence *biology educator*
West, Ralph Leland *veterinarian*

Denver
Barz, Richard L. *microbiologist*
Ehret, Josephine Mary *microbiologist, researcher*
Freiheit, Clayton Fredric *zoo director*
Heifets, Leonid *microbiologist, researcher*
Hildebrand, Verna Lee *human ecology educator*
Holmes, Randall Kent *microbiology educator, physician, university administrator*
Horowitz, Isaac M. *control research consultant, writer*
Mitchell, Jerry Michael *biologist*
Pfenninger, Karl H. *cell biology and neuroscience educator*
Puck, Theodore Thomas *geneticist, biophysicist, educator*
Richardson, Elizabeth Hall *ecologist*
Talmage, David Wilson *microbiology and medical educator, physician, former university administrator*

Durango
Steinhoff, Harold William *retired research institute executive*

Englewood
Albrecht, Duane Taylor *veterinarian*
Brierley, James Alan *research administrator*

Estes Park
Jones, A. Durand *park administrator*

Fort Collins
Benjamin, Stephen Alfred *veterinary medicine educator, environmental pathologist, researcher*
Burns, Denver P. *forestry research administrator*
Follett, Ronald Francis *soil scientist*
Halvorson, Ardell David *soil scientist*
Keim, Wayne Franklin *retired agronomy educator, plant geneticist*
Lumb, William Valjean *veterinarian*
Maga, Joseph Andrew *food science educator*
Mortvedt, John Jacob *soil scientist*
Ogg, James Elvis *microbiologist, educator*
Peterson, Gary Andrew *agronomics researcher*
Roos, Eric Eugene *plant physiologist*
Seidel, George Elias, Jr. *animal scientist, educator*
Smith, Dwight Raymond *ecology and wildlife educator, writer*
Smith, Gary Chester *meat scientist, researcher*
Smith, Ralph Earl *virologist*
†Snyder, Carol Jeanne *agricultural economist*
Williamson, Samuel Chris *research ecologist*

Golden
Bergeron, Sheila Diane *retired science educator, educational consultant*
Hubbard, Harold Mead *retired research executive*

Littleton
Vail, Charles Daniel *veterinarian, consultant*

Longmont
Dierks, Richard Ernest *veterinarian, educational administrator*
Ulrich, John August *microbiology educator*

Telluride
Groeneveld, David Paul *plant ecologist, hydrologist*

CONNECTICUT

East Glastonbury
Smith, David Clark *research scientist*

Farmington
Bronner, Felix *physiologist, biophysicist, educator, painter*
Rothfield, Lawrence I. *microbiology educator*

Groton
Routien, John Broderick *mycologist*
Tassinari, Melissa Sherman *toxicologist*

Hamden
Delehant, Raymond Leonard *botanist, educator*

Middle Haddam
Dart, John Robert *horticulturist*

Middletown
Morris, Jonathan Ira *biology educator*

Milford
Calabrese, Anthony *marine biologist*

Monroe
Turko, Alexander Anthony *biology educator, hypnotherapist*

New Haven
Altman, Sidney *biology educator*
Anderson, John Frederick *science administrator, entomologist, researcher*
Aronson, Peter Samuel *medical scientist, physiology educator*
Buss, Leo William *biologist, educator*
Chandler, William Knox *physiologist*
Cohen, Lawrence Baruch *neurobiologist, educator*
DuBois, Arthur Brooks *physiologist, educator*
Galston, Arthur William *biology educator*
Giebisch, Gerhard Hans *physiology educator*
Gordon, John Charles *forestry educator*
Hoffman, Joseph Frederick *physiology educator*
Slayman, Carolyn Walch *geneticist, educator*
Smith, David Martyn *forestry educator*
Smith, William Hulse *forestry and environmental studies educator*
Stolwijk, Jan Adrianus Jozef *physiologist, biophysicist*
Stowe, Bruce Bernot *biology educator*
Summers, William Cofield *science educator*
Trinkaus, John Philip *cell and developmental biologist*
Waggoner, Paul Edward *agricultural scientist*
Wagner, Günter Paul *biologist educator*

New London
Goodwin, Richard Hale *botany educator*
Haas, Thomas Joseph *chemistry educator*

Norwalk
Nishikida, Koichi *research scientist*

Southport
Hill, David Lawrence *research corporation executive*

Storrs Mansfield
Anderson, Gregory Joseph *botanical sciences educator*
Cyr, Juliette Mary *molecular biology researcher*
Koths, Jay Sanford *floriculture educator*
Laufer, Hans *developmental biologist, educator*
Marcus, Philip Irving *virology educator, researcher*
Romano, Antonio *microbiologist*
Slater, James Alexander *entomologist, educator*

Wallingford
Molinoff, Perry Brown *biologist, science administrator*

Waterford
Hinerfeld, Lee Ann *veterinarian*

West Haven
Debeyssey, Mark Sammer *molecular and cellular biologist*
Linemeyer, David Lee *molecular biologist*

Westport
Altman, Lawrence Gene *biologist*

Willington
Rogers, Diana Florence *research scientist*

DELAWARE

Delmar
Tasker, John Baker *veterinary medical educator, college dean*

Hockessin
Mills, George Alexander *retired science administrator*

Newark
Buchanan, Thomas Steven *biomechanics educator*
Campbell, Linzy Leon *molecular biology researcher, educator*
DeCherney, George Stephen *research scientist, research facility administrator*
Sparks, Donald Lewis *soil chemistry educator*
Threen, Dean Richard *molecular biologist*
Yan, Xiao-Hai *science center director, educator*

Wilmington
Eleuterio, Marianne Kingsbury *retired genetics educator*
Howard, Richard James *mycology researcher*

DISTRICT OF COLUMBIA

Washington
Abernathy, Charles Owen *toxicologist*
Affronti, Lewis Francis, Sr. *microbiologist, educator*
Ahl, Alwynelle Self *zoology, ecology and veterinary medical executive*
Anderson, Donald Morgan *entomologist*
Apple, Martin Allen *scientific federation executive, educator*
Batdorf, Lynn Robert *horticulturist*
Bernthal, Frederick Michael *association executive*
Bishop, William Peter *research scientist*
Boright, John Phillips *science administrator*
Brandt, Carl David *research virologist*
Brown, Lester Russell *research institute executive*
Carhart, Homer W(alter) *research scientist*
Case, Larry D. *agricultural education specialist*
Chan, Wai-Yee *molecular geneticist*
Coleman, Bernell *physiologist, educator*
Colglazier, E. William *science academy administrator, physicist*
Cooper, Chester Lawrence *research administrator*
Crawford, Lester Mills, Jr. *veterinarian*
Crum, John Kistler *chemical society director*
Davis, Donald Ray *entomologist*
DeGiovanni-Donnelly, Rosalie Frances *biology researcher, educator*
Dickey, John Sloan, Jr. *science association director*
Dombeck, Michael Paul *fisheries biologist*
Elias, Thomas Sam *botanist, author*
Falci, Kenneth Joseph *food and nutrition scientist*
Feulner, Edwin John, Jr. *research foundation executive*
Frahm, Veryl Harvey, Jr. *laboratory manager*
†Gonzalez, I. Miley *agriculture administrator*
Goslin, David Alexander *research administrator, sociologist*
Hammonds, Timothy Merrill *scientific association executive, economist*
Harding, Fann *health scientist, administrator*
Hazen, Robert Miller *research scientist, musician*
Henkin, Robert Irwin *neurobiologist, internal medicine, nutrition and neurology educator, scientific products company executive, taste and smell disease physician*
Henry, Thomas Joseph *research entomologist*
Holmes, George Edward *molecular biologist, educator*
Hope, William Duane *zoologist, curator*
Huntoon, Carolyn Leach *physiologist*
Huntress, Wesley Theodore, Jr. *scientist*
James, Charles Clinton *science education educator, consultant*
Kapetanakos, Christos Anastasios *science administrator, physics educator*
Kennedy, Eugene Richard *microbiologist, university dean*
Kleiman, Devra Gail *zoologist, zoological park research scientist*
Kramer, Jay Harlan *physiologist, researcher, educator*
Krombein, Karl vonVorse *entomologist*
Malcom, Shirley Mahaley *science association executive*
†Mallan, John Powers *retired educator*
Menzer, Robert Everett *toxicologist, educator*
Meyers, Wayne Marvin *microbiologist*
Miller, Alan Stanley *ecology center administrator, law educator*
†Moritz-Ridenour, Amy *research center administrator*
Moss, Thomas Henry *science association administrator*
Nabholz, Joseph Vincent *biologist, ecologist*
Nightingale, Elena Ottolenghi *geneticist, physician, administrator*
O'Neil, Joseph Francis *association executive*
Palmer, Robert E. *science administrator*
Putzrath, Resha Mae *toxicologist*
Pyke, Thomas Nicholas, Jr. *government science and engineering administrator*
Ralls, Katherine *zoologist*
Ritter, Donald Lawrence *environmental policy institute executive*
Robinson, Michael Hill *zoological park director, biologist*
Rubinoff, Ira *biologist, research administrator, conservationist*
Sass, Neil Leslie *toxicologist*
Schad, Theodore MacNeeve *science research administrator, consultant*
Schiff, Stefan Otto *zoologist, educator*
Schram, Susan Gale *agriculturist, consultant*
Schultz, Todd R. *science administrator*
Shands, Henry Lee *plant geneticist, administrator*
Smith, Philip Meek *science policy consultant, writer*
Tidball, M. Elizabeth Peters *physiologist, educator, research director*
Todhunter, John Anthony *toxicologist*
Torrey, Barbara Boyle *research council administrator*
Train, Russell Errol *environmentalist*
Vandiver, Pamela Bowren *research scientist*
Walmsley, James Naylor *hydroponic farming executive*
Wasshausen, Dieter Carl *systematic botanist*
†Watkins, Shirley R. *agriculture department administrator*
West, Robert MacLellan *science education consultant*
†Wilf, Peter Daniel *paleobiologist*
Wilkinson, Ronald Sterne *science administrator, environmentalist, historian*

FLORIDA

Belle Glade
Waddill, Van Hulen *entomology educator*

Boca Raton
Reid, George Kell *biology educator, researcher, author*
Samuels, William Mason *physiology association executive*

Bonita Springs
Dacey, George Clement *retired laboratory administrator, consultant*

Bradenton
Maynard, Donald Nelson *horticulturist, educator*

Chuluota
Hatton, Thurman Timbrook, Jr. *retired horticulturist, consultant*

Clearwater
Bramante, Pietro Ottavio *physiology educator, retired pathology specialist*

Coral Gables
Schaiberger, George Elmer *microbiologist educator*

Coral Springs
Furman, Mark Evan *human performance scientist*

Daytona Beach
Duma, Richard Joseph *microbiologist, physician, pathologist, researcher, educator*
Scott, John Brooks *research institute executive, retired*

Delray Beach
Chavin, Walter *biological science educator and researcher*
†Lucà-Moretti, Maurizio *scientist, nutrition researcher*

Englewood
Urka, Martin C. *soil scientist*

Fort Pierce
Calvert, David Victor *soil science educator*
Rice, Mary Esther *biologist*

Gainesville
Besch, Emerson Louis *physiology educator, past academic administrator*
Burridge, Michael John *veterinarian, educator, research administrator*
Conrad, Joseph Henry *animal nutrition educator*
Dilcher, David Leonard *paleobotany educator, research scholar*
Drury, Kenneth Clayton *biological scientist*
Edwardson, John Richard *retired agronomist*
Gelband, Craig Harris *physiologist, pharmacologist*
Green, Eleanor Myers *veterinarian, educator*
Gutekunst, Richard Ralph *microbiology educator*
Hall, David Walter *botanist*
Himes, James Albert *veterinary medicine educator emeritus*
Hoy, Marjorie Ann *entomology educator*
Jaeger, Marc Julius *physiology educator, researcher*
Jones, David Alwyn *geneticist, botany educator*
Jones, Richard Lamar *entomology educator*
Mead, Frank Waldreth *taxonomic entomologist*
Meredith, Julia Alice *nematologist, biologist, researcher*
†Nell, Terril A. *horticulturalist, educator*
†Nichols, Linda Rose *educator, program administrator*
Nicoletti, Paul Lee *veterinarian, educator*
Oberlander, Herbert *insect physiologist, educator*
Odum, Howard T. *emeritus environmental science educator*
Popenoe, Hugh Llywelyn *soils educator*
Purcifull, Dan Elwood *plant virologist, educator*
Quesenberry, Kenneth Hays *agronomy educator*
Schelske, Claire L. *limnologist, educator*
Schmidt-Nielsen, Bodil Mimi (Mrs. Roger G. Chagnon) *physiologist*
Smith, Wayne Hilry *forest resources and conservation educator*
Stern, William Louis *botanist, educator*
Teixeira, Arthur Alves *food engineer, educator, consultant*
Tumlinson, James H., III *agriculturist*
Wilcox, Charles Julian *geneticist, educator*

Hollywood
Matasa, Claude George *researcher, science administrator, educator*

Homestead
Roberts, Larry Spurgeon *biological sciences educator, zoologist*

Jacksonville
Hartzell, Charles R. *research administrator, biochemist, cell biologist*
Lluberas, Manuel F. *biologist*
Tardona, Daniel Richard *ethologist, naturalist, writer, park ranger, educator*

Jay
Brecke, Barry John *weed scientist, researcher, educator*

Lake Alfred
Kender, Walter John *horticulturist, educator*

Lake Buena Vista
†Stevens, Elizabeth Franke *zoologist*

Lake Placid
Layne, James Nathaniel *vertebrate biologist*

Largo
Mandelker, Lester *veterinarian*

Melbourne
Helmstetter, Charles Edward *microbiologist*
Storrs, Eleanor Emerett *research institute consultant*

Miami
Chen, Chun-fan *biology educator*
Colwin, Arthur Lentz *biologist, educator*
†Lokeshwar, Balakrishna Loknath *cancer biologist, educator*
Muench, Karl Hugo *clinical geneticist*
Stone, Ronald William *veterinarian*

Micanopy
Cripe, Wyland Snyder *veterinary medicine educator, consultant*

North Miami
Polley, Richard Donald *microbiologist, polymer chemist*

Ona
Rechcigl, Jack Edward *soil and environmental sciences educator*

Orlando
Barros, Nélio Baptista *biological oceanographer*
Quinn, Sondra *science center executive*
Wutscher, Heinz Konrad *horticulturist*

Palm Beach
Hopper, Arthur Frederick *biological science educator*

Palm Harbor
Banwart, George Junior *food microbiology educator*

Pensacola
Foster, Virginia *retired botany educator*

Punta Gorda
Beever, James William, III *biologist*

Ramrod Key
Clark, John Russell *marine biologist*

Saint Augustine
Greenberg, Michael John *biologist, editor*

Saint Petersburg
Byrd, Isaac Burlin *fishery biologist, fisheries administrator*
Mueller, O. Thomas *molecular geneticist, pediatrics educator*

Sarasota
Byron, H. Thomas, Jr. *veterinarian, educator*
Gilbert, Perry Webster *emeritus educator*
Mahadevan, Kumar *marine laboratory director, researcher*
Pierce, Richard Harry *research director for laboratory*
Seibert, Russell Jacob *botanist, research associate*

Sunny Isles Beach
Adrian, Manuella *research scientist, administrator*

Tallahassee
Abele, Lawrence Gordon *biology educator, university administrator*
Adams, James Alfred *natural science educator*
Brennan, Leonard Alfred *research scientist, administrator*
Dall, Sasha Raoul Xola *evolutionary ecologist, researcher*
Friedmann, E(merich) Imre *biologist, educator*
Koontz, Christine Miller *research faculty*
Lipner, Harry *retired physiologist, educator*
Long, Michael Christian *forester*
Meredith, Michael *science educator, researcher*
Onokpise, Oghenekome Ukrakpo *agronomist, educator, forest geneticist, agroforester*

Tampa
Hickman, Hugh V. *science educator, researcher*
Hinsch, Gertrude Wilma *biology educator*
Lim, Daniel Van *microbiology educator*

Vero Beach
Baker, Richard H. *retired geneticist, educator*
Grobman, Arnold Brams *retired biology educator and academic administrator*
Grobman, Hulda Gross (Mrs. Arnold B. Grobman) *retired health sciences educator*

West Palm Beach
Freudenthal, Ralph Ira *toxicology consultant*
Sturrock, Thomas Tracy *botany educator, horticulturist*

Winter Park
Fluno, John Arthur *entomologist, consultant*

Yulee
†Citino, Scott Bradley *wildlife veterinarian*

Zephyrhills
†McGavern, Melanie Lynn *veterinarian*

GEORGIA

Alpharetta
Balows, Albert *microbiologist, educator*
Rettig, Terry *veterinarian, wildlife consultant*

Athens
Agosin, Moises Kankolsky *zoology educator*
Albersheim, Peter *biology educator*
Anderson, Wyatt Wheaton *biology educator*
Avise, John Charles *geneticist, educator*
Baile, Clifton A. *biologist, researcher*
Giles, Norman Henry *educator, geneticist*
Hildebrand, Don *science foundation executive*
Langdale, George Wilfred *soil scientist, researcher*
Marks, Henry Lewis *poultry scientist*
Miller, Lois Kathryn *virology educator*
Payne, William Jackson *microbiologist, educator*
Plummer, Gayther L(ynn) *climatologist, ecologist, researcher*
Sumner, Malcom Edward *agronomist, educator*
Swayne, David Eugene *avian pathologist, researcher*
Tyler, David Earl *veterinary medical educator*

Atlanta
Carey, Gerald John, Jr. *research institute director, former air force officer*
Cavallaro, Joseph John *microbiologist*
Clifton, David Samuel, Jr. *research executive, economist*
Compans, Richard W. *microbiology educator*
Gunn, Robert Burns *physiology educator*
Jeffery, Geoffrey Marron *medical parasitologist*
La Farge, Timothy *plant geneticist*
Langdale, Noah Noel, Jr. *research educator, former university president*
Long, Leland Timothy *geophysics educator, seismologist*
McGowan, John Edward, Jr. *clinical microbiology educator, epidemiologist, infectious diseases specialist*
Pratt, Harry Davis *retired entomologist*
Spitznagel, John Keith *microbiologist, immunologist*
Zumpe, Doris *ethologist, researcher, educator*

Bainbridge
Goodyear, Nancy L. *biology educator*

Baldwin
Smith, John Andrew *veterinarian*

Bogart
Butts, David Phillip *science educator*

Columbus
†Fluellen, Abraham P. *researcher*
Gore, James Arnold *biology educator, aquatic ecologist, hydrologist*
Kilgore, J. Donald *coroner*

Duluth
Johnston, William David *biotechnology executive*

Dunwoody
La Motte, Louis Cossitt, Jr. *medical scientist, consultant*

Griffin
Doyle, Michael Patrick *food microbiologist, educator, administrator*
Duncan, Ronny Rush *agriculturist, turf researcher, consultant*
Shuman, Larry Myers *soil chemist*

Kennesaw
Jones, J. Todd *veterinarian*
Lain, David Cornelius *health scientist, researcher*

Macon
Adkison, Linda Russell *geneticist, consultant*
Harrison, James Ostelle *ecologist*
Volpe, Erminio Peter *biologist, educator*

Martinez
Chaudhary, Shaukat Ali *ecologist, plant taxonomist*

Newton
Walton, William Robert *academic administrator*

Norcross
Darst, Bobby Charles *soil chemist, administrator*
Dibb, David Walter *research association administrator*
McDonald, James *science foundation executive*
Wagner, Robert Earl *agronomist*

Savannah
Eaves, George Newton *lecturer, consultant, research administrator*

Statesboro
Parrish, John Wesley, Jr. *biology educator*

Summerville
Wright, Kevin Douglas *veterinarian*

Tifton
Austin, Max Eugene *horticulture educator*

Valdosta
Grissino-Mayer, Henri Dee *research scientist*

HAWAII

Aiea
Munechika, Ken Kenji *research center administrator*

Hawaii National Park
Gray, Elizabeth Marie *biologist*

Honolulu
Abbott, Isabella Aiona *biology educator, retired*
Ashton, Geoffrey Cyril *geneticist, educator*
Carson, Hampton Lawrence *geneticist, educator*
Greenfield, David W. *zoology educator*
Kamemoto, Fred Isamu *zoologist*
Kay, Elizabeth Alison *zoology educator*
Lamoureux, Charles Harrington *botanist, arboretum administrator*
Laughlin, Charles William *agriculture educator, research administrator*
Mandel, Morton *molecular biologist*
Sagawa, Yoneo *horticulturist, educator*
Smith, Albert Charles *biologist, educator*
Zaleski, Halina Maria *animal scientist*

Kamuela
Young, Ernest *park administrator*

Kapaa
Chimoskey, John Edward *physiologist, medical educator*

Pearl City
Hodgson, Lynn Morrison *marine biologist*
Kanenaka, Rebecca Yae *microbiologist*

Tripler Army Medical Center
Uyehara, Catherine Fay Takako (Yamauchi) *physiologist, educator, pharmacologist*

IDAHO

Boise
Brownfield, Shelby Harold *soil scientist*
Burton, Lawrence DeVere *agriculturist, educator*
Nelson, Willard Gregory *veterinarian, mayor*

Coeur D Alene
Adams, Elinor Ruth *retired laboratory technician*

Moscow
Roberts, Lorin Watson *botanist, educator*
Scott, James Michael *research biologist*

Nampa
Redfield, David Allen *chemistry educator*

Pocatello
McCune, Mary Joan Huxley *microbiology educator*
Seeley, Rod Ralph *physiology educator*

Post Falls
Brede, Andrew Douglas *research director, plant breeder*

ILLINOIS

Abbott Park
Allen, Steven Paul *microbiologist*
Frazier, Douglas Byron *health care consultant*

Argonne
Schriesheim, Alan *research administrator*

Bloomington
Godt, Earl Wayne, II *technology education educator*
Harms, David Jacob *agricultural consultant*

Bridgeview
Parmer, Dan Gerald *veterinarian*

Brookfield
Rabb, George Bernard *zoologist*

Burr Ridge
Rosenberg, Robert Brinkmann *technology organization executive*

Carbondale
Burr, Brooks Milo *zoology educator*

Champaign
Batzli, George Oliver *ecology educator*
Levin, Geoffrey Arthur *botanist*
Ridlen, Samuel Franklin *agriculture educator*
Sanderson, Glen Charles *science director*
Smith, Robert Lee *agriculturalist*

Chicago
Beattie, Ted Arthur *zoological gardens and aquarium administrator*
Beecher, William John *zoologist, museum director*
Bell, Kevin J. *zoological park administrator*
Buss, Daniel Frank *environmental scientist*
Chakrabarty, Ananda Mohan *microbiologist*
Cohen, Edward Philip *microbiology and immunology educator, physician*
Crane, Peter Robert *botanist, geologist, paleontologist, educator*
Davidson, Richard Laurence *geneticist, educator*
Desjardins, Claude *physiologist, dean, administrator*
Ernest, J. Terry *ocular physiologist, educator*
Fisher, Lester Emil *zoo administrator*
Fuchs, Elaine V. *molecular biologist, educator*
Gindilis, Viktor Mironovitch *geneticist, researcher*
Greenberg, Bernard *entomologist, educator*
Haselkorn, Robert *virology educator*
Helms, Byron Eldon *associate director of research, biology and physiology administrator*
Houk, James Charles *physiologist, educator*
Kass, Leon Richard *educator*
Kopec, John William *research scientist*
Lewert, Robert Murdoch *microbiologist, educator*
Lindquist, Susan Lee *biology and microbiology educator*
†Lohmiller, Jeffrey Joseph *veterinarian, educator*
Mahowald, Anthony Peter *geneticist, developmental biologist, educator*
Mateles, Richard Isaac *biotechnologist*
McCrone, Walter Cox *research institute executive*
McKinley, Vicky Lynn *biology educator*
Melikian, Grigory Borisovich *science educator*
Miller, Patrick William *research administrator, educator*
Mullins, Obera *microbiologist*
Overton, Jane Vincent Harper *biology educator*
Park, Thomas Joseph *biology researcher, educator*
Pick, Ruth *research scientist, physician, educator*
Pumper, Robert William *microbiologist*
Roizman, Bernard *virologist, educator*
Rothman-Denes, Lucia Beatriz *biology educator*
Rymer, William Zev *research scientist, administrator*
Shott, Susan *medical biostatistician, educator*
Solaro, Ross John *physiologist, biophysicist*
Van Valen, Leigh *biologist, educator*
Willson, Mary F. *ecology researcher, educator*

Danville
Craig, Hurshel Eugene *agronomist*

Decatur
Forster, Lance Allen *technical researcher animal science*

Dekalb
Zar, Jerrold H(oward) *biology educator, university dean, statistician*

Des Plaines
Lee, Bernard Shing-Shu *research company executive*
Stokes, Robert Allan *science research facility executive, physicist*

Evanston
Dallos, Peter John *neurobiologist, educator*
King, Robert Charles *biologist, educator*
Novales, Ronald Richards *zoologist, educator*
Villa-Komaroff, Lydia *molecular biologist, educator, university official*
Wu, Tai Te *biological sciences and engineering educator*

Forest Park
Orland, Frank J. *oral microbiologist, educator*

Glenview
Kinigakis, Panagiotis *research scientist, engineer, author*

Harvey
Liem, Khian Kioe *medical entomologist*

Hinsdale
Pawley, Ray Lynn *zoological park and environmental consultant*
†Smith, Jared Russell William *research executive*

Lake Forest
†Zamer, William E. *biologist, educator*

Libertyville
Munson, Norma Frances *biologist, ecologist, nutritionist, educator*

Lisle
Ware, George Henry *botanist*

Lombard
Velardo, Joseph Thomas *molecular biology and endocrinology educator*

Long Grove
Beach, Robert Mark *biologist*

Macomb
Anderson, Richard Vernon *ecology educator, researcher*

Maywood
Blumenthal, Harold Jay *microbiologist, educator*
Cera, Lee Marie *veterinarian*

Mount Prospect
Garvin, Paul Joseph, Jr. *toxicologist*

Naperville
Perez-Reyes, Edward *molecular physiologist*

North Chicago
Albach, Richard Allen *microbiology educator*

Northbrook
Glabe, Elmer Frederick *food scientist*

Oak Brook
Morello, Josephine A. *microbiology and pathology educator*

Rockford
Steffan, Wallace Allan *entomologist, educator, museum director*

Schaumburg
Parker, Norman W. *scientist*

Springfield
Munyer, Edward A. *zoologist, museum administrator*

Urbana
Banwart, Wayne Lee *agronomy, environmental science educator*
Becker, Donald Eugene *animal science educator*
Berenbaum, May Roberta *entomology educator*
Buetow, Dennis Edward *physiology educator*
Burger, Ambrose William *agronomy educator*
Chow, Poo *wood technologist, scientist*
Crang, Richard Francis Earl *plant and cell biologist, research center administrator*
Dziuk, Philip John *animal scientist educator*
Endress, Anton G. *horticulturist, educator*
Frazzetta, Thomas Henry *evolutionary biologist, functional morphologist, educator*
Friedman, Stanley *insect physiologist, educator*
Garrigus, Upson Stanley *animal science and international agriculture educator*
Garrow, Timothy Alan *nutrition science educator*
Greenough, William Tallant *psychobiologist, educator*
Harper, James Eugene *plant physiologist*
Heath, James Edward *physiology educator, retired*
Heichel, Gary Harold *crop sciences educator*
Hixon, James Edward *physiology educator*
Hoeft, Robert Gene *agriculture educator*
Hoffmeister, Donald Frederick *zoology educator*
Hymowitz, Theodore *plant geneticist, educator*
Isaacson, Richard Evan *microbiologist*
Mc Glamery, Marshal Dean *agronomy, weed science educator*
Meyer, Richard Charles *microbiologist*
Nanney, David Ledbetter *genetics educator*
Parker, Alan John *veterinary neurologist, educator, researcher*
Prosser, C. Ladd *physiology educator, researcher*
Rebeiz, Constantin A. *plant physiology educator*
Ricketts, Gary Eugene *retired animal scientist*
Ridgway, Marcella Davies *veterinarian*
Seigler, David Stanley *botanist, chemist, educator*
Sinclair, James Burton *plant pathology educator, consultant*
Small, Erwin *veterinarian, educator*
Stout, Glenn Emanuel *retired science administrator*
Waldbauer, Gilbert Peter *entomologist, educator*
†Wallig, Matthew Alan *veterinary pathologist*

Whitt, Gregory Sidney *molecular phylogenetics, evolution educator*
Wolfe, Ralph Stoner *microbiology educator*

Watseka
Neumann, Frederick Lloyd *plant breeder*

West Chicago
Hauptmann, Randal Mark *biotechnologist*

Wheaton
Pun, Pattle Pak Toe *microbiologist, educator*

INDIANA

Bloomington
Clevenger, Sarah *botanist, computer consultant*
Gest, Howard *microbiologist, educator*
Hammel, Harold Theodore *physiology and biophysics educator, researcher*
Hegeman, George Downing *microbiology educator*
Heiser, Charles Bixler, Jr. *botany educator*
Hites, Ronald Atlee *environmental science educator, chemist*
Mc Clung, Leland Swint *microbiologist, educator*
Moran, Emilio Federico *anthropology and ecology educator*
Nolan, Val, Jr. *biologist, lawyer*
Preer, John Randolph, Jr. *biology educator*
Ruesink, Albert William *biologist, plant sciences educator*
Weinberg, Eugene David *microbiologist, educator*

Carmel
Gehring, Perry James *toxicologist, chemical company executive*

Crawfordsville
Simmons, Emory G. *mycologist*

Evansville
Denner, Melvin Walter *retired life sciences educator*

Fort Wayne
†Cooper, William Edgar *animal behaviorist, educator*

Greensburg
Ricke, David Louis *agricultural and environmental consultant*

Hobart
Seeley, Mark *agronomist*

Indianapolis
Borst, Philip Craig *veterinarian, councilman*
Christian, Joe Clark *medical genetics researcher, educator*
Daily, Fay Kenoyer *retired botany educator*
Hodes, Marion Edward *genetics educator, physician*
Jones, Robert Brooke *microbiologist, educator, associate dean*
McDonald, Clement J. *biomedical engineer*
Ochs, Sidney *neurophysiology educator*
Rhoades, Rodney Allen *physiologist, educator*
Storhoff, Diana Carmack *research scientist*
Thomas, Jerry Arthur *soil scientist*

Lafayette
Achgill, Ralph Kenneth *retired research scientist*
Claflin, Robert Malden *retired veterinary educator, university dean*
Harris, Donald Wayne *research scientist*
Nicholson, Ralph Lester *botanist, educator*

Muncie
Hendrix, Jon Richard *biology educator*
Henzlik, Raymond Eugene *zoophysiologist, educator*
Mertens, Thomas Robert *biology educator*

New Albany
Baker, Claude Douglas *biology educator, researcher, environmental activist*

Notre Dame
Bender, Harvey A. *biology educator*
Jensen, Richard Jorg *biology educator*

Purdue University
Guo, Peixuan *molecular virology educator*

Terre Haute
Dusanic, Donald Gabriel *parasitology educator, microbiologist*

West Lafayette
Albright, Jack Lawrence *animal science and veterinary educator*
Amstutz, Harold Emerson *veterinarian, educator*
Axtell, John David *genetics educator, researcher*
Borgens, Richard *biologist*
†Brush, F(ranklin) Robert *psychobiology educator*
Cochrane, Thomas Thurston *tropical soil scientist, agronomist*
Edwards, Charles Richard *entomology and pest management educator*
Ferris, Virginia Rogers *nematologist, educator*
Franzmeier, Donald Paul *agronomy educator, soil scientist*
Harmon, Bud Gene *animal sciences educator, consultant*
Hoover, William Leichliter *forestry and natural resources educator, financial consultant*
Hunt, Michael O'Leary *wood science and engineering educator*
Johannsen, Chris Jakob *agronomist, educator, administrator*
Le Master, Dennis Clyde *natural resource economics and policy educator*
McFee, William Warren *soil scientist*
Nelson, Philip Edwin *food scientist, educator*
Ohm, Herbert Willis *agronomy educator*
Ortman, Eldon E. *entomologist, educator*
Schreiber, Marvin Mandel *agronomist, educator*
Sherman, Louis Allen *biology educator*
Stob, Martin *physiology educator*
White, Joe Lloyd *soil scientist, educator*

IOWA

Amana
Vorhies, Mahlon Wesley *veterinary pathologist, educator*

Ames
Ahrens, Franklin Alfred *veterinary pharmacology educator*
Anderson, Lloyd Lee *animal science educator*
Beran, George Wesley *veterinary microbiology educator*
Berger, P(hilip) Jeffrey *animal science educator, quantitative geneticist*
Burris, Joseph Stephen *agronomy educator*
Cao, Heping *biologist, researcher*
Frederick, Lloyd Randall *soil microbiologist*
Freeman, Albert E. *agricultural science educator*
Ghoshal, Nani Gopal *veterinary anatomist, educator*
Greve, John Henry *veterinary parasitologist, educator*
Hallauer, Arnel Roy *geneticist*
Hatfield, Jerry Lee *plant physiologist, biometeorologist*
Johnson, Lawrence Alan *cereal technologist, educator, administrator*
Karlen, Douglas Lawrence *soil scientist*
Keeney, Dennis Raymond *soil science educator*
Kelly, James Michael *plant and soil scientist*
†Martin, Paul A. *veterinary educator and researcher*
Mengeling, William Lloyd *veterinarian, virologist, researcher*
Mertins, James Walter *entomologist*
Moon, Harley William *veterinarian*
Moore, Kenneth James *agronomy educator*
O'Berry, Phillip Aaron *veterinarian*
Pearson, Phillip Theodore *veterinary clinical sciences and biomedical engineering educator*
Ross, Richard Francis *veterinarian, microbiologist, educator*
Seaton, Vaughn Allen *retired veterinary pathology educator*
Snow, Joel Alan *research director*
Thompson, Louis Milton *agronomy educator, scientist*
Voss, Regis Dale *agronomist, educator*
Wallin, Jack Robb *research plant pathology educator*
Wass, Wallace Milton *veterinarian, clinical science educator*
Willham, Richard Lewis *animal science educator*
Young, Jerry Wesley *animal nutrition educator*

Cedar Rapids
Dvorak, Clarence Allen *microbiologist*

Coon Rapids
Shirbroun, Richard Elmer *veterinarian, cattleman*

Des Moines
Arvidson, Robert Benjamin, Jr. *geneticist, consultant*
Rosen, Matthew Stephen *botanist, consultant*

Eldora
Kerns, Steve *geneticist*

Estherville
Klepper, Robert Rush *plant physiologist*

Grinnell
Campbell, David George *ecologist, researcher, author*
Walker, Waldo Sylvester *biology educator, academic administrator*

Iowa City
Cruden, Robert William *botany educator*
Daniels, Lacy *microbiology educator*
Hausler, William John, Jr. *microbiologist, educator, public health laboratory administrator*
Husted, Russell Forest *research scientist*
Kessel, Richard Glen *zoology educator*
Milkman, Roger Dawson *genetics educator, molecular evolution researcher*
Osborne, James William *radiation biologist*
Pessin, Jeffrey E. *physiology educator*
Reynolds, David G(eorge) *retired physiologist, educator*
Wunder, Charles C(ooper) *physiology and biophysics educator, gravitational biologist*

Johnston
Duvick, Donald Nelson *plant breeder*

Wever
Lodwick, Seeley Griffiths *agriculturist, consultant*

KANSAS

Emporia
Sundberg, Marshall David *biology educator*

Hays
Coyne, Patrick Ivan *physiological ecologist*
Talbott, Nancy Costigan *science educator*

Junction City
Ling, Robert William, Jr. *biologist, educator*

Kansas City
Behbehani, Abbas M. *clinical virologist, educator*
Goldberg, Ivan D. *microbiologist, educator*
Greenwald, Gilbert Saul *physiologist*

Kiowa
Conrad, Melvin Louis *biology educator*

Lawrence
Armitage, Kenneth Barclay *biology educator, ecologist*
Bovee, Eugene Cleveland *protozoologist, emeritus educator*
Byers, George William *retired entomology educator*
Johnston, Richard Fourness *biologist*
Lichtwardt, Robert William *mycologist*
Michener, Charles Duncan *entomologist, researcher, educator*
O'Brien, William John *ecology researcher*
Shankel, Delbert Merrill *microbiology and biology educator*

Leawood
Vetter, James Louis *food research association administrator*

Manhattan
Erickson, Howard Hugh *veterinarian, physiology educator*
Johnson, Terry Charles *biologist, educator*
Kaufman, Donald Wayne *research ecologist*
Kirkham, M. B. *plant physiologist, educator*
Mengel, David Bruce *agronomy and soil science educator*
Posler, Gerry Lynn *agronomist, educator*
Richard, Patrick *science research administrator, nuclear scientist*

Neosho Falls
Bader, Robert Smith *biology, zoology educator and researcher*

Parsons
Lomas, Lyle Wayne *agricultural research administrator, educator*

Shawnee Mission
Goetz, Kenneth Lee *cardiovascular physiologist, research consultant*

Topeka
Mara, John Lawrence *veterinarian, consultant*

KENTUCKY

Lexington
Barnhart, Charles Elmer *animal sciences educator*
Frye, Wilbur Wayne *soil science educator, researcher, administrator*
Goodman, Norman Loyal *microbiologist, educator*
Grabau, Larry J. *crop physiologist, educator*
Kasperbauer, Michael John *plant physiology educator, researcher*
†Love, Harold Gibson *agricultural economics educator*
Mitchell, George Ernest, Jr. *animal scientist, educator*
Palmer, Brent David *environmental physiology educator, biologist*
Pirone, Thomas Pascal *plant pathology educator*
Rangnekar, Vivek Mangesh *molecular biologist, researcher*
Reed, Michael Robert *agricultural economist*
Thrift, Frederick A. *zoologist, educator*
Timoney, Peter Joseph *veterinarian, virologist, educator, consultant*

Louisville
Harris, Patrick Donald *physiology educator*
Heinicke, Ralph Martin *consultant*
Roisen, Fred Jerrold *neurobiologist, educator, researcher, anatomy educator*

Murray
Keller, Randal Joseph *toxicology educator*

Prestonsburg
Pridham, Thomas Grenville *retired research microbiologist*

Richmond
Branson, Branley Allan *biology educator*

LOUISIANA

Baton Rouge
Besch, Everett Dickman *veterinarian, university dean emeritus*
Burns, Paul Yoder *forester, educator*
Hansel, William *biology educator*
Head, Jonathan Frederick *cell biologist*
Klei, Thomas Ray *parasitology educator*
Liuzzo, Joseph Anthony *food science educator*
Patrick, William Hardy, Jr. *wetland biogeochemist, educator, laboratory director*

Boyce
Chilton, St. John Poindexter *retired plant pathology educator, farm owner*

Chauvin
Sammarco, Paul William *ecologist, researcher*

Gretna
Simoneaux, Sandi Sue *veterinarian*

Hammond
Shepherd, David Preston *biology educator, researcher*

New Iberia
Janssen, Christopher Frank *veterinarian*

New Orleans
Beard, Elizabeth Letitia *physiologist, educator*
Brody, Arnold Ralph *research scientist, educator*
Fingerman, Milton *biologist, educator*
Ivens, Mary Sue *microbiologist, mycologist*
Levitzky, Michael Gordon *physiology educator, researcher*
Lingle, Sarah Elizabeth *research scientist*
Mitchell, Kenneth D. *physiologist, medical educator*
Navar, Luis Gabriel *physiology educator, researcher*
Orihel, Thomas Charles *parasitology educator, research scientist*
Rossowska, Magdalena Joanna *physiology educator, research scientist*
Spurlock, Jimmie Paul, Jr. *veterinarian, educator*
Superneau, Duane William *geneticist, physician*
Welden, Arthur Luna *biology educator*
Whidden, Stanley John *physiologist, physician*

Saint Gabriel
Berggren, Gerard T. *plant pathologist*

Shreveport
Jamison, Richard Melvin *virologist, educator*
Rust, John McNeil *veterinarian*

MAINE

Bar Harbor
Hoppe, Peter Christian *biologist, geneticist*
Leiter, Edward Henry *scientist*
Paigen, Kenneth *geneticist, research director*

Damariscotta
Fuller, Melvin Stuart *botany educator*

Falmouth
Eno, Amos Stewart *natural resource foundation administrator*

Greenville
Sommerman, Kathryn Martha *retired entomologist*

Jonesport
Radomski, Jack London *toxicology consultant*

Lewiston
Chute, Robert Maurice *retired biologist, educator, poet*

Mount Desert
Crawford, Richard Bradway *biologist, biochemist, educator*

New Vineyard
West, Arthur James, II *biologist*

Orono
Campana, Richard John *retired plant pathology educator, writer, consultant*
Chute, Harold LeRoy *veterinary pathologist, former chemical company executive*
Knight, Fred Barrows *forester, entomologist, educator*

Wells
Neilson, Elizabeth Anastasia *health sciences educator, association executive, author, editor*

MARYLAND

Aberdeen Proving Ground
Evans, Edward Spencer, Jr. *entomologist*
Powers, Nelson Roger *entomologist*

Annapolis
†Anderson, William Carl *association executive, environmental engineer, consultant*
Kushlan, James A. *biologist, research administrator, author, educator*

Baltimore
Brady, Joseph Vincent *behavioral biologist, educator*
Brown, Donald David *biology educator*
Clark, Patricia *molecular biologist*
DeTolla, Louis James *research veterinarian*
Dubner, Ronald *neurobiologist, educator*
Fowler, Bruce Andrew *toxicologist*
Gall, Joseph Grafton *biologist, researcher, educator*
Goldberg, Alan Marvin *toxicologist, educator*
Grollman, Sigmund Sidney *physiology educator*
Habermann, Helen Margaret *plant physiologist, educator*
Hansen, Barbara Caleen *physiology educator, scientist*
Littlefield, John Walley *geneticist, cell biologist, pediatrician*
McKusick, Victor Almon *geneticist, educator, physician*
†Nammour, Henri Habib *internist, pulmonologist, critical care physician*
Nathans, Daniel *molecular biology and genetics educator*
Permutt, Solbert *physiologist, physician*
Rubin, Robert Jay *toxicologist*
Sack, George Henry, Jr. *molecular geneticist*
Salters, Charles Robert *biology educator, dean*
Smith, Hamilton Othanel *molecular biologist, educator*
Suskind, Sigmund Richard *microbiology educator*
Trpis, Milan *vector biologist, scientist, educator*
†Turner, Thomas Bourne *retired microbiology educator*
†Warner, Christine Marie *researcher*
Weng, Han-Rong *physiologist, researcher*
†Xiao, Yan *science educator*

Beltsville
Abdul-Baki, Aref Asad *physiologist, researcher*
Collins, Anita Marguerite *research geneticist*
Hackett, Kevin James *insect pathologist*
Murrell, Kenneth Darwin *microbiologist, parasitologist*
Norman, H. Duane *dairy geneticist*
Palm, Mary Egdahl *mycologist*
Terrill, Clair Elman *animal scientist, geneticist, consultant*
Zarlenga, Dante Sam, Jr. *molecular biologist*

Berlin
Buchholz, Bernard *retired research manager*

Bethesda
Ahmed, S. Basheer *research company executive, educator*
Bennink, Jack Richard *microbiologist, researcher*
Brady, Roscoe Owen *neurogeneticist, educator*
Bunger, Rolf *physiology educator*
Burg, Maurice Benjamin *renal physiologist, physician*
Chen, Liping *molecular biologist, researcher, biochemist*
Collins, Francis S. *medical research scientist*
Felsenfeld, Gary *government official, scientist*
Frank, Martin *physiology educator, health scientist, association executive*
Fraumeni, Joseph Francis, Jr. *scientific researcher, medical educator, physician, military officer*
Gartland, William Joseph, Jr. *research institute administrator*
Gilbert, Daniel Lee *physiologist*
Gordis, Enoch *science administrator, internist*
Gruber, Jack *medical virologist, biomedical research administrator*

Guttman, Helene Nathan *biomedical research consultant, transpersonal counselor, regression therapist*
Hancock, Charles Cavanaugh, Jr. *scientific association administrator*
Hausman, Steven Jack *health science administrator*
Hodgdon, Harry Edward *association executive, wildlife biologist*
Horakova, Zdenka Zahutova *retired toxicologist, pharmacologist*
Jackson, Michael John *physiologist, association executive*
Jones, John Courts *wildlife biologist*
Jordan, Elke *molecular biologist, government medical research institute executive*
Law, Lloyd William *geneticist*
Lorber, Mortimer *retired physiology educator*
Martino, Robert Louis *computational scientist and engineer, researcher*
Miller, Louis Howard *biologist, researcher*
Monjan, Andrew Arthur *health science administrator*
Moss, Bernard *virologist, researcher*
†Pakaluk, Debra Lorraine Behm *science educator*
Piatigorsky, Joram Paul *research scientist, molecular biologist*
Potter, Michael *genetics researcher, medical researcher*
Purcell, Robert Harry *virologist*
Salmoiraghi, Gian Carlo *physiologist, educator*
Sewell, Rodney Milton *biologist*
Shulman, Lawrence Edward *biomedical research administrator, rheumatologist*
Slavkin, Harold Charles *biologist*
Sokoloff, Louis *physiologist, neurochemist*
Sponsler, George Curtis, III *research administrator, lawyer*
Underwood, Brenda S. *microbiologist, grants administrator*
Walleigh, Robert Shuler *retired consultant*
Woolley, George Walter *biologist, geneticist, educator*
Yamada, Kenneth Manao *cell biologist*
Zierdt, Charles Henry *microbiologist*

Chevy Chase
Choppin, Purnell Whittington *research administrator, virology researcher, educator*
Cowan, William Maxwell *neurobiologist*
Harter, Donald Harry *research administrator, medical educator*

Clarksburg
Gonano, J. Roland *technology research and development manager*

College Park
Clark, Eugenie *zoologist, educator*
Diener, Theodor Otto *plant pathologist*
Fanning, Delvin Seymour *soil science educator*
Gantt, Elisabeth *plant biology educator, researcher*
Heath, James Lee *food science educator, researcher*
Jeffery, William Richard *developmental biology educator, researcher*
Miller, Raymond Jarvis *agronomy educator*
Olver, Frank William John *retired research educator*
Stark, Francis C(io), Jr. *horticulturist, educator*
Vandersall, John Henry *dairy science educator*
Weil, Raymond Richard *soil scientist*

Columbia
Bond, Gorman Morton *ornithologist, researcher*
†Ranasinghe, John Ananda *ecologist, researcher*

Frederick
Aiuto, Russell *science education consultant*
Creasia, Donald Anthony *toxicologist, researcher*
Knisely, Ralph Franklin *retired microbiologist*

Fulton
Johnson, Virgil Evans, Jr. *research scientist*

Gaithersburg
Carter, Kenneth Charles *geneticist*
Rollence, Michele Lynette *molecular biologist*
Semerjian, Hratch Gregory *research and development executive*

Garrett Park
Baldwin, Calvin Benham, Jr. *retired medical research administrator*

Germantown
Norcross, Marvin Augustus *veterinarian, retired government agency official*

Greenbelt
Thomas, Lindsey Kay, Jr. *research ecology biologist, educator, consultant*
Whitlock, Laura Alice *research scientist*

Hancock
Popenoe, John *horticultural consultant, retired botanical garden administrator*

Ijamsville
Vickers, James Hudson *veterinarian, research pathologist*

Jefferson
Beall, James Robert *toxicologist*

Kensington
Jackson, William David *research executive*

Laurel
Rorie, Conrad Jonathan *scientist, naval officer*
†Spjut, Richard Wayne *botanist, consultant*

Leonardtown
McIntosh, Heather Aileen *biologist*

Libertytown
Lindblad, Richard Arthur *retired health services administrator, drug abuse epidemiologist*

North Bethesda
Anderson, Owen Raymond *scientific and educational organization executive*

Potomac
Brewer, Nathan Ronald *veterinarian, consultant*

Princess Anne
Joshi, Jagmohan *agronomist, consultant*

Rockville
Adams, Mark David *molecular biologist*
Bayne, Kathryn Ann Louise *veterinarian*
Bollum, Frederick James *biotechnology executive*
Erwin, Joseph Marvin *neurobiologist, primatologist*
Gail, Mitchell H. *science foundation executive*
Ginsberg, Harold Samuel *virologist, educator*
Gluckstein, Fritz Paul *veterinarian, biomedical information specialist*
Gougé, Susan Cornelia Jones *microbiologist*
Landon, John Campbell *medical research company executive*
Leef, James Lewis *biology educator, immunology research executive*
Lewis, Andrew Morris, Jr. *virologist*
MacGregor, James Thomas *toxicologist*
MacPhee, Martin James *medical researcher, immunologist*
Mertz, Walter *retired government research executive*
Poljak, Roberto J(uan) *research director, biotechnology educator*
Rafajko, Robert Richard *medical research company executive*
Rosen, Saul Woolf *research scientist, health facility administrator*
Ryan, Kevin William *research virologist, educator, administrator*
†Sundlof, Stephen Frederick *veterinary administrator*
Thompson, Barry Hammond *medical geneticist*

Salisbury
Moultrie, Fred *geneticist*

Silver Spring
Kohler, Max Adam *consulting hydrologist, weather service administrator*
Leedy, Daniel Loney *ecologist*
Lynt, Richard King *microbiologist*

Towson
Wubah, Daniel Asua *microbiologist, educator*

MASSACHUSETTS

Amherst
Belt, Edward Scudder *sedimentologist, educator*
Coppinger, Raymond Parke *biologist, educator*
Godfrey, Paul Joseph *science foundation director*
Holmes, Francis William *plant pathologist*
Margulis, Lynn (Lynn Alexander) *biologist*
Marrett, Cora B. *university educator, science educator*
Palmer, John Derry *physiology educator*
Palser, Barbara F. *botany researcher, retired educator*
Stein, Otto Ludwig *botany educator*
Tippo, Oswald *botanist, educator, university administrator*

Bedford
Chung-Welch, Nancy Yuen Ming *biologist*
Griffin, Donald R(edfield) *zoology educator*
Slechta, Robert Frank *biologist, educator*

Belmont
Kety, Seymour S(olomon) *physiologist, neuroscientist*

Beverly
Roberts, Richard John *molecular biologist, consultant, research director*

Billerica
Kolb, Charles Eugene *research corporation executive*

Boston
Beckwith, Jonathan Roger *geneticist*
Carradini, Lawrence *comparative biologist, science administrator*
Coffin, John Miller *molecular biologist, educator*
Cohen, Jonathan Brewer *molecular neurobiologist, biochemist*
Collier, R(obert) John *biomedical researcher, academic dean*
Essex, Myron Elmer *microbiology educator*
Faller, Douglas V. *cancer research scientist, physician*
Green, Howard *cellular physiologist, educator, administrator*
Hubel, David Hunter *physiologist, educator*
Kahn, Carl Ronald *research laboratory administrator*
Kaminer, Benjamin *physician, educator*
Lees, Sidney *research facility administrator, bioengineering educator*
Malamy, Michael H(oward) *molecular biology and microbiology educator*
McLinden, James Hugh *molecular biologist*
Nichols, Guy Warren *retired institute executive, utilities executive*
Park, James Theodore *microbiologist, educator*
Schubel, Jerry Robert *marine science educator, scientist, university dean*
Sonenshein, Abraham Lincoln *microbiology educator*
Streilein, J. Wayne *research scientist*
Tosteson, Daniel Charles *physiologist, medical school dean emeritus*
Yang, Zhen *research scientist, chemistry educator*

Boxborough
Li, Yao Tzu *science educator*

Cambridge
Anker, Peder Johan *historian of sicence*
Bazzaz, Fakhri A. *plant biology educator, administrator*
Berg, Howard C. *biology educator*
Bogorad, Lawrence *biologist, educator*
Branton, Daniel *biology educator*
Demain, Arnold Lester *microbiologist, educator*
Dowling, John Elliott *biology educator*
Erikson, Raymond Leo *biology educator*
Forman, Richard T. T. *ecology educator*
Fox, Maurice Sanford *molecular biologist, educator*
Freed, Lisa Ernestine *research scientist*
Friedman, Orrie Max *biotechnology company executive*
Gilbert, Walter *molecular biologist, educator*
Goldberg, Ray Allan *agribusiness educator*
Goldblith, Samuel Abraham *food science educator*
Hartl, Daniel Lee *genetics educator*
Hastings, John Woodland *biologist, educator*
Horvitz, Howard Robert *biology educator, researcher*
Hubbard, Ruth *biology educator*
Hynes, Richard Olding *biology researcher and educator*
Knoll, Andrew Herbert *biology educator*
Lerman, Leonard Solomon *science educator, scientist*
Levi, Herbert Walter *biologist, educator*
Liu, Guosong *neurobiologist*
Lodish, Harvey Franklin *biologist, educator*
Lynch, Harry James *biologist*
Magasanik, Boris *microbiology educator*
Magee, John Francis *research company executive*
Maniatis, Thomas Peter *molecular biology educator*
Mayr, Ernst *retired zoologist, philosopher*
McMahon, Thomas Arthur *biology and applied mechanics educator*
Melton, Douglas A. *molecular and cell biology educator*
Pardue, Mary-Lou *biology educator*
Pentland, Alex P. *research scientist, educator, administrator*
Pierce, Naomi Ellen *biology educator, researcher*
Rich, Alexander *molecular biologist, educator*
Shultz, Leila McReynolds *botanist, educator*
†Springett, Gregory M. *molecular biologist, physician*
Tannenbaum, Steven Robert *toxicologist, chemist*
Tonegawa, Susumu *biology educator*
Torriani-Gorini, Annamaria *microbiologist*
Vincent, James Louis *biotechnology company executive*
Wilson, Edward Osborne *biologist, educator, author*
Wogan, Gerald Norman *toxicology educator*
Wurtman, Judith Joy *research scientist*

Canton
Lyman, Charles Peirson *comparative physiologist*

Charlestown
Gusella, James F. *geneticist, educator*

Concord
Huxley, Hugh Esmor *molecular biologist, educator*

Falmouth
Schlesinger, Robert Walter *microbiologist, microbiology educator emeritus*

Framingham
Goldman, Ralph Frederick *research physiologist, educator*

Grafton
Haggerty, John Edward *research center administrator, former army officer*

Great Barrington
Stonier, Tom *theoretical biologist, educator*

Jamaica Plain
Cook, Robert Edward *plant ecology educator, research director*

Lexington
Drouilhet, Paul Raymond, Jr. *science laboratory director, electrical engineer*
Fillios, Louis Charles *retired science educator*
Gibbs, Martin *biologist, educator*
Melngailis, Ivars *solid state researcher*

Lincoln
Payne, Roger Searle *zoology researcher and administrator, conservationist*

Lowell
Coleman, Robert Marshall *biology educator*

Natick
Lachica, R(eynato) Victor *microbiologist*
Sahatjian, Ronald Alexander *science foundation executive*

Newton
West, Doe *bioethicist, social justice activist*

North Falmouth
Morse, Robert Warren *research administrator*

North Grafton
Schwartz, Anthony *veterinary surgeon, educator*

Norwood
Pence, Robert Dudley *biomedical research administrator, hospital administrator*

Quincy
Hagar, William Gardner, III *photobiology educator*

Raynham
Jelley, Scott Allen *microbiologist*

Southborough
Gauduin, Marie-Claire Elisabeth *microbiologist, immunologist, pilot*

Waban
Farber, Neal Mark *biotech executive, molecular biologist*

Waltham
Galinat, Walton Clarence *research scientist*

Wayland
Blair, John *consulting scientist*

Wellesley
Gerety, Robert John *microbiologist, pharmaceutical company executive, pediatrician, vaccinologist*
Samuels, Linda Sue *science educator*

West Falmouth
Vaccaro, Ralph Francis *marine biologist*

Williamstown
Lee, Arthur Virgil, III *biotechnology company executive*

Woburn
Gelb, Arthur *science association executive, electrical and systems engineer*

Woods Hole
Burris, John Edward *biologist, educator, administrator*
Copeland, Donald Eugene *research marine biologist*
Ebert, James David *research biologist, educator*
Inoué, Shinya *microscopy and cell biology scientist, educator*
Loewenstein, Werner Randolph *physiologist, biophysicist, educator*
Woodwell, George Masters *ecology research director, lecturer*

Worcester
Bagshaw, Joseph Charles *molecular biologist, educator*

MICHIGAN

Ann Arbor
Alexander, Richard Dale *zoology educator*
Allen, Sally Lyman *biologist*
Anderson, William R. *botanist, educator, curator, director*
Beeton, Alfred Merle *laboratory director, limnologist, educator*
Bryant, Barbara Everitt *academic researcher, market research consultant, former federal agency administrator*
Cochran, Kenneth William *toxicologist*
Dawson, William Ryan *zoology educator*
Drach, John Charles *scientist, educator*
Easter, Stephen Sherman, Jr. *biology educator*
Evans, Francis Cope *ecologist*
Faulkner, John Arthur *physiologist, educator*
Gelehrter, Thomas David *medical and genetics educator, physician*
Ginsburg, David *human genetics educator, researcher*
Hartung, Rolf *environmental toxicology educator, researcher, consultant*
Hasan, Ahmed Abdul Kashem *biomedical researcher, research scientist*
Hawkins, Joseph Elmer, Jr. *retired acoustic physiologist, educator*
Horowitz, Samuel Boris *biomedical researcher, educational consultant*
Kaufman, Peter Bishop *biological sciences educator*
Kostyo, Jack Lawrence *physiology educator*
†Liang, Junfeng *research scientist*
Lowe, John Burton *molecular biology educator, pathologist*
Moore, Thomas Edwin *biology educator, museum director*
Neidhardt, Frederick Carl *microbiologist*
Petty, Elizabeth Marie *geneticist*
Richardson, Rudy James *toxicology and neurosciences educator*
Savageau, Michael Antonio *microbiology and immunology educator*
Shappirio, David Gordon *biologist, educator*
Stoermer, Eugene Filmore *biologist, educator*
Wagner, Warren Herbert, Jr. *botanist, educator*
Walker, Jack L. *environmental scientist*
†Wang, Shixin *research scientist*
Whitehouse, Frank, Jr. *microbiologist*
Williams, John Andrew *physiology educator, consultant*

Augusta
Johnson, Wilbur Corneal (Joe Johnson) *biologist*

Big Rapids
Barnes, Isabel Janet *microbiology educator, college dean*

Dearborn
Schneider, Michael Joseph *biologist*

Detroit
DeRoo, Sally A. *biology, geology and environmental science educator*
Edwards, Brian Francis Peregrine *science educator*
Krawetz, Stephen Andrew *molecular medicine and genetics scientist*
Novak, Raymond Francis *toxicology research institute director, pharmacology educator*
Phillis, John Whitfield *physiologist, educator*
Singh, Kameshwar Prasad *toxicologist, researcher*
†Van Dyke, Daniel L. *geneticist*

East Lansing
Bukovac, Martin John *horticulturist, educator*
Dennis, Frank George, Jr. *retired horticulture educator*
Fischer, Lawrence Joseph *toxicologist, educator*
Fromm, Paul Oliver *physiology educator*
Gerhardt, Philipp *microbiologist, educator*
Hackel, Emanuel *science educator*
Hollingworth, Robert Michael *toxicology researcher*
Isleib, Donald R. *retired agricultural researcher*
Kamrin, Michael Arnold *toxicology educator*
Kende, Hans Janos *plant physiology educator*
Knobloch, Irving William *retired biology educator, author*
Lenski, Richard Eimer *evolutionary biologist, educator*
Liu, Jianguo *ecologist*
Lockwood, John LeBaron *plant pathologist*
Lucas, Robert Elmer *soil scientist*
McMeekin, Dorothy *botany, plant pathology educator*
Nelson, Ronald Harvey *animal science educator, researcher*
Patterson, Maria Jevitz *microbiology-pediatric infectious disease educator*
Petrides, George Athan *ecologist, educator*
Root-Bernstein, Robert Scott *biologist, educator*
Witter, Richard Lawrence *veterinarian, educator*

Edwardsburg
Floyd, Alton David *cell biologist, consultant*

Farmington Hills
Dragun, James *soil chemist*

Flint
Wigston, David Laurence *biologist, university dean*

Hickory Corners
Lauff, George Howard *biologist*

Highland Park
Crittenden, Mary Lynne *science educator*

Hopkins
Irish, Diana Maria *wildlife rehabilitation agent*

Kalamazoo
Enyedi, Alexander Joseph *plant physiologist, researcher*
Marshall, Vincent de Paul *industrial microbiologist, researcher*
Tsai, Ti-Dao *electrophysiologist*

Lansing
Carlotti, Ronald John *food scientist*
Venable, Robert Ellis *crop scientist*

Midland
Bus, James Stanley *toxicologist*
Davidson, John Hunter *agriculturist*

Mount Pleasant
Novitski, Charles Edward *biology educator*

Okemos
Gast, Robert Gale *agriculture educator, experiment station administrator*

Portage
Elliott, George Algimon *pathologist, toxicologist, veterinarian*

Rochester
Unakar, Nalin Jayantilal *biological sciences educator*

Saginaw
Faubel, Gerald Lee *agronomist, golf course superintendent*

Sanford
Wilmot, Thomas Ray *medical entomologist, educator*

Southfield
Colmery, Benjamin Herring, III *veterinarian*

Ypsilanti
Caswell, Herbert Hall, Jr. *retired biology educator*

MINNESOTA

Adrian
Hanson, Jim Henry *veterinarian*

Duluth
Heller, Lois Jane *physiologist, educator, researcher*
Johnson, Arthur Gilbert *microbiology educator*
Whitmyer, Robert Wayne *soil scientist, consultant, researcher*

Grand Rapids
†Nyvall, Robert Frederick *plant pathologist, educator*

Mapleton
John, Hugo Herman *natural resources educator*

Marcell
Aldrich, Richard John *agronomist, educator*

Minneapolis
†Cox, J. Allen *physicist*
Danielson, James Walter *research microbiologist*
Dworkin, Martin *microbiologist, educator*
Ederer, Grace Mary *clinical laboratory scientist, retired*
Frestedt, Joy Louise *scientist*
Gorham, Eville *ecologist, biogeochemist*
Gudmundson, Barbara Rohrke *ecologist*
Haase, Ashley Thomson *microbiology educator, researcher*
Howe, Craig Walter Sandell *medical organization executive, internist*
Huang, Victor Tsangmin *food scientist, researcher*
Meyer, Maurice Wesley *physiologist, dentist, neurologist*
Miller, Robert Francis *physiologist, educator*
Rahman, Yueh-Erh *biologist*
Serstock, Doris Shay *retired microbiologist, educator, civic worker*
Smyrl, William Hiram *chemical engineering educator*
Symosek, Peter Frank *research scientist*
Watson, Dennis Wallace *microbiology educator, scientist*

Moorhead
Gee, Robert LeRoy *agriculturist, dairy farmer*

Prior Lake
Tufte, Obert Norman *retired research executive*

Rochester
Maher, L. James, III *molecular biologist*
Shepherd, John Thompson *physiologist*
Wood, Earl Howard *physiologist, educator*

Roseville
Marten, Gordon Cornelius *research agronomist, educator, federal agency administrator*

Saint Cloud
Musah, Al-Hassan Issah *reproductive physiologist*

Saint Joseph
Kirick, Daniel John *agronomist*

Saint Paul
Baker, Donald Gardner *retired soil science educator*
Barnwell, Franklin Hershel *zoology educator*
Cheng, H(wei) H(sien) *soil scientist, agronomic and environmental science educator*
Chiang, Huai Chang *entomologist, educator*
Davis, Margaret Bryan *paleoecology researcher, educator*
Dee, Scott Allen *veterinarian*
Diesch, Stanley La Verne *veterinarian, educator*
Ek, Alan Ryan *forestry educator*
Johnson, Kenneth Harvey *veterinary pathologist*
Jones, Charles Weldon *biologist, educator, researcher*
Kommedahl, Thor *plant pathology educator*
Leonard, Kurt John *plant pathologist, university program director*
Lyubimov, Aleksandr Vladimirovich *toxicologist*
Magee, Paul Terry *geneticist and molecular biologist, college dean*
Marini, John Joseph *medical scientist, educator, physician*
McKinnell, Robert Gilmore *zoology, genetics and cell biology educator*
Munson, Robert Dean *agronomist, soil scientist, consultant*
Phillips, Ronald Lewis *plant geneticist, educator*
Pomeroy, Benjamin Sherwood *veterinary medicine educator*
Roy, Robert Russell *toxicologist*
Sentz, James Curtis *agriculturist, agricultural developer*
Stadelmann, Eduard Joseph *plant physiologist, educator*
Tordoff, Harrison Bruce *retired zoologist, educator*
Wendt, Hans W(erner) *life scientist*
Zeyen, Richard John *plant pathology educator*

MISSISSIPPI

Biloxi
Deegen, Uwe Frederick *marine biologist*

Lorman
Ezekwe, Michael Obi *animal science educator*

Meridian
Blackwell, Cecil *science association executive*

Mississippi State
Cooper, Robert Carl, Jr. *veterinary medicine educator*
Jenkins, Johnie Norton *research geneticist, research administrator*
Reddy, Kambham Raja *plant physiology educator*
White, Charles H. *food science and technology educator*

Oxford
Duke, Stephen Oscar *physiologist, researcher, educator*

Stoneville
Ranney, Carleton David *plant pathology researcher, administrator*

University
Keiser, Edmund Davis, Jr. *biologist, educator*

Vicksburg
Marcuson, William F. *research administrator*
Mather, Bryant *research administrator*

MISSOURI

Ballwin
Sidoti, Daniel R. *food technologist*

Bridgeton
Hemming, Bruce Clark *microbiologist*

Canton
Glover, Albert Downing *retired veterinarian*

Cape Girardeau
Blackwelder, Richard E(liot) *entomologist, zoology educator, archivist*

Chesterfield
de Figueiredo, Mario Pacheco *food scientist*

Columbia
Blevins, Dale Glenn *agronomy educator*
Brown, Olen Ray *medical microbiology research educator*
Constantinescu, Gheorghe M. *veterinarian*
Darrah, Larry Lynn *plant breeder*
David, John Dewood *biology educator*
Davis, James O(thello) *physician, educator*
Duncan, Donald Pendleton *retired forestry educator*
Finkelstein, Richard Alan *microbiologist*
Ignoffo, Carlo Michael *insect pathologist-virologist*
Mitchell, Roger Lowry *retired agronomy educator*
Morehouse, Georgia Lewis *microbiologist, researcher*
Morehouse, Lawrence Glen *veterinarian, educator*
†Nelson, C. Jerry *agronomy educator*
Poehlmann, Carl John *agronomist, researcher*
Vogt, Albert Ralph *forester, educator, program director*
Wagner, Joseph Edward *veterinarian, educator*
Yanders, Armon Frederick *biological sciences educator, research administrator*
Youmans, William Barton *physiologist*

Eureka
Lindsey, Susan Lyndaker *zoologist*

Fayette
†Porneluzi, Paul A. *biologist, educator*

Greenwood
Klaus, Suzanne Lynne *horticulturist, production specialist*

Jefferson City
Reidinger, Russell Frederick, Jr. *fish and wildlife scientist*

Kansas City
Mc Kelvey, John Clifford *research institute executive*

Kirksville
Peterson, Donald Fred *physiologist, educator*

Mexico
Hudson, Harold Don *veterinarian*

Mount Vernon
Witty, Thomas Ezekiel *psychologist, researcher*

Saint Charles
Radke, Rodney Owen *agricultural research executive, consultant*

Saint Louis
Allen, Garland Edward *biology educator, science historian*
Asa, Cheryl Suzanne *biologist*
Croat, Thomas Bernard *botanical curator*
Curran, Michael Walter *management scientist*
Curtiss, Roy, III *biology educator*
Green, Maurice *molecular biologist, virologist, educator*
Hamburger, Viktor *retired biology educator*
Hoessle, Charles Herman *zoo director*
Laskowski, Leonard Francis, Jr. *microbiologist*
†Peck, Carol King *physiologist, educator*
Pikaard, Craig Stuart *biology educator*
Raven, Peter Hamilton *botanical garden director, botany educator*
Schlesinger, Milton J. *virology educator, researcher*
Sexton, Owen James *vertebrate ecology educator, conservationist*
Templeton, Alan Robert *biology educator*
Wold, William Sydney *molecular biology educator*
Zhuo, Min *neurobiology educator*

Wentzville
Garrett, Dwayne Everett *veterinary clinic executive*

West Plains
Wilcoxson, Roy Dell *plant pathology educator and researcher*

Windyville
Condron, Barbara O'Guinn *metaphysics educator, school administrator, publisher*

Winigan
†Smith, Wayne Delarmie *veterinarian, farmer*

MONTANA

Bozeman
Costerton, John William Fisher *microbiologist*
Hovin, Arne William *agronomist, educator*
Lavin, Matthew T. *horticultural educator*
Todd, Kenneth S., Jr. *parasitologist, educator*

Gardiner
Halfpenny, James Carson *scientist, educator, author*

Great Falls
Paulson-Ehrhardt, Patricia Helen *sales executive*

Hamilton
Munoz, John Joaquin *research microbiologist*
Rudbach, Jon Anthony *biotechnical company executive*

Havre
Clouse, Vickie Rae *biology and paleontology educator*

Miles City
Heitschmidt, Rodney Keith *rangeland ecologist*

Missoula
Jenni, Donald Alison *zoology educator*

Polson
Stanford, Jack Arthur *biological station administrator*

Red Lodge
Kauffman, Marvin Earl *geoscience consultant*

NEBRASKA

Clay Center
Laster, Danny Bruce *animal scientist*

Gering
Weihing, John Lawson *plant pathologist, state senator*

Humboldt
Rumbaugh, Melvin Dale *geneticist, agronomist*

Lincoln
Adams, Charles Henry *retired animal scientist, educator*
Gardner, Charles Olda *plant geneticist and breeder, design consultant, analyst*
Genoways, Hugh Howard *systematic biologist, educator*
Hanway, Donald Grant *retired agronomist, educator*
Johnson, Virgil Allen *retired agronomist*
Louda, Svata M. *ecologist, educator*
Massengale, Martin Andrew *agronomist, university president*
McClurg, James Edward *research laboratory executive*
Morris, M(ary) Rosalind *cytogeneticist, educator*
Sander, Donald Henry *soil scientist, researcher*
Swartzendruber, Dale *soil physicist, educator*

Omaha
Badeer, Henry Sarkis *physiology educator*
Fawcett, James Davidson *herpetologist, educator*
Nipper, Henry Carmack *toxicologist, educator*
Simmons, Lee Guyton, Jr. *zoological park director*

NEVADA

Fallon
Isidoro, Edith Annette *horticulturist*

Las Vegas
Alexander, John Bradfield *scientist, retired army officer*
Hess, John Warren *scientific institute administrator, educator*

Reno
Bohmont, Dale Wendell *agricultural consultant*
Gifford, Gerald Frederic *education educator*
Qualls, Robert Gerald *ecologist*
Smith, Aaron *research director, clinical psychologist*
Von Bartheld, Christopher Stephen *neurobiologist*

NEW HAMPSHIRE

Durham
Aber, John David *global ecosystem research scientist*
Harter, Robert Duane *soil scientist, educator*
Pistole, Thomas Gordon *microbiology educator, researcher*

Hanover
Gilbert, John Jouett *aquatic ecologist, educator*
Roos, Thomas Bloom *biological scientist, educator*
Spiegel, Evelyn Sclufer *biology educator, researcher*
Spiegel, Melvin *retired biology educator*

Lebanon
Mc Cann, Frances Veronica *physiologist, educator*
Munck, Allan Ulf *physiologist, educator*
Ou, Lo-Chang *physiology educator*

Manchester
Stahl, Barbara J. *biologist, educator*

Sanbornton
Weiant, Elizabeth Abbott *retired biology educator*

Silver Lake
Pallone, Adrian Joseph *research scientist*

NEW JERSEY

Annandale
Drakeman, Donald Lee *biotechnology company executive, lawyer*

Clifton
Yau, Edward Tintai *toxicologist, pharmacologist*

Cranford
Jenssen, Warren Donald *microbiologist*

East Hanover
Foley, James Edward *scientist, pharmaceutical company executive*
Nemecek, Georgina Marie *molecular pharmacologist*

East Millstone
†Rodwell, Dean Edward *toxicologist*

Flemington
Wiedl-Kramer, Sheila Colleen *biologist*

Hoboken
Abel, Robert Berger *science administrator*

Holmdel
†Kashyap, Satchitanand *research scientis*

Kenilworth
Kravec, Cynthia Vallen *microbiologist*

Kinnelon
Richardson, Joseph Blancet *former biology educator, educational facilities planning consultant*

Lakewood
Gross, Michael Fred *biologist, educator, researcher*

Livingston
Schlesinger, Stephen Lyons *horticulturist*

Madison
Campbell, William Cecil *biologist*

Montclair
Chinard, Francis Pierre *physiologist, physician, preventive medicine consultant*

Murray Hill
†Li, Qi *researcher*

New Brunswick
Ballou, Janice Donelon *research director*
Day, Peter Rodney *geneticist, educator*
Day-Salvatore, Debra Lynn *medical geneticist*
Ehrenfeld, David William *biology educator, author*
Funk, Cyril Reed, Jr. *agronomist, educator*
†Grassle, Judith Payne *marine biology educator*
Hayakawa, Kan-Ichi *food science educator*
Lachance, Paul Albert *food science educator, clergyman*
Maramorosch, Karl *virologist, educator*
Montville, Thomas Joseph *food microbiologist, educator*
Murray, Bertram George *biology educator*
Psuty, Norbert Phillip *marine sciences educator*
Solberg, Myron *food scientist, educator*
Tedrow, John Charles Fremont *soils educator*
Wang, Tsuey Tang *science educator, venture capitalist*

Newark
Geskin, Ernest S(amuel) *science administrator, consultant*

Nutley
Dennin, Robert Aloysius, Jr. *pharmaceutical research scientist*

Paterson
Greidanus, Ida *biology educator*

Piscataway
Denhardt, David Tilton *molecular and cell biology educator*
Essien, Francine B. *geneticist, educator*
Liu, Alice Y. C. *biology educator*
Pramer, David *microbiologist, educator, research administrator*
Trivedi, Harsh Mahendra *research scientist, educator*
Witkin, Evelyn Maisel *geneticist*

Plainfield
Frost, David *former biology educator, medical editor, consultant*

Port Norris
Canzonier, Walter Jude *shellfish aquaculturist*

Princeton
Altmann, Stuart Allen *biologist, educator*
Collins, Amy Amanda *research assistant*
Crandall, David LeRoy *research scientist*
Feder, John Nathan *molecular biologist*
Gould, James L. *biology educator*
Jacobs, William Paul *botanist, educator*
Merrill, Leland Gilbert, Jr. *retired environmental science educator*
Shenk, Thomas Eugene *molecular biology educator, academic administrator*
Steinberg, Malcolm Saul *biologist, educator*
Swenson, Christine Erica *microbiologist*
Thompson, Ellen Kubacki *microbiologist, medical writer, consultant*
Tilghman, Shirley Marie *biology educator*
Wieschaus, Eric F. *molecular biologist, educator*

Rahway
Dombrowski, Anne Wesseling *microbiologist, researcher*
Reynolds, Glenn Franklin *medicinal research scientist*
Strack, Alison Merwin *neurobiologist*

Red Bank
Fred, Rogers Murray, III *veterinary oncologist*

Rutherford
Aberman, Harold Mark *veterinarian*
Bertone, Andrew E. *biological scientist, environmental scientist*

Shrewsbury
Westerman, Liane Marie *research scientist executive*

Sparta
Buist, Jean Mackerley *veterinarian*

Stanton
Frascella, Daniel William, Jr. *scientist*
Kille, John William, Jr. *toxicology and biomedical product consultant*

Stockton
Seizinger, Bernd Robert *molecular geneticist, physician, researcher*

Stratford
Li, David Wan-Cheng *cell biologist*

Teterboro
Gambino, S(alvatore) Raymond *medical laboratory executive, educator*

Vineland
Kazam, Abdul Raoof *veterinarian*

Wayne
White, Doris Gnauck *science educator, biochemical and biophysics researcher*

Wyckoff
Cropper, Susan Peggy *veterinarian*

NEW MEXICO

Albuquerque
†Fisher, Don Carlton *toxicologist*
Henderson, Rogene Faulkner *toxicologist, researcher*
Hsi, David Ching Heng *plant pathologist and geneticist, educator*
Mauderly, Joe Lloyd *pulmonary toxicologist*
O'Neil, Daniel Joseph *science research executive, research educator*
Perez-Castro, Ana Veronica *developmental biology researcher*

Alto
Thrasher, Jack Dwayne *toxicologist, researcher, consultant*

Carlsbad
Deckert, Frank *park administrator*
Goldstein, Barry Bruce *biologist, food company executive, lawyer*

Cedar Crest
Rypka, Eugene Weston *microbiologist*

Las Cruces
Schemnitz, Sanford David *wildlife biology educator*

Los Alamos
Gregg, Charles Thornton *research company executive*
McComas, David John *science administrator, space physicist*
Wallace, Terry Charles, Sr. *technical administrator, researcher, consultant*

Santa Fe
Harding, Marie *ecological executive, artist*
†McCarthy, Laura Falk *forester*
Moore, Jay Winston *director cytogenetics laboratory*
Myers, Charlotte Will *biology educator*

Tijeras
Van Arsdel, Eugene Parr *tree pathologist, meteorologist*

NEW YORK

Albany
Able, Kenneth Paul *biology educator*
Bawa, Sukhdev Raj *biomedical researcher, educator, administrator*
Csiza, Charles Karoly *veterinarian, microbiologist*
D'Elia, Christopher Francis *marine biologist*
Demerjian, Kenneth Leo *atmospheric science educator, research center director*
Hitchcock, Karen Ruth *biology educator, university dean, academic administrator*
Schmidt, John Thomas *neurobiologist*
Stevens, Roy W. *microbiologist*
Stewart, Margaret McBride *biology educator, researcher*
†Taber, Harry Warren *research scientist*
Toombs, Russ William *laboratory director*

Annandale On Hudson
Ferguson, John Barclay *biology educator*

Baldwin
Lister, Bruce Alcott *food scientist, consultant*

Bronx
Conway, William Gaylord *zoologist, zoo director, conservationist*
Frenz, Dorothy Ann *cell and developmental biologist*
Friedman, Ronald Marvin *cellular biologist*
Kaul, Dhananjaya Kumar *physiologist*
Lattis, Richard Lynn *zoo director*
Long, Gregory R. *botanic garden administrator*
Pettoello-Mantovani, Massimo *pediatrician, educator, microbiologist, researcher*
Scheuer, James *physician, educator, researcher*

Bronxville
Hutchison, Dorris Jeannette *retired microbiologist, educator*

Brooklyn
Altura, Bella T. *physiologist, educator*
Altura, Burton Myron *physiologist, educator*
Carswell, Lois Malakoff *botanical gardens executive, consultant*
†Cunningham, John Thomas *science educator*
Freijoso, Ricardo *microbiologist*
Gabriel, Mordecai Lionel *biologist, educator*
Garibaldi, Louis E. *aquarium administrator*
Kramer, Allan Franklin, II *botanical garden official, researcher*
MacFarland, Craig George *natural resource management professional*
Pagala, Murali Krishna *physiologist*
Schiffman, Gerald *microbiologist, educator*
Verma, Ram Sagar *geneticist, educator, author, administrator*
Zuk, Judith *botanic garden administrator*

Buffalo
Duax, William Leo *biological researcher*
He, Guang Sheng *research scientist*
Keem, Michael Dennis *veterinarian*
Kite, Joseph Hiram, Jr. *microbiologist, educator*
Tomasi, Thomas B. *cell biologist, administrator*

Cazenovia
Bump, Karin Diann *animal scientist, educator*

Chenango Bridge
Fisher, Dale Dunbar *animal scientist, dairy nutritionist*

Cobleskill
Ingels, Jack Edward *horticulture educator*

Cold Spring Harbor
Watson, James Dewey *molecular biologist, educator*
Wigler, Michael H. *molecular biologist*

Cooperstown
Harman, Willard Nelson *malacologist, educator*

Cutchogue
Bidwell, Robert Ernest *inventor*

Depew
Koch, Ronald Peter *retired biologist*

East Hampton
Murbach, David Paul *horticulturist*

East Setauket
Briggs, Philip Terry *biologist*

Flushing
Commoner, Barry *biologist, educator*

Franklin
Young, William Donald, Jr. *bacteriologist, artist-blacksmith, photographer*

Fredonia
Benton, Allen Haydon *biology educator*

Garden City
Eickelberg, W. Warren Barbour *academic administrator*
Podwall, Kathryn Stanley *biology educator*

Geneseo
†Spicka, Edwin J. *biology educator*

Great Neck
Puttlitz, Donald Herbert *medical microbiologist*

Hamilton
Kessler, Dietrich *biology educator*

Hauppauge
Wang, Chang Yi *biomedical company executive*

Hawthorne
Frischmuth, Robert Alfred *landscape planner, filmmaker*

Hempstead
Blumenthal, Ralph Herbert *natural science educator*
Cassidy, David C. *science educator*

Highland
Rosenberger, David A. *research scientist, cooperative extension specialist*

Homer
Gustafson, John Alfred *biology educator*

Irvington
Lyons, Michael Joseph *microbiologist, research, educator*

Ithaca
Adler, Kraig (Kerr) *biology educator*
Alexander, Martin *environmental toxicologist, consultant*
Arntzen, Charles Joel *bioscience educator*
Baylor, Harry Brooks *microbiologist*
Blackler, Antonie William Charles *biologist*
Calnek, Bruce Wixson *veterinary virologist*
Davies, Peter John *plant physiology educator, researcher*
Dobson, Alan *veterinary physiology educator*
Earle, Elizabeth Deutsch *biology educator*
Eisner, Thomas *biologist, educator*
Fick, Gary Warren *agronomy educator, forage crops researcher*
Foote, Robert Hutchinson *animal physiology educator*
Fox, Francis Henry *veterinarian*
Gillett, James Warren *ecotoxicology educator*
Grunes, David Leon *research soil scientist, educator, editor*
Hudler, George *plant pathologist, educator*
Jagendorf, Andre Tridon *plant physiologist*
Kallfelz, Francis A. *veterinary medicine educator*
Kennedy, Wilbert Keith, Sr. *agronomy educator, retired university official*
Kingsbury, John Merriam *botanist, educator*
Korf, Richard Paul *mycology educator*
Kramer, John Paul *entomologist, educator*
Krueger, Charles Conrad *fishery science educator*
Lengemann, Frederick William *physiology educator, scientist*
Lopez, Jorge Washington *veterinary virologist*
Lund, Daryl Bert *food science educator*
Mai, William Frederick *plant nematologist, educator*
Mortlock, Robert Paul *microbiologist, educator*
Novak, Joseph Donald *science educator, knowlege studies specialist*
Phemister, Robert David *veterinary medical educator*
Pimentel, David *entomologist, educator*
†Polack, Evelyne Weber *veterinarian, pathologist*
Poppensiek, George Charles *veterinary scientist, educator*
Schlafer, Donald Hughes *veterinary pathologist*
Scott, Fredric Winthrop *veterinarian*
Seeley, John George *horticulture educator*
Steingraber, Sandra Kathryn *biologist, ecologist, writer*
Viands, Donald Rex *plant breeder and educator*
Walcott, Charles *neurobiology and behvior educator*
Wasserman, Robert Harold *biology educator*
Welch, Ross Maynard *plant physiologist, researcher, educator*
Wootton, John Francis *physiology educator*

Larchmont
Sklarew, Robert Jay *biomedical research educator, consultant*

Lewiston
Gallo, Mark Allen *microbiology educator*

Liverpool
†Schuehler, Kathleen H. *biology educator*

Macedon
McGee, Dennis Emmett *research technologist*

Manhasset
Bialer, Martin George *geneticist*
Lipson, Steven Mark *clinical virologist, educator*

Manorville
Esp, Barbara Ann Lorraine *research scientist, educator*

Millbrook
Likens, Gene Elden *biology and ecology educator, administrator*

New Hyde Park
Isenberg, Henry David *microbiology educator*

New Paltz
Huth, Paul Curtis *ecosystem scientist, botanist*

New Rochelle
Beardsley, Robert Eugene *microbiologist, educator*

New York
Akingbemi, Benson Tokunbo *biomedical scientist, veterinarian, educator*
Anderson, O(rvil) Roger *biology educator, marine biology and protozoology, researcher*
Anderson, Sydney *biologist, museum curator*
Basilico, Claudio *molecular biologist, educator*
Bernstein, Jonine Lisa *biometry researcher, epidemiologist, educator*
Blobel, Günter *cell biologist, educator*
Bock, Walter Joseph *zoology educator*
Calame, Kathryn Lee *microbiologist, educator*
Carlson, Marian Bille *geneticist, researcher, educator*
Catanzaro, Daniel Frank *molecular biologist, educator*
Chaganti, Raju S. *geneticist, educator, researcher*
Cherksey, Bruce David *physiology educator*
Chua, Nam-Hai *plant molecular biologist, educator*
Cohen, Joel Ephraim *scientist, educator*
Cranefield, Paul Frederic *physiology educator, physician, scientist*
Cronholm, Lois S. *biology educator*
Dales, Samuel *microbiologist, virologist, educator*
Darnell, James Edwin, Jr. *molecular biologist, educator*
Desnick, Robert John *human geneticist*
Despommier, Dickson Donald *microbiology educator, parasitologist, researcher*
Garvey, Michael Steven *veterinarian, educator*
Grafstein, Bernice *physiology and neuroscience educator, researcher*
Hanafusa, Hidesaburo *virologist*
Hirschhorn, Rochelle *genetics educator*
Hudspeth, Albert James *biomedical researcher, educator*
Hutner, Seymour Herbert *microbiologist, protozoologist*
Jacobson, Leslie Sari *biologist, educator*
King, Marvin *research executive*
Lederberg, Joshua *geneticist, educator*
Levine, Arnold Jay *molecular biology educator*
Maas, Werner Karl *microbiology educator*
Manski, Wladyslaw Julian *microbiology educator, medical scientist*
Moroz, Pavel Emanuel *research scientist*
Morse, Stephen Scott *virologist, immunologist*
†Mourad, Boaz Aaron *researcher, psychology educator*
Pietruski, John Michael, Jr. *biotechnology company executive, pharmaceuticals executive*
Pollack, Robert Elliot *biologist, educator*
Poshni, Iqbal Ahmed *microbiologist*
Rothman, James Edward *cell biologist, educator*
Rozen, Jerome George, Jr. *research entomologist, museum curator and research administrator*
Rutishauser, Urs Stephen *cell biologist*
Sabatini, David Domingo *cell biologist, biochemist*
Silverstein, Samuel Charles *cellular biology and physiology educator, researcher*
Stotzky, Guenther *microbiologist, educator*
Stutman, Leonard Jay *research scientist, cardiologist*
Sun, Ji *research scientist*
Telang, Nitin T. *cancer biologist, educator*
Tierno, Philip Mario, Jr. *microbiologist, educator, researcher*
Tietjen, John Henry *retired biology and oceanography educator*
Tomasz, Alexander *cell biologist*
Trager, William *biology educator*
Underwood, Joanna DeHaven *environmental research and education organizations president*
Wharton, Danny Carroll *zoo biologist*
Windhager, Erich Ernst *physiologist, educator*
Young, Michael Warren *geneticist, educator*
Zinder, Norton David *genetics educator, university dean*

Orangeburg
Squires, Richard Felt *research scientist*

Owego
Kemp, Eugene Thomas *veterinarian*

Patchogue
Gibbons, Edward Francis *psychobiologist*

Pearl River
Barik, Sudhakar *microbiologist, research scientist*
Projan, Steven Jay *microbiologist*

Pittsford
Thorndike, Elizabeth *educator*

Port Jefferson
Arnaboldi, Joseph Paul *retired veterinarian*

Purchase
Ehrman, Lee *geneticist*

Riverhead
Kent, Robert John *marine biologist*

Rochester
Chang, Jack Che-man *imaging materials and media administrator*
Clarkson, Thomas William *toxicologist, educator*
Coleman, Paul David *neurobiology researcher, educator*
Cropper, André Dominic *research scientist*
Mittermeyer, Paul F. *laser energetics technician, writer*
Morrow, Paul Edward *toxicology educator*
Muchmore, William Breuleux *zoologist, educator*
Rustchenko, Elena *geneticist*

Saranac Lake
North, Robert John *biologist*

Schenectady
Bedard, Donna Lee *environmental microbiologist*
Cerne, Gerald John *biology educator*
Sternlicht, Beno *research and development company executive*

Southold
Callis, Jerry Jackson *veterinarian*

Stanley
Jones, Gordon Edwin *horticulturist*

Staten Island
Fishman, Brian Scott *research assistant*
Wisniewski, Henryk Miroslaw *pathology and neuropathology educator, research facility administrator, research scientist*

Stone Ridge
Terpening, Donald Lester *science educator, medical technologist*

Stony Brook
Erk, Frank Chris *biologist, educator*
Lennarz, William Joseph *research biologist, educator*
Levinton, Jeffrey S. *biology educator, oceanographer*
Rohlf, F. James *biometrician, educator*
Williams, George Christopher *biologist, ecology and evolution educator*
Wurster, Charles Frederick *environmental scientist, educator*

Suffern
Kromidas, Lambros *cell biologist, physical scientist, toxicologist*

Syracuse
Burgess, Robert Lewis ecologist, educator
Delmar, Mario cardiac physiology educator
Dunham, Philip Bigelow biology educator, physiologist
Kriebel, Mahlon Edward physiology educator, inventor
Russell-Hunter, Gus W(illiam) D(evigne) zoology educator, research biologist, writer
Tanenbaum, Stuart William biotechnologist, educator
Turner, Christopher Edward cell biology educator

Troy
Ehrlich, Henry Lutz biology educator
Murarka, Shyam Prasad science educator, administrator
Watson, Edward Bruce science educator

Tuxedo Park
Heusser, Calvin John biology educator, researcher
†Lippmann, Morton environmental health science researcher
Rossman, Toby Gale genetic toxicology educator, researcher

Upton
Petrakis, Leonidas research scientist, educator, administrator

Utica
Antzelevitch, Charles research center executive

Valhalla
Hommes, Frits Aukustinus biology educator
Kilbourne, Edwin Dennis virologist, educator
Wolin, Michael Stuart physiology educator

White Plains
Peyton, Donald Leon retired standards association executive

Woodbury
Doering, Charles Henry research scientist, educator, editor, publisher

Woodside
Kekatos, Deppie-Tinny Z. microbiologist, researcher, lab technologist

NORTH CAROLINA

Asheboro
Jones, David M. zoological park director

Atlantic Beach
Barnes, James Thomas, Jr. aquarium director

Beaufort
Ramus, Joseph S. marine biologist

Burlington
Turanchik, Michael research and development director

Cary
Mochrie, Richard D. physiology educator

Chapel Hill
Andrews, Richard Nigel Lyon environmental policy educator, environmental studies administrator
Farber, Rosann Alexander geneticist, educator
Gilbert, Lawrence Irwin biologist, educator
Hackenbrock, Charles R. cell biologist, educator
Huang, Eng-Shang virology educator, biomedical engineer
Judd, Burke Haycock geneticist
Kuenzler, Edward Julian ecologist and environmental biologist
McBay, Arthur John toxicologist, consultant
Scott, Tom Keck biologist, educator
Smithies, Oliver geneticist, educator
Stiven, Alan Ernest population biologist, ecologist
Stumpf, Walter Erich cell biology educator, researcher
Warren, Donald William physiology educator, dentistry educator
Weiss, Charles Manuel environmental biologist

Charlotte
Cornell, James Fraser, Jr. entomologist, educator

Durham
Abdel-Rahman, Mohamed international agribusiness consultant
Blum, Jacob Joseph physiologist, educator
Bolognesi, Dani Paul virologist, educator
Bond, Enriqueta Carter science administrator
Cook, Clarence Edgar research facility scientist
Cruze, Alvin M. research institute executive
Culberson, William Louis botany educator
Gillham, Nicholas Wright geneticist, educator
Keene, Jack Donald molecular genetics and microbiology educator
Malindzak, George Steve, Jr. cardiovascular physiology, biomedical engineer
Naylor, Aubrey Willard botany educator
Nicklas, Robert Bruce cell biologist
Pearsall, Samuel Haff, III landscape ecologist, geographer, foundation administrator
Raetz, Christian R. H. biochemistry educator
Richardson, Curtis John ecology educator
Richardson, Stephen Giles biotechnology company executive
Rouse, Doris Jane physiologist, research administrator
Schmidt-Nielsen, Knut physiologist, educator
Searles, Richard Brownlee botany educator, marine biology researcher
Sheetz, Michael Patrick cell biology educator
Somjen, George Gustav physiologist
Terborgh, John J. natural science educator

Greenville
Thurber, Robert Eugene physiologist, researcher

Hendersonville
Brittain, James Edward science and technology educator, researcher
Kehr, August Ernest geneticist, researcher

Kinston
Arcino, Manuel Dagan microbiologist, consultant

Kitty Hawk
Sjoerdsma, Albert research institute executive

Kure Beach
Lanier, James Alfred, III aquarium administrator

Little Switzerland
Gross, Samson Richard geneticist, biochemist, educator

New Bern
Ash, William James geneticist

Pfafftown
Radford, Kathy Ann veterinarian

Pinehurst
Burris, Kenneth Wayne biologist, educator

Raleigh
Aronson, Arthur Lawrence veterinary pharmacology and toxicology educator
Atchley, William Reid geneticist, evolutionary biologist, educator
Benson, D(avid) Michael plant pathologist
Cook, Maurice Gayle soil science educator, consultant
Cooper, Arthur Wells ecologist, educator
Cummings, Ralph Waldo soil scientist, educator, researcher
Dunphy, Edward James crop science extension specialist
Goodman, Major Merlin botanical sciences educator
Gordon, Morris Aaron medical mycologist, microbiologist
Hardin, James W. botanist, herbarium curator, educator
Hassan, Hosni Moustafa microbiologist, biochemist, toxicologist and food scientist, educator
Havlin, John Leroy soil scientist, educator
Hodgson, Ernest toxicology educator
Kelman, Arthur plant pathologist, educator
Moreland, Donald Edwin plant physiologist
Sanders, Douglas Charles horticulturist, researcher, educator
Scandalios, John George geneticist, educator
Sederoff, Ronald Ross geneticist
Stuber, Charles William genetics educator, researcher
Timothy, David Harry biology educator
Triantaphyllou, H. H. plant pathologist
Wollum, Arthur George, II microbiologist, researcher, educator
Zeng, Zhao-Bang geneticist, educator

Research Triangle Park
de Serres, Frederick Joseph genetic toxicologist
McClellan, Roger Orville toxicologist
Mumford, Stephen Douglas population growth control research scientist
Ross, Jeffrey Alan research biologist

Washington
Heck, Henry D'Arcy toxicologist

Wilmington
Bolen, Eric George biology educator
Roer, Robert David physiologist, educator
Watanabe, Wade Osamu marine biologist

Winston Salem
Dodd, Virginia Marilyn veterinarian
Ganz, Charles laboratory executive
Laxminarayana, Dama geneticist, researcher, educator

Wrightsville Beach
Phull, Bopinder S. research scientist

NORTH DAKOTA

Fargo
Schmidt, Claude Henri retired research administrator
Williams, Norman Dale geneticist, researcher

Grand Forks
Fox, Carl Alan research executive
Long, William McMurray physiology educator

Jamestown
Kirby, Ronald Eugene fish and wildlife research administrator

Minot
†Clark, Brandi M. veterinary technician
Morgan, Rose Marie retired biology educator

OHIO

Ada
†Keiser, Terry D. biologist, educator

Ashland
Rueger, Daniel Scott horticulture educator

Athens
Ungar, Irwin Allan botany educator

Avon Lake
†Zurcher, Vickie Lee geneticist

Bay Village
Stanbery, Robert Charles veterinarian

Bowling Green
Clark, Eloise Elizabeth biologist, educator
Heckman, Carol A. biology educator

Cincinnati
Etges, Frank Joseph parasitology educator
†Huether, Carl A. biology educator
†Kothari, Ravi science educator
†Lindquist, H.D. Alan parasitologist, restaurateur
Maruska, Edward Joseph zoo administrator
Nebert, Daniel Walter molecular geneticist, research administrator
Saal, Howard Max clinical geneticist, pediatrician, educator
Safferman, Robert Samuel microbiologist
Schaefer, Frank William, III microbiologist, researcher
Sperelakis, Nicholas, Sr. physiology and biophysics educator, researcher
Stanberry, Lawrence Raymond virologist, vaccinologist, pediatrician, educator

Cleveland
Lakshmanan, Mark Chandrakant physiologist, physician
†Starkman, Glenn David physicist, educator
Steinberg, Arthur G(erald) geneticist
Taylor, Steve Henry zoologist

Columbus
Boerner, Ralph E. J. forest soil ecologist, plant biology educator
Capen, Charles Chabert veterinary pathology educator, researcher
Disinger, John Franklin natural resources educator
Fausey, Norman Ray soil scientist
Fawcett, Sherwood Luther research laboratory executive
Floyd, Gary Leon plant cell biologist
Fry, Donald Lewis physiologist, educator
Glaser, Ronald microbiology educator, scientist
Kapral, Frank Albert medical microbiology and immunology educator
Lal, Rattan soil scientist, researcher
Marushige-Knopp, Yuka food scientist
Needham, Glen Ray entomology and acarology educator, researcher
Olesen, Douglas Eugene research institute executive
Peterle, Tony John zoologist, educator
Pieper, Heinz Paul physiology educator
Quinn, Robert David research institute executive
Reeve, John Newton molecular biology and microbiology educator
Roth, Robert Earl environmental educator
Triplehorn, Charles A. entomology educator, insects curator
von Recum, Andreas F. veterinarian, bioengineer
Warmbrod, James Robert agriculture educator, university administrator
Wood, Jackie Dale physiologist, educator, researcher
Yohn, David Stewart virologist, science administrator
Zartman, David Lester animal sciences educator, researcher

Cumberland
Reece, Robert William zoological park administrator

Dayton
Isaacson, Milton Stanley research and development company executive, engineer
Tan, Seng C. research scientist, materials research executive

Delaware
Fry, Anne Evans zoology educator

Fairborn
Byczkowski, Janusz Zbigniew toxicologist

Granville
Haubrich, Robert Rice biology educator

Kent
Cooperrider, Tom S. botanist

Kirtland
Munson, Richard Howard horticulturist

Loveland
Reynolds, Robert Gregory toxicologist, management consultant

Mason
Leusch, Mark Steven microbiologist

Milford
Comstock, Walter biologist, educator

Oxford
Eshbaugh, W(illiam) Hardy botanist, educator
MacKenzie, Ann Haley science educator
Williamson, Clarence Kelly microbiologist, educator

Powell
Borin, Gerald W. zoological park administrator

Rootstown
†Jamison, James Mark cell biologist

Springfield
Hobbs, Horton Holcombe, III biology educator
Ryu, Kyoo-Hai Lee physiologist

Toledo
Thomas, Lewis Edward laboratory executive, retired petroleum company executive

Upper Arlington
Snyder, Susan Leach science educator

Wooster
Ferree, David Curtis horticultural researcher
Grewal, Parwinder S. biologist, researcher
Lafever, Howard Nelson plant breeder, geneticist, educator
Madden, Laurence Vincent plant pathology educator

OKLAHOMA

Ardmore
Aldridge, Charles Douglas veterinarian

Durant
Rice, Stanley Arthur biology educator

Edmond
Caire, William biologist, educator

El Reno
Phillips, William Allison research animal scientist

Langston
Mallik, Muhammad Abdul-Bari soil microbiologist

Lawton
Buckley, Gary Steven science educator

Newcastle
Mudroch, Kimberly Ann veterinarian

Norman
Carpenter, Charles Congden zoologist, educator
Hutchison, Victor Hobbs biologist, educator

Ochelata
Hitzman, Donald Oliver microbiologist

Oklahoma City
Alexander, Patrick Byron zoological society executive
†Sauer, Brian molecular geneticist, researcher
Scott, Lawrence Vernon microbiology educator

Pawhuska
Strahm, Samuel Edward veterinarian

Ponca City
Bolene, Margaret Rosalie Steele bacteriologist, civic worker
Wann, Laymond Doyle retired petroleum research scientist

Spiro
Aishman, Sharon Kay science educator

Stillwater
Campbell, John Roy animal scientist educator, academic administrator
Confer, Anthony Wayne veterinary pathologist, educator
Ewing, Sidney Alton veterinary medical educator, parasitologist
Grischkowsky, Daniel Richard research scientist, educator
Langwig, John Edward retired wood science educator
Quinn, Art Jay veterinarian, retired educator
Whitcomb, Carl Ervin horticulturist, researcher

Tulsa
Johnson, Gerald, III cardiovascular physiologist, researcher
Korstad, John Edward biology educator

OREGON

Ashland
Christianson, Roger Gordon biology educator
MacMillen, Richard Edward biological sciences educator, researcher

Beaverton
Machida, Curtis A. research molecular neurobiologist, educator

Corvallis
Brown, George research forester and educator
Castle, Emery Neal agricultural and resource economist, educator
Chambers, Kenton Lee botany educator
Farkas, Daniel Frederick food science and technology educator
Frakes, Rod Vance plant geneticist, educator
Ho, Iwan research plant pathologist
Liegel, Leon Herman soil scientist, research forester
Moore, Thomas Carrol botanist, educator
Morita, Richard Yukio microbiology and oceanography educator
Rounds, Donald Edwin retired cell biologist
Schmidt, Bruce Randolph science administrator, researcher
Trappe, James Martin mycologist
Westwood, Melvin Neil horticulturist, pomologist
Young, J. Lowell soil chemist, biologist

Eugene
Lande, Russell Scott biologist, educator
Matthews, Brian W. molecular biology educator
Stahl, Franklin William biology educator

Hillsboro
Bhagwan, Sudhir computer industry and research executive, consultant
Matlock, John Hudson science administrator, materials engineer

Mcminnville
Roberts, Michael Foster biology educator

Newport
Weber, Lavern John marine science administrator, educator

Pendleton
Klepper, Elizabeth Lee physiologist
Smiley, Richard Wayne research center administrator, researcher

Phoenix
Blackman, David Lee research scientist

Portland
Button, Jerry Edward biologist
Gillette, Richard Gareth neurophysiology educator, researcher
Glass, Laurel Ellen gerontologist, developmental biologist, physician, retired educator
Grimsbo, Raymond Allen forensic scientist
Hagenstein, William David forester, consultant
Marshall, David Brownell biologist, consultant
Stafford, Helen Adele retired biology educator
Vecchio, Tony zoological park administrator
Wilson, Thomas Woodrow, III research scientist, consultant

Prineville
Demmer, Richard James *biologist*

Salem
Bellman, Michael Stanley *forester, freelance writer*

Yachats
Gerdemann, James Wessel *plant pathologist, educator*

PENNSYLVANIA

Allentown
†Schaeffer, Robert L. *retired biology educator*

Ambler
Crowell, Richard Lane *microbiology educator*

Apollo
Burks, Brian Scott *veterinarian*

Bala Cynwyd
Corliss, John Ozro *zoology educator*

Boalsburg
Rashid, Kamal A. *program director, researcher*

Boyertown
Thomas, Richard Earl, Jr. *biologist*

Cochranton
Baldwin, Anthony Blair *systems theoretician, agricultural executive*

Doylestown
Marino, Paul Michael *science education educator*
Mishler, John Milton (Yochanan Menashsheh ben Shaul) *natural sciences educator, administrator, artist*

Edinboro
Miller, G(erson) H(arry) *research institute director, mathematician, computer scientist, chemist*

Elizabethville
Romberger, John Albert *scientist, historian*

Exton
Molloy, Christopher John *molecular/cellular biologist, pharmacist*

Gettysburg
Hendrix, Sherman Samuel *biology educator, researcher*

Grantham
Falk, Noel Wesley *biology educator, radio and television program host, horticultural consultant*

Harrisburg
DuBrock, Calvin William *wildlife program administrator*

Hershey
Demers, Laurence Maurice *science educator, consultant, editor*
Lang, Carol Max *veterinarian, educator*
Leventhal, Ruth *parasitology educator, former university official*

Holland
Umbreit, Wayne William *bacteriologist, educator*

Holtwood
Liebman, Shirley Anne *analytical research scientist*

Kennett Square
Allam, Mark Whittier *veterinarian, former university administrator*

King Of Prussia
Ladunga, Istvan (Steve Ladunga) *computational molecular biologist*
Wang, Xin-Min *molecular biologist*

Lewisburg
Candland, Douglas Keith *educator*
Sojka, Gary Allan *biologist, educator, university official*

Narberth
Nathanson, Neal *virologist, epidemiologist, educator*

New Kensington
Lederman, Frank L. *scientist, research center administrator*

Philadelphia
Brinster, Ralph Lawrence *biologist*
Brobeck, John Raymond *physiology educator*
Davis, Robert Harry *physiology educator*
Detweiler, David Kenneth *veterinary physiologist, educator*
DiBerardino, Marie Antoinette *developmental biologist, educator*
Eisenstein, Toby K. *microbiology educator*
Erickson, Ralph O. *botany educator*
Faber, Donald Stuart *neurobiology and anatomy educator*
Fisher, Aron Baer *physiology and medicine educator*
Franzini-Armstrong, Clara *biologist*
Furth, John Jacob *molecular biologist, pathologist, educator*
Hammond, Benjamin Franklin *microbiologist, educator*
Hand, Peter James *neurobiologist, educator*
Harvey, Colin Edwin *veterinary medicine educator*
Hinshaw, Keith C. *veterinarian*
Hoskins, Alexander L. (Pete Hoskins) *zoological park administrator*
Knudson, Alfred George, Jr. *medical geneticist*
Koprowski, Hilary *microbiologist, educator*
Lefer, Allan Mark *physiologist*
Lu, Ponzy *molecular biology educator*
Medvec, Stephen Edward *research manager, educator*
Meyer, Paul William *arboretum director, horticulturist*
Mintz, Beatrice *biologist*
Niewiarowski, Stefan *physiology educator, biomedical research scientist*
Patrick, Ruth (Mrs. Ruth Hodge Van Dusen) *limnologist, diatom taxonomist, educator*
Patterson, Donald Floyd *human, medical and veterinary genetics educator*
Peachey, Lee DeBorde *biology educator*
Pepe, Frank A. *cell and developmental biology educator*
Perry, Robert Palese *molecular biologist, educator*
Porter, Roger John *medical research administrator, neurologist, pharmacologist*
†Robertson, Robert *biologist, malacologist*
Shockman, Gerald David *microbiologist, educator*
Silvers, Willys Kent *geneticist*
Stevens, Rosemary A. *public health and social history educator*
Tammen, James F. *plant pathologist, educator*
Xin, Li *physiologist*
Young, Robert Crabill *medical researcher, science facility administrator, internist*

Pipersville
Erickson, Edward Leonard *biotechnology company executive, consultant*

Pittsburgh
Boyce, Alfred Warne *analytical laboratory executive*
Brunson, Kenneth Wayne *cancer biologist*
Edmonds, Mary Patricia *biological sciences educator*
Feingold, David Sidney *microbiology educator*
Fletcher, Ronald Darling *microbiologist educator*
Henry, Susan Armstrong *biology educator, university dean*
Jones, Elizabeth Winifred *biology educator*
Kanade, Takeo *science educator, institute administrator*
Keleti, Georg *retired microbiologist, researcher*
Kiger, Robert William *botanist, science historian, educator*
LaJohn, Lawrence Anthony *research scientist*
Li, Mengfeng *molecular biologist, virologist, educator*
Maxwell, Bonnie K. *science educator*
McGovern, John Joseph *retired air pollution control executive*
McWilliams, Betty Jane *science administrator, communication disorders educator, researcher*
Murphy, Robert Francis *biology educator and researcher*
Murray, Sandra Ann *biology research scientist, educator*
Parkes, Kenneth Carroll *ornithologist*
Partanen, Carl Richard *biology educator*
Slifkin, Malcolm *clincal microbiologist, educator*
Taylor, D. Lansing *cell biology educator*
Wang, Allan Zuwu *cell biologist, pharmacologist*
Youngner, Julius Stuart *microbiologist, educator*

Quakertown
de Limantour, Clarice Barr *food scientist*

Ridley Park
Logan, Thomas Joseph *molecular biologist, pharmaceutical researcher*

Saint Davids
Gage, (Leonard) Patrick *research company executive*

Sayre
May, Lisa Gregory *cell biologist, researcher*

Schuylkill Haven
Sarno, Patricia Ann *biology educator*

Scranton
Clymer, Jay Phaon, III *science educator*

Selinsgrove
†Richard, David Seward *biology educator*

State College
Hettche, L. Raymond *research director*
Morrow, David Austin, III *veterinary medical educator*

Swarthmore
Gilbert, Scott Frederick *biologist, educator, author*
Sawyers, Claire Elyce *arboretum administrator*

Swiftwater
Melling, Jack *biotechnologist*

Titusville
Peaslee, Margaret Mae Hermanek *zoology educator*

University Park
Bollag, Jean-Marc *soil biochemistry educator, consultant*
Brenchley, Jean Elnora *microbiologist, researcher*
Buskirk, Elsworth Robert *physiologist, educator*
Buss, Edward George *geneticist*
Fowler, H(oratio) Seymour *retired science educator*
Hagen, Daniel Russell *physiologist, educator*
Kuhns, Larry J. *horticulturist, educator*
Ma, Hong *plant molecular biologist, educator*
Manbeck, Harvey B. *agricultural and biological engineer, wood engineer, educator*
Stern, Robert Morris *gastrointestinal psychophysiology researcher, psychology educator*
Stinson, Richard Floyd *retired horticulturist, educator*
Tukey, Loren Davenport *pomology educator, researcher*

Villanova
Steg, Leo *research and development executive*

Warminster
Jesberg, Robert Ottis, Jr. *science educator*

Wayne
Krutsick, Robert Stanley *retired science center executive*
Thelen, Edmund *research executive*

West Mifflin
Clayton, John Charles *scientist, researcher*

West Point
Caskey, Charles Thomas *biology and genetics educator*
Hilleman, Maurice Ralph *virus research scientist*
Scolnick, Edward Mark *science administrator*

Wilkes Barre
Hayes, Wilbur Frank *biology educator*
Ogren, Robert Edward *biologist, educator*

RHODE ISLAND

Cranston
Mruk, Charles Karzimer *agronomist*

Kingston
Goos, Roger Delmon *mycologist*
Harlin, Marilyn Miler *marine botany educator, researcher, consultant*
Harrison, Robert William *zoologist, educator*

Newport
Koch, Robert Michael *senior research scientist, consultant, educator*

North Scituate
Dupree, Thomas Andrew *forester, state official*

Providence
†Cao, Weibiao *physiologist, researcher*
Lederberg, Seymour Samuel *molecular biologist, educator*
Marshall, Jean McElroy *physiologist*
Rothman, Frank George *biology educator, biochemical genetics researcher*
Schmitt, Johanna Marie *plant population biologist, educator*

SOUTH CAROLINA

Aiken
Wood, Susan *applied technology center executive*

Charleston
Burrell, Victor Gregory, Jr. *marine scientist*
Cheng, Thomas Clement *parasitologist, immunologist, educator, author*

Clemson
Birrenkott, Glen P., Jr. *poultry science educator*
Caldwell, Judith *horticultural educator*
Gangemi, J(oseph) David *microbiology educator, biomedical researcher, research administrator, hospital administrator*
Wilkinson, T. Ross *microbiologist, educator*

Columbia
Abel, Francis Lee *physiology educator*
Baker, Carleton Harold *physiology educator*
Best, Robert Glen *geneticist*
Corey, David Thomas *invertebrate zoology specialist*
Dawson, Wallace Douglas, Jr. *geneticist*
Henderson, Robert Edward *research institute director*
Rhoades, Donald Scott *zoo and botanical park curator, biology educator*
Vernberg, Frank John *marine and biological sciences educator*
Watabe, Norimitsu *biology and marine science educator*

Easley
Spearman, David Hagood *veterinarian*

Gaffney
Jones, Nancy Gale *retired biology educator*

Greenville
Cureton, Claudette Hazel Chapman *biology educator*
LaFleur, Karen Meredith *science educator*

Hilton Head Island
Adams, William Hensley *ecologist, educator*
Flemister, Launcelot Johnson *physiologist, educator*
Rapp, Fred *virologist*

Spartanburg
Leonard, Walter Raymond *retired biology educator*

Sumter
†Eberl, James J. *consultant*

SOUTH DAKOTA

Brookings
Sword, Christopher Patrick *microbiologist, university dean*

Vermillion
Langworthy, Thomas Allan *microbiologist, educator*

Volga
Moldenhauer, William Calvin *soil scientist*

TENNESSEE

Chattanooga
Zimmerman, Ray Arthur *naturalist*

Collegedale
†Perumal, John *biologist, educator*

Cookeville
†Coe, Felix Gilmore *science educator*
Forest, Herman Silva *biology educator*
Harris, John Wallace *biology educator*

Franklin
Schuerer, Paula Ann *veterinarian, biology educator*

Gatlinburg
Cave, Kent R. *national park ranger*

Knoxville
Anderson, Ilse Janell *clinical geneticist*
Caponetti, James Dante *botany educator*
Carroll, Roger Clinton *medical biology educator*
Chen, James Pai-fun *biology educator, researcher*
Conger, Bob Vernon *plant and soil science educator*
Harris, William Franklin, III *biologist, environmental science director and educator*
Holton, Raymond William *botanist, educator*
Mazur, Peter *cell physiologist, cryobiologist*
Mc Hargue, Carl Jack *research laboratory administrator*
Roddy, Patrick *zoological park administrator*
Swingle, Homer Dale *horticulturist, educator*
White, David Cleaveland *microbial ecologist, environmental toxicologist*

Maryville
Hall, Marion Trufant *botany educator, arboretum director*

Memphis
Chung, King-Thom *microbiologist, educator*
Curran, Thomas *molecular biologist, educator*
Freeman, Bob A. *retired microbiology educator, retired dean*
Hofmann, Polly A. *physiology educator*
Howe, Martha Morgan *microbiologist, educator*
Knox, Roger *zoological park administrator*
Wilson, Charles Glen *zoo administrator*

Nashville
Hogan, Brigid L. *molecular biologist*
Orgebin-Crist, Marie-Claire *biology educator*
Phillips, John A(tlas), III *geneticist, educator*
Pincus, Theodore *microbiologist, rheumatologist, educator*
Snyders, Dirk Johan *electrophysiologist, biophysicist, educator*
Sutcliffe, James Sheldon *human genetics educator, researcher*
Wang, Taylor Gunjin *science administrator, astronaut, educator*

Oak Ridge
Auerbach, Stanley Irving *ecologist, environmental scientist, educator*
Boyle, William R. *science administrator*
Luxmoore, Robert John *soil and plant scientist*
Russell, Liane Brauch *geneticist*
Slusher, Kimberly Goode *researcher*

Sewanee
Yeatman, Harry Clay *biologist, educator*

Seymour
Garren, Lisa Ann *veterinarian*

TEXAS

Alvarado
Evans, Garen Lee *laboratory director, regulatory compliance officer*

Amarillo
Myers, Terry Lewis *clinical geneticist, educator*
Sprowls, Robert Wayne *veterinarian, laboratory administrator*

Arlington
Smatresk, Neal Joseph *physiologist, biology educator, science education consultant*

Austin
Biesele, John Julius *biologist, educator*
Bronson, Franklin H. *zoology educator*
Delevoryas, Theodore *botanist, educator*
Drummond Borg, Lesley Margaret *clinical geneticist*
Gans, Carl *zoologist, educator*
Grant, Verne Edwin *biology educator*
Hubbs, Clark *zoologist, researcher*
Jacobson, Antone Gardner *zoology educator*
Patterson, Donald Eugene *research scientist*
Poulsen, Lawrence LeRoy *research scientist*
Simpson, Beryl Brintnall *botany educator*
Sutton, Harry Eldon *geneticist, educator*
Thornton, Joseph Scott *research institute executive, materials scientist*
Turner, Billie Lee *botanist, educator*
Walker, James Roy *microbiologist*

Borger
Chisum, Matthew Eual *laboratory manager*

Brownsville
Farst, Don David *zoo director, veterinarian*

Bushland
Unger, Paul Walter *soil scientist*

Cedar Park
Albin, Leslie Owens *biology educator*

Cibolo
Newsom, Melvin Max *retired research company executive*

College Station
Armstrong, Robert Beall *physiologist*
Beaver, Bonnie Veryle *veterinarian, educator*
Black, Samuel Harold *microbiology and immunology educator*
Borlaug, Norman Ernest *agricultural scientist*
Fisher, Richard Forrest *soils educator*
Hall, Timothy Couzens *biology educator, consultant*
Heidelbaugh, Norman Dale *veterinary medicine educator, consultant, author, inventor*
Howe, Lisa Marie *veterinarian, educator*
Kohel, Russell James *geneticist*
McCrady, James David *veterinarian, educator*
Milford, Murray Hudson *soil science educator*
Neill, William Harold, Jr. *biological science educator and researcher*
Nightingale, Arthur E. *retired horticulture sciences educator*
Rosberg, David William *plant sciences educator*
Sis, Raymond Francis *veterinarian, educator*
Storey, J. Benton *horticulturalist, educator*
Wilding, Lawrence Paul *pedology educator, soil science consultant*

PROFESSIONAL INDEX 6193 SCIENCE: LIFE SCIENCE

Wu, Guoyao *animal science, nutrition and physiology educator*

Conroe
†Vinson, Judith Paull *veterinarian*

Corpus Christi
Berkebile, Charles Alan *geology educator, hydrogeology researcher*
Parker, Roy Denver, Jr. *entomologist*
Schake, Lowell Martin *animal science educator*

Corsicana
Carroll, Ray Dean, Sr. *veterinarian*

Dallas
Brown, Michael Stuart *geneticist, educator, administrator*
Denur, Jack Boaz *scientific researcher, scientific consultant*
Land, Geoffrey Allison *science administrator*
McKnight, Steven Lanier *molecular biologist*
Neaves, William Barlow *cell biologist, educator*
Read, James Carroll *geneticist educator*
Reinert, James A. *entomologist, educator*
Sudhof, Thomas C. *molecular genetics educator, neuroscientist*
Vitetta, Ellen Shapiro *microbiologist educator, immunologist*

Denison
Brar, Gurdarshan Singh *soil scientist, researcher*

Denton
Garcia-Heras, Jaime *clinical cytogeneticist, researcher*
Schwalm, Fritz Ekkehardt *biology educator*

El Paso
Harris, Arthur Horne *biology educator*
Johnson, Jerry Douglas *biology educator*

Fort Worth
Keck, Michael Brian *biologist, educator*

Galveston
Giam, Choo-Seng *marine science educator*
Prakash, Satya *biology educator*
Smith, Eric Morgan *virology educator*
Thompson, Edward Ivins Brad *biological chemistry and genetics educator, molecular endocrinologist, department chairman*
Würsig, Bernd Gerhard *marine biology educator*
Zimmerman, Roger Joseph *fishery biologist*

Georgetown
Girvin, Eb Carl *biology educator*

Hamilton
†Freeman, Michael Lee *veterinarian*

Harlingen
Dittman, Kathryn Anne *veterinarian*

Hempstead
Propst, Catherine Lamb *biotechnology company executive*

Houston
Abbey, George W. S. *space center executive*
Baughn, Robert Elroy *microbiology educator*
Brown, Jack Harold Upton *physiology educator, university official, biomedical engineer*
Butel, Janet Susan *virology educator*
†Carson, Arch Irwin *toxicology educator, preventive medicine physician*
DeBakey, Lois *science communications educator, writer, editor*
DeBakey, Selma *science communications educator, writer, editor, lecturer*
Garcia, Hector David *toxicologist*
Goldstein, Margaret Ann *biologist*
Jurtshuk, Peter, Jr. *microbiologist*
Kimbrell, Deborah Ann *geneticist, educator*
Konisky, Jordan *microbiology educator*
Louderback, Truman Eugene *environmental project manager*
Nelson, David Loren *geneticist, educator*
Northington, David Knight, III *research center director, botanist, educator*
O'Malley, Bert William *cell biologist, educator, physician*
Röller, Herbert Alfred *biology and medical scientist, educator*
Sass, Ronald Lewis *biology and chemistry educator*
Schultz, Stanley George *physiologist, educator*
Seaton, Alberta Jones *biologist, educator, consultant*
Steele, James Harlan *former public health veterinarian, educator*

Hunt
Price, Donald Albert *veterinarian, consultant*

Irving
Fukui, George Masaaki *microbiology consultant*

Lackland AFB
Burghardt, Walter Francis, Jr. *veterinarian*

Laguna Park
Folkens, Alan Theodore *clinical and pharmaceutical microbiologist*

Longview
Martin, Ulrike Balk *laboratory technician*

Lubbock
Hentges, David John *microbiology educator*
Jackson, Raymond Carl *cytogeneticist*
Skoog, Gerald Duane *science educator*
Wendt, Charles William *soil physicist, educator*

Midland
Coombs, Kerry Leland *veterinarian, educator*

Nacogdoches
Worrell, Albert Cadwallader *forest economics educator*

Pearland
Shurtleff, Malcolm C. *plant pathologist, consultant, educator, extension specialist*

Port Aransas
Wohlschlag, Donald Eugene *zoologist, marine ecologist, educator emeritus*

Richardson
Gray, Donald Melvin *molecular and cell biology educator*
Rutford, Robert Hoxie *geoscience educator*

Round Rock
Schneider, Dennis Ray *microbiology educator*

San Antonio
Burch, James Leo *science research institute executive*
Deviney, Marvin Lee, Jr. *research institute scientist, program manager*
Donaldson, Willis Lyle *research institute administrator*
Gates, Mahlon Eugene *applied research executive, former government official, former army officer*
Irving, George Washington, III *veterinarian, research director, consultant*
Kalter, Seymour Sanford *virologist, educator*
Kittle, Joseph S. *science administrator, consultant*
Masoro, Edward Joseph, Jr. *physiology educator*
McIntosh, Dennis Keith *veterinary practitioner, consultant*
Polan-Curtain, Jodie Lea *physiologist researcher*
Spannagel, Alan Wayne *physiologist*
Springer, Karl Josef *science administrator*
Stone, William Harold *geneticist, educator*

San Marcos
Longley, Glenn *biology educator, research director*

Stephenville
Simpson, Charles Edmond *crop science educator*

Uvalde
Ramsey, Frank Allen *veterinarian, retired army officer*

Vernon
Slosser, Jeffery Eric *research entomologist*

Waco
Hillis, William Daniel *biology educator*

Warda
Kunze, George William *retired soil scientist*

UTAH

Logan
Rasmussen, Harry Paul *horticulture and landscape educator*
Sharik, Terry Lane *forest resources educator*
Vest, Hyrum Grant, Jr. *horticultural sciences educator*

Provo
Blake, George Rowland *soil science educator, water resources research administrator*
Crookston, R. Kent *agronomy educator*
McArthur, Eldon Durant *geneticist, researcher*
Smith, H(oward) Duane *zoology educator*

Salt Lake City
†Brown, Rulon Spilsbury *agricultural consultant*
Capecchi, Mario Renato *genetecist, educator*
Emerson, Sharon B. *biology researcher and educator*
King, R. Peter *science educator, academic center director*
Roth, John Roger *geneticist, biology educator*
Salisbury, Frank Boyer *plant physiologist, educator, author*
Straight, Richard Coleman *photobiologist, natural philosopher*
Warner, Homer R. *physiologist, educator*
White, Raymond Leslie *geneticist*

VERMONT

Burlington
Bartlett, Richmond Jay *soil chemistry educator, researcher*
Forcier, Lawrence Kenneth *natural resource educator*
Heinrich, Bernd *biologist, educator*
Hendley, Edith Di Pasquale *physiology and neuroscience educator*
Ross, Donald Savage *soil chemist, laboratory director*

Charlotte
Melby, Edward Carlos, Jr. *veterinarian*

Middlebury
Landgren, Craig Randall *academic administrator*
Saul, George Brandon, II *biology educator*

Morrisville
Lechevalier, Hubert Arthur *microbiology educator*
Lechevalier, Mary Pfeil *retired microbiologist, educator*

Norwich
Naumann, Robert Bruno Alexander *chemistry and physics educator*

Shelburne
Lynch, Peter *biology educator*

South Burlington
Johnson, Robert Eugene *physiologist*

VIRGINIA

Abingdon
Roberts, John Bennett, Jr. *veterinarian*

Alexandria
Walton, Thomas Edward *research scientist, educator, administrator*
Woolley, Mary Elizabeth *research administrator*

Arlington
Adams, Donald Edward *biotechnology and pharmaceutical patent examiner*
Basu, Sunanda *scientific administrator, researcher in space physics*
Bridgewater, Albert Louis *science foundation administrator*
Cameron, Maryellen *science association administrator, geologist, educator*
Colwell, Rita Rossi *microbiologist, molecular biologist, educator, federal agency administrator*
Cooper, Jon Charles *environmental science educator, lawyer*
Corell, Robert Walden *science administration educator*
Goforth, Wayne Reid *research administrator, biologist*
Haq, Bilal Ul *national science foundation program director, researcher*
Harris, William James, Jr. *research administrator, educator*
Held, Joe Roger *veterinarian, epidemiologist*
Junker, Bobby Ray *research and development executive, physicist*
Knipling, Edward Fred *retired research entomologist, agricultural administrator*
Lynch, John Thomas *science foundation administrator, physicist*
O'Neill, Brian *research organization administrator*
Williams, Luther Steward *science foundation administrator*

Blacksburg
Buhyoff, Gregory J. *forestry specialist, educator*
Burkhart, Harold Eugene *forestry educator*
Cheramie, Lesley Goyette *veterinarian*
Cowles, Joe Richard *biology educator*
De Datta, Surajit Kumar *soil scientist, agronomist, educator*
Haney, Harry L., Jr. *forestry specialist, educator*
McKenna, James Richard *agronomy educator*
Minckler, Leon Sherwood *forestry and conservation educator, author*

Charlottesville
Berne, Robert Matthew *physiologist, educator*
Friesen, Wolfgang Otto *biology educator*
Garrett, Reginald Hooker *biology educator, researcher*
Hamilton, Howard Laverne *zoology educator*
Hornberger, George Milton *environmental science educator*
Kadner, Robert Joseph *microbiology educator*
Kelly, Thaddeus Elliott *medical geneticist*
Murray, Joseph James, Jr. *zoologist*
Somlyo, Andrew Paul *physiology, biophysics and cardiology educator*
Wagner, Robert Roderick *microbiologist, oncology educator*
Wilbur, Henry Miles *zoologist, educator*
Wright, Theodore Robert Fairbank *biologist, educator*

Crozet
Gordon, Ronald Clayton *biomedical engineer*

Fairfax
Howard-Peebles, Patricia N. *clinical cytogeneticist*
Isbister, Jenefir Diane Wilkinson *microbiologist, researcher, educator, consultant*
Peters, Esther Caroline *aquatic toxicologist, pathobiologist, consultant*

Falls Church
Gorges, Heinz August *retired research engineer*
Hart, C(harles) W(illard), Jr. *zoologist, curator*
Simpson, John Arol *retired government executive, physicist*

Fort Belvoir
Severin, Scott Robert *veterinarian*

Fredericksburg
Moorman, William Jacob *agronomist, consultant*

Front Royal
Douglas, J(ocelyn) Fielding *toxicologist, consultant*

Hampton
Creedon, Jeremiah F. *aeronautical research laboratory administrator*

Haymarket
Katz, Alan Charles *toxicologist*

Leesburg
Mokhtarzadeh, Ahmad Agha *agronomist, consultant*

Lexington
Hickman, Cleveland Pendleton, Jr. *biology educator*

Mc Lean
Krugman, Stanley Liebert *science administrator, geneticist*
Layson, William McIntyre *research consulting company executive*
Shank, Fred Ross *food scientist*
Talbot, Lee Merriam *ecologist, educator, association executive*

Richmond
Boadle-Biber, Margaret Clare *physiology educator*
Wolf, Barry *genetics, pediatric educator*
Yu, Robert Kuan-jen *biochemistry educator*

Roanoke
Woods, Walter Ralph *retired agricultural scientist, administrator*

Vienna
Giovacchini, Robert Peter *toxicologist, manufacturing executive, retired*
Jahn, Laurence Roy *retired biologist, institute executive*

Virginia Beach
Merchant, Donald Joseph *retired microbiologist and educator*
Simmons, Marsha Thrift *science and reading educator, musician*

Warrenton
Henricson, Beth Ellen *microbiologist*
Lutz, Elaine Elizabeth *veterinarian*

Williamsburg
Griffith, Melvin Eugene *entomologist, public health official*
Hoegerman, Stanton Fred *cytogeneticist*

WASHINGTON

Centralia
Kyte, Lydiane *retired botanist*

Edmonds
Paul, Ronald Stanley *research institute executive*

Friday Harbor
Brookbank, John W(arren) *retired microbiology educator*

Kent
Schneider, Eugene Saul *microbiologist, laboratory administrator*
†White, Dana Eileen *public health research and evaluation assistant*

Olympia
Raphael, Martin George *research wildlife biologist*
Steiger, Gretchen Helene *marine mammalogist, research biologist*

Poulsbo
Tozer, William Evans *entomologist, educator*

Prosser
Miller, David Eugene *soil scientist, researcher*
Proebsting, Edward Louis, Jr. *retired research horticulturist*

Pullman
Carlson, James Roy *animal science educator*
Gustafsson, Borje Karl *veterinarian, educator*
Henson, James Bond *veterinary pathologist*
Hosick, Howard Lawrence *cell biology educator, academic administrator*
Wilson, Robert Burton *veterinary and medical educator*

Redmond
Kelman, Bruce Jerry *toxicologist, consultant*

Richland
†Bacon, Diana Holford *hydrologist, researcher*
Bian, Randy Xindi *research scientist*
Colson, Steven Douglas *research director, chemistry educator*

Seattle
Bassingthwaighte, James Bucklin *physiologist, educator, medical researcher*
Boersma, P. Dee *zoology educator*
Brownstein, Barbara Lavin *geneticist, educator, university official*
Buffington, John Douglas *ecologist, researcher*
Byers, Peter H. *geneticist*
Cleland, Robert Erskine *plant physiologist, educator*
Daniel, Thomas L. *zoology educator*
Edmondson, W(allace) Thomas *retired limnologist, educator*
Evans, Charles Albert *microbiology educator*
Groman, Neal Benjamin *microbiology educator*
Hartwell, Leland Harrison *geneticist, educator*
†Henderson, Scottie Yvette *researcher*
Hendrickson, Anita Elizabeth *biology educator*
Hille, Bertil *physiology educator*
Hood, Leroy Edward *molecular biologist, educator*
Karr, James Richard *ecologist, educator, research director*
Kohn, Alan J. *zoology educator*
Kruckeberg, Arthur Rice *botanist, educator*
Kuhl, Patricia K. *science educator*
Lee, Qwihee Park *plant physiologist*
Livingston, Patricia Ann *marine biologist, researcher*
Miller, Robert Carmi, Jr. *microbiology educator, university administrator*
Motulsky, Arno Gunther *geneticist, physician, educator*
Nester, Eugene William *microbiology educator*
Ning, Xue-Han (Hsueh-Han Ning) *physiologist, researcher*
Olstad, Roger Gale *science educator*
Orians, Gordon Howell *biology educator*
Ratner, Buddy Dennis *bioengineer, educator*
Smith, Gerald R. *molecular geneticist*
Smith, Orville Auverne *physiology educator*
Towne, David L. *zoological park administrator*
Tukey, Harold Bradford, Jr. *horticulture educator*
Woods, James Sterrett *toxicologist*
Wooster, Warren S(criver) *marine science educator*
Wott, John Arthur *arboretum and botanical garden executive, horticulture educator*

Spokane
Shaw, Margery Wayne Schlamp *geneticist, physician, lawyer*

Tacoma
Champ, Stanley Gordon *scientific company executive*
McLaughlin, Peter Donald *staff scientist, program manager*
Otten, Thomas *zoological park director*

Wenatchee
Elfving, Don C. *horticulturist*
Schrader, Lawrence Edwin *plant physiologist, educator*

WEST VIRGINIA

Beaver
Baligar, Virupax C. *research soil scientist*

Voigt, Paul Warren *research geneticist*

Charleston
Gillespie, William Harry *forestry executive, geology educator*

Falling Waters
Schellhaas, Linda Jean *toxicologist, consultant*

Kearneysville
Biggs, Alan Richard *plant pathologist, educator*

Morgantown
Cochrane, Robert Lowe *biologist*
Gladfelter, Wilbert Eugene *physiology educator*
Nath, Joginder *genetics and biology educator, researcher*

South Charleston
Britton, Laurence George *research scientist*

WISCONSIN

Bayfield
Gallinat, Michael Paul *fisheries biologist*

Fond Du Lac
Hayes, Elizabeth Lamb *biology educator*

Madison
Armstrong, Gregory Davenport *arboretum administrator*
Barnes, Robert F. *agronomist*
Beyer-Mears, Annette *physiologist*
Bisgard, Gerald Edwin *biosciences educator, researcher*
Brock, Thomas Dale *microbiology educator*
Bula, Raymond J. *agronomist*
Burkholder, Wendell Eugene *retired entomology educator, researcher*
Crow, James Franklin *retired genetics educator*
Dick, Elliot Colter *virologist, epidemiologist, educator*
Easterday, Bernard Carlyle *veterinary medicine educator*
Ensign, Jerald C. *bacteriology educator*
Goodman, Robert Merwin *microbiologist, plant biologist, educator*
Graham, James Miller *physiology researcher*
Greaser, Marion Lewis *science educator*
Hagedorn, Donald James *phytopathologist, educator, agricultural consultant*
Hall, David Charles *zoo director, veterinarian*
Helgeson, John Paul *plant physiologist, researcher*
Hopen, Herbert John *horticulture educator*
Iltis, Hugh Hellmut *plant taxonomist-evolutionist, educator*
Jackson, Marion Leroy *agronomist, soil scientist*
Jarrell, Wesley Michael *soil and ecosystem science educator, researcher*
Jeanne, Robert Lawrence *entomology educator*
Kaesberg, Paul Joseph *virology researcher*
Kimble, Judith E. *molecular biologist, cell biologist*
Kirk, Thomas Kent *research scientist*
Kore, Anita Maureen *veterinary toxicologist*
Lillesand, Thomas Martin *remote sensing educator*
Magnuson, John Joseph *zoology educator*
Moss, Richard L. *physiology educator*
Nelson, Oliver Evans, Jr. *geneticist, educator*
Newcomb, Eldon Henry *retired botany educator*
Olson, Norman Fredrick *food science educator*
Pariza, Michael Willard *research institute executive, microbiology and toxicology educator*
Pella, Milton Orville *retired science educator*
Peterson, David Maurice *plant physiologist, research leader*
Ris, Hans *zoologist, educator*
Rueckert, Roland Rudyard *retired virologist, educator*
Sharkey, Thomas David *educator, botanist*
Skoog, Folke Karl *botany educator*
Smalley, Eugene Byron *plant pathology educator, forest pathologist, mycologist*
Sunde, Milton Lester *retired poultry science educator*
Susman, Millard *geneticist, educator*
Szybalski, Waclaw *molecular geneticist, educator*
Walker, Duard Lee *medical educator*
Welker, Wallace Irving *neurophysiologist, educator*
Zedler, Joy Buswell *ecological sciences educator*

Middleton
Hinsdill, Ronald Dwight *bacteriology educator, immunotoxicologist*

Milwaukee
Besharse, Joseph Culp *cell biologist, researcher*
Boese, Gilbert Karyle *cultural organization executive*
Friday, Gerald Edmund *biologist, educator*
†Smith, James John *physiologist*
Wilkenhauser, Charles *zoological park administrator*

Oconomowoc
Luedke, Patricia Georgianne *microbiologist*

Rhinelander
Newman, Linnaea Rose *interior horticulturist consultant*

Shawano
Heikes, Keith *science administrator*

Sheboygan
Marr, Kathleen Mary *biologist, educator*

WYOMING

Cheyenne
Schuman, Gerald Eugene *soil scientist*

Jackson
Davis, Randy Lee *soil scientist*

Laramie
Christensen, Martha *mycologist, educator*
Lewis, Randolph Vance *molecular biologist, researcher*

Moose
Craighead, Frank Cooper, Jr. *ecologist*

TERRITORIES OF THE UNITED STATES

PUERTO RICO

San Juan
Fernández-Coll, Fred *microbiologist, food technology laboratory director*
Orkand, Richard Kenneth *neurobiologist, researcher, educator*

CANADA

ALBERTA

Calgary
Jones, Geoffrey Melvill *physiology research educator*
Mossop, Grant Dilworth *geological institute director*
Yoon, Ji-Won *virology, immunology and diabetes educator, research administrator*

Edmonton
Cossins, Edwin Albert *biology educator, academic administrator*
Hiruki, Chuji *plant virologist, science educator*

Lethbridge
Cho, Hyun Ju *veterinary research scientist*

BRITISH COLUMBIA

Bamfield
Druehl, Louis Dix *biology educator*

Burnaby
Borden, John Harvey *entomologist, educator*

Nanaimo
Ricker, William Edwin *biologist*

Sidney
Bigelow, Margaret Elizabeth Barr (M.E. Barr) *mycology educator*
Kendrick, William Bryce *biology educator, author, publisher*
Mann, Cedric Robert *retired institute administrator, oceanographer*

Vancouver
Blair, Robert *animal science administrator, educator, researcher*
Campbell, Jack James Ramsay *microbiology educator*
Chitty, Dennis Hubert *zoology educator*
Hoar, William Stewart *zoologist, educator*
Jones, David Robert *zoology educator*
Lindsey, Casimir Charles *zoologist*
Maclachlan, Gordon Alistair *biology educator, researcher*
March, Beryl Elizabeth *animal scientist, educator*
McBride, Barry Clarke *microbiology and oral biology educator, research microbiologist*
Mc Lean, Donald Millis *microbiology, pathology educator, physician*
Newman, Murray Arthur *aquarium administrator*
Phillips, Anthony George *neurobiology educator*
Phillips, John Edward *zoologist, educator*
Randall, David John *physiologist, zoologist, educator*
Rennie, Paul Steven *research scientist*
Shaw, Michael *biologist, educator*
†Stephens, William Thomas *forestry products executive*
Wellington, William George *plant science and ecology educator*

West Vancouver
Donaldson, Edward Mossop *research scientist emeritus, aquaculture consultant*

MANITOBA

Winnipeg
Eales, John Geoffrey *zoology educator*
Findlay, Glen Marshall *agrologist*
Suzuki, Isamu *microbiology educator, researcher*

NEWFOUNDLAND

Saint John's
Davis, Charles Carroll *aquatic biologist, educator*

NOVA SCOTIA

Dartmouth
Mann, Kenneth Henry *marine ecologist*

Halifax
Hall, Brian Keith *biology educator, author*
O'Dor, Ron *physiologist, marine biology educator*

Wolfville
Toews, Daniel Peter *zoologist*

ONTARIO

Caledon East
Fallis, Albert Murray *microbiology educator*

Deep River
Newcombe, Howard Borden *biologist, consultant*

Downsview
Forer, Arthur H. *biology educator, researcher, editor*

Guelph
Benn, Denna M. *veterinarian*
Beveridge, Terrance James *microbiology educator, researcher*
Bewley, John Derek *botany researcher, educator*
Jorgensen, Erik *forest pathologist, educator, consultant*
Kasha, Kenneth John *agriculturist, educator*
Oaks, B. Ann *plant physiologist, educator*
Sells, Bruce Howard *biomedical sciences educator*

Kingston
Leggett, William C. *biology educator, academic administrator*
Turpin, David Howard *biologist, educator*
Wyatt, Gerard Robert *biology educator, researcher*

London
Locke, Michael *zoology educator*

Nepean
Beare-Rogers, Joyce Louise *former research executive*
Bishop, Claude Titus *retired biological sciences research administrator, editor*

North York
Davey, Kenneth George *biologist, university official*

Ottawa
Batra, Tilak Raj *research scientist*
Bhartia, Prakash *defense research management executive, researcher, educator*
Bisby, Mark Ainley *physiology educator*
Carty, Arthur John *science policy advisor, research administrator*
Davis, John Christopher *zoologist, aquatic toxicologist*
Dence, Michael Robert *retired research director*
Hughes, Stanley John *mycologist*
Lister, Earle Edward *animal science consultant*
Perry, Malcolm Blythe *biologist*
Sinha, Ramesh Chandra *plant pathologist*
Storey, Kenneth Bruce *biology educator*
Topp, George Clarke *soil physicist*

Peterborough
Hutchinson, Thomas Cuthbert *ecology and environmental educator*

Port Rowan
Francis, Charles MacKenzie *wildlife biologist*

Sault Sainte Marie
Kondo, Edward Shinichi *plant pathologist, researcher*

Scarborough
White, Calvin John *zoo executive, financial manager, zoological association executive*

Stittsville
MacLeod, Robert Angus *microbiology educator, researcher*

Toronto
Atwood, Harold Leslie *physiology and zoology educator*
Heath, Michele Christine *botany educator*
Kerr, David Wylie *natural resource company executive*
Kushner, Donn Jean *microbiologist, children's author*
Liversage, Richard Albert *cell biologist*
MacLennan, David Herman *research scientist, educator*
McNeill, John *botanist*
Moens, Peter B. *biology researcher and educator*
Pawson, Anthony J. *molecular biologist*
Sigal, Israel Michael *scientist*
Stadelman, William Ralph *chemical institution executive*
Tobe, Stephen Solomon *zoology educator*
Tsui, Lap-Chee *molecular genetics educator*

Waterloo
Hynes, Hugh Bernard Noel *biology educator*

Yarker
Smallman, Beverley N. *biology educator*

QUEBEC

Ile Perrot
Tomlinson, George Herbert *retired industrial company research executive*

Laval
Kluepfel, Dieter *microbiologist*
Pavilanis, Vytautas *microbiology educator, physician*

Montreal
Carroll, Robert Lynn *biology educator, vertebrate paleontologist, museum curator*
Chang, Thomas Ming Swi *medical scientist, biotechnologist*
Dansereau, Pierre *ecologist*
Gibbs, Sarah Preble *biologist, educator*
Goldstein, Sandu *biotechnology executive, researcher*
Guindon, Yvan *science administrator, research scientist*
Jolicoeur, Paul *molecular biologist*
Stangel, Ivan *biomaterials scientist, educator*
Stanners, Clifford Paul *molecular and cell biologist, biochemistry educator*

Quebec
Bourget, Edwin Robert *marine ecologist, educator*
Potvin, Pierre *physiologist, educator*
Trudel, Marc J. *botanist*

Sainte Anne de Bellevue
Grant, William Frederick *geneticist, educator*
Steppler, Howard Alvey *agronomist*

SASKATCHEWAN

Regina
Davis, Gordon Richard Fuerst *retired biologist, translator*
Sonntag, Bernard H. *agrologist, public service executive*

Saskatoon
Babiuk, Lorne Alan *virologist, immunologist, research administrator*
Harvey, Bryan Laurence *crop science educator*
Huang, Pan Ming *soil science educator*
Shokeir, Mohamed Hassan Kamel *medical geneticist, educator*

MEXICO

Mexico City
Baer, George Martin *veterinarian, researcher*

AUSTRALIA

Randwick
Hall, Peter Francis *physiologist*

CHINA

Hong Kong
Chang, Shu Ting *fungal geneticist, mushroom biologist*
Kung, Shain-dow *molecular biologist, academic administrator*

ENGLAND

Cambridge
Huxley, Sir Andrew (Fielding) *physiologist, educator*
Klug, Aaron *molecular biologist*
Milstein, César *molecular biologist*
Sanger, Frederick *retired molecular biologist*

Cranbrook
Hattersley-Smith, Geoffrey Francis *retired government research scientist*

Leeds
Phillips, Oliver *tropical biodiversity scientist*

London
Katz, Sir Bernard *physiologist*
May, Robert McCredie *biology educator*
Morris, Desmond (John) *zoologist, author, artist*
Pecorino, Lauren Teresa *biologist*

Oxford
Gowans, James Learmonth (Sir) *science administrator, immunologist*
Thomson, Keith Stewart *biologist, author*

FRANCE

Marnes-la-Coquette
Plotkin, Stanley Alan *medical virologist*

Paris
Jacob, François *biologist*
LeGoffic, Francois *biotechnology educator*

GERMANY

Düsseldorf
Stuhl, Oskar Paul *scientific and regulatory consultant*

Stuttgart
Klitzing, Klaus von *research facility administrator, physicist*

Würzburg
Hölldobler, Berthold Karl *zoologist, educator*

ISRAEL

Rehovot
Sachs, Leo *geneticist, educator*

ITALY

Frascati
Haegi, Marcel *scientist, physicist*

Milan
Dulbecco, Renato *biologist, educator*

Naples
Tarro, Giulio *virologist*

Rome
†Levi-Montalcini, Rita *neurobiologist, researcher*

JAPAN

Chiba
Arai, Toshihiko *retired microbiology and immunology educator*

Kanagawa
Okui, Kazumitsu *biology educator*

Kobe
Tochikura, Tatsurokuro *applied microbiologist, home economics educator*

Tokyo
Ishii, Akira *medical parasitologist, malariologist, allergologist*
Ueno, Tomiko F. *forestry company executive*

PAKISTAN

Faisalabad Punjab
†Siddique, Muhammad *poultry pathobiologist*

PERU

Lima
French, Edward Ronald *plant pathologist*

POLAND

Warsaw
Koscielak, Jerzy *scientist, science administrator*

SAUDI ARABIA

Abha
Gedebou, Messele *microbiologist, educator*

SCOTLAND

Gullane
Collins, Jeffrey Hamilton *research facility administrator, electrical engineering educator*

SWITZERLAND

Basel
Arber, Werner *microbiologist*
Gehring, Walter Jakob *biology and genetics educator*

Geneva
Hearn, John Patrick *biologist, educator*

Zurich
Wüthrich, Kurt *molecular biologist, biophysical chemist*

TAIWAN

Hualien
Lin, Jung-Chung *microbiologist, researcher*

THAILAND

Nakorn Pathom
†Chanthanom-Good, Suvajee *science educator*

WEST INDIES

Roseau
Jeffries, Charles Dean *microbiology educator, scientist*

ADDRESS UNPUBLISHED

Agrios, George Nicholas *plant pathology educator*
Ahearne, John Francis *scientific research administrator, researcher*
Ahlquist, Paul Gerald *molecular biology researcher, educator*
Alexander, Edward Russell *retired disease research administrator, educator*
Allen, Lew, Jr. *laboratory executive, former air force officer*
Andrews, Richard Vincent *physiologist, educator*
Armstrong, Thomas Newton, III *American art and garden specialist, consultant*
Arnott, Howard Joseph *biology educator, university dean*
Baker, Joseph Roderick, III *aviculturist*
Barabino, William Albert *science and technology researcher, inventor*
Barrett, Izadore *retired fisheries research administrator*
Bautista, Anthony Hernandez *biomedical company executive*
Berlowitz Tarrant, Laurence *biotechnologist, university administrator*
Bernard, Richard Lawson *geneticist, retired*
Bers, Donald Martin *physiology educator*
Bidwell, Roger Grafton Shelford *biologist, educator*
Block, Barbara Ann *biology educator*
Bonner, John Tyler *biology educator*
Bormann, Frederick Herbert *forestry and environmental science educator*
Bremner, John McColl *agronomy and biochemistry educator*
Breslin, Elizabeth Walker *biological scientist, biomedical consultant*
Brill, Winston Jonas *microbiologist, educator, research director, publisher and management consultant*
†Brondizio, Eduardo Sonnewend *ecological researcher, consultant*
Bullock, Theodore Holmes *biologist, educator*
Burnside, Orvin Charles *agronomy educator, researcher*
Caldwell, Elwood Fleming *food scientist*
Carlquist, Sherwin *biology and botany educator*
Carter, David LaVere *soil scientist, researcher, consultant*
Caulder, Jerry Dale *weed scientist*
Champlin, William Glen *clinical microbiologist-immunologist*
Cheng, Liangsheng *engineer, researcher, educator*
Clayton, David A(lvin) *biology educator*
Cole, Jerome Foster *research company executive*
†Courbis, Sarah Shelby *marine biologist*
Creech, John Lewis *retired scientist, consultant*
Cross, Harold Zane *agronomist, educator*
D'Alesandro, Philip Anthony *parasitologist, immunologist, retired educator*
De Antoni, Edward Paul *cancer control research scientist*
Decker, Walter Johns *toxicologist*
Dubesa, Elaine J. *biotechnology company executive*
Dugan, Patrick Raymond *microbiologist, university dean*
Durham, Thena Monts *microbiologist, researcher, management executive*
Eicher, George John *aquatic biologist*
Ellner, Paul Daniel *clinical microbiologist*
Elson, Hannah Friedman *research biologist*
Engel, Michael Scott *entomologist, paleontologist*
Erlenmeyer-Kimling, L. *psychiatric and behavior genetics researcher, educator*
Evans, Charles Wayne, II *biologist, researcher*
Feir, Dorothy Jean *entomologist, physiologist, educator*
†Fernandez, Carmen Lucy *biologist, mental health counselor*
Flemming, David Paul *biologist*
Fox, Michael Wilson *veterinarian, animal behaviorist*
Foy, Charles Daley *retired soil scientist*
Freeman, Arthur *veterinarian, retired association administrator*
Gallo, Robert Charles *research scientist*
Garruto, Ralph Michael *research anthropologist, educator, biologist*
Gay, William Ingalls *veterinarian, health science administrator*
Gennaro, Antonio L. *biology educator*
Gill, William Robert *soil scientist*
Gilmore, Gail Pearsall *consultant, writer*
Glick, J. Leslie *biotechnology entrepreneur*
Glover, Lisa Marie *research analyst*
Goldman, Robert David *cell biologist, educator*
Green, Bennett Donald *biotechnologist*
Greenman, David Lewis *consultant physiologist and toxicologist*
Hamilton, William Howard *laboratory executive*
Harlan, Jack Rodney *geneticist, emeritus educator*
Harriman, Philip Darling *geneticist, science foundation executive*
Harris, Elliott Stanley *toxicologist*
Hartman, Margaret J. *biologist, educator, university official*
Hayashi, Teru *zoologist, educator*
Hendricks, Gilbert L., III *physiologist, researcher*
†Herbers, Joan Marie *biology educator*
Honour, Lynda Charmaine *research scientist, educator, psychotherapist*
Hough, Janet Gerda Campbell *research scientist*
Hsiao, Kwang-Jen *genetics and biochemistry educator*
Hunt, Ronald Duncan *veterinarian, educator, pathologist*
Jackson, Victor Louis *retired naturalist*
Jacobs, Hyde Spencer *soil chemistry educator*
Karr, Gerald Lee *agricultural economist, state senator*
Katz, Anne Harris *biologist, educator, writer, aviator*
Key, Dana Lynn *English education and biology educator*
†Khoury, Jehad *research scientist*
King, John Quill Taylor *science center administrator, college administrator emeritus*
Kinzley, Colleen Elizabeth *zoological park curator*
Kipnis, Nahum S. *science educator*
Kirsteuer, Ernst Karl Eberhart *biologist, curator*
Koller, Loren D. *veterinary medicine educator*
Kurtz, Myra Berman *microbiologist*
Lacey, Howard Raymond *food technologist*
Lambert, Richard Bowles, Jr. *festival administrator*
Leath, Kenneth Thomas *research plant pathologist, educator, agricultural consultant*
Leder, Philip *geneticist, educator*
Lewis, Robert Alan *physiologist, environmental toxicologist*
Lindsay, Dale Richard *research administrator*
Lindstedt-Siva, (Karen) June *marine biologist, environmental consultant*
Livingston, Gideon (Guy) Eleazar *food and nutrition scientist, consultant*
Maier, Robert Hawthorne *biology educator*
Mannering, Jerry Vincent *agronomist, educator*
Markovitz, Alvin *molecular biologist, geneticist, educator*
Martino, Joseph Paul *research scientist*
Maslansky, Carol Jeanne *toxicologist*
Maunder, Addison Bruce *agronomic research company executive*
McConnaughey, Bayard Harlow *retired biology educator*
McFarland, Victor Alan *toxicologist*
McShefferty, John *retired research company executive, consultant*
Mehta, Peshotan Rustom *magnetotherapist and holisticologist*
Menn, Julius Joel *scientist*
Moran, Nancy A. *ecology educator*
Moreland, Alvin Franklin *veterinarian*
Moscona, Aron Arthur *biology educator, scientist*
Myers, Jack Edgar *biologist, educator*
Narath, Albert *retired laboratory administrator*
Navalkar, Ramchandra Govindrao *microbiologist, immunologist*
Neel, James Van Gundia *geneticist, educator*
Nelson, Wallace Warren *retired superintendent experimental station, agronomy educator*
O'Brien, Stephen James *geneticist*
Oswald, Robert Bernard *science administrator, nuclear engineer*
Paganelli, Charles Victor *physiologist*
Palade, George Emil *biologist, educator*
Peter, Richard Ector *zoology educator*
Pettit, Ghery DeWitt *retired veterinary medicine educator*
Pielou, Evelyn C. *biologist*
Pierce, John Thomas *industrial hygienist, clinical toxicologist*
Pinter, Gabriel George *physiolog educator*
Pionke, Harry Bernhard *research leader and soil scientist*
Pitrella, Francis Donald *human factors professional*
Pollack, Sylvia Byrne *retired educator, researcher, counselor*
Pollock, Roy Van Horn *animal health researcher*
Prescott, John Hernage *aquarium executive*
Pyle, Robert Michael *naturalist, writer*
Rabson, Robert *plant physiologist, retired science administrator*
Reetz, Harold Frank, Jr. *industrial agronomist*
Rogers, Jack David *plant pathologist, educator*
†Rothman, Robert *science educator*
Sattler, Rolf *retired plant morphologist, educator*
Schaertl, Gary Richard *forester, forest management educator*
Schaller, George Beals *zoologist*
Schwab, John Harris *microbiology and immunology educator*
Scott, David Clinton *research scientist*
Scott, Jane Vicroy *microbiologist*
Sears, Rollin George *wheat geneticist, small grains researcher*
Simon, Melvin I. *molecular biologist, educator*
Simpson, Frederick James *retired research administrator*
Sjostrand, Fritiof Stig *biologist, educator*
Skinner, James Stanford *physiologist, educator*
Sokal, Robert Reuven *biology educator, author*
Soper, James Herbert *botanist, curator*
Southwick, Charles Henry *zoologist, educator*
Speight, James Glassford *research company executive*
Sprague, George Frederick *geneticist*
Stavroulakis, Anthea Merrie *biology educator*
Stebbins, George Ledyard *research botanist, retired educator*
Stefano, George B. *neurobiologist, researcher*
Steinberg, Marshall *retired toxicologist*
Stickle, David Walter *microbiologist*
Stone, John Floyd *soil physics researcher and educator*
Stroud, Richard Hamilton *aquatic biologist, scientist, consultant*
Stump, John Edward *veterinary anatomy educator, ethologist*
Tandler, Bernard *cell biology educator*
Tenney, Stephen Marsh *physiologist, educator*
Thomas, Teresa Ann *microbiologist, educator*
Tipples, Keith Howard *retired research director*
Tung, Yeishin *research scientist*
Vaughan, John Charles, III *horticultural products executive*
Wiatr, Christopher Louis *microbiologist*
Wilkinson, Stanley Ralph *agronomist*
Woo, Savio Lau Ching *molecular medical geneticist*
Wooten, Frank Thomas *retired research facility executive*
Wormwood, Richard Naughton *retired naturalist, writer*
Yang, Xiangzhong *research scientist, administrator, educator*
Yunis, Jorge Jose *anatomy, pathology, and microbiology educator*
Zhu, Yong *research scientist*
Zwain, Ismail Hassan *molecular endocrinologist*

SCIENCE: MATHEMATICS AND COMPUTER SCIENCE

UNITED STATES

ALABAMA

Auburn
Govil, Narendra Kumar *mathematics educator*

Birmingham
Peeples, William Dewey, Jr. *mathematics educator*

Florence
Foote, Avon Edward *webmaster, communications educator*
Johnson, Johnny Ray *mathematics educator*

Huntsville
Freas, George Wilson, II *computer consultant*
McAuley, Van Alfon *aerospace mathematician*

Mobile
McCleery, Winston Theodore *computer consulting company executive*
†Simpkins, Christen, Jr. *systems engineer, educator*
Yett, Fowler Redford *mathematics educator*

Pelham
Turner, Malcolm Elijah *biomathematician, educator*

Tuscaloosa
Drake, Albert Estern *retired statistics educator, farming administrator*
Fechner, Roy Fredric *mathematics educator*

ALASKA

Anchorage
Mann, Lester Perry *mathematics educator*

ARIZONA

Avondale
SantaVicca, Edmund Frank *information scientist*

Chandler
Rudibaugh, Melinda Campbell *mathematics educator*
Sue, Lawrence Gene *statistician*

Fort Huachuca
Clark, Brian Thomas *mathematical statistician, operations research analyst*

Mesa
Stott, Brian *software company executive*

Phoenix
†Baugh, James A. *mathematics educator, retired army officer*
Doto, Irene Louise *statistician*

Prescott
Anderson, Arthur George *laboratory director, former computer company executive, consultant*

Scottsdale
Friesen, Oris Dewayne *software engineer, historian*

Sierra Vista
Sizemore, Nicky Lee *computer scientist*

Sun City
Jackson, Randy *computer networking executive*

Tempe
Bristol, Stanley David *mathematics educator*
Downs, Floyd L. *mathematics educator*
Golshani, Forouzan *computer science and engineering educator*
Hoppensteadt, Frank Charles *educator, mathematician, university administrator*
Ihrig, Edwin Charles, Jr. *mathematics educator*
Smith, Harvey Alvin *mathematics educator, consultant*
Yau, Stephen Sik-sang *computer science and engineering educator, computer scientist, researcher*

Tucson
Karson, Catherine June *computer programmer, consultant*
Weller, Cheryl K. *Internet service provider executive, educator*
Willoughby, Stephen Schuyler *mathematics educator*

Yuma
Jack, Dixie Lynn *software consultant, social worker*

ARKANSAS

Batesville
Carius, Robert Wilhelm *mathematics and science educator, retired naval officer*

Fayetteville
Madison, Bernard L. *mathematics educator*

Little Rock
Jones, William Richard *database administrator*

CALIFORNIA

Alameda
Mewhinney, Bruce Harrison Nicholas *internet developer*

Azusa
Sambasivam, Samuel E. *computer science and mathematics educator*

Banning
Swick, Sean Bowman *software developer*

Berkeley
Arveson, William Barnes *mathematics educator*
Bergman, George Mark *mathematician, educator*
Berlekamp, Elwyn Ralph *mathematic educator, electronics company executive,*
Bickel, Peter John *statistician, educator*
Blackwell, David H. *statistics educator*
Brayton, Robert K. *computer science educator*
Chern, Shiing-Shen *mathematics educator*
Chorin, Alexandre Joel *mathematician, educator*
Cooper, William Secord *information science educator*
Freedman, David Amiel *statistics educator, consultant*
Frenkel, Edward Vladimir *mathematician, educator*
Henkin, Leon Albert *mathematician, educator*
Henzinger, Thomas Anton *computer science educator*
Kaplansky, Irving *mathematician, educator, research institute director*
Le Cam, Lucien Marie *mathematics educator*
Lehmann, Erich Leo *statistics educator*
Osserman, Robert *mathematician, educator, author*
Patterson, David Andrew *computer scientist, educator, consultant*
Ratner, Marina *mathematician, educator, researcher*
Sequin, Carlo H. *computer science educator*
Shvidler, Mark Joseph *mathematician*
Smith, Alan Jay *computer science educator, consultant*
Tarter, Michael Ernest *biostatistician, educator*
Thomas, Paul Emery *mathematics educator*
Vojta, Paul Alan *mathematics educator*
Wehausen, John Vrooman *mathematician, educator*
Wolf, Joseph Albert *mathematician, educator*
Xie, Ganquan *mathematician, computational geophysical scientist, educator*

Brea
Natsuyama, Harriet Hatsune *mathematician*

Calabasas
Hosseiniyar, Mansour M. *software engineer, financial consultant*

Camarillo
Vannix, C(ecil) Robert *programmer, systems analyst*

Carlsbad
Halberg, Charles John August, Jr. *mathematics educator*

Carmichael
Givant, Philip Joachim *mathematics educator, real estate investment executive*

Carson
Kowalski, Kazimierz *computer science educator, researcher*

Castroville
Guglielmo, Eugene Joseph *software engineer, consultant*

Claremont
Coleman, Courtney Stafford *mathematician, educator*
Cooke, Kenneth Lloyd *mathematician, educator*
Henriksen, Melvin *mathematician, educator*
Mullikin, Harry Copeland *mathematics educator*

Costa Mesa
DeMille-Camacho, Dianne Lynne *mathematics educator, administrator*

Panaccione, Bruce Roy *systems analyst, geographer*

Cupertino
Holmes, Richard Albert *software engineer, consultant*
Togasaki, Shinobu *computer scientist*

Cypress
Sillman, George Douglas *computer programmer analyst*

Davis
Olsson, Ronald Arthur *computer science educator*
†Thurston, William Paul *mathematician*

El Cajon
Rose, Raymond Allen *computer scientist*

Elk Grove
McDavid, Douglas Warren *systems consultant*

Encinitas
Burgin, George Hans *computer scientist, educator*

Escondido
Collins, George Timothy *computer software consultant*

Fountain Valley
Berman, Steven Richard *software engineer*

Fresno
Diestelkamp, Dawn Lea *county superior court manager*
Michael, James Daniel *computer scientist*

Fullerton
†Morton, Michael James *software engineer*

Gilroy
McCarty, Robert Clarke *mathematician*

Glendale
Kay, Alan *computer scientist*

Hayward
Duncan, Doris Gottschalk *information systems educator*

Irvine
Abu-Mostafa, Ayman Said *computer consultant*
Bennett, Bruce Michael *mathematician, educator, musician*
Chacon, Michael Ernest *computer networking specialist*
Hoffman, Donald David *cognitive and computer science educator*

La Crescenta
Klint, Ronald Vernon *math educator, financial consultant*

La Honda
Henderson, D. Austin *computer scientist*
Melvin, Jay Wayne *computer programmer*

La Jolla
†Freedman, Michael Hartley *mathematician, educator*
Goguen, Joseph Amadee *computer science educator*
Halkin, Hubert *mathematics educator, research mathematician*
Longuet-Higgins, Michael Selwyn *mathematician, physicist*
Martin, James John, Jr. *retired consulting research firm executive, systems analyst*
Rosen, Judah Ben *computer scientist*
Rosenblatt, Murray *mathematics educator*
Terras, Audrey Anne *mathematics educator*
Wulbert, Daniel Eliot *mathematician, educator*
Zyroff, Ellen Slotoroff *information scientist, classicist, educator*

La Mesa
Allen, David Charles *computer science educator*

Long Beach
Palacios, Alana Sue *computer programmer*

Los Angeles
Afifi, Abdelmonem A. *biostatistics educator, academic dean*
Arbib, Michael Anthony *neuroscientist, educator, cybernetician*
Bekey, George Albert *computer scientist, educator, engineer*
Boehm, Barry William *computer science educator*
Chacko, George Kuttickal *systems science educator, consultant*
†Dyer, Michael George *educator in computer science*
Estrin, Gerald *computer scientist, engineering educator, academic administrator*
Golomb, Solomon Wolf *mathematician, electrical engineer, educator, university official*
Gordon, Basil *mathematics educator*
Greenberger, Martin *computer and information scientist, educator*
Harris, Theodore Edward *mathematician, educator*
Jacobsen, Laren *programmer, analyst*
Kalaba, Robert Edwin *applied mathematician*
Kleinrock, Leonard *computer scientist*
Pearl, Judea *computer scientist, educator*
Petak, William John *systems management educator*
Port, Sidney Charles *mathematician, educator*
Pottenger, Mark McClelland *computer programmer*
Rodriguez, Edward John *educational software developer*
Schmitz, John Anthony *systems analyst*
Shapley, Lloyd Stowell *mathematics and economics educator*
Stormes, John Max *instructional systems developer*
Touber, Joshua Samuel *technology consultant*
Waterman, Michael Spencer *mathematics educator, biology educator*

Los Gatos
Rissanen, Jorma Johannes *computer scientist*

Malibu
Crawford, Natalie Wilson *applied mathematician*

Stalzer, Mark Anthony *computer scientist*

Manhattan Beach
Lucas, Suzanne *statistician, entrepreneur*

Marina Del Rey
Touch, Joseph Dean *computer scientist, educator*

Martinez
Tong, Siu Wing *computer programmer*

Menlo Park
Bourne, Charles Percy *information scientist, educator*
Neumann, Peter Gabriel *computer scientist*

Milpitas
Wheeler, William R. *technical advisor*

Moffett Field
Baldwin, Betty Jo *computer specialist*

Moss Landing
Lange, Lester Henry *mathematics educator*

Newport Beach
Cook, Marcy Lynn *mathematics educator, consultant*

Northridge
Stratton, Gregory Alexander *computer specialist, administrator, mayor*

Oakland
Lepowsky, William Leonard *mathematics and statistics educator*
Long, William Joseph *software engineer*
Lubliner, Irving *mathematics educator, consultant*
Zelmanowitz, Julius Martin *mathematics educator, university administrator*

Oxnard
Hayashi, Alan T. *mathematics educator*

Palo Alto
Beretta, Giordano Bruno *computer scientist, researcher*
Kolarov, Krasimir Dobromirov *computer scientist, researcher*
Lamport, Leslie B. *computer scientist*
Mahmood, Aamer *computer system architect*
Martin, Roger John *computer scientist*
Oki, Brian Masao *software engineer*
Rejman, Diane Louise *manufacturing systems applications analyst*

Pasadena
Chandy, K. Mani *computer science educator*
Franklin, Joel Nicholas *mathematician, educator*
Marsden, Jerrold Eldon *mathematician, educator, engineer*
Mead, Carver Andress *computer science educator*
Patterson, Mark Jerome *computer software designer*
Saffman, Philip G. *mathematician*
Todd, John *mathematician, educator*
Whitham, Gerald Beresford *mathematics educator*

Pico Rivera
Donoghue, John Charles *software management consultant*

Pomona
Bernau, Simon John *mathematics educator*

Portola Valley
Kuo, Franklin F. *computer scientist, electrical engineer*

Ramona
Bennett, James Chester *computer consultant, real estate developer*

Redondo Beach
Woike, Lynne Ann *computer scientist*

Redwood City
Itnyre, Jacqueline Harriet *systems analyst*

Riverside
Howe, Vernon Wesley *mathematics educator*
Przytycki, Józef Henryk *mathematician*
Ratliff, Louis Jackson, Jr. *mathematics educator*

Rolling Hills Estates
Clewis, Charlotte Wright Staub *mathematics educator*

Roseville
†Reichmann, Péter Iván *mathematician*

Sacramento
Sawiris, Milad Youssef *statistician, educator*

San Bruno
Olson, Julie Ann *systems consultant, educator*

San Carlos
Komissarchik, Edward *computer scientist*

San Diego
Burke, John *science technology company executive*
Garrison, Betty Bernhardt *retired mathematics educator*
Hales, Alfred Washington *mathematics educator, consultant*
Huang, Kun Lien *software engineer, scientist*
Legrand, Shawn Pierre *computer systems programmer*
Loper, Warren Edward *computer scientist*
Romano, Albert *retired educator, statistical consultant*
Schwertly, Harvey Kenneth, Jr. *computer electronics educator*
Wadlington, W. M. *software company executive*
Willerding, Margaret Frances *mathematician*

San Francisco
Backus, John *computer scientist*

Cruse, Allan Baird *mathematician, computer scientist, educator*
Fitzpatrick, William Peter *computer programmer, analyst, state legislator*
Leung, Kason Kai Ching *computer specialist*
Lowndes, David Alan *programmer analyst*

San Gabriel
Kettemborough, Clifford Russell *computer scientist, consultant, manager*

San Jose
Eyerman, David John *software engineer*
Geschke, Charles M. *computer scientist, computer company executive*
Gilmore, Helen Carol *computer specialist, executive*
Morgridge, John P. *computer business executive*

San Juan Capistrano
Botway, Lloyd Frederick *computer scientist, consultant*

San Leandro
Ley, David Chanpannha *secondary mathematics and ESL educator*

San Luis Obispo
Lang, Martin Traugott *mathematics educator*

San Marino
Lashley, Virginia Stephenson Hughes *retired computer science educator*

San Ramon
Rose, Joan L. *computer security specialist*
Schofield, James Roy *computer programmer*

Santa Barbara
Johnsen, Eugene Carlyle *mathematician and educator*
Marcus, Marvin *mathematician, educator*
Minc, Henryk *mathematics educator*
Newman, Morris *mathematician*
Simons, Stephen *mathematics educator, researcher*

Santa Clara
Halmos, Paul Richard *mathematician, educator*
Klosinski, Leonard Frank *mathematics educator*
Lawrence, Deborah Jean *statistician*
Lin, Tao *software engineer*

Santa Cruz
Huskey, Harry Douglas *information and computer science educator*

Santa Monica
Anderson, Robert Helms *information scientist*
Ware, Willis Howard *computer scientist*

Santee
Peters, Raymond Eugene *computer systems company executive*

Saratoga
Park, Joseph Chul Hui *computer scientist*

Scotts Valley
Janssen, James Robert *consulting software engineer*

South Pasadena
†Lima, Donald Roger *computer programmer*

Stanford
Anderson, Theodore Wilbur *statistics educator*
Brown, Byron William, Jr. *biostatistician, educator*
Cover, Thomas M. *statistician, electrical engineer, educator*
Dantzig, George Bernard *applied mathematics educator*
Efron, Bradley *mathematics educator*
Feigenbaum, Edward Albert *computer science educator*
Keller, Arthur Michael *computer science researcher*
Keller, Joseph Bishop *mathematician, educator*
Knuth, Donald Ervin *computer sciences educator*
Lieberman, Gerald J. *statistics educator*
McCarthy, John *computer scientist, educator*
Moses, Lincoln E. *statistician, educator*
Olshen, Richard A. *statistician, educator*
Ornstein, Donald Samuel *mathematician, educator*
Schoen, Richard Melvin *mathematics educator, researcher*
Ullman, Jeffrey David *computer science educator*
Whittemore, Alice *biostatistician*

Thousand Oaks
†Johnson, Shirley Amagna *systems analyst*
Sladek, Lyle Virgil *mathematician, educator*

Torrance
Houston, Samuel Robert *statistics educator, consultant*

Walnut Creek
Barnett, David Hughes *software engineer, computer systems architect*

West Hills
Koerber, John Robert *computer programmer*

Westlake Village
Munson, John Backus *computer systems consultant, retired computer engineering company executive*

Woodland Hills
Fitzpatrick, Dennis Michael *information systems executive*

Woodside
Taylor, Robert William *research director*

COLORADO

Boulder
Beylkin, Gregory *mathematician*
Crow, Edwin Louis *mathematical statistician, consultant*
Glover, Fred William *artificial intelligence and optimization research director, educator*
Monarchi, David Edward *management scientist, information scientist, educator*
Mycielski, Jan *mathematician, educator*

Colorado Springs
Heffron, Michael Edward *software engineer, computer scientist*
Simmons, George Finlay *mathematics educator*

Denver
Coffelt, Janice Litherland *contracting officer*
Cutter, Gary Raymond *biostatistician*
Kirslis, Peter Andre Christopher *computer science research and development specialist*
Kushner, Todd Roger *computer scientist, software engineer*
Larsen, Gwynne E. *computer information systems educator*
Mendez, Celestino Galo *mathematics educator*

Divide
Trench, William Frederick *mathematics educator*

Durango
Spencer, Donald Clayton *mathematician*

Fort Collins
Edgeman, Rick Lee *statistics educator, consultant*
Mielke, Paul William, Jr. *statistician*

Golden
Bradley, James Alexander *software engineer, researcher*
Kuehn, Carl Peter *information technology consultant, statistician*

Lakewood
Priest, Terrance Lee *logistics professional*

Littleton
Riley, Mary Jane *computer scientist*

Longmont
Ford, Byron Milton *computer consultant*
McEachern, Susan Mary *information technology specialist*

Louisville
Tetlow, William Lloyd *infotech consultant*

Pueblo
Chandler, Kris *computer consultant, educator*

Westminster
Wade, Rodger Grant *financial systems analyst*

CONNECTICUT

Ansonia
Kerpa, Gary J. *computer science consultant*

Bloomfield
Johnson, Linda Thelma *information specialist*

Bridgeport
Sobh, Tarek Mahmoud *computer science educator, researcher*

Burlington
Sonn, Gay *mathematics educator*

Danbury
Fuller, Cassandra Miller *applications specialist*
Scalzo, Robert Edward *middle school mathematics educator*
Wright, Marie Anne *management information systems educator*

East Hartford
Murphy, Ann Burke *retired systems analyst*

Fairfield
Eigel, Edwin George, Jr. *mathematics educator, retired university president*
Shaffer, Dorothy Browne *retired mathematician, educator*

Hamden
†Saulnier, Bruce Melburn *computer science educator*

Middletown
Comfort, William Wistar *mathematics educator*
Hager, Anthony Wood *mathematics educator*
Reid, James Dolan *mathematics educator, researcher*

New Britain
Margiotta, Mary-Lou Ann *software engineer*

New Haven
Fischer, Michael John *computer science educator*
Howe, Roger Evans *mathematician, educator*
Jacobson, Nathan *mathematics educator*
Mandelbrot, Benoit B. *mathematician, scientist, educator*
Margulis, Gregory A. *mathematics educator, researcher*
Massey, William S. *mathematician, educator*
Mostow, George Daniel *mathematics educator*
Rickart, Charles Earl *mathematician, educator*
Seligman, George Benham *mathematics educator*
Szczarba, Robert Henry *mathematics educator, mathematician*
Tufte, Edward Rolf *statistics educator, publisher*
Zhang, Heping *biostatistician*

Rocky Hill
Tietjen, Scott Phillips *computer programmer, analyst*

Stamford
Frank, Laura Jean *computer scientist*

Vernon Rockville
Roden, Jon-Paul *computer science educator*

Rice, John Rischard *computer scientist, researcher, educator*

IOWA

Algona
Burrow, David Michael *mathematics educator, academic administrator*

Ames
Dahiya, Rajbir Singh *mathematics educator, researcher*
David, Herbert Aron *statistics educator*
Fuller, Wayne Arthur *statistics educator*

Cedar Falls
Wirth, David Eugene *software designer, consultant*

Center Junction
Antons, Pauline Marie *mathematics educator*

Des Moines
Wilson, Sally Ann *computer systems analyst, business executive*

Dubuque
Decker, Judith Ann *computer science educator*

Grinnell
Adelberg, Arnold Melvin *mathematics educator, researcher*
Ferguson, Pamela Anderson *mathematics educator, educational administrator*

Iowa City
Broffitt, James Drake *professor statistics and actuarial science*
Hogg, Robert Vincent, Jr. *mathematical statistician, educator*
Johnson, Eugene Walter *mathematician, editor*
Kleinfeld, Erwin *mathematician, educator*
Robertson, Timothy Joel *statistician, educator*
Woolson, Robert Francis *biostatistician*

West Burlington
Polley, Michael Glen *mathematics educator*

KANSAS

Lawrence
Gay, Aleda Susan *mathematician, educator*
Himmelberg, Charles John, III *mathematics educator, researcher*

Manhattan
Higgins, James Jacob *statistics educator*

Shawnee
Delay, Susan Lyne *software trainer*

Wichita
Aelmore, Donald K. *systems engineer*
Hostetler, John Jay *systems consultant*
Palmer, Ada Margaret *systems accountant, computer consultant*

KENTUCKY

Bardstown
Kibiloski, Floyd Terrance *business and computer consultant, editor, educator*

Corbin
Steenbergen, Gary Lewis *computer aided design educator*

Frankfort
Mosier, Jo Ann *mathematics educator*

Lexington
Stockbridge, Richard H. *probability and statistics educator*

Louisville
Greaver, Joanne Hutchins *mathematics educator, author*
Hoye, Robert Earl *systems science educator*
Schneider, Arthur *computer graphics specialist*

Madisonville
†Hougland, Virginia Lee *mathematics educator*

Morehead
Mann, James Darwin *mathematics educator*

Nicholasville
McMullin, Shertina A. *mathematics and English teacher*

Richmond
King, Amy Cathryne Patterson *mathematics educator, researcher*

LOUISIANA

Baton Rouge
Zhu, Jianchao *computer and control scientist, engineer, educator*

Monroe
Cage, Bobby Nyle *research and statistics educator*

Natchitoches
Webb, Randall Joseph *mathematics educator, university president*

New Orleans
Adams, Darlene W. *computer services administrator*
Birtel, Frank Thomas *mathematician, philosopher, educator*
LaValle, Irving Howard *decision analysis educator*

Shreveport
Becker, Roger Vern *information science educator*

MAINE

Brunswick
Tucker, Allen Brown, Jr. *computer science educator*

Liberty
Anderson, Alfred Oliver *mathematician, consultant*

Standish
†Balcomb, Scott Hull *mathematics educator*

Yarmouth
Grover, Mark Donald *computer scientist*

MARYLAND

Annapolis
†Konkowski, Deborah Ann *mathematics educator*

Baltimore
Arsham, Hossein *operations research analyst*
Bard, James F., Jr. *information systems professional*
Bausell, R. Barker, Jr. *research methodology educator*
Boardman, John Michael *mathematician, educator*
Chen, Tar Timothy *biostatistician*
Goldman, Alan Joseph *mathematician*
Igusa, Jun-Ichi *mathematician, educator*
Karow, Charles Stanley *computer consultant*
Kosaraju, S. Rao *computer science educator, researcher*
Masson, Gerald M. *computer science educator*
Meyer, Jean-Pierre Gustave *mathematician, educator*
Potra, Florian Alexander *mathematics educator*
Sherman, Alan Theodore *computer science educator*
Shiffman, Bernard *mathematician, educator*
Slepian, Paul *mathematician, educator*
Wierman, John Charles *mathematician, educator*
Wilson, Peter Mason *computer programmer*

Bel Air
Eichelberger, Robert John *retired government research and development administrator, consultant*

Bethesda
Cohn, Murray Steven *information technology administrator*
Friestedt, Amédée Chabrisson *medical genetics database manager*
Gilford, Dorothy Morrow *statistician, researcher*
Heller, Daniel Robert *investment banker, portfolio manager*
Lipkin, Bernice Sacks *computer science educator*
Moshman, Jack *statistical consultant*
Navarro, Joseph Anthony *statistician, consultant*
Sammet, Jean E. *computer scientist*
Smith, Kent Ashton *scientific and technical information executive*
Stokes, Arnold Paul *mathematics educator*
Taylor, John Darryl *computer scientist*
Weiss, George Herbert *mathematician, consultant*

Bowie
Cohn, Harvey *mathematician*

Chevy Chase
Hoffman, Kenneth Myron *mathematician, educator*

College Park
Antman, Stuart Sheldon *mathematician, educator*
†Iozzi, Alessandra *mathematician, educator*
Miller, Raymond Edward *computer science educator*
Minker, Jack *computer scientist, educator*
Rosenfeld, Azriel *computer science educator, consultant*
White, Marilyn Domas *information science educator*
Yorke, James Alan *chaos mathematician*

Columbia
Gregorie, Corazon Arzalem *operations supervisor*
Kendrick, John Lawrence *software engineer*
Spohn, William Gideon, Jr. *mathematician, musician*
Straja, Sorin Radu *chemical engineer, mathematician, computer programmer*

Elliott City
Morris, Stephen Brent *mathematician*

Fort Washington
Gleason, John Thomas *consultant software development planner*
Wilcox, Richard Hoag *information scientist*

Frederick
Alvord, W. Gregory *statistician*

Gaithersburg
Carasso, Alfred Sam *mathematician*
Gilsinn, David Edmund *mathematician, researcher*
Hoferek, Mary Judith *database administrator*
Jefferson, David *computer scientist*
Olejar, Paul Duncan *former information science administrator*
Rosenblatt, Joan Raup *mathematical statistician*

Garrett Park
McDowell, Eugene Charles *systems analyst, bioethicist*

Huntingtown
†Emberland, Gorm Petter *software developer, computer programmer*

Hyattsville
Bender, Howard Jeffrey *software engineering educator*
Embody, Daniel Robert *biometrician*

Kensington
Lisle, Martha Oglesby *retired mathematics educator*

Lanham Seabrook
Brasoveanu, Dan *systems analyst*

Laurel
Gieszl, Louis Roger *mathematician*

Potomac
DiPentima, Renato Anthony *systems executive*
Frieder, Gideon *computer science and engineering educator*

Rockville
Basinger, William Daniel *computer programmer*
Kalton, Graham *survey statistician*
Lin, Jonathan Chung-Shih *computer scientist*
Menkello, Frederick Vincent *computer scientist*
Nevin, Joseph Francis *computer systems engineer*
Waksberg, Joseph *statistical company executive, researcher*
Yao, Andy Shunchi *computer science educator*

Silver Spring
Hetzel, Alice M. *statistician, researcher*
Hoch, Peggy Marie *computer scientist*
Sirken, Monroe Gilbert *statistician*

Simpsonville
Bluher, Gregory *computer scientist, mathematician*

MASSACHUSETTS

Amherst
Weems, Charles Chilton *computer science educator*

Andover
Leyva, Christine Marie *information specialist*

Arlington
Nahigian, Russell Ara *mathematician*
Whitehead, George William *retired mathematician*

Auburn
Hahn, Robert Simpson *computer scientist, mechanical engineer*

Bedford
Hantman, Barry G. *software engineer*

Belmont
Hooker, Richard Arthur *computer scientist*
Lange, Nicholas Theodore *biostatistician*
Reynolds, William Francis *mathematics educator*

Boston
Berkey, Dennis D. *mathematics educator*
†Carlson, Neil Ryan *computer scientist*
Falb, Peter Lawrence *mathematician, educator, investment company executive*
Gilmore, Maurice Eugene *mathematics educator*
Henry, Christopher Joel *software consultant*
Moseby, LeBaron Clarence, Jr. *mathematics and computer science educator*
Nyberg, Stanley Eric *cognitive scientist*
Previato, Emma *mathematics educator*
Rand, William Medden *biostatistics educator*
Sabbag, Douglas Walter *computer consultant company executive*
Schribman, Shelley Iris *database engineer, consultant*
Stallman, Richard Matthew *software developer*
Stone, Arthur Harold *mathematics educator*
Warga, Jack *mathematician, educator*
Zelen, Marvin *statistics educator*

Brockton
Parcels, Burtis George *computer consultant, educator*

Cambridge
Anderson, Donald Gordon Marcus *mathematics educator*
Artin, Michael *mathematics educator*
Bartee, Thomas Creson *computer scientist, educator*
Bott, Raoul *mathematician, educator*
Carrier, George Francis *applied mathematics educator*
Chernoff, Herman *statistics educator*
Cho, John Yungdo Nagamichi *atmospheric research scientist*
Conrades, George Henry *information systems company executive*
Dertouzos, Michael Leonidas *computer scientist, electrical engineer, educator*
Dudley, Richard Mansfield *mathematician, educator*
Elkies, Noam D. *mathematics educator*
Foley, James David *computer science educator, consultant*
Gagliardi, Ugo Oscar *systems software architect, educator*
Greenspan, Harvey Philip *applied mathematician, educator*
Grosz, Barbara Jean *computer science educator*
Helgason, Sigurdur *mathematician, educator*
Kac, Victor G. *mathematician, educator*
Kazhdan, David *mathematician, educator*
Kung, Hsiang-Tsung *computer architect*
Lampson, Butler Wright *computer scientist*
Light, Richard Jay *statistician, education educator*
Lusztig, George *mathematician*
Lynch, Nancy Ann *computer scientist, educator*
Mack, Robert Whiting *computer consultant*
Mackey, George Whitelaw *mathematician, educator*
Mazur, Barry Charles *mathematician*
†McMullen, Curtis T. *mathematics educator*
Minsky, Marvin Lee *mathematician, educator*
Moses, Joel *computer scientist, educator*
Mosteller, Frederick *mathematical statistician, educator*
Oettinger, Anthony Gervin *mathematician, educator*
Orlin, James Berger *mathematician, management scientist, educator*
Pratt, John Winsor *statistics educator*
Roberts, Edward Baer *technology management educator*
Rockart, John Fralick *information systems reseacher*
Rubin, Donald Bruce *statistician, educator, research company executive*
Singer, Isadore Manuel *mathematician, educator*
Stanley, Richard P. *mathematics educator*
Strang, William Gilbert *mathematician, educator*
Stroock, Daniel Wyler *mathematician, educator*
†Suhm, Bernhard *scientist*
Tian, Gang *mathematics educator*
Toomre, Alar *applied mathematician, theoretical astronomer*
Valiant, Leslie Gabriel *computer scientist*
Welsch, Roy Elmer *statistician*
Yantosca, Robert Michael *scientific programmer*
Yau, Shing-Tung *mathematics educator*

Framingham
Lavin, Philip Todd *biostatistician executive*
Scherr, Allan Lee *computer scientist, executive*

Greenfield
Robinson, John Alan *logic and computer science educator*

Lexington
Guivens, Norman Roy, Jr. *mathematician, engineer*
Schafer, Alice Turner *retired mathematics educator*

Lincoln
LeGates, John Crews Boulton *information scientist*

Medford
Quinto, Eric Todd *mathematics educator*

Medway
Yonda, Alfred William *mathematician*

Milford
Williams, Richard Charles *computer programmer, consultant*

Natick
Moler, Cleve Barry *mathematician*

Quincy
Hayes, Bernardine Frances *computer systems analyst*

Sharon
Dunham, Barbara Jean *administrator*

Shrewsbury
Garabedian, Charles, Jr. *mathematics educator*

Somerville
Adams, Jonathan L. *computer programmer*

Tewksbury
Andersson, Allen Arvid *computer scientist*

Waltham
Brown, Edgar Henry, Jr. *mathematician, educator*
O'Donnell, Teresa Hohol *software development engineer, antennas engineer*

Wellesley
Hildebrand, Francis Begnaud *mathematics educator*
Kottas, James Alan *computer scientist*

Westborough
Crosby, Thomas W. *computer scientist*

Westfield
Buckmore, Alvah Clarence, Jr. *computer scientist, ballistician*

Westford
Selesky, Donald Bryant *software developer*

Westwood
Smith, Denis Joseph *mathematics educator*

Winchester
Dalton, Robert Edgar *mathematician, computer scientist*
Jackson, Francis Joseph *research and development company executive*
Shannon, Claude Elwood *mathematician, educator*
Tisdale, Phebe Alden *cryptographer*

Woburn
Hatch, Mark Bruce *software engineer*

Worcester
Malone, Joseph James *mathematics educator, researcher*

MICHIGAN

Ann Arbor
Bartle, Robert Gardner *retired mathematics educator*
Beutler, Frederick Joseph *information scientist*
Brown, Morton B. *biostatistics educator*
Conway, Lynn *computer scientist, electrical engineer, educator*
Fulton, William *mathematics educator*
Gehring, Frederick William *mathematician, educator*
Hill, Bruce Marvin *statistician, scientist, educator*
Leabo, Dick A. *retired statistics educator*
Lewis, Donald John *mathematics educator*
Mallory, Steven Reece *software engineering executive*

Auburn Hills
Mukundan, Gopalan *information technologist*

Bellevue
Hamel, Louis Reginald *systems analysis consultant*

Bloomfield Hills
Graff, Robert Alan *computer consultant*
Nuss, Shirley Ann *computer coordinator, educator*

Clarkston
Gibson, Toby Allen *systems analyst, poet*

Dearborn
Brown, James Ward *mathematician, educator, author*

Detroit
Dwyer, John M. *mathematician, statistician, computer scientist*
Rajlich, Vaclav Thomas *computer science educator, researcher, consultant*
Schreiber, Bertram Manuel *mathematics educator*
Spansky, Robert Alan *computer systems analyst, retired*

East Lansing
†Li, Tien-Yien *mathematics educator*
Moran, Daniel Austin *mathematician*
Stapleton, James Hall *statistician, educator*
Weng, John Juyang *computer science educator, researcher*

Farmington
Ginsberg, Myron *computer scientist*

Farmington Hills
Karniotis, Stephen Paul *computer scientist*

Flint
McCartin, Brian James *mathematician, educator*

Grand Rapids
Timpe, Michael Wayne *systems analyst*

Harrison Township
Childress, Janet Lynn *logistician*

Jackson
Ross, Lorraine Sumiko *mathematics and science educator, bookkeeper*

Kalamazoo
Calloway, Jean Mitchener *mathematician, educator*
Clarke, Allen Bruce *mathematics educator, retired academic administrator*

Mount Pleasant
Rubin, Stuart Harvey *computer science educator, researcher*

Northville
Hansen, Jean Marie *math and computer educator*

Novi
Chow, Chi-Ming *retired mathematics educator*

Rochester
†Shillor, Meir *mathematics educator*

Rochester Hills
Graves, Vashti Sylvia *computer analyst, EDP auditor, consultant*

Saline
Cornell, Richard Garth *biostatistics educator*

Southfield
Erickson, Garwood Elliott *computer consulting company executive*

Sterling Heights
†Chrzanowski, Winifred Helene *data management specialist*

Troy
Grewell, Judith Lynn *computer services executive*

Warren
Bley, Ann *program analyst*
†Johnson, Leonard Gustave *research mathematician, consultant*
Lamb, David Alan *mathematician*

West Bloomfield
Miller, Nancy Ellen *computer consultant*

Ypsilanti
Gledhill, Roger Clayton *statistician, engineer, mathematician, educator*
Gunasekera, Thilak Wijenayaka *mathematician, educator*
Ullman, Nelly Szabo *statistician, educator*

MINNESOTA

Burnsville
†Anderson, Eril W.L. *web designer*

Inver Grove Heights
Evans, Roger Lynwood *scientist, patent liaison*

Mankato
Morrow, Steven Roger *computer scientist*

Minneapolis
Aris, Rutherford *applied mathematician, educator*
Brasket, Curt Justin *systems analyst, chess player*
Du, Ding-Zhu *mathematician, educator*
Friedman, Avner *mathematician, educator*
Garfield, Joan Barbara *statistics educator*
Gersemehl, William Terry *information systems manager*
Kahn, Donald William *mathematics educator*
Markus, Lawrence *retired mathematics educator*
Miller, Willard, Jr. *mathematician, educator*
Nitsche, Johannes Carl Christian *mathematics educator*
Pour-El, Marian Boykan *mathematician, educator*
Serrin, James Burton *mathematics educator*
Slagle, James Robert *computer science educator*
Warner, William Hamer *applied mathematician*

Moorhead
Heuer, Gerald Arthur *mathematician, educator*

New Brighton
Shier, Gloria Bulan *mathematics educator*

Northfield
Appleyard, David Frank *mathematics and computer science educator*
Steen, Lynn Arthur *mathematician, educator*

Rochester
Grosset, Jessica Ariane *computer analyst*
Van Norman, Willis Roger *computer systems researcher*

Roseville
Kane, George Francis *systems analyst*

Saint Cloud
Guster, Dennis Charles *computer scientist, educator*

Saint Paul
Bingham, Christopher *statistics educator*
Spellmire, Sandra Marie *systems analyst, programmer*

MISSISSIPPI

Jackson
Galloway, Patricia Kay *systems analyst, ethnohistorian*

Mississippi State
Ahmad, Shair *mathematics educator*

University
Roach, David Giles *information technology administrator*

MISSOURI

Columbia
Basu, Asit Prakas *statistician*
Beem, John Kelly *mathematician, educator*
Schrader, Keith William *mathematician*
Williams, Frederick *statistics educator*
Wright, Farroll Tim *statistics educator, researcher*

Grain Valley
Flora, Jairus Dale, Jr. *statistician*

Kansas City
Mazza-Deblauwe, Tania Sue *software engineer, technology educator*
Peake, Candice K. Loper *data processing professional*

Maryville
King, Terry Lee *statistician, mathematician*

Nevada
Hornback, Joseph Hope *mathematics educator*

Rolla
Grimm, Louis John *mathematician, educator*
Zobrist, George Winston *computer scientist, educator*

Saint Louis
Baernstein, Albert, II *mathematician*
Boothby, William Munger *mathematics educator*
Burleski, Joseph Anthony, Jr. *information technology executive*
Cawns, Albert Edward *computer systems consultant*
Corbett, James Joseph *retired computer programmer*
Freese, Raymond William *mathematics educator*
Haskins, James Leslie *mathematics educator*
Kempf, Kenneth Charles *computer drafting professional*
Key, Marcella Ann *computer information specialist*
Nussbaum, A(dolf) Edward *mathematician, educator*
Pollack, Seymour Victor *computer science educator*
Raeuchle, John Steven *computer analyst*
Schmidt, Douglas Craig *computer science educator, consultant*
†Sikic, Hrvoje *mathematician*
Thompson, Rodney Marlin *computer consultant*
Wilson, Edward Nathan *mathematician, educator*

Springfield
Robertson, Ruth Ann *systems analyst, engineer*

Trenton
Myntti, Jon Nicholas *software engineer*

MONTANA

Helena
Johnson, Qulan Adrian *software engineer*

NEBRASKA

Kearney
Fredrickson, Scott Alfred *instructional technology educator, consultant*

Lincoln
Westphal, Dorothy Mae *systems analyst*
Wiegand, Sylvia Margaret *mathematician, educator*

Omaha
Chen, Zhengxin *computer scientist*
Gessaman, Margaret Palmer *mathematics educator, college dean*
†Reek, John Christian *market analyst*

NEVADA

Carson City
Palmer, Roger Cain *information scientist*

Henderson
Jackson, Robert Loring *science and mathematics educator, academic administrator*

Las Vegas
†Bein, Wolfgang Walter *computer science educator*
Komm, Kermit Matthew *software engineer*

Yerington
Price, Thomas Munro *computer consultant*

NEW HAMPSHIRE

Durham
Appel, Kenneth I. *mathematician, educator*
Van Osdol, Donovan Harold *mathematics educator*

Hanover
Baumgartner, James Earl *mathematics educator*
Kurtz, Thomas Eugene *mathematics educator*
Lamperti, John Williams *mathematics educator*
Snell, James Laurie *mathematician, educator*

Nashua
Meagher, Robert Michael *software engineer*
Smith, Thomas Raymond, III *software engineer*

Plymouth
Drexel, Peter George *computer science educator*

NEW JERSEY

Allendale
Bai, Nina Beate *senior software engineer, consultant*

Camden
Gerver, Joseph Leonide *mathematics educator*

Cinnaminson
Kauffmann, Robert Fredrick *software engineer*

Clark
Burtnick, Ronald *sales executive*

Clinton
†Quandt, Michael T. *manager systems analysis*

Edison
Doherty, Patricia Ann *computer systems analyst*
Tyrl, Paul *mathematics educator, researcher, consultant*

Englewood
Lapidus, Arnold *mathematician*

Flemington
Bieri, Barbara Normile *systems analyst, consultant*

Florham Park
Graham, Ronald Lewis *mathematician*
Rabinovich, Michael *computer scientist*
Sloane, Neil James Alexander *mathematician, researcher*

Haddonfield
Enfield, Ronald Lee *Internet software company executive*

Jersey City
Poiani, Eileen Louise *mathematics educator, college administrator, higher education planner*

Lakewood
Houle, Joseph E. *mathematics educator*
Sloyan, Sister Stephanie *mathematics educator*

Lawrenceville
Hester, Kara-Lyn Annette *software engineer*

Liberty Corner
Bergeron, Robert Francis, Jr. (Terry Bergeron) *software engineer*

Lincroft
Orost, Joseph Martin *computer scientist*

Marlton
Flacco, Elaine Germano *computer programmer*

Middletown
Mannepalli, Yellamandeswara Rao *software engineer, consultant*

Moorestown
Benjamin, Milton Kemp *computer scientist, engineer, physicist*

Murray Hill
Kruskal, Joseph B. *mathematician, statistician, researcher*

Neshanic Station
Muckenhoupt, Benjamin *retired mathematics educator*

New Brunswick
Amarel, Saul *computer scientist, educator*
Kruskal, Martin David *mathematical physicist, educator*
Kulikowski, Casimir Alexander *computer science educator*
Saracevic, Tefko *information science educator*
Scanlon, Jane Cronin *mathematics educator*
Strawderman, William E. *statistics educator*

New Providence
Mumick, Inderpal Singh *computer scientist, engineer*

Newark
Wang, Jason Tsong-Li *computer science educator*

Parsippany
Reiley, Thomas Phillip *consultant*

Piscataway
Gelfand, Israel Moseevich *mathematician, biologist*
Kenney, Mary R. *software engineer*

Princeton
Aizenman, Michael *mathematics and physics educator, researcher*
Bombieri, Enrico *mathematician, educator*
Borel, Armand *mathematics educator*
Browder, William *mathematician, educator*
Christodoulou, Demetrios *mathematics educator*
Deligne, Pierre René *mathematician*
Fefferman, Charles Louis *mathematics educator*
Gear, Charles William *computer scientist*
Griffiths, Phillip A. *mathematician, academic administrator*
Gunning, Robert Clifford *mathematics educator*
Kohn, Joseph John *mathematics educator*
Langlands, Robert Phelan *mathematician*

Hanover
Levin, Simon Asher *mathematician, ecologist, educator*
MacPherson, Robert Duncan *mathematician, educator*
Musinguzi, Hannington Rwabazaire *software engineer*
Nash, John Forbes, Jr. *research mathematician*
Umscheid, Ludwig Joseph *computer specialist*
Wiles, Andrew J. *mathematician, educator*
Zierler, Neal *retired mathematician*

Ridgefield Park
Jurasek, John Paul *mathematics educator, counselor*
Litwinowicz, Anthony *information specialist, researcher*

Roseland
Rivero, Jose Antonio *computer company executive*

Somerset
†Mazzeo, Christine M. *computer and mathematics educator*
Schoen, Howard Franklin *computer programmer, analyst*

Summit
Slepian, David *mathematician, communications engineer*

Teaneck
Zwass, Vladimir *information systems educator*

Trenton
Kell, Deborah Ellen Harvey *mathematics educator*

Vineland
Steward, Mollie Aileen *mathematics and computer science educator*

Watchung
Schaefer, Jacob Wernli *military systems consultant*

Westwood
Dorner-Andelora, Sharon Agnes Haddon *computer technical consultant, educator*

Willingboro
Ingerman, Peter Zilahy *infosystems consultant*

NEW MEXICO

Albuquerque
Bell, Stoughton *computer scientist, mathematician, educator*
Krostag, Diane Theresa Michaels *clinical informatics analyst*
†Roth, Frank J. *computer scientist*
Sobolewski, John Stephen *computer scientist, consultant*

Aztec
†Van Auken, Ginger Suzanne *mathematics educator*

Belen
Gutjahr, Allan Leo *mathematics educator, researcher*

Farmington
Doig, Beverly Irene *systems specialist*

Jemez Springs
Sigler, Marjorie Diane *computer programming executive, analyst*

Kirtland AFB
Anderson, Christine Marlene *software engineer*

Los Alamos
Kellner, Richard George *mathematician, computer scientist*

Santa Fe
Sciame, Donald Richard *computer systems analyst, dentist, magician, locksmith*
Stringer, Gail Griffin *information systems consultant*

NEW YORK

Albany
Derderian, John A. *systems analyst*
Hsia, Franklin Wen-Hai *computer programmer, systems analyst, consultant*
Richbart, Carolyn Mae *mathematics educator*
Rosenkrantz, Daniel J. *computer science educator*
Wilson, Brian Eugene *computer scientist*

Amherst
Brown, Stephen Ira *mathematics educator*

Aurora
Shilepsky, Arnold Charles *mathematics educator, computer consultant*

Ballston Lake
McCann, Chris (Christian David McCann) *software engineer, educator*

Batavia
Rigerman, Ruth Underhill *mathematics educator*

Binghamton
Hilton, Peter John *mathematician, educator*
Klir, George Jiri *systems science educator*

Brockport
Michaels, John G. *mathematics educator*

Bronx
Koranyi, Adam *mathematics educator*
Rose, Israel Harold *mathematics educator*
Seltzer, William *statistician, social researcher, former international organization director*
Tong, Hing *mathematician, educator*
Wigsten, Paul Bradley, Jr. *computer and financial consultant*

Brooklyn
Bachman, George *mathematics educator*
Pennisten, John William *computer scientist, linguist, actuary*
Weill, Georges Gustave *mathematics educator*

Buffalo
Berner, Robert Frank *managerial statistics educator, administrator*
Bross, Irwin Dudley Jackson *biostatistician*
Coburn, Lewis Alan *mathematics educator*
Eberlein, Patricia James *mathematician, computer scientist, educator*
Goodberry, Diane Jean (Oberkircher) *mathematics educator, tax accountant*
Hauptman, Herbert Aaron *mathematician, educator, researcher*
Priore, Roger L. *biostatistics educator, consultant*
Seitz, Mary Lee *mathematics educator*
Selman, Alan Louis *computer science educator*
Shapiro, Stuart Charles *computer scientist, educator*
Wiesenberg, Russel John *statistician*

Chappaqua
Glazer, Richard Basil *university program director*

Corning
Johnson, Janet LeAnn Moe *statistician, engineering professional*
†Neubauer, Dean Veral *statistician*

Delmar
Houghton, Raymond Carl, Jr. *computer science educator*

Farmingdale
Sandler, Gerald Howard *computer science educator, company executive*

Flushing
Mendelson, Elliott *mathematician, educator*

Hamilton
Tucker, Thomas William *mathematics professor*

Hawthorne
Green, Paul Eliot, Jr. *communications scientist*
Karnaugh, Maurice *computer scientist, educator*

Hempstead
Hastings, Harold Morris *mathematics educator, researcher, author*

Hicksville
†Whitlock, Prentice Earle *retired mathematics educator, clergyman*
Yen, Henry Chin-Yuan *computer systems programmer, software engineer, consulting company executive*

Ithaca
Conway, Richard Walter *computer scientist, educator*
Dynkin, Eugene B. *mathematics educator*
Earle, Clifford John, Jr. *mathematician*
Hartmanis, Juris *computer scientist, educator*
Morgenstern, Matthew *computer scientist*
Nerode, Anil *mathematician, educator*
Pingali, Keshav Kumar *computer scientist*
Shore, Richard Arnold *mathematics educator*
Trotter, Leslie Earl *operations research educator, consultant*

Kenmore
Kenny, John Edward *computer analyst*

Long Island City
Goldstein, Katherine H. *technology educator, computer consultant*

Massapequa
Batt, Alyse Schwartz *technical officer*

Middleport
Travers, Carol *mathematics educator*

Middletown
Edelhertz, Helaine Wolfson *mathematics educator*

Monroe
Lifshitz, Kenneth Bernard *computer programmer*

New Paltz
Fleisher, Harold *computer scientist*

New York
Adams, Jeffrey Alan *web developer, writer*
Aschoff, Lawrence Michael *computer information scientist*
Bass, Hyman *mathematician, educator*
Chichilnisky, Graciela *mathematician, economist, educator, consultant*
Derman, Cyrus *mathematical statistician*
Di Paola, Robert Arnold *mathematics and computer science educator*
Edwards, Harold Mortimer *mathematics educator*
Fiorino, Anthony Saverio (Tony Eitan) *research analyst*
Frankel, Martin Richard *statistician, educator, consultant*
Gilmore, Jennifer A.W. *computer specialist*
Gomory, Ralph Edward *mathematician, manufacturing company executive, foundation executive*
Gross, Jonathan Light *computer scientist, mathematician, educator*
Hedbring, Charles *computer consultant, writer*
Kurnow, Ernest *statistician, educator*
Lax, Peter David *mathematician, educator*
Levitt, Norman Jay *mathematician*
Lucas, Henry Cameron, Jr. *information systems educator, writer, consultant*
Lunin, Lois F. *information scientist, artist*
Majda, Andrew J. *mathematician, educator*
McKean, Henry P. *mathematics institute administrator*
Moise, Edwin Evariste *mathematician, educator*
Morawetz, Cathleen Synge *mathematics educator*
Moyne, John Abel *computer scientist, linguist, educator*
Nirenberg, Louis *mathematician, educator*
O'Connor, Kevin *computer programing executive*
Padberg, Manfred Wilhelm *mathematics educator*
Posamentier, Alfred Steven *mathematics educator, university administrator*
Rajkumar, Ajay *computer scientist, consultant*
Schain, Randy David *computer software executive, venture capitalist*
Sellers, Peter Hoadley *mathematician*
Shionoiri, Hideo *computer technologist*
Sohmer, Bernard *mathematics educator, administrator*
Traub, J(oseph) F(rederick) *computer scientist, educator*
Varadhan, Srinivasa S. R. *mathematics educator*
Weitzner, Harold *mathematics educator*
Widlund, Olof Bertil *computer science educator*
Wyn-Jones, Alun (William Wyn-Jones) *software developer, mathematician*

New York Mills
Blank, William Russell *mathematics educator*

Niskayuna
Stanard, Christopher Leon *statistician*

North Syracuse
Nilsen, Matthew Scott *computer programer*

Northport
Gelfand, Andrew *software developer, consultant*

Ozone Park
Gebaide, Stephen Elliot *mathematics and computer science educator*

Pearl River
Galante, Joseph Anthony, Jr. *computer programmer*

Pittsford
Hollingsworth, Jack Waring *mathematics and computer science educator*

Plattsburgh
Helinger, Michael Green *mathematics educator*

Poughkeepsie
Thomas, Sarah Rebecca *computer science educator*

Rhinebeck
Hellerman, Leo *retired computer scientist and mathematician*

Rochester
Angel, Allen Robert *mathematics educator, author, consultant*
Bergeron, Ronald Jay *computer programmer, analyst*
Simon, William *biomathematician, educator*

Rome
Romeu, Jorge Luis *mathematics educator, writer*

Sleepy Hollow
Maun, Mary Ellen *computer consultant*

Somers
Chen, Shuang *computer science professional*

Staten Island
Friederwitzer, Fredda J(oy) *mathematics educator*
Shullich, Robert Harlan *systems analyst*

Stony Brook
Anderson, Michael Thomas *mathematics researcher, educator*
Glimm, James Gilbert *mathematician, educator*
Laspina, Peter Joseph *computer resource educator*
Lawson, H(erbert) Blaine, Jr. *mathematician, educator*
Michelsohn, Marie-Louise *mathematician, educator*
Tewarson, Reginald Prabhakar *mathematics educator, consultant*
Tucker, Alan Curtiss *mathematics educator*

Syracuse
Church, Philip Throop *mathematician, educator*
Covillion, Jane Tanner *mathematics educator*
Graver, Jack Edward *mathematics educator*
Hansen, Per Brinch *computer scientist*
Pardee, Otway O'Meara *computer science educator*
Peters, Christopher Allen *computer consultant*

Troy
Berg, Daniel *science and technology educator*
Drew, Donald Allen *mathematical sciences educator*

Valley Stream
De Mita, Francis Anthony *mathematics educator*

Wallkill
Bittner, Ronald Joseph *computer systems analyst, magician*

West Hempstead
Guggenheimer, Heinrich Walter *mathematician, educator*

West Point
Barr, Donald Roy *statistics and operations research educator, statistician*

West Seneca
Krist, Betty Jane *mathematics educator, researcher*

White Plains
Cheng, Alexander Lihdar *computer scientist, researcher*
Machover, Carl *computer graphics consultant*

Yonkers
Goon, Gilbert *software consultant*

Yorktown Heights
d'Heurle, François Max *research scientist, engineering educator*
Hoffman, Alan Jerome *mathematician, educator*
†Masullo, Miriam Julia *computer scientist*
Winograd, Shmuel *mathematician*

NORTH CAROLINA

Apex
Rawlings, John Oren *statistician, researcher*

Boone
Johnson, Phillip Eugene *mathematics educator*

Cape Carteret
Mullikin, Thomas Wilson *mathematics educator*

Cary
Goodnight, James *software company executive*

Chapel Hill
Brooks, Frederick Phillips, Jr. *computer scientist*
Coulter, Elizabeth Jackson *biostatistician, educator*
Fuchs, Henry *computer science educator*
Stasheff, James Dillon *mathematics educator*
Wogen, Warren Ronald *mathematics educator*

Charlotte
Gardner, Robert Charles *systems analyst, administrator*
Zytkow, Jan Mikolaj *computer science educator*

Clyde
Codd, Richard Trent, Jr. *computer scientist, educator*

Cullowhee
Willis, Ralph Houston *mathematics educator*

Durham
Allard, William Kenneth *mathematician*
Loveland, Donald William *computer science educator*
Reif, John Henry *computer science educator*
Rose, Donald James *computer science educator*
Woodbury, Max Atkin *polymath, educator, researcher*

Greensboro
Blanchet-Sadri, Francine *mathematician*
Kurepa, Alexandra *mathematician, educator*
Sadri, Fereidoon *computer science educator*

Hertford
Sutton, Louise Nixon *retired mathematics educator*

Murfreesboro
McLawhorn, Rebecca Lawrence *mathematics educator*

Pine Knoll Shores
Thatcher, Muriel Burger *mathematics education educator, consultant*

Raleigh
Chou, Wushow *computer scientist, educator*
McAllister, David Franklin *computer science educator*
McPherson, Samuel Dace, III *computer scientist, instructor, consultant*
Nelson, Larry A. *statistics educator, consultant*
Wesler, Oscar *mathematician, educator*
Wetsch, John Robert *information systems specialist*

West Jefferson
Merrion, Arthur Benjamin *mathematics educator, tree farmer*

Winston Salem
Baxter, Lawrence Gerald *strategic analyst, law educator, business consultant*
Lu, Dan *systems analyst, mathematician, consultant*

NORTH DAKOTA

Jamestown
†Cox, Robert Ripley, Jr. *biology statistician*

OHIO

Akron
Hollis, William Frederick *information scientist*
Powell, Robert Eugene *computer operator*
Quesada, Antonio Rettschlag *mathematics educator*

Athens
Wen, Shih-Liang *mathematics educator*

Berea
Little, Richard Allen *mathematics and computer science educator*

Bowling Green
Newman, Elsie Louise *mathematics educator*

Cincinnati
Flick, Thomas Michael *mathematics educator, educational administrator*
Semon, Warren Lloyd *retired computer sciences educator*
Wilsey, Philip Arthur *computer science educator*
Wolford, Ronald Eugene *computer operations professional*

Cleveland
Clark, Robert Arthur *mathematician, educator*
de Acosta, Alejandro Daniel *mathematician, educator*
Goffman, William *mathematician, educator*
Lange, Frederick Edward, Jr. *computer information systems architect*
Szarek, Stanislaw Jerzy *mathematics educator*
†Vayner, Ellen B. *analyst*
Waren, Allan David *computer information scientist, educator*
Woyczynski, Wojbor Andrzej *mathematician, educator*
Zheng, Yao *computational scientist*

Columbia Station
Pingatore, Sam Robert *systems analyst, consultant, business executive*

Columbus
Baker, Gregory Richard *mathematician*
Chandrasekaran, Balakrishnan *computer and information science educator*
Dowling, Thomas Allan *mathematics educator*
Gartner, Daniel Lee *computer information executive*
Kindig, Fred Eugene *statistics educator, arbitrator*
Kirwan, William English, II *mathematics educator, university official*

Dayton
Berra, P. Bruce *computer educator*
Garcia, Oscar Nicolas *computer science educator*
Rucker, Richard Sim *information systems executive*
Staker, Robert Dale *cost analyst, computer scientist, biologist, educator*

Dublin
Miller, Charles *business management research and measurements consultant*

Granville
†Bonar, Daniel Donald *mathematics educator*

Hamilton
Fein, Thomas Paul *software support specialist*

Kent
Cummins, Kenneth Burdette *retired science and mathematics educator*
Varga, Richard Steven *mathematics educator*

Lima
Johnson, Patricia Lyn *mathematics educator*

Loveland
Glover, Robert Caldwell *computer graphics specialist, artist*

Mansfield
Gregory, Thomas Bradford *mathematics educator*

Marion
Rowe, Lisa Dawn *computer programmer/analyst, computer consultant*

Milford
Zimov, Bruce Steven *software engineer*

New Carlisle
Hansford, Larry Clarence *computer consultant company executive*

Painesville
Taylor, Norman Floyd *computer educator, administrator*

Rockford
Thompson, Robert Douglas *computer science educator, banker, consultant*

Uniontown
Lucas, Jeffrey A. *computer analyst*

Upper Sandusky
Baker, Harrison Scott *computer consultant*

Warren
Perera, Vicumpriya Sriyantha *mathematics educator*

Westlake
Whitehouse, John Harlan, Jr. *systems software consultant, diagnostician*

OKLAHOMA

Edmond
French, Dana Lewis *computer consultant*
Loman, Mary LaVerne *retired mathematics educator*

Jones
Jones, Jeffery Lynn *software engineer*

Lawton
McKellips, Terral Lane *mathematics educator, university administrator*

Norman
Lakshmivarahan, Sivaramakrishnan *computer science educator*
MacFarland, Miriam Katherine (Mimi) (Mimi MacFarland) *computer science consultant, writer*

Oklahoma City
Philipp, Anita Marie *computer sciences educator*

Stillwater
Provine, Lorraine *mathematics educator*

Tulsa
Preston, Kenneth Marshall *computer and business educator*
Thompson, Carla Jo Horn *mathematics educator*

OREGON

Albany
Yu, Kitson Szewai *computer science educator*

Beaverton
Bilow, Steven Craig *computer and video systems specialist*

Bend
Taylor, Gene Raymond *computer and information systems educator*

Corvallis
Parks, Harold Raymond *mathematician, educator*

PROFESSIONAL INDEX 6201 SCIENCE: MATHEMATICS AND COMPUTER SCIENCE

Eugene
Andrews, Fred Charles *mathematics educator*

Florence
Gray, Augustine Heard, Jr. *computer consultant*

Monmouth
Forcier, Richard Charles *information technology educator, computer applications consultant*

Portland
Ahuja, Jagdish Chand *mathematics educator*
Lambert, Richard William *mathematics educator*

Tualatin
Brown, Robert Wallace *mathematics educator*

West Linn
†Zielinski, Adam Steven *systems administrator*

PENNSYLVANIA

Allentown
Russell, Alan Harold *computer specialist, educator*

Aston
Horvath, David Bruce *computer consultant, writer, educator*

Audubon
†Palmer, Christine M. *mathematics educator*

Berwyn
Swank, Annette Marie *software designer*

Bethlehem
Ghosh, Bhaskar Kumar *statistics educator, researcher*
McAulay, Alastair D. *electrical and computer engineer, educator*
Rivlin, Ronald Samuel *mathematics educator emeritus*
Schattschneider, Doris Jean *mathematics educator*
Styer, Jane M. *computer consultant*

Blue Bell
Halas, Cynthia Ann *business information specialist*
Young, Charles Randall *software professional*

Bristol
Bush, Harold Ehrig *computer consultant*

Bryn Mawr
Ackoff, Russell Lincoln *systems sciences educator*

Cashtown
Saliu, Ion *software developer, computer programmer*

Chalfont
Schott, Jeffrey Brian *software engineer*

Coatesville
Burton, Mary Louise Himes *computer specialist*

Coraopolis
Skovira, Robert Joseph *information scientist, educator*

Exton
†Romeo, Joseph Anthony *computer programmer*

Harrisburg
Shatto, Ellen Latherow *mathematics educator*

Johnstown
Mehlman, Marc Harvey *mathematician, educator*

Lansdale
Lafredo, Stephen *systems associate*

Large
Allen, David Woodroffe *computer scientist*

Malvern
Everhart, Rodney Lee *software industry executive*
Fitch, Mary Jane Early *lawyer, computer consultant, writer*

Marion Center
Bomboy, John David *mathematics educator*

Meadville
Cable, Charles Allen *mathematician*

Mercer
Brady, Wray Grayson *mathematician, educator*

Middletown
†Richards, Winston Ashton *mathematics educator, statistician*

North Wales
Kleiman, Keith Jeffrey *computer consultant*

Palmyra
Singer, William Harry *interactive multimedia architect, software engineer, expert systems designer, consultant, entrepreneur*

Philadelphia
Badler, Norman Ira *computer and information science educator*
Banerji, Ranan Bihari *mathematics and computer science educator*
Brown, Ronald Rea *software engineer, artist*
Calabi, Eugenio *mathematician, educator*
Collons, Rodger Duane *decision sciences educator*
Cowles, Roger E. *computer consultant*
de Cani, John Stapley *statistician, educator*
Freyd, Peter John *mathematician, computer scientist, educator*
Harbater, David *mathematician*
Hildebrand, David Kent *statistics educator*
Iglewicz, Boris *statistician, educator*
Joshi, Aravind Krishna *computer educator, information scientist*
Kadison, Richard Vincent *mathematician, educator*
†Kimchuk, Amy Lynn *mathematics educator*
Knopp, Marvin Isadore *mathematics educator*
Lee, Insup *computer science educator*
Mode, Charles J. *mathematician, educator*
Porter, Gerald Joseph *mathematician, educator*
Scandura, Joseph Michael *mathematics educator, researcher, software engineer*
Scedrov, Andre *mathematics and computer science researcher, educator*
Shatz, Stephen Sidney *mathematician, educator*
Smith, Jonathan M. *computer science educator*
Sztandera, Les Mark *computer science educator*
Warner, Frank Wilson, III *mathematics educator*
White, Howard D. *information science educator*

Phoenixville
Koenig, Michael Edward Davison *information science educator*

Pittsburgh
Balas, Egon *applied mathematician, educator*
Bryant, Randal Everitt *computer science educator, consultant*
Byrnes, Paul David *software engineer, consultant*
Caginalp, Gunduz *mathematician, educator, researcher*
Carney, David John *computer scientist, music theorist*
Chrysanthis, Panos Kypros *computer science educator, researcher*
Cohen, Henry Bruce *mathematics educator*
Dannenberg, Roger Berry *computer scientist*
Deskins, Wilbur Eugene *mathematician, educator*
Fienberg, Stephen Elliott *statistician*
Grover, Carole Lee *mathematics educator*
Gurtin, Morton Edward *mathematics educator*
Kadane, Joseph B. *statistics educator*
†Larget, Bret *statistics educator*
Lehoczky, John Paul *statistics educator*
Rheinboldt, Werner Carl *mathematics educator, researcher*
Shaw, Mary M. *computer science educator*
Thompson, Gerald Luther *operations research and applied mathematics educator*

Plymouth Meeting
Shindledecker, Joseph Gregory *programmer, analyst*

Reading
Rochowicz, John Anthony, Jr. *mathematician, mathematics and physics educator*

Rydal
Bacon, George Hughes, Jr. *systems analyst, consultant*

Scranton
Powell, Robert Ellis *mathematics educator, college dean*

Swarthmore
Kelemen, Charles F. *computer science educator*

University Park
Andrews, George Eyre *mathematics educator*
Antle, Charles Edward *statistics educator*
†Ayoub, Raymond George *mathematics educator*
Lindsay, Bruce George *statistics educator*
Rao, Calyampudi Radhakrishna *statistician, educator*
Rosenberger, James Landis *statistician, educator, consultant*

Vandergrift
Kulick, Richard John *computer scientist, researcher*

Villanova
Beck, Robert Edward *computer scientist, educator*
Scheffler, Barbara Jane *statistician, business executive*

Wallingford
Morrison, Donald Franklin *statistician, educator*

Warrendale
†Mullig, Michael Brendan *systems administrator*

West Mifflin
Starmack, John Robert *mathematics educator*

RHODE ISLAND

Kingston
Roxin, Emilio Oscar *mathematics educator*

Newport
Clark, Cathy Ann *mathematician*
Piepgrass, Daniel James *logistics manager*

Providence
Banchoff, Thomas Francis *mathematics educator*
Charniak, Eugene *computer scientist, educator*
Chauvin, Charlotte Ann *computer science educator*
Dafermos, Constantine Michael *applied mathematics educator*
Davis, Philip J. *mathematician*
Ewing, John Harwood *mathematics educator*
Fleming, Wendell Helms *mathematician, educator*
Freiberger, Walter Frederick *mathematics educator, actuarial science consultant, educator*
Gottschalk, Walter Helbig *mathematician, educator*
Hsieh, Din-Yu *applied mathematics educator*
Kushner, Harold Joseph *mathematics educator*
Mumford, David Bryant *mathematics educator*
Savage, John Edmund *computer science educator, researcher*
Silverman, Joseph Hillel *mathematics educator*
Tabenkin, Alexander Nathan *metrologist*
van Dam, Andries *computer scientist, educator*

SOUTH CAROLINA

Charleston
†Chen, Mei-Qin *mathematics educator*
Plichta, Thomas Edward *software engineering company executive*

Clemson
Hare, Eleanor O'Meara *computer science educator*

Columbia
Eastman, Caroline Merriam *computer science educator*

Conway
Saxena, Subhash Chandra *mathematics educator, researcher, administrator*

Florence
Whitaker, Wilma Neuman *mathematics instructor*

Gaffney
Wilde, Edwin Frederick *mathematics educator*

Lancaster
Carter, Richard Bonner *systems specialist*

Orangeburg
Champy, William, Jr. *mathematician, educator, researcher, scientist*
Clark, Paul Buddy *management information systems educator, consultant*

Spartanburg
Codespoti, Daniel Joseph *computer science educator*
Hilton, Theodore Craig *computer scientist, computer executive*

SOUTH DAKOTA

Aberdeen
Markanda, Raj Kumar *mathematics educator*

TENNESSEE

Brownsville
Kalin, Robert *retired mathematics educator*

Chattanooga
Ebiefung, Aniekan Asukwo *mathematics educator and researcher*

Cleveland
Laws, Charles George *mathematics educator, quality engineer*

Franklin
Smotherman, Carolyn *mathematics educator*

Hermitage
†Greenleaf, Douglas A. *information specialist*

Johnson City
Pumariega, JoAnne Buttacavoli *mathematics educator*

Knoxville
Barrett, Lida Kittrell *mathematics educator*
Tenopir, Carol *information science educator*
Ward, Robert Cleveland *computer science researcher, administrator*

Martin
Gathers, Emery George *computer science educator*
†Petty, James Alan *mathematics educator, consultant*

Memphis
Franklin, Stanley Phillip *computer scientist, cognitive scientist, mathematician, educator*
Goldstein, Jerome Arthur *mathematics educator*

Nashville
Blair, Joyce Allsmiller *computer science educator*
Dupont, William Dudley *biostatistician, educator*
Fischer, Patrick Carl *computer scientist, retired educator*
Infante, Ettore Ferrari *mathematician, educator, university administrator*
Jonsson, Bjarni *mathematician, educator*
Williams, Marsha Rhea *computer scientist, educator, researcher, consultant*

Oak Ridge
Bugg, Keith Edward *computer software developer, software company executive*
Kliewer, Kenneth Lee *computational scientist, research administrator*
Penniman, W. David *information scientist, educator, consultant*
Raridon, Richard Jay *computer specialist*

Sewanee
Puckette, Stephen Elliott *mathematics educator, mathematician*

TEXAS

Arlington
†Baldwin, Donald James, II *software developer*
Greenspan, Donald *mathematician, educator*
Han, Chien-Pai *statistics educator*
Kendall, Jillian D. *information systems specialist, program developer, educator, consultant*
Raisinghani, Mahesh (Mike) Sukhdev *software consultant*
Reyes, Arthur Alexander *computer science educator*

Austin
†Beckner, William *mathematician*
Bona, Jerry Lloyd *mathematician, educator*
Clark, Charles T(aliferro) *retired business statistics educator*
Dijkstra, Edsger Wybe *computer science educator, mathematician*
Garner, Harvey Louis *computer scientist, consultant, electrical engineering educator*
Gillman, Leonard *mathematician, educator*
Knudsen, John Roland *retired mathematics educator, consultant*
Kozmetsky, George *computer science educator*
Lam, Simon Shin-Sing *computer science educator*
Misra, Jayadev *computer science educator*
Moyers, Robert Charles *systems analyst, state official, microcomputer consultant*
Pixley, Carl Preston *mathematician*
Sadun, Lorenzo Adlai *mathematician*
Sager, Thomas William *statistics research administrator*
Tate, John T. *mathematics educator*
Turney, James Edward *computer scientist*
Uhlenbeck, Karen Keskulla *mathematician, educator*
Williamson, Hugh Jackson *statistician*

Beeville
Lamm, Harriet A. *mathematics educator*

Brownsville
Xu, Zhong Ling *mathematician, educator*

College Station
Chui, Charles K. *mathematics educator*
Ewing, Richard Edward *mathematics, chemical and petroleum engineering educator*
Parzen, Emanuel *statistical scientist*
Sanchez, David Alan *mathematics educator*

Dallas
Barr, Richard Stuart *computer science and management science educator*
Browne, Richard Harold *statistician, consultant*
Chen, Zhangxin John *mathematics educator*
Conger, Sue Ann *computer information systems educator*
Gensheimer, Elizabeth Lucille *software specialist*
Kruse, Ann Gray *computer programer*

De Soto
Ball, Millicent Joan (Penny Ball) *multimedia developer*

Denton
Das, Sajal Kumar *computer science educator, researcher*
Renka, Robert Joseph *computer science educator, consultant*

El Paso
Foged, Leslie Owen *mathematician*

Grapevine
Gibbons, Michael Lawrence *software engineer*

Houston
Brown, Sharon Elizabeth *software engineer*
Crutchfield, Robert Alan *computer scientist*
Fenn, Sandra Ann *programmer, analyst*
Freeman, Marjorie Schaefer *mathematics educator*
Gardner, Everette Shaw, Jr. *information sciences educator, consultant, author*
Glowinski, Roland *mathematics educator*
Harvey, F. Reese *mathematics educator*
Hempel, John P. *mathematics educator*
Hoang, Hung Manh *information systems analyst, consultant*
Ilin, Andrew V. *software engineer*
Kennedy, Ken *computer science educator*
Kimmel, Marek *biomathematician, educator*
Parker, Norman Neil, Jr. *software systems analyst, mathematics educator*
Scott, David Warren *statistics educator*
Wang, Chao-Cheng *mathematician, engineer*
Wells, Raymond O'Neil, Jr. *mathematics educator, researcher*
†Westberry, John Elliott *mathematics educator*
Woo, Walter *computer systems consultant*

Irving
Anastasi, Richard Joseph *computer software consultant*
Anderson, Michael Curtis *computer industry analyst*
Kaufman, Sanders *computer programmer*
†McClinton, Travis Victor, II *mathematics educator*

Kingsville
Cecil, David Rolf *mathematician, educator*

Kingwood
Burghduff, John Brian *mathematics educator*

Lewisville
Ferguson, R. Neil *computer systems consultant*

Lubbock
Conover, William Jay *statistics educator*
Hennessey, Audrey Kathleen *computer researcher, educator*

Mcallen
Cox, George Sherwood *computer science educator*

Richardson
Pervin, William Joseph *computer science educator*
Wiorkowski, John James *mathematics educator*

San Antonio
†Azuaje, Rafael *computer scientist, educator*
†Beauford, Judith Elaine *mathematics educator*
Bennett, Gerard Paul *computer scientist*
Blaylock, Neil Wingfield, Jr. *applied statistics educator*
Estep, Myrna Lynne *systems analyst, philosophy educator*
Hall, Douglas Lee *computer science educator*
Traylor, Donald Reginald *mathematics educator*

Snyder
Anderson, Elsie Miners *mathematics educator*

Temple
Rajab, Mohammad Hasan *biostatistician, educator*

The Woodlands
Ulin, Samuel Alexander *computer systems developer*

Waco
Mathews, Cameron Anthony *internet design consultant*
Odell, Patrick Lowry *mathematics educator*
Rolf, Howard Leroy *mathematician, educator*

†Walbesser, Henry Herman *computer science educator*

UTAH

Layton
Gregson, Garry Evan *network administrator, information consultant*

North Logan
Chen, Li *computer scientist, software engineer*

Orem
Moore, Hal G. *mathematician, educator*

Provo
Lang, William Edward *mathematics educator*

VERMONT

Burlington
Crouse, Roger Leslie *information analyst, quality consultant, facilitator*
Haugh, Larry Douglas *statistics professor*

Colchester
Moore, Mitchell Steven *computer consultant*

North Bennington
Adler, Irving *mathematician*

Randolph
Calter, Paul Arthur *mathematics educator, mechanical engineer*

VIRGINIA

Alexandria
†DePiro, Michael Francis *program analyst*
Engler, Brian David *systems operations executive*
Perchik, Benjamin Ivan *operations research analyst*

Arlington
Ciment, Melvyn *mathematician*
Clema, Joe Kotouc *computer scientist*
Coles, Bertha Sharon Giles *visual information specialist*
Cummings, John William, Jr. *logistician, systems analyst*
Golladay, Mary Jean *statistician*
Long, Madeleine J. *mathematics and science educator*
Murray, Jeanne Morris *computer scientist, educator, consultant, researcher*
†Osterholz, John Louis *information administrator*
†Salisbury, Gary LeRoy *corporate information manager, military officer*
Shrier, Stefan *mathematician, educator*
Swartz, Roger Donald *computer scientist*
Zgonc, Janice Ann *technical information specialist*

Blacksburg
Good, Irving John *statistics educator, mathematician, philosopher of science*
Olin, Robert Floyd *mathematics educator and reseacher*

Centreville
Bucciero, Joseph Mario, Jr. *executive consulting firm*

Charlottesville
Catlin, Avery *engineering and computer science educator, writer*
Mansfield, Lois Edna *mathematics educator, researcher*
Martin, Nathaniel Frizzel Grafton *mathematician, educator*
Pang, Maybeline Miusze (Chan) *software testing and systems engineer, analyst*
Rosenblum, Marvin *mathematics educator*
Thomas, Lawrence Eldon *mathematics educator*

Clifton
Hoffman, Karla Leigh *mathematician*

Dahlgren
Banerjee, Marianne Heafield *systems analyst*

Fairfax
Denning, Peter James *computer scientist, engineer*
Sage, Andrew Patrick, Jr. *systems information and software engineering educator*
Schneck, Paul Bennett *computer scientist*
Tucker, Dewey Duane *systems analyst*

Falls Church
Flory, Robert Mikesell *computer systems analyst, personnel management specialist*

Fort Belvoir
Raymond, George Edward, Jr. (Chip Raymond) *operations research analyst*

Fort Lee
Johnson, Harry Watkins *defense analyst*

Fredericksburg
Hajek, Otomar *mathematics educator*
Lipscomb, Stephen Leon *mathematics educator, researcher*

Glen Allen
Wright, Sylvia Hoehns *computer systems specialist*

Heathsville
Stubbs, Susan Conklin *statistician*

Herndon
Hermansen, John Christian *computational linguist*

Lexington
Tierney, Michael John *mathematics and computer science educator*

Lynchburg
Moorman, Steve Thomas *systems analyst*

Manakin Sabot
Thompson, Walter David, Jr. *systems analyst*

Manassas
McCormick, Ferris Ellsworth *computer technology consultant*
Smith, Todd Lawrence *computer scientist*

Mc Lean
Allison, George Burgess *systems analyst*
Loatman, Robert Bruce *computer scientist*

Newport News
Phinazee, Henry Charles *systems analyst, educator*
Summerville, Richard M. *mathematician, retired academic administrator*

Norfolk
Maly, Kurt John *computer science educator*
Marchello, Joseph Maurice *mathematics and physical science educator*

Richmond
Charlesworth, Arthur Thomas *mathematics and computer science educator*
Hamlett, Robert Barksdale *systems engineer*
Jones, Jerry Lee *computer educator*
Malone, Nicholas Sherlon *systems analyst, consultant*

Springfield
Lautzenheiser, Marvin Wendell *computer software engineer*
Quick, Danny Richard *computer systems engineer*

Stafford
†Humphrey, Matthew Cameron *computer scientist, consultant*

Sterling
Heberling, Timothy Alan *information systems engineer*

Suffolk
†English, Betty Jo Boone *programming educator*

Sweet Briar
Wassell, Stephen Robert *mathematics educator, researcher*

Vienna
Croog, Roslyn Zeporah *senior systems engineer*
de Planque, Emile, III *computer consultant*
†Frakes, Ronald LaVerne, Jr. *systems analyst*
Lillard, Mark Hill, III *computer consulting executive, former air force officer*
Vachher, Sheila Ann *information systems consultant*

Virginia Beach
Brennan, Patrick Jeremiah *software developer*
Vita, James Paul *software engineer*

Warrenton
Gullace, Marlene Frances *information engineer, systems analyst, consultant*

Williamsburg
Rodman, Leiba *mathematics educator*
Zhang, Xiaodong *computer scientist, educator, researcher*

WASHINGTON

Bellevue
Schuiski, Larry Leroy *information scientist*

Ellensburg
Comstock, Dale Robert *mathematics educator*

Everett
Labayen, Louie Anthony Lopez *information analyst, consultant*

Federal Way
Cunningham, John Randolph *systems analyst*

Lacey
Wells, Roger Stanley *software engineer*

Pullman
Hildebrandt, Darlene Myers *information scientist*
Kallaher, Michael Joseph *mathematics educator*

Redmond
Kimmich, Jon Bradford *computer science program executive*
Yagi, Fumio *mathematician, systems engineer*
Zhang, Zhengyou *computer scientist*

Richland
Cochran, James Alan *mathematics educator*

Seattle
Breslow, Norman Edward *biostatistics educator, researcher*
Brown, William John *computer scientist*
Criminale, William Oliver, Jr. *applied mathematics educator*
Gates, Theodore Allan, Jr. *database administrator*
Gillispie, Steven Brian *systems analyst, researcher*
Klee, Victor La Rue *mathematician, educator*
Lee, John Marshall *mathematics educator*
Michael, Ernest Arthur *mathematics educator*
Murray, James Dickson *mathematical biology educator*
Nelson, Walter William *computer programmer, consultant*
Nijenhuis, Albert *mathematician, educator*
O'Malley, Robert Edmund, Jr. *mathematics educator*
Pyke, Ronald *mathematics educator*
Segal, Jack *mathematics educator*
Smith, Teresa Ann *computer consultant*
Wegelin, Jacob Andreas *statistician*

Shoreline
Reddecliffe, Karin Linnae Ellis *educator*

Spokane
Mayer, Herbert Carleton, Jr. *computer consultant*

Tacoma
Burns, Robin C(arol) *mathematics theoretician, accountant*

White Salmon
Verry, William Robert *retired mathematics researcher*

Woodinville
Lanter, Sean Keith *software engineer*

WEST VIRGINIA

Elkins
Reed, Elizabeth May Millard *mathematics and computer science educator, publisher*

Morgantown
De Vore, Paul Warren *technology educator*

WISCONSIN

Franklin
Bui, Ty Van *computer programmer, systems analyst*

Madison
Abualsamid, Ahmad Zuhair *software scientist, researcher*
Askey, Richard Allen *mathematician*
Beck, Anatole *mathematician, educator*
Cravens, Stanley H. *software development manager*
de Boor, Carl *mathematician*
Harvey, John Grover *mathematics educator*
Hickman, James Charles *business and statistics educator, business school dean*
Johnson, Millard Wallace, Jr. *mathematics and engineering educator*
Johnson, Richard Arnold *statistics educator, consultant*
Moore, Edward Forrest *computer scientist, mathematician, former educator*
Robinson, Stephen Michael *applied mathematician, educator*

Milwaukee
Solomon, Donald William *mathematics and computer science educator, consultant*

Sheboygan
Cecil, Louis Anton *mathematics educator*

TERRITORIES OF THE UNITED STATES

PUERTO RICO

Mayaguez
Collins, Dennis Glenn *mathematics educator*

CANADA

ALBERTA

Edmonton
Davis, Wayne Alton *computer science educator*

BRITISH COLUMBIA

Burnaby
Borwein, Peter Benjamin *mathematician*

Vancouver
Boyd, David William *mathematician, educator*
Clark, Colin Whitcomb *mathematics educator*
Feldman, Joel Shalom *mathematician*
Granirer, Edmond Ernest *mathematician, educator*
Miura, Robert Mitsuru *mathematician, researcher, educator*
Seymour, Brian Richard *mathematics educator, researcher*
Sion, Maurice *mathematics educator*
Swanson, Charles Andrew *mathematics educator*

Victoria
Manning, Eric *computer science and engineering educator, university dean, researcher*

NOVA SCOTIA

Halifax
Fillmore, Peter Arthur *mathematician, educator*

ONTARIO

Hamilton
Banaschewski, Bernhard *mathematics educator*

Kingston
Campbell, L(ouis) Lorne *mathematics educator*

London
Bauer, Michael Anthony *computer scientist, educator*
Borwein, David *mathematics educator*
Ehrman, Joachim Benedict *mathematics educator*

Ottawa
Csörgő, Miklós *mathematics and statistics educator*

Dlab, Vlastimil *mathematics educator, researcher*
Fellegi, Ivan Peter *statistician*
Macphail, Moray St. John *mathematics educator emeritus*

Toronto
Arthur, James Greig *mathematics educator*
Cook, Stephen Arthur *mathematics and computer science educator*
Coxeter, Harold Scott Macdonald *mathematician*
Dawson, Donald Andrew *mathematics educator, researcher*
Fraser, Donald Alexander Stuart *mathematics educator*
Friedlander, John Benjamin *mathematics educator*
Gotlieb, Calvin Carl *computer scientist, educator*
Greiner, Peter Charles *mathematics educator, researcher*
Halperin, John Stephen *mathematics educator*
Rooney, Paul George *mathematics educator*
Tall, Franklin David *mathematics educator*

Waterloo
Aczél, János Dezsö *mathematics educator*
Cowan, Donald Douglas *mathematician, educator, computer scientist*
Gladwell, Graham Maurice Leslie *mathematician, civil engineering educator*
Paldus, Josef *mathematics educator*
Sprott, David Arthur *statistics and psychology educator*
Stewart, Cameron Leigh *mathematics educator*

QUEBEC

Montreal
Dubuc, Serge *mathematics educator*
Maag, Urs Richard *statistics educator*
Moser, William Oscar Jules *mathematics educator*
Suen, Ching Yee *computer scientist and educator, researcher*

Quebec
Theodorescu, Radu Amza Serban *mathematician, educator*

AUSTRALIA

Canberra
Gani, Joseph Mark *statistics educator, administrator, researcher*

BRAZIL

Rio de Janeiro
Lin, Frank Chiwen *computer science educator*

São José dos Campos
Berman, Marcelo Samuel *mathematics and physics educator, cosmology researcher*

CHINA

Hong Kong
Xu, Lei *computer scientist, educator*

ENGLAND

Leicester
Harijan, Ram *computer scientist, technology transfer researcher*

London
Ralston, Anthony *computer scientist, mathematician, educator*

FRANCE

Angers
Chauvet, Gilbert André *mathematics educator*

Avignon
De Mori, Renato *computer science educator, researcher*

Bures sur Yvette
Gromov, Mikhael *mathematician*

Paris
Lions, Jacques Louis *mathematician, educator*
Serre, Jean-Pierre *mathematician, scholar*
Yuechiming, Roger Yue Yuen Shing *mathematics educator*

GERMANY

Darmstadt
Hofmann, Karl Heinrich *mathematics educator*

Schwerte
Rosenberg, Alex *mathematician, educator*

HONG KONG

Hong Kong
Smale, Stephen *retired mathematics educator*

INDIA

Bahadurgarh
Garg, Ajay *systems administrator*

JAPAN

Chiba
Yamada, Shinichi *mathematician, computer scientist, educator*

Hiroshima
Kasami, Tadao *information science educator*

Nagoya
Kimura, Miyoshi *statistics educator, researcher*

Tokyo
Eto, Hajime *information scientist, educator*

THE NETHERLANDS

Hengelo
†Cruz, Wilfredo Vargas *software safety and reliability consultant*

NORWAY

Kolbotn
†Skow, Rune *telecommunication specialist*

PAKISTAN

Multan
†Khan, Abdul Rahim *mathematics educator, researcher and author*

RUSSIA

Moscow
Arnold, Vladimir Igorevich *mathematics researcher*

SCOTLAND

Edinburgh
Atiyah, Sir Michael Francis *mathematician*

SWITZERLAND

Zurich
Kalman, Rudolf Emil *research mathematician, system scientist*
Lanford, Oscar Erasmus, III *mathematics educator*
Moser, Jürgen Kurt *mathematician, educator*
Nievergelt, Jurg *computer science educator*

WALES

Aberystwyth
Walters, Kenneth *applied mathematics educator*

ADDRESS UNPUBLISHED

Allison, Robert Clyde *business and computers consultant*
Altheide, Phyllis Sage *computer scientist, software engineer*
Ancheta, Caesar Paul *software developer*
Auslander, Marc Alan *computer scientist*
Bajcsy, Ruzena Kucerova *computer science educator*
Balsamello, Joseph Vincent *information services manager*
Barrett, Christine Khan *engineering project management coordinator*
Basch, Reva *information services company executive*
Benson, Sharon Joan *mathematics educator*
Borwein, Jonathan Michael *mathematics educator*
Bowlby, Richard Eric *retired computer systems analyst*
Box, George Edward Pelham *statistics educator*
Browder, Felix Earl *mathematician, educator*
Buck, Alison Jennifer *computer programmer*
†Cameron, Kirk MacGregor Drummond *statistician*
Chaloner, Alice Brainerd *mathematics educator*
Choi, Man-Duen *mathematics educator*
Colvin, Burton Houston *mathematician, government official*
†Colwell, David Russell *software engineer*
†Combs, Roy James, Jr. *analyst, researcher*
Covin, Carol Louise *computer consultant*
†Dar, Huma Bashir *computer scientist, researcher, educator*
Davenport, William Harold *mathematics educator*
Downey, Deborah Ann *systems specialist*
Edwards, Elwood Gene *mathematician, educator*
Efros, Leonid *computer software scientist and developer*
†El-Bakry, Amr Saad *mathematician, researcher*
Elliott, David LeRoy *mathematician, educator, engineering educator*
Ezell, Margaret Prather *information systems executive*
Ferguson, James Clarke *mathematician, algorithmist*
Ferino, Christopher Kenneth *computer information scientist*
Fisher, Gordon McCrea *mathematician*
Freitag, Harlow *retired computer scientist and corporate executive*
Fuller, Nancy MacMurray *mathematics educator, tutor*
Gibson, Beatrice Ann *retired systems analyst, artist*
Goldberg, Samuel *retired mathematician, foundation officer*
Graham, Parker Lee, II *computer systems manager*
Grebb, Michael D. *systems analyst*
Greever, Margaret Quarles *retired mathematics educator*
Grenander, Ulf *mathematics educator*
Halberstam, Heini *mathematics educator*
Haley, Richard Edward, Jr. *computer scientist*
Heinicke, Peter Hart *computer consultant*
Henderson, Gary Allen *computer scientist, educator, consultant*
Hendrick, Arnold J. *game designer*
Hill, Shirley Ann *mathematics educator*
Horton, Wilfred Henry *mathematics educator*
House, Stephen Eugene *information systems consultant*
Hunte, Beryl Eleanor *mathematics educator, consultant*
Husain, Taqdir *mathematics educator*
Israel, Robert Allan *statistician*
Jaw, Andrew Chung-Shiang *software analyst*
Johnson, Deborah Crosland Wright *mathematics educator*
Johnson, Kevin Rogers *systems analyst, journalist*
Jones, Anita Katherine *computer scientist, educator*
Jones, Deanna Elaine *mathematics educator*
Kadota, Takashi Theodore *mathematician, electrical engineer*
Kelley, Mary Elizabeth (LaGrone) *computer specialist*
Kiser, M.L. *computer programmer*
Kister, James Milton *retired mathematician, educator*
Knight, Thomas Jefferson, Jr. *computer consultant, trainer*
Krantz, Steven George *mathematics educator, writer*
Kurfehs, Joseph Morris *investment company systems manager*
Laning, J. Halcombe *retired computer scientist*
Lerner, Vladimir Semion *computer scientist, educator*
Levine, Maita Faye *mathematics educator*
LIndsey, Mack Clay *computer programmer*
Liskov, Barbara Huberman *software engineering educator*
Low, Emmet Francis, Jr. *mathematics educator*
Lynch, Robert Emmett *mathematics educator*
Mahoney, Linda Kay *mathematics educator*
Main, Myrna Joan *mathematics educator*
Maisel, Herbert *computer science educator*
Makepeace, Coline M. *computer scientist*
Mangan, Patricia Ann Pritchett *statistician*
Mansour, Stephen Malik *software developer, mathematician*
†Mattson, Harold Frazyer, Jr. *mathematics educator*
Maxwell, Barbara Sue *systems analyst consultant, educator*
McLaughlin, Robert Bruce *software designer*
Miller, Allen Richard *mathematician*
†Murff, Elizabeth Jane Tipton *mathematician, statistician, educator*
Norman, E. Gladys *business computer educator, consultant*
Norton, Robert Michael *mathematician, educator, statistician*
Padberg, Harriet Ann *mathematics educator*
Paris, Steven Mark *software engineer*
Pattison, Jon Allen *computer scientist, consultant*
Paul, Vera Maxine *mathematics educator*
Pendleton, Joan Marie *microprocessor designer*
Perko, Walter Kim *computer consultant, songwriter, poet*
Pickle, Linda Williams *biostatistician*
Pizzuto, Debra Kay *mathematics educator*
Pollock, Karen Anne *computer analyst*
Porter, Hayden Samuel *computer science educator*
Potts, Ronald Clyde *computer programmer, analyst*
Probasco, Patricia Lou *software quality consultant*
Ramesh, Nagarajan *computer scientist*
†Reddy, Kishore P. *internet services company executive*
Reese, Edward James, Jr. *computer scientist*
Richgels, Glen William *mathematics educator*
Robold, Alice Ilene *retired mathematician, educator*
†Sauers, Todd Alan *statistician*
Simmons, James Gregg *statistician*
Smith, M. Tacy *computer applications trainer, consultant*
Southward, Glen Morris *statistician, educator*
Spence, Dianna Jeannene *software engineer, educator*
Spinrad, Robert Joseph *computer scientist*
Stern, Nancy Fortgang *mathematics and computer science, educator*
Stuart, Sandra Joyce *computer information scientist*
Suppes, Patrick *statistics, education, philosophy and psychology educator*
Tan, Hui Qian *computer science and civil engineering educator*
†Tietz, Dietmar Juergen *computer Web engineer, scientist*
Tuul, Johannes *physics educator, researcher*
Vasily, John Timothy *information systems executive, state government official*
Voigt, Robert Gary *numerical analyst*
Wagner, Ellyn S(anti) *mathematics educator*
Waller, Ray Albert *statistician*
Williams, David Keith *technical trainer*
Winder, Robert Owen *retired mathematician, computer engineer executive*
Winthrop-St.Gery, Rhett *computer specialist*
Wong, Rebecca Kimmae *mathematics educator, consultant*
Woodside, George Robert *computer software developer*
Yntema, Mary Katherine *retired mathematics educator*
Young, Sharon Laree *mathematics educator*
Yung, Yiu Fai *statistician, educator*
Zendle, Howard Mark *software development researcher*

SCIENCE: PHYSICAL SCIENCE

UNITED STATES

ALABAMA

Birmingham
Bugg, Charles Edward *biochemistry educator, scientist*
Elgavish, Gabriel Andreas *physical biochemistry educator*
Montgomery, John Atterbury *research chemist, consultant*
Robinson, Edward Lee *retired physics educator, consultant*

Daphne
Baugh, Charles Milton *biochemistry educator, college dean*

Dauphin Island
Porter, John Finley, Jr. *physicst, conservationist, retired educator*

Dothan
Mocker, Hans Walter *physicist*

Gordo
McKnight, William Baldwin *physics educator*

Harvest
Norman, Ralph Louis *physicist, consultant*

Huntsville
Allan, Barry David *research chemist, government official*
Campbell, Jonathan Wesley *astrophysicist, aerospace engineer*
Cornatzer, William Eugene *retired biochemistry educator*
Costes, Nicholas Constantine *aerospace technologist, university educator, retired government official*
Decher, Rudolf *physicist*
Dimmock, John Oliver *university research center director*
Gillani, Noor Velshi *atmospheric scientist, researcher, educator*
†Jedlovic, Gary J. *meteorologist, remote sensing scientist*
Johnson, Charles Leslie *aerospace physicist, consultant*
Miller, Walter Edward *physical scientist, researcher*
Parnell, Thomas Alfred *physicist*
Smith, Robert Earl *space scientist*
Stuhlinger, Ernst *physicist*
Vaughan, William Walton *atmospheric scientist*
Wright, John Collins *retired chemistry educator*

Mobile
Perry, Nelson Allen *radiation safety engineer, radiological consultant*

Montgomery
Tan, Boen Hie *analytical biochemist, biomedical scientist*

New Market
Roberts, Thomas George *retired physicist*

Selma
Collins, Eugene Boyd *medical chemist, molecular pathologist, consultant*

Tuscaloosa
Cava, Michael Patrick *chemist, educator*
Coulter, Philip Wylie *physicist, educator*
LaMoreaux, Philip Elmer *geologist, hydrogeologist, consultant*
Mancini, Ernest Anthony *geologist, educator, researcher*
Moore, James Daniel *hydrogeologist*

ALASKA

Anchorage
Patrick, Leslie Dayle *hydrologist*

Fairbanks
Duffy, Lawrence Kevin *biochemist, educator*
Fathauer, Theodore Frederick *meteorologist*
Fischer, Robert Edward *meteorologist*
Hopkins, David Moody *geologist*
Lingle, Craig Stanley *glaciologist, educator*
McNutt, Stephen Russell *volcanologist, geophysical scientist*
Roederer, Juan Gualterio *physics educator*
Weller, Gunter Ernst *geophysics educator*

ARIZONA

Flagstaff
Colbert, Edwin Harris *paleontologist, museum curator*
Millis, Robert Lowell *astronomer*
Shoemaker, Carolyn Spellmann *planetary astronomer*
†Tanaka, Kenneth Lloyd *planetary geologist*
Venedam, Richard Joseph *chemist, educator*

Green Valley
Bates, Charles Carpenter *oceanographer*
Dingle, Albert Nelson *meteorology educator*
Ramette, Richard Wales *chemistry educator*

Page
Leus McFarlen, Patricia Cheryl *water chemist*

Peoria
Lichtenberg, Larry Ray *chemist, consultant, researcher*

Phoenix
Allen, John Rybolt L. *chemist, biochemist*
Bolin, Vladimir Dustin *chemist*
Hudson, Laura Lyn Whitaker *scientific researcher*
McKeighen, Ronald Eugene *physicist*

Scottsdale
Hockmuth, Joseph Frank *physicist, psychotherapist*
McPherson, Donald J. *metallurgist*

Taylor
Kerr, Barbara Prosser *solar device designer*

Tempe
Bauer, Ernst Georg *physicist, educator*
Blankenship, Robert Eugene *chemistry educator*
Buseck, Peter Robert *geochemistry educator*
Cowley, John Maxwell *physics educator*
Glick, Milton Don *chemist, university administrator*
Goronkin, Herbert *physicist*
†Hestenes, David *physics educator*
Juvet, Richard Spalding, Jr. *chemistry educator*
Mahajan, Subhash *electronic materials educator*
McKelvy, Michael John *materials chemist, research scientist*
Moore, Carleton Bryant *geochemistry educator*
Nigam, Bishan Perkash *physics educator*
Pettit, George Robert *chemistry educator, cancer researcher*
Péwé, Troy Lewis *geologist, educator*
Presley-Holloway, Marsha Ann *planetary scientist*
Quadt, Raymond Adolph *metallurgist, cement company executive*
Smith, David John *physicist, educator*
Starrfield, Sumner Grosby *astrophysics educator, researcher*
Vandenberg, Edwin James *chemist, educator*
Wehinger, Peter Augustus *astronomer, educator*

Tucson
Angel, James Roger Prior *astronomer*
Barrett, Bruce Richard *physics educator*
Broadfoot, Albert Lyle *physicist*
Code, Arthur Dodd *astrophysics educator*
Crawford, David L. *astronomer*
Davies, Roger *geoscience educator*
Davis, Stanley Nelson *hydrologist, educator*
Dessler, Alexander Jack *space physics and astronomy educator, scientist*
De Young, David Spencer *astrophysicist, educator*
Dickinson, Robert Earl *atmospheric scientist, educator*
Dodd, Charles Gardner *physical chemist*
Fang, Li-Zhi *physicist, educator*
Grayeski, Mary Lynn *chemist, foundation administrator*
Green, Richard Frederick *astronomer*
Gruhl, James *energy scientist*
Harrison, Edward Robert *physicist, educator*
Hartmann, William Kenneth *astronomy scientist*
Hay, Richard Le Roy *geology educator*
Haynes, Caleb Vance, Jr. *geology and archaeology educator*
Hays, James Fred *geologist, educator*
Hill, Henry Allen *physicist, educator*
Hoffmann, William Frederick *astronomer*
Howard, Robert Franklin *observatory administrator, astronomer*
Hruby, Victor Joseph *chemistry educator*
Hubbard, William Bogel *planetary sciences educator*
Hunten, Donald Mount *planetary scientist, educator*
Jackson, Kenneth Arthur *physicist, researcher*
Jeffay, Henry *biochemistry educator*
Jefferies, John Trevor *astronomer, astrophysicist, observatory administrator*
Karkoschka, Erich *planetary science researcher, writer*
Kessler, John Otto *physicist, educator*
Kiersch, George Alfred *geological consultant, retired educator*
Krider, E. Philip *atmospheric scientist, educator*
Lamb, Willis Eugene, Jr. *physicist, educator*
Law, John Harold *biochemistry educator*
Lunine, Jonathan Irving *planetary scientist, educator*
Macleod, Hugh Angus McIntosh *optical science educator, physicist, consultant*
Marcialis, Robert Louis *planetary astronomer*
McEwen, Alfred Sherman *planetary geologist*
Nanz, Robert A. *biochemist*
Parmenter, Robert Haley *physics educator*
Powell, Richard C. *physicist, educator, researcher*
Roemer, Elizabeth *astronomer, educator*
Rountree, Janet Caryl *astrophysicist*
Schaefer, John Paul *chemist, corporate executive*
Scotti, James Vernon *astronomer*
Sewell, Charles Robertson *geologist, exploration company executive, investor*
Sprague, Ann Louise *space scientist*
Strittmatter, Peter Albert *astronomer, educator*
Swalin, Richard Arthur *scientist, company executive*
Tifft, William Grant *astronomer*
Wolff, Sidney Carne *astronomer, observatory administrator*

ARKANSAS

Bella Vista
Johnson, A(lyn) William *chemistry educator, writer, researcher, consultant*

Fayetteville
Lacy, Claud H. Sandberg *astronomer*
Lieber, Michael *physics educator*
Wilkins, Charles L. *chemistry educator*

Little Rock
Braithwaite, Wilfred John *physics educator*
Darsey, Jerome Anthony *chemistry educator, consultant*
Sorenson, John Robert Joseph *chemistry educator*

Marianna
Carroll, Stephen Douglas *chemist, research specialist*

Pine Bluff
Walker, Richard Brian *chemistry educator*

Russellville
Albert, Milton John *retired chemist, microbiologist*

CALIFORNIA

Anaheim
Loeblich, Helen Nina Tappan *paleontologist, educator*

Apple Valley
Mays, George Walter, Jr. *educational technology educator, consultant, tutor*

Atascadero
Ogier, Walter Thomas *retired physics educator*

Auburn
Hess, Patrick Henry *chemist*

Bakersfield
Dorer, Fred Harold *chemistry educator*

Banning
Holmes, John Richard *physicist, educator*

Bayside
Cocks, George Gosson *retired chemical microscopy educator*

Bellflower
Martin, Melissa Carol *radiological physicist*

Bereley
Chamberlain, Owen *nuclear physicist*

Berkeley
Alpen, Edward Lewis *biophysicist, educator*
Alvarez, Walter *geology educator*
Ames, Bruce N(athan) *biochemist, molecular biologist*
Barker, Horace Albert *biochemist, microbiologist*
Barnett, R(alph) Michael *theoretical physicist, educational agency administrator*
Bartlett, Neil *chemist, educator*
Bartlett, Paul A. *organic chemist*
Bergman, Robert George *chemist, educator*
Berry, William Benjamin Newell *geologist, educator, former museum administrator*
Birman, Alexander *physicist, researcher*
Bolt, Bruce Alan *seismologist, educator*
Bragg, Robert Henry *physicist, educator*
Brewer, Leo *physical chemist, educator*
Bukowinski, Mark Stefan Tadeusz *geophysics educator*
Carmichael, Ian Stuart Edward *geologist, educator*
Cerny, Joseph, III *chemistry educator, scientific laboratory administrator, university dean and official*
Chamberlin, Michael John *biochemistry educator*
Chandler, David *scientist, educator*
Chew, Geoffrey Foucar *physicist*
Clarke, John *physics educator*
Cohen, Marvin Lou *physics educator*
Curtis, Garniss Hearfield *geology educator*
Davis, Marc *astrophysics educator*
Diamond, Richard Martin *nuclear chemist*
Ely, Robert Pollock, Jr. *physics educator, researcher*
Fleming, Graham Richard *chemistry educator*
Fowler, Thomas Kenneth *physicist*
Fréchet, Jean Marie Joseph *chemistry educator*
Gaillard, Mary Katharine *physics educator*
Glaser, Donald Arthur *physicist*
Goldhaber, Gerson *physicist, educator*
Hahn, Erwin Louis *physicist, educator*
Haller, Eugene Ernest *materials scientist, educator*
Heathcock, Clayton Howell *chemistry educator, researcher*
Heiles, Carl Eugene *astronomer, educator*
Helmholz, August Carl *physicist, educator emeritus*
Hoffman, Darleane Christian *chemistry educator*
Jackson, J(ohn) David *physicist, educator*
Johnston, Harold S(ledge) *chemistry educator*
Kerth, Leroy T. *physics educator*
Kim, Sung-Hou *chemistry educator, biophysical and biological chemist*
King, Ivan Robert *astronomy educator*
Kittel, Charles *physicist, educator emeritus*
Klinman, Judith Pollock *biochemist, educator*
Knight, Walter David *physics educator*
Koshland, Daniel Edward, Jr. *biochemist, educator*
Kurtzman, Ralph Harold *retired biochemist, researcher, consultant*
Langridge, Robert *scientist, educator*
Leopold, Luna Bergere *geology educator*
Lester, William Alexander, Jr. *chemist, educator*
Linn, Stuart Michael *biochemist, educator*
Lipps, Jere Henry *paleontology educator*
Mandelstam, Stanley *physicist*
Marg, Elwin *physiological optics, optometry educator*
McKee, Christopher Fulton *astrophysics and astronomy educator*
Miller, William Hughes *theoretical chemist, educator*
Moore, C. Bradley *chemistry educator*
Nero, Anthony Vincent, Jr. *physicist, environmental scientist, writer*
Pavlath, Attila Endre *research chemist*
Perez-Mendez, Victor *physics educator*
Perry, Dale Lynn *chemist*
Pines, Alexander *chemistry educator, researcher, consultant*
Rasmussen, John Oscar *nuclear scientist*
Raymond, Kenneth Norman *chemistry educator, research chemist*
Reynolds, John Hamilton *physicist, educator*
Ritchie, Robert Oliver *materials science educator*
Schultz, Peter G. *chemistry educator*
Sessler, Andrew Marienhoff *physicist*
Shen, Yuen-Ron *physics educator*
Shu, Frank Hsia-San *astronomy educator, researcher, author*
Shugart, Howard Alan *physicist, educator*
Smith, Kirk Robert *environmental health sciences educator, researcher*
Smith, Neville Vincent *physicist*
Smoot, George Fitzgerald, III *astrophysicist*
Somorjai, Gabor Arpad *chemist, educator*
Spinrad, Hyron *astronomer*
Steiner, Herbert Max *physics educator*
Strauss, Herbert Leopold *chemistry educator*
Streitwieser, Andrew, Jr. *chemistry educator*
Symons, Timothy James McNeil *physicist*
Thompson, Anthony Wayne *metallurgist, educator, consultant*
Tjian, Robert Tse Nan *bichemistry educator, biology resercher, virology researcher*
Townes, Charles Hard *physics educator*
Trilling, George Henry *physicist, educator*
Tsina, Richard Vasil *chemistry educator*
Valentine, James William *paleobiology educator, author*
Weber, Eicke Richard *physicist*

Bonita
Wood, Fergus James *geophysicist, consultant*

Bradbury
Greenstein, Jesse Leonard *astronomer, educator*

Brea
Shen, Gene Giin-Yuan *organic chemist*

Burbank
Razouk, Rashad Elias *retired chemistry educator*

Burlingame
Hotz, Henry Palmer *physicist*

Canyon Lake
Schilling, Frederick Augustus, Jr. *geologist, consultant*

Carlsbad
Smith, Warren James *optical scientist, consultant, lecturer*

Carmel
Vagnini, Livio Lee *chemist, forensic consultant*

Carpinteria
Fisher, John Crocker *physicist*

China Lake Nwc
Bennett, Jean Louise McPherson *physicist, research scientist*

Chino
Koestel, Mark Alfred *geologist, photographer*

Chula Vista
Smith, Peggy O'Doniel *physicist, educator*
Wolk, Martin *physicist, electronics engineer*

Claremont
Helliwell, Thomas McCaffree *physicist, educator*
Kubota, Mitsuru *chemistry educator*

Concord
Hearst, John Eugene *chemistry educator, researcher, consultant*

Corona Del Mar
Britten, Roy John *biophysicist*

Costa Mesa
Bender, Edward Erik *geology educator, researcher*

Crescent City
Carter, Neville Louis *geophysicist, educator*

Culver City
Tang, Yin Sheng *physicist*

Cupertino
Nelson, Richard Burton *physicist, engineer, former patent consultant*

Davis
Black, Arthur Leo *biochemistry educator*
Cahill, Thomas Andrew *physicist, educator*
Conn, Eric Edward *plant biochemist*
Day, Howard Wilman *geology educator*
Feeney, Robert Earl *research biochemist*
Hedrick, Jerry Leo *biochemistry and biophysics educator*
Jungerman, John Albert *physics educator*
Keizer, Joel Edward *theoretical scientist, educator*
Mukherjee, Amiya K *metallurgy and materials science educator*
Nash, Charles Presley *chemistry educator*
Painter, Ruth Robbins *retired environmental biochemist*
Shelton, Robert Neal *physics educator, researcher*
Stumpf, Paul Karl *biochemistry educator emeritus*
Troy, Frederic Arthur, II *medical biochemistry educator*
Volman, David Herschel *chemistry educator*
Woodruff, Truman O(wen) *physicist, emeritus educator*
Wooten, Frederick (Oliver) *applied science educator*

El Cerrito
Griffith, Ladd Ray *retired chemical research director*
Siri, William E. *physicist*

El Segundo
Kostoulas, Ioannis Georgiou *physicist*

Emeryville
Masri, Merle Sid *biochemist, consultant*

Encinitas
Goldberg, Edward Davidow *geochemist, educator*

Encino
Hawthorne, Marion Frederick *chemistry educator*
Phelps, Michael Edward *biophysics educator*
Thorpe, Gary Stephen *chemistry educator*

Escondido
Tomomatsu, Hideo *chemist*

Fallbrook
Tess, Roy William Henry *chemist*

Flintridge
Otte, Carel *geologist*
Pickering, William Hayward *physics educator, scientist*

Foster City
Brankamp, Robert George *biosystems specialist*
Zaidi, Iqbal Mehdi *biochemist, scientist*

Fountain Valley
Davis, Jeremy Matthew *chemist*

Fremont
Gill, Stephen Paschall *physicist, mathematician*
Lee, Chan-Yun *physicist, process engineer, educator*
Li, Wenbin *physicist, engineer*

Fresno
Gump, Barry Hemphill *chemistry and food science educator*
Kauffman, George Bernard *chemistry educator*

Fullerton
Shapiro, Mark Howard *physicist, educator, academic dean, consultant*
†Wan, Julia Chang *science educator*

Glendale
Levy, Ezra Cesar *aerospace scientist, real estate broker*

Hayward
Pearce-Percy, Henry Thomas *physicist, electronics executive*

Hemet
Berger, Lev Isaac *physicist, educator*

Hollister
Smith, George Larry *analytical and environmental chemist*
Spencer, Douglas Lloyd *chemist, manufacturing executive*

Inglewood
Lewis, Roy Roosevelt *physicist*

Irvine
Bander, Myron *physics educator, university dean*
Bradshaw, Ralph Alden *biochemistry educator*
Bron, Walter Ernest *physics educator*
Clark, Bruce Robert *geology consultant*
Dzyaloshinskii, Igor Ekhielievich *physicist*
Knight, Patricia Marie *optics researcher*
Maradudin, Alexei A. *physics educator*
McLaughlin, Calvin Sturgis *biochemistry educator*
Nalcioglu, Orhan *physics educator, radiological sciences educator*
Nomura, Masayasu *biological chemistry educator*
Overman, Larry Eugene *chemistry educator*
Phalen, Robert Franklynn *environmental scientist*
Rentzepis, Peter M. *chemistry educator*
Rowland, Frank Sherwood *chemistry educator*
Rynn, Nathan *physics educator, consultant*
Wallis, Richard Fisher *physicist, educator*
White, Stephen Halley *biophysicist, educator*

Kensington
Appelman, Evan Hugh *retired chemist*
Connick, Robert Elwell *retired chemistry educator*

La Canada
Baines, Kevin Hays *planetary scientist, astronomer*

La Habra
Woyski, Margaret Skillman *retired geology educator*

La Jolla
Andre, Michael Paul *physicist, educator*
Arnold, James Richard *chemist, educator*
Asmus, John Fredrich *physicist*
Backus, George Edward *theoretical geophysicist*
Benson, Andrew Alm *biochemistry educator*
Berger, Wolfgang H. *oceanographer, marine geologist*
Boger, Dale L. *chemistry educator*
Buckingham, Michael John *oceanography educator*
Burbidge, E. Margaret *astronomer, educator*
Burbidge, Geoffrey *astrophysicist, educator*
Case, Kenneth Myron *physics educator*
Continetti, Robert E. *chemistry educator*
Cox, Charles Shipley *oceanography researcher, educator*
Cunningham, Bruce Arthur *biochemist*
Davis, Russ Erik *oceanographer, educator*
Doolittle, Russell Francis *biochemist, educator*
Driscoll, Charles Frederick *physics educator*
Edelman, Gerald Maurice *biochemist, neuroscientist, educator*
Fisher, Robert Lloyd *retired marine geologist and oceanographer*
Geiduschek, E(rnest) Peter *biophysics and molecular biology educator*
Gilbert, James Freeman *geophysics educator*
Itano, Harvey Akio *biochemistry educator*
Kadonaga, James Takuro *biochemist*
Kitada, Shinichi *biochemist*
Knox, Robert Arthur *oceanographer, academic administrator*
Kolodner, Richard David *biochemist, educator*
Lal, Devendra *nuclear geophysics educator*
Lauer, James Lothar *physicist, educator*
Lerner, Richard Alan *chemistry educator, scientist*
Lobert, Jürgen Michael *research chemist*
MacDougall, John Douglas *earth science educator*
McCammon, James Andrew *chemistry educator*
McIlwain, Carl Edwin *physicist*
Miller, Stanley Lloyd *chemistry and biochemistry educator*
Mullin, Michael Mahlon *Biology and oceanography educator*
Mullis, Kary Banks *biochemist*
Nicolaou, K. C. *chemistry educator*
Nierenberg, William Aaron *oceanography educator*
Ohkawa, Tihiro *physicist*
O'Neil, Thomas Michael *physicist, educator*
Onuchic, José Nelson *biophysics educator, electrical engineer*
Patton, Stuart *biochemist, educator*
Peterson, Laurence E. *physics educator*
Rebek, Julius, Jr. *chemistry educator, consultant*
Ride, Sally Kristen *physics educator, scientist, former astronaut*
Rosenbluth, Marshall Nicholas *physicist, educator*
Schimmel, Paul Reinhard *biochemist, biophysicist, educator*
Sclater, John George *geophysics educator*
Seegmiller, Jarvis Edwin *biochemist, educator*
Sham, Lu Jeu *physics educator*
Sharpless, K. Barry *chemist, educator*
Shor, George G., Jr. *geophysicist, oceanographic administrator, engineer*
Shuler, Kurt Egon *chemist, educator*
Somerville, Richard Chapin James *atmospheric scientist, educator*
Spiess, Fred Noel *oceanographer, educator*
Stone, William Ross *research and development company executive, physicist*
Taylor, Susan Serota *biochemistry researcher*
Tietz, Norbert Wolfgang *clinical chemistry educator, administrator*
Tsien, Roger Yonchien *chemist, cell biologist*
Van Lint, Victor Anton Jacobus *physicist*
Wall, Frederick Theodore *retired chemistry educator*
Watson, Kenneth Marshall *physics educator*
York, Herbert Frank *physics educator, government official*

La Verne
Hwang, Cordelia Jong *chemist*

Lafayette
Reynolds, Harry Lincoln *physicist*

Laguna Beach
Batdorf, Samuel B(urbridge) *physicist*

Laguna Hills
Iberall, Arthur Saul *physicist, publisher*

Livermore
Alder, Berni Julian *physicist*
Bjorkholm, John Ernst *physicist*
Campbell, John Hyde *laser materials researcher, consultant*
Cook, Robert Crossland *research chemist*
Ellsaesser, Hugh Walter *retired atmospheric scientist*
Futch, Archer Hamner *retired physicist*
Hooper, Edwin Bickford *physicist*
Kidder, Ray Edward *physicist, consultant*
Kirkwood, Robert Keith *applied physicist*
Leith, Cecil Eldon, Jr. *retired physicist*
Max, Claire Ellen *physicist*
Nuckolls, John Hopkins *physicist, researcher*
Schock, Robert Norman *geophysicist*
Shotts, Wayne J. *nuclear scientist, federal agency administrator*
Tarter, Curtis Bruce *physicist, science administrator*
Wilson, James Ricker *physicist, consultant*
Wong, Joe *physical chemist*

Loma Linda
Slattery, Charles Wilbur *biochemistry educator*
Wilcox, Ronald Bruce *biochemistry educator, researcher*

Long Beach
Bauer, Roger Duane *chemistry educator, science consultant*
McGaughey, Charles Gilbert *retired research biochemist*
Scott, Bruce Laurence *physicist, educator*
Snow, James Harry *metallurgist, educator, aircraft planning executive*

Los Altos
Barker, William Alfred *physics educator*
Hall, Charles Frederick *space scientist, government administrator*
Jones, Robert Thomas *aerospace scientist*

Los Altos Hills
van Tamelen, Eugene Earle *chemist, educator*

Los Angeles
Adamson, Arthur Wilson *chemistry educator*
Aller, Lawrence Hugh *astronomy educator, researcher*
Allerton, Samuel Ellsworth *biochemist*
Anderson, W. French *biochemist, physician*
Benson, Sidney William *chemistry researcher*
Bhaumik, Mani Lal *physicist*
Billig, Franklin Anthony *chemist*
Bird, Peter *geology educator*
Bottjer, David John *earth sciences educator*
†Boyer, Paul D. *biochemist, educator*
Brown, Elliott Rowe *physicist*
Byers, Nina *physics educator*
Campbell, Kenneth Eugene, Jr. *vertebrate paleontologist*
Carter, Emily Ann *physical chemist, researcher, educator*
Chapman, Orville Lamar *chemist, educator*
Coleman, Charles Clyde *physicist, educator*
Coleman, Paul Jerome, Jr. *physicist, educator*
Cornwall, John Michael *physics educator, consultant, researcher*
Coroniti, Ferdinand Vincent *physics educator, consultant*
Cram, Donald James *chemistry educator*
Dawson, John Myrick *plasma physics educator*
Dows, David Alan *chemistry educator*
Dunn, Arnold Samuel *biochemistry educator*
Dunn, Bruce Sidney *materials science educator*
Fischer, Alfred George *geology educator*
Foote, Christopher Spencer *chemist, educator*
Fried, Burton David *physicist, educator*
Fulco, Armand John *biochemist*
Ganas, Perry Spiros *physicist*
Ghez, Andrea Mia *astronomy and physics educator*
Ghil, Michael *atmospheric scientist, geophysicist*
Glitz, Dohn George *biochemistry educator*
Hall, Clarence Albert, Jr. *geologist, educator*
Houk, Kendall Newcomb *chemistry educator*
Igo, George Jerome *physics educator*
Jaffe, Sigmund *chemist, educator*
Kaplan, Isaac Raymond *chemistry educator, corporate executive*
Kaula, William Mason *geophysicist, educator*
Kivelson, Margaret Galland *physicist*
Knopoff, Leon *geophysics educator*
Kobe, Lan *medical physicist*
Koga, Rokutaro *physicist*
Krupp, Edwin Charles *astronomer*
Kunc, Joseph Anthony *physics and engineering educator, consultant*
Laaly, Heshmat Ollah *chemist, roofing materials executive, consultant*
Levine, Raphael David *chemistry educator*
Maki, Kazumi *physicist, educator*
Markland, Francis Swaby, Jr. *biochemist, educator*
Neufeld, Elizabeth Fondal *biochemist, educator*
Olah, George Andrew *chemist, educator*
Onak, Thomas Philip *chemistry educator*
Paulson, Donald Robert *chemistry educator*
Reiss, Howard *chemistry educator*
Roberts, Sidney *biological chemist*
Scott, Robert Lane *chemist, educator*
Simkhovich, Boris Zalman *biochemist, researcher*
Smathers, James Burton *medical physicist, educator*
Smith, Emil L. *biochemist, consultant*
Smith, William Ray *retired biophysicist, engineer*
Stellwagen, Robert Harwood *biochemistry educator*
Szwarc, Michael *polymer scientist*
Thorne, Richard Mansergh *physicist*
Trimble, Stanley Wayne *hydrology and geography educator*
Ufimtsev, Pyotr Yakovlevich *physicist, electrical engineer, educator*
Whitten, Charles Alexander, Jr. *physics educator*
Wudl, Fred *chemistry educator*
Wurtele, Morton Gaither *meteorologist, educator*
Yanai, Michio *meteorologist, educator*

Los Osos
Topp, Alphonso Axel, Jr. *environmental scientist, consultant*

Magalia
Sincoff, Steven Lawrence *chemistry educator*

Malibu
Chester, Arthur Noble *physicist*
Margerum, J(ohn) David *chemist*

Pepper, David M. *physicist, educator, author, inventor*

Marina
Shane, William Whitney *astronomer*

Menlo Park
Boyarski, Adam Michael *physicist*
Bukry, John David *geologist*
Friend, David Robert *chemist*
Funkhouser, Lawrence William *retired geologist*
Holzer, Thomas Lequear *geologist*
Kuwabara, James Shigeru *research hydrologist*
Lachenbruch, Arthur Herold *geophysicist*
Luepke, Gretchen *geologist*
Shen, Nelson Mu-Ching *fiber optics communications scientist*
Tokheim, Robert Edward *physicist*
Vickers, Roger Spencer *physicist, environmental mapping director*

Milpitas
Duque, Ricardo German *analytical chemist*

Modesto
Gunter, William Dayle, Jr. *physicist*
Morrison, Robert Lee *physical scientist*

Moffett Field
Lissauer, Jack Jonathan *astronomy educator*
Ragent, Boris *physicist*
Salama, Farid *astrophysicist, spectroscopist, research scientist*

Monrovia
Andary, Thomas Joseph *biochemist*
Edwards, Kenneth Neil *chemist, consultant*

Montecito
Wheelon, Albert Dewell *physicist*

Monterey
Collins, Curtis Allan *oceanographer*
Shull, Harrison *chemist, educator*

Moss Landing
Brewer, Peter George *ocean geochemist*
Clague, David A. *geologist*

Mountain View
Loew, Gilda Harris *research biophysicist, biology research executive*
McCormac, Billy Murray *physicist, research institution executive, former army officer*

Napa
Chung, Dae Hyun *retired geophysicist*

North Hollywood
Patterson, James Franklyn *physics educator*

Novato
Simon, Lee Will *astronomer*

Oakland
Brust, David *physicist*
Harpster, Robert Eugene *engineering geologist*
Jukes, Thomas Hughes *biological chemist, educator*
Linford, Rulon Kesler *physicist, engineer*
Mikalow, Alfred Alexander, II *deep sea diver, marine surveyor, marine diving consultant*
Wong, Ivan Gynmun *seismologist*

Oceanside
L'Annunziata, Michael Frank *chemist, consultant*

Orange
Korb, Lawrence John *metallurgist*
Talbott, George Robert *physicist, mathematician, educator*

Orinda
Baker, Don Robert *chemist, inventor*
Heftmann, Erich *biochemist*

Pacific Palisades
Abrams, Richard Lee *physicist*
Csendes, Ernest *chemist, corporate and financial executive*

Palmdale
Smith, Maureen McBride *laboratory administrator*

Palo Alto
Andersen, Torben Brender *optical researcher, astronomer, software engineer*
Breiner, Sheldon *geophysics educator, business executive*
Cohen, Karl Paley *nuclear energy consultant*
Cutler, Leonard Samuel *physicist*
Datlowe, Dayton Wood *space scientist, physicist*
Eng, Lawrence Fook *biochemistry educator, neurochemist*
Ernst, Wallace Gary *geology educator*
Flory, Curt Alan *research physicist*
Gliner, Erast Boris *theoretical physicist*
Haisch, Bernhard Michael *astronomer*
Loewenstein, Walter Bernard *nuclear power technologist*
McHugh, Stuart Lawrence *research scientist*
Panofsky, Wolfgang Kurt Hermann *physicist, educator*
Saxena, Arjun Nath *physicist*
Schreiber, Everett Charles, Jr. *chemist, educator*
Spira-Solomon, Darlene Joy *industrial chemist, researcher, department manager*
Taimuty, Samuel Isaac *physicist*
Theeuwes, Felix *physical chemist*
Varney, Robert Nathan *retired physicist, researcher*

Palos Verdes Estates
Joshi, Satish Devdas *organic chemist*
Paulikas, George Algis *retired physicist*

Paradise
Wilder, James D. *geology and mining administrator*

Pasadena
Ahrens, Thomas J. *geophysicist*
Albee, Arden Leroy *geologist, educator*
Allen, Clarence Roderic *geologist, educator*
Anderson, Don Lynn *geophysicist, educator*
Baldeschwieler, John Dickson *chemist, educator*
Barnes, Charles Andrew *physicist, educator*
Beauchamp, Jesse Lee (Jack Beauchamp) *chemistry educator*
Beaudet, Robert Arthur *chemistry educator*
Bejczy, Antal Károly *research scientist, research facility administrator*
Bercaw, John Edward *chemistry educator, consultant*
Blandford, Roger David *astronomy educator*
Boehm, Felix Hans *physicist, educator*
Chahine, Moustafa Toufic *atmospheric scientist*
Chan, Sunney Ignatius *chemist*
Cohen, Marshall Harris *astronomer, educator*
Culick, Fred Ellsworth Clow *physics and engineering educator*
Davidson, Norman Ralph *biochemistry educator*
Dervan, Peter Brendan *chemistry educator*
Dougherty, Dennis A. *chemistry educator*
Duxbury, Thomas Carl *planetary scientist*
Epstein, Samuel *geologist, educator*
Ferber, Robert Rudolf *physics researcher, educator*
Frautschi, Steven Clark *physicist, educator*
Friedl, Randall Raymond *environmental scientist*
Fu, Lee-Lueng *oceanographer*
Fultz, Brent Thomas *materials scientist, educator, researcher*
Goodstein, David Louis *physics educator*
Gray, Harry Barkus *chemistry educator*
Grubbs, Robert Howard *chemistry educator*
Gurnis, Michael Christopher *geological sciences educator*
Heindl, Clifford Joseph *physicist*
Hitlin, David George *physicist, educator*
Ingersoll, Andrew Perry *planetary science educator*
Jastrow, Robert *physicist*
Koonin, Steven Elliot *physicist, educator, academic administrator*
Leonard, Nelson Jordan *chemistry educator*
Lewis, Nathan Saul *chemistry educator*
Liepmann, Hans Wolfgang *physicist, educator*
Marcus, Rudolph Arthur *chemist, educator*
Mc Koy, Basil Vincent Charles *theoretical chemist, educator*
Neugebauer, Gerry *retired astrophysicist, educator*
Neugebauer, Marcia *physicist, administrator*
Oemler, Augustus, Jr. *astronomer*
Politzer, Hugh David *physicist, educator*
Roberts, John D. *chemist, educator*
Samson, Sten Otto *x-ray crystallographer, consultant, researcher*
Sandage, Allan Rex *astronomer*
Sargent, Wallace Leslie William *astronomer, educator*
Schieldge, John Philip *physicist, researcher*
Schmidt, Maarten *astronomy educator*
Schwarz, John Henry *theoretical physicist, educator*
Sekanina, Zdenek *astronomer*
Sharp, Robert Phillip *geology educator, researcher*
Stevenson, David John *planetary scientist, educator*
Stone, Edward Carroll *physicist, educator*
Thorne, Kip Stephen *physicist, educator*
Tombrello, Thomas Anthony, Jr. *physics educator, consultant*
Vogt, Rochus Eugen *physicist, educator*
Wasserburg, Gerald Joseph *geology and geophysics educator*
Westphal, James Adolph *planetary science educator*
Yau, Kevin Kam-ching *astronomer*
Yeomans, Donald Keith *astronomer*
Zewail, Ahmed Hassan *chemistry and physics educator, editor, consultant*
Zirin, Harold *astronomer, educator*

Petaluma
Eck, Robert Edwin *physicist*

Placerville
Beneš, Norman Stanley *meteorologist*

Pleasanton
Denavit, Jacques *retired physicist*

Pomona
Aurilia, Antonio *physicist, educator*
Bidlack, Wayne Ross *nutritional biochemist, toxicologist, food scienti*

Poway
†Yousefian, Shahram *chemist*

Rancho Santa Fe
Creutz, Edward Chester *physicist, museum consultant*

Redondo Beach
Ball, William Paul *physicist, engineer*
Foster, John Stuart, Jr. *physicist, former defense industry executive*
Lake, Bruce Meno *applied physicist*

Redwood City
Nacht, Sergio *biochemist*

Richmond
Barashkov, Nickolay Nickolayevich *polymer chemist, researcher*
Thomas, John Richard *chemist*

Ridgecrest
Lepie, Albert Helmut *chemist, researcher*

Riverside
Green, Harry Western, II *geology-geophysics educator, university official*
Norman, Anthony Westcott *biochemistry educator*
Orbach, Raymond Lee *physicist, educator*
Rabenstein, Dallas Leroy *chemistry educator*
Van Dalen, Gordon John *physicist*
White, Robert Stephen *physics educator*
Wild, Robert Lee *physics educator*

Rohnert Park
Trowbridge, Dale Brian *educator*

Sacramento
Dedrick, Kent Gentry *retired physicist, researcher*
Nussenbaum, Siegfried Fred *chemistry educator*

San Diego
Bussard, Robert William *physicist*
Cantor, Charles Robert *biochemistry educator*
Clauson, Gary Lewis *chemist*
Cobble, James Wikle *chemistry educator*
Fisher, Frederick Hendrick *oceanographer emeritus*
Gastil, Russell Gordon *geologist, educator*
Greene, John M. *physicist*
Hayes, Claude Quinten Christopher *research scientist*
Lao, Lang Li *nuclear fusion research physicist*
Mohan, Chandra *research biochemistry educator*
Morgan, Mark Quenten *astronomer, astrophysics educator*
Orgel, Leslie Eleazer *chemist*
Pecsok, Robert Louis *chemist, educator*
Pincus, Howard Jonah *geologist, engineer, educator*
Roeder, Stephen Bernhard Walter *chemistry and physics educator*
Seegall, Manfred Ismar Ludwig *retired physicist, educator*
Shackelford, Gordon Lee, Jr. *physics educator*
Shneour, Elie Alexis *biochemist*
Springer, Wayne Richard *research biochemist, healthcare system official*
Wright, Jon Alan *physicist, researcher*

San Francisco
Bourne, Henry R. *biochemistry professor*
Boyer, Herbert Wayne *biochemist*
Burlingame, Alma Lyman *chemist, educator*
Cluff, Lloyd Sterling *earthquake geologist*
Dickinson, Wade *physicist, oil company executive, educator*
Dill, Kenneth Austin *pharmaceutical chemistry educator*
Düzgünes, Nejat A. *biophysicist, microbiologist*
Grodsky, Gerold Morton *biochemistry educator*
Kelly, Regis Baker *biochemistry educator, biophysics educator*
Landahl, Herbert Daniel *biophysicist, mathematical biologist, researcher, consultant*
Mandra, York T. *geology educator*
Nguyen, Ann Cac Khue *pharmaceutical and medicinal chemist*
Raedeke, Linda Dismore *geologist*
Sussman, Brian Jay *meteorologist, weather broadcaster*
Watanabe, Larry Geo *biomaterials scientist*

San Jose
Castellano, Joseph Anthony *chemist, management consulting firm executive*
Craford, M. George *physicist, research administrator*
Dafforn, Geoffrey Alan *biochemist*
Eigler, Donald Mark *physicist*
Forster, Julian *physicist, consultant*
Gruber, John Balsbaugh *physics educator, university administrator*
Mee, C(harles) Denis *physicist*
Morawitz, Hans *physicist*
Neptune, John Addison *chemistry educator, consultant*
Nimmagadda, Rao Rajagopala *materials scientist, researcher*
Parkin, Stuart S. P. *materials scientist*
Pitts, William Clarence *physicist*
Winters, Harold Franklin *physicist*

San Leandro
Stallings, Charles Henry *physicist*

San Luis Obispo
Grismore, Roger *physics educator, researcher*
Hafemeister, David Walter *physicist*

San Mateo
Gombocz, Erich Alfred *biochemist*

San Pedro
Simmons, William *physicist, retired aerospace research executive*

Santa Barbara
Ahlers, Guenter *physicist, educator*
Atwater, Tanya Maria *marine geophysicist, educator*
Bruice, Thomas C. *chemist, educator*
Christman, Arthur Castner, Jr. *scientific advisor*
Crowell, John C(hambers) *geology educator, researcher*
Dunne, Thomas *geology educator*
Fisher, Matthew P. A. *physicist*
Ford, Peter C. *chemistry educator*
Gossard, Arthur Charles *physicist*
Heeger, Alan Jay *physicist*
Hubbard, Arthur Thornton *chemistry educator, electro-surface chemist*
Kennedy, John Harvey *chemistry educator*
Kohn, Walter *educator, physicist*
Kram, Mark Lenard *hydrogeologist, environmental geochemist*
Langer, James Stephen *physicist, educator*
Luyendyk, Bruce Peter *geophysicist, educator, institution administrator*
Macdonald, Ken Craig *geophysicist*
Martzen, Philip D. *physicist, software developer*
Meinel, Aden Baker *optics scientist*
Peale, Stanton Jerrold *physics educator*
Pilgeram, Laurence Oscar *biochemist*
Scalapino, Douglas James *physics educator*
Strahler, Arthur Newell *former geology educator, author*
Tilton, George Robert *geochemistry educator*
Veigele, William John *physicist*
Wilson, Leslie *biochemist, cell biologist, biology educator*

Santa Clara
Gozani, Tsahi *nuclear physicist*
Wang, Liang-guo *research scientist*

Santa Cruz
Bunnett, Joseph Frederick *chemist, educator*
Drake, Frank Donald *radio astronomer, educator*
Faber, Sandra Moore *astronomer, educator*
Flatté, Stanley Martin *physicist, educator*
Goldbeck, Robert Arthur, Jr. *physical chemist*
Griggs, Gary Bruce *earth sciences educator, oceanographer, geologist, consultant*
Heusch, Clemens August *physicist, educator*
Hill, Terrell Leslie *chemist, biophysicist*
Kostic, Petar Jovan *physicist*
Kraft, Robert Paul *astronomer, educator*
Lay, Thorne *geosciences educator*
Nelson, Jerry Earl *astrophysics educator*
Noller, Harry Francis, Jr. *biochemist, educator*
Osterbrock, Donald E(dward) *astronomy educator*
Sands, Matthew Linzee *physicist, educator*
Silver, Mary Wilcox *oceanography educator*
Williams, Quentin Christopher *geophysicist, educator*
Wipke, W. Todd *chemistry educator*

Santa Maria
Ellis, Emory Leon *retired biochemist*

Santa Monica
Davies, Merton Edward *planetary scientist*
Intriligator, Devrie Shapiro *physicist*
Park, Edward Cahill, Jr. *retired physicist*
Shipbaugh, Calvin LeRoy *physicist*

Santa Rosa
Belmares, Hector *chemist*

Solana Beach
Agnew, Harold Melvin *physicist*

South San Francisco
Canova-Davis, Eleanor *biochemist, researcher*

Stanford
Allen, Matthew Arnold *physicist*
Andersen, Hans Christian *chemistry educator*
Baldwin, Robert Lesh *biochemist, educator*
Berg, Paul *biochemist, educator*
Bonner, William Andrew *chemistry educator*
Brauman, John I. *chemist, educator*
Bube, Richard Howard *materials scientist*
Coleman, Robert Griffin *geology educator*
Collman, James Paddock *chemistry educator*
Deal, Bruce Elmer *physical chemist, educator*
Djerassi, Carl *chemist, educator, writer*
Fetter, Alexander Lees *theoretical physicist, educator*
Harbaugh, John Warvelle *applied earth sciences educator*
Harrison, Walter Ashley *physicist, educator*
Herring, William Conyers *physicist, emeritus educator*
Kennedy, Donald *environmental science educator, former academic administrator*
Kornberg, Arthur *biochemist*
Kornberg, Roger David *biochemist, structural biologist*
Kovach, Robert Louis *geophysics educator*
Krauskopf, Konrad Bates *geology educator*
†Laughlin, Robert B. *physics educator*
Lehman, (Israel) Robert *biochemistry educator, consultant*
Levinthal, Elliott Charles *physicist, educator*
Little, William Arthur *physicist, educator*
Matson, Pamela Anne *environmental science educator*
McConnell, Harden Marsden *biophysical chemistry researcher, chemistry educator*
†Osheroff, Douglas Dean *physicist, researcher*
Perl, Martin Lewis *physicist, engineer, educator*
Richter, Burton *physicist, educator*
Ross, John *physical chemist, educator*
Schneider, Stephen Henry *climatologist, environmental policy analyst, researcher*
Shaw, Herbert John *physics educator emeritus*
Spicer, William Edward, III *physicist, educator, engineer*
Stryer, Lubert *biochemist, educator*
Taube, Henry *chemistry educator*
Taylor, Richard Edward *physicist, educator*
Teller, Edward *physicist*
Thompson, George Albert *geophysics educator*
Trost, Barry Martin *chemist, educator*
Wagoner, Robert Vernon *astrophysicist, educator*
Walt, Martin *physicist, consulting educator*
Wang, Suwen *physicist, consultant*
Waymouth, Robert *chemistry educator*
Wender, Paul Anthony *chemistry educator*
Wojcicki, Stanley George *physicist, educator*
Zare, Richard Neil *chemistry educator*

Stockton
Whiteker, Roy Archie *retired chemistry educator*

Sunnyvale
DeMello, Austin Eastwood *astrophysicist, concert artist, poet, writer*
Majumder, Sabir Ahmed *physical and analytical chemist*
Thissell, James Dennis *physicist*

Tarzana
Meyers, Robert Allen *chemist, publisher*

Thousand Oaks
Sherman, Gerald *nuclear physicist, financial estate adviser, financial company executive*

Torrance
Rogers, Howard H. *chemist*
Zhao, Mingjun *physicist, research scientist*

Truckee
Todd, Linda Marie *nutrition researcher, financial consultant, pilot*

Tustin
Zhu, Peter Chaoquan *chemist*

Van Nuys
Freiberg, Robert Jerry *laser physicist, engineer, technology administrator, consultant*

Walnut Creek
Wu, Tse Cheng *research chemist*

Woodland Hills
Harris, Sigmund Paul *physicist*

Woodside
Ashley, Holt *aerospace scientist, educator*

COLORADO

Arvada
Knight, William V. *geologist*
Martin, Robert Gregory *chemist*

Aspen
Pullen, Margaret I. *genetic physicist*

Aurora
Sherlin, Jerry Michael retired hydro meteorological technician

Boulder
Albritton, Daniel Lee atmospheric scientist
Alldredge, Leroy Romney retired geophysicist
Bailey, Dana Kavanagh radiophysicist, botanist
Baker, Daniel Neil physicist
Bartlett, David Farnham physics educator
Begelman, Mitchell Craig astrophysicist, educator
Brown, Jack D(elbert) chemist, researcher
Calvert, Jack George atmospheric chemist, educator
Cech, Thomas Robert chemistry and biochemistry educator
Chappell, Charles Franklin meteorologist, consultant
Clark, Alan Fred physicist
Conti, Peter Selby astronomy educator
Cornell, Eric Allin physics educator
Cristol, Stanley Jerome chemistry educator
Dryer, Murray physicist
Fleming, Rex James meteorologist
Garstang, Roy Henry astrophysicist, educator
Gossard, Earl Everett physicist
Hall, John Lewis physicist, researcher
Hermann, Allen Max physics educator
Hildner, Ernest Gotthold, III solar physicist, science administrator
Hofmann, David John atmospheric science researcher, educator
Hogg, David Clarence physicist
Holzer, Thomas E. physicist
Joselyn, Jo Ann space scientist
Kapteyn, Henry Cornelius physics and engineering educator
Kellogg, William Welch meteorologist
King, Edward Louis retired chemistry educator
Kisslinger, Carl geophysicist, educator
Koch, Tad Harbison chemistry educator, researcher
Lally, Vincent Edward atmospheric scientist
LeMone, Margaret Anne atmospheric scientist
Leone, Stephen Robert chemical physicist, educator
Lineberger, William Carl chemistry educator
Little, Charles Gordon geophysicist
Low, Boon Chye physicist
MacDonald, Alexander Edward meteorologist
Malde, Harold Edwin retired federal government geologist
McCray, Richard Alan astrophysicist, educator
Meagher, James Francis atmospheric research executive
Miller, Harold William nuclear geochemist
Ostrovsky, Lev Aronovich physicist, oceanographer, educator
Pankove, Jacques Isaac physicist
Peterson, Roy Jerome physics educator
Robinson, Peter paleontology educator, consultant
Roellig, Leonard Oscar physics educator
Schneider, Nicholas McCord planetary scientist, educator, textbook author
Schnell, Russell Clifford atmospheric scientist, researcher
Snow, Theodore Peck astrophysics educator
Spangler, Timothy Chester meteorologist, program director
Tatarskii, Valerian Il'Ich physics researcher
Tolbert, Bert Mills biochemist, educator
Trenberth, Kevin Edward atmospheric scientist
Washington, Warren Morton meteorologist
Wieman, Carl E. physics educator
Zavorotny, Valery Ustimovich physicist, researcher

Canon City
Fair, Annie May geological computer specialist

Colorado Springs
Corry, Charles Elmo geophysicist, consultant
Hoffman, John Raleigh physicist
Rogers, Steven Ray physicist
Schwartz, Donald chemistry educator

Denver
Barker, Fred research geologist, scientific editor
Chappell, Willard Ray physics educator, environmental scientist
†Clark, Lori DeVito environmental scientist
Cobban, William Aubrey paleontologist
Eaton, Gareth Richard chemistry educator, university dean
Foster, Norman Holland geologist
Hetzel, Fredrick William biophysicist, educator
Iona, Mario retired physics educator
Johnson, Walter Earl geophysicist
Klipping, Robert Samuel geophysicist
Landon, Susan Melinda petroleum geologist
Mullineaux, Donal Ray geologist
Neumann, Herschel physics educator
Pakiser, Louis Charles, Jr. geophysicist
Peregrine, David Seymour astronomer, consultant
Quinn, John Michael physicist, geophysicist
Smith, Dwight Morrell chemistry educator
Thordarson, William retired hydrogeologist
Weihaupt, John George geosciences educator, scientist, university administrator

Durango
†Prowse, Allen Bennie chemist

Englewood
Brown, Steven Harry corporation health physicist, consultant
Dahl, Gardar Godfrey, Jr. geologist, consultant

Evergreen
Haun, John Daniel petroleum geologist, educator
Heyl, Allen Van, Jr. geologist
Phillips, Adran Abner (Abe Phillips) geologist, oil and gas exploration consultant

Fort Collins
Bamburg, James Robert biochemistry educator
Bernstein, Elliot Roy chemistry educator
Curthoys, Norman P. biochemistry educator, consultant
Elkind, Mortimer Murray biophysicist, educator
Fixman, Marshall chemist, educator
Johnson, Robert Britten geology educator
Ladanyi, Branka Maria chemist, educator
Meyers, Albert Irving chemistry educator
Mosier, Arvin Ray chemist, researcher
Patton, Carl Elliott physics educator
Schumm, Stanley Alfred geologist, educator

Golden
Freeman, Val LeRoy geologist
Furtak, Thomas Elton physicist, educator, author, consultant
Hutchinson, Richard William geology educator, consultant
Kennedy, George Hunt chemistry educator
Krauss, George metallurgist
Tilton, John Elvin mineral economics educator
Wei, Su-Huai physicist
Weimer, Robert Jay geology educator, energy consultant, civic leader
White, James Edward geophysicist

Grand Junction
Duray, John Robert physicist
Rutz, Richard Frederick physicist, researcher

Greeley
Fadner, Willard Lee physics educator, researcher
Jones, Loretta Lucek chemistry educator, writer
†Walch, Robert Anton physics educator

Lakewood
Parker, John Marchbank consulting geologist

Littleton
Choquette, Philip Wheeler geologist, educator
Paull, Richard Allen geologist, educator
Rinkenberger, Richard Krug physical scientist, geologist, consultant

Louisville
Brault, James William physicist

Ridgway
Lathrop, Kaye Don nuclear scientist, educator

Silverthorne
Ponder, Herman geologist

CONNECTICUT

Bridgeport
Chih, Chung-Ying physicist, consultant
Ettre, Leslie Stephen chemist

Brookfield
Schetky, Laurence McDonald metallurgist, researcher

Danbury
Joyce, William H. chemist
Pastor, Stephen Daniel chemistry educator, researcher

Durham
Hicks, Norman William physical science educator

Fairfield
Simpson, W(ilburn) Dwain physicist, corporate executive, computer systems, telecommunications, environmental, and advanced fueling systems consultant

Farmington
Osborn, Mary Jane Merten biochemist
Spencer, Richard Paul biochemist, educator, physician

Greenwich
Davenport, Lee Losee physicist

Groton
Lewis, Ralph Stanton geologist
Swindell, Archie Calhoun, Jr. research biochemist, statistician
†Xu, Zuoyu biochemist, researcher

Hartford
Kung, Pang-Jen materials scientist, electrical engineer

Manchester
Galasso, Francis Salvatore materials scientist
Stull, Daniel Richard retired research thermochemist, educator, consultant

Middletown
Fry, Albert Joseph chemistry educator
Haake, Paul chemistry, biochemistry and history of science educator
Novick, Stewart Eugene physical chemist, educator
Sease, John W(illiam) chemistry educator
Upgren, Arthur Reinhold, Jr. astronomer, educator

Mystic
Chiang, Albert Chinfa polymer chemist

New Britain
Baskerville, Charles Alexander geologist, educator
Dimmick, Charles William geology educator

New Haven
Adair, Robert Kemp physicist, educator
Aylor, Donald Earl biophysicist, research meteorologist, plant pathology educator and reseacher
Bennett, William Ralph, Jr. physicist, educator
Berner, Robert Arbuckle geochemist, educator
Berson, Jerome Abraham chemistry educator
Bromley, David Allan physicist, engineer, educator
Brünger, Axel Thomas biophysicist, researcher, educator
Casten, Richard Francis physicist
Chupka, William Andrew chemical physicist, educator
Coleman, Joseph Emory biophysics and biochemistry educator
Crothers, Donald Morris biochemist, educator
Garen, Alan biophysics professor
Gordon, Robert Boyd geophysics educator
Graedel, Thomas Eldon chemist, researcher
Handschumacher, Robert Edmund biochemistry educator
Haskins, Caryl Parker scientist, author
Herzenberg, Arvid physicist, educator
Hoffleit, Ellen Dorrit astronomer
Hohenberg, Pierre Claude research physicist
Hughes, Vernon Willard physics educator, researcher
Jorgensen, William L. chemistry educator
Klein, Martin Jesse physicist, educator, science historian
Mac Dowell, Samuel Wallace physics educator
Marchesi, Vincent T. biochemist, educator
Moore, Peter Bartlett biochemist, educator
Ostrom, John H. vertebrate paleontologist, educator, museum curator
Reifsnyder, William Edward meteorologist
Richards, Frederic Middlebrook biochemist, educator
Rodgers, John geologist, educator
Saltzman, Barry meteorologist, educator
Sandweiss, Jack physicist, educator
Shulman, Robert Gerson biophysics educator
Skinner, Helen Catherine Wild biomineralogist
Slayman, Clifford Leroy biophysicist, educator
Sofia, Sabatino astronomy educator
Steitz, Joan Argetsinger biochemistry educator
Tully, John Charles research chemical physicist
Turekian, Karl Karekin geochemistry educator
Wasserman, Harry Hershal chemistry educator
Wolf, Werner Paul physicist, educator
Zeller, Michael Edward physicist, educator

New Milford
Fabricand, Burton Paul physicist, educator

Newtown
Bockelman, Charles Kincaid physics educator

Ridgefield
Grozinger, Karl Georg chemist, researcher
Nodland, Borge Heming physicist
Sen, Pabitra N. physicist, researcher

Rocky Hill
Chu, Hsien-Kun chemist, researcher
Griesé, John William, III astronomer, mental health advocate

Southbury
Morehead, Frederick Ferguson retired physical chemist

Stamford
Courter, Jeanne Lynn materials scientist

Stonington
Mantz, Arlan W. physics educator

Storrs Mansfield
Azaroff, Leonid Vladimirovitch physics educator
Bartram, Ralph Herbert physicist
Bobbitt, James McCue chemist
Devereux, Owen Francis metallurgy educator
Kattamis, Theodore Zenon metallurgy educator, material engineering
Klemens, Paul Gustav physicist, educator
Marcus, Harris Leon materials science educator
Schuster, Todd Mervyn biophysics educator, biotechnology company executive
Stwalley, William Calvin physics and chemistry educator

Waterford
Johnson, Gary William environmental scientist

West Hartford
Markham, Sister M(aria) Clare chemistry educator, educational director

West Hartland
Perkins, Bob(by) F(rank) geologist, dean

Windsor
Garde, Anand Madhav materials scientist

Woodbury
Skinner, Brian John geologist, educator

DELAWARE

Dover
Wasfi, Sadiq Hassan chemistry educator

Greenville
Levitt, George retired chemist

Lewes
Boyer, John Strickland biochemist, biophysics

New Castle
Bellenger, George Collier, Jr. physics educator

Newark
Burmeister, John Luther chemistry educator, consultant
Daniels, William Burton physicist, educator
Esrey, Elizabeth Gove Goodier chemist, biologist
Evans, Dennis Hyde chemist, educator
Evenson, Paul Arthur physics educator
Hutton, David Glenn environmental scientist, consultant, chemical engineer
Jordan, Robert Reed geologist, educator
Kasprzak, Lucian Alexander physicist, researcher, technical manager
Mather, John Russell climatologist, educator
Murray, Richard Bennett physics educator
Ness, Norman Frederick astrophysicist, educator, administrator
Trofimenko, Swiatoslaw chemist, researcher, consultant
Wetlaufer, Donald Burton biochemist, educator
Wu, Jin oceanographer, educator, engineer
Zank, Gary Paul phyicist

Newport
Kirkland, Joseph J. research chemist

Wilmington
Crittenden, Eugene Dwight, Jr. chemical company executive
Jezl, Barbara Ann chemist, automation consultant
Kwolek, Stephanie Louise chemist
Marcali, Jean Gregory chemist, retired
Moore, Carl Gordon chemist, educator
Parshall, George William research chemist
Smook, Malcolm Andrew chemist, chemical company executive
†Wasserman, Edel scientist, executive

DISTRICT OF COLUMBIA

Washington
Abelson, Philip Hauge physicist
Alexander, Joseph Kunkle, Jr. physicist
†Armstrong, Spence M. aerospace technology administrator
†Baker, D. James oceanographic and atmospheric administrator
Berendzen, Richard astronomer, educator, author
Bienenstock, Arthur Irwin physicist, educator, government official
Bierly, Eugene Wendell meteorologist, science administrator
Boyd, Francis R. geophysicists
Brown, Louis physicist, researcher
Callahan, Debra Jean environmental organization executive
Charlton, Gordon Randolph physicist
Cheetham, Alan Herbert paleontologist
Chubb, Talbot Albert physicist
Coffey, Timothy physicist, think-tank executive
Davidson, Eugene Abraham biochemist, university administrator
Devine, Katherine environmental consultant, educator
Domning, Daryl Paul paleontologist, educator
Donohue, Joyce Morrissey biochemist, toxicologist, nutritionist, educator
Dusold, Laurence Richard chemist, computer specialist
Dutro, John Thomas, Jr. geologist, paleontologist
El Khadem, Hassan Saad chemistry educator, researcher
Fainberg, Anthony physicist
Fogleman, Guy Carroll physicist, mathematician, educator
Friedman, Herbert physicist
Garavelli, John Stephen biochemistry research scientist
Giacconi, Riccardo astrophysicist, educator
Ginsburg, Mitchell Paul international economist
Goldstein, Allan Leonard biochemist, educator
Hallgren, Richard Edwin meteorologist
Hamilton, Robert Morrison geophysicist
Harwit, Martin Otto astrophysicist, writer, educator, museum director
Haslam, Charles Linn aerospace executive, lawyer, educator
Heineman, Heinz chemist
Heinemann, Heinz chemist, educator, researcher, consultant
Higgins, Peter Thomas technology consultant
Holland, Christie Anna biochemist, virologist
Holloway, John Thomas physicist
Imam, M. Ashraf materials scientist, educator
Johnston, Kenneth John astronomer, scientific director naval observatory
Karle, Isabella L. chemist
Karle, Jerome physicist, researcher
†Kimble, Melinda L. environmental administrator
Klein, Philipp Hillel electronic materials consultant
Knopman, Debra Sara hydrologist, policy analyst
Kouts, Herbert John Cecil physicist
Krebs, Martha physicist, federal science agency administrator
Labandeira, Conrad Christopher paleobiologist
Lash, Jonathan non-profit environment/development executive
Ledley, Robert Steven biophysicist
Lehman, Donald Richard physicist, educator
Lehmberg, Robert Henry research physicist
Mao, Ho-kwang geophysicist, educator
Mark, Hans Michael physicist, government official
Mason, Brian Harold geologist, curator
McEwen, Gerald Noah, Jr. bio scientist executive
Mead, Gilbert D(unbar) geophysicist, lawyer
Meijer, Paul Herman Ernst educator, physicist
Mielke, James Edward geochemist
Morehouse, David Frank geologist
Nelson, Alan Phillip nuclear energy scientist
Nelson, George Driver astronomy and education educator, former astronaut
O'Connor, Thomas Edward petroleum geologist, world bank officer
Oertel, Goetz K. H. physicist, professional association administrator
Oliver, William Albert, Jr. paleontologist
Oran, Elaine Surick physicist, engineer
Perros, Theodore Peter chemist, educator
Pojeta, John, Jr. geologist
Pope, Michael Thor chemistry educator
Preer, James Randolph academic administrator, science educator
Press, Frank geophysicist, educator
Prewitt, Charles Thompson geochemist
Roscher, Nina Matheny chemistry educator
Rosenberg, Jerome David physicist
Rosenberg, Norman Jack agricultural meteorologist, educator
Sansalone, William Robert biochemistry educator, researcher
Sayre, Edward Vale chemist
Scott, Raymond Peter William chemistry research educator, writer
†Selinger, Robin L.B. physics educator
Shapero, Donald Campbell physicist, government official
Siegel, Frederic Richard geology educator
Singer, Maxine Frank biochemist, scientific research company executive
Solomon, Sean Carl geophysicist, lab administrator
Spilhaus, Athelstan Frederick, Jr. oceanographer, association executive
Stanley, Daniel Jean geological oceanographer, senior scientist
Stewart, John Cameron environmental scientist
Strand, Kaj Aage astronomer
Sundaresan, P. Ramnathan research chemist, consultant
Uberall, Herbert Michael Stefan physicist, educator
Villforth, John Carl health physicist
Walker, Bailus, Jr. environmental scientist, dean, health facility administrator
Watters, Thomas Robert geologist, museum administrator
Werntz, Carl Weber physics educator
Wetherill, George West geophysicist, planetary scientist
White, John Arnold physics educator, research scientist
White, Robert Mayer meteorologist
Whitmore, Frank Clifford, Jr. geologist
Wilson, William Stanley oceanographer

Yochelson, Ellis L(eon) *paleontologist*
Yoder, Hatten Schuyler, Jr. *petrologist*
Youtcheff, John Sheldon *physicist*

FLORIDA

Alachua
Schneider, Richard T(heodore) *optics research executive, engineer*

Boca Raton
Resnick, Robert *physicist, educator*
Ross, Fred Michael *organic chemist*
Weissbach, Herbert *biochemist*
Wiesenfeld, John Richard *chemistry educator*

Boynton Beach
Balis, Moses Earl *biochemist, educator*
Fields, Theodore *consulting medical radiation physicist*

Cape Coral
West, John Merle *retired physicist, nuclear consultant*

Cocoa
Maddison, Ronald Charles *physicist*

Coral Gables
Criss, Cecil M. *chemistry educator*
Einspruch, Norman Gerald *physicist, educator*
Leblanc, Roger Maurice *chemistry educator*

Dania
Dodge, Richard Eugene *oceanographer, educator, marine life administrator*

Delray Beach
Drimmer, Bernard E. *research physicist*
Zarwyn, Berthold *physical scientist*

Fort Lauderdale
Zikakis, John P. *consultant, educator, researcher, biochemist*

Fort Myers
Horecker, Bernard Leonard *retired biochemistry educator*
Missimer, Thomas Michael *geologist*

Fort Pierce
Solon, Leonard R(aymond) *physicist, educator, consultant*

Gainesville
Andrew, Edward Raymond *physicist*
Carr, Thomas Deaderick *astronomer/physics educator, science administrator*
Cousins, Robert John *nutritional biochemist, educator*
Davis, George Kelso *nutrition biochemist, educator*
Hanrahan, Robert Joseph *chemist, educator*
Hanson, Harold Palmer *physicist, government official, editor, academic administrator*
Holloway, Paul Howard *materials science educator*
Hope, George Marion *vision scientist*
Jacobs, Alan Martin *physicist, educator*
Katritzky, Alan Roy *chemistry educator, consultant*
Klauder, John Rider *physics educator*
Micha, David Allan *chemistry and physics educator*
Ohrn, Nils Yngve *chemistry and physics educator*
Opdyke, Neil Donald *geology educator*
Person, Willis Bagley *chemistry educator*
Pop, Emil *research chemist*
Sisler, Harry Hall *chemist, educator*
Smith, Alexander Goudy *physics and astronomy educator*
Stehli, Francis Greenough *geologist, educator*
Sullivan, Neil Samuel *physicist, researcher, educator*
Trickey, Samuel Baldwin *physics educator, researcher, university administrator*
Yost, Richard Alan *chemistry educator*
Young, David Michael *biochemistry and molecular biology educator, physician*
Zerner, Michael Charles *chemistry and physics educator, consultant, researcher*

Hialeah Gardens
Stewart, Burch Byron *laboratory director*

Indialantic
Button, Kenneth John *physicist*

Jacksonville
Beattie, Donald A. *energy scientist, consultant*

Jupiter
Jacobson, Jerry Irving *biophysicist, theoretical physicist*

Key West
Trammell, Herbert Eugene *physicist, laboratory executive*

Lakeland
McFarlin, Richard Francis *industrial chemist, researcher*

Largo
Rester, Alfred Carl, Jr. *physicist*

Longboat Key
Brown, Henry *chemist*
Stapleton, Harvey James *physics educator*

Marco Island
Hyde, James Franklin *chemist, consultant*

Melbourne
Nelson, Gordon Leigh *chemist, educator*

Miami
Blanco, Luciano-Nilo *physicist*
Cai, Yong *chemist*
Donelan, Mark Anthony *physicist*
Glaser, Luis *biochemistry educator*
Mooers, Christopher Northrup Kennard *physical oceanographer, educator*
Ostlund, H. Gote *atmospheric and marine scientist, educator*
Rosenthal, Stanley Lawrence *meteorologist*
Rotenberg, Don Harris *chemist*
Van Vliet, Carolyne Marina *physicist, educator*
Wells, Daniel Ruth *physics educator*

Mount Dora
Foote, Nathan Maxted *retired physical science educator*

Naples
Leitner, Alfred *mathematical physicist, educator, educational film producer*
Stewart, Harris Bates, Jr. *oceanographer*

Ocala
Forgue, Stanley Vincent *physics educator*
Fredericks, William John *chemistry educator*

Orange Park
Walsh, Gregory Sheehan *optical systems professional*

Orlando
Baker, Peter Mitchell *laser scientist and executive, educator*
Barlow, Nadine Gail *planetary geoscientist*
Blue, Joseph Edward *physicist*
Llewellyn, Ralph Alvin *physics educator*
Silfvast, William T. *laser physics educator, consultant*
Ting, Robert Yen-ying *physicist*

Ormond Beach
Kanfer, Julian Norman *biochemist, educator*

Palm Beach Gardens
Bonifazi, Stephen *chemist*

Palmetto
Compton, Charles Daniel *chemistry educator*

Panama City Beach
Shugart, Cecil Glenn *retired physics educator*

Pembroke Pines
Herzog, Richard F. *retired science educator*

Pensacola
Steinhoff, Raymond O(akley) *consulting geologist*

Pompano Beach
Shang, Charles Yulin *medical physicist*

Punta Gorda
†Rohrbach, David Franklin *chemistry educator*

Saint Petersburg
Hansel, Paul George *physicist, consultant*

Sanibel
Herriott, Donald Richard *optical physicist*

Sarasota
Myerson, Albert Leon *physical chemist*
White, Jeffrey Lloyd *radiotherapy physicist*

Sun City Center
Calviello, Joseph Anthony *research electrophysicist, consultant*

Tallahassee
Caspar, Donald Louis Dvorak *biophysics and structural biology educator*
Choppin, Gregory Robert *chemistry educator*
Crow, Jack E. *physics administrator*
Herndon, Roy Clifford *physicist*
Ivlev, Boris Ivanovich *physicist*
Kemper, Kirby Wayne *physics educator*
Loper, David Eric *geophysics educator, mathematics educator*
Mandelkern, Leo *biophysics and chemistry educator*
Marshall, Alan George *chemistry and biochemistry educator*
Moulton, Grace Charbonnet *physics educator*
Owens, Joseph Francis, III *physics educator*
Pfeffer, Richard Lawrence *geophysics educator*
Rikvold, Per Arne *physics researcher and educator*
Robson, Donald *physics educator*
Schrieffer, John Robert *physics educator, science administrator*
Sushko, Yuri *physicist researcher*
Walborsky, Harry M. *chemistry educator, consultant*

Tampa
Binford, Jesse Stone, Jr. *chemistry educator*
Johnson, Anthony O'Leary (Andy Johnson) *meteorologist, consultant*

Venice
Leidheiser, Henry, Jr. *retired chemistry educator, consultant*

West Palm Beach
Witt, Gerhardt Meyer *hydrogeologist*

Weston
Atlas, David *meteorologist, research scientist*

GEORGIA

Albany
McManus, James William *chemist, researcher*

Athens
Allinger, Norman Louis *chemistry educator*
Black, Clanton Candler, Jr. *biochemistry educator, researcher*
Darvill, Alan G. *biochemist, botanist, educator*
DerVartanian, Daniel Vartan *biochemistry educator*
Eriksson, Karl-Erik Lennart *biochemist, educator*
Johnson, Michael Kenneth *chemistry educator*
Landau, David Paul *physics educator*
Pelletier, S. William *chemistry educator*
Schaefer, Henry Frederick, III *chemistry educator*
Shaw, James Scott *astronomy educator*
Yamaguchi, Yukio *chemistry research scientist*
Yen, William Mao-Shung *physicist*

Atlanta
Ashby, Eugene Christopher *chemistry educator*
Blankenship, Samuel Max *physicist*
Copeland, John Alexander, III *physicist*
Cramer, Howard Ross *geologist, environmental consultant*
Dennison, Daniel Bassel *chemist*
El-Sayed, Mostafa Amr *chemistry educator*
Finkelstein, David Ritz *physicist, educator, consultant*
Fox, Ronald Forrest *physics educator*
Goldstein, Jacob Herman *retired physical chemist*
Harmer, Don Stutler *physics and nuclear engineering educator*
Iacobucci, Guillermo Arturo *chemist*
Johnson, Ronald Carl *chemistry educator*
Kahn, Bernd *radiochemist, educator*
Lin, Ming-Chang *physical chemistry educator, researcher*
Long, Maurice Wayne *physicist, electrical engineer, radar consultant*
Massey, Walter Eugene *physicist, science foundation administrator*
McCormick, Donald Bruce *biochemist, educator*
Strekowski, Lucjan *chemistry educator*
Wartell, Roger Martin *biophysics educator*
Wiesenfeld, Kurt Arn *physicist, educator*
Wong, Ching-Ping *chemist, materials scientist, engineer, educator*

Conyers
Hungerford, Lugene Green *physicist*

Griffin
Georgiev, Goshko Atanasov *agrometeorologist, researcher*

Grovetown
Muzik, Nancy Lynn *chemist*

Hull
Melton, Charles Estel *retired physicist, educator*

Marietta
Bridges, Alan Lynn *physicist, computer scientist, systems software engineer*

Peachtree City
Roobol, Norman Richard *industrial painting consultant, educator*

Riverdale
Awachie, Peter Ifeacho Anazoba *chemistry educator, research chemist*

Savannah
Anantha Narayanan, Venkataraman *physics educator*
Froelicher, Franz *chemist, geologist, environmental consultant*
Simonaitis, Richard Ambrose *chemist*
Walter, Paul Hermann Lawrence *chemistry educator*
Windom, Herbert Lynn *oceanographer, environmental scientist*

Statesboro
Mobley, Cleon Marion, Jr. (Chip Mobley) *physics educator, real estate executive*

Suwanee
†White, Gregory Dale *environmental consultant*

Tucker
Valk, Henry Snowden *physicist, educator*

Warner Robins
Lavdas, Leonidas G. *meteorologist, religion educator*

HAWAII

Camp H M Smith
Surface, Stephen Walter *water treatment chemist, environmental protection specialist*

Hawaii National Park
Swanson, Donald Alan *geologist*

Hickam AFB
Miller, David Allen *air force officer, observatory administrator*

Hilo
Griep, David Michael *astronomical scientist, researcher*

Honolulu
Chambers, Kenneth Carter *astronomer*
Hawke, Bernard Ray *planetary scientist*
Herbig, George Howard *astronomer, educator*
Ihrig, Judson La Moure *chemist*
Joseph, Robert David *astronomer, educator*
Keil, Klaus *geology educator, consultant*
Khan, Mohammad Asad *geophysicist, educator, former energy minister and senator of Pakistan*
Kong, Laura S. L. *geophysicist*
Mader, Charles Lavern *chemist*
Meech, Karen Jean *astronomer*
Ogburn, Hugh Bell *chemical engineer, consultant*
Raleigh, Cecil Baring *geophysicist*
Rosendal, Hans Erik *meteorologist*
Yamamoto, Harry Yoshimi *biochemist, educator*

Kahului
Nishimoto, Marc Makoto *research chemist*

Pukalani
Fredericksen, Walter Mailand *behavioral and ocean sciences educator emeritus*

IDAHO

Moscow
Bitterwolf, Thomas Edwin *chemistry educator*
Goszczynski, Stefan *chemistry educator*
Miller, Maynard Malcolm *geologist, educator, research institute director, explorer, state legislator*
Shreeve, Jean'ne Marie *chemist, educator*
Stumpf, Bernhard Josef *physicist*

Pocatello
Hazen, Dean Scott *meteorologist*

ILLINOIS

Abbott Park
Jeng, Tzyy-Wen *biochemist*

Argonne
Blander, Milton *chemist*
Carpenter, John Marland *engineer, physicist*
Derrick, Malcolm *physicist*
DiMelfi, Ronald J. *materials scientist*
Fields, Paul Robert *retired research nuclear chemist, consultant*
Green, David William *chemist, educator*
Herzenberg, Caroline Stuart Littlejohn *physicist*
Katz, Joseph Jacob *chemist, educator*
Lawson, Robert Davis *theoretical nuclear physicist*
Morss, Lester Robert *chemist*
Perlow, Gilbert J(erome) *physicist, editor*
Peshkin, Murray *physicist*
Sabau, Carmen Sybile *chemist*
Schiffer, John Paul *physicist*
†Sedlet, Jacob *chemist*
Steindler, Martin Joseph *chemist*
Stock, Leon Milo *chemist, educator*

Arlington Heights
Lewin, Seymour Zalman *chemistry educator, consultant*
Smith, Norman Obed *physical chemist, educator*
Walter, Robert Irving *chemistry educator, chemist*

Batavia
Bardeen, William Allan *research physicist*
Chrisman, Bruce Lowell *physicist, administrator*
Jonckheere, Alan Mathew *physicist*
Lach, Joseph Theodore *physicist*
Peoples, John, Jr. *physicist, researcher*
†Quigg, Chris *physicist*
Witherell, Michael S. *physicist*

Brookfield
Stejskal, Joseph Frank, Jr. *carbohydrate chemist*

Carbondale
Wotiz, John Henry *chemist, educator*

Champaign
Buschbach, Thomas Charles *geologist, consultant*
Cartwright, Keros *hydrogeologist, researcher*
Gross, David Lee *geologist*
Herendeen, Robert Albert *environmental scientist*
Herzog, Beverly Leah *hydrogeologist*
Simmons, Ralph Oliver *physics educator*
Slichter, Charles Pence *physicist, educator*
Whitaker, Stephen Taylor *geologist, oil exploration consultant*
Wolfram, Stephen *physicist, computer company executive*

Chicago
Blumberg, Avrom Aaron *physical chemistry educator*
Bonham, Russell Aubrey *chemistry educator*
†Chambers, Donald Arthur *biochemistry and molecular medicine educator*
Clayton, Robert Norman *chemist, educator*
Collins, Harvey Taliaferro *chemist*
Coppersmith, Susan Nan *physicist*
Cronin, James Watson *physicist, educator*
Epstein, Wolfgang *biochemist, educator*
Erber, Thomas *physics educator*
Evans, Earl Alison, Jr. *biochemist*
Fano, Ugo *physicist, educator*
Fanta, Paul Edward *chemist, educator*
Freed, Karl Frederick *chemistry educator*
Fried, Josef *chemist, educator*
Frisch, Henry Jonathan *physics educator*
†Frydman, Lucio *chemist, researcher, educator*
Fultz, Dave *meteorology educator*
Gislason, Eric Arni *chemistry educator*
Goldsmith, Julian Royce *geochemist, educator*
Goldwasser, Eugene *biochemist, educator*
Gomer, Robert *chemistry educator*
Halpern, Jack *chemist, educator*
Harvey, Ronald Gilbert *research chemist*
Hildebrand, Roger Henry *astrophysicist, physicist*
Huston, John Lewis *chemistry educator*
Hutchison, Clyde Allen, Jr. *chemistry educator*
Iqbal, Zafar Mohd *cancer researcher, biochemist, pharmacologist, toxicologist, consultant, molecular biologist*
Jain, Nemi Chand *chemist, coating scientist, educator*
Kleppa, Ole J. *chemistry educator*
Kouvel, James Spyros *physicist, educator*
Lederman, Leon Max *physicist, educator*
Levi-Setti, Riccardo *physicist, director*
Levy, Donald Harris *chemistry educator*
Liao, Shutsung *biochemist, oncologist*
Makinen, Marvin William *biophysicist, educator*
Margoliash, Emanuel *biochemist, educator*
Meyer, Peter *physicist, educator*
Mintzer, David *physics educator*
Nagel, Sidney Robert *physics educator*
Nambu, Yoichiro *physics educator*
Oehme, Reinhard *physicist, educator*
Oka, Takeshi *physicist, chemist, astronomer, educator*
Olsen, Edward John *geologist, educator*
Oxtoby, David William *chemistry educator*
Palmer, Patrick Edward *radio astronomer, educator*
Platzman, George William *geophysicist, educator*
Reiffel, Leonard *physicist, scientific consultant*
Robbins, Kenneth Carl *biochemist*
Rosner, Jonathan Lincoln *physicist, educator*
Rosner, Robert *astrophysicist*
Sachs, Robert Green *physicist, educator, laboratory administrator*
Sager, William Frederick *retired chemistry educator*
Schillinger, Edwin Joseph *physics educator*
Schug, Kenneth Robert *chemistry educator*
Sibener, Steven Jay *chemistry educator*
Sills, Thomas W. *physical science educator*
Simpson, John Alexander *physicist*
Skilling, Thomas Ethelbert, III *meteorologist, meteorology educator*
Steck, Theodore Lyle *biochemistry and molecular biology educator, physician*
Steiner, Donald Frederick *biochemist, physician, educator*

Tao, Mariano *biochemistry educator*
Trenary, Michael *chemistry educator*
Truran, James Wellington, Jr. *astrophysicist*
Turkevich, Anthony Leonid *chemist, educator*
Turner, Michael Stanley *physics educator*
Williams-Ashman, Howard Guy *biochemist, educator*
Winston, Roland *physicist, educator*
Wolf-Chase, Grace Annamarie *astronomer, astrophysicist*
York, Donald Gilbert *astronomy educator, researcher*

Deerfield
Guttman, Arnold R. *chemist, educator*

Dekalb
Kimball, Clyde William *physicist, educator*
Rossing, Thomas D. *physics educator*

Des Plaines
Arena, Blaise Joseph *research chemist*

Downers Grove
Hubbard, Lincoln Beals *medical physicist, consultant*

Elmhurst
Betinis, Emanuel James *physics and mathematics educator*

Evanston
Allred, Albert Louis *chemistry educator*
Basolo, Fred *chemistry educator*
Bordwell, Frederick George *chemistry educator*
Cohen, Jerome Bernard *materials science educator*
Freeman, Arthur J. *physics educator*
Ibers, James Arthur *chemist, educator*
Johnson, David Lynn *materials scientist, educator*
Klotz, Irving Myron *chemist, educator*
Lambert, Joseph Buckley *chemistry educator*
Letsinger, Robert Lewis *chemistry educator*
Meshii, Masahiro *materials science educator*
Oakes, Robert James *physics educator*
†Okal, Emile Andre *geophysicist, educator*
Olson, Gregory Bruce *materials science and engineering educator, academic director*
Pople, John Anthony *chemistry educator*
Sachtler, Wolfgang Max Hugo *chemistry educator*
Seidman, David N(athaniel) *materials science and engineering educator*
Shriver, Duward Felix *chemistry educator, researcher, consultant*
Silverman, Richard Bruce *chemist, biochemist, educator*
Spears, Kenneth George *chemistry educator*
Taam, Ronald Everett *physics and astronomy educator*
Ulmer, Melville Paul *physics and astronomy educator*
Vaynman, Semyon *materials scientist, educator*
Wang, Jian-Sheng *materials scientist*
Weertman, Johannes *materials science educator*
Weertman, Julia Randall *materials science and engineering educator*
Wessels, Bruce W. *materials scientist, educator*

Glen Ellyn
Mooring, F. Paul *physics editor*

Glencoe
Grossweiner, Leonard Irwin *physicist, educator*

Glenview
Rorig, Kurt Joachim *chemist, research director*

Hinsdale
Kaminsky, Manfred Stephan *physicist*

Homewood
Parker, Eugene Newman *retired physicist, educator*

Lake Forest
Weston, Arthur Walter *chemist, scientific and business executive*

Lemont
Williams, Jack Marvin *research chemist*

Lisle
Staab, Thomas Eugene *chemist*

Lockport
Bhatti, Neeloo *environmental scientist*

Marseilles
Van Horn, John Kenneth *health physicist, consultant*

Mount Carmel
Fornoff, Frank J(unior) *retired chemistry educator, consultant*

Naperville
Arzoumanidis, Gregory G. *chemist*
Rosenmann, Daniel *physicist, educator*
Sellers, Gregory Jude *physicist*
Sherren, Anne Terry *chemistry educator*

North Chicago
Loga, Sanda *physicist, educator*

Northbrook
Colton, Frank Benjamin *retired chemist*

Northfield
Shabica, Charles Wright *geologist, earth science educator*

O'Fallon
Jenner, William Alexander *meteorologist, educator*

Palos Hills
Vasiliauskas, Edmund *chemistry educator*

Peoria
Chamberlain, Joseph Miles *retired astronomer, educator*
Cunningham, Raymond Leo *research chemist, retired*
Nielsen, Harald Christian *retired chemist*
Rankin, John Carter *consulting chemist*
Saha, Badal Chandra *biochemist*

Philo
Wood, Susanne Griffiths *environmental chemist, microbiologist*

Rock Island
Anderson, Richard Charles *geology educator*
Hammer, William Roy *paleontologist, educator*
Sundelius, Harold W. *geology educator*

Rockford
Walhout, Justine Simon *chemistry educator*

Round Lake
Breillatt, Julian Paul, Jr. *biochemist, biomedical engineer*

Savoy
Lane, Russell Watson *water treatment consultant retired, chemist*

Skokie
Becker, Daniel Paul *medicinal chemist, researcher*

South Holland
Capriglione, Ralph Raymond *geologist, educator*

Springfield
Gallina, Charles Onofrio *nuclear scientist*
Noyce, James Roger *chemist, consultant*

Urbana
Beak, Peter Andrew *chemistry educator*
Birnbaum, Howard Kent *materials science educator*
Brown, Theodore Lawrence *chemistry educator*
Crofts, Antony Richard *biophysics educator*
Drickamer, Harry George *retired chemistry educator*
Dunn, Floyd *biophysicist, bioengineer, educator*
Ehrlich, Gert *science educator, researcher*
Fantini, Sergio *physical science researcher, educator*
Forbes, Richard Mather *biochemistry educator*
Ginsberg, Donald Maurice *physicist, educator*
Goldwasser, Edwin Leo *physicist*
Govindjee *biophysics and biology educator*
Greene, Laura Helen *physicist*
Gruebele, Martin *chemistry educator*
Gutowsky, Herbert Sander *chemistry educator*
Hager, Lowell Paul *biochemistry educator*
Iben, Icko, Jr. *astrophysicist, educator*
Jonas, Jiri *chemistry educator*
Kirkpatrick, R(obert) James *geology educator*
Klein, Miles Vincent *physics educator*
Kushner, Mark Jay *physics and engineering educator*
Lauterbur, Paul C(hristian) *chemistry educator*
Lazarus, David *physicist, educator*
Makri, Nancy *chemistry educator*
Mapother, Dillon Edward *physicist, university official*
Raheel, Mastura *textile scientist, educator*
Rowland, Theodore Justin *physicist, educator*
Salamon, Myron Ben *physicist, educator*
Satterthwaite, Cameron B. *physics educator*
Schweizer, Kenneth Steven *physics educator*
Simon, Jack Aaron *geologist, former state official*
Snyder, Lewis Emil *astrophysicist*
Suslick, Kenneth Sanders *chemistry educator*
Switzer, Robert Lee *biochemistry educator*
Woese, Carl R. *biophysicist, microbiology educator*
Wolynes, Peter Guy *chemistry researcher, educator*

Wheaton
Wolfram, Thomas *physicist*

Wilmette
Rocek, Jan *chemist, educator*

Woodridge
Hedge, Jeanne Colleen *computer programmer*

Worth
Ammeraal, Robert Neal *biochemist*

INDIANA

Bloomington
Bent, Robert Demo *physicist, educator*
Bundy, Wayne M. *retired geologist, consultant*
Cameron, John M. *nuclear scientist, educator, science administrator*
Chisholm, Malcolm Harold *chemistry educator*
Davidson, Ernest Roy *chemist, educator*
Day, Harry Gilbert *nutritional biochemist, consultant*
Edmondson, Frank Kelley *astronomer*
Goodman, Charles David *physicist, educator*
Hattin, Donald Edward *geologist, educator*
Hendry, Archibald Wagstaff *physics educator*
Johnson, Hollis Ralph *astronomy educator*
Macfarlane, Malcolm Harris *physics educator*
Parmenter, Charles Stedman *chemistry educator*
Peters, Dennis Gail *chemist*
Pollock, Robert Elwood *nuclear physicist*
Putnam, Frank William *biochemistry and immunology educator*
Schaich, William L. *physics educator*

Carmel
Watson, Ian Allen *chemist*

Chesterton
Crewe, Albert Victor *physicist, artist, business executive*

Elkhart
Free, Helen Mae *chemist, consultant*
Rand, Phillip Gordon *chemist*

Fort Wayne
Cox, David Jackson *biochemistry educator*
Stevenson, Kenneth Lee *chemist, educator*

Greenfield
Myerholtz, Ralph W., Jr. *retired chemical company executive, research chemist*

Hammond
Vojcak, Edward Daniel *metallurgist*

Indianapolis
Aprison, Morris Herman *biochemist, experimental and theoretical neurobiologist, emeritus educator*
Bulloff, Jack John *physical chemist, consultant*
Fife, Wilmer Krafft *chemistry educator*
†Henry, Kenneth James, Jr. *medicinal chemist, anti-infectives researcher*
Hermann, Robert Bell *physical chemist, consultant*
Mihelich, Edward David *chemist*
Mirsky, Arthur *geologist, educator*
Riggin, Leh-daw Alice *analytical chemist*
Scriven, Eric Frank Vaughan *chemist, researcher*
Wong, David T. *biochemist*

Lafayette
Brewster, James Henry *retired chemistry educator*
Feuer, Henry *chemist, educator*
Gartenhaus, Solomon *physicist*
Judd, William Robert *engineering geologist, educator*
Loeffler, Frank Joseph *physicist, educator*
Porile, Norbert Thomas *chemistry educator*

Mishawaka
Braunsdorf, James Allen *physics educator*

Notre Dame
Browne, Cornelius Payne *physics educator*
Feigl, Dorothy Marie *chemistry educator, university official*
Helquist, Paul M. *chemistry educator, researcher*
Huber, Paul William *biochemistry educator, researcher*
Marshalek, Eugene Richard *physics educator*
Scheidt, W. Robert *chemistry educator, researcher*
Schuler, Robert Hugo *chemist, educator*
Thomas, John Kerry *chemistry educator*

Purdue University
Brown, Herbert Charles *chemistry educator*

Terre Haute
Guthrie, Frank Albert *chemistry educator*
Taylor, Dean Alan *physicist*

West Lafayette
Adelman, Steven Allen *theoretical physical chemist, chemistry educator*
Amy, Jonathan Weekes *scientist, educator*
Barnes, Virgil Everett, II *physics educator*
BeMiller, James Noble *biochemist, educator*
Cramer, William Anthony *biochemistry and biophysics researcher, educator*
Diamond, Sidney *chemist, educator*
Grimley, Robert Thomas *chemistry educator*
Hanks, Alan R. *chemistry educator*
Laskowski, Michael, Jr. *chemist, educator*
Leap, Darrell Ivan *hydrogeologist*
Lipschutz, Michael Elazar *chemistry educator, consultant, researcher*
Margerum, Dale William *chemistry educator*
McMillin, David Robert *chemistry educator*
Melhorn, Wilton Newton *geosciences educator*
Morrison, Harry *chemistry educator, university dean*
Overhauser, Albert Warner *physicist*
Rossmann, Michael George *biochemist, educator*
Truce, William Everett *chemist, educator*

IOWA

Ames
Barnes, Richard George *physicist, educator*
Barton, Thomas Jackson *chemistry educator, researcher*
Bowen, George Hamilton, Jr. *astrophysicist, educator*
Clem, John Richard *physicist, educator*
Corbett, John Dudley *chemistry educator*
Fritz, James Sherwood *chemistry educator*
Gschneidner, Karl Albert, Jr. *metallurgist, educator, editor, consultant*
Horowitz, Jack *biochemistry educator*
Jacobson, Robert Andrew *chemistry educator*
Moyer, James Wallace *physicist, consultant*
Peterson, Francis *physicist, educator*
Ruedenberg, Klaus *theoretical chemist, educator*
Russell, Glen Allan *chemist, educator*
Smith, John Francis *materials science educator*
Svec, Harry John *chemist, educator*
Thompson, Donald Oscar *physicist*
Yeung, Edward Szeshing *chemist*

Cedar Falls
†Koob, Robert Duane *chemistry educator, educational administrator*

Cedar Rapids
Boettcher, Norbe Birosel *chemist*

Coralville
Bell, Raymond Martin *retired physics educator*

Iowa City
Baker, Richard Graves *geology educator, palynologist*
Burton, Donald Joseph *chemistry educator*
Donelson, John Everett *biochemistry educator, molecular biologist*
Grabbe, Crockett Lane *physicist, researcher, writer*
Gurnett, Donald Alfred *physics educator*
Koch, Donald LeRoy *geologist, state agency administrator*
Linhardt, Robert John *medicinal chemistry educator*
Montgomery, Rex *biochemist, educator*
Nair, Vasu *chemist, educator*
Plapp, Bryce Vernon *biochemistry educator*
Routh, Joseph Isaac *biochemist*
Tallent, William Hugh *chemist, research administrator*
Titze, Ingo Roland *physics educator*
Van Allen, James Alfred *physicist, educator*

North Liberty
Glenister, Brian Frederick *geologist, educator*

Spirit Lake
Brett, George Wendell *retired geologist, philatelist*

KANSAS

Kansas City
Ebner, Kurt Ewald *biochemistry educator*
Noelken, Milton Edward *biochemistry educator, researcher*

Lawrence
Ammar, Raymond George *physicist, educator*
Angino, Ernest Edward *retired geology educator*
Dreschhoff, Gisela Auguste Marie *physicist, educator*
Enos, Paul *geologist, educator*
Gerhard, Lee Clarence *geologist, educator*
Harmony, Marlin Dale *chemistry educator*
Landgrebe, John Allan *chemistry educator*
Mitscher, Lester Allen *chemist, educator*
Olea, Ricardo Antonio *mathematical geologist, petroleum engineer*

Lebanon
Colwell, John Edwin *retired aerospace scientist*

Manhattan
Setser, Donald Wayne *chemistry educator*
Taketomi, Susamu *physicist, researcher*

North Newton
Quiring, Frank Stanley *chemist, educator*

Overland Park
Ostby, Frederick Paul, Jr. *meteorologist, retired government official*

Shawnee Mission
Billings, Patricia Jean *inventor*
Stanton, Gary Charles *research chemist*

Silver Lake
Nuzman, Carl Edward *retired hydrologist*

Topeka
Barton, Janice Sweeny *chemistry educator*
Cohen, Sheldon Hersh *chemistry educator, university official*

Wichita
Andrew, Kenneth L. *research physicist, physics educator*
Cowdery, Robert Douglas *consulting geologist*

KENTUCKY

Ashland
Mitchell, Maurice McClellan, Jr. *chemist*

Bowling Green
Slocum, Donald Warren *chemist*

Carrollton
Tatera, James Frank *chemist, process analysis specialist*

Danville
Muzyka, Jennifer Louise *chemist, educator*

Florence
†Lawson, Harry Wilbur *chemist, consultant, writer*

Highland Heights
Redding, Rogers Walker *physics educator*

Lexington
Brown, William Randall *geology educator*
Cheniae, George Maurice *plant biochemist*
DeLong, Lance Eric *physics educator, researcher*
Elitzur, Moshe *physicist, educator*
Hamilton-Kemp, Thomas Rogers *organic chemist, educator*
Kern, Bernard Donald *retired educator, physicist*
Liu, Keh-Fei Frank *physicist, educator*
Lodder, Robert Andrew *chemistry and pharmaceutics educator*
Meier, Mark Stephan *chemistry educator*
Ng, Kwok-Wai *physics educator*

Louisville
Belanger, William Joseph *chemist, polymer applications consultant*
Cohn, David V(alor) *oral biology and biochemistry educator*
Furka, Árpád *organic chemist, educator*
Prough, Russell Allen *biochemistry educator*
Taylor, Kenneth Grant *chemistry educator*

Murray
Loganathan, Bommanna Gounder *environmental chemist, biologist, researcher, educator*
Mateja, John Frederick *science educator*

Sturgis
Thornsberry, Willis Lee, Jr. *chemist*

Williamsburg
†Newquist, Lawrence Allen *physics educator*

LOUISIANA

Alexandria
Rogers, James Edwin *geology and hydrology consultant*

Baton Rouge
Coleman, James Malcolm *marine geology educator*
†Frank, Juhan *astrophysicist*
Hazel, Joseph Ernest *geology educator, stratigrapher*
Lambremont, Edward Nelson, Jr. *nuclear science educator*
†Mainkar, Neeraj Arvind *simulation modeler, physicist*
Mc Glynn, Sean Patrick *physical chemist, educator*
O'Connell, Robert Francis *physics educator*
Omoike, Isaac Irabor *chemist, publisher, author*
Pryor, William Austin *chemistry educator*
Roberts, Harry Heil *geological research administrator*
Traynham, James Gibson *chemist, educator*

West, Philip William chemistry educator

Covington
Vercellotti, John Raymond research chemist

Kenner
deMonsabert, Winston Russel chemist, consultant

Metairie
Hartman, James Austin retired geologist
Horkowitz, Sylvester Peter chemist

New Orleans
Benerito, Ruth Rogan (Mrs. Frank H. Benerito) chemist
Bertoniere, Noelie Rita research chemist
Dribus, John Robert geologist
Perdew, John Paul physics educator, condensed matter and density functional theorist
Rondeau, Clement Robert petroleum geologist
Rosensteel, George Thomas physics educator, nuclear physicist
Roskoski, Robert, Jr. biochemist, educator, author
Seab, Charles Gregory astrophysicist
Thomas, Robert Allen environmental communications educator

MAINE

Chebeague Island
Allen, Clayton Hamilton physicist, acoustician

Friendship
Owen, Wadsworth oceanographer, consultant

Kittery
McNally, James Henry physicist, defense consultant

Orono
Borns, Harold William, Jr. geologist, educator
Norton, Stephen Allen geological sciences educator

Waterford
Cutler, Cassius Chapin physicist, educator

MARYLAND

Aberdeen
Russell, William Alexander, Jr. environmental scientist

Annapolis
Bontoyan, Warren Roberts chemist, state laboratories administrator
Brunk, William Edward astronomer
Clotworthy, John Harris oceanographic consultant
Hammer, Jacob Myer physicist, consultant
Johnson, David Simonds meteorologist
Rowell, Charles Frederick chemistry educator

Baltimore
Albinak, Marvin Joseph chemistry educator
Allen, Ronald John astrophysics educator, researcher
Bowen, Kit Hansel, Jr. chemistry educator
Chien, Chia-Ling physics educator
Crippen, Raymond Charles chemist, consultant
Dagdigian, Paul Joseph chemistry educator
Dicello, John Francis, Jr. physicist, educator
Djordjevic, Borislav Boro materials scientist, researcher
Eichhorn, Gunther Louis chemist
Englund, Paul Theodore biochemist, educator
Feldman, Gordon physics educator
Freire, Ernesto biophysicist, educator
Fulton, Thomas theoretical physicist, educator
Green, Robert Edward, Jr. physicist, educator
Grossman, Lawrence biochemist, educator
Haig, Frank Rawle physics educator, clergyman
Hauser, Michael George astrophysicist
Helm, Donald Cairney hydrogeologist, engineer, educator
Henry, Richard Conn astrophysicist, educator
Huang, Pien Chien biochemistry educator, scientist
Judd, Brian Raymond physicist, educator
Koski, Walter S. chemistry educator, scientist
Krolik, Julian Henry astrophysicist, educator
Kruger, Jerome materials science educator, consultant
Lane, Malcolm Daniel biological chemistry educator
Larrabee, Martin Glover biophysics educator
Lee, Yung-Keun physicist, educator
Madansky, Leon particle physicist, educator
Marsh, Bruce David geologist, educator
McCarty, Richard Earl biochemist, biochemistry educator
Moos, H. Warren physicist, astronomer, educator, administrator
Newman, William Louis geologist
Nickon, Alex chemist, educator
Pettijohn, Francis John geology educator
Posner, Gary Herbert chemist, educator
Roseman, Saul biochemist, educator
Roth, George Stanley research biochemist, physiologist
†Ruknudin, Abdul biophysicist, researcher, educator
Shamoo, Adil Elias biochemist, biophysicist, educator
Silverstone, Harris J. chemistry educator
Stanley, Steven Mitchell paleobiologist, educator
Storrs, Alexander David astronomer
Weaver, Kenneth Newcomer geologist, state official
Westerhout, Gart retired astronomer
Williams, Robert Eugene astronomer

Bel Air
Cash, (Cynthia) LaVerne physicist

Beltsville
Johnson, Phyllis Elaine chemist

Berlin
Passwater, Richard Albert biochemist, author

Bethesda
Ahmad, Imad Aldean astronomer, consultant
Ashwell, G. Gilbert biochemist
Azaryan, Anahit Vazgenovna biochemist, researcher
Backus, Robert Coburn biophysical chemist
Becker, Edwin Demuth chemist, laboratory director
Cantoni, Giulio Leonardo biochemist, government official
Cassman, Marvin biochemist
Daly, John W. chemistry research administrator
Ehrenstein, Gerald biophysicist
Fales, Henry Marshall chemist
Gelboin, Harry Victor biochemistry educator, researcher
Gellert, Martin Frank biochemist
Gerwin, Brenda Isen research biochemist
Huebner, John Stephen geologist
Kaufman, Seymour biochemist
Kindt, Thomas James chemist
Korn, Edward David biochemist
†Livermore, Arthur Hamilton chemist, consultant
Murayama, Makio biochemist
Nash, Howard Allen biochemist, researcher
Nirenberg, Marshall Warren biochemist
Rice, Kenner Cralle medicinal chemist
Silberberg, Rein nuclear astrophysicist, researcher
Sinclair, Warren Keith radiation biophysicist, organization executive, consultant
Stadtman, Earl Reece biochemist
Tabor, Herbert biochemist
Trus, Benes Louis structural chemist
†Tuorkowski, Robert John hydrogeologist
Vaughan, Martha biochemist
Witkop, Bernhard chemist
Wright, James Roscoe chemist
Zimmerberg, Joshua Jay cellular biophysicist
Zwanzig, Robert Walter chemist, physical science educator

Cabin John
Shropshire, Walter, Jr. biophysicist emeritus, pastor
Townsend, John William, Jr. physicist, retired federal aerospace agency executive

Cambridge
Koch-Eilers, Evamaria Wysk oceanographer, researcher

Catonsville
Vanderlinde, Raymond Edward clinical chemist

Chevy Chase
Gavin, James Raphael, III biochemist
Hudson, Ralph P. physicist
Promisel, Nathan E. materials scientist, metallurgical engineer
Sinclair, Rolf Malcolm retired physicist

Cobb Island
Vanderslice, Joseph Thomas chemist

College Park
Benesch, William Milton molecular physicist, atmospheric researcher, educator
Brodsky, Marc Herbert physicist, research and publishing executive
Carton, James Alfred oceanographer, educator
DeSilva, Alan W. physics educator, researcher
Dragt, Alexander James physicist
Fenselau, Catherine Clarke chemistry educator
Fisher, Michael Ellis mathematical physicist, chemist
Franz, Judy R. physics educator
Gluckstern, Robert Leonard physics educator
Greenberg, Oscar Wallace physicist, educator
Griem, Hans Rudolf physicist, educator
Grim, Samuel Oram chemistry educator
Helz, George Rudolph chemistry educator, research center director
Irwin, George Rankin physicist, mechanical engineering educator
Kearney, Philip Charles biochemist
Kundu, Mukul Ranjan physics and astronomy educator
Lubkin, Gloria Becker physicist
Mc Donald, Frank Bethune physicist
Misner, Charles William physics educator
Rabin, Herbert physics educator, university official
Rasmusson, Eugene Martin meteorology researcher
Redish, Edward Frederick physicist, educator
Silverman, Joseph chemistry educator, scientist
Skuja, Andris physics educator
Snow, George Abraham physicist
Thirumalai, Devarajan physical sciences researcher, educator
Webb, Richard Alan physicist
Zen, E-an research geologist, educator

Columbia
Bareis, Donna Lynn biochemist, pharmacologist
Clark, Billy Pat physicist
Deutsch, Robert William physicist
Fisher, Dale John chemist, instrumentation and medical diagnostic device investigator
Khare, Mohan chemist
Lijinsky, William biochemist

Crofton
Watson, Robert Tanner retired physical scientist

Darnestown
Hoffer, James Brian physicist, consultant

Dayton
Fischell, Robert Ellentuch physicist

Forest Hill
Stuempfle, Arthur Karl physical science manager

Fort Washington
Behrens, James William physicist, administrator, author

Frederick
Carton, Robert John environmental scientist
Cragg, Gordon Mitchell government chemist
Garver, Robert Vernon research physicist
Smith, Sharron Williams chemistry educator
Szeliga, Jan Stefan chemist

Frostburg
Tam, Francis Man Kei physics educator

Gaithersburg
Adams, James Michael nuclear physicist
Cahn, John Werner metallurgist, educator
Caplin, Jerrold Leon health physicist
Caswell, Randall Smith physicist
Celotta, Robert James physicist
Chi, Peter Howard physicist
Costrell, Louis physicist
Hamer, Walter Jay chemical consultant, science writer
Harman, George Gibson physicist, consultant
Hougen, Jon Torger physical chemist, researcher
Hsu, Stephen Ming materials scientist, chemical engineer
Hubbell, John Howard radiation physicist
Jacox, Marilyn Esther chemist
Phillips, William Daniel physicist
Pierce, Daniel Thornton physicist
Reader, Joseph physicist
Sengers, Johanna M. H. Levelt thermophysicist
Taylor, Barry Norman physicist
Verkouteren, Robert Michael chemist
Wiese, Wolfgang Lothar physicist

Garrett Park
Melville, Robert Seaman chemist

Germantown
Nazarian, Ashot chemical physicist, consultant, researcher
Steadman, Stephen Geoffrey physicist

Glenelg
Williams, Donald John research physicist

Greenbelt
Degnan, John James, III physicist
Häkkinen, Sirpa Marja Anneli oceanographer
Hollis, Jan Michael astrophysicist, scientific computer analyst
Holt, Stephen S. astrophysicist
Krueger, Arlin James physicist
Maran, Stephen Paul astronomer
Mather, John Cromwell astrophysicist
Mumma, Michael Jon physicist
Ormes, Jonathan Fairfield astrophysicist, science administrator, researcher
Parkinson, Claire L. climatologist
Ramaty, Reuven Robert physicist, researcher
Simpson, Joanne Malkus meteorologist
Stief, Louis John chemist
Wood, H(oward) John, III astrophysicist, astronomer

Hunt Valley
Moore, Jeffrey chemical information scientist

Laurel
Avery, William Hinckley physicist, chemist
Babin, Steven Michael atmospheric scientist, researcher
Kossiakoff, Alexander chemist
Lui, Anthony Tat Yin physicist
Maurer, Richard Hornsby physicist

Mechanicsville
Henderson, Madeline Mary (Berry) (Berry Henderson) chemist, researcher, consultant

Monrovia
Tokar, John Michael retired oceanographer, ocean engineer

Montgomery Village
Kushner, Lawrence Maurice physical chemist

Parkton
Fitzgerald, Edwin Roger physicist, educator

Parkville
Jensen, Arthur Seigfried consulting engineering physicist

Pasadena
Young, Russell Dawson physics consultant

Potomac
Baer, Ledolph oceanographer, meteorologist
Engelmann, Rudolf Jacob meteorologist
Epstein, Edward S. meteorologist

Queenstown
Denton, Lawrence Monette consultant meteorologist, historian

Reisterstown
Tannenbaum, Harvey defense technology consultant

Rockville
Berger, Robert Lewis retired biophysicist, researcher
Buchanan, John Donald retired health physicist, radiochemist
Finlayson, John Sylvester biochemist
Grady, Lee Timothy pharmaceutical chemist
Jamieson, Graham A. biochemist, organization official
Luo, Ray physical chemist, biochemist
McClamroch, Donal Lee, Jr. forensic chemist, educator
Murray, Peter metallurgist, manufacturing company executive
Schindler, Albert Isadore physicist, educator
Zoon, Kathryn Egloff biochemist

Salisbury
Mulligan, Joseph Francis physicist, historian of science, educator

Silver Spring
Douglass, Carl Dean biochemistry consultant, former government official
Gibson, William Michael oceanographer
Leonard, Dorothy Louise environmental analyst
Rueger, Lauren John retired physicist, consultant
Scheer, Milton David chemical physicist
White, Herbert Laverne meterologist, federal agency administrator
Young, Jay Alfred chemical safety and health consultant, writer, editor

Suitland
Rao, Desiraju Bhavanarayana meteorologist, oceanographer, educator

Temple Hills
Strauss, Simon Wolf chemist, materials scientist

Upper Marlboro
Hunt, James Christopher physics and astronomy educator, history of science researcher

West Bethesda
Stoyanov, Aleksandr John physicist, researcher

MASSACHUSETTS

Acton
Conoby, Joseph Francis chemist

Amherst
Archer, Ronald Dean chemist, educator
Byron, Frederick William, Jr. physicist, educator, university vice chancellor
Ehrlich, Paul chemist, educator
Fink, Richard David chemist, educator
Goldstein, Joseph Irwin materials scientist, educator
†Hallock, Robert Bruce physics educator
Kantor, Simon William chemistry educator
MacKnight, William John chemist, educator
Peterson, Gerald Alvin physics educator
Rabin, Monroe Stephen Zane physicist
Romer, Robert Horton physicist, educator
Scott, David Knight physicist, university administrator
Slakey, Linda Louise biochemistry educator
Stein, Richard Stephen chemistry educator

Andover
Africk, Steven Allen physicist

Ayer
†Namin, Reza chemistry educator, consultant

Bedford
Carr, Paul Henry physicist
Sizer, Irwin Whiting biochemistry educator

Belmont
Hauser, George biochemist, educator

Beverly
Harris, Miles Fitzgerald meteorologist
Rose, Peter Henry nuclear physicist
Wan, Zhimin physicist

Billerica
Miller, Dawn Marie meteorologist

Boston
Anselme, Jean-Pierre Louis Marie chemist
Aronow, Saul radiological physicist, consultant
Blout, Elkan Rogers biological chemistry educator, university dean
Brecher, Kenneth astrophysicist
Brownell, Gordon Lee physicist, educator
Cohen, Robert Sonné physicist, philosopher, educator
Deutsch, Thomas Frederick physicist
El-Baz, Farouk research director, educator
Guertin, Robert Powell physics educator, university dean
Hegedüs, Zoltán Louis retired chemist, researcher
Kaplan, Michael Daniel physics and chemistry researcher, educator
Kennedy, Eugene Patrick biochemist, educator
Kornberg, Sir Hans Leo biochemist
Le Quesne, Philip William chemistry educator, researcher
Lichtin, Norman Nahum chemistry educator
Malenka, Bertram Julian physicist, educator
Miliora, Maria Teresa chemist, psychotherapist, psychoanalyst, educator
Nanji, Amin Akbarali biochemist, clinical pathologist, educator
Ondrechen, Mary Jo chemistry educator, consultant, researcher
Pardee, Arthur Beck biochemist, educator
Prabakaran, Daniel biochemist, researcher
Stanley, H(arry) Eugene physicist, educator
Stollar, Bernard David biochemist, educator
Strominger, Jack Leonard biochemist
Trackman, Philip Charles biochemist, researcher
Vallee, Bert Lester biochemist, physician, educator
Walsh, Christopher Thomas biochemist, department chairman
Webster, Edward William medical physicist
White, Morris Francis biochemistry educator
Yu, Yong Ming physiological biochemist, surgeon

Brookline
Ferrell, Robert Craig computational physicist, consultant
Lynton, Ernest Albert physicist, educator, former university official
Saini, Gulshan Rai soil physicist, agricultural hydrologist
Tuchman, Avraham physicist, researcher

Cambridge
Abban, Andrew Paul laboratory coordinator
Alberty, Robert Arnold chemistry educator
Anderson, James Gilbert chemistry educator
Barger, James Edwin physicist
Benedek, George Bernard physicist, educator
Biemann, Klaus chemistry educator
Birgeneau, Robert Joseph physicist, educator
Bloch, Konrad Emil biochemist
Bloembergen, Nicolaas physicist, educator
Boyle, Edward Allen oceanography educator
Bradt, Hale Van Dorn physicist, x-ray astronomer, educator
Branscomb, Lewis McAdory physicist
Brooks, Harvey physics educator
Burchfiel, Burrell Clark geology educator
Burke, Bernard Flood physicist, educator
Burnham, Charles Wilson mineralogy educator
Butler, James Newton chemist, educator
Cameron, Alastair Graham Walter astrophysicist, educator
Canizares, Claude Roger astrophysicist, educator
Carter, Ashton Baldwin physicist, educator, government agency executive
Ceyer, Sylvia T. chemistry educator
Clark, George Whipple physics educator
Coleman, Sidney Richard physicist, educator
Corey, Elias James chemistry educator
Covert, Eugene Edzards aerophysics educator
Dame, Thomas Michael radio astronomer
Danheiser, Rick Lane organic chemistry educator

Deutsch, Martin emeritus physics professor
Doering, William von Eggers organic chemist, educator
Doty, Paul Mead biochemist, educator, arms control specialist
Dresselhaus, Mildred Spiewak physics and engineering educator
Durant, Graham John medicinal chemist, drug researcher
Dziewonski, Adam Marian earth science educator
Eagar, Thomas Waddy metallurgist, educator
Eagleson, Peter Sturges hydrologist, educator
Edsall, John Tileston biological chemistry educator
Ehntholt, Daniel James chemist
†Ehrenfeld, John Roos environmental policy educator
Ehrenreich, Henry physicist, educator
Emanuel, Kerry Andrew earth sciences educator
Evans, Anthony Glyn materials scientist
Evans, David A(lbert) chemistry educator
†Evans, James Brian geophysics educator
Feld, Michael Stephen physics educator
Feshbach, Herman physicist, educator
Field, George Brooks theoretical astrophysicist
Foner, Simon research physicist
French, Anthony Philip physicist, educator
Frey, Frederick August geochemistry researcher, educator
Friedman, Jerome Isaac physics educator, researcher
Garland, Carl Wesley chemist, educator
Garrelick, Joel Marc acoustical scientist, consultant
Geller, Margaret Joan astrophysicist, educator
Gingerich, Owen Jay astronomer, educator
Goldstone, Jeffrey physicist
Gordon, Roy Gerald chemistry educator
Gould, Stephen Jay paleontologist, educator
Greene, Frederick D., II chemistry educator
Grindlay, Jonathan Ellis astrophysics educator
Grove, Timothy Lynn geology educator
Guth, Alan Harvey physicist, educator
Halperin, Bertrand Israel physics educator
Herschbach, Dudley Robert chemistry educator
Hoffman, Paul Felix geologist, educator
Holdren, John Paul energy and resource educator, researcher, author, consultant
Holm, Richard Hadley chemist, educator
Holton, Gerald physicist, science historian
Horwitz, Paul physicist
Houtchens, Robert Austin, Jr. biochemist
Huang, Kerson physics educator
Huchra, John Peter astronomer, educator
Ingard, Karl Uno physics educator
Jackiw, Roman physicist, educator
Jaffe, Arthur Michael physicist, mathematician, educator
Jordan, Thomas Hillman geophysicist, educator
Joss, Paul Christopher astrophysicist, atmospheric physicist, educator
Kamentsky, Louis Aaron biophysicist
Karplus, Martin chemistry educator
Keck, James Collyer physicist, educator
Kerman, Arthur Kent physicist, educator
Khorana, Har Gobind chemist, educator
Kim, Peter Sungbai biochemistry educator
King, Ronold Wyeth Percival physics educator
Kistiakowsky, Vera physics researcher, educator
Klemperer, William chemistry educator
Kleppner, Daniel physicist, educator
Klibanov, Alexander Maxim chemistry and biotechnology educator, researcher
Lee, Patrick A. physics educator
Lightman, Alan Paige physicist, writer, educator
Lindzen, Richard Siegmund meteorologist, educator
Lippard, Stephen James chemist, educator
Lipscomb, William Nunn, Jr. retired physical chemistry educator
Litster, James David physics educator, dean
Livingston, James Duane physicist, educator
Loeb, Abraham astrophysics educator, researcher
Lomon, Earle Leonard physicist, educator, consultant
Lorenz, Edward Norton meteorologist, educator
Low, Francis Eugene physics educator
Lyon, Richard Harold physicist educator,
Marsden, Brian Geoffrey astronomer
Martin, Paul Cecil physicist, educator
Marvin, Ursula Bailey geologist
McElroy, Michael physicist, researcher, educator
Meselson, Matthew Stanley biochemist, educator
Molina, Mario Jose physical chemist, educator
Moran, James Michael, Jr. astronomer, educator
Narayan, Ramesh astronomy educator
Negele, John William physics educator, consultant
Nelson, David Robert physics educator
Nelson, Keith Adam chemistry educator
Newell, Reginald Edward physics educator
Oppenheim, Irwin chemical physicist, educator
Orme-Johnson, William Henry, III chemist, educator
Paul, William physicist, educator
Pershan, Peter Silas physicist, educator
Petersen, Ulrich geology educator
Pettengill, Gordon H(emenway) physicist, educator
Ramsey, Norman F. physicist, educator
Redwine, Robert Page physicist, educator
Rice, James Robert engineering scientist, geophysicist
Roedder, Edwin Woods geologist
Rose, Robert Michael materials science and engineering educator
Rosen, Richard David research meteorologist, educator
Rosenblith, Walter Alter scientist, educator
†Ross, Caroline Anne materials science educator
Rubin, Lawrence Gilbert physicist, laboratory manager
Sadoway, Donald Robert materials science educator
Salzmann, George Stephen biochemist, priest
Schild, Rudolph Ernst astronomer, educator
Schreiber, Stuart L. chemist, educator
Schrock, Richard Royce chemistry educator
Seyferth, Dietmar chemist, educator
Shapiro, Irwin Ira physicist, educator
Silbey, Robert James chemistry educator, researcher, consultant
Solomon, Arthur Kaskel biophysics educator
Spaepen, Frans August applied physics researcher, educator
Steinfeld, Jeffrey Irwin chemistry educator, consultant, writer
Steinmetz, Michael biochemist
Strandberg, Malcom Woodrow Pershing physicist
Thaddeus, Patrick physicist, educator
Thompson, James Burleigh, Jr. geologist, educator
Ting, Samuel Chao Chung physicist, educator
Tinkham, Michael physicist, educator
Verdine, Gregory Lawrence chemist, educator
Vessot, Robert Frederick Charles physicist
Villars, Felix Marc Hermann physicist, educator
Wang, James Chuo biochemistry and molecular biology educator
Waugh, John Stewart chemist, educator
Weinberg, Robert Allan biochemist, educator
Westheimer, Frank Henry chemist, educator
Whipple, Fred Lawrence astronomer
Whitesides, George McClelland chemistry educator
Wiley, Don Craig biochemistry and biophysics educator
Wilson, Robert Woodrow radio astronomer
Wisdom, Jack Leach physicist, educator
Wood, John Armstead planetary scientist, geological sciences educator
Wunsch, Carl Isaac oceanographer, educator

Chestnut Hill
Fourkas, John T. chemistry educator
Nisonoff, Alfred biochemist, educator

Concord
Valley, George Edward, Jr. physicist, educator

Cotuit
Miller, Robert Charles retired physicist

East Longmeadow
Skutnik, Bolesh J. optics scientist, lay worker, lawyer

Eastham
Miller, Gabriel Lorimer physicist, researcher

Fall River
†Guillemette, Mark Edgar textile technologist

Falmouth
Goody, Richard Mead geophysicist

Framingham
Hopkins, Esther Arvilla Harrison retired chemist, patent lawyer

Great Barrington
Lane-Zucker, Laurie John executive

Hanscom AFB
Mailloux, Robert Joseph physicist
Straka, Ronald Morris physicist

Holden
Gordon, Steven B. chemist

Leominster
Marro, Matthew Shawn chemist

Lexington
Buchanan, John Machlin biochemistry educator
Cathou, Renata Egone chemist, consultant
Champion, Kenneth Stanley Warner physicist
Dionne, Gerald Francis research physicist, educator, consultant
Kanter, Irving mathematical physicist
Kirkpatrick, Francis H(ubbard), Jr. biophysicist, intellectual property practitioner, consultant
Mollo-Christensen, Erik Leonard oceanographer
Nash, Leonard Kollender chemistry educator
Shull, Clifford G. physicist, educator
Silverman, Sam Mendel physicist, lawyer
Williamson, Richard Cardinal physicist

Lowell
Carr, George Leroy physicist, educator
Israel, Stanley C. chemistry educator
Tripathy, Sukant Kishore chemistry educator

Marblehead
Cohen, Merrill chemist

Mashpee
LeBaron, Francis Newton biochemistry educator

Medford
Gunther, Leon physicist
Mc Carthy, Kathryn A. physicist
Milburn, Richard Henry physics educator
Schneps, Jack physics educator
Thornton, Ronald physicist, educator
Urry, Grant Wayne chemistry educator

Melrose
Sullivan, Charles Irving polymer chemist

Newton
Dunlap, William Crawford physicist
Heyn, Arno Harry Albert retired chemistry educator
Jarchow, Craig McHugh technology manager
Weisskopf, Victor Frederick physicist

North Dartmouth
Sauro, Joseph Pio physics educator
Zuo, Yuegang chemist, educator

Northampton
Fleck, George Morrison chemistry educator

Pittsfield
Wheelock, Kenneth Steven chemist

Roxbury
Franzblau, Carl biochemist, consultant, researcher
MacNichol, Edward Ford, Jr. biophysicist, educator
Simons, Elizabeth R(eiman) biochemist, educator
Small, Donald MacFarland biophysics educator, gastroenterologist

Salem
Brown, Walter Redvers John physicist

South Hadley
Campbell, Mary Kathryn chemistry educator
Leal, Joseph Rogers chemist

Stow
Becherer, Richard Joseph science consulting firm executive, physicist

Sturbridge
Feller, Winthrop Bruce physicist
McMahon, Maribeth Lovette physicist

Zhong, William Jiang Sheng glass scientist

Sudbury
Blackey, Edwin Arthur, Jr. geologist

Waltham
Cohen, Saul G. chemist, educator
De Rosier, David John biophysicist, educator
Deser, Stanley physicist, educator
Epstein, Irving Robert chemistry educator
Fasman, Gerald David biochemistry educator
Foxman, Bruce Mayer chemist, educator
Jeanloz, Roger William biochemist, educator
Jencks, William Platt biochemist, educator
Lees, Marjorie Berman biochemist, neuroscientist
Petsko, Gregory Anthony chemistry and biochemistry educator
Schweber, Silvan Samuel physics and history educator
Snider, Barry B. organic chemist

Watertown
Lin, Alice Lee Lan physicist, researcher, educator

Wayland
Clark, Melville, Jr. physicist, electrical engineer
Statz, Hermann physicist

Wellesley
Charpie, Robert Alan physicist
Kato, Walter Yoneo physicist
Kobayashi, Yutaka biochemist, consultant

Wenham
Herrmann, Robert Lawrence biochemistry, science and religion educator

Westford
Salah, Joseph Elias research scientist, educator

Weston
Schloemann, Ernst Fritz (Rudolf August) physicist, engineer
Wang, Chia Ping physicist, educator
Whitehouse, David Rempfer physicist

Westwood
Bernfeld, Peter Harry William biochemist

Williamstown
Crampton, Stuart Jessup Bigelow physicist, educator
Markgraf, J(ohn) Hodge chemist, educator
Park, David Allen physicist, educator
Pasachoff, Jay Myron astronomer, educator
Wobus, Reinhard Arthur geologist, educator

Woods Hole
Berggren, William Alfred geologist, research micropaleontologist, educator
Butman, Bradford oceanographer
Cohen, Seymour Stanley biochemist, educator
Fofonoff, Nicholas Paul oceanographer, educator
Gagosian, Robert B. chemist, educator
Hart, Stanley Robert geochemist, educator
Steele, John Hyslop marine scientist, oceanographic institute administrator
Uchupi, Elazar geologist, researcher
Von Herzen, Richard Pierre research scientist, consultant

Worcester
Hohenemser, Christoph physics educator, researcher
Pavlik, James William chemistry educator

Yarmouth Port
Darby, Joseph Branch, Jr. retired metallurgist, government official

MICHIGAN

Ann Arbor
Agranoff, Bernard William biochemist, educator
Akerlof, Carl William physics educator
Ashe, Arthur James, III chemistry educator
Atreya, Sushil Kumar space science educator, astrophysicist, researcher
Banks, Peter Morgan enviromental research business executive
Bartell, Lawrence Sims chemist, educator
Blinder, Seymour Michael chemistry educator
Chupp, Timothy Edward physicist, educator, nuclear scientist, academic administrator
Clarke, John Terrel astrophysicist
Cordes, Eugene Harold pharmacy and chemistry educator
Crane, Horace Richard physicist, educator
Dekker, Eugene Earl biochemistry educator
Dixon, Jack Edward biological chemistry educator, consultant
Donahue, Thomas Michael physics educator
Drake, Richard Paul physicist, educator
Duff, Michael James physicist
Elste, Guenther Heino Erich astrophysicist
Farrand, William Richard geology educator
Fisk, Lennard Ayres physicist, educator
Freese, Katherine physicist, educator
Haddock, Fred Theodore, Jr. astronomer, educator
Jones, Lawrence William educator, physicist
Kesler, Stephen Edward economic geology educator
Krimm, Samuel physicist, educator
Krisch, Alan David physics educator
Lee, Stephen chemist, educator
Longone, Daniel Thomas chemistry educator
Marletta, Michael biochemistry educator, researcher, protein chemist
Matthews, Rowena Green biological chemistry educator
Neal, Homer Alfred physics educator, researcher, university administrator
Nordman, Christer Eric chemistry educator
Nriagu, Jerome Okon environmental geochemist
Parkinson, William Charles physicist, educator
Pollack, Henry Nathan geophysics educator
Rea, David K. geology and oceanography educator
Roe, Byron Paul physics educator
Roush, William R. chemistry educator
Samson, Perry J. environmental scientist, educator
Schacht, Jochen Heinrich biochemistry educator
Shaw, Jiajiu chemist
Steel, Duncan Gregory physics educator
Tamres, Milton chemistry educator
Townsend, LeRoy B. chemistry educator, university administrator, researcher
Van der Voo, Rob geophysicist
Weinreich, Gabriel physicist, minister, educator
Wharton, John James, Jr. research physicist
Wong, Victor Kenneth physics educator, academic administrator
Woo, Peter Wing Kee organic chemist
Zhang, Youxue geology educator

Big Rapids
Mathison, Ian William chemistry educator, academic dean

Cross Village
Stowe, Robert Allen catalytic and chemical technology consultant

Dearborn
Rokosz, Michael John research scientist
Xu, Bing Chang physicist

Detroit
Bohm, Henry Victor physicist
Frade, Peter Daniel chemist, educator
Gupta, Suraj Narayan physicist, educator
†Harr, Robert Francis physicist
Johnson, Carl Randolph chemist, educator
Kirschner, Stanley chemist
Oliver, John Preston chemistry educator, academic administrator
Orton, Colin George medical physicist
Stewart, Melbourne George, Jr. physicist, educator

East Lansing
Abolins, Maris Arvids physics researcher and educator
Austin, Sam M. physics educator
Benenson, Walter nuclear physics educator
Blosser, Henry Gabriel physicist
Burnett, Jean Bullard (Mrs. James R. Burnett) biochemist
Case, Eldon Darrel materials science educator
Cross, Aureal Theophilus geology and botany educator
D'Itri, Frank Michael environmental research chemist
Dye, James Louis chemistry educator
Gelbke, Claus-Konrad nuclear physics educator
Harrison, Michael Jay physicist, educator
†Hyndman, David William geological sciences educator
Luecke, Richard William biochemist
Macrakis, Kristie Irene history of science educator
Preiss, Jack biochemistry educator
Summitt, (William) Robert chemist, educator
Tien, H. Ti biophysics and physiology educator, scientist
Wolterink, Lester Floyd biophysicist, educator
Yussouff, Mohammed physicist, educator

Farmington Hills
Hodjat, Yahya metallurgist
Theodore, Ares Nicholas research chemist

Ferndale
Pence, Leland Hadley organic chemist

Flint
†Phelps, Janet Ann environmental health coordinator

Highland
Brown, Ray Kent biochemist, physician, educator

Holland
Inghram, Mark Gordon physicist, educator

Houghton
McGinnis, Gary David chemist, science educator

Kalamazoo
Bannister, Brian retired organic chemist
Cheney, Brigham Vernon physical chemist
Chou, Kuo-Chen biophysical chemist
Greenfield, John Charles bio-organic chemist

Lake Linden
Campbell, Wilbur Harold research plant biochemist, educator

Leland
Small, Hamish chemist

Madison Heights
Chapman, Gilbert Bryant physicist
Koshy, Vettithara Cherian chemistry educator, technical director and formulator
Murphy, Donald Paul research chemist

Midland
Chao, Marshall chemist
Crummett, Warren Berlin analytical chemistry consultant
Dorman, Linneaus Cuthbert retired chemist
Dreyfuss, Patricia chemist, researcher
Leng, Marguerite Lambert regulatory consultant, biochemist
Nowak, Robert Michael chemist

Mount Pleasant
Dietrich, Richard Vincent geologist, educator

Saginaw
Wierzbicki, Jacek Gabriel physicist, researcher

Three Rivers
Boyer, Nicodemus Elijah organic-polymer chemist, consultant

Troy
Fritzsche, Hellmut physics educator
Ovshinsky, Stanford Robert physicist, inventor, energy and information company executive

Warren
Deak, Charles Karol chemist
Herbst, Jan Francis physicist, researcher
Heremans, Joseph Pierre physicist
Schwartz, Shirley E. chemist

Smith, George Wolfram *physicist, educator*
Smith, John Robert *physicist*
Taylor, Kathleen (Christine) *physical chemist*

West Bloomfield
Ben, Manuel *chemist*
Harwood, Julius J. *metallurgist, educator*

Wyandotte
Aslam, Syed *chemist, research*

Ypsilanti
Barnes, James Milton *physics and astronomy educator*

MINNESOTA

Austin
Holman, Ralph Theodore *biochemistry and nutrition educator*
Schmid, Harald Heinrich Otto *biochemistry educator, academic director*

Duluth
Rapp, George Robert, Jr. (Rip Rapp) *geology and archeology educator*
Zhdankin, Viktor Vladimirovich *chemistry educator*

Lake Elmo
Vivona, Daniel Nicholas *chemist*

Lakeville
Phinney, William Charles *retired geologist*

Minneapolis
Ackerman, Eugene *biophysics educator*
Berg, Stanton Oneal *firearms and ballistics consultant*
Carr, Robert Wilson, Jr. *chemistry educator*
Crawford, Bryce Low, Jr. *chemist, educator*
Goldman, Allen Marshall *physics educator*
Halley, James Woods *physics educator*
Hamermesh, Morton *physicist, educator*
Heller, Kenneth Jeffrey *physicist*
Hogenkamp, Henricus Petrus Cornelis *biochemistry researcher, biochemistry educator*
Hooke, Roger LeBaron *geomorphology and glaciology educator*
Johnson, Robert Glenn *geology and geophysics educator*
Jones, Thomas Walter *astrophysics educator, researcher*
Kruse, Paul Walters, Jr. *physicist, consultant*
Kuhi, Leonard Vello *astronomer, university administrator*
Marshak, Marvin Lloyd *physicist, educator*
Portoghese, Philip Salvatore *medicinal chemist, educator*
Prager, Stephen *chemistry educator*
Rubens, Sidney Michel *physicist, technical advisor*
Siepmann, Joern Ilja *chemistry educator*
Truhlar, Donald Gene *chemist, educator*
Usacheva, Marina Nikolaevna *photochemist, researcher*
Wood, Wellington Gibson, III *biochemistry educator*
Wright, Herbert E(dgar), Jr. *geologist*

Northfield
Casper, Barry Michael *physics educator*
Cederberg, James *physics educator*
Henrickson, Eiler Leonard *retired geologist, educator*
Noer, Richard J. *physics educator, researcher*
Ramesh, Kalahasti Subrahmanyam *materials scientist*

Rochester
Pang, Yuan-Ping *synthetic and computational chemist*

Saint Paul
Clapp, C(harles) Edward *research chemist, soil biochemistry educator*
Hobbie, Russell Klyver *physics educator*
Newmark, Richard Alan *chemist*
Nicholson, Morris Emmons, Jr. *metallurgist, educator*
Southwick, David Leroy *geology researcher*
Thompson, Mary Eileen *chemistry educator*
Walton, Matt Savage *retired geologist, educator*

Wayzata
Bremel, Thomas John *biochemist, researcher*

White Bear Lake
Holmen, Reynold Emanuel *chemist*

Woodbury
Bicking, Merlin Kim Lambert *consulting chemist, medical products executive*

MISSISSIPPI

Bay Saint Louis
Zeile, Fred Carl *oceanographer, meteorologist*

Jackson
Leszczynski, Jerzy Ryszard *chemistry educator, researcher*
Read, Virginia Hall *biochemistry educator*
Smith, Edgar Eugene *biochemist, university administrator*

Mississippi State
Alley, Earl Gifford *chemist*

Pascagoula
Corben, Herbert Charles *physicist, educator*

Picayune
Lowrie, Allen *geologist, oceanographer*

Stennis Space Center
Hurlburt, Harley Ernest *oceanographer*

MISSOURI

Ballwin
Stevens, James Edward *chemistry educator*

Cape Girardeau
Hathaway, Ruth Ann *chemist*

Clinton
†Kelsay, David Roland *chemist*

Columbia
Bauman, John E., Jr. *chemistry educator*
Decker, Wayne Leroy *meteorologist, educator*
Ethington, Raymond Lindsay *geology educator, researcher*
Plummer, Patricia Lynne Moore *chemistry and physics educator*
Rabjohn, Norman *chemistry educator emeritus*
Rhyne, James Jennings *condensed matter physicist*
Shelton, Kevin L. *geology educator*
Unklesbay, Athel Glyde *geologist, educator*
Weisman, Gary Andrew *biochemist*

Creve Coeur
Bockserman, Robert Julian *chemist*

Independence
Hopkins, Earl Norris *metallurgist*

Jackson
Close, Edward Roy *hydrogeologist, environmental engineer, physicist*

Kansas City
Ching, Wai Yim *physics educator, researcher*
Coveney, Raymond Martin, Jr. *educator*
Gier, Audra May Calhoon *environmental chemist*
Hasan, Syed Eqbal *environmental geologist, educator*
†McGhee, Flin Cameron, III *chemistry educator, consultant*
Parizek, Eldon Joseph *geologist, college dean*
Rost, William Joseph *chemist*
Wilkinson, Ralph Russell *biochemistry educator, toxicologist*

Kirksville
Festa, Roger Reginald *chemist, educator*

Rolla
Adawi, Ibrahim Hasan *physics educator*
Alexander, Ralph William, Jr. *physics educator*
Armstrong, Daniel Wayne *chemist, educator*
Leventis, Nicholas *chemistry educator, consultant*
Mc Farland, Robert Harold *physicist, educator*
O'Keefe, Thomas Joseph *metallurgical engineer*
Rueppel, Melvin Leslie *environmental research director and educator*
Sabnis, Ram Wasudeo *research chemist*

Saint Charles
Beste, Robert Culbertson *geologist*

Saint Louis
Bender, Carl Martin *physics educator, consultant*
Burgess, James Harland *physics educator, researcher*
Callis, Clayton Fowler *research chemist*
Frieden, Carl *biochemist, educator*
Friedlander, Michael Wulf *physicist, educator*
Gibbons, Patrick Chandler *physicist, educator*
Hawkins, Pamela Leigh Huffman *biochemist*
Israel, Martin Henry *astrophysicist, educator, academic administrator*
Kornfeld, Rosalind Hauk *research biochemist*
Lipkin, David *chemist*
Macias, Edward S. *chemistry educator, university official and dean*
Marshall, Garland Ross *biochemist, biophysicist, medical educator*
Miller, James Gegan *research scientist, physics educator*
Murray, Robert Wallace *chemistry educator*
Profeta, Salvatore, Jr. *chemist*
Purdy, James Aaron *medical physics educator*
Rosenthal, Harold Leslie *biochemistry educator*
Sikorski, James Alan *research chemist*
Sly, William S. *biochemist, educator*
Takano, Masaharu *physical chemist*
Walker, Robert Mowbray *physicist, educator*
Weber, Morton M. *microbial biochemist, educator*
Welch, Michael John *chemistry educator, researcher*
Will, Clifford Martin *physicist, educator*
Wrighton, Mark Stephen *chemistry educator*
Zinner, Ernst K. *physics educator, earth and planetary science educator, researcher*

Springfield
Thompson, Clifton C. *retired chemistry educator, university administrator*
Toste, Anthony Paim *chemistry educator, researcher*

Wildwood
Colletti, Teresa Ann *polymer chemist*

MONTANA

Billings
Darrow, George F. *natural resources company owner, consultant*

Bozeman
Anacker, Edward William *retired chemistry educator*
Grieco, Paul Anthony *chemistry educator*
Horner, John Robert *paleontologist, researcher*
Lapeyre, Gerald J. *physics educator, researcher*
Mertz, Edwin Theodore *retired biochemist, emeritus educator*

Butte
Zeihen, Lester Gregory *geology educator*

Dayton
Volborth, Alexis von *geochemistry and geological engineering educator*

Missoula
Murray, Raymond Carl *forensic geologist, educator*
Osterheld, R(obert) Keith *chemistry educator*

Rollins
Zelezny, William Francis *retired physical chemist*

NEBRASKA

Crete
Brakke, Myron Kendall *retired research chemist, educator*

Kearney
Kinsinger, Jack Burl *chemist, educator*
Wubbels, Gene Gerald *chemistry educator*

Lincoln
Blad, Blaine L. *agricultural meteorology educator, consultant*
Eckhardt, Craig Jon *chemistry educator*
Hubbard, Kenneth Gene *climatologist*
Jones, Lee Bennett *chemist, educator, university official*
Treves, Samuel Blain *geologist, educator*
Yoder, Bruce Alan *chemist*

Omaha
Watt, Dean Day *retired biochemistry educator*
Zepf, Thomas Herman *physics educator, researcher*

NEVADA

Carson City
Crawford, John Edward *geologist, scientist*
Holmes, Richard Brooks *mathematical physicist*

Las Vegas
Kenny, Ray *geology and geochemistry educator, researcher*
Kielhorn, Richard Werner *chemist*
Nacht, Steve Jerry *geologist*

Reno
Bonham, Harold Florian *research geologist, consultant*
Horton, Robert Carlton *geologist*
Johnson, Arthur William, Jr. *planetarium executive*
Leipper, Dale Frederick *physical oceanographer, meteorologist, educator*
Pierson, William Roy *chemist*
Sladek, Ronald John *physics educator*
Taranik, James Vladimir *geologist, educator*

NEW HAMPSHIRE

Colebrook
Peterson, John O.H. *chemist, researcher*

Durham
Tischler, Herbert *geologist, educator*

Freedom
Keith, Barry Harold *environmental scientist*

Glen
Zager, Ronald I. *chemist, consultant*

Hanover
Braun, Charles Louis *chemistry educator, researcher*
Kantrowitz, Arthur *physicist, educator*
Montgomery, David Campbell *physicist, educator*
Perrin, Noel *environmental studies educator*
Stockmayer, Walter H(ugo) *chemistry educator*
Sturge, Michael Dudley *physicist*
Wegner, Gary Alan *astronomer*

Jaffrey
Walling, Cheves Thomson *chemistry educator*

Lee
Blidberg, D. Richard *marine engineer*

Rumney
Smith, F(rederick) Dow(swell) *physicist, retired college president*

Salem
Simmons, Marvin Gene *geophysics educator*

Wolfeboro
Varnerin, Lawrence John *physicist, retired educator*

NEW JERSEY

Annandale
Cohen, Morrel Herman *physicist, biologist, educator*
Gorbaty, Martin Leo *chemist, researcher*
Sinfelt, John Henry *chemist*

Bergenfield
Kramer, Bernard *physicist, educator*

Berkeley Heights
Geusic, Joseph Edward *physicist*
Mac Rae, Alfred Urquhart *physicist, electrical engineer*

Blairstown
Martin, James Walter *chemist, technology executive*

Bogota
Condon, Francis Edward *retired chemistry educator*

Bound Brook
Karol, Frederick John *industrial chemist*

Brick
Myers, Howard *aerospace scientist, systems analyst*

Budd Lake
Khazen, Aleksandr Moiseyevich *physicist*

Camden
Beck, David Paul *biochemist*

Cherry Hill
Stern, Howard S. *chemistry educator*

Cliffside Park
Ginos, James Zissis *retired research chemist*

Columbia
Timcenko, Lydia Teodora *biochemist, chemist*

Edison
Firstenberg, Donald Elliott *chemist*

Ewing
Brown, Richard Alexander *chemist*

Far Hills
McCall, David Warren *retired chemistry research director, consultant*

Freehold
Kwon, Joon Taek *retired chemistry researcher*

Hamilton
Barclay, Robert, Jr. *chemist*

Highland Park
Brudner, Harvey Jerome *physicist*
Feigenbaum, Abraham Samuel *nutritional biochemist*

Hoboken
Fajans, Jack *physics educator*
Schmidt, George *physicist*

Holmdel
Burrus, Charles Andrew, Jr. *research physicist*
Gordon, James Power *optics scientist*
Kaminow, Ivan Paul *physicist*
Mollenauer, Linn Frederick *physicist*

Jersey City
Koster, Emlyn Howard *geologist, educator*
Nakhla, Atif Mounir *scientist, biochemist*

Kenilworth
Cayen, Mitchell Ness *biochemist*
Evans, Charlie Anderson *chemist*
Krishna, Gopal *scientist, pharmacokineticist*

Lawrenceville
Sheats, John Eugene *chemistry educator*

Madison
Udenfriend, Sidney *biochemist*

Mahwah
Yeh, Lun-Shu Ray *electrochemist*

Manahawkin
Logan, Ralph Andre *physicist*

Maplewood
Johnson, Dewey, Jr. *biochemist*
Leeds, Norma Sterne *chemistry educator*
Newmark, Harold Leon *biochemist, researcher, educator*
Tatyrek, Alfred Frank *consultant, materials and environmental engineer, analytical and research chemist*

Marlton
†Kimelman, Adam S. *journalist*

Mays Landing
Doughty, Mark Edward *environmental consultant*

Merchantville
Wilson, H(arold) Fred(erick) *chemist, research scientist*

Middletown
Lundgren, Carl William, Jr. *physicist*

Millburn
Wernick, Jack Harry *chemist*

Millington
Glockmann, Walter Friedrich *physicist, consultant*

Milltown
Sacharow, Stanley *chemist, consultant, writer*

Montclair
Kowalski, Stephen Wesley *chemistry educator*

Morris Plains
Presslitz, Joseph Edwin *biochemist*

Morristown
Baughman, Ray Henry *materials scientist*
de Mauret, Kevin John *geologist*
Golecki, Ilan *physicist, researcher, educator*
Harbison, James Prescott *research physicist*
Morgan, Samuel P(ope) *physicist, applied mathematician*
Van Uitert, LeGrand Gerard *retired chemist*

Murray Hill
Chu, Sung Nee George *materials scientist*
White, Alice Elizabeth *physicist, researcher*

Neptune
Aguiar, Adam Martin *chemist, educator*

New Brunswick
Eisenreich, Steven John *chemistry educator, environmental scientist*
Fisher, Hans *nutritional biochemistry educator*
Ho, Chi-Tang *food chemistry educator*
Liao, Mei-June *biopharmaceutical company executive*
Robock, Alan *meteorology educator*
Rosen, Robert Thomas *analytical and food chemist*
Strauss, Ulrich Paul *chemist, educator*

New Providence
Bishop, David John *physicist*
Brinkman, William Frank *physicist, research executive*

Capasso, Federico *physicist, research administrator*
Gaylord, Norman Grant *chemical and polymer consultant*
Glass, Alastair Malcolm *physicist, research director*
Helfand, Eugene *chemist*
Johnson, David Wilfred, Jr. *ceramic scientist, researcher*
Lanzerotti, Louis John *physicist*
Laudise, Robert Alfred *research chemist*
MacChesney, John Burnette *materials scientist, researcher*
Murray, Cherry Ann *physicist, researcher*
Passner, Albert *physicist, researcher*
Sivco, Deborah Lee *research materials scientist*
Stillinger, Frank Henry *chemist, educator*
van Dover, Robert Bruce *physicist*

Newark
Fu, Shou-Cheng Joseph *biomedicine educator*
Murnick, Daniel Ely *physicist, educator*
Spruch, Grace Marmor *physics educator*
Waelde, Lawrence Richard *chemist*

North Caldwell
Piel, Emil J. *retired science educator*

Northvale
Ruderman, Warren *chemist*

Paulsboro
Chang, Clarence Dayton *chemist*

Piscataway
Champe, Pamela Chambers *biochemistry educator, writer*
Devlin, Thomas Joseph *physicist*
Gotsch, Audrey Rose *environmental health sciences educator, researcher*
Kear, Bernard Henry *materials scientist*
Lebowitz, Joel Louis *mathematical physicist, educator*
Lindenfeld, Peter *physics educator*
Madey, Theodore Eugene *physics educator*
Manowitz, Paul *biochemist, researcher, educator*
Plano, Richard James *physicist, educator*
Pond, Thomas Alexander *physics educator, university official*
Robbins, Allen Bishop *physics educator*
Rokhvarger, Anatoly Efim *materials science and ceramic technology scientist*
Shatkin, Aaron Jeffrey *biochemistry educator*
Snitzer, Elias *physicist*
Witz, Gisela *chemist, educator*
Yacowitz, Harold *biochemist, nutritionist*

Pomona
Lessie, Douglas Louis *physics educator*
Sharon, Yitzhak Yaakov *physicist, educator*

Port Murray
Kunzler, John Eugene *physicist*

Pottersville
Mellberg, James Richard *dental research chemist*

Princeton
Adler, Stephen Louis *physicist*
Bahcall, Neta Assaf *astrophysicist*
Bonini, William Emory *geophysics educator*
Bryan, Kirk, Jr. *research meteorologist, research oceanographer*
Christman, Edward Arthur *physicist*
Davidson, Ronald Crosby *physicist, educator*
Dyson, Freeman John *physicist*
Fisch, Nathaniel Joseph *physicist*
Fitch, Val Logsdon *physics educator*
Florey, Klaus Georg *chemist, pharmaceutical consultant*
Gott, J. Richard, III *astrophysicist*
Grisham, Larry Richard *physicist*
Groves, John Taylor, III *chemist, educator*
Happer, William, Jr. *physicist, educator*
Harford, James Joseph *aerospace historian*
Hawryluk, Richard Janusz *physicist*
Hopfield, John Joseph *biophysicist, educator*
Hulse, Russell Alan *physicist*
Hut, Piet *astrophysics educator*
Jenkins, Edward Beynon *research astronomer*
Kauzmann, Walter Joseph *chemistry educator*
Kyin, Saw William *chemist, consultant*
Lemonick, Aaron *physicist, educator*
Lieb, Elliott Hershel *physicist, mathematician, educator*
Long, Frank Wesley, Jr. *chemist*
Mahlman, Jerry David *research meteorologist*
McClure, Donald Stuart *physical chemist, educator*
Morgan, William Jason *geophysics educator*
Novotny, Jiri *biophysicist*
Ondetti, Miguel Angel *chemist, consultant*
Ostriker, Jeremiah Paul *astrophysicist, educator*
Page, Lyman Alexander, Jr. *physicist*
Peebles, Phillip James E. *physicist, educator*
Potasek, Mary Joyce *physicist, researcher*
Rebenfeld, Ludwig *chemist, educator*
Rodwell, John Dennis *biochemist*
Royce, Barrie Saunders Hart *physicist, educator*
Rutherford, Paul Harding *physicist*
Seiberg, Nathan *physics educator*
Seman, Charles Jacob *research meteorologist*
Shoemaker, Frank Crawford *physicist, educator*
Smagorinsky, Joseph *meteorologist*
Smith, Arthur John Stewart *physicist, educator*
Spiro, Thomas George *chemistry educator*
Sterzer, Fred *research physicist*
Stix, Thomas Howard *physicist, educator*
Tang, Chao *physicist*
Taylor, Joseph Hooton, Jr. *radio astronomer, physicist*
Treiman, Sam Bard *physics educator*
Tremaine, Scott Duncan *astrophysicist*
Van Houten, Franklyn Bosworth *geologist, educator*
Wheeler, John Archibald *physicist, educator*
Wightman, Arthur Strong *physicist, educator*
Wilczek, Frank Anthony *physics educator*
Wilkinson, David Todd *physics educator*
Williams, Robert H. *environmental scientist*
Witten, Edward *mathematical physicist*
Wood, Eric Franklin *earth and environmental sciences educator*
Yang, Hong *chemistry researcher*
Yao, Kuo Wei *biochemist*

Rahway
Garcia, Maria Luisa *biochemist, researcher*
Kaczorowski, Gregory John *biochemist, researcher, science administrator*
Patchett, Arthur Allan *medicinal chemist, pharmaceutical executive*
Shapiro, Bennett Michaels *biochemist, educator*

Raritan
Haller, William Paul *analytical chemist, robotics specialist*

Red Bank
Eiselt, Michael Herbert *optics scientist*

Ridgefield
Goldman, Arnold Ira *biophysicist, statistical analyst*

Somerville
Khanna, Dinesh Narain *chemist*
Singman, Charles Neil *chemist*

Springfield
Panish, Morton B. *physicial chemist, consultant*

Stirling
Walsh, Peter Joseph *physics educator*

Summit
Burbank, Robinson Derry *crystallographer*
Gonnella, Nina Celeste *biophysical chemist*
Phillips, James Charles *physicist, educator*
Rosensweig, Ronald Ellis *scientist consultant*
Wissbrun, Kurt Falke *chemist, consultant*
Ziegler, John Benjamin *chemist, lepidopterist*

Teaneck
Nagy, Christa Fiedler *biochemist*
Tamir, Theodor *electrophysics researcher, educator*

Tenafly
Feigelson, Philip *biochemist, educator*

Titusville
Godly, Gordon Thomas *retired chemist, consultant*

Trenton
Cushman, David Wayne *research biochemist*
Parsa, Bahman *nuclear chemist*

Union
Zois, Constantine Nicholas Athanasios *meteorology educator*

West Caldwell
Berenfeld, Mark M. *chemist*

Westfield
Bartok, William *environmental technologies consultant*

Westwood
Schutz, Donald Frank *geochemist, environmental corporate executive*

NEW MEXICO

Albuquerque
Beckel, Charles Leroy *physics educator*
†Button, Luella Mary Watkins (Lue) *retired physicist, dog trainer, coach rescue team*
Chronister, Richard Davis *physicist*
†Cutchen, J. Thomas *physicist*
Evans, Pauline D. *physicist, educator*
Freiwald, David Allen *physicist, mechanical engineer*
Gander, John Edward *biochemistry educator*
Garland, James Wilson, Jr. *retired physics educator*
Harrison, Charles Wagner, Jr. *applied physicist*
Hylko, James Mark *health physicist, certified quality auditor*
Johnson, Ralph Theodore, Jr. *physicist*
Loftfield, Robert Berner *biochemistry educator*
Papike, James Joseph *geology educator, science institute director*
Romig, Alton Dale, Jr. *materials scientist, educator*
Seiler, Fritz Arnold *physicist*
Vianco, Paul Thomas *metallurgist*

Deming
Snyder, Charles Theodore *geologist*

Las Cruces
Coburn, Horace Hunter *retired physics educator*
Kemp, John Daniel *biochemist, educator*
Lease, Jane Etta *environmental science consultant, retired librarian*

Los Alamos
Becker, Stephen A. *physicist, designer*
Bell, George Irving *biophysics researcher*
Colgate, Stirling Auchincloss *physicist*
Engelhardt, Albert George *physicist*
Friar, James Lewis *physicist*
Garvey, Doris Burmester *environmental administrator*
Gibson, Benjamin Franklin *physicist*
Grilly, Edward Rogers *physicist*
Jagnow, David Henry *petroleum geologist*
Johnson, Mikkel Borlaug *physicist*
Judd, O'Dean P. *physicist*
Keepin, George Robert, Jr. *physicist*
Kubas, Gregory Joseph *research chemist*
†Lee, David Mallin *physicist*
Makaruk, Hanna Ewa *theoretical physicist*
Matlack, George Miller *radiochemist*
Mihalas, Dimitri Manuel *astronomer, educator*
Mitchell, Terence Edward *materials scientist*
Mjolsness, Raymond Charles *retired physicist, researcher*
Nix, James Rayford *nuclear physicist, consultant*
O'Brien, Harold Aloysius, Jr. *nuclear chemist, physics researcher, consultant*
Pack, Russell T. *theoretical chemist*
Penneman, Robert Allen *retired chemist*
Press, William Henry *astrophysicist, computer scientist*
Rosen, Louis *physicist*
Selden, Robert Wentworth *physicist, science advisor*
Smith, James Lawrence *research physicist*
Snell, Charles Murrell *physicist, astrophysicist*
Terrell, (Nelson) James *physicist*
Trewhella, Jill *biophysicist*
Wahl, Arthur Charles *retired chemistry educator*
Whitten, David George *chemistry educator*
Williams, Joel Mann *polymer material scientist*
WoldeGabriel, Giday *research geologist*
Zweig, George *physicist, neurobiologist*

Los Lunas
Graham, Robert Albert *research physicist*

Santa Fe
Cowan, George Arthur *chemist, bank executive, director*
Fisher, Robert Alan *laser physicist*
Gell-Mann, Murray *theoretical physicist, educator*
Giovanielli, Damon Vincent *physicist, consulting company executive*
Jones, Walter Harrison *chemist, educator*
Leibowitz, Jack Richard *physicist, educator*
Ratliff, Floyd *biophysics educator, scientist*
Romanowski, Thomas Andrew *physics educator*
Schoenborn, Benno P. *biophysicist, educator*
White, David Hywel *physics educator*

Socorro
Broadhead, Ronald Frigon *petroleum geologist, geology educator*
Kottlowski, Frank Edward *geologist*

Sunspot
Altrock, Richard Charles *astrophysicist*
Beckers, Jacques Maurice *astrophysicist*

NEW YORK

Albany
Fakundiny, Robert Harry *geologist, educator, consultant*
Frost, Robert Edwin *chemistry educator*
Kim, Jai Soo *physics educator*
Morris, Margretta Elizabeth *conservationist*
Reichert, Leo Edmund, Jr. *biochemist, endocrinologist*
Schneider, Allan Stanford *biochemistry neurosience and pharmacology educator, biomedical research scientist*

Alfred
Pye, Lenwood David *materials science educator, researcher, consultant*
Rossington, David Ralph *physical chemistry educator*

Aurora
†Schwab, Linda S. *chemistry educator*

Ballston Spa
Westbrook, Jack Hall *metallurgist, consultant*

Binghamton
Coates, Donald Robert *geology educator, scientist*
Eisch, John Joseph *chemist, educator, consultant*
Whittingham, M(ichael) Stanley *chemist*

Briarcliff Manor
Bhargava, Rameshwar Nath *physicist*
Jepsen, Mary Lou *optical scientist, business executive*

Bronx
Shamos, Morris Herbert *physicist educator*
Siddons, Sarah Mae *chemist*
Thysen, Benjamin *biochemist, health science facility administrator, researcher*
Yalow, Rosalyn Sussman *medical physicist*

Brooklyn
Castleman, Louis Samuel *metallurgist, educator*
Charton, Marvin *chemist, educator*
Choudhury, Deo Chand *physicist, educator*
Eirich, Frederick Roland *chemist, educator*
Franco, Victor *theoretical physics educator*
Friedman, Gerald Manfred *geologist, educator*
Friedman, Paul *chemistry educator*
Grimblatov, Valentin *physicist, biomedical engineer*
Kjeldaas, Terje, Jr. *physics educator emeritus*
Ma, Tsu Sheng *chemist, educator, consultant*
Mook, Sarah *retired chemist*
Morawetz, Herbert *chemistry educator*
Oliner, Arthur Aaron *physicist, educator*
Pearce, Eli M. *chemistry educator, administrator*
Ronn, Avigdor Meir *chemical physics educator, consultant, researcher*
Stracher, Alfred *biochemistry educator*
Wolf, Edward Lincoln *physics educator*

Buffalo
Amborski, Leonard Edward *chemist*
Anbar, Michael *biophysics educator*
Bardos, Thomas Joseph *chemist, educator*
Coppens, Philip *chemist*
Jain, Piyare Lal *physics educator*
Patel, Mulchand Shambhubhai *biochemist, researcher*
Reitan, Paul Hartman *geologist, educator*
Treanor, Charles Edward *scientist*
Wang, Jui Hsin *biochemistry educator*

Canandaigua
Lowther, Frank Eugene *research physicist*

Canton
Romey, William Dowden *geologist, educator*

Cazenovia
Clarke, George Alton *chemist, acdemic administrator, retired*

Chestnut Ridge
Huntoon, Robert Brian *chemist, food industry consultant*

Clinton
Ring, James Walter *physics educator*

Cooperstown
Peters, Theodore, Jr. *research biochemist, consultant*

Corning
Keck, Donald Bruce *physicist*
Maurer, Robert Distler *retired industrial physicist*
Miller, Roger Allen *physicist*
Williams, Jimmie Lewis *research chemist*

Dobbs Ferry
Triplett, Kelly B. *chemist*

East Hampton
Garrett, Charles Geoffrey Blythe *physicist*

Farmingdale
Marcuvitz, Nathan *electrophysics educator*
Nolan, Peter John *physics educator*

Flushing
Coch, Nicholas Kyros *geologist, educator*
Finks, Robert Melvin *paleontologist, educator*
Gafney, Harry D. *chemistry educator*
Goldman, Norman Lewis *chemistry educator*
Speidel, David Harold *geology educator*

Freeport
Pullman, Maynard Edward *biochemist*

Geneva
Roelofs, Wendell Lee *biochemistry educator, consultant*

Getzville
†Schulman, Diane R. *chemistry educator*

Glen Cove
Dehn, Joseph William, Jr. *chemist*

Hamilton
Holbrow, Charles Howard *physicist, educator*

Hannacroix
Schwebler, Stephen *retired chemist*

Hawthorne
Batstone, Joanna L. *physicist*

Hempstead
Sparberg, Esther B. *chemist, educator*

Hopewell Junction
Anandan, Munisamy *physicist*

Horseheads
Josbeno, Larry Joseph *physics educator*

Irvington
Devons, Samuel *educator, physicist*
Elbaum, Marek *electro-optical sciences executive, researcher*

Ithaca
Ashcroft, Neil William *physics educator, researcher*
Bassett, William Akers *geologist, educator*
Batterman, Boris William *physicist, educator, academic director*
Bauer, Simon Harvey *chemistry educator*
Bauman, Dale Elton *nutritional biochemistry educator*
Berkelman, Karl *physics educator*
Bethe, Hans Albrecht *physicist, educator*
Burns, Joseph Arthur *planetary science educator*
Carpenter, Barry Keith *chemistry educator, researcher*
Clardy, Jon Christel *chemistry educator, consultant*
Craighead, Harold G. *physics educator*
Fay, Robert Clinton *chemist, educator*
Fitchen, Douglas Beach *physicist, educator*
Freed, Jack Herschel *chemist, educator*
Gold, Thomas *astronomer, educator*
Goldsmith, Paul Felix *physics and astronomy educator*
Gottfried, Kurt *physicist, educator*
Greisen, Kenneth Ingvard *physicist, emeritus educator*
Hart, Edward Walter *physicist*
Hess, George Paul *biochemist, educator*
Hoffmann, Roald *chemist, educator*
Holcomb, Donald Frank *physicist, academic administrator*
Kinoshita, Toichiro *physicist*
Lee, David Morris *physics educator*
Liboff, Richard Lawrence *physicist, educator*
Lumley, John Leask *physicist, educator*
McDaniel, Boyce Dawkins *physicist, educator*
McLafferty, Fred Warren *chemist, educator*
McMurry, John Edward *chemistry educator*
Meinwald, Jerrold *chemist, educator*
Mermin, N. David *physicist, educator, essayist*
Morrison, George Harold *chemist, educator*
Oliver, Jack Ertle *geophysicist*
Pohl, Robert Otto *physics educator*
Reppy, John David, Jr. *physicist*
†Richardson, Robert Coleman *physics educator, researcher*
Ruoff, Arthur Louis *physicist, educator*
Salpeter, Edwin Ernest *physical sciences educator*
Scheraga, Harold Abraham *physical chemistry educator*
Slate, Floyd Owen *chemist, materials scientist, civil engineer, educator, researcher*
Terzian, Yervant *astronomy and astrophysics educator*
Thomas, J. Earl *physicist*
Tigner, Maury *retired physicist, educator*
Turcotte, Donald Lawson *geophysical sciences educator*
Webb, Watt Wetmore *physicist, educator*
Widom, Benjamin *chemistry educator*
Wilson, Robert Rathbun *retired physicist*
Zilversmit, Donald Berthold *nutritional biochemist, educator*

Jamaica
Greenberg, Jacob *biochemist, educator, consultant*
Lengyel, István *chemist, educator*
Sun, Siao Fang *chemistry educator*

Larchmont
Guttenplan, Joseph B. *biochemist*

Levittown
Mader, Bryn John *vertebrate paleontologist*

PROFESSIONAL INDEX 6213 SCIENCE: PHYSICAL SCIENCE

Lewiston
Dexter, Theodore Henry chemist

Lynbrook
Yee, David chemist, pharmaceutical company executive

Mamaroneck
Mazzola, Claude Joseph physicist, small business owner

Manhasset
Pam, Eleanor behavioral sciences educator

Manlius
Martonosi, Anthony Nicholas biochemistry educator, researcher

Melville
Damadian, Raymond Vahan biophysicist
Pelle, Edward Gerard biochemist
Price, Howard Charles chemist

New Hartford
Maurer, Gernant Elmer metallurgical executive, consultant

New Paltz
†Lavallee, David Kenneth chemistry educator, researcher

New Rochelle
Margolin, Harold metallurgical educator

New York
Allison, Michael David space scientist, astronomy educator
Asch, Arthur Louis environmental company executive
Ashen, Philip chemist
Bederson, Benjamin physicist, educator
Berne, Bruce J. chemistry educator
Borowitz, Sidney retired physics educator
Breslow, Esther May Greenberg biochemistry educator, researcher
Breslow, Ronald Charles chemist, educator
Campbell, George, Jr. physicist, administrator
Chargaff, Erwin biochemistry educator emeritus, writer
Cheng, Chuen Yan biochemist, educator
Chevray, Rene physics educator
Cohen, Ezechiel Godert David physicist, educator
Colby, Frank Gerhardt scientific consultant
Courant, Ernest David physicist
Cross, George Alan Martin biochemistry educator, researcher
Cummins, Herman Zachary physicist
Dailey, Benjamin Peter chemistry educator
Danishefsky, Samuel J. chemistry educator
de Duve, Christian René chemist, educator
Doorish, John Francis physicist, mathematician, educator
Edelman, Isidore Samuel biochemist and medical educator
Eisenthal, Kenneth B. physical chemistry educator
Erlanger, Bernard Ferdinand biochemist, educator
Ferrier, Joseph John atmospheric physicist
Flynn, George William chemistry educator, researcher
Fox, Jack Jay chemist, educator
Fraenkel, George Kessler chemistry educator
Glassgold, Alfred Emanuel physicist, educator
Goulianos, Konstantin physics educator
Grunberger, Dezider biochemist, researcher
Gudas, Lorraine Jean biochemist, molecular biologist, educator
Guillen, Michael Arthur mathematical physicist, educator, writer, television journalist
Guo, Chu chemistry educator
Hajjar, David Phillip biochemist, educator
Hallberg, Bengt O. systems strategy director, fiber optic specialist
Halpern, Alvin Michael physicist, educator
Hansen, James E. physicist, meteorologist, federal agency administrator
Harris, Cyril Manton physicist, engineering and architecture educator, consulting acoustical engineer
Hoffert, Martin Irving applied science educator
Hoffman, Linda M. chemist, educator
†Johnston, Ronald Charles chemistry educator
Kaku, Michio theoretical nuclear physicist, educator
Katsoyannis, Panayotis George biochemist, educator
Katz, Thomas J. chemistry educator
Kellogg, Herbert Humphrey metallurgist, educator
Khuri, Nicola Najib physicist, educator
Krasna, Alvin Isaac biochemist, educator
Kuo, John Tsungfen geophysicist, educator, researcher
Laughlin, John Seth physicist, educator
Lax, Melvin theoretical physicist
Lee, Tsung-Dao physicist, educator
Lieberman, Seymour biochemistry educator emeritus
Low, Barbara Wharton biochemist, biophysicist
Machlin, Eugene Solomon metallurgy educator, consultant
Marshall, Thomas Carlisle applied physics educator
McKenna, Malcolm Carnegie vertebrate paleontologist, curator, educator
Merrifield, Robert Bruce biochemist, educator
Middleton, David physicist, applied mathematician, educator
Nakanishi, Koji chemistry educator, research institute administrator
Newell, Norman Dennis paleontologist, geologist, museum curator, educator
Norell, Mark Allen paleontology educator
Nowick, Arthur Stanley metallurgy and materials science educator
Oppenheimer, Michael physicist
Oreskes, Irwin biochemistry educator
Osgood, Richard Magee, Jr. applied physics and electrical engineering educator, research administrator
Pais, Abraham physicist, educator
Parkin, Gerard Francis Ralph chemistry educator, researcher
Pechukas, Philip chemistry educator
Percus, Jerome Kenneth physicist, educator
Peskin, Charles physicist, educator
Pinczuk, Aron physicist
Piore, Emanuel Rueven physicist
Rhodes, Yorke E(dward) organic chemist, educator
Robinson, Enders Anthony geophysics educator, writer
Sakita, Bunji physicist, educator
Sarachik, Myriam Paula physics educator
Saxena, Brij B. biochemist, endocrinologist, educator
Schwartz, Melvin physics educator, laboratory administrator
Shalit, Hanoch imaging scientist, executive
Simon, Eric Jacob neurochemist, educator
Sonenberg, Martin biochemistry educator, physician
Spector, Abraham ophthalmic biochemist, educator, laboratory administrator
Spielman, Andrew Ian biochemist
Stork, Gilbert chemistry educator, investigator
Störmer, Horst Ludwig physicist
Stroke, Hinko Henry physicist, educator
Szer, Wlodzimierz biochemist, educator
Tomashefsky, Philip biomedical researcher, educator
Turro, Nicholas John chemistry educator
Verdol, Joseph Arthur chemist
Von Foerster, Thomas physicist, editor
Werthamer, N. Richard physicist
Worgul, Basil Vladimir radiation scientist
Zakim, David biochemist

Niagara Falls
Bharadwaj, Prem Datta physics educator
Knowles, Richard Norris chemist

Niskayuna
Billmeyer, Fred Wallace, Jr. chemist, educator
Burke, Joseph Eldrid materials scientist
Edelheit, Lewis S. research physicist
Katz, Samuel geophysics educator
Lafferty, James Martin physicist
Mihran, Theodore Gregory retired physicist

Oneonta
Horner, Carl Matthew chemistry educator
Merilan, Michael Preston astrophysicist, dean, educator

Oswego
Silveira, Augustine, Jr. chemistry educator

Palisades
Broecker, Wallace S. geophysics educator
Cane, Mark Alan oceanography and climate researcher
Hayes, Dennis Edward geophysicist, educator
Richards, Paul Granston geophysics educator, seismologist
Sykes, Lynn Ray geologist, educator

Potsdam
Fendler, Janos Hugo chemistry educator
Mackay, Raymond Arthur chemist
Matijevic, Egon chemistry educator
Siiman, Olavi chemist

Poughkeepsie
Beck, Curt Werner chemist, educator
Deiters, Sister Joan Adele psychotherapist, nun, chemistry educator
Lang, William Warner physicist
Maling, George Croswell, Jr. physicist
Pliskin, William Aaron physicist

Rochester
Bigelow, Nicholas Pierre physicist, educator
Boeckman, Robert Kenneth, Jr. chemistry educator, organic chemistry researcher
Duarte, Francisco Javier physicist, researcher
Eisenberg, Richard S. chemistry educator
Elder, Fred Kingsley, Jr. physicist, educator
Farrar, James Martin chemistry educator
Ferbel, Thomas physics educator, physicist
Gates, Marshall DeMotte, Jr. chemistry educator
Hall, Dennis Gene optics educator
Hilf, Russell biochemist
Kampmeier, Jack August Carlos chemist, educator
Kende, Andrew Steven chemistry educator
Kingslake, Rudolf retired optical designer
Knauer, James Philip physicist
Knox, Robert Seiple physicist, educator
Kreilick, Robert W. chemist, educator
Langner, Andreas chemistry educator, consultant
Lever, O. William, Jr. chemist
Luckey, George William research chemist
Makous, Walter Leon visual scientist, educator
Mandel, Leonard physics and optics educator, researcher
McCrory, Robert Lee physicist, mechanical engineering educator
Salamone, Joseph Charles polymer chemistry educator
Sherman, Fred biochemist, educator
Skupsky, Stanley laser fusion scientist
Smith, Harold Charles biochemistry educator, academic administrator
Thomas, John Howard astrophysicist, engineer, educator
Thorndike, Edward Harmon physicist
Wolf, Emil physics educator

Roslyn
Stein, Theodore Anthony biochemist, educator

Rouses Point
Weierstall, Richard Paul retired pharmaceutical chemist

Saint James
Bigeleisen, Jacob chemist, educator

Scarborough
Wittcoff, Harold Aaron chemist

Scarsdale
Porosoff, Harold chemist, research and development director

Schenectady
Alpher, Ralph Asher physicist
Anthony, Thomas Richard research physicist
Cline, Harvey Ellis metallurgist
Fleischer, Robert Louis physics educator
Hebb, Malcolm Hayden physicist
Kambour, Roger Peabody polymer physical chemist, researcher
Luborsky, Fred Everett research physicist
Tiemann, Jerome J. physicist
Zheng, Maggie (Xiaoci) materials scientist, turbine coating specialist

Sea Cliff
Rich, Charles Anthony hydrogeologist, consultant

Shelter Island
Cerami, Anthony biochemistry educator

Sherburne
Dodd, Jack Gordon, Jr. physicist, educator

Smithtown
Friedlander, Gerhart nuclear chemist

Southold
Bachrach, Howard L. biochemist

Spencerport
Vizy, Kalman Nicholas research physicist

Staten Island
Minotti, Mark Anthony chemistry educator
Yang, Song-Yu research biochemist

Stony Brook
Alexander, John Macmillan, Jr. chemistry educator
Bonner, Francis Truesdale chemist, educator, university dean
Brown, Gerald Edward physicist, educator
Chen Ning Yang physicist, educator
Hanson, Gilbert Nikolai geochemistry educator
Herman, Herbert materials science educator
Kahn, Peter B. physics educator
Krikorian, Abraham Der biochemistry and cell biology educator
Ojima, Iwao chemistry educator
Scarlata, Suzanne Frances biophysical chemist
Swanson, Robert Lawrence oceanographer, academic program administrator
†Waliser, Duane Edward atmospheric science educator, consultant
Weidner, Donald J. geophysicist educator

Syracuse
Baldwin, John Edwin chemistry educator
Birge, Robert Richards chemistry educator
Conan, Robert James, Jr. chemistry educator, consultant
†Griffin, David mycologist
Honig, Arnold physics educator, researcher
Lemon, Leslie Roy radar meteorologist
Levy, Hans Richard biochemistry educator
McDonnell, Jeffrey John hydrology educator
Muller, Ernest H. geology educator
Nafie, Laurence Allen chemistry educator
Prucha, John James geologist, educator
Robinson, Joseph Edward geology educator, consulting petroleum geologist
Smith, Kenneth Judson, Jr. chemist, theoretician, educator
Wellner, Marcel Nahum physics educator, researcher

Tarrytown
Gross, Stanislaw environmental sciences educator, activist
Singer, Jeffrey Michael organic analytical chemist

Troy
Bunce, Stanley Chalmers chemist, educator
Daves, Glenn Doyle, Jr. science educator, chemist, researcher
Ferris, James Peter chemist, educator
Giaever, Ivar physicist
Krause, Sonja chemistry educator
Levinger, Joseph Solomon physicist, educator
Medicus, Heinrich Adolf physicist, educator
Potts, Kevin T. emeritus chemistry educator
Sperber, Daniel physicist
White, Frederick Andrew physics educator, physicist

Tuxedo Park
Hall, Frederick Keith chemist

Upton
Blume, Martin physicist
Bond, Peter Danford physicist
Chrien, Robert Edward retired physicist
Goldhaber, Maurice physicist
Harbottle, Garman chemist
Hendrie, Joseph Mallam physicist, nuclear engineer, government official
Holroyd, Richard Allen research scientist
Lindenbaum, S(eymour) J(oseph) physicist
Lowenstein, Derek Irving physicist
Marr, Robert Bruce physicist, educator
McWhan, Denis Bayman physicist
Ozaki, Satoshi physicist
Pandey, Sanjeev Ulrich physicist
Rau, Ralph Ronald retired physicist
Ruckman, Mark Warren physicist
Samios, Nicholas Peter physicist
Setlow, Jane Kellock biophysicist
Setlow, Richard Burton biophysicist
Shutt, Ralph P. research physicist
Studier, Frederick William biophysicist
Sutherland, John Clark physicist, researcher
Sutin, Norman chemistry educator, scientist

Utica
Iodice, Arthur Alfonso biochemist

Wappingers Falls
Maissel, Leon Israel physicist, engineer
McCamy, Calvin Samuel optics scientist

Webster
Conwell, Esther Marly physicist

West Point
Leupold, Herbert August physicist
Oldaker, Bruce Gordon physicist, military officer

White Plains
Flanigen, Edith Marie materials scientist, consultant

Yonkers
Levatino, Thomas, Jr. physics and chemistry educator
Roth, Howard chemist, engineer, consultant

Yorktown Heights
Chaudhari, Praveen materials physicist
Fang, Frank Fu physicist, electronics engineer
Fowler, Alan Bicksler retired physicist
Garwin, Richard Lawrence physicist
Gutzwiller, Martin Charles theoretical physicist, research scientist
Keyes, Robert W. physicist
Kirkpatrick, Edward Scott physicist
Landauer, Rolf William physicist
Lang, Norton David physicist
Ning, Tak Hung physicist, microelectronic technologist
Sorokin, Peter Pitirimovich physicist
Spiller, Eberhard Adolf physicist

NORTH CAROLINA

Apex
Liu, Andrew Tze Chiu chemical researcher and developer

Asheville
Haggard, William Henry meteorologist
Meyerson, Seymour retired chemist

Black Mountain
Lathrop, Gertrude Adams chemist, consultant

Chapel Hill
Brookhart, Maurice S. chemist
Buck, Richard Pierson chemistry educator, researcher
Bursey, Maurice M. chemistry educator
Davis, Morris Schuyler astronomer
Eliel, Ernest Ludwig chemist, educator
Forman, Donald T. biochemist
Frampton, Paul Howard physics researcher, educator
Fullagar, Paul David geology educator, geochemical consultant
Lee, Kuo-Hsiung medicinal chemistry educator
Ligett, Waldo Buford chemist
Macdonald, James Ross physicist, educator
McKay, Kenneth Gardiner physicist, electronics company executive
Merzbacher, Eugen physicist, educator
Meyer, Thomas J. chemistry educator
Miller, Daniel Newton, Jr. retired geologist, consultant
Mitchell, Earl Nelson physicist, educator
Murray, Royce Wilton chemistry educator
Neumann, Andrew Conrad geological oceanography educator
Parr, Robert Ghormley chemistry educator
Rogers, John James William geology educator
St. Jean, Joseph, Jr. micropaleontologist, educator
Sancar, Aziz research biochemist
Slifkin, Lawrence Myer physics educator
Wolfenden, Richard Vance biochemistry educator
York, James Wesley, Jr. theoretical physicist, educator

Charlotte
Hall, Peter Michael physics educator, electronics researcher
Roels, Oswald Albert oceanographer, educator, business executive

Davidson
Burnett, John Nicholas retired chemistry educator

Duck
Majewski, Theodore Eugene chemist

Durham
Chesnut, Donald Blair chemistry educator
Cocks, Franklin Hadley materials scientist
Evans, Ralph Aiken physicist, consultant
Fridovich, Irwin biochemistry educator
†Hajcak, Catherine geologist, consultant
Hammes, Gordon G. chemistry educator
Han, Moo-Young physicist
Jaszczak, Ronald Jack physicist, researcher, consultant
Joklik, Wolfgang Karl biochemist, virologist, educator
Kay, Richard Frederick paleontology and biological anthropology educator
Meyer, Horst physics educator
Modrich, Paul L. biochemistry educator
Opara, Emmanuel Chukwuemeka biochemistry educator
Pearsall, George Wilbur materials scientist, mechanical engineer, educator, consultant
Perkins, Ronald Dee geologist, educator
Roberson, Nathan Russell physicist, educator
Smith, Peter chemist, educator, consultant
Stroscio, Michael Anthony physicist, educator
Walter, Richard Lawrence physicist, educator

Fayetteville
Resnick, Paul R. research chemist

Greensboro
Banegas, Estevan Brown environmental biotechnology executive
Clark, Clifton Bob physicist
Williams, Irving Laurence physics educator

Hendersonville
Halm, James Maurice retired chemist, poet
Kratz, Howard Russel physicist, researcher
Saby, John Sanford physicist

High Point
Bowman, Gray chemist, educator

Linwood
Barnes, Melver Raymond retired chemist

New Hill
Goncarovs, Gunti radiation chemist
Weber, Michael Howard senior nuclear control operator

Pinehurst
Huizenga, John Robert nuclear chemist, educator

Pittsboro
Quinn, Jarus William physicist, former association executive

Raleigh
Arya, Satya Pal *meteorology educator*
Aspnes, David Erik *physicist, educator*
Droessler, Earl George *geophysicist educator*
Ebisuzaki, Yukiko *chemistry educator*
Fox, Marye Anne *university chancellor, chemistry educator*
Goldstein, Irving Solomon *chemistry educator, consultant*
Horton, Horace Robert *biochemistry educator*
Mitchell, Gary Earl *physicist, educator*
Owens, Tyler Benjamin *chemist*
Stiles, Phillip John *physicist, educator*
Swaisgood, Harold Everett *biochemist, educator*
Whitten, Jerry Lynn *chemistry educator*

Research Triangle Park
Chao, James Lee *chemist*
Selkirk, James Kirkwood *biochemist*
Senzel, Alan Joseph *analytical chemistry consultant, music critic*
Wiener, Russell Warren *environmental scientist, researcher*

Wilmington
Bissette, Samuel Delk *astronomer, artist, financial executive*
Hansen, Steven Michael *fiber scientist, researcher*
Humphreys, Charles Raymond, Jr. *retired research chemist*
Quin, Louis DuBose *chemist, educator*

Winston Salem
Dobbins, James Talmage, Jr. *analytical chemist, researcher*
Mokrasch, Lewis Carl *neurochemist, educator*
Rodgman, Alan *chemist, consultant*

NORTH DAKOTA

Bismarck
†Ness, Gary Robert *administrator*

Grand Forks
Jacobs, Francis Albin *biochemist, educator*
Nordlie, Robert Conrad *biochemistry educator*

OHIO

Akron
Abraham, Tonson *chemist, researcher*
Bohm, Georg G. A. *physicist*
Cheng, Stephen Zheng Di *chemistry educator, polymeric material researcher*
Gent, Alan Neville *physicist, educator*
Kennedy, Joseph Paul *polymer scientist, researcher*
Maximovich, Michael Joseph *chemist, consultant*
Piirma, Irja *chemist, educator*

Alliance
Berthold, John William, III *physicist*

Archbold
Bergman, Jerry Rae *science educator*

Beavercreek
Gupta, Vijay Kumar *chemistry educator*

Berea
Jensen, Adolph Robert *former chemistry educator*

Bowling Green
Brecher, Arthur Seymour *biochemistry educator*
Steel, Steven Chesney *environmental scientist, educator*

Bratenahl
Dunn, Horton, Jr. *organic chemist*

Brecksville
Farkas, Julius *chemist*

Burbank
Koucky, Frank Louis *geology educator, archeogeology researcher*

Chardon
Dietrich, Joseph Jacob *retired chemist, research executive*
Uscheek, David Petrovich *chemist*

Cincinnati
Alexander, John J. *chemistry educator*
Benjamin, Lawrence *retired research chemist*
Crable, John V. *chemist*
Ford, Emory A. *chemist, researcher*
Francis, Marion David *consulting chemist*
Goodman, Bernard *physics educator*
Kawahara, Fred Katsumi *research chemist*
Martin, Daniel William *acoustical physicist*
Meal, Larie *chemistry educator, researcher, consultant*
Menyhert, Stephan *retired chemist*
Merchant, Mylon Eugene *physicist, engineer*
Relyea, Carl Miller *hydrologist*
Rockwell, R(onald) James, Jr. *laser and electro-optics consultant*
Sullivan, James F. *physicist, educator*
Williams, James Case *metallurgist*
Witten, Louis *physics educator*

Cleveland
Bidelman, William Pendry *astronomer, educator*
Blackwell, John *polymers scientist, educator*
Carey, Paul Richard *biophysicist*
Chamis, Christos Constantinos *aerospace scientist, educator*
Deissler, Robert George *fluid dynamicist, researcher*
Dowell, Michael Brendan *chemist*
Eakman, Mark *chemist*
Hanson, Richard Winfield *biochemist, educator*
Jenkins, Thomas Llewellyn *physics educator*
Klopman, Gilles *chemistry educator*
Koenig, Jack L. *chemist, educator*
Kowalski, Kenneth Lawrence *physicist, educator*
Krieger, Irvin Mitchell *chemistry educator, consultant*
Landau, Bernard Robert *biochemistry educator, physician*
Lando, Jerome Burton *macromolecular science educator*
Litt, Morton Herbert *macromolecular science educator, researcher*
Mawardi, Osman Kamel *plasma physicist*
McGervey, John Donald *physics educator, researcher*
Rogers, Charles Edwin *physical chemistry educator*
Schuele, Donald Edward *physics educator*
Troiano, Alexander Robert *metallurgist, educator*

Columbus
Behrman, Edward Joseph *biochemistry educator*
Bergstrom, Stig Magnus *geology educator*
Brierley, Gerald P. *physiological chemistry educator*
Brown, Susan Thomas *research scientist*
Corbato, Charles Edward *geology educator*
Cornwell, David George *biochemist, educator*
Daehn, Glenn Steven *materials scientist*
De Lucia, Frank Charles *physicist, educator*
Denniss, Juliet Dawn *environmental specialist, geologist*
Elliot, David Hawksley *geologist*
Faure, Gunter *geology educator*
Firestone, Richard Francis *chemistry educator*
Foland, Kenneth A. *geological sciences educator*
Goodridge, Alan Gardner *research biochemist, educator*
Gordon, Sydney Michael *research chemist*
Herbst, Eric *physicist, astronomer*
Kolattukudy, Pappachan Ettoop *biochemist, educator*
Ling, Ta-Yung *physics educator*
†Madia, William Juul *chemist*
Marzluf, George Austin *biochemistry educator*
Mayer, Victor James *earth system science educator*
Meites, Samuel *clinical chemist, educator*
Milford, Frederick John *retired research company executive*
Miller, Terry Alan *chemistry educator*
Newsom, Gerald Higley *astronomy educator*
Paquette, Leo Armand *chemistry educator*
Reibel, Kurt *physicist, educator*
Relle, Ferenc Matyas *chemist*
Rosenberg, Paul *physicist, consultant*
Smail, Harry E(ugene) *environmental planner and administrator*
Soloway, Albert Herman *medicinal chemist*
Voss, Anne Coble *nutritional biochemist*
Wali, Mohan Kishen *environmental science and natural resources educator*
Webb, Thomas Evan *biochemistry educator*
Wilkins, John Warren *physics educator*
Wojcicki, Andrew Adalbert *chemist, educator*

Dayton
Battino, Rubin *chemistry educator, retired*
Chuck, Leon *materials scientist*
Fang, Zhaoqiang *research physicist*
Janning, John Louis *research scientist, consultant*
Nielsen, Philip Edward *physicist, research manager*
Weathington, Billy Christopher *analytical chemist*

Fairborn
Workman, John Mitchell *chemist*

Highland Hills
Brathwaite, Ormond Dennis *chemistry educator*

Huron
†Herdendorf, Charles Edward, III *retired oceanographer, limnologist, consultant*

Kent
Doane, J. William *physics educator and researcher, science administrator*
Heimlich, Richard Allen *geologist, educator*
†Keller, John David *earth science educator*
Myers, R(alph) Thomas *chemist, educator*
Tuan, Debbie Fu-Tai *chemistry educator*

Kettering
Clark, Leland Charles, Jr. *biochemist, medical products executive*

Liberty Township
Conditt, Margaret Karen *scientist, policy analyst*

Mansfield
Beiter, Thomas Albert *crystallographer, research scientist, consultant*

Mason
Colson, Anny-Odile *chemist*

Middletown
Marine, Susan Sonchik *analytical chemist, educator*

Norwalk
Germann, Richard Paul *pharmaceutical company chemist, executive*

Oberlin
Carlton, Terry Scott *chemist, educator*
Simonson, Bruce Miller *geologist, educator*
Warner, Robert Edson *physics educator*
Weinstock, Robert *physics educator*

Oxford
Gordon, Gilbert *chemist, educator*
Macklin, Philip Alan *physics educator*

Painesville
Scozzie, James Anthony *chemist*

Piketon
Manuta, David Mark *research chemist, consultant*

Sheffield Lake
Friend, Helen Margaret *chemist*

Toledo
Saffran, Murray *biochemist*

West Chester
Mack, Mark Philip *chemical company executive*

Wickliffe
Kornbrekke, Ralph Erik *colloid chemist*

Willoughby
†Krause, Marjorie N. *biochemist, computer scientist*

Wright Patterson AFB
Eastwood, DeLyle *chemist*
Fernelius, Nils Conard *physicist*
Garscadden, Alan *physicist*
Voevodin, Andrey Aleksejevich *material scientist*

Yellow Springs
Spokane, Robert Bruce *biophysical chemist*

OKLAHOMA

Ada
Stafford, Donald Gene *chemistry educator*
Wilkin, Richard Thomas *geochemist*

Bartlesville
Dwiggins, Claudius William, Jr. *chemist*
Hogan, J(ohn) Paul *chemistry researcher, consultant*
Welch, M. Bruce *research chemist*

Edmond
Aclin, Keith Andrew *technicial service executive, educator*

Fort Towson
Pike, Thomas Harrison *plant chemist*

Muskogee
Kendrick, Thomas Rudolph *chemist*

Norman
Atkinson, Gordon *chemistry educator*
Bluestein, Howard Bruce *meteorology educator*
Christian, Sherril D. *chemistry educator, administrator*
Ciereszko, Leon Stanley, Sr. *chemistry educator*
Eilts, Michael Dean *research meteorologist, manager*
Kessler, Edwin *meteorology educator, consultant*
Lamb, Peter James *meteorology educator, researcher, consultant*
Mankin, Charles John *geology educator*
Pigott, John Dowling *geologist, geophysicist, geochemist, educator, consultant*
Roberts, Raymond Url *geologist*
†Xue, Ming *meteorologist, researcher*

Nowata
Osborn, Ann George *retired chemist*

Oklahoma City
Alaupovic, Petar *biochemist, educator*
Dunn, Parker Southerland *retired chemical company consultant*
Johnson, B(ruce) Connor *biochemist, educator, consultant*
Magarian, Robert Armen *medicinal chemist, researcher, educator, inventor*
Matsumoto, Hiroyuki *biochemistry educator, researcher*

Stillwater
Berlin, Kenneth Darrell *chemistry educator, consultant, researcher*
Gorin, George *retired chemistry educator*
†Rooney, John F., Jr. *geography educator, researcher*

Tulsa
Bennison, Allan Parnell *geological consultant*
Blais, Roger Nathaniel *physics educator*
Horn, Myron Kay *consulting petroleum geologist, author, educator*
Smothers, William Edgar, Jr. *geophysical exploration company executive*

OREGON

Albany
Dooley, George Joseph, III *metallurgist*

Ashland
Addicott, Warren Oliver *retired geologist, educator*
Grover, James Robb *chemist, editor*

Beaverton
Hammond, George Simms *chemist, consultant*

Bend
Gustafson, Lewis Allan *engineering geologist*

Chiloquin
Siemens, Richard Ernest *retired metallurgy administrator, researcher*

Corvallis
Arp, Daniel James *biochemistry educator*
Baird, William McKenzie *chemical carcinogenesis researcher, biochemistry educator*
Dalrymple, Gary Brent *research geologist*
Drake, Charles Whitney *physicist*
Evans, Harold J. *plant physiologist, biochemist, educator*
Huyer, Adriana *oceanographer, educator*
Moore, George W(illiam) *geologist*
Shoemaker, Clara Brink *retired chemistry educator*
Sleight, Arthur William *chemist*
Thomas, Thomas Darrah *chemistry educator*
Van Holde, Kensal Edward *biochemistry educator*
Yeats, Robert Sheppard *geologist, educator*

Eugene
Boekelheide, Virgil Carl *chemistry educator*
Crasemann, Bernd *physicist, educator*
Diwu, Zhenjun *chemist*
Donnelly, Russell James *physicist, educator*
Girardeau, Marvin Denham *physics educator*
Griffith, Osbie Hayes *chemistry educator*
Mazo, Robert Marc *chemistry educator, retired*
Retallack, Gregory John *geologist educator*
Schellman, John A. *chemistry educator*
von Hippel, Peter Hans *chemistry educator*
Youngquist, Walter Lewellyn *consulting geologist*

Hillsboro
Carruthers, John Robert *scientist*
Yang, Lin *chemist*

Medford
Bouquet, Francis Lester *physicist*

Monmouth
White, Donald Harvey *physics educator emeritus*

Otter Rock
Kassner, Michael Ernest *materials science educator, researcher*

Portland
Claycomb, Cecil Keith *biochemist, educator*
Cohen, Norm *chemist*
Jones, Richard Theodore *biochemistry educator*
Marsh, John Harrison *environmental planner, lawyer*
Pearson, David Petri *chemist*
Weeks, Wilford Frank *retired geophysics educator, glaciologist*
Wetzel, Karl Joseph *physics educator, university official and dean*

Salem
Gillette, (Philip) Roger *physicist, systems engineer*

PENNSYLVANIA

Allentown
Goldey, James Mearns *physicist*
Orphanides, Gus George *research chemist*
Pez, Guido Peter *research chemist*

Ardmore
Stanley, Edward Alexander *geologist, forensic scientist, technical and academic administrator*

Bellefonte
Betz, William Robert *chemist*

Berwyn
Whittington, Cathy Dee *chemist*

Bethlehem
Alhadeff, Jack Abraham *biochemist, educator*
Eades, J. A. *electron microscopist, physicist, consultant*
Evenson, Edward Bernard *geology educator*
Gunton, James Douglas *physics educator*
Heindel, Ned Duane *chemistry educator*
Hertzberg, Richard Warren *materials science and engineering educator, researcher*
Lyman, Charles Edson *materials scientist, educator*
Smyth, Donald Morgan *chemical educator, researcher*
Watkins, George Daniels *physics educator*
Weidner, Richard Tilghman *physicist, educator*

Bryn Mawr
Crawford, Maria Luisa Buse *geology educator*
Mallory, Frank Bryant *chemistry educator*

Carlisle
Laws, Kenneth L. *physics educator, author*
Long, Howard Charles *physics educator emeritus*

Chadds Ford
Webster, Owen Wright *chemist*

Cheltenham
Shmukler, Herman William *retired biochemist, consultant*

Clearfield
Haag, Harvey Eugene *physics educator*

Collegeville
Holder, Neville Lewis *chemist*

Conshohocken
Fletcher, Jeffrey Edward *editor, biochemist, medical writer*
Kirkpatrick, John Alger *organic chemist, food scientist*

Dallas
Rockensies, Kenneth Jules *physicist, educator*

Doylestown
Brink, Frank, Jr. *biophysicst, former educator*
Tabachnick, Michael Neil *physicist, educator*

Elkins Park
Prince, Morton Bronenberg *physicist*

Erie
Karlson, Eskil Leannart *biophysicist*

Feasterville Trevose
Dickstein, Jack *chemist*

Harrisburg
Dodge, Clifford Howle *geologist*
Mowery, J. Ronald *geologist, physicist, educator*
Zook, Merlin Wayne *meteorologist*

Haverford
Lazar, Anna *chemist*

Hershey
King, Steven Harold *health physicist*

Huntingdon Valley
Leibholz, Stephen Wolfgang *physicist, engineering company executive, entrepreneur*

Kennett Square
Lippincott, Sarah Lee *astronomer, graphologist*
Wilson, Armin *chemist, retired*

Lincoln University
Roberts, Lynn Ernest *theoretical physicist, educator*
Williams, Willie, Jr. *physicist, educator*

Lock Haven
Sweeny, Charles David *chemist*

Malvern
Fisher, Sallie Ann *chemist*

Media
Voltz, Sterling Ernest *physical chemist, researcher*

Merion Station
Amado, Ralph David *physics educator*

Mont Alto
Toothacker, William Sanford, III *physics educator*

Mount Joy
Lodde, Gordon Maynard *health physics consultant*

Moylan
Eberl, James Joseph *physical chemist, consultant*

Narberth
Fenichel, Richard Lee *retired biochemist*

New Holland
Papadakis, Emmanuel Philippos *physicist, consultant*

Philadelphia
Ajzenberg-Selove, Fay *physicist, educator*
Burstein, Elias *physicist, educator*
Chance, Britton *biophysics and physical chemistry educator emeritus*
Childress, Scott Julius *medicinal chemist*
Cohn, Mildred *biochemist, educator*
Creech, Hugh John *chemist*
Davis, Raymond, Jr. *physical chemistry researcher*
Devlin, Thomas McKeown *biochemist, educator*
Dutton, Peter Leslie *biochemist, educator*
Dymicky, Michael *retired chemist*
Farber, Emmanuel *pathology and biochemistry educator*
Fitts, Donald Dennis *chemist, educator*
Glick, Jane Mills *biochemistry educator*
Glusker, Jenny Pickworth *chemist*
Hameka, Hendrik Frederik *chemist, educator*
Havas, Peter *physicist, educator*
Hochstrasser, Robin M. *chemist, educator*
Hossain, Murshed *physicist*
Intemann, Robert Louis *physics educator, researcher*
Karathanasis, Sotirios Konstantinou *biochemist*
Klein, Abraham *physics educator, researcher*
Klein, Michael Lawrence *research chemist, educator*
Kritchevsky, David *biochemist, educator*
Lande, Kenneth *physicist, astronomer, educator*
Langacker, Paul George *physics educator*
Levitt, Israel Monroe *astronomer*
Litwack, Gerald *biochemistry researcher, educator, administrator*
Ma, Chung-Pei Michelle *astronomer, educator*
Malamud, Daniel *biochemistry educator*
Marinelli, Joseph Marcello *aerospace advisor*
Maurer, Paul Herbert *biochemist, educator*
Muzykantov, Vladimir Rurick *immunochemist, researcher*
Nixon, Eugene Ray *chemist, educator*
Noordergraaf, Abraham *biophysics educator*
Otvos, Laszlo Istvan, Jr. *organic chemist*
Prairie, Celia Esther Freda *biochemistry educator*
Prockop, Darwin Johnson *biochemist, physician*
Rosen, Gerald Harris *physicist, consultant, educator*
Rutman, Robert Jesse *biochemist, educator*
Shen, Benjamin Shih-Ping *scientist, engineer, educator*
Takashima, Shiro *biophysics educator*
Vitek, Vaclav *materials scientist*
Wales, Walter D. *physicist, educator*
Wilcots, David N. *consulting and environmental geologist, artist*

Pittsburgh
Berry, Guy Curtis *polymer science educator, researcher*
Biondi, Manfred Anthony *physicist, educator*
Bothner-By, Aksel Arnold *chemist, horseman*
Caretto, Albert Alexander *chemist, educator*
Carr, Walter James, Jr. *research physicist, consultant*
Cassidy, William Arthur *geology and planetary science educator*
Choyke, Wolfgang Justus *physicist*
Chu, Deh-Ying *chemist, researcher*
Coltman, John Wesley *physicist*
Emmerich, Werner Sigmund *physicist*
Feller, Robert Livingston *chemist, art conservation scientist*
Fetkovich, John G. *physics educator*
Finn, Frances Mary *biochemistry researcher*
Friedberg, Simeon Adlow *physicist, educator*
Gerjuoy, Edward *physicist, lawyer*
Huang, Mei Qing *physics educator, researcher*
Janis, Allen Ira *retired physicist, educator*
Kumta, Prashant Nagesh *materials science educator, engineering educator, consultant*
Laughlin, David Eugene *materials science educator, metallurgical consultant*
MaŠka, Rudolf *retired chemist, financial executive*
Massalski, Thaddeus Bronislaw *material scientist, educator*
Matyjaszewski, Krzysztof *chemist, educator*
Mortimer, James Winslow *analytical chemist*
Mullins, William Wilson *physical metallurgist*
Page, Lorne Albert *physicist, educator*
Plazek, Donald John *materials science educator*
Rosenberg, Jerome Laib *chemist, educator*
Rosenkranz, Herbert S. *environmental toxicology educator*
Sashin, Donald *pet physicist, radiological physicist, educator*
Sekerka, Robert Floyd *physics educator, scientist*
Sorensen, Raymond Andrew *physics educator*
Wallenberger, Frederick T. *materials scientist*
White, Robert Marshall *physicist, government official, educator*
Yates, John Thomas, Jr. *chemistry educator, research director*
Young, Hugh David *physics educator, writer, organist*

Plymouth Meeting
Mitchell, Matthew Dunlap *medical research analyst*

Pottstown
Hergert, Herbert Lawrence *consultant*

Quakertown
McDaniel, Robert Stephen *technical professional*

Reading
Feeman, James Frederic *chemist, consultant*
Richart, Douglas Stephen *chemist*

Spring House
Klotz, Wendy Lynnett *analytical chemist*
Reitz, Allen Bernard *organic chemist*

State College
Atchley, Anthony Armstrong *physicist, educator*
Garrett, Steven Lurie *physicist*
German, Randall Michael *materials engineering educator, consultant*
Ginoza, William *retired biophysics educator*
†Henisch, Heinz Kurt *retired physics educator*
Zhao, Hequan *chemist, researcher*

Swarthmore
Bilaniuk, Oleksa Myron *physicist, educator*
Hammons, James Hutchinson *chemistry educator, researcher*
Oneal, Glen, Jr. *retired physicist*
Pasternack, Robert Francis *chemistry educator*

Swiftwater
Six, Howard R. *microbiologist*

University Park
Allcock, Harry R. *chemistry educator*
Badding, John Victor *chemistry educator*
Barnes, Hubert Lloyd *geochemistry educator*
Barron, Eric *earth scientist*
Benkovic, Stephen James *chemist*
Biederman, Edwin Williams, Jr. *petroleum geologist*
Blackadar, Alfred Kimball *meteorologist, educator*
†Brandt, William Nielsen *astronomer*
Cahir, John Joseph *meteorologist, educational administrator*
Castleman, Albert Welford, Jr. *physical chemist, educator*
†Clothiaux, Eugene Edmund *climate research scientist, meteorology educator*
Coleman, Michael Murray *polymer science educator*
Dutton, John Altnow *meteorologist, educator*
Frankl, Daniel Richard *physicist, educator*
Hogg, Richard *mineral/particle process engineering educator*
Hosler, Charles Luther, Jr. *meteorologist, educator*
Howell, Benjamin Franklin, Jr. *geophysicist, educator*
Jackman, Lloyd Miles *chemistry educator*
Kasting, James Fraser *research meteorologist, physicist*
Lampe, Frederick Walter *chemistry educator, consultant*
Larson, Daniel John *physics educator*
†Liu, Zi-Kui *materials science and engineering educator*
Newnham, Robert Everest *materials scientist, educator, research director*
Pazur, John Howard *biochemist, educator*
Roy, Rustum *interdisciplinary educator, materials researcher*
Rusinko, Frank, Jr. *fuels and materials scientist*
Song, Chunshan *chemist, chemical engineer, educator*
Taylor, William Daniel *biophysics educator, university dean*
White, William Blaine *geochemist, educator*
Winograd, Nicholas *chemist*

Valley Forge
Erb, Doretta Louise Barker *polymer applications scientist*
Erb, Robert Allan *physical scientist*

Villanova
Edwards, John Ralph *chemist, educator*
Phares, Alain Joseph *physicist, educator*

Wyndmoor
Pfeffer, Philip Elliot *biophysicist*

Wynnewood
Weinhouse, Sidney *biochemist, educator*

York
Burness, James Hubert *chemistry educator*

RHODE ISLAND

Coventry
Traficante, Daniel Dominick *chemist*

Kingston
Nixon, Scott West *oceanography science educator*

Narragansett
Pilson, Michael Edward Quinton *oceanography educator*

Newport
Piquette, Jean Conrad *physicist*

Portsmouth
Hostetler, Dean Bryan *industry environmental compliance consultant*

Providence
Avery, Donald Hills *metallurgist, educator, ethnographer*
Bray, Philip James *physicist*
Briant, Clyde Leonard *metallurgist, educator*
Carpenter, Gene Blakely *crystallography and chemistry educator*
Cooper, Leon N. *physicist, educator*
Dahlberg, Albert Edward *biochemistry educator*
Elbaum, Charles *physicist, educator, researcher*
Gerritsen, Hendrik Jurjen *physics educator, researcher*
Greene, Edward Forbes *chemistry educator*
†Head, James W., III *geological sciences educator*
Hermance, John Francis *geophysics educator, environmental geophysics and hydrology consultant*
Houghton, Anthony *physics educator, research scientist*
Imbrie, John *oceanography educator*
Lanou, Robert Eugene, Jr. *physicist, educator*
Levin, Frank S. *physicist, educator*
Parmentier, E. M. (Marc) *geophysics educator*
Pieters, Carle McGetchin *geology educator, planetary scientist, researcher*
Rieger, Philip Henri *chemistry educator*
Risen, William Maurice, Jr. *chemistry educator*
Tauc, Jan *physics educator*
Webb, Thompson *geological sciences educator, researcher*
Widgoff, Mildred *physicist, educator*

Wakefield
Moore, George Emerson, Jr. *geologist, educator*

West Greenwich
Anderson, Theodore Robert *physicist*

SOUTH CAROLINA

Aiken
Noah, John Christopher *scientist, planner, educator*

Anderson
Elzerman, Alan William *environmental chemistry educator*

Clemson
Clayton, Donald Delbert *astrophysicist, nuclear physicist, educator*
Davies, Brian Ewart *environmental sciences educator*
Griffin, Villard Stuart, Jr. *geology educator*
Krause, Lois Ruth Breur *chemistry educator*

Columbia
Edge, Ronald Dovaston *physics educator*
Paleologos, Evangelos *hydrologist, educator*
Schuette, Oswald Francis *physics educator*
Secor, Donald Terry, Jr. *geologist, educator*

Fair Play
Apinis, John *chemist*

Greer
Fantry, John Joseph *chemist*

Hilton Head Island
Ballantine, Todd Henry *environmental scientist*

Irmo
Gandy, James Thomas *meteorologist, entrepreneur*

Kiawah Island
Norton, Norman James *exploration geologist*

Pendleton
Spain, James Dorris, Jr. *biochemist, educator*

Spartanburg
Kuhn, Hans Heinrich *chemist*

SOUTH DAKOTA

Brookings
Duffey, George Henry *physics educator*
Jensen, William Phelps *chemistry educator*

Sioux Falls
Viste, Arlen Ellard *chemistry educator*

Spearfish
Erickson, Richard Ames *physicist, emeritus educator*

Vermillion
Neuhaus, Otto Wilhelm *biochemistry educator*

TENNESSEE

Chattanooga
Kiser, Thelma Kay *analytical chemist*

Cookeville
Kumar, Krishna *physics educator*

Cornersville
Caulfield, Henry John *physics educator*

Fayetteville
Wolfhard, Hans Georg *research scientist*

Gray
Terry, Glenn A. *retired nuclear chemist*

Greenback
Weeks, Robet Andrew *materials science researcher, educator*

Kingston
Manly, William Donald *metallurgist*

Knoxville
Alexeff, Igor *physicist, electrical engineer, educator emeritus*
Borie, Bernard Simon, Jr. *physicist, educator*
Dean, John Aurie *chemist, author, chemistry educator emeritus*
Mahan, Gerald Dennis *physics educator, researcher*
Schweitzer, George Keene *chemistry educator*
Williams, Thomas Ffrancon *chemist, educator*
Wunderlich, Bernhard *physical chemistry educator*

Memphis
Crane, Laura Jane *research chemist*
Desiderio, Dominic Morse, Jr. *chemistry and neurochemistry educator*
Fain, John Nicholas *biochemistry educator*
Lasslo, Andrew *medicinal chemist, educator*
Wildman, Gary Cecil *chemist*

Morristown
Culvern, Julian Brewer *retired chemist, educator*

Nashville
Barton, Neal, Jr. *meteorologist*
Bayuzick, Robert J. *materials scientist*
Chappell, Charles Richard *space scientist*
Chytil, Frank *biochemist*
Cohen, Stanley *biochemistry educator*
Cunningham, Leon William *biochemist, educator*
Dettbarn, Wolf-Dietrich *neurochemist, pharmacologist, educator*
Fort, Tomlinson *chemist, chemical engineering educator*
Hall, Douglas Scott *astronomy educator*
Heiser, Arnold Melvin *astronomer*
Hercules, David Michael *chemistry educator, consultant*
Kono, Tetsuro *biochemist, physiologist, educator*
Lukehart, Charles Martin *chemistry educator*
Silberman, Enrique *physics researcher and administrator*
Stubbs, Gerald *biochemist, educator*
Surowiec, Andrew Julius *biophysicist, researcher*
Wert, James Junior *materials scientist, educator*

Oak Ridge
Carlsmith, Roger Snedden *chemistry and energy conservation researcher*
Dickens, Justin Kirk *nuclear physicist*
Gifford, Franklin Andrew, Jr. *meteorologist*
Horak, James Albert *materials scientist, nuclear engineer, educator*
Huff, Dale Duane *hydrologist, educator*
Krause, Manfred Otto *physicist*
Larson, Bennett Charles *solid state physicist, researcher*
Maienschein, Fred C. *physicist*
Pinnaduwage, Lal Ariyaritna *physicist, educator*
Plasil, Franz *physicist*
Postma, Herman *physicist, consultant*
Satchler, George Raymond *physicist*
Totter, John Randolph *biochemist*
Trivelpiece, Alvin William *physicist, corporate executive*
Weinberg, Alvin Martin *physicist*
Whealton, John H. *physicist, educator*
Young, Jack Phillip *chemist*
Zucker, Alexander *physicist, administrator*

Powell
Gentry, Robert Vance *physicist, researcher, writer*

Signal Mountain
Howe, Lyman Harold, III *chemist*

Tullahoma
Dahotre, Narendra Bapurao *materials scientist, researcher, educator*

TEXAS

Abilene
Pickens, Jimmy Burton *earth and life science educator, military officer*

Amarillo
Malcolm, Steven Bryan *chemist, laboratory manager*

Arlington
Burkart, Burke *geology educator, researcher*
Damuth, John Erwin *marine geologist*
Pomerantz, Martin *chemistry educator, researcher*
Rajeshwar, Krishnan *chemist, educator*
Smith, Charles Isaac *geology educator*

Austin
Ancker-Johnson, Betsy *physicist, engineer, retired automotive company executive*
Bard, Allen Joseph *chemist, educator*
Bash, Frank Ness *astronomer, educator*
Bengtson, Roger Dean *physicist*
Boggs, James Ernest *chemistry educator*
Campion, Alan *chemistry educator*
Clark, Roy Thomas, Jr. *chemistry educator, administrator*
DeWitt-Morette, Cécile *physicist*
Dicus, Duane A. *physicist, educator*
Duncombe, Raynor Lockwood *astronomer*
Erskine, James Lorenzo *physics educator*
†Faulkner, Larry Ray *chemistry educator, university official*
Fisher, William Lawrence *geologist, educator*
Folk, Robert Louis *geologist, educator*
Fonken, Gerhard Joseph *retired chemistry educator, academic administrator*
Gardiner, William Cecil, Jr. *chemist, educator*
Gavenda, J(ohn) David *physicist*
Gentle, Kenneth William *physicist*
Griffy, Thomas Alan *physics educator*
Heller, Adam *chemist, researcher*
Hilburn, John Charles *geologist, geophysicist*
Ho, Paul Siu-Chung *physics educator*
Horton, Claude Wendell *physicist, educator*
Hudspeth, Emmett LeRoy *physicist, educator*
Maxwell, Arthur Eugene *oceanographer, marine geophysicist, educator*
Nguyen, Truc Chinh *analytical chemist*
Posey, Daniel Earl *analytical chemist*
Pradzynski, Andrzej Henryk *chemist*
Reed, Lester James *biochemist, educator*
Snell, Esmond Emerson *biochemist*
Stewart, Kent Kallam *analytical biochemistry educator*
Swinney, Harry Leonard *physics educator*
Trafton, Laurence Munro *astronomer*
Tyler, Noel *geological researcher and educator*
Udagawa, Takeshi *physicist, educator*
Wheeler, John Craig *astrophysicist, writer*
White, John Michael *chemistry educator*
Willson, C. Grant *chemistry educator, engineering educator*
Ziegler, Daniel Martin *chemistry educator*

Baytown
Mendelson, Robert Allen *polymer scientist, rheologist*

Brazoria
Jones, Lawrence Ryman *retired research chemist*

Carrollton
Wang, Peter Zhenming *physicist*

College Station
Arnowitt, Richard Lewis *physics educator, researcher*
Berg, Robert Raymond *geologist, educator*
Berner, Leo De Witte, Jr. *retired oceanographer*
Conway, Dwight Colbur *chemistry educator*
Cotton, Frank Albert *chemist, educator*
Duce, Robert Arthur *atmospheric chemist, university administrator*
Fackler, John Paul, Jr. *chemistry educator*
Goodman, David Wayne *research chemist, educator*
Hardy, John Christopher *physicist, educator*
Laane, Jaan *chemistry educator*
McIntyre, John Armin *physics educator*
McIntyre, Peter Mastin *physicist, educator*
Nachman, Ronald James *research chemist*
Natowitz, Joseph B. *chemistry educator, research administrator*
O'Connor, Rod *chemist, consultant, inventor*
Prescott, John Mack *biochemist, retired university administrator*
Reid, Robert Osborne *oceanographer*
Scott, Alastair Ian *chemistry educator*
Stanton, Robert James, Jr. *geologist, educator*
Stipanovic, Robert Douglas *chemist, researcher*
Wild, James Robert *biochemistry and genetics educator*

Crosby
Griffin, John Joseph, Jr. *chemist, video producer*

Dallas
Blattner, Wolfram Georg Michael *meteorologist*
Brooks, James Elwood *geologist, educator*
Estabrook, Ronald Winfield *chemistry educator*
Frank, Steven Neil *chemist*
Gibbs, James Alanson *geologist*
Green, Cecil Howard *geophysicist, consultant, educator*
Hensell, Linda Marie *environmental scientist*
Marshall, John Harris, Jr. *geologist, oil company executive*
Ray, Bradley Stephen *petroleum geologist*
Ries, Edward Richard *petroleum geologist, consultant*
Robertson, Herbert Chapman, Jr. *geoscience consulting company executive*
Sharp, William Wheeler *geologist*
Shaw, Don Wayne *physical chemist*
Stratton, Robert *financial company executive, physicist*
Vega, Roberto *physics educator*
†Woolley, (Lowell) Bryan *author, journalist*

Denton
Marchand, Alan Philip *chemistry educator*
Saleh, Farida Yousry *chemistry educator*

El Paso
Cook, Clarence Sharp *physics educator*
Hardaway, Robert Morris, III *physician, educator, retired army officer*

Fort Worth
Caldwell, Billy Ray *geologist*
Gutsche, Carl David *chemistry educator*
Mills, John James *research director*
Quarles, Carroll Adair, Jr. *physicist, educator*
Reinecke, Manfred G. *chemistry educator*
Smith, William Burton *retired chemist, educator*
Webb, Theodore Stratton, Jr. *aerospace scientist, consultant*

Galveston
Bonchev, Danail Georgiev *chemist, educator*
Gorenstein, David G. *chemistry and biochemistry educator*
Kurosky, Alexander *biochemist, educator*
LaGrone, Lavenia Whiddon *chemist, real estate broker*

Hawkins
Scott, Thomas Gordon *chemistry educator, writer*

Highland Village
Coogan, Melinda Ann Strank *chemistry educator*

Horseshoe Bay
Ramey, James Melton *chemist*

Houston
Ahmad, Salahuddin *nuclear scientist*
Anderson, Richard Carl *geophysical exploration company executive*
Baker, Stephen Denio *physics educator*
Barron, Andrew Ross *chemistry educator, consultant*
Bennett, George Nelson *biochemistry educator*
Black, David Charles *astrophysicist*
Bonner, Billy Edward *physics educator*
Brandt, I. Marvin *chemist, engineer*
Brooks, Philip Russell *chemistry educator, researcher*
Brotzen, Franz Richard *materials science educator*
Burke, Kevin Charles Antony *geologist*
Cameron, William Duncan *plastics company executive*
Cantwell, Thomas *geophysicist, electrical engineer*
Chu, Paul Ching-Wu *physicist*
Chu, Wei-Kan *physicist, educator*
Concilio, Charles Bennett *retired chemist, educator*
Curl, Robert Floyd, Jr. *chemistry educator*
Dasgupta, Amitava *chemist, educator*
Downs, Hartley H., III *chemist*
Estle, Thomas Leo *physicist, educator*
Freeman, John Clinton *meteorologist, oceanographer*
Gibson, Everett Kay, Jr. *space scientist, geochemist*
Goloby, George William, Jr. *environmental scientist, ornithologist, aviculturist*
Gordon, William Edwin *physicist, engineer, educator, university official*
Haas, Merrill Wilber *geologist, oil company executive*
Hackerman, Norman *chemist, academic administrator*
Ignatiev, Alex *physics researcher*
Iliev, Milko Nikolov *physicist, researcher*
Kevan, Larry *chemistry educator*
Kinsey, James Lloyd *chemist, educator*
Kit, Saul *biochemist, educator*
Klein, George D. *geologist, executive*
Kochi, Jay Kazuo *chemist, educator*
Kouri, Donald Jack *chemist, educator*
Krakower, Terri Jan *biochemist, researcher*
Liang, Edison Parktak *astrophysicist, educator, researcher*
Lucid, Shannon W. *biochemist, astronaut*
Mamedov, Edouard Akhmed *chemist, researcher*
Margrave, John Lee *chemist, educator, university administrator*
Mateker, Emil Joseph, Jr. *geophysicist*
Matthews, Kathleen Shive *biochemistry educator*
McCleary, Henry Glen *geophysicist*
Mehra, Jagdish *physicist*
†Nordlander, Peter Jan Arne *physics educator, researcher*
Phillips, Joseph Daniel *geomagneticist, oceanographer*
Powell, Michael Robert *biophysicist, physicist, chemist*
Reiff, Patricia Hofer *space physicist, educator*
Reso, Anthony *geologist, earth resources economist*
Robison, Buena Chambers, III *environmental scientist*
Rudolph, Frederick Byron *biochemistry educator*
Scuseria, Gustavo Enrique *theoretical chemist*
Sheriff, Robert *geophysicist, educator, consultant*
Sisson, Virginia Baker *geology educator*
Slaugh, Lynn H. *chemist*
Smalley, Richard Errett *chemistry and physics educator, researcher*
Smith, Ken A. *physicist*
Soileau, Kerry Michael *aerospace technologist, researcher*
Stankiewicz, Bogdan Artur *geologist*
Swezey, Christopher Stephen *geologist*
Talwani, Manik *geophysicist, educator*
Tatham, Robert Haines *geophysicist*
†Taylor, William Lansing *geologist*
Wakil, Salih Jawad *biochemistry educator*
Weinstein, Roy *physics educator, researcher*
Wilson, Thomas Leon *physicist*
Winzeler, Ted J. *geologist*
Yang, Chao Yuh *chemistry educator*
Zlatkis, Albert *chemistry educator*

Humble
Brinkley, Charles Alexander *geologist*

Irving
Hendrickson, Constance Marie McRight *chemist, consultant*
Holdar, Robert Martin *chemist*

Kerrville
Shaw, Alan Bosworth *geologist, paleontologist, retired*

La Porte
Darby, Barbara Ann-Lofthouse *chemical technician*

Lackland A F B
Rodgers, Robert Aubrey *physicist*

Lake Jackson
Tasa, Kendall Sherwood *college administrator*

Lubbock
Laing, Malcolm Brian *geologist, consultant*
Robinson, G. Wilse *molecular physicist, educator*

Marathon
Kurie, Andrew Edmunds *mining geologist*

New Braunfels
Wilson, James Lee *retired geology educator, consultant*

Plano
Dahiya, Jai Bhagwan *chemist*

Richardson
Johnson, Francis Severin *physicist*
Khan, Riaz Hussain *geophysicist, earth sciences educator*
Nevill, William Albert *chemistry educator*

Rockport
Mulle, George Ernest *petroleum geologist*

San Antonio
Budalur, Thyagarajan Subbanarayan *chemistry educator*
Burton, Russell Rohan *aerospace scientist, researcher*
Gladstone, George Randall *planetary scientist*
Hamm, William Joseph *retired physics educator*
Hammond, Weldon Woolf, Jr. *hydrogeologist*
Hanahan, Donald James *biochemist, educator*
Lyle, Robert Edward *chemist*
Markwell, Dick R(obert) *retired chemist*
Masters, Bettie Sue Siler *biochemist, educator*
Rafelson, Max Emanuel, Jr. *biochemist, medical school administrator*
Sablik, Martin John *research physicist*
Sinkin, Fay Marie *environmentalist*
Sutherland, Berry *geologist, educator*
Synek, Miroslav *physicist, chemist, world affairs consultant, researcher*
Tsin, Andrew Tsang Cheung *biochemistry educator*

Southlake
Herrmann, Debra McGuire *chemist, educator*

Spring
Jones, Katharine Jean *research physicist*

Sugar Land
Odegard, Mark Erie *geophysicist, consultant*

Tyler
Walsh, Kenneth Albert *chemist*

Waco
Pedrotti, Leno Stephano *physics educator*

UTAH

Bingham Canyon
Callender, Jonathan Ferris *environmental geologist, consultant*

Logan
Aust, Steven Douglas *biochemistry, biotechnology and toxicology educator*
Bowles, David Stanley *engineering educator, consultant*
Emert, George Henry *biochemist, academic administrator*
Schunk, Robert Walter *space physics research administrator*
Scouten, William Henry *chemistry educator, academic administrator*

North Logan
Sunderland, Norman Ray (Norm Sunderland) *health physicist, nuclear engineer educator*

Ogden
Welch, Garth Larry *chemistry educator, retired*

Provo
Hall, Howard Tracy *chemist*

Salt Lake City
Anspaugh, Lynn Richard *research biophysicist*
Dick, Bertram Gale, Jr. *physics educator*
Foltz, Rodger Lowell *chemistry educator, mass spectroscopist*
Gortatowski, Melvin Jerome *retired chemist*
Hill, George Richard *chemistry educator*
Kanes, William Henry *geology educator, research center administrator*
Kenison, Lynn T. *chemist*
Loh, Eugene C. *physicist, educator*
Miller, Jan Dean *metallurgy educator*
Moe, Scott Thomas *chemist*
O'Halloran, Thomas Alphonsus, Jr. *physicist, educator*
Olson, Ferron Allred *metallurgist, educator*
Parry, Robert Walter *chemistry educator*
Poulter, Charles Dale *chemist, educator, consultant*
Vardeny, Zeev Valy *physicist educator*
Velick, Sidney Frederick *research biochemist, educator*
Wall, Lloyd L. *geological engineer*

VERMONT

Burlington
Chiu, Jen-Fu *biochemistry educator*
Nyborg, Wesley Lemars *physics educator*
Weed, Lawrence L. *biochemist, educator*
White, William North *chemistry educator*

Hartland
Oort, Abraham Hans *meteorologist, researcher, educator*

Killington
Laing, David *natural science educator*

Middlebury
Winkler, Paul Frank, Jr. *astrophysicist, educator*

Thetford
Hoagland, Mahlon Bush *biochemist, educator*

VIRGINIA

Abingdon
Taylor, Alfred Raleigh *geologist*

Alexandria
Baker, George Harold, III *physicist*
Berman, Alan *physicist*
Biberman, Lucien Morton *physicist*
Brenner, Alfred Ephraim *physicist*
Campbell, Francis James *retired chemist*
Masterson, Kleber Sanlin, Jr. *physicist*
Milling, Marcus Eugene, Sr. *geologist*
Muir, Warren Roger *chemist, toxic substances specialist*
Ray, Terrill Wylie *physical scientist*
Shapiro, Maurice Mandel *astrophysicist*
Toulmin, Priestley *geologist*
Wolicki, Eligius Anthony *nuclear physicist, consultant*
Yaworsky, George Myroslaw *physicist, technical and management consultant*
Zook, Theresa Fuetterer *gemologist, consultant*

Annandale
Matuszko, Anthony Joseph *research chemist, administrator*

Arlington
Akkara, Joseph Augustine *biochemist*
Bautz, Laura Patricia *astronomer*
Berg, John Richard *chemist, former federal government executive*
Carter, William Harold, Sr. *physicist, researcher, electrical engineer*
Cavanaugh, Margaret Anne *chemist*
Dickman, Robert Laurence *physicist, researcher*
Dorman, Craig Emery *oceanographer, academic administrator*
Ensminger, Luther Glenn *chemist*
Johnson, Charles Nelson, Jr. *physicist*
Ordway, Frederick Ira, III *educator, consultant, researcher, author*
Reynolds, Peter James *physicist*
Romney, Carl F. *seismologist*
Schwartz, Lyle Howard *materials scientist, science administrator*
Van Horn, Hugh M. *physicist, astronomer*
Weber, Alfons *physicist*
Whitcomb, James Hall *geophysicist, foundation administrator*
Wodarczyk, Francis John *chemist*
Yankwich, Peter Ewald *chemistry educator*
Zirkind, Ralph *physicist, educator*

Ashburn
Bennett, Lawrence Herman *physicist*

Blacksburg
Bauer, Henry Hermann *chemistry and science educator*
Cairns, John, Jr. *environmental science educator, researcher*
Graybeal, Jack Daniel *chemist, educator*
Langel, Robert Allan, III *geophysicist*
McGrath, James Edward *chemistry educator*
Mo, Luke Wei *physicist, educator*
Ogliaruso, Michael Anthony *chemist, educator*
Terhune, Robert William *optics scientist*

Broad Run
Peters, William Nelson *physicist*

Charlottesville
Biltonen, Rodney Lincoln *biochemistry and pharmacology educator*
Bloomfield, Louis Aub *physicist, educator*
Bradbeer, Clive *biochemistry and microbiology educator, research scientist*
Brill, Arthur Sylvan *biophysics educator*
Chevalier, Roger Alan *astronomy educator, consultant*
Fredrick, Laurence William *astronomer, educator*
Gallagher, Thomas Francis *physicist*
Gaskin, Felicia *biochemist, educator*
Grimes, Russell Newell *chemistry educator, inorganic chemist*
Gugelot, Piet Cornelis *physics educator*
Hereford, Frank Loucks, Jr. *physicist, educator*
Hunt, Donald Frederick *chemistry educator*
Kellermann, Kenneth Irwin *astrophysicist*
Kerr, Anthony Robert *scientist*
Kuhlmann-Wilsdorf, Doris *physics and materials science educator*
Kumar, Rajesh *biochemist researcher*
MacDonald, Timothy Lee *chemistry educator*
Martin, Robert Bruce *chemistry educator*
Rastinejad, Fraydoon *biophysicist, structural biologist, educator*
Roberts, Morton Spitz *astronomer*
Sarazin, Craig Leigh *astronomer, educator*
Shen, Tsung Ying *medicinal chemistry educator*
Sundberg, Richard Jay *chemistry educator*
Vanden Bout, Paul Adrian *astronomer, physicist, educator*

Dahlgren
Walters, Robert Ancil *physicist, mathematician*

Fairfax
Morowitz, Harold Joseph *biophysicist, educator*
Singer, S(iegfried) Fred *geophysicist, educator*

Falls Church
Benson, William Edward (Barnes) *geologist*
Berg, Lillian Douglas *chemistry educator*
Spindel, William *chemist, consultant*

Farmville
Moon, William Arthur, Jr. *petroleum geologist, consultant*

Floyd
Clemens, Donald Faull *chemistry educator*

Front Royal
Dengel, Ottmar Hubert *physicist*

Gainesville
Steger, Edward Herman *chemist*

Galax
Sense, Karl August *physicist, educator*

Hampden Sydney
Kniffen, Donald Avery *astrophysicist, educator, researcher*

Hampton
Deepak, Adarsh *meteorologist, aerospace engineer, atmospheric scientist*
Houbolt, John Cornelius *physicist*
Saqib, Mohammad *materials scientist*

Harrisonburg
White, Larry Hartford *chemistry educator*

Herndon
Crossfield, Albert Scott *aeronautical science consultant, pilot*

Lexington
Spencer, Edgar Winston *geology educator*

Lynchburg
Morgan, Evan *chemist*

Manassas
Tidman, Derek Albert *physics researcher*

Mc Lean
Braddock, Joseph Vincent *physicist*
Carter, William Walton *physicist*
Doyle, Frederick Joseph *retired government research scientist*
Theon, John Speridon *meteorologist*
Waesche, R(ichard) H(enley) Woodward *combustion research scientist*
Watt, William Stewart *physical chemist*

Newington
Sebastian, Richard Lee *physicist, executive*

Newport News
Isgur, Nathan Gerald *physicist, educator*

Norfolk
Sanders, James Grady *biogeochemist*
Schellenberg, Karl Abraham *biochemist*

Petersburg
Stronach, Carey Elliott *physicist, educator*

Reston
Burton, James Samuel *physical chemist*
†Groat, Charles *geologist*
Kramish, Arnold *physicist, historian, author*
Peck, Dallas Lynn *retired geologist*
Ross, Malcolm *mineralogist, crystallographer*

Richmond
Suleymanian, Mirik *biophysicist*
Wakeham, Helmut Richard Rae *chemist, consulting company executive*

PROFESSIONAL INDEX 6217 SCIENCE: PHYSICAL SCIENCE

Roanoke
Al-Zubaidi, Amer Aziz *physicist, educator*

Springfield
†Malmberg, Kenneth Brian *environmentalist*

Sweet Briar
McClenon, John Raymond *chemistry educator*

Toano
Carlson, David Emil *physicist*

Vienna
Zehl, Otis George *optical physicist*

Warm Springs
Orem, Henry Philip *retired chemist, chemical engineer, consultant*

Williamsburg
Goodwin, Bruce Kesseli *retired geology educator, researcher*
Kossler, William John *physics educator*
Muller, Julius Frederick *chemist, business administrator*
Siegel, Robert Ted *physicist*
Starnes, William Herbert, Jr. *chemist, educator*

Winchester
Ludwig, George Harry *physicist*

Wytheville
†DiYorio, John Salvatore *chemistry educator*

WASHINGTON

Battle Ground
Morris, William Joseph *paleontologist, educator*

Bellevue
Benveniste, Jacob *retired physicist*
Fremouw, Edward Joseph *physicist*
Rossi, Amadeo Joseph *chemist*

Bellingham
Morse, Joseph Grant *chemistry educator*

Bothell
Alvi, Khisal Ahmed *chemist*

Clinton
Forward, Robert L(ull) *physicist, businessman, consultant, writer*

Coupeville
Eaton, Gordon Pryor *geologist*

Eastsound
Fowles, George Richard *physicist, educator*

Edmonds
Galster, Richard W. *engineering geologist*

Ellensburg
Rosell, Sharon Lynn *physics and chemistry educator, researcher*
Yu, Roger Hong *physics educator*

Friday Harbor
Agosta, William Carleton *chemist, educator*

Hamilton
Anderson, Duwayne Marlo *earth and polar scientist, university administrator*

Independence
Feng, Xiangdong Shawn *chemist*

Lake Forest Park
Favorite, Felix *oceanographer*

Lopez Island
Whetten, John Theodore *geologist*

Lynnwood
Olsen, Kenneth Harold *geophysicist, astrophysicist*

Oak Harbor
Crampton, George Harris *neuroscientist, retired army officer*
Daugherty, Kenneth Earl *research company executive, educator*

Olympia
Bloomquist, Rodney Gordon *geologist*
Yake, William Ellsworth *environmental scientist, poet*

Pullman
Crosby, Glenn Arthur *chemistry educator*
Hamilton, Charles Howard *metallurgy educator*
Ryan, Clarence Augustine, Jr. *biochemistry educator*

Redmond
Wang, Lin *physicist, computer science educator, computer software consultant*

Renton
Hu, John Chih-An *retired chemist, research engineer*

Richland
Bevelacqua, Joseph John *physicist, researcher*
Bush, Spencer Harrison *metallurgist*
Dunning, Thom H., Jr. *environmental molecular science executive*
Elderkin, Charles Edwin *retired meteorologist*
Fruchter, Jonathan Sewell *research scientist, geochemist*
Huang, Fan-H Frank *materials scientist, researcher*
Jacobsen, Gerald Bernhardt *biochemist*
Moore, Emmett Burris, Jr. *physical chemist, educator*
Rebagay, Teofila Velasco *chemist, chemical engineer*
Stenner, Robert David *environmental and health research engineer, toxicologist*
Sundaram, Shanmugavelayutham Kamakshi *materials scientist, consultant*
Xantheas, Sotiris Stavros *chemist, researcher*

Seattle
Andersen, Niels Hjorth *chemistry educator, biophysics researcher, consultant*
Anderson, Arthur G., Jr. *chemistry educator*
Arons, Arnold Boris *physicist, educator*
Banse, Karl *retired oceanography educator*
Baum, William Alvin *astronomer, educator*
Bernard, Eddie Nolan *oceanographer*
Bichsel, Hans *physicist, consultant, researcher*
Bodansky, David *physicist, educator*
Borden, Weston Thatcher *chemistry educator*
Brown, Craig William *physical chemist*
Brown, Frederick Calvin *physicist, educator*
Brown, Lowell Severt *physicist, educator*
Brownlee, Donald Eugene, II *astronomer, educator*
Charlson, Robert Jay *atmospheric sciences educator, scientist*
Christian, Gary Dale *chemistry educator*
Clark, Kenneth Courtright *retired physics and geophysics educator*
Cramer, John Gleason, Jr. *physics educator, experimental physicist*
Creager, Joe Scott *geology and oceanography educator*
Dalton, Larry Raymond *chemistry educator, researcher, consultant*
Dash, J. Gregory *physicist, educator*
Dehmelt, Hans Georg *physicist*
Erdmann, Joachim Christian *physicist*
Evans, Bernard William *geologist, educator*
Felton, Samuel Page *biochemist*
Fischer, Edmond Henri *biochemistry educator*
Fischer, Fred Walter *physicist, engineer, educator*
Floss, Heinz G. *chemistry educator, scientist*
Fortson, Edward Norval *physics educator*
Geballe, Ronald *physicist, university dean*
Gerhart, James Basil *physics educator*
Gordon, Milton Paul *biochemist, educator*
Gouterman, Martin Paul *chemistry educator*
Gregory, Norman Wayne *chemistry educator, researcher*
Halver, John Emil *nutritional biochemist*
Harrison, Don Edmunds *oceanographer, educator*
Heath, George Ross *oceanographer*
Henley, Ernest Mark *physics educator, university dean emeritus*
Hodge, Paul William *astronomer, educator*
Ingalls, Robert Lynn *physicist, educator*
Krebs, Edwin Gerhard *biochemistry educator*
Kwiram, Alvin L. *physical chemistry educator, university official*
Lackie, Kenneth William *physical scientist*
Lingafelter, Edward Clay, Jr. *chemistry educator*
Lord, Jere Johns *retired physics educator*
Lubatti, Henry Joseph *physicist, educator*
Malins, Donald Clive *biochemistry, researcher*
Mallory, V(irgil) Standish *geologist, educator*
Margon, Bruce Henry *astrophysicist, educator*
Mulally, Alan R. *aerospace company executive*
Neurath, Hans *biochemist, educator*
Olmstead, Marjorie Ann *physics educator*
Pocker, Yeshayau *chemistry, biochemistry educator*
Porter, Stephen Cummings *geologist, educator*
Rabinovitch, Benton Seymour *chemist, educator emeritus*
Reed, Richard John *retired meteorology educator*
Reinhardt, William Parker *chemical physicist, educator*
Rhines, Peter Broomell *oceanographer, atmospheric scientist*
Robertson, Robert Graham Hamish *physicist*
†Sarachik, Edward S. *atmospheric sciences educator*
Spinrad, Bernard Israel *physicist, educator*
Stern, Edward Abraham *physics educator*
Stubbs, Christopher W. *physics educator*
Szkody, Paula *astronomy educator, researcher*
Thouless, David James *physicist, educator*
Varanasi, Usha *environmental scientist*
Wallerstein, George *astronomer, educator*
Walsh, Kenneth Andrew *biochemist*
Weitkamp, William George *retired nuclear physicist*
Wilets, Lawrence *physics educator*
Williams, Robert Walter *physics educator*

Silverdale
Walske, M(ax) Carl, Jr. *physicist*

Spokane
Campbell, Harry Woodson *geologist, mining engineer*
Segal, Vladimir M. *metallurgist, researcher*

WEST VIRGINIA

Charleston
Bhasin, Madan Mohan *chemical research scientist*
Bryant, George Macon *chemist*

Institute
DasSarma, Basudeb *chemistry educator*

Logan
Galya, Thomas Andrew *geologist*

Morgantown
Beattie, Diana Scott *biochemistry educator*
Butcher, Fred R. *biochemistry educator, university administrator*
Das, Kamalendu *chemist*
Fodor, Gábor Béla *chemistry educator, researcher*
Seehra, Mohindar Singh *physics educator, researcher*

WISCONSIN

Cottage Grove
Hesse, Thurman Dale *welding and metallurgy educator, consultant*

Elkhorn
O'Brien, Francis Joseph *environmental services company executive*

Green Bay
Pearson, Carol Ann *chemistry educator*

La Crosse
Rozelle, Lee Theodore *physical chemist*

Lake Mills
Roselle, Paul Lucas *material scientist*

Madison
Adler, Julius *biochemist, biologist, educator*
Anderson, Louis Wilmer, Jr. *physicist, educator*
Barger, Vernon Duane *physicist, educator*
Beinert, Helmut *biochemist*
Bentley, Charles Raymond *geophysics educator*
Botez, Dan *physicist*
Bretherton, Francis P. *atmospheric and oceanic sciences educator*
Bryson, Reid Allen *earth sciences educator*
Burris, Robert Harza *biochemist, educator*
Cassinelli, Joseph Patrick *astronomy educator*
Christensen, Nikolas Ivan *geophysicist, educator*
Churchwell, Edward Bruce *astronomer, educator*
Clark, David Leigh *marine geologist, educator*
Clay, Clarence Samuel *acoustical oceanographer*
Cleland, W(illiam) Wallace *biochemistry educator*
Connors, Kenneth Antonio *retired chemistry educator*
Craddock, (John) Campbell *geologist, educator*
Curtiss, Charles Francis *chemist, educator*
Dahl, Lawrence Frederick *chemistry educator*
Dahlberg, James E(ric) *biochemist, molecular biologist*
Deutsch, Harold Francis *biochemist, researcher, educator*
DeWerd, Larry Albert *medical physicist, educator*
Dott, Robert Henry, Jr. *geologist, educator*
Ediger, Mark D. *chemistry educator*
Ellis, Arthur Baron *chemist, educator*
Evenson, Merle Armin *chemist, educator*
Farrar, Thomas C. *chemist, educator*
Fennema, Owen Richard *food chemistry educator*
Ferry, John Douglass *retired chemist, educator*
Gorski, Jack *biochemistry educator*
Hamers, Robert J. *chemistry educator, researcher*
Hedden, Gregory Dexter *environmental science educator, consultant*
Hokin, Lowell Edward *biochemist, educator*
Houghton, David Drew *meteorologist, educator*
Lagally, Max Gunter *physics educator*
Lardy, Henry A(rnold) *biochemistry educator*
Lawler, James Edward *physics educator*
Maher, Louis James, Jr. *geologist, educator*
Moore, John Ward *chemistry educator*
Morton, Stephen Dana *chemist*
Mukerjee, Pasupati *chemistry educator*
Pondrom, Lee Girard *physicist, educator*
Pray, Lloyd Charles *geologist, educator*
Rich, Daniel Hulbert *chemistry educator*
Richards, Hugh Taylor *physics educator*
Robertson, James Magruder *geological research administrator*
Rowe, John Westel *retired organic chemist*
Satter, Larry Dean *biochemist, scientific research administrator*
Savage, Blair deWillis *astronomer, educator*
Sih, Charles John *pharmaceutical chemistry educator*
Skinner, James Lauriston *chemist, educator*
Suttie, John Weston *biochemist*
Vaughan, Worth Edward *chemistry educator*
West, Robert Culbertson *chemistry educator*
Whitford, Albert Edward *astronomer*
Young, Raymond Allen *chemist, educator*
Zimmerman, Howard Elliot *chemist, educator*

Middleton
Ferry, James Allen *physicist, electrostatics company executive*
Ostrom, Meredith Eggers *retired geologist*

Milwaukee
Bader, Alfred Robert *chemist*
Baker, John Edward *cardiac biochemist, educator*
Greenler, Robert George *physics educator, researcher*
Griffith, Owen Wendell *biochemistry educator*
Haworth, Daniel Thomas *chemistry educator*
Hendee, William Richard *medical physics educator, university official*
Jache, Albert William *retired chemistry educator, scientist*
Karkheck, John Peter *physics educator, researcher*
Miller, David Hewitt *environmental scientist, writer*
Muñoz, Amalia *biochemical researcher*

Neenah
Workman, Jerome James, Jr. *chemist*

Racine
†Engelman, John Herrick *chemist*

Schofield
Adams, James William *retired chemist*

Stevens Point
George, Thomas Frederick *chemistry educator*

Stoughton
Huber, David Lawrence *physicist, educator*

Washington Island
Raup, David Malcolm *paleontology educator*

Williams Bay
Hobbs, Lewis Mankin *astronomer*

WYOMING

Casper
Seese, William Shober *chemistry educator*
Wold, John Schiller *geologist, former congressman*

Laramie
Grandy, Walter Thomas, Jr. *physicist, educator*
Hausel, William Dan *economic geologist, martial artist*
Meyer, Edmond Gerald *energy and natural resources educator, resources scientist, entrepreneur, former chemistry educator, university administrator*
Roark, Terry Paul *astronomer, educator*

Wapiti
Sowerwine, Elbert Orla, Jr. *chemist, chemical engineer*

TERRITORIES OF THE UNITED STATES

PUERTO RICO

Mayaguez
Souto Bachiller, Fernando Alberto *chemistry educator*

San Juan
Pabon-Perez, Heidi *medical physicist, educator*

MILITARY ADDRESSES OF THE UNITED STATES

EUROPE

APO
Bikales, Norbert M. *chemist, science administrator*

CANADA

Sherbrooke
Deslongchamps, Pierre *chemistry educator*

ALBERTA

Calgary
Armstrong, David Anthony *physical chemist, educator*
Campbell, Finley Alexander *geologist*
Hyne, James Bissett *chemistry educator, industrial scientist, consultant*
Thorsteinsson, Raymond *geology research scientist*
Walker, Roger Geoffrey *geology educator, consultant*

Drumheller
Currie, Philip John *research paleontologist, museum curator*

Edmonton
Gough, Denis Ian *geophysics educator*
Harris, Walter Edgar *chemistry educator*
Jones, Richard Norman *physical chemist, researcher*
Kay, Cyril Max *biochemist*
Khanna, Faqir Chand *physics educator*
Kratochvil, Byron George *chemistry educator, researcher*
Lemieux, Raymond Urgel *chemistry educator*
Rostoker, Gordon *physicist, educator*
Rutter, Nathaniel Westlund *geologist, educator*
Stelck, Charles Richard *geology educator*
Sykes, Brian Douglas *biochemistry educator, researcher*

BRITISH COLUMBIA

Burnaby
Wainwright, David Stanley *intellectual property professional*

Sidney
Petrie, William *physicist*
van den Bergh, Sidney *astronomer*

Vancouver
Bloom, Myer *physicist, educator*
Clarke, Garry Kenneth Connal *geophysics educator*
Hardy, Walter Newbold *physics educator, researcher*
James, Brian Robert *chemistry educator*
Ozier, Irving *physicist, educator*
Pickard, George Lawson *physics educator*
Pincock, Richard Earl *chemistry educator*
Russell, Richard Doncaster *geophysicist, educator, geoscientist*
Sinclair, Alastair James *geology educator*
Smith, Michael *biochemistry educator*
Snider, Robert F. *chemistry educator, researcher*
Stewart, Ross *chemistry educator*
Underhill, Anne Barbara *astrophysicist*
Vogt, Erich Wolfgang *physicist, academic administrator*
Wheeler, John Oliver *geologist*

Victoria
Barnes, Christopher Richard *geologist*
Batten, Alan Henry *astronomer*
Best, Melvyn Edward *geophysicist*
Hutchings, John Barrie *astronomer, researcher*
Israel, Werner *physics educator*
Leffek, Kenneth Thomas *chemist, educator*
MacLeod, John Munroe *radio astronomer*
Mc Carter, John Alexander *biochemistry educator*
Morton, Donald Charles *astronomer*
Oke, John Beverley *astronomy educator*
Stetson, Peter Brailey *astronomer*
Wiles, David McKeen *chemist*

West Vancouver
Wynne-Edwards, Hugh Robert *entrepreneur, scientist*

MANITOBA

Winnipeg
Barber, Robert Charles *physics educator*
Bigelow, Charles Cross *biochemist, university administrator*
Ferguson, Robert Bury *mineralogy educator*
Mantsch, Henry Horst *chemistry educator*
Schaefer, Theodore Peter *chemistry educator*
Smith, Ian Cormack Palmer *biophysicist*

NEWFOUNDLAND

Saint John's
Rochester, Michael Grant *geophysics educator*
Williams, Harold *geology educator*

NOVA SCOTIA

Antigonish
Gillis, John William *retired geologist, retired provincial government legislator*

Dartmouth
Elliott, James A. *oceanographer, researcher*
Keen, Charlotte Elizabeth *marine geophysicist, researcher*
Platt, Trevor Charles *oceanographer, scientist*

Halifax
Dahn, Jeff Raymond *physics educator*
Gold, Edgar *marine affairs educator, mariner, lawyer*

Tatamagouche
Roach, Margot Ruth *retired biophysicist, educator*

Wallace
Boyle, Willard Sterling *physicist*

Wolfville
Bishop, Roy Lovitt *physics and astronomy educator*

ONTARIO

Ancaster
Brockhouse, Bertram Neville *physicist, retired educator*

Chalk River
Milton, John Charles Douglas *nuclear physicist*
Torgerson, David Franklyn *chemist, research facility administrator*

Deep River
Davies, John Arthur *physics and engineering educator, scientist*

Downsview
Ribner, Herbert Spencer *physicist, educator*
Tennyson, Roderick C. *aerospace scientist*

Gloucester
Marsters, Gerald Frederick *retired aerospace science and technology executive*

Guelph
Dickinson, William Trevor *hydrologist, educator*
Karl, Gabriel *physics educator*

Hamilton
Basinski, Zbigniew Stanislaw *metal physicist, educator*
Datars, William Ross *physicist, educator*
Garland, William James *engineering physics educator*
Gillespie, Ronald James *chemistry educator, researcher, writer*
MacLean, David Bailey *chemistry educator, researcher*
Schwarcz, Henry Philip *geologist, educator*
Spenser, Ian Daniel *chemist educator*
Sprung, Donald Whitfield Loyal *physics educator*
Welch, Douglas Lindsay *physics educator*

Kingston
Ewan, George Thomson *physicist, educator*
McDonald, Arthur Bruce *physics educator*
Sayer, Michael *physics educator*
Spencer, John Hedley *biochemistry educator*
Stewart, Alec Thompson *physicist*
Szarek, Walter Anthony *chemist, educator*

Lions Bay
Bartholomew, Gilbert Alfred *retired physicist*

London
Bancroft, George Michael *chemical physicist, educator*
Dreimanis, Aleksis *emeritus geology educator*
Fyfe, William Sefton *geochemist, educator*
Stewart, Harold Brown *biochemist*
Stillman, Martin J. *physical science research administrator, bioinorganic chemist*
Stothers, John B. *chemistry educator*

Manotick
Hobson, George Donald *retired geophysicist*

Ottawa
Alper, Howard *chemistry educator*
Andrew, Bryan Haydn *astronomer*
Bright, M. W. A. *physical science administrator*
Fallis, Alexander Graham *chemistry educator*
Halliday, Ian *astronomer*
Harington, Charles Richard *vertebrate paleontologist*
Haworth, Richard Thomas *geophysicist, science director*
Himms-Hagen, Jean Margaret *biochemist*
Holmes, John Leonard *chemistry educator*
Ingold, Keith Usherwood *chemist, educator*
Kates, Morris *biochemist, educator*
Marmet, Paul *physicist*
McLaren, Digby Johns *geologist, educator*
Ramsay, Donald Allan *physical chemist*
Redhead, Paul Aveling *physicist*
St-Onge, Denis Alderic *geologist, research scientist*
Schneider, William George *chemist, research consultant*
Templeton, Ian Malcolm *retired physicist*
Varshni, Yatendra Pal *physicist*
Veizer, Ján *geology educator*
Whitehead, J. Rennie *science consultant*

Owen Sound
Morley, Lawrence Whitaker *geophysicist, remote sensing consultant*

Palgrave
Kieffer, Susan Werner *research geologist and development consultant*

Richmond Hill
Fernie, John Donald *astronomer, educator*
Garrison, Robert Frederick *astronomer, educator*

Toronto
Alcock, Charles Benjamin *materials science consultant*
Baines, Andrew DeWitt *medical biochemist*
Bohme, Diethard Kurt *chemistry educator*
Brook, Adrian Gibbs *chemistry educator*
Carswell, Allan Ian *physics educator*
Dunlop, David John *geophysics educator, researcher*
Goldberg, David Meyer *biochemistry educator*
Hofmann, Theo *biochemist, educator*
Ivey, Donald Glenn *physics educator*
Jervis, Robert E. *chemistry educator*
Kresge, Alexander Jerry *chemistry educator*
List, Roland *physicist, educator, former UN official*
Litherland, Albert Edward *physics educator*
MacRae, Donald Alexander *astronomy educator*
Moffat, John William *physics educator*
Naldrett, Anthony James *geology educator*
Norris, Geoffrey *geology educator, consultant*
Packham, Marian Aitchison *biochemistry educator*
Pilliar, Robert Mathews *metallurgy educator, materials scientist*
Polanyi, John Charles *chemist, educator*
Pritchard, Huw Owen *chemist, educator*
Prugovecki, Eduard *mathematical physicist, educator, author*
Rowe, David John *physics educator*
Seaquist, Ernest Raymond *astronomy educator*
Siminovitch, Louis *biophysics educator, scientist*
Spooner, Ed Thornton Casswell *geology educator and researcher*
Stoicheff, Boris Peter *physicist, educator*
Tidwell, Thomas Tinsley *chemistry educator*
Whittington, Stuart Gordon *chemistry educator*
Wicks, Frederick John *research mineralogist, museum curator*
Yip, Cecil Cheung-Ching *biochemist, educator*

Waterloo
Morgan, Alan Vivian *geologist, educator*

Windsor
Drake, Gordon William Frederic *physics educator*
Jones, William Ernest *chemistry educator*
Thibert, Roger Joseph *clinical chemist, educator*

QUEBEC

Laval
David, Michel Louis *geostatistician, consultant*

Montreal
Chan, Tak Hang *chemist, educator*
Das Gupta, Subal *physics educator, researcher*
Derome, Jacques Florian *meteorology educator*
de Takacsy, Nicholas Benedict *physicist, educator*
Edward, John Thomas *chemist, educator*
Eisenberg, Adi *chemist*
Gaudry, Roger *chemist, university official*
Hay, Allan Stuart *chemist, educator*
Johnstone, Rose Mamelak (Mrs. Douglas Johnstone) *biochemistry educator*
Langleben, Manuel Phillip *physics educator*
Michaud, Georges Joseph *astrophysics educator*
Mysak, Lawrence Alexander *oceanographer, climatologist, mathematician, educator*
Perlin, Arthur Saul *chemistry educator*
Podgorsak, Ervin B. *medical physicist, educator, administrator*
Purdy, William Crossley *chemist, educator*
Solomon, Samuel *biochemistry educator, administrator*
Sourkes, Theodore Lionel *biochemistry educator*
Taras, Paul *physicist, educator*
Whitehead, Michael Anthony *chemistry educator*

Outremont
Levesque, Rene Jules Albert *retired physicist*

Pointe Claire
Bachynski, Morrel Paul *physicist*
Bolker, Henry Irving *retired chemist, research institute director, educator*

Quebec
Engel, Charles Robert *chemist, educator*
Page, Michel *biochemist*

Sainte Foy
Legendre, Louis *biological oceanography educator, researcher*

Sherbrooke
Tremblay, André-Marie *physicist*

Wakefield
Roots, Ernest Frederick *scientific advisor emeritus*

SASKATCHEWAN

Saskatoon
Hirose, Akira *physics educator, researcher*
Kupsch, Walter Oscar *geologist*

MEXICO

Cuernavaca
†Bolivar Zapata, Francisco *biochemist*

Mexico City
Peimbert, Manuel *astronomer*

Puebla
Zehe, Alfred Fritz Karl *physics educator*

AUSTRALIA

Canberra
Philip, John Robert *physicist, mathematician, researcher*
Sargeson, Alan McLeod *chemistry educator*
Taylor, Stuart Ross *geochemist, author*

AUSTRIA

Laxenburg
MacDonald, Gordon James Fraser *geophysicist*

Vienna
Pohl, Adolf Leopold *clinical chemist, quality assurance consultant*

BELGIUM

Brussels
Prigogine, Vicomte Ilya *physics educator*

Drongen
Charlier, Roger Henri *oceanography, geography, and geology educator*

Liège
Mosora, Florentina Ioana *physics educator*

BRAZIL

Sorocaba
Martins, Nelson *physics educator*

CHINA

Beijing
Ni, Jun *physics educator*
Zhou, Zhigang *materials scientist, educator*

Chengdu
Zhou, Kang-Wei *physics educator*

DENMARK

Copenhagen
Bohr, Aage Niels *physicist, educator*
Hansen, Ole *physicist*
†Mottelson, Ben R. *physicist*
Pethick, Christopher John *physicist*

ENGLAND

Brighton
Kroto, Harold Walter *chemistry researcher, educator*

Cambridge
Buckingham, Amyand David *chemistry educator*
Edwards, Sir Samuel Frederick *physicist, educator*
Rees, Martin John *astronomy educator*

Cranfield
Richardson, Ian Malcolm *research physicist*

Falmer
Cornforth, Sir John Warcup *chemist*

London
Hoyle, Sir Fred *astronomer, mathematician*

Oxford
Williams, William Stanley Cossom *physics educator and researcher*

FEDERAL REPUBLIC OF GERMANY

Bonn
Sage, Leslie John *astronomer*

FINLAND

Tampere
Ovtchinnikov, Alexander Vladimirovich *physicist*

FRANCE

Creteil
Renoux, André *physicist, educator*

Lyon
Rice, Jerry Mercer *biochemist*

Marseille
Azzopardi, Marc Antoine *astrophysicist, scientist*

Meudon
Neel, Louis Eugene Felix *physicist*

Orsay
Deutsch, Claude David *physicist, educator*
Friedel, Jacques *physics educator*

Paris
de Gennes, Pierre-Gilles *physicist, educator*
Lehn, Jean-Marie Pierre *chemistry educator*
Lucas, Georges *physicist, researcher*

GERMANY

Erlangen
Gladysz, John Andrew *chemistry educator*

Frankfurt
Michel, Hartmut *biochemist*

Garching
Fischer, Ernst Otto *chemist, educator*
Mössbauer, Rudolf Ludwig *physicist, educator*

Göttingen
Eigen, Manfred *physicist*
Neher, Erwin *biophysicist*
Sheldrick, George Michael *chemistry educator, crystallographer*

Groebenzell
Chandrasekhar, B(ellur) S(ivaramiah) *physics educator*

Hamburg
Lehne, Pascal Horst *chemistry educator, consultant*

Munich
Huber, Robert *biochemist, educator*

Stuttgart
Cardona, Manuel *physics educator*

HONG KONG

Kowloon
Chang, Leroy L. *physicist*

HUNGARY

Budapest
Evans, Myron Wyn *physicist*

ISRAEL

Ra'ananna
Hayon, Elie M. *chemist, educator*

Rehovot
Sharon, Nathan *biochemist*

Tel Aviv
Jortner, Joshua *physical chemistry scientist, educator*

ITALY

Assergi
Berezinsky, Veniamin Sergeevich *physicist*

JAPAN

Gyoda
Shibasaki, Yoshio *chemistry educator, researcher*

Koganei
Akiyama, Masayasu *chemistry educator*

Nagoya
Hayashi, Mitsuhiko *retired physics educator*
Kaneyoshi, Takahito *physicist*

Okayama
Ubuka, Toshihiko *biochemistry educator, dean*

Osaka
Ikeda, Kazuyosi *physicist, poet*

Sakyo
Ueno, Hiroshi *biochemist*

Shimizu
Uyeda, Seiya *geophysics educator*

Shinjuku
Shimada, Haruo *physical chemistry educator*

Tokyo
Fuketa, Toyojiro *physicist*
Iida, Shuichi *physicist, educator*
Ishii, Yoshinori *geophysics educator*
Manabe, Syukuro *climatologist*

Tsukuba Ibaraki
Esaki, Leo *physicist, foundation executive*

Yamaguchi
Suzuki, Nobutaka *chemistry educator*

THE NETHERLANDS

Amsterdam
Averill, Bruce Alan *chemistry educator*

Goor
Bonting, Sjoerd Lieuwe *biochemist, priest*

NORWAY

Sandvika
Christensen, Hans Christian *retired chemist*

REPUBLIC OF KOREA

Pohang
Choi, Sang-il *physics educator, researcher*

RUSSIA

Moscow
Basov, Nikolai Gennadievich *physicist*
Ginzburg, Vitaly Lazarevich *physicist*
Goldanskii, Vitalii Iosifovich *chemist, physicist*

Novosibirsk
Aleksandrov, Leonid Naumovitsh *physicist, educator, researcher*

SCOTLAND

Peebles
Hooper, John Edward *retired physicist, researcher*

SWEDEN

Huddinge
Jensen, Elwood Vernon *biochemist*

Österskär
Bolin, Bert Richard Johannes *atmospheric physicist, research meteorologist*

Stockholm
Hillert, Mats *materials scientist, educator*
Peskov, Vladimir Dmitrievich *physicist, educator, consultant*

SWITZERLAND

Bäch
Rohrer, Heinrich *physicist*

Geneva
Charpak, Georges *physicist, nuclear scientist*
Overseth, Oliver Enoch *physicist, educator*
Steinberger, Jack *physicist, educator*

Küsnacht
Eschenmoser, Albert *chemist*

Zurich
Binnig, Gerd Karl *physicist*
Diederich, Francois Nico *chemistry educator*
Dunitz, Jack David *retired chemistry educator, researcher*
Ernst, Richard Robert *chemist, educator*

TAIWAN

Hsinchu
Huang, Jia-Hong *materials science educator*

Taipei
Lee, Yuan Tseh *chemistry educator*
Yin, Shih-Jiun *biochemist*

VENEZUELA

Caracas
Mendelovici, Efraim Eliahu *materials chemistry and earth sciences researcher*

WALES

Powys
Seaton, Michael John *physicist*

ADDRESS UNPUBLISHED

Adams, John Andrew *physicist, engineering company executive*
Aharonov, Yakir *physicist, educator*
Akasofu, Syun-Ichi *geophysicist*
Almond, Joan *retired chemist*
Anders, Edward *chemist, educator*
Anderson, Philip Warren *physicist*
Arenstein, Walter Alan *environmental scientist*
Arnett, Edward McCollin *chemistry educator, researcher*
Baldwin, George Curriden *physicist, educator*
Bandeen, William Reid *retired meteorologist*
Barr, John Baldwin *chemist, research scientist*
Basford, Robert Eugene *retired biochemistry educator, researcher*
Baym, Gordon Alan *physicist, educator*
Behrendt, John Charles *research geophysicist*
Berry, Richard Stephen *chemist*
Bersin, Richard Lewis *physicist, plasma process technologist*
Blush, Steven Michael *nuclear scientist, safety consultant*
Bodanszky, Miklos *chemist, educator*
Bondar, Richard Jay Laurent *biochemist*
Boyes, Stephen Richard *hydrogeologic consultant*
Braden, Charles Hosea *physicist, university administrator*
Brand, John Charles *chemistry educator*
Bratsch, Steven Gary *chemistry educator*
Bretthauer, Erich Walter *chemist, educator*
Brown, Barbara S. *environmental scientist*
Brown, Rhonda Rochelle *chemist, health facility administrator, lawyer*
Bundy, Hallie Flowers *biochemist, educator*
Bunyan, Ellen Lackey Spotz *chemist, educator*
Cahn, Robert Nathan *physicist*
Caldwell, Karin D. *biochemist educator*
Cane, David E. *chemistry educator*
Cardman, Lawrence Santo *physics educator, research administrator*
Carlson, Marguerite T. *science educator*
Carr, Albert Anthony *retired organic chemist*
Christoffersen, Ralph Earl *chemist*
Chu, Benjamin Thomas Peng-Nien *chemistry educator*
Chu, Steven *physics educator*
Church, Eugene Lent *physicist, consulting scientist*
Clark, Carolyn Archer *aerosopace technologist, life scientist*
Clayton-Townsend, JoAnn *aerospace analyst*
Clement, Robert Alton *retired chemist*
Cohen, Philip *retired hydrogeologist*
Compton, W. Dale *physicist*
Conerly-Perks, Erlene Brinson *retired chemist*
†Connors, Christopher *geology educator*
Critoph, Eugene *retired physicist, nuclear research company executive*
Crutzen, Paul Josef *research meteorologist, chemist*
Cuatrecasas, Pedro Martin *research biochemist, pharmaceutical executive*
Dale, Wesley John *chemistry educator*
Daniels, James Maurice *physicist*
Deisenhofer, Johann *biochemistry educator, researcher*
De Loach, Bernard Collins, Jr. *retired physicist*
de Planque, E. Gail *physicist*
Detert, Miriam Anne *chemical analyst*
Dickinson, William Richard *retired geologist and educator*
Diehl, Harry Alfred *chemist, genealogist*
Dixon, Gordon Henry *biochemist*
Driggers, L. Eley *clinical metaphysicist*
Eberly, Joseph Henry *physics educator, consultant*
Edwards, Helen Thom *physicist*
Engeler, William Ernest *retired physicist*
English, Bruce Vaughan *environmental consultant*
Englund, Kenneth John *retired geologist*
Esquivel, Agerico Liwag *retired research physicist*
Ewen, H.I. *physicist*
Farmer, Crofton Bernard *atmospheric physicist*
Farquhar, James *geochemist, researcher*
Fischel, David *astrophysicist, remote sensing specialist*
Fisher, Charles Harold *chemistry educator, researcher*
Flor, Loy Lorenz *chemist, corrosion engineer, consultant*
Ford, Kenneth William *physicist*
Formo, Jerome Lionel *chemist*
Fox, John David *educator, physicist*
Fradkin, David Milton *physicist, educator*
Franz, John E. *bio-organic chemist, researcher*
Frauenfelder, Hans *physicist, educator*
Galison, Peter Louis *history of science educator*
Gardner, Wilford Robert *physicist, educator*
Gass, Arthur Edward, Jr. *chemist*
Geller, Seymour *retired educator, researcher*
Getting, Ivan Alexander *physicist, former aerospace company executive*
Gilinsky, Victor *physicist*
Glashow, Sheldon Lee *physicist, educator*
Glesk, Ivan *physicist, educator, researcher*
Gloeckler, George *physics educator*
Goldberger, Marvin Leonard *physicist, educator*
Golden, David Edward *physicist*
Gounaris, Anne Demetra *biochemistry educator, researcher*
Greaves, William Webster *chemist, patent analyst*
Grosset, Anne Marie *biophysicist, researcher*
Gummel, Hermann Karl *retired physicist, laboratory administrator*
Gundlach, Robert William *retired physicist*
Gutsch, William Anthony, Jr. *astronomer*
Hagemier, Herman Frederick *chemist*
Hall, Grace Rosalie *physicist, educator, literary scholar*
Hardy, Ralph W. F. *biochemist, biotechnology executive*
Hart, Howard Roscoe, Jr. *retired physicist*
Haskin, Larry Allen *earth and planetary scientist, educator*
Hatcher, Herbert John *biochemist, microbiologist*
Heeschen, David Sutphin *astronomer, educator*
Herzfeld, Charles Maria *physicist*
Hinkley, Everett David, Jr. *physicist, business executive*
Ho, Chih-Ming *physicist, educator*
Ho, John Wing-Shing *biochemistry educator, researcher*
Hoeg, Donald Francis *chemist, consultant, former research and development executive*
Holmes, Jerry Dell *retired organic chemist*
Hook, Vivian Yuan-Wen Ho *biochemist, neuroscientist*
Hubbard, Stevan Ralph *biophysicist, educator*
Ingle, James Chesney, Jr. *geology educator*
Inlow, Rush Osborne *chemist*
James, Harold L(loyd) *geologist*
Jan, Yuh Nung *biochemistry and physiology educator*
Jarmie, Nelson *physicist, consultant*
Jiang, Bai-Chuan *optical educator*
Jones, Thornton Keith *research chemist*
Jordan, Thomas Fredrick *physics educator*
Kamen, Martin David *physical biochemist*
Kastner, Marc Aaron *physics educator*
Kennel, Charles Frederick *physics educator, government official*
Kerr, Donald MacLean, Jr. *physicist*
Kerwin, Larkin *retired physics educator*
Klema, Ernest Donald *nuclear physicist, educator*
Knudsen, William Claire *geophysicist*
Kraichnan, Robert Harry *theoretical physicist, consultant*
Kress, Albert Otto, Jr. *polymer chemist*
Kropschot, Richard Henry *retired physicist, science laboratory administrato*
Kumar, Kaplesh *materials scientist*
Kustin, Kenneth *chemist*
Langerak, Esley Oren *retired research chemist*
Laporte, Leo Frederic *earth sciences educator*
Lau, Albert Man-Fai *physicist*
LeBlond, Paul Henri *oceanographer, educator*
Le Mehaute, Bernard Jean *marine physics educator*
Lemke, James Underwood *physicist*
Levenson, Marc David *optics and lasers specialist, scientist, editor*
Levi, Barbara Goss *physicist, editor*
Lippincott, James Andrew *biochemistry and biological sciences educator*
Liu, Shengzhong (Frank) *chemist, researcher*
Lloyd, Joseph Wesley *physicist, researcher*
Loach, Paul Allen *biochemist, biophysicist, educator*
Los, Marinus *retired agrochemical researcher*
Lugt, Hans Josef *physicist*
†Luo, Li-Shi *physics scientist*
Lurix, Paul Leslie, Jr. *chemist*
Lynds, Beverly Turner *retired astronomer*
MacQueen, Robert Moffat *solar physicist*
Maddin, Robert *metallurgist educator*
Maglich, Bogdan Castle *physicist*
Maiman, Theodore Harold *physicist*
Maniloff, Jack *biophysicist, educator*
March, Jacqueline Front *retired chemist*
Marcuse, Dietrich *retired physicist*
Marinetti, Guido V. *biochemistry educator*
Martin, Archer John Porter *retired chemistry educator*
McKinstry, Lydia *chemistry educator*
McLendon, George Leland *chemistry educator, researcher*
Meiling, Gerald Stewart *materials scientist*
Miller, Jeffrey Veach *biochemist, researcher*
Mil'shtein, Samson *semiconductor physicist*
Mislow, Kurt Martin *chemist, educator*
Nash, Susan Smith *geologist*
Nemec, Josef *retired organic chemist, researcher*
Neumark, Gertrude Fanny *materials science educator*
Nobles, Laurence Hewit *retired geology educator*
Noyes, H(enry) Pierre *physicist*
Obushenko, Ivan Makarovich *chemist*
Olsen, Clifford Wayne *retired physical chemist, consultant*
†Opsahl-Ong, Beale Hibbs *physicist*
Orttung, William Herbert *chemistry educator*
Osborn, Terry Wayne *biochemist, executive*
Pall-Pallant, Teri *paleontologist, inventor, behavioral scientist, design engineer, advertising agency executive*
Palmer, Larry George *chemist*
Palmer, Ricky Samuel *physicist*
Parreira, Helio Correa *physical chemist*
Pautler, Maria Christine Sadusky *environmental scientist*
Pearson, Ralph Gottfrid *chemistry educator*
Petersen, Arne Joaquin *chemist*
Phillips, Julia Mae *physicist*
Piehl, Donald Herbert *chemist, consultant*
Pocock, Frederick James *environmental scientist, engineer, consultant*
Portis, Alan Mark *physicist, educator*
Pound, Robert Vivian *physics educator*
Price, Clifford Warren *retired metallurgist, researcher*
Price, Paul Buford *physicist, educator*
Proctor, Richard J. *geologist, consultant*
Pursey, Derek Lindsay *physics educator*
Putnam, Robert Ervin *chemist*
Pyper, James William *chemist*
Qutub, Musa Yacub *hydrogeologist, educator, consultant*
Rabó, Jule Anthony *chemical researcher, consultant*
Rasmusson, Gary Henry *medicinal chemist*
Redfield, Alfred Guillou *physics and biochemistry educator*
Reichmanis, Elsa *chemist*
Rice, Stuart Alan *chemist, educator*
Richards, Paul Linford *physics educator, researcher*
Richardson, Charles Clifton *biochemist, educator*
Richardson, Jasper Edgar *nuclear physicist*
Rider, Paul Edward *physicist, educator*
Robbins, Jessie Earl *metallurgist*
Robertson, John Archibald Law *nuclear scientist*
Robinson, Bruce Butler *physicist*
Rose, Marian Henrietta *physics researcher*
Rosenkilde, Carl Edward *physicist*
Ross, Alberta Barkley *retired chemist*
Rubin, Vera Cooper *research astronomer*
Salzer, Louis William *chemist*
Sandorfy, Camille *chemistry educator*
Saxena, Vinod Kumar *meteorology educator*
Sayre, David *physicist*
Schelar, Virginia Mae *chemistry consultant*
Schmidt, Ruth A(nna) M(arie) *geologist*
Schonhorn, Harold *chemist, researcher*
Sellin, Ivan Armand *physicist, educator, researcher*
Sellmyer, David Julian *physicist, educator*
Setters, Paula Louise Henderson *physics educator*
Shapiro, Zalman Mordecai *chemist, consultant*
Sharon, Timothy Michael *physicist*
Shaw, Melvin Phillip *physicist, engineering educator, psychologist*
Sheinin, Rose *biochemist, educator*
Shirley, David Arthur *chemistry educator, science administrator*
Smith, Charles Haddon *geoscientist, consultant*
Souw, Bernard Eng-Kie *physicist, consultant*
Speier, John Leo, Jr. *retired chemist*
Spejewski, Eugene Henry *physicist, educator*
Spencer, David Anthony *geologist, researcher*
Squibb, Samuel Dexter *chemistry educator*
Steinert, Leon Albert *mathematical physicist*
Steinmetz, John Charles *geologist, paleontologist*
Stevenson, Paul Michael *physics educator, researcher*
Strouth, Baron Howard Steven *geologist, mining engineer*
Sturtevant, Julian Munson *biophysical chemist, educator*
Sullivan, Nicholas G. *science educator, speleologist*
Sundaresan, Mosur Kalyanaraman *physics educator*
Sunderman, Duane Neuman *chemist, research institute executive*
Symchowicz, Samson *biochemist*
Taylor, Hugh Pettingill, Jr. *geologist, educator*
Teal, Edwin Earl *retired engineering physicist, consultant*
Thuillier, Richard Howard *meteorologist*
†Trautvetter, Lois Calian *chemistry educator, consultant*
Turco, Richard Peter *atmospheric scientist*
Ullman, Edwin Fisher *research chemist*
van der Meer, Simon *physicist*
Vanderwalker, Diane Mary *materials scientist*
Vanier, Jacques *physicist*
Veronis, George *geophysicist, educator*
Vilenchik, Michael Marc *biophysicist, physician, virologist, radiobiologist*
Vitaliano, Charles J(oseph) *geologist, educator*
Vook, Frederick Ludwig *physicist, consultant*
Wahl, Floyd Michael *geologist*
Wallace, Jane House *retired geologist*
Wallace, Robert Earl *geologist*
Warshawsky, Isidore *physicist, consultant*
Washington, Josephine Harriet *biologist, endocrinologist, educator*
Watko, Julie Anne *astrophysicist, actor*
Wattenberg, Albert *physicist, educator*
Waymouth, John Francis *physicist, consultant*
Weinberg, Steven *physics educator*
Weisburger, Elizabeth Kreiser *retired chemist, editor*
Weiss, Michael James *chemistry educator*
Weissman, Samuel Isaac *chemistry educator*
Wells, Robert Hartley *chemistry professional*
Whistler, Roy Lester *chemist, educator, industrialist*
Wickner, William Tobey *biochemistry educator*
Wilhelms, Don Edward *geologist*
Wilson, Kenneth Geddes *physics research administrator, educator*
Wolff, Manfred Ernst *medicinal chemist, pharmaceutical company executive*
Wolff, Peter Adalbert *physicist, educator*
Woo, Jonathan C. G. *chemist, management consultant*
Wroblowa, Halina Stefania *electrochemist*
Wyrtki, Klaus *oceanography educator*
Yates, David John C. *chemist, researcher*
Yearian, Mason Russell *retired physicist*
Zaffaroni, Alejandro C. *biochemist, medical research company executive*
Zaleski, Jan Franciszek *biochemist*
Zellmer, Darwin Llewelyn *radiation biophysicist*
Zimm, Bruno Hasbrouck *physical chemistry educator*

SOCIAL SCIENCE

UNITED STATES

ALABAMA

Arab
Hall, Atlee Burpee *researcher*

Auburn
Clark, Janet Eileen *political scientist, educator*

Birmingham
Hawk, Beverly Gale *political scientist, educator*
McCarl, Henry Newton *economics and geology educator*
Morrisey, Michael A. *health economics educator*
Nunn, Grady Harrison *political science educator emeritus*
Pedersen, Paul Bodholdt *psychologist, educator*
Ramey, Craig T. *psychology educator*
Refinetti, Roberto *psychologist*
Taub, Edward *psychology researcher*

Collinsville
Beasley, Mary Catherine *home economics educator, administrator, researcher*

Dothan
Wright, Burton *sociologist*

Fairhope
Brumback Patterson, Cathy Jean *psychologist*

Fort Rucker
Caldwell, John Alvis, Jr. *experimental psychologist*

Hartselle
Slate, Joe Hutson *psychologist, educator*

Hoover
†Anyanwu, Victor O. *criminologist, political scientist*

Huntsville
Kestle, Wendell Russell *cost and economic analyst, consultant*

Jacksonville
Dunaway, Carolyn Bennett *retired sociology educator*

Lillian
Moyer, Kenneth Evan *psychologist, educator*

Maxwell AFB
Wendzel, Robert Leroy *political science educator*

Mobile
Suess, James Francis *clinical psychologist*
Vitulli, William Francis *psychology educator*

Montevallo
McChesney, Robert Michael, Sr. *political science educator*

Montgomery
†Fisher, Gerald Patrick *criminal justice educator*

Pell City
Passey, George Edward *psychology educator*

Phenix City
Greathouse, Patricia Dodd *retired psychometrist, counselor*

Tuscaloosa
Abdel-Ghany, Mohamed *family economics educator*
Baklanoff, Eric Nicholas *economist, educator*
Bills, Robert E(dgar) *emeritus psychology educator*
Cramer, Dale Lewis *economics educator*
Fish, Mary Martha *economics educator*
Weaver, David *geography educator*

ALASKA

Anchorage
Fisher, Margaret Eleanor *psychologist, lawyer, arbitrator, mediator, educator*
Kernodle, Una Mae *family and consumer sciences curriculum specialist, retired secondary education educator*
Mattison, Elisa Sheri *organizational psychologist*
Risley, Todd Robert *psychologist, educator*

Fairbanks
Kunz, Michael Lenney *archaeologist*

ARIZONA

Flagstaff
Block, M. Juliann McCarthy *school psychologist*
Maxwell, Mary Susanna *psychology educator*

McDonald, Craydon Dean *psychologist*
Smith, Zachary Alden *political science and public administration educator*
†Walka, Joseph J. *economics educator*

Glendale
Sims, Glenn *sociologist, educator*

Phoenix
†Berman, Tressa Lynn *anthropologist, writer*
Bostwick, Todd William *city archaeologist*
Leonard, Elizabeth Lipman *psychologist*
Lyon, William James *sociology educator*
Roe, William Thomas *behaviorial engineer, educator, researcher*
Wolf, Irna Lynn *psychologist*

Sacaton
Stephenson, Larry Kirk *stategic planner, management, geography educator*

Scottsdale
Braun, Stephen Hughes *psychologist*
Henry, Lois Hollender *psychologist*
Kizziar, Janet Wright *psychologist, author, lecturer*

Sedona
Becker, Wesley Clemence *psychology educator emeritus*
Eggert, Robert John, Sr. *economist*

Sierra Vista
Lutes, Todd Oakley *political science educator*

Sun City West
Pipitone, Phyllis L. *psychologist, educator, author*

Tempe
Alisky, Marvin Howard *political science educator*
Farber, Bernard *sociologist, educator*
Gordon, Leonard *sociology educator*
Guinouard, Donald Edgar *psychologist*
Hackett, Edward John *sociology educator and researcher*
Johanson, Donald Carl *physical anthropologist*
Lounsbury, John Frederick *geographer, educator*
Metcalf, Virgil Alonzo *economics educator*
Miller, Warren Edward *political scientist*
Montero, Darrel Martin *social worker, educator*
O'Neil, Michael Joseph *opinion survey executive, marketing consultant*
Rice, Ross R(ichard) *political science educator*
Simon, Sheldon Weiss *political science educator*
Uttal, William R(eichenstein) *psychology and engineering educator, research scientist*
Weigend, Guido Gustav *geographer, educator*

Tucson
Beach, Lee Roy *psychologist, educator, academic administrator*
Billings, Richard Bruce *economics educator, consultant*
Birkby, Walter Hudson *forensic anthropologist, consultant*
Block, Michael Kent *economics and law educator, public policy association executive, former government official, consultant*
Brainerd, Charles J(on) *experimental psychologist, applied mathematician, educator*
Clarke, James Weston *political science educator, writer*
Fontana, Bernard Lee *retired anthropologist, writer, consultant*
Jacome, Felipe Carlos *anthropologist*
Milward, Hendree Brinton, Jr. *management and public administration educator*
Mishler, William, II *political science educator*
Rogers, John Alvin *retired technical educator, writer, publisher*
Sampliner, Linda Hodes *psychologist, consultant*
Smith, David Wayne *psychologist, educator*
Smith, Vernon Lomax *economist, researcher*
Soren, David *archaeology educator, cinema author*
Stini, William Arthur *anthropologist, educator*
Thompson, Raymond Harris *retired anthropologist, educator*
Underwood, Jane Hainline Hammons *anthropologist, educator*
Volgy, Thomas John *political science educator, organization official*
Wahlke, John Charles *political science educator*
Whiting, Allen Suess *political science educator, writer, consultant*

Yuma
Norton, Dunbar Sutton *economic developer*

ARKANSAS

Arkadelphia
Sandford, Juanita Dadisman *sociologist, educator, writer*

Bentonville
Glover, Deborah Joyce *school psychologist, consultant*

Blytheville
†Davidson, Michael W. *psychologist*

Conway
Mc New, Bennie Banks *economics and finance educator*

Fayetteville
Green, Thomas James *archaeologist*
Mc Gimsey, Charles Robert, III *anthropologist*

Jonesboro
King, Dorothy Jackson *psychologist, marriage-family counselor, therapist*

Little Rock
Ledbetter, Calvin Reville, Jr. (Cal Ledbetter) *political science educator, university dean, former legislator*
Wepfer, Julia M. *psychologist*
Worley, Karen Boyd *psychologist*

Morrilton
Thompson, Robert Lee *agricultural economist, nonprofit executive*

Pine Bluff
Tai, Chong-Soo Stephen *political scientist, educator*

Scott
Rolingson, Martha *research archeologist*

State University
Marlay, Ross *political scientist, educator*
Power, Mary Susan *political science educator*

CALIFORNIA

Alameda
Boyer, Ford Sylvester *relationship consultant, minister*

Apple Valley
Fisher, Weston Joseph *economist*

Arcata
Emenhiser, JeDon Allen *political science educator, academic administrator*

Atascadero
Cotter, Cornelius Philip *political scientist, educator*

Azusa
†Palm, Daniel Carl *political science educator*

Bakersfield
Hamann, Janet Marian *educational psychology educator*
Osterkamp, Dalene May *psychology educator, artist*
Singer, George Milton *clinical psychologist*

Belmont
Orszag, Peter Richard *economist*

Benicia
Nelson, Elmer Kingsholm, Jr. *educator, writer, mediator, consultant*

Berkeley
Adelman, Irma Glicman *economics educator*
Alhadeff, David Albert *economics educator*
Auerbach, Alan Jeffrey *economist*
Bellah, Robert Neelly *sociologist, educator*
Brandes, Stanley Howard *anthropology educator, writer*
Breslauer, George William *political science educator*
Canfield, Judy Ohlbaum *psychologist*
Cheit, Earl Frank *economist, educator*
Chodorow, Nancy Julia *sociology educator*
Clark, John Desmond *anthropology educator*
Colson, Elizabeth Florence *anthropologist*
Dekel, Eddie *economics educator*
Foster, George McClelland, Jr. *anthropologist*
Freedman, Mervin Burton *psychologist, educator*
Gilbert, Richard Joseph *economics educator*
Graburn, Nelson Hayes Henry *anthropologist, educator*
Harsanyi, John Charles *economics educator*
Howell, Francis Clark *anthropologist, educator*
Jensen, Arthur Robert *psychology educator*
Kallgren, Joyce Kislitzin *political science educator*
Kirch, Patrick Vinton *anthropology educator, archaeologist*
Lambert, Nadine Murphy *psychologist, educator*
Landau, Martin *political science educator*
Lazarus, Richard Stanley *psychology educator*
Lee, Ronald Demos *demographer, economist, educator*
Leonard, David King *political science educator*
Letiche, John Marion *economist, educator*
Lipson, Leslie Michael *political science educator*
Maisel, Sherman Joseph *economist, educator*
Maslach, Christina *psychology educator*
Muir, William Ker, Jr. *political science educator*
Quigley, John Michael *economist, educator*
Ranney, (Joseph) Austin *political science educator*
Rosenzweig, Mark Richard *psychology educator*
Shack, William Alfred *anthropology educator, researcher, consultant*
Shapiro, Carl *economics educator and consultant*
Smolensky, Eugene *economics educator*
Stewart, Patricia Rhodes *retired clinical psychologist, researcher*
Turner, Weld W(inston) *industrial psychologist*
Varian, Hal Ronald *economics educator*
Wilensky, Harold L. *political science and industrial relations educator*
Williamson, Oliver Eaton *economics and law educator*
Wolfinger, Raymond Edwin *political science educator*

Beverly Hills
Aguilera, Donna Conant *psychologist, researcher*
Himelstein, Susan *psychologist*
Yaryan, Ruby Bell *psychologist*

Blythe
Hansen, Randall Glenn *school psychologist, consultant*

Bonita
Deane, Debbe *psychologist, journalist, editor, consultant*

Burlingame
Schwantes, Robert Sidney *international relations executive*

Carmel
Parker, Donald Henry *psychologist, author*
Reese, William Albert, III *psychologist, clinical neuropsychologist*

Carpinteria
Schmidhauser, John Richard *political science educator*
Wheeler, John Harvey *political scientist*

Cayucos
Hedlund, James Lane *retired psychologist, educator*

Chico
McNall, Scott Grant *sociology educator*
Rodrigue, Christine M(ary) *geography educator, business consultant*

Claremont
Bjork, Gordon Carl *economist, educator*
Borcherding, Thomas Earl *economist*
†Brint, Steven Gregory *sociologist, educator*
Jaffa, Harry Victor *political philosophy educator emeritus*
Leeb, Charles Samuel *clinical psychologist*
Likens, James Dean *economics educator*
McClelland, Harold Franklin *economics educator*
Phelps, Orme Wheelock *economics educator emeritus*
Rossum, Ralph Arthur *political science educator*
Wents, Doris Roberta *psychologist*
Wykoff, Frank Champion *economics educator*

Compton
Drew, Sharon Lee *sociologist*

Corona Del Mar
Hinderaker, Ivan *political science educator*

Corte Madera
Kratka-Schneider, Dorothy Maryjohanna *psychotherapist*

Costa Mesa
Gardin, John George, II *psychologist*

Culver City
Maltzman, Irving Myron *psychology educator*

Cypress
Friess, Donna Lewis *children's rights advocate, writer*

Davis
Cohen, Lawrence Edward *sociology educator, criminologist*
Cook, Roberta Lynn *agricultural economist, educator*
Goldstone, Jack Andrew *sociologist*
Groth, Alexander Jacob *political science educator*
Harper, Lawrence Vernon *human development educator*
Hawkes, Glenn Rogers *psychology educator*
Jett, Stephen Clinton *geography and textiles educator, researcher*
Lofland, Lyn Hebert *sociology educator*
Mason, William A(lvin) *psychologist, educator, researcher*
McHenry, Henry Malcolm *anthropologist, educator*
Musolf, Lloyd Daryl *political science educator, institute administrator*
Owings, Donald Henry *psychology educator*
†Rothchild, Donald Sylvester *political science educator*
Skinner, G(eorge) William *anthropologist, educator*
Smith, Michael Peter *social science educator, researcher*
Spindler, George Dearborn *anthropologist, educator, author, editor*
Storm, Donald John *archaeologist, historian*
Sumner, Daniel Alan *economist, educator*
Wegge, Leon Louis François *retired economics educator*

Del Mar
Boynton, Robert Merrill *retired psychology educator*

El Cajon
Spiegel, Charles (Louis S.J. Spiegel) *psychology educator*

Elk Grove
Weagraff, Patrick James *psychology educator, writer*

Encino
Gross, Sharon Ruth *forensic psychologist, researcher*

Fallbrook
Bryant, Don Estes *economist, scientist*

Foster City
Thomlinson, Ralph *demographer, educator*

Fremont
Baker, Paul Thornell *anthropology educator*
Feinberg, Richard Alan *clinical psychologist*

Fresno
Dackawich, S. John *sociology educator*
Huddleston, Forest Willis *retired mental healing counselor*
Kus, James Stedry *geography educator, archaeologist*
O'Brien, John Conway *economist, educator, writer*
O'Connor, Kevin John *psychologist*

Fullerton
Boyum, Keith Orel *political scientist, consultant*
Hershey, Gerald Lee *psychologist*
†Junn, Ellen N. *psychology educator*
Kaisch, Kenneth Burton *psychologist, priest*
†Traphagan, John Willis *anthropologist*

Glendale
Hadley, Paul Ervin *international relations educator*

Glendora
Cerullo, Rudy Michael, II *psychology, theology educator, minister*

Granada Hills
Aller, Wayne Kendall *psychology educator, researcher, computer education company executive, property manager*

Granite Bay
Hartmann, Frederick Howard *political science educator emeritus*

Hayward
Jun, Jong Sup *public administration educator*

Healdsburg
Glad, Joan Bourne *clinical psychologist, educator*

Hermosa Beach
Wickwire, Patricia Joanne Nellor *psychologist, educator*

Hollywood
Fisher, Joel Marshall *political scientist, legal consultant, educator*

Irvine
Aigner, Dennis John *economics educator, consultant*
Burton, Michael Ladd *anthropology educator*
Cushman, Robert Fairchild *political science educator, author, editor*
Danziger, James Norris *political science educator*
Freeman, Linton Clarke *sociology educator*
Greenberger, Ellen *psychologist, educator*
Huff, C(larence) Ronald *public policy and criminology educator*
Lave, Charles Arthur *economics educator*
Luce, R(obert) Duncan *psychology educator*
Margolis, Julius *economist, educator*
Mason, Roger Deen *archaeologist*
†Ranjan, Priya *economist*
Schonfeld, William Rost *political science educator, researcher*
Sperling, George *cognitive scientist, educator*
†Sunoo, Harold W. *Asian studies educator*
White, Douglas Richie *anthropology educator*

Kenwood
Podboy, John Watts *clinical, forensic psychologist*

La Jolla
Attiyeh, Richard Eugene *economics educator*
Cain, William Stanley *psychologist, educator*
Coburn, Marjorie Foster *psychologist, educator*
Erie, Steven Philip *political science educator*
Farson, Richard Evans *psychologist*
Harris, Philip Robert *management and space psychologist*
Hoston, Germaine Annette *political science educator*
Lane, Sylvia *economist, educator*
Mandler, George *psychologist*
Mandler, Jean Matter *psychologist, educator*
Pratt, George Janes, Jr. *psychologist, author*
Schiller, Herbert Irving *social scientist, author*
Spiro, Melford Elliot *anthropology educator*
Starr, Ross Marc *economist, educator*
Timmer, Charles Peter *agricultural and development economist*
White, Halbert Lynn, Jr. *economist, educator, consultant*

La Mirada
Pike, Patricia Louise *psychology educator*

La Verne
†Somvichian, Kamol *political science educator*

Laguna Beach
Bent, Alan Edward *political science educator, administrator*

Laguna Hills
Noble, Marion Ellen *retired home economist*

Lake Arrowhead
Beckman, James Wallace Bim *economist, marketing executive*

Larkspur
Saxton, Lloyd *psychologist, author*

Loma Linda
Betancourt, Hector Mainhard *psychology scientist, educator*

Los Altos
Carr, Jacquelyn B. *psychologist, educator*

Los Angeles
Alexander, Jeffrey Charles *sociology educator*
Allen, William Richard *retired economist*
Álvarez, Rodolfo *sociology educator, consultant*
Anawalt, Patricia Rieff *anthropologist*
Anderson, Austin Gilman *economics research company consultant*
Arnold, Jeanne Eloise *anthropologist, archaeologist, educator*
Basch, Darlene Chakin *clinical social worker*
Bennett, Charles Franklin, Jr. *biogeographer, educator*
Blakely, Edward James *economics educator*
Brubaker, William Rogers *sociology educator*
Butterworth, Robert Roman *psychologist, researcher, media therapist*
Cerrell, Joseph R. *political scientist, consultant*
Champagne, Duane Willard *sociology educator*
Clark, Burton Robert *sociologist, educator*
Clark, William Arthur V. *geographer, demographer*
Coombs, Robert Holman *behavioral scientist, medical educator, therapist, author*
Darby, Michael Rucker *economist, educator*
Dawson, Adam *private investigator, former newspaper editor*
Dekmejian, Richard Hrair *political science educator*
Demsetz, Harold *economist, educator*
Dosamantes-Beaudry, Irma *psychology educator*
Ellickson, Bryan Carl *economics educator*
Elliott, John Ed *economics educator*
Forness, Steven Robert *educational psychologist*
Goldberg, Herb *psychologist, educator*
Goldschmidt, Walter Rochs *anthropologist, educator*
Greenberg, Ira Arthur *psychologist*
Griffiths, Barbara Lorraine *psychologist, writer*
Harberger, Arnold Carl *economist, educator*
Hoffenberg, Marvin *political science educator, consultant*
Ilanit, Tamar *psychologist*
Intriligator, Michael David *economist, educator*
Jamison, Dean Tecumseh *economist*
Kandal, Terry R. *sociology educator, consultant*
Kelley, Harold Harding *psychology educator*
Klein, Benjamin *economics educator, consultant*
La Force, James Clayburn, Jr. *economist, educator*
Landen, Sandra Joyce *psychologist, educator*
Lasswell, Marcia Lee *psychologist, educator*
Leijonhufvud, Axel Stig Bengt *economics educator*
Levine, Robert Arthur *economist, policy analyst*
Lowenthal, Abraham Frederic *international relations educator*
Lyman, John *psychology and engineering educator*

PROFESSIONAL INDEX 6221 SOCIAL SCIENCE

Mack, Brenda Lee *sociologist, public relations consulting company executive, media executive*
†MacLeod, William Bentley *economics and law educator*
†Maida, Carl Albert *anthropologist*
Malamuth, Neil Moshe *psychology and communication educator*
Malecki, Edward Stanley, Jr. *political science educator*
Maquet, Jacques Jerome Pierre *anthropologist, writer*
Michael, William Burton *psychologist, educator*
Montoya, Velma *economist, policy consultant*
Morgner, Aurelius *economist, educator*
Nelson, Howard Joseph *geographer, educator*
Orme, Antony Ronald *geography educator*
Raven, Bertram H(erbert) *psychology educator*
Rodnick, Eliot Herman *psychologist, educator*
Seeman, Melvin *sociologist, educator*
Sheinbaum, Stanley K. *economist*
Shneidman, Edwin S. *psychologist, educator, thanatologist, suicidologist*
†Sokoloff, Kenneth Lee *economics educator*
Squire, Molly Ann *organizational psychologist*
Strack, Stephen Naylor *psychologist*
Thompson, Earl Albert *economics educator*
Thompson, Richard Frederick *psychologist, neuroscientist, educator*
Thrower, Norman Joseph William *geographer, educator*
Totten, George Oakley, III *political science educator*
Turner, Ralph Herbert *sociologist, educator*
Vuckovic, Gojko Milos *public administration scholar*
Watson, Sharon Gitin *psychologist, executive*
Williams, Robert Martin *economist, consultant*
Wittrock, Merlin Carl *educational psychologist*
Wong, James Bok *economist, engineer, technologist*
Zeitlin, Maurice *sociology educator, author*

Malibu
Aiken, Lewis Roscoe, Jr. *psychologist, educator*
Monsma, Stephen Vos *political scientist, educator*

Marina Del Rey
Heisser-Metoyer, Patricia *psychologist, organizational consultant*

Menlo Park
Clair, Theodore Nat *educational psychologist*
Lindzey, Gardner *psychologist, educator*
Vane, Sylvia Brakke *anthropologist, publisher, cultural resource management company executive, writer*

Mill Valley
Benezet, Louis Tomlinson *retired psychology educator, former college president*
Harner, Michael James *anthropologist, educator, author*

Modesto
Berry, John Charles *clinical psychologist, educational administrator*

Moffett Field
Cohen, Malcolm Martin *psychologist, researcher*
Haines, Richard Foster *psychologist*

Monarch Beach
de Beixedon, S(usan) Yvette *psychologist*

Monterey
Boger, Dan Calvin *statistical and economic consultant, educator*
Caldwell, Joni *psychology educator, small business owner*

Monterey Park
Amezcua, Charlie Anthony *social science counselor*

Newport Beach
Lawson, Thomas Cheney *fraud examiner*
Whittemore, Paul Baxter *psychologist*

Northridge
Harwick, Betty Corinne Burns *sociology educator*

Oakland
Anderson, Robert Thomas *anthropologist, researcher, physician*
Elgin, Gita *psychologist*
Farrell, Kenneth Royden *economist*
†Hamer, Forrest Michael *psychologist*
Nathan, Laura E. *sociology educator*
Nebelkopf, Ethan *psychologist*

Oceanside
Hertweck, Alma Louise *sociology and child development educator*
Hertweck, E. Romayne *psychology educator*
Stewart, Kenneth Malcolm *retired anthropologist, researcher*

Orange
Becker, Juliette *psychologist, marriage and family therapist*

Orinda
Sprainqs, Violet Evelyn *psychologist*

Oroville
Shelton, Joel Edward *clinical psychologist*

Pacific Palisades
Longaker, Richard Pancoast *political science educator emeritus*

Palo Alto
Eulau, Heinz *political scientist, educator*
Flanagan, Robert Joseph *economics educator*
Rosaldo, Renato Ignacio, Jr. *cultural anthropology educator*
Scitovsky, Anne Aickelin *economist*

Pasadena
Davis, Lance Edwin *economics educator*
Helander, Terrill Webb *educational psychologist*
Horner, Althea Jane *psychologist*
Ledyard, John Odell *economics educator, consultant*
Munger, Edwin Stanton *political geography educator*
Plott, Charles Raymond *economics educator*

Scudder, Thayer *anthropologist, educator*

Paso Robles
Rocha, Marilyn Eva *clinical psychologist*

Petaluma
Carr, Les *psychologist, educator*

Pico Rivera
Harwick, Wayne Thomas *economist*

Placentia
Gobar, Alfred Julian *economic consultant, educator*
Linnan, Judith Ann *psychologist*

Pleasant Hill
Richard, Robert Carter *psychologist*
Stevenson, James D(onald), Jr. *psychologist, counselor*

Pomona
Garrity, Rodman Fox *psychologist, educator*

Portola Valley
Ward, Robert Edward *retired political science educator and university administrator*

Rancho Cucamonga
Shields, Andrea Lyn *psychologist, educator*

Rancho Mirage
Deiter, Newton Elliott *clinical psychologist*
Lacey, John Irving *psychologist, physiologist, educator*

Redding
Drake, Patricia Evelyn *psychologist*

Redondo Beach
Naples, Caesar Joseph *law/public policy educator, lawyer, consultant*

Riverside
Adrian, Charles Raymond *political science educator*
Burgess, Curt *psychologist, computer scientist, educator*
Eyman, Richard Kenneth *psychologist, educator*
Griffin, Keith Broadwell *economics educator*
†Kauffman, Kristina Marie *political science educator*
Petrinovich, Lewis Franklin *psychology educator*
Rosenthal, Robert *psychology educator*
Turk, Austin Theodore *sociology educator*

Rohnert Park
Byrne, Noel Thomas *sociologist, educator*
Criswell, Eleanor Camp *psychologist*
†Merril, Charles Hall *social science educator*
Phillips, Peter Martin *sociologist, educator, media researcher*

Sacramento
Bennett, Lawrence Allen *psychologist, criminal justice researcher*
Boylan, Richard John *psychologist, hypnotherapist, researcher, behavioral scientist, educator*
Chapman, Loring *psychology, physiology educator, neuroscientist*
Gottfredson, Don Martin *criminal justice educator*
Harris, Wilson *psychiatrist, research scientist*
Majesty, Melvin Sidney *psychologist, consultant*
Newland, Chester Albert *public administration educator*
Post, August Alan *economist, artist*
Tashjian, Gregory Kimball Thaddeus *political consultant, writer*
Wender, Deborah Elizabeth *policy consultant, social worker*
Zeman, Valerie Denise *home economics educator*

San Bernardino
Maul, Terry Lee *psychologist, educator*

San Diego
Bales, Robert Freed *social psychologist, educator*
Blade, Melinda Kim *archaeologist, educator, researcher*
Callahan, LeeAnn Lucille *psychologist*
Carleson, Robert Bazil *public policy consultant, corporation executive*
Clague, Christopher K(arran) *economics educator*
Edwards, Darrel *psychologist*
Emerick, Robert Earl *sociologist, educator*
Getis, Arthur *geography educator*
†Johnson, Grace Alexander *anthropologist, curator*
Kiesler, Charles Adolphus *psychologist, academic administrator*
Lewis, Shirley Jeane *psychology educator*
McEvoy, Pamela T. *clinical psychologist*
Nagao, Norris Sadato *political science educator, consultant*
Rea, Amadeo Michael *ethnobiologist, ornithologist*
Storer, Norman William *sociology educator*
Vaughn, Billy Eldridge *psychology educator, publisher*
Weeks, John Robert *geographer, sociology educator*

San Francisco
Adamson, Mary Anne *geographer, systems engineer*
Adler, Nancy Elinor *psychologist, educator*
Burgess, Leonard Randolph *business administration and economics educator, writer*
Butz, Otto William *political science educator*
†Clementi, Mark Anthony *clinical and sport psychologist, educator*
Estes, Carroll Lynn *sociologist, educator*
†Hawthorne, Mark R. *investigator, educator*
Hoadley, Walter Evans *economist, financial executive, lay worker*
Krippner, Stanley Curtis *psychologist*
Luft, Harold S. *health economist*
Marston, Michael *urban economist, asset management executive*
Marvin, David Keith *international relations educator*
Meister, Gerry Smith *social studies educator*
†Munroe, Tapan *economist, educator, consultant*
Rice, Dorothy Pechman (Mrs. John Donald Rice) *medical economist*
Smith, Robert Charles *political science educator, researcher*
Warner, Rollin Miles, Jr. *economics educator, real estate broker*

Wilson, Robert Llewellyn *clinical psychologist, educator*

San Jose
Cedolini, Anthony John *psychologist*
Chastain, Robert Lee *educational psychologist*
Cohen, D. Ashley *clinical neuropsychologist*
McDowell, Jennifer *sociologist, composer, playwright, publisher*
Patnoe, Shelley Elizabeth *psychologist, writer*
†Van Selst, Mark G.A. *psychology educator*

San Luis Obispo
Culbertson, James Thomas *psychologist*
Seeber, James J. *sociology educator*

San Rafael
†Sybinsky, Estrella Besinga *political science educator*
Tosti, Donald Thomas *psychologist, consultant*

Santa Ana
Foster, Julian Francis Sherwood *political science educator*

Santa Barbara
Beutler, Larry Edward *psychology educator*
Clinard, Marshall Barron *sociologist, educator*
Comanor, William S. *economist, educator*
Davidson, Roger H(arry) *political scientist, educator*
Erasmus, Charles John *anthropologist, educator*
Jochim, Michael Allan *archaeologist*
Kendler, Howard H(arvard) *psychologist, educator*
Mayer, Richard Edwin *psychology educator*
Turner, Henry A. *retired political science educator, author*

Santa Clara
Field, Alexander James *economics educator*

Santa Cruz
Kline, Sybil Rose *researcher*
Pettigrew, Thomas Fraser *social psychologist, educator*
Roby, Pamela Ann *sociology educator*
Rorer, Leonard George *psychologist, writer*
Smith, M(ahlon) Brewster *psychologist, educator*
Tharp, Roland George *psychology, education educator*
Tonay, Veronica Katherine *psychology educator*

Santa Monica
†Cullen, Frank W. *government relations consultant*
Lindsley, Donald Benjamin *physiological psychologist, educator*
Russell, Marlou *psychologist*
Smith, James Patrick *economist*
Veit, Clairice Gene Tipton *measurement psychologist*
Wolf, Charles, Jr. *economist, educator*
Yago, Glenn Harvey *economist, educator, entrepreneur*
†Zimmerman, Bill *political consultant*

Simi Valley
Whitley, David Scott *archaeologist*

Stanford
Almond, Gabriel Abraham *political science educator*
Amemiya, Takeshi *economist, statistician*
Anderson, Annelise Graebner *economist*
Anderson, Martin Carl *economist*
Arrow, Kenneth Joseph *economist, educator*
Bandura, Albert *psychologist*
Boskin, Michael Jay *economist, government official, university educator, consultant*
†Brody, Richard Alan *political science educator, researcher*
Bunzel, John Harvey *political science educator, researcher*
Carlsmith, James Merrill *psychologist, educator*
Damon, William Van Buren *developmental psychologist, educator, writer*
Enthoven, Alain Charles *economist, educator*
Friedman, Milton *economist, educator emeritus, author*
Fuchs, Victor Robert *economics educator*
Gage, Nathaniel Lees *psychologist, educator*
George, Alexander Lawrence *political scientist, educator*
Greenberg, Joseph H. *anthropologist, linguist*
Hall, Robert Ernest *economics educator*
Harris, Donald J. *economics educator*
Hickman, Bert George, Jr. *economist, educator*
Hilgard, Ernest Ropiequet *psychologist*
Holloway, David James *political science educator*
Howell, James Edwin *economist, educator*
Huntington, Hillard Griswold *economist*
Inkeles, Alex *sociology educator*
Johnston, Bruce Foster *economics educator*
Krueger, Anne O. *economics educator*
Krumboltz, John Dwight *psychologist, educator*
Kurz, Mordecai *economics educator*
Laitin, David Dennis *political science educator*
Lau, Lawrence Juen-Yee *economics educator, consultant*
Lazear, Edward Paul *economics and industrial relations educator, researcher*
Lepper, Mark Roger *psychology educator*
Lewis, John Wilson *political science educator*
Lipset, Seymour Martin *sociologist, political scientist, educator*
Maccoby, Eleanor Emmons *psychology educator*
Manley, John Frederick *political scientist, educator*
March, James Gardner *social scientist, educator*
Mc Lure, Charles E., Jr. *economist*
Meier, Gerald Marvin *economics educator*
Noll, Roger Gordon *economist, educator*
North, Robert Carver *political science educator*
Paul, Benjamin David *anthropologist, educator*
Rakove, Jack Norman *history educator*
Reynolds, Clark Winton *economist, educator*
Ricardo-Campbell, Rita *economist, educator*
Roberts, Donald John *economics and business educator, consultant*
†Rowen, Henry Stanislaus *economics educator*
Scott, W(illiam) Richard *sociology educator*
Shepard, Roger Newland *psychologist, educator*
Smelser, Neil Joseph *sociologist*
Solomon, Ezra *economist, educator*
Sulloway, Frank Jones *psychologist, historian*
Taylor, John Brian *economist, educator*
Triska, Jan Francis *retired political science educator*
Van Horne, James Carter *economist, educator*
Zajonc, Robert B(oleslaw) *psychology educator*

Zimbardo, Philip George *psychologist, educator, writer*

Sylmar
Yguado, Alex Rocco *economics educator*

Torrance
Talmo-Wang, Regina Marie *social studies educator*

Turlock
Ahlem, Lloyd Harold *psychologist*

Ventura
Kent, Theodore Charles *psychologist*
Naurath, David Allison *engineering psychologist, researcher*

Vista
Beversdorf, Anne Elizabeth *astrologer, Jyotishi, author, educator*

Walnut Creek
Keith, Bruce Edgar *political analyst, genealogist*

Whittier
McKenna, Jeanette Ann *archaeologist*

Woodland Hills
Blanchard, William Henry *psychologist*
Nierenberg, Norman *urban land economist, retired state official*

COLORADO

Boulder
Borysenko, Joan *psychologist, biologist*
Bourne, Lyle Eugene, Jr. *psychology educator*
Brues, Alice Mossie *physical anthropologist, educator*
Greenberg, Edward Seymour *political science educator, writer*
Greene, David Lee *physical anthropologist, educator*
Healy, Alice Fenvessy *psychology educator, researcher*
Jessor, Richard *psychologist, educator*
Kintsch, Walter *psychology educator, director*
Menken, Jane Ava *demographer, educator*
Sutton, Philip D(ietrich) *psychologist*
White, Gilbert F(owler) *geographer, educator*

Colorado Springs
Brooks, Glenn Ellis *political science educator, educational administrator*
Plunkett, Michael C. *psychotherapist*
Shafer, Dallas Eugene *psychology gerontology educator, minister*

Denver
Adelman, Jonathan Reuben *political science educator, consultant*
Berland, Karen Ina *psychologist*
Conger, John Janeway *psychologist, educator*
Hashimoto, Jerry Shigeru *child psychologist*
Hill, Diane Seldon *corporate psychologist*
Kestenbaum, Richard *clinical and school psychologist, consultant adolescent, family and child psychology, biofeedback*
Lefly, Dianne Louise *research psychologist*
Markman, Howard J. *psychology educator*
Mendelsohn, Harold *sociologist, educator*
Mills, Kathleen Claire *anthropology and mathematics educator*
Moeller, Richard Robert *political science educator*
Muth, John William *economics educator*
Nelson, Sarah Milledge *archaeology educator*
Purcell, Kenneth *psychology educator, university dean*
Snyder, Charles Royce *sociologist, educator*
Winters, Richard Allen *mineral economist*
Yamamoto, Kaoru *psychology and education educator*
Zimet, Carl Norman *psychologist, educator*

Englewood
Haupenthal, Laura Ann *clinical psychologist*
Hendrick, Hal Wilmans *human factors educator*

Estes Park
Moore, Omar Khayyam *experimental sociologist*

Fort Carson
Chomko, Stephen Alexander *archaeologist*

Fort Collins
Bennett, Jacqueline Beekman *school psychologist*
Bennett, Thomas LeRoy, Jr. *clinical neuropsychology educator*
Eitzen, David Stanley *sociologist, educator*
Guest, Richard Eugene *psychologist*
Suinn, Richard Michael *psychologist*
Walsh, Richard George *agricultural economist*

Golden
Petrick, Alfred, Jr. *mineral economics educator, consultant*
Wellisch, William Jeremiah *social psychology educator*
Woolsey, Robert Eugene Donald *mineral economics, mathematics and business administration educator*

Grand Junction
Bacon, Phillip *geographer, author, consultant*
Butcher, Duane Clemens *economist, consultant*

La Junta
Strong, Mayda Nel *psychologist, educator*

Lakewood
Thomson, Marjorie Belle Anderson *sociology educator, consultant*

Littleton
Anderson, Darrell Edward *psychologist, educator*
Greenspan, Stephen Howard *retired psychology educator*
Milliken, John Gordon *research economist*

Pueblo
Alt, Betty L. *sociology educator*

Vega, Jose Guadalupe *psychologist, clinical director*

CONNECTICUT

Bloomfield
†Carstensen, Fred V. *economics educator*

Branford
Glick, Marion Shepherd *psychology, educator*
Hayes, Samuel Perkins *social scientist, educator*

Bridgeport
Stokes, Charles Junius *economist, educator*
van der Kroef, Justus Maria *political science educator*

Brookfield
Stern, Michael Lawrence *psychologist*

Chester
Feldmann, Shirley Clark *psychology educator*

Colebrook
Fuller, Renee Nuni *psychologist, educational publisher*

Danbury
Tolor, Alexander *psychologist, educator*

Fairfield
†Morehouse, Sarah McCally *political science educator*

Falls Village
Purcell, Mary Louise Gerlinger *retired educator*

Guilford
Chatt, Allen Barrett *psychologist, neuroscientist*

Hamden
Abelson, Robert Paul *psychologist, educator*

Hartford
Giannaros, Demetrios Spiros *economist, educator, politician*
Gunderson, Gerald Axel *economics educator, administrator*
Vohra, Ranbir *political scientist, educator*

Higganum
de Brigard, Emilie *anthropologist, consultant*

Mansfield Center
Liberman, Alvin Meyer *psychology educator*

Meriden
Muzyczka, Kathleen Ann *family and consumer sciences educator*

Middletown
Miller, Richard Alan *economist, educator*
Scheibe, Karl Edward *psychology educator*

Milford
Haigh, Charles *criminal justice educator*
Taylor, Charles Henry *psychoanalyst, educator*

New Britain
Cline, John Carroll *clinical psychologist*
Cotten-Huston, Annie Laura *psychologist, educator*

New Canaan
Marcus, Edward *economist, educator*

New Haven
Apter, David Ernest *political science and sociology educator*
Bell, Wendell *sociologist, educator, futurist*
Benjamin, Martin *anthropologist*
Blatt, Sidney Jules *psychology educator, psychoanalyst*
Bracken, Paul *political science educator*
Brainard, William Crittenden *economist, educator, university official*
Brownell, Kelly David *psychologist, educator*
Bruder, Charles Irwin *psychologist, researcher*
Child, Irvin Long *psychologist, educator*
Coe, Michael Douglas *anthropologist, educator*
Conklin, Harold Colyer *anthropologist, educator*
Crakes, Gary Michael *economics educator*
Crowder, Robert George *psychology educator*
Doob, Leonard William *psychology educator, academic administrator*
Ember, Carol R. *anthropology educator, author*
Erikson, Kai *sociologist, educator*
†Evenson, Robert Eugene *economics educator*
Garner, Wendell Richard *psychology educator*
Geselowitz, Michael Norman *anthropologist*
Hoge, Michael Alan *psychologist*
Joy, Stephen Patrick *psychology educator, psychotherapist*
Kessen, William *psychologist, educator*
LaPalombara, Joseph *political science educator*
Marks, Lawrence Edward *psychologist, educator*
Mayhew, David Raymond *political educator*
McGuire, William James *social psychology educator*
Miller, Neal Elgar *psychologist, emeritus educator*
Nemerson, Matthew Lewis *economic developer, civic leader*
Phillips, Peter Charles Bonest *economist, educator, researcher*
Pospisil, Leopold Jaroslav *anthropology and law educator*
Ranis, Gustav *economist, educator*
Reynolds, Lloyd George *economist, educator*
†Richard, Alison Fettes *anthropology educator*
Rosenstone, Steven Jay *political science educator*
Rouse, Irving *anthropologist, emeritus educator*
Russett, Bruce Martin *political science educator*
Scarf, Herbert Eli *economics educator*
Schultz, T. Paul *economics educator*
†Shapiro, Ian *political science educator*
Shubik, Martin *economics educator*
Stevens, Joseph Charles *psychology educator*
Tobin, James *economics educator*
Wagner, Allan Ray *psychology educator, experimental psychologist*
Westerfield, Holt Bradford *political scientist, educator*
Zigler, Edward Frank *psychologist, educator*

North Haven
Dahl, Robert Alan *political science educator*
Mahl, George Franklin *psychoanalyst, psychologist, educator*

Norwalk
Rosado, Rodolfo Jose *psychologist, educator*

Old Lyme
Johnson, James Myron *psychologist, educator*

Ridgefield
Stoddard, William Bert, Jr. *economist*

Southbury
Atwood, Edward Charles *economist, educator*
Wescott, Roger Williams *anthropologist*
Wilson, Geraldine O'Connor *psychologist*

Stamford
Teeters, Nancy Hays *economist*

Storrs Mansfield
Allen, John Logan *geographer*
Britner, Preston Arthur, IV *developmental psychologist, educator*
Gilmour, Robert S. *political science educator*
Katz, Leonard *psychology educator*
†Ladd, Everett Carll *political science educator, author*
McEachern, William Archibald *economics educator*
Zirakzadeh, Cyrus Ernesto *political science educator*

Suffield
Charkiewicz, Mitchell Michael, Jr. *economics and finance educator*

Voluntown
Thevenet, Patricia Confrey *social studies educator*

Waterbury
Phillips, Walter Mills, III *psychologist, educator*

West Haven
†L'Heureux, Amy Elizabeth *school psychologist*

Westport
Nolte, Richard Henry *political science researcher, consultant*
O'Leary, James John *economist*

Willimantic
Mann, Prem Singh *economics educator*

DELAWARE

Camden Wyoming
Porterfield, Craig Allen *psychologist, consultant*

Dover
Hoff, Samuel Boyer *political science educator*
Streetman, Lee George *sociology educator, criminology educator*

Newark
Bunkše, Edmunds Valdemārs *geographer, educator, consultant*
DiRenzo, Gordon James *sociologist, psychologist, educator*
Graham, Frances Keesler (Mrs. David Tredway Graham) *psychologist, educator*
Gulick, Walter Lawrence *psychologist, former college president*
Mangone, Gerard J. *international and maritime law educator*
Palley, Marian Lief *political science educator*
†Unger, Donald G. *psychologist, educator*

Wilmington
Kneavel, Thomas Charles, Jr. *psychologist*
†Lazar, Kathleen Ellen *clinical psychologist*
Reeder, Charles Benton *economic consultant*

DISTRICT OF COLUMBIA

Washington
Aaron, Henry Jacob *economics educator*
Abler, Ronald Francis *geography educator*
Abraham, Katharine Gail *economics educator*
Alexander, Arthur Jacob *economist*
Amling, Frederick *economist, educator, investment manager*
Arend, Anthony Clark *international relations educator*
Aschheim, Joseph *economist, educator*
Åslund, Anders *economist*
Bader, John Burkhardt *political scientist, educator*
Baer, Michael Alan *political scientist, educator*
Ballentine, J. Gregory *economist*
Barnett, Arthur Doak *political scientist, educator*
†Beck, Peter Michael *economics researcher*
Becker, Mary Louise *political scientist*
Bergmann, Barbara Rose *economics educator*
Bergsten, C. Fred *economist*
Besen, Stanley Martin *economist*
Blair, Margaret Mendenhall *research economist, consultant*
Blasier, Cole *political scientist*
Bluth, B. J. (Elizabeth Jean Catherine Bluth) *sociologist, aerospace technologist*
Boucher, Wayne Irving *policy analyst*
Boughton, James Murray *economist*
Bramson, Leon *social scientist, educator*
Breed, Joseph Illick *financial economist*
Brimmer, Andrew Felton *economic and financial consultant*
Brzezinski, Zbigniew *political science educator, author*
Burtless, Gary Thomas *economist, consultant*
Caldwell, Willard E. *psychologist, educator*
Carpenter, Ted Galen *political scientist*
Carter, Jean Anne *psychologist*
Cavanagh, John Henry *political economist*
Cazan, Matthew John *political science educator*
†Cha, Victor D. *government educator, consultant*
Checchi, Vincent Victor *economist*
Chu, David S. C. *economist*
Cline, William Richard *economist, educator*
Clodius, Robert LeRoy *economist, educator*
Cobble, Steven Bruce *political consultant, strategist*
Cohen, David *public affairs specialist, educator*
Cohen, Marc Jacob *researcher*
Cohen, Stephen Philip *political science and history educator*
Corbet, Richard Hugh *trade policy specialist, educator, writer*
Danziger, Raphael *political scientist, researcher*
Davis, Lynn Etheridge *political scientist*
Dickens, William Theodore *economic researcher*
Dillon, Wilton Sterling *anthropologist, foundation administrator*
Dizard, Wilson Paul, Jr. *international affairs consultant, educator*
Donovan, Molly Walsh *clinical psychologist*
Downs, Anthony *urban economist, real estate consultant*
Eads, George Curtis *economic consultant*
East, Maurice Alden *political scientist, educator*
Ehrenreich, Robert Marc *archaeologist, materials scientist, museum administrator*
Ershler, William Baldwin *biogerontologist, educator*
Etzioni, Amitai *sociologist, educator*
Faux, Jeff (Geoffrey Peter Faux) *economist, writer*
Feshbach, Murray *demographer, educator*
Fischer, Stanley *economist, educator*
Flattau, Pamela Ebert *research psychologist, consultant*
Franco, Robert *economist*
Frank, Isaiah *economist, educator*
Gallo, Anthony Ernest *economist, agribusiness author*
Gelbard, Alene H. *demographer, policy analyst*
Genia, Vicky *psychologist*
Gernert, Jeffrey Jared *psychologist*
Godson, Roy Simon *political scientist, think tank executive*
†Goode, Ann *civil rights administrator*
Goode, Richard Benjamin *economist, educator*
Greenberg, Milton *political scientist, educator*
Gubser, Peter Anton *political scientist, writer, educator*
Halperin, Morton H. *political scientist*
Harper, Robert Allan *consulting psychologist, retired*
Harris, Charles Wesley *political science educator*
Helms, Robert Brake *economist, research director*
Hess, Stephen *political scientist, author*
Hickman, R(obert) Harrison *political pollster, strategist*
†Hollerbach, Paula Elizabeth *demographer, researcher*
Holliday, Bertha Garrett *psychologist*
Horowitz, Herbert Eugene *educator, consultant, former ambassador*
†Howe, Herbert Marshall, Jr. *political science educator*
Hudson, Michael Craig *political science educator*
Hufbauer, Gary Clyde *economist, lawyer, educator*
Hughes, Kent Higgon *economist*
Jacobson, Allen H. *economist*
James, Estelle *economics educator*
Jamme, Albert Joseph *archaeologist, educator*
Jaspersen, Frederick Zarr *economist*
Johnson, Omotunde Evan George *economist*
Johnson, Robert Henry *political science educator*
Jones, William Bowdoin *political scientist, retired diplomat, lawyer*
Joyner, Christopher Clayton *international relations educator*
Katson, Roberta Marina *economist*
Kemp, Geoffrey Thomas Howard *international affairs specialist*
Kendrick, John Whitefield *economist, educator, consultant*
Khadduri, Majid *international studies educator*
Kibler, Virginia Mary *economist*
Kirkpatrick, Jeane Duane Jordan *political scientist, government official*
Knapp, Charles Boynton *economist, educator, institute president*
Korologos, Tom Chris *government affairs consultant, former federal official*
Kristol, Irving *social sciences educator, editor*
Krulfeld, Ruth Marilyn *anthropologist, educator*
Kuh, Charlotte Virginia *economist*
Kybal, Elba Gómez del Rey *economist, non-profit organization executive*
Laden, Ben Ellis *economist*
Lardy, Nicholas Richard *economics educator*
Lenczowski, John *political science educator*
LeoGrande, William Mark *political science educator, writer*
†Libin, Alexander Viktorovich *psychologist, researcher, writer*
Liebenson, Herbert *economist, trade association executive*
Lieber, Robert James *political science educator, writer*
Lin, William Wen-Rong *economist*
Lindsey, Lawrence Benjamin *economist*
Littig, Lawrence William *psychologist, educator*
Lustig, Nora Claudia *researcher*
Luttwak, Edward Nicolae *academic, writer policy and business consultant*
Mann, Thomas Edward *political scientist*
Marcuss, Rosemary Daly *economist*
Martinez, Herminia S. *economist, banker*
McGinnies, Elliott Morse *psychologist, educator*
Meggers, Betty J(ane) *anthropologist*
Mellor, John Williams *economist, policy consultant firm executive*
Metz, Helen Chapin *Middle East analyst*
Millar, James Robert *economist, educator, university official*
Miller, James Clifford, III *economist*
Minarik, Joseph John *economist, researcher*
Muldrow, Tressie Wright *psychologist*
Munasinghe, Mohan *development economist*
Nagorski, Zygmunt *political scientist*
Nakhleh, Emile A. *political science educator*
Nelson, Candice Jean *political science educator*
Newman, Monroe *retired economist, educator*
Niskanen, William Arthur, Jr. *economist, think tank executive*
Noland, Marcus *economist, educator*
O'Dell, Michael James *social sciences specialist*
Offutt, Susan Elizabeth *economist*
Ogg, Clayton Wallace *economist*
Oh, John Kie-Chiang *political science educator, university official*
Olson, Charles Eric *economist*
†O'Neill, Richard P. *economist, director*
Ooms, Van Doorn *economist*
Ortner, Donald J. *biological anthropologist, educator*
Oweiss, Ibrahim Mohamed *economist, educator*
Ozer, Martha Ross *school psychologist*
Perry, George Lewis *research economist, consultant*
Phillips, Susan Meredith *financial economist, university administrator*
Pickenpaugh, Thomas Edward *archaeologist*
†Pirchner, Herman, Jr. *foreign policy specialist*
†Pollock, Jefrey Ian *pollster, political consultant*
Preeg, Ernest Henry *strategic and international studies center executive*
†Prestowitz, Clyde Vincent *economist, research administrator*
Prewitt, Kenneth *political science educator, foundation executive*
Randall, Robert L(ee) *ecological economist*
Raslear, Thomas Gregory *psychologist*
Ravenal, Earl Cedric *international relations educator, author*
Reich, Bernard *political science educator*
Reining, Priscilla Copeland *anthropologist*
Reynolds, Robert Joel *economist, consultant*
Ridley, Stanley Eugene *clinical psychologist, consultant*
Roberts, Markley *economist, educator*
Roberts, Walter Ronald *political science educator, former government official*
†Robinson, Daniel N. *psychology educator*
Rodriguez, Rita Maria *economist*
Roett, Riordan *political science educator, consultant*
Rosenau, James Nathan *political scientist, author*
Rosenberg, Joel Barry *government economist*
†Rundquist, Paul Stanley *government policy analyst, educator*
Ryn, Claes Gösta *political science educator, author, research institute administrator*
Sanderson, Fred Hugo *economist*
Sawhill, Isabel Van Devanter *economist*
Scheppach, Raymond Carl, Jr. *association executive, economist*
Scheraga, Joel Dov *economist*
Schlesinger, James Rodney *economist*
Schley, Wayne Arthur *political consultant*
Schultze, Charles Louis *economist, educator*
†Shapiro, Robert J. *economic affairs executive*
†Silvia, Stephen John *political science educator*
Simes, Dimitri Konstantin *international affairs expert and educator*
†Sitilides, John *government relations executive, policy analyst*
†Smith, Amy Capen *economist*
Smith, Bruce David *archaeologist*
Smythe-Haith, Mabel Murphy *consultant on African economic development, speaker, writer*
Solomon, Elinor Harris *economics educator*
Solomon, Richard Harvey *political scientist*
Stein, Herbert *economist*
Steiner, Gilbert Yale *political scientist*
Stelzer, Irwin Mark *economist*
Sterner, Michael Edmund *international affairs consultant*
Stiglitz, Joseph Eugene *economist*
Stone, Russell A. *sociology educator*
Sundquist, James Lloyd *political scientist*
Sunley, Emil McKee *economist*
Sweeney, Richard James *economics educator*
Teele, Thurston Ferdinand *economist*
Toder, Eric Jay *economist*
Turner, John Andrew *economist*
†Valenzuela, Arturo Arms *political science educator, writer, consultant*
VandenBos, Gary Roger *psychologist, publisher*
Voll, Sarah Potts *economic consultant*
Walinsky, Louis Joseph *economic consultant, writer*
Weintraub, Sidney *economist, educator*
Weiss, David Alan *international trade consultant*
†Weissman, Stephen Richard *political scientist, policy analyst, advocate*
White, John Kenneth *politics educator*
Wilensky, Gail Roggin *economist*
Wilson, Ewen Maclellan *economist*
Wolf, Patrick John *political science educator*
†Wood, Bernard Anthony *anthropology educator*
Yellen, John Edward *archaeologist*

FLORIDA

Boca Raton
Brennan, Teresa Mary Isabel *social theory educator, writer*
Feuerlein, Willy John Arthur *economist, educator*
†Franklin, Ronald *neuropsychologist*
Latané, Bibb *social psychologist*

Boynton Beach
Mittel, John J. *economist, corporate executive*

Bradenton
Ellman, Norman Kenneth *psychologist, psychoanalyst*

Clearwater
Davidson, Joan Gather *psychologist*
Peterson, James Robert *retired engineering psychologist*

Cocoa
McLendon, Dorothy *school psychologist*

Coral Gables
Shipley, Vergil Alan *political science educator*

Davie
Morris, Joseph Raymond *business and economics educator*

Daytona Beach
Patterson, Roger Lewis *psychologist*

Delray Beach
Blankenheimer, Bernard *economics consultant*
Borkosky, Bruce Glenn *psychologist*
Dye, Thomas Roy *political science educator*
Levinson, Harry *psychologist, educator*

Dunnellon
Dixon, W(illiam) Robert *retired educational psychology educator*

Fort Lauderdale
Azrin, Nathan Harold *psychologist*
Bartelstone, Rona Sue *gerontologist*
Cash, Ralph Eugene *psychologist*

Collins, Ronald William *psychologist, educator*
Maxwell, Sara Elizabeth *psychologist, educator, speech pathologist, director*
McGreevy, Mary *retired psychology educator*

Gainesville
Bernard, H. Russell *anthropology educator, scientific editor*
Capaldi, Elizabeth Ann Deutsch *psychological sciences educator*
Carr, Glenna Dodson *economics educator*
Catasus, Jose Magin Perez *school psychologist*
Dewsbury, Donald Allen *historian of psychology, comparative psychologist*
Hornberger, Robert Howard *psychologist*
Jackson, LaTrelle D. *psychologist, educator*
Milanich, Jerald Thomas *archaeologist, museum curator*
Shaeff, Gary William *anthropologist, computer consultant*
Teitelbaum, Philip *psychologist*
von Mering, Otto Oswald *anthropology educator*
Wagner, Eric Armin *sociology educator*
White, Susie Mae *school psychologist*

Greenacres
Diaz, Raul *psychologist*

Hollywood
Foreman, Edwin Francis *economist, real estate broker*
Valdes, Jacqueline Chehebar *neuropsychologist, consultant, researcher*
Weinberg, Marcy *psychologist*

Jacksonville
Brady, James Joseph *economics educator*
Ejimofor, Cornelius Ogu *political scientist, educator*
Godfrey, John Munro *economic consultant*
Moore, David Graham *sociologist, educator*

Juno Beach
Penn, Sherry Eve *communication psychologist, educator*

Key West
Bond, Alma Halbert *psychoanalyst, author*

Largo
Ellis, Susan Gottenberg *psychologist*

Longboat Key
Albee, George Wilson *psychology educator*

Maitland
Blackburn, John Oliver *economist, consultant*
Von Hilsheimer, George Edwin, III *neuropsychologist*

Miami
†Burnett, Keitha Denise *social studies educator*
Chirovsky, Nicholas Ludomir *economics educator, historian, author*
Escotet, Miguel-Angel *psychologist, educator*
Fuertes, Raul A. *psychologist, educator*
Humphries, Joan Ropes *psychologist, educator*
Kanet, Roger Edward *political science educator, university administrator*
Mau, James Anthony *sociologist, academic administrator, educator*
Rosenberg, Mark B. *political science educator, university official*
Routh, Donald K(ent) *psychology educator*
Russell, Elbert Winslow *neuropsychologist*
Salazar-Carrillo, Jorge *economics educator*
†Taylor, Dorothy Lee *sociology educator*

Mount Dora
Myren, Richard Albert *criminal justice consultant*

Naples
Clark, Kenneth Edwin *psychologist, former university dean*
Conrad, Kelley Allen *industrial and organizational psychologist*
Gillespie, Jacquelyn Randall *psychologist*
Gilman, John Richard, Jr. *management consultant*

North Miami
Averch, Harvey Allan *economist, educator, academic administrator*
Sundel, Martin *social work educator, psychologist*

Orlando
†Koonce, Jefferson Michael *psychologist, university official, consultant*

Palm Bay
Seifer, Ronald Leslie *psychologist*

Palm Harbor
Slorah, Patricia Perkins *anthropologist*

Panama City Beach
Roberts, Paul Craig, III *economics educator, author, columnist*

Pensacola
DeMaria, Michael Brant *psychologist*
Long, H. Owen *retired economics educator, fiction writer*

Plantation
Appel, Antoinette Ruth *neuropsychologist*
†Fish, Michael *psychologist*
†Maingot, Anthony Peter *sociology educator*

Pompano Beach
Gilchrist, William Risque, Jr. *economist*
Pigott, Melissa Ann *social psychologist*
Wilson, Arthur Jess *psychologist, educator*

Ponte Vedra Beach
Wu, Hsiu Kwang *economist, educator*

Port Charlotte
Von Holden, Martin Harvey *psychologist*

Port Richey
Mueller, Lois M. *psychologist*

Port Saint Lucie
Augelli, John Pat *geography educator, author, consultant, rancher*

Roseland
Canterbury-Counts, W. Douglas *psychologist*

Saint Augustine
Theil, Henri *economist, educator*

Saint Cloud
Shuman, Barbara *social studies educator*

Saint Petersburg
Serrie, Hendrick *anthropology and international business educator*

Sanibel
Crown, David Allan *criminologist, educator*

Sarasota
†Ainslie, Kimble Fletcher *scholar, research consultant, writer*
Gordon, Sanford Daniel *economics educator*
Gurvitz, Milton Solomon *psychologist*

Summerland Key
Muth, John Fraser *economics educator*

Sun City Center
Hall, John Fry *psychologist, educator*

Tallahassee
Holcombe, Randall Gregory *economics educator*
Hult, Gert Tomas Mikael *international business executive, educator*
Laird, William Everette, Jr. *economics educator, administrator*
Nam, Charles Benjamin *sociologist, demographer, educator*
Paredes, James Anthony *anthropologist, educator*
Serow, William John *economics educator*
Standley-Burt, Nancy Vilma *psychologist, educator*
Thompson, Gregory Lee *social sciences educator*
Whitney, Glayde Dennis *psychologist, educator, geneticist*
Zirps, Fotena Anatolia *psychologist, researcher*

Tampa
Clark, Michael Earl *psychologist*
†Graham, Laurel Diane *sociology educator*
†Heide, Kathleen Margaret *criminology educator, psychotherapist*
Jreisat, Jamil Elias *public administration and political science educator, consultant*
Mellish, Gordon Hartley *economist, educator*
Piper, John Richard *political science educator*
Tykot, Robert Howard *social sciences educator, archaeologist*
Vanden, Harry Edwin *political science educator*
Weiner, Irving Bernard *psychologist*

Tarpon Springs
Padberg, Daniel Ivan *agricultural economics educator, researcher*

Tequesta
Swets, John Arthur *psychologist, researcher*

Vero Beach
†Duncan, Joseph Wayman *business economist*
Thomas, Milton John, Jr. *economist*

West Palm Beach
McCluskey, Neil Gerard *gerontologist, educator, literary agent*

Winter Garden
Clifford, Margaret Louise *psychologist*

GEORGIA

Albany
Barnes, David Benton *school psychologist*

Athens
Clute, Robert Eugene *political and social science educator*
Dunn, Delmer Delano *political science educator*
Garbin, Albeno Patrick *sociology educator*
Kamerschen, David Roy *economist, educator*
O'Toole, Laurence Joseph *political science educator, researcher*
Pavlik, William Bruce *psychologist, educator*
Rosen, Sidney *psychologist*
Tesser, Abraham *social psychologist*

Atlanta
†Anthony, Jacquelyn A. *political scientist, educator*
Bahl, Roy Winford *economist, educator, consultant*
Cameron, Rondo *economic history educator*
Curran, Christopher *economics educator*
Endicott, John Edgar *international relations educator*
Ferriss, Abbott Lamoyne *sociology educator emeritus*
Kerr, Nancy Helen *psychology educator*
Kieh, George Klay *political science educator, consultant*
†Klehr, Harvey *political science educator*
L'Abate, Luciano *psychologist*
Levy, Daniel *economics educator*
Muth, Richard Ferris *economics educator*
†Papp, Daniel Stephen *international affairs educator*
Payne, Maxwell Carr, Jr. *retired psychology educator*
Rollins, Howard Alonzo, Jr. *psychology educator*
Snarey, John Robert *psychologist, researcher, educator*
Tillman, Mary Norman *urban affairs consultant*
Wald, Michael Leonard *economist*
Weiss, Jay M(ichael) *psychologist, educator*
†Woodard, John Leonard *neuropsychologist, researcher*

Augusta
†Davies, Kimberly Ann *sociology educator*

Brunswick
†Willis, Faith M. *sociology educator, researcher*

Carrollton
Aanstoos, Christopher Michael *psychology educator*
Arons, Myron Milford *psychology educator*
†Caress, Stanley Malcolm *political science educator*
Gustin, Ann Winifred *psychologist*

Cleveland
†Harris, Kevin J. *political science educator, consultant*

Columbus
Kerr, Allen Stewart *psychologist*

Dahlonega
Friedman, Barry David *political scientist, educator*

Kennesaw
Jeffrey, Christina Fawcett *political scientist, educator*
Ziegler, Christine Bernadette *psychology educator, consultant*

Lawrenceville
Carter, Dale William *psychologist*

Milledgeville
Isaac, Walter Lon *psychology educator*
Peterson, Dave Leonard *psychologist*

Norcross
Conway, Hobart McKinley, Jr. *geo-economist*

Oxford
Cody, William Bermond *political science educator*

Rome
Johnson, Alberta Clark *psychology educator*

Savannah
†Kalantari, Behrooz *political science educator*

Smyrna
Murray, Barry Wayne *economics educator*

Statesboro
Brown, John Howard *economics educator*

Stockbridge
Grimes, Richard Allen *economics educator*

Stone Mountain
Nelson, Larry Keith *document investigation laboratory executive*

Watkinsville
Nichols, William Curtis *psychologist, family therapist, consultant*

HAWAII

Honolulu
Bitterman, Morton Edward *psychologist, educator*
Brennan, Jerry Michael *economics educator, statistician, researcher, clinical and forensic psychologist*
Cattell, Heather Birkett *psychologist*
Cho, Lee-Jay *social scientist, demographer*
Flannelly, Kevin J. *psychologist, research analyst*
Fullmer, Daniel Warren *psychologist, educator, retired*
Hatfield, Elaine Catherine *psychology educator*
Ishikawa-Fullmer, Janet Satomi *psychologist, educator*
Kuroda, Yasumasa *political science educator, researcher*
Laney, Leroy Olan *economist, banker, educator*
Mark, Shelley Muin *economist, educator, government official*
Marsella, Anthony Joseph *psychologist, educator*
Morse, Richard *social scientist*
Nordyke, Eleanor Cole *population researcher, public health nurse*
Ogawa, Dennis Masaaki *American studies educator*
Paige, Glenn Durland *political scientist, educator*
Rambo, A. Terry *anthropologist, researcher*
Riggs, Fred Warren *political science educator*
Steinhoff, Patricia Gayle *sociology educator*
Suh, Dae-Sook *political science educator*
Szumotalska Stamper, Ewa *psychologist*
Weiner, Ferne *psychologist*

Kahului
Shaw, Virginia Ruth *clinical psychologist*

Kailua
†Johnson, Ronald Charles *psychology educator*

Kailua Kona
Ashley, Darlene Joy *psychologist*
Scarr, Sandra Wood *psychology educator, researcher*

Wahiawa
Kiyota, Heide Pauline *clinical psychologist*

Waianae
Pinckney, Neal Theodore *psychologist, educator*

IDAHO

Boise
Huckstead, Charlotte Van Horn *retired home economist, artist*
Overgaard, Willard Michele *retired political scientist, jurisprudent*

Caldwell
Lonergan, Wallace Gunn *economics educator, management consultant*

Pocatello
Spadafore, Gerald Joseph *psychology educator*

Wilder
Culton, Sarah Alexander *psychologist, writer*

ILLINOIS

Addison
†Kelsay, Bruce D. *school psychologist*

Arlington Heights
Tongue, William Walter *economics and business consultant, educator emeritus*

Barrington
Chung, Joseph Sang-hoon *economics educator*
Wood, Andrée Robitaille *archaeologist, researcher*

Carbondale
Eynon, Thomas Grant *sociology educator*
Hofling, Charles Andrew *anthropologist, linguist, educator*
Johnson, Elmer Hubert *sociologist, researcher in criminology*
Lit, Alfred *experimental psychologist, vision science educator, engineering psychology consultant*
Rubin, Harris B. *psychology educator*
Somit, Albert *political educator*

Champaign
Arnould, Richard Julius *economist, educator, consultant*
†Arwine, Alan Troy *political educator*
Davis, James Henry *retired psychology educator*
Due, John Fitzgerald *economist, educator emeritus*
Eriksen, Charles Walter *psychologist, educator*
Humphreys, Lloyd Girton *research psychologist, educator*
Kanfer, Frederick H. *psychologist, educator*
Miller, Gregory Allen *psychology educator*
Orr, Daniel *educator, economist*
Sprenkle, Case Middleton *economics educator*
Tracey, Terence John *psychology educator*
Triandis, Harry Charalambos *psychology educator*

Charleston
Havey, J. Michael *psychologist, educator*

Chicago
Aliber, Robert Z. *economist, educator*
Annable, James Edward *economist*
Arditti, Fred D. *economist, former educator*
Baum, Bernard Helmut *sociologist, educator*
Becker, Gary Stanley *economist, educator*
Bidwell, Charles Edward *sociologist, educator*
Boyce, David Edward *transportation and regional science educator*
Boyer, John William *history educator, dean*
Bradburn, Norman M. *behavioral science educator*
Braidwood, Robert John *archaeologist, educator*
Butler, Robert Allan *psychologist, educator*
Cacioppo, John Terrance *psychology educator, researcher*
Carlton, Dennis William *economics educator*
Coase, Ronald Harry *economics educator*
Cohen, Jerome *psychology educator, electrophysiologist*
Cohler, Bertram Joseph *social sciences educator, clinical psychologist*
Cohn, Bernard Samuel *anthropologist, historian, educator*
Cox, Charles C. *economist*
Cropsey, Joseph *political science educator*
Dietler, Michael David *archaeologist, educator*
Fogel, Robert William *economist, educator, historian*
Freeman, Leslie Gordon *anthropologist, educator*
Freeman, Susan Tax *anthropologist, educator, culinary historian*
Friedrich, Paul *anthropologist, linguist, poet*
Fromm, Erika (Mrs. Paul Fromm) *clinical psychologist*
Genetski, Robert James *economist*
Gibson, McGuire *archaeologist, educator*
Ginsburg, Norton Sydney *geography educator*
†Gittins, Anthony J. *anthropologist, theology educator*
Gould, John Philip *economist, educator*
Graber, Doris Appel *political scientist, editor, author*
Greeley, Andrew Moran *sociologist, author*
Grossman, Lisa Robbin *clinical psychologist, lawyer*
Gutmann, David Leo *psychology educator*
Harris, Chauncy Dennison *geographer, educator*
Hayes, William Aloysius *economics educator*
Hebel, Doris A. *astrologer*
Heckman, James Joseph *economist, econometrician, educator*
Huyck, Margaret Hellie *psychology educator*
Johnson, Janet Helen *Egyptology educator*
Kaplan, Kalman Joel *psychologist, educator*
Kaplan, Morton A. *political science and philosophy educator*
Kennedy, Eugene Cullen *psychology educator, writer*
Larson, Allan Louis *political scientist, educator, lay church worker*
Laumann, Edward Otto *sociology educator*
Levine, Donald Nathan *sociologist, educator*
Lippman, Jessica G. *clinical psychologist, educator*
Liu, Ben-chieh *economist*
Lucas, Robert Emerson, Jr. *economist, educator*
Madden, Bartley Joseph *economist*
Malik, Raymond Howard *economist, scientist, corporate executive, inventor, educator*
McNeill, G. David *psychologist, educator*
Mikesell, Marvin Wray *geography educator*
Miller, Oscar *economics educator*
Mirza, David Brown *economist, educator*
Moretti, Robert James *psychologist, educator*
Morewitz, Stephen John *behavioral scientist, consultant, educator*
Mugnaini, Enrico *neuroscience educator*
Nicholas, Ralph Wallace *anthropologist, educator*
O'Connell, Daniel Craig *psychology educator*
Osowiec, Darlene Ann *clinical psychologist, educator, consultant*
Peltzman, Sam *economics educator*
Pugh, Roderick Wellington *psychologist, educator*
†Rieger, Pearl Beverly *psychoeducational diagnostician, consultant*
Rosen, George *economist, educator*
Rosen, Sherwin *economist, educator*
Rosenblum, Victor Gregory *political science and law educator*
Rychlak, Joseph Frank *psychology educator, theoretician*
Sanders, Jacquelyn Seevak *psychologist, educator*

Scheinkman, José Alexandre *economics educator*
Silvia, John Edwin *economist*
Sladen, Bernard Jacob *psychologist*
Smith, Raymond Thomas *anthropology educator*
Smith, Stan Vladimir *economist, financial service company executive*
Stocking, George Ward, Jr. *anthropology educator*
Stover, Leon (Eugene) *anthropology educator, writer, critic*
Sumner, William Marvin *anthropology and archaeology educator*
Swonk, Diane Catherine *economist*
Taccarino, John Robert *psychology educator*
Taub, Richard Paul *social sciences educator*
Tekmetarovic, Lisa *economics educator*
Tipp, Karen Lynn Wagner *school psychologist*
Trapani, Catherine *special education and educational psychologist*
Tsou, Tang *political science educator, researcher*
Upshaw, Harry Stephan *psychology educator*
Walberg, Herbert John *psychologist, educator, consultant*
Walker, Ronald Edward *psychologist, educator*
Zellner, Arnold *economics and statistics educator*
Zonis, Marvin *political scientist, educator*

Dekalb
Lippold, Neal William *criminal justice educator*
Quinney, Richard *sociology educator*
Skeels, Jack William *economics educator, consultant*

Downers Grove
Feeney, Don Joseph, Jr. *psychologist*
Gioioso, Joseph Vincent *psychologist*

Edwardsville
†Drucker, Mark Lewis *public administration educator, consultant*

Evanston
Bienen, Henry Samuel *political science educator, university executive*
Braeutigam, Ronald Ray *economics educator*
Gordon, Robert James *economics educator*
Howard, Kenneth Irwin *psychology educator*
Hurter, Arthur Patrick *economist, educator*
Irons, William George *anthropology educator*
Moskos, Charles C. *sociology educator*
Myerson, Roger Bruce *economist, game theorist, educator*
Porter, Robert Hugh *economics educator*
Reiter, Stanley *economist, educator*
Shanas, Ethel *sociology educator*

Glen Ellyn
Carson, Andrew Doyle *research psychologist*
Frateschi, Lawrence Jan *economist, statistician, educator*

Hinsdale
Dederick, Robert Gogan *economist*

Hoffman Estates
Fitzpatrick, Ellen *economist, consultant*

Homewood
Lyttle, Christopher Sherman *medical sociologist*

Joliet
Holmgren, Myron Roger *social sciences educator*

Lockport
McIntyre, John Andrew *environmental and economic planner, geography educator*

Macomb
Rao, Vaman *economics educator*
Walzer, Norman Charles *economics educator*

Maryville
Stark, Patricia Ann *psychologist, educator*

Maywood
Bilek, Arthur John *criminologist*

Morton Grove
Farber, Isadore E. *psychologist, educator*

Mundelein
Kincaid, Cynthia June *school psychologist*

Normal
Skibo, James M. *anthropologist, educator*
†Strand, David Arthur *psychologist*
†Veney, Cassandra *political science educator*

Oak Park
†Goergen, Juana Iris *Latin American studies educator*
Reed, Charles Allen *retired anthropologist*

Olympia Fields
Sprinkel, Beryl Wayne *economist, consultant*

Palatine
Rembusch, Joseph John *psychologist, management consulting company executive*

Peoria
†Curtis, R. Craig *political science educator*

Pontiac
Milanowski, Tanya Jane *school psychologist*

Rockford
Mc Nelly, Frederick Wright, Jr. *psychologist*

Romeoville
Houlihan, James William *criminal justice educator*

Springfield
Mills, Jon K. *psychologist, educator, philosopher*
Phillips, John Robert *political scientist, educator*
Reyman, Jonathan Eric *archaeologist, anthropologist, researcher*
†Sisneros, Anthony *political science educator*
Wehrle, Leroy Snyder *economist, educator*
Whitney, John Freeman, Jr. *political science educator*

Tinley Park
Antia, Kersey H. *industrial and clinical psychologist, consultant*

Urbana
Baer, Werner *economist, educator*
†Banich, Marie T. *psychology educator*
Brems, Hans Julius *economist, educator*
Carmen, Ira Harris *political scientist, educator*
Due, Jean Margaret *agricultural economist, educator*
Gabriel, Michael *psychology educator*
Giertz, J. Fred *economics educator*
Giles, Eugene *anthropology educator*
Gove, Samuel Kimball *political science educator*
†Knott, Jack H. *political science educator, administrator*
Kolodziej, Edward Albert *political scientist, educator*
Leuthold, Raymond Martin *agricultural economics educator*
Linowes, David Francis *political economist, educator, corporate executive*
Nettl, Bruno *anthropology and musicology educator*
Resek, Robert William *economist*
Rich, Robert F. *law and political science educator*
Schmidt, Stephen Christopher *agricultural economist, educator*
Spitze, Robert George Frederick *agricultural economics educator*
Wirt, Frederick Marshall *political scientist*
Yu, George Tzuchiao *political science educator*

Waggoner
Matthews, Beverly J. *psychologist*

Waukegan
†Jumisko, Marci Kay *economics educator*

Wilmette
Espenshade, Edward Bowman, Jr. *geographer, educator*
Schloss, Nathan *economist*

Wood River
Boger, Gena Cecile *school psychologist*

INDIANA

Angola
†Dobbert, Duane Lloyd *forensic psychologist, educator, consultant*

Bloomington
Braden, Samuel Edward *economics educator*
Conrad, Geoffrey Wentworth *archaeologist, educator*
Conway, Dennis *geography educator*
Dinsmoor, James Arthur *psychology educator*
Estes, William Kaye *psychologist, educator*
Guth, Sherman Leon (S. Lee Guth) *psychologist, educator*
Karkut, Richard Theodore *clinical psychologist*
Ostrom, Vincent A(lfred) *political science educator*
Patrick, John Joseph *social sciences educator*
Peebles, Christopher Spalding *anthropologist, dean, academic administrator*
Risinger, C. Frederick *social studies educator*
Saunders, W(arren) Phillip, Jr. *economics educator, consultant, author*
Shiffrin, Richard M. *psychologist, educator*
Smith, Frederick Robert, Jr. *social studies educator*
Stolnitz, George Joseph *economist, educator, demographer*
Stryker, Sheldon *sociologist, educator*
†Timberlake, William David *psychology educator*
Vincent, Jeffrey Robert *labor studies educator*
von Furstenberg, George Michael *economics educator, researcher*

Columbus
Hackett, John Thomas *economist*

Gary
†Assibey-Mensah, George Ossei *political science educator*
Szarleta, Ellen Jean *economics educator*

Indianapolis
Garrett, Deloris Brink (Dee) *school psychologist, psychology educator*
Hingtgen, Joseph Nicholas *psychologist, neuroscientist, educator*
Krauss, John Landers *public policy, urban affairs consultant, mediator*
Labsvirs, Janis *economist, educator*
Plascak-Craig, Faye Dene *psychology educator, researcher*
Richardson, Mildred Tourtillott *retired psychologist*
Strain, Edward Richard *psychologist*

Jasper
Hayes, Mary Ann *social studies educator*

Lafayette
Hardin, Lowell Stewart *retired economics educator*
Kofmehl, Kenneth Theodore *political science educator*
Schönemann, Peter Hans *psychology educator*

Michigan City
Burgwald, Beryle Alan *political science educator*

Morgantown
Jones, Barbara Ewer *school psychologist, occupational therapist*

Muncie
†Bowers-Bienkowski, Evelyn Joy *physical anthropologist, educator*
Carmin, Robert Leighton *retired geography educator*
Church, Jay Kay *psychologist, educator*
McIntosh, David Eugene, Jr. *psychologist, educator*
Sargent, Thomas Andrew *retired political science educator*
Swartz, B(enjamin) K(insell), Jr. *archaeologist, educator*

North Manchester
Harshbarger, Richard B. *economics educator*

Notre Dame
Arnold, Peri Ethan *political scientist*
Bartell, Ernest *economist, educator, priest*
Craypo, Charles *labor economics educator*
Despres, Leo Arthur *sociology and anthropology educator, academic administrator*
Dowty, Alan Kent *political scientist, educator*
Ghilarducci, Teresa *economist, educator*
Leege, David Calhoun *political scientist, educator*
†Nordstrom, Carolyn Rebecca *anthropology and peace studies educator*
Swartz, Thomas R. *economist, educator*
Weigert, Andrew Joseph *sociology educator*

Purdue University
Schweickert, Richard Justus *psychologist, educator*

South Bend
Keen, Mike Forrest *sociologist, educator*

Terre Haute
Drummond, Dorothy Weitz *geography education consultant, educator, author*
Snow, Richard Kenneth *geographer, educator*

West Lafayette
Anderson, James George *sociologist, educator*
Cicirelli, Victor George *psychologist*
Connor, John Murray *agricultural economics educator*
Farris, Paul Leonard *agricultural economist*
Gruen, Gerald Elmer *psychologist, educator*
Horwich, George *economist, educator*
Jagacinski, Carolyn Mary *psychology educator*
Perrucci, Robert *sociologist, educator*
Schrader, Lee Frederick *agricultural economist*
Swensen, Clifford Henrik, Jr. *psychologist, educator*
Theen, Rolf Heinz-Wilhelm *political science educator*
Thursby, Jerry Gilbert *economics educator, consultant*
Tyner, Wallace Edward *economics educator*
Weinstein, Michael Alan *political science educator*
Wright, Gordon Pribyl *management, operations research educator*

IOWA

Ames
Ahmann, John Stanley *psychology educator*
Finn, Brendan Peter *school psychologist*
Fox, Karl August *economist, eco-behavioral scientist*
Harl, Neil Eugene *economist, lawyer, educator*
†James, Patrick *political science educator*
Klonglan, Gerald Edward *sociology educator*
Orazem, Peter Francis *economics educator*

Cedar Rapids
Hensley, Robert Bruce *psychology educator*

Clive
Miller, Kenneth Edward *sociologist, educator*

Coggon
Hammer, Robert Eugene *psychologist*

Coralville
†Lueder, Barbara Ann *school psychologist*

Des Moines
Hill-Davis, Deborah Ann *school psychologist*

Dubuque
Barker, Richard Alexander *organizational psychologist*

Glenwood
Paul, Harva Hall *school psychologist*

Iowa City
Albrecht, William Price *economist, educator, government official*
Barkan, Joel David *political science educator, consultant*
Block, Robert I. *psychologist, researcher, educator*
Elardo, Richard *psychology and education educator*
Forsythe, Robert Elliott *economics educator*
Green, William *archaeologist*
Kim, Chong Lim *political science educator*
Krause, Walter *retired economics educator, consultant*
Loewenberg, Gerhard *political science educator*
Nathan, Peter E. *psychologist, educator*
Pogue, Thomas Franklin *economics educator, consultant*
Shannon, Lyle William *sociology educator*
Siebert, Calvin D. *economist, educator*
Wasserman, Edward Arnold *psychology educator*

Knoxville
Joslyn, Wallace Danforth *retired psychologist*

Mount Vernon
Ruppel, Howard James, Jr. *sociologist, sexologist, educator*

Oskaloosa
Porter, David Lindsey *history and political science educator, author*

Pella
Baker-Roelofs, Mina Marie *retired home economics educator*
Racheter, Donald Paul *political science educator*

Sioux City
Hatfield, Susan Williams *school psychologist, psychologist, consultant*

KANSAS

El Dorado
Stone, Duane Snyder *school psychologist, clergyman*

Kansas City
Tröster, Alexander Ivo *neuropsychologist, educator*

Lawrence
Gerner, Deborah Jeanne *political scientist, educator*
Heller, Francis H(oward) *law and political science educator emeritus*
Sheridan, Richard Bert *economics educator*
†Thurmaier, Kurt Michael *public administration educator*
Weiss, Thomas Joseph *economics educator*

Leavenworth
Sumerall, Scott Wright *psychologist*

Manhattan
†Herspring, Dale R. *political science educator, consultant*
Hoyt, Kenneth Boyd *educational psychology educator*
Lemire, David Stephen *school psychologist, educator*
Murray, John Patrick *psychologist, educator, researcher*
Nafziger, Estel Wayne *economics educator*
Phares, E. Jerry *psychology educator*
Prins, Harald Edward Lambert *anthropologist, educator*
Stunkel, Edith Leverenz *gerontologist, consultant*

Overland Park
Burger, Henry G. *anthropologist, vocabulary scientist, publisher*
FitzGerald, Thomas Joe *psychologist*

Pittsburg
Behlar, Patricia Ann *political science educator*

Saint John
Robinson, Alexander Jacob *clinical psychologist*

Topeka
†Cann, Steven J. *political science educator*
Jervis, David Thompson *political science educator*
Lyon, Joanne B. *psychologist*
Richardson, Jacqueline Sue *school psychologist*
Spohn, Herbert Emil *psychologist*

Wichita
Clark, Susan Matthews *psychologist*
Dorr, Stephanie Tilden *psychologist*

Winfield
Schul, Bill Dean *psychological administrator, author*

KENTUCKY

Barbourville
Dabbagh, Mohamed Abdul-Hay *financial economist, oil-capital flow researcher*

Bowling Green
Cangemi, Joseph Peter *psychologist, consultant, educator*
Cravens, Raymond Lewis *retired political science educator*

Corbin
Doby, John Thomas *social psychologist*

Frankfort
McCarthy, Lynn Cowan *professional genealogist*

Highland Heights
Hopgood, James F. *anthropologist*
Littleton, Nan Elizabeth Feldkamp *psychologist, educator*

Hopkinsville
Cooley-Parker, Sheila Leanne *psychologist, consultant*

Lexington
Davis, Vincent *political science educator*
Hochstrasser, Donald Lee *cultural anthropologist, community health and public administration educator*
Hultman, Charles William *economics educator*
Straus, Robert *behavioral sciences educator*
Worell, Judith P. *psychologist, educator*

Louisville
Baron, Martin Raymond *psychology educator*
Edgell, Stephen Edward *psychology educator, statistical consultant*
†Ziegler, Charles Edward *political science educator*

Prestonsburg
Mc Aninch, Robert Danford *philosophy and government affairs educator*

Versailles
Stober, William John, II *economics educator*

LOUISIANA

Alexandria
Thevenot, Maude Travis *retired home economist*

Baton Rouge
Riopelle, Arthur Jean *psychologist*
Speier, Karen Rinardo *psychologist*
†Thayer, Frederick Clifton *public policy educator*
Timmons, Edwin O'Neal *psychologist*
Tolbert, Charles Madden, II *sociology educator*

Grambling
†El-Baghdadi, Mahdi Abbas *public administration educator*

Lafayette
Dur, Philip Francis *political scientist, educator, retired foreign service officer*

Lake Charles
Middleton, George, Jr. *clinical child psychologist*

Metairie
Falco, Maria Josephine political scientist, academic administrator

New Orleans
Balée, William L. anthropology educator
Boudreaux, Kenneth Justin economics and finance educator, consultant
Bricker, Harvey Miller anthropology educator
Bricker, Victoria Reifler anthropology educator
Freudenberger, Herman retired economics educator
Jacobsen, Thomas Warren archaeologist, educator
†Jordan, Robert Smith political science educator
Lee, Silas, III sociologist, public opinion research consultant
Moely, Barbara E. psychology researcher, educator
Olson, Richard David psychology educator
O'Neal, Edgar Carl psychology educator
Paradise, Louis Vincent educational psychology educator, university official
Robins, Robert Sidwar political science educator, administrator

Shreveport
Holt, Edwin Joseph psychology educator
Staats, Thomas Elwyn neuropsychologist

MAINE

Augusta
Nickerson, John Mitchell political science educator
†Schlenker, Jon Arlin sociology and anthropology educator

Bangor
Ward, Debora Elliott psychologist

Bath
Stoudt, Howard Webster biological anthropologist, human factors specialist, consultant

Blue Hill
Mills, David Harlow psychologist, association executive

Brunswick
Fuchs, Alfred Herman psychologist, college dean, educator
Morgan, Richard Ernest political scientist, educator

Canaan
Walker, Willard Brewer anthropology educator, linguist

Kennebunkport
McLaughlin, Charles James, IV social sciences scholar

Kittery Point
Howells, William White anthropology educator

Lewiston
Dennison, Gerard Francis economic analyst
Murray, Michael Peter economist, educator

Orono
Boyle, Kevin John economics educator, consultant
Cohn, Steven Frederick sociology educator, consultant
Devino, William Stanley economist, educator
Erdley, Cynthia Anne psychology educator
Goldstone, Sanford psychology educator
Munson, Henry Lee, Jr. anthropologist, educator

Portland
Hatem, Michael Thomas child psychology educator

Surry
†Doty, Maxene Stansell psychologist, retired
Pickett, Betty Horenstein psychologist

Waterville
Gemery, Henry Albert economics educator
Mavrinac, Albert Anthony political scientist, educator, lawyer

MARYLAND

Arnold
Powers, Tyrone criminal justice and sociology educator, writer

Baltimore
Anderson, Gerard Fenton economist, university program administrator
Bellack, Alan Scott clinical psychologist
Bright, Margaret sociologist
Bucher, Richard David sociology educator
Catania, A(nthony) Charles psychology educator
Cooper, Joseph political scientist, educator
Crawford, Edward E. psychologist
Davis, Carole Joan psychologist
Dickey, George Edward water resources consultant, economics educator
Dietze, Gottfried political science educator
Entwisle, Doris Roberts sociology educator
Ginsberg, Benjamin political science educator
Goedicke, Hans archeology educator
Green, Bert Franklin, Jr. psychologist
Groenheim, Henri Arnold psychologist, consultant
Grossman, Joel B(arry) political science educator
Henderson, Lenneal Joseph, Jr. political science educator
Howard, J. Woodford, Jr. political science educator
Karni, Edi economics educator
Klarman, Herbert Elias economist, educator
Maccini, Louis John economic educator
Mintz, Sidney Wilfred anthropologist
Money, John William psychologist
Nathanson, Josef economist, urban planner, municipal official
Rose, Hugh retired economics educator
Rubinstein, Robert Lawrence anthropologist, gerontologist
Salamon, Lester Milton political science educator
Shabsin, Harry Stewart psychologist
Stanley, Julian Cecil, Jr. psychology educator
Stenberg, Carl W(aldamer), III public administration educator, university dean
Wolman, M. Gordon geography educator
Wong, Wing-Chun Godwin philosopher
Yantis, Steven George psychology educator
Young, Hobart Peyton economist, mathematician, educator

Beltsville
Ehrle, Raymond Albert retired psychologist and university official

Bethesda
Banik, Sambhu Nath psychologist
Dommen, Arthur John agricultural economist
Duncan, Constance Catharine psychologist, educator, researcher
Ferris, Frederick Joseph gerontologist, social worker
Galston, William Arthur political scientist, educator
Guadagno, Mary Ann Noecker social scientist, consultant
Haugan, Gertrude M. clinical psychologist
Holland, Robert Carl economist
†Hutchinson, David Michael economist
Kleine, Herman economist
Lystad, Mary Hanemann (Mrs. Robert Lystad) sociologist, author
Mirsky, Allan Franklin psychologist, researcher
Mishkin, Mortimer neuropsychologist
Papaioannou, Evangelia-Lilly psychologist, researcher
Riley, Matilda White (Mrs. John W. Riley, Jr.) sociologist
Schwartz, Charles Frederick retired economist, consultant
Solomon, Robert economist
Spangler, Miller Brant science and technology analyst, planner, consultant
Striner, Herbert Edward economics educator
Taylor, William Jesse, Jr. international studies educator, research center executive
Wheeler, Porter King economist
Willner, Dorothy anthropologist, educator
Wolfbein, Seymour Louis economist, educator
Yager, Joseph Arthur, Jr. economist

Cabin John
Gallagher, Hugh Gregory government affairs author, consultant

Chestertown
Wendel, Richard Frederick economist, educator, consultant

Chevy Chase
Cody, Peter Malcolm economics, development, management consultant
Norwood, Bernard economist
Norwood, Janet Lippe economist
Riley, John Winchell, Jr. consulting sociologist
Sapin, Burton Malcolm political science educator, foreign policy analyst
Walk, Richard David retired psychology educator
Willner, Ann Ruth political scientist, educator

Cobb Island
†Hedrick, Terry Elizabeth psychologist, researcher

College Park
Burns, James MacGregor political scientist, historian
Czujko, Roman psychologist, survey researcher
Fago, David Paul psychologist, educator
Feldman, Robert Harry health psychology educator
Gaylin, Ned L. psychology educator
†Gurr, Ted Robert political science educator, author
Just, Richard Eugene agricultural and resource economics educator consultant
Locke, Edwin Allen, III psychologist, educator
Nerlove, Marc Leon economics educator
Piper, Don Courtney political science educator
Presser, Stanley sociology educator
Quester, George Herman political science educator
Schelling, Thomas Crombie economist, educator
Schneider, Benjamin psychology educator
Sigall, Harold Fred psychology educator
†Skroban, Stacy Brooke criminology educator
Sperling, Mindy Toby social sciences and bilingual education educator
Struna, Nancy L. social historian
Szymanski, Edna Mora rehabilitation psychology and special education educator
Ulmer, Melville Jack economist, educator
Williams, Aubrey Willis anthropology educator

Columbia
May, John Raymond clinical psychologist
Queen, Sandy (Sandra Jane Queen) psychologist, trainer

Cumberland
Heckert, Paul Charles sociologist, educator

Ellicott City
Alonso, Diane Lindwarm cognitive psychologist
†Cole, Deborah S. psychologist
Robison, Susan Miller psychologist, speaker, consultant
Webster, Sharon B. economist

Fort Washington
McCafferty, James Arthur sociologist
Schlotzhauer, Virginia Hughes parliamentary consultant

Frederick
†Zielinski, John Paul archeologist, educator

Gaithersburg
Ross, Sherman psychologist, educator

Greenbelt
Ervin, David Eugene economist, educator, researcher

Hagerstown
Thomas, Yvonne Shirey family and consumer science educator

Lanham Seabrook
Corrothers, Helen Gladys criminal justice official

Lexington Park
Donely, George Anthony Thomas, III economist, consultant

Lutherville
Eisenberg, Joseph Martin psychologist

Lutherville Timonium
Muuss, Rolf Eduard retired psychologist, educator

Mitchellville
Blough, Roy retired economist

Newark
Stidman, John Scales school psychologist

Olney
Lee, Daniel Kuhn economist

Potomac
Fischetti, Michael public administration educator, arbitrator
Jones, Sidney Lewis economist, government official
Smallwood, Grahame Thomas, Jr. genealogist
Vadus, Gloria A. scientific document examiner
Walker, Charls Edward economist, consultant
Weiss, Michael David mathematician, mathematical economist

Rockville
Donahue, Mary Rosenberg psychologist
Feingold, S. Norman psychologist
George, Kathryn Elaine economist, financial writer
Niewiaroski, Trudi Osmers (Gertrude Niewiaroski) social studies educator
Noll, Richard Dean, Jr. psychologist, educator and historian

Royal Oak
Israel, Lesley Lowe political consultant

Saint Marys City
Hill, Walter Watson, Jr. political science educator
Stabile, Donald Robert economics educator, consultant economic history

Saint Michaels
Wilson, Jerry Vernon criminology consultant, writer, educator

Silver Spring
Alexander, Herbert E. political scientist
Bardon, Jane Elias economist
Goodall, Jane anthropologist
Hsueh, Chun-tu political scientist, historian, foundation executive
Nehmer, Stanley economics consultant
Oswald, Rudolph A. economist
Rayburn, Carole (Mary Aida) Ann psychologist, researcher, writer

Takoma Park
Saint, Wilfred, Jr. sociology educator

Upper Marlboro
Callens, Charlotte psychology educator

MASSACHUSETTS

Amherst
Aizen, Rachel K. clinical psychologist
Alfange, Dean, Jr. political science educator
Averill, James Reed psychology educator
Beals, Ralph E. economist, educator
Benson, Lucy Peters Wilson political and diplomatic consultant
Berger, Seymour Maurice social psychologist
Demerath, Nicholas Jay, III sociology educator
Grose, Robert Freeman psychology educator
Halpern, Joel Martin anthropologist, photographer
Ingle, Grant M. organizational psychologist, consultant
Klare, Michael Thomas social science educator, program director
Mc Donagh, Edward Charles sociologist, university administrator
Mills, Patricia Jagentowicz political philosophy educator, writer
Rossi, Alice S. sociology educator, author
Strickland, Bonnie Ruth psychologist, educator
Taubman, William Chase political science educator
Woodbury, Richard Benjamin anthropologist, educator

Andover
Mac Neish, Richard Stockton archaeologist, educator

Auburn
Alexander, Judith Elaine psychologist, consultant

Babson Park
Genovese, Francis Charles (Frank Genovese) economist, consultant, editor, writer
Jones, Kent Albert economist

Barnstable
Randolph, Robert Lee economist, educator

Belmont
Bergson, Abram economist, educator
Feldstein, Kathleen Foley economist, consultant
Levendusky, Philip George clinical psychologist, administrator
Ronningstam, Elsa Frideborg psychologist
Youngberg, Robert Lovett psychologist

Boston
Berger, Harvey Robert psychologist
Bustin, Edouard Jean political scientist, educator
Carliner, Geoffrey Owen economist, director
†Clark, Kim Bryce business educator
Coulter, Jeffrey Philip sociology educator, writer
Crotty, William political science educator
Dentler, Robert Arnold sociologist, educator
Dimmitt, Cornelia psychologist, educator
Gamst, Frederick Charles anthropology educator
Gleason, Jean Berko psychology educator
Gordon, Thomas Joseph psychologist
Greenwood, Joen Elizabeth economist, consultant
Hammond, Norman David Curle archaeology educator, researcher
Hogarty, Richard Anthony political scientist, educator
Kubzansky, Philip Eugene environmental and organizational psychologist
Kurzweil, Edith sociology educator, editor
Markham, Jesse William economist
Mason, Emanuel Joel psychology educator
Merton, Robert C. economist, educator
Miller, Bradley Adam economist
Murphy, Evelyn Frances economist
Newbrander, William Carl health economist, management consultant
Newhouse, Joseph Paul economics educator
Norman, Dennis Keith psychologist, educator
O'Hern, Jane Susan psychologist, educator
Rossell, Christine Hamilton political science educator
Roth, Alvin Eliot economics educator
Sanders, Irwin Taylor sociology educator
Sass, Steven Arthur economist, editor
Sinai, Allen Leo economist, educator
†Tuchscherer, Konrad Timothy anthropologist, historian, linguist
Upshur, Carole Christofk psychologist, educator
Wechsler, Henry research psychologist
Welch, Garry William psychologist, consultant, educator
Woerner, Frederick Frank international relations educator

Braintree
Salloway, Josephine Plovnick school psychologist, marriage and family therapist, mental health counselor, psychology educator, college counselor

Bridgewater
Faiman-Silva, Sandra Lynne anthropologist

Brighton
†Garrison, Jean Anne social science educator

Brookline
Beaudoin, Carol Ann psychologist
Buchin, Jacqueline Chase clinical psychologist
Cromwell, Adelaide M. sociology educator
Kanin, Doris May political scientist, consultant

Burlington
Harding, Wayne Michael sociologist, researcher

Cambridge
Abt, Clark C. social scientist, executive, engineer, publisher, educator
Alt, James Edward political science educator
Appley, Mortimer Herbert psychologist, university president emeritus
†Bacigalupo, Ana Mariella anthropology educator
Baker, Susan Lowell psychologist
Bane, Mary Jo political science educator
Berliner, Joseph Scholom economics educator
Berndt, Ernst Rudolf economist, educator
Bishop, Robert Lyle economist, educator
Blackmer, Donald Laurence Morton political scientist
Borjas, George J(esus) economics educator
Brown, Edgar Cary retired economics educator
Chall, Jeanne Sternlicht psychologist, educator
Champion, (Charles) Hale political science educator, former public official
Cooper, Richard Newell economist, educator
Coser, Lewis Alfred sociology educator
Dominguez, Jorge Ignacio government educator
Dorfman, Robert economics educator
Dornbusch, Rudiger economics educator
Drago-Severson, Eleanor Elizabeth developmental psychologist, educator, researcher
Dunlop, John Thomas economics educator, former secretary of labor
Eckaus, Richard Samuel economist, educator
Ellwood, David Tabor public policy educator
Feldstein, Martin Stuart economist, educator
Fisher, Franklin Marvin economist
Fountain, Jane Ellen public policy educator
Frankel, Jeffrey Alexander economist
Friedman, Benjamin Morton economics educator
†Galbraith, John Kenneth retired economist
Gardner, Howard Earl psychologist, author
Gilligan, Carol F. psychologist, writer
Goodwin, Neva R. economist
Griliches, Zvi economist, educator
Hausman, Jerry Allen economics educator, consultant
Henninger, Polly neuropsychologist, researcher and clinician
Holzman, Philip Seidman psychologist, educator
Horowitz, Morris A. economist
Huntington, Samuel Phillips political science educator
Jacoby, Henry Donnan economist, educator
Jencks, Christopher Sandys public policy educator
Johnson, Willard Raymond political science educator, consultant
Jorgenson, Dale Weldeau economist, educator
Joskow, Paul Lewis economist, educator
Kagan, Jerome psychologist, educator
Katz, Lawrence Francis economics educator
Kaysen, Carl economics educator
Kelman, Herbert Chanoch psychology educator
Keniston, Kenneth psychologist, educator
Kennedy, Stephen Dandridge economist, researcher
Keyfitz, Nathan sociologist, demographer, educator
Khoury, Philip S. social sciences educator, historian
Kleinman, Arthur Michael medical anthropologist, psychiatrist, educator
Kosslyn, Stephen M. psychologist educator
Lamberg-Karlovsky, Clifford Charles anthropologist, archaeologist
Langer, Ellen Jane psychologist, educator, writer
Lieberson, Stanley sociologist, educator
Maass, Arthur political science and environmental studies educator
Maher, Brendan Arnold psychology educator, editor
Mansbridge, Jane Jebb political scientist, educator
Marder, William David health economist
Meyer, John Robert economist, educator
Mitten, David Gordon classical archaeologist
Montgomery, John Dickey political science educator
Moore, Mark Harrison criminal justice and public policy educator
Neustadt, Richard Elliott political scientist, educator
Nichols, Albert L. economics consultant
†Ostrowski, Donald Gary social sciences educator
Oye, Kenneth A. political scientist, educator

Patterson, Orlando *sociologist*
Peattie, Lisa Redfield *urban anthropology educator*
Perkins, Dwight Heald *economics educator*
Pfaltzgraff, Robert Louis, Jr. *political scientist, educator*
Pinker, Steven A. *cognitive science educator*
Plotkin, Irving H(erman) *economist, consultant*
Plummer, Michael Justin *sociology educator*
Poterba, James Michael *economist, educator*
Pye, Lucian Wilmot *political science educator*
Rathjens, George William *political scientist, educator*
Rayman, Paula M. *economics educator*
Robinson, Marguerite Stern *anthropologist, educator, consultant*
Rodrik, Dani *economics and international affairs educator*
Rogoff, Kenneth Saul *economics educator*
Rosovsky, Henry *economist, educator*
Rotemberg, Julio Jacobo *economist, educator, consultant*
Samuelson, Paul Anthony *economics educator*
Sapolsky, Harvey Morton *political scientist, educator*
Scherer, Frederic Michael *economics educator*
Skolnikoff, Eugene B. *political science educator*
Solow, Robert Merton *economist, educator*
Stager, Lawrence E. *archaeologist, educator*
Tambiah, Stanley Jeyarajah *anthropologist*
Thompson, Dennis Frank *political science and ethics educator, consultant*
Ulam, Adam B. *history and political science educator*
van der Merwe, Nikolaas Johannes *archaeologist*
Verba, Sidney *political scientist, educator*
Vernon, Raymond *economist, educator*
Vogt, Evon Zartman, Jr. *anthropologist*
Weiner, Myron *political science educator*
Willie, Charles Vert *sociology educator*
Wilson, William Julius *sociologist, educator*
Zeckhauser, Richard Jay *economist, educator*
Zeidenstein, George *population educator*
Zinberg, Dorothy Shore *science policy educator*

Chestnut Hill
Baum, Christopher Frederick *economics educator, consultant*
Collins, Allan Meakin *cognitive scientist, psychologist, educator*
†James, Kane *economics educator*
Siegel, Richard Allen *economist*
Smith, David Horton *social sciences educator*

Cohasset
Campbell, John Coert *political scientist, author*

Concord
Codere, Helen Frances *anthropologist, educator, university dean*

Fairhaven
†Heskett, Robert Earl *psychologist*

Feeding Hills
Norris, Pamela *school psychologist*

Framingham
Dube, Beatrice Dorothy *psychologist*
Tischler, Henry Ludwig *sociology educator*

Haverhill
Ruiz-Rodriguez, Eduardo Antonio *psychology and sociology educator*

Ipswich
Jennings, Frederic Beach, Jr. *economist, consultant, saltwater flyfishing guide*

Lancaster
McDowell, David Jamison *clinical psychologist*

Leverett
Barkin, Solomon *economist*

Lexington
Bell, Carolyn Shaw *economist, educator*
Holzman, Franklyn Dunn *economics educator*
Jordan, Judith Victoria *clinical psychologist, educator*
Kindleberger, Charles P., II *economist, educator*
Manganello, James Angelo *psychologist*
Nye, Joseph S(amuel), Jr. *political science educator, administrator*
Papanek, Gustav Fritz *economist, educator*
Shapiro, Marian Kaplun *psychologist*
Washburn, Barbara Polk *cartographer, researcher, explorer*

Lunenburg
Pomeroy, Leon Ralph *psychologist*

Marshfield
†Cunio, Maria T. Muñoz *psychologist*

Medford
Conklin, John Evan *sociology educator*
DeBold, Joseph Francis *psychology educator*
Elkind, David *psychology educator*
Luria, Zella Hurwitz *psychology educator*
Miczek, Klaus Alexander *psychology educator*
Montgomery, Tommie Sue *political scientist, educator*

Melrose
Henken, Bernard Samuel *clinical psychologist, speech pathologist*

Nantucket
Sangree, Walter Hinchman *social anthropologist, educator*

Natick
Bensel, Carolyn Kirkbride *psychologist*
Davis, Teresa Agnes *school psychologist, educator*

Needham
McEvoy, Michael Joseph *economist*

Newton
Carton, Lonnie Caming *educational psychologist*
Holbik, Karel *economics educator*
White, Burton Leonard *educational psychologist, author*

Newton Center
Adams, F. Gerard *economist, educator*
†Everett, William Johnson *ethics educator, writer*

Newton Hlds
Fanger, Mark *psychologist, psychotherapist, consultant*

North Dartmouth
Barrow, Clyde Wayne *political scientist, educator*

Northampton
Lehmann, Phyllis Williams *archaeologist, educator*
Robinson, Donald Leonard *social scientist, educator*
Rose, Peter Isaac *sociologist, writer*
Volkmann, Frances Cooper *psychologist, educator*

Orleans
Rappaport, Margaret M.W.E. *physician, psychologist, author, aviation consultant*

Quincy
O'Brien, John Steininger *clinical psychologist*
Spangler, Arthur Stephenson, Jr. *psychologist*

Raynham
Kaplan, Kenneth Barry *psychologist*

Salem
Goss, Laurence Edward, Jr. *geographer, educator*

Shrewsbury
Sassen, Georgia *psychologist, educator*

Siasconset
Emerson, Alice Frey *political scientist, educator emerita*

South Dartmouth
Stern, T. Noel *political scientist, educator*

Springfield
Napolitan, Joseph *political consultant*

Stockbridge
†Tillman, Jane Guion *clinical psychologist*

Stoughton
Gallant, George William *political scientist*
†Lowe, David Adam *psychologist*

Swampscott
Trant, Robert Paul *school psychologist*

Tewksbury
Huvos, Christopher L. *psychologist*

Waltham
Brown, Seyom *international relations educator, government consultant*
Conrad, Peter *sociology educator*
Evans, Robert, Jr. *economics educator*
Flynn, Patricia Marie *economics educator*
†Kahana, Michael Jacob *cognitive neuroscientist*
McCulloch, Rachel *economics researcher, educator*
Morant, Ricardo Bernardino *psychology educator*
†Petri, Peter Alexander *economist, educator, director*
Ross, George William *social scientist, educator*
Sekuler, Robert William *psychology educator, scientist*
†Simon, Laurence Roger *international development educator, philosopher*
Unger, Rhoda Kesler *psychology educator*
Zebrowitz, Leslie Ann *psychology educator*

Wayland
Boulding, Elise Marie *sociologist, educator*
Wolf, Irving *clinical psychologist*

Wellesley
Eilts, Hermann Frederick *international relations educator, former diplomat*
Giddon, Donald B(ernard) *psychologist, educator*
Miller, Linda B. *political scientist*
†Paarlberg, Robert L. *political science educator*
Rich, Wilbur Cornelius *political scientist, educator*

West Tisbury
Smith, Henry Clay *retired psychology educator*

Westborough
Staffier, Pamela Moorman *psychologist*
Tobias, Lester Lee *psychological consultant*

Weston
Kraft, Gerald *economist*

Williamstown
Bolton, Roger Edwin *economist, educator*
Cramer, Phebe *psychologist*
Crider, Andrew Blake *psychologist*
Kassin, Saul *psychology educator*
McGill, Thomas Emerson *psychology educator*
Sabot, Richard Henry *economics educator, researcher, consultant, entrepreneur*
Sheahan, John Bernard *economist, educator*
Solomon, Paul Robert *neuropsychologist, educator*

Woburn
Faro, Patricia Baker *school psychologist, consultant*

Worcester
Latham, Eleanor Ruth Earthrowl *neuropsychology therapist*
Rosenbaum, Alan *psychologist, educator*
Turner, Billie Lee, II *geography educator*
Wapner, Seymour *psychologist, educator, administrator*

MICHIGAN

Ann Arbor
Apperson, Jean *psychologist*
Arlinghaus, Sandra Judith Lach *mathematical geographer, educator*
Barbarin, Oscar Anthony *psychologist*
Behling, Charles Frederick *psychology educator*
Berent, Stanley *psychologist, educator, researcher, consultant*
Bishop, Elizabeth Shreve *psychologist*
Bornstein, Morris *economist, educator*
Cain, Albert Clifford *psychology educator*
Campbell, John Creighton *political science educator, association administrator*
Cannell, Charles Frederick *psychologist, educator*
Cohen, Malcolm Stuart *economist, research institute director*
Converse, Philip Ernest *social science educator*
Courant, Paul Noah *economist, educator, university official*
Dominguez, Kathryn Mary *educator*
Douvan, Elizabeth *social psychologist, educator*
Eron, Leonard David *psychology educator*
Freedman, Ronald *sociology educator*
Fusfeld, Daniel Roland *economist*
Garn, Stanley Marion *physical anthropologist, educator*
Gomberg, Edith S. Lisansky *psychologist, educator*
House, James Stephen *social psychologist, educator*
Howrey, Eugene Philip *economics educator, consultant*
Hunger, Jenny Ruth *geographer*
Inglehart, Ronald Franklin *political science educator*
Jackson, James Sidney *psychology educator*
Jacobson, Harold Karan *political science educator, researcher*
Johnston, Lloyd Douglas *social scientist*
Kingdon, John Wells *political science educator*
Manis, Melvin *psychologist, educator*
Mc Cracken, Paul Winston *retired economist, business educator*
McKeachie, Wilbert James *psychologist, educator*
Mitchell, Edward John *economist, retired educator*
Nisbett, Richard Eugene *psychology educator*
Paige, Jeffery Mayland *sociologist, educator*
Parsons, Jeffrey Robinson *anthropologist, educator*
Pedley, John Griffiths *archaeologist, educator*
Pierce, Roy *political science educator*
Saxonhouse, Arlene W. *political scientist, educator*
Shapiro, Matthew David *economist*
Singer, Eleanor *sociologist, editor*
Singer, Joel David *political science educator*
Smith, Dean Gordon *economist, educator*
Smith, Edward E. *psychologist*
Stafford, Frank Peter, Jr. *economics educator, consultant*
Steiner, Peter Otto *economics educator, dean*
Steiss, Alan Walter *research administrator, educator*
Stolper, Wolfgang Friedrich *retired economist, educator*
Whitman, Marina Von Neumann *economist, educator*
Zucker, Robert A(lpert) *psychologist*

Battle Creek
Andert, Jeffrey Norman *clinical psychologist*

Berkley
Brewer, Garry Dwight *social scientist, educator*

Big Rapids
Santer, Richard Arthur *geography educator*

Bingham Farms
Gass, Gertrude Zemon *psychologist, researcher*
Toll, Roberta Darlene (Mrs. Sheldon S. Toll) *clinical psychologist*

Birmingham
Harms, Deborah Gayle *psychologist*

Bloomfield Hills
Belavek, Debra Louise *school psychologist*

Canton
Schulz, Karen Alice *psychologist, medical psychotherapist, vocational case manager*

Detroit
Baba, Marietta Lynn *business anthropologist*
Cantoni, Louis Joseph *psychologist, poet, sculptor*
Goodman, Allen Charles *economics educator*
Gould, Wesley Larson *political science educator*
Kaplan, Bernice Antoville *anthropologist, educator*
Lasker, Gabriel Ward *anthropologist, educator*
Marx, Thomas George *economist*
†Stack, Steven John, Jr. *criminal justice educator*
Weiss, Mark Lawrence *anthropology educator*

East Lansing
Abeles, Norman *psychologist, educator*
Abramson, Paul Robert *political scientist, educator*
Allen, Bruce Templeton *economics educator*
Axinn, George Harold *rural sociology educator*
Fisher, Ronald C. *economics educator*
Ilgen, Daniel Richard *psychology educator*
Kreinin, Mordechai Eliahu *economics educator*
Majors, Richard George *psychology educator*
Manderscheid, Lester Vincent *agricultural economics educator*
Manning, Peter Kirby *sociology educator*
McKinley, Camille Dombrowski *psychologist*
Menchik, Paul Leonard *economist, educator*
Papsidero, Joseph Anthony *social scientist, educator*
Poland, Robert Paul *business educator, consultant*
Press, Charles *retired political science educator*
Ricks, Donald Jay *agricultural economist*
Robbins, Lawrence Harry *anthropologist*
Rubner, Michael *international relations educator, university administrator*
Schlesinger, Joseph Abraham *political scientist*
Sommers, Lawrence Melvin *geographer, educator*
Strassmann, W. Paul *economics educator*
Suits, Daniel Burbidge *economist*
Useem, John Hearld *sociologist, anthropologist*
Useem, Ruth Hill *sociology educator*
Winder, Clarence Leland *psychologist, educator*
Woodbury, Stephen Abbott *economics educator*

Farmington
Baker, Edward Martin *engineering and industrial psychologist*

Farmington Hills
Birdsong, Emil Ardell *clinical psychologist*
Sobczak, Judy Marie *clinical psychologist*

Flint
Amy, Patricia Eleen *psychologist*

Grand Haven
PreFontaine, Ronald Louis *school psychologist, human resources consultant*

Grand Rapids
Jansma, Theodore John, Jr. *psychologist*
Kooistra, William Henry *clinical psychologist*
Tafelski, Michael Dennis *psychologist*

Grosse Pointe
Kerns, Gertrude Yvonne *psychologist*

Hancock
Dresch, Stephen Paul *economist, state legislator*

Harbor Springs
Ketcham, Warren Andrew *psychologist, educator*

Hillsdale
Wolfram, Gary Lee *economics educator, consultant*

Kalamazoo
Forsleff, Louise Stewart *psychologist*
Nassaney, Michael Shakir *anthropology educator*

Lansing
†Fletcher, Mark Robert *political scientist*
Heater, William Henderson *retired psychology educator*

Mount Pleasant
Croll, Robert Frederick *economist, educator*

Northport
Thomas, Philip Stanley *economics educator*

Okemos
Berkman, Claire Fleet *psychologist*
Solo, Robert Alexander *economist, educator*

Rochester
Maines, David Russell *sociology educator*

Sandusky
Keeler, Lynne Livingston Mills *psychologist, educator, consultant*

Sault Sainte Marie
Johnson, Gary Robert *political scientist, editor*

Shelby Township
Kinkel, R. John *research company executive, educator*

Southfield
Anderson, Mark Brian *psychologist*
Gregory, Karl Dwight *economist, educator, consultant*
Ross, Dale Garand *therapist, programming consultant, speaker, writer*
Thimotheose, Kadakampallil George *psychologist*

University Center
Hoerneman, Calvin A., Jr. *economics educator*

West Bloomfield
Dvorkin, Louis *neuropsychologist*

Ypsilanti
deSouza, Joan Melanie *psychologist*
†Friedman, Monroe *psychologist, educator*
Weinstein, Jay A. *social science educator, researcher*

MINNESOTA

Dent
Kosler, Sonja Raye *political consultant, artist*

Duluth
Hoffman, Richard George *psychologist*
Morris, Katherine Lang *counseling psychologist*

Eagan
Goh, Michael Pik-Bien *counseling, psychology educator, consultant*

Excelsior
Hoyt, Richard Comstock *economics consulting company executive*

Forest Lake
Marchese, Ronald Thomas *ancient history and archaeology educator*

Minneapolis
Adams, John Stephen *geography educator*
Bancroft, Ann *polar explorer*
Bouchard, Thomas Joseph, Jr. *psychology educator, researcher*
Chipman, John Somerset *economist, educator*
Dawis, René V. *psychology educator, research consultant*
Erickson, W(alter) Bruce *business and economics educator, entrepreneur*
Geweke, John Frederick *economics educator*
Gray, Virginia Hickman *political science educator*
Gudeman, Stephen Frederick *anthropology educator*
Holt, Robert Theodore *political scientist, dean, educator*
Hurwicz, Leonid *economist, educator*
Jeffrey-Smith, Lilli Ann *biofeedback specialist, educator, administrator*
Johnson, Badri Nahvi *sociology educator, real estate business owner*
Johnson, David Wolcott *psychologist, educator*
Knoke, David Harmon *sociology educator*
Kozberg, Steven Freed *psychologist*
Kudrle, Robert Thomas *economist, educator*
Meehl, Paul Everett *psychologist, educator*
Narvaez, Darcia Fe *educational psychologist*
Nightingale, Edmund Joseph *clinical psychologist, educator*
Porter, Philip Wayland *geography educator*
Reiss, Ira Leonard *retired sociology educator, writer*

Reuss, Carl Frederick sociologist
Rogers, William Cecil political science educator
Schreiner, John Christian economics consultant, software publisher
Schwartzberg, Joseph Emanuel geographer, educator
Scoville, James Griffin economics educator
Shively, William Phillips political scientist, educator
†Strommen, Merton Peter research psychologist, clergyman
Ward, David Allen sociology educator
Wiener, Daniel Norman psychologist
Ysseldyke, James Edward psychology educator, research center administrator

Moorhead
Follingstad, Carol C. psychologist, consultant, educator
Noblitt, Harding Coolidge political scientist, educator
Trainor, John Felix retired economics educator

Morris
Kahng, Sun Myong economics educator

Northfield
Clark, William Hartley political science educator
Lamson, George Herbert economics educator
Lewis, Stephen Richmond, Jr. economist, academic administrator

Pipestone
Smith, Nancy Ann school psychologist

Saint Cloud
Frank, Stephen Ira political science educator
Reha, Rose Krivisky retired business educator

Saint Joseph
Bye, Lynn Ellen social work educator

Saint Louis Park
Schlutter, Lois Cochrane psychologist

Saint Paul
†Anton, Danilo Jose geographer, writer
Dahl, Reynold Paul applied economics educator
D'Aurora, James Joseph psychologist, consultant
Jessup, Paul Frederick financial economist, educator
Peterson, Willis Lester economics educator
Rossmann, Jack Eugene psychology educator
Ruttan, Vernon Wesley agricultural economist
Schultz, David A. political science educator, editor, writer, lawyer

Saint Peter
Leitch, Richard political science educator
Mc Rostie, Clair Neil economics educator
Ostrom, Don political science educator

Scandia
Borchert, John Robert geography educator

Winona
Beyer, Susan Kelley school psychologist
Holm, Joy Alice psychology educator, art educator, artist, goldsmith

MISSISSIPPI

Biloxi
Crumbaugh, James Charles psychologist

Clarksdale
Cline, Beth Marie school psychologist

Grenada
†Kincaide, Donald Lewis political science educator

Gulfport
Olivier, Michael Joseph economic development executive

Hattiesburg
Burrus, John N(ewell) sociology educator
Davis, Charles Raymond political scientist, educator

Jackson
†Simmons, Donna Addkison political consultant

Mississippi State
Clynch, Edward John political science educator, researcher
Wall, Diane Eve political science educator

Natchez
Dunnell, Robert Chester archaeologist, educator

Ridgeland
O'Neill, Paul John retired psychology educator

MISSOURI

Bolivar
Brown, Autry psychology educator, clergyman

Cape Girardeau
Gerber, Mitchel political scientist, educator

Clayton
McCann-Turner, Robin Lee psychoanalyst

Columbia
Biddle, Bruce Jesse social psychologist, educator
Breimyer, Harold Frederick agricultural economist
Bunn, Ronald Freeze political science educator, lawyer
Dolliver, Robert Henry psychology educator
LoPiccolo, Joseph psychologist, educator, author
†Morrison, Minion K. C. political science educator
Multon, Karen Diane psychologist, educator
Ratti, Ronald Andrew economics educator
Rowlett, Ralph Morgan archaeologist, educator
Salter, Christopher Lord geography educator
Twaddle, Andrew Christian sociology educator
Yarwood, Dean Lesley political science educator

Fulton
Jefferson, Kurt Wayne political science educator

Grandview
Justesen, Don Robert psychologist

Half Way
Graves, Jerrell Loren demographic studies researcher

Kansas City
Alarid, Leanne Fiftal criminal justice educator
Bernstein, Phyliss Louise psychologist
Eddy, William Bahret psychology educator, university dean
Fry-Wendt, Sherri Diane psychologist
Graham, Charles research psychologist
Kahn, George Arnett economist
Lubin, Bernard psychologist, educator

Raytown
Smith, Robert Francis psychologist, consultant

Rolla
Irion, Arthur Lloyd psychologist, educator

Saint Joseph
Boor, Myron Vernon psychologist, educator

Saint Louis
Anderson, Odin Waldemar sociologist, educator
Barnett, William Arnold economics educator
Beck, Lois Grant anthropologist, educator
Browman, David L(udvig) archaeologist
Etzkorn, K. Peter sociology educator, author
Fox, Richard Gabriel anthropologist, educator
Gfeller, Donna Kvinge clinical psychologist
†Harvey, Richard Diamond psychology educator
Hirsh, Ira Jean psychology educator, researcher
Kagan, Sioma economics educator
Kling, Merle political scientist, university official
Laster, Atlas, Jr. psychologist
Leguey-Feilleux, Jean-Robert political scientist, educator
Leven, Charles Louis economics educator
Le Vine, Victor Theodore political science educator
Miller, Gary J. political economist
Neuefeind, Wilhelm economics educator, university administrator
North, Douglass Cecil economist, educator
Pittman, David Joshua sociologist, educator, researcher, consultant
Roediger, Henry L., III psychology educator
Rosenzweig, Saul psychologist, educator, administrator
Salisbury, Robert Holt political science educator
Schwier, Ann Stranquist economics educator
Smith, Arthur E. counseling educator, vocational psychologist
Storandt, Martha psychologist
Thompson, Vetta Lynn Sanders psychologist, educator
Virgo, John Michael economist, researcher, educator
Watson, Patty Jo anthropology educator
Weidenbaum, Murray Lew economics educator
Williams, Mary Alice Baldwin retired home economist, volunteer consultant
Witherspoon, William investment economist
Woodward, Robert Simpson, IV economics educator

Springfield
†Qiao, Yuhua public administration educator
Stone, Allan David economics educator
Van Cleave, William Robert international relations educator

MONTANA

Bozeman
Gray, Philip Howard retired psychologist, educator
Spencer, Robert C. retired political science educator
Stroup, Richard Lyndell economics educator, writer

Missoula
Gallagher, Tonya Marie family support specialist
Lopach, James Joseph political science educator
Power, Thomas Michael economist, educator
Wollersheim, Janet Puccinelli psychology educator
Yee, Albert Hoy retired psychologist, educator

NEBRASKA

Alliance
Haefele, Edwin Theodore political theorist, consultant

Grand Island
Buettner, Anne Ramona Wing-mui Yu psychologist

Harrison
Knudson, Ruthann environmental consultant

Lincoln
Auld, James S. educational psychologist
Deegan, Mary Jo sociology educator
Dittmer, Billie Spruill school psychologist
Gonzalez, Jorge E. psychologist, researcher
†Kathlene, Lyn political science edcuator
Ottoson, Howard Warren agricultural economist, former university administrator
Peterson, Wallace Carroll, Sr. economics educator
Stoddard, Robert H. geography educator
Whitt, Hugh P. sociology educator

Omaha
Justice, Bob Joe corporate development executive
Rousseau, Mark Owen sociologist
Wunsch, James Stevenson political science educator

Peru
Smith, Terry Bruce political science educator, college vice president

NEVADA

Carson City
Anderson, Bernard Joseph social studies educator

East Ely
Alderman, Minnis Amelia psychologist, educator, small business owner

Incline Village
Jones, Robert Alonzo economist

Las Vegas
Benbow, Richard Addison psychological counselor
Goldstein, Steven Edward psychologist
Goodall, Leonard Edwin public administration educator
Rich, Ray human behavior educator
Weeks, Gerald psychology educator

Reno
Chapman, Samuel Greeley political science educator, criminologist
Chu, Shih-Fan (George Chu) economics educator
Cummings, Nicholas Andrew psychologist
Davis, Paul Bryan political science educator
Guinn, Janet Martin psychologist, consultant
Haynes, Gary Anthony archaeologist
Leland, Joy Hanson anthropologist, alcohol research specialist
Webster, Michael Anderson experimental psychologist
Weinberg, Leonard Burton political scientist

NEW HAMPSHIRE

Bedford
Collins, Diana Josephine psychologist

Concord
Rogers, Katherine Diane political consultant, commissioner

Dover
Charos, Evangelos Nikolaou economics educator

Durham
Palmer, Stuart Hunter sociology educator
Romoser, George Kenneth political science educator
Rosen, Sam economics educator emeritus

Goffstown
Oktavec, Eileen M. anthropologist, artist

Hanover
Clement, Meredith Owen economist, educator
Demko, George Joseph geographer
Fischel, William Alan economics educator
Hall, Raymond sociology educator
†Heatherton, Todd Frederick psychology educator
Kleck, Robert Eldon psychology educator
Logue, Dennis Emhardt financial economics educator, consultant
Lyons, Gene Martin political scientist, educator
Masters, Roger Davis government educator
Riggs, Lorrin Andrews psychologist, educator
Rutter, Jeremy Bentham archaeologist, educator
Starzinger, Vincent Evans political science educator

Henniker
Braiterman, Thea Gilda economics educator, state legislator, selectman

Hudson
Dumond, Robert Wilfred mental health consultant, lay pastoral worker

Keene
Baldwin, Peter Arthur psychologist, educator, author, minister

Lebanon
Emery, Virginia Olga Beattie psychologist, researcher
Silberfarb, Peter Michael psychiatrist, educator

Litchfield
Niccoli, Anne Marie social sciences educator

Manchester
Piotrowski, Thaddeus Marian sociology educator

West Lebanon
Bower, Richard Stuart economist, educator

Windham
Hurst, Michael William psychologist

NEW JERSEY

Bayonne
Masella, Robert Thomas political science educator, funeral service

Belmar
De Santo, Donald James psychologist, educational administrator

Camden
Mandelbaum, Dorothy Rosenthal psychologist, educator
†Worrall, John D. economics educator, consultant, writer

Cherry Hill
Metzman, Frances Schuman gerontologist

Cranford
Herz, Sylvia Beatrice clinical and community psychologist

Denville
Breed, Ria anthropologist

East Orange
Wolff, Derish Michael economist, company executive

Englewood
Farrell, Patricia Ann psychologist, educator

Englewood Cliffs
†Haber, Barbara Fran psychologist

Ewing
McGowan, Joan Yuhas development researcher

Flemington
Jackson, Ryno Marshall forensic psychologist, consultant

Florham Park
Brodkin, Adele Ruth Meyer psychologist

Fort Lee
Kadish, Lori Gail clinical psychologist

Gillette
Pfafflin, Sheila Murphy psychologist

Glassboro
Mukhoti, Bela Banerjee economics educator

Green Village
Riemer, Neal political scientist

Hackensack
Ciccone, Joseph Lee criminal justice educator

Hasbrouck Heights
Perham, Roy Gates, III industrial psychologist

Hawthorne
Cole, Leonard Aaron political scientist, dentist

Highland Park
†Baker, Ross Kenneth political science educator, columnist

Hightstown
Fitch, Lyle Craig economist, administrator

Jersey City
D'Amico, Thomas F. economist, educator

Kingston
Blank, Leonard psychologist

Lakewood
Quinn, Evelyn Saul social work educator

Lawrenceville
Baer, John Metz, Jr. psychology educator
Moser, Rosemarie Scolaro psychologist

Livingston
Friedman, Merton Hirsch retired psychologist, educator

Lyndhurst
Bunda, Stephen Myron political advisor, consultant, lawyer, classical philosopher

Madison
Woolley, Peter James political scientist
†Wright, Rosemary Ann sociologist, consultant

Mahwah
Frundt, Henry John sociologist, educator

Manahawkin
Pulz, Gary Edward psychologist

Marlboro
Leveson, Irving Frederick economist

Medford
Klugman, Peter Jay psychologist, consultant

Milltown
Sacharow, Beverly Lynn gerontologist

Mine Hill
Robertiello, Gina Marie criminal justice educator

Montclair
Haupt, Edward J. psychology educator
McMillan, Robert Lee psychology educator

Montvale
Baba, Thomas Frank corporate economist, economics educator

New Brunswick
Alexander, Robert Jackson economist, educator
Flaherty, Charles Foster, Jr. psychology educator, researcher
†Gatta, Mary Lizabeth sociologist
Glasser, Paul Harold sociologist, educator, university administrator, social worker
Glickman, Norman Jay economist, urban policy analyst
Killingsworth, Mark R. economics educator, consultant
Mechanic, David social sciences educator
Pallone, Nathaniel John psychologist, educator
Reock, Ernest C., Jr. retired government services educator, academic director
Rosenberg, Seymour psychologist, educator
Russell, Louise Bennett economist, educator
Tiger, Lionel social scientist, anthropology consultant
Toby, Jackson sociologist, educator
Voos, Paula Beth economics educator
Wilkinson, Louise Cherry psychology educator, dean

New Egypt
Erbe, Edward Robert social studies educator, music percussion educator

Newark
Carroll, John Douglas mathematical and statistical psychologist
Cheng, Mei-Fang psychobiology educator, neuroethology researcher
Gordon, Jonathan David psychologist, lawyer
Hallard, Wayne Bruce economist

Hiltz, Starr Roxanne *sociologist, educator, computer scientist, writer, lecturer, consultant*
Holzer, Marc *public administrator educator*
Patrick, Robert Herbert, Jr. *economist, educator*

Piscataway
Alderfer, Clayton Paul *organizational psychologist, educator, author, consultant, administrator*
Julesz, Bela *experimental psychologist, educator, electrical engineer*
Kovach, Barbara Ellen *management and psychology educator*
Lichtig, Leo Kenneth *health economist*
Mitchell, James Kenneth *geography educator*
Peterson, Donald Robert *psychologist, educator, university administrator*
Schwebel, Milton *psychologist, educator*
†Waxman, Chain I. *educator in sociology, researcher*

Plainboro
†Stathatos, Peter Anthony *industrial psychologist*

Port Elizabeth
Ficcaglia, Leslie M. *psychologist, portrait artist*

Princeton
Ashenfelter, Orley Clark *economics educator*
Barlow, Walter Greenwood *public opinion analyst, management consultant*
Berry, Charles Horace *economist, educator*
Bogan, Elizabeth Chapin *economist, educator*
Bogucki, Peter Ignatius *archaeologist*
Bradford, David Frantz *economist*
Chow, Gregory Chi-Chong *economist, educator*
Coffey, Joseph Irving *international affairs educator*
Cook, Michael Allan *social sciences educator*
Cooper, Joel *psychology educator*
†de Grazia, Alfred *philosopher, behavioral scientist*
Deneen, Patrick John *political scientist, educator*
Doig, Jameson Wallace *political science educator*
Friedberg, Aaron Louis *political science educator*
Geertz, Clifford James *anthropology educator*
Geertz, Hildred Storey *anthropology educator*
Gilpin, Robert George, Jr. *political science educator*
Glucksberg, Sam *psychology educator*
Gordenker, Leon *political sciences educator*
Greenstein, Fred Irwin *political science educator*
Gross, Charles Gordon *psychology educator, neuroscientist*
Halpern, Manfred *political science educator*
Hawver, Dennis Arthur *psychological consultant*
Hirschman, Albert Otto *political economist, educator*
†Hochschild, Jennifer L. *political scientist, educator*
Issawi, Charles Philip *economist, educator*
Kateb, George Anthony *political science educator*
Kenen, Peter Bain *economist, educator*
Kuenne, Robert Eugene *economics educator*
Lazarus, Arnold Allan *psychologist, educator*
Lewis, John Prior *economist, educator*
Malkiel, Burton Gordon *economics educator*
Miller, George Armitage *psychologist, educator*
Montagu, Ashley *anthropologist, social biologist*
Parry, Scott Brink *psychologist*
†Prodromou, Elizabeth Helen *political science educator*
Rosenthal, Howard Lewis *political science educator*
Rozman, Gilbert Friedell *sociologist, educator*
Shear, Theodore Leslie, Jr. *archaeologist, educator*
Starr, Paul Elliot *sociologist, writer, editor, educator*
Ullman, Richard Henry *political science educator*
Von Hippel, Frank Niels *public and international affairs educator*
Walzer, Michael Laban *political science educator*
Warren, Kay B. *anthropology educator*
Wenglinsky, Harold Heidt *research scientist*
Westoff, Charles Francis *demographer, educator*
Willig, Robert Daniel *economics educator*
Willingham, Warren Willcox *psychologist, testing service executive*

Red Bank
McWhinney, Madeline H. (Mrs. John Denny Dale) *economist*

Roosevelt
Warren, Peter Beach *economist*

Saddle River
Lasser, Gail Maria *psychologist, educator*

Scotch Plains
†Dazzo, Nicholas John *economist*

Short Hills
Mack, Judith Cole Schrim *political science educator*
Rosenblum, Jeffrey Ira *consulting economist*

Springfield
Shilling, A. Gary *economic consultant, investment advisor*

Teaneck
Brudner, Helen Gross *social sciences educator*
Cassimatis, Peter John *economics educator*
Westin, Alan Furman *political science educator*

Tenafly
Blank, Marion Sue *psychologist*

Tinton Falls
Butler, Nancy Taylor *gender equity specialist, program director*
Sager, Lawrence Cooper *psychologist*

Toms River
Shawl, S. Nicole *hypnobehavioral scientist*

Trenton
Rusciano, Frank Louis *political science educator, consultant*
Saraf, Komal C. *psychologist*

Union
Sigmon, Scott B. *psychologist*

Upper Montclair
Cordasco, Francesco *sociologist, educator, author*

Verona
Aronow, Edward *psychologist, educator*

Vineland
Hunt, Howard F(rancis) *psychologist, educator*

Wayne
Salny, Abbie Feinstein *psychologist*

NEW MEXICO

Albuquerque
Basso, Keith Hamilton *cultural anthropologist, linguist, educator*
Elliott, Charles Harold *clinical psychologist*
Harris, Fred R. *political science educator, former senator*
May, Philip Alan *sociology educator*
†Nagengast, Carole *anthropology educator*
Schwerin, Karl Henry *anthropology educator, researcher*
Sickels, Robert Judd *political science educator*
Straus, Lawrence Guy *anthropology educator, editor-in-chief*
Stuart, David Edward *anthropologist, author, educator*
Tainter, Joseph Anthony *archaeologist*

Corrales
Adams, James Frederick *psychologist, educational administrator*

Las Cruces
Lease, Richard Jay *police science educator, former police officer*
Roscoe, Stanley Nelson *psychologist, aeronautical engineer*
Ward, James D. *government educator, writer*

Las Vegas
Riley, Carroll Lavern *anthropology educator*

Portales
Agogino, George Allen *anthropologist, educator*

Santa Fe
Kingman, Elizabeth Yelm *anthropologist*
Noble, Merrill Emmett *retired psychology educator, psychologist*
Perry, Nancy Estelle *psychologist*
Schaafsma, Polly Dix *archaeologist, researcher*
Struever, Stuart McKee *archaeologist*
Williams, Stephen *anthropologist, educator*

Taos
Pasternack, Robert Harry *school psychologist*
Young, Jon Nathan *archeologist*

NEW YORK

Albany
Harris, Eric R. *policy analyst, county official*
†Hart, John P. *archaeologist*
Ley, Ronald *psychologist, educator*
Moore, Gwen Lova *social sciences educator*
Nathan, Richard P(erle) *political scientist, educator*
Schwartz, M. Myles *neuropsychologist*
Smith, Michael Ernest *archaeologist, educator*
Spitze, Glenna D. *sociology educator*
Teevan, Richard Collier *psychology educator*
Thompson, Frank Joseph *political science educator*
Thornberry, Terence Patrick *criminologist, educator*
Wright, Theodore Paul, Jr. *political science educator*
Zimmerman, Joseph Francis *political scientist, educator*

Albertson
Michaels, Craig Adam *psychologist*

Alfred
Keith, Timothy Zook *psychology educator*

Amherst
Cramer, Stanley Howard *psychology educator, author*

Annandale On Hudson
Papadimitriou, Dimitri Basil *economist, college administrator*

Averill Park
Haines, Walter Wells *retired economics educator*

Beacon
Moreno, Zerka Toeman *psychodrama educator*

Bellport
Moeller, Mary Ella *retired home economist, educator, radio commentator*

Binghamton
Babb, Harold *psychology educator*
Isaacson, Robert Lee *psychology educator, researcher*
James, Gary Douglas *biological anthropologist, educator, researcher*
Levis, Donald James *psychologist, educator*
O'Neil, Patrick Michael *political scientist, educator*
Wallerstein, Immanuel *sociologist*

Brentwood
Connors, William Francis, Jr. *psychology educator*

Brockport
Flanagan, Timothy James *criminal justice educator, university official*

Bronx
Fishman, Joshua Aaron *sociolinguist, educator*
Hooker, Olivia J. *psychologist, educator*
Kelly, Mary Susan *psychologist, educator*
Soulé, Charles Raymond, Jr. *psychologist*

Bronxville
Franklin, Margery Bodansky *psychology educator, researcher*

Brooklyn
†Barton, Halbert Everett *anthropology educator, consultant*
Boloker, Rose L. *school psychologist*
Bowers, Patricia Eleanor Fritz *economist*
Chesler, Phyllis *psychology educator*
†Darrison, Cynthia R. *political consultant*
James, Milton Garnet *economist*
Kaplan, Lawrence Rice *psychologist*
Kaplan, Mitchell Alan *sociologist, researcher*
Lieberman, Morris Baruch *psychologist, educator, researcher*
Martinez-Pons, Manuel *psychology educator*
Minkoff, Jack *economics educator*
Reinisch, June Machover *psychologist, educator*
Ricciardi, Christopher Gerard *archaeologist, educator*
Rothenberg, Mira Kowarski *clinical psychologist and psychotherapist*
†Siegelman, Kenneth Barry *social studies educator*
Spivack, Frieda Kugler *psychologist, administrator, educator, researcher*
Steiner, Robert S. *psychologist*
Weinstein, Marie Pastore *psychologist*
†Weinstock, Deborah *psychologist*

Buffalo
Abrahams, Athol Denis *geography researcher, educator*
Aurbach, Herbert Alexander *sociology educator*
Bromley, Hank J. *sociologist, educator*
Floss, Frederick George *economics and finance educator, consultant*
Gort, Michael *economics educator*
Hetzner, Donald Raymund *social studies educator, forensic social scientist*
Hull, Elaine Mangelsdorf *psychology educator*
Levine, Murray *psychology educator*
Levy, Kenneth Jay *psychology educator, academic administrator*
†Norvilitis, Jill Marie *psychology educator*
Pruitt, Dean Garner *psychologist, educator*
†Rusting, Cheryl Lenorre *psychology educator*
†Schuetze, Pamela *psychology educator, researcher*
†Singer, Simon Isaac *sociology educator*
Tedlock, Barbara Helen *anthropologist, educator, academic administrator*
Tedlock, Dennis *anthropology and literature educator*
†Weisstein, Naomi *neuroscientist, psychology educator, writer*

Centerport
Carll, Elizabeth Kassay *psychologist*

Chittenango
Brady, Don Paul *school psychologist, therapist, consultant*

Clayton
Schmidt, Karl M., Jr. *political science educator*

Conesus
Dadrian, Vahakn Norair *sociology educator*

Coram
Helmer, Carol A. *psychologist, school psychologist*

Cortland
Swartwood, Michie Odle *psychology educator*

De Witt
Pearl, Harvey *rehabilitation psychologist*

Delmar
Mancuso, James Carmin *psychologist, educator*

Dobbs Ferry
Sutton, Francis Xavier *social scientist, consultant*

East Hampton
Merton, Robert K. *sociologist, educator*

Fairport
Badenhop, Sharon Lynn *psychologist, educator, entrepreneur*
Fisher, Jerid Martin *neuropsychologist*

Feura Bush
Byrne, Donn Erwin *psychologist, educator*

Fishkill
Stein, Paula Nancy *psychologist, educator*

Flushing
Amsterdam, David Erik *school psychologist*
Hacker, Andrew *political science educator*
†Liang, Zai *sociology educator*
Psomiades, Harry John *political science educator*
Smith, Charles William *social sciences educator, sociologist*

Fredonia
Klonsky, Bruce Gary *educator*

Garden City
†Koenig, Louis William *political science educator, author*
Ohrenstein, Roman Abraham *economics educator, economist, rabbi*

Garrison
Murray, Thomas Henry *bioethics educator, writer*

Geneseo
Battersby, Harold Ronald *anthropologist, archaeologist, linguist*
Olczak, Paul Vincent *psychology educator*

Great Neck
†Aronson, Margaret R. *school psychologist*
Hamovitch, William *economist, educator, university official*
Joskow, Jules *economic research company executive*
†Rossi, Ino *anthropology educator*

Guilderland
Gordon, Leonard Victor *psychologist, educator emeritus*

Hamilton
Farnsworth, Frank Albert *retired economics educator*
Johnston, (William) Michael *political science educator, university administrator*

Hampton Bays
Baker, Donald G. *social sciences educator*

Hempstead
Block, Jules Richard *psychologist, educator, university official*
Levinthal, Charles Frederick *psychologist, psychology educator, writer*
Wattel, Harold Louis *economics educator*

Henrietta
Carmel, Simon J(acob) *anthropologist*

Ithaca
Ascher, Robert *anthropologist, archaeologist, educator, filmmaker*
Beneria, Lourdes *economist, educator*
Blau, Francine Dee *economics educator*
Brownstein, Martin Lewis *political science educator*
Darlington, Richard Benjamin *psychology educator*
Easley, David *economics educator*
Ehrenberg, Ronald Gordon *economist, educator*
Fireside, Harvey Francis *political scientist, educator*
Forker, Olan Dean *agricultural economics educator*
Haltom, Cristen Eddy *psychologist*
Hockett, Charles Francis *anthropology educator*
Isard, Walter *economics educator*
Jarrow, Robert Alan *economics and finance educator, consultant*
Kahin, George McTurnan *political science and history educator*
Kahn, Alfred Edward *economist, educator, government official*
Kennedy, Kenneth Adrian Raine *biological anthropologist, forensic anthropologist*
Kirsch, A(nthony) Thomas *anthropology and Asian studies educator, researcher*
Lowi, Theodore J(ay) *political science educator*
Lyons, Thomas Patrick *economics educator*
Neisser, Ulric *psychology educator*
Shell, Karl *economics educator*
Smith, Robert John *anthropology educator*
Stycos, Joseph Mayone *demographer, educator*
Tomek, William Goodrich *agricultural economist*

Lewiston
Whitney, Stewart Bowman *sociology educator and program director*

Massapequa
Bogorad, Barbara Ellen *psychologist*
†McCann, John W., III *psychologist, consultant*

Mexico
Sade, Donald Stone *anthropology educator*

Mill Neck
Grieve, William Roy *psychologist, educator, educational administrator, researcher,*

Millbrook
Turndorf, Jamie *clinical psychologist*

Mount Kisco
Schwarz, Wolfgang *psychologist*

Mount Vernon
Ben-Dak, Joseph David *political scientist, educator, consultant*

Nanuet
†Faustino, Peter J. *school psychologist*

New City
Spalding, Mary Branch *psychologist, psychotherapist*
Wechman, Robert Joseph *economist, educator*

New Paltz
Schnell, George Adam *geographer, educator*
Smiley, Albert Keith *economist, resort executive*

New Rochelle
Berlage, Gai Ingham *sociologist, educator*
Golub, Sharon Bramson *psychologist, educator*

New York
Abu-Lughod, Janet Lippman *sociologist, educator*
Adler, Freda Schaffer (Mrs. G. O. W. Mueller) *criminologist, educator*
Alford, Robert Ross *sociologist*
Allison, David Bradley *psychologist*
Andersen, Marianne Singer *clinical psychologist*
Angell, Wayne D. *economist, banker*
Anspach, Ernst *economist, lawyer*
†Arnold, Dieter Karl Heinrich *Egyptologist*
Baldwin, David Allen *political science educator*
Bardach, Joan Lucile *clinical psychologist*
Barron, Susan *clinical psychologist*
Betts, Richard Kevin *political science educator*
Bond, George Clement *anthropologist, educator*
Boodey, Cecil Webster, Jr. *political science educator*
Boorstein, Laurence *economist*
Bowen, William Gordon *economist, educator, foundation administrator*
Braham, Randolph Lewis *political science educator*
Brams, Steven John *political scientist, educator, game theorist*
Browne, Joy *psychologist*
Brusca, Robert Andrew *economist*
Bryant, Coralie Marcus *political science educator*
Buck, Louise Zierdt *psychologist*
Burnham, Lem *psychologist*
Caraley, Demetrios James *political scientist, educator, author*
Carr, Arthur Charles *psychologist, educator*
Charney, Craig Russell *pollster, political scientist*
†Clark, Harry Warren *public policy consultant*
Clear, Todd *criminal justice educator*
Cochrane, James Louis *economist*
Cohen, Michael *psychologist*
Cohen, Stephen Frand *political scientist, historian, educator, author, broadcaster*
Cole, Ann Harriet *psychologist, communications consultant*
Cole, Jonathan Richard *sociologist, academic administrator*

Comitas, Lambros *anthropologist*
Cookson, Peter Willis, Jr. *sociologist, writer*
Dalton, Dennis Gilmore *political science educator*
deMause, Lloyd *psychohistorian*
Denoon, David Baugh Holden *economist, educator, consultant*
Dhrymes, Phoebus James *economist, educator*
Diaz, William Adams *political scientist*
Dowling, Edward Thomas *economics educator*
†Duke, Anthony Drexel *sociologist, educator, philanthropist*
Edinger, Lewis Joachim *political science educator*
Edwards, Franklin R. *economist, educator, consultant*
Elinson, Jack *sociology educator*
Ellis, Albert *clinical psychologist, educator, author*
Engler, Robert *political science educator, author*
Epstein, Cynthia Fuchs *sociology educator, writer*
Fancher, Edwin Crawford *psychologist, educator*
Feinberg, Mortimer Robert *psychologist, educator*
Felgran, Steven David *economist*
Finger, Seymour Maxwell *political science educator, former ambassador*
†Firestone, Marsha L. *economic organization executive*
Franklin, Julian Harold *political science educator*
Freund, William Curt *economist*
Gans, Herbert J. *sociologist, educator*
Gerber, Gwendolyn Loretta *psychologist, educator*
Gerson, Kathleen *sociology educator*
Ginzberg, Eli *economist, emeritus educator, government consultant, author*
Glass, David Carter *psychology educator*
Gluck, Andrew Lee *vocational economic analyst, counselor, philosopher*
Goldman, Leo *psychologist, educator*
†Goldstein, Walter *economics educator*
Goss, Mary E. Weber *sociology educator*
Gould, Jay Martin *economist, consultant*
Green, Miriam Blau *psychologist*
Greene, Kay C. *psychologist, author*
Gross, Feliks *sociologist, educator, author*
Guyot, James Franklin *political science educator*
Habachy, Suzan Salwa Saba *development economist, non profit administrator*
Hahn, Fred *retired political science and history educator*
Halper, Thomas *political science educator*
Hamilton, Linda Helen *clinical psychologist*
Hammer, Emanuel Frederick *clinical psychologist, psychoanalyst*
Haywood, H(erbert) Carl(ton) *psychologist, educator*
Heal, Geoffrey Martin *economics educator*
Heber, Ruth R. *psychologist, consultant*
Heilbroner, Robert Louis *economist, author*
Heilbrun, James *economist, educator*
Helmreich, William Benno *sociology educator, consultant*
†Herman, Barry Martin *international economist*
Heyde, Martha Bennett (Mrs. Ernest R. Heyde) *psychologist*
Heydebrand, Wolf Von *sociology educator*
Hochman, David *economic development consultant*
Hoffman, Martin Leon *psychology educator*
Hollander, Edwin Paul *psychologist, educator*
Holloway, Ralph Leslie *anthropology educator*
Hormats, Robert David *economist, investment banker*
Hoxter, Curtis Joseph *international economic adviser, public relations and affairs counselor*
Hubbard, Robert Glenn *economics educator*
Ianni, Francis Anthony James *anthropologist, psychoanalyst, educator*
Ivanovitch, Michael Steve *economist*
Jacoby, Jacob *consumer psychology educator*
Jaeger, David Allen *economics educator*
†Jasso, Guillermina *sociologist, educator*
Jervis, Robert *political science educator*
Jonas, Ruth Haber *psychologist*
Jones, David Milton *economist, educator*
Jordan, Theresa Joan *psychologist, educator*
Jurman, Elisabeth Antonie *economist*
Kaplan, Leo Sylvan *social scientist, former college administrator*
Kasinitz, Philip *sociologist*
Kavaler-Alder, Susan *clinical psychologist*
Kavesh, Robert A. *economist, educator*
Kazemi, Farhad *political science educator*
Kesselman, Mark Jonathan *political science educator, writer*
Koppenaal, Richard John *psychology educator*
Krauss, Herbert Harris *psychologist*
Kronen, Jerilyn *psychologist*
Kvint, Vladimir Lev *economist, educator, mining engineer*
Laderman, Carol C. *anthropologist, educator*
Lakah, Jacqueline Rabbat *political scientist, educator*
Lancaster, Kelvin John *economics educator*
Leahey, Miles Cary *economist*
Lee, Robert Sanford *psychologist*
Lefkowitz, Joel M. *psychologist, educator*
Lehman, Edward William *sociology educator, researcher*
Leibow, David B. *psychiatrist, writer*
Levison, Peggy Lee *psychologist*
Lewis, Hylan Garnet *sociologist, educator*
Lichtblau, John H. *economist*
Lieberman, Charles *economist*
Lipsey, Robert Edward *economist, educator*
Logue, Alexandra Woods *higher education administrator, psychologist*
Low, Setha Marilyn *anthropology and psychology educator, consultant*
Lubin, Carol Riegelman *political scientist*
†Luthar, Suniya Sunanda *psychologist, educator*
Marlin, John Tepper *economist, writer, consultant*
Martin, Linda Gaye *demographer, economist*
†McCarthy, Jonathan Paul *economist*
Mc Cullough, J. Lee *industrial psychologist*
McKesson, John Alexander, III *international relations educator*
Meyer-Bahlburg, Heino F. L. *psychologist, educator*
Mincer, Jacob *economics educator*
Mintz, Donald Edward *psychologist, educator*
Molz, Redmond Kathleen *public administration educator*
Moore, Geoffrey Hoyt *economist*
Moskowitz, Arnold X. *economist, strategist, educator*
Muller, Charlotte Feldman *economist, educator*
Murphy, Austin de la Salle *economist, educator, banker*
Nadiri, M. Ishaq *economics educator, researcher, lecturer, consultant*
Nakamura, James I. *economics educator*
Nathan, Andrew James *political science educator*
Nelkin, Dorothy *sociology and science policy educator*
Netzer, Dick *economics educator*
Newman, Alexander *psychologist*
†Omolade, Barbara *sociology educator*
O'Neill, June Ellenoff *economist*
Papalia, Diane Ellen *human development educator*
Patrick, Hugh Talbot *economist, educator*
Persell, Caroline Hodges *sociologist, educator, author, researcher, consultant*
Petchesky, Rosalind Pollack *political science and women's studies educator*
Phelps, Edmund Strother *economics educator*
Piombino, Nicholas *psychotherapist*
Piven, Frances Fox *political scientist, educator*
Presser, Harriet Betty *sociology educator*
Pye, Gordon Bruce *economist*
Quackenbush, Margery Clouser *psychoanalyst, administrator*
Radner, Roy *economist, educator, researcher*
Rieber, Robert W. *psychology educator, linguistics educator*
Riss, Eric *psychologist*
Rivlin, Benjamin *political science educator*
Rothschild, Joseph *political science educator*
Ruggie, John Gerard *political science educator, diplomat*
Ryder, John George *psychologist*
Sands, Harry *psychologist, health administrator, researcher*
Sarnoff, Irving *retired psychology educator, author*
Sartori, Giovanni *political scientist*
Saxe, Leonard *social psychologist, educator*
Scelsa, Joseph Vincent *sociologist*
Schilling, Warner Roller *political scientist, educator*
†Schlesinger, Yaffa *sociology educator*
Schneider, Greta Sara *economist, financial consultant*
Schotter, Andrew Roye *economics educator, consultant*
Schwab, George David *social science educator, author*
Schwartz, Anna Jacobson *economic historian*
Schwedler, Jillian Marie *researcher*
Sennett, Richard *sociologist, writer*
Shamberg, Barbara A(nn) *psychologist*
Shapiro, Judith R. *anthropology educator, academic administrator*
Sheldon, Eleanor Harriet Bernert *sociologist*
Sherry, George Leon *political science educator*
Silver, Morris *economist, educator*
Silverman, Sydel Finfer *anthropologist*
Simon, Jacqueline Albert *political scientist, journalist*
Simon, Norma Plavnick *psychologist*
†Skinner, Elliott Percival *anthropology educator*
Small, George LeRoy *geographer, educator*
Snow, Karl Nelson, Jr. *public management educator, university administrator, former state senator*
Snyder, Jack L. *social sciences administrator*
†Stroessner, Steven John *psychology educator*
Sylla, Richard Eugene *economics educator*
Tallmer, Margot Sallop *psychologist, psychoanalyst, gerontologist*
Taylor, Lance Jerome *economics educator*
Tepper, Lynn Marsha *gerontology educator*
Terris, Lillian Dick *psychologist, association executive*
Tester, Leonard Wayne *psychology educator*
†Toguc, Nurhan *economics educator, researcher*
Tronto, Joan Claire *political science educator*
VanBurkalow, Anastasia *retired geography educator*
Velayo, Richard Soriano *psychologist, educator, researcher*
Vora, Ashok *financial economist*
Walder, Eugene *psychologist*
Walter, Ingo *economics educator*
Watts, Harold Wesley *economist, educator*
Weinstein, Irving *psychologist*
Wellisz, Stanislaw *economics educator*
Wenglowski, Gary Martin *economist*
Westheimer, (Karola) Ruth Siegel *psychologist, television personality*
White, Lawrence J. *economics educator*
Wojnilower, Albert Martin *economist*
Wrong, Dennis Hume *sociologist, educator*
Zarnowitz, Victor *economist, educator*
Zawistowski, Stephen Louis *psychologist, educator*

Newburgh
Fallon, Rae Mary *psychology educator, early childhood consultant*
Rubin, Jeffrey Michael *psychologist*

Newtonville
Apostle, Christos Nicholas *social psychologist*

Niagara University
Osberg, Timothy Michael *psychologist, educator, researcher*
Sarkees, Meredith Reid *political scientist, educator*

North Woodmere
Aviles, Alice Alers *psychologist*

Nyack
Frawley-O'Dea, Mary Gail *clinical psychologist, psychoanalyst, educator*

Old Westbury
†Ehrenreich, John Herman *psychologist*
Ozelli, Tunch *economics educator, consultant*

Oneonta
Bergstein, Harry Benjamin *psychology educator*

Oswego
Gooding, Charles Thomas *psychology educator, retired college provost*
Gordon, Norman Botnick *psychology educator*
Thibault, Edward A. *criminology educator*

Oyster Bay
Trevor, Bronson *economist*

Plattsburgh
Bethlen, Francis R. *business and economics educator, food distribution engineering specialist*

Pleasant Valley
Marshall, Natalie Junemann *economics educator*

Pleasantville
Black, Percy *psychology educator*

Pomona
Gordon, Edmund Wyatt *psychologist, educator*

Potsdam
Chugh, Ram L. *economics educator*

Poughkeepsie
Johnson, M(aurice) Glen *political science educator*
Skojec, William Charles *clinical psychologist*

Purchase
Ryan, Edward W. *economics educator*
Siegel, Nathaniel Harold *sociology educator*

Rhinebeck
Flexner, Kurt Fisher *economist, educator*

Riverdale
De La Cancela, Victor *psychologist*

Rochester
Alpert-Gillis, Linda Jayne *clinical psychologist*
Bluhm, William Theodore *political scientist, educator*
Deci, Edward Lewis *psychologist, educator*
DuBrin, Andrew John *behavioral sciences, management educator, author*
Fenno, Richard Francis, Jr. *political science educator*
Fox, Mary Maselli *psychologist*
Freeman, Leslie Jean *neuropsychologist, researcher*
Hanushek, Eric Alan *economics educator*
Johnston, Frank C. *psychologist*
Jones, Ronald Winthrop *economics educator*
Laties, Victor Gregory *psychology educator*
Levy, Harold David *psycholinguist*
Long, John Broaddus, Jr. *economist, educator*
Mc Kenzie, Lionel Wilfred *economist, educator*
Mueller, John Ernest *political science educator, dance critic and historian*
Niemi, Richard Gene *political science educator*
Pearse, Robert Francis *psychologist, educator*
Phelps, Charles Elliott *economics educator*
Regenstreif, S(amuel) Peter *political scientist, educator*
Rosett, Richard Nathaniel *economist, educator*
Rothman-Marshall, Gail Ann *psychology educator*
Stanley, Harold Watkins *political science educator*
Steamer, Robert Julius *political science educator*
Vernarelli, Michael Joseph *economics educator, consultant*
Zax, Melvin *psychologist, educator*

Rome
†Kuhn, Jill Marie *school psychologist*

Sag Harbor
Baer, Jon Alan *political scientist*

Scarborough
Parks, Robert Henry *consulting economist, educator*

Scarsdale
Cohen, Irwin *economist*
Wesely, Yolanda Thereza *retired sociologist, marketing professional, researcher*
Wolfzahn, Annabelle Forsmith *psychologist*

Schenectady
Board, Joseph Breckinridge, Jr. *political scientist, educator*
Terry, Richard Allan *consulting psychologist, former college president*

Shoreham
Ciborowski, Paul John *counseling psychology educator*

Sleepy Hollow
Schippa, Joseph Thomas, Jr. *psychologist, educational consultant, hypnotherapist*

Somers
Joerger, Jay Herman *psychologist, entrepreneur*
Trzasko, Joseph Anthony *psychologist*

South Salem
Saurwein, Virginia Fay *international affairs specialist*

Sparkill
Joyce, Ursula Mary *psychologist*

Staten Island
McEwan, Gordon Francis *archaeologist, educator*
Popler, Kenneth *behavioral healthcare executive, psychologist*
†Popper, Deborah Epstein *geography educator*

Stony Brook
†Arens, William Edward *social anthropology educator, writer*
Goodman, Norman *sociologist, researcher*
Katkin, Edward Samuel *psychology educator*
Neuberger, Egon *economics educator*
Schneider, Mark *political science educator*
Stolzberg, Mark Elliott *psychologist*
Stone, Elizabeth Caecilia *anthropology educator*
Travis, Martin Bice *political scientist, educator*

Syracuse
Andersen, Kristi Jean *political scientist*
Birkhead, Guthrie Sweeney, Jr. *political scientist, university dean*
Braungart, Margaret Mitchell *psychology educator*
Braungart, Richard Gottfried *sociology and international relations educator*
Burgess, Norma J. *sociology educator*
Frohock, Fred Manuel *political science educator*
Jensen, Robert Granville *geography educator, university dean*
Jump, Bernard, Jr. *economics educator*
Kriesberg, Louis *sociologist, educator*
Lambright, William Henry *political science-public administration educator*
Mazur, Allan Carl *sociologist, engineer, educator*
Meinig, Donald William *geography educator*
Monmonier, Mark *geographer, graphics educator, essayist*
Palmer, John L. *social sciences researcher, educator*
Schwartz, Richard Derecktor *sociologist, educator*
Wadley, Susan Snow *anthropologist*
Zito, George Vincent *sociologist, sociology educator*

Tarrytown
Marcus, Sheldon *social sciences educator*
Weiner, Max *educational psychology educator*

Troy
Brazil, Harold Edmund *political science educator*
Breyman, Steve *political science educator*
Diwan, Romesh Kumar *economics educator*

Utica
Baller, William Warren *school psychologist*

Wappingers Falls
Sucich, Diana Catherine *school psychologist, counselor*

Warwick
†Kaminsky, Anatol *educator, writer*

West Seneca
Wolfgang, Jerald Ira *economic development educator*

White Plains
Bloom, Adam I. *psychologist*
Kaushik, Surendra Kumar *economist*
†Raue, Patrick J. *psychologist*
Scott, Nancy Ellen *psychologist*

Whitestone
Juszczak, Nicholas Mauro *psychology educator*

Woodmere
Levine, Solomon *clinical psychologist*

Yonkers
Lupiani, Donald Anthony *psychologist*
Monegro, Francisco *psychology educator, alternative medicine consultant*
Varma, Baidya Nath *sociologist, broadcaster, poet*

NORTH CAROLINA

Asheville
Dickens, Charles Henderson *retired social scientist, consultant*

Beaufort
Hardee, Luellen Carroll Hooks *school psychologist*

Boiling Springs
Rainer, Jackson Patten *psychologist, educator*

Boone
Jones, Dan Lewis *psychologist*

Calabash
Strunk, Orlo Christopher, Jr. *psychology educator*

Carrboro
†Brunet, James Robert *public administration research associate*

Cashiers
O'Connell, Edward James, Jr. *psychology educator, computer applications and data analysis consultant*

Chapel Hill
Akin, John Stephen *economics educator*
Baroff, George Stanley *psychologist, educator*
Barton, Allen Hoisington *sociologist*
Blau, Peter Michael *sociologist, educator*
Brockington, Donald Leslie *anthropologist, archaeologist, educator*
Brown, Frank *social science educator*
Crane, Julia Gorham *anthropology educator*
Dahlstrom, William Grant *psychologist, educator*
Fieleke, Norman Siegfried *economist, educator*
Fox, Ronald Ernest *psychologist*
Friedman, James Winstein *economist, educator*
Gottlieb, Gilbert *psychobiologist, educator*
Graham, George Adams *political scientist, emeritus educator*
Handy, Rollo Leroy *philosopher, research executive*
Hochbaum, Godfrey Martin *retired behavioral scientist*
Huber, Evelyne *political science educator*
Jones, Lyle Vincent *psychology educator*
Lowman, Robert Paul *psychology educator, academic administrator*
Lunde, Anders Steen *demographer*
Page, Ellis Batten *psychologist, educator, corporate officer*
Pfouts, Ralph William *economist, consultant*
Reed, John Shelton, Jr. *sociologist, writer*
Richardson, Richard Judson *political science educator*
Rindfuss, Ronald Richard *sociology educator*
Schopler, John Henry *psychologist, educator*
Schoultz, Lars *political scientist, educator*
Simpson, Richard Lee *sociologist, educator*
Snyder, Glenn Herald *political science educator, writer*
Steponaitis, Vincas Petras *archaeologist, anthropologist, educator*
Treml, Vladimir Guy *economist, educator*
Udry, Joe Richard *sociology educator*
Wilson, Glenn *economist, educator*
Wilson, Robert Neal *sociologist, educator*
Wright, Deil Spencer *political science educator*

Charlotte
†Dorin, Dennis Daniel *political science educator, researcher*
Goolkasian, Paula A. *psychologist, educator*
†Greer, Scott L. *economist*
Kidda, Michael Lamont, Jr. *psychologist, educator*
Neel, Richard Eugene *economics and business educator*
Webster, Murray Alexander, Jr. *sociologist, educator*

Clemmons
†Church, Avery Grenfell *retired anthropology educator, poet*

Durham
Aldrich, John Herbert *political science educator*
Behn, Robert Dietrich *public policy educator, writer*
Braibanti, Ralph John *political scientist, educator*
Burmeister, Edwin *economics educator*
Cartmill, Matt *anthropologist, anatomy educator*
Elliot, Jeffrey M. *political science educator, author*
Gittler, Joseph Bertram *sociology educator*

†Guseh, James Sawalla *public administration educator*
Holsti, Ole Rudolf *political scientist, educator*
Kelley, Allen Charles *economist, educator*
Keohane, Robert Owen *political scientist, educator*
Kreps, Juanita Morris *economics educator, former government official*
Land, Kenneth Carl *sociology educator, demographer, statistician, consultant*
Leach, Richard Heald *political scientist, educator*
Lockhead, Gregory Roger *psychology educator*
Mickiewicz, Ellen Propper *political science educator*
Simons, Elwyn LaVerne *physical anthropologist, primatologist, paleontologist, educator*
Sloan, Frank Allen *economics educator*
Staddon, John Eric Rayner *psychology, zoology, neurobiology educator*
Surwit, Richard Samuel *psychology educator*
Tiryakian, Edward Ashod *sociology educator*

Franklin
Earhart, Eileen Magie *retired child and family life educator*

Greensboro
†Amponsah, William Appiah *international economics educator*
Gill, Diane Louise *psychology educator, university official*
Goble, Alan Keith *psychology educator*
Goldman, Bert Arthur *psychologist, educator*
Hidore, John Junior *geographer, educator*
Shelton, David Howard *economics educator*
Zopf, Paul Edward, Jr. *sociologist*

Greenville
Webster, Raymond Earl *psychology educator, director, psychotherapist*
Williams, Melvin John *sociologist, educator*

Hertford
Guyer, Charles Grayson, II *psychologist*

Hillsborough
Goodwin, Craufurd David *economics educator*

Jonas Ridge
Faunce, William Dale *clinical psychologist, researcher, consultant*

Pittsboro
Doenges, Byron Frederick *economist, educator, former government official*

Raleigh
Corder, Billie Farmer *clinical psychologist, artist*
Hayes, Charles Austin *economic development executive, consultant*
Hiday, Virginia Aldigé *sociologist educator*
Johnson, Charles Lavon, Jr. *clinical neuropsychologist, consultant*
†Leiter, Jeffrey Carl *sociologist, educator*
Newman, Slater Edmund *psychologist, educator*
†Seater, John Joseph *economics educator*
†Ward, Thomas Gregory *history and social science educator, curriculum developer and consultant*

Research Triangle Park
Dunteman, George Henry *psychologist*

Salisbury
Tseng, Howard Shih Chang *business and economics educator, investment company executive*

Wilson
†Hardy-Braz, Steven Thomas *psychologist*

Winston Salem
†Lee, Wei-Chin *political scientist*

NORTH DAKOTA

Bismarck
Sperry, James Edward *anthropologist, retired state official*

Fargo
†Kloberdanz, Timothy J. *educator in social sciences, writer*
Riley, Thomas Joseph *anthropologist, educational administrator*

Grand Forks
Ferraro, F. Richard *psychologist, educator*
Penland, James Granville *psychologist*

OHIO

Akron
Coyne, Thomas Joseph *economist, finance educator*
Sam, David Fiifi *political economist, educator*
†Siebert, Loren J. *geography educator*
†Su, Dongwei *economist, educator*

Ashland
Ford, Lucille Garber *economist, educator*
Rogers, Robert P. *economist, educator*

Athens
†Baum, Edward *political science educator*
Brehm, Sharon Stephens *psychology educator, university administrator*
Klare, George Roger *psychology educator*

Beachwood
Boyle, Kammer *management psychologist*
Wolf, Milton Albert *economist, former ambassador, investor*

Berea
Miller, Dennis Dixon *economics educator*

Bowling Green
Anderson, Thomas Dale *retired geography educator, consultant, writer*
Guion, Robert Morgan *psychologist, educator*
Hakel, Milton Daniel, Jr. *psychology educator, consultant, publisher*
McCaghy, Charles Henry *sociology educator*

Centerville
Shaffer, Jill *clinical psychologist*

Cincinnati
Baracskay, Daniel John *political scientist, educator*
Bieliauskas, Vytautas Joseph *clinical psychologist, educator*
Bishop, George Franklin *political scientist, educator*
Bluestein, Venus Weller *retired psychologist, educator*
Dember, William Norton *psychologist, educator*
Katz, Robert Langdon *human relations educator, rabbi*
Rosenthal, Susan Leslie *psychologist*
†Zucker, David I. *psychologist*

Cleveland
Beall, Cynthia *anthropologist, educator*
Binstock, Robert Henry *public policy educator, writer, lecturer*
Burke, John Francis, Jr. *economist*
Carlsson, Bo Axel Vilhelm *economics educator*
Carter, John Dale *organizational development executive*
Davidson, James Wilson *clinical psychologist*
Deal, William Thomas *school psychologist*
Goldstein, Melvyn C. *anthropologist, educator*
Green, Barbara Buckstein *political scientist, educator*
Grundy, Kenneth William *political science educator*
Kolb, David Allen *psychology educator*
†Lucker, Andrew M. *political science educator, computer consultant*
Mayland, Kenneth Theodore *economist*
McHale, Vincent Edward *political science educator*
Myers, Eddie Earl *clinical psychologist*
Rosegger, Gerhard *economist, educator*
Sibley, Willis Elbridge *anthropology educator, consultant*
Stein, Herman David *social sciences educator, past university provost*
†Stoller, Eleanor Palo *sociology educator*

Columbus
Alger, Chadwick Fairfax *political scientist, educator*
Arnold, Kevin David *psychologist, educational researcher*
Beck, Paul Allen *political science educator*
Becker, Ralph Leonard *psychologist*
Bourguignon, Erika Eichhorn *anthropologist, educator*
Gilliom, Morris Eugene *social studies and global educator*
†Glass, Amy Jocelyn *economist*
Huber, Joan Althaus *sociology educator*
Ichiishi, Tatsuro *economics and mathematics educator*
Jackson, Randall W. *geography educator*
Kessel, John Howard *political scientist, educator*
Ladman, Jerry R. *economist, educator*
Lebow, Richard Ned *political science, history and psychology educator*
Lee, Anne Beatrice *archaeologist, forensic anthropologist*
Lundstedt, Sven Bertil *behavioral and social scientist, educator*
Lynn, Arthur Dellert, Jr. *economist, educator*
Marble, Duane Francis *geography educator, researcher*
Meyer, Patricia Morgan *neuropsychologist, educator*
Millett, Stephen Malcolm *futurist, consultant, historian*
Morrison, Joel Lynn *cartographer, geographer*
Namboodiri, Krishnan *sociology educator*
Naylor, James Charles *psychologist, educator*
Newman, Barbara Miller *psychologist, educator*
Newman, Philip Robert *psychologist*
Osipow, Samuel Herman *psychology educator*
Patterson, Samuel Charles *political science educator*
Petty, Richard Edward *psychologist, educator, researcher*
Ray, Edward John *economics educator, administrator*
Reichwein, Jeffrey Charles *archaeologist*
Richardson, Laurel Walum *sociology educator*
Steckel, Richard Hall *economist*
Taaffe, Edward James *geography educator*
Tuckman, Bruce Wayne *educational psychologist, educator, researcher*
Viezer, Timothy Wayne *economist*
Weisberg, Herbert Frank *political science educator*

Dayton
Jones, Reginald Lorrin *clinical psychologist, consultant*
Lentz, Linda Kay *school psychologist, learning disability educator*
Williams, Michael Alan *psychologist*

Delaware
Gierhart, Mary Kelbley *school psychologist*

Findlay
Peters, Milton Eugene *educational psychologist*

Gambier
Macionis, John Johnston *professor, writer*

Georgetown
Conway, Dorothy Jean Williams *economist*

Hamilton
New, Rosetta Holbrock *home economics educator, nutrition consultant*

Hudson
Sorgi, Mercedes Prieto *psychologist*

Kent
Feinberg, Richard *anthropologist, educator*
McKee, David Lannen *economics educator*
Thapar, Neela *geographer*
Williams, Harold Roger *economist, educator*

Maumee
Mohler, Terence John *psychologist*

Moreland Hills
Tolchinsky, Paul Dean *organization design psychologist*

Oberlin
Friedman, William John *psychology educator*
Layman, Emma McCloy (Mrs. James W. Layman) *psychologist, educator*
Taylor, Richard Wirth *political science educator*
†Vujavic, Veljko *sociology educator*

Oxford
Rejai, Mostafa *political science educator*
Stevens, Brenda Anita *psychologist, educator*
Wagenaar, Theodore Clarence *sociology educator*

Parma
Bate, Brian R. *psychologist*

Powell
Spangler, Edra Mildred *clinical psychologist*

Toledo
Al-Marayati, Abid A. *political science educator*
Bernieri, Frank John *social psychology educator*
Heintz, Carolinea Cabaniss *retired home economics educator*

Troy
Szoke, Joseph Louis *psychologist, mental health facility administrator*

Worthington
Wasserman, Karen Boling *clinical psychologist, nursing consultant*

Wright Patterson AFB
Boff, Kenneth Richard *engineering research psychologist*

Youngstown
†Sweeney, Christopher John *psychology educator, consultant*

Zanesville
Hartman, Julie Marie *school psychologist*
Workman, James E. *retired school psychologist*

OKLAHOMA

Choctaw
†Linduff, James Virgil *criminologist*

Durant
Kennedy, Elizabeth Carol *psychologist, educator*

Edmond
Smock, Donald Joe *governmental liaison, political consultant*

Norman
Affleck, Marilyn *sociology educator*
Bell, Robert Eugene *anthropologist educator*
†Gaddie, Ronald Keith *political science educator, writer*
Henderson, George *educational sociologist, educator*
Hiner, Gladys Webber *psychologist*
Hufnagel, Glenda Ann Lewin *human relations educator and administrator*
†Raadschelders, Jozef Cornelis Nicolaas *political science educator*
Wallis, Robert Ray *psychologist*

Oklahoma City
Allbright, Karan Elizabeth *psychologist, consultant*
Bell, Thomas Eugene *psychologist, educational administrator*
Craig, George Dennis *economics educator, consultant*
Rundell, Orvis Herman, Jr. *psychologist*
Shaw, William James *psychologist*

Stillwater
Wilkinson, J(anet) Barbara *psychologist, educator*

Tulsa
Cooke, Marvin Lee *sociologist, consultant, urban planner*
Thompson, Harold Jerome *counselor, mental retardation professional*

OREGON

Corvallis
Gillis, John Simon *psychologist, educator*
Harter, Lafayette George, Jr. *economics educator emeritus*

Eugene
Aikens, C(lyde) Melvin *anthropology educator, archaeologist*
†Blonigen, Bruce Aloysius *economics educator*
Burris, Vallon Leon, Jr. *sociologist, educator*
Davis, Richard Malone *economics educator*
Gwartney, Patricia Anne *sociology educator*
Khang, Chulsoon *economics educator*
Littman, Richard Anton *psychologist, educator*

Forest Grove
Gibby-Smith, Barbara *psychologist, nurse*

Newberg
Adams, Wayne Verdun *pediatric psychologist, educator*

Portland
Blodgett, Forrest Clinton *economics educator*
Broughton, Ray Monroe *economic consultant*
Davis, James Allan *gerontologist, educator*
Heart, Tracy *therapist, counselor*
Kristof, Ladis Kris Donabed *political scientist, author*
Matarazzo, Joseph Dominic *psychologist, educator*
†Peck, Richard L. *social sciences educator*
Ricks, Mary F(rances) *archaeologist, anthropologist, consultant*
Wiens, Arthur Nicholai *psychology educator*
Wineberg, Howard *social studies educator, researcher*

Salem
Thompson, George Frederick, Jr. *public management educator*

Woodburn
Miles, Donald Geoffrey *economist*

PENNSYLVANIA

Abington
Schwartz, Lita Linzer *psychologist, educator*

Alburtis
Stafford, William Butler *retired psychology educator*

Allentown
Bednar, Charles Sokol *political scientist, educator*

Annville
Cullari, Salvatore Santino *clinical psychologist, educator, writer*
Tom, C. F. Joseph *economics educator*

Bala Cynwyd
Bersh, Philip Joseph *psychologist, educator*

Berwyn
Weinberg, Michael *psychologist*

Bethlehem
Aronson, Jay Richard *economics educator, researcher, academic administrator*
Filipos, Xenia Elizabeth Lychos *political scientist*
Heath, Douglas Edwin *geography educator*
†Lasker, Judith N. *sociologist, educator*
†Scanlon, Edward Charles *clinical psychologist*
Schwartz, Eli *economics educator, writer*

Bryn Mawr
Hoffman, Howard Stanley *experimental psychologist, educator*
†Needleman, Carolyn Emerson *sociology educator, researcher*
Porter, Judith Deborah Revitch *sociologist, educator*

Carlisle
Jacobs, Norman G(abriel) *sociologist, educator*
Jones, Oliver Hastings *consulting economist*
Streidl, Isabelle Roberts Smiley *economist*

Collegeville
Fago, George Clancy *psychology educator*

Devon
Heebner, Albert Gilbert *economist, banker, educator*

Dickson City
Carluccio, Sheila Cook *psychologist*

Doylestown
Ginsberg, Barry Gavrille *psychologist, consultant, trainer*

Dunmore
†Zawistowski, Theodore L. *sociology educator, editor*

Easton
Hagar, Susan Mack *school psychologist, school counselor*
Kincaid, John *political science educator, editor*

Edinboro
Antley, Eugene Brevard *sociology and religion educator*

Elkins Park
Goode, Paul *psychologist, educator, consultant*

Erie
Adovasio, J. M. *anthropologist, archeologist, educator*
Cocco, Karen Jean *school psychologist*

Fairless Hills
Rosella, John Daniel *clinical psychologist, educator*

Fleetwood
Buckalew, Robert Joseph *psychologist, consultant*

Gettysburg
Heisler, Barbara Schmitter *sociology educator*

Grantham
†Eby, John W. *sociology educator*

Greensburg
Anderson, Linda D. *psychologist*
Ramm, Douglas Robert *psychologist*

Harmony
Baldwin, Carla Suzann *psychologist*

Harrisburg
Hyle, Jack Otto *orthomolecular psychologist*

Haverford
de Laguna, Frederica *anthropology educator emeritus, author, consultant*
Mellink, Machteld Johanna *archaeologist, educator*
Northrup, Herbert Roof *economist, business executive*

Huntingdon
McLaughlin, Ronald Keith *psychologist, educator*

Indiana
Mc Cauley, R. Paul *criminologist, educator*
Miller, Vincent Paul, Jr. *geography and regional planning educator*
Tobin, Lois Moore *home economist, educator, retired*
Walker, Donald Anthony *economist, educator*

PROFESSIONAL INDEX 6231 SOCIAL SCIENCE

King Of Prussia
Manfredi, Deanna Ann *psychologist*

Lancaster
Auster, Carol Jean *sociology educator*
†Kenien, Nicholas N. *psychologist*

Lansdale
Wittreich, Warren James *psychologist, consultant*

Latrobe
Watson, Bradley Charles Stephen *political science educator, lawyer, writer*

Lewisburg
Bannon, George *retired economics educator, department chairman*
Blair, Harry Wallace *political science educator, consultant*

Lincoln University
Favor, Kevin Eli *psychology educator*

Meadville
Adams, Earl William, Jr. *economics educator*
Wharton, William Polk, Jr. *consulting psychologist, retired educator*

Media
Lewandowski, Theodore Charles *psychology educator*
Smith, David Gilbert *political science educator*

Nanticoke
†Stankovich, Joseph George, Jr. *social science researcher*

New Castle
Grzebieniak, John Francis *psychologist*

New Kensington
Bonzani, Renée Marie *anthropologist, researcher*
Hahn, William Orr *psychologist, consultant*

Newtown
Coale, Ansley Johnson *economics educator*
Richard, James Thomas *psychologist, educator*

Norristown
Leigh, Nanette Marie *psychologist*

Philadelphia
Botwinick, Milton Edward *genealogist, researcher*
Buerkle, Jack Vincent *sociologist, educator*
Cass, David *economist, educator*
Clark, John J. *economics and finance educator*
Coché, Judith *psychologist, educator*
Dubrow-Eichel, Steve Kenneth *psychologist*
Erdmann, James Bernard *educational psychologist*
Evan, William Martin *sociologist, educator*
Fox, Renée Claire *sociology educator*
Frankel, Francine Ruth *political science educator*
Gelles, Richard James *sociology and psychology educator*
Goodenough, Ward Hunt *anthropologist, educator*
Grossman, Sanford Jay *economics educator*
Harvey, John Adriance *psychology and pharmacology educator, researcher, consultant*
Klausner, Samuel Zundel *sociologist, educator*
Klein, Lawrence Robert *economist, educator*
Lang, Richard Warren *economist*
Lee, Chong-Sik *political scientist, educator*
Michael, Henry N. *geographer, anthropologist*
Miller, Ronald Eugene *regional science educator*
Newman, Cory Frank *clinical psychologist*
Orne, Emily Carota *research psychologist*
†Persico, Nicola Giuseppe *economics educator*
Preston, Samuel Hulse *demographer*
Rescorla, Robert Arthur *psychology educator*
Rima, Ingrid Hahne *economics educator*
Rosnow, Ralph Leon *psychology researcher and educator*
Ruane, Joseph William *sociologist*
Sabloff, Jeremy Arac *archaeologist*
Seligman, Martin E. P. *psychologist*
Seltzer, Vivian Center *clinical psychologist, educator*
†Shachmurove, Yochanan *economics educator*
Steinberg, Laurence *psychology educator*
Summers, Anita Arrow *public policy and management educator*
Summers, Robert *economics educator*
Tominaga, Masatoshi *anthropologist, consulting company executive*
Trulear, Harold Dean *minister, theological educator, social researcher*
Van De Walle, Etienne *demographer*
Wadden, Thomas Antony *psychologist, educator*
†Waldron, Arthur Nelson *international relations educator*
Wallace, Anthony Francis Clarke *anthropologist, educator*
†Weinraub, Marsha A. *psychology educator*
†Williams-Witherspoon, Kimmika Lyvette *anthropology educator*

Pittsburgh
Anderson, John Robert *psychology and computer science educator*
Barry, Herbert, III *psychologist*
Blumstein, Alfred *urban and public affairs educator*
Burston, Daniel *psychology educator*
Carroll, Holbert Nicholson *political science educator*
Cohen, Jacqueline *university researcher, sociology educator*
Davis, Otto Anderson *economics educator*
Dawes, Robyn Mason *psychology educator*
Drennan, Robert D. *archeology educator, researcher*
Eaton, Joseph W. *sociology educator*
Fararo, Thomas John *sociologist, educator*
Farrow, Robert Scott *economist, educator*
Fischhoff, Baruch *psychologist, educator*
†Foerster, Schuyler *political science educator, consultant*
Hammond, Paul Young *political scientist, educator*
Holzner, Burkart *sociologist, educator*
Keefe, William Joseph *political science educator*
†Kim, Minseong *economics educator*
Lave, Judith Rice *economics educator*
Levit, Herbert Irving *clinical and forensic psychologist*
Matchett, Janet Reedy *psychologist*
McCallum, Bennett Tarlton *economics educator*
McClelland, James Lloyd *psychology educator, cognitive scientist*
McGuire, Timothy William *economics and management educator, dean, management executive*
Meltzer, Allan H. *economist, educator*
Mesa-Lago, Carmelo *economist, educator*
Ogul, Morris Samuel *political science educator, consultant*
Perloff, Robert *psychologist, educator*
Ramsey, David Allen *psychologist*
Reich, Simon Francis *political scientist, educator*
Schorr-Ribera, Hilda Keren *psychologist*
Schulze, Karen Joyce *clinical psychologist*
Simon, Herbert A(lexander) *social scientist*
Strauss, Robert Philip *economics educator*
Sussna, Edward *economist, educator*

Plymouth Meeting
Friedman, Philip Harvey *psychologist*

Reading
Millar, Robert James *social science educator*

Rosemont
Connally, Andrew David *historian, educator*

Scranton
Parente, William Joseph *political science educator*
Sebastianelli, Carl Thomas *clinical psychologist*

Shippensburg
Kaluger, George *clinical psychologist, educator*

State College
Gould, Peter Robin *geographer, educator*
La Porte, Robert, Jr. *political science educator, researcher*
Plut, Richard Robert *psychologist, psychometrician*

Swarthmore
Hopkins, Raymond Frederick *political science educator*
Keith, Jennie *anthropology educator and administrator, writer*
Saffran, Bernard *economist, educator*

University Park
Domowitz, Ian *economics educator*
Epp, Donald James *economist, educator*
Ford, Donald Herbert *psychologist, educator*
Friedman, Robert Sidney *political science educator*
Klein, Philip Alexander *economist*
Marshall, Robert Clifford *economics educator*
Nelsen, Hart Michael *sociologist, educator*
Ray, William Jackson *psychologist*
Rose, Adam Zachary *economist, educator*
Schaie, K(laus) Warner *human development and psychology educator*
Snow, Dean Richard *anthropology educator, archaeologist*
Walden, Daniel *humanities and social sciences educator*

Villanova
Johannes, John Roland *political science educator, academic administrator*
Lesch, Ann Mosely *political scientist, educator*
Malik, Hafeez *political scientist, educator*

Waymart
Willis, Ellen Debora *psychiatric nurse*

Wayne
MacNeal, Edward Arthur *economic consultant*
†Perrott, Lenore Catherine *psychologist*

West Chester
Benzing, Cynthia Dell *economics educator*
Green, Andrew Wilson *economist, lawyer, educator*

Wynnewood
Khouri, Fred John *political science educator*
Phillips, Almarin *economics educator, consultant*

Yardley
Kaska, Charles Powers *psychologist*

York
McMillan, Wendell Marlin *agricultural economist*

RHODE ISLAND

Barrington
Paolino, Ronald Mario *clinical psychologist, consultant, psychopharmacologist, pharmacist*

Kingston
Alexander, Lewis McElwain *geographer, educator*
Seifer, Marc Jeffrey *psychology educator*
Sharif, Mohammed *economics educator, researcher*
Turnbaugh, William Arthur *archeologist, educator*

Peace Dale
Brennan, Noel-Anne Gerson *anthropology educator, writer*

Providence
Anton, Thomas Julius *political science and public policy educator, consultant*
Borts, George Herbert *economist, educator*
Church, Russell Miller *psychology educator*
Goldstein, Sidney *sociology educator, demographer*
Goodman, Elliot Raymond *political scientist, educator*
Groden, Gerald *psychologist*
Grossman, Herschel I. *economics educator*
Heath, Dwight Braley *anthropologist, educator*
Jones, Ferdinand Taylor, Jr. *psychologist, educator*
Krech, Shepard, III *anthropology educator*
†Lindstrom, David Philip *sociology educator*
Marsh, Robert Mortimer *sociologist, educator*
Modell, John *social sciences educator*
Perkins, Whitney Trow *political science educator emeritus*
Rueschemeyer, Dietrich *sociology educator*
Shepp, Bryan Eugene *psychologist, educator*
Siqueland, Einar *psychology educator*
Stein, Jerome Leon *economist, educator*
Stout, Robert Loren *psychologist*
Stultz, Newell Maynard *political science educator*

Smithfield
Morahan-Martin, Janet May *psychologist, educator*

SOUTH CAROLINA

Beaufort
McCaslin, F. Catherine *consulting sociologist*

Camden
Reich, Merrill Drury *intelligence consultant, writer*

Charleston
Barclay, James Ralph *psychologist, educator*
Falsetti, Sherry Ann *psychologist, medical educator*
Jacobs, Walter Darnell *political scientist, educator*
Lovinger, Sophie Lehner *child psychologist*

Columbia
Booth, Hilda Earl Ferguson *clinical psychologist, Spanish language educator*
Davis, Keith Eugene *psychologist, educator, consultant*
Feinn, Barbara Ann *economist*
Harrison, Faye Venetia *anthropologist, educator*
Hatch, David Lincoln *sociology educator*
Kiker, Billy Frazier *economics educator*
McAbee, Thomas Allen *psychologist*
Melton, Gary Bentley *psychology and law educator*
Rippeteau, Bruce Estes *archaeologist, administrator*
Starr, Harvey *political scientist*
Wilder, Ronald Parker *economics educator*
Zaepfel, Glenn Peter *psychologist*

Florence
Thigpen, Neal Dorsey *political science educator*

Georgetown
Hopkins, Linda Ann *school psychologist*

Greenville
Armstrong, Joanne Marie *clinical and consulting psychologist, business advisor, mediator*
†Khandke, Kailash *economics educator*

Hilton Head Island
Cox, Albert Harrington, Jr. *economist*

Laurens
Martin, Margaret McNeill *home economist, educator*

Rock Hill
Prus, Joseph Stanley *psychology educator, consultant*

SOUTH DAKOTA

Aberdeen
Hedges, Mark Stephen *clinical psychologist*

Brookings
Janssen, Larry Leonard *economics educator, researcher*

Canton
Perkinson, Robert Ronald *psychologist*

Keystone
Wagner, Mary Kathryn *sociology educator, former state legislator*

Lennox
Brendtro, Larry Kay *psychologist, organization administrator*

Madison
†Talley, Daniel Alfred *economics educator*

Rapid City
Kennedy, Judith Mary *school psychologist*

Sioux Falls
Williams, W. Vail *psychologist*

Vermillion
Carlson, Loren Merle *political science educator*
Clem, Alan Leland *political scientist*

TENNESSEE

Chattanooga
Clark, Jeff Ray *economist*
Rabin, Alan Abraham *economics educator*
Wilson, Richard Lee *political science educator*

Germantown
Nottingham, Edgar Jameson, IV *clinical psychologist*

Henderson
†Schwartz, Robert Marc *psychology educator*

Johnson City
Larkin, Donald Wayne *clinical psychologist*

Knoxville
Cole, William Edward *economics educator, consultant*
†Perrin, Robert George *sociology educator*

Maryville
Crisp, Polly Lenore *psychologist*

Memphis
†Bracken, Bruce A. *psychologist, educator*
Daniel, Coldwell, III *economist, educator*
Depperschmidt, Thomas Orlando *economist, educator*
Jacobson, Gerald *psychologist*
†Kemme, David Michael *economics educator*
Pohlmann, Marcus D. *political science educator*
Ward, Jeannette Poole *psychologist, educator*

Millington
Melcher, Jerry William Cooper *clinical psychologist, army officer*

Mount Juliet
Masters, John Christopher *psychologist, educator, writer*

Nashville
Benbow, Camilla Persson *psychology educator, researcher*
Buckles, Stephen Gary *economist, educator*
Burish, Thomas Gerard *psychology educator*
Gove, Walter R. *sociology educator*
Graham, George J., Jr. *political scientist, educator*
Guinsburg, Philip Fried *alcohol and substance abuse counselor*
Hancock, M(arion) Donald *political science educator*
Hargrove, Erwin Charles, Jr. *political science educator*
Jamison, Connie Joyce *sociology educator*
Kaas, Jon H. *psychology educator*
Klein, Christopher Carnahan *economist*
†Lubinski, David John *psychologist, educator*
Russell, Clifford Springer *economics and public policy educator*
Scheffman, David Theodore *economist, management educator, consultant*
Schoggen, Phil H(oward) *psychologist, educator*
Sekwat, Alex Sube *public administration educator*
Smith, Dani Allred *sociologist, educator*
Strupp, Hans Hermann *psychologist, educator*
Westfield, Fred M. *economics educator*

Oak Ridge
Johnson, Ruth Crumley *economics educator*

Sewanee
Mohiuddin, Yasmeen Niaz *economics educator*

TEXAS

Abilene
Bridges, Julian Curtis *sociologist educator, department head*
Hennig, Charles William *psychology educator*

Amarillo
Ayad, Joseph Magdy *psychologist*

Arlington
Cole, Richard Louis *political scientist, educator*
Ericson, Phyllis Jane *psychologist, psychotherapist, consultant*
Mullendore, Walter Edward *economist*
Ramsey, Charles Eugene *sociologist, educator*

Austin
Blake, Robert Rogers *psychologist, behavioral science company executive*
Blodgett, Warren Terrell *public affairs educator*
Buchanan, Bruce, II *political science educator*
Burnham, Walter Dean *political science educator*
Cleland, Charles Carr *psychologist, educator*
Dalton, Caryl *school psychologist*
Drake, Stephen Douglas *clinical psychologist, health facility administrator*
Dusansky, Richard *economist, educator*
Epstein, Jeremiah Fain *anthropologist, educator*
Glade, William Patton, Jr. *economics educator*
Grangaard, Daniel Robert *psychologist*
Hamermesh, Daniel Selim *economics educator*
Hansen, Niles Maurice *economics educator*
Hester, Thomas Roy *anthropologist*
Holtzman, Wayne Harold *psychologist, educator*
Holz, Robert Kenneth *geography educator*
Huff, David L. *geography educator*
Huston, Ted Laird *psychology educator*
Iscoe, Ira *psychology educator*
Jordan-Bychkov, Terry Gilbert *geography educator*
Kendrick, David Andrew *economist, educator*
Lariviere, Richard Wilfred *Asian studies educator, university administrator, consultant*
Loehlin, John Clinton *psychologist, educator*
Lopreato, Joseph *sociology educator, author*
Manosevitz, Martin *psychologist*
McFadden, Dennis *experimental psychology educator*
†Mennell Putman, T. Elizabeth *anthropologist, researcher*
Phelps, Gerry Charlotte *economist, minister*
Pingree, Dianne *sociologist, educator, mediator, consultant*
Prentice, Norman Macdonald *clinical psychologist*
Reid, Jackson Brock *psychologist, educator*
Roach, James Robert *retired political science educator*
Rostow, Elspeth Davies *political science educator*
Rostow, Walt Whitman *economist, educator*
Sayrak, Akin *economics educator*
†Schmandt, Jurgen Augustinus *public affairs educator*
Schmandt-Besserat, Denise *archaeologist, educator*
Schmitt, Karl Michael *retired political scientist*
†Shepperd, Jerry Wayne *sociology educator*
Smith, Alfred Goud *anthropologist, educator*
Smith, Todd Malcolm *political consultant*
†Sparrow, Bartholomew Huntington *political scientist, educator*
Thiessen, Delbert Duane *psychologist*

Baytown
Coker, Sally Jo *sociology educator*

Bedford
Walther, Richard Ernest *psychology educator, library administrator*

Brooks AFB
Patterson, John C. *clinical psychology researcher*
Wilde, James Dale *archaeologist, educator*

College Station
Arnold, J(ames) Barto, III *marine archaeologist*
Bass, George Fletcher *archaeology educator*
Bond, Jon Roy *political science educator*
†Burk, James Steven *sociologist*
Copp, James Harris *sociologist, educator*
Furubotn, Eirik Grundtvig *economics educator*
Greenhut, Melvin Leonard *economist, educator*
Jansen, Dennis William *economics educator, consultant*

Knutson, Ronald Dale *economist, educator, academic adminstrator*
Luepnitz, Roy Robert *psychologist, consultant, small business owner, entrepreneur*
Murphy, Kathleen Jane *psychologist, educator*
Solecki, R. Stefan *anthropologist, educator*
Steffy, John Richard *nautical archaeologist, educator*
Van Riper, Paul Pritchard *political science educator*

Corpus Christi
Cutlip, Randall Brower *retired psychologist, college president emeritus*

Cuero
Stubbs, Janine LaVelle *social science educator*

Dallas
Berkeley, Betty Life *gerontology educator*
Betts, Dianne Connally *economist, educator*
†Cortese, Anthony Joseph *sociologist*
Farrar, Beverly Jayne *psychologist*
Free, Mary Moore *biological and medical anthropologist*
Fry, Edward Irad *anthropology educator*
Goodson, Shannon Lorayn *behavioral scientist, author*
Kemper, Robert Van *anthropologist, educator*
Reagan, Barbara Benton *economics educator*
Williams, Martha Spring *psychologist*

Denton
Belfiglio, Valentine John *political science educator, pharmacist*

Egypt
Krenek, Mary Louise *political science researcher, educator*

El Paso
Cuevas, David *psychologist*

Fort Worth
Becker, Charles McVey *economics and finance educator*
Dees, Sandra Kay Martin *psychologist, research scientist*
Durham, Floyd Wesley, Jr. *economist, educator*
†Giles-Sims, Jean G. *sociology educator*
Horsfall, Sara *sociology educator*
Hurley, Linda Kay *psychologist*
Simpson, Dennis Dwayne *psychologist, educator*

Galveston
Barratt, Ernest Stoelting *psychologist, educator*
Fisher, Seymour *psychologist, educator*

Georgetown
Camp, Thomas Harley *economist*
Elder, John Blanton *psychologist, clergyman*

Grapevine
Ketter, Ronald George *political science educator, consultant*

Houston
Brito, Dagobert Llanos *economics educator*
Bryant, John Bradbury *economics educator, consultant*
Condit, Linda Faulkner *economist*
Cuthbertson, Gilbert Morris *political science educator*
Davidson, Chandler *sociologist, educator*
Dougan, Deborah Rae *neuropsychology professional*
Ebaugh, Helen Rose *sociology educator, researcher*
Ewoh, Andrew Ikeh Emmanuel *political science educator*
Foster, Dale Warren *political scientist, educator, management consultant, real estate*
Grossett, Deborah Lou *psychologist, behavior analyst, consultant*
Haymond, Paula J. *psychologist, diagnostician, hypnotherapist*
Justice, (David) Blair *psychology educator, author*
Kershaw, Carol Jean *psychologist*
Kimmel, Herbert David *psychology educator*
Martin, Randi Christine *psychology educator*
Martin, William C. *sociology educator, writer*
McIntosh, Susan Keech *anthropology educator*
Miller, Janel Howell *psychologist*
Paul, Gordon Lee *behavioral scientist, psychologist*
†Pomerantz, James Robert *psychology educator, academic administrator*
Prather, Rita Catherine *psychology educator*
Schneider, David J. *psychology educator, academic administrator*
Williams, Wright *psychologist, educator*
Wilson, Rick Keith *political science educator*

Huntsville
Payne, Richard Harold *political science educator*

Irving
Cooper, Kathleen Bell *economist*

Lancaster
Wendorf, Denver Fred, Jr. *anthropology educator*

Llano
Walter, Virginia Lee *psychologist, educator*

Lubbock
Gilliam, John Charles *economist, educator*
Havens, Murray Clark *political scientist, educator*
Stein, William Warner *anthropology educator*

Mc Dade
Carson, David Costley *psychologist, health care administrator*

Mcallen
†Rebuelta, Avelino Luis *public administration educator*

Meadows Place
Greco, Janice Teresa *psychology educator*

Nacogdoches
Clagett, Arthur F(rank) *psychologist, sociologist, qualitative research writer, retired sociology educator*

Olney
Timmons, Gordon David *economics educator*

Plano
MacAlpine, Michelle Lewis *psychologist*
MacKinnon, John Jefferson *archaeologist, anthropology and history educator*

Post
Earl, Lewis Harold *economics and management consultant, lawyer*

Prairie View
Prestage, Jewel Limar *political science educator*
Server, Ronald Douglas *political scientist, lawyer, educator*

Richardson
Andrews, Melinda Wilson *human development researcher*
Berry, Brian Joe Lobley *geographer, political economist, urban planner*

Rusk
Harper, James Howard *psychologist, hospital official*

San Antonio
Bellows, Thomas John *political scientist, educator*
Benz, George Albert *economic consultant, retired educator*
Firestone, Juanita Marlies *sociology educator*
Harris, Richard John *social sciences educator*
Hazuda, Helen Pauline *sociologist, educator*
Henington, C. Dayle *retired economist*
Palmer, J(ohn) David *politcal science educator*
Ribble, Ronald George *psychologist, educator, writer*
Rogers, William *psychologist, behavior specialist, writer, lecturer, journalist*
†Schurr, Theodore George *molecular anthropologist, human geneticist*
Spiro, Herbert John *political scientist, politician, educator, ambassador*

San Marcos
Fletcher, John Lynn *psychology educator*

Spicewood
Robbins, Eugene Weldon *genealogist*

Temple
Swartz, Jon David *psychologist, educator*

Tyler
Ramirez, Enrique Rene *social sciences educator*

Waco
Osborne, Harold Wayne *sociology educator, consultant*

Weatherford
Buckner-Reitman, Joyce *psychologist, educator*

UTAH

North Salt Lake
Barden, Robert Christopher *lawyer, psychologist, educator, analyst, author*

Ogden
Bailey, Charles Richard *political consultant*
Holt, Ronald Lawrence *anthropologist, educator*

Provo
Bahr, Howard Miner *sociologist, educator*
Christiansen, John Rees *sociologist, educator*
Fry, Earl Howard *political scientist, educator*
Kunz, Phillip Ray *sociologist, educator*
Manning, Richard L *economics educator*
Porter, Blaine Robert Milton *sociology and psychology educator*

Salt Lake City
Benjamin, Lorna Smith *psychologist*
†DiPadova, Laurie Newman *educator*
Goodey, Ila Marie *psychologist*
Harpending, Henry Cosad *anthropologist, educator*
Lease, Ronald Charles *financial economics educator*
Mangum, Garth Leroy *economist, educator*
Swaner-Smoot, Paula Margetts *clinical psychologist*
Weigel, Richard George *psychologist, educator*

Sandy
Smith, Willard Grant *psychologist*

South Jordan
Rowley, Maxine Lewis *home economics educator, writer*

VERMONT

Brattleboro
Kotkov, Benjamin *clinical psychologist*

Burlington
Cutler, Stephen Joel *sociologist*
Lawson, Robert Bernard *psychology educator*
Sampson, Samuel Franklin *sociology educator*
Smallwood, Franklin *political science educator*

Essex Junction
Dietzel, Louise A. *psychologist*

Flushing
Krasner, Michael Alan *political science educator*

Middlebury
Gibson, Eleanor Jack (Mrs. James J. Gibson) *retired psychology educator*
Robison, Olin Clyde *political science educator, former college president*
Wonnacott, (Gordon) Paul *economics educator*

Shelburne
Little, George Thomas *international relations educator, retired*

South Pomfret
Arkin, William Morris *military and political analyst, writer, consultant*

VIRGINIA

Alexandria
Carvalho, Julie Ann *psychologist*
Corson, Walter Harris *sociologist*
Johnson, Edgar McCarthy *psychologist*
Lytle, Michael Allen *criminologist, consultant*
Mann, Seymour Zalmon *political science and public administration educator emeritus, union official*
Parsons, Henry McIlvaine *psychologist*
Phillips, Karen Borlaug *economist, association executive*
Puscheck, Herbert Charles *social sciences educator*
Revere, Virginia Lehr *clinical psychologist*
Snyder, Jed C. *foreign affairs specialist*
Spar, Edward Joel *demographer*
Tucker, John Robert *financial executive*

Annandale
Downen, Robert Lynn *international affairs analyst and consultant, editor, writer*

Arlington
Brown, Robert Lyle *foreign affairs consultant*
Chipman, Susan Elizabeth *psychologist*
Coleman, Rodney Albert *government affairs consultant*
Frantz, Cecilia Aranda *psychologist*
Fuchs, Roland John *geography educator, university science official*
Funseth, Robert Lloyd Eric Martin *international consultant, lecturer, retired senior foreign service officer*
Henderson, John Brown *economist*
Henle, Peter *retired economic consultant, arbitrator*
Kerns, Wilmer Lee *social science researcher*
Marshall, Charles Burton *political science consultant*
Morgan, Bruce Ray *international consultant*
Weidemann, Celia Jean *social scientist, international business and financial development consultant*
Zakheim, Dov Solomon *economist, government official*

Blacksburg
Ash, Philip *psychologist*
Bryant, Clifton Dow *sociologist, educator*
Morgan, George Emir, III *financial economics educator*
Sgro, Joseph Anthony *psychologist, educator*
Shepard, Jon Max *sociologist*
Sweeney, Lucy Graham *psychologist*

Bluemont
Kobetz, Richard William *criminologist, consultant*

Charlotte Court House
Prophett, Andrew Lee *political science educator*

Charlottesville
Abraham, Henry Julian *political science educator*
Bovet, Eric David *economist, consultant*
Epstein, William *experimental psychologist*
Gold, Paul Ernest *psychology educator, behavioral neuroscience educator*
Gottesman, Irving Isadore *psychology educator*
Handler, Jerome Sidney *anthropology educator*
Henry, Laurin Luther *public affairs educator*
Hetherington, Eileen Mavis *psychologist, educator*
Holt, Charles Asbury *economics educator*
Hymes, Dell Hathaway *anthropologist, educator*
Kiewra, Gustave Paul *psychologist, educator*
Lynch, Allen Charles *political science researcher*
McCarty, Richard Charles *psychology educator*
McClain, Paula Denice *political scientist*
Meiburg, Charles Owen *business administration educator*
Menaker, Shirley Ann Lasch *psychology educator, academic administrator*
Perdue, Charles L., Jr. *anthropology and English educator*
Quandt, William Bauer *political scientist*
Reppucci, Nicholas Dickon *psychologist, educator*
Rhoads, Steven Eric *political science educator*
Sabato, Larry Joseph *political science educator*
Sherman, Roger *economics educator*
Sykes, Gresham M'Cready *sociologist, educator, artist*
Turner, Edith Lucy Brocklesby *anthropology educator, researcher*
†Vining, Daniel Rutledge *economics educator*
Wagner, Roy *anthropology educator, researcher*
Whitaker, John King *economics educator*
Wilson, Melvin Nathaniel *psychology educator*

Chesapeake
McCarthy, Mary Elizabeth *psychologist*

Churchville
Chester, Francis *political science educator, lawyer*

Claremont
Seward, Troilen Gainey *psychologist*

Earlysville
Caplow, Theodore *sociologist*

Eastville
Williams, Ida Jones *consumer and home economics educator, writer*

Fairfax
Barth, Michael Carl *economist*
Bennett, James Thomas *economics educator*
Boneau, C. Alan *psychology educator, researcher*
Buchanan, James McGill *economist, educator*
Cahill, Anne Pickford *economist, demographer*
†Fleishman, Edwin Alan *psychologist, author*
Goode, William Josiah *sociology educator*
Kash, Don Eldon *political science educator*
†Lehman, Elyse Brauch *psychology educator*
†Pfiffner, James Price *political science educator*
Rowley, Charles Kershaw *economics educator*

Steele, Howard Loucks *economic development consultant, author*
Wan, Ming *political scientist, educator*
†Weiss, Joshua Noah *political science educator, consultant, researcher*

Fairfax Station
Sielicki-Korczak, Boris Zdzislaw *political educator, investigative consultant*

Falls Church
Blaydes, Stephanie Anne *policy analyst*
Calkins, Susannah Eby *retired economist*
Clizbe, John Anthony *psychologist, organization administrator*
Kling, William *economist, retired foreign service officer*
Waud, Roger Neil *economics educator*
Weiss, Armand Berl *economist, association management executive*

Farmville
Dorrill, William Franklin *political scientist, educator*

Fredericksburg
Mercer, Monique Yvette *social sciences researcher*

Great Falls
Crook, Frederick W. *economist*

Harrisonburg
Ivory, Ming Marie *political scientist*
Zehr, Howard *social sciences educator*

Herndon
Abdullah, Nina Junaina *psychologist*
Spragens, William Clark *public policy educator, consultant*

Lancaster
Beane, Judith Mae *psychologist*

Lexington
Elmes, David Gordon *psychologist, educator*
Jarrard, Leonard Everett *psychologist, educator*
John, Lewis George *political science educator*
Phillips, Charles Franklin, Jr. *economist, educator*
Winfrey, John Crawford *economist, educator*

Lorton
Sun, Li-Teh *economics educator*

Lynchburg
Morland, John Kenneth *sociology and anthropology educator*
Whittemore, Linda Genevieve *clinical psychologist*

Mc Lean
Deardourff, John D. *political consultant*
Hjort, Howard Warren *consultant, economist*
†Whitehead, Clay Thomas *business executive*
Zeleny, Marjorie Pfeiffer (Mrs. Charles Ellingson Zeleny) *psychologist*

Midlothian
Stringham, Luther Winters *economist, administrator*

Montross
Fountain, Elizabeth Bean *home economist, musician, philanthropist*

Norfolk
Ahrari, M. Ehsan *political science educator, researcher, consultant*
Glickman, Albert Seymour *psychologist, educator*
Peterson-Vita, Elizabeth Ann *psychologist*

Potomac Falls
Payne, Roger Lee *geographer*

Reston
Watson, William Downing, Jr. *economist, educator*

Richmond
Campbell, Thomas Corwith, Jr. *economics educator*
Chmura, Christine *economist*
Heiss, Frederick William *political science educator, public administrator, policy researcher*
Murdoch-Kitt, Norma Hood *clinical psychologist*
O'Neal, Robert Steven *criminologist, consultant*

Roanoke
Gardner, Marvin Allen, Jr. *pastoral and clinical psychologist*

Round Hill
Pugh, Marion Stirling *archaeologist, author*

Sperryville
Armor, David J. *sociologist*

Spotsylvania
Arnhoff, Franklyn Nathaniel *psychologist, sociologist, educator*

Springfield
Chatelier, Paul Richard *aviation psychologist, training company officer*

Sterling
Henshaw, Barbara Louise Hanby *retired psychology tester, counselor*

Suffolk
Tritten, James John *national security educator*

Sweet Briar
Miller, Reuben George *economics educator*
Shea, Brent Mack *social science educator*

Vienna
Schneider, Peter Raymond *political scientist*

Virginia Beach
Caplan, Helene Moses *psychologist*

Warrenton
Malmgren, Harald Bernard *economist*

Williamsburg
Blouet, Brian Walter *geography educator*
Johnston, Robert Atkinson *psychologist, educator*
Lange, Carl James *psychology educator*
Price, Richard *anthropologist, author*
Rosen, Ellen Freda *psychologist, educator*
Smith, Roger Winston *political theorist, educator*

Winchester
Butler, Scot *economist, researcher*

WASHINGTON

Bellevue
Akutagawa, Donald *psychologist, educator*

Bellingham
Burdge, Rabel James *sociology educator*
Haensly, Patricia Anastacia *psychology educator*
Hoover, Kenneth Ray *political science educator, writer*
Nugent, Frank Anthony *psychology educator*

Camano Island
de Vries, Rimmer *economist*

Des Moines
Ortmeyer, Carl Edward *retired demographer*

Ellensburg
Collins, Fuji *mental health professional*

Everett
Van Ry, Ginger Lee *school psychologist*

Freeland
Freehill, Maurice F. *retired educational psychology educator*

Gig Harbor
Canter, Ralph Raymond *psychology educator, research director*

Hansville
Blalock, Ann Bonar *policy analyst, evaluation researcher*

Kirkland
Goldman, Ralph Morris *political science educator*
Look, Janet K. *psychologist*

La Conner
Knopf, Kenyon Alfred *economist, educator*

Mount Vernon
Garcia, John *psychologist, educator*

Olympia
Blake, Ann Beth *psychologist*

Port Angeles
Osborne, Richard Hazelet *anthropology and medical genetics educator*

Pullman
Dillman, Donald Andrew *sociologist, educator, survey methodologist*
Dunlap, Riley Eugene *sociologist*
McSweeney, Frances Kaye *psychology educator*
Warner, Dennis Allan *psychology educator*

Renton
Johnson, Benjamin Erskine *psychologist, health care administrator, consultant*

Richland
Roop, Joseph McLeod *economist*

Seattle
Beyers, William Bjorn *geography educator*
Borgatta, Edgar F. *social psychologist, educator*
Brammer, Lawrence Martin *psychology educator*
Butler, Keith Arnold *psychologist, software researcher*
Chirot, Daniel *sociology and international studies educator*
Cowhey, Peter Francis *international relations educator, consultant*
Ellings, Richard James *political and economic research institution executive*
Evans, Ellis Dale *psychologist, educator*
Gore, William Jay *political science educator*
Gross, Edward *retired sociologist, educator, lawyer*
Hirschman, Charles, Jr. *sociologist, educator*
Lang, Kurt *sociologist, educator, writer*
†Langford, Jean Marie *cultural anthropologist*
Mah, Feng-hwa *economics educator*
Matthews, Donald Rowe *political scientist, educator*
Morrill, Richard Leland *geographer, educator*
Narver, John Colin *business administration educator*
Olson, David John *political science educator*
Patrick, Donald Lee *social scientist, health services researcher*
Sarason, Irwin G. *psychology educator*
Schall, Lawrence Delano *economics educator, consultant*
Startz, Richard *economist*
Turnovsky, Stephen John *economics educator*
van den Berghe, Pierre Louis *sociologist, anthropologist*
†Wheeler, Deborah Lynn *educator*
Wolfle, Dael Lee *public affairs educator*
Woods, Ronald Earl *foreign policy educator*

Sequim
Mc Hugh, Margaret Ann Gloe *psychologist*

Spokane
Novak, Terry Lee *public adminstration educator*

Tacoma
Ernst, John Allan *clinical neuropsychologist*
Schauss, Alexander George *psychologist, researcher*
Strege, Timothy Melvin *economic consultant*

University Place
Bourgaize, Robert G. *economist*

Vancouver
Craven, James Michael *economist, educator*

Walla Walla
†Apostolidis, Paul C. *political science educator*

Yakima
Landreau, Anthony Norman (Tony Landreau) *anthropologist, museologist*

WEST VIRGINIA

Bethany
Cooey, William Randolph *economics educator*

Fairmont
Fulda, Michael *political science educator, space policy researcher*

Martinsburg
Yoe, Harry Warner *retired agricultural economist*

Morgantown
Brisbin, Richard A., Jr. *political scientist, educator*
†Claar, Victor Vyron *economics educator*
McAvoy, Rogers *educational psychology educator, consultant*
Peterson, Sophia *international studies educator*
Reese, Hayne Waring *psychologist*
Witt, Tom *economics researcher, educator*

Salem
Frasure, Carl Maynard *political science educator*

WISCONSIN

Beloit
Davis, Harry Rex *political science educator*
Kreider, Leonard Emil *economics educator*

Cascade
Baumann, Carol Edler *retired political science educator*

Eau Claire
Dick, Raymond Dale *psychology educator*
Hugo, Miriam Jeanne *educator, counselor*

Elm Grove
Bielke, Patricia Anne *psychologist*

Fond Du Lac
Bespalec, Dale Anthony *clinical psychologist*
Kaufman, Harvey Isidore *neuropsychology consultant*
Reed, Jeffrey Garth *organizational psychologist, educator*

Green Bay
Butler, Robert Andrews *clinical psychologist*
Kraft, Michael Eugene *political science educator*

Hartland
Burrus, Daniel Allen *research company executive, consultant*

Kenosha
Cyr, Arthur I. *political science and economics educator*
Statham, Anne Adele *sociology educator*

La Crosse
Albrechtson, Rick *psychologist*

Madison
Andreano, Ralph Louis *economist, educator*
†Baldwin, Robert Edward *economics educator*
Barrows, Richard Lee *economics educator, academic administrator*
†Beissinger, Mark Richard *political scientist, educator*
Bennett, Kenneth Alan *retired biological anthropologist*
Brock, William Allen, III *economics educator, consultant*
Chapman, Loren J. *psychology educator*
Cohen, Bernard Cecil *political scientist, educator*
Downs, Donald Alexander, Jr. *political scientist, educator*
Freudenburg, William R. *sociology educator*
Goldberger, Arthur Stanley *economics educator*
Graf, Truman Frederick *agricultural economist, educator*
Greenfield, Norman Samuel *psychologist, educator*
Haller, Archibald Orben *sociologist, educator*
Hansen, W. Lee *economics educator, author*
Hester, Donald Denison *economics educator*
Luening, Robert Adami *agricultural economics educator emeritus*
Mueller, Willard Fritz *economics educator*
Nichols, Donald Arthur *economist, educator*
†Ohnuki-Tierney, Emiko *social sciences educator*
Owens, Robert George *psychologist, researcher*
Rice, Joy Katharine *psychologist, educational policy studies and women's studies educator*
Robinson, Arthur Howard *geography educator*
Schmidt, John Richard *agricultural economics educator*
Sewell, William Hamilton *sociologist*
Slesinger, Doris Peyser *sociology educator*
Strasma, John Drinan *economist, educator*
Strier, Karen Barbara *anthropology educator*
Taylor, Fannie Turnbull *social education and arts administration educator*
Thiesenhusen, William Charles *agricultural economist*
Wilson, Franklin D. *sociology educator*
Young, Merwin Crawford *political science educator*

Menomonee Falls
Griswold, Paul Michael *clinical psychologist, consultant*

Mequon
Woessner, William Craig *school psychologist*

Milwaukee
Handelman, Howard *political scientist, educator*
Hawkins, Brett William *political science educator*
Kuchan, Anthony Mark *psychologist, educator*
Kupst, Mary Jo *psychologist, researcher*
LaMalfa, Joachim Jack *clinical psychologist*
Moberg, David Oscar *sociology educator*
Quade, Quentin Lon *political science educator*
Quereshi, Mohammed Younus *psychology educator, consultant*
Warren, Richard M. *experimental psychologist, educator*
Wolfe, Christopher *political science educator*

Oak Creek
†Rivera, Mario Angelo *anthropologist, consultant, researcher*

Oregon
Dorner, Peter Paul *retired economist, educator*

Oshkosh
Gruberg, Martin *political science educator*

Plymouth
Woythal, Constance Lee *psychologist*

Prescott
†Kees, Mary Adele *school psychologist*

Ripon
Steinbring, John Henry (Jack Steinbring) *archaeologist*

Schofield
Gontarz, Michael Joseph *school psychologist*

Stevens Point
Doherty, Patricia Anne *psychologist*

Verona
Waldron, Ellis Leigh *retired political science educator*

Wausau
Ament, Richard Rand *psychologist*

Whitewater
Culbertson, Frances Mitchell *psychology educator*

WYOMING

Gillette
Mathers, Earl Frank *economic developer*

Laramie
Chai, Winberg *political science educator*
Crocker, Thomas Dunstan *economics educator*
†Forsling, Peter J. *defense analyst*
Gill, George Wilhelm *anthropologist*
Harkin, Michael Eugene *anthropologist, educator, writer*
Shaffer, Sherrill Lynn *economist*

Powell
Brophy, Dennis Richard *psychology and philosophy educator, administrator, clergyman*

TERRITORIES OF THE UNITED STATES

PUERTO RICO

Bayamon
Herrans-Perez, Laura Leticia *psychologist, educator, research consultant*

Caguas
Rivera-Urrutia, Beatriz Dalila *psychology and rehabilitation counseling educator*

Guaynabo
Barquin, Ramón Carlos, III *political scientist, consultant*

Hormigueros
Acosta, Ursula *psychologist*

Rio Piedras
Davila, Norma *developmental psychologist and program evaluator*

San Juan
Diaz de Gonzalez, Ana Maria *psychologist, educator*

MILITARY ADDRESSES OF THE UNITED STATES

PACIFIC

APO
Calder, Kent Eyring *political science educator, diplomat*

CANADA

ALBERTA

Calgary
Forbis, Richard George *archaeologist*
Kelley, Jane Holden *archaeology educator*
Stebbins, Robert Alan *sociology educator*

Edmonton
Freeman, Milton Malcolm Roland *anthropology educator*
Krotki, Karol Jozef *sociology educator, demographer*
Lechelt, Eugene Carl *psychology educator*
†Mardon, Austin Albert *geographer, writer, researcher*

BRITISH COLUMBIA

Burnaby
Brantingham, Patricia Louise *criminology educator*
Brantingham, Paul Jeffrey *criminology educator*
Copes, Parzival *economist, researcher*
Kimura, Doreen *psychology educator, researcher*

Vancouver
Aberle, David Friend *anthropologist, educator*
Craig, Kenneth Denton *psychologist, educator, researcher*
Cynader, Max Sigmund *psychology, physiology, brain research educator, researcher*
Elkins, David J. *political science educator*
Ericson, Richard Victor *social science-law educator, university official*
Feaver, George Arthur *political science educator*
Holsti, Kalevi Jacque *political scientist, educator*
Kesselman, Jonathan Rhys *economics educator, public policy researcher*
Langdon, Frank Corriston *political science educator, researcher*
Laponce, Jean Antoine *political scientist*
Lipsey, Richard George *economist, educator*
Marchak, Maureen Patricia *anthropology and sociology educator*
Pearson, Richard Joseph *archaeologist, educator*
Robinson, John Lewis *geography educator*
Shearer, Ronald Alexander *economics educator*
Slaymaker, Herbert Olav *geography educator*
Suedfeld, Peter *psychologist, educator*
Tees, Richard Chisholm *psychology educator, researcher*

Victoria
Barber, Clarence Lyle *economics educator*
Payne, Robert Walter *psychologist, educator*

NEW BRUNSWICK

Charters Settlement
Easterbrook, James Arthur *psychology educator*

Fredericton
Kenyon, Gary Michael *gerontology educator, researcher*

NOVA SCOTIA

Halifax
Borgese, Elisabeth Mann *political science educator, author*
Shaw, Timothy Milton *political science educator*
Stairs, Denis Winfield *political science educator*
Winham, Gilbert Rathbone *political science educator*

ONTARIO

Downsview
Endler, Norman Solomon *psychology educator*

Hamilton
George, Peter James *economist, educator*
King, Leslie John *geography educator*
Ryan, Ellen Bouchard *psychology educator, gerontologist*

Kingston
Kaliski, Stephan Felix *economics educator*
Meisel, John *political scientist*

London
Laidler, David Ernest William *economics educator*
Wonnacott, Ronald Johnston *economics educator*

Nepean
Cornell, Peter McCaul *economic consultant, former government official*

Niagara-on-the-Lake
Olley, Robert Edward *economist, educator*

North York
Richmond, Anthony Henry *sociologist, emeritus educator*

Ottawa
Brooks, David Barry *resource economist*
Cappe, Melvin Samuel *economist*
Griller, David *economics and technology consultant*
Ives, John David (Jack Ives) *geography and environmental sciences educator*

Toronto
Clark, Samuel Delbert *sociology educator*
Dean, William George *geography educator*
Ferguson, Kingsley George *psychologist*
Goldfarb, Martin *sociologist*
Grayson, Albert Kirk *Near Eastern studies educator*
Grinspun, Ricardo *economist, educator*
Helleiner, Gerald Karl *economics educator*
Hollander, Samuel *economist, educator*
Munro, John Henry Alexander *economics educator, writer*
Pratt, Robert Cranford *political scientist, educator*
Rapoport, Anatol *peace studies educator, mathematical biologist*
Rose, Jeffrey Raymond *economist, educator, negotiator*
Ross, Murray George *social science educator, university president emeritus*
Tulving, Endel *psychologist, educator*
Wilson, Thomas Arthur *economics educator*

Waterloo
Falding, Harold Joseph *sociology educator*
Nelson, J. Gordon *geography educator*
Warner, Barry Gregory *geographer, educator*

Windsor
Auld, Frank psychologist, educator
Minton, Henry Lee psychology educator

QUEBEC

Ile des Soeurs
Dagenais, Marcel Gilles economist, educator

Montreal
Brecher, Irving economics educator
Brecher, Michael political science educator
Dufour, Jean-Marie economics researcher, educator
Ikawa-Smith, Fumiko anthropologist, educator
Jonassohn, Kurt sociologist, educator
Melzack, Ronald psychology educator
Milner, Brenda Atkinson Langford neuropsychologist
Milner, Peter Marshall psychology educator
Nayar, Baldev Raj political science educator
Normandeau, Andre Gabriel criminologist, educator
Orban, Edmond Henry political science educator
Raynauld, Andre economist, educator
Smith, Philip Edward Lake anthropology educator
Stewart, Jane psychology educator
Szabo, Denis criminologist, educator
Tremblay, Rodrigue economics educator
Trigger, Bruce Graham anthropology educator
Vaillancourt, Jean-Guy sociology educator
Vikis-Freibergs, Vaira psychologist, educator
Waller, Harold Myron political science educator

Quebec
Belanger, Gerard economics educator
Migue, Jean Luc economics educator
Tremblay, Marc Adélard anthropologist, educator

SASKATCHEWAN

Saskatoon
Randhawa, Bikkar Singh psychologist, educator

MEXICO

Jalisco
Wolf, Charlotte Elizabeth sociologist

BRAZIL

Rio Claro
Christofoletti, Antonio geography educator

CZECH REPUBLIC

Prague
Dine, Thomas Alan foreign policy expert

DENMARK

Copenhagen
Bundesen, Claus Mogens psychologist, educator

EGYPT

Cairo
†Sullivan, Earl Le Roy political science educator, academic administrator

ENGLAND

Birmingham
Fry, Maxwell John economist, educator

Cambridge
Renfrew, Andrew Colin (Lord Renfrew of Kaimsthorn) archaeologist, academic administrator

Claverton Down
Buchanan, Robert Angus archaeology educator

Devon
Rossmiller, George Eddie agricultural economist

London
Batty, J. Michael geographer, educator
Douglas, Mary Tew anthropology and humanities educator
Junz, Helen B. economist
Kuper, Adam Jonathan anthropologist, educator

FRANCE

Fontainebleu
Ayres, Robert Underwood environmental economics and technology educator

Paris
Allais, Maurice-Felix economist
Mayor Zaragoza, Federico United Nations official, former university official

GERMANY

Bonn
Selten, Reinhard retired economist, educator

Munich
Whetten, Lawrence Lester international relations educator

GREECE

Athens
Kalamotousakis, George John economist

HONG KONG

Kowloon
Banister, Judith demographer, educator

ISRAEL

Tel Aviv
Rubin, Barry Mitchel foreign policy analyst, writer

ITALY

Pisa
Settis, Salvatore archaeologist, art historian

Rome
Meyers, William Henry economics educator
Westley, John Richard economist

JAPAN

Tokyo
Ginkel, Johannes Auguste van geographer, educator
Nishiyama, Chiaki economist, educator

NORWAY

Oslo
Haavelmo, Trygve economics educator

PANAMA

Panama
Roussel, Lee Dennison economist

PORTUGAL

Lisbon
Thore, Sten Anders economics and aerospace engineering educator

SRI LANKA

Colombo
Spain, James William political scientist, writer, investor

SWITZERLAND

Geneva
Twarog, Sophia Nora economist, international civil servant

TAIWAN

Hualien
Shieh, John Ting-chung economics educator

ADDRESS UNPUBLISHED

†Aarstol, Michael Patrick economics educator
Abel, Harold psychologist, educator, academic administrator
Adams, John Quincy economist, educator
Adams, Robert McCormick anthropologist, educator
Adelman, Richard Charles gerontologist, educator
Ahmed, Syed Z. anthropologist
Albagli, Louise Martha psychologist
†Albert, Sarah Cathleen public policy specialist
Alker, Hayward Rose political science educator
Allen, John Lyndon social studies educator
Allen, Leatrice Delorice psychologist
Alpher, Victor Seth retired clinical psychologist, consultant,
Altman, Irwin psychology educator
Altshuler, Alan Anthony political scientist
Anderson, Bernard E. economist
Anderson, Louise Stout crime analyst
Axilrod, Stephen Harvey global economic consultant, economist
Bambrick, James Joseph labor economist, labor relations executive
Barber, James David political scientist, retired educator
Bergin, Allen Eric clinical psychologist, educator
Bishop, J. Joe social studies educator
†Bocskor, Nancy Leah political consultant
Bohannan, Paul James anthropologist, writer, former university administrator
Boling, Patricia Ann political science educator, researcher, writer
†Borum, Bradford R. policy analyst
Boyer, Heidi Hild public policy consultant
Bracey, Earnest Norton political science educator
Braen, Bernard Benjamin psychology educator
Bredfeldt, John Creighton economist, financial analyst, retired air force officer
Broberg, Merle retired social worker
Buchin, Jean psychologist
Calleo, David Patrick political science educator
Canjar, Patricia McWade psychologist
Cantril, Albert H(adley) public opinion analyst
Carlsen, Mary Baird clinical psychologist
Carlson, Gustav Gunnar anthropology educator
Carlson, Janet Frances psychologist, educator
Cavin, Susan Elizabeth sociologist, writer
Chapman, Richard LeRoy public policy researcher
Chase, Clinton Irvin psychologist, educator, business executive
Chew, Margaret Sarah geography educator, retired
Chinitz, Benjamin economics educator
†Chiswick, Barry Raymond economics educator
Christian, James Wayne economist
Ciullo, Rosemary psychologist
†Coates-Shrider, Lisa Nicole psychology educator
†Cohen, Barbara L. clinical neuropsychologist
Collins, Harker economist, manufacturing executive, publisher, marketing, financial, business and legal consultant
Conaway, Mary Ann behavioral studies educator
†Coover, Roderick Luis anthropologist
Cozan, Lee clinical research psychologist
Crampton, Esther Larson sociology and political science educator
Daniels, Arlene Kaplan sociology educator
D'Antonio, William Vincent sociology educator
†Davis, Robert Scott criminal justice educator
Dawkins, Marva Phyllis psychologist
Dean, Leslie Alan (Cap Dean) economic and social development consultant
de Blij, Harm Jan geography educator, editor
Debreu, Gerard economics and mathematics educator
Dellere, Diana Marie school psychologist
Del Rosario, Rose Marie clinical sociologist, educator, consultant
Denevan, William Maxfield geographer, educator, ecologist
†DiLeo, Daniel social sciences educator
Dole, Arthur Alexander psychology educator
Donnelly, Leslie Faye Harris psychologist, psychology educator
Dowd, Morgan Daniel political science educator
Dwyer, Gerald Paul, Jr. economist, educator
Earle, Timothy Keese anthropology educator
Edwards, Ward Dennis psychology and industrial engineering educator
Egnor, Joanne McClellan psychology educator
Eley, Lynn W. political science educator, former mayor
Engel, Bernard Theodore psychologist, educator
Evans, Frederick John psychologist
†Everly, George Stotelmyer, Jr. psychophysiologist, educator
Field, Julia Allen futurist, strategist, writer
Finnberg, Elaine Agnes psychologist, editor
Frankel, Judith Jennifer Mariasha clinical psychologist, consultant
Fritz, Jan Marie planning educator
Frost, Ellen Louise political economist
Gabel, Creighton retired anthropologist, educator
Gerlach, Luther Paul anthropologist
†Gershman, John Jeremy research analyst, consultant
Gleach, Frederic Wright anthropologist
Goldston, Stephen Eugene community psychologist, educator, consultant
Gootee, Tara Renee educational counselor, family therapist
Gottschalk, Charles M. international energy consultant
Grassmuck, George Ludwig political science educator
Greene, Beverly Ann clinical psychologist
Greenwood, Janet Kae Daly psychologist, educational administrator
Grindea, Daniel international economist
Grow, Robert Theodore economist, association executive
Guthrie, Robert Val retired psychologist and educator
Haber, Ralph Norman psychology consultant, researcher, educator
Hage, George Campbell social studies educator, minister, and counselor
Haining, Jeane psychologist
Hall, Jay social psychologist
Hare, Frederick Kenneth geography and environmental educator, university official
Hargrove, Erwin C. political scientist, educator
Hartzell, Irene Janofsky psychologist
†Heatherley, James Lawrence psychologist, educator
Hefferan, Colien Joan economist
Helfgott, Roy B. economist, educator
Hewlett-Kierstead, Nancy Carrick psychologist
Hilliard, Sam Bowers geography educator
Hires, William Leland psychologist, consultant
Hirsch, Walter economist, researcher
Holleb, Doris B. urban planner, economist
Hosek, James Robert economist
Hughes, Ann Hightower retired economist, international trade consultant
Igbineweka, Andrew Osabuohien public administration/political science educator
Jannuzi, F. Tomasson economics educator
Jayne, Cynthia Elizabeth psychologist
Johnson, Albert Wesley consultant on governance
Johnson, Claudia Anderson psychologist
Jones, Joan Megan anthropologist
Juviler, Peter Henry political scientist, educator
Kahana, Eva Frost sociology educator
Kaplan, Candia Post psychologist
Karczmar, Mieczyslaw economist
Karson, Samuel psychologist, educator
Kaslow, Florence Whiteman psychologist, educator
Kates, Robert William geographer, educator, independent scholar
Katz, Phyllis Alberts developmental research psychologist
Katznelson, Ira Isaac social sciences educator, writer
Kellner, Irwin L. economist
Kendrick, Budd Leroy psychologist
Kennedy, Marla Catherine psychologist
Kenyon, Daphne Anne economics educator
Keyes, Margaret Naumann home economics educator
Klass, Morton anthropology educator, consultant
Kohan, Dennis Lynn international trade educator, consultant
Komiya, Noboru psychology educator
Kostere, Kim Martin psychologist, consultant
Kottler, Raymond George Michael economist, researcher
Kramer, Karen Sue mind-body psychologist
Lanzillotti, Robert Franklin economist, educator
Larson, Patricia Joan clinical therapist
Lauber, John K. research psychologist
Lazorchak, Joseph Michael economist
Lease, Martin Harry, Jr. retired political science educator
LeBlanc, Hugh Linus political science educator, consultant
Lee, Aldora G. social psychologist
Leith, Karen Pezza psychologist, educator
Levi, Maurice David economics educator
†Lewis, Carla S. retired psychology educator
Lewis, Charles Leonard psychologist
Lewis, Robert Turner retired psychologist
Lewis Mill, Barbara Jean school psychologist, educator
Lichtenberg, Byron K. futurist, manufacturing executive, space flight consultant, pilot
Lief, Thomas Parrish sociologist, educator
Lipsitt, Lewis Paeff psychology educator
Lisovskaya, Elena Borisovna sociologist, educator
Lucas, Wayne Lee sociologist, educator
Lyman, Ruth Ann psychologist
MacLennan, Beryce Winifred psychologist
Maehr, Martin Louis psychology educator
Manchester, Carol Ann Freshwater psychologist
Marini, Frank Nicholas political science and public administration educator
Martin, Catherine Elizabeth anthropology educator
Martin, Sally S. family studies educator
Massa, Salvatore Peter psychologist
Matheny, Adam Pence, Jr. child psychologist, educator, consultant, researcher
Matthews, Wendy Schempp psychologist, researcher
Mc Clellan, Catharine anthropologist, educator
McCoy, Patricia A. clinical special educator, writer, art critic
McGough, Duane Theodore economist, retired government official
Mehlman, Benjamin psychologist, educator
Michael, Donald Nelson social scientist, educator
Modigliani, Franco economics and finance educator
Moore, Ruth Lambert Bromberg retired clinical psychologist
Nardi, Thomas James psychologist
Naylor, Thomas Herbert economist, educator, consultant
Nearine, Robert James educational psychologist
Newborn, Jud anthropologist, writer, lyricist
Norsworthy, John Randolph economist, educator
Obligacion, Freddie Rabelas sociology educator, researcher
O'Brien, John Wilfrid economist, emeritus university president, educator
Oksas, Joan Kay economist, educator
Olson, William Clinton international affairs educator, author, lecturer
O'Neal, Harriet Roberts psychologist, psycholegal consultant
†O'Neill, James Benjamin economics educator
Pace, Charles Robert psychologist, educator
Palisi, Anthony Thomas psychologist, educator
†Pappas, Christine Jean psychologist
Parker, Harry John retired psychologist, educator
Patel, Roshni social studies educator
Pearlmutter, Florence Nichols psychologist, therapist
Pedersen, Knud George economics educator, academic administrator
Perez, Luz Lillian psychologist
Phillips, Carla Rahn history educator
Pilisuk, Marc community psychology educator
Piore, Nora Kahn economist, health policy analyst
Pollack, Gerald Alexander economist, government official
†Porro-Salinas, Patricia Maria clinical psychologist
Potts, Nancy Dee Needham psychologist
Ragusea, Stephen Anthony psychologist, educator
Ramsey, Patricia Gale psychology and education educator
Randall, Richard Rainier geographer
Reed, Diane Marie psychologist
Renfro, William Leonard futurist, lawyer, inventor, entrepreneur
Riecken, Henry William psychologist, research director
Ringler, Lenore educational psychologist, educator
Roche de Coppens, Peter George sociologist, educator
Rosen, Lawrence anthropology educator
Rossi, Peter Henry sociology educator
Rubin, Zick psychology educator, lawyer, writer
Ruchelman, Leonard Isadore urban studies and public administration educator
Ruderman, Armand Peter health economics educator, consultant, volunteer
Rusch, Kathy Lynn school psychologist, educational advisor
Sameroff, Arnold Joshua developmental psychologist, educator, research scientist
Schenkel, Susan psychologist, educator, author
Schubert, Glendon political scientist, educator
Sebastian, Peter international affairs consultant, former ambassador
Shapiro, Leo J. social researcher
Sharpe, William Forsyth economics educator
Shaw-Mutz, Bernadette Jane jury sociologist
Shure, Myrna Beth psychologist, educator
Sills, Richard Reynolds scientist, educator
Sims, Kent Otway economist
Smith, Edward K. economist, consultant
Smith, Ethel Farrington retired social worker, editor
Smith, V. Kerry economics educator
Snyder, Marvin neuropsychologist
Sonderegger, Theo Brown psychology educator
Spencer, Milton Harry economics and finance educator
Spinweber, Cheryl Lynn psychologist, sleep specialist
Spring, Michael Gerard international relations specialist
Sprinthall, Norman Arthur psychology educator
Stallone, Thomas Michael clinical psychologist
Stalon, Charles Gary retired economics educator, institute administrator
Steffens, Dorothy Ruth political economist
Steinhauser, Sheldon Eli sociology and gerontology educator, consultant
Stinson, Thomas Franklin economist, educator
†Stone, Douglas Bryan financial economist
Stratton, Julius Augustus psychologist, consultant
Striker, Cecil Leopold archaeologist, educator
Studness, Charles Michael economist
Stufano, Thomas Joseph criminologist, author, inventor
Suraci, Patrick Joseph clinical psychologist
Sutton, Willis Anderson, Jr. sociology educator
Swanstrom, Thomas Evan economist
Swindler, Daris Ray physical anthropologist, forensic anthropologist
Tarrance, Vernon Lance, Jr. public opinion research executive
†Tartakoff, Laura Ymayo political science educator
Ter Horst, Jerald Franklin public affairs counsel
Textor, Robert Bayard cultural anthropology writer, consultant, educator
Theobald, H Rupert retired political scientist
Tonello-Stuart, Enrica Maria political economist
Tremblay, Richard Ernest psychology educator
†van de Zilver, Peter A.L. economist, business executive

Vaughan, Nadine *psychologist*
Verplanck, William Samuel *psychologist, educator*
Volcker, Paul A. *economist*
†Waisman, Carlos H. *sociologist*
Wallerstein, Judith Saretsky *marriage and divorce researcher*
Waltz, Kenneth Neal *political science educator*
Weber, Mary Ellen Healy *economist*
†Weber, William L. *economics educator*
Weil, Rolf Alfred *economist, university president emeritus*
Werner-Jacobsen, Emmy Elisabeth *developmental psychologist*
White, Larry D. *political science educator*
Whitener, Lawrence Bruce *political consultant, consumer advocate, educator, paralegal*
Wilkinson, Doris *medical sociology educator*
Willey, Gordon Randolph *retired anthropologist, archaeologist, educator*
Williams, David Vandergrift *organizational psychologist*
Williamson, Jo Ann *psychologist*
Wolfe, Gregory Baker *international relations educator*
Wonders, William Clare *geography educator*
Wood, Robert Coldwell *political scientist*
Woodcock, Richard Wesley *educational psychologist*
Wright, James David *sociology educator, writer*
Yost, William Albert *psychology educator, hearing researcher*
Zavala, Albert *research psychologist*
Zeigler, L(uther) Harmon *political science educator*
Zuckerman, Harriet *sociologist, educator*

UNCLASSIFIED

UNITED STATES

ARIZONA

Phoenix
†Nielsen, George B.

CALIFORNIA

Los Angeles
†Kornwasser, Joseph K.

Tustin
†Del Campo, C. Alicia *theater scholar*

CONNECTICUT

Vernon Rockville
†Obroski, Paulo *public administration coordinator*

DELAWARE

Newark
†Cole, Peter *linguistics educator*

DISTRICT OF COLUMBIA

Washington
Campbell, Bruce James
†Gentry, Pamela

FLORIDA

Deland
†Pleus, Michael P.

Naples
Lichtwardt, Harry E.

Tallahassee
†McCarty, Ann Darice *scientist*

GEORGIA

Atlanta
†Edson, Margaret *playwright*

ILLINOIS

Des Plaines
†Henrikson, Arthur Allen *political cartoonist, educator*

Quincy
†Preston, Ann Elizabeth *media and communication educator*

Springfield
†Pilapil, Deborah Ann *legislative liaison*

INDIANA

Bloomington
†Yang, Seong-Deog *educator*

LOUISIANA

New Orleans
†Lupo, Thomas J.

MARYLAND

Annapolis
†Riddick, Major F., Jr.

North Bethesda
†McCarn, Davis Barton *computer company executive, mathematician*

MASSACHUSETTS

Boston
†Ainsworth, Kimberly E. *federal employee*

North Billerica
†Panditi, Surya

Northampton
Betlyon, John Wilson

MICHIGAN

Farmington
†Kadi, Osama

MISSOURI

Saint Louis
†Clemens, Robert *violin maker*

NEBRASKA

North Platte
†Bauer, Mary Jane

NEW JERSEY

Hightstown
†Viola, Albert T. *arts center administrator, author, composer, actor*

NEW YORK

Albany
Bee, Clair Francis Jr.

New York
†Denison, Dwight Val *educator*
†Francisco, Roma Mercedes *educator*
†Kastrup, Dieter *United Nations official*
†Penland, Diane Robinson *educator*

Rochester
†Braun, Wilhelm *retired educator*
†Ninfo, John C., II

OHIO

Cincinnati
Draper, Sharon M. *educator, author*

Yellow Springs
†Moinzadeh, Sadie *institutional researcher, educator*

OREGON

Salem
†Wyatt, Bill *government staff*

PENNSYLVANIA

Harrisburg
†Holman, Mark *state official*

Mechanicsburg
†Van Zile, Susan J.

Pittsburgh
†Colosimo, Steven Francis *counselor*

TEXAS

Austin
†Knowles, Harry Jay *internet personality*

Dallas
†Edmondson, James Howard *former insurance executive, investor*

UTAH

Salt Lake City
†Griggs, John Bronson *technology executive*

WASHINGTON

Yakima
†Ullas, Yvonne L.

ITALY

Bosisio Parini
Buttram, Debra Doris *dog trainer, apparel executive*

MADAGASCAR

Antananarivo
†Rajaonarivony, Narisoa *program chief, researcher*

ADDRESS UNPUBLISHED

Bradley, William Bryan *cable television regulator*
†Colgan, Ann K. *educator*
†DiEdwardo, Mary Ann Pasda *artist, writer*
†Hapka, Catherine M. *internet executive*
†Richter, Mary Persis (Polly Richter) *broadcast assistant*

Retiree Index

The index below lists the names of those individuals whose biographical sketches last appeared in the 51st, 52nd, or 53rd Edition of *Who's Who in America*. The latest volume containing a full sketch is indicated by *51, 52,* or *53* following each name. The listees have since retired from active participation in their

A

Abell, Millicent Demmin, *52*
Adams, W. G., *53*
Aebersold, Robert Neil, *52*
Agria, John Joseph, *52*
Aguilar, Robert P., *51*
Aikens, Joan Deacon, *53*
Alexander, David Lee, *52*
Allen, Frederic W., *51*
Allen, Ronald W., *51*
Alm, Alvin Leroy, *52*
Almen, Louis Theodore, *52*
Alpern, Robert Zellman, *51*
Altenstadter, Shelley G., *51*
Andrew, Gwen, *51*
Andrews, Bethlehem Kottes, *53*
Andrews, Henry Nathaniel, Jr., *52*
Andrews, James Edgar, *51*
Andrews, Robert Frederick, *52*
Ansell, George Stephen, *52*
Asselin, Martial, *51*
Athanassiades, Ted, *52*
Atkinson, Robert Poland, *51*

B

Badgley, William S., *53*
Baker, Clifford Cornell, *51*
Barlick, Al, *53*
Barnett, Robert James, *51*
Barr, Robert Alfred, Jr., *51*
Bartels, Gerald Lee, *51*
Bassett, Edward Powers, *52*
Bassist, Donald Herbert, *51*
Bates, George Edmonds, *51*
Baughn, Juan R., *51*
Bauman, Robert Poe, *52*
Baxter, Thomas Gregory, *52*
Beeners, Wilbert John, *52*
Begley, Michael Joseph, *51*
Belew, David Owen, Jr., *51*
Bell, Daniel Long, Jr., *51*
Bell, David Gus (Buddy Bell), *53*
Bembridge, John Anthony, *51*
Benzel, Brian L., *52*
Berger, Arthur Victor, *51*
Bergeron, R. Thomas, *52*
Bergman, Klaus, *52*
Bernstein, Lionel M., *51*
Betz, Charles W., *51*
Billman, Jennifer, *52*
Black, Kent March, *52*
Blacker, Coit Dennis, *51*
Blaire, Stephen E., *53*
Blake, Larry Jay, *51*
Bloede, Victor Gustav, *52*
Blount, Don H., *52*
Bodow, Warren G., *52*
Bolstad, D. D., *51*
Bond, Thomas Alden, *51*
Bonney, M. Doane, *51*
Bookner, Becci Jane, *51*
Booth, Paul Wayne, *53*
Boren, Arthur Rodney, *51*
Boudreaux, Warren Louis, *51*
Bourdo, G. F., *51*
Bowe, Riddick Lamont, *51*
Bowen, James, *51*
Bowen, Jerry Wayne, *53*
Bowron, Eljay B., *53*
Boyd, William Beaty, *51*
Boylan, David Ray, *52*
Bozone, Billie Rae, *51*
Bradfield, Richard Harold, *52*
Bratton, Ronald B., *51*
Braxton, Janice Lawrence, *53*
Brennan, Edward A., *51*
Brennan, Oscar A., *51*
Brewer, Warren Wesley, *51*
Briscoe, Keith G., *51*
Brophy, Theodore Frederick, *52*
Brown, Corrick, *51*
Brown, Dale Duward, *52*
Brown, George J., *51*
Brown, Nicholas, *51*
Brownell, John Arnold, *52*
Burke, Daniel Barnett, *52*
Burklew, Donald R., *52*

C

Calloway, D. Wayne, *51*
Canfield, William Newton, *52*
Cantrell, Joseph Doyle, *52*
Carlson, Rolland S., *52*
Carmody, John, *53*
Carmody, Thomas Roswell, *52*
Carpenter, Bruce H., *51*
Carpenter, William Levy, *51*
Carr, Charles Lee Glenn, Jr. (Chuck Carr), *53*
Carrington, Betty Watts, *52*
Carstens, Harold Henry, *51*
Carter, Anthony, *52*
Case, Andrew J., *51*
Cassiday, Paul Richard, *53*
Cavenar, Jesse Oscar, Jr., *51*
Cerveny, Frank Stanley, *51*
Chalfant, Edward Cole, *52*
Chang, Kung-Li (Charlie), *52*
Chappuie, Louis Edward, *52*
Chiasson, Donat, *51*
Chiat, Jay, *52*
Chilstrom, Herbert Walfred, *51*
Choate, Jerry D., *51*
Christie, Richard Gary, *52*
Chubb, Harold D., *51*
Ciriacy, Edward Walter, *52*
Clabby, William Robert, *51*
Clanon, Thomas Lawrence, *52*
Clarie, T. Emmet, *51*
Clark, Jonathan Montgomery, *52*
Clark, Richard Harry Jr., *52*
Clarke, Don R., *51*
Clayton, Constance, *51*
Clendenin, John L., *52*
Cline, Ned Aubrey, *51*
Cochran, George Van Brunt, *52*
Coffey, C. Shelby, III, *52*
Cole, Jay N., *51*
Collins, Jerry Allan, *51*
Comparin, Robert Anton, *51*
Compton, Robert D., *52*
Conley, Clare Dean, *53*
Connolly, Eugene B., Jr., *51*
Cook, Samuel DuBois, *51*
Cornstein, David B., *53*
Correu, James M., *51*
Corry, Charles Albert, *51*
Cotliar, George J., *51*
Cournoyea, Nellie J., *51*
Coyne, Mary Jeanne, *51*
Craig, Andrew Billings, III, *52*
Crawford, William Basil, Jr., *51*
Creedon, John J., *52*
Crim, Reuben Sidney, *51*
Croom, John Henry, III, *51*
Croxton, Fred(erick) E(mory), Jr., *52*
Cryer, Eugene Edward, *51*
Cuatrecasas, Pedro Martin, *51*
Cunningham, Arthur Francis, *52*
Cunningham, James Everett, *52*
Curran-Smith, Anita Stiles, *52*
Cushman, Aaron D., *51*
Cuthill, Robert T., *51*

D

Dahl, John Anton, *51*
Daly, James Joseph, *51*
Daly, John Francis, *52*
Dameron, William H., III, *51*
Dane, Paul Nelson, *51*
Daniell, Robert F., *53*
Danilova, Alexandra, *51*
Danly, Donald Robert, *52*
Daughtry, Sylvester, *52*
Daughtry, Sylvia, *51*
Davis, John Massey, *51*
Dawson, Andre Nolan, *51*
Day, Thomas Brennock, *51*
Dear, Joseph A., *51*
DeBruler, Roger O., *51*
Deegan, Derek James, *52*
Deering, Joseph William, *52*
Delaquis, Noel, *51*
Del Santo, Lawrence A., *51*
Deputy, Byard Sanford, *51*
Dickenson, H. H., *52*
Dickson Alex Dockery, *51*
Di Co...o, Joanne Violet, *51*
Dillingham, Robert Bulger, *52*
Doherty, James Edward, III, *52*
Dolson, Franklin Robert, *51*
Donnahoe, Alan Stanley, *51*
Donnelly, John, *52*

Dorius, Kermit Parrish, *51*
D'Ornellas, Robert W., *51*
Doyle, Francis Xavier, *51*
Doyle, Wilfred Emmett, *51*
Drennen, William Miller, *51*
Drew, James Vandervort, *51*
Drexler, Clyde, *52*
Dreyfus, Daniel, *51*
Dudick, Michael Joseph, *51*
Duran, Roberto, *53*
Dutko, H.J., *51*

E

Eastman, Albert Theodore, *51*
Ebert, Richard J., *52*
Edgar, William H., *53*
Effa, Herman, *51*
Eickelberg, John Edwin, *52*
Eidt, Clarence Martin, Jr., *52*
Elder, Mark Lee, *52*
Elmer, William Morris, *52*
Elzay, Richard Paul, *52*
Emerich, Donald Warren, *51*
Emery, Sherman Raymond, *52*
Engel, Joel Stanley, *52*
Englander, Roman, *51*
Epp, Telfer L., *51*
Erdmann, August, *51*
Ernsberger, Fred Martin, *53*
Estill, Robert Whitridge, *51*
Etheridge, James Edward, Jr., *51*
Everson, Leonard Charles, *52*

F

Faget, Maxime A(llan), *52*
Feaster, Robert K., *51*
Fenters, James Dean, *52*
Ferrara, Arthur Vincent, *51*
Ferris, Thomas Francis, *51*
Finesilver, Sherman Glenn, *51*
Fink, Howard David, *52*
Finnegan, John Robert, Sr., *51*
Fisher, Robert Allison, *51*
Fitzgerald, Michael J., *52*
Fleming, Thomas Crawley, *52*
Fletcher, Anne Bosshard, *51*
Flores, Thomas R., *51*
Flower, Joseph Reynolds, *51*
Flynn, Donald F., *52*
Fowler, Earle Cabell, *52*
Fox, Bernard Michael, *52*
Frame, John Timothy, *51*
Frappier, Gilles, *51*
Frederick, William Sherrad, *53*
Fricke, H. Walter, *51*
Friedman, Herbert, *51*
Frisque, Gilles, *52*
Fry, Hayden, *51*
Fryar, Irving Dale, *51*
Frye, Richard Nelson, *52*

G

Gaines, Clarence Edward, Sr., *52*
Galbis, Ignacio Ricardo Maria, *51*
Gallagher, Richard Hugo, *51*
Galloway, Gerald Edward, Jr., *51*
Ganter, Bernard J., *51*
Gariepy, Corinne, *51*
Garrett, Dennis Andrew, *52*
Garrison, U. Edwin, *52*
Gartner, Michael Alfred, *53*
Gass, Raymond William, *52*
Gates, William H., *53*
Gault, Stanley Carleton, *51*
Gelber, Herbert Donald, *51*
Gelineau, Louis Edward, *52*
Genge, Kenneth Lyle, *51*
Georges, John A., *51*
Giannini, Margaret Joan, *51*
Gilbert, Donald Floyd, *51*
Gilliland, James S., *52*
Glaskowsky, Elizabeth Pope, *51*
Glavin, William Francis, *52*
Gleason, Andrew Mattei, *52*
Glotzer, Marilyn, *51*
Golbus, Mitchell S., *51*
Goldblatt, David Ira, *52*
Gonzalez, Ruben, *51*
Goodman, Louis Sanford, *52*
Goodrich, Maurice Keith, *52*

Goodridge, Noel Herbert Alan, *51*
Goodwin, Samuel McClure, *53*
Gossage, Thomas Layton, *51*
Gossett, Oscar Milton, *52*
Graf, Edward Louis, Jr., *52*
Graham, Otto Everett, Jr., *53*
Grant, Lester Howard, *52*
Green, George, *51*
Greendorfer, Terese Grosman, *51*
Greenleaf, Richard Edward, *52*
Grieve, Pierson MacDonald, *52*
Griffin, Gwyn, *51*
Griffiths, Arthur R., *53*
Grodus, Edward T., *51*
Groennert, Charles Willis, *53*
Gross, Michael S., *53*
Grossman, Elizabeth Korn, *52*
Grove, William Boyd, *51*
Gulbrandsen, Christian L., *52*
Gutmann, Max, *52*

H

Hackett, Bruce Clayton, *53*
Hagen, Arthur Ainsworth, *53*
Haley, Charles Lewis, *52*
Hall, John Richard, *51*
Halling, Leonard William, *52*
Halverson, Richard Christian, *51*
Handelsman, Jacob Charles, *52*
Handelsman, M. Gene, *51*
Hardy, Duane Horace, *51*
Hardy, Randall Webster, *52*
Harr, Joseph, *51*
Harrison, Lou Silver, *51*
Harvey, Cynthia, *51*
Harvey, George Burton, *51*
Harvey, J. Ernest, Jr., *52*
Haslam, Robert B., *51*
Hastings, Donald F., *52*
Hathaway, Alden Moinet, *51*
Hause, Jesse George, *51*
Hawkinson, John, *53*
Hayes, Webb Cook, III, *52*
Head, Edward Dennis, *51*
Heatherington, J. Scott, *52*
Hedgepeth, Leroy J., *52*
Heidrick, Gardner Wilson, *51*
Heistand, Joseph Thomas, *51*
Hendrix, Dennis Ralph, *52*
Hennigan, George R., *52*
Henry, James B., *51*
Herder, Robert H., *51*
Herrin, Frances Sudomier, *51*
Herring, Leonard Gray, *52*
Herzel, Leo, *52*
Hewes, Henry, *51*
Hickcox, Curtiss Bronson, *52*
Hickey, Robert Philip, Jr., *51*
Highleyman, Samuel Locke, III, *51*
Hill, Edward G., *52*
Hill, Errol Gaston, *51*
Himstead, Scott, *51*
Hinton, Christopher Jerrod, *51*
Hirsch, Joe Elbe, *53*
Hohage, Frederick William, *52*
Holden, Gwen Adams, *51*
Holland, Darrell Wendell, *51*
Holm, Jeanne Marjorie, *51*
Holt, Jack Wilson, Jr., *51*
Holthouse, Rita J., *51*
Honderich, Beland Hugh, *51*
Honea, T. Milton, *52*
Hood, Howard Allison, *52*
Hoover, William R(ay), *51*
Horowitz, Lewis Jay, *53*
Howard, Joseph Clemens, *51*
Howell, James Theodore, *53*
Huang, Elsie Lee, *51*
Hughes, Author E., *51*
Hughes, Everett Clark, *52*
Hughes, Harold Hasbrouck, Jr., *51*
Hughes, Roger K., *52*
Hughes, William Anthony, *51*
Hull, Kent, *52*
Hulst, John B., *51*
Hunt, Donald R., *52*
Huntley, Robert Edward Royall, *52*
Hunziker, Robert McKee, *52*
Hutchinson, Frederick Edward, *51*
Hytche, William Percy, *51*

I

Ianni, Lawrence Albert, *51*
Iversen, James Delano, *51*

J

Jacey, Charles Frederick, Jr., *52*
Jackson, Keith Jerome, *51*
Jahadi, Mohammad Reza, *52*
Jefferson, Bernard S., *51*
Jelinek, Fran, *51*
Johnson, Charles Christopher, Jr., *51*
Johnson, Raymond A., *51*
Jones, Alan C., *52*
Jones, Bob Gordon, *51*
Jones, Brent Michael, *52*
Jones, Thomas Curtis, *51*
Jones, Walk Claridge, III, *52*
Jordan, David Loran, *51*
Joseph, Stephen Carl, *52*
Jossem, Edmund Leonard, *52*

K

Kapioltas, John, *52*
Katz, Leon, *52*
Kauffman, Robert Craig, *51*
Keller, George Matthew, *52*
Kelly, Patrick Farrell, *51*
Kelsey, John Walter, *53*
Key, Jimmy (James Edward Key), *53*
Kiley, James P., *52*
Kirkendall, Richard Stewart, *52*
Klein, Anton J., *51*
Klein, Willie, *51*
Klobuchar, James John, *51*
Knight, Charles Field, *53*
Knowlton, Richard L., *52*
Knox, James Lloyd, *51*
Koester, Charles R., *51*
Komidar, Joseph Stanley, *52*
Korner, Jules Gilmer, III, *52*
Kosich, George John, *52*
Kraus, Michael, *51*
Krickstein, Aaron, *53*
Kross, Walter, *53*
Krowe, Allen Julian, *52*
Kundert, Alice E., *51*

L

Lam, David C., *51*
Lanzoni, Vincent, *51*
Larson, Dayl Andrew, *52*
Lawson, David Jerald, *51*
Lawson, David Lewis, *52*
Lehman, Edwin, *51*
Lehovec, Kurt, *51*
Lennon, Elizabeth Marie, *53*
Leone, Lucile P., *52*
Leonis, John Michael, *52*
Lerner, Aaron Bunsen, *51*
Levowitz, Bernard Samuel, *52*
Lewis, Norman, *52*
Liebe, Hans J., *51*
Liebowitz, Harold, *53*
Ling, Dwight L., *51*
Link, William P., *51*
Litzsinger, Paul Richard, *52*
Longaker, Nancy, *53*
Longerbone, Doug, *52*
Loomis, Worth (Alfred Worthington Loomis), *51*
Lovelace, Alan Mathieson, *52*
Lowden, Suzanne, *51*

M

MacAulay, Colin Alexander, *51*
MacBurney, Edward Harding, *51*
Mackey, Sally Schear, *51*
MacLeod, John, *53*
Madden, Joseph Michael, *52*
Majors, Johnny (John Terrill Majors), *53*
Makowka, Leonard, *52*
Mancheski, Frederick John, *51*
Maple, John E., *51*
Marchioni, Allen, *52*
Marsh, Caryl Glenn, *51*
Marshall, John Aloysius, *51*

Marshall, Nancy Haig, *52*
Marteau, Kimberly K., *51*
Martin, Bruce Douglas, *51*
Martin, William Aubert, *53*
Mason, Bruce, *53*
Mason, Steven Charles, *52*
Massa, Paul Peter, *51*
Massion, Walter Herbert, *52*
Mate, Martin, *51*
Matthews, Bruce Rankin, *53*
Mattingly, Donald Arthur, *51*
Maurer, Theodore A., *52*
McAninch, Harold D., *51*
McCaffrey, William Thomas, *53*
McClure, Lucretia Walker, *52*
McConnell, Elliott Bonnell, Jr., *52*
McCowan, Rodney A., *51*
McCraw, Leslie G., *52*
McCullough, R. Michael, *52*
McDonnell, John Finney, *52*
McDowell, Marion, *51*
McElroy, Charlotte Ann, *51*
McGlinchey, Joseph Dennis, *52*
McGonigal, Pearl, *51*
McIntyre, Guy Maurice, *52*
McLaughlin, Audrey, *51*
McLaughlin, Bernard J., *53*
McMillan, John A., *52*
McNamara, John F., *51*
McNeill, Alfred Thomas, Jr., *51*
McPhee, Richard S., *51*
McSweeney, Michael Terrence, *52*
Meadows, Donald Frederick, *53*
Mellor, James Robb, *52*
Menk, Louis Wilson, *52*
Merachnik, Donald, *52*
Metzler, Cynthia A., *51*
Meyer, John, *51*
Miller, Donald Eugene, *52*
Miller, Edward David, *53*
Miller, Gerald E., *51*
Miller, John Henry, *53*
Minnick, Carlton Printess, Jr., *51*
Moffet, Hugh Lamson, *52*
Monachino, Francis Leonard, *51*
Monk, Art, *51*
Monroe, Russell Ronald, *52*
Montgomery, John E., *51*
Moody, James L., Jr., *52*
Moore, David Lowell, *52*
Moore, Michael Thomas, *52*
Moore, Penelope, *52*
Moore, Walter Bruce, *52*
Moos, Eugene, *51*
Moose, Richard M., *51*
Morgan, Howard Edwin, *52*
Morgan, Lewis Render, *52*
Morton, Leland Clure, *51*
Mouch, Frank Messman, *51*
Mowatt, Wayne L., *51*
Mullaney, Joseph E., *52*
Mulvoy, Mark, *51*
Murphy, Reg, *53*
Murphy, Robert C(harles), *51*

N

Nef, Evelyn Stefansson, *52*
Nelson, Kent C. (Oz Nelson), *53*
Neugarten, Bernice Levin, *51*
Newman, Ron, *53*
Newton, Nate, *53*
Nicholas, Robert Leon, *52*
Nichols, Horace Elmo, *52*
Nieves, Joesphine, *51*
Nix, Robert N(elson) C(ornelius), Jr., *52*
Nofsinger, William Morris, *52*
Nolan, Robert, *52*
Norris, John Windsor, Jr., *53*
Nuchia, Samuel M., *51*
Nurcombe, Barry, *51*

O

O'Byrne, Paul J., *52*
O'Connell, Kenneth John, *52*
O'Connor, Richard Donald, *51*
Odegaard, Charles Edwin, *51*
O'Grady, Thomas B., *52*
Oishi, Satoshi, *51*
O'Keefe, Joseph Thomas, *51*
O'Kelly, Bernard, *51*
Oliver, Thomas K., Jr., *51*
O'Niel, John, Jr., *53*
Ontiveros, Steven, *51*
Orozco, Raymond E., *51*
Ottenberg, James Simon, *52*
Overton, Stanley Dixon, *53*
Owens, Donald D., *52*
Owens, Lewis E., *51*
Owens, William Arthur, *51*
Ozbun, Jim L., *51*

P

Page, Austin P., *51*
Palmer, Alice Eugenia, *52*
Palmer, Lester Davis, *51*
Parish, Robert Lee (Chief Parish), *52*
Patten, John W., *51*
Pearson, Donna Sutherland, *52*
Peirce, George Leighton, *52*
Pelton, Joan Elisabeth Mason, *52*
Peña, Federico Fabian, *52*
Penney, Alphonsus Liguori, *51*
Penzias, Arno Allan, *52*
Perschino, Arthur J., *52*
Pershing, Richard Wilson, *52*
Peters, Douglas Dennison, *52*
Peters, Frank Lewis, Jr., *51*
Peters, Lauralee Milberg, *53*
Petersen, Gary N., *52*
Peterson, Esther, *51*
Phillips, Jack Carter, *51*
Pietra, Giuseppe Giovanni, *52*
Pilla, Felix Mario, *52*
Pinch, John G., *51*
Pincus, George, *51*
Pister, Karl Stark, *51*
Posin, Daniel Q., *52*
Poulos, Gary Peter, *51*
Powell, Lewis Franklin, Jr., *52*
Prezio, Joseph Anthony, *51*
Pritchard, Paul C(lement), *51*
Prude, Elaine S., *51*

Pruitt, Albert W., *52*

Q

Quinn, John R., *52*
Quinn, Robert Henry, *52*
Quirico, Francis Joseph, *52*

R

Ramos, Melvin John, *52*
Randall, William Theodore, *51*
Ransom, William Harrison, *52*
Rasco, Carol Hampton, *51*
Rave, James A., *52*
Redeker, Allan Grant, *52*
Reed, William G., Jr., *51*
Reeds, Roger, *51*
Reese, Errol Lynn, *51*
Reeves, Michael Stanley, *52*
Reiss, John C., *52*
Remy, Ray, *51*
Rensi, Edward Henry, *52*
Reveiz, Fuad, *52*
Rice, Robert H., *51*
Rich, Clayton, *51*
Richardson, Bruce LeVoyle, *52*
Richardson, Frank H., *52*
Richardson, Maurice M., *52*
Richman, Joan F., *52*
Ridder, Bernard Herman, Jr., *52*
Riley, Dorothy Comstock, *51*
Rimmereid, Arthur V., *51*
Rindlaub, John Wade, *52*
Roberts, Cecil Kenneth, *52*
Robillard, Donald J., *51*
Robinson, Sumner Martin, *51*
Rodman, Oliver, *51*
Roedel, Paul Robert, *52*
Rosenow, John Henry, *52*
Ross, Henry Raymond, *53*
Rostagno, Derrick, *52*
Rotch, William, *52*
Roth, Herbert, Jr., *52*
Roth, William George, *52*
Rothwell, Robert Clark, *52*
Roy, Raymond, *52*
Rubottom, Donald Julian, *52*
Rugge, Hugo Robert, *52*
Ruiz-Petrich, Elena, *52*
Russell, George Albert, *51*
Ryan, Buddy (James Ryan), *51*
Ryan, John Franklin, *52*

S

Sack, Burton Marshall, *53*
Sackett, Joseph Frederic, *52*
Saenger, Theodore Jerome, *52*
Sago, Paul Edward, *51*
Sams, W(iley) Mitchell, Jr., *52*
Sanchez, Robert Fortune, *51*
Sandler, Marion Osher, *53*
Sapolu, Manase Jesse, *52*
Sauer, Kenneth H., *51*
Sauer, Robert C., *51*
Sayers, Roger, *51*
Schad, James L., *51*
Schein, Harvey L., *52*
Schlarman, Stanley Gerard, *52*
Schlosberg, Richard T., III, *52*
Schmidt, Allen Edward, *52*
Schnack, Larry Gene, *52*
Schorzman, Clarice B., *51*
Schuiling, William E., *51*
Schumacher, Hans H., *52*
Schwartz, Harry Kane, *52*
Schweig, Margaret Berris, *52*
Schwenger, Frances, *52*
Scott, John William, *52*
Sears, William Rees, *52*
Sebastian, Michael James, *52*
Sevetson, Donald James, *53*
Sfat, Michael Rudolph, *52*
Shapero, Harold (Samuel), *51*
Shapiro, Howard Alan, *52*
Shaw, James, *51*
Shay, John E., Jr., *52*
Shea, Donald Francis, *51*
Shea, John J., *52*
Sheng, Jack Tse-liang, *51*
Shepherd, R. F., *52*
Sherratt, Gerald Robert, *52*
Shill, Victor Lamar, *51*
Shipley, Lucia Helene, *53*
Siegler, Thomas Edmund, *53*
Sigler, Andrew Clark, *51*
Silins, Ints M., *53*
Silverman, William A., *52*
Simon, David, *51*
Simonett, John E., *52*
Simonson, Ted, *52*
Simpson, Ocleris C., *52*
Sinclair, Joseph Samuels, *52*
Singleton, Henry Earl, *52*
Sinner, George Albert, *51*
Skeete, F. Herbert, *51*
Skiles, Paul, *51*
Skinner, Stanley Thayer, *52*
Slade, Gerald Jack, *52*
Slane, Henry Pindell, *52*
Slater, Oliver Eugene, *51*
Smith, Charles, *51*
Smith, Clodus Ray, *52*
Smith, Daniel R., *51*
Smith, G. Elaine, *52*
Smith, Gordon E., *51*
Smith, Hamilton Othanel, *51*
Smith, James Stephen, *51*
Smith, Jeffrey P., *52*
Smith, Joe Mauk, *51*
Smith, Leo Gilbert, *52*
Smith, Raymond Victor, *51*
Smith, Roy Jordan, *52*
Smith, William K., *52*
Speaks, Ruben Lee, *51*
Speed, John Sackett, *51*
Speicher, Opal, *51*
Spencer, Geoffrey F., *51*
Stallings, Gene Clifton, *51*
Starr, Frederick Brown, *52*
Stauffer, John H., *51*
Steele, Kurt D., *52*
Stegemoeller, Harvey A., *51*
Stein, Paul E., *52*
Stephens, Olin James, II, *52*

Stephens, William Richard, *52*
Stevens, William Louis, *51*
Stith, Forrest Christopher, *51*
Stockton, Thomas B., *51*
Stofft, William A., *51*
Stone, David Deaderick, *52*
Stone, Warren R., *51*
Strandquist, John Herbert, *53*
Strang, Charles Daniel, *52*
Strickland, William James, *51*
Stull, G. Alan, *51*
Suckling, Robert McCleary, *51*
Suggs, James C., *51*
Sullivan, Donald, *51*
Sullivan, Thomas John, *51*
Sullivan, William James, *51*
Swails, Norman E., *52*
Swenson, Daniel Lee, *51*
Symons, J. Keith, *52*
Symons, James Martin, *52*

T

Tait, John Edwin, *51*
Talley, Robert Boyd, *51*
Taylor, Frederick Rankin, *53*
Taylor, Joyce, *53*
Tcherkassky, Marianna Alexsavena, *51*
Teague, Wayne, *51*
Tempel, Thomas Robert, *51*
Tennis, Calvin Cabell, *52*
Terrill, James E., *51*
Thatcher, Rex Howard, *52*
Theis, Francis William, *52*
Thelen, Max, Jr., *51*
Theodore, Nick Andrew, *51*
Thomas, Dudley Breckinridge, *51*
Thomas, Nathaniel Charles, *53*
Thomas, Robert Dean, *51*
Thomas, Roy Lee, *51*
Thompson, Emmett Frank, *52*
Thompson, Granville Berry, *51*
Thomsen, Mark William, *51*
Thorne, Frank Leadley, *52*
Toller, William Robert, *51*
Tomlinson, Kenneth Y., *51*
Toumey, Hubert John (Hugh Toumey), *52*
Triplett, Loren O., *52*
Tumminello, Stephen Charles, *52*
Turbeville, Gus, *51*
Turkin, Marshall William, *52*
Turnbull, Renaldo, *53*
Tusher, Thomas William, *52*

U

Underwood, Bernard Edward, *52*

V

Van de Wetering, John E(dward), *52*
Vest, Frank Harris, Jr., *52*
Vienne, Dorothy Titus, *52*
Vincenti-Brown, Crispin Rufus William, *52*
Vittoria, Joseph V., *51*
Voell, Richard Allen, *51*
Voet, Paul C., *52*
Vredenburg, Dwight Charles, *52*

W

Waddell, R. Eugene, *53*
Wagoner, William Hampton, *51*
Waldman, Diane, *51*
Walker, LeRoy, *51*
Walker, Phillip R., *52*
Wallace, David Dunsmore, *52*
Walmsley, Arthur Edward, *51*
Warlick, Charles Henry, *52*
Warner, Homer R., *51*
Warren, Gerald Lee, *51*
Watkins, Stanley, *51*
Watts, Charles DeWitt, *52*
Watts, Heather, *51*
Weber, David C(arter), *51*
Weber, Julian L., *53*
Weber, Ronald Gilbert, *51*
Weigel, Stanley Alexander, *52*
Weimer, Paul K(essler), *51*
Weingarten, Murray, *52*
Weismiller, David R., *52*
Weiss, Richard Ronald, *52*
Weissenbuehler, Wayne, *51*
Weitzel, Peter Andre, *51*
Welsh, Thomas J., *52*
Wendell, Earl W., *52*
Wenz, Richard L., *51*
Werger, Paul Myron, *51*
Werner, Charles George, *51*
White, H. Blair, *52*
Whitfield, Princess D., *51*
Wilkinson, John Burke, *51*
Wilks, Ivor Gordon Hughes, *51*
Williams, Phillip L., *51*
Williams, Richard David, III, *51*
Williams, Willie, *52*
Willis, Carl Bertram, *51*
Wilsnack, Roger E., *51*
Wilson, Marjorie Price, *51*
Windle, Joseph Raymond, *51*
Woeste, John Theodore, *51*
Woitach, Richard, *51*
Woodland, N. Joseph, *52*
Woodruff, Harrison D., Jr., *51*
Woods, James Dudley, *51*
Wulf, Jerold W., *52*

Y

Yamaoka, Seigen Haruo, *51*
Yeakel, Joseph Hughes, *51*

Z

Zarazoga, Daniel, *53*
Zatuchni, Gerald Irving, *52*
Zlatoper, Ronald Joseph, *51*

Necrology

Biographees of the 53rd Edition of *Who's Who in America* whose deaths have been reported to the editors prior to the close of compilation of this edition are listed below. For those individuals whose deaths were reported prior to July 1998, complete biographical information, including date of death and place of interment, can be found in Volume XI of *Who Was Who in America*.

A

Abrahams, William Miller
Abrams, Samuel K.
Abrams, William Bernard
Adams, Richard Towsley
Aden, Arthur Laverne
Albaugh, Fred William
Albrecht, Felix Robert
Albright, Archie Earl, Jr.
Alden, Douglas William
Aldrich, Robert Anderson
Alfred, William
Allen, Howard Pfeiffer
Allin, John Maury
Altimari, Frank Xavier
Ambler, Eric
Amory, Cleveland
Anastasi, Gaspar Walter
Andrews, Frederick Newcomb
Antler, Morton
Appel, John J.
Arkus, Leon Anthony
Arnold, Kenneth James
Arrington, Leonard James
Arron, Judith Hagerty
Atkins, William Theodore
Autry, Gene (Orvon Gene Autry)
Avallone, Michael Angelo
Axelrad, Irving Irmas
Axelrod, Daniel Isaac

B

Babson, David Leveau
Bagwell, Cecil Ray
Bailey, Orville Taylor
Bakay, Louis
Baker, Norman Henderson
Baldwin, Velma Neville Wilson
Barber, Andrew Bollons
Bardon, Marcel
Barger, James Daniel
Barnum, William Laird
Bart, Georgiana Cray
Bart, Lionel
Barton, Alexander James
Barton, Derek Harold Richard
Basham-Tooker, Janet Brooks
Batzer, R. Kirk
Baur, Isolde Nacke
Baxter, William Francis
Beadle, Alfred Newman
Bechtol, William Milton
Beck, Joan Wagner
Beebe, Richard Townsend
Beeching, Charles Train, Jr.
Behrens, Richard John
Bell, John Milton
Benson, George Charles Sumner
Benson, Morton
Berger, Curtis Jay
Bergman, Harry
Bergman, (Ernst) Ingmar
Bernstein, Isadore Abraham
Bernstein, Zalman C.
Bessey, William Higgins
Bettmann, Otto Ludwig
Biesenberger, Joseph A.
Bigelow, David Skinner, III
Blackburn, Jack Bailey
Blackmun, Harry Andrew
Blakeslee, Alton Lauren
Blandau, Richard Julius
Bloland, Paul Anson
Bloomfield, Arthur Irving
Blum, Lawrence Philip
Bogash, Richard
Bogle, Hugh Andrew
Bohne, Carl John, Jr.
Bonnycastle, Lawrence Christopher
Boudreaux, Warren Louis
Bourke, Vernon Joseph
Boutillier, Robert John
Bowman, Edward Harry
Box, Dwain D.
Boyd, William Douglas, Jr.
Brassell, Roselyn Strauss
Breffeilh, Louis Andrew
Breindel, Eric Marc
Brice, William Jules
Brichta, Paul
Brickhouse, John B. (Jack Brickhouse)
Bright, Harold Frederick

Briner, William H.
Broudy, Harry Samuel
Brown, Ann L.
Brown, George Edward, Jr.
Brown, George Hay
Brown, Ralph Sharp
Bruck, Ferdinand Frederick
Bryan, David Tennant
Brydon, Harold Wesley
Buckley, Victoria
Budiansky, Bernard
Buscaglia, (Felice) Leo(nardo)
Busse, Wilbur Edward
Bustad, Leo Kenneth
Butler, George Harrison
Buxton, Jorge Norman
Byrnes, Robert Francis

C

Cannon, Daniel Willard
Carberry, John J. Cardinal
Carelli, Gabor Paul
Carney, Richard Edgar
Carroll, Charles Lemuel, Jr.
Carroll, Kenneth Kitchener
Cartwright, Howard E(ugene)
Cassilly, Richard
Caudill, Howard Edwin
Celebrezze, Anthony
Cella, Francis Raymond
Chandler, Robert Flint, Jr.
Chiles, Lawton Mainor
Ching, Lawrence Lin Tai
Chinn, Thomas Wayne
Christensen, Julien Martin
Church, John Trammell
Clark, Thomas Lloyd
Clarkson, Max Boydell Elliott
Clifford, Clark McAdams
Cohen, Arthur Abram
Cohen, Max
Cohen, Melvin Joseph
Cohen, Norton Jacob
Cohen, Richard Stockman
Cole, Julian D.
Coleman, John Macdonald
Collier, Oscar
Conger, Stephen Halsey
Connelly, Kathleen Fitzgerald
Conover, Robert Fremont
Cook, Charles Emerson
Cook, James Winfield Clinton
Cooper, Terry O.
Corcoran, Eileen Lynch
Corker, Charles Edward
Cotter, Richard Vern
Couger, James Daniel
Coulter, Wallace Henry
Covalt, Genevieve
Crain, Cullen Malone
Crain, William Henry
Crompton, Arnold
Crowley, Daniel John
Crozier, Lucille Breeding
Culver, Robert Elroy
Cummings, Walter J.
Curley, Arthur
Currier, Frederick Plumer
Curtis, Alva Marsh
Curtis, Walter W.
Cutler, Robert Porter
Cyert, Richard Michael

D

Dabney, Seth Mason, III
Daggett, Robert Sherman
Dalrymple, Jean Van Kirk
Danforth, Louis Fremont
D'Arcangelo, Allan Matthew
Davidson, Robert Laurenson Dashiell
Davis, Bruce Livingston, Jr.
Day, Billie Ann
Deavers, Karl Alan
DeBock, Florent Alphonse
Deese, James Earle
Defliese, Philip Leroy
De Frank, Vincent
Degler, Carl Neumann
Deitcher, Herbert
DeLashmet, Gordon Bartlett
del Regato, Juan Angel
DeMascio, Robert Edward

Denoon, Clarence England, Jr.
DeuPree, Robert Marshall
Devany, Joseph Aloysius
Devol, Kenneth Stowe
Dewey, David Lawrence
Dickerson, Ernest
Dickerson, William Roy
Dickie, Margaret McKenzie
Dickson, Brian
Dietz, Alma
Dill, William Joseph
Di Maggio, Joseph Paul
Dixon, Ernest Thomas, Jr.
Dixon, Thomas Francis
Dokoudovsky, Ludmila
Dolch, William Lee
Dolin, Albert Harry
Donaldson, Lauren R.
Dorwart, Robert Alan
Doty, Brant Lee
Dovring, Folke
Doyle, John Robert, Jr.
Drury, Allen Stuart
Du Bois, Philip Hunter
Duca, Alfred Milton
Dunnington, Walter Grey, Jr.
Duprat, Jo Ann
Durwood, Stanley H.
Dwyer, Edward James
Dyer, David William
Dyson, Raymond Clegg

E

Eames, Earl Ward, Jr.
Earle, Richard H.
Eckardt, Arthur Roy
Eddy, Edward Danforth
Edelman, Harold
Edwards, F(loyd) Kenneth
Edwards, Page Lawrence, Jr.
Eichhorn, Heinrich Karl
Elion, Gertrude Belle
Ellingwood, Herbert Eugene
Ellis, William Harold
Ellis, William Hartshorne
Elrod, Harold Glenn
Emerson, Marvin Chester
Emery, Kenneth Orris
Emmons, Howard Wilson
Enns, Mark Kynaston
Enright, Arthur Joseph
Ensminger, Marion Eugene
Estrin, Herman Albert
Evankovich, George Joseph
Evans, Edwin Curtis
Evans, Trevor Heiser
Ewert, Richard H(uckeby)
Exton, Inez Pauline

F

Fadiman, Clifton
Fairbanks, Harold Vincent
Farage, Donald J.
Farmer, James
Farquhar, Norman
Fascell, Dante B.
Feininger, Andreas Bernhard Lyonel
Fine, Donald Irving
Finnie, C(larence) Herbert (Herb Finnie)
Fischer, Eugene H.
Fishman, Jacob Robert
Fleischer, Michael
Fletcher, Riley Eugene
Flick, Gervase Mead
Flora, Karl Philip
Flynn, James Rourke
Flynn, Richard James
Ford, Kenneth
Fosholt, Sanford Kenneth
Foster, Edson L.
Fowle, Frank Fuller
Frame, Clarence George
Frankel, Arnold J.
Fredericks, Marshall Maynard
Freedman, Audrey Willock
Freeman, Montine McDaniel
Freitag, Robert Frederick
French, Charles Ferris, Jr.
Freund, Norman Lawrence
Frisell, Wilhelm Richard
Fromm, Alfred
Fuller, Lawrence Joseph

Fulton, Darrell Nelson
Fuzak, Victor Thaddeus

G

Gallaway, Marthine S.
Galletti, Pierre Marie
Gallman, Robert Emil
Garibay-Gutierrez, Luis
Garratt, Graham
Gerking, Shelby Delos, Jr.
Giffen, Lawrence Everett, Sr.
Gillette, Stanley C.
Gilman, Peter Augustus
Glidden, Germain G.
Godden, Rumer
Goldbach, Ray
Goldfarb, Mark Leonard
Goldhaber, Gertrude Scharff
Goldscheider, Sidney
Goldstein, Bernard Herbert
Goldstein, Louis Lazarus
Golnick, Leon Shaffer
Good, Lee T.
Goodman, Hubert Thorman
Goodson, Louie Aubrey, Jr.
Grade, Lord Lew
Granbery, Edwin Carleton, Jr.
Gray, John E.
Graybeal, Sidney Norman
Green, Marshall
Greenberg, Frank
Greene, Donald Johnson
Greenfield, Meg
Grenander, M. E.
Grier, Herbert Earl
Griffin, Bryant Wade
Griffith Joyner, Florence DeLorez
Grillo, Joann Danielle
Gross, Ernest Arnold
Gross, Ludwik
Grossman, Morton S.
Grotowski, Jerzy
Groupe, Vincent
Grover, Robert Lawrence
Gunter, Gordon P.
Gurahian, Vincent

H

Haake, Arthur C.
Haenszel, William Manning
Hagan, Alfred Chris
Hagan, Richard Francies
Hall, Kathryn Evangeline
Hall, Kenneth Keller
Halle, Louis Joseph
Ham, William Taylor, Jr.
Hamilton, Howard Britton
Hampton, Henry Eugene
Hampton, Mark
Hancock, Walker Kirtland
Handy, William Talbot, Jr.
Hanna, Geoffrey Chalmers
Hansen, Robert Suttle
Hanson, Charles Easton, Jr.
Harker, Robert Twaites
Harley, William Gardner
Harney, David Moran
Harrer, Gustave Adolphus
Harris, Frances Alvord (Mrs. Hugh W. Harris)
Harris, Henry Hiter, Jr.
Harrison, Anna Jane
Hart, Paul
Harvey, Abner McGehee
Hatcher, Robert Douglas
Hausser, Robert Louis
Hayes, Edward F.
Hayes, Peter Lind
Haynes, Robert Hall
Hayward, John Tucker
Heilig, David
Heinlein, Oscar Allen
Henneman, John Bell, Jr.
Henry, Paul James
Herzberg, Gerhard
Hess, Leon
Hiatt, Robert Worth
Hickman, Leon Edward
Higginbotham, A. Leon, Jr.
Higgins, James Henry
Higgins, William Henry Clay, III
Hindus, Milton

Hinshaw, Lerner Brady
Hios, Theodore
Hitchings, George Herbert
Hodara, Eden
Hodge, Carleton Taylor
Hodgkin, Sir Alan Lloyd
Hoff, Nicholas John
Hole, Fred
Hollenbeck, Marynell
Holliman, John
Holmes, Paul Kinloch, Jr.
Holzman, William (Red)
Hook, Edward Watson, Jr.
Hopper, Robert William
Horner, William Harry
Hottel, Hoyt Clarke
Howe, John Perry
Howell, Thomas Edwin
Huang, Kee Chang
Hudson, Donald Ellis
Hughes, Joe Kenneth
Hughes, Ted
Husted, John Edwin
Huston, Harris Hyde
Huvos, Kornel
Huyett, Daniel Henry, III
Hyman, Milton

I

Iselin, Sally Cary
Ivan, Thomas Nathaniel

J

Jameson, Dorothea
Jannasch, Holger Windekilde
Janssen, Orville Henry
Jasper, Herbert Henri
Jebsen, Joan Helene
Jenner, Lois Polin
Johnson, Frank Minis, Jr.
Johnson, Hal Harold Gustav
Jones, Harvie Paul
Jones, Henry
Jones, Richard Cyrus
Jones, Robert Lee
Jones, Wilbur Boardman, Jr.
Joseph, David J., Jr.
Josephs, Melvin Jay
Joslyn, Jay Thomas
Juba, George E.

K

Kaminer, Peter H.
Kanin, Garson
Karls, John B.
Karmin, Monroe William
Kelley, Jackson DeForest
Kelley, Robb Beardsley
Kelly, Francis W.
Kendall, Henry Way
Kenealy, Matthew H., III
Kennedy, Peter Smithson
Kennedy, Richard Thomas
Kidd, William Matthew
Kiley, Richard Paul
Kimbrough, Ralph Bradley
King, Arnold Kimsey, Jr.
Kirk, Maurice Blake
Kirkpatrick, Forrest Hunter
Knepper, William Edward
Kness, Richard Maynard
Knox, Ernest Rudder
Knox, Northrup Rand
Knudsen, Semon Emil
Kober, Carl Leopold
Koch, Peter
Korth, Fred
Kramer, Morton
Kramer, Philip
Krieble, Robert H.
Kring, Walter Donald
Kristeller, Paul Oskar
Kroch, Carl Adolph
Kronstadt, Arnold Mayo
Kuyatt, Chris E(rnie) (Earl)
Kyle, John Hamilton

L

LaGrone, Alfred Hall

Lake, William Thomas
Landry, G. Yves
Lane, Harold Edwin
Lane, Robert Gerhart
Lang, Hans Joachim
Lanham, Urless Norton
Larson, Clarence Edward
Lassers, Willard J.
LaVeck, Gerald DeLoss
Lavenson, James H.
Lehmann, Heinz Edgar
Leighton, Joseph
Lele, Padmakar Pratap
Leonard, Roy Junior
Leontief, Wassily
Le Van, Daniel Hayden
Levine, Rachmiel
Lewis, Bernard Leroy
Lewis, Shari
Leydet, François Guillaume
Lieberman, Harvey Michael
Lillehei, C. Walton
Lipowski, Zbigniew Jerzy
List, Noel David
Lister, Keith Fenimore
Livingood, Clarence S.
Lomax, Harvard
Lord, Jere Williams, Jr.
Lord, Marion Manns
Love, Franklin Sadler
Lowell, Juliet
Luckman, Charles
Lund, Bert Oscar, Jr.
Lunsford, Marvin Carl

M

Macdonald, Katharine March
Mac Vicar, Robert William
Mahler, Harry Bez
Mann, Jonathan Max
Marquardt, Kathleen Patricia
Marshall, E. G.
Martin, Maurice John
Martin, Murray Simpson
Masterson, Kleber Sandlin
Mayer, Henry Michael
Mayer, Robert Wallace
Mays, Kate S.
McCord, William Charles
Mc Coy, Robert Baker
McCracken, Alexander Walker
Mc Cue, Carolyn Moore
Mc Cullough, Helen Craig
McDaniels, B. T.
Mc Dowall, Roddy
Mc Goon, Dwight Charles
McGurn, George William
McLaren, James Clark
McLaughlin, Edward David
McLaughlin, Linda Lee Hodge
Meisinger, Henry Peter
Mellon, Paul
Menuhin, Yehudi
Meredith, George (Marlor)
Michaud, Howard Henry
Mickelson, Arnold Rust
Micks, Don Wilfred
Migden, Chester L.
Miller, Calvin Francis
Miller, Judith Ann
Miller, Paul Lukens
Miller, Richard Jerome
Miller, Robert William
Minsker, Robert Stanley
Mirsky, Jeffrey
Modlin, George Matthews
Monberg, Jay Peter
Montone, Liber Joseph
Moore, Brian
Moore, Robert Edward
Moore, Walter Parker, Jr.
Morgan, David Ernest
Morrin, Thomas Harvey
Morris, Charles Elliot
Morris, Edwin Alexander
Morris, James Aloysius
Morris, John E.
Morris, Willie
Morton, Malvin
Mow, Douglas Farris
Mullaley, Robert Charles
Müller-Eberhard, Hans Joachim
Mullis, Madeline Gail Herman

N

Nadel, Ethan Richard
Naimoli, Raymond Anthony
Nastasi, Kathleen Patricia
Ness, Frederic William
Nesson, H. Richard
Neustadt, Barbara Mae
Newburger, Frank L., Jr.
Newell, Frank William
Newsome, George Marvin
Newton, George Addison
Nikiforuk, Peter N.
Nodine, Loren L.
Nolan, John Gavin
North, Phil Record
Nussdorf, Bernard

O

Ogren, Carroll Woodrow
Old, Lloyd John
Oldfather, Charles Eugene
Oler, Wesley Marion, III
Oliver, Robert Warner
Organski, Abramo Fimo Kenneth
Orlen, Joel
O'Rourke, Dennis
Orton, Stewart
Owen, James Churchill, Jr.
Owings, Margaret Wentworth

P

Pai, Shih I.
Pakula, Alan J.
Panaro, Victor Anthony
Panitz, Lawrence Herbert
Paredes, Americo
Parker, Donald Howard
Parker, Maynard Michael

Parkinson, Ethelyn Minerva
Paschang, John Linus
Passano, Edward Magruder
Pattison, Abbott Lawrence
Patty, R. Bruce
Pearson, Albert Marchant
Peebles, Carter David
Perdue, James Everett
Phifer, J. Reese
Philips, David Evan
Piel, William, Jr.
Pierce, George Foster, Jr.
Pincus, Joseph
Poe, Douglas Allan
Polzin, John Theodore
Powers, James Earl
Price, Charles Eugene
Pritzker, Jay
Prochnow, Herbert Victor
Prystowsky, Harry
Puckett, James Manuel, Jr.
Putnam, Peter Brock
Puzo, Mario

Q

Quigley, Jack Allen
Quinn, Betty Nye
Quintero, Jose

R

Radell, Nicholas John
Radley, Virginia Louise
Raymond, Arthur Emmons
Raynor, John Patrick
Reed, Dwayne Milton
Reedy, George Edward
Reichard, Hugo Manley
Reichard, John Francis
Reifler, Clifford Bruce
Reilly, Peter C.
Reines, Frederick
Ricca, Joseph John
Rich, Giles Sutherland
Richards, Kenneth Edwin
Rieser, Leonard Moos
Riles, Wilson Camanza
Riseley, Martha Suzannah Heater (Mrs.
    Charles Riseley)
Roberts, David Glendenning
Rockelman, Georgia F(owler) Benz
Rockwell, Alvin John
Rodbell, Martin
Roemer, Edward Pier
Rolle, Esther
Rollins, Lanier
Ronald, William
Rose, Robert R., Jr.
Rosenthal, Richard Laurence
Ross, Bernard Harris
Ross, Joseph Foster
Rothwarf, Allen
Rubin, Irving
Rubright, Royal Cushing
Ruttenberg, Harold Joseph

S

Salony, John, III
Salzer, John Michael
Samter, Max
Sanders, Lawrence
Sandson, John I.
Sarian, Jirair Nerses
Saunders, Adah Wilson
Schaaf, Miv
Schawlow, Arthur Leonard
Schiff, John Jefferson
Schilling, Sylvester Paul
Schneider, Melvin Frederick
Schrader, Harry Christian, Jr.
Schrader, Martin Harry
Schroepfer, George John, Jr.
Schwann, William Joseph
Schwartz, Henry Gerard
Scibelli, Anthony M.
Scopp, Irwin Walter
Seaborg, Glenn Theodore
Sears, George Ames
Segal, Irving Ezra
Seitz, Collins Jacques
Shapira, Emmanuel
Shapiro, Alvin Philip
Shapiro, George M.
Shaw, Robert Lawson
Shelton, Wayne Vernon
Shepard, Elaine Elizabeth
Shriver, Garner Edward
Shumate, Charles Albert
Sibley, Charles Gald
Sidney, Sylvia (Sophia Kossow)
Silverman, Alvin Michaels
Silverstein, Shelby (Shel Silverstein)
Siskel, Gene (Eugene Kal Siskel)
Slettebak, Arne
Smith, Carlton Myles
Smith, Wilfred Irvin
Smyth, Reginald (Reggie Smythe)
Snider, Ruth Atkinson
Snyder, Robert Martin
Sonneborn, Henry, III
Spears, Monroe Kirk
Speas, Robert Dixon
Stahr, Elvis J(acob), Jr.
Stair, Frederick Rogers
Starr, Richard Cawthon
Steiner, Erich Ernst
Stephens, Woodford Cefis (Woody
    Stephens)
Stevens, Clyde Benjamin, Jr.
Stevens, Joseph Edward, Jr.
Stevens, William John
Stewart, Eugene Lawrence
Stewart, Harold Leroy
Stoneman, Samuel Sidney
Stout, Juanita Kidd
Strassmeyer, Mary
Streibich, Harold Cecil
Strongin, Theodore
Sugarman, Matthew S.
Summitt, Robert Layman
Sutherland, Raymond Carter
Suzuki, Michio
Swaim, Joseph Carter, Jr.

T

Talbot, Matthew J.
Tawil, Joseph E.
Taylor, J(ames) Herbert
Taylor, Telford
Teague, Peyton Clark
Terry, Frank Jeffrey
Thomas, Charles Howard, II
Thurber, Donald MacDonald Dickinson
Tiecke, Richard William
Tilberis, Elizabeth
Tilton, James Floyd
Timmins, Richard Haseltine
Torme, Mel(vin) (Howard Torme)
Torrey, Henry Cutler
Tour, Robert Louis
Townsend, Palmer Wilson
Toyomura, Dennis Takeshi
Treffinger, Karl Edward
Tresmontan-Stitt, Olympia Davis
Trostel, Michael Frederick
Trueblood, Paul Graham
Tullos, John Baxter
Tupper, Charles John
Turner, William Wilson
Tuttleton, James Wesley
Twersky, Victor

U

Underberg, Alan Jack

V

Van den Akker, Johannes Archibald
Van Landingham, Leander Shelton, Jr.
Van Valkenburg, Mac Elwyn
Vaughan, Joseph Lee
Verger, Morris David
Vest, Marvin Lewis
Veysey, Arthur Ernest
Vigil, Charles S.
Visser, John Evert
Voell, Richard Allen

W

Wacker, Frederick Glade, Jr.
Wagner, John Garnet
Wait, James Richard
Wallace, George Corley
Wallis, W(ilson) Allen
Walls, Benjamin Carmage
Wardwell, Allen
Warlick, Roger Kinney
Warren, Harry Verney
Warren, Robert Willis
Wasson, Richard Howard
Weatherby, Susan Moormann
Webb, William John
Weightman, Judy Mae
Weiner, Annette Barbara
Weins, Leo Matthew
Weissman, Norman
Welsh, Lawrence H.
Wentorf, Robert Henry
West, Dorothy
Weyenberg, Donald Richard
Whallon, Evan Arthur, Jr.
White, Ralph David
White, W(illiam) Arthur
Whitten, Dolphus, Jr.
Whittingham, Charles Edward
Widmer, Kemble
Wilber, Charles Grady
Williams, Alan Davison
Williams, Chester Arthur, Jr.
Williams, Robert Roy
Williams, Thomas Allison
Wilson, Margaret Dauler
Wisdom, John Minor
Wistisen, Martin J.
Wolf, Eric Robert
Wolken, Jerome Jay
Wood, Raymund Francis
Woods, Richard Seavey
Woodside, Robert Elmer
Worthy, James Carson
Wyner, Aaron Daniel
Wynn, Early
Wyss, Norma Rose Topping

Y

Yates, Elton Gottlieb
Yoggerst, James Paul
Youngdahl, James Edward

Z

Zienty, Ferdinand Benjamin
Zipprodt, Patricia
Zucker, Jean Maxson